A Complete
CONCORDANCE
to
Science and Health
with Key to the Scriptures

*Together with an Index to the Marginal Headings
and a List of the Scriptural Quotations contained in that
book as finally revised by its author*

MARY BAKER EDDY
Discoverer and Founder of Christian Science

Marcas Registradas

Published by

THE FIRST CHURCH OF CHRIST, SCIENTIST

in Boston, Massachusetts, U.S.A.

A Complete

CONCORDANCE

to the Writings of

MARY BAKER EDDY

ISBN 0-87952-092-2

Preface

For many years there have been calls for a more complete index to "SCIENCE AND HEALTH WITH KEY TO THE SCRIPTURES," and although the index prepared by the late Rev. J. H. Wiggin about the year 1885 was quite large, neither it nor subsequent indices fully met the requirements of the students of our textbook. It finally became apparent that the only satisfactory way to meet this need was to prepare a complete Concordance, which should include all prominent words and phrases which the student may desire to find. I am confident that this work will fully meet his demands.

Following this is a preface prepared by the individual whom I employed as compiler of this Concordance, in which he sets forth his plan of arrangement, with an explanation of abbreviations used in this work.

MARY BAKER EDDY

PLEASANT VIEW, CONCORD, N.H.
May 15, 1903

Compiler's Preface

This Concordance contains every noun, verb, adjective, and adverb in Science and Health, together with certain pronouns, prepositions, and conjunctions, which were deemed of sufficient importance to be introduced.

The numbers indicating page and line refer to the word under consideration and not necessarily to the beginning of the line quoted.

The letters preceding the numbers are abbreviations of the chapters where the references are to be found. A * following a page number indicates that the reference is in the quotation in italics at the head of the chapter indicated.

A special feature of the work is to be found in the fact that every noun of frequent occurrence is provided with sub-titles. These sub-titles are arranged in alphabetical order, under their respective nouns, and consist of adjectives or other qualifying words or phrases, preserving in every case the exact phraseology of Science and Health. By this method, all that the author of the Christian Science textbook has said on any given subject will be found grouped in one place. For example: the spiritual man is often referred to as the "idea of God." More than twenty references to this subject will be found in the sub-title "idea of" under the principal word "God." The sub-titles also enable those who are familiar with the text to look up passages by means of such words as God, Life, Truth, Love, Mind, matter, error, etc., without searching through several hundred references.

A few adjectives also, such as human, material, mortal, spiritual, etc., are furnished with sub-titles.

Certain words occurring in some places as nouns, are used in other places as verbs or adjectives. For example: the word "healing" is used as a noun, an adjective, and a participle. All such words appearing more than fifty times are classified and grouped under their respective parts of speech. If used less than fifty times in all, these words are not so separated.

Every reference to the author of Science and Health will be found under the heading "Eddy, Mrs. Mary Baker."

An index to the Marginal Headings in Science and Health will be found in Appendix A.

Every Scriptural quotation is indexed under every important word in it, in the same manner as other words, and is followed by the book, chapter, and verse where it may be found in the Bible. A separate list of all the books, chapters, and verses of the Bible from which quotations have been taken for use in SCIENCE AND HEALTH will be found in Appendix B.

In the hope that this work may be of service to the many thousand students of our beloved textbook, and an incentive to a more profound study of the life-giving Science elucidated therein, and in grateful acknowledgment of the loving wisdom of its Founder and our Leader, which has alone made this book a possibility, the following pages are committed to the public.

THE COMPILER

Preface to the New Edition

In this edition of the Concordance, compiled from the 1908 edition of SCIENCE AND HEALTH, the plan of the original Concordance has been retained in its entirety. In preparing the references great care has been exercised to select the context which would most successfully suggest the entire sentence in which the indexed word occurs, and increased facilities for the topical study of the textbook have been provided in a rearrangement of some of the sub-titles. All references not found in the current edition of SCIENCE AND HEALTH have been omitted; and about five thousand new references have been inserted. Of these nearly sixteen hundred were needed for new words not hitherto indexed; and more than thirty-four hundred were required to index the changes in SCIENCE AND HEALTH which have been made by its author since the first Concordance was printed.

Mrs. Eddy has said: "I have revised SCIENCE AND HEALTH only to give a clearer and fuller expression of its original meaning" (SCIENCE AND HEALTH, 361-21). Some idea of the extent of her recent revisions may be gained from the above figures, which thus serve to enhance an appreciative recognition of the indefatigable labors of our Leader in the interests of humanity.

ALBERT F. CONANT
Compiler

This edition of the Concordance to SCIENCE AND HEALTH has been compiled from the 1910 edition of the Christian Science textbook as finally revised by its author. It therefore includes the changes and additions made by Mrs. Eddy subsequent to 1908, the date of the former compilation, and agrees with the current editions.

BOSTON, MASSACHUSETTS, January, 1916

List of Abbreviations

The abbreviations made use of in this Concordance are as follows:—

CHAPTER TITLES IN SCIENCE AND HEALTH

pref. Preface
pr. . . .Prayer
a. . . . .Atonement and Eucharist
m. . . . .Marriage
sp. . .Christian Science versus Spiritualism
an. . .Animal Magnetism Unmasked
s. . . . .Science, Theology, Medicine
ph. . . .Physiology
f. . . . .Footsteps of Truth
c. . . . .Creation

b. . . . .Science of Being
o. . . . .Some Objections Answered
p. . . . .Christian Science Practice
t. . . . .Teaching Christian Science
r. . . . .Recapitulation
k. . . . .Key to the Scriptures
g. . . . .Genesis
ap. . . .The Apocalypse
gl. . . .Glossary
fr. . . .Fruitage

The words "Christian Science" have been abbreviated in the lines to C.S.

BOOKS OF THE BIBLE

Gen. . . . . .Genesis	*Ezek.* . . . . .Ezekiel	*Eph.* . . . . .Ephesians
Exod. . . . . . . .Exodus	*Dan.* . . . . .Daniel	*Phil.* . . . . .Philippians
Lev. . . . . .Leviticus	*Hos.* . . . . .Hosea	*Col.* . . . . .Colossians
Deut. . . . . . . .Deuteronomy	*Hab.* . . . . .Habakkuk	*I Thess.* . . . . . .I Thessalonians
I Kings . . . . . .I Kings	*Matt.* . . . . . . .Matthew	*II Thess.* . . . . .II Thessalonians
Job . . . . .Job	*Mark* . . . . . .Mark	*I Tim.* . . . . . .I Timothy
Psal. . . . . .Psalms	*Luke* . . . . . . .Luke	*II Tim.* . . . . .II Timothy
Prov. . . . . . . .Proverbs	*John* . . . . . . .John	*Heb.* . . . . .Hebrews
Eccl. . . . . .Ecclesiastes	*Acts* . . . . . . .Acts	*Jas.* . . . . .James
Song. . . . . .Song of Solomon	*Rom.* . . . . . . .Romans	*I Pet.* . . . . . .I Peter
Isa. . . . . .Isaiah	*I Cor.* . . . . .I Corinthians	*II Pet.* . . . . . .II Peter
Jer. . . . . .Jeremiah	*II Cor.* . . . . . .II Corinthians	*I John* . . . . . .I John
Lam. . . . . .Lamentations	*Gal.* . . . . .Galatians	*Rev.* . . . . .Revelation

A Complete
CONCORDANCE
to
Science and Health with Key to the Scriptures

A

Aaron's
gl 595–13 The Urim and Thummim, . . . on A· breast
abandon
s 129–21 We must a· pharmaceutics, and take up
f 254–21 a· so fast as practical the material,
o 348–23 would it not be well to a· the defence,
p 400–11 and a· their material beliefs.
g 534– 1 Hence she is first to a· the belief in the
abandoned
pref x–18 a· as hopeless by regular medical attendants.
b 304–32 is a· to conjectures, left in the hands of
p 382–30 medicines I had taken only a· me to
abandonment
p 374–31 expels it through the a· of a belief,
abashed
p 439–15 turned from the a· witnesses,
g 532–19 Ashamed before Truth, error shrank a·
abate
ph 196–24 help to a· sickness and to destroy it.
p 373–25 decomposition, or deposit will a·,
406–14 Sin and sickness will a· and seem less real
abatement
f 219–31 but we may look for an a· of these evils ;
Abel (see also **Abel's**)
g 540–26 And A·, he also brought of the— Gen. 4 : 4.
540–31 A· takes his offering from the firstlings
541– 7 [Jehovah] had respect unto A·,— Gen. 4 : 4.
541–11 Cain rose up against A· his brothor, Gen. 4 : 8.
541–20 Where is A· thy brother?— Gen. 4 : 9.
gl 579– 8 definition of
Abel's
g 541– 4 Cain seeks A· life, instead of
abetted
p 439–24 You aided and a· Fear and Health-laws.
abeyance
p 405– 6 to hold hatred in a· with kindness,
abide
a 50–16 They must a· in him and he in them,
55–28 that he may a· with you forever."— John 14 : 16.
b 274–12 The senses of Spirit a· in Love,
p 381–27 a· by the rule of perpetual harmony,
t 456–19 One must a· in the morale of truth
456–23 understand and a· by the divine Principle
462–14 a· strictly by its rules, heed every statement,
r 495–16 Allow nothing but His likeness to a· in your
abides
b 304–17 produced by its Principle, . . . and a· with it.
p 384–25 fear subsides and the conviction a· that
abideth
b 325– 5 Such a one a· in Life,
abiding
b 289–11 To suppose that sin, . . . revenge, have life a·
327– 1 there is no a· pleasure in evil,
p 390–21 Dismiss it with an a· conviction that
405–24 The a· consciousness of wrong-doing tends
r 495–30 a· steadfastly in wisdom, Truth, and Love.
abiding-place
f 244– 9 goodness would have no a·
b 282–14 straight line finds no a· in a curve,

abilities
s 128–15 the latent a· and possibilities of man.
ability
God-given
ph 182–26 God-given a· to demonstrate Mind's sacred
healing
p 410–29 until the practitioner's healing a· is
t 449–12 registers his healing a· and fitness to teach.
human
a 52–25 speaking of human a· to reflect divine power,
infinite
r 494–17 Jesus demonstrated . . . the infinite a· of Spirit,
lesser
sp 95–14 greater or lesser a· of a Christian Scientist
one's
c 260–15 distrust of one's a· . . . often hampers
your
ph 182– 1 will diminish your a· to become a Scientist,

_____

sp 92–24 the a· to make nothing of error will be
s 128–11 a· to exceed their ordinary capacity.
130–22 a· of Spirit to make the body harmonious,
ph 187– 9 attributes to some material god . . . an a·
f 218–18 without faith in God's willingness and a·
p 393–14 nothing can vitiate the a· and power
404–25 increases his a· to master evil
405–25 wrong-doing tends to destroy the a· to do right.
428–19 We must realize the a· of mental might
g 524–29 Could Spirit . . . give matter a· to sin and suffer?
555–27 or that Truth confers the a· to

able
a 49–23 a·, through Truth, Life, and Love, to triumph
sp 85–10 a· to read the human mind after this manner
93– 1 substantial and a· to control the body?
95– 9 a· to discern the thought of the sick
s 127–27 Science . . . is alone a· to interpret God aright.
137–10 Who or what is it that is a· to do the work,
145– 3 caught its sweet tones, . . . without being a· to
161– 6 a· to nullify the action of the flames,
ph 191–31 Truth is a· to cast out the ills of the flesh.
196–11 "Fear him which is a· to— Matt. 10 : 28.
f 217–24 you will be a· to demonstrate this
235–24 physicians should be a· to teach it.
249– 8 no mortal nor material power as a· to destroy.
253–13 there is no cause . . . a· to make you sick
b 304– 8 nor any other creature, shall be a·— Rom. 8 : 39.
323– 2 will not be a· to glean . . . without striving
329–16 until one is a· to prevent bad results,
o 343– 9 one might not be a· to say with the apostle,
345–21 Anybody, who is a· to perceive the incongruity
345–22 ought to be a· to discern the distinction
352– 2 did not sufficiently understand God to be a·
359–24 "God is a· to raise you up from sickness ;"
p 385– 3 a· to undergo without sinking fatigues and
387–11 we are a· to rest in Truth, refreshed by
423– 2 and may not be a· to mend the bone,
r 488– 4 a· to banish a severe malady, the cure shows
493–18 Mind must be found . . . a· to destroy all ills.
g 530–11 as a· to feed and clothe man as He doth the
547–12 Agassiz was a· to see in the egg the
555–16 Jesus was a· to present himself unchanged
ap 568– 4 Science is a· to destroy this lie, called evil.

ablest
  g 553–10   One of our *a·* naturalists has said :

ablutions
  p 413–12   daily *a·* of an infant are no more natural
  431–29   I practise daily *a·* and perform my

abnormal
  s 120–14   health is normal and disease is *a·*.
  p 423–27   Ossification or any *a·* condition

abnormally
  p 377–13   suddenly weak or *a·* strong,

abode
  b 280– 5   light and harmony which are the *a·* of Spirit,
  292–23   and *a·* not in the truth, because— *John* 8 : 44.

abolish
  m 58–30   nothing can *a·* the cares of marriage.
  f 225–19   *a·* the whipping-post and slave market ;
  225–23   Legally to *a·* unpaid servitude

abolished
  f 224–29   the Soul-inspired motto, "Slavery is *a·*."
  226– 1   African slavery was *a·* in our land.

abolition
  f 225–24   *a·* of mental slavery is a more difficult task.

abomination
  gl 588– 4   "worketh *a·* or maketh a lie." — *Rev.* 21 : 27.

abortive
  t 459–14   Any attempt to . . . must prove *a·*.

abound
  f 202–26   Truth should "much more *a·*." — *Rom.* 5 : 20.
  223–29   sin will much more *a·* as truth urges
  b 320– 4   Metaphysics *a·* in the Bible,
  g 512–11   *a·* in the spiritual atmosphere of Mind,

abounds
  f 202–25   Error *a·* where Truth should

about
  pref xi–27   *a·* the year 1867.
  pr 9–28   Then why make long prayers *a·* it
  13–16   before we tell Him . . . *a·* it.
  a 25– 9   went daily *a·* his Father's business.
  33–13   their Master was *a·* to suffer violence
  41–18   *a·* three centuries after the crucifixion.
  41–26   his apostles still went *a·* doing good
  43–29   beliefs *a·* life, substance, and
  52– 1   From early boyhood he was *a·* his
  an 105–26   will be millstones *a·* his neck,
  s 121–26   revolves *a·* the sun once a year,
  125–19   material theories *a·* laws of health
  132–16   their materialistic beliefs *a·* God.
  134–12   and so it came *a·* that human rights
  137–15   the common report *a·* him.
  153–30   loquacious tattling *a·* disease,
  155– 2   forgets all *a·* the accident,
  ph 169– 9   it always came *a·* as I had foretold.
  172– 3   Theorizing *a·* man's development
  176– 7   taking no thought *a·* food
  193–13   In *a·* ten minutes he opened his eyes
  197–12   *a·* moral and spiritual law,
  f 201–16   we shall not hug our tatters close *a·* us.
  202–24   Our beliefs *a·* a Supreme Being
  222–14   Taking less thought *a·* what he should **eat**
  222–15   *a·* the economy of living
  230–13   so as to bring *a·* certain evil results,
  232– 5   The beliefs we commonly entertain *a·*
  237– 3   On being questioned *a·* it she answered
  237–17   theories or thoughts *a·* sickness.
  237–24   to hear *a·* the fallacy of matter
  238–28   no time for gossip *a·* false law
  c 260–26   by conversation *a·* the body,
  261–14   walking *a·* as actively as the
  b 305–31   The Sadducees reasoned falsely *a·* the
  328– 6   Understanding little *a·* the divine
  328–12   destroys human delusions *a·* Him
  o 352–30   not irrational to tell the truth *a·* ghosts.
  357–18   false notions *a·* the Divine Being
  357–20   wrong notions *a·* God must have
  p 363– 6   which hung loosely *a·* her shoulders,
  372– 6   One theory *a·* this mortal mind is,
  374– 8   I never thought of and knew nothing *a·*,
  389– 6   The less we know or think *a·* hygiene,
  389–16   metaphors *a·* the fount and stream,
  396– 7   a discouraging remark *a·* recovery,
  413–27   *a·* disease, health-laws, and death,
  414–30   is not brought *a·* by divine Love.
  416–27   If they ask *a·* their disease,
  416–29   they think too much *a·* their ailments,
  419–13   with which to move itself *a·*
  424–23   while others are thinking *a·* your patients
  425–32   Discard all notions *a·* lungs,
  t 445–30   Recalling Jefferson's words *a·* slavery,
  g 521–19   *a·* creation in the book of Genesis.
  529– 4   It came *a·*, also, that instruments were
  536–23   hedge *a·* their achievements with thorns.

about
  g 544–17   The first statement *a·* evil,
  548–20   statements now current, *a·* birth and
  553–27   ancient superstition *a·* the creation
  555– 8   not comprehend what you say *a·* error."

above
  pr 11–24   but if we desire holiness *a·* all else, we shall
  16–20   Only as we rise *a·* all material sensuousness
  a 18–18   could conciliate no nature *a·* his own,
  34–25   ascend far *a·* their apprehension.
  35–17   his spiritual and final ascension *a·* matter,
  44–26   a method infinitely *a·* that of human invention.
  46–21   his exaltation *a·* all material conditions ;
  46–28   rose *a·* the physical knowledge of his disciples,
  49–22   is *a·* the reach of human wrath,
  53–12   *a·* and contrary to the world's religious sense.
  sp 74– 8   a sprout which has risen *a·* the soil.
  77–26   The departed would gradually rise *a·* ignorance
  98– 3   elevation of existence *a·* mortal discord
  98–15   *a·* the loosening grasp of creeds,
  99–19   may possess natures *a·* some others
  s 118– 3   an inference far *a·* the merely ecclesiastical
  123–13   Divine Science, rising *a·* physical theories,
  147–20   lifts you high *a·* the perishing fossils
  153–12   highest attenuation . . . rises *a·* matter into
  ph 167– 7   only as we live *a·* corporeal sense
  174– 9   rising *a·* material standpoints,
  189– 6   raises the human thought *a·* the cruder theories
  f 238–29   place the fact *a·* the falsehood,
  240–10   the Principle is *a·* what it reflects,
  246– 8   by no means a material germ rising . . . *a·* his
  c 262–12   rise *a·* the testimony of the material senses,
  262–13   *a·* the mortal to the immortal idea of God.
  266–30   He is *a·* sin or frailty.
  b 269–11   Metaphysics is *a·* physics,
  302–16   always beyond and *a·* the mortal illusion
  307–31   *A·* error's awful din, blackness, and chaos,
  313– 8   With the oil of gladness *a·* thy— *Heb.* 1 : 9.
  318–16   Is the sick man sinful *a·* all others?
  p 365– 9   enable them to rise *a·* the supposed necessity
  373–21   you must rise *a·* both fear and sin.
  379–14   Had he known . . . he would have risen *a·* the
  385– 7   divine law, rising *a·* the human.
  394–16   that he should not try to rise *a·* his
  400–18   By lifting thought *a·* error, or disease,
  405– 3   any man, who is *a·* the lowest type
  407–14   lifting humanity *a·* itself
  437–30   bar of Truth, which ranks *a·* the lower Court
  t 448–12   C. S. rises *a·* the evidence of the
  448–13   but if you have not risen *a·* sin yourself,
  450–19   evil will boast itself *a·* good.
  451–17   If . . . spiritual, they come from *a·*,
  r 471–26   interprets God as *a·* mortal sense.
  493–13   A full answer to the *a·* question
  g 505–15   which were *a·* the firmament :— *Gen.* 1 : 7.
  511–20   and fowl that may fly *a·* the earth— *Gen.* 1 : 20.
  511–29   The fowls, which fly *a·* the earth
  512– 2   aspirations soaring beyond and *a·* corporeality
  520–28   immortal creating thought is from *a·*,
  521– 1   Knowledge of this lifts man *a·* the sod,
  521– 2   *a·* earth and its environments,
  523–11   comes from beneath, not from *a·*.
  531–11   rise *a·* all material and physical sense,
  ap 558–15   it has for you a light *a·* the sun,
  569–18   not struggling to lift their heads *a·* the

Abraham
  b 333–23   *A·*, Jacob, Moses, and the prophets
  333–29   "Before *A·* was, I am ;"— *John* 8 : 58.
  334– 2   and therefore antedated *A·* ;
  t 444–24   part from these opponents as did *A·*
  g 501– *   *appeared unto A·, unto Isaac, and*— *Exod.* 6 : 3.
  gl 579–10   definition of

abroad
  a 29– 2   take up arms against error at home and *a·*.

abscess
  f 251– 3   an *a·* should not grow more painful

absence
of law
  p 391–18   Injustice declares the *a·* of law.
of light
  f 215–17   only a mortal sense of the *a·* of light,
of other proofs
  p 363–28   In the *a·* of other proofs, was her grief
of pain
  ph 186–26   If pain is as real as the *a·* of pain,
of solar time
  g 504–18   words which indicate, in the *a·* of solar time,
of something
  ph 186–12   It is nothing, because it is the *a·* of something.
of soul
  b 311–16   sense of temporary loss or *a·* of soul,
of truth
  sp 92–30   when it is merely the *a·* of truth,
  ph 186–11   a negation, because it is the *a·* of truth.

absence

suppositional

f 215–20   the suppositional *a·* of Life, God,

---

ph 173–14   Spirit's contrary, the *a·* of Spirit.
    186–13   because it presupposes the *a·* of God,
f 207–25   errors, which presuppose the *a·* of Truth,
b 282–29   the opposite of God or God's *a·*,
    287– 9   We call the *a·* of Truth, *error.*
    287–15   how can He be absent or suggest the *a·* of
g 504–31   supposition of the *a·* of Spirit.
    555– 2   and that health attends the *a·* of
gl 584–28   the *a·* of substance, life, or intelligence.

absent

pr 14– 3   "*a·* from the body" — *II Cor.* 5 : 8.
    14–21   because the Ego is *a·* from the body,
sp 82– 2   We think of an *a·* friend as easily as
    82– 4   It is no more difficult to read the *a·* mind
s 130–32   no longer imagine evil to be . . . and good *a·*?
ph 179– 5   Science can heal the sick, who are *a·* from
f 216–29   *a·* from the body, — *II Cor.* 5 : 8.
    250–21   and the mind seems to be *a·*.
b 287–14   how can He be *a·* or suggest the absence of
p 383–10   *a·* from the body, — *II Cor.* 5 : 8.
    439– 6   Death testified that he was *a·* from
gl 581–25   *a·* from the body, — *II Cor.* 5 : 8.

absolute

pr 1– 2   *a·* faith that all things are possible to God,
    3–16   demands *a·* consecration of thought,
a 41–21   the divine healing of *a·* Science.
sp 72–11   (in *a·* Science) Soul, or God, is the only
s 107– 5   final revelation of the *a·* divine Principle
    109– 9   and thus proved *a·* and divine.
    109–20   I won my way to *a·* conclusions
    116–31   Mind in a finite form is an *a·* impossibility.
    142–10   Truth, alone can furnish us with *a·* evidence.
    151– 6   erring, finite, human mind has an *a·* need of
ph 177– 5   divine Mind's healing power and *a·* control
f 219– 4   Mind should be, and is, supreme, *a·*, and final.
    254–16   During the sensual ages, *a·* C. S. may not
c 262 15   the *a·* centre and circumference of his being.
b 269–21   testimony of the material senses is neither *a·*
    274–23   Divine Science is *a·*, and permits no
    283–11   Principle is *a·*.
    325–15   *a·* meaning of the apostolic words
o 341–17   facts are so *a·* and numerous in support of
    344– 2   it claims God as the only *a·* Life and Soul,
p 388–22   food does not affect the *a·* Life of man,
    423–26   which ultimately asserts its *a·* supremacy.
t 448–24   pursuit of instructions opposite to *a·* C. S.
    454–12   the doctrine of *a·* C. S.,
r 465– 4   *A·* C. S. pervades its statements,
    465–12   They refer to one *a·* God.
    483–21   The spirit of C. S., if not the *a·* letter.
    484– 2   until its *a·* Science is reached.
g 507– 2   the *a·* formations instituted by Mind,
    520– 7   The *a·* ideal, man, is no more seen nor
ap 573 28   This is indeed a foretaste of *a·* C. S.

absolutely

pr 14–10   to be *a·* governed by divine Love,
s 123– 9   the most *a·* weak and inharmonious creature
ph 167–29   timid conservatism is *a·* inadmissible.
    182–10   for one *a·* destroys the other,
o 355–21   statement that the teachings . . . are "*a·* false,
p 372–14   When man demonstrates C. S. *a·*,
g 549–30   He *a·* drops from his summit,
ap 565–17   will eventually rule . . . imperatively, *a·*,

absoluteness

o 345– 7   When . . . His *a·* is set forth,

absolution

p 364–12   declaring the *a·* of the penitent.

absorb

s 147–15   never . . . can *a·* the whole meaning
g 556–13   C. S. may *a·* the attention of sage and

absorbed

a 52– 7   their senses . . . *a·* the material evidence of sin,
sp 74– 7   the acorn, already *a·* into a sprout
    91–16   *A·* in material selfhood we discern . . . but faintly
c 259– 1   Man is not *a·* in Deity,
    261–10   turns away from the body with such *a·* interest
b 309–31   never *a·* nor limited by its own formations.
    331– 7   God would not be reflected but *a·*,

absorption

c 265–11   by no means suggests man's *a·* into Deity

abstinence

f 220–24   Finding his health failing, he gave up his *a·*,

abstract

t 459–24   To mortal sense C. S. seems *a·*,
r 470–11   Divine Science explains the *a·* statement
ap 558–11   To mortal sense Science seems . . . obscure, *a·*,

absurd

m 67–19   The notion . . . is too *a·* for consideration,
f 208–14   *a·* to suppose that matter can both cause and
    217– 3   notion of such a possibility is more *a·* than
r 485– 3   *Material sense* is an *a·* phrase,
    495– 7   and it would be *a·* to try.
g 550–29   not so hideous and *a·* as the supposition

absurdities

o 354– 3   Are the protests of C. S. . . . *a·*,"
g 551– 1   material senses must father these *a·*,

absurdity

s 163–28   humiliating view of so much *a·*,
r 472–21   and we should have a self-evident *a·*

abundant

ph 188–25   and you have an *a·* or scanty crop

abundantly

g 511–20   Let the waters bring forth *a·* — *Gen.* 1 : 20.
    512– 6   which the waters brought forth *a·*, — *Gen.* 1 : 21.
    548–25   he would have blessed the human race more *a·*.

abuse

ph 175– 9   What an *a·* of natural beauty to say that a rose,
t 446–32   oftentimes subjects you to its *a·*.
    455–22   renders any *a·* of the mission an impossibility.
ap 560–22   *A·* of the motives and religion of St. Paul

abused

an 102–27   is much more likely to be *a·* by its possessor,
s 110–22   and its ideas may be temporarily *a·* and
p 410–26   If mental practice is *a·*
    430 32   was personally *a·* on those occasions.
    432–23   protested that the prisoner had *a·* him,
t 460–19   If Christian healing is *a·* by mere smatterers

abyss

ph 199–26   to walk the rope over Niagara's *a·* of waters,

academic

f 235–12   not so much *a·* education,

academics

ph 195–19   *A·* of the right sort are requisite.

accelerated

ap 569–23   comes back to him at last with *a·* force,

accept

pr 2–28   pouring forth more than we *a·*
a 54–19   would not *a·* his meek interpretation of life
sp 78–13   Then why . . . *a·* them as oracles?
    91– 9   difficult for the sinner to *a·* divine Science,
s 130– 6   and therefore they cannot *a·*.
ph 182– 8   Which, then, are we to *a·* as legitimate
f 227–24   *a·* the "glorious liberty of the — *Rom.* 8 : 21.
    231–17   Therefore we *a·* the conclusion that discords
    249– 1   Let us *a·* Science, relinquish all theories
    254–20   This task God demands us to *a·* lovingly
c 266–12   Love will force you to *a·* what best promotes
b 272–16   teachings which . . . grossness could not *a·*.
p 420–11   if they will only *a·* Truth, they can
r 494–26   Which of these . . . are you ready to *a·*?

acceptable

pr 3–31   In such a case, the only *a·* prayer
a 34– 4   "holy, *a·* unto God," — *Rom.* 12 : 1.
f 221–21   Hence semi-starvation is not *a·* to wisdom,
b 325–22   holy, *a·* unto God, — *Rom.* 12 : 1.

acceptance

f 202–12   the perception and *a·* of Truth.
b 330– 7   would meet with immediate and universal *a·*.
o 343–23   meekness and . . . are the conditions of its *a·*,
    355–22   ever offered for *a·*,"

accepted

a 39–18   "*Now*," . . . "is the *a·* time ; — *II Cor.* 6 : 2.
sp 93– 8   "Behold, *now* is the *a·* time ; — *II Cor.* 6 : 2.
s 131–24   not *a·* until the hearts of men are made ready
    132–10   it has not yet been generally *a·*.
f 248–17   Have you *a·* the mortal model?
b 316– 2   way of salvation to all who *a·* his word.
o 344–20   not included in the commonly *a·* systems ;
p 386– 2   evidence of the senses is not to be *a·*
t 461– 5   C. S. must be *a·* at this period by induction.
r 469–19   claimed no other Mind and *a·* no other,
g 552– 5   was once an *a·* theory.

accepting

s 129–23   look deep into realism instead of *a·* only
o 357– 5   not by *a·*, but by rejecting a lie.

accepts

pr 8–16   If we feel the aspiration, . . . this God *a·* ;
s 148–17   drops the true tone, and *a·* the discord.
g 520–14   thought *a·* the divine infinite calculus.
    536–24   Mortal mind *a·* the erroneous.
gl 585–20   human belief before it *a·* sin, sickness,

access

s 128–17   giving mortals *a·* to broader and higher realms.

accident

s	155– 2	Presently the child forgets all about the a·,
f	214–29	Neither age nor a· can interfere with the
	252–26	says : . . . But a touch, an a·, the law of
b	304–24	would lose harmony, if time or a· robbed
o	342–18	If . . . truth becomes an a·.
p	392–29	exercise, heredity, contagion, or a·,
	397–12	When an a· happens, you think or exclaim,
	397–15	Your thought is . . . more powerful than the a·
r	486– 4	Suppose one a· happens to the eye,

accidents

p	402–16	You say that a·, injuries, and disease kill man,
	424– 5	A· are unknown to God,
	424–10	Under divine Providence there can be no a·,

accommodate

ph	195–29	lowering the intellectual standard to a·
b	280–13	to a· its finite sense of the divisibility
	313–26	To a· himself to immature ideas

accompanied

sp	94– 8	with the demonstration which a· it,

accompanies

b	287–17	Neither understanding nor truth a· error,
g	514–18	Tenderness a· all the might imparted by Spirit.

accompaniment

f	249–28	The night-dream has less matter as its a·.

accompaniments

sp	78–16	Spiritualism with its material a·
b	310– 8	but without material a·.

accompany

f	223–21	Spiritual rationality and free thought a·
	243–11	must always a· the letter of Science
p	375– 4	belief that inflammation and pain must a·
g	553– 1	and a· their descriptions with important

accompanying

ap	573–13	A· this scientific consciousness was

accomplish

sp	77– 3	Neither do other mortals a· the
	96–32	to find means by which to a· more evil ;
o	352–31	To a· a good result, it is certainly not irrational
p	394– 8	Knowledge that we can a· the good
t	448–22	impossible for error, . . . to a· the grand results

accomplished

pref	vii–26	must declare what the pioneer has a·.
a	51–13	but when his earth-mission was a·,
b	322–10	in view of the immense work to be a·
p	365–16	healing work will be a· at one visit,
t	457– 6	than has been a· by other books.
r	484– 3	When this is a·, neither pride, prejudice,

accomplishes

g	546–28	resides in the good this system a·,

accomplishing

pr	1– 7	God's gracious means for a·
ap	571– 2	evil's hidden mental ways of a· iniquity.

accomplishment

pr	13– 8	striving for the a· of all we ask,
p	429– 7	The final demonstration takes time for its a·.

accord

m	63–16	marvel why usage should a· woman less rights
s	129– 9	be it in a· with your preconceptions or
f	202–16	immortal man, in a· with the divine Principle
b	314–31	submissive to death as being in supposed a·
	337– 9	the Son must be in a· with the Father,
p	408–16	Can drugs go of their own a· to the brain
t	455– 1	auxiliaries to aid in bringing thought into a·
g	515–23	moves in a· with Him,
	515–28	the lips of this likeness move in a· with yours.
	545–15	and do not a· infinity to Deity.

accordance

a	27–11	in strict a· with his scientific statement :
	36– 8	not in a· with God's government,
sp	96–26	shaped his course in a· with divine Science
ph	168–22	in a· with God's law, the law of Mind.
f	208–12	not in a· with the goodness of God's character
	231–26	is in a· with divine Science.
b	276– 7	in a· with the Scriptural command :
p	440–26	in a· with the divine statutes,
g	557–25	in a· with the first chapter of the
gl	597– 1	in a· with Pharisaic notions.

accorded

r	474– 4	reception a· to Truth in the early Christian era

according

pr	5–18	giving us strength a· to our day.
	6–20	To suppose that God forgives or punishes sin a·
	7–12	"a zeal . . . not a· to knowledge" — Rom. 10 : 2.
	15– 8, 9	rewards a· to motives, not a· to speech.
a	22–19	and receive a· to your deserving.
	27–32	a· to certain assumed material laws.
m	57–31	Marriage is unblest or blest, a· to the
sp	77–17	longer or shorter duration a· to the tenacity
	97– 7	A· to human belief, the lightning is fierce

according

an	100– 2	A· to the American Cyclopædia,
	105–15	courts reasonably pass sentence, a· to the
s	108– 3	A· to St. Paul, it was "the gift of the — Eph. 3 : 7.
	110–28	and demonstrated a· to Christ's command,
	113–23	A· to the Scripture, I find that God is true,
	127–11	a· to the requirements of the context.
	131–17	a· to the Scriptural saying,
	149–31	and demonstrate truth a· to Christ.
	155– 5	a· to this faith will the effect be.
	157–16	(a· to the narrative in Genesis)
	158– 5	the first prescription, a· to the "History of
	161–25	treating the case a· to his physical diagnosis,
ph	168–10	When sick (a· to belief) you rush after drugs,
	170– 1	and a· to belief, poisons the human system.
	173–22	Phrenology makes man knavish or honest a·
	175–22	was not discussed a· to Cutter
	183– 8	Can the agriculturist, a· to belief, produce
	183–10	awaiting its germination a· to the laws of
	188–26	a· to the seedlings of fear.
	189–16	it is as truly mortal mind, a· to its degree,
	189–27	A· to mortal thought, the development of
	199–16	a· as they influence them through mortal mind
f	208–28	harmonious or discordant a· to the images of
	213–28	a· as the hand, which sweeps over it,
	230–22	A· to Holy Writ, the sick are never
	233–25	When numbers have been divided a· to
	236–16	"a· to the pattern showed to thee — Heb. 8 : 5.
	239– 9	let worth be judged a· to wisdom,
	242–21	A· to the Bible, the facts of being are
	245–30	decrepitude is not a· to law,
	250–17	a· to the dream he entertains in sleep.
c	256–20	"doeth a· to His will — Dan. 4 : 35.
b	284–28	A· to C. S., the only real senses of
	320–22	for a· to that error man is mortal.
	327– 3	gaining an affection for good a· to Science,
	334–22	a· to the testimony of the corporeal senses,
	337–10	A· to divine Science, man is
o	341–15	demonstrated a· to a divine given rule,
	342–19	a system which works a· to the Scriptures
	342–30	practising pharmacy or obstetrics a· to the
	344–16	a· to the rules which disclose its merits or
	355–15	One, a· to the commands of our Master, heals
	357–23	a· to the vision of St. John in the Apocalypse.
p	362–12	A· to the custom of those days,
	370–23	A· to both medical testimony and
	404– 2	judge the case a· to C. S.
	416–19	and been developed a· to it,
	423–12	A· to Scripture, it searches
	423–17	a· to the evidence which matter presents.
	423–25	a· to the law of Mind, which ultimately asserts
	425– 7	leading points included (a· to belief)
	429–23	a· to the calculations of natural science.
	435–26	a· to the law of Spirit, God.
t	443–11	A· to our statute, Material Law is a liar
	449–23	attracted or repelled a· to personal merit
	457–16	both sides were beautiful a· to their degree ;
r	473–22	test its unerring Science a· to his rule,
	478– 4	Even a· to the teachings of natural science,
	490–16	since he is so already, a· to C. S.
g	502–19	a· to the teachings of C. S.
	516– 1	note how true, a· to C. S.,
	519–28	a· to the apprehension of divine Science.
	520–11	a· to the calendar of time.
	523–14	a· to the best scholars, there are clear evidences
	526–29	The name Eden, a· to Cruden, means pleasure,
	528–28	a· to this narrative, surgery was first performed
	533–17	A· to this belief, the rib taken from
	543–22	found, a· to divine Science, to be the
	545– 4	a· to the record, material man was
	549–13	A· to recent lore, successive generations
ap	565–19	This immaculate idea, . . . a· to the Revelator,
gl	584– 6	Mind measures time a· to the good that is

accordingly

s	152–19	and he recovered a·.
p	385–29	and you are thirsty a·,

accords

ph	192–18	this teaching a· with Science and harmony.

account

all

f	245– 6	became insane and lost all a· of time.

continued

g	521–20	but the continued a· is mortal and material.

its own

m	65–25	is never desirable on its own a·.

scientific

g	523–24	spiritually scientific a· of creation,

Scriptural

g	523– 2	perusal of the Scriptural a·

second

g	526–24	second biblical a· is a picture of error
	537–20	second a· in Genesis — is to depict the falsity of

account
  this
  g 538–26   This *a·* is given, not of immortal man, but
  gl 579– 4   On this *a·* this chapter is added.
  your
  p 405–16   until you have balanced your *a·* with God.

  sp 90– 2   how then can we *a·* for their primal origin?
  s 123–31   but not on that *a·* is it less scientific.
  b 290– 6   on *a·* of that single experience,
  o 357–11   or makes man capable of suffering on *a·* of
  p 379–20   not dying on *a·* of the state of her blood,
  386–11   not because of the climate, but on *a·* of the
  392– 5   broken moral law should be taken into *a·*
  396–18   on *a·* of the tenacity of belief in its truth,
  g 553–21   theory . . . to *a·* for human origin,

accounted
  m 69–27   But they which shall be *a·* worthy — *Luke* 20 : 35.
  b 316–26   That man was *a·* a criminal
  o 343–31   is often *a·* a heretic.

accounts
  a 30– 8   This *a·* for his struggles in Gethsemane
  s 139– 5   Scriptures are full of *a·* of the triumph of
  g 523–27   *a·* become more . . . closely intertwined

accredited
  a 18–10   Jesus acted boldly, against the *a·* evidence
  o 358–32   than they have in their own *a·* . . . pastors,

accretion
  m 68–27   C. S. presents unfoldment, not *a·* ;

accumulated
  p 380–23   evidence of which has *a·* to prove

accumulates
  p 399– 8   No gastric gas *a·*, . . . apart from

accurate
  sp 92–17   The portrayal is still graphically *a·*,
  c 255– 9   afforded no foundation for *a·* views

accurately
  sp 84–32   we can know the truth more *a·* than the
  s 129– 3   the reasoning of an *a·* stated syllogism
  b 283–26   unless its Science be *a·* stated.
  o 349–14   conveying the teachings of divine Science *a·*
  t 447– 9   incapable of knowing or judging *a·*

accursed
  a 25– 8   shed upon "the *a·* tree," — *see Gal.* 3 : 13.
  b 338–20   when matter, as that which is *a·*,
  338–27   Jehovah declared the ground was *a·* ;

accusation
  a 53– 2   latter *a·* was true, but not in their meaning.
  f 203– 9   The *a·* of the rabbis,

accusations
  a 52–29   The *a·* of the Pharisees were
  s 133–25   one of the Jewish *a·* against him
  ap 564–10   The author is convinced that the *a·* against

accused
  ap 568–16   *a·* them before our God — *Rev.* 12 : 10.

accuser
  t 459–25   Neither is he a false *a·*.
  ap 568–16   *a·* of our brethren is cast down, — *Rev.* 12 : 10.
  568–29   the *a·* is not there, and Love sends forth

accusers
  a 50–21   what would his *a·* have said?

accustomed
  c 261–13   noted actor was *a·* night after night
  t 452– 7   Walking in the light, we are *a·* to
  452– 8   eyes *a·* to darkness are pained by the light.

ache
  p 393–18   Have no fear that matter can *a·*,

aches
  f 212– 3   tooth . . . extracted sometimes *a·* again in belief,

achieved
  f 254–17   may not be *a·* prior to the change

achievement
  m 63–25   the *a·* of a nobler race for legislation,
  ph 199–21   devotion of thought to an honest *a·*
  199–22   makes the *a·* possible.
  t 456– 2   adverse to its highest hope and *a·*.

achievements
  g 536–23   and hedge about their *a·* with thorns.

achieves
  t 459– 5   as mortal man *a·* no worldly honors except by

achieving
  c 260–13   Science reveals the possibility of *a·*

aching
  ph 165–17   distressed stomachs and *a·* heads.
  c 261–17   sat *a·* in his chair till his cue was spoken,
  b 295– 1   The belief that a severed limb is *a·*

acid
  p 401– 9   (as when an alkali is destroying an *a·*,)
  422–14   As when an *a·* and alkali meet and

acknowledge
  a 20–24   Material belief is slow to *a·*
  25– 1   Thomas was forced to *a·* how complete
  sp 94–22   but one returned . . . to *a·* the divine Principle
  s 151–29   narrow way is to see and *a·* this fact,
  ph 166–20   waiting for the hour . . . in which to *a·* Him,
  169–30   Whatever teaches man to . . . *a·* other powers
  f 228–26   to *a·* any other power is to dishonor God.
  239–17   and whom we *a·* and obey as God.
  p 400–10   *a·* the supremacy of divine Mind,
  425–21   the less we *a·* matter or its laws,
  t 450–16   many are reluctant to *a·* that they have yielded ;
  461–19   If you commit a crime, should you *a·* to yourself
  r 497– 5   We *a·* and adore one supreme and infinite God
  497– 6   We *a·* His Son, one Christ ;
  497– 9   We *a·* God's forgiveness of sin in the
  497–13   We *a·* Jesus' atonement as the
  497–16   we *a·* that man is saved through Christ,
  497–20   We *a·* that the crucifixion of Jesus
  g 551–14   it does not *a·* the method of divine Mind,

acknowledged
  pr 4–15   if not *a·* in audible words,
  a 31– 4   Jesus *a·* no ties of the flesh.
  54– 5   The world *a·* not his righteousness,
  f 227– 2   and the rights of man are fully known and *a·*.
  233– 9   perfection is seen and *a·* only by degrees.
  239–23   Mortal mind is the *a·* seat of human motives.
  p 385– 1   power of Mind . . . will be *a·*.
  402– 3   branch of its healing which will be last *a·*.
  408– 3   not *a·* nor discovered to be error
  427–24   Mind, governing all, must be *a·* as supreme
  r 492–17   until one is *a·* to be the victor.
  ap 572–18   seen and *a·* that matter must disappear.
  gl 587– 3   The rights of woman *a·*
  588– 6   Divine Science understood and *a·*.

acknowledging
  s 157– 9   *a·* that the divine Mind has all power,
  r 491–13   only by *a·* the supremacy of Spirit,
  g 521–10   *a·* now and forever God's supremacy,

acknowledgment
  sp 91–15   but is the *a·* of them.
  f 226– 8   asking a fuller *a·* of the rights of man
  p 372–28   a just *a·* of Truth and of what it has done for us

acme
  ap 577–30   his vision is the *a·* of this Science

Aconitum
  s 152–30   Jahr, from *A·* to *Zincum oxydatum,*

acorn
  sp 74– 7   the *a·*, already absorbed into a sprout

acquaint
  s 107–13   thoughts *a·* themselves intelligently with God.
  b 324–12   "*a·* now thyself with Him, — *Job* 22 : 21.
  p 403–24   Never . . . and then *a·* your patient with it.

acquaintance
  a 24– 4   *A·* with the original texts,
  sp 84–14   *A·* with the Science of being enables us

acquainted
  p 432– 3   *a·* with the plaintiff, Personal Sense,

acquiescence
  a 48–26   Pilate was drawn into *a·* with the demands

acquires
  s 158–21   *a·* an educated appetite for strong drink,

acquit
  pr 11– 9   The moral law, which has the right to *a·*

across
  pref vii– 9   *a·* a night of error should dawn the morning
  sp 74–26   There is no bridge *a·* the gulf which divides

act
  motive and
  p 376–14   more life . . . in one good motive and *a·*,
  natural
  a 44–24   On the contrary, it was a divinely natural *a·*,
  not a supernatural
  a 44–23   but it was not a supernatural *a·*.
  of commending
  sp 92–13   represents the serpent in the *a·* of commending
  of describing
  sp 79– 1   The *a·* of describing disease — its symptoms,
  of doing good
  f 202–32   in the *a·* of doing good,
  of healing
  ph 182– 1   The *a·* of healing the sick through divine Mind
  of homicide
  p 440–13   disobedience to God, or an *a·* of homicide.
  of reading
  sp 83–31   *a·* of reading mortal mind investigates

act

of yielding
p 413– 3 The a· of yielding one's thoughts to the
slain in the
b 290–28 murderer, though slain in the a·, does not
wicked
an 104–32 human mind must move the body to a wicked a·?

———

pr 12– 7 making it a· more powerfully on the body
s 160– 3 systems of physics a· against metaphysics,
160–24 If muscles can cease to a· and become rigid
ph 176– 8 left the stomach and bowels free to a·
185–28 This is because erroneous methods a·
f 250– 4 suppose . . . unintelligence to a· like
c 264–11 we must a· as possessing all power
b 283– 9 states of mortal mind which a·, react,
p 368–25 matter has no consciousness . . . it cannot a· ;
384– 2 Can matter, . . . a· without mind?
394– 9 stimulates the system to a· in the direction
397–25 than when they a·, walk, see,
402–25 believe that they cannot a· voluntarily
424–17 should not a· against your influence
435– 9 an a· which should result in good to himself
gl 582– 8 strength, animation, and power to a·.

acted

a 18–10 a· boldly, against the accredited evidence
20– 4 a· and spake as he was moved, . . . by Spirit.
s 148– 5 a· in direct disobedience to them.

acting

a 43–25 a· under spiritual law in defiance of matter
m 67–11 a· up to his highest understanding,
s 160–23 never capable of a· contrary to mental
ph 172–32 a· through the five physical senses
178–18 Mortal mind, a· from the basis of sensation
p 397– 2 a· beneficially or injuriously on the health,
417–13 all causation is Mind, a· through spiritual law.
435–23 to punish a man for a· justly.
436– 8 a· within the limits of the divine law,
t 452–25 by right talking and wrong a·,
452–28 A· from sinful motives destroys your power
r 495–11 life-giving power of Truth a· on human belief,

action

all
ph 187–23 divine Mind includes all a· and volition,
p 419–20 Mind produces all a·.
basis of
s 160– 5 forsake the material for the spiritual basis of a·,
being and its
s 151–18 Fear never stopped being and its a·.
belief and
f 253–23 you can alter this wrong belief and a·
call into
ph 173–32 call into a· less faith than Buddhism
cause
s 160–15 and so cause a· ; but what does anatomy say
changed the
ph 185– 4 My metaphysical treatment changed the a· of
classify
ph 187–25 The human mind tries to classify a· as
devoid of
p 399–21 Without this force the body is devoid of a·,
diminishes the
p 420–20 It increases or diminishes the a·,
discordant
f 239–25 produces every discordant a· of the body.
diseased
p 428– 1 no inaction, diseased a·, overaction,
divine
an 104–15 which indicates the rightness of all divine a·,
effect or
t 463–30 Such seeming medical effect or a· is
entire
r 494– 2 and to govern man's entire a·?
error in
f 207– 7 Error of statement leads to error in a·.
error of
g 550–15 Error of thought is reflected in error of a·.
every
p 407–24 perfect, harmonious in every a·.
excited
p 377–23 the morbid or excited a· of any organ.
feeling and
p 393–11 and govern its feeling and a·.
form, and
b 301– 3 mirror, repeats the color, form, and a·
God rests in
g 519–25 God rests in a·.
harmonious
b 283– 6 its perpetual and harmonious a·.
p 420– 3 no metastasis, no stoppage of harmonious a·,
r 480–14 Harmonious a· proceeds from Spirit, God.
higher plane of
c 256– 2 Advancing to a higher plane of a·,
impedes
ph 166– 4 Mind is all that feels, acts, or impedes a·.

action

injurious
t 451–28 It is the injurious a· of one mortal mind
is erroneous
r 480–15 its a· is erroneous and presupposes
is harmonious
f 239–26 If . . . a· is harmonious.
latter
ph 187–17 Anatomy allows the mental cause of the
latter a·,
law of this
p 422–14 explain to them the law of this a·.
life or
ph 187–28 body loses all appearance of life or a·,
materialistic
ph 187–19 the cause of all materialistic a·?
mental
an 104–13 C. S. goes to the bottom of mental a·,
p 401–22 effect . . . is dependent upon mental a·.
404– 1 physician should be familiar with mental a·
modus and
f 213– 1 would reverse the immortal modus and a·,
muscular
s 152–10 Anatomy describes muscular a· as produced
no involuntary
ph 187–22 There is no involuntary a·.
normal
f 212–30 The realities of being, its normal a·, and
nullify the
s 161– 7 able to nullify the a· of the flames,
of a water-wheel
p 399–18 the a· of a water-wheel is but a derivative
of divine Principle
s 121–29 imitates the a· of divine Principle ;
of error
r 484–22 voluntary or involuntary a· of error
of man
f 207–28 The spiritual fact, repeated in the a· of man
of mortal mind
ph 176– 2 The a· of mortal mind on the body
p 423–28 is as directly the a· of mortal mind
of mortal thought
p 399–10 apart from the a· of mortal thought,
of Soul
sp 89–23 a· of Soul confers a freedom, which explains
of the divine Mind
f 225–28 rooted out through the a· of the divine Mind.
of the human mind
pref xi– 3 a phase of the a· of the human mind,
f 234–30 the a· of the human mind, unseen to the senses.
of the lungs
p 415–20 the a· of the lungs, of the bowels,
of the mortal body
s 108–31 the organism and a· of the mortal body,
ph 187–20 a· of the mortal body is governed by
of the system
p 378– 9 no inflammatory nor torpid a· of the system.
415– 6 quickens or impedes the a· of the system,
t 447–14 The recuperative a· of the system,
of this Mind
g 519–27 No exhaustion follows the a· of this Mind,
of thought
p 384–13 Through this a· of thought and its results
of Truth
ph 169–27 Only the a· of Truth, Life, and Love can give
183–18 legitimate and only possible a· of Truth
p 386–13 the a· of Truth on the minds of mortals,
organic
s 126– 1 through its supposed organic a·
160–10 the organic a· and secretion of the viscera.
or stagnation
s 159–27 how much pain or pleasure, a· or stagnation,
physical
p 420–27 power over every physical a· and condition.
power of
s 157–15 power of a· is proportionately increased.
represent the
p 415–23 represent the a· of all the organs
reverse this
c 261– 1 Now reverse this a·.
ripen into
ph 188– 9 hatred, revenge ripen into a·,
salutary
p 414– 6 it yields . . . to the salutary a· of truth,
scientific
f 210–14 the scientific a· of the divine Mind
speech and
t 454–21 strength and freedom to speech and a·.
spring into
gl 597– 9 crime, . . . which was ready to spring into a·
thought and
c 265–13 a wider sphere of thought and a·,

———

pref xi– 3 which a· in some unexplained way
pr 3–26 A· expresses more gratitude than speech.
an 104–17 wrongness of the opposite so-called a·,

action

s 136– 6	no intelligence, a·, nor life separate
ph 167–21	can no more unite in a·,
199– 1	If matter were the cause of a·,
199–31	before his power of putting resolve into a·
f 211–17	and this a· shows the nature of
239–25	If a· proceeds from the divine Mind,
p 400–26	The a· of so-called mortal mind must be
401–26	or restore will and a· to cerebrum
419–20	If the a· proceeds from Truth,
r 480–10	Consciousness, as well as a·, is governed by
gl 586– 8	FAN. . . . that which gives a· to thought.

actions

p 393– 5	ignorant of itself, of its own a·,
413–28	these a· convey mental images to

active

b 327–29	Reason is the most a· human faculty.
p 387– 3	Because mortal mind is kept a·, must it pay
387– 8	when we realize that immortal Mind is ever a·,
ap 570– 5	certain a· yet unseen mental agencies

actively

c 261–14	walking about as a· as the youngest member

activities

ph 185–31	material mentality and its suppositional a·.
ap 562–15	yield to the a· of the divine Principle

activity

b 268– 3	With like a· have thought's swift

actor

c 261–12	a noted a· was accustomed
p 399–15	If Mind is the only a·, how can mechanism

acts

pr 12–11	which a· through blind belief,
s 155–22	a· more powerfully . . . in proportion as
162– 6	C. S. a· as an alterative,
ph 166– 4	Mind is all that feels, a·, or impedes action.
187–31	holds in belief a body, through which it a·
f 206– 8	erring, human thought a· injuriously
238– 1	Motives and a· are not rightly valued
251–21	a· upon the so-called human mind
b 273–26	His a· were the demonstration of Science,
p 436–13	Such a· bear their own justification,
r 473–27	his a· of higher importance than his words.
g 520–30	Spirit a· through the Science of Mind,
gl 595–18	limits, in which are summed up all human a·,

actual

pr 14– 7	but the a· demonstration and
s 110– 3	contradict . . . the belief that matter can be a·.
122– 6	the a· reign of harmony on earth.
ph 183–27	casts out all evils . . . with the a· spiritual law,
f 254–31	which determines the outward and a·.
b 281–23	sin and mortality are without a· origin
297–30	has little relation to the a· or divine.
p 347– 4	Who dares to say that a· Mind can
410–12	showing that Truth is the a· life of man ;
r 478–24	this belief is mortal and far from a·.
491– 4	a belief without a· foundation or

actuality

a 52–20	the mighty a· of all-inclusive God, good.
s 130– 9	you can demonstrate the a· of Science.
b 296–16	spiritual sense, and the a· of being.
321–12	In this incident was seen the a· of Science.
r 481–22	then assume . . . because of their admitted a·.
g 502–13	reflection of God and the spiritual a· of man,

actually

p 397– 6	a· injuring those whom we mean to bless.

acute

sp 85–23	Jew and Gentile may have had a· corporeal
s 162–18	in cases of both a· and chronic disease
ph 176–29	Hence decided types of a· disease
f 246–32	A· and chronic beliefs reproduce their own
247– 1	The a· belief of physical life comes on at
p 369–16	Jesus never asked if disease were a· or chronic,
390–28	approaching symptoms of chronic or a· disease,

acuteness

s 128–10	gives them a· and comprehensiveness

Adam (see also Adam's)

alias error

g 528–24	A·— alias error— gives them names.

and Eve

sp 92–12	serpent . . . speaking to A· and Eve.

and his progeny

g 532–10	A· and his progeny were cursed, not blessed ;

as in

g 545–31	"As in A· [error] all die,— I Cor. 15: 22.

called unto

g 532–14	Lord God [Jehovah] called unto A·,— Gen. 3: 9.

hypnotic state in

g 528–16	inducing a sleep or hypnotic state in A·

innocent as

ph 175–29	They were as innocent as A·, before he

Adam

knew it not

g 532–29	the body had been naked, and A· knew it not;

like

f 214–11	The material senses, like A·, originate in

name

b 338–14	Divide the name A· into two syllables,
gl 580–21	The name A· represents the false

or error

ph 177–16	A· or error, . . . had the naming of
g 534–13	unfolded the remedy for A·, or error ;

prior to

c 267–10	must have had children prior to A·.

race of

o 345–25	and the sinning race of A·.

where art thou

ph 181–24	"A·, where art thou?"— Gen. 3: 9.
b 307–32	Truth still calls : "A·, where art thou?
308– 8	demand, "A·, where art thou?"— Gen. 3: 9.

---

f 214– 9	A·, represented in the Scriptures as formed
249–23	Mortals are the A· dreamers.
b 338–12	The word A· is from the Hebrew adamah,
338–28	from this ground, or matter, sprang A·,
338–30	it follows that A· was not the ideal man
o 346– 2	such criticism confounds man with A·.
g 506–28	Upon A· devolved the pleasurable task
506–29	A· has not yet appeared in the narrative.
527–23	and brought them unto A·— Gen. 2: 19.
527–24	whatsoever A· called every living— Gen. 2: 19.
528– 4	That A· gave the name and nature of animals,
528–10	caused a deep sleep to fall upon A·,— Gen. 2: 21.
529–30	A·, the synonym for error, stands for a belief
532– 1	Did God . . . create one man unaided,— that is, A·,
533– 4	This had never been bestowed on A·.
533–14	A·, alias mortal error, charges God and woman
533–23	bone and flesh which came from A·
535 10	And unto A· He said,— Gen. 3: 17.
538–23	And A· knew Eve his wife ;— Gen. 4: 1.
553–17	A· was created before Eve.
553–18	the maternal egg never brought forth A·.
556–18	the deep sleep which fell upon A·?
ap 560– 4	typical of six thousand years since A·,
gl 579–15	definition of

adamah

b 338–12	word Adam is from the Hebrew a·,

adamant

f 242–17	a· of error,— self-will, self-justification,

Adam-belief

g 556–23	Even so goes on the A·

Adam-dream

b 282–29	the A·, which is neither Mind nor man,
306–32	parent of all human discord was the A·,

Adamic

g 525– 5	mankind represents the A· race,

Adam's

g 533–18	the rib taken from A· side has grown into
553–19	Eve was formed from A· rib,
554–24	This he said of Judas, one of A· race.

Adams

ph 176– 4	and unmanly A· attributed their own downfall

adaptation

pr 13– 2	Love is impartial and universal in its a·
s 116–11	correct view of C. S. and of its a·

adapted

m 58– 1	intercourse with those a· to elevate it,
an 101–14	had been promised . . . as conclusive, and as a·
s 146–32	comprehensible by and a· to the thought of
b 318–27	and are not a· to elevate mankind.
p 403–22	and this is best a· for healing the sick.
ap 574– 3	The Revelator also takes in another view, a·

add

s 130–19	cannot a· to the contents of a vessel already full.
ph 180–15	invalid may unwittingly a· more fear to
t 462– 6	and a· continually to his store of spiritual

added

a 50– 6	a· to an overwhelming sense of the magnitude
51– 5	This dread a· the drop of gall to his cup.
m 56– 3	Jesus a·: "Suffer it to be so now :— Matt. 3: 15.
f 237– 5	with laughing eyes, she presently a·,
b 295– 3	a· proof of the unreliability of
o 342–11	to which command was a· the promise
344– 4	It should be a· that this is claimed
p 398– 4	It is a· that "the spirit— Mark 9: 26.
t 454– 1	It need not be a· that the use of tobacco
gl 579– 4	On this account this chapter is a·.

adding

p 375–18	a· to his patient's mental . . . power,

addition
pr 16–13 whether the last line is not an *a·* to the prayer
s 128–29 The *a·* of two sums in mathematics
b 329–18 To be discouraged, is to resemble a pupil in *a·*,
g 524–24 Is this *a·* to His creation real or unreal?

additional
m 58–14 With *a·* joys, benevolence should grow

address
s 160– 1 should *a·* himself to the work of destroying it

addresses
p 433– 3 *a·* the jury of Mortal Minds.

addressing
a 38–12 He was *a·* his disciples, yet he did not say,
p 400–20 When we remove disease by *a·* the

adds
sp 99– 7 he straightway *a·* : "for it is God— *Phil.* 2 : 13.
g 551–11 but he *a·* that mankind has ascended

adequate
f 234–23 *a·* to the right education of human thought.
c 256–24 No form nor physical combination is *a·* to
p 412–14 It is indeed *a·* to unclasp the hold

adhere
s 112– 9 and *a·* to some particular system of
141– 5 Few understand *a·* to Jesus' divine
ph 181–23 if you *a·* to error and are afraid to trust
t 459–32 Scientist should understand and *a·* strictly
r 471–24 tried to *a·* to it until she caught the first gleam
495–28 *A·* to the divine Principle of C. S. and follow

adhered
a 54–22 There *a·* to him only a few unpretentious

adherence
m 65–28 permanence and peace in a more spiritual *a·*.
ph 166–23 Failing to recover health through *a·* to
f 222–18 as was believed, only by the strictest *a·* to
p 382–31 *A·* to hygiene was useless.
t 456– 5 Strict *a·* to the divine Principle and

adherents
s 112– 7 become *a·* of the Socratic, the Platonic,
r 497– 3 As *a·* of Truth, we take the inspired Word

adheres
t 448–26 If the student *a·* strictly to the teachings of
462– 3 any student, who *a·* to the divine rules

adhering
p 387–19 By *a·* to the realities of eternal existence,

adhesion
s 124–20 *A·*, cohesion, and attraction are properties of
b 293–15 whose *a·* and cohesion are Life,

adjective
r 466– 2 *Omni* is adopted from the Latin *a·* signifying

adjudged
p 442– 1 There, Man is *a·* innocent of

adjusted
a 40– 8 adjusts the balance as Jesus *a·* it.
ph 168– 4 If the scales are evenly *a·*,

adjustment
b 282–15 a curve finds no *a·* to a straight line.
p 401–29 *a·* of broken bones and dislocations

adjusts
a 40– 8 *a·* the balance as Jesus adjusted it.
t 449– 8 Right *a·* the balance sooner or later.

administer
s 153–20 Now *a·* mentally to your patient
ph 174–26 why treat the body alone and *a·* a dose of
p 424–13 if one doctor should *a·* a drug to counteract

administered
s 153– 9 a teaspoonful of the water *a·* at intervals of
p 416– 6 A hypodermic injection of morphine is *a·*

administers
p 399– 6 Mortal mind prescribes the drug, and *a·* it.

admission
another
b 278–17 requires another *a·*,— namely, that Spirit
p 388–14 and there follows the necessity for another *a·*
proportionate
ph 167– 8 Our proportionate *a·* of the claims of

sp 75–15 not by an *a·* that his body had died
90–24 *a·* to one's self that man is God's own likeness
f 224–25 stands at the door of this age, knocking for *a·*.
b 278–16 The *a·* that there can be material substance
308– 9 is met by the *a·* from the head, heart,
p 394–10 The *a·* that any bodily condition is
t 450–18 but unless this *a·* is made, evil will boast
gl 596–18 only fit preparation for *a·* to the presence

admissions
f 220– 4 Such *a·* ought to open people's eyes
244–28 Such *a·* cast us headlong into darkness
p 394–13 such *a·* are discouraging,

admit
pr 3–17 We *a·* theoretically that God is
a 24–31 his own disciples could not *a·*
26–23 makes us *a·* its Principle to be Love.
39–32 once *a·* that evil confers no pleasure,
an 105– 7 to contradict precedent and to *a·* that
s 120– 2 never understand this while we *a·* that soul is in
130–12 since you *a·* that God is omnipotent ;
143–18 You *a·* that mind influences the body
ph 172–32 When we *a·* that matter (heart, blood,
182–30 To *a·* that sickness is a condition over which
f 202–27 We *a·* that God has almighty power,
237–28 more for them than they are willing to *a·*
244–16 If man were dust . . . we might *a·* the hypothesis
250–31 nor will Science *a·* that happiness is ever the
b 298–22 and *a·* no materialistic beliefs.
339–30 never to *a·* that sin can have intelligence
o 347– 2 Who is ready to *a·* this?
348– 3 Medical theories virtually *a·* the nothingness
353–10 All must *a·* that Christ is
353–20 We must not continue to *a·* that
355–17 declines to *a·* that Christ's religion
357– 1 In common justice, we must *a·* that God
p 368–27, 28 *A·* the existence of matter, and you *a·*
369– 1 is liable to *a·* also the reality of
376–30 To fear and *a·* the power of disease,
388–12 *A·* the common hypothesis that food is
389–13 Our dietetic theories first *a·* that food sustains
393– 2 we *a·* the intruding belief, forgetting
395– 2 They *a·* its reality, whereas they should deny it.
t 461– 5 We *a·* the whole, because a part is proved
461–21 to *a·* that you are sick, renders your case
r 466–17 the point you will most reluctantly *a·*,
469–22 bury the sense of infinitude, when we *a·*
479–27 We *a·* that black is not a color, because
g 530–22 and saying, . . . Only *a·* that I am real,
555–25 We lose our standard . . . when we *a·*

admits
s 148–31 the guidance of a theology which *a·*
ph 174–23 Anatomy *a·* that mind is somewhere in man,
f 202–31 Common opinion *a·* that a man may take cold
229–12 and at the same time *a·* that Spirit is God,
b 283–12 *a·* of no error, but rests upon understanding.
p 401–27 Until the advancing age *a·* the efficacy
g 551–10 Mr. Darwin *a·* this, but he adds that

admitted
f 204–12 The first power is *a·* to be good,
b 270–12 it is generally *a·* that this intelligence is
276–17 If God is *a·* to be the only Mind
p 428–29 and the immortal facts of being are *a·*.
r 471–13 facts of divine Science should be *a·*,
481–22 assume . . . because of their *a·* actuality.

admittedly
ph 187–15 the hand, *a·* moved by the will.

admitting
p 376–29 you cannot check a fever after *a·*
392–25 *A·* only such conclusions as you wish realized
397–10 You cause bodily sufferings . . . by *a·* their
r 469–26 *a·* that God, or good, is omnipresent

admonition
a 25–20 Hence the force of his *a·*,

adopt
sp 99–18 individuals, who *a·* theosophy, spiritualism,
s 112– 9 they *a·* and adhere to some particular
145–14 It matters not what . . . method one may *a·*,
154–32 method for any mother to *a·*
f 248–23 and *a·* into your experience the
p 441–21 recommend that Materia Medica *a·* C. S.
t 452–31 and then should *a·* C. S.,

adopted
an 101–19 This report was *a·* by the Royal Academy
s 164– 7 none can be *a·* as a safe guidance in practice."
f 220–22 clergyman once *a·* a diet of bread and water
221– 1 I knew a person who when quite a child *a·*
p 378–19 hygienic drilling and drugging, *a·* to cure
r 466– 2 *Omni* is *a·* from the Latin adjective
g 553–20 Whatever theory may be *a·* by

adoption
s 141–27 The *a·* of scientific religion and of
c 255– * the *a·*, to wit, the redemption— *Rom.* 8 : 23.

adopts
g 547–29 Inspired thought . . . *a·* the spiritual and

adorable
pr 16–29 *A·* One.

adoration
sp 88–22 and the individual manifests profound *a·*.
p 363– 8 Did he repel her *a·*?

adore
a 26– 1 While we *a·* Jesus, and the heart overflows
s 140– 9 We shall obey and *a·* in proportion
r 497– 5 We acknowledge and *a·* one supreme and

adored
 r 472– 2 that God is to be understood, a·,
adorned
 f 235–17 though a· with gems of scholarly attainment,
adornment
 m 60–22 passion, frivolous amusements, personal a·,
adroitness
 g 515– 8 a wise idea, charming in its a·,
adult (*see also* **adult's**)
 ph 178–13 Perhaps an a· has a deformity produced
 p 371–14 The a·, in bondage to his beliefs,
 371–16 the a· must be taken out of his darkness,
adulterated
 t 457– 4 Other works, . . . have a· the Science.
 r 482– 3 Human thought has a· the meaning
adulterating
 t 464–25 A· C. S., makes it void.
adulteries
 an 100– * *evil thoughts, murders, a·,* — *Matt.* 15 : 19.
adulterous
 pr 11– 3 When forgiving the a· woman he said,
 sp 85–25 Jesus knew the generation to be wicked and a·,
adultery
 m 56–19 "Thou shalt not commit a·," — *Exod.* 20 : 14.
 an 106–21 A·, fornication, uncleanness, — *Gal.* 5 : 19.
 f 252–19 says : . . . I can cheat, lie, commit a·, rob,
 b 330–30 hypocrisy, slander, hate, theft, a·,
adult's
 s 130–20 Laboring long to shake the a· faith in matter
adults
 f 236–25 Children are more tractable than a·,
 o 352–17 Children, like a·, *ought* to fear a reality which
advance
 pr 10–20 But the a· guard of progress has
 a 41– 3 this a· beyond matter must
 m 61–30 must greatly improve to a· mankind.
 s 158–28 Homœopathy, a step in a· of allopathy,
 f 207– 3 proportionately as we a· spiritually,
 239– 3 lay it upon those who are in a· of creeds.
 o 361–23 Spiritual ideas unfold as we a·.
 p 371–24 because this teaching is in a· of the age,
 412– 3 to a· and destroy the human fear of
 430– 8 he will a· more rapidly towards God,
 t 449–14 a· in proportion to your honesty and fidelity,
 457–23 To pursue other vocations and a· rapidly
 462–15 heed every statement, and a· from the rudiments
 g 542 25 to a· itself, breaks God's commandments.
advanced
 pr 16– 2 must precede this a· spiritual understanding.
 a 23–18 Faith, a· to spiritual understanding,
 40– 2 The a· thinker and devout Christian,
 45 32 Jesus' students, not sufficiently a·
 sp 76–12 When a· to spiritual being and
 77–24 with every a· stage of existence.
 84– 7 When sufficiently a· in Science to be
 ph 200– 4 Moses a· a nation to the worship of God in
 f 230– 7 coming of Christ, the a· appearing of Truth,
 b 324– 2 renders thought receptive of the a· idea.
 p 391 8 the incipient or a· stages of disease,
 t 461– 8 taught only by those who are morally a·
advancement
 m 56– 5 Jesus' concessions . . . were for the a· of
 b 326–20 nothing but wrong intention can hinder your a·.
 p 429–10 in the line of spiritual a·.
 t 459– 9 Judge not the future a· of C. S. by
advances
 sp 95–32 Humanity a· slowly out of sinning sense
advancing
 a 21– 9 If the disciple is a· spiritually,
 55– 2 The a· century, from a deadened sense
 m 65–15 struggling against the a· spiritual era.
 s 134– 2 At every a· step, truth is still opposed
 c 256– 2 A· to a higher plane of action,
 p 401–27 Until the a· age admits the efficacy
 t 452–11 Your a· course may provoke envy,
 g 513– 6 A· spiritual steps in the teeming universe
 536– 7 human concepts a· and receding,
advantage
 a 42– 5 The universal belief in death is of no a·.
 sp 77–18 Of what a·, then, would it be to us,
 s 145–16 Scientific healing has this a· over other
 b 269–18 they have this a· over the objects and
 279–12 and they have the a· of being eternal.
 t 443– 2 as to the propriety, a·, and consistency of
advantages
 p 369–29 of the a· of Mind and immortality?
advent
 a 30– 5 Born of a woman, Jesus' a· in the flesh
 43– 7 The a· of this understanding is
 b 333–16 The a· of Jesus of Nazareth marked

adversary
 s 161–32 agrees with his "a· quickly," — *Matt.* 5 : 25.
 p 390–19 "Agree with thine a· quickly, — *Matt.* 5 : 25.
 391–23 your a· will deliver you to the judge
 gl 580–28 definition of
 580–28 An a· is one who opposes, denies,
 581– 2 name . . . in Scripture, the "a·." — *I Pet.* 5 : 8.
adverse
 p 419–16 Meet every a· circumstance as its master.
 t 456– 1 to influence mankind a· to its highest
adversity
 m 64–12 some noble woman, struggling alone with a·,
 66– 3 Sweet are the uses of a· ;
advertisements
 ph 179–32 Descriptions of disease . . . and a· of quackery
advertises
 p 439– 5 and a· largely for his employers.
advice
 p 394–14 a· to a man who is down in the world,
 424–19 either by giving antagonistic a· or
advise
 s 149–19 a· our patients to be hopeful and cheerful
advised
 f 220–24 and a· others never to try dietetics for
 t 444–13 Students are a· by the author to be
advising
 pr 3– 3 not sufficient to warrant him in a· God.
advocate
 s 154– 2 and certainly we should not be error's a·.
advocates
 ph 179–12 Every medical method has its a·.
advocating
 s 153–31 as we would avoid a· crime.
Æon
 b 335–11 the Logos, the Λ· or Word of God,
aëriform
 g 511–23 To mortal mind, the universe is . . . and a·.
Æsculapius
 s 150–31 The hosts of A· are flooding the world
 152– 6 endeavored to make this book the A· of mind
afar
 g 538– 8 the sword of Truth gleams a· and indicates
affairs
 p 430–31 the superintendence of human a·,
affect
 pr 16–14 this does not a· the meaning of the prayer itself.
 a 55– 5 but this does not a· the invincible facts.
 s 123– 5 Ptolemaic blunder could not a· the harmony of
 125–24 find that these changes cannot a· his crops.
 125–32 mortal belief, wholly inadequate to a· a man
 p 379–23 so-called vital current does not a· the
 383–13 does not a· his happiness, because
 388–22 food does not a· the absolute Life of man,
 395–31 brain-lobes cannot . . . a· the functions of
 401–25 remove paralysis, a· organization,
 402–21 and in this way a· the body,
 408–19 Drugs do not a· a corpse,
 g 553–31 you may also ask how belief can a· a result
affected
 b 310–13 sun is not a· by the revolution of the earth.
 p 380–17 The body is a· only with the belief of disease
affection
Christly
 p 365–19 If the Scientist has enough Christly a· to
flowers of
 m 57–25 may uproot the flowers of a·, and scatter them
grave of
 m 68– 9 Jealousy is the grave of a·.
higher
 m 65–19 human mind will at length demand a higher a·.
human
 m 57–22 Human a· is not poured forth vainly,
 65– 7 If the foundations of human a· are consistent
 p 364–28 expressed by meekness and human a·,
 366–13 physician who . . . is deficient in human a·,
ineffable
 p 364– 8 the higher tribute to such ineffable a·,
justice and
 gl 592–13 the union of justice and a·,
kindly
 gl 594–14 SHEM . . . A corporeal mortal ; kindly a· ;
links of
 m 60– 7 welding indissolubly the links of a·.
maternal
 m 60–11 maternal a· lives on under whatever
mother's
 m 60– 8 A mother's a· cannot be weaned from
one
 f 201– 4 knowing too that one a· would be supreme

affection

practical
a 24–27 efficacy of the crucifixion lay in the practical *a·*
promotes
an 103– 1 promotes *a·* and virtue in families
pure
a 54– 3 Out of the amplitude of his pure *a·*,
s 147–29 A pure *a·* takes form in goodness,
gl 589–21 pure *a·* blessing its enemies.
purity and
pr 15–27 purity, and *a·* are constant prayers.
a 36– 1 They, who know not purity and *a·*
spiritual
p 366–17 Not having this spiritual *a·*, the physician
unrequited
a 49–12 sublime courage, and unrequited *a·*?

pr 8–29 learn what is the *a·* and purpose of the heart,
9–20 surrender of all merely material sensation, *a·*,
s 115–26 MORAL. Humanity, honesty, *a·*, compassion,
ph 183–22 demands man's entire obedience, *a·*, and
b 327– 2 and also by gaining an *a·* for good
p 363–32 the mere fact that she was showing her *a·*

affections

and aims
c 265– 6 their *a·* and aims grow spiritual,
centre for the
m 60–18 strength to man, and a centre for the *a·*.
famished
pr 17– 5 *Give us grace for to-day ; feed the famished a·*;
her
s 154–24 and her *a·* need better guidance,
his
a 52– 4 His *a·* were pure ; theirs were carnal.
human
m 61– 4 good in human *a·* must have ascendency
interests and
m 59–15 hallowing the union of interests and *a·*,
renewal of
gl 582– 9 Renewal of *a·* ; self-offering ;
sensualist's
f 241– 8 The sensualist's *a·* are as imaginary,
transplant the
c 265–32 transplant the *a·* from sense to Soul,
understanding and
pr 5–18 riches of His love into the understanding and *a·*,
unselfish
p 365–11 but if the unselfish *a·* be lacking,
whole
b 326–10 his whole *a·* on spiritual things,
worldling's
t 459– 8 have nothing in common with the worldling's *a·*,

a 18– * *crucified the flesh with the a· and — Gal. 5 : 24.*
m 57–16 incompetent to meet the demands of the *a·*,
58–23 the centre, though not the boundary, of the *a·*.
ph 182–11 must be supreme in the *a·*.
f 239–17 we must learn where our *a·* are placed
t 451–16 If our hopes and *a·* are spiritual,
gl 587–23 HEART. Mortal feelings, motives, *a·*,
597– 4 The motives and *a·* of a man

affects

pr 12–16 Prayer to a corporeal God *a·* the sick like
s 149–18 remarked . . . "We know that mind *a·* the body
ph 17– 3 *a·* people like a Parisian name for a
f 222– 4 This person learned that food *a·* the body only
b 297–10 a change in either . . . *a·* the physical
p 397– 2 not seeing how mortal mind *a·* the body,
423– 6 oftentimes *a·* a sensitive patient
r 483–11 Moral ignorance or sin *a·* your demonstration,

affiliation

sp 81– 9 maintain their *a·* with mortal flesh ;

affinities

ph 191–28 illusive senses may fancy *a·* with their

affinity

ph 191–30 Mind has no *a·* with matter,

affirm

s 140– 4 That God is a corporeal being, nobody can truly
a·.
f 219–14 When this is understood, we shall never *a·*
c 255–15 That God is . . . material, no man should *a·*.
b 274–19 beliefs of mortal mind, which *a·* that life,

affirmation

p 392– 1 The physical *a·* of disease should
429–16 mortal mind's *a·* is not true.

affirmations

s 149–30 to understand the *a·* of divine Science,
p 394–20 their denials are better than their *a·*.

affirmative

s 132– 1 an *a·* reply, recounting his works
p 418–20 Truth is *a·*, and confers harmony.
432–19 and Governor Mortality replies in the *a·*.
r 489–21 An *a·* reply would contradict the

affirmed

a 42– 2 whereas priest and rabbi *a·* God to be a
r 483– 2 It may be *a·* that they do not heal,

affirms

f 215–16 but Science *a·* darkness to be
218– 2 that which *a·* weariness, made that weariness.
b 307– 7 Evil still *a·* itself to be mind,
p 429–13 Mortal mind *a·* that mind is subordinate
t 456–10 Whoever *a·* that there is more than
g 549–32 he virtually *a·* that the germ of humanity is

affixed

r 483–13 she *a·* the name "Science" to Christianity,

affixes

ph 184– 7 the penalties it *a·* last so long as the belief

affliction

m 64– 6 visit the fatherless . . . in their *a·*, — *Jas. 1 : 27.*
p 377– 4 *a·* is often the source of joy,
gl 586–13 *a·* purifying and elevating man.

afflictions

a 41– 5 as well as through their sorrows and *a·*.

afflictive

ap 574–29 suffering sense deems wrathful and *a·*,

affluence

a 54– 4 With the *a·* of Truth, he vanquished error.
s 140–11 but rejoicing in the *a·* of our God.

afford

pr 8– 1 A wordy prayer may *a·* a quiet sense of
m 64–16 aid her sympathy and charity would *a·*.
sp 99– 3 ethics, and superstition *a·* no
s 144–10 and *a·* faint gleams of God, or Truth.
f 232– 6 beliefs . . . *a·* no scatheless and permanent
b 268–15 semi-metaphysical systems *a·* no . . . aid
t 443–19 other systems they fancy will *a·* relief.
r 471– 8 corporeal senses, *a·* no indication of the
492–21 Matter can *a·* you no aid.

afforded

c 255– 9 *a·* no foundation for accurate views
258– 5 craving for something . . . holier, than is *a·* by
t 460–28 through the meagre channel *a·* by language

affording

r 473–19 *a·* the proof of Christianity's truth

affords

sp 81–10 this fact *a·* no certainty of everlasting life.
s 112–24 *a·* no foundation upon which to establish
ph 194–31 The light which *a·* us joy gave him a belief of
f 208– 1 suppositional error, which *a·* no proof of God,
o 356– 4 material existence *a·* no evidence of
gl 583–14 Church is that institution, which *a·* proof of

affrighted

p 366–26 sinners should be *a·* by their sinful beliefs ;

aflame

p 367– 8 legitimate C. S., *a·* with divine Love.

aforesaid

p 412–30 on the *a·* basis of C. S.

aforethought

p 437– 7 It indicates malice *a·*, a determination to
t 451–27 malpractice arises from ignorance or malice *a·*.

aforetime

pref xi–18 coming now as was promised *a·*,
s 131–22 As *a·*, the spirit of the Christ,
b 271–28 have the opportunity now, as *a·*, to learn

afraid

ph 181–23 if you adhere to error and are *a·* to trust
b 308– 6 mortal belief will be *a·* as it was in the
o 352–16 but you must not be *a·* of them"?
p 410–30 keynote of . . . "Be not *a·* !" — *Mark 6 : 50.*
t 447–30 A sinner is *a·* to cast the first stone.
g 532–15 I was *a·*, because I was naked ; — *Gen. 3 : 10.*

African

f 225–32 when *A·* slavery was abolished in our land.
226– 5 The voice of God in behalf of the *A·* slave

after

pref xii– 2 No charters were granted . . . *a·* 1883,
pr 2– 5 goes forth hungering *a·* righteousness
16– 8 one brief prayer, which we name *a·* him
16– 9 "*A·* this manner therefore — *Matt. 6 : 9.*
a 21–29 *A·* following the sun for six days,
24–32 *A·* the resurrection, even the unbelieving
27–11 proved by his reappearance *a·* the crucifixion
41–18 lost, about three centuries *a·* the crucifixion.
43– 2 did understand it *a·* his bodily departure.
45–13 Three days *a·* his bodily burial
45–22 saw Jesus *a·* the resurrection
46– 2 until they saw him *a·* his crucifixion
46–14 and *a·* his resurrection he proved
46–20 Jesus' unchanged physical condition *a·*
47– 5 *A·* gaining the true idea of their glorified
m 59–23 *A·* marriage, it is too late to grumble
59–25 exist before this union and continue ever *a·*,

after

m	62–10	those parents should not, in a· years, complain
sp	74– 5	a· having once left it, would be
	85–11	able to read the human mind a· this manner
	85–18	A· the same method, events of great moment
	94–15	belief that the infinite is formed a· the pattern
s	107– *	*preached of me is not a· man.— Gal.* 1 : 11.
	109–11	For three years a· my discovery, I sought
	111–26	A· a lengthy examination of my discovery
	131–15	a· the manner of God's appointing,
	137– 4	even by them, until a· the crucifixion,
s	156–21	A· trying this, she informed me that
	159– 2	A· the autopsy, her sister testified that the
ph	168–11	you rush a· drugs, search out the
	180–10	bearing fruit a· its kind,
	195– 2	A· the babbling boy had been taught to speak
f	217–14	know we no man a· the flesh !"— II Cor. 5 : 16.
	221–10	until three hours a· eating.
	222–11	a· he had availed himself of the fact that
	234–22	the weary searcher a· a divine theology,
	236–15	either a· a model odious to herself
c	259–23	and forms its offspring a· human illusions.
	261–13	was accustomed night a· night to go
	265–24	aspiration a· heavenly good comes
b	317–21	a· his resurrection from the grave,
	333–20	both before and a· the Christian era,
o	344– 8	man in His own image and a· His likeness.
p	372–23	Its false supports fail one a· another.
	376–29	you cannot check a fever a· admitting
	427–16	Man is the same a· as before a bone is broken
	429–20	exist a· the body is disintegrated.
	431– 8	going to sleep immediately a· a heavy meal.
	432–21	I was called for, shortly a· the report of
	434– 8	A· much debate and opposition,
	435–30	to judge . . . a· the law,— Acts 23 : 3.
	436– 3	A· betraying him into the hands of your law,
	438– 3	man in our image, a· our likeness ;— Gen. 1 : 26.
r	465– 2	A· much labor and increased spiritual
	469–26	a· admitting that God, or good, is
	475–12	man in our image, a· our likeness ;— Gen. 1 : 26.
	483–13	A· the author's sacred discovery,
	487– 6	before and a· that which is called death.
g	507–13	yielding fruit a· his kind,— Gen. 1 : 11.
	508–10	herb yielding seed a· his kind,— Gen. 1 : 12.
	508–11	seed was in itself, a· his kind : — Gen. 1 : 12.
	512– 6	abundantly, a· their kind,— Gen. 1 : 21.
	512– 6	every winged fowl a· his kind : — Gen. 1 : 21.
	513–15	the living creature a· his kind,— Gen. 1 : 24.
	513–16	and beast of the earth a· his kind : — Gen. 1 : 24.
	513–22	beast of the earth a· his kind,— Gen. 1 : 25.
	513–23	and cattle a· their kind,— Gen. 1 : 25.
	513–24	upon the earth a· his kind : — Gen. 1 : 25.
	515–12	man in our image, a· our likeness ;— Gen. 1 : 26.
	516– 9	fashions all things, a· His own likeness.
	523–29	a· which the distinction is not definitely
	524– 7	constantly went a· "strange gods."— Jer. 5 : 19.
	525–12	And God said, Let us make man a· our mind
	525–14	and God shaped man a· His mind ;
	525–14	a· God's mind shaped He him ;
	543– 2	This error, a· reaching the climax of
	549– 5	supposition that life . . . must decay a· it has
	555–31	present himself unchanged a· the crucifixion.
ap	565–23	A· the stars sang together
	570– 9	as a flood, a· the woman,— Rev. 12 : 15.
gl	584–24, 25	not a· the image and likeness of Spirit, but a·
	595–20	and continues a·, what is termed death,
		(see also **death**)

after-dinner

ph	175–20	selfishness, coddling, and sickly a· talk.

afternoon

ph	193–15	between three and four o'clock in the a·

afterward

s	163– 2	marking Nature with his name, and a· letting

afterwards

pr	6–10	supposition . . . that a· we shall be free to
a	42–24	A· he would show it to them unchanged.
s	110–16	a· the truth of C. S. was demonstrated.
	132–32	yet a· he seriously questioned
ph	188– 7	but a· it governs the so-called man.
	190– 2	embryonic mortal mind, a· mortal men
	190–16	a· to . . . return to its native nothingness.
	196–29	mental state, which is a· outlined on the body.
	198–13	a· to appear on the body;
f	230–19	Does wisdom make blunders which must a· be
p	374–21	it is resolved into its primitive mortal
	386–30	assertion might a· be proved to you.
	421– 8	a· make known to the patient your motive
t	452–21	and a· we must wash them clean.
g	514– 2	recreate persons or things upon its
	528–25	A· he is supposed to become the basis
	531–16	If, . . . mind was a· put into body by
	532– 2	but a· require the union of the
	547–21	and a· must either return to Mind or
ap	562– 5	the idea . . . which Jesus a· manifested,

again

pr	5–12	"shall be measured to you a·,"— Luke 6 : 38.
a	31– 6	A· he asked : "Who is my mother,— Matt. 12 : 48.
	31–28	A·, foreseeing the persecution which
	34–24	rise a· in the spiritual realm of reality,
	37– 4	it shall be measured to you a·."— Matt. 7 : 2.
	46–11	and is a· seen casting out evil and
	52–17	To-day, as of old, error and evil a·
	55– 9	gospel of healing is a· preached by the
	55–13	although it is a· ruled out of the synagogue.
sp	71–14	Close your eyes a·, and you may see
	75–16	that his body had died and then lived a·.
	97–29	Christianity is a· demonstrating the Life
s	110–27	and must a· be spiritually discerned,
	132– 5	"Go and show John a·— Matt. 11 : 4.
	152–14	contradicts another over and over a·.
	156–23	but on the third day she a· suffered,
ph	167–16	A·, an error in the premise must appear in
	185– 5	and she never suffered a· from east winds,
	198–18	A·, giving another direction to faith,
f	212– 3	tooth . . . extracted sometimes aches a· in belief,
	232–16	In our age Christianity is a· demonstrating
b	306–15	brought together a· at some uncertain
	310–12	when the earth has a· turned upon its axis.
p	425–26	You will never fear a· except to offend God,
	436–13	Mortal Man should find it a·.
t	444–21	Fear not that he will smite thee a·
r	480–19	A·, God, or good, never made
	489– 3	lobster loses its claw, the claw grows a·.
g	529– 3	not woman a· taken from man.
	556–11	to live a· in renewed forms,
ap	560–17	A·, without a correct sense of its
	570–20	nor a· sink the world into the deep waters of

against

a	18–10	a· the accredited evidence of the senses,
	18–11	a· Pharisaical creeds and practices,
	29– 2	a· error at home and abroad.
	47–10	Judas conspired a· Jesus.
	48–29	a· human rights and divine Love,
	52–18	common cause a· the exponents of truth.
m	57–17	a· the better claims of intellect,
	60–17	becoming a barrier a· vice,
	65–15	struggling a· the advancing spiritual era.
sp	79– 2	Warning people a· death is an error
	97–21	array the most falsities a· themselves,
an	106– 3	to work a· the free course of honesty
	106– 4	to push vainly a· the current
	106–28	a· such there is no law."— Gal. 5 : 23.
s	116–15	nor do they carry the day a· physical enemies,
	118–27	a kingdom necessarily divided a· itself,
	130–17	beliefs which war a· spiritual facts;
	131–10	enmity a· God."— Rom. 8 : 7.
	133–25	Jewish accusations a· him who
	138– 1	shall not prevail a· it."— Matt. 16 : 18.
	155–15	belief in physics weighs a· the
	155–18	general belief, . . . works a· C. S.,
	159– 4	protected a· inhaling the ether
	160– 3	act a· metaphysics, and vice versa,
	160–19	Can muscles, bones, blood, and nerves rebel a·
ph	167–20	lusteth a· the Spirit."— Gal. 5 : 17.
	168– 9	belief militates a· your health,
	177–23	a· God, Spirit and Truth.
	182–24	working a· themselves and their prayers
	200–22	the flesh that warreth a· Spirit.
f	234–10	guard a· false beliefs as watchfully as
	234–11	bar our doors a· the approach of
	236–13	either for or a· crime.
	238–11	who can be a· us?"— Rom. 8 : 31.
	242–19	which wars a· spirituality
	246–19	so many conspiracies a· manhood
	252– 2	divided a· itself,— Mark 3 : 24.
	253–20	no opposition to right endeavors a·
b	269– 2	a house divided a· itself.
	274–22	the flesh wars a· Spirit.
	307–23	weighs a· our course Spiritward.
	339–14	a· the day of wrath."— Rom. 2 : 5.
	339–15	He is joining in a conspiracy a·
	339–16	a· his own awakening to the
o	347– 1	"The flesh lusteth a·— Gal. 5 : 17.
	347– 1	Spirit a· the flesh."— Gal. 5 : 17.
	354– 1	protests of C. S. a· the notion
	354– 5	obey the Scriptures and war a·
	358–16	verdict of Truth a· error,
	358–31	a· whom they have been warned,
p	368–10	A· the fatal beliefs that error is as real as
	374–18	no argument a· the mental origin of disease.
	380– 9	a· the control of Mind over body,
	380–14	will be turned a· himself.
	380–31	a· Himself, a· Life, health, harmony.
	384–12	enter his protest a· this belief
	388–19	divided a· itself,"— Matt. 12 : 25.
	389–18	kingdom divided a· itself.
	391– 2	arrayed a· the supremacy of Spirit.
	391– 8	rise in rebellion a· them.
	392– 9	take antagonistic grounds a·

against
p 394–22 a· whom mortals should not contend?
395– 1 The sick . . . argue for suffering, instead of a· it.
395–25 while you argue a· their reality,
401– 2 and works a· itself ;
405–10 army of conspirators a· health,
405–12 the arbiter of truth a· error.
411– 5 when he argued a· it,
412–20 array your mental plea a· the
414–18 lest you array the sick a· their
417–16 When you silence the witness a· your plea,
419–31 If it is found necessary to treat a·
420–16 when they will not array themselves a· it,
424–17 should not act a· your influence
425–31 mental protest a· the opposite belief
433–11 the evidence of Personal Sense a·
434–26 foul conspiracy a· the liberty and
436– 6 a witness a· Mortal Man
438–12 bearing false witness a· Man.
438–17 a· the rights and life of man.
439–22 in his struggles a· liver-complaint
440–28 I ask that he be forbidden to enter a·
441–14 cannot bear witness a· Mortal Man,
441–20 in favor of Man and a· Matter.
t 445– 3 defend themselves a· sin, and to guard a· the
446–30 be watched and guarded a·.
449– 7 reacts most heavily a· one's self.
449–21 understood and guarded a·.
452– 1 bar the door of his thought a· this
r 481–13 a· which wisdom warns man,
489–20 the medium for sinning a· God,
g 531–28 since flesh wars a· Spirit
534–19 is enmity a· God ;— Rom. 8 : 7.
541–14 rose up a· Abel— Gen. 4 : 8.
543–14 a· which divine Science is engaged in a
ap 564–10 accusations a· Jesus of Nazareth
564–14 the dragon as warring a· innocence.
565– 3 inflamed with war a· spirituality,
566–26 fought a· the dragon ;— Rev. 12 : 7.
566–32 a· the power of sin, Satan, and
567– 9 A· Love, the dragon warreth not long,
567–11 Truth and Love prevail a· the dragon
568–31 in our warfare a· error,
gl 581–18 a kingdom divided a· itself,
584–12 The flesh, warring a· Spirit ;

agamogenesis
m 68–17 one individual who believed in a· ;
68–25 but I discredit the belief that a· applies to

Agassiz
Louis
g 547– 9 Louis A·, by his microscopic examination
_____
an 104– 8 A·, the celebrated naturalist and author,
g 547–11 A· was able to see in the egg the
548–29 A· declares . . . "Certain animals,
549–24 In one instance a celebrated naturalist, A·,
ap 561– 5 A·, through his microscope, saw

age
advance of the
p 371–24 this teaching is in advance of the a·,
advancing
p 401–27 Until the advancing a· admits the efficacy
anathemas of the
b 315–10 brought upon him the anathemas of the a·.
and blight
f 246–31 rather than into a· and blight.
and decay
f 247–30 resplendent and eternal over a· and decay.
any
b 325–30 When first spoken in any a·, Truth,
ensnare the
an 102–22 they ensnare the a· into indolence,
every
a 46–10 has spoken . . . in every a· and clime.
f 243– 7 can heal the sick in every a· and triumph over
r 482–25 to the hungering heart in every a·.
exempt from
f 247–14 Immortality, exempt from a· or decay,
her
f 245–16 Asked to guess her a·, those unacquainted
ignorant
r 474– 8 To the ignorant a· in which it first appears,
malice of the
f 215–32 The ignorance and malice of the a· would
material
a 36–15 earthly price of spirituality in a material a·
sp 98– 9 Christianity is misinterpreted by a material a·,
o 350–17 it was difficult in a material a· to apprehend
g 546–23 C. S. is dawning upon a material a·.
materiality of the
a 31–10 Referring to the materiality of the a·,
nor accident
f 214–28 Neither a· nor accident can interfere with the
our
f 232–16 In our a· Christianity is again demonstrating

age
pictures
f 244–29 Shakespeare's poetry pictures a· as infancy,
present
ap 560– 5 has reference to the present a·.
seems ready
ph 170–24 The a· seems ready to approach this subject,
sensualism of the
m 65–15 in the materialism and sensualism of the a·,
tendency of the
s 111–22 calculated to offset the tendency of the a· to
that
b 332–30 He expressed the highest type . . . in that a·.
this
pref xi–23 to proclaim His Gospel to this a·,
an 106–15 Let this a·, which sits in judgment on
f 224–24 stands at the door of this a·, knocking
b 317– 6 lives most the life of Jesus in this a·
p 364–17 indicated by one of the needs of this a·.
367–25 the Christ-cure has come to this a·
372–10 The Science . . . would be clearer in this a·,
t 456–28 Because it is the voice of Truth to this a·,
ap 570–22 In this a· the earth will help the woman ;
thought of the
s 147– 1 the thought of the a· in which we live.
ugliness to
f 246–11 robs youth and gives ugliness to a·.
warn the
m 65– 9 Divorces should warn the a·
_____
ph 194–23 at the a· of seventeen Kaspar was still a
f 236–30 While a· is halting between two opinions
245–25 could not a· while believing herself young,
247– 3 I have seen a· regain two of the
o 353–13 The a· has not wholly outlived the sense of
r 473–18 In an a· of ecclesiastical despotism,
ap 562–18 lamps in the spiritual heavens of the a·,

agencies
ap 570– 5 certain active yet unseen mental a·

agency
s 150–22 This human view infringes man's free moral a· ;

agent
pref x– 7 They regard the human mind as a healing a·,
an 100–10 susceptible to the influence of this a·,
101–23 it is not a remedial a·,
s 112– 1 the most effective curative a·
146–17 Science, the curative a· of God,
b 338–19 dust was deemed the a· of Deity
p 435–16 the a· of those laws is an outlaw,
t 444– 4 suffering is oft the divine a· in this

agents
sp 78–27 claimed to be the a· of God's government.
s 164– 6 classification of diseases or of therapeutic a·,
r 485–26 delineates foreign a·, called disease and sin.

ages
all
sp 98–18 It is imperious throughout all a·
b 271– 3 Christ's Christianity . . . reappearing in all a·,
bygone
s 134– 1 To-day the cry of bygone a· is repeated,
future
pref vii–25 Future a· must declare what the pioneer
sensual
f 254–16 During the sensual a·, absolute C. S. may not
_____
s 118–10 A· pass, but this leaven of Truth is
141– 2 theological and ritualistic religion of the a·
ph 174–18 are pursuing and will overtake the a·,
f 204–20 When will the a· understand the Ego,
233– 9 The a· must slowly work up to
241–17 error of the a· is preaching without practice.
246–17 Never record a·.
b 303–15 All the vanity of the a· can never
p 380– 5 Truth is the rock of a·, the headstone
ap 560–26 not only obscured the light of the a·, but

aggravate
p 401–12 This fermentation should not a· the

aggravated
p 422– 7 certain moral and physical symptoms seem a·,
g 540–12 when the symptoms of evil, illusion, are a·,

aggravation
an 105–27 The a· of error foretells its doom,
s 156–14 began to fear an a· of symptoms
ph 169– 3 Whenever an a· of symptoms has occurred

aggregated
f 209–16 a· substances composing the earth,

aggression
t 451– 5 They must renounce a·, oppression and

aggressive
an 102–17 its a· features are coming to the front.

aghast
ap 563– 7 why should we stand a· at nothingness?

agnosticism
s 111– 1 vague hypotheses of *a·*, pantheism,
129–17 spiritualism, theosophy, *a·*,
139–28 theosophy, and *a·* are opposed to
gl 596– 3 *a·* may define Deity as "the great unknowable ;"

ago
a 46– 9 which identified Jesus thus centuries *a·*,
sp 80–23 French toy which years *a·* pleased so many
82– 5 Chaucer wrote centuries *a·*, yet we still
87–29 may reproduce voices long *a·* silent.
93– 3 Jesus, who nearly nineteen centuries *a·*
s 122– 9 exposed nineteen hundred years *a·*
138–26 as readily as it was proved centuries *a·*.
f 224–12 Centuries *a·* religionists were ready to hail
232–18 as it did over nineteen hundred years *a·*,
p 380–22 Many years *a·* the author
r 487–12 gave . . . hearing to the deaf centuries *a·*,
495– 3 as surely as it did nineteen centuries *a·*.

agony
a 26– 4 in speechless *a·* exploring the way
48– 6 struggling in voiceless *a·*,
48–10 Remembering the sweat of *a·*
b 327–14 to be effaced by the sweat of *a·*.
p 416– 1 At last the *a·* also vanishes.
g 548–13 Every *a·* of mortal error helps error to
gl 588– 3 self-imposed *a·* ; effects of sin ;

agree
s 113–12 these propositions will be found to *a·*
b 320– 6 theologians in Europe and America *a·* that
p 390–18 "*A·* with thine adversary quickly, — *Matt.* 5 : 25.
390–27 "*A·* to disagree" with approaching symptoms

agreeable
s 128–20 An odor becomes beneficent and *a·*

agreed
p 442– 5 The Jury of Spiritual Senses *a·* at once

agreement
b 333– 1 illustrates the coincidence, or spiritual *a·*,

agreements
m 63–31 enter into business *a·*, hold real estate,

agrees
s 161–31 *a·* with his "adversary quickly," — *Matt.* 5 : 25.
162– 2 the matter-physician *a·* with the disease,
162– 2 the metaphysician *a·* only with health
b 313– 9 With this *a·* another passage
g 553–24 If consentaneous human belief *a·* upon

agriculture
r 485–29 controlled war and *a·* as much as

agriculturist
s 125–22 The *a·* will find that these changes
ph 183– 8 Can the *a·*, according to belief, produce a

aid
divine
o 354– 6 Why do they invoke the divine *a·* to enable
no
s 132–17 received no *a·* nor approval from other sanitary
r 492–21 Matter can afford you no *a·*.
of Mind
ph 182–23 forthwith shut out the *a·* of Mind
outside
sp 89– 9 Destroy her belief in outside *a·*, and
ready
m 64–15 debarred, . . . from giving the ready *a·*
receive
t 444– 7 If Christian Scientists ever fail to receive *a·*
r 483–26 if any system honors God, it ought to receive *a·*,
without the
sp 80–20 mind, without the *a·* of hands,
your
p 439–22 unfortunate Mortal Man who sought your *a·*

a 19–19 to understand . . . and *a·* its efficacy ;
22– 1 thinking with the *a·* of this to drug
sp 86– 6 mortal mind, whose touch called for *a·*.
97– 2 They will *a·* in the ejection of error.
b 268–15 systems afford no substantial *a·* to
307–10 It says : . . . I *a·* Him.
p 420– 6 call an experienced Christian Scientist to *a·*
t 447–10 heal the sick when called upon for *a·*,
454–32 human auxiliaries to *a·* in bringing
457–28 as if the non-intelligent could *a·* Mind !

aided
a 19– 6 Jesus *a·* in reconciling man to God
p 394–24 unless it can be *a·* by a drug or
406–12 spiritual perception, *a·* by Science,
439–24 You *a·* and abetted Fear and Health-laws.

aiding
c 266–22 material sense, *a·* evil with evil,
t 458–12 to think of *a·* the divine Principle

aids
sp 91–18 denial of material selfhood *a·* the discernment
ph 186–21 *a·* in peremptorily punishing the evil-doer.
b 296–29 and *a·* in taking the next step
p 385– 9 surpassing all other *a·*,
t 461–23 to recognize your sin, *a·* in destroying it.
g 533–19 *a·* man to make sinners more rapidly
548–14 so *a·* the apprehension of immortal Truth.

ailed
s 135– 1 "What *a·* thee, O thou sea, — *Psal.* 114 : 5.

ailment
ph 179–19 The epizoötic is a humanly evolved *a·*,
197– 3 A new name for an *a·* affects people like a
p 381–24 that you are quite free from some *a·*.
382–32 The *a·* was not bodily, but mental,
392– 4 To cure a bodily *a·*,
412–19 find the type of the *a·*, get its name,
423–16 He regards the *a·* as weakened or

ailments
s 140– 3 effectual in the treatment of moral *a·*.
ph 174–23 to cure mortal *a·*.
f 219– 3 My method . . . applies to all bodily *a·*,
p 398–28 faith removes bodily *a·* for a season,
413–31 reproduced in the very *a·* feared.
416–29 they think too much about their *a·*,
421– 3 physical *a·* (so-called) arise from the belief

ails
t 460–23 superficial and cold assertion, "Nothing *a·* you."

aim
f 241–23 One's *a·*, a point beyond faith, should be
g 547–23 Our *a·* must be to have them understood

aimed
a 51–26 *a·* at the divine Principle, Love,

aims
m 61– 8 and give higher *a·* to ambition.
63–26 a race having higher *a·* and motives.
sp 95– 3 His holy motives and *a·* were traduced
f 234–31 Evil thoughts and *a·* reach no farther and
c 265– 6 their affections and *a·* grow spiritual,
p 405– 3 The indulgence of evil motives and *a·*
t 459– 8 the worldling's affections, motives, and *a·*.

air
and exercise
ph 166–27 less than in drugs, *a·*, and exercise,
f 232–19 never taught that drugs, food, *a·*, and exercise
change of
f 219–27 impute their recovery to change of *a·* or diet,
draught of
p 384–16 If exposure to a draught of *a·*
exercise and
ph 174– 6 baths, diet, exercise, and *a·* ?
fowl of the
(see fowl)
fowls of the
s 125–27 the fish of the sea and the fowls of the *a·*.
f 237–13 like "the fowls of the *a·*,"   *Luke* 8 : 5.
native
s 128–18 It raises the thinker into his native *a·* of insight
of Eden
ph 176–18 would load with disease the *a·* of Eden,
open
f 220– 1 said : "I exercise daily in the open *a·*.
pure
a 44–14 He did not depend upon food or pure *a·*
undulations of the
f 212–27 that the undulations of the *a·* convey sound,
wind or
gl 598–13 It might be translated *wind* or *a·*,

sp 90–19 through the *a·* and over the ocean.
p 375– 3 painlessly as gas dissipates into the *a·*
392–28 whether it be *a·*, exercise, heredity, contagion,
gl 598–15 What Jesus gave up was indeed *a·*,

alabaster
p 363– 1 She bore an *a·* jar containing

alarm
b 321–16 The illusion of Moses lost its power to *a·*
o 352–29 The objects of *a·* will then vanish
p 424–18 such opinions as may *a·* or discourage,
t 446– 7 may either arise from the *a·* of the physician,

alarmed
s 130– 1 The petty intellect is *a·* by
p 422–12 ignorant that it is a favorable omen, may be *a·*.

alarming
p 395–29 and it may appear in a more *a·* form.

albeit
g 512–30 *a·* God is ignorant of the existence of

alchemy
p 422–20 C. S., by the *a·* of Spirit,

alcoholic
p 406–28 The depraved appetite for a· drinks,

alias
ph 172–20 obtains in mortals, a· mortal mind,
p 391– 2 the plea of mortal mind, a· matter,
399–10 mortal thought, a· mortal mind.
400–14 conscious thought, a· the body,
409– 9 Unconscious mortal mind — a· matter,
432– 8 from my residence in matter, a· brain,
432–27 justice, a· nature's so-called law ;
g 528–24 Adam — a· error — gives them names.
533–15 Adam, a· mortal error, charges God
gl 591–27 suppositional material sense, a· the belief that

alienate
b 303–32 declared that nothing could a· him from God,

alike
sp 71–27 and structure of spiritualism are a· material
s 135–24 and they are a· in demonstration.
b 279–25 this belief contradicts a· revelation and

alive
a 44–29 a·, demonstrating within the narrow tomb
ph 200– 1 through his verse the gods became a· in a
f 216– 3 Who shall say that man is a· to-day, but
222–18 he had been kept a·, as was believed, only by
b 334–27 and, behold, I am a· for evermore, — *Rev.* 1 : 18.
p 373– 4 and be more a· to His promises.
g 545–32 shall all be made a·." — *I Cor.* 15 : 22.

alkali
p 401– 9 (as when an a· is destroying an acid),
422–14 As when an acid and a· meet and

All
eternal
b 280– 3 not products of the . . . eternal A·.
God as
p 397–21 confidence in God as A·,
God is
b 339– 7 Since God is A·, there is no room for
p 366–29 Life is God and God is A·.
g 532–24 God is A· and He is Mind
infinite
ap 576– 4 this New Jerusalem, this infinite A·,
Mind is
s 109– 2 the proposition that Mind is A·
g 508– 3 Mind is A· and reproduces all

———

pr 17–15 *Life, Truth, Love, over all, and A·.*
p 399– 2 therefore good is infinite, is A·.

all
pref x–19 Few invalids will turn to God till a· physical
xl– 5 a· other pathological methods are the fruits of
pr 2–14 for He already knows a·.
2–18 is not a· that is required.
3– 8 Shall we ask the divine Principle of a· goodness
3–28 and yet return thanks to God for a· blessings,
4– 8 evidence of our gratitude for a· that he has
5–32 seek the destruction of a· evil works,
8– 9 full . . . of a· uncleanness." — *Matt.* 23 : 27.
9– 5 The test of a· prayer lies in the answer to
9–17 with a· thy heart, — *Matt.* 22 : 37.
9–18 and with a· thy soul, — *Matt.* 22 : 37.
9–18 and with a· thy mind" — *Matt.* 22 : 37.
9–20 surrender of a· merely material sensation,
9–25 Are you willing to leave a· for Christ,
10–25 misapprehension of the source and means of a·
11–24 but if we desire holiness above a· else,
11–31 will bring us into a· Truth.
12–32 a· may avail themselves of God as
13– 8 striving for the accomplishment of a· we ask,
13–26 divine Principle, Love, the Father of a·
16–11 prayer which covers a· human needs.
16–19 the first lie and a· liars.
16–20 Only as we rise above a· material sensuousness
17–14 *For God is infinite, all-power, a· Life,*
17–15 *Life, Truth, Love, over a·,*
a 18–12 refuted a· opponents with his healing power.
20–25 The truth is the centre of a· religion.
20–32 divine Principle and Science of a· healing.
23–31 spiritual understanding and confides a· to God.
24–21 chiefly as providing a ready pardon for a·
25–27 a· the emotional love . . . will never alone
26– 6 a· have the cup of sorrowful effort
26– 8 till a· are redeemed through divine Love.
26–29 It was the divine Principle of a· real being
28– 9 While respecting a· that is good in the Church
31–11 He recognized Spirit, . . . as the Father of a·.
31–16 resurrection and the life" to a·— *John* 11 : 25.
32–18 saying, Drink ye a· of it." — *Matt.* 26 : 27.
33– 9 Their Master had explained it a· before,
33–17 and said, "Drink ye a· of it." — *Matt.* 26 : 27.
33–22 It gives a· for Christ, or Truth.

all
a 33–31 Are a· who eat bread and drink wine
34– 1 and leave a· for the Christ-principle?
34–10 If a· who ever partook of the sacrament
34–13 If a· who seek his commemoration
34–18 Through a· the disciples experienced,
36–12 He was forsaken by a· save
37–17 learn to emulate Jesus in a· his ways
37–29 "Go ye into a· the world, — *Mark* 16 : 15.
38–14 in a· time to come.
39–26 divine Principle of a· that really exists
42–13 followed by the desertion of a· save a few
43– 4 a· enabled the disciples to understand
43–29 must triumph over a· material beliefs
44–11 a· the claims of medicine, surgery,
45–23 the final proof of a· that he had taught,
46– 4 the truthfulness of a· that he had taught.
46–21 his exaltation above a· material conditions ;
46–31 by a· they had witnessed and suffered,
49– 8 Were a· conspirators save eleven?
49–17 Forsaken by a· whom he had blessed,
50–23 Even what they did say, . . . that a· evidence of
51–20 was for the salvation of us a·,
51–24 in a· that he said and did.
52–26 not for their day only but for a· time :
53–29 had not conquered a· the beliefs of the flesh
54– 8 A· must . . . plant themselves in Christ,
55–23 divine healing is throughout a· time ;
55–24 whosoever layeth his earthly a· on the altar
m 56– 4 to fulfil a· righteousness." — *Matt.* 3 : 15.
56–16 Infidelity . . . is the social scourge of a· races,
58–14 selfish exaction of a· another's time and
59– 5 should wait on a· the years of married life.
59– 9 not be required to participate in a· the
64–26 Until it is learned that God is the Father of a·,
64–31 will ultimately claim its own, — a· that really is,
67–23 Grace and Truth are potent beyond a· other
69–14 unfolds a· creation, confirms the Scriptures,
sp 70–12 The divine Mind maintains a· identities,
71– 5 idea, of a· reality continues forever ;
71– 6 Principle of a·, is not *in* Spirit's formations.
72–10 and in the place of darkness a· is light,
75–22 waken . . . out of the belief that a· must die,
76– 4 forgets a· else and breathes aloud his rapture.
79–27 Science objects to a· this, contending that
83–23 Between C. S. and a· forms of
84–28 A· we correctly know of Spirit comes from God,
86–27 can a· be taken from pictorial thought
87– 1 So is it with a· material conceptions.
87–23 yet these are a· there.
89–19 It possesses of itself a· beauty and poetry,
89–22 We are a· capable of more than we do.
91– 7 point of departure for a· true spiritual growth.
93–22 belief that Spirit is finite . . . has darkened a·
          history.
94– 5 includes a· that is implied by the
95– 8 in that ratio we know a· human need
96–19 a· discord will be swallowed up in spiritual
96–23 until a· errors of belief yield to understanding.
97–19 until divine Spirit, . . . dominates a· matter,
97–27 indicates that a· matter will disappear
98–18 It is imperious throughout a· ages
an 102– 2 God governs a· that is real, harmonious,
104–15 indicates the rightness of a· divine action,
s 108– 8 show the falsity of a· material things ;
108–22 a· real being is in God, the divine Mind,
108–31 mortal, misnamed *mind* produces a· the
109–17 Principle of a· harmonious Mind-action
110– 2 filling all space, constituting a· Science,
110– 6 God's creation, in which a· that He has made
113– 2 one divine Principle of a· Science ;
113–18 God, Spirit, being a·, nothing is matter.
114–23 C. S. explains a· cause and effect as mental,
116–16 even to the extinction of a· belief in matter,
116–18 They never . . . insist upon the fact that God
          is a·,
118–20 In a· mortal forms of thought,
119–12 to make Him responsible for a· disasters,
124– 2 based on Truth, the Principle of a· science.
126– 8 A· Science is divine.
126–18 Or shall a· that is beyond the cognizance
130– 8 Science, which destroys a· discord,
130–12 demonstrated, will destroy a· discord,
132–13 divine Principle which brings out a· harmony
136–30 they did not comprehend a· that he said
138–18 the precedent for a· Christianity,
138–27 "Go ye into a· the world, — *Mark* 16 : 15.
141– 9 to leave a· for Christ.
141–10 A· revelation (such is the popular thought !)
141–20 The Bible declares that a· believers are
142– 6 modern religions generally omit a· but one of
146–29 It lives through a· Life, and extends
148–16 Anatomy takes up man at a· points materially,
149–26 divine Mind, governs a·, not partially but
150–27 doctrine that man's harmony . . . a· his earthly
          days,

all

all

all

o 349–15 like a· other languages, English is inadequate
349–29 equally true of a· learning, even that which
350– 6 To understand a· our Master's sayings
353–10 A· must admit that Christ is
353–16 A· the real is eternal.
353–20 We must give up the spectral at a· points.
353–22 but we must yield up a· belief in it
354– 7 to leave a· for Christ, Truth?
360– 2 nothing is lost, and a· is won, by
361–14 conflicts not at a· with another of his sayings :
p 363–10 Nor was this a·.
363–21 and so brought home the lesson to a·,
364– 5 lay down his mortal existence in behalf of a·
365– 6 than a· cries of "Lord, Lord !"
367–16 with those hairs a· numbered by the Father.
368– 6 time will prove a· this.
368–27 the source of a· seeming sickness.
369– 2 a· discordant conditions,
369– 5 loses to human sense a· entity
369–10 A· these deeds manifested Jesus' control
371–13 looks for relief in a· ways except the right
372– 9 Science of being, in which a· is divine Mind,
373– 1 If we are Christians on a· moral questions,
373– 9 Under a· modes of pathological treatment,
374–16 we can destroy a· ills which proceed from
375–15 A· unscientific mental practice is erroneous
376–14 than in a· the blood which ever flowed
377–10 they can be healthy in a· climates,
377–26 cause of a· so-called disease is mental,
379– 7 recognizing a· causation as vested in divine
384–28 a· the evidence before the senses can never
385– 9 and endurance surpassing a· other aids,
385–13 exempts man from a· penalties but those
385–15 a· untoward conditions, if without sin,
386–22 Thus it is with a· sorrow, sickness, and
386–25 Error, . . . produces a· the suffering on earth.
388–17 ambiguous nature of a· material health-theories.
390– 2 she said, "My food is a· digested,
390–10 Truth will at length compel us a· to exchange
391–15 Truth, will destroy a· other supposed suffering,
391–31 as a· that is pure, and bearing the fruits
392– 9 take antagonistic grounds against a· that
393– 7 remote, and exciting cause of a· bad effects
393–12 resist a· that is unlike good.
394– 3 to understand that . . . is best of a·,
394–21 assuring him that a· misfortunes
395–12 destroys a· faith in sin and
396– 3 efface from thought a· forms and types of
396–20 wrong side,— a· teaching that the body suffers,
399–28 A· that is real is included in this
400–23 Mortal mind rules a· that is mortal.
403–26 so-called mind produces a· that is unlike
404–10 Lust, malice, and a· sorts of evil are
404–17 The temperance reform, felt a· over our land,
406– 1 The Bible contains the recipe for a· healing.
406–16 a· that is unlike the true likeness disappears.
411–20 procuring cause and foundation of a· sickness
412– 2 The great fact that God lovingly governs a·,
413–22 need not wash his little body a· over each day
415–23 represent the action of a· the organs
417–13 a· causation is Mind, acting through
418– 3 depends on mentally destroying a· belief
418–21 A· metaphysical logic is inspired by this simple
418–22 rule of Truth, which governs a· reality.
418–27 Cast out a· manner of evil.
419– 4 Errors of a· sorts can enter in this direction.
419–20 Mind produces a· action.
421– 6 true definition of a· human belief
421–17 God, Spirit, is a·, and there is none beside Him,
425–32 Discard a· notions about lungs, tubercles,
426–23 The relinquishment of a· faith in death
426–32 human concepts . . . are a·that can be destroyed,
427–24 Mind, governing a·, must be acknowledged
427–27 when a· such remedies have failed?
429–27 have faith in a· the sayings of our Master,
430– 1 includes a· the phenomena of existence.
431– 5 During a· this time the prisoner
431–16 a· these assistants resigned to me,
434–24 A· the testimony has been on the side of
436–10 Upon this statute hangs a· the law
438– 5 over a· the power of the enemy :— Luke 10 : 19.
439–27 Our higher statutes declare you a·,
441– 1 comprehending and defining a· law
442–10 a· sallowness and debility had disappeared.
t 443–10 a· are privileged to work out their
443–21 with a· longsuffering— II Tim. 4 : 2.
444– 3 a· must rise superior to materiality,
447–21 the claims of evil and disease in a· their forms,
451–26 A· mental malpractice arises from ignorance or
454–13 truth which strips a· disguise from error.
454–27 loving care . . . support a· their feeble footsteps,
456–26 so do a· his students and patients.
458– 1 on the same platform as a· other quackery.
459– 6 gain . . . by forsaking a· worldliness.
460– 4 necessary constituents and relations of a·

all

t 460– 5 and it underlies a· metaphysical practice.
460–12 to the material thought a· is material,
r 466– 2 adopted from the Latin adjective signifying a·.
466–26 the outcome of a· man-made beliefs.
468–10 A· is infinite Mind and its infinite
469– 3 which includes in itself a· substance
471– 3 a· that He creates are perfect and eternal,
471–28 gave the spiritual import, . . . of a· that proceeds
472– 7 making it coordinate with a· that is real
472–24 A· reality is in God, and His creation,
472–26 and He makes a· that is made.
473– 1 a· inharmony of mortal mind or body is
473–13 more than a· other men, has presented
474–17 they must a· be from the same source ;
474–26 Truth spares a· that is true.
474–29 while a· that is real is eternal.
475– 2 To Truth there is no error,— a· is Truth.
475– 3 a· is Spirit, divine Principle and its idea.
475–15 compound idea of God, including a· right ideas ;
475–16 generic term for a· that reflects God's image
475–22 reflects spiritually a· that belongs to his Maker.
476–22 outside of a· material selfhood.
479–10 image of mortal thought, . . . is a· that the eye
480–12 origin and governor of a· that Science reveals.
481–23 human verdicts are the procurers of a· discord.
483– 7 Mind transcends a· other power,
483– 8 supersede a· other means in healing.
483–26 to receive aid, . . . from a· thinking persons.
484–23 involuntary action of error in a· its forms ;
484–26 hypotheses involved in a· false theories and
486–23 a· the spiritual senses of man, are eternal.
488–24 Mind alone possesses a· faculties,
488–29 reproduce them in a· their perfection ;
489–13 it breaks a· the commands of the
489–29 Outside the material sense of things, a· is
490–24 destroy a· material sense with immortal
491–12 facts of being, in which a· must end.
492–19 fight it out on this line, if it takes a· summer."
493– 6 A· the evidence of physical sense and a·
493–17 superior to a· the beliefs of the five corporeal
493–18 Mind must be found . . . able to destroy a· ills.
495– 3 A· of Truth is not understood ;
496– 9 We a· must learn that Life is God.
496–19 overlying, and encompassing a· true being.
g 504– 6 A· questions as to the divine creation
505– 9 divine Mind, not matter, creates a· identities,
506–29 task of finding names for a· material things,
507– 7 Spirit names and blesses a·.
507–21 reflect the Mind which includes a·.
507–24 Infinite Mind creates and governs a·,
507–25 divine Principle of a· expresses Science
508– 3 Mind is All and reproduces a·
508– 7 Mind is the Soul of a·.
508– 8 Mind is Life, . . . which governs a·.
509– 3 is discerned to be the Life of a·,
510–11 reflected spiritually by a· who walk in the light
512–22 a· form, color, quality, and quantity,
513–17 classifies, and individualizes a· thoughts,
513–20 continuity of a· individuality
513–26 God creates a· forms of reality.
514–19 Tenderness accompanies a· the might
514–26 the control which Love held over a·,
514–28 A· of God's creatures, moving in the
515–22 family name for a· ideas,
515–22 A· that God imparts moves in accord with
516–13 bathes a· in beauty and light.
517–19 they a· have one Principle and parentage.
518–16 a· having the same Principle, or Father ;
518–21 which shine through a· as the blossom
518–21 A· the varied expressions of God reflect
518–28 Spirit, comprehends and expresses a·,
518–28 a· must therefore be as perfect as the
519– 2 who from a· eternity knoweth His own
519– 8 and a· the host of them.— Gen. 2 : 1.
519–18 "we a· come in the unity of— Eph. 4 : 13.
519–24 a· His work which He had made.— Gen. 2 : 2.
520–13 in which a· sense of error forever disappears
520–23 emphatic declaration that God creates a·
520–29 Because Mind makes a·, there is
521–5, 6 A· that is made is the work of God, and a· is
522– 5 assigns a· might and government to God.
523–12 A· is material myth, instead of
524–23 God is reflected in a· His creation.
526– 8 namely, that a· Life is God.
526–16 God pronounced good a· that He created.
526–17 Scriptures declare that He created a·.
529–28 faith to fight a· claims of evil,
530–11 recognizing God, the Father and Mother of a·,
531– 4 maintained in a· the subsequent forms of belief.
531–11 rise above a· material and physical sense,
532– 4 God makes and governs a·.
532– 5 A· human knowledge and material sense
533–10 an attempt to trace a· human errors
535–23 eat of it a· the days of thy life :— Gen. 3 : 17.
536– 9 The divine understanding reigns, is a·,

all

g 538– 3   drive error out of *a·* selfhood.
539–18   the serpent, to grovel beneath *a·* the beasts
540– 6   I the Lord do *a·* these things ;"— *Isa.* 45 : 7.
540–15   that Truth may annihilate *a·* sense of evil
543–13   with *a·* its sin, sickness, and death,
543–25   When Spirit made *a·*, did it leave aught for
544–16   A· is under the control of the one Mind,
545–14   errors send falsity into *a·* human doctrines
545–18   Outside of C. S. *a·* is vague and hypothetical,
545–31   "As in Adam [error] *a·* die,— *I Cor.* 15 : 22.
545–32   shall *a·* be made alive."— *I Cor.* 15 : 22.
546–30   Principle which *a·* may understand.
547– 1   one example would authenticate *a·* the others.
547– 3   contains the proof of *a·* here said of C. S.
551–11   through *a·* the lower grades of existence.
551–16   *a·* Science is of God, not of man.
551–20   by which *a·* peculiarities of ancestry,
551–27, 28   A· must be Mind, or else *a·* must be matter.
552– 6   geology, and *a·* other material hypotheses
554– 2   even the cause of *a·* that exists,
554–26   A· these sayings were to show that
556– 7   destroys forever *a·* belief in
ap 559– 2   open for *a·* to read and understand.
559– 6   the source of *a·* error's visible forms?
560–24   *a·* who have spoken something new
562–12   The twelve tribes of Israel with *a·* mortals,
564–15   Since Jesus must have been tempted in *a·* points,
565– 7   rule *a·* nations with a rod of iron :— *Rev.* 12 : 5.
565–16   God's idea, will eventually rule *a·* nations and
565–23   and *a·* was primeval harmony,
566– 6   so shall the spiritual idea guide *a·* right desires
567– 7   To infinite, ever-present Love, *a·* is Love,
568–31   Self-abnegation, by which we lay down *a·* for
571–11   At *a·* times and under *a·* circumstances,
571–20   higher humanity will unite *a·* interests
573–31   and *a·* tears will be wiped away.
574– 4   weary pilgrim, journeying "uphill *a·* the way."
575–20   shall not be shut at *a·* by day :— *Rev.* 21 : 25.
577–22   A· who are saved must walk in this light.
577–25   *a·* is good, and nothing can enter that
578–16   mercy shall follow me *a·* the days— *Psal.* 23 : 6.
gl 583–21   divine Principle of *a·* that is real and good ;
583–24   God, who made *a·* that was made
587– 7   Life ; Truth ; Love ; *a·* substance ;
588–15   A· the objects of God's creation reflect
592–23   the immortality of *a·* that is spiritual.
593–21   demonstrated as supreme over *a·* ;
594–20   *a·* that is good ; God ;
595–18   limits, in which are summed up *a·* human acts,
596–15   reveals Spirit, . . . as the illuminator of *a·*.
fr 600– *   *worthy of the Lord unto a· pleasing,— Col.* 1 : 10.
(*see also* **being, disease, earth, error, evil, existence, good, mankind, men, Mind, others, power, sin, space, things, truth**)

all-absorbing

c 264–27   peace which comes from an *a·* spiritual love.

all-acting

gl 587– 6   *a·*, all-wise, all-loving, and eternal ;

allay

a 44–13   He took no drugs to *a·* inflammation.

allayed

s 159–18   They would either have *a·* her fear

allaying

p 411–27   begin your treatment by *a·* the fear
422– 9   *a·* the tremor which Truth often brings to error

alleged

sp 81–14   Nor is the case improved when *a·* spirits
o 345–32   as is *a·* by one critic.
p 434–28   shows the *a·* crime never to have been
436– 8   on the night of the *a·* offence

allegiance

a 32– 4   soldier was required to swear *a·*
f 226–21   man's birthright of sole *a·* to his Maker

allegorical

ap 564–31   this *a·*, talking serpent typifies mortal mind,
575–16   Taken in its *a·* sense,

allegory

ph 177–15   Scriptural *a·* of the material creation,
b 280–21   The argument of the serpent in the *a·*,
p 430–13   I here present to my readers an *a·*
430–15   an *a·* in which the plea of C. S. heals
g 531– 7   The order of this *a·*— the belief that
532–28   In the *a·* the body had been naked,
533–12   The *a·* shows that the snake-talker utters the
537–20   the purpose of this *a·*— this second account
540–22   Hebrew *a·*, representing error as assuming
544–26   Therefore man, in this *a·*, is neither a

all-embracing

an 102–10   pointing of the needle . . . symbolizes this *a·*

alleviate

an 101–26   If animal magnetism seems to *a·*

alleviates

p 411–31   it *a·* the symptoms of every disease.

alleviating

an 100– 6   as a means of *a·* disease.

all-harmonious

pr 16–27   Our Father-Mother God, *a·*,

all-hearing

pr 7–24   It is the *a·* and all-knowing Mind,

allied

s 121–31   and is *a·* to divine Science as displayed in
g 512–14   their natures are *a·* to God's nature ;

All-in-all

God being
s 142–28   God being *A·*, He made medicine ;
God is
    (*see* **God**)
Mind is
s 109– 5   reveals incontrovertibly that Mind is *A·*,

— — —

sp 72–24   derived from God, the infinite *A·*,
an 103–16   God and His idea, the *A·*.
s 127– 4   If God, the *A·*, be the creator
b 275– 7   starting-point . . . is that God, Spirit, is *A·*,
gl 596– 6   makes Him better known as the *A·*,

all-in-all

g 552–17   emerge from this notion of material life as *a·*.

all-inclusive

a 52–21   the mighty actuality of *a·* God, good.
s 116–10   is and must of necessity be,— *a·*.
b 287–14   God being everywhere and *a·*,
331–20   He is *a·*, and is reflected by
g 514– 4   nothing exists beyond the range of *a·* infinity,

all-inclusiveness

o 351–25   the *a·* of harmonious Truth.

all-knowing

pr 7–25   It is the all-hearing and *a·* Mind,
ph 187– 4   how ignorant must they be of the *a·* Mind
r 487–15   Spirit is *a·* ;
gl 587– 5   The great I AM ; the *a·*, all-seeing,

All-loving

pr 2–12   the *A·* does not grant them simply on the

all-loving

gl 587– 6   all-acting, all-wise, *a·*, and eternal ;

all-might

b 319–11   must yield to the *a·* of infinite Spirit.

allness

pr 15–18   we must deny sin and plead God's *a·*.
c 267– 6   The *a·* of Deity is His oneness.
b 328–13   the grand realities of His *a·*.
336–23   A· is the measure of the infinite,
o 346–12   to prove the somethingness— yea, the *a·*— of
p 424–25   the oneness and the *a·* of divine Love ;
t 450–21   by understanding . . . the *a·* of God,
r 497–22   even the *a·* of Soul, Spirit,
ap 563–17   the nothingness of evil and the *a·* of God.

allopathic

p 416– 9   Yet any physician— *a·*, homœopathic,

allopathy

s 158–28   Homœopathy, a step in advance of *a·*,
o 344–30   Is it because *a·* and homœopathy are more

allow

a 30–27   to *a·* Soul to hold the control,
c 259–10   higher than their poor thought-models would *a·*,
p 433– 8   urges the jury not to *a·* their judgment to be
r 495–15   A· nothing but His likeness to abide

allowed

a 51– 9   but he *a·* men to attempt the
m 62–17   Children should be *a·* to remain children
63–30   woman should be *a·* to collect her own wages,
p 431– 2   *a·* to testify in the case.
434–10   where C. S. is *a·* to appear as counsel
437–15   Spirit not *a·* a hearing ;
437–30   unjust usages were not *a·* at the bar of Truth,

allowing

s 108–12   My conclusions were reached by *a·* the evidence
159–28   how much . . . one form of matter is *a·*

allows

ph 187–16   Anatomy *a·* the mental cause of the
o 343–28   Hence the mistake which *a·* words, rather than
g 549–29   and *a·* matter and material law to usurp

All-power

f 231–10   no lesser power equals the infinite *A·* ;
t 454– 6   The understanding, . . . of the divine *A·*
gl 581– 3   ALMIGHTY. A· ; infinity ; omnipotence.

all-power

pr	17–14	*For God is infinite, a*,
s	130–14	good and its sweet concords have *a*.
f	203– 4	omnipotence— has *a*, assigns sure rewards
	228–26	Omnipotence has *a*,
r	466– 3	Hence God combines *a* or potency,
	469–27	after admitting that God, . . . has *a*,

all-powerful

s	108–23	Life, Truth, and Love are *a*
t	450– 4	belief . . . in a natural, *a* devil.

all-presence

b	278–22	Spirit is supreme and *a*.
r	466– 4	all-science or true knowledge, *a*.

all-science

r	466– 3	God combines all-power or potency, *a*

all-seeing

gl	587– 5	The great I AM ; the all-knowing, *a*,

alludes

b	333–10	*a* to the spirituality which is taught,
o	342– 1	*a* to "doubtful disputations."— *Rom.* 14 : 1.

alluring

a	21–28	The company is *a* and the pleasures exciting.

allusion

g	510–21	There is no Scriptural *a* to solar light until
	510–23	and the *a* to fluids . . . indicates

All-wise

t	455–23	The *A* does not bestow

all-wise

gl	587– 6	all-acting, *a*, all-loving, and eternal ;

almanacs

ph	171– 9	not needing to consult *a* for the probabilities

almightiness

r	487–29	reality of Life, its *a* and immortality.

Almighty (*see also* Almighty's)

s	119– 4	When we . . . we disown the *A*,
g	501– *	*by the name of God A*;— *Exod.* 6 : 3.
ap	576–10	the Lord God *A* and the Lamb— *Rev.* 21 : 22.
gl	581– 3	definition of

almighty

f	202–27	admit that God has *a* power,
o	348–15	when we ascribe to Him *a* Life and Love?
	357–27	Can Deity be *a*, if another mighty

Almighty God

f	228–15	assert their freedom in the name of *A* *G*.
p	438–15	I ask your arrest in the name of *A* *G*

Almighty's

f	218–20	why do you substitute drugs for the *A* power,

almost

f	221–11	in hunger and weakness, *a* in starvation,
o	350– 2	They think of matter as something and *a*
p	376– 7	and does its work *a* self-deceived.
g	502– 3	is so brief that it would *a* seem,
	524–10	the true idea of God seems *a* lost.
gl	590–17	the word *kurios a* always has this lower sense,

aloft

p	426–27	hold the banner of Christianity *a*

alone

pr	6– 4	this divine Principle *a* reforms the sinner.
	11–28	nor can prayer *a* give us an
a	25–28	will never *a* make us imitators of him.
	26– 2	treading *a* his loving pathway
	49–15	met his earthly fate *a* with God.
	51–22	His purpose in healing was not *a* to
m	57–20	it cannot exist *a*, but requires all mankind
	60–13	selfishness and impurity *a* are fleeting,
	60–32	Higher enjoyments *a* can satisfy
	64–11	some noble woman, struggling *a* with
sp	86– 2	to be occasioned by physical contact *a*,
	86–23	Education *a* determines the difference.
	90– 8	earth's motion . . . sustained by Mind *a*.
	92–29	instead of urging the claims of Truth *a*.
s	117– 4	not one of a series, but one *a*
	117– 9	mortals *a* do this.
	127–10	The terms . . . C. S., or Science *a*,
	127–27	and is *a* able to interpret God aright.
	135– 9	Spiritual evolution *a* is worthy of
	142– 9	Truth, *a* can furnish us with absolute
	147–30	but Science *a* reveals the divine Principle
	157– 9	rests on Mind *a* as the curative Principle,
ph	173–28	error which the human mind *a* has created.
	174–25	if . . . sick, why treat the body *a*
	182– 2	healing the sick through divine Mind *a*,
	184–21	Mortal mind *a* suffers,
	194–31	a belief formed by education *a*.
	196– 9	Sin *a* brings death, is sin is the only
	199–10	great fact that Mind *a* enlarges and
f	203–32	for God *a* is man's life.
	212–22	God *a* makes and clothes the lilies
	219–28	not rendering to God the honor due to Him *a*.
	251–14	an error that Christ, Truth, *a* can destroy.

alone

c	263– 6	Immortal spiritual man *a* represents the
b	270–26	Truth and Love *a* can unmake them.
	270–29	the fact that the human mind *a* suffers,
	270–30	the divine Mind *a* heals.
	271–17	"Neither pray I for these *a*,— *John* 17 : 20.
	272–31	C. S., . . . *a* reveals the natural, divine
	279–28	not two bases of being, . . . but one *a*,
	285– 4	Science of being obtains not *a* hereafter
	292– 4	Divine Science *a* can compass the heights
	308–16	Jacob was *a* wrestling with error,
	339– 8	Spirit, *a* created all, and called it good.
p	366–19	Love which *a* confers the healing power.
	382– 7	this *a* would usher in the millennium.
	389– 4	a victory which Science *a* can explain.
	391–26	Mortal mind *a* sentences itself.
	400–22	thought *a* creates the suffering.
	402– 6	cure, . . . through mental surgery *a*,
	409–20	should be governed by God *a*.
	410–10	"Man shall not live by bread *a*,— *Matt.* 4 : 4.
	419– 6	God and His ideas *a* are real
	424–26	to be *a* with God and the sick when
	435– 6	Mortal Mind, which *a* is capable of sin and
t	456– 8	This *a* entitles them to the high standing
	462–18	self-denial, sincerity, . . . and persistence *a*
r	483–24	wrestle with material observations *a*,
	488–23	Mind *a* possesses all faculties,
g	510–18	Love *a* can impart the limitless idea of
	518– 3	himself subordinate *a* to his Maker.
	533–20	more rapidly than he can *a*.
	543–26	Ideas of Truth *a* are reflected in the
	546– 3	this belief *a* is mortal.
	556–15	but the Christian *a* can fathom it.
gl	595–15	which *a* can fit us for the office of
	596– 1	That which spiritual sense *a* comprehends,

along

s	129–27	some of the leading illusions *a* the path
	141–11	the line of scholarly and ecclesiastical
	156–22	she could get *a* two days without globules ;
o	343–31	first . . . to press *a* the line of gospel-healing,
p	373–28	languidly creeps *a* its frozen channels,
	415–30	whole frame will sink from sight *a* with
r	490–22	*a* with the dissolving elements of clay.

aloof

s	109–13	kept *a* from society, and devoted time

aloud

sp	76– 5	forgets all else and breathes *a* his rapture.
p	396– 9	avoid speaking *a* the name of the disease.

Alpine

m	61–17	like tropical flowers born amid *A* snows.

already

pr	2– 9	to do more than He has *a* done,
	2–14	for He *a* knows all.
	2–25	anything He does not *a* comprehend?
	3– 6	The rule is *a* established, and it is our task
	3–23	really grateful for the good *a* received?
	8–26	do we not *a* know more of this heart
	11–15	if indeed, he has not *a* suffered sufficiently
m	69– 7	God's children *a* created will be cognized
sp	74– 7	acorn, *a* absorbed into a sprout
	80–20	when we *a* know that it is mind-power which
s	108–20	*a* within the shadow of the death-valley,
	112–24	*a* been stated and proved to be true,
	130–20	cannot add to the contents of a vessel *a* full.
	131–15	This Science has come *a*,
	137–12	In his rejection of the answer *a* given
	147–21	perishing fossils of theories *a* antiquated,
	161–28	if it were not *a* determined by mortal mind.
	163–17	it has *a* destroyed more lives than
ph	168–13	have *a* brought yourself into the slough of
	175– 2	efface the outlines of disease *a* formulated
	180–15	reservoir *a* overflowing with that emotion.
	198– 7	his fear, which has *a* developed the disease
f	201–13	We cannot fill vessels *a* full.
	206–22	Is God creating anew what He has *a* created?
	229– 2	it is *a* proved that matter has not destroyed
	233–16	*A* the shadow of His right hand rests upon
c	260–14	to discover what God has *a* done;
	266– 9	this seeming vacuum is *a* filled
b	274–31	This suppositional partnership is *a* obsolete,
	291– 8	till mortals have *a* yielded to each lesser call
	323–14	must put into practice what we *a* know.
p	402– 4	the author has *a* in her possession
	416–30	have *a* heard too much on that subject.
t	459–10	Judge not . . . by the steps *a* taken,
r	490–16	since he is so *a*, according to C. S.
	492– 7	It is *a* proved that a knowledge of this,
g	510–22	*a* divided into evening and morning ;
	521–24	presented in the verses *a* considered,
	528– 3	God has *a* created man, both male and
	533–21	is *a* found in the rapid deterioration
	533–31	She has *a* learned that corporeal sense
ap	572–24	he *a* saw a new heaven and a new earth.

also

pref	ix– 1	She *a·* began to jot down her thoughts
	xi–23	there came *a·* the charge to plant and
pr	6– 2	"he *a·* will deny us." — *II Tim.* 2 : 12.
	11– 2	specified *a·* the terms of forgiveness.
	14–20	works that I do shall he do *a·* ; — *John* 14 : 12.
a	23–32	Hebrew verb *to believe* means *a·* to be firm
	34–20	His resurrection was *a·* their resurrection.
	40–13	opposite is *a·* true, While there's sin there's
	42–31	works that I do shall he do *a·*." — *John* 14 : 12.
	52–28	works that I do shall he do *a·* ;" — *John* 14 : 12.
m	60– 6	The beautiful in character is *a·* the good,
sp	71–16	Thus you learn that these *a·* are images,
	71–18	From dreams *a·* you learn that
	92– 5	*a·* capable of imparting these sensations.
	93– 5	works that I do shall he do *a·*," — *John* 14 : 12.
	93– 5	*a·* said, "But the hour cometh, — *John* 4 : 23.
an	106–25	as I have *a·* told you in time past, — *Gal.* 5 : 21.
s	112–26	*A·*, if any so-called new school claims to be
	117– 1	term *individuality* is *a·* open to objections,
	133– 5	There was *a·* a certain centurion of whose
	135–11	same power which heals sin heals *a·* sickness.
	137–29	"And I say *a·* unto thee, — *Matt.* 16 : 18.
	158– 7	Apollo was *a·* regarded as the sender of
	162–15	*a·* without the false beliefs of a so-called
ph	169–19	*a·* declares that all disease is cured by
	181–29	there will your heart be *a·*." — *Matt.* 6 : 21.
	186–24	If . . . evil is *a·* as immortal.
f	221– 8	His physician *a·* recommended that he
	222– 7	He learned *a·* that mortal mind
	222–13	he *a·* had less faith in the so called
	243–10	which was *a·* in Christ Jesus" — *Phil.* 2 : 5.
	253–22	*A·*, if you believe yourself diseased,
c	255– *	*not only they, but ourselves a·*, — *Rom.* 8 : 23.
	202–20	there will your heart be *a·*." — *Matt.* 6. 21.
b	268– *	*a· may have fellowship with* — *I John* 1 : 3.
	271–18	for them *a·* which shall believe — *John* 17 : 20.
	276– 9	which was *a·* in Christ Jesus." — *Phil.* 2 : 5.
	286–29	error must *a·* say, "I am true."
	305–12	Gender *a·* is a quality, not of God,
	305–19	these *a·* doeth the Son likewise." — *John* 5 : 19.
	320–13	for that he *a·* is flesh," — *Gen.* 6 : 3.
	325–11	then shall ye *a·* appear — *Col.* 3 : 4.
	326– 5	works that I do shall he do *a·*." — *John* 14 : 12.
	327– 2	and *a·* by gaining an affection for good
	331–14	Scriptures *a·* declare that God is Spirit.
	332– 1	They *a·* indicate the divine Principle
	332– 8	"For we are *a·* His offspring." — *Acts* 17 : 28.
	334–29	and is *a·* a reference to the human sense of
o	341– *	*a· quicken your mortal bodies* — *Rom.* 8 : 11.
	343–13	he *a·* scientifically demonstrates this great fact,
p	364–23	it must be said of them *a·* that they
	366–22	The physician must *a·* watch, lest he
	369– 1	and he is liable to admit *a·* the reality of
	370–26	Hygienic treatment *a·* loses its efficacy.
	372–25	*a·* deny before my Father *Matt.* 10 : 33.
	373–17	Scriptures *a·* declare, through the exalted
	377–23	You *a·* remove in this way what are termed
	377–28	*a·* a fear that Mind is helpless
	398–25	So *a·* faith, cooperating with a belief
	405–17	that shall he *a·* reap." — *Gal.* 6 : 7.
	414–11	*a·* the fact that truth and love will
	414–24	*a·* that matter neither feels, suffers, nor enjoys.
	416– 1	At last the agony *a·* vanishes.
	426–15	*a·* learning the necessity of working out his
	426–23	and *a·* of the fear of its sting
	429–23	it must *a·* have an ending,
	437– 2	*a·* testified that he was on intimate terms
	439– 2	*A·*, be it known that False Belief,
	441– 5	He *a·* decided that the plaintiff, Personal Sense,
	441–32	speaks of him *a·* as "a murderer — *John* 8 : 44.
t	444–18	but let us *a·* be careful always to
	444–20	turn to him the other *a·*." — *Matt.* 5 : 39.
	445– 2	*A·* the teacher must thoroughly fit his students
	451–16	there will his heart be *a·*.
	452–12	but it will *a·* attract respect.
	463– 5	Teacher and student should *a·* be familiar with
r	465–13	They are *a·* intended to express the nature,
	467–16	having that Mind which was *a·* in Christ.
	469– 6	it would *a·* have an ending.
	490–10	From this *a·* comes its powerlessness,
	494–31	It should be said of his followers *a·*,
	496– 1	You will *a·* learn that in Science there is no
	497–25	that Mind to be in us which was *a·* in Christ
g	504–12	This *a·* shows that there is no place where
	510–15	He made the stars *a·*. — *Gen.* 1 : 16.
	512– 9	*a·* by holy thoughts, winged with Love.
	514–22	wolf *a·* shall dwell with the lamb, — *Isa.* 11 : 6.
	515–26	lift a weight, your reflection does this *a·*.
	517– 1	the word for *man* is used *a·* as the synonym
	524– 6	It was *a·* found among the Israelites.
	526– 1	the tree of life *a·*, in the midst of — *Gen.* 2 : 9.
	527–15	It is plain *a·* that material perception,
	529– 4	It came about, *a·*, that instruments were needed
	535–24	thorns *a·* and thistles shall it — *Gen.* 3 : 18.
	537– 2	and take *a·* of the tree of life, — *Gen.* 3 : 22.

also

g	537–14	that shall he *a·* reap." — *Gal.* 6 : 7.
	540–26	And Abel, he *a·* brought of the — *Gen.* 4 : 4.
	548–31	*a·* increase their numbers naturally
	553–31	may *a·* ask how belief can affect a result
	554–22	*a·* said, "Have not I chosen — *John* 6 : 70.
ap	561–11	saw *a·* the spiritual ideal as a woman
	562–24	*A·* the spiritual idea is typified by
	563–16	but he *a·* sees the nothingness of evil
	566–19	we may *a·* offer the prayer which concludes
	568–11	Here, *a·*, the Revelator first exhibits the
	570–28	They should *a·* know the great delusion of
	574– 3	The Revelator *a·* takes in another view,
	574–21	brought *a·* the experience which at last
	576–14	The word *temple a·* means *body.*
gl	579– 6	which is *a·* their original meaning.
	598– 1	Greek word for *wind (pneuma)* is used *a·*

altar

a	55–24	on the *a·* of divine Science,
m	65– 4	May Christ, Truth, be present at every bridal *a·*
t	454–21	Love is priestess at the *a·* of Truth.
gl	596– 7	Paul saw in Athens an *a·* dedicated

alter

f	253–23	you can *a·* this wrong belief and action
b	297– 4	no circumstance can *a·* the situation, until
p	382– 8	bathing and rubbing to *a·* the secretions

alterative

s	162– 6	C. S. acts as an *a·*, neutralizing error
f	224– 2	the world feels the *a·* effect of truth
p	371–30	Truth is an *a·* in the entire system,
	420–21	better than any drug, *a·*, or tonic.
	421–22	chemicalization, which is the *a·* effect
	423–11	This corrective is an *a·*, reaching to every part

altered

p	408– 2	This view is not *a·* by the fact that

alternating

b	298–16	This human belief, *a·* between a

alternative

f	221–14	informed him that death was indeed his only *a·*.
p	436–21	You have left Mortal Man no *a·*.

although

a	19–14	*a·* his teaching set households at variance,
	19–28	*a·* God is good.
	30– 6	*a·* he was endowed with the Christ,
	55–13	*a·* it is again ruled out of the synagogue.
s	112–10	*A·* these opinions may have occasional gleams
	147–14	*A·* this volume contains the complete
	148–32	*a·* our great Master demonstrated that
	152– 8	*a·* they know not how the work is done.
	158–32	*a·* her physicians insisted that it would be
o	343– 8	*a·*, without this cross-bearing, one might not
p	386–29	you would not have understood him, *a·* the
	430–31	*A·* I have the superintendence of
	431–28	*a·* nothing on my part has occasioned
r	466–17	*a·* . . . it is the most important to understand.
	469–22	when we admit that, *a·* God is infinite,
	471–14	*a·* the evidence as to these facts
	492– 2	*a·* the so-called dreamer is unconscious?
g	523– 6	*A·* presenting the exact opposite of
	546–16	*a·* the material senses can take no cognizance

altitudes

f	215–11	not subordinate to geometric *a·*.

altogether

pr	3–14	the One "*a·* lovely ;" — *Song* 5 : 16.
sp	87–32	or *a·* gone from physical sight
g	538– 1	Love infinitely wise and *a·* lovely,

alway

b	317–14	"Lo, I am with you *a·*," — *Matt.* 28 : 20.
t	446–22	"Lo, I am with you *a·*, — *Matt.* 28 : 20.

always

pr	4–12	The habitual struggle to be *a·* good
	5–14	but not *a·* in this world.
	7–18	If spiritual sense *a·* guided men,
	7–26	to whom each need of man is *a·* known
	8–21	does not *a·* mean a desire for it.
	10–22	Experience teaches us that we do not *a·* receive
	10–29	it is not *a·* best for us to receive.
	11– 9	*a·* demands restitution before mortals can
	12– 5	no power to gain more . . . than is *a·* at hand.
m	62– 9	to b *a·* fed, rocked, tossed, or talked to,
	66–26	If one is better than the other, as must *a·*
sp	86–16	though we can *a·* feel their influence.
	95– 1	The effect of his Mind was *a·* to heal and
	98–22	For centuries — yea, *a·* — natural science has
an	104–12	Lastly, they say they have *a·* believed it."
s	125– 5	Moral conditions will be found *a·* harmonious
	128–30	must *a·* bring the same result.
	134– 8	and so has come *a·* to mean one who
	134–26	Thou hearest me *a·* ;" — *John* 11 : 42.
	145–22	mystery which godliness *a·* presents to
	145–22	mystery *a·* arising from ignorance of the

always
ph 169– 8 But it *a·* came about as I had foretold.
170–20 *a·* in opposition, never in obedience, to physics.
184–27 *a·* breathed with great difficulty when the
189–30 keeping *a·* in the direct line of matter,
200– 9 Life is, *a·* has been, and ever will be
f 225–12 There is *a·* some tumult, but there is a
225–26 *a·* germinating in new forms of tyranny,
243–11 must *a·* accompany the letter of Science
246–24 is *a·* beautiful and grand.
c 267–28 "let thy garments be *a·* white."— *Eccl.* 9 : 8.
b 277–31 mortal phenomenon, . . . *a·* erroneous.
282–24 *a·* governing itself erroneously.
284–32 intercommunication is *a·* from God to
302–16 is *a·* beyond and above the mortal illusion
309–29 so-called life *a·* ends in death.
320–13 My spirit shall not *a·* strive— *Gen.* 6 : 3.
326–25 spiritual sense, which is *a·* right.
329–23 A· right, its divine Principle never repents,
334–19 as the Christ has *a·* done,
336–17 never was material, but *a·* spiritual
p 375–26 Consumptive patients *a·* show . . . courage,
377– 5 he should rejoice *a·* in ever-present Love.
380– 4 Truth is *a·* the victor.
392–11 should *a·* be met with the mental negation.
402– 1 C. S. is *a·* the most skilful surgeon,
411–21 Disease is *a·* induced by a false sense
411–27 A· begin your treatment by allaying the fear
417– 4 A· support their trust in the power of Mind
425–30 be *a·* ready with the mental protest against
426– 6 when she has the high goal *a·* before her
t 443–10 she *a·* has felt, that all are privileged to
444–18 *a·* to "judge righteous— *John* 7 : 24.
448–25 must *a·* hinder scientific demonstration.
458–14 Divinity is *a·* ready.
r 482– 6 proper use of the word *soul* can *a·* be
492–32 would keep truth and error *a·* at war.
494–10 Divine Love *a·* has met and *a·* will meet
g 508–20 grammars *a·* recognize a neuter gender,
518–14 in return, the higher *a·* protects the lower.
523–20 Deity therein is *a·* called Jehovah,
530–17 myth represents error as *a·* asserting its
537–32 God, who is Love *a·*,
552–30 matter *a·* surrenders its claims when
554– 8 Error is *a·* error.
ap 575–14 Spiritual teaching must *a·* be by symbols.
gl 590–17 the word *kurios* almost *a·* has

amalgamation
f 207–17 such as the *a·* of Truth and error
g 550–27 A· is deemed monstrous

amazement
c 263–25 peers from its cloister with *a·*

ambiguities
s 114–26 disentangles the interlaced *a·* of being,

ambiguity
o 355– 2 and then the *a·* will vanish.

ambiguous
p 388–17 *a·* nature of all material health-theories.

ambition
m 58– 8 Unselfish *a·*, noble life-motives, and purity,
61– 8 and give higher aims to *a·*.
61–21 What hope of happiness, what noble *a·*,
t 462–28 It teaches the control of mad *a·*.

ambush
ap 571–11 Who is telling mankind of the foe in *a·*?

ameliorate
s 141–28 divine healing will *a·* sin, sickness, and death.
t 458–22 but Science will *a·* mortal malice.

Amen
b 268– * *I can do no otherwise; so help me God! A· !*
o 343– 1 The people are taught in such cases to say, A·.

amenable
p 434–31 God made Man immortal and *a·* to Spirit

America
b 320– 6 theologians in Europe and A· agree that

American
f 245–12 Some A· travellers saw her when she was

American Cyclopædia
an 100– 3 According to the A· C·, he regarded this

amid
a 37–14 not *a·* the smoke of battle is merit seen
m 61–17 like tropical flowers born *a·* Alpine snows.
67– 8 Can you steer safely *a·* the storm?"
sp 95–23 Led by a solitary star *a·* the darkness,
f 220–12 snowbird sings and soars *a·* the blasts;
b 306–25 Undisturbed *a·* the jarring testimony of the

amidst
m 66–17 A· gratitude for conjugal felicity,
66–18 A· conjugal infelicity, it is well to hope, pray,
ap 563–28 subtlety, winding its way *a·* all evil,

amiss
pr 10–28 receive not, because ye ask *a·*,— *Jas.* 4 : 3.
10–32 Then "ye ask *a·*."— *Jas.* 4 : 3.

among
pref ix–13 still in circulation *a·* her first pupils ;
pr 9–26 and so be counted *a·* sinners?
16–12 some doubt *a·* Bible scholars,
a 24–29 The truth had been lived *a·* men ;
32– 6 A· the Jews it was an ancient custom
m 56– 8 generation *a·* human kind.
65–22 impurity and error are left *a·* the lees.
65–26 which was once a fixed fact *a·* us,
an 101– 9 *a·* whom were Roux, Bouillaud, and
106– 8 *a·* which are self-government, reason,
s 129–28 reformatory mission *a·* mortals.
133–16 in captivity *a·* foreign nations,
150–10 a permanent dispensation *a·* men ;
161–17 *a·* which are life, liberty, and
ph 196–32 diseases *a·* the human family.
200–26 not to know anything *a·* you,— *I Cor.* 2 : 2.
200–28 not to know anything *a·* you,
f 237–16 C. S., *a·* their first lessons,
238– 7 "Come out from *a·* them,— *II Cor.* 6 : 17.
242–23 parted my raiment *a·*— *John* 19 : 24.
c 256–21 *a·* the inhabitants of the earth ; — *Dan.* 4 : 35.
t 453– 2 *a·* the examples on the blackboard,
460–29 her manuscript circulated *a·* the students.
463– 2 The material physician gropes *a·*
g 524– 6 It was also found *a·* the Israelites,
535–17 into the heritage of the first born *a·* men?

Amorites
g 524– 3 in the Moloch of the A·,

amount
ph 175–21 The exact *a·* of food the stomach could digest

amounts
ph 172– 5 *a·* to nothing in the right direction and
p 375–31 fear so excessive that it *a·* to fortitude.
g 551–23 question of the naturalist *a·* to this :

ample
s 163–26 so *a·* an exhibition of human invention

amplification
g 501–10 that *a·* of wonder and glory

amplitude
a 54– 3 Out of the *a·* of his pure affection,

amputate
ph 172–26 when you *a·* a limb ;

amputated
f 212– 5 A limb which has been *a·* has continued

amusement
m 58–20 a wandering desire for incessant *a·*
62– 9 create in their babes a desire for incessant *a·*,
ph 195–30 to meet a frivolous demand for *a·*

amusements
m 60–22 frivolous *a·*, personal adornment,

analogous
g 510–25 *a·* to the suppositional resolving of

analogy
s 110–32 No *a·* exists between the vague hypotheses of

analyzes
p 433– 3 He *a·* the offence, reviews the testimony,

anathemas
b 315–10 brought upon him the *a·* of the age.

Anatomy
p 430–23 Materia Medica, A·, Physiology,
437–22 Materia Medica, A·, Physiology,

anatomy
admits
ph 174–23 A· admits that mind is somewhere in man,
allows
ph 187–16 A· allows the mental cause of the latter action,
and theology
s 148–13 *a·* and theology define man as
148–17 A· and theology reject the divine Principle
declares
ph 173–17 A· declares man to be structural.
describes
s 152–10 A· describes muscular action as
finds
s 160–14 A· finds a necessity for nerves to
learn from
s 160–29 only to learn from *a·* that muscle is not
mental
t 462–32 Scientist, through understanding mental *a·*,
nor theology
s 148– 7 Neither *a·* nor theology has ever
of Christian Science
t 462–25 *a·* of C. S. teaches when and how to probe the
takes up man
s 148–15 A· takes up man at all points materially.

anatomy
treatises on
ph 179–21 Treatises on a·, physiology, and health,

s 160–16 what does a· say when the cords contract
160–27 Why then consult a· to learn how
ph 173– 2 we fail to see how a· can distinguish
173–23 a·, physiology, phrenology, do not define
t 462–20 A·, when conceived of spiritually, is

ancestors
m 61–20 the grosser traits of their a·.
ph 175–27 empurpled the plump cheeks of our a·,

ancestry
m 63– 6 The beautiful, good, and pure constitute his a·.
g 551–20 by which all peculiarities of a·,

anchor
a 40–32 the a· of hope must be cast beyond the

ancient
a 32– 3 In a· Rome a soldier was required to
32– 7 Among the Jews it was an a· custom
41–18 No a· school of philosophy, *materia medica*,
43–10 and is now repeating its a· history.
sp 84– 3 The a· prophets gained their foresight
an 105–28 and confirms the a· axiom :
s 126–26 found nothing in a· or in modern systems
139–17 manifest mistakes in the a· versions ;
144–30 It is a question to-day, whether the a·
146– 2 The a· Christians were healers.
146–28 It is as a· as "the Ancient of days."— *Dan. 7 : 9.*
f 243–12 to confirm and repeat the a· demonstrations
b 319–16 are so many a· and modern mythologies.
o 349– 3 As Paul asked of the unfaithful in a· days,
p 389–24 the a· error that there is fraternity between
r 469–30 a· mythology and pagan idolatry.
483–19 To . . . the a· worthies, and to Christ Jesus,
g 514–31 source of strength to the a· worthies.
516–31 In one of the a· languages
551–32 The a· and hypothetical question,
553–26 supersede the more a· superstition
ap 567–18 That false claim— that a· belief,

anciently
s 142– 4 A· the followers of Christ, or Truth,
c 255– 7 a· classified as the higher criticism,
o 343–25 A· those apostles who were

Ancient of days
s 146–28 It is as ancient as "the A· of d·."— *Dan. 7 : 9.*

anew
pr 4–22 will mould and fashion us a·,
a 20–22 saves retracing and traversing a· the path
35– 6 Discerning Christ, Truth, a·
m 66–13 Love propagates a· the higher joys
s 150– 7 Its appearing is the coming a· of the gospel of
f 206–21 Is God creating a· what He has already created?
p 425–26 and Spirit will form you a·.
g 528– 6 cannot be true that man was ordered to create man a·

angel
f 224–26 Will you open or close the door upon this a·
h 308–10 an a·, a message from Truth and Love,
g 521–17 point of a diamond" and the pen of an a·.
ap 558– 3 And I saw another mighty a·— *Rev. 10 : 1.*
558– 9 This a· or message which comes from
559– 1 a· had in his hand "a little book,"— *Rev. 10 : 2.*
561– 8 saw an "a· standing in the— *Rev. 19 : 17.*
574–29 Love can make an a· entertained unawares.

angelic
sp 93–19 may clothe it with a· vestments,
ap 574–18 the seven a· vials full of seven plagues,

angel's
ap 559– 6 The a· left foot was upon the earth ;

angels
confers upon
b 298–30 Human conjecture confers upon a· its own
His
o 360–27 And His a· He chargeth with— *see Job 4 : 18.*
his
ap 566–26 Michael and his a· fought— *Rev. 12 : 7.*
566–27 the dragon fought, and his a·,— *Rev. 12 : 7.*
567–17 his a· were cast out with him.— *Rev. 12 : 9.*
567–26 His a·, or messages, are cast out with
my
b 299– 7 My a· are exalted thoughts,
seven
ap 574– 6 came unto me one of the seven a·— *Rev. 21 : 9.*
these
g 512– 9 These a· of His presence, which have the
ap 567– 3 These a· deliver us from the depths.

m 56– * as the a· of God in heaven.— *Matt. 22 : 30.*
64–21 but man would be as the a·.
ph 174–11 a· of His presence— the spiritual intuitions

angels
b 298–25 A· are not etherealized human beings,
298–28 A· are pure thoughts from God,
299–11 A· are God's representatives.
299–17 we entertain "a· unawares."— *Heb. 13 : 2.*
p 372–17 Therefore he will be as the a· in heaven.
r 482–23 A· announced to the Wisemen of old
482–24 and a· whisper it, through faith,
g 501–11 glory which a· could only whisper
548–16 by which men may entertain a·,
ap 566–29 The Old Testament assigns to the a·,
gl 581– 4 definition of

anger
b 293–25 "The a· of the Lord."— *Deut. 29 : 20.*
gl 595– 4 The idea of Truth ; justice. Revenge ; a·.
597–29 Destruction ; a· ; mortal passions.

angry
p 369–32 to murmur or to be a· over sin.

anguish
ph 195– 6 Every sound convulsed him with a·.
p 386–19 You think that your a· is occasioned by your

angular
f 248–23 a· outline and deformity of matter models.

animal
magnetism
(see **magnetism**)
———

a 28–32 There is too much a· courage in society
48–23 rebuking resentment or a· courage.
m 61– 5 and the spiritual over the a·,
67–18 notion that a· natures can possibly give
sp 90– 1 or if one a· can originate another,
an 100– 9 A· bodies are susceptible to
100–20 no proof of the existence of the a· magnetic
102– 3 His power is neither a· nor human.
102– 4 Its basis being a belief and this belief a·,
104–20 revenge, malice, are a· propensities
ph 173– 5 farther than his a· progenitors.
179–17 the wild a·, . . . sniffs the wind with delight.
f 222–25 if eating a bit of a· flesh could overpower
252–20 A· in propensity, deceitful in sentiment,
b 298–36 not . . . evolving a· qualities in their wings ;
309–28 to suppose that there can be . . . organic a· or
327–25 the man who has more a· than moral courage,
p 374–30 Mortal mind produces a· heat,
378–12 An a· may infuriate another by
t 450–32 electricity, a· nature, and organic life,
r 490– 5 Human will is an a· propensity,
g 500–20 So-called mineral, vegetable, and a· substances
512–26 confers a· names and natures upon its
529–24 nothing in the a· kingdom which represents the
541–10 the homage bestowed through a gentle a·
548–24 far apart from his material sense of a· growth
ap 563–31 It is the a· instinct in mortals,
564– 4 This malicious a· instinct, of which the dragon
564–26 are typified by a serpent, or a· subtlety.
gl 597–20 mortal belief ; a· power.

animality
ap 569–12 masters his mortal beliefs, a·, and hate,

animals
b 277–13 Natural history presents vegetables and a·
g 511–25 A· and mortals metaphorically present
528– 5 Adam gave the name and nature of a·,
531–20 Who will say that minerals, vegetables, and a·
548–30 "Certain a·, besides the ordinary
549– 3 multiplication of certain a· takes place
550– 7 the individuality and identity of a·
554–29 It is the general belief that the lower a·
557– 8 many a· suffer no pain in multiplying ;

animate
ph 189–26 belief of inanimate, and then of a· matter.
f 243–32 Perfection does not a· imperfection.
p 409– 6 its final statement,— a· error
409–19 The a· should be governed by God alone.
g 541– 2 A lamb is a more a· form of existence,

animated
a 26–14 the godliness which a· him.
an 100– 9 the celestial bodies, the earth, and a· things.
t 459–19 Whether a· by malice or ignorance,
g 525– 2 a mortal sinner, a· by the breath of God?

animating
gl 583–20 the a· divine Principle of all

animation
gl 582– 8 life, strength, a·, and
599– 4 ZEAL. The reflected a· of Life,

ankylosed
s 162–21 a· joints have been made supple,

annihilate
an 103–25 they a· the fables of mortal mind,
ph 172–27 and worms a· it.
f 252–27 the law of God, may at any moment a·

annihilate
t 451– 1 the errors which Truth must and will *a·*
r 490–21 would, by fair logic, *a·* man
g 540–15 that Truth may *a·* all sense of evil

annihilated
f 246– 1 Mind and its formations can never be *a·*.
b 292–28 man would be *a·*, were it not
310–28 then Spirit, . . . would be *a·*.
r 477–18 Were it otherwise, man would be *a·*.
486–27 If this were not so, man would be speedily *a·*.
493–19 Sickness is a belief, which must be *a·*
g 536–16 governed by corporeality . . . man would be *a·*.

annihilates
b 330–26 delusion of material sense, which Science *a·*.
340–25 *a·* pagan and Christian idolatry,

annihilation
f 243–28 a law of *a·* to everything unlike themselves,
b 278–26 logic which would prove his *a·*.
310–25 If . . . the *a·* of Spirit would be inevitable.
gl 582–22 physical sense put out of sight and hearing ; *a·*.

announce
s 119–13 but to *a·* Him as their source,
p 391–25 Disease has no intelligence to . . . *a·* its name.

announced
b 298–19 When the real is attained, which is *a·* by
p 379– 3 *a·* as partners in the beginning.
r 482–23 Angels *a·* to the Wisemen of old

announcing
p 386–16 blundering despatch, mistakenly *a·*

annoyances
m 59– 9 *a·* and cares of domestic economy,

annually
b 328–20 hundreds of persons die there *a·* from

annul
pr 11–19 not to *a·* the divine sentence
s 139–25 nor *a·* the healing by the prophets,
f 229–28 should not if we could, *a·* the decrees of
b 273–21 God never ordained a material law to *a·*
p 381–29 man's moral right to *a·* an unjust sentence.
384–12 has only to enter his protest . . . in order to *a·*
385–12 though it can never *a·* the law which
389–20 cannot *a·* these regulations by an

annulled
m 59–27 The nuptial vow should never be *a·*,
o 349– 7 our Master *a·* material law
p 382– 1 he *a·* supposed laws of matter,

annuls
b 340–28 *a·* the curse on man,
r 491–13 Spirit, which *a·* the claims of matter,

anodynes
s 143–17 and quiets pain with *a·*.
p 374– 2 *A·*, counter-irritants, and depletion

anoint
p 364–14 wash and *a·* his guest's feet,

anointed
a 42–22 glory which God bestowed on His *a·*,
f 201– * *the footsteps of Thine a·.— Psal.* 89 : 51.
b 313– 4 may be rendered "Jesus the *a·*,"
313– 7 even thy God, hath *a·* thee— *Heb.* 1 : 9.
p 363–28 before she *a·* them with the oil.
gl 597–10 which was ready to . . . crucify God's *a·*.

anointeth
ap 578–14 [LOVE] *a·* my head with oil ; — *see Psal.* 23 : 5.

anointing
p 367–26 through silent utterances, and divine *a·*

anomalous
p 375–29 This state of mind seems *a·* except to the

anon
g 513–10 *a·* the veil is lifted, and the scene shifts

another (*see also* another's)
pr 1– 4 Regardless of what *a·* may say
12– 9 This, however, is one belief casting out *a·*,
12–28 *a·* who offers the same measure of prayer?
16–19 is but *a·* name for the first lie
a 23–25 *A·* kind of faith understands divine Love
36– 4 simply through translation into *a·* sphere.
37–10 connect one stage with *a·* in the history of
38–13 At *a·* time Jesus prayed, not for the twelve only,
40– 5 *A·* will say : "Go thy way— *Acts* 24 : 25.
55–27 "He shall give you *a·* Comforter, — *John* 14 : 16.
m 58–27 because *a·* supplies her wants.
sp 73– 4 but *a·*, who has died . . . it terms a *spirit.*
73– 8 belief that one man, as spirit, can control *a·*
75–30 pass from one dream to *a·* dream,
88–16 and at *a·* are called spirits.
89– 4 in the belief that *a·* mind is
90– 1 if one animal can originate *a·*,
an 100– 5 exerted by one living organism over *a·*,
104–23 hypnotizer employs one error to destroy *a·*.

another
s 110–10 brought to light *a·* glorious proposition,
112–28 and yet uses *a·* author's discoveries
122–15 optical focus is *a·* proof of the illusion
125–12 As human thought changes from one stage to *a·*
130– 5 One has a farm, *a·* has merchandise.
143–14 human mind uses one error to medicine *a·*.
149– 8 succeeds in one instance fails in *a·*.
152–11 in one instance and not in *a·*.
152–13 in which one statement contradicts *a·*
159–28 allowing *a·* form of matter.
160–20 in one instance and not in *a·*,
ph 176–25 One disease is no more real than *a·*.
187–11 and then impute this result to *a·* illusive
198–18 Again, giving *a·* direction to faith,
f 211–22 transfer of the thoughts . . . to *a·*,
220–21 and thinking it sees *a·* kitten.
221–31 brings with it *a·* lesson,
229–14 declaring Him good in one instance and evil in *a·*.
235– 2 cannot go . . . from one human mind to *a·*,
236–13 Her thoughts form the embryo of *a·*
247– 5 *A·* woman at ninety had new teeth,
250–29 Mortal thoughts chase one *a·* like snowflakes.
b 276– 6 in which one mind is not at war with *a·*,
278–17 requires *a·* admission, — namely,
313– 9 With this agrees *a·* passage
o 348– 9 one disease can be just as much a delusion as *a·*
357–27 Can Deity be almighty, if *a·* mighty
361–14 conflicts not at all with *a·* of his sayings :
p 372–23 Its false supports fail one after *a·*.
378–13 An animal may infuriate *a·* by
383–31 *a·* medical mistake, resulting from
386–19 *A·* despatch, correcting the mistake,
388–13 there follows the necessity for *a·* admission
402–20 We say that one human mind can influence *a·*
418–16 one disease would be as readily destroyed as *a·*
419–14 or to change itself from one form to *a·*.
420– 1 nor go from one part to *a·*, for Truth destroys
424–14 a remedy prescribed by *a·* doctor.
427–13 Death is but *a·* phase of the dream
431–25 *A·* witness takes the stand and testifies :
432– 9 *A·* witness is called for by the
432–20 *A·* witness takes the stand and testifies :
438–19 *A·* witness, equally inadequate, said
t 445– 6 No hypothesis as to the existence of *a·* power
449– 1 to free *a·* from the fetters of disease.
449– 7 The wrong done *a·* reacts most heavily
450– 4 *A·* class, still more unfortunate,
451–29 one mortal mind controlling *a·*
458– 8 *A·* plank in the platform is this,
r 469–27 believe there is *a·* power, named *evil.*
483– 4 exchanging one disease for *a·*;
486– 4 Suppose one accident happens to the eye, *a·*
486–10 and one error will not correct *a·*.
489–20 at *a·* the medium for obeying God?
491–18 awake at one time and asleep at *a·*,
491–20 this belief culminates in *a·* belief,
496– 3 no transfer of evil suggestions . . . to *a·*,
496– 7 to have one Mind, and to love *a·* as
g 504–21 Here we have the explanation of *a·* passage
529– 6 *A·* change will come as to the nature and
530–21 saying, . . . Bow down to me and have *a·* god
552– 2 *A·* question follows : Who or what produces
554–14 *a·* false claim, that of self-conscious matter,
ap 558– 3 And I saw *a·* mighty angel— *Rev.* 10 : 1.
562–29 And there appeared *a·* wonder— *Rev.* 12 : 3.
570– 6 will finally be shocked into *a·* extreme
570– 7 for one extreme follows *a·*.
572– 6 Love one *a·*"— *I John* 3 : 23.
573– 8 while to *a·*, the unillumined human mind,
573–13 *a·* revelation, even the declaration
574– 3 The Revelator also takes in *a·* view,
gl 583–28 one belief preying upon *a·*.
584–14 free from one belief only to be fettered by *a·*,
591– 8 *a·* name for mortal mind ; illusion ;
594–10 claim . . . that there was *a·* power,

another's
a 21– 7 *a·* goodness, suffering, and triumph,
22–26 nor by pinning one's faith . . . to *a·* vicarious
40–14 *A·* suffering cannot lessen our own liability.
m 58–14 selfish exaction of all *a·* time and thoughts.
t 449– 2 manacled, it is hard to break *a·* chains.
g 518–19 seeking his own in *a·* good.

answer (noun)
pr 9– 5 test of all prayer lies in the *a·* to these
136–10 His *a·* to this question the world rejected.
137–12 In his rejection of the *a·* already given
ph 183–10 The *a·* is no, and yet the Scriptures inform us
b 284–19 The *a·* to all these questions must forever be
p 363–21 Jesus approved the *a·*.
399–14 matter can return no *a·* to immortal Mind.
r 465– 9 *A·*.— God is incorporeal, divine,
465–12 *A·*.— They are. They refer to one absolute
465–17 *A·*.— There is not. Principle and its idea
466– 8 *A·*.— To human belief, they are

answer (noun)
r 467– 3   A·.— The first demand of this Science is,
468– 9   A·.— There is no life, truth, . . . in matter.
468–17   A·.— Substance is that which is
468–26   A·.— Life is divine Principle, Mind,
469– 8   A·.— Intelligence is omniscience,
469–13   A·.— Mind is God.
471–23   A·.— The author subscribed to an orthodox
472–14   A·.— Error is a supposition that pleasure
472–24   A·.— All reality is in God and His creation,
475– 6   A·.— Man is not matter;
477–20   A·.— Identity is the reflection of Spirit,
478–16   A·.— No, not if God is true
482–15   A·.— It is, since Christ is . . . the truth
484– 9   A·.— Not one of them is included in it.
485– 1   A·.— If error is necessary to define
485– 2   If error is necessary . . . the a· is yes ;
487–15   A·.— Spirit is all-knowing ;
488–16   A·.— C. S. sustains with immortal proof
493–11   A·.— The method of C. S. Mind-healing
493–13   A full a· to the above question involves
495–27   A·.— Study thoroughly the letter
496–30   A·.— They have not, if by that term

answer (verb)
s 132– 3   the divine power to heal would fully a·
f 223–20   The efforts of error to a· this question
o 342–24   and they a· with rejoicing.
p 440– 5   to a· for his crime.
g 551–24   We a· that it cannot.

answered
pref viii–12   What is Truth, is a· by demonstration,
pr 15–21   Such prayer is a·, in so far as we
a 49– 1   The women at the cross could have a·
sp 86– 3   a·, "The multitude throng thee."— Luke 8 : 45.
86– 6   Repeating his inquiry, he was a· by
f 237– 3   she a· ingenuously, "There is no sensation in
b 305 16   "Then a· Jesus and said— John 5 : 19.
308–29   he straightway a· ; and then his name
p 364–10   Jesus a· by rebuking self-righteousness
374– 9   The author has a· this question
g 504– 7   are a· in this passage,
552– 1   is a·, if the egg produces the parent.

answers
m 67– 9   He a· bravely, but even the dauntless seaman
r 465– 7   chapter sub-title

antagonism
s 145–26   and thus they increase the a· of
145–29   By this a· mortal mind must continually weaken
o 345–30   the main cause of the carnal mind's a·.

antagonistic
sp 83– 9   Nothing is more a· to C. S. than
s 108– 1   a conviction a· to the testimony of the
129–18   pantheism, and infidelity are a· to true
ph 182–15   The hypotheses of mortals are a· to
f 204– 7   a· entities and beings,
204–16   the first and second a· powers,
231–14   but there are no a· powers nor laws,
o 353– 4   physical senses and Science have ever been a·,
356– 2   so a· that the material thought must
p 392– 9   take a· grounds against all that
424–19   either by giving a· advice or
g 522– 5   the other is false, for they are a·.

antecedent
b 290 5   but which has no physical a· reality
o 356–30   Does subsequent follow its a·?

antedated
b 334– 2   and therefore a· Abraham ;

Antediluvians
pref viii–21   the reputed longevity of the A·,

anterior
s 146–27   far a· to the period in which Jesus lived.

anthropomorphic
f 224–13   were ready to hail an a· God,
c 257–17   and would say that an a· God, instead of
b 317– 5   and proclaimed an a· God.
337– 1   but not in any a· sense.
o 351–19   a personal devil and an a· God
g 517–3, 4   The word a·, in such a phrase as "an a· God,"

anthropomorphism
g 517– 2   This definition has been weakened by a·,

anti-Christian
ph 169–31   Whatever teaches man to . . . is a·.

anticipating
a 33– 3   a· the hour of their Master's betrayal,
s 132–24   A· this rejection of idealism,
ap 566– 5   and a· the promised joy,

antidote
s 155–29, 30   if drugs are an a· to disease, why lessen the a·?
b 274– 1   Truth and Love a· this mental miasma,
o 346–20   because Truth is error's a·.
r 495–10   and find a sovereign a· for error

antidotes
g 270–28   and a sense of ease a· suffering,

antipathies
s 163–32   the fixed and repulsive a· of nature.

antipode
sp 72–18   not made manifest through matter, the a· of
ph 200–20   suppositional a· of divine infinite Spirit,
f 208–10   It is the very a· of immortal Mind,
215–25   Mortal man is the a· of immortal man
c 257–24   mind in matter to be the a· of Mind.
r 484–23   it is the human a· of divine Science.
gl 580–12   the a· of God, or Spirit ;

antipodes
b 286–27   Transitory thoughts are the a· of
335 30   the suppositional a· of Spirit,
g 544–23   the very a· of immortal and spiritual being.

antiquated
s 147–21   perishing fossils of theories already a·,

antithesis
s 133–19   Judaism was the a· of Christianity,

anvil
ph 199– 2   lift the hammer and strike the a·,

anxiety
gl 586–11   FEAR. Heat ; inflammation ; a· ; ignorance ;

any
pref x–23   personal experience of a· sincere seeker of Truth.
x–25   than that of a· other sanitary method.
pr 7–10   But does it produce a· lasting benefit?
9– 4   the falsehood which does no one a· good.
a 47 32   belief in a· possible material intelligence.
55– 1   if he entertained a· other sense of being
m 67–31   rebuked the suffering from a· such cause
sp 73–11   A· other control or attraction of so-called
73–16   electricity or a· other form of matter,
73–26   mistake to suppose that matter is a· part
76–14   more than a tree can return to its seed.
87–24   Do not suppose that a· mental concept is gone
87–27   by friendship or by a· intense feeling
95–11   Error of a· kind cannot hide from the
98–23   has not been considered a part of a· religion,
an 101–31   A· seeming benefit derived from it
103–13   wholly separate from a· half-way
s 112–23   A· theory of C. S., which departs from
112–26   Also, if a· so-called new school claims
115– 6   make them comprehensible to a· reader,
120–25   A· conclusion pro or con, deduced from
132–10   gave his benediction to a· one who should not
132–23   if it is wrought in a· but a material
145–20   If there is a· mystery in Christian healing,
149–12   If you fail to succeed in a· case, it is because
154– 1   to cherish error in a· form,
154–31   more successful method for a· mother
ph 167–28   impossible to gain control . . . in a· other way
169–22   drug or a· other means toward which
175–12   and dissuade a· sense of fear or fever.
177–23   in a· direction against God,
181–13   when you resort to a· except spiritual means.
181–31   A· hypnotic power you may exercise will
183–23   for a· lesser loyalty.
f 206–25   Can there be a· birth or death for man,
207–21   there can be no effect from a· other cause,
217–26   or a· illusion of physical weariness,
228–26   to acknowledge a· other power is to
230–23   drugs, hygiene, or a· material method.
233– 1   nor opportunity in Science for error of a· sort.
233–29   counter fact relative to a· disease
244– 6   never fearing nor obeying error in a· form.
249–10   A· other theory of Life, or God,
250–22   Now I ask, Is there a· more reality in
252–27   may at a· moment annihilate
253–25   Do not believe in a· supposed necessity for
c 255–17   finiteness, cannot be made the basis of a· true
b 276–18   ceases to be a· opportunity for sin and death.
280– 9   belief can never do justice to Truth in a·
283– 2   belief that there is a· true existence apart from
297–17   only fact concerning a· material concept is,
301–20   belief that man has a· other substance,
302–17   illusion of a· life, substance, . . . in matter.
302–27   not in a· bodily or personal likeness
304– 8   nor depth, nor a· other creature,— Rom. 8 : 39.
315– 7   and laid no claim to a· other.
325–30   When first spoken in a· age, Truth,
328–24   and if they drink a· deadly thing,— Mark 16 : 18.
337– 1   but not in a· anthropomorphic sense.
339– 5   God's pardon, destroying a· one sin,
339–29   divest sin of a· supposed mind or reality
o 342–14   heal the sick in a· town where they
348– 6   Ought we not, then, to approve a· cure,

any

o	348–18	to have no faith in evil or in *a·* power but God,
	350–20	lest at *a·* time they should see— *Matt.* 13 : 15.
	352–19	for at *a·* moment they may become
	354–13	opponents . . . neither give nor offer *a·* proofs
	355–18	*a·* systematic healing power
	356–14	not contributing in *a·* way to
	356–27	Would *a·* one call it wise and good
	359– 3	Let *a·* clergyman try to cure his friends by
p	362– *	*if they drink a· deadly thing,— Mark* 16 : 18.
	369–12	or the constructor of *a·* form of existence.
	369–31	*a·* more than he is morally saved in or by sin.
	372–19	How, then, in Christianity *a·* more than in C. S.,
	372–30	If pride, superstition, or *a·* error
	375–14	by yielding his mentality to *a·* mental
	377–23	the morbid or excited action of *a·* organ.
	377–30	Without this . . . *a·* circumstance is
	384–26	consumption, nor *a·* other disease
	385–31	*A·* supposed information, coming from
	386– 3	*a·* more than it is in the case of sin.
	387–23	cannot suffer as the result of *a·* labor of love,
	393–20	as the result of a law of *a·* kind,
	394–10	admission that *a·* bodily condition
	401– 1	*A·* human error is its own enemy,
	401–23	could you produce *a·* effect upon the brain
	404– 4	*a·* one of the myriad forms of sin,
	406–26	Inharmony of *a·* kind involves
	410–26	or is used in *a·* way except to
	413–30	probable at *a·* time that such ills
	413–32	or *a·* other malady, timorously held
	414–14	dementia, hatred, or *a·* other discord.
	415–14	Opiates do not remove the pain in *a·*
	416– 8	To him there is no longer *a·* pain.
	416– 9	Yet *a·* physician — allopathic, homœopathic,
	419– 8	If your patient from *a·* cause suffers a
	419–22	mortal mind is liable to *a·* phase of belief
	420–21	better than *a·* drug, alterative, or tonic.
	423–27	Ossification or *a·* abnormal condition
	424–21	divine Mind can remove *a·* obstacle,
	425–27	never believe that heart or *a·* portion
	426– 1	or disease arising from *a·* circumstance,
	429–23	for if Life ever had *a·* beginning,
	438– 6	nothing shall by *a·* means— *Luke* 10 : 19.
	440–15	what greater justification can *a·* deed
	440–29	forbidden to enter . . . *a·* more suits
	441– 3	*a·* so-called law, which undertakes to
	441– 6	not permitted to enter *a·* suits at the bar of
t	445–17	or limit in *a·* direction of thought
	446–31	and the ultimate triumph of *a·* cause.
	448–30	nothing short of right-doing has a· claim to
	455–22	renders *a·* abuse of the mission an
	456–16	*A·* dishonesty in your theory and practice
	457– 9	never used this newly discovered power in *a·*
	459–12	*A·* attempt to heal mortals with erring
	459–30	than *a·* other healer on the globe.
	462– 2	*a·* student, who adheres to the divine rules
	464–13	If from an injury or from *a·* cause,
r	479– 4	be uttered by *a·* mother,
	479–16	or use *a·* of the physical senses?
	483–25	but if *a·* system honors God,
	485–32	The notion of *a·* life or intelligence
	488–17	the impossibility of *a·* material sense,
	489– 8	*A·* hypothesis which supposes life
	493–23	just as it removes *a·* other sense of
	493–26	*A·* sense of soul in matter is not the
	495–19	can destroy *a·* painful sense of,
	496–28	Have Christian Scientists *a·* religious creed?
g	507–19	do not yield fruit because of *a·*
	525– 9	In the Saxon, *mankind, a woman, a· one ;*
	529–14	more subtle than *a·* beast of the— *Gen.* 3 : 1.
	542–17	lest *a·* finding him should kill him.— *Gen.* 4 : 15.
	550–20	If Life has *a·* starting-point
	554– 5	nor are there properly *a·* mortal beings,
	554– 8	*A·* statement of life, following from a
	554–10	because it is destitute of *a·* knowledge
	554–12	destitute of *a·* knowledge of life
ap	564–32	"more subtle than *a·* beast of the— *Gen.* 3 : 1.
	566–28	found *a·* more in heaven.— *Rev.* 12 : 8.
gl	584–15	*A·* material evidence of death is false,

(*see also* **man**)

anybody

o	345–21	*A·,* who is able to perceive the

anyone

t	461– 1	I do not maintain that *a·* can
ap	560–16	or entertain a false estimate of *a·* whom God

anything

pr	2–24	*a·* He does not already comprehend?
s	164– 7	or *a·* like the truth,
ph	200–25	not to know *a·* among you,— *I Cor.* 2 : 2.
	200–28	not to know *a·* among you,
f	232– 1	without Him was not *a·* made— *John* 1 : 3.
b	335–11	"was not *a·* made that was made."— *John* 1 : 3.
o	347– 8	This writer infers that if *a·* needs
p	381–11	cannot in reality suffer from breaking *a·*
t	458–11	It is *a·* but scientifically Christian

anything

r	477–24	can never reflect *a·* inferior to Spirit.
	480–27	without Him was not *a·* made— *John* 1 : 3.
g	501– *	*without Him was not a· made— John* 1 : 3.
	525–19	was not *a·* made that was made."— *John* 1 : 3.

apace

c	265–17	as if man were a weed growing *a·*

apart

a	30–11	Had his origin and birth been wholly *a·*
	52– 2	His pursuits lay far *a·* from theirs.
sp	87–10	Though bodies are leagues *a·*
	91–26	postulate of belief . . . something *a·* from God.
s	114–32	*A·* from the usual opposition to
f	213– 8	spiritual facts exist *a·* from this mortal and
	228–25	There is no power *a·* from God.
b	270–11	Few deny . . . that intelligence, *a·* from man
	283– 3	belief that there is any true existence *a·* from
p	399– 9	*a·* from the action of mortal thought,
r	473– 9	nothing *a·* from Him is present or has power.
	480–13	Material sense has its realm *a·* from Science
	488–22	*a·* from what belief bestows upon them,
g	544– 2	a creation so wholly *a·* from God's,
	548–23	so far *a·* from his material sense
	549– 3	takes place *a·* from sexual conditions.

apathy

an	102–22	produce the very *a·* on the subject which
f	249–24	Sleep and *a·* are phases of the
ap	570– 4	The present *a·* as to the tendency of

apehood

g	543–21	May not Darwin be right in thinking that *a·*

aphorisms

o	358–14	C. S. is neither made up of contradictory *a·*

Aphrodite

g	524– 4	in the Hindoo Vishnu, in the Greek *A·,*

Apocalypse

m	56–11	as in the vision of the *A·,*
o	357–24	according to the vision of St. John in the *A·.*
g	536– 1	In the *A·* it is written :
	546–18	Genesis and the *A·* seem more obscure
ap	559–32	The twelfth chapter of the *A·,*
	561–22	The woman in the *A·* symbolizes
	564–24	From Genesis to the *A·,* sin, sickness, and
	565– 1	In the *A·,* when nearing its doom,
	568– 5	The twelfth chapter of the *A·* typifies
	572– 4	in Genesis and in the *A·,*
	572–15	furnish the vision of the *A·,*
	575– 7	This sacred city, described in the *A·*

apodictical

s	107– 7	This *a·* Principle points to the revelation

Apollo

s	158– 3	designated *A·* as "the god of medicine."
	158– 7	*A·* was also regarded as the sender of disease,
	158–13	*A·,* who was banished from heaven

apostle (*see also* **apostle's**)

pr	5–29	An *a·* says that the Son of God [Christ]
a	28–29	encountered by prophet, disciple, and *a·,*
	39–18	"*Now,*" cried the *a·,* "is the— *II Cor.* 6 : 2.
sp	99– 7	"Work out your . . . says the *a·,— Phil.* 2 : 12.
ph	172–21	to which the *a·* refers when he says
b	303–32	the *a·* declared that nothing could alienate
	332– 6	As the *a·* expressed it in words which
o	343– 9	one might not be able to say with the *a·,*
	345–26	*a·* says : "For if a man think himself— *Gal.* 6 : 3.
r	474–29	The *a·* says that the mission of Christ is
g	519–18	till, in the language of the *a·,*
ap	577–30	St. John's Revelation as recorded by the great *a·*

Apostle James

m	64– 3	taught by the *A· J·,* when he said :
r	487–25	*A· J·* said, "Show me thy faith— *Jas.* 2 : 18.
g	527–12	*A· J·* says : "God cannot be tempted— *Jas.* 1 : 13.

Apostle John

p	388– 7	The *A· J·* testified to the divine basis of
	410–17	*A· J·* says : "There is no fear in— *I John* 4 : 18.

Apostle Paul

sp	79–17	*A· P·* bade men have the Mind that was
an	103– 2	*A· P·* refers to the personification of evil as
p	383– 9	like the *A· P·,* is "willing rather— *II Cor.* 5 : 8.
g	534–14	and the *A· P·* explains this warfare

apostle's

ap	560–23	hid from view the *a·* character,

apostles

Christian

o	349–22	the prophecy concerning the Christian *a·,*

floral

f	240– 6	The floral *a·* are hieroglyphs of Deity.

his

a	40–27	follow the example of our Master and his *a*
	41–26	Persecuted from city to city, his *a·* still
b	269–23	on the teachings of Jesus, of his *a·,*
o	358–17	illustrated by the prophets, by Jesus, by his *a·,*

apostles

lesser
a 40–21   lesser *a·* of Truth may endure human brutality
those
o 343–25   Anciently those *a·* who were Jesus' students,

s 126–29   and the lives of prophets and *a·*.
f 243–13   the ancient demonstrations of prophets and *a·*.

apostolic
sp 97–30   *a·* work of casting out error and healing the
b 325–15   The absolute meaning of the *a·* words is
o 347–19   namely, *a·*, divine healing?
p 366–14   and we have the *a·* warrant for asking :
t 443–20   may learn the value of the *a·* precept :
451– 3   constant pressure of the *a·* command

apothecary
s 163–10   surgeon, *a·*, man-midwife, chemist,

apparent
a 42– 6   It cannot make Life or Truth *a·*.
f 207– 2   evil becomes more *a·* and obnoxious
251– 3   belief of mortal mind *a·* as an abscess
b 324– 8   Unless the . . . are becoming more *a·*,
o 345–15   at least none which are *a·* to those
359–16   is not or to the material senses,
p 374–11   before it is consciously *a·* on the body,
390– 8   which produces *a·* discord,
428–27   immortality will become more *a·*, as
r 467–12   perfect in proportion as this fact becomes *a·*,
g 505–11   the ideas of Spirit *a·* only as Mind,
543– 7   becomes more beautifully *a·* at error's demise.
552– 8   and as necessarily *a·* to the

apparently
pr 8–10   If a man, though *a·* fervent and prayerful,
12–21   to be *a·* either poisonous or sanative.
s 108–19   When *a·* near the confines of mortal existence,
109–23   gradually and *a·* through divine power.
122–17   sky and tree-tops *a·* join hands,
152–14   Sir Humphry Davy once *a·* cured a case of
b 321–17   when he discovered that what he *a·* saw
p 415–27   Etherization will *a·* cause the body
r 491–25   *a·* with their own separate embodiment.

apparitions
sp 86–14   These may appear to the ignorant to be *a·* ;
86–18   *a·* brought out in dark seances

appeal
a 50– 9   This despairing *a·*, if made to a human parent,
50–12   The *a·* of Jesus was made both to his
ph 182– 5   The demands of God *a·* to thought only ;
b 319–10   the lower *a·* to the general faith in
o 351–32   They might *a·* to Jehovah, but their prayer
p 405–32   and to *a·* to divine sources outside of
440–20   Mortal Man has his *a·* to Spirit, God,
440–30   *a·* to the just and equitable decisions of

appealed
s 136 11   Ho *a·* to his students !
p 403–11   but matter is *a·* to in the other.

appeals
s 130– 2   is alarmed by constant *a·* to Mind.

appear
pref ix–21   but it did not *a·* in print until 1876,
a 40– 2   Remove error from thought, and it will not *a·* in
m 60– 2   and man, not of the earth earthly . . . will *a·*.
sp 86–13   These may *a·* to be apparitions ;
91–12   the sooner man's great reality will *a·*
97–12   the more its nothingness will *a·*,
s 123– 4   The true idea and Principle of man will then *a·*.
164–17   If you or I should *a·* to die,
ph 167–17   error in the premise must *a·* in the conclusion.
168–28   sensation would not *a·* if the error of belief
191– 6   man in God's likeness will *a·*,
198–13   afterwards to *a·* on the body ;
199–31   before his power . . . could *a·*.
f 211–11   does not *a·* in the spiritual understanding
211–17   Without mortal mind, the tear could not *a·* ;
216–23   evil would *a·* to be the master of good,
249– 5   Let the "male and female" . . . *a·*.— *Gen.* 1 : 27.
c 264– 3   before the permanent facts . . . *a·*.
b 295–15   and the real sense of being, . . . will *a·*.
297–23   begins to *a·*, and Truth, the ever-present,
312–17   without Love, God, immortality cannot *a·*.
325–11   "When Christ, who is our life, shall *a·* — *Col.* 3 : 4.
325–12   then shall ye also *a·* — *Col.* 3 : 4.
332–24   *a·* to mortals in such a form of humanity
o 341– 7   *a·* contradictory when subjected to such usage.
347–30   The harmonious will *a·* real,
348– 6   making the disease *a·* to be— what it really is
p 378– 2   and causes the two to *a·* conjoined,
390–12   When the first symptoms of disease *a·*,
395–29   it may *a·* in a more alarming form.
410–24   Selfishness does not *a·* in the
417–22   Disease should not *a·* real to the physician,

appear
p 428–10   that the spiritual facts of being may *a·*,
430– 5   immortal manhood, the Christ ideal, will *a·*.
434–10   where C. S. is allowed to *a·* as counsel
434–13   now summoned to *a·* before the bar of Justice
t 450– 6   so depraved that they *a·* to be innocent.
r 476–12   immortals, or the children of God, will *a·*
485– 8   If the unimportant and evil *a·*,
485–12   disease, and death *a·* more and more unreal
488–11   *a·* in our common version to approve
g 502–16   Christian views of the universe *a·*,
506–17   and let the dry land *a·* :— *Gen.* 1 : 9.
506–21   in order that the purpose may *a·*.
507–29   and must ever continue to *a·*
509–27   *a·* in man and the universe
520–12   These days will *a·* as mortality disappears,
537–26   the text is made to *a·* contradictory
550–13   its eternal perfection should *a·* now,
556– 8   Then will the new heaven and new earth *a·*,
ap 573–30   this reality of being will surely *a·* sometime
fr 600– *   *whether the tender grape a·*,— *Song* 7 : 12.

appearance
an 101–27   this *a·* is deceptive, since error cannot
ph 168–26   before the so-called disease made its *a·*
187–28   body loses all *a·* of life or action,
f 215–18   darkness loses the *a·* of reality.
p 416–23   body is no longer the parent, even in *a·*.
432–28   but my *a·* with a message from
r 491–19   sometimes presenting no *a·* of mind,
g 553–22   sure to become the signal for the *a·* of

appearances
s 121–22   Science shows *a·* often to be erroneous,

appeared
s 138–10   his cures, which *a·* miraculous to outsiders.
154–12   symptoms of this disease *a·*,
b 308–20   a message from Truth and Love, *a·* to him
309– 7   The result of Jacob's struggle thus *a·*.
324–20   When the truth first *a·* to him in Science,
334–11   Jesus *a·* as a bodily existence.
p 374– 9   and knew nothing about, until it *a·*
r 477– 1   the perfect man, who *a·* to him
g 501– *   *And I a· unto Abraham,* — *Exod.* 6 : 3.
507 1   Adam has not yet *a·* in the narrative.
ap 560– 6   And there *a·* a great wonder in— *Rev.* 12 : 1.
562–29   And there *a·* another wonder in— *Rev.* 12 : 3.
gl 597– 5   if only he *a·* unto men to fast.

appearing
Messianic
s 133– 1   questioned the signs of the Messianic *a·*,

s 118– 7   foretelling the second *a·* in the flesh
150– 6   Its *a·* is the coming anew of the gospel of
f 224–16   but this was not the manner of truth's *a·*.
224–21   the harbingers of truth's full-orbed *a·*.
230– 7   the advanced *a·* of Truth, which
b 299– 7   *a·* at the door of some sepulchre,
r 482 24   announced to the Wisemen of old this dual *a·*,
g 504–16   The successive *a·* of God's ideas
507 28   Creation is ever *a·*, and must ever continue
507–30   Mortal sense inverts this *a·*
gl 589–25   spiritual understanding of God and man *a·*.

appears
m 69– 9   the real, ideal man *a·* in proportion as
sp 76–31   must be overcome, . . . before immortality *a·*.
92–23   Until the fact concerning error . . . *a·*,
96–18   until their nothingness *a·*,
s 116– 5   and man as God's image *a·*.
ph 187–31   which *a·* to the human mind to live,
f 210–27   and *a·* . . . to make good its claim.
250–24   whatever *a·* to be a mortal man is a
b 271–22   When the Science of Christianity *a·*, it will
281– 5   When one *a·*, the other disappears.
289–18   what *a·* to the senses to be death is but
295–20   through which Truth *a·* most vividly
312– 7   sense-dream vanishes and reality *a·*.
320–20   (however transcendental such a thought *a·*),
o 353–19   until perfection *a·* and reality is reached.
354–32   If the letter of C. S. *a·* inconsistent,
p 415–10   Inflammation never *a·* in a part which
r 474– 9   To the ignorant age in which it first *a·*,
477– 2   where sinning mortal man *a·* to mortals.
477–10   *a·* to be matter and mind united ;
480– 1   When the substance of Spirit *a·*
493– 3   To corporeal sense, the sun *a·* to rise and set,
g 507– 4   feeds and clothes every object, as it *a·*
516– 2   As the reflection of yourself *a·*
542– 5   whenever and wherever it *a·*.
gl 595–21   mortal disappears and spiritual perfection *a·*.

appeased
a 22–28   or that divinity is *a·* by human suffering,
22–32   Wrath which is only *a·* is not destroyed,

appellation
b 309– 1   but this *a·* was withheld,

appellative
  c 267–14 the same authority for the *a·* mother,
appertain
  ph 182– 7 what are termed laws of nature, *a·* to matter.
appetite
  s 158–22 acquires an educated *a·* for strong drink,
  f 218–11 and say, "I am malice, lust, *a·*, envy, hate."
  b 327– 4 neither pleasure nor pain, *a·* nor passion,
  p 398–23 *A·* and disease reside in mortal mind,
  406–28 The depraved *a·* for alcoholic drinks,
  r 490– 9 cooperates with *a·* and passion.
appetites
  a 53– 5 so far removed from *a·* and passions
  s 115–21 Evil beliefs, passions and *a·*, fear,
  ph 188– 8 Passion, depraved *a·*, dishonesty,
  f 201–10 false *a·*, hatred, fear, all sensuality,
  b 327– 7 all the sinful *a·* of the human mind.
  p 404– 8 there is no real pleasure in false *a·*.
  g 526–11 The *a·* and passions, sin, sickness,
  536–20 Passions and *a·* must end in pain.
applause
  pr 7–16 may embrace too much love of *a·*
apples
  ph 165– 1 Physiology is one of the *a·* from
applicable
  t 463–27 There is a law of God *a·* to healing,
application
  s 126–22 its *a·* to the treatment of disease
  126–32 If Christendom resists the author's *a·* of the
  147– 4 the sacred rules for its present *a·*
  ph 198–17 by the *a·* of caustic or croton oil,
  b 271–16 Hence the universal *a·* of his saying :
  o 341–13 Sneers at the *a·* of the word *Science*
  p 421–29 or by employing a single material *a·*
applications
  s 118– 4 and formal *a·* of the illustration.
applied
  s 116–25 words *person* and *personal* . . . when *a·* to
  116–28 If the term personality, as *a·* to God,
  127–16 relates especially to Science as *a·* to
  147– 8 and everywhere, when honestly *a·*
  150– 2 Truth, as *a·* through this Christian system
  o 344–32 the word *Spirit* is so commonly *a·* to Deity,
  t 457–30 Let this Principle be *a·* to the cure of disease
  gl 597–26 *a·* to Mind or to one of God's qualities.
  599– 3 You. As *a·* to corporeality, a mortal ;
applies
  a 24– 1 This certainly *a·* to Truth and Love
  m 68–26 I discredit the belief that agamogenesis *a·* to
  sp 93–24 and *a·* exclusively to God.
  f 219– 3 My method of treating fatigue *a·* to
apply
  an 105–17 and no longer *a·* legal rulings wholly to
applying
  f 218–30 that passage is not perverted by *a·* it literally
  p 401–24 by *a·* the drug to either?
appointed
  an 100–15 Under this order a commission was *a·*,
  101– 8 In 1837, a committee of nine persons was *a·*,
  c 261–14 to go upon the stage and sustain his *a·* task,
  b 332–23 He was *a·* to speak God's word
  ap 560–17 whom God has *a·* to voice His word.
appointing
  s 131–15 has come already, after the manner of God's *a·*,
  b 326– 4 it must be in the way of God's *a·*.
  r 483–29 and it does this in the way of His *a·*,
apportion
  g 505–30 human beliefs, which *a·* to themselves a task
appreciable
  a 30–12 Jesus would not have been *a·* to
appreciated
  a 37–14 not . . . seen and *a·* by lookers-on.
appreciating
  m 60–24 calls discord harmony, not *a·* concord.
appreciation
  s 136–22 That a wicked king . . . should have no high *a·*
  b 300– 3 Finite sense has no true *a·* of
apprehend
  a 31–18 following his demonstration so far as we *a·*
  s 140– 9 as we *a·* the divine nature and love Him
  ph 167– 6 We *a·* Life in divine Science only as
  179– 8 the spiritual capacity to *a·* thought
  f 222– 2 as we better *a·* our spiritual existence
  231–28 To fear them is impossible, when you fully *a·*
  b 280–12 belief can neither *a·* nor worship the
  323–13 In order to *a·* more, we must
  o 350–17 difficult in a material age to *a·* spiritual Truth.
  353–32 nor *a·* the reality of Life.
  g 510– 2 How much more should we seek to *a·*

apprehend
  g 545–25 could not *a·* the nature and operation of
apprehended
  a 39–28 This thought is *a·* slowly,
  m 56– 9 is discerned intact, is *a·* and understood,
  sp 91–24 that the spiritual facts may be better *a·*.
  96–29 real objects will be *a·* mentally
  s 110–30 Its Science must be *a·* by as many as believe
  136–29 The disciples *a·* their Master better than
  b 288–11 When the . . . effects of C. S. are fully *a·*,
  p 402–10 Mind and its formations will be *a·*
  g 513–13 reflections of deific power cannot be *a·* until
apprehension
  clear
    t 459– 4 Paul and John had a clear *a·* that,
  deific
    ap 576–29 not yet elevated to deific *a·*
  human
    r 471–30 reduced to human *a·*, she has named C. S.
  of divine Principle
    sp 90–30 through an *a·* of divine Principle.
  of divine Science
    g 519–28 according to the *a·* of divine Science.
  of mortals
    p 368– 7 nearer than ever before to the *a·* of mortals,
  our
    sp 80– 1 in proportion to our *a·* of the truth,
    93–31 This belief tends to becloud our *a·* of the
  quick
    sp 86– 7 His quick *a·* of this mental call
  rejoice in the
    o 354–28 I rejoice in the *a·* of this grand verity.
  rests on the
    t 460– 6 Mind-healing rests on the *a·* of the
  right
    pref vii–19 only guarantee of obedience is a right *a·* of
    t 460–17 to be dealt with through right *a·* of
  scientific
    pr 16–17 This reading strengthens our scientific *a·*
  spiritual
    o 349–28 as thought is educated up to spiritual *a·*.
    g 506–12 calm and exalted thought or spiritual *a·*
  their
    a 34–26 and ascend far above their *a·*.
    g 509– 5 to their *a·* he rose from the grave,

    r 487–10 The *a·* of this gave sight to the blind
    g 548–14 and so aids the *a·* of immortal Truth.
    gl 583–16 to the *a·* of spiritual ideas
approach
  sp 95– 6 We *a·* God, or Life, in proportion to
  ph 170–25 The age seems ready to *a·* this subject,
  f 234–11 as we bar our doors against the *a·* of
  b 278–15 Hence, as we *a·* Spirit and Truth,
  p 374–17 Ignorance of the cause or *a·* of disease
  406–14 seem less real as we *a·* the scientific period,
  t 450–10 open to the *a·* and recognition of Truth.
  r 483–12 hinders its *a·* to the standard in C. S.
  ap 559–24 When you *a·* nearer and nearer to
approached
  p 362–12 this woman (Mary Magdalene, . . . *a·* Jesus.
approaches
  m 67–32 The epoch *a·* when the understanding
  sp 97–14 The nearer a false belief *a·* truth
  p 402– 8 The time *a·* when mortal mind will
  409– 5 and the nearer matter *a·* its final statement,
  r 496–10 Am I living the life that *a·* the supreme good?
  ap 576–30 the word gradually *a·* a higher meaning.
approaching
  a 47–16 A period was *a·* which would reveal
  f 223–22 accompany *a·* Science
  241–29 and are *a·* spiritual Life
  p 390–27 "Agree to disagree" with *a·* symptoms
approbation
  m 59– 5 and mutual attention and *a·*
  b 332– 7 quoted with *a·* from a classic poet :
appropriates
  f 242–27 superstition *a·* no part of the
  t 459– 2 Man then *a·* those things which
approval
  a 42–11 endorsed pre-eminently by the *a·* of God,
  s 132–17 received no aid nor *a·* from other
  p 382– 3 having only human *a·* for their sanction.
approve
  o 348– 5 Ought we not, then, to *a·* any
  r 488–12 Scriptures often appear . . . to *a·* and
approved
  p 363–20 Jesus *a·* the answer, and so brought
approves
  a 22–31 Mercy cancels the debt only when justice *a·*.
approximation
  sp 94–30 An *a·* of this discernment

a priori
r 467–25　*a· p·* reasoning shows material existence to be

apt
p 384–21　are not *a·* to follow exposure ;

arbiter
p 369–12　belief that matter . . . can be the *a·* of life
405–12　the *a·* of truth against error.

arbitrament
g 555– 4　human belief, and not the divine *a·*,

arbutus
g 516–15　The modest *a·* sends her sweet breath

arch
a 40–23　through the triumphal *a·* of Truth and Love.

arches
f 247–25　*a·* the cloud with the bow of beauty,

architect
m 68– 5　learn how Spirit, the great *a·*,

architectural
s 142–11　*a·* skill, making dome and spire

archpriests
r 481– 5　Like the *a·* of yore, man is free

arctic
f 240– 2　*A·* regions, sunny tropics, giant hills,

Arcturus
c 257–21　guideth "*A·* with his sons."— *Job* 38 : 32.

arduous
p 396–16　refutation becomes *a·*, not because the

arena
sp 96–12　material world is even now becoming the *a·*
g 538–20　Until that . . . enters into the *a·*,

Argentum nitratum
s 156– 9　prescribed the fourth attenuation of *A· n·*

argue
p 380–12　as though the defendant should *a·* for the
395– 1　The sick unconsciously *a·* for suffering,
395–25　while you *a·* against their reality,
412–20　*A·* at first mentally, not audibly.

argued
p 411– 5　If the student . . . when he *a·* against it,
435– 5　False Belief has *a·* that the body should die,

argues
g 551– 9　One distinguished naturalist *a·* that

arguing
p 376–23　by both silently and audibly *a·*
g 539 23　*a·* for the Science of creation,

argument
mental
t 454–32　the letter and mental *a·* are only
no
p 374–18　no *a·* against the mental origin of

b 280–21　The *a·* of the serpent in the allegory,
o 343–15　By parable and *a·* he explains the
p 412–18　To heal by *a·*, find the type of
412–22　conform the *a·* so as to destroy the evidence
414–20　The Christian Scientist's *a·* rests on the
434–20　and opens the *a·* for the defence :
g 530–20　In parable and *a·*, this falsity is exposed

arguments
b 268–16　their *a·* are based on the
o 355– 7　proofs are better than mere verbal *a·*
p 307– 7　borrowed speeches, and the doling of *a·*,
411– 9　and needed the *a·* of truth for reminders.
412– 5　You may vary the *a·* to meet the
414– 7　The *a·* to be used in curing insanity
418–17　if *a·* are used to destroy it,
418–23　By the truthful *a·* you employ,

aright
pref vii–19　whom to know *a·* is Life eternal.
pr 15–14　In order to pray *a·*, we must
a 18– 7　He did life's work *a·* not only in
28–18　Not a . . . did the material world measure *a·*.
53–16　The world could not interpret *a·* the
sp 94–26　enabled him to direct those thoughts *a·* ;
s 127–27　and is alone able to interpret God *a·*.
f 254–13　to *begin a·* and to continue the strife
c 256–15　nor can He be understood *a·* through
b 326–16　The purpose and motive to live *a·* can be
r 466–28　Science will declare God *a·*,
490– 6　Hence it cannot govern man *a·*.

arise
sp 80–26　*a·* from the volition of human belief,
88–25　for both *a·* from mortal belief.
94–15　*a·* from the belief that the infinite is
s 145–18　From this fact *a·* its ethical as well as its
f 288–23　Attempts to conciliate society . . . *a·* from
b 301–25　sin, disease, and death *a·* from the
p 398–13　"Damsel, I say unto thee, *a·* !"— *Mark* 5 : 41.

arise
p 421– 3　*a·* from the belief that other portions
t 446– 7　may either *a·* from the alarm of the physician,
g 523– 8　The creations of matter *a·* from a mist
544– 7　Birth, decay, and death *a·* from the
ap 575– 1　*A·* from your false consciousness

arises
pref viii–18　question *a·*, Is there less sickness because of
a 53–20　*a·* from the great distance between
sp 92– 7　From the illusion . . . *a·* the decomposition of
s 120–10　Then the question inevitably *a·* :
154– 3　Disease *a·*, like other mental conditions, from
ph 166–16　From it *a·* the inharmonious body.
f 243–14　*a·* not so much from lack of desire as from
p 433– 2　Judge Medicine *a·*, and with great solemnity
t 451–27　*a·* from ignorance or malice aforethought.
r 490–10　From this cooperation *a·* its evil.

arising
sp 94–20　betrayal, *a·* from sensuality.
s 145–23　the mystery always *a·* from ignorance
p 426– 1　or disease *a·* from any circumstance,

arithmetic
s 129– 4　a properly computed sum in *a·*.

ark
gl 581– 8　definition of
581–13　*a·* indicates temptation overcome

arm
a 24–11　"the *a·* of the Lord" is revealed— *Isa.* 53 : 1.
49–17　No human eye was there to pity, no *a·* to save.
s 160– 9　motion of the *a·* is no more dependent
ph 198–29　Because the muscles of the blacksmith's *a·*
198–32　it does not follow that . . . a less used *a·*
199–13　by reason of the blacksmith's faith . . . his *a·*
p 365–14　to evoke healing from the outstretched *a·*
379–12　warm water was trickling over his *a·*.

armed
a 52–23　which *a·* him with Love.
b 298– 7　cannot destroy Science *a·* with faith,

arms
a 29– 1　Christians must take up *a·* against error
m 61–15　promising children in the *a·* of gross parents,
b 322–28　turn us like tired children to the *a·* of

army
c 256–21　in the *a·* of heaven, and among— *Dan.* 4 : 35.
p 405–10　if you would not cherish an *a·* of conspirators

aroma
ph 191–32　Mind, God, sends forth the *a·* of Spirit,

around
a 32–32　with shadows fast falling *a·* ;
sp 92–11　a serpent coiled *a·* the tree of knowledge
s 163–31　the fleeting vapors *a·* us,
164– 2　the groping of Homer's Cyclops *a·* his cave."
b 310–16　*a·* which circle harmoniously all things
p 363–10　Knowing what those *a·* him were saying

arouse
p 404 00　*A·* the sinner to this new and true view

arouses
ap 559–13　It *a·* the "seven thunders" of evil, — *Rev.* 10 : 3.

arraigned
ap 564–20　spiritual idea was *a·* before the

arraigns
p 440– 4　whom Truth *a·* before the supreme bar

arrange
s 163–31　as impracticable as to *a·* the fleeting vapors

arranges
ph 190–11　and *a·* itself into five so-called senses,

arranging
f 230–12　to suppose Him capable of first *a·*

array
sp 97–21　broadest facts *a·* the most falsities against
ph 176–10　ghastly *a·* of diseases was not paraded
f 224–14　and *a·* His vicegerent with pomp and splendor ;
c 260–28　If we *a·* thought in mortal vestures,
p 412–19　*a·* your mental plea against the physical.
414–18　lest you *a·* the sick against their own interests
420–15　when they will not *a·* themselves against it,

arrayed
p 391– 2　*a·* against the supremacy of Spirit.

arrest
an 105–24　God will *a·* him.
p 431–13　At the time of the *a·* the prisoner
436–15　Prior to the night of his *a·*, the prisoner
436–18　and thus save him from *a·*.
438–15　I ask your *a·* in the name of Almighty God
441–14　neither can Fear *a·* Mortal Man

arrested
p 431–10　*a·* Mortal Man in behalf of the state
t 452– 5　The wrong thought should be *a·*

arrive

    s 120– 8 *a·* at the fundamental facts of being.
    f 233–11 before we *a·* at the demonstration of
    c 260– 1 one can no more *a·* at the
    o 359–19 when shall we *a·* at the goal which
    p 406–24 until we *a·* at the fulness of God's idea,
    r 468– 1 Thus we *a·* at Truth, or intelligence,
    g 543–12 *a·* at the understanding that material life,

arrived

    p 432–26 Materia Medica, was present when I *a·*,

arrogance

    f 252–17 Material sense lifts its voice with the *a·* of
    p 367–12 with the *a·* of rank and display of scholarship,

arsenic

    ph 178– 2 *a·*, the strychnine, or whatever the drug

art

    a 44–23 It was a method of surgery beyond material *a·*,
    g 507–26 expresses Science and *a·* throughout His crea-
            tion,

article

    s 145–32 Our Master's first *a·* of faith propounded to
    b 320–11 and in the learned *a·* on Noah

articulata

    g 556– 3 Vertebrata, *a·*, mollusca, and radiata

articulations

    g 501– 4 spiritual import of the Word, in its earliest *a·*,

artifice

    sp 83– 4 *a·* and delusion claimed that they could equal

artificial

    r 489– 7 not with an *a·* limb, but with the genuine

artist (*see also* artist's)

    sp 86–32 before the *a·* can convey them to canvas.
    ph 198– 9 materialistic doctor, . . . is an *a·* who outlines
    b 310– 1 The *a·* is not in his painting.
    o 360– 4 The other *a·* replies: "You wrong my

artist's

    b 299– 5 save in the *a·* own observation and
     310– 2 picture is the *a·* thought objectified.

artists

    o 359–30 Scientist and an opponent are like two *a·*.

arts

    p 369–24 preventive . . . *a·* belong emphatically to

ascend

    a 34–25 and *a·* far above their apprehension.
    ph 189–24 we constantly *a·* in infinite being.
    f 222– 2 and *a·* the ladder of life.
    p 407–19 *a·* a degree in the scale of health,

ascended

    a 46–16 was not changed until he himself *a·*,
    g 551–11 but he adds that mankind has *a·*

ascendency

    m 61– 4 good in human affections must have *a·*
     67–20 remember that through spiritual *a·*

ascending

    ph 189–30 goes on in an *a·* scale by evolution,
    c 265–27 brightens the *a·* path of many a heart.
    g 508–22 last in the *a·* order of creation,
     509– 6 on the third day of his *a·* thought,

ascends

    g 509–16 rarefaction of thought as it *a·* higher.

ascension

    a 34–28 which has since been called the *a·*.
     35–17 his spiritual and final *a·* above matter,
     46–23 explained his *a·*, and revealed
     46–26 his final demonstration, called the *a·*,
    b 292–31 In his resurrection and *a·*, Jesus showed
     314– 2 and no less material until the *a·*
     334–15 continued until the Master's *a·*,
    g 509–25 periods of spiritual *a·* are the days

ascertain

    s 152–17 to *a·* the temperature of the patient's body ;
     159–25 to *a·* how much harmony, or health,
    f 239–16 To *a·* our progress, we must learn
    b 337–31 you *a·* that this Science is demonstrably true,
    r 495–31 you will soon *a·* that error cannot destroy error.
    g 547– 7 and so *a·* if the author has given

ascetic

    a 53– 3 Jesus was no *a·*.

ascribe

    a 34– 2 why *a·* this inspiration to a dead rite,
    o 348–15 when we *a·* to Him almighty Life and

ascribes

    c 262– 7 but it *a·* to Him the entire glory.

ashamed

    a 21–32 By-and-by, *a·* of his zigzag course,
    g 532–19 *A·* before Truth, error shrank abashed

Asher

    gl 581–15 definition of

Asia Minor

    b 324–25 A· M·, Greece, and even in imperial Rome.

aside

    a 20–28 "Let us lay *a·* every weight,— *Heb.* 12 : 1.
     20–30 put *a·* material self and sense,
     44– 2 before the thorns can be laid *a·* for a crown,
     49–31 turned "*a·* the right of a man— *Lam.* 3 : 35.
     52–15 Herod and Pilate laid *a·* old feuds
    sp 83–18 belief . . . that occasionally Spirit sets *a·* these
    s 141– 8 to set *a·* even the most cherished beliefs
    ph 166–18 Instead of thrusting Him *a·* in times of
    f 237– 8 before her parents would have laid *a·* their drugs,
    b 286–12 Physical causation was put *a·*
     304–31 thrusting *a·* his divine Principle
     338–26 *a·* from their metaphysical derivation,
    p 409–23 to be laid *a·* for the pure reality.
    g 521–30 would set *a·* the omnipotence of Spirit ;
     555–24 and set *a·* the proper conception of Deity,

ask

    pr 1– * before ye *a·* Him.— *Matt.* 6 : 8.
     2–23 God is Love. Can we *a·* Him to be more?
     3– 8 Shall we *a·* the divine Principle of all
     6– 9 supposition that we have nothing to do but to *a·*
     6–17 More than this we cannot *a·*,
     7–31 or mean to *a·* forgiveness at some later day.
     8–25 and *a·* that it may be laid bare before us,
     9–28 Then why . . . *a·* to be Christians, since you
     10–23 the blessings we *a·* for in prayer.
     10–26 or we should certainly receive that for which
          we *a·*,
     10–27 The Scriptures say : Ye *a·*, and— *Jas.* 4 : 3.
     10–27 receive not, because ye *a·* amiss,— *Jas.* 4 : 3.
     10–29 and for which we *a·* ;
     10–31 Do you *a·* wisdom to be merciful and not
     10–32 Then "ye *a·* amiss."— *Jas.* 4 : 3.
     13– 8 striving for the accomplishment of all we *a·*,
     13–11 we labor for what we *a·* ;
    a 24–22 sinners who *a·* for it and are willing
    m 67– 7 We *a·* the helmsman : "Do you know your
     69–20 Some day the child will *a·* his parent :
     69–23 the child may *a·*, "Do you teach that
    ph 177–28 does human belief, you *a·*, cause this death?
     181– 4 one should *a·*, "Who art thou that
     191–18 It should no longer *a·* of the head,
    f 250–22 Now I *a·*, Is there any more reality in
    o 349– 4 rabbis of the present day *a·* concerning
     355–32 Strangely enough, we *a·* for material theories
    p 371–22 No impossible thing do I *a·* when urging
     416–27 If they *a·* about their disease,
     435–34 I *a·* that the prisoner be restored to
     437–18 I *a·* that the Supreme Court of Spirit reverse
     438–15 I *a·* your arrest in the name of Almighty God
     440–28 I *a·* that he be forbidden to
    r 496– 9 *A·* yourself : Am I living the life that
    g 521–18 will naturally *a·* if there is nothing more
     551–17 Naturalists *a·* : "What can there be, of a
     553–31 may also *a·* how belief can affect a result

asked

    a 31– 6 Again he *a·* : "Who is my mother,— *Matt.* 12 : 48.
    sp 86– 1 Jesus once *a·*, "Who touched— *Luke* 8 : 45.
    s 132–26 Jesus *a·*, "When the Son of man— *Luke* 18 : 8.
    ph 195– 3 he *a·* to be taken back to his dungeon,
    f 216–26 Paul *a·* : What concord hath— *II Cor.* 6 : 15.
     245–15 *A·* to guess her age, those unacquainted with
    b 308–29 was *a·*, "What is thy name?"— *Gen.* 32 : 27.
    o 349– 3 As Paul *a·* of the unfaithful
    p 369–16 Jesus never *a·* if disease were acute or chronic,
     395–15 Prayers, in which God is not *a·* to heal
     399–29 Our Master *a·* : "How can one— *Matt.* 12 : 29.
     411–13 It is recorded that once Jesus *a·*
    g 539–24 Paul *a·* : "What communion— *II Cor.* 6 : 14.

asking

    pr 2–31 *A·* God to *be* God is a vain repetition.
     4–17 Simply *a·* that we may love God will never
     9– 7 Do we love . . . better because of this *a·*?
     9–14 shall never meet this great duty simply by *a·*
    s 135–19 limiting the Holy One of Israel and *a·* :
    f 222–30 "*a·* no question for conscience— *I Cor.* 10 : 25.
     226– 8 *a·* a fuller acknowledgment of the rights of
    p 366–14 we have the apostolic warrant for *a·* :
    g 527–27 and *a·* a prospective sinner to help

asks

    b 281– 9 Science . . . rebukes mortal belief, and *a·* :
    p 432–16 The Judge *a·* if by doing good to his neighbor,

asleep

    sp 95–28 the world is *a·* in the cradle of infancy,
    ph 193–13 the breathing became natural ; he was *a·*.
    b 291–22 As man falleth *a·*, so shall he awake.
    p 416–18 in twenty minutes the sufferer is quietly *a·*.
     442–31 either when *a·* or when awake.
    r 491–18 awake at one time and *a·* at another,

aspect
t 457–17 no good *a·*, either silvern or golden.

aspersion
p 437– 5 This is a foul *a·* on man's Maker.

aspiration
pr 8–14 If we feel the *a·*, humility, gratitude,
16–21 reach the heaven-born *a·* and
c 265–24 The *a·* after heavenly good comes even before

aspirations
m 60– 4 Kindred tastes, motives, and *a·*
c 257–26 to still the desires, to satisfy the *a·*?
g 512– 1 correspond to *a·* soaring beyond and above

assassin
p 419–26 the mental *a·*, who, in attempting to rule
t 445– 4 the attacks of the would-be *mental a·*,

assassins
s 164–20 or produced by mental *a·*,
t 447–11 and save the victims of the mental *a·*.

assent
r 471–11 but yield *a·* to astronomical propositions

assert
f 228–14 Mortals will some day *a·* their freedom
253–16 *a·* your prerogative to overcome the belief in
p 395– 9 *a·* its claims over mortality and disease.

asserting
sp 79–28 *a·* that Mind controls body and brain.
p 421–30 like *a·* that the products of eight multiplied by
g 530–17 myth represents error as always *a·* its

assertion
sp 80–10 the *a·* that spirit-communications are
81–11 A man's *a·* that he is immortal no more proves
81–13 than the opposite *a·*, that he is mortal,
s 136–26 Hence Herod's *a·* : "John have I— *Luke* 9 : 9·.
137–21 This *a·* elicited from Jesus the benediction,
p 383–24 Does his *a·* prove the use of tobacco to be
386–30 although the correctness of the *a·* might
t 460–23 superficial and cold *a·*, "Nothing ails you."
r 478–17 *a·* that there can be pain or

asserts
ph 166–30 but when Mind at last *a·* its mastery
f 226–21 birthright of sole allegiance to his Maker *a·*
b 277–19 Error . . . *a·* that Spirit produces matter
p 423–26 which ultimately *a·* its absolute supremacy.

assiduously
f 233–14 the goal of goodness is *a·* earned

assigning
s 122– 3 *a·* seeming power to sin, sickness,
f 244–30 instead of *a·* to man the everlasting grandeur

assigns
s 123– 7 reverses the order of Science and *a·*
f 203– 4 *a·* sure rewards to righteousness,
p 400–17 except what mortal mind *a·* to it.
g 522– 5 The first record *a·* all might and government
ap 566–29 The Old Testament *a·* to the angels,

assimilate
pr 4–20 striving to *a·* more of the divine character,
t 462– 2 Some individuals *a·* truth more readily
r 466–13 which neither dwell together nor *a·*.

assimilated
b 272– 4 This sense is *a·* only as we are honest,

assist
p 432–26 endeavoring to *a·* the prisoner to escape
g 529– 5 were needed to *a·* the birth of mortals.

assistants
p 431–16 all these *a·* resigned to me,

associates
p 377–32 *a·* sickness with certain circumstances
t 449–19 baneful effect of evil *a·* is less seen than

association
s 154– 3 like other mental conditions, from *a·*.
154– 6 this law obtains credit through *a·*,

associations
sp 87–10 leagues apart and their *a·* forgotten,
87–11 their *a·* float in the general atmosphere

assume
sp 96–17 sin, sickness, and death, which *a·* new phases
s 119– 7 they *a·* that matter is the product of Spirit.
b 313–15 we may *a·* that the author of this
o 344– 8 Is it sacrilegious to *a·* that God's likeness
t 447–32 To *a·* that there are no claims of evil and yet
r 481–20 Human hypotheses first *a·* the reality of
481–21 *a·* the necessity of these evils
g 553–11 "We have no right to *a·* that

assumed
a 27–32 according to certain *a·* material laws.
s 145–30 continually weaken its own *a·* power.
b 326–26 Thought *a·* a nobler outlook,
r 470– 7 *a·* the loss of spiritual power,

assumes
p 421–28 not build it up by wishing to see the forms it *a·*

assuming
g 540–22 representing error as *a·* a divine character,

assumption
sp 75– 1 truth lays bare the mistaken *a·*
g 546– 7 this *a·* of error would dethrone the
552– 9 proof requisite to sustain this *a·*

assurance
m 69–15 brings the sweet *a·* of no parting,
ph 176–32 Truth handles . . . contagion with perfect *a·*.
f 223–15 the *a·* which comes of understanding ;

assurances
p 387–12 the *a·* of immortality, opposed to mortality.

assure
p 416–28 *A·* them that they think too much about

assured
a 38– 2 men are *a·* that this command was
sp 98– 2 spiritual recompense of the persecuted is *a·*
o 352–23 should be *a·* that their fears are groundless,
358–24 Sometimes it is said : "Rest *a·* that

assuredly
pr 15–30 they *a·* call down infinite blessings.
m 65–30 will *a·* throw off this evil,

assures
r 489–32 It *a·* mortals that there is

assuring
ph 169– 5 *a·* me that danger was over,
p 394–21 *a·* him that all misfortunes are
t 447–23 A sinner is not reformed merely by *a·* him

Assyrian
an 103– 5 Sin was the *A·* moon-god.

astonished
ap 563– 3 We may well be *a·* at sin,

astonishing
s 134–19 its *a·* and unequalled success in the

astounded
m 56– 2 came to him for baptism, John was *a·*.
s 130–29 *a·* at the vigorous claims of evil
ap 563– 5 and still more *a·* at hatred,

astray
b 309–17 If these children should go *a·*,

astrography
s 121– 5 before he spake, *a·* was chaotic,

astronomer
sp 84–32 more accurately than the *a·* can read the stars
s 125–28 The *a·* will no longer look up to the stars,

astronomical
s 121–28 As thus indicated, *a·* order
122–32 *A·* science has destroyed the false theory
f 209–25 mundane formations, *a·* calculations,
r 471–11 but yield assent to *a·* propositions
493– 4 but *a·* science contradicts this,

astronomy
s 119–27 As *a·* reverses the human perception
ph 188–31 *A·* gives the desired information
189– 2 willing to leave with *a·* the explanation
195–16 Through *a·*, natural history, chemistry,
f 235–16 will reach higher than the heavens of *a·* ;
r 471–11 of the earth's motions or of the science of *a·*,

astutely
p 378–26 nor a self-constituted. . .power, which copes *a·*

asunder
m 56– * *let not man put a·.— Matt.* 19 : 6.
60–14 wisdom will ultimately put *a·* what she hath not
f 226–20 Science rends *a·* these fetters,

asylum
ph 193–26 threatened with incarceration in an insane *a·*

asylums
p 408–11 people who are committed to insane *a·*

ate
a 32–28 Passover, which Jesus *a·* with his disciples
ph 175–29 before he *a·* the fruit of false knowledge,
195– 7 All that he *a·*, except his black crust,
197–21 the simple food our forefathers *a·*
f 221– 3 he *a·* only bread and vegetables,
221–24 and he *a·* without suffering,

atheism
s 139–28 *A·*, pantheism, theosophy, and
gl 580–27 and then disappeared in the *a·* of matter.

atheistic
s 139–31 does not follow that the profane or *a·* invalid

Athenians
gl 596– 8   Referring to it, he said to the *A* :
Athens
gl 596– 7   Paul saw in *A* an altar dedicated
athirst
ap 570–15   weary wanderers, *a* in the desert
athlete
ph 172–30   may present more nobility than the . . . *a*,
atmosphere
damp
  ph 175–26   Damp *a* and freezing snow empurpled the
earth's
  g 547–12   was able to see in the egg the earth's *a*,
general
  sp 87–11   float in the general *a* of human mind.
immoral
  t 452–15   Never breathe an immoral *a*, unless
of intelligence
  ph 192– 1   aroma of Spirit, the *a* of intelligence.
of Mind
  g 512–11   abound in the spiritual *a* of Mind,
of Soul
  gl 587–26   HEAVEN. . . . bliss ; the *a* of Soul.
of Spirit
  sp 70– 6   can never enter the *a* of Spirit.
  gl 590– 3   the *a* of Spirit, where Soul is supreme.
surrounding
  s 128–21   its escape into the surrounding *a*.
this
  b 273–31   this *a* . . . cannot be destructive to morals

  a 37–11   cleanse and rarefy the *a* of material sense
  s 125–26   mariner will have dominion over the *a*
  128–16   It extends the *a* of thought,
  f 220–14   The *a* of the earth,
  220–14   kinder than the *a* of mortal mind,
  p 386– 9   mortals declare that certain states of the *a*
  392–21   If you decide that climate or *a* is unhealthy,
  gl 585–19   *a* of human belief before it accepts sin,
atom
  c 263–29   A sensual thought, like an *a* of dust
  gl 583–25   could not create an *a* . . . the opposite of
atone
  a 19– 4   Man cannot exceed divine Love, and so *a* for
atonement
in the
  a 19–21   has little part in the *a*,
  24–13   This is having part in the *a* ;
Jesus'
  a 19–19   will help us to understand Jesus' *a* for sin
  r 497–13   We acknowledge Jesus' *a* as the
of Christ
  a 18–13   *a* of Christ reconciles man to God,
requires
  a 23– 4   The *a* requires constant self-immolation
views of
  a 24–16   ordinary theological views of *a* will

  a 18– 1   *A* is the exemplification of man's unity with
  23– 8   The *a* is a hard problem in theology,
at-one-ment
  a 19–22   in the *a* with God,
  21– 5   This is having our part in the *a*
  45–20   hath elevated them to possible *a* with
atrocities
  an 105–23   to commit fresh *a* as opportunity occurs
attach
  p 385–10   penalty which our beliefs would *a* to our best
  440–11   to which you *a* penalties ;
attached
  a 31–13   He *a* no importance to dead ceremonies.
attaches
  s 117– 7   C. S. *a* no physical nature and significance to
attack
  a 27–30   Jesus' persecutors made their strongest *a* upon
  p 379– 1   If disease can *a* and control the body
  392–16   liable to an *a* from that source.
attacks
  f 236– 8   infuriated *a* on individuals, who
  t 445– 4   to guard against the *a* of the
attain
  pr 9–27   Do you really desire to *a* this point?
  m 57– 3   without it one cannot *a* the Science of
  ph 181–20   till you finally *a* the understanding of C. S.
  f 251–29   corrected before we can *a* harmony.
  254– 5   or *a* slowly and yield not to discouragement.
  c 262–22   and *a* the bliss of loving unselfishly,
  p 366– 5   and thus *a* the spiritual freedom which will
  g 536–27   Through toil, . . . what do mortals *a* ?

attainable
  r 487– 4   never *a* through death, but gained by
attained
  m 60–30   and happiness would be more readily *a*
  s 117–12   the spiritual meaning of which is *a*
  ph 167– 4   If . . . the Science of healing is not *a*,
  167–27   must be *a* through the divine Mind.
  f 237– 9   mental height their little daughter . . . *a*.
  b 297–16   Thus the reality of being is *a*
  298–19   When the real is *a*, which is announced by
  o 356– 3   before the spiritual fact is *a*.
attaining
  c 260– 9   human beliefs will be *a* diviner conceptions,
  b 273–14   impossibility of *a* perfect understanding till
attainment
  a 39–28   interval before its *a* is attended with doubts
  m 61– 6   *a* of this celestial condition would
  f 235–17   though adorned with gems of scholarly *a*,
  p 428–11   the great *a* by means of which
  t 455–31   The higher your *a* in the Science of
attainments
  pr 10–15   Spiritual *a* open the door to a
  p 367–29   student's higher *a* in this line of light.
  g 505–27   is not the result of scholarly *a* ;
attains
  pr 2–16   Goodness *a* the demonstration of
attempt
any
  t 459–12   Any *a* to heal mortals with erring
every
  ph 186–20   Every *a* of evil to destroy good
mental
  g 517– 6   mental *a* to reduce Deity to corporeality.
to purify
  t 452–15   Never . . . unless in the *a* to purify it.
to trace
  g 533–10   an *a* to trace all human errors
unwitting
  f 212–11   I have seen an unwitting *a* to

  a 51– 9   he allowed men to *a* the destruction of
  ph 178–29   may *a* to unite with it hypnotism,
  182–13   If we *a* it, we shall presently
  187–26   and suffers from the *a*.
  f 230– 2   Would you *a* with drugs, or without,
  231– 8   What God cannot do, man need not *a*.
  238–16   when we *a* to claim the benefits of an
  o 357–15   how dare we *a* to destroy what
  p 395–22   and then to *a* its cure through Mind.
  439–11   manacling . . . in the *a* to save him.
  t 447– 4   no moral right to *a* to influence the
attempted
  o 351–28   in their *a* worship of the spiritual.
  g 513– 3   and is an *a* infringement on infinity.
attempting
  p 419–26   assassin, who, in *a* to rule mankind,
  r 480–18   thus *a* to separate Mind from God.
attempts
  pref ix– 7   *a* to convey his feeling.
  ix–14   but they are feeble *a* to state the Principle
  f 238–22   *A* to conciliate society and so gain
  c 263–25   and *a* to pattern the infinite.
  b 300– 1   Human logic is awry when it *a* to
  318–25   *a* to heal it, with matter.
  329–18   *a* to solve a problem of Euclid,
  t 445– 5   *assassin*, who *a* to kill morally and
  447– 7   ignorant *a* to do good may render you
attend
  pr 13–22   doubts and fears which *a* such a belief,
  a 31–29   would *a* the Science of Spirit,
  33–29   the persecutions which *a* a new and
  sp 98– 1   which *a* a new step in Christianity ;
  f 235– 4   doctor infected with smallpox to *a* you
  t 463– 6   To *a* properly the birth of the new child,
  g 549–22   such vague hypotheses as must necessarily *a*
attendants
  pref x–19   abandoned as hopeless by regular medical *a*.
attended
  a 39–29   interval before its attainment is *a* with doubts
  s 133–13   miracles *a* the successes of the Hebrews ;
  139– 9   Reforms have commonly been *a* with
  f 224– 9   *a* by life and peace instead of discord and
  p 422–23   and *a* by the same symptoms.
  431– 6   During all this time the prisoner *a* to
attends
  g 555– 2   and that health *a* the absence of
attention
  m 59– 5   mutual *a* and approbation should
  ph 198–14   but to do this requires *a*.
  p 369–17   never recommended *a* to laws of health,

attention
p	382– 5	If half the a· given to hygiene were
	396– 8	nor draw a· to certain symptoms as
g	556–14	C. S. may absorb the a· of sage and
	556–25	Ontology receives less a· than physiology.

attenuated
s	153– 1	is frequently a· to such a degree that
	153– 5	the author has a· Natrum muriaticum

attenuation
s	153– 8	with one drop of that a· in a goblet of water,
	153–11	The highest a· of homœopathy
	153–21	a high a· of truth,
	156– 9	the fourth a· of Argentum nitratum
	156–10	occasional doses of a high a· of Sulphuris.
	158–29	mortal mind, of a higher a· than the drug,

attest
pr	4–15	a· our worthiness to be partakers of
	15–24	and let our lives a· our sincerity.
s	150–15	to a· the reality of the higher mission
ph	193–28	I cannot a· the truth of that report,
p	272–24	which really a· the divine origin and

attested
sp	80–23	a· the control of mortal mind over its

attorney
p	430–22	False Belief is the a· for Personal Sense.
	437–32	The a·, C. S., then read from the
	438–23	False Belief, the a· for Personal Sense,
	440– 8	Mortal Minds were deceived by your a·,
	441–28	Your a·, False Belief, is an impostor,

attract
t	452–12	may provoke envy, but it will also a· respect.

attracted
a	21–26	and will be a· thitherward.
t	449–23	a mind which is a· or repelled according to

attracting
ph	169–12	fosters disease by a· the mind to the subject

attraction
m	57–11	a· between native qualities will be
sp	73–12	Any other control or a· of so-called spirit
an	102– 9	There is but one real a·,
	102–11	or the a· of God, divine Mind.
s	124–20	Adhesion, cohesion, and a· are properties of
f	213–13	Material theories partially paralyze this a·
	213–14	by an opposite a· towards the finite,
b	293–15	whose potency is Truth, whose a· is Love,
g	536 12	spiritual gravitation and a· to one Father,

attractive
p	407– 4	a· to no creature except a loathsome worm,
r	491–27	may have an a· personality.

attribute
m	62–20	must not a· more and more intelligence
s	111–22	tendency of the age to a· physical effects to
ph	199–29	the unscientific might a· to a lubricating oil.
p	319–30	for instance, to name Love as merely an a·

attributed
ph	176– 5	unmanly Adams a· their own downfall
b	284–27	the effects commonly a· to them

attributes
ph	187– 9	With pagan blindness, it a· to
f	210–11	Knowing that Soul and its a· were
b	275–16	These are His a· the eternal
	301– 1	yea, which manifests God's a·
r	465–14	The a· of God are justice, mercy,
	473–11	the ideal Truth . . . a· all power to God.
g	555–13	C. S. a· to error neither entity nor power,

attuned
p	411– 8	was not perfectly a· to divine Science,

audible
pr	4–15	which, even if not acknowledged in a· words,
	4–27	A· prayer can never do the works of
	7– 8	A· prayer is impressive;
	8–18	Professions and a· prayers are like
	11–31	Such a desire has little need of a· expression.
ap	559– 8	exercised upon visible error and a· sin.
gl	594– 9	first a· claim that God was not omnipotent

audibly
pr	12–30	because they pray or are prayed for a·,
p	376–22	silently and a· arguing the true facts
	412–11	but by naming it a·, you are liable
	412–21	at first mentally, not a·,
	412–30	through the parent's thought, silently or a·
	417–27	Explain a· to your patients, as soon as

audience
pr	15–12	that man may have a· with Spirit,

audience-chamber
p	442– 6	resounded throughout the vast a·

auditor
p	424–22	you need the ear of your a·.

auditory
pr	7–24	The "divine ear" is not an a· nerve.
ph	194–10	Destruction of the a· nerve and

aught
sp	93–13	nor creates a· that can cause evil.
s	120–18	impossible for a· but Mind to testify truly
ph	181–25	It is unnecessary to resort to a· besides Mind
f	203–14	destroys reliance on a· but God,
	207–22	no reality in a· which does not proceed from
b	284–14	or know a· unlike the infinite?
	291– 4	a· but the destruction of sin,
	302– 9	It is impossible that man should lose a·
p	391–14	It is error to suffer for a· but your own sins.
	412– 2	never punishing a· but sin,
	419–17	lest a· unfit for development enter
	429– 1	It is a sin to believe that a· can overpower
	441– 4	which undertakes to punish a· but sin,
r	479– 6	On the contrary, if a· comes from God,
g	504– 2	never reflected by a· but the good.
	543–25	did it leave a· for matter to create?
	553–30	before they think or know a· of their origin,
	555–25	author of a· that can become

augury
m	58–20	a poor a· for the happiness of wedlock.

Australia
sp	82–29	When wandering in A·, do we look

authentic
ph	194–17	The a· history of Kaspar Hauser is

authenticate
g	547– 1	proving of one example would a· all

author (see also Eddy, Mrs. Mary Baker)
called the
pref	xi–22	God called the a· to proclaim His Gospel

cannot be, the
f	230–16	cannot be, the a· of experimental sins.

naturalist and
an	104– 8	Agassiz, the celebrated naturalist and a·,

not as the
s	127–17	C. S. reveals God, not as the a· of sin, sickness,

not the
sp	89–26	The tree is not the a· of itself.
f	231–16	God is not the a· of mortal discords.
	249–12	Mind is not the a· of matter,
o	349–12	God is not the a· of sickness.
p	381–16	He is not the a· of barbarous codes.

of all things
g	519– 1	eternal Mind, the a· of all things,

of the unreal
r	474–28	error, not Truth, is the a· of the unreal,

started by the
pref	xi–26	Mind-healing was started by the a·

the only
a	29–10	perception that God is the only a· of man.
b	313–15	we may assume that the a· of this
p	390–23	God is no more the a· of sickness than
r	474–18	If . . . God must be their a·.
	100 24	God is not its a·
g	512–30	and claims God as their a·;
	538–31	supposes God to be the a· of sin and
	546–21	To the a·, they are transparent,
	554–27	is the a· of itself, and is simply a falsity
	555–25	when we admit that the perfect is the a· of
ap	567–27	are cast out with their a·.

authorities
a	29–13	tradition that Publius Lentulus wrote to the a·

authority
better
p	438– 1	remarking that the Bible was better a· than

divine
   (see divine)

my only
s	126–29	The Bible has been my only a·.

no
t	447– 3	We have no a· . . . to attempt to

of this science
ph	189– 1	yield to the a· of this science,

Scriptural
o	342–30	Shall it be denied that . . . has Scriptural a·?
ap	573–24	This is Scriptural a· for concluding
pr	14–30	speak "as one having a·." — Matt. 7 : 29.
a	26–15	gave Jesus a· over sin, sickness, and death.
ph	168–18	Are we to believe an a· which denies
	168–19	an a· which Jesus proved to be false
c	267–14	the same a· for the appellative mother,
o	357–14	the creativeness and a· of Deity,
p	393–10	Exercise this God-given a·.
	395– 7	should speak to disease as one having a·
r	471–12	but yield . . . to the a· of natural science.
g	517–11	not as much a· for considering

author's (see Eddy, Mrs. Mary Baker)

authors
c	263– 2	independent workers, personal a·, and
p	387–15	If printers and a· have the shortest span of

automatic
p 399–16 how can mechanism be a·?
autopsy
s 159– 2 After the a·, her sister testified that
auxiliaries
t 454–32 letter and mental argument are only human a·
auxiliary
pref xii–19 as a· to her church.
avail
pr 3– 9 we have only to a· ourselves of God's rule
3–23 Then we shall a· ourselves of the blessings we
12–32 all may a· themselves of God as
ph 167–18 To have one God and a· yourself of the
183– 2 so-called laws . . . would render Spirit of no a·,
p 406–21 We can, and ultimately shall, so rise as to a·
g 550–10 Of what a· is it to investigate what
availability
f 236–19 a· of good as the remedy for every woe.
available
s 143–30 deprives you of the a· superiority of
f 237–22 This makes C. S. early a·.
availed
f 222–10 a· himself of the fact that Mind governs man,
avenue
b 280–22 urges through every a· the belief
avenues
b 293–32 The five physical senses are the a· and
aver
o 348–29 this I do a·, that, as a result of teaching C. S.,
354– 3 "utter falsities and absurdities," as some a·?
359–11 a· that the material senses are indispensable
r 474–20 a·, "I am not come to destroy, — Matt. 5 : 17.
avers
b 320–20 a· that this fact is not forever to be humbled
avert
a 40–20 could not a· a felon's fate,
avoid
s 153–30 we shall a· loquacious tattling about
153–31 as we would a· advocating crime.
ph 169–14 and by dosing the body in order to a· it.
f 230–15 for doing what they could not a· doing.
234–14 a· casting pearls before those who
b 329–16 he should a· their occasion.
p 396– 5 A· talking illness to the patient.
396– 9 a· speaking aloud the name of the disease.
avoidance
g 542–10 The a· of justice and the denial of truth
ap 571– 5 necessary to ensure the a· of the evil?
await
a 28–30 a·, in some form, every pioneer of truth.
m 66–22 It is better to a· the logic of events
sp 97– 3 a· the certainty of ultimate perfection.
awaited
a 20–20 scourge and the cross a· the great Teacher.
awaiting
ph 183– 9 a· its germination according to the laws of
p 439–28 a· the sentence which General Progress
awaits
m 67–13 the mariner works on and a· the issue.
b 291–26 No resurrection from the grave a· Mind
291–28 No final judgment a· mortals,
awake
pr 4–22 until we a· in His likeness.
sp 75–13 that I may a· him out of sleep."— John 11 : 11.
75–31 when we a· from earth's sleep to the
ph 190–29 when I a·, with Thy likeness.— Psal. 17 : 15.
f 249–27 than are the thoughts of mortals when c·.
b 291–23 As man falleth asleep, so shall he a·.
323–19 When the sick or the sinning a· to realize
p 420–30 tell your patient that he must a·.
442–32 either when asleep or when a·.
r 491–18 that matter is a· at one time and
491–28 a·, we dream of the pains and pleasures of
awaken
b 291–10 need not fancy that . . . death will a· them
327–30 a· the man's dormant sense of moral
g 553– 3 which should a· thought to a higher and
awakened
p 417–21 from which the patient needs to be a·.
r 493–18 If Jesus a· Lazarus from the dream,
awakening
f 230– 4 the a· from this mortal dream, or illusion,
230– 6 This a· is the forever coming of Christ,
b 339–16 against his own a· to the awful unreality
g 556–29 when that a· comes, existence will be
awakenings
sp 82–27 Different dreams and different a·

awakens
ph 196– 6 Better the suffering which a· mortal mind
o 342–21 C. S. a· the sinner, reclaims the
award
pr 5–14 Saints and sinners get their full a·,
away
pref vii–17 Contentment with . . . are crumbling a·.
pr 8–22 If we turn a· from the poor,
a 21–10 He constantly turns a· from material sense,
22–18 When the smoke of battle clears a·,
27–26 They fell a· from grace because they
35– 5 turned a· from material things,
39–24 material pains and material pleasures to pass a·,
45–17 Christ hath rolled a· the stone from
48– 8 turned forever a· from earth to heaven,
sp 87– 8 Though individuals have passed a·,
87–31 which are thousands of miles a·
89–29 had the right to take it a·.
95–29 dreaming a· the hours.
s 122–25 To material sense, the severance . . . takes a·
131–23 which taketh a· the ceremonies and doctrines
147–12 centuries had passed a· since Jesus practised
150–16 to take a· the sins of the world.
152– 4 Mind takes a· all its supposed sovereignty,
155– 6 Even when you take a· the
ph 168– 7 you take a· from Mind,
172–25 you take a· a portion of the
187–27 If you take a· this erring mind,
191–15 Truth . . . chasing a· the darkness of error.
f 201– 8 a new creature, in whom old things pass a·
206–20 and then taking it a· by death?
212–15 take a· this so-called mind instead of a piece of
232–29 so-called pleasures and pains of sense pass a·
237–13 snatches a· the good seed before it has
238–12 To fall a· from Truth in times of persecution,
239– 5 Take a· wealth, fame, and social
241–10 revenge, and so forth, steal a· the treasures of
241–14 Take a· the spiritual signification of
247–11 the beauty of material things passes a·,
250–25 Take a· the mortal mind, and matter has no
c 261– 2 Look a· from the body into Truth and
261– 9 If one turns a· from the body
261–24 Breaking a· from the mutations of time
265–31 if they wrench a· false pleasurable beliefs
b 268– 8 looking a· from matter to Mind
273–11 and thus tears a· the foundations of error.
276–22 a· from materiality to the Principle
278– 3 Divine metaphysics explains a· matter.
288–16 the tumult dies a· in the distance.
294– 7 loss of one finger would take a· some quality
296–26 foundations which time is wearing a·.
299–29 will melt a· the shadow
312–28 and so turns a· from the intelligent and
323–21 towards Soul and a· from material sense,
323–26 takes a· all sin and the delusion that
323–30 We are either turning a· from this utterance,
334–18 taking a· the sins of the world,
o 347–23 If C. S. takes a· the popular gods,
p 362–14 and his bare feet a· from it.
365– 3 the heavenly homesick looking a· from earth,
376–10 whom you declare to be wasting a·
376–12 blood never gave life and can never take it a·,
377– 8 come back no better than when they went a·.
401–19 forcing impurities to pass a·,
403–20 sweeps a· the gossamer web of mortal illusion.
416–31 Turn their thoughts a· from their bodies
428–12 sweep a· the false and give place to the true.
439–10 frightening a· Materia Medica, who was then
t 462– 9 If the student goes a· to practise
r 479–13 Take a· so-called mortal mind, which constitutes
484– 4 bigotry, nor envy can wash a· its foundation,
493–22 takes a· this physical sense of discord,
g 510–12 and turn a· from a false material sense.
521–13 should look a· from the opposite supposition
522– 9 as having broken a· from Deity
536– 4 and the first earth were passed a· ;— Rev. 21 : 1.
536– 8 the sea, . . . is represented as having passed a·.
539– 7 as if . . . matter can both give and take a·.
548–11 only as the clouds of corporeal sense roll a·.
556– 9 for the former things will have passed a·.
ap 570–10 to be carried a· of the flood.— Rev. 12 : 15.
571–31 He takes a· mitre and sceptre.
572–21 and the first earth were passed a· ;— Rev. 21 : 1.
573–31 and all tears shall be wiped a·.
574–11 carried John a· in spirit.

awful
a 48–28 ignorant of the consequences of his a· decision
50– 7 wrung from Jesus' lips the a· cry,
s 110– 8 I beheld, as never before, the a· unreality
151–14 the a· and oppressive bondage now enforced
f 207– 9 We must learn that evil is the a· deception
223–30 but the a· daring of sin destroys sin,
226–30 I saw before me the a· conflict,
b 307–31 Above error's a· din, blackness, and chaos,

bayonet
f 225–11 Science, heeding not the pointed b·, marches on.
226–12 not through human warfare, not with b· and

beam
f 205–28 Selfishness tips the b· of human existence
t 455–14 "First cast out the b· out of — *Matt.* 7 : 5.

beaming
p 442–12 countenance b· with health and happiness.

beams
pref vii– 3 beholds the first faint morning b·,
vii–10 should dawn the morning b·
g 504– 8 solar b· are not yet included in the record

bear
pref xii–24 is joyful to b· consolation to the sorrowing
a 31– 2 Pride and fear are unfit to b· the standard of
s 120–16 nor can the material senses b· reliable
f 201– * b· *in my bosom the reproach* — *Psal.* 89 : 50.
202– 6 If men would bring to b· upon the study of
254–30 Take it up and b· it, for through it you win
b 298–10 spiritual sense can b· witness only to Truth
330– 9 and the letter and the spirit b· witness,
p 411–10 b· witness to the truth,
417–28 Explain . . . as soon as they can b· it,
436–13 Such acts b· their own justification,
441–13 Material Law is a liar who cannot b· witness
t 451–18 they b· as of old the fruits of the Spirit.
ap 561–31 to b· witness of that Light." — *John* 1 : 8.

beards
g 549–25 and b· the lion of materialism in its den.

beareth
b 272– 7 else it b· not much fruit, for the

bearing
ph 180– 9 the seed within itself b· fruit
f 252–31 Spirit, b· opposite testimony, saith :
b 299–19 a tree, b· the fruits of sin,
p 391–31 and b· the fruits of Spirit.
438–12 and b· false witness against Man.
r 494–28 b· Truth's signet, its lap piled high with
g 518– 6 given you every herb b· seed, — *Gen.* 1 : 29.

bears
ph 197– 9 which b· the fruit of sin, disease, and
f 207–31 which b· no resemblance to spirituality,
225– 7 time b· onward freedom's banner.
b 271– 1 seed of Truth springs up and b· much fruit.
o 361–29 That which when sown b· immortal fruit,

beast
any
g 529–14 more subtle than any b· of the — *Gen.* 3 : 1.
ap 564–32 "more subtle than any b· of the — *Gen.* 3 : 1.
every
g 518– 9 And to every b· of the earth, — *Gen.* 1 : 30.
597–22 formed every b· of the field, — *Gen.* 2 : 19.
ferocious
sp 78– 2 the gnarled oak, the ferocious b·,
p 378–15 man's gaze, fastened fearlessly on a ferocious b·,

f 244–24 not a b·, a vegetable, nor a migratory mind.
b 327–14 Sin is the image of the b·
p 378–15 often causes the b· to retreat in terror.
g 513–16 b· of the earth after his kind : — *Gen.* 1 : 24.
513–22 God made the b· of the earth — *Gen.* 1 : 25.
542– 9 sets upon error the mark of the b·.
551– 7 the bird is not the product of a b·.
ap 567–27 b· and the false prophets are lust and

beasts
f 244–14 is like the b· and vegetables,
g 539–18 the serpent, to grovel beneath all the b·

beat
f 203–30 sin, sorrow, and death b· in vain.

beatific
c 266–28 he reflects the b· presence,

beatified
b 303–19 b· understanding of the Science of Life.

beatitudes
t 446–25 divine b·, reflect the spiritual light

Beaumont's "Medical Experiments"
ph 175–24 B· "M· E·'" did not govern the digestion.

beautifies
g 516–19 b· the landscape, blesses the earth.

beautiful
a 32–25 it was natural and b·.
m 60– 6 The b· in character is also the good,
61–15 often these b· children early droop and die,
63– 5 The b·, good, and pure constitute his ancestry.
sp 74–17 The caterpillar, transformed into a b· insect,
ph 190–15 springing from the soil with b· green blades,
f 240– 8 The stars make night b·,
246–21 and limiting all that is good and b·,
246–24 is always b· and grand.
248– 5 that a friend can ever seem less than b·.

beautiful
f 248– 9 supplying it with b· images of thought
b 276–14 and presents them as b· and immortal.
277–31 mortal phenomenon, . . . sometimes b·,
280– 6 All things b· and harmless are ideas of Mind.
304–20 Harmony in man is as b· as in music,
p 442–14 feet "b· upon the mountains," — *Isa.* 52 : 7.
t 457–16 both sides were b· according to their degree ;
r 477–28 when they called a certain b· lake
485–25 its own b· images, but it effaces them
g 527– 3 to make it b· or to cause it to live and grow.
527– 5 but ever b· and complete.
ap 561–12 the b· description which Sir Walter Scott
575–22 "B· for situation, the joy of the. — *Psal.* 48 : 2.
gl 593– 1 The love of the good and b·,

beautifully
sp 77–24 would grow b· less
g 543– 7 becomes more b· apparent at error's demise.

beauty
all
sp 89–19 It possesses of itself all b· and poetry,
and fragrance
ph 175–11 The joy of its presence, its b· and fragrance,
and goodness
sp 76–23 possessing unlimited divine b· and goodness
b 304– 4 which hide spiritual b· and goodness.
g 503–22 immortal forms of b· and goodness.
and holiness
f 246–25 unfolds wisdom, b·, and holiness.
bathes all in
g 510–13 bathes all in b· and light.
bow of
f 247–26 arches the cloud with the bow of b·,
demonstrates the
a 26–19 musician demonstrates the b· of the music
goodness and
s 121–13 So we have goodness and b· to gladden the
grace and
c 263–14 when he would outline grace and b·,
grow in
o 341– 7 Scriptures, which grow in b· and consistency
natural
ph 175– 9 an abuse of natural b· to say that a rose,
of holiness
s 135–12 This is "the b· of holiness," — *Psal.* 29 : 2.
f 253– 2 The b· of holiness, the perfection of being,
of this text
ap 574–16 b· of this text is, that the sum total of
recipe for
f 247–31 recipe for b· is to have less illusion
secret
pr 15–25 Christians rejoice in secret b· and bounty,
sense of
f 246–14 the transient sense of b· fades,
tremulous with
s 142–13 making dome and spire tremulous with b·,

m 57–15 B·, wealth, or fame is incompetent
f 247–10 B·, as well as truth, is eternal ;
247–10 but the b· of material things passes away,
247–21 B· is a thing of life, which dwells forever in
g 509–26 in which b·, sublimity, purity, and holiness

became
a 34–18 they b· more spiritual and understood better
47– 6 they b· better healers, leaning no longer on
s 111–27 this fact b· evident to me,
ph 193–12 the breathing b· natural ; he was asleep.
200– 1 the gods b· alive in a nation's belief.
f 245– 5 she b· insane and lost all account of time.
b 314–28 the more odious he b· to sinners
316– 1 he b· the way of salvation to all who
321–26 the inward voice b· to him the voice of God,
326–27 and his life b· more spiritual.
o 351– 8 The author b· a member of the orthodox
p 411–17 and straightway b· whole.
t 460–31 the teaching b· clearer, until finally the
g 524–15 and man b· a living soul. — *Gen.* 2 : 7.
544– 4 In God's creation ideas b· productive,
ap 574–11 It exalted him till he b· conscious of the

because
pref viii–19 b· of these practitioners?
x–20 b· there is so little faith in
pr 5–28 b· he fancies himself forgiven.
9– 6 Do we love our neighbor better b· of
10–27 b· ye ask amiss, — *Jas.* 4 : 3.
11–20 b· sin brings inevitable suffering.
12–19 b· it has no intelligence.
12–29 If the sick recover b· they
13–25 B· of human ignorance of the
14–20 I go unto my — *John* 14 : 12.
14–21 b· the Ego is absent from the body,
a 21– 3 b· you are a better man.
21– 7 b· of another's goodness,
27–26 They fell away from grace b· they

because

a 28–27 *b·* it is honored by sects and societies,
  29– 9 *b·* then our labor is more needed.
  32– 1 *b·* they have not known— *John* 16 : 3.
  38– 1 *B·* men are assured that
  39–24 unreal, *b·* impossible in Science.
  41–29 *B·* it demanded more than they
  42–21 *B·* of the wondrous glory which
  43–21 rose higher in demonstration *b·* of
  53– 6 *b·* he was their friend ;
  53– 9 *B·* the divine Principle and practice
  53–12 were unknown to the world *b·*
m 58–27 *b·* another supplies her wants.
  60– 9 *b·* the mother-love includes purity
  60–20 *B·* the education of the higher
  62–31 *B·* mortals believe in material laws
sp 82–10 *b·* different states of consciousness are
  82–15 *b·* both of us are either unconscious or
  86–15 *b·* it is unusual to see thoughts,
  87–24 *b·* you do not think of it.
  91–10 *b·* Science exposes his nothingness ;
  94–10 *b·* he made himself the Son of God.''— *John*
        19 : 7.
  95–20 *b·* even human invention must
  99–16 errs *b·* it is human.
an 103–13 *b·* Mind-science is of God
s 117– 1 *b·* an individual may be one of
  117–25 *b·* of opacity to the true light,
  118–28 *b·* these definitions portray law as
  119–23 *b·* it is opposed to the nature of Spirit,
  129– 2 *b·* its logic is as harmonious as the
  133–19 *b·* Judaism engendered the
  134–23 not *b·* this Science is supernatural
  134–24 nor *b·* it is an infraction of
  134–25 *b·* it is the immutable law of God,
  141– 6 *B·* his precepts require the
  144–23 *B·* divine Science wars with so-called
  146– 4 *B·* our systems of religion are governed
  146–18 *B·* truth divests material drugs of
  149–13 it is *b·* you have not demonstrated the
  149–14 *b·* you have not obeyed the rule
  150–32 *b·* they are ignorant that the human mind
  153–25 We weep *b·* others weep, we yawn *b·* they yawn,
  153–26 we have smallpox *b·* others have it ;
  154–14 *b·* no cholera patient had been in that bed.
  157– 4 *b·* its one recognized Principle of healing is
ph 168–15 *B·* man-made systems insist that
  178– 9 is not dangerous *b·* of its priority
  181–16 you manipulate *b·* you are ignorant of
  184–21 not *b·* a law of matter has been
  184–22 *b·* a law of this so-called mind has been
  185–28 *b·* erroneous methods act on and through
  186–11 *b·* it is the absence of truth.
  186–12 *b·* it is the absence of something.
  186–13 *b·* it presupposes the absence of God,
  198–29 *B·* the muscles of the blacksmith's arm
  199– 6 *B·* nobody believes that mind is producing
  199–12 Not *b·* of muscular exercise.
f 205– 5 all *b·* of their blindness,
  207– 2 *B·* God is Spirit, evil becomes
  210–21 *B·*, in obedience to the immutable law
  210–30 *B·* immortal sense has no error of sense,
  212– 9 *B·* the memory of pain is more vivid
  212–25 *B·* all the methods of Mind are not
  215– 9 *b·* matter and mortality do not reflect
  215–27 *B·* he understood the superiority and
  216– 1 *b·* of his faith in Soul and his
  227–10 *b·* some public teachers permit
  231–20 To hold yourself superior to sin, *b·*
  236–28 Jesus loved little children *b·* of their
  238–20 *b·* we suffer severely from error.
  243–28 *b·* they declare nothing except God.
  245–21 Years had not made her old, *b·*
  253– 8 *b·* I AM THAT I AM.
c 263–10 *b·* he has not tasted heaven.
b 273– 9 *b·* they are not based on the divine law.
  274– 8 not really natural nor scientific, *b·*
  278–29 We define matter as error, *b·* it is the
  289–32 *B·* Life is God, Life must be eternal,
  291–16 immortal, *b·* sin is not there
  292–13 *b·* this so-called mind has no
  292–21 Even *b·* ye cannot— *John* 8 : 43.
  292–24 *b·* there is no truth in— *John* 8 : 44.
  301–14 seems to mortal sense transcendental, *b·*
  302–20 *b·* the Soul, or Mind, of the spiritual man
  302–22 *b·* this real man is governed by
  305–27 *B·* man is the reflection of his
  310–30 *b·* Mind is Spirit, which
  311– 7 Soul is immortal *b·* it is Spirit,
  312– 2 *b·* such so-called knowledge is reversed
  314– 1 no more perfect *b·* of death
  314–23 *B·* of mortals' material and sinful belief,
  316–18 rose higher to human view *b·* of the
  317–16 no less tangible *b·* it is spiritual
  317–17 *b·* his life is not at the mercy of
  329– 7 *B·* you cannot walk on the water

because

b 329–19 denies the rule of the problem *b·*
  330–23 one Mind only, *b·* there is one God.
  335– 2 no evil in Spirit, *b·* God is Spirit.
  335–20 *B·* Soul is immortal, it does not
o 341– * *b·* I tell you the truth,— *John* 8 : 45.
  343–21 *b·* meekness and spirituality are
  344– 6 and that this claim is made *b·*
  344–29 Is it *b·* allopathy and homœopathy
  346–20 *b·* Truth is error's antidote.
  346–23 *b·* matter has no sensation,
  348–17 *b·* I desire to have no faith in evil
  349–17 *b·* one is obliged to use material terms
  350–16 often refused to explain his words, *b·*
  351–22 *B·* such starting-points are neither
  352– 1 *b·* they did not sufficiently understand
  352–27 *b·* there are no such things.
  355–27 *b·* . . . are God's immortal keynotes,
  358–21 *b·* there are few who have gained a
  359– 6 Is this *b·* the patients have more faith
  360– 1 *b·* drawn from Truth,
p 364–30 *b·* much is forgiven them.
  367–30 *B·* Truth is infinite,
  367–31 *B·* Truth is omnipotent
  368–24 *B·* matter has no consciousness
  371–23 *b·* this teaching is in advance
  373– 7 partly *b·* they were willing to
  374– 6 *B·* mortal mind seems to be conscious,
  374–24 your steps are less firm *b·* of your
  375–31 *b·* it is a stage of fear so excessive
  376–18 *B·* the so-called material body
  377–16 *B·* a belief originates unseen,
  379–10 and died *b·* of that belief,
  383–13 *b·* mind and body rest on the
  385–27 *b·* you have partaken of salt fish,
  386–11 not *b·* of the climate, but
  387– 3 *B·* mortal mind is kept active,
  387–13 *b·* they faithfully perform the
  387–16 it is not *b·* they occupy the most
  387–24 but grows stronger *b·* of it.
  388– 6 *b·* it knows less of material law.
  388–24 *B·* sin and sickness are not qualities of
  390– 6 *b·*, to the mortal senses, there is
  390–22 *b·* you know that God is no
  393– 4 *b·* mortal mind is ignorant of itself,
  396–17 not *b·* the testimony of sin . . . is true,
  397–27 *b·* they combine as one.
  401– 1 ''*b·* of their unbelief''— *Matt.* 13 : 58.
  401– 9 *b·* the truth of being must
  402–27 *b·* their belief is not better instructed
  407–31 *b·* its method of madness is in
  411– 8 *b·* the student was not perfectly attuned
  415– 7 *b·* thought moves quickly or slowly,
  426–30 *b·* matter has no life to surrender.
  433–19 *B·* he has loved his neighbor as himself,
  442– 2 *b·* there are no such laws.
t 447–23 *b·* there is no sin.
  456–27 *B·* it is the voice of Truth
  456–30 *B·* it was the first book . . . containing
  457– 4 *B·* this book has done more for
  457–15 *b·* each of them could see but one face
  461– 6 *b·* a part is proved and that
  461–13 *b·* Science reverses the evidence before
  461–20 *b·* of the different effects
  464–26 ''The hireling fleeth, *b·* — *John* 10 : 13.
r 468– 4 *b·* it kills itself.
  468– 5 *b·* error is unlike Truth.
  468– 6 *B·* Soul is immortal,
  469–18 *b·* there is but one God ;
  471–15 *b·* the evidence . . . is fully sustained by
  472–19 Error is unreal *b·* untrue.
  472–30 *b·* they are not of God.
  475–11 *b·* he is spiritual and perfect,
  479–27 *b·* it reflects no light.
  479–29 *b·* it has none of the divine hues.
  481–21 *b·* of their admitted actuality.
  483–22 *B·* the Science of Mind seems to
  485– 8 *b·* of their uselessness or their
  489–25 *b·* matter has no sensation,
g 501– 3 *b·* the spiritual import of the Word,
  507–19 do not yield fruit *b·* of any
  507–20 *b·* they reflect the Mind which
  517–16 *b·* there is but one God.
  520–25 not *b·* of seed or soil,
  520–25 *b·* growth is the eternal mandate of Mind.
  520–28 *B·* Mind makes all,
  523– 3 *B·* of its false basis, the mist of
  523–17 *b·* the Supreme Being is therein called
  523–19 *b·* Deity therein is always called Jehovah,
  527–20 Evil is unreal *b·* it is a lie,
  529–28 *b·* we know that they are worthless
  532–16 *b·* I was naked ;— *Gen.* 3 : 10.
  535–19 *B·* thou hast hearkened— *Gen.* 3 : 17.
  544–11 man exists *b·* God exists.
  546–19 *b·* they cannot possibly be
  554– 6 *b·* being is immortal, like Deity,

because

g	554–10	b· it is destitute of any knowledge
	555–14	b· error is neither mind nor the
	556–26	B· mortal mind must waken to
	557–10	has its suffering b· it is a false belief.
ap	559–27	b· you must share the hemlock cup
	560–27	B· it has hid from them the true idea
	561– 6	B· of his more spiritual vision,
	567–11	b· the dragon cannot war with them.
	568–22	b· he knoweth that— Rev. 12 : 12.
	571– 5	B· people like you better when
	573–19	B· St. John's corporeal sense of the

beck

a	21–26	the worldly man is at the b· and call of error,

beckons

sp	76– 3	and the hand which b· them,

becloud

sp	93–31	This belief tends to b· our apprehension

beclouds

b	315–17	sin, which b· the spiritual sense of Truth ;

become

pr	7–28	By it we may b· involuntary hypocrites,
	14–12	B· conscious for a single moment that Life
a	22–16	go not back to error, nor b· a sluggard in
m	59– 8	compact which might otherwise b· unbearable
	61–18	b· parents in their turn,
	62–18	should b· men and women only through
	65–31	marriage will b· purer when the scum
sp	73–31	nor the finite b· the channel of the infinite.
	84– 9	men b· seers and prophets
	89– 5	the devotee may b· unwontedly eloquent.
	96– 8	Earth will b· dreary and desolate,
	97–10	the blow of the other will b· harmless.
an	105–19	words of Judge Parmenter . . . will b·
s	112– 7	b· adherents of the Socratic,
	139–26	b· "the head of the corner."— Matt. 21 : 42.
	158–23	until . . . men and women b· loathsome sots.
	160–16	when the cords contract and b· immovable?
	160–20	Can muscles, . . . b· cramped despite the
	160–24	and b· rigid of their own preference,
ph	172–16	in order to b· man.
	182– 1	will diminish your ability to b· a
f	201– 9	"all things are b· new."— II Cor. 5 : 17.
	234– 9	b· more familiar with good than with evil,
	240–23	we must b· dissatisfied with it.
	251– 5	neither should a fever b· more severe
c	264–15	multitudinous objects . . . will b· visible.
b	270–25	They think sickly thoughts, and so b· sick.
	282–20	nor can non-intelligence b· Soul.
	295–22	in order to b· a better transparency for Truth.
	309–12	He was to b· the father of those, who
	311–23	it will b· the law of Life to man,
	321– 9	When, . . . he saw it b· a serpent,
	323–32	Willingness to b· as a little child
	336–22	lose the deific character, and b· less than
o	352–19	at any moment they may b· its helpless victims ;
	354 26	Sin should b· unreal to every one.
	356– 2	material thought must b· spiritualized
p	368– 8	truth will b· still clearer
	369– 6	in that proportion does man b· its master.
	380– 2	b· a fever case, which ends in a belief called
	397–30	b· more manly or womanly.
	409– 7	the more prolific it is likely to b· in sin and
	420–16	ready to b· receptive to the new idea.
	422– 9	the book will b· the physician,
	428–27	man's immortality will b· more apparent,
	431–28	testifies :—. . . I have lost my healthy hue and b·
	432–17	Judge asks if . . . it is possible for man to b·
t	455–32	the more impossible it will b· for
r	467–11	Mankind will b· perfect in proportion as this
g	523–27	The different accounts b· more and more closely
	524–16	Did the . . . infinite Principle b· a finite deity,
	524–20	How then could a material organization b· the
	524–21	How could the non-intelligent b· the medium of
	525– 1	Does Mind, God, enter matter to b· there a
	528– 1	Was it requisite. . . that dust should b· sentient,
	528–25	Afterwards he is supposed to b· the basis of
	530– 2	increases in falsehood and his days b· shorter.
	536–31	the man is b· as one of us,— Gen. 3 : 22.
	537–31	lest man should improve it and b· better ;
	545– 3	the man is b· as one of us."— Gen. 3 : 22.
	547–21	implies that the great First Cause must b·
	550– 8	God cannot b· finite, and be limited
	550– 9	Spirit cannot b· matter, nor can
	552–20	may b· wild with freedom
	553– 9	or . . . harmony will never b· the standard of
	553–22	that theory is sure to b· the signal for
	555–26	of aught that can b· imperfect.
ap	573–26	we can b· conscious, here and now, of
gl	587–17	God . . . cannot b· finite and imperfect.
	590–26	statements of the Scriptures b· clouded

becomes

sp	72–28	The joy of intercourse b· the jest of sin, when
	97– 7	the more impotent error b· as a belief.
	97–11	The more destructive matter b·, the more
	97–16	the riper it b· for destruction.
s	123– 8	reverses the order of Science . . . so that man b·
	128–12	b· more elastic, is capable of greater
	128–20	An odor b· beneficent and agreeable only
	146–11	is made the servant of Science and religion b·
	157–12	the drug b· more like the human mind than
	160– 7	the inanimate drug b· powerless.
	160–12	the heart b· as torpid as the hand.
ph	168–15	man-made systems insist that man b·
	199–13	his arm b· stronger.
f	207– 2	evil b· more apparent and obnoxious
c	263–15	He b· a general mis-creator, who
b	290–26	b· thus only when he reaches perfection.
	291–25	Mind never b· dust.
	297–29	Until belief b· faith, and faith b·
	312– 6	b· nothingness, as the sense-dream vanishes
	319–18	when it b· fairly understood that the
	327–12	and it b· his torment.
o	342–17	then there is no . . . law, and truth b·
p	377–12	Through different states of mind, the body b·
	388–23	and this b· self-evident, when we learn that
	396–16	refutation b· arduous, not because the
	400–15	This task b· easy, if you understand
	400–25	the image which b· visible to the senses.
	420–28	If it b· necessary to startle mortal mind
	424– 2	the child b· a separate, individualized
t	460–19	it b· a tedious mischief-maker.
r	467–12	perfect in proportion as this fact b· apparent,
	480– 4	Where the spirit of God is, . . . evil b· nothing,
g	513–13	until divine Science b· the interpreter.
	524–10	God b· " a man of war,"— Exod. 15 : 3.
	531– 1	it supposes that . . . matter b· living,
	531– 6	error, . . . that non-intelligence b·
	543– 6	b· . . . apparent at error's demise.
	544–31	It declares . . . that matter b· spiritual.
ap	565– 2	and b· the great red dragon,

becometh

m	56– 3	it b· us to fulfil all.— Matt. 3 : 15.

becoming

m	60–16	b· a barrier against vice,
sp	96–12	even now b· the arena for conflicting forces.
f	239–18	If divine Love is b· nearer, dearer,
b	297–24	and Truth, . . . is b· understood.
	324– 7	Unless the harmony and immortality of man are b·
p	395–32	would prevent the brain from b· diseased,
	406–32	b· a fool or an object of loathing ;
t	458–24	thus b· a law unto himself.

bed

sp	90–17	The looker-on sees the body in b·,
s	154–11	made to believe that he occupied a b· where
	154 15	because no cholera patient had been in that b·.
	156– 7	and yet, as she lay in her b·, the patient
ph	193– 1	Mr. Clark . . . had been confined to his b·
p	390–17	nor laid upon a b· of suffering in payment of
	427–26	Called to the b· of death, what material remedy

bedside

ph	193–10	I went to his b·.

Beelzebub

a	28–20	saying : . B· is his patron.
	53– 1	casteth out devils through B·,"— Luke 11 : 15.
p	422– 2	Jesus said : "If I by B· cast out — Matt. 12 : 27.
ap	564– 2	and cast out devils through B·.

Beethoven

f	213–23	This was even more strikingly true of B·,

befogged

f	205–15	B· in error (the error of believing that

befool

p	440– 6	is taught how to make sleep b· reason

before

pref	ix–23	b· a work on the subject could be
	ix–26	B· writing this work,
	xi–11	b· which sin and disease lose their
pr	1– *	b· ye ask Him.— Matt. 6 : 8.
	1–13	exalted b· they take form in words
	3– 4	Who would stand b· a blackboard, and pray
	6–23	b· he cast it out.
	8–25	that it may be laid bare b· us,
	9–15	b· we can enjoy the fruition
	11–10	demands restitution b· mortals can
	13–15	knows our need b· we tell Him
a	19–30	no other gods b· me,"— Exod. 20 : 3.
	20– 8	kingdom of God b· you."— Matt. 21 : 31.
	20–30	race that is set b· us ;"— Heb. 12 : 1.
	32–29	on the night b· his crucifixion,
	33– 9	Their Master had explained it all b·,
	35–12	They bow b· Christ, Truth,
	36– 5	sufficient suffering, either b· or after
	37– 8	falls only b· the sword of Spirit.

before

a	39–28	the interval *b·* its attainment
	41– 2	into which Jesus has passed *b·* us ;
	41–23	*b·* it was understood,
	43– 4	his material disappearance *b·* their eyes
	44– 1	*b·* the thorns can be laid aside
	44–19	that he might employ his feet as *b·*.
	45–29	same body that he had *b·* his crucifixion,
	48–20	was silent *b·* envy and hate.
	49–26	priests and rabbis, *b·* whom he
	49–31	*b·* the face of the— *Lam.* 3 : 35.
	50– 2	a sheep *b·* her shearers— *Isa.* 53 : 7.
	50–20	*b·* the evidence of the bodily senses,
m	59–25	understanding should exist *b·* this union
	64– 4	undefiled *b·* God— *Jas.* 1 : 27.
sp	76– 1	those who have gone *b·*.
	76–31	must be overcome, . . . *b·* immortality appears.
	82–20	*b·* the change we call death,
	86–32	*b·* the artist can convey them to canvas.
	87–31	forms rise *b·* us, which are
	89–16	tongue grows mute which *b·* was eloquent.
	96– 5	*B·* error is wholly destroyed,
	97–27	all matter will disappear *b·* the
an	104–11	they say it has been discovered *b·*.
	104–27	leaving the case worse than *b·*
	106–24	I tell you *b·*,— *Gal.* 5 : 21.
s	110– 8	I beheld, as never *b·*,
	116– 6	*b·* the corporeal human senses,
	119–26	the evidence *b·* the senses
	121– 4	*b·* he spake, astrography was
	125–30	will find his flower *b·* its seed.
	129–16	torment us *b·* the time?"— *Matt.* 8 : 29.
	131– 7	false evidence *b·* the corporeal senses
	137– 5	immaculate Teacher stood *b·* them,
	137–26	*B·* this the impetuous disciple had
	143–12	*b·* it could be considered as medicine.
	161–21	she knelt *b·* a statue of Liberty,
	164–14	*b·* all mankind is saved
ph	168–25	*b·* the so-called disease made its
	169– 5	*b·* the patient felt the change ;
	174–29	holding it *b·* the thought of both
	175–29	as innocent as Adam, *b·* he
	176– 3	*b·* inquisitive modern Eves took
	176–11	was not paraded *b·* the imagination.
	180–19	even *b·* they go to work to
	181– 2	*B·* deciding that the body, matter, is
	185– 7	*B·* this book was published,
	187–32	a body like the one it had *b·* death.
	191–20	is not mute *b·* non-intelligence.
	196–28	and from the image brought *b·* the mind ;
	198–15	is formed *b·* one sees a doctor
	198–15	*b·* the doctor undertakes to
	199–30	fear must have disappeared *b·* his
f	213–30	*B·* human knowledge dipped to its
	214– 6	evidence *b·* his material senses,
	215–20	flee as phantoms of error *b·* truth
	219–18	*b·* it can be made manifest on the body,
	222–30	and eat what is set *b·* you,
	226–22	I saw *b·* me the sick,
	226–29	I saw *b·* me the awful conflict,
	233–11	*b·* we arrive at the demonstration of
	234–14	avoid casting pearls *b·* those who
	234–25	Sin and disease must be thought *b·* they
	237– 7	It might have been months or years *b·*
	237–13	snatches away the good seed *b·* it
	238– 1	not rightly valued *b·* they are understood.
	238–27	People with mental work *b·* them
	245– 9	she stood daily *b·* the window
	247–20	*b·* they are perceived humanly.
	248–15	What is the model *b·* mortal mind?
	248–21	The world is holding it *b·* your gaze
	251– 4	should not grow more painful *b·* it suppurates,
	251– 5	neither should a fever become more severe *b·*
	251–29	*b·* we can attain harmony,
	254– 9	*b·* the spiritual facts of existence are
c	264– 2	*b·* the permanent facts and their
	264–14	which *b·* were invisible,
	265–25	*b·* we discover what belongs to
b	272– 3	*b·* Truth can be understood.
	272–18	your pearls *b·* swine."— *Matt.* 7 : 6.
	280–19	no other gods *b·* me !"— *Exod.* 20 : 3.
	290– 4	are not in the least understood *b·*
	290– 7	as material as *b·* the transition,
	297–13	that disappears which *b·* seemed real
	303–31	*b·* the material senses yielded to
	314–21	presented to her, more than ever *b·*,
	317–13	*b·* it hated you ;"— *John* 15 : 18.
	317–23	had loved *b·* the tragedy on Calvary.
	320–32	in celestial perfection *b·* Elohim,
	321– 9	Moses fled *b·* it ;
	322– 8	*b·* harmonious and immortal man
	322–10	*b·* this recognition of divine Science
	324–17	certainly *b·* we can reach the goal
	333–19	and after the Christian era,
	333–29	"*B·* Abraham was,— *John* 8 : 58.
	334–19	*b·* the human Jesus was incarnate

before

b	340–15	no other gods *b·* me."— *Exod.* 20 : 3.
o	350–26	*b·* the Science of being can be demonstrated.
	356– 3	*b·* the spiritual fact is attained.
p	363–27	*b·* she anointed them with the oil.
	365–18	like dew *b·* the morning sunshine.
	368– 5	Error is a coward *b·* Truth.
	368– 7	nearer than ever *b·* to the apprehension
	371–17	*b·* he can get rid of the illusive
	372–25	shall deny me *b·* men,— *Matt.* 10 : 33.
	372–26	deny *b·* my Father— *Matt.* 10 : 33.
	374–11	*b·* it is consciously apparent on the
	384–29	the evidence *b·* the senses
	384–30	*b·* the divine rights of intelligence,
	389–26	This belief totters to its falling *b·* the
	396–12	*b·* a crisis is passed.
	397–32	You will understand . . . better than *b·*.
	400– 5	must be held in subjection *b·* its
	400–13	*b·* it has taken tangible shape in
	415–28	*B·* the thoughts are fully at rest,
	417–18	The evidence *b·* the corporeal senses
	418–32	flee *b·* the light of Truth.
	426– 6	when she has the high goal always *b·* her
	427–11	*b·* Life can be understood
	427–17	the same after as *b·* a bone is broken
	429– 8	We look *b·* our feet, and
	429–19	If man did not exist *b·* the
	429–22	must have lived *b·* birth,
	434–13	to appear *b·* the bar of Justice
	437– 9	*b·* the Judge of our higher tribunal,
	437–10	*b·* its jurors, the Spiritual Senses,
	440– 5	*b·* the supreme bar of Spirit
	440– 7	*b·* sacrificing mortals to their false gods.
	441–33	*b·* the tribunal of divine Spirit.
t	452– 5	*b·* it has a chance to manifest itself.
	453–14	*b·* he can know others and
	461–13	because Science reverses the evidence *b·* the
	464–24	ignorance, envy, fall *b·* an honest heart.
r	467– 4	no other gods *b·* me."— *Exod.* 20 : 3.
	471– 7	evidence *b·* the five corporeal senses,
	480–31	As vapor melts *b·* the sun,
	480–32	would vanish *b·* the reality of good.
	486–15	the same immediately after death as *b·*.
	487– 5	both *b·* and after that which is called death.
	492– 3	there should be but one fact *b·* the
k	499– *	*I have set b· thee an— Rev.* 3 : 8.
g	509–24	*b·* it was in the earth."— *Gen.* 2 : 5.
	515–28	compare man *b·* the mirror to his
	520–19	*b·* it was in the earth,— *Gen.* 2 : 5.
	520–20	herb of the field *b·* it— *Gen.* 2 : 5.
	521–29	opposite of scientific truth as *b·* recorded.
	526– 4	*b·* it was in the earth."— *Gen.* 2 : 5.
	532–19	*b·* Truth, error shrank abashed
	535–13	other creations must go down *b·* C. S.
	543–17	evidence *b·* the material senses.
	548–12	*b·* Life is spiritually learned.
	549– 5	after it has grown to maturity, if not *b·*,
	553–17	Adam was created *b·* Eve.
	553–29	*b·* they think or know aught of their
	556–27	*b·* it cares to solve the problem of
ap	563–25	stood *b·* the woman— *Rev.* 12 : 4.
	564–21	*b·* the tribunal of so-called mortal mind,
	566–10	moves *b·* them, a pillar of cloud
	566–17	Her fathers' God *b·* her moved,
	568–17	*b·* our God day and night.— *Rev.* 12 : 10.
	568–27	than has ever *b·* reached high heaven,
	578–13	preparest a table *b·* me— *see Psal.* 23 : 5.
gl	579– *	*I have set b· thee an— Rev.* 3 : 8.
	585–20	human belief *b·* it accepts sin,
	593– 5	*b·* the conscious facts of spiritual Truth.
	595–14	when he went *b·* Jehovah,
	595–19	TIME. . . . that which begins *b·*, and

beforehand

p	396–10	Never say *b·* how much you have to

began

pref	viii–28	As early as 1862 she *b·* to write down and
	ix– 1	She also *b·* to jot down her thoughts on the
s	133–15	when . . . their demoralization *b·*.
	156–14	*b·* to fear an aggravation of symptoms
ph	200– 2	Pagan worship *b·* with muscularity,
f	245–32	The infinite never *b·* nor will it ever end.
	249–15	God is the infinite, and infinity never *b·*,
p	429–20	before the material organization *b·*,
g	532–27	error *b·* and will end the dream of matter.
	534–26	since the Christian era *b·*.
	557–23	as if he *b·* materially right,

begets

ph	169–12	faith in rules of health or in drugs *b·*
g	550–26	A serpent never *b·* a bird,

begin

f	234–19	We must *b·* with this so-called mind and
	246–27	and *b·* the demonstration thereof.
	252– 8	they *b·* to disappear.
	254–13	but to *b·* aright and to continue the strife

begin

c	258–32	and thus *b·* to comprehend in Science
	262–28	To *b·* rightly is to end rightly.
	262–29	Every concept which seems to *b·* with the
b	275–11	you must *b·* by reckoning God as the
	283– 1	As mortals *b·* to understand Spirit, they
	322–29	Then we *b·* to learn Life in divine Science.
p	411–27	Always *b·* your treatment by allaying the
	429– 4	We must *b·*, however, with the more simple
	429– 6	and the sooner we *b·* the better.
r	467–30	we *b·* with Mind, which must be understood
g	531–26	Does Life *b·* with Mind or with matter?
	549–14	successive generations do not *b·* with the

beginning

and end

b	282– 8	which has both *b·* and end.
	338– 5	belief — that man . . . has *b·* and end,
gl	580–22	supposition that Life . . . has *b·* and end ;

any

p	429–23	for if Life ever had any *b·*,

from the

sp	89–31	"a murderer from the *b·*." — *John* 8 : 44.
ph	186–32	human mind has been an idolater from the *b·*,
b	268– *	*That which was from the b·,* — *I John* 1 : 1.
	202 23	a murderer from the *b·*, — *John* 8 : 44.
	296–31	Mortal belief is a liar from the *b·*,
p	409–23	are counterfeits from the *b·*,
	441–33	"a murderer from the *b·*." — *John* 8 : 44.
r	476–16	They were, from the *b·* of mortal history,
g	539– 3	"a murderer from the *b·*." — *John* 8 : 44.
ap	564–29	From the *b·* to the end, the serpent
	567–26	he must be a lie from the *b·*.
	580–31	a murderer from the *b·*, — *John* 8 : 44.

in the

an	103– 9	As in the *b·*, however, this liberation
s	140–28	In the *b·* God created man
ph	188– 6	is an unconscious error in the *b·*,
b	308– 7	belief will be afraid as it was in the *b·*,
p	379– 3	announced as partners in the *b·*.
r	479–18	"In the *b·* God created the — *Gen.* 1 : 1.
g	502–22	In the *b·* God created the — *Gen.* 1 : 1.
	531–15	If, in the *b·*, man's body originated in

its

t	403–15	Its *b·* will be meek, its growth sturdy,

no

b	307–25	Truth has no *b·*.
g	502–24	The infinite has no *b·*.

of the Old Testament

g	501– 2	starts with the *b·* of the Old Testament,

of the world

s	129–14	not since the *b·* of the world ;" — *Matt.* 24 : 21.

of wisdom

p	373–16	fear of the Lord is the *b·* of wisdom," — *Psal.* 111 : 10.

scientific

f	219–31	this scientific *b·* is in the right direction.

this word

g	502–24	This word *b·* is employed to signify *the only,*

to end

s	130– 4	From *b·* to end, the Scriptures are full of
r	478–24	From *b·* to end, whatever is mortal
ap	559–21	Read this book from *b·* to end.

with Genesis

g	502– 1	A second necessity for *b·* with Genesis is

without

f	253– 6	life, without *b·* and without end,
b	282– 7	represents the infinite without *b·* or end ;
	333–18	without *b·* of years or end of days.
p	399–32	without *b·* with so-called mortal mind,
r	468–27	Life is without *b·* and without end.
g	521– 5	narrative of being that is without *b·* or end.
gl	585– 6	which are likewise without *b·* or end.

b	331– 9	falsely testifies to a *b·* and an end.
r	469– 6	If Life ever had a *b·*, it would also have
g	528–19	*B·* creation with darkness instead of
	538–28	As both mortal man and sin have a *b·*,
	550–17	as *b·* and ending, and with birth, decay,
gl	585–23	Eve. A *b·* ; mortality ;
	592– 4	the belief that life has a *b·*

beginnings

p	384–14	will prove to himself, by small *b·*,

begins

m	57–29	and *b·* to unfold its wings for heaven.
f	216–12	*b·* at once to destroy the errors of mortal sense
c	262–30	concept which seems to begin with the brain *b·* falsely.
b	297–23	in which spiritual evidence, ... *b·* to appear,
p	410–29	Christian scientific practice *b·* with
r	476– 3	declares that man *b·* in dust or as
g	529–31	*b·* his reign over man somewhat mildly,
	539– 3	Error *b·* by reckoning life as separate
	544–31	Error *b·* with corporeality as the producer
	550–11	ends, even as it *b·*, in nameless nothingness?
gl	595–19	that which *b·* before, . . . what is termed death,

begotten

c	257–19	"who hath *b·* the drops of dew," — *Job* 38 : 28.
b	282–30	for it is not *b·* of the Father.
	325–24	But he, who is *b·* of the beliefs of the

beguiled

g	533–28	She says, "The serpent *b·* me, — *Gen.* 3 : 13.

beguiles

g	533–14	first voluble lie, which *b·* the woman

begun

sp	96–22	This mental fermentation has *b·*,
b	326–18	You have *b·* at the numeration-table of C. S.,

behalf

pr	12–27	Does Deity interpose in *b·* of one worshipper,
f	226– 5	The voice of God in *b·* of the African slave
p	364– 5	to lay down his mortal existence in *b·* of
	389– 3	given in *b·* of the control of Mind over
	431–11	arrested Mortal Man in *b·* of the state
t	455–13	to use the energies of Mind in your own *b·*,

behavior

p	441– 8	to give heavy bonds for good *b·*.

beheaded

s	136–27	"John have I *b·* : but who is this?" — *Luke* 9 : 9.

beheld

a	45–23	*b·* the final proof of all that he had taught,
s	110– 8	Thus it was that I *b·*, as never before,
c	259–16	then mortals have never *b·* in man the
b	326–23	Saul of Tarsus *b·* the way — the Christ, or
	326–30	He *b·* for the first time the true idea of Love,
r	476–32	Jesus *b·* in Science the perfect man,
	478– 5	never *b·* Spirit or Soul leaving a body or
ap	561– 9	The Revelator *b·* the spiritual idea
gl	583– 8	some of the ideas of God *b·* as men,

behest

iii– *		This is Thy high *b·* :
g	533– 2	Had he lost man's rich inheritance and God's *b·*,

behests

r	495–29	and follow the *b·* of God,

behind

pr	7– 2	"Get thee *b·* me, Satan." — *Matt.* 16 : 23.
s	138– 4	lay *b·* Peter's confession of the
b	299– 1	It has *b·* it no more reality than
o	353–24	those things which are *b·*." — *Phil.* 3 : 13.
p	362–15	to come *b·* the couch
g	542– 6	Though error hides *b·* a lie

behold

pref	vii–11	The Wisemen were led to *b·* and to follow
a	39–18	*b·*, now is the day of salvation," — *II Cor.* 6 : 2.
sp	93– 7	"*B·*, now is the accepted time :— *II Cor.* 6 : 2.
	93– 8	*b·*, now is the day of salvation," — *II Cor.* 6 : 2.
ph	190–28	As for me, I will *b·* Thy face — *Psal.* 17 : 15.
f	243–23	"of purer eyes than to *b·* evil," — *Hab.* 1 : 13.
c	264– 5	sometimes *b·* in the camera of divine Mind,
	264–29	we shall *b·* and understand God's creation,
b	280–10	*b·* the zeal of belief to establish the
	334–27	*b·*, I am alive for evermore, — *Rev.* 1 : 18.
o	346–18	"fraught with falsities painful to *b·*"?
	347–13	they would *b·* the signs of Christ's coming.
	347–28	mortals will *b·* the nothingness of sickness
	357– 5	"of purer eyes than to *b·* evil." — *Hab.* 1 : 13.
	360–26	*B·*, He putteth no trust in — see *Job* 4 : 18.
p	438– 5	*B·*, I give unto you power — *Luke* 10 : 19.
k	499– *	*b·* I have set before thee an open — *Rev.* 3 : 8.
g	517–21	Who shall *b·* it?
	518– 5	And God said, *B·*, I have given — *Gen.* 1 : 29.
	518–25	and, *b·*, it was very good. — *Gen.* 1 : 31.
	525–24	"and, *b·*, it was very good." — *Gen.* 1 : 31.
	534– 3	and to *b·* at the sepulchre the risen Saviour,
	536–31	*B·*, the man is become as — *Gen.* 3 : 22.
	545– 3	"*B·*, the man is become as — *Gen.* 3 : 22.
ap	562–30	and *b·* a great red dragon, — *Rev.* 12 : 3.
	574–22	at last lifted the seer to *b·* the great city,
	574–26	and you will *b·* the soft-winged dove
	575– 2	and *b·* the Lamb's wife, — Love wedded to
gl	579– *	*b·*, I have set before thee an open — *Rev.* 3 : 8.
	585–11	of whatever the material senses *b·* ;

beholding

m	65–16	*B·* the world's lack of Christianity
b	323– 9	*B·* the infinite tasks of truth,
g	528–22	*B·* the creations of his own dream
ap	573– 4	*b·* what the eye cannot see,

beholds

pref	vii– 2	wakeful shepherd *b·* the first
sp	95–26	when he *b·* the light which heralds
	98– 4	prophet of to-day *b·* in the mental horizon
s	126– 5	when man *b·* himself God's reflection,
r	479–10	image of mortal thought, . . . is all that the eye *b·*,
ap	563–16	and *b·* its awful character ;
	571–26	thoughts which he *b·* in mortal mind.

Being

Divine
pr 3–12   The Divine *B·* must be reflected by man,
   o 357–18   false notions about the Divine *B·*
omnipresent
   r 466– 1   omniscient, and omnipresent *B·*,
Supreme
   sp 93–23   the name of the Supreme *B·*.
   s 117– 9   the Supreme *B·* or His manifestation ;
   127–18   Supreme *B·*, Mind, exempt from all evil.
   f 202–24   Our beliefs about a Supreme *B·* contradict
   b 285–22   the Supreme *B·*, or divine Principle,
   g 523–18   the Supreme *B·* is therein called Elohim.
   524– 8   They called the Supreme *B·* by the
   527–29   Is the Supreme *B·* retrograding,

   b 290– 1   Life is the everlasting I AM, the *B·*

being

actuality of
   b 296–16   spiritual sense, and the actuality of *b·*.
all
   s 131– 5   God, the divine Principle of all *b·*.
   f 244– 1   God is good and the fount of all *b·*,
   b 302–22   God, the divine Principle of all *b·*,
   p 407–23   In Science, all *b·* is eternal,
   414–27   God, in whom all *b·* is painless and permanent.
   t 460– 7   the nature and essence of all *b·*,
   g 528– 1   all *b·* is the reflection of the eternal Mind,
ambiguities of
   s 114–27   disentangles the interlaced ambiguities of *b·*,
and Deity
   g 554– 6   *b·* and Deity are inseparable.
basis of
   p 414–21   rests on the Christianly scientific basis of *b·*.
cannot be lost
   f 215– 6   *b·* cannot be lost while God exists.
capacities of
   ph 200– 6   illustrated the grand human capacities of *b·*
celestial
   a 26–17   to reveal the Science of celestial *b·*,
   b 337–18   and perfection is the order of celestial *b·*
charms of
   f 247–29   are poor substitutes for the charms of *b·*,
circumference of
   f 204– 1   is at once the centre and circumference of *b·*.
circumference of his
   c 262–16   the absolute centre and circumference of his *b·*.
coexists with
   f 246–12   radiant sun of virtue and truth coexists with *b·*.
conception of
   sp 84–24   true conception of *b·* destroys the belief of
   s 148–12   instead of from the highest, conception of *b·*.
   c 260–12   seen as the only true conception of *b·*.
   b 324–29   which is the true conception of *b·*,
concord of
   s 129–26   or learn from discord the concord of *b·*?
consciousness of
   c 261–28   you will rise to the spiritual consciousness of *b·*,
continuity of
   s 123–29   the scientific order and continuity of *b·*.
corporeal
   sp 71–31   a corporeal *b·*, a finite form,
   s 140– 4   That God is a corporeal *b·*, nobody can truly
   b 309– 2   for the messenger was not a corporeal *b·*,
   ap 577– 8   God as Father-Mother, not as a corporeal *b·*.
deflection of
   g 502–11   This deflection of *b·*, rightly viewed, serves to
demonstration of man's
   b 290– 3   Principle, rule, and demonstration of man's *b·*
divine Principle of
   g 530– 6   sustained by God, the divine Principle of *b·*.
economy of
   p 423–25   Both...are now at work in the economy of *b·*
entire
   s 151–27   the entire *b·* is found harmonious
eternal
   f 232– 8   the claims of harmonious and eternal *b·*
   g 521– 3   spiritual harmony and eternal *b·*.
fact of
   f 228– 5   if this great fact of *b·* were learned,
   249–26   night-dream is sometimes nearer the fact of *b·*
   b 285– 5   the great fact of *b·* for time and eternity.
   320–18   text declares plainly the spiritual fact of *b·*,
facts of
   s 120– 9   arrive at the fundamental facts of *b·*.
   147–22   enables you to grasp the spiritual facts of *b·*
   f 221–18   beliefs of mortals, and not the facts of *b·* ;
   242–12   the facts of *b·* are commonly misconstrued,
   b 279–18   the immortal facts of *b·* are seen,
   293–16   perpetuating the eternal facts of *b·*.
   312– 3   reversed by the spiritual facts of *b·*
   315–22   enabled him to demonstrate the facts of *b·*,
   323– 3   not . . . glean from C. S. the facts of *b·* without
   p 370– 4   gather the facts of *b·* from the divine Mind.
   428–10   in order that the spiritual facts of *b·* may

being

facts of
   p 428–28   and the immortal facts of *b·* are admitted.
   r 471– 9   afford no indication of the grand facts of *b·* ;
   491–12   cannot connect mortals with the . . . facts of *b·*,
   g 546–24   facts of *b·*, ... shine in the darkness,
   ap 574–12   became conscious of the spiritual facts of *b·*
   gl 584–16   for it contradicts the spiritual facts of *b·*.
functions of
   p 387–14   faithfully perform the natural functions of *b·*.
glorified
   b 291–11   not . . . death will awaken them to glorified *b·*.
God's
   r 470–24   Man is the expression of God's *b·*.
   481– 3   God's *b·* is infinity, freedom, harmony,
happiness of
   m 60–26   not discerning the true happiness of *b·*,
   b 286– 1   relates most nearly to the happiness of *b·*.
harmonious
   m 68–32   the unbroken links of eternal, harmonious *b·*
   p 376–24   the true facts in regard to harmonious *b·*,
   412–25   Realize . . . the fact of harmonious *b·*,
harmony of
   (*see* **harmony**)
his original
   sp 97–20   in the likeness of Spirit, his original *b·*.
human
   pr 2–20   as one pleads with a human *b·*,
   sp 82–27   as it would be between a mole and a human *b·*.
idea of (*see also* **true idea of**)
   a 55– 8   the healing Christ and spiritual idea of *b·*.
   r 477–17   the immortal idea of *b·*, indestructible
identity of
   r 475–17   conscious identity of *b·* as found in Science,
image of His
   b 313–22   and an image of His *b·*." — *see Heb.* 1 : 3.
immortal
   ph 178–27   understanding of the status of immortal *b·*.
   190–18   it never merges into immortal *b·*,
   p 420–32   harmonious facts of Soul and immortal *b·*.
individual
   p 427– 5   Man's individual *b·* can no more die nor
infinite
   ph 189–24   constantly ascend in infinite *b·*.
is eternal
   s 122–27   Life goes on unchanged and *b·* is eternal.
is holiness
   r 492– 7   *B·* is holiness, harmony, immortality.
is immortal
   g 554– 6   because *b·* is immortal, like Deity,
is Spirit
   a 29–26   the full recognition that *b·* is Spirit.
is sustained
   f 221–22   Science, in which *b·* is sustained by God,
keynote of
   f 240–14   and you lose the keynote of *b·*,
law of
   ph 186–27   and if so, harmony cannot be the law of *b·*.
   r 485–22   by fulfilling the spiritual law of *b·*,
law of his
   m 63–11   and Life is the law of his *b·*.
Life and
   an 103–31   Life and *b·* are of God.
   o 355–13   the harmonious and true sense of Life and *b·*
material
   ph 172–11   this supposed chain of material *b·*.
   172–15   If man was first a material *b·*,
mysteries of
   sp 90–29   improve our time in solving the mysteries of *b·*
narrative of
   g 521– 4   inspired record closes its narrative of *b·*
one's
   m 60– 2   Science inevitably lifts one's *b·* higher
our
   f 208– 6   and move, and have our *b·*." — *Acts* 17 : 28.
   c 264–12   in whom we have our *b·*.
   o 361–20   and move, and have our *b·*." — *Acts* 17 : 28.
   p 381–19   we live, move, and have our *b·* in
   g 536–13   and move, and have our *b·*," — *Acts* 17 : 28.
perfection of
   f 253– 2   The beauty of holiness, the perfection of *b·*,
perpetuates
   f 235–23   divine Truth which is Life and perpetuates *b·*,
possibilities of
   f 203–14   brings out the possibilities of *b·*,
Principle of
   pr 6–16   we must understand the divine Principle of *b·*.
   a 25–19   demonstrated . . . the Principle of *b·*.
   b 286–10   [the divine Principle of *b·*]
   gl 579–11   faith in the divine Life and . . . Principle of *b·*.
Principle of his
   f 202–16   in accord with the divine Principle of his *b·*,
problem of
   (*see* **problem**)

being

real
- *a* 26–29   It was the divine Principle of all real *b·*
- *s* 108–22   all real *b·* is in God, the divine Mind,
-   129–22   ontology, — "the science of real *b·*."
- *p* 371–15   no more comprehends his real *b·* than
- *r* 491–22   material man as never the real *b·*.

realism of
- *s* 144–20   and is not a factor in the realism of *b·*.

realities of
- *f* 212–29   The realities of *b·*, its normal action, and
-   229– 6   but if sin and suffering are realities of *b·*,
- *c* 264–20   Spirit and . . . are the only realities of *b·*.

reality of
-   (*see* **reality**)

reality or
- *g* 538–14   is significant of eternal reality or *b·*.

recognition of
- *ap* 573–25   such a recognition of *b·* is, . . . possible

Science of
-   (*see* **Science**)

scientific
- *f* 233–12   the demonstration of scientific *b·*,
- *c* 259–12   The Christlike understanding of scientific *b·*
- *b* 271– 2   chain of scientific *b·* reappearing in all ages,
-   332– 2   indicate the divine Principle of scientific *b·*,
- *r* 494–24   unbroken reality of scientific *b·*.

scientific statement of
- *r* 468– 8   What is the scientific statement of *b·*?

sense of
- *a* 41– 7   into the spiritual sense of *b·*.
-   55– 1   any other sense of *b·* and religion than theirs?
- *ph* 172–14   only as the false sense of *b·* disappears.
-   191–13   the spiritual sense of *b·*
- *c* 205–10   This scientific sense of *b·*, forsaking matter
- *b* 205 14   the real sense of *b·*, perfect and forever intact,
-   298–24   and to the spiritual sense of *b·*.
-   309– 5   gave him the spiritual sense of *b·*
- *r* 490–26   ushers in the spiritual sense of *b·*,
- *g* 545–22   entertained a false sense of *b·*.
-   548–17   true ideas of God, the spiritual sense of *b·*.
-   550–12   The true sense of *b·* and its eternal perfection

solution of
- *b* 314– 8   Our Master gained the solution of *b·*,

source of
- *m* 63–10   Spirit is his primitive and ultimate source of *b·* ;
- *f* 213–32   the one Mind and true source of *b·*,

spiritual
-   (*see* **spiritual**)

star of
- *pref* vii–10   and shine the guiding star of *b·*.

state of
- *r* 476–14   They never had a perfect state of *b·*,

superabundance of
- *f* 201–11   superabundance of *b·* is on the side of God,

true
- *s* 126– 9   never projected the least portion of true *b·*.
-   129–19   are antagonistic to true *b·*
- *r* 496–19   overlying, and encompassing all true *b·*.

true idea of
- *b* 325– 8   Jesus gave the true idea of *b·*,
- *o* 353–29   true idea of *b·* is spiritual and immortal,

truth of
-   (*see* **truth**)

understanding of
- *f* 211–12   in the spiritual understanding of *b·* ?
- *b* 330– 2   understanding of *b·* supersedes mere belief.
- *r* 495–22   Let C. S., . . . support your understanding of *b·*,

universal
- *g* 519– 9   the ideas of God in universal *b·*

verities of
- *p* 397–24   familiar with the great verities of *b·*.

verity of
- *p* 414–26   Keep in mind the verity of *b·*,
- *r* 468– 7   for sin is not the eternal verity of *b·*.

will be recognized
- *sp* 90–12   *b·* will be recognized as spiritual,

will be understood
- *sp* 91–13   his genuine *b·* will be understood.
- *f* 214–16   *b·* will be understood and found to be

your
- *f* 227–29   and defaced the tablet of your *b·*.

- *sp* 76– 6   When *b·* is understood, Life will
-   76–26   constitutes . . . man, whose *b·* is spiritual.
- *s* 151–18   Fear never stopped *b·* and its action.
- *f* 215– 4   then *b·* and immortality will be lost,
-   228– 6   nothing inharmonious can enter *b·*,
-   244–20   If man . . . springs from matter into *b·*,
-   247–19   *B·* possesses its qualities before they
- *c* 265– 7   must near the broader interpretations of *b·*,
- *b* 275–10   To grasp the reality and order of *b·*
-   275–14   All substance, intelligence, wisdom, *b·*,
-   279–28   there are not two bases of *b·*,
-   292– 5   compass the heights and depths of *b·*
-   305– 8   Man, . . . reflects the central light of *b·*,

being

- *o* 351–21   especially if we consider Satan as a *b·* coequal
-   361–18   Father and son, are one in *b·*.
- *p* 416–32   Teach them that their *b·* is sustained by
- *g* 531–14   will recognize his God-given dominion and *b·*.

being (ppr.)

- *pr* 3– 1   without *b·* reminded of His province.
- *a* 21–25   *B·* in sympathy with matter,
-   45–12   *b·* reconciled, we shall be saved — *Rom.* 5 : 10.
- *m* 68– 3   for fear of *b·* thought ridiculous.
- *sp* 72–21   God, good, *b·* ever present, it follows
-   75–29   the moment when the link . . . is *b·* sundered.
-   81–18   Man . . . cannot help *b·* immortal.
-   98–29   and *b·* practical and complete,
- *an* 102– 4   Its basis *b·* a belief and this belief
- *s* 113–18   God, Spirit, *b·* all, nothing is matter.
-   124– 1   *b·* based on Truth, the Principle of
-   126–17   Shall Science explain cause and effect as *b·*
-   142–28   God *b·* All-in-all, He made medicine ; but
-   145– 2   without *b·* able to explain them.
-   163–23   we cannot help *b·* disgusted with
- *ph* 168–27   Disease *b·* a belief, a latent illusion
-   184– 2   The premises *b·* erroneous.
- *f* 203– 7   If God were understood instead of *b·* merely
-   206–17   Spirit, not matter, *b·* the source of supply.
-   209– 1   Man, *b·* immortal, has a perfect . . . life.
-   210–25   What is termed matter, *b·* unintelligent,
-   222–22   far from *b·* the image and likeness of
-   230–31   *b·* the remote, predisposing, and
-   237– 3   On *b·* questioned about it
-   250–30   not *b·* at the mercy of death,
-   254– 8   To stop eating, drinking, or *b·* clothed
- *c* 257–13   is very far from *b·* the supposed substance of
- *b* 279–12   and they have the advantage of *b·* eternal.
-   280–27   *b·* perpetual in His own individuality,
-   287–14   God *b·* everywhere and all-inclusive,
-   293–19   the great difference *b·* that electricity is not
-   295–12   but infinite Spirit *b·* all,
-   308–22   and Truth, *b·* thereby understood,
-   313–21   "Who, *b·* a brightness from His — *see Heb.* 1 : 3.
-   314–31   as *b·* in supposed accord with the
-   315–30   *b·* conceived by a human mother,
-   316– 4   The real man *b·* linked by Science to
-   325– 4   is *b·* ushered into the undying realities of
-   334–31   Spirit *b·* God, there is but one Spirit,
-   335–16   Soul and Spirit *b·* one,
-   337–27   *b·* the opposite of the real or the spiritual
-   339– 3   *B·* destroyed, sin needs no other
- *o* 339– 9   evil, *b·* contrary to good,
-   341–14   cannot prevent that from *b·* scientific
- *p* 363–12   they were wondering why, *b·* a prophet,
-   413–26   that mind *b·* laden with illusions
-   430–27   evidence for the prosecution *b·* called for,
-   433– 1   testimony for the plaintiff, . . . *b·* closed,
-   438– 9   Instead of *b·* a traitor in the Province of
- *t* 455– 7   Hence the necessity of *b·* right yourself
- *r* 472– 9   Sickness, sin, and death, *b·* inharmonious,
-   477– 7   Soul, *b·* Spirit, is seen in nothing imperfect
-   479–31   *b·* understood by the things that — *Rom.* 1 : 20.
- *g* 504– 6   questions as to the divine creation *b·*
-   506 1   matter, not *b·* the reflection of Spirit,
-   513–27   So-called mortal mind — *b·* non-existent
-   516– 3   so you, *b·* spiritual, are the reflection
-   525–10   the primary sense *b· image, form ;*
-   544– 6   Mind, instead of matter, *b·* the producer,
-   557–25   *b·* in accordance with the first chapter of the
- *ap* 562–22   And she *b·* with child cried, — *Rev.* 12 : 2.
-   567–25   therefore, in his pretence of *b·* a talker,
- *fr* 600– *   *b· fruitful in every good work,* — *Col.* 1 : 10.

beings

all
- *t* 460– 4   necessary constituents and relations of all *b·*,"

corporeal
- *sp* 70–10   supposition that corporeal *b·* are spirits,

entities and
- *f* 204– 8   antagonistic entities and *b·*,

exalted
- *g* 513– 7   lead on to spiritual spheres and exalted *b·*.

human
- *b* 298–25   Angels are not etherealized human *b·*,

inhabited by
- *sp* 91– 3   inhabited by *b·* under the control of supreme

mortal
- *g* 554– 5   nor are there properly any mortal *b·*,

spiritual
- *c* 264–32   universe of Spirit is peopled with spiritual *b·*

upward-soaring
- *b* 299–12   These upward-soaring *b·* never lead towards

Belial

- *ph* 171–24   than between *B·* and Christ.
- *f* 216–26   "What concord hath Christ with *B·*?" — *II Cor.* 6 : 15.
- *g* 539–26   what concord hath Christ with *B·*?" — *II Cor.* 6 : 15.

belied
 an 104– 6 and *b·* by wolves in sheep's clothing.

belief
 abandonment of a
  p 374–31 expels it through the abandonment of a *b·*,
 abandon the
  g 534– 1 Hence she is first to abandon the *b·* in the
 according to
  ph 168–10 When sick (according to *b·*)
  170– 1 according to *b·*, poisons the human system.
  183– 8 Can the agriculturist, according to *b·*,
  p 425– 7 the leading points included (according to *b·*)
 aches again in
  f 212– 3 sometimes aches again in *b·*,
 acute
  f 247– 1 acute *b·* of physical life comes on at a remote
 all
  s 116–16 even to the extinction of all *b·* in matter,
  o 353–22 we must yield up all *b·* in it and be wise.
  p 418– 4 depends on mentally destroying all *b·* in
  g 556– 7 destroys forever all *b·* in
 ancient
  ap 567–18 That false claim— that ancient *b·*,
 another
  r 491–20 this belief culminates in another *b·*,
 arise from the
  sp 94–15 arise from the *b·* that the infinite is
  p 421– 4 physical ailments . . . arise from the *b·* that
 ask how
  g 553–31 you may also ask how *b·* can affect
 banish the
  p 391– 9 Banish the *b·* that you can possibly
 basis of
  p 424– 6 and we must leave the mortal basis of *b·*
 believer and
  r 487–18 The believer and *b·* are one and are mortal.
 bestows
  r 488–22 apart from what *b·* bestows upon them,
 better
  p 442–21 changes a belief of sin . . . into a better *b·*,
 blind
  pr 12–11 which acts through blind *b·*,
  12–23 The common custom . . . finds help in blind *b·*
  a 34–22 dulness and blind *b·* in God
  sp 83–10 a blind *b·* without understanding,
  s 124– 4 a law of mortal mind, a blind *b·*,
  132–21 blind *b·* shuts the door upon it,
 blindness of
  r 486–18 Alas for the blindness of *b·*, which
 called death
  p 380– 2 fever case, which ends in a *b·* called death,
 change of
  ph 169– 1 change of *b·* from a material to a spiritual
 changes in
  pr 12–24 Changes in *b·* may go on indefinitely,
 change the
  p 398–27 change the *b·* of disease to a
  r 491– 5 Change the *b·*, and the sensation changes.
 chronic
  f 247– 2 is not so disastrous as the chronic *b·*.
 cling to a
  f 237–26 They . . . cling to a *b·* in the life and
 controlled by
  b 304–28 Controlled by *b·*, instead of understanding,
 corporeal
  gl 587–21 HAM (Noah's son). Corporeal *b·* ;
  589– 1 ISSACHAR (Jacob's son). A corporeal *b·* ;
 coupled with the
  p 389– 2 for the penalty is coupled with the *b·*.
 customary
  f 229–17 This customary *b·* is misnamed material law,
 darkness of
  ap 569–17 dwellers still in the deep darkness of *b·*.
 defined as a
  s 129–11 Pantheism may be defined as a *b·* in the
 destroys the
  a 37– 1 which destroys the *b·* called sin
  sp 84–24 true conception of being destroys the *b·* of
 destroy the
  p 368–30 can destroy the *b·* in material conditions,
  375–23 Destroy the *b·*, show mortal mind that
  424–29 you must destroy the *b·* in these ills
  r 473– 7 Christ came to destroy the *b·* of sin.
  491– 6 Destroy the *b·*, and the sensation disappears.
 destruction of the
  f 219–19 the destruction of the *b·* will be the
 disease being a
  ph 168–27 Disease being a *b·*, a latent illusion
 doctor's
  ph 198–24 moulded and formed by his doctor's *b·*
 doctrine, or
  a 26–28 Our Master taught no mere . . . doctrine, or *b·*.
 dream or
  r 491–22 The dream or *b·* goes on,
 drive
  f 251– 8 as to drive *b·* into new paths.

belief
 educated
  a 39–10 The educated *b·* that Soul is in the body
  r 489– 9 Any hypothesis which . . . is an educated *b·*.
 element of the
  r 480– 8 Nerves are an element of the *b·* that
 embodied in the
  sp 93–29 this is the error embodied in the *b·* that
 erring
  r 472–29 seem real to human, erring *b·*,
 erroneous
  ph 184–11 never honoring erroneous *b·* with the
  b 297–12 Erroneous *b·* is destroyed by truth.
  p 389– 5 every erroneous *b·*, or material condition.
  415–16 till it can master an erroneous *b·*.
  420–23 but erroneous *b·*, taken at its best,
  g 541–16 erroneous *b·* that life, substance, and
  544–28 erroneous *b·* reverses understanding and
 error of
  (see **error**)
 error of a
  a 47–32 Jesus realized the utter error of a *b·* in
  g 526–12 error of a *b·* in intelligent matter.
 errors of
  sp 96–23 until all errors of *b·* yield to understanding.
  t 450–25 knows that they are errors of *b·*,
 evolves, in
  s 108–27 this false sense evolves, in *b·*, a
 experiences of
  b 322–26 The sharp experiences of *b·* in the
 faith and
  pr 12–18 borrows its power from human faith and *b·*.
 false
  sp 97–14 The nearer a false *b·* approaches truth
  an 103–20 the false *b·* that mind is in matter,
  ph 168–14 through just this false *b·*.
  184–17 Whatever is governed by a false *b·*
  194– 8 When one's false *b·* is corrected,
  f 222–32 We must destroy the false *b·* that
  b 283–21 false *b·* as to what really constitutes life
  297–14 seemed real to this false *b·*,
  298– 5 false *b·* silences for a while the voice of
  298– 6 false *b·* cannot destroy Science
  304– 3 It is ignorance and false *b·*,
  o 346–24 hence pain in matter is a false *b·*,
  p 370– 4 turn from the lie of false *b·* to Truth,
  376–22 destroy the patient's false *b·* by
  379–14 he would have risen above the false *b·*.
  383–27 the illusive physical effect of a false *b·*,
  393–30 A false *b·* is both the tempter and the tempted,
  r 480–24 Evil is a false *b·*.
  g 546– 1 false *b·* that spirit is now submerged in
  557–10 human propagation . . . is a false *b·*.
  gl 582– 7 pride ; envy ; fame ; illusion ; a false *b·* ;
 finite
  b 280– 9 Finite *b·* can never do justice to Truth
  280–10 Finite *b·* limits all things,
  322–12 that finite *b·* may be prepared to relinquish
  gl 585–24 a finite *b·* concerning life, substance, and
 formed by education
  ph 194–30 material sense . . . a *b·* formed by education
 forms of
  g 531– 4 in all the subsequent forms of *b·*.
 freed from the
  ph 178–24 freed from the *b·* of heredity,
 fulfils
  b 297–32 A mortal *b·* fulfils its own conditions.
 general
  s 155– 4 it is the law of a general *b·*,
  155–11 When the general *b·* endorses the inanimate
  155–17 This erroneous general *b·*, which
  g 554–29 general *b·* that the lower animals are less sickly
 give up the
  b 283– 2 they give up the *b·* that there is
  p 397–28 Give up the *b·* that mind is,
 her
  sp 89– 9 Destroy her *b·* in outside aid,
  89–10 The former limits of her *b·* return.
  ph 185– 4 changed the action of her *b·* on the lungs,
  f 245–23 bodily results of her *b·* that she was young
  p 379–21 from her *b·* that blood is destroying her life.
  379–23 her *b·* produces the very results she dreads.
  389–29 In her *b·* . . . . had chronic liver-complaint,
 his
  ph 197–31 his *b·* in its reality and fatality will harm his
  199–27 His *b·* that he could do it gave
  b 325– 2 loses his *b·* in death.
  o 346–23 there is no reality in his *b·* of pain,
  p 425–21 God is more to a man than his *b·*
 human
  (see **human**)
 illusion of
  r 490–31 Under the mesmeric illusion of *b·*,
 improved
  b 296–28 An improved *b·* is one step out of error,

belief

improved
  p 442–19 An improved *b·* cannot retrograde.
in a bodily soul
  c 257– 9 it is the *b·* in a bodily soul and
in a diseased brain
  p 421– 2 insanity implies *b·* in a diseased brain,
in a human doctrine
  b 286– 2 To seek Truth through *b·* in a human doctrine
in a material basis
  b 268– 6 *B·* in a material basis, from which
in a self-made
  b 282–10 a *b·* in a self-made and temporary
in consumption
  p 375–32 *b·* in consumption presents to mortal thought
in death
  (*see* **death**)
in disease
  s 145–12 Christ, Truth, subdues the human *b·* in disease.
  p 377–31 It is latent *b·* in disease, as well as
  414– 2 the foundations of the *b·* in disease
  419– 3 or even create the *b·* in disease.
  r 482–31 mortal mind . . . causes the *b·* in disease.
in error
  b 297–27 A belief in Truth is better than a *b·* in error,
in evil
  g 540– 7 stirring up the *b·* in evil to its utmost,
in feebleness
  f 219–17 for the *b·* in feebleness must obtain in
in illusion
  g 555–32 not the *b·* in illusion or error.
in many gods
  gl 591– 2 mythology,— *b·* in many gods,
in material life
  pr 6–13 until *b·* in material life and sin is destroyed.
  g 533–23 *b·* in material life and intelligence is
in material origins
  f 213–31 into *b·* in material origins
in material suffering
  p 405–30 *B·* in material suffering causes mortals to
in matter
  gl 581–10 understanding . . . destroying *b·* in matter.
in "original sin"
  gl 579–15 a falsity ; the *b·* in "original sin,"
in other gods
  g 535–12 A *b·* in other gods, other creators,
in pain
  s 153–19 The boil simply manifests, . . . a *b·* in pain,
  153–24 that is, its own *b·* in pain.
in sickness
  pr 12– 9 casting out a *b·* in sickness.
  14–15 If suffering from a *b·* in sickness,
  f 218–24 Treat a *b·* in sickness as you would sin,
  b 297–10 a health-belief or a *b·* in sickness
  p 430– 9 *B·* in sickness and death, as certainly as
in sin
  f 219–29 Entire immunity from the *b·* in sin, suffering,
  253–16 overcome the *b·* in sin, disease, or
  253–28 *b·* in sin and death is destroyed
  b 289– 3 *débris* of error, *b·* in sin, sickness, and
  290–16 destroyed the *b·* in sin,
  p 430–10 *b·* in sin, tends to shut out the true sense
  r 407–11 But the *b·* in sin is punished
  gl 584–14 a *b·* in sin, sickness, and death ;
in something
  sp 92–26 is laid on a *b·* in something besides God.
in the experience
  b 291–10 need not fancy that *b·* in the experience of
in their reality
  o 352–27 If *b·* in their reality is destroyed,
in the material origin
  g 549–31 coming down to a *b·* in the material origin of
in the necessity
  f 251–18 a *b·* in the necessity of sickness and death,
in the plagues
  s 133– 9 saved the Israelites from *b·* in the plagues.
in the unknown
  pr 12– 9 a *b·* in the unknown casting out a
intruding
  p 393– 2 we admit the intruding *b·*, forgetting
in Truth
  b 297–26 A *b·* in Truth is better than a belief in error,
involves
  g 526– 9 *B·* involves theories of material hearing,
is changeable
  sp 96–23 *B·* is changeable, but
Jew's
  o 361–11 Thus he virtually unites with the Jew's *b·*
latent
  p 377–31 It is latent *b·* in disease, as well as
leads to
  sp 92–30 leads to *b·* in the superiority of error.
lord of the
  g 518– 2 He is lord of the *b·* in earth and heaven,
lost in the
  t 455–11 If you are yourself lost in the *b·* and fear of

belief

man's
  s 159–30 Ignorant of the fact that a man's *b·* produces
  ph 175–23 A man's *b·* in those days was not so severe upon
material
  (*see* **material**)
matter is a
  ph 190– 3 all this while matter is a *b·*,
melts
  p 442–21 *b·* melts into spiritual understanding,
mere
  a 23–16 Faith, if it be mere *b·*, is as a pendulum
  b 330– 2 understanding of being supersedes mere *b·*.
  r 487–22 Mere *b·* is blindness without Principle
mistaken
  p 377–27 a mistaken *b·* or conviction of the
  g 554–19 Mind sets at naught such a mistaken *b·*.
Mohammedan's
  ph 166–12 Mohammedan's *b·* is a religious delusion ;
mortal
  (*see* **mortal**)
mortal in
  r 486–22 will continue mortal in *b·* and subject to chance
nation's
  ph 200– 2 the gods became alive in a nation's *b·*.
new
  f 251–11 they have but passed the portals of a new *b·*.
no
  a 19–31 Thou shalt have no *b·* of Life as mortal ;
not
  pr 15–29 Practice not profession, understanding not *b·*,
nourishes the
  pr 5–25 If prayer nourishes the *b·* that sin is
of corporeal sense
  sp 77– 5 continues to be a *b·* of corporeal sense
of danger
  p 374–23 You cannot forget the *b·* of danger,
of disease
  ph 178– 8 remote cause or *b·* of disease is not
  p 380–18 The body is affected only with the *b·* of disease
  398–27 change the *b·* of disease to a belief of health.
of grief
  p 386–27 under the influence of the *b·* of grief,
of having died
  sp 74–14 the *b·* of having died and left a material body
of health
  p 398–27 change the belief of disease to a *b·* of health.
of intense pain
  ph 195– 1 gave him a *b·* of intense pain.
of life
  sp 74–10 When here or hereafter the *b·* of life in matter
  89–30 incident shows that the *b·* of life in matter was
  f 203–21 when evil has overtaxed the *b·* of life
  t 450–31 all evil combines in the *b·* of life,
  g 542– 1 The *b·* of life in matter sins
  gl 584–14 until every *b·* of life where Life is not
of material mind
  g 529–30 Adam, . . . stands for a *b·* of material mind.
of mortal mind
  f 229–29 transgression of a *b·* of mortal mind,
  251– 3 The so-called *b·* of mortal mind
  b 292–13 Matter is the primitive *b·* of mortal mind,
  p 384–10 this is but a *b·* of mortal mind,
of pain
  f 247–32 to retreat from the *b·* of pain or pleasure
  o 346–23 there is no reality in his *b·* of pain,
  p 416– 3 the *b·* of pain will presently return, unless
  t 464–18 when the *b·* of pain was lulled,
of sickness
  f 229–30 which causes the *b·* of sickness.
of sin
  a 38–27 To those buried in the *b·* of sin and self,
  ph 188– 4 The *b·* of sin, which has grown terrible in
  b 318–14 brought the *b·* of sin and death
  p 442–20 Christ changes a *b·* of sin or of sickness into
  r 473– 7 Christ came to destroy the *b·* of sin.
of substance-matter
  b 314– 4 had relinquished the *b·* of substance-matter.
of the disease
  p 377–20 when the *b·* of the disease had gone.
of the eternity
  b 278–23 *b·* of the eternity of matter contradicts
of the flesh
  b 310–22 It is the *b·* of the flesh . . . which sins.
old
  b 281–30 The old *b·* must be cast out
one
  pr 12– 8 This, however, is one *b·* casting out another,
  p 370–16 produces through one *b·*,
  gl 583–28 one *b·* preying upon another.
  584–13 that which frets itself free from one *b·*
one's
  f 234–32 and do no more harm than one's *b·* permits.
only in
  b 328– 8 mortals get rid of . . . only in *b·*.

belief

only in
gl 591–15 feels, hears, tastes, and smells only in *b·*.

opposite
f 205–11 the opposite *b·* is the prolific source of
b 338– 4 opposite *b·* — that man originates in matter
p 370–16 it removes through an opposite *b·*,
   385–30 opposite *b·* would produce the opposite result.
   425–31 protest against the opposite *b·* in heredity.
   427– 2 can never change in Science to the opposite *b·*

originates unseen
p 377–16 Because a *b·* originates unseen, the

palsy is a
p 375–21 Palsy is a *b·* that matter governs mortals,

pantheistic
b 279–24 infected with the pantheistic *b·* that

patient's
ph 198–23 A patient's *b·* is more or less moulded

perpetuates the
pr 2–20 perpetuates the *b·* in God as humanly

phase of
p 419–22 mortal mind is liable to any phase of *b·*.

physical
p 395–27 erroneous . . . to feel these ills in physical *b·*.
   418–26 Include moral as well as physical *b·* in
gl 582– 4 BENJAMIN . . . A physical *b·* as to life,
   586–18 FLESH. An error of physical *b·* ;

plane of
sp 75–19 would have stood on the same plane of *b·*

popular
s 155–21 must mightily outweigh the power of popular *b·*
b 316–15 and the blindness of popular *b·*,

postulate of
sp 91–25 The first erroneous postulate of *b·* is,

potent
g 553–25 this potent *b·* will immediately supersede

proceeds from the
sp 88–32 When eloquence proceeds from the *b·* that

produces the
ph 184– 6 *B·* produces the results of belief,

product of
r 490– 3 Will-power is but a product of *b·*,

relinquish the
o 357– 9 If mankind would relinquish the *b·* that

removing the
p 421–14 removing the *b·* that this chemicalization

results of
ph 184– 6 Belief produces the results of *b·*,

reverse the
p 408–26 Reverse the *b·*, and the results would be

sensual
gl 590–11 LEVI . . . A corporeal and sensual *b·* ;

sensuous
gl 582–24 CANAAN (the son of Ham). A sensuous *b·* ;
   592–27 PHARISEE. Corporeal and sensuous *b·* ;

separated by
ap 562–13 separated by *b·* from man's divine origin

separate from the
pr 14–25 Entirely separate from the *b·* and dream of

sickness is a
r 493–19 Sickness is a *b·*, which must be annihilated

simply a
sp 71– 3 simply a *b·*, an illusion of material sense.

sinful
b 314–23 Because of mortals' material and sinful *b·*,

strays into a sense
b 311–15 *b·* strays into a sense of temporary loss

such
b 280–11 Such *b·* can neither apprehend nor worship

such a
pr 13–22 doubts and fears which attend such a *b·*,
sp 83–11 for such a *b·* hides Truth
s 155–14 such a *b·* is governed by the majority.
f 245–24 manifested the influence of such a *b·*.

tenacity of
p 396–18 on account of the tenacity of *b·* in its truth,

that
a 41–31 that *b·*, . . . has never made a disciple who
p 379–11 and died because of that *b·*,
g 553–32 precedes the development of that *b·*.

that all must die
sp 75–21 out of the *b·* that all must die,

that another mind
sp 89– 4 in the *b·* that another mind is speaking

that everything
g 531– 2 the *b·* that everything springs from dust

that existence
p 427– 9 The *b·* that existence is contingent on matter

that God
f 204–30 *b·* that God lives in matter is pantheistic.
o 357– 9 the *b·* that God makes sickness,

that he dies
r 486–11 The *b·* that he dies will not establish his

that inflammation
p 375– 3 the *b·* that inflammation and pain must

belief

that life
sp 76– 8 the *b·* that life, or mind, was ever in
f 222–32 *b·* that life and intelligence are in
b 289– 4 *b·* that life and sensation are in the body
   318–20 error — or *b·* that life is in matter
r 485–19 The *b·* that life can be in matter
   487–23 The *b·* that life is sentient and
g 541–16 erroneous *b·* that life, substance, and
gl 587– 9 Mythology ; a *b·* that life, substance,
   588–17 even the *b·* that life, substance, and
   592– 1 *b·* that life, substance, and intelligence are
   592– 4 the *b·* that life has a beginning

that man
a 42–19 *b·* that man has existence or mind separate
sp 91– 5 rid ourselves of the *b·* that man is separated
b 301–20 The *b·* that man has any other substance,
   320–21 the *b·* that man is flesh and matter,
p 427– 2 the opposite *b·* that man dies.
gl 592– 5 *b·* that man is the offspring of mortals ;

that material bodies
sp 73–19 The *b·* that material bodies return to dust,

that matter
s 110– 3 contradict forever the *b·* that matter can
b 289–21 The *b·* that matter has life results,
   294– 9 The *b·* that matter thinks, sees, or feels
   294–10 *b·* that matter enjoys and suffers.
p 360–11 the *b·* that matter is substance,
   372–10 the *b·* that matter is the medium of man,
   375–21 Palsy is a *b·* that matter governs mortals,
r 491–17 The *b·* that matter and mind are one,
g 543–28 The *b·* that matter supports life
ap 563–11 the *b·* that matter has power of its own,
gl 586–20 a *b·* that matter has sensation.

that Mind
b 292– 8 the *b·* that Mind, . . . can be fettered

that mind
an 103–20 It is the false *b·* that mind is in matter,
b 298–15 expresses the *b·* that mind is in matter.
   308– 1 the *b·* that mind is in matter,
p 379–31 through the *b·* that mind is in matter
   397–28 Give up the *b·* that mind is, . . . compressed
gl 587– 1 a *b·* that mind is outlined and limited ;

that one man
sp 73– 8 The *b·* that one man, as spirit, can

that pain
b 303–21 The *b·* that pain and pleasure, . . . mingle

that sensation
gl 591–27 the *b·* that sensation is in matter,

that Soul
a 39–10 educated *b·* that Soul is in the body
b 280–22 the *b·* that Soul is in body,

that Spirit
sp 93–21 The *b·* that Spirit is finite as well as infinite

that spirit
sp 73–22 Equally incorrect is the *b·* that spirit is confined
g 546– 1 *b·* that spirit is now submerged in

that substance
ap 563– 8 the *b·* that substance, . . . can be material.

that the body governed
f 226–23 the *b·* that the body governed them,

that the human race
gl 585–25 *b·* that the human race originated materially

that the universe
sp 83–16 The *b·* that the universe, including man,

their
sp 81– 6 their *b·* in mediumship would vanish.
p 389–23 Their *b·* in material laws and in
   402–27 because their *b·* is not better instructed
g 536–28 They give up their *b·* in perishable life

this
sp 80–30 This *b·* rests on the common conviction that
   83–18 this *b·* belittles omnipotent wisdom,
   89–16 the body responds to this *b·*,
   92–27 This *b·* tends to support two opposite powers,
   93–30 This *b·* tends to becloud our apprehension of
an 102– 4 Its basis being a belief and this *b·* animal,
   103–22 This *b·* has not one quality of Truth.
s 124– 8 this *b·* mistakes effect for cause
   143–21 Controlled by this *b·*, you continue in the
   153–19 this *b·* is called a boil.
c 257–10 This *b·* is shallow pantheism.
   258– 7 The insufficiency of this *b·* to supply the
b 279–25 this *b·* contradicts alike revelation and
   302–12 and this *b·* is all that will ever be lost.
p 374–20 this *b·* helps rather than hinders disease.
   384–12 has only to enter his protest against this *b·*
   389– 4 control of Mind over this *b·*
   389–26 This *b·* totters to its falling before the
   389–31 symptoms connected with this *b·*.
   423– 2 this *b·* should not be communicated to the
r 469–28 This *b·* that there is more than one mind
   478–24 this *b·* is mortal and far from actual.
   489– 9 In infancy this *b·* is not equal to guiding the
   489–11 as consciousness develops, this *b·* goes out
   490– 3 this *b·* commits depredations on harmony.

belief

this
r 491–20 this b· culminates in another belief,
g 533–17 According to this b·, the rib taken from
546– 3 this b· alone is mortal.

understanding and
b 288–12 the conflict between . . . understanding and b·,

understanding or
b 324–11 understanding or b·, Spirit or matter.

unexpressed
p 423– 6 Remember that the unexpressed b· oftentimes

universal
a 42– 5 The universal b· in death is of no advantage.
s 155–15 The universal b· in physics weighs against

unreal
o 353–30 the ghost, some unreal b·.

until the
b 297– 2 nothing can change this state, until the b· changes.
297– 4 until the b· on this subject changes.

whatever the
p 418–17 Whatever the b· is, if arguments are used

which breeds
m 62– 7 a b· which breeds disease.

which unites
f 229– 9 the b· which unites such opposites as

without understanding
sp 83–10 a blind b· without understanding,
r 472–18 Error is a b· without understanding.

wrong
f 253–23 you can alter this wrong b· and action

your
ph 168– 8 Your b· militates against your health,
p 384–24 to destroy the bad effects of your b·.
385–24 will suffer in proportion to your b· and fear.
386–22 your suffering was merely the result of your b·.
t 461–17 you should tell your b· sometimes,

zeal of
b 280–20 zeal of b· to establish the opposite error

m 62– 6 master the b· in so-called physical laws,
68–25 the b· that agamogenesis applies to the
sp 74–11 error which has held the b·
74–12 dissolves with the b·,
74–15 b· of still living in an organic, material body.
78– 6 How unreasonable is the b· that we are
97– 7 the more impotent error becomes as a b·.
97–17 The more material the b·, the more
an 102– 4 Its basis being a b· and this belief animal,
104–24 If he heals sickness through a b·,
104–24 and a b· originally caused the sickness,
s 129–12 Pantheism . . . a b· which Science overthrows.
144–11 The more material a b·, the more obstinately
155–13 a b· held by a minority,
164–22 mortal thoughts in b· rule the materiality
ph 172–19 The b· that there is Soul in sense or Life in
184– 7 penalties it affixes last so long as the b·
187–30 the human mind still holds in b· a body,
189–26 first the b· of inanimate, and then of
192– 1 The b· that a pulpy substance under the skull
198– 2 has in b· more power to harm
f 205–24 a b· in many ruling minds hinders man's
212– 1 limb . . . amputated has continued in b· to pain
220–26 The b· that either fasting or feasting makes
b 279–16 In proportion as the b· disappears that life
285–16 The b· that a material body is man
286– 5 We must not . . . depend upon b· instead of
295– 1 The b· that a severed limb is aching in the
297–20 Faith is higher and more spiritual than b·.
297–29 Until b· becomes faith, and faith becomes
312–11 The b· of that mortal that he must die
321–13 Matter was shown to be a b· only.
o 340–14 the b· that we suffer from the sins of others.
358–26 a b· that in the removal of disease
p 380– 3 which b· must be finally conquered by
386– 5 b· says that you may catch cold
386–12 not because of the climate, but on account of the b·.
392–17 You will call it neuralgia, but we call it a b·.
398–25 faith, cooperating with a b· in the healing
402–32 a b· without a real cause.
409–11 The b·, that the unconscious substratum
416–13 unless the b· which occasions the pain has
418–18 the b· must be repudiated,
422–32 The b· that he has met his master in
425–20 What if the b· is consumption?
t 450– 3 b· in a mysterious, supernatural God,
r 467–19 The b· that the greater can be in the lesser
487–13 You speak of b·. Who or what is it that
488– 7 Hebrew and Greek words often translated b·
488–12 appear . . . to approve and endorse b·,
491– 4 a b· without actual foundation
495–20 b· in, that which Life is not.
497–12 punished so long as the b· lasts.
g 526– 8 B· is less than understanding.
535– 2 The seed . . . of b· and of understanding,
gl 579–17 a curse ; a b· in intelligent matter,

belief
gl 587–11 the b· that infinite Mind is in finite forms ;
592– 6 the b· that there can be more than one creator ;
594– 3 the b· in more than one God ;

beliefs

all the
a 53–29 had not conquered all the b· of the flesh
r 493–17 superior to all the b· of the five corporeal senses,

and opinions
gl 590– 5 mortality ; b· and opinions ;

begotten of the
b 325–24 begotten of the b· of the flesh

carnal
c 263–11 Carnal b· defraud us.

changes its
s 125– 2 as mortal mind changes its b·.

cherished
s 141– 8 to set aside even the most cherished b·

chronic
f 246–32 Acute and chronic b· reproduce their own types.

different
sp 74–22 different b·, which never blend.

diseased
p 404–10 all sorts of evil are diseased b·,

dismal
b 272–27 the dismal b· of sin, sickness, and death.

doctrinal
r 496–31 if by that term is meant doctrinal b·.

dying
sp 76–18 Suffering, sinning, dying b· are unreal.

erroneous
c 267–21 inverted thoughts and erroneous b·

evil
s 115–31 Evil b·, passions and appetites, fear,
115–25 Second Degree: Evil b· disappearing.
f 206–32 There are evil b·, often called evil spirits ;
c 266–26 evil b· which originate in mortals are hell.

false
sp 79–17 Jesus cast out evil spirits, or false b·.
99–20 some others who eschew their false b·.
s 162–16 false b· of a so-called material existence.
ph 171–25 so-called laws of matter are nothing but false b·
171–27 These false b· are the procuring cause
f 234–10 and guard against false b· as watchfully
236–31 or battling with false b·,
237–31 they had false b· and suffer the delusive
b 274–21 These false b· and their products
278–13 one of the false b· of mortals,
327– 6 destroy the false b· of pleasure, pain,
p 421– 1 the insane suffer, from false b·.
g 556– 5 These false b· will disappear,

fatal
p 368–10 Against the fatal b· that error is as

former
t 400–30 As former b· were gradually expelled

ghostly
o 353–14 not wholly outlived the sense of ghostly b·.

held in the
p 413–32 malady, timorously held in the b·

his
p 371 15 The adult, in bondage to his b·,

his own
p 372–12 bind himself with his own b·,

human
(see **human**)

inharmonious
f 251–30 Inharmonious b·, which rob Mind,

in sickness
p 391– 3 Blot out . . . its b· in sickness and sin,

insidious
p 376– 9 hidden, undefined, and insidious b·.

man-made
r 466–26 the outcome of all man-made b·.

material
(see **material**)

materialistic
s 132–16 retained their materialistic b· about God.
b 298–22 and admit no materialistic b·.
316–28 spiritualizing materialistic b·,

mortal
(see **mortal**)

of mortal mind
sp 89– 3 shows that the b· of mortal mind are loosed.
b 274–19 simply the manifested b· of mortal mind,
p 425–14 this is but one of the b· of mortal mind.

of the human mind
ph 187–10 b· of the human mind rob and enslave it,

opinions and
b 273–30 conflicting mortal opinions and b·

opposite
sp 75–29 when the link between their opposite b·

other
f 208–32 and of other b· included in matter.

our
f 202–24 Our b· about a Supreme Being contradict
p 385–10 forestalls the penalty which our b· would

beliefs

outgrow their
sp 77–27 Spiritualists would outgrow their *b·*

outgrown
a 28–12 we cannot hold to *b·* outgrown ;

perilous
t 450–27 Who, that has felt the perilous *b·* in

pleasurable
c 265–32 if they wrench away false pleasurable *b·*

present
f 228–17 Dropping their present *b·*, they

remove its
p 421– 8 in order to remove its *b·*,

self-imposed
f 221–18 the self-imposed *b·* of mortals,

sick
p 366–25 The sick are terrified by their sick *b·*,

sinful
a 53–32 Had he shared the sinful *b·* of others,
f 241–32 than for sinful *b·* to enter the kingdom of
p 366–26 sinners should be affrighted by their sinful *b·* ;

stubborn
f 237–10 more stubborn *b·* and theories of parents

their
p 396–23 explain to the sick the power which their *b·*
403– 1 So the sick through their *b·* have

their own
f 226–27 I wished to save from the slavery of their own *b·*

these
sp 79–12 C. S. removes these *b·* and

those
a 54– 1 he would have been less sensitive to those *b·*.

traditional
o 352–24 ghosts are not realities, but traditional *b·*,

unjust
p 440–22 The false and unjust *b·* of your

a 43–31 errors growing from such *b·*.
sp 88–14 *B·* proceed from the so-called material senses,
99–26 until the *b·* of material existence are
s 155–10 and the *b·* which are in the majority rule.
f 232– 4 The *b·* we commonly entertain about happiness
o 343–19 that sin, sickness, and death are *b·*
p 425–10 hemorrhage, and decomposition are *b·*,
gl 595–18 thoughts, *b·*, opinions, knowledge ;

believe

pr 1– * *but shall b· that those things— Mark 11 : 23.*
1– * *b· that ye receive them,— Mark 11 : 24.*
a 23–27 "Lord, I *b·* ; help thou mine— *Mark 9 : 24.*
23–29 "*B·* . . . and thou shalt be saved !"— *Acts 16 : 31.*
23–32 Hebrew verb *to b·* means also *to be firm*
24–12 He . . . will *b·* our report,
29–13 "The disciples of Jesus *b·* him the Son
38–10 signs shall follow them that *b·* ;— *Mark 16 : 17.*
38–14 but *them*— "them that *b·*"— *Mark 16 : 17.*
38–19 as should *b·* "through their word."— *John*
17 : 20.
41–30 enough for them to *b·* in a national Deity ;
52–28 signs shall follow them that *b·*."— *Mark 16 : 17.*
m 62–31 Because mortals *b·* in material laws
sp 71–26 I never could *b·* in spiritualism.
93–10 If we *b·* otherwise, we may be
s 110–30 apprehended by as many as *b·* on Christ
119–26 to *b·* that the earth is in motion
147–15 never *b·* that you can absorb the
150–18 would have one *b·* that both matter and
154–10 A man was made to *b·* that he
ph 168–17 are we to *b·* it?
168–18 Are we to *b·* an authority which denies God's
177–31 In such cases a few persons *b·* the potion
178– 2 *b·* the arsenic, the strychnine, or
186–30 Since it must *b·* in something besides itself,
189– 4 we still *b·* that there is solar light and heat.
f 203–17 We are prone to *b·* either in more than one
203–22 then mortals *b·* that the deathless Principle,
212–21 In legerdemain and . . . mortals *b·*
215–15 We are sometimes led to *b·* that darkness is
218–19 If you do *b·* in God, why do you substitute
218–25 Resist the temptation to *b·* in
222– 6 to *b·* that proper food supplies nutriment
253–18 If you *b·* in and practise wrong knowingly,
253–22 Also, if you *b·* yourself diseased,
253–25 Do not *b·* in any supposed necessity for sin,
c 263– 1 They *b·* themselves to be independent workers,
b 271–18 for them also which shall *b·*— *John 17 : 20.*
277–29 Nothing we can say or *b·* regarding
285–32 essential to understand, instead of *b·*,
302–30 though mortal sense would fain have us so *b·*.
311–20 So long as we *b·* that soul can sin
312–18 Mortals try to *b·* without understanding
312–20 Mortals *b·* in a finite personal God ;
318– 1 For him to *b·* in matter was no task,
321–27 if they will not *b·* thee,— *Exod. 4 : 8.*
321–28 will *b·* the voice of the latter sign."— *Exod. 4 : 8.*
328–23 signs shall follow them that *b·*,— *Mark 16 : 17.*
o 341– * *ye b· me not.— John 8 : 45.*

believe

o 341– * *why do ye not b· me? — John 8 : 46.*
346–26 when you *b·* that nitrous-oxide gas has
349–32 the opponents of C. S. *b·* substance to be
352–26 should be told not to *b·* in ghosts,
359–27 signs shall follow them that *b·* ;— *Mark 16 : 17.*
p 362– * *signs shall follow them that b· : — Mark 16 : 17.*
368–32 Once let the mental physician *b·* in the
372–20 How, then, . . . can we *b·* in the reality and
380–28 Nothing is more disheartening than to *b·* that
381–23 or you will never *b·* that you are quite free
384–22 but if you *b·* in laws of matter
392–15 If you *b·* in inflamed and weak nerves,
395–24 to *b·* in the real existence of a tumor,
402–25 operator would make his subjects *b·* that they
425– 4 You will have humors, just so long as you *b·*
425–27 you will never *b·* that heart . . . can destroy
428–32 It is a sin to *b·* that aught can overpower
429–25 Do you *b·* this?
t 461– 2 but I do *b·* that the real man is immortal
461–16 If you *b·* that you are sick,
463–29 sick are not healed by . . . drugs, as they *b·*
r 469–27 still *b·* there is another power,
474–21 Is it possible, then, to *b·* that the
487–16 Matter cannot *b·*, and Mind understands.
487–17 The body cannot *b·*,
488– 9 the English verb *b·* ;
494– 5 infidelity to *b·* that so great a work
g 540–23 is to teach mortals never to *b·* a lie.

believed

pr 6–29 It is *b·* by many that a certain magistrate,
a 43– 6 Heretofore they had only *b·* ;
44–28 His disciples *b·* Jesus to be dead
45–26 for they *b·* his body to be dead.
53–13 Mortals *b·* in God as humanly mighty,
m 68–16 one individual who *b·* in agamogenesis ;
sp 75–17 Had Jesus *b·* that Lazarus had
95–25 Is the wise man of to-day *b·*,
an 104–12 Lastly, they say they have always *b·* it."
s 133–11 and straightway *b·* that they were healed
136–18 some of the people *b·* that Jesus was a
154–22 Then it is *b·* that exposure to the
ph 199–25 Had Blondin *b·* it impossible
f 203– 7 understood instead of being merely *b·*,
222–18 had been kept alive, as was *b·*, only by
b 305–32 Pharisees, who *b·* error to be as immortal as
328–26 It were well had Christendom *b·*
339–27 Mind must be not merely *b·*,
o 348–28 would not be *b·* for an indefinite
359– 9 I as a Christian Scientist *b·* in the Holy Spirit,
p 371– 9 are *b·* to be here without their consent
403– 9 it is *b·* that the misfortune is a material effect.
409–16 conscious mortal mind is *b·* to be superior
425– 2 His parents . . . have so *b·*.
r 492–29 The conservative theory, long *b·*, is
g 545–22 They *b·* in the existence of matter,
gl 596–12 The rabbins *b·* that the stones in

believer

r 487–18 The *b·* and belief are one and are mortal.

believers

s 141–20 The Bible declares that all *b·* are

believes

a 38–12 Who *b·* him?
39–31 so long as he *b·* in the pleasures of sin?
sp 80–29 *b·* that this wonder emanates from spirits
86–29 Mortal mind sees what it *b·*
86–30 as certainly as it *b·* what it sees.
89–14 If one *b·* that he cannot be an orator without
ph 166– 8 Mohammedan *b·* in a pilgrimage to Mecca
166– 9 The popular doctor *b·* in his prescription,
166–10 pharmacist *b·* in the power of his drugs
171–17 man *b·* himself to be combined matter and
171–18 He *b·* that Spirit is sifted through matter,
199– 6 nobody *b·* that mind is producing such a
f 250–10 Spirit . . . never *b·*, but knows ;
c 263–15 mis-creator, who *b·* he is a semi-god.
b 294–28 inebriate *b·* that there is pleasure in
294–29 thief *b·* that he gains something by stealing,
o 360–32 The Jew *b·* that the Messiah or Christ
361– 1 the Christian *b·* that Christ is God.
361– 6 The Jew who *b·* in the First Commandment
361– 9 Christian who *b·* in the First Commandment
p 375–10 *b·* that matter, not mind, has helped him.
377– 1 If your patient *b·* in taking cold,
402–19 manifests only what mortal mind *b·*,
422–30 he *b·* that something stronger than Mind
427– 7 If man *b·* in death now, he
r 487–14 Who or what is it that *b·*?
g 517–15 The world *b·* in many persons ;

believeth

pr 14–19 "He that *b·* on me,— *John 14 : 12.*
a 22–27 Whosoever *b·* that wrath is righteous
42–30 "He that *b·* on me,— *John 14 : 12.*
52–27 "He that *b·* on me,— *John 14 : 12.*

believeth
sp 93– 4 "He that *b·* on me,— *John* 14 : 12.
ph 170–11 "Whosoever liveth and *b·* in me— *John* 11 : 26.
b 315– 1 "Whosoever liveth and *b·* in me— *John* 11 : 26.
324–32 "He that *b·* in me— *see John* 11 : 26.
326– 4 "He that *b·* on me,— *John* 14 : 12.

believing
m 69– 6 can never . . . while *b·* that man is a creator.
sp 89– 6 *b·* that somebody else possesses her tongue
s 134–29 There is divine authority for *b·* in the
156–11 *B·* then somewhat in the ordinary theories
ph 187– 1 *b·* in more than the one Mind.
f 205– 7 When will the error of *b·* that there is
205–15 the error of *b·* that matter can
218–14 *b·* that the body can be sick independently
245– 6 *B·* that she was still living in the same hour
245–25 She could not age while *b·* herself young,
b 290–29 no more spiritual for *b·* that his body died
p 385–23 Saying this and *b·* it,
388– 9 Idolaters, *b·* in more than one mind,
397–11 by *b·* them to be real and continuous.
r 487–16 this precludes the need of *b·*.
gl 582– 1 definition of

belittle
c 255–11 to *b·* Deity with human conceptions.
g 536–22 Their narrow limits *b·* their gratifications,

belittles
sp 83–19 this belief *b·* omnipotent wisdom,

belly
ap 559–18 it shall make thy *b·* bitter,— *Rev.* 10 : 9.

belong
s 112– 7 forfeit their claims to *b·* to its school,
123–25 did not specially *b·* to a dispensation now ended,
124–21 They *b·* to divine Principle, and support the
124–29 they *b·* wholly to divine Mind,
130–25 such as they *b·* to the heavenly kingdom.
ph 192–17 Moral and spiritual might *b·* to Spirit,
f 207–24 disease, and death *b·* not to the Science of being.
b 275–15 immortality, cause, and effect *b·* to God.
286–32 and *b·* not to the divine Mind.
287– 2 but *b·*, . . . to the nothingness of error,
p 369–24 preventive and curative) arts *b·* emphatically to
r 472–10 nor *b·* to His government.
476–19 the facts which *b·* to immortal man.

belonged
b 333– 5 *b·* to him in common with other Hebrew

belonging
sp 73–25 the sensations *b·* to the body.
g 529–11 *b·* to no lesser parent.
551–21 all peculiarities of ancestry, *b·* to either sex,

belongs
a 28–25 To suppose that persecution . . . *b·* to the past,
s 144–14 Human will *b·* to the so-called
f 230– 1 If sickness is real, it *b·* to immortality ;
c 258–27 To him *b·* eternal Life.
265–20 even before we discover what *b·* to wisdom
r 475–22 reflects spiritually all that *b·* to his Maker.
490–11 since all power *b·* to God, good.
ap 572–10 *b·* not to His children,

beloved
a 23– 6 That God's wrath should be vented upon His *b·*
36–13 forsaken by all save John, the *b·* disciple,
b 319–32 meaning by that what the *b·* disciple meant
ap 566–15 When Israel, of the Lord *b·*,
576– 9 describing this holy city, the *b·* Disciple writes :

bench
p 430–26 and Judge Medicine is on the *b·*.

beneath
a 36–14 in silent woe *b·* the shadow of his cross.
55–16 gathering *b·* its wings the sick and sinning.
b 280–11 would compress Mind, which is infinite, *b·* a
281–18 supposed to exist in matter or *b·* a skull bone
313–24 He plunged *b·* the material surface of things,
t 451–17 they come from above, not from *b·*,
g 516–13 The grass *b·* our feet silently exclaims,
520–28 creating thought is from above, not from *b·*.
523–11 In error everything comes from *b·*,
539–18 to grovel *b·* all the beasts of the field.

benediction
a 44– 2 laid aside for a crown, the *b·* follow,
48–11 fell in holy *b·* on the grass of Gethsemane,
s 132–10 In other words, he gave his *b·* to
137–22 This assertion elicited from Jesus the *b·*,

benedictions
b 317–11 blessed *b·* rest upon Jesus' followers :

benefactions
pr 3–22 for a liberal outpouring of *b·*.

benefactor
t 450– 8 they never fail to stab their *b·* in the back.

beneficent
s 128–20 An odor becomes *b·* and agreeable
p 394–31 till they feel its *b·* influence.

beneficial
pr 12– 5 The *b·* effect of such prayer for the sick
s 156– 3 what made them . . . *b·* or injurious?
p 367–27 increase the *b·* effects of Christianity.

beneficially
p 397– 2 acting *b·* or injuriously on the health,

benefit
any lasting
pr 7–10 But does it produce any lasting *b·*?
any seeming
an 101–31 Any seeming *b·* derived from it is
great
ap 570–27 the great *b·* which Mind has wrought.
to man
r 471–22 Are doctrines and creeds a *b·* to man?

pr 2– 2 or to *b·* those who hear us,
11– 6 this may be no moral *b·* to the criminal,
s 151–12 enlarged power it confers to *b·* the race
ph 185–26 may seem for a time to *b·* the sick,
f 238– 3 wait till those whom you would *b·* are ready
p 392–12 Whatever *b·* is produced on the body,
395–16 Prayers, in which . . . do not *b·* the sick.
t 447– 5 except it be to *b·* them.
449–10 than for you to *b·* yourself by injuring others.
ap 567–20 either to *b·* or to injure men

benefited
pr 2– 4 Are we *b·* by praying?
b 324–30 if . . . you cannot be *b·* by what I say.
p 375–14 No person is *b·* by yielding his
t 443–15 and think they can be *b·* by
463–32 said to the author, "The world is *b·* by you,

benefiting
ap 571–10 for the sake of doing right and *b·* our race.

benefits
s 149–28 Whatever guides thought spiritually *b·*
f 238–17 when we attempt to claim the *b·* of
245– 2 *b·* of destroying that illusion, are illustrated
p 372–31 prevents the honest recognition of *b·* received,

benevolence
m 58–15 With additional joys, *b·* should grow more
p 433–21 guilty of *b·* in the first degree,

benighted
pref vii– 7 would make plain to *b·* understanding

benign
p 365– 7 The *b·* thought of Jesus,
440–34 the Chief Justice . . . with *b·* and imposing

Benjamin
gl 582– 4 definition of

Benjamin Franklin
an 100–15 *B· F·* was one of the commissioners.

bereft
p 374–27 body, when *b·* of mortal mind, at first cools,

Berna, Monsieur
an 101–14 facts which had been promised by Monsieur *B·*

beset
a 20–29 sin which doth so easily *b·* us,— *Heb.* 12 : 1.
22–15 If your endeavors are *b·* by fearful odds,
s 152–12 Such errors *b·* every material theory,

besets
p 426–21 destroy the great fear that *b·* mortal existence.

beside
p 414–22 none else *b·* Him."— *Deut.* 4 : 35.
421–17 and that there is none *b·* Him.
435–19 Watching *b·* the couch of pain
g 514–13 *b·* the still waters."— *Psal.* 23 : 2.
ap 578– 7 *b·* the still waters.— *Psal.* 23 : 2.

besides
sp 92–27 a belief in something *b·* God.
s 121–26 *b·* turning daily on its own axis.
ph 181–25 unnecessary to resort to aught *b·*
186–31 Since it must believe in something *b·* itself,
g 548–31 *b·* the ordinary process of generation,

besottedness
b 322–19 cannot make the inebriate leave his *b·*, until

besought
s 158– 2 pagan priests, who *b·* the gods to heal the
p 395–15 but is *b·* to take the patient to Himself,

best
pref viii–15 confers the most health and makes the *b·* men.
pr 10–30 it is not always *b·* for us to receive.
11– 6 at *b·*, it only saves the criminal from
11–32 It is *b·* expressed in thought and in life.
a 52–16 putting to shame and death the *b·* man that
52–19 "man of sorrows" *b·* understood— *Isa.* 53 : 3.

best

sp 81– 7	At the very b· and on its own theories,
s 111–20	for the b· essay on Natural Science,
125– 2	What is now considered the b· condition for
ph 170–15	The b· interpreter of man's needs said :
176–20	while divine Mind is its b· friend.
f 201– 1	The b· sermon ever preached is
c 259– 7	was b· expressed in Christ Jesus,
266–12	to accept what b· promotes your growth.
b 317– 7	Whosoever . . . declares b· the power of C. S.,
o 360–29	the Galilean Prophet, the b· Christian on earth,
p 364– 2	rightfully regarded as the b· man that ever
383– 8	takes the b· care of his body when he
385–10	penalty which our beliefs would attach to our b·
394– 3	is b· of all, for this understanding is
403–22	and this is b· adapted for healing the sick.
416–28	tell them only what is b· for them to know.
420–23	erroneous belief, taken at its b·, is not
439–31	We send our b· detectives to whatever
g 523–15	according to the b· scholars, there are
556–16	to him who understands b· the divine Life.

bestial

b 293–22	wind, wave, lightning, fire, b· ferocity

bestow

pr 2–10	nor can the infinite do less than b· all good,
a 25–27	and all the emotional love we can b· on him,
25–31	our Master worked and suffered to b·
36–23	as for this world to b· on the righteous their
48–15	Truth and Love b· few palms until
f 202– 7	half the faith they b· upon the so-called pains
t 455–23	does not b· His highest trusts upon the

bestowals

pr 13– 3	universal in its adaptation and b·.

bestowed

a 42–22	glory which God b· on His anointed,
55– 7	than the later centuries have b· upon
ph 200– 6	capacities of being b· by immortal Mind.
p 387–28	protecting power b· on man by
393–14	the ability and power divinely b· on man.
g 533– 3	This had never been b· on Adam.
541– 9	the homage b· through a gentle animal

bestows

pr 6– 6	God is not separate from the wisdom He b·.
11–17	Truth b· no pardon upon error,
14–19	Hence the hope of the promise Jesus b· :
b 275–19	no good is, but the good God b·.
r 488–22	apart from what belief b· upon them,
g 555–26	when we admit . . . that God b· the power to
ap 573– 8	that consciousness which God b·,

Bethlehem

pref vii– 6	the B· babe, the human herald of

betoken

sp 82–27	different awakenings b· a differing

betray

c 266–13	Friends will b· and enemies will slander,
g 542– 8	Truth causes sin to b· itself, and

betrayal

a 33– 4	anticipating the hour of their Master's b·,
47–11	hatred towards that just man effected his b·
47–23	and so he plotted the b· of Jesus
sp 94–19	evoked denial, ingratitude, and b·,

betrayed

p 439–25	You b· Mortal Man, meanwhile declaring

betrayer

a 43–14	the treason and suicide of his b·,
47–19	placed a gulf between Jesus and his b·,

betraying

p 436– 3	After b· him into the hands of your law,

betrays

ph 192–25	b· its weakness and falls, never to rise.
t 456–16	dishonesty in your theory and practice b· a
r 485– 6	which ever b· mortals into sickness, sin, and
ap 560–30	b· at once a greater ignorance

better

pr 2– 2	Do we pray to make ourselves b·
4–18	but the longing to be b· and holier,
5–26	and that man is made b· merely by
7–20	a higher experience and a b· life
9– 6	Do we love our neighbor b· because of this
9– 9	prayed for something b·, though we give no
a 21– 4	can finally say, . . . because you are a b· man.
25–16	Jesus presented the ideal of God b· than
34–19	and understood b· what the Master had taught.
47– 6	they became b· healers, leaning no longer on
47–23	world generally loves a lie b· than Truth ;
m 57–17	should never weigh against the b· claims of
61–12	b· balanced minds, and sounder constitutions.
63– 2	would never think that flannel was b· for
66–22	It is b· to await the logic of events
66–25	If one is b· than the other, as must always
sp 91–23	that the spiritual facts may be b· apprehended.

better

sp 94–25	this insight b· enabled him to direct
s 114–18	if a b· word or phrase could be suggested, it
136–29	apprehended their Master b· than did others ;
154–25	her affections need b· guidance,
154–31	The b· and more successful method
155–32	is it safe to say that the less . . . the b·?
157–32	Mankind is the b· for this spiritual and
ph 168–31	which will be b· understood hereafter,
175– 5	there will be b· constitutions and less disease.
186–29, 30	If mortal mind knew how to be b·, it would be b·.
194– 7	and determines a case for b· or for worse.
196– 6	B· the suffering which awakens
198–12	It is b· to prevent disease from forming
f 210–16	a b· understanding of Soul and salvation.
220– 8	than his misguided reason,
220–27	belief that either fasting or feasting makes men b·
222– 1	as we b· apprehend our spiritual existence
224– 5	we shall b· understand the Science
235– 4	B· suffer a doctor infected with smallpox to
239– 9	and we get b· views of humanity.
c 258– 5	unsatisfied human craving for something b·,
260–16	and to bring out b· and higher results,
b 285–21	the b· understanding that Science gives
286– 8	is b· than all burnt offerings.
295–22	become a b· transparency for Truth.
297–26	Some thoughts are b· than others.
297–26	belief in Truth is b· than a belief in error,
315– 5	His b· understanding of God was a rebuke to
323–24	contemplation of something b· than disease or
333–14	but Christ Jesus b· signifies the Godlike.
o 355– 6	proofs are b· than mere verbal arguments
p 367– 5	b· than hecatombs of gushing theories,
370– 1	To be . . . whole, man must be b· spiritually
375– 9	proves this when his patient says, "I am b·,"
377– 7	they come back no b· than when they went
383–25	Does his assertion prove . . . man to be the b·
389–11	the b· results of Mind's opposite evidence.
394– 1	to be hopeful is still b·?
394–19	their denials are b· than their affirmations.
397–31	understand yourself and your Maker b·
401–28	it is b· for Christian Scientists to leave
402–27	their belief is not b· instructed by
404–32	unless it makes him b· mentally,
405–22	b· to be exposed to every plague on earth than
407–18	he will get the b· of that desire,
420–21	b· than any drug, alterative, or tonic.
425–23	Consciousness constructs a b· body when
429– 6	and the sooner we begin the b·.
438– 1	was b· authority than Blackstone :
442–21	changes a belief of sin or . . . into a b· belief,
t 452–15	B· is the frugal intellectual repast
r 466–30	making mankind b· physically, morally, and
473–23	a b· understanding of God
485–16	come naturally into Spirit through b· health
486–17	If . . . then death is not an enemy but a b·
489– 1	less mind there is manifested in matter the b·.
g 537–31	lest man should improve it and become b· ;
553– 7	Mortal thought must obtain a b· basis,
554–21	Jesus defined this . . . b· than we can,
557–15	the less a mortal knows of sin, . . . the b·
ap 560–25	all who have spoken something new and b·
571– 6	Because people like you b· when you
gl 583– 2	whose b· originals are God's thoughts,
596– 5	makes Him b· known as the All-in-all,

between

pr 16– 5	distinguishes b· Truth that is sinless and
a 22– 3	b· sin and the hope of forgiveness,
23–16	swinging b· nothing and something,
30–10	mediator, or way-shower, b· God and
30–23	difference b· the offspring of Soul and
34–29	contrast b· our Lord's last supper and
36–16	distance b· Christianity and sensualism
47–17	distance b· Judas and his Master.
47–19	a gulf b· Jesus and his betrayer,
53–21	distance b· the individual and Truth.
m 57–12	The attraction b· native qualities will
63–12	establishes very unfair differences b·
sp 73–32	b· so-called material existence and
74–13	b· persons in such opposite dreams
75–28	the link b· their opposite beliefs
81– 2	b· the so-called dead and the living,
82–23	Communion b· them and ourselves would
82–26	b· a mole and a human being.
83–22	B· C. S. and all forms of
83–24	impassable as that b· Dives and Lazarus.
an 100– 8	"There exists a mutual influence b· the
s 110–32	No analogy exists b· the vague hypotheses
126–15	b· C. S. on the one hand and
141– 1	This indicates the distance b· the
143–14	Driven to choose b· two difficulties,
145– 9	not b· material methods, but b·
145–28	the warfare b· Spirit and the flesh
ph 171–23	No more sympathy exists b· the flesh and

between

ph 171–24	than *b·* Belial and Christ.
173– 2	*b·* humanity and the brute,
193–15	It was *b·* three and four o'clock
f 202– 3	unity which exists *b·* God and man
236–30	While age is halting *b·* two opinions
240–31	how to divide *b·* sense and Soul.
244– 8	is seen *b·* the cradle and the grave,
246– 2	swinging *b·* evil and good,
254– 7	not until the battle *b·* Spirit and flesh is
b 273–12	the enmity *b·* Science and the senses,
288– 3	suppositional warfare *b·* truth and error
288– 4	the mental conflict *b·* the evidence of
288– 6	this warfare *b·* the Spirit and flesh
288–11	the conflict *b·* truth and error,
293– 5	forms no link *b·* matter and Mind,
294–19	*b·* immortal man, representing Spirit, and
298–16	This human belief, alternating *b·* a
312–27	divides faith and understanding *b·*
315–31	the mediator *b·* Spirit and the flesh,
315–32	*b·* Truth and error.
316–13	warfare *b·* this spiritual idea and
316–14	*b·* spiritual clear-sightedness and
332–16	one mediator *b·* God and men, — *I Tim.* 2 : 5.
333– 1	*b·* God and man in His image.
338–24	would impose *b·* man and his creator.
o 345–21	incongruity *b·* God's idea and
345–24	*b·* God's man, made in His image, and
356–18	*b·* error and Truth, *b·* flesh and Spirit.
360–20	swinging *b·* the real and the unreal.
p 389–25	*b·* pain and pleasure, good and evil,
403– 2	*b·* voluntary and involuntary mesmerism
t 444–26	*b·* me and thee, and *b·* my herdmen — *Gen.* 13 : 8.
457–14	led to a quarrel *b·* two knights
462–10	dividing his interests *b·* God and
g 505–21	line of demarcation *b·* the real and
506– 2	*b·* the false and the true.
523–10	which God erects *b·* the true and false.
534– 9	put enmity *b·* thee and— *Gen.* 3 : 15.
534–10	*b·* thy seed and her seed ;— *Gen.* 3 : 15.
534–14	Apostle Paul explains this warfare *b·* the
538– 8	distance *b·* Truth and error,
538– 9	*b·* the material and spiritual,
ap 567–12	conflict *b·* the flesh and Spirit.
gl 586–16	*b·* Truth and error, *b·* Spirit and

beware

s 117–29	Jesus bade his disciples *b·* of the
ph 196–14	The command was a warning to *b·*, not of Rome,
p 382–11	*b·* of making clean merely the outside of

beyond

pr 13– 5	In public prayer we often go *b·* our
13– 6	*b·* the honest standpoint of fervent desire.
27– 2	was intended to prove *b·* a question
41– 1	hope must be cast *b·* the veil of matter
41– 3	this advance *b·* matter must come
44–22	It was a method of surgery *b·* material art,
46–24	and progressive state *b·* the grave.
a 50–26	was terrible *b·* human conception.
m 67–23	Grace and Truth are potent *b·* all
sp 98 15	*B·* the frail premises of human beliefs,
s 116–18	matter is nothing *b·* an image in mortal mind.
125– 7	Neither . . . nor overaction is *b·* God's control ;
126–19	*b·* the cognizance of the material senses
127– 8	there can be nothing *b·* illimitable divinity.
151– 6	has an absolute need of something *b·* itself
156–29	the next stately step *b·* homœopathy.
ph 177– 4	I have demonstrated this *b·* all cavil.
187–10	it attributes to . . . an ability *b·* itself.
194–19	It proves *b·* a doubt that education
f 213–22	He was a musician *b·* what the world knew.
241–23	One's aim, a point *b·* faith, should be
c 264– 7	Mortals must look *b·* fading, finite forms,
b 284–25	*b·* the cognizance of these senses,
298–18	never reaches *b·* the boundary of the
302–16	is always *b·* and above the mortal illusion
306– 6	and demonstrated this *b·* cavil.
312–24	which cannot penetrate *b·* matter.
328–32	reaching *b·* the pale of a single period
p 388–26	it would be foolish to venture *b·* our
394–10	admission that any bodily condition is *b·* the
409–30	and expect to find *b·* the grave
413– 5	A single requirement, *b·* what is necessary
426–25	would raise the standard of health . . . far *b·* its
429– 9	we look *b·* a single step in the line of
g 512– 1	aspirations soaring *b·* and above corporeality
514– 4	nothing exists *b·* the range of

bias

p 381– 3	the *b·* of education enforces this slavery.

Bible

pref viii–30	the *B·* was her sole teacher ;
pr 16–12	some doubt among *B·* scholars, whether the
a 24– 8	make the *B·* the chart of life,
39–13	The *B·* calls death an enemy,

Bible

m 58–32	"She that is married . . . says the *B·* ;" — *I Cor.* 7 : 34.
sp 99– 5	is what the *B·* demands.
an 104–10	First, people say it conflicts with the *B·*.
s 110–14	the *B·* was my only textbook.
126–29	The *B·* has been my only authority.
131–11	The central fact of the *B·* is the
140– 5	The *B·* represents Him as saying :
141–20	The *B·* declares that all believers are
146–23	derives its sanction from the *B·*,
161– 7	nullify the . . . flames, as in the *B·* case of
f 241–13	The *B·* teaches transformation of the
242–21	According to the *B·*, the facts of being
c 263–17	He might say in *B·* language :
b 319–22	the original language of the *B·*
319–24	the spiritual meaning of the *B·*,
320– 4	Metaphors abound in the *B·*,
328–18	Our missionaries carry the *B·* to India,
335–10	as the *B·* declares, without the Logos, the
o 342– 9	in the face of *B·* history and in defiance
344–32	In the *B·* the word *Spirit* is so commonly
p 406– 1	The *B·* contains the recipe for all healing.
435–29	To him I might say, in *B·* language,
437–33	read from the supreme statute-book, the *B·*,
438– 1	remarking that the *B·* was better authority
441– 3	explained from his statute-book, the *B·*,
r 480–26	The *B·* declares : "All things were — *John* 1 : 3.
497– 4	we take the inspired Word of the *B·* as our
g 537–22	Subsequent *B·* revelation is coordinate with
546–22	for they contain the deep divinity of the *B·*.
ap 572– 4	both the first and last books of the *B·*,
577–31	the acme of this Science as the *B·* reveals it.
gl 579– 5	the metaphysical interpretation of *B·* terms,

biblical

g 526–24	This second *b·* account is a

bicuspids

f 247– 6	incisors, cuspids, *b·*, and one molar.

bid

p 363–14	the woman's immoral status and *b·* her depart,
394–20	Will you *b·* a man let evils overcome him,

bidden

s 130– 4	When all men are *b·* to the feast,
160–18	or has it *b·* them to be impotent?
b 307–28	nor *b·* to obey material laws which

bidding

b 321–14	The serpent, evil, under wisdom's *b·*, was

bids

pr 5– 8	Temptation *b·* us repeat the offence,
a 29– 8	It *b·* us work the more earnestly in times of

big

pref vii– 2	to-day is *b·* with blessings.

bigot

a 52–30	The *b·*, the debauchee, the hypocrite,

bigoted

a 48– 2	staves of *b·* ignorance smote him sorely.
p 366–21	swallow the camels of *b·* pedantry.

bigotry

t 450– 1	whose *b·* and conceit twist every fact
464–23	weapons of *b·*, ignorance, envy, fall
r 484– 3	neither pride, prejudice, *b·*, nor envy, can
gl 597–13	tore from *b·* and superstition their coverings,

Bill of Rights

s 161–14	harmony with our Constitution and *B· of R·*,

billows

f 240– 4	giant hills, winged winds, mighty *b·*,

bind

a 44–16	*b·* up the wounded side and lacerated feet,
f 229–16	to *b·* mortals to sickness, sin, and death.
p 366–31	we must first learn to *b·* up the broken-hearted.
372–12	*b·* himself with his own beliefs,
399–31	first *b·* the strong man?" — *Matt.* 12 : 29.

binds

sp 96– 2	unwillingness . . . *b·* Christendom with chains.
f 225– 1	What is it that *b·* man with iron shackles
ap 575–31	which *b·* human society into solemn union ;

biographical

pref viii–25	*b·* sketch, narrating experiences which

bird

s 121–11	*b·* and blossom were glad in God's . . . sunshine,
c 261–28	even as the *b·* which has burst from the egg
g 550–26	A serpent never begets a *b·*,
551– 7	the *b·* is not the product of a beast.
552– 1	question, Which is first, the egg or the *b·* ?

birth

any

f 206–25	Can there be any *b·* or death for man,

as untimely

c 265–16	senses represent *b·* as untimely

birth

before
p 429–22   If . . . we must have lived before b˙,
human
ph 190–14   Human b˙, growth, maturity, and decay
new
t 463–17   When this new b˙ takes place,
g 548–15   This is the new b˙ going on hourly,
origin and
a 30–11   Had his origin and b˙ been wholly apart
prior to his
ph 178–14   produced prior to his b˙ by the fright
spiritual
t 463–12   this idea . . . in the travail of spiritual b˙.
time-tables of
f 246–18   Time-tables of b˙ and death are

ph 185–13   They have their b˙ in mortal mind,
191–12   even to the b˙ of a new-old idea,
f 244–13   Man undergoing b˙, maturity, and decay
244–24   He has neither b˙ nor death.
b 288–25   spiritual real man has no b˙,
302–11   the b˙, sin, sickness, and death of
305–28   not subject to b˙, growth, maturity, decay.
t 463– 7   To attend properly the b˙ of the new child,
463– 9   that the b˙ will be natural and safe.
g 529– 5   instruments . . . assist the b˙ of mortals.
539–31   Science of creation, so conspicuous in the b˙ of
544– 7   B˙, decay, and death arise from the
548–20   statements now current, about b˙ and
549–14   not begin with the b˙ of new individuals,
550–18   as beginning and ending, and with b˙, decay,
ap 562–23   travailing in b˙, and— Rev. 12 : 2.
562–27   joy that the b˙ goes on ;

birthright

f 226–20   man's b˙ of sole allegiance to his Maker
g 518– 1   His b˙ is dominion, not subjection.

birth-throes

g 557– 6   Mind controls the b˙ in the lower realms

bit

f 222–25   if eating a b˙ of animal flesh could
237– 6   "Mamma, my finger is not a b˙ sore."

bite

g 534–27   The serpent, material sense, will b˙ the heel
ap 563–20   that he may b˙ the heel of truth

bites

f 216– 7   Error b˙ the heel of truth, but cannot kill

bitter

a 32–12   The cup shows forth his b˙ experience,
b 287–13   sweet water and b˙?"— Jas. 3 : 11.
t 455–30   cannot send forth both sweet waters and b˙.
r 489–23   fountain sendeth not forth sweet waters and b˙.
ap 518– 8   and it shall make thy belly b˙, — Rev. 10 : 9.
559–23   murmur not . . . if you find its digestion b˙,
559–28   share the hemlock cup and eat the b˙ herbs ;

bitterness

a 43–22   because of the cup of b˙ he drank.
54–21   His earthly cup of b˙ was drained
s 139–13   wisely to stem the tide of sectarian b˙,

black

ph 195– 5   All that he ate, except his b˙ crust,
r 479–27   We admit that b˙ is not a color,

blackboard

pr 3– 4   Who would stand before a b˙, and
t 453– 2   among the examples on the b˙,

blackness

b 307–31   Above error's awful din, b˙, and chaos,

blacksmith's

ph 198–29   Because the muscles of the b˙ arm
199–13   but by reason of the b˙ faith in

Blackstone

p 438– 2   the Bible was better authority than B˙ :

blade

sp 70–12   from a b˙ of grass to a star,
ph 191–21   By its own volition, not a b˙ of grass springs

blades

ph 190–15   grass . . . with beautiful green b˙,

blameworthy

p 414–30   whereas imperfection is b˙,

blanches

p 433–14   His sallow face b˙ with fear,

blandly

t 450– 7   while looking you b˙ in the face,

blank

c 266– 7   Would existence . . . be to you a b˙?

blanket

ph 179–17   that he will take cold without his b˙,

blasphemer

sp 94–27   what would be said . . . of an infidel b˙

blasphemes

sp 88–23   Excite the opposite development, and he b˙.

blasphemies

an 100– *   thefts, false witness, b˙ :— Matt. 15 : 19.

blast

t 451–32   malpractice tends to b˙ moral sense,

blasts

m 57–25   The wintry b˙ of earth may uproot the
f 220–12   snowbird sings and soars amid the b˙ ;

blaze

b 296–15   and they must go out under the b˙ of Truth,

blazons

f 247–26   b˙ the night with starry gems,

bleeding

pr 10– 2   even though with b˙ footsteps,
a 41– 9   though it be with b˙ footprints,
p 379–10   fancied himself b˙ to death,
379–13   Had he known his sense of b˙ was an

blend

m 58– 7   they should be concordant in order to b˙
59–13   their sympathies should b˙ in sweet confidence
sp 74–23   different beliefs, which never b˙.
gl 588–14   numbers which never b˙ with each other,

blending

b 308–11   a b˙ of false claims, false pleasure,
316–22   Christ illustrates that b˙ with God,
g 552–25   b˙ tints of leaf and flower show the

blends

c 263– 7   When mortal man b˙ his thoughts of

bless

pr 9–12   and b˙ them that curse us ;
13–17   God will b˙ it, and we shall incur less
a 30–29   Only in this way can we b˙ our enemies,
50–11   to sustain and b˙ so faithful a son.
m 60–29   infinite resources with which to b˙ mankind,
c 263–14   injuring those whom he would b˙.
p 397– 7   actually injuring those whom we mean to b˙.
t 453–19   You uncover sin, . . . in order to b˙ the

blessed

pr 2– 6   is b˙ of our Father,
32–15   Jesus took bread, and b˙ it— Matt. 26 : 26.
36– 2   in the b˙ company of Truth and Love
40–31   nature of Christianity is peaceful and b˙,
49–18   Forsaken by all whom he had b˙,
s 132– 9   And b˙ is he, whosoever— Matt. 11 : 6.
137–22   "B˙ art thou, Simon Bar-jona :— Matt. 16 : 17.
c 267–28   "B˙ is the man that endureth— Jas. 1 : 12.
b 317–11   b˙ benedictions rest upon Jesus' followers :
324– 5   "B˙ are the pure in heart :— Matt. 5 : 8.
338–29   notwithstanding God had b˙ the earth
338–31   not the ideal man for whom the earth was b˙.
o 341– 9   "B˙ are the pure in heart :— Matt. 5 : 8.
g 512–17   And God b˙ them, saying,— Gen. 1 : 22.
517–25   And God b˙ them, and— Gen. 1 : 28.
518–17   b˙ is that man who seeth his brother's need
532–10   Adam and his progeny were cursed, not b˙ ;
537–28   b˙ the earth and gave it to man
548–25   would have b˙ the human race more
ap 558– *   B˙ is he that readeth, and— Rev. 1 : 3.
571– 8   requires the spirit of our b˙ Master
573–18   but as the b˙ child of God.

blessedness

pr 2–30   the source of all existence and b˙.
10–25   the source and means of all goodness and b˙,
c 264–25   Spiritual living and b˙ are the only
b 329–27   their real spiritual source to be all b˙,

blesses

pr 8–23   the reward of Him who b˙ the poor.
a 30–18   which b˙ even those that curse it.
33–23   It b˙ its enemies, heals the sick,
sp 78–28   Spirit b˙ man, but man
an 103– 8   b˙ the whole human family.
f 206–16   we find that whatever b˙ one b˙ all,
234– 5   b˙ the human family with crumbs of comfort
g 507– 6   Spirit names and b˙ all.
512–20   Spirit b˙ the multiplication of its own
516–19   beautifies the landscape, b˙ the earth.
517–30   Divine Love b˙ its own ideas,

blessing

pr 3–10   in order to receive His b˙,
a 20–17   returning b˙ for cursing, he taught mortals
50–17   be shorn of its mighty b˙ for the human race.
f 238– 3   wait till those . . . are ready for the b˙,
r 488– 6   you receive the b˙ of Truth.
g 545–20   yet this opposite, . . . impudently demands a b˙.
ap 570–23   Those ready for the b˙ you impart
gl 589–21   pure affection b˙ its enemies.

blessings
all
  pr 3–28   yet return thanks to God for all *b·*,
great
  a 25–30   else we are not improving the great *b·*
infinite
  pr 15–30   and they assuredly call down infinite *b·*.
  b 325– 8   which results in infinite *b·* to mortals.
our
  pr 3–32   put the finger on the lips and remember our *b·*.
spiritual
  a 53–17   spiritual *b·* which might flow from such
  g 512–15   spiritual *b·*, thus typified, are the

  pref vii– 2   to-day is big with *b·*.
  pr 3–24   shall avail ourselves of the *b·* we have,
     4–14   are made manifest in the *b·* they bring,
     4–14   *b·* which, even if not acknowledged in
     10–23   we do not always receive the *b·* we ask for
  c 266–16   the foregoing prophecy and its *b·*.
  o 343–11   and the blind look up to C. S. with *b·*,
  r 489–16   channel to man of divine *b·*
  gl 597– 7   long petitions for *b·* upon material methods,

blest
  iii– *   And I am *b·* !
  m 57–31   Marriage is unblest or *b·*, according to

blight
  f 246–31   rather than into age and *b·*.

blighted
  sp 77–29   a state resembling that of *b·* buds,
     78– 1   The decaying flower, the *b·* bud,

blighting
  f 236–22   *b·* the buddings of self-government.

blind
  pref xi–20   And recovering of sight to the *b·*,— *Luke* 4 : 18.
  pr 12– 7   through a *b·* faith in God.
     13–30   *b·* to the reality of man's existence,
  a 23–28   expresses the helplessness of a *b·* faith ;
     27– 4   how that the *b·* see,— *Luke* 7 : 22.
  s 124–11   In a word, human belief is a *b·* conclusion
     132– 6   the *b·* receive their sight.— *Matt.* 11 : 5.
  ph 167– 4   If we rise no higher than *b·* faith,
     183–28   the law which gives sight to the *b·*,
     192–11   a *b·* miscalled force, the offspring of will
     194–12   if mortal mind says, "I am deaf and *b·*,"
     196– 2   It is but a *b·* force.
  f 210–13   gave sight to the *b·*, hearing to the deaf,
     223–18   "If the *b·* lead the *b·*,— *Matt.* 15 : 14.
     226–25   The lame, the deaf, the dumb, the *b·*,
  b 316–31   *b·* to the possibilities of Spirit
     324–21   was made *b·*, and his blindness was felt ;
     337– 7   *b·* mortals do lose sight of spiritual
  o 342–25   the lame to walk, and the *b·* to see.
     343–11   The sick, the halt, and the *b·* look up to C. S.
     350–15   Unless the works are . . . the words are *b·*.
  p 391– 7   Instead of *b·* and calm submission
     398–27   a *b·* faith removes bodily ailments for a season,
     439–18   the *b·* Hypnotism, and the masked
  t 444– 2   these very failures may open their *b·* eyes
     450–17   putting a sharp knife into the hands of a *b·* man
  r 487–11   apprehension of this gave sight to the *b·*
     490– 8   Will— *b·*, stubborn, and headlong
  g 536–19   The *b·* leading the *b·*, both would fall.
  gl 582– 2   not a faltering nor a *b·* faith,
     599– 5   *B·* enthusiasm ; mortal will.
  (*see also* **belief**)

blinded
  f 223–17   but more are *b·* by their old illusions,

blindly
  b 305–32   not so *b·* as the Pharisees,
  p 377–18   that it may not produce *b·* its bad effects.

blindness
mortal
  p 374–13   This mortal *b·* and its sharp consequences
pagan
  ph 187– 8   With pagan *b·*, it attributes to

  ph 194–11   not necessary to ensure deafness and *b·* ;
  f 205– 5   all because of their *b·*,
  c 263–30   A sensual thought, . . . is dense *b·*
  b 316–15   between spiritual clear-sightedness and the *b·*
     324–22   Paul was made blind, and his *b·* was felt ;
  t 448– 2   *B·* and self-righteousness cling fast to
     448–15   upon your *b·* to evil or upon the
  r 486–18   Alas for the *b·* of belief, which
     486–29   then palsy, *b·*, and deafness would
     487–22   Mere belief is *b·* without Principle

bliss
all
  f 253– 5   include and impart all *b·*,
attain the
  c 262–22   and attain the *b·* of loving unselfishly,

bliss
boundless
  r 481– 4   freedom, harmony, and boundless *b·*.
eternal
  ap 577–10   there is no impediment to eternal *b·*,
spiritual
  gl 582–15   a sense of Soul, which has spiritual *b·*

  a 36– 2   never find *b·* . . . simply through translation
     39–12   out of mortality into immortality and *b·*.
  ph 175–32   "Where ignorance is *b·*, 't is folly to be wise,"
  f 203–25   not a stepping-stone to Life, immortality, and *b·*.
  b 328– 1   the grandeur and *b·* of a spiritual sense,
     337– 7   Sensualism is not *b·*, but bondage.
  ap 574–15   the spiritual outpouring of *b·* and glory,
  gl 587–26   spirituality ; *b·*; the atmosphere of Soul.

blister
  ph 198–17   by a counter-irritant,— perhaps by a *b·*,

Blondin
  ph 199–25   Had *B·* believed it impossible to walk the rope

blood
all the
  p 376–14   than in all the *b·* which ever flowed through
and nerves
  s 160–19   Can muscles, bones, *b·*, and nerves rebel
bayonet and
  f 226–12   won, . . . not with bayonet and *b·*,
brother's
  g 541–28   The voice of thy brother's *b·*— *Gen.* 4 : 10.
consumption of the
  p 376–11   with consumption of the *b·*,
drink his
  a 25–11   they truly eat his flesh and drink his *b·*,
essence of
  a 25– 3   The spiritual essence of *b·* is sacrifice.
flesh and
  a 25–10   His true flesh and *b·* were his Life ;
  s 137–23   flesh and *b·* hath not revealed it— *Matt.* 16 : 17.
  b 321– 4   "Flesh and *b·* cannot inherit the— *I Cor.* 15 : 50.
  r 478–29   conferred not with flesh and *b·*."— *Gal.* 1 : 16.
her
  p 379–15   inspecting the hue of her *b·*
     379–21   not dying on account of the state of her *b·*,
his
  a 30–16   by man shall his *b·* be shed."— *Gen.* 9 : 0.
  p 379–18   when not a drop of his *b·* was shed.
human
  a 25– 6   than can be expressed by our sense of human *b·*.
humor in the
  p 424–32   may tell you that he has a humor in the *b·*,
man's
  a 30–15   "Whoso sheddeth man's *b·*,— *Gen.* 9 : 6.
material
  a 25– 6   The material *b·* of Jesus was no more efficacious
of the Lamb
  ap 568–18   by the *b·* of the Lamb,— *Rev.* 12 : 11.
of the martyrs
  a 37– 5   "The *b·* of the martyrs is the seed of
passage of the
  ph 187–14   opening and closing for the passage of the *b·*,
rushes madly
  p 373–27   When the *b·* rushes madly through the veins
shared the
  a 33–28   Have you shared the *b·* of the New Covenant,
went down in
  f 225–20   but oppression neither went down in *b·*,

  s 143–19   but you conclude that the stomach, *b·*,
     151–19   *b·*, heart, . . . have nothing to do with Life,
  ph 172–23   Brain, heart, *b·*, . . . the material structure?
     172–32   (heart, *b·*, brain, acting through the
  f 220–31   controls the stomach, bones, lungs, heart, *b·*,
  b 308–10   the head, heart, stomach, *b·*, nerves,
  p 372– 8   can form *b·*, flesh, and bones.
     376–11   should be told that *b·* never gave life
     379–21   her belief that *b·* is destroying her life.
     408–20   does not distribute drugs through the *b·*,
  r 475– 7   brain, *b·*, bones, and other material elements.

bloodshed
  sp 94–14   Tyranny, intolerance, and *b·*, wherever found,
  s 139–10   Reforms have commonly been attended with *b·*

blossom
  m 62–23   The divine Mind, which forms the bud and *b·*,
  s 121–11   bird and *b·* were glad
  g 518–21   as the *b·* shines through the bud.
  gl 596–27   maketh the valley to bud and *b·* as the rose.

blot
  p 391– 3   *B·* out the images of mortal thought

blots
  p 437– 6   It *b·* the fair escutcheon of omnipotence.

blow

sp 97–10 the flight of one and the *b·* of the other
f 201–15 Then, when the winds of God *b·*,
g 535–10 Divine Science deals its chief *b·* at

bloweth

gl 598– 3 *b·* where it listeth. — *John* 3 : 8.

blue

f 220– 9 violet lifts her *b·* eye to greet the early spring.

blunder

s 123– 5 Ptolemaic *b·* could not affect the harmony of
g 549– 7 a *b·* which will finally give place to

blundering

p 386–16 A *b·* despatch, mistakenly announcing

blunders

f 230–19 Does wisdom make *b·*

bluntly

pref x–12 *b·* and honestly given the text of Truth.

blush

sp 92–25 We should *b·* to call that real which

Board of Health

p 432–22 by the officer of the *B· of H·*,
432–28 with a message from the *B· of H·*

boast

t 450–18 evil will *b·* itself above good.

bodies

animal
an 100– 9 Animal *b·* are susceptible to the influence of
celestial
an 100– 9 celestial *b·*, the earth, and animated things.
s 123– 1 theory as to the relations of the celestial *b·*,
f 209–20 and revolutions of the celestial *b·*,
g 509–13 creates no other than heavenly or celestial *b·*,
material
sp 73–19 The belief that material *b·* return to dust,
minds and
s 110–26 power of C. S. to heal mortal minds and *b·*.
f 210–15 action of . . . Mind on human minds and *b·*
p 408–13 effects of illusion on mortal minds and *b·*.
mortal
sp 92– 8 decomposition of mortal *b·* in what is termed
o 341– * *shall also quicken your mortal b· — Rom.* 8 : 11.
organic
sp 74– 4 must be free from organic *b·* ;
our
c 261–31 We should forget our *b·* in remembering good
our own
p 402–22 we rarely remember that we govern our own *b·*.
spiritual
sp 73–20 belief that . . . rise up as spiritual *b·*
terrestrial
s 123– 3 the greater error as to our terrestrial *b·*.
their
sp 90–21 yet their *b·* stay in one place.
p 396–23 which their beliefs exercise over their *b·*.
409–15 knowing how to govern their *b·*.
416–31 Turn their thoughts away from their *b·*
their own
ph 199–15 Mortals develop their own *b·*
f 228–16 Then they will control their own *b·*
these
g 551–18 transmitted through these *b·* called eggs,
unseen
p 429–17 with *b·* unseen by those who think that
your
b 325–22 "Present your *b·* a living — *Rom.* 12 : 1.

sp 87–10 Though *b·* are leagues apart
87–22 the *b·* which lie buried in its sands :

bodiless

s 116–22 God is not *corporeal,* but *incorporeal,* . . . *b·*.

bodily

a 43– 2 they did understand it after his *b·* departure.
45–13 Three days after his *b·* burial
50–20 before the evidence of the *b·* senses,
sp 76–24 without a single *b·* pleasure or pain,
80– 5 for the support of *b·* endurance.
s 136– 8 divine power to save men both *b·* and spiritually.
161–24 ordinary practitioner, examining *b·* symptoms,
ph 166–19 thrusting Him aside in times of *b·* trouble,
172– 1 which he has through the *b·* senses,
f 217–10 unnatural mental and *b·* conditions,
219– 3 applies to all *b·* ailments,
228–21 we shall never depend on *b·* conditions,
245–23 The *b·* results of her belief that she was young
c 257– 9 belief in a *b·* soul and a material mind,
b 302–27 not in any *b·* or personal likeness
334–12 Jesus appeared as a *b·* existence.
p 368–20 That Life is not contingent on *b·* conditions
382–32 The ailment was not *b·*, but mental,
387–32 to defend himself, . . . from *b·* suffering.
389– 9 Matter does not inform you of *b·* derangements ;

bodily

p 392– 4 To cure a *b·* ailment, every broken moral law
should
392–26 conclusions as you wish realized in *b·* results,
394–10 The admission that any *b·* condition
397– 9 You cause *b·* sufferings and increase them
398–28 faith removes *b·* ailments for a season,
413–20 I insist on *b·* cleanliness within and without.
416– 1 as if it were a separate *b·* member.
t 448– 5 Evil which obtains in the *b·* senses,

Body

p 432–11 I am Mortality, Governor of the Province of *B·*,
437– 1 Nerve, testified that he was a ruler of *B·*,
438–10 Instead of being a ruler in the Province of *B·*,
439– 7 absent from the Province of *B·*,

body

absent from the
pr 14– 4 are not "absent from the *b·*" — *II Cor.* 5 : 8.
14–22 because the Ego is absent from the *b·*,
f 216–29 to be absent from the *b·*, — *II Cor.* 5 : 8.
p 383–10 to be absent from the *b·*, — *II Cor.* 5 : 8.
gl 581–25 to be absent from the *b·*, — *II Cor.* 5 : 8.
action of the
f 239–25 and produces every discordant action of the *b·*.
affects the
s 149–18 "We know that mind affects the *b·*
f 222– 4 learned that food affects the *b·* only as
p 397– 2 not seeing how mortal mind affects the *b·*,
affect the
p 402–21 and in this way affect the *b·*,
and mind
ph 190– 5 producing mortals, both *b·* and mind ;
b 302– 3 The material *b·* and mind are temporal,
and Soul
r 477–19 *Question.* — What are *b·* and Soul?
apparent on the
p 374–12 before it is consciously apparent on the *b·*,
appearance in the
ph 168–26 made its appearance in the *b·*.
argued that the
p 435– 5 False Belief has argued that the *b·* should
as matter
f 214–31 evident that the *b·* as matter has no sensation
belief that the
f 226–23 in the belief that the *b·* governed them,
believing that the
f 218–15 believing that the *b·* can be sick independently
better
p 425–23 Consciousness constructs a better *b·* when
brain or
p 401–24 produce any effect upon the brain or *b·*
brings to the
s 162– 4 C. S. brings to the *b·* the sunlight of Truth,
buried the
sp 75–19 plane of belief as those who buried the *b·*,
bury the
p 429–18 unseen by those who think that they bury the *b·*.
called man
sp 81–21 give to the worms the *b·* called man,
ph 190–13 and the bulk of a *b·*, called man.
called the
b 313–29 Jesus called the *b·*, which by
cannot believe
r 487–17 The *b·* cannot believe.
cannot be saved
sp 98– 7 *B·* cannot be saved except through Mind.
cannot die
p 426–30 Man is immortal, and the *b·* cannot die,
cannot suffer
p 392–32 then the *b·* cannot suffer from them.
cause the
p 415–27 will apparently cause the *b·* to disappear.
clean
p 383– 3 We need a clean *b·* and a clean mind,
coming from the
p 385–31 coming from the *b·* or from inert matter
complaint from the
p 391–29 contradict every complaint from the *b·*,
concerning the
f 219–15 never affirm concerning the *b·* what we
condition of the
f 217–17 conquered a diseased condition of the *b·* through
p 408–30 that condition of the *b·* which we call sensation
control over the
ph 166– 7 thus the conscious control over the *b·* is lost.
p 406–27 a loss of control over the *b·*.
controls the
p 400– 1 mind, which directly controls the *b·*
control the
sp 93– 2 recognize Soul as . . . able to control the *b·*
p 379– 1 If disease can attack and control the *b·*
conversation about the
c 260–26 by conversation about the *b·*,
corresponds with
p 412–26 until the *b·* corresponds with the

body

corrupt
p 404– 9 A corrupt mind is manifested in a corrupt *b*·.
dead
s 113– 7 the letter is but the dead *b*· of Science,
p 416–21 only in mortal mind, as the dead *b*· proves ;
derangement of the
p 423–28 abnormal condition or derangement of the *b*·
detach sense from the
c 261–21 Detach sense from the *b*·, or matter,
divine
ap 559–25 when you eat the divine *b*· of
dosing the
ph 169–14 and by dosing the *b*· in order to avoid it.
effects on the
o 350–25 known by its effects on the *b*·
p 370–20 very direct and marked effects on the *b*·.
374– 5 Hatred and its effects on the *b*· are removed
effects upon the
ph 176–10 seen in its glorious effects upon the *b*·.
effect upon the
p 398–21 and produces a new effect upon the *b*·.
even in
p 404–31 nor Mind can help him . . . even in *b*·, unless
experiences no pain
c 261–10 the *b*· experiences no pain.
explanation of
ph 200– 9 wise not to undertake the explanation of *b*·.
expose the
p 380– 5 Expose the *b*· to certain temperatures,
feeds the
f 248– 8 Immortal Mind feeds the *b*· with
fettered by the
b 292–10 belief that Mind, . . . can be fettered by the *b*·,
finite
b 309–25 impossible for . . . Soul to be in a finite *b*·
flee from
p 405–31 to flee from *b*· to Spirit,
foe of the
ph 176–20 Mortal mind is the worst foe of the *b*·,
functions of the
p 373–22 expressed . . . in the functions of the *b*·.
governed by the
c 257–10 belief in . . . a soul governed by the *b*·
governing the
p 370– 8 proves that fear is governing the *b*·.
government of the
ph 167–27 scientific government of the *b*· must be attained
182–18 Mind's government of the *b*· must supersede
t 462–30 It urges the government of the *b*·
governs the
s 111–28 Mind governs the *b*·, not partially but wholly.
162–13 the fact that Mind governs the *b*·,
ph 180–14 Ignorant that the human mind governs the *b*·,
govern the
f 251–15 learn how mankind govern the *b*·,
251–18 should learn whether they govern the *b*·
greater than
f 223–12 Soul is Spirit, and Spirit is greater than *b*·.
guillotined
p 427–17 bone is broken or the *b*· guillotined.
had been naked
g 532–28 In the allegory the *b*· had been naked,
healer of the
b 326–15 healer of mortal mind is the healer of the *b*·.
heal the
s 146–14 even the might of Mind — to heal the *b*·
p 399–32 In other words : How can I heal the *b*·, without
his
a 45–26 for they believed his *b*· to be dead.
46–15 his *b*· was not changed until he
53–25 Jesus bore our sins in his *b*·.
sp 75–16 not by an admission that his *b*· had died
75–18 that Lazarus had lived or died in his *b*·,
ph 188–16 the dreamer thinks that his *b*· is material
f 216–17 his *b*· is in submission to everlasting Life
b 290–29 no more spiritual for believing that his *b*· died
290–31 His *b*· is as material as his mind, and *vice versa*.
314–13 When Jesus spoke of reproducing his *b*·,
314–16 their material temple instead of his *b*·,
320–31 if disease and worms destroyed his *b*·, yet
p 383– 8 takes the best care of his *b*· when he
388– 9 when dire inflictions failed to destroy his *b*·.
414– 1 held in the beliefs concerning his *b*·.
416–22 mortal has resigned his *b*· to dust,
r 486–14 his *b*· was the same immediately after death
his own
s 150–28 doctrine . . . then thrust out of his own *b*·
human
m 62–24 will care for the human *b*·, even as it
s 125– 4 now considered . . . health in the human *b*·
t 458–31 trying to sustain the human *b*·
imaged on the
p 379–31 the fever-picture, . . . imaged on the *b*·
improves under
p 370– 5 The *b*· improves under the same regimen

body

indifference to the
f 216– 2 his faith in Soul and his indifference to the *b*·.
influences the
s 143–18 You admit that mind influences the *b*·
inharmonious
ph 166–16 From it arises the inharmonious *b*·.
innocent
p 437–16 the helpless innocent *b*· tortured,
instead of
f 223– 5 illusion that he lives in *b*· instead of in Soul,
b 315– 8 He knew that the Ego was Mind instead of *b*·
p 419–17 Observe mind instead of *b*·,
g 536–15 governed . . . by *b*· instead of by Soul,
intact in
r 492– 1 the dream leaves mortal man intact in *b*·
is affected
p 380–17 *b*· is affected only with the belief of disease
is controlled
pr 14–17 when the *b*· is controlled by spiritual Life,
is devoid
p 399–21 Without this force the *b*· is devoid of action,
is disintegrated
p 429–20 after the *b*· is disintegrated.
is not controlled
s 143–24 *b*· is not controlled scientifically by a
is not first
f 207–15 B· is not first and Soul last,
is the substratum
p 371– 2 The *b*· is the substratum of mortal mind,
its own
ph 196– 5 power of mortal mind over its own *b*·
justice to the
p 434–32 Denying justice to the *b*·,
keeping the
p 413–18 only for the purpose of keeping the *b*· clean.
keep the
p 383–19 mind must be clean to keep the *b*· in proper
leaving a
r 478– 6 has never beheld Spirit or Soul leaving a *b*·
lies listless
f 250–20 To the observer, the *b*· lies listless,
light of the
p 393–25 "the light of the *b*· is the eye," — *Matt.* 6 : 22.
limited
b 284– 7 would seem to spring from a limited *b*· ;
335–18 never . . . in a limited mind or a limited *b*·.
little
p 413 22 need not wash his little *b*· all over each day
look away from the
c 261– 2 Look away from the *b*· into Truth and Love,
lost from the
r 491–24 memory and consciousness are lost from the *b*·,
makes . . . tributary
s 119–31 C. S. . . . makes *b*· tributary to Mind.
making the
u 34– 4 making the *b*· "holy, acceptable — *Rom.* 12 : 1.
manifestation in the
s 154– 8 and its consequent manifestation in the *b*·.
manifest on the
f 219–18 before it can be made manifest on the *b*·,
r 493–22 It is fear made manifest on the *b*·.
man's
f 216–28 When you say, "Man's *b*· is material,"
f 531–15 If, in the beginning, man's *b*· originated in
masters of the
f 228 23 but we shall be masters of the *b*·,
mastery of the
p 406–30 destroyed only by Mind's mastery of the *b*·.
material
(*see* **material**)
Mind and
b 285–13 Spirit and matter, Mind and *b*·,
mind and
s 149–29 benefits mind and *b*·.
151– 1 ignorant that the human mind and *b*· are myths.
157–27 but they leave both mind and *b*· worse
157–29 the entire corporeality, — namely, mind and *b*·,
158–12 truth which heals both mind and *b*·.
ph 169– 1 process which mortal mind and *b*· undergo
177– 8 Mortal mind and *b*· are one.
b 293– 9 This so-called mind and *b*· is the
316–10 manifest . . . upon the human mind and *b*·,
p 383–13 because mind and *b*· rest on the same basis.
388–32 the harmonious functions of mind and *b*·,
405–15 will be executed upon mortal mind and *b*·,
406– 9 healing of mortals, both mind and *b*·.
409– 4 *Mortal mind* and *b*· combine as one,
Mind controls
sp 79–28 asserting that Mind controls *b*· and brain.
mind or
p 365–31 unchristian practitioner is not giving to mind
or *b*·
r 473– 1 inharmony of mortal mind or *b*· is illusion,

body
Mind over
  ph 169–16 understood the control of Mind over *b·*,
  p 380–10 against the control of Mind over *b·*,
mortal
  (*see* **mortal**)
mortality of the
  ph 191–27 infers the mortality of the *b·*.
move the
  a 104–32 human mind must move the *b·* to a wicked act
my
  a 32–17 Take, eat ; this is my *b·*.— *Matt.* 26 : 26
  p 374– 9 until it appeared on my *b·* ?''
  383– 5 One says : "I take good care of my *b·*.''
no heed to the
  p 400–21 giving no heed to the *b·*,
not in
  pr 13–32 not cognizant of life in Soul, not in *b·*.
not in the
  r 467–17 Science reveals Spirit, Soul, as not in the *b·*,
outlined on the
  ph 196–30 which is afterwards outlined on the *b·*.
outline on the
  r 485–25 If thought yields . . . it cannot outline on the *b·*
outside the
  g 510–17 representation of Soul outside the *b·*,
over the
  ph 167–28 to gain control over the *b·*
  194– 9 Truth sends a report of health over the *b·*.
  f 217–26 learn the power of Mind over the *b·*
  218–16 no jurisdiction over the *b·*.
  p 382–27 supporting the power of Mind over the *b·*
  417–29 control which Mind holds over the *b·*.
parted from the
  p 401–22 If the mind were parted from the *b·*,
pass from the
  p 375– 2 Heat would pass from the *b·* as painlessly as
patient's
  s 152–17 to ascertain the temperature of the patient's *b·* ;
physical
  s 124–32 The elements and functions of the physical *b·*
poor
  p 383–30 pinching and pounding the poor *b·*,
portion of the
  p 425–28 or any portion of the *b·*
portions of the
  p 421– 4 belief that other portions of the *b·*
possible for the
  sp 90–12 will be found to be equally possible for the *b·*.
produced on the
  p 392–13 Whatever benefit is produced on the *b·*,
puts the
  p 399– 7 and puts the *b·* through certain motions.
reach the
  ph 170–15 and reach the *b·* through Mind.
reconstruct the
  p 422–19 changes . . . serve to reconstruct the *b·*.
redemption of our
  c 255– * to wit, the redemption of our *b·*.— *Rom.* 8 : 23.
relieve the
  s 157–26 quiet mortal mind, and so relieve the *b·* ;
rendered pure
  p 383– 3 a *b·* rendered pure by Mind
responds
  sp 89–15 the *b·* responds to this belief,
results upon the
  p 384–13 and its results upon the *b·*.
same
  a 45–29 He presented the same *b·* that he had before
says of the
  f 218– 5 what the human mind says of the *b·*,
sees the
  sp 90–17 The looker-on sees the *b·* in bed,
sensationless
  b 280–26 man has a sensationless *b·* ;
senses and the
  b 317–26 testimony of the material senses and the *b·*,
sensibly with the
  pr 14– 1 If we are sensibly with the *b·*
sensuous
  f 203–19 We imagine that Mind can be . . . in a sensu-
          ous *b·*.
sick
  c 260–20 sick *b·* is evolved from sick thoughts.
slave to the
  gl 582–27 and would make mortal mind a slave to the *b·*.
solid
  f 242–15 Self-love is more opaque than a solid *b·*.
Soul and
  s 114–25 It lifts the veil of mystery from Soul and *b·*.
  119–30 reverses the seeming relation of Soul and *b·*.
  122–30 make the same mistake regarding Soul and *b·*
soul and
  s 123– 6 as does the error relating to soul and *b·*,
  ph 196–11 able to destroy both soul and *b·*.— *Matt.* 10 : 28.
  b 338– 6 belief . . . that he is both soul and *b·*,

body
steers the
  p 426– 4 divine power, which steers the *b·* into health.
stimulus of the
  p 420–22 Mind is the natural stimulus of the *b·*,
stimulus to the
  p 420–19 It imparts a healthy stimulus to the *b·*,
superimposed upon the
  p 425–11 images . . . superimposed upon the *b·* ;
sustain the
  p 417– 5 power of Mind to sustain the *b·*.
teaching that the
  p 396–21 all teaching that the *b·* suffers,
temple also means
  ap 576–15 The word *temple* also means *b·*.
temple, or
  p 428–13 establish in truth the temple, or *b·*,
termed the
  p 409–12 substratum of mortal mind, termed the *b·*,
that
  sp 72– 5 that *b·* would disappear to mortal sense,
  73–25 belief . . . sensations belonging to that *b·*.
  90–18 but the supposed inhabitant of that *b·*
  ph 188–17 thinks . . . the suffering is in that *b·*.
  r 478–18 That *b·* is most harmonious in which the
this
  ph 187–32 This *b·* is put off only as
  f 208–27 A mortal man possesses this *b·*,
  p 368–22 when we learn that life and man survive this *b·*.
this temple
  a 27–12 "Destroy this temple [*b·*],— *John* 2 : 19.
  r 494– 2 " Destroy this temple [*b·*],— *John* 2 : 19.
transformation of the
  f 241–13 transformation of the *b·* by the renewal of
treat the
  ph 174–25 Then, if . . . sick, why treat the *b·* alone
triumph over
  a 42–16 the proof of his final triumph over *b·*
triumph over the
  f 242– 8 and the final triumph over the *b·*.
washing the
  f 241–27 washing the *b·* of all the impurities of flesh,
when bereft
  p 374–26 *b·*, when bereft of mortal mind, at first cools,
when the
  p 391–18 When the *b·* is supposed to say, "I am sick,"
whole
  f 219–12 makes the whole *b·* "sick,— *Isa.* 1 : 5.
will reflect
  b 324– 9 the *b·* will reflect what governs it,
will then utter
  pr 14–14 the *b·* will then utter no complaints.
would respond
  p 411– 5 the *b·* would respond more quickly,
your
  m 62–14 less thought "for your *b·* what ye— *Matt.* 6 : 25.
  sp 79–24 says : . . . Your *b·* is weak, and it must be
  ph 165– * *nor yet for your b·, what ye*— *Matt.* 6 : 25.
  f 208–30 You embrace your *b·* in your thought,
  227–28 crippled your capacities, enfeebled your *b·*,
  p 393–11 Take possession of your *b·*,
  393–21 Your *b·* would suffer no more from tension

  pr 12– 7 making it act more powerfully on the *b·*
  a 39–10 The educated belief that Soul is in the *b·*
  42–24 Let men think they had killed the *b·* !
  sp 89–29 Cain . . . concluded that if life was in the *b·*,
  an 105–12 Can you separate the mentality from the *b·*
  s 107–16 false consciousness that life inheres in the *b·*,
  120– 2 never . . . while we admit that soul is in *b·*
  122–31 They insist that soul is in *b·*
  130–22 ability of Spirit to make the *b·* harmonious,
  151– 3 this one factor they represent to be *b·*,
  152– 7 Æsculapius of mind as well as of *b·*,
  160–12 When this so-called mind quits the *b·*,
  164–23 miscalled life in the *b·* or in matter.
  ph 165– * *and the b· than raiment?*— *Matt.* 6 : 25.
  174–27 Why declare that the *b·* is diseased,
  176– 2 The action of mortal mind on the *b·*
  177–10 Matter, or *b·*, is but a false concept
  177–13 the *b·* is a sensuous, human concept.
  179–14 the *b·* then seems to require such treatment.
  180– 3 it should be taught to do the *b·* no harm
  181– 3 Before deciding that the *b·*, matter,
  187–30 the human mind still holds in belief a *b·*,
  187–32 a *b·* like the one it had before death.
  189–10 to explain the effect of mortal mind on the *b·*,
  194–21 mortal mind manifests itself in the *b·*
  198–14 afterwards to appear on the *b·*,
  f 204–31 The error, which says that Soul is in *b·*,
  206– 9 both upon the *b·* and through it.
  209– 3 belief which makes the *b·* discordant
  211– 7 The sensations of the *b·* must either be the
  211–26 then, when the *b·* is dematerialized,
  216–15 understanding makes the *b·* harmonious ;
  217–20 When mentality gives rest to the *b·*,

body
- *f* 218– 3   the *b·* is as material as the wheel.
- 218– 5   the *b·*, like the inanimate wheel.
- 218– 9   The *b·* is supposed to say, "I am ill."
- 219–16   We shall not call the *b·* weak,
- 223–12   If Spirit were once within the *b·*,
- 240–13   to be governed by matter or Soul in *b·*,
- 248– 1   belief of pain or pleasure in the *b·*
- 253–24   without hindrance from the *b·*.
- *c* 260–31   If we look to the *b·* for pleasure, we find pain ;
- 261– 9   If one turns away from the *b·*
- *b* 280–23   the belief that Soul is in *b·*,
- 288–23   Soul is sinless, not to be found in the *b·* ;
- 289– 5   belief that life and sensation are in the *b·*
- 291– 3   that the so-called death of the *b·*
- 293– 8   substratum is named matter or *b·* ;
- 297– 6   this testimony manifests itself on the *b·*
- 302–28   the *b·* presents no proper likeness of divinity,
- 308–11   looking for happiness and life in the *b·*
- 313–31   and the *b·* no more perfect because of death
- 314–18   the *b·*, which they laid in a sepulchre,
- 318–32   The *b·* does not include soul,
- 323–22   removes thought from the *b·*, and elevates
- 325– 6   life obtained not of the *b·* incapable of
- 329–14   not tarry in the storm if the *b·* is freezing,
- 337– 3   as material sensation, or a soul in the *b·*,
- *p* 375– 5   the separation of heat from the *b·*.
- 375–22   belief that matter . . . can paralyze the *b·*,
- 376–17   If the *b·* is material, it cannot, . . . suffer
- 377–12   Through different states of mind, the *b·*
- 379–28   pictures drawn of the *b·* by a mortal mind.
- 380–32   Every law of . . . the *b·*, supposed to govern,
- 382–11   no thought . . . for the *b·*."— *Luke* 12 : 22.
- 383– 7   influence of the divine Mind on the *b·*
- 386–14   corresponding effects of Truth on the *b·*,
- 388–10   thought that they could kill the *b·* with matter,
- 391–12   prevent the development of pain in the *b·*.
- 393– 4   The *b·* seems to be self-acting, only because
- 396–29   never giving the *b·* life and sensation.
- 399–12   mortal mind sends its despatches over its *b·*,
- 400–14   before it has taken tangible shape in . . . the *b·*,
- 400–23   We see in the *b·* the images of this mind,
- 400–31   baneful influence of sinful thought on the *b·*.
- 411–26   is imaged forth on the *b·*.
- 416–17   even as the *b·*, which has
- 416–22   *b·* is no longer the parent, even in
- 425–14   If the *b·* is diseased, this is but one of the
- 429–14   affirms that mind is subordinate to the *b·*,
- 429–14   affirms . . . that the *b·* is dying,
- 431–11   in behalf of the state (namely, the *b·*)
- 432– 8   my residence in matter, *alias* brain, to *b·*.
- 435– 3   Has the *b·* . . . committed a criminal deed?
- 435– 7   The *b·* committed no offence.
- *r* 476– 7   Error will cease to claim that soul is in *b·*,
- 478–13   Who can see a soul in the *b·*?
- 485–20   belief that life can be in matter or soul in *b·*,
- *g* 531–16   If . . . mind was afterwards put into *b·*
- *ap* 576–20   with "no temple [*b·*] therein"— *Rev.* 21 : 22.
- *gl* 595– 7   TEMPLE.   *B·* ; the idea of Life, substance,

boil
- *s* 153–16   You say a *b·* is painful ;
- 153–17   The *b·* simply manifests, . . . a belief in pain,
- 153–20   and this belief is called a *b·*.
- 153–21   and it will soon cure the *b·*.

boiling
- *f* 243– 5   which delivered men from the *b·* oil,

boldly
- *a* 18–10   Jesus acted *b·*, against the accredited evidence

bondage
- **continued**
- *f* 227–12   ignorance . . . the foundation of continued *b·*
- **human**
- *f* 227– 8   law of the divine Mind must end human *b·*,
- **land of**
- *ap* 566–16   Out of the land of *b·* came,
- **oppressive**
- *s* 151–15   oppressive *b·* now enforced by false theories,
- **out of**
- *ap* 559–30   prefigured this perilous passage out of *b·*

- *ph* 191–17   from self-imposed materiality and *b·*.
- *f* 225–30   are still in *b·* to material sense,
- 226–29   hold the children of Israel in *b·*.
- 227–22   Escape from the *b·* of sickness, sin, and
- *b* 337– 7   Sensualism is not bliss, but *b·*.
- *p* 368–13   hope of freedom from the *b·* of sickness
- 371–14   The adult, in *b·* to his beliefs,

bonds
- *b* 284– 9   It can never be in *b·*,
- *p* 372–12   and then call his *b·* material and
- 434–29   not proved "worthy of death, or of *b·*."— *Acts* 23 : 29.
- 441– 8   to give heavy *b·* for good behavior.

bone
- *ph* 193– 5   said the *b·* was carious for several inches.
- 193– 7   the evidence of this condition of the *b·*.
- *b* 280–11   would compress Mind, . . . beneath a skull *b·*.
- 281–19   mind supposed to exist . . . beneath a skull *b·*
- *p* 402–19   whether it be a broken *b·*, disease, or sin.
- 423– 2   and may not be able to mend the *b·*,
- 423–32   The so-called substance of *b·* is formed first by
- 427–17   Man is the same after as before a *b·* is broken
- *g* 533–22   the rapid deterioration of the *b·* and flesh

bone-disease
- *p* 422–22   Let us suppose two parallel cases of *b·*,

bones
- **broken**
- *p* 401–29   adjustment of broken *b·* and dislocations
- 402– 6   broken *b·*, dislocated joints, and
- **carious**
- *s* 162– 9   restores carious *b·* to soundness.
- 162–22   carious *b·* have been restored to healthy
- **flesh and**
- *a* 45–27   "Spirit hath not flesh and *b·*,— *Luke* 24 : 39.
- *b* 313–30   Jesus called . . . "flesh and *b·*."— *Luke* 24 : 39.
- *o* 352– 7   a mortal and material belief of flesh and *b·*
- *p* 372– 8   One theory about . . . blood, flesh, and *b·*.
- **muscles and**
- *sp* 84–21   nor upon muscles and *b·* for locomotion,
- **nerves nor**
- *f* 219–11   Not muscles, nerves, nor *b·*,

- *s* 143–19   the stomach, blood, nerves, *b·*,
- 160–19   Can muscles, *b·*, blood, and nerves rebel
- *ph* 172–23   Brain, heart, blood, *b·*, etc.,
- 173–19   measuring human strength by *b·* and sinews,
- *f* 216–16   makes the nerves, *b·*, brain, etc., servants,
- 220–31   controls the stomach, *b·*, lungs, heart,
- *p* 423–29   *B·* have only the substance of thought
- 424– 4   and its own thoughts of *b·*.
- *r* 475– 7   made up of brain, blood, *b·*, and

Book
- *p* 441–31   is recorded in our *B·* of books as a liar.

book
- **little**
- *ap* 558– 6   he had in his hand a little *b·* open :— *Rev.* 10 : 2.
- 559– 1   angel had in his hand "a little *b·*,"— *Rev.* 10 : 2.
- 559–17   "Go and take the little *b·*.— *Rev.* 10 : 8.
- **of Ecclesiastes**
- *b* 340– 4   This text in the *b·* of Ecclesiastes
- **of Genesis**
- *g* 502– 9   Spiritually followed, the *b·* of Genesis is
- 521–19   about creation in the *b·* of Genesis.
- 523–16   in the early part of the *b·* of Genesis.
- **of Hebrews**
- *ap* 575–12   as we read in the *b·* of Hebrews ;
- **of Job**
- *b* 321– 2   as may be seen by studying the *b·* of Job.
- **of Revelation**
- *ap* 558– 1   in the tenth chapter of his *b·* of Revelation :
- **perusal of the**
- *t* 446– 9   Perseverance in the perusal of the *b·*
- **same**
- *ap* 559– 2   Did this same *b·* contain the revelation of
- **this**
- *pref* x–10   books, however, which are based on this *b·*
- xii–21   she had never read this *b·* throughout
- *an* 104– 5   it will be seen why the author of this *b·*
- *s* 110–18   contained in this *b·*, SCIENCE AND HEALTH ;
- 110–20   This *b·* may be distorted by shallow criticism
- 129–32   in the system taught in this *b·*,
- 138–32   It is his theology in this *b·*
- 147–17   never . . . by a simple *perusal* of this *b·*.
- 152– 6   endeavored to make this *b·* the Æsculapius of
- *ph* 185– 7   Before this *b·* was published,
- *b* 330– 3   Until the author of this *b·* learned the
- *p* 422– 5   If the reader of this *b·* observes a great stir
- *t* 446– 7   sometimes seem worse while reading this *b·*,
- 457– 3   borrowed from this *b·* without giving it credit,
- 457– 4   this *b·* has done more for teacher and
- *g* 546–27   the system stated in this *b·*
- 547– 4   If one of the statements in this *b·* is true,
- *ap* 559–20   Read this *b·* from beginning to end.

- *pref* vii–22   A *b·* introduces new thoughts,
- *s* 147–17   The *b·* needs to be *studied*,
- *p* 422– 8   Continue to read, and the *b·* will become
- *t* 456–30   Because it was the first *b·* known,

booked
- *p* 382–19   A patient thoroughly *b·* in medical theories

books
- *pref* x– 4   Various *b·* on mental healing have
- x– 9   A few *b·*, however, which are based on
- *sp* 88–30   it is said to be a gift . . . obtained from *b·*
- *ph* 176–12   There were fewer *b·* on digestion
- 185– 7   other *b·* were in circulation, which discussed
- 196–20   Such *b·* as will rule disease out of mortal mind,

ooks
- *p* 441–31 is recorded in our Book of *b·* as a liar.
- *t* 457– 6 than has been accomplished by other *b·*.
- *ap* 572– 3 in both the first and last *b·* of the Bible,

borders
- *p* 430– 6 Faith should enlarge its *b·*

bore
- *a* 20–14 Jesus *b·* our infirmities ;
- 50–30 The real cross, which Jesus *b·* up the hill of grief,
- 53–25 Jesus *b·* our sins in his body.
- *p* 363– 1 She *b·* an alabaster jar

born
- *a* 30– 5 *B·* of a woman, Jesus' advent in the flesh
- *m* 57–19 Happiness is spiritual, *b·* of Truth and Love.
- 61–17 like tropical flowers *b·* amid Alpine snows.
- *s* 109–26 "Unto us a child is *b·*,— *Isa.* 9 : 6.
- *f* 227–17 Paul said, "I was free *b·*."— *Acts* 22 : 28.
- 250–10 which is never *b·* and never dies.
- *c* 258–27 Never *b·* and never dying,
- *b* 274–10 Ideas, on the contrary, are *b·* of Spirit,
- 295–32 error theorizes that spirit is *b·* of matter
- 296– 4 Progress is *b·* of experience.
- 332– 9 Jesus was *b·* of Mary.
- *t* 463–14 conceived and *b·* of Truth and Love,
- 463–18 the C. S. infant is *b·* of the Spirit, *b·* of God,
- *g* 529– 3 that man should be *b·* of woman,
- 535–17 the heritage of the first *b·* among men
- 552–15 "Man that is *b·* of a woman—*Job* 14 : 1.
- 557–20 lifts the curtain on man as never *b·*
- *ap* 563–26 her child as soon as it was *b·*.— *Rev.* 12 : 4.
- *gl* 598– 4 every one that is *b·* of the Spirit—*John* 3 : 8.

borne
- *a* 33–10 had *b·* this bread from house to house,
- *s* 109–24 When a new spiritual idea is *b·* to earth,
- *p* 383–18 could not be *b·* by the refined.

borrow
- *a* 21–32 would *b·* the passport of some wiser pilgrim,

borrowed
- *s* 112–12 *b·* from that truly divine Science
- *c* 267–22 Thought is *b·* from a higher source
- *p* 367– 6 better than . . . stereotyped *b·* speeches,
- *t* 457– 3 *b·* from this book without giving it credit,
- *g* 511– 2 and radiates their *b·* light,

borrows
- *pr* 12–17 *b·* its power from human faith and belief.
- *ap* 562– 9 the universe *b·* its reflected light,

bosom
- *a* 29–27 dwelt forever an idea in the *b·* of God,
- *sp* 87–22 of the tall ships that float on its *b·*,
- *f* 201– * *how I do bear in my b·*— *Psal.* 89 : 50.
- *b* 321–21 when Moses first put his hand into his *b·*
- 334– 5 Christ, dwells forever in the *b·* of the Father,
- *ap* 569–22 sin, which one has made his *b·* companion,

Boston
- *pref* xi–29 Massachusetts Metaphysical College in *B·*,
- *an* 105–19 these words of Judge Parmenter of *B·*

Boston Herald
- *an* 102–24 an extract from the *B· H·* :

botanic
- *p* 416–10 allopathic, homœopathic, *b·*, eclectic

botanist
- *s* 155– 8 The chemist, the *b·*, the druggist,
- *ap* 560–19 The *b·* must know the genus

both
- *pref* viii– 9 physics teach that *b·* Spirit and matter
- viii–13 by healing *b·* disease and sin ;
- *a* 18– 5 His mission was *b·* individual and collective.
- 23–10 eventually *b·* sin and suffering will fall
- 24–26 Then we must differ from them *b·*.
- 39–24 *b·* are unreal, because impossible in Science.
- 50–12 The appeal of Jesus was made *b·* to
- *m* 57–10 *B·* sexes should be loving, pure, tender,
- 59– 3 enduring obligations on *b·* sides.
- 59–32 it never would, if *b·* husband and wife were
- 60–10 purity and constancy, *b·* of which are immortal.
- *sp* 73– 9 *b·* the individuality and the Science of man,
- 77– 7 *b·* here and hereafter,
- 80–21 mind-power which moves *b·* table and hand.
- 80–31 *b·* visibly and invisibly,
- 82–15 because *b·* of us are either unconscious or
- 85–23 *B·* Jew and Gentile may have had
- 85–30 great Teacher knew *b·* cause and effect,
- 88–25 for *b·* arise from mortal belief.
- 91–27 erroneous postulate is, that man is *b·*
- 91–29 erroneous postulate is, that mind is *b·*
- 99– 8 worketh in you *b·* to will and—*Phil.* 2 : 13.
- *an* 103–11 a knowledge of *b·* good and evil,
- 103–21 false belief that mind is . . . *b·* evil and good ;
- 104– 4 are *b·* comprehended, as they will be
- *s* 113–22 *B·* are not, cannot be, true.
- 114– 1 Usage classes *b·* evil and good together

both
- 114– 8 and calls *mind b·* human and divine.
- 126–18 as being *b·* natural and spiritual?
- 128–31 If *b·* the major and the minor propositions
- 136– 5 and heal *b·* the sick and the sinning.
- 136– 8 power to save men *b·* bodily and spiritually.
- 148–12 *B·* anatomy and theology define
- 148–13 define man as *b·* physical and mental,
- 150–19 would have one believe that *b·* matter and
- 157–27 but they leave *b·* mind and body worse
- 157–31 Science *b·* neutralizes error and destroys it.
- 158–11 truth which heals *b·* mind and body.
- 162–18 in cases of *b·* acute and chronic disease
- *ph* 167–15 If God made man *b·* good and evil,
- 170–28 or as *b·* material and spiritual,
- 174–29 the thought of *b·* physician and patient?
- 177– 9 *b·* must be destroyed by immortal Mind.
- 180– 1 are *b·* prolific sources of sickness.
- 182– 9 We cannot obey *b·* physiology and Spirit,
- 186–26 If pain is as real as . . . *b·* must be immortal ;
- 188–15 In *b·* the waking and the sleeping dream,
- 190– 5 producing mortals, *b·* body and mind ;
- 196–11 able to destroy *b·* soul and body—*Matt.* 10 : 28.
- *f* 206– 8 *b·* upon the body and through it.
- 208–14 absurd to suppose that matter can *b·* cause and
- 216–20 to suppose that man, . . . is *b·* matter and Spirit,
- 216–20 to suppose that man, . . . *b·* good and evil.
- 218–12 What renders *b·* sin and sickness difficult of
- 223–18 *b·* shall fall into the ditch."—*Matt.* 15 : 14.
- 229–11 calls *b·* the offspring of spirit,
- 234–15 robbing *b·* themselves and others.
- *b* 270– 6 hence *b·* cannot be real.
- 281– 7 presupposes man to be *b·* mind and matter.
- 282– 8 the finite, which has *b·* beginning and end.
- 283–15 They speak of *b·* Truth and error as *mind*,
- 287– 6 supposes man to be *b·* mental and material.
- 287–29 *b·* good and evil.
- 293–11 *b·* strata, mortal mind and
- 294– 6 If man is *b·* mind and matter,
- 303–13 *b·* spiritually and materially,
- 303–13 or by *b·* God and man,
- 303–15 can never make *b·* these contraries true.
- 307–21 as *b·* good and evil,
- 320– 7 Scriptures have *b·* a spiritual and literal
- 320–10 must rest upon *b·* the literal and moral ;"
- 330–22 Mind is not *b·* good and bad,
- 330–25 The notion that *b·* evil and good
- 333–19 *b·* before and after the Christian era,
- 338– 5 belief . . . that he is *b·* soul and body,
- 338– 6 *b·* good and evil, *b·* spiritual and material
- *o* 346–30 We cannot serve *b·* God and mammon
- 350–12 *b·* of which must be understood.
- 355–24 misapprehension *b·* of the divine Principle and
- 360– 5 those which are *b·* mental and material.
- 360–15 *B·* you cannot have.
- *p* 366–28 calm in the presence of *b·* sin and disease,
- 368– 6 *B·* truth and error have come nearer
- 370–17 but it uses the same medicine in *b·* cases.
- 370–23 According to *b·* medical testimony and
- 372–20 can we believe in the reality and power of *b·*
- 373–21 you must rise above *b·* fear and sin.
- 376–22 by *b·* silently and audibly arguing the
- 378–14 and *b·* will fight for nothing.
- 379– 2 for *b·* are errors,
- 393–30 false belief is *b·* the tempter and the tempted,
- 395–10 same Principle cures *b·* sin and sickness.
- 396– 3 *b·* for one's own sake and for that of the patient.
- 399–12 so-called mind is *b·* the service and message
- 402–30 cannot produce *b·* disorder and order.
- 403–12 *b·* have their origin in the human mind,
- 404–27 *B·* cures require the same method
- 405–15 *B·* will be manacled until the last farthing is
- 406– 3 Sin and sickness are *b·* healed by the same
- 406– 9 healing of mortals, *b·* mind and body.
- 420–17 Truth overcomes *b·* disease and sin
- 421–32 are *b·* forty, and that their combined sum
- 422–22 cases of bone-disease, *b·* similarly produced
- 423–15 as *b·* his foe and his remedy.
- 423–24 *B·* Science and consciousness are now at work
- 427– 7 for *b·* are immortal.
- *t* 450–23 heals them *b·* by understanding God's power
- 454–18 the true incentive in *b·* healing and teaching.
- 455–30 cannot send forth *b·* sweet waters and bitter.
- 456–23 you must *b·* understand and abide by the
- 457–12 we cannot scientifically *b·* cure and
- 457–15 *b·* sides were beautiful
- 458– 7 *b·* a mental and a material standpoint.
- 461–23 *B·* sin and sickness are error,
- 462–30 *b·* in health and in sickness.
- *r* 482– 4 hypothesis that soul is *b·* an evil and a good
- 487– 5 *b·* before and after that which is called death.
- *g* 504– 6 *b·* spiritual and material
- 512–23 are mental, *b·* primarily and secondarily.
- 513– 1 *b·* this mortal mentality, so-called, and its
- 524–19 Mind had made man, *b·* male and female.
- 523– 3 already created man, *b·* male and female

both

g	529–10	*b·* man and woman proceed from God
	531– 7	error, . . . that mind and soul are *b·* right and
	531–27	Certainly not by *b·*, since
	536–19	The blind leading the blind, *b·* would fall.
	538–27	As *b·* mortal man and sin have a
	539– 6	as if . . . matter can *b·* give and take away.
	542–21	*b·* for what it is and for what it does.
	551– 1	*b·* the material senses and their reports are
	555–21	as if man were the offspring of *b·* Mind and
	555–22	of *b·* Deity and humanity.
ap	561– 3	destroys *b·* faith in evil and the
	572– 3	in *b·* the first and last books of the Bible,
	577–25	*b·* within and without,
gl	587–10	belief that . . . are *b·* mental and material ;
	588–18	belief that . . . are *b·* mental and material.
	598– 5	the original word is the same in *b·* cases,

bottles

s	114–21	poured into the old *b·* of the letter.
b	281–27	does not put new wine into old *b·*,

bottom

an	104–13	C. S. goes to the *b·* of mental action,
ph	184– 9	probing the trouble to the *b·*,

Bouillaud

an	101– 9	among whom were Roux, *B·*, and Cloquet,

bound

pr	6–24	he said that Satan had *b·* her,
sp	77– 4	Neither do other mortals . . . at a single *b·*.
f	227–27	The illusion . . . has *b·* you,
r	495–10	"whom Satan hath *b·*," — *Luke* 13 : 16.
	495–12	opens the prison doors to such as are *b·*,
ap	559–10	to the globe's remotest *b·*.

boundary

m	58–22	the centre, though not the *b·*, of the affections.
sp	97–15	without passing the *b·* where,
b	298–18	never reaches beyond the *b·* of the
ap	577–12	This spiritual, holy habitation has no *b·*

bounded

sp	84–19	Mind is infinite, not *b·* by corporeality,
c	250–13	The everlasting I AM is not *b·* nor
b	301–32	Immortality is not *b·* by mortality.

bounding

f	207– 4	*B·* off with laughing eyes,

boundless

u	22–24	*b·* freedom, and sinless sense,
c	258–15	higher and higher from a *b·* basis.
b	323–11	until *b·* thought walks enraptured,
r	481– 4	freedom, harmony, and *b·* bliss.

bounds

g	550– 8	cannot . . . be limited within material *b·*.

bounty

pr	15–25	Christians rejoice in secret beauty and *b·*,
a	36–11	pour his dear-bought *b·* into barren lives.

bow

a	35 13	They *b·* before Christ, Truth,
ph	174– 5	that man should *b·* down to a flesh-brush,
f	214–18	We *b·* down to matter, . . . like the pagan
	247–26	arches the cloud with the *b·* of beauty,
g	530–21	saying, . . . *B·* down to me and

bowed

a	32–13	he *b·* in holy submission to the divine decree.
	36–13	a few women who *b·* in silent woe
gl	598–11	"He *b·* his head, — *John* 19 : 30.

bowels

ph	176– 8	left the stomach and *b·* free to act,
	179–28	to move the *b·*, or to produce sleep
p	413– 7	Mind regulates the condition of the stomach, *b·*,
	415–21	the action of the lungs, of the *b·*,

box

ph	170–30	is the Pandora *b·*, from which

boy

ph	193– 2	caused by a fall . . . when quite a *b·*.
	195– 2	After the babbling *b·* had been taught to
p	398– 2	as when he said to the epileptic *b·*,

boyhood

a	52– 1	From early *b·* he was about his
ph	193–23	ever since the injury was received in *b·*.

boys

b	333– 6	in common with other Hebrew *b·* and men,
p	379–16	think of the experiment of those Oxford *b·*,

Brahman

p	362–11	the household of a high-caste *B·*,

brain

and nerves

s	122–12	sections of matter, such as *b·* and nerves,
b	290–11	manifested through *b·* and nerves, is false.

and viscera

p	415–24	including *b·* and viscera.

body and

sp	79–28	Mind controls body and *b·*.

brain

called

ph	185–29	material stratum of the human mind, called *b·*,

can give no idea

ph	191– 1	The *b·* can give no idea of God's man.

congestion of the

p	408–23	as would congestion of the *b·*,

consult your

ph	165–18	Then you consult your *b·* in order to

diseased

p	421– 3	insanity implies belief in a diseased *b·*,

effect upon the

p	401–23	could you produce any effect upon the *b·* or

is not mind

p	372– 1	Remember, *b·* is not mind.

named

b	295–26	The theoretical mind is matter, named *b·*,

or matter

c	259–24	*B·* or matter never formed a human concept.

portions of the

g	531– 8	It is well that the upper portions of the *b·*

prevent the

p	395–31	would prevent the *b·* from becoming diseased,

proceeding from the

sp	88–12	proceeding from the *b·* or from matter,

size of a

ph	190–12	presently measure mind by the size of a *b·*

size of the

ph	165– 7	To measure . . . by the size of the *b·*

softened

p	387– 4	must it pay the penalty in a softened *b·*?

substratum of

p	408–29	thought in the corporeal substratum of *b·*

your

sp	79–24	says : . . . Your *b·* is overtaxed,

s	127–20	nerves, *b·*, stomach, lungs, and so forth,
	151–19	The blood, heart, lungs, *b·*, etc.,
ph	172–23	*B·*, heart, blood, . . . the material structure?
	172–32	heart, blood, *b·*, acting through the
	189–16	it is as truly mortal mind, . . . as is the material *b·*
	189–29	the lower, basal portion of the *b·*,
	190– 7	neither . . . is found in *b·* or elsewhere in
f	211– 1	If *b·*, nerves, stomach, are intelligent,
	216–16	it makes . . . bones, *b·*, etc., servants,
c	262 29	Every concept which seems to begin with the *b·*
b	294–13	saying : . . . Nerves feel. *B·* thinks and sins.
p	408–17	Can drugs go of their own accord to the *b·*
	408–25	with the mind than is the *b·*.
	409– 6	animate error called nerves, *b·*, mind,
	409– 9	mortal mind — *alias* matter, *b·*,
	414–10	impossibility that matter, *b·*, can control
	432– 8	for I convey messages from . . . *b·*, to body.
r	475– 7	Man is not matter ; he is not made up of *b·*,
	478–14	Does *b·* think, and do nerves feel,
gl	587–13	theories that hold mind . . . existing in *b·*,

brain-lobes

p	395 30	The knowledge that *b·* cannot kill
r	478–22	and *b·* cannot think

brainology

ph	171–10	not needing to study *b·*
b	295–28	*B·* teaches that mortals are created to suffer

brake

a	32–16	*b·* it, and gave it to the disciples, — *Matt.* 26 : 26.

branch

p	402– 2	surgery is the *b·* of its healing which
t	160 24	This *b·* of study is indispensable

brave

s	120–32	chained the limbs of the *b·* old navigator,
	144– 7	when dawns the sun's *b·* light.

bravely

m	67– 9	He answers *b·*, but even the dauntless

brazen

s	133–11	The Israelites looked upon the *b·* serpent,

breach

s	112–30	inculcates a *b·* of that divine commandment
p	382–18	"more honored in the *b·* than the observance,"

bread

and vegetables

f	221– 3	he ate only *b·* and vegetables,

breaking of

a	46– 7	and by the breaking of *b·*.

daily

pr	17– 4	Give us this day our daily *b·* ; — *Matt.* 6 : 11.

diet of

f	220–22	clergyman once adopted a diet of *b·* and water

Jesus took

a	32–15	Jesus took *b·*, and blessed it. — *Matt.* 26 : 26.

of Life

f	222–10	feeds thought with the *b·* of Life.

our

a	35–26	Our *b·*, "which cometh down — *John* 6 : 33.

bread

slice of
f 221– 7   only a thin slice of *b·* without water.
their
a 33– 6   Their *b·* indeed came down from heaven.
this
a 31–23   "As often as ye eat this *b·*,— *I Cor.* 11 : 26.
   33–10   this *b·* was feeding and sustaining them.
   33–11   They had borne this *b·* from house to house,
use of
a 32–21   lost, if . . . confined to the use of *b·* and wine.

a 31–19   we drink of his cup, partake of his *b·*,
   32–23   yet Jesus prayed and gave them *b·*.
   33–32   Are all who eat *b·* and drink wine
m 68–20   when casting my *b·* upon the waters,
p 410–10   "Man shall not live by *b·* alone,— *Matt.* 4 : 4.
g 535–26   sweat of thy face shalt thou eat *b·*,— *Gen.* 3 : 19.

breadth

g 520– 3   The depth, *b·*, height, might, majesty,

break

a 39–25   To *b·* this earthly spell, mortals must
   41–12   cannot forever *b·* the Golden Rule
f 225–18   potent to *b·* despotic fetters
   234–29   to look with desire . . . was to *b·* a moral precept.
   239– 7   *B·* up cliques, level wealth with honesty,
p 412–17   must *b·* the dream of the material senses.
   420–28   to *b·* its dream of suffering,
t 448–27   ventures not to *b·* its rules,
   449– 2   With . . . wrists manacled, it is hard to *b·*
ap 569–15   Alas for those who *b·* faith with divine Science

breakage

p 402–15   no *b·* nor dislocation can really occur.

breaketh

b 308–24   "Let me go, for the day *b·* ;"— *Gen.* 32 : 26.

breakfast

a 34–30   his last spiritual *b·* with his disciples

breaking

a 33–11   *b·* (explaining) it to others,
   46– 7   and by the *b·* of bread.
sp 96–15   The *b·* up of material beliefs
c 261–24   *B·* away from the mutations of time and sense,
o 349– 5   "Through *b·* the law,— *Rom.* 2 : 23.
p 363– 3   *B·* the sealed jar, she perfumed Jesus' feet
   381–11   cannot in reality suffer from *b·* anything

breaks

f 241– 6   Sin *b·* in upon them,
b 301–21   belief . . . *b·* the First Commandment,
p 396–30   It *b·* the dream of disease
r 489–13   it *b·* all the commands of the
   494–23   *b·* their illusion with the unbroken reality of
g 542–25   to advance itself, *b·* God's commandments.

breast

gl 595–14   which were to be on Aaron's *b·*

breast-plate

gl 596–12   the *b·* of the high-priest

breath

pr 2– 8   God is not moved by the *b·* of praise
s 120–30   When Columbus gave freer *b·* to the globe,
ph 175–13   and the *b·* of new-mown hay
   184–30   Her *b·* came gently.
   192–15   the devouring flame, the tempest's *b·*.
f 225–21   nor did the *b·* of freedom come from
g 516–15   sends her sweet *b·* to heaven.
   524–15   into his nostrils the *b·* of life ;— *Gen.* 2 : 7.
   525– 2   animated by the *b·* of God?

breathe

t 452–14   Never *b·* an immoral atmosphere, unless

breathed

ph 184–28   always *b·* with great difficulty when
g 524–14   and *b·* into his nostrils — *Gen.* 2 : 7.
gl 598–14   common statement, "He *b·* his last."

breathes

sp 76– 4   forgets all else and *b·* aloud his rapture.
g 548– 3   and *b·* through the sacred pages

breathing

ph 185– 2   her difficulty in *b·* had gone.
   193–12   and the *b·* became natural ;
f 225–17   *b·* the omnipotence of divine justice,

breeds

m 62– 7   master the belief . . . which *b·* disease.

brethren

a 31– 7   and who are my *b·*,"— *Matt.* 12 : 48.
s 107– *   But I certify you, *b·*, that— *Gal.* 1 : 11.
   137–17   Simon replied for his *b·*,
t 444– 8   their *b·* upon whom they may call,
   444–27   for we be *b·*."— *Gen.* 13 : 8.
   444–30   are discordant and ofttimes false *b·*.
r 470– 2   the whole family of man would be *b·* ;
ap 568–16   accuser of our *b·* is cast down,— *Rev.* 12 : 10.

bridal

m 65– 3   May Christ, Truth, be present at every *b·* altar
f 238–13   From out the *b·* chamber of wisdom

bride

m 58–24   Said the peasant *b·* to her lover :
g 548– 1   Spirit and the *b·* say, Come !— *Rev.* 22 : 17.
ap 561–12   a *b·* coming down from heaven,
   561–13   "the *b·*" and "the Lamb"— *see Rev.* 21 : 9.
   574– 8   I will show thee the *b·*,— *Rev.* 21 : 9.
gl 582–14   definition of

bridegroom

gl 582–17   definition of

bridge

sp 74–26   There is no *b·* across the gulf which
gl 598–26   would *b·* over with life discerned spiritually

brief

pr 16– 7   taught his disciples one *b·* prayer,
a 42–12   his *b·* triumphal entry into Jerusalem
ph 194– 3   Reviewing this *b·* experience,
f 206–20   for the *b·* space of a few years
b 334– 9   Jesus, whose earthly career was *b·*.
p 433–16   A *b·* consultation ensues,
r 496–31   a *b·* exposition of the important points,
g 502– 3   real prelude of the older Scriptures is so *b·*
   521– 7   We leave this *b·*, glorious history
ap 565–14   had a *b·* history in the earthly

briefly

g 547–17   *B·*, this is Darwin's theory,

bright

a 34–31   in the *b·* morning hours at the joyful meeting
s 121–11   earth and heaven were *b·*,
f 246–15   dawn . . . with *b·* and imperishable glories.
ap 558–12   but a *b·* promise crowns its brow

brightens

c 265–27   *b·* the ascending path of many a heart.
g 516–18   *b·* the flower, beautifies the landscape,

brighter

a 32–26   refresh his heart with *b·*, with spiritual views.
r 496–13   *b·* "unto the perfect day."— *Prov.* 4 : 18.

brightness

s 139–11   even when the end has been *b·* and peace ;
b 313–10   "the *b·* of His [God's] glory,— *Heb.* 1 : 3.
   313–21   "Who, being a *b·* from His glory,— *see Heb.* 1 : 3.
ap 565– 5   loathing the *b·* of divine glory.

brim

pr 5–16   Ingratitude and persecution filled it to the *b·* ;

bring

pr 2–16   but it tends to *b·* us into harmony with it.
   2–29   The unspoken desire does *b·* us nearer the
   4–14   are made manifest in the blessings they *b·*,
   4–25   and patience must *b·* experience.
   11–21   Petitions to mortals only the results of
   11–30   will *b·* us into all Truth.
a 34–16   they will *b·* in the millennium.
sp 97–22   they *b·* error from under cover.
s 128–30   addition of two sums . . . must always *b·*
f 202– 6   If men would *b·* to bear upon the
   212–19   *b·* the rose into contact with the olfactory
   230– 5   will *b·* us into health, holiness, and
   230–13   so as to *b·* about certain evil results,
c 260–16   and to *b·* out better and higher results,
   261– 5   you will *b·* these into your experience
b 300–10   will *b·* to light the true reflection of God
o 351–16   cannot *b·* out the practical proof . . . while
p 374– 4   but the truth of being, . . . will *b·* relief.
   386–18   same grief that the friend's real death would *b·*.
   392– 3   Only while . . . remains can it *b·* forth death.
   400–27   to *b·* out the harmony of being.
   405–29   penalties you incur and the ills they *b·*.
   422–15   meet and *b·* out a third quality,
   424– 9   to change the . . . and thus *b·* out harmony.
r 483–22   seems to *b·* into dishonor the ordinary scientific
   492–12   and *b·* immortality to light.
g 504–24   The rays of infinite Truth, . . . *b·* light
   507–11   Let the earth *b·* forth grass,— *Gen.* 1 : 11.
   511–19   Let the waters *b·* forth— *Gen.* 1 : 20.
   513–14   Let the earth *b·* forth— *Gen.* 1 : 24.
   535– 8   in sorrow shalt *b·* forth— *Gen.* 3 : 16.
   535–24   thistles shall it *b·* forth to thee ;— *Gen.* 3 : 18.
   550–27   nor does a lion *b·* forth a lamb.
   557–18   "In sorrow thou shalt *b·* forth— *Gen.* 3 : 16.
ap 570– 2   will *b·* the hour when the people will chain,

bringeth

c 257–20   *b·* "forth Mazzaroth in his season,"— *Job* 38 : 32.
p 442–15   as of one "that *b·* good tidings."— *Isa.* 52 : 7.

bringing

a 35–23   by *b·* forth the fruits of Love,
m 57–13   *b·* sweet seasons of renewal
f 210–14   *b·* to light the scientific action of
   249– 6   *b·* us into newness of life
o 360–15   You are *b·* out your own ideal.

bringing

p 435–12 b· joy instead of grief,
t 454–32 auxiliaries to aid in b· thought into accord
g 529– 1 b· forth fruit of its own kind,
540– 8 when b· it to the surface and
ap 561–15 God and his Christ, b· harmony to earth.
gl 589–17 and b· to light man's immortality.

brings

pr 11–11 Broken law b· penalty . . . to compel this
11–20 because sin b· inevitable suffering.
a 37– 2 Does not Science show that sin b· suffering
37–13 Consciousness of right-doing b· its own reward ;
m 69–15 b· the sweet assurance of no parting,
sp 72–13 Truth . . . b· to light immortality.
77– 6 Error b· its own self-destruction
s 132–13 divine Principle which b· out all harmony.
157–29 b· out the proof that Life is continuous
162– 4 C. S. b· to the body the sunlight of Truth,
ph 169–24 mortal mind, not matter, which b· to the sick
196– 9 Sin alone b· death, for sin is the only
f 203–13 Spiritual perception b· out the possibilities of
206–27 He destroys them, and b· to light immortality.
221–31 b· with it another lesson,
224–28 Truth b· the elements of liberty.
224–30 power of God b· deliverance to the
248–11 which each day b· to a nearer tomb.
b 272–10 spiritual sense of the Scriptures b· out the
276–12 b· objects and thoughts into human view
293–29 C. S. b· to light Truth and its supremacy,
305–26 destroys all error and b· immortality to light.
336–28 Science of being . . . b· immortality to light.
338– 2 b· to light the only living and true God
o 348–23 while complaining of the suffering disease b·,
p 401–18 b· sin and sickness to the surface,
404– 7 suffering which his submission to such habits b·,
404–19 cuts down every tree that b· not forth good fruit.
407–27 b· the divine Mind, Life not death,
422–10 tremor which Truth often b· to error
t 446–27 exercise of will b· on a hypnotic state,
r 487–31 b· out the enduring and harmonious phases
496–14 what the understanding of God b· to man.
g 530– 6 The earth, . . . b· forth food for man's use.
540–31 he b· a material offering to God.
555– 4 b· the physical organism under the yoke of
ap 558–17 It b· the baptism of the Holy Ghost,
gl 596– 4 but C. S. b· God much nearer to man,

brink

f 235–22 To the tremblers on the b· of death,

broad

t 451–13 "wide is the gate, and b· is — Matt. 7 : 13.

broadcast

m 65–13 b· powers of evil so conspicuous to-day
ph 197–18 departments of knowledge now b· in the earth,

broaden

f 235–32 their listeners will . . . b· their concepts.

broadening

o 258–14 developing itself, b· and rising

broader

s 128–17 access to b· and higher realms.
c 265– 7 must near the b· interpretations of being,

broadest

sp 97–21 b· facts array the most falsities against
s 111–30 submitted . . . to the b· practical tests.
147– 8 submitted to the b· practical test,

broken

pr 11–10 B· law brings penalty
a 38– 8 b· by the demands of divine Science.
m 66– 7 a b· reed, which pierces the heart.
ph 184–25 what is termed a fatally b· physical law.
p 364–27 by their genuine repentance, by their b· hearts,
384–25 that you have b· no law,
385–26 not the penalty for having b· a law of
392– 4 b· moral law should be taken into account
401–29 adjustment of b· bones and dislocations
402– 6 b· bones, dislocated joints, and
402–19 whether it be a b· bone, disease, or sin.
427–17 the same after as before a bone is b·
t 447– 1 heavenly law is b· by trespassing upon
g 522– 9 as having b· away from Deity
ap 563–14 belief . . . the Ten Commandments can be b·.

broken-hearted

p 366–31 must first learn to bind up the b·.

bronchial

ph 175–28 the refinement of inflamed b· tubes.

brood

f 234–18 b· of evils which infest it would be cleared out.

brother (see also brother's)

c 267–15 as for that of b· and sister.
267–17 my b·, and sister, and mother." — Matt. 12 : 50.
p 366–15 "He that loveth not his b· — I John 4 : 20.

brother

g 541–14 rose up against Abel his b·, — Gen. 4 : 8.
541–20 Where is Abel thy b·? — Gen. 4 : 9.
541–26 the human duty of man towards his b·.

brotherhood

b 340–24 constitutes the b· of man ;
r 467–12 true b· of man will be established.
470– 3 b· of man would consist of Love and
g 518–16 The rich in spirit help the poor in one grand b·,
541–17 ruptures the life and b· of man

brother's

t 455–16 mote out of thy b· eye." — Matt. 7 : 5.
g 518–18 seeth his b· need and supplieth it,
541– 4 Jealous of his b· gift,
541–21 Am I my b· keeper? — Gen. 4 : 9.
541–28 The voice of thy b· blood — Gen. 4 : 10.

brought

a 19–15 b· to material beliefs not peace,
29–22 b· forth her child by the revelation of Truth,
44–25 divinity b· to humanity the understanding
50– 1 b· as a lamb to the slaughter, — Isa. 53 : 7.
m 61–10 every mountain of selfishness be b· low,
65–29 mental chemicalization, which has b·
sp 86–18 apparitions b· out in dark seances
an 100– 1 b· into notice by Mesmer in Germany
s 110– 9 equipollence of God b· to light
115– 7 C. S. as b· forth in my discovery.
121–30 thus b· nearer the spiritual fact,
136– 7 Despite the persecution this b· upon him,
148– 1 When his students b· to him a case
159– 7 The case was b· to trial.
164–27 then shall be b· to pass the saying — I Cor. 15 : 54.
ph 168–13 b· yourself into the slough of disease
196–28 from the image b· before the mind ;
f 240–29 until all error is finally b· into subjection
b 268– 1 In the material world, thought has b· to light
292–30 connection with his God, which Jesus b· to light.
303–12 spiritually conceived and b· forth ;
306–15 to be b· together again at some . . . time
309–20 to be b· back through great tribulation,
315–10 b· upon him the anathemas of the age.
318–14 b· the belief of sin and death
335–24 Life as immortality b· to light.
o 351–32 their prayer b· down no proof that it was heard,
p 363–21 and so b· home the lesson to all,
388–20 which is "b· to desolation." — Matt. 12 : 25.
414–30 unreal, and is not b· about by divine Love.
426–28 Sin b· death, and death will disappear with
428–22 The great spiritual fact must be b· out
420– 2 this Life must be b· to light
436–18 But they b· with them Fear,
r 476–17 "conceived in sin and b· forth in iniquity."
490–20 then shall be b· to pass the saying — I Cor. 15 : 54.
g 505–28 it is the reality of all things b· to light.
508– 9 the earth b· forth grass, — Gen. 1 : 12.
512– 5 which the waters b· forth — Gen. 1 : 21.
527–23 and b· them unto Adam — Gen. 2 : 19.
529–13 and b· her unto the man. — Gen. 2 : 22.
532– 7 when eating its first fruits b· death?
538–21 b· into view only as the unreal
540–25 Cain b· of the fruit of the — Gen. 4 : 3.
540–27 b· of the firstlings of his flock, — Gen. 4 : 4.
548–27 Modern discoveries have b· to light
551–21 b· down from generation to generation?"
553–18 the maternal egg never b· forth Adam.
ap 565– 6 And she b· forth a man child, — Rev. 12 : 5.
569–31 b· forth the man child. — Rev. 12 : 13.
574–21 b· also the experience which at last
gl 582–23 immortality b· to light.

brow

ph 193– 9 The dew of death was on his b·.
f 245–15 youth sat gently on cheek and b·
t 451– 6 with the crown of Love upon her b·,
ap 558–12 a bright promise crowns its b·.

bruise

g 534–11 it shall b· thy head, — Gen. 3 : 15.
534–11 and thou shalt b· his heel. — Gen. 3 : 15.
534–29 the woman, this idea, will b· the head of

bruised

pref xi–21 To set at liberty them that are b·. — Luke 4 : 18.

bruises

f 216– 8 Truth b· the head of error

brusque

p 365– 1 and the b· business visitor

brutal

a 43–13 The malignity of b· persecutors,
p 405– 2 Hatred inflames the b· propensities.
ap 564–16 b· barbarity of his foes could emanate from

brutality

a 40–22 lesser apostles of Truth may endure human b·

brute
m 63– 7 His origin is not, . . . in b· instinct,
ph 173– 3 distinguish between humanity and the b·,
b 277–16 nor the man by the b·.

bud
m 62–23 which forms the b· and blossom,
68–24 perpetuation of the floral species by b· or
sp 78– 1 The decaying flower, the blighted b·,
g 518–21 as the blossom shines through the b·.
gl 596–26 maketh the valley to b· and blossom as the rose.
fr 600– * *and the pomegranates b· forth.— Song* 7 : 12.

Buddhism
ph 173–32 call into action less faith than B·

budding
p 413–28 convey . . . to children's b· thoughts,

buddings
f 236–22 blighting the b· of self-government.

buds
sp 77–29 a state resembling that of blighted b·,
ph 191–22 not a spray b· within the vale,
g 549–12 sometimes through eggs, sometimes through b·,

buffeting
t 460–22 b· them with the . . . cold assertion,

build
sp 84–27 spiritualism has no basis upon which to b·.
s 137–31 I will b· my church ;— *Matt.* 16 : 18.
f 201– 7 We cannot b· safely on false foundations.
235– 3 if virtue and truth b· a strong defence.
p 421–27 you should not b· it up by
t 450– 9 A third class of thinkers b· with solid masonry.

builder
b 314–14 knowing, as he did, that Mind was the b·,
p 428–13 "whose b· and maker is God."— *Heb.* 11 : 10.
428–17 the eternal b·, the everlasting Father,
ap 575–10 b· and maker of this New Jerusalem is God,

builders
s 139–26 stone which the b· rejected"— *Matt.* 21 : 42.

building
f 241–26 corner-stone of all spiritual b· is purity.

builds
sp 83–11 hides Truth and b· on error.
ph 177–11 so-called mind b· its own superstructure,
gl 581–19 The higher false knowledge b·

built
a 35–20 Our church is b· on the divine Principle, Love.
s 127–31 in so far as this is b· on the false hypotheses
138–15 the foundation on which Jesus b·.
f 226–14 God has b· a higher platform of human rights,
226–15 and He has b· it on diviner claims.
b 269–28 not houses b· on the rock.
t 454– 8 path which leads to the house b· without hands
r 484– 4 for it is b· upon the rock, Christ.

bulk
ph 190–12 and the b· of a body, called man.

bullet
o 358– 2 Can a leaden b· deprive a man of Life,

bundle
s 149– 6 a b· of speculative human theories?

buoyant
s 109–16 search was sweet, calm, and b· with hope,

buoys
a 24– 9 the b· and healing currents of Truth

burden
a 50–26 The b· of that hour was terrible

burial
a 35– 8 or the b· of mind in matter,
45–13 Three days after his bodily b·
f 232–30 unquestionable signs of the b· of error
gl 582–21 definition of

buried
a 38–26 To those b· in the belief of sin and self,
sp 75–19 same plane . . . as those who b· the body,
87 –23 the bodies which lie b· in its sands :
b 299– 8 has b· its fondest earthly hopes.
p 429–15 affirms . . . that it must be b·

buries
g 537–16 and b· itself in the ground,

burlesque
sp 92–18 a b· of God's man

burn
a 46– 6 by the words, which made their hearts b·
ap 565–20 fiery baptism will b· up the chaff of error

burned
s 134–11 the followers of Christ were b·, crucified, and
161– 3 You say, "*I* have b· my finger."
g 535– 4 the one to be b·, the other to be garnered

burning
ap 566–24 A b· and a shining light !

burns
s 161– 5 mortal mind, and not matter, b· it.

burnt
b 286– 8 is better than all b· offerings.

burst
c 261–29 even as the bird which has b· from the egg
b 288–15 lightnings and thunderbolts of error may b·

bursting
f 252–28 Like b· lava, I expand but to my own despair,

bury
o 355–11 let the dead b· their dead."— *Matt.* 8 : 22.
p 367– 2 nor b· the *morale* of C. S.
429–18 unseen by those who think that they b· the
r 469–21 We b· the sense of infinitude, when we admit

business
Father's
a 25– 9 as he went daily about his Father's b·.
52– 1 he was about his "Father's b·."— *Luke* 2 : 49.
neighbor's
m 64–13 never well to interfere with your neighbor's b·."
———
m 63–30 enter into b· agreements, hold real estate,
s 128– 7 b· men and cultured scholars
p 365– 1 the cook, and the brusque b· visitor

busy
ph 180– 6 when he sees his would-be healers b·,

buyer
p 439– 3 False Belief, . . . is a b· for this firm.

by-and-by
a 21–31 B·, ashamed of his zigzag course,

bygone
s 134– 1 To-day the cry of b· ages is repeated,

byways
s 158–19 the b· of this wilderness world,

C

Cæsar
a 20– 1 He rendered "unto C·— *Matt.* 22 : 21.
g 540–17 Science renders "unto C·— *Matt.* 22 : 21.

Cæsar's
a 20– 2 the things which are C· ;— *Matt.* 22 : 21.
g 540–18 the things which are C· ; — *Matt.* 22 : 21.

Cain (*see also* **Cain's**)
sp 89–27 C· . . . concluded that if life was in the body,
g 538–24 she conceived, and bare C·,— *Gen.* 4 : 1.
540–25 C· brought of the fruit— *Gen.* 4 : 3.
540–28 C· is the type of mortal and material man,
541– 4 Jealous . . . C· seeks Abel's life,
541– 7 but unto C·, and to his offering,— *Gen.* 4 : 5.
541–14 C· rose up against Abel— *Gen.* 4 : 8.
541–19 the Lord [Jehovah] said unto C·,— *Gen.* 4 : 9.
542–15 Therefore whosoever slayeth C·— *Gen.* 4 : 15.
542–17 set a mark upon C·,— *Gen.* 4 : 15.
542–27 C· went out from the presence— *Gen.* 4 : 16.

Cain's
g 541– 3 more . . . than does C· fruit.
541–10 than for the worship expressed by C· fruit?

calamities
f 223–28 Marvels, c·, and sin will much more abound
r 486–32 these c· often drive mortals to seek and

calculate
sp 85– 1 read the stars or c· an eclipse.
s 162–32 "it is impossible to c· the mischief which
b 319– 5 To c· one's life-prospects from a

calculated
s 111–21 an essay c· to offset the tendency of the age

calculations
f 209–26 mundane formations, astronomical c·,
p 429–24 even according to the c· of natural science.

calculus
f 209–29 swallowed up in the infinite c· of Spirit.
g 520–15 and thought accepts the divine infinite c·.

calendar
a 20– 9 Jesus' history made a new c·,
g 520–11 according to the c· of time.

calendars
f 246– 5 Life and its faculties are not measured by c·.

calf

g 514–24 And the *c·* and the young lion,— *Isa.* 11 : 6.

California

a 21–16 while I am *en route* for *C·*,

call

last
b 291– 7 but this last *c·* of wisdom cannot come till
lesser
b 291– 8 till mortals have . . . yielded to each lesser *c·*
mental
sp 86– 8 His quick apprehension of this mental *c·*
midnight
p 365– 6 preparing their helpers for the "midnight *c·*,"
of error
a 21–26 worldly man is at the beck and *c·* of error,

pr 15–30 they assuredly *c·* down infinite blessings.
a 20– 9 which we *c·* the Christian era ;
31– 4 "*C·* no man your father upon— *Matt.* 23 : 9.
40– 7 I will *c·* for thee."— *Acts* 24 : 25.
sp 82–20 as before the change we *c·* death,
87–13 The Scotch *c·* such vision "second sight,"
92–25 We should blush to *c·* that real which
98–25 multitudes consider that which they *c· science*
s 157–14 the substratum . . . which we *c·* matter ;
ph 172– 9 if man passes through what we *c·* death
173–27 and so continue to *c·* upon matter
173–32 *c·* into action less faith than Buddhism
189–15 We *c·* the body material ; but
f 219–16 We shall not *c·* the body weak,
b 285– 4 not alone hereafter in what men *c·* Paradise,
287– 9 We *c·* the absence of Truth, *error*.
307–12 It says : . . . put spirit into what I *c·* matter,
o 356–27 Would any one *c·* it wise and good
p 372– 4 What you *c·* matter was originally
372–12 and then *c·* his bonds material and
373–28 When . . . we *c·* these conditions disease.
392–16, 17 You will *c·* it neuralgia, but we *c·* it a belief.
408–30 condition of the body which we *c·* sensation
411–14 a disease which moderns would *c· dementia.*
412–10 may *c·* the disease by name when you mentally
416–16 The material body, which you *c· me,*
420– 6 they should early *c·* an experienced
t 444– 9 their brethren upon whom they may *c·*,
464–16 the sufferer could *c·* a surgeon,
r 479–16 Does that which we *c·* dead ever see
g 504–27 Did infinite Mind create matter, and *c·* it
515–29 *C·* the mirror divine Science,
515–30 and *c·* man the reflection.
527–24 to see what he would *c·* them :— *Gen.* 2 : 19.
549–20 including those which we *c·* human,
555–20 and *c·* this sham unity *man,*

called

pref xi–22 When God *c·* the author to proclaim His Gospel
a 27 25 "Many are *c·*, but few are— *Matt.* 22 : 14.
34–28 which has since been *c·* the ascension.
61– 1 which destroys the belief *c·* sin
44–20 Could it be *c·* supernatural for the
45–25 disciples at first *c·* him a spirit, ghost,
46–26 his final demonstration, *c·* the ascension,
52–31 *c·* Jesus a glutton and a wine-bibber.
sp 75–26 one possible moment, when . . . those *c·* dead,
80–24 over its lower substratum, *c·* matter.
81–22 give to the worms the body *c·* man,
84–26 material personalities *c·* spirits,
86– 5 mortal mind, whose touch *c·* for aid.
88–17 and at another are *c·* spirits.
90– 6 the imaginary line *c·* the equator
an 101–30 animal magnetism, recently *c·* hypnotism,
s 108–24 the opposite of Truth,— *c·* error,
109–27 his name shall be *c·* Wonderful."— *Isa.* 9 : 6.
110– 9 I beheld, . . . the awful unreality *c·* evil.
126–19 Or shall all that . . . be *c·* supernatural,
127–30 C. S. eschews what is *c·* natural science,
135–14 and when Truth casts out the evil *c·* disease,
137–26 the impetuous disciple had been *c·*
139– 7 by what men *c·* miracles ;
143–10 The divine Mind never *c·* matter *medicine,*
153–19 and this belief is *c·* a boil.
162–23 restored what is *c·* the lost substance of lungs,
162–26 as surely as it heals what is *c·* functional,
ph 168–21 in defiance of what is *c·* material law,
185–29 material stratum of the human mind, *c·* brain,
190– 8 human belief *c·* mortal man
190–13 and the bulk of a body, *c·* man.
192–32 I was *c·* to visit Mr. Clark in Lynn,
199–28 belief . . . gave his thought-forces, *c·* muscles,
f 204–13 an intelligence or Mind *c·* God.
204–15 cannot therefore be mind, though so *c·*.
206–32 There are evil beliefs, often *c·* evil spirits ;
213– 2 supposition of reality is *c·* a deceiver,
245– 4 the London medical magazine *c·* The Lancet
250–14 and that one is *c·* man ;
254–17 prior to the change *c·* death,
b 274– 7 *Natural science,* as it is commonly *c·*,

called

b 274–26 The conventional firm, *c·* matter and mind,
281–14 The one Ego, the one Mind or Spirit *c·* God,
285–10 the *unlikeness c·* sin, sickness, and
290–16 If the change *c· death* destroyed the
293– 9 the more ethereal is *c·* mind.
293–10 the illusion *c·* a mortal,
293–25 The manifestations of evil, . . . are *c·*
295–25 All that is *c·* mortal thought
302–26 infinite Principle, *c·* Person or God.
309–10 He was no longer *c·* Jacob, but Israel,
309–15 were to be *c·* the children of Israel,
313–29 Jesus *c·* the body, which by spiritual power
319–11 material means (commonly *c·* nature)
331–27 constitute the triune Person *c·* God,
339– 8 Spirit, alone created all, and *c·* it good.
o 343–18 proving by what are wrongly *c·* miracles,
p 362–12 (Mary Magdalene, as she has since been *c·*)
374–13 state of mortal mind, though it is *c·* matter.
380– 2 which ends in a belief *c·* death,
398– 1 Sometimes Jesus *c·* a disease by name,
398–11 synagogue ruler's daughter, whom they *c·* dead
409– 6 animate error *c·* nerves, brain, mind,
411– 4 If the student silently *c·* the disease by
411–24 The mental state is *c·* a material state.
414–14 whether it is *c·* dementia, hatred,
427–26 *C·* to the bed of death, what material remedy
430–27 The evidence for the prosecution being *c·*
431– 1 must remain silent until *c·* for at this trial,
431–20 The next witness is *c·* :
432– 9 Another witness is *c·* for by the
432–21 I was *c·* for, shortly after the
436–19 result which they were *c·* to prevent.
437–20 False Belief, *c·* C. S. to order
t 447–10 heal the sick when *c·* upon for aid,
r 469–16 opposite of infinite Mind— *c· devil*
477–28 when they *c·* a certain beautiful lake
478–28 and *c·* me by His grace,— *Gal.* 1 : 15.
482–16 Jesus *c·* himself "the Son of man,"— *Matt.* 9 : 6.
483–16 Science has *c·* the world to battle
485–27 delineates foreign agents, *c·* disease and sin.
487– 6 both before and after that which is *c·* death.
g 504– 3 God *c·* the light Day,— *Gen.* 1 : 5.
504– 4 and the darkness He *c·* Night.— *Gen.* 1 : 5.
506– 8 God *c·* the firmament Heaven.— *Gen.* 1 : 8.
506–22 God *c·* the dry land Earth ;— *Gen.* 1 : 10.
506–23 the waters *c·* He Seas :— *Gen.* 1 : 10.
508– 1 human or material belief, *c·* mortal man.
520–10 The numerals of infinity, *c· seven days,*
522–13 *c·* life and intelligence in matter.
523–17 One is *c·* the Elohistic,
523–18 Supreme Being is therein *c·* Elohim.
523–19 The other document is *c·* the Jehovistic,
523–20 Deity therein is always *c·* Jehovah,
523–26 the creator is *c·* Jehovah, or the Lord.
524– 7 *c·* the Supreme Being by the national name of
524–17 that He should now be *c·* Jehovah?
527 24 Adam *c·* every living creature,— *Gen.* 2 : 19.
532–13 Lord God [Jehovah] *c·* unto Adam,— *Gen.* 3 : 9.
534–16 material intelligence *c· energy*
535–30 God *c·* the dry land Earth :— *Gen.* 1 : 10.
536– 1 the waters *c·* He Seas "— *Gen.* 1 : 10.
551– 5 cannot produce its opposite . . . *c·* matter.
551–18 transmitted through these bodies *c·* eggs,
ap 567–15 that old serpent, *c·* the devil,— *Rev.* 12 : 9.
568– 5 Science is able to destroy this lie, *c·* evil.
572–24 stage in human experience *c·* death,
gl 580–17 the opposite of Love, *c·* hate ;
580–18 usurper of Spirit's creation, *c·* . . . matter ;
586–10 the divine Principle, commonly *c·* God.

calling

pr 6– 7 *C·* on Him to forgive our work
a 31– 9 no record of his *c·* any man by the name of
s 148–20 *c·* that *man* which is not the counterpart,
154– 6 *c·* up the fear that creates the image of disease
ph 175–16 If a random thought, *c·* itself dyspepsia,
f 251–31 beliefs, which rob Mind, *c·* it matter,
b 283–30 by *c·* a curve a straight line
p 422– 1 and then *c·* the process mathematics.
491– 9 the latter *c·* itself right.
g 528–23 and *c·* them real and God-given,
528–26 *c·* them *mankind,* — that is, a kind of man.
532–20 the divine voice *c·* out to the corporeal senses.

calls

a 39–13 The Bible *c·* death an enemy,
m 60–24 An ill-attuned ear *c·* discord harmony,
sp 73– 3 Spiritualism *c·* one person, . . . *material,*
s 114– 2 *c·* sick and sinful humanity *mortal mind,*
114– 8 and *c· mind* both human and divine.
124–27 Human knowledge *c·* them forces of matter ;
ph 170– 4 The discord which *c·* for material methods
187–29 this so-called mind then *c·* itself dead ;
f 229–11 *c·* both the offspring of spirit,
b 287–18 Evil *c·* itself something, when it is nothing.
307–32 the voice of Truth still *c·* :

calls

b	311–28	They are only what mortal belief c· them.
	312– 4	That which material sense c· intangible,
p	399–18	manages it, and then c· it material.
g	507–30	inverts this appearing and c· ideas material.

calm

sp	99–23	The c·, strong currents of true spirituality,
s	109–15	c·, and buoyant with hope,
ph	198– 5	The patient may seem c· under it, but he is not.
f	248– 1	unchanging c· and glorious freedom of
o	358–15	It presents the c· and clear verdict of Truth
p	366–27	c· in the presence of both sin and disease,
	391– 7	Instead of blind and c· submission to
	393–32	It is well to be c· in sickness ;
	415–25	c· and instruct mortal mind with immortal
	421–21	C· the excitement sometimes induced
r	495–18	nor doubt overshadow your . . . c· trust,
g	506–11	The c· and exalted thought or

calmly

a	41– 8	The God-inspired walk c· on

calomel

ph	198– 1	harm his patients even more than his c·

Calvary

a	30– 9	his struggles in Gethsemane and on C·,
b	317–23	whom they had loved before the tragedy on C·.
ap	575–31	Cross of C·, which binds human society

cambric

p	379–15	the hue of her blood on a c· handkerchief,

came

pref	vii– 5	yet it traversed the night, and c· where,
	ix–12	she "lisped in numbers, for the numbers c·."
	ix–31	she c· at length to its solution ;
	xi–23	c· the charge to plant and water His
pr	5–29	c· to "destroy the works of the— I John 3 : 8.
	6–26	He c· teaching and showing men how to
a	27–29	the essential religion he c· to establish
	30–19	Christ Jesus c· to rebuke rabbinical error
	33– 7	Their bread indeed c· down from heaven.
	47–28	each one c· to a violent death except
m	56– 1	When our great Teacher c· to him for baptism,
s	108– 1	Whence c· to me this heavenly conviction,
	109–23	The revelation . . . c· to me gradually
	131–17	"He c· unto his own,— John 1 : 11.
	134–12	it c· about that human rights were
	135–16	"it c· to pass, when the devil was— Luke 11 : 14.
ph	169– 8	But it always c· about as I had foretold.
	184–30	Her breath c· gently.
f	214– 2	they c· as sound to the primitive prophets.
	214–13	They go out as they c· in,
	224–27	as he c· of old to the patriarch at noonday
b	319–22	The divine Science . . . c· through inspiration,
p	362– 7	A "strange woman" c· in.— Prov. 23 : 27.
	364–21	spiritual purgation which c· through the
	389–28	case of convulsions, . . . c· under my
	398– 5	rent him sore and c· out of him,— Mark 9 : 26.
	439– 7	when a message c· from False Belief,
	439–23	You c· to his rescue, only to
r	473– 7	Christ c· to destroy the belief of sin.
	474–18	Jesus c· to destroy sin, sickness, and death ;
g	529– 2	there c· a suggestion of change in the
	529– 4	It c· about, also, that instruments were
	533–22	which c· from Adam to form Eve.
ap	566–16	Out of the land of bondage c·,
	572–26	Through what sense c· this vision to St. John?
	574– 6	c· unto me one of the seven angels— Rev. 21 : 9.

camel

f	241–31	"easier for a c· to go through the— Matt. 19 : 24.
t	449– 9	"easier for a c· to go through the— Matt. 19 : 24.

camels

s	140–15	straining out gnats and swallowing c·.
f	202– 2	straining out gnats and swallowing c·.
p	366–20	while they swallow the c· of bigoted pedantry.

camera

c	264– 6	we sometimes behold in the c· of
b	305– 5	A picture in the c· . . . is not the original,

campaign

r	492–17	Discussing his c·, General Grant said :

Canaan

gl	582–24	definition of

cancel

pr	5–22	not to be used as a confessional to c· sin.

cancelled

pr	5–26	If prayer nourishes the belief that sin is c·,

cancels

a	22–31	Mercy c· the debt only when justice approves.
o	361– 3	c· the disagreement, and settles the
p	404–15	and reformation c· the crime.

cancer

p	390–28	whether it is c·, consumption, or smallpox.
	395–25	a tumor, a c·, or decayed lungs,

cannibal

f	214–25	spread their table with c· tidbits

cannon's

f	225–21	nor did . . . freedom come from the c· mouth.

canon

p	382–18	so-called law of matter a c· "more honored

canvas

sp	86–32	before the artist can convey them to c·.

capabilities

b	312–25	A personal sense of God and of man's c·
	322– 9	is obtained and his c· revealed.

capable

sp	89–22	We are all c· of more than we do.
	92– 5	c· of experiencing pleasure and pain
	92– 6	c· of imparting these sensations.
s	128–13	is c· of greater endurance,
	160–23	never c· of acting contrary to
ph	174– 7	Nothing save divine power is c· of
	179– 2	the sudden cures of which it is c· ;
	182– 8	c· of producing the highest human good?
f	206–10	Will-power is c· of all evil.
	230–12	to suppose Him c· of
o	355–27	Without this . . . no one is c· of impartial or
	357– 3	for doing what He created man c· of
	357–11	or makes man c· of suffering
p	393–13	God has made man c· of this,
	432– 5	whereas Mortal Man, . . . is c· of falsehood.
	435– 6	Mortal Mind, which alone is c· of sin
r	480–20	never made man c· of sin.
	480–22	seems to make men c· of wrong-doing.
	481–15	declaring . . . good and evil to be c· of
g	532–23	Is Mind c· of error as well as of truth,

capacious

p	425–29	If you have sound and c· lungs

capacities

sp	94–31	union with the infinite c· of the one Mind.
ph	200– 6	and illustrated the grand human c·
f	202–22	the finity of error and the infinite c· of Truth,
	227–28	crippled your c·, enfeebled your body,
c	258–22	The human c· are enlarged and perfected
t	445– 8	Unfold the latent energies and c·

capacity

sp	85– 3	which demonstrates the c· of Soul,
s	128–11	ability to exceed their ordinary c·.
ph	165– 6	To measure intellectual c· by
	179– 8	the spiritual c· to apprehend thought
f	209–31	a conscious, constant c· to understand God.
	223– 4	fetters of man's finite c· are forged by
o	357– 8	Truth creates neither a lie, a c· to lie, nor a liar.
r	475–31	nor can God, . . . engender the c· or freedom to
g	519–12	Human c· is slow to discern and to grasp

capitalization

b	319–31	by special and proper c·

captive

f	224–30	power of God brings deliverance to the c·.
p	434– 1	open wide those prison doors and set the c· free.
r	495–13	sets the c· free physically and morally.

captives

pref	xi–19	deliverance to the c· [of sense].— Luke 4 : 18.
s	161– 8	Bible case of the three young Hebrew c·,

captivity

s	133–15	Even in c· among foreign nations,
f	227–20	but evil and error lead into c·.

cardinal

a	52–22	These were the two c· points of Mind-healing,
ap	577–13	but its four c· points are :

care

best

p	383– 8	Scientist takes the best c· of his body when he

God's

m	66–11	Trials are proofs of God's c·.

good

p	383– 5	One says : "I take good c· of my body."

His

gl	589–11	man is His idea, the child of His c·.

loving

t	454–27	Let your loving c· and counsel support all their

omnipotent

f	231–25	To fear sin is to . . . distrust His omnipotent c·.

unselfish

m	59–17	Tender words and unselfish c·

pr	9–29	since you do not c· to tread in the footsteps of
m	62–23	divine Mind, . . . will c· for the human body,
ph	188–20	sickness and c·, are traced upon mortals
b	272–13	the c· our Master took not to impart to dull ears

career
devious
s 164– 1   said : . . . Dark and perplexed, our devious c·
earthly
a 30–23   throughout the whole earthly c· of Jesus,
b 334– 8   the fleshly Jesus, whose earthly c· was brief.
glorious
a 32–32   in the twilight of a glorious c·
his
a 51– 4   the sublimest influence of his c·.
sacred
a 37–20   would gladly have turned his sacred c· into
sinless
a 26–24   the precious import of our Master's sinless c·
that
a 37–22   take up the more practical import of that c· !

a 40–19   If a c· so great and good as that of Jesus
careful
s 153–29   we shall be more c· of our mental conditions,
ph 196–12   A c· study of this text shows
t 444–18   be c· always to "judge righteous— John 7 : 24.
careless
s 110–21   or by c· or malicious students,
p 364–32   Did the c· doctor, the nurse, the cook,
care-lined
f 245–14   She had no c· face,
cares
m 58–30   but nothing can abolish the c· of marriage
   59–10   the annoyances and c· of domestic economy.
sp 78–25   not in the medley where matter c· for matter,
g 556–27   before it c· to solve the problem of being,
careth
m 58–31   "She that is married c·— I Cor. 7 : 34.
t 464–27   and c· not for the sheep."— John 10 : 13.
caring
p 413–21   but in c· for an infant
t 445–29   and c· only for the fees.
carious
s 162– 9   restores c· bones to soundness.
  162–22   c· bones have been restored to healthy
ph 193– 5   said the bone was c· for several inches.
carnal
a 52– 5   His affections were pure ; theirs were c·.
an 105– 6   over the c· or mortal mind,
s 131–10   "The c· mind is enmity— Rom. 8 : 7.
c 263–11   C· beliefs defraud us.
b 292–27   This c· material mentality, misnamed mind,
  311– 3   What we term mortal mind or c· mind,
  315–13   Their c· minds were at enmity with it.
o 345–29   enrages the c· mind and is the main cause of
  345–30   cause of the c· mind's antagonism.
p 395–11   overcomes faith in a c· mind,
g 534–18   "The c· mind is enmity— Rom. 8 : 7.
carnivorous
g 514–20   The individuality created by God is not c·,
carpet
s 154–29   thinks she has hurt her face by falling on the c·,
carried
s 130–29   c· out in special theories
ph 171–19   sifted through matter, o· on a nerve,
b 314–25   c· the problem of being,
p 387– 7   that intellectual labor has been c·
ap 570–10   to be c· away of the flood. — Rev. 12 : 15.
  574–11   ministry of Truth, . . . c· John away in spirit.
carries
sp 90–18   c· it through the air and over the ocean.
s 153–27   mortal mind, . . . contains and c· the infection.
f 204–10   (mortal man) who c· out the delusions
  241– 7   and c· off their fleeting joys.
b 294– 5   c· within itself the seeds of all error.
carry
pr 10–17   One of the forms of worship in Thibet is to c·
s 116–15   nor do they c· the day against physical enemies,
ph 176–26   can c· its ill-effects no farther than
f 243–21   Neither . . . can c· on such telegraphy ;
b 328–18   Our missionaries c· the Bible to India,
g 514–17   They c· the baggage of stern resolve,
carve
f 248–28   c· them out in grand and noble lives.
carves
b 299– 2   when he c· his "Statue of Liberty,"
case
any
s 149–13   If you fail to succeed in any c·, it is because
belief in the
ph 198–24   formed by his doctor's belief in the c·,
Bible
s 161– 7   as in the Bible c· of the three young Hebrew

case
chronic
ph 178–16   that chronic c· is not difficult to cure.
cope with the
p 423–22   strong, instead of weak, to cope with the c· ;
determines a
ph 194– 7   determines a c· for better or for worse.
difficult
t 449–18   than it does to heal the most difficult c·.
either
sp 73– 1   In either c·, one does not support the other.
ph 170–29   but in either c· dependent upon his
  181–18   In either c· you must improve your mental
every
an 105–13   Mortal mind, . . . is the criminal in every c· ;
s 149– 5   more excellent way is divine Science in every c·.
p 415– 3   Mind in every c· is the eternal God,
factor in the
s 151– 2   as if there was but one factor in the c· ;
fever
p 380– 2   a fever c·, which ends in a belief called
governs the
p 422–31   he believes that . . . matter— governs the c·.
his
ph 194–30   His c· proves material sense to be but
his own
t 464–18   he could handle his own c·
hopeless
ph 196–25   Many a hopeless c· of disease is induced by a
however obstinate the
p 414– 5   However obstinate the c·, it yields more readily
individual
p 408– 9   cannot, . . . shield the individual c·
injures the
p 403–29   improves or injures the c· in proportion
judge the
p 404– 1   in order to judge the c· according to C. S.
leaving the
an 104–27   leaving the c· worse than before it was grasped
mental
p 430–17   Suppose a mental c· to be on trial,
nature of a
p 403–28   The human mind determines the nature of a c·,
of convulsions
p 389–28   A c· of convulsions, produced by
of dropsy
s 156– 5   A c· of dropsy, given up by the faculty,
of paralysis
s 152–15   apparently cured a c· of paralysis simply by
of sickness
p 386– 3   not to be accepted in the c· of sickness,
of sin
p 386– 4   any more than it is in the c· of sin.
of temptation
p 441– 7   and in c· of temptation, to give heavy bonds
one
p 403–11   is employed to remove the illusion in one c·,
  422–24   A surgeon is employed in one c·,
one side of the
f 238–20   listening only to one side of the c·.
particular
ph 178– 2   though they know nothing of this particular c·
plead the
p 412– 4   plead the c· scientifically for Truth.
renders your
t 461–22   to admit that . . . renders your c· less curable.
reverse the
p 392–24   Reverse the c·.
single
s 155–21   in order to heal a single c· of disease.
such a
pr 3–30   In such a c·, the only acceptable prayer is
symptoms of the
p 412– 6   to meet the . . . symptoms of the c· you treat,
take the
t 458–14   the divine Mind is ready to take the c·.
terrible
s 156– 6   It was a terrible c·.
testimony in the
p 434–27   The only valid testimony in the c·
this
pr 10–30   In this c· infinite Love will not grant the
p 435–29   what jurisdiction had his Honor, . . . in this c· ?
treating the
s 161–25   treating the c· according to his physical diag-
    nosis,
your own
p 384–23   if . . . you are not fit to conduct your own c·

m 66–26   as must always be the c·,
  68–20   I have named her c· to individuals,
sp 81–14   Nor is the c· improved when alleged spirits
  81–23   in the c· of man as truly as
  81–24   in the c· of numbers and of music,
an 104–25   it is a c· of the greater error overcoming the
  135–31   as must be the c· in the cycles of

case

s	148– 1	When his students brought to him a c·
	159– 7	The c· was brought to trial.
ph	189–21	The reverse is the c· with all the formations of
	193–30	and what his physician said of the c·,
p	396–11	Never say . . . how much you have to contend
		with in a c·,
	401–19	as is the c· with a fermenting fluid.
	412–28	If the c· is that of a young child or an infant,
	420–20	or diminishes . . . as the c· may require,
	422–13	If such be the c·, explain to them the
	425– 6	If the c· to be mentally treated is consumption,
	431– 2	would be allowed to testify in the c·.
	433–15	The c· is given to the jury.
	434–15	the c· for Mortal Man *versus* Personal Sense
	434–24	Mortal Man has had no proper counsel in the c·.
	436–27	Judge Medicine sat in judgment on the c·,
	438–21	the facts in the c· show that this fur is a

cases

all
ph	176–21	Should all c· of organic disease be treated by

both
p	370–17	but it uses the same medicine in both c·.
gl	598– 6	the original word is the same in both c·,

certain
m	56– 5	Jesus' concessions (in certain c·)

majority of
m	60–19	This, however, in a majority of c·,
r	482– 2	gives the exact meaning in a majority of c·.

most
s	140– 2	more than it is needed in most c· ;

other
r	482– 8	In other c·, use the word *sense*,

parallel
p	422–22	suppose two parallel c· of bone-disease,

same
o	359– 5	Yet Scientists will take the same c·,

such
s	177–31	In such c· a few persons believe the potion
o	343– 1	The people are taught in such c· to say, Amen.
p	394–32	faith is not the healer in such c·.
	433–11	The jury must regard in such c· only the
t	443–18	should give up such c·,
	446–10	has generally completely healed such c·.

these
pref	x–17	These c· for the most part have been

well-authenticated
pref	x–16	thousands of well-authenticated c· of healing,

s	162–18	in c· of both acute and chronic disease
ph	176–23	c· of hysteria, hypochondria, and
p	430–17	as c· are tried in court.

cast

pr	1– *	*and be thou c· into the sea ;— Mark* 11 : 23.
	6–23	uncovered and rebuked sin before he c· it out.
a	35– 5	and c· their net on the right side.
	41– 1	hope must be c· beyond the veil of matter
s	161– 8	captives, c· into the Babylonian furnace ;
ph	168– 6	Whatever influence you c· on the side of matter,
f	242–24	for my vesture they did c· lots." — *John* 19 : 24.
	244–28	Such admissions c· us headlong into darkness
b	271–26	or to c· them on the right side for Truth,
	272–17	neither c· ye your pearls before — *Matt.* 7 : 6.
	321– 8	When, led by wisdom to c· down his rod,
p	362– *	*Why art thou c· down,— Psal.* 42 : 11.
	366– 4	first c· moral evils out of himself
	366– 6	enable him to c· physical evils out of his patient;
	422– 3	by whom do your children c· them out ?" — *Matt.*
		12 : 27.
	431–11	arrested Mortal Man . . . and c· him into
	441–15	nor can Disease c· him into prison.
t	447–30	A sinner is afraid to c· the first stone.
	460–32	shadow of old errors was no longer c· upon
r	494–31	should be said . . . they c· fear and all evil
ap	563–24	and did c· them to the earth :— *Rev.* 12 : 4.
	567–23	The words "c· unto the earth"— *Rev.* 12 : 13.
	568–16	accuser of our brethren is c· down, — *Rev.* 12 : 10.
	569–30	saw that he was c· unto the earth,— *Rev.* 12 : 13.

cast out

pr	7– 5	when he c· out devils and healed the sick
a	34–15	heal the sick, c· out evils,
	41–32	c· out evils and heal the sick.
	49– 4	healed the sick, c· out evil,
	51–31	c· out evil, and raise the dead.
m	56–12	the corporeal sense of creation was c· out,
sp	79–17	Jesus c· out evil spirits, or false beliefs.
s	130–18	beliefs must be denied and c· out
	135–15	When Christ c· out the devil of dumbness,
	136– 4	a divine Principle, which would c· out error
	137– 2	c· out evil, raise the dead ;
	138–11	diseases were c· out neither by corporeality,
	138–22	easier for Christianity to c· out sickness than
ph	170–20	Jesus healed the sick and c· out error,
	185–22	Jesus c· out evil and healed the sick,
	188–27	must be uprooted and c· out.

cast out

ph	191–31	Truth is able to c· out the ills of the flesh.
b	281–31	The old belief must be c· out
	322– 1	to heal the sick, and c· out evils
o	342–12	should c· out evils and heal the sick.
	348–12	delusions, were c· out and the dumb spake.
p	362– *	*In my name shall they c· out devils :— Mark* 16 : 17.
	392– 6	must be c· out to readjust the balance for God.
	411–16	Thereupon Jesus c· out the evil,
	418–27	C· out all manner of evil.
	422– 3	"If I by Beelzebub c· out devils, — *Matt.* 12 : 27.
	442–13	Divine Love had c· out fear.
t	445–23	hatred, and revenge are c· out by the
	455–14	"First c· out the beam — *Matt.* 7 : 5.
	455–15	shalt thou see clearly to c· out — *Matt.* 7 : 5.
	462– 5	c· out error, heal the sick,
r	494–30	Our Master c· out devils (evils) and healed the
ap	564– 1	and c· out devils through Beelzebub.
	567–14	And the great dragon was c· out,— *Rev.* 12 : 9.
	567–16	he was c· out into the earth,— *Rev.* 12 : 9.
	567–17	his angels were c· out with him.— *Rev.* 12 : 9.
	567–22	and it is c· out by Christ, Truth,
	567–27	His angels, . . . are c· out with their author.
	570– 8	c· out of his mouth water— *Rev.* 12 : 15.
	570–12	the dragon c· out of his mouth.— *Rev.* 12 : 16.

casteth

a	52–32	"He c· out devils through— *Luke* 11 : 15.
ph	180–24	influence of divine Love which c· out fear.
p	373–18	"perfect Love c· out fear."— *I John* 4 : 18.
	406–10	"Perfect Love c· out fear."— *I John* 4 : 18.
	410–19	perfect Love c· out fear.— *I John* 4 : 18.

casting

pr	12– 8	This, however, is one belief c· out another,
	12– 9	a belief in the unknown c· out a
a	33– 8	healing the sick and c· out error.
	34– 3	by c· out error and making the
	35–24	c· out error and healing the sick.
	41–15	c· out error and healing the sick,
	42–32	by c· out error, healing the sick,
	46–11	again seen c· out evil and healing the sick.
m	68–20	when c· my bread upon the waters,
sp	97–31	apostolic work of c· out error and healing the
s	135–29	c· out error and healing the sick,
	136–13	c· out evils and healing the sick?
	138–13	c· out the errors of mortal mind.
ph	182– 2	The act . . . of c· out error with Truth,
	184– 9	finding and c· out by denial the error
f	210– 8	c· out evils, and destroying death,
	234–14	avoid c· pearls before those who trample them
b	271–10	Truth, c· out all inharmony.
	316–28	healing the sick, c· out evils,
	332–15	healing the sick and c· out evils,
o	347–17	healing the sick, and c· out evils.
p	392– 7	C· out evil and fear enables
r	482–16	the truth c· out all error.
gl	583– 8	c· out error and healing the sick ;
	583–18	c· out devils, or error, and healing the sick.

casts

pr	14–28	understanding c· out error and heals the sick,
a	25–15	c· out error, and triumphs over death.
	33–24	c· out error, raises the dead from trespasses
s	135–13	when Truth heals the sick, it c· out evils,
	135–14	and when Truth c· out the evil called disease,
	143– 3	Christ c· out evils and heals the sick.
ph	183–26	Truth c· out all evils and
	189– 7	above the cruder theories . . . and c· out a fear.
f	230– 8	which c· out error and heals the sick.
b	275–32	It c· out error and heals the sick.
	282– 1	Truth c· out evils and heals the sick.
o	350–11	Truth c· out error and heals the sick.
t	448–10	and c· thee down from the pinnacle.
r	472– 3	c· out suppositional error and heals the sick.
	473–30	which heals the sick and c· out error,
	482–26	Sickness is part of the error which Truth c· out.
	495– 2	Truth c· out error now as surely as it did
	497–11	spiritual understanding that c· out evil

catalepsy

f	217–11	even of c· and hysteria ;

cataleptic

s	128–24	waking him from a c· nightmare,

cataplasms

s	158–16	Drugs, c·, and whiskey are

cataract

ph	192–14	It is the headlong c·, the devouring flame,

catarrh

f	220– 4	have continual colds, c·, and cough."
	220–12	he has no c· from wet feet,
	220–15	leaves c· to the latter.
p	386– 6	belief says that you may catch cold and have c·;
	386– 9	c·, fever, rheumatism, or consumption,

catch

f 205–16 we can *c·* clear glimpses of God only as
o 349–26 Mortal thought does not at once *c·* the higher
p 386– 6 belief says that you may *c·* cold
427–32 will waken . . . to *c·* this trumpet-word

catches

s 145– 2 natural musician *c·* the tones of harmony,

categories

b 269–13 *c·* of metaphysics rest on one basis,

caterpillar

sp 74–17 The *c·*, transformed into a beautiful insect,

Catholic

f 238– 9 Losing her crucifix, the Roman *C·* girl said,

cattle

f 222–25 and over the *c·*,"— *Gen.* 1 : 26.
r 475–25 and over the *c·*,— *Gen.* 1 : 26.
g 513–15 *c·*, and creeping thing,— *Gen.* 1 : 24.
513–23 and *c·* after their kind,— *Gen.* 1 : 25.
514–16 "the *c·* upon a thousand hills."— *Psal.* 50 : 10.
515–14 and over the *c·*,— *Gen.* 1 : 26.

caught

s 145– 1 or whether they *c·* its sweet tones,
154–13 had not *c·* the cholera by material contact,
ph 171– 2 mankind has *c·* their moral contagion.
b 304–22 If mortals *c·* harmony through
333–24 *c·* glorious glimpses of the Messiah, or Christ,
r 471–25 until she *c·* the first gleam of that which
477–26 Indians *c·* some glimpses of the underlying
ap 565– 8 *c·* up unto God, and to His throne.— *Rev.* 12 : 5.
565–27 and to be *c·* up unto God,

causation

all
ph 180–12 nor take the ground that all *c·* is
p 379– 7 recognizing all *c·* as vested in divine Mind.
417–13 all *c·* is Mind, acting through spiritual law.
mental
p 423– 9 Scientist, . . . commences with mental *c·*,
physical
b 286–12 Physical *c·* was put aside
spiritual
ph 170–22 Spiritual *c·* is the one question
170–23 spiritual *c·* relates to human progress.

f 208–25 Mind, not matter, is *c·*.
230–12 arranging law and *c·* so as to
g 552– 7 material hypotheses deal with *c·* as

causative

ph 195–12 whether it is mortal mind . . . that is *c·*.

Cause

g 547–20 evolution implies that the great First *C·* must

cause (noun)

and cure
f 220– 6 to look in other directions for *c·* and cure.
and effect
sp 83–31 from which *c·* and effect are interpreted.
85–30 The great Teacher knew both *c·* and effect,
s 114–23 C. S. explains all *c·* and effect as mental,
126–17 Shall Science explain *c·* and effect as being
161–30 looked as deeply for *c·* and effect into
f 211–18 nature of all so-called material *c·* and effect.
b 275–15 immortality, *c·*, and effect belong to God.
p 370– 9 law of *c·* and effect, or like producing like.
374–25 and ignorance of mental *c·* and effect.
g 556–20 In sleep, *c·* and effect are mere illusions.
any
p 419– 8 If your patient from any *c·* suffers a relapse,
t 446–31 will prevent . . . the ultimate triumph of any *c·*.
464–13 If from an injury or from any *c·*,
any other
f 207–21 there can be no effect from any other *c·*,
common
a 52–18 error and evil again make common *c·*
divine
b 286–24 they lack a divine *c·*.
exciting
ph 178–11 predisposing cause and the exciting *c·* are
f 230–32 the exciting *c·* of all suffering,
p 393– 7 remote, and exciting *c·* of all bad effects
from effect to
r 467–24 We reason imperfectly from effect to *c·*,
main
o 345–30 the main *c·* of the carnal mind's antagonism.
material
f 211–18 nature of all so-called material *c·*
p 416–11 will tell you that the troublesome material *c·*
meet the
p 419– 9 meet the *c·* mentally and courageously,
mental
s 157– 2 C. S. deals wholly with the mental *c·*
ph 187–17 Anatomy allows the mental *c·* of the latter
p 374–25 ignorance of mental *c·* and effect.

cause (noun)

no
f 253–12 you see there is no *c·* . . . able to
p 386–23 learn at length that there is no *c·* for grief,
of disease
ph 174–30 should understand that the *c·* of disease
f 230–32 *c·* of disease must be obliterated
p 370–21 since mortal mind must be the *c·* of disease
t 445–26 is the *c·* of disease rather than its cure.
463– 1 deals with the real *c·* of disease.
one primal
f 207–20 There is but one primal *c·*.
only
f 207–23 this great and only *c·*.
c 262–30 Divine Mind is the only *c·*
b 286–24 and since God, Spirit, is the only *c·*,
p 415– 2 Immortal Mind is the only *c·* ;
or approach
p 374–17 Ignorance of the *c·* or approach of disease
or effect
m 67–32 from any such *c·* or effect.
f 207–18 amalgamation of Truth and error in *c·* or effect.
predisposing
ph 178–11 predisposing *c·* and the exciting cause are
procuring
ph 171–27 the procuring *c·* of all sin and disease.
p 411–20 procuring *c·* and foundation of all sickness
real
p 402–32 a belief without a real *c·*.
t 463– 1 deals with the real *c·* of disease.
remote
ph 178– 8 The remote *c·* or belief of disease
seeks
b 279–31 Pantheism . . . seeks *c·* in effect,
shows the
a 53–19 Science shows the *c·* of the shock
spiritual
s 111–23 rather than to a final spiritual *c·*,
b 268– 5 to the spiritual *c·* of those lower things
313–26 and found the spiritual *c·*.
their
p 421–24 sometimes explain the symptoms and their *c·*
to effect
r 467–29 Reasoning from *c·* to effect
universal
b 331–19 divine Principle, Love, the universal *c·*,
without
p 386–28 had said, . . . "Your sorrow is without *c·*,"
without a
ap 504–28 "They hated me without a *c·*."— *John* 15 : 25.

s 124– 9 this belief mistakes effect for *c·*
ph 187–19 the *c·* of all materialistic action?
189–10 though the *c·* be unseen,
195–18 thought passes naturally from effect back to *c·*.
198–32 If matter were the *c·* of action,
c 262–31 *C·* does not exist in matter,
b 268– 9 looking . . . to Mind as the *c·* of every effect.
310–17 and the *c·* given for the exaltation of Jesus.
o 357–28 if another mighty and self creative *c·* exists
p 377–22 and you remove the *c·* of all disease
377–26 The *c·* of all so-called disease is mental,
393–32 the sin and the sinner, the disease and its *c·*.
415– 3 disease is neither a *c·* nor an effect.
422–11 Patients, unfamiliar with the *c·* of this
r 480–17 would make matter the *c·* as well as the effect
g 554– 2 even the *c·* of all that exists,

cause (verb)

pr 6–11 To *c·* suffering as the result of sin,
sp 93–14 nor creates aught that can *c·* evil.
s 160–15 to convey the mandate of mind . . . and so *c·*
ph 165–16 You say that . . . *c·* distressed stomachs and
175–14 to fancy that the perfume of clover . . . can *c·*
177–28 does human belief, you ask, *c·* this death?
f 206–30 God does not *c·* man to sin, to be sick, or to die.
208–15 to suppose that matter can both *c·* and cure
230–18 no more . . . than goodness can *c·* evil
b 318–13 We must *c·* the error to cease
p 370–13 by using the same drug which might *c·* the
374– 7 say : "How can my mind *c·* a disease I never
397– 9 You *c·* bodily sufferings and increase them by
403– 5 should and does *c·* the perpetrator to suffer,
414–10 impossibility that matter, . . . can suffer or *c·*
415–27 apparently *c·* the body to disappear.
419–12 nor fear has the power to *c·* disease or a relapse.
t 457–13 cannot . . . both cure and *c·* disease
463–18 can *c·* the mother no more suffering.
g 527– 3 to make it beautiful or to *c·* it to live and grow.
ap 570–10 that he might *c·* her to— *Rev.* 12 : 15.

caused

a 46–18 Jesus *c·* him to examine the nail-prints and the
49– 4 and *c·* the disciples to say to their Master :
51–29 *c·* the selfish materialist to hate him ;
m 64– 1 *c·* by the selfishness and inhumanity of man.
68–21 it may have *c·* the good to ponder

caused

an 104–24 and a belief originally c· the sickness,
s 164–18 c· by a majority of human beliefs
ph 183–12 first c· the condemnation of man to till the
193– 1 c· by a fall upon a wooden spike
b 312–13 you say that matter has c· his death.
p 377–15 A sudden joy or grief has c· what is termed
379–17 Oxford boys, who c· the death of a man,
399– 5 can matter cure what matter has c· ?
411–19 Jesus c· the evil to be self-seen
r 484–19 are really c· by the faith in them
g 520–21 had not c· it to rain — Gen. 2 : 5.
528–10 c· a deep sleep to fall upon Adam, — Gen. 2 : 21.

causeless

p 386–32 that lamentation is needless and c·.

causes

pr 12–20 It is a mortal belief, . . . which c· a drug to
a 22– 7 This c· them, even as drowning men,
39–10 c· mortals to regard death as a friend,
m 68–23 salutary c· sometimes incur these effects.
sp 93–13 Good never c· evil,
s 111–23 to attribute physical effects to physical c·
139– 1 the wicked to "forsake his way, — Isa. 55 : 7.
142–17 c· the left to let go its grasp
ph 170–19 what then c· it?   Not divine law,
188–23 What c· disease cannot cure it.
198–20 c· a vigorous reaction upon itself,
f 208– 7 this seeming power, . . . which c· disease
211–25 If . . . organism c· the eyes to see
229–23 If God c· man to be sick,
229–30 which c· the belief of sickness.
b 278–20 it would follow that there are two eternal c·,
318– 7 senses are saying that matter c· disease
o 342–25 It c· the deaf to hear,
344–12 understood . . . that error c· disease,
p 377– 3 If grief c· suffering, convince the sufferer that
378– 1 and c· the two to appear conjoined,
378–15 often c· the beast to retreat in terror.
379– 5 where the ordinary physician looks for c·.
387–25 mortal mind, . . . c· all things discordant.
399– 4 but if the material body c· disease,
401– 8 If faith in the truth . . . c· chemicalization
405–30 Belief in material suffering c· mortals to
t 449– 3 A little leaven c· the whole mass to ferment.
458–32 Christianity c· men to turn naturally from
r 482–31 but c· the belief in disease.
g 517–30 c· them to multiply, — to manifest His power.
542– 8 Truth c· sin to betray itself,
550–19 and c· our standard to trail in the dust.

causeth

s 140–26 c· no evil, disease, nor death.

causing

a 22– 4 selfishness and . . . c· constant retrogression,
sp 93–15 does not create a mind susceptible of c· evil,
p 415–18 c· a pale or flushed cheek.
422–17 c· it to depend less on material evidence.
g 520–31 never c· man to till the ground,

caustic

ph 198–17 by the application of c· or croton oil,

caution

gl 586–12 ignorance ; error ; desire ; c·.

cave

s 164– 2 groping of Homer's Cyclops around his c·."

caverns

sp 87–20 ignorant of the gems within its c·,

cave's

a 45– 1 great stone must be rolled from the c· mouth ;

cavil

ph 177– 4 I have demonstrated this beyond all c·.
b 306– 6 and demonstrated this beyond c·.

cavity

f 247– 9 upper and lower teeth without a decaying c·.

cease

s 126– 5 for mortality will c· when man beholds
140–16 only as we c· to worship materially.
160–24 If muscles can c· to act and become rigid
f 204–32 must unsay it and c· from such utterances ;
216– 5 Here theories c·, and Science unveils the
219– 2 and the mortal dream will forever c·.
228–12 It will c· when man enters into his heritage
234–21 or sin and sickness will never c·.
c 262–20 supposed pain and pleasure of matter c· to
b 288–14 conflict between truth and error, . . . will c·,
290–24 sin and error . . . do not c· at that moment,
318–14 We must cause the error to c·
327–13 way to escape the misery of sin is to c· sinning.
o 346–14 only as we c· to manifest evil or the belief that
p 370–28 and then they c· to improve.
391–16 will c· in proportion as the sin ceases.
418–14 sickness, sin, and death should c· through C. S.
r 467–12 as this fact becomes apparent, war will c·
476– 7 Error will c· to claim that soul is in body,

ceased

s 160–17 Has mortal mind c· speaking to them,

ceaseless

b 322–27 disappointments and c· woes,

ceases

m 57–28 until it c· to sigh over the world
68–31 Proportionately as human generation c·,
sp 97–16 without passing the boundary where, . . . it c·
b 276–18 c· to be any opportunity for sin and death.
o 346–20 If a dream c·, it is self-destroyed,
p 391–16 will cease in proportion as the sin c·.
r 468–29 One c· in proportion as the other is recognized.

ceasing

pr 15–21 We must "pray without c·." — I Thess. 5 : 17.

celebrate

a 35–14 They c· their Lord's victory over death,

celebrated

an 104– 8 Agassiz, the c· naturalist and author,
g 549–24 In one instance a c· naturalist, Agassiz,

celestial

a 26–17 to reveal the Science of c· being,
m 61– 7 The attainment of this c· condition would
an 100– 8 c· bodies, the earth, and animated things.
s 123– 1 theory as to the relations of the c· bodies,
f 209–19 distances, and revolutions of the c· bodies,
c 267–25 all error disappears in c· Truth.
b 298–26 Angels . . . are c· visitants,
299–29 and reveal the c· peaks.
320–32 stand in c· perfection before Elohim,
337–17 perfection is the order of c· being
g 509–11 Spirit creates no other than . . . c· bodies,
509–14 stellar universe is no more c· than our earth.
ap 572–29 terrestrial or c·, material or spiritual?

cell

ph 191–23 not a flower starts from its cloistered c·.
p 433–27 The prisoner is then remanded to his c·

cell-division

m 68–24 perpetuation of the floral species by bud or c·

cement

m 57– 1 Chastity is the c· of civilization
ap 571–19 The c· of a higher humanity will

censure

pr 3–29 the sharp c· our Master pronounces on
9– 3 The wrong lies in unmerited c·,

central

s 121–25 The sun is the c· stillness,
131–10 The c· fact of the Bible is the
f 209– 6 the c· sun of its own systems of ideas,
224–16 Of old the cross was truth's c· sign,
238–31 The cross is the c· emblem of history.
b 305– 7 Man, . . . reflects the c· light of being,
310–15 God, . . . as the c· Life and intelligence
t 454–30 the c· point of C. S.

centre

a 20–25 The truth is the c· of all religion.
m 58–22 c·, though not the boundary, of the affections.
60–18 Marriage . . . a c· for the affections.
f 204– 1 God is at once the c· and circumference of being.
c 262–15 absolute c· and circumference of his being.

centred

o 351–27 Israelites c· their thoughts on the material

centuries

ago
a 46– 8 which identified Jesus thus c· ago,
sp 82– 5 Chaucer wrote c· ago,
93– 2 Remember Jesus, who nearly nineteen c· ago
s 138–26 to-day as readily as it was proved c· ago.
f 224–12 C· ago religionists were ready to hail an
r 487–11 gave . . . hearing to the deaf c· ago,
495– 3 as surely as it did nineteen c· ago.
coming
b 321–30 And so it was in the coming c·,
labor of
m 67–27 does not put to silence the labor of c·.
later
a 55– 7 no more injustice than the later c· have
three
a 41–18 lost, about three c· after the crucifixion.

pref viii–17 Sickness has been combated for c· by doctors
a 55–15 immortal idea is sweeping down the c·,
sp 98–22 For c· — yea, always — natural science
s 147–11 though c· had passed away since
f 224–11 In the record of nineteen c·,
b 328–16 For c· it has been dormant,

centurion

s 133– 5 There was also a certain c· of whose faith

century

a 55– 2 advancing c·, . . . to-day subjects to
s 134–20 and unequalled success in the first c·.
147– 6 Late in the nineteenth c· I demonstrated

century

b	333–17	marked the first *c·* of the Christian era,
o	355–19	systematic healing power since the first *c·*.
p	383–22	eating or smoking poison for half a *c·*,
ap	560– 2	in connection with the nineteenth *c·*.

cerebellum

p	401–26	or restore will . . . to cerebrum and *c·*?

cerebro-spinal

ph	175– 7	*c·* meningitis, hay-fever, and rose-cold?

cerebrum

p	401–26	or restore will and action to *c·* and

ceremonies

a	31–14	He attached no importance to dead *c·*.
m	64– 9	seems on most occasions to be the master of *c·*,
s	131–23	which taketh away the *c·* and doctrines
	135–27	was not a creed, nor a system of *c·*,
f	228–32	excel the influence of their dead faith and *c·*.
gl	597– 3	consisted mostly of rites and *c·*.

ceremony

s	152–18	sick man supposed this *c·* was intended to

certain

pref	ix–10	As a *c·* poet says of himself,
	ix–12	*C·* essays written at that early date
pr	6–29	It is believed by many that a *c·* magistrate,
a	27–32	to kill him according to *c·* assumed
m	56– 4	Jesus' concessions (in *c·* cases)
	57– 6	through *c·* elements of the feminine,
sp	81– 8	can only prove that *c·* individuals
	91–22	*C·* erroneous postulates should be
s	122–11	so-called senses . . . ordain *c·* sections of
	133– 5	There was also a *c·* centurion of whose faith
	154– 4	a law of mortal mind that *c·* diseases
	161–16	"Man is endowed by his Maker with *c·*
ph	177– 6	as *c·* as the evidence of my own existence.
	179–13	preference of mortal mind for a *c·* method
f	228– 3	*c·* idiosyncrasies of mortal mind
	230–13	to bring about *c·* evil results,
	251– 7	Fright is so great at *c·* stages of
o	349–28	To a *c·* extent this is equally true of
p	362– 2	was once the honored guest of a *c·* Pharisee,
	370–11	which might be produced by a *c·* drug,
	375–22	making *c·* portions of it motionless.
	378– 1	associates sickness with *c·* circumstances
	379– 9	on whom *c·* English students experimented,
	386– 5	Expose the body to *c·* temperatures,
	386– 9	So long as mortals declare that *c·* states of
	396– 8	nor draw attention to *c·* symptoms
	399– 3	You say that *c·* material combinations
	399– 8	and puts the body through *c·* motions.
	400–32	recorded that in *c·* localities he did not
	417–30	by *c·* fears and false conclusions,
	418– 9	unerring, and *c·* effect of divine Science.
	422– 6	and *c·* moral and physical symptoms seem
	422–27	and renders them fatal at *c·* points,
	424–20	While it is *c·* that the divine Mind can
	430–29	I was present on *c·* nights
	437–33	*c·* extracts on the Rights of Man,
t	443–16	*c·* ordinary physical methods of
	449–24	*C·* minds meet only to separate
	459–30	treats disease with more *c·* results
r	477–28	when they called a *c·* beautiful lake
	478– 9	and by a *c·* class of persons,
	484–17	*C·* results, supposed to proceed from drugs.
g	500– 7	presented to them the *c·* sense of eternal Life.
	548–30	"*C·* animals, besides the ordinary
	549– 3	the multiplication of *c·* animals
ap	569–14	in a sweet and *c·* sense that God is Love.
	570– 5	*c·* active yet unseen mental agencies
gl	581–21	the more *c·* is the downfall of its structure.

certainly

pr	10–26	or we should *c·* receive that for which we ask.
a	24– 1	This *c·* applies to Truth and Love
m	63–28	*c·* the wronged, and perchance impoverished,
sp	80–28	produces table-tipping as *c·* as table-setting,
	86–30	as *c·* as it believes what it sees.
	90–31	*c·* shall know this when man reflects God.
an	101–16	*c·* not conclusive in favor of the doctrine of
s	154– 1	and *c·* we should not be error's advocate.
ph	170– 8	Christian ideas *c·* present
	177– 2	as *c·* as it produces hysteria, and
f	233– 7	demands of us only what we can *c·* fulfil.
b	324–17	*c·* before we can reach the goal of Spirit,
o	352–31	*c·* not irrational to tell the truth about ghosts.
	353–11	omnipotent Truth *c·* does destroy error.
p	363–31	*C·* there was encouragement in
	393–26	he *c·* means that light depends upon Mind,
	430–10	Belief in sickness . . . as *c·* as belief in sin,
r	483–20	God *c·* revealed the author of C. S.,
g	531–27	*C·* not by both, since flesh wars against Spirit

certainty

sp	81–11	this fact affords no *c·* of everlasting life.
	97– 4	cheerfully await the *c·* of ultimate perfection.
s	108–13	to multiply with mathematical *c·*

certainty

f	245–19	a Franklin might work with more *c·*
p	389–14	then discuss the *c·* that food can kill man.
r	496–17	enables you to demonstrate, with scientific *c·*,

certify

s	107– *	*But I c· you, brethren,— Gal.* 1 : 11.

cessation

ap	573–27	a *c·* of death, sorrow, and pain.

chafed

p	383–16	symbolized, and not *c·*, by its surroundings ;

chaff

b	269– 6	Jesus' demonstrations sift the *c·* from the wheat.
r	466–28	to separate the *c·* from the wheat.
ap	565–21	fiery baptism will burn up the *c·* of error

chain

ph	172–11	this supposed *c·* of material being.
	172–12	divine Science reveals the eternal *c·*
b	271– 2	the *c·* of scientific being reappearing
ap	570– 2	people will *c·*, with fetters of some sort,

chained

s	120–31	*c·* the limbs of the brave old navigator,
p	380–16	Gazing at a *c·* lion, crouched for a spring,

chains

sp	96– 3	unwillingness . . . binds Christendom with *c·*.
p	380–19	ignorant of the truth which *c·* disease.
t	449– 2	manacled, it is hard to break another's *c·*.

chair

c	261–17	and sat aching in his *c·* till his cue was spoken.

Chaldean Wisemen

s	121– 7	The *C· W·* read in the stars the fate of

challenge

b	268–10	Materialistic hypotheses *c·* metaphysics

challenges

s	162– 3	agrees only with health and *c·* disease.

chamber

f	238–14	From out the bridal *c·* of wisdom

chambers

b	299– 6	artist's own observation and "*c·* of imagery."
p	365–26	finds its way into the *c·* of disease

chance

m	58–29	Wealth may obviate . . . the *c·* for ill-nature
ph	176– 9	and gave the gospel a *c·* to be seen
p	424– 8	in order to change the notion of *c·*
t	452– 6	before it has a *c·* to manifest itself.
r	486–22	subject to *c·* and change.

chances

sp	77–30	where the *c·* of the departed for improvement
p	394–25	material means the only refuge from fatal *c·*?

change (noun)

accomplish the

sp	77– 3	Neither do other mortals accomplish the *c·*

another

g	529– 7	Another *c·* will come as to

as radical

a	34–17	a *c·* as radical as that which has come

before the

sp	82–20	as before the *c·* we call death,

called death

f	254–17	may not be achieved prior to the *c·* called death,
b	290–16	If the *c·* called *death* destroyed the

chance and

r	486–22	mortal in belief and subject to chance and *c·*.

great

a	24–17	views of atonement will undergo a great *c·*,

needed

b	291–25	and growth shall effect the needed *c·*.

of air

f	219–27	impute their recovery to *c·* of air or diet,

of base

s	162–10	stir the human mind to a *c·* of base,

of belief

ph	169– 1	*c·* of belief from a material to a spiritual basis.

subject to

b	297–18	but subject to *c·* and dissolution.

suggestion of

g	529– 2	a suggestion of *c·* in the *modus operandi*,

this

p	431–29	nothing on my part has occasioned this *c·*.

what produces the

p	398–18	What produces the *c·*?

a	34–27	*c·* which has since been called the ascension.
ph	169– 6	before the patient felt the *c·* ;
	194– 6	A *c·* in human belief changes all the
b	297– 9	is either a health-belief or,
t	446– 7	the *c·* may either arise from the

change (verb)

pr	2–15	Prayer cannot *c·* the Science of being,
	2–26	Do we expect to *c·* perfection?
	11–27	Prayer cannot *c·* the unalterable Truth,

change (verb)

s 125– 1 physical body and of the physical world will c·
125–25 "As a vesture shalt Thou c·— *Psal.* 102 : 26.
f 240–11 C· this statement, suppose Mind to be
253–19 you can at once c· your course
c 260–19 Mortals must c· their ideals
b 281–32 which is to c· our standpoint,
297– 1 nothing can c· this state, until
297–12 C· the evidence, and that disappears which
307–11 It says : . . . Truth shall c· sides
o 359–13 must c· the human concept of life,
p 370–30 naturally and genuinely c· our basis
375– 7 C· the mental state, and the
398–26 c· the belief of disease to a belief of health.
419–13 or to c· itself from one form to another.
419–32 disease or its symptoms cannot c· forms,
424– 8 in order to c· the notion of chance
427– 1 this fact can never c· in Science to
r 481–11 contradictions . . . do not c· the unseen Truth,
491– 5 C· the belief, and the sensation changes.
g 522–32 Does the unerring Principle . . . c· or repent?
544–10 Matter cannot c· the eternal fact

changeable

sp 96–24 Belief is c·,
g 537–29 and divine Love, . . . is represented as c·.

changeableness

s 140–24 wrath, repentance, and human c·.

changed

pref x– 2 she would not have them c·.
a 35– 4 they c· their methods,
46–15 proved . . . that his body was not c·
sp 96– 9 seedtime and harvest (though in c· forms),
s 125– 8 normal and natural to c· mortal thought,
125–25 and they shall be c·."— *Psal.* 102 : 26.
162–19 Secretions have been c·,
ph 185– 1 The wind had not c·,
185– 3 My metaphysical treatment c· the action of
193–10 In a few moments his face c· ;
b 291– 6 We know that all will be c·
308–30 then his name was c· to Israel,
309– 9 This c· the man.
326–26 Then the man was c·.
p 373–32 when by mental means the circulation is c·,
411–17 and the insane man was c·
416–14 unless the belief . . . has meanwhile been c·.
432–29 but my appearance . . . c· the purpose
g 529– 6 suggestive obstetrics has c·.
531–23 Has man . . . c· the method of his Maker?
548–21 will be c· with the progress of information."

changeless

sp 96–24 spiritual understanding is c·.

changes

pr 12–24 C· in belief may go on indefinitely,
s 118–23 c· the whole of mortal thought,
118–24 as yeast c· the chemical properties of meal.
125– 1 as mortal mind c· its beliefs.
125–12 As human thought c· from one stage to
125–21 with c· of time and tide, cold and heat,
125–23 will find that these c· cannot affect his crops.
153– 3 or c· one of the symptoms of disease.
162– 7 It c· the secretions, expels humors,
ph 194– 6 A change in human belief c· all the physical
f 224– 6 the Science which governs these c·,
238– 4 Science is working c· in personal character
b 297– 2 until the belief c·.
297– 5 until the belief on this subject c·.
310–32 These c· are the mutations of material sense,
319–28 A misplaced word c· the sense
322– 3 When understanding c· the standpoints
p 398–29 hypnotism c· such ills into new and
422–16 c· the material base of thought,
422–18 These c· which go on in mortal mind
442–20 Christ c· a belief of sin or of sickness
r 491– 5 Change the belief, and the sensation c·.
g 543– 6 it is the idea of Truth and c· not,

changeth

s 140–26 divine Love, which c· not and
b 310–18 Soul c· not.
g 515– 9 the power which c· the serpent into a staff.

changing

sp 78– 4 the c· deflections of mortal mind ;
79– 6 by c· the patient's thoughts regarding death.
c 255– 1 Eternal Truth is c· the universe.
255– 5 c· chaos into order
b 279– 1 the erring, c·, and dying,
321–32 by c· water into wine,
r 494–26 the mortal testimony, c·, dying, unreal.
g 511–17 The c· glow and full effulgence

channel

sp 73–31 nor can the finite become the c· of the infinite.
t 460–28 through the meagre c· afforded by language
r 489–16 How then can this sense be the God-given c·
gl 593–14 RIVER. C· of thought.

channels

s 108–32 set my thoughts to work in new c·,
f 205–26 and leads human thought into opposite c·
b 276–21 is turned into new and healthy c·,
p 373–28 languidly creeps along its frozen c·,
g 506–19 gathers unformed thoughts into their proper c·,

chaos

c 255– 5 changing c· into order
b 307–31 Above error's awful din, blackness, and c·,
p 372– 6 likened by Milton to "c· and old night."
r 479–23 Darkness and c· are the imaginary opposites of
ap 570–21 the deep waters of c· and old night.

chaotic

s 121– 5 and before he spake, astrography was c·,

Chapman, Dr.

s 163–19 Dr. C·, . . . in a published essay said :

chapter

first

b 313– 6 said of him in the first c· of Hebrews :
g 502–13 as given in the first c· of Genesis.
505– 3 have no record in the first c· of Genesis.
521– 8 (as stated in the first c· of Genesis)
523–22 Throughout the first c· of Genesis
526– 7 contradicts the teaching of the first c·,
535–29 In the first c· of Genesis we read :
537–10 In the first c· of Genesis,
537–24 recorded in the first c· of Genesis.
557–26 the first c· of the Old Testament,
ap 561–29 In the first c· of the Fourth Gospel
gl 590–21 not used in the first c· of Genesis,

last

s 117–11 in the last c· of Mark's Gospel
b 272–11 referred to in the last c· of Mark's Gospel.

previous

r 493–12 is touched upon in a previous c·

same

b 313– 9 another passage in the same c·,
gl 598– 7 as in other passages in this same c·

second

g 521–26 second c· of Genesis contains a statement
522–25 latter part of the second c· of Genesis,
526–15 the second c· of Genesis.

seventh

p 362– 1 in the seventh c· of Luke's Gospel

tenth

ap 558– 1 in the tenth c· of his book of Revelation :

third

gl 598– 2 John's Gospel, the third c·, where we read :

this

r 465– 1 This c· is from the first edition of
gl 579– 4 On this account this c· is added.

twelfth

ap 559–32 The twelfth c· of the Apocalypse,
568– 5 The twelfth c· of the Apocalypse typifies

twelve

g 523–28 to the end of c· twelve,

g 523–26 fourth verse of c· two to c· five,
gl 585–15 ERROR. See c· on Recapitulation, page 472.
588–26 See c· on Recapitulation, page 469.
590–14 LIFE. See c· on Recapitulation, page 468.
593– 3 PRINCIPLE. See c· on Recapitulation, page 465.
594–18 SOULS. See c· on Recapitulation, page 466.
594–25 SUBSTANCE. See c· on Recapitulation, page 468.

chapters

ap 568– 7 following c· depict the fatal effects
gl 590–23 introduced in the second and following c·,

character

apostle's

ap 560–23 hid from view the apostle's c·,

awful

ap 563–16 and beholds its awful c· ;

beautiful in

m 60– 6 The beautiful in c· is also the good,

Christian

b 291– 9 in the growth of Christian c·.

deific

b 336–22 lose the deific c·, and become less than God.

divine

pr 4–21 to assimilate more of the divine c·,
g 540–23 representing error as assuming a divine c·,

elevate

r 492–11 will purify and elevate c·.

finite in

sp 71–29 limited and finite in c· and quality.

God's

f 208–12 not in accordance with the goodness of God's c·.
b 283–22 detracts from God's c· and nature,

his

a 53– 9 was the very opposite of his c·.

human

ap 565–22 melting and purifying even the gold of human c·,

individual

t 449–24 a good detective of individual c·.

character
  infinite
  c 257–28   or Mind would lose its infinite *c·*
  lovely
  m 68–17   she was unmarried, a lovely *c·*,
  no
  p 400–17   disease . . . has no *c·* nor type,
  nurseries of
  f 235–10   Nurseries of *c·* should be strongly garrisoned
  of Judas
  c 260– 5   while holding in thought the *c·* of Judas.
  of Mind
  s 142–31   the nature and *c·* of Mind, God.
  origin and
  g 539–17   this lie as to man's origin and *c·*
  perception of
  s 128– 9   enlarges their perception of *c·*,
  personal
  f 238– 4   Science is working changes in personal *c·*
  straightforward
  ph 168– 1   fair seeming for straightforward *c·*,
  this
  pref xii– 3   hers was the only College of this *c·*

  pr 8– 7   indexes which do not correspond with their *c·*.
  a 28–15   Neither the origin, the *c·*, nor the work
  m 67–19   notion that animal natures . . . give force to *c·*
  b 313–14   is, in the Greek Testament, *c·*.
  o 357–18   false notions about the Divine Being and *c·*

characteristic
  s 152–31   the general symptoms, the *c·* signs,
  b 305–12   Gender also is a quality, . . . a *c·* of
  ap 566–30   Michael's *c·* is spiritual strength.

characteristics
  sp 95–18   and is one of the special *c·* thereof.
  g 512–12   consequently reproduce their own *c·*.

characterized
  sp 76–17   *c·* by the divine Spirit as idea, not matter.
  s 112–21   *c·* in the epistle to the Hebrews.

characters
  f 235–18   will degrade the *c·* it should inform and elevate.
  gl 588–13   unchanged forever in their individual *c·*,

charge
  pref xi–23   the *c·* to plant and water His vineyard.
  m 61–25   more solemn *c·*, than the culture of your
  o 355– 3   The *c·* of inconsistency
  p 398– 3   I *c·* thee, come out of him, — *Mark* 9: 25.
  441– 9   He concluded his *c·* thus :
  g 512–11   angels of His presence, which have the holiest *c·*,
  ap 564– 7   to *c·* the innocent with the crime.

charged
  a 49–19   *c·* with the grandest trust of heaven,
  p 430 18   *c·* with having committed liver-complaint.
  436–27   and substantially *c·* the jury, . . . to find

charges
  f 220–19   and then *c·* them to something else,
  b 307–16   Error *c·* its lie to Truth
  p 438–16   on three distinct *c·* of crime,
  g 533–15   *c·* God and woman with his own dereliction,
  ap 564– 3   evil still *c·* the spiritual idea with

chargeth
  o 360–27   His angels He *c·* with frailty. — *see Job* 4 : 18.

charitable
  o 354–31   opponents of divine Science must be *c·*, if
  t 444–13   Students are advised . . . to be *c·* and kind,

charity
  pref xii–23   In the spirit of Christ's *c·*,
  pr 8–19   are like *c·* in one respect,
  m 64–15   aid her sympathy and *c·* would afford.
  b 270–23   Meekness and *c·* have divine authority.
  p 405– 8   to conquer . . . revenge with *c·*,
  t 447–12   Ignorance, subtlety, or false *c·*
  gl 592–25   OIL. Consecration ; *c·* ; gentleness ;

charming
  g 515– 7   a wise idea, *c·* in its adroitness,

charms
  f 247–23   reflects the *c·* of His goodness
  247–29   poor substitutes for the *c·* of being,

chart
  a 24– 8   and make the Bible the *c·* of life,

charter
  pref xii–18   She retained her *c·*, and as its President,

chartered
  pref xi–31   enabled her to get this institution *c·*

charters
  pref xii– 1   No *c·* were granted . . . after 1883,

chase
  f 250–29   Mortal thoughts *c·* one another like snowflakes,

chasing
  ph 191–15   *c·* away the darkness of error.

chastened
  a 35– 2   hearts *c·* and pride rebuked.
  f 241– 4   he who refuses obedience to God, is *c·* by Love.

chasteneth
  f 241– 1   "Whom the Lord loveth He *c·*." — *Heb.* 12 : 6.

chastisements
  b 323– 6   Through the wholesome *c·* of Love,

chastity
  m 57– 1   *C·* is the cement of civilization
  b 272–21   it is *c·* and purity, in contrast with the
  p 405– 7   to conquer lust with *c·*,

chattering
  ph 194–25   a mental infant, crying and *c·*

Chaucer
  sp 82– 5   *C·* wrote centuries ago,

cheat
  f 252–19   *c·*, lie, commit adultery, rob, murder,
  b 298–20   joy is no longer a trembler, nor is hope a *c·*.

cheats
  g 536–22   Their supposed joys are *c·*.

check
  sp 97– 2   those who discern C. S. will hold crime in *c·*.
  f 203– 2   as though evil could . . . *c·* the reward
  b 283– 5   and there is no inertia to retard or *c·*
  p 376–28   inquire when it will be safe to *c·* a fever.
  376–29   you cannot *c·* a fever after admitting

checked
  ph 165–13   has not *c·* sickness.

cheek
  f 245–15   youth sat gently on *c·* and brow.
  p 415–19   causing a pale or flushed *c·*.
  t 444–20   shall smite thee on thy right *c·*, — *Matt.* 5 : 39.

cheeks
  ph 175–27   empurpled the plump *c·* of our ancestors,

cheer
  m 59–13   blend in sweet confidence and *c·*,

cheerful
  s 149–20   advise our patients to be hopeful and *c·*
  p 395–19   The nurse should be *c·*, orderly,

cheerfully
  sp 97– 3   *c·* await the certainty of ultimate perfection.

chemical
  s 118–24   as yeast changes the *c·* properties of meal.

chemicalization
  mental
  m 65–29   The mental *c·*, which has brought
  ph 169– 4   has occurred through mental *c·*,
  p 401–18   Mental *c·* brings sin and sickness to the surface,
  t 453– 8   Mental *c·* follows the explanation of Truth,
  moral
  sp 96–21   Mortal error will vanish in a moral *c·*.
  g 540–11   In moral *c·*, when the symptoms of evil,
  this
  p 421–15   by removing the belief that this *c·* produces

  ph 168–31   Here let a word be noticed . . . *c·*.
  168–32   By *c·* I mean the process which mortal mind
  p 401– 8   If faith in the truth of being, . . . causes *c·*
  401–16   What I term *c·* is the upheaval produced
  421–21   Calm the excitement sometimes induced by *c·*,

chemist
  s 155– 8   The *c·*, the botanist, the druggist,
  163–10   surgeon, apothecary, man-midwife, *c·*,

chemistry
  ph 195–17   astronomy, natural history, *c·*, music,
  p 422–16   mental and moral *c·* changes the

Chemosh
  g 524– 3   in the Moabitish god *C·*,

cherish
  pr 13–16   If we *c·* the desire honestly and silently
  m 68– 7   *c·* nothing which hinders our highest selfhood.
  s 153–32   nor society should ever tempt us to *c·* error
  p 405–10   if you would not *c·* an army of conspirators

cherished
  s 141– 8   to set aside even the most *c·* beliefs
  b 330– 5   *c·* sanguine hopes that C. S. would meet with
  p 411–25   Whatever is *c·* in mortal mind

cherishing
  p 401– 4   *c·* evil passions and malicious purposes,

cherub
  g 538– 5   Truth places the *c·* wisdom at the gate

Cherubims
  g 537– 6   He placed at the east . . . *C·*, — *Gen.* 3 : 24.

chewing
  p 407– 4   *c·* a leaf naturally attractive to no

chide
   o 347–32 which they *c·* us for naming nothing

chief
   b 288–20 The *c·* stones in the temple of C. S.
   o 349–13 The *c·* difficulty . . . lies in this,
   t 458– 2 The *c·* plank in this platform is the doctrine
   g 535–10 Divine Science deals its *c·* blow at the

Chief Justice
   p 440–33 the *C· J·* of the Supreme Court,

chiefly
   a 24–21 *c·* as providing a ready pardon for
   p 401–31 mental healer confines himself *c·* to
   g 501– 3 *c·* because the spiritual import of the Word,

child (*see also* child's; Eddy, Mrs. Mary Baker)
at prayer
   s 119–20 or prostrates in death the *c·* at prayer,
being with
   ap 562–22 And she being with *c·* cried, — *Rev.* 12 : 2.
every
   a 37–23 duty and privilege of every *c·*, man, and
her
   a 29–22 brought forth her *c·* by the revelation of Truth,
   m 60– 9 affection cannot be weaned from her *c·*,
   s 154–19 govern her *c·* more than the child's mind
   154–25 not a Christian Scientist, . . . who says to her *c·* :
   154–30 moaning more childishly than her *c·*,
   f 206–19 giving the mother her *c·*
   o 352–12 Would a mother say to her *c·*,
   ap 563–26 to devour her *c·* as soon as — *Rev.* 12 : 4.
   565– 8 her *c·* was caught up unto God, — *Rev.* 12 : 5.
inspire the
   m 61–21 what noble ambition, can inspire the *c·*
is born
   s 109–26 "Unto us a *c·* is born, — *Isa.* 9 : 6.
is exposed
   s 154–16 If a *c·* is exposed to contagion or infection,
little
   b 323–32 Willingness to become as a little *c·*
   p 382–23 the kingdom of God as a little *c·*, — *Luke* 18 : 17.
   g 514–25 And a little *c·* shall lead them. — *Isa.* 11 : 6.
male
   ap 565–10 Herod decreed the death of every male *c·*
new
   t 463– 7 To attend properly the birth of the new *c·*,
of God
   b 288–32 man's real existence as a *c·* of God
   ap 573–18 but as the blessed *c·* of God.
of His care
   gl 589–10 man is His idea, the *c·* of His care.
parent and
   p 416–20 This materialism of parent and *c·* is
quite a
   f 221– 1 I knew a person who when quite a *c·*
until the
   g 557– 1 until the *c·* could remain under water
young
   ph 191–11 "where the young *c·* was," — *Matt.* 2 : 9.
   p 412–28 If the case is that of a young *c·* or an infant,

   pref ix– 3 A *c·* drinks in the outward world
   m 62– 6 with which the *c·* can meet and master
   69–20 Some day the *c·* will ask his parent :
   69–23 the *c·* may ask, "Do you teach that
   s 154–17 and says, "My *c·* will be sick."
   155– 1 the *c·* forgets all about the accident,
   p 371–16 no more comprehends . . . than does the *c·* ;
   413–31 A *c·* may have worms, if you say so,
   424– 2 the *c·* becomes a separate, . . . mortal mind,
   r 479– 1 If a *c·* is the offspring of physical sense
   479– 2 If . . . the *c·* must have a material,

childhood
   o 359–22 In *c·*, she often listened with joy to

childhood's
   f 221–27 feeling *c·* hunger

childish
   o 352–22 watering the very roots of *c·* timidity,

childishly
   s 154–30 moaning more *c·* than her child,

childless
   b 306–12 and the Father would be *c·*, — no Father.

children (*see also* children's)
beautiful
   m 61–16 often these beautiful *c·* early droop and die,
bring forth
   g 535– 8 in sorrow thou shalt bring forth *c·* ; — *Gen.* 3 : 16.
   557–18 thou shalt bring forth *c·*." — *Gen.* 3 : 16.
education of
   m 62– 4 The entire education of *c·* should be
God's
   m 69– 7 God's *c·* already created will be cognized
   b 303– 5 Multiplication of God's *c·* comes from
   t 444–28 Immortals, or God's *c·* in divine Science,
   r 476–28 When speaking of God's *c·*,

children
health of
   p 413–11 good or bad effects on the health of *c·*.
her
   m 63–32 and own her *c·* free from interference.
   b 317–11 "wisdom is justified of her *c·*." — *Matt.* 11 : 19.
His
   ap 572–10 belongs not to His *c·*,
His eternal
   g 529–11 and are His eternal *c·*,
in knowledge
   m 62–17 should be allowed to remain *c·* in knowledge,
little
   s 130–24 our Master's love for little *c·*,
   f 236–28 Jesus loved little *c·* because of
of divine Love
   g 529–22 to tempt the *c·* of divine Love?
of earth
   b 309–14 *c·* of earth who followed his example
of God
   f 227–25 liberty of the *c·* of God," — *Rom.* 8 : 21.
   r 470–16 The *c·* of God have but one Mind.
   476–12 immortals, or the *c·* of God, will appear
   476–13 Mortals are not fallen *c·* of God.
   ap 572– 8 In Science we are *c·* of God ;
of Israel
   f 226–29 hold the *c·* of Israel in bondage.
   b 309–16 were to be called the *c·* of Israel,
   ap 566– 1 As the *c·* of Israel were guided
   gl 583– 5 definition of
of men
   s 107– 9 delivering the *c·* of men from every ill
   148– 9 men of *men*, or the "*c·* of men," — *Psal.* 14 : 2.
   p 409–22 imperfect so-called "*c·* of men" — *Psal.* 14 : 2.
   t 444–29 but mortals, or the "*c·* of men" — *Psal.* 14 : 2.
   r 476–28 God's children, not the *c·* of men,
of the wicked one
   r 476– 2 They are the *c·* of the wicked one,
produced on
   p 371– 6 similar to that produced on *c·*
promising
   m 61–14 promising *c·* in the arms of gross parents,
should be allowed
   m 62–16 *C·* should be allowed to remain
should be assured
   o 352–22 *c·* should be assured that
should be taught
   f 237–15 *C·* should be taught the Truth-cure,
should be told
   o 352–26 *c·* should be told not to believe in ghosts,
should obey
   f 236–21 *C·* should obey their parents ;
temperature of
   p 413– 8 the temperature of *c·* and of men,
their
   f 236–23 Parents should teach their *c·* . . . the truths of
   g 557– 4 learn how to develop their *c·* properly
these
   b 309–17 If these *c·* should go astray,
tired
   b 322–28 turn us like tired *c·* to the arms of divine Love.
transmitted to
   m 61–28 Nothing unworthy . . . should be transmitted
       to *c·*.
your
   f 237–19 keep out of the minds of your *c·*
   p 422– 3 by whom do your *c·* cast — *Matt.* 12 : 27.

   m 69–26 "The *c·* of this world marry, — *Luke* 20 : 34.
   f 230–25 soothing syrups to put *c·* to sleep,
   236–25 *C·* are more tractable than adults,
   c 267–10 forever Father must have had *c·* prior to Adam.
   o 352–17 *C·*, . . . *ought* to fear a reality which can harm
   p 371–11 As frightened *c·* look everywhere for the
   414– 2 and thus are *c·* educated into discord.
   gl 582–28 definition of

children's
   m 62–11 their *c·* fretfulness or frivolity,
   f 211–20 the *c·* teeth are set on edge." — *Ezek.* 18 : 2.
   o 352–20 instead of increasing *c·* fears
   p 413–28 these actions convey . . . to *c·* budding thoughts,

child's
   pref x– 1 the memorials of a *c·* growth,
   s 154–19 more than the *c·* mind governs itself,

chill
   p 378–28 to *c·* harmony with a long and cold night of

chilled
   p 431–26 dry, hot, and *c·* by turns

chills
   c 256–26 it *c·* the spirit of Christianity.
   p 366–10 mental penury *c·* his faith and understanding
   375– 6 *C·* and heat are often the form in which
   375– 7 and the *c·* and fever disappear.
   384–17 followed by *c·*, dry cough, influenza,

chiseling
f 248–14 moulding and *c·* thought.

chloroform
c 261–19 as if he had inhaled *c·*,

choice
p 409–19 except through fear or *c·*.

choke
f 237–11 often *c·* the good seed in the minds of
p 405– 9 *C·* these errors in their early stages,

cholera
s 154–11 where a *c·* patient had died.
154–14 had not caught the *c·* by material contact,
154–14 no *c·* patient had been in that bed.

choose
a 30–30 We cannot *c·* for ourselves,
s 143–14 Driven to *c·* between two difficulties,
r 481– 1 How important, then, to *c·* good

chords
b 304–25 To be master of *c·* and discords,

chose
a 47–13 He *c·* his time, when the
48–18 and *c·* not the world's means of defence.

chosen
a 27–26 "Many are called, but few are *c·*." — *Matt.* 22 : 14.
g 554–23 "Have not I *c·* you twelve, — *John* 6 : 70.

Christ (*see also* **Christ's**)
also in
r 467–16 having that Mind which was also in *C·*.
atonement of
a 18–13 atonement of *C·* reconciles man to God,
Belial and
ph 171–24 than between Belial and *C·*.
believe on
s 110–31 apprehended by as many as believe on *C·*
bow before
a 35–12 They bow before *C·*, Truth, to receive more of
came to destroy
r 473– 6 *C·* came to destroy the belief of sin.
cast out by
ap 567–22 cast out by *C·*, Truth, the spiritual idea,
cast out the devil
s 135–15 When *C·* cast out the devil of dumbness,
casts out evils
s 143– 3 *C·* casts out evils and heals the sick.
coming of
f 230– 7 This awakening is the forever coming of *C·*,
consecration to
a 28–10 one's consecration to *C·* is more on the
deathless
a 28–13 the divine Principle of the deathless *C·*,
demonstrated
b 332–19 Jesus demonstrated *C·* ;
demonstrate the
b 285–30 how to demonstrate the *C·*, Truth,
destroyed by
pr 5–24 Sin is forgiven only as it is destroyed by *C·*,
discerning
a 35– 6 Discerning *C·*, Truth, anew on the shore of
divine idea or
b 334– 2 but that the divine idea or *C·* was and is so
divine Principle of
a 18–14 for the divine Principle of *C·* is God,
divinity of the
a 25–31 The divinity of the *C·* was made manifest in the
doctrines of
s 134–16 how can they illustrate the doctrines of *C·*
dwells forever
b 334– 4 *C·*, dwells forever in the bosom of the Father,
dwelt forever
a 29–26 The *C·* dwelt forever an idea in the
endowed with the
a 30– 7 although he was endowed with the *C·*,
eternal
a 38–23 The eternal *C·*, . . . never suffered.
b 334–14 the eternal *C·* and the corporeal Jesus
eternity of the
b 334–29 a mystical statement of the eternity of the *C·*,
even
a 19– 5 Even *C·* cannot reconcile Truth to error,
even so in
g 545–31 even so in *C·* [Truth] shall all be — *I Cor.* 15 : 22.
faith in the
s 134– 9 The new faith in the *C·*, Truth, so roused the
follow
a 27–28 those who profess to follow *C·*
b 326– 3 If we wish to follow *C·*, Truth, it must be
p 434– 7 Others say, . . . let us follow *C·*."
followers of
pr 5–15 The followers of *C·* drank his cup.
s 134–11 the followers of *C·* were burned, crucified,
142– 4 Anciently the followers of *C·*, or Truth,
following
ph 179– 3 and following *C·* in the daily life.

Christ
fulness of
g 519–21 the stature of the fulness of *C·*'"? — *Eph.* 4 : 13.
gain the
b 326–13 if we would gain the *C·* as our only Saviour.
God's idea
ap 565–16 for *C·*, God's idea, will eventually rule
had come
a 27– 2 intended to prove . . . that the *C·* had come :
hath rolled away
a 45–17 *C·* hath rolled away the stone from the door
heart of
ap 568–28 and nearer to the great heart of *C·* ;
herald of
pref vii– 7 the human herald of *C·*, Truth,
hid with
b 325–18 "hid with *C·* in God," — *Col.* 3 : 3.
t 445–14 "hid with *C·* in God," — *Col.* 3 : 3.
His
ap 561–15 God and His *C·*, bringing harmony to earth.
568–15 and the power of His *C·* : — *Rev.* 12 : 10.
if we deny
pr 6– 2 The Scriptures say, that if we deny *C·*,
illustrates
b 316–21 *C·* illustrates that blending with God,
332–32 Thus it is that *C·* illustrates the coincidence,
inseparable from
r 482–21 He was inseparable from *C·*, the Messiah,
invisible
b 334–10 The invisible *C·* was imperceptible
is the divine idea
b 332–19 he proved that *C·* is the divine idea of God
r 473–16 Jesus is the human man, and *C·* is the divine idea ;
is the ideal
r 473–10 *C·* is the ideal Truth,
is the true idea
b 332– 9 *C·* is the true idea voicing good,
is "the way
o 353–10 admit that *C·* is "the way, — *John* 14 : 6.
r 482–15 It is, since *C·* is "the way" — *John* 14 : 6.
is Truth
a 18–15 *C·* is Truth, which reaches no higher than
is without beginning
b 333–17 the *C·* is without beginning of years
Jesus the
b 313– 2 The term Christ Jesus, or Jesus the *C·*
333–14 name of our Master, . . . was Jesus the *C·* ;
r 473–17 hence the duality of Jesus the *C·*.
law of
ph 182–32 law of *C·*, or Truth, makes all things possible
p 434– 6 "The law of *C·* supersedes *our* laws ;
learned through
sp 84–29 and is learned through *C·* and C. S.
leave all for
pr 9–25 Are you willing to leave all for *C·*,
s 141– 9 that is, . . . to leave all for *C·*.
ph 192– 6 not . . . Scientists until we leave all for *C·*.
o 354– 7 to enable them to leave all for *C·*, Truth?
leaves all for
f 238–24 He who leaves all for *C·*
life of
s 149–14 have not demonstrated the life of *C·*,
like
f 249–18 Life is, like *C·*, "the same — *Heb.* 13 : 8.
living
u 31–15 It is the living *C·*, the practical Truth,
manifestation of
s 141–24 Neither can this manifestation of *C·* be
merits of
f 202–12 redeemed through the merits of *C·*,
Messiah or
b 333–24 glorious glimpses of the Messiah, or *C·*,
o 361– 1 The Jew believes that the Messiah or *C·*
gl 594–16 SON. The Son of God, the Messiah or *C·*.
Mind of
pref ix–19 still . . . waiting for the Mind of *C·*.
mission of
r 474–30 The apostle says that the mission of *C·* is
nothing left but
f 238–10 said, "I have nothing left but *C·*."
one
r 497– 6 we acknowledge His Son, one *C·* ;
or Truth
a 33–23 It gives all for *C·*, or Truth.
34–15 cast out evils, and preach *C·*, or Truth,
s 135–30 not merely in the *name* of *C·*, or Truth,
142– 4 Anciently the followers of *C·*, or Truth,
ph 182–32 law of *C·*, or Truth, makes all things possible
b 289–14 *C·*, or Truth, overcame . . . death
326–23 Saul . . . beheld the way — the *C·*, or Truth
p 391–14 *C·*, or Truth, will destroy all other
r 485–21 mortal error which *C·*, or Truth, destroys
plainly declared
b 320– 2 *C·* plainly declared, "I am the way, — *John* 14 : 6.

Christ

plant themselves in
a 54– 9 All must sooner or later plant themselves in *C·*,
presence of
o 351–14 the living, palpitating presence of *C·*,
presents
b 316–20 *C·* presents the indestructible man,
profess to follow
a 27–28 Why do those who profess to follow *C·* reject
raiment of
c 267–27 glistering,'' like the raiment of *C·*.— *Luke* 9 : 29.
raised up
o 341– * *He that raised up C· from the dead* — *Rom.* 8 : 11.
receive
b 333–23 to all prepared to receive *C·*, Truth.
regarded
b 313–16 regarded *C·* as the Son of God,
represented
b 316–12 Jesus represented *C·*, the true idea of God.
ruling of the
s 141–22 do not now, understand this ruling of the *C·* ;
says
b 286–11 for *C·* says, ''I am the way.''— *John* 14 : 6.
Science of
a 55–18 when man shall recognize the Science of *C·*
s 118– 2 the spiritual leaven signifies the Science of *C·*
spirit of
t 462– 5 and imbibes the spirit of *C·*,
spirit of the
s 131–23 As aforetime, the spirit of the *C·*,
the healing
a 55– 8 the healing *C·* and spiritual idea of being.
the way through
ph 171– 5 even the way through *C·*, Truth,
t 444–17 be faithful in pointing the way through *C·*,
this
a 26–12 This *C·*, or divinity of the man Jesus,
Thou art the
s 137–18 ''Thou art the *C·*,— *Matt.* 16 : 16.
to find
b 316– 6 lose sight of mortal selfhood to find *C·*,
understanding of
sp 76–28 the final understanding of *C·* in divine Science.
unveiled the
a 38–25 He unveiled the *C·*, the spiritual idea of
we need
a 39– 7 We need ''*C·*, and him crucified.''— *I Cor.* 2 : 2.
what concord hath
f 216–26 ''What concord hath *C·* with— *II Cor.* 6 : 15.
g 539–26 what concord hath *C·* with— *II Cor.* 6 : 15.
will command
ap 570–25 and *C·* will command the wave.

---

pr 5–29 An apostle says that the Son of God [*C*] came
a 18– * *For C· sent me not to baptize,*— *I Cor.* 1 : 17.
18–17 *C·*, Truth, could conciliate no nature above his
26–10 The *C·* was the Spirit which Jesus implied
34– 5 If *C·*, Truth, has come to us in demonstration,
49–21 He was to prove that the *C·* is not subject
m 65– 3 May *C·*, Truth, be present at every bridal altar
sp 79–18 bade men have the Mind that was in the *C·*.
85–14 is not this the *C·*?''— *John* 4 : 29.
s 107– * *but by the revelation of Jesus C·.*— *Gal.* 1 : 12.
107– 1 In the year 1866, I discovered the *C·* Science
118– 8 second appearing in the flesh of the *C·*,
127– 9 The terms . . . *C·* Science or C. S.,
132–30 with the truest conception of the *C·*?
133– 4 ''Is not this the *C·*?''— *John* 4 : 29.
137–20 *C·*, the spirit of God, of Truth, Life, and Love,
142– 8 seek the undivided garment, the whole *C·*,
142– 9 *C·*, Truth, alone can furnish us with
145–12 as immortal Mind through *C·*, Truth,
149–31 and demonstrate truth according to *C·*.
ph 200–26 Jesus *C·*, and him crucified.''— *I Cor.* 2 : 2.
200–28 Jesus *C·*, and him glorified.
f 231– 1 must be obliterated through *C·*
242– 9 and *C·* in divine Science shows us this way.
251–13 is an error that *C·*, Truth, alone can destroy.
b 268– * *and with His Son Jesus C·.*— *I John* 1 : 3.
270–23 It has nothing in *C·*.
286–10 *C·*, Life, Truth, Love ;
290–21 shall be unrighteous still, until . . . *C·*, Truth,
316– 7 *C·*, Truth, was demonstrated through Jesus
324–27 ''If *C·* [Truth] be not risen,— *I Cor.* 15 : 14.
325–10 *C·*, who is our life, shall appear— *Col.* 3 : 4.
331–30 *C·* the spiritual idea of sonship ;
332–11 The *C·* is incorporeal, spiritual,
333– 3 word *C·* is not properly a synonym for Jesus,
333– 8 *C·* is not a name so much as the divine title of
333– 9 *C·* expresses God's spiritual, eternal nature.
333–20 the *C·*, as the spiritual idea,
333–26 The divine image, idea, or *C·* was, is, and
334–17 while the spiritual self, or *C·*, continues
334–19 taking away the sins of the world, as the *C·*
337–10 in conformity with *C·*.

Christ

b 337–18 demonstrates Life in *C·*, Life's spiritual ideal.
o 347–14 *C·*, as the spiritual or true idea of God,
347–24 it is *C·*, Truth, who destroys these
361– 2 the Christian believes that *C·* is God.
361– 4 *C·*, as the true spiritual idea, is the ideal of
361–12 Jesus *C·* is not God, as Jesus himself declared,
p 364–26 do they show their regard for Truth, or *C·*,
367–10 This is what is meant by seeking Truth, *C·*,
391– 5 delivered to the judgment of Truth, *C·*,
410– 9 the only true God, and Jesus *C·*,— *John* 17 : 3.
428–25 sooner or later, through *C·* and C. S.,
430– 5 immortal manhood, the *C·* ideal, will appear.
433–31 Ah ! but *C·*, Truth, the spirit of Life
442–20 *C·* changes a belief of sin or of sickness
442–22 *C·*, Truth, gives mortals temporary food
r 473–13 *C·*, the true idea of God,
484– 5 for it is built upon the rock, *C·*.
493–29 the *C·* could improve on a false sense.
496–16 *C·*, which enables you to demonstrate,
497–16 we acknowledge that man is saved through *C·*,
g 540– 1 *C·* is the offspring of Spirit,
ap 568–31 by which we lay down all for Truth, or *C·*,
575–18 the Word, *C·*, Christianity, and divine Science ;
577–15 second, the *C·*, the spiritual idea of God ;
gl 583–10 definition of
(*see also* **Messiah, Saviour, Son**)

Christ-cure

p 367–24 The infinite Truth of the *C·* has come
t 456–17 gross ignorance of the method of the *C·*.

Christ-element

b 288–29 The *C·* in the Messiah made him the

Christendom

sp 96– 2 unwillingness . . . binds *C·* with chains.
s 126–32 If *C·* resists the author's application
b 328–26 It were well had *C·* believed and
o 343–23 *C·* generally demands so much less.

Christ-example

s 138–21 to follow the *C·*, and to heal the sick

Christ-healing

a 44–25 the understanding of the *C·*
s 136– 2 a spiritual foundation of *C·*.

Christian (*see also* **Christian's**)

pr 7–23 ventilation of fervent sentiments never makes
a *C·*.
a 40– 3 The advanced thinker and devout *C·*,
s 138–25 The *C·* can prove this to-day
148–22 tries to explain how to make this man a *C·*,
f 203–11 to the *C·* the only true spirit is Godlike.
238– 9 enables one to be *C·*.
o 353– 7 How can a *C·*, . . . think of the latter as real
360–29 the Galilean Prophet, the best *C·* on earth,
360–30 while to-day, Jew and *C·* can unite in
361– 1 the *C·* believes that Christ is God.
361– 9 *C·* who believes in the First Commandment
g 556–15 but the *C·* alone can fathom it.

Christian (adj.)

apostles
o 349–22 the prophecy concerning the *C·* apostles,
character
b 291– 9 each lesser call in the growth of *C·* character.
churches
s 131–13 Must C. S. come through the *C·* churches
conversion
f 217– 7 Paul's peculiar *C·* conversion and experience,
demand
a 37–32 Why has this *C·* demand so little inspiration
m 66–22 if there is no *C·* demand for it.
demonstration
s 141– 4 requisite for *C·* demonstration.
duties
a 31–12 First in the list of *C·* duties,
effort
a 38– 1 to stir mankind to *C·* effort?
encouragement
p 367– 3 *C·* encouragement of an invalid,
era
(*see* **era**)
evidence
r 487–19 *C·* evidence is founded on Science
experience
a 29– 7 *C·* experience teaches faith in the right
explanations
r 490–23 scientifically *C·* explanations of the
healing
(*see* **healing**)
history
b 328–15 has sadly disappeared from *C·* history.
ap 577–17 the Christ-idea in *C·* history ;
ideas
ph 170– 8 *C·* ideas certainly present . . . the Principle
idolatry
b 340–26 annihilates pagan and *C·* idolatry,

Christian (adj.)

martyr
a 28–22 Remember, thou *C·* martyr,
martyrs
p 388– 1 The *C·* martyrs were prophets of C. S.
marvels
r 474–11 *C·* marvels . . . will be misunderstood
meaning
g 506–27 the scientifically *C·* meaning of the text.
metaphysics
s 155–16 high and mighty truths of *C·* metaphysics.
Mind-healing
sp 98–16 demonstration of *C·* Mind-healing stands
opponents
o 354–12 On the other hand, the *C·* opponents of C. S.
perfection
f 201–18 *C·* perfection is won on no other basis.
power
f 233– 2 rather than professions of *C·* power.
record
g 531–30 the scientifically *C·* record of man
scientific practice
p 410–29 *C·* scientific practice begins with
Scientist
(*see* **Scientist**)
Scientists
(*see* **Scientists**)
sentiment
pr 7–16 to induce or encourage *C·* sentiment.
sermons
o 345– 8 *C·* sermons will heal the sick.
service
p 436–11 Giving a cup of cold water . . . is a *C·* service.
state
p 403–21 The most *C·* state is one of rectitude and
system
s 150– 2 this *C·* system of healing disease.
thought
pref x–26 unbiased *C·* thought is soonest touched
views
g 502–16 scientifically *C·* views of the universe

sp 94– 6 *C·* and scientific statement of personality
98–32 is not ecclesiastical but *C·*,
s 112–15 and are not scientifically *C·*.
o 354–31 must be charitable, if they would be *C·*.
p 365–21 then he is *C·* enough to practise
t 458–11 It is anything but scientifically *C·* to
459–29 the *C·* and scientific expounder

Christian Church
a 41–16 in the *C·* *C·* this demonstration of

Christianity (*see also* **Christianity's**)
all
s 138–18 precedent for all *C·*, theology, and healing.
antithesis of
s 133–19 Judaism was the antithesis of *C·*,
banner of
p 426–27 would enable us to hold the banner of *C·* aloft
causes men
t 458–32 *C·* causes men to turn naturally from
Christ's
b 271– 2 Christ's *C·* is the chain of scientific being
demonstration of
f 228–31 when they saw the demonstration of *C·*
easier for
s 138–22 It is easier for *C·* to cast out sickness than sin,
effects of
p 367–27 and increase the beneficial effects of *C·*.
El Dorado of
pr 9–21 This is the El Dorado of *C·*.
element of
s 146– 3 Why has this element of *C·* been lost?
b 328–17 a lost element of *C·*.
o 347–18 restoring an essential element of *C·*,
faith in
s 127– 2 she will not therefore lose faith in *C·*,
gains
f 238–24 forsakes popularity and gains *C·*.
history of
p 387–27 The history of *C·* furnishes sublime proofs
is not false
f 232–13 *C·* is not false,
is the basis
ph 192–29 *C·* is the basis of true healing.
lack of
m 65–17 Beholding the world's lack of *C·*
left out of
a 55–13 curative mission, . . . cannot be left out of *C·*,
love of
f 235–32 Love of *C·*, rather than love of popularity,
measured
s 142– 5 measured *C·* by its power over sickness, sin,
more
r 487– 7 more *C·* in seeing and hearing spiritually

Christianity
must be Science
s 135–21 It has been said, . . . that *C·* must be Science,
nature of
a 40–31 The nature of *C·* is peaceful and blessed,
new step in
sp 98– 1 persecutions which attend a new step in *C·* ;
not proceed from
sp 88–24 These effects, however, do not proceed from *C·*,
opponents of
s 134–10 roused the hatred of the opponents of *C·*,
our
ph 167–10 our health, our longevity, and our *C·*.
perceive
b 322– 6 perceive *C·*, or Truth, in its divine Principle.
popular
m 67–26 the limited demonstration of popular *C·*
practical
f 224–22 A higher and more practical *C·*,
o 341– 4 from a theoretical to a practical *C·*.
practice of
r 473–19 introduced the teaching and practice of *C·*,
preaching
b 324–24 healing the sick and preaching *C·*
primitive
m 64– 9 master of ceremonies, ruling out primitive *C·*.
proof of
(*see* **proof**)
pure
b 329– 2 healing elements of pure *C·* will be
reappearance of the
sp 98– 5 reappearance of the *C·* which heals the sick
robs
s 134–18 robs *C·* of the very element, which gave
Science and
f 231–13 If God makes sin, . . . Science and *C·* are
helpless ;
p 371–26 Mankind will improve through Science and *C·*.
Science must be
s 135–22 and Science must be *C·*,
Science of
(*see* **Science**)
Science to
s 127– 1 application of the word Science to *C·*,
o 341–13 the application of the word *Science* to *C·*
r 483–14 she affixed the name "Science" to *C·*,
soul of
s 140–17 Spiritual devoutness is the soul of *C·*.
spirit of
c 256–27 it chills the spirit of *C·*.
statement in
f 207– 6 every scientific statement in *C·* has its proof.
support of
o 342– 4 are summoned to the support of *C·*,
true
o 359–18 True *C·* is to be honored wherever found,
will demonstrate
r 466–29 *C·* will demonstrate this declaration

a 28–28 and that *C·* to-day is at peace with the world
36–16 moral distance between *C·* and sensualism
sp 97–29 *C·* is again demonstrating the Life that is
98–23 *C·* not excepted.
s 127– 3 nor will *C·* lose its hold upon her.
133–25 planted *C·* on the foundation of Spirit,
135–26 *C·* as Jesus taught it was not a creed,
f 224–12 sects many but not enough *C·*.
232–16 In our age *C·* is again demonstrating
b 274–13 *C·* and the Science which expounds it
o 342–16 If *C·* is not scientific,
353–31 Mortal beliefs can neither demonstrate *C·*
358–22 the great import to *C·* of those works
p 372–18 C. S. and *C·* are one.
372–19 How, then, in *C·* any more than in C. S.,
373– 2 the physical exemption which *C·* includes,
t 451– 6 *C·*, with the crown of Love upon her brow,
462–17 *C·*, and persistence alone win the prize,
464–21 In founding a pathological system of *C·*,
r 483–32 *C·* will never be based on a divine . . . until
ap 575–18 the Word, Christ, *C·*, and divine Science ;
577–16 *C·*, which is the outcome of the divine Principle

Christianity's
a 39– 3 until *C·* last triumph.
r 473–20 the proof of *C·* truth and love ;

Christianization
pr 1– 8 the *C·* and health of mankind.
b 272–19 It is the spiritualization of thought and *C·*

Christianly
o 353– 1 *C·* scientific real is the sensuous unreal.
355– 3 *C·* scientific methods of dealing with sin
p 414–20 rests on the *C·* scientific basis of being.
421–25 It is no more *C·* scientific to see disease
t 448–16 A dishonest position is far from *C·* scientific.
458–23 The *C·* scientific man reflects the divine law,
g 546–27 system stated in this book is *C·* scientific
ap 572– 5 *C·* and scientifically reduced to its native

Christian's
o 361– 8   Thus the Jew unites with the C· doctrine

Christians
pr   9–28   Then why . . . ask to be C·, since
15–25   C· rejoice in secret beauty and bounty,
a   21– 6   C· do not continue to labor . . . because of
29– 1   C· must take up arms against error
33–27   C·, are you drinking his cup?
37–21   May the C· of to-day take up the
37–25   C· claim to be his followers,
s 138–18   C· are under as direct orders now,
146– 2   The ancient C· were healers.
f 242–31   and require of C· the proof which he gave,
b 326–28   wrong that he had done in persecuting C·,
o 354– 4   Why then do C· try to obey the Scriptures
p 373– 1   If we are C· on all moral questions,

Christian Science
(see Science)

Christian Science Journal
pref xii–12   sole editor and publisher of the C· S· J·,

Christian Scientist
(see Scientist)

Christian Scientist Association
pref xii– 9   President of the first C· S· A·,

Christian Scientists
(see Scientists)

Christ-idea
s 112–21   divine Principle of healing and the C·
b 316–17   The C·, . . . rose higher to human view
ap 570–19   to drown the C·?
577–17   the C· in Christian history ;

Christ Jesus
pref vii– 8   the way of salvation through C· J·,
a   30–19   C· J· came to rebuke rabbinical error
ph 180–29   as taught and demonstrated by C· J·.
f 235–26   C· J·, the true idea of spiritual power.
243–10   which was also in C· J·.''— Phil. 2 : 5.
244–11   law of the Spirit of life in C· J·— Rom. 8 : 2.
c 259– 7   The divine nature was best expressed in C· J·,
b 270–31   The life of C· J· was not miraculous,
276– 9   which was also in C· J·.''— Phil. 2 : 5.
313– 2   The term C· J·, or Jesus the Christ
315–16   God's spiritual idea as presented by C· J·.
332–17   one mediator . . . the man C· J·.''— I Tim. 2 : 5.
332–29   incarnate in the good and pure C· J·.
333–12   life of which C· J· was the embodiment.
333–14   but C· J· better signifies the Godlike.
338–32   The ideal man was . . . known as C· J·.
o 350– 9   grow into that stature of manhood in C· J·
p 381–31   C· J· overruled the error which would impose
r 483–20   the ancient worthies, and to C· J·,
497–15   man's unity with God through C· J·,
497–25   which was also in C· J· ;

Christlike
s 138–20   to be C·, to possess the Christ-spirit,
146–12   and religion becomes C·.
c 259–11   The C· understanding of scientific being

Christliness
o 342–26   Who would be the first to disown the C· of

Christly
f 242–28   restores every part of the C· garment
p 365–19   If the Scientist has enough C· affection

Christ-man
b 316–17   the C·, rose higher to human view

Christ-power
s 134–15   Devoid of the C·,
150–16   C· to take away the sins of the world.

Christ-principle
a   34– 2   and leave all for the C·?

Christ's
pref xii–23   In the spirit of C· charity,
a   18– *   they that are C· have crucified — Gal. 5 : 24.
19– 1   C· purpose to reconcile man to God,
22– 6   Waking to C· demand, mortals experience
22– 9   through C· precious love these efforts are
55–24   drinketh of C· cup now,
sp   95–26   the light which heralds C· eternal dawn
98–19   C· revelation of Truth, of Life, and of Love,
98–27   Mystery does not enshroud C· teachings,
s 110–29   and demonstrated according to C· command,
f 226–13   but through C· divine Science.
234– 6   crumbs of comfort from C· table,
236– 9   attacks on . . . who reiterate C· teachings
b 271– 1   C· Christianity is the claim of scientific being
315–12   hid from their sense C· sonship with God.
o 347–14   they would behold the signs of C· coming.
355–17   declines to admit that C· religion has
p 410–30   C· keynote of harmony,
436–11   Giving a cup of cold water in C· name,
t 458–29   C· way is the only one by which mortals are

Christ's
ap 569–12   He that touches the hem of C· robe
570–17   Give them a cup of cold water in C· name,
gl 583– 9   CHILDREN OF ISRAEL. . . . C· offspring.

Christ-spirit
s 138–20   to be Christlike, to possess the C·,
141–16   the C· which governed the corporeal Jesus.

chronic
s 162–18   in cases of both acute and c· disease
ph 176–30   the less distinct type and c· form of disease.
178–16   that c· case is not difficult to cure.
f 246–32   Acute and c· beliefs reproduce their own types.
247– 2   and is not so disastrous as the c· belief.
p 369–17   Jesus never asked if disease were acute or c·,
373– 9   to lift a student out of a c· sin.
389–30   In her belief the woman had c· liver-complaint,
390–28   approaching symptoms of c· or acute disease,

chronicles
g 522– 8   second record c· man as mutable and

chronological
f 246–17   C· data are no part of the vast forever.

chronologically
s 143–28   If Mind was first c·, is first potentially,

chrysalis
b 297–21   It is a c· state of human thought,

Church
a   28– 9   While respecting all that is good in the C·
37– 6   blood of the martyrs is the seed of the C·.''
41–16   in the Christian C· this demonstration of
o 351– 9   a member of the orthodox Congregational C·
gl 583–12   definition of
583–14   The C· is that institution, which affords proof

church
her
pref xii–20   as auxiliary to her c·.
his
s 136– 1   Jesus established his c· and
my
s 137–32   upon . . . I will build my c· ;— Matt. 16 : 18.
our
a   35–20   Our c· is built on the divine Principle,
this
a   35–21   We can unite with this c· only as

f 224–20   opposition from c·, state laws, and the press,
o 351–11   prayers of her devout parents and the c· ;

Church Councils
s 139–15   The decisions by vote of C· C·

church-dome
g 516–17   The sunlight glints from the c·,

churches
s 131–14   Must C. S. come through the Christian c·
131–16   but the c· seem not ready to receive it,
f 235– 7   and the readers in c·

church-members
o 358–29   Is it likely that c· have more faith in

Church of Christ, Scientist
pref xii– 8   pastor of the first established C· of C·, S· ;

circle
m   58–20   amusement outside the home c·
b 282– 5   a c· or sphere and a straight line.
282– 6   The c· represents the infinite
310–16   around which c· harmoniously all things

circulated
t 460–29   by her manuscript c· among the students.

circulation
pref ix–13   are still in c· among her first pupils ;
ix–25   copies were, however, in friendly c·.
ph 185– 8   other books were in c·, which discussed
p 373–32   when by mental means the c· is changed,
415–18   It either retards the c· or quickens it,

circumference
f 204– 1   is at once the centre and c· of being.
c 262–15   the absolute centre and c· of his being.

circumscribe
m   61– 1   We cannot c· happiness within the

circumscribed
pr   2–21   perpetuates the belief in God as humanly c·,
b 284– 5   if the infinite could be c· within the finite,
g 550– 1   a c· and non-intelligent egg.

circumstance
m   61–14   If some fortuitous c· places
f 250–32   nor . . . that happiness is ever the sport of c·.
b 297– 3   no c· can alter the situation, until
p 377–30   any c· is of itself powerless to produce
378– 6   and meet every c· with truth.
419–16   Meet every adverse c· as its master.
426– 1   or disease arising from any c·,
ap 574–28   c·, which your suffering sense deems

circumstances

pr	5– 7	we are placed under the stress of *c*.
m	66–28	patience salutary under such *c*,
s	147– 9	under *c* where demonstration was
b	319– 9	sustains man under all *c*;
p	378– 1	which associates sickness with certain *c*
	412–12	liable under some *c* to impress it
	440–14	under stress of *c*,
t	443– 5	under ordinary *c* a resort to
	448– 8	Under such *c*, to say that there is no evil,
g	553–12	have grown or been formed under *c* which
ap	571–15	under all *c*, overcome evil with good.

citation

s	137–14	their *c* of the common report about him.

cited

sp	79– 5	Thousands of instances could be *c*
o	358–19	Why are the words . . . more frequently *c*

cities

b	300– 6	which makes trees and *c* seem to be

citizen

p	438–11	Nerve was an insubordinate *c*,

citizens

f	227–24	*C* of the world, accept the

city
great

ap	574–22	lifted the seer to behold the great *c*,

heavenly

ap	576– 3	This heavenly *c*, . . . this New Jerusalem,
	577–24	their honors within the heavenly *c*.

holy

ap	576– 8	describing this holy *c*, the beloved Disciple

of Lynn

s	158–31	A woman in the *c* of Lynn, Massachusetts,

of our God

ap	558– *	*to be praised in the c of our God,— Psal.* 48 : 1.
	577–19	This *c* of our God has no need of sun

of the Spirit

ap	575–25	It is indeed a *c* of the Spirit,

our

ap	575–18	The four sides of our *c* are

sacred

ap	575– 7	This sacred *c*, described in the Apocalypse

a	41–26	Persecuted from *c* to *c*, his apostles
s	149–32	there is hardly a *c*, village, or hamlet,
p	367–20	A *c* that is set on an hill— *Matt.* 5 : 14.
t	459–19	in the crowded streets of a *c*.
ap	574–15	the *c* which "lieth foursquare." — *Rev.* 21 :16.
	575–12	"a *c* which hath foundations." — *Heb.* 11 : 10.
	575–17	the description of the *c* as foursquare
	575–21	This *c* is wholly spiritual, as its four sides
	575–24	the *c* of the great King." — *Psal.* 48 : 2.
	577–26	and nothing can enter that *c*, which

civil

pr	7– 1	The only *c* sentence which he had for error
m	63–12	*C* law establishes very unfair differences
b	340–27	whatever is wrong in social, *c*, criminal,

civilization

m	57– 1	Chastity is the cement of *c*
	63–14	*c* mitigates it in some measure.
	63–17	than does either C. S. or *c*.
ph	179–30	idols of *c* are far more fatal to health
	173–32	idols of *c* call into action less faith
	174– 4	Is *c* only a higher form of idolatry,

civilized

ph	174– 2	as consciously as do *c* practitioners

civilly

gl	587– 4	rights of woman acknowledged morally, *c*,

clad

b	320–32	still *c* in material flesh,
t	463–15	The new idea, . . . is *c* in white garments.
ap	561–26	The spiritual idea is *c* with the radiance of
	571–18	*C* in the panoply of Love,

claim
any

t	448–30	nothing short of right-doing has any *c* to

audible

gl	594– 9	first audible *c* that God was not omnipotent

false

f	233–13	false *c* of error continues its delusions
g	523– 4	mist of obscurity . . . deepens the false *c*,
	523– 8	arise from a mist or false *c*,
	554–14	as he grows up into another false *c*,
ap	564–22	the false *c* of mind in matter
	567–18	That false *c* — that ancient belief,

first

gl	594– 5	the first *c* that there is an opposite of Spirit,
	594– 7	the first *c* that sin, sickness, and death

his

s	131–30	established his *c* to the Messiahship.

claim
its

f	210–28	and appears to itself to make good its *c*.
g	513– 2	this mortal mentality, so-called, and its *c*,

knowing the

t	450–29	Knowing the *c* of animal magnetism,

of sin

p	390–20	Suffer no *c* of sin or of sickness to grow
t	447–24	To put down the *c* of sin, you must detect it,
	461–27	must first see the *c* of sin, and then destroy it.

strong

s	130–26	If thought is startled at the strong *c* of Science

this

o	344– 6	this *c* is made because the Scriptures say

unreality of the

b	285–11	The unreality of the *c* that a mortal

usurps

g	513– 2	the *c* usurps the deific prerogatives

a	37–26	Christians *c* to be his followers,
m	64–30	Spirit will ultimately *c* its own,
ph	186–23	If we . . . discord has as lasting a *c* upon us
f	238–16	when we attempt to *c* the benefits of an
b	283–16	They *c* that to be life which is but the
	311–29	lose all supposed consciousness or *c* to life
	312–19	Mortals *c* that death is inevitable ;
	315– 7	and laid no *c* to any other.
	329–25	maintains the *c* of Truth by quenching error.
r	476– 7	Error will cease to *c* that soul is in body,
	478– 8	except the *c* of mortal belief?

claimants

s	104–11	more scientific than are false *c*

claimed

a	28– 1	Pharisees *c* to know and to teach the divine will,
sp	78–26	*c* to be the agents of God's government.
	83– 4	*c* that they could equal the work of wisdom.
s	136– 5	He *c* no . . . action, nor life separate from God.
o	344– 4	should be added that this is *c* to represent
r	469–19	and if mortals *c* no other Mind

claiming

b	330–29	nothing *c* to be something,
p	436–32	*C* to protect Mortal Man
ap	567–19	*c* that there is intelligence in matter
gl	591–25	Nothing *c* to be something,

claims
assert its

p	395– 9	assert its *c* over mortality and disease.

better

m	57–17	the better *c* of intellect, goodness, and virtue.

confirms its

sp	94–17	The progress of truth confirms its *c*,

diviner

f	226–15	He has built it on diviner *c*.

false

pr	7– 7	deprives material sense of its false *c*.
b	273–27	the false *c* of material sense or law.
	308–12	a blending of false *c*,
	357–23	They are false *c*, which will eventually
p	438–12	putting in false *c* to office
g	538–16	the false *c* that misrepresent God, good.

forfeit their

s	112– 6	forfeit their *c* to belong to its school,

of Christian Science

p	371–23	when urging the *c* of C. S. ;

of evil

s	130–29	astounded at the vigorous *c* of evil
t	447–20	Expose and denounce the *c* of evil
	448– 1	To assume that there are no *c* of evil
g	529–28	have faith to fight all *c* of evil,

of God

a	23–20	and establishes the *c* of God.

of good

ph	167– 8	Our proportionate admission of the *c* of good

of matter

f	242– 6	Denial of the *c* of matter
r	491–14	which annuls the *c* of matter,

of medicine

a	44–11	all the *c* of medicine, surgery, and hygiene.

of mortality

ph	182– 6	the *c* of mortality, . . . appertain to matter.

of mortal mind

an	103– 6	The destruction of the *c* of mortal mind

of Truth

sp	92–28	instead of urging the *c* of Truth alone.

parental

m	63–20	property, and parental *c* of the two sexes.

resisted

f	223–30	as truth urges upon mortals its resisted *c* ;

surrenders its

g	552–30	matter always surrenders its *c* when

these

f	226–15	These *c* are not made through code or **creed**,

claims

your
t 455–10 and support your c· by demonstration.

s 112–27 if any so-called new school c· to be C. S.,
148–25 c· to rule man by material law,
151–31 mortal mind c· to govern every organ
ph 171– 1 Matter, which . . . c· to be a creator, is a fiction,
193–25 his physician c· to have cured him,
f 227– 6 the c· of the enslaving senses must be denied
232– 7 the c· of harmonious and eternal being
b 273– 1 Matter and its c· of sin, sickness, and death
o 344– 1 it c· God as the only absolute Life and Soul,
g 512–29 and c· God as their author ;
523– 7 the lie c· to be truth.
529–28 have faith to fight all c· of evil,

clairvoyance
sp 85– 2 This Mind-reading is the opposite of c·.
95–16 This kind of mind-reading is not c·,

clairvoyant
sp 87–17 to read the human mind, but not as a c·.
an 101–11 the phenomena exhibited by a reputed c·.

clamor
b 327–15 rushes forth to c· with midnight and tempest.

clap
f 220–10 The leaves c· their hands

Clark, Mr.
ph 192–32 I was called to visit Mr. C· in Lynn,
193– 8 Mr. C· lay with his eyes fixed and sightless.

class
s 151– 9 philanthropy of the higher c· of physicians.
161–30 if this old c· of philanthropists looked
164– 9 the cultured c· of medical practitioners
b 290–14 To the spiritual c·, relates the Scripture :
t 450– 1 There is a large c· of thinkers whose
450– 5 Another c·, still more unfortunate, are
450– 8 A third c· of thinkers build with solid masonry.
454–25 at the close of a c· term,
r 478–10 and by a certain c· of persons,

class-book
r 465– 2 the author's c·, copyrighted in 1870.

classes
s 114– 1 Usage c· both evil and good together
g 549–10 are supposed to have, as c·,

classic
sp 82– 6 What is c· study, but discernment of
b 332– 7 quoted with approbation from a c· poet :

classification
s 124–31 so restores them to their rightful home and c·.
127– 6 everything entitled to a c· as truth,
164– 5 "No systematic or theoretical c· of diseases
p 407–31 Sin is spared from this c·, only because

classified
c 255– 7 anciently c· as the higher criticism,
r 473– 6 are to be c· as effects of error.
g 556– 4 mortal and material concepts c·,

classifies
f 213– 7 and then c· it materially.
g 513–17 Spirit diversifies, c·, and individualizes

classify
an 106–17 c· all others as did St. Paul
ph 187–24 The human mind tries to c· action
r 483– 5 We c· disease as error,
495– 8 c· sickness and error as our Master did,
ap 560–20 in order to c· it correctly.

clauses
o 341– 5 generally based on detached sentences or c·

claw
r 489– 2 When the unthinking lobster loses its c·,
489– 2 the c· grows again.
489– 7 would be replaced as readily as the lobster's c·,

clay
ph 173– 7 supposition, . . . the potter is subject to the c·,
f 243–16 The c· cannot reply to the potter.
b 310– 9 The potter is not in the c· ;
310– 9 else the c· would have power over the potter.
r 490–23 along with the dissolving elements of c·.

clean
p 382–12 beware of making c· merely the outside
383– 3 We need a c· body and a c· mind,
383–19 This shows that the mind must be c·
413–18 only for the purpose of keeping the body c·,
t 452–22 and afterwards we must wash them c·.

cleanliness
p 413–16 "C· is next to godliness,"
413–20 I insist on bodily c· within and without.

cleanse
a 25– 7 no more efficacious to c· from sin
37–11 c· and rarefy the atmosphere of material sense

cleansed
a 27– 5 the lame walk, the lepers are c·,— Luke 7 : 22.
s 132– 7 the lame walk, the lepers are c·,— Matt. 11 : 5.
133–32 Creeds and rituals have not c· their hands

clear
a 50–11 who could withhold a c· token of his presence
m 65–21 until we get at last the c· straining of truth,
an 104–31 Is it not c· that the human mind must
ph 182–16 c· to those who heal the sick on the basis of
f 205–16 we can catch c· glimpses of God only as
b 325–20 Paul had a c· sense of the demands of Truth
o 358–15 It presents the calm and c· verdict of Truth
p 388–28 a c· comprehension of the living Spirit.
398– 6 c· evidence that the malady was not material.
418– 8 and a c· perception of the unchanging,
418–12 It must be c· to you that sickness
t 444–31 The teacher must make c· to students
459– 4 Paul and John had a c· apprehension that,
r 495–17 Let neither fear nor doubt overshadow your c· sense
g 523–15 c· evidences of two distinct documents

cleared
f 234–18 brood of evils which infest it would be c· out.
b 288–16 may burst and flash till the cloud is c·

clearer
a 55–12 in a c· light than mere words can possibly do,
s 121–20 rebuked by c· views of the everlasting facts,
f 239– 7 Take away wealth, . . . and we get c· views
c 262–14 These c·, higher views inspire the Godlike man
b 313–20 The passage is made even c· in
o 361–22 to give a c· and fuller expression
p 368– 8 truth will become still c·
372– 9 Science of being, . . . would be c· in this age,
t 460–31 the teaching became c·, until
g 501– 7 whereas the New Testament narratives are c·
504–19 spiritually c· views of Him,
553– 5 This c· consciousness must precede an
ap 568–28 rises c· and nearer to the great heart of Christ ;

clearest
g 517–13 Love imparts the c· idea of Deity.

clearly
b 275–21 shows c· that all is Mind,
t 455–15 then shalt thou see c·— Matt. 7 : 5.
r 479–31 invisible things . . . are c· seen,— Rom. 1 : 20.
ap 568–32 This rule c· interprets God as divine Principle,

clearness
p 380–26 this evidence will gather momentum and c·,

clears
a 22–18 When the smoke of battle c· away,

clear-sightedness
b 316–14 between spiritual c· and the blindness of

cleave
o 354–15 Surely it is not enough to c· to barren and

clergy
a 20–12 partake of the Eucharist, support the c·,
o 348–10 It is a pity that the medical faculty and c·

clergyman
f 220–22 A c· once adopted a diet of bread and water
o 359– 3 Let any c· try to cure his friends by their faith

clergymen
f 235–28 C·, occupying the watchtowers of the world,

clerical
f 236– 1 should stimulate c· labor and progress.

climate
p 377–10 when their fear of c· is exterminated.
386–11 not because of the c·, but on account of the
392–21 If you decide that c· or atmosphere is unhealthy,
394–24 unless it can be aided by a drug or c·?

climates
p 377– 6 Invalids flee to tropical c·
377–10 prove that they can be healthy in all c·,

climax
b 322– 7 This must be the c·
g 543– 2 error, after reaching the c· of suffering,

climb
b 326– 7 must not try to c· the hill of Science by
g 514– 8 In humility they c· the heights of holiness.

clime
a 46–10 has spoken . . . in every age and c·.

climes
f 225–29 Men and women of all c· and races

cling
f 237–26 c· to a belief in the life and intelligence of
c 263– 9 c· to earth because he has not tasted heaven.
266–11 even if you c· to a sense of personal joys,
b 283–23 lost to all who c· to this falsity.
328– 9 and must therefore c· to mortals until,
t 448– 2 Blindness and self-righteousness c· fast to
r 495–14 c· steadfastly to God and His idea.

clings
s 146–15 Scholasticism *c·* for salvation to the person,

clip
pr 4–31 creeds *c·* the strong pinions of love,

cliques
f 239– 8 Break up *c·*, level wealth with honesty,

cloaked
gl 597– 8 but *c·* the crime, latent in thought,

clock
o 360–19 Like a pendulum in a *c·*,

cloister
c 263–25 peers from its *c·* with amazement

cloistered
ph 191–23 not a flower starts from its *c·* cell.

Cloquet
an 101– 9 among whom were Roux, Bouillaud, and *C·*,

close
pr 15–15 must *c·* the lips and silence the material senses.
u 32–31 a sad supper taken at the *c·* of day,
sp 71–10 *C·* your eyes, and you may dream that you
71–14 *C·* your eyes again, and you may see
87–30 *c·* the eyes, and forms rise before us,
f 201–16 we shall not hug our tatters *c·* about us.
224–25 Will you open or *c·* the door upon this
p 431–18 getting Mortal Man into *c·* confinement
t 454–25 at the *c·* of a class term,
ap 564–29 The serpent is . . . *c·* upon the heel of harmony.

closed
pref xii–14 She *c·* her College, October 29, 1889,
pr 15– 5 *C·* to error, it is open to Truth,
15–11 the door of the erring senses must be *c·*.
a 33– 1 and this supper *c·* forever Jesus' ritualism
46–27 which *c·* the earthly record of Jesus,
ph 165– 4 *c·* the eyes of mortals to man's God-given
171– 7 gates of Paradise which human beliefs have *c·*,
193–12 The eyelids *c·* gently and
o 350–20 and their eyes they have *c·* ;— *Matt.* 13 : 15.
p 433– 2 testimony for the plaintiff, . . . being *c·*,
440–33 Here the counsel for the defence *c·*,
r 491–23 belief goes on, whether our eyes are *c·* or open.
g 528–11 and *c·* up the flesh instead — *Gen.* 2 : 21.

closely
m 57–27 serves to unite thought more *c·* to God,
sp 97– 5 In reality, the more *c·* error simulates truth
g 523–28 become more and more *c·* intertwined

closes
m 69–11 neither *c·* man's continuity nor his sense of
s 144–26 pride, or prejudice *c·* the door
g 521– 4 Here the inspired record *c·* its narrative
ap 577–29 *c·* with St. John's Revelation

closet
pr 14–31 enter into thy *c·*, — *Matt.* 6 : 6.
15– 3 The *c·* typifies the sanctuary of Spirit,
15–15 to pray aright, we must enter into the *c·*

closing
ph 187–13 opening and *c·* for the passage of the blood,

clothe
pr 4–32 and *c·* religion in human forms.
sp 93–19 human faith may *c·* it with angelic vestments,
g 530–11 as able to feed and *c·* man as He doth the lilies.

clothed
f 254– 0 To stop eating, drinking, or being *c·* materially
p 442–25 and man is *c·* and fed spiritually.
ap 558– 4 *c·* with a cloud :— *Rev.* 10 : 1.
558– 9 This angel . . . *c·* with a cloud, prefigures
560– 7 a woman *c·* with the sun, — *Rev.* 12 : 1.
561–11 the spiritual ideal as a woman *c·* in light,

clothes
m 62–24 even as it *c·* the lily ;
s 146–19 truth . . . *c·* Spirit with supremacy.
f 212–23 God alone makes and *c·* the lilies of the field,
g 507– 4 Spirit duly feeds and *c·* every object,

clothing
an 104– 7 belied by wolves in sheep's *c·*.
p 442–23 Truth, gives mortals temporary food and *c·*
ap 567–29 These wolves in sheep's *c·* are detected

cloud
f 210–21 as a sunbeam penetrates the *c·*.
247–26 arches the *c·* with the bow of beauty,
b 288–16 may burst and flash till the *c·* is cleared
295–23 like a *c·* melting into thin vapor,
298– 4 As a *c·* hides the sun it cannot extinguish,
ap 558– 4 clothed with a *c·* :— *Rev.* 10 : 1.
558–10 This angel . . . clothed with a *c·*, prefigures
566–10 a pillar of *c·* by day and of fire by night,

clouded
gl 590–26 statements of the Scriptures become *c·*

clouds
gathering
g 547–13 the gathering *c·*, the moon and stars,
murky
s 122–21 in the midst of murky *c·* and drenching rain.
varying
b 311– 1 the varying *c·* of mortal belief,

---

m 67– 4 the *c·* lower, the wind shrieks
s 122–17 On the eye's retina, . . . *c·* and ocean meet
f 245–21 coaxed the enamoured lightning from the *c·*.
o 354–20 which are like *c·* without rain.
g 548– 9 when *c·* cover the sun's face !
548–11 seen only as the *c·* of corporeal sense roll away.
557–19 Divine Science rolls back the *c·* of error

clover
ph 175–13 profane to fancy that the perfume of *c·*

coalesce
s 143–32 may try to make Mind and drugs *c·*,

coalition
f 218–10 The reports of sickness may form a *c·* with

coated
f 379–26 The quickened pulse, *c·* tongue, febrile heat,

Coated Tongue
p 431–21 I am *C· T·*. I am covered with a

coaxed
f 245–20 *c·* the enamoured lightning from the clouds.

coddling
ph 175–20 people had less time for selfishness, *c·*,

code
f 226–16 These claims are not made through *c·* or creed,

codes
ph 183– 3 and demand obedience to materialistic *c·*,
f 226–18 Human *c·*, scholastic theology,
234–21 The present *c·* of human systems disappoint
b 340–27 civil, criminal, political, and religious *c·* ;
p 381–16 but He is not the author of barbarous *c·*.

coequal
o 351–21 if we consider Satan as a being *c·* in power

coeternal
b 336–11 coexistent and *c·* with that Mind.

coexist
c 267–12 man and the spiritual universe *c·* with
b 270– 1 theory, . . . that Mind and matter *c·*
279–13 Spirit and matter can neither *c·* nor cooperate,
336–30 God and man *c·* and are eternal.
r 471–16 the evidence that God and man *c·*

coexistence
b 269– 3 supposed *c·* of Mind and matter

coexistent
m 69– 1 not of the earth earthly but *c·* with God,
b 336–11 *c·* and coeternal with that Mind.
r 478– 1 for man is *c·* with God.
g 516–21 Man . . . as *c·* and eternal with God
520– 9 Principle and its idea, man, are *c·*
557–21 as never dying, but as *c·* with his creator.
gl 581–11 God and man *c·* and eternal ;

coexists
s 120– 5 and man *c·* with and reflects Soul,
f 246–12 sun of virtue and truth *c·* with being.
c 266–31 but he *c·* with God and the universe.

coffee
sp 80– 3 A cup of *c·* or tea is not the equal of truth,
p 406–29 tobacco, tea, *c·*, opium,

cognizable
sp 86–28 as readily as from objects *c·* by the senses.

cognizance
beyond the
s 126–19 beyond the *c·* of the material senses
b 284–25 beyond the *c·* of these senses,
cannot take
g 543–10 corporeal senses cannot take *c·* of Spirit.
has no
b 292–14 this so-called mind has no *c·* of Spirit.
have no
c 258–21 so-called senses have no *c·* of either
of good or evil
ph 171–32 error . . . that the *c·* of good or evil,
take
an 105–16 When our laws eventually take *c·* of
taken no
f 245–22 she had taken no *c·* of passing time
take no
sp 72– 2 of which corporeal sense can take no *c·*.
75– 7 or the material senses could take no *c·* of
ph 191– 2 It can take no *c·* of Mind.
b 273– 4 physical senses can take no *c·* of God
r 479–15 and matter can take no *c·* of matter.

cognizance

take no
r 488–21 corporeal senses can take no *c·* of spiritual
g 531–29 the corporeal senses can take no *c·* of Spirit.
546–17 the material senses can take no *c·* of Spirit

takes no
gl 591–14 that of which immortal Mind takes no *c·* ;

cognizant
pr 13–32 is not *c·* of life in Soul,
sp 88– 6 The mind may even be *c·* of a present flavor
b 276–11 consciousness is *c·* only of the things of God.
285– 1 cannot be *c·* of good or of evil,

cognize
o 359–17 *c·* only that which is the opposite of Spirit.

cognized
m 69– 8 God's children already created will be *c·*
sp 75– 4 the existence *c·* by the physical senses,
b 311–26 The objects *c·* by the physical senses

cognizes
b 306–24 which *c·* Life as permanent.

cohesion
s 124–20 *c·*, and attraction are properties of Mind.
b 293–16 whose adhesion and *c·* are Life,

coiled
sp 92–11 a serpent *c·* around the tree of knowledge.

coincide
sp 80–13 but I cannot *c·* with their views.
93–10 Divine logic and revelation *c·*.
ph 167–21 can no more unite . . . than good can *c·* with
g 522–23 convince reason and *c·* with revelation

coincidence
ph 194– 4 I cannot fail to discern the *c·* of
b 332–32 illustrates the *c·*, or spiritual agreement,
ap 561–16 John saw the human and divine *c·*,
561–23 illustrates the *c·* of God and man

coincides
o 358– 9 C. S., understood, *c·* with the Scriptures,

cold

and heat
s 125–22 *c·* and heat, latitude and longitude.

effects of
ph 184–19 We say man suffers from the effects of *c·*,

heat and
p 374–26 Heat and *c·* are products of mortal mind.

matter cannot take
p 377– 2 convince him that matter cannot take *c·*,

this
f 202–32 Common opinion admits . . . that this *c·* may

——

pref vii–16 and the *c·* conventionality of materialism
s 113– 8 is but the dead body of Science, — pulseless, *c·*,
ph 179–16 that he will take *c·* without his blanket,
195– 5 Outside of dismal darkness and *c·* silence
f 202–31 Common opinion admits that a man may take *c·*
220– 2 We hear it said : . . . I take *c·* baths,
220– 3 to overcome a predisposition to take *c·* ;
224–19 *C·* disdain, stubborn resistance,
p 377– 1 If your patient believes in taking *c·*,
378–28 a long and *c·* night of discord.
384– 9 though they expose him to fatigue, *c·*, heat,
386– 6 belief says that you may catch *c·* and
429–11 corpse, deserted by thought, is *c·* and decays,
436–11 Giving a cup of *c·* water in Christ's name,
t 460–22 *c·* assertion, "Nothing ails you."
ap 570–17 Give them a cup of *c·* water in Christ's name,

coldness
gl 593–18 Rock. . . . *C·* and stubbornness.

colds
f 220– 3 We hear it said : . . . I have continual *c·*,
220–16 *C·*, coughs, and contagion are engendered solely

collapse
s 124–27 Withdraw them, and creation must *c·*.
f 209–10 The world would *c·* without Mind,

collect
m 63–30 should be allowed to *c·* her own wages,

collective
a 18– 6 His mission was both individual and *c·*.

collectively
m 58–10 constitute individually and *c·*

College
pref xii– 3 hers was the only *C·* of this character
xii– 7 were taught by the author in this *C·*.
xii–14 She closed her *C·*, October 29, 1889,
xii–19 reopened the *C·* in 1899

colleges
pref xi–30 a law relative to *c·* having been passed,

color
f 247–24 in expression, form, outline, and *c·*.
b 301– 3 mirror, repeats the *c·*, form, and action
310– 7 seen in all form, substance, and *c·*,
338–13 signifying the *red c· of the ground*,
r 479–27 We admit that black is not a *c·*,
g 512–22 From . . . the one Mind emanate all form, *c·*,

Colossians
b 325–10 In *C·* (iii. 4) Paul writes :

Columbus
s 120–30 When *C·* gave freer breath to the globe,

combat
b 268–11 challenge metaphysics to meet in final *c·*.
269–29 The theories I *c·* are these :
p 396–25 to *c·* their erroneous sense,

combated
pref viii–17 Sickness has been *c·* for centuries

combination
c 256–24 No form nor physical *c·* is adequate to
p 399– 9 not a secretion nor *c·* can operate, apart from

combinations
p 399– 3 You say that certain material *c·* produce

combine
b 275–13 Spirit, Life, Truth, Love, *c·* as one,
288– 9 Superstition and understanding can never *c·*.
p 397–28 because they *c·* as one.
409– 4 *Mortal mind* and body *c·* as one,

combined
pr 1– 6 Prayer, watching, and working, *c·* with
s 163–18 war, pestilence, and famine, all *c·*."
ph 171–18 believes himself to be *c·* matter and Spirit.
p 421–32 and that their *c·* sum is fifty,

combines
t 450–30 all evil *c·* in the belief of life, . . . in matter,
r 466– 3 Hence God *c·* all-power or potency,

combustion
s 161–10 might produce spontaneous *c·*.

come
pref vii–13 The time for thinkers has *c·*.
x–29 or discerning the truth, *c·* not to the light
pr 1– * *shall c· to pass; — Mark* 11 : 23.
8– 4 little hope for those who *c·* only spasmodically
12–23 should *c·* from the enlightened understanding.
13– 4 *c·* ye to the waters." — Isa.* 55 : 1.
16–30 Thy kingdom *c·*. — *Matt.* 6 : 10.
16–31 *Thy kingdom is c·*;
a 18– * *until the kingdom of God shall c·.— Luke* 22 : 18.
22–13 "Occupy till I *c·* !" — *Luke* 19 : 13.
24–18 change as radical as that which has *c·* over
27– 3 intended to prove . . . that the Christ had *c·* :
31–24 show the Lord's death till he *c·*." — *I Cor.* 11 : 26.
34– 5 Truth has *c·* to the understanding
34– 6 If Christ, Truth, has *c·* to us in demonstration,
38–14 in all time to *c·*.
40–29 has *c·* so generally to mean public worship
41– 3 must *c·* through the joys and triumphs of the
m 56–10 and His kingdom is *c·*
sp 80– 6 A communication purporting to *c·* from the
85–12 "*C·*, see a man, which — *John* 4 : 29.
86–11 Opposites *c·* from contrary directions,
90– 5 from which loaf or fish could *c·*?
90–28 recognition of Spirit must finally *c·*,
92–32 Do you say the time has not yet *c·*
an 100–19 we have *c·* to the unanimous conclusions
s 112–18 with this infinitude *c·* spiritual rules,
125–21 The seasons will *c·* and go
129–16 *c·* hither to torment us — *Matt.* 8 : 29.
130– 5 bidden to the feast, the excuses *c·*.
131–13 Must C. S. *c·* through the Christian churches
131–14 This Science has *c·* already,
131–31 "Art thou he that should *c·*," — *Matt.* 11 : 3.
133– 2 "Art thou he that should *c·*?" — *Matt.* 11 : 3.
134– 8 and so has *c·* always to mean
141–10 revelation (such is the popular thought !) must *c·*
144– 2 Why should we . . . since no good can *c·* of it?
ph 173–26 Human reason and religion *c·* slowly to the
182–27 Pleas for drugs and laws of health *c·* from
192– 7 They *c·* from the hearing of the ear,
f 212– 8 Why need pain, . . . *c·* to this mortal sense?
223–32 until "He *c·* whose right it is." — *Ezek.* 21 : 27.
225–21 nor did the breath of freedom *c·* from the
238– 6 " *C·* out from among them, — *II Cor.* 6 : 17.
238–14 there will *c·* the warning,
c 266– 7 Then the time will *c·* when
b 280– 6 only reflections of good can *c·*.
283–10 which act, react, and then *c·* to a stop.
285–17 time has *c·* for a finite . . . to give place
291– 8 last call of wisdom cannot *c·* till
304– 7 nor things present, nor things to *c·*, — *Rom.* 8 : 38.
321–10 bade him *c·* back and handle the serpent,
321–27 " It shall *c·* to pass, — *Exod.* 4 : 8.
322–11 before this recognition of divine Science can *c·*

come

b 324–30	if the idea . . . . *c·* not to your thought,
333–21	has *c·* with some measure of power and grace
o 361– 1	Jew believes that . . . Christ has not yet *c·* ;
361– 8	God is *c·* and is present now and forever.
p 362–15	to *c·* behind the couch and reach his feet.
367–24	Truth of the Christ-cure has *c·* to this age
368– 6	Both truth and error have *c·* nearer than ever
368–15	When we *c·* to have more faith in the truth
376– 8	diseases deemed dangerous sometimes *c·* from
377– 7	they *c·* back no better than when they went
393– 1	issues of pain or pleasure must *c·* through
398– 3	I charge thee, *c·* out of him, — *Mark* 9 : 25.
398–30	The Science of Mind must *c·* to the rescue,
411– 1	thing which I greatly feared is *c·* — *Job* 3 : 25.
t 451– 3	to *c·* out from the material world
451–17	they *c·* from above, not from beneath,
r 474–20	"I am not *c·* to destroy, — *Matt.* 5 : 17.
478–11	to go into the house or to *c·* out of it,
485–15	*c·* naturally into Spirit through better health
g 501– 7	and *c·* nearer the heart.
519–18	"we all *c·* in the unity of the faith, — *Eph.* 4 : 13.
529– 7	Another change will *c·* as to the
543–10	They cannot *c·* into His presence,
548– 1	The Spirit and the bride say, C· ! — *Rev.* 22 : 17.
556–17	*c·* from the deep sleep which
556–22	Oblivion and dreams, not realities, *c·* with sleep.
ap 558– 3	mighty angel *c·* down from heaven, — *Rev.* 10 : 1.
567– 4	Truth and Love *c·* nearer in the hour of woe,
568–14	Now is *c·* salvation, and strength, — *Rev.* 12 : 10.
568–22	the devil is *c·* down unto you, — *Rev.* 12 : 12.
574– 8	C· hither, I will show thee — *Rev.* 21 : 9.
575– 1	thought gently whispers : "C· hither !
gl 585–13	"Elias truly shall first *c·* — *Matt.* 17 : 11.
585–18	a type of the glory which is to *c·* ;

comeliness

f 247–19	C· and grace are independent of matter.
b 281–15	supplies all form and *c·*

comes

pr 5– 8	and woe *c·* in return for what is done.
a 42– 8	*c·* in darkness and disappears with the light.
sp 75– 2	assumption that man dies . . . but *c·* to life as
76–32	recognition of Spirit . . . *c·* not suddenly
84–28	All we correctly know of Spirit *c·* from God,
85– 5	This Soul-sense *c·* to the human mind when
s 112–16	*c·* one Principle and its infinite idea,
113– 5	but its spirit *c·* only in small degrees.
115– 3	through which the understanding . . . *c·*,
118–32	the natural order of heaven *c·* down to earth.
ph 174–31	its cure *c·* from the immortal divine
178–20	this so-called mind, from which *c·* all evil,
188–28	When darkness *c·* over the earth,
180–25	From mortal mind *c·* the reproduction of the
f 202–19	when God's kingdom *c·* on earth ;
223–16	the assurance which *c·* of understanding ;
230 9	salvation which *c·* through God,
238–26	Justice often *c·* too late to secure a verdict.
239–27	If it *c·* from erring mortal mind,
247– 1	acute belief of physical life *c·* on at a remote
250–12	a ray of light which *c·* from the sun,
c 264–27	which *c·* from an all-absorbing spiritual love.
265–25	The aspiration after heavenly good *c·*
266–10	When this hour of development *c·*,
b 280–16	belief *c·* to have "gods many — *I Cor.* 8 : 5.
289– 1	real existence as a child of God *c·* to light.
290–12	Hence Truth *c·* to destroy this error
291–20	judgment-day of wisdom *c·* hourly
303– 6	*c·* from no power of propagation in
318–19	beliefs, from which *c·* so much suffering,
327– 1	Reform *c·* by understanding that
339–24	gives place to . . . and God's kingdom *c·*
o 347–15	Christ, . . . *c·* now as of old,
358–25	*c·* through rousing within the sick
p 382–16	the devotee . . . who *c·* to teach the
387–21	supposition that death *c·* in obedience to the
434– 2	on the wings of divine Love, there *c·* a despatch :
r 466–27	Science of Christianity *c·* with fan in hand
473–10	that *c·* to heal sickness and sin
479– 6	On the contrary, if aught *c·* from God,
483– 1	Then *c·* the question,
490–10	From this also *c·* its powerlessness,
g 523–11	In error everything *c·* from beneath,
529–21	Whence *c·* a talking, lying serpent
556–29	but when that awakening *c·*,
ap 558– 9	message which *c·* from God,
569–22	back to him at last with accelerated force,
gl 583–10	*c·* to the flesh to destroy incarnate error.

comet

s 121–15	is as the wandering *c·* or the desolate star

cometh

pref vii– 3	ere *c·* the full radiance of a risen day.
a 31–26	"The hour *c·*, and now is, — *John* 4 : 23.
31–31	yea, the time *c·*, — *John* 16 : 2.
35–26	"which *c·* down from heaven," — *John* 6 : 33.

cometh

m 64–18	the time *c·* of which Jesus spake,
sp 78–29	cannot "tell whence it *c·*." — *John* 3 : 8.
93– 6	"But the hour *c·*, and now is, — *John* 4 : 23.
s 132–27	"When the Son of man *c·*, — *Luke* 18 : 8.
f 224–26	who *c·* in the quiet of meekness,
225– 1	Whence *c·* it?
b 286– 9	Master said, "No man *c·* unto — *John* 14 : 6.
325–26	time *c·* when the spiritual origin of man,
g 550– 3	If this be so, whence *c·* Life, or Mind,
ap 575– 4	Then *c·* the marriage feast,
575– 8	and *c·* "down from God, — *Rev.* 21 : 2.

comfort

an 101–29	Discomfort under error is preferable to *c·*.
ph 197– 6	costs many a man his earthly days of *c·*.
f 234– 6	crumbs of *c·* from Christ's table,
ap 578–12	[LOVE's] rod and [LOVE's] staff they *c·* me. — *Psal.* 23 : 4.

comforted

a 33–12	and now it *c·* themselves.
sp 78–30	By it the sick are healed, the sorrowing are *c·*,

Comforter

a 55–28	"He shall give you another C·, — *John* 14 : 16.
55–29	This C· I understand to be Divine Science.
s 123–22	through the teachings of the C·,
127–29	the C· which leadeth into all truth.
b 271–20	Our Master said, "But the C· — *John* 14 : 26.
331–31	divine Science or the Holy C·.
332–21	the Holy Ghost, or C·, revealing the
r 497– 7	the Holy Ghost or divine C· ;

comforts

gl 582–12	that which *c·*, consoles, and supports.

coming

pref xi–18	*c·* now as was promised aforetime,
a 52–14	word concerning the *c·* Prince of Peace.
sp 83– 7	good and evil elements now *c·* to the surface.
an 102–17	its aggressive features are *c·* to the front.
s 132–11	such effects, *c·* from divine Mind,
150 7	Its appearing is the *c·* anew of the gospel of
150– 8	This *c·*, as was promised by the Master,
f 215–17	at the *c·* of which darkness loses the
230– 7	This awakening is the forever *c·* of Christ,
245–10	before the window watching for her lover's *c·*.
b 321–29	And so it was in the *c·* centuries,
o 347–14	would behold the signs of Christ's *c·*.
p 385–31	Any supposed information, *c·* from the body
g 549–31	*c·* down to a belief in the material origin of
ap 561–12	the spiritual ideal . . . *c·* down from heaven,
561–32	John the Baptist prophesied the *c·* of the
574–13	*c·* down from God, out of heaven," — *Rev.* 21 : 2.

command

apostolic
t 451– 3	the constant pressure of the apostolic *c·*

Christ's
s 110–29	demonstrated according to Christ's *c·*,

direct
o 342–10	in defiance of the direct *c·* of Jesus,

first
b 280–18	as Jehovah's first *c·* of the Ten :

follow the
f 228–20	If we follow the *c·* of our Master,

God's
g 530– 6	The earth, at God's *c·*, brings forth food

Scriptural
f 238– 6	To obey the Scriptural *c·*,
b 276– 8	in accordance with the Scriptural *c·* :

single
g 524–18	With a single *c·*, Mind had made man,

spiritual
ph 168–19	spiritual *c·* relating to perfection,

this
pr 9–19	This *c·* includes much,
a 38– 2	Because men are assured that this *c·*

ph 196–14	The *c·* was a warning to beware,
f 225– 9	*c·* their sentinels not to let truth pass
o 342–11	to which *c·* was added the promise
p 403–14	You *c·* the situation if you understand
r 467– 5	Therefore the *c·* means this :
ap 570–25	and Christ will *c·* the wave.

commanded

a 37–27	do they follow him in the way that he *c·*?
m 67–22	and *c·* even the winds and waves
g 527– 6	And the Lord God [Jehovah] *c·* — *Gen.* 2 : 16.
533– 7	whereof I *c·* thee — *Gen.* 3 : 11.
535–21	which I *c·* thee, saying, — *Gen.* 3 : 17.

commandest

p 435–30	and *c·* . . . to be smitten — *Acts* 23 : 3.

commanding

p 439– 7	*c·* him to take part in the homicide.
442–11	His form was erect and *c·*,

Commandment
m 69–21 "Do you keep the First C·?
b 301–22 not spiritual and breaks the First C·,
340–16 The First C· is my favorite text.
340–21 The divine Principle of the First C·
o 361– 6 The Jew who believes in the First C·
361–10 The Christian who believes in the First C·

commandment
a 19–29 Jesus urged the c·,
m 56–18 c·, "Thou shalt not commit — Exod. 20 : 14.
s 112–30 inculcates a breach of that divine c·
b 308– 4 art thou . . . keeping His c·?''

Commandments
ap 563–13 belief that . . . the Ten C· can be broken.

commandments
pr 4– 5 To keep the c· of our Master
4–11 "If ye love me, keep my c·." — John 14 : 15.
a 25–20 "If ye love me, keep my c·." — John 14 : 15.
f 241–22 "If ye love me, keep my c·." — John 14 : 15.
b 340– 8 Fear God, and keep His c· : — Eccl. 12 : 13.
340–11 love God and keep His c· :
g 542–26 to advance itself, breaks God's c·.

commands
a 20–26 It c· sure entrance into the realm of Love.
26– 6 if we follow his c· faithfully ;
37–27 Hear these imperative c· :
f 222–28 contrary to His c·.
o 355–16 according to the c· of our Master,
p 405– 5 C. S. c· man to master the propensities,
r 489–14 it breaks all the c· of the Mosaic Decalogue

commemorate
a 32– 9 Eucharist does not c· a Roman soldier's oath,
35–12 the morning meal which Christian Scientists c·.

commemorated
a 33–31 can you then say that you have c· Jesus
34–11 If all . . . had really c· the sufferings of Jesus

commemoration
a 34– 6 no other c· is requisite,
34–13 If all who seek his c· through material symbols

commences
ph 189–29 c· in the lower, basal portion of the brain,
p 423– 9 c· with mental causation,
430–20 patient feels ill, ruminates, and the trial c·.

commend
t 457–25 some learners c· diet and hygiene.

commendation
p 365–20 such c· as the Magdalen gained from Jesus,

commended
a 35–28 draught our Master drank and c· to his
p 434–32 that court c· man's immortal Spirit

commending
sp 92–14 serpent in the act of c· to

comment
pr 8–12 what must be the c· upon him?
8–14 there would be no occasion for c·.
a 55– 3 subjects to unchristian c· and usage
g 523– 2 of the Scriptural account now under c·.

commercialism
ph 195–28 Literary c· is lowering the intellectual

commingle
ph 198–26 His thoughts and his patient's c·,
f 211– 3 if . . . Truth and error, c·
b 281– 4 Spirit and matter no more c· than light and
296–24 When the evidence . . . seems to c·,
r 492–22 The notion that mind and matter c·
g 539–20 false to say that Truth and error c·

commingling
r 481–15 declaring . . . good and evil to be capable of c·.

commission
a 54–13 In witness of his divine c·,
an 100–14 Under this order a c· was appointed,
100–16 This c· reported to the government
104–30 as well as the c· of a crime.
p 433–22 this has led him into the c· of the

Commissioner
p 432– 2 the State C·.

commissioners
an 100–15 Benjamin Franklin was one of the c·.

commissions
t 455–24 When He c· a messenger,

commit
m 56–18 "Thou shalt not c· adultery," — Exod. 20 : 14.
an 105– 2 The hands, without . . . could not c· a murder.
105–10 Can matter c· a crime?
105–23 to c· fresh atrocities as opportunity occurs
f 252–19 cheat, lie, c· adultery, rob, murder,
o 356–25 Does divine Love c· a fraud on humanity
p 406–17 moral man has no fear that he will c· a murder,
432– 7 I knew the prisoner would c· it,

commit
436–30 deeds which the divine law compels man to c·
t 461–18 If you c· a crime, should you acknowledge

commits
pref xii–26 she c· these pages to honest seekers for Truth.
r 490– 4 this belief c· depredations on harmony.

committed
s 161–22 "Liberty, what crimes are c· in thy name!"
p 408–11 people who are c· to insane asylums
430–18 is charged with having c· liver-complaint.
431– 8 At last he c· liver-complaint,
434–28 shows the alleged crime never to have been c·
435– 4 Has the body or has Mortal Mind c· a
435– 7 The body c· no offence.
435–14 If liver-complaint was c· by trampling on

committee
an 101– 8 a c· of nine persons was appointed,

committing
p 436–17 to prevent his c· liver-complaint,
t 459–14 C· the bare process of mental healing to

common
pr 12–22 c· custom of praying for the recovery
a 52–18 make c· cause against the exponents of truth.
sp 80–30 This belief rests on the c· conviction that
92–17 for the c· conception of mortal man
an 101–17 nothing in c· with either physiology or
106– 2 to drop from the platform of c· manhood
s 137–14 implied in their citation of the c· report
137–27 had been called only by his c· names,
153– 5 Natrum muriaticum (c· table-salt)
f 202–31 C· opinion admits that a man may take cold
b 294– 2 These senses indicate the c· human belief,
333– 5 in c· with other Hebrew boys and men,
o 342–30 according to the c· theories,
357– 1 In c· justice, we must admit that God
p 363– 3 which is in such c· use in the East.
363–17 were released . . . by their c· creditor.
365–11, 12 and c· sense and c· humanity are
383–32 c· notion that health depends on inert matter
388–12 Admit the c· hypothesis
407–32 in consonance with c· mortal belief.
t 459– 7 Then he will have nothing in c· with
r 488–12 Scriptures often appear in our c· version
g 523–20 or Lord God, as our c· version translates it.
540– 9 reducing it to its c· denominator.
gl 598–14 the phrase is equivalent to our c· statement,

commonly
s 116–24 As the words . . . are c· and ignorantly
139– 9 Reforms have c· been attended with bloodshed
ph 183–20 mortals c· recognize as law that which hides
f 232– 4 The beliefs we c· entertain about happiness
242–22 the facts of being are c· misconstrued,
243–13 That those wonders are not more c· repeated
b 274– 7 Natural science, as it is c· called,
284–26 by the effects c· attributed to them.
310–18 We are c· taught that there is a human soul
319–11 material means (c· called nature)
333– 4 though it is c· so used.
o 344–20 are not included in the c· accepted systems;
344–32 the word Spirit is so c· applied to Deity,
gl 586–10 the divine Principle, c· called God.

Common Version
b 313–13 "express image" in the C· V· — Heb. 1 : 3.

Commonwealth
pref xi–29 under the seal of the C·,

commotion
p 422–11 Patients, unfamiliar with the cause of this c·

commune
a 35–13 and silently to c· with the divine Principle,
sp 73–29 mistake to suppose that . . . can c· together.
74–31 so-called dead and living cannot c· together,
75–26 one possible moment, when those . . . can c·
76–13 can no longer c· with matter;
84–15 to c· more largely with the divine Mind,

communed
sp 73–15 If Spirit, or God, c· . . . through electricity

communicable
sp 72–25 but evil is neither c· nor scientific
72–29 when evil and suffering are c·.
74– 3 To be on c· terms with Spirit,

communicate
sp 78–22 How then can it c· with man through
82–14 we do not c· with the dreamer by our side

communicated
f 212– 2 is not c· through a nerve.
213–18 as c· through the senses of Soul
p 423– 3 this belief should not be c· to the patient,

communicates
sp 85–31 truth c· itself but never imparts error.

communicating
t 446– 2 perhaps c· his own bad morals,

communication
sp 73–32 There is no *c·* between so-called material
78–12 even were *c·* possible
80– 6 A *c·* purporting to come from

communications
sp 77–22 Even if *c·* from spirits to mortal consciousness
77–23 such *c·* would grow beautifully less
78–13 *C·* gathered from ignorance are pernicious

communicator
sp 72–30 divine law is the *c·* of truth,
81–32 deceased person, supposed to be the *c·*,

communicators
sp 72– 9 So-called *spirits* are but corporeal *c·*.

communing
sp 78– 8 belief . . . that at the same time we are *c·* with

communion
a 30– 1 Mary's self-conscious *c·* with God.
35–25 Our Eucharist is spiritual *c·* with the one God.
sp 72– 7 condition precedent to *c·* with Spirit
74–13 No correspondence nor *c·* can exist between
82–23 *C·* . . . would be prevented by this difference.
g 539–24 "What *c·* hath light with— *II Cor.* 6 : 14.

community
an 103– 2 in families and therefore in the *c·*.
t 446– 3 a *c·* unprepared for self-defence.
456– 9 which most of them hold in the *c·*,

commute
p 378– 5 will enable you to *c·* this self-sentence,

compact
m 59– 7 compromises will often maintain a *c·*

companion
ap 569–22 The sin, which one has made his bosom *c·*,

companionship
a 21–24 and our *c·* may continue.
m 60– 5 formation of a happy and permanent *c·*.

company
a 21–28 *c·* is alluring and the pleasures exciting.
36– 2 in the blessed *c·* of Truth and Love
m 66–27 the other pre-eminently needs good *c·*.
c 261–15 actively as the youngest member of the *c·*.

compare
g 515–28 Now *c·* man before the mirror

comparison
c 256–17 in *c·* with the sublime question,
b 297–25 Human thoughts have their degrees of *c·*.

comparative
pref ix–29 her *c·* ignorance of the stupendous

compass
f 233–19 *c·* the destruction of sin and sickness
b 292– 5 Divine Science alone can *c·* the heights

compassed
b 302– 1 Soul is not *c·* by finiteness.

compassion
s 115–26 MORAL. Humanity, honesty, affection, *c·*,

compassionately
p 363– 9 He regarded her *c·*.
365–22 and deal with his patients *c·* ;

compel
pr 11–11 in order to *c·* this progress.
p 390–10 Truth will at length *c·* us all to exchange the
440–23 human mental legislators *c·* them to

compelled
s 159– 5 she was *c·* by her physicians to take it.
p 436–25 they were *c·* to let him be taken

compels
p 436–30 deeds which the divine law *c·* man to commit.

compensated
s 163–27 if it were not more than *c·* by

compensation
ap 574–19 has full *c·* in the law of Love.
gl 581–15 Hope and faith ; spiritual *c·* ;

compilation
f 241–15 that *c·* can do no more for mortals

complain
m 62–11 those parents should not, in after years, *c·*
62–30 and produce the ills of which we *c·*.

complaining
o 348–22 while *c·* of the suffering disease brings,
p 395–17 An ill-tempered, *c·*, or deceitful person

complaint
f 221–16 without a vestige of the old *c·*.
p 391–29 Mentally contradict every *c·*

complaints
pr 14–15 the body will then utter no *c·*.
f 237–31 would rid them of their *c·*,

complete
pref ix–15 and are not *c·* nor satisfactory expositions
a 25– 1 Thomas was forced to acknowledge how *c·*
sp 98–28 not . . . fragmentary, but practical and *c·* ;
98–29 and being practical and *c·*,
s 147–14 this volume contains the *c·* Science of
o 353–15 eternity, immortality, *c·* reality.
p 417–28 the *c·* control which Mind holds over the
t 457–27 which they mean to *c·* with Mind,
g 519– 9 the ideas of God in universal being are *c·*
527– 5 but ever beautiful and *c·*.

completed
a 41–15 *c·* his earthly mission ;
ap 562– 5 Revelator *c·* this figure with woman,

completely
s 137–13 Jesus *c·* eschewed the narrow opinion
t 446–10 has generally *c·* healed such cases.

completeness
m 57– 5 Union of . . . qualities constitutes *c·*.

complex
p 393–27 not upon the *c·* humors, lenses, muscles,

compliance
p 433– 7 In *c·* with a stern duty, his Honor,

complicated
an 102–20 weaving webs more *c·* and subtle.
g 549–19 the most *c·* corporeal structures,

complication
p 389–31 suffering from a *c·* of symptoms

component
a 28–16 Not a single *c·* part of his nature
g 550–18 decay and dissolution as its *c·* stages

composed
r 478–25 is *c·* of material human beliefs
g 551–19 *c·* of the simplest material elements,

composing
f 200–17 aggregated substances *c·* the earth,

compositions
pref viii–30 but these *c·* were crude,

compound
r 468–23 universe, . . . is a *c·* idea,
475–14 He is the *c·* idea of God,
g 507–18 multiplication of the *c·* idea man.
gl 585– 8 to spiritual sense, it is a *c·* idea.
591– 5 MAN. The *c·* idea of infinite Spirit ;

compounded
f 209–16 *c·* minerals or aggregated substances
ap 577– 7 this *c·* spiritual individuality reflects

comprehend
pr 2 25 anything He does not already *c·*?
sp 98–11 which the material senses cannot *c·*,
s 136–24 for how could such a sinner *c·*
136–30 but they did not *c·* all that he said
ph 187– 3 mortals do not *c·* even mortal existence,
f 210– 4 the language which human thought can *c·*.
c 258–32 and thus begin to *c·* in Science
b 301– 5 Few persons *c·* what C. S. means by
g 555– 8 said . . . I do not *c·* what you say about error."

comprehended
an 104– 4 When C. S. and animal magnetism are both *c·*,
s 141–24 Neither can this manifestation . . . be *c·*, until
149– 9 These states are not *c·*,
ph 167– 5 and Soul-existence, . . . is not *c·*.
b 303– 9 and are *c·* in and formed by Spirit,
325–31 the darkness *c·* it not."— *John* 1 : 5.
o 350–13 Unless the works are *c·* which his
g 520– 8 is no more seen nor *c·* by mortals,

comprehending
f 219–25 not *c·* the Principle of the cure,
p 441– 1 *c·* and defining all law and evidence,
g 546–25 though the darkness, *c·* them not,

comprehends
o 347–21 which the darkness *c·* not.
p 369– 8 and *c·* the theology of Jesus
371–15 no more *c·* his real being than
r 481– 8 Through spiritual sense only, man *c·* . . . Deity.
g 518–27 divine Principle, or Spirit, *c·* and expresses
gl 596– 1 That which spiritual sense alone *c·*,

comprehensible
s 115– 6 to make them *c·* to any reader,
146–32 to a form *c·* by and adapted to

comprehension
p 388–28 and a clear *c·* of the living Spirit.
t 462– 1 requisite for a thorough *c·* of C. S.
r 488–24 Mind alone possesses . . . perception, and *c·*.

comprehensiveness
s 128–10 gives them acuteness and *c·*

compress
280–10 limits all things, and would *c·* Mind,

compressed
c 256–13 nor *c·* within the narrow limits of
p 397–29 Give up the belief that mind is, . . . *c·* within

comprised
s 127– 7 *c·* in a knowledge or understanding of God,
b 286–31 Sin, sickness, and death are *c·* in

compromise
t 443– 6 those, who make such a *c·*,

compromised
pref x–11 The author has not *c·* conscience

compromises
m 59– 7 Mutual *c·* will often maintain a compact

computed
s 129– 4 or of a properly *c·* sum in arithmetic

con
s 120–25 Any conclusion *pro* or *c·*,
129– 9 be the fable *pro* or *c·*,—

conceal
pr 4– 1 we cannot *c·* the ingratitude of barren lives.
t 447–13 false charity does not forever *c·* error;
g 542–10 disposition to excuse guilt or to *c·* it

concealed
g 542– 7 error cannot forever be *c·*.

concealment
gl 596–28 VEIL. A cover; *c·*; hiding; hypocrisy.

conceals
b 326– 1 false sense . . . *c·* scientific demonstration.

concede
ph 186–22 If we *c·* the same reality to discord as to

conceded
ph 166–28 balance of power is *c·* to be with matter by
c 267– 8 It is generally *c·* that God is Father,
p 396–15 is not a difficult task in view of the *c·* falsity

conceding
p 394– 5 By *c·* power to discord,

conceit
t 450– 2 whose bigotry and *c·* twist every fact
ap 571–27 Thus he rebukes the *c·* of sin,

conceive
b 318– 2 for him to *c·* of the substantiality of Spirit
331–23 to *c·* of such omnipresence and individuality

conceived
a 29–17 Virgin-mother *c·* this idea of God,
f 211–30 be *c·* of as immortal.
b 303–11 is spiritually *c·* and brought forth;
303–12 statement that man is *c·* and evolved
315–30 being *c·* by a human mother,
t 462–20 Anatomy, when *c·* of spiritually, is
463–14 *c·* and born of Truth and Love,
r 476–16 "*c·* in sin and brought forth in iniquity."
g 538–24 and she *c·*, and bare Cain,— *Gen. 4: 1.*
540–28 mortal and material man, *c·* in sin
545– 6 never had been divinely *c·*.

conceives
f 213– 6 Mortal mind *c·* of something as

conceiving
g 513–19 are as eternal as the Mind *c·* them;
gl 582–14 *c·* man in the idea of God;

concept
  corporeal
  gl 589–16 JESUS. The highest human corporeal *c·*
  every
  c 262–29 Every *c·* which seems to begin with the brain
  false
  ph 177–10 Matter, or body, is but a false *c·*
  human
  (see **human**)
  Jewish
  ap 576–28 The term Lord, . . . expresses the Jewish *c·*,
  material
  b 297–17 only fact concerning any material *c·* is,
  334–16 material *c·*, or Jesus, disappeared,
  mental
  sp 87–24 Do not suppose that any mental *c·* is gone
  p 376–19 the so-called material body is a mental *c·*
  perfect
  t 454–23 and form the perfect *c·*.
  true
  sp 87–25 The true *c·* is never lost.
  unreal
  an 102– 7 an unreal *c·* of the so-called mortal mind.
  your
  o 346–27 in your *c·*, the tooth, the operation,

conception
  common
  sp 92–17 the common *c·* of mortal man
  divine
  b 315–25 The divine *c·* of Jesus pointed to this
  faint
  a 47– 3 gave them a faint *c·* of the Life which
  false
  b 281–20 false *c·* as to man and Mind.
  285–16 is a false *c·* of man.

conception
  finite
  c 258– 2 A mortal, corporeal, or finite *c·* of God
  b 285–18 time has come for a finite *c·* . . . to give place
  highest
  s 148–12 instead of from the highest, *c·* of being.
  b 327– 9 Evil is sometimes a man's highest *c·* of right,
  his
  f 248–13 in order to perfect his *c·*.
  b 299– 3 embodies his *c·* of an unseen quality
  human
  a 50–27 The burden . . . was terrible beyond human *c·*.
  ph 185–14 puts forth a human *c·* in the name of Science
  g 505– 7 by which human *c·*, material sense,
  Mary's
  b 332–26 Mary's *c·* of him was spiritual,
  material
  f 213– 9 apart from this mortal and material *c·*.
  g 536–24 erroneous, material *c·* of life and joy,
  mental
  p 403–31 mental *c·* and development of disease
  of God
  s 133–29 Jewish *c·* of God, as Yawah,
  ph 185–19 rests on the *c·* of God as the only Life,
  of mortal mind
  b 274– 4 *c·* of mortal mind, the offspring of sense,
  proper
  g 555–24 and set aside the proper *c·* of Deity,
  thy
  g 535– 7 thy sorrow and thy *c·* :— *Gen. 3: 16.*
  true
  sp 84–24 true *c·* of being destroys the belief of
  c 258–23 gains the true *c·* of man and God.
  260– 2 the true *c·* or understanding of man,
  260–12 as the only true *c·* of being.
  b 324–29 which is the true *c·* of being,
  t 456–14 separates himself from the true *c·* of C. S
  truest
  s 132–29 or endow him with the truest *c·* of the Christ ?
  unconfined
  b 323–11 *c·* unconfined is winged to reach the divine

conceptions
  diviner
  c 260–10 human beliefs will be attaining diviner *c·*,
  erroneous
  s 116–26 confused and erroneous *c·* of divinity
  finite
  g 545– 1 through mortal and finite *c·*.
  higher
  f 247–17 reflecting those higher *c·* of loveliness
  human
  c 255–12 to belittle Deity with human *c·*.
  257–16 material senses and human *c·* would
  material
  sp 87– 1 So is it with all material *c·*.
  t 463– 9 detach mortal thought from its material *c·*,
  our
  pr 3–17 How empty are our *c·* of Deity !
  f 244– 7 If we were to derive all our *c·*
  spiritual
  o 349–16 inadequate to the expression of spiritual *c·*

  c 260– 7 The *c·* of mortal, erring thought

concepts
  m 62–26 thrusting in the laws of erring, human *c·*.
  f 235–32 and broaden their *c·*.
  239–24 It forms material *c·* and
  c 256–15 nor can He be understood . . . through mortal *c·*.
  259–30 demands spiritual thoughts, divine *c·*,
  264– 1 the fleeting *c·* of the human mind.
  p 426–31 human *c·* named matter, death, disease,
  g 516–31 genders are human *c·*,
  531–13 exchanging human *c·* for the divine
  536– 7 as a symbol of tempest-tossed human *c·*
  556– 4 mortal and material *c·* classified,

concern
  sp 84–16 foretell events which *c·* the universal

concerned
  s 121–25 so far as our solar system is *c·*,

concerning
  a 47–14 people were in doubt *c·* Jesus' teachings.
  52–14 word *c·* the coming Prince of Peace.
  sp 89–13 Scriptural word *c·* a man,
  92–22 Until the fact *c·* error . . . appears,
  s 133–22 *c·* God, man, sanitary methods, and
  f 205– 6 their false sense *c·* God and man.
  219–14 never affirm *c·* the body what we do not wish
  220–28 *c·* which God said,
  b 297–17 The only fact *c·* any material concept is,
  o 349– 4 rabbis of the present day ask *c·* our healing
  349–22 the prophecy *c·* the Christian apostles,
  p 383–27 confirming the Scriptural conclusion *c·* a man,
  412– 7 *c·* the truth which you think or speak.

concerning
p 413–32 held in the beliefs *c·* his body.
t 448– 9 tell the truth *c·* the lie.
r 481–16 *c·* this "tree of the knowledge— *Gen.* 2 : 17.
494–25 Which of these two theories *c·* man
g 524–25 or is it a lie *c·* man and God?
gl 585–24 a finite belief *c·* life, substance, and

concession
sp 84–25 for without the *c·* of material personalities

concessions
a 33– 1 closed forever Jesus' ritualism or *c·* to matter.
m 56– 4 Jesus' *c·* . . . to material methods were
p 398– 7 the *c·* which Jesus was willing to make
t 456–18 Science makes no *c·* to persons or

conciliate
a 18–18 Christ, . . . could *c·* no nature above his own,
f 238–22 Attempts to *c·* society and so gain

conclude
s 143–19 but you *c·* that the stomach, blood, nerves,
f 217– 4 than to *c·* that individual musical tones
p 387– 6 we *c·* that intellectual labor
r 467–24 We reason imperfectly . . . when we *c·* that

concluded
sp 89–28 Cain very naturally *c·* that if life
f 222–26 *c·* that God never made a dyspeptic,
p 441– 9 He *c·* his charge thus :

concludes
ap 566–19 we may also offer the prayer which *c·* the

concluding
ap 573–24 This is Scriptural authority for *c·*

conclusion
any
s 120–25 Any *c·* *pro* or *con*, deduced from supposed
blind
s 124–11 In a word, human belief is a blind *c·*
fair
g 555– 3 A fair *c·* from this might be,
false
g 525–27 the false *c·* of the material senses.
no other
s 109–10 This proof once seen, no other *c·* can be reached.
premise or
s 129– 6 can tolerate no error in premise or *c·*.
scientific
b 279–26 A logical and scientific *c·* is reached
Scriptural
p 383–27 the Scriptural *c·* concerning a man,
this
p 425– 2 Mortal mind, not matter, induces this *c·*

s 128–32 *c·*, if properly drawn, cannot be false.
ph 167 17 error in the premise must appear in the *c·*.
f 231–17 Therefore we accept the *c·* that discords
b 277–28 error in the premise leads to errors in the *c·*
278–24 and leads to the *c·* that if man is
279– 6 The doom of matter establishes the *c·*
010 16 which led to the *c·* that the
340– 7 "Let us hear the *c·* of the whole— *Eccl.* 12 . 10.
340– 9 Let us hear the *c·* of the whole matter :
o 347–10 the *c·* would be that there is nothing
433– 6 His *c·* is, that laws of nature render

conclusions
absolute
s 109–21 and I won my way to absolute *c·*
doctrines and
g 545–14 into all human doctrines and *c·*,
false
s 121–22 deluded the judgment and induced false *c·*.
f 204– 3 All forms of error support the false *c·*
p 417–30 by certain fears and false *c·*,
his
403–30 truth or error which influences his *c·*.
human
b 298– 1 are the vague realities of human *c·*.
logical
b 270–10 are scientific and logical *c·* reached.
my
s 108–12 My *c·* were reached by allowing the
one's
c 259–32 Deducing one's *c·* as to man from
our
p 397– 5 By not perceiving . . . we are misled in our *c·*
spiritual
b 300– 2 it attempts to draw correct spiritual *c·*
such
p 392–25 Admitting only such *c·* as you wish
their own
p 418– 2 the baneful effects of their own *c·*.
unanimous
an 100–19 we have come to the unanimous *c·*

sp 84– 2 nor with the *c·* of mortal beliefs.
ph 184– 2 premises being erroneous, the *c·* are wrong.

conclusions
b 269–13 does not enter into metaphysical premises or *c·*.
338–10 premises and *c·* of material and mortal
g 547–10 strengthens the thinker's *c·* as to the

conclusive
an 101–14 promised by Monsieur Berna . . . as *c·*,
101–16 are certainly not *c·* in favor of the doctrine
s 159– 8 The evidence was found to be *c·*,

conclusively
s 108–16 proves *c·* that three times three
123–11 The verity of Mind shows *c·*
f 204– 6 that mortal error is as *c·* mental

concomitant
r 484–28 *Question.—* Is materiality the *c·*

concomitants
ph 196–16 sin, and death are not *c·* of Life or Truth.

concord
pref viii– 7 and gives sweet *c·* to sound.
m 60–25 calls discord harmony, not appreciating *c·*.
s 129–25 Can we . . . learn from discord the *c·* of being?
148–23 *c·* and unity of Spirit and His likeness.
f 216–26 "What *c·* hath Christ with— *II Cor.* 6 : 15.
240–11 In the order of Science, . . . all is one grand *c·*.
t 453– 4 when he distinguishes *c·* from discord.
g 539–25 what *c·* hath Christ with— *II Cor.* 6 : 15.

concordant
m 58– 6 they should be *c·* in order to blend properly.

concords
s 130–14 good and its sweet *c·* have all-power.

concur
b 319–14 Spirit and matter neither *c·* in man nor in

condemn
pr 11– 9 which has the right to acquit or *c·*,
o 341– 1 strictures on this volume would *c·*
p 433–23 which material laws *c·* as homicide.
435–33 If they *c·* him not, neither shall
435–34 neither shall Judge Medicine *c·* him ;
437– 7 a determination to *c·* Man
t 444–19 and never to *c·* rashly.
g 522–31 Does the creator *c·* His own creation?

condemnation
sp 85–28 never spared hypocrisy the sternest *c·*.
ph 183–12 error, first caused the *c·* of man
f 232–24 sealed God's *c·* of sin, sickness, and death.
g 545– 7 The *c·* of mortals to till the ground

condemnations
o 342– 5 unqualified *c·* of scientific Mind-healing,

condemned
a 43–22 Human law had *c·* him,
s 144–15 belongs to the . . . senses, and its use is to be *c·*,
p 436–26 taken into custody, tried, and *c·*.
440– 2 when it *c·* Mortal Man on the ground of
t 443– 9 at times severely *c·* by some Scientists,
459–10 *c·* for failing to take the first step.
g 539–16 God *c·* this lie as to man's origin

condemning
g 539–17 by *c·* its symbol, the serpent,

condemns
s 132–22 and *c·* the cure of the sick and sinning if it
t 448– 6 but which the heart *c·*, has no foundation ;
g 532–11 *c·* material man and remands him to dust.

condition
abnormal
p 423–27 Ossification or any abnormal *c·*
action and
p 420–27 power over every physical action and *c·*.
best
s 125– 2 What is now considered the best *c·*
bodily
p 394–10 The admission that any bodily *c·*
celestial
m 61– 7 The attainment of this celestial *c·*
diseased
ph 193–22 The diseased *c·* had continued there
f 217–17 have once conquered a diseased *c·*
earthly
a 30– 6 partook partly of Mary's earthly *c·*,
elastic
s 161– 1 the supple and elastic *c·* of the healthy limb,
material
sp 74– 5 and their return to a material *c·*,
p 389– 5 and every erroneous belief, or material *c·*.
410–15 The more difficult seems the material *c·*
mental
ph 181–19 you must improve your mental *c·*
p 397– 8 Suffering is no less a mental *c·* than
moral
s 139–32 The moral *c·* of such a man demands
natural
b 321–23 restored his hand to its natural *c·*

condition

negative
ph 173–15 to pass through a negative c· would be
of matter
s 120–15 Health is not a c· of matter, but of Mind ;
b 321–20 and not a c· of matter,
p 371– 1 to discover the c· of matter,
of mortality
f 215–23 Every quality and c· of mortality is lost,
old
sp 74–12 and never returns to the old c·.
original
sp 74– 7 the restoration to its original c· of the
our own
o 348–24 by so doing our own c· can be improved
physical
a 46–20 Jesus' unchanged physical c· after what
b 297–11 change in . . . affects the physical c·.
p 411–25 cherished in mortal mind as the physical c·
primitive
f 244–17 hypothesis that he returns . . . to his primitive c· ;
proper
p 383–20 must be clean to keep the body in proper c·.
quality or
f 230– 3 to destroy a quality or c· of Truth?
b 299– 4 his conception of an unseen quality or c·,
regulates the
p 413– 7 Mind regulates the c· of the stomach,
sinless
o 344– 5 sinless c· of man in divine Science,
source and
ph 181– 2 God, is the source and c· of all existence
spiritual
t 460–27 to impart, . . . from her own spiritual c·,
subjective
ph 189–32 matter is the subjective c· of mortal mind.
superinduced
sp 89–15 without study or a superinduced c·,
that
f 217–18 that c· never recurs,
p 408–29 that c· of the body which we call sensation
their
f 211– 2 if they talk to us, tell us their c·,
p 394–23 Will you tell the sick that their c· is hopeless,
this
ph 193– 7 the evidence of this c· of the bone.
o 349–21 Out of this c· grew the prophecy,
p 371–19 the only way out of this c·.

sp 72– 6 A c· precedent to communion with Spirit
ph 182–30 To admit that sickness is a c· over which
188–14 recognizes his c· to be wholly a state of
p 392–27 When the c· is present which you say induces

conditional
r 486–19 belief, which makes harmony c· upon death

conditions
all
f 220–30 Mortal mind forms all c· of the mortal body,
bodily
f 217–10 unnatural mental and bodily c·,
228–22 never depend on bodily c·, structure, or
p 368–20 That Life is not contingent on bodily c·
can make no
s 120–12 No ! for matter can make no c· for man.
discordant
p 369– 2 he is liable to admit also . . . discordant c·,
diseased
p 403– 2 induced their own diseased c·.
excited
p 417–10 there will be no reaction from . . . excited c·.
false
p 368–26 and these false c· are the source of
healthy
s 162–22 carious bones have been restored to healthy c·.
its own
b 297–32 A mortal belief fulfils its own c·.
p 422–26 holding that matter forms its own c·
material
(see **material**)
mental
s 153–29 we shall be more careful of our mental c·,
154– 3 Disease arises, like other mental c·,
159–12 Is it skilful . . . to take no heed of mental c·
moral
s 125– 5 Moral c· will be found always harmonious
c 260–23 evolves bad physical and moral c·.
normal
p 412–26 corresponds with the normal c· of health
of matter
s 162–15 faculties of Spirit exist without the c· of matter
of sin
g 556–10 Mortal belief infolds the c· of sin.
opposite
sp 74–27 the gulf which divides two such opposite c·

conditions
physical
sp 77– 8 mortal mind creates its own physical c·.
s 150–27 physical c· all his earthly days,
these
p 373–29 we call these c· disease.
unsuitable
t 455– 5 unsuitable c· for healing the sick.
untoward
p 385–16 and all untoward c·, *if without sin*,
ways and
b 317–15 not only in all time, but in *all ways* and c·.

o 343–22 the c· of its acceptance,
p 368–26 its c· are illusions,
413– 4 contemplation of physical wants or c·
413– 5 induces these very c·.
g 549– 3 takes place apart from sexual c·.

conduct
p 384–23 if . . . you are not fit to c· your own case

confer
m 61– 2 The senses c· no real enjoyment.
s 132–28 Did the doctrines . . . c· healing power

conferred
r 478–29 I c· not with flesh—*Gal.* 1 : 16.
gl 581– 1 the name often c· upon him in Scripture,

confers
pref viii–14 Christian healing c· the most health and
a 40– 1 once admit that evil c· no pleasure,
sp 89–23 influence or action of Soul c· a freedom,
s 151–11 the enlarged power it c· to benefit the race
157–24 Erring mortal mind c· the power
f 217– 2 through the understanding which Science c·
c 265–12 but c· upon man enlarged individuality,
b 298–30 Human conjecture c· upon angels its own forms
p 366–19 Love which alone c· the healing power.
404–23 show him that sin c· no pleasure,
418–20 Truth is affirmative, and c· harmony.
g 512–26 c· animal names and natures upon its
555–27 or that Truth c· the ability to

confess
pr 8–24 We c· to having a very wicked heart
p 374–18 You c· to ignorance of the future
g 533–27 finds woman the first to c· her fault.

confesseth
t 448–18 whoso c· and forsaketh them— *Prov.* 28 : 13.

confession
s 138– 4 Peter's c· of the true Messiah.

confessional
pr 5–22 Prayer is not to be used as a c·

confidence
m 58–18 the sweet interchange of c· and love ;
59–13 their sympathies should blend in sweet c·
68–10 The presence of mistrust, where c· is due,
s 155– 7 individual c· in the drug,
p 368– 3 The c· inspired by Science lies in the fact
397–21 in exact proportion to your . . . c· in God
t 443– 7 tends to deter those, . . . from entire c· in

confident
s 132– 2 c· that this exhibition of the divine power

confides
a 23–31 and c· all to God.

confine
m 58–17 jealousy, which would c· a wife or a husband

confined
a 32–21 if the sacrament is c· to the use of bread and
sp 73–22 incorrect is the belief that spirit is c·
ph 193– 1 c· to his bed six months with hip-disease,
f 214– 5 If Enoch's perception had been c· to the
b 331– 1 Life is no more c· to the forms
p 390–16 and then you will not be c· to a sick-room
429–32 That statement is not c· to spiritual life,
r 467–23 Spirit, Soul, is not c· in man,
g 508–19 The word is not c· to sexuality,

confinement
p 431–18 getting Mortal Man into close c·

confines
s 108–19 When apparently near the c· of
p 401–31 c· himself chiefly to mental reconstruction

confirm
ph 199–22 Exceptions only c· this rule,
f 243–12 in order to c· and repeat the
p 432–24 was required to c· his testimony.

confirmation
r 488– 2 result of our teachings is their sufficient c·.

confirmed
a 54–27 and history has c· the prediction.
sp 94–18 our Master c· his words by his works.
s 131–26 The mission of Jesus c· prophecy,
gl 581– 1 This view of Satan is c· by the

confirming
p 383–27   c· the Scriptural conclusion concerning a man,
confirms
pr   6–32   language of our Master c· this description.
m 69–14   unfolds all creation, c· the Scriptures,
sp 94–17   The progress of truth c· its claims,
an 105–28   and c· the ancient axiom :
s 120–28   c· that testimony as legitimate
p 370–13   This c· my theory that
conflict
m 69–19   and not c· with the scientific sense of God's
sp 96–31   During this final c·, wicked minds will
f 226–30   I saw before me the awful c·,
b 288– 4   the mental c· between the evidence of the
288–11   the c· between truth and error,
ap 567–12   Thus endeth the c· between the
conflicting
sp 96–13   even now becoming the arena for c· forces.
b 273–29   c· mortal opinions and beliefs
o 355–14   relative value of the two c· theories
t 447– 7   c· selfish motives, and ignorant attempts
conflicts
an 104–10   First, people say it c· with the Bible.
o 361–14   This declaration of Jesus, understood, c· not
conform
p 412–22   c· the argument so as to destroy the evidence
t 445– 1   Scientist must c· to God's requirements.
conformity
b 337– 9   in c· with Christ.
confounded
o 358– 6   Such doctrines are "confusion worse c·."
gl 567–25   hence it should not be c· with the
confounds
o 346– 1   I regret that such criticism c· man with Adam.
confronts
t 452–13   When error c· you, withhold not the rebuke
confused
s 116–26   c· and erroneous conceptions of divinity
g 506 25   the human concept and divine idea seem c·
confusion
b 304–28   liable to be misapprehended and lost in c·,
o 358– 5   Such doctrines are "c· worse confounded."
gl 581–21   higher false knowledge builds . . . the more c·
congestion
p 408–23   as perceptibly as would c· of the brain,
congestive
p 384–18   c· symptoms in the lungs, or hints of
congratulate
t 448–14   do not c· yourself upon your
congregate
gl 595– 9   superstructure, where mortals c· for worship.
Congregational Church
o 551– 8   author became a member of the orthodox C· C·
conjectural
ph 176–19   weigh down mankind with . . . c· evils.
f 229–20   law of mortal mind, c· and speculative,
conjecture
b 298–30   Human c· confers upon angels its own forms
330–17   knowledge of it is left either to human c· or
conjectured
f 245–16   c· that she must be under twenty.
conjectures
b 304–32   So man, . . . is abandoned to c·,
g 504–26   human doctrines, hypotheses, and vague c·
conjoin
m 57– 9   These different elements c· naturally
conjoined
p 378– 2   and causes the two to appear c·,
conjugal
m 65–29   has brought c· infidelity to the surface,
66–17   Amidst gratitude for c· felicity,
66–18   Amidst c· infelicity, it is well to hope,
conjure
p 403–23   Never c· up some new discovery from
connate
pref viii–20   the response deducible from two c· facts,
connect
a 37– 9   human links which c· one stage with another
r 491–11   Matter cannot c· mortals with the true origin
connected
s 145–20   Indeed, its . . . effects are indissolubly c·.
p 389–31   complication of symptoms c· with this belief.
408–25   less intimately c· with the mind than

connection
sp 98–25   that which they call *science* has no proper c· with
ph 178–10   c· of past mortal thoughts with present.
b 292–30   real man's indissoluble c· with his God,
o 350–28   that life-link forming the c· through which
ap 560– 1   in c· with the nineteenth century.
conquer
b 317–20   enables him to c· sin, disease, and
324–16   in which we must c· sin, sickness, and death,
339–31   You c· error by denying its verity.
p 393– 9   and can c· sickness, sin, and death.
394–26   Is there no divine permission to c· discord
405– 7   to c· lust with chastity,
419–28   you must c· your own fears
conquered
a 53–29   he had not c· all the beliefs of the flesh
f 217–16   When you have once c· a diseased condition
231– 4   Unless an ill is rightly met . . . the ill is never c·.
b 309– 8   He had c· material error with
p 380– 3   must be finally c· by eternal Life.
400– 6   This error c·, we can despoil
405–27   You are c· by the moral penalties you incur
407– 7   is c· only by a mighty struggle.
425–24   when faith in matter has been c·.
ap 564–16   met and c· sin in every form
conquering
f 253–14   I hope that you are c· this false sense.
c 262–23   and c· all that is unlike God.
conquers
p 378–26   and finally c· it.
conquest
p 418– 2   Show them that the c· over sickness,
ap 568–26   What shall we say of the mighty c· over all sin?
conscience
pref x–11   The author has not compromised c·
a 28–11   In c·, we cannot hold to beliefs outgrown ;
an 106– 9   self-government, reason, and c·.
f 222–31   "asking no question for c· sake."—*I Cor.* 10 : 25.
p 405–23   to endure the cumulative effects of a guilty c·.
conscientious
pr 12–13   prayers were deep and c· protests of Truth,
s 163– 8   said : "I declare my c· opinion,
t 451–19   every c· teacher of the Science of Mind-healing.
conscientiously
o 343–30   Whoever is the first meekly and c·
conscious
pr 14–12   Become c· for a single moment that
sp 82–19   and were in as c· a state of existence
s 125–13   of c· pain and painlessness,
ph 166– 6   thus the c· control over the body is lost.
f 209–31   a c· constant capacity to understand God.
213–25   Mental melodies . . . supersede c· sound.
250– 9   which never errs, and is ever c· ;
b 302– 6   c· infinitude of existence and of all identity
p 374– 6   Because mortal mind seems to be c·,
379–29   images, . . . frighten c· thought,
390–32   Rise in the c· strength of the spirit of Truth
400–14   before it has taken tangible shape in c· thought,
409–13   independently of this so-called c· mind,
409–16   c· mortal mind is believed to be superior
423–24   the stimulus of courage and c· power.
435– 6   would console c· Mortal Mind,
r 475–16   c· identity of being as found in Science,
484–14   the c· and unconscious thoughts of mortals.
g 521– 2   above earth . . . to c· spiritual harmony
ap 569– 8   when we are c· of the supremacy of Truth,
573–26   can become c·, here and now, of a cessation of
574–12   It exalted him till he became c· of the
gl 593– 5   the c· facts of spiritual Truth.
consciously
sp 87– 6   to be individually and c· present.
ph 174– 6   as c· as do civilized practitioners by their
199–18   whether this development is produced c· or
b 308–15   talked with God as c· as man talks with man.
p 374–11   before it is c· apparent on the body,
403– 4   voluntary mesmerism is induced c·
ap 576–24   man possesses this recognition of harmony c·
consciousness
abiding
p 405–24   The abiding c· of wrong-doing
corporeal
m 67–27   Spiritual, not corporeal, c· is needed.
develops
r 489–10   and as c· develops, this belief goes out,
differing
sp 82–28   Different dreams . . . betoken a differing c·.
disappear from
o 347–29   and sickness will disappear from c·.
divine
g 531–13   exchanging human concepts for the divine c·
gl 598–23   One moment of divine c·,

consciousness
eternal
  c 263–31   instead of a scientific eternal *c·* of creation.
false
  s 107–15   Feeling so perpetually the false *c·* that life
  ap 575– 1   Arise from your false *c·*
full
  gl 598–28   and man would be in the full *c·* of
holier
  p 419–30   rise into higher and holier *c·*.
human
    (*see* **human**)
illusive
  b 293– 4   the least material form of illusive *c·*,
immortal
  b 279–11   Ideas are tangible and real to immortal *c·*,
  r 486– 9   in order to possess immortal *c·*.
individual
  sp 76–16   but he will be an individual *c·*,
is cognizant
  b 276–10   *c·* is cognizant only of the things of God.
man's
  b 336–14   man's *c·* and individuality are reflections
  ap 576–22   is within reach of man's *c·* here,
material
  ph 196–14   the word *soul* means . . . material *c·*.
  b 295–27   *material c·*, the exact opposite of real Mind,
mazes of
  sp 82–17   different mazes of *c·*.
memory and
  r 491–23   memory and *c·* are lost from the body,
mortal
  sp 77–22   if communications from spirits to mortal *c·* were
  b 278–14   exists only in a supposititious mortal *c·*.
    295–13   mortal *c·* will at last yield to the
no
  f 206– 2   no *c·* of the existence of matter or error.
    243–25   Truth has no *c·* of error.
    245–11   Having no *c·* of time,
  p 368–25   Because matter has no *c·* or Ego,
no other
  f 242–11   to have no other *c·* of life
  c 264–19   finding all in God, . . . needing no other *c·*.
  b 323– 5   and to possess no other *c·* but good.
  g 536– 9   and there is no other *c·*.
of existence
  p 428–24   We must hold forever the *c·* of existence,
of right-doing
  a 37–13   *C·* of right-doing brings its own reward ;
of Truth
  f 218– 7   The *c·* of Truth rests us
pure
  gl 582–17   the pure *c·* that God, . . . creates man
Science and
  p 423–24   Both Science and *c·* are now at work
scientific
  ap 573–13   Accompanying this scientific *c·*
spiritual
    (*see* **spiritual**)
stages of
  ap 573–11   indicates states and stages of *c·*.
state of
  sp 82–21   their state of *c·* must be different from ours.
states of
  sp 82–11   because different states of *c·* are involved,
    82–13   cannot exist in two different states of *c·* at the
supposed
  s 120–26   matter's supposed *c·* of health or disease,
  b 311–29   all supposed *c·* or claim to life or existence,
that
  ap 573– 7   that *c·* which God bestows,
this clearer
  g 553– 5   This clearer *c·* must precede an understanding
true
  b 302–26   Man's true *c·* is in the mental,
  p 391–30   rise to the true *c·* of Life as Love,
uplifts
  g 505–16   understanding which uplifts *c·*
vanish from
  sp 77–15   for this dream . . . to vanish from *c·*,
  p 415–29   the limbs will vanish from *c·*.

   ———

  pr 14–27   the *c·* of man's dominion over the whole earth.
  sp 74–32   for they are in separate states of existence, or *c·*.
  b 278– 4   Spirit is the only substance and *c·*
    278–16   we lose the *c·* of matter.
    283–32   Are mentality, immortality, *c·*,
    307–32   *C·*, where art thou?
  p 407–28   brings . . . Life not death, into your *c·*.
    409–10   cannot dictate terms to *c·*
    422–17   giving more spirituality to *c·*
    425–23   *C·* constructs a better body when
  r 480–10   *C·*, as well as action, is governed by Mind,
  ap 573–23   involve the spiritual idea and *c·* of reality.
    578–17   [the *c·*] of [LOVE] for ever.— *Psal.* 23 : 6.

consecrate
  p 428–15   We should *c·* existence, . . . to the eternal
consecrating
  p 388– 2   Through the uplifting and *c·* power of
consecration
  pr 3–16   demands absolute *c·* of thought, energy, and
  a 28–10   one's *c·* to Christ is more on the ground of
  c 262– 1   *C·* to good does not lessen man's dependence
    262– 3   Neither does *c·* diminish man's obligations
  p 367–14   from the summit of devout *c·*,
  gl 592–25   OIL.   *C·* ; charity ; gentleness ;
consecutively
  pref xii–21   she had never read this book throughout *c·*
consent
  s 152– 1   and must by its own *c·* yield to Truth.
  f 221–30   without the *c·* of mortal mind,
    229–15   By universal *c·*, mortal belief has
  p 371–10   Mortals are believed to be here without their *c·*
    379– 2   without the *c·* of mortals,
consentaneous
  g 553–23   If *c·* human belief agrees upon an ovum
consequence
  sp 81–30   and follows as a necessary *c·*
  s 158–32   was etherized and died in *c·*,
  o 352–13   and sick in *c·* of the fear :
consequences
  a 48–28   ignorant of the *c·* of his awful decision
  f 237–32   they hug false beliefs and suffer the delusive *c·*.
  b 322–24   refraining from it only through fear of *c·*
  p 374–14   This mortal blindness and its sharp *c·*
    436–22   He must obey your law, fear its *c·*,
  ap 570–18   and never fear the *c·*.
consequent
  an 104–16   and the *c·* wrongness of the opposite
  s 115– 4   the *c·* difficulty of so expressing
    154– 7   and its *c·* manifestation in the body.
  o 355–25   a *c·* inability to demonstrate this Science.
  r 474–10   and *c·* maltreatment which it receives.
consequently
  an 103–29   and *c·* no transference of mortal thought
  ph 178– 5   *C·*, the result is controlled by
  b 270–24   Mortals think wickedly ; *c·* they
  r 470–27   and *c·* a time when Deity was
  g 512–12   and *c·* reproduce their own characteristics.
    513–28   *c·* not within the range of immortal existence
    538–29   have a beginning, they must *c·* have an end,
conservatism
  ph 167–29   timid *c·* is absolutely inadmissible.
  p 364–19   through material *c·* and for personal homage?
  t 452–20   We soil our garments with *c·*,
conservative
  r 492–29   The *c·* theory, long believed,
consider
  m 68–13   *C·* its obligations, its responsibilities,
  sp 83– 1   it is wise earnestly to *c·* whether it is the
    98–24   Even now multitudes *c·* that which they call
  s 119– 8   and *c·* matter . . . in and of itself,
  f 214–20   to fear and to obey what they *c·* a material body
  o 347–12   Critics should *c·* that the so-called mortal man
    351–20   if we *c·* Satan as a being coequal in power
  p 382–17   *c·* the so-called law of matter
consideration
  m 67–19   The notion . . . is too absurd for *c·*,
  s 157– 1   Homœopathy takes mental symptoms largely into *c·*
  t 445–32   for the petty *c·* of money,
  g 532– 9   the prediction in the story under *c·*.
considerations
  m 60–21   the higher nature is neglected, and other *c·*,
considered
  a 38– 7   and so it will be *c·*, when the
  m 66–27   Socrates *c·* patience salutary under such
  sp 91–22   Certain erroneous postulates should be here *c·*
    98–23   has not been *c·* a part of any religion,
  s 125– 2   What is now *c·* the best condition
    136–17   These prophets were *c·* dead,
    139–16   what should and should not be *c·* Holy Writ ;
    143–12   before it could be *c·* as medicine.
    159–16   they would have *c·* the woman's state of
  ph 170–22   Spiritual causation is the one question to be *c·*,
  p 431– 9   *c·* criminal, inasmuch as this offence is
    436–24   the penalty they *c·* justly due,
  g 521–24   presented in the verses already *c·*,
considering
  o 352– 6   evidently *c·* it a mortal and material belief
  g 517–11   not as much authority for *c·* God masculine,
    517–12   as we have for *c·* Him feminine.

consigns

sp 77–28   Spiritism *c·* the so-called dead to a
g 542–24   To envy's own hell, justice *c·* the lie

consist

f 233– 3   These proofs *c·* solely in the destruction of sin,
r 470– 3   brotherhood of man would *c·* of Love and Truth,

consisted

gl 597– 3   Judaic religion *c·* mostly of rites and

consistency

f 242–26   one web of *c·* without seam or rent.
o 341– 7   grow in beauty and *c·* from one grand root,
354–18   *C·* is seen in example more than in precept.
t 443– 3   as to the propriety, advantage, and *c·* of

consistent

pr 9–32   *C·* prayer is the desire to do right.
m 65– 7   If the foundations of human affection are *c·*
f 254– 2   Individuals are *c·* who, watching and
t 458–27   honest and *c·* in following the leadings of
g 547–16   Darwin's theory . . . is more *c·* than most

consistently

pr 9–10   by living *c·* with our prayer?

consisteth

g 544– 9   Life *c·* not of the things which a man eateth.

consisting

f 221– 7   this meal *c·* of only a thin slice of bread

consists

s 123–19   The revelation *c·* of two parts :
ph 184– 8   remedy *c·* in probing the trouble to the bottom
b 323– 3   This strife *c·* in the endeavor to forsake error
t 462–21   and *c·* in the dissection of thoughts
g 503– 1   *c·* of the unfolding of spiritual ideas

consolation

pref xii–25   and is joyful to bear *c·* to the sorrowing

console

p 435– 6   Reverend Theology would *c·*
ap 574– 4   adapted to *c·* the weary pilgrim,

consoles

gl 582–12   that which comforts, *c·*, and supports

consolidation

ph 185–30   which is but a mortal *c·* of

consoling

pr 7–29   and *c·* ourselves in the midst of

consonance

ph 168–16   all in *c·* with the laws of God,
p 407–32   is in *c·* with common mortal belief.

consonant

g 501–13   is *c·* with ever-present Love.

conspicuous

m 65–13   broadcast powers of evil so *c·* to-day
g 539–31   so *c·* in the birth of Jesus,

conspiracies

f 246–19   *c·* against manhood and womanhood.

conspiracy

b 339–15   He is joining in a *c·* against himself,
p 434–26   we shall unearth this foul *c·*
438–16   *c·* against the rights and life of man.

conspirators

a 49– 8   Were all *c·* save eleven?
p 405–10   if you would not cherish an army of *c·*

conspired

u 47–10   Judas *c·* against Jesus.

constancy

m 60– 9   mother-love includes purity and *c·*,
r 488–10   understanding, trust, *c·*, firmness.
gl 582– 1   BELIEVING.   Firmness and *c·* ;

constant

pr 15–27   purity, and affection are *c·* prayers.
a 22– 4   sensuality causing *c·* retrogression,
23– 5   The atonement requires *c·* self-immolation
24– 1   to *believe* means also *to be firm* or *to be c·*.
m 58– 1   To happify existence by *c·* intercourse
s 130– 1   petty intellect is alarmed by *c·* appeals to Mind.
f 209–31   conscious, *c·* capacity to understand God.
p 382– 8   *C·* bathing and rubbing to alter the
385–15   *C·* toil, deprivations, exposures, and
t 451– 2   the *c·* pressure of the apostolic command

constantly

a 21–10   He *c·* turns away from material sense,
ph 189–23   we *c·* ascend in infinite being.
f 235–14   uplifting thoughts . . . *c·* imparted to pupils
p 403–16   Mortal mind is *c·* producing on mortal body
413–25   *c·* directing the mind to such signs,
t 453–11   with some . . . symptoms *c·* reappear.
r 492–14   New thoughts are *c·* obtaining the floor.
g 524– 6   *c·* went after "strange gods."— *Jer.* 5 : 19.
548–32   increase their numbers naturally and *c·*
gl 598– 8   our Master had *c·* to employ words of

consternation

p 434– 3   *C·* fills the prison-yard.

constituent

f 209–17   relations which *c·* masses hold to each other,

constituents

m 58– 9   these *c·* of thought, mingling,
t 460– 4   the necessary *c·* and relations of all beings,"

constitute

a 53–26   mortal errors which *c·* the material body,
m 58– 9   *c·* individually and collectively true happiness,
63– 6   The beautiful, good, and pure *c·* his ancestry.
b 274–21   false beliefs and their products *c·* the flesh,
331–26   Life, Truth, and Love *c·* the triune
p 430–24   Greed and Ingratitude, *c·* the jury.
r 470– 5   unity of Principle and spiritual power which *c·*
488–14   Do the five corporeal senses *c·* man?
g 503– 9   divine Principle and idea *c·* spiritual harmony,
516– 5   Life, intelligence, Truth, and Love, which *c·*

constituted

f 229–15   mortal belief has *c·* itself a law
p 437–27   judicial proceedings of a regularly *c·* court.
r 466– 9   personalities *c·* of mind and matter,

constitutes

m 57– 4   Union of the . . . qualities *c·* completeness.
sp 76–25   the only veritable, indestructible man,
85– 7   Such intuitions reveal whatever *c·* and
ph 172– 1   *c·* his happiness or misery.
173– 1   When we admit that matter . . . *c·* man,
183– 5   To suppose that God *c·* laws of inharmony
194–19   education *c·* this so-called mind,
b 283–21   false belief as to what really *c·* life
289– 6   overcome by the understanding of what *c·* man
297– 9   the understanding of what *c·* health ;
301–13   *c·* the only real and eternal entity.
305–15   the underlying reality of reflection.
316–21   whom Spirit creates, *c·*, and governs.
340–23   *c·* the brotherhood of man ;
r 479–14   which *c·* matter's supposed selfhood,
g 527–16   *c·* evil and mortal knowledge.
ap 560–14   *c·* the kingdom of heaven in man.

constituting

s 110– 2   filling all space, *c·* all Science,
p 388–19   *c·* a "kingdom divided against— *Matt.* 12 : 25.
393–28   iris and pupil, *c·* the visual organism.

Constitution

s 161–14   in harmony with our *C·* and Bill of Rights,

constitutions

m 61–13   better balanced minds, and sounder *c·*.
ph 175– 6   there will be better *c·* and less disease.
197–26   Many of the effeminate *c·* of our time

constructing

g 522–27   supposedly cooperating with matter in *c·*

construction

f 400–27   no organic *c·* can give it hearing

constructor

p 369–12   or the *c·* of any form of existence.

constructs

p 399–17   It *c·* a machine, manages it,
402–14   mortal mind *c·* the mortal body
425–23   Consciousness *c·* a better body when
gl 580–29   not one who *c·* and sustains reality

construe

a 30–30   though they may not so *c·* our words.

construed

p 436–31   *c·* obedience to the law of divine Love as

consult

a 21–17   We have separate time-tables to *c·*,
s 160–27   Why then *c·* anatomy to learn
ph 165–18   Then you *c·* your brain in order to
171– 9   not needing to *c·* almanacs for the
f 222–29   *c·* matter not at all,

consultation

p 433–16   A brief *c·* ensues,

consulted

s 159–14   as if matter were the only factor to be *c·*?
t 443– 1   When the discoverer of C. S. is *c·*

consulting

s 163–22   "*C·* the records of our science,
f 222–15   *c·* the stomach less about the

consume

pr 10–28   that ye may *c·* it upon your lusts."— *Jas.* 4 : 3.
f 205– 4   drop with drunkenness, *c·* with disease,
p 425–19   and know that there is nothing to *c·*,

consuming

f 252–30   shine with the resplendency of *c·* fire.
ap 558–19   described by John the Baptist as *c·* error.

consummate
　　a 51–19　His *c·* example was for the salvation of
　　r 493–30　Who dares to doubt this *c·* test
consummation
　　a 48–15　until the *c·* of a life-work.
　　sp 96–25　As this *c·* draws nearer,
　　p 367–28　I long to see the *c·* of my hope,
consumption
　　ph 184–27　A woman, whom I cured of *c·*,
　　p 375–32　The belief in *c·* presents to mortal thought
　　376–11　whom you declare to be wasting away with *c·*
　　384–26　neither rheumatism, *c·*, nor any other
　　386–10　catarrh, fever, rheumatism, or *c·*,
　　390–28　whether it is cancer, *c·*, or smallpox.
　　392–17　If you think that *c·* is hereditary in your
　　425– 6　If the case to be mentally treated is *c·*,
　　425–20　What if the belief is *c·*?
　　426– 1　Discard all notions about . . . inherited *c·*,
consumptive
　　f 243–18　dizzy, diseased, *c·*, or lame.
　　p 375–26　*C·* patients always show great hopefulness
contact
　　sp 86– 2　Supposing this . . . occasioned by physical *c·*
　　s 154–14　he had not caught the cholera by material *c·*,
　　ph 196–27　not from infection nor from *c·* with material
　　f 212–19　bring the rose into *c·* with the olfactory nerves
contagion
　　s 153–28　When this mental *c·* is understood,
　　154–16　If a child is exposed to *c·* or infection,
　　154–22　Then it is believed that exposure to the *c·*
　　ph 171– 3　mankind has caught their moral *c·*.
　　176–31　Truth handles the most malignant *c·*
　　f 220–16　Colds, coughs, and *c·* are engendered
　　p 384– 9　though they expose him to fatigue, cold, heat, *c·*.
　　392–29　whether it be air, exercise, heredity, *c·*,
contagious
　　s 154– 5　that certain diseases should be regarded as *c·*,
contain
　　c 257–30　require an infinite form to *c·* infinite Mind.
　　b 271–29　The Scriptures *c·* it.
　　g 546–21　for they *c·* the deep divinity of the Bible.
　　ap 559– 2　Did this same book *c·* the revelation of
contained
　　sp 93–30　belief that the infinite can be *c·* in the finite.
　　s 110–18　the Science *c·* in this book,
containing
　　sp 80– 9　Yet the very periodical *c·* this sentence
　　p 363– 2　*c·* costly and fragrant oil,
　　398–16　sometimes not *c·* a particle of medicine,
　　t 456–31　*c·* a thorough statement of C. S.
contains
　　s 147–14　this volume *c·* the complete Science
　　153–27　mortal mind, ... *c·* and carries the infection.
　　p 399–27　The one Mind, God, *c·* no mortal opinions.
　　406– 1　The Bible *c·* the recipe for all healing.
　　t 456–28　voice of Truth to this age, and *c·* the
　　r 466–16　*c·* the point you will most reluctantly admit,
　　g 521–27　The second chapter of Genesis *c·*
　　547– 2　*c·* the proof of all here said of C. S.
　　gl 579– 4　It *c·* the metaphysical interpretation
contaminated
　　b 287–32　Truth cannot be *c·* by error.
　　304–20　Truth is not *c·* by error.
contemplate
　　g 536–10　The way of error is awful to *c·*.
contemplates
　　p 415– 8　leaps or halts when it *c·* unpleasant things,
contemplation
　　b 276–22　towards the *c·* of things immortal
　　323–23　*c·* of something better than disease or sin.
　　p 376– 3　patient turns involuntarily from the *c·* of it,
　　413– 3　undue *c·* of physical wants
　　g 550–16　continual *c·* of existence as material
　　553– 4　a higher and purer *c·* of man's origin.
contempt
　　p 437–21　called C. S. to order for *c·* of court.
contend
　　p 380– 9　we virtually *c·* against the control of Mind
　　394–22　against whom mortals should not *c·*
　　396–11　Never say . . . how much you have to *c·* with
contending
　　sp 79–27　*c·* for the rights of intelligence
　　p 380– 8　*C·* for the evidence or indulging the
　　400–18　*c·* persistently for truth, you destroy error.
content
　　f 240–23　If at present *c·* with idleness,
contentment
　　pref vii–15　*C·* with the past and the cold conventionality
　　t 452–16　Better is the frugal intellectual repast with *c·*

contents
　　s 130–19　cannot add to the *c·* of a vessel already full.
contest
　　sp 99–20　Therefore my *c·* is not with the individual,
contests
　　ap 567– 7　The Gabriel of His presence has no *c·*.
context
　　s 127–12　according to the requirements of the *c·*.
　　o 341– 6　clauses separated from their *c·*.
　　g 501– 5　seems so smothered by the immediate *c·*
continent
　　ap 559– 9　scientific thought reaches over *c·* and ocean
contingent
　　p 368–20　Life is not *c·* on bodily conditions
　　427–10　belief that existence is *c·* on matter
　　g 509–21　are no more *c·* now on time or
　　552– 7　hypotheses deal with causation as *c·* on matter
continual
　　f 220– 3　We hear it said : . . . I have *c·* colds,
　　240–14　and there is *c·* discord.
　　g 550–16　*c·* contemplation of existence as material
continually
　　s 144–19　Will-power . . . produces evil *c·*,
　　145–29　mortal mind must *c·* weaken its own
　　f 248–21　The world is holding it before your gaze *c·*.
　　248–27　and look at them *c·*,
　　b 291–29　judgment-day of wisdom comes hourly and *c·*,
　　320–29　whereas this passage is *c·* quoted
　　p 377–17　mental state should be *c·* watched
　　424–17　by *c·* expressing such opinions as may
　　t 462– 6　add *c·* to his store of spiritual understanding,
continuance
　　p 397–10　by admitting their reality and *c·*,
continuation
　　p 399–19　*c·* of, the primitive mortal mind.
continue
　　a 21– 6　not *c·* to labor and pray, expecting because of
　　21–24　and our companionship may *c·*.
　　29– 4　*c·* this warfare until they have finished their
　　m 56–13　marriage will *c·*, subject to
　　59–25　should exist before this union and *c·* ever after,
　　64–27　Until . . . marriage will *c·*.
　　sp 96–10　will *c·* unto the end,
　　96–19　disturbances will *c·* until the end of error,
　　96–22　fermentation has begun, and will *c·* until
　　99–22　and shall *c·* to labor and to endure.
　　s 124–19　is, and must *c·* to be, an enigma.
　　143–21　by this belief, you *c·* in the old routine.
　　ph 173–27　and so *c·* to call upon matter to
　　f 203–26　will *c·* to kill him so long as he sins.
　　205– 1　else God will *c·* to be hidden from humanity,
　　227– 8　or mortals will *c·* unaware of man's inalienable
　　254–13　but to *begin* aright and to *c·* the strife
　　c 267– 5　are in and of Spirit, . . . and so forever *c·*.
　　b 285–24　shall *c·* to seek salvation
　　o 353– 5　and they will so *c·*, till the testimony of
　　353–18　All things will *c·* to disappear, until
　　353–20　We must not *c·* to admit the somethingness
　　353–27　so long will ghosts seem to *c·*.
　　p 403–18　and it will *c·* to do so, until
　　422– 8　*C·* to read, and the book will become the
　　　　　　physician,
　　t 449– 6　in order to *c·* in well doing.
　　r 472–22　we should *c·* to lose the standard of
　　486–21　So long as . . . mortals will *c·* mortal in belief
　　g 507–28　and must ever *c·* to appear
continued
　　sp 81– 8　have a *c·* existence after death
　　s 156–19　I did so, and she *c·* to gain.
　　ph 193–22　The diseased condition had *c·* there
　　f 212– 5　amputated has *c·* in belief to pain the
　　222–19　and yet he *c·* ill all the while.
　　227–12　ignorance . . . the foundation of *c·* bondage
　　b 334–15　*c·* until the Master's ascension,
　　p 438–14　Turning suddenly to Personal Sense, . . . C.S. *c·*:
　　438–18　Then C. S. *c·*:
　　g 521–20　but the *c·* account is mortal and material.
continues
　　pr 5–27　He grows worse who *c·* in sin
　　a 19–20　but if the sinner *c·* to pray and repent,
　　sp 71– 5　identity, or idea, of all reality *c·* forever ;
　　77– 5　Existence *c·* to be a belief of corporeal sense
　　s 118–23　This *c·* until the leaven of Spirit
　　ph 173–18　Physiology *c·* this explanation,
　　f 233–13　false claim of error *c·* its delusions
　　b 334–17　*c·* to exist in the eternal order of
　　gl 595–20　*c·* after, what is termed death, until
continuing
　　b 302–14　*C·* our definition of *man,*

continuity
m 69–11 neither closes man's *c·* nor his sense of
s 123–29 the scientific order and *c·* of being.
124–25 Spirit is the life, substance, and *c·* of
f 246–30 loveliness, freshness, and *c·*,
b 325–14 understood in all its perfection, *c·*, and might,
g 513–20 existence and *c·* . . . remain in God,

continuous
s 157–30 proof that Life is *c·* and harmonious.
p 397–12 by believing them to be real and *c·*.

contract
m 58–12 Never *c·* the horizon of a worthy outlook
s 160–16 when the cords *c·* and become immovable?

contracted
s 160–31 Is a stiff joint or a *c·* muscle

contradict
an 105– 7 would be to *c·* precedent
s 110– 2 *c·* forever the belief that
118–29 Therefore they *c·* the divine decrees
122– 5 great facts of Life, . . . *c·* their false witnesses,
149–22 The logic is lame, and facts *c·* it.
f 202–24 *c·* the practice growing out of them.
232–14 but religions which *c·* its Principle are false.
b 277–22 suppositions *c·* even the order of material
o 358– 6 If two statements directly *c·* each other
p 389–22 Materialists *c·* their own statements.
391–29 Mentally *c·* every complaint from the body,
407–21 If delusion says, "I have lost my memory," *c·* it.
r 489–21 An affirmative reply would *c·* the Scripture,

contradicting
b 297–22 *c·* the testimony of material sense,
298–13 Spiritual sense, *c·* the material senses,
gl 596–26 C. S., *c·* sense, maketh the valley to bud

contradiction
s 163–28 so much absurdity, *c·*, and falsehood.
c 257–31 phrase *infinite form* involves a *c·* of terms.
r 472–17 Error is the *c·* of Truth.
g 504–28 and the *c·* of Spirit is matter,
526–23 in *c·* of the first creation?
545–26 Hence the seeming *c·* in that Scripture,

contradictions
s 129– 2 So in C. S., there are no discords nor *c·*,
b 289–26 spiritual fact and the . . . are *c·* ;
335–31 and must be *c·* of reality.
r 481– 9 The various *c·* of the Science of Mind

contradictory
o 341– 8 appear *c·* when subjected to such usage.
345–14 in this volume of mine there are no *c·*
358– 8 Is Science thus *c·*?
358–13 C. S. is neither made up of *c·* aphorisms
r 492–15 These two *c·* theories
g 537–27 made to appear *c·* in some places,
546– 9 Is C. S. *c·*?

contradicts
sp 93–18 Whatever *c·* the real nature of the divine
s 119–25 one finds that it *c·* the evidence before the senses
152–13 in which one statement *c·* another
ph 170–11 not only *c·* human systems, but points to
178–20 but this so-called mind, . . . *c·* itself,
f 213– 1 Whoever *c·* this mortal mind supposition
b 278–20 *c·* the demonstration of life as Spirit,
279–25 *c·* alike revelation and right reasoning.
281– 8 Divine Science *c·* the corporeal senses,
287– 7 Divine Science *c·* this postulate
303–14 but the statement . . . *c·* this
o 345–11 mind which *c·* itself neither knows itself nor
353– 8 Truth which *c·* the evidence of error,
r 485– 5 Whatever *c·* this statement is the false sense,
493– 4 science *c·* this, and explains the solar system
g 526– 7 *c·* the teaching of the first chapter,
529–26 and should rejoice that evil, . . . *c·* itself
538–20 Until that which *c·* the truth of being
gl 584–16 for it *c·* the spiritual facts of being.

contradistinction
s 114– 5 in *c·* to the divine Mind, or Truth
p 418– 5 Stick to the truth of being in *c·* to the error
g 522– 1 it is the false history in *c·* to the true.
538–22 the unreal in *c·* to the real and eternal.

contraries
b 303–15 can never make both these *c·* true.
p 372–21 and hope to succeed with *c·*?
r 466–11 contrasting pairs of terms represent *c·*,

contrarieties
s 163–29 To harmonize the *c·* of medical doctrines is

contrariwise
s 130–28 ought we not, *c·*, to be astounded at the

contrary
pref xi– 4 On the *c·*, C. S. rationally explains
a 21–20 On the *c·*, if my friends pursue my course,
44–24 On the *c·*, it was a divinely natural act,
53–13 above and *c·* to the world's religious sense.

contrary
sp 71–31 a theory *c·* to C. S.
83–21 It is *c·* to C. S. to suppose that life
86–11 Opposites come from *c·* directions,
s 123–32 On the *c·*, C. S. is pre-eminently scientific,
129–10 with your preconceptions or utterly *c·* to them.
150–21 and *c·* to the law of divine Mind.
160–23 never capable of acting *c·* to mental direction.
ph 172–18 On the *c·*, man is the image and likeness of
173–14 Matter is Spirit's *c·*,
183– 7 however much is said to the *c·*.
f 222–28 *c·* to His commands.
230–11 It would be *c·* to our highest ideas of God
b 270– 5 One is *c·* to the other
273– 2 claims of sin, sickness, and death are *c·* to God,
274– 9 Ideas, on the *c·*, are born of Spirit,
275–30 *c·* to the one Spirit.
339– 9 evil, being *c·* to good, is unreal,
o 349– 8 annulled material law by healing *c·* to it.
p 431– 3 Notwithstanding my rules to the *c·*,
434– 4 Some exclaim, "It is *c·* to law and justice."
435–31 to be smitten *c·* to the law?"— *Acts* 23 : 3.
441–29 a verdict *c·* to law and gospel.
t 456– 3 but *c·* to its spirit or rules,
r 479– 5 On the *c·*, if aught comes from God,

contrast
a 34–29 What a *c·* between our Lord's last supper and
b 272–20 in *c·* with the results of the ghastly farce
272–22 in *c·* with the downward tendencies and

contrasting
r 466–10 these *c·* pairs of terms represent

contrasts
f 252–15 *c·* strikingly with the testimony of Spirit.

contributing
o 356–13 not *c·* in any way to each other's happiness

contribution
gl 595–22 Tithe. *C·* ; tenth part ; homage ;

contrition
p 364– 9 or the *c·* of the Magdalen?

control (noun)
absolute
ph 177– 6 divine Mind's healing power and absolute *c·*
attested the
sp 80–23 attested the *c·* of mortal mind over its
complete
p 417–28 the complete *c·* which Mind holds over the body.
conscious
ph 166– 6 thus the conscious *c·* over the body is lost.
despotic
an 102–27 It implies the exercise of despotic *c·*,
divine
pr 9–23 recognizes only the divine *c·* of Spirit,
p 400–28 Without divine *c·* there is discord,
God's
s 125– 7 Neither . . . is beyond God's *c·* ;
his
a 25–22 Though demonstrating his *c·* over sin and
r 482–22 enabled Jesus to demonstrate his *c·* over matter.
hypnotic
p 402–31 the person under hypnotic *c·*
Jesus'
p 369–11 All these deeds manifested Jesus' *c·*
loss of
p 400–27 a loss of *c·* over the body.
Mind's
ph 171–12 Mind's *c·* over the universe, including man,
no
s 151–22 it has no *c·* over God's man.
ph 182–31 To admit that . . . God has no *c·*,
normal
p 406–30 normal *c·* is gained through divine strength
other
sp 73–12 Any other *c·* or attraction of so-called spirit
took
p 431–23 hypnotized the prisoner and took *c·* of his mind,

a 30–27 allow Soul to hold the *c·*, we shall loathe sin
sp 91– 3 beings under the *c·* of supreme wisdom?
ph 167–28 impossible to gain *c·* over the body in any
169–16 If we understood the *c·* of Mind over body,
f 217–22 as you understand the *c·* which Mind has over
217–24 will be able to demonstrate this *c·*.
b 322– 5 gain the reality of Life, the *c·* of Soul over sense,
p 380–10 we virtually contend against the *c·* of Mind
389– 4 it will be given in behalf of the *c·* of Mind
394–11 that any bodily condition is beyond the *c·*
429– 5 the more simple demonstrations of *c·*,
t 462–28 It teaches the *c·* of mad ambition.
g 514–26 Understanding the *c·* which Love held
544–16 under the *c·* of the one Mind.

control (verb)
sp 73– 8 belief that one man, as spirit, can c· another
    74–19 nor . . . return to fraternize with or c· the worm.
    93– 1 as substantial and able to c· the body?
f 228–15 Then they will c· their own bodies
   228–23 and form and c· it with Truth.
   234–26 You must c· evil thoughts
   234–27 or they will c· you in the second.
p 375–13 while the hypnotist . . . in order to c· him.
   377–29 and incompetent to c· it.
   378– 7 Disease is less than mind, and Mind can c· it.
   379– 1 If disease can attack and c· the body
   392–26 you will c· yourself harmoniously.
   414–10 impossibility that matter, brain, can c·
r 485–29 as much as nerves c· sensation

controlled
pr 14–17 c· by spiritual Life, Truth, and Love.
sp 73–15 communed with mortals or c· them
    84– 9 c· not by demons, spirits, or demigods,
s 125–18 man cannot be c· by sin or death,
   136–19 believed that Jesus was a medium, c· by
   136–25 Herod doubted if Jesus was c· by the
   143–20 C· by this belief, you continue in the old routine.
   143–24 body is not c· scientifically by a negative mind.
ph 178– 5 c· by the majority of opinions,
   184–16 C· by the divine intelligence,
b 292–10 belief that . . . Life be c· by death.
   303– 4 c· by Mind, the Principle
   304–16 Harmony is produced by its Principle, is c· by it
   304–28 C· by belief, instead of understanding,
   318–30 as numbers are c· and proved by
o 356– 9 and c· sickness, sin, and death
r 485–28 heathen gods of mythology c· war . . . as much as

controlling
m 63– 3 never think that flannel was better . . . than
           the c·
p 379– 6 jurisdiction of the world is in Mind, c· every
t 451–28 action of one mortal mind c· another
gl 583–27 so-called mortal mind c· mortal mind ;

controls
sp 73–11 God c· man, and God is the only Spirit.
    79–28 asserting that Mind c· body and brain.
s 121–24 simple rule that the greater c· the lesser.
   145–17 that in it Truth c· error.
f 220–31 c· the stomach, bones, lungs, heart,
b 319–19 Mind c· man and man has no Mind but God.
p 400– 1 mortal mind, which directly c· the body?
g 557– 6 Mind c· the birth-throes in the lower

convenient
a 40– 6 when I have a c· season — *Acts* 24 : 25.
sp 72–19 Error is not a c· sieve through which

convening
pref xii–10 Christian Scientist Association, c· monthly ;

conventional
b 274–25 The c· firm, called matter and mind,

conventionality
pref vii–16 and the cold c· of materialism

conversation
a 21– 2 overcoming error in your daily walk and c·,
c 260–26 by c· about the body,

conversing
p 424–24 thinking about your patients or c· with them,

conversion
f 217– 7 Paul's peculiar Christian c· and experience,

convert
b 272– 1 how shall they preach, c·, and heal multitudes,
p 365–27 c· into a den of thieves the temple

converted
a 38–30 and be c·, and I might heal you.
o 350–22 should be c·, and I should heal — *Matt.* 13 : 15.

convey
pref ix– 7 stammeringly attempts to c· his feeling.
sp 86–32 before the artist can c· them to canvas.
s 160–14 to c· the mandate of mind to muscle
f 212–26 the lips or hands . . . in order to c· thought,
   212–27 we say . . . the undulations of the air c· sound,
p 413–28 these actions c· mental images to
   432– 7 c· messages from my residence in matter,

conveyed
f 243–19 If this information is c·,
r 488– 8 c· by the English verb *believe ;*

conveying
o 349–13 The chief difficulty in c· the teachings

conveys
f 214–15 c· the impressions of Mind to man,
   243–19 mortal mind c· it.
b 340– 4 This text . . . c· the C. S. thought,
p 421– 5 c· the true definition of all human belief in

conviction
abiding
  p 390–21 Dismiss it with an abiding c· that it
common
  sp 80–30 common c· that mind and matter cooperate
deep-lying
  pref xii–15 with a deep-lying c· that the next two years
heavenly
  s 108– 1 Whence came to me this heavenly c·,
honest
  p 418– 7 Plead with an honest c· of truth
solid
  t 460–16 is more than fancy ; it is solid c·.

sp 90–25 This c· shuts the door on death,
s 108– 1 a c· antagonistic to the testimony of the
p 377–27 c· of the necessity and power of
   384–25 When the fear subsides and the c· abides
   404–19 This c·, that there is no real pleasure in sin,

convictions
pr 13– 5 In public prayer we often go beyond our c·,
s 134– 8 one who suffers for his c·.
r 494–18 helping . . . human sense to flee from its own c·

convince
a 46–17 To c· Thomas of this, Jesus caused him
an 101–22 c· her that it is not a remedial agent,
b 327–27 c· the mortal of his mistake
p 377– 1 mentally c· him that matter cannot take cold,
   377– 3 If grief causes suffering, c· the sufferer that
g 522–23 c· reason and coincide with revelation

convinced
pref x–27 soonest touched by Truth, and c· of it.
a 35– 2 C· of the fruitlessness of their toil
   46– 3 This c· them of the truthfulness of
f 240–25 c· of the error that is to be overcome.
o 346–22 When a sufferer is c· that
ap 564–10 The author is c· that the accusations

convinceth
o 341– * *Which of you c· me of sin? — John* 8 : 46.

convincing
a 43–11 Jesus' last proof was the highest, the most c·,
p 404– 7 c· him that there is no real pleasure in

convivial
a 32–10 wine, used on c· occasions and in Jewish rites,

convulsed
ph 195– 6 Every sound c· him with anguish.

convulses
sp 80–25 It is mortal mind which c· its
f 223–14 The question, . . . c· the world.

convulsions
p 389–28 A case of c·, produced by

cook
p 364–32 Did the careless doctor, the nurse, the c·,

cools
p 374–27 body, when bereft of mortal mind, at first c·,

cooperate
sp 80–31 belief . . . that mind and matter c·
b 270– 2 theory, . . . that Mind and matter coexist and c·.
   279–13 Spirit and matter can neither coexist nor c·,

cooperates
r 490– 9 Will . . . c· with appetite and passion.

cooperating
p 398–25 So also faith, c· with a belief in
g 522–26 Spirit as supposedly c· with matter

cooperation
s 144– 4 needs no c· from lower powers,
o 348–16 I deny His c· with evil,
r 490–10 From this c· arises its evil.

coordinate
sp 84– 1 Science is immortal and c· neither with
r 468– 2 never can be c· with human illusions.
   472– 7 making it c· with all that is real
g 537–22 c· with the Science of creation

copartnership
b 274–28 destroy the imaginary c·,
o 356–17 There is neither a present nor an eternal c·

cope
p 423–22 has rendered himself strong, . . . to c· with

Copernicus
s 121– 4 C· mapped out the stellar system,

copes
p 378–26 Sickness is not a . . . power, which c· astutely

copies
pref ix–25 c· were, however, in friendly circulation.

copious
pref ix–27 she made c· notes of Scriptural exposition,

copy
sp 87– 2 They c· or reproduce them, even when

copyist
pr 16–13 addition to the prayer by a later *c·* ;
copyrighted
pref ix–20 Her first pamphlet on C. S. was *c·* in 1870.
r 465– 2 the author's class-book, *c·* in 1870.
corals
sp 87–21 the sea is ignorant . . . of the *c·*,
cords
s 142–20 The strong *c·* of scientific demonstration,
160–16 what does anatomy say when the *c·* contract
r 474– 7 worse *c·* than those which cut the flesh.
Corinthians
b 321– 3 As Paul says, in his first epistle to the *C·*,
corner
s 139–27 become "the head of the *c·*." — *Matt.* 21 : 42.
p 380– 6 Truth is the rock of ages, the headstone of the *c·*,
corner-stone
f 241–26 *c·* of all spiritual building is purity.
corporeal
pr 12–16 Prayer to a *c·* God affects the sick like
13–20 If we pray to God as a *c·* person,
13–26 is represented as a *c·* creator ;
14– 2 If we . . . regard omnipotence as a *c·*,
m 67–27 Spiritual, not *c·*, consciousness is needed.
sp 70–10 The supposition that *c·* beings are spirits,
71–31 a *c·* being, a finite form,
72– 9 So-called *spirits* are but *c·* communicators,
74–28 and the physical, or *c·*.
76–16 Neither will man seem to be *c·*,
s 116– 6 the evidence before the *c·* human senses,
116–21 God is not *c·*, but *incorporeal*,
116–22 Mortals are *c·*, but God is incorporeal.
140– 4 That God is a *c·* being, nobody can truly affirm.
141–10 the Christ-spirit which governed the *c·* Jesus.
144–21 Truth, and not *c·* will, is the divine power
ph 107– 1 Should we implore a *c·* God to heal
c 255–14 That God is *c·* or material, no man should
258– 1 A mortal, *c·*, or finite conception of God
b 284– 6 If God were limited . . . God would be *c·*,
285–23 By interpreting God as a *c·* Saviour
309– 2 the messenger was not a *c·* being,
312–14 People go into ecstasies over the sense of a *c·*
328– 2 silences the material or *c·*.
332–17 The *c·* man Jesus was human.
334– 3 not that the *c·* Jesus was one with the
334–14 the eternal Christ and the *c·* Jesus
p 402– 9 forsake its *c·*, structural, and material basis,
408–28 in the *c·* substratum of brain
t 443– 5 a resort to faith in *c·* means
453–19 You uncover sin, . . . to bless the *c·* man ;
g 549–19 the most complicated *c·* structures,
550–16 contemplation of existence as material and *c·*
ap 561–20 material and *c·* selfhood disappear,
577– 8 God as Father-Mother, not as a *c·* being.
gl 587–21 HAM (Noah's son). *C·* belief ;
580 1 ISSACHAR (Jacob's son). A *c·* belief ;
589–16 JESUS. The highest human *c·* concept
589–23 JUDAH. A *c·* material belief
590–11 LEVI (Jacob's son). A *c·* and sensual belief ;
591– 1 physical sense of God as finite and *c·*.
592–27 PHARISEE. *C·* and sensuous belief ;
(see also **mortal, sense, senses**)
corporealities
sp 71–28 Its spirits are so many *c·*,
corporeality
above
g 512– 2 aspirations soaring beyond and above *c·*
applied to
gl 599– 3 You. As applied to *c·*, a mortal ; finity.
entire
s 157–28 C. S. impresses the entire *c·*,
governed by
g 536–15 governed by *c·* instead of divine Principle,
groundwork of
sp 84– 6 a groundwork of *c·* and human belief.
inability of
r 494–16 Jesus demonstrated the inability of *c·*,
no
b 305– 8 there is no *c·* in the mirrored form,
nor mind
gl 584–17 error ; neither *c·* nor mind ;
not bounded by
sp 84–20 Mind is infinite, not bounded by *c·*,

s 138–12 diseases were cast out neither by *c·*, . . . nor
140–11 warring no more over the *c·*,
ph 192– 8 from *c·* instead of from Principle,
b 284–10 nor be fully manifested through *c·*.
g 517– 7 mortally mental attempt to reduce Deity to *c·*.
544–32 Error begins with *c·* as the producer
gl 582–21 *C·* and physical sense put out of sight and
593–12 REUBEN (Jacob's son). *C·* ; sensuality ;
594–22 SPIRITS. Mortal beliefs ; *c·* ;

corporeally
s 148–10 as created *c·* instead of spiritually
corpse
b 312– 8 The senses regard a *c·*, not as man,
p 408–19 Drugs do not affect a *c·*,
429–11 *c·*, deserted by thought, is cold and decays,
correct
m 60–27 Science will *c·* the discord,
s 116–11 A *c·* view of C. S.
128–32 If both . . . are *c·*, the conclusion, if properly
ph 167– 7 only as we live above corporeal sense and *c·* it.
180–22 to *c·* this turbulent element of mortal mind
f 206–30 Mind does not make mistakes and . . . *c·* them.
219– 7 and then say the product is *c·*.
235– 9 their learning or their *c·* reading.
c 264–13 As mortals gain more *c·* views of God
b 284–17 *c·* testimony as to spiritual life, truth, and
300– 2 it attempts to draw *c·* spiritual conclusions
o 355–27 capable of impartial or *c·* criticism,
361–24 must be *c·* in order to be Science
p 408–14 supposition that we can *c·* insanity by
425–24 *C·* material belief by spiritual
t 453– 1 to distinguish the *c·* from the incorrect
r 477– 3 this *c·* view of man healed the sick.
486–13 and one error will not *c·* another.
492–13 a statement proved to be good must be *c·*.
494–20 serves to *c·* the errors of corporeal sense ;
g 547– 8 given you the *c·* interpretation of Scripture.
ap 500–18 without a *c·* sense of its highest visible idea,
corrected
pr 11 14 never pardons our sins . . . till they are *c·*
ph 194– 8 When one's false belief is *c·*,
f 251–29 Ignorance must be seen and *c·*
b 298–11 until this sense is *c·* by C. S.
correcting
p 386–20 *c·* the mistake, heals your grief,
corrective
p 423–10 This *c·* is an alterative,
correctly
sp 84–28 All we *c·* know of Spirit comes from God,
o 347–10 Had he stated his syllogism *c·*,
t 449–17 to teach this subject properly and *c·*
ap 560–21 in order to classify it *c·*.
correctness
a 50–23 and that all evidence of their *c·*
p 386–29 although the *c·* of the assertion
corrects
pref viii– 7 science of music *c·* false tones and gives
pr 6– 3 Divine Love *c·* and governs man.
a 121–23 and *c·* these errors by the simple rule that
f 233–22 the spiritual idea which *c·* and destroys them.
c 259–28 *c·* error with truth and demands
b 294–31 The Science of Mind *c·* such mistakes,
correlated
b 276–10 Man and his Maker are *c·* in divine Science,
288– 1 the *c·* statement, that *error*, . . . is unreal.
correlation
ap 561–14 the *c·* of divine Principle and spiritual idea,
correlative
b 316–31 blind to the possibilities of Spirit and its *c·* truth.
correspond
pr 8– 6 indexes which do not *c·* with their character.
s 158–13 history of material medicine may *c·* with
294– 1 physical senses . . . *c·* with error.
b 365–23 the result will *c·* with the spiritual intent.
g 512– 1 *c·* to aspirations soaring beyond and above
correspondence
sp 74–13 No *c·* nor communion can exist between
b 271– 3 maintaining its obvious *c·* with
corresponding
a 23–22 words *c·* thereto have these two definitions,
p 386–14 and the *c·* effects of Truth on the body,
corresponds
p 412–26 until the body *c·* with the
g 509– 1 This period *c·* to the resurrection,
517– 9 The ideal man *c·* to creation,
517–10 The ideal woman *c·* to Life and to Love.
552–14 Human experience . . . *c·* with that of Job,
corroborative
g 549– 1 This discovery is *c·* of the Science of Mind,
corrupt
f 204–20 Judging them by their fruits, they are *c·*.
241– 6 "where moth and rust doth *c·*." — *Matt.* 6 : 19 .
p 404– 9 A *c·* mind is manifested in a *c·* body.
corruptible
s 164–25 "When this *c·* shall have — *I Cor.* 15 : 54.
r 496–24 "when this *c·* shall have — *I Cor.* 15 : 54.

cost
ph 197– 8 But the price does not exceed the original *c·*.
costly
p 363– 2 *c·* and fragrant oil,— sandal oil perhaps,
costs
ph 197– 6 *c·* many a man his earthly days of comfort.
couch
o 342–22 from the *c·* of pain the helpless invalid.
p 362–13 he reclined on a *c·*
363– 1 to come behind the *c·* and reach his feet.
435–19 Watching beside the *c·* of pain
cough
f 220– 4 continual colds, catarrh, and *c·*."
p 384–17 followed by chills, dry *c·*, influenza,
coughs
f 220–16 Colds, *c·*, and contagion are engendered
Councils
s 139–15 The decisions by vote of Church *C·*
counsel (*see also* **counsel's**)
his
p 442– 9 We noticed, as he shook hands with his *c·*,
Master's
t 443–12 our motto should be the Master's *c·*,
no proper
p 434–24 Mortal Man has had no proper *c·* in the case.
opposing
p 437–20 Here the opposing *c·*, False Belief, called
profound
ap 572– 8 simple and profound *c·* of the inspired writer.

p 434–10 where C. S. is allowed to appear as *c·*
434–16 Mortal Man's *c·* regards the prisoner
439– 3 the *c·* for the plaintiff, Personal Sense,
440– 4 machinations of the *c·*, False Belief,
440–33 Here the *c·* for the defence closed,
t 454–27 Let your loving care and *c·* support all their
counsellor
p 435– 4 *C·* False Belief has argued that
counsel's
p 434–17 The *c·* earnest, solemn eyes,
counted
pr 9–26 for Truth, and so be *c·* among sinners?
countenance
p 362– * *Who is the health of my c·—Psal.* 42 : 11.
442–12 his *c·* beaming with health and happiness.
counter
f 233–28 The *c·* fact relative to any disease
counteract
p 424–13 if one doctor should administer a drug to *c·*
counteracting
gl 581– 6 purity, and immortality, *c·* all evil,
counteracts
p 414– 7 salutary action of truth, which *c·* error.
counterfeit
s 148–21 but the *c·*, of God's man.
b 285– 9 man's *c·*, the inverted likeness,
293–24 manifestations of evil, which *c·* divine justice,
gl 580–16 Life's *c·*, which ultimates in death ;
counterfeits
c 267–22 beliefs must be *c·* of Truth.
b 286–26 They are but *c·* of the spiritual
293–13 so-called gases and forces are *c·* of
293–17 *c·* the true essence of spirituality
337–23 poor *c·* of the invisible universe and
p 409–22 are *c·* from the beginning,
r 476– 1 Mortals are the *c·* of immortals.
gl 583– 1 *c·* of creation, whose better originals are
counter-irritant
ph 198–16 undertakes to dispel it by a *c·*,
counter-irritants
p 374– 2 Anodynes, *c·*, and depletion
counterpart
s 148–20 calling that *man* which is not the *c·*,
counterpoise
p 368– 1 Evil is but the *c·* of nothingness.
countless
g 503–17 reflecting Him in *c·* spiritual forms.
517–18 God has *c·* ideas, and they all have
country
f 225–14 The history of our *c·*, like all history,
counts
p 426– 7 than when she *c·* her footsteps
coupled
pr 11–29 prayer, *c·* with a fervent habitual desire
p 389– 1 for the penalty is *c·* with the belief.
gl 590–18 unless specially *c·* with the name God.

courage
animal
a 28–32 There is too much animal *c·* in society
48–23 thus rebuking resentment or animal *c·*.
moral
a 29– 1 and not sufficient moral *c·*.
b 327–23 Moral *c·* is requisite to meet the wrong
327–26 man who has more animal than moral *c·*,
p 404–24 this knowledge strengthens his moral *c·*
g 514–10 Moral *c·* is "the lion of the tribe—Rev.* 5 : 5.
gl 592–11 Moses. A corporeal mortal ; moral *c·* ;
more
p 417– 6 Never tell the sick that they have more *c·* than
sublime
a 49–11 his divine patience, sublime *c·*,
their
p 417– 8 their strength is in proportion to their *c·*.

m 57– 7 while the feminine mind gains *c·* and strength
sp 97–23 It requires *c·* to utter truth ;
p 375–27 always show great hopefulness and *c·*,
423–23 the stimulus of *c·* and conscious power.
courageously
p 419– 9 meet the cause mentally and *c·*,
course
advancing
t 452–11 Your advancing *c·* may provoke envy,
free
an 106– 4 to work against the free *c·* of honesty
his
a 21–14 till at last he finishes his *c·* with joy.
sp 96–26 he who has shaped his *c·* in accordance
t 458–26 The Christian Scientist wisely shapes his *c·*,
its
p 376–30 after admitting that it must have its *c·*.
my
a 21–21 On the contrary, if my friends pursue my *c·*,
only
p 392– 8 The only *c·* is to take antagonistic grounds
our
b 307–23 and so weighs against our *c·* Spiritward.
such a
t 453–27 for such a *c·* increases fear,
their
a 29– 5 until they have finished their *c·*.
ph 174–19 rebuking in their *c·* all error
true
p 419– 4 Your true *c·* is to destroy the foe,
your
m 67– 8 "Do you know your *c·*?
f 253–19 you can at once change your *c·*
zigzag
a 21–32 By-and-by, ashamed of his zigzag *c·*, he would

s 119– 2 of *c·* we cannot really endow matter with
t 443– 8 While a *c·* of medical study is
gl 593–15 River. . . . it typifies the *c·* of Truth ;
court
m 58–26 a wife ought to be on trial, as cases are tried in *c·*.
p 430–18 case to be on trial, as cases are tried in *c·*.
434–30 the lower *c·* has sentenced Mortal Man to die,
434–32 Denying justice to the body, that *c·* commended
436–33 that *c·* pronounced a sentence of death
437–21 called C. S. to order for contempt of *c·*.
437–27 proceedings of a regularly constituted *c·*.
courtesy
p 364–15 a special sign of Oriental *c·*.
Court of Error
p 432– 9 Another witness is called for by the *C· of E·*
434–12 who were at the previous *C· of E·*,
436–30 the *C· of E·* construed obedience to the
437–17 the terrible records of your *C· of E·*,
437–31 bar of Truth, which ranks above the lower
C· of E·.
441–18 the decrees of the *C· of E·* in favor of Matter,
441–27 Your personal jurors in the *C· of E·*
Court of Material Error
p 440–29 suits to be tried at the *C· of M· E·*.
Court of Spirit
p 434– 9 permission is obtained for a trial in the *C· of S·*,
437–10 our higher tribunal, the Supreme *C· of S·*,
437–18 I ask that the Supreme *C· of S·* reverse this
437–28 But Judge Justice of the Supreme *C· of S·*
Court of Truth
p 438–26 When the *C· of T·* summoned Furred Tongue
court-room
p 430–24 The *c·* is filled with interested spectators,
courts
an 104–20 *c·* recognize evidence to prove the motive
105– 3 *C·* and juries judge and sentence mortals
105–12 the body over which *c·* hold jurisdiction?
105–14 *c·* reasonably pass sentence, according to

covenant
m 56–15 Infidelity to the marriage *c·* is the
64–30 ensure the stability of the marriage *c·*.
c 255–11 Mortal man has made a *c·* with his eyes

cover
pr 8–19 they "*c·* the multitude of sins."— *I Pet.* 4 : 8.
sp 97–22 they bring error from under *c·*.
g 548–10 when clouds *c·* the sun's face !
gl 596–28 VEIL. A *c·* ; concealment ; hiding ; hypocrisy.

covered
pr 8–17 "there is nothing *c·* that shall— *Matt.* 10 : 26.
p 431–21 I am Coated Tongue. I am *c·* with a

covereth
t 448–17 "He that *c·* his sins shall not— *Prov.* 28 : 13.

covering
p 413–14 *c·* it with dirt in order to make it thrive
t 446–30 *C·* iniquity will prevent prosperity

coverings
f 241–11 Stripped of its *c·*, what a mocking
gl 597–14 tore from bigotry and superstition their *c·*,

covers
pr 16–11 gave that prayer which *c·* all human needs.
f 247–27 and *c·* earth with loveliness.
p 421–16 great fact which *c·* the whole ground,

covetous
m 64–14 debarred by a *c·* domestic tyrant

coward
p 368– 5 Error is a *c·* before Truth.

cowering
p 378–12 sent it *c·* back into the jungle.

cradle
sp 95–29 the world is asleep in the *c·* of infancy,
f 244– 8 is seen between the *c·* and the grave,

cradled
pref vii– 6 in *c·* obscurity, lay the Bethlehem babe,

craftiness
an 103– 5 defines it as dishonesty and *c·*.

cramped
s 160–20 become *c·* despite the mental protest?

cranium
sp 92– 9 Mind is not an entity within the *c·*
ph 173–23 according to the development of the *c·* ;

craving
c 258 4 unsatisfied human *c·* for something better,

cravings
m 60–32 Higher enjoyments alone can satisfy the *c·*
s 108– 8 immortal *c·*, "the price of learning love,"
g 501–17 more native to their immortal *c·*

craze
p 408– 8 general *c·* cannot, in a scientific diagnosis,

create
m 62– 8 If parents *c·* in their babes a desire for
sp 93–15 Good does not *c·* a mind susceptible of
s 151– 4 could not possibly *c·* a remedy outside of itself,
157–18 If He could *c·* drugs intrinsically bad, then
ph 177–21 and *c·* the so-called laws of the flesh,
f 203– 6 shows that matter can neither . . . *c·* nor
204–24 the notion that they can *c·*
251 33 imprison themselves in what they *c·*.
c 263– 4 would not or could not *c·*.
263–12 producing evil when he would *c·* good,
b 278– 2 nothing in Spirit out of which to *c·* matter.
279–14 and one can no more *c·* the other
279–15 than Truth can *c·* error, or *vice versa*.
287–12 Did God, Truth, *c·* error? No !
o 356–21 is it possible for Him to *c·* man subject to
356–24 Does God *c·* a material man out of Himself,
356–28 to *c·* the primitive, and then punish its
357–31 can Life, or God, dwell in evil and *c·* it?
p 419– 3 hate will perpetuate or even *c·* the
g 504–27 Did infinite Mind *c·* matter, and call it *light*?
522–21 represented as entering matter in order to *c·*
526–23 Did He *c·* this fruit-bearer of sin
528– 6 cannot be true that man was ordered to *c·*
528–17 and thereby *c·* woman?
532– 1 Did God at first *c·* one man unaided,
532– 3 in order to *c·* the rest of the human family?
540– 5 "I make peace, and *c·* evil. — *Isa.* 45 : 7.
543–26 did it leave aught for matter to *c·*?
544–15 No mortal mind has the might or right . . . to *c·* or
gl 579–12 the purpose of Love to *c·* trust in good,
583–25 could not *c·* . . . an element the opposite of

created
m 68– 6 we shall learn how Spirit, . . . has *c·* men and
69– 7 God's children already *c·* will be cognized
s 125–10 the prior states which human belief *c·* and
140–29 In the beginning God *c·* man in His,
148– 8 described man as *c·* by Spirit,

created
s 148–10 as *c·* corporeally instead of spiritually
161– 6 Holy inspiration has *c·* states of mind which
ph 173–29 the error which the human mind alone has *c·*.
f 205–12 God *c·* all through Mind,
206–22 Is God creating anew what He has already *c·*?
252–12 the eternal verity, man *c·* by and of Spirit,
c 256– 6 All things are *c·* spiritually.
263–20 but one creator, who has *c·* all.
b 279– 9 Matter is neither *c·* by Mind nor
294–27 God *c·* man.
295–12 immortals, *c·* in God's own image ;
295–29 Brainology teaches that mortals are *c·* to suffer
306–30 God's man, spiritually *c·*, is not material
307–27 Man was not *c·* from a material basis,
335– 7 Spirit, God, has *c·* all
335– 8 Spirit never *c·* matter.
339– 8 Spirit, alone *c·* all, and called it good.
o 344– 7 God has *c·* man in His own image
357– 2 for doing what He *c·* man capable of doing,
r 479–18 "In the beginning God the— *Gen.* 1 : 1.
g 502–22 In the beginning God *c·* the— *Gen.* 1 : 1.
507–23 Mind and the universe *c·* by God.
512– 4 And God *c·* great whales,— *Gen.* 1 : 21.
514–20 individuality *c·* by God is not carnivorous,
516–24 So God *c·* man— *Gen.* 1 : 27.
516–25 in the image of God *c·* He him ;— *Gen.* 1 : 27.
516–26 male and female *c·* He them.— *Gen.* 1 : 27.
520–17 when they were *c·*,— *Gen.* 2 : 4.
521–14 supposition that man is *c·* materially,
526–16 God pronounced good all that He *c·*,
526–17 and the Scriptures declare that He *c·* all.
528– 3 record declares that God has already *c·* man,
531–31 *c·* by Mind in the image and likeness of God
536–16 *C·* by flesh instead of by Spirit,
543–24 man, whom God *c·* with a word,
545–10 Man, *c·* by God, was given dominion
553–17 Adam was *c·* before Eve.
gl 580–14 image and likeness of what God has not *c·*,
580–26 supposition . . . creator entered what He *c·*,
581–12 spiritual realities of all things are *c·* by Him
584–22 self-made or *c·* by a tribal god

creates
m 69–22 If the father replies, "God *c·* man through
69–24 "Do you teach that Spirit *c·* materially,
sp 77– 8 mortal mind *c·* its own physical conditions.
93–13 nor *c·* aught that can cause evil.
s 122– 2 and so *c·* a reign of discord,
154– 7 calling up the fear that *c·* the image of disease
157–20 If He *c·* drugs at all
ph 173– 7 supposition, that Spirit is within what it *c·*
179–13 *c·* a demand for that method,
187– 6 so-called material sense *c·* its own forms of
c 257–12 Mind *c·* His own likeness in ideas,
b 280– 7 Mind *c·* and multiplies them,
280–14 divine Principle, Love, *c·* and governs all
295– 5 God *c·* and governs the universe,
316–20 man, whom Spirit *c·*, constitutes, and governs.
331– 7 If He dwelt within what He *c·*,
o 357– 8 Truth *c·* neither a lie, a capacity to lie, nor a liar.
p 400–22 we prove that thought alone *c·* the suffering.
r 471– 3 all that He *c·* are perfect and eternal,
472–25 That which He *c·* is good,
g 503–23 Mind *c·* no element nor symbol of discord and
503–24 God *c·* neither erring thought, mortal life,
505– 9 divine Mind, not matter, *c·* all identities,
507–24 Infinite Mind *c·* and governs all,
509–13 Spirit *c·* no other than heavenly
513–26 God *c·* all forms of reality.
520–23 God *c·* all through Mind, not through matter,
523–25 it is Elohim (God) who *c·*.
538–19 in which God *c·* the heavens, earth, and man.
540– 2 Spirit *c·* neither a wicked nor a mortal man,
546– 5 If Mind, God, *c·* error,
gl 582–18 *c·* man as His own spiritual idea,

creating
f 206–21 Is God *c·* anew what He has already created?
231–15 *c·* and governing man through perpetual
249– 5 "male and female" of God's *c·* — *Gen.* 1 : 27.
b 338–19 was deemed the agent of Deity in *c·* man,
g 515– 6 serpent of God's *c·* is neither subtle nor
520–27 the immortal *c·* thought is from above,
534– 5 to manifest the deathless man of God's *c·*.
gl 591–26 mythology ; error *c·* other errors ;

creation
account of
g 523–24 the spiritually scientific account of *c·*,
accurate views of
c 255– 9 accurate views of *c·* by the divine Mind.
all
m 69–14 unfolds all *c·*, confirms the Scriptures,
basis of the
g 528–26 supposed to become the basis of the *c·* of
consciousness of
c 263–31 scientific eternal consciousness of *c·*.

creation

corresponds to
g 517– 9   The ideal man corresponds to *c*·,
counterfeits of
gl 583– 1   Sensual and mortal beliefs ; counterfeits of *c*·,
divine
(*see* **divine**)
divine Principle of
g 546–10   Is the divine Principle of *c*· misstated?
existence and
gl 580–11   opposed to . . . spiritual existence and *c*· ;
fact of
r 471–20   spirituality . . . is the only fact of *c*·.
g 529–10   usher in . . . the glorious fact of *c*·,
facts of
g 539–28   power to expound the facts of *c*·,
544–19   The facts of *c*·, as previously recorded,
first
g 526–24   in contradiction of the first *c*·?
God's
m 69– 6   Mortals can never understand God's *c*· while
69–19   not conflict with the scientific sense of God's *c*·.
s 110– 5   the radiant reality of God's *c*·,
157–16   If drugs are part of God's *c*·,
c 260–11   the immortal and perfect model of God's *c*·
262–10   the nature and quality of God's *c*·
264–30   we shall behold and understand God's *c*·,
b 307–23   seems . . . a part of God's *c*·,
g 519–13   slow to discern and to grasp God's *c*·
544– 3   In God's *c*· ideas became productive,
ap 577–11   the perfectibility of God's *c*·.
gl 588–16   All the objects of God's *c*· reflect one Mind,
590–12   denial of the fulness of God's *c*· ;
His
f 231–29   and know that they are no part of His *c*·.
r 472–24   All reality is in God and His *c*·,
g 502– 8   inverted images of the creator and His *c*·.
507–27   expresses Science and art throughout His *c*·,
516– 5   are reflected by His *c*· ;
523– 6   declares . . . that error can improve His *c*·.
524–24   yet God is reflected in all His *c*·.
524–24   Is this addition to His *c*· real or unreal?
554–20   defined this opposite of God and His *c*·
gl 579–17   opposite of good,— of God and His *c*· ;
His own
g 522–31   Does the creator condemn His own *c*·?
527–19   the tree of death to His own *c*·?
illustration of
b 315–26·   and presented an illustration of *c*·.
line of
g 557–12   as the line of *c*· rises towards spiritual man,
man, and
r 489–30   wrong sense of God, man, and *c*· is *non-sense*,
material
ph 177–15   Scriptural allegory of the material *c*·,
g 522–24   declaring this material *c*· false.
544– 1   record of a material *c*· which followed the
material view of
g 521–25   opposite error, a material view of *c*·,
method of
ap 568–10   first the true method of *c*· is set forth
Mind's
g 509–26   the days and seasons of Mind's *c*·,
new
c 263–21   Whatever seems to be a new *c*·, is but
not
c 263–28   mortal sense of persons and things is not *c*·.
objects of
c 264–14   multitudinous objects of *c*·, which before
of the world
r 479–31   from the *c*· of the world,— Rom. 1 : 20.
one
g 502–29   There is but one creator and one *c*·.
order of
g 508–23   in the ascending order of *c*·.
record of
g 504– 9   not yet included in the record of *c*·,
521–15   turn our gaze to the spiritual record of *c*·,
526– 3   previous and more scientific record of *c*·
reflects the
b 305–14   though he reflects the *c*· of Mind,
Science of
g 509–29   Knowing the Science of *c*·,
537–23   Science of *c*· recorded in the first chapter
539–23   arguing for the Science of *c*·,
539–30   The Science of *c*·, . . . inspired his wisest
scientific
g 545–21   translators of this record of scientific *c*·
sense of
m 56–11   the corporeal sense of *c*· was cast out,
Spirit's
gl 580–18   the usurper of Spirit's *c*·,
spiritual
(*see* **spiritual**)
theories of
c 255– 7   The mythical human theories of *c*·,

creation

theory of
g 547–11   conclusions as to the scientific theory of *c*·.
this
g 502–29   This *c*· consists of the unfolding of spiritual
truth of
sp 93–17   and not the truth of *c*·.
c 263– 6   spiritual man alone represents the truth of *c*·.
vast
f 209– 7   the life and light of all its own vast *c*· ;
whole
c 255– *   *we know that the whole c· groaneth* — Rom. 8 : 22.
would simulate
b 281–25   out of which error would simulate *c*·

s 124–27   Withdraw them, and *c*· must collapse.
c 256–32   *c*· is the infinite . . . idea emanating from this
b 321–20   leprosy was a *c*· of mortal mind
g 504–15   a revelation instead of a *c*·
507– 8   and *c*· would be full of nameless offspring,
507–28   *C*· is ever appearing,
521–19   if there is nothing more about *c*· in the book of
527–26   the lie represents God as repeating *c*·,
528–19   Beginning *c*· with darkness instead of light,
537–11   *C*· is there represented as spiritual,
539–20   false to say that Truth and error commingle in *c*·.
544– 2   a *c*· so wholly apart from God's,
551–25   so long as it bases *c*· on materiality.
553–27   superstition about the *c*· from dust
554–18   the *c*· of whatever is sinful and mortal ;
555–22   *C*· rests on a spiritual basis.

creations

crude
c 264– 3   The crude *c*· of mortal thought
His
ph 187– 5   ignorant . . . of the all-knowing Mind and of
His *c*·.
b 331– 6   Life is Mind, the creator reflected in His *c*·.
gl 580– 4   the opposite of Spirit and His *c*· ;
innumerable
r 479–23   the only facts are Spirit and its innumerable *c*·.
of God
f 205– 8   error . . . that sin, sickness, and death are *c*· of
God,
c 266– 1   Soul, where the *c*· of God are good,
of matter
b 287– 5   but *c*· of matter must return to dust.
g 523– 7   The *c*· of matter arise from a mist
of Spirit
b 286–25   temporal and material are not then *c*· of Spirit.
287– 4   All *c*· of Spirit are eternal ;
of Truth
b 287– 4   error, which simulates the *c*· of Truth.
other
g 535–13   belief in . . . other *c*· must go down
Spirit's
g 525– 4   not the validity of Spirit or Spirit's *c*·.

c 263– 4   The *c*· of mortal mind are material.
g 528–23   Beholding the *c*· of his own dream
543–23   the *c*· of erroneous thought, not of

creative

sp 71– 8   God, the *c*·, governing, infinite Principle
89–25   Matter is neither intelligent nor *c*·.
b 302–32   is but the reflection of the *c*· power
317– 3   usurped the throne of the *c*· divine Principle,
r 475–21   no life, intelligence, nor *c*· power of his own,
g 502–27   *c*· Principle — Life, Truth, and Love — is God.
507–15   universe of Spirit reflects the *c*· power
513–21   God, who is the divinely *c*· Principle thereof.
531–23   Has man sought out other *c*· inventions,
549–29   forsakes Spirit as the divine origin of *c*· Truth,
556–19   Sleep is darkness, but God's *c*· mandate was,
gl 582–19   God is the only *c*· power.

creativeness

o 357–14   the *c*· and authority of Deity,

creator

but one
m 69–14   to understand that there is but one *c*·,
c 263–20   There can be but one *c*·, who has created all.
g 502–29   There is but one *c*· and one creation.
coexistent with his
g 557–21   as never dying, but as coexistent with his *c*·.
corporeal
pr 13–27   Father of all is represented as a corporeal *c*· ;
grand
s 143–26   Mind is the grand *c*·,
infinite Mind is the
c 256–32   Infinite Mind is the *c*·,
inseparable from his
r 491–16   man . . . inseparable from his *c*·.
is called
g 523–26   the *c*· is called Jehovah, or the Lord.

creator
man and his
  b 338–25 would impose between man and his *c·*.
not a
  c 259–26 Vibration is not intelligence ; hence it is not a *c·*.
  b 305–14 The verity that God's image is not a *c·*,
not the
  f 207– 8 God is not the *c·* of an evil mind.
of ideas
  f 249–12 the *c·* of ideas is not the creator of illusions.
of illusions
  f 249–13 the creator of ideas is not the *c·* of illusions.
of man
  r 470–21 God is the *c·* of man,
one
  o 356–32 Then there must have been more than one *c·*,
  gl 592– 7 belief that there can be more than one *c·* ;
prerogative of his
  g 530–10 presuming not on the prerogative of his *c·*,
substance and
  c 257– 7 theory that Spirit is not the only substance and *c·*
the only
  a 31–10 He recognized Spirit, God, as the only *c·*,
  b 331–19 the universal cause, the only *c·*,
wisdom of the
  b 273–24 and impugn the wisdom of the *c·*.

  m 69– 7 never . . . while believing that man is a *c·*.
  69–21 Do you have one God and *c·*,
  69–22 or is man a *c·* ?"
  s 119– 9 to leave the *c·* out of His own universe ;
  119–11 and regard God as the *c·* of matter,
  127– 4 the *c·* of the spiritual universe,
  ph 171– 1 Matter, which . . . claims to be a *c·*, is a fiction,
  c 256– 7 Mind, not matter, is the *c·*.
  b 277–10 and error has no *c·*.
  278– 1 Is Spirit the source or *c·* of matter?
  303–24 belief that . . . man . . . is himself a *c·*,
  331– 5 Life is Mind, the *c·* reflected in
  g 502– 7 inverted images of the *c·* and His creation.
  507–22 implies a mortal mind and man a *c·*.
  508– 6 substance of . . . a flower is God, the *c·* of it.
  514– 6 in which and of which God is the same *c·*.
  522–31 Does the *c·* condemn His own creation?
  531–17 If, . . . afterwards put into body by the *c·*,
  533–12 as if He were the *c·* of evil.
  gl 579– 9 surrendering to the *c·* the early fruits of
  580–26 supposition that . . . *c·* entered what He created,
  583–20 definition of

creators
  g 535–12 A belief in other gods, other *c·*,
creature
any other
  b 001 8 nor any other *c·*,— *Rom.* 8 : 39.
every
  a 37–30 preach the gospel to every *c·* !"— *Mark* 16 : 15
  s 138–28 preach the gospel to every *c·* !— *Mark* 16 : 15.
  p 418–28 "Preach the gospel to every *c·*."— *Mark* 16 : 15.
inharmonious
  s 123– 9 weak and inharmonious *c·* in the universe.
living
  g 512– 5 and every living *c·* that moveth,— *Gen.* 1 : 21.
  513–15 bring forth the living *c·* after his— *Gen.* 1 : 24.
  527 25 whatsoever Adam called every living *c·*,— *Gen.* 2 : 19.
moving
  g 511–20 moving *c·* that hath life,— *Gen.* 1 : 20.
new
  f 201– 8 Truth makes a new *c·*,

  b 299–31 If man were solely a *c·* of the
  p 407– 4 attractive to no *c·* except a loathsome
creatures
  b 298–32 human *c·* with suggestive feathers ;
  g 514–28 All of God's *c·*, . . . are harmless,
  549– 9 *C·* of lower forms of organism
credit
  pr 8–32 do we listen . . . and *c·* what is said?
  s 112–29 without giving that author proper *c·*,
  154– 6 this law obtains *c·* through association,
  p 417– 3 Give sick people *c·* for sometimes knowing
  t 457– 3 borrowed from this book without giving it *c·*,
creditor
  p 363–18 released . . . by their common *c·*.
credits
  a 27–23 Tradition *c·* him with two or three hundred
  g 528–15 Here falsity, error, *c·* Truth, God, with
credulity
  p 370–27 fails at length to inspire the *c·* of the sick,
credulous
  f 212–21 In legerdemain and *c·* frenzy,

creed
highest
  r 471–29 her highest *c·* has been divine Science,
orthodox
  r 471–24 The author subscribed to an orthodox *c·*
religious
  r 496–29 Have Christian Scientists any religious *c·* ?

  s 135–27 Christianity as Jesus taught it was not a *c·*,
  f 226–16 These claims are not made through code or *c·*,
  234– 2 as ritualism and *c·* hamper spirituality.
  o 351–12 spiritual sense of the *c·* was discerned
  t 450– 2 Their *c·* teaches belief in a
  458–21 ritualism and *c·* are summoned to give place
creeds
  pr 4–31 Long prayers, superstition, and *c·*
  a 18–11 against Pharisaical *c·* and practices,
  sp 98–12 *C·*, doctrines, and human hypotheses
  98–16 above the loosening grasp of *c·*,
  s 133–32 *C·* and rituals have not cleansed their
  f 239– 4 those who are in advance of *c·*.
  r 471–22 Are doctrines and *c·* a benefit to man?
creepeth
  r 475–27 that *c·* upon the earth."— *Gen.* 1 : 26.
  g 513–24 everything that *c·* upon the earth— *Gen.* 1 : 25.
  515–15 that *c·* upon the earth. — *Gen.* 1 : 26.
  518–10 everything that *c·* upon the earth,— *Gen.* 1 : 30.
creeping
  r 475–26 over every *c·* thing— *Gen.* 1 : 26.
  g 513–15 cattle, and *c·* thing,— *Gen.* 1 : 24.
  515– 4 *c·* over lofty summits,
  515–14 over every *c·* thing — *Gen.* 1 : 26.
creeps
  p 373–28 languidly *c·* along its frozen channels,
cried
  a 39–18 "*Now,*" *c·* the apostle,— *II Cor.* 6 : 2.
  p 398– 5 *c·*, and rent him sore— *Mark* 9 : 26.
  ap 562–22 And she being with child *c·*,— *Rev.* 12 : 2.
cries
  pr 13– 3 It is the open fount which *c·*,
  f 227–22 C. S. raises the standard of liberty and *c·* :
  p 365– 6 than all *c·* of "Lord, Lord !"
crieth
  g 541–28 *c·* unto Me from the ground.— *Gen.* 4 : 10.
crime
advocating
  s 153–31 as we would avoid advocating *c·*.
alleged
  p 434–28 alleged *c·* never to have been committed.
cloaked the
  gl 597– 8 but cloaked the *c·*, latent in thought,
diminish
  m 61– 8 would improve our progeny, diminish *c·*,
invoke
  g 542–12 tend to perpetuate sin, invoke *c·*,
looms of
  a 102 18 The looms of *c·*, hidden in the dark
mental
  an 105–17 laws eventually take cognizance of mental *c·*
second
  p 433–23 led him into the commission of the second *c·*,
this
  an 106–14 incurs the divine penalty due this *c·*.
  p 433 24 For this *c·* Mortal Man is sentenced

  sp 97– 1 will hold *c·* in check.
  an 104–30 motive as well as the commission of a *c·*.
  105– 4 in order to restrain *c·*,
  105–10 Can matter commit a *c·* ?
  105–14 and human law rightly estimates *c·*,
  f 236–13 strongest educator, either for or against *c·*.
  p 404–15 as . . . reformation cancels the *c·*.
  432– 6 I was witness to the *c·* of liver-complaint.
  432–22 shortly after the report of the *c·*,
  438–16 on three distinct charges of *c·*,
  438–20 on the night of the *c·*
  440– 5 Truth arraigns . . . to answer for his *c·*.
  440–25 render obedience to these laws punishable as *c·*.
  t 461–19 If you commit a *c·*, should you acknowledge
  ap 564– 7 to charge the innocent with the *c·*.
  564–23 its own *c·* of defying immortal Mind.
crimes
  a 40–16 *c·* of his implacable enemies less criminal?
  s 161–22 "Liberty, what *c·* are committed in thy name !"
  p 440–10 Good deeds are transformed into *c·*,
criminal
  pr 11– 6 this may be no moral benefit to the *c·*,
  11– 7 it only saves the *c·* from one form of
  a 40–16 crimes of his implacable enemies less *c·* ?
  an 102–23 apathy on the subject which the *c·* desires.
  105–13 Mortal mind, not matter, is the *c·*
  106– 1 *c·* misuse of human will-power,

criminal

ph 198– 4   as a *c·* hears his death-sentence.
b 316–26   That man was accounted a *c·*
  340–27   *c·*, political, and religious codes ;
p 431– 9   which I considered *c·*, inasmuch as
  432–14   treated as a *c·* and punished with death.
  435– 4   or has Mortal Mind committed a *c·* deed?
  437– 5   He also testified that . . . Man . . . was a *c·*.
  437–15   Soul a *c·* though recommended to
t 461–20   acknowledge to yourself that you are a *c·*?
ap 564–12   instigated by the *c·* instinct

cripple

ph 172–29   the unfortunate *c·* may present more
b 294–14   saying : . . . Injury can *c·* and matter can kill
t 460–21   it starts a petty crossfire over every *c·*

crippled

f 227–28   *c·* your capacities, enfeebled your body,

cripples

t 448–10   Evasion of Truth *c·* integrity,

crisis

p 396–12   growing worse before a *c·* is passed.
  421–11   If a *c·* occurs in your treatment,
t 446– 8   or it may mark the *c·* of the disease.

critic

o 346– 1   as is alleged by one *c·*.
  347– 3   It is said by one *c·*, that to verify this

criticising

o 345–10   It is sometimes said, in *c·* C. S.,

criticism

s 110–20   This book may be distorted by shallow *c·*
c 255– 7   anciently classified as the higher *c·*,
o 346– 1   such *c·* confounds *man* with Adam.
  355–27   capable of impartial or correct *c·*,

criticisms

o 341– 4   These *c·* are generally based on

critics

o 347–12   *C·* should consider that the so-called mortal man
  347–31   *c·* will then see that error is indeed the

crop

ph 183– 9   Can the agriculturist, . . . produce a *c·* without
  188–25   you have an abundant or scanty *c·*

crops

s 125–24   these changes cannot affect his *c·*.

cross

cup is the
a 35–27   Our cup is the *c·*.
foot of the
a 42–14   sadly followed him to the foot of the *c·*.
gallows and the
s 134–13   hallowed by the gallows and the *c·*.
his
a 34– 1   willing truly to drink his cup, take his *c·*,
  36–14   beneath the shadow of his *c·*.
manger and the
s 142–15   In vain do the manger and the *c·* tell their
material
a 50–32   Not the spear nor the material *c·*
on the
a 49–28   mocked him on the *c·*, saying derisively,
real
a 50–30   The real *c·*, which Jesus bore up the hill of grief,
scourge and the
a 20–20   scourge and the *c·* awaited the great Teacher.
take up the
pr 15–19   We must resolve to take up the *c·*,
a 34–14   If all who seek . . . will take up the *c·*,
taking up the
ph 179– 3   this can be done only by taking up the *c·*
women at the
a 49– 1   The women at the *c·* could have answered

pr 9–15   There is a *c·* to be taken up
f 224–16   Of old the *c·* was truth's central sign,
  238–31   The *c·* is the central emblem of history.
  254–30   Your good will be evil spoken of. This is the *c·*.
c 266–30   He does not *c·* the barriers of time
b 294–14   saying : . . . The stomach can make a man *c·*.

cross-bearing

a 36–28   toil, sacrifice, *c·*, multiplied trials,
o 343– 8   without this *c·*, one might not

crossfire

t 460–21   it starts a petty *c·* over every cripple

Cross of Calvary

ap 575–31   *C·* of *C·*, which binds human society

cross-questioning

g 533–26   Truth, *c·* man as to his

croton oil

ph 198–18   by the application of caustic or *c· o·*,

crouched

p 380–16   Gazing at a chained lion, *c·* for a spring,

crowded

t 459–19   turning him loose in the *c·* streets of a city.

crown

a 29– 6   they will have the *c·* of rejoicing.
  44– 2   before the thorns can be laid aside for a *c·*,
s 116–14   They never *c·* the power of Mind as the Messiah,
f 254–31   for through it you win and wear the *c·*.
c 267–30   he shall receive the *c·* of life,— *Jas.* 1 : 12.
t 451– 6   with the *c·* of Love upon her brow,
ap 560– 8   upon her head a *c·* of twelve stars.— *Rev.* 12 : 1.
  562–16   These are the stars in the *c·* of rejoicing.
  565–13   and deprive Herod of his *c·*.

crowned

a 22– 9   these efforts are *c·* with success.
  45– 4   *c·* with the glory of a sublime success,
s 141–12   as kings are *c·* from a royal dynasty.
  141–18   Its only *c·* head is immortal sovereignty.
f 243– 8   It *c·* the demonstrations of Jesus
ap 562–11   The spiritual idea is *c·* with twelve stars.

crowning

s 117–22   his mighty, *c·*, unparalleled, and

crowns

ap 558–12   but a bright promise *c·* its brow.
  562–31   and seven *c·* upon his heads. — *Rev.* 12 : 3.

crucified

a 18– *   *have c· the flesh*— *Gal.* 5 : 24.
  28– 6   he would not have been *c·*.
  39– 7   We need "Christ, and him *c·*."— *I Cor.* 2 : 2.
  43–18   which Jesus taught, and for which he was *c·*,
s 134–11   burned, *c·*, and otherwise persecuted ;
ph 200–26   Jesus Christ, and him *c·*."— *I Cor.* 2 : 2.
b 334–30   a reference to the human sense of Jesus *c·*,

crucifix

f 238– 9   Losing her *c·*, the Roman Catholic girl said,

crucifixion

a 24–20   Does erudite theology regard the *c·* of Jesus
  24–27   The efficacy of the *c·* lay in the
  27–11   proved by his reappearance after the *c·*
  32–29   on the night before his *c·*,
  41–18   lost, about three centuries after the *c·*.
  45–29   the same body that he had before his *c·*,
  46– 2   until they saw him after his *c·*
s 137– 5   not spiritually discerned, . . . until after the *c·*,
b 316–18   rose higher to human view because of the *c·*,
  317–29   proof that he was unchanged by the *c·*.
r 497–20   the *c·* of Jesus and his resurrection
g 555–31   able to present himself unchanged after the *c·*.
ap 564–11   author is convinced that . . . even his *c·*

crucify

sp 94– 9, 10   said : "*C·* him, *c·* him— *John* 19 : 6.
s 134– 2   the cry . . . is repeated, "*C·* him !"— *John* 19 : 6.
gl 597– 9   to spring into action and *c·* God's anointed.

crucifying

b 316–17   by *c·* the flesh.

crude

pref viii–31   but these compositions were *c·*,
f 224– 4   As the *c·* footprints of the past disappear
c 264– 3   The *c·* creations of mortal thought
g 502–14   thus the *c·* forms of human thought

Cruden

g 526–29   The name Eden, according to *C·*,

cruder

ph 189– 6   raises the human thought above the *c·* theories

cruel

b 290–30   and learning that his *c·* mind died not.

cruelty

a 51–25   pride, envy, *c·*, and vengeance,

crumbling

pref vii–16   and the cold conventionality . . . are *c·* away.

crumbs

f 234– 6   with *c·* of comfort from Christ's table,

crusade

f 226– 7   the voice of the herald of this new *c·*

crush

p 407–10   they *c·* out happiness, health, and manhood.

crust

ph 195– 7   All that he ate, except his black *c·*,

cry

a 50– 8   wrung from Jesus' lips the awful *c·*,
  51– 1   wrung from his faithful lips the plaintive *c·*,
s 129–15   and earth will echo the *c·*,
  134– 1   To-day the *c·* of bygone ages is repeated,
ph 194–29   And with no language but a *c·*.
p 442– 7   and there resounded . . . the *c·*, Not guilty.
ap 559–17   Then will a voice from harmony *c·* :

crying
m 64– 1 Want of uniform justice is a c· evil
ph 194–24 a mental infant, c· and chattering
194–27 An infant c· in the night,
194–28 An infant c· for the light,
f 208–19 voice of one c· in the wilderness"— *Matt.* 3 : 3.

cue
c 261–17 sat aching in his chair till his c· was spoken,

culminate
g 549–21 Here these material researches c·

culminates
r 491–20 this belief c· in another belief,

culminating
s 155– 4 law of a general belief, c· in individual faith,
gl 597–10 martyrdom of Jesus was the c· sin of Pharisaism.

culmination
p 380–27 reaches its c· of scientific statement and

cultivated
b 271–14 the result of their c· spiritual understanding

cultivating
ph 197–16 We should master fear, instead of c· it.

cultivation
g 527– 5 Man is God's reflection, needing no c·,

culture
m 61–25 a more solemn charge, than the c· of your
sp 95–12 Whoever reaches this point of moral c·
f 235–13 spiritual c·, which lifts one higher.

cultured
s 128– 7 business men and c· scholars
164– 9 the c· class of medical practitioners
c 255– 8 c· scholars in Rome and in Greece,

cultus
s 133–23 sanitary methods, and a religious c·.

cumulative
p 405–23 the c· effects of a guilty conscience.

cup
Christ's
a 55–25 drinketh of Christ's c· now,
drink this
a 31–23 and drink this c·,— *I Cor.* 11 : 26.
earthly
a 54–21 His earthly c· of bitterness was drained
hemlock
ap 559–28 you must share the hemlock c·
his
pr 5–15 The followers of Christ drank his c·.
10– 9 and are willing to drink his c·,
a 31–19 we drink of his c·, partake of his bread,
33–14 drain to the dregs his c· of sorrow.
33–27 Christians, are you drinking his c·?
33–31 have commemorated Jesus in his c·?
34– 1 willing truly to drink his c·,
34 1? and drunk of his c·,
51– 5 This dread added the drop of gall to his c·.
54–27 those who followed him should drink of his c·,
Jesus'
pr 10– 6 If good enough to profit by Jesus' c·
Master's
b 317– 8 will drink of his Master's c·.
my
ap 578–14 my c· runneth over.— *Psal.* 23 : 5.
of bitterness
a 43 21 because of the c· of bitterness he drank.
of coffee
sp 80– 3 A c· of coffee or tea is not the equal of truth,
of cold water
p 436–11 Giving a c· of cold water in Christ's name,
ap 570–17 Give them a c· of cold water in Christ's name,
of our Lord
a 32–11 nor was the wine, used . . . the c· of our Lord.
of wine
a 32– 8 to pass each guest a c· of wine.
our
a 35–27 Our c· is the cross.
same
a 48–13 when he drinks from the same c·,

a 26– 7 all have the c· of sorrowful effort to drink
32–11 The c· shows forth his bitter experience,
32–12 the c· which he prayed might pass from him,
32–17 took the c·, and gave thanks,— *Matt.* 26 : 27.
53– 7 hence the c· he drank.
m 67– 1 The c· our Father hath given,

cups
b 322–20 Then he turns from his c·,

curable
t 461–22 renders your case less c·,

curative
a 55–11 that c· mission, . . . cannot be left out
s 112– 1 the most effective c· agent in medical practice.
145–15 or reliance on some other minor c·.

curative
s 146–17 Science, the c· agent of God,
152–29 skeptical as to material c· methods.
156– 1 If drugs possess . . . intelligent c· qualities,
157– 9 rests on Mind alone as the c· Principle,
p 369–24 (that is, the preventive and c·) arts

cure (noun)
any
o 348– 6 Ought we not, then, to approve any c·, which
cause and
f 220– 7 to look in other directions for cause and c·.
effecting a
t 460–21 Instead of scientifically effecting a c·,
its
ph 174–31 and its c· comes from the immortal divine Mind.
p 395–23 and then to attempt its c· through Mind.
t 445–26 and is the cause of disease rather than its c·.
of disease
pref xi– 4 results in the c· of disease.
s 147– 4 its present application to the c· of disease.
149– 3 as far outweighs drugs in the c· of disease
t 457–31 Let this Principle be applied to the c· of disease
of sin
s 149– 4 as in the c· of sin.
of the sick
s 132–22 and condemns the c· of the sick and sinning if it
b 285–27 and resort to matter . . . for the c· of the sick.
Principle of the
f 219–26 not comprehending the Principle of the c·,
radical
p 398–31 come to the rescue, to work a radical c·.

———

f 218–13 What renders . . . sickness difficult of c· is,
222–29 In seeking a c· for dyspepsia
p 370–15 faith in the drug is the sole factor in the c·.
402– 5 well-authenticated records of the c·,
t 457–13 cannot . . . both c· and cause disease
457–27 intending thereby to initiate the c·
r 488– 4 the c· shows that you understand this

cure (verb)
an 101–26 seems to alleviate or to c· disease,
s 149–21 remarked . . . mind can never c· organic
151–22 human mind has no power to kill or to c·.
153–21 and it will soon c· the boil.
161–27 the very disease he is trying to c·,
ph 174–22 belief is all that enables a drug to c·
178–17 that chronic case is not difficult to c·.
180–31 dissolve a tumor, or c· organic disease,
188–24 What causes disease cannot c· it.
197–23 would not c· dyspepsia at this period.
f 208–15 to suppose that matter can both cause and c·
221– 2 adopted the Graham system to c· dyspepsia.
233–29 The counter fact . . . is required to c· it.
o 359– 3 Let any clergyman try to c· his friends by
p 366– 3 to c· his patient, the metaphysician must
373– 5 easier to c· the most malignant disease than
373– 6 easier . . . to c· than to c· sin.
375–25 and you c· the palsy,
377– 8 Then is the time to c· them through C. S.,
378–20 drilling and drugging, adopted to c· matter,
392– 4 To c· a bodily ailment,
399– 5 can matter c· what matter has caused?
412–16 To prevent disease or to c· it,
417–24 since it is demonstrable that the way to c·
417–31 divine Mind can c· by opposite thoughts.
424–28 To prevent or c· scrofula

cured
m 68–19 and a Christian Scientist c· her.
s 149–23 author has c· what is termed organic disease
149–24 as readily as she has c· purely functional disease,
152–15 once apparently c· a case of paralysis
153–10 c· a patient sinking in the last stage of typhoid
156–27 employing no other means, and she was c·.
ph 169–19 all disease is c· by divine Mind.
181–27 if they are c·, they generally know it
184–27 A woman, whom I c· of consumption,
193–25 his physician claims to have c· him,
o 355–30 and evidenced by the sick who are c·
p 373–19 The fear occasioned by ignorance can be c·;
383– 1 was c· when I learned my way in C. S."
389–32 I c· her in a few minutes.
398–10 Often he gave no name to the distemper he c·.
400– 4 and therefore the disease is thoroughly c·.

cures
s 109–18 c· were produced in primitive Christian healing
138–10 explained his c·, which appeared miraculous
ph 179– 1 perform the sudden c· of which it is capable ;
f 208– 8 which causes disease and c· it?
o 344–29 while C. S. c· its hundred ?
359– 5 will take the same cases, and c· will follow.
p 395–10 The same Principle c· both sin and sickness.
404–27 Both c· require the same method
g 546–29 for it c· on a divine demonstrable Principle

curing
p 414– 8 The arguments to be used in c· insanity

current
sp 97– 9 and the electric c· swift,
an 106– 5 push vainly against the c· running heavenward.
p 379–22 The so-called vital c· does not affect
g 548–20 many general statements now c·,

currents
a 24– 9 healing c· of Truth are pointed out.
sp 99–23 The calm, strong c· of true spirituality,
ph 185–10 discussed . . . the earth's magnetic c·

curse
pr 9–13 and bless them that c· us ;
a 30–18 Love, which blesses even those that c· it.
b 340–28 equalizes the sexes ; annuls the c· on man,
g 557–17 the c· will be removed which says to woman,
gl 579–17 ADAM. Error ; . . . a c· ;

cursed
g 532–10 Adam and his progeny were c·,
535–22 c· is the ground for thy sake ;— Gen. 3 : 17.
541–29 And now art thou c· from the earth.— Gen. 4 : 11.

curses
g 524–27 for God presently c· the ground.

cursing
a 20–17 returning blessing for c·, he taught mortals

curtain
g 557–20 and lifts the c· on man as never born

curve
b 282–14 finds no abiding-place in a c·,
282–15 a c· finds no adjustment to a straight line.
282–22 Even though they seem to touch, one is still a c·
283–30 by calling a c· a straight line

cuspids
f 247– 6 incisors, c·, bicuspids, and one molar.

custody
p 436–25 compelled to let him be taken into c·,
439–13 Health-officer had Mortal Man in c·,

custom
pr 12–22 The common c· of praying for the recovery of
a 32– 7 Among the Jews it was an ancient c·
ph 176– 7 The primitive c· of taking no thought about
f 247–12 C·, education, and fashion form the
p 362–13 According to the c· of those days,

customary
f 229–17 This c· belief is misnamed material law,
p 363– 6 as was c· with women of her grade.

cut
pref vii–24 and to c· the rough granite.
a 27–19 to c· down the false doctrine of pantheism,
s 141– 7 c· off the right hand and pluck out the right
f 212–11 a finger which had been c· off for months.
r 474– 8 worse cords than those which c· the flesh.

cuticle
p 382–10 or to remove unhealthy exhalations from the c·

cuts
p 404–18 c· down every tree that brings not forth

Cutter
ph 170– 8 Did Jesus . . . less than Graham or C·?
175–22 was not discussed according to C·

cutting
f 224–19 modern lash is less material . . . but it is equally as c·.

cycles
s 135–31 as must be the case in the c· of divine light.
b 319–13 the infinite c· of eternal existence,

Cyclops
s 164– 2 the groping of Homer's C· around his cave."

D

daily
pr 4–19 expressed in d· watchfulness and in
17– 4 Give us this day our d· bread ;— Matt. 6 : 11.
a 21– 1 If Truth is overcoming error in your d· walk
25– 9 as he went d· about his Father's business.
40–30 public worship instead of d· deeds.
s 121–27 besides turning d· on its own axis.
ph 179– 3 and following Christ in the d· life.
f 220– 1 We hear it said : "I exercise d· in the open air.
245– 9 she stood d· before the window watching
b 272–20 It is the . . . Christianization of d· life,
283–28 We must . . . live it in d· life ;
o 350– 4 or as very far removed from d· experience,
p 413–12 d· ablutions of an infant are no more natural
413–19 without scrubbing the whole surface d·.
431– 6 the prisoner attended to his d· labors,
431–29 testifies : . . . I practise d· ablutions
g 557– 1 and repeated this operation d·,

dam
b 338–15 it reads, a d·, or obstruction.
338–21 Here a d· is not a mere play upon words ;

damnation
s 150–25 predestination of souls to d· or salvation.

damned
a 38– 6 doctrine . . . few to be saved, while the rest are d· ;

damp
ph 175–26 D· atmosphere and freezing snow

damsel
p 398–12 "D·, I say unto thee, arise !"— Mark 5 : 41.

Dan
gl 583–26 definition of

dance
f 250–28 Upon this stage . . . goes on the d· of mortal mind.

danger
belief of
p 374–23 You cannot forget the belief of d·,
disease and
p 411–29 their exemption from disease and d·.
great
t 445–27 great d· in teaching Mind-healing indiscriminately,
hopeless
p 375–28 when they are supposed to be in hopeless d·.
humanity sees
p 371–12 sick humanity sees d· in every direction,
seen the
ap 571–14 unfaithful stewards who have seen the d·

pr 7–27 The d· from prayer is that it may

danger
s 135–17 d· of repeating the offence of the Jews
ph 169– 5 mental signs, assuring me that d· was over,
p 381– 9 you say that there is d·.
381– 9 This fear is the d· and induces

dangerous
s 147–32 Jesus never spoke of disease as d·
ph 178– 9 is not d· because of its priority
f 228– 9 we shall have no d· inheritances,
b 299–22 judge the knowledge . . . to be untrue and d·.
p 376– 8 diseases deemed d· sometimes come from the
t 445–10 Teach the d· possibility of dwarfing the
446–17 or his demonstration is protracted, d·,
456– 4 is most d· quackery.

Daniel
g 514–27 D· felt safe in the lions' den,

dare
o 357–14 how d· we attempt to destroy what He

dares
p 387– 4 Who d· to say that actual Mind can be over worked?
r 489–19 Who d· to say that the senses of man
493–30 Who d· to doubt this consummate test
g 531–21 Who d· to say either that God is in

daring
f 223–30 but the awful d· of sin destroys sin,

dark
a 35– 3 the fruitlessness of their toil in the d·
47–25 His d· plot fell to the ground,
sp 86–18 apparitions brought out in d· seances
an 102–18 hidden in the d· recesses of mortal thought,
s 163–32 said : . . . D· and perplexed, our devious career
ph 200– 1 When Homer sang . . . Olympus was d·,
c 263– 9 he will no longer grope in the d·
p 371– 7 telling ghost-stories in the d·.
403–24 d· forebodings regarding disease
418–31 d· images of mortal thought,
428– 4 resolves the d· visions of material sense
g 502– 6 the light over the d·,
ap 558–12 seems at first obscure, abstract, and d· ;
559–12 It is heard in the desert and in d· places of fear.
566– 2 d· ebbing and flowing tides of human fear,
gl 596–23 Though the way is d· in mortal sense,

darkened
sp 93–22 belief that Spirit is finite . . . has d· all history.

darkening
s 139–21 d· to some extent the inspired pages.

darkest
sp 96–11 "The d· hour precedes the dawn."

darkness

accustomed to
t 452– 9   eyes accustomed to *d·* are pained by
amid the
sp 95–24   Led by a solitary star amid the *d·*,
and chaos
r 479–23   *D·* and chaos are the imaginary opposites
and dogma
f 244–28   cast us headlong into *d·* and dogma.
and doubt
g 551–24   *D·* and doubt encompass thought,
and light
sp 74–21   *D·* and light, infancy and manhood,
believe that
f 215–15   sometimes led to believe that *d·* is
cannot see in
t 452– 8   we cannot see in *d·*.
comes in
a 42– 8   comes in *d·* and disappears with the light.
deep
ap 569–17   They are dwellers still in the deep *d·* of belief.
dismal
ph 195– 5   Outside of dismal *d·* and cold silence
fall in the
t 463– 4   and so he may stumble and fall in the *d·*.
flees
b 310–11   *d·* flees when the earth has again turned
gives place
pref xi–13   as necessarily as *d·* gives place to light
induces fear
p 371–14   *D·* induces fear.
light and
ph 186–10   light and *d·*, cannot mingle.
b 281– 5   no more commingle than light and *d·*.
r 474–32   for light and *d·* cannot dwell together.
light destroys
sp 72–10   As light destroys *d·*
loses the appearance
f 215–18   *d·* loses the appearance of reality.
material
g 504–20   not implied by material *d·* and dawn.
obscures light
g 504–29   and *d·* obscures light.
of error
ph 191–15   chasing away the *d·* of error.
of vacuity
r 480– 6   there remains only the *d·* of vacuity
or gloom
f 248– 7   instead of lapsing into *d·* or gloom.
saith to the
g 503–13   saith to the *d·* upon the face of error,
Science affirms
f 215–16   Science affirms *d·* to be only a
shine in the
g 546–25   like rays of light, shine in the *d·*,
shineth in
b 325–31   the light, "shineth in *d·*,— *John* 1 : 5.
shining in
o 347–21   and is the light shining in *d*,
sleep is
g 556–19   Sleep is *d·*, but God's creative mandate was, ,
turns from
t 459– 1   as the flower turns from *d·* to light.
walketh in
m 56–16   pestilence that walketh in *d·*,— *Psal.* 91 : 6.
walking in
p 374–22   It is like walking in *d·*
was upon the face
r 479–20   *d·* was upon the face of — *Gen.* 1 : 2.
g 503– 7   *d·* was upon the face of — *Gen.* 1 : 2.

———

sp 72–10   and in the place of *d·* all is light,
   74–24   that *d·* can represent light,
ph 188–28   When *d·* comes over the earth,
b 325–31   *d·* comprehended it not." — *John* 1 : 5.
   338–18   "*d·* . . . upon the face of — *Gen.* 1 : 2.
o 347–31   which the *d·* comprehends not.
p 371–17   adult must be taken out of his *d·*,
   373– 2   but are in *d·* as to the physical exemption which
r 475– 1   Light extinguishes the *d·*,
g 503–27   divided the light from the *d·*.— *Gen.* 1 : 4.
   504– 4   and the *d·* He called Night.— *Gen.* 1 : 5.
   504–29   contradiction of Spirit is matter, *d·*,
   511–10   to divide the light from the *d·* — *Gen.* 1 : 18.
   528–19   Beginning creation with *d·* instead of light,
   539–25   "What communion hath light with *d·*? — *II Cor.* 6 : 14.
g 546–25   though the *d·*, . . . may deny their reality.
gl 592–21   NIGHT. *D·*; doubt; fear.
   596–20   VALLEY. Depression; meekness; *d·*.
   597–16   WILDERNESS. Loneliness; doubt; *d·*.

Darwin

g 543–20   May not *D·* be right in thinking that
   551–10   Mr. *D·* admits this, but he

Darwin's

g 547–15   *D·* theory of evolution
   547–17   Briefly, this is *D·* theory,

dashing

gl 593–16   muddy, foaming, and *d·*, it is a type of error.

data

f 246–17   Chronological *d·* are no part of the vast forever.

date

pref ix–12   Certain essays written at that early *d·*
   xii– 3   up to that *d·*, hers was the only College of
an 104– 4   as they will be at no distant *d·*,

dates

1775
an 100– 2   first brought into notice by Mesmer . . . in 1775.
1784
an 100–12   In 1784, the French government ordered the
1837
an 101– 8   In 1837, a committee of nine persons was
1862
pref viii–28   As early as 1862 she began to write down
1866
pref viii–26   experiences which led her, in the year 1866,
s 107– 1   In the year 1866, I discovered the Christ Science
1867
pref ix–24   From 1867 until 1875, copies were,
   ix–29   This was during the years 1867 and 1868.
   xi–27   in Lynn, Massachusetts, about the year 1867.
1868
pref ix–29   This was during the years 1867 and 1868.
1870
pref ix–21   Her first pamphlet, . . . copyrighted in 1870 ;
r 465– 2   the author's class-book, copyrighted in 1870.
1875
pref ix–24   From 1867 until 1875, copies were,
   x– 4   SCIENCE AND HEALTH was published in 1875.
r 465– 4   she revised that treatise for this volume in 1875
1876
pref ix–22   but it did not appear in print until 1876,
1880
s 161–11   In 1880, Massachusetts put her foot on a
1881
pref xi–27   In 1881, she opened the Metaphysical College
1883
pref xii– 2   No charters were granted . . . after 1883,
1889, October 29
pref xii–14   She closed her College, October 29, 1889,
1891
pref xii–18   preparation of the revision . . . in 1891.
1899
pref xii–19   reopened the College in 1899
1907, June 10
pref xii–20   Until June 10, 1907, she had never

daughter

f 237– 9   mental height their little *d·* . . . attained.
p 398–10   To the synagogue ruler's *d·*,

daughters

g 503– 5   highest ideas are the sons and *d·* of God
   515–22   family name for all ideas,— the sons and *d·* of

dauntless

m 67– 9   even the *d·* seaman is not sure of his safety ;

David

ph 200– 4   law of Sinai lifted thought into the song of *D·*.
k 499– *   He that hath the key of *D·*,— *Rev.* 3 : 7.
gl 579– *   He that hath the key of *D·*,— *Rev.* 3 : 7.

Davy, Sir Humphry

s 152–14   It is related that Sir Humphry *D·*

dawn

pref vii– 9   across a night of error should *d·* the morning beams
a 35–10   in the *d·* of a new light
sp 95–23   Midnight foretells the *d·*.
   95–26   the light which heralds Christ's eternal *d·*
   96–11   "The darkest hour precedes the *d·*."
f 246–15   should *d·* upon the enraptured sense
b 298– 3   They *d·* in faith and glow full-orbed
o 354–24   with the *d·* Truth will waken men spiritually
g 504–20   not implied by material darkness and *d·*.
   506–13   Thus the *d·* of ideas goes on,

dawned

t 457– 7   Since the divine light of C. S. first *d·*

dawning

g 546–23   C. S. is *d·* upon a material age.

dawns

s 144– 7   Withdraws the star, when *d·* the sun's brave
ph 191–10   Principle of man *d·* upon human thought,
b 308–25   the light of Truth and Love *d·* upon thee.

Day

a 43–10   which so illuminated the Pentecostal *D·*
g 504– 3   And God called the light *D·*,— *Gen.* 1 : 5.

day

and night
ap 568–17   before our God *d·* and night.— *Rev.* 12 : 10.
close of
a 32–31   a sad supper taken at the close of *d·*,
each
a 21–13   gain a little each *d·* in the right direction,
f 248–11   which each *d·* brings to a nearer tomb.
p 413–23   need not wash his little body all over each *d·*
every
sp 70– 1   Every *d·* is a mystery.
f 233– 1   Every *d·* makes its demands upon us
c 261–16   he hobbled every *d·* to the theatre,
p 413–14   taking a fish out of water every *d·*
fifth
g 513– 5   and the morning were the fifth *d·*.— *Gen.* 1 : 23.
first
g 504– 5   and the morning were the first *d·*.— *Gen.* 1 : 5.
gl 584– 3   and the morning were the first *d·*."— *Gen.* 1 : 5.
fourth
g 511–16   and the morning were the fourth *d·*.— *Gen.* 1 : 19.
future
s 150–24   and will be to all others at some future *d·*,
gala
f 252–23   says: . . . make my short span of life one gala *d·*,
God's
gl 584– 7   This unfolding is God's *d·*,
happy
a 55–17   My weary hope tries to realize that happy *d·*,
its
sp 95–21   even human invention must have its *d·*,
later
pr 7–32   or mean to ask forgiveness at some later *d·*.
next
ph 193–18   The next *d·* I saw him in the yard.
of salvation
a 39–19   now is the *d·* of salvation,"— *II Cor.* 6 : 2.
sp 93– 8   now is the *d·* of salvation,"— *II Cor.* 6 : 2.
of Spirit
g 505– 1   No . . . . planetary revolutions form the *d·* of Spirit.
of wrath
b 339–15   "wrath against the *d·* of wrath."— *Rom.* 2 : 5.
one
s 156–20   she would give up her medicine for one *d·*,
g 504–22   "one *d·* is with the Lord as — *II Pet.* 3 : 8.
gl 598–21   "One *d·* is with the Lord as— *II Pet.* 3 : 8.
orb of
ph 188–31   The human eye knows not where the orb of *d·* is,
189–12   when the orb of *d·* disappears,
our
pr 5–18   giving us strength according to our *d·*.
perfect
p 388–29   In that perfect *d·* of understanding,
r 496–13   brighter "unto the perfect *d·*."— *Prov.* 4 : 18.
ap 562–20   shines "unto the perfect *d·*"— *Prov.* 4 : 18.
present
o 349– 4   the rabbis of the present *d·* ask
risen
pref vii– 4   ere cometh the full radiance of a risen *d·*.
second
g 506– 9   and the morning were the second *d·*.— *Gen.* 1 : 8.
seventh
g 519–22   And on the seventh *d·* God ended His—*Gen.* 2 : 2.
519–24   He rested on the seventh *d·*— *Gen.* 2 : 2.
sixth
g 518–26   and the morning were the sixth *d·*.— *Gen.* 1 : 31.
some
m 69–20   Some *d·* the child will ask his parent :
f 228–14   Mortals will some *d·* assert their freedom
suppositional
g 533–25   but error has its suppositional *d·*
that
sp 95–21   we want that *d·* to be succeeded by C. S.,
b 292– 3   "but of that *d·* and hour,— *Matt.* 24 : 36.
their
a 52–26   speaking not for their *d·* only
c 264– 2   They have their *d·* before the permanent facts
third
s 156–23   but on the third *d·* she again suffered,
g 508–27   and the morning were the third *d·*.— *Gen.* 1 : 13.
509– 6   he rose from the grave,— on the third *d·*
this
pr 17– 4   Give us this *d·* our daily bread ;— *Matt.* 6 : 11.

s 116–15   nor do they carry the *d·* against physical
ph 174–13   the *d·* is at hand"— *Rom.* 13 : 12.
197–10   "In the *d·* that thou eatest— *Gen.* 2 : 17.
b 308–24   "Let me go, for the *d·* breaketh ;"— *Gen.* 32 : 26.
310–11   *D·* may decline and shadows fall,
r 481–18   "In the *d·* that thou eatest— *Gen.* 2 : 17.
g 509–10   to divide the *d·* from the night ;— *Gen.* 1 : 14.
510–14   the greater light to rule the *d·*,— *Gen.* 1 : 16.
511– 9   and to rule over the *d·*— *Gen.* 1 : 18.
520–17   in the *d·* that the Lord God— *Gen.* 2 : 4.
527– 9   in the *d·* that thou eatest— *Gen.* 2 : 17.

day

g 530–14   in the *d·* ye eat thereof,— *Gen.* 3 : 5.
532– 8   "In the *d·* that thou eatest— *Gen.* 2 : 17.
543–31   "In the *d·* that the Lord God— *Gen.* 2 : 4.
ap 566–10   a pillar of cloud by *d·* and of fire by night,
575–20   shall not be shut at all by *d·* :— *Rev.* 21 : 25.
gl 584– 1   definition of

day-dreams

sp 88– 1   In our *d·* we can recall

Day of Pentecost

a 47– 9   an overwhelming power as on the *D· of P·*.

days (see also days')

ancient
o 349– 3   As Paul asked of the unfaithful in ancient *d·*,
Ancient of
s 146–29   as ancient as "the Ancient of *d·*."— *Dan.* 7 : 9.
and seasons
g 509–25   the *d·* and seasons of Mind's creation,
and years
g 509–11   and for *d·*, and years.— *Gen.* 1 : 14.
earthly
s 150–27   by physical conditions all his earthly *d·*,
ph 197– 6   costs many a man his earthly *d·* of comfort.
few
g 536–21   "of few *d·*, and full of trouble."— *Job* 14 : 1.
552–15   of few *d·*, and full of trouble."— *Job* 14 : 1.
his
ph 190–23   As for man, his *d·* are as grass :— *Psal.* 103 : 15.
r 476–24   "As for man, his *d·* are as grass :— *Psal.* 103 : 15.
g 530– 1   increases in falsehood and his *d·* become
latter
sp 83– 9   in order to escape the error of these latter *d·*.
b 320–31   yet in the latter *d·* he should stand
length of
b 283–25   demonstrated in length of *d·*,
of my life
ap 578–16   follow me all the *d·* of my life ;— *Psal.* 23 : 6.
our
p 409–29   We cannot spend our *d·* here in ignorance of
r 487–28   lengthens our *d·* by strengthening our trust
seven
g 520–10   The numerals of infinity, called *seven d·*,
six
a 21–30   After following the sun for six *d·*,
these
g 520–12   These *d·* will appear as mortality disappears,
those
s 107–18   the prospect of those *d·* in which we must say,
129–13   In those *d·* there will be
ph 175–23   man's belief in those *d·* was not so severe upon
p 362–13   According to the custom of those *d·*,
ap 562– 1   John saw in those *d·* the spiritual idea
three
a 27–13   in three *d·* I [Spirit] will raise it up."—*John* 2 : 19.
45–13   Three *d·* after his bodily burial he
b 314–15   in three *d·* I will raise it up,"— *John* 2 : 19.
r 494– 3   in three *d·* I [Mind] will— *John* 2 : 19.
two
s 156–22   she could get along two *d·* without globules ;
f 202–17   The *d·* of our pilgrimage will multiply
b 333–18   without beginning of years or end of *d·*.
g 535–23   all the *d·* of thy life :— *Gen.* 3 : 17.

days'

a 44– 7   His three *d·* work in the sepulchre

daystar

pref vii–11   follow this *d·* of divine Science,

dead

are raised
a 27– 5   the deaf hear, the *d·* are raised,— *Luke* 7 : 22.
s 132– 7   the deaf hear, the *d·* are raised— *Matt.* 11 : 5.
Lazarus from the
s 134–27   and he raised Lazarus from the *d·*,
raised the
m 67–22   raised the *d·*, and commanded even the wind
b 273–26   healed the sick, and raised the *d·*
raises the
a 33–24   raises the *d·* from trespasses and sins,
raise the
a 51–32   cast out evil, and raise the *d·*.
s 137– 3   cast out evil, raise the *d·* ;
b 329– 8   Because you cannot . . . raise the *d·*,
raising the
a 43– 1   healing the sick, and raising the *d·*,
b 316–29   casting out evils, . . . and raising the *d·*,
p 369– 9   raising the *d·*, and walking over the wave.
430– 3   healing the dying and raising the *d·*.
so-called
sp 74–30   so-called *d·* and living cannot commune
75– 3   The so-called *d·*, in order to reappear
75– 7   could take no cognizance of the so-called *d·*.
77–28   Spiritism consigns the so-called *d·* to a
81– 2   between the so-called *d·* and the living,

a 23–15   "Faith without works is *d·*."— *Jas.* 2 : 26.

dead

a	31–14	He attached no importance to *d·* ceremonies.
	34– 3	Then why ascribe this inspiration to a *d·* rite,
	44–28	His disciples believed Jesus to be *d·* while he
	45–26	for they believed his body to be *d·*.
m	69–29	and the resurrection from the *d·*,— *Luke* 20 : 35.
sp	75–26	those living on the earth and those called *d·*,
s	113– 7	Without this, the letter is but the *d·* body
	136–17	These prophets were considered *d·*,
	164–18	we should not be *d·*.
ph	187–29	this so-called mind then calls itself *d·* ;
f	216– 3	Who shall say that man . . . may be *d·* to-morrow?
	228–31	excel the influence of their *d·* faith and
	251–10	(1) that they are not *d·* ;
b	295–30	It further teaches that when man is *d·*,
	312– 9	People say, "Man is *d·* ;"
	316–29	those *d·* in trespasses and sins,
	334–26	I am he that liveth, and was *d·*— *Rev.* 1 : 18.
o	341– *	*raised up Jesus from the d·* — *Rom.* 8 : 11.
	341– *	*He that raised up Christ from the d·* — *Rom.* 8 : 11.
	355–10, 11	let the *d·* bury their *d·*." — *Matt.* 8 : 22.
p	369–27	Unscientific methods are finding their *d·* level.
	398– 6	and he was as one *d·*," — *Mark* 9 : 26.
	398–11	synagogue ruler's daughter, whom they called *d·*
	398–12	"she is not *d·*, but sleepeth," — *Luke* 8 : 52.
	416–21	only in mortal mind, as the *d·* body proves ;
	427–32	its own material declaration, "I am *d·*,"
	433–25	sentenced to be tortured until he is *d·*.
r	479–16	Does that which we call *d·* ever see,

deadened
a	55– 2	from a *d·* sense of the invisible God,

deadly
b	328–24	if they drink any *d·* thing,— *Mark* 16 : 18.
p	362– *	*if they drink any d· thing,— Mark* 16 : 18.
t	458–20	Sin makes *d·* thrusts at the Christian Scientist

deadness
p	399–21	this *d·* shows that so-called mortal life

deaf
a	27– 5	the *d·* hear, the dead are raised,— *Luke* 7 : 22.
s	132– 7	*d·* hear, the dead are raised— *Matt.* 11 : 5.
ph	183–28	hearing to the *d·*, voice to the dumb,
	194–12	if mortal mind says, "I am *d·* and blind,"
f	210–13	hearing to the *d·*, feet to the lame,
	213–24	Beethoven, who was so long hopelessly *d·*.
	226–25	The lame, the *d·*, the dumb, the blind,
o	342–25	causes the *d·* to hear, the lame to walk,
p	398– 2	"Thou dumb and *d·* spirit,— *Mark* 9 : 25.
t	444–23	If . . . medical schools turn a *d·* ear to
r	487–11	gave . . . hearing to the *d·* centuries ago,

deafness
ph	194–11	not necessary to ensure *d·* and blindness ;
r	486–29	then palsy, blindness, and *d·* would

deal
s	148–19	and *d·* — the one wholly, the other primarily
p	005–22	and *d·* with his patients compassionately ;
g	552– 7	hypotheses *d·* with causation as contingent on

dealer
p	438–28	is not an importer or *d·* in fur,

dealing
o	349–18	in *d·* with spiritual ideas.
	355– 4	methods of *d·* with sin and disease
t	446– 3	and in this way *d·* pitilessly with

deals
s	157– 2	C. S. *d·* wholly with the mental cause
p	423–15	The matter-physician *d·* with matter
t	463– 1	discerns and *d·* with the real cause of disease.
g	535–10	Divine Science *d·* its chief blow at the

dealt
b	329– 3	will be fairly *d·* with ; they will be sought and
t	460–17	*d·* with through right apprehension of

dear
pr	9–30	in the footsteps of our *d·* Master?
a	34–24	for soon their *d·* Master would rise
f	253– 9	I hope, *d·* reader, I am leading you into
o	360–13	*D·* reader, which mind-picture or
p	366– 1	sense of the *d·* Father's loving-kindness.
g	547– 6	You can prove for yourself, *d·* reader,
ap	573–29	Take heart, *d·* sufferer, for this reality
	574–25	Think of this, *d·* reader, for it will

dear-bought
a	36–11	that he might pour his *d·* bounty into
	54–11	liberally pour his *d·* treasures

dearer
f	239–19	If divine Love is becoming nearer, *d·*,

dearest
m	58–21	Home is the *d·* spot on earth,

Death
p	432–21	I am *D·*. I was called for,
	439– 6	*D·* testified that he was absent

Death
p	439– 9	At this request *D·* repaired to the spot
	439–22	his struggles against liver-complaint and *D·*.
	440–10	a verdict delivering Mortal Man to *D·*.

death
after
a	24–24	only for the presentation, after *d·*,
	35–16	his probation in the flesh after *d·*,
	36– 6	sufficient suffering, either before or after *d·*,
sp	81– 9	a continued existence after *d·*
b	291–24	so shall he be after *d·*, until
p	409–28	will not depend on it after *d·*.
	429–21	If we live after *d·* and are immortal,
r	486–15	body was the same immediately after *d·*

and finiteness
r	469– 5	*D·* and finiteness are unknown to Life.

and matter
r	486–19	conditional upon *d·* and matter,

and mortality
b	295–31	resurrected from *d·* and mortality.

and the grave
a	39–14	Jesus overcame *d·* and the grave
	45– 7	in his victory over *d·* and the grave.
	49–24	over sin, sickness, *d·*, and the grave.
s	137– 6	sickness, sin, disease, *d·*, and the grave.

an enemy
a	39–13	The Bible calls *d·* an enemy,

announcing the
p	386–17	mistakenly announcing the *d·* of a friend,

because of
b	314– 1	no more perfect because of *d·*

bed of
p	427–26	Called to the bed of *d·*, what material

before
ph	187–32	a body like the one it had before *d·*.

belief called
p	380– 3	which ends in a belief called *d·*,

belief in
a	42– 5	The universal belief in *d·* is of no advantage.
b	289–22	law of mortal mind, in a belief in *d·*.
	325– 2	he who perceives . . . loses his belief in *d·*.
p	426–11	If the belief in *d·* were obliterated,
	430– 8	When man gives up his belief in *d·*,

birth and
f	246–18	Time-tables of birth and *d·* are so many

birth nor
f	244–24	He has neither birth nor *d·*.

birth or
f	206–25	Can there be any birth or *d·* for man,

bleeding to
p	379–10	fancied himself bleeding to *d·*,

bring forth
p	392– 3	Only while . . . sin remains can it bring forth *d·*.

brink of
f	235–22	To the tremblers on the brink of *d·* ,

brought
p	426–28	Sin brought *d·*, and death will disappear with
g	532– 7	when eating its first fruits brought *d·* ?

called
f	254–17	prior to the change called *d·*,
b	290–16	If the change called *d·* destroyed the belief
r	487– 6	both before and after that which is called *d·*.
ap	572–24	stage in human experience called *d·*,

can never
sp	76–29	*D·* can never hasten this state of

caused the
p	379–17	Oxford boys, who caused the *d·* of a man,

cessation of
ap	573–27	conscious, here and now, of a cessation of *d·*,

decay, and
g	544– 7	Birth, decay, and *d·* arise from the

decreed the
ap	565–10	Herod decreed the *d·* of every male child

deny
s	113–19	Life, God, omnipotent good, deny *d·*,

despair and
p	433–15	a look of despair and *d·* settles upon it.

destroyed by his
a	50–24	and that all evidence . . . was destroyed by his *d·*.

destroying
f	210– 8	casting out evils, and destroying *d·*,

dew of
ph	193– 9	The dew of *d·* was on his brow.

discord and
s	124–10	and holding fast to discord and *d·*.
f	224–10	life and peace instead of discord and *d·*.

disease and
(see disease)

disease, nor
s	140–27	causeth no evil, disease, nor *d·*.
p	368–22	disease, nor *d·* can be spiritual,

disease, sin, and
sp	78– 3	like the discords of disease, sin, and *d·*,
b	275–29	such as matter, disease, sin, and *d·*,
p	412–15	and to destroy disease, sin, and *d·*.

death

dream of
p 427–29   dream of *d·* must be mastered by Mind
429–17   Mortals waken from the dream of *d·*

end in
b 331– 5   subject to their limitations and would end in *d·*.

ends in
b 307–16   false sense of an existence which ends in *d·*.
309–29   such so-called life always ends in *d·*.

error and
a 44– 1   must seal the victory over error and *d·*,
gl 539–10   such as evil, matter, error, and *d·*?

evidence of
gl 584–15   Any material evidence of *d·* is false,

experience of
b 291–10   belief in the experience of *d·*

faith in
p 426–23   The relinquishment of all faith in *d·*

fear of
gl 596–25   destroy . . . the fear of *d·*,

foundations of
ph 171–16   destroying the foundations of *d·*.

frighten into
sp 79– 4   error that tends to frighten into *d·*

has no dominion
o 347– 5   all is Life, and *d·* has no dominion.

hastening to
sp 78– 7   belief that we are . . . hastening to *d·*,

health-laws, and
p 413–27   illusions about disease, health-laws, and *d·*,

ignominy and
an 105–27   down to the depths of ignominy and *d·*.

illusion
f 251– 9   In the illusion of *d·*, mortals wake to the
r 493–29   awakened Lazarus from the dream, illusion, of *d·*,

instantaneous
p 377–16   has caused what is termed instantaneous *d·*.

instant of
b 290–24   which possess us at the instant of *d·*

instead of
f 253–30   which is the law of Life instead of *d·*,
p 435–14   and life instead of *d·*.

interval of
gl 598–27   would bridge over . . . the interval of *d·*,

is not the result
r 486–12   *D·* is not the result of Truth

is swallowed up
s 164–28   *D·* is swallowed up in victory"— *I Cor.* 15 : 54.
r 496–27   *D·* is swallowed up in victory."— *I Cor.* 15 : 54.

is the illusion
p 428– 3   Life is real, and *d·* is the illusion.

Jesus'
a 24–23   Does spiritualism find Jesus' *d·* necessary

Jesus overcame
a 39–14   Jesus overcame *d·* and the grave

life and
(see **life**)

Life destroys
b 339– 2   Divine Life destroys *d·*,

Life over
p 406–23   Life over *d·*, and good over evil,

master of
b 316–19   proved that Truth was the master of *d·*.

matter and
b 289–29   Matter and *d·* are mortal illusions.

must be overcome
sp 76–30   for *d·* must be overcome, not submitted to,

never see
sp 70– *   *he shall never see d·.*— *John* 8 : 51.
f 217–13   he shall never see *d·* !"— *John* 8 : 51.
p 428– 8   he shall never see *d·*."— *John* 8 : 51.
429–32   he shall never see *d·*."— *John* 8 : 51.
438– 7   he shall never see *d·*.— *John* 8 : 51.

no
b 288–26   no birth, no material life, and no *d·*.
331–16   all is Life, and there is no *d·*.
p 387– 2   and know that there is no *d·*.
426–13   understanding obtained that there is no *d·*,
428– 1   "There is no *d·*, no inaction,
429– 3   by the understanding that there is no *d·*,

no partnership with
f 243–27   Life has no partnership with *d·*.

no reality in
p 427– 9   learning that there is no reality in *d·*,

not
r 485–18   Not *d·*, but the understanding of Life,

not subject to
sp 74– 2   spiritual life which is not subject to *d·*.
b 288–25   that Life is not subject to *d·* ;

not the
b 271–14   the eternal life, not the *d·*, of Jesus,
296–11   not the *d·* of organic matter,

of these errors
b 290–25   but endure until the *d·* of these errors.

overcome
p 427–18   If man is never to overcome *d·*, why do the

death

overcomes
b 289–15   Truth, overcame and still overcomes *d·*
315–24   heals sickness, and overcomes *d·*,

persecuted unto
s 134– 6   were so often persecuted unto *d·*,

physical
an 101–25   lead to moral and to physical *d·*.

power of
r 473–15   and destroying the power of *d·*.

power over
a 26–25   and of his demonstration of power over *d·*.

punishable with
p 431–10   this offence is deemed punishable with *d·*.

punished with
p 432–15   treated as a criminal and punished with *d·*.

regarding
sp 79– 6   changing the patient's thoughts regarding *d·*.

resort to
b 306– 4   and then resort to *d·* to reproduce

resulted in the
o 342–32   if their treatment resulted in the *d·* of a patient.

resulting in
gl 591–10   MATTER. . . . life resulting in *d·*,

second
sp 77–12   "the second *d·* hath no power."— *Rev.* 20 : 6.
b 290–14   the second *d·* hath no power."— *Rev.* 20 : 6.

seemed to be
a 46–21   unchanged . . . after what seemed to be *d·*

[seeming]
a 45–11   by the [seeming] *d·* of His Son,— *Rom.* 5 : 10.

sentence of
p 433–19   the solemn sentence of *d·* upon the prisoner.
436– 3   for which Mortal Man is under sentence of *d·*.
436–33   pronounced a sentence of *d·* for doing right.

shadow of
ap 578–11   valley of the shadow of *d·*,— *Psal.* 23 : 4.
gl 596–22   valley of the shadow of *d·*,— *Psal.* 23 : 4.

shall not see
b 325– 1   "He . . . shall not see *d·*."— see *John* 11 : 26.

shame and
a 52–16   putting to shame and *d·* the best man that

shuts the door on
sp 90–26   This conviction shuts the door on *d·*,

sickness and
(see **sickness**)

sickness, sin, and
(see **sickness**)

sickness, sin, nor
p 381–18   In . . . Love there is no sickness, sin, nor *d·*,

sickness, sin, or
t 463–23   manifested in forms of sickness, sin, or *d·*

sin and
(see **sin**)

sin, disease, and
(see **sin**)

sin, disease, or
f 253–17   overcome the belief in sin, disease, or *d·*.
253–26   Do not believe in . . . sin, disease, or *d·*,
p 330– 9   the demands of sin, disease, or *d·*,

sin or
s 125–19   cannot be controlled by sin or *d·*,

sin, sickness, and
(see **sin**)

sin, sickness, nor
ap 567– 8   there is no error, no sin, sickness, nor *d·*.

sin, sickness, or
r 472–27   the only reality of sin, sickness, or *d·* is
gl 585–21   before it accepts sin, sickness, or *d·* ;

so-called
b 291– 3   suppositions. . . that the so-called *d·* of the body

sorrow and
f 203–30   waves of sin, sorrow, and *d·* beat in vain.

spiritual
b 310–24   and spiritual *d·* is oblivion.

sting of
r 496–20   "The sting of *d·* is sin ;— *I Cor.* 15 : 56.

stung to
ap 569–26   The dragon is at last stung to *d·*

submissive to
b 314–31   submissive to *d·* as being in supposed accord

suffering, and
f 219–30   from the belief in sin, suffering, and *d·*

supposed
gl 598–11   In the record of Jesus' supposed *d·*, we read :

supposition that
p 387–21   supposition that *d·* comes in obedience to

termed
sp 92– 8   decomposition . . . in what is termed *d·*.
b 290– 4   before what is termed *d·* overtakes mortals,
gl 595–20   continues after, what is termed *d·*, until

this
ph 177–28   does human belief, you ask, cause this *d·*?
b 312– 9   but this *d·* is the departure of a mortal's mind,

tree of
g 527–18   the tree of *d·* to His own creation?

death

triumphing over
  f 232–19   healing the sick and triumphing over *d·*.

triumph over
  a 54–16   and triumph over *d·* through Mind,

triumphs over
  a 25–16   casts out error, and triumphs over *d·*.
     31–22   the divine Principle which triumphs over *d·*.

ultimates in
  gl 580–17   Life's counterfeit, which ultimates in *d·* ;

until
  m 68–12   "until *d·* do us part."

unto the
  ap 568–19   loved not their lives unto the *d·.— Rev.* 12 : 11.

vanish in
  g 555–30   which seemed to vanish in *d·*.

victory over
  a 35–15   They celebrate their Lord's victory over *d·*,
     45– 7   in his victory over *d·* and the grave.
  p 427–21   shall obtain the victory over *d·* in proportion

violent
  a 47–29   each one came to a violent *d·* except

warning people against
  sp 79– 3   Warning people against *d·* is an error

was occasioned
  s 159– 9   *d·* was occasioned, not by the ether,

we call
  sp 82–20   as before the change we call *d·*,
  ph 172– 9   if man passes through what we call *d·*

we find
  c 260–32   If we look to the body . . . for Life, we find *d·* ;

will be found
  a 42– 6   *D·* will be found at length to be a

will be obsolete
  sp 90–13   and *d·* will be obsolete,

will disappear
  p 426–28   *d·* will disappear with the disappearance of sin.

will occur
  sp 77– 9   *D·* will occur on the next plane of existence

---

  a 31–24   the Lord's *d·* till he come."— *I Cor.* 11 : 26.
     39–11   causes mortals to regard *d·* as a friend,
     39–15   To him, therefore, *d·* was not the threshold
     47–29   except St. John, of whose *d·* we have no record.
  sp 73–23   belief that spirit . . . is freed by *d·*,
     90–14   some insist that *d·* is the necessary prelude to
  s 108–25   called error, sin, sickness, disease, *d·*,
     113–20   sin, evil, *d·*, deny good, omnipotent God,
     115–24   hatred, revenge, sin, sickness, disease, *d·*.
     119–20   or prostrates in *d·* the child at prayer,
     151–17   Mortal belief says that *d·* has
  ph 172–10   and *d·* is the Rubicon of spirituality?
     186–25   If *d·* is as real as Life, immortality is a myth.
     190– 9   Sin alone brings *d·*, for sin is the only
  f 202 30   true way leads to Life instead of to *d·*,
     203–24   *D·* is not a stepping-stone to Life,
     206–21   and then taking it away by *d·*?
     216–25   while health would seem the exception, *d·* the
     219– 1   sorrow, sin, *d·*, will be unknown,
     221–13   informed him that *d·* was indeed his only
     239–28   it is discordant and ends in sin, sickness, *d·*.
     244–19   If man flickers out in *d·*
     250–31   reveals Life as not being at the mercy of *d·*,
     251–24   the healer of sin, disease, *d·*.
  c 265–16   The senses represent . . . *d·* as irresistible,
  b 289–18   what appears to the senses to be *d·* is but
     291–23   As *d·* findeth mortal man, so shall he be . . . until
     292–10   belief that . . . Life be controlled by *d·*,
     296–10   The *d·* of a false material sense and of sin,
     304– 6   "Neither *d·*, nor life,— *Rom.* 8 : 38.
     304–14   can never produce mind nor life result in *d·*.
     306– 3   They would first make life result in *d·*,
     306– 5   taught them how *d·* was to be overcome
     312–13   you say that matter has caused his *d·*.
     312–19   Mortals claim that *d·* is inevitable ;
  o 360–28   the Jews put to *d·* the Galilean Prophet,
  p 386–18   same grief that the friend's real *d·* would bring.
     407–27   and brings . . . Life not *d·*, into
     409–31   *D·* will not make us harmonious and immortal
     426–18   are not saved from sin or sickness by *d·*.
     426–31   human concepts named matter, *d·*, disease,
     427– 7   If man believes in *d·* now, he must disbelieve
         in it
     427–13   *D·* is but another phase of the dream
     427–19   that shall be destroyed is *d·*''— *I Cor.* 15 : 26.
     433–30   to prepare the frightened sense . . . for *d·*.
     434–29   not proved "worthy of *d·*, or— *Acts* 26 : 31.
  r 481–14   declaring existence to be at the mercy of *d·*,
     486–15   If *d·* restores sight, sound, and strength
     486–17   If . . . then *d·* is not an enemy
     487– 4   never attainable through *d·*, but gained by
  g 522–30   Does Life, Truth, and Love produce *d·*,
  gl 584– 9   definition of
     588– 2   revenge ; sin ; sickness ; *d·* ;
     591–11   MATTER. Mythology ; . . . *d·* in life ;

death
  gl 592–10   MORTAL MIND. . . . sin ; sickness ; *d·*.
     595– 6   TARES. . . . sin ; sickness ; disease ; *d·*.

deathless
  a 28–13   the divine Principle of the *d·* Christ,
     44– 9   He proved Life to be *d·*
  m 69–16   and of man *d·* and perfect
  sp 72– 6   would disappear to mortal sense, would be *d·*.
  f 203–22   that the *d·* Principle, or Soul,
  c 266–29   Man is *d·*, spiritual.
  b 335–32   The Ego is *d·* and limitless,
  p 427– 9   since the truth of being is *d·*.
  r 487– 3   Life is *d·*.   Life is the origin and
     487–28   trust in the *d·* reality of Life,
  g 509– 3   the *d·* Life, or Mind,
     534– 5   to manifest the *d·* man of God's creating.

death-pallor
  ph 193–11   its *d·* gave place to a natural hue.

death-process
  b 289–20   to . . . the real universe there is no *d·*.

death-sentence
  ph 198– 4   as a criminal hears his *d·*.

death-valley
  s 108–20   within the shadow of the *d·*,

debarred
  m 64–14   A wife is sometimes *d·*
  p 362– 7   Heedless of the fact that she was *d·*

debars
  p 366– 8   *d·* him from giving drink to the thirsty

debased
  f 235–16   while the *d·* and unscrupulous mind,
  b 318–10   all that is material, untrue, selfish, or *d·*.

debate
  p 434– 8   After much *d·* and opposition,

debauched
  s 136–21   That a wicked king and *d·* husband

debauchee
  a 52–30   The bigot, the *d·*, the hypocrite,

debility
  p 442–10   all sallowness and *d·* had disappeared.

débris
  b 289– 2   can never rise from the temporal *d·* . . . until

debt
  pr 4– 7   our proper *d·* to him and the only worthy
  a 22–31   Mercy cancels the *d·* only when justice
     23– 4   One sacrifice, . . . is insufficient to pay the *d·*
  p 363 24   Why did he thus summarize her *d·*

debtors
  pr 17– 6   as we forgive our *d·.— Matt.* 6 : 12.
  p 363–16   He described two *d·*, one for a large sum

debts
  pr 11– 2   "Forgive us our *d·*,"— *Matt.* 6 : 12.
     17– 6   And forgive us our *d·*, — *Matt.* 6 : 12.

decadence
  f 244–30   pictures age as . . . helplessness and *d·*,

Decalogue
  s 112–31   commandment in the Hebrew *D·*,
  r 489–14   it breaks all the commands of the Mosaic *D·*

decapitates
  c 266– 3   sword of Science, with which Truth *d·* error,

decay

age and
  f 247 30   shining resplendent and eternal over age and *d·*.

age or
  f 247–14   Immortality, exempt from age or *d·*,

and death
  g 544– 7   Birth, *d·*, and death arise from the

and dissolution
  g 550–18   *d·*, and dissolution as its component stages

discord and
  b 280– 2   Symbols and elements of discord and *d·*
  r 468–18   eternal and incapable of discord and *d·*.
  g 503–24   creates no element nor symbol of discord and *d·*.

laws of
  f 244–14   beasts and vegetables,— subject to laws of *d·*.

maturity, and
  s 124–18   represented as subject to growth, maturity, and
         d·,
  ph 190–14   Human birth, growth, maturity, and *d·*
  f 244–13   Man undergoing birth, maturity, and *d·*

maturity, nor
  b 310–31   neither growth, maturity, nor *d·* in Soul.

not subject to
  ph 200–13   and not subject to *d·* and dust.

  m 66–13   when these *d·*, Love propagates anew the
     68–11   and scatters love's petals to *d·*.
  b 305–28   not subject to birth, growth, maturity, *d·*.
     318–12   and doom all things to *d·*.

decay
g 549– 5   germinates in eggs and must *d·*
551–30   the material seed must *d·*

decayed
p 395–25   a tumor, a cancer, or *d·* lungs,

decaying
sp 78– 1   The *d·* flower, the blighted bud,
f 247– 9   upper and lower teeth without a *d·* cavity.

decays
b 323–18   the one unused talent *d·* and is lost.
p 429–11   corpse, deserted by thought, is cold and *d·*,

decease
s 164–18   The seeming *d·*, caused by a

deceased
sp 81–32   somebody, . . . must have known the *d·*
s 159– 3   her sister testified that the *d·* protested

deceit
s 115–22   pride, envy, *d·*, hatred, revenge,
p 405– 8   and to overcome *d·* with honesty.
t 448–31   To talk the right and live the wrong is foolish *d·*,

deceitful
f 252–21   Animal in propensity, *d·* in sentiment,
p 395– 4   the testimony of the *d·* senses,
395–17   *d·* person should not be a nurse.

deceive
pr 8–16   it is wise not to try to *d·* ourselves
c 266–23   material sense, . . . would *d·* the very elect.

deceived
f 213– 3   or is said to be *d·*.
b 339–17   awful unreality by which he has been *d·*.
p 440– 8   *d·* by your attorney, False Belief,
t 451–26   subtle degree of evil, *d·* and deceiving.

deceiver
f 213– 3   Whoever contradicts this . . . is called a *d·*,

deceiveth
o 345–27   he *d·* himself." — *Gal.* 6 : 3.
ap 567–15   *d·* the whole world : — *Rev.* 12 : 9.

deceiving
t 451–26   subtle degree of evil, deceived and *d·*.

deception
m 59–25   for *d·* is fatal to happiness.
f 207– 9   evil is the awful *d·* and unreality of existence.

deceptive
an 101–27   this appearance is *d·*, since

decide
a 50– 3   Who shall *d·* what truth and love are?
ph 195–11   The point for each one to *d·* is,
p 392–21   If you *d·* that climate . . . is unhealthy,
t 463–21   To *d·* quickly as to the proper treatment of

decided
ph 176–29   Hence *d·* types of acute disease
f 221– 5   he *d·* that his diet should be more rigid,
p 374– 1   which mortal mind has *d·* upon as essential
432–29   he *d·* at once that the prisoner should die.
441– 5   He also *d·* that the plaintiff, Personal Sense,
t 453–12   I have never witnessed so *d·* effects from

decides
p 385–20   Mind *d·* whether or not the flesh shall
418–19   and to whatever *d·* its type and symptoms.
435–24   *d·* what penalty is due for the sin,
441–19   Spirit *d·* in favor of Man and against Matter.
441–25   Supreme Bench *d·* in favor of intelligence,

deciding
ph 181– 2   Before *d·* that the body, matter, is disordered,

decision
a 48–29   his awful *d·* against human rights and
f 216–22   If the *d·* were left to the corporeal senses,
p 380–13   *d·* which the defendant knows will be
389– 2   If this *d·* be left to C. S.,
437–19   I ask that the Supreme Court . . . reverse this *d·*.

decisions
s 139–15   The *d·* by vote of Church Councils
b 304–26   Left to the *d·* of material sense,
p 392–22   Your *d·* will master you,
440–30   the just and equitable *d·* of divine Spirit

Declaration
an 106– 6   C. S. has its *D·* of Independence.
s 161–16   that immortal sentiment of the *D·*,

declaration
o 361–13   This *d·* of Jesus, understood, conflicts not
p 363–22   that remarkable *d·* to the woman,
427–31   Thought will waken from its own material *d·*,
r 466–29   Christianity will demonstrate this *d·*
478– 9   What would be thought of the *d·* that a
g 520–23   Here is the emphatic *d·* that God creates all
526– 6   This opposite *d·*, . . . contradicts the
538–30   Eve's *d·*, "I have gotten a man — *Gen.* 4 : 1.
ap 573–14   even the *d·* from heaven, supreme harmony,

declare
pref vii–25   Future ages must *d·* what the pioneer has
a 50– 3   "Who shall *d·* his generation?" — *Isa.* 53 : 8.
m 69–24   or do you *d·* that Spirit is infinite,
s 163– 8   said : "I *d·* my conscientious opinion,
ph 174–26   Why *d·* that the body is diseased,
181–14   It is foolish to *d·* that you
f 243–29   because they *d·* nothing except God.
b 268– *   *d· we unto you,* — *I John* 1 : 3.
286–17   The Scriptures *d·* all that He made to be good.
287–21   Scriptures *d·* that man was made in God's
307– 9   It says : . . . I *d·* that God makes evil minds
318– 6   Scriptures *d·* that God made all,
320–30   as if Job intended to *d·*
330–19   God is what the Scriptures *d·* Him to be,
331–14   Scriptures also *d·* that God is Spirit.
p 373–17   Scriptures also *d·*, through the exalted thought
376–10   invalid, whom you *d·* to be wasting away
381–18   Scriptures *d·* that we live, move, and
386– 8   So long as mortals *d·* that certain states of the
391–25   Disease has no intelligence to *d·* itself
397–17   *D·* that you are not hurt and understand . . . why,
397–22   which the Scriptures *d·* Him to be.
400–30   Scriptures plainly *d·* the baneful influence of
439–27   Our higher statutes *d·* you all,
r 466–28   Science will *d·* God aright,
g 519–17   How shall we *d·* Him, till,
525–25   The corporeal senses *d·* otherwise ;
526–17   the Scriptures *d·* that He created all.
539–16   Scriptures *d·* that God condemned this lie
546–11   Has God no Science to *d·* Mind,
ap 569–24   Scriptures *d·* that evil is temporal,
gl 596– 9   Him *d·* I unto you." — *Acts* 17 : 23.

declared
m 64–19   when he *d·* that in the resurrection
s 133– 6   centurion of whose faith Jesus himself *d·*,
137–19   The Messiah is what thou hast *d·*,
162–32   He *d·* that "it is impossible to calculate the
163– 5   *d·* himself "sick of learned quackery."
ph 165– 2   Evil *d·* that eating this fruit would
f 234–28   that to look with desire on
b 280–17   Moses *d·* as Jehovah's first command
303–32   *d·* that nothing could alienate him from God,
320– 3   Christ plainly *d·*, "I am the way, — *John* 14 : 6.
338–27   Jehovah *d·* the ground was accursed ;
o 352– 5   Our Master *d·* that his material body
361–13   Jesus Christ is not God, as Jesus himself *d·*,
p 437–25   They *d·* that C. S. was overthrowing
g 522–16   this state of things is *d·* to be temporary
525–17   In the Gospel of John, it is *d·* that

declares
s 124–28   *d·* that they belong wholly to divine Mind,
141–20   The Bible *d·* that all believers are
151–26   must be put off, as St. Paul *d·*.
ph 169–19   *d·* that all disease is cured by divine Mind.
173–17   Anatomy *d·* man to be structural.
f 220– 9   Instinct is better . . . as even nature *d·*.
b 307– 7   *d·* that there is more than one intelligence
317– 7   Whosoever . . . *d·* best the power of C. S.,
320–17   Here the original text *d·* plainly the
335–10   for, as the Bible *d·*, without the Logos,
o 347– 4   C. S. *d·* that whatever is mortal or discordant
p 391–17   Injustice *d·* the absence of law.
393–25   When Jesus *d·* that "the light of — *Matt.* 6 : 22.
414–21   *d·*, "The Lord He is God — *Deut.* 4 : 35.
414–23   C. S. *d·* that Mind is substance,
429–12   Science *d·* that man is subject to Mind.
r 475– 1   Scripture *d·* that there is "no night — *Rev.* 22 : 5.
476– 3   which *d·* that man begins in dust or
477–12   *d·* the corporeal senses to be . . . illusions.
480–26   Bible *d·* : "All things were made by — *John* 1 : 3.
485– 4   *d·* that Mind, not matter, sees, hears, feels,
g 507–23   The scientific divine creation *d·*
522–29   Scripture . . . *d·* God's work to be finished.
523– 4   and finally *d·* that God knows error
526– 4   more scientific record of creation *d·*
528– 2   the record *d·* that God has already created man,
544–29   It *d·* mind to be in and of matter,
548–29   Agassiz *d·* . . . "Certain animals,
551–29   error *d·* that the material seed must

declaring
a 19–12   *d·* precisely what would destroy sickness,
ph 180–18   by *d·* disease to be a fixed fact,
f 206–23   *d·* that His work was *finished*,
229–13   *d·* Him good in one instance and evil in another.
o 352–20   increasing children's fears by *d·* ghosts to be
p 364–11   and *d·* the absolution of the penitent.
439–26   meanwhile *d·* Disease to be God's servant
t 447–28   by *d·* there is no sickness,
r 481–14   *d·* existence to be at the mercy of death,
g 522–24   *d·* this material creation false.
528–21   and *d·* what great things error has done.

decline
b 310–11   Day may *d·* and shadows fall,

declines
 o 355–17 popular religion, *d·* to admit that
declining
 f 246–13 Manhood is . . . undimmed by a *d·* sun.
decomposed
 p 429–11 affirms . . . that it must be buried and *d·*
decomposition
 sp 92– 7 the *d·* of mortal bodies in what is termed death.
 p 373–24 The inflammation, *d·*, or deposit will abate,
 425–10 tubercles, hemorrhage, and *d·* are beliefs,
 r 488–26 not at the mercy of organization and *d·*,
decree
 a 32–14 he bowed in holy submission to the divine *d·*.
 p 440–20 You cannot trample upon the *d·* of the
decreed
 f 221–19 He learned . . . that God never *d·* disease,
 ap 565–10 Herod *d·* the death of every male child
decrees
 s 118–31 they contradict the divine *d·*
 f 229–28 should not if we could, annul the *d·* of
 p 381– 3 Ignorant of . . . we submit to unjust *d·*,
 435–11 The law of our Supreme Court *d·* that
 441–18 the *d·* of the Court of Error in favor of Matter,
decrepitude
 f 245–30 plain that *d·* is not according to law,
decries
 o 342– 8 He that *d·* this Science
dedicated
 gl 596– 7 *d·* "to the unknown God."— *Acts* 17 : 23.
deduced
 s 120–25 Any conclusion *pro* or *con*, *d·* from
 b 268– 7 from which may be *d·* all rationality,
 274– 8 *d·* from the evidence of the material senses.
deducible
 pref viii–20 the response *d·* from two connate facts,
deducing
 c 259–32 *D·* one's conclusions as to man
deductions
 b 273– 7 *D·* from material hypotheses are not scientific.
 g 553–16 why are his *d·* generally material?
deed
any
 p 440–15 what greater justification can any *d·* have,
criminal
 p 435– 4 Has the body . . . committed a criminal *d·* ?
good
 p 435–15 trampling on Laws of Health, this was a good *d·*,
 436–12 Laying down his life for a good *d·*,
Jesus'
 a 15– 8 Jesus' *d·* was for the enlightenment of men
my
 o 343– 3 and for proving my word by my *d·*
thought and
 a 19–18 every good thought and *d·*, will help us
 gl 595–15 holiness and purification of thought and *d·*,
word or
 m 59–21 how slight a word or *d·* may renew the
 f 205–19 some word or *d·* which indicates the true idea,

 a 31–17 to all who follow him in *d·*.
 f 203–16 man the image of his Maker in *d·* and in truth.
deeds
best
 p 385–11 penalty which our beliefs would attach to our best *d·*.
daily
 a 40–30 public worship instead of daily *d·*.
good
 pr 4– 5 patience, meekness, love, and good *d·*.
 a 41–27 his apostles still went about doing good *d·*,
 p 435–12 but good *d·* are immortal, bringing joy
 436– 2 he was an eye-witness to the good *d·*
 440–10 Good *d·* are transformed into crimes,
his
 a 26–26 proved by his *d·* that C. S. destroys sickness,
 c 262– 8 the old man with his *d·*,"— *Col.* 3 : 9.
 b 296– 9 The old man with his *d·* must be put off.
 o 350–12 His words were the offspring of his *d·*,
of kindness
 p 384– 8 for honest labor, or for *d·* of kindness,
of violence
 an 105– 4 to prevent *d·* of violence or to punish them.
our
 o 354–21 If our words fail to express our *d·*,
these
 p 369–10 All these *d·* manifested Jesus' control
the very
 p 436–29 the very *d·* which the divine law compels
wicked
 b 314–12 material views were the parents of their wicked *d·*.

deeds
without
 o 354–19 Inconsistency is shown by words without *d·*,

 pr 1–14 before they take form in words and in *d·*.
 o 354–10 find their immortality in *d·*,
 p 430– 4 must put off itself with its *d·*,
deem
 b 283–19 and *d·* this the manifestation of the one Life,
 p 441–10 plea of False Belief we *d·* unworthy of
deemed
 s 158–10 This was *d·* progress in medicine ;
 b 338–19 dust was *d·* the agent of Deity
 p 376– 8 diseases *d·* dangerous sometimes come from
 431–10 this offence is *d·* punishable with death.
 g 525–28 death must be *d·* as devoid of reality
 550–27 Amalgamation is *d·* monstrous
deems
 ap 574–29 which your suffering sense *d·* wrathful
deep
 pr 12–13 *d·* and conscientious protests of Truth,
 s 125–27 dominion over the atmosphere and the great *d·*,
 129–22 We must look *d·* into realism
 ph 184–30 The inspirations were *d·* and natural.
 b 307– 1 the Adam-dream, the *d·* sleep,
 338–18 upon the face of the *d·*."— *Gen.* 1 : 2.
 r 479–20 upon the face of the *d·*."— *Gen.* 1 : 2.
 g 503– 7 upon the face of the *d·*.— *Gen.* 1 : 2.
 528–10 caused a *d·* sleep to fall upon Adam,— *Gen.* 2 : 21.
 546–21 for they contain the *d·* divinity of the Bible.
 556–18 the *d·* sleep which fell upon Adam?
 ap 569–17 are dwellers still in the *d·* darkness of belief.
 570–21 the *d·* waters of chaos and old night.
deepen
 sp 99–25 spirituality, . . . must *d·* human experience,
deepens
 g 523– 4 mist of obscurity . . . *d·* the false claim,
deeper
 b 329–29 the *d·* the error into which mortal mind
deeply
 pr 7–10 Looking *d·* into these things, we find
 s 161–30 looked as *d·* for cause and effect
 t 453–28 impresses more *d·* the wrong mind-picture.
deep-lying
 pref xii–15 with a *d·* conviction that the next two years
defaced
 f 227–28 and *d·* the tablet of your being.
defeat
 s 122– 5 great facts of Life, . . . *d·* this triad of errors,
 f 239–13 success in error is *d·* in Truth.
 o 357–32 Can matter . . . *d·* omnipotence?
 p 390–31 to *d·* the passage of an inhuman law.
 422–32 This mental state invites *d·*.
 t 446–18 A wrong motive involves *d·*.
defeats
 a 99–30 attended with doubts and *d·* as well as triumphs.
defence
 a 48–18 and chose not the world's means of *d·*.
 f 235– 3 if virtue and truth build a strong *d·*,
 o 348–23 would it not be well to abandon the *d·*,
 p 434–21 and opens the argument for the *d·* :
 440–33 Here the counsel for the *d·* closed,
defend
 p 377–29 a fear that Mind is helpless to *d·* the
 387–31 faith and understanding whereby to *d·* himself,
 t 445– 2 students to *d·* themselves against sin,
 451–22 in order to *d·* himself from the influence of
defendant
 p 380–12 as though the *d·* should argue for the plaintiff
 380–13 decision which the *d·* knows will be
 430–21 Mortal Man is the *d·*.
defending
 o 348–21 *d·* the supposed rights of disease,
defiance
 a 43–25 acting under spiritual law in *d·* of matter
 ph 168–21 in *d·* of what is called material law,
 f 228– 1 and in *d·* of all material conditions.
 o 342– 9 and in *d·* of the direct command of Jesus,
deficiency
 p 388–16 a *d·* or an excess, a quality or a quantity.
deficient
 p 366–13 is *d·* in human affection,
defies
 an 105– 9 *d·* justice and is recommended to mercy.
defile
 an 100– * *the things which d· a man.*— *Matt.* 15 : 20.
defileth
 ap 577–26 "*d·*, . . . or maketh a lie."— *Rev.* 21 : 27.

define

sp 81–25 so-called laws of matter, which *d·* man as
s 148–13 anatomy and theology *d·* man as
ph 173–24 physiology, phrenology, do not *d·* the
b 278–29 We *d·* matter as error, because it is the
318– 5 Corporeal senses *d·* diseases as realities ;
r 485– 1 If error is necessary to *d·* or to reveal
gl 596– 3 Paganism and agnosticism may *d·* Deity as

defined

a 54– 3 Out of . . . his pure affection, he *d·* Love.
s 117–30 which he *d·* as human doctrines.
129–11 Pantheism may be *d·* as a belief in the
p 408–12 distinctly *d·* instances of the baneful
t 460– 3 Ontology is *d·* as "the science of
g 507– 7 Without natures particularly *d·*,
517– 6 may be *d·* as a mortally mental attempt
554–20 Jesus *d·* this opposite of God and His creation

defines

an 103– 4 *d·* it as dishonesty and craftiness.
ph 191–25 Physical sense *d·* mortal man as based on matter,
f 208– 2 Material sense *d·* all things materially,
p 410– 5 *d·* everlasting life as a present knowledge of
r 488–17 *d·* these so-called senses as *mortal beliefs*,

defining

p 441– 1 comprehending and *d·* all law and evidence,

definite

pref ix– 8 the tongue voices the more *d·* thought,
s 147–26 but he left no *d·* rule for
f 206–22 The Scriptures are *d·* on this point,
p 410–20 Here is a *d·* and inspired proclamation of C. S.

definitely

g 523–29 after which the distinction is not *d·* traceable.

definition

s 114– 6 spiritually unscientific *d·* of mind
c 257– 3 then all is Mind ; and this *d·* is scientific.
b 270–20 establish the *d·* of omnipotence,
302–14 Continuing our *d·* of *man*,
338–25 The dissection and *d·* of words,
p 421– 6 the true *d·* of all human belief in ill-health,
g 517– 2 *d·* has been weakened by anthropomorphism,
gl 579– 2 material *d·* of a Scriptural word

definitions

a 23–22 two *d·*, *trustfulness* and *trustworthiness*.
s 118–26 The *d·* of material law, as given
118–28 these *d·* portray law as physical,

deflection

g 502–11 This *d·* of being, rightly viewed,

deflections

sp 78– 4 changing *d·* of mortal mind ;
b 305–20 the *d·* of matter as opposed to the Science of

deformed

s 160–25 If muscles can cease to act . . . be *d·* or
p 418–30 tubercles, inflammation, pain, *d·* joints,

deformity

ph 178–13 Perhaps an adult has a *d·*
f 244– 2 He does not produce moral or physical *d·* ;
244– 2 therefore such *d·* is not real,
248–24 the angular outline and *d·* of matter models.
c 263–13 forming *d·* when he would outline grace

defraud

c 263–11 Carnal beliefs *d·* us.

defrauds

r 489–13 Corporeal sense *d·* and lies ;

defying

ap 564–23 uncover its own crime of *d·* immortal

degenerating

g 545– 5 material man was fast *d·*

degrade

f 235–18 will *d·* the characters it should inform

degree

first

s 115–20 *First D· :* Depravity.
p 433–17 "Guilty of liver-complaint in the first *d·*."
433–21 guilty of benevolence in the first *d·*,

highest

s 163–16 are in the highest *d·* uncertain ;
ap 564–18 the highest *d·* of human depravity.

limited

b 313–28 was possessed only in a limited *d·*

second

s 115–25 *Second D· :* Evil beliefs disappearing.

small

r 492– 8 knowledge of this, even in small *d·*,

some

a 37–24 It is possible, . . . to follow in some *d·*

subtle

t 451–26 especially any subtle *d·* of evil,

sufficient

t 454–14 He, who understands in a sufficient *d·*

degree

their

t 457–16 both sides were beautiful according to their *d·* ;

third

s 116– 1 *Third D· :* Understanding.
116– 4 In the third *d·* mortal mind disappears,

s 153– 1 frequently attenuated to such a *d·* that
ph 189–16 it is as truly mortal mind, according to its *d·*,
b 337–10 man is in a *d·* as perfect as
p 407–19 and ascend a *d·* in the scale of health,
t 454– 6 The understanding, even in a *d·*,

degrees

pref ix–31 *d·* by which she came at length to its solution ;
s 113– 5 but its spirit comes only in small *d·*.
f 233– 9 is seen and acknowledged only by *d·*.
b 297–25 Human thoughts have their *d·* of comparison.
327–31 by *d·* he will learn the nothingness of the
p 407–30 All sin is insanity in different *d·*.

deific

b 334–24 but undying in the *d·* Mind.
336–22 else God would . . . lose the *d·* character,
r 482– 7 where the *d·* meaning is required.
g 513– 2 for the claim usurps the *d·* prerogatives
513–12 the motions and reflections of *d·* power
514– 1 could not by simulating *d·* power
ap 576–29 not yet elevated to *d·* apprehension

deify

f 251–31 and *d·* their own notions,

deities

s 524– 5 and in a thousand other so-called *d·*.

Deity

allness of

c 267– 6 The allness of *D·* is His oneness.

a national

a 41–31 enough for them to believe in a national *D·* ;

and humanity

g 555–22 of both *D·* and humanity.

applied to

s 116–26 *person* and *personal* . . . when applied to *D·*,
o 345– 1 word *Spirit* is so commonly applied to *D·*,

authority of

o 357–14 the creativeness and authority of *D·*,

being and

g 554– 7 being and *D·* are inseparable.

conception of

g 555–24 and set aside the proper conception of *D·*,

conceptions of

pr 3–17 How empty are our conceptions of *D·* !

constitute

g 516– 5 Truth, and Love, which constitute *D·*,

define

gl 596– 3 Paganism and agnosticism may define *D·* as

explains

g 545– 1 Error . . . explains *D·* through mortal and

faith in

s 146– 7 faith in drugs the fashion, rather than faith in
      D·.

hieroglyphs of

f 240– 7 The floral apostles are hieroglyphs of *D·*.

humanization of

g 517– 3 anthropomorphism, or a humanization of *D·*.

human sense of

ap 576–31 human sense of *D·* yields to the divine sense,

idea of

b 339–21 has yielded to a more spiritual idea of *D·*,
g 517–14 for Love imparts the clearest idea of *D·*.

loves

r 481– 9 Through . . . man comprehends and loves *D·*.

misconceptions of

sp 94–13 the misconceptions of *D·* there prevalent.

name for

b 332– 4 Father-Mother is the name for *D·*,

perfection of

g 546– 8 error would dethrone the perfection of *D·*.

seal of

g 511–11 divine Science, which is the seal of *D·*

signifies

r 466–20 Soul or Spirit signifies *D·* and nothing else.

Spirit, or

gl 588–23 if used with reference to Spirit, or *D·*.

spiritual sense of

ap 578– 3 the incorporeal or spiritual sense of *D·* :

was satisfied

g 519– 3 *D·* was satisfied with His work.

wholeness of

r 465–14 the nature, essence, and wholeness of *D·*.

pr 12–27 Does *D·* interpose in behalf of one worshipper,
s 111–15 physical hypotheses as to *D·*,
c 255–12 to belittle *D·* with human conceptions.
259– 1 Man is not absorbed in *D·*,
263– 3 orginators of something which *D·* would not
265–11 by no means suggests man's absorption into *D·*

Deity
b 284–15 Can *D·* be known through the material senses?
338–19 matter or dust was deemed the agent of *D·*
o 351–21 if we consider Satan . . . coequal in power with *D·*,
357–27 Can *D·* be almighty, if another mighty and
r 470–27 and consequently a time when *D·* was
475–20 has not a single quality underived from *D·* ;
g 517– 7 attempt to reduce *D·* to corporeality.
522– 9 as having broken away from *D·*
523– 9 because *D·* therein is always called Jehovah,
531– 3 springs from dust instead of from *D·*
545–15 and do not accord infinity to *D·*.
550–24 An egg is an impossible enclosure for *D·*.
554– 6 because being is immortal, like *D·*,
gl 591–19 *D·*, which outlines but is not outlined.

deity
ph 186–31 it enthrones matter as *d·*.
g 524–17 Did the . . . infinite Principle become a finite *d·*,

delay
p 407– 9 Every hour of *d·* makes the struggle more
434– 2 "*D·* the execution ; the prisoner is not guilty."

delicious
r 491– 2 A *d·* perfume will seem intolerable.

delight
pn 179–18 the wild animal, . . . sniffs the wind with *d·*.
g 526–30 The name Eden, . . . means *pleasure, d·*.

delineate
f 208–30 should *d·* upon it thoughts of health,

delineates
b 310– 3 fancies that it *d·* thought on matter,
r 485–26 *d·* foreign agents, called disease and sin.

delineations
ph 198–11 and then fills in his *d·* with

deliver
pr 16–15 In the phrase, "*D·* us from evil," — *Matt.* 6 : 13.
16–16 "*D·* us from the evil one."
17– 8 but *d·* us from evil ; — *Matt.* 6 : 13.
a 22–20 Love is not hasty to *d·* us from temptation,
s 151–14 Even this . . . would ultimately *d·* mankind
p 391–23 your adversary will *d·* you to the judge
405–11 They will *d·* you to the judge,
405–13 The judge will *d·* you to justice,
ap 567– 3 These angels *d·* us from the depths.

deliverance
pref xi–19 *d·* to the captives [of sense], *Luke* 4 : 18.
a 22–23 Final *d·* from error, whereby we
f 224–30 power of God brings *d·* to the captive.

delivered
m 67–28 Man *d·* from sin, disease, and death
ph 165– * *d· them from their destructions.* — *Psal.* 107 : 20.
f 243– 5 which *d·* men from the boiling oil,
p 391– 4 Then, when thou art *d·* to the judgment
ap 562–23 and pained to be *d·*. — *Rev.* 12 : 2.
562–25 waiting to be *d·* of her sweet promise ;
563–26 which was ready to be *d·*, — *Rev.* 12 : 4.

deliverer
f 226–32 trusting Truth, the strong *d·*,
b 308–32 Then Jacob questioned his *d·*,

delivereth
pr 17–10 but *d·* us from sin, disease, and death.

delivering
s 107– 9 *d·* the children of men from every ill
p 440– 9 a verdict *d·* Mortal Man to Death.

delivers
p 404–32 and so *d·* him from his destroyers.

deluded
s 121–21 *d·* the judgment and induced false conclusions

delusion
artifice and
sp 83– 4 artifice and *d·* claimed that they could equal
first
gl 594– 7 the first *d·* that error exists as fact ;
give up the
ph 191– 4 As mortals give up the *d·* that
great
ap 570–28 should also know the great *d·* of mortal mind,
of material sense
b 330–26 a *d·* of material sense,
of suffering
ph 184–24 by destroying the *d·* of suffering
pure
ap 567–21 That false claim . . . is pure *d·*, the red dragon ;
religious
ph 166–13 Mohammedan's belief is a religious *d·* ;

b 301–24 *D·*, sin, disease, and death arise from
307– 1 *d·* that life and intelligence proceeded from
319– 1 The *d·* that there is life in matter
323–26 the *d·* that there are other minds,

delusion
o 348– 9 one disease can be just as much a *d·* as another.
p 407–21 If *d·* says, "I have lost my memory,"
g! 593–12 *d·* ; mortality ; error.

delusions
f 204–10 carries out the *d·* of sin, sickness, and death.
233–14 error continues its *d·* until
b 328–12 the Science which destroys human *d·*
o 348–12 *d·*, were cast out and the dumb spake.

delusive
sp 70– 3 cannot inform us what is real and what is *d·*,
f 237–32 hug false beliefs and suffer the *d·* consequences.
249–11 Any other theory . . . is *d·* and mythological.

demand
awful
b 308– 8 This awful *d·*, . . . is met by the admission
Christian
a 37–32 Why has this Christian *d·* so little inspiration
m 66–22 if there is no Christian *d·* for it.
Christ's
a 22– 6 Waking to Christ's *d·*, mortals experience
divine
f 253–32 divine *d·*, "Be ye therefore— *Matt.* 5 : 48.
b 329–23 Science is a divine *d·*, not a human.
eternal
gl 595–11 the eternal *d·* of divine Science.
first
r 467– 3 The first *d·* of this Science is,
frivolous
ph 195–30 to meet a frivolous *d·* for amusement
its
ph 199–11 by reason of its *d·* for and supply of power.
moral
sp 92–23 Until . . . the moral *d·* will not be met,
no
p 435–22 no *d·*, human or divine, renders it just to
perpetual
c 255– 4 the perpetual *d·* of Truth and Love,
spiritual
p 385– 8 spiritual *d·*, . . . supplies energy and endurance

a 22–11 the *d·* of Life and Love,
m 65–18 human mind will at length *d·* a higher affection.
s 152–32 signs, which *d·* different remedies ;
ph 179–13 creates a *d·* for that method,
183– 3 *d·* obedience to materialistic codes,
b 308– 7 hide from the *d·*, "Where art thou?" — *Gen.* 3 · 9.
p 386– 7 no such result occurs without mind to *d·* it
g 524–30 and eventually ejected at the *d·* of matter?

demanded
a 41–29 *d·* more than they were willing to practise.
p 390–18 the last penalty *d·* by error.

demanding
f 226– 9 *d·* that the fetters of sin, sickness, and

demands
acquiescence with the
u 48–27 acquiescence with the *d·* of Jesus' enemies.
different
m 59–12 the different *d·* of their united spheres,
eternal
ph 184–13 the only legitimate and eternal *d·* on man,
he uttered the
b 314–27 he uttered the *d·* of its divine Principle,
its
f 233– 1 Every day makes its *d·* upon us
its own
r 489–14 to meet its own *d·*.
meet the
m 57–16 fame is incompetent to meet the *d·* of the
c 257–25 to meet the *d·* of human want and woe,
of Christian Science
b 327–17 the strict *d·* of C. S. seem peremptory ;
of divine Science
a 38– 8 is broken by the *d·* of divine Science.
f 241– 2 the *d·* of divine Science
of God
s 129–32 the *d·* of God must be met.
ph 182– 5 The *d·* of God appeal to thought only ;
of Truth
ph 170–14 The *d·* of Truth are spiritual,
b 325–20 Paul had a clear sense of the *d·* of Truth
t 450–13 They do not . . . whine over the *d·* of Truth,
spiritual
r 483–10 not be ignorant of the moral and spiritual *d·*

pr 3–15 *d·* absolute consecration of thought, energy, and
11– 9 The moral law, . . . always *d·* restitution
a 23–30 *d·* self-reliant trustworthiness,
40–25 *d·* that all men should follow the example
sp 99– 5 to escape from sin, is what the Bible *d·*.
s 139–32 *d·* the remedy of Truth
ph 183–21 rightly *d·* man's entire obedience,
f 233– 6 *d·* of us only what we can certainly fulfil.
254–20 This task God *d·* us to accept lovingly

demands

c 256–19	Who is it that *d·* our obedience?
259–29	*d·* spiritual thoughts, divine concepts,
261–32	Good *d·* of man every hour,
o 343–23	Christendom generally *d·* so much less.
p 380– 8	indulging the *d·* of sin, disease, or death,
r 467– 1	What are the *d·* of the Science of
g 532–30	but now error *d·* that *mind* shall
545–20	impudently *d·* a blessing.
gl 592–15	justice *d·* penalties under the law.

demarcation

b 294–19	The lines of *d·* between
g 505–21	Understanding is the line of *d·*
gl 586–16	line of *d·* between Truth and error,

dematerialization

f 211–29	only through *d·* and spiritualization

dematerialized

f 211–27	then, when the body is *d·*, these faculties

dementia

b 330–31	*d·*, insanity, inanity, devil,
p 411–14	a disease which moderns would call *d·*.
414–14	*d·*, hatred, or any other discord.
423–29	as directly the action of mortal mind as is *d·*

demerit

t 449–23	according to personal merit or *d·*,

demerits

o 344–16	rules which disclose its merits or *d·*,

demigods

sp 84–10	controlled not by demons, spirits, or *d·*,

demise

g 543– 7	more beautifully apparent at error's *d·*.

demon

p 411–15	*d·*, or evil, replied that his name was Legion.

demons

sp 84–10	controlled not by *d·*, spirits, or demigods,

demonstrable

sp 99– 3	ethics, and superstition afford no *d·*
an 106–16	sanction only such methods as are *d·*
s 108– 6	unfolding to me the *d·* fact that
111– 2	and the *d·* truths of C. S.;
112– 4	C. S. is *d·*.
ph 171–13	Mind's control over the universe, . . . is *d·*
b 323–15	Truth is *d·* when understood,
o 344–12	the opponents of a *d·* Science
p 417–23	it is *d·* that the way to cure the patient
r 487–20	is founded on Science or *d·* Truth,
g 546–29	it cures on a divine *d·* Principle

demonstrably

s 134–21	The true Logos is *d·* C. S.,
b 337–31	you ascertain that this Science is *d·* true,

demonstrate

a 19–24	Those who cannot *d·*, at least in part,
25–25	that they might *d·* this power as he did
30– 3	and could *d·* the Science of Love
51–22	to *d·* his divine Principle.
sp 98–14	much less can they *d·* it.
s 111–13	its rules *d·* its Science.
130– 8	when you can *d·* the actuality of Science.
141–23	they cannot *d·* God's healing power.
147– 2	This system enables the learner to *d·*
149–31	dismiss superstition, and *d·* truth
150–14	these signs are only to *d·* its divine origin,
162–28	to *d·* the higher rule.
ph 182–26	ability to *d·* Mind's sacred power.
f 217–24	you will be able to *d·* this control.
254–18	not the power to *d·* what we do not
b 274–12	and they *d·* Truth and Life.
283–29	unless we so do, we can no more *d·*
285–30	will seek to learn, . . . how to *d·* the Christ,
315–22	enabled him to *d·* the facts of being,
o 352– 2	to *d·* His power to heal,
353–31	Mortal beliefs can neither *d·* Christianity nor
355–25	a consequent inability to *d·* this Science.
p 429–26	and do not *d·* the facts it involves.
t 447–32	to know it, he must *d·* his statement.
452–26	Such a practice does not *d·* the Science
456–20	or he cannot *d·* the divine Principle.
460–12	is the one most difficult to understand and *d·*,
462– 5	any student, . . . can *d·* C. S.,
462–13	Whoever would *d·* the healing of C. S.
r 466–29	Christianity will *d·* this declaration
482–22	enabled Jesus to *d·* his control over matter.
493–15	enables the healer to *d·* . . . the Principle
496–17	enables you to *d·*, with scientific certainty,
g 539–28	more than human power to . . . *d·* the one Mind

demonstrated

pref ix–23	this Science must be *d·* by healing,
a 18– 3	taught and *d·* man's oneness with the Father,
24–28	affection and goodness it *d·* for mankind.
25–18	he *d·* more spiritually than all others
30–22	*d·* throughout the whole earthly career of Jesus,

demonstrated

a 41–20	or *d·* the divine healing of absolute Science.
44– 4	and the supremacy of Spirit be *d·*.
45– 6	Our Master fully and finally *d·* divine Science
54– 2	he *d·* the divine Life.
sp 77–11	Then, and not until then, will it be *d·*
93– 3	Jesus, who . . . *d·* the power of Spirit
s 109– 8	its divine Principle is *d·* by healing the sick
110–17	afterwards the truth of C. S. was *d·*.
110–25	will forever remain to be discerned and *d·*.
110–25	Jesus *d·* the power of C. S.
110–28	spiritually discerned, taught, and *d·*
115– 7	any reader, who has not personally *d·* C. S.
126–24	I have *d·* through Mind the effects of Truth
130–11	if Science, when understood and *d·*, will
146–24	the divine origin of Science is *d·*
147– 6	I *d·* the divine rules of C. S.
149– 1	our great Master *d·* that Truth could save
149–13	because you have not *d·* the life of Christ,
150– 4	the healing power of Truth is widely *d·*
ph 177– 4	I have *d·* this beyond all cavil.
180–29	as taught and *d·* by Christ Jesus.
184–23	I have *d·* this as a rule of divine Science
193–32	It has been *d·* to me that Life is God
f 201– 2	*d·* by the destruction of sin, sickness, and
230–10	the divine Principle, Love, as *d·* by Jesus.
244– 5	On their basis Jesus *d·* Life,
b 271–15	the divine Science, which their Master *d·*
272–31	C. S., as *d·* by Jesus,
274–16	Jesus *d·* this great verity.
283–25	practically *d·* in length of days,
289– 1	Truth *d·* is eternal life.
306– 6	and *d·* this beyond cavil.
316– 8	Christ, Truth, was *d·* through Jesus
321–19	It was scientifically *d·* that leprosy
321–30	the Science of being was *d·* by Jesus,
323–16	good is not understood until *d·*.
325–29	Science . . . will be understood and *d·*.
330–10	infallibility of divine metaphysics will be *d·*.
332–19	*d·* Christ;
333–12	*d·* in the life of which Christ Jesus was
o 341–15	*d·* according to a divine given rule,
346–11	its nothingness is not saved, but must be *d·*
350–26	before the Science of being can be *d·*.
360–30	for the truth he spoke and *d·*,
p 369– 9	*d·* in healing the sick, raising the dead,
406– 8	the power of God is understood and *d·*
430– 2	Jesus *d·* this, healing the dying
r 472– 3	God is to be understood, adored, and *d·*;
494–11	to imagine that Jesus *d·* . . . only for a
494–16	Jesus *d·* the inability of corporeality,
495– 5	hence its healing power is not fully *d·*.
497–17	as *d·* by the Galilean Prophet
g 547– 2	statement of C. S., if *d·* by healing,
ap 559–15	Then is the power of Truth *d·*,
564–19	Until the majesty of Truth should be *d·*
572–13	this divine Principle, understood and *d·*,
gl 593–21	understood and *d·* as supreme over all;

demonstrates

a 26–19	musician *d·* the beauty of the music
42–25	This *d·* that in C. S. the true man
sp 85– 3	which *d·* the capacity of Soul,
an 103–14	is of God and *d·* the divine Principle,
s 147–31	divine Principle of goodness and *d·* its rules.
b 294–31	Truth *d·* the falsity of error.
306– 7	Life *d·* Life.
337–14	C. S. *d·* that none but the pure in heart
337–18	*d·* Life in Christ, Life's spiritual ideal.
339–12	Science *d·* the unreality of evil,
340–17	my favorite text. It *d·* C. S.
340–22	by which man *d·* health, holiness, and life
o 343–17	he also scientifically *d·* this great fact,
351– 4	divine Principle which *d·* C. S.,
p 372–14	When man *d·* C. S. absolutely,
375–11	*d·* that divine Mind heals,
405–20	*d·* the government of God,
g 505–23	and *d·* the divine sense,

demonstrating

pr 5– 2	keeps him from *d·* his power over error.
a 25–22	Though *d·* his control over sin and disease,
29–23	*d·* God as the Father of men.
43–23	but he was *d·* divine Science.
44–29	*d·* within the narrow tomb the power of Spirit
sp 97–29	Christianity is again *d·* the Life that
s 117–17	and *d·* Life and Truth in himself
137– 1	teaching and *d·* the truth of being.
147–27	but he left no definite rule for *d·* this
f 224–22	*d·* justice and meeting the needs of mortals
232–16	Christianity is again *d·* the power of
254–14	to *begin* aright and to continue the strife of *d·*
b 314– 8	*d·* the existence of but one Mind
315–32	Explaining and *d·* the way of divine Science,
o 351–25	*d·* the all-inclusiveness of harmonious Truth.
t 456–12	Principle and method of *d·* C. S.
456–32	it gave the first rules for *d·* this Science,

demonstrating
  r 492–28   *d·* harmony and immortality.
     496–11   *d·* the healing power of Truth and Love?
  g 519–14   *d·* its spiritual origin.

demonstration
actual
  pr 14– 7   the actual *d·* and understanding of Life
alike in
  s 135–25   and they are alike in *d·*.
and spiritual understanding
  o 355–27   *d·* and spiritual understanding are. . .keynotes,
answered by
  pref viii–13   question, What is Truth, is answered by *d·*,
begin the
  f 246–28   We should find this out, and begin the *d·*
Christian
  s 141– 4   More . . . is requisite for Christian *d·*.
earlier
  s 150–11   now, as in the time of its earlier *d·*,
fatal to its
  s 129–19   and fatal to its *d·* ;
final
  a 43–17   final *d·* of the truth which Jesus taught,
     46–26   his final *d·*, called the ascension,
     48–30   hastening the final *d·* of what life is
     53–30   nor had he risen to his final *d·*
  p 429– 6   final *d·* takes time for its accomplishment.
ground of
  a 28–11   is more on the ground of *d·* than
higher in
  a 43–21   Jesus rose higher in *d·* because of
highest
  a 50–15   Had . . . Love forsaken him in his highest *d·* ?
his
  a 26–25   his *d·* of power over death.
     31–18   following his *d·* so far as we apprehend it,
  b 309–13   followed his *d·* of the power of Spirit
    312–31   and his *d·* of divine Principle
    314–25   The higher his *d·* of divine Science
  t 446–16   or his *d·* is protracted, dangerous, and
    460– 1   and rest his *d·* on this sure basis.
instead of
  b 286– 5   and so depend upon belief instead of *d·*,
  o 342– 2   proof and *d·*, instead of opinion
its
  s 111–27   and its *d·* in healing the sick,
  f 241–30   approaching spiritual Life and its *d·*.
  r 483–17   to battle over this issue and its *d·*,
  ap 561–18   divinity embracing humanity in Life and its *d·*,
judgment and
  t 455–19   may be mistaken in judgment and *d·*,
lesser
  s 108–14   and the lesser *d·* to prove the greater,
limited
  m 67–25   the limited *d·* of popular Christianity
mar the
  s 139–24   could neither . . . mar the *d·* of Jesus, nor
my
  s 109– 1   led up to my *d·* of the proposition
of Christian healing
  f 238–32   lodestar in the *d·* of Christian healing,
of Christianity
  f 228–30   when they saw the *d·* of Christianity
of Christian Science
  t 445– 7   to hinder the *d·* of C. S.
of divine Love
  s 135–28   but it was the *d·* of divine Love
  f 241–20   the reflection and *d·* of divine Love,
of divine power
  a 27– 7   Tell John what the *d·* of divine power is,
of divine Principle
  b 312–31   and his *d·* of divine Principle
of divine Science
  b 314–25   The higher his *d·* of divine Science
  gl 583–17   and the *d·* of divine Science,
of eternal Life
  b 279–20   *d·* of eternal Life and Truth and Love.
of healing
  a 41–17   this *d·* of healing was early lost,
of life
  a 45–19   through the revelation and *d·* of life in God,
  f 214– 7   nor been guided into the *d·* of life eternal.
  b 278–24   the *d·* of life as Spirit,
of power
  pr 10–11   the unction of Spirit in *d·* of power
  a 26–25   and of his *d·* of power over death.
of Science
  b 273–27   His acts were the *d·* of Science,
of scientific being
  f 233–11   the *d·* of scientific being,
of Spirit
  pr 14– 5   in the *d·* of Spirit.
of the divine nature
  pr 4–23   through *d·* of the divine nature ;
of the facts
  p 428– 3   A *d·* of the facts of Soul in Jesus' way

demonstration
of this Science
  t 457–23   and advance rapidly in the *d·* of this Science,
of Truth
  pr 2–17   Goodness attains the *d·* of Truth.
  a 37–24   the *d·* of Truth and Life, of health and holiness.
  s 135–30   not merely in the *name* . . . but in *d·* of Truth,
  t 445–12   spiritual understanding and *d·* of Truth
possible
  t 456–15   separates himself . . . from its possible *d·*.
present
  s 123–24   The proof, by present *d·*, that the
proof and
  o 342– 2   The hour has struck when proof and *d·*,
reason, and
  s 109–21   through divine revelation, reason, and *d·*.
rules for the
  s 113– 2   rules for the *d·* of this divine Principle.
Science and
  f 243– 2   the Science and *d·* of spiritual good
scientific
  sp 99–28   the scientific *d·* of divine Spirit
  s 142–21   The strong cords of scientific *d·*,
  b 326– 2   A false sense . . . conceals scientific *d·*.
  p 376–32   to paralyze mental and scientific *d·*.
  t 448–25   must always hinder scientific *d·*.
Scientist's
  t 457–29   The Scientist's *d·* rests on one Principle,
subject to
  o 361–25   must be correct . . . and subject to *d·*.
teaching and
  b 270–18   nature of the teaching and *d·* of God,
their
  a 26– 8   in proportion to their *d·* of his love,
  s 112–18   spiritual rules, laws, and their *d·*,
this
  pref viii–14   this *d·* shows that Christian healing
  a 41–17   this *d·* of healing was early lost,
  o 346–17   How then can this *d·* be
thought and
  c 259–14   the basis of thought and *d·*.
your
  t 456–24   and abide by the divine Principle of your *d·*,
  r 483–11   Moral ignorance or sin affects your *d·*,
zenith of
  ap 565–26   impelled the idea to rise to the zenith of *d·*.

  pr 16– 3   The highest prayer . . . is *d·*.
  a 25–13   Jesus taught the way of Life by *d·*,
    34– 6   If Christ, Truth, has come to us in *d·*,
    34– 7   for *d·* is Immanuel, or *God with us*,
  sp 94– 8   with the *d·* which accompanied it,
    98–16   *d·* of Christian Mind-healing stands
  s 147– 9   under circumstances where *d·* was
    147–18   the *d·* of the rules of scientific healing
  f 226–16   in *d·* of "on earth peace,— *Luke 2 : 14*.
    239– 1   the *d·* by which sin and sickness are destroyed.
  b 270–19   the *d·* which was to destroy sin,
    274–25   establishing it by *d·*.
    000 3   If the Principle, rule, and *d·* of man's being
    329–13   We must prove our faith by *d·*.
  t 455–10   and support your claims by *d·*.
  r 473–26   Jesus established what he said by *d·*,
  gl 592–12   a type of moral law and the *d·* thereof ;

demonstrations
ancient
  f 243–12   the ancient *d·* of prophets and apostles.
his
  c 266–24   his *d·*, which dominate the flesh.
Jesus'
  f 210– 6   are set forth in Jesus' *d·*,
  b 269– 5   Jesus' *d·* sift the chaff from the wheat,
marvellous
  g 540– 1   and was the basis of his marvellous *d·*.
natural
  s 131–28   natural *d·* of the divine power,
of Jesus
  s 122– 9   practically exposed . . . by the *d·* of Jesus ;
  f 243– 8   It crowned the *d·* of Jesus with
simple
  p 429– 5   We must begin, . . . with the more simple *d·*

  a 47– 2   discernment of Jesus' teachings and *d·*,
  s 126–28   the teachings and *d·* of our great Master
    131–28   *d·* which were not understood.
  g 549– 8   give place to higher theories and *d·*.

demonstratively
  o 358–10   sustains logically and *d·* every point

demonstrator
  a 42–15   The resurrection of the great *d·*
    48–19   great *d·* of Truth and Love was silent
    49–14   The meek *d·* of good,
  b 329–10   Be thankful that Jesus, who was the true *d·* of

demoralization
  s 133–15   when they departed from . . . their *d·* began

demoralized
p 407–25   the perfect model . . . instead of its d· opposite.
demoralizes
g 533–14   beguiles the woman and d· the man.
den
p 365–28   convert into a d· of thieves
g 514–27   Daniel felt safe in the lions' d·,
549–26   and beards the lion of materialism in its d·.
denial
evoked
sp 94–19   His healing-power evoked d·, ingratitude,
of Truth
p 372–27   In C. S., a d· of Truth is fatal,
g 542–11   The avoidance of justice and the d· of truth tend
———
sp 91–17   d· of material selfhood aids the discernment
s 134–17   D· of the possibility of Christian healing
ph 184– 9   casting out by d· the error of belief
f 205–29   D· of the oneness of Mind
242– 6   D· of the claims of matter is a great step
gl 590–12   d· of the fulness of God's creation ;
denials
s 113–22   Which of the d· in proposition four is true?
p 394–19   their d· are better than their affirmations.
denied
s 130–18   these material beliefs must be d· and cast out
f 227– 6   claims of the enslaving senses must be d·
o 342–18   Shall it be d· that a system which
r 479–28   So evil should be d· identity or power,
denies
s 120–23   and thus Science d· all disease,
ph 168–18   Are we to believe an authority which d·
b 318–22   The Science of Mind d· the error of
329–19   and d· the rule of the problem
r 492–25   Science of Mind, which d· this notion.
gl 580–28   An adversary is one who opposes, d·, disputes,
denominated
pref viii–27   the discovery of the system that she d· C. S.
denomination
o 360–31   can unite in doctrine and d·
denominator
g 540– 9   reducing it to its common d·, nothingness.
denounce
t 447–20   Expose and d· the claims of evil and disease
dense
c 263–30   A sensual thought, . . . is d· blindness
denunciation
o 341–18   misrepresentation and d· cannot overthrow it.
denunciations
o 342–31   no d· would follow them, even if
g 522–18   God's glowing d· of man when not found in
deny
pr 6– 2   The Scriptures say, that if we d· Christ,
6– 2   "he also will d· us."— II Tim. 2 : 12.
15–18   we must d· sin and plead God's allness.
a 54–32   Would they not d· him even the rights of
s 111–10   some may d· its right to the name of Science.
113–19   Life, God, omnipotent good, d· death, evil,
113–20   Disease, sin, evil, death, d· good,
132–11   any one who should not d· that
ph 189– 8   mortals should no more d· the power of C. S.
189–11   than they should d· the existence of the sunlight
f 232–11   prevalent theories practically d· this,
b 270–10   Few d· the hypothesis that
309–22   led to d· material sense, or mind in matter,
o 348–16   I d· His cooperation with evil,
354– 8   Why do they use this phraseology, and yet d·
             C. S.
357–15   to d· that God made man evil
p 368–29   D· the existence of matter, and
371–25   we should not d· our need of its spiritual
372–25   "Whosoever shall d· me— Matt. 10 : 33.
372–26   him will I also d· before my— Matt. 10 : 33.
380–10   and d· the power of Mind to heal.
390– 4   We cannot d· that Life is self-sustained,
390– 5   never d· the everlasting harmony of Soul,
395– 2   They admit . . . whereas they should d· it
412–11   call the disease by name when you mentally
             d· it ;
t 450–32   who will d· that these are the errors which
453– 1   You do not d· the mathematician's right
g 546–26   though the darkness, . . . may d· their reality.
denying
a 53–23   weep over the warning, instead of d· the truth
s 122–19   d· the testimony of the senses,
ph 182–25   by . . . d· man's God-given ability to
b 339–32   You conquer error by d· its verity.
o 342– 7   the sad effects on the sick of d· Truth.
p 390–25   divine authority for d· that necessity
434–32   D· justice to the body,

depart
a 41– 6   we must d· from material sense
s 112– 5   Those who d· from this method
o 352–28   terror of ghosts will d· and health be restored.
p 363–14   detect the woman's immoral status and bid
             her d·,
r 475–29   The real man cannot d· from holiness,
departed
sp 72–25   may flow from the d· to mortals ;
77–19   Of what advantage, . . . to us, or to the d·,
77–25   The d· would gradually rise above ignorance
77–30   chances of the d· for improvement
78– 9   If the d· are in rapport with mortality,
82– 9   If spiritual life has been won by the d·,
82–18   even if our d· friends were near us
88–31   said to be . . . received from . . . d· spirits.
88–32   the belief that a d· spirit is speaking,
s 133–14   but when they d· from the true idea,
b 321–11   handle the serpent, and then Moses' fear d·.
departing
sp 75–32   the d· may hear the glad welcome of
76– 1   The ones d· may whisper this vision,
s 111– 8   though d· from the realm of the physical,
ph 183– 3   thus d· from the basis of one God,
t 457–24   D· from C. S., some learners commend diet and
department
t 462–19   as they usually do in every d· of life.
departments
ph 197–17   d· of knowledge now broadcast in the earth,
departs
s 112–23   Any theory of C. S., which d· from
142–30   d· from the nature and character of Mind,
g 547– 5   not one d· from the stated system and rule.
departure
a 43– 2   they did understand it after his bodily d·.
sp 91– 7   great point of d· for all true spiritual growth.
f 213–11   Every step towards goodness is a d· from
b 312–10   death is the d· of a mortal's mind,
312–12   belief of that mortal . . . occasioned his d· ;
depend
a 44–14   He did not d· upon food or pure air
ph 168–12   and d· upon them to heal you,
181–18   not sufficiently spiritual to d· on Spirit.
f 228–21   we shall never d· on bodily conditions,
b 286– 5   and so d· upon belief instead of
p 409–28   will not d· on it after death.
422–17   causing it to d· less on material evidence.
ap 569–27   periods of torture . . . must d· upon sin's obdu-
             racy.
dependence
s 152–23   Every material d· had failed her
c 262– 2   Consecration to good does not lessen man's d·
dependency
b 335– 5   would reduce God to d· on matter,
dependent
sp 84–20   not d· upon the ear and eye for sound or sight
89–18   Mind is not necessarily d· upon
s 160– 9   motion of the arm is no more d· upon
ph 170–29   but in either case d· upon his
b 292–17   so-called life of mortals is d· on matter.
311– 3   d· on matter for manifestation,
p 401–21   medicine is d· upon mental action.
r 489–17   How can man, . . . be d· on material means
g 509– 3   d· upon no material organization.
depending
b 314–29   those who, d· on doctrines and material laws
depends
sp 81–28   man's immortality d· upon that of God,
95–15   d· upon his genuine spirituality.
ph 192–22   Your influence for good d· upon
b 296–20   d· upon the tenacity of error.
p 383–32   notion that health d· on inert matter
393–26   certainly means that light d· upon Mind,
409–27   no right to say that life d· on matter
418– 3   d· on mentally destroying all belief in
depict
c 260– 4   or the painter can d· the form and face of Jesus,
g 537–20   this second account . . . is to d· the falsity of
ap 568– 8   The following chapters d· the fatal effects of
depicts
b 319– 3   Science d· disease as error,
ap 571–25   In significant figures he d· the thoughts
depleted
p 416–25   the mental process by which they are d·,
depletion
p 374– 2   Anodynes, counter-irritants, and d·
deplorably
s 143– 8   The sick are more d· lost than the sinning, if
deplore
ph 195–24   barbarisms of learning which we d·,

deport
m 67–13 Thus should we *d·* ourselves on the
ph 180–11 Physicians should not *d·* themselves as if

deposed
p 436– 2 *d·* that he was an eye-witness

deposit
m 63–31 allowed to . . . hold real estate, *d·* funds,
p 373–25 decomposition, or *d·* will abate,

depraved
s 115–22 *d·* will, self-justification, pride, envy,
ph 188– 8 Passion, *d·* appetites, dishonesty,
p 406–28 The *d·* appetite for alcoholic drinks,
t 450– 5 so *d·* that they appear to be innocent.

depraving
f 226– 4 under more subtle and *d·* forms.

depravity
s 115–20 *First Degree: D·.*
ph 195–27 impossible ideals, and specimens of *d·*,
ap 564–18 the highest degree of human *d·*.

depredations
r 490– 4 this belief commits *d·* on harmony.

depress
p 394– 6 majority of doctors *d·* mental energy,

depressed
p 420–18 The fact . . . reassures *d·* hope.

depressing
s 109–16 The search was sweet, . . . not selfish nor *d·*,
p 384– 3 relieve our minds from the *d·* thought

depression
gl 596–20 VALLEY. *D·* ; meekness ; darkness.

deprivations
ph 172–31 teaching us by his very *d·*,
p 385–15 Constant toil, *d·*, exposures, and

deprive
o 358– 2 Can a leaden bullet *d·* a man of Life,
ap 565–12 and *d·* Herod of his crown.

deprived
sp 98–29 are not *d·* of their essential vitality.
f 215–13 is never for an instant *d·* of the light and
b 304–10 Love cannot be *d·* of its manifestation,
p 403–19 *d·* of its imaginary powers by Truth,
435–35 liberty of which he has been unjustly *d·*.
440–32 the rights of which he has been *d·*.
r 490–13 mortals are more or less *d·* of Truth.

deprives
pr 7– 6 *d·* material sense of its false claims.
s 143–22 *d·* you of the available superiority of divine

depth
b 304– 7 nor height, nor *d·*,— *Rom.* 8 : 39.
g 520– 3 The *d·*, breadth, height, might, majesty,

depths
an 105–27 down to the *d·* of ignominy and death.
f 213–30 Before human knowledge dipped to its *d·*
b 902– 5 compass the heights and *d·* of being
ap 567– 3 These angels deliver us from the *d·*.

De Quincey
s 113–14 *De Q·* says mathematics has not a

derange
p 414–10 impossibility that matter, brain, can . . . *d·*
mind,

deranged
p 421– 4 belief that other portions . . . are *d·*.

derangement
p 421– 4 *D·*, . . . is a word which conveys the
423–27 abnormal condition or *d·* of the body

derangements
p 389– 9 Matter does not inform you of bodily *d·* ;

dereliction
g 533–16 charges God and woman with his own *d·*,

derisively
a 49–29 mocked him on the cross, saying *d·*,

derivation
b 338–26 aside from their metaphysical *d·*,

derivative
o 356–29 to create the primitive, and then punish its *d·* ?
p 399–19 is but a *d·* from, and continuation of,

derivatives
sp 93–25 The modifying *d·* of the word *spirit*

derive
f 244– 7 If we were to *d·* all our conceptions of man
p 408–21 *d·* a supposed effect on intelligence

derived
a 18–18 *d·* from the eternal Love.
32– 6 our English word *sacrament* is *d·* from
44–21 in his proof of man's truly *d·* power
sp 72–23 In Science, individual good *d·* from God,
88–28 the possibilities *d·* from divine Mind,

derived
an 101–31 Any seeming benefit *d·* from it is
s 143–27 no power except that which is *d·* from Mind.
o 354–16 *d·* from the traditions of the elders
358–28 power, *d·* from the Holy Ghost.''
p 385– 6 support which they *d·* from the divine law,
g 517– 5 is *d·* from two Greek words,
539–12 possesses nothing which he has not *d·* from God.

derives
s 146–23 Divine Science *d·* its sanction from the Bible,

descending
ap 574–27 soft-winged dove *d·* upon you.

descent
a 43– 8 is what is meant by the *d·* of the Holy Ghost,
s 141–12 line of scholarly and ecclesiastical *d·*,

describe
pref ix– 6 yet he cannot *d·* the world.
g 552–32 Naturalists *d·* the origin of mortal and

described
sp 79–20 He never *d·* disease, . . . but he healed disease.
87– 9 remains to be discerned, *d·*, and transmitted.
s 148– 7 Neither anatomy nor theology has ever *d·*
ph 197– 5 A minutely *d·* disease costs many a man his
p 363–15 *d·* two debtors, one for a large sum and
g 529–25 the species *d·*,— a talking serpent,
ap 558–18 whose flames of Truth were prophetically *d·*
564–12 instigated by the criminal instinct here *d·*.
575– 7 This sacred city, *d·* in the Apocalypse

describes
sp 95–27 when he beholds . . . and *d·* its effulgence?
s 152–10 Anatomy *d·* muscular action as
b 279– 3 A New Testament writer plainly *d·* faith,
g 551–12 *d·* the gradations of human belief,
ap 574–15 which he *d·* as the city which

describing
sp 79– 1 The act of *d·* disease
ap 576– 8 further *d·* this holy city,

description
pr 6–32 strong language of our Master confirms this *d·*.
ph 170–28 The *d·* of man as purely physical, or
194–26 and realizing Tennyson's *d·* :
ap 566–12 If we remember the beautiful *d·*
575–13 The *d·* is metaphoric.
575–16 *d·* of the city as foursquare has a profound

descriptions
ph 179–32 *D·* of disease given by physicians
196–23 forcible *d·* and medical details,
197– 1 and by printing long *d·* which
g 553– 2 and accompany their *d·* with

desert
ap 559–12 heard in the *d·* and in dark places of fear.
566– 5 through the great *d·* of human hopes,
570–15 weary wanderers, athirst in the *d·*

deserted
p 429–11 The corpse, *d·* by thought, is cold

desertion
a 42–13 followed by the *d·* of all save a few friends,
47–27 The disciples' *d·* of their Master
50– 5 last supreme moment of mockery, *d·*,

deserts
m 63–28 If a dissolute husband *d·* his wife,

deserves
f 251–26 nothing is left which *d·* to perish or

deserving
a 22–20 and receive according to your *d·*.
b 296–31 a liar from the beginning, not *d·* power.

design
a 35–30 The *d·* of Love is to reform the sinner.
b 271– 4 uniting all periods in the *d·* of God.

designate
s 114–17 to *d·* that which has no real existence.
123–17 to *d·* the scientific system of divine healing.
ap 571–13 *d·* those as unfaithful stewards who

designated
s 158– 3 *d·* Apollo as "the god of medicine."

designates
t 454–19 inspires, illumines, *d·*, and leads the way.

designed
f 233–30 *d·* to rebuke and destroy error.

designs
s 157–20 If He . . . *d·* them for medical use,
gl 583–28 error, working out the *d·* of error ;

desirable
pref x–31 but sound morals are most *d·*.
a 27–23 but only eleven left a *d·* historic record.
m 65–25 never *d·* on its own account.
p 426– 9 When the destination is *d·*,

desire

cherish the
pr 13–16   If we cherish the *d·* honestly and
energy, and
pr 3–16   consecration of thought, energy, and *d·*.
fervent
pr 4– 3   prayer of fervent *d·* for growth in grace,
13– 6   beyond the honest standpoint of fervent *d·*.
for holiness
pr 11–22   a *d·* for holiness is requisite
habitual
pr 11–30   prayer, coupled with a fervent habitual *d·*
heart's
sp 88– 3   the poet Tennyson expressed the heart's *d·*,
humble
t 448– 5   the Publican's wail . . . won his humble *d·*.
lack of
f 243–15   arises not so much from lack of *d·*
look with
f 234–28   Jesus declared that to look with *d·* on
no
t 445–14   there will be no *d·* for other healing methods.
such a
pr 11–31   Such a *d·* has little need of audible expression.
that
p 407–18   and he will get the better of that *d·*,
thy
g 535– 8   thy *d·* shall be to thy husband,— *Gen.* 3 : 16.
to do right
pr 9–32   Consistent prayer is the *d·* to do right.
unspoken
pr 2–28   The unspoken *d·* does bring us nearer the
wandering
m 58–19   a wandering *d·* for incessant amusement
wrong
p 407–17   Let the slave of wrong *d·* learn the

---

pr 1– *   *What things soever ye d·* — *Mark* 11 : 24.
1–11   *D·* is prayer ; and no loss can occur
2– 5   the *d·* which goes forth hungering after
8–22   does not always mean a *d·* for it.
9–26   Do you really *d·* to attain this point?
10– 1   Prayer means that we *d·* to
10–29   That which we *d·* and for which we ask,
11–24   but if we *d·* holiness above all else,
m 62– 8   If parents create in their babes a *d·*
c 261–12   Under the strong impulse of a *d·* to perform
b 322–32   easier to *d·* Truth than to rid one's self of
o 348– 1   and which we *d·* neither to honor nor to fear.
348–17   I *d·* to have no faith in evil or in
p 398–22   and the *d·* for strong drink is gone.
426–20   It will master either a *d·* to die or a dread of
gl 586–12   ignorance ; error ; *d·* ; caution.

desired

s 136–28   No wonder Herod *d·* to see the new Teacher.
ph 188–32   Astronomy gives the *d·* information
c 260–16   distrust of one's ability to gain the goodness *d·*
g 530–23   saying, . . . more to be *d·* than Truth,

desires

our
pr 1–12   no loss can occur from trusting God with our *d·*,
13–12   public expression of our *d·* increase them?
15–22   in so far as we put our *d·* into practice.
purer
p 407–15   lifting humanity above itself into purer *d·*,
real
pr 10– 4   leave our real *d·* to be rewarded by Him.
right
ap 566– 6   the spiritual idea guide all right *d·*
stronger
c 265–24   gained stronger *d·* for spiritual joy?

---

pr 7–29   uttering *d·* which are not real
sp 73–21   with material sensations and *d·*,
an 102–23   apathy on the subject which the criminal *d·*.
c 257–26   to still the *d·*, to satisfy the aspirations?
t 458–16   the author *d·* to keep it out of C. S.

desolate

sp 96– 8   Earth will become dreary and *d·*,
s 121–15   as the wandering comet or the *d·* star

desolation

p 388–20   which is "brought to *d·*."— *Matt.* 12 : 25.
gl 599– 8   Emptiness ; unfaithfulness ; *d·*.

despair

pr 8– 3   We never need to *d·* of an honest heart ;
ph 170–31   all ills have gone forth, especially *d·*.
174–26   administer a dose of *d·* to the mind?
f 252–29   says : . . . I expand but to my own *d·*,
p 376– 4   latent fear and the *d·* of recovery
382–31   hopeless suffering and *d·*.
433–14   a look of *d·* and death settles upon it.

despaired

b 321– 6   *d·* of making the people understand

---

despairing

a 50– 9   This *d·* appeal, if made to a
ph 166–24   the *d·* invalid often drops them,
p 379–14   Let the *d·* invalid, . . . think of the experiment

despairingly

p 389–32   One instant she spoke *d·* of herself.

despatch

p 386–16   A blundering *d·*, mistakenly announcing
386–20   Another *d·*, correcting the mistake,
434– 2   on the wings of divine Love, there comes a *d·* :

despatches

p 399–11   mortal mind sends its *d·* over its body,

despise

ph 182–14   "hold to the one, and *d·* the— *Matt.* 6 : 24.
r 490–19   *D·* not prophesyings."— *I Thess.* 5 : 20.

despised

a 20–16   "*D·* and rejected of men,"— *Isa.* 53 : 3.
52–13   "*D·* and rejected of men,"— *Isa.* 53 : 3.

despite

sp 81–24   *d·* the so-called laws of matter,
82–14   *d·* his physical proximity, because both of us
s 136– 6   *D·* the persecution this brought
160–21   and become cramped *d·* the mental protest?
r 474–24   *D·* the hallowing influence of Truth

despoil

p 400– 7   we can *d·* "the strong man"— *Matt.* 12 : 29.

despoils

an 102–32   C. S. *d·* the kingdom of evil,

despondent

p 431–24   took control of his mind, making him *d·*.

despotic

an 102–27   It implies the exercise of *d·* control,
f 225–18   potent to break *d·* fetters
225–25   *d·* tendencies, inherent in mortal mind

despotism

an 102–31   Its so-called *d·* is but a phase of
p 375–15   yielding his mentality to any mental *d·*
r 473–18   In an age of ecclesiastical *d·*,
gl 590–13   LEVI (Jacob's son). . . . ecclesiastical *d·*

destination

p 426– 8   When the *d·* is desirable,

destiny

c 266– 5   man's higher individuality and *d·*.
b 281–10   whence its origin and what its *d·*?

destitute

b 275–25   human theories are *d·* of Science.
p 437–12   *d·* of intelligence and truth
g 554–10   *d·* of any knowledge of the so-called
554–11   *d·* of any knowledge of its origin

destroy

pr 5–30   "*d·* the *works* of the devil." — *I John* 3 : 8.
6–27   how to *d·* sin, sickness, and death.
16– 5   and must *d·* sin and death.
a 19–13   declaring precisely what would *d·* sickness,
27–12   "*D·* this temple [body],— *John* 2 : 19.
53–27   and could *d·* those errors ;
sp 73–30   This error Science will *d·*.
78–17   would *d·* the supremacy of Spirit.
81–27   cannot *d·* the divine Principle of Science.
85–12   and discern the error you would *d·*.
89– 9   *D·* her belief in outside aid,
an 104–23   hypnotizer employs one error to *d·* another.
105–29   "Whom the gods would *d·*, they first
s 118–11   It must *d·* the entire mass of error,
123– 2   will surely *d·* the greater error
130–12   and demonstrated, will *d·* all discord,
139– 3   theology which the impious sought to *d·*.
146– 8   By trusting matter to *d·* its own discord,
ph 181–12   You weaken or *d·* your power
186–19   The only power of evil is to *d·* itself.
186–20   It can never *d·* one iota of good.
186–21   Every attempt of evil to *d·* good is a failure,
196–11   able to *d·* both soul and body— *Matt.* 10 : 28.
196–24   help to abate sickness and to *d·* it.
f 203– 6   matter can neither . . . create nor *d·*.
216–13   begins at once to *d·* the errors
217–27   and so *d·* this illusion,
222–32   We must *d·* the false belief that
230– 3   Would you attempt . . . to *d·* a quality
231–19   beliefs which divine Truth and Love *d·*.
232–20   or that they could *d·* human life ;
233–30   designed to rebuke and *d·* error.
249– 8   no mortal nor material power as able to *d·*.
251–14   an error that Christ, Truth, alone can *d·*.
b 270–20   *d·* sin, sickness, and death,
274–28   *d·* the imaginary copartnership,
290–12   Hence Truth comes to *d·* this error
296– 7   suffering or Science must *d·* all illusions
298– 6   belief cannot *d·* Science armed with faith,
299–25   which cannot *d·* the right reflection.

destroy

b 303–18 Science will eventually d· this illusion
  314–14 and said, "D· this temple, — *John* 2 : 19.
  327– 6 Mind can and does d· the false beliefs of
o 343–20 illusive errors— which he could and did d·.
  353–12 omnipotent Truth certainly does d· error.
  357–15 how dare we attempt to d· what
p 374–16 can d· all ills which proceed from mortal mind.
  376–22 d· the patient's false belief
  376–26 D· fear, and you end fever.
  378–10 Remove the error, and you d· its effects.
  378–18 exercised over mortal beliefs to d· them ;
  384–24 or to d· the bad effects of your belief.
  388– 8 when dire inflictions failed to d· his body.
  388–15 admission . . . that food has power to d·
  388–21 If food was prepared by Jesus . . . it cannot d·
  390–14 Let your higher sense of justice d· the
  391–14 Truth, will d· all other supposed suffering,
  394– 2 Truth can d· its seeming reality,
  398–21 d· the illusion of pleasure in intoxication,
  400–19 contending persistently for truth, you d· error.
  404– 5 d· these errors with the truth of being,
  404–11 d· them only by destroying the wicked motives
  405–19 This is sin's necessity, — to d· itself.
  405–25 tends to d· the ability to do right.
  408–17 d· the so-called inflammation of
  412– 3 and d· the human fear of sickness.
  412–15 to unclasp the hold and to d· disease,
  412–22 so as to d· the evidence of disease.
  414–13 d· all error, whether it is called
  417–17 you d· the evidence, for the disease disappears.
  418–17 If arguments are used to d· it,
  418–27 in your efforts to d· error.
  419– 5 Your true course is to d· the foe,
  421–26 If you would d· the sense of disease,
  423–10 the truth of being, to d· the error.
  425–17 can never d· God, who is man's Life.
  425–28 will never believe that heart . . . can d· you.
  426–17 learned that disease cannot d· life,
  426–21 d· the great fear that besets mortal existence.
  428–19 mortal sense cannot impair nor mortal belief d·.
t 447–19 truth and . . . understanding, which d· disease.
  450–26 errors of belief, which Truth can and will d·.
  461–27 first see the claim of sin, and then d· it.
r 474– 2 d· all error, evil, disease, and death.
  474–19 Jesus came to d· sin, sickness,
  474–20 "I am not come to d·, but to— *Matt.* 5 : 17.
  474–21 the evils which Jesus lived to d·
  474–30 "d· the works of the devil."— *I John* 3 : 8.
  490–24 d· all material sense with immortal testimony.
  492–11 progress will finally d· all error,
  493–18 and able to d· all ills.
  494– 2 "D· this temple [body], — *John* 2 : 19.
  495– 7 If sickness is true . . . you cannot d·
  495–19 can d· any painful sense of, or belief in,
  496– 1 will soon ascertain that error cannot d· error.
g 529– 8 will d· the *dream* of existence,
  534–28 will struggle to d· the spiritual idea of Love ;
  540–19 Let Truth uncover and d· error
  544–15 No mortal mind has the might . . . to d·.
  545–10 so improve material belief . . . as to d·
  548–14 helps error to d· error,
ap 568– 4 Science is able to d· this lie, called evil.
  575– 4 this revelation will d· forever the
gl 583–11 comes to the flesh to d· incarnate error.
  596–24 d· the unrest of mortal thought,

    (*see also* **belief**)

destroyed

pr 5–24 Sin is forgiven only as it is d· by Christ,
  6–14 belief in material life and sin is d·.
a 23– 1 Wrath which is only appeased is not d·,
  27–16 The I . . . is not in matter to be d·.
  39– 9 We must have trials . . . until all error is d·.
  50–24 was d· by his death.
sp 73–18 If . . . omnipotent Spirit would be d·.
  76–10 and the belief . . . will be d·.
  81– 4 this latter evidence is d· by Mind-science.
  96– 6 Before error is wholly d·,
  97–15 having been d· by divine Love,
s 122–32 Astronomical science has d· the false theory
  131– 6 When once d· by divine Science,
  163–17 except, indeed, that it has already d·
ph 168–29 if the error of belief was met and d·
  177– 9 both must be d· by immortal Mind.
f 203–21 overtaxed the belief . . . and d· it,
  210– 9 last enemy that shall be d·," — *I Cor.* 15 : 26.
  229– 3 proved that matter has not d· them,
  231– 5 not d· in the mind of mortals, but seem
  233– 5 by the power of Spirit, as Jesus d· them.
  239– 1 by which sin and sickness are d·.
  253–28 The belief in sin and death is d· by the
c 267– 1 Every object in material thought will be d·,
b 274–29 formed only to be d· in a manner . . . unknown.
  290–16 If the change called *death* d· the belief
  292– 1 When the last mortal fault is d·,

destroyed

b 294–17 d· by Truth through spiritual sense
  297–12 Erroneous belief is d· by truth.
  311–13 Evil is d· by the sense of good.
  320–31 if disease and worms d· his body,
  321–14 serpent, . . . was d· through understanding
  328– 9 These errors are not thus really d·,
  338– 8 error which must be d· by Truth.
  339– 3 Being d·, sin needs no other form of forgiveness.
  340–29 leaves nothing that can . . . be punished or d·.
o 352–28 If belief in their reality is d·,
p 369–21 man has not two lives, one to be d·
  370 32 is d· through Science,
  381–13 The so-called laws of mortal belief arc d· by
  389–11 pseudo-mental testimony can be d· only by
  400– 2 When disease is once d· in
  400–27 must be d· by the divine Mind
  406–29 d· only by Mind's mastery of the body.
  411–19 caused the evil to be self-seen and so d·.
  411–22 false sense mentally entertained, not d·.
  418–16 one disease would be as readily d· as another.
  421–20 and when the fear is d·,
  426–32 The human concepts . . . are all that can be d·.
  427–19 last enemy that shall be d· — *I Cor.* 15 : 26.
t 452–32 the wrong power would be d·.
  461–30 you will not feel it, and it is d·.
r 488–30 but they cannot be disturbed nor d·,
gl 593–22 sin, sickness, and death d·.

destroyer

a 48–14 exalting ordeal of sin's revenge on its d· ?
p 435–16 a d· of Mortal Man's liberty

destroyers

p 405– 1 and so delivers him from his d·.

destroying

pr 6–12 is the means of d· sin.
  10–13 overcoming . . . and thus d· all error.
a 40–12 God's method of d· sin.
s 157– 3 mental cause in judging and d· disease.
  160– 1 should address himself to the work of d· it
ph 171–16 and d· the foundations of death.
  184–24 by d· the delusion of suffering
f 210– 8 casting out evils, and d· death,
  241–21 healing sickness and d· sin.
  245– 2 the benefits of d· that illusion,
  248–10 and d· the woes of sense.
b 316–11 healing sickness and d· sin.
  332–15 d· sin, disease, and death.
  339– 5 Does not God's pardon, d· any one sin,
p 368–19 healing the sick and d· error.
  369– 2 and this hinders his d· them.
  379–22 her belief that blood is d· her life.
  401– 8 which you impart mentally while d· error,
  401– 9 (as when an alkali is d· an acid),
  401–17 d· erroneous mortal belief,
  404–11 d· the wicked motives which produce them.
  418– 3 d· all belief in material pleasure or pain.
  422–10 which Truth often brings to error when d· it.
t 446–14 d· his own power to heal and his own health.
  461–29 to recognize your sin, aids in d· it.
  469–23 is the first step towards d· error.
r 473–14 and d· the power of death.
ap 565–26 d· sin, sickness, and death,
gl 581–10 understanding of Spirit, d· belief in matter.
  589–17 d· error and bringing to light man's

destroys

pr 15–13 divine Principle, Love, which d· all error.
a 23–10 an error of sinful sense which Truth d·,
  26–26 He proved by his deeds that C. S. d· sickness,
  36–32 the law of righteousness which d· the
sp 72–10 As light d· darkness
  72–12 Truth d· mortality, and brings
  84–24 d· the belief of spiritualism at its very
  91–19 d· the erroneous knowledge gained from
  98– 6 Christianity which heals the sick and d· error,
s 128–25 d· with the higher testimony of Spirit
  130– 8 divine Science, which d· all discord,
  143– 1 Truth d· only what is untrue.
  157–31 Science both neutralizes error and d· it.
ph 171–29 The opposite truth, . . . d· sin, sickness,
  172–26 If . . . the surgeon d· manhood,
  182–10 for one absolutely d· the other,
  186– 5 C. S. d· material beliefs
f 203–14 d· reliance on aught but God,
  206–27 d· them, and brings to light immortality.
  216– 8 Truth . . . d· error.
  223–30 but the awful daring of sin d· sin,
  231– 4 If God d· not sin, sickness, and death, they
  233–22 the spiritual idea which corrects and d· them.
  243–31 They are inharmonies which Truth d·.
  252–10 understanding of Truth which d· error,
b 275–27 It d· the false evidence that misleads
  276–26 The latter d· the former.
  286–30 But by this saying error, the lie, d· itself.
  288–31 d· what mortals seem to have learned

destroys
b 289–16 a mortal belief, or error, which Truth *d·*
292– 8 only as it *d·* all error and
293– 6 material mindlessness, . . . *d·* itself.
299–24 Truth never *d·* God's idea.
305–26 *d·* all error and brings immortality to light.
315–23 spiritual Truth *d·* material error,
323–27 The true idea of God . . . *d·* mortality.
328–11 *d·* human delusions about Him
339– 2 Divine Life *d·* death, Truth *d·* error,
339– 3 and Love *d·* hate.
o 346–15 Disbelief in error *d·* error,
347–24 Christ, Truth, who *d·* these evils,
350–30 Soul rebukes sense, and Truth *d·* error.
358– 1 axe, which *d·* a tree's so-called life,
p 395–12 faith in God *d·* all faith in sin
420– 1 nor go from one part to another, for Truth *d·*
422–20 Thus C. S., . . . *d·* sin and death.
t 452–14 withhold not the . . . explanation which *d·* error.
452–28 Acting from sinful motives *d·* your power
454– 6 *d·* fear, and plants the feet in the true path,
r 472–11 His law, rightly understood, *d·* them.
474–31 Truth *d·* falsity and error,
483–18 heals the sick, *d·* error, and
485–22 error which Christ, or Truth, *d·*
g 556– 7 *d·* forever all belief in intelligent matter.
ap 561– 3 *d·* both faith in evil and the

destructible
o 360– 7 renders these ideals imperfect and *d·* ;

destruction
attempt the
a 51– 9 to attempt the *d·* of the mortal body
element of
ph 196–10 sin is the only element of *d·*.
error's
o 357–12 and error's *d·* ensured ;
final
b 339– 6 and involve the final *d·* of all sin?
of all evil works
pr 5–31 seek the *d·* of all evil works,
of error
sp 91–13 The *d·* of error is by no means the
b 272–26 triumphs of C. S. are recorded in the *d·* of error
329–26 pardon of divine mercy is the *d·* of error.
r 474–24 hallowing influence of Truth in the *d·* of error,
ap 559–16 made manifest in the *d·* of error.
of evil
a 53–24 sacrifice which goodness makes for the *d·* of evil.
of sin
pr 5–20 the *d·* of sin through suffering.
f 201– 2 the *d·* of sin, sickness, and death.
233– 3 proofs . . . in the *d·* of sin, sickness, and
233–19 compass the *d·* of sin and sickness
b 291– 4 aught but the *d·* of sin,
339– 1 *d·* of sin is the divine method of pardon.
r 497–10 God's forgiveness of sin in the *d·* of sin
pangs of
b 296–20 how long they will suffer the pangs of *d·*,
ripe for
ap 565– 4 against spirituality, and ripe for *d·*.
that wasteth
m 56–17 *d·* that wasteth at noonday.'' — *Psal.* 91 : 6.

sp 91–14 is by no means the *d·* of Truth or Life,
97–17 the riper it becomes for *d·*.
an 103– 6 The *d·* of the claims of mortal mind
ph 173–16 For positive Spirit to . . . would be Spirit's *d·*.
194–10 *D·* of the auditory nerve
f 219–19 *d·* of the belief will be the removal of its effects.
t 451–13 the way, that leadeth to *d·*. — *Matt.* 7 : 13.
gl 586–13 remorse ; lust ; hatred ; *d·* ;
597–29 *D·* ; anger; mortal passions.

destructions
ph 165– * *delivered them from their d·.* — *Psal.* 107 : 20.

destructive
sp 93–17 *D·* electricity is not the offspring of
97–11 The more *d·* matter becomes,
f 210–32 it is without a *d·* element.
b 273–31 atmosphere of mortal mind cannot be *d·*
t 445–25 The human will . . . is *d·* to health,
g 545–17 false view, *d·* to existence and happiness.

desultory
o 354–15 to cleave to barren and *d·* dogmas,

detach
c 261–21 *D·* sense from the body, or matter,
t 463– 8 you should so *d·* mortal thought from its

detached
o 341– 5 criticisms are generally based on *d·* sentences

detail
pref x–14 or treat in full *d·* so infinite a theme.

details
ph 196–23 forcible descriptions and medical *d·*,

detect
p 363–13 *d·* the woman's . . . status and bid her depart,
363–26 did his insight *d·* this unspoken moral uprising?
t 447–25 To put down the claim of sin, you must *d·* it,

detected
c 267–20 more than is *d·* upon the surface,
ap 567–29 *d·* and killed by innocence, the Lamb of Love

detection
f 252–20 elude *d·* by smooth-tongued villainy.

detective
t 449–24 a good *d·* of individual character.

detectives
p 439–31 We send our best *d·* to whatever locality

deter
t 443– 6 tends to *d·* those, who make such a

deterioration
g 533–22 the rapid *d·* of the bone and flesh

determination
a 28– 6 *d·* to hold Spirit in the grasp of matter
p 437– 7 It indicates . . . a *d·* to condemn Man

determine
ph 173– 3 or *d·* when man is really *man*

determined
s 161–28 even if it were not already *d·* by mortal mind.
ph 200–25 "For I *d·* not to know — *I Cor.* 2 : 2.
200–27 I am *d·* not to know

determines
sp 86–23 Education alone *d·* the difference.
ph 167– 8 *d·* the harmony of our existence,
186– 7 the thoroughness of this work *d·* health.
194– 7 and *d·* a case for better or for worse.
f 254–22 the spiritual which *d·* the outward and actual.
p 403–27 The human mind *d·* the nature of a case,
g 508–13 God *d·* the gender of His own ideas.

dethrone
p 378–23 to dispute the empire of Mind or to *d·*
g 546– 7 would *d·* the perfection of Deity.

dethrones
s 148–25 Physiology exalts matter, *d·* Mind, and

detracts
b 283–22 so *d·* from God's character and nature,

detrimental
t 446–28 *d·* to health and integrity of thought.

develop
pref viii– 4 To *d·* the full might of this Science,
ph 199–15 Mortals *d·* their own bodies
g 557– 4 learn how to *d·* their children properly

developed
a 29–29 though at first faintly *d·*.
an 105–22 Whoever uses his *d·* mental powers like an
ph 198– 7 which has already *d·* the disease
198–30 muscles of the blacksmith's arm are strongly *d·*,
p 416–19 and been *d·* according to it,
g 550– 9 nor can Spirit be *d·* through its opposite.

developing
c 258–13 forever *d·* itself, broadening and
p 381– 5 or that some disease is *d·* in the system,

development
explanation and
an 102–26 not . . . an easy explanation and *d·*.
greater
sp 82–32 hastening to a greater *d·* of power,
hour of
c 266–10 When this hour of *d·* comes,
man's
ph 172– 3 Theorizing about man's *d·* from
of disease
p 400–15 and you prevent the *d·* of disease.
403–31 mental conception and *d·* of disease
of pain
p 391–12 you can prevent the *d·* of pain in the body.
opposite
sp 88–22 Excite the opposite *d·*, and he blasphemes.
precedes the
g 553–32 which precedes the *d·* of that belief.
spiritual
m 66–11 Spiritual *d·* germinates not from
g 547–27 not in material history but in spiritual *d·*.
this
ph 199–17 whether this *d·* is produced consciously or
g 530– 2 In this *d·*, the immortal, spiritual law

ph 173–23 according to the *d·* of the cranium ;
189–28 the *d·* of embryonic mortal mind
f 244–31 everlasting grandeur and immortality of *d·*,
p 392–19 liable to the *d·* of that thought
419–17 lest aught unfit for *d·* enter thought.
gl 588– 7 the *d·* of eternal Life, Truth, and Love.

develops
 s 128–15 *d·* the latent abilities . . . of man.
 r 489–11 as consciousness *d·*, this belief goes out,

deviations
 g 502– 7 mortal *d·* and inverted images

devil
 cast out the
  s 135–15 When Christ cast out the *d·* of dumbness,
 flesh, and the
  o 354– 5 "the world, the flesh, and the *d·"*
 hast a
  sp 70– * *Now we know that thou hast a d .— John* 8 : 52.
 is come down
  ap 568–21 the *d·* is come down unto you,— *Rev.* 12 : 12.
 knoweth
  ap 569–23 for the *d·* knoweth his time is short.
 or evil
  r 469–16 *d·* or evil— is not Mind,
  ap 563–19 serpent, whose name is *d·* or evil,
 personal
  o 351–19 a personal *d·* and an anthropomorphic God
 works of the
  pr 5–30 "destroy the *works* of the *d·."— I John* 3 : 8.
  r 474–31 "destroy the works of the *d·."— I John* 3 : 8.

 s 135–16 when the *d·* was gone out,— *Luke* 11 : 14.
 b 292–22 Ye are of your father, the *d·— John* 8 : 44.
 330–31 dementia, insanity, inanity, *d·*,
 t 450– 4 belief . . . in a natural, all-powerful *d·*.
 g 539– 2 In the words of Jesus, it (evil, *d·*) is
 554–23 and one of you is a *d·?"— John* 6 : 70.
 554–25 Jesus never intimated that God made a *d ,*
 554–26 "Ye are of your father, the *d·."— John* 8 : 44.
 ap 567–15 that old serpent, called the *d·,— Rev.* 12 : 9.
 567–19 that old serpent whose name is *d·* (evil),
 gl 580–30 Jesus said of the *d·*, "He was— *John* 8 : 44.
 584–17 definition of

devils
 pr 7– 5 he cast out *d·* and healed the sick and sinning.
 a 49– 5 "Even the *d·* are subject unto us — *Luke* 10 : 17.
 52–32 "He casteth out *d·* through— *Luke* 11 : 15.
 o 348–12 when *d·*, delusions, were cast out
 p 363– * *In my name shall they cast out d· :—Mark* 16 : 17.
 422– 3 "If I by Beelzebub cast out *d·,— Matt.* 12 : 27.
 r 494–30 Our Master cast out *d·* (evils) and healed the
 ap 564– 1 and cast out *d·* through Beelzebub.
 gl 583–18 casting out *d·*, or error, and healing the sick.

devious
 s 164– 1 said : . . . our *d·* career resembles

devised
 s 142– 2 the old systems, *d·* for subduing them,
 ph 183–14 nor *d·* a law to perpetuate error.

devoid
 s 134–15 *D·* of the Christ-power,
 p 300–21 Without this force the body is *d·* of action,
 r 480– 9 whereas matter is *d·* of sensation.
 g 525–29 as *d·* of reality as they are of good,
 549–22 false systems, . . . are *d·* of metaphysics.

devolved
 g 506–28 Upon Adam *d·* the pleasurable task

devote
 f 237–25 They *d·* themselves a little longer to their

devoted
 s 109–14 *d·* time and energies to discovering a
 gl 582– 6 so-called mortal mind, *d·* to matter ;

devotee
 sp 89– 5 the *d·* may become unwontedly eloquent.
 p 382–15 than is the *d·* of supposed hygienic law,

devotion
 a 49– 2 They knew what had inspired their *d·*,
 ph 199–21 *d·* of thought to an honest achievement
 f 241–19 The substance of all *d·* is

devour
 ap 563–26 for to *d·* her child as soon as— *Rev.* 12 : 4.
 564– 1 which would impel them to *d·* each other

devouring
 ph 192–14 It is the headlong cataract, the *d·* flame,
 b 329–15 nor should he remain in the *d·* flames.

devout
 pr 4–29 silent prayer, watchfulness, and *d·* obedience
 7–21 with more *d·* self-abnegation and purity.
 40– 3 The advanced thinker and *d·* Christian,
 o 351–11 as did the prayers of her *d·* parents
 p 367–14 from the summit of *d·* consecration,

devoutness
 s 140–17 Spiritual *d·* is the soul of Christianity.

dew
 ph 193– 9 The *d·* of death was on his brow.
 c 257–20 hath begotten the drops of *d·,"— Job* 38 : 28.
 p 365–18 like *d·* before the morning sunshine.

diagnosis
 s 157– 1 Homœopathy . . . in its *d·* of disease.
 161–26 treating the case according to his physical *d·*,
 p 370–20 A physical *d·* of disease
 408– 9 this general craze cannot, in a scientific *d·*,
 t 463– 3 under influences not embraced in his *d·*,

diametrically
 o 352– 8 the Jews took a *d·* opposite view.

diamond
 g 521–16 the point of a *d·"* and the pen of an angel.
 — *Jer.* 17 : 1.

diapason
 ap 559–14 to utter the full *d·* of secret tones.

diathesis
 p 424–32 a humor in the blood, a scrofulous *d·*.

dictate
 f 228–23 we shall be masters of the body, *d·* its terms,
 p 409–10 matter, . . . cannot *d·* terms to consciousness

dictated
 s 158– 4 supposed to have *d·* the first prescription,

Dictionary, Smith's Bible
 b 320– 8 In Smith's Bible *D·* it is said :

dictum
 t 444– 6 is the *d·* of Scripture.

did
 a 18– 6 He *d·* life's work aright
 25–26 demonstrate this power as he *d·*
 26– 2 gratitude for what he *d·* for mortals,
 30–16 Not so *d·* Jesus, the new executor
 51–20 only through doing the works which he *d·*
 51–24 in all that he said and *d .*
 53– 3 as *d·* the Baptist's disciples ;
 55– 6 Perhaps the early Christian era *d·*
 sp 79–19 Jesus *d·* his own work
 83– 3 What the prophets of Jehovah *d·*,
 85–13 all things that ever I *d· :— John* 4 : 29.
 86– 4 Jesus knew, as others *d·* not,
 an 106–18 classify all others as *d·* St. Paul
 s 130–30 apprehended their Master better than *d·* others ;
 136–31 *d·* not comprehend all that he said and *d·*,
 139– 7 so *d·* Joshua, Elijah, and Elisha.
 141–21 outsiders *d·* not then, and do not now,
 152–16 This he *d·* merely to ascertain the
 156–18 I *d·* so, and she continued to gain.
 ph 168–20 He *d·* the will of the Father.
 193–18 and take supper with his family. He *d·* so.
 193–29 but what I saw and *d·* for that man,
 f 232–17 demonstrating . . . as it *d·* over nineteen
 hundred
 b 314–13 knowing, as he *d·*, that Mind was the builder,
 328–19 explain it practically, as Jesus *d·*,
 329–11 Be thankful that Jesus, . . . *d·* these things,
 o 351–10 as *d·* the prayers of her devout parents
 359–10 while they, the patients, *d·* not.
 p 364–28 show their regard . . . as *d·* this woman?
 400–32 in certain localities had *d·* not many
 t 444–24 part from these opponents as *d·* Abraham
 r 494– 3 and he *d·* this for tired humanity's reassurance.
 495– 3 as surely as it *d·* nineteen centuries ago.
 495– 8 classify sickness and error as our Master *d·*,

die
 m 61–16 often these beautiful children early droop and *d·*,
 sp 75–22 waken . . . out of the belief that all must *d·*,
 94–10 by our law he ought to *d·,— John* 19 : 7.
 o 164–17 If you or I should appear to *d·*,
 164–19 human beliefs that man must *d·*,
 ph 170–11 believeth in me shall never *d·,"— John* 11 : 26.
 197–10 thou shalt surely *d·."— Gen.* 2 : 17.
 f 206–31 does not cause man to sin, to be sick, or to *d·*.
 210–26 cannot say, "I suffer, I *d·*, I am sick,
 221–12 and finally made up his mind to *d·*,
 b 277– 3 "Thou shalt surely *d· ;"— Gen.* 2 : 17.
 289–23 So man, tree, and flower are supposed to *d·* ;
 295–29 teaches that mortals are created to . . . *d·*.
 310–23 If Soul sinned, Soul would *d·*.
 312–12 The belief of that mortal that he must *d·*
 315– 2 believeth in me shall never *d·."— John* 11 : 26.
 328–20 *d·* there annually from serpent-bites
 p 375– 1 mortal mind, not matter, which says, "I *d·*."
 381–15 types of disease, with which mortals *d·*.
 387–13 Our thinkers do not *d·* early because they
 406–25 no more fear that we shall be sick and *d·*.
 426–20 It will master either a desire to *d·* or a dread
 426–30 Man is immortal, and the body cannot *d·*,
 427– 6 Man's individual being can no more *d·* nor
 432–30 he decided at once that the prisoner should *d·*.
 434–31 lower court has sentenced Mortal Man to *d·*,
 435– 5 argued that the body should *d·*,
 435–12 whosoever *sinneth* shall *d·* ;
 435–18 Laws of Health should be sentenced to *d·*.
 436–29 His Honor sentenced Mortal Man to *d·*
 r 481–19 thou shalt surely *d·."— Gen.* 2 : 17.
 486– 6 To *d·*, that he may regain these senses?

die
  g 527–10   thou shalt surely *d*·.— *Gen.* 2 : 17.
       529–20   neither shall ye touch it, lest ye *d*·.— *Gen.* 3 : 3.
       530–14   Ye shall not surely *d*· :— *Gen.* 3 : 4.
       532– 9   thou shalt surely *d*·,'' — *Gen.* 2 : 17.
       545–31   "As in Adam [error] all *d*·, — *I Cor.* 15 : 22.
  gl 580–20   saith, "Thou shalt surely *d*·." — *Gen.* 2 : 17.

died
  a 46– 3   until they . . . learned that he had not *d*·.
  sp 73– 4   but another, who has *d*· to-day
      74–15   belief of having *d*· and left a material body
      75–15   the understanding that Lazarus had never *d*·,
      75–16   not by an admission that his body had *d*·
      75–17   Had Jesus believed that Lazarus had . . . *d*·
      75–24   those who have thought they *d*·,
  s 154–11   a bed where a cholera patient had *d*·.
     154–13   the symptoms . . . appeared, and the man *d*·.
     158–32   was etherized and *d*· in consequence,
     159–20   sequel proved that this Lynn woman *d*· from
  b 290–29   believing that his body *d*·
     290–30   learning that his cruel mind *d*· not.
  p 379–10   fancied himself bleeding to death, and *d*·
     382–26   wrote to me : "I should have *d*·, but for the

dies
  sp 75– 2   mistaken assumption that man *d*· as matter
  ph 168–16   becomes sick and useless, suffers and *d*·,
     177–26   swallowed through mistake, and the patient *d*·
  f 202–17   God, neither sins, suffers, nor *d*·.
     204– 2   It is evil that *d*· ; good *d*· not.
     250–11   which is never born and never *d*·.
  b 275– 1   Matter has no life to lose, and Spirit never *d*·.
     285– 8   material personality which suffers, sins, and *d*· ?
     288–16   the tumult *d*· away in the distance.
  o 349–11   neither Life nor man *d*·, and that God is not the
  p 374–29   Nothing that lives ever *d*·, and *vice versa.*
     427– 2   the opposite belief that man *d*·.
  r 486–11   In reality man never *d*·.
     486–11   The belief that he *d*· will not establish his
     491–21   another belief, that man *d*·.
  g 543– 5   not the real man, who *d*·.
     556–11   *d*· to live again in renewed forms,

diet
  ph 174– 6   to baths, *d*·, exercise, and air?
     197–23   Their *d*· would not cure dyspepsia at this
  f 219–28   and impute their recovery to . . . *d*·,
     220–22   once adopted a *d*· of bread and water
     221– 5   decided that his *d*· should be more rigid,
  t 457–25   some learners commend *d*· and hygiene.

dietetic
  p 389–13   *d*· theories first admit that food sustains

dietetics
  f 220–25   never to try *d*· for growth in grace.

differ
  a 24–26   Then we must *d*· from them both.
  b 273– 8   They *d*· from real Science because they
  t 461–20   Your responses should *d*· because
  r 488– 8   words often translated *belief d*· somewhat

difference
  a 30–23   showing the *d*· between the offspring
  sp 82–24   would be prevented by this *d*·.
     86–23   Education alone determines the *d*·.
  b 293–19   *d*· being that electricity is not
  p 403– 2   *d*· between voluntary and involuntary
     421– 2   The only *d*· is, that insanity implies

differences
  m 63–12   Civil law establishes very unfair *d*·

different
  a 21–18   separate time-tables to consult, *d*· routes
  m 57– 9   These *d*· elements conjoin naturally
     58– 6   Tones of the human mind may be *d*·,
     59–12   *d*· demands of their united spheres,
  sp 74–22   *d*· beliefs, which never blend.
     82–10   *d*· states of consciousness are involved,
     82–12   cannot exist in two *d*· states of consciousness
     82–16   through *d*· mazes of consciousness.
     82–21   their state of consciousness must be *d*·
     82–27   *D*· dreams and *d*· awakenings
  s 139–18   the thirty thousand *d*· readings in the
     149– 8   the *d*· mental states of the patient.
     152–32   symptoms, . . . which demand *d*· remedies ;
     161–32   upon *d*· terms than does the metaphysician ;
     163–24   hypotheses obtruded upon us at *d*· times.
  b 293– 7   are but *d*· strata of human belief.
  p 377–12   Through *d*· states of mind,
     407–30   All sin is insanity in *d*· degrees.
     408–27   and the results would be perceptibly *d*·.
  t 461–21   because of the *d*· effects they produce.
  r 493– 5   the solar system as working on a *d*· plan.
  g 523–27   The *d*· accounts become more and
     525– 8   the term *man* in *d*· languages.
     546–31   a thousand *d*· examples of one rule,
  549–10   three *d*· methods of reproduction

different
  g 552–27   The intermixture of *d*· species,
  ap 566–30   assigns to the angels, . . . *d*· offices.
  gl 598– 6   yet it has received *d*· translations,

differing
  sp 82–28   betoken a *d*· consciousness.
  t 444–14   towards *d*· forms of religion and medicine,
     444–15   those who hold these *d*· opinions.

differs
  s 123–30   C. S. *d*· from material science,

difficult
  sp 82– 3   It is no more *d*· to read the absent mind
     86–22   why is it more *d*· to see a thought than
     91– 9   *d*· for the sinner to accept divine Science,
  s 147–32   Jesus never spoke of disease as . . . *d*· to heal.
  ph 178–17   that chronic case is not *d*· to cure.
  f 218–13   renders both sin and sickness *d*· of cure
     225–25   abolition of mental slavery is a more *d*· task.
  b 318– 4   but for him to conceive of, . . . was more *d*·.
  o 350–17   *d*· in a material age to apprehend spiritual
  p 382–20   more *d*· to heal through Mind than one who
     396–15   not a *d*· task in view of the conceded falsity
     398–29   changes such ills into new and more *d*· forms
     410–15   The more *d*· seems the material condition
     424–22   *d*· to make yourself heard mentally while
     426– 6   finds the path less *d*· when she
  t 448–32   Fettered by sin yourself, it is *d*· to
     449–18   than it does to heal the most *d*· case.
     452– 2   a task not *d*·, when one understands
     460–11   the one most *d*· to understand and
     462–16   There is nothing *d*· nor toilsome in this task,

difficulties
  m 60–11   maternal affection lives on under whatever *d*·.
     63–22   without encouraging *d*· of greater magnitude,
  s 143–14   Driven to choose between two *d*·,
     149–21   remarked . . . mind can never cure organic *d*·."
  p 377–25   organic diseases as readily as functional *d*·.
     394–16   that he should not try to rise above his *d*·.

difficulty
  s 115– 5   and the consequent *d*· of so expressing
     115– 9   The great *d*· is to give the right impression,
  ph 184–28   breathed with great *d*· when the wind was
     185– 1   so her *d*· in breathing had gone.
     185– 3   The wind had not produced the *d*·.
  o 348– 8   Here is the *d*· : it is not generally
     349–13   chief *d*· in conveying the teachings of
  p 403– 8   the *d*· is a mental illusion,
     427–22   great *d*· lies in ignorance of what God is.

diffusive
  m 58–16   benevolence should grow more *d*·.

dig
  sp 79–10   *d*· up every seed of error's sowing.

digest
  ph 175–21   The exact amount of food the stomach could *d*·

digested
  sp 84–31   If . . . thoroughly learned and properly *d*·,
  p 390– 2   she said, "My food is all *d*·,

digestible
  ph 197–25   and the most *d*· food in the stomach,

digestion
  ph 175–25   "Medical Experiments" did not govern the *d*·,
     176–12   There were fewer books on *d*·
  ap 559–23   if you find its *d*· bitter.

dignified
  s 118–21   In all mortal forms of thought, dust is *d*· as

dignify
  s 149–27   predicting disease does not *d*· therapeutics.

dignity
  s 158–17   stupid substitutes for the *d*· and potency
  f 236– 7   emolument rather than the *d*· of God's laws,
  g 527–30   and is man giving up his *d*· ?

dilemma
  s 119– 8   To seize the first horn of this *d*·
     119–11   while to grasp the other horn of the *d*·

diligence
  g 514–15   *d*·, promptness, and perseverance

dim
  s 147–23   hitherto unattained and seemingly *d*·.
  g 513– 8   To material sense, this divine universe is *d*·

diminish
  m 61– 8   *d*· crime, and give higher aims to ambition.
  ph 181–32   will *d*· your ability to become a Scientist,
  f 202–18   The days . . . will multiply instead of *d*·,
     248–31   sin, disease, and death will *d*·
  c 262– 3   Neither does consecration *d*· man's obligations
  p 410–28   will *d*·, until the practitioner's

diminished
  s 155–29   homœopathy, and . . . have *d*· drugging ;

diminishes
sp 96–28 As material knowledge *d·* and
s 155–25 Homœopathy *d·* the drug,
p 415–20 thought increases or *d·* the secretions,
420–20 It increases or *d·* the action, as the case may
423– 4 this fear greatly *d·* the tendency towards a

diminishing
f 224– 1 and the power of sin *d·*,

dimly
s 117–26 human reason *d·* reflects and

din
b 307–31 Above error's awful *d·*, blackness, and chaos,

dipped
f 213–30 Before human knowledge *d·* to its depths

dire
ph 196– 4 can save him from the *d·* effects of knowledge.
p 388– 8 *d·* inflictions failed to destroy his body.

direct
sp 94–25 enabled him to *d·* those thoughts aright ;
an 105– 1 The hands, without mortal mind to *d·* them,
s 138–19 under as *d·* orders now, as they were then,
148– 5 but acted in *d·* disobedience to them.
ph 189–31 keeping always in the *d·* line of matter,
f 228– 1 by healing in *d·* opposition to them
235– 8 selected with as *d·* reference to their morals
249–31 He is the *d·* opposite of material sensation,
b 273–26 in *d·* opposition to material laws.
284–17 which receive no *d·* evidence of Spirit,
o 342– 9 in defiance of the *d·* command of Jesus,
p 370–19 produce very *d·* and marked effects on
t 457–20 no excellence without labor in a *d·* line.

directed
ph 169–23 towards which human faith or endeavor is *d·*.
p 378–30 if such a power could be divinely *d·*,
r 494–19 Reason, rightly *d·*, serves to correct

directing
p 413–25 constantly *d·* the mind to such signs,

direction
another
ph 198–19 Again, giving another *d·* to faith,
any
ph 177–23 in any *d·* against God,
b 280– 9 can never do justice to Truth in any *d·*.
t 445–17 or limit in any *d·* of thought the omnipresence
457– 9 this newly discovered power in any *d·*
every
p 371–19 sick humanity sees danger in every *d·*,
406–21 to avail ourselves in every *d·*
t 458–18 sword of Truth must turn in every *d·*
mental
s 160–24 never capable of acting contrary to mental *d·*.
of mortal mind
s 160–10 no more dependent upon the *d·* of mortal mind,
opposite
ph 195–10 those very senses, trained in an opposite *d·*.
p 388–14 another admission in the opposite *d·*,
right
a 21–13 gain a little each day in the right *d·*,
21–31 imagine himself drifting in the right *d·*.
ph 172– 5 amounts to nothing in the right *d·*
f 219–32 this scientific beginning is in the right *d·*.
248–26 we must first turn our gaze in the right *d·*,
p 401– 3 it does nothing in the right *d·* and
this
p 419– 4 Errors of all sorts tend in this *d·*.
unerring
p 424– 9 the proper sense of God's unerring *d·*
whichever
p 392–23 Your decisions . . . whichever *d·* they take.

m 64– 3 in the *d·* taught by the Apostle James,
p 394– 9 to act in the *d·* which Mind points out.
t 451–15 walks in the *d·* towards which he looks,

directions
sp 86–11 Opposites come from contrary *d·*,
f 220– 6 to look in other *d·* for cause and cure.
b 329– 9 great might of divine Science in these *d·*.

directly
ph 177–29 as *d·* as if the poison had been
187–15 as *d·* as does the hand,
192–31 receives *d·* the divine power.
f 220–32 as *d·* as the volition or will moves the hand.
b 311–19 *d·* opposite to the immortal reality of being.
o 358– 6 If two statements *d·* contradict each other
p 397–11 as *d·* as you enhance your joys by
400– 1 mortal mind, which *d·* controls the body
423–28 as *d·* the action of mortal mind as is dementia
g 533–11 to trace all human errors *d·* or indirectly

directs
s 160–26 as they please or as disease *d·*,
f 254–11 seek Truth righteously. He *d·* our path

dirt
p 383–14 To the mind equally gross, *d·* gives no uneasiness.
413–14 and covering it with *d·* in order to
413–21 I am not patient with a speck of *d·* ;
gl 595–24 UNCLEANLINESS. Impure thoughts ; error;
sin; *d·*.

disable
p 378–27 never endowed matter with power to *d·* Life

disabled
p 373–25 the *d·* organ will resume its healthy functions.

disabuse
s 130–15 would *d·* the human mind of material beliefs

disagree
p 390–27 "Agree to *d·*" with approaching symptoms

disagreement
o 361– 3 cancels the *d·*, and settles the question.

disappear
pref xi–12 and *d·* as naturally and as
a 34–27 he would *d·* to material sense
sp 72– 6 that body would *d·* to mortal sense,
97–27 will *d·* before the supremacy of Spirit.
f 203–29 should *d·* on the shore of time ;
211–21 Sympathy with error should *d·*.
224– 4 As the crude footprints of the past *d·*
228–10 and fleshly ills will *d·*.
248–32 will diminish until they finally *d·*.
252– 8 human beliefs . . . begin to *d·*.
b 295–14 mortal consciousness will at last . . . *d·*,
319–18 Mystery, miracle, sin, and death will *d·*
324– 3 and joy to see them *d·*,
o 347–29 and sickness will *d·* from consciousness.
353–18 All things will continue to *d·*, until
357–23 are false claims, which will eventually *d·*,
p 375– 8 and the chills and fever *d·*.
395–14 sin, disease, and death will *d·*.
415–27 will apparently cause the body to *d·*.
425–13 Then these ills will *d·*.
426–28 death will *d·* with the disappearance of sin.
427– 6 can no more die nor *d·* in unconsciousness
442–22 and sin, disease, and death *d·*.
r 476–11 Mortals will *d·*, and immortals, . . . will appear
476–18 Sin, sickness, and death must *d·*
480–30 understood as nothingness, they would *d·*.
485– 8 soon to *d·* because of their uselessness
g 509–28 appear in man and the universe never to *d·*.
556– 6 These false beliefs will *d·*, when the
ap 561–21 material and corporeal selfhood *d·*,
572–18 seen and acknowledged tha' matter must *d·*,
gl 584– 4 The objects of time and sense *d·*

disappearance
a 43– 3 his material *d·* before their eyes
p 426–29 death will disappear with the *d·* of sin.
gl 593– 4 *d·* of material sense

disappeared
ph 199–30 His fear must have *d·* before his
b 333–18 has sadly *d·* from Christian history.
334–10 material concept, or Jesus, *d·*,
p 436– 5 the Health-agent *d·*,
438–27 he *d·* and was never heard of more.
442–10 all sallowness and debility had *d·*.
gl 580–27 and then *d·* in the atheism of matter.

disappearing
an 102–16 mild forms of animal magnetism are *d·*,
s 115–25 *Second Degree:* Evil beliefs *d·*.
gl 580–24 material belief progressing and *d·* ;
590–24 is *d·* from the recorder's thought,

disappears
a 42– 8 comes in darkness and *d·* with the light.
m 69–10 as the false and material *d·* .
sp 89–10 Destroy her belief . . . and her eloquence *d·*.
97–13 its mortal zenith in illusion and forever *d·*.
s 116– 4 In the third degree mortal mind *d·*,
131– 7 false evidence before the corporeal senses *d·*.
155–27 the potency . . . increases as the drug *d·*.
156–30 matter *d·* from the remedy entirely,
ph 172–14 only as the false sense of being *d·*.
189–12 existence of the sunlight when the orb of day *d·*,
190–18 This mortal seeming . . . finally *d·*,
f 207– 4 until it *d·* from our lives.
222– 1 this phantasm of mortal mind *d·*
230–27 We think that we are healed when a disease *d·*,
251–26 improves mankind until error *d·*,
252–11 until the entire mortal, material error finally *d·*,
c 264–21 Matter *d·* under the microscope of Spirit.
267–25 in which all error *d·* in celestial Truth.
b 274–32 matter, . . . in the light of divine metaphysics, *d·*,
279–16 In proportion as the belief *d·* that life
281– 5 When one appears, the other *d·*.
293– 1 mortality *d·* in presence of the reality.
297–13 that *d·* which before seemed real

disappears
p 368–23   material belief in them *d·*
368–31   When fear *d·*, the foundation of disease is gone.
406–13   Then error *d·*.   Sin and sickness will abate
406–16   all that is unlike the true likeness *d·*.
417–17   you destroy the evidence, for the disease *d·*.
442–24   material, transformed with the ideal, *d·*,
r 491– 6   Destroy the belief, and the sensation *d·*.
g 520–12   These days will appear as mortality *d·*,
520–14   in which all sense of error forever *d·*
gl 595–21   mortal *d·* and spiritual perfection appears.
597–18   in which a material sense of things *d·*,

disappoint
f 234–22   The present codes of human systems *d·*

disappointed
f 245– 5   *D·* in love in her early years,
t 452–25   and you will be *d·*.

disappointments
m 57–31   *d·* it involves or the hopes it fulfils.
b 322–27   as well as our *d·* and ceaseless woes,

disarm
ph 178–25   and we *d·* sin of its imaginary power

disarmed
b 290–31   until evil is *d·* by good.

disarms
p 394–11   *d·* man, prevents him from helping himself,

disarrangement
p 421– 5   *d·*, is a word which conveys the true definition

disasters
s 119–12   to make Him responsible for all *d·*,

disastrous
f 247– 2   is not so *d·* as the chronic belief.

disbelief
a 29– 7   faith in the right and *d·* in the wrong.
o 346–15   *D·* in error destroys error,
p 397–20   in exact proportion to your *d·* in physics,

disbelieve
p 427– 8   If man believes in death now, he must *d·* in it
t 453– 3   You do not . . . .*d·* the musician when he

disbelieving
a 50–27   The distrust of mortal minds, *d·* the purpose

discard
f 213–32   which *d·* the one Mind and true source of
p 425–32   *D·* all notions about lungs, tubercles,

discern
a 22–18   you will *d·* the good you have done,
sp 84–23   by which we *d·* man's nature and existence.
85–11   and *d·* the error you would destroy.
85–21   ye can *d·* the face of the sky ;— *Matt.* 16 : 3.
85–22   not *d·* the signs of the times?"— *Matt.* 16 : 3.
91–16   Absorbed in material selfhood we *d·* . . . faintly
95– 9   able to *d·* the thought of the sick
95–14   to *d·* thought scientifically, depends upon
97– 1   those who *d·* C. S. will hold crime in check.
ph 194– 3   I cannot fail to *d·* the coincidence of
f 233–17   Ye who can *d·* the face of the sky,
233–19   how much more should ye *d·* the sign
c 258–31   you can *d·* the heart of divinity,
b 310–30   which material sense cannot *d·*.
315–13   They could not *d·* his spiritual existence.
o 345–23   ought to be able to *d·* the distinction
t 455–27   if he is taught of God to *d·* it.
g 509–31   can *d·* the face of the sky ;— *Matt.* 16 : 3.
510– 1   not *d·* the signs of the times?"— *Matt.* 16 : 3.
510– 4   To *d·* the rhythm of Spirit and to be holy,
519–12   Human capacity is slow to *d·* and to grasp
534– 2   and to *d·* spiritual creation.

discerned
m 56– 9   Until the spiritual creation is *d·* intact,
65– 6   spiritual and eternal existence may be *d·*.
68–32   the unbroken links . . . will be spiritually *d·* ;
sp 85–17   In like manner he *d·* disease
87– 9   to be *d·*, described, and transmitted.
98–12   which can only be spiritually *d·*.
s 110–23   forever remain to be *d·* and demonstrated.
110–27   and must again be spiritually *d·*,
137– 4   not spiritually *d·*, even by them, until
ph 168–24   I have *d·* disease in the human mind,
f 210– 5   Principle and proof of Christianity are *d·* by
b 275–31   Truth, spiritually *d·*, is scientifically
302– 7   thereby *d·* and remains unchanged.
330–15   nor . . . can be *d·* by the material senses.
o 351–12   spiritual sense of the creed was *d·*
t 461–10   nor is it *d·* from the standpoint of
g 509– 2   Spirit is *d·* to be the Life of all,
512–24   *d·* only through the spiritual senses.
gl 585–10   with which can be *d·* the spiritual fact
598–27   bridge over with life *d·* spiritually

discernible
sp 76–27   a perfection *d·* only by those who

discerning
pref x–28   or *d·* the truth, come not to the light
a 35– 6   *D·* Christ, Truth, anew on the shore
m 60–25   not *d·* the true happiness of being,
s 143–22   never *d·* how this deprives you
f 227–14   *D·* the rights of man, we cannot

discernment
a 47– 1   *d·* of Jesus' teachings and
sp 82– 6   *d·* of the minds of Homer and Virgil,
91–18   aids the *d·* of man's spiritual and
94–30   An approximation of this *d·*
ph 171– 4   Through *d·* of the spiritual opposite
o 346–16   and leads to the *d·* of Truth.
g 505–20   Spiritual sense is the *d·* of spiritual good.
ap 561– 4   leads to the *d·* of the divine idea.
gl 586– 3   EYES. Spiritual *d·*,

discerns
t 462–32   *d·* and deals with the real cause of disease.

discharge
ph 193–20   The *d·* from the sore stopped,
r 478–19   *d·* of the natural functions is least noticeable

Disciple
ap 576– 9   the beloved *D·* writes:

disciple (*see also* **Eddy, Mrs. Mary Baker**)
beloved
a 36–13   the beloved *d·*, and a few women
b 319–32   what the beloved *d·* meant in one of his
doubting
b 317–30   To this dull and doubting *d·* Jesus remained a
impetuous
s 137–26   Before this the impetuous *d·* had
mightiest
a 48–12   shall the humblest or mightiest *d·* murmur
Simon the
p 362– 4   though he was quite unlike Simon the *d·*.

a 21– 9   If the *d·* is advancing spiritually,
28–29   encountered by prophet, *d·*, and apostle,
41–32   belief, . . . never made a *d·* who could cast out
s 141– 6   Because his precepts require the *d·* to
b 271–11   In Latin the word rendered *d·* signifies
324–19   Paul was not at first a *d·* of Jesus

disciples (*see also* **disciples'**)
Baptist's
a 53– 4   He did not fast as did the Baptist's *d·* ;
his
pr 16– 7   Our Master taught his *d·* one brief prayer,
a 32–28   The Passover, which Jesus ate with his *d·*
34–30   his last spiritual breakfast with his *d·*
38–13   He was addressing his *d·*, yet he did not say,
42–28   Jesus had taught his *d·* the Science of
44–28   His *d·* believed Jesus to be dead while he
45–14   after his bodily burial he talked with his *d·*.
45–24   Even his *d·* at first called him a spirit,
46–28   above the physical knowledge of his *d·*,
52–26   prophetically said to his *d·*,
sp 86– 3   his *d·* answered, "The multitude— *Luke* 8 : 45.
s 117–29   Jesus bade his *d·* beware of the leaven of
132–31   once pointed his *d·* to Jesus as
b 271– 7   Jesus instructed his *d·* whereby to heal the sick
313–28   only in a limited degree even by his *d·*,
317–21   presented himself to his *d·* after his
p 367–18   of which Jesus spoke to his *d·*,
388–21   If food was prepared by Jesus for his *d·*,
his immediate
b 328–29   Had it been given only to his immediate *d·*,
his own
a 24–31   his own *d·* could not admit such an
its
o 349–20   this sense must be gained by its *d·*
of Jesus
a 29–13   "The *d·* of Jesus believe him the Son of God."
other
a 27–24   credits him with two or three hundred other *d·*
seventy
o 342–13   He bade the seventy *d·*, as well as

a 32–16   brake it, and gave it to the *d·*,— *Matt.* 26 : 26.
32–21   The *d·* had eaten, yet Jesus prayed and
34–18   Through all the *d·* experienced,
43– 5   all enabled the *d·* to understand
49– 4   and caused the *d·* to say to their Master :
sp 86–10   more spiritual susceptibility than the *d·*.
s 136–24   what the *d·* did not fully understand?
136–29   The *d·* apprehended their Master better

disciples'
a 35– 1   and his *d·* grief into repentance,
47–27   The *d·* desertion of their Master
sp 86– 8   The *d·* misconception of it uncovered

discipline
m 66–28   Xantippe a *d·* for his philosophy.

disciplined
  f 202–10 until *d·* by the prison and the scaffold ;
disclose
  o 344–16 rules which *d·* its merits or demerits,
  t 447–13 evil will in time *d·* and punish itself.
discloses
  f 202–21 experience *d·* the finity of error
discolored
  p 385–21 *d·*, painful, swollen, and inflamed.
discomfiture
  ph 169– 7 to his *d·*, when he was incredulous.
discomfort
  a 53–16 The world could not interpret aright the *d·*
  53–18 which might flow from such *d·*.
  an 101–28 *D·* under error is preferable to comfort.
discontented
  b 305– 2 A *d·*, discordant mortal is no more a *man* than
  ap 559–27 do not be surprised nor *d·* because you must
discord
 accepts the
  s 148–17 drops the true tone, and accepts the *d·*.
 all
  sp 96–20 all *d·* will be swallowed up in spiritual Truth.
  s 130– 8 divine Science, which destroys all *d·*,
  130–12 Science, . . . will destroy all *d·*,
  r 481–23 human verdicts are the procurers of all *d·*.
 and death
  s 124–10 limiting Life and holding fast to *d·* and death.
  f 224–10 life and peace instead of *d·* and death.
 and decay
  b 280– 2 Symbols and elements of *d·* and decay
  r 468–18 eternal and incapable of *d·* and decay.
  g 503–24 no element nor symbol of *d·* and decay.
 and dismay
  sp 96–13 On one side there will be *d·* and dismay ;
 and mortality
  b 338– 7 terminates in *d·* and mortality,
 any other
  p 414–14 dementia, hatred, or any other *d·*.
 apparent
  p 390– 8 ignorance . . . which produces apparent *d·*,
 calls
  m 60–24 An ill-attuned ear calls *d·* harmony,
 can never establish
  o 356– 7 *D·* can never establish the facts of harmony.
 conceding power to
  p 394– 5 By conceding power to *d·*,
 continual
  f 240–14 and there is continual *d·*.
 division and
  s 148–23 how from this basis of division and *d·*
 educated into
  p 414– 3 and thus are children educated into *d·*.
 error and
  p 423–21 superior to error and *d·*,
 fearful
  m 65–11 The union of the sexes suffers fearful *d·*.
 forsake
  p 400–10 only as they forsake *d·*,
 human
  b 306–32 parent of all human *d·* was the Adam-dream,
 instead of
  f 224–10 life and peace instead of *d·* and death.
  253–30 law of . . . harmony instead of *d·*,
 is the nothingness
  b 276–26 *D·* is the *nothingness* named error.
 is unnatural
  b 304–21 and *d·* is unnatural, unreal.
 is unreal
  b 276–15 *D·* is unreal and mortal.
  p 414–23 harmony is universal, and *d·* is unreal.
 its own
  s 146– 8 By trusting matter to destroy its own *d·*,
 learn from
  s 129–25 or learn from *d·* the concord of being?
 marvel at
  ap 563– 1 Human sense may well marvel at *d·*,
 mortal
  sp 98– 3 the elevation of existence above mortal *d·*
  c 262–27 foundation of mortal *d·* is a false sense
 night of
  p 378–28 chill harmony with a . . . night of *d·*.
 no
  b 331–16 in Spirit . . . there can be no *d·* ;
 no rule of
  f 219–20 Science includes no rule of *d·*,
 of every kind
  p 394–26 conquer *d·* of every kind with harmony,
 of every name
  o 355–11 Let *d·* of every name and nature
 opposite
  f 207–30 the opposite *d·*, . . . is not real.

discord
 or harmony
  f 213–28 discoursing either *d·* or harmony
 overcomes
  s 134–22 natural law of harmony which overcomes *d·*,
 physical sense of
  r 493–23 takes away this physical sense of *d·*,
 produce
  m 58– 5 Ill-arranged notes produce *d·*.
 reign of
  s 122– 2 and so creates a reign of *d·*,
 seeming
  p 390– 7 to the mortal senses, there is seeming *d:*
 silence
  r 495–23 and silence *d·* with harmony.
 the unreal
  ap 563– 2 harmony is the real and *d·* the unreal.
 the unreality
  o 352– 3 to make . . . *d·* the unreality.
 will correct the
  m 60–27 Science will correct the *d·*,

  ───

  ph 170– 4 The *d·* which calls for material methods
  186–23 If we concede the same reality to *d·* as to
  186–23 If . . . *d·* has as lasting a claim
  f 228–18 and *d·* as the material unreality.
  c 255– 5 and *d·* into the music of the spheres.
  b 305– 2 subjected to material sense which is *d·*.
  305– 3 mortal is no more a *man* than *d·* is music.
  o 351–24 proves the nothingness of error, *d·*,
  p 368–12 beliefs . . . that *d·* is as normal as harmony
  379–32 belief that . . . *d·* is as real as harmony,
  400–28 Without divine control there is *d·*,
  t 453– 4 when he distinguishes concord from *d·*.
discordant
  ph 184–18 Whatever is governed by a false belief is *d·*
  f 208–28 and he makes it harmonious or *d·*
  209– 3 mortal belief which makes the body *d·*
  213–15 towards the finite, temporary, and *d·*.
  239–25 produces every *d·* action of the body.
  239–27 it is *d·* and ends in sin, sickness, death.
  b 305– 3 *d·* mortal is no more a *man* than
  318–17 so far as he is *d·*, he is not the image of God.
  337–13 while error is mortal and *d·*.
  o 347– 5 whatever is mortal or *d·* has no origin,
  p 369– 2 to admit also the reality of all *d·* conditions,
  387–26 which causes all things *d·*.
  t 444–30 mortals, . . . are *d·* and ofttimes
discords
  pref viii– 5 *d·* of corporeal sense must yield to
  sp 78– 2 like the *d·* of disease, sin, and death,
  s 129– 2 So in C. S. there are no *d·*
  155–22 to offset the *d·* of matter and the ills of flesh,
  ph 183– 5 *d·* have no support from nature or divine law
  f 231–16 God is not the author of mortal *d·*.
  231–17 *d·* have only a fabulous existence,
  b 304–25 To be master of chords and *d·*,
discount
  pr 5–10 there is no *d·* in the law of justice
discourage
  p 424–18 such opinions as may alarm or *d·*,
discouraged
  s 130– 2 *d·* over its slight spiritual prospects.
  b 329–17 To be *d·*, is to resemble a
discouragement
  f 254– 6 or attain slowly and yield not to *d·*.
discouraging
  p 394–13 such admissions are *d·*,
  396– 7 Never startle with a *d·* remark
  t 447–18 without frightening or *d·* the patient
discoursing
  f 213–27 *d·* either discord or harmony
discover
  s 129– 7 *d·* it by reversing the material fable,
  c 260–14 at work to *d·* what God has already done ;
  265–25 we *d·* what belongs to wisdom and Love.
  p 369–15 in order to *d·* some means of healing it.
  370–32 to *d·* the condition of matter,
  t 462–22 to *d·* their quality, quantity, and origin.
  g 548– 5 we *d·* man in the image and likeness of God.
discoverable
  sp 87– 4 lost to . . . the mind in which they are *d·*.
discovered
  pref viii–31 the first steps of a child in the newly *d·*
  an 104–11 Next, they say it has been *d·* before.
  s 107– 1 In the year 1866, I *d·* the Christ Science
  126–23 just as I have *d·* them.
  147–28 This rule remained to be *d·* in C. S.
  b 321–17 when he *d·* that what he apparently saw
  p 408– 4 nor *d·* to be error by many who are sick,
  t 457– 8 this newly *d·* power in any direction

discoverer of Christian Science
(see **Eddy, Mrs. Mary Baker**)

discoveries
s 112–28 and yet uses another author's d·
g 548–27 Modern d· have brought to light important

discovering
s 109–14 devoted . . . energies to d· a positive rule.

discovers
g 549–24 d· the pathway leading to divine Science,

discovery
author's
pref vii–27 Since the author's d· of the might of
his
s 121– 2 if his d· had undermined the
my
s 107– 3 and named my d· C. S.
108–30 My d·, that erring, mortal, misnamed *mind*
109–11 For three years after my d·,
111–26 After a lengthy examination of my d·
115– 8 as brought forth in my d·.
new
p 403–23 Never conjure up some new d·
of the system
pref viii–26 d· of the system that she denominated C. S.
sacred
r 483–13 After the author's sacred d·,
spiritual
p 380–22 Many years ago the author made a spiritual d·,
this
s 153–13 This d· leads to more light.
g 549– 1 This d· is corroborative of the Science
549– 2 this d· shows that the multiplication of

s 123–20 d· of this divine Science of Mind-healing,
c 263–21 the d· of some distant idea of Truth ;
p 411– 3 My first d· in the student's practice

discredit
m 68–25 I d· the belief that agamogenesis applies to

discrimination
m 63–19 d· as to the person, property, and

discuss
p 389–14 then d· the certainty that food can kill man.

discussed
ph 175–22 was not d· according to Cutter
185– 8 which d· "mental medicine" and "mind-cure,"

discussing
f 237–16 kept from d· or entertaining theories or
r 492–17 D· his campaign, General Grant said :

disdain
f 224–19 Cold d·, stubborn resistance,

Disease
p 439–26 meanwhile declaring D· to be God's servant
439–32 reported to be haunted by D·,
439–33 they learn that D· was never there,
441–15 nor can D· cast him into prison.

disease
acute
ph 176–29 Hence decided types of acute d·
p 390–28 approaching symptoms of chronic or acute d·,
advanced stages of
p 391– 8 the incipient or advanced stages of d·,
affirmation of
p 392–11 physical affirmation of d· should always
agrees with the
s 162– 2 the matter-physician agrees with the d·,
all
s 120–23 and thus Science denies all d·, heals the sick,
ph 169–18 not only reveals the origin of all d·
169–19 declares that all d· is cured by divine Mind.
176–25 All d· is the result of education,
f 218–32 all d·, pain, weakness, weariness,
p 377–22 you remove the cause of all d·
392– 6 Fear, which is an element of all d·,
alleviating
an 100– 6 as a means of alleviating d·.
and death
s 116–17 belief in matter, evil, d·, and death,
ph 176–15 d· and death, will lose their foothold.
f 207–23 d·, and death belong not to the Science of
215–19 So sin and sorrow, d· and death,
c 260–21 d·, and death proceed from fear.
p 401– 6 but it engenders d· and death.
414– 2 foundations of the belief in d· and death,
t 450–20 enlisted to lessen evil, d·, and death ;
r 474– 3 destroy all error, evil, d·, and death,
g 547–32 lifts humanity out of d· and death
and its cause
p 393–32 the sin and the sinner, the d· and its cause.
and mortality
g 557–15 the less a mortal knows of sin, d·, and mortality,

disease
and sin
pref viii–13 by healing both d· and sin ;
f 208–32 banish all thoughts of d· and sin
p 420–17 Truth overcomes both d· and sin
r 485–27 and delineates foreign agents, called d· and sin.
antidote to
s 155–30 if drugs are an antidote to d·, why lessen the
any
f 233–29 The counter fact relative to any d·
any other
p 384–27 rheumatism, consumption, nor any other d·
appetite and
p 398–23 Appetite and d· reside in mortal mind,
approach of
p 374–17 Ignorance of the cause or approach of d·
arises
s 154– 3 D· arises, like other mental conditions,
being a belief
ph 168–26 D· being a belief, a latent illusion
belief in
(see **belief**)
belief of
ph 178– 9 The remote cause or belief of d· is not
p 380–18 body is affected only with the belief of d·
398–27 and change the belief of d· to a belief of health.
belief of the
p 377–20 when the belief of the d· had gone.
belief produces
s 159–30 belief produces d· and all its symptoms,
breeds
m 62– 7 master the belief . . . which breeds d·.
called a
p 398– 1 Sometimes Jesus called a d· by name,
called the
p 411– 4 student silently called the d· by name,
call the
p 412–10 call the d· by name when you mentally deny it ;
case of
s 155–21 in order to heal a single case of d·.
ph 196–25 Many a hopeless case of d· is induced by
cause a
p 374– 7 the sick say : "How can my mind cause a d·
cause of
(see **cause**)
causes
ph 188–24 What causes d· cannot cure it.
f 208– 7 What then is this . . . which causes d·
b 318– 8 senses are saying that matter causes d·
o 344–12 understood . . . that error causes d·,
p 399– 4 but if the material body causes d·,
chains
p 380–19 mind ignorant of the truth which chains d·.
challenges
s 162– 3 agrees only with health and challenges d·.
chambers of
p 365–26 finds its way into the chambers of d·
chronic
s 162–18 in cases of both acute and chronic d·
chronic form of
ph 176–31 less distinct type and chronic form of d·.
classify
r 483– 5 We classify d· as error,
consume with
f 205– 4 drop with drunkenness, consume with d·,
consumption, or
p 426– 1 notions about . . . consumption, or d·
crisis of the
t 446– 8 or it may mark the crisis of the d·.
crop of
ph 188–25 an abundant or scanty crop of d·,
cure
an 101–26 seems to alleviate or to cure d·,
f 208–15 absurd to suppose that matter can . . . cure d·,
cure of
pref xi– 4 results in the cure of d·.
s 147– 5 its present application to the cure of d·.
149– 3 far outweighs drugs in the cure of d·
t 457–31 Let this Principle be applied to the cure of d·
declaring
ph 180–18 by declaring d· to be a fixed fact,
depicts
b 319– 3 Science depicts d· as error,
describing
sp 79– 1 The act of describing d· . . . is not scientific.
descriptions of
ph 179–32 Descriptions of d· given by physicians
destroy
p 412–15 and to destroy d·, sin, and death.
t 447–20 truth and . . . which destroy d·.
destroying
s 157– 3 in judging and destroying d·.
destroys
p 420– 1 nor go from one part to another, for Truth destroys d·.

disease

developed the
ph 198– 7 his fear, which has already developed the *d·*

development of
p 400–15 you prevent the development of *d·*.
403–31 mental conception and development of *d·*

diagnosis of
s 157– 1 Homœopathy . . . in its diagnosis of *d·*.
p 370–20 A physical diagnosis of *d·* . . . tends to

disappears
f 230–27 We think that we are healed when a *d·* disappears,
p 417–17 you destroy the evidence, for the *d·* disappears.

discords of
sp 78– 2 like the discords of *d·*, sin, and death,

disquisitions on
p 371– 5 Disquisitions on *d·* have a mental effect

dread
b 321–23 white as snow with the dread *d·*,

dream of
p 396–30 It breaks the dream of *d·*

eradicate the
ph 180–20 before they go to work to eradicate the *d·*

error and
pr 5–32 all evil works, error and *d·* included.

error, or
p 400–18 By lifting thought above error, or *d·*, and

every
p 400–16 if you understand that every *d·* is an error,
411–32 it alleviates the symptoms of every *d·*.

evidence of
p 412–23 so as to destroy the evidence of *d·*.

evil and
t 447–21 Expose . . . the claims of evil and *d·*

evil called
s 135–14 and when Truth casts out the evil called *d·*,

exemption from
p 411–29 their exemption from *d·* and danger.

expels the
s 153– 3 it is not the drug which expels the *d·*

explanation of
p 374–10 The author . . . in her explanation of *d·*

fastens
p 395–28 fastens *d·* on the patient,

fear of
ph 169–13 by exciting fear of *d·*,
188–27 Sin and the fear of *d·* must be uprooted
197–31 should suppress his fear of *d·*,
p 373–14 The fear of *d·* and the love of sin are
377–32 fear of *d·*, which associates sickness with
400– 3 the fear of *d·* is gone, and therefore
t 455–11 lost in the belief and fear of *d·* or sin,

fear of the
ph 196–28 but from the fear of the *d·*

feelings or
p 396– 6 inquiries relative to feelings or *d·*.

fetters of
t 449– 1 to free another from the fetters of *d·*.

forms of
p 398–29 more difficult forms of *d·*.

fosters
ph 169–12 faith . . . in drugs begets and fosters *d·*

foundation of
p 368–31 When fear disappears, the foundation of *d·* is gone.
t 453–27 increases fear, the foundation of *d·*,

functional
s 149–24 as readily as she has cured purely functional *d·*,

God never decreed
f 221–19 that God never decreed *d·*,

has no intelligence
p 378– 3 *D·* has no intelligence.
391–24 *D·* has no intelligence to declare itself
419–12 *D·* has no intelligence with which to move

heal
pref x–21 His disposition and power to heal *d·*.
f 202–29 and yet we rely on . . . to heal *d·*, as if

healed
sp 79–22 He never described . . . but he healed *d·*.
p 386–13 healed *d·* through the action of Truth.

healing
s 150– 3 through this Christian system of healing *d·*.

heals
t 445–24 cast out by the divine Mind which heals *d·*.

health or
s 120–27 matter's supposed consciousness of health or *d·*,

he discerned
sp 85–17 In like manner he discerned *d·*

hinders
p 374–21 this belief helps rather than hinders *d·*.

holds
p 395–27 Mental practice, which holds *d·* as a

illusions about
p 413–27 illusions about *d·*, health-laws, and death,

disease

image of
s 154– 7 the fear that creates the image of *d·*
p 400–12 Eradicate the image of *d·* from the

images of
ph 175– 1 We should prevent the images of *d·* from
197– 2 which mirror images of *d·* distinctly in thought.

imbecility or
ph 197–15 removed from imbecility or *d·*.

incipient stages of
p 390–30 Meet the incipient stages of *d·* with

increase
s 159–32 is liable to increase *d·* with his own mind,

induce
p 370–22 physical diagnosis . . . tends to induce *d·*.
417–30 Show them how mortal mind seems to induce *d·*

induces
p 392–28 the condition . . . which you say induces *d·*,

injuries, and
p 402–17 You say that accidents, injuries, and *d·* kill

insist that
p 409– 3 insist that *d·* is formed by mortal mind

is abnormal
s 120–14 health is normal and *d·* is abnormal.

is an experience
r 493–20 *D·* is an experience of so-called mortal mind.

is an image
p 411–23 *D·* is an image of thought externalized.

is expressed
p 373–21 *D·* is expressed not so much by the lips as in

is less than mind
p 378– 7 *D·* is less than mind, and Mind can control it.

is mental
b 270–28 *d·* is mental, not material.
p 377–26 cause of all so-called *d·* is mental,

is unreal
f 229–32 the truth that *d·* is *unreal.*

itself
p 419–11 Neither *d·* itself, sin, nor fear has the power

leads to
s 120–29 confirms that testimony . . . and so leads to *d·*.

less
ph 175– 6 there will be better constitutions and less *d·*.
g 554–32 This would indicate that there is less *d·*

less for the
p 421–12 treat the patient less for the *d·* and

load with
ph 176–17 Human fear of miasma would load with *d·*

malignant
p 373– 6 It is easier to cure the most malignant *d·* than

method of treating
o 344–26 to investigate this method of treating *d·*?

methods of treating
o 344–19 There are various methods of treating *d·*,

minutely described
ph 197– 5 A minutely described *d·* costs many

mortality and
p 395–10 its claims over mortality and *d·*.

name of a
p 411–13 once Jesus asked the name of a *d·*,

name of the
p 396–10 avoid speaking aloud the name of the *d·*.

never described
sp 79–21 He never described *d·*,

never spoke of
s 147–32 Jesus never spoke of *d·* as dangerous

no hereditary
p 412–32 knows that there can be no hereditary *d·*,

nor death
s 140–27 causeth no evil, *d·*, nor death.
p 368–22 Neither evil, *d·*, nor death can be

not aggravate the
p 401–12 This fermentation should not aggravate the *d·*,

one
ph 176–24 One *d·* is no more real than another.
o 348– 9 one *d·* can be just as much a delusion as another.
p 418–15 one *d·* would be as readily destroyed as another.
r 483– 4 exchanging one *d·* for another.

organic
s 149–23 The author has cured what is termed organic *d·*
162–25 C. S. heals organic *d·* as surely
ph 176–21 Should all cases of organic *d·* be treated by
177– 1 Human mind produces what is termed organic *d·*
180–32 dissolve a tumor, or cure organic *d·*,
p 428–30 The author has healed hopeless organic *d·*,

origin of
p 374–18 no argument against the mental origin of *d·*.

origin of all
ph 169–18 reveals the origin of all *d·* as mental,

or its symptoms
p 419–32 *d·* or its symptoms cannot change forms,

or sin
b 323–24 contemplation of something better than *d·* or sin
p 402–19 whether it be a broken bone, *d·*, or sin.
t 455–11 the belief and fear of *d·* or sin,

disease

outlines of
ph 175– 2 we should efface the outlines of *d·*
pain or
p 421–15 belief that . . . produces pain or *d·*.
physical
s 150–14 the metaphysical healing of physical *d·* ;
power of
p 376–31 To fear and admit the power of *d·*,
predicting
s 149–27 predicting *d·* does not dignify therapeutics.
prevent
ph 170–18 If there are material laws which prevent *d·*,
198–12 It is better to prevent *d·* from forming in
p 412–16 To prevent *d·* or to cure it,
preventing
s 147–28 this Principle of healing and preventing *d·*.
produce
p 399– 4 You say . . . material combinations produce *d·* ;
produces
f 228–16 absurd to suppose that . . . God, produces *d·*
b 270–27 If a sense of *d·* produces suffering
pulmonary
m 63– 2 for warding off pulmonary *d·*
f 203– 1 that this cold may produce fatal pulmonary *d·* ;
p 392–20 in the form of what is termed pulmonary *d·*,
question of
p 406–18 he should be as fearless on the question of *d·*.
regarding
p 403–24 Never conjure up . . . forebodings regarding *d·*
432–13 says : . . . there is a statute regarding *d·*,
relative to
ph 198–10 who outlines his thought relative to *d·*,
removal of
o 358–27 in the removal of *d·*
remove
p 400–20 When we remove *d·* by addressing the
render
p 433– 6 that laws of nature render *d·*
reports
p 409–13 belief, that . . . body, suffers and reports *d·*
resist
p 420–11 they can resist *d·* and ward it off,
says to
s 144–22 says to *d·*, "Peace, be still." — *Mark* 4 : 39.
sender of
s 158– 8 Apollo was also regarded as the sender of *d·*,
sense of
b 270–27 If a sense of *d·* produces suffering
p 421–27 If you would destroy the sense of *d·*,
should not implant
ph 180–17 Doctors should not implant *d·* in the thoughts
sickness and
ph 179–23 the promoters of sickness and *d·*.
sin and
    (*see* **sin**)
sin, and death
sp 78– 2 like the discords of *d·*, sin, and death,
b 275–29 so-called powers, such as . . . *d·*, sin, and death,
p 412–15 and to destroy *d·*, sin, and death.
sin, . . . and death
    (*see* **sin**)
sin or
p 396–17 not because the testimony of sin or *d·* is true,
sin, . . . or death
f 253–16 overcome the belief in sin, *d·*, or death.
253–25 supposed necessity for sin, *d·*, or death,
p 380– 9 the demands of sin, *d·*, or death,
slough of
ph 168–13 already brought yourself into the slough of *d·*
so-called
ph 168–26 before the so-called *d·* made its appearance
p 377–26 cause of all so-called *d·* is mental,
soil of
ph 188–24 The soil of *d·* is mortal mind,
some
p 381– 5 or that some *d·* is developing
speak to
p 395– 7 speak to *d·* as one having authority over it,
subject to
s 150–19 believe that both . . . are subject to *d·*,
suffering and
f 221–17 He learned that suffering and *d·* were the
supposed
p 418–19 the negation must extend to the supposed *d·*
supposed rights of
o 348–22 defending the supposed rights of *d·*,
symptoms of
s 153– 4 or changes one of the symptoms of *d·*.
p 390–12 When the first symptoms of *d·* appear,
398–18 are known to relieve the symptoms of *d·*.
system of treating
s 111–30 my metaphysical system of treating *d·*
tattling about
s 153–31 we shall avoid loquacious tattling about *d·*,

disease

their
p 416–27 If they ask about their *d·*,
the very
s 161–27 would naturally induce the very *d·*
this
s 154–12 Immediately the symptoms of this *d·* appeared,
ph 174–27 Why . . . picture this *d·* to the mind,
p 425– 8 leading points included . . . in this *d·*.
thought of
ph 198–15 The thought of *d·* is formed before
p 396– 2 never hold in mind the thought of *d·*,
thoughts of
ph 196–21 so efface the images and thoughts of *d·*,
f 208–32 banish all thoughts of *d·* and sin
to see
p 421–25 It is no more Christianly scientific to see *d·*
transmission of
f 228– 3 The transmission of *d·* or of certain
treatment of
pref viii– 1 in the treatment of *d·* as well as of sin,
s 126–23 its application to the treatment of *d·*
157–22 and recommend them for the treatment of *d·*?
p 369– 4 is unfitted for the successful treatment of *d·*.
treats
b 318–24 Medical science treats *d·* as though
t 459–30 treats *d·* with more certain results
types of
p 381–15 cannot legislate the times, . . . and types of *d·*,
396– 3 all forms and types of *d·*,
unreal
p 417–24 the way to cure . . . is to make *d·* unreal
unreality of
p 417–26 understand the unreality of *d·* in Science.
t 461–29 to prove . . . the error or unreality of *d·*,
unsee the
t 461–29 you must mentally unsee the *d·* ;
weariness and
ph 183–16 supposed laws which result in weariness and *d·*
what is termed
ph 188– 3 What is termed *d·* does not exist.
when treating
p 424–27 well to be alone with . . . when treating *d·*.
will vanish
p 365–17 *d·* will vanish into its native nothingness
yoke of
g 555– 5 physical organism under the yoke of *d·*.
you overcome
p 392– 2 it is through divine Mind that you overcome *d·*.

————

s 108–25 called error, sin, sickness, *d·*, death,
113–20 omnipotent good, deny death, evil, sin, *d·*.
113–20 *D·*, sin, evil, death, deny good, omnipotent God,
115–23 hatred, revenge, sin, sickness, *d·*, death.
137– 6 the victor over sickness, sin, *d·*, death,
159–21 and not from the *d·* or the operation.
160–26 If muscles can cease to act . . . as *d·* directs,
162–24 I have restored . . . where *d·* was organic.
ph 168–24 I have discerned *d·* in the human mind,
169–10 *d·* has a mental, mortal origin,
176–26 *d·* can carry its ill-effects no farther than
196–20 Such books as will rule *d·* out of mortal mind,
f 230–18 no more . . . than . . . and health occasion *d·*.
251–24 the healer of sin, *d·*, death.
b 318–24 as though *d·* were real,
318–25 If *d·* is right it is wrong to heal it.
320–30 even if *d·* and worms destroyed his body,
o 345–32 not . . . to "educate the idea of God, or treat it for *d·*,"
348– 4 even while treating them as *d·* ;
348– 6 making the *d·* appear to be . . . an illusion?
348–22 complaining of the suffering *d·* brings,
353– 2 Sin, *d·*, whatever seems real to
p 368–28 mortality (and therefore *d·*)
369–15 never . . . made a reality of *d·*
369–16 Jesus never asked if *d·* were acute
371–30 and health instead of *d·*.
373–11 the sick recover more rapidly from *d·* than
373–29 we call these conditions *d·*.
378–22 *D·* is not an intelligence to dispute
379– 1 If *d·* can attack and control the body
395–21 It is mental quackery to make *d·* a reality
400– 2 When *d·* is once destroyed
400– 3 therefore the *d·* is thoroughly cured.
409– 2 "But if *d·* obtains in matter, why do you insist
411–14 a *d·* which moderns would call *dementia*.
411–21 *D·* is always induced by a false sense
412–21 Argue . . . that the patient has no *d·*,
415– 2 *d·* is neither a cause nor an effect.
417–21 *D·* should not appear real to the physician,
419–12 Neither . . . has the power to cause *d·* or a
419–14 If *d·* moves, mind, not matter, moves it ;
420–25 they can meet *d·* fearlessly, if
421–18 There is *no d·*.
426–17 *d·* cannot destroy life,

disease

p 426–31 human concepts named matter, death, d·,
  432–14 he upon whose person d· is found
t 457–13 cannot . . . both cure and cause d·
gl 595– 5 Mortality ; error ; sin ; sickness ; d· ;

disease-beliefs

p 409– 7 the more prolific it is likely to become in sin and d·.

diseased

s 164–15 and all d· thought-germs are exterminated.
ph 174–27 Why declare that the body is d·,
  193–21 The d· condition had continued there ever since
f 209– 3 belief which makes the body discordant and d·
  217–17 When you have once conquered a d· condition
  237–20 either sinful or d· thoughts.
  243–18 dizzy, d·, consumptive, or lame.
  253–22 Also, if you believe yourself d·,
p 376–24 representing man as healthy instead of d·,
  395–32 would prevent the brain from becoming d·,
  403– 2 induced their own d· conditions.
  404–10 malice, and all sorts of evil are d· beliefs,
  421– 2 insanity implies belief in a d· brain,
  425–14 If the body is d·, this is but one of the
  428– 1 no inaction, d· action, overaction, nor
  432–17 become d·, transgress the laws, and
r 487–31 This Principle makes whole the d·,

diseases

array of
ph 176–11 A ghastly array of d· was not paraded
certain
s 154– 5 Since it is a law of mortal mind that certain d·
classification of
s 164– 5 "No systematic . . . classification of d·
define
b 318– 5 Corporeal senses define d· as realities ;
hereditary
p 424–29 scrofula and other so-called hereditary d·,
most
p 414– 6 it yields more readily than do most d· to the
organic
p 377–24 You also remove. . .what are termed organic d·
other
p 376– 2 more terrifying than that of most other d·.
  414– 9 The arguments . . . are the same as in other d· :
our
b 320–29 hope in Him who healeth all our d· ;
violence of
pref viii–23 increased violence of d· since the flood.
worst of
p 396– 1 a moral offence is indeed the worst of d·.

––––––

s 138–11 He showed that d· were cast out
  150–32 are flooding the world with d·,
ph 165–13 D· have multiplied, since man-made material
  196–32 sorrows and d· among the human family.
  197– 1 It does this by giving names to d·
p 376– 7 d· deemed dangerous sometimes come from
t 453–26 nor give names to d·,

disentangles

s 114–26 d· the interlaced ambiguities of being,

disgrace

s 120–32 d· and starvation stared him in the face ;

disguise

f 254–26 What is there to strip off error's d· ?
o 343–14 Jesus strips all d· from error,
l 454–10 the great truth which strips all d· from error.
r 472–29 until God strips off their d·.

disgusted

s 163–23 we cannot help being d· with the

disgusting

p 407– 5 Puffing the obnoxious fumes . . . is at least d·.

disheartening

p 380–28 Nothing is more d· than to believe

dishonest

ph 192–16 all that is selfish, wicked, d·, and impure.
f 252–18 and says : I am wholly d·,
t 448–16 A d· position is far from Christianly

dishonestly

s 130– 7 It is vain to speak d· of

dishonesty

an 103– 4 further defines it as d· and craftiness.
  104–19 d·, sensuality, falsehood, revenge,
ph 188– 9 Passion, depraved appetites, d·, envy,
b 330–29 d·, selfishness, envy, hypocrisy,
p 404–29 envy, d·, fear, . . . make a man sick,
t 453–16 D· is human weakness,
  456–16 Any d· in your theory and practice
  464–28 Neither d· nor ignorance ever founded,

dishonor

f 228–26 to acknowledge any other power is to d· God.
r 483–22 Science of Mind seems to bring into d· the

dishonorest

o 349– 6 breaking the law, d· thou God?"— Rom. 2: 23.

dishonors

ph 183–30 If C. S. d· human belief,

disinclined

f 218–14 sinner, d· to self-correction,

disintegrated

p 429–20 he could not exist after the body is d·.

dislocated

p 402– 6 broken bones, d· joints, and spinal vertebræ.

dislocation

p 402–15 no breakage nor d· can really occur.
  408–22 d· of the tarsal joint would produce

dislocations

p 401–30 the adjustment of broken bones and d·

dismal

ph 195– 5 Outside of d· darkness and cold silence
b 272–27 the d· beliefs of sin, sickness, and death.

dismay

sp 96–14 On one side there will be discord and d· ;

dismiss

s 149–30 d· superstition, and demonstrate truth
p 390–21 D· it with an abiding conviction
t 454–25 Do not d· students at the close of a

dismissal

f 218–25 Treat a belief in sickness . . . with sudden d·.

disobedience

a 19–27 If living in d· to Him, we ought to feel no
s 148– 6 but acted in direct d· to them.
f 227–31 d· to which would have made man ill,
p 436–31 construed . . . as d· to the law of Life.
  440– 3 on the ground of hygienic d·,
  440–12 d· to the so-called laws of Matter
  440–13 d· to God, or an act of homicide.

disobey

p 372–16 nor d· the law of God.
r 483–10 you must not be ignorant of . . . nor d·

disobeyed

ph 184–23 a law of this so-called mind has been d·.
p 385–27 a law of mortal mind which you have d·.

disorder

s 135– 7 The miracle introduces no d·,
ph 184–10 belief which produces a mortal d·,
p 402–30 Science cannot produce both d· and order.
  404–14 you can remove this d· as God's law is
  415–25 To remove the error producing d·, you must

disordered

ph 181– 3 Before deciding that the body, matter, is d·,
p 408–18 the so-called inflammation of d· functions,

disown

s 119– 4 When we endow matter. . .we d· the Almighty,
o 342–26 Who would be the first to d· the Christliness of

dispel

ph 198–16 and before the doctor undertakes to d· it

dispelling

b 332–13 d· the illusions of the senses ;

dispels

sp 80–15 Science d· mystery and explains
b 283– 1 Truth is the light which d· error.

dispensation

s 123–26 did not specially belong to a d· now ended,
  150–10 for its establishment as a permanent d·
b 270–16 hence their foresight of the new d· of Truth.

dispensed

p 389– 1 the food or this thought must be d· with,

disperse

f 205–17 catch clear glimpses of God only as the mists d·,

display

m 60–23 personal adornment, d·, and pride,
b 317–32 Nothing but a d· of matter
p 367–12 the arrogance of rank and d· of scholarship,

displayed

s 121– 9 d· upon the empyrean,
  121–31 d· in the . . . government of the universe.
  163–25 Nowhere is the imagination d· to a greater
p 378–31 less wisdom than we usually find d· in

displeasure

g 542– 2 It incurs divine d·, and it would kill Jesus
ap 571– 9 to tell a man his faults, and so risk human d·

disport

g 514– 7 infinite ideas run and d· themselves.

disposal

b 304–19 is not, therefore, at the d· of physical sense.
  305– 1 placed at the d· of illusions,

disposes

r 473– 4 The Science of Mind d· of all evil.

disposition
pref x–21 so little faith in His *d·* and power to heal
 m 59–24 to grumble over incompatibility of *d·*.
 s 130– 2 The licentious *d·* is discouraged
 b 324– 1 this *d·* helps to precipitate the
 g 542– 9 the *d·* to excuse guilt . . . is punished.
dispossesses
 p 375–12 *d·* the patient of his individuality
disprove
 s 164–20 does not in the least *d·* C. S. ;
disputations
 o 342– 1 Paul alludes to "doubtful *d·*."— *Rom.* 14 : 1.
dispute
 p 378–22 Disease is not an intelligence to *d·* the
 390–12 *d·* the testimony of the material senses
 r 490– 2 but the grand truths of C. S. *d·* this error.
 492–16 will *d·* the ground, until one is
disputed
 f 227– 4 and that, even as oppressive laws are *d·*
disputes
 gl 580–29 An adversary is one who opposes, denies, *d·*,
disputing
 g 539–22 *D·* these points with the Pharisees
disquieted
 p 362– * *And why art thou d· within me?*— *Psal.* 42 : 11.
disquisitions
 p 371– 5 *D·* on disease have a mental effect similar to
 387–20 instead of reading *d·* on the
disregard
 m 64–27 Let not mortals permit a *d·* of law
 f 210–10 his *d·* of matter and its so-called laws.
disregarded
 f 227–32 Jesus would not have *d·* those laws
 p 365–12 if . . . common sense and common humanity are *d·*,
disregarding
 t 445–28 thus *d·* the morals of the student
disrobe
 f 201–14 Let us *d·* error.
dissatisfied
 f 240–23 we must become *d·* with it.
dissection
 b 338–25 The *d·* and definition of words,
 t 462–21 and consists in the *d·* of thoughts
disseminating
 an 100–10 *d·* itself through the substance of the
dissent
 s 155–12 individual *d·* or faith, unless it rests on Science,
dissimulation
 r 483–31 fulfil one's mission without timidity or *d·*,
dissipates
 sp 79–30 It *d·* fatigue in doing good.
 p 375– 2 as painlessly as gas *d·* into the air
dissolute
 m 63–28 If a *d·* husband deserts his wife,
dissolution
 b 290–18 If . . . happiness would be won at the moment of *d·*,
 297–18 but subject to change and *d·*.
 g 550–18 birth, decay, and *d·* as its component stages
dissolve
 ph 180–31 To reduce inflammation, *d·* a tumor,
 f 242–16 *d·* with the universal solvent of Love
dissolves
 sp 74–11 the error which has held the belief *d·*
 s 162– 8 *d·* tumors, relaxes rigid muscles,
dissolving
 f 224– 5 disappear from the *d·* paths
 r 490–22 along with the *d·* elements of clay.
dissuade
 ph 175–12 and *d·* any sense of fear or fever.
distance
 focal
 b 301–27 supposed standpoint outside the focal *d·* of
 great
 a 53–21 the great *d·* between the individual and Truth.
 infinite
 a 47–17 the infinite *d·* between Judas and his Master.
 g 538– 8 the infinite *d·* between Truth and error,
 moral
 a 36–16 moral *d·* between Christianity and sensualism
 not
 f 209–15 Nearness, not *d·*, lends enchantment
 spiritual
 a 47–20 this spiritual *d·* inflamed Judas' envy.

 an 105–30 The *d·* from ordinary medical practice to C. S. is

distance
 s 141– 1 This indicates the *d·* between the
 b 288–17 the tumult dies away in the *d·*.
distances
 f 209–19 *d·*, and revolutions of the celestial bodies,
distant
 a 24–15 The time is not *d·* when the
 sp 82– 1 it is as easy to read *d·* thoughts as near.
 an 104– 4 comprehended, as they will be at no *d·* date,
 c 263–22 the discovery of some *d·* idea of Truth ;
 g 513– 9 To . . . sense, this divine universe is dim and *d·*,
distemper
 p 398–10 Often he gave no name to the *d·* he cured.
distinct
 sp 70–13 divine Mind maintains all identities, . . . as *d·*
 ph 176–30 the less *d·* type and chronic form of disease.
 f 204–28 never . . . has a mind of his own, *d·* from God,
 214– 2 the impressions from Truth were as *d·* as sound,
 217– 9 prove Mind to be scientifically *d·* from matter,
 b 306–22 not more *d·* nor real to the material senses
 335– 3 theory, that Spirit is *d·* from matter
 p 438–16 on three *d·* charges of crime, to wit :
 g 523–15 clear evidences of two *d·* documents
distinction
 s 116–27 and its *d·* from humanity.
 o 345–23 ought to be able to discern the *d·*
 g 523–29 after which the *d·* is not definitely traceable.
distinctive
 ap 560– 4 the *d·* feature has reference to
distinctly
 sp 83–30 are *d·* opposite standpoints,
 ph 197– 2 which mirror images of disease *d·* in thought.
 b 314–26 and the more *d·* he uttered the demands of
 p 396–26 Keep *d·* in thought that man is
 408–11 so many *d·* defined instances of the
 415–32 leaving the pain standing forth as *d·* as
distinguish
 ph 173– 2 we fail to see how anatomy can *d·*
 t 453– 1 to *d·* the correct from the incorrect
distinguished
 sp 88– 9 How are veritable ideas to be *d·*
 b 320– 5 *d·* theologians in Europe and America
 g 551– 9 One *d·* naturalist argues that
distinguishes
 pr 16– 5 It *d·* between Truth . . . and the falsity of
 t 453– 3 when he *d·* concord from discord.
distinguishing
 g 506– 1 *d·* between the false and the true.
distorted
 s 110–20 This book may be *d·* by shallow criticism
 b 322–22 incurred through the pains of *d·* sense.
distressed
 ph 165–17 *d·* stomachs and aching heads.
distribute
 p 408–20 Truth does not *d·* drugs through the blood,
distrust
 a 50–27 *d·* of mortal minds, disbelieving the purpose
 f 231–25 and *d·* His omnipotent care.
 234– 3 If we trust matter, we *d·* Spirit.
 c 260–15 *d·* of one's ability to gain the goodness
 o 351– 3 When we lose faith . . . we *d·* the divine
distrusted
 t 459–22 when the latter is *d·* and thwarted
disturb
 f 254–25 what is there to *d·* the waters?
disturbance
 p 421–13 the mental *d·* or fermentation,
disturbances
 sp 96–18 These *d·* will continue until the end of error,
disturbed
 p 379–29 The images, held in this *d·* mind,
 400–20 by addressing the *d·* mind,
 421– 6 human belief in ill-health, or *d·* harmony.
 r 488–29 but they cannot be *d·* nor destroyed,
disturbs
 p 388–31 If mortals think that food *d·* the
ditch
 f 223–19 both shall fall into the *d·*."— *Matt.* 15 : 14.
diurnal
 s 121–17 The earth's *d·* rotation is invisible
diverged
 a 21–19 Our paths have *d·* at the very outset,
diversifies
 g 513–17 Spirit *d·*, classifies, and individualizes
Dives
 sp 83–25 as impassable as that between *D·* and Lazarus.

divest

   sp 90– 8 *D·* yourself of the thought that
    b 339–29 to *d·* sin of any supposed mind or reality,
    p 428– 8 To *d·* thought of false trusts

divested

    b 291–30 by which mortal man is *d·* of all material error.

divests

    s 146–18 *d·* material drugs of their imaginary power,

divide

    f 240–31 how to *d·* between sense and Soul.
     250– 1 run into error when we *d·* Soul into souls,
    b 280–14 seeks to *d·* the one Spirit into persons and
    338–14 *D·* the name Adam into two syllables,
    g 505– 5 and let it *d·* the waters from— *Gen.* 1 : 6.
    509–10 to *d·* the day from the night ;— *Gen.* 1 : 14.
    511– 9 *d·* the light from the darkness :— *Gen.* 1 : 18.

divided

    s 118–27 a kingdom necessarily *d·* against itself,
    f 233–25 When numbers have been *d·* according to
    252– 2 "If a kingdom be *d·* against— *Mark* 3 : 24.
    b 269– 2 Pandemonium, a house *d·* against itself.
    294–24 represented as *d·* into intelligent gods.
    o 354–27 It is in itself inconsistent, a *d·* kingdom.
    p 388–19 "kingdom *d·* against itself,"— *Matt.* 12 : 25.
    389–17 and the kingdom *d·* against itself.
    g 503–27 *d·* the light from the darkness.— *Gen.* 1 : 4.
    505–13 *d·* the waters which were under— *Gen.* 1 : 7.
    510–22 already *d·* into evening and morning ;
    gl 581–17 kingdom *d·* against itself, which cannot stand ;

divides

    sp 74–26 There is no bridge across the gulf which *d·*
    b 312–27 It *d·* faith and understanding

dividing

    t 462–10 *d·* his interests between God and mammon

Divine

Being

    pr 3–12 The *D·* Being must be reflected by man,
    o 357–18 false notions about the *D·* Being

Love

    p 439–29 sentence which . . . *D·* Love will pronounce.

Science

    a 55–29 This Comforter I understand to be *D·* Science.
    s 127– 9 The terms *D·* Science, Spiritual Science,

    sp 99–16 C. S. is unerring and *D·* ;
    f 205–32 When we fully understand our relation to the *D·*,

divine

action

    an 104–15 indicates the rightness of all *d·* action,

agent

    t 444– 4 suffering is oft the *d·* agent in this elevation.

aid

    o 354– 6 Why do they invoke the *d·* aid to enable them to

All-power

    t 454– 6 The understanding, . . . of the *d·* All-power

anointing

    p 367–26 through silent utterances and *d·* anointing

arbitrament

    g 555– 4 human belief, and not the *d·* arbitrament,

authority

    sp 76–21 man is immortal and lives by *d·* authority.
    s 134–29 There is *d·* authority for believing in the
    b 270–23 Meekness and charity have *d·* authority.
    o 354–28 Its supposed realism has no *d·* authority,
    p 381–30 a sentence never inflicted by *d·* authority.
    382– 2 lacking *d·* authority and having only
    390–23 have *d·* authority for denying that necessity

basis

    p 388– 7 Apostle John testified to the *d·* basis of C. S.,

beatitudes

    t 446–25 Not human platitudes, but *d·* beatitudes,

beauty

    sp 76–23 possessing unlimited *d·* beauty and goodness

blessings

    r 489–16 channel to man of *d·* blessings

body

    ap 559–25 when you eat the *d·* body of this Principle,

cause

    b 286–24 they lack a *d·* cause.

character

    pr 4–21 to assimilate more of the *d·* character,
    g 540–23 error as assuming a *d·* character,

coincidence

    ap 561–16 John saw the human and *d·* coincidence,

Comforter

    r 497– 7 the Holy Ghost or *d·* Comforter ;

commandment

    s 112–30 inculcates a breach of that *d·* commandment

commission

    a 54–13 In witness of his *d·* commission,

conception

    b 315–25 The *d·* conception of Jesus pointed to

divine

concepts

    c 259–29 demands spiritual thoughts, *d·* concepts,

consciousness

    g 531–13 human concepts for the *d·* consciousness.
    gl 598–23 One moment of *d·* consciousness, or the

control

    pr 9–23 recognizes only the *d·* control of Spirit,
    p 400–28 Without *d·* control there is discord,

creation

    g 504– 6 All questions as to the *d·* creation
    507–22 The scientific *d·* creation declares
    514– 2 could not . . . invert the *d·* creation,
    521–23 The Science and truth of the *d·* creation
    525– 6 a human, not a *d·*, creation.

decree

    a 32–14 bowed in holy submission to the *d·* decree.

decrees

    s 118–30 they contradict the *d·* decrees

demand

    f 253–32 *d·* demand, "Be ye therefore— *Matt.* 5 : 48.
    b 329–23 Science is a *d·* demand, not a human.

displeasure

    g 542– 2 incurs *d·* displeasure, and it would kill Jesus

ear

    pr 7–23 The "*d·* ear" is not an auditory nerve.

economy

    b 327–21 place nor power in the human or the *d·* economy.

Ego

    b 336– 6 The *d·* Ego, or individuality, is reflected

energies

    ph 186– 4 filling it with the *d·* energies of Truth.

energy

    f 249– 6 Let us feel the *d·* energy of Spirit,
    t 445–21 the unlabored motion of the *d·* energy

Esse

    sp 93–19 contradicts the real nature of the *d·* Esse,

Exemplar

    pr 5–31 We should follow our *d·* Exemplar,

force

    s 134–19 the very element, which gave it *d·* force

glory

    b 323–12 is winged to reach the *d·* glory.
    ap 565– 5 loathing the brightness of *d·* glory.

good

    f 203–31 *d·* good, does not kill a man in order to

goodness

    m 66–15 unfolds new views of *d·* goodness and love.

government

    f 225– 3 is opposed to the *d·* government.

healing

    a 41–20 the *d·* healing of absolute Science.
    55–22 The time for the reappearing of the *d·* healing
    s 123–17 the scientific system of *d·* healing.
    141–27 The adoption of . . . *d·* healing will
    c 259–12 understanding of . . . *d·* healing includes
    o 347–19 namely, apostolic, *d·* healing?

heights

    b 305–26 the *d·* heights of our Lord.
    ap 566–11 Science . . . leading to *d·* heights.

help

    p 393– 3 through *d·* help we can forbid this entrance.
    t 453–17 Dishonesty . . . which forfeits *d·* help.

hues

    r 479–29 because it has none of the *d·* hues.

idea

    sp 88–18 To love one's neighbor as one's self, is a *d·* idea ;
    b 332–20 Christ is the *d·* idea of God
    334– 1 the *d·* idea or Christ was and is so
    t 463– 7 birth of the new child, or *d·* idea,
    r 470–22 the *d·* idea or reflection, man,
    473–16 Jesus is the human man, and Christ is the *d·* idea;
    482–21 the *d·* idea of God outside the flesh.
    g 506–25 Here the human concept and *d·* idea seem
    507–31 misinterpreted, the *d·* idea seems to fall
    ap 560–29 ignorant of the *d·* idea he taught.
    560–30 Ignorance of the *d·* idea betrays at once
    561– 4 leads to the discernment of the *d·* idea.
    561–25 as the divine Principle and *d·* idea.
    gl 589–17 JESUS. . . . corporeal concept of the *d·* idea.

ideal

    s 119–20 is not the *d·* ideal of omnipresent Love.

image

    f 205–19 perceive the *d·* image in some word or deed
    c 258–17 man as the true *d·* image and likeness,
    b 301–17 man is the *d·* image and likeness,
    332–12 yea, the *d·* image and likeness,
    333–26 The *d·* image, idea, or Christ

individuality

    b 303– 8 reflect the one *d·* individuality

influence

    pref xi–16 a *d·* influence ever present in
    f 236–16 or through *d·* influence,

intelligence

    ph 184–16 Controlled by the *d·* intelligence,

divine

Justice
p 437– 9 in the presence of d· Justice,

justice
an 105–24 D· justice will manacle him.
f 225–18 breathing the omnipotence of d· justice,
b 293–25 manifestations of evil, which counterfeit d· justice,

law
a 30–17 Not so did Jesus, . . . present the d· law of Love,
sp 72–30 d· law is the communicator of truth,
s 108– 5 It was the d· law of Life and Love,
134–25 nor because it is an infraction of d· law,
ph 170–19 Not d· law, for Jesus healed the sick
183– 6 discords have no support from nature or d· law,
f 205–22 the d· law of loving our neighbor as ourselves
227–27 The illusion of material sense, not d· law,
b 273– 9 because they are not based on the d· law.
p 372–13 and then . . . name them d· law.
385– 7 the d· law, rising above the human.
436– 9 acting within the limits of the d· law,
436–29 deeds which the d· law compels man to commit.
440–19 in obedience to d· law?
t 445–15 You render the d· law of healing obscure
458–24 Christianly scientific man reflects the d· law,
459–29 (that is, the student . . . of the d· law)
g 522–32 Does the unerring Principle of d· law change
540– 7 the prophet referred to d· law

laws
s 107– 2 the Christ Science or d· laws of Life,

Life
pr 10–16 a higher understanding of the d· Life.
14–26 Life d·, revealing spiritual understanding
a 25–11 and they . . . who partake of that d· Life.
54– 2 he demonstrated the d· Life.
s 138– 6 It was now evident to Peter that d· Life,
b 331– 1 God is d· Life, and Life is
339– 2 D· Life destroys death,
g 538–12 a figure of d· Life and Love,
556–16 to him who understands best the d· Life.
gl 579–10 ABRAHAM. Fidelity ; faith in the d· Life
596–23 d· Life and Love illumine it,

light
s 135–32 as must be the case in the cycles of d· light.
t 457– 7 Since the d· light of C. S. first dawned

likeness
b 300–22 and of man as reflecting the d· likeness.
o 356–23 man who is made in the d· likeness
r 491–16 establishes man forever in the d· likeness,

logic
sp 72–21 it follows in d· logic that evil,
93–10 D· logic and revelation coincide.

Love
pr 6– 3 D· Love corrects and governs man.
14–11 to be absolutely governed by d· Love,
a 19– 4 Man cannot exceed d· Love.
19–10 by the law of Spirit, — the law of d· Love.
23–25 understands d· Love and how to
26– 9 till all are redeemed through d· Love.
38–26 the Christ, the spiritual idea of d· Love.
40–25 d· Love, demands that all men should
43–14 were overruled by d· Love
48–29 decision against human rights and d· Love,
54–17 highest proof he could have offered of d· Love.
55–20 and the healing power of the d· Love
sp 97–15 having been destroyed by d· Love,
98– 3 above mortal discord and in the gift of d· Love.
s 135–29 demonstration of d· Love casting out error
140–26 The C. S. God is universal, eternal, d· Love,
ph 180–23 influence of d· Love which casteth out fear.
f 218–23 turning in time of need to God, d· Love,
224–31 No power can withstand d· Love.
239–18 If d· Love is becoming nearer, dearer,
240– 1 Nature voices natural, . . . law and d· Love,
241–20 reflection and demonstration of d· Love,
243– 4 The d· Love, which made harmless the
c 256–18 What is infinite Mind or d· Love?
257–18 d· Love, — is the father of the rain,
266– 9 seeming vacuum is already filled with d· Love.
b 285–24 not as the saving Principle, or d· Love,
288– 8 faith in and the understanding of d· Love.
304–10 d· Love cannot be deprived of its manifestation,
309– 3 incorporeal impartation of d· Love to man,
322–29 turn us like tired children to the arms of d· Love.
325–18 with Truth in d· Love,
337– 8 harmonize with his Principle, d· Love ;
340–12 D· Love is infinite.
o 356–25 Does d· Love commit a fraud on humanity
p 363–24 Why did he thus summarize her debt to d· Love?
365–15 reaches his patient through d· Love,
367– 9 parodies on . . . C. S., aflame with d· Love.
375–20 restoring him physically through d· Love.
411–10 If Spirit or the power of d· Love bear witness
412–14 power of C. S. and d· Love is omnipotent.
414–30 unreal, and is not brought about by d· Love.
417– 2 health, peace, and harmony in God, d· Love.

divine

Love
p 420–26 d· Love gives them all power over
424–25 the oneness and the allness of d· Love ;
434– 1 Swift on the wings of d· Love, there comes
436–31 construed obedience to the law of d· Love
442–12 D· Love had cast out fear.
t 454–22 Wait patiently for d· Love to move upon
r 494–10 D· Love always has met and always will
494–14 in every hour, d· Love supplies all good.
g 517–30 D· Love blesses its own ideas,
529–22 serpent to tempt the children of d· Love?
537–27 d· Love, which blessed the earth
ap 560–12 great miracle, to human sense, is d· Love,
574–10 this message from d· Love, carried John
578– 5 [D· LOVE] is my shepherd ; — Psal. 23 : 1.

manifestation
gl 583–10 CHRIST. The d· manifestation of God,

mercy
b 329–26 The pardon of d· mercy is the destruction of
g 542–12 jeopardize self-control, and mock d· mercy.

message
b 332–10 the d· message from God to men

messages
ap 566–29 assigns to the angels, God's d· messages,

metaphysics
s 111–11 The Principle of d· metaphysics is God ;
111–12 the practice of d· metaphysics is the
111–14 D· metaphysics reverses perverted and
112–32 God is the Principle of d· metaphysics.
113– 9 fundamental propositions of d· metaphysics
113–26 d· metaphysics of C. S., like the method in
146–31 D· metaphysics is now reduced to a system,
ph 192–29 in the understanding of d· metaphysics.
f 217–21 the problem of being in d· metaphysics ;
b 274–32 in the light of d· metaphysics,
275–20 D· metaphysics, as revealed to
278– 3 D· metaphysics explains away matter.
330– 9 the infallibility of d· metaphysics will be
p 374–14 show our need of d· metaphysics.
397–20 your fidelity to d· metaphysics,
t 459–32 rules of d· metaphysics as laid down
g 549– 6 shown by d· metaphysics to be a mistake,

method
f 240–29 The d· method of paying sin's wages
b 339– 1 The destruction of sin is the d· method
ap 568– 6 typifies the d· method of warfare in Science,

Mind
pr 1–10 are not unknown to the d· Mind.
2–19 The mere habit of pleading with the d· Mind,
a 36–20 d· Mind is the immortal law of justice
m 62–22 The d· Mind, which forms the bud
68–29 an impartation of the d· Mind to man
sp 70–12 The d· Mind maintains all identities,
83– 1 whether it is the human mind or the d· Mind
84–11 prerogative of the ever-present, d· Mind,
84–15 to commune more largely with the d· Mind,
85– 6 when the latter yields to the d· Mind.
88–11 Ideas are emanations from the d· Mind.
88–28 It shows the possibilities derived from d· Mind,
an 102–11 or the attraction of God, d· Mind.
104–15 as the emanation of d· Mind,
104–19 The medicine of Science is d· Mind ;
s 108–10 for the d· Mind cannot suffer.
108–22 all real being is in God, the d· Mind,
109– 5 the only realities are the d· Mind and idea.
111– 5 the human mind, to be opposed to the d· Mind,
114– 5 in contradistinction to the d· Mind,
124–29 they belong wholly to d· Mind,
127–24 all truth proceeds from the d· Mind.
127–27 Science is an emanation of d· Mind,
128– 2 the might of d· Mind.
132–11 such effects, coming from d· Mind, prove
140– 8 we know Him as d· Mind, as Life,
143–10 The d· Mind never called matter medicine,
143–23 the available superiority of d· Mind.
149–25 with no power but the d· Mind.
149–26 Since God, d· Mind, governs all,
150–21 contrary to the law of d· Mind.
151–21 the real man is governed by the d· Mind.
151–23 The d· Mind that made man maintains His
151–26 All that really exists is the d· Mind and its
152– 3 The immortal d· Mind takes away all its
153–14 the d· Mind is the healer
157–10 acknowledging that the d· Mind has all power.
158–17 the dignity and potency of d· Mind
160– 2 through the power of d· Mind.
162–11 may yield to the harmony of the d· Mind.
ph 166–26 invalid's faith in the d· Mind is less than in
167–27 must be attained through the d· Mind.
169–20 all disease is cured by d· Mind,
169–30 other powers than the d· Mind, is anti-Christian.
174–32 and its cure comes from the immortal d· Mind.
176–14 human mind gives place to the d· Mind,
176–20 while d· Mind is its best friend.
178–15 based on Science or the d· Mind,

divine

Mind

ph.	178–22	yield to the eternal Truth, or the d· Mind
	180–29	found in the Science of d· Mind as taught
	182– 2	healing the sick through d· Mind alone,
	182–22	Mortals entreat the d· Mind to heal
	183–21	D· Mind rightly demands man's entire
	187–22	The d· Mind includes all action and volition,
	189–22	all the formations of the immortal d· Mind.
	194– 4	the spiritual idea of man with the d· Mind.
f	204–26	the image or reflection of d· Mind ;
	209– 8	and man is tributary to d· Mind.
	210–15	scientific action of the d· Mind on human
	216–17	governed by the law of d· Mind,
	218–16	believing . . . that the d· Mind has no
	219–13	whereas d· Mind heals.
	225–28	rooted out through the action of the d· Mind.
	227– 7	law of the d· Mind must end human bondage,
	229–30	not of a law of matter nor of d· Mind,
	236–10	d· Mind heals sickness as well as sin
	239–26	If action proceeds from the d· Mind,
	251–20	understanding that the d· Mind makes perfect,
	251–23	find the d· Mind to be the only Mind,
c	255–10	views of creation by the d· Mind.
	259–28	are transmitted by the d· Mind
	262–30	D· Mind is the only cause or Principle
	264– 6	sometimes behold in the camera of d· Mind,
	267– 5	They are in and of Spirit, d· Mind,
b	269–14	rest on one basis, the d· Mind.
	270–21	demonstration of God, d· Mind,
	270–30	the d· Mind alone heals.
	284–29	are spiritual, emanating from d· Mind.
	286–32	belong not to the d· Mind.
	293–14	counterfeits of the spiritual forces of d· Mind,
	307–25	The d· Mind is the Soul of man,
	310– 6	but all might is d· Mind.
	318– 8	saying . . . that the d· Mind cannot or will not
	319–19	understood that the d· Mind controls man
	327– 5	d· Mind can and does destroy the false beliefs
	331–13	except the d· Mind and His ideas.
p	366–17	lacks faith in the d· Mind.
	370– 5	gather the facts of being from the d· Mind.
	372– 9	Science of being, in which all is d· Mind,
	375–12	Scientist demonstrates that d· Mind heals,
	379– 8	all causation as vested in d· Mind.
	380–24	the d· Mind produces in man health,
	383– 7	exalting influence of the d· Mind on the body
	392– 1	you master fear and sin through d· Mind ;
	392– 2	through d· Mind that you overcome disease.
	393–16	firm in your understanding that the d· Mind
	396–32	not by matter nor by the d· Mind
	400–10	acknowledge the supremacy of d· Mind,
	400–27	must be destroyed by the d· Mind
	403–13	and can be healed only by the d· Mind.
	407–27	brings the d· Mind, Life not death,
	417–31	and how d· Mind can cure by opposite thoughts.
	424–21	the d· Mind can remove any obstacle,
	400 11	allegory illustrative of the law of d· Mind
	441 26	no law outside of d· Mind can punish
t	445–23	hatred, and revenge are cast out by the d· Mind
	452–27	the Science by which d· Mind heals the sick.
	458–13	the d· Mind is ready to take the case.
	458–27	consistent in following the leadings of d· Mind.
	459–14	resting on the omnipotence of the d· Mind,
	460– 7	on the d· Mind and Love's essential qualities.
r	460– 4	Life is d· Mind.
	470–29	his perfect Principle, the d· Mind.
	471–29	import, . . . of all that proceeds from the d· Mind.
	484–16	Drugs . . . oppose the supremacy of the d· Mind.
	493–20	belief, which must be annihilated by the d· Mind.
	493–31	willingness of d· Mind to hold man forever intact
g	503–20	Immortal and d· Mind presents the idea of God :
	505– 9	The d· Mind, . . . creates all identities,
	508– 2	only as the d· Mind is All and reproduces all
	508–15	the pure thought emanating from d· Mind.
	511– 5	The d· Mind supports the sublimity,
	519–26	can never impoverish, the d· Mind.
	546– 6	If . . . error must exist in the d· Mind,
	551–14	does not acknowledge the method of d· Mind,
ap	570–31	the power of good resident in d· Mind,
	577–21	and d· Mind is its own interpreter.

name

r	483–30	through the d· name and nature.

nature

pr	4–24	through demonstration of the d· nature ;
a	26–13	his d· nature, the godliness which
sp	83–14	manifestation of power is from the d· nature
s	140–10	as we apprehend the d· nature
ph	179–11	but reflecting the d· nature.
c	259– 7	d· nature was best expressed in Christ Jesus,
b	333–25	the d· nature, the essence of Love.
g	509–27	purity, and holiness — yea, the d· nature
	524–31	lose therein the d· nature and omnipotence?

order

a	20–21	well knowing that to obey the d· order

divine

order

sp	73–17	the d· order and the Science of
an	106–12	when the d· order is interfered with,
r	471– 2	but holds the d· order or spiritual law,
g	531–17	If, . . . why is not this d· order still maintained

origin

s	146–22	practically prove its d· origin and efficacy.
	146–24	d· origin of Science is demonstrated through
	150–15	these signs are only to demonstrate its d· origin,
b	272–24	d· origin and operation of C. S.
	298–23	Spiritual ideas lead up to their d· origin,
g	539–27	The d· origin of Jesus gave him more than
	549–28	forsakes Spirit as the d· origin of
ap	562–13	separated by belief from man's d· origin

pardon

a	40–11	This is my sense of d· pardon,

patience

a	49–11	privations, sacrifices, his d· patience,

penalty

an	106–13	incurs the d· penalty due this crime.

perfection

r	470–25	did not express the d· perfection,

permission

p	378–29	Such a power, without the d· permission, is
	394–25	Is there no d· permission to conquer discord

possibilities

b	326– 1	A false sense . . . hides the d· possibilities,

power

a	27– 7	Tell John what the demonstration of d· power
	49–28	had given the highest proofs of d· power,
	52–25	human ability to reflect d· power,
s	109–23	gradually and apparently through d· power.
	131–28	natural demonstrations of the d· power,
	132– 3	exhibition of the d· power to heal
	135–10	alone is worthy of the exercise of d· power.
	136– 7	he used his d· power to save men
	144–21	Truth, . . . is the d· power which says to disease,
ph	169–26	except by means of the d· power.
	170 32	which takes d· power into its own hands
	174– 6	Nothing save d· power is capable of
	192–31	receives directly the d· power.
f	227–11	an ignorance of d· power,
b	309–19	thus losing the d· power which heals the sick
	316–27	could prove God's d· power by healing
	320–26	gives a profound idea of the d· power to heal
p	426– 3	d· power, which steers the body into health.
r	494–12	Jesus demonstrated the d· power to heal
g	519–13	grasp God's creation and the d· power
	534–15	the idea of d· power, which Jesus presented,
	541–23	At first it usurps d· power.

powers

f	249– 9	subject to the d· "powers that be." — Rom. 13 : 1.

precepts

s	141– 5	Few understand or adhere to Jesus' d· precepts
b	276– 4	When the d· precepts are understood,

presence

r	12– 4	no power to gain more of the d· presence than

Principle

pref	viii– 4	live in obedience to its d· Principle.
	x–22	The d· Principle of healing is proved
	xi–10	d· Principle, before which sin and disease
pr	3– 8	Shall we ask the d· Principle
	6– 4	d· Principle alone reforms the sinner.
	6–16	we must understand the d· Principle of being.
	11–12	d· Principle never pardons our sins . . . till
	12–20	not d· Principle or Love, which causes a
	13–25	human ignorance of the d· Principle.
	15–12	d· Principle, Love, which destroys all error.
a	18–14	d· Principle of Christ is God,
	19– 8	Love, the d· Principle of Jesus' teachings,
	19–25	d· Principle of the teachings and practice
	20–31	seek the d· Principle and Science
	25–14	understand how this d· Principle heals
	25–26	understand its d· Principle.
	26–29	It was the d· Principle of all real being
	28–13	by understanding more of the d· Principle
	29–27	d· Principle of the man Jesus,
	30– 3	demonstrate the Science . . . or d· Principle.
	31–21	d· Principle which triumphs over death.
	35–14	commune with the d· Principle, Love.
	35–20	Our church is built on the d· Principle, Love.
	39–26	d· Principle of all that really exists
	45–21	at-one-ment with . . . his d· Principle,
	47– 7	leaning . . . on the d· Principle of their work.
	50–13	appeal . . . was made both to his d· Principle,
	51–23	but to demonstrate his d· Principle.
	51–26	aimed at the d· Principle, Love,
	53– 9	the d· Principle and practice of Jesus
sp	71– 6	d· Principle of all, is not in Spirit's
	72– 3	The d· Principle of man speaks through
	79–14	resting on d· Principle, . . . in its revelation of
	81–22	producing, governing, d· Principle lives on,
	81–27	cannot destroy the d· Principle of Science.
	83–28	gains the d· Principle and explanation of
	84–28	All . . . comes from God, d· Principle,

divine

Principle

sp	90–30	through an apprehension of *d·* Principle.
	91– 6	obey only the *d·* Principle, Life and Love.
	94–22	acknowledge the *d·* Principle which had healed
	99– 3	afford no demonstrable *d·* Principle by which
an	103–14	is of God and demonstrates the *d·* Principle,
s	107– 6	revelation of the absolute *d·* Principle
	109– 8	until its *d·* Principle is demonstrated
	112–21	the *d·* Principle of healing and the Christ-idea
	113– 1	can be but one *d·* Principle of all Science ;
	113– 3	rules for the demonstration of this *d·* Principle.
	115–13	GOD : *D·* Principle, Life, Truth, Love, Soul,
	117–20	inadequate to interpret the *d·* Principle
	120–20	the *d·* Principle of Science, reversing the
	121–29	imitates the action of *d·* Principle,
	123–27	illustrated an ever-operative *d·* Principle.
	124–15	interpreted by Science from its *d·* Principle,
	124–21	They belong to *d·* Principle, and support the
	127–18	C. S. reveals God, ... as *d·* Principle,
	130–10	in perfect harmony with God, *d·* Principle,
	131– 5	in harmony with God, the *d·* Principle
	132–12	*d·* Principle which brings out all harmony.
	133–16	*d·* Principle wrought wonders for the people
	136– 3	his religion had a *d·* Principle,
	141–15	followed the understanding of the *d·* Principle
	141–25	until its *d·* Principle is scientifically
	146–16	to the person, instead of to the *d·* Principle,
	147– 2	to demonstrate the *d·* Principle,
	147–25	taught the generalities of its *d·* Principle
	147–30	Science alone reveals the *d·* Principle
	148–18	Anatomy and theology reject the *d·* Principle
	162–27	a fuller understanding of the *d·* Principle
ph	167– 3	should we understand the . . . . *d·* Principle
	171–14	Jesus illustrated the *d·* Principle
	191– 9	*d·* Principle of man dawns upon human thought,
	195–14	metaphysical Science and its *d·* Principle.
f	202–16	in accord with the *d·* Principle of his being,
	207–14	perfect Father, or the *d·* Principle of man.
	230– 9	the *d·* Principle, Love, as demonstrated by
	232–17	demonstrating the power of *d·* Principle,
c	256– 7	Love, the *d·* Principle, is the Father and
b	270–13	is the eternal Mind or *d·* Principle,
	272–28	The *d·* Principle of the universe must
	272–29	God is the *d·* Principle of all
	272–32	reveals the natural, *d·* Principle of Science.
	273– 6	without the *d·* Principle of divine Science.
	275– 9	God is Love, and therefore He is *d·* Principle.
	275–11	the *d·* Principle of all that really is.
	275–17	the infinite *d·* Principle, Love.
	281–12	perfect Mind, Spirit, *d·* Principle.
	283–24	The *d·* Principle, or Life, cannot be
	283–27	We must receive the *d·* Principle
	285–22	the Supreme Being; or *d·* Principle,
	285–30	seek to learn, . . . from the *d·* Principle, God,
	286–10	[the *d·* Principle of being]
	286–14	He knew that the *d·* Principle, Love, creates
	299–14	guide to the *d·* Principle of all good,
	302–21	God, the *d·* Principle of all being,
	303– 1	the creative power of the *d·* Principle
	303–30	nor separated from its *d·* Principle.
	304–17	*D·* Principle is the Life of man.
	304–31	So man, . . . thrusting aside his *d·* Principle
	305–10	his *d·* Principle, not in a mortal body.
	305–25	Love, the *d·* Principle that obtains in
	306–27	the immutable, harmonious, *d·* Principle,
	312–31	and his demonstration of *d·* Principle
	314–27	uttered the demands of its *d·* Principle,
	316–22	blending with God, his *d·* Principle,
	317– 3	the throne of the creative *d·* Principle,
	318–29	In Science man is governed by God, *d·* Principle,
	319– 8	Having faith in the *d·* Principle of health
	322– 7	perceive Christianity, . . . in its *d·* Principle.
	322–12	turn our thoughts towards *d·* Principle,
	328– 6	Understanding little about the *d·* Principle
	329–24	its *d·* Principle never repents,
	330–20	Spirit is *d·* Principle,
	330–20	*d·* Principle is Love,
	331–18	He is *d·* Principle, Love, the universal
	331–27	that is, the triply *d·* Principle, Love.
	332– 1	indicate the *d·* Principle of scientific being,
	332–21	revealing the *d·* Principle, Love,
	333–27	inseparable from the *d·* Principle, God.
	335–25	Mind is the *d·* Principle, Love,
	336–25	God, the *d·* Principle of man,
	340–20	The *d·* Principle of the First Commandment
o	341–15	that . . . which is based on *d·* Principle,
	345–18	can heal the sick on the *d·* Principle of
	351– 4	the *d·* Principle which demonstrates C. S.,
	355–24	the *d·* Principle and practice of C. S.
p	390– 8	ignorance of God, the *d·* Principle,
	406– 4	tree is typical of man's *d·* Principle,
	419–27	tramples upon the *d·* Principle
t	445–21	hiding the *d·* Principle of harmony,
	456– 5	Strict adherence to the *d·* Principle and
	456–20	or he cannot demonstrate the *d·* Principle.

divine

Principle

t	456–24	the *d·* Principle of your demonstration.
	458–12	to think of aiding the *d·* Principle of healing
	464–22	has labored to expound *d·* Principle.
r	466–30	this declaration and its *d·* Principle,
	468–26	Life is *d·* Principle, Mind, Soul, Spirit.
	470–21	the *d·* Principle of man remaining perfect,
	470–32	The relations of . . . *d·* Principle and idea,
	473–23	God as *d·* Principle, Love,
	475– 3	all is Spirit, *d·* Principle and its idea.
	476– 5	inseparable as *d·* Principle and idea.
	481–28	Soul is the *d·* Principle of man
	484– 1	based on a *d·* Principle and so found to be
	490–17	reduce to practice the real man's *d·* Principle,
	495–28	Adhere to the *d·* Principle of C. S.
	496–18	based upon its *d·* Principle, Love,
g	503– 9	The *d·* Principle and idea constitute
	507–16	the creative power of the *d·* Principle,
	507–25	This *d·* Principle of all expresses Science
	512– 3	incorporeal and *d·* Principle, Love.
	515–29	Now compare man . . . to his *d·* Principle, God.
	518–27	The *d·* Principle, or Spirit, comprehends
	518–29	be as perfect as the *d·* Principle is perfect.
	524–11	the *d·* Principle to be lived and loved.
	530– 5	sustained by God, the *d·* Principle of being.
	536–15	by corporeality instead of *d·* Principle,
	544–32	Error begins with . . . instead of *d·* Principle,
	546– 9	Is the *d·* Principle of creation misstated?
ap	559–24	When you approach . . . this *d·* Principle,
	560–19	without . . . we can never understand the *d·* Principle.
	560–31	a greater ignorance of the *d·* Principle
	561–14	*d·* Principle and spiritual idea,
	561–24	as the *d·* Principle and divine idea.
	562–15	yield to the activities of the *d·* Principle
	565–27	be found in its *d·* Principle.
	567–10	he is killed by the *d·* Principle.
	569– 1	This rule clearly interprets God as *d·* Principle,
	572–13	this *d·* Principle, understood and demonstrated,
	573–15	the *d·* Principle of harmony, is ever with men,
	577–16	which is the outcome of the *d·* Principle
gl	582–18	God, the *d·* Principle, creates man
	583–13	rests upon and proceeds from *d·* Principle.
	583–21	*d·* Principle of all that is real and good ;
	586– 9	the *d·* Principle, commonly called God.
	587–26	HEAVEN. . . . government by *d·* Principle ;
	588– 9	I, or EGO. *D·* Principle ; Spirit ;
	588–11	There is but one I, or Us, but one *d·* Principle,
	588–20	incorporeal and eternal Mind ; *d·* Principle ;
	589– 9	God is the *d·* Principle of all existence,
	591–16	the only Spirit, Soul, *d·* Principle,
	591–18	not that which is *in* man, but the *d·* Principle,
	594–19	Divine substance ; Mind ; *d·* Principle ;
	595–25	UNGODLINESS. Opposition to the *d·* Principle

proof

f	215–22	With its *d·* proof, Science reverses the

Providence

p	424–10	Under *d·* Providence there can be no accidents,

purpose

sp	83–27	The latter is a revelation of *d·* purpose

reality

sp	95–22	to be succeeded by C. S., by *d·* reality.

record

s	139–21	material sense stole into the *d·* record,

reflection

c	259–18	true likeness cannot be lost in *d·* reflection.

remedy

b	326– 7	and find the *d·* remedy for every ill,

revelation

s	109–21	*d·* revelation, reason, and demonstration.
ap	561–20	In *d·* revelation, . . . the spiritual idea is

right

f	227–26	be free ! This is your *d·* right.

rights

f	253–10	into the understanding of your *d·* rights,
p	384–31	quail before the *d·* rights of intelligence,

rock

b	297–28	no mortal testimony is founded on the *d·* rock.

rules

s	147– 6	the *d·* rules of C. S.
t	462– 3	any student, who adheres to the *d·* rules

Science

(see **Science***)*

sense

g	505–24	the *d·* sense, giving the spiritual proof
ap	576–31	human sense of Deity yields to the *d·* sense,

sentence

pr	11–19	not to annul the *d·* sentence

service

a	40–28	It is sad that the phrase *d· service* has

sonship

b	316– 7	and to recognize the *d·* sonship.

source

ph	167–14	the *d·* source of all health and perfection.
	189–23	They proceed from the *d·* source ;

divine
sources
  p 405–32 appeal to *d·* sources outside of themselves.
sovereign
  g 523–31 the *d·* sovereign of the Hebrew people,
Spirit
  a 29–24 The Holy Ghost, or *d·* Spirit, overshadowed the
    30– 7 endowed with the Christ, the *d·* Spirit,
    46– 7 The *d·* Spirit, which identified Jesus thus
  sp 76–17 characterized by the *d·* Spirit as idea,
    97–18 until *d·* Spirit, supreme in its domain,
    99–28 the scientific demonstration of *d·* Spirit
  s 125–18 When subordinate to the *d·* Spirit,
    138–13 nor by hygiene, but by the *d·* Spirit,
    148–28 it ignores the *d·* Spirit as unable
  p 412–17 power of . . . *d·* Spirit, must break the dream
    440–30 the just and equitable decisions of *d·* Spirit
    442– 1 before the tribunal of *d·* Spirit.
  g 516–29 God made man . . . to reflect the *d·* Spirit.
    522–15 opposed to the supremacy of *d·* Spirit ;
    532–11 this indicates that the *d·* Spirit, or Father,
state
  b 291–14 a *d·* state of Mind in which all
statutes
  ph 184–14 enforcing obedience through *d·* statutes.
  p 440–26 in accordance with the *d·* statutes,
strength
  p 406–31 normal control is gained through *d·* strength
student
  s 117–16 As a *d·* student he unfolded God to man,
substance
  b 300–28 reflects and expresses the *d·* substance
  r 468–24 reflecting the *d·* substance of Spirit.
  gl 594–19 SPIRIT. *D·* substance ; Mind ;
theology
  f 234–22 the weary searcher after a *d·* theology,
  r 469–29 as pernicious to *d·* theology as
thought
  s 118–14 means of *d·* thought, which include
  g 514–15 figurative transmission from the *d·* thought
title
  b 333– 8 not a name so much as the *d·* title of
Truth
  pr 4– 1 While the heart is far from *d·* Truth
  a 18– 2 whereby man reflects *d·* Truth, Life, and Love.
    26–14 *D·* Truth, Life, and Love gave Jesus authority
  an 106–11 governed by his Maker, *d·* Truth and Love.
  ph 180–32 I have found *d·* Truth more potent than
  f 231–18 mortal beliefs which *d·* Truth and Love destroy.
    235–23 *d·* Truth which is Life and perpetuates being,
  o 350–14 *D·* Truth must be known by its effects
  p 388– 3 uplifting and consecrating power of *d·* Truth,
  t 453–29 the *d·* Truth that makes man free.
    459–27 Guided by *d·* Truth and not guesswork,
  r 472– 3 *d·* Truth casts out suppositional error and heals
understanding
  g 536– 8 The *d·* understanding reigns, is *all*,
universe
  g 513– 8 To material sense, this *d·* universe is dim
utterance
  s 127–28 It is a *d·* utterance, — the Comforter
vesture
  f 242–27 appropriates no part of the *d·* vesture,
voice
  g 532–20 error shrank abashed from the *d·* voice
way
  c 266–19 Universal Love is the *d·* way in C. S.
will
  a 28– 1 Pharisees claimed to know and to teach the *d·* will,
  r 474–22 real or the offspring of the *d·* will?
wisdom
  m 66–20 wait patiently on *d·* wisdom to point out
  p 386–24 *d·* wisdom will then be understood.
Word
  r 480–27 were made by Him [the *d·* Word] ; — *John* 1 : 3.

  pr 12–12 the *d·* healing Principle as manifested in
  a 33–19 human element in him struggled with the *d·*,
    43–27 The *d·* must overcome the human at every point.
    51– 8 identity in the likeness of the *d·* ;
    53–14 as humanly mighty, rather than as *d·*,
  sp 98–32 not human but *d·*, not physical but
    99–15 that which is spiritual and *d·*,
  s 109– 9 and thus proved absolute and *d·*.
    114– 9 and calls *mind* both human and *d·*.
    126– 8 All Science is *d·*.
    142–17 causes the left to let go its grasp on the *d·*.
    147–11 Truth had lost none of its *d·* and healing
  ph 177– 5 The evidence of *d·* Mind's healing power
    200–20 suppositional antipode of *d·* infinite Spirit,
  f 213–29 hand, which sweeps over it, is human or *d·*.
  b 269–22 testimony of . . . neither absolute nor *d·*.
    275–19 no life is Life but the *d·* ;
    277–25 the opposite of the real is not *d·*,
    287–10 In Science, Truth is *d·*,

divine
  b 297–31 has little relation to the actual or *d·*.
    301–12 He reflects the *d·*,
    302–25 He is therefore the *d·*, infinite
    305–30 mortal dreams are of human origin, not *d·*.
    312–29 the intelligent and *d·* healing Principle
    335–18 Spirit is eternal, *d·*.
    335–28 immutable, immortal, *d·*, eternal.
  o 341–16 according to a *d·* given rule,
  p 396–23 Give them *d·* and wholesome understanding,
    435–22 no demand, human or *d·*, renders it just
    442– 3 our Government is *d·*.
  t 445–17 when you weigh the human in the scale with the *d·*,
    462–23 Are thoughts *d·* or human?
  r 465– 9 God is incorporeal, *d·*,
    473–31 Jesus *proved* the Principle, . . . to be *d·*.
    483– 6 and this Mind must be *d·*, not human.
    492–27 the Principle of this Science is *d·*,
    497–14 the evidence of *d·*, efficacious Love,
  g 520–14 accepts the *d·* infinite calculus.
    524–16 Did the *d·* and infinite Principle become a
    542–21 let human justice pattern the *d·*.
    546–29 for it cures on a *d·* demonstrable Principle
    554– 4 God, who is its *d·* immortal Principle.
  gl 586–24 the human yielding to the *d·* ;
    590– 6 hypotheses ; that which is not *d·*
    592–16 MOTHER. God ; *d·* and eternal Principle ;
divinely
  pr 10– 8 Until we are thus *d·* qualified
  a 23– 7 *d·* unnatural. Such a theory is man-made.
    42– 1 Jesus' life proved, *d·* and scientifically,
    44–24 On the contrary, it was a *d·* natural act,
  sp 84–17 to be *d·* inspired, — yea, to reach the
  s 145– 3 So *d·* imbued were they with the spirit of
    152–26 by which mortals are *d·* driven to a
  b 313– 5 Jesus the God-crowned or the *d·* royal man,
  p 378–30 if such a power could be *d·* directed,
    393–14 the ability and power *d·* bestowed
  g 513–21 the *d·* creative Principle thereof.
    545– 6 and never had been *d·* conceived.
  ap 577– 9 In this *d·* united spiritual consciousness,
  gl 591–21 MIRACLE. That which is *d·* natural, but
diviner
  s 107–12 are inspired with a *d·* nature and essence ;
  f 226–15 He has built it on *d·* claims.
  c 260–10 beliefs will be attaining *d·* conceptions,
  b 285–20 give place to a *d·* sense of intelligence
  p 369– 7 He enters into a *d·* sense of the facts,
  g 548–23 Had the naturalist, . . . gained the *d·* side
  ap 563– 2 to a *d·* sense, harmony is the real
diving
  c 262–10 *d·* into the shallows of mortal belief.
divinity
conceptions of
  s 116–26 confused and erroneous conceptions of *d·*
deep
  g 546–22 they contain the deep *d·* of the Bible.
essence of
  g 537– 9 knowledge of evil was never the essence of *d·*
gleams of
  s 112–12 opinions may have occasional gleams of *d·*,
illimitable
  s 127– 8 there can be nothing beyond illimitable *d·*.
likeness of
  b 302–29 the body presents no proper likeness of *d·*,
one
  ap 571–21 will unite all interests in the one *d·*.
raindrops of
  b 288–17 the raindrops of *d·* refresh the earth.

  a 22–28 believeth . . . that *d·* is appeased by
    25–31 The *d·* of the Christ was made manifest in
    26–13 This Christ, or *d·* of the man Jesus,
    44–24 *d·* brought to humanity the understanding
  s 116– 9 may be to us what *d·* really is
    132–19 from doctrines of physics or of *d·* ;
  c 258–32 you can discern the heart of *d·*,
  b 281–16 reflects reality and *d·* in individual
    306–10 If . . . there would be no *d·* reflected.
    332–30 He expressed the highest type of *d·*,
  t 458–14 *D·* is always ready.
  g 522–10 Existence, separate from *d·*, . . . impossible.
  ap 561–17 in the man Jesus, as *d·* embracing humanity
divisibility
  b 280–13 finite sense of the *d·* of Soul
division
  s 148–23 from this basis of *d·* and discord
  r 478– 1 But there is, there can be, no such *d·*,
divisor
  gl 598–30 mortal thought, the *d·* of which is the solar year.

divorce
m 59–29 but the frequency of d· shows
b 306–14 and then are separated as by a law of d·

divorced
s 155– 7 have not yet d· the drug from the general faith.
r 477–31 man, d· from Spirit, would lose his entity.

divorces
m 65– 8 D· should warn the age of some

dizzy
f 243–17 do not inform us that they are d·,

do
pr 2– 1 D· we pray to make ourselves better
2– 8 to d· more than He has already done,
2– 9 nor can the infinite d· less than
2–11 We can d· more for ourselves by
3– 1 He who is immutably right will d· right
3– 8 Shall we ask the divine Principle . . . to d· His
4–27 Audible prayer can never d· the works of
6– 9 supposition that we have nothing to d· but
8– 6 which d· not correspond with their character.
8–32 D· we not rather give thanks that
9– 6 D· we love our neighbor better because of this
9– 7 D· we pursue the old selfishness,
9–26 D· you really desire to attain this point?
9–32 Consistent prayer is the desire to d· right.
10–22 we d· not always receive the blessings we ask for
10–31 D· you ask wisdom to be merciful
11–25 We must be willing to d· this,
11–30 desire to know and d· the will of God,
13–13 D· we gain the omnipotent ear sooner by
14–20 works that I d· shall he d· also ;— John 14 : 12.
a 18– 8 to show them how to d· theirs,
18– 8 but not to d· it for them
19–24 enables man to d· the will of wisdom.
21– 6 Christians d· not continue to
25–29 We must go and d· likewise,
27–28 Why d· those who profess to follow Christ
31– 8 they who d· the will of his Father.
32– 1 these things will they d· unto you,— John 16 : 3.
42–31 works that I d· shall he d· also.”— John 14 : 12.
48–31 what the true knowledge of God can d·
51–21 which he did and taught others to d·.
52–27 works that I d· shall he d· also ;”— John 14 : 12.
55–12 clearer light than mere words can possibly d·,
m 59– 1 and this is the pleasantest thing to d·.
62–15 will d· much more for the health of
sp 82– 2 as we d· of one present.
83– 3 the worshippers of Baal failed to d· ;
85– 8 enabling one to d· good,
89–22 We are all capable of more than we d·.
93– 5 works that I d· shall he d· also,”— John 14 : 12.
95–13 cannot injure others, and must d· them good.
99– 8 both to will and to d· of His— Phil. 2 : 13.
an 103–32 In C. S., man can d· no harm,
106–27 they which d· such things— Gal. 5 : 21.
s 109–29 If any man will d· His will,— John 7 : 17.
117– 9 mortals alone d· this.
119– 2 that is, when we d· so in our theories,
135–20 What cannot God d·?
137–10 what is it that is able to d· the work,
141–22 did not then, and d· not now, understand
141–29 Let our pulpits d· justice to C. S.
144– 2 Why should we wish to make them d· so,
151–20 brain, etc., have nothing to d· with Life,
161–15 then will d· less violence to that immortal
ph 166–21 He can d· all things for us in sickness
169–32 The good that a poisonous drug seems to d·
174– 2 as consciously as d· civilized practitioners
174– 8 doing so much for man as he can d· for himself.
180– 3 should be taught to d· the body no harm
180–18 as they so frequently d·, by declaring
192–23 The good you d· and embody gives you
198–14 but to d· this requires attention.
199–27 His belief that he could d· it gave
f 214–21 more than they d· a spiritual God.
231– 8 What God cannot d·, man need not attempt.
234–31 d· no more harm than one's belief permits.
237–27 and expect this error to d· more for them
237–29 the only living and true God can d·.
241–15 can d· no more for mortals than
249–19 nothing to d· with Life.
253–19 change your course and d· right.
c 263–18 “The good that I would, I d· not :— Rom. 7 : 19.
263–19 evil which I would not, that I d·.”— Rom. 7 : 19.
267–16 whosoever shall d· the will of— Matt. 12 : 50.
b 268– * Here I stand. I can d· no otherwise ;
280– 9 Finite belief can never d· justice to
283–28 unless we so d·, we can no more demonstrate
292–23 lusts of your father ye will d·.— John 8 : 44.
305–17 Son can d· nothing of himself,— John 5 : 19.
305–18 what he seeth the Father d· :— John 5 : 19.
322–23 A man who likes to d· wrong
326– 5 works that I d· shall he d· also.”— John 14 : 12.
o 346–32 what frail mortals are trying to d·?

do
o 349–27 can d· so only as thought is educated
357– 4 and knew from the outset that man would d·.
359–32 When others see them as I d·,
p 364–14 his rich entertainer had neglected to d·,
365– 4 this knowledge would d· much more
370–25 and d· no more for the patient.
371–28 father to the fact that Mind can d· it ;
379– 2 If disease can attack . . . sin can d· the same,
383– 6 To d· this, the pure and exalting influence
385–17 Whatever it is your duty to d·,
385–18 you can d· without harm to yourself.
389–10 it is supposed to d· so.
402–26 handle themselves as they should d·.
403–18 and it will continue to d· so, until
405–25 tends to destroy the ability to d· right.
414– 6 yields more readily than d· most diseases
417–25 To d· this, the physician must
420– 7 If they are unwilling to d· this
435–21 that they should d· unto you,”
442– 4 “Shall not the Judge. . .d· right?”— Gen. 18 : 25.
t 447– 8 ignorant attempts to d· good may render you
448–16 the good you know and d· not.
448–29 It is C. S. to d· right,
454–26 feeling that you have no more to d· for them.
456–26 and so d· all his students and patients.
460–27 to d· this orally through the meagre channel
462–18 as they usually d· in every
464– 9 not take her place, even if willing so to d·.
r 497–26 to d· unto others as we would have them d·
g 530–20 saying, . . . I can d· what God has not done
539–14 the propensity or power to d· evil?
540– 6 I the Lord d· all these things ;”— Isa. 45 : 7.

doctor (see also **doctor's**)
another
p 424–14 a remedy prescribed by another d·.
faith of
p 398–19 It is the faith of the d·
materialistic
ph 198– 9 The materialistic d·, though humane,
one
p 424–13 if one d· should administer a drug to
popular
ph 166– 9 popular d· believes in his prescription,
s 155– 9 the d·, and the nurse equip the medicine with
ph 193– 8 The d· went out.
197–31 The d· should suppress his fear
198–15 is formed before one sees a d·
198–16 before the d· undertakes to dispel it
198–24 even though the d· says nothing to support
f 235– 4 Better suffer a d· infected with smallpox
p 364–32 Did the careless d·, the nurse, the cook,

doctored
o 347– 8 infers that if anything needs to be d·,
347–11 there is nothing left to be d·.

doctoring
p 365–10 physical thought-taking and d· ;

doctor's
ph 166–13 the d· and pharmacist's is a medical
197–30 The d· mind reaches that of his patient.
198– 4 A patient hears the d· verdict
198–24 moulded and formed by his d· belief

doctors
pref viii–17 by d· using material remedies ;
ph 180–17 D· should not implant disease in the
198–27 importance that d· be Christian Scientists.
f 221–12 having exhausted the skill of the d·,
p 394– 6 majority of d· depress mental energy,
417– 4 sometimes knowing more than their d·.

doctrinal
a 37–20 into a mutilated d· platform.
s 132–23 on any but a material and a d· theory.
o 361– 3 C. S. intervenes, explains these d· points,
r 496–31 if by that term is meant d· beliefs.

doctrine
Christian's
o 361– 8 Thus the Jew unites with the Christian's d·
erroneous
g 526–20 erroneous d· that the knowledge of evil
false
a 27–20 to cut down the false d· of pantheism,
forms of
a 20– 3 He at last paid no homage to forms of d·
his
s 132– 2 his works instead of referring to his d·,
human
b 286– 2 To seek Truth through belief in a human d·
my
s 109–28 “My d· is not mine, but His— John 7 : 16.
old
a 38– 5 than the old d· of foreordination,
one
a 23–12 “He that taketh one d·, firm in faith,

doctrine
rejected
s 150–25 rejected d· of the predestination of
  ———
a 26–28 Our Master taught no mere theory, d·,
an 101–16 not conclusive in favor of the d·
s 109–30 he shall know of the d·,—*John* 7: 17.
  150–26 The d· that man's harmony is governed by
  150–29 d· of the superiority of matter
b 279–22 Every system of human philosophy, d·,
  304– 9 This is the d· of C. S. :
o 360–31 Jew and Christian can unite in d·
t 443–22 all longsuffering and d·."—*II Tim.* 4: 2.
  454–12 is the d· of absolute C. S.,
  458– 3 The chief plank in this platform is the d·
doctrines
and creeds
r 471–22 Are d· and creeds a benefit to man?
human
s 117–31 which he defined as human d·.
g 504–25 a thousand years of human d·,
  545–14 errors send falsity into all human d·
man-made
a 38– 8 lethargy of mortals, produced by man-made d·,
s 134–14 Man-made d· are waning.
medical
s 163–30 To harmonize the contrarieties of medical d·
of Christ
s 134–16 how can they illustrate the d· of Christ
of John
s 132–28 Did the d· of John the Baptist confer
of men
s 131–24 taketh away the ceremonies and d· of men,
of physics
s 132–18 from d· of physics or of divinity ;
old
o 360–12 my old d· or human opinions."
such
o 358– 5 Such d· are "confusion worse confounded."
varied
b 319–15 varied d· and theories which presuppose
  ———
pref vii–14 Truth, independent of d· . . . knocks at the
sp 98–12 Creeds, d·, and human hypotheses
b 314–29 to those who, depending on d·
gl 590– 6 human theories, d·, hypotheses ;
document
g 523–19 The other d· is called the Jehovistic,
documents
g 523–16 evidences of two distinct d·
does
pr 9– 4 the falsehood which d· no one any good.
  12–18 The drug d· nothing, because it has no
a 26–17 to prove what God is and what He d· for man.
m 63–17 than d· either C. S. or civilization.
s 123– 6 as d· the error relating to soul and
  102– 1 but upon different terms than d· the
ph 187–15 as directly as d· the mind,
  196–32 It d· this by giving names to diseases
f 212–23 and this He d· by means of Mind,
  218– 1 Mortal mind d· the false talking,
b 335–20 Soul . . . d· not exist in mortality.
o 342– 8 decries this Science d· it presumptuously,
  356–30 follow its antecedent? It d·.
p 366–28 knowing, as he d·, that Life is God
  371–16 no more comprehends . . . than d· the child ;
  373–11 than d· the sinner from his sin.
  376– 7 and d· its work almost self-deceived.
  379–22 The so-called vital current d· not affect
  387–19 That man . . . who d· the most good.
  401– 3 it d· nothing in the right direction
  413– 9 Mind regulates . . . and matter d· not.
t 449– 4 A grain of C. S. d· wonders for mortals,
  449–17 than it d· to heal the most difficult case.
  456–22 Truth d· the work,
  458–24 He d· violence to no man.
r 483–28 it d· this in the way of His appointing,
g 515–26 lift a weight, your reflection d· this also.
  541– 3 more nearly resembles . . . than d· Cain's
  542–22 penalty, both for what it is and for what it d·.
  550–27 nor d· a lion bring forth a lamb.
  551–13 but it d· not acknowledge the method
gl 585–23 that which d· not last forever ;
doest
c 256–23 What d· Thou?"—*Dan.* 4: 35.
doeth
a 31–32 think that he d· God service ;—*John* 16: 2.
c 256–20 "d· according to His will—*Dan.* 4: 35.
b 305–18 what things soever He d·,—*John* 5: 19.
  305–19 these also d· the Son likewise."—*John* 5: 19.
dogma
ph 195–24 the mere d·, the speculative theory,
f 244–28 cast us headlong into darkness and d·.
o 342– 3 demonstration, instead of opinion and d·,

dogmas
o 354–16 to cleave to barren and desultory d·,
dogs
b 272–17 not that which is holy unto the d·,—*Matt.* 7: 6.
doing
a 22–14 and "be not weary in well d·."—*II Thess.* 3: 13.
  36–29 in return for our efforts at well d·.
  41–27 apostles still went about d· good deeds,
  51–20 only through d· the works which he did
  55–21 what it has done and is d· for mankind.
sp 79–30 need "not be weary in well d·."—*Gal.* 6: 9.
  79–30 It dissipates fatigue in d· good.
s 155–12 inanimate drug as d· this or that,
  158–28 Homœopathy, . . . is d· this.
ph 165– 4 Instead of so d·, it closed the eyes of mortals
  174– 7 Nothing save divine power is capable of d·
  181–26 that you are d· something for them,
f 202–32 in the act of d· good.
  203– 2 and check the reward for d· good.
  230–15 for d· what they could not avoid d·.
  254–15 demonstrating the great problem . . . is d· much.
c 266–20 sinner makes his own hell by d· evil,
  266–21 and the saint his own heaven by d· right.
o 348–24 by so d· our own condition can be improved'
  357–2, 3 for d· what He created man capable of d·,
p 384– 7 God never punishes man for d· right,
  387–22 supposition . . . that God punishes man for d· good,
  410–27 to promote right thinking and d·,
  432–16 The Judge asks if by d· good to his neighbor,
  435–20 d· "unto others as ye would that they should
  436–31 pronounced a sentence of death for d· right.
t 448–31 d· one's self the most harm.
  449– 6 in order to continue in well d·.
r 483–29 by d· many wonderful works
g 527–27 but d· so materially, not spiritually,
ap 563–28 but d· this in the name of good.
  571– 9 d· right and benefiting our race.
doleful
f 203–28 and of fearful and d· dying
doling
p 367– 7 and the d· of arguments,
dolorous
g 552–12 no member of this d· and fatal triad.
domain
sp 80–17 d· of reason into the realm of mysticism.
  97–18 until divine Spirit, supreme in its d·,
dome
s 142–12 making d· and spire tremulous with beauty,
domestic
m 59–10 annoyances and cares of d· economy,
  64–14 debarred by a covetous d· tyrant
dominant
ap 559– 4 d· power of which was upon the sea,
dominate
c 266–25 the demonstrations, which d· the flesh.
t 446–16 Good must d· in the thoughts of the healer,
dominates
sp 97–19 until divine Spirit, . . . d· all matter,
dominion
and power
s 143–30 give to Mind the glory, honor, d·, and power
God-given
ph 165– 5 man's God-given d· over the earth.
f 228–13 God-given d· over the material senses.
p 381–21 will sooner grasp man's God-given d·.
g 531–14 recognize his God-given d· and being.
its
r 485–24 If thought yields its d· to other powers,
over all the earth
an 102–14 has d· over all the earth
f 202–22 God gives man d· over all the earth.
b 316–23 gives man d· over all the earth.
g 516–20 reflects God's d· over all the earth.
  531–32 and having d· over all the earth.
  533– 2 God's behest, d· over all the earth?
over all things
b 307–26 gives man d· over all things.
over error
p 380–21 and prove man's d· over error.
over the atmosphere
s 125–26 mariner will have d· over the atmosphere
over the fish
f 222–23 "d· over the fish of the sea,—*Gen.* 1: 26.
r 475–42 d· over the fish of the sea,—*Gen.* 1: 26.
g 515–12 d· over the fish of the sea,—*Gen.* 1: 26.
  517–27 d· over the fish of the sea,—*Gen.* 1: 28.
over the whole earth
pr 14–27 man's d· over the whole earth.
g 545–11 was given d· over the whole earth.

dominion

over the works
ph 200–14 d· over the works of Thy hands.— *Psal.* 8 : 6.

f 238–22 and so gain d· over mankind,
o 347– 7 all is Life, and death has no d·.
p 438– 4 and let them have d·.— *Gen.* 1 : 26.
g 515–21 "Let *them* have d·."— *Gen.* 1 : 26.
518– 1 His birthright is d·, not subjection.

done

pr 1– 8 whatever has been successfully d· for the
2– 9 to do more than He has already d·,
3– 9 His work is d·,
4– 9 our gratitude for all that he has d·.
5– 9 woe comes in return for what is d·.
6– 8 badly d· or left undone,
9–14 simply by asking that it may be d·.
17– 1 Thy will be d· in earth, as it is— *Matt.* 6 : 10.
a 22–19 you will discern the good you have d·,
33–20 "Not my will, but Thine, be d· !"— *Luke* 22 : 42.
38–18 otherwise the healing could not have been d·
44– 3 "Well d·, good and faithful— *Matt.* 25 : 23.
55–20 what it has d· and is doing for mankind.
sp 85–29 "These ought ye to have d·,— *Matt.* 23 : 23.
s 152– 8 although they know not how the work is d·.
163– 1 mischief which Hippocrates has d·,
164–14 Much yet remains to be said and d·
ph 179– 2 can be d· only by taking up the cross
187–18 We say,"My hand hath d· it."
199–27 he could never have d· it.
f 202– 5 God's will must be universally d·.
209–23 In proportion as this is d·, man and the
c 260–15 to discover what God has already d· ;
266–18 This is d· through self-abnegation.
b 326–28 He learned the wrong that he had d·
334–19 as the Christ has always d·,
p 364–13 He even said that this poor woman had d·
372–29 acknowledgment of Truth and of what it has d·
373–13 if the teaching is faithfully d·.
t 449– 7 The wrong d· another reacts most heavily
457– 5 this book has d· more for teacher and student,
r 483–32 to be well d·, the work must be d· unselfishly.
494– 6 that so great a work as the Messiah's was d·
g 528–22 declaring what great things error has d·.
530–21 saying, . . . I can do what God has not d·
557–27 Mind, spake and it was d·.

doom

foresee the
f 227–15 cannot fail to foresee the d· of all oppression.
foreshadows its
ap 571–27 rebukes . . . sin, and foreshadows its d·.
foretells its
an 105–28 The aggravation of error foretells its d·,
moral
p 405–27 hastening on to physical and moral d·.
nearing its
ap 565– 1 when nearing its d·, this evil increases
of matter
b 279– 6 d· of matter establishes the conclusion
precipitates his
m 67–16 precipitates his d· or sunshine gladdens

a 40–14 While there's sin there's d·.
f 241– 6 Mortality is their d·.
b 318–11 They would . . . d· all things to decay.

doomed

g 551–31 the resulting germ is d· to the same routine.

dooms

g 535–11 It d· idolatry.

door

bar the
t 452– 1 Instruct him how to bar the d· of his thought
closes the
s 144–26 Ignorance, pride, or prejudice closes the d·
close the
f 224–25 Will you open or close the d· upon this angel
of this age
f 224–24 stands at the d· of this age, knocking
of thought
p 392–24 Stand porter at the d· of thought.
open
k 499– * *I have set before thee an open d·,— Rev.* 3 : 8.
gl 579– * *I have set before thee an open d·,— Rev.* 3 : 8.
opened the
sp 99–11 has opened the d· of the human understanding.
open the
pr 10–15 Spiritual attainments open the d· to a
shuts the
sp 90–26 This conviction shuts the d· on death,
s 132–22 blind belief shuts the d· upon it,
shut the
pr 15–15 enter into the closet and shut the d·.
s 142–14 they . . . shut the d· on progress.

door

shut thy
pr 14–32 when thou hast shut thy d·,— *Matt.* 6 : 6.
some other
sp 99–12 None may pick the lock nor enter by some other
d·.

pr 15– 4 the d· of which shuts out sinful sense
15–10 the d· of the erring senses must be closed.
a 45–17 hath rolled away the stone from the d·
b 299– 7 appearing at the d· of some sepulchre,

doors

pr 10–19 stop at the d· to earn a penny by
f 234–11 as watchfully as we bar our d· against
p 366–30 If we would open their prison d· for the sick,
433–32 can open wide those prison d·
r 495–12 opens the prison d· to such as are bound,

dormant

b 327–30 man's d· sense of moral obligation,
328–16 For centuries it has been d·,
gl 583–16 rousing the d· understanding

dose

ph 174–26 and administer a d· of despair to the
177–25 If a d· of poison is swallowed through mistake,

doses

s 156–10 d· of a high attenuation of *Sulphuris.*

dosing

ph 169–13 and by d· the body in order to avoid it.

dost

pr 9–17 D· thou "love the Lord thy God — *Matt.* 22 : 37.

double

gl 590–21 This d· term is not used in the first chapter

doubly

o 343– 7 This makes it d· unfair to impugn

doubt

pr 1– * *and shall not d· in his heart,— Mark* 11 : 23.
16–11 some d· among Bible scholars, whether
47–14 were in d· concerning Jesus' teachings.
sp 80–12 I entertain no d· of the humanity
82– 8 of whose personal existence we may be in d· ?
s 130– 9 unwise to d· if reality is in perfect harmony
130–30 astounded at the vigorous claims of evil and d·
ph 189–12 or d· that the sun will reappear.
194–19 It proves beyond a d· that education
f 231–24 To fear sin is . . . to d· His government
p 429–26 This is why you d· the statement
t 445– 7 No hypothesis . . . should interpose a d· or
r 493–30 Who dares to d· this consummate test
495–17 Let neither fear nor d· overshadow
g 537–19 No one can reasonably d· that the purpose
551–25 Darkness and d· encompass thought, so long as
gl 592–21 NIGHT. Darkness ; d· ; fear.
597–16 WILDERNESS. Loneliness ; d· ; darkness.

doubted

s 136–25 But even Herod d· if Jesus was controlled by

doubtful

o 342– 1 alludes to "d· disputations."— *Rom.* 14 : 1.

doubting

b 317–29 To this dull and d· disciple
t 455– 4 a faltering and d· trust in Truth

doubts

pr 13–21 d· and fears which attend such a belief,
a 39–29 d· and defeats as well as triumphs.
s 130–27 If thought is startled at the . . . and d· the
p 422–28 d· as to the ultimate outcome of the injury.

dove

ap 574–27 and you will behold the soft-winged d·
gl 584–26 definition of

down

pref viii–28 As early as 1862 she began to write d·
ix– 1 She also began to jot d· her thoughts
pr 6–28 "[It] is hewn d·."— *Matt.* 7 : 19.
15–30 they assuredly call d· infinite blessings.
a 27–19 cut d· the false doctrine of pantheism,
31–20 we shall rest, sit d· with him,
33– 7 Their bread indeed came d· from heaven.
35–26 "which cometh d· from heaven,"— *John* 6 : 33.
41–25 sat d· at the right hand of the Father.
51– 7 power to lay d· a human sense of life
55–15 Truth's immortal idea is sweeping d· the
an 105–26 d· to the depths of ignominy and death.
s 118–32 natural order of heaven comes d· to earth.
ph 174– 5 idolatry, that man should bow d· to a
176–18 weigh d· mankind with superimposed
178– 4 for it is set d· as a poison by
f 214–18 We bow d· to matter, . . . like the pagan
223–22 Spiritual rationality . . . cannot be put d·.
225–20 oppression neither went d· in blood, nor
c 266–17 Thus He teaches mortals to lay d· their
b 301–29 inverted . . . with everything turned upside d·.
319–27 who only wrote d· what an inspired

down

b	321– 8	led by wisdom to cast *d·* his rod,
o	351–32	brought *d·* no proof that it was heard.
p	362– *	*Why art thou cast d·, O my soul — Psal.* 42 : 11.
	364– 5	to lay *d·* his mortal existence in behalf
	394–15	advice to a man who is *d·* in the world,
	404–18	cuts *d·* every tree that brings not forth
	436–12	Laying *d·* his life for a good deed,
t	447–24	To put *d·* the claim of sin, you must
	448–10	and casts thee *d·* from the pinnacle.
	460– 1	metaphysics as laid *d·* in this work,
	462–15	and advance from the rudiments laid *d·*.
r	470–19	Has God taken *d·* His own standard,
g	514–23	leopard shall lie *d·* with the kid ;— *Isa.* 11 : 6.
	530–21	saying, through the material senses : . . . Bow
		d· to me
	535–13	A belief in other gods, . . . must go *d·*
	547–22	or go *d·* into dust and nothingness.
	549–31	coming *d·* to a belief in the material origin
	551–21	brought *d·* from generation to generation?"
ap	558– 3	angel come *d·* from heaven,— *Rev.* 10 : 1.
	561–12	a bride coming *d·* from heaven,
	568–16	accuser of our brethren is cast *d·*,— *Rev.* 12 : 10.
	568–22	the devil is come *d·* unto you,— *Rev.* 12 : 12.
	568–31	by which we lay *d·* all for Truth,
	574–13	"New Jerusalem, coming *d·* from— *Rev.* 21 : 2.
	575– 8	"*d·* from God, out of heaven,"— *Rev.* 21 : 2.
	577–23	will lay *d·* their honors within the
	578– 6	to lie *d·* in green pastures :— *Psal.* 23 : 2.

downfall

ph	176– 5	unmanly Adams attributed their own *d·*
gl	581–21	more certain is the *d·* of its structure.

downward

b	272–22	in contrast with the *d·* tendencies and

Dragon, Red

gl	593– 7	definition of

dragon

against the

ap	567–11	Truth and Love prevail against the *d·*

cannot war

ap	567–11	the *d·* cannot war with them.

cast out

ap	570–12	the *d·* cast out of his mouth.— *Rev.* 12 : 16.

fought

ap	566–27	*d·* fought, and his angels,— *Rev.* 12 : 7.

fought against the

ap	566–26	his angels fought against the *d·* ;— *Rev.* 12 : 7.

great

ap	567–14	the great *d·* was cast out,— *Rev.* 12 : 9.

horns of the

ap	563–11	The ten horns of the *d·* typify the belief

old

ap	570–18	What if the old *d·* should send forth

red

ap	562–30	and behold a great red *d·*,— *Rev.* 12 : 3.
	563– 8	The great red *d·* symbolizes a lie,
	565– 2	and becomes the great red *d·*,
	567–21	false claim . . . is pure delusion, the red *d·* ;

show the

ap	567–24	show the *d·* to be nothingness,

stood before the

ap	563–25	and the *d·* stood before the woman— *Rev.* 12 : 4.

this

ap	563–10	This *d·* stands for the sum total of human error.

warreth not long

ap	567– 9	Against Love, the *d·* warreth not long,

ap	564– 5	animal instinct, of which the *d·* is the type,
	564–14	the *d·* as warring against innocence.
	569–25	The *d·* is at last stung to death by his own
	569–29	And when the *d·* saw that he was— *Rev.* 12 : 13.

drain

a	33–14	and *d·* to the dregs his cup of sorrow.

drained

a	54–21	cup of bitterness was *d·* to the dregs.

drank

pr	5–15	The followers of Christ *d·* his cup.
a	35–28	draught our Master *d·* and commended
	43–22	because of the cup of bitterness he *d·*.
	52– 5	His senses *d·* in the spiritual evidence
	53– 7	hence the cup he *d·*.
f	221– 3	*d·* nothing but water.

draught

pref	ix– 4	A child drinks . . . and rejoices in the *d·*.
a	35–28	*d·* our Master drank and commended
p	384–16	If exposure to a *d·* of air while in a

draughts

f	234– 1	Spiritual *d·* heal,

draw

b	300– 2	it attempts to *d·* correct spiritual conclusions
p	396– 8	nor *d·* attention to certain symptoms as

drawn

a	48–26	Pilate was *d·* into acquiescence with the
s	117–24	Evidence *d·* from the five physical senses
	129– 1	conclusion, if properly *d·*, cannot be false.
f	247–16	models of spiritual sense, *d·* by perfect Mind
b	274–11	not mere inferences *d·* from material premises.
o	360– 1	real and eternal because *d·* from Truth,
p	379–27	pictures *d·* on the body by a
	379–30	the fever-picture, *d·* by millions of mortals

draws

sp	96–25	As this consummation *d·* nearer,

dread

a	51– 5	This *d·* added the drop of gall to his cup.
b	321–22	white as snow with the *d·* disease,
p	426–20	master either a desire to die or a *d·* of the grave,

dreads

p	379–24	her belief produces the very results she *d·*.
	415– 9	looks upon some object which he *d·*.

dream

according to the

f	250–17	according to the *d·* he entertains in sleep.

another

sp	75–30	we pass from one dream to another *d·*,

ceases

o	346–20	If a *d·* ceases, it is self-destroyed,

dreamer and

g	530–28	therefore the dreamer and *d·* are one,

erroneous

f	223–26	startle . . . thought from its erroneous *d·*

fleshly

ph	196– 7	awakens mortal mind from its fleshly *d·*,

has no reality

g	530–26	The *d·* has no reality, no intelligence,

his own

g	528–23	Beholding the creations of his own *d·*

illusion or

r	490–30	oblivion, nothingness, or an illusion or *d·*.

leaves mortal man

r	492– 1	when the *d·* leaves mortal man intact in body

mortal

(see **mortal***)*

of death

p	427–29	The *d·* of death must be mastered by Mind
	429–17	Mortals waken from the *d·* of death

of disease

p	396–30	It breaks the *d·* of disease to understand that

of existence

g	529– 8	destroy the *d·* of existence, reinstate reality,

of material life

sp	77–13	period required for this *d·* of material life,

of material living

pr	14–25	separate from the . . . *d·* of material living,

of matter

g	532–27	error began and will end the *d·* of matter.

of mortal existence

f	250–23	in the waking *d·* of mortal existence

of pain

ph	188–11	Mortal existence is a *d·* of pain and

of sin

ph	188–12	a *d·* of sin, sickness, and death ;

of suffering

p	420–29	to break its *d·* of suffering,

one

sp	75–30	we pass from one *d·* to another dream,

or belief

r	491–22	The *d·* or belief goes on, whether our eyes are

phase of the

p	427–13	Death is but another phase of the *d·* that

phases of the

f	249–24	Sleep and apathy are phases of the *d·* that

pleasure of a

ph	188–19	produced physically by the pleasure of a *d·*.

sickness is a

p	417–20	To the C. S. healer, sickness is a *d·*

sleeping

ph	188–15	In both the waking and the sleeping *d·*,
f	250–23	any more reality in . . . than in the sleeping *d·* ?
r	494–22	as the experiences of the sleeping *d·* seem real

temporal

p	412–24	and that sickness is a temporal *d·*.

that matter

o	347–26	The *d·* that matter and error are something

this

sp	77–13	this *d·* of material life, embracing its
ph	196– 8	which tend to perpetuate this *d·*.
r	491–31	that this *d·* . . . may not be mortal man?

vanishes

f	250–18	When that *d·* vanishes, the mortal finds

m	62–16	will do much more . . . than you *d·*.
sp	71–10	Close your eyes, and you may *d·* that you
ph	188–13	is like the *d·* we have in sleep,
f	250– 6	Mortal existence is a *d·* ;
p	412–17	break the *d·* of the material senses.
r	491–28	awake, we *d·* of the pains and pleasures

dream
r 493–28 awakened Lazarus from the d·,
g 528– 7 this supposition was a d·, a myth.
556–24 of which mortal and material life is the d·.

dreamed
f 249–20 You say, "I d· last night."

dreamer
sp 82–14 not communicate with the d· by our side
ph 188–16 the d· thinks that his body is material
b 322–21 as the startled d· who wakens from an
r 491–31 this dream — rather than the d·
492– 2 the so-called d· is unconscious?
g 530–28 therefore the d· and dream are one,

dreamers
f 249–23 Mortals are the Adam d·.

dreaming
sp 95–29 in the cradle of infancy, d· away the hours.

dream-land
g 543–11 and must dwell in d·, until mortals

dream-narrative
g 530–26 The history of error is a d·.

dreams
different
sp 82–27 Different d· and different awakenings betoken
mortal
b 305–29 These mortal d· are of human origin,
opposite
sp 74–14 between persons in such opposite d· as
our
sp 82–16 unconscious or are wandering in our d·
f 212– 1 We suffer or enjoy in our d·,

sp 71–18 From d· also you learn that
90–16 In d· we fly to Europe and meet a
f 249–22 and His likeness never d·.
250– 8 Spirit is the Ego which never d·,
p 386– 1 an illusion of mortal mind, — one of its d·.
397–26 when they . . . enjoy, or suffer in d·.
g 505– 2 mortal mind, sleep, d·, sin,
556–22 Oblivion and d·, not realities, come with sleep.

dream-sensations
f 250–19 experiencing none of these d·.

dream-shadows
p 418–31 pain, deformed joints, are waking d·,

dreamy
sp 88– 1 and this not in d· sleep.

dreary
sp 96– 8 Earth will become d· and desolate,

dregs
a 33–14 drain to the d· his cup of sorrow.
54–22 cup of bitterness was drained to the d·.

drenching
s 122–21 midst of murky clouds and d· rain.

dress
ph 193–17 I told him to rise, d· himself, and take supper
g 526–27 into the garden of Eden, to d· it — Gen. 2 : 15.
527– 2 God could not put Mind into matter . . . to d· it

drew
b 321–22 and d· it forth white as snow
ap 563–23 And his tail d· the third part — Rev. 12 : 4.

drift
pref x–12 has not compromised . . . to suit the general d·
f 205–25 hinders man's normal d· towards the one Mind,
250–30 like snowflakes, and d· to the ground.

drifting
a 21–31 if he can only imagine himself d· in the

drilling
p 378–19 d· and drugging, adopted to cure matter,

drink
pr 10– 9 Until we are . . . willing to d· his cup,
a 18– * I will not d· of the fruit of — Luke 22 : 18.
25–11 they truly eat his flesh and d· his blood,
26– 7 all have the cup of sorrowful effort to d·
31–18 we d· of his cup, partake of his bread,
31–23 and d· this cup, — I Cor. 11 : 26.
32–18 D· ye all of it." — Matt. 26 : 27.
33–17 "D· ye all of it." — Matt. 26 : 27.
33–32 Are all who eat bread and d· wine in memory
34– 1 Are all . . . willing truly to d· his cup,
54–27 those who followed him should d· of his cup,
m 62–14 or what ye shall d·" ; — Matt. 6 : 25.
67– 2 shall we not d· it and learn the lessons
s 158–22 acquires an educated appetite for strong d·,
ph 165– * or what ye shall d·; — Matt. 6 : 25.
170–17 or what ye shall d·." — Matt. 6 : 25.
f 222–15 less thought about what he should eat or d·,
b 317– 8 will d· of his Master's cup.
328–24 and if they d· any deadly thing, — Mark 16 : 18.
p 362– * and if they d· any deadly thing, — Mark 16 : 18.

drink
p 366– 8 debars him from giving d· to the thirsty
398–22 and the desire for strong d· is gone.
431– 5 the prisoner gave him d·.
g 530– 9 or what ye shall d·," — Matt. 6 : 25.
ap 570–16 waiting and watching for rest and d·.

drinketh
a 55–24 d· of Christ's cup now,

drinking
a 33–27 Christians, are you d· his cup?
f 254– 8 To stop eating, d·, or being clothed

drinks
pref ix– 3 child d· in the outward world through the eyes
a 48–12 when he d· from the same cup,
p 406–28 The depraved appetite for alcoholic d·,
t 454– 2 the use of tobacco or intoxicating d· is not

drive
f 251– 8 to d· belief into new paths.
o 357–31 Can matter d· Life, Spirit, hence, and so defeat
r 487– 1 these calamities often d· mortals to seek
g 538– 3 d· error out of all selfhood.

driven
s 135– 3 Jordan, that thou wast d· back? — Psal. 114 : 5.
143–14 D· to choose between two difficulties,
152–26 mortals are divinely d· to a spiritual source

droop
m 61–16 often these beautiful children early d· and die,

drooping
m 58– 3 or else joy's d· wings trail in dust.

drop
a 51– 5 This dread added the d· of gall to his cup.
an 106– 2 to d· from the platform of common manhood
s 153– 8 and yet, with one d· of that attenuation
f 205– 4 stumble with lameness, d· with drunkenness.
c 255– 2 d· off their mental swaddling-clothes,
262–21 They will then d· the false estimate of life
o 361–16 As a d· of water is one with the ocean,
p 379–17 when not a d· of his blood was shed.

dropped
f 222–20 Now he d· drugs and material hygiene,
b 296– 5 the mortal is d· for the immortal.

dropping
f 228–17 D· their present beliefs, they will recognize

drops
s 148–16 d· the true tone, and accepts the discord.
ph 166–24 the despairing invalid often d· them,
c 257–20 "who hath begotten the d· of dew," — Job 38 : 28.
g 520–27 Mortal thought d· into the ground,
549–31 He absolutely d· from his summit,

dropsy
s 156– 5 A case of d·, . . . fell into my hands.

dross
m 66–32 furnace separates the gold from the d·

drove
g 537– 5 So He d· out the man : — Gen. 3 : 24.

drown
ap 570–19 a new flood to d· the Christ-idea?
570–20 He can neither d· your voice with its roar,

drowning
a 22– 7 This causes them, even as d· men,
ap 569–19 to lift their heads above the d· wave.

drug (see also **drug's**)
administer a
p 424–13 if one doctor should administer a d· to
any
p 420–21 better than any d·, alterative, or tonic.
applying the
p 401–24 by applying the d· to either?
causes a
pr 12–21 which causes a d· to be apparently
certain
p 370–11 might be produced by a certain d·,
confidence in the
s 155– 7 take away the individual confidence in the d·,
diminishes the
s 155–26 Homœopathy diminishes the d·,
disappears
s 155–27 the potency . . . increases as the d· disappears.
divorced the
s 155– 7 you have not yet divorced the d· from
does nothing
pr 12–18 The d· does nothing, because it has no
enables a
ph 174–22 belief is all that enables a d· to
exterminates the
s 157– 8 C. S. exterminates the d·,
faith in the
p 370–14 faith in the d· is the sole factor in the cure.

drug

inanimate
s 155–12   When the general belief endorses the inanimate d·
160– 7   the inanimate d· becomes powerless.
b 312–30   and so turns . . . to the inanimate d·.
like a
pr 12–17   affects the sick like a d·,
may eventually lose
p 370–24   a d· may eventually lose its supposed power
mentalizes a
s 157–11   Homœopathy mentalizes a d·
no efficacy in a
s 153–15   learned . . . that there is no efficacy in a d·.
poisonous
ph 169–32   good that a poisonous d· seems to do is evil,
prescribes the
p 399– 6   Mortal mind prescribes the d·, and
rely on a
f 202–28   yet we rely on a d· . . . to heal disease,
same
p 370–12   are removed by using the same d·
whatever the
ph 178– 3   the strychnine, or whatever the d· used,

----

s 152–32   but the d· is frequently attenuated
153– 2   it is not the d· which expels the disease
157–12   d· becomes more like the human mind
157–24   the power which the d· seems to possess.
158–30   of a higher attenuation than the d·,
163–11   man-midwife, chemist, druggist, or d·
ph 169–22   however much we trust a d·
p 394–24   unless it can be aided by a d·
401–25   Would the d· remove paralysis,

drugging

s 155–29   homœopathy, and . . . have diminished d· ;
p 378–19   hygienic drilling and d·, adopted to

druggist

s 155– 9   The chemist, the botanist, the d·,
163–11   chemist, d·, or drug on the face of the earth,

drug's

s 157–14   and the d· power of action is

drugs

and hygiene
ph 167–12   D· and hygiene cannot successfully usurp
r 484–15   D· and hygiene oppose the supremacy of the
and inert matter
r 484–17   D· and inert matter are unconscious, mindless.
does not distribute
p 408–20   Truth does not distribute d· through the blood,
does not employ
s 143– 5   God does not employ d· or hygiene,
do not affect
p 408–19   D· do not affect a corpse,
faith in
s 145–14   whether faith in d·, trust in hygiene,
146– 7   have rendered faith in d· the fashion,
ph 181–30   If you have more faith in d· than in Truth,
giving
p 413–24   Giving d· to infants, noticing every symptom
hygiene and
f 222–19   the strictest adherence to hygiene and d·,
inanimate
an 106– 1   from the use of inanimate d· to the
lose their
s 160– 5   d· lose their healing force, for they have no
material
s 146–18   truth divests material d· of their
matter or
t 463–29   are not healed by inanimate matter or d·,
Mind and
s 143–32   may try to make Mind and d· coalesce,
mineral
s 158– 9   from image-gods to vegetable and mineral d·
never gave
p 369–18   never gave d·, never prayed to know if
never taught that
f 232–19   Jesus never taught that d·, food, air,
outweighs
s 149– 3   Mind as far outweighs d· in the cure of
physician prescribes
ph 198–19   the physician prescribes d·, until the
pleas for
ph 182–27   Pleas for d· and laws of health come from
prescribed no
s 148– 4   prescribed no d·, urged no obedience to
rush after
ph 168–11   When sick (according to belief) you rush after d·,
substitute
f 218–20   why do you substitute d· for the
substitutes
s 146–13   Material medicine substitutes d· for the
their
f 237– 8   before her parents would have laid aside their d·,

drugs

through
o 345– 6   and work through d· to heal the sick?
took no
a 44–13   He took no d· to allay inflammation.
use of
sp 79– 8   more sanitary than the use of d·,
s 155– 3   When the sick recover by the use of d·,
with
f 230– 2   Would you attempt with d·, or without,
without
ph 185–23   not only without d·, but without hypnotism,

----

s 155–29   but if d· are an antidote to disease,
155–30   If d· are good things, is it safe to
155–32   If d· possess intrinsic virtues or
156– 2   Who named d·, and what made them good
157–16   If d· are part of God's creation,
157–18   then d· cannot be poisonous.
157–19   If He could create d· intrinsically bad,
157–20   If He creates d· at all . . . why did Jesus not
158–16   D·, cataplasms, and whiskey are
ph 166–11   believes in the power of his d·
166–27   less than in d·, air, and exercise,
169–11   faith in rules of health or in d· begets
f 222–20   he dropped d· and material hygiene,
230–23   never really healed by d·, hygiene,
251–16   faith in hygiene, in d·, or in will-power.
p 408–16   Can d· go of their own accord to the brain
t 463–26   nor did he use d·.
r 483– 1   Then comes the question, how do d·,
484–18   results, supposed to proceed from d·,

drug-systems

s 158–25   D· are quitting their hold on matter

drunk

a 34–11   If all who ever partook of . . . and d· of his cup,
p 406–32   There is no enjoyment in getting d·,

drunkard

b 322–17   The d· thinks he enjoys drunkenness,

drunkenness

an 106–23   d·, revellings and such like : — Gal. 5 : 21.
f 205– 4   drop with d·, consume with disease,
b 322–18   The drunkard thinks he enjoys d·,

dry

p 379–26   coated tongue, febrile heat, d· skin,
384–17   followed by chills, d· cough, influenza,
431–26   I am Sallow Skin. I have been d·, hot,
r 491– 1   swimming when he is on d· land.
g 506–16   and let the d· land appear : — Gen. 1 : 9.
506–22   And God called the d· land Earth ; — Gen. 1 : 10.
507– 1   In metaphor, the d· land illustrates
535–30   And God called the d· land Earth ;   Gen. 1 : 10.
557– 4   develop their children properly on d· land.

dual

b 334–12   This d· personality of the unseen and the seen,
r 482–24   Angels announced . . . this d· appearing,

duality

r 473–16   hence the d· of Jesus the Christ.

due

pr 6– 1   We cannot escape the penalty d· for sin.
a 36– 7   To remit the penalty d· for sin, would be
41–13   he cannot forever . . . escape the penalty d·.
m 68–10   mistrust, where confidence is d·,
sp 88–27   It is d· to inspiration rather than to
an 101– 2   are d· to manipulations,
106–14   incurs the divine penalty d· this crime.
s 143–30   everlastingly d· its holy name.
151– 8   Great respect is d· the motives and
162–29   With d· respect for the faculty,
ph 184–32   She looked and saw that it pointed d· east.
f 219–28   not rendering to God the honor d· to Him
b 338–32   The ideal man was revealed in d· time,
o 341–12   Proof is essential to a d· estimate of this subject.
355–23   wholly d· to a misapprehension
p 385–14   from all penalties but those d· for wrong-doing.
396–19   d· to the force of education
435–25   decides what penalty is d· for the sin,
436–24   from the penalty they considered justly d·,

dull

b 272–14   not to impart to d· ears and gross hearts the
317–29   To this d· and doubting disciple
o 350–19   and their ears are d· of hearing, — Matt. 13 : 15.

dulness

a 34–22   raise themselves and others from spiritual d·
b 272–15   which d· and grossness could not accept.

duly

g 507– 3   Spirit d· feeds and clothes every object,

dumb

a 50– 2   sheep before her shearers is d·, — Isa. 53 : 7.
s 135–17   "it came to pass, . . . the d· spake." — Luke 11 : 14.
ph 183–29   voice to the d·, feet to the lame.
f 226–25   The lame, the deaf, the d·, the blind,

dumb

o 342–23   It speaks to the *d·* the words of Truth,
348–13   when devils,. . . were cast out and the *d·* spake.
p 398– 2   "Thou *d·* and deaf spirit, — *Mark* 9 : 25.

dumbness

s 135–16   When Christ cast out the devil of *d·*,

dungeon

ph 194–22   Incarcerated in a *d·*, where neither sight nor
195– 3   he asked to be taken back to his *d·*,

duodecillions

s 108–17   three times three *d·* must be nine *d·*,

duplicity

gl 589– 4   JACOB.   A corporeal mortal embracing *d·*,

duration

sp 77–17   will be of longer or shorter *d·*

during

pref ix–28   This was *d·* the years 1867 and 1868.
xii– 6   *D·* seven years over four thousand students
pr 9– 2   *D·* many years the author has been most grateful
a 47–31   *D·* his night of gloom and glory
sp 96–31   *D·* this final conflict, wicked minds will
an 101–10   which tested *d·* several sessions
s 107– 4   graciously preparing me *d·* many
f 254–16   *D·* the sensual ages, absolute C. S.
b 306– 9   *d·* that moment there would be no
p 431– 5   *D·* all this time the prisoner attended to

dust

and nothingness
g 547–22   or go down into *d·* and nothingness.
atom of
c 263–29   like an atom of *d·* thrown into the
decay and
ph 200–13   and not subject to decay and *d·*.
decomposed into
p 429–16   buried and decomposed into *d·* ;
dust to
s 126– 3   The problem of nothingness, or "dust to *d·*,"
ap 567–25   show the dragon to be nothingness, dust to *d·* ;
gl 580– 1   "dust to *d·* ;" red sandstone ; nothingness ;
ephemeral
c 267– 4   start not from matter or ephemeral *d·*.
fall into
an 103–28   singe their own wings and fall into *d·*.
formed from
f 214–10   represented in the Scriptures as formed from *d·*,
b 281–26   through a man formed from *d·*.
ground and
g 537–17   since ground and *d·* stand for nothingness.
injected into
g 524–30   Is Spirit, God, injected into *d·*,
matter or
ph 172–18   If . . . he is a portion of matter, or *d·*.
b 338–19   matter or *d·* was deemed the agent of Deity
non-intelligent
g 531–16   If, . . . body originated in non-intelligent *d·*,
primarily
g 543–20   who shall say that he is not primarily *d·* ?
remands him to
g 532–12   condemns material man and remands him to *d·*.
returning to
g 522–17   this man to be mortal, — *d·* returning to *d·*.
returns to
b 277– 4   the Scripture says that *d·* returns to *d·*.
g 543– 3   error, . . . yields to Truth and returns to *d·* ;
return to
sp 73–19   The belief that material bodies return to *d·*,
f 214–12   originate in matter and return to *d·*,
b 278–26   originated in matter and must return to *d·*,
287– 5   but creations of matter must return to *d·*.
g 536–29   the mortal and material return to *d·*,
trail in
m 58– 4   or else joy's drooping wings trail in *d·*.
trail in the
g 550–20   causes our standard to trail in the *d·*.
turns hope to
c 263–16   His "touch turns hope to *d·*,

s 118–20   In all mortal forms of thought, *d·* is
f 244–15   If man were *d·* in his earliest stage
c 263–16   the *d·* we all have trod."
b 291–25   Mind never becomes *d·*.
296– 1   error . . . man has a resurrection from *d·* ;
338–13   red color of the ground, *d·*, nothingness.
p 416–22   has resigned his body to *d·*,
r 476– 3   declares that man begins in *d·*
485–20   belief . . . that man springs from *d·*
g 524–14   formed man of the *d·* of the ground, — *Gen.* 2 : 7.
524–31   Does Spirit enter *d·*, and lose therein the
528– 1   Was it requisite . . . that *d·* should become
531– 3   the belief that everything springs from *d·*

dust

g 535–27   *d·* thou art, and unto *d·* — *Gen.* 3 : 19.
545–29   "*D·* [nothingness] thou art, — *Gen.* 3 : 19.
545–29   unto *d·* [nothingness] shalt thou — *Gen.* 3 : 19.
552–24   is not in egg nor in *d·*.
553–27   superstition about the creation from *d·*
gl 584–28   definition of
585–27   belief . . . that man started first from *d·*,

duties

a 31–12   First in the list of Christian *d·*, he taught

duty

pr 9–14   we shall never meet this great *d·* simply by
a 37–22   it is the *d·* and privilege of every
m 67–12   firm at the post of *d·*, the mariner works on
b 340– 6   especially when the word *d·*, which is not in the
340– 9   for this is the whole *d·* of man." — *Eccl.* 12 : 13.
p 385–17   Whatever it is your *d·* to do, you can do
433– 7   In compliance with a stern *d·*, his Honor,
r 496– 6   in C. S. the first *d·* is to obey God,
g 541–25   Now it repudiates even the human *d·* of man

dwarfing

t 445–11   *d·* the spiritual understanding

dwell

sp 82–23   nor are they in the mental realm in which we *d·*.
b 284–14   Can the infinite *d·* in the finite
o 341– *   *But if the spirit . . . d· in you,* — *Rom.* 8 : 11.
357–30   if so, can Life, or God, *d·* in evil
r 466–12   which neither *d·* together nor
474–32   light and darkness cannot *d·* together.
478–21   How can intelligence *d·* in matter
g 510– 3   more . . . than to *d·* on the objects of sense !
514–22   wolf also shall *d·* with the lamb, — *Isa.* 11 : 6.
534–22   that the spirit of God *d·* in you." — *Rom.* 8 : 9.
543–11   must *d·* in dream-land, until mortals
550–31   originate the impure . . . and *d·* in it.
ap 568–20   heavens, and ye that *d·* in them. — *Rev.* 12 : 12.
578–17   and I will *d·* in the house — *Psal.* 23 : 6.

dweller

b 301–31   an unsubstantial *d·* in material forms,

dwellers

ap 569–16   *d·* still in the deep darkness of belief.

dwelleth

o 341– *   *by His spirit that d· in you.* — *Rom.* 8 : 11.

dwelling

a 23–13   has the Holy Ghost *d·* in him."
sp 78–31   the invisible good *d·* in eternal Science.
b 308– 1   Art thou *d·* in the belief that mind is
311–14   false estimates of soul as *d·* in sense
311–15   and of mind as *d·* in matter,
o 349–24   while *d·* on a material plane,
g 503–28   God, Spirit, *d·* in infinite light and

dwelling-places

s 142–24   meet *d·* for the Most High.

dwells

f 247–22   which *d·* forever in the eternal Mind
b 284– 2   It is not rational to say that Mind . . . *d·* in
334– 5   Christ, *d·* forever in the bosom of the Father,
g 514– 6   Mind, joyous in strength, *d·* in the realm of Mind.
gl 580–24   supposition . . . Soul *d·* in material sense ;

dwelt

a 29–26   The Christ *d·* forever an idea
b 331– 6   If He *d·* within what He creates,
g 542–28   and *d·* in the land of Nod. — *Gen.* 4 : 16.

dying

a 42–20   existence . . . separate from God is a *d·* error.
sp 76–18   Suffering, sinning, *d·* beliefs are unreal.
78–11   mortal, sinning, suffering, and *d·*.
ph 193– 4   physician, who said that the patient was *d·*.
f 203–28   and of fearful and doleful *d·*
c 258–28   Never born and never *d·*,
259–11   presented man as fallen, sick, sinning, and *d·*.
b 279– 1   the erring, changing, and *d·*,
292–11   A sinful, sick, and *d·* mortal is not
p 368–17   more faith in living than in *d·*,
373– 7   The author has raised up the *d·*,
379–20   not *d·* on account of the state of her blood,
428–31   and raised the *d·* to life and health
429–15   Mortal mind affirms . . . that the body is *d·*,
430– 2   healing the *d·* and raising the dead.
441–16   refuses to recognize Man as sick or *d·*,
r 494–27   mortal testimony, changing, and *d·*, unreal.
g 556–13   is not to be gained by *d·*.
557–21   man as never born and as never *d·*,

dynasties

ap 577–23   Mighty potentates and *d·* will lay down

dynasty

s 141–13   as kings are crowned from a royal *d·*.
141–17   For this Principle there is no *d·*,

dyspepsia

ph 175- 7 In old times who ever heard of *d*·,
175-16 If a random thought, calling itself *d*·,
197-23 Their diet would not cure *d*· at this period.
f 221- 2 adopted the Graham system to cure *d*·.
221- 4 His *d*· increasing, he decided that his diet
222-29 In seeking a cure for *d*·

dyspeptic

f 222-22 He learned that a *d*· was very far from
222-27 finally concluded that God never made a *d*·,

dyspeptics

ph 197-26 With rules of health . . . there would still be *d*·

E

each

pr 7-25 to whom *e*· need of man is always known
a 21-13 gain a little *e*· day in the right direction,
32- 8 to pass *e*· guest a cup of wine.
47-28 *e*· one came to a violent death except St. John,
m 59- 4 most tender solicitude for *e*· other's happiness,
59-13 *e*· partner sustaining the other,
66-14 *E*· succesive stage of experience unfolds new
sp 88-10 By learning the origin of *e*·.
ph 195-11 The point for *e*· one to decide is,
f 246-25 *E*· succeeding year unfolds wisdom,
248-10 which *e*· day brings to a nearer tomb.
b 291- 8 *e*· lesser call in the growth of Christian
o 356-14 not contributing in any way to *e*· other's
p 413-22 need not wash his little body all over *e*· day
l 457- 15 *e*· of them could see but one face of it,
g 502-18 *e*· text is followed by its spiritual
506-13 forming *e*· successive stage of progress.

each other

a 21-20 little opportunity to help *e*· other
m 57- 9 conjoin naturally with *e*· other,
f 209-18 which constituent masses hold to *e*· other,
b 278-21 warring forever with *e*· other ;
o 358- 7 If two statements directly contradict *e*· other
ap 564- 1 which would impel them to devour *e*· other
gl 588-14 numbers which never blend with *e*· other,

ear

and eye
sp 84-20 not dependent upon the *e*· and eye
deaf
t 444-23 a deaf *e*· to the teachings of C. S.,
divine
pr 7-24 The "divine *e*·" is not an auditory nerve.
gain the
pr 15-29 gain the *e*· and right hand of omnipotence
hath not heard
s 117-14 *E*· hath not heard, nor hath lip spoken, the
heard
c 255-18 Eye hath not seen Spirit, nor hath *e*· heard His
t 459- 3 "eye hath not seen nor *e*· heard." —*I Cor.* 2 : 9.
hearing of the
ph 192- 8 They come from the hearing of the *e*·,
c 262-18 by the hearing of the *e*· : —*Job* 42 : 5.
ill-attuned
m 60-24 An ill-attuned *e*· calls discord harmony,
need the
p 424-22 you need the *e*· of your auditor.
omnipotent
pr 13-13 Do we gain the omnipotent *e*· sooner by words
through the
b 284-23 through the eye nor hear it through the *e*·,
trieth words
s 115- 8 "The *e*· trieth words, —*Job* 34 : 3.
whispered into the
p 374- 4 whispered into the *e*· of mortal mind,

pr 14- 2 material person, whose *e*· we would gain,
f 213-17 The *e*· does not really hear.
r 486- 5 accident happens . . . to the *e*·,

earlier

s 150-11 as in the time of its *e*· demonstration,

earliest

a 45-22 They who *e*· saw Jesus after the resurrection
f 236-24 should teach their children at the *e*·
244-15 If man were dust in his *e*· stage
g 501- 4 the Word, in its *e*· articulations,

early

pref viii-28 As *e*· as 1862 she began to write down
ix-12 Certain essays written at that *e*· date
a 41-17 this demonstration of healing was *e*· lost,
52- 1 From *e*· boyhood he was about his
55- 6 Perhaps the *e*· Christian era
m 61-16 often these beautiful children *e*· droop
f 220-10 lifts her blue eye to greet the *e*· spring.
237-22 This makes C. S. *e*· available.
245- 5 Disappointed in love in her *e*· years,
o 351- 9 became a member . . . in *e*· years.
359-21 *e*· received her religious education.
p 387-13 Our thinkers do not die *e*· because they
405- 9 Choke these errors in their *e*· stages,
420- 6 they should *e*· call an experienced

early

r 471-24 subscribed to an orthodox creed in *e*· youth,
474- 4 accorded to Truth in the *e*· Christian era
g 523-16 in the *e*· part of the book of Genesis.
gl 579- 9 surrendering to the creator the *e*· fruits
fr 600- * *Let us get up e· to the vineyards ;* —*Song* 7 : 12.

earn

pr 10-19 and stop at the doors to *e*· a penny

earned

f 233-15 goal of goodness is assiduously *e*·

earnest

pr 15-17 In the quiet sanctuary of *e*· longings,
a 21-12 If honest, he will be in *e*· from the start,
b 299-16 By giving *e*· heed to these spiritual guides
309-13 those, who through *e*· striving followed
317-27 to Soul, for an *e*· of immortality,
p 434-17 *e*·, solemn eyes, kindling with hope

earnestly

a 29- 8 It bids us work the more *e*· in times of
sp 82-32 it is wise *e*· to consider whether it is the
r 476-21 Learn this, O mortal, and *e*· seek the

ears

a 38-29 and having *e*· ye hear not ;
f 211-26 the eyes to see and the *e*· to hear,
b 272-14 not to impart to dull *e*· and gross hearts
o 350-19 and their *e*· are dull of hearing, —*Matt.* 13 : 15.
350-21 and hear with their *e*·, —*Matt.* 13 : 15.
gl 585- 1 definition of
585- 4 "Having *e*·, hear ye not?" —*Mark* 8 : 18.

Earth

g 506-22 And God called the dry land *E*· ; —*Gen.* 1 : 10.
535-30 "And God called the dry land *E*· ; —*Gen.* 1 : 10.

earth (see also earth's)

above
g 521- 2 above the sod, above *e*· and its environments,
above the
g 511-21 fowl that may fly above the *e*· —*Gen.* 1 : 20.
511-29 fowls, which fly above the *e*· in the open
all the
an 102-14 has dominion over all the *e*· and its hosts.
f 202-23 gives man dominion over all the *e*·.
b 316-23 which gives man dominion over all the *e*·.
p 442- 4 Judge of all the *e*· do right?" —*Gen.* 18 : 25.
r 475-26 the cattle, and over all the *e*·, —*Gen.* 1 : 26.
g 515-11 the cattle, and over all the *e*·, —*Gen.* 1 : 26.
516-21 and reflects God's dominion over all the *e*·.
518- 7 upon the face of all the *e*·, —*Gen.* 1 : 29.
531-32 and having dominion over all the *e*·.
533- 3 Had he lost . . . dominion over all the *e*·?
and heaven
s 121-10 *e*· and heaven were bright,
c 204 30 all the glories of *e*· and heaven and
g 518- 2 lord of the belief in *e*· and heaven,
and man
g 538-19 God creates the heavens, *e*·, and man.
and the heavens
g 520-18 made the *e*· and the heavens, —*Gen.* 2 : 4.
543-31 made the *e*· and the heavens," —*Gen.* 2 : 4.
at God's command
g 530- 6 The *e*·, at God's command, brings forth food
atmosphere of the
f 220-14 The atmosphere of the *e*·, kinder than
away from
p 365- 3 the heavenly homesick looking away from *e*·,
beast of the
g 513-16 beast of the *e*· after his kind : —*Gen.* 1 : 24.
513-22 beast of the *e*· after his kind, —*Gen.* 1 : 25.
518- 9 And to every beast of the *e*·, —*Gen.* 1 : 30.
blasts of
m 57-25 The wintry blasts of *e*· may uproot the
blessed the
b 338-29 notwithstanding God had blessed the *e*·
g 537-28 which blessed the *e*· and gave it to man
blesses the
g 516-19 beautifies the landscape, blesses the *e*·.
borne to
s 109-24 When a new spiritual idea is borne to *e*·,
broadcast in the
ph 197-18 knowledge now broadcast in the *e*·,
brought forth
g 508- 9 And the *e*· brought forth grass, —*Gen.* 1 : 12.

earth

cast unto the
ap 567–24　The words "cast unto the *e*·"— *Rev.* 12 : 13.
　569–30　saw that he was cast unto the *e*·,— *Rev.* 12 : 13.
children of
b 309–15　the children of *e*· who followed his example
cling to
c 263–10　cling to *e*· because he has not tasted heaven.
composing the
f 209–17　aggregated substances composing the *e*·,
covers
f 247–27　and covers *e*· with loveliness.
dearest spot on
m 58–22　Home is the dearest spot on *e*·,
dominion over the
ph 165– 5　man's God-given dominion over the *e*·.
down to
s 118–32　natural order of heaven comes down to *e*·.
every plague on
p 405–22　better to be exposed to every plague on *e*·
face of the
s 163–11　druggist, or drug on the face of the *e*·,
faith on the
s 132–27　shall he find faith on the *e*·?"— *Luke* 18 : 8.
first
g 536– 3　the first heaven and the first *e*·— *Rev.* 21 : 1.
ap 572–21　the first heaven and the first *e*·— *Rev.* 21 : 1.
from
a 48– 8　turned forever away from *e*· to heaven,
from the
g 521–21　went up a mist from the *e*·,— *Gen.* 2 : 6.
　541–29　now art thou cursed from the *e*·.— *Gen.* 4 : 11.
　546–13　went up a mist from the *e*·."— *Gen.* 2 : 6.
glories of
c 264–30　all the glories of *e*· and heaven and man.
harmony on
s 122– 7　the actual reign of harmony on *e*·.
harmony to
sp 72–31　communicator of . . . harmony to *e*· and
ap 561–15　God and His Christ, bringing harmony to *e*·.
has no repayment
sp 97–32　E· has no repayment for the persecutions
heaven and
　(see **heaven**)
heaven and the
r 479–19　created the heaven and the *e*·.— *Gen.* 1 : 1.
g 502–23　created the heaven and the *e*·.— *Gen.* 1 : 1.
heaven on
s 110–12　establishment of the kingdom of heaven on *e*·.
ph 174–20　proclaiming the kingdom of heaven on *e*·.
heavens and
ap 573– 7　heavens and *e*· to one human consciousness,
　573–20　John's corporeal sense of the heavens and *e*·
heavens and the
g 519– 7　heavens and the *e*· were finished,— *Gen.* 2 : 1.
helped the woman
ap 570–10　And the *e*· helped the woman,— *Rev.* 12 : 16.
inhabitant of the
b 317–31　the Master remained an inhabitant of the *e*·.
inhabitants of the
c 256–22　the inhabitants of the *e*· ;— *Dan.* 4 : 35.
inhabiters of the
ap 568–21　inhabiters of the *e*· and of the sea !— *Rev.* 12 : 12.
inherit the
g 516–15　"The meek shall inherit the *e*·."— *Psal.* 37 : 11.
instead of the
s 121–19　instead of the *e*· from west to east.
in the
g 509–24　before it was in the *e*·."— *Gen.* 2 : 5.
　520–19　before it was in the *e*·,— *Gen.* 2 : 5.
　526– 5　before it was in the *e*·."— *Gen.* 2 : 5.
launched
s 124–23　which launched the *e*· in its orbit
let the
g 507–11　Let the *e*· bring forth grass,— *Gen.* 1 : 11.
　513–14　Let the *e*· bring forth the living— *Gen.* 1 : 24.
material
c 264– 1　the mortal body and material *e*·, are the
melted
sp 97–26　uttered His voice, the *e*· melted."— *Psal.* 46 : 6.
multiply in the
g 512–19　let fowl multiply in the *e*·.— *Gen.* 1 : 22.
new
sp 91– 2　"a new heaven and a new *e*·."— *Rev.* 21 : 1.
g 536– 2　a new heaven and a new *e*· :— *Rev.* 21 : 1.
　556– 8　Then will the new heaven and new *e*· appear,
ap 572–20　a new heaven and a new *e*· :— *Rev.* 21 : 1.
　572–25　he already saw a new heaven and a new *e*·.
　572–29　Were this new heaven and new *e*· terrestrial
　573–22　he could see the new heaven and new *e*·,
opened her mouth
ap 570–11　and the *e*· opened her mouth,— *Rev.* 12 : 16.
our
g 509–14　stellar universe is no more celestial than our *e*·.
　548– 9　How little light or heat reach our *e*· when

earth

over the
ph 188–28　When darkness comes over the *c*·,
　189– 3　explanation of the sun's influence over the *e*·.
pilgrim on
f 254–31　Pilgrim on *e*·, thy home is heaven ;
received the harmony
a 54– 6　*e*· received the harmony his . . . example
refresh the
b 288–18　Then the raindrops of divinity refresh the *e*·.
replenish the
g 511– 5　"multiply and replenish the *e*·."— *Gen.* 1 : 28.
　517–26　multiply, and replenish the *e*·,— *Gen.* 1 : 28.
return to
a 24–25　as a proof that spirits can return to *e*·?
sp 73– 5　and supposedly will return to *e*· to-morrow,
revolution of the
b 310–13　not affected by the revolution of the *e*·.
revolves
s 121–26　the *e*· revolves about the sun once a year,
salt of the
p 367–19　"Ye are the salt of the *e*·."— *Matt.* 5 : 13.
suffering on
p 386–25　Error, . . . produces all the suffering on *e*·.
sufferings upon
s 158–15　and endured great sufferings upon *e*·.
taint of
m 66–14　joys of Spirit, which have no taint of *e*·.
thou
s 135– 5　Tremble, thou *e*·, at the— *Psal.* 114 : 7.
to believe that the
s 119–26　to believe that the *e*· is in motion
Truth on
b 281– 3　enter into the kingdom of Truth on *e*·
upon the
a 31– 5　no man your father upon the *e*· :— *Matt.* 23 : 9.
r 475–27　that creepeth upon the *e*·."— *Gen.* 1 : 26.
g 507–13　seed is in itself, upon the *e*· :— *Gen.* 1 : 11.
　510– 7　to give light upon the *e*· :— *Gen.* 1 : 15.
　511– 8　to give light upon the *e*·,— *Gen.* 1 : 17.
　513–24　that creepeth upon the *e*·— *Gen.* 1 : 25.
　515–15　that creepeth upon the *e*·— *Gen.* 1 : 26.
　517–29　that moveth upon the *e*·.— *Gen.* 1 : 28.
　518–10　that creepeth upon the *e*·,— *Gen.* 1 : 30.
　520–21　not caused it to rain upon the *e*·,— *Gen.* 2 : 5.
ap 559– 7　The angel's left foot was upon the *e*· ;
was blessed
b 338–31　not the ideal man for whom the *e*· was blessed.
was without form
r 479–19　the *e*· was without form,— *Gen.* 1 : 2.
g 503– 6　the *e*· was without form,— *Gen.* 1 : 2.
whole
pr 14–28　man's dominion over the whole *e*·.
ph 191–14　Thus the whole *e*· will be transformed by
g 545–11　was given dominion over the whole *e*·.
ap 575–23　the joy of the whole *e*·,— *Psal.* 48 : 2.
will become dreary
sp 96– 7　E· will become dreary and desolate,
will echo
s 129–15　and *e*· will echo the cry,
will help the woman
ap 570–22　In this age the *e*· will help the woman ;

pr 17– 1　Thy will be done in *e*·,— *Matt.* 6 : 10.
　17– 2　*as in heaven, so on e*·,
a 54–30　glorified man were physically on *e*· to-day,
m 69– 1　and man, not of the *e*· earthly
sp 72–28　nor the medium through which truth passes to *e*·.
　75–26　those living on the *e*·
an 100– 9　celestial bodies, the *e*·, and animated things.
s 150– 7　"on *e*· peace, good-will toward— *Luke* 2 : 14.
f 202–19　when God's kingdom comes on *e*· ;
　226–17　"on *e*· peace, good-will toward— *Luke* 2 : 14.
　310–12　when the *e*· has again turned upon its axis.
　339–25　"in *e*·, as it is in heaven."— *Matt.* 6 : 10.
o 360–29　the Galilean Prophet, the best Christian on *e*·,
　361–27　is the higher hope on *e*·,
r 493– 3　and the *e*· to stand still ;
g 520–17　of the heavens and of the *e*·— *Gen.* 2 : 4.
　522–20　as the life-giving principle of the *e*·.
　538–11　The sun, giving light and heat to the *e*·,
　548–12　E· has little light or joy for mortals before
　552– 4　That the *e*· was hatched from the
ap 558– 8　and his left foot on the *e*·.— *Rev.* 10 : 2.
　563–24　and did cast them to the *e*· :— *Rev.* 12 : 4.
　567–16　he was cast out into the *e*·,— *Rev.* 12 : 9.
gl 585– 5　definition of
　585– 7　To material sense, *e*· is matter ;

earthly

pr 10– 7　to profit by Jesus' cup of *e*· sorrows,
a 30– 6　partook partly of Mary's *e*· condition,
　30–23　throughout the whole *e*· career of Jesus,
　36–12　What was his *e*· reward?
　36–14　*e*· price of spirituality in a material age
　39–25　To break this *e*· spell,

earthly

a	41–16	completed his e· mission ;
	46–27	which closed the e· record of Jesus,
	47–28	in his last e· struggle
	49–15	met his e· fate alone with God.
	52–24	The highest e· representative of God,
	54–21	His e· cup of bitterness was drained to the
	55–23	whosoever layeth his e· all on the altar
m	69– 1	and man, not of the earth e·
sp	72–26	A sinning, e· mortal is not the reality of
s	150–27	The doctrine that . . . all his e· days,
ph	197– 6	costs many a man his e· days of comfort.
f	202–20	e· experience discloses the finity of error
c	265–27	The loss of e· hopes and pleasures
b	299– 9	buried its fondest e· hopes.
	314– 5	spiritual sense had quenched all e· yearnings.
	315–28	more spiritual than all other e· personalities.
	334– 8	fleshly Jesus, whose e· career was brief.
p	387–15	If . . . authors have the shortest span of e·
ap	565–14	a brief history in the e· life of our Master ;

earth-mission

a	51–13	but when his e· was accomplished,

earthquake

b	293–22	expressed in e·, wind, wave,

earth's

a	37–10	They are e· luminaries, which serve to
sp	75–31	from e· sleep to the grand verities of Life,
	90– 6	The e· orbit and the imaginary line called
	90– 7	e· motion and position are sustained by Mind
s	121–17	The e· diurnal rotation is invisible
ph	185–10	the e· magnetic currents
r	471–10	the e· motions or of the science of astronomy,
	486– 9	E· preparatory school must be improved
g	510–20	Geology has never explained the e· formations;
	547–12	able to see in the egg the e· atmosphere,

earthward

b	272–23	e· gravitation of sensualism and impurity,

ease

m	58–27	a wife ought not to court . . . stupid e·,
f	220–13	procures a summer residence with more e· than
b	270–28	and a sense of e· antidotes suffering,

easier

s	138–22	e· for Christianity to cast out sickness than
f	241–31	"e· for a camel to go through— Matt. 19 : 24.
b	322–31	It is e· to desire Truth than to
p	373– 5	It is e· to cure the most malignant disease than
	373–12	Healing is e· than teaching,
t	449– 9	"e· for a camel to go through— Matt. 19 : 24.

easiest

pr	5– 4	Sorrow for wrong-doing is . . . the very e· step.

casily

a	20–29	the sin which doth so e· beset us,— Heb. 12 : 1.
sp	82– 2	We think of an absent friend as e· as
	94–24	Our Master e· read the thoughts of mankind,

East

p	363– 3	which is in such common use in the E·.

east

a	21–30	he turns e· on the seventh, satisfied if
s	121–18	the sun seems to move from e· to west,
	121–19	instead of the earth from west to e·
ph	184–29	when the wind was from the e·.
	184–32	She looked and saw that it pointed due e·.
	185– 5	she never suffered again from e· winds,
g	537– 5	He placed at the e· of the garden— Gen. 3 : 24.

eastern

sp	94–12	The e· empires and nations owe their

eastward

ap	575–27	e·, to the star seen by the Wisemen

easy

sp	82– 1	as e· to read distant thoughts as near.
an	102–25	not lending itself to an e· explanation
f	236–31	youth makes e· and rapid strides towards Truth.
p	362–15	It was therefore e· for the Magdalen
	400–15	This task becomes e·, if you understand

eat

a	25–10	they truly e· his flesh and drink his blood,
	31–22	"As often as ye e· this bread,— I Cor. 11 : 26.
	32–17	Take, e· ; this is my body.— Matt. 26 : 26.
	33–32	Are all who e· bread and drink wine in memory
m	58–24	"Two e· no more together
	58–25	than they e· separately."
	62–13	what ye shall e·, or what ye shall— Matt. 6 : 25.
ph	165– *	what ye shall e·, or what ye shall— Matt. 6 : 25.
	170–16	what ye shall e·, or what ye shall— Matt. 6 : 25.
f	220–29	"Thou shalt not e· of it."— Gen. 2 : 17.
	222–15	less thought about what he should e· or drink,
	222–30	and e· what is set before you,
p	388–30	we shall neither e· to live nor live to e·,
	390– 3	and I should like something more to e·."
g	527– 8	thou mayest freely e· :— Gen. 2 : 16.
	527– 9	thou shalt not e· of it :— Gen. 2 : 17.

eat

g	529–16	Ye shall not e· of every tree— Gen. 3 : 1.
	529–17	We may e· of the fruit of— Gen. 3 : 2.
	529–19	Ye shall not e· of it,— Gen. 3 : 3.
	530– 9	what ye shall e·, or what ye shall— Matt. 6 : 25.
	530–15	in the day ye e· thereof,— Gen. 3 : 5.
	533– 7	that thou shouldst not e·?— Gen. 3 : 11.
	533– 9	she gave me of the tree, and I did e·.— Gen. 3 : 12.
	533–29	beguiled me, and I did e· ;"— Gen. 3 : 13.
	535–22	Thou shalt not e· of it :— Gen. 3 : 17.
	535–23	in sorrow shalt thou e· of it— Gen. 3 : 17.
	535–25	and thou shalt e· the herb— Gen. 3 : 18.
	535–26	shalt thou e· bread,— Gen. 3 : 19.
	537– 2	and e·, and live forever ;— Gen. 3 : 22.
ap	559–17	Take it, and e· it up ;— Rev. 10 : 9.
	559–25	when you e· the divine body
	559–28	share the hemlock cup and e· the bitter herbs ;

eaten

a	32–22	The disciples had e·,
f	211–20	"the fathers have e· sour grapes,— Ezek. 18 : 2.
g	533– 6	Hast thou e· of the tree,— Gen. 3 : 11.
	535–21	and hast e· of the tree— Gen. 3 : 17.

eaters

sp	90–20	Opium and hashish e· mentally travel far

eatest

ph	197–10	"In the day that thou e· thereof— Gen. 2 : 17.
r	481–19	"In the day that thou e· thereof— Gen. 2 : 17.
g	527–10	in the day that thou e· thereof— Gen. 2 : 17.
	532– 8	"In the day that thou e· thereof— Gen. 2 : 17.

eateth

g	544–10	consisteth not of the things which a man e·.

eating

a	32–15	"As they were e·, Jesus took— Matt. 26 : 26.
ph	165– 2	Evil declared that e· this fruit
f	221–10	until three hours after e·.
	222–15	if e· a bit of animal flesh could overpower him.
	254– 8	To stop e·, drinking, or being clothed
p	383–21	e· or smoking poison for half a century,
	388–27	foolish to stop e· until we gain perfection
g	532– 7	when e· its first fruits brought death?

ebbing

ap	566– 2	dark e· and flowing tides of human fear,

Ecclesiastes

b	291–20	So we read in E·.
	340– 4	This text in the book of E·

ecclesiastical

sp	98–32	The way . . . is not e· but Christian,
s	118– 4	far above the merely e·
	141–11	along the line of scholarly and e· descent,
	141–17	For this Principle there is . . . no e· monopoly.
t	444–22	If e· sects or medical schools turn
r	473–18	In an age of e· despotism,
gl	590–13	LEVI (Jacob's son). . . . e· despotism.

echo

s	126–11	and interpreted in its own way the e· of Spirit,
	129–15	and earth will e· the cry,
c	202–18	Mortals will e· Job's thought,

echoing

f	226– 6	voice of God . . . was still e· in our land,

eclectic

p	416–10	allopathic, homœopathic, botanic, e·

eclipse

sp	85– 1	read the stars or calculate an e·.

economy

m	59–10	the annoyances and cares of domestic e·,
	59–11	nor . . . be expected to understand political e·.
ph	170– 7	Did Jesus understand the e· of man less
f	222–16	consulting the stomach less about the e· of
	228–22	bodily conditions, structure, or e·,
b	327–21	in the human or the divine e·.
p	423–25	now at work in the e· of being

ecstasies

b	312–14	People go into e· over the sense of a

ecstasy

pr	7–17	sensation, not Soul, produces material e·
	14– 7	is to have, not mere emotional e· or faith,

ecstatic

pr	7–19	there would grow out of e· moments

Eddy, Mrs. Mary Baker

pref	xii–27	MARY BAKER EDDY

author

pref	ix–10	So was it with the a·.
	x–11	The a· has not compromised conscience
	xi–22	When God called the a· to
	xi–26	first school of C. S. . . . was started by the a·
	xii– 7	four thousand students were taught by the a·
pr	9– 2	During many years the a· has been most grateful
an	104– 5	will be seen why the a· of this book has
s	112–29	without giving that a· proper credit,

Eddy, Mrs. Mary Baker

author

s 114– 2   a· calls sick and sinful humanity *mortal mind*,
114–31   what is termed by the a· *mortal mind*.
123–17   The term C. S. was introduced by the a·
130–23   a· has often remembered our Master's love
149–22   a· has cured what is termed organic disease
150–23   it is as evidently erroneous to the a·,
152– 5   The a· has endeavored to make this book the
153– 5   The a· has attenuated *Natrum muriaticum*
162–17   a· has restored health in cases of
c 266–15   The a· has experienced the foregoing
b 330– 3   Until the a· . . . learned the vastness of C. S.,
o 351– 8   The a· became a member of the orthodox
p 373– 6   The a· has raised up the dying,
374– 9   The a· has answered this question
377–19   a· never knew a patient who did not
380–22   years ago the a· made a spiritual discovery,
386–12   The a· has in too many instances
394–17   Experience has proved to the a· the fallacy
402– 4   it is but just to say that the a· has already
428–30   The a· has healed hopeless organic disease,
t 444–13   Students are advised by the a· to be
445–31   the a· trembles whenever she sees a
446–11   Whoever practises the Science the a· teaches,
453– 5   a· understands what she is saying.
457– 8   Since the divine light . . . dawned upon the a·,
458–16   a· desires to keep it out of C. S.
460–25   When . . . was a fresh revelation to the a·,
463–32   It has been said to the a·,
464– 4   Could her friends know how little time the a·
464–22   the a· has labored to expound
r 471–23   a· subscribed to an orthodox creed in early
g 546–21   To the a·, they are transparent,
547– 7   so ascertain if the a· has given you the correct
ap 564–10   The a· is convinced that the accusations

author's

pref vii–27   Since the a· discovery of the
viii–24   In the a· work, RETROSPECTION AND
an 101–21   The a· own observations of the workings of
s 112–28   and yet uses another a· discoveries
126–32   If Christendom resists the a· application
129–30   a· small estimate of the pleasures of the table.
152–21   The a· medical researches and experiments
t 446– 5   thorough perusal of the a· publications
452–24   simply by repeating the a· words,
r 465– 1   from the first edition of the a· class-book,
483–13   After the a· sacred discovery,
g 556–28   hence the a· experience ;

child

pref viii–31   the first steps of a c· in the newly

disciple

pref ix–17   finds herself a willing d· at the heavenly gate,

discoverer of Christian Science

o 359–20   the d· of C. S. early received
p 426– 5   The d· of C. S. finds the path less difficult
t 443– 1   When the d· of C. S. is consulted by
g 555– 6   An inquirer once said to the d· of C. S. :

editor

pref xii–12   sole e· and publisher of the C. S. Journal,

her

pref viii– 1   h· system has been fully tested
viii–26   experiences which led h·, in the year 1866, to
viii–29   the results of h· Scriptural study,
viii–30   the Bible was h· sole teacher ;
ix– 1   She also began to jot down h· thoughts
ix–13   still in circulation among h· first pupils ;
ix–20   H· first pamphlet on C. S. was copyrighted
ix–29   h· comparative ignorance of the stupendous
x–16   she and h· students have proved
x–17   proved the worth of h· teachings.
x–27   Only those quarrel with h· method who
x–28   do not understand h· meaning,
xl–31   enabled h· to get this institution chartered
xii–11   publisher of h· own works ;
xii–14   She closed h· College, October 29, 1889,
xii–16   conviction that the next two years of h· life
xii–18   She retained h· charter,
xii–20   as auxiliary to h· church.
xii–22   in order to elucidate h· idealism.
an 101–22   convince h· that it is not a remedial agent,
s 127– 1   or questions h· use of the word Science,
127– 4   nor will Christianity lose its hold upon h·.
152–22   prepared h· thought for the metaphysics of
152–24   material dependence had failed h· in h· search
152–28   H· experiments in homœopathy
152–28   had made h· skeptical as to
o 351–10   h· own prayers failed to heal h·
351–11   as did the prayers of h· devout parents
359–21   early received h· religious education.
359–23   falling from the lips of h· saintly mother,
p 374–10   The author . . . in h· explanation of disease
402– 4   the author has already in h· possession
402– 5   records of the cure, by herself and h· students
426– 6   when she has the high goal always before h·

her

p 426– 7   than when she counts h· footsteps
t 443– 2   consulted by h· followers as to the
457–10   H· prime object, since entering this field
460–26   impart, . . . from h· own spiritual condition,
460–29   by h· manuscript circulated among the students.
460–30   beliefs were gradually expelled from h· thought,
464– 3   Could h· friends know how little time
464– 5   except through h· laborious publications,
464– 9   Others could not take h· place,
464–10   She therefore remains unseen at h· post,
r 471–29   Since then h· highest creed has been

hers

pref xii– 3   h· was the only College of this character

herself

pref ix–17   she still finds h· a willing disciple
p 402– 5   records of the cure, by h· and her students
464– 5   in which to make h· outwardly known

I am blest

iii– *   And *I* am blest !

I am leading

f 253– 9   I hope, dear reader, *I* am leading you

I am not patient with

p 413–21   *I* am not patient with a speck of dirt ;

I as a Christian Scientist

o 359– 8   *I* as a Christian Scientist believed in the

I ask

f 250–22   Now *I* ask, Is there any more reality in the
p 371–22   No impossible thing do *I* ask

I began

s 156–13   Believing then somewhat in . . . *I* began to

I beheld

s 110– 8   Thus it was that *I* beheld, as never before,

I cannot attest

ph 193–28   *I* cannot attest the truth of that report,

I cannot coincide

sp 80–13   but *I* cannot coincide with their views.

I cannot fail to

ph 194– 3   *I* cannot fail to discern the coincidence

I combat

b 269–29   The theories *I* combat are these :

I cured

ph 184–27   A woman, whom *I* cured of consumption,
p 389–31   *I* cured her in a few minutes.

I demonstrated

s 147– 6   *I* demonstrated the divine rules of C. S.

I deny

o 348–16   *I* deny His cooperation with evil,

I desire

o 348–17   *I* desire to have no faith in evil

I did so

s 156–18   *I* did so, and she continued to gain.

I discovered

s 107– 1   In the year 1866, *I* discovered the Christ Science

I discredit

m 68–25   *I* discredit the belief that agamogenesis

I do aver

o 348–29   *I* do aver, that, as a result of teaching C. S.,

I do believe

t 461– 2   but *I* do believe that the real man is immortal

I do not maintain

t 461– 1   *I* do not maintain that anyone can

I entertain no

sp 80–12   *I* entertain no doubt of the humanity

I find

s 111– 3   *I* find the will, . . . opposed to the divine Mind
113–24   *I* find that God is true,

I had foretold

ph 169– 9   But it always came about as *I* had foretold.

I have been informed

ph 193–24   Since his recovery *I* have been informed that

I have demonstrated

s 126–24   *I* have demonstrated . . . the effects of Truth
ph 177– 4   *I* have demonstrated this beyond all cavil.
184–23   *I* have demonstrated this as a rule

I have discerned

ph 168–24   *I* have discerned disease in the human mind,

I have discovered

s 126–23   just as *I* have discovered them.

I have found

s 126–26   *I* have found nothing in ancient or in
ph 180–32   *I* have found divine Truth more potent

I have had

s 126–30   *I* have had no other guide

I have healed

o 359– 7   *I* have healed infidels

I have made

f 233–27   tests *I* have made of the effects of truth

I have named

m 68–19   *I* have named her case to individuals,

I have narrated

ph 193–30   occurred just as *I* have narrated.

I have never supposed

o 348–26   *I* have never supposed the world would

Eddy, Mrs. Mary Baker

I have never witnessed
  t 453–11 *I* have never witnessed so decided effects from
I have not seen
  ph 193–19 Since then *I* have not seen him,
I have restored
  s 162–22 *I* have restored what is called the
I have revised
  o 361–21 *I* have revised SCIENCE and HEALTH only to
I have said
  ph 169– 6 and *I* have said to the patient,
I have seen
  ph 169– 4 *I* have seen the mental signs,
  f 212–10 *I* have seen an unwitting attempt
  247– 3 *I* have seen age regain two of the elements
I have set forth
  s 126–22 *I* have set forth C. S.
I here present
  p 430–13 *I* here present to my readers an allegory
I hope
  f 253– 9 *I* hope, dear reader, I am leading you into
  253–14 *I* hope that you are conquering this false
I insist
  p 413–20 *I* insist on bodily cleanliness
I keep
  p 371–21 nor would *I* keep the suckling a
I kindly quote
  s 162–29 *I* kindly quote from Dr. Benjamin Rush,
I knew
  s 109–16 *I* knew the Principle of all harmonious
  f 221– 1 *I* knew a person who when quite a child
  247– 4 A woman of eighty-five, whom *I* knew,
I learned
  s 108–21 *I* learned these truths in divine Science :
  ph 194–14 (as *I* learned in metaphysics)
I long to see
  p 367–27 *I* long to see the consummation of my hope,
I love
  sp 99–21 *I* love mankind, and shall continue
I mean
  ph 168–32 By chemicalization *I* mean the process
I met
  ph 193– 3 On entering the house *I* met his physician,
I must know
  s 109–19 but *I* must know the Science of
I name
  ph 169–10 *I* name these facts to show that
  f 210–23 *I* name it mortal.
I never could
  sp 71–25 *I* never could believe in spiritualism.
I never knew
  m 68– 6 *I* never knew more than one individual who
I prescribed
  s 156– 8 *I* prescribed the fourth attenuation of
I pressed on
  f 226–31 but *I* pressed on through faith in God,
I regret
  o 346– 1 *I* regret that such criticism confounds
I rejoice
  o 354–28 *I* rejoice in the apprehension of this grand
I rescued
  p 382–24 One whom *I* rescued from seeming…oblivion,
I sat
  ph 184–29 *I* sat silently by her side a few moments.
I saw
  ph 193–18 The next day *I* saw him in the yard.
  193–29 what *I* saw and did for that man,
  f 226–22 *I* saw before me the sick,
  226–29 *I* saw before me the awful conflict,
  227– 3 *I* saw that the law of mortal belief
I say
  b 329– 7 proves the truth of all that *I* say of it.
I say with Paul
  f 216–28 *I* say with Paul : Be "willing— *II Cor.* 5 : 8.
I should appear
  s 164–17 If you or *I* should appear to die,
I sought
  s 109–11 *I* sought the solution of this problem
I speak
  pr 1– 5 *I* speak from experience.
I submitted
  s 111–29 *I* submitted my metaphysical system
I term
  p 401–16 What *I* term *chemicalization* is the upheaval
I then
  o 343– 1 Shall *I* then be smitten for healing
I then requested
  ph 184–31 *I* then requested her to look at the
I therefore
  b 269–22 *I* therefore plant myself unreservedly on the
I told
  ph 193–17 *I* told him to rise, dress himself,

Eddy, Mrs. Mary Baker

I understand
  pr 16–24 let me give what *I* understand to be the
  a 40–11 which *I* understand to mean God's method
  55–29 This Comforter *I* understand to be Divine
       Science.
I was called
  ph 192–32 *I* was called to visit Mr. Clark
I went
  ph 193– 9 *I* went to his bedside.
I wished
  f 226–26 *I* wished to save from the slavery of
I won my way
  s 109–20 *I* won my way to absolute conclusions
I would not transform
  p 371–20 *I* would not transform the infant at once into
me
  pr 16–24 let *m·* give what I understand to be the
  s 107– 4 God had been graciously preparing *m·*
  108– 1 Whence came to *m·* this heavenly conviction,
  108– 5 unfolding to *m·* the demonstrable fact that
  109–23 revelation of Truth . . . came to *m·* gradually
  110–18 No human pen nor tongue taught *m·* the Science
  111–28 this fact became evident to *m·*,
  113–10 in the four following, to *m·*, *self-evident*
  156–17 It then occurred to *m·* to give her
  156–21 After trying this, she informed *m·* that
  156–26 and receiving occasional visits from *m·*,
  ph 169– 5 assuring *m·* that danger was over,
  177– 6 is to *m·* as certain as the
  193–32 It has been demonstrated to *m·*
  f 226 22 I saw before *m·* the sick,
  226–30 I saw before *m·* the awful conflict,
  226–32 to guide *m·* into the land of C. S.,
  p 382–25 One whom I rescued . . . wrote to *m·* :
messenger
  t 455–24 When He commissions a *m·*, it is one who
mine
  o 345–14 but in this volume of *m·* there are no
my
  *iii– *** OH ! Thou hast heard *m·* prayer ;
  a 40–10 This is *m·* sense of divine pardon,
  55–16 *M·* weary hope tries to realize
  m 68–20 when casting *m·* bread upon the waters,
  sp 99–20 *m·* contest is not with the individual,
  s 108–12 *M·* conclusions were reached by
  108–30 *M·* discovery, that erring, mortal . . . *mind*
  108–32 set *m·* thoughts to work in new channels,
  109– 1 and led up to *m·* demonstration of the
  109–11 For three years after *m·* discovery,
  109–20 I won *m·* way to absolute conclusions
  110–14 the Bible was *m·* only textbook.
  111–26 After a lengthy examination of *m·* discovery
  111–29 I submitted *m·* metaphysical system
  115– 8 C. S. as brought forth in *m·* discovery.
  126–27 nothing . . . on which to found *m·* own, except
  126–29 The Bible has been *m·* only authority.
  156– 6 A case of dropsy, . . . fell into *m·* hands.
  ph 177– 6 as certain as the evidence of *m·* own existence.
  185– 3 *M·* metaphysical treatment changed the
  f 219– 2 *M·* method of treating fatigue applies
  237– 1 little girl, . . . listened to *m·* explanations,
  b 299– 7 *M·* angels are exalted thoughts,
  340–16 The First Commandment is *m·* favorite text.
  o 343– 3 and for proving *m·* word by *m·* deed
  p 367–28 I long to see the consummation of *m·* hope,
  370–14 This confirms *m·* theory that faith in the drug
  389–29 case of convulsions, . . . under *m·* observation.
  411– 3 *M·* first discovery in the student's practice
  t 456–25 requires *m·* work SCIENCE AND HEALTH
myself
  b 269–22 I therefore plant *m·* unreservedly on the
one
  t 455–21 *o·* who has grown into such a fitness for it
  455–25 When He commissions a messenger, it is *o·* who
pastor
  pref xii– 8 *p·* of the first established Church of Christ,
President
  pref xii– 9 *P·* of the first Christian Scientist Association,
  xii–19 and as its *P·*, reopened the College
publisher
  pref xii–10 *p·* of her own works ;
  xii–12 sole editor and *p·* of the C. S. Journal,
she
  pref viii–27 the system that *s·* denominated C. S.
  viii–28 As early as 1862 *s·* began to write
  ix– 1 *S·* also began to jot down her thoughts on the
  ix–11 *s·* "lisped in numbers, for the numbers came."
  ix–17 *s·* still finds herself a willing disciple
  ix–22 *s·* had learned that this Science must
  ix–26 *s·* made copious notes of Scriptural exposition,
  ix–31 *s·* came at length to its solution :
  ix–32 *s·* values them as a parent may treasure the
  x– 2 and *s·* would not have them changed.
  x–13 *S·* has made no effort to embellish,
  x–16 *s·* and her students have proved

Eddy, Mrs. Mary Baker
she
pref xi–28 In 1881, *s·* opened the . . . College
xii– 8 Meanwhile *s·* was pastor of the
xii–13 *S·* closed her College, October 29, 1889,
xii–18 *S·* retained her charter,
xii–20 *s·* had never read this book throughout
xii–26 *s·* commits these pages to honest seekers
s 127– 2 *s·* will not therefore lose faith in
127–10 The terms . . . *s·* employs interchangeably,
149–23 as readily as *s·* has cured purely functional
152–24 and *s·* can now understand why,
153–10 *s·* has cured a patient sinking in the last stage
b 330– 5 *s·* cherished sanguine hopes
o 351– 9 *s·* learned that her own prayers
359–22 In childhood, *s·* often listened with joy
359–25 *s·* pondered the meaning of that Scripture
359–26 that Scripture *s·* so often quotes :
p 373– 8 while *s·* has struggled long, and
426– 6 when *s·* has the high goal always before her
426– 7 than when *s·* counts her footsteps
t 443– 4 *s·* tries to show them that
443– 9 *s·* feels, as *s·* always has felt, that all are
445–32 the author trembles whenever *s·* sees a
453– 5 author understands what *s·* is saying.
457– 8 *s·* has never used this newly discovered power in
457– 9 never used . . . in any direction which *s·*
460–25 *s·* had to impart, while teaching its grand facts,
460–27 and *s·* had to do this orally
464– 8 would understand why *s·* is so secluded.
464–10 *S·* therefore remains unseen at her post,
r 465– 3 *s·* revised that treatise for this volume
471–24 until *s·* caught the first gleam of
471–31 which, . . . *s·* has named C. S.
483–13 *s·* affixed the name "Science" to Christianity,
writer's
ap 577–28 The *w·* present feeble sense of C. S.
you
p 382–26 but for the glorious Principle *y·* teach,
t 464– 1 "The world is benefited by *y·*,
464– 2 it feels your influence without seeing *y·*.
464– 2 Why do *y·* not make yourself more widely known?"
g 555– 8 I do not comprehend what *y·* say about error."
your
t 464– 1 it feels *y·* influence without seeing you.
g 555– 7 "I like *y·* explanations of truth,
yourself
t 464– 2 Why do you not make *y·* more widely known?"

Eden
m 68–11 mistrust, . . . withers the flowers of *E·*
ph 176–18 would load with disease the air of *E·*,
g 526–27 put him into the garden of *E·*, — *Gen.* 2 : 15.
526–29 name *E·*, according to Cruden, means *pleasure*,
526–30 In this text *E·* stands for the mortal, . . . body.
537– 4 forth from the garden of *E·*, — *Gen.* 3 : 23.
537– 6 at the east of the garden of *E·* — *Gen.* 3 : 24.

edge
f 211–21 the children's teeth are set on *e·*." — *Ezek.* 18 : 2.
p 374–22 walking in darkness on the *e·* of a precipice.

Edinburgh
f 208–17 John Young of *E·* writes :

edition
pref x– 3 The first *e·* of SCIENCE AND HEALTH was
r 465– 1 This chapter is from the first *e·* of

editor
(*see* **Eddy, Mrs. Mary Baker**)

educate
m 69–17 If Christian Scientists *e·* their own offspring
69–18 they can *e·* others spiritually
ph 179–15 You can even *e·* a healthy horse so far
o 345–31 not . . . to "*e·* the idea of God,

educated
a 39–10 *e·* belief that Soul is in the body
s 158–22 acquires an *e·* appetite for strong drink,
ph 195– 8 All that gives pleasure to our *e·* senses
c 260–24 Selfishness and sensualism are *e·* in
o 349–27 as thought is *e·* up to spiritual apprehension.
p 414– 2 and thus are children *e·* into discord.
r 484–20 false human consciousness is *e·* to feel.
489– 9 hypothesis which supposes . . . is an *e·* belief.

education
academic
f 235–12 it is not so much academic *e·*,
bias of
p 381– 3 the bias of *e·* enforces this slavery.
entire
m 62– 4 The entire *e·* of children should be
force of
p 396–19 due to the force of *e·*
formed by
ph 194–31 a belief formed by *e·* alone.

education
religious
o 359–22 early received her religious *e·*.
right
f 234–23 adequate to the right *e·* of human thought.
this
c 260–27 this *e·* is at the expense of spiritual growth.
———
m 60–20 the *e·* of the higher nature is neglected,
sp 86–23 *E·* alone determines the difference.
ph 176–26 All disease is the result of *e·*,
194–19 *e·* constitutes this so-called mind,
f 247–12 *e·*, and fashion form the transient standards of

educational
sp 89–18 not necessarily dependent upon *e·* processes.
f 226–27 the *e·* systems of the Pharaohs,

educator
f 236–12 A mother is the strongest *e·*,

efface
ph 175– 2 we should *e·* the outlines of disease
196–21 *e·* the images and thoughts of disease,
b 318– 3 to know that nothing can *e·* Mind
318–15 would *e·* the pure sense of omnipotence.
p 396– 2 *e·* from thought all forms and types of
396–25 *e·* the images of sickness from mortal mind.

effaced
f 240–20 until all wrong work is *e·* or rectified.
b 327–14 to be *e·* by the sweat of agony.
g 543– 5 The image of Spirit cannot be *e·*,

effaces
r 485–26 *e·* them and delineates foreign agents,

effect
alterative
f 224– 2 the world feels the alterative *e·* of truth
p 421–22 alterative *e·* produced by Truth upon error,
any
p 401–23 If . . . could you produce any *e·* upon the brain
appear in
a 40– 2 and it will not appear in *e·*.
baneful
t 449–19 The baneful *e·* of evil associates is
beneficial
pr 12– 5 The beneficial *e·* of such prayer for the sick
cause and
(*see* **cause**)
cause or
m 67–32 from any such cause or *e·*.
f 207–18 amalgamation of Truth and error in cause or *e·*.
cause to
r 467–29 Reasoning from cause to *e·* in the Science
certain
p 418– 9 unerring, and certain *e·* of divine Science.
every
b 268– 9 Mind as the cause of every *e·*.
p 379– 7 controlling every *e·* and recognizing all
healing
s 141–14 the healing *e·* followed the understanding
152– 9 Truth has a healing *e·*, even when
its
p 404– 1 familiar with mental action and its *e·*
material
p 403– 9 believed that the misfortune is a material *e·*.
medical
t 463–30 Such seeming medical *e·* or action is
mental
p 371– 5 Disquisitions on disease have a mental *e·*
mistakes
s 124– 8 this belief mistakes *e·* for cause
new
p 398–20 and produces a new *e·* upon the body.
no
f 207–21 there can be no *e·* from any other cause,
p 408–29 unconscious thought . . . produces no *e·*,
none
f 232–23 never tried to make of none *e·* the sentence
of illusion
an 101–31 In no instance . . . other than the *e·* of illusion.
of mortal mind
ph 189–10 explain the *e·* of mortal mind on the body,
c 261– 8 The *e·* of mortal mind on health and happiness
of this Science
s 162– 9 The *e·* of this Science is to stir the
only
p 401–21 The only *e·* produced by medicine is
physical
p 383–26 prove the illusive physical *e·* of a false belief,
produce the
f 211–15 produce the *e·* seen in the lachrymal gland?
same
t 458– 9 will finally have the same *e·* as
seeks cause in
b 279–31 Pantheism, . . . seeks cause in *e·*,
supposed
p 408–21 derive a supposed *e·* on intelligence

effect

whatever
o 358–25   it is said : "Rest assured that whatever *e·*

sp 95– 1   The *e·* of his Mind was always to heal
an 101–29   In no instance is the *e·* of animal magnetism,
s 155– 5   according to this faith will the *e·* be.
ph 179–30   may erelong reap the *e·* of this mistake.
195–18   passes naturally from *e·* back to cause.
b 291–24   until probation and growth shall *e·* the
p 370–15   The *e·*, which mortal mind produces through
415– 3   disease is neither a cause nor an *e·*.
r 467–24   We reason imperfectly from *e·* to cause,
467–25   when we conclude that matter is the *e·* of Spirit ;
480–17   would make matter the cause as well as the *e·*

effected
a 47–11   hatred towards that just man *e·* his betrayal.
o 348– 6   any cure, which is *e·* by making the
p 413–18   *e·* without scrubbing the whole surface daily.

effecting
t 460–20   Instead of scientifically *e·* a cure,

effective
s 112– 1   most *e·* curative agent in medical practice.

effects

bad
p 377–18   that it may not produce blindly its bad *e·*.
384–24   or to destroy the bad *e·* of your belief.
393– 7   remote, and exciting cause of all bad *e·*
413–10   good or bad *e·* on the health of children.
baneful
ph 181–17   ignorant of the baneful *e·* of magnetism,
p 498–12   baneful *e·* of illusion on mortal minds
418– 1   the baneful *e·* of their own conclusions.
beneficial
p 367–27   increase the beneficial *e·* of Christianity.
cumulative
p 405–23   the cumulative *e·* of a guilty conscience.
decided
t 453–12   I have never witnessed so decided *e·* from
different
t 461–21   because of the different *e·* they produce.
dire
ph 196– 4   save him from the dire *e·* of knowledge.
elevating
s 146–21   elevating *e·* practically prove its divine origin
fatal
p 384–22   if you believe in laws of matter and their fatal *e·*
ap 568– 8   the fatal *e·* of trying to meet error with error.
glorious
ph 176–10   In its glorious *e·* upon the body.
good
p 397–19   good *e·* to be in exact proportion to your
healing
p 398–26   belief in the healing *e·* of time and
its
an 101–23   its *e·* upon those who practise it,
f 219–20   will be the removal of its *e·*.
b 283– 8   Matter and its *e·* — sin, sickness, and
290–13   and its *e·*, — sickness, sin, and death.
310–10   manifest by its *e·* upon the human mind and
o 360–25   known by its *e·* on the body
p 374– 5   Hatred and its *e·* on the body
378–10   Remove the error, and you destroy its *e·*.
404–13   while its *e·* still remain on the individual,
g 540–15   uncovers so-called sin and its *e·*,
material
sp 78–22   communicate with man through . . . material *e·*?
of Christian Science
b 288–10   When the . . . *e·* of C. S. are fully apprehended,
323–28   *e·* of C. S. are not so much seen as felt.
of error
an 101–28   error cannot remove the *e·* of error.
b 273–30   beliefs emit the *e·* of error at all times,
r 473– 6   are to be classified as *e·* of error.
g 537–21   the falsity of error and the *e·* of error.
of fear
p 373–20   to remove the *e·* of fear produced by sin,
of medicine
s 163–15   Professor in London, said : "The *e·* of medicine
of sin
gl 588– 3   HELL. . . . self-imposed agony ; *e·* of sin ;
of Truth
s 126–24   the *e·* of Truth on the health, longevity,
p 386–14   the corresponding *e·* of Truth on the
of truth
f 233–27   scientific tests I have made of the *e·* of truth
only
p 379– 5   Christian Scientist finds only *e·*, where the
on the body
o 350–25   known by its *e·* on the body
p 370–19   produce very direct and marked *e·* on the body.
374– 5   Hatred and its *e·* on the body are removed

effects

physical
    (see **physical**)
qualities and
ph 177–21   qualities and *e·* of what is termed matter,
sad
o 342– 7   the sad *e·* on the sick of denying Truth.
such
s 132–11   any one who should not deny that such *e·*,
suffers from the
ph 184–19   We say man suffers from the *e·* of cold,
their
f 217–16   are superior to others, is seen by their *e·*.
p 409– 1   errors it includes and of their *e·*.
these
m 68–23   salutary causes sometimes incur these *e·*.
sp 88–23   These *e·*, however, do not proceed from
those
p 386–10   those *e·* will follow, — not because of the climate
violent
an 101– 1   that the violent *e·*, which are observed

sp 78–31   These are the *e·* of one universal God,
s 156–21   give up her medicine for one day, and risk the *e·*.
159–21   died from *e·* produced by mortal mind,
ph 181–22   satisfied with good words instead of *e·*,
b 284–26   the *e·* commonly attributed to them.

effectual
pr 11–18   but wipes it out in the most *e·* manner.
s 108– 4   *e·* working of His power." — *Eph.* 3 : 7.
140– 2   *e·* in the treatment of moral ailments.
p 372–29   acknowledgment of Truth . . . is an *e·* help.

effeminate
ph 197–26   Many of the *e·* constitutions of our time

efficacious
a 25– 7   The material blood of Jesus was no more *e·*
r 497–14   the evidence of divine, *e·* Love,

efficaciously
t 456–21   *e·* treated by the metaphysical process.

efficacy

admits the
p 401–27   Until the advancing age admits the *e·*
aid its
a 19–20   understand Jesus' atonement for sin and aid its *e·* ;
healing
s 147–11   had lost none of its divine and healing *e·*,
loses its
p 370–26   Hygienic treatment also loses its *e·*.
no
pr 12–17   has no *e·* of its own but borrows
s 153–15   and that there is no *e·* in a drug.
origin and
s 146–22   practically prove its divine origin and *e·*.
test its
o 344–15   until the enemies of C. S. test its *e·*

a 24–27   The *e·* of the crucifixion lay in the
25– 3   The *e·* of Jesus' spiritual offering is
s 158–17   divine Mind and its *e·* to heal.

efficient
f 233–31   Why should truth not be *e·* in sickness,
p 376–21   Therefore the *e·* remedy is to destroy the

effort
pref x 13   She has made no *e·* to embellish,
a 19–17   every *e·* for reform, every good thought
22–27   pinning one's faith . . . to another's vicarious *e·*.
26– 7   all have the cup of sorrowful *e·* to drink
38– 1   to stir mankind to Christian *e·* ?
ph 166– 5   the healing *e·* is made on the wrong side,
c 262–25   even as light emits light without *e·* ;
b 329–20   because he fails in his first *e·*.
g 554–17   The first *e·* of error has been and is to

efforts

our
a 36–29   in return for our *e·* at well doing.
c 262–11   reverse our feeble flutterings — our *e·* to
their
ph 180– 6   faith in their *e·* is somewhat helpful
t 456–10   reputation experimentally justified by their *e·*
these
pref ix–29   These *e·* show . . . the degrees by which
a 22– 9   these *e·* are crowned with success.
vigorous
a 22– 8   to make vigorous *e·* to save themselves ;
your
p 418–26   in your *e·* to destroy error.

f 223–20   The *e·* of error to answer this question

effulgence
sp 95–27   he beholds the light . . . and describes its *e·*
g 504–26   vague conjectures emit no such *e·*.
511–17   The changing glow and full *e·* of

egg

maternal
g 553–18 the maternal *e·* never brought forth Adam.
non-intelligent
g 550– 2 a circumscribed and non-intelligent *e·*.
nor in dust
g 552–24 redeeming power, . . . is not in *e·* nor in dust.
nucleus, or
g 549–16 with the formation of the nucleus, or *e·*,
of night
g 552– 5 That the earth was hatched from the "*e·* of night"
parent of the
g 552– 4 Who or what produces the parent of the *e·*?

c 261–29 even as the bird which has burst from the *e·*
r 485–20 belief . . . man springs from dust or from an *e·*,
g 543–19 If man is material and originates in an *e·*,
543–25 Did man, whom God created . . . originate in an *e·*?
547–12 able to see in the *e·* the earth's atmosphere,
550–23 An *e·* is an impossible enclosure for Deity.
552– 1 Which is first, the *e·* or the bird?
552– 1 is answered, if the *e·* produces the parent.
552–14 mortal life, which starts from an *e·*,
ap 561– 6 Agassiz, . . . saw the sun in an *e·*
gl 585–28 second from a rib, and third from an *e·*.

eggs

g 549– 4 The supposition that life germinates in *e·*
549–12 sometimes through *e·*, sometimes through buds,
551–10 naturalist argues that mortals spring from *e·*
551–18 transmitted through these bodies called *e·*,

Ego

but one
f 249–32 and there is but one *E·*.
divine
b 336– 6 The divine *E·*, or individuality, is reflected
eternal
b 314– 6 Thus he found the eternal *E·*, and proved that
is deathless
b 335–32 The *E·* is deathless and limitless,
is Mind
f 216–11 The understanding that the *E·* is Mind,
one
b 281–14 The one *E·*, the one Mind or Spirit called God,
understand the
f 204–21 When will the ages understand the *E·*,

pr 14–21 [because the *E·* is absent from the body,
sp 70– 9 the *E·* and the Father are inseparable.
f 250– 7 Spirit is the *E·* which never dreams,
250–11 Spiritual man is the likeness of this *E·*.
b 281– 9 What is the *E·*, whence its origin
306–11 The *E·* would be unexpressed,
315– 7 He knew that the *E·* was Mind instead of
p 368–25 Because matter has no consciousness or *E·*,
gl 588– 9 definition of
588–21 I AM. . . . divine Principle ; the only *E·*.

Ego-God
b 281–11 Ego-man is the reflection of the *E·* ;

Ego-man
b 281–11 *E·* is the reflection of the Ego-God ;
281–11 *E·* is the image and likeness of

egotism
t 452–17 than the luxury of learning with *e·* and vice.

egotists
c 263– 1 Mortals are *e·*.

egregious
o 355–22 the most *e·* fallacies ever offered

Egypt
s 133– 8 In *E·*, it was Mind which saved the Israelites
ph 185–16 the necromancers of *E·* strove to emulate
f 221–27 he thought of the flesh-pots of *E·*,

eight
p 421–31 asserting that the products of *e·* multiplied by

eighty-five
f 247– 4 A woman of *e·*, . . . had a return of sight.

either
pr 12–21 drug to be apparently *e·* poisonous or sanative
a 36– 5 suffering, *e·* before or after death,
m 61–22 propensities that must be *e·* overcome or
63–17 less rights than does *e·* C. S. or civilization.
sp 73– 1 In *e·* case, one does not support the other.
77–20 the illusion *e·* of a soul inert or of a
82–15 because both of us are *e·* unconscious or
83–22 to suppose that life is *e·* material or
86–19 *e·* involve feats by tricksters, or
93–11 *e·* our logic is at fault or
an 101–18 nothing in common with *e·* physiology or
103–23 It is *e·* ignorant or malicious.

either
s 119– 6 They *e·* presuppose the self-evolution
153–14 From it may be learned that *e·*
159–17 They would *e·* have allayed her fear or
ph 168– 5 removal of a single weight from *e·* scale
170–29 but in *e·* case dependent upon his
171– 9 *e·* of his life or of the weather,
181–18 In *e·* case you must improve your
f 203–17 We are prone to believe *e·* in more than one
211– 7 The sensations of the body must *e·* be
213– 6 conceives of something as *e·* liquid or solid,
213–28 discoursing *e·* discord or harmony
220–26 The belief that *e·* fasting or feasting makes
232– 7 no scatheless and permanent evidence of *e·*.
236–12 strongest educator, *e·* for or against crime.
236–15 *e·* after a model odious to herself or
237–20 keep out . . . *e·* sinful or diseased thoughts,
240–24 sooner or later, *e·* by suffering or by Science,
249–13 *E·* there is no omnipotence, or omnipotence is
c 258–21 so-called senses have no cognizance of *e·*
b 291–27 for the grave has no power over *e·*.
296– 6 *E·* here or hereafter, suffering or Science must
297–10 a change in *e·* a health-belief or a
323–30 We are *e·* turning away from this utterance, or
324–16 conquer sin, sickness, and death, *e·* here or
330–17 knowledge of it is left *e·* to human conjecture or
o 353– 9 *e·* in the form of sickness or of sin?
360–16 This ideal is *e·* temporal or eternal.
360–17 *E·* Spirit or matter is your model.
p 384– 2 Can matter, . . . *e·* feel or act without
385–32 coming from . . . as if *e·* were intelligent,
388–32 *e·* the food or this thought must be
390–24 no law of His to support the necessity *e·* of sin or
401–24 by applying the drug to *e·*?
415–17 *e·* retards the circulation or quickens it,
423– 3 not to be communicated to the patient, *e·* verbally or
424–18 *e·* by giving antagonistic advice or
426–20 master *e·* a desire to die or a dread of the grave
442–31 *e·* when asleep or when awake.
t 446– 7 may *e·* arise from the alarm of the physician, or
451– 9 will *e·* make shipwreck of their faith or
451–29 *e·* with a mistaken or a wicked purpose.
457–18 there is no good aspect, *e·* silvern or golden.
r 488–19 cannot be true *e·* of man nor of his
490–29 Sleep shows material sense as *e·* oblivion,
g 508–18 does not necessarily refer *e·* to masculinity or
531–21 Who dares to say *e·* that God is in matter or
547–21 must *e·* return to Mind or
551– 3 *E·* Mind produces, or it is produced.
551–21 peculiarities of ancestry, belonging to *e·* sex,
ap 567–20 claiming that there is intelligence in matter *e·*

ejected
g 524–30 and eventually *e·* at the demand of matter?

ejection
sp 97– 2 They will aid in the *e·* of error.
ph 171–20 exposed to *e·* by the operation of

elaborate
pref x–14 She has made no effort to embellish, *e·*,

elaborated
s 141–14 Jesus *e·* the fact that the healing effect

elastic
s 128–13 becomes more *e·*, is capable of greater
161– 1 supple and *e·* condition of the healthy limb,

elasticity
ph 198–20 until the *e·* of mortal thought haply causes a

elders
a 41–28 The truth taught by Jesus, the *e·* scoffed at.
o 354–16 derived from the traditions of the *e·*

El Dorado
pr 9–21 This is the *E· D·* of Christianity.
ap 559–30 into the *E· D·* of faith and hope.

elect
c 266–23 material sense, . . . would deceive the very *e·*.

election
a 38– 5 old doctrine of . . . the *e·* of a few to be saved,

elective
m 63–20 If the *e·* franchise for women will remedy

electric
sp 78–22 through *e·*, material effects?
97– 9 and the *e·* current swift,
p 393–23 or the *e·* wire which you stretch,

electricity

destructive
sp 93–17 Destructive *e·* is not the offspring of
hypnotism and
sp 78–26 hypnotism and *e·* are claimed to be
spirits and
sp 80–29 believes that . . . emanates from spirits and *e·*
trust in
ph 181– 9 When you manipulate patients, you trust in *e·*

electricity

wires nor
sp 78–19 Spirit needs no wires nor *e·* in order to

---

sp 73–16 through *e·* or any other form of matter,
ph 178–30 may attempt to unite with it hypnotism, . . . *e·*;
b 293– 3 *E·* is not a vital fluid,
293–17 *e·* is the sharp surplus of materiality
293–19 *e·* is not intelligent,
t 450–32 *e·*, animal nature, and organic life,

element

destructive
f 210–32 it is without a destructive *e·*.
essential
o 347–18 restoring an essential *e·* of Christianity,
fleshly
b 332–31 Into the real and ideal man the fleshly *e·* cannot
grossest
ap 565– 9 Led on by the grossest *e·* of mortal mind,
human
a 33–18 When the human *e·* in him struggled with
lost
b 328–17 has been dormant, a lost *e·* of Christianity.
mental
s 157– 5 whole force of the mental *e·* is employed
native
p 383–15 It is the native *e·* of such a mind,
no
b 311– 7 it is Spirit, which has no *e·* of self-destruction.
g 503–23 no *e·* nor symbol of discord and decay.
no material
ph 191– 7 will include in that likeness no material *e·*.
of error
t 463–12 has not a single *e·* of error,
of evil
g 539–11 God could never impart an *e·* of evil,
of progress
f 233– 5 This is an *e·* of progress,
only
ph 196– 9 for sin is the only *e·* of destruction.
swinish
b 272– 8 the swinish *e·* in human nature uproots it.
the very
s 134–19 robs Christianity of the very *e·*, which
this
s 146– 3 Why has this *e·* of Christianity been lost?
turbulent
ph 180–23 they should try to correct this turbulent *e·*

---

b 310–24 Sin is the *e·* of self-destruction,
p 392– 6 Fear, which is an *e·* of all disease,
413–16 more vigorously in its own *e·*.
r 480– 8 Nerves are an *e·* of the belief
t 583–25 not create an atom or an *e·* the opposite of

elementary

p 372– 5 error in solution, *e·* mortal mind,
ap 559– 5 upon the sea,— upon *e·*, latent error,

elements

certain
m 57– 6 through certain *e·* of the feminine,
different
m 57– 9 These different *e·* conjoin naturally
dissolving
r 490–22 along with the dissolving *e·* of clay.
evil
sp 83– 7 evil *e·* now coming to the surface.
healing
b 329– 2 the healing *e·* of pure Christianity will be
infinite
g 512–21 From the infinite *e·* of the one Mind
material
b 284–25 Even the more subtile and misnamed material *e·*
r 475– 7 blood, bones, and other material *e·*.
g 551–20 composed of the simplest material *e·*,
mortal
p 374–29 is resolved into its primitive mortal *e·*.
primal
ap 559–26 partaking of the nature, or primal *e·*, of Truth
symbols and
b 280– 2 Symbols and *e·* of discord

---

s 124–32 The *e·* and functions of the physical body
f 224–28 Truth brings the *e·* of liberty.
247– 3 two of the *e·* it had lost, sight and teeth.
b 309–18 not in *e·* which are not spiritual,
r 479–25 and they are the *e·* of nothingness.
481–24 Sin has the *e·* of self-destruction,
g 507– 3 while *water* symbolizes the *e·* of Mind.

elevate

m 58– 2 intercourse with those adapted to *e·* it,
f 235–18 will degrade the characters it should . . . *e·*.
b 318–27 and are not adapted to *e·* mankind.
r 492–11 will purify and *e·* character.

elevated

a 45–20 hath *e·* them to possible at-one-ment
ap 576–28 Jewish concept, not yet *e·* to deific apprehension

elevates

b 323–22 *e·* even mortal mind to the contemplation

elevating

m 57–24 enlarging, purifying, and *e·* it.
s 146–21 *e·* effects practically prove its divine origin
o 341– 9 *e·* them from a theoretical to a practical
gl 583–15 and is found *e·* the race,
586–14 FIRE. . . . affliction purifying and *e·* man.

elevation

pr 7– 9 it gives momentary solemnity and *e·* to thought.
m 63–24 the *e·* of society in general
sp 98– 2 the *e·* of existence above mortal discord
p 426–25 health and morals far beyond its present *e·*,
t 444– 4 suffering is oft the divine agent in this *e·*.

eleven

a 27–23 but only *e·* left a desirable historic record.
49– 8 Were all conspirators save *e·*?

Elias

s 136–15 some, *E·* ; and others, Jeremias,— *Matt.* 16 : 14.
136–19 controlled by the spirit of John or of *E·*.
ap 562– 3 As *E·* presented the idea of the fatherhood
gl 585– 9 definition of
585–13 "*E·* truly shall first come and— *Matt.* 17 : 11.

elicited

s 137–21 This assertion *e·* from Jesus the benediction,

Elijah

s 139– 7 so did Joshua, *E·*, and Elisha.

eliminate

o 348–18 Is it not well to *e·* from so-called mortal mind

eliminated

b 273–15 till the errors of sense are *e·*

Elisha

s 139– 8 so did Joshua, Elijah, and *E·*.

Elohim

b 320–32 stand in celestial perfection before *E·*,
g 515–16 The eternal *E·* includes the
515–17 The name *E·* is in the plural,
523 18 the Supreme Being is therein called *E·*.
523–25 it is *E·* (God) who creates.
gl 591– 4 one Spirit, or intelligence, named *E·*, or God.

Elohistic

g 523–17 One is called the *E·*, because
538–18 no record in the *E·* introduction of Genesis,

Eloi, Eloi, lama sabachthani

a 51– 1 the plaintive cry, "*E·*, *E·*, l· s·?"— *Mark* 15 : 34.

elongated

s 162–21 shortened limbs have been *e·*,

eloquence

sp 88–26 *E·* re-echoes the strains of Truth and Love.
88–31 When *e·* proceeds from the belief that a
89– 9 Destroy her belief in . . . and her *e·* disappears.

eloquent

sp 89– 5 the devotee may become unwontedly *e·*.
89–17 the tongue grows mute which before was *e·*.

else

pr 3–12 reflected by man,— *e·* man is not the image
11–24 if we desire holiness above all *e·*,
a 25–29 *e·* we are not improving the great blessings
m 58– 3 or *e·* joy's drooping wings trail in dust.
sp 76– 4 forgets all *e·* and breathes aloud his rapture.
89– 7 believing that somebody *e·* possesses her tongue
s 109–13 searched the Scriptures and read little *e·*,
119– 7 or *e·* they assume that matter is the product of
135–22 *e·* one or the other is false and useless ;
143– 6 *e·* Jesus would have recommended and
ph 168– 8 which would otherwise outweigh all *e·*.
182–28 or *e·* from ignorance of C. S. and its
197–31 *e·* his belief in its reality and fatality will
f 205– 1 *e·* God will continue to be hidden from
206– 5 *e·* it will misguide the judgment
208–18 "God is the father of mind, and of nothing *e·*."
220–19 and then charges them to something *e·*,
c 263–22 *e·* it is a new multiplication or self-division
b 272– 7 *e·* it beareth not much fruit,
289– 9 He is little *e·* than the expression of error.
310– 9 *e·* the clay would have power over the potter.
331–22 reflected by . . . and by nothing *e·*.
335–20 for Spirit is more than all *e·*.
336–21 *e·* God would be manifestly finite,
p 414–22 there is none *e·* beside Him."— *Deut.* 4 : 35.
435–26 For naught *e·* can he be punished,
r 466–20 Soul or Spirit signifies Deity and nothing *e·*.
478–26 of material human beliefs and of nothing *e·*,
481– 3 tributary to God, Spirit, and to nothing *e·*.
g 551–28 All must be Mind, or *e·* all must be matter.

elsewhere
ph 190– 7　neither . . . is found in brain or e· in matter
　195– 4　said that he should never be happy e·.
　b 277– 3　and e· the Scripture says that
　gl 598– 7　and e· in the New Testament.

elucidate
pref xii–21　in order to e··her idealism.
　r 465– 5　to e· scientific metaphysics.

elucidates
gl 579– 3　often e· the meaning of the inspired

elucidation
o 349–18　The e· of C. S. lies in its spiritual sense,

elude
f 252–19　and says: . . . I e· detection by smooth-tongued
p 440– 1　he could not possibly e· their search.

emanate
f 229– 7　whence did they e·?
　236– 2　Truth should e· from the pulpit,
b 273– 2　contrary to God, and cannot e· from Him.
g 512–22　From . . . Mind e· all form, color,
ap 564–17　barbarity of his foes could e· from

emanates
sp 80–29　believes that this wonder e· from spirits
g 504– 1　from which e· the true idea,

emanating
s 118–15　e· from the invisible and infinite power
c 257– 1　infinite image or idea e· from this Mind.
b 284–29　spiritual, e· from divine Mind.
g 508–15　the pure thought e· from divine Mind.

emanation
an 104–15　as the e· of divine Mind,
s 127–26　Science is an e· of divine Mind,
g 519– 5　the e·, of His infinite self-containment

emanations
sp 88–11　Ideas are e· from the divine Mind.
b 336–16　They are the e· of Him who is Life,

emancipate
f 223–23　They will e· humanity, and supplant

emancipated
g 546– 2　at some future time to be e· from it,

emasculation
b 271– 5　Neither e·, illusion, nor insubordination

embellish
pref x–14　She has made no effort to e·,

embellishments
f 247–28　e· of the person are poor substitutes

emblem
f 238–31　The cross is the central e· of history.

embodied
sp 93–29　this is the error e· in the belief that
p 372–11　belief . . . that man can enter his own e·

embodies
b 299– 3　which e· his conception of an unseen quality

embodiment
f 225–16　proportionate to its e· of right thinking.
b 333–13　the life of which Christ Jesus was the e·.
o 350–27　Hence its e· in the incarnate Jesus,
r 491–25　apparently with their own separate e·.
ap 563–15　lifts the veil from this e· of all evil,

embody
ph 192–23　good you do and e· gives you the only power

embrace
pr 7–15　may e· too much love of applause
f 208–29　You e· your body in your thought,
c 258– 2　finite conception of God cannot e· the

embraced
t 463– 3　under influences not e· in his diagnosis,
g 503– 2　which are e· in the infinite Mind

embracing
sp 77–14　e· its so-called pleasures and pains,
f 208–10　e· sin, sickness, and death
ap 561–17　in the man Jesus, as divinity e· humanity
gl 589– 4　A corporeal mortal e· duplicity,

embryo
f 236–13　Her thoughts form the e· of another
r 476– 4　declares that man begins . . . as a material e·.
gl 583– 2　God's thoughts, not in e·, but in maturity ;

embryology
g 550–25　E· supplies no instance of one species
　553– 1　in the various forms of e·,

embryonic
ph 188– 6　an e· thought without motive ;
　189–28　the development of e· mortal mind.
　190– 1　formation of so-called e· mortal mind,
　190– 8　This e· and materialistic human belief
g 547–14　the germinating speck of so-called e· life

embryonic
g 548–29　facts in regard to so-called e· life.
　550–22　If Life is God, . . . then Life is not e·,
ap 561– 6　at a point of so-called e· life.

emeralds
sp 87–19　The mine knows naught of the e· within

emerge
r 485–14　E· gently from matter into Spirit.
g 549–17　one or more individualities subsequently e· ;
　552–16　Mortals must e· from this notion

emergence
g 553–25　as the point of e· for the human race,

emergency
p 406– 5　which is equal to every e·,

emerging
s 148–11　as e· from the lowest, instead of from

emigrant
p 383–12　A hint may be taken from the e·,

emit
b 273–30　beliefs e· the effects of error at all times,
g 504–26　vague conjectures e· no such effulgence.

emits
c 262–25　even as light e· light without effort ;

Emmaus
a 46– 5　In the walk to E·, Jesus was known

emolument
f 236– 6　e· . . . which many leaders seek?

emotion
pr 7–18　produces material ecstasy and e·.
ph 180–16　reservoir already overflowing with that e·.

emotional
pr 14– 7　is to have, not mere e· ecstasy or faith,
a 25–27　all the e· love we can bestow on him, will never

emphasize
g 516–27　To e· this momentous thought,

emphasizes
s 116–20　C. S. strongly e· the thought that

emphatic
g 520–23　Here is the e· declaration that God

emphatically
p 369–24　preventive and curative) arts belong e· to C. S.

empire
p 378–22　not an intelligence to dispute the e· of Mind

empires
pref vii–20　Though e· fall, "the Lord shall — Exod. 15 : 18.
sp 94–12　The eastern e· and nations owe their
s 121– 8　the fate of e· and the fortunes of men.

employ
a 44–18　that he might e· his feet as before.
s 143– 5　God does not e· drugs or hygiene,
　157–21　why did Jesus not e· them
ph 181–11　and for that reason, you e· matter
f 218–21　and e· means which lead only into
　235–19　Physicians, whom the sick e· in their
p 390–31　as a legislator would e· to defeat the passage of
　418–23　By the truthful arguments you e·,
gl 598– 9　to e· words of material significance

employed
an 102–28　abused by its possessor, than otherwise e·,
s 112– 1　proved itself, whenever scientifically e·,
　116–25　are commonly and ignorantly e·,
　143– 7　else Jesus would have . . . e· them
　156– 7　Tapping had been e·, and yet,
　157– 5　whole force of the mental element is e·
ph 186– 8　under whatever name . . . they are e·;
o 349–25　material terms must be generally e·.
p 403–10　The human mind is e· to remove the illusion
　422–24　A surgeon is e· in one case,
g 502–25　word beginning is e· to signify the only,
gl 590–15　this term is sometimes e· as a title,

employers
p 439– 5　advertises largely for his e·.

employing
s 156–26　e· no other means, and she was cured.
p 421–29　or by e· a single material application

employs
an 104–23　The hypnotizer e· one error to destroy
s 127–10　The terms . . . C. S., or Science alone, she e·

empowers
ph 199–10　and e· man through its mandate,

emptied
f 201–14　They must first be e·.

emptiness
gl 599– 7　E· ; unfaithfulness ; desolation.

empty
pr 3–17 How *e·* are our conceptions of Deity !
a 54–11 *e·* or sin-filled human storehouses,
f 234–20 and *e·* it of sin and sickness,

emptying
ph 186– 2 *e·* his thought of the false stimulus

empurpled
ph 175–26 *e·* the plump cheeks of our ancestors,

empyrean
s 121–10 was to them displayed upon the *e·*,

emulate
a 37–16 learn to *e·* him in *all* his ways
ph 185–17 strove to *e·* the wonders wrought by Moses.
g 515– 2 enables its possessor to *e·* the example of

emulations
an 106–22 hatred, variance, *e·*, wrath,— *Gal.* 5 : 20.

enable
pr 4–29 watchfulness, and devout obedience *e·* us to
17– 2 *E· us to know,* — *as in heaven, so on earth,*
a 42–29 He was here to *e·* them to test his
o 354– 6 to *e·* them to leave all for Christ,
p 365– 9 *e·* them to rise above the supposed necessity
366– 5 *e·* him to cast physical evils out of his patient ;
378– 5 *e·* you to commute this self-sentence,
426–26 would *e·* us to hold the banner of Christianity

enabled
pref xi–30 *e·* her to get this institution chartered
a 24–30 *e·* their Master to triumph over the grave,
28–14 *e·* to heal the sick and to triumph over sin.
30– 9 this *e·* him to be the mediator,
35– 7 *e·* to rise somewhat from mortal sensuousness,
43– 4 *e·* the disciples to understand what Jesus
51–30 which *e·* Jesus to heal the sick,
54–24 it *e·* them to understand the Nazarene
sp 94–25 *e·* him to direct those thoughts aright ;
b 315–21 *e·* him to demonstrate the facts of things,
324–23 *e·* him to follow the example and teachings
r 482–22 *e·* Jesus to demonstrate his control over matter.
g 534– 3 This hereafter *e·* woman to be the
534– 5 This *e·* woman to be first to interpret

enables
pr 3–11 *e·* us to work out our own salvation.
10–14 It is striving that *e·* us to enter.
a 19–23 and *e·* man to do the will of wisdom.
sp 84–14 Acquaintance with the Science of being *e·*
87–15 Science *e·* one to read the human mind,
87–17 It *e·* one to heal through Mind,
s 147– 1 This system *e·* the learner to demonstrate
147–21 and *e·* you to grasp the spiritual facts
ph 174–22 belief is all that *e·* a drug to cure
f 298– 8 *e·* one to be Christian.
b 317–19 and *e·* him to conquer sin,
o 350– 9 *e·* them to interpret his spiritual meaning.
p 392– 8 *e·* truth to outweigh error.
r 493–14 *e·* the healer to demonstrate . . . the Principle
496–16 *e·* you to demonstrate, with scientific certainty,
g 515– 1 *e·* its possessor to emulate the example of Jesus.

enabling
sp 85– 8 *e·* one to do good, but not evil.

enact
p 440–23 beliefs . . . compel them to *e·* wicked laws of

enactment
p 384–11 belief of mortal mind, not an *e·* of wisdom,

enactments
p 381–20 Think less of the *e·* of mortal mind,

enamoured
f 245–20 coaxed the *e·* lightning from the clouds.

enchantment
f 209–15 Nearness, not distance, lends *e·* to this view.

enclosure
g 550–23 An egg is an impossible *e·* for Deity.

encompass
g 551–25 Darkness and doubt *e·* thought, so long as

encompassing
r 496–19 overlying, and *e·* all true being.
gl 585–16 Divine Science *e·* the universe and man ;
597–29 God's spiritual government, *e·* all things.

encounter
f 254–28 If you launch your bark . . . you will *e·* storms.

encountered
a 28–29 The trials *e·* by prophet, disciple, and

encourage
pr 7–16 to induce or *e·* Christian sentiment.
p 396–11 nor *e·* in the patient's thought the

encouragement
b 339–11 sinner can receive no *e·* from the
p 363–31 there was *e·* in the mere fact that
367– 4 tender word and Christian *e·* of an invalid,

encourages
b 320–28 and *e·* mortals to hope in Him

encouraging
m 63–22 without *e·* difficulties of greater

end (noun)
beginning and
b 282– 8 the finite, which has both beginning and *e·*.
338– 5 belief — that man . . . has beginning and *e·*,
gl 580–22 supposition that Life . . . has beginning and *e·* ;
beginning or
b 282– 7 represents the infinite without beginning or *e·*,
g 521– 5 narrative of being that is without beginning or *e·*.
gl 585– 6 which are likewise without beginning or *e·*.
beginning to
s 139– 4 From beginning to *e·*, the Scriptures
r 478–25 From beginning to *e·*, whatever is mortal
ap 559–21 Read this book from beginning to *e·*.
no
ap 565–15 there shall be no *e·*,'' — *Luke* 1 : 33.
of error
sp 95–19 We welcome . . . the *e·* of error,
96–19 disturbances will continue until the *e·* of error,
their
pr 5–20 the Psalmist could see their *e·*,
this
pr 5– 6 To this *e·* we are placed under the
a 22–12 for to this *e·* God worketh with you.
until the
sp 96–19 disturbances will continue until the *e·* of error,
g 533–25 and multiplies until the *e·* thereof.
unto the
sp 96–10 will continue unto the *e·*,
t 446–23 even unto the *e·* of the world.'' — *Matt.* 28 : 20.
without
f 253– 6 life, without beginning and without *e·*,
r 468–27 Life is without beginning and without *e·*.

sp 96–27 he . . . will endure to the *e·*.
s 139–10 even when the *e·* has been brightness
f 212–11 attempt to scratch the *e·* of a finger which
c 259–30 to the *e·* that they may produce harmonious
b 331–10 testifies to a beginning and an *e·*.
333–18 without beginning of years or *e·* of days.
p 401–11 to the *e·* of producing a higher
r 484–26 thus putting an *e·* to the hypotheses
g 501–14 which subserve the *e·* of natural good,
523–28 intertwined to the *e·* of chapter twelve,
538–29 they must consequently have an *e·*,
ap 564–30 From the beginning to the *e·*, the serpent
569–20 What must the *e·* be?
gl 592– 5 a beginning and therefore an *e·* ;

end (verb)
f 214–27 when a wound on the retina may *e·* the
227– 8 law of the divine Mind must *e·* human bondage,
245–32 infinite never began nor will it ever *e·*.
249–15 infinity never began, will never *e·*,
c 262–28 To begin rightly is to *e·* rightly.
b 292– 2 will *e·* the battle of Truth with error
331– 5 subject to their limitations and would *e·* in death.
p 376–27 Destroy fear, and you *e·* fever.
427–15 Nothing can . . . *e·* the existence of man
r 491–12 facts of being, in which all must *e·*.
g 532–27 error began and will *e·* the dream of matter.
536–20 Passions and appetites must *e·* in pain.

endeavor
sp 96–31 wicked minds will *e·* to find means
ph 169–23 towards which human faith or *e·* is directed.
b 323– 4 This strife consists in the *e·* to forsake error
p 368–14 has little inspiration to nerve *e·*.

endeavored
a 27–31 *e·* to hold him at the mercy of matter
s 152– 5 author has *e·* to make this book the Æsculapius of

endeavoring
f 246– 7 and *e·* to reach Spirit
p 426– 8 in *e·* to reach it.
432–26 *e·* to assist the prisoner to escape

endeavors
a 22–15 If your *e·* are beset by fearful odds,
f 253–20 right *e·* against sin or sickness,
p 426–14 Man should renew his energies and *e·*.

ended
s 123–26 not specially belong to a dispensation now *e·*,
g 519–22 God *e·* His work which — *Gen.* 2 : 2.

endeth
ap 567–12 Thus *e·* the conflict between the flesh and

ending
p 429–23 it must also have an *e·*,
r 469– 6 it would also have an *e·*.
g 550–17 as beginning and *e·*, and with birth, decay, and

endless
a 18– 5 and for this we owe him e· homage.
endorse
r 488–12 appear . . . to approve and e· belief,
endorsed
a 42–11 e· pre-eminently by the approval of God,
endorses
s 155–11 When the general belief e· the
endow
s 119– 1 When we e· matter with vague spiritual power,
119– 3 of course we cannot really e· matter with
132–29 or e· him with the truest conception of the
o 357–13 but if we theoretically e· mortals with
endowed
a 30– 6 e· with the Christ, the divine Spirit,
an 106– 7 God has e· man with inalienable rights,
s 161–16 "Man is e· by his Maker with
b 312–32 Jesus' spiritual origin . . . richly e· him
p 378–27 God never e· matter with power to disable Life
t 461– 9 morally advanced and spiritually e·,
g 548–26 Natural history is richly e· by the labors
endowment
sp 88–29 said to be a gift whose e· is obtained from
endowments
r 488–25 mental e· are not at the mercy of
endows
p 380–30 to believe . . . that God e· this opposing power
g 522– 6 e· man out of God's perfection and power.
ends
f 239–28 discordant and e· in sin, sickness, death.
251– 6 neither should a fever . . . before it e·.
c 261–26 the solid objects and e· of life
307–16 false sense of an existence which e· in death.
309–29 so-called life always e· in death.
340–24 constitutes the brotherhood of man ; e· wars ;
p 380– 2 which e· in a belief called death,
g 550–11 which e·, even as it begins,
ap 561– 2 which works out the e· of eternal good
endued
a 55–25 e· with the spirit . . . of Christian healing.
t 445–10 possibilities of man e· with divine Science.
endues
g 547–18 Darwin's theory,— that Mind. . .e· matter with
endurance
sp 80– 5 or for the support of bodily e·.
s 128– 8 C. S. enhances their e· and mental powers,
128–13 more elastic, is capable of greater e·,
p 385– 8 supplies energy and e· surpassing all other
387– 6 When we reach our limits of mental e·,
endure
a 39– 3 indignities as he received, his followers will e·
40–21 e· human brutality without murmuring,
sp 96–27 he . . . will e· to the end.
99–22 and shall continue to labor and to e·.
b 290–24 but e· until the death of these errors.
p 385– 5 which ordinary people could not e·.
405–23 than to e· the cumulative effects of a
endured
a 36–10 Jesus e· the shame, that he might
s 158–14 Apollo, . . . e· great sufferings upon earth.
b 239– 2 e· the lash of their predecessors,
endureth
pref xii–24 "hopeth all things, e· all things,"— I Cor. 13 : 7.
c 267–28 "Blessed is the man that e·— Jas. 1 : 12.
enduring
m 59– 2 a full recognition of its e· obligations
65– 8 they will be strong and e·.
c 259–27 Immortal ideas, pure, perfect, and e·,
261– 4 Hold thought steadfastly to the e·,
r 488– 1 e· and harmonious phases of things.
enemies (see also **enemies'**)
blessing its
gl 589–22 pure affection blessing its e·.
bless our
a 30–29 Only in this way can we bless our e·,
his
a 43–24 Out of reach of the barbarity of his e·,
51– 6 Jesus could have withdrawn himself from his e·.
implacable
a 40–16 the crimes of his implacable e·
Jesus'
a 48–27 acquiescence with the demands of Jesus' e·.
love our
f 234–12 We should love our e·
mine
ap 578–14 in the presence of mine e· :— Psal. 23 : 5.
of Christian Science
o 344–15 until the e· of C. S. test its efficacy
physical
s 116–16 nor do they carry the day against physical e·,

enemies
Thine
f 201– * Thine e· have reproached,— Psal. 89 : 51.

a 33–23 It blesses its e·, heals the sick,
45–11 "For if, when we were e·,— Rom. 5 : 10.
48–21 Peter would have smitten the e· of
c 266–13 Friends will betray and e· will slander,
t 449–26 They are e· without the preliminary offence.
enemies'
a 51–13 could give his temporal life into his e· hands ;
enemy
a 39–13 The Bible calls death an e·,
f 210– 9 last e· that shall be destroyed,"— I Cor. 15 : 26.
p 401– 2 Any human error is its own e·,
427–19 last e· that shall be destroyed— I Cor. 15 : 26.
438– 6 over all the power of the e· :— Luke 10 : 19.
r 486–17 If . . . then death is not an e·
energies
divine
ph 186– 4 filling it with the divine e· of Truth.
his
p 426–14 Man should renew his e· and endeavors,
latent
t 445– 8 Unfold the latent e· and
recuperative
f 252– 5 and of the recuperative e· of Truth
spiritual
p 387– 9 spiritual e· can neither wear out nor
wasted
a 44–15 to resuscitate wasted e·.

s 109–14 devoted time and e· to discovering
t 455–12 and if, . . . you fail to use the e· of Mind
energy
pr 3–16 absolute consecration of thought, e·, and
f 249– 6 Let us feel the divine e· of Spirit,
p 385– 8 The spiritual demand, . . . supplies e·
394– 6 majority of doctors depress mental e·,
t 445–21 the unlabored motion of the divine e·
463–10 Though gathering new e·, this idea cannot
g 534–16 material intelligence called e·
enfeebled
f 227–28 crippled your capacities, e· your body,
enforce
r 488–13 to e· the necessity of understanding.
enforced
s 151–15 bondage now e· by false theories,
enforces
p 381– 3 the bias of education e· this slavery.
enforcing
ph 184–14 e· obedience through divine statutes.
engaged
p 385– 2 philanthropists e· in humane labors
g 543–14 against which divine Science is e· in a
engender
r 475–30 nor can God, . . . e· the capacity or freedom
to sin.
engendered
s 133–20 e· the limited form of a national
f 220–16 are e· solely by human theories.
engenders
t 401– 6 not a healer, but it e· disease and death.
England
s 111–20 offered in Oxford University, E·,
163– 7 William IV, King of E·,
English
a 23–21 In Hebrew, Greek, Latin, and E·, faith and
32– 5 our E· word sacrament is derived from it.
ph 176– 1 "Where ignorance is bliss, . . . says the E· poet,
f 245– 3 a sketch from the history of an E· woman,
o 349–10 like all other languages, E· is inadequate
p 379– 9 on whom certain E· students experimented,
r 488– 9 conveyed by the E· verb believe ;
engraved
g 521–15 should be e· on the understanding
engulfed
p 382–25 in which the senses had e· him,
enhance
p 397–11 as directly as you e· your joys by
enhances
s 128– 8 C. S. e· their endurance and mental powers,
f 209–14 immanent sense of Mind-power e· the glory of
enigma
sp 70– 1 Mortal existence is an e·.
s 124–19 is, and must continue to be, an e·.
enigmatical
r 467–26 shows material existence to be e·.

enjoined
a 55– 4 the idea of Christian healing e· by Jesus ;
p 441– 7 but be e· to keep perpetual silence,
t 463–25 He never e· obedience to the laws of nature,

enjoy
pr 9–15 before we can e· the fruition of our hope
ph 176–28 human mind, . . . is supposed to feel, suffer, e·.
181– 7 Matter, which can neither suffer nor e·,
f 212– 1 We suffer or e· in our dreams,
246–22 would e· more than threescore years and ten
250–16 A mortal may be weary or pained, e· or suffer,
p 397–26 walk, see, hear, e·, or suffer in dreams.

enjoyed
f 221–25 but he never e· his food as he had

enjoyment
m 61– 3 The senses confer no real e·.
p 397– 8 Suffering is no less a mental condition than is e·.
406–32 There is no e· in getting drunk,

enjoyments
m 60–32 Higher e· alone can satisfy the cravings

enjoys
b 294–10 belief that matter e· and suffers.
322–17 drunkard thinks he e· drunkenness,
p 414–25 matter neither feels, suffers, nor e·.
gl 582–16 has spiritual bliss and e· but cannot suffer.

enlarge
ph 199– 3 might be thought true that hammering would e·
p 430– 6 Faith should e· its borders

enlarged
a 46–32 they were roused to an e· understanding
s 151–11 and were in possession of the e· power
c 258–22 The human capacities are e· and perfected
265– 5 treasures of Truth and Love are e·.
265–12 but confers upon man e· individuality,
g 557–13 towards e· understanding and intelligence ;

enlarges
s 128– 9 e· their perception of character,
ph 199–10 Mind alone e· and empowers man

enlarging
m 57–23 Love enriches the nature, e·,

enlighten
pr 2– 3 Do we pray . . . to e· the infinite
g 510– 9 Truth and Love e· the understanding,

enlightened
pr 12–24 help should come from the e· understanding.
15–31 Trustworthiness is the foundation of e· faith.

enlightening
g 538–12 e· and sustaining the universe.

enlightenment
a 45– 8 Jesus' deed was for the e· of men
t 462– 7 understanding, potency, e·, and success.
g 556–17 Did . . . the e· of the race come from the

enlisted
ph 168– 9 when it ought to be e· on the side of health,
t 450–19 Christian Scientist has e· to lessen evil,

enmity
s 131–10 carnal mind is e· against God."— Rom. 8 : 7.
b 273–12 Hence the e· between Science and the senses,
315–14 Their carnal minds were at e· with it.
g 534– 9 I will put e· between thee and— Gen. 3 : 15.
534–19 carnal mind is e· against God ;— Rom. 8 : 7.

Enoch's
f 214– 5 If E· perception had been confined to the

enough
pr 10– 6 If good e· to profit by Jesus' cup
a 28–22 it is e· if thou art found worthy to unloose the
41–30 It was e· for them to believe in a national Deity ;
f 224–12 sects many but not e· Christianity.
o 345–16 well e· to pass judgment upon them.
354–15 Surely it is not e· to cleave to
355–32 Strangely e·, we ask for material
p 365–19 If the Scientist has e· Christly affection to
365–21 Christian e· to practise scientifically
g 520– 5 That is e· !

enrages
o 345–29 e· the carnal mind and is the main cause

enraptured
f 246–15 should dawn upon the e· sense
b 323–11 until boundless thought walks e·,

enrich
sp 79–32 neither does withholding e· us.

enriches
m 57–23 Love e· the nature, enlarging, purifying,
o 361–29 e· mankind only when it is understood,

en route
a 21–15 to Europe, while I am e· r· for California,

enshroud
sp 98–27 Mystery does not e· Christ's teachings,

enslave
ph 187–11 beliefs of the human mind rob and e· it,

enslavement
f 228–11 The e· of man is not legitimate.
p 373–15 are the sources of man's e·.
407– 6 Man's e· to the most relentless masters

enslaves
f 225– 2 Whatever e· man is opposed to the

enslaving
f 227– 6 claims of the e· senses must be denied

ensnare
an 102–21 they e· the age into indolence,

ensue
m 65–20 There will e· a fermentation over this

ensues
p 433–16 A brief consultation e·, and the jury
gl 581–21 confusion e·, and the more certain is the

ensuing
p 397–19 you will find the e· good effects to be

ensure
m 64–29 e· the stability of the marriage covenant.
ph 194–11 are not necessary to e· deafness
ap 571– 5 necessary to e· the avoidance of the evil

ensured
o 357–13 and error's destruction e· ;

ensures
c 260–17 and e· failure at the outset.

entangled
f 227–27 bound you, e· your free limbs,

enter
pr 10–15 It is striving that enables us to e·.
14–31 e· into thy closet,— Matt. 6 : 6.
15– 9 To e· into the heart of prayer,
15–14 we must e· into the closet and shut the door.
a 21–10 he is striving to e· in.
40–22 rejoicing to e· into fellowship with him
40–32 but in order to e· into the kingdom,
m 63–30 e· into business agreements, hold real estate,
66–10 Through great tribulation we e· the kingdom,
sp 70– 6 can never e· the atmosphere of Spirit.
99–12 None may pick the lock nor e· by some other
f 228– 6 nothing inharmonious can e· being,
238–18 to e· unlawfully into the labors of others.
241–32 than for sinful beliefs to e· the kingdom of
b 269–12 matter does not e· into metaphysical premises
281– 2 by which we e· into the kingdom of Truth
332–32 Into the . . . ideal man the fleshly element cannot e·.
336–20 A portion of God could not e· man ;
p 372–11 belief . . . that man can e· his own embodied
382–23 shall in no wise e· therein."— Luke 18 : 17.
384–11 and man has only to e· his protest
398– 3 and e· no more into him."— Mark 9 : 25.
399–22 "How can one e· into a— Matt. 12 : 29.
419–18 lest aught unfit for development e· thought.
440–28 forbidden to e· against Mortal Man
441– 6 not permitted to e· any suits at the bar of Soul,
t 451–12 strive, to e· the narrow path of Life,
r 481– 6 free "to e· into the holiest,"— Heb. 10 : 19.
g 524–31 Does Spirit e· dust, and lose therein
525– 1 Does Mind, God, e· matter
544–30 to e· man's nostrils so that
ap 577–26 nothing can e· that city, which

entered
m 59– 1 Matrimony should never be e· into without
sp 76–11 understood that Spirit never e· matter
gl 580–26 supposition . . . creator e· what He created,

entering
ph 193– 2 On e· the house I met his physician,
t 457–11 Her prime object, since e· this field of labor,
r 478– 6 never beheld Spirit . . . leaving a body or e· it.
g 522–20 Spirit is represented as e· matter

enters
f 228–12 It will cease when man e· into his heritage
b 277–28 in every statement into which it e·.
336– 2 Mind never e· the finite.
336– 4 Good never e· into evil,
p 369– 7 He e· into a diviner sense of the facts,
442–16 Neither animal magnetism nor hypnotism e·
g 503–12 No supposition of error e· there.
529–22 e· into the metaphor only as evil.
530–31 Second, it supposes that mind e· matter,
538–20 Until that . . . e· into the arena,
gl 580–23 supposition . . . that the infinite e· the

entertain
sp 80–12 I e· no doubt of the humanity and
f 214–18 We bow down to matter, and e· finite thoughts
232– 5 beliefs we commonly e· about happiness
b 299–17 and we e· "angels unawares."— Heb. 13 : 2.

entertain
p 391–10 Banish the belief that you can possibly e· a
418–24 spirit of Truth and Love which you e·,
g 548–16 by which men may e· angels,
ap 560–16 or e· a false estimate of anyone whom

entertained
a 54–32 if he e· any other sense of being
p 411–22 always induced by a false sense mentally e·,
g 545–22 The translators . . . e· a false sense of being.
ap 574–30 an angel e· unawares.

entertainer
p 364–13 had done what his rich e· had neglected to do,

entertaining
f 237–17 kept from discussing or e· theories
b 280–31 The only excuse for e· human opinions

entertains
f 250–17 according to the dream he e· in sleep.
p 422–27 e· fears and doubts as to the ultimate

enthroned
f 252–25 and says : . . . I am e· in the gorgeousness of
c 266–26 infinite Mind e· is heaven.
b 306–26 Science, still e·, is unfolding to mortals
t 454–10 hate has . . . no kingdom. Love is e·.

enthrones
ph 186–31 it e· matter as deity.
p 394–12 and e· matter through error.
t 446–21 To understand God . . . e· faith in Truth,
ap 571–32 He e· pure and undefiled religion,

enthusiasm
gl 599– 5 ZEAL. . . . Blind e· ; mortal will.

entire
m 62– 4 The e· education of children should be
s 118–11 It must destroy the e· mass of error,
151–27 e· being is found harmonious
157–28 C. S. impresses the e· corporeality,
ph 183–21 man's e· obedience, affection, and strength.
f 219–29 E· immunity from the belief in sin,
244–21 If . . . God is without His e· manifestation,
252–11 e· mortal, material error finally disappears,
c 262– 7 ascribes to Him the e· glory.
b 277–17 throughout the e· round of nature.
p 371–31 Truth is an alterative in the e· system,
384–32 over the e· functions and organs of the
408– 7 throughout the e· round of the material senses,
t 443– 7 e· confidence in omnipotent Mind
461– 7 illustrates and proves the e· Principle.
r 494– 1 and to govern man's e· action?
496– 5 and governs the e· universe.
g 502– 4 preponderance of unreality in the e·
537–12 represented as spiritual, e·, and good.

entirely
pr 14–25 E· separate from the belief and dream of
s 156–30 matter disappears from the remedy e·,
o 353– 6 testimony of the physical senses yields e·
g 545–16 material theory, which is e· a false view,

entireness
b 293–30 the e· of God, good, and the nothingness of evil.

entities
f 204– 8 antagonistic e· and beings,

entitled
a 42–10 Though e· to the homage of the world
s 127– 6 e· to a classification as truth,
ph 183–31 the one Mind only is e· to honor.
b 312–32 richly endowed him and e· him to
r 493–12 in a previous chapter e· C. S. Practice.

entitles
t 456– 8 This alone e· them to the high standing

entity
all
p 369– 5 loses to human sense all e· as man,
eternal
b 301–13 constitutes the only real and eternal e·.
lose his
r 477–31 man, divorced from Spirit, would lose his e·.
man's
o 356– 6 sickness, and death do not prove man's e·
no real
f 250– 7 mortal existence has no real e·,
g 506– 4 Therefore matter, . . . has no real e·.
nor power
g 555–13 C. S. attributes to error neither e· nor power,
real
ph 186–17 It says : "I am a real e·,
without
r 470–28 If . . . Deity was unexpressed — that is, without e·.

sp 92– 9 Mind is not an e· within the cranium
o 359–12 to man's existence or e·,
p 399–25 This misnamed mind is not an e·.

entrance
a 20–26 It commands sure e· into the realm of Love.
p 393– 3 through divine help we can forbid this e·.

entreat
ph 182–22 Mortals e· the divine Mind to heal the sick,

entry
a 42–12 his brief triumphal e· into Jerusalem

enumerates
s 152–30 Jahr, . . . e· the general symptoms,

enunciator
g 524–22 How could . . . error be the e· of Truth?

environment
sp 87– 8 their mental e· remains

environments
c 258–10 which must escape from its e·
g 521– 2 lifts man above the sod, above earth and its e·

Envy
p 430–23 Hypnotism, E·, Greed and Ingratitude,

envy (see also envy's)
and hate
a 48–21 was silent before e· and hate.
t 462–27 selfishness, malice, e·, and hate.
bigotry, nor
r 484– 4 neither pride, prejudice, bigotry, nor e·
or jealousy
m 64– 8 Pride, e·, or jealousy seems on most occasions

a 47–20 this spiritual distance inflamed Judas' e·.
51–25 motives of his persecutors were pride, e·,
s 115–22 pride, e·, deceit, hatred, revenge,
ph 188– 9 dishonesty, e·, hatred, revenge
f 218–11 malice, lust, appetite, e·, hate."
241– 3 incurs the hostility of e· ;
241– 9 Falsenood, e·, hypocrisy, malice, hate,
b 289–10 To suppose that sin, lust, hatred, e·,
330–30 dishonesty, selfishness, e·, hypocrisy,
p 404–29 e·, dishonesty, fear, . . . make a man sick,
407– 7 passion, selfishness, e·, hatred,
419– 2 Lurking error, lust, e·, revenge, malice, or
t 445–22 Self-seeking, e·, passion, pride, hatred,
452–12 Your advancing course may provoke e·,
464–24 weapons of bigotry, ignorance, e·, fall
ap 564–25 death, e·, hatred, and revenge, — all evil,
gl 582– 6 pride ; e· ; fame ; illusion ;
589– 2 e· ; hatred ; selfishness ; self-will ; lust.
589–14 sensuality ; e· ; oppression ; tyranny.
593– 8 animal magnetism ; e· ; revenge.

envyings
an 106–23 e·, murders, drunkenness, — Gal. 5 : 21.

envy's
g 542–24 To e· own hell, justice consigns the

ephemeral
c 267– 4 offspring of God start not from matter or e· dust.
r 485– 9 e· views of error ought to be obliterated

epileptic
p 398– 2 as when he said to the e· boy,

epistle
an 106–18 in his great e· to the Galatians,
s 112–22 characterized in the e· to the Hebrews.
b 313–16 the author of this remarkable e·
321– 3 Paul says, in his first e· to the Corinthians,
g 534–18 Paul says in his e· to the Romans :

epistles
b 319–32 what the beloved disciple meant in one of his e·,

epizoötic
ph 179–18 The e· is a humanly evolved ailment,

epoch
m 67–32 The e· approaches when the understanding

equal
m 67–10 nautical science is not e· to the Science of
sp 80– 3 A cup of coffee or tea is not the e· of truth,
83– 4 artifice and delusion claimed that they could e·
s 117– 5 one alone and without an e·.
133–24 made "himself e· with God," — John 5 : 18.
b 314– 9 but one Mind without a second or e·.
368–11 beliefs . . . that evil is e· in power to good
406– 5 is e· to every emergency,
418–10 if your fidelity is half e· to the
r 489– 9 In infancy this belief is not e· to
ap 560–23 made him e· to his great mission.
574–23 the four e· sides of which were heaven-bestowed

equalizes
b 340–28 e· the sexes ; annuls the curse on man,

equalling
s 108–16 three multiplied by three, e· nine,

equally
sp 73–21　E· incorrect is the belief that spirit
90–11　will be found to be e· possible for the body
ph 167–24　or to expect to work e· with Spirit and matter,
f 211–11　Is it not e· true that matter does not
221–21　and it is e· far from Science,
224–18　is less material . . . but it is e· as cutting.
231–26　To hold yourself superior to . . . is e· wise,
o 349–29　To a certain extent this is e· true of all
p 383–14　To the mind e· gross, dirt gives no uneasiness.
424–15　It is e· important in metaphysical practice
438–19　Another witness, e· inadequate, said

equals
f 231– 9　no lesser power e· the infinite All-power ;

equator
sp 90– 7　the imaginary line called the e·

equip
s 155– 9　e· the medicine with their faith,

equipoise
s 124–22　support the e· of that thought-force,

equipollence
s 110– 9　The e· of God brought to light another

equipped
b 328–15　man's power, when he is e· by God,

equitable
p 440–30　just and e· decisions of divine Spirit

equity
p 435–24　Supreme Judge in o· decides what penalty

equivalent
pr 6–13　will furnish more than its e· of pain,
gl 598–13　e· to our common statement,

equivalents
g 525– 7　some of the e· of the term *man*

era
Christian
a 20– 9　which we call the Christian e· ;
55– 6　Perhaps the early Christian e· did Jesus
s 138–17　Jesus established in the Christian o·
139– 8　The Christian e· was ushered in with
b 333–17　marked the first century of the Christian e·,
333–20　both before and after the Christian e·,
r 474– 5　accorded to Truth in the early Christian e·
g 534–26　since the Christian e· began.
new
a 43–18　opened a new e· for the world.
spiritual
m 65–16　struggling against the advancing spiritual e·.

eradicate
s 142– 1　and it will e· sickness and sin
ph 180–20　even before they go to work to e· the disease
p 400–12　E· the image of disease from the

eradicated
t 446–32　Ignorance of the error to be e·

erase
sp 81–20　E· the figures which express number,
b 290– 2　was and is and shall be, whom nothing can e·.

ere
pref vii– 3　e· cometh the full radiance of a

erect
p 442–11　His form was o· and commanding,

erected
s 161–21　a statue of Liberty, e· near the guillotine :

erects
g 523–10　which God e· between the true and false.

erelong
ph 179–30　may e· reap the effect of this mistake.
192–25　which e· betrays its weakness and falls,

err
b 272– 9　"Ye do e·, not knowing the— *Matt.* 22 : 29.
g 555–27　or . . . confers the ability to e·.

erring
pr 15–10　the door of the e· senses must be closed.
m 62–26　the laws of e·, human concepts.
s 108–30　My discovery, that e·, mortal, . . . *mind*
151– 5　e·, finite, human mind has an absolute need
157–23　E· mortal mind confers the power which
ph 166–15　The e· human mind is inharmonious
186– 7　E· human mind-forces can work only evil
187–27　If you take away this e· mind,
188– 1　only as the mortal, e· mind yields to God,
192–11　E· power is a material belief,
f 202–29　senseless matter or e· mortal mind
206– 8　e·, human thought acts injuriously
211–22　the thoughts of one e· mind
239–27　If it comes from e· mortal mind,
253–12　outside of e·, mortal, material sense
c 260– 7　The conceptions of mortal, e· thought
b 279– 1　the e·, changing, and dying,

erring
t 447– 6　you must not forget that e· human opinions,
459–12　Any attempt to heal mortals with e·
r 472–28　seem real to human, e· belief,
477–13　corporeal senses to be mortal and e· illusions.
494–17　thus helping e· human sense to flee from
g 503–24　God creates neither e· thought, mortal life,
505–30　The mortal, e·, and finite are human beliefs,
gl 587–14　supposititious minds, . . . e· and mortal ;

erroneous
sp 71–22　spiritualism will be found mainly e·,
91–19　and destroys the e· knowledge
91–22　Certain e· postulates should be
s 112–29　is e·, for it inculcates a breach of
116–26　confused and e· conceptions of divinity
121–23　Science shows appearances often to be e·,
150–23　it is as evidently e· to the author,
155–16　e· general belief, which sustains medicine
ph 177–16　e· theory of life and intelligence in matter,
184– 2　The premises being e·, the conclusions
185–26　because e· mental practice may seem
185–28　because e· methods act on and through the
f 204–18　Such theories are evidently e·.
223–26　slumbering thought from its e· dream
c 267–21　inverted thoughts and e· beliefs
b 277–32　sometimes beautiful, always e·.
o 352–24　traditional beliefs, e· and man-made.
p 372– 2　mortal body is only an e· mortal belief
375–16　unscientific mental practice is e·
378–20　represented by two material e· bases.
395–23　It is no less e· to believe in the
396–25　with which to combat their e· sense,
401–17　Truth is destroying e· mortal belief.
r 472–21　absurdity — namely, e· *truth.*
478–18　The assertion that there can be . . . is e·.
480–15　Inharmony has no Principle ; its action is e·
487–24　The belief that life is sentient . . . is e·.
g 522–18　In this e· theory, matter takes the place of
526–20　e· doctrine that the knowledge of evil is
536–24　Mortal mind accepts the e·,
543–24　creations of e· thought, not of matter.
554– 9　following from a misconception of life, is e·,
gl 588–17　whatever reflects not this one Mind, is . . . e·,
(*see also* **belief, postulate**)

erroneously
b 274–17　what we e· term the five physical
282–25　mortal thought, always governing itself e·.

Error (*see also* **Error's**)
Court of
(*see* Court)

p 438 24　Personal Sense, who is in partnership with E·
438–31　the firm of Personal Sense, E·, & Co.,
error (*see also* **error's**)
abounds
f 202–25　E· abounds where Truth should
above
p 400–18　By lifting thought above e·, or disease,
accompanies
b 287–17　Neither . . . nor truth accompanies e·,
action of
r 484–22　the voluntary or involuntary action of e·
Adam — alias
g 528–24　Adam — *alias* e· — gives them names.
adamant of
f 242–18　the adamant of e·, self-will,
Adam or
ph 177–16　Adam or e·, . . . had the naming of
g 534–13　unfolded the remedy for Adam, or e· ;
adhere to
ph 181–23　if you adhere to e· and are afraid to trust
against
a 29– 2　take up arms against e· at home and abroad.
aggravation of
an 105–27　The aggravation of e· foretells its doom,
all
pr 10–13　and thus destroying all e·.
15–13　divine Principle, Love, which destroys all e·.
a 35–19　Our baptism is a purification from all e·.
39– 5　He overcame the world, the flesh, and all e·,
39– 9　until all e· is destroyed.
s 132–25　salvation from all e·, physical and mental,
ph 174–19　rebuking in their course all e·
f 227– 3　the law of mortal belief included all e·,
240–28　until all e· is finally brought into
251–23　leads the human mind to relinquish all e·,
c 267–25　all e· disappears in celestial Truth.
b 292– 8　only as it destroys all e·
294– 5　carries within itself the seeds of all e·.
303–19　through the self-destruction of all e·
305–26　destroys all e· and brings immortality to light.
p 414–13　destroy all e·, whether it is called
r 474– 2　destroy all e·, evil, disease, and death.

error

all
r 482–16 the truth casting out all *e*.
492–12 Thus progress will finally destroy all *e*,
g 543–17 All *e* proceeds from the evidence before the
545–28 Truth has but one reply to all *e*,
ancient
p 389–24 the ancient *e* that there is fraternity between
and death
g 539–10 such as evil, matter, *e*, and death?
and discord
p 423–21 superior to *e* and discord,
and disease
pr 5–32 destruction of all evil works, *e* and disease
and evil
a 52–17 *e* and evil again make common cause
b 272–26 in the destruction of *e* and evil,
and hatred
g 522–30 produce death, *e*, and hatred?
and mortality
b 292– 3 the battle of Truth with *e* and mortality ;
and sin
b 296–17 lose all satisfaction in *e* and sin
and Truth
o 356–13 as the two opposites, — as *e* and Truth,
356–18 between *e* and Truth, between flesh and Spirit.
animate
p 409– 6 its final statement, — animate *e*
antidote for
r 495–10 and find a sovereign antidote for *e*
any
p 372–30 If pride, superstition, or any *e*
assumption of
g 546– 7 this assumption of *e* would dethrone the
attributes to
g 555–13 C. S. attributes to *e* neither entity nor power,
back to
a 22–16 go not back to *e*, nor become a sluggard in the
basic
p 405– 1 The basic *e* is mortal mind.
r 470– 6 was the basic *e* of idolatry.
befogged in
f 205–15 Befogged in *e* (the error of believing that
begins
g 539– 3 *E* begins by reckoning life as separate
544–31 *E* begins with corporeality as the producer
belief in
b 297–27 belief in Truth is better than a belief in *e*,
belief, or
b 289–16 a mortal belief, or *e*, which Truth destroys
gl 589–20 Truth rebuking mortal belief, or *e*,
beliefs that
p 368–10 Against the fatal beliefs that *e* is as real
believed
b 306– 1 believed *e* to be as immortal as Truth.
bites the heel
f 216– 7 *E* bites the heel of truth, but cannot kill truth.
brings to
p 422–10 tremor which Truth often brings to *e*
builds on
sp 83–11 belief hides Truth and builds on *e*.
burial of
f 232–30 unquestionable signs of the burial of *e*
called
s 108–24 that the opposite of Truth, — called *e*,
call of
a 21–26 the worldly man is at the beck and call of *e*,
cannot produce
p 420– 8 *e* cannot produce this unnatural reluctance.
cannot remove
an 101–27 *e* cannot remove the effects of error.
cannot support
r 481–27 since Truth cannot support *e*.
capable of
g 532–23 Is Mind capable of *e* as well as of truth,
casting out
a 33– 8 healing the sick and casting out *e*.
34– 4 instead of showing, by casting out *e*
35–24 casting out *e* and healing the sick.
41–15 casting out *e* and healing the sick,
43– 1 must understand . . . by casting out *e*,
sp 97–31 apostolic work of casting out *e* and healing
s 135–29 casting out *e* and healing the sick,
ph 182– 3 The act of . . . casting out *e* with Truth, shows
gl 583– 9 casting out *e* and healing the sick ;
cast out
s 136– 4 divine Principle, which would cast out *e*
ph 170–20 Jesus healed the sick and cast out *e*,
t 462– 6 can demonstrate C. S., cast out *e*,
casts out
pr 14–29 This understanding casts out *e*
a 25–15 casts out *e*, and triumphs over death.
33–24 casts out *e*, raises the dead from trespasses
f 230– 8 casts out *e* and heals the sick.
b 275–32 It casts out *e* and heals the sick.

error

casts out
o 350–11 Truth casts out *e* and heals the sick.
r 473–30 which heals the sick and casts out *e*,
495– 2 Truth casts out *e* now as surely as
causes disease
o 344–12 understood . . . that *e* causes disease,
chaff of
ap 565–21 fiery baptism will burn up the chaff of *e*
charges its lie
b 307–16 *E* charges its lie to Truth
claim of
f 233–13 false claim of *e* continues its delusions
closed to
pr 15– 6 Closed to *e*, it is open to Truth,
clouds of
g 557–19 Divine Science rolls back the clouds of *e*
conquer
b 339–31 You conquer *e* by denying its verity.
conquered
p 400– 6 This *e* conquered, we can despoil
consuming
ap 558–19 prophetically described . . . as consuming *e*.
contaminated by
b 287–32 Truth cannot be contaminated by *e*.
convinced of the
f 240–25 convinced of the *e* that is to be overcome.
corrects
c 259–29 which corrects *e* with truth
correspond with
b 294– 1 physical senses . . . correspond with *e*.
counteracts
p 414– 7 salutary action of truth, which counteracts *e*.
create
b 279–15 no more . . . than Truth can create *e*,
287–12 Did God, Truth, create *e*?
creates
g 546– 6 If Mind, God, creates *e*, that . . . would
darkness of
ph 191–15 chasing away the darkness of *e*.
débris of
b 289– 3 temporal *débris* of *e*, belief in sin, sickness,
deliverance from
a 22–23 Final deliverance from *e*,
delusion that
gl 594– 7 first delusion that *e* exists as fact ;
demanded by
p 390–18 the last penalty demanded by *e*.
demands
g 532–29 *e* demands that *mind* shall see and feel through
designs of
gl 583–28 DAN . . . error, working out the designs of *e* ;
destroy
f 233–30 is designed to rebuke and destroy *e*.
o 353–12 omnipotent Truth certainly does destroy *e*.
p 400–19 lifting thought above . . . you destroy *e*.
418–27 in your efforts to destroy *e*.
r 496– 1 error cannot destroy *e*.
g 542–19 Let Truth uncover and destroy *e*
548–14 Every agony of . . . helps error to destroy *e*,
destroying
p 368–19 healing the sick and destroying *e*.
401– 8 If . . . destroying *e*, causes chemicalization
t 463–24 first step towards destroying *e*.
gl 589–17 rebuking and destroying *e* and bringing
destroys
sp 98– 6 which heals the sick and destroys *e*,
f 216– 8 Truth . . . destroys *e*.
252–10 understanding of Truth which destroys *e*,
b 339– 3 Truth destroys *e*, and Love destroys hate.
o 346–15 Disbelief in error destroys *e*,
350–30 Soul rebukes sense, and Truth destroys *e*.
t 452–14 the explanation which destroys *e*.
r 483–18 heals the sick, destroys *e*,
destroy the
p 423–10 the truth of being, to destroy the *e*.
destruction of
(*see* **destruction**)
devils, or
gl 583–18 thereby casting out devils, or *e*,
disappears
f 251–26 improves mankind until *e* disappears,
c 267–25 *e* disappears in celestial Truth.
p 406–13 Then *e* disappears. Sin and sickness will abate
disbelief in
o 346–15 Disbelief in *e* destroys error,
discern the
sp 85–11 and discern the *e* you would destroy.
discomfort under
an 101–28 Discomfort under *e* is preferable to comfort.
disease as
b 319– 3 Science depicts disease as *e*,
r 483– 5 We classify disease as *e*,
disease is an
p 400–16 if you understand that every disease is an *e*,

error

dispels
b 283– 1 Truth is the light which dispels *e·*.
dominion over
p 380–21 and prove man's dominion over *e·*.
drive
g 538– 3 drive *e·* out of all selfhood.
dying
a 42–20 belief . . . separate from God is a dying *e·*.
effects of
an 101–28 error cannot remove the effects of *e·*.
b 273–30 beliefs emit the effects of *e·* at all times,
r 473– 6 are to be classified as effects of *e·*.
g 537–21 to depict . . . the effects of *e·*.
effort of
g 554–17 first effort of *e·* has been and is to impute
efforts of
f 223–20 The efforts of *e·* to answer this question
ejection of
sp 97– 2 They will aid in the ejection of *e·*.
element of
t 463–12 has not a single element of *e·*,
end of
sp 95–20 We welcome . . . the end of *e·*,
96–19 disturbances will continue until the end of *e·*,
escape the
sp 83– 8 to escape the *e·* of these latter days.
every form of
p 418–29 Speak the truth to every form of *e·*.
evidence of
o 353– 8 Truth which contradicts the evidence of *e·*,
evil and
f 227–19 evil and *e·* lead into captivity.
evil or
r 489–25 the only source of evil or *e·*.
evolved by
g 523– 4 the mist of obscurity evolved by *e·*
excision of
t 462–25 indispensable to the excision of *e·*.
excludes itself
g 537–14 E· excludes itself from harmony,
experience of
f 237–18 To prevent the experience of *e·*
expression of
b 289– 9 He is little else than the expression of *e·*.
exterminator of
r 469–13 The exterminator of *e·* is
face of
g 503–13 saith to the darkness upon the face of *e·*,
fact concerning
sp 92–22 Until the fact concerning *e·* . . . appears,
falls
a 37– 8 *e·* falls only before the sword of Spirit.
falsity and
r 474–31 Truth destroys falsity and *e·*,
falsity of
b 294–32 Truth demonstrates the falsity of *e·*.
g 537–21 to depict the falsity of *e·*
fatal
b 303–24 The belief that . . . is a fatal *e·*.
fear of
p 380–21 Truth can prevent the fear of *e·*,
felt the power
a 20–19 when *e·* felt the power of Truth,
finity of
f 202–21 earthly experience discloses the finity of *e·*
forms of
f 204– 3 All forms of *e·* support the false conclusions
c 264–24 proved them to be forms of *e·*.
forsake
b 323– 4 in the endeavor to forsake *e·*
foundations of
b 273–12 tears away the foundations of *e·*.
o 357–12 the foundations of *e·* would be sapped
from . . . to Truth
p 370–31 from *e·* to Truth, from matter to Spirit.
from . . . to truth
sp 77– 3 the change from *e·* to truth
fundamental
m 65– 9 some fundamental *e·* in the marriage state.
ph 171–31 fundamental *e·* lies in the supposition
give up
b 330– 1 in proportion as mortals give up *e·*
greater
an 104–25 the greater *e·* overcoming the lesser.
104–26 greater *e·* thereafter occupies the ground,
s 123– 2 will surely destroy the greater *e·*
greater than
f 223–10 Remember that truth is greater than *e·*,
growth of
ph 188–22 Sickness is a growth of *e·*,
guilt and
ap 568– 1 Innocence and Truth overcome guilt and *e·*.
has no creator
b 277–10 and *e·* has no creator.

error

has no foothold
b 282–18 *e·* has no foothold in Truth.
head of
f 216– 8 Truth bruises the head of *e·*
helps
g 548–14 helps *e·* to destroy error,
he vanquished
a 54– 5 With the affluence of Truth, he vanquished *e·*
hides
g 542– 5 *e·* hides behind a lie and excuses guilt,
his
b 308–21 smote the sinew, or strength, of his *e·*,
308–26 perceiving his *e·* and his need of help,
history of
g 521–29 history of *e·* or matter, if veritable, would
522–13 the history of *e·* in its externalized forms,
525–26 if we give the same heed to the history of *e·*
530–26 The history of *e·* is a dream-narrative.
human
b 294– 1 the avenues and instruments of human *e·*,
p 401– 2 Any human *e·* is its own enemy,
ap 563–10 dragon stands for the sum total of human *e·*.
husbandman of
ph 180– 2 mortal mind is the husbandman of *e·*,
hypothesis of
g 522–28 is based on some hypothesis of *e·*,
ignorance of the
t 446–31 Ignorance of the *e·* to be eradicated
illusion of
g 523–16 is significant of the illusion of *e·*,
illusion or
g 556– 1 and not the belief in illusion or *e·*.
impossible for
t 448–22 well knowing it to be impossible for *e·*, evil,
impotence of
t 454– 5 which illustrates the impotence of *e·*.
impotent
sp 97– 7 the more impotent *e·* becomes as a belief.
g 555–18 Only impotent *e·* would seek to unite
impurity and
m 65–22 impurity and *e·* are left among the lees.
in action
f 207– 7 Error of statement leads to *e·* in action.
incarnate
gl 583–11 comes to the flesh to destroy incarnate *e·*.
infers from
b 282–32 rule of inversion infers from *e·* its opposite,
in solution
p 372– 4 matter was originally *e·* in solution,
in the premise
ph 167–16 an *o·* in the premise must appear in the
b 277–27 This *e·* in the premise leads to errors in
involves
b 301– 8 but his sense of substance involves *e·*
involving
b 286–23 temporal thoughts are human, involving *e·*,
is a coward
p 308– 4 E· is a coward before Truth.
is always
g 554– 8 E· is always *e·*. It is no *thing*,
is a supposition
r 472–14 E· is a supposition that pleasure and pain,
is false
b 287–22 E· is false, mortal belief ;
is limited
r 466–14 Truth is limitless ; *e·* is limited.
is mortal
b 337–12 while *e·* is mortal and discordant.
r 466–13 Truth is immortal ; *e·* is mortal.
is non-intelligent
r 466–14 *e·* is non-intelligent.
is nothing
o 346–10 we need to understand that *e·* *is* nothing,
is not real
f 251– 1 E· is not real, hence it is not
is not true
t 461–25 *e·* is not true, hence it is unreal.
is opposed
p 406–20 E· is opposed to Life.
is reduced
sp 91–11 *e·* is reduced to its native nothingness,
is self-destroyed
p 368– 8 still clearer as *e·* is self-destroyed.
is unlike Truth
r 468– 5 because *e·* is unlike Truth.
is unreal
c 265–21 the *e·* is unreal and obsolete.
p 368– 4 in the fact that Truth is real and *e·* **is unreal.**
r 466–15 Truth is real, and *e·* is unreal.
472–18 E· is unreal because untrue.
its
sp 97–18 the more obvious its *e·*,
s 144–12 the more obstinately tenacious its *e·* ;
ph 197–29 belief loses some portion of its *e·*.
b 322–13 belief may be prepared to relinquish its *e·*.

error

knowledge of
  f 252– 9   A knowledge of *e·* and of its operations
  g 533–27   cross-questioning man as to his knowledge of *e·*,
latent
  ap 559– 5   upon elementary, latent *e·*,
leading
  p 377–21   Remove the leading *e·* or governing fear
learned from
  b 288–32   what mortals seem to have learned from *e·*,
level of
  ph 173– 9   supposition, . . . Truth is reduced to the level of *e·*,
love rebuking
  gl 594–15   love rebuking *e·* ; reproof of sensualism.
lurking
  p 419– 2   Lurking *e·*, lust, envy, revenge, malice,
made up of
  b 295–25   mortal thought is made up of *e·*.
make nothing of
  sp 92–24   the ability to make nothing of *e·* will be
manifestation of the
  g 532–26   Fear was the first manifestation of the *e·*
mass of
  s 118–11   It must destroy the entire mass of *e·*,
material
  f 252–11   mortal, material *e·* finally disappears,
  b 291–31   mortal man is divested of all material *e·*.
  309– 8   He had conquered material *e·* with the
  315–23   spiritual Truth destroys material *e·*,
matter and
  ph 181–31   will incline you to the side of matter and *e·*.
  o 347–26   dream that matter and *e·* are something
matter as
  b 278–29   We define matter as *e·*, because it is the
matter or
  s 145–27   towards other forms of matter or *e·*,
  f 206– 3   no consciousness of the existence of matter or *e·*.
methods of
  t 451–25   may perceive the nature and methods of *e·*
mirage of
  f 244– 3   is not real, but is illusion, the mirage of *e·*.
mortal
  (*see* **mortal**)
motive-power of
  gl 597–20   WILL.   The motive-power of *e·* ;
much
  b 295–21   lost much materiality— much *e·*
must be mortal
  r 468– 5   If Truth is immortal, *e·* must be mortal,
named
  b 276–27   the *nothingness* named *e·*.
  r 471– 6   The unlikeness of Truth,— named *e·*,
  gl 594– 2   the opposite of Truth, named *e·* ;
nature of
  g 555– 9   This is the nature of *e·*.
neutralizes
  s 157–31   Science both neutralizes *e·* and destroys it.
neutralizing
  s 162– 6   alterative, neutralizing *e·* with Truth.
never imparts
  sp 85–32   truth communicates itself but never imparts *e·*.
never made
  ph 183–14   Truth never made *e·* necessary,
night of
  pref vii– 9   till across a night of *e·*
no
  s 129– 5   can tolerate no *e·* in premise or conclusion.
  131– 3   There is no *e·* in Science,
  f 210–31   immortal sense has no *e·* of sense,
  b 278– 8   even as in Truth there is no *e·*,
  283–12   It admits of no *e·*, but rests upon
  t 450–29   Who, . . . can say that there is no *e·* of belief?
  r 475– 2   To Truth there is no *e·*,— all is Truth.
  ap 567– 8   there is no *e·*, no sin, sickness, nor death.
no consciousness of
  f 243–25   Truth has no consciousness of *e·*.
no home in
  b 282–18   Truth has no home in *e·*,
nor obeying
  f 244– 6   never fearing nor obeying *e·* in any form.
no sense of
  f 210–31   it has no sense of *e·* ;
not
  p 420– 3   Truth not *e·*, Love not hate, . . . governs man.
not contaminated by
  b 304–20   Truth is not contaminated by *e·*.
nothingness of
  (*see* **nothingness**)
not Truth
  p 386–25   E·, not Truth, produces all the suffering
  r 474–27   *e·*, not Truth, is the author of the unreal,
now simulates
  g 528–20   *e·* now simulates the work of Truth,
of action
  g 550–15   Error of thought is reflected in *e·* of action.

error

of any kind
  sp 95–11   E· of any kind cannot hide from the law of God.
of any sort
  f 232–32   nor opportunity in Science for *e·* of any sort.
of belief
  ph 168–28   if the *e·* of belief was met and destroyed
  184–10   casting out by denial the *e·* of belief
  f 208– 8   What is it but an *e·* of belief,
  t 450–29   Who, . . . can say that there is no *e·* of belief?
  r 486–21   So long as this *e·* of belief remains,
of believing
  f 205– 7   When will the *e·* of believing that there is
  205–15   *e·* of believing that matter can be intelligent
offspring of
  gl 589– 2   A corporeal belief ; the offspring of *e·* ;
of measuring
  f 246–20   Except for the *e·* of measuring and limiting
of mortal belief
  a 20–14   he knew the *e·* of mortal belief,
of physical belief
  gl 586–18   FLESH.   An *e·* of physical belief ;
of sensation
  b 318–22   denies the *e·* of sensation in matter,
of statement
  f 207– 6   E· of statement leads to error in action.
  b 277–26   Matter is an *e·* of statement.
of the ages
  f 241–17   *e·* of the ages is preaching without practice.
of thought
  g 550–15   E· of thought is reflected in error of action.
one
  an 104–23   hypnotizer employs one *e·* to destroy another.
  s 143–13   the human mind uses one *e·* to
  r 486–13   one *e·* will not correct another.
only
  gl 585–21   the only *e·* of which is limitation ;
oppose
  s 145–25   Other methods undertake to oppose *e·* with
opposing
  sp 93–16   evil is the opposing *e·* and not the truth
opposite
  b 280–20   the opposite *e·* of many minds.
  g 521–25   now the opposite *e·*, . . . is to be set forth.
or unreality
  t 461–26   the *e·* or unreality of sin,
  461–28   the *e·* or unreality of disease,
out of
  b 296–28   An improved belief is one step out of *e·*,
outweigh
  p 392– 8   enables truth to outweigh *e·*.
overcoming
  a 21– 1   If Truth is overcoming *e·* in your daily walk
  an 104–25   the greater *e·* overcoming the lesser.
overruled the
  p 381–31   Christ Jesus overruled the *e·* which would
pantheistic
  b 307– 3   This pantheistic *e·*, or so-called *serpent*,
partakes of its own
  b 307–19   Thus *e·* partakes of its own nature
part of the
  r 482–26   Sickness is part of the *e·* which Truth casts out.
part with
  p 430– 4   Mortal mind must part with *e·*,
phantoms of
  f 215–20   and flee as phantoms of *e·* before truth
picture of
  g 526–25   second biblical account is a picture of *e·*
pierces the
  f 210–20   Truth pierces the *e·* of mortality
policy of
  t 452–23   take no risks in the policy of *e·*.
power over
  pr 5– 2   from demonstrating his power over *e·*.
practical
  t 452– 4   Incorrect reasoning leads to practical *e·*.
proves that
  b 338– 9   proves that *e·* has been ingrafted into the
quenching
  b 329–25   maintains the claim of Truth by quenching *e·*.
rabbinical
  a 30–20   Christ Jesus came to rebuke rabbinical *e·*
reap the
  t 462–12   he will inevitably reap the *e·* he sows.
rejection of
  a 20–15   [the rejection of *e·*]
relies
  b 277–19   E· relies upon a reversal of this order,
relinquish its
  b 322–13   belief may be prepared to relinquish its *e·*.
relinquishment of
  pr 7– 6   relinquishment of *e·* deprives material sense
remedy for
  s 143– 1   Truth is God's remedy for *e·* of every kind,
remove
  a 40– 1   Remove *e·* from thought,

error

remove the
ph 173–28 to remove the *e·* which the human mind
p 378–10 Remove the *e·*, and you destroy its effects.
415–25 To remove the *e·* producing disorder,
repeats
a 28–28 E· repeats itself.
replies
g 554–16 E· replies, "God made you."
representing
g 540–22 representing *e·* as assuming a divine character,
representing the
b 294–20 representing the *e·* that life and intelligence
represents
g 530–17 myth represents *e·* as always asserting its
546–13 represents *e·* as starting from an idea of good
reversed
b 319– 4 *e·* reversed as subserving the facts
reverse of
p 442–18 but the reverse of *e·* is true.
run into
f 250– 1 We run into *e·* when we divide Soul into souls,
says
r 478–23 E· says, "I am man ;"
sea of
ap 569–18 They are in the surging sea of *e·*,
seed of
g 535– 2 The seed of Truth and the seed of *e·*,
self-destroying
gl 581–17 Badel. Self-destroying *e·* ;
self-destruction of
b 293–27 they show the self-destruction of *e·*
self-evident
b 309–27 It is a self-evident *e·* to suppose that there
sense of
g 520–14 in which all sense of *e·* forever disappears
serpents of
gl 587–15 the serpents of *e·*, which say,
seven seals of
ap 572–15 open the seven seals of *e·* with Truth,
should not seem
s 131– 1 *e·* should not seem so real as truth.
shrank abashed
g 532–19 Ashamed before Truth, *e·* shrank abashed
sickness and
r 495– 8 classify sickness and *e·* as our Master did,
side of
f 205–29 Selfishness tips the beam . . . towards the side of *e·*,
signet of
gl 593–23 Seal. The signet of *e·* revealed by Truth.
simulates truth
sp 97– 5 the more closely *e·* simulates truth
sin and
b 290–23 sin and *e·* which possess us at the instant of
sin, or
ph 183–11 Scriptures inform us that sin, or *e·*,
soweth the wind
f 210–24 E· soweth the wind
standpoint of
g 545–24 From that standpoint of *e·*, they could not
state of
b 311–17 This state of *e·* is the mortal dream of life
states of
gl 592– 7 idolatry ; the subjective states of *e·* ;
still the
f 214–13 still the *e·*, not the truth of being.
stronger
an 104–28 before it was grasped by the stronger *e·*.
submission to
ph 183–24 Submission to *e·* superinduces loss of power.
such an
pr 5–23 Such an *e·* would impede true religion.
suffering is an
a 23– 9 suffering is an *e·* of sinful sense
suffer severely from
f 238–21 because we suffer severely from *e·*.
supplant
r 495–22 understanding will supplant *e·* with Truth,
suppose
f 250– 2 and suppose *e·* to be mind,
supposed reality of
gl 596–25 and the supposed reality of *e·*.
supposes man
b 287– 6 E· supposes man to be both mental and material.
suppositional
f 208– 1 obtained from suppositional *e·*,
r 472– 4 casts out suppositional *e·* and heals
supposition of
g 503–11 No supposition of *e·* enters there.
surface of
f 254–24 If you venture upon the quiet surface of *e·*
sympathy with
f 211–21 Sympathy with *e·* should disappear.
254–25 and are in sympathy with *e·*,

error

synonym for
g 529–30 Adam, the synonym for *e·*, stands for a
tenacity of
sp 77–18 according to the tenacity of *e·*.
b 296–21 depends upon the tenacity of *e·*.
termed
gl 580–16 the opposer of Truth, termed *e·* ;
term for
an 103–19 hypnotism is the specific term for *e·*,
testimony of
r 481–14 forbidden fruit . . . is the testimony of *e·*,
that
b 320–22 according to that *e·* man is mortal.
g 546– 6 that *e·* must exist in the
their
b 320–16 [or, in their *e·* they are]
p 405–31 causes mortals to retreat from their *e·*,
theorizes
b 295–31 *e·* theorizes that spirit is born of matter
this
a 42–20 This *e·* Jesus met with divine Science
sp 73–29 This *e·* Science will destroy.
f 237–27 and expect this *e·* to do more for them than
b 277–27 This *e·* in the premise leads to errors in
280–16 Through this *e·*, human belief comes to have
290–12 Hence Truth comes to destroy this *e·*
295–11 to escape from the mortality of this *e·*.
307–14 This *e·* has proved itself to be error.
p 400– 6 This *e·* conquered, we can despoil
r 470– 7 This *e·* assumed the loss of
486–21 So long as this *e·* of belief remains,
490– 2 grand truths of C. S. dispute this *e·*.
g 526–12 sickness, and death, follow in the train of this *e·*
543– 2 This *e·*, . . . yields to Truth
this is the
sp 93–29 and this is the *e·* embodied in the belief
g 531– 5 This is the *e·*, — that mortal man
thunderbolts of
b 288–15 lightnings and thunderbolts of *e·* may burst
treated
t 463–24 Our Master treated *e·* through Mind.
treated as
p 425–12 they should be treated as *e·*
treatment of
t 463–21 as to the proper treatment of *e·*
Truth against
o 358–16 calm and clear verdict of Truth against *e·*,
truth against
p 405–12 the arbiter of truth against *e·*.
Truth and
(*see* **Truth**)
truth and
(*see* **truth**)
Truth controls
s 145–17 in it Truth controls *e·*.
Truth decapitates
c 266– 3 sword . . . with which Truth decapitates *e·*,
Truth destroys
b 350– 9 Truth destroys *e·*, and Love destroys hate.
o 350–30 Soul rebukes sense, and Truth destroys *e·*.
Truth or
f 211– 5 say whether Truth or *e·* is the greater?
b 324–10 whether it be Truth or *e·*,
truth or
p 403–30 in proportion to the truth or *e·* which
Truth over
s 111–13 the power of Truth over *e·* ;
p 378–17 represents the power of Truth over *e·*,
406–22 the supremacy of Truth over *e·*,
r 484–25 Science . . . over material sense, and Truth over *e·*,
truth regarding
t 461–25 The truth regarding *e·* is, that
Truth upon
p 421–23 alterative effect produced by Truth upon *e·*,
trying to meet
ap 568– 8 fatal effects of trying to meet *e·* with error.
type of
gl 593–17 foaming, and dashing, it is a type of *e·*.
unconscious
ph 188– 6 is an unconscious *e·* in the beginning,
uncover
sp 92–21 Uncover *e·*, and it turns the lie upon you.
unnatural as
s 131– 1 Truth should not seem so . . . unnatural as *e·*,
unveils
g 542– 8 Truth, through her eternal laws, unveils *e·*.
utter
a 47–32 Jesus realized the utter *e·* of a belief in any
victory over
a 44– 1 Truth and Life must seal the victory over *e·*
views of
r 485–10 ephemeral views of *e·* ought to be obliterated
visible
ap 559– 8 exercised upon visible *e·* and audible sin.

error
voluntary
 r 491– 8 made up of involuntary and voluntary *e*·,
warfare against
 ap 568–32 in our warfare against *e*·,
wars with
 s 144–24 even as Truth wars with *e*·,
waves of
 t 455– 9 in order to walk over the waves of *e*·
way of
 g 536–10 The way of *e*· is awful to contemplate.
way to extract
 f 201–17 The way to extract *e*· from mortal mind
we find
 c 260–32 If we look to the body . . . for Truth, we find *e*· ;
we treat
 o 346–19 We treat *e*· through the understanding of Truth,
what is
 r 472–13 *Question.*— What is *e*·?
which impedes
 pr 2–21 an *e*· which impedes spiritual growth.
which prevents
 p 409–14 the *e*· which prevents mortals from knowing
wilful
 p 369–30 No man is physically healed in wilful *e*·
will cease
 r 476– 7 *E*· will cease to claim that soul is in body,
will never save
 a 24– 2 Firmness in *e*· will never save from sin,
will not expel
 r 482–27 *E*· will not expel *e*·.
world of
 pr 13–30 world of *e*· is ignorant of the world of Truth,
would establish
 ap 568– 2 ever since *e*· would establish material belief,
would simulate
 b 281–25 out of which *e*· would simulate creation
wrestled with
 gl 583– 7 who, having wrestled with *e*·, sin, and
wrestling with
 b 308–16 Jacob was *alone*, wrestling with *e*·,
yields
 b 329–31 till *e*· yields to Truth.

---

 pr 7– 1 The only civil sentence which he had for *e*·
   11–17 Truth bestows no pardon upon *e*·,
 a 19– 5 cannot reconcile Truth to *e*·,
   30–25 between the offspring . . . of Truth and of *e*·.
   36– 7 would be for Truth to pardon *e*·.
   52–12 foresight of the reception *e*· would give him.
 sp 72–19 *E*· is not a convenient sieve
   74–11 the *e*· which has held the belief dissolves
   77– 6 *E*· brings its own self-destruction
   79– 3 Warning people against death is an *e*· that
   92–29 The mistake of thinking that *e*· can be real,
   92–31 leads to belief in the superiority of *e*·.
   96– 5 Before *e*· is wholly destroyed, there will be
   97–22 they bring *e*· from under cover.
   97–24 the louder will *e*· scream,
 s 123– 6 the *e*· relating to soul and body,
   126– 2 *E*· will be no longer used in stating truth.
   145–25 Other methods . . . oppose error with *e*·,
   154– 1 Neither . . . should ever tempt us to cherish *e*·
 ph 183–15 nor devised a law to perpetuate *e*·.
   188–23 *E*· rehearses *e*·.
   191–30 Truth never mingles with *e*·.
 f 201–14 Let us disrobe *e*·.
   204–31 The *e*·, which says that Soul is in body,
   231–13 If . . . truth results in *e*·, then
   239–12 success in *e*· is defeat in Truth.
   245– 1 The *e*· of thinking that we are growing old,
   251–13 Sickness, as well as sin, is an *e*·
 b 269–10 The first is *e*· ; the latter is truth.
   281– 7 *E*· presupposes man to be both mind and
   282–26 *E*· is the so-called intelligence of mortal mind.
   286–29 *e*· must also say, "I am true."
   286–30 *e*·, the lie, destroys itself.
   287– 9 We call the absence of Truth, *e*·.
   287–18 nor is *e*· the offshoot of Mind.
   287–25 The supposition that . . . is an *e*·.
   288– 2 *e*·, *Truth's unlikeness, is unreal.*
   291–31 As for spiritual *e*· there is none.
   294–11 This mortal belief, misnamed *man*, is *e*·,
   299–26 Corporeal sense, or *e*·, may seem to hide Truth,
   307– 5 that is, I will make *e*· as
   307–14 This error has proved itself to be *e*·.
   318–14 We must cause the *e*· to cease
   318–20 as the *e*· . . . yields to the reality of
   322–32 than to rid one's self of *e*·.
   329–29 *e*· into which mortal mind is plunged,
   338– 8 the *e*· which must be destroyed by Truth.
   338–22 it stands for obstruction, *e*·,
 o 343–14 Jesus strips all disguise from *e*·,
   347–15 Is it *e*· which is restoring our
   347–31 These critics will then see that *e*· is
   351–17 while *e*· seems as potent and real

error
 o 353–22 When we learn that *e*· is not real.
 p 367–30 *e*· should be known as nothing.
   367–32 *e*·, Truth's opposite, has no might.
   368–16 more faith in the truth of being than . . . in *e*
   369–32 It is *e*· even to murmur
   391–13 It is *e*· to suffer for aught but your own sins.
   392– 5 taken into account and the *e*· be rebuked.
   394–12 enthrones matter through *e*·.
   398– 5 spirit [*e*·] cried, and rent him — *Mark* 9 : 26.
   401–11 truth of being must transform the *e*·
   402–22 The *e*·, mesmerism — or hypnotism,
   406–19 Resist evil — *e*· of every sort — and it will
   408– 1 Every sort of sickness is *e*·,
   408– 4 nor discovered to be *e*·
   418– 6 in contradistinction to the *e*· that life,
 t 447–13 false charity does not forever conceal *e*· ;
   450–13 They do not incline longingly to *e*·,
   452–12 When *e*· confronts you, withhold not the rebuke
   454–13 truth which strips all disguise from *e*·.
   454–15 points out to his student *e*· as well as truth,
   458– 9 Another plank in the platform is this, that *e*·
   461–24 Both sin and sickness are *e*·,
   463–22 whether *e*· is manifested in forms of
 r 467–20 belief that the greater can be in the lesser is an *e*·
   469–17 evil — is not Mind, is not Truth, but *e*·,
   472–16 *E*· is neither Mind nor one of Mind's faculties.
   472–17 *E*· is the contradiction of Truth.
   472–18 *E*· is a belief without understanding.
   472–20 If *e*· were true, its truth would be *e*·,
   473– 5 Truth, God, is not the father of *e*·.
   474–25 must *e*· still be immortal?
   476– 6 *E*·, urged to its final limits, is
   483–14 affixed . . . the name "*e*" to corporeal sense,
   485– 1 If *e*· is necessary to define or to reveal
   486–13 Death is not the result of Truth but of *e*·,
   496– 1 soon ascertain that *e*· cannot destroy error.
 g 523– 5 and finally declares that God knows *e*·
   523– 5 and that *e*· can improve His creation.
   523–11 In *e*· everything comes from beneath,
   524–22 How could . . . *e*· be the enunciator of Truth?
   528–15 Here falsity, *e*·, credits Truth, God, with
   528–22 and declaring what great things *e*· has done.
   532–27 *e*· began and will end the dream of matter.
   533–24 but *e*· has its suppositional day
   537–16 *E*· tills its own barren soil
   542– 6 cannot forever be concealed.
   542– 9 sets upon *e*· the mark of the beast.
   545–15 *E*· tills the whole ground
   545–31 "As in Adam [*e*·] all die, — *I Cor.* 15 : 22.
   548– 3 C. S. separates *e*· from truth,
   551–29 *e*· declares that the material seed must
   555– 8 not comprehend what you say about *e*·."
   555–11 *E*· would have itself received as mind,
   555–14 *e*· is neither mind nor the outcome of Mind.
 ap 568– 8 fatal effects of trying to meet error with *e*·.
 gl 579–15 ADAM. *E*· ; a falsity ;
   582– 7 *e*· masquerading as the possessor of life,
   582–25 the *e*· which would make man mortal
   583–27 *e*·, working out the designs of error ;
   584–17 DEVIL. Evil ; a lie ; *e*· ;
   585–15 definition of
   585–25 *e*· ; the belief that the human race
   586–11 ignorance ; *e*· ; desire ; caution.
   588– 1 Mortal belief ; *e*· ; lust ; remorse ; hatred ;
   591–26 *e*· creating other errors ;
   593– 6 PURSE. Laying up treasures in matter ; *e*·.
   593– 7 RED DRAGON. *E*· ; fear ; inflammation ;
   593–13 sensuality ; delusion ; mortality ; *e*·.
   595– 5 TARES. Mortality ; *e*· ; sin ; sickness ;
   595–19 beliefs, opinions, knowledge ; matter ; *e*· ;
   595–24 Impure thoughts ; *e*· ; sin ; dirt.
   598–17 *E*· ; fornication ; temptation ; passion.

Error's
 p 438–24 and smuggles *E*· goods into market
error's
 sp 79–10 dig up every seed of *e*· sowing.
 s 154– 1 we should not be *e*· advocate.
 f 254–26 What is there to strip off *e*· disguise?
 b 307–31 Above *e*· awful din, blackness, and chaos,
 o 346–20 because Truth is *e*· antidote.
   357–12 and *e*· destruction ensured ;
 g 543– 7 more beautifully apparent at *e*· demise.
 ap 559– 5 the source of all *e*· visible forms
   564– 3 *e*· own nature and methods.

errors
all its
 ph 177– 3 it must relinquish all its *e*·,
all sorts of
 c 257–22 Finite mind manifests all sorts of *e*·,
both are
 p 379– 3 both are *e*·, announced as partners
casting out the
 s 138–13 casting out the *e*· of mortal mind.

errors

correct the
r 494–20 serves to correct the *e·* of corporeal sense ;
destroy the
f 216–13 begins at once to destroy the *e·* of mortal sense
destroy those
a 53–26 He knew . . . and could destroy those *e·* ;
fevers are
p 379–25 Fevers are *e·* of various types.
fundamental
g 545–13 Such fundamental *e·* send falsity into all
history of the
an 101– 5 in the history of the *e·* of the human mind,
human
g 533–10 Here there is an attempt to trace all human *e·*
ignorant of the
p 408–32 ignorant of the *e·* it includes
illusive
o 343–19 illusive *e·* — which he could and did destroy.
leads to
b 277–27 This error in the premise leads to *e·* in
mortal
a 53–26 mortal *e·* which constitute the material body,
multitudinous
a 43–30 and the multitudinous *e·* growing from
of all sorts
p 419– 3 *E·* of all sorts tend in this direction.
of belief
sp 96–23 until all *e·* of belief yield to
t 450–25 knows that they are *e·* of belief,
offending
p 392–31 Exclude from mortal mind the offending *e·* ;
of sense
f 240–27 In trying to undo the *e·* of sense
b 273–14 till the *e·* of sense are eliminated,
p 406–11 The Science of being unveils the *e·* of sense,
old
t 460–32 finally the shadow of old *e·* was no longer cast
other
gl 591–27 mythology ; error creating other *e·* ;
such
s 152–11 Such *e·* beset every material theory,
these
s 121–23 and corrects these *e·* by the simple rule that
f 232–21 nor did he illustrate these *e·* by his practice.
b 290–25 but endure until the death of these *e·*.
328– 8 These *e·* are not thus really destroyed,
o 356–21 as He is of experiencing these *e·*.
p 404– 5 meet and destroy these *e·* with the truth
405– 9 Choke these *e·* in their early stages,
triad of
s 122– 5 facts of Life, . . . defeat this triad of *e·*,
o 356–22 subject to this triad of *e·*,

———

a 30–26 If we have triumphed sufficiently over the *e·*
f 207–25 They are the *e·*, which presuppose
c 267–24 by reversal, *e·* serve as waymarks to the
b 294–17 even the *e·* that are destroyed by Truth
t 451– 1 the *e·* which Truth must and will annihilate
gl 594–24 the opposites of God , *e·* ; hallucinations,

errs

sp 99–16 the human sense of things *e·*
f 250– 9 which never *e·*, and is ever conscious ;
t 456–12 greatly *e·*, ignorantly or intentionally,

erudite

a 24–20 Does *e·* theology regard the crucifixion

erudition

sp 88–27 It is due to inspiration rather than to *e·*.

escape

pr 6– 1 We cannot *e·* the penalty due for sin.
a 36– 7 *E·* from punishment is not in accordance with
41–12 cannot forever break the Golden Rule and *e·* the
48–13 or even wish. to *e·* the exalting ordeal
sp 83– 8 to *e·* the error of these latter days.
99– 4 divine Principle by which mortals can *e·*
99– 5 to *e·* from sin, is what the Bible demands.
an 103– 7 by which man can *e·* from sin
s 128–21 its *e·* into the surrounding atmosphere.
151–16 from which multitudes would gladly *e·*.
f 227–22 *E·* from the bondage of sickness, sin, and
c 258–10 which must *e·* from its environments
b 295–10 in order to *e·* from the mortality
316– 3 mortals may learn how to *e·* from evil.
327–12 way to *e·* the misery of sin is to cease sinning.
p 432–26 endeavoring to assist the prisoner to *e·*
ap 571–12 *E·* from evil, and designate those as unfaithful

escaped

an 105–22 Whoever uses his . . . powers like an *e·* felon

escapes

s 128–13 *e·* . . . from itself, and requires less repose.
f 203–23 then mortals believe that . . . Soul, *e·* from

eschew

sp 99–20 some others who *e·* their false beliefs.

eschewed

s 137–13 Jesus completely *e·* the narrow opinion

eschews

s 112–13 divine Science which *e·* man-made systems,
127–30 C. S. *e·* what is called natural science,

escutcheon

p 437– 6 It blots the fair *e·* of omnipotence.

esoteric

an 101–32 proportional to one's faith in *e·* magic.

Esoteric Magic

p 441–22 Hypnotism, Oriental Witchcraft, and *E· M·*

especially

s 117–21 miracles (marvels) wrought by Jesus and *e·*
127–15 term C. S. relates to *e·*
ph 170–31 all ills have gone forth, *e·* despair.
b 340– 5 conveys the C. S. thought, *e·* when the
o 348–24 *e·* when by so doing our own condition
351–20 *e·* if we consider Satan as a
p 362– 8 *e·* under the stern rules of rabbinical law,
363–11 those around him . . . *e·* his host,
414– 4 treatment of insanity is *e·* interesting.
418–23 *e·* by the spirit of Truth and Love
t 444–32 the Science of healing, *e·* its ethics,
451–25 *e·* any subtle degree of evil,
g 554–31 *e·* those of the human form.

Esquimaux

sp 82–29 do we look for help to the *E·*
ph 174– 1 *E·* restore health by incantations

essay

s 111–20 for the best *e·* on Natural Science,
111–21 an *e·* calculated to offset the tendency
163–21 Dr. Chapman, . . . in a published *e·* said :

essays

pref ix–12 Certain *e·* written at that early date

Esse

sp 93–19 the real nature of the divine *E·*,

essence

nature and
s 107–12 inspired with a diviner nature and *e·* ;
b 270– 6 in its very nature and *e·* ;
t 460– 7 the nature and *e·* of all being,
of divinity
g 537– 9 was never the *e·* of divinity
of Love
b 333–25 in the divine nature, the *e·* of Love.
of this Science
b 271–23 Sermon on the Mount is the *e·* of this Science,
real
b 292–32 mortal man is not the real *e·* of manhood,
resembles its
sp 97– 6 resembles its *e·*, mortal mind,
same in
b 331–29 same in *e·*, though multiform in office :
spiritual
a 25– 3 The spiritual *e·* of blood is sacrifice,
true
b 293–18 counterfeits the true *e·* of spirituality or

———

r 465–13 the nature, *e·*, and wholeness of Deity.

essential

a 27–30 the *e·* religion he came to establish
sp 98–30 they are not deprived of their *e·* vitality.
s 117–10 God's *e·* language is spoken of in
b 285–20 It is *e·* to understand, instead of believe,
331–32 the threefold, *e·* nature of the infinite.
o 341–12 Proof is *e·* to a due estimate of this subject.
347–18 restoring an *e·* element of Christianity,
349–10 Two *e·* points of C. S. are,
p 374– 1 mortal mind has decided upon as *e·* for health.
t 460– 8 the divine Mind and Love's *e·* qualities.
g 553–13 *e·* to their maintenance and reproduction,

establish

a 27–29 the essential religion he came to *e·*
s 108– 9 *e·* the truism that the only sufferer is
112–25 affords no foundation upon which to *e·* a
ph 189– 9 the power of C. S. to *e·* harmony
196–18 no relation to God wherewith to *e·*
f 203– 8 this understanding would *e·* health.
b 270–20 *e·* the definition of omnipotence.
280–20 But behold the zeal of belief to *e·*
335– 5 would . . . *e·* a basis for pantheism.
o 356– 7 Discord can never *e·* the facts of harmony.
p 373–22 *E·* the scientific sense of health,
414–11 truth and love will *e·* a healthy state,
428–13 Thus we may *e·* in truth the temple, or body,
t 464– 7 to *e·* the stately operations of C. S.,
r 486–11 The belief that he dies will not *e·* his
ap 568– 3 ever since error would *e·* material belief,

established

pref xii– 4   which had been e· in the United States,
     xii– 8   pastor of the first e· Church of Christ, Scientist ;
 pr   3– 6   The rule is already e·, and it is our task
  a 20–10   but he e· no ritualistic worship.
     24– 5   (e· by hierarchies, and instigated
  s 131–30   e· his claim to the Messiahship.
    136– 1   Jesus e· his church and maintained
    138–17   Jesus e· in the Christian era the
    162–24   healthy organizations have been e·
  c 255– *   Thy throne is e· of old :— Psal. 93 : 2.
  o 348–11   Jesus e· this foundational fact,
  p 384–28   In Science this is an e· fact
  r 467–13   true brotherhood of man will be e·.
    473–26   Jesus e· what he said by demonstration,

establishes

  a 23–19   and e· the claims of God.
  m 63–12   civil law e· very unfair differences
  b 279– 6   The doom of matter e· the conclusion
  r 491–15   e· man forever in the divine likeness,

establishing

  s 135– 8   e· the Science of God's unchangeable law.
  b 274–24   e· it by demonstration.

establishment

  s 110–11   the e· of the kingdom of heaven on earth.
    150– 9   for its e· as a permanent dispensation

estate

  c 258–30   impossible . . . to fall from his high e·.
  g 514–21   the millennial e· pictured by Isaiah :
    548– 7   man has never lost his spiritual e·

esteemed

  a 49–32   e· Jesus as "stricken, smitten— Isa. 53 : 4.

estimate

  s 129–31   small e· of the pleasures of the table.
  c 262–21   will then drop the false e· of life and
  o 341–12   Proof is essential to a due e· of this subject.
    360– 3   all is won, by a right e· of what is real."
 ap 560–16   or entertain a false e· of anyone whom

estimates

 an 105–14   and human law rightly e· crime,
  b 311–14   false e· of soul as dwelling in sense

estimation

  a 47–24   in order to raise himself in popular e·.

etceteras

  b 330–32   with all the e· that word includes.

eternal

and harmonious
  b 320–18   man's e· and harmonious existence as image,
and real
  b 300–13   temporal and unreal never touch the e· and real.
  r 494–27   The other is the e· and real evidence,
as God
  g 554– 3   universe, inclusive of man, is as e· as God,
as the Mind
  g 513–18   as e· as the Mind conceiving them ;
being
  f 232– 8   the claims of harmonious and e· being
  g 521– 3   conscious spiritual harmony and e· being.
being is
  s 122–27   Life goes on unchanged and being is e·.
  p 407–23   In Science, all being is e·, spiritual,
bliss
 ap 577–10   no impediment to e· bliss,
builder
  p 428–16   the e· builder, the everlasting Father,
causes
  b 278–20   it would follow that there are two e· causes,
chain
 ph 172–12   divine Science reveals the e· chain
children
  g 529–11   His e· children, belonging to
Christ
  a 38–23   The e· Christ, . . . never suffered.
  b 334–14   the e· Christ and the corporeal Jesus
coexistent and
  g 516–22   Man . . . as coexistent and e· with God
    520–10   Principle and . . . are coexistent and e·.
 gl 581–11   God and man coexistent and e· ;
consciousness
  c 263–30   a scientific e· consciousness of creation.
copartnership
  o 356–17   neither a present nor an e· copartnership
dawn
 sp 95–26   the light which heralds Christ's e· dawn
demand
 gl 595–11   the e· demand of divine Science.
demands
 ph 184–13   the only legitimate and e· demands
distinct and
 sp 70–13   maintains all identities, . . . as distinct and e·.
Ego
  b 314– 6   Thus he found the e· Ego,

eternal

Elohim
  g 515–16   The e· Elohim includes the
entity
  b 301–13   constitutes the only real and e· entity.
ever present and
  b 306–29   Life and the universe, ever present and e·.
existence
  m 65– 6   spiritual and e· existence may be discerned.
  b 319–13   the infinite cycles of e· existence,
  p 387–20   adhering to the realities of e· existence,
fact
  g 544–10   Matter cannot change the e· fact
facts
  b 293–16   Life, perpetuating the e· facts
Father-Mother
  b 335–26   nothing unlike the e· Father-Mother, God.
God
  p 415– 4   Mind in every case is the e· God,
good
  f 213–14   attraction towards infinite and e· good
  b 340–19   have no other spirit or mind but God, e· good,
 ap 561– 2   which works out the ends of e· good
good and
  b 269–20   this advantage . . . they are good and e·.
harmonious and
 sp 88–14   Ideas are spiritual, harmonious, and e·.
 an 102– 2   all that is real, harmonious, and e·,
  s 114–29   man, is spiritual, harmonious, and e·.
    151–28   is found harmonious and e·.
 ph 184–17   man is harmonious and e·.
  f 209–24   the universe will be found harmonious and e·.
    232– 8   the claims of harmonious and e· being
  b 336–26   are inseparable, harmonious, and e·.
  r 472– 8   that which is harmonious and e·.
    472–25   All reality is . . . harmonious and e·.
harmony
   (see **harmony**)
history
  r 471– 5   unchanged in its e· history.
honors
  a 39– 4   He won e· honors.
indestructible and
  a 51–14   his spiritual life, indestructible and e·,
  p 402–13   Man is indestructible and e·.
  r 477–17   immortal idea of being, indestructible and e·.
individuality
 sp 91–19   man's spiritual and e· individuality,
  b 282– 9   self-existent and e· individuality or Mind ;
interpretation
  t 461–14   the e· interpretation of God and man.
in the heavens
  l 454– 9   "e· in the heavens."— II Cor. 5 : 1.
law
  p 385–11   Let us remember that the e· law of right,
laws
  g 542– 7   Truth, through her e· laws, unveils error.
Life
   (see **Life**)
life
   (see **life**)
Life is
  f 246–27   Life is e·. We should find this out,
likeness
  f 246– 5   are the e· likeness of their Maker.
  p 395– 5   immortality and e· likeness to God.
Love
  a 19– 1   derived from the e· Love
man
  a 29–32   Spirit is harmonious and man e·.
 ph 191– 6   this e· man will include in that likeness
  b 311–31   the spiritual, e· man is not touched by
mandate
  g 520–26   growth is the e· mandate of Mind.
manifestations
  b 275–16   the e· manifestations of the infinite divine
man is
  g 538–30   the sinless, real man is e·.
means
  t 444–10   right use of temporary and e· means.
Mind
   (see **Mind**)
nature
  b 333– 9   Christ expresses God's spiritual, e· nature.
noon
  f 246–12   Manhood is its e· noon,
not
  b 279– 9   and is therefore not e·.
 ap 569–25   Scriptures declare that evil is temporal, not e·.
order
  b 334–18   exist in the e· order of divine Science,
perfect and
  m 69–16   and of man . . . perfect and e·.
  f 205–13   and made all perfect and e·.
  c 260– 8   the ideal of all that is perfect and e·.

eternal

perfect and
b 280– 3 not products of the . . . perfect, and e· *All.*
286–21 God's thoughts are perfect and e·,
292–12 not the likeness of God, the perfect and e·.
r 471– 4 all that He creates are perfect and e·,
gl 583–22 that which is perfect and e· ;
perfection
g 550–13 The true sense of being and its e· perfection
Principle
b 299–32 If . . . he would have no e· Principle
312–20 man's e· Principle is ever-present Life.
gl 579–11 faith in the divine Life and in the e· Principle
592–16 MOTHER. God ; divine and e· Principle ;
pure and
r 467–15 man is the likeness of God, pure and e·,
quality
r 469– 9 It is the primal and e· quality of
real and
(see **real**)
real is
o 353–16 All the real is e·.
r 474–29 while all that is real is e·.
realities
sp 78– 5 they are not the e· realities of Mind.
reality
g 538–14 significant of e· reality or being.
reflection
b 296– 3 man is the spiritual, e· reflection of God.
resplendent and
f 247–29 shining resplendent and e· over age and decay.
Science
sp 78–32 the invisible good dwelling in e· Science.
s 150– 5 demonstrated as an immanent, e· Science,
c 258–29 under the government of God in e· Science,
scientific nor
b 297–18 it is neither scientific nor e·,
self-existent and
b 278–19 self-creative, self-existent, and e·.
282– 0 self-existent and e· individuality or Mind ;
g 555–18 God, the self-existent and e·,
sinless and
b 304–15 The perfect man . . . is sinless and e·.
spiritual and
m 65– 9 spiritual and e· existence may be discerned.
sp 91–19 man's spiritual and e· individuality,
ph 190–19 immortal man, spiritual and e·, is found to be
c 264– 7 mental picture is spiritual and e·.
b 286–26 but counterfeits of the spiritual and e·.
302– 4 the real man is spiritual and e·.
335–14 Things spiritual and e· are substantial.
336–18 Immortal man is . . . always spiritual and e·.
337–28 the opposite of the real or the spiritual and e·.
o 356– 1 in support of spiritual and e· truths,
p 410– 2 heed to C. S., which is spiritual and e·,
substance
b 290–25 e· substance, which cannot destroy the
301–11 and reflects the e· substance, or Spirit,
temporal or
o 360–17 This ideal is either temporal or e·.
things
b 337–24 E· things (verities) are God's thoughts
Truth
(see **Truth**)
truth
b 303–14 statement . . . contradicts this e· truth.
unchangeable and
s 120– 4 Spirit, is God, unchangeable and e· ;
unfallen and
r 476–32 man in God's image is unfallen and e·.
unfolding
b 335–23 we gain the e· unfolding of Life
verities
s 110– 4 These e· verities reveal primeval existence
r 476–13 the only and e· verities of man.
verity
f 252–12 the e· verity, man created by
b 296– 2 whereas Science unfolds the e· verity,
r 468– 7 sin is not the e· verity of being.
480–28 This is the e· verity of divine Science.
g 502–25 e· verity and unity of God and man,
wonder
g 503–15 Hence the e· wonder,

pr 13–29 ignorant . . . of man's e· incorporeal existence.
m 68–31 the unbroken links of e·, harmonious being
s 115–16 spiritual idea, individual, perfect, e·.
140–25 C. S. God is universal, e·, divine Love,
145–23 ignorance of the laws of e· and unerring Mind.
ph 173–20 Man is spiritual, individual, and e· ;
f 247–10 Beauty, as well as truth, is e· ;
c 267– 2 the spiritual idea, . . . is e·.
267– 8 God is Father, e·, self-created, infinite.
b 275– 5 This shows that matter . . . is not e·.
278–32 Spirit is substantial and e·.

eternal

b 279–12 and they have the advantage of being e·.
287– 5 All creations of Spirit are e· ;
290– 1 Because Life is God, Life must be e·,
334– 1 not that the human Jesus was or is e·,
335–18 Spirit is e·, divine.
335–28 immutable, immortal, divine, e·.
335–29 Nothing unspiritual can be real, . . . or e·.
336– 5 never . . . the e· into the temporal,
336–30 God and man coexist and are e·.
r 468–17 *Answer.* — Substance is that which is e·
475–18 the reflection of God, . . . and therefore is e· ;
486–24 spiritual senses of man, are e·.
gl 580–22 false supposition that Life is not e·,
587– 6 all-acting, all-wise, all-loving, and e· ;
590– 2 the realm of unerring e·, and

eternality

s 123–28 indicates the e· of the scientific order

eternally

s 118–11 e· glorified in man's spiritual freedom.
143–29 If Mind was . . . and must be first e·,
f 240–17 revolutions of the universe of Mind go on e·.
b 302– 9 when God is all and e· his.
r 495–19 life harmonious — as Life e· is

eternity

all
g 519– 2 from all e· knoweth His own ideas.
belief of the
b 278–23 The belief of the e· of matter
foretaste of
gl 598–24 spiritual understanding . . . a foretaste of e·.
glory of
g 502–17 illuminating time with the glory of e·.
heaven and
g 503–10 spiritual harmony, — heaven and e·.
no part of
r 468–29 and time is no part of e·.
seal of
a 44– 8 His three days' work. . .set the seal of e· on time.
statement of the
b 334–20 statement of the e· of the Christ,
time and
b 285– 6 the great fact of being for time and e .
type of
gl 585– 5 a type of e· and immortality,
will reveal
g 520–13 and they will reveal e·, newness of Life,
work of
pr 3–15 to understand God is the work of e·,

o 353–15 Time has not yet reached e·,
r 468–28 E·, . . . expresses the thought of Life,
469– 1 e· is forever infinite.
g 517–22 Even e· can never reveal the whole of God,
gl 599– 1 E· is God's measurement of

ether

s 159– 2 a needed surgical operation without the e·
159– 4 protested against inhaling the e·
159– 9 occasioned, not by the e·, but by fear
159–19 would have performed the operation without e·.

ethereal

f 249–30 makes its mundane flights quite e·.
b 293– 9 the more e· is called mind.

etherealized

b 298–25 Angels are not e· human beings,
gl 598–15 was indeed air, an e· form of matter,

etherization

p 415–27 E· will apparently cause the body to

etherized

s 158–32 A woman in the city of Lynn, . . . was e·

ethical

s 145–18 From this fact arise its e· as well as its
145–19 its e· and physical effects are
ph 185–24 the reverse of e· and pathological Truth-power.
p 429–30 not understood generally by our e· instructors.

ethics

sp 99– 2 e·, and superstition afford no demonstrable
o 348–30 e· and temperance have received an impulse,
t 444–32 the Science of healing, especially its e·,
404–29 a scientific system of e·.

Eucharist

a 20–11 partake of the E·, support the clergy,
32– 9 But the E· does not commemorate a
35–25 Our E· is spiritual communion with

Euclid

b 329–18 who attempts to solve a problem of E·,

Euphrates

gl 585–16 definition of

Europe
a 21–15   If my friends are going to E·,
sp 74–25   that we are in E· when we are in
90–16   In dreams we fly to E· and meet a
b 320– 6   distinguished theologians in E· and America

evade
f 230–24   These merely e· the question.

evangel
b 308–24   Then said the spiritual e· :
ap 559–20   Mortals, obey the heavenly e·.

Evangelist's
f 231–31   planted on the E· statement that

evangelized
f 254–19   But the human self must be e·.

evaporates
p 375– 3   as painlessly as gas . . . when it e·
g 557–16   When the mist of mortal mind e·,

evasion
t 448–10   E· of Truth cripples integrity,

Eve (see also Eve's)
sp 92–12   serpent . . . speaking to Adam and E·.
g 533–23   which came from Adam to form E·.
538–23   And Adam knew E· his wife ;— Gen. 4 : 1.
553–17   Adam was created before E·.
553–19   E· was formed from Adam's rib,
gl 585–23   definition of

even
pref viii– 6   e· as the science of music
pr 4–14   blessings which, e· if not acknowledged in
9–19   e· the surrender of all merely material
10– 2   e· though with bleeding footsteps,
13–14   E· if prayer is sincere,
a 19– 5   E· Christ cannot reconcile Truth to error,
20– 1   there is one Life, — e· God, good.
20–18   e· the nature of God ;
22– 7   causes them, e· as drowning men,
24–32   After the resurrection, e· . . . Thomas
28– 3   E· many of his students stood in his way.
28–18   E· his righteousness and purity
30–18   which blesses e· those that curse it.
37–28   e· as your Father which is in — Matt. 5 : 48.
38– 4   e· more pernicious than the old doctrine of
43– 1   e· as they did understand it
45–24   E· his disciples at first called him a spirit,
46–16   or, in other words, rose e· higher
47– 1   e· to the spiritual interpretation and
48–13   or e· wish, to escape the exalting ordeal
49– 5   "E· the devils are subject — Luke 10 : 17.
50–21   E· what they did say, — that Jesus' teachings
54–32   Would they not deny him e· the
m 57–22   e· though it meet no return.
62–24   e· as it clothes the lily :
65–23   fermentation e· of fluids is not pleasant.
67– 9   but e· the dauntless seaman
67–22   commanded e· the winds and waves
sp 77–22   E· if communications from spirits to
78–12   e· were communication possible
80–22   E· planchette — the French toy
82–18   e· if our departed friends were near us
87– 3   e· when they are lost to the memory of
88– 6   The mind may e· be cognizant of a
95–20   e· human invention must have its day,
96–12   This material world is e· now becoming
97–16   it ceases to be e· an illusion,
98–24   E· now multitudes consider that which they call
s 111–15   e· as the explanation of optics rejects
113–11   E· if reversed, these propositions will
116–16   e· to the extinction of all belief in matter,
126– 6   e· as man sees his reflection in a glass.
131–21   e· so, Father, for so it seemed — Luke 10 : 21.
133–15   E· in captivity among foreign nations,
136–25   But e· Herod doubted if Jesus
137– 4   not spiritually discerned, e· by them,
139–10   e· when the end has been brightness
141– 8   to set aside e· the most cherished beliefs
144– 4   e· if these so-called powers are real.
144–24   e· as Truth wars with error,
146–14   e· the might of Mind
146–21   e· when its elevating effects
147–11   e· though centuries had passed away
150–29   e· the doctrine of the superiority of matter
151–13   E· this one reform in medicine
152– 9   e· when not fully understood.
155– 6   E· when you take away the individual confidence
161–28   e· if it were not already determined
ph 171– 5   e· the way through Christ, Truth,
177–26   e· though physician and patient are
177–28   E· so, and as directly as if
179–15   You can e· educate a healthy horse so far
180–19   e· before they go to work to eradicate
185–16   e· as the necromancers of Egypt
187– 3   mortals do not comprehend e· mortal existence,
191–12   e· to the birth of a new-old idea,

even
ph 193– 6   He e· showed me the probe,
197–32   will harm his patients e· more than
198–24   e· though the doctor says nothing
f 213–23   e· more strikingly true of Beethoven,
215–29   E· the faith of his philosophy spurned
216–32   and have but one Mind, e· God ;
217–11   e· of catalepsy and hysteria ;
220– 8   Instinct is better . . . as e· nature declares.
227– 4   e· as oppressive laws are disputed
233–12   not e· "the Son but the Father ;" — Mark 13 : 32.
234– 2   e· as ritualism and creed hamper
244–29   E· Shakespeare's poetry pictures age as
252– 7   When false human beliefs learn e· a little
c 255– *   e· we ourselves groan — Rom. 8 : 23.
259–20   e· as your Father which is in — Matt. 5 : 48.
261–28   e· as the bird which has burst from the egg
262–25   e· as light emits light without effort ;
263– 2   and e· privileged originators
265–25   e· before we discover what belongs to wisdom
266–10   e· if you cling to a sense of personal joys,
267–27   E· in this world, therefore,
b 276–20   e· as our Father in heaven is perfect,
277–22   contradict e· the order of material so-called
278– 7   e· as in Truth there is no error,
282–21   E· though they seem to touch,
284–24   E· the more subtile and misnamed
291–30   e· the judgment by which mortal man
292–21   e· because ye cannot hear my — John 8 : 43.
294–17   e· the errors that are destroyed by
301– 1   e· as the human likeness
302–20   e· as the Father is perfect,
302–31   E· in C. S., reproduction
309–23   e· as the gospel teaches.
311–23   e· the higher law of Soul,
313– 7   e· thy God, hath anointed thee — Heb. 1 : 9.
313–20   e· clearer in the translation of the
313–28   only in a limited degree e· by his disciples,
318– 6   e· while the corporeal senses are saying
320–18   e· man's eternal and harmonious existence
320–30   e· if disease and worms destroyed his body,
323–23   and elevates e· mortal mind to the
324–25   Asia Minor, Greece, and e· in imperial Rome.
334–19   e· before the human Jesus was incarnate
336–10   e· the infinite expression of infinite Mind,
338–22   e· the supposed separation of
o 341– 6   E· the Scriptures, . . . appear contradictory when
342–31   e· if their treatment resulted in death
348– 4   e· while treating them as disease ;
349–29   all learning, e· that which is wholly material.
357–15   or e· to deny that God made
359–11   E· though you aver that the
361–17   e· so God and man, Father and son,
p 364–12   He e· said that this poor woman
368–12   e· the hope of freedom from the
369–32   It is error e· to murmur
375–27   e· when they are supposed to be in hopeless
378– 2   e· as poetry and music are reproduced
397–29   belief that mind is, e· temporarily,
398–27   E· a blind faith removes
400–24   e· as in optics we see painted on the retina
400–31   E· our Master felt this.
404–31   e· in body, unless it makes him better mentally,
407–15   e· into spiritual power and good-will to man.
414–22   E· so, harmony is universal,
416–17   e· as the body, . . . is material.
416–23   no longer the parent, e· in appearance.
419– 3   hate will perpetuate or e· create the
427– 3   e· the law of the spirit of Truth,
429–23   e· according to the calculations of
440–13   E· penal law holds homicide, . . . to be
t 446–22   e· unto the end of the world." — Matt. 28 : 20.
454– 6   The understanding, e· in a degree,
457–26   They e· practise these, intending
464– 9   could not take her place, e· if willing so to do.
r 470– 1   With one Father, e· God,
471– 9   e· as these so-called senses receive no
478– 4   E· according to the teachings of natural science,
478–12   nor were they e· visible through the windows?
485–23   in which man is perfect, e· as the
486– 7   E· then he must gain spiritual understanding
491–29   e· though he does not understand C. S.,
492– 8   a knowledge of this, e· in small degree,
494–21   e· as the experiences of the sleeping dream
496–22   e· with the spiritual law which says
497–22   e· the allness of Soul, Spirit,
g 502–16   E· thus the crude forms of human thought
506–20   e· as He opens the petals of a
509–18   e· as nebulæ indicate the immensity of
517–22   E· eternity can never reveal the whole of God,
520– 1   sweetest rest, e· from a human standpoint,
541–12   e· the human concept of Love
541–25   Now it repudiates e· the human duty
542– 9   E· the disposition to excuse guilt
544–17   under the control of the one Mind, e· God.
545–31   e· so in Christ — I Cor. 15 : 22.

even

g 549–27   e· this great observer mistakes nature,
   550–11   ends, e· as it begins, in nameless nothingness?
   550–13   should appear now, e· as it will hereafter.
   552– 8   e· where the proof requisite to sustain this
   554– 2   e· the cause of all that exists,
   556–22   E· so goes on the Adam-belief,
ap 564– 6   to kill . . . e· their fellow-mortals,
   564–11   and e· his crucifixion
   565–22   purifying e· the gold of human character.
   573–14   e· the declaration from heaven,
   577– 1   e· as the material sense of personality
gl 588–13   e· as numbers which never blend
   588–17   e· the belief that life, substance, and

evening

and morning
g 510–22   already divided into e· and morning ;
and the morning
g 504– 4   e· and the morning were the first — Gen. 1 : 5.
   506– 9   e· and the morning were the second — Gen. 1 : 8.
   508–26   e· and the morning were the third — Gen. 1 : 13.
   511–15   e· and the morning were the fourth — Gen. 1 : 19.
   513– 4   e· and the morning were the fifth — Gen. 1 : 23.
   518–25   e· and the morning were the sixth — Gen. 1 : 31.
gl 584– 3   e· and the morning were the first — Gen. 1 : 5.

gl 586– 1   definition of

evenings
g 504–17   taking place on so many e· and mornings,

evenly
ph 168– 4   If the scales are e· adjusted,

event
a 24–31   could not admit such an e· to be possible.
  45–24   misconstrued that e·.

events
m 60–12   From the logic of e· we learn that
  66–23   It is better to await the logic of e·
sp 84–16   to foresee and foretell e· which concern the
  85–18   e· of great moment were foretold by the

eventually
a 23–10   e· both sin and suffering will fall at the feet of
an 105–16   When our laws e· take cognizance of
f 244–17   hypothesis that he returns e· to his
b 303–18   will e· destroy this illusion
o 357–23   false claims, which will e· disappear,
p 370–24   a drug may e· lose its supposed power
r 492–23   must e· submit to the Science of Mind,
g 524–30   and e· ejected at the demand of matter?
ap 565–16   will e· rule all nations and peoples
  569–20   must e· expiate their sin through suffering.

ever
pref xi–17   e· present in human consciousness
pr 5– 9   So it will e· be, till we learn that
u 04 10   If all who e· partook of the sacrament
  41–20   No ancient school . . . e· taught or
  52–16   the best man that e· trod the globe.
m 59–25   before this union and continue e· after,
sp 71–30   presupposes Spirit, which is e· infinite,
  72–21   God, good, being e· present, it follows
  76– 9   belief that life, . . . was e· in a finite form,
  85–13   told me all things that e· I did : — John 4 : 29.
  91– 2   Have you e· pictured this heaven and
s 118–10   this leaven of Truth is e· at work.
  129– 5   Truth is e· truthful,
  148– 7   Neither anatomy nor theology has e· described
  153–32   Neither sympathy nor society should e· tempt
  164– 6   e· yet promulgated, is true,
ph 175– 7   In old times who e· heard of dyspepsia,
  193–22   e· since the injury was received in boyhood.
  200–10   Life is, . . . and e· will be independent of
  200–17   the real man was, is, and e· shall be perfect,
f 201– 1   The best sermon e· preached is
  219–21   "The wish," . . . "is e· father to the thought."
  245–32   infinite never began nor will it e· end.
  248– 4   One marvels that a friend can e· seem less
  250– 9   which never errs, and is e· conscious ;
  250–32   nor . . . e· the sport of circumstance.
c 260–25   by the thoughts e· recurring to one's self,
b 277– 1   but matter is e· non-intelligent
  300–21   the realization of God as e· present
  302–13   this belief is all that will e· be lost.
  306–28   Life and the universe, e· present
  313–24   Jesus . . . was the most scientific man that e·
  314–21   presented to her, more than e· before,
  333–27   and e· will be inseparable from the
o 353– 4   senses and Science have e· been antagonistic,
  355–22   e· offered for acceptance,"
p 364– 2   the best man that e· trod this planet.
  368– 7   truth and error have come nearer than e·
  374–29   Nothing that lives e· dies.
  376–14   than in all the blood which e· flowed
  384–27   neither . . . will e· result from exposure to the
  387– 8   immortal Mind is e· active,

ever
p 429–22   for if Life e· had any beginning,
t 444– 7   If Christian Scientists e· fail to receive
  464–28   Neither dishonesty nor ignorance e· founded,
r 469– 6   If Life e· had a beginning,
  470– 9   the loss of Love as e· present and
  470–24   If there e· was a moment when
  470–30   If man e· existed without this
  471–18   God is infinite, therefore e· present,
  478–10   when no such persons were e· seen to go into
  479–16   Does that which we call dead e· see, hear,
  485– 6   which e· betrays mortals into sickness, sin, and
g 507–28   Creation is e· appearing,
  507–28   and must e· continue to appear
  527– 5   but e· beautiful and complete.
  531– 9   as if hope were e· prophesying thus :
  534–26   than there has e· been since the
ap 568– 1   E· since the foundation of the world,
  568– 2   e· since error would establish material belief,
  568–27   A louder song, sweeter than has e· before
  572–14   can e· furnish the vision of the Apocalypse,
  573–16   the divine Principle of harmony, is e· with men,
  578–18   in the house . . . of [LOVE] for e·. — Psal. 23 : 6.

ever-agitated
f 254–27   the e· but healthful waters of truth,

everlasting
a 23–11   will fall at the feet of e· Love.
  33–15   With the great glory of an e· victory
  45– 4   sublime success, an e· victory.
sp 81–11   this fact affords no certainty of e· life.
  99–27   sin, disease, and death give e· place to
s 121–20   clearer views of the e· facts,
  121–31   the e· government of the universe.
f 216–18   in submission to e· Life and Truth and Love.
  244–31   e· grandeur and immortality of development,
c 255– *   Thou art from e·. — Psal. 93 : 2.
  256–13   The e· I AM is not bounded nor
b 286–27   are the antipodes of e· Truth,
  290– 1   the e· I AM, the Being who was and is
p 390– 5   should never deny the e· harmony of Soul,
  410– 5   defines e· life as a present knowledge of
  428–17   the eternal builder, the e· Father,
r 489–12   yields to the reality of e· Life.
g 556–12   life e· is not to be gained by dying.
ap 568–30   Love sends forth her primal and e· strain.
gl 594–20   God ; that only which is perfect, e·,

everlastingly
s 143–30   power e· due its holy name.

evermore
b 334–27   and, behold, I am alive for e·, — Rev. 1 : 18.

ever-operative
s 123 27   they illustrated an e· divine Principle.

ever-presence
s 107– 8   e·, delivering the children of men
ap 567– 2   the e· of ministering Love.

ever-present
pr 16 21   Thy kingdom is come ; Thou art e·.
a 52– 9   the e· rebuke of his perfection and purity.
sp 84–11   prerogative of the e·, divine Mind,
s 108–23   Truth, and Love are all-powerful and e· ;
  130–32   no longer imagine evil to be e·
ph 180–25   the e· Mind who understands all things,
f 218–23   divine Love, who is an e· help
c 256–11   rather than the one e· I AM.
b 207–24   and Truth, the e·, is becoming understood.
  312–20   man's eternal Principle is e· Life.
p 377– 5   he should rejoice always in e· Love.
r 496– 4   this e· omnipotent Mind is reflected
g 501–13   is consonant with e· Love.
  503–14   light of e· Love illumines the universe.
  504–14   fill immensity and are e·.
ap 567– 7   To infinite, e· Love, all is Love,

every
pr 6–12   E· supposed pleasure in sin
  13– 4   "Ho, e· one that thirsteth, — Isa. 55 : 1.
a 19–17   E· pang of repentance and suffering,
  19–17   e· effort for reform,
  19–18   e· good thought and deed,
  20–28   "Let us lay aside e· weight, — Heb. 12 : 1.
  23–19   Spirit, which rebukes sin of e· kind
  28–31   await, in some form, e· pioneer of truth.
  30–28   loathe sin and rebuke it under e· mask.
  37–23   privilege of e· child, man, and woman,
  37–30   preach the gospel to e· creature !" — Mark 16 : 15.
  43–27   divine must overcome the human at e· point.
  45– 2   but Jesus vanquished e· material obstacle,
  45– 2   overcame e· law of matter,
  46–10   spoken . . . in e· age and clime.
m 61– 9   E· valley of sin must be exalted,
  61– 9   and e· mountain of selfishness be brought low,
  65– 3   May Christ, Truth, be present at e· bridal altar
sp 70– 1   E· day is a mystery.
  77–24   less with e· advanced stage of existence.

every

sp 79–10 and dig up e· seed of error's sowing.
98–20 for e· man to understand and to practise.
an 102–19 e· hour weaving webs more complicated
104– 9 "E· great scientific truth goes through three
105–13 Mortal mind, . . . is the criminal in e· case ;
s 107–10 delivering the children of men from e· ill
113–24 "but e· [mortal] man a liar."— *Rom.* 3 : 4.
122–22 instances . . . which e· thinker can recall
134– 2 At e· advancing step,
138–27 Our Master said to e· follower :
138–28 preach the gospel to e· creature !— *Mark* 16 : 15.
143– 1 Truth is God's remedy for error of e· kind,
144–28 e· man will be his own physician.
148–14 e· function, formation, and manifestation.
149– 5 more excellent way is divine Science in e· case.
151–20 E· function of the real man is governed by the
151–31 mortal mind claims to govern e· organ
152–12 Such errors beset e· material theory,
152–23 E· material dependence had failed her
158–25 Evidences of progress . . . greet us on e· hand.
162–13 not in one instance, but in e· instance.
ph 179–12 E· medical method has its advocates.
186–15 E· mortal must learn that there is neither
186–20 E· attempt of evil to destroy good
188–13 e· one recognizes his condition to be
194–13 E· theory opposed to this fact
195– 6 E· sound convulsed him with anguish.
197– 4 E· one hastens to get it.
f 207– 5 e· scientific statement in Christianity has
208– 9 a law of mortal mind, wrong in e· sense,
213–11 E· step towards goodness is a departure from
215–23 E· quality and condition of mortality
224– 2 feels the . . . effect of truth through e· pore.
224– 7 E· sensuous pleasure or pain is self-destroyed
233– 1 E· day makes its demands upon us
236–20 availability of good as the remedy for e· woe.
239–24 produces e· discordant action of the body.
242–28 while inspiration restores e· part of the
243– 7 can heal the sick in e· age
c 261–16 he hobbled e· day to the theatre,
261–32 Good demands of man e· hour,
262–28 E· concept which seems to begin with the brain
267– 1 E· object in material thought
b 268– 9 Mind as the cause of e· effect.
277–28 e· statement into which it enters.
279–22 E· system of human philosophy,
280–22 urges through e· avenue the belief
299–14 e· real individuality, image, or
307–21 e· sin or supposed material pain
323– 4 the endeavor to forsake error of e· kind
326– 7 and find the divine remedy for e· ill,
o 354–26 Sin should become unreal to e· one.
355–11 Let discord of e· name and nature
358–11 and sustains . . . e· point it presents.
p 370– 1 To be e· whit whole,
371–13 sick humanity sees danger in e· direction,
371–32 and can make it "e· whit whole."— *John* 7 : 23.
378– 6 and meet e· circumstance with truth.
379– 7 Mind, controlling e· effect
380–32 E· law of matter or the body,
389– 4 e· erroneous belief, or material condition.
391–29 Mentally contradict e· complaint
392– 4 e· broken moral law should be taken into account
394–26 conquer discord of e· kind with harmony,
400–16 understand that e· disease is an error,
405–22 better to be exposed to e· plague on earth
406– 5 equal to e· emergency,
406–19 Resist evil— error of e· sort
406–21 to avail ourselves in e· direction
407– 8 E· hour of delay makes the
407–24 perfect, harmonious in e· action.
408– 1 E· sort of sickness is error,
410–10 e· word that proceedeth out — *Matt.* 4 : 4.
410–14 E· trial of our faith in God makes us
411–31 alleviates the symptoms of e· disease.
413–14 taking a fish out of water e· day
413–24 noticing e· symptom of flatulency,
415– 3 Mind in e· case is the eternal God,
418–28 "Preach the gospel to e· — *Mark* 16 : 15.
418–29 Speak the truth to e· form of error.
419–16 Meet e· adverse circumstance as its master.
420–26 e· physical action and condition.
423–11 reaching to e· part of the human system.
431– 4 prisoner watched with the sick e· night
t 448–19 Try to leave on e· student's mind
450– 2 twist e· fact to suit themselves.
451–19 E· Christian Scientist, e· conscientious teacher
451–25 nature and methods of error of e· sort,
458–18 sword of Truth must turn in e· direction
460–21 starts a petty crossfire over e· cripple
462–14 abide strictly by its rules, heed e· statement,
462–18 as they . . . do in e· department of life.
463– 2 phenomena, which fluctuate e· instant
r 471–21 but e· [material] man a liar."— *Rom.* 3 : 4.

every

r 475–26 and over e· creeping thing — *Gen.* 1 : 26.
482–25 to the hungering heart in e· age.
486– 5 until e· corporeal sense is quenched.
494–10 and always will meet e· human need.
494–14 in e· hour, divine Love supplies all good.
g 507– 4 Spirit duly feeds and clothes e· object,
512– 4 e· living creature that moveth,— *Gen.* 1 : 21.
512– 6 e· winged fowl after his kind :— *Gen.* 1 : 21.
515–14 and over e· creeping thing — *Gen.* 1 : 26.
517–28 and over e· living thing — *Gen.* 1 : 28.
518– 6 e· herb bearing seed,— *Gen.* 1 : 29.
518– 8 And to e· beast of the earth,— *Gen.* 1 : 30.
518– 9 and to e· fowl of the air,— *Gen.* 1 : 30.
518–11 I have given e· green herb — *Gen.* 1 : 30.
520–19 and e· plant of the field — *Gen.* 2 : 5.
520–19 and e· herb of the field — *Gen.* 2 : 5.
526– 4 "e· plant of the field — *Gen.* 2 : 5.
527–20 Evil is . . . false in e· statement.
527–22 formed e· beast of the field,— *Gen.* 2 : 19.
527–22 and e· fowl of the air ;— *Gen.* 2 : 19.
527–24 Adam called e· living creature,— *Gen.* 2 : 19.
533–24 belief . . . is growing worse at e· step,
537– 7 sword which turned e· way,— *Gen.* 3 : 24.
542– 1 The belief of life in matter sins at e· step.
547– 4 e· one must be true, for not one departs from
548–13 E· agony of mortal error helps error to
ap 564–16 met and conquered sin in e· form.
565–10 decreed the death of e· male child
569– 3 E· mortal at some period,
gl 584–14 e· belief of life where Life is not yields to
598– 4 So is e· one that is born of the— *John* 3 : 8.
fr 600– * *being fruitful in e· good work,*— *Col.* 1 : 10.
(see also **tree**)

everything

belief that
g 531– 2 the belief that e· springs from dust
God saw
g 518–24 And God saw e· that He had made,— *Gen.* 1 : 31.
good in
ph 176–13 "sermons in stones, and good in e·."
He saw
g 525–23 He saw e· which He had made,
opposition to
s 114–32 the usual opposition to e· new,
relating to God
s 127–13 stand for e· relating to God,
sacrifice
pr 11–25 we shall sacrifice e· for it.
that creepeth
g 513–23 and e· that creepeth upon — *Gen.* 1 : 25.
518–10 and to e· that creepeth — *Gen.* 1 : 30.

s 127– 5 e· entitled to a classification as truth,
f 243–28 annihilation to e· unlike themselves,
b 269–32 The first theory, that matter is e·,
270– 3 (1) that e· is matter ; (2) that e· is Mind.
301–28 with e· turned upside down.
331–16 E· in God's universe expresses Him.
g 523–11 In error e· comes from beneath,
525–20 E· good or worthy, God made.

everywhere

iii– * Thou here, and e·.
s 147– 8 e·, when honestly applied
f 223– 8 If Spirit is *all* and is e·,
b 287–14 God being e· and all-inclusive,
o 361– 5 now and forever, here and e·.
p 371–11 As frightened children look e· for the
r 473– 8 God is e·, and nothing apart from Him is present
g 516– 8 shall see this true likeness and reflection e·.

Eve's

g 538–30 E· declaration, "I have gotten — *Gen.* 4 : 1.

Eves

ph 176– 3 modern E· took up the study of medical works

evidence

absolute
s 142–10 Truth, alone can furnish us with absolute e·.
according to the
p 423–17 according to the e· which matter presents.
accredited
a 18–10 against the accredited e· of the senses,
all
a 50–23 and that all e· of their correctness
all the
p 384–28 all the e· before the senses can never overrule.
basis of
gl 581–19 on the basis of e· obtained from the
change the
b 297–13 Change the e·, and that disappears
Christian
r 487–19 Christian e· is founded on Science

evidence

clear
  p 398– 6 clear *e·* that the malady was not material.
contradicts the
  s 119–26 contradicts the *e·* before the senses
  o 353– 8 which contradicts the *e·* of error,
destroy the
  p 412–22 conform the argument so as to destroy the *e·*
  417–17 you destroy the *e·*, for the disease disappears.
false
  s 120–24 heals the sick, overthrows false *e·*,
  131– 6 false *e·* before the corporeal senses disappears.
  f 252–15 The false *e·* of material sense contrasts
  b 275–27 It destroys the false *e·* that misleads
  287–29 false *e·* will finally yield to Truth,
  p 420–31 Turn his gaze from the false *e·* of the senses
feasible
  o 345–20 the only feasible *e·* that one does understand
full
  a 42–17 and gave full *e·* of divine Science,
furnish the
  ph 189–17 is supposed to furnish the *e·* of
immediate
  ph 188–29 physical senses have no immediate *e·* of
immortal
  a 29–31 immortal *e·* that Spirit is harmonious
latter
  sp 81– 4 this latter *e·* is destroyed by Mind-science.
law and
  p 441– 1 comprehending and defining all law and *e·*,
material
  a 52– 7 the material *e·* of sin, sickness, and death.
  p 422–18 causing it to depend less on material *e·*.
  gl 584–15 Any material *e·* of death is false,
no
  pr 9– 9 though we give no *e·* of the sincerity of
  o 356– 4 material existence affords no *e·* of spiritual
no direct
  b 284–17 which receive no direct *e·* of Spirit,
not so much
  sp 81– 1 There is not so much *e·* to prove
of matter
  s 128–26 the so-called *e·* of matter.
of Personal Sense
  p 433–11 *e·* of Personal Sense against Mortal Man.
of Spirit
  b 296–23 When the *e·* of Spirit and matter,
of the material senses
  b 274– 9 deduced from the *e·* of the material senses.
of the physical senses
  s 114– 7 based on the *e·* of the physical senses,
  122– 1 *e·* of the physical senses often reverses
of the senses
  a 18–10 against the accredited *e·* of the senses,
  p 386– 2 the *e·* of the senses is not to be accepted
  420–31 Turn his gaze from the false *e·* of the senses
of the spiritual senses
  b 200 4 the *e·* of the spiritual senses
of things
  r 468–21 the *e·* of things not seen "— *Heb.* 11 : 1.
of this condition
  ph 193– 7 *e·* of this condition of the bone.
of this revelation
  s 108–12 allowing the *e·* of this revelation to multiply
only
  f 207–32 The only *e·* of this inversion is
permanent
  f 232– 6 no scatheless and permanent *e·* of either.
real
  r 494–27 The other is the eternal and real *e·*,
recognize
  an 104–29 Our courts recognize *e·* to prove the
reverses the
  s 116– 5 Science so reverses the *e·* before the
  f 215–22 reverses the *e·* of material sense.
  t 461–13 because Science reverses the *e·* before the
rises above the
  t 448–12 rises above the *e·* of the corporeal senses ;
scientific
  p 380–23 scientific *e·* of which has accumulated
sensible
  s 109– 7 not, . . . seen to be supported by sensible *e·*,
spiritual
  a 52– 6 drank in the spiritual *e·* of health,
  b 297–22 spiritual *e·*, contradicting the testimony of
  gl 585– 9 spiritual *e·* opposed to material sense ;
stronger
  pr 7– 2 stronger *e·* that Jesus' reproof was pointed
  o 353– 7 having the stronger *e·* of Truth
sufficient
  p 363–29 was her grief sufficient *e·* to warrant
this
  p 380–26 this *e·* will gather momentum
to the senses
  p 370–10 furnishes the *e·* to the senses,

evidence

worthy
  pr 4– 8 the only worthy *e·* of our gratitude
  a 23–18 Faith, . . . is the *e·* gained from Spirit,
  42–18 *e·* so important to mortals.
  50–20 before the *e·* of the bodily senses,
  s 117–24 *E·* drawn from the five physical senses
  159– 7 The *e·* was found to be conclusive,
  164–21 rather does it *e·* the truth of
  ph 177– 5 The *e·* of divine Mind's healing power
  177– 6 as certain as the *e·* of my own existence.
  f 214– 5 *e·* before his material senses,
  b 303–30 When the *e·* before the material senses yielded
  o 359–14 The *e·* of the existence of Spirit,
  p 380– 8 Contending for the *e·* or indulging the
  389–12 better results of Mind's opposite *e·*.
  417–18 The *e·* before the corporeal senses
  428–26 The *e·* of man's immortality will become
  430–27 *e·* for the prosecution being called for,
  r 471– 7 *e·* before the five corporeal senses,
  471–14 the *e·* as to these facts is not supported by
  471–16 the *e·* that God and man coexist
  478– 3 What *e·* of Soul or of immortality
  493– 6 All the *e·* of physical sense
  497–13 the *e·* of divine, efficacious Love,
  g 543–17 All error proceeds from the *e·* before the
  gl 590– 4 *E·* obtained from the five corporeal senses;

evidenced
  o 355–29 and *e·* by the sick who are cured

evidences
  s 158–24 *E·* of progress and of spiritualization
  c 264–25 the only *e·*, by which we can recognize
  b 289–17 destroys with the spiritual *e·* of Life;
  p 395– 8 master the false *e·* of the corporeal senses
  428– 9 false trusts and material *e·*
  g 523–15 clear *e·* of two distinct documents

evident
  m 68–25 perpetuation of the floral species by bud . . .
           is *e·*
  sp 82– 1 must have known the deceased . . . is *e·*,
  s 111–27 became *e·* to me, — that Mind governs
  138– 6 It was now *e·* to Peter that divine Life,
  f 214–30 *e·* that the body as matter has no sensation
  o 345– 4 As it is *e·* that the likeness of Spirit cannot

evidently
  s 150–23 and it is as *e·* erroneous to the author,
  f 204–18 Such theories are *e·* erroneous.
  o 352– 6 *e·* considering it a mortal and material belief

evil (*see also* evil's)

all
  s 127–19 Supreme Being, Mind, exempt from all *e·*.
  ph 178–20 this so called mind, from which comes all *e·*,
  f 206–10 Will-power is capable of all *e·*.
  t 450–30 claim of animal magnetism, that all *e·*
  r 473– 4 The Science of Mind disposes of all *e·*.
  494–32 they cast fear and all *e·* out of themselves
  ap 561–10 lifts the veil from this embodiment of all *e·*,
  569–28 winding its way amidst all *e·*,
  564–25 hatred, and revenge, — all *e·*, — are typified
  gl 581– 6 counteracting all *e·*, sensuality, and
all manner of
  p 418–27 Cast out all manner of *e·*.
all sorts of
  p 404–10 Lust, malice, and all sorts of *e·*
and error
  f 227–19 but *e·* and error lead into captivity.
and fear
  p 392– 7 Casting out *e·* and fear enables
and good
  sp 91–29 postulate is, that mind is both *e·* and good
  an 103–21 belief that mind is . . . both *e·* and good ;
  s 114– 1 Usage classes both *e·* and good together
  f 246– 2 not a pendulum, swinging between *e·* and good,
  b 330–25 The notion that both *e·* and good are real
and hate
  t 448–22 impossible for error, *e·*, and hate to accomplish
and materiality
  b 277–11 *e·* and materiality are unreal
and matter
  b 277– 9 *e·* and matter, are mortal error,
and suffering
  sp 72–29 when *e·* and suffering are communicable.
ascendency over the
  m 61– 5 must have ascendency over the *e·*
attempt of
  ph 186–20 Every attempt of *e·* to destroy good is a failure,
avoidance of the
  ap 571– 5 necessary to ensure the avoidance of the *e·*
becomes more apparent
  f 207– 2 *e·* becomes more apparent and obnoxious
becomes nothing
  r 480– 4 *e·* becomes nothing, — the opposite of

evil

behold
f 243–23 "of purer eyes than to behold *e*·,"— *Hab.* 1 : 13.
o 357– 5 "of purer eyes than to behold *e*·."— *Hab.* 1 : 13.

belief in
g 540– 7 stirring up the belief in *e*· to its utmost,

blindness to
t 448–15 upon your blindness to *e*·

calls itself
b 287–18 *E*· calls itself something, when it is nothing.

cannot be
sp 91–30 whereas the real Mind cannot be *e*·

can only seem
r 470–14 *e*· can only seem to be real by giving reality to

casting out
a 46–11 again seen casting out *e*· and healing the sick.
p 392– 7 Casting out *e*· and fear enables

cast out
a 49– 4 healed the sick, cast out *e*·,
51–31 enabled Jesus to heal the sick, cast out *e*·,
s 137– 2 heal the sick, cast out *e*·, raise the dead ;
ph 185–22 Jesus cast out *e*· and healed the sick,

cast out the
p 411–16 Thereupon Jesus cast out the *e*·,

casts out
r 497–11 understanding that casts out *e*· as unreal.

casts out the
s 135–14 when Truth casts out the *e*· called disease,

causing
sp 93–16 not create a mind susceptible of causing *e*·,

cease to manifest
o 346–14 only as we cease to manifest *e*·

claims of
s 130–30 astounded at the vigorous claims of *e*·
t 447–21 Expose and denounce the claims of *e*·
448– 1 To assume that there are no claims of *e*·
g 529–28 faith to fight all claims of *e*·,

coincide with
ph 167–22 no more . . . than good can coincide with *e*·.

confers no pleasure
a 40– 1 once admit that *e*· confers no pleasure,

constitutes
g 527–17 constitutes *e*· and mortal knowledge.

create
g 540– 5 "I make peace, and create *e*·.— *Isa.* 45 : 7.

crying
m 64– 1 Want of uniform justice is a crying *e*·

declared
ph 165– 2 *E*· declared that eating this fruit would open

degree of
t 451–26 subtle degree of *e*·, deceived and deceiving.

deliver us from
pr 16–15 "Deliver us from *e*·,"— *Matt.* 6 : 13.
17– 9 deliver us from *e*· ;— *Matt.* 6 : 13.

demon, or
p 411–15 demon, or *e*·, replied that his name was Legion.

destruction of
a 53–24 sacrifice . . . for the destruction of *e*·.

devil or
r 469–16 *devil* or *e*· — is not Mind, is not Truth,
ap 563–19 that old serpent, whose name is devil or *e*·,

element of
g 539–11 God could never impart an element of *e*·,

error and
a 52–17 error and *e*· again make common cause
b 272–26 recorded in the destruction of error and *e*·,

escape from
b 316– 3 may learn how to escape from *e*·.
ap 571–12 Escape from *e*·, and designate those as

flesh, and
pr 10–13 overcoming the world, the flesh, and *e*·,

foreshadowing
sp 84– 5 not by foreshadowing *e*· and mistaking fact

foundation of
sp 92–26 The foundation of *e*· is laid on a belief in

from good to
sp 77– 2 said : "I cannot turn at once from good to *e*·."

good and
(see **good**)

good or
ph 172– 1 and that the cognizance of good or *e*·,
f 205–16 believing that matter can be . . . good or *e*·),
240–18 Mortals move onward towards good or *e*·
b 340– 1 their imaginary power for good or *e*·,

good over
p 406–23 Life over death, and good over *e*·,

has no history
g 538–21 *e*· has no history,

has no power
p 398–32 *E*· has no power, no intelligence,

has no reality
sp 71– 2 *E*· has no reality.

has tried
ap 568– 3 *e*· has tried to slay the Lamb ;

evil

inventions of
ap 563– 7 showing its horns in the many inventions of *e*·.

is a negation
ph 186–11 *E*· is a negation, because it is the absence of

is but an illusion
r 480–23 Hence, *e*· is but an illusion,

is destroyed
b 311–13 *E*· is destroyed by the sense of good.

is nothing
b 330–27 *E*· is nothing, no thing, mind, nor power.

is not Mind
f 207– 8 Indeed, *e*· is not Mind.
r 469–16 *e*· — is not Mind, is not Truth,

is not mind
p 398–32 fact remains that *e*· is not mind.

is not power
an 102–30 Mankind must learn that *e*· is not power.
ph 192–24 *E*· is not power.

is not supreme
f 207–10 *E*· is not supreme ; good is not helpless ;

is self-assertive
ph 186–17 *E*· is self-assertive.

is sometimes
b 327– 9 *E*· is sometimes a man's highest conception

is temporal
ap 569–25 *e*· is temporal, not eternal.

is unreal
t 447–31 He may say, as a subterfuge, that *e*· is unreal,
g 527–19 *E*· is unreal because it is a lie,

its
r 490–10 From this cooperation arises its *e*·.

knowledge of
g 526–21 erroneous doctrine that the knowledge of *e*· is
527–14 a knowledge of *e*· would make man mortal.
537– 9 knowledge of *e*· was never the essence of

lapse into
r 470–17 How can good lapse into *e*·,

lessen
t 450–20 has enlisted to lessen *e*·,

lie, called
ap 568– 5 Science is able to destroy this lie, called *e*·.

manifestations of
b 293–24 manifestations of *e*·, which counterfeit divine

master
p 404–25 increases his ability to master *e*·

matter and
gl 583–23 CREATOR. . . . the opposite of matter and *e*·,

matter, or
sp 92–16 knowledge gained from matter, or *e*·,
gl 594– 6 claim that there is . . . matter, or *e*· ;

medium of
sp 91–31 Mind cannot be evil nor the medium of *e*·,

mention of
g 526–14 first mention of *e*· is in the legendary

named
r 469–28 believe there is another power, named *e*·.
gl 594–10 claim . . . there was another power, named *e*·,

never causes
sp 93–13 Good never causes *e*·,

never enters into
b 336– 4 Good never enters into *e*·,

never produce
b 304–13 good can never produce *e*· ;

no
s 140–27 Love, . . . causeth no *e*·, disease, nor
f 207– 1 for there is no *e*· in Spirit.
210–30 immortal sense includes no *e*· nor pestilence.
b 278– 8 in Truth there is no error, and in good no *e*·.
335– 2 There is no *e*· in Spirit, because God is Spirit.
t 448– 8 Under such circumstances, to say that there is no *e*·,
453–22 thanks God that there is no *e*·, yet serves evil
ap 578–11 I will fear no *e*· :— *Psal.* 23 : 4.
gl 596–22 I will fear no *e*·."— *Psal.* 23 : 4.

no longer imagine
s 130–32 no longer imagine *e*· to be ever-present

nothingness of
b 269– 8 the unreality, the nothingness, of *e*·.
293–31 entireness of God, good, and the nothingness of *e*·.
ap 563–17 but he also sees the nothingness of *e*·

not supported by
r 471–15 evidence . . . is not supported by *e*·,

one
pr 16–19 one *e*·, is but another name for
r 476– 2 children of the wicked one, or the one *e*·,

only
ph 186– 8 Erring human mind-forces can work only *e*·

only as
g 529–23 enters into the metaphor only as *e*·.

or matter
t 454–11 *e*· or matter has neither intelligence nor power.

overcome
ap 571–16 under all circumstances, overcome *e*· with

evil
  parent of
    r 480–25   The supposititious parent of *e·* is a lie.
  personification of
    an 103– 3   Paul refers to the personification of *e·* as
  personified
    o 357– 7   Jesus said of personified *e·*, that it was
  point out the
    ap 571– 1   they are not so willing to point out the *e·*
  produces
    s 144–19   It produces *e·* continually,
    f 231–12   If God makes sin, if good produces *e·*,
  producing
    c 263–12   producing *e·* when he would create good,
    o 343–16   impossibility of good producing *e·* ;
  prolific of
    t 457–17   mental malpractice, prolific of *e·*,
  remedy the
    m 63–21   If . . . franchise for women will remedy the *e·*
  repetition of
    sp 73–14   known by its fruit, — the repetition of *e·*.
  represents
    b 282–10   the straight line represents *e·*,
  resist
    p 406–19   Resist *e·* — error of every sort
  resisting
    t 446–24   Resisting *e·*, you overcome it
  sense of
    b 325– 3   He . . . loses all sense of *e·*,
    g 540–15   that Truth may annihilate all sense of *e·*
  serves
    t 453–22   yet serves *e·* in the name of good.
  shalt not know
    a 19–32   thou shalt not know *e·*, for there is one Life,
  sin, and
    b 315– 8   matter, sin, and *e·* were not Mind ;
  source of
    r 489–24   The corporeal senses are the only source of *e·*
  statement about
    g 544–17   The first statement about *e·*,
  still charges
    ap 564– 3   *e·* still charges the spiritual idea with
  symptoms of
    g 540–12   when the symptoms of *e·*, illusion, are aggra-
            vated,
  tempted with
    g 527–13   "God cannot be tempted with *e·*,— *Jas.* 1 : 13
  this
    m 65–31   will assuredly throw off this *e·*,
    ap 565– 2   nearing its doom, this *e·* increases
  to accomplish more
    sp 96–32   wicked minds will endeavor . . . to accomplish
            more *e·* ;
  unimportant and
    r 485– 8   If the unimportant and *e·* appear,
  unreality called
    s 110– 9   the awful unreality called *e·*.
  unreality of
    f 206–21   the nothingness and unreality of *e·*.
    b 339–12   Science demonstrates the unreality of *e·*,
    339–19   Only those, . . . understand the unreality of *e·*.
  victory over
    ap 571–18   the occasion for a victory over *e·*.
  will boast
    t 450–18   unless . . . *e·* will boast itself above good.
  would appear
    f 216–22   *e·* would appear to be the master of good,
  would vanish
    r 480–31   *e·* would vanish before the reality of good.

    pr 5–27   If prayer nourishes the . . . prayer is an *e·*.
    a 42–27   governed by God — by good, not *e·* — and is
    m 65–13   powers of *e·* so conspicuous to-day
    68–22   and the *e·* to hatch their silly innuendoes
    sp 72–22   the suppositional opposite of good,
    72–25   *e·* is neither communicable nor scientific.
    76–10   belief . . . in a finite form, or good in *e·*,
    93–14   nor creates aught that can cause *e·*.
    93–16   *e·* is the opposing error and not the truth
    an 102–32   C. S. despoils the kingdom of *e·*,
    103–17   *E·* is a suppositional lie.
    103–21   false belief . . . that *e·* is as real as good
    104–17   *e·*, occultism, necromancy, mesmerism,
    105– 9   *e·*, which is the real outlaw,
    s 113–19   deny death, *e·*, sin, disease.
    113–20   *e·*, death, deny good, omnipotent God, Life.
    114– 5   human mind and *e·* in contradistinction to
    116–17   extinction of all belief in matter, *e·*,
    119–22   *e·* should be regarded as unnatural,
    ph 167– 8   admission of the claims of good or of *e·*
    169–32   good that a poisonous drug seems to do is *e·*,
    186–16   there is neither power nor reality in *e·*.
    186–18   should strip *e·* of all pretensions.
    186–19   The only power of *e·* is to destroy itself.
    186–24   If *e·* is as real as good, *e·* is also as

evil
    f 203– 1   as though *e·* could overbear the law of Love,
    203–20   when *e·* has overtaxed the belief of life
    204– 1   It is *e·* that dies ; good dies not.
    204–13   *e·*, is the unlikeness of good.
    204–32   The error, which says . . . good is in *e·*,
    207– 9   *e·* is the awful deception and unreality
    207–15   nor is *e·* mightier than good.
    229–13   declaring Him good in one instance and *e·* in
    230–18   no more . . . than goodness can cause *e·*
    234–10   more familiar with good than with *e·*,
    236–32   insubordination is an *e·*,
    244–27   He does not pass . . . from *e·* to good,
    244–27   He does not pass . . . from good to *e·*.
    c 263–18   the *e·* which I would not, *that I do.*"— *Rom.* 7 : 19.
    266–20   sinner makes his own hell by doing *e·*,
    266–22   material sense, aiding *e·* with *e·*,
    b 277– 7   Good cannot result in *e·*.
    277–21   asserts . . . that good is the origin of *e·*.
    285– 2   cannot be cognizant of good or of *e·*,
    288–22   that Life is God, good, and not *e·* ;
    290–31   no purer until *e·* is disarmed by good.
    292–15   To mortal mind, . . . *e·* is real.
    292–22   of your father, the devil [*e·*],— *John* 8 : 44.
    307– 7   *E·* still affirms itself to be mind,
    308– 2   Art thou dwelling in the belief . . . that *e·* is
            mind,
    311– 6   Hence *e·* is not made and is not real.
    321–13   The serpent, *e·*, under wisdom's bidding, was
    327– 2   there is no abiding pleasure in *e·*,
    327–20   *e·* has in reality neither place nor power
    339– 9   *e·*, being contrary to good, is unreal,
    o 348–16   I deny His cooperation with *e·*,
    348–17   I desire to have no faith in *e·*
    356–25   Does *e·* proceed from good?
    357–16   deny that God made man evil and made *e·* good
    357–30   can Life, or God, dwell in *e·*
    p 367–32   *E·* is but the counterpoise of nothingness.
    368–11   beliefs . . . that *e·* is equal in power to good
    368–22   Neither *e·*, disease, nor death can be
    404–12   If the *e·* is over in the repentant mortal mind,
    411–19   Jesus caused the *e·* to be self-seen
    t 447–13   *e·* will in time disclose and punish itself.
    448– 5   *E·* which obtains in the bodily senses,
    448– 7   if *e·* is uncondemned, it is undenied
    448– 8   Under such circumstances, to say . . . is an *e·*
    452– 3   *e·* has in reality no power.
    r 469–22   when we admit that, . . . *e·* has a place
    469–23   *e·* can have no place, where
    470–13   *e·*, the unlikeness of God, is unreal.
    474– 3   destroy all error, *e·*, disease, and death.
    474–26   If *e·* is real, Truth must make it so ;
    479–28   *e·* should be denied identity or power,
    480–21   the opposite of good — that is, *e·*
    480–23   *E·* is a false belief.
    g 501–18   the history of perpetual *e·*.
    526–22   Was *e·* instituted through God, Love?
    527–19   Has *e·* the reality of good?
    529–26   should rejoice that *e·*, . . . contradicts itself
    532–23   Is Mind capable . . . of *e·* as well as of good,
    536–12   as if He were the creator of *e·*.
    537–10   *e·* has no local habitation nor
    538–21   *e·* is brought into view only as the unreal
    539– 2   In the words of Jesus, it (*e·*, devil) is
    539– 9   such as *e·*, matter, error, and death
    540–13   may think . . . the Lord hath wrought an *e·* ;
    555–20   error would seek to unite . . . good with *e·*,
    ap 559–13   the "seven thunders" of *e·*,— *Rev.* 10 : 3.
    561– 3   destroys both faith in *e·* and
    561– 4   and the practice of *e·*,
    567–19   serpent, whose name is devil (*e·*),
    gl 579–16   *e·* ; the opposite of good, — of God
    584–17   DEVIL. *E·* ; a lie ; error ;

evil (adj., adv.)
    pr 4–25   goodness will "be *e·* spoken of,"— *Rom.* 14 : 16.
    5–32   seek the destruction of all *e·* works,
    sp 70–11   that there are good and *e·* spirits, is a mistake.
    79–17   Jesus cast out *e·* spirits, or false beliefs.
    83– 6   incredible good and *e·* elements
    85– 9   enabling one to do good, but not *e·*.
    an 100– *   *out of the heart proceed e· thoughts,* — *Matt.* 15 : 19.
    s 115–21   *E·* beliefs, passions and appetites, fear,
    115–25   *Second Degree: E·* beliefs disappearing.
    f 206–32   There are *e·* beliefs, often called *e·* spirits ;
    207– 8   God is not the creator of an *e·* mind.
    229–24   If . . . its opposite, health, must be *e·*,
    230–13   so as to bring about certain *e·* results,
    234–26   You must control *e·* thoughts in the
    234–31   *E·* thoughts and aims reach no farther and
    234–32   *E·* thoughts, lusts, and malicious purposes
    254–29   Your good will be *e·* spoken of.
    c 266–26   *e·* beliefs which originate in mortals are hell.
    b 274– 6   symbolizes all that is *e·* and perishable.
    307–10   It says : . . . God makes *e·* minds and *e·* spirits,
    o 357–16   deny that God made man *e·*

evil (adj., adv.)

p 401– 5	cherishing e· passions and malicious purposes,
405– 3	The indulgence of e· motives and aims
413– 1	and cannot transmit good or e· intelligence
t 449–19	The baneful effect of e· associates
449–20	The inoculation of e· human thoughts
458– 4	one good and the other e·,
r 482– 4	hypothesis that soul is both an e· and a good
496– 2	there is no transfer of e· suggestions
g 533–18	the rib . . . has grown into an e· mind,
539–14	the propensity or power to do e·?
ap 563–13	and that by means of an e· mind in matter
gl 594–22	Mortal beliefs ; corporeality ; e· minds ;

evil-doer

ph 186–22	aids in peremptorily punishing the e·.

evil one

pr 16–16	"Deliver us from the e· o·."
16–18	C. S. teaches us that "the e· o·,"

evil's

ap 571– 2	expose e· hidden mental ways of

evils

all

ph 183–26	Truth casts out all e· and

brood of

f 234–18	the brood of e· which infest it

casting out

s 136–14	casting out e· and healing the sick
f 210– 8	casting out e·, and destroying death,
b 316–28	healing the sick, casting out e·,
332–15	healing the sick and casting out e·,
o 347–17	healing the sick, and casting out e·.

cast out

a 34–15	cast out e·, and preach Christ, or Truth,
41–32	cast out e· and heal the sick.
b 322– 1	to heal the sick and cast out e·
o 342–12	students should cast out e· and heal the sick.

casts out

s 135–13	when Truth heals the sick, it casts out e·,
143– 3	Christ casts out e· and heals the sick.
b 282– 1	Truth casts out e· and heals the sick.

conjectural

ph 176–19	superimposed and conjectural e·.

moral

p 366– 4	must first cast moral e· out of himself

physical

p 366– 6	cast physical e· out of his patient ;

these

f 207– 1	but these e· are not Spirit,
219–31	may look for an abatement of these e· ;
o 347–25	it is Christ, Truth, who destroys these e·,
r 481–21	hypotheses . . . assume the necessity of these e·

p 394–20	Will you bid a man let e· overcome him,
r 474–21	Is it possible, then, to believe that the e·
494–30	Our Master cast out devils (e·)

evince

o 355– 7	prayers which e· no spiritual power to heal.

evoke

p 365–13	with which to e· healing from the

evoked

sp 94–19	His healing-power e· denial, ingratitude,

evolution

s 135– 9	Spiritual e· alone is worthy of
ph 189–30	e·, keeping always in the direct line of matter,
g 547–16	Darwin's theory of e· from a material basis
547–20	Material e· implies that the great First Cause
551–12	E· describes the gradations of human belief,

evolve

sp 86–13	Mortals e· images of thought.
b 335–19	Nothing but Spirit, Soul, can e· Life,
524–28	Could Spirit e· its opposite, matter,

evolved

m 69– 3	man and the universe are e· from Spirit,
sp 86–20	e· involuntarily by mortal mind.
ph 179–19	The epizoötic is a humanly e· ailment,
c 260–20	A sick body is e· from sick thoughts.
b 303–13	statement that man is conceived and e·
r 475–30	nor can God, by whom man is e·,
g 523– 3	the mist of obscurity e· by error
532–17	e· through material sense,
544–22	these gods must be e· from materiality
545–13	the theory of man as e· from Mind.

evolves

sp 71–16	images, which mortal mind holds and e·
s 108–27	e·, in belief, a subjective state
c 260–22	e· bad physical and moral conditions.
b 295– 7	filled with spiritual ideas, which He e·,
r 468– 1	intelligence, which e· its own unerring idea

evolving

b 298–25	e· animal qualities in their wings ;

exact

s 113–13	showing mathematically their e· relation
161– 4	an e· statement, more e· than you suppose ;
ph 175–20	The e· amount of food the stomach could digest
b 295–27	The theoretical mind is . . . the e· opposite
p 397–19	in e· proportion to your disbelief in physics,
r 482– 1	gives the e· meaning in a majority of cases.
g 521–28	which is the e· opposite of scientific truth
523– 6	Although presenting the e· opposite of Truth,

exaction

m 58–13	the selfish e· of all another's time

exactly

o 350– 5	C. S. takes e· the opposite view.

exaggerated

ph 195–26	Novels, remarkable only for their e· pictures,

exalt

c 266–14	until the lesson is sufficient to e· you ;
t 464–23	not to e· personality.

exaltation

a 46–21	was followed by his e· above all
46–22	and this e· explained his ascension,
b 313–17	the cause given for the e· of Jesus,
314– 2	(his further injury)
gl 581–14	temptation overcome and followed by e·.

exalted

pr 1–13	that they may be moulded and e·
a 38–16	right hand of the Lord is e·." — Psal. 118 : 16.
m 61– 9	Every valley of sin must be e·,
f 203–12	This thought incites to a more e· worship
b 299– 7	My angels are e· thoughts,
p 363–13	wondering why, being a prophet, the e· guest
373–17	through the e· thought of John,
g 506–11	e· thought or spiritual apprehension
513– 7	lead on to spiritual spheres and e· beings.
ap 574–11	It e· him till he became conscious of the
gl 598–25	This e· view, obtained and retained

exalting

a 48–13	e· ordeal of sin's revenge on its destroyer
p 383– 6	the pure and e· influence of the divine Mind

exalts

s 148–25	Physiology e· matter, dethrones Mind,

examination

s 111–26	After a lengthy e· of my discovery
ph 196–26	induced by a single post mortem e·,
p 438–26	summoned Furred Tongue for e·,
g 547– 9	microscopic e· of a vulture's ovum,

examine

pr 8–28	We should e· ourselves and
a 46–18	caused him to e· the nail-prints and the
s 159–24	They e· the lungs, tongue, and pulse
p 370–32	Physicians e· the pulse, tongue, lungs,

examined

c 267–19	e· in the light of divine Science,
b 274–31	e· in the light of divine metaphysics,

examining

s 161–24	ordinary practitioner, e· bodily symptoms,

example

consummate

a 51–19	His consummate e· was for the

emulate the

g 515– 2	to emulate the e· of Jesus.

following the

ph 192–28	following the e· of our Master

follow the

a 40–26	all men should follow the e· of our Master
b 324–23	to follow the e· and teachings of Jesus,

glorified

a 54– 7	the harmony his glorified e· introduced.

great

g 555–28	Our great e·, Jesus, could restore
ap 577–19	forever interprets this great e·

his

pr 4– 7	To keep the commandments. . .and follow his e·,
9–30	If unwilling to follow his e·,
a 51–20	They would not accept . . . nor follow his e·.
b 309–15	the children of earth who followed his e·
329–11	and left his e· for us.
r 473–21	but to reach his e· and to test its

Jesus'

pr 4–30	enable us to follow Jesus' e·.
r 494– 7	God, who needed no help from Jesus' e·

Master's

o 349– 9	We propose to follow the Master's e·.

one

g 546–32	proving of one e· would authenticate

teaching and

a 54– 8	Who is ready to follow his teaching and e·?

this

s 161–13	If her sister States follow this e·

a 37–24	to follow . . . the e· of the Master
s 113–28	For e· : There is no pain in Truth,

EXAMPLE 167 EXERCISE

example

f 236–10	in support of his proof by *e·*
b 320–25	For *e·*, the text, "In my flesh— *Job.* 19 : 26.
o 354–18	Consistency is seen in *e·* more than in

examples

o 343–29	which allows words, . . . to follow such *e·* !
t 453– 2	among the *e·* on the blackboard,
g 546–32	a thousand different *e·* of one rule,

exceed

a 19– 4	Man cannot *e·* divine Love,
s 128–11	ability to *e·* their ordinary capacity.
ph 197– 7	But the price does not *e·* the original cost.

excel

f 228–31	*e·* the influence of their dead faith and

excellence

f 249– 4	producing His own models of *e·*.
t 457–20	no *e·* without labor in a direct line.

excellent

s 149– 4	The more *e·* way is divine Science
o 360–22	as given in the *e·* translation of the

except

a 47–29	each one came to a violent death *e·* St. John,
sp 98– 8	Body cannot be saved *e·* through Mind.
s 126–27	*e·* the teachings and demonstrations of
143–27	no power *e·* that which is derived from
149–10	they are left without explanation *e·* in C. S.
163–16	*e·*, indeed, that it has already destroyed
ph 169–20	There can be no healing *e·* by this Mind,
169–26	sick are never really healed *e·* by means of the
181–13	when you resort to any *e·* spiritual means.
195– 7	All that he ate, *e·* his black crust,
f 243–29	they declare nothing *e·* God.
246–20	*E·* for the error of measuring
b 271–32	*e·* they be sent?"— *Rom.* 10 : 15.
272– 2	how shall they preach, . . . *e·* the people hear?
331–13	nothing possesses reality. . . *e·* the divine Mind
331–24	*e·* as infinite Spirit or Mind.
o 360– 5	replies : . . . I have no mind-ideals *e·* those which
p 371–13	looks for relief in all ways *e·* the right one.
375–29	seems anomalous *e·* to the expert in C. S.
381–11	*e·* a moral or spiritual law.
399–30	*e·* he first bind the strong man?"— *Matt.* 12 : 29.
400–17	*e·* what mortal mind assigns to it.
407– 5	no creature *e·* a loathsome worm,
409–18	*e·* through fear or choice.
410–26	in any way *e·* to promote right thinking
425–26	You will never fear again *e·* to offend God,
t 447– 5	*e·* it be to benefit them.
453–25	*e·* that you must not tell the patient that he is
459– 5	achieves no worldly honors *e·* by sacrifice,
464– 5	*e·* through her laborious publications,
r 473–31	Few, however, *e·* his students
478– 7	*e·* the claim of mortal belief?
ap 564–17	*e·* the highest degree of human depravity.

excepted

sp 98–24	not . . . a part of any religion, Christianity not *e·*

exception

f 216–25	health would seem the *e·*,
t 457–19	C. S. is not an *e·* to the general rule,

exceptions

ph 199–22	*E·* only confirm this rule,

excess

p 388–16	through a deficiency or an *e·*,

excessive

p 375–31	fear so *e·* that it amounts to fortitude.

exchange

o 360– 7	replies : . . . yet I would not *e·*
p 390–10	to *e·* the pleasures and pains of sense for the

exchanges

b 269–15	*e·* the objects of sense for the

exchanging

r 483– 4	*e·* one disease for another.
g 531–11	*e·* it for spiritual perception,
531–12	*e·* human concepts for the divine consciousness.

excision

t 462–25	indispensable to the *e·* of error.

excite

sp 88–20	*E·* the organ of veneration or religious faith,
88–22	*E·* the opposite development, and he

excited

p 377–23	the morbid or *e·* action of any organ.
415– 1	Inflammation is fear, an *e·* state of mortals
417–10	no reaction . . . from *e·* conditions.

excitement

an 101– 3	or to the *e·* of the imagination
p 421–21	Calm the *e·* sometimes induced by

exciting

a 21–29	The company is alluring and the pleasures *e·*.
ph 169–13	by *e·* fear of disease, and by dosing the body
178–11	predisposing cause and the *e·* cause are mental.
f 230–32	the *e·* cause of all suffering,
p 393– 7	remote, and *e·* cause of all bad effects

exclaim

p 397–13	you think or *e·*, "I am hurt !"
434– 4	Some *e·*, "It is contrary to law

exclaims

g 516–14	grass beneath our feet silently *e·*,

exclude

ph 170– 9	certainly present what human theories *e·*
p 392–31	*E·* from mortal mind the offending errors ;

excluded

f 237–21	should be *e·* on the same principle
g 543–16	are never *e·* by falsity.

excludes

s 123–13	*e·* matter, resolves *things* into *thoughts*,
ph 185–20	*e·* the human mind as a spiritual factor
g 537–14	Error *e·* itself from harmony.

exclusively

sp 93–24	It means quantity . . . and applies *e·* to God.

excuse

b 280–30	The only *e·* for entertaining human opinions,
g 542–10	Even the disposition to *e·* guilt or to

excuses

s 130– 4	bidden to the feast, the *e·* come.
g 542– 6	hides behind a lie and *e·* guilt,

executed

p 405–14	will be *e·* upon mortal mind and body.
441–23	*e·* at the hands of our sheriff, Progress.

execution

p 434– 2	there comes a despatch : "Delay the *e·* ;

executioner

p 385–13	the law which makes sin its own *e·*,

executor

a 30–17	Not so did Jesus, the new *e·* for God,
p 439–27	and the righteous *e·* of His laws.

Exegesis

g 502–21	chapter sub-title

exegesis

g 502–18	In the following *e·*, each text is

Exemplar

pr 5–31	We should follow our divine *E·*,
p 395– 6	Like the great *E·*, the healer should
ap 577–19	this great example and the great *E·*.

exemplification

a 18– 1	the *e·* of man's unity with God,
35–16	its *e·* of human probation, and

exempt

s 127–18	Mind, *e·* from all evil.
t 247–18	Immortality, *e·* from age or decay,

exemption

p 373– 2	physical *e·* which Christianity includes,
411–28	their *e·* from disease and danger.

exempts

p 385–13	*e·* man from all penalties but those due

exercise

air, and

ph 166–27	less than in drugs, air, and *e·*,
f 232–19	Jesus never taught that drugs, food, air, and *e·*

and air

ph 174– 6	to flannels, to baths, diet, *e·*, and air?

faith in

ph 199–13	the blacksmith's faith in *e·*,

muscular

ph 199–12	Not because of muscular *e·*, but

of despotic control

an 102–26	It implies the *e·* of despotic control,

of divine power

s 135– 9	worthy of the *e·* of divine power.

of faith

ph 170– 5	result of the *e·* of faith in material

of will

t 446–27	*e·* of will brings on a hypnotic state,

perpetual

r 487– 9	the perpetual *e·* of the Mind-faculties

plans the

p 399– 7	Mortal mind plans the *e·*,

sp 75–22	can then *e·* Jesus' spiritual power
ph 165– 7	To measure . . . strength by the *e·* of muscle,
181–32	Any hypnotic power you may *e·* will diminish
198–31	does not follow that *e·* has produced this
199– 5	trip-hammer is not increased in size by *e·*.
f 206–12	while the *e·* of the sentiments
220– 1	We hear it said : "I *e·* daily

exercise

p 392–28 whether it be air, e·, heredity, contagion,
393–10 E· this God-given authority.
396–23 power which their beliefs e· over their
435–19 in the e· of a love that
t 455–13 if, . . . you can e· little or no power for

exercised

m 64– 3 Our forefathers e· their faith in the
f 206– 4 e· only in subordination to Truth ;
o 355–18 has e· any systematic healing power
p 378–18 e· over mortal beliefs to destroy them ;
ap 559– 7 e· upon visible error and audible sin.

exerted

an 100– 4 so-called force, which he said could be e·

exhalations

p 382– 9 or to remove unhealthy e· from the

exhausted

f 221–12 having e· the skill of the doctors,
p 416–12 when the soporific influence of the opium is e·,

exhaustion

g 519–27 No e· follows the action of this Mind,

exhibit

s 120–19 or to e· the real status of man.

exhibited

an 101–11 phenomena e· by a reputed clairvoyant.

exhibiting

p 404– 6 e· to the wrong-doer the suffering which

exhibition

s 132– 3 e· of the divine power to heal
150– 6 Science, instead of a phenomenal e·.
163–26 so ample an e· of human invention

exhibits

ap 568–11 first e· the true warfare and then the false.

exhort

t 443–21 "Reprove, rebuke, e· — II Tim. 4 : 2.

exist

m 57–20 It is unselfish ; therefore it cannot e· alone,
59–25 A mutual understanding should e·
sp 70–15 Does life or soul e· in the thing formed?
74–13 No correspondence nor communion can e· between
82–12 cannot e· in two different states of
s 153–22 The fact that pain cannot e· where
162–14 indestructible faculties of Spirit e· without
ph 188– 3 What is termed disease does not e·.
f 213– 8 Immortal and spiritual facts e· apart from
c 262–31 Cause does not e· in matter, in mortal mind,
b 281–18 The mind supposed to e· in matter
310– 4 Did it e· prior to thought?
319–16 presuppose life and intelligence to e· in
327– 5 neither . . . e· in or of matter,
334–17 continues to e· in the eternal order
335–21 Soul . . . does not e· in mortality.
337–25 as they e· in the spiritual realm of the real.
o 352–14 Would a mother say . . . They e·, and are to be
feared ;
p 429–19 If man did not e· before the material
429–20 If . . . he could not e· after the body
t 461– 1 I do not maintain that anyone can e· in the
r 488–30 since they e· in immortal Mind, not in matter.
g 546– 5 If . . . error must e· in the divine Mind,
gl 581–13 the spiritual realities . . . e· forever.

existed

b 302–15 harmonious and immortal man has e· forever,
r 470–30 If man ever e· without this perfect Principle

existence

all
pr 2–29 the source of all e· and blessedness.
ph 181– 2 God, is the source and condition of all e·
b 280–27 God, the Soul of man and of all e·,
gl 588–12 Mind, governing all e· ;
589–10 God is the divine Principle of all e·,
and continuity
g 513–19 e·, and continuity of all individuality
and happiness
g 545–29 destructive to e· and happiness.
and intelligence
g 510–17 giving e· and intelligence to the universe.
and utility
an 100–18 "In regard to the e· and utility of
belief that
p 427–10 belief that e· is contingent on matter
bodily
b 334–12 Jesus appeared as a bodily e·.
chain of
ph 172–12 Science reveals the eternal chain of e·
consciousness of
p 428–24 must hold forever the consciousness of e·,
consecrate
p 428–15 We should consecrate e·,

existence

contemplation of
g 550–16 contemplation of e· as material
continued
sp 81– 9 a continued e· after death
continues to be
sp 77– 5 E· continues to be a belief . . . until
declaring
r 481–14 declaring e· to be at the mercy of death,
demonstrating the
b 314– 9 demonstrating the e· of but one Mind
deny the
ph 189–11 than they should deny the e· of the sunlight
p 368–29 Deny the e· of matter, and you can
dream of
g 529– 8 will destroy the dream of e·,
dream that
p 427–13 the dream that e· can be material.
earthly
p 387–15 the shortest span of earthly e·,
elevation of
sp 98– 2 the elevation of e· above mortal discord
eternal
m 65– 6 spiritual and eternal e· may be discerned.
b 319–13 the infinite cycles of eternal e·,
p 387–20 By adhering to the realities of eternal e·,
evidence of the
o 359–15 The evidence of the e· of Spirit,
fabulous
f 231–18 discords have only a fabulous e·,
facts of
sp 95–31 Material sense does not unfold the facts of e· ;
f 254– 9 before the spiritual facts of e· are gained
g 552–11 spiritual scientific facts of e· include no
gl 597–19 spiritual sense unfolds the great facts of e·.
form of
p 369–13 or the constructor of any form of e·,
g 541– 2 A lamb is a more animate form of e·,
grades of
g 551–12 through all the lower grades of e·.
happiness and
o 356–14 each other's happiness and e·.
p 407–20 the scale of health, happiness, and e·.
r 487– 2 find a higher sense of happiness and e·.
harmonious
b 320–19 man's eternal and harmonious e· as image,
harmony of our
ph 167– 9 determines the harmony of our e·,
has no real
s 114–17 to designate that which has no real e·.
b 287–23 it is illusion, . . . and it has no real e·.
gl 584–11 Matter has no life, hence it has no real e·.
human
ph 190–22 saddening strains on human e· :
f 205–28 Selfishness tips the beam of human e·
ignorant of the
g 512–30 albeit God is ignorant of the e· of both
immortal
g 514– 1 not within the range of immortal e·
incorporeal
pr 13–29 man's eternal incorporeal e·.
infantile
g 554–13 unconscious of his fœtal and infantile e· ;
infinitude of
b 302– 7 conscious infinitude of e· and of all identity
inimical to
p 389–21 cannot . . . be inimical to e·.
intelligent
sp 73–27 any part of the reality of intelligent e·,
life or
b 311–29 lose all . . . claim to life or e·,
manifestation of
g 555–29 individualized manifestation of e·,
man's
pr 13–31 blind to the reality of man's e·,
b 306–20 Science proves man's e· to be intact.
o 352– 9 spirituality, was the reality of man's e·,
359–12 you aver that . . . are indispensable to man's e·
r 470–31 If . . . then man's e· was a myth.
material
(see material)
misapprehension of
ph 191– 9 is found to be a misapprehension of e·,
mortal
(see mortal)
my own
ph 177– 7 certain as the evidence of my own e·.
nature and
sp 84–23 by which we discern man's nature and e·.
necessity of
ap 560–13 the grand necessity of e· is to gain the
no other
b 310–28 Spirit, which has no other e·,
r 492– 5 In reality there is no other e·,
no proof of the
an 100–20 no proof of the e· of the animal magnetic

existence

nor realness
o 347– 5 has no origin, *e·*, nor realness.
not the fact, of
s 127–20 matter is the falsity, not the fact, of *e·* ;
of man
p 427–15 Nothing can . . . end the *e·* of man in Science.
origin or
b 287– 1 They are without a real origin or *e·*.
g 554–12 of its origin or *e·*.
or mind
a 42–19 belief that man has *e·* or mind separate
personal
sp 82– 7 of whose personal *e·* we may be in doubt?
phenomena of
p 430– 2 includes all the phenomena of *e·*.
plane of
sp 77– 9 Death will occur on the next plane of *e·*
ap 573– 3 The Revelator was on our plane of *e·*,
planes of
f 226– 3 found on higher planes of *e·*
primeval
s 110– 4 These eternal verities reveal primeval *e·*
Principle of
c 262–31 the only cause or Principle of *e·*.
real
b 288–32 man's real *e·* as a child of God
317–32 Nothing but . . . could make *e·* real to Thomas.
p 395–24 to believe in the real *e·* of a tumor,
reality nor
b 331–12 nothing possesses reality nor *e·* except
reality of
f 215– 9 Mortals are unacquainted with the reality of *e·*,
reflected in
g 516–10 Life is reflected in *e·*,
rightful
b 281–24 without actual origin or rightful *e·*.
scale of
b 290– 6 no higher spiritually in the scale of *e·*
sense of
sp 75– 9 from the spiritual sense of *e·*
s 122–28 Temporal life is a false sense of *e·*.
g 539– 1 This false sense of *e·* is fratricidal.
ap 566– 8 from a material sense of *e·* to the
spiritual
(*see* **spiritual**)
stage of
sp 77–25 less with every advanced stage of *e·*.
f 244–15 If man were dust in his earliest stage of *e·*,
250–28 Upon this stage of *e·* goes on the dance of
state of
(*see* **state**)
states of
sp 74–32 they are in separate states of *e·*,
still in the
sp 75– 4 still in the *e·* cognized by the physical senses,
supposed
s 126– 1 its supposed organic action or supposed *e·*.
r 470– 5 supposed *e·* of more than one mind
sustain
b 274– 2 and thus invigorate and sustain *e·*.
thoughts of
c 263– 7 blends his thoughts of *e·* with
to happify
m 58– 1 To happify *e·* by constant intercourse with
true
c 264–26 by which we can recognize true *e·*
b 283– 2 belief that there is any true *e·* apart from God.
unreality of
p 207–10 evil is the awful deception and unreality of *e·*.
verities of
g 543–15 great verities of *e·* are never excluded by
views of
f 246–29 shape our views of *e·* into loveliness,
world's
pref ix– 5 He is as sure of the world's *e·* as
your own
p 374–20 and incapacity to preserve your own *e·*,

ph 175–30 of the *e·* of tubercles and troches,
f 206– 3 no consciousness of the *e·* of matter or error.
215–25 antipode of immortal man in origin, in *e·*, and
216–24 would appear . . . to be the rule of *e·*,
c 266– 6 Would *e·* without personal friends be
b 307–15 transient, false sense of an *e·* which
p 368–27 Admit the *e·* of matter, and
425–16 matter never sustained *e·*
t 445– 6 No hypothesis as to the *e·* of another power
g 522–10 *E·*, separate from divinity, . . . impossible.
545–23 They believed in the *e·* of matter,
556–29 *e·* will be on a new standpoint.

existent
s 120–22 reveals man as harmoniously *e·* in Truth,
b 302–18 illusion of any life, . . . as *e·* in matter.
308–18 a mortal sense of life, . . . as *e·* in matter
311–18 mortal dream of life . . . as *e·* in matter,
r 472–15 supposition that pleasure and pain, . . . are *e·* in

existing
gl 587–13 theories that hold mind to be . . . *e·* in brain,

exists
a 39–26 divine Principle of all that really *e·*
m 64–29 a worse state of society than now *e·*.
an 100– 8 propositions . . . "There *e·* a mutual influence
s 110–32 No analogy *e·* between the vague hypotheses
151–26 All that really *e·* is the divine Mind
ph 171–23 No more sympathy *e·* between the flesh and
177– 8 Neither *e·* without the other,
188–31 knows not where the orb of day is, nor if it *e·*.
f 202– 3 The scientific unity which *e·* between
215– 6 being cannot be lost while God *e·*.
253–28 for no such law *e·*.
c 258–15 Mind manifests all that *e·*
b 271– 6 Neither . . . *e·* in divine Science.
272–30 the divine Principle . . . of all that really *e·*.
278–13 *e·* only in a supposititious . . . consciousness.
311–10 Sin *e·* . . . only so long as the
340–13 all that really *e·* is in and of God,
o 357–28 if another mighty and self-creative cause *e·*
g 514– 4 nothing *e·* beyond the range of . . . infinity,
520– 7 can repeat only an infinitesimal part of what *e·*.
531–22 Who dares to say . . . that matter *e·* without
544–11 fact that man *e·* because God *e·*.
554– 2 even the cause of all that *e·*,
gl 592– 8 that which neither *e·* in Science nor
594– 7 the first delusion that error *e·* as fact ;

exit
s 117–22 and triumphant *e·* from the flesh.

expand
f 252–28 and says : . . . Like bursting lava, I *e·*
c 264–17 this understanding will *e·* into

expands
c 255– 3 thought *e·* into expression.

expansive
ph 195–20 study, and original thought are *e·*
c 265–14 confers upon man . . . a more *e·* love,

expect
pr   2–26 Do we *e·* to change perfection?
ph 167–23 or to *e·* to work equally with Spirit and matter,
f 219–10 and then *e·* that the result will be harmony.
237–27 and *e·* this error to do more for them than
p 409–30 cannot . . . *e·* to find beyond the grave a
t 452–23 *E·* to heal simply by . . . and you will be disappointed.

expectation
c 260–26 and by the *e·* of perpetual pleasure or pain
p 363–30 sufficient evidence to warrant the *e·*
396–12 nor encourage . . . the *e·* of growing worse
426– 9 *e·* speeds our progress.

expected
m 59–10 nor should woman be *e·* to understand political

expecting
a 21– 6 not . . . to labor and pray, *e·* because of
ph 177–27 though physician and patient are *e·* favorable

expedients
t 443–22 If the sick find these material *e·* unsatisfactory,

expel
r 482–27 Error will not *e·* error.

expelled
o 346–29 Material beliefs must be *e·*
t 460–30 As former beliefs were gradually *e*

expelling
p 437–24 rose to the question of *e·* C. S. from the bar,

expels
s 153– 3 it is not the drug which *e·* the disease
162– 7 It changes the secretions, *e·* humors,
p 374–31 then *e·* it through the abandonment of a belief,

expense
c 260–28 this education is at the *e·* of spiritual growth.

experience
author's
g 556–28 hence the author's *e·* ;
bitter
a 32–12 The cup shows forth his bitter *e·*,
brief
ph 194– 3 Reviewing this brief *e·*,
Christian
a 29– 7 Christian *e·* teaches faith in the right
daily
o 350– 4 or as very far removed from daily *e·*.
earthly
f 202–21 earthly *e·* discloses the finity of error
fruits of
gl 579– 9 surrendering to the creator the early fruits of *e·*.
higher
pr   7–20 a higher *e·* and a better life

experience
human
sp 99–25 spirituality, . . . must deepen human *e·*,
g 552–13 Human *e·* in mortal life,
ap 572–24 transitional stage in human *e·* called death,
individual
a 26– 5 yet Jesus spares us not one individual *e·*,
p 370–24 medical testimony and individual *e·*,
in practice
t 461–32 student's spiritual growth and *e·* in practice
my
o 360– 4 other artist replies : "You wrong my *e·*.
of death
b 291–10 belief in the *e·* of death
of error
f 237–18 To prevent the *e·* of error and its sufferings,
personal
pref x–23 in the personal *e·* of any sincere seeker
single
b 290– 7 on account of that single *e·*,
speak from
pr 1– 5 I speak from *e·*.
stage of
m 66–15 Each successive stage of *e·* unfolds new views
teaches us
pr 10–22 *E·* teaches us that we do not always
your
f 248–23 and adopt into your *e·* the angular
c 261– 6 and you will bring these into your *e·*

pr 4–26 and patience must bring *e·*.
a 22– 7 Waking to Christ's demand, mortals *e·* suffering.
36– 2 They, who know not purity and affection by *e·*,
39–22 now is the time in which to *e·* that salvation
m 65– 1 *E·* should be the school of virtue,
s 122–21 *E·* is full of instances of similar illusions,
f 217– 8 Paul's peculiar Christian conversion and *e·*,
238–11 an *e·* we have not made our own,
240–31 learning from *e·* how to divide between
b 296– 4 Progress is born of *e·*.
p 394–17 *E·* has proved to the author the
421–26 than it is to *e·* it.
t 443–14 If patients fail to *e·* the
r 493–20 Disease is an *e·* of so-called mortal mind.
ap 574–21 brought also the *e·* which

experienced
a 34–18 Through all the disciples *e·*,
38–21 Jesus *e·* few of the pleasures
f 213–20 Mozart *e·* more than he expressed.
c 266–15 The author has *e·* the foregoing prophecy
p 385–16 can be *e·* without suffering.
420– 6 should early call an *e·* Christian Scientist

experiences
pref viii–26 *e·* which led her, in the year 1866,
s 108– 7 human *e·* show the falsity of all material things ;
c 261–11 If one turns away from . . . the body *e·* no pain.
b 322–26 The sharp *e·* of belief in the
r 494–21 as the *e·* of the sleeping dream seem real

experiencing
sp 92– 5 is not only capable of *e·*
f 250–19 *e·* none of these dream-sensations.
o 356–20 as He is of *e·* these errors.

experiment
an 101– 6 an important *e·* upon the power of
p 379–16 think of the *e·* of those Oxford boys,

experimental
f 230–16 cannot be, the author of *e·* sins.

experimentally
t 456– 9 reputation *e·* justified by their efforts.

experimented
p 379– 9 A felon, on whom certain English students *e·*,

Experiments, Beaumont's Medical
ph 175–24 Beaumont's "Medical *E·*" did not govern the

experiments
s 152–21 The author's medical researches and *e·*
152–28 Her *e·* in homœopathy had made her skeptical
162–12 *E·* have favored the fact that Mind governs

expert
p 375–29 seems anomalous except to the *e·* in C. S.

expiate
ap 569–20 eventually *e·* their sin through suffering.

explain
a 27–17 Jesus' parables *e·* Life as never mingling with
sp 83– 6 Science only can *e·* the incredible good
s 126–17 Shall Science *e·* cause and effect
145– 3 sweet tones, . . . without being able to *e·* them.
148–22 Then theology tries to *e·* how to make
ph 189– 9 to *e·* the effect of mortal mind
200– 8 Whoever is incompetent to *e·* Soul
b 328–19 can it be said that they *e·* it practically,
o 350–16 The Master often refused to *e·* his words,
p 388– 4 a victory which Science alone can *e·*.

explain
p 396–22 At the right time *e·* to the sick the
414–15 *e·* C. S. to them, but not too soon,
417–27 *E·* audibly to your patients,
421–23 sometimes *e·* the symptoms and their cause
422–13 *e·* to them the law of this action.
438–29 we have heard Materia Medica *e·* how
r 487–22 without Principle from which to *e·* the
490–28 Sleep and mesmerism *e·* the mythical nature
493– 9 *Question.* — Will you *e·* sickness
g 510–20 it cannot *e·* them.

explained
a 33– 9 Their Master had *e·* it all before,
46–22 and this exaltation *e·* his ascension,
s 124–16 but when *e·* on the basis of physical sense
131–26 *e·* the so-called miracles of olden time
138–10 On this spiritually scientific basis Jesus *e·*
b 334–28 [Science has *e·* me]."
o 350–14 Unless the works . . . which his words *e·*,
350–31 the Word was materially *e·*,
p 420–14 This fact of C. S. should be *e·* to invalids when
441– 2 *e·* from his statute-book, the Bible,
g 501–15 *e·* by that Love for whose rest the
510–20 Geology has never *e·* the earth's formations ;

explaining
a 33–11 *breaking* (*e·*) it to others,
b 292–19 *E·* the origin of material man
315–32 *E·* and demonstrating the way

explains
pref xi– 5 C. S. rationally *e·* that all other
sp 80–16 and *e·* extraordinary phenomena ;
89–23 *e·* the phenomena of improvisation
s 114–23 C. S. *e·* all cause and effect as mental,
148– 8 The former *e·* the man of *men*,
b 278– 3 Divine metaphysics *e·* away matter.
o 343–15 the impossibility of good producing evil ;
361– 2 Here C. S. intervenes, *e·* these
p 433– 5 *e·* the law relating to liver-complaint.
r 470–11 Divine Science *e·* the abstract statement
493– 5 science contradicts this, and *e·* the
g 511– 3 and so *e·* the Scripture phrase,
522–11 Science *e·* as impossible.
534–14 and the Apostle Paul *e·* this warfare
545– 1 Error . . . *e·* Deity through mortal and finite

explanation
easy
an 102–26 not lending itself to an easy *e·*
her
p 374–10 in her *e·* of disease as originating in
of body
ph 200– 9 would be wise not to undertake the *e·* of body.
of optics
s 111–15 even as the *e·* of optics rejects the
Principle and
sp 83–28 gains the divine Principle and *e·* of all things.
scientific
a 23– 9 but its scientific *e·* is, that
this
ph 173–18 Physiology continues this *e·*,
b 302– 6 not lost, but found through this *e·* ;
without
s 149–10 they are left without *e·* except in C. S.
your
f 237–29 Impatient at your *e·*,

ph 189– 2 the *e·* of the sun's influence over the earth.
p 385– 5 *e·* lies in the support which they derived from
414–17 until your patients are prepared for the *e·*,
t 452–13 withhold not the rebuke or the *e·* which destroys
453– 9 chemicalization follows the *e·* of Truth,
g 504–21 Here we have the *e·* of another passage

explanations
f 237– 1 had occasionally listened to my *e·*,
r 482–13 Is it important to understand these *e·*
490–23 The scientifically Christian *e·* of the
g 555– 7 said . . . "I like your *e·* of truth,

explication
sp 83–16 since Science is an *e·* of nature.
g 501– 6 often seems so smothered . . . as to require *e·* ;

exploiting
t 457–31 without *e·* other means.

explored
s 121– 6 the heavenly fields were incorrectly *e·*.

exploring
a 26– 4 in speechless agony *e·* the way for us,

exponent
a 49– 9 Had they forgotten the great *e·* of God?

exponents
a 52–18 common cause against the *e·* of truth.

expose
p 384– 8   though they e· him to fatigue, cold, heat,
386– 5   E· the body to certain temperatures, and
t 447–20   E· and denounce the claims of evil
ap 571– 2   e· evil's hidden mental ways of

exposed
s 122– 8   e· nineteen hundred years ago
154–16   If a child is e· to contagion or infection,
ph 171–19   e· to ejection by the operation of
p 405–22   better to be e· to every plague on earth
g 539–21   this falsity is e· by our Master

exposes
sp 91–10   because Science e· his nothingness ;

exposition
pref ix–27   she made copious notes of Scriptural e·,
r 496–31   The following is a brief e· of

expositions
pref ix–16   not complete nor satisfactory e· of Truth.

exposure
s 154–22   Then it is believed that e· to the contagion
p 384–16   If e· to a draught of air while in a
384–21   such symptoms are not apt to follow e· ;
384–27   nor any other disease will ever result from e·
ap 571– 4   Why this backwardness, since e· is necessary

exposures
p 385– 4   have been able to undergo . . . fatigues and e·
385–15   Constant toil, deprivations, e·,

expound
t 464–22   has labored to e· divine Principle,
g 539–28   gave him more than human power to e·

expounder
t 459–29   the Christian and scientific e·

expounds
b 274–14   Christianity and the Science which e· it

express
pr 4–10   is not of itself sufficient to e· loyal and
8–15   gratitude, and love which our words e·,
sp 81–20   Erase the figures which e· number,
98–13   human hypotheses do not e· C. S. ;
f 223– 7   Matter does not e· Spirit.
b 313–11   and the e· [expressed] image— Heb. 1 : 3.
313–12   the phrase "e· image"— Heb. 1 : 3.
331–32   e· in divine Science the threefold,
332–30   highest type . . . which a fleshly form could e·
336–24   and nothing less can e· God.
o 354–21   If our words fail to e· our deeds,
r 465–13   also intended to e· the nature, essence,
470–25   If there ever was a moment when man did not e·
470–26   then there was a moment when man did not e

expressed
pr 4– 4   e· in patience, meekness, love, and
4–19   e· in daily watchfulness and in striving
11–32   It is best e· in thought and in life.
a 25– 5   infinitely greater than can be e· by our
88– 2   for which the poet Tennyson e·
sp 72–17   Perfection is not e· through imperfection.
s 111– 5   as e· through divine Science.
119–18   spiritual and is not e· in matter.
ph 178–20   divine Mind, e· in Science.
f 210 1   Its ideas are e· only in
213–20   Mozart experienced more than he e·.
c 259– 7   divine nature was best e· in Christ Jesus,
b 293–21   fury of mortal mind— e· in earthquake,
304–30   music is, must be, imperfectly e·.
313–11   and the express [e·] image— Heb. 1 : 3.
332– 6   As the apostle e· it in words which
332–29   He e· the highest type of divinity,
p 364–27   e· by meekness and human affection,
373–21   Disease is e· not so much by the lips as in
392–13   must be e· mentally,
423– 7   more strongly than the e· thought.
r 471–28   the spiritual import, e· through Science,
g 508–16   The feminine gender is not yet e·
519–10   are complete and forever e·,
520– 3   Unfathomable Mind, e·,
541–10   the worship e· by Cain's fruit?

expresses
pr 3–26   Action e· more gratitude than speech.
a 23–28   e· the helplessness of a blind faith ;
38–16   It e· spiritual power ;
f 208–26   A material body only e· a material and
c 258–13   God e· in man the infinite idea
b 298–15   Material sense e· the belief that
300–28   reflects and e· the divine substance
310–10   God is His own infinite Mind, and e· all.
331–17   Everything in God's universe e· Him.
333– 9   Christ e· God's spiritual, eternal nature.
p 376–21   only what that so-called mind e·
r 467–31   understood through the idea which e· it
468–28   Eternity, not time, e· the thought of Life,
477–30   Separated from man, who e· Soul, Spirit would
484–13   The physical universe e· the conscious

expresses
g 507–26   This divine Principle of all e· Science
518–27   Spirit, comprehends and e· all,
ap 576–27   The term Lord, . . . e· the Jewish concept,

expressing
sp 89–20   beauty and poetry, and the power of e· them.
s 114–19   in e· the new tongue we must
115– 5   difficulty of so e· metaphysical ideas
p 424–17   e· such opinions as may alarm
g 507– 5   tenderly e· the fatherhood and

expression
audible
pr 11–32   Such a desire has little need of audible e·.
fervency of
pr 8–21   with whatever fervency of e·
fuller
o 361–22   to give a clearer and fuller e·
infinite
b 336–10   even the infinite e· of infinite Mind,
of Soul
r 477–26   Man is the e· of Soul.
of Spirit
r 484–30   the understanding and e· of Spirit?
perfect
gl 591–19   of whom man is the full and perfect e· ;
public
pr 13–12   Can the mere public e· of our desires
verbal
pr 3–25   Gratitude is much more than a verbal e· of

sp 86–26   peculiarities of e·, recollected sentences,
f 210–19   The e· mortal mind is really a solecism,
247–23   reflects the charms of His goodness in e·,
c 255– 3   thought expands into e·.
b 289– 9   He is little else than the e· of error.
o 349–16   English is inadequate to the e· of
r 470–23   Man is the e· of God's being.

expressions
g 518–22   All the varied e· of God

expressive
b 320– 5   names are often e· of spiritual ideas.

extend
p 418–18   negation must e· to the supposed disease

extended
a 43–20   perpetuated and e· it.

extends
s 128–16   It e· the atmosphere of thought,
146–29   and e· throughout all space.
b 328–31   purpose of his great life-work e· through time

extent
s 139–22   darkening to some e· the inspired pages.
163–25   Nowhere is . . . displayed to a greater e· ;
o 349–28   To a certain e· this is equally

exterminated
s 164–16   diseased thought-germs are e·.
p 377–11   when their fear of climate is e·.

exterminates
s 157– 8   C. S. e· the drug, and rests on Mind

extermination
g 543–15   is engaged in a warfare of e·.

exterminator
r 469–13   The e· of error is the great truth

externalized
o 360–13   which mind-picture or e· thought
p 411–23   an image of thought e·.
g 512–15   e·, yet subjective, states of faith and
522–13   gives the history of error in its e· forms,

externals
pr 8– 8   such e· are spoken of by Jesus as

extinct
sp 74–11   When . . . the belief of life in matter is e·,
b 309–30   Life is never for a moment e·.

extinction
s 116–16   even to the e· of all belief in matter,

extinguish
b 298– 5   As a cloud hides the sun it cannot e·,

extinguished
a 51–18   no more . . . than God could be e·.

extinguishes
r 474–32   Light e· the darkness,

extract
an 102–24   an e· from the Boston Herald :
f 201–17   The way to e· error from mortal mind is to

extracted
f 212– 3   tooth . . . e· sometimes aches again in belief,

extracts
p 437–33   certain e· on the Rights of Man,

extraordinary
   sp 80–16 dispels mystery and explains e· phenomena ;
extravagance
   m 58–26 a wife ought not to court vulgar e·
extreme
   ap 570– 6 shocked into another e· mortal mood,
       570– 7 for one e· follows another.
extremity
   ph 166–25 in his e· and only as a last resort,
  · *c* 266–14 "man's e· is God's opportunity."
eye (*see also* **eye's**)
  beholds
   r 479–10 An image . . . is all that the e· beholds.
  blue
   f 220– 9 The violet lifts her blue e· to greet the
  brother's
   t 455–16 mote out of thy brother's e·."— *Matt.* 7: 5.
  ear and
   sp 84–20 not dependent upon the ear and e· for
  guided by the
   p 429– 8 When walking, we are guided by the e·.
  hath not seen
   ph 179– 7 Immortal Mind heals what e· hath not seen ;
   c 255–18 E· hath not seen Spirit, nor hath ear heard
   t 459– 2 "e· hath not seen nor ear heard."— *I Cor.* 2: 9.
   g 554– 1 reveals what "e· hath not seen,"— *I Cor.* 2: 9.
  human
   a 49–16 No human e· was there to pity,
   ph 188–30 The human e· knows not where the orb of day is,
  mine
   c 262–18 but now mine e· seeth Thee."— *Job.* 42: 5.
  of a needle
   f 241–31 to go through the e· of a needle,"— *Matt.* 19: 24.
   t 449–10 to go through the e· of a needle,"— *Matt.* 19: 24.
  physical
   s 121–18 is invisible to the physical e·,
  right
   s 141– 7 cut off the right hand and pluck out the right e·,
  testimony of the
   s 121–21 false testimony of the e· deluded the
  thine own
   t 455–15 the beam out of thine own e· ;— *Matt.* 7: 5.
  through the
   b 284–22 They can neither see Spirit through the e· nor
  twinkling of an
   b 291– 6 "in the twinkling of an e·,"— *I Cor.* 15: 52.

   a 30–15 "An e· for an e·,"— *Matt.* 5: 38.
   b 330–13 E· hath neither seen God nor His image
   p 378–11 By looking a tiger fearlessly in the e·,
      378–13 may infuriate another by looking it in the e·,
     393–26 "the light of the body is the e·,"— *Matt.* 6: 22.
   r 486– 4 Suppose one accident happens to the e·,
   ap 573– 4 while yet beholding what the e· cannot see,
eyelids
   ph 193–11 e· closed gently and the breathing became
eye's
   s 122–16 On the e· retina, sky and tree-tops

eyes
  blind
   t 444– 2 these very failures may open their blind e·.
  causes the
   f 211–25 If . . . material organism causes the e· to see
  close the
   sp 87–30 We have but to close the e·, and forms rise
  close your
   sp 71–10 Close your e·, and you may dream that you
     71–14 Close your e· again, and you may
  having
   a 38–28 Having e· ye see not,
   gl 586– 6 "Having e·, see ye not?"— *Mark* 8: 18.
  his
   ph 193– 8 Mr. Clark lay with his e· fixed and sightless.
     193–13 In about ten minutes he opened his e·
     195– 1 His e· were inflamed by the light.
   f 221–23 These truths, opening his e·,
   c 255–11 Mortal man has made a covenant with his e·
  laughing
   f 237– 5 Bounding off with laughing e·, she presently
  man's
   ph 165– 3 declared . . . this fruit would open man's e·
  mortal
   b 334–20 Jesus was incarnate to mortal e·.
  of purer
   f 243–22 "of purer e· than to behold evil,"— *Hab.* 1: 13.
   o 357– 4 "of purer e· than to behold evil."— *Hab.* 1: 13.
  opened the
   a 49– 3 opened the e· of their understanding,
  open the
   t 451–24 obligated to open the e· of his students
   ap 570–30 willing to open the e· of the people to the
  our
   b 268– * *which we have seen with our e·,*— *I John* 1: 1.
   r 491–22 goes on, whether our e· are closed or open.
  people's
   f 220– 5 Such admissions ought to open people's e·
  solemn
   p 434–18 earnest, solemn e·, kindling with hope
  their
   a 43– 4 his material disappearance before their e·
   o 350–19 and their e· they have closed ;— *Matt.* 13: 15.
     350–21 they should see with their e·,— *Matt.* 13: 15.
  through the
   pref ix– 4 drinks in the outward world through the e·
  your
   g 530–15 then your e· shall be opened ;— *Gen.* 3: 5.
     530–20 and saying, . . . "I can open your e·.
   ap 574–26 it will lift the sackcloth from your e·,

   sp 76– 3 at Niagara, with e· open only to that wonder,
   ph 165– 4 it closed the e· of mortals
     189– 3 If the e· see no sun for a week, we still
   t 452– 8 e· accustomed to darkness are pained by
   g 530–23 saying, . . . more pleasant to the e·
   gl 586– 3 definition of
eye-witness
   p 436– 2 he was an e· to the good deeds

F

fable
   s 129– 8 by reversing the material f·,
     129– 9 be the f· *pro* or *con*,
   b 302–19 This statement is based on fact, not f·.
   p 408– 7 a universal insanity . . . mistakes f· for fact
   g 544–18 suggestion of more than the one Mind,— is in
        the f·
   gl 586– 7 Fan. Separator of f· from fact ;
fables
   an 103–26 they annihilate the f· of mortal mind,
fabulous
   f 231–18 discords have only a f· existence,
face
  before the
   a 49–31 before the f· of the Most High,"— *Lam.* 3: 35.
  her
   s 154–29 little one, who thinks she has hurt her f·
  his
   ph 193–10 In a few moments his f· changed ;
   ap 558– 5 and his f· was as it were the sun,— *Rev.* 10: 1.
  My
   s 140– 6 "Thou canst not see My f· ;— *Exod.* 33: 20.
  name the
   sp 76– 2 name the f· that smiles on them
  of Jesus
   c 260– 5 or the painter can depict the form and f· of Jesus,
  of the sky
   sp 85–21 can discern the f· of the sky ;— *Matt.* 16: 3.
   f 233–17 Ye who can discern the f· of the sky,
   g 509–31 can discern the f· of the sky ;— *Matt.* 16: 3.

face
  one
   t 457–15 each of them could see but one f· of it,
  pallid
   p 415–17 Note how thought makes the f· pallid.
  sallow
   p 433–14 His sallow f· blanches with fear,
  sun's
   g 548–10 when clouds cover the sun's f· !
  Thy
   ph 190–28 As for me, I will behold Thy f·— *Psal.* 17: 15.
  thy
   g 535–25 in the sweat of thy f· shalt thou— *Gen.* 3: 19.
  whole
   g 521–22 the whole f· of the ground.— *Gen.* 2: 6.

   pr 8– 5 f· to f· with their wickedness
   s 121– 1 and starvation stared him in the f· ;
     163–11 druggist, or drug on the f· of the earth,
   f 245–14 She had no care-lined f·,
   c 263–29 thrown into the f· of spiritual immensity,
   b 305– 5 a f· reflected in the mirror is not the original,
     338–18 upon the f· of the deep,"— *Gen.* 1: 2.
   o 342– 9 presumptuously, in the f· of Bible history
   t 450– 7 while looking you blandly in the f·,
   r 479–20 upon the f· of the deep."— *Gen.* 1: 2.
   g 503– 7 upon the f· of the deep.— *Gen.* 1: 2.
     503– 8 moved upon the f· of the waters.— *Gen.* 1: 2.
     503–13 saith to the darkness upon the f· of error,
     518– 6 upon the f· of all the earth,— *Gen.* 1: 29.
   ap 558–14 When you look it fairly in the f·,

faces

p 439–16 in the perturbed f· of these worthies,
gl 596–29 The Jewish women wore veils over their f·

facilitate

p 421–10 showing him that it was to f· recovery.

fac-similes

sp 86–25 Portraits, landscape-paintings, f· of

fact

awful
r 472–28 the awful f· that unrealities seem real
based on
b 302–18 This statement is based on f·, not fable.
central
s 131–10 The central f· of the Bible is the
concerning error
sp 92–22 Until the f· concerning error — namely,
counter
f 233–28 The counter f· relative to any disease
demonstrable
s 108– 6 unfolding to me the demonstrable f· that
elaborated the
s 141–14 Jesus elaborated the f· that the healing effect
established
p 384–28 In Science this is an established f·
eternal
g 544–10 Matter cannot change the eternal f·
every
t 450– 2 twist every f· to suit themselves.
figure or in
b 282–13 Mind and . . . never unite in figure or in f·.
fixed
m 65–26 Matrimony, which was once a fixed f· among us,
ph 180–19 by declaring disease to be a fixed f·,
foundational
o 348–12 Jesus established this foundational f·,
glorious
g 529– 9 usher in Science and the glorious f· of creation,
great
s 109– 6 This great f· is not, however, seen to be
137–17 and his reply set forth a great f· :
ph 199– 9 Hence the great f· that Mind alone
f 228– 4 impossible if this great f· of being were learned,
b 285– 5 the great f· of being for time and eternity.
339–26 the great f· that God is the only Mind ;
o 343–18 scientifically demonstrates this great f·,
p 398–32 The great f· remains that
412– 1 The great f· that God lovingly governs all,
421–16 great f· which covers the whole ground,
430–12 When will mankind wake to this great f·
harmony is the
p 412–23 Mentally insist that harmony is the f·,
heedless of the
p 362– 7 Heedless of the f· that she was debarred
ignorant of the
s 159–30 Ignorant of the f· that a man's belief produces
illustrates the
p 402–24 mesmerism . . . illustrates the f· just stated.
immortal
b 327– 4 Science, which reveals the immortal f·
in metaphysics
s 154– 9 This f· in metaphysics is illustrated by
in Science
ap 573– 6 This testimony . . . sustains the f· in Science,
knowledge of the
ph 199–19 of less importance than a knowledge of the f·.
matter of
r 486–32 as a matter of f·, these calamities often
mere
p 363–32 there was encouragement in the mere f·
mistaking
sp 84– 5 not by foreshadowing evil and mistaking f·
of being
f 228– 4 if this great f· of being were learned,
249–26 is sometimes nearer the f· of being than
b 285– 5 the great f· of being for time and eternity.
320–18 declares plainly the spiritual f· of being,
one
r 492– 3 should be but one f· before the thought,
one more
an 101– 5 one more f· to be recorded in the history of
only
b 297–17 The only f· concerning any material concept is,
r 471–20 spirituality of the universe is the only f·
remains
s 164–23 the forever f· remains paramount
b 289–23 the f· remains, that God's universe is
scientific
m 69– 2 The scientific f· that man and the universe
f 207–27 The spiritual reality is the scientific f·
b 295–13 will at last yield to the scientific f·
spiritual
(see **spiritual**)
such a
s 152–19 Such a f· illustrates our theories.

fact

this
sp 81–10 this f· affords no certainty of
s 111–27 this f· became evident to me,
134–32 This f· at present seems more mysterious than
145–17 From this f· arise its ethical as well as
151–29 acknowledge this f·, yield to this power,
154– 9 This f· in metaphysics is illustrated by
ph 194–14 theory opposed to this f· . . . would presuppose
f 207– 5 This f· proves our position,
320–21 avers that this f· is not forever to be humbled
p 420–13 This f· of C. S. should be explained to invalids
427– 1 If it is true that man lives, this f· can never
r 467–11 in proportion as this f· becomes apparent,
whereas the
pref viii–10 whereas the f· is that Spirit is good and real,
f 211–28 whereas the f· is that only through

———

sp 73– 6 The f· is that neither the one nor the other
s 116–17 They never . . . insist upon the f· that God is all,
127–20 It teaches that matter is the falsity, not the f·,
143– 2 Hence the f· that, to-day, as yesterday, Christ
153–22 The f· that pain cannot exist where there is no
154–13 f· was, that he had not caught the cholera by
162–12 Experiments have favored the f· that Mind
f 222–12 availed himself of the f· that Mind governs
238–29 To reconstruct timid justice and place the f·
b 270–29 Hence the f· that the human mind
289–14 the f· that the Christ, or Truth, overcame
339–11 can receive no encouragement from the f·
p 368– 3 confidence inspired by Science lies in the f·
368–29 has a foundation in f·.
371– 1 when in f· all is Mind,
371–28 father to the f· that Mind can do it ;
374–12 is in f· the objective state of mortal mind,
388–22 The f· is, food does not affect the absolute
408– 2 This view is not altered by the f· that
408– 7 mistakes fable for f· throughout the entire
412–25 Realize the presence of health and the f·
414–11 the f· that truth and love will establish a
420–17 f· that Truth overcomes both disease and
r 486– 1 matter is without foundation in f·,
gl 606 7 F·N. Separator of fable from f· ;
594–11 the first delusion that error exists as f· ;

factor

pref x– 8 this mind not a f· in the Principle of C. S.
s 109– 2 as the leading f· in Mind-science,
144–20 is not a f· in the realism of being.
151– 2 as if there was but one f· in the case ;
151– 3 but this one f· they represent to be body,
159–14 as if matter were the only f· to be consulted
ph 185–21 excludes the human mind as a spiritual f·
p 370–14 faith in the drug is the sole f· in the cure.

factors

r 492–30 theory, . . . is that there are two f·,

facts

broadest
op 97–21 The broadest f· array the most falsities
connate
pref viii–21 the response deducible from two connate f·,
conscious
gl 593– 5 the conscious f· of spiritual Truth.
demonstrate the
p 429–27 and do not demonstrate the f· it involves.
eternal
b 293–16 perpetuating the eternal f·
everlasting
s 121–20 rebuked by clearer views of the everlasting f·,
fundamental
s 120– 9 arrive at the fundamental f· of being.
grand
f 244– 4 Divine Science reveals these grand f·.
t 460–26 she had to impart, while teaching its grand f·,
r 471– 9 afford no indication of the grand f· of being ;
great
s 122– 4 the great f· of Life, rightly understood,
gl 597–19 spiritual sense unfolds the great f· of
immortal
b 279–17 the immortal f· of being are seen,
p 428–28 the immortal f· of being are admitted.
important
g 548–28 important f· in regard to so-called embryonic
invincible
a 55– 5 but this does not affect the invincible f·.
maintain the
p 417–11 Maintain the f· of C. S., — that Spirit is God,
of being
(see **being**)
of creation
g 539–28 power to expound the f· of creation,
544–19 The f· of creation, as previously recorded,
of divine Science
r 471–13 f· of divine Science should be admitted,

facts
of existence
  sp 95–30   does not unfold the *f·* of existence ;
  g 552–11   spiritual scientific *f·* of existence
  gl 597–19   unfolds the great *f·* of existence.
of harmony
  o 356– 7   Discord can never establish the *f·* of harmony.
of Mind
  b 268–18   as well as on the *f·* of Mind.
  283–10   They are not *f·* of Mind.
of Science
  g 516– 7   subordinate . . . to the *f·* of Science,
of Soul
  p 420–31   the harmonious *f·* of Soul and immortal being.
  428– 4   demonstration of the *f·* of Soul in Jesus' way
of Spirit
  f 215–10   matter and mortality do not reflect the *f·* of Spirit.
  b 281–30   as we grasp the *f·* of Spirit.
only
  r 479–22   the only *f·* are Spirit and its innumerable
permanent
  c 264– 2   before the permanent *f·* . . . appear.
primal
  sp 87–15   for it presents primal *f·* to mortal mind.
spiritual
  (*see* **spiritual**)
subserving the
  b 319– 4   error reversed as subserving the *f·*
these
  s 139–20   these *f·* show how a mortal and material sense
  ph 169–10   I name these *f·* to show that disease has
  r 471–14   the evidence as to these *f·* is not
true
  p 376–23   true *f·* in regard to harmonious being,
two
  f 251–10   mortals wake to the knowledge of two *f·* :

  an 101–13   "The *f·* which had been promised by
  s 149–32   The logic is lame, and *f·* contradict it.
  f 237–23   Some invalids are unwilling to know the *f·*
  o 341–17   The *f·* are so absolute and numerous
  343– 8   unfair to impugn and misrepresent the *f·*,
  p 369– 8   He enters into a diviner sense of the *f·*,
  438–21   the *f·* in the case show that this fur
  r 476–19   the *f·* which belong to immortal man.
  496–22   belief, at war with the *f·* of immortal Life,

faculties
  s 162–14   The indestructible *f·* of Spirit exist without
  f 211–27   then, when the body is dematerialized, these *f·*
  211–30   these *f·* be conceived of as immortal,
  214–32   there is no oblivion for Soul and its *f·*.
  215– 5   with all the *f·* of Mind ;
  246– 4   Life and its *f·* are not measured by
  r 472–17   Error is neither Mind nor one of Mind's *f·*.
  488–24   Mind alone possesses all *f·*,

faculty
  an 100–13   ordered the medical *f·* of Paris to
  s 156– 5   A case of dropsy, given up by the *f·*,
  162–29   With due respect for the *f·*,
  b 327–29   Reason is the most active human *f·*.
  o 348–10   It is a pity that the medical *f·* and clergy
  p 407–22   No *f·* of Mind is lost.
  r 490– 5   Human will is . . . not a *f·* of Soul.
  g 528–31   this may be a useful hint to the medical *f·*.

fade
  sp 81–19   grass seemeth to wither and the flower to *f·*,

fades
  f 246–14   the transient sense of beauty *f·*,

fading
  s 150–30   the doctrine of . . . is *f·* out.
  f 247–11   *f·* and fleeting as mortal belief.
  c 263–32   The *f·* forms of matter,
  264– 7   Mortals must look beyond *f·*, finite forms,
  o 357–22   wrong notions . . . are *f·* out.

fail
  s 149–12   If you *f·* to succeed in any case, it is because
  ph 173– 1   we *f·* to see how anatomy can
  194– 3   I cannot *f·* to discern the coincidence
  f 227–14   cannot *f·* to foresee the doom of all oppression.
  o 354–21   If our words *f·* to express our deeds,
  p 372–22   Its false supports *f·* one after another.
  t 443–14   If patients *f·* to experience the
  444– 7   If Christian Scientists ever *f·* to receive
  448–28   he cannot *f·* of success in healing.
  450– 8   never *f·* to stab their benefactor in the back.
  455–12   and if, knowing the remedy, you *f·* to use the
  ap 569–15   and *f·* to strangle the serpent of sin

failed
  pref x–20   till all physical supports have *f·*,
  a 45–14   persecutors had *f·* to hide immortal Truth
  sp 83– 3   the worshippers of Baal *f·* to do ;
  s 148– 2   brought to him a case they had *f·* to heal,

failed
  s 152–24   Every material dependence had *f·* her
  o 351–10   learned that her own prayers *f·* to heal her
  p 388– 8   when dire inflictions *f·* to destroy his body.
  427–27   when all such remedies have *f·*
  t 464–15   and the Scientists had *f·* to relieve him,

failing
  ph 166–23   F· to recover health through adherence to
  f 220–23   Finding his health *f·*, he gave up his
  t 459–10   lest you yourself be condemned for *f·* to

fails
  s 148–27   When physiology *f·* to give health or life
  149– 8   succeeds in one instance *f·* in another,
  157– 3   It succeeds where homœopathy *f·*,
  b 329–19   because he *f·* in his first effort.
  p 370–27   Quackery likewise *f·* at length to

failure
  ph 186–21   Every attempt of evil to destroy good is a *f·*,
  199–23   *f·* is occasioned by a too feeble faith.
  c 260–17   distrust . . . ensures *f·* at the outset.

failures
  f 240–19   past *f·* will be repeated until all wrong work is
  t 444– 2   these very *f·* may open their blind eyes.

fain
  b 302–29   mortal sense would *f·* have us so believe.

faint
  pref vii– 3   beholds the first *f·* morning beams,
  a 47– 3   a *f·* conception of the Life which is God.
  s 144–10   and afford *f·* gleams of God, or Truth.
  f 218–29   they shall walk, and not *f·*."— *Isa.* 40 : 31.
  219–12   "sick, and the whole heart *f·* ;"— *Isa.* 1 : 5.
  254– 4   walk, and not *f·*,"— *Isa.* 40 : 31.

faintly
  a 29–29   though at first *f·* developed.
  sp 91–17   and reflect but *f·* the substance of Life or
  ap 577–32   one word shows, though *f·*, the light which C. S.

fair
  pref viii–16   On this basis C. S. will have a *f·* fight.
  s 122–20   barometer, . . . points to *f·* weather in
  141–30   Let it have *f·* representation by the press.
  ph 167–32   *f·* seeming for straightforward character,
  191–22   not a leaf unfolds its *f·* outlines,
  p 437– 6   It blots the *f·* escutcheon of omnipotence.
  r 490–21   would, by *f·* logic, annihilate man
  g 555– 3   A *f·* conclusion from this might be,
  ap 575–25   a city of the Spirit, *f·*, royal, and square.

fairly
  f 231– 3   Unless an ill is rightly met and *f·* overcome
  240–28   one must pay fully and *f·* the
  b 319–19   when it becomes *f·* understood that the divine
  329– 2   elements of pure Christianity will be *f·*
  t 457–10   never . . . fears to have *f·* understood.
  ap 558–14   When you look it *f·* in the face,

fairness
  f 248– 9   feeds the body with supernal freshness and *f·*,

faith
absolute
  pr 1– 2   absolute *f·* that all things are possible to God,
all
  p 395–12   destroys all *f·* in sin and in
  426–23   The relinquishment of all *f·* in death
and belief
  pr 12–18   borrows its power from human *f·* and belief.
and piety
  sp 98–26   no proper connection with *f·* and piety.
and understanding
  s 107–13   fresh pinions are given to *f·* and understanding,
  b 312–27   It divides *f·* and understanding between
  p 366–10   mental penury chills his *f·* and understanding.
  387–30   gives man *f·* and understanding whereby to
armed with
  b 298– 7   Science armed with *f·*, hope, and fruition.
article of
  s 145–32   Our Master's first article of *f·* propounded to
blacksmith's
  ph 199–13   but by reason of the blacksmith's *f·* in
blind
  pr 12– 8   through a blind *f·* in God.
  a 23–28   expresses the helplessness of a blind *f·* ;
  ph 167– 4   If we rise no higher than blind *f·*,
  p 398–28   blind *f·* removes bodily ailments for a season,
  gl 582– 2   not a faltering nor a blind *f·*, but the
break
  ap 569–15   Alas for those who break *f·* with divine Science
dawn in
  b 298– 3   They dawn in *f·* and glow full-orbed
dead
  f 228–32   influence of their dead *f·* and ceremonies.
describes
  b 279– 4   New Testament writer plainly describes *f·*,
dissent or
  s 155–12   individual dissent or *f·*, unless it rests on

faith

ecstasy or
  pr 14– 7 is to have, not mere emotional ecstasy or *f·*,
El Dorado of
  ap 559–30 out of bondage into the El Dorado of *f·* and
enlightened
  pr 15–31 the foundation of enlightened *f·*.
feeble
  ph 199–24 failure is occasioned by a too feeble *f·*.
fetter
  f 226–19 fetter *f·* and spiritual understanding.
firm in
  a 23–13 said : "He that taketh one doctrine, firm in *f·*,
general
  a 155– 8 not yet divorced the drug from the general *f·*.
  b 319–10 lower appeal to the general *f·*
great
  s 133– 7 "I have not found so great *f·*,— *Matt.* 8 : 10.
half the
  f 202– 7 half the *f·* they bestow upon the
his
  s 146– 1 he proved his *f·* by his works.
  ph 180– 6 his *f·* in their efforts is somewhat helpful
  f 216– 1 his *f·* in Soul and his indifference to the body.
  p 366–10 mental penury chills his *f·*
hope and
  pr 9–16 enjoy the fruition of our hope and *f·*.
  a 45–18 from the door of human hope and *f·*,
  gl 581–15 ASHER (Jacob's son).   Hope and *f·* ;
  584–27 DOVE. . . . purity and peace ; hope and *f·*.
human
  (*see* **human**)
implicit
  a 25–26 Implicit *f·* in the Teacher and all the
in a carnal mind
  p 395–11 Science overcomes *f·* in a carnal mind,
in Deity
  s 146– 7 faith in drugs the fashion, rather than *f·* in Deity.
individual
  s 155– 4 general belief, culminating in individual *f·*,
in drugs
  s 145–14 whether *f·* in drugs, trust in hygiene,
  146– 7 have rendered *f·* in drugs the fashion,
  ph 181–30 If you have more *f·* in drugs than in Truth,
in God
  (*see* **God**)
in hygiene
  f 251–16 whether through *f·* in hygiene,
in matter
  pref xi– 7 the fruits of human *f·* in matter,
  s 130–21 Laboring long to shake the adult's *f·* in matter
  146– 6 The first idolatry was *f·* in matter.
  ph 170– 6 *f·* in matter instead of in Spirit.
  p 425–24 when *f·* in matter has been conquered.
inspires
  g 547–32 which lifts humanity . . . and inspires *f·*.
in the divine Principle
  b 319– 7 Having *f·* in the divine Principle
in the drug
  p 370–14 *f·* in the drug is the sole factor in the cure.
in the right
  a 29– 7 Christian experience teaches *f·* in the right
in the truth
  p 368–15 When we come to have more *f·* in the truth
  401– 7 If *f·* in the truth of being, which you impart
in Truth
  b 286– 7 gives full *f·* in Truth,
  t 446–21 strengthens hope, enthrones *f·* in Truth,
invalid's
  ph 166–26 The invalid's *f·* in the divine Mind
in words
  f 210– 1 superiority of faith by works over *f·* in words.
is higher
  b 297–20 F· is higher and more spiritual than belief.
John's
  s 133– 3 Was John's *f·* greater than that of the
keep the
  a 29– 5 If they keep the *f·*, they will have the
kept the
  a 21– 3 I have kept the *f·*,"— *II Tim.* 4 : 7.
lacks
  p 366–17 physician lacks *f·* in the divine Mind
less
  ph 173–32 call into action less *f·* than Buddhism
  f 222–13 he also had less *f·* in the so-called pleasures
little
  pref x–21 because there is so little *f·* in His
  p 394–30 the sick usually have little *f·* in it till they
living
  b 308– 3 art thou in the living *f·* that there is
lose
  s 127– 2 she will not therefore lose *f·* in Christianity,
  o 351– 3 When we lose *f·* in God's power to heal,
material
  ph 180–21 through the material *f·* which they inspire.

faith

more
  sp 89– 6 Having more *f·* in others than in herself,
  ph 181–30 If you have more *f·* in drugs than in Truth,
  o 358–29 Is it likely that church-members have more *f·* in
  359– 6 Is this because the patients have more *f·* in
  p 368–15 When we come to have more *f·* in the truth
  368–16 more *f·* in Spirit than in matter,
  368–16 more *f·* in living than in dying,
  368–17 more *f·* in God than in man,
  373– 3 we must have more *f·* in God on this subject
my
  o 343– 5 show thee my *f·* by my works."— *Jas.* 2 : 18.
  r 487–26 show thee my *f·* by my works."— *Jas.* 2 : 18.
new
  s 134– 9 The new *f·* in the Christ, Truth,
no
  ph 169–17 we should put no *f·* in material means.
  o 348–17 I desire to have no *f·* in evil or
  r 486– 2 you can have no *f·* in falsehood when
one kind of
  a 23–24 One kind of *f·* trusts one's welfare to others.
one's
  a 22–26 nor by pinning one's *f·* without works
  an 101–32 proportional to one's *f·* in esoteric magic.
our
  b 329–13 We must prove our *f·* by demonstration.
  340– 2 until we lose our *f·* in them
  p 410–14 Every trial of our *f·* in God makes us stronger.
  410–17 the stronger should be our *f·*
point beyond
  f 241–23 One's aim, a point beyond *f·*, should be
prayer of
  pr 12– 1 "The prayer of *f·* shall save— *Jas.* 5 : 15.
religious
  sp 88–21 Excite the organ of veneration or religious *f·*,
  s 139–12 reform in religious *f·* will teach men
resort to
  t 443– 5 a resort to *f·* in corporeal means
shall he find
  s 132–27 shall he find *f·* on the earth?"— *Luke* 18 : 8.
significance of
  r 488–10 they have more the significance of *f·*,
stepping-stone to
  pref vii–18 no longer the stepping stone to *f·*
strong
  ap 567– 5 strong *f·* or spiritual strength wrestles
superiority of
  f 209–32 It shows the superiority of *f·* by works
that
  o 359– 4 Will that *f·* heal them?
their
  a 49– 3 inspired their devotion, winged their *f·*,
  m 64– 3 Our forefathers exercised their *f·*
  s 155–10 equip the medicine with their *f·*,
  o 350– 4 try to cure his friends by their *f·* in him.
  t 451–10 will either make shipwreck of their *f·* or
this
  s 155– 5 according to this *f·* will the effect be.
  ph 181–30 this *f·* will incline you to the side of
  r 497–30 This *f·* relies upon an understood Principle.
thy
  o 343– 4 "Show me thy *f·* without thy— *Jas.* 2 : 18.
  r 487–25 "Show me thy *f·* without thy— *Jas.* 2 : 18.
to uplift
  r 497–21 served to uplift *f·* to
unflinching
  p 426–27 with unflinching *f·* in God,
unity of the
  g 519–19 come in the unity of the *f·*, *Eph.* 4 : 13.
uplifting
  s 109–19 Christian healing by holy, uplifting *f·* ;
without works
  a 22–26 nor by pinning one's *f·* without works
  23–15 "F· without works is dead."— *Jas.* 2 : 26.

  pref xi– 7 *f·* in the workings, not of Spirit, but
  pr 11–22 only the results of mortals' own *f·*.
  16– 3 The highest prayer is not one of *f·* merely ;
  a 23–16 F·, if it be mere belief, is as a pendulum
  23–17 F·, advanced to spiritual understanding,
  23–21 *f·* and the words corresponding thereto
  23–25 Another kind of *f·* understands divine Love
  sp 86– 7 he was answered by the *f·* of a sick woman.
  an 106–28 gentleness, goodness, *f·*,— *Gal.* 5 : 22.
  s 115–27 compassion, hope, *f·*, meekness, temperance.
  125–14 changes . . . from *f·* to understanding,
  133– 6 also a certain centurion of whose *f·*
  160– 7 Unsupported by the *f·* reposed in it,
  ph 169–11 *f·* in rules of health or in drugs begets
  169–14 The *f·* reposed in these things should find
  170– 5 the exercise of *f·* in material modes,
  198–19 giving another direction to *f·*, the physician
  f 206–12 hope, *f·*, love— is the prayer of the righteous
  215–29 Even the *f·* of his philosophy spurned

faith

f	218–18	if you are without f· in God's willingness
b	288– 7	settle all questions through f· in
	297–29	Until belief becomes f·, and f· becomes
	298–14	involves intuition, hope, f·, understanding,
	312–26	limits f· and hinders spiritual
p	382–14	more receptive of spiritual power and of f·
	394–32	shows that f· is not the healer in such cases.
	395–20	punctual, patient, full of f·,
	398–19	It is the f· of the doctor and the
	398–25	So also f·, cooperating with a belief in
	424–30	f· in the possibility of their transmission.
	429–27	We must have f· in all the sayings of our Master,
	430– 6	F· should enlarge its borders
r	482–25	angels whisper it, through f·, to the hungering
	484–19	are really caused by the f· in them
g	512–16	externalized, yet subjective, states of f·
	529–28	f· to fight all claims of evil,
ap	561– 3	destroys both f· in evil and the practice
gl	579–10	f· in the divine Life and in the eternal Principle

faithful

a	44– 3	"Well done, good and f· servant,"—Matt. 25 : 23.
	49–18	this f· sentinel of God at the highest post
	50–12	to sustain and bless so f· a son.
	50–32	wrung from his f· lips the plaintive cry,
c	267–30	when he is tried, [proved f·],—Jas. 1 : 12.
b	314–20	but the f· Mary saw him,
	323–17	"f· over a few things,"—Matt. 25 : 21.
t	444–16	Let us be f· in pointing the way
ap	569– 6	"Thou hast been f· over a few—Matt. 25 : 23.

faithfully

a	26– 6	if we follow his commands f· ;
p	373–12	if the teaching is f· done.
	387–13	do not die early because they f· perform the

faithfulness

a	34–26	As the reward for his f·, he would disappear to
f	225– 6	the fewness and f· of its followers.

faithless

s	148– 2	"O f· generation,"—Mark 9 : 19.

fall

pref	vii–20	Though empires f·, "the Lord shall—Exod. 15 :18.
a	23–11	will f· at the feet of everlasting Love.
an	103–28	singe their own wings and f· into dust.
ph	193– 2	caused by a f· upon a wooden spike
f	223–18	both shall f· into the ditch."—Matt. 15 : 14.
	227– 1	into the land of C. S., where fetters f·
	238–12	To f· away from Truth in times of persecution,
c	258–29	it were impossible for man, . . . to f· from his
b	282–28	Whatever indicates the f· of man
	310–11	Day may decline and shadows f·,
p	380– 4	Sickness and sin f· by their own weight.
	380– 6	on whomsoever it shall f·,—Matt. 21 : 44.
	441–11	now and forever, f· into oblivion,
t	463– 4	he may stumble and f· in the darkness.
	464–24	weapons of bigotry, . . . f· before an
g	507–31	misinterpreted, the divine idea seems to f·
	528–10	a deep sleep to f· upon Adam,—Gen. 2 : 21.
	536–19	The blind leading the blind, both would f·.

fallacies

o	355–22	and the most egregious f· ever offered

fallacy

f	237–24	the f· of matter and its supposed laws.
p	394–17	the f· of material systems in general,
r	466–24	have perpetuated the f· that intelligence,

fallen

c	259–10	thoughts which presented man as f·,
r	470–20	Has God taken down His . . . and has man f·?
	476–13	Mortals are not f· children of God.

faileth

b	291–19	"In the place where the tree f·,—Eccl. 11 : 3.
	291–22	As man f· asleep, so shall he awake.

falling

a	32–32	with shadows fast f· around ;
s	154–29	thinks she has hurt her face by f·
o	359–23	f· from the lips of her saintly mother,
p	389–26	This belief totters to its f·
t	449–12	Man's moral mercury, rising or f·,

falls

a	37– 8	error f· only before the sword of Spirit.
ph	192–26	betrays its weakness and f·, never to rise.
f	249–26	It f· short of the skies, but makes its
b	291–22	"As the tree f·, so it must lie."
g	543– 1	f· back upon itself.

false

pref	viii– 7	as the science of music corrects f· tones
a	27–20	to cut down the f· doctrine of pantheism,
	50–23	they did say,—that Jesus' teachings were f·,
m	60–26	physical sense, . . . places it on a f· basis.
	62–29	f· views of life hide eternal harmony,
	68– 7	We ought to weary of the fleeting and f·
	69–10	as the f· and material disappears.

false

sp	70– 5	Whatever is f· or sinful can never enter
	94–12	owe their f· government to the misconceptions
	99–21	not with the individual, but with the f· system.
an	100– *	thefts, f· witness, blasphemies :— Matt. 15 : 19.
s	107–15	Feeling so perpetually the f· consciousness
	108–25	testimony of f· material sense,
	121–22	deluded the . . . and induced f· conclusions.
	122– 5	contradict their f· witnesses, and reveal
	123– 1	science has destroyed the f· theory
	127–31	f· hypotheses that matter is its own lawgiver,
	128–28	not upon the judgment of f· sensation.
	129– 1	conclusion, if properly drawn, cannot be f·.
	135–23	else one or the other is f· and useless ;
	151–15	bondage now enforced by f· theories.
	164–11	more scientific than are f· claimants
ph	168–20	authority which Jesus proved to be f·
	175–30	before he ate the fruit of f· knowledge,
	177–10	body, is but a f· concept of mortal mind.
	180– 3	and to uproot its f· sowing.
	186– 2	by emptying his thought of the f· stimulus
	192– 5	quit our reliance upon that which is f·
	196– 7	f· pleasures which tend to perpetuate this
f	201– 7	We cannot build safely on f· foundations.
	201–10	f· appetites, hatred, fear, all sensuality,
	204– 3	All forms of error support the f· conclusions
	204–23	F· and self-assertive theories have given
	218– 1	Mortal mind does the f· talking,
	229–21	f· law should be trampled under foot.
	232–14	Christianity is not f·,
	232–15	religions which contradict its Principle are f·.
	238–28	no time for gossip about f· law or testimony.
	242– 3	their material beliefs and f· individuality.
	252– 7	When f· human beliefs learn even a little
c	262–21	They will then drop the f· estimate of life
	265–32	if they wrench away f· pleasurable beliefs
b	278– 9	a f· supposition, the notion that there is
	281–19	f· conception as to man and Mind.
	281–29	Our f· views of matter perish
	285–16	is a f· conception of man.
	287–22	Error is f·, mortal belief ;
	290–12	That Life or Mind is finite . . . is f·.
	293–12	both strata, . . . are f· representatives of man.
	296–11	The death of a f· material sense
	308–12	f· pleasure, pain, sin, sickness, and death."
	308–18	matter with its f· pleasures and pains,
	311–14	f· estimates of soul as dwelling in sense
	315–11	The opposite and f· views of the people
	324– 2	Gladness to leave the f· landmarks
o	355–21	"absolutely f·, and the most egregious fallacies
	357–17	f· notions about the Divine Being
	357–21	must have originated in a f· supposition,
	358– 7	one is true, the other must be f·.
p	368–26	these f· conditions are the source of all seeming
	372–22	Its f· supports fail one after another.
	380–11	This f· method is as though the defendant
	389–15	This f· reasoning is rebuked
	390–14	the f· process of mortal opinions
	395– 8	leaving Soul to master the f· evidences
	403–17	producing . . . the results of f· opinions ;
	404– 8	there is no real pleasure in f· appetites.
	417–30	by certain fears and f· conclusions,
	428– 9	To divest thought of f· trusts
	428–12	we shall sweep away the f·
	437–13	Nerve, . . . to be a f· witness.
	438–12	and bearing f· witness against Man.
	440– 7	before sacrificing mortals to their f· gods.
	440–22	The f· and unjust beliefs of your
t	444–30	are discordant and ofttimes f· brethren.
	447–12	Ignorance, subtlety, or f· charity
	458–25	Neither is he a f· accuser.
	459–20	a f· practitioner will work mischief,
r	484–19	f· human consciousness is educated to feel.
	484–26	involved in all f· theories and practices.
	489–25	C. S. shows them to be f·,
g	506– 2	distinguishing between the f· and the true.
	510–12	turn away from a f· material sense.
	522– 1	f· history in contradistinction to the true.
	522– 4	If one is true, the other is f·,
	522–24	in declaring this material creation f·.
	523– 3	Because of its f· basis, the mist of
	523–10	which God erects between the true and f·.
	525–27	favors the f· conclusion of the
	527–20	it is a lie,—f· in every statement.
	539–19	It is f· to say that Truth and error commingle
	545–17	a f· view, destructive to existence
	545–19	this opposite, in its f· view of God and man,
	549–22	as must necessarily attend f· systems,
ap	560–16	a f· estimate of anyone whom God has appointed
	567–28	The beast and the f· prophets are lust and
	568–11	first the true method . . . and then the f·.
	568–12	exhibits the true warfare and then the f·.
	575– 1	Arise from your f· consciousness
gl	580–21	The name Adam represents the f· supposition
	581–19	The higher f· knowledge builds

false
 gl 584–16 Any material evidence of death is *f·*,
 588–17 whatever reflects not this one Mind, is *f·*
 597–12 It revealed the *f·* foundations
 (*see also* **belief, beliefs, claim, claims, evidence, sense, testimony**)

False Belief
 p 430–21 *F· B·* is the attorney for Personal Sense.
 435– 4 Counsellor *F· B·* has argued that
 437–20 Here the opposing counsel, *F· B·*,
 438–22 a foreign substance, imported by *F· B·*,
 439– 2 *F· B·*, the counsel for the plaintiff,
 439– 7 when a message came from *F· B·*,
 440– 4 machinations of the counsel, *F· B·*,
 440– 8 deceived by your attorney, *F· B·*,
 441–10 The plea of *F· B·* we deem unworthy
 441–11 Let what *F· B·* utters, . . . fall into oblivion,
 441–28 Your attorney, *F· B·*, is an impostor,

falsehood
 capable of
 p 432– 5 the prisoner at the bar, is capable of *f·*.
 no faith in
 r 486– 2 you can have no faith in *f·*

 pr 9– 4 the *f·* which does no one any good.
 an 104–20 sensuality, *f·*, revenge, malice,
 s 163–29 so much absurdity, contradiction, and *f·*.
 ph 186–18 This *f·* should strip evil of all pretensions.
 f 238–30 and place the fact above the *f·*,
 241– 9 *F·*, envy, hypocrisy, malice,
 t 450– 6 They utter a *f·*, while looking you blandly
 g 530– 1 increases in *f·* and his days become shorter.

falsehood's
 r 486– 3 when you have learned *f·* true nature.

falsely
 c 262–30 which seems to begin with the brain begins *f·*.
 b 305–31 The Sadducees reasoned *f·* about the
 331– 9 *f·* testifies to a beginning and an
 p 372–24 *f·* parading in the vestments of law.

falsities
 sp 78– 3 They are the *f* of sense,
 97–21 The broadest facts array the most *f·*
 b 307–20 partakes of its own nature and utters its own *f·*.
 o 346–18 "fraught with *f·* painful to behold"?
 354– 3 "utter *f·* and absurdities,"

falsity
 and illusion
 g 554–28 and is simply a *f·* and illusion.
 conceded
 p 396–15 not a difficult task in view of the conceded *f·*
 matter is the
 s 127–19 It teaches that matter is the *f·*,
 of error
 b 294–32 Truth demonstrates the *f·* of error.
 of material belief
 c 258– 8 proves the *f·* of material belief.
 send
 g 545–14 errors send *f·* into all human doctrines
 their own
 f 252– 8 learn even a little of their own *f·*,
 this
 b 283–24 lost to all who cling to this *f·*.
 301–30 This *f·* presupposes soul to be an
 g 539–21 this *f·* is exposed by our Master

 pr 16– 6 Truth that is sinless and the *f·* of sinful sense.
 s 108– 7 experiences show the *f·* of all material things ;
 f 253–15 Knowing the *f·* of so-called material sense,
 b 317– 4 insisted on the might of matter, the force of *f·*,
 t 464–26 *F·* has no foundation.
 r 474–31 Truth destroys *f·* and error,
 g 522– 3 proves the *f·* of the second.
 528–15 Here *f·*, error, credits Truth, God, with
 537–21 to depict the *f·* of error
 543–16 are never excluded by *f·*.
 gl 579–15 a *f·* ; the belief in "original sin,"

faltering
 t 455– 4 a *f·* and doubting trust in Truth
 gl 582– 1 not a *f·* nor a blind faith, but the perception

fame
 m 57–15 Beauty, wealth, or *f·* is incompetent to meet
 f 239– 5 Take away wealth, *f·*, and social organizations,
 gl 582– 6 pride ; envy ; *f·* ; illusion ; a false belief ;

familiar
 sp 70– * them that have f· spirits,— Isa. 8 : 19.*
 89–12 This *f·* instance reaffirms the
 f 234– 9 become more *f·* with good than with evil,
 b 320–11 the *f·* text, Genesis vi. 3,
 p 397–23 To heal the sick, one must be *f·* with
 403–32 *f·* with mental action and its effect
 t 463– 5 should also be *f·* with the obstetrics
 ap 576–15 was *f·* with Jesus' use of this word,

families
 an 103– 1 promotes affection and virtue in *f·*

family
 harmonious
 t 444–29 God's children . . . are one harmonious *f·* ;
 his
 ph 193–18 dress himself, and take supper with his *f·*.
 human
 (*see* **human**)
 universal
 ap 577– 4 one Father with His universal *f·*,
 whole
 r 470– 1 the whole *f·* of man would be brethren ;
 your
 p 392–18 If you think that . . . is hereditary in your *f·*,

 g 515–21 Man is the *f·* name for all ideas,

famine
 sp 96–16 may seem to be *f·* and pestilence,
 s 163–18 war, pestilence, and *f·*, all combined."

famished
 pr 17– 5 *feed the f· affections ;*

famous
 s 161–20 the words of the *f·* Madame Roland,
 162–30 I kindly quote from Dr. Benjamin Rush, the *f·*
 g 548–18 of the origin of mortals, a *f·* naturalist says :

fan
 r 466–27 Science of Christianity comes with *f·* in hand
 gl 586– 7 definition of

fancied
 f 252–28 and says : . . . all my *f·* joys are fatal.
 p 379–10 *f·* himself bleeding to death,

fancies
 pr 5–28 because he *f·* himself forgiven.
 b 310– 2 The human belief *f·* that it delineates

fancy
 s 136–20 This ghostly *f·* was repeated by Herod
 ph 175–13 profane to *f·* that the perfume of clover
 191–28 illusive senses may *f·* affinities with
 b 291–10 Mortals need not *f·* that belief in the
 299– 1 suggestive feathers ; but this is only *f·*.
 t 443–19 other systems they *f·* will afford relief.
 460–16 Sickness is more than *f·* ;

far
 pr 3–32 While the heart is *f·* from divine Truth
 10– 2 walk in the light so *f·* as we receive it,
 15–22 in so *f·* as we put our desires into practice.
 a 31–18 so *f·* as we apprehend it,
 34–25 ascend *f·* above their apprehension.
 52– 2 His pursuits lay *f·* apart from theirs.
 53– 4 so *f·* removed from appetites and passions
 sp 70–21 so *f·* as can be learned from the Gospels,
 90–21 mentally travel *f·* and work wonders,
 s 118– 3 an inference *f·* above the merely
 121–25 so *f·* as our solar system is concerned,
 124–24 "Thus *f·* and no farther."
 127–31 in so *f·* as this is built on the false
 146–27 *f·* anterior to the period in which Jesus lived,
 149– 3 Mind as *f·* outweighs drugs in the cure of
 ph 173–30 The idols of civilization are *f·* more fatal
 174–12 "the night is *f·* spent,— Rom. 13 : 12.
 179–16 educate a healthy horse so *f·* in physiology
 f 221–22 and it is equally *f·* from Science,
 222–22 He learned that a dyspeptic was very *f·* from
 222–23 *f·* from having "dominion— Gen. 1 : 26.
 229– 9 Not *f·* removed from infidelity is the belief
 257–13 the substance of an idea is very *f·* from
 b 300– 9 So *f·* as the scientific statement as to
 318–17 so *f·* as he is discordant, he is not the image
 o 350– 4 very *f·* removed from daily experience.
 354–23 The night of materiality is *f·* spent,
 p 387– 7 has been carried sufficiently *f·* ;
 426–25 *f·* beyond its present elevation.
 t 448–16 A dishonest position is *f·* from Christianly
 r 478–24 this belief is mortal and *f·* from actual.
 g 548–23 so *f·* apart from his material sense of

farce
 b 272–20 the ghastly *f·* of material existence ;

farm
 s 130– 5 One has a *f·*, another has merchandise,

far-off
 sp 90–16 we fly to Europe and meet a *f·* friend.

farther
 pr 5–19 looking *f·*, the Psalmist could see their end,
 6–18 higher we cannot look, *f·* we cannot go.
 s 124–24 "Thus far and no *f·*."
 ph 173– 4 or determine when man . . . has progressed *f·*
 176–27 can carry its ill-effects no *f·* than
 197–14 the *f·* mortals will be removed from imbecility
 f 234–31 reach no *f·* and do no more harm than
 p 425– 1 or some of his progenitors *f·* back

farthing

pr	5–11	"the uttermost *f·*." — *Matt.* 5 : 26.
f	240–28	one must pay fully and fairly the utmost *f·*,
p	390–17	in payment of the last *f·*,
	405–15	will be manacled until the last *f·* is paid,

fashion

pr	4–21	will mould and *f·* us anew,
m	68– 4	They are slaves to *f·*, pride, and sense.
s	146– 7	have rendered faith in drugs the *f·*,
f	247–12	Custom, education, and *f·* form the

fashionable

o	344–30	more *f·* and less spiritual?

fashions

g	516– 9	God *f·* all things, after His own

fast

a	32–32	with shadows *f·* falling around ;
	53– 3	He did not *f·* as did the Baptist's disciples ;
s	124–10	and holding *f·* to discord and death.
f	254–21	abandon so *f·* as practical the material,
p	392–14	thought should be held *f·* to this ideal.
t	448– 3	Blindness and . . . cling *f·* to iniquity.
	464–20	hold *f·* that which is good." — *I Thess.* 5 : 21.
g	545– 5	material man was *f·* degenerating
gl	597– 5	if only he appeared unto men to *f·*.

fasten

p	439–23	to *f·* upon him an offence

fastened

p	378–14	*f·* fearlessly on a ferocious beast,

fastens

p	395–28	*f·* disease on the patient,

fasting

f	220–26	The belief that either *f·* or feasting makes
	221–20	never ordained a law that *f·* should be

fat

g	540–27	his flock, and of the *f·* thereof. — *Gen.* 4 : 4.

fatal

pr	7–32	Hypocrisy is *f·* to religion.
m	59–26	for deception is *f·* to happiness.
	59–30	*f·* mistakes are undermining its foundations.
s	129–19	and *f·* to its demonstration ;
ph	173–30	The idols of civilization are far more *f·*
f	203– 1	admits . . . that this cold may produce *f·*
	252–28	and says : . . . all my fancied joys are *f·*.
b	286– 6	this is *f·* to a knowledge of Science.
	303–24	The belief that . . . is a *f·* error.
p	368–10	*f·* beliefs that error is as real as Truth,
	372–27	a denial of Truth is *f·*,
	384–22	if you believe in laws of matter and their *f·*
	394–25	Are material means the only refuge from *f·*
	422–27	holding that matter . . . renders them *f·*
g	552–12	no member of this dolorous and *f·* triad.
ap	560–26	but has been *f·* to the persecutors.
	568– 8	*f·* effects of trying to meet error with error.

fatality

sp	79– 2	its symptoms, locality, and *f·*
ph	197–32	his belief in its reality and *f·* will harm

fatally

ph	184–25	termed a *f·* broken physical law.

fate

a	40–21	could not avert a felon's *f·*,
	49–15	met his earthly *f·* alone with God.
s	121– 2	but sterner still would have been his *f·*, if
	121– 7	read in the stars the *f·* of empires
ph	176– 5	attributed their own downfall and the *f·* of

Father (*see also* Father's)

and Mother

c	256– 7	the *F·* and Mother of the universe,
g	530–11	recognizing God, the *F·* and Mother of all,

and son

o	361–18	*F·* and son, are one in being.

bosom of the

b	334– 5	dwells forever in the bosom of the *F·*,

cometh unto the

b	286– 9	"No man cometh unto the *F·* — *John* 14 : 6.

Ego and the

sp	70– 9	the Ego and the *F·* are inseparable.

everlasting

p	428–17	the eternal builder, the everlasting *F·*,

God and the

m	64– 5	undefiled before God and the *F·*, — *Jas.* 1 : 27.

God as the

a	29–23	demonstrating God as the *F·* of men.

God is his

m	63–10	God is his *F·*, and Life is the law of his being.

heavenly

a	40–25	Our heavenly *F·*, divine Love, demands that
p	387–29	bestowed on man by his heavenly *F·*,

Father

his

a	30– 3	his *F·* or divine Principle.
	31– 8	they who do the will of his *F·*.
m	63–10	God is his *F·*, and Life is the law of his being.
p	410– 6	knowledge of his *F·* and of himself,

in secret

pr	15– 7	The *F·* in secret is unseen to the

inspired by the

s	133–27	taught as he was inspired by the *F·*

is perfect

b	302–20	man as perfect, even as the *F·* is perfect,

my

pr	14–21	because I go unto my *F·*," — *John* 14 : 12.
a	26–12	"I and my *F·* are one." — *John* 10 : 30.
sp	79–20	"My *F·* worketh hitherto, — *John* 5 : 17.
s	137–24	my *F·* which is in heaven ;" — *Matt.* 16 : 17.
c	267–16	the will of my *F·* which is in — *Matt.* 12 : 50.
b	315– 3	"I and my *F·* are one," — *John* 10 : 30.
	333–29	"I and my *F·* are one ;" — *John* 10 : 30.
	333–30	"My *F·* is greater than I." — *John* 14 : 28.
o	361–15	"I and my *F·* are one," — *John* 10 : 30.
p	372–26	before my *F·* which is in heaven." — *Matt.* 10 : 33.

not known the

a	32– 1	they have not known the *F·* — *John* 16 : 3.

numbered by the

p	367–16	with those hairs all numbered by the *F·*.

of all

pr	13–26	the *F·* of all is represented as a corporeal
a	31–11	the only creator, and therefore as the *F·* of all.
m	64–26	Until it is learned that God is the *F·* of all,

our

pr	2– 6	the desire . . . is blessed of our *F·*,
	13–11	our *F·*, who seeth in secret, will reward
	16–26	Our *F·* which art in heaven, — *Matt.* 6 : 9.
m	67– 1	The cup our *F·* hath given,
b	276–20	even as our *F·* in heaven is perfect,

the perfect

f	207–14	the perfect *F·*, or the divine Principle of man.

will of the

ph	168–21	He did the will of the *F·*.

with the

a	18– 4	demonstrated man's oneness with the *F·*,
b	334– 4	not that the corporeal Jesus was one with the *F·*,
	337– 9	the Son must be in accord with the *F·*,

worship the

a	31–27	shall worship the *F·* in spirit — *John* 4 : 23.
sp	93– 7	shall worship the *F·* in spirit — *John* 4 : 23.
s	140–21	shall worship the *F·* in spirit — *John* 4 : 23.

your

pr	1– *	*Your F· knoweth what things ye* — *Matt.* 6 : 8.
a	31– 5	one is your *F·*, which is in heaven." — *Matt.* 23:9.
	37–28	your *F·* which is in heaven — *Matt.* 5 : 48.
c	259–20	your *F·* which is in heaven — *Matt.* 5 : 48.
b	326–21	your *F·* will open the way.

---

pr	14–32	pray to thy *F·* which is in secret ; — *Matt.* 6 : 6.
	15– 1	and thy *F·*, which seeth in secret, — *Matt.* 6 : 6.
a	41–25	then sat down at the right hand of the *F·*.
sp	77–16	neither the Son, but the *F·*." — *Mark* 13 : 32.
s	131–19	"I thank Thee, O *F·*, Lord of — *Luke* 10 : 21.
	131–22	even so, *F·*, for so it seemed good — *Luke* 10 : 21.
f	233–13	not even "the Son but the *F·* ;" — *Mark* 13 : 32.
c	257–14	Hence the *F·* Mind is not the father of matter.
	267– 8	It is generally conceded that God is *F·*,
	267– 9	If this is so, the forever *F·* must have
b	268– *	*our fellowship is with the F·*, — *I John* 1 : 3.
	282–31	for it is not begotten of the *F·*.
	305–18	but what he seeth the *F·* do ; — *John* 5 : 19.
306–11, 12		and the *F·* would be childless, — no *F·*.
	314– 6	proved that he and the *F·* were inseparable
	325–17	found, in His likeness, perfect as the *F·*,
	334– 6	not that the *F·* is greater than Spirit,
o	357–29	Has the *F·* "Life in Himself," — *John* 5 : 26.
r	467–10	all men have one Mind, one God and *F·*,
	470– 1	With one *F·*, even God, the whole family of man
	485–23	"*F·* which is in heaven — *Matt.* 5 : 48.
g	518–17	all having the same Principle, or *F·* ;
	532–11	the divine Spirit, or *F·*, condemns material man
	536–12	gravitation and attraction to one *F·*,
ap	569– 2	Life, represented by the *F·* ;
	577– 3	as one *F·* with His universal family,
gl	586– 9	definition of

father

name of

a	31–10	no record of his calling any man by the name of *f·*.

not the

sp	89–27	and man is not the *f·* of man.
c	257–15	the Father Mind is not the *f·* of matter.
r	473– 5	Truth, God, is not the *f·* of error.

of mind

f	208–17	John Young, . . . writes: "God is the *f·* of mind,

of mythology

b	294–23	belief in them to be the *f·* of mythology,

father

primeval
g 553–28　or from the rib of our primeval *f·*.

your
a 31– 5　"Call no man your *f·* upon — *Matt.* 23 : 9.
b 292–22　Ye are of your *f·*, the devil — *John* 8 : 44.
　292–22　the lusts of your *f·* ye will do. — *John* 8 : 44.
g 554–26　"Ye are of your *f·*, the devil." — *John* 8 : 44.

---

a 50–10　would impugn the justice and love of a *f·* who
m 69–22　If the *f·* replies, "God creates man through
f 219–21　"is ever *f·* to the thought."
c 257–19　divine Love, — is the *f·* of the rain,
b 292–26　a liar, and the *f·* of it." — *John* 8 : 44.
　309–12　He was to become the *f·* of those, who
o 357– 8　"a liar, and the *f·* of it." — *John* 8 : 44.
p 371–27　is *f·* to the fact that Mind can do it ;
g 533–30　"Neither man nor God shall *f·* my fault."
　551– 1　the material senses must *f·* these
　554–22　"He is a liar, and the *f·* of it." — *John* 8 : 44.
　556–31　It is related that a *f·* plunged his infant
gl 580–31　he is a liar and the *f·* of it." — *John* 8 : 44.

fatherhood

g 507– 5　the *f·* and motherhood of God.
　519–11　the *f·* and motherhood of Love.
ap 562– 4　As Elias presented the idea of the *f·* of God,

fatherless

m 64– 5　To visit the *f·* and widows — *Jas.* 1 : 27.

Father-Mother

pr 16 27　Our *F·* God, all-harmonious,
b 331–30　God the *F·* ; Christ the spiritual idea
　332– 4　*F·* is the name for Deity,
　335–26　nothing unlike the eternal *F·*, God.
g 516–23　the infinite *F·* God.
ap 577– 8　reflects God as *F·*, not as a

Father's

a 25– 9　as he went daily about his *F·* business.
　52– 1　he was about his "*F·* business." — *Luke* 2 : 49.
p 366– 2　sense of the dear *F·* loving-kindness.
　442–27　it is your *F·* good pleasure — *Luke* 12 : 32.

fathers

f 211–19　"the *f·* have eaten sour grapes, — *Ezek.* 18 : 2.

fathers'

ap 566–17　Her *f·* God before her moved,

fathom

c 262– 9　We cannot *f·* the nature and quality of
g 519–17　What can *f·* infinity !
　556–15　the Christian alone can *f·* it.

fatigue

sp 79 30　It dissipates *f·* in doing good.
ph 165–16　You say that indigestion, *f·*, sleeplessness,
　184–19　We say man suffers from the effects of . . . *f·*.
f 217–20　the next toil will *f·* you less,
　217–25　scientific and permanent remedy for *f·*
　218–30　applying it literally to moments of *f·*,
　219– 5　My method of treating *f·* applies to
p 384– 8　though they expose him to *f·*, cold, heat,

fatigued

f 218– 3　You do not say a wheel is *f·* ;

fatigues

f 217–29　You say, "Toil *f·* me."
p 385– 4　undergo without sinking *f·* and exposures

falling

g 514–24　young lion, and the *f·* together ; — *Isa.* 11 · 6

fault

pr 8–31　If a friend informs us of a *f·*,
sp 93–12　otherwise, . . . our logic is at *f·*
b 292– 1　When the last mortal *f·* is destroyed,
g 533–27　finds woman the first to confess her *f·*.
　533–30　"Neither man nor God shall father my *f·*."

faults

ap 571– 9　to tell a man his *f·*, and so risk

favor

a 36–17　preclude C. S. from finding *f·* with the
an 101–16　not conclusive in *f·* of the doctrine of
p 380–13　in *f·* of a decision which the defendant
　441–19　decrees of the Court of Error in *f·* of Matter,
　441–19　Spirit decides in *f·* of Man
　441–25　The Supreme Bench decides in *f·* of
t 458– 7　This theory is supposed to *f·*

favorable

ph 177–27　physician and patient are expecting *f·*
p 422– 8　these indications are *f·*.
　422–12　ignorant that it is a *f·* omen,
　423– 5　tendency towards a *f·* result.

favored

s 162–12　Experiments have *f·* the fact that

favorite

s 121– 2　if his discovery had undermined the *f·*
b 340–16　The First Commandment is my *f·* text.

favors

g 525–27　*f·* the false conclusion of the

Fear

p 436–18　they brought with them *F·*, the sheriff,
　436–20　It was *F·* who handcuffed Mortal Man
　439–24　You aided and abetted *F·*
　441–14　neither can *F·* arrest Mortal Man

fear (noun)

and sin
p 373–21　you must rise above both *f·* and sin.
　392– 1　you master *f·* and sin through divine

and trembling
a 23–26　with *f·* and trembling." — *Phil.* 2 : 12.
sp 99– 6　with *f·* and trembling," — *Phil.* 2 : 12.
p 442–26　with *f·* and trembling :" — *Phil.* 2 : 12.

belief and
p 385–25　will suffer in proportion to your belief and *f·*.
t 455–11　lost in the belief and *f·* of disease

blanches with
p 433–14　His sallow face blanches with *f·*,

calling up the
s 154– 6　calling up the *f·* that creates the

casteth out
ph 180–24　divine Love which casteth out *f·*.
p 373–18　"perfect Love casteth out *f·*." — *I John* 4 : 18.
　406–10　"Perfect Love casteth out *f·*." — *I John* 4 : 18.
　410–19　perfect Love casteth out *f·*. — *I John* 4 : 18.

cast out
p 442–13　Divine Love had cast out *f·*.

darkness induces
p 371–14　Darkness induces *f·*.

dark places of
ap 559–12　heard in the desert and in dark places of *f·*.

destroy
p 376–26　Destroy *f·*, and you end fever.

destroys
t 454– 7　destroys *f·*, and plants the feet in the true

disappears
p 368–31　When *f·* disappears, the foundation of

doubt or
t 445– 7　No hypothesis . . . should interpose a doubt or *f·*

effects of
p 373–20　the effects of *f·* produced by sin,
　380–15　The physical effects of *f·* illustrate

evil and
p 392– 7　Casting out evil and *f·* enables

exciting
ph 169–13　by exciting *f·* of disease, and by dosing the body

fruits of
g 532–18　the immediate fruits of *f·* and shame.

governing
p 377–21　Remove the leading error or governing *f·*

great
p 426–21　and thus destroy the great *f·* that besets

her
s 159–18　They would either have allayed her *f·* or

his
ph 197–31　should suppress his *f·* of disease,
　198– 6　his *f·*, which has already developed the
　199–30　His *f·* must have disappeared before his
p 405–18　good man finally can overcome his *f·* of
　423– 2　The belief . . . increases his *f·* ;
　436–23　and be punished for his *f·*.

hope and
b 298–17　hope and *f·*, life and death,

human
ph 176–17　Human *f·* of miasma would load with disease
p 412– 3　and destroy the human *f·* of sickness.
ap 563– 5　We may well be perplexed at human *f·* ;
　566– 3　dark ebbing and flowing tides of human *f·*,

ignorance or
ph 188–23　springing from mortal ignorance or *f·*.

increases
t 453–27　for such a course increases *f·*,

inflammation is
p 414–32　Inflammation is *f·*, an excited state

latent
p 376– 4　the latent *f·* and the despair of recovery

made manifest
r 493–21　It is *f·* made manifest on the body.

master
ph 197–16　We should master *f·*, instead of cultivating
p 392– 1　you master *f·* and sin through divine

more
ph 180–15　may unwittingly add more *f·* to the

mortal
p 377–27　disease is mental, a mortal *f·*,

Moses'
b 321–11　and then Moses' *f·* departed.
　321–25　God had lessened Moses' *f·*

no
p 393–18　Have no *f·* that matter can ache,
　406–17　has no *f·* that he will commit a murder,
　410–18　"There is no *f·* in Love, — *I John* 4 : 18.

fear (noun)
  nor doubt
    r 495–17   Let neither *f·* nor doubt overshadow
  of climate
    p 377–10   when their *f·* of climate is exterminated.
  of consequences
    b 322–24   only through *f·* of consequences
  of death
    gl 596–25   destroy . . . the *f·* of death,
  of disease
    (*see* **disease**)
  of error
    p 380–20   power of Truth can prevent the *f·* of error,
  of its sting
    p 426–24   and also of the *f·* of its sting
  of patients
    p 411–27   by allaying the *f·* of patients.
  of punishment
    b 327–22   *F·* of punishment never made man truly honest.
  of the disease
    ph 196–27   induced . . . from the *f·* of the disease
  of the Lord
    p 373–15   "The *f·* of the Lord is the— *Psal.* 111 : 10.
  or fever
    ph 175–12   and dissuade any sense of *f·* or fever.
  or sin
    p 392– 3   Only while *f·* or sin remains can it
  patient's
    ph 168–25   and recognized the patient's *f·* of it,
  pride and
    a 31– 1   Pride and *f·* are unfit to bear the standard of
  proceed from
    c 260–22   disease, and death proceed from *f·*.
  removing the
    p 411–32   If you succeed in wholly removing the *f·*,
  seedlings of
    ph 188–26   according to the seedlings of *f·*.
  stage of
    p 375–31   a stage of *f·* so excessive that it amounts to
  this
    p 381– 9   This *f·* is the danger
    423– 4   this *f·* greatly diminishes the tendency
  will soothe
    p 398–26   will soothe *f·* and change the belief of disease to
  your
    p 374–24   your steps are less firm because of your *f·*,

    m 68– 3   for *f·* of being thought ridiculous.
    s 115–21   Evil beliefs, passions and appetites, *f·*,
    125–14   changes . . . from *f·* to hope
    151–18   *F·* never stopped being and its action.
    159– 9   not by the ether, but by *f·* of inhaling it.
  ph 180–22   Instead of furnishing thought with *f·*,
    189– 7   and casts out a *f·*.
  f 201–10   false appetites, hatred, *f·*, all sensuality,
    209– 4   in proportion as ignorance, *f·*, or
    222–27   while *f·*, hygiene, physiology, and physics
    230–26   satisfy mortal belief, and quiet *f·*.
  b 327– 6   destroy the false beliefs of pleasure, pain, or *f·*
  o 352–13   sick in consequence of the *f·* :
    352–30   no longer seeming worthy of *f·* or honor.
  p 370– 8   proves that *f·* is governing the body.
    373–19   The *f·* occasioned by ignorance can be cured ;
    377–28   also a *f·* that Mind is helpless
    384–24   the *f·* subsides and the conviction abides
    391–32   *F·* is the fountain of sickness,
    392– 5   *F·*, which is an element of all disease,
    404–29   envy, dishonesty, *f·*, . . . make a man sick,
    409–19   never yields to the weaker, except through *f·* or
    411–21   foundation of all sickness is *f·*, ignorance, or
    419–11   Neither disease itself, sin, nor *f·* has the power
    421–20   when the *f·* is destroyed, the inflammation
  t 445–19   C. S. silences human will, quiets *f·*
  r 494–31   they cast *f·* and all evil out of
  g 532–26   *F·* was the first manifestation of the error of
  gl 586–11   definition of
    586–13   *F·* ; remorse ; lust ; hatred ; destruction ;
    592–21   NIGHT.   Darkness ; doubt ; *f·*.
    593– 7   RED DRAGON.   Error ; *f·* ; inflammation ;

fear (verb)
  s 156–14   to *f·* an aggravation of symptoms from
  ph 196–11   "*F·* him which is able to— *Matt.* 10 : 28.
  f 214–20   to *f·* . . . . what they consider a material body
    231–22   To *f·* sin is to misunderstand the power of Love
    231–27   To *f·* them is impossible, when you
  b 340– 7   *F·* God, and keep His— *Eccl.* 12 : 13.
  o 348– 2   and which we desire neither to honor nor to *f·*.
    352–17   Children, like adults, *ought* to *f·* a
  p 376–30   To *f·* and admit the power of disease,
    406–25   and no more *f·* that we shall be sick
    419–25   Never *f·* the mental malpractitioner,
    425–26   You will never *f·* again except to offend God,
    436–22   He must obey your law, *f·* its consequences,
    442–27   "*F·* not, little flock ;— *Luke* 12 : 32.
  t 444–21   *F·* not that he will smite thee again
    452–10   you should not *f·* to put on the new.

fear (verb)
  ap 570–18   and never *f·* the consequences.
    578–11   I will *f·* no evil :— *Psal.* 23 : 4.
  gl 596–22   I will *f·* no evil."— *Psal.* 23 : 4.
feared
  f 215–28   Socrates *f·* not the hemlock poison.
  o 352–15   Would a mother say . . . They exist, and **are**
        to be *f·* ;
  p 411– 1   "The thing which I greatly *f·*— *Job* 3 : 25.
    413–31   may be reproduced in the very ailments *f·*.
feareth
  p 410–19   He that *f·* is not made perfect— *I John* 4 : 18.
fearful
  pr 6–31   left this record : "His rebuke is *f·*."
  a 22–15   If your endeavors are beset by *f·* odds,
  m 65–11   The union of the sexes suffers *f·* discord.
  f 203–28   of *f·* and doleful dying
  p 415–15   render mortal mind temporarily less *f·*,
fearing
  f 244– 6   never *f·* nor obeying error in any form.
fearless
  p 406–18   should be as *f·* on the question of disease.
  g 514–11   Free and *f·* it roams in the forest.
fearlessly
  p 378–11   By looking a tiger *f·* in the eye,
    378–15   man's gaze, fastened *f·* on a ferocious beast,
    420–25   Tell the sick that they can meet disease *f·*, if
fears
  certain
    p 417–30   seems to induce disease by certain *f·*
  children's
    o 352–20   but instead of increasing children's *f·*
  doubts and
    pr 13–22   doubts and *f·* which attend such a belief,
  entertains
    p 422–27   entertains *f·* and doubts as to the ultimate
  her own
    s 154–18   The law of mortal mind and her own *f·*
  his
    p 367– 5   patience with his *f·* and the removal of them,
  mental
    ph 199–20   latent mental *f·* are subdued by him.

    ph 187– 8   and then worships and *f·* them.
    o 352–23   assured that their *f·* are groundless,
    p 392–30   shut out these unhealthy thoughts and *f·*.
    419–29   you must conquer your own *f·*
    t 457– 9   never . . . in any direction which she *f·*
feasible
  m 63–23   A *f·* as well as rational means of improvement
  o 345–19   practical proof is the only *f·* evidence
feast
  a 32– 8   ancient custom for the master of a *f·*
  s 130– 4   When all men are bidden to the *f·*,
  ap 575– 4   Then cometh the marriage *f·*,
feasting
  f 220–26   The belief that either fasting or *f·*
feathers
  b 299– 1   with suggestive *f·* ; but this is only fancy.
feats
  sp 86–19   either involve *f·* by tricksters, or
  ph 199–19   The *f·* of the gymnast prove that
feature
  ap 560– 4   the distinctive *f·* has reference to
features
  an 102–17   its aggressive *f·* are coming to the front.
febrile
  p 379–26   coated tongue, *f·* heat, dry skin,
fed
  a 33– 5   heavenly manna, which of old had *f·*
  m 62– 9   to be always *f·*, rocked, tossed, or talked to,
  b 273–25   *f·* the multitude, healed the sick,
  p 442–25   until . . . man is clothed and *f·* spiritually.
feeble
  pref ix–14   *f·* attempts to state the Principle
  ph 199–23   failure is occasioned by a too *f·* faith.
  c 262–11   We must reverse our *f·* flutterings
  t 454–27   loving care and counsel support all their *f·*
  ap 577–28   The writer's present *f·* sense of C. S.
feebleness
  f 219–17   for the belief in *f·* must
feebly
  s 117–27   dimly reflects and *f·* transmits Jesus' works
feed
  pr 17– 5   *f·* the famished affections;
  g 530–11   as able to *f·* and clothe man
feeding
  a 33–10   this bread was *f·* and sustaining them.
  f 234– 7   *f·* the hungry and giving living waters

feeds

f 222– 9 and *f·* thought with the bread of Life.
248– 8 Mind *f·* the body with supernal
g 507– 4 Spirit duly *f·* and clothes every object,

feel

pr 8–14 If we *f·* the aspiration, humility, gratitude,
a 19–27 in disobedience . . . we ought to *f·* no security,
sp 86–16 though we can always *f·* their influence.
86–22 more difficult to see a thought than to *f·* one?
s 153–23 where there is no mortal mind to *f·* it
ph 176–28 The human mind, not matter, is supposed to *f·*,
193–14 and said : "I *f·* like a new man.
f 211– 2 if they . . . report how they *f·*,
249– 6 Let us *f·* the divine energy of Spirit,
c 264–26 and *f·* the unspeakable peace which comes
b 284–23 nor can they *f·*, taste, or smell Spirit.
294–13 error, saying : . . . Nerves *f·*. Brain thinks
o 346–25 Do you *f·* the pain of tooth-pulling, when you
p 376–26 impossible for matter to suffer, to *f·* pain
384– 2 Can matter, . . . either *f·* or act without
394–31 till they *f·* its beneficent influence.
395–26 to *f·* these ills in physical belief.
t 461–30 unsee the disease ; then you will not *f·* it,
r 478–14 Does brain think, and do nerves *f·*,
479–11 Matter cannot see, *f·*, hear, taste,
479–12 cannot *f·* itself, see itself, nor understand
479–16 see, hear, *f·*, or use any of the
484–20 human consciousness is educated to *f·*.
g 532–30 error demands that *mind* shall . . . *f·* through matter,

feeling

pref ix– 8 attempts to convey his *f·*.
sp 86–21 is no less a quality of physical **sense** than *f·*.
87–27 by friendship or by any intense *f·*
s 107–15 F· so perpetually the false consciousness
f 221–27 *f·* childhood's hunger and undisciplined by
p 393–11 and govern its *f·* and action.
t 454–26 Do not dismiss students . . . *f·* that you

feelings

p 396– 6 Make no unnecessary inquiries relative to *f·*
gl 587–23 HEART. Mortal *f·*, motives, affections,

feels

sp 86–30 It *f·*, hears, and sees its own thoughts.
ph 166– 3 Mind is all that *f·*, acts, or impedes action.
f 224– 2 the world *f·* the alterative effect of truth
b 294– 9 The belief that matter thinks, sees, or *f·*
p 401–14 and mortal mind only *f·* and sees materially.
414–25 matter neither *f·*, suffers, nor enjoys.
430–19 The patient *f·* ill, ruminates,
t 443– 9 she *f·*, as she always has felt, that all
451–23 He *f·* morally obligated to open the eyes of
464– 1 *f·* your influence without seeing you.
r 467–28 Matter neither sees, hears, nor *f·*,
485– 5 Science declares that Mind, . . . sees, hears, *f·*,
gl 591–15 *f·*, hears, tastes, and smells only in belief.

fees

t 445–29 danger in . . . caring only for the *f·*.

feet

bare

p 362–14 and his bare *f·* away from it.

guest's

p 364–14 wash and anoint his guest's *f·*,

his

a 44–19 that he might employ his *f·* as before.
p 363– 1 to come behind the couch and reach his *f·*.
363–27 She bathed his *f·* with her tears
442–14 his *f·* "beautiful upon the—*Isa.* 52 : 7.
ap 558– 5 and his *f·* as pillars of fire :—*Rev.* 10 : 1.
    (*see also sub-title* **under his**)

its

ap 558–16 Its *f·* are pillars of fire, foundations of Truth

Jesus'

p 363– 4 she perfumed Jesus' *f·* with the oil,

lacerated

a 44–17 bind up the wounded side and lacerated *f·*,

Master's

a 28–24 to unloose the sandals of thy Master's *f·* !

of everlasting Love

a 23–11 will fall at the *f·* of everlasting Love.

our

f 224– 7 and shall plant our *f·* on firmer ground.
p 429– 8 We look before our *f·*,
g 516–14 The grass beneath our *f·* silently exclaims,

patient's

f 235–25 the patient's *f·* may be planted on the rock

to the lame

ph 183–29 voice to the dumb, *f·* to the lame.
f 210–13 hearing to the deaf, *f·* to the lame,

under her

ap 560– 8 and the moon under her *f·*,—*Rev.* 12 : 1.
561–27 and matter is put under her *f·*.
562– 7 The moon is under her *f·*.

under his

ph 200–15 hast put all things under his *f·*."—*Psal.* 8 : 6.
f 230–21 and can man put that law under his *f·*

under the

ph 182–22 puts matter under the *f·* of Mind.

wet

f 220–12 he has no catarrh from wet *f·*,

———

t 454– 7 and plants the *f·* in the true path,

felicity

m 66–17 Amidst gratitude for conjugal *f·*,

fell

a 27–26 They *f·* away from grace because
47–25 His dark plot *f·* to the ground,
47–26 and the traitor *f·* with it.
48–10 Remembering the sweat of agony which *f·*
s 133–10 and manna *f·* from the sky.
156– 5 A case of dropsy, . . . *f·* into my hands.
g 556–18 the deep sleep which *f·* upon Adam?
557–32 but immediately *f·* into mental sin ;

fellow-being

p 366–12 physician who lacks sympathy for his *f·*

fellow-beings

pr 13–16 before we tell Him or our *f·* about it.

fellow-countrymen

g 509–31 Jesus rebuked the material thought of his *f·* :

fellow-man

s 128–23 If one would not quarrel with his *f·*
p 435– 8 in obedience to higher law, helped his *f·*,
440–18 for ministering to the wants of his *f·*

fellow-men

t 447– 9 or judging accurately the need of your *f·*.

fellow-mortals

ap 564– 6 incites mortals to kill . . . even their *f·*,

Fellow of the Royal College of Physicians

s 164– 3 F· of the R· C· of P·, London.

fellows

b 313– 8 oil of gladness above thy *f·*.— *Heb.* 1 : 9.

fellowship

pr 8– 7 They hold secret *f·* with sin,
a 40–23 rejoicing to enter into *f·* with him
b 268– * *may have f· with us :— I John* 1 : 3.
268– * *our f· is with the Father,— I John* 1 : 3.
276– 5 unfold the foundation of *f·*,

felon

an 105–23 like an escaped *f·* to commit fresh atrocities
p 379– 9 A *f·*, on whom certain English students

felon's

a 40–21 If a career so great . . . could not avert a *f·* fate,

felt

a 20–19 and when error *f·* the power of Truth,
52– 9 Their imperfections and impurity *f·* the
53–28 but at the time when Jesus *f·* our infirmities,
sp 88–19 can never be seen, *f·*, nor understood through
ph 109– 0 before the patient *f·* the change ;
c 205–23 Who that had *f·* the loss of human peace
b 323–29 The effects of C. S. are not so much seen as *f·*.
324–22 was made blind, and his blindness was *f·* ;
p 395–22 to hold it as something seen and *f·*
400–31 Even our Master *f·* this.
404–17 The temperance reform, *f·* all over our land,
t 443–10 she always has *f·*, that all are privileged to
449–20 baneful effect . . . is less seen than *f·*.
450–27 Who, that has *f·* the perilous beliefs in
g 514–27 Daniel *f·* safe in the lions' den,

female

f 249– 5 "male and *f·*" of God's creating—*Gen.* 1 : 27.
g 508–21 a neuter gender, neither male nor *f·*.
508–22 Mind . . . names the *f·* gender last
508–28 The . . . individual idea, be it male or *f·*,
516–25 male and *f·* created He them.—*Gen.* 1 : 27.
524–19 Mind had made man, both male and *f·*.
525–16 and He shaped them male and *f·*.
528– 4 has already created man, both male and *f·*
ap 577– 5 presents the unity of male and *f·*

feminine

m 57– 7 Union of the masculine and *f·* qualities
57– 7 through certain elements of the *f·*,
57– 7 the *f·* mind gains courage and strength
64–24 masculine wisdom and *f·* love,
g 508–16 *f·* gender is not yet expressed in the text.
511–28 taking form in masculine, *f·*, or neuter gender.
516–30 Masculine, *f·*, and neuter genders
517–13 as we have for considering Him *f·*,

femininity

g 508–19 does not necessarily refer to either . . . or *f·*.

ferment

t 449– 3 A little leaven causes the whole mass to *f·*.

fermentation
m 65–20 There will ensue a *f·* over this
   65–23 The *f·* even of fluids is not pleasant.
sp 96–22 This mental *f·* has begun,
p 401–12 This *f·* should not aggravate the disease,
  421–13 more for the mental disturbance or *f·*,

fermenting
p 401–20 as is the case with a *f·* fluid.

ferocious
sp 78– 2 the blighted bud, the gnarled oak, the *f·* beast,
p 378–15 fastened fearlessly on a *f·* beast,

ferocity
b 293–22 lightning, fire, bestial *f·*

fervency
pr 8–21 Praying for humility with whatever *f·*

fervent
pr 2–12 We can do more for ourselves by humble *f·*
   4– 3 the prayer of *f·* desire for growth in grace,
   7–22 A self-satisfied ventilation of *f·* sentiments
   8–10 If a man, though apparently *f·* and prayerful,
  11–29 prayer, coupled with a *f·* habitual desire
  13– 6 beyond the honest standpoint of *f·* desire.
ap 565–21 with the *f·* heat of Truth and Love,

fervor
sp 89–24 and the *f·* of untutored lips.

festive
f 240– 4 *f·* flowers, and glorious heavens,

festivity
p 362– 6 as if to interrupt the scene of Oriental *f·*.

fetter
f 226–19 material medicine and hygiene, *f·* faith

fettered
sp 77–21 a so-called mind *f·* to matter.
b 292– 9 belief that Mind, . . . can be *f·* by the body,
t 448–32 *F·* by sin yourself, it is difficult to
gl 584–13 free from one belief only to be *f·* by another,

fetterless
sp 84–17 yea, to reach the range of *f·* Mind.

fetters
f 223– 4 the *f·* of man's finite capacity are forged by
  225–19 potent to break despotic *f·*
  226–10 demanding that the *f·* of sin, sickness,
  226–20 Science rends asunder these *f·*,
  227– 1 to guide me into the land of C. S., where *f·* fall
  249–29 It throws off some material *f·*.
t 449– 1 to free another from the *f·* of disease.
ap 570– 2 the people will chain, with *f·* of some sort,

feuds
a 52–15 Herod and Pilate laid aside old *f·* in order to

fever
chills and
p 375– 8 Change the . . . and the chills and *f·* disappear.
fear or
ph 175–12 and dissuade any sense of fear or *f·*.
typhoid
s 153–11 patient sinking in the last stage of typhoid *f·*.
you end
p 376–27 Destroy fear, and you end *f·*.

f 251– 5 neither should a *f·* become more severe
p 375– 6 often the form in which *f·* manifests itself.
  376–18 cannot, for that very reason, suffer with a *f·*.
  376–28 when it will be safe to check a *f·*.
  376–29 in Science you cannot check a *f·* after admitting
  380– 2 a *f·* case, which ends in a belief called
  386–10 catarrh, *f·*, rheumatism, or consumption,

fever-picture
p 379–30 the *f·*, drawn by millions of mortals

fevers
p 379–25 *F·* are errors of various types.

few
pref ix– 6 He finds a *f·* words, and with these he
   x– 9 A *f·* books, however, which are based on this
   x–19 *F·* invalids will turn to God till with
a 27–26 "Many are called, but *f·* are— *Matt.* 22: 14.
  36–13 He was forsaken by all save . . . a *f·* women
  38– 6 old doctrine . . . the election of a *f·* to be saved,
  38–21 Jesus experienced *f·* of the pleasures of the
  42–13 the desertion of all save a *f·* friends,
  48–15 Truth and Love bestow *f·* palms until
  54–22 adhered to him only a *f·* unpretentious friends,
s 141– 4 *F·* understand or adhere to Jesus' divine
ph 177–31 In such cases a *f·* persons believe the potion
  184–29 I sat silently by her side a *f·* moments.
  193–10 In a *f·* moments his face changed ;
  195– 3 babbling boy . . . taught to speak a *f·* words,
f 206–20 for the brief space of a *f·* years
  225–17 A *f·* immortal sentences, breathing the omni-
             potence of
b 270–10 *F·* deny the hypothesis that

few
b 301– 5 *F·* persons comprehend what C. S. means by
  323–17 If "faithful over a *f·* things,"— *Matt.* 25: 21.
o 358–21 *f·* who have gained a true knowledge of
p 389–32 I cured her in a *f·* minutes.
t 450–15 *F·* yield without a struggle,
r 473–31 *F·*, however, except his students understood
g 536–21 "of *f·* days, and full of trouble."— *Job* 14: 1.
  552–15 of *f·* days, and full of trouble."— *Job* 14: 1.
  556–32 plunged his infant babe, only a *f·* hours old,
ap 569– 6 faithful over a *f·* things,— *Matt.* 25: 23.

fewer
ph 175– 4 When there are *f·* prescriptions,
  176–12 There were *f·* books on digestion

fewness
f 225– 5 the *f·* and faithfulness of its followers.

fibres
r 488–23 Nerves have no more sensation, . . . than the *f·*

fiction
sp 84– 5 foreshadowing evil and mistaking fact for *f·*,
ph 171– 1 Matter, which . . . claims to be a creator, is a *f·*,
  195–25 the speculative theory, the nauseous *f·*.

fidelity
a 49–13 gratify his last. . . yearning with one sign of *f·*?
sp 95– 7 our *f·* to Truth and Love ;
p 397–20 and your *f·* to divine metaphysics,
  418–10 if your *f·* is half equal to the truth of
t 449–15 in proportion to your honesty and *f·*,
gl 579–10 ABRAHAM. *F·* ; faith in the divine Life

field
beast of the
g 527–22 formed every beast of the *f·*,— *Gen.* 2: 19.
  529–14 more subtle than any beast of the *f·* — *Gen.* 3: 1.
ap 565– 1 "more subtle than any beast of the *f·*." — *Gen.*
             3: 1.
beasts of the
g 539–19 to grovel beneath all the beasts of the *f·*.
flower of the
ph 190–24 As a flower of the *f·*, so he— *Psal.* 103: 15.
r 476–25 as a flower of the *f·*, so he— *Psal.* 103: 15.
herb of the
g 520–20 herb of the *f·* before it grew :— *Gen.* 2: 5.
  535–25 thou shalt eat the herb of the *f·* :— *Gen.* 3: 18.
leave the
p 419– 5 leave the *f·* to God, Life, Truth, and Love,
lilies of the
f 212–23 makes and clothes the lilies of the *f·*,
open
g 514–13 Undisturbed it lies in the open *f·*, or rests in
plant of the
g 509–24 the "plant of the *f·* before it— *Gen.* 2: 5.
  520–19 every plant of the *f·* before it— *Gen.* 2: 5.
  526– 4 "every plant of the *f·* before it— *Gen.* 2: 5.
this
t 457–11 since entering this *f·* of labor,

fields
s 121– 5 the heavenly *f·* were incorrectly explored.

fierce
sp 97– 8 According to human belief, the lightning is *f·*

fiery
s 133–17 in the *f·* furnace and in kings' palaces.
f 243– 6 from the *f·* furnace, from the jaws of the lion,
ap 565–20 *f·* baptism will burn up the chaff of error

fifth
sp 92– 3 *f·* erroneous postulate is, that matter holds
g 513– 5 and the morning were the *f·* day.— *Gen.* 1: 23.

fifty
p 422– 1 and that their combined sum is *f·*,

fight
pref viii–16 On this basis C. S. will have a fair *f·*.
a 21– 3 "I have fought a good *f·* — *II Tim.* 4: 7.
f 225– 8 The powers of this world will *f·*, and
b 309–12 a soldier of God, who had fought a good *f·*.
p 378–14 and both will *f·* for nothing.
r 492–18 "I propose to *f·* it out on this line,
  492–20 You must *f·* it out on this line.
g 529–28 faith to *f·* all claims of evil,

fighting
f 216–10 On which side are we *f·*?

fights
ap 567– 1 He leads the hosts . . . and *f·* the holy wars.

figs
b 276–31 grapes from thorns nor *f·* from thistles.

figurative
g 514–14 In the *f·* transmission from the divine thought

figuratively
b 299–18 is *f·* represented in Scripture as a tree,

FIGURE 183 FINGERS

figure
- b 282-13 never unite in f· or in fact.
- g 529-26 evil, by whatever f· presented,
- 538-11 The sun, . . . is a f· of divine Life and Love,
- ap 562- 6 completed this f· with woman, typifying the

figured
- b 282- 4 are f· by two geometrical symbols,

figures
- sp 81-20 Erase the f· which express number,
- ap 571-25 In significant f· he depicts the thoughts which

fill
- ph 195-27 f· our young readers with wrong tastes and
- f 201-13 We cannot f· vessels already full.
- g 504-13 Truth, Life, and Love f· immensity
- 512-18 and f· the waters in the seas ;— Gen. 1: 22.
- 520- 4 majesty, and glory of infinite Love f· all space.

filled
- pref x- 6 f· with plagiarisms from Science and Health.
- pr 5-16 Ingratitude and persecution f· it to the brim ;
- c 266- 9 but this seeming vacuum is already f·
- b 295- 6 The universe is f· with spiritual ideas,
- 315-15 Their thoughts were f· with mortal error,
- p 430-25 court-room is f· with interested spectators,
- r 469-24 where all space is f· with God.

filling
- s 110- 2 Spirit possessing all power, f· all space,
- ph 186- 3 f· it with the divine energies of Truth.

fills
- ph 190- 9 f· itself with thoughts of pain and pleasure,
- 198-11 f· in his delineations with sketches from
- b 331-22 He f· all space, and it is impossible to
- p 434- 3 Consternation f· the prison-yard.

filth
- p 383-12 whose f· does not affect his happiness,

final
- a 22-23 F· deliverance from error, whereby we
- 35-17 spiritual and f· ascension above matter,
- 42-16 proof of his f· triumph over body and
- 43-17 f· demonstration of the truth which Jesus
- 45 23 f· proof of all that he had taught,
- 46-26 In his f· demonstration, called the
- 48-30 hastening the f· demonstration of what life is
- 53-30 nor had he risen to his f· demonstration
- sp 76-28 those who have the f· understanding of Christ
- 96-10 until the f· spiritualization of all things.
- 96-31 During this f· conflict, wicked minds
- s 107- 5 for the reception of this f· revelation of the
- 111-23 rather than to a f· spiritual cause,
- 128- 1 material conditions, and that these are f·
- ph 188-10 from shame and woe to their f· punishment.
- f 219- 5 Mind should be, and is, supreme, . . . and f·.
- 242- 7 and the f· triumph over the body.
- b 268-10 challenge metaphysics to meet in f· combat.
- 268-14 In this f· struggle for supremacy,
- 288 10 When the f· physical and moral effects of C. S.
- 291-28 No f· judgment awaits mortals,
- 292- 1 then the f· trump should sound
- 339- 6 and involve the f· destruction of all sin?
- p 409- 5 the nearer matter approaches its f· statement,
- 429- 6 The f· demonstration takes time for its
- r 476- 6 Error, urged to its f· limits, is
- g 506- 7 and makes Truth f·.

finally
- a 21- 2 can f· say, "I have fought a— II Tim. 4: 7.
- 45- 6 Our Master fully and f· demonstrated
- sp 90-28 recognition of Spirit must f· come,
- 96- 4 Love will f· mark the hour of harmony,
- s 125-31 will f· be proved nothing more than
- 156-19 F· she said that she would give up her
- ph 178-21 must f· yield to the eternal Truth.
- 181-19 till you f· attain the understanding of C. S.
- 190-18 This mortal seeming . . . f· disappears,
- f 221-11 and f· made up his mind to die,
- 222-26 f· concluded that God never made a dyspeptic,
- 240-28 error is f· brought into subjection
- 248-32 will diminish until they f· disappear,
- 252-11 entire mortal, material error f· disappears,
- c 260-11 God's creation will f· be seen as the
- 264- 4 must f· give place to the glorious forms which
- b 287-29 false evidence will f· yield
- 310- 6 Thought will f· be understood and seen
- p 371- 3 this so-called mind must f· yield to the
- 378-26 and f· conquers it.
- 380- 3 death, which belief must be f· conquered by
- 405-18 The good man f· can overcome his fear of
- t 458- 9 that error will f· have the same effect as
- 460-31 f· the shadow of old errors was no longer cast
- r 476-17 Mortality is f· swallowed up in immortality.
- 492-11 Thus progress will f· destroy all error,
- g 523- 4 and f· declares that God knows error
- 549- 7 a blunder which will f· give place to
- ap 565-17 imperatively, absolutely, f·
- 570- 5 will f· be shocked into another extreme

find
- pr 7-11 Looking deeply into these things, we f· that
- 14-16 you will f· yourself suddenly well.
- a 22- 2 thinking with the aid of this to f· and follow the
- 24-23 Does spiritualism f· Jesus' death necessary
- 36- 2 can never f· bliss in the blessed company of
- m 65-27 f· permanence and pleasure in a more spiritual
- sp 83- 7 Mortals must f· refuge in Truth
- 96-32 wicked minds will endeavor to f· means
- s 111- 3 I f· the will, or sensuous reason of the
- 113-24 According to the Scripture, I f· that God is
- 124- 9 seeks to f· life and intelligence in matter,
- 125-23 agriculturist will f· that these changes cannot
- 125-30 florist will f· his flower before its seed.
- 132-27 shall he f· faith on the earth?" — Luke 18: 8.
- ph 169-15 should f· stronger supports and a higher home.
- 171- 8 and will f· himself unfallen, upright, pure,
- f 206-15 we f· that whatever blesses one blesses all,
- 232-29 we f· unquestionable signs of the burial of error
- 241-23 One's aim, . . . should be to f· the footsteps of
- 246-27 Life is eternal. We should f· this out,
- 251-23 to f· the divine Mind to be the only Mind,
- c 260-31 If we look to the body for pleasure, we f· pain ;
- 260-32 for Life, we f· death ; for Truth, we f· error ;
- 261- 1 for Spirit, we f· its opposite, matter.
- 262-11 efforts to f· life and truth in matter
- b 316- 6 lose sight of mortal selfhood to f· Christ,
- 322-31 "Canst thou by searching f· out — Job. 11: 7.
- 326- 6 and f· the divine remedy for every ill,
- o 354- 9 words of divine Science f· their immortality in
- 360- 2 they will f· that nothing is lost,
- p 378-31 less wisdom than we usually f· displayed in
- 397-18 and you will f· the ensuing good effects to be
- 409-30 cannot . . . expect to f· beyond the grave a
- 411-31 will f· that it alleviates the symptoms
- 412-18 f· the type of the ailment, get its name,
- 416-13 will f· himself in the same pain, unless
- 417- 1 and that they f· health, peace, and
- 426- 2 will f· that mortal mind, when instructed
- 436- 7 Your Supreme Court must f· the prisoner
- 436-13 Mortal Man should f· it again.
- 436-28 charged the jury, . . . to f· the prisoner guilty.
- t 443-22 If the sick f· these material expedients
- 444-11 Step by step will those who trust Him f·
- r 487- 1 f· a higher sense of happiness and existence.
- 491-15 f· the indissoluble spiritual link which
- 495-10 and f· a sovereign antidote for error
- g 551-27 "Canst thou by searching f· out — Job. 11: 7.
- ap 559-23 murmur not . . . if you f· its digestion bitter.

findeth
- b 291-23 As death f· mortal man, so shall he be after

finding
- a 36-17 from f· favor with the worldly-minded.
- ph 184- 9 in f· and casting out by denial the error
- f 220-23 F· his health failing, he gave up his
- 235- 2 cannot go forth, . . . f· unsuspected lodgment,
- c 264-18 f· all in God, good, and needing no other
- h 308-11 f· only an illusion, a blending of false claims,
- 322-23 likes to do wrong f· pleasure in it
- 327- 8 malice, f· pleasure in revenge!
- p 365- 7 f· utterance in such words as
- 369-27 Unscientific methods are f· their
- g 506-28 task of f· names for all material things,
- 542-17 lest any f· him should kill him. — Gen. 4: 15.

finds
- pref ix- 6 He f· a few words, and with these he
- ix-17 she still f· herself a willing disciple at
- pr 12-23 The common custom . . . f· help in blind belief,
- m 59-15 in which the heart f· peace and home.
- 69- 8 only as man f· the truth of being.
- s 119-25 viewing the sunrise, one f· that it contradicts
- 160-14 Anatomy f· a necessity for nerves
- f 250-18 f· himself experiencing none of these
- b 282-14 straight line f· no abiding-place in a curve,
- 282-15 a curve f· no adjustment to a straight line.
- 322-14 Man's wisdom f· no satisfaction in sin,
- p 365-25 If . . . inhumanity, or vice f· its way into the
- 379- 4 The Christian Scientist f· only effects, where
- 426- 5 The discoverer of C. S. f· the path less
- g 533-27 f· woman the first to confess her fault.

finger
- pr 3-31 put the f· on the lips and remember our
- s 161- 3 You say, "I have burned my f·."
- f 212-11 attempt to scratch the end of a f· which
- 237- 2 A little girl, . . . badly wounded her f·.
- 237- 6 "Mamma, my f· is not a bit sore."
- b 294- 6 the loss of one f· would take away

finger-posts
- f 242-30 The f· of divine Science show the way

fingers
- b 299- 9 With white f· they point upward to a
- p 401-30 to the f· of a surgeon,

finished
a	29– 4	until they have *f·* their course.
f	206–23	declaring that His work was *f·*,
g	519– 8	the heavens and the earth were *f·*,— *Gen.* 2 : 1.
	522–29	the Scripture . . . declares God's work to be *f·*.

finishes
a	21–14	till at last he *f·* his course with joy.

finite
sp	71–29	limited and *f·* in character and quality.
	72–22	belief that spirit is confined in a *f·*,
	73–31	nor can the *f·* become the channel of the infinite.
	76– 7	as neither material nor *f·*, but as infinite,
	93–21	belief that Spirit is *f·* as well as infinite
	93–28	*F·* spirit would be mortal,
	93–30	belief that the infinite can be . . . in the *f·*.
s	133–21	It was a *f·* and material system,
	151– 5	erring, *f·*, human mind has an absolute need of
f	213–15	towards the *f·*, temporary, and discordant.
	214–18	and entertain *f·* thoughts of God
	223– 4	the fetters of man's *f·* capacity are forged by
	223–13	If . . . Spirit would be *f·*,
c	256– 1	The *f·* must yield to the infinite.
	256–25	A *f·* and material sense of God leads to
	256–31	originating from a *f·* or material source
	256–32	must be limited and *f·*.
	257–22	*F·* mind manifests all sorts of errors,
	257–24	Who hath found *f·* life or love sufficient
	257–32	*F·* man cannot be the image and likeness of
	258– 2	A mortal, corporeal, or *f·* conception of God
	264– 8	Mortals must look beyond fading, *f·* forms,
b	280– 9	*F·* belief can never do justice to Truth
	280–10	*F·* belief limits all things,
	280–24	and that infinite Spirit, and Life, is in *f·* forms.
	281–28	does not put . . . the infinite into the *f·*.
	282– 8	the *f·*, which has both beginning and end.
	284– 5	if the infinite could be circumscribed within the *f·*,
	284–14	Can the infinite dwell in the *f·*?
	285–18	The time has come for a *f·* . . . to give place
	286– 4	through the *f·*, mutable, and mortal,
	290–10	That Life or Mind is *f·* and physical, . . . is false.
	309–25	impossible for . . . Soul to be in a *f·* body
	312–21	Mortals believe in a *f·* personal God ;
	312–23	theories are based on *f·* premises,
	312–28	matter and Spirit, the *f·* and the infinite,
	322–12	that *f·* belief may be prepared to relinquish
	335–22	for Spirit is not *f·*.
	336– 2	Mind never enters the *f·*.
	336–22	else God would be manifestly *f·*,
	339–22	until the *f·* gives place to the infinite,
o	343– 6	Is not *f·* mind ignorant of God's method?
r	466–21	There is no *f·* soul nor spirit.
	468–30	Time is *f·* ; eternity is forever infinite.
g	505–30	mortal, erring, and *f·* are human beliefs,
	524–16	Did the divine . . . become a *f·* deity,
	545– 1	through mortal and *f·* conceptions.
	550– 8	God cannot become *f·*, and be limited
	553–23	appearance of its method in *f·* forms
gl	580– 7	a so-called *f·* mind, producing other minds,
	580–23	supposition . . . that the infinite enters the *f·*,
	585–24	a *f·* belief concerning life, substance, and
	587– 2	GHOST. . . . a supposition that spirit is *f·*.
	587–12	belief that infinite Mind is in *f·* forms ;
	587–18	and cannot become *f·* and imperfect.
	591– 1	a physical sense of God as *f·* and corporeal.
		(*see also* **form, sense**)

finiteness
c	255–16	physical *f·*, cannot be made the basis of
	256–29	*F·* cannot present the idea or the vastness of
b	284– 2	not rational to say that Mind . . . dwells in *f·*,
	302– 1	Soul is not compassed by *f·*.
r	469– 5	Death and *f·* are unknown to Life.
gl	580– 1	a belief in intelligent matter, *f·*, and mortality ;

finity
f	202–21	earthly experience discloses the *f·* of error
	229– 8	Mind signifies God,— infinity, not *f·*.
gl	585–22	*f·* ; the opposite of infinity.
	594– 5	the first lie of limitation ; *f·* ;
	599– 3	As applied to corporeality, a mortal ; *f·*.

fire
sp	72–32	As readily can you mingle *f·* and frost as
f	252–30	with the resplendency of consuming *f·*.
b	293–22	wind, wave, lightning, *f·*, bestial ferocity
t	457–32	One cannot scatter his *f·*, and
ap	558– 6	and his feet as pillars of *f·* :— *Rev.* 10 : 1.
	558–16	Its feet are pillars of *f·*, foundations of
	565–20	This immaculate idea, . . . will baptize with *f·* ;
	566–10	a pillar of cloud by day and of *f·* by night,
gl	586–13	definition of

firm
a	23–13	"He that taketh one doctrine, *f·* in faith,
	23–32	Hebrew verb *to believe* means also *to be f·*
m	67–12	*f·* at the post of duty, the mariner works on
s	138– 8	a *f·* foundation in the realm of harmony.

firm
b	274–25	The conventional *f·*, called matter and mind,
p	374–24	your steps are less *f·* because of your fear,
	393–16	Be *f·* in your understanding that the
	438–31	the *f·* of Personal Sense, Error, & Co.,
	439– 4	Personal Sense, is a buyer for this *f·*.

firmament
above the
g	505–15	waters which were above the *f·* :— *Gen.* 1 : 7.

God called the
g	506– 8	God called the *f·* Heaven.— *Gen.* 1 : 8.

God made the
g	505–13	And God made the *f·*,— *Gen.* 1 : 7.

of the heaven
g	509–10	lights in the *f·* of the heaven,— *Gen.* 1 : 14.
	510– 6	lights in the *f·* of the heaven,— *Gen.* 1 : 15.
	511– 7	set them in the *f·* of the heaven,— *Gen.* 1 : 17.

open
g	511–21	in the open *f·* of heaven.— *Gen.* 1 : 20.
	511–29	fly above the earth in the open *f·*

or understanding
g	523– 9	and not from the *f·*, or understanding,

under the
g	505–14	waters which were under the *f·* — *Gen.* 1 : 7.

g	505– 4	God said, Let there be a *f·* — *Gen.* 1 : 6.
	505– 8	Spiritual understanding, . . . is the *f·*.
gl	586–15	definition of

firmer
f	224– 7	and shall plant our feet on *f·* ground.

firmly
s	147–19	demonstration of the rules . . . will plant you *f·*
t	454–28	until your students tread *f·* in the straight and

firmness
a	24– 2	*F·* in error will never save from sin, disease,
r	488–11	understanding, trust, constancy, *f·*.
gl	582– 1	BELIEVING. *F·* and constancy ;

first
pref	vii– 3	beholds the *f·* faint morning beams,
	viii–31	*f·* steps of a child in the newly discovered
	ix–13	still in circulation among her *f·* pupils ;
	ix–20	Her *f·* pamphlet on C. S. was
	x– 3	The *f·* edition of SCIENCE AND HEALTH was
	xi–25	The *f·* school of C. S. Mind-healing
	xii– 5	the United States, where C. S. was *f·* introduced.
	xii– 8	the *f·* established Church of Christ, Scientist ;
	xii– 9	the *f·* Christian Scientist Association,
	xii–13	the *f·* periodical issued by Christian Scientists.
pr	16–19	is but another name for the *f·* lie
a	29–29	though at *f·* faintly developed.
	31–12	*F·* in the list of Christian duties, he taught
	40– 9	*f·* removing the sin which incurs the penalty.
	45–25	Even his disciples, at *f·* called him a spirit,
m	62–32	this does not make materiality *f·*
sp	87–14	when really it is *f·* sight instead of
	91–25	The *f·* erroneous postulate of belief is,
	92–14	commending to our *f·* parents the knowledge of
an	100– 1	Mesmerism . . . was *f·* brought into notice by
	104–10	*F·*, people say it conflicts with the Bible.
	105–29	"Whom the gods would destroy, they *f·*
s	115–20	*F·* Degree: Depravity.
	116– 8	"The last shall be *f·*, and the *f·* last,"— *Matt.* 20 : 16.
	116–12	includes vastly more than is at *f·* seen.
	119– 8	To seize the *f·* horn of this dilemma
	134–20	its astonishing . . . success in the *f·* century.
	142– 9	the whole Christ, as our *f·* proof of Christianity,
	142–26	Which was *f·*, Mind or medicine?
	142–27	If Mind was *f·* and self-existent,
	142–28	Mind, . . . must have been the *f·* medicine.
	143–28	was *f·* chronologically, is *f·* potentially,
	143–29	and must be *f·* eternally,
	145–32	Our Master's *f·* article of faith propounded to
	146– 5	The *f·* idolatry was faith in matter.
	158– 5	He was supposed to have dictated the *f·*
	163– 1	*f·* marking Nature with his name,
ph	166–28	or he would have resorted to Mind *f·*.
	172–15	If man was *f·* a material being,
	177–13	from *f·* to last, the body is a
	183–11	sin, or error, *f·* caused the condemnation of
	189–26	*f·* the belief of inanimate, and then of
f	201–13	They must *f·* be emptied.
	204–12	The *f·* power is admitted to be good,
	204–16	a supposed mixture of the *f·* and second
	207–15	Body is not *f·* and Soul last,
	225– 5	You may know when *f·* Truth leads by
	230–12	to suppose Him capable of *f·* arranging
	234–26	control evil thoughts in the *f·* instance,
	237–16	taught . . . C. S., among their *f·* lessons,
	248–25	must *f·* turn our gaze in the right direction,
b	269– 2	From *f·* to last the supposed coexistence of
	269–10	The *f·* is error ; the latter is truth.
	269–32	The *f·* theory, that matter is everything.
	280–18	Jehovah's *f·* command of the Ten :

first

b 286–12 Physical causation was put aside from *f·* to
306– 3 They would *f·* make life result in death,
321– 3 Paul says, in his *f·* epistle to the
321–21 when Moses *f·* put his hand into his bosom
321–28 to the voice of the *f·* sign,— *Exod.* 4 : 8.
324–19 Paul was not at *f·* a disciple of Jesus
324–20 When the truth *f·* appeared to him in Science,
325–30 When *f·* spoken in any age, Truth,
326–31 He beheld for the *f·* time the true idea of Love,
329–19 because he fails in his *f·* effort.
333–17 the *f·* century of the Christian era,
334–26 "I am the *f·* and the last :— *Rev.* 1 : 17.
o 342–26 Who would be the *f·* to disown the Christliness
343–30 *f·* . . . to press along the line of gospel-healing,
355–18 any . . . healing power since the *f·* century.
p 366– 4 must *f·* cast moral evils out of himself
366–31 we must *f·* learn to bind up the broken-hearted.
374–27 body, when bereft of mortal mind, at *f·* cools,
389–13 Our dietetic theories *f·* admit that food sustains
390–12 When the *f·* symptoms of disease appear,
399–30 *f·* bind the strong man?"— *Matt.* 12 : 29.
403– 7 In the *f·* instance it is understood
411– 3 My *f·* discovery in the student's practice
412–20 Argue at *f·* mentally, not audibly,
423–32 so-called substance of bone is formed *f·* by
427–28 but it should have been his *f·* and only resort.
433–17 "Guilty of liver-complaint in the *f·* degree."
433–21 guilty of benevolence in the *f·* degree.
t 447–30 A sinner is afraid to cast the *f·* stone.
449–22 The *f·* impression, made on a mind which
455–14 "F· cast out the beam out of— *Matt.* 7 : 5.
456–27 *F·* : Because it is the voice of Truth
456–30 *Second:* Because it was the *f·* book
456–32 Hence it gave the *f·* rules for
457– 7 Since the divine light of C. S. *f·* dawned
459–11 condemned for failing to take the *f·* step.
461–27 you must *f·* see the claim of sin,
463–23 the *f·* step towards destroying error.
r 465– 1 This chapter is from the *f·* edition of
466–17 although *f·* and last it is the most
467– 3 The *f·* demand of this Science is,
471–25 until she caught the *f·* gleam of that which
474– 8 To the ignorant age in which it *f·* appears,
481–20 Human hypotheses *f·* assume the reality of
496– 6 in C. S. the *f·* duty is to obey God,
g 503–21 *f·*, in light ; *second,* in reflection ;
503– 5 and the morning were the *f·* day.— *Gen.* 1 : 5.
522– 3 The Science of the *f·* record proves the
522– 5 The *f·* record assigns all might and
526–14 *f·* mention of evil is in the legendary
526–24 in contradiction of the *f·* creation?
528–18 This is the *f·* record of magnetism.
528–28 surgery was *f·* performed mentally
520– 5 The *f·* system of suggestive obstetrics has
530–29 *F·*, this narrative supposes that
532– 1 Did God at *f·* create one man unaided,
532– 7 when eating its *f·* fruits brought death?
532–26 Fear was the *f·* manifestation of the error of
532–31 The *f·* impression material man had of himself
533–13 the snake-talker utters the *f·* voluble lie,
533–27 finds woman the *f·* to confess her fault.
534– 1 Hence she is *f·* to abandon the belief
534– 6 enabled woman to be *f·* to interpret the
535–17 the heritage of the *f·* born among men
536– 3 the *f·* heaven and the *f·* earth— *Rev.* 21 : 1.
541–22 At *f·* it usurps divine power.
541–24 It is supposed to say in the *f·* instance,
544–17 The *f·* statement about evil,
544–17 the *f·* suggestion of more than the one Mind,
551– 4 If Mind is *f·*, it cannot produce its opposite
551– 5 If matter is *f·*, it cannot produce Mind.
551–32 Which is *f·*, the egg or the bird?
553–14 or important to their origin and *f·*
554–17 *f·* effort of error has been and is
ap 558–11 To mortal sense Science seems at *f·* obscure,
559–22 It will be indeed sweet at its *f·* taste,
565–18 represented *f·* by man and,. . .last by woman,
568–10 *f·* the true method of creation is set forth
568–11 the Revelator *f·* exhibits the true warfare
572– 3 in both the *f·* and last books of the Bible,
572–20, 21 the *f·* heaven and the *f·* earth— *Rev.* 21 : 1.
577–13 *f·*, the Word of Life, Truth, and Love ;
gl 580– 2 nothingness ; the *f·* god of mythology ;
584– 3 and the morning were the *f·* day."— *Gen.* 1 : 5.
585–13 "Elias truly shall *f·* come and— *Matt.* 17 : 11.
585–27 *f·* from dust, second from a rib,
594– 3 the *f·* statement of mythology and idolatry ;
594– 4 animal magnetism ; the *f·* lie of limitation ;
594– 5 *f·* claim that there is an opposite of Spirit,
594– 6 *f·* delusion that error exists as fact ;
594– 7 *f·* claim that sin, sickness, and death are
594– 8 *f·* audible claim that God was not omnipotent
(see also **chapter**)

First Cause

g 547–20 evolution implies that the great *F· C·*

First Commandment

m 69–20 "Do you keep the *F· C·* ?
b 301–22 is not spiritual and breaks the *F· C·*,
340–16 The *F· C·* is my favorite text.
340–21 The divine Principle of the *F· C·*
o 361– 6 The Jew who believes in the *F· C·*
361–10 The Christian who believes in the *F· C·*

firstfruits

c 255– * *which have the f· of the Spirit,— Rom.* 8 : 23.

firstlings

g 540–27 Abel, he also brought of the *f·*— *Gen.* 4 : 4.
541– 1 Abel takes his offering from the *f·* of the

fish

of the sea

s 125–27 *f·* of the sea and the fowls of the air.
f 222–24 "dominion over the *f·* of the sea,— *Gen.* 1 : 26.
r 475–24 dominion over the *f·* of the sea,— *Gen.* 1 : 26.
g 515–13 dominion over the *f·* of the sea,— *Gen.* 1 : 26.
517–27 dominion over the *f·* of the sea,— *Gen.* 1 : 28.

salt

p 385–28 because you have partaken of salt *f·*,

———

sp 90– 5 from which loaf or *f·* could come?
p 413–13 taking a *f·* out of water every day
g 557– 3 moving and playing without harm, like a *f·*.

fishes

sp 90– 3 How were the loaves and *f·* multiplied
f 206–17 as Jesus showed with the loaves and the *f·*,
p 367–11 not "for the loaves and *f·*,"— *see John* 6 : 26.

fists

ph 192–18 who holds the "wind in His *f·* ;"— *Prov.* 30 : 4.

fit

p 384–23 if . . . you are not *f·* to conduct your own case
420–15 when they are in a *f·* mood to receive it,
t 445– 2 teacher must thoroughly *f·* his students
gl 595–15 alone can *f·* us for the office of spiritual teaching.
596–17 the only *f·* preparation for admission to the

fitness

pr 15–32 Without a *f·* for holiness, we cannot receive
t 440–12 registers his healing ability and *f·* to teach.
455–22 one who has grown into such a *f·* for it as

fitted

pr 3–24 and thus be *f·* to receive more.

five

s 117–24 Evidence drawn from the *f·* physical senses
ph 173– 1 brain, acting through the *f·* physical senses
190–11 and arranges itself into *f·* so-called senses,
200–22 in other words the *f·* senses,
b 274– 4 knowledge gained from the *f·* senses
274–17 what we erroneously term the *f·* physical senses
287–27 *f·* material senses testify to truth and error
293–32 The *f·* physical senses are the avenues and
p 421–31 asserting that the products of eight multiplied
by *f·*,
r 471– 7 the evidence before the *f·* corporeal senses,
477– 9 To the *f·* corporeal senses, man appears to be
486–28 If the *f·* corporeal senses were the medium
488–14 Do the *f·* corporeal senses constitute man?
493–18 all the beliefs of the *f·* corporeal senses,
g 523–26 fourth verse of chapter two to chapter *f·*,
526–10 involves theories of . . . termed the *f·* senses.
532– 6 gained from the *f·* corporeal senses.
532–31 through matter, the *f·* senses.
543– 9 *f·* corporeal senses cannot take cognizance of
gl 581–20 obtained from the *f·* corporeal senses,
589–13 obtained from the *f·* corporeal senses ;
590– 4 obtained from the *f·* corporeal senses ;

fix

p 414–15 To *f·* truth steadfastly in your

fixed

m 65–26 Matrimony, which was once a *f·* fact
69– 3 as *f·* in divine Science as is the proof that
sp 83–24 great gulf is. . .as impassable as that between
s 113– 2 there must be *f·* rules for the demonstration of
128–27 It rests on *f·* Principle
163–32 or to reconcile the *f·* and repulsive antipathies
ph 180–19 by declaring disease to be a *f·* fact,
193– 8 Mr. Clark lay with his eyes *f·* and sightless.
f 233–25 divided according to a *f·* rule,

fixedness

b 330– 4 the *f·* of mortal illusions,

fixing

c 261–27 *F·* your gaze on the realities supernal,

fixity

a 23–17 between nothing and something, having no *f·*.

flame

ph 192–14 It is the headlong cataract, the devouring *f·*,
ap 566–18 An awful guide, in smoke and *f·*,

flames
  s 161– 7   able to nullify the action of the *f*·,
  b 329–15   nor should he remain in the devouring *f*·.
  g 504–10   not from the sun nor from volcanic *f*·,
  ap 558–18   *f*· of Truth were prophetically described

flaming
  g 537– 6   a *f*· sword which turned every way, — *Gen.* 3 : 24.

flannel
  m 63– 2   You would never think that *f*· was

flannels
  ph 174– 5   to *f*·, to baths, diet, exercise, and air?

flash
  b 288–15   burst and *f*· till the cloud is cleared

flashing
  p 439–16   his words *f*· as lightning

flatteries
  f 238– 8   this frown, more than *f*·,

flatulency
  p 413–25   noticing every symptom of *f*·,

flavor
  sp 88– 6   mind may even be cognizant of a present *f*·

fled
  b 321– 9   When, . . . he saw it become a serpent, Moses *f*·
  ap 565–29   woman *f*· into the wilderness, — *Rev.* 12 : 6.

fleddest
  s 135– 2   O thou sea, that thou *f*·? — *Psal.* 114 : 5.

flee
  f 215–20   *f*· as phantoms of error before truth and
  p 377– 6   Invalids *f*· to tropical climates
  405–31   causes mortals . . . to *f*· from body to
  406–19   Resist evil . . . and it will *f*· from you.
  418–32   dark images . . . which *f*· before the light of
  r 494–18   thus helping erring human sense to *f*· from

flees
  b 310–11   darkness *f*· when the earth has again

fleeth
  t 464–26   "The hireling *f*·, because he is an — *John* 10 : 13.

fleeting
  m 60–13   selfishness and impurity alone are *f*·,
  66–18   it is well to remember how *f*· are human joys.
  68– 7   We ought to weary of the *f*· and false
  s 163–31   as to arrange the *f*· vapors around us,
  f 241– 7   Sin . . . carries off their *f*· joys.
  247–11   fading and *f*· as mortal belief.
  c 264– 1   *f*· concepts of the human mind.

flesh
  advent in the
  a 30– 5   Born of a woman, Jesus' advent in the *f*·
  and all error
  a 39– 5   He overcame the world, the *f*·, and all error,
  and blood
  a 25–10   His true *f*· and blood were his Life ;
  s 137–23   *f*· and blood hath not revealed it — *Matt.* 16 : 17.
  b 321– 4   "*F*· and blood cannot inherit the — *I Cor.* 15 : 50.
  r 478–29   conferred not with *f*· and blood." — *Gal.* 1 : 16.
  and bones
  a 45–27   "Spirit hath not *f*· and bones, — *Luke* 24 : 39.
  b 313–30   Jesus called the body, . . . "*f*· and bones." — *Luke* 24 : 39.
  o 352– 7   mortal and material belief of *f*· and bones,
  p 372– 8   can form blood, *f*·, and bones.
  and evil
  pr 10–13   overcoming the world, the *f*·, and evil,
  and matter
  b 320–22   the belief that man is *f*· and matter,
  and Spirit
  ph 167–20   The *f*· and Spirit can no more unite
  171–23   No more . . . between the *f*· and Spirit
  o 356–12   spoke of *f*· and Spirit as the two opposites,
  356–18   between error and Truth, between *f*· and Spirit.
  ap 567–12   endeth the conflict between the *f*· and Spirit.
  and the devil
  o 354– 5   "the world, the *f*·, and the devil"
  animal
  f 222–25   if eating a bit of animal *f*· could overpower
  belief of the
  b 310–22   It is the belief of the *f*· and of
  beliefs of the
  a 53–29   he had not conquered all the beliefs of the *f*·
  b 325–25   But he, who is begotten of the beliefs of the *f*·
  bone and
  g 533–22   rapid deterioration of the bone and *f*· which
  comes to the
  gl 583–11   comes to the *f*· to destroy incarnate error.
  constitute the
  b 274–21   beliefs and their products constitute the *f*·,
  crucified the
  a 18– *   *crucified the f· with the affections and* — *Gal.* 5 : 24.
  crucifying the
  b 316–17   conclusion that . . . by crucifying the *f*·.

flesh
  cut the
  r 474– 8   worse cords than those which cut the *f*·.
  dominate the
  c 266–25   his demonstrations, which dominate the *f*·.
  exit from the
  s 117–23   and triumphant exit from the *f*·.
  ills of
  s 155–23   the discords of matter and the ills of *f*·,
  b 277–21   produces all the ills of *f*·,
  ills of the
  ph 191–32   able to cast out the ills of the *f*·.
  b 320–27   divine power to heal the ills of the *f*·,
  gl 581–16   the ills of the *f*· rebuked.
  impurities of
  f 241–28   washing the body of all the impurities of *f*·,
  in my
  b 320–25   "In my *f*· shall I see God," — *Job* 19 : 26.
  let not the
  a 33–20   Let not the *f*·, but the Spirit, be represented
  lust of the
  f 223– 3   shall not fulfil the lust of the *f*·." — *Gal.* 5 : 16.
  gl 584–20   hypnotism ; the lust of the *f*·,
  manifest in
  b 334–15   the corporeal Jesus manifest in *f*·,
  material
  b 321– 1   still clad in material *f*·,
  matter, or the
  a 35–17   final ascension above matter, or the *f*·,
  mortal
  sp 81–10   their affiliation with mortal *f*· ;
  not in the
  g 534–22   But ye are not in the *f*·, — *Rom.* 8 : 9.
  not the offspring of
  b 289–31   Man is not the offspring of *f*·, but of Spirit,
  offspring of the
  gl 594–17   The son of man, the offspring of the *f*·.
  opposed to
  s 114– 4   meaning . . . the *f*· opposed to Spirit,
  outside the
  r 482–22   the divine idea of God outside the *f*·.
  overcome the
  b 289– 7   Then Spirit will have overcome the *f*·.
  piece of the
  f 212–16   this so-called mind instead of a piece of the *f*·,
  pierced his
  a 50–30   sharper than the thorns which pierced his *f*·.
  probation in the
  a 35–15   his probation in the *f*· after death,
  Spirit against the
  o 347– 2   and the Spirit against the *f*·." — *Gal.* 5 : 17.
  Spirit and
  f 254– 7   until the battle between Spirit and *f*· is fought
  b 288– 7   and this warfare between the Spirit and *f*·
  g 530–25   Thus Spirit and *f*· war.
  Spirit and the
  s 145–28   warfare between Spirit and the *f*· goes on.
  b 315–31   the mediator between Spirit and the *f*·,
  Spirit over the
  b 316– 9   to prove the power of Spirit over the *f*·,
  strength and
  f 222–17   he recovered strength and *f*· rapidly.
  warfare with the
  b 324–15   It is a warfare with the *f*·,
  Word was made
  o 350–24   "The Word was made *f*·." — *John* 1 : 14.
  works of the
  an 106–20   the works of the *f*· are manifest, — *Gal.* 5 : 19.
  wound the
  p 385–19   If you sprain the muscles or wound the *f*·,

  ——

  a 25–11   they truly eat his *f*· . . . who partake of
  31– 4   Jesus acknowledged no ties of the *f*·.
  s 107–10   from every ill "that *f*· is heir to."
  118– 7   second appearing in the *f*· of the Christ,
  ph 167–20   The "*f*· lusteth against the Spirit." — *Gal.* 5 : 17.
  177–22   create the so-called laws of the *f*·,
  200–22   the *f*· that warreth against Spirit.
  f 217–14   know we no man after the *f*· !" — *II Cor.* 5 : 16.
  235–25   when the soul is willing and the *f*· weak,
  244–10   the worms would rob him of the *f*·
  253–31   of Spirit instead of the *f*·.
  b 274–22   and the *f*· wars against Spirit.
  310–21   If Soul could sin, Spirit, Soul, would be *f*·
  311–10   All sin is of the *f*·.
  316–30   satisfied with the *f*·, resting on the basis
  320–13   with man, for that he also is *f*·," — *Gen.* 6 : 3.
  320–17   they are [or, in their error they are] but *f*·."
  o 347– 1   "The *f*· lusteth against the Spirit, — *Gal.* 5 : 17.
  356–15   the *f*· profiteth nothing." — *John* 6 : 63.
  p 385–21   Mind decides whether or not the *f*· shall
  t 461– 1   not . . . exist in the *f*· without food
  g 528–11   closed up the *f*· instead thereof ; — *Gen.* 2 : 21.
  531–27   since *f*· wars against Spirit

flesh
g 534–21 they that are in the *f* cannot— *Rom.* 8 : 8.
536–16 Created by *f* instead of by Spirit,
gl 584–12 The *f*, warring against Spirit ;
586–18 definition of

flesh-brush
ph 174– 5 that man should bow down to a *f*,

fleshliness
c 266–17 teaches mortals to lay down their *f*

fleshly
pref xi– 8 not of Spirit, but of the *f* mind
m 57–27 severance of *f* ties serves to unite thought
s 155–24 less weight into the material or *f* scale
ph 196– 7 awakens mortal mind from its *f* dream,
f 222– 9 whereas Truth regenerates this *f* mind
228– 9 and *f* ills will disappear.
314– 3 waited until the mortal or *f* sense
317–30 remained a *f* reality, so long as
332–30 highest type . . . which a *f* form could express
332–31 Into the . . . ideal man the *f* element cannot
334– 8 infinitely greater, than the *f* Jesus,

flesh-pots
f 221–26 he thought of the *f* of Egypt,

flexibility
ph 199–28 gave his . . . muscles, their *f*

flickers
f 244–19 If man *f* out in death or

flight
sp 07–10 yet in C. S. the *f* of one and the blow of the
c 261–30 and preens its wings for a skyward *f*.

flights
f 249–30 but makes its mundane *f* quite ethereal.

flimsy
an 103–26 whose *f* and gaudy pretensions,

float
sp 87–11 *f* in the general atmosphere of
87–22 of the tall ships that *f* on its bosom,

flock
p 442–27 "Fear not, little *f* :— *Luke* 12 : 32.
g 540–27 brought of the firstlings of his *f*,— *Gen.* 4 : 4.
541– 1 offering from the firstlings of the *f*.

flocks
m 61–26 stock to increase your *f* and herds?

flood
pref viii–23 increased violence of diseases since the *f*.
ap 570– 9 cast out of his mouth water as a *f*,— *Rev.* 12 : 15.
570–10 to be carried away of the *f*.— *Rev.* 12 : 15.
570–19 swallowed up the *f* which the— *Rev.* 12 : 16.
570–19 What if the old dragon should send forth a new *f*

flooding
s 150–31 hosts of Æsculapius are *f* the world

flood-tides
f 201–18 pour in truth through *f* of Love.

floor
r 492–14 New thoughts are constantly obtaining the *f*.

floral
m 68–24 The perpetuation of the *f* species by bud or
f 240– 6 The *f* apostles are hieroglyphs of Deity.

florist
s 125–30 the *f* will find his flower before its seed.

flour
sp 90– 1 and wheat to produce *f*,

flourish
pr 5–19 *f* "like a green bay tree ;"— *Psal.* 37 : 35.
fr 600– * *let us see if the vine f*,— *Song* 7 : 12.

flourisheth
ph 190–24 a flower of the field, so he *f*.— *Psal.* 103 : 15.
r 476–25 a flower of the field, so he *f*.— *Psal.* 103 : 15.

flow
a 53–18 spiritual blessings which might *f* from
sp 72–24 individual good . . . may *f* from the departed

flowed
s 133– 9 In the wilderness, streams *f* from the rock,
p 376–15 than in all the blood which ever *f* through

flower
brightens the
g 516–19 brightens the *f*, beautifies the landscape,
decaying
sp 78– 1 The decaying *f*, the blighted bud,
his
s 125–30 the florist will find his *f* before its seed.
leaf and
g 552–25 The blending tints of leaf and *f*
new-blown
p 413–23 in order to keep it sweet as the new-blown *f*.

flower
tree, and
b 289–23 So man, tree, and *f* are supposed to die ;
———
sp 71–11 you may dream that you see a *f*,
71–12 the *f* is a product of the so-called mind,
81–19 seemeth to wither and the *f* to fade,
ph 190–24 As a *f* of the field, so he— *Psal.* 103 : 15.
191–23 not a *f* starts from its cloistered cell.
c 265–18 or a *f* withered by the sun
t 459– 1 as the *f* turns from darkness to light.
r 476–25 as a *f* of the field,— *Psal* 103 : 15.
g 508– 6 substance of a thought, a seed, or a *f*

flowers
a 22–25 is not reached through paths of *f*
m 57–25 may uproot the *f* of affection,
61–17 like tropical *f* born amid Alpine snows.
68–10 mistrust, . . . withers the *f* of Eden
f 212–22 credulous frenzy, . . . spirits produce the *f*.
240– 4 festive *f*, and glorious heavens,

flowery
a 41–11 hypocrite may have a *f* pathway here, but

flowing
a 25– 8 than when it was *f* in his veins
r 487–20 Truth, *f* from immortal Mind,
ap 566– 2 the dark ebbing and *f* tides of human fear,
gl 589– 8 spiritual peace, *f* from the understanding

flows
s 139–13 sectarian bitterness, whenever it *f* inward.
g 552–22 From a material source *f* no remedy for

fluctuate
t 463– 2 among phenomena, which *f* every instant

fluid
an 101– 1 no proof . . . of the animal magnetic *f* ;
b 293– 3 Electricity is not a vital *f*,
338–16 This suggests the thought of something *f*,
p 401–13 should be as painless to man as to a *f*,
401–20 as is the case with a fermenting *f*.

fluids
m 65–23 The fermentation even of *f* is not pleasant.
g 510–23 and the allusion to *f*
510–24 by the resolving of *f* into solids,

flushed
p 415–19 causing a pale or *f* cheek.

flutterings
c 262–11 We must reverse our feeble *f*

fly
sp 90–16 In dreams we *f* to Europe
g 511–20 fowl that may *f* above the earth— *Gen.* 1 : 20.
511–29 The fowls, which *f* above the earth

flying
b 298–27 *f* on spiritual, not material, pinions.

foam
f 203–27 The *f* and fury of illegitimate living

foaming
gl 593–16 *f*, and dashing, it is a type of error.

focal
b 301–27 supposed standpoint outside the *f* distance

focus
s 122–15 The optical *f* is another proof of the
g 504–24 when gathered into the *f* of ideas,

foe
ph 176–19 Mortal mind is the worst *f* of the body,
p 419– 5 Your true course is to destroy the *f*,
423–15 as both his *f* and his remedy.
ap 571–11 Who is telling mankind of the *f* in ambush?
571–12 Is the informer one who sees the *f* ?

foes
a 44– 6 the tomb gave Jesus a refuge from his *f*,
ap 564–17 The brutal barbarity of his *f*

foetal
g 553–20 from Adam's rib, not from a *f* ovum.
554–13 unconscious of his *f* and infantile existence ;

foetus
m 62– 2 The *f* must be kept mentally pure

follow
pref vii–11 The Wisemen were led to behold and to *f*
pr 4– 6 and *f* his example, is our proper debt to him
4–30 enable us to *f* Jesus' example.
5–31 We should *f* our divine Exemplar,
9–30 If unwilling to *f* his example,
a 22– 2 to find and *f* the right road.
26– 6 if we *f* his commands faithfully :
27–28 Why do those who profess to *f* Christ
31–16 to all who *f* him in deed.
37–23 It is possible, . . . to *f* in some degree
37–26 do they *f* him in the way that he commanded?
38–10 "These signs shall *f* them that— *Mark* 16 : 17.

follow

a	38–13	he did not say, "These signs shall *f·* you,"
	40–26	should *f·* the example of our Master
	44– 2	laid aside for a crown, the benediction *f·*,
	52–28	"These signs shall *f·* them that — *Mark* 16 : 17.
	54– 8	Who is ready to *f·* his teaching and example?
	54–20	would not accept . . . *f·* his example.
sp	82–18	In like manner it would *f·*, even if our
	96– 5	spiritualization will *f·*, for Love is Spirit.
s	138–21	to *f·* the Christ-example, and to heal the sick
	139–30	it does not *f·* that the profane or atheistic
	151–30	yield to this power, and *f·* the leadings of
	161–13	If her sister States *f·* this example
ph	198–30	does not *f·* that exercise has produced this
f	227–22	and cries: "*F·* me!
	228–20	If we *f·* the command of our Master,
	248–22	are liable to *f·* those lower patterns,
c	266–24	Mortals must *f·* Jesus' sayings and
b	278–20	From this it would *f·* that there are
	324–23	spiritual light soon enabled him to *f·* the
	326– 3	If we wish to *f·* Christ, Truth, it must be
	328–22	"These signs shall *f·* them that — *Mark* 16 : 17.
o	342–31	no denunciations would *f·* them, even if
	343–29	mistake which allows words, . . . to *f·* such
	345– 5	does it not *f·* that God cannot be in His
	349– 8	We propose to *f·* the Master's example.
	355–10	"*F·* me; and let the dead bury — *Matt.* 8 : 22.
	356–30	Does subsequent *f·* its antecedent?
	359– 5	will take the same cases, and cures will *f·*.
	359–26	"And these signs shall *f·* them — *Mark* 16 : 17.
p	362– *	*And these signs shall f· them — Mark* 16 : 17.
	384–21	such symptoms are not apt to *f·* exposure;
	386–11	effects will *f·*, . . . on account of the belief.
	434– 6	law of Christ supersedes *our* laws; let us *f·*
r	495–29	and *f·* the behests of God,
g	526–12	sickness, and death, *f·* in the train of this error
ap	578–16	goodness and mercy shall *f·* me — *Psal.* 23 : 6.
gl	591– 2	From this *f·* idolatry and mythology,
	594–12	SHEEP. . . . those who *f·* their leader.

followed

a	42–13	was *f·* by the desertion of all save a few
	42–14	who sadly *f·* him to the foot of the cross.
	46–21	was *f·* by his exaltation above all
	54–26	He said that those who *f·* him should
s	141–15	*f·* the understanding of the divine Principle
b	309–13	those, who through earnest striving *f·* his
	309–15	the children of earth who *f·* his example
p	384–17	*f·* by chills, dry cough, influenza,
g	502– 9	Spiritually *f·*, the book of Genesis is the
	502–18	*f·* by its spiritual interpretation
	524– 1	The idolatry which *f·* this material
	544– 1	record of material creation which *f·* the
ap	575–28	who *f·* it to the manger of Jesus ;
gl	581–14	temptation overcome and *f·* by exaltation.

follower

s	138–27	Our Master said to every *f·* :

followers

her

t	443– 2	consulted by her *f·* as to the

his

a	31–12	he taught his *f·* the healing power of
	33– 3	His *f·*, sorrowful and silent,
	35–29	draught our Master . . . commended to his *f·*.
	37–26	Christians claim to be his *f·*,
	39– 2	Such indignities . . . his *f·* will endure until
s	136– 3	He taught his *f·* that his religion
o	350– 8	his *f·* must grow into that stature
r	494–31	It should be said of his *f·* also,

its

f	225– 6	by the fewness and faithfulness of its *f·*.

Jesus'

b	317–12	benedictions rest upon Jesus' *f·* :
	324–20	but a persecutor of Jesus' *f·*.

of Christ

pr	5–15	The *f·* of Christ drank his cup.
s	134–10	the *f·* of Christ were burned, crucified, and
	142– 4	Anciently the *f·* of Christ, or Truth,

persecuted

a	33– 6	the persecuted *f·* of Truth.

professed

a	37–16	When will Jesus' professed *f·* learn to
a	38– 3	a select number of *f·*.

following

pr	10–11	and "with signs *f·*." — *Mark* 16 : 20.
a	21–29	After *f·* the sun for six days,
	31–17	*f·* his demonstration so far as we
an	102–23	The *f·* is an extract from the Boston Herald :
s	110–13	In *f·* these leadings of scientific
	110–29	with "signs *f·*." — *Mark* 16 : 20.
	113–10	are summarized in the four *f·*,
	117–13	attained through "signs *f·*." — *Mark* 16 : 20.
	154– 9	fact in metaphysics is illustrated by the *f·*

following

ph	179– 3	*f·* Christ in the daily life.
	192–27	*f·* the example of our Master
b	270– 2	One only of the *f·* statements can be true :
	288–21	are to be found in the *f·* postulates :
	329– 1	of a single period or of a limited *f·*.
	330– 8	When the *f·* platform is understood
p	363–21	*f·* it with that remarkable declaration
t	458–27	honest and consistent in *f·* the leadings of
r	470–12	the *f·* self-evident proposition :
	496–31	The *f·* is a brief exposition of
g	502–18	In the *f·* exegesis, each text is
	525– 7	The *f·* are some of the equivalents of
	525–12	*f·* translation is from the Icelandic :
	554– 9	*f·* from a misconception of life,
ap	568– 7	*f·* chapters depict the fatal effects of
	577–32	In the *f·* Psalm one word shows,
gl	590–23	introduced in the second and *f·* chapters,

follows

sp	72–21	God, good, being ever present, it *f·*
	80– 7	communication purporting to . . . reads as *f·* :
	81–29	and *f·* as a necessary consequence
an	100– 7	His propositions were as *f·* :
	100–17	reported to the government as *f·* :
	101–12	Their report stated the results as *f·* :
	106–19	when he wrote as *f·* :
s	128– 6	From this it *f·* that business men
	130–13	for from this premise it *f·* that
b	320–14	quoted as *f·*, from the original Hebrew :
	331–12	From this it *f·* that nothing possesses
	338–30	From this it *f·* that Adam was not the
o	353–29	from this it *f·* that whatever is laid off is
p	388–13	there *f·* the necessity for another admission
t	449–31	and unless this result *f·*, the teacher is
	453– 8	chemicalization *f·* the explanation of Truth,
g	516–29	It *f·* that *man* is a generic term.
	519–27	No exhaustion *f·* the action of this Mind,
	552– 3	Another question *f·* : Who or what
ap	568– 9	narrative *f·* the order used in Genesis.
	570– 7	for one extreme *f·* another.

folly

ph	175–32	"Where ignorance is bliss, 't is *f·* to be wise,"
p	426–15	and see the *f·* of hypocrisy,

fondest

b	299– 9	has buried its *f·* earthly hopes.

food

amount of

ph	175–21	exact amount of *f·* the stomach could digest

and clothing

p	442–23	Truth, gives mortals temporary *f·* and clothing

and raiment

t	461– 2	without *f·* and raiment ;

brings forth

g	530– 7	earth, at God's command, brings forth *f·*

digestible

ph	197–25	and the most digestible *f·* in the stomach,

good for

g	526– 1	pleasant to the sight, and good for *f·* ; — *Gen.* 2 : 9.

my

p	390– 2	she said, "My *f·* is all digested, and

partaking of

p	431– 6	partaking of *f·* at irregular intervals,

proper

f	222– 6	one of which is to believe that proper *f·*

simple

ph	197–21	told that the simple *f·* our forefathers ate
a	44–14	He did not depend upon *f·* or pure air
ph	176– 8	custom of taking no thought about *f·*
	195–16	furnishes *f·* for thought.
f	221–25	but he never enjoyed his *f·* as he
	221–29	understanding, that neither *f·* nor
	222– 4	This person learned that *f·*
	222–11	*F·* had less power to help or to hurt
	232–19	Jesus never taught that drugs, *f·*,
p	388–12	Admit the common hypothesis that *f·*
	388–15	another admission . . . that *f·* has power
	388–20	If *f·* was prepared by Jesus for his
	388–22	The fact is, *f·* does not affect the absolute
	388–31	If mortals think that *f·* disturbs
	388–32	either the *f·* or this thought must be
	389– 8	mortal mind, which reports *f·* as undigested.
	389–13	theories first admit that *f·* sustains
	389–14	theories . . . discuss the certainty that *f·* can
	389–19	If God has, . . . instituted laws that *f·*
	389–21	cannot annul . . . by an opposite law that *f·*
	413– 8	regulates the condition of the . . . bowels, and *f·*,

fool

p	407– 1	becoming a *f·* or an object of loathing ;

foolish

a	32–23	This would have been *f·* in a literal sense ;
ph	181–14	It is *f·* to declare that you
f	202– 1	*f·* as straining out gnats and swallowing camels.
	238–25	Society is a *f·* juror, listening only to one side

foolish
p 388–26   but it would be *f·* to venture beyond our
388–27   *f·* to stop eating until we gain perfection
t 448–31   To talk the right and live the wrong is *f·* deceit,

foot
a 42–14   who sadly followed him to the *f·* of the cross.
s 113–14   not a *f·* to stand upon which is not purely
161–11   put her *f·* on a proposed tyrannical law,
f 229–22   should be trampled under *f·*,
234–15   those who trample them under *f·*,
ap 558– 7   his right *f·* upon the sea, — *Rev.* 10 : 2.
558– 7   and his left *f·* on the earth. — *Rev.* 10 : 2.
559– 4   "right *f·*" or dominant power— *Rev.* 10 : 2.
559– 6   The angel's left *f·* was upon the earth ;

foothold
ph 176–16   disease and death, will lose their *f·*.
b 282–18   and error has no *f·* in Truth.
g 535– 1   has given the understanding a *f·* in C. S.

footing
m 65–26   must lose its present slippery *f·*,

footprints
a 41– 9   walk calmly on though it be with bleeding *f·*,
f 224– 4   As the crude *f·* of the past disappear

footsteps
bleeding
pr 10– 3   even though with bleeding *f·*,
her
p 420– 7   than when she counts her *f·*
human
f 254– 1   the human *f·* leading to perfection
of thought
ph 174– 9   The *f·* of thought, rising above
of Truth
ph 192–27   We walk in the *f·* of Truth and Love
f 241–24   should be to find the *f·* of Truth,
tread in the
pr 9–29   since you do not care to tread in the *f·*

f 201– *   *the f· of Thine anointed.— Psal.* 89 : 51.
t 454–28   care and counsel support all their feeble *f·*,

forbade
a 48–22   Jesus *f·* him, thus rebuking resentment

forbearance
t 444–21   Fear not that he will smite thee again for thy *f·*.

Forbes, Sir John
s 164– 3   Sir John *F·*, M.D., F.R.S.,

forbid
p 393– 3   forgetting that . . . we can *f·* this entrance.

forbidden
f 234–28   to look with desire on *f·* objects
p 440–28   I ask that he be *f·* to enter
r 481–12   *f·* fruit of knowledge, . . . is the testimony of
g 528–31   when the *f·* fruit was bringing forth

forbore
a 19–12   The Master *f·* not to speak the whole truth,

force
accelerated
ap 560–23   comes back to him at last with accelerated *f·*,
blind
ph 190– 2   It is but a blind *f·*.
divine
s 134–19   the very element, which gave it divine *f·*
healing
s 160– 5   drugs lose their healing *f·*,
physical
r 484–15   Physical *f·* and mortal mind are one.
whole
s 157– 5   the whole *f·* of the mental element is
without this
p 399–20   Without this *f·* the body is devoid of action,

a 25–20   Hence the *f·* of his admonition,
m 67–18   notion that animal natures . . . give *f·* to char-
    acter
sp 80–15   It is mysticism which gives spiritualism its *f·*.
an 100– 4   he regarded this so-called *f·*, which he said
ph 192–11   a material belief, a blind miscalled *f·*,
c 266–12   Love will *f·* you to accept what best promotes
b 317– 4   insisted on the might of matter, the *f·* of falsity,
p 396–19   due to the *f·* of education
g 555– 1   in proportion as the *f·* of mortal mind is less

forced
a 25– 1   unbelieving Thomas was *f·* to acknowledge
s 159– 6   Her hands were held, and she was *f·* into

forceps
o 346–28   the operation, and the *f·* are unchanged.

forces
sp 96–13   becoming the arena for conflicting *f·*.
s 124–26   We tread on *f·*.
124–28   Human knowledge calls them *f·* of matter ;
b 293–13   The material so-called gases and *f·*
293–14   counterfeits of the spiritual *f·* of divine Mind,
ap 559–14   stirs their latent *f·* to utter the

forcible
pr 7– 5   showing the necessity for such *f·* utterance,
ph 196–22   *f·* descriptions and medical details,

forcing
p 401–19   *f·* impurities to pass away,

forebodings
p 403–24   Never conjure up some new discovery from
    dark *f·*

forefathers
m 64– 2   Our *f·* exercised their faith
ph 175–17   had tried to tyrannize over our *f·*,
197–17   It was the ignorance of our *f·*
197–21   We are told that the simple food our *f·* ate

foregoing
f 245–28   One instance like the *f·* proves
c 266–16   The author has experienced the *f·* prophecy

forehead
g 555–10   The mark of ignorance is on its *f·*,

foreign
s 133–16   Even in captivity among *f·* nations,
p 438–22   show that this fur is a *f·* substance,
r 485–26   and delineates *f·* agents, called disease and sin,

foreknowledge
a 41–23   but this *f·* hindered him not.

foremost
s 144– 3   If Mind is *f·* and superior, let us rely

foreordination
a 38– 5   more pernicious than the old doctrine of *f·*,

foresaw
a 41–22   Jesus *f·* the reception C. S. would have
s 139–25   *f·* that "the stone which the— *Matt.* 21 : 42.

foresee
sp 84–15   to *f·* and foretell events which
f 227–14   we cannot fail to *f·* the doom of all oppression.

foreseeing
a 31–28   *f·* the persecution which would attend the

foreshadowed
b 288–13   *f·* by the prophets and inaugurated by Jesus,
322–16   necromancy of yesterday *f·* the mesmerism

foreshadowing
sp 84– 4   not by *f·* evil and mistaking fact for

foreshadows
f 223–31   and *f·* the triumph of truth.
ap 571–27   rebukes the conceit of sin, and *f·* its doom.

foresight
a 52–12   prophet's *f·* of the reception error would give
sp 84– 3   ancient prophets gained their *f·* from
b 270–15   hence their *f·* of the new dispensation

forest
g 514–12   Free and fearless it roams in the *f·*.

forestalls
p 385– 9   *f·* the penalty which our beliefs would attach to

foretaste
ap 573–28   This is indeed a *f·* of absolute C. S.
gl 598–24   understanding of Life and Love, is a *f·* of

foretell
sp 84–16   *f·* events which concern the universal welfare,

foretelling
s 118– 7   *f·* the second appearing in the flesh of

foretells
sp 95–23   Midnight *f·* the dawn.
an 105–28   The aggravation of error *f·* its doom,

foretold
sp 85–19   events of great moment were *f·* by the
95–24   the Magi of old *f·* the Messiahship of Truth.
ph 169– 9   But it always came about as I had *f·*.

forever
at peace
f 215– 1   Spirit's senses . . . are *f·* at peace.
cease
f 219– 2   and the mortal dream will *f·* cease.
Christ dwelt
a 29–26   The Christ dwelt *f·* an idea in the bosom
closed
a 33– 1   and this supper closed *f·* Jesus' ritualism
continue
c 267– 5   They are in and of Spirit, . . . and so *f·* continue.
continues
sp 71– 5   identity, or idea, of all reality continues *f·* ;

forever

contradict
s 110– 3　contradict *f·* the belief that

destroys
s 128–25　*f·* destroys with the higher testimony of Spirit
g 556– 7　destroys *f·* all belief in intelligent matter.

disappears
sp 97–13　its mortal zenith in illusion and *f·* disappears.
g 520–14　in which all sense of error *f·* disappears

dwells
f 247–22　Beauty . . . dwells *f·* in the eternal Mind
b 334– 5　Christ, dwells *f·* in the bosom of the Father,

exist
gl 581–13　are created by Him and exist *f·*.

expressed
g 519–10　ideas of God . . . are complete and *f·* expressed,

intact
b 295–15　the real sense of being, perfect and *f·* intact,
r 481–12　Truth, which remains *f·* intact.
493–31　*f·* intact in his perfect state,

lost
b 331– 8　and the Science of being would be *f·* lost

man has existed
b 302–15　harmonious and immortal man has existed *f·*,

near
gl 596– 6　better known as the All-in-all, *f·* near.

not
b 320–15　said, My spirit shall not *f·* rule
320–21　this fact is not *f·* to be humbled by

now and
sp 92–10　not an entity . . . sinning now and *f·*.
o 361– 5　the ideal of God now and *f·*,
361– 9　God is come and is present now and *f·*.
p 441–11　Let what False Belief utters, now and *f·*,
g 521–10　joyfully acknowledging now and *f·*

opposed
g 530– 4　*f·* opposed to mortal, material sense.

permanent
b 290–18　happiness would be . . . *f·* permanent ;

reflected
g 503– 3　in the infinite Mind and *f·* reflected.

remain
s 110–23　the Science and truth therein will *f·* remain
f 208–24　which cannot be lost nor remain *f·* unseen.

silenced
sp 97–25　inarticulate sound is *f·* silenced in oblivion.

silences
s 124–13　which immortal Spirit silences *f·*.

the same
a 51–15　his spiritual life, . . . was found *f·* the same.

to-day and
(see **to-day**)

unchanged
gl 588–13　unchanged *f·* in their individual characters,

unlimited
b 288–28　*f·* unlimited by the mortal senses.

vast
f 246–18　Chronological data are no part of the vast *f·*.
c 266–31　into the vast *f·* of Life,
r 479–21　In the vast *f·*, in the Science and truth of

warring
b 278–20　warring *f·* with each other ;

will destroy
ap 575– 5　will destroy *f·* the physical plagues

will stand
f 229–25　all that He makes is good and will stand *f·*.

———

pref vii–21　"the Lord shall reign *f·*." — *Exod.* 15 : 18.
pr 17–13　the power, and the glory, *f·*. — *Matt.* 6 : 13.
a 41–12　cannot *f·* break the Golden Rule and escape the
48– 8　turned *f·* away from earth to heaven,
55–28　that he may abide with you *f·*." — *John* 14 : 16.
m 58–17　which would confine . . . *f·* within four walls,
64–32　the voices of physical sense will be *f·* hushed.
s 164–23　the *f·* fact remains paramount
210–11　Soul and its attributes were *f·* manifested
230– 6　This awakening is the *f·* coming of Christ,
c 258–13　the infinite idea *f·* developing itself,
267– 9　If this is so, the *f·* Father must have
b 284–19　The answer to all these questions must *f·* be
336–12　He has been *f·* in the eternal Mind,
o 343–12　Truth will not be *f·* hidden by
p 428–24　We must hold *f·* the consciousness of
441–16　*f·* in the image and likeness of his Maker.
t 447–12　subtlety, or false charity does not *f·* conceal
r 469– 1　Time is finite ; eternity is *f·* infinite.
471–17　Man is, and *f·* has been, God's reflection.
491–16　establishes man *f·* in the divine likeness,
g 515–16　eternal Elohim includes the *f·* universe.
516–22　Man and woman . . . *f·* reflect,
537– 2　and eat, and live *f·* ; — *Gen.* 3 : 22.
542– 6　error cannot *f·* be concealed.
556–12　only to go out at last *f·* ;
gl 585–24　that which does not last *f·* ;

forfeit
s 112– 6　*f·* their claims to belong to its school,

forfeits
t 453–17　Dishonesty is human weakness, which *f·*

forgave
p 363–20　"He to whom he *f·* most." — *Luke* 7 : 43.

forged
f 223– 4　the fetters of man's finite capacity are *f·* by

forget
c 261–10　with such absorbed interest as to *f·* it,
261–31　We should *f·* our bodies in remembering good
b 309–17　and *f·* that Life is God, good,
p 374–23　You cannot *f·* the belief of danger,
t 447– 6　In mental practice you must not *f·* that

forgets
sp 76– 4　*f·* all else and breathes aloud his rapture.
s 155– 1　Presently the child *f·* all about the accident,

forgetting
sp 89– 3　*F·* her ignorance in the belief that
ph 165–19　your remedy lies in *f·* the whole thing ;
o 353–23　"*f·* those things which — *Phil.* 3 : 13.
p 393– 2　*f·* that through divine help we can forbid

forgive
pr 6– 7　Calling on Him to *f·* our work badly done
11– 2　Jesus' prayer, "*F·* us our debts," — *Matt.* 6 : 12.
17– 6　*f·* us our debts, as we *f·* our — *Matt.* 6 : 12.

forgiven
pr 5–23　Sin is *f·* only as it is destroyed
5–28　because he fancies himself *f·*.
a 24–22　and are willing to be *f·* ?
f 202– 1　supposing that sin can be *f·* when
p 363–23　"Thy sins are *f·*." — *Luke* 7 : 48.
364–31　because much is *f·* them.

forgiveness
pr 7–31　or mean to ask *f·* at some later day.
11– 3　specified also the terms of *f·*.
a 22– 4　Vibrating . . . between sin and the hope of *f·*,
b 339– 4　Being destroyed, sin needs no other form of *f·*.
r 497– 9　We acknowledge God's *f·* of sin in the

forgives
pr 6–19　To suppose that God *f·* or punishes sin according

forgiving
pr 11– 3　When *f·* the adulterous woman he said,

forgotten
a 49– 8　Had they *f·* the great exponent of God?
sp 87–10　leagues apart and their associations *f·*,

form (noun)

alarming
p 395–29　may appear in a more alarming *f·*.

all
b 281–15　supplies all *f·* and comeliness
310– 7　seen in all *f·*, substance, and color,
g 512–22　all *f·*, color, quality, and quantity,

and action
b 301– 3　repeats the color, *f·*, and action

and face
c 260– 4　or the painter can depict the *f·* and face of Jesus,

animate
g 541– 2　A lamb is a more animate *f·* of existence.

another
s 159–28　allowing another *f·* of matter.

any
s 154– 1　to cherish error in any *f·*,
f 244– 6　never fearing nor obeying error in any *f·*.
p 369–13　or the constructor of any *f·* of existence.

any other
sp 73–16　electricity or any other *f·* of matter,

chronic
ph 176–31　less distinct type and chronic *f·* of disease.

etherealized
gl 598–15　was indeed air, an etherealized *f·* of matter,

every
p 418–29　Speak the truth to every *f·* of error.
ap 564–16　Jesus . . . met and conquered sin in every *f·*.

finite
sp 71– 8　infinite Principle outside of finite *f·*,
71–31　a corporeal being, a finite *f·*,
76– 9　belief that life, or mind, was ever in a finite *f·*,
s 116–30　An infinite Mind in a finite *f·* is an
c 257–27　Infinite Mind cannot be limited to a finite *f·*,
g 527– 2　God could not put . . . Spirit into finite *f·*

fleshly
b 332–30　highest type of divinity, which a fleshly *f·* could

higher
ph 174– 4　Is civilization only a higher *f·* of idolatry,

his
p 442–11　His *f·* was erect and commanding,

human
c 255–16　The human *f·*, or physical finiteness, cannot
b 315–29　Wearing in part a human *f·*
g 554–31　especially those of the human *f·*.

form (noun)

infinite
c 257–30   It would require an infinite *f·* to contain
257–31   phrase *infinite f·* involves a contradiction
limited
s 133–20   limited *f·* of a national or tribal religion.
malicious
an 103–24   malicious *f·* of hypnotism ultimates in
man and
g 517– 6   two Greek words, signifying *man* and *f·*,
material
c 258– 9   Man is more than a material *f·* with a mind
b 280–26   instead of possessing a sentient material *f·*,
293– 4   least material *f·* of illusive consciousness,
mirrored
b 305– 9   As there is no corporeality in the mirrored *f·*,
new
sp 74– 9   has a new *f·* and state of existence.
no
a 26–31   His proof of Christianity was no *f·* or system
c 256–24   No *f·* nor physical combination is adequate
no other
b 339– 4   sin needs no other *f·* of forgiveness.
of matter
   (*see* matter)
one
pr 11– 7   it only saves the criminal from one *f·* of
s 145–26   they increase the antagonism of one *f·*
159–28   how much . . . one *f·* of matter is
p 419–14   or to change itself from one *f·* to another.
precise
c 256–16   precise *f·* of God must be of small importance
serpentine
ap 563–27   The serpentine *f·* stands for subtlety,
some
a 28–31   await, in some *f·*, every pioneer of truth.
taking
ph 175– 1   prevent the images of disease from taking *f·*
g 511–28   taking *f·* in masculine, feminine, or neuter
without
s 126– 5   mortal mind will be without *f·* and void,
r 479–19   And the earth was without *f·*, — *Gen.* 1 : 2.
g 503– 6   And the earth was without *f·*, — *Gen.* 1 : 2.

pr 1–13   exalted before they take *f·* in words
s 119–15   in the *f·* and under the name of natural law.
146–32   to a *f·* comprehensible by and adapted to
147–29   A pure affection takes *f·* in goodness,
f 247–23   in expression, *f·*, outline, and color.
c 261–22   which is only a *f·* of human belief,
b 332–25   appear to mortals in such a *f·*
o 353– 9   either in the *f·* of sickness or of sin?
p 367– 1   under the napkin of its *f·*,
375– 6   often the *f·* in which fever manifests itself.
392–19   in the *f·* of what is termed pulmonary disease,
g 525–10   the primary sense being *image*, *f·*;

form (verb)

m 02– 5   such as to *f·* habits of obedience
ph 170– 3   Modes of matter *f·* neither a moral nor a
172–10   Spirit can *f·* no real link in this supposed
f 218–10   The reports of sickness may *f·* a coalition with
228–23   and *f·* and control it with Truth.
236–13   *f·* the embryo of another mortal mind,
247–13   *f·* the transient standards of mortals.
248–26   We must *f·* perfect models in thought
p 372– 7   can *f·* blood, flesh, and bones.
425–25   and Spirit will *f·* you anew.
t 454–23   and *f·* the perfect concept.
g 505– 1   No solar rays . . . *f·* the day of Spirit.
533–23   bone and flesh which came from Adam to *f·*

formal

s 118– 4   above the merely ecclesiastical and *f·*

formalism

c 256–26   material sense of God leads to *f·*

formation

m 60– 5   *f·* of a happy and permanent companionship.
61–29   *f·* of mortals must greatly improve
sp 71–13   a *f·* of thought rather than of matter.
s 148–15   for every function, *f·*, and manifestation.
ph 190– 1   the *f·* of so-called embryonic mortal mind,
g 510–23   indicates a supposed *f·* of matter
527–30   Was it requisite for the *f·* of man
549–15   with the *f·* of the nucleus, or egg,

formations

all the
ph 189–22   The reverse is the case with all the *f·* of
earth's
g 510–20   Geology has never explained the earth's *f·*;
harmonious
ph 198–22   a picture of healthy and harmonious *f·*.

formations

its
f 209– 5   Mind, supreme over all its *f·*
246– 1   Mind and its *f·* can never be annihilated.
c 264–20   Spirit and its *f·* are the only realities
p 402–10   its *f·* will be apprehended in Science,
g 557–25   proclaims the Science of Mind and its *f·*
its own
b 309–32   never absorbed nor limited by its own *f·*.
mundane
f 209–25   Material substances or mundane *f·*,
not in Spirit's
sp 71– 7   divine Principle of all, is not *in* Spirit's *f·*.

g 507– 2   the absolute *f·* instituted by Mind,

formed

sp 70–16   Does life or soul exist in the thing *f·*?
86–31   Pictures are mentally *f·* before the artist can
94–15   belief that the infinite is *f·* after the pattern
ph 194–30   a belief *f·* by education alone.
198–15   thought of disease is *f·* before
198–23   moulded and *f·* by his doctor's belief
200–12   man is the idea of God, not *f·* materially
f 214– 9   represented in the Scriptures as *f·* from
c 259–25   Brain . . . never *f·* a human concept.
b 274–26   firm, called matter and mind, God never *f·*.
274–29   *f·* only to be destroyed
281–25   through a man *f·* from dust.
303– 9   *f·* by Spirit, not by material sensation.
303–17   illusion that life, or mind, is *f·* by
p 396–31   understand that sickness is *f·* by the human mind,
409– 3   why do you insist that disease is *f·* by
423–32   so-called substance of bone is *f·* first by the
g 524–13   *f·* man of the dust of the ground, — *Gen.* 2 : 7.
527–22   *f·* every beast of the field, — *Gen.* 2 : 19.
553–12   *f·* under circumstances which
553–19   Eve was *f·* from Adam's rib,
553–29   You may say that mortals are *f·* before they

former

sp 89–10   The *f·* limits of her belief return.
s 148– 8   The *f·* explains the men of *men*,
156–13   her *f·* physician had prescribed these remedies,
ph 187–17   of the latter action, but not of the *f·*.
f 237–21   excluded on the same principle as the *f·*.
b 276–26   The latter destroys the *f·*.
l 460–29   As *f·* beliefs were gradually expelled
g 556– 8   for the *f·* things will have passed away.
ap 573– 1   They could not be the *f·*,

formidable

b 317–19   more real, more *f·* in truth,

forming

ph 198–13   to prevent disease from *f·* in mortal mind
c 263–13   *f·* deformity when he would outline grace
o 350–28   Jesus, — that life-link *f·* the connection
g 506–13   *f·* each successive stage of progress.

forms (noun)

all
sp 83–23   Between C. S. and all *f·* of superstition
f 204– 3   All *f·* of error support the false conclusions
p 396– 3   efface from thought all *f·* and types of disease,
g 513–26   God creates all *f·* of reality.
cannot change
p 419–32   disease or its symptoms cannot change *f·*,
changed
sp 96– 9   seedtime and harvest (though in changed *f·*),
crude
g 502–14   Even thus the crude *f·* of human thought
depraving
f 226– 4   under more subtle and depraving *f·*.
differing
t 444–14   not only towards differing *f·* of religion
difficult
p 398–29   changes such ills into new and more difficult *f·*
externalized
g 522–13   history of error in its externalized *f·*,
finite
c 264– 8   Mortals must look beyond fading, finite *f·*,
b 280–24   belief that . . . Life, is in finite *f·*.
g 553–23   appearance of its method in finite *f·*
gl 587–12   belief that infinite Mind is in finite *f·* ;
glorious
c 264– 5   must finally give place to the glorious *f·*
hideous
f 248–19   vicious sculptors and hideous *f·*.
human
pr 4–32   and clothe religion in human *f·*.
immortal
g 503–22   immortal *f·* of beauty and goodness.
in all their
t 447–21   evil and disease in all their *f·*,
individual
g 512–13   Their individual *f·* we know not,

forms (noun)

its
r 484–23   action of error in all its *f·* ;
lower
g 549– 9   Creatures of lower *f·* of organism are
material
b 301–31   presupposes soul . . . in material *f·*,
mild
an 102–16   The mild *f·* of animal magnetism are
modes and
p 406– 8   in place of modes and *f·*,
multifarious
r 477–21   in multifarious *f·* of the living Principle,
myriad
b 306–21   The myriad *f·* of mortal thought,
p 404– 4   servant of any one of the myriad *f·* of sin,
new
f 225–27   always germinating in new *f·* of tyranny,
g 541–22   Here the serpentine lie invents new *f·*.
of doctrine
a 20– 3   He at last paid no homage to *f·* of doctrine
of error
f 204– 3   All *f·* of error support the false conclusions
c 264–24   who proved them to be *f·* of error.
of matter
s 145–27   towards other *f·* of matter or error,
ph 172–16   must have passed through all the *f·* of matter
c 263–32   fading *f·* of matter, the mortal body
of Mind
b 303– 3   reflection, . . . of the multitudinous *f·* of Mind
g 505–10   they are *f·* of Mind, the ideas of Spirit
507–17   reproduces the multitudinous *f·* of Mind
of sickness
t 463–22   whether error is manifested in *f·* of sickness,
of sin
o 348–20   will show itself in *f·* of sin, sickness, and
p 404– 4   servant of any one of the myriad *f·* of sin,
of thought
s 118–20   In all mortal *f·* of thought, dust is
ph 187– 7   material sense creates its own *f·* of thought,
b 298–31   confers upon angels its own *f·* of thought,
of worship
pr 10–17   One of the *f·* of worship in Thibet
physical
c 262–32   Cause does not exist . . . in physical *f·*.
qualities, and
ph 177–19   indicated matter's properties, qualities, and *f·*.
renewed
g 556–11   dies to live again in renewed *f·*,
severest
s 162–19   chronic disease in their severest *f·*.
Soul-created
b 306–23   than are the Soul-created *f·* to spiritual sense,
spiritual
g 503–17   reflecting Him in countless spiritual *f·*.
subsequent
g 531– 4   maintained in all the subsequent *f·* of belief.
various
f 248–14   We are all sculptors, working at various *f·*,
g 553– 1   in the various *f·* of embryology,
visible
ap 559– 6   the source of all error's visible *f·*?

---

sp 71– 9   outside of finite form, which *f·* only reflect.
87–30   close the eyes, and *f·* rise before us,
b 331– 2   Life is no more confined to the *f·* which reflect
p 421–28   should not build it up by wishing to see the *f·*

forms (verb)

m 62–22   divine Mind, which *f·* the bud and blossom,
f 216–32   this Mind *f·* its own likeness,
220–30   *f·* all conditions of the mortal body,
239–24   It *f·* material concepts and
c 259–22   *f·* its offspring after human illusions.
b 293– 5   *f·* no link between matter and Mind,
337–11   as perfect as the Mind that *f·* him.
p 422–14   holding that matter *f·* its own conditions
423–30   the substance of thought which *f·* them.
g 509–16   God *f·* and peoples the universe.
511– 1   This Mind *f·* ideas, its own images,
515– 9   subject to the Mind which *f·* them,
550– 5   God is the Life, or intelligence, which *f·* and

formulated

s 144– 8   mortal beliefs *f·* in human philosophy,
ph 175– 2   efface the outlines of disease already *f·*

fornication

an 106–21   Adultery, *f·*, uncleanness,— *Gal.* 5 : 19.
gl 598–17   Error ; *f·* ; temptation ; passion.

fornications

an 100– *   *murders, adulteries, f·,— Matt.* 15 : 19.

forsake

s 130–31   no longer think it . . . unnatural to *f·* it,
139– 1   causes the wicked to "*f·* his way,— *Isa.* 55 : 7.
160– 4   When mortals *f·* the material for the
ph 195–13   We should *f·* the basis of matter

forsake

f 239–14   "Let the wicked *f·* his way,— *Isa.* 55 : 7.
b 290–28   The murderer, . . . does not thereby *f·* sin.
323– 4   strife consists in the endeavor to *f·*
326–12   We must *f·* the foundation of
339–18   Only those, who repent of sin and *f·* the
p 370– 2   we must *f·* the mortal sense of things,
400–10   only as they *f·* discord,
402– 8   mortal mind will *f·* its corporeal, structural,

forsaken

a 36–12   He was *f·* by all save
49–17   *F·* by all whom he had blessed,
50– 8   "My God, why hast Thou *f·* me?"— *Mark* 15 : 34.
50–14   Had Life, Truth, and Love *f·* him
f 202– 1   supposing that sin . . . when it is not *f·*,

forsakes

f 238–24   *f·* popularity and gains Christianity.
g 549–28   this great observer mistakes nature, *f·* Spirit

forsaketh

t 448–18   whoso confesseth and *f·* them— *Prov.* 28 : 13.

forsaking

c 265–10   This scientific sense of being, *f·* matter for
p 393– 2   like a watchman *f·* his post,
t 459– 6   gain heavenly riches by *f·* all worldliness.

forth

pr 2– 5   the desire which goes *f·* hungering after
2–28   which is pouring *f·* more than we accept?
15–19   and go *f·* with honest hearts to work
a 27–22   Jesus sent *f·* seventy students at one time,
29–22   brought *f·* her child by the revelation of Truth,
32–12   The cup shows *f·* his bitter experience,
35–23   by bringing *f·* the fruits of Love,
45– 3   and stepped *f·* from his gloomy resting-place,
49– 7   Where were the seventy whom Jesus sent *f·*?
m 57–22   Human affection is not poured *f·* vainly,
s 115– 7   C. S. as brought *f·* in my discovery.
126–13   nor sent *f·* a positive sound.
126–22   I have set *f·* C. S. and its application to
127–21   nerves, brain, stomach, lungs, and so *f·*,
137–17   and his reply set *f·* a great fact :
ph 170–31   from which all ills have gone *f·*,
185–14   puts *f·* a human conception in the name of
191–32   Mind, God, sends *f·* the aroma of Spirit,
196–31   The press unwittingly sends *f·* many sorrows
f 210– 6   They are set *f·* in Jesus' demonstrations,
235– 1   cannot go *f·*, like wandering pollen,
239–30   The perfect Mind sends *f·* perfection,
239–31   Imperfect mortal mind sends *f·* its own
241–10   hypocrisy, malice, hate, revenge, and so *f·*,
c 257–20   bringeth "*f·* Mazzaroth in his— *Job* 38 : 32.
b 268–12   woman goes *f·* to battle with Goliath.
287–13   "Doth a fountain send *f·* at the— *Jas.* 3 : 11.
303–12   is spiritually conceived and brought *f·*;
321–22   drew it *f·* white as snow with the dread disease,
327–15   rushes *f·* to clamor with midnight and tempest.
o 345– 8   When . . . His absoluteness is set *f·*,
360–20   Like a pendulum . . . you will be thrown back
  and *f·*,
p 392– 3   Only while . . . sin remains can it bring *f·* death.
398–14   "Stretch *f·* thine hand,"— *Matt.* 12 : 13.
404–19   every tree that brings not *f·* good fruit.
404–29   envy, dishonesty, fear, and so *f·*,
411–26   Whatever is cherished . . . is imaged *f·* on the
  body.
415–31   leaving the pain standing *f·* as distinctly as
440–24   wicked laws of sickness and so *f·*,
442–14   Mortal Man, no longer sick . . . walked *f·*,
t 455–29   the same fountain cannot send *f·* both
r 476–17   "conceived in sin and brought *f·* in iniquity."
489–23   sendeth not *f·* sweet waters and bitter.
g 507–11   Let the earth bring *f·* grass,— *Gen.* 1 : 11.
508– 9   And the earth brought *f·* grass,— *Gen.* 1 : 12.
511–19   Let the waters bring *f·*— *Gen.* 1 : 20.
512– 5   which the waters brought *f·*— *Gen.* 1 : 21.
512–29   this so-called mind puts *f·* its own qualities,
513–14   Let the earth bring *f·*— *Gen.* 1 : 24.
521–26   a material view of creation, is to be set *f·*.
529– 1   bringing *f·* fruit of his own kind,
530– 7   The earth, at God's command, brings *f·* food
535– 8   in sorrow thou shalt bring *f·*— *Gen.* 3 : 16.
535–24   thistles shall it bring *f·*— *Gen.* 3 : 18.
537– 1   lest he put *f·* his hand,— *Gen.* 3 : 22.
537– 3   sent him *f·* from the garden— *Gen.* 3 : 23.
g 550–27   nor does a lion bring *f·* a lamb.
553–18   the maternal egg never brought *f·* Adam.
557–18   "In sorrow thou shalt bring *f·*— *Gen.* 3 : 16.
ap 565– 6   And she brought *f·* a man child,— *Rev.* 12 : 5.
568–10   first the true method of creation is set *f·*
568–29   Love sends *f·* her primal and everlasting strain,
569–31   which brought *f·* the man child.— *Rev.* 12 : 13.
570–19   What if the old dragon should send *f·* a new
574–21   which poured *f·* hatred and torment,
fr 600– *   *and the pomegranates bud f·.— Song* 7 : 12.

forthwith
     ph 182–23   and *f·* shut out the aid of Mind

fortitude
     ph 198– 6   His *f·* may sustain him, but his fear,
     p 375–32   fear so excessive that it amounts to *f·*.

fortuitous
     m 61–14   If some *f·* circumstance places

fortunes
     s 121– 8   the fate of empires and the *f·* of men.

forty
     p 421–32   asserting that the products . . . are both *f·*,

fossils
     s 147–21   the perishing *f·* of theories already antiquated,

fosters
     ph 169–12   *f·* disease by attracting the mind to the
     g 555–32   Truth *f·* the idea of Truth,

fought
     a 21– 2   "I have *f·* a good fight— *II Tim. 4 : 7.*
     f 254– 7   not until the battle between Spirit and flesh is *f·*
     b 309–11   a soldier of God, who had *f·* a good fight.
     ap 566–26   Michael and his angels *f·* — *Rev. 12 : 7.*
     566–27   the dragon *f·*, and his angels, — *Rev. 12 : 7.*

foul
     p 431–21   covered with a *f·* fur,
     434–26   we shall unearth this *f·* conspiracy against the
     437– 5   This is a *f·* aspersion on man's Maker.
     438–20   a garment of *f·* fur was spread over him

found
     pref viii– 2   fully tested and has not been *f·* wanting ;
     viii–25   may be *f·* a biographical sketch, narrating
     pr 7– 3   is *f·* in his own words,
     a 28–23   if thou art *f·* worthy to unloose the sandals
     30–32   In meekness and might, he was *f·* preaching
     42– 7   Death will be *f·* at length to be a mortal dream,
     51–15   his spiritual life, . . . was *f·* forever the same.
     m 66–31   It never leaves us where it *f·* us.
     sp 71–22   spiritualism will be *f·* mainly erroneous,
     90–11   will be *f·* to be equally possible for the body.
     94–14   intolerance, and bloodshed, wherever *f·*,
     97–19   and man is *f·* in the likeness of Spirit,
     s 113–12   these propositions will be *f·* to agree in
     125– 4   may no longer be *f·* indispensable to health.
     125– 5   Moral conditions will be *f·* always harmonious
     125– 8   man will be *f·* normal and natural
     126–26   I have *f·* nothing in ancient or in modern
     126–27   nothing . . . on which to *f·* my own, except
     128– 7   have *f·* that C. S. enhances their
     133– 6   "I have not *f·* so great faith, — *Matt. 8 : 10.*
     150– 1   hardly a . . . hamlet, in which are not to be *f·*
     151–27   the entire being is *f·* harmonious
     159– 8   The evidence was *f·* to be conclusive,
     ph 166–31   *f·* to be harmonious and immortal.
     170–10   as man is *f·*, . . . reflecting the divine nature.
     180–28   The only way to this living Truth, . . . is *f·* in
     180–32   I have *f·* divine Truth more potent than
     188– 2   and man is *f·* in His image.
     190– 7   and yet neither . . . is *f·* in brain
     190–19   immortal man, . . . is *f·* to be the real man.
     191– 8   theoretical life-basis is *f·* to be a
     195– 5   Outside of dismal darkness . . . he *f·* no peace.
     196– 3   but he has not yet *f·* it true that
     f 209–24   man and the universe will be *f·* harmonious
     214–16   will be understood and *f·* to be harmonious.
     226– 3   a world-wide slavery, *f·* on higher planes
     232– 8   Security . . . is *f·* only in divine Science,
     c 257–24   Who hath *f·* finite life or love sufficient
     b 270– 4   "I have *f·* a ransom." — *Job 33 : 24.*
     288–21   are to be *f·* in the following postulates :
     288–23   Soul is sinless, not to be *f·* in the body ;
     291–17   man is *f·* having no righteousness of his own,
     297–16   and man *f·* to be immortal.
     302– 2   Principle is not to be *f·* in fragmentary ideas.
     302– 5   The identity of the real man is not lost, but *f·*
     307–14   Its life is *f·* to be not Life, but only a transient,
     312– 5   is *f·* to be substance.
     313–25   He . . . *f·* the spiritual cause.
     314– 5   Thus he *f·* the eternal Ego,
     325–14   then shall man be *f·* in God's image.
     325–16   Then shall man be *f·*, in His likeness,
     o 344– 9   God's likeness is not *f·* in matter,
     359–18   Christianity is to be honored wherever *f·*,
     p 419–31   If it is *f·* necessary to treat against relapse,
     432–14   he upon whose person disease is *f·* shall be
     r 475–17   conscious identity of being as *f·* in Science,
     481–31   *f·* that it is the sense of sin which is lost,
     484– 1   and so *f·* to be unerring,
     489– 4   it would be *f·* that the senses of Mind are
     493–17   Mind must be *f·* superior to all the beliefs
     g 522–22   denunciations of man when not *f·* in His image,
     524– 6   It was also *f·* among the Israelites,
     533–21   *f·* in the rapid deterioration of the
     543–22   Minerals and vegetables are *f·*,

found
     ap 565–27   be *f·* in its divine Principle.
     566–28   neither was their place *f·* any more— *Rev. 12 : 8.*
     gl 580–12   are *f·* to be the antipode of God,
     583–15   The Church . . . is *f·* elevating the race,

foundation
cause and
     p 411–20   procuring cause and *f·* of all sickness
firm
     s 138– 8   a firm *f·* in the realm of harmony.
its
     r 484– 4   nor envy can wash away its *f·*,
no
     s 112–25   affords no *f·* upon which to establish
     c 255– 9   they afforded no *f·* for
     t 448– 6   Evil . . . which the heart condemns, has no *f·* ;
     464–26   Falsity has no *f·*.
no scientific
     an 102– 1   Animal magnetism has no scientific *f·*,
of disease
     p 368–31   When fear disappears, the *f·* of disease is gone.
     t 453–27   such a course increases fear, the *f·* of disease,
of evil
     sp 92–26   The *f·* of evil is laid on a belief
of Spirit
     s 133–26   planted Christianity on the *f·* of Spirit,
spiritual
     s 136– 2   a spiritual *f·* of Christ-healing.
     gl 593–18   Rock. Spiritual *f·* ; Truth.
     599– 6   Zion. Spiritual *f·* and superstructure ;
without
     sp 93–20   Whatever contradicts the . . . is without *f·*.
     r 486– 1   is without *f·* in fact,
without actual
     r 491– 4   shows it to be a belief without actual *f·*

     pr 15–31   the *f·* of enlightened faith.
     s 138–14   the *f·* on which Jesus built.
     f 227–12   the *f·* of continued bondage
     c 262–27   The *f·* of mortal discord is a false sense
     b 276– 5   they unfold the *f·* of fellowship,
     287–23   without spiritual identity or *f·*,
     317– 9   "secret from the *f·* of the— *Matt. 13 : 35.*
     326–12   forsake the *f·* of material systems,
     334–21   slain from the *f·* of the world," — *Rev. 13 : 8.*
     p 368–29   has a *f·* in fact.
     ap 568– 2   Ever since the *f·* of the world,

foundational
     o 348–12   Jesus established this *f·* fact,

foundations
false
     f 201– 7   We cannot build safely on false *f·*.
     gl 597–12   It revealed the false *f·* and
its
     m 59–31   fatal mistakes are undermining its *f·*.
     s 124– 6   When . . . its *f·* are gone.
material
     g 525–11   supposed material *f·* of life and intelligence.
no
     p 415– 5   Sin, disease, and death have no *f·* in Truth.
of death
     ph 171–16   and destroying the *f·* of death.
of error
     b 273–11   thus tears away the *f·* of error.
     o 357–12   the *f·* of error would be sapped
of Truth
     ap 558–16   Its feet are pillars of fire, *f·* of Truth and Love.
other
     b 269–25   Other *f·* there are none.

     m 65– 7   If the *f·* of human affection
     b 296–25   *f·* which time is wearing away.
     p 414– 1   the *f·* of the belief in disease and death,
     g 539– 5   thus sapping the *f·* of immortality,
     ap 575–12   "a city which hath *f·*." — *Heb. 11 : 10.*

founded
     s 127–32   hypotheses . . . that law is *f·* on material
     163– 8   *f·* on long observation and reflection,
     b 297–27   no mortal testimony is *f·* on the divine rock.
     t 464–28   Neither dishonesty nor ignorance ever *f·*,
     r 487–19   Christian evidence is *f·* on Science

founding
     s 138– 2   Jesus purposed *f·* his society,
     t 464–21   in *f·* a pathological system of Christianity,

fount
     pr 2–27   Shall we plead for more at the open *f·*,
     13– 3   It is the open *f·* which cries,
     f 239–29   opposite sources never mingle in *f·* or stream.
     244– 1   God is good and the *f·* of all being,
     p 389–16   the metaphors about the *f·* and stream,

fountain
a 18–17   The *f·* can rise no higher than its source.
ph 190–30   For with Thee is the *f·* of life; — *Psal.* 36 : 9.
b 287–12   "Doth a *f·* send forth — *Jas.* 3 : 11.
p 391–32   Fear is the *f·* of sickness,
t 455–29   the same *f·* cannot send forth both
r 489–22   same *f·* sendeth not forth sweet waters and

four
pref xii– 6   During seven years over *f·* thousand students
m 58–17   which would confine. . .forever within *f·* walls,
s 113–10   *f·* following, to me, *self-evident* propositions.
113–22   Which of the denials in proposition *f·* is true?
ph 193–15   between three and *f·* o'clock in the afternoon
ap 574–23   city, the *f·* equal sides of which were
575–18   The *f·* sides of our city are
575–21   wholly spiritual, as its *f·* sides indicate.
577–13   its *f·* cardinal points are :

foursquare
ap 574–16   city which "lieth *f·*." — *Rev.* 21 : 16.
575– 8   as one that "lieth *f·*" — *Rev.* 21 : 16.
575–17   description of the city as *f·* has a profound

fourth
sp 91–32   The *f·* erroneous postulate is,
s 156– 9   the *f·* attenuation of *Argentum nitratum*
g 511–16   and the morning were the *f·* day. — *Gen.* 1 : 19.
523–25   From the *f·* verse of chapter two
ap 577–17   *f·*, C. S., which to-day and forever interprets

Fourth Gospel
ap 561–30   In the first chapter of the *F· G·* it is written,

fowl
of the air
f 222–24   and over the *f·* of the air, — *Gen* 1 : 26.
r 475–25   and over the *f·* of the air, — *Gen.* 1 : 26.
g 515–13   and over the *f·* of the air, — *Gen.* 1 : 26.
517–28   and over the *f·* of the air, — *Gen.* 1 : 28.
518– 9   and to every *f·* of the air, — *Gen.* 1 : 30.
527–22   and every *f·* of the air ; — *Gen.* 2 : 19.
winged
g 512– 6   every winged *f·* after his kind : — *Gen.* 1 : 21.

g 511–20   *f·* that may fly above the earth — *Gen.* 1 : 20.
512–19   let *f·* multiply in the earth. — *Gen.* 1 : 22.

fowls
s 125–27   over the fish of the sea and the *f·* of the air.
f 237–13   "the *f·* of the air," — *Luke* 8 : 5.
g 511–29   The *f·*, which fly above the earth

fraction
s 108–18   not a *f·* more, not a unit less.

fragmentary
sp 98–28   they are not theoretical and *f·*,
b 302– 2   Principle is not to be found in *f·* ideas.

fragrance
ph 175–11   The joy of its presence, its beauty and *f·*,

fragrant
o 363– 2   jar containing costly and *f·* oil,

frail
sp 98–15   Beyond the *f·* premises of human beliefs,
o 346–32   is not this what *f·* mortals are trying to do?
t 459–15   *f·* mortals, untaught and unrestrained by C. S.,

frailty
ph 194–18   the *f·* and inadequacy of mortal mind.
c 266–30   He is above sin or *f·*.
o 360–27   His angels He chargeth with *f·*. — *see Job* 4 : 18.

frame
p 415–30   the whole *f·* will sink from sight

franchise
m 63–20   If the elective *f·* for women will remedy

Franklin
f 245–19   useful hint, upon which a *F·* might work

Franklin, Benjamin
an 100–15   Benjamin *F·* was one of the commissioners.

fraternity
p 389–24   error that there is *f·* between pain and pleasure,

fraternize
sp 74–19   nor does the insect return to *f·* with or

fratricidal
g 539– 2   This false sense of existence is *f·*.

fraud
o 356–26   Does divine Love commit a *f·* on humanity

fraudulent
f 252–22   deceitful in sentiment, *f·* in purpose,

fraught
o 346–17   How then can this . . . be "*f·* with falsities

free
iii– *   the truth shall make you *f·*. — *John* 8 : 32.
pr 6–10   supposition that . . . we shall be *f·* to repeat
11–14   leaves the offender *f·* to repeat the offence,
m 63–32   and own her children *f·* from interference.

free
sp 74– 4   To be . . . persons must be *f·* from organic
90–25   sets man *f·* to master the infinite idea.
an 106– 3   to work against the *f·* course of honesty
s 114–27   and sets *f·* the imprisoned thought.
150–22   human view infringes man's *f·* moral agency ;
ph 171– 8   find himself unfallen, upright, pure, and *f·*,
176– 8   left the stomach and bowels *f·* to act
191–16   The human thought must *f·* itself from
f 206– 6   else it will misguide the judgment and *f·* the
223–21   Spiritual rationality and *f·* thought accompany
225– 4   Truth makes man *f·*.
227–16   God made man *f·*.
227–17   Paul said, "I was *f·* born." — *Acts* 22 : 28.
227–18   All men should be *f·*.
227–19   Love and Truth make *f·*,
227–25   Citizens of the world, accept the. . .and be *f·* !
227–27   has bound you, entangled your *f·* limbs,
244–12   hath made me *f·* from the law of — *Rom.* 8 : 2.
p 381–24   quite *f·* from some ailment.
434– 1   can . . . set the captive *f·*.
442– 8   prisoner rose up regenerated, strong, *f·*.
t 443–18   leave invalids *f·* to resort to whatever
448–32   to *f·* another from the fetters of disease.
453–30   the divine Truth that makes man *f·*.
r 481– 6   *f·* "to enter into the holiest," — *Heb.* 10 : 19.
495–13   sets the captive *f·* physically and morally.
g 514–11   F· and fearless it roams in the forest.
gl 584–13   that which frets itself *f·* from one belief

freed
sp 73–23   belief that spirit . . . is *f·* by death,
73–24   belief . . . that, when it is *f·* from the
ph 178–24   we are *f·* from the belief of heredity,

freedom (*see also* **freedom's**)
assert their
f 228–14   Mortals will some day assert their *f·*
boundless
a 22–24   boundless *f·*, and sinless sense,
breath of
f 225–21   nor did the breath of *f·* come from the cannon's
capacity or
r 475–31   nor . . . engender the capacity or *f·* to sin.
confers a
sp 89–23   influence or action of Soul confers a *f·*,
glorious
f 248– 1   and glorious *f·* of spiritual harmony.
heritage of
f 228– 7   when man enters into his heritage of *f·*,
hope of
p 368–13   even the hope of *f·* from the bondage
human
f 242– 7   towards the joys of Spirit, towards human *f·*
moral
m 58–12   There is moral *f·* in Soul.
right to
f 227– 5   and mortals are taught their right to *f·*,
spiritual
s 118–12   eternally glorified in man's spiritual *f·*.
p 366– 5   and thus attain the spiritual *f·*
strength and
t 454–20   strength and *f·* to speech and action.
universal
f 226– 8   sounded the keynote of universal *f·*,
wild with
g 552–21   may become wild with *f·*

f 225–31   ignorant how to obtain their *f·*.
226–11   and that its *f·* be won,
236–28   because of their *f·* from wrong
r 481– 3   God's being is infinity, *f·*, harmony,

freedom's
f 225– 7   time bears onward *f·* banner.

freely
sp 89– 8   believing that . . . she talks *f·*.
g 527– 8   thou mayest *f·* eat : — *Gen.* 2 : 16.
548– 2   take the water of life *f·*." — *Rev.* 22 : 17.

freer
s 120–30   When Columbus gave *f·* breath to the globe,

frees
b 291– 3   suppositions . . . death of the body *f·* from sin,

freezing
ph 175–26   Damp atmosphere and *f·* snow
b 329–14   should not tarry in the storm if the body is *f·*,
r 490–32   will think that he is *f·* when he is warm,

French
sp 80–22   Even planchette — the *F·* toy which
an 100–12   In 1784, the *F·* government ordered

frenzy
f 212–21   In legerdemain and credulous *f·*,

frequency
m 59–28   the *f·* of divorce shows that the

frequent
  ap 566–22 In shade and storm the *f·* night,
frequently
  s 153– 1 *f·* attenuated to such a degree that
  ph 180–18 Doctors should not . . . as they so *f·* do,
  o 358–19 more *f·* cited for our instruction
fresh
  an 105–23 to commit *f·* atrocities as opportunity occurs
  s 107–12 *f·* pinions are given to faith and understanding,
  t 460–24 Science of Mind was a *f·* revelation
freshness
  f 246–23 still maintain his vigor, *f·*, and promise.
  246–30 into loveliness, *f·*, and continuity,
  248– 9 Mind feeds the body with supernal *f·*
fretfulness
  m 62–11 their children's *f·* or frivolity,
frets
  gl 584–13 that which *f·* itself free from one belief only to
friend
  absent
    sp 82– 2 We think of an absent *f·* as easily as
  best
    ph 176–20 while divine Mind is its best *f·*.
  better
    r 486–17 If. . .then death is not an enemy but a better *f·*
  far-off
    sp 90–16 In dreams we fly to Europe and meet a far-off *f·*.
  of man
    a 49–15 the highest instructor and *f·* of man,
  of Mortal Man
    p 433–32 the spirit of Life and the *f·* of Mortal Man,
  of publicans
    a 53– 1 and is the "*f·* of publicans and— *Luke* 7 : 34.
  our
    sp 75–12 "Our *f·* Lazarus sleepeth ;— *John* 11 : 11.
  sick
    p 430–30 when the prisoner, . . . watched with a sick *f·*.
  their
    a 53– 7 He rebuked sinners. . .because he was their *f·* ;

    pr 8–31 If a *f·* informs us of a fault,
    a 28–20 a glutton and a *f·* of the impure,
    34– 8 if a *f·* be with us,
    34– 9 why need we memorials of that *f·*?
    39–11 causes mortals to regard death as a *f·*,
    f 248– 4 One marvels that a *f·* can ever seem less than
    p 386–17 mistakenly announcing the death of a *f·*,
friendly
  pref ix–25 copies were, however, in *f·* circulation.
  p 438–31 to be on *f·* terms with the firm of
friend's
  p 386 17 grief that the *f·* real death would bring.
friends
  departed
    sp 82–19 even if our departed *f·* were near us
  few
    a 42–13 the desertion of all save a few *f·*,
  give to
    pref viii–29 give to *f·* the results of her Scriptural study,
  her
    t 404– 3 Could her *f·* know how little time
  his
    a 46– 5 Jesus was known to his *f·* by the words, which
    o 350– 3 Let any clergyman try to cure his *f·* by
    p 436–23 His *f·* struggled hard to rescue the
  make
    g 552–10 Mortal theories make *f·* of sin,
  my
    a 21–15 If my *f·* are going to Europe,
    21–21 On the contrary, if my *f·* pursue my course,
  our
    p 386–31 So, when our *f·* pass from our sight
  personal
    c 266– 6 Would existence without personal *f·* be
  prisoner's
    p 432–25 One of the prisoner's *f·*, Materia Medica,
  professed
    p 436–16 professed *f·*, Materia Medica and Physiology,
  unpretentious
    a 54–23 only a few unpretentious *f·*,

    c 266–13 *F·* will betray and enemies will slander,
friendship
  sp 87–26 by *f·* or by any intense feeling
fright
  s 151–18 belief says that death has been occasioned by *f·*.
  ph 178–14 by the *f·* of his mother.
  f 251– 7 *F·* is so great at certain stages of
frighten
  sp 79– 3 is an error that tends to *f·*
  p 379–29 The images, held . . . *f·* conscious thought.

frightened
  s 154–17 the mother is *f·* and says,
  o 352–12 child, who is *f·* at imaginary ghosts
  p 371–11 As *f·* children look everywhere for
  433–28 to prepare the *f·* sense . . . for *death.*
  t 460–15 to the *f·*, false sense of the patient.
frightening
  p 439–10 *f·* away Materia Medica,
  t 447–18 without *f·* or discouraging the patient
frivolity
  m 62–11 their children's fretfulness or *f·*,
frivolous
  m 60–22 *f·* amusements, personal adornment,
  ph 195–30 to meet a *f·* demand for amusement
front
  an 102–17 its aggressive features are coming to the *f·*.
  b 301– 3 form, and action of the person in *f·* of the
frost
  sp 72–32 As readily can you mingle fire and *f·*
frosts
  c 265–19 and nipped by untimely *f·* ;
frown
  f 238– 8 To obey . . . is to incur society's *f·* ;
  238– 8 but this *f·*, more than flatteries,
frozen
  p 373–28 languidly creeps along its *f·* channels,
frugal
  t 452–16 Better is the *f·* intellectual repast
fruit
  bearing
    ph 180–10 seed within itself bearing *f·* after its kind,
  bears the
    ph 197– 9 bears the *f·* of sin, disease, and death,
  bringing forth
    g 529– 1 bringing forth *f·* of its own kind,
  Cain's
    g 541– 3 more nearly resembles . . . than does Cain's *f·*.
    541–11 than for the worship expressed by Cain's *f·*?
  forbidden
    r 481–12 The forbidden *f·* of knowledge,
    g 529– 1 when the forbidden *f·* was bringing forth
  good
    p 404–19 every tree that brings not forth good *f·*.
    t 459–27 tree must be good, which produces good *f·*.
  immortal
    o 361–29 That which when sown bears immortal *f·*,
  known by his
    b 299–23 tree is known by his *f·*"— *Matt.* 12 : 33.
  known by its
    sp 73–13 belief, which ought to be known by its *f·*,
  known by their
    an 106–17 demonstrable in Truth and known by their *f·*,
  much
    b 271– 1 seed of Truth springs up and bears much *f·*.
  not much
    b 272– 7 else it beareth not much *f·*,
  of false knowledge
    ph 175–30 Adam, before he ate the *f·* of false knowledge,
  of the ground
    g 540–25 brought of the *f·* of the ground— *Gen.* 4 : 3.
  of the Spirit
    an 106–27 the *f·* of the Spirit is love,— *Gal.* 5 : 22.
  of the tree
    g 529–18 but of the *f·* of the tree which— *Gen.* 3 : 3.
  of the trees
    g 529–17 We may eat of the *f·* of the trees— *Gen.* 3 : 2.
  of the vine
    a 18– * I will not drink of the f· of the vine,— Luke* 22 : 18.
  this
    ph 165– 2 Evil declared that eating this *f·* would open
  yield
    g 507–19 tree and herb do not yield *f·* because of
  yielding
    g 507–13 yielding *f·* after his kind,— *Gen.* 1 : 11.
    508–11 and the tree yielding *f·*,— *Gen.* 1 : 12.

    p 389–17 the fount and stream, the tree and its *f·*,
    g 507–12 the *f·* tree yielding fruit— *Gen.* 1 : 11.
    518– 7 the *f·* of a tree yielding seed ;— *Gen.* 1 : 29.
fruitage
  o 348–27 the full *f·* of C. S.,
fruit-bearer
  g 526–23 Did He create this *f·* of sin
fruitful
  g 512–17 Be *f·*, and multiply,— *Gen.* 1 : 22.
  517–26 Be *f·*, and multiply,— *Gen.* 1 : 28.
  550–28 Amalgamation . . . is seldom *f·*,
  fr 600– * being f· in every good work,— Col.* 1 : 10.

fruition
pr	9–15	before we can enjoy the *f·* of our hope
b	298– 7	Science armed with faith, hope, and *f·*.
	298–14	faith, understanding, *f·*, reality.

fruitless
pr	6–28	He said of the *f·* tree,
p	375–17	should be understood and so rendered *f·*.

fruitlessness
a	35– 3	Convinced of the *f·* of their toil

fruits
early
gl	579– 9	surrendering to the creator the early *f·* of

first
g	532– 7	when eating its first *f·* brought death

immediate
g	532–18	produced the immediate *f·* of fear and shame.

immortal
r	494–29	its lap piled high with immortal *f·*.

its
p	426–14	this would be . . . known by its *f·*.

of human faith
pref	xi– 6	the *f·* of human faith in matter,

of Love
a	35–24	by bringing forth the *f·* of Love,

of sin
b	299–19	bearing the *f·* of sin, sickness, and death.

of Spirit
p	391–32	and bearing the *f·* of Spirit.

of the Spirit
t	451–18	they bear as of old the *f·* of the Spirit.

present
o	349– 1	If such are the present *f·*, what will the

their
f	204–19	Judging them by their *f·*, they are corrupt.
o	342–28	"By their *f·* ye shall know them"— *Matt.* 7 : 20.
fr	600– *	*by their f· ye shall know them.*— *Matt.* 7 : 20.

your
r	496–13	Your *f·* will prove what the

a	38–22	the *f·* of other people's sins, not of his own.
f	220–27	The belief that . . . is one of the *f·*
	243–30	sin, and death are not of the *f·* of Life.

fulfil
m	56– 4	to *f·* all righteousness."— *Matt.* 3 : 15.
f	223– 3	not *f·* the lust of the flesh."— *Gal.* 5 : 16.
	233– 7	demands of us only what we can certainly *f·*.
r	474–20	not come to destroy, but to *f·*."— *Matt.* 5 : 17.
	483–30	One must *f·* one's mission without timidity

fulfilled
a	41–24	He *f·* his God-mission, and then
	55–21	The promises will be *f·*.
s	109–25	Scripture of Isaiah is renewedly *f·* :
p	404–15	can remove this disorder as God's law is *f·*
i	463–10	Truth is here and has *f·* its perfect work.
g	534–12	This prophecy has been *f·*.
ap	569– 7	literally *f·*, when we are conscious of

fulfilling
m	59–11	*F·* the different demands of their united
p	435–20	"is the *f·* of the law,"— *Rom.* 13 : 10.
r	485–22	by *f·* the spiritual law of being,

fulfils
m	57–32	disappointments it involves or the hopes it *f·*.
s	134–31	A miracle *f·* God's law, but does not violate
b	276– 2	and *f·* these sayings of Scripture,
	297–32	A mortal belief *f·* its own conditions.
	340–24	ends wars ; *f·* the Scripture,
ap	572–12	Love *f·* the law of C. S.,

full
pref	vii– 3	ere cometh the *f·* radiance of a risen day.
	viii– 4	To develop in *f·* might of this Science.
	x–14	or treat in *f·* detail so infinite a theme.
pr	5–12	*f·* "and running over."— *Luke* 6 : 38.
	5–14	Saints and sinners get their *f·* award,
	8– 9	*f·* . . . of all uncleanness."— *Matt.* 23 : 27.
a	29–25	with the *f·* recognition that being is Spirit.
	31–20	a *f·* understanding of the divine Principle
	36–22	*f·* punishment this side of the grave
	36–24	bestow on the righteous their *f·* reward.
	37– 5	History is *f·* of records of suffering.
	39– 6	a *f·* salvation from sin, sickness, and death.
	42–17	and gave *f·* evidence of divine Science.
	50–19	If his *f·* recognition of eternal Life had
m	59– 2	a *f·* recognition of its enduring obligations
an	105–31	*f·* many a league in the line of light ;
s	122–21	Experience is *f·* of instances of similar
	130–20	cannot add to the contents of a vessel already *f·*.
	139– 4	the Scriptures are *f·* of accounts of the
ph	182–20	Obedience to material law prevents *f·*
f	201–13	We cannot fill vessels already *f·*.
	244–21	when there is no *f·* reflection of the
	247– 8	his *f·* set of upper and lower teeth
c	261–19	he was in the *f·* possession of his

full
b	286– 7	gives *f·* faith in Truth,
	313– 2	the *f·* and proper translation of the Greek),
o	348–27	the *f·* fruitage of C. S.,
p	395–19	The nurse should be cheerful, . . . *f·* of faith,
	406– 6	*f·* salvation from sin, sickness, and death.
t	456–28	contains the *f·* statement of C. S.,
r	493–13	A *f·* answer to the above question
g	507– 8	creation would be *f·* of nameless offspring,
	511–17	The changing glow and *f·* effulgence of
	536–21	few days, and *f·* of trouble."— *Job* 14 : 1.
	542–21	Sin will receive its *f·* penalty,
	552–16	few days, and *f·* of trouble."— *Job* 14 : 1.
ap	559–14	to utter the *f·* diapason of secret tones.
	565– 4	It is *f·* of lust and hate, loathing the
	574– 7	*f·* of the seven last plagues,— *Rev.* 21 : 9.
	574–18	the seven angelic vials *f·* of seven plagues,
	574–18	has *f·* compensation in the law of Love.
gl	591– 6	MAN. . . . the *f·* representation of Mind.
	591–19	of whom man is the *f·* and perfect expression ;
	598–28	man would be in the *f·* consciousness of

fuller
s	162–27	it requires only a *f·* understanding of the
f	226– 8	a *f·* acknowledgment of the rights of man
o	361–22	to give a clearer and *f·* expression

full-orbed
f	224–21	the harbingers of truth's *f·* appearing.
b	298– 3	and glow *f·* in spiritual understanding.

fully
pref	viii– 2	her system has been *f·* tested
a	42–32	must understand more *f·* his Life-principle
	45– 6	Our Master *f·* and finally demonstrated
	45–32	not sufficiently advanced *f·* to understand
s	132– 3	to heal would *f·* answer the question.
	136–24	what the disciples did not *f·* understand?
	152– 9	a healing effect, even when not *f·* understood.
f	205–32	When we *f·* understand our relation to the Divine,
	227– 2	fetters fall and the rights of man are *f·* known
	231–28	impossible, when you *f·* apprehend God
	240–27	one must pay *f·* and fairly the
b	284–10	nor be *f·* manifested through corporeality.
	288–11	When the . . . effects of C. S. are *f·* apprehended,
	326–14	Not partially, but *f·*, the great healer of
	339–18	Only those, . . . can *f·* understand the unreality of evil.
o	343–15	when his teachings are *f·* understood.
	344–11	Were it more *f·* understood that Truth heals
p	415–28	Before the thoughts are *f·* at rest,
r	471–16	evidence . . . is *f·* sustained by spiritual sense.
	495– 5	hence its healing power is not *f·* demonstrated.
g	556–16	It is made known most *f·* to him who

fulness
b	336–20	neither could God's *f·* be reflected by a single
p	406–24	until we arrive at the *f·* of God's idea,
g	519–20	the stature of the *f·* of Christ"— *Eph.* 4 : 13.
gl	590–12	denial of the *f·* of God's creation ;

fumes
p	407– 3	Puffing the obnoxious *f·* of tobacco,

function
s	148–15	every *f·*, formation, and manifestation.
	151–20	Every *f·* of the real man is governed by the

functional
s	125– 3	considered the best condition for . . . *f·* health
	149–24	as readily as she has cured purely *f·* disease,
	162–26	as surely as it heals what is called *f·*,
p	377–25	organic diseases as readily as *f·* difficulties.

functions
disordered
p	408–18	inflammation of disordered *f·*,

elements and
s	124–32	elements and *f·* of the physical body

entire
p	384–32	entire *f·* and organs of the human system

healthy
p	373–26	disabled organ will resume its healthy *f·*.

my
p	431–30	and perform my *f·* as usual,

natural
p	387–14	perform the natural *f·* of being.
r	478–20	the discharge of the natural *f·* is least noticeable.

of Mind
r	478–23	Matter cannot perform the *f·* of Mind.

of mind
p	388–32	the harmonious *f·* of mind and body,
	395–31	cannot kill a man nor affect the *f·* of mind

of the body
p	373–22	Disease is expressed . . . in the *f·* of the body.

vital
p	387–17	and perform the most vital *f·* in society.

fundamental

m	65– 9	some f· error in the marriage state.
s	113– 9	f· propositions of divine metaphysics
	120– 8	arrive at the f· facts of being.
ph	167–29	On this f· point, timid conservatism is
	171–31	f· error lies in the supposition that
t	460–10	Yet this most f· part of metaphysics
g	545–13	Such f· errors send falsity into

funds

m	63–31	deposit f·, and own her children free from

fungus

s	160–30	Is man a material f· without Mind

fur

p	431–21	covered with a foul f·,
	438–10	said that . . . a garment of foul f·
	438–22	this f· is a foreign substance,
	438–28	is not an importer or dealer in f·,
	438–29	explain how this f· is manufactured,

furnace

m	66–31	f· separates the gold from the dross
s	133–17	in the fiery f· and in kings' palaces.
	161– 8	captives, cast into the Babylonian f· ;
f	243– 6	from the fiery f·, from the jaws of the lion,

furnish

pr	6–13	will f· more than its equivalent of pain,
a	51–10	that he might f· the proof of immortal life.
s	135–19	"Can God f· a table in the— Psal. 78 : 19.
	142–10	Truth, alone can f· us with absolute evidence.
ph	189–17	is supposed to f· the evidence of
ap	572–14	f· the vision of the Apocalypse,

furnished

sp	99– 9	Truth has f· the key to the kingdom,
b	317–28	to him Jesus f· the proof
r	472–11	Jesus f· proofs of these statements.

furnishes

m	63–13	C. S. f· no precedent for such injustice,
ph	195–15	Whatever f· the semblance of an idea
	195–16	f· food for thought.
f	245–18	This instance of youth preserved f·
b	336–27	The Science of being f· the rule of

furnishes

p	370–10	Homœopathy f· the evidence to the
	387–27	The history of Christianity f· sublime
t	461–14	f· the eternal interpretation of God and
ap	571–23	f· the mirror in which mortals may see

furnishing

ph	180–21	Instead of f· thought with fear, they should
p	439– 4	keeps a f· store, and advertises

Furred Tongue

p	438–26	summoned F· T· for examination,

further

an	103– 4	and f· defines it as dishonesty
f	226– 2	f· steps towards the banishment of
b	295–29	It f· teaches that when man is
	314– 2	(his f· spiritual exaltation),
	338–17	It f· suggests the thought of that
p	441–20	We f· recommend that Materia Medica
ap	576– 8	f· describing this holy city,
	576–18	What f· indication need we of the

furthermore

m	64–17	F·, the time cometh of which

fury

f	203–27	The foam and f· of illegitimate living
b	293–21	There is no vapid f· of mortal mind

fustian

s	142–16	tell their story to pride and f·.

future

pref	vii–25	F· ages must declare what the pioneer has
a	24–19	in regard to predestination and f· punishment.
sp	84– 6	predicting the f· from a groundwork of
	84–13	to know the past, the present, and the f·.
s	150–24	and will be to all others at some f· day,
b	306–15	at some uncertain f· time and in a manner
p	374–19	You confess to ignorance of the f·
t	459– 9	Judge not the f· advancement of C. S. by the
g	546– 2	at some f· time to be emancipated

future-world

a	39–20	not that now men must prepare for a f·

G

Gabriel

ap	567– 1	G· has the more quiet task
	567– 6	The G· of His presence has no contests.

Gad

gl	586–21	definition of

gain

pr	11–23	a desire for holiness is requisite in order to g·
	12– 4	mere request . . . has no power to g·
	13–13	Do we g· the omnipotent ear sooner by words
	14– 3	whose ear we would g·,
	15–29	g· the ear and right hand of omnipotence
	21–13	g· a little each day in the right direction,
m	65–11	To g· C. S. and its harmony,
	69– 4	g· the sense of health only as
sp	72– 7	is the g· of spiritual life.
s	156–19	I did so, and she continued to g·.
ph	167–28	impossible to g· control over the body in
f	238–22	Attempts to . . . g· dominion over mankind,
	254– 4	g· good rapidly and hold their position,
c	260–15	distrust of one's ability to g· the goodness
	264– 8	if they would g· the true sense of things.
	264–13	As mortals g· more correct views of God
	265– 7	g· some proper sense of the infinite,
	266–17	lay down their fleshliness and g·
b	322– 5	we shall g· the reality of Life,
	326–13	if we would g· the Christ as our only Saviour.
	328–10	they g· the true understanding of God
	335–23	we g· the eternal unfolding of Life
o	355– 1	they should g· the spiritual meaning of C. S.,
p	388–28	foolish to stop eating until we g·
t	459– 6	he must g· heavenly riches by
r	486– 7	Even then he must g· spiritual understanding
g	501–10	recompensing human want . . . with spiritual g·.
ap	560–13	necessity of existence is to g· the true idea

gained

a	23–18	the evidence g· from Spirit,
sp	84– 3	ancient prophets g· their foresight from
	91–20	erroneous knowledge g· from matter
	92–15	a knowledge g· from matter, or evil,
s	111–32	this system has gradually g· ground,
f	254–10	facts of existence are g· step by step,
c	265–23	g· stronger desires for spiritual joy?
b	269–27	knowledge g· through the material senses
	272– 3	spiritual sense of truth must be g·
	274– 3	knowledge g· from the five senses
	290–19	Perfection is g· only by perfection.

gained

b	299–18	Knowledge g· from material sense is
	314– 8	Our Master g· the solution of being,
	326–16	purpose and motive to live aright can be g·
o	349–20	this sense must be g· by its disciples
	358–21	Is it not because there are few who have g·
p	365–21	such commendation as the Magdalen g·
	400–30	normal control is g· through divine strength
t	449– 6	but more of C. S. must be g·
r	474–15	glorious Principle of these marvels is g·.
	482– 7	g· by substituting the word God,
	487– 4	g· by walking in the pathway of Truth
	490 20	knowledge g· from the so-called material senses
g	532– 6	g· from the five corporeal senses.
	536–25	the true idea is g· from the immortal side.
	547–25	only by this understanding can truth be g·.
	548–22	g· the diviner side in C. S.,
	556–13	life everlasting is not to be g· by dying.

gaining

a	47– 5	After g· the true idea of their glorified Master,
ph	198– 7	already developed the disease that is g·
b	324– 8	are not g· the true idea of God ;
	327– 2	also by g· an affection for good
	327–28	seeking material means for g· happiness.

gains

m	57– 7	the feminine mind g· courage and strength
sp	83–28	man g· the divine Principle and explanation
f	238–24	forsakes popularity and g· Christianity.
c	258–23	in proportion as humanity g· the true
b	294–29	thief believes that he g· something by stealing,

gala

f	252–23	says : . . . my short span of life one g· day.

Galatians

an	106–19	St. Paul in his great epistle to the G·,

Galilean Prophet

o	360–28	the Jews put to death the G· P·,
r	497–18	as demonstrated by the G· P·

Galilean Sea

a	34–32	joyful meeting on the shore of the G· S· !

Galilee

sp	90– 4	on the shores of G·,
s	147–13	and in the valleys of G·.

gall

a	51– 5	This dread added the drop of g· to his cup.

gallows
s 134–13   hallowed by the *g·* and the cross.

garden
culture of your
m   61–26   the culture of your *g·* or the raising of stock
of Eden
g   526–27   and put him into the *g·* of Eden, — *Gen.* 2 : 15.
537– 3   forth from the *g·* of Eden, — *Gen.* 3 : 23.
537– 6   at the east of the *g·* of Eden — *Gen.* 3 : 24.

a   47–31   night of gloom and glory in the *g·*,
g   526– 2   in the midst of the *g·*, — *Gen.* 2 : 9.
527– 7   Of every tree of the *g·* — *Gen.* 2 : 16.
529–16   of every tree of the *g·* ? — *Gen.* 3 : 1.
529–18   fruit of the trees of the *g·* : — *Gen.* 3 : 2.
529–19   in the midst of the *g·* — *Gen.* 3 : 3.
532–15   I heard Thy voice in the *g·*, — *Gen.* 3 : 10.

garment
s   142– 8   We must seek the undivided *g·*,
ph   170–27   at least to touch the hem of Truth's *g·*.
197– 4   Parisian name for a novel *g·*.
f   242–28   every part of the Christly *g·* of righteousness.
p   438–20   said that . . . a *g·* of foul fur

garments
c   267–27   "let thy *g·* be always white." — *Eccl.* 9 : 8.
t   452–20   We soil our *g·* with conservatism,
463–15   The new idea, . . . clad in white *g·*.

garnered
g   535– 5   the other to be *g·* into heavenly places.

garrisoned
f   235–11   should be strongly *g·* with virtue.

gas
o   346–26   when you believe that nitrous-oxide *g·* has
p   375– 2   painlessly as *g·* dissipates into the air
399– 8   No gastric *g·* accumulates, . . . apart from

gases
b   293–13   The material so-called *g·* and forces

gash
p   393–23   than the trunk of a tree which you *g·*

gastric
ph   175–24   not so severe upon the *g·* juices.
p   399– 8   No *g·* gas accumulates, . . . apart from

gate
pref   ix–18   a willing disciple at the heavenly *g·*,
s   142–14   the poor and the stranger from the *g·*,
t   451–12   for "wide is the *g·*, — *Matt.* 7 : 13.
g   535–16   When will man pass through the open *g·* of C. S.
538– 5   Truth places the cherub wisdom at the *g·* of

gates
s   137–32   and the *g·* of hell — *Matt.* 16 : 18.
146–20   "stranger that is within thy *g·*," — *Exod.* 20 : 10.
ph   171– 6   man will reopen . . . the *g·* of Paradise
ap   571–28   has opened wide the *g·* of glory,
575–19   "and the *g·* of it shall not be shut — *Rev.* 21 : 25.
575–26   Northward, its *g·* open to the North Star,
577–24   Its *g·* open towards light and glory

gateway
g   537–15   Truth guards the *g·* to harmony.

gather
s   129–24   Can we *g·* peaches from a pine-tree,
b   276–30   Divine Science does not *g·* grapes from
p   370– 4   *g·* the facts of being from the divine Mind.
380–26   Gradually this evidence will *g·* momentum
g   539–24   "Do men *g·* grapes of thorns?" — *Matt.* 7 : 16.

gathered
sp   78–14   Communications *g·* from ignorance are
g   504–23   when *g·* into the focus of ideas,
506–16   *g·* together unto one place, — *Gen.* 1 : 9.
527–16   perception, *g·* from the corporeal senses,

gathering
a   55–16   *g·* beneath its wings the sick and sinning.
t   463–10   Though *g·* new energy, this idea cannot
g   506–23   the *g·* together of the waters — *Gen.* 1 : 10.
535–30   the *g·* together of the waters — *Gen.* 1 : 10.
547–13   the *g·* clouds, the moon and stars,

gathers
b   299–15   whither every real individuality, . . . *g·*.
g   506–18   Spirit, God, *g·* unformed thoughts into

gaudy
an   103–26   whose flimsy and *g·* pretensions,

gave
pr   16–10   then he *g·* that prayer which covers all
a   26–15   Truth, Life, and Love *g·* Jesus authority over
29–18   and *g·* to her ideal the name of Jesus
32–16   and *g·* it to the disciples, — *Matt.* 26 : 26.
32–18   *g·* thanks, and *g·* it to them — *Matt.* 26 : 27.
32–22   yet Jesus prayed and *g·* them bread.
33–16   he *g·* thanks and said,
41–14   proofs of Truth, . . . which Jesus *g·*
42– 4   *g·* no hint of the unchanging love of God.

gave
a   42–17   and *g·* full evidence of divine Science,
44– 5   lonely precincts of the tomb *g·* Jesus a refuge
47– 2   *g·* them a faint conception of the Life
sp   89–29   if life was in the body, and man *g·* it,
s   120–30   When Columbus *g·* freer breath to the globe,
132–10   In other words, he *g·* his benediction to
134–19   the very element, which *g·* it divine force
137–28   the Master *g·* him a spiritual name
ph   176– 9   and *g·* the gospel a chance to be seen
193–11   its death-pallor *g·* place to a natural hue.
194–31   *g·* him a belief of intense pain.
195– 9   *g·* him pain through those very senses,
199–27   His belief that he could do it *g·*
f   210–13   *g·* sight to the blind, hearing to the deaf,
220–24   he *g·* up his abstinence,
242–32   require of Christians the proof which he *g·*,
b   308–22   *g·* him spiritual strength in this Peniel of
309– 4   *g·* him the spiritual sense of being
325– 8   Jesus *g·* the true idea of being,
p   364–20   such seekers as he *g·* small reward
369–18   never *g·* drugs, never prayed to know if
376–12   should be told that blood never *g·* life
398– 9   Often he *g·* no name to the distemper
431– 5   the prisoner *g·* him drink.
t   456–32   it *g·* the first rules for demonstrating this
r   471–27   and *g·* the spiritual import,
487–11   apprehension of this *g·* sight to the blind
g   528– 4   That Adam *g·* the name and nature of animals,
533– 8   she *g·* me of the tree, — *Gen.* 3 : 12.
537–28   and *g·* it to man for a possession,
539–27   The divine origin of Jesus *g·* him
gl   598–11   and *g·* up the ghost ;" — *John* 19 : 30.
598–15   What Jesus *g·* up was indeed air,

gavest
g   533– 8   The woman whom Thou *g·* to be — *Gen.* 3 : 12.
533–16   "The woman, whom Thou *g·* me, is responsible."

gaze
f   248–21   holding it before your *g·* continually.
248–25   first turn our *g·* in the right direction,
c   261–27   Fixing your *g·* on the realities supernal,
264– 9   Where shall the *g·* rest but in the
p   378–14   A man's *g·*, fastened fearlessly on a
420–30   Turn his *g·* from the false evidence of the
g   521–14   turn our *g·* to the spiritual record of creation,

gazing
p   380–15   *G·* at a chained lion, crouched for a spring,

gems
sp   87–20   the sea is ignorant of the *g·* within
f   235–17   adorned with *g·* of scholarly attainment,
247–27   blazons the night with starry *g·*,

gender
b   305–12   *G·* also is a quality, not of God, but
g   508–13   God determines the *g·* of His own ideas.
508–13   *G·* is mental, not material.
508–16   feminine *g·* is not yet expressed in the text.
508–17   *G·* means simply *kind* or *sort*,
508–20   grammars always recognize a neuter *g·*,
508–22   names the female *g·* last in the ascending
511–28   masculine, feminine, or neuter *g·*.

genders
g   516–30   Masculine, feminine, and neuter *g·* are

genera
r   482–18   As woman is but a species of the *g·*,

general
pref   x–12   to suit the *g·* drift of thought,
a   32– 4   required to swear allegiance to his *g·*.
m   63–25   the elevation of society in *g·*
sp   83–17   belief that . . . man, is governed in *g·* by
87–11   in the *g·* atmosphere of human mind.
96– 7   interruptions of the *g·* material routine.
s   152–31   Jahr, . . . enumerates the *g·* symptoms,
155– 4   it is the law of a *g·* belief,
155– 8   not yet divorced the drug from the *g·* faith.
155–11   When the *g·* belief endorses the
155–17   erroneous *g·* belief, . . . works against C. S.
c   263–15   He becomes a *g·* mis-creator,
b   306–16   this is the *g·* religious opinion of mankind,
319–10   the *g·* faith in material means
p   394–18   the fallacy of material systems in *g·*,
408– 8   this *g·* craze cannot, . . . shield the
411– 5   as a *g·* rule the body would respond more quickly,
412– 6   the peculiar or *g·* symptoms of the case
t   457–19   C. S. is not an exception to the *g·* rule,
g   548–19   " It is very possible that many *g·* statements
553–21   adopted by *g·* mortal thought
554–29   It is the *g·* belief that the lower animals

General Grant
r   492–18   Discussing his campaign, *G· G·* said :

generalities
s   147–25   taught the *g·* of its divine Principle

generally

a	28–16	nor the work of Jesus was g· understood.
	40–29	has come so g· to mean public worship
	47–22	world g· loves a lie better than Truth ;
s	132–19	and it has not yet been g· accepted.
	142– 6	modern religions g· omit all but one of these
	164– 9	It is just to say that g· the
ph	181–27	if they are cured, they g· know it
c	267– 8	It is g· conceded that God is Father,
b	270–12	it is g· admitted that this intelligence is
o	341– 5	criticisms are g· based on detached sentences
	343–23	Christendom g· demands so much less.
	348– 8	it is not g· understood how
	349– 2	when this Science is more g· understood
	349–25	material terms must be g· employed.
p	429–29	not understood g· by our ethical instructors.
t	446– 9	has g· completely healed such cases.
g	553–16	why are his deductions g· material?

General Progress
p	439–29	awaiting the sentence which G· P· and

generating
m	62– 1	only be permitted for the purpose of g·.

generation

a	29–21	put to silence material law and its order of g·,
	50– 3	"Who shall declare his g·?" — Isa. 53 : 8.
m	56– 7	the legal and moral provision for g·
	62–16	will do much more for the health of the rising g·
	68–31	Proportionately as human g· ceases,
sp	85–25	Jesus knew the g· to be wicked
s	148– 2	"O faithless g·," — Mark 9 : 19.
t	446–13	pours light and healing upon this g·,
g	548–20	general statements . . . about birth and g·,
	548–31	besides the ordinary process of g·,
	551–22	are brought down from g· to g·?"

generations

ph	174–15	marking out the path for g· yet unborn.
c	260– 9	Through many g· human beliefs will
b	333–19	Throughout all g· both before and after
g	520–16	These are the g· of the heavens — Gen. 2 : 4.
	549–14	successive g· do not begin with the birth

generic

c	259– 1	begin to comprehend . . . the g· term man.
r	475–15	g· term for all that reflects God's image
g	516–29	It follows that man is a g· term.
ap	561–22	woman in the Apocalypse symbolizes g· man,

generically
c	267– 6	G· man is one, and specifically man means

generous
s	129–30	The g· liver may object to the
t	450–10	They are sincere, g·, noble,

Genesis
and the Apocalypse
g	546–18	G· and the Apocalypse seem more obscure

beginning with
g	502– 1	second necessity for beginning with G· is

book of
g	502– 9	Spiritually followed, the book of G· is the
	521–19	more about creation in the book of G·.
	523–17	in the early part of the book of G·.

first chapter of
g	502–14	as given in the first chapter of G·
	505– 3	have no record in the first chapter of G·.
	521– 8	(as stated in the first chapter of G·)
	523–22	Throughout the first chapter of G·
	535–29	In the first chapter of G· we read :
	537–10	In the first chapter of G·, evil has no
	537–28	recorded in the first chapter of G·.
gl	590–22	not used in the first chapter of G·,

narrative in
s	157–17	(according to the narrative in G·)

order used in
ap	568– 9	The narrative follows the order used in G·.

Science of
g	525–22	In the Science of G· we read

second account in
g	537–20	this second account in G·

second chapter of
g	521–26	second chapter of G· contains a statement of
	522–25	latter part of the second chapter of G·,
	526–15	is in the . . . second chapter of G·.

spoken of in
ph	180–10	the seed within itself . . . spoken of in G·.

to Revelation
s	139–24	seen from G· to Revelation,

to the Apocalypse
ap	564–24	From G· to the Apocalypse,

g	538–18	in the Elohistic introduction of G·,
ap	564–31	In G·, this allegorical, talking serpent
	568–10	In G·, first the true method of creation is
	572– 4	Thus we see, . . . in G· and in the Apocalypse,

genial
ap	575–30	southward, to the g· tropics,

genius
g	548–27	endowed by the labors and g· of great men.

Gentile
sp	85–23	Both Jew and G· may have had acute

gentle
g	541–10	the homage bestowed through a g· animal

gentleness
an	106–28	longsuffering, g·, goodness, faith, — Gal. 5 : 22.
gl	592–25	OIL. Consecration ; charity ; g· ;

gently
ph	184–30	Her breath came g·.
	193–12	The eyelids closed g· and
f	245–15	youth sat g· on cheek and brow.
r	485–14	Emerge g· from matter into Spirit.
ap	574–30	Then thought g· whispers : "Come hither !

genuine
m	60– 1	if both . . . were g· Christian Scientists.
sp	91–13	his g· being will be understood.
	95– 2	only g· Science of reading mortal mind.
	95–15	depends upon his g· spirituality.
s	112–26	to establish a g· school of this Science.
b	291– 2	suppositions . . . that happiness can be g· in
	294–25	Man's g· selfhood is recognizable only in
p	364–26	by their g· repentance, by their broken hearts,
	375–17	g· Christian Scientist is adding to his
r	477–16	the g· and perfect man,
	489– 7	not with an artificial limb, but with the g·

genuinely
p	370–29	should naturally and g· change our basis

genus
b	277–16	the order of g· and species is preserved
ap	560–20	botanist must know the g· and species

geology
g	510–19	G· has never explained the earth's formations ;
	552– 6	Heathen philosophy, modern g·, and

geometric
f	215–11	not subordinate to g· altitudes.

geometrical
b	282– 4	are figured by two g· symbols,

geometry
b	283–30	than we can teach and illustrate g· by

germ
f	246– 7	Man is by no means a material g·
o	361–20	A g· of infinite Truth, . . . is the
g	549–18	simple ovum as the g·, the starting-point,
	550– 1	he virtually affirms that the g· of humanity
	551–31	resulting g· is doomed to the same routine.

Germany
an	100– 2	brought into notice by Mesmer in G·

germinated
sp	74– 9	The seed which has g· has

germinates
m	66–11	Spiritual development g· not from seed
g	546– 4	Spirit, God, never g·,
	549– 4	supposition that life g· in eggs

germinating
f	225–26	always g· in new forms of tyranny,
g	547–14	g· speck of so-called embryonic life

germination
ph	183– 9	g· according to the laws of nature?

gestation
m	62– 3	the period of g· have the sanctity of virginity.

get
pref	xi–31	enabled her to g· this institution chartered
pr	5–14	Saints and sinners g· their full award,
	7– 2	"G· thee behind me, Satan." — Matt. 16 : 23.
	12–31	If . . . only petitioners . . . should g· well.
a	39–25	mortals must g· the true idea and
m	65–21	we g· at last the clear straining of truth,
s	156–22	informed me that she could g· along two days
ph	197– 5	Every one hastens to g· it.
f	231– 2	or the so-called physical senses will g· the
	239– 7	and we g· clearer views
	239– 9	and we g· better views of humanity.
b	328– 7	mortals g· rid of sin, sickness, and death only
	339–28	To g· rid of sin through Science,
p	371–17	before he can g· rid of the illusive sufferings
	407–18	and he will g· the better of that desire,
	412–19	g· its name, and array your mental plea against
t	447–26	and thus g· the victory over sin
g	553– 7	g· nearer the truth of being,
fr	600– *	Let us g· up early to the vineyards ; — Song 7 : 12.

Gethsemane
a	30– 9	This accounts for his struggles in G·
	48–11	in holy benediction on the grass of G·,
gl	586–23	definition of

getting
p	406–32	There is no enjoyment in g· drunk,
	431–17	g· Mortal Man into close confinement

ghastly
ph 176–10   A g· array of diseases was not paraded
b 272–20   the g· farce of material existence ;

ghost
a 45–25   disciples at first called him a spirit, g·, or
o 353–25   grave does not banish the g· of materiality.
353–30   the g·, some unreal belief.
p 371–12   children look everywhere for the imaginary g·,
g, 587– 1   definition of
598–12   and gave up the g· ;"— John 19 : 30.
598–12   but this word g· is pneuma.

ghostly
sp 86–17   Haunted houses, g· voices,
s 136–20   This g· fancy was repeated by Herod
o 353–13   not wholly outlived the sense of g· beliefs.

ghosts
o 352–13   child, who is frightened at imaginary g·
352–14   Would a mother say . . . "I know that g· are
352–21   by declaring g· to be real, merciless, and
352–23   that g· are not realities,
352–26   should be told not to believe in g·,
352–28   terror of g· will depart
352–32   not irrational to tell the truth about g·.
353–27   so long will g· seem to continue.

ghost-stories
p 371– 6   by telling g· in the dark.

giant
f 240– 3   Arctic regions, sunny tropics, g· hills,

gift
sp 88–29   though it is said to be a g·
98– 3   assured . . . in the g· of divine Love.
s 108– 3   "the g· of the grace of God— Eph. 3 : 7.
135–27   nor a special g· from a ritualistic Jehovah ;
b 271–13   was not a supernatural g· to those learners,
g 541– 4   Jealous of his brother's g·,
541– 5   instead of making his own g· a higher tribute

Gihon
gl 587– 3   definition of

girl
f 237– 1   A little g·, who had occasionally listened to
238–10   Losing her crucifix, the Roman Catholic g· said,

give
pref viii–29   began to write down and g· to friends the
pr 3–19   we try to g· information to this infinite Mind.
9– 1   Do we not rather g· thanks that we
9– 9   though we g· no evidence of the sincerity of
11–28   nor can prayer alone g· us an understanding
16–24   Here let me g· what I understand to be the
17– 4   G· us this day our daily bread ;— Matt. 6 : 11.
17– 5   G· us grace for to-day;
a 24– 5   willingness to g· up human beliefs
30– 1   could g· a more spiritual idea of life than other
51–12   Jesus could g· his temporal life into his
52–13   foresight of the reception error would g· him.
55–27   "He shall g· you another— John 14 : 16.
m 61– 8   celestial condition would . . . g· higher aims
65– 4   and to g· to human life an inspiration
67–18   notion that animal natures can possibly g· force
sp 81–21   g· to the worms the body called man,
94–21   but one returned to g· God thanks,
99–27   g· everlasting place to the scientific
s 115– 9   difficulty is to g· the right impression,
138–24   more willing . . . than are sinners to g· up the
141–30   G· to it the place in our institutions of learning
143–29   g· to Mind the glory, honor, dominion, and
148–27   When physiology fails to g· health or life by
152– 7   that it may g· hope to the sick
156–16   unwilling to g· up the medicine
156–17   occurred to me to g· her unmedicated pellets
156–20   she would g· up her medicine for one day,
ph 169–27   the action of Truth, . . . can g· harmony.
191– 1   The brain can g· no idea of God's man.
191– 4   As mortals g· up the delusion that
192–21   senses must g· up their false testimony.
f 203–31   does not kill a man in order to g· him eternal
214–25   would spread their table . . . and g· thanks.
216–30   G· up your material belief of mind in matter,
219– 8   No more can we say . . . muscles g· strength,
219– 9   No more can we say . . . nerves g· pain or
223–17   and try to "g· it pause."
249– 2   g· up imperfect models and illusive ideals ;
253– 4   saith : . . . I g· immortality to man,
253– 6   saith : . . . I g· life, without beginning
253– 7   saith : . . . I am supreme and g· all,
c 260– 7   conceptions of mortal, erring thought must g·way
b 268– 5   things which g· impulse to inquiry.
272–17   "G· not that which is holy— Matt. 7 : 6.
283– 2   they g· up the belief that there is
284–17   Can the . . . g· correct testimony
313– 2   to g· the full and proper translation of
330– 1   as mortals g· up error for Truth
o 353–19   We must g· up the spectral at all points.
354–13   opponents of C. S. neither g· nor offer any

give
o 360– 8   replies : . . . mine g· me such personal pleasure,
361–21   to g· a clearer and fuller expression
p 396–23   G· them divine and wholesome understanding,
397–28   G· up the belief that mind is,
410– 1   If here we g· no heed to C. S.,
417– 3   G· sick people credit for sometimes knowing
417–31   G· your patients an underlying understanding
438– 5   Behold, I g· unto you power— Luke 10 : 19.
440– 9   were influenced to g· a verdict
441– 8   to g· heavy bonds for good behavior.
442–28   to g· you the kingdom." — Luke 12 : 32.
t 443– *   G· instruction to a wise man,— Prov. 9 : 9.
443–18   g· up such cases, and leave invalids free to
453–26   nor g· names to diseases,
454–20   Right motives g· pinions to thought,
464–17   would g· him a hypodermic injection,
r 489–27   no organic construction can g· it hearing
g 510– 7   to g· light upon the earth :— Gen. 1 : 15.
511– 8   to g· light upon the earth,— Gen. 1 : 17.
524–28   Could Spirit . . . g· matter ability to sin and
525–25   if we g· the same heed to the history of
536–27   They g· up their belief in perishable life
539– 6   as if . . . matter can both g· and take away.
ap 568–24   For victory over a single sin, we g· thanks
570–16   G· them a cup of cold water
570–24   Those ready for the blessing . . . will g· thanks.
gl 596–15   illuminations of Science g· us a sense of the
598–16   for never did he g· up Spirit, or Soul.
(see also **place**)

given
pref x–13   bluntly and honestly g· the text of Truth.
xii–16   next two years of her life should be g· to
pr 9–11   If selfishness has g· place to kindness,
a 49–27   to whom he had g· the highest proofs
50–20   If his full recognition . . . had for a moment g· way
m 56– *   nor are g· in marriage,— Matt. 22 : 30.
67– 2   The cup our Father hath g·, shall we not drink
69–11   or to be "g· in marriage" — Matt. 22 : 30.
69–27   and are g· in marriage :— Luke 20 : 34.
69–29   nor are g· in marriage." — Luke 20 : 35.
sp 98– 7   no other sign shall be g·.
s 107–13   fresh pinions are g· to faith
108– 4   the grace of God g· unto me by the— Eph. 3 : 7.
118–26   definitions of material law, as g·
133–31   Jewish conception of God, . . . has not quite g· place
137–12   rejection of the answer already g·
156– 5   case of dropsy, g· up by the faculty,
ph 175– 5   and less thought is g· to sanitary subjects,
179–32   Descriptions of disease g· by physicians
f 204–23   theories have g· sinners the notion that
b 313–17   the cause g· for the exaltation of Jesus,
328–28   Had it been g· only to his immediate disciples,
o 341–16   demonstrated according to a divine g· rule,
360–22   as g· in the excellent translation of
361–30   hence the many readings g· the Scriptures,
p 382– 5   If half the attention g· to hygiene were g· to
389– 3   it will be g· in behalf of the control of Mind
428–28   more apparent, as material beliefs are g· up
433–15   The case is g· to the jury.
g 502–13   as g· in the first chapter of Genesis.
518– 5   Behold, I have g· you— Gen. 1 : 29.
518–11   I have g· every green herb— Gen. 1 : 30.
534–30   The spiritual idea has g· the understanding
538–26   This account is g·, ... of mortal man,
545–11   Man, . . . was g· dominion over the whole
547– 8   so ascertain if the author has g· you the
ap 571–14   and yet have g· no warning.

Giver
s 112–19   like the great G·, are "the same— Heb. 13 : 8.

gives
pref viii– 7   g· sweet concord to sound.
xi–13   as necessarily as darkness g· place to light
pr 6– 6   talents He g· we must improve.
7– 8   g· momentary solemnity and elevation to
7–12   g· occasion for reaction unfavorable to
a 33–22   It g· all for Christ, or Truth.
m 58– 3   Unity of spirit g· new pinions to joy,
sp 80–14   It is mysticism which g· spiritualism its force.
83–19   belittles omnipotent wisdom, and g· to matter
s 128–10   C. S. . . . . g· them acuteness and
ph 168– 5   g· preponderance to the opposite.
176–14   human mind g· place to the divine Mind,
183–23   Obedience to Truth g· man power and strength.
183–27   the law which g· sight to the blind,
187– 7   material sense . . . g· them material names,
188–31   Astronomy g· the desired information
192–23   g· you the only power obtainable.
195– 8   All that g· pleasure to our educated senses
f 202–22   God g· man dominion over all the earth.
217–19   When mentality g· rest to the body,
246–11   robs youth and g· ugliness to age.
b 285–21   the better understanding that Science g·

gives

b 286– 7 understanding of Truth g· full faith in Truth,
307–26 and g· man dominion over all things.
316–22 g· man dominion over all the earth.
320–26 g· a profound idea of the divine power
323–25 true idea of God g· the true understanding
339–23 until the finite g· place to the infinite,
p 383–15 To the mind equally gross, dirt g· no uneasiness.
387–30 g· man faith and understanding
420–26 divine Love g· them all power over
430– 8 When man g· up his belief in death,
442–12 Christ, Truth, g· mortals temporary food
r 467–26 Spirit g· the true mental idea.
482– 1 g· the exact meaning in a majority of cases.
g 509–15 This text g· the idea of the rarefaction of
509–18 understanding g· gleams of the infinite only,
516–16 The great rock g· shadow and shelter.
518–13 God g· the lesser idea of Himself
522–12 This second record unmistakably g· the
528–24 Adam— alias error— g· them names.
gl 586– 7 that which g· action to thought.

giveth

g 518–19 Love g· to the least spiritual idea.

giving

pr 5–18 g· us strength according to our day.
a 19– 7 reconciling man to God by g· man
25–23 g· the requisite proofs of their own piety.
36–27 g· us only toil, sacrifice, cross-bearing,
m 64 15 g· the ready aid her sympathy and
64–20 no more marrying nor g· in marriage,
sp 79–31 G· does not impoverish us in the service
80– 2 strength is not lessened by g· utterance
s 112–28 without g· that author proper credit,
128–17 g· mortals access to broader and higher
ph 196–32 It does this by g· names to diseases
198–18 Again, g· another direction to faith,
f 206–19 g· the mother her child
210–15 g· a better understanding of Soul
221–24 "g· God thanks ;"— see Eph. 5 : 20.
234– 7 and g· living waters to the thirsty.
c 266– 4 g· place to man's higher individuality
b 299–15 By g· earnest heed to these spiritual guides
p 365–30 unchristian practitioner is not g·
366– 8 debars him from g· drink to the thirsty
396–29 never g· the body life and sensation.
400–21 g· no heed to the body,
407–12 g· strength to the weakness of mortal mind,
413–24 G· drugs to infants,
422–16 g· more spirituality to consciousness
424–19 either by g· antagonistic advice or
436–11 G· a cup of cold water in Christ's name,
t 457– 3 borrowed from this book without g· it credit,
r 470–15 seem to be real by g· reality to the unreal.
g 505 24 g· the spiritual proof of the universe
510–17 g· existence and intelligence to the universe.
527–29 and is man g· up his dignity?
530–18 error . . . g· the lie to divine Science
538–11 The sun, g· light and heat to the earth,
gl 579– 6 Bible terms, g· their spiritual sense,

glad

sp 75–32 g· welcome of those who have gone before.
s 121–11 bird and blossom were g·

gladden

s 121–13 goodness and beauty to g· the heart ;

gladdens

m 67–16 or sunshine g· the troubled sea.

gladly

a 37–19 would g· have turned his sacred career into
s 151–16 from which multitudes would g· escape.

gladness

b 313– 8 the oil of g· above thy fellows.— Heb. 1 : 9.
324– 2 G· to leave the false landmarks
p 367–14 the oil of g· and the perfume of gratitude,

glances

f 247–25 Love . . . g· in the warm sunbeam,
g 516–17 The sunlight . . . g· into the prison-cell,

glancing

f 220–20 a kitten g· into the mirror at itself

gland

f 211–16 the effect seen in the lachrymal g·?

glandular

ph 175–14 g· inflammation, sneezing, and nasal pangs.

glass

s 126– 7 even as man sees his reflection in a g·.
b 295–18 The light and the g· never mingle,
295–18 the g· is less opaque than the walls.

gleam

r 471–25 until she caught the first g· of
gl 582–11 a g· of the infinite idea of the

gleams

s 112–11 opinions may have occasional g· of divinity,
144–10 and afford faint g· of God, or Truth.
g 509–18 understanding gives g· of the infinite only,
538– 8 the sword of Truth g· afar

glean

b 323– 2 they will not be able to g· from C. S. the

glides

f 240–19 towards good or evil as time g· on.
g 516–18 The sunlight . . . g· into the sick-chamber,

glimpses

f 205–17 we can catch clear g· of God only as
b 333–24 caught glorious g· of the Messiah,
r 477–27 Indians caught some g· of the underlying

glints

g 516–17 The sunlight g· from the church-dome,

glistering

c 267–26 "white and g·," like the raiment— Luke 9 : 29.

gloaming

p 371–18 illusive sufferings which throng the g·.

gloat

a 36–25 g· over their offences to the last

globe

a 52–17 the best man that ever trod the g·.
s 120–31 When Columbus gave freer breath to the g·,
b 313–24 the most scientific man that ever trod the g·.
t 459–31 than any other healer on the g·.

globe's

ap 559–10 to the g· remotest bound.

globules

s 156–22 she could get along two days without g· ;

gloom

a 34–32 His g· had passed into glory,
47–31 During his night of g· and glory
ph 174–14 are our guardians in the g·.
f 248– 8 instead of lapsing into darkness or g·.

gloomy

a 45– 3 stepped forth from his g· resting-place,

glories

f 246–16 with bright and imperishable g·.
c 258– 2 the g· of limitless, incorporeal Life and Love.
264–30 all the g· of earth and heaven and man.

glorification

a 43–15 to the g· of the man

glorified

a 45–30 and so g· the supremacy of Mind
47– 5 After gaining the true idea of their g· Master,
54– 6 the harmony his g· example introduced.
54–29 If that Godlike and g· man were
s 118–12 eternally g· in man's spiritual freedom.
ph 200–29 Jesus Christ, and him g·.
b 291–11 not fancy that . . . will awaken them to g· being
299–10 they point upward to a new and g· trust,
g 516–22 forever reflect, in g· quality,

glorious

a 29–15 g· perception that God is the only author
32–32 in the twilight of a g· career
s 110–10 brought to light another g· proposition,
ph 176–10 seen in its g· effects upon the body.
f 202–13 For this g· result C. S. lights the torch
227–24 "g· liberty of the children of— Rom. 8 : 21.
240– 5 festive flowers, and g· heavens,
248– 1 g· freedom of spiritual harmony.
c 264– 5 must finally give place to the g· forms
b 288–27 Science reveals the g· possibilities of
308–27 did not loosen his hold upon this g· light until
333–24 caught g· glimpses of the Messiah,
o 359–31 spiritual ideals, indestructible and g·.
p 382–26 but for the g· Principle you teach,
r 473–32 his teachings and their g· proofs,
474–14 until the g· Principle of these marvels is gained.
g 521– 7 We leave this brief, g· history of
529– 9 usher in Science and the g· fact of creation,
545–27 so g· in its spiritual signification.
ap 568– 7 warfare in Science, and the g· results

glory

bliss and
ap 574–15 the spiritual outpouring of bliss and g·,
crowned with the
a 45– 4 crowned with the g· of a sublime success,
divine
b 323–12 is winged to reach the divine g·.
ap 565– 5 loathing the brightness of divine g·.
entire
c 262– 7 but it ascribes to Him the entire g·.
gates of
ap 571–29 he has opened wide the gates of g·,
gloom and
a 47–31 During his night of gloom and g·

glory
God's
b 313–11 "the brightness of His [God's] g·,— *Heb.* 1 : 3.
great
a 33–15 With the great g· of an everlasting victory
imperishable
f 253– 3 the perfection of being, imperishable g·,
His
b 313–21 being a brightness from His g·,— *see Heb.* 1 : 3.
light and
ap 575–10 represents the light and g· of divine Science.
577–25 Its gates open towards light and g·
living
a 39–17 was not the threshold . . . into living g·.
noontide
p 367–23 but radiate and glow into noontide g·.
of eternal life
a 54–26 and to share the g· of eternal life.
of eternity
g 502–17 illuminating time with the g· of eternity.
of infinite Love
g 520– 4 majesty, and g· of infinite Love fill all space.
of Mind
f 209–14 sense of Mind-power enhances the g· of Mind.
throne of
a 26– 4 his loving pathway up to the throne of g·,
type of the
gl 585–18 a type of the g· which is to come;
wonder and
g 501–11 that amplification of wonder and g·
wondrous
a 42–22 the wondrous g· which God bestowed on

pr 17–13 and the power, and the g·, forever.— *Matt.* 6 : 13.
a 35– 1 His gloom had passed into g·,
45–16 G· be to God, and peace to the
s 143–30 the g·, honor, dominion, and power
f 247–14 Immortality, . . . has a g· of its own,
b 325–12 [be manifested] with him in g·."— *Col.* 3 : 4.
ap 566– 8 the g· prepared for them who love God.

glow
sp 89–11 She says, "I am incapable of words that g·,
b 298– 3 and g· full-orbed in spiritual understanding.
329– 3 will g· in all the grandeur of universal goodness.
p 367–23 but radiate and g· into noontide glory.
g 511–17 The changing g· and full effulgence of

glowing
g 522–21 God's g· denunciations of man when not

glutton
a 28–20 saying: He is a g·
52–31 the hypocrite, called Jesus a g· and a

gluttony
f 221–32 g· is a sensual illusion,

gnarled
sp 78– 1 the g· oak, the ferocious beast,

gnats
s 140–14 straining out g· and swallowing camels.
f 202– 2 straining out g· and swallowing camels.
p 366–20 Such so-called Scientists will strain out g·,

go
pr 6–18 farther we cannot g·.
11– 4 "G·, and sin no more."— *John* 8 : 11.
11–10 before mortals can "g· up higher."— *Luke* 14 : 10.
12–25 Changes in belief may g· on indefinitely,
13– 5 we often g· beyond our convictions,
14–21 because I g· unto my Father,"— *John* 14 : 12.
15–19 and g· forth with honest hearts
a 20– 7 publicans and the harlots g·— *Matt.* 21 : 31.
22–16 g· not back to error,
25–29 We must g· and do likewise,
27– 3 "G· your way, and tell John— *Luke* 7 : 22.
37–29 "G· ye into all the world,— *Mark* 16 : 15.
40– 6 "G· thy way for this time;— *Acts* 24 : 25.
sp 75–13 but I g·, that I may awake him— *John* 11 : 11.
79– 9 Science must g· over the whole ground,
an 105–32 to g· in healing from the use of inanimate drugs
s 125–21 The seasons will come and g·
132– 4 "G· and show John again those— *Matt.* 11 : 4.
138–27 "G· ye into all the world,— *Mark* 16 : 15.
142–17 causes the left to let g· its grasp on the
ph 180–19 even before they g· to work to eradicate
f 202– 9 they would not g· on from bad to worse,
214–13 They g· out as they came in,
235– 1 cannot g· forth, like wandering pollen,
240–16 revolutions of the universe of Mind g· on
241–31 to g· through the eye of a needle,"— *Matt.* 19 : 24.
c 261–13 to g· upon the stage and sustain his
b 296–15 they must g· out under the blaze of Truth,
308–24 "Let me g·, for the day breaketh;"— *Gen.* 32 : 26.
309–17 If these children should g· astray,
312–14 People g· into ecstasies over the sense of a
o 342–10 "G· ye into all the world,— *Mark* 16 : 15.
p 406–23 and this growth will g· on until

go
p 408–16 Can drugs g· of their own accord to the brain
420– 1 nor g· from one part to another,
422–18 These changes which g· on in mortal mind
t 449– 9 to g· through the eye of a— *Matt.* 19 : 24.
451–14 many there be which g· in— *Matt.* 7 : 13.
r 478–11 ever seen to g· into the house
g 519–14 the divine power and presence which g· with it,
535–13 belief . . . must g· down before C. S.
547–22 or g· down into dust and nothingness.
556–11 only to g· out at last forever;
ap 559–17 "G· and take the little book.— *Rev.* 10 : 8.

goal
m 61–32 If the . . . is requisite to reach this g·,
f 233–14 until the g· of goodness is . . won.
b 324–17 certainly before we can reach the g· of Spirit,
o 359–19 but when shall we arrive at the g· which
p 426– 6 when she has the high g· always before her
ap 560–15 g· is never reached while we hate our

goblet
s 153– 8 one drop of that attenuation in a g· of water,

God (*see also* **God's**)
acceptable unto
a 34– 4 "holy, acceptable unto G·,"— *Rom.* 12 : 1.
b 325–23 holy, acceptable unto G·,— *Rom.* 12 : 1.
account with
p 405–17 until you have balanced your account with G·.
advising
pr 3– 3 not sufficient to warrant him in advising G·.
affluence of our
s 140–12 but rejoicing in the affluence of our G·.
agent of
s 146–17 his Science, the curative agent of G·, is silenced.
alienate him from
b 304– 1 nothing could alienate him from G·,
all-inclusive
a 52–21 the mighty actuality of all-inclusive G·,
allness of
t 450–22 understanding . . . the allness of G·,
ap 563–18 the nothingness of evil and the allness of G·.
alone with
a 49–16 met his earthly fate alone with G·.
p 424–26 well to be alone with G· and the sick when
and His Christ
ap 561–15 G· and His Christ, bringing harmony to earth.
and His creation
r 472–24 All reality is in G· and His creation,
g 554–20 opposite of G· and His creation
gl 579–16 the opposite of good,— of G· and His creation;
and His idea
sp 71– 2 nothing is Spirit,— but G· and His idea.
an 103–16 good is the infinite G· and His idea,
s 116– 8 so that G· and His idea may be to us
ph 167–25 but one way— namely, G· and His idea
p 372– 9 all is divine Mind, or G· and His idea,
r 495–15 cling steadfastly to G· and His idea.
and His reflection
b 314– 7 inseparable as G· and His reflection
and His thoughts
s 114–11 noumenon and phenomena, G· and His thoughts.
and mammon
o 346–31 We cannot serve both G· and mammon
t 462–10 dividing his interests between G· and mammon
and man
s 111– 7 Science of G· and man is no more supernatural
f 202– 3 unity which exists between G· and man
205– 6 their false sense concerning G· and man.
232– 3 Many theories relative to G· and man
c 258– 6 material belief in a physical G· and man.
264–13 gain more correct views of G· and man,
b 303–14 or by both G· and man,
333– 1 agreement, between G· and man in His image.
336–28 G· and man are not the same,
336–30 G· and man coexist and are eternal.
338– 3 the only living and true G· and man
o 361–17 even so G· and man, Father and son,
t 454–17 Love for G· and man is the true incentive
461–14 the eternal interpretation of G· and man.
r 470–19 standard of perfection was originally G· and man.
470–32 relations of G· and man, . . . are indestructible
471–16 evidence that G· and man coexist
g 502–26 the eternal verity and unity of G· and man,
545–20 in its false view of G· and man,
546–15 It supposes G· and man to be
ap 561–24 G· and man as the divine Principle and
577– 2 the incorporeal sense of G· and man
gl 581–11 G· and man coexistent and eternal;
589–24 spiritual understanding of G· and man
and men
a 30–10 mediator, or *way-shower*, between G· and men.
b 332–17 mediator between G· and men,— *I Tim.* 2 : 5.
and Satan
p 389–25 pain and pleasure, good and evil, G· and Satan.
and Soul
b 335–16 G· and Soul are one,

God

and the real man
  r 476– 4   G· and the real man are inseparable
angels of
  m 56– *   *as the angels of G· in heaven.— Matt.* 22 : 30.
anthropomorphic
  f 224–14   were ready to hail an anthropomorphic G·,
  c 257–18   would say that an anthropomorphic G·,
  b 317– 5   and proclaimed an anthropomorphic G·.
  o 351–19   a personal devil and an anthropomorphic G·
  g 517– 5   such a phrase as "an anthropomorphic G·,"
apart from
  sp 91–26   belief . . . something apart from G·.
  f 228–25   There is no power apart from G·.
  b 283– 3   belief . . . true existence apart from G·.
applied to
  s 116–28   If the term personality, as applied to G·, means
approval of
  a 42–12   endorsed pre-eminently by the approval of G·,
at-one-ment with
  a 19–22   in the atonement, — in the *at-one-ment* with G·,
attraction of
  an 102–11   or the attraction of G·, divine Mind.
attribute of
  b 319–30   to name Love as merely an attribute of G· ;
attributes of
  r 465–14   attributes of G· are justice, mercy, wisdom,
avail themselves of
  pr 13– 1   *all* may avail themselves of G·
becomes
  g 524–10   G· becomes "a man of war," — *Exod.* 15 : 3.
before
  m 64– 5   before G· and the Father, — *Jas.* 1 : 27.
before our
  ap 568–17   before our G· day and night. — *Rev.* 12 : 10.
behests of
  r 495–29   and follow the behests of G·,
belief in
  pr 2–20   belief in G· as humanly circumscribed,
  a 34–22   from spiritual dulness and blind belief in G·
beliefs about
  s 132–10   retained their materialistic beliefs about G·.
belief that
  f 204–10   belief that G· lives in matter is pantheistic.
  o 357–10   relinquish the belief that G· makes sickness,
believe in
  f 218–19   If you do believe in G·,
believed in
  a 53–14   Mortals believed in G· as humanly mighty,
belong to
  b 275–15   cause, and effect belong to G·.
belongs to
  r 490–11   since all power belongs to G·, good.
bestowed
  a 42–22   glory which G· bestowed on His anointed,
bestows
  b 275–19   no good is, but the good G· bestows.
  g 555–26   when we admit . . . that G· bestows the power to
  ap 573– 8   that consciousness which G· bestows,
blending with
  b 316–19   illustrates that blending with G·,
blessed them
  g 512–17   And G· blessed them, saying, — *Gen.* 1 : 22.
  517–25   And G· blessed them, — *Gen.* 1 : 28.
born of
  t 463–18   born of the Spirit, born of G·,
bosom of
  a 29–27   dwelt forever an idea in the bosom of G·,
brings
  gl 596– 4   C. S. brings G· much nearer to man,
called
  pref xi–22   When G· called the author to proclaim His
  f 204–13   good, an intelligence or Mind called G·.
  b 281–14   The one Ego, the one Mind or Spirit called G·,
  331–27   constitute the triune Person called G·,
  g 504– 3   And G· called the light Day, — *Gen.* 1 : 5.
  506– 8   And G· called the firmament — *Gen.* 1 : 8.
  506–22   G· called the dry land Earth ; — *Gen.* 1 : 10.
  535–29   G· called the dry land Earth ; — *Gen.* 1 : 10.
  gl 586–10   the divine Principle, commonly called G·.
can never destroy
  p 425–17   can never destroy G·, who is man's Life.
cannot become
  g 550– 7   G· cannot become finite, and be limited
cannot be tempted
  g 527–12   "G· cannot be tempted with evil, — *Jas.* 1 : 13.
cannot mistake
  t 455–20   but G· cannot mistake.
cannot please
  g 534–21   in the flesh cannot please G·. — *Rom.* 8 : 8.
caught up unto
  ap 565– 5   child was caught up unto G·, — *Rev.* 12 : 5.
  565–27   and to be caught up unto G·,
certainly revealed
  r 483–20   to Christ Jesus, G· certainly revealed the spirit

God

charges
  g 533–15   Adam, . . . charges G· and woman with
child of
  b 289– 1   man's real existence as a child of G·
  ap 573–18   regarded . . . as the blessed child of G·.
children of
  (*see* children)
Christian Science
  s 140–25   The C. S. G· is universal, eternal,
city of our
  ap 558– *   *to be praised in the city of our G·, — Psal.* 48 : 1.
  577–20   This city of our G· has no need of sun or
claims
  o 344– 1   claims G· as the only absolute Life and Soul,
  g 512–30   and claims G· as their author ;
claims of
  a 23–20   and establishes the claims of G·.
claim that
  gl 594– 9   first audible claim that G· was not omnipotent
coexistent with
  m 69– 1   not of the earth earthly but coexistent with G·,
  r 478– 2   for man is coexistent with G·.
coexists with
  c 266–32   but he coexists with G· and the universe.
coexist with
  c 267–12   man and the spiritual universe coexist with G·.
combines all-power
  r 466– 3   Hence G· combines all-power or potency,
comes from
  sp 84–28   All we correctly know of Spirit comes from G·,
  r 479– 6   if aught comes from G·, it cannot be mortal
  ap 558– 9   This angel or message which comes from G·,
communion with
  a 30– 1   Mary's self-conscious communion with G·.
conception of
  s 133–29   The Jewish conception of G·, as Yawah,
  ph 185–19   rests on the conception of G· as the only Life,
  c 258– 2   mortal, corporeal, or finite conception of G·
confides all to
  a 23–31   includes. . . .understanding and confides all to G·.
connection with his
  b 202–30   real man's indissoluble connection with his G·,
contrary to
  b 273– 2   Matter and its claims . . . are contrary to G·
controls man
  sp 73–10   G· controls man, and
created
  s 140–29   In the beginning G· created man
  b 294–27   G· created man.
  r 479–18   "In the beginning G· created the — *Gen.* 1 : 1.
  g 502–22   In the beginning G· created the— *Gen.* 1 : 1.
  512– 4   And G· created great whales, — *Gen.* 1 : 21.
  516–24   So G· created man in His own — *Gen.* 1 : 27.
  543–24   Did man, whom G· created with a word,
created all
  f 205–12   G· created all through Mind,
created by
  g 507–23   Mind and the universe created by G·.
  514–20   individuality created by G· is not carnivorous,
  545–10   Man, created by G·, was given dominion
creates
  m 69–22   If the father replies, "G· creates man through
  b 295– 5   G· creates and governs the universe,
  g 503–24   G· creates neither erring thought, mortal life,
  513–26   G· creates all forms of reality.
  520–23   declaration that G· creates all through Mind,
  538–19   G· creates the heavens, earth, and man.
creations of
  c 266– 1   where the creations of G· are good,
daughters of
  g 503– 5   highest ideas are the sons and daughters of G·.
  515–22   the sons and daughters of G·.
declare that
  b 307– 9   It says : . . . I declare that G· makes evil minds
  318– 6   Scriptures declare that G· made all,
  331–14   Scriptures also declare that G· is Spirit.
  g 539–16   Scriptures declare that G· condemned this lie
demands
  f 254–20   This task G· demands us to accept lovingly
demands of
  s 130– 1   the demands of G· must be met.
  ph 182– 5   The demands of G· appeal to thought only ;
demonstrating
  a 29–23   demonstrating G· as the Father of men.
demonstration of
  b 270–18   nature of the teaching and demonstration of G·,
deny that
  o 357–16   to deny that G· made man evil
dependence on
  c 262– 2   does not lessen man's dependence on G·,
derived from
  sp 72–24   In Science, individual good derived from G·,
  g 539–12   nothing which he has not derived from G·.
design of
  b 271– 5   uniting all periods in the design of G·.

God

determines
g 508–13 *G·* determines the gender of His own ideas.
did not express
r 470–27 If . . . a moment when man did not express *G·*,
dishonor
f 228–27 to acknowledge any other power is to dishonor *G·*.
dishonorest thou
o 349– 6 dishonorest thou *G·* ?''— *Rom.* 2 : 23.
disobedience to
p 440–13 disobedience to *G·*, or an act of homicide.
distinct from
f 204–28 never . . . distinct from *G·*, the *all* Mind.
divided the light
g 503–27 *G·* divided the light from the— *Gen.* 1 : 4.
does not cause
f 206–30 *G·* does not cause man to sin, to be sick, or
does not employ
s 143– 5 It is plain that *G·* does not employ drugs
down from
ap 574–14 coming down from *G·*,— *Rev.* 21 : 2.
575– 9 ''down from *G·*, out of heaven,''— *Rev.* 21 : 2.
ended His work
g 519–22 *G·* ended His work which He— *Gen.* 2 : 2.
enmity against
s 131–10 carnal mind is enmity against *G·*.''— *Rom.* 8 : 7.
g 534–19 carnal mind is enmity against *G·* ;— *Rom.* 8 : 7.
entireness of
b 293–30 universal harmony, the entireness of *G·*,
equipollence of
s 110– 9 The equipollence of *G·* brought to light
equipped by
b 328–15 man's power, when he is equipped by *G·*,
erects
g 523–10 which *G·* erects between the true and false.
eternal
p 415– 4 Mind in every case is the eternal *G·*,
eternal as
g 554– 3 universe, inclusive of man, is as eternal as *G·*,
gl 594–11 claim that . . . was as real and eternal as *G·*,
eternal with
g 516–22 woman as coexistent and eternal with *G·*
even
a 20– 1 for there is one Life,— even *G·*, good.
f 216–32 and have but one Mind, even *G·* ;
r 470– 1 With one Father, even *G·*, the whole family of
g 544–17 All is under the control of the one Mind, even *G·*.
exclusively to
sp 93–25 and applies exclusively to *G·*.
executor for
a 30–17 Not so did Jesus, the new executor for *G·*,
exists
f 215– 6 but being cannot be lost while *G·* exists.
g 544–11 man exists because *G·* exists.
exponent of
a 49– 9 Had they forgotten the great exponent of *G·* ?
expresses
c 258–13 *G·* expresses in man the infinite idea
expressions of
g 518–22 All the varied expressions of *G·* reflect
faith in
pr 12– 8 through a blind faith in *G·*.
s 130–21 and to inculcate a grain of faith in *G·*,
f 226–31 but I pressed on through faith in *G·*,
p 368–17 more faith in *G·* than in man,
373– 4 then we must have more faith in *G·*
395–12 and faith in *G·* destroys all faith in sin
410–14 Every trial of our faith in *G·* makes us
426–27 with unflinching faith in *G·*,
fashions
g 516– 9 *G·* fashions all things, after His own
fatherhood of
ap 562– 4 the idea of the fatherhood of *G·*,
Father-Mother
pr 16–27 Our *Father-Mother G·*, all-harmonious,
g 516–23 the infinite Father-Mother *G·*.
fear
b 340– 7 Fear *G·*, and keep His— *Eccl.* 12 : 13.
filled with
r 469–24 where all space is filled with *G·*.
forms
g 509–16 *G·* forms and peoples the universe.
fully apprehend
f 231–28 impossible, when you fully apprehend *G·*
gives man
f 202–22 *G·* gives man dominion over all
gives the lesser
g 518–13 *G·* gives the lesser idea of Himself
gleams of
s 144–10 and afford faint gleams of *G·*, or Truth.
glimpses of
f 205–17 we can catch clear glimpses of *G·* only as
glory be to
a 45–16 Glory be to *G·*, and peace to the

God

governed by
a 42–27 in C. S. the true man is governed by *G·*
ph 180–25 When man is governed by *G·*,
f 215–12 Whatever is governed by *G·*, is never . . .
deprived
b 304–15 governed by *G·*, his perfect Principle
318–29 In Science man is governed by *G·*,
p 409–20 The animate should be governed by *G·*
r 495– 2 whenever man is governed by *G·*.
government of
c 258–29 under the government of *G·* in eternal Science,
p 405–20 demonstrates the government of *G·*,
governs all
an 102– 2 *G·* governs all that is real, harmonious, and
governs the universe
an 102–13 since *G·* governs the universe ;
grace of
s 108– 4 grace of *G·* given unto me by the— *Eph.* 3 : 7.
guest of
f 254–32 stranger, thou art the guest of *G·*.
had blessed
b 338–29 notwithstanding *G·* had blessed the earth
harmony and
b 340– 3 make life its own proof of harmony and *G·*.
harmony in
p 417– 2 peace, and harmony in *G·*,
harmony with
s 130–10 reality is in perfect harmony with *G·*,
131– 5 in order to be in harmony with *G·*,
has almighty power
f 202–27 We admit that *G·* has almighty power,
has appointed
ap 560–17 false estimate of anyone whom *G·* has appointed
has built
f 226–14 *G·* has built a higher platform of human rights,
has countless ideas
g 517–18 *G·* has countless ideas, and they all have
has created
o 344– 7 Scriptures say that *G·* has created man in His
has endowed man
an 106– 7 *G·* has endowed man with inalienable rights,
has sentenced
b 322–14 *G·* has sentenced sin to suffer.
has set His signet
r 472– 6 *G·* has set His signet upon Science,
hath said
g 529–19 *G·* hath said, Ye shall not eat of it,— *Gen.* 3 : 3.
have mercy
p 433–25 ''May *G·* have mercy on your soul,'' is the
heals the sick
ap 570–26 When *G·* heals the sick or the sinning,
her fathers'
ap 566–17 Her fathers' *G·* before her moved,
he served
a 52– 4 He served *G·* ; they served mammon.
highway of our
m 61–11 that the highway of our *G·* may be prepared
honor
r 483–27 And C. S. does honor *G·*
honors
r 483–26 if any system honors *G·*, it ought to receive aid,
hope thou in
p 362– * *Hope thou in G·; for I shall yet— Psal.* 42 : 11.
ideal of
a 25–16 Jesus presented the ideal of *G·* better than
o 361– 5 Christ, . . . is the ideal of *G·* now and forever,
idea of
a 29–17 The Virgin-mother conceived this idea of *G·*,
43–15 glorification of the man and of the true idea of *G·*,
54–10 plant themselves in Christ, the true idea of *G·*.
s 132–25 this rejection . . . of the true idea of *G·*,
ph 200–12 man is the idea of *G·*, not formed materially
c 258–12 this reflection is the true idea of *G·*.
262–14 above the mortal to the immortal idea of *G·*.
b 289– 8 A wicked mortal is not the idea of *G·*.
303–29 Spiritual man is the image or idea of *G·*,
316–12 Jesus represented Christ, the true idea of *G·*.
316–24 The spiritual idea of *G·*, as presented by Jesus,
323–24 true idea of *G·* gives the true understanding
324– 9 are not gaining the true idea of *G·* ;
332–20 Christ is the divine idea of *G·*
o 345–32 not the purpose of C.S. to ''educate the idea of *G·*,
347–15 as the spiritual or true idea of *G·*,
r 473–14 has presented Christ, the true idea of *G·*,
475–15 He is the compound idea of *G·*,
476–10 and man is the idea of *G·*
477–12 C. S. reveals man as the idea of *G·*,
482–21 the divine idea of *G·* outside the flesh.
g 503–20 divine Mind presents the idea of *G·* :
524– 9 true idea of *G·* seems almost lost.
ap 561–23 generic man, the spiritual idea of *G·* ;
577–15 the Christ, the spiritual idea of *G·* ;
gl 582–15 conceiving man in the idea of *G·* ;
585–17 EUPHRATES . . . the true idea of *G·* ;

God

ideas of
 f 230–11 It would be contrary to our highest ideas of G·
 g 510– 3 seek to apprehend the spiritual ideas of G·,
 519– 9 ideas of G· in universal being are complete
 548–17 true ideas of G·, the spiritual sense of being.
 gl 583– 8 some of the ideas of G· beheld as men,
illustrated
 g 501–12 and which G· illustrated by light and harmony,
image of
 m 67– 1 may be graven with the image of G·.
 ph 173–24 image of G·, the real immortal man.
 c 259– 6 In divine Science, man is the true image of G·.
 259–17 never beheld in man the reflex image of G·.
 b 285–12 claim that a mortal is the true image of G·
 289– 6 what constitutes man as the image of G·.
 300– 8 who cannot be the image of G·.
 318–17 so far as he is discordant, he is not the image of G·.
 p 437– 4 Man was made in the image of G·,
 g 502–10 the history of the untrue image of G·,
 516–25 in the image of G· created He him ;— *Gen.* 1 : 27.
imparts
 g 515–23 All that G· imparts moves in accord
imply that
 b 331–11 Scriptures imply that G· is All-in-all.
 g 537–30 would imply that G· withheld from man
impute to
 g 554–17 to impute to G· the creation of whatever is sinful
infinite
 an 103–16 The maximum of good is the infinite G·
 c 258– 1 the image and likeness of the infinite G·.
 b 277–12 and cannot be the outcome of an infinite G·,
 287–11 and the *infinite* G· can have no unlikeness.
 335–13 invisible and indivisible infinite G·.
 340–23 One infinite G·, good, unifies men and nations ;
 p 381–19 and have our being in the infinite G·,
 r 497– 6 one supreme and infinite G·.
inspired by
 a 51–3 He was inspired by G·, by Truth and Love,
intelligence or
 b 307– 8 declares . . . more than one intelligence or G·.
interpret
 s 127–27 and is alone able to interpret G· aright.
interprets
 r 471–26 that which interprets G· as above mortal sense.
 ap 569– 1 clearly interprets G· as divine Principle,
in the hands of
 g 521– 9 in the hands of G·, not of man,
invisible
 a 55– 3 a deadened sense of the invisible G·,
 b 305– 8 the central light of being, the invisible G·.
 337–21 man, as the reflection of the invisible G·,
is able
 o 359–24 "G· is able to raise you up from sickness ;"
is All
 b 339– 7 Since G· is All, there is no room for
 p 366–29 knowing, . . . that Life is God and G· is All,
 g 532–24 G· is All and He is Mind
is all
 s 116–18 They never . . . insist upon the fact that G· is all,
 b 302– 9 when G· is all and eternally his.
is All-in-all
 s 113–16 G· is All-in-all.
 b 331–11 The Scriptures imply that G· is All-in-all.
 p 425–20 since Spirit, G·, is All-in-all.
 r 468–11 for G· is All-in-all.
 g 503–13 Word of God, saith . . . "G· is All-in-all,"
is come
 o 361– 8 the Christian's doctrine that G· is come
is divine Life
 b 331– 1 G· is divine Life,
is everywhere
 r 473– 8 G· is everywhere, and nothing apart from
is Father
 c 267– 8 It is generally conceded that G· is Father,
is good
 pr 3–18 G· is good, omnipotent, omnipresent,
 a 19–28 although G· is good.
 s 113–17 G· is good. Good is Mind.
 f 243–32 G· is good and the fount of all being,
 b 328– 5 G· is good and the only real Life.
 p 399– 1 G· is good, and therefore good is
is his Father
 m 63–10 G· is his Father, and Life is the law of his being.
is incorporeal
 s 116–22 Mortals are corporeal, but G· is incorporeal.
 r 465– 9 G· is incorporeal, divine, supreme,
is individual
 b 331–18 G· is individual, incorporeal.
 336–32 G· is individual and personal in a scientific
is indivisible
 b 336–19 G· is indivisible. A portion of God could not
is infinite
 pr 17–14 For G· is infinite, all-power,
 f 223– 7 G· is infinite omnipresent Spirit.

God

is infinite
 b 278–10 Spirit, G·, is infinite, all.
 312–21 G· is infinite Love, which must be unlimited.
 330–11 G· is infinite, the only Life, substance,
 r 469–22 when we admit that, although G· is infinite,
 471–18 G· is infinite, therefore ever present,
 492–25 G· *is infinite ; hence all is Mind.*
is intelligence
 pr 2–23 G· is intelligence. Can we inform the infinite
is just
 t 445–31 when I remember that G· is just,"
is Love
 pr 2–23 G· is Love. Can we ask Him to be more?
 6–17 "G· is Love."— *I John* 4 : 8.
 a 42– 1 Jesus' life proved, . . . that G· is Love,
 b 275– 8 G· is Love, and therefore He is divine
 302–25 G· is Love. He is therefore the divine
 312–16 G· *is* Love, and without Love, God, immortality
 cannot
 ap 569–14 in a sweet and certain sense that G· is Love.
is love
 b 320– 1 "G· is love."— *1 John* 4 : 8.
is Mind
 f 239–30 Mind sends forth perfection, for G· is Mind.
 b 311– 4 G· is Mind : all that Mind, God, is, or
 330–22 Mind is not both good and bad, for G· is Mind ;
 r 492–25 G· *is Mind, and God is infinite;*
is more
 p 425–21 G· is more to a man than his belief,
is natural good
 s 119–21 G· is natural good, and is represented only by
is not corporeal
 s 116–21 G· is not *corporeal*, but *incorporeal*,
is not influenced
 pr 7–23 G· is not influenced by man.
is not man
 r 480–19 Man is not God, and G· is not man.
is not moved
 pr 2– 8 G· is not moved by the breath of praise
is not separate
 pr 6– 5 G· is not separate from the wisdom He bestows.
is "of purer eyes
 f 243–22 G· is "of purer eyes than— *Hab.* 1 : 13.
 o 357– 4 G· is "of purer eyes than— *Hab.* 1 : 13.
is omnipotent
 pr 17– 2 G· *is omnipotent, supreme.*
 s 130–12 since you admit that G· is omnipotent ;
 p 394–28 Life is God, and that G· is omnipotent.
is One
 s 117– 3 whereas G· is One,— not one of a series, but
is one
 c 267– 5 G· is one. The allness of Deity is His oneness.
 gl 587–17 G· is one God, infinite and perfect,
is our Life
 s 107–17 in reality G· is our Life,
 p 388–24 self-evident, when we learn that G· is our Life.
is our refuge
 t 444–11 "G· is our refuge and strength,— *Psal.* 46 : 1.
is reflected
 g 524–23 yet G· is reflected in all His creation.
is revealed
 f 241–25 the Horeb height where G· is revealed ;
 b 300–31 G· is revealed only in that which
 g 511–12 G· is revealed as infinite light.
is seen
 b 300–29 G· is seen only in the spiritual universe
is Spirit
 s 117– 6 G· is Spirit ; therefore the language of
 f 207– 2 Because G· is Spirit, evil becomes
 b 331–14 Scriptures also declare that G· is Spirit,
 335– 2 There is no evil in Spirit, because G· is Spirit.
is substance
 b 301–17 G· is substance and man is the divine image
is the creator
 r 470–21 G· is the creator of man,
is the Father
 m 64–26 Until it is learned that G· is the Father of all,
is the infinite
 f 249–14 G· is the infinite, and infinity never began,
is the lawmaker
 p 381–15 G· is the lawmaker,
is the Life
 g 550– 5 G· is the Life, or intelligence, which forms
is the light
 ap 558–15 for G· "is the light thereof."— *Rev.* 21 : 23.
is the only Life
 b 289– 4 until he learns that G· is the only Life.
 324–14 the understanding that G· is the only Life.
 r 472– 1 Science teaches man that G· is the only Life,
is the only Mind
 b 308– 5 the lesson is learned that G· is the only Mind
 339–26 the great fact that G· is the only Mind ;
is the only power
 p 419–27 for G· is the only power.

God

is the only Spirit
sp 73–11 *G·* is the only Spirit.

is the power
a 27– 8 *G·* is the power in the Messianic work.

is the Principle
s 112–32 *G·* is the Principle of divine metaphysics.
r 476– 9 *G·* is the Principle of man,

is to be understood
r 472– 2 *G·* is to be understood, adored, and

is true
s 113–24 I find that *G·* is true,

is Truth
b 312–18 yet *G· is* Truth.

Jehovah
g 543–32 the Lord God [Jehovah *G·*] made — *Gen.* 2 : 4.

kingdom of
(*see* **kingdom**)

kingdom of our
ap 568–15 and the kingdom of our *G·*, — *Rev.* 12 : 10.

knowledge of
a 48–31 what the true knowledge of *G·* can do for man.
s 133–31 not quite given place to the true knowledge of *G·*,
g 540–21 a false sense which hath no knowledge of *G·*."
fr 600– * *increasing in the knowledge of G·.* — *Col.* 1 : 10.

known to
pr 15–26 hidden from the world, but known to *G·*.

knows our need
pr 13–15 *G·* knows our need before we tell Him

Lamb of
s 132–32 Jesus as "the Lamb of *G·* ;" — *John* 1 : 29.
ap 564–13 speaks of Jesus as the Lamb of *G·*
gl 590– 9 definition of

law of
(*see* **law**)

laws of
s 128– 5 refers only to the laws of *G·*
ph 168–17 all in consonance with the laws of *G·*,

leadeth us
pr 17–10 *And G· leadeth us not into temptation,*

leave the field to
p 419– 5 leave the field to *G·*, Life, Truth, and Love,

less than
f 203–18 to believe . . . in some power less than *G·*.
b 336–23 else God would . . . become less than *G·*.
g 543– 1 misconception of Life as something less than *G·*,

Life as
sp 79– 4 those who are ignorant of Life as *G·*.
b 310–27 and if Spirit should lose Life as *G·*,

life in
a 45–19 the revelation and demonstration of life in *G·*,
b 324–18 the goal of Spirit, or life in *G·*.

Life is
(*see* **Life**)

Life, or
f 249–11 Any other theory of Life, or *G·*, is delusive
b 283–14 They insist that Life, or *G·*, is
o 357–30 and, if so, can Life, or *G·*, dwell in evil
g 543–29 belief . . . would make Life, or *G·*, mortal.

Life which is
a 47– 3 faint conception of the Life which is *G·*.
ap 561–20 understanding the Life which is *G·*.

likeness of
sp 71–19 neither . . . is the image or likeness of *G·*,
81–17 Man in the likeness of *G·*
f 206–26 the spiritual image and likeness of *G·* ?
222–23 far from being the image and likeness of *G·*,
b 285– 9 not man, the image and likeness of *G·*,
287–20 not the image and likeness of *G·* ;"
292–11 sick, and dying mortal is not the likeness of *G·*,
299–15 individuality, image, or likeness of *G·*,
303–23 belief . . . material man is the likeness of *G·*
315–17 The likeness of *G·* we lose sight of through
p 414–27 man is the image and likeness of *G·*,
r 467–15 man is the likeness of *G·*, pure and eternal,
475– 9 man is made in the image and likeness of *G·*.
g 531–32 man . . . in the image and likeness of *G·*
548– 6 man in the image and likeness of *G·*,
gl 591– 6 the spiritual image and likeness of *G·* ;

likeness to
pr 12–15 man's likeness to *G·* and of man's unity
p 395– 5 man's immortality and eternal likeness to *G·*.

Lord our
c 256–12 the Lord our *G·* is one Lord." — *Deut.* 6 : 4.

love
pr 4–17 Simply asking that we may love *G·* will never
ph 167–19 you must love *G·* supremely.
b 326– 9 man cannot love *G·* supremely . . . while
340–10 love *G·* and keep His commandments :
t 444– 5 to them that love *G·*," — *Rom.* 8 : 28.
ap 566– 9 glory prepared for them who love *G·*.

love of
a 42– 4 gave no hint of the unchanging love of *G·*.
b 304–9 from the love of *G·*." — *Rom.* 8 : 39.

God

lovingly governs
p 412– 1 great fact that *G·* lovingly governs all,

made
f 231–20 because *G·* made you superior to it
g 505–13 And *G·* made the firmament, — *Gen.* 1 : 7.
510–13 And *G·* made two great lights ; — *Gen.* 1 : 16.
513–22 And *G·* made the beast of — *Gen.* 1 : 25.
525–20 Everything good or worthy, *G·* made.
526– 4 *G·* made "every plant — *Gen.* 2 : 5.

made all
f 229– 7 *G·* made all that was made,
b 318– 6 Scriptures declare that *G·* made all,

made Man
p 434–31 but *G·* made Man immortal

made man
ph 167–15 If *G·* made man both good and evil,
f 227–16 *G·* made man free.
g 516–28 *G·* made man in His own image,

maintained by
g 531–18 divine order still maintained by *G·*

maker is
p 428–14 "whose builder and maker is *G·*." — *Heb.* 11 : 10.

makes
g 532– 3 *G·* makes and governs all.

man and
c 258–24 gains the true conception of man and *G·*.
g 524–26 or is it a lie concerning man and *G·* ?

manifestation of
b 295–16 manifestation of *G·* through mortals is as
gl 583–10 Christ. The divine manifestation of *G·*,

man is not
f 250–12 Man is not *G·*, but like a ray of
r 480–19 Man is not *G·*, and God is not man.

man nor
g 533–30 "Neither man nor *G·* shall father my fault."

man of
b 314–10 Jews, who sought to kill this man of *G·*,

man-projected
s 140–23 tribal Jehovah was a man-projected *G·*,

man to
a 18–13 reconciles man to *G·*, not God to man ;
19– 2 Christ's purpose to reconcile man to *G·*,
19– 7 Jesus aided in reconciling man to *G·*
sp 94– 8 and of the relation of man to *G·*,
s 114–26 It shows the scientific relation of man to *G·*,

material view of
g 521–27 this material view of *G·* and the universe,

meaning of
c 261–23 you may learn the meaning of *G·*,

message from
b 332–10 the divine message from *G·* to men

Mind is
sp 91–31 nor the medium of evil, for Mind is *G·*.
b 275–22 that all is Mind, and that Mind is *G·*,
310–29 Mind is *G·*, and God is not seen by
r 469–13 *Answer.* — Mind is *G·*.

Mind or
p 372– 9 all is divine Mind, or *G·* and His idea,
r 482–29 on the basis of the one Mind or *G·*.

misrepresent
g 538–17 the false claims that misrepresent *G·*,

motherhood of
g 507– 6 the fatherhood and motherhood of *G·*.

mouth of
p 410–11 proceedeth out of the mouth of *G·*," — *Matt.* 4 : 4.

named
ph 200–24 the infinite Spirit, named *G·*.
r 469–11 Life, Truth, and Love, — named *G·*.

nature and
s 118–31 the law of Love, in which nature and *G·* are

nature of
a 20–18 even the nature of *G·* ;
g 537–32 but this is not the nature of *G·*,

never decreed disease
f 221–19 that *G·* never decreed disease,

never endowed matter
p 378–26 *G·* never endowed matter with power to

never made
f 222–26 concluded that *G·* never made a dyspeptic,
g 540–20 "*G·* never made you, and you are a false sense

never slumbers
f 249–21 *G·* never slumbers, and His likeness

no law of
p 391–13 No law of *G·* hinders this result.

no part in
a 19–26 Those who cannot . . . have no part in *G·*.

no relation to
ph 196–17 They have no relation to *G·* wherewith

nothing except
f 243–29 because they declare nothing except *G·*.

notions about
o 357–20 wrong notions about *G·* must have

not originate in
r 472–10 sin, and death, . . . do not originate in *G·*

God

obedience to
  a 25–18   By his obedience to *G·*, he demonstrated
  ph 183–13   obedience to *G·* will remove this necessity.
  f 241– 4   he who refuses obedience to *G·*, is chastened
obey
  r 496– 7   first duty is to obey *G·*,
obeying
  r 489–21   at another the medium for obeying *G·*?
obligations to
  c 262– 4   Neither does . . . diminish man's obligations
      to *G·*,
obnoxious to
  g 533–21   Materiality, so obnoxious to *G·*, is
offend
  p 425–27   You will never fear again except to offend *G·*,
offering to
  g 540–31   he brings a material offering to *G·*.
offspring of
  a 29–30   Man as the offspring of *G·*, as the idea of Spirit,
  c 267– 3   offspring of *G·* start not from matter or
  p 396–27   man is the offspring of *G·*, not of man ;
of Jacob
  s 135– 6   presence of the *G·* of Jacob."— *Psal.* 114 : 7.
of nature
  a 44–20   for the *G·* of nature to sustain Jesus
omnipotence of
  o 345– 7   When the omnipotence of *G·* is preached
  l 445–18   omnipresence and omnipotence of *G·*.
omnipotent
  s 113–21   evil, death, deny good, omnipotent *G·*,
one
  a 35–26   spiritual communion with the one *G·*.
  m 69–21   Do you have one *G·* and creator,
  sp 94– 1   Jesus taught but one *G·*, one Spirit,
  s 113– 1   As there is but one *G·*, there can be but
  ph 167–18   To have one *G·* and avail yourself of the
  183– 4   thus departing from the basis of one *G·*,
  191– 5   delusion that there is more than . . . one *G·*,
  f 204–21   When will the ages . . . realize only one *G·*,
  205–26   hinders man's normal drift towards the . . .
      one *G·*,
  249– 3   let us have one *G·*, one Mind,
  c 256– 9   The theory of three persons in one *G·*
  b 276– 1   Having one *G·*, . . . unfolds the power that
  301–22   Thou shalt have one *G·*, one Mind.
  308– 4   there is and can be but one *G·*,
  330–24   one Mind only, because there is one *G·*.
  332–16   one *G·*, and one mediator— *I Tim.* 2 : 5.
  334–32   but one infinite and therefore one *G·*
  o 347– 9   writer infers that . . . it must be the one *G·*,
  356–32   Then there must have been . . . more than one *G·*.
  357–20   As there is in reality but one *G·*, one Mind,
  361–11   unites with the Jew's belief in one *G·*,
  p 382–15   of spiritual power and of faith in one *G·*,
  419–25   for there is but one Mind, one *G·*.
  r 465–16   is there more than one *G·*
  467–10   all men have one Mind, one *G·* and Father,
  469–18   but one Mind, because there is but one *G·*,
  g 515–18   does not imply more than one *G·*,
  517–17   because there is but one *G·*.
  532–25   and there is but one *G·*, hence one Mind
  544–27   nor the image and likeness of the one *G·*.
  gl 580– 3   not God's man, who represents the one *G·*
  580–26   that the one *G·* and creator entered
  587–17   God is one *G·*, infinite and perfect,
  591–17   substance, Life, Truth, Love ; the one *G·* ;
  594– 4   the belief in more than one *G·* ;
one absolute
  r 465–12   They refer to one absolute *G·*.
one omnipresent
  o 361– 7   a monotheist ; he has one omnipresent *G·*.
on the side of
  f 201–12   superabundance of being is on the side of *G·*,
opposed to
  s 151–25   The human mind is opposed to *G·*
  ph 192–20   can have no power opposed to *G·*,
  ap 569– 5   mortal belief in a power opposed to *G·*.
opposes
  o 357–25   If what opposes *G·* is real,
opposite of
  b 282–29   the fall of man or the opposite of *G·*
  g 554–20   Jesus defined this opposite of *G·*
  gl 591–13   the opposite of *G·* ;
  592– 4   and therefore the opposite of *G·*,
opposites of
  gl 594–23   the opposites of *G·* ; errors ; hallucinations.
opposite to
  p 380–29   to believe that there is a power opposite to *G·*,
or good
  (see **good**)
origin of
  g 555–17   is like inquiring into the origin of *G·*,
or Spirit
  gl 580–13   the antipode of *G·*, or Spirit ;

God

our ignorance of
  p 390– 7   It is our ignorance of *G·*, the divine Principle,
outcome of
  f 250–13   man, the outcome of *G·*, reflects God.
patient
  f 242–16   In patient obedience to a patient *G·*,
people of
  s 133–17   wrought wonders for the people of *G·*
  b 288–19   a rest to the people of *G·*."— *Heb.* 4 : 9.
perfect
  c 259–13   perfect *G·* and perfect man,— as the basis
  b 337– 0   not the . . . likeness of Spirit, the perfect *G·*
perfection of
  c 262– 6   C. S. takes naught from the perfection of *G·*,
Person or
  b 302–26   infinite Principle, called Person or *G·*.
possible to
  pr 1– 3   faith that all things are possible to *G·*,
pours the riches
  pr 5–16   *G·* pours the riches of His love into the
power of
  s 146–14   medicine substitutes drugs for the power of *G·*
  f 224–30   The power of *G·* brings deliverance to
  p 406– 8   the power of *G·* is understood
power with
  b 308–31   "power with *G·* and with men."— *Gen.* 32 : 28.
pray to
  pr 13–20   If we pray to *G·* as a corporeal person, this will
prepared of
  ap 565–30   she hath a place prepared of *G·*.— *Rev.* 12 : 6.
prepares the soil
  o 361–28   until *G·* prepares the soil
presence of
  g 543– 9   shut out from the presence of *G·*.
priests unto
  s 141–21   "kings and priests unto *G·*."— *Rev.* 1 : 6.
prince of
  b 309–11   Israel,— a prince of *G·*, or a soldier of God,
proceed from
  g 529–11   both man and woman proceed from *G·*
pronounced good
  g 526–15   *G·* pronounced good all that He created,
prove what
  a 26–17   to prove what *G·* is and what He does for man.
quality of
  g 506– 5   Understanding is a quality of *G·*,
realization of
  b 300–21   through the realization of *G·* as ever present
realm of
  r 481– 6   the holiest,"— the realm of *G·*.— *Heb.* 10 : 19.
recognizing
  g 530–10   recognizing *G·*, the Father and Mother of all,
reconciled to
  a 45–11   we were reconciled to *G·* by— *Rom.* 5 : 10.
reflecting
  b 337– 2   man, reflecting *G·*, cannot lose his
  r 489–17   How can man, reflecting *G·*, be dependent on
reflection of
  (see **reflection**)
reflections of
  b 336–15   man's . . . are reflections of *G·*.
reflects
  sp 70– 8   man, made in God's likeness, reflects *G·*.
  90–32   shall know this when man reflects *G·*.
  f 250–13   man, the outcome of God, reflects *G·*.
  b 286–20   spiritual universe is good, and reflects *G·*
  305–10   man, like all things real, reflects *G·*,
  306–19   cannot be separated . . . if man reflects *G·*.
  r 478–27   That only is real which reflects *G·*.
  g 502–28   The universe reflects *G·*.
  525– 5   Man reflects *G·* ;
  ap 577– 8   reflects *G·* as Father-Mother,
relating to
  s 127–13   terms stand for everything relating to *G·*,
relation to
  f 215–26   in existence, and in his relation to *G·*.
  231–24   Science of being in man's relation to *G·*,
  b 316– 7   the real man and his relation to *G·*,
reliance on
  ph 170– 1   it robs man of reliance on *G·*,
remain in
  g 513–20   continuity of all individuality remain in *G·*,
remembering that
  p 419– 6   remembering that *G·* and His ideas alone are
rendering to
  f 219–28   not rendering to *G·* the honor due to Him
representative of
  a 52–24   The highest earthly representative of *G·*,
represents
  g 527–11   Here the metaphor represents *G·*, Love, as
  527–26   the lie represents *G·* as repeating creation,
requires
  f 254– 6   *G·* requires perfection, but not until the
rests in
  g 519–25   *G·* rests in action.

God

return thanks to
pr 3–28 and yet return thanks to G· for all blessings,
reveals
s 127–17 C. S. reveals G·, not as the author of sin,
said
ph 197– 8 G· said of the tree of knowledge,
f 220–29 G· said, "Thou shalt not eat of it." — Gen. 2 : 17.
r 475–23 And G· said : "Let us make man — Gen. 1 : 26.
g 503–18 And G· said, Let there be light : — Gen. 1 : 3.
505– 4 And G· said, Let there be a — Gen. 1 : 6.
506–15 And G· said, Let the waters — Gen. 1 : 9.
507–11 And G· said, Let the earth — Gen. 1 : 11.
509– 9 And G· said, Let there be lights — Gen. 1 : 14.
511–19 And G· said, Let the waters — Gen. 1 : 20.
513–14 And G· said, Let the earth — Gen. 1 : 24.
515–11 And G· said, Let us make man — Gen. 1 : 26.
517–25 G· said unto them, Be fruitful, — Gen. 1 : 28.
518– 5 And G· said, Behold, I have given — Gen. 1 : 29.
525–13 G· said, Let us make man after our mind
529–15 Yea, hath G· said, Ye shall not eat — Gen. 3 : 1.
saw everything
g 518–24 And G· saw everything that He — Gen. 1 : 31.
saw that it
g 506–24 and G· saw that it was good. — Gen. 1 : 10.
508–11 and G· saw that it was good. — Gen. 1 : 12.
511–10 and G· saw that it was good. — Gen. 1 : 18.
512– 7 and G· saw that it was good. — Gen. 1 : 21.
513–24 and G· saw that it was good. — Gen. 1 : 25.
515– 2 "And G· saw that it was good." — Gen. 1 : 25.
saw the light
g 503–26 And G· saw the light, — Gen. 1 : 4.
Science is of
g 551–16 all Science is of G·, not of man.
Science of
s 111– 7 Science of G· and man is no more supernatural
111–10 as the Science of G·, Spirit, must,
seek unto their
sp 70– * Should not a people seek unto their G·? — Isa. 8 : 19.
selects
t 455–20 G· selects for the highest service
sense of
c 256–25 material sense of G· leads to formalism
b 279–30 starting from a material sense of G·,
312–24 A personal sense of G· and of man's
r 489–30 A wrong sense of G·, man, and creation is
ap 577– 2 incorporeal sense of G· and man
gl 590–24 when the spiritual sense of G· and of infinity
591– 1 a physical sense of G· as finite and corporeal.
sentence of
f 232–24 the sentence of G·, which sealed
sent from
ap 561–31 "There was a man sent from G· — John 1 : 6.
sentinel of
a 49–18 faithful sentinel of G· at the highest post
separate from
a 42–20 belief that man has . . . mind separate from G·
s 136– 6 He claimed no . . . life separate from G·.
shaped man
g 525–14 and G· shaped man after His mind ;
smile of
ph 175–10 to say that a rose, the smile of G·, can produce
soldier of
b 309–11 Israel, — a prince of God, or a soldier of G·,
Son of
(see **Son**)
sonship with
b 315–12 hid from their sense Christ's sonship with G·.
sons of
b 315–20 the liberty of the sons of G·.
Soul as
b 310–14 Science reveals Soul as G·, untouched by sin
Soul, or
sp 72–11 Soul, or G·, is the only truth-giver to man.
r 468–22 the synonym of Mind, Soul, or G·,
Spirit and
o 345– 1 Spirit and G· are often regarded as
Spirit is
(see **Spirit**)
spirit of
s 137–20 Christ, the spirit of G·, of Truth, Life, and
r 480– 3 Where the spirit of G· is,
g 503– 8 the spirit of G· moved upon the — Gen. 1 : 2.
534–22 the spirit of G· dwell in you." — Rom. 8 : 9.
Spirit, or
sp 73–15 If Spirit, or G·, communed with mortals
r 482–11 Soul is properly the synonym of Spirit, or G· ;
spiritual
f 214–21 more than they do a spiritual G·.
supernatural
t 450– 4 belief in a mysterious, supernatural G·,
supposes
g 538–31 supposes G· to be the author of sin

God

supremacy of
s 130–27 claim of Science for the supremacy of G·,
sustained by
f 221–22 in which being is sustained by G·,
g 530– 5 In divine Science, man is sustained by G·,
symbol of
g 517–20 The only proper symbol of G· as person is
talked with
b 308–15 talked with G· as consciously as man talks with
taught of
t 455–26 if he is taught of G· to discern it.
term for
b 286–17 In the Saxon . . . good is the term for G·.
thanks
t 453–21 masquerader in this Science thanks G· that
the All-in-all
s 127– 4 If G·, the All-in-all, be the creator of the
the Father-Mother
b 331–30 G· the Father-Mother ; Christ the
the living
s 137–18 the Son of the living G· !" — Matt. 16 : 16.
theories concerning
s 133–23 special theories concerning G·,
those who scoff at
o 358–15 nor of the inventions of those who scoff at G·.
thoughts from
b 298–28 Angels are pure thoughts from G·, winged with
to ignore
ph 166–17 To ignore G· as of little use in sickness is a
to man
a 18–14 reconciles man to God, not G· to man ;
19– 2 to reconcile man to God, not G· to man.
an 104– 1 true thoughts, passing from G· to man.
s 117–17 As a divine student he unfolded G· to man,
f 206–15 In the scientific relation of G· to man,
b 284–30 Thought passes from G· to man,
332– 2 relation of G· to man and the universe.
to suppose that
pr 6–19 To suppose that G· forgives . . . according
ph 183– 5 To suppose that G· constitutes laws of
towards
f 213–12 and is a tendency towards G·, Spirit.
p 430– 9 he will advance more rapidly towards G·,
tributary to
r 481– 2 is tributary to G·, Spirit, and to nothing else.
tri-unity of
b 340–18 It inculcates the tri-unity of G·, Spirit,
true
f 237–29 the only living and true G· can do.
b 338– 3 brings to light the only living and true G·
p 410– 8 know Thee, the only true G·, — John 17 : 3.
trust
a 20–21 to obey the divine order and trust G·,
understand
pr 3–15 to understand G· is the work of eternity,
a 22–29 does not understand G·.
f 209–32 constant capacity to understand G·.
o 352– 2 they did not sufficiently understand G·
t 446–21 To understand G· strengthens hope,
r 486–29 If . . . medium through which to understand G·,
understanding of
a 33–30 a new and higher understanding of G·
sp 76–13 When advanced to . . . the understanding of G·,
79–13 through the higher understanding of G·,
s 127– 7 a knowledge or understanding of G·,
b 275–26 The true understanding of G· is spiritual.
315– 5 His better understanding of G· was a rebuke to
328–11 they gain the true understanding of G·
p 428–32 the understanding of G· as the only Life.
r 473–23 a better understanding of G· . . . is required.
496–14 prove what the understanding of G· brings
ap 567– 6 prevails through the understanding of G·.
576–25 in proportion to his understanding of G·.
gl 589–24 understanding of G· and man appearing.
understanding that
b 324–14 the understanding that G· is the only Life.
gl 589– 9 the understanding that G· is the divine
unity of
s 132–12 coming from divine Mind, prove the unity of G·,
g 502–26 eternal verity and unity of G· and man,
unity with
a 18– 2 exemplification of man's unity with G·,
r 497–15 unfolding man's unity with G·
universal
sp 78–31 These are the effects of one universal G·,
unknown
p 428–16 not "to the unknown G·" — Acts 17 : 23.
gl 596– 8 dedicated "to the unknown G·." — Acts 17 : 23.
unknown to
p 424– 5 Accidents are unknown to G·,
unlike
f 249–16 and includes nothing unlike G·.
c 262–23 and conquering all that is unlike G·.

God

unlikeness of
r 470–14   the unlikeness of *G·*, is unreal.
unsustained by
f 212–18   undirected and unsustained by *G·*.
unto
a 20– 2   unto *G·* the things that — *Matt.* 22 : 21.
g 540–18   unto *G·* the things that — *Matt.* 22 : 21.
verities of
a 28– 5   and taught the unseen verities of *G·*,
voice of
f 226– 5   voice of *G·* in behalf of the African slave
b 321–26   became to him the voice of *G·*,
wait on
b 323–10   we pause, — wait on *G·*.
walked with
f 214– 7   "walked with *G·*," — *Gen.* 5 : 24.
waymarks of
g 542–24   not to remove the waymarks of *G·*.
we approach
sp 95– 7   We approach *G·*, or Life, in proportion to
what is
r 465– 8   *Question.* — What is *G·*?
whole of
g 517–23   can never reveal the whole of *G·*,
will arrest
an 105–24   *G·* will arrest him.
will bless
pr 13–17   *G·* will bless it, and we shall incur less risk
will heal
pr 12– 3   A mere request that *G·* will heal the sick
r 495– 1   *G·* will heal the sick through man,
will never place
a 31– 2   *G·* will never place it in such hands.
will not punish
o 357– 1   we must admit that *G·* will not punish man for
will of
pr 11–30   habitual desire to know and do the will of *G·*,
gl 597–22   "For this is the will of *G·*." — *I Thess.* 4 : 3.
will overturn
f 223–31   *G·* will overturn, until
will redeem
o 354–21   *G·* will redeem that weakness,
will save us
pr 2–18   A request that *G·* will save us
will smite
p 439–20   *G·* will smite you, O whited walls,
will still guide
t 444– 9   *G·* will still guide them into the right use of
will supply
ap 571–16   Know thyself, and *G·* will supply the wisdom
will sustain
pr 10– 7   *G·* will sustain us under these sorrows.
will turn to
pref x–19   Few invalids will turn to *G·* till all
winds of
f 201–15   Then, when the winds of *G·* blow,
wisdom of
gl 597–21   The might and wisdom of *G·*.
without
r 480–31   "having no hope, and without *G·* — *Eph.* 2 : 12.
g 531–22   or that matter exists without *G·*?
with us
pref xl–16   Immanuel, or "*G·* with us," — *Matt.* 1 : 23.
a 34– 8   Immanuel, or *G· with us*;
s 107– 8   Immanuel, "*G·* with us," — *Matt.* 1 : 23.
Word of
f 231–32   made by Him [the Word of *G·*] ; — *John* 1 : 3.
b 335–11   the Logos, the Æon or Word of *G·*,
g 503–13   Divine Science, the Word of *G·*, saith to the
   525–18   all things were made through the Word of *G·*,
worketh with you
a 22–12   to this end *G·* worketh with you.
work of
g 521– 6   All that is made is the work of *G·*,
works
c 263– 8   When mortal man . . . works only as *G·* works,
worship
ap 576–13   no material structure in which to worship *G·*,
worship of
ph 200– 5   the worship of *G·* in Spirit instead of matter,
would reduce
b 335– 5   would reduce *G·* to dependency on matter,
would rob
f 214–23   for mortal illusions would rob *G·*,
yields to
ph 188– 1   only as the mortal, erring mind yields to *G·*,

———

pref vii–17   Ignorance of *G·* is no longer the stepping-stone
pr 1–12   no loss can occur from trusting *G·* with
   2–31   Asking *G·* to *be G·* is a vain repetition.
   2–31   *G·* is "the same yesterday, and — *Heb.* 13 : 8.
   8–16   If we feel the aspiration, . . . this *G·* accepts ;
   9–17   "love the Lord thy *G·* — *Matt.* 22 : 37.
   12–16   Prayer to a corporeal *G·* affects the sick like a

God

a 18–14   the divine Principle of Christ is *G·*,
   18–15   how can *G·* propitiate Himself?
   27–20   doctrine of pantheism, — that *G·*, or Life,
   29–16   *G·* is the only author of man.
   31–10   He recognized Spirit, *G·*, as the only creator,
   31–32   will think that he doeth *G·* service ; — *John* 16 : 2.
   36–31   Can *G·* therefore overlook the law of
   42– 2   priest and rabbi affirmed *G·* to be
   46–17   higher in the understanding of Spirit, *G·*.
   49–32   "stricken, smitten of *G·*." — *Isa.* 53 : 4.
   50– 8   "My *G·*, why hast Thou forsaken — *Mark* 15 : 34.
   50–13   his divine Principle, the *G·* who is Love,
   51–17   no more . . . than *G·* could be extinguished.
m 56– *   *What therefore G· hath joined* — *Matt.* 19 : 6.
   57–28   unite thought more closely to *G·*,
   69–14   to understand that there is but one creator, *G·*.
sp 70– 7   Man is never *G·*,
   71– 7   Soul is synonymous with Spirit, *G·*,
   72–21   *G·*, good, being ever present, it follows
   76– 7   Life will be recognized . . . as *G·*,
   78–24   *G·* is not in the medley where matter
   81–29   man's immortality depends upon that of *G·*,
   89–21   *G·*, is heard when the senses are silent.
   91– 6   belief that man is separated from *G·*,
   92–27   a belief in something besides *G·*.
   93–26   refer only to quality, not to *G·*.
   93–27   He is not *G·*, Spirit.
   94–21   but one returned to give *G·* thanks,
   99– 7   it is *G·* which worketh in you — *Phil.* 2 : 13.
an 103–14   because Mind-science is of *G·*
   103–32   Life and being are of *G·*.
s 107– 3   *G·* had been graciously preparing me
   107–14   acquaint themselves intelligently with *G·*.
   108–22   all real being is in *G·*,
   109–17   I knew the Principle . . . to be *G·*,
   109–30   whether it be of *G·*, or whether — *John* 7 : 17.
   111–12   The Principle of divine metaphysics is *G·* ;
   113–18   *G·*, Spirit, being all, nothing is matter.
   113–19   Life, *G·*, omnipotent good, deny death, evil,
   115–13   *G·* ; Divine Principle, Life, Truth, Love,
   116–28   *G· is infinite Person*, — in the sense of
   119–11   other horn of the dilemma and regard *G·* as
   119–17   In one sense *G·* is identical with nature,
   119–24   it is opposed to the nature of Spirit, *G·*.
   120– 5   man coexists with and reflects Soul, *G·*,
   124–15   interpreted . . . from its divine Principle, *G·*.
   133–24   he made "himself equal with *G·*," — *John* 5 : 18.
   133–28   no . . . substance outside of *G·*.
   135–19   "Can *G·* furnish a table in the — *Psal.* 78 : 19.
   135–20   What cannot *G·* do?
   140– 4   That *G·* is a personal being, nobody can truly
   140–30   would . . . make *G·* in their own human image.
   142–28   *G·* being All-in-all, He made medicine ;
   142–31   the nature and character of Mind, *G·*.
   143– 9   if the sick cannot rely on *G·* for help
   148–31   admits *G·* to be the healer of sin but not
   149–26   Since *G·*, divine Mind, governs all,
   151–20   nothing to do with Life, *G·*.
   161– 1   Is *G·* the lawgiver?
ph 166–26   only as a last resort, turns to *G·*,
   167– 1   Should we implore a corporeal *G·* to heal
   177–23   against *G·*, Spirit and Truth.
   180–27   with *G·* all things are possible.
   181– 1   since Mind, *G·*, is the source
   182–30   To admit that . . . is a condition over which *G·*
   186–14   it presupposes the absence of *G·*,
   191–32   *G·*, sends forth the aroma of Spirit,
   192–10   Spirit is not separate from *G·*.
   193–27   "It was none other than *G·* and
   196–5   beware, not of Rome, Satan, nor of *G·*, but of
f 202–17   with the divine Principle of his being, *G·*,
   203– 7   If *G·* were understood instead of being merely
   203–15   destroys reliance on aught but *G·*,
   203–31   *G·*, divine good, does not kill a man in order to
   203–32   *G·* alone is man's life.
   203–32   *G·* is at once the centre and
   204–24   notion that they can create what *G·* cannot,
   205– 1   else *G·* will continue to be hidden
   205– 9   error of believing that . . . are creations of *G·*
   205–31   not of Spirit, *G·*, good, but of
   206–19   Does *G·* send sickness,
   206–21   Is *G·* creating anew what He has already
   206–24   nothing is new to *G·*,
   206–26   Instead of *G·* sending sickness and death,
   207– 8   *G·* is not the creator of an evil mind.
   208– 1   error, which affords no proof of *G·*,
   208– 7   this seeming power, independent of *G·*,
   208–15   absurd to suppose . . . *G·*, produces disease
   208–17   John Young . . . writes : "*G·* is the father of
   212–22   *G·* alone makes and clothes the lilies
   213– 9   *G·*, good, is self-existent and self-expressed,
   214–19   finite thoughts of *G·* like the pagan idolater.
   215–20   are the suppositional absence of Life, *G·*,
   216– 4   What has touched Life, *G·*, to such strange

God

f 218–23   turning in time of need to G·,
221–24   "giving G· thanks ;"— see Eph. 5 : 20.
222–16   consulting the stomach less . . . and G· more,
224–32   supposed power, which opposes itself to G·?
227–30   If G· had instituted material laws
229– 8   Mind signifies G·,— infinity,
229–23   If G· causes man to be sick,
230– 9   salvation which comes through G·,
230–16   G·, good, can no more produce sickness than
231– 4   If G· destroys not sin, sickness, and death,
231– 7   What G· cannot do, man need not attempt.
231– 8   If G· heals not the sick, they are not healed,
231–10   G·, Truth, . . . does heal the sick
231–12   If G· makes sin, if good produces evil,
231–16   G· is not the author of mortal discords.
232– 4   neither make man harmonious nor G· lovable.
232– 9   "with G· all things are— Mark 10 : 27.
238–10   "If G· be for us, who can be— Rom. 8 : 31.
239– 6   weigh not one jot in the balance of G·,
239–18   whom we acknowledge and obey as G·.
241–29   signifies that the pure in heart see G·
242– 5   "they shall all know Me [G·],— Jer. 31 : 34.
242–12   no other consciousness of life— than good, G·
244–20   If . . . there must be an instant when G·
253– 4   saith : . . . all are Mine, for I am G·.
253–26   G· never requires obedience to a so-called
254–11   When we wait patiently on G·
c 255–14   That G· is corporeal . . . no man should affirm.
256–16   precise form of G· must be of small importance
258–18   no more . . . than we know of G·.
259–23   G·, Spirit, works spiritually, not materially.
260–14   to discover what G· has already done ;
264–18   finding all in G·, good,
b 268– *   *I can do no otherwise ; so help me G· !*
269– 9   Human philosophy has made G· manlike.
272–29   G· is the divine Principle of all
273– 4   physical senses can take no cognizance of G·
273–21   G· never ordained a material law to annul
273–23   would oppose the supremacy of Spirit, G·,
274–26   firm, called matter and mind, G· never formed.
275– 4   matter did not originate in G·, Spirit,
275– 7   G·, Spirit, is All-in-all,
275–11   begin by reckoning G· as the divine Principle
275–14   are the Scriptural names for G·.
276– 7   all have one Spirit, G·,
276–11   is cognizant only of the things of G·.
276–17   If G· is admitted to be the only Mind
277– 7   As G· Himself is good and is Spirit,
279–19   their only idea or intelligence is in G·.
280–26   G·, the Soul of man and of all existence,
283–20   deem this the manifestation of the one Life, G·.
284– 4   If G· were limited to man or matter, or if the
284– 5   If G· were limited . . . G· would be corporeal,
284–21   The physical senses can obtain no proof of G·.
284–32   intercommunication is always from G· to
285–15   Is G· a physical personality?
285–23   By interpreting G· as a corporeal Saviour
285–30   seek to learn, . . . from the divine Principle, G·,
286–23   since G·, Spirit, is the only cause,
287–11   Did G·, Truth, create error? No !
287–13   G· being everywhere and all-inclusive,
298–23   lead up to their divine origin, G·,
300– 4   no true appreciation of infinite Principle, G·,
300–24   If . . . G· would have no representative,
300–25   and matter would be identical with G·.
302–21   Soul, or Mind, of the spiritual man is G·,
303–25   G·, without the image and likeness of Himself,
305–12   Gender also is a quality, not of G·, but a
305–14   he reflects the creation of Mind, G·,
305–22   deflections of . . . are all unlike Spirit, G·.
306– 8   If G·, . . . were parted for a moment from
306–19   cannot be separated for an instant from G·,
307–13   as much as G·, Spirit, who *is* the only Life."
310–10   G· is His own infinite Mind, and expresses all.
310–29   Mind, God, and G· is not seen by
311– 5   all that Mind, G·, is, or hath made,
312–17   without Love, G·, immortality cannot appear.
312–21   Mortals believe in a finite personal G· ;
313– 7   Therefore G·, even thy G·, hath— Heb. 1 : 9.
319– 9   understanding G·, sustains man
319–20   Mind controls man and man has no Mind but G·.
320–26   "In my flesh shall I see G·,"— Job 19 : 26.
321–24   G· had lessened Moses' fear by this proof in
322–31   by searching find out G·?"— Job 11 : 7.
324– 6   for they shall see G·."— Matt. 5 : 8.
325–18   "hid with Christ in G·,"— Col. 3 : 3.
330–13   Eye hath neither seen G· nor His
330–14   Neither G· nor the perfect man can
330–19   G· is what the Scriptures declare Him to be,
331– 7   If . . . G· would not be reflected but absorbed,
333–27   inseparable from the divine Principle, G·,
334– 5   dwells forever in the bosom of the Father, G·,
334– 7   Spirit, which is G·,
334–31   Spirit being G·, there is but one Spirit,

God

b 335– 7   Spirit, G·, has created all in and of Himself.
335–26   can produce nothing unlike the eternal . . . G·.
336–13   He has been forever in the eternal Mind, G· ;
336–19   A portion of G· could not enter man ;
336–21   else G· would be manifestly finite,
336–24   and nothing less can express G·.
336–25   G·, the divine Principle of man,
336–30   G· is the parent Mind, and man is
337–15   none but the pure in heart can see G·,
338–23   the supposed separation of man from G·,
339– 8   G·, Spirit, alone created all,
339–10   Therefore evil, . . . cannot be the product of G·.
340–13   all that really exists is in and of G·,
340–19   man shall have no other spirit or mind but G·,
o 341–10   for they shall see G·"— Matt. 5 : 8.
342–17   If . . . Science is not of G·, then there is no
345– 5   G· cannot be in His unlikeness
347– 6   Nothing really has Life but G·,
348–15   Are we . . . imputing too much power to G·,
348–18   no faith . . . in any power but G·,
349–11   G· is not the author of sickness.
356–19   G· is as incapable of producing sin, sickness,
356–24   Does G· create a material man out of Himself,
357–26   If . . . G· is not supreme and infinite.
358– 3   Can a leaden bullet deprive a man of . . . G·,
358– 4   If G· is at the mercy of matter, then matter is
360–24   mortal man be more just than G·?— Job 4 : 17.
361– 2   the Christian believes that Christ is G·.
361–12   Jesus Christ is not G·, as Jesus himself declared,
p 362– *   *health of my countenance and my G·.— Psal.* 42:11.
366–16   G· whom he hath not seen?"— I John 4 : 20.
369–19   to know if G· were willing that a man should
369–26   psychology, or the Science of Spirit, G·,
380–30   to believe that . . . G· endows this opposing
381– 1   null and void by the law of Life, G·.
384– 6   G· never punishes man for doing right,
387–22   supposition . . . that G· punishes man for doing
388–15   hypothesis . . . food has power to destroy
     Life, G·,
389–18   If G· has, . . . instituted laws that food shall
390–22   G· is no more the author of sickness than
392– 7   must be cast out to readjust the balance for G·.
393–13   G· has made man capable of this,
394–22   G·, against whom mortals should not contend
395–15   Prayers, in which G· is not asked to heal
397–21   confidence in G· as All,
399–27   G·, contains no mortal opinions.
413– 2   G·, the only Mind, does not produce pain
414–21   "The Lord He is G·— Deut. 4 : 35.
421–17   G·, Spirit, is all, and that there is none beside
427–22   in ignorance of what G· is.
427–22   G·, Life, Truth, and Love make man undying.
433–29   to prepare the frightened sense of Life, G·,
435– 2   Spirit which is G· Himself
435–27   according to the law of Spirit, G·.
440–21   Mortal Man hath his appeal to Spirit, G·,
t 445–14   "hid with Christ in G·,"— Col. 3 : 3.
450–28   beliefs in . . . intelligence separated from G·,
r 465–18   and this one is G·, omnipotent, omniscient,
466–28   Science will declare G· aright,
467–18   G· as not in man but as reflected by man.
469–14   the great truth that G·, good, is the *only* Mind,
470–17   G·, the Mind of man, never sins
470–19   Has G· taken down His own standard,
471– 3   G· and all that He creates are perfect
471–21   "Let G· be true, but every— Rom. 3 : 4.
472–29   until G· strips off their disguise.
472–30   not true, because they are not of G·.
473– 4   Truth, G·, is not the father of error.
473–12   and attributes all power to G·.
474–18   If . . . G· must be their author.
475–19   that which has no separate mind from G· ;
475–30   nor can G·, by whom man is evolved,
478–16   No, not if G· is true and mortal man a liar.
478–27   "But when it pleased G·,— Gal. 1 : 15.
480– 3   and there is no place where G· is not,
480–11   Consciousness, as well as action, . . . is in G·,
480–14   Harmonious action proceeds from Spirit, G·.
480–18   thus attempting to separate Mind from G·.
480–24   G· is not its author.
481– 8   never helps mortals to understand Spirit, G·.
481–26   If sin is supported, G· must uphold it,
482– 7   gained by substituting the word G·,
489–20   the medium for sinning against G·,
494– 6   G·, who needed no help from Jesus' example
g 501– *   *by the name of G· Almighty ;— Exod.* 6 : 3.
502–28   The creative Principle . . . is G·.
503–28   G·, Spirit, dwelling in infinite light and
506–10   G·, unites understanding to eternal harmony.
506–18   Spirit, G·, gathers unformed thoughts
508– 6   The only intelligence or substance . . . is G·,
511– 7   And G· set them in the firmament— Gen. 1 : 17.
512–30   albeit G· is ignorant of the existence of both
514– 5   of which G· is the sole creator.

God

g 515–29 Now compare man before the mirror to . . . G·.
516–10 Truth in truthfulness, G· in goodness,
517–12 not as much . . . for considering G· masculine,
517–15 if G· is personal, there is but one person,
522– 6 assigns all might and government to G·,
523– 5 and finally declares that G· knows error
523–25 it is Elohim (G·) who creates.
524–27 for G· presently curses the ground.
524–29 Is Spirit, G·, injected into dust,
525– 1 Does Mind, G·, enter matter to become there a
525– 3 animated by the breath of G·?
525–29 as devoid of reality as they are of good, G·.
526–22 Was evil instituted through G·, Love?
527– 1 G· could not put Mind into matter nor
527–17 But is it true that G·, good, made
528– 3 G· has already created man,
528– 7 cannot be . . . in partnership with G· ;
528–15 error, credits Truth, G·, with inducing
530–14 for G· doth know that in the day — Gen. 3 : 5.
530–20 saying, . . . I can do what G· has not done
531–21 Who dares to say either that G· is in matter or
532– 1 Did G· at first create one man unaided,
536–11 The illusion of sin is without hope or G·.
536–18 starting from matter instead of from G·,
539–10 G· could never impart an element of evil,
541– 9 Had G· more respect for the homage
546– 4 Spirit, G·, never germinates, but is
546– 5 If Mind, G·, creates error, that error must
546–10 Has G· no Science to declare Mind,
551–27 by searching find out G·?" — Job 11 : 7.
554–16 Error replies, "G· made you."
554–25 Jesus never intimated that G· made a devil,
555–30 Knowing that G· was the Life of man,
557–26 when G·, Mind, spake and it was done.
ap 560–25 something new and better of G·
573–15 G·, the divine Principle of harmony,
575–11 builder and maker of this New Jerusalem is G·,
gl 580–14 image and likeness of what G· has not created,
582–18 pure consciousness that G·, . . . creates man
582–19 G· is the only creative power.
583–24 G·, who made all that was made
587– 5 definition of
587–19 Goop. G· ; Spirit ; omnipotence ;
588–20 I Am. G· ; incorporeal and eternal Mind ;
590–19 unless specially coupled with the name G·.
591– 4 Spirit, or intelligence, named Elohim, or G·.
591–18 the divine Principle, or G·,
592–16 Mother. G· ; divine and eternal Principle ;
504–20 G· ; that only which is perfect,

(see also All, All-in all, All-loving, All-power, All-wise, Almighty, Being, Cause, Comforter, creator, Deity, Ego, Ego-God, Elohim, Esse, Father, Father Mother, First Cause, Giver, Godhead, God-power, God-principle, He, Him, Himself, His, Holy Ghost, Holy One, Holy Spirit, I, I AM, Immanuel, Justice, King, Life, Life-principle, Light, Logos, Lord, Love, Maker, Me, Mind, Most High, Mother, My, One, Person, Principle, Providence, Ruler, Soul, Spirit, Sun of Righteousness, Supreme Being, Supreme Lawgiver, Supreme Ruler, Thee, Thou, Thy, Truth, Us, wisdom, Wonderful, Word)

god

a 103– 3 "the g· of this world," — II Cor. 4 : 4.
s 140–31 What is the g· of a mortal, but
158– 3 designated Apollo as "the g· of medicine."
158– 8 also regarded as . . . "the g· of pestilence."
158–13 may correspond with that of its material g·,
ph 165– 3 would open man's eyes and make him as a g·.
187– 9 attributes to some material g· or medicine
g 524– 3 in the Moabitish g· Chemosh,
524–11 "a man of war," a tribal g· — Exod. 15 : 3.
530–21 saying, . . . and have another g·.
544–26 man, in this allegory, is neither a lesser g· nor
gl 580– 2 the first g· of mythology ;
584–22 saith : "I am . . . created by a tribal g·

God-bestowed

g 526–21 doctrine . . . evil is as real, hence as G·, as

God-created

g 555–12 as if it were as real and G· as

God-crowned

b 313– 4 Jesus the G· or the divinely royal man,

God-given

ph 165– 4 man's G· dominion over the earth.
182–25 denying man's G· ability to
f 228–13 his G· dominion over the material senses.
p 378–24 Sickness is not a G·, . . . material power,
381– 1 Ignorant of our G· rights,
381–21 will sooner grasp man's G· dominion.
387–10 nor . . . trespass upon G· powers
393–10 Exercise this G· authority.

God-given

r 489–15 can this sense be the G· channel to
g 528–24 calling them real and G·.
531–14 man will recognize his G· dominion

Godhead

c 255–17 true idea of the infinite G·.

God-inspired

a 41– 8 The G· walk calmly on

Godlike

a 54–29 If that G· and glorified man were
ph 200–19 man is . . . upright and G·.
f 203–12 the only true spirit is G·.
c 262–14 higher views make the G· man to reach
b 269–10 C. S. makes man G·.
333–15 but Christ Jesus better signifies the G·.

godliness

a 26–14 the g· which animated him.
s 145–21 the mystery which g· always presents to
p 413–16 "Cleanliness is next to g·,"

God-mission

a 41–24 He fulfilled his G·, and then

God-power

s 138– 3 the G· which lay behind Peter's confession

God-principle

r 473– 7 The G· is omnipresent and omnipotent.

God's

allness
pr 15–18 we must deny sin and plead G· allness.
anointed
gl 597– 9 which was ready to . . . crucify G· anointed.
appointing
s 131–15 after the manner of G· appointing,
b 326– 4 in the way of G· appointing.
attributes
b 301– 1 which manifests G· attributes and power,
behest
g 533– 2 Had he lost man's rich inheritance and G· behest,
being
r 470–24 Man is the expression of G· being.
481– 3 G· being is infinity, freedom, harmony, and
care
m 66–11 Trials are proofs of G· care.
character
f 208–12 the goodness of G· character
b 283–22 false belief . . . detracts from G· character and
children
m 69– 7 G· children already created will be cognized
b 003– 5 Multiplication of G· children comes from
t 444–28 Immortals, or G· children in divine Science,
r 476–28 speaking of G· children, not the children of
command
g 530– 6 the earth, at G· command, brings forth
commandments
g 542–25 to advance itself, breaks G· commandments.
condemnation
f 232–24 G· condemnation of sin, sickness, and
control
s 125– 7 Neither . . . is beyond G· control ;
creation
(see creation)
creative mandate
g 556–19 G· creative mandate was,
creatures
g 514–28 All of G· creatures, . . . are harmless,
day
gl 584– 7 This unfolding is G· day,
divine messages
ap 566–29 to the angels, G· divine messages,
divine power
b 316–27 prove G· divine power by healing the sick,
dominion
g 516–20 reflects G· dominion over all the earth.
forgiveness
r 497– 9 We acknowledge G· forgiveness of sin in the
fulness
b 336–20 neither could G· fulness be reflected by
glory
b 313–10 "the brightness of His [G·] glory, — Heb. 1 : 3.
government
(see government)
gracious means
pr 1– 7 G· gracious means for accomplishing
healing
s 141–23 they cannot demonstrate G· healing power.
idea
b 299–24 Truth never destroys G· idea.
o 345–22 incongruity between G· idea and poor humanity,
p 406–24 until we arrive at the fulness of G· idea,
ap 565–16 G· idea will eventually rule all nations

God's

ideas
g 503–16   infinite space is peopled with *G·* ideas,
    504–16   The successive appearing of *G·* ideas is
    505–28   *G·* ideas reflect the immortal,
    511– 4   *G·* ideas "multiply and—*Gen.* 1 : 28.
identities
sp 70–14   The questions are : What are *G·* identities?
image
    (*see* **image**)
infinite ideas
g 511–17   full effulgence of *G·* infinite ideas,
infinite plan
m 69–12   sense of increasing number in *G·* infinite plan.
kingdom
f 202–19   when *G·* kingdom comes on earth ;
b 339–24   *G·* kingdom comes "in earth, as—*Matt.* 6 : 10.
law
    (*see* **law**)
laws
f 236– 7   emolument rather than the dignity of *G·* laws,
light
g 504–12   no place where *G·* light is not seen,
likeness
    (*see* **likeness**)
love
b 326– 8   All nature teaches *G·* love to man,
man
    (*see* **man**)
method
a 40–11   *G·* method of destroying sin.
o 343– 6   Is not finite mind ignorant of *G·* method?
mind
g 525–15   after *G·* mind shaped He him ;
motherhood
ap 562– 6   the spiritual idea of *G·* motherhood.
nature
g 512–14   their natures are allied to *G·* nature ;
omnipotence
a 55–19   when he shall realize *G·* omnipotence
opportunity
c 266–15   "man's extremity is *G·* opportunity."
own image
b 295–12   immortals, created in *G·* own image ;
g 517–22   This ideal is *G·* own image, spiritual and
own likeness
sp 90–24   The admission . . . that man is *G·* own likeness
r 477– 3   the Saviour saw *G·* own likeness,
own way
g 542–19   destroy error in *G·* own way,
pardon
b 291– 4   The suppositions . . . that *G·* pardon is
   339– 5   Does not *G·* pardon, destroying any one sin,
perfection
g 522– 7   endows man out of *G·* perfection
power
a 42–15   great demonstrator of *G·* power
an 102–14   but man, reflecting *G·* power, has dominion
o 351– 3   When we lose faith in *G·* power to heal,
t 450–24   heals them both by understanding *G·* power
qualities
gl 597–26   not be confounded with . . . one of *G·* qualities.
reflection
s 126– 6   when man beholds himself *G·* reflection,
r 471–17   Man is, and forever has been, *G·* reflection.
g 527– 4   Man is *G·* reflection, needing no cultivation,
remedy
s 143– 1   Truth is *G·* remedy for error of every kind,
representatives
b 299–12   Angels are *G·* representatives.
requirements
pr 7–14   wholesome perception of *G·* requirements.
t 445– 1   the Scientist must conform to *G·* requirements.
rule
pr 3–10   we have only to avail ourselves of *G·* rule
servant
p 439–26   meanwhile declaring Disease to be *G·* servant
spiritual idea
s 115–15   MAN : *G·* spiritual idea, individual,
b 315–15   *G·* spiritual idea as presented by Christ Jesus.
supremacy
g 521–10   acknowledging now and forever *G·* supremacy,
thoughts
b 286–21   *G·* thoughts are perfect and eternal,
   337–25   Eternal things (verities) are *G·* thoughts
gl 581– 4   ANGELS. *G·* thoughts passing to man ;
   583– 2   whose better originals are *G·* thoughts,
unchangeable law
s 135– 8   the Science of *G·* unchangeable law.
universe
b 289–24   *G·* universe is spiritual and immortal.
   331–17   Everything in *G·* universe expresses Him.
will
f 202– 4   *G·* will must be universally done.
   241– 2   He, who knows *G·* will . . . and obeys

God's

willingness
f 218–18   if you are without faith in *G·* willingness
word
b 332–24   He was appointed to speak *G·* word
work
ph 167–16   What can improve *G·* work?
g 522–29   declares *G·* work to be finished.
wrath
a 23– 6   That *G·* wrath should be vented upon

a 20– 3   unto God the things that are *G·*."— *Matt.* 22 : 21.
sp 99–29   and to *G·* spiritual, perfect man.
s 117–10   *G·* essential language is spoken of
   121–11   glad in *G·* perennial and happy sunshine,
ph 168–18   *G·* spiritual command relating to perfection,
f 249– 5   "male and female" of *G·* creating—*Gen.* 1 : 27.
b 282–29   Whatever indicates . . . *G·* absence, is the
   333– 9   Christ expresses *G·* spiritual, eternal nature.
   336–31   man is *G·* spiritual offspring.
o 355–28   *G·* immortal keynotes, proved to be such
p 424– 9   the proper sense of *G·* unerring direction
g 515– 6   serpent of *G·* creating is neither subtle nor
   522–21   *G·* glowing denunciations of man when not
   534– 5   to manifest the deathless man of *G·* creating.
   540–18   unto God the things that are *G·*."— *Matt.* 22 : 21.
   544– 2   a creation so wholly apart from *G·*,
gl 597–28   the movements of *G·* spiritual government,
   599– 1   Eternity is *G·* measurement of Soul-filled years.

gods

besought the
s 158– 2   pagan priests, who besought the *g·* to heal
false
p 440– 7   before sacrificing mortals to their false *g·*.
Grecian
ph 199–32   When Homer sang of the Grecian *g·*,
heathen
r 485–28   The heathen *g·* of mythology
many
sp 78–26   where spiritism makes many *g·*,
b 280–16   "*g·* many and lords many."— *I Cor.* 8 : 5.
   307– 9   It says : "There shall be lords and *g·* many.
   335– 1   There are neither spirits many nor *g·* many.
p 388–10   believing in . . . "*g·* many,"— *I Cor.* 8 : 5.
gl 580– 8   "*g·* many and lords many"— *I Cor.* 8 : 5.
   591– 2   mythology,— belief in many *g·*,
material
f 237–26   devote themselves . . . to their material *g·*,
no other
a 19–30   "Thou shalt have no other *g·*— *Exod.* 20 : 3.
b 280–19   "Thou shalt have no other *g·*— *Exod.* 20 : 3.
   340–15   "Thou shalt have no other *g·*— *Exod.* 20 : 3.
r 467– 4   "Thou shalt have no other *g·*— *Exod.* 20 : 3.
   467–13   Having no other *g·*, turning to no other but
other
ph 187– 1   having other *g·* and believing in more than
b 275–28   misleads thought and points to other *g·*,
g 535–12   A belief in other *g·*, other creators,
popular
o 347–23   If C. S. takes away the popular *g·*,
sacrifice to the
gl 595–23   TITHE . . . . A sacrifice to the *g·*.
shall be as
b 280–22   "Ye shall be as *g·*,"— *Gen.* 3 : 5.
   307– 5   "Ye shall be as *g·* ;"— *Gen.* 3 : 5.
g 530–16   and ye shall be as *g·*,— *Gen.* 3 : 5.
   541–24   "Ye shall be as *g·*."— *Gen.* 3 : 5.
   544–21   "Ye shall be as *g·*,"— *Gen.* 3 : 5.
gl 587–16   "Ye shall be as *g·*."— *Gen.* 3 : 5.
strange
g 524– 7   went after "strange *g·*."— *Jer.* 5 : 19.
these
g 544–22   these *g·* must be evolved from materiality

sp 93–28   then men would be spirits, *g·*.
an 105–29   "Whom the *g·* would destroy, they first
ph 200– 1   the *g·* became alive in a nation's belief.
b 294–24   represented as divided into intelligent *g·*.
r 466–20   is as improper as the term *g·*.
gl 587– 9   definition of
   594–23   supposed intelligences, or *g·* ;

Godward

c 265– 5   Mortals must gravitate *G·*,

goes

pr 2– 5   the desire which *g·* forth hungering after
an 104– 9   "Every great scientific truth *g·* through three
   104–13   C. S. *g·* to the bottom of mental action,
   122–26   in Science, Life *g·* on unchanged
   145– 8   struggle for the recovery of invalids *g·* on,
   145–29   warfare between Spirit and the flesh *g·* on.
ph 189–30   *g·* on in an ascending scale by evolution,
f 250–28   Upon this stage of existence *g·* on the dance of
b 268–12   woman *g·* forth to battle with Goliath.
   284–31   neither sensation nor report *g·* from

goes

b	300–31	the ray of light which g· out from it.
t	447–16	The recuperative action . . . g· on naturally.
	462– 9	If the student g· away to practise
r	489–11	as consciousness develops, this belief g· out,
	491–22	belief g· on, whether our eyes are closed or
g	506–13	the dawn of ideas g· on,
	556–22	Even so g· on the Adam-belief,
ap	562–27	for joy that the birth g· on ;

going

a	21–15	If my friends are g· to Europe,
	21–27	He is like a traveller g· westward
s	158–28	Matter is g· out of medicine ;
b	323–31	or we are listening to it and g· up higher.
p	431– 7	sometimes g· to sleep immediately after
g	548–15	This is the new birth g· on hourly,
gl	587–14	suppositious minds, . . . g· in and out

gold

a	47–21	greed for g· strengthened his ingratitude,
m	66–32	separates the g· from the dross
ap	565–22	purifying even the g· of human character.

golden

s	121–12	happy sunshine, g· with Truth.
t	457–18	no good aspect, either silvern or g·.

Golden Rule

u	41–12	cannot forever break the G· R· and escape the
f	234–13	on the basis of the G· R· ;

Golden Shore

ap	576– 1	to the grand realization of the G· S· of Love

Goliath

b	268–13	woman goes forth to battle with G·.

gone

m	65–32	will become purer when the scum is g·.
sp	76– 1	the glad welcome of those who have g· before.
	87–24	Do not suppose that any mental concept is g·
	87–32	or altogether g· from physical sight
s	124– 6	When . . . its foundations are g·.
	135–16	when the devil was g· out,— Luke 11 : 14.
ph	170–31	from which all ills have g· forth,
	185– 2	her difficulty in breathing had g·.
	190–25	passeth over it, and it is g· ;— Psal. 103 : 16.
	193–14	said : . . . My suffering is all g·."
f	203–20	When the material body has g· to ruin,
	212–12	When the nerve is g·,
b	305–24	illusion of life that is here to-day and g· to-morrow.
p	368–32	the foundation of disease is g·.
	377–20	when the belief of the disease had g·.
	398–23	the desire for strong drink is g·.
	400– 3	once destroyed . . . the fear of disease is g·,
	421–19	When the supposed suffering is g·
r	476–26	passeth over it, and it is g· ;— Psal. 103 : 16.

good

accomplish the

p	394– 8	Knowledge that we can accomplish the g·

according to the

gl	584– 6	measures time according to the g· that

affection for

b	327– 9	by gaining an affection for g·

all

pr	2–10	nor can the infinite do less than bestow all g·,
f	232–10	all g· is possible to Spirit ;
c	260–13	the possibility of achieving all g·,
b	299–14	but guide to the divine Principle of all g·,
r	494–14	in every hour, divine Love supplies all g·.

all is

g	521– 6	the work of God, and all is g·.
ap	577–25	all is g·, and nothing can enter that city, which

all that is

gl	594–20	divine Principle ; all that is g· ;

already received

pr	3–22	Are we . . . grateful for the g· already received?

and beautiful

gl	593– 1	The love of the g· and beautiful,

and evil

sp	92–15	the knowledge of g· and evil,
an	103–11	in a knowledge of both g· and evil,
ph	167–15	If God made man both g· and evil,
	186– 9	Spirit and matter, g· and evil,
f	211– 4	sickness and health, g· and evil,
	216–20	both matter and Spirit, both g· and evil.
	220–28	the knowledge of g· and evil,"— Gen. 2 : 17.
b	269– 4	the supposed coexistence of g· and evil
	283–16	They speak of both . . . g· and evil as spirit.
	287–29	material senses testify to . . . both g· and evil.
	307–21	If we regard . . . Mind as both g· and evil,
	338– 6	g· and evil, both spiritual and material
p	389–25	g· and evil, God and Satan.
r	466–10	truth and error, g· and evil ;
	481–15	declaring . . . g· and evil to be capable of
	481–17	the knowledge of g· and evil,"— Gen. 2 : 17.
g	526– 2	tree of knowledge of g· and evil.— Gen. 2 : 9.

good

and evil

g	527– 8	the knowledge of g· and evil,— Gen. 2 : 17.
	530–16	as gods, knowing g· and evil.— Gen. 3 : 5.
	536–31	to know g· and evil :— Gen. 3 : 22.

and pure

m	63– 6	The beautiful, g·, and pure constitute his

another's

g	518–19	seeking his own in another's g·.

availability of

f	236–19	availability of g· as the remedy for every woe.

capacities for

t	445– 9	Unfold the . . . capacities for g· in your pupil.

choose

r	481– 1	How important, then, to choose g· as

claims of

ph	167– 8	Our . . . admission of the claims of g· or of evil

consecration to

c	262– 2	Consecration to g· does not lessen man's

contrary to

b	339– 9	evil, being contrary to g·, is unreal,

demands

c	261–32	G· demands of man every hour,

demonstrator of

a	49–14	The meek demonstrator of g·,

dies not

f	204– 2	It is evil that dies ; g· dies not.

disarmed by

b	290–31	until evil is disarmed by g·.

discern the

a	22–10	you will discern the g· you have done,

divine

f	203–31	God, divine g·, does not kill a man

doing

sp	79–31	It dissipates fatigue in doing g·.
f	202–32	in the act of doing g·,
	203– 3	and check the reward for doing g·.
p	387–23	supposition . . . God punishes man for doing g·,
	432–16	The Judge asks if by doing g· to his neighbor,

eternal

f	213–14	attraction towards infinite and eternal g·
b	340–19	have no other spirit or mind but God, eternal g·,
ap	561– 3	which works out the ends of eternal g·

evil and

(see evil)

gain

f	254– 4	who gain g· rapidly and hold their position,

God is

(see God)

God, or

c	261–23	you may learn the meaning of God, or g·,
p	380–29	opposite to God, or g·,
t	450–22	understanding . . . the allness of God, or g·.
r	469–26	admitting that God, or g·, is omnipresent
	470– 2	with one Mind and that God, or g·,
	470–13	If God, or g·, is real, then evil, . . . is unreal.
	480–20	God, or g·, never made man capable of sin.
g	533–11	directly or indirectly to God, or g·,
gl	592– 4	and therefore the opposite of God, or g· ;

grasp on

b	327–10	until his grasp on g· grows stronger.

heavenly

c	265–25	The aspiration after heavenly g· comes

highest human

ph	192– 9	capable of producing the highest human g·

idea of

b	325– 3	He who has the true idea of g·
	327–26	the man . . . who has not the true idea of g·?
g	546–14	represents error as starting from an idea of g·

immortality of

sp	81–30	consequence of the immortality of g·.
f	215–28	the superiority and immortality of g·,

individual

sp	72–23	In Science, individual g· derived from God,

infinite

sp	93–18	not the offspring of infinite g·.

in the name of

t	453–23	yet serves evil in the name of g·.
ap	563–28	but doing this in the name of g·.

invisible

sp	78–31	the invisible g· dwelling in eternal Science.

is infinite

p	399– 2	and therefore g· is infinite,

is Mind

s	113–17	God is good. G· is Mind.

is natural

s	128– 2	G· is natural and primitive.

is self-existent

f	213– 9	God, g·, is self-existent and self-expressed,

is the term

b	286–16	In the Saxon . . . g· is the term for God.

knowledge of

g	526–22	as the knowledge of g·.

maximum of

an	103–16	The maximum of g· is the infinite God

good

must dominate
t 446–15   G· must dominate in the thoughts of the healer,
natural
s 119–21   God is natural *g·*, and is represented only by
g 501–15   which subserve the end of natural *g·*,
no
s 113–32   no matter in good, and no *g·* in matter.
  144– 2   since no *g·* can come of it?
b 275–19   no *g·* is, but the good God bestows.
no matter in
s 113–32   no matter in *g·*, and no good in matter.
of one's neighbor
p 440–16   than that it is for the *g·* of one's neighbor?
omnipotent
s 113–19   Life, God, omnipotent *g·*, deny death,
opposite of
sp 72–22   evil, the suppositional opposite of *g·*,
r 480–21   It is the opposite of *g·* — that is, evil
gl 579–16   evil ; the opposite of *g·*,
or evil
ph 171–32   the cognizance of *g·* or evil,
f 205–16   error . . . matter can be intelligent for *g·* or evil
  240–18   Mortals move onward towards *g·* or evil
b 340– 1   their imaginary power for *g·* or evil,
over evil
p 406–23   the supremacy of . . . *g·* over evil,
power of
ap 570–31   the power of *g·* resident in divine Mind,
purposes of
an 103–15   working out the purposes of *g·* only.
reality of
f 205–21   the supremacy and reality of *g·*,
b 269– 7   unfold the unity and the reality of *g·*,
r 480–32   evil would vanish before the reality of *g·*.
g 527–19   Has evil the reality of *g·* ?
reflections of
b 280– 6   From Love . . . only reflections of *g·* can come.
represents
b 282– 9   The sphere represents *g·*,
resides in the
g 546–28   resides in the *g·* this system accomplishes,
result in
p 435– 9   an act which should result in *g·* to himself
sense of
b 311–13   Evil is destroyed by the sense of *g·*.
spiritual
m 56– 6   for the advancement of spiritual *g·*.
f 243– 3   and demonstration of spiritual *g·*
g 505–21   Spiritual sense is the discernment of spiritual *g·*.
standard of
g 539– 8   What can be the standard of *g·*, of Spirit,
substance of
b 301–19   man . . . in reality has, only the substance of *g·*,
supremacy of
s 130–28   and doubts the supremacy of *g·*,
supreme
r 496–10   living the life that approaches the supreme *g·* ?
Truth and
s 114– 6   the divine Mind, or Truth and *g·*.
g 529–27   has neither origin nor support in Truth and *g·*.
universal
sp 76– 8   will be recognized . . . as God, universal *g·* ;
unlike
p 393–13   to resist all that is unlike *g·*.
unlikeness of
f 204–14   evil, is the unlikeness of *g·*.
voicing
b 332–10   Christ is the true idea voicing *g·*,
your
f 254–29   Your *g·* will be evil spoken of.
your influence for
ph 192–22   Your influence for *g·* depends upon the

a 20– 1   for there is one Life, — even God, *g·*.
  42–27   true man is governed by God — by *g·*,
  52–21   the mighty actuality of all-inclusive God, *g·*.
m 60– 7   The beautiful in character is also the *g·*,
  61– 4   The *g·* in human affections must
  68–21   it may have caused the *g·* to ponder
sp 72–21   God, *g·*, being ever present, it follows
  76– 9   belief that . . . was ever in a finite form, or *g·* in evil,
  77– 2   "I cannot turn at once from *g·* to evil."
  81–29   man's immortality depends upon that of God, *g·*,
  85– 8   enabling one to do *g·*, but not evil.
  93–13   G· never causes evil,
  93–15   G· does not create a mind susceptible of
  95–13   cannot injure others, and must do them *g·*.
an 103–22   belief . . . that evil is as real as *g·*
s 113–30   Disease, sin, evil, death, deny *g·*,
  130–13   *g·* and its sweet concords have all-power.
  130–32   imagine evil to be ever-present and *g·* absent?
  134–26   because it is the immutable law of God, *g·*.
ph 167–21   no more . . . than *g·* can coincide with evil.

good

ph 169–24   whatever *g·* they may seem to receive from
  176–13   "sermons in stones, and *g·* in everything."
  186–18   It says : "I am a real entity, overmastering *g·*."
  186–20   It can never destroy one iota of *g·*.
  186–21   Every attempt . . . to destroy *g·* is a failure,
  186–24   If evil is as real as *g·*, evil is also as immortal.
  192–23   The *g·* you do and embody gives you
f 201–12   superabundance of being is on the side of God, *g·*.
  204–22   The first power is admitted to be *g·*,
  204–32   The error, which says . . . *g·* is in evil,
  205–31   not of Spirit, God, *g·*, but of
  207–11   Evil is not supreme ; *g·* is not helpless ;
  207–16   nor is evil mightier than *g·*.
  216–23   evil would appear to be the master of *g·*,
  230–15   G· is not, cannot be, the author of
  230–17   God, *g·*, can no more produce sickness
  231–12   If God makes sin, if *g·* produces evil,
  234– 9   become more familiar with *g·* than with evil,
  242–12   It is to know no other reality . . . than *g·*
  244–27   He does not pass . . . from evil to *g·*,
  244–27   He does not pass . . . from *g·* to evil.
c 261– 5   the enduring, the *g·*, and the true,
  261–31   should forget our bodies in remembering *g·*
  263–13   producing evil when he would create *g·*,
  263–18   "The *g·* that I would, I do not :— *Rom.* 7 : 19.
  264–18   finding all in God, *g·*, and needing no other
  275–19   no good is, but the *g·* God bestows.
b 277– 7   G· cannot result in evil.
  277–21   asserts . . . that *g·* is the origin of evil.
  278– 8   in Truth there is no error, and in *g·* no evil.
  285– 1   cannot be cognizant of *g·* or of evil,
  288–22   Life is God, *g·*, and not evil ;
  293–30   universal harmony, the entireness of God, *g·*,
  304–12   *g·* can never produce evil ;
  309–18   and forget that Life is God, *g·*,
  309–18   *g·* is not in elements which are not spiritual,
  310–27   if Spirit should lose Life as God, *g·*, then
  323– 5   possess no other consciousness but *g·*.
  323–16   *g·* is not understood until demonstrated.
  327–19   hastening to learn that Life is God, *g·*,
  336– 4   G· never enters into evil,
  340–23   One infinite God, *g·*, unifies men and nations ;
o 343–16   impossibility of *g·* producing evil ;
  348–18   or in any power but God, *g·*.
  356–25   Does evil proceed from *g·* ?
p 368–11   fatal beliefs . . . that evil is equal in power to *g·*
  387–19   That man . . . who does the most *g·*.
  404–25   ability to master evil and to love *g·*.
  405–20   demonstrates the government of God, *g·*,
  414–22   "The Lord He is God [*g·*] ; — *Deut.* 4 : 35.
  415– 4   Mind in every case is the eternal God, *g·*.
t 444– 5   "All things work together for *g·* — *Rom.* 8 : 28.
  447– 8   ignorant attempts to do *g·*
  448–15   or upon the *g·* you know and *do* not.
  450–19   evil will boast itself above *g·*.
r 469–14   truth that God, *g·*, is the *only* Mind,
  470–17   How can *g·* lapse into evil,
  490–11   since all power belongs to God, *g·*.
g 504– 2   God, . . . is never reflected by aught but the *g·*
  525–29   as devoid of reality as they are of *g·*,
  527–18   But is it true that God, *g·*, made
  532–24   Is Mind capable . . . of evil as well as of *g·*,
  538–17   false claims that misrepresent God, *g·*.
  555–19   error would seek to unite . . . *g·* with evil,
ap 571–16   At all times . . . overcome evil with *g·*,
gl 579–13   the purpose of Love to create trust in *g·*,
  580– 5   that which is not the image and likeness of *g·*,
  587–19   definition of
  594– 6   claim that there is an opposite of Spirit, or *g·*,
  594–11   claim that . . . was as real and eternal as God, *g·*

good (adj., adv.)

pref viii–10   and physics teach that both . . . are real and *g·*,
  viii–11   the fact is that Spirit is *g·* and real,
  x–24   Its purpose is *g·*, and its practice is
pr 4–12   The habitual struggle to be always *g·*
  9– 4   the falsehood which does no one any *g·*.
  10– 6   If *g·* enough to profit by Jesus' cup
a 19–18   every *g·* thought and deed, will help us
  21– 3   "I have fought a *g·* fight — *II Tim.* 4 : 7.
  28– 9   While respecting all that is *g·* in the Church
  35–32   *g·* man's heaven would be a hell to the sinner.
  40–20   If a career so great and *g·* as that of Jesus
  44– 3   *g·* and faithful servant," — *Matt.* 25 : 23.
m 66–26   the other pre-eminently needs *g·* company.
sp 70–11   that there are *g·* and evil spirits, is a mistake.
  83– 6   the incredible *g·* and evil elements
  99– 8   to do of His *g·* pleasure" — *Phil.* 2 : 13.
s 110– 7   is pronounced by His wisdom *g·*.
  120–11   indicate that he is in *g·* health?
  131–22   for so it seemed *g·* in Thy sight." — *Luke* 10 : 21.
  155–31   If drugs are *g·* things, is it safe to say
  156– 3   and what made them *g·* or bad
  157–17   If drugs are . . . , *g·*, then drugs cannot be poisonous.

good (adj., adv.)

ph	167–32	Substituting *g·* words for a *g·* life,
	169–31	*g·* that a poisonous drug seems to do is evil,
	181–22	are satisfied with *g·* words instead of effects,
	189–13	sins of others should not make *g·* men suffer.
f	206–24	His work is *finished*, . . . and that it was *g·*.
	210–28	appears . . . to make *g·* its claim.
	229–13	declaring Him *g·* in one instance and
	229–23	If God causes man to be sick, sickness must be *g·*,
	229–25	all that He makes is *g·* and will stand forever.
	236–27	that will make them happy and *g·*.
	237–11	theories of parents often choke the *g·* seed
	237–13	snatches away the *g·* seed before it has
	246–21	and limiting all that is *g·* and beautiful,
	252–24	where the *g·* purpose waits!
c	266– 1	where the creations of God are *g·*,
b	269–19	this advantage . . . they are *g·* and eternal.
	270–32	the *g·* soil wherein the seed of Truth
	272– 6	"honest and *g·* heart" — *Luke* 8 : 15.
	277– 8	As God Himself is *g·*
	286–18	all that He made to be *g·*, like Himself,
	286–18	like Himself, — *g·* in Principle and in idea.
	286–20	Therefore the spiritual universe is *g·*,
	294–26	recognizable only in what is *g·* and true.
	309–12	a soldier of God, who had fought a *g·* fight.
	311– 5	all that Mind, God, is, or hath made, is *g·*,
	330–22	Mind is not both *g·* and bad,
	332–28	incarnate in the *g·* and pure Christ Jesus.
	339– 9	God, . . . created all, and called it *g·*.
o	342–27	to disown the Christliness of *g·* works,
	352–31	To accomplish a *g·* result, it is certainly
	356–28	Would any one call it wise and *g·* to
	357–16	deny that God made man evil and made evil *g·*
p	376–14	more . . . immortality in one *g·* motive and act,
	383– 5	One says: "I take *g·* care of my body."
	397–19	you will find the ensuing *g·* effects to be
	404–19	every tree that brings not forth *g·* fruit.
	405–18	The *g·* man finally can overcome his fear of
	413– 1	and cannot transmit *g·* or evil intelligence
	413–10	*g·* or bad effects on the health of children.
	431–31	testifies: . . . I am robbed of my *g·* looks
	435–15	this was a *g·* deed,
	436–12	Laying down his life for a *g·* deed,
	441– 8	to give heavy bonds for *g·* behavior.
	442–15	one "that bringeth *g·* tidings." — *Isa.* 52 : 7.
	442–27	it is your Father's *g·* pleasure — *Luke* 12 : 32.
t	449–24	a *g·* detective of individual character.
	457–17	to mental malpractice, . . . there is no *g·* aspect,
	458– 4	one *g·* and the other evil,
	459–26, 27	The tree must be *g·*, which produces *g·* fruit.
	464–20	hold fast that which is *g·*." — *I Thess.* 5 : 21.
r	472–25	That which He creates is *g·*,
	489– 5	hypothesis that soul is both an evil and a *g·*
	480–32	sometimes *g·* and sometimes bad.
	492–13	statement proved to be *g·* must be
g	503–26	saw the light, that it was *g·*: — *Gen.* 1 : 4.
	506–24	God saw that it was *g·*. — *Gen.* 1 : 10.
	508–12	God saw that it was *g·*. — *Gen.* 1 : 12.
	511–10	God saw that it was *g·*. — *Gen.* 1 : 18.
	512– 7	God saw that it was *g·*. — *Gen.* 1 : 21.
	513–25	God saw that it was *g·*. — *Gen.* 1 : 25.
	515– 3	God saw that it was *g·*." — *Gen.* 1 : 25.
	518–25	and, behold, it was very *g·*. — *Gen.* 1 : 31.
	525–20	Everything *g·* or worthy, God made.
	525–24	"and, behold, it was very *g·*." — *Gen.* 1 : 31.
	526– 1	pleasant to the sight, and *g·* for food; — *Gen.* 2 : 9.
	526–16	God pronounced *g·* all that He created,
	537–13	represented as spiritual, entire, and *g·*.
gl	583–21	divine Principle of all that is real and *g·*;
fr	600– *	being *fruitful in every g· work*, — *Col.* 1 : 10.

(see also **deeds**)

Good, Dr. Mason

s	163–13	Dr. Mason *G·*, a learned Professor in London,

goodness

affection and

a	24–28	lay in the practical affection and *g·*

and beauty

s	121–13	So we have *g·* and beauty to gladden the

and blessedness

pr	10–25	source and means of all *g·* and blessedness,

and mercy

ap	578–16	*g·* and mercy shall follow me — *Psal.* 23 : 6.

and power

g	515–23	reflecting *g·* and power.

and purity

p	364– 1	a man of undoubted *g·* and purity,

and spirituality

b	277– 8	*g·* and spirituality must be immortal.
	277–10	If *g·* and spirituality are real,

and virtue

m	57–17	the better claims of intellect, *g·*, and virtue.

another's

a	21–7	another's *g·*, suffering, and triumph,

attains

pr	2–16	*G·* attains the demonstration of Truth.

goodness

beauty and

sp	76–23	possessing unlimited divine beauty and *g·*
b	304– 4	which hide spiritual beauty and *g·*.
g	503–22	immortal forms of beauty and *g·*.

charms of His

f	247–23	and reflects the charms of His *g·*

culture and

sp	95–12	reaches this point of moral culture and *g·*

divine

m	66–16	unfolds new views of divine *g·* and love.

goal of

f	233–14	until the goal of *g·* is . . . won.

great

a	47–18	He knew that the great *g·* of that Master

happiness and

f	244– 9	happiness and *g·* would have no

idea of

s	119–22	God . . . is represented only by the idea of *g·*;

immortality, and

g	518–20	Love giveth . . . immortality, and *g·*,

inspiration of

gl	581– 5	inspiration of *g·*, purity, and

Life and

f	246–28	Life and *g·* are immortal.

of God's character

f	208–12	not in accordance with the *g·* of God's character

omnipotent in

p	367–31	Because Truth is omnipotent in *g·*,

Principle of

s	147–31	Science alone reveals the divine Principle of *g·*.

Principle of all

pr	3– 8	Shall we ask the divine Principle of all *g·* to

towards

f	213–11	Every step towards *g·* is a departure from

universal

b	329– 4	glow in all the grandeur of universal *g·*.

without

b	328– 4	suppose that they can live without *g·*,

pr	4–24	*g·* will "be evil spoken of," — *Rom.* 14 : 16.
a	53–24	the lifelong sacrifice which *g·* makes for
an	106–28	longsuffering, gentleness, *g·*, — *Gal.* 5 : 22,
s	147–29	A pure affection takes form in *g·*,
ph	196–19	Sin makes its own hell, and *g·* its own heaven.
f	230–17	no more . . . than *g·* can cause evil
	248–29	Let unselfishness, *g·*, mercy,
c	260–15	distrust of one's ability to gain the *g·*
r	465–15	justice, mercy, wisdom, *g·*,
g	516–11	Life is reflected in existence, . . . God in *g·*,

goods

p	399–30	and spoil his *g·*, — *Matt.* 12 : 29.
	400– 7	of his *g·*, — namely, of sin and disease.
	438–24	and smuggles Error's *g·* into market
	439 1	introducing their *g·* into the market.

good-will

s	150– 8	"on earth peace, *g·* toward men." — *Luke* 2 : 14.
f	226 17	"on earth peace, *g·* toward men." — *Luke* 2 : 14.
p	407–16	even into spiritual power and *g·* to man,

gorgeousness

f	252–25	and says: . . . I am enthroned in the *g·* of matter

Gospel

John's

gl	598– 2	in John's *G·*, the third chapter,

Luke's

p	362– 1	in the seventh chapter of Luke's *G·*

Mark's

s	117–11	in the last chapter of Mark's *G·*
b	272–12	referred to in the last chapter of Mark's *G·*.

pref	xi–22	called the author to proclaim His *G·*
	525–17	In the *G·* of John, it is declared that
ap	561–30	In the first chapter of the Fourth *G·*

gospel

is preached

a	27– 6	to the poor the *g·* is preached." — *Luke* 7 : 22.

law and

p	441–30	a verdict contrary to law and *g·*.

of healing

a	55– 9	the *g·* of healing is again preached

of Love

ap	577– 4	His universal family, held in the *g·* of Love.

preaches the

a	33–25	and preaches the *g·* to the poor,

preaching the

a	31– 1	he was found preaching the *g·* to the poor,
o	347–16	preaching the *g·* to the poor,

preach the

a	18– *	but to preach the *g·*. — *I Cor.* 1 : 17.
	37–30	preach the *g·* to every — *Mark* 16 : 15.
s	138–28	preach the *g·* to every — *Mark* 16 : 15.

gospel

preach the

  o 342–11 and preach the *g·*,"— *Mark* 16 : 15.

  p 418–28 "Preach the *g·* to every— *Mark* 16 : 15.

  s 107– * the g· which was preached of me— Gal.* 1 : 11.

  132– 8 the poor have the *g·* preached — *Matt.* 11 : 5.

  150– 7 the coming anew of the *g·* of

  ph 176– 9 gave the *g·* a chance to be seen

  b 309–23 and led to deny . . . even as the *g·* teaches.

  337–15 can see God, as the *g·* teaches.

  o 349– 6 We have the *g·*, however,

  gl 592–13 MOSES. . . . the proof that, without the *g·*,

gospel-healing

  o 343–31 to press along the line of *g·*,

Gospels

  sp 79–21 so far as can be learned from the *G·*,

gossamer

  p 403–20 the *g·* web of mortal illusion.

gossip

  f 238–28 no time for *g·* about false law or testimony.

gotten

  r 479– 5 "I have *g·* a man from the Lord"— *Gen.* 4 : 1.

  g 538–24 I have *g·* a man from the Lord— *Gen.* 4 : 1.

  538–30 "I have *g·* a man from the Lord,"— *Gen.* 4 : 1.

govern

  s 151–31 mortal mind claims to *g·* every organ

  154–18 and her own fears *g·* her child more than

  ph 175–25 Beaumont's . . . did not *g·* the digestion.

  f 206– 7 It is the province of spiritual sense to *g·* man.

  227–30 If God had instituted material laws to *g·* man,

  251–15 learn how mankind *g·* the body,

  251–17 learn whether they *g·* the body through a

  251–19 or *g·* it from the higher understanding

  p 380–32 Every law of matter . . . supposed to *g·* man,

  393–11 and *g·* its feeling and action.

  402–22 we rarely remember that we *g·* our own bodies.

  409–15 prevents . . . knowing how to *g·* their bodies.

  414–12 guide and *g·* mortal mind

  r 490– 6 Hence it cannot *g·* man aright.

  494– 1 and to *g·* man's entire action?

governed

  pr 14–10 to be absolutely *g·* by divine Love,

  a 42–26 in C. S. the true man is *g·* by God

  m 62–27 The higher nature of man is not *g·* by the lower ;

  sp 83–17 belief that . . . man, is *g·* in general by

  an 106–10 *g·* by his Maker, divine Truth and Love.

  s 125–15 *g·* by Soul, not by material sense.

  131– 4 our lives must be *g·* by reality

  141–16 the Christ-spirit which *g·* the corporeal Jesus.

  146– 4 our systems of religion are *g·* more or less by

  150–26 The doctrine that man's harmony is *g·* by

  151–21 Every function of the real man is *g·* by the

  155–14 such a belief is *g·* by the majority.

  160–29 only to learn . . . that muscle is not so *g·*?

  ph 180–25 When man is *g·* by God, the ever-present

  184–17 Whatever is *g·* by a false belief is discordant

  187–21 is *g·* by this so-called mind, not by matter.

  187–23 man in Science is *g·* by this Mind.

  195–15 an idea *g·* by its Principle,

  f 206–13 prayer, *g·* by Science instead of the senses,

  215–12 Whatever is *g·* by God, is never . . . deprived of

  216–17 If man is *g·* by the law of divine Mind,

  226–23 belief that the body *g·* them, rather than Mind.

  231–30 Man, *g·* by his Maker, having no other Mind,

  240–12 suppose Mind to be *g·* by matter

  245–26 for the mental state *g·* the physical.

  246–24 Man, *g·* by immortal Mind, is always

  c 257–10 it is the belief in . . . soul *g·* by the body

  b 273–18 Man is harmonious when *g·* by Soul.

  274–27 *g·* by the unerring and eternal Mind,

  302–22 this real man is *g·* by Soul instead of sense,

  304–14 The perfect man— *g·* by God,

  318–28 The governor is not subjected to the *g·*.

  318–29 man is *g·* by God, divine Principle,

  p 376–19 a mental concept and *g·* by mortal mind,

  409–20 The animate should be *g·* by God alone.

  r 480–10 Consciousness, as well as action, is *g·* by

  495– 2 whenever man is *g·* by God.

  g 536–14 if man should be *g·* by corporeality

  536–18 mortal man would be *g·* by himself.

  546–11 while matter is *g·* by

  gl 583– 7 who, . . . are *g·* by divine Science ;

  588–15 though they are *g·* by one Principle.

governing

  sp 71– 8 God, the creative, *g·*, infinite Principle

  81–22 the producing, *g·*, divine Principle lives on,

  s 158–30 and mortal mind, . . . is *g·* the pellet.

  ph 174– 1 less faith . . . in a supreme *g·* intelligence.

  f 209– 5 Mind, . . . *g·* them all, is the central sun

  231–15 no antagonistic powers . . . *g·* man through

  b 282–25 mortal thought, always *g·* itself erroneously.

governing

  b 303– 5 the Principle *g·* the reflection.

  308– 5 God is the only Mind *g·* man,

  p 370– 8 proves that fear is *g·* the body.

  377–21 Remove the leading error or *g·* fear

  427–24 Immortal Mind, *g·* all, must be acknowledged

  g 510–30 *g·* the universe, including man,

  gl 588–12 Mind, *g·* all existence ;

  595– 1 SUN. The symbol of Soul *g·* man,

Government

  p 442– 3 Our statute is spiritual, our *G·* is divine.

government

by divine Principle

  gl 587–25 reign of Spirit ; *g·* by divine Principle ;

divine

  f 225– 3 opposed to the divine *g·*.

false

  sp 94–12 owe their false *g·* to the misconceptions of

French

  an 100–12 In 1784, the French *g·* ordered the

God's

  a 36– 8 not in accordance with God's *g·*,

  m 62–25 but let no mortal interfere with God's *g·*

  sp 78–27 claimed to be the agents of God's *g·*.

  s 125–17 Reflecting God's *g·*, man is self-governed.

  p 393–17 in Science man reflects God's *g·*.

His

  s 128– 5 His *g·* of the universe, inclusive of man.

  f 231–24 To fear sin is . . . to doubt His *g·*

  r 472–10 do not originate in God nor belong to His *g·*.

might and

  g 522– 6 first record assigns all might and *g·* to God,

of God

  c 258–29 man, under the *g·* of God in eternal Science,

  p 405–20 demonstrates the *g·* of God,

of the body

  ph 167–26 scientific *g·* of the body must be

  182–18 Mind's *g·* of the body must supersede the

  t 462–30 It urges the *g·* of the body

of the universe

  s 121–32 in the everlasting *g·* of the universe.

  128– 5 His *g·* of the universe, inclusive of man.

  g 539–15 resigned to matter the *g·* of the universe?

reins of

  p 422–29 Not holding the reins of *g·* in his own hands,

spiritual

  gl 597–28 the movements of God's spiritual *g·*,

---

  an 100–16 reported to the *g·* as follows :

  c 265– 1 and its *g·* is divine Science.

  p 378–23 not . . . take the *g·* into its own hands,

  438–25 without the inspection of Soul's *g·* officers.

governments

  p 378–32 usually find displayed in human *g·*.

Governor

  p 432–11 I am Mortality, *G·* of the Province of Body,

governor

  b 318–28 The *g·* is not subjected to the governed.

  r 480–11 origin and *g·* of all that Science reveals.

Governor Mortality

  p 432–18 and *G· M·* replies in the affirmative.

governs

  pr 6– 3 Divine Love corrects and *g·* man.

  a 39–27 and *g·* the universe harmoniously.

  an 102– 2 God *g·* all that is real, harmonious, and

  102–13 since God *g·* the universe ;

  s 111–28 Mind *g·* the body, not partially but wholly.

  149–26 Mind, *g·* all, not partially but supremely,

  154–19 more than the child's mind *g·* itself,

  160–28 to learn how mortal mind *g·* muscle,

  162–12 Mind *g·* the body, . . . in every instance.

  ph 180–14 Ignorant that the human mind *g·* the body,

  188– 8 but afterwards it *g·* the so-called man.

  f 209– 4 in proportion as ignorance, . . . *g·* mortals.

  219–10 No more can we say . . . that matter *g·*,

  219–20 Science . . . *g·* harmoniously.

  219–24 and yet misunderstand the science that *g·* it.

  222–12 availed himself of the fact that Mind *g·*

  224– 6 the Science which *g·* these changes,

  231–21 God made you superior to it and *g·* man,

  b 270–11 intelligence, . . . *g·* the universe,

  286–14 divine Principle, Love, creates and *g·* all

  295– 5 God creates and *g·* the universe,

  304–22 The science of music *g·* tones.

  316–21 Spirit creates, constitutes, and *g·*.

  324– 9 the body will reflect what *g·* it,

  p 375–21 a belief that matter *g·* mortals,

  377– 3 convince him . . . that thought *g·* this liability.

  393–17 in your understanding that the divine Mind *g·*,

  412– 2 great fact that God lovingly *g·* all,

  418–22 this simple rule of Truth, which *g·* all reality

  420– 4 Spirit not matter, *g·* man.

governs

p 422–31 he believes that . . . matter— g· the case.
r 496– 5 Mind is reflected by man and g· the entire
g 507–17 Life, . . . g· the multiplication of the
507–24 Infinite Mind creates and g· all,
508– 7 and Love which g· all.
532– 4 No! God makes and g· all.
539–29 makes and g· man and the universe.

grace

pr 4– 4 prayer of fervent desire for growth in g·,
17– 5 Give us g· for to-day ;
a 27–26 They fell away from g· because they
m 67–23 G· and Truth are potent beyond all other
s 108– 3 "the gift of the g· of God — Eph. 3 : 7.
118–16 the invisible and infinite power and g·,
134–17 doctrines of Christ or the miracles of g·
f 220–25 never to try dietetics for growth in g·.
247–19 Comeliness and g· are independent of matter.
c 263–13 forming deformity when he would outline g·
b 333–22 has come with some measure of power and g·
r 478–29 called me by His g·,— Gal. 1 : 15.
494–15 miracle of g· is no miracle to Love.

graces

p 429– 4 as well as by other g· of Spirit.

gracious

pr 1– 7 God's g· means for accomplishing

graciously

s 107– 4 God had been g· preparing me

gradation

g 511–26 metaphorically present the g· of

gradations

g 551–13 Evolution describes the g· of human belief,

grade

p 303– 7 as was customary with women of her g·.

grades

ph 172– 7 Materialism g· the human species as
g 551– 12 through all the lower g· of existence.

gradually

sp 77–25 The departed would g· rise above ignorance
s 109–23 The revelation of Truth . . . came to me g·
111–31 this system has g· gained ground,
p 380–25 G· this evidence will gather momentum
t 460–30 As former beliefs were g· expelled
ap 576–30 Yet the word g· approaches a higher meaning.

grafting

f 201–20 G· holiness upon unholiness,

Graham

ph 170– 8 Did Jesus understand . . . less than G· or Cutter?
f 221– 2 adopted the G· system to cure dyspepsia.

grain

s 130–21 and to inculcate a g· of faith in God,
t 449– 3 A g· of C S. does wonders for mortals,

grammars

g 508–20 g· always recognize a neuter gender,

grand

sp 75–31 from earth's sleep to the g· verities of Life,
s 116–13 Works on metaphysics leave the g· point
143–26 Mind is the g· creator, and there can be
164–10 generally . . . are g· men and women,
ph 200– 6 illustrated the g· human capacities of being
f 240– 7 Suns and planets teach g· lessons.
240–11 In the order of Science, . . . all is one g· concord.
244– 4 Divine Science reveals these g· facts.
246–25 Man, . . . is always beautiful and g·.
248–28 carve them out in g· and noble lives.
b 328–12 reveals the g· realities of His allness.
o 341– 7 grow in beauty . . . from one g· root,
354–29 I rejoice in the apprehension of this g· verity.
p 384–15 prove to himself, . . . the g· verities of C. S.
t 448–23 accomplish the g· results of Truth and Love.
460–25 she had to impart, while teaching its g· facts,
r 471– 8 senses, afford no indication of the g· facts,
490– 1 the g· truths of C. S. dispute this error.
g 511–25 mountains stand for solid and g· ideas.
514–30 A realization of this g· verity was a source of
518–16 The rich in spirit help the poor in one g·
ap 560–13 the g· necessity of existence is to gain the
575–32 g· realization of the Golden Shore of Love

grandest

a 49–19 charged with the g· trust of heaven,
f 213–21 rapture of his g· symphonies was never heard.

grandeur

a 39– 2 met the mockery of his unrecognized g·.
f 244–31 g· and immortality of development,
b 328– 1 the g· and bliss of a spiritual sense,
329– 4 glow in all the g· of universal goodness.
ap 571–30 the sublime g· of divine Science,

granite

pref vii–25 and to cut the rough g·.

Grant, General

r 492–18 Discussing his campaign, General G· said :

grant

pr 2–13 the All-loving does not g· them simply on the
10–31 In this case infinite Love will not g· the request.

granted

pref xii– 1 No charters were g· . . . after 1883,
m 63–23 let us hope it will be g·.
t 453– 4 should be g· that the author understands

grape

fr 600– * whether the tender g· appear,— Song 7 : 12.

grapes

f 211–20 "the fathers have eaten sour g·,— Ezek. 18 : 2.
b 276–30 Divine Science does not gather g· from thorns
g 539–24 "Do men gather g· of thorns ?"— Matt. 7 : 16.

graphic

a 52–14 Isaiah's g· word concerning the coming

graphically

sp 92–17 The portrayal is still g· accurate,

grapple

a 29– 2 They must g· with sin in themselves and in
f 235–31 love to g· with a new, right idea
ap 569– 4 Every mortal . . . must g· with and overcome

grasp

pr 13–23 and so we cannot g· the wonders wrought
a 28– 7 determination to hold Spirit in the g· of matter
sp 98–16 above the loosening g· of creeds,
s 119 10 to g· the other horn of the dilemma
142–17 and causes the left to let go its g· on the
147–22 enables you to g· the spiritual facts
ph 192– 5 only as we . . . g· the true.
f 209–11 intelligence which holds the winds in its g·.
254–12 mortals g· the ultimate . . . slowly ;
b 275–10 To g· the reality and order of being
281–29 as we g· the facts of Spirit.
327–10 until his g· on good grows stronger.
o 349–20 in order to g· the meaning of this Science.
p 381–21 will sooner g· man's God-given dominion.
g 519–12 is slow to discern and to g· God's creation
ap 573– 2 is unable to g· such a view.

grasped

an 104–27 leaving the case worse than before it was g· by

grass

blade of

sp 70–13 from a blade of g· to a star,
ph 191–21 By its own volition, not a blade of g· springs up,

days are as

ph 190–23 As for man, his days are as g· :—Psal. 103 : 15.
r 476–24 "As for man, his days are as g· :— Psal. 103 : 15.

of Gethsemane

a 48–11 fell in holy benediction on the g· of Gethsemane,

sp 81 18 the g· seemeth to wither and the flower to
ph 190 15 is as the g· springing from the soil
s 507–12 Let the earth bring forth g·,— Gen. 1 : 11.
508– 9 the earth brought forth g·,— Gen. 1 : 12.
516–13 The g· beneath our feet silently exclaims,

grateful

pr 3–22 Are we really g· for the good
9– 2 the author has been most g· for

gratification

a 38–27 living only for pleasure or the g· of the senses,

gratifications

g 536–22 Their narrow limits belittle their g·,

gratify

a 49–12 O, why did they not g· his last human yearning
s 163–26 exhibition of human invention might g·

gratitude

pr 3–25 G· is much more than a verbal expression of
3–26 Action expresses more g· than speech.
4– 8 worthy evidence of our g· for all that he has
4–10 to express loyal and heartfelt g·,
8–15 If we feel the aspiration, humility, g·,
a 26– 2 heart overflows with g· for what he did
m 66–17 Amidst g· for conjugal felicity, it is well to
p 367–15 oil of gladness and the perfume of g·,
gl 595–22 Tithe. Contribution ; tenth part ; homage ; g·.

grave

beyond the

a 46–24 and progressive state beyond the g·.
p 409–30 cannot . . . expect to find beyond the g· a

death and the

a 39–14 Jesus overcame death and the g·
45– 7 in his victory over death and the g·.
49–25 triumph over sin, sickness, death, and the g·.
s 137– 7 victor over sickness, sin, . . . death, and the g·.

grave

from the
b 291–26 No resurrection from the g· awaits Mind
  313–30 which by spiritual power he raised from the g·,
  317–22 after his resurrection from the g·,
g 509– 6 to their apprehension he rose from the g·,
has no power
b 291–26 for the g· has no power over either.
of affection
m 68– 9 Jealousy is the g· of affection.
robs the
b 275–27 It robs the g· of victory.
  323–26 The true idea . . . robs the g· of victory,
this side of the
a 36–23 punishment this side of the g·

a 24–30 enabled their Master to triumph over the g·,
sp 73–26 g· mistake to suppose that matter is
s 138– 1 [hades, the under-world, or the g·]
f 244– 8 seen between the cradle and the g·,
b 291– 5 these are g· mistakes.
o 353–25 The g· does not banish the ghost of
p 426–20 either a desire to die or a dread of the g·,
r 496–23 the spiritual law which says to the g·,

grave-clothes
p 367– 2 nor bury the morale of C. S. in the g· of its

graven
m 67– 1 may be g· with the image of God.

gravitate
c 265– 5 Mortals must g· Godward,

gravitates
b 323–21 g· towards Soul and away from

gravitation
b 272–23 earthward g· of sensualism and impurity,
g 536–12 If man's spiritual g· and attraction to

gravity
s 149–18 A physician . . . remarked with great g· :

gray
f 245–14 no care-lined face, no wrinkles nor g· hair,
g 513– 9 g· in the sombre hues of twilight ;

great
pr 5– 4 The next and g· step required by wisdom
  9–13 we shall never meet this g· duty simply by
  16– 1· A g· sacrifice of material things must precede
a 23– 3 One sacrifice, however g·, is insufficient to
  24–17 views of atonement will undergo a g· change,
  25– 1 complete was the g· proof of Truth and Love.
  25–30 else we are not improving the g· blessings
  29–10 G· is the reward of self-sacrifice,
  33– 7 It was the g· truth of spiritual being,
  33–15 With the g· glory of an everlasting victory
  36–15 g· moral distance between Christianity and
  40–19 If a career so g· and good as that of Jesus
  42–15 The resurrection of the g· demonstrator
  44– 6 place in which to solve the g· problem of being.
  44–32 a g· stone must be rolled from the cave's mouth ;
  47–18 He knew that the g· goodness of that Master
  48–19 g· demonstrator of Truth and Love was silent
  49– 9 Had they forgotten the g· exponent of God?
  53–21 g· distance between the individual and Truth.
m 66– 1 immortal Shakespeare, g· poet of humanity :
  66–10 Through g· tribulation we enter the
  68– 5 shall learn how Spirit, the g· architect,
sp 83–24 Between C. S. and . . . superstition a g· gulf
  85–18 events of g· moment were foretold by the
  91– 7 Here is the g· point of departure for all true
  91–12 the sooner man's g· reality will appear
an 104– 9 "Every g· scientific truth goes through three
  106–18 in his g· epistle to the Galatians,
s 109–32 The three g· verities of Spirit,
  112–19 which, like the g· Giver,
  115– 1 the one g· obstacle to the reception of
  115– 9 g· difficulty is to give the right impression,
  122– 4 the g· facts of Life, rightly understood,
  125–26 dominion over the atmosphere and the g· deep,
  126–28 demonstrations of our g· Master
  129–13 there will be "g· tribulation— Matt. 24 : 21.
  133– 6 "I have not found so g· faith,— Matt. 8 : 10.
  136–22 and the g· work of the Master,
  148–32 our g· Master demonstrated that Truth could
  149–17 A physician . . . remarked with g· gravity :
  151– 8 G· respect is due the motives and
  158–14 and endured g· sufferings upon earth.
ph 184–28 always breathed with g· difficulty when the
  200–16 The g· truth in the Science of being,
f 207–23 does not proceed from this g· and only cause.
  216–19 The g· mistake of mortals is to suppose that
  234–29 laid g· stress on the action of the human mind,
  242– 6 Denial of the claims of matter is a g· step

great
f 251– 7 Fright is so g· at certain stages of
  254–14 demonstrating the g· problem of being,
c 267–10 The g· I AM made all
b 268– 2 brought to light with g· rapidity
  274–16 Jesus demonstrated this g· verity.
  293–19 g· difference being that electricity is not
  309–21 to be brought back through g· tribulation,
  326–14 the g· healer of mortal mind is the healer of
  328–30 his g· life-work extends through time
  329– 9 the g· might of divine Science
o 358–22 g· import to Christianity of those works
p 375–26 g· hopefulness and courage, even when
  395– 6 Like the g· Exemplar, the healer should
  397–23 familiar with the g· verities of being.
  403– 2 The g· difference between voluntary and
  417– 9 If you make the sick realize this g· truism,
  422– 5 If the reader of this book observes a g· stir
  426–21 destroy the g· fear that besets mortal existence.
  427–21 The g· difficulty lies in ignorance of
  428–11 this is the g· attainment by means of which
  428–22 The g· spiritual fact must be brought out
  433– 2 with g· solemnity addresses the jury
t 445– 9 Teach the g· possibilities of man
  445–27 g· danger in teaching . . . indiscriminately,
  448– 4 went out to the g· heart of Love,
  454–13 g· truth which strips all disguise from error.
r 469–14 the g· truth that God, good, is the only Mind,
  494– 5 so g· a work as the Messiah's
g 510–13 And God made two g· lights ;— Gen. 1 : 16.
  512– 4 And God created g· whales,— Gen. 1 : 21.
  516–16 The g· rock gives shadow and shelter.
  528–22 declaring what g· things error has done.
  543–15 The g· verities of existence are never excluded
  546–24 g· spiritual facts of being, like rays of light,
  547–20 evolution implies that the g· First Cause
  548–27 endowed by the labors and genius of g· men.
  549–27 even this g· observer mistakes nature,
  550–21 If . . . then the g· I AM is a myth.
  555–28 Our g· example, Jesus, could restore
ap 558– * G· is the Lord, and greatly to be— Psal. 48 : 1.
  560– 6 And there appeared a g· wonder— Rev. 12 : 1.
  560–11 The g· miracle, to human sense, is divine Love,
  560–24 which made him equal to his g· mission.
  562–27 g· is the idea, and the travail portentous.
  562–30 and behold a g· red dragon,— Rev. 12 : 3.
  563– 8 The g· red dragon symbolizes a lie,
  565– 2 and becomes the g· red dragon, swollen with sin,
  566– 4 walking wearily through the g· desert
  567–14 And the g· dragon was cast out,— Rev. 12 : 9.
  568–22 having g· wrath, because he— Rev. 12 : 12.
  568–28 clearer and nearer to the g· heart of Christ;
  570–27 should know the g· benefit which Mind has
      wrought.
  570–28 also know the g· delusion of mortal mind,
  574–22 lifted the seer to behold the g· city,
  575–24 the city of the g· King."— Psal. 48 : 2.
  577–19 interprets this g· example and the g· Exemplar.
  577–30 as recorded by the g· apostle,
gl 580–10 an unreality as opposed to the g· reality
  587– 5 GOD. The g· I AM ; the all-knowing, all-seeing,
  596– 4 may define Deity as "the g· unknowable ;"
  597– 6 The g· Nazarene, as meek as he was mighty,
  597–19 spiritual sense unfolds the g· facts of existence.

(see also **fact, Teacher***)*

greater
a 25– 4 infinitely g· than can be expressed by
m 61–24 a g· responsibility, a more solemn charge,
  63–22 difficulties of g· magnitude,
sp 82–32 hastening to a g· development of power,
  95–14 g· or lesser ability of a Christian Scientist
an 104–25 case of the g· error overcoming the lesser.
  104–26 g· error thereafter occupies the ground,
s 108–15 the lesser demonstration to prove the g·,
  121–24 rule that the g· controls the lesser.
  123– 2 will surely destroy the g· error
  128–13 is capable of g· endurance,
  133– 3 Was John's faith g· than that of the
  143–16 takes the lesser to relieve the g·.
  163–25 Nowhere is . . . displayed to a g· extent ;
f 211– 6 who shall say whether Truth or error is the g·?
  223–10 Remember that truth is g· than error,
  223–11 and we cannot put the g· into the less.
  223–11 Soul is Spirit, and Spirit is g· than body.
b 333–30 "My Father is g· than I."— John 14 : 28.
  334– 7 not that the Father is g· than Spirit,
  334–7, 8 but g·, infinitely g·, than the fleshly Jesus,
p 440–15 what g· justification can any deed have,
r 467–18 The g· cannot be in the lesser.
  467–20 belief that the g· can be in the lesser
g 508–24 rising from the lesser to the g·,
  510–14 the g· light to rule the day,— Gen. 1 : 16.
  518–14 lesser idea of Himself for a link to the g·,
  534–24 will be g· mental opposition to the
ap 560–31 a g· ignorance of the divine Principle

greatest
   f 242– 5   the least of them unto the *g*·."— *Jer.* 31 : 34.
   p 368– 1   The *g*· wrong is but a supposititious opposite
     376– 6   Just so is it with the *g*· sin.

greatly
   m 61–29   formation of mortals must *g*· improve
   p 411– 1   "The thing which I *g*· feared — *Job* 3 : 25.
     423– 4   for this fear *g*· diminishes the
   t 156–12   *g*· errs, ignorantly or intentionally,
   g 535– 6   I will *g* multiply thy sorrow — *Gen.* 3 : 16.
   ap 558– *   and *g*· to be praised — *Psal.* 48 : 1.

Great Spirit
   r 477–29   "the smile of the *G· S*·."

Grecian
   ph 199–32   When Homer sang of the *G*· gods,

Greece
   c 255– 8   cultured scholars in Rome and in *G*·,
   b 324–25   Asia Minor, *G*·, and even in imperial Rome.

Greed
   p 430–24   *G*· and Ingratitude, constitute the jury.

greed
   a 47–21   *g*· for gold strengthened his ingratitude,

Greek
   a 23–21   In Hebrew, *G*·, Latin, and English,
   s 134– 4   The word *martyr*, from the *G*·,
     137–31   [the meaning of the *G*· word *petros*, or *stone*]
   b 313– 3   the full and proper translation of the *G*·),
     313–13   is, in the *G*· Testament, *character*.
     333–14   proper name of our Master in the *G*· was
   r 474–12   *marvel* is the simple meaning of the *G*· word
     488– 7   The Hebrew and *G*· words
   g 517– 5   derived from two *G*· words, signifying
     524– 4   seen . . . in the *G*· Aphrodite.
   gl 590–17   In the *G*·, the word *kurios* almost always has
     594– 1   (*ophis*, in *G*· ; *nacash*, in Hebrew).
     598– 1   The *G*· word for *wind* (*pneuma*) is used also

green
   pr 5–19   flourish "like a *g*· bay tree ;" — *Psal.* 37 : 35.
   ph 190–15   the grass . . . with beautiful *g*· blades,
   g 514–13   or rests in "*g*· pastures, — *Psal.* 23 : 2.
     518–11   I have given every *g*· herb — *Gen.* 1 : 30.
   ap 578– 6   to lie down in *g*· pastures : — *Psal.* 23 : 2.

greet
   s 158–24   Evidences of progress . . . *g*· us on every hand.
   f 220– 9   violet lifts her blue eye to *g*· the early spring.

grew
   f 245–11   she literally *g*· no older.
   o 349–21   Out of this condition *g*· the prophecy
   g 520–20   herb of the field before it *g*· · — *Gen.* 2 : 5.

grief
   a 35– 1   and his disciples' *g*· into repentance,
     50–31   real cross, which Jesus bore up the hill of *g*·,
   p 363–29   was her *g*· sufficient evidence to warrant the
     377– 3   If *g*· causes suffering, convince the
     377–15   sudden joy or *g*· has caused what is termed
     386–17   occasions the same *g*· that the friend's
     386–20   correcting the mistake, heals your *g*·,
     386–24   learn at length that there is no cause for *g*·,
     386–27   under the influence of the belief of *g*·,
     435–13   bringing joy instead of *g*·,

grind
   p 380– 7   it will *g*· him to powder." — *Matt.* 21 : 44.

grinding
   pr 10–19   to earn a penny by *g*· out a prayer.

groan
   c 255– *   *g*· within ourselves, waiting for — *Rom.* 8 : 23.

groaneth
   c 255– *   we know that the whole creation *g*· — *Rom.* 8 : 22.

grope
   c 263– 9   he will no longer *g*· in the dark

gropes
   t 463– 2   The material physician *g*· among phenomena,

groping
   s 164– 1   resembles the *g*· of Homer's Cyclops

gross
   m 61–15   promising children in the arms of *g*· parents,
   sp 75– 9   *g*· materialism is scientifically impossible,
   b 272–14   not to impart to dull ears and *g*· hearts the
   o 350–18   "This people's heart is waxed *g*·, — *Matt.* 13 : 15.
   p 383–14   To the mind equally *g*·, dirt gives no uneasiness.
     383–18   impurity and . . . which do not trouble the *g*·,
   t 456–17   betrays a *g*· ignorance of the method

grosser
   m 61–19   the *g*· traits of their ancestors.
   ph 177–13   material body is the *g*· portion ;
   b 293– 8   The *g*· substratum is named matter

grossest
   ap 565– 9   Led on by the *g*· element of mortal mind,

grossness
   b 272–15   which dulness and *g*· could not accept.

ground
   and dust
   g 537–17   since *g*· and dust stand for nothingness.
   cursed is the
   g 535–22   cursed is the *g*· for thy sake ; — *Gen.* 3 : 17.
   curses the
   g 524–27   for God presently curses the *g*·.
   dispute the
   r 492–16   will dispute the *g*·, until one is acknowledged
   drift to the
   f 250–30   like snowflakes, and drift to the *g*·.
   drops into the
   g 520–27   Mortal thought drops into the *g*·,
   dust of the
   g 524–14   formed man of the dust of the *g*·, — *Gen.* 2 : 7.
   face of the
   g 521–22   watered the whole face of the *g*·. — *Gen.* 2 : 6.
   fell to the
   a 47–25   His dark plot fell to the *g*·,
   firmer
   f 224– 7   shall plant our feet on firmer *g*·.
   fruit of the
   g 540–25   Cain brought of the fruit of the *g*· — *Gen.* 4 : 3.
   gained
   s 111–32   this system has gradually gained *g*·,
   herbs of the
   g 541–13   more spiritual type . . . than the herbs of the *g*·
   hold your
   p 417–14   hold your *g*· with the unshaken understanding
   occupies the
   an 104–26   This greater error thereafter occupies the *g*·,
   of demonstration
   a 28–10   more on the *g*· of demonstration than
   till the
   ph 183–12   condemnation of man to till the *g*·,
   g 520–22   there was not a man to till the *g*·. — *Gen.* 2 : 5.
     520–31   never causing man to till the *g*·,
     537– 4   to till the *g*· from whence — *Gen.* 3 : 23.
     544– 5   and "not a man to till the *g*·." — *Gen.* 2 : 5.
     545– 7   condemnation of mortals to till the *g*·
   was accursed
   b 338–27   Jehovah declared the *g*· was accursed ;
   whole
   sp 79–10   Science must go over the whole *g*·,
   p 421–16   the great fact which covers the whole *g*·,
   g 545–16   Error tills the whole *g*· in this material theory,

   pr 2–13   does not grant them simply on the *g*· of
   ph 180–12   nor take the *g*· that all causation is matter,
   b 338–13   signifying the *red color of the g*·,
     338–28   from this *g*·, or matter, sprang Adam,
   p 381– 7   on the *g*· that sin has its necessities.
     437–29   on the *g*· that unjust usages were not allowed
     440– 2   on the *g*· of hygienic disobedience,
   g 525–30   And out of the *g*· made the   *Gen.* 2 : 9.
     527–21   And out of the *g*· the Lord God — *Gen.* 2 : 19.
     535–20   till thou return unto the *g*· ; — *Gen.* 3 : 19.
     537–17   Error . . . buries itself in the *g*·,
     541–28   crieth unto Me from the *g*·. — *Gen.* 4 : 10.

groundless
   o 352–23   should be assured that their fears are *g*·,

grounds
   p 392– 9   take antagonistic *g*· against all that is

groundwork
   sp 84– 6   from a *g*· of corporeality and human belief.
   s 147–19   plant you firmly on the spiritual *g*· of

grovel
   g 539–18   to *g*· beneath all the beasts of the field.

grow
   pr 7–19   there would *g*· out of ecstatic moments
     10– 5   world must *g*· to the spiritual understanding
   m 58–15   benevolence should *g*· more diffusive.
   sp 77–24   would *g*· beautifully less with every
   ph 197–27   will never *g*· robust until
   f 251– 4   an abscess should not *g*· more painful
   c 265– 6   their affections and aims *g*· spiritual,
   b 300–19   (to mortal sight) they *g*· side by side until
     318–19   invalids *g*· more spiritual, as the
   o 341– 7   Even the Scriptures, which *g*· in beauty
     350– 8   his followers must *g*· into that stature
   p 387– 1   when we *g*· into the understanding of Life,
     390–20   Suffer no claim of sin or of sickness to *g*·
   r 496–13   *g*· brighter "unto the perfect day." — *Prov.* 4 : 18.
   g 525–31   to *g*· every tree that is pleasant — *Gen.* 2 : 9.
     527– 4   to make it beautiful or to cause it to live and *g*·.

growing
   a 43–30   the multitudinous errors *g*· from
   f 202–25   contradict the practice *g*· out of them.
     245– 1   error of thinking that we are *g*· old,
     245–23   nor thought of herself as *g*· old.
   c 265–17   as if man were a weed *g*· apace

growing
　p 396–12　nor encourage . . . the expectation of *g·* worse
　g 533–24　The belief . . . is *g·* worse at every step,
　ap 570– 3　the people will chain, . . . the *g·* occultism

grown
　ph 188– 4　The belief of sin, which has *g·* terrible
　t 455–21　one who has *g·* into such a fitness for it
　g 533–18　According to this belief, the rib . . . has *g·*
　549– 5　after it has *g·* to maturity,
　553–11　to assume that individuals have *g·* or

grows
　pr 5–27　He *g·* worse who continues in sin because
　sp 89–16　tongue *g·* mute which before was eloquent.
　b 327–10　until his grasp on good *g·* stronger.
　p 387–24　but *g·* stronger because of it.
　433–13　As the Judge proceeds, the prisoner *g·* restless.
　r 489– 2　loses its claw, the claw *g·* again.
　g 520–25　the plant *g·*, not because of seed or soil, but
　554–14　as he *g·* up into another false claim,

growth
　and organization
　g 548–24　material sense of animal *g·* and organization,
　child's
　pref x– 1　may treasure the memorials of a child's *g·*,
　in grace
　pr 4– 4　prayer of fervent desire for *g·* in grace,
　f 220–25　never to try dietetics for *g·* in grace.
　in wisdom
　p 363–30　repentance, reformation, and *g·* in wisdom
　material
　m 68–28　it manifests no material *g·* from molecule to
　of error
　ph 188–22　Sickness is a *g·* of error,
　only through
　m 62–18　only through *g·* in the understanding of
　probation and
　b 291–24　until probation and *g·* shall effect the
　promotes your
　c 266–12　to accept what best promotes your *g·*.
　promote the
　ph 195–21　promote the *g·* of mortal mind out of itself,
　spiritual
　　(*see* **spiritual**)
　subject to
　s 124–18　represented as subject to *g·*, maturity, and
　this
　p 406–23　and this *g·* will go on until
　r 481–17　this *g·* of material belief,

　m 68–14　to your *g·* and to your influence on other lives.
　ph 190–14　Human birth, *g·*, maturity, and decay
　b 291– 9　in the *g·* of Christian character.
　305–28　not subject to birth, *g·*, maturity, decay.
　310–31　neither *g·*, maturity, nor decay in Soul.
　t 463–16　Its beginning will be meek, its *g·* sturdy,
　g 520–26　*g·* is the eternal mandate of Mind.

grumble
　m 59–23　After marriage, it is too late to *g·*

guarantee
　pref vii–18　only *g·* of obedience is a right apprehension of

guard
　pr 10–20　the advance *g·* of progress has
　a 48– 6　held uncomplaining *g·* over a world
　f 225–10　not to let truth pass the *g·* until
　234–10　and *g·* against false beliefs as watchfully
　t 445– 3　to *g·* against the attacks of the
　458–10　to *g·* "the tree of life." — *Gen.* 3 : 24.

guarded
　t 446–29　This must therefore be watched and *g·* against.
　449–21　ought to be understood and *g·* against.

guardians
　ph 174–13　spiritual intuitions . . . are our *g·* in the gloom.

guarding
　g 538– 4　two-edged sword, *g·* and guiding.

guards
　g 526–19　sword which *g·* it is the type of
　537–15　Truth *g·* the gateway to harmony.

guess
　f 245–15　Asked to *g·* her age, those unacquainted with

guesswork
　t 459–28　Guided by divine Truth and not *g·*,

guest
　a 32– 8　ancient custom . . . to pass each *g·* a cup of
　f 254–32　stranger, thou art the *g·* of God.
　p 362– 2　Jesus was once the honored *g·* of a
　363–13　wondering why, . . . the exalted *g·* did not at once

guest's
　p 364–14　wash and anoint his *g·* feet,

guests
　g 538– 6　at the gate . . . to note the proper *g·*.

guidance
　a 25–25　He worked for their *g·*, that they might
　s 148–31　leaves them to the *g·* of a theology which admits
　154–25　and her affections need better *g·*,
　164– 8　said : . . . none can be adopted as a safe *g·*

guide
　s 126–30　I have had no other *g·* in
　r 226–32　trusting Truth, the strong deliverer, to *g·* me
　b 299–13　*g·* to the divine Principle of all good,
　p 414–12　love will . . . *g·* and govern mortal mind
　t 444– 9　God will still *g·* them into the right use of
　r 467–14　the one perfect Mind to *g·* him,
　497– 4　the Bible as our sufficient *g·* to eternal Life.
　ap 566– 6　so shall the spiritual idea *g·* all right desires
　566–18　An awful *g·*, in smoke and flame,

guided
　pr 7–18　If spiritual sense always *g·* men,
　an 106–10　self-governed only when he is *g·* rightly
　f 214– 7　*g·* into the demonstration of life eternal.
　p 429– 8　When walking, we are *g·* by the eye.
　t 459–27　*G·* by divine Truth and not guesswork,
　ap 566– 1　As the children of Israel were *g·*

guides
　a 21–22　we have the same railroad *g·*,
　s 149–28　Whatever *g·* thought spiritually benefits
　f 235–21　They should be wise spiritual *g·* to
　b 299–16　giving earnest heed to these spiritual *g·*

guideth
　c 257–21　*g·* "Arcturus with his sons." — *Job* 38 : 32.

guiding
　pref vii–10　and shine the *g·* star of being.
　r 489–10　not equal to *g·* the hand to the mouth ;
　g 538– 4　a two-edged sword, guarding and *g·*.

guillotine
　s 161–22　knelt before a statue . . . erected near the *g·* :

guillotined
　p 427–17　same after as before . . . the body *g·*.

guilt
　t 455– 3　mental state of self-condemnation and *g·*
　g 542– 6　error hides behind a lie and excuses *g·*,
　542–10　disposition to excuse *g·* . . . is punished.
　ap 568– 1　Innocence and Truth overcome *g·* and error.

guilty
　s 119–14　thereby making Him *g·* of maintaining
　p 391–19　supposed to say, "I am sick," never plead *g·*.
　391–22　If you say, "I am sick," you plead *g·*.
　405–23　the cumulative effects of a *g·* conscience.
　433–17　"*G·* of liver-complaint in the first degree."
　433–21　*g·* of benevolence in the first degree,
　434– 3　"Delay the execution ; the prisoner is not *g·*."
　436–28　charged the jury, . . . to find the prisoner *g·*.
　442– 7　and there resounded . . . the cry, Not *g·*.

gulf
　a 47–19　placed a *g·* between Jesus and his betrayer,
　sp 74–26　There is no bridge across the *g·* which
　83–24　Between C. S. and . . . superstition a great *g·*

gushing
　p 367– 6　better than hecatombs of *g·* theories,

gymnast
　ph 199–19　The feats of the *g·* prove

H

habit
　pr 2–19　The mere *h·* of pleading with the divine Mind,
　p 383–25　Does his assertion prove the use . . . a salubrious *h·*,

habitat
　p 413–19　Water is not the natural *h·* of humanity.

habitation
　r 477– 6　Man is not a material *h·* for Soul ;
　g 537–11　In the first chapter . . . evil has no local *h·*
　ap 577–12　This spiritual, holy *h·* has no boundary

habits
　m 62– 5　*h·* of obedience to the moral and spiritual law,
　p 404– 7　suffering which his submission to such *h·* brings,

habitual
　pr 4–12　The *h·* struggle to be always good
　11–29　*h·* desire to know and do the will of God,

hades
　s 137–32　[*h·*, the *under-world*, or the *grave*]

hail
　f 224–13　were ready to *h·* an anthropomorphic God,

hair
f 245–14 no care-lined face, no wrinkles nor gray *h*·,
p 363– 5 her long *h*·, which hung loosely

hairs
p 367–16 with those *h*· all numbered by the Father.

half
m 66– 8 We do not *h*· remember this in the sunshine of
f 202– 7 *h*· the faith they bestow upon the so-called
p 382– 5 If *h* the attention given to hygiene were
383–21 eating or smoking poison for *h*· a century,
418–10 Then, if your fidelity is *h* equal to the

half-hidden
o 351– 1 sprang from *h*· Israelitish history

half-way
an 103–13 separate from any *h*· impertinent knowledge,
ph 167–23 It is not wise to take a halting and *h*· position
b 274–23 permits no *h*· position in learning its Principle

hallowed
pr 16–28 *H*· be Thy name.— *Matt.* 6 : 9.
s 134–12 were *h*· by the gallows and the cross.
t 462–29 It unfolds the *h*· influences of unselfishness,

hallowing
m 59–14 thus *h*· the union of interests and affections,
r 474–24 Despite the *h*· influence of Truth in the

hallucination
ph 176–24 in cases of hysteria, hypochondria, and *h*·?

hallucinations
o 348– 4 virtually admit the nothingness of *h*·,
gl 594–24 the opposites of God ; errors ; *h*·.

halo
f 248– 3 Its *h*· rests upon its object.

halt
o 343–10 The sick, the *h*·, and the blind look up to C. S.

halting
ph 167–22 It is not wise to take a *h*· and half-way position
f 236–30 While age is *h*· between two opinions

halts
p 415– 7 leaps or *h*· when it contemplates unpleasant

Ham
gl 582–24 CANAAN (the son of *H*·). A sensuous belief ;
587–21 definition of

hamlet
s 149–32 there is hardly a city, village, or *h*·, in which

hammer
ph 199– 2 if . . . could lift the *h*· and strike the anvil,
199– 7 producing such a result on the *h*·.

hammering
ph 199– 3 it might be thought true that *h*· would

hamper
f 234– 2 even as ritualism and creed *h*· spirituality.

hampers
c 260–17 often *h*· the trial of one's wings

hand
at
pr 12– 5 no power to gain more . . . than is always at *h*·.
ph 174–13 far spent, the day is at *h*·"— *Rom.* 13 : 12.
p 385–20 you sprain the muscles . . . your remedy is at *h*·.
ap 558– * *for the time is at h*·.— *Rev.* 1 : 3.
every
s 158–25 Evidences of progress . . . greet us on every *h*·.
fan in
r 466–27 Science of Christianity comes with fan in *h*·
guiding the
r 489–10 not equal to guiding the *h*· to the mouth ;
helping
m 64–10 lends a helping *h*· to some noble woman,
His
c 256–22 and none can stay His *h*·, or say— *Dan.* 4 : 35.
his
b 321–21 when Moses first put his *h*· into his bosom
321–23 restored his *h*· to its natural condition
g 537– 1 and now, lest he put forth his *h*·,— *Gen.* 3 : 22.
ap 558– 6 had in his *h*· a little book open :— *Rev.* 10 : 2.
559– 1 had in his *h*· "a little book,"— *Rev.* 10 : 2.
moves the
f 220–32 as directly as the volition or will moves the *h*·.
my
ph 187–18 We say, "My *h*· hath done it."
of Love
a 36–27 or that the *h*· of Love is satisfied with
on the other
m 58–19 on the other *h*·, a wandering desire for
an 103–12 On the other *h*·, Mind-science is wholly
b 301–10 On the other *h*·, the immortal, spiritual man
333– 8 On the other *h*·, Christ is not a name so much as
o 354–12 On the other *h*·, the Christian opponents
p 364–25 On the other *h*·, do they show their regard
t 452–29 On the other *h*·, if you had the inclination
r 493– 1 On the other *h*·, C. S. speedily shows

hand
right
pr 15–29 gain the ear and right *h*· of omnipotence
a 38–16 right *h*· of the Lord is exalted."— *Psal.* 118 : 16.
41–25 then sat down at the right *h*· of the Father.
s 141– 7 to cut off the right *h*· and pluck out the
142–17 Sensuality palsies the right *h*·, and causes
f 233–16 Already the shadow of His right *h*· rests upon
table and
sp 80–22 mind-power which moves both table and *h*·,
thine
p 398–14 "Stretch forth thine *h*·,"— *Matt.* 12 : 13.
vanished
sp 88– 4 the touch of a vanished *h*·,
which beckons
sp 76– 3 and the *h*· which beckons them,
withered
p 398–13 To the sufferer with the withered *h*·

---

s 126–16 The point at issue between C. S. on the one *h*·
160–13 the heart becomes as torpid as the *h*·.
ph 179 27 with homœopathic pellet and powder in *h*·,
187–15 the *h*·, admittedly moved by the will.
f 213–28 as the *h*·, which sweeps over it, is human or

handcuffed
p 436–20 It was Fear who *h*· Mortal Man and would now

handkerchief
p 379–15 inspecting the hue of her blood on a cambric *h*·,

handle
b 321–11 wisdom bade him come back and *h*· the serpent
321–32 taught them how to *h*· serpents unharmed,
p 402–26 *h*· themselves as they should do.
t 464–18 he could *h*· his own case

handled
b 268– * *our hands have h*·, of the Word— *I John* 1 : 1.

handles
ph 176–31 Truth *h*· the most malignant contagion

handmaid
a 36– 9 since justice is the *h*· of mercy.

hands
at the
p 441–23 executed at the *h*· of our sheriff, Progress.
clap their
f 220–10 The leaves clap their *h*· as nature's untired
cleansed their
s 133–32 Creeds and rituals have not cleansed their *h*·
enemies'
a 51–13 give his temporal life into his enemies' *h*· ;
her
s 150– 6 Her *h*· were held, and she was forced into
his own
p 422–29 Not holding the reins of government in his
own *h*·,
into the
p 436– 4 After betraying him into the *h*· of your law,
t 480–17 like putting a sharp knife into the *h*· of a
its own
ph 170–32 which takes divine power into its own *h*·
p 378–24 and take the government into its own *h*·.
join
s 122–17 sky and tree-tops apparently join *h*·,
lips or
f 212–26 we say the lips or *h*· must move in order to
my
s 156– 6 A case of dropsy, . . . fell into my *h*·.
of God
g 521– 8 in the *h*· of God, not of man,
of ignorance
b 305– 1 left in the *h*· of ignorance,
on the sick
a 38–11 they shall lay *h*· on the sick,— *Mark* 16 : 18.
b 328–25 They shall lay *h*· on the sick,— *Mark* 16 : 18.
o 359–27 they shall lay *h*· on the sick,— *Mark* 16 : 18.
p 362– * *they shall lay h*· *on the sick,— Mark* 16 : 18.
our
b 268– * *our h*· *have handled, of the Word— I John* 1 : 1.
shook
p 442– 9 We noticed, as he shook *h*· with his counsel,
such
a 31– 3 God will never place it in such *h*·.
Thy
ph 200–15 dominion over the works of Thy *h*·.— *Psal.* 8 : 6.
use those
a 44–17 that he might use those *h*· to remove the
without
t 454– 8 path which leads to the house built without *h*·

---

a 38–15 Here the word *h*· is used metaphorically,
sp 80–20 that mind, without the aid of *h*·,
an 105– 1 The *h*·, without mortal mind to direct them,
p 432–27 prisoner to escape from the *h*· of justice,

hangs
  p 436–10   Upon this statute *h·* all the law

haply
  ph 198–20   *h·* causes a vigorous reaction upon itself,

happens
  p 397–13   When an accident *h·*, you think
  r 486– 4   Suppose one accident *h·* to the eye,

happify
  m 57–32   To *h·* existence by constant intercourse with

happiness
all
  c 261– 3   Principle of all *h·*, harmony, and immortality.
and existence
  o 356–14   to each other's *h·* and existence.
  p 407–19   in the scale of health, *h·*, and existence.
  r 487– 1   find a higher sense of *h·* and existence.
and goodness
  f 244– 8   *h·* and goodness would have no abiding-place
and life
  f 232– 5   beliefs we commonly entertain about *h·* and life
  b 308–10   looking for *h·* and life in the body,
and success
  p 405–11   conspirators against health, *h·*, and success.
circumscribe
  m 61– 1   We cannot circumscribe *h·* within the
crush out
  p 407–11   they crush out *h·*, health, and manhood.
each other's
  m 59– 4   most tender solicitude for each other's *h·*,
  o 356–14   to each other's *h·* and existence.
existence and
  q 545–17   false view, destructive to existence and *h·*.
fatal to
  m 59–26   for deception is fatal to *h·*.
gaining
  b 327–28   seeking material means for gaining *h·*.
harmony and
  m 60– 3   higher in the scale of harmony and *h·*.
health and
  s 152–27   driven to a spiritual source for health and *h·*.
  c 261– 8   The effect of mortal-mind on health and *h·* is
  p 442–12   his countenance beaming with health and *h·*.
health or
  p 420–24   at its best, is not promotive of health or *h·*.
his
  ph 172– 2   constitutes his *h·* or misery.
  p 383–13   emigrant, whose filth does not affect his *h·*,
hope of
  m 61–20   What hope of *h·*, . . . can inspire the child who
human
  m 65– 2   human *h·* should proceed from man's highest
is spiritual
  m 57–18   *H·* is spiritual, born of Truth and Love.
life and
  c 262–21   will then drop the false estimate of life and *h·*,
  q 536–28   give up their belief in perishable life and *h·* ;
man's
  b 304–18   Man's *h·* is not, therefore, at the disposal of
of being
  m 60–26   not discerning the true *h·* of being,
  b 286– 1   relates most nearly to the *h·* of being.
of mortals
  p 397– 4   on the morals and the *h·* of mortals,
of wedlock
  m 58–21   a poor augury for the *h·* of wedlock.
of your wife
  m 59–18   the welfare and *h·* of your wife
or misery
  s 122–14   its status of *h·* or misery.
  ph 172– 2   constitutes his *h·* or misery.
pursuit of
  s 161–18   life, liberty, and the pursuit of *h·*."
still seeking
  b 290– 8   still seeking *h·* through a material,
true
  m 58–10   true *h·*, strength, and permanence.
      60–26   not discerning the true *h·* of being,
  b 337– 7   For true *h·*, man must harmonize with his
would be won
  b 290–17   *h·* would be won at the moment of dissolution,

---

  m 60–30   and *h·* would be more readily attained
      61– 5   or *h·* will never be won.
  f 250–31   nor will Science admit that *h·* is ever the sport of
  b 291– 2   that *h·* can be genuine in the midst of

happy
  a 55–17   My weary hope tries to realize that *h·* day,
  m 60– 5   a *h·* and permanent companionship.
      65–18   powerlessness of vows to make home *h·*,
  s 121–12   glad in God's perennial and *h·* sunshine,
  ph 195– 4   said that he should never be *h·* elsewhere.
  f 236–27   verities that will make them *h·* and good.
  b 297– 2   Mortal belief says, "You are *h·* !"

harbingers
  f 224–20   the *h·* of truth's full-orbed appearing.

hard
  a 23– 8   The atonement is a *h·* problem in theology,
  f 225–24   Legally to abolish unpaid servitude . . . was *h·*
  p 436–23   His friends struggled *h·* to rescue the prisoner
  t 449– 2   your own wrists manacled, it is *h·* to break

hardened
  p 404–16   The healthy sinner is the *h·* sinner.

hardier
  ph 197–19   that made them *h·* than our trained

hardly
  s 149–32   To-day there is *h·* a city, village, or hamlet,

harlots
  a 20– 7   publicans and the *h·* go into the— *Matt.* 21 : 31

harm
  an 103–32   In C. S., man can do no *h·*,
  ph 180– 3   should be taught to do the body no *h·*
      197–32   will *h·* his patients even more than
      198– 2   has in belief more power to *h·* man than
  f 234–32   and do no more *h·* than one's belief permits.
  o 344–14   misrepresentations, which *h·* the sick ;
      352–18   *ought* to fear a reality which can *h·* them
  p 385–18   you can do without *h·* to yourself.
      442–31   mental malpractice cannot *h·* you
  t 448–32   foolish deceit, doing one's self the most *h·*.
  g 557– 3   moving and playing without *h·*, like a fish.

harmful
  p 405–29   pains of sinful sense are less *h·* than its
      413– 6   A single requirement, beyond . . . is *h·*.
  t 459–21   ignorance is more *h·* than

harmless
  sp 97–11   and the blow of the other will become *h·*.
  ph 177–32   a few persons believe the potion . . . to be *h·*.
  f 243– 4   The divine Love, which made *h·* the
  b 280– 6   All things beautiful and *h·* are ideas of Mind.
  g 514–28   Paul proved the viper to be *h·*.
      514–29   God's creatures, . . . are *h·*,

harmonies
  m 60–28   and teach us life's sweeter *h·*.
  p 382– 2   matter, opposed to the *h·* of Spirit,
  t 452–23   spiritual sense of Truth unfolds its *h·*,

harmonious
  a 29–31   immortal evidence that Spirit is *h·*
  m 68–31   the unbroken links of eternal, *h·* being
  sp 88–14   Ideas are spiritual, *h·*, and eternal.
  an 102– 2   God governs all that is real, *h·*, and
  s 109–17   I knew the Principle of all *h·* Mind-action to be
      114–28   universe, including man, is spiritual, *h·*, and
      125– 5   Moral conditions will be found always *h·*
      125– 9   and therefore more *h·* in his manifestations
      129– 3   its logic is as *h·* as the reasoning of an
      130–22   ability of Spirit to make the body *h·*,
      151–27   entire being is found *h·* and
      157–30   proof that Life is continuous and *h·*.
  ph 166–31   man found to be *h·* and immortal.
      184–16   man is *h·* and eternal.
      198–22   a picture of healthy and *h·* formations.
  f 207–29   is *h·* and is the ideal of Truth.
      208–28   he makes it *h·* or discordant according to
      209–24   man and the universe will be found *h·* and
      214–17   being will be understood and found to be *h·*.
      216–15   This understanding makes the body *h·* ;
      232– 7   Security for the claims of *h·* and eternal being
      239–26   If . . . from the divine Mind, action is *h·*.
  c 259–30   to the end that they may produce *h·* results.
  b 273–17   never made mortals whole, *h·*, and immortal.
      273–18   Man is *h·* when governed by Soul.
      283– 5   to retard or check its perpetual and *h·* action.
      291–15   manifestations of Mind are *h·* and immortal,
      296–12   reveals man and Life, *h·*, real, and eternal.
      300–16   The inharmonious and . . . never touch the *h·*
      302–15   *h·* and immortal man has existed forever,
      306–27   is unfolding to mortals the immutable, *h·*,
      320–18   man's eternal and *h·* existence as image,
      322– 8   before *h·* and immortal man is obtained
      335–27   Reality is spiritual, *h·*, immutable,
      335–29   Nothing unspiritual can be real, *h·*, or eternal.
      336–26   are inseparable, *h·*, and eternal.
  o 346–13   we are *h·* only as we cease to
      347–30   The *h·* will appear real,
      351–25   demonstrating the all-inclusiveness of *h·* Truth.
      355–12   let the *h·* and true sense of Life
  p 376–23   the true facts in regard to *h·* being,
      388–31   If mortals think that food disturbs the *h·*
      407–23   spiritual, perfect, *h·* in every action.
      409–32   Death will not make us *h·* and immortal
      412–25   and the fact of *h·* being,
      419– 7   His ideas alone are real and *h·*.
      420– 2   no metastasis, no stoppage of *h·* action,
      420–31   to the *h·* facts of Soul and immortal being.
  t 444–28   Immortals, . . . are one *h·* family ;

harmonious

r 472– 8 with that which is h and eternal.
472–24 God and His creation, h and eternal.
478–19 That body is most h in which the
480–13 H action proceeds from Spirit, God.
488– 1 brings out the enduring and h phases of things.
495–18 calm trust, that the recognition of life h
(see also **man**)

harmoniously

a 39–27 divine Principle . . . governs the universe h.
s 120–21 reveals man as h existent in Truth,
f 219–21 includes no rule of discord, but governs h.
b 310–16 around which circle h all things in
p 392–26 you will control yourself h.

harmonize

s 163–29 To h the contrarieties of medical doctrines
b 337– 3 man must h with his Principle,

Harmony

ap 576– 2 and the Peaceful Sea of H.

harmony

all is
b 331–15 Therefore in Spirit all is h,
r 489–29 Outside the material sense of things, all is h.
and happiness
m 60– 3 higher in the scale of h and happiness.
and immortality
sp 76–22 the perfect h and immortality of Life,
c 261– 3 all happiness, h, and immortality.
b 280– 4 His own individuality, h, and immortality,
311–24 prevails . . . through h and immortality.
324– 7 Unless the h and immortality of man
p 380–25 produces in man health, h, and immortality.
381–24 The h and immortality of man
428– 5 resolves . . . into h and immortality.
r 492–28 is divine, demonstrating h and immortality.
g 521–12 The h and immortality of man are intact.
and reward
a 21– 9 that they shall reach his h and reward.
and Science
b 299–27 hide Truth, health, h, and Science,
attain
f 251–30 before we can attain h.
bringing
ap 561–15 God and His Christ, bringing h to earth.
bring out
p 424– 9 in order to . . . bring out h.
brings out all
s 132–13 divine Principle which brings out all h,
chill
p 378–28 or to chill h with a long and cold night of discord.
confers
p 418–21 Truth is affirmative, and confers h.
depredations on
r 490– 4 this belief commits depredations on h.
determines the
ph 167– 9 determines the h of our existence,
discord or
f 213–28 discoursing either discord or h according as
disturbed
p 421– 7 human belief in ill-health, or disturbed h.
divine Principle of
t 445–25 hiding the divine Principle of h,
ap 573–10 God, the divine Principle of h,
establish
ph 189– 9 no more deny the power of C. S. to establish h
eternal
pref vii–12 this daystar . . . lighting the way to eternal h.
m 62–29 Our false views of life hide eternal h,
f 242– 1 than for sinful beliefs to enter . . . eternal h.
b 338– 2 C. S., rightly understood, leads to eternal h.
r 479–25 light, understanding, and eternal h,
494– 8 needed no help . . . to preserve the eternal h
494–23 the Science of man's eternal h breaks their
g 506–11 God, unites understanding to eternal h.
548– 8 man has never lost his . . . eternal h.
gl 598–29 consciousness of his immortality and eternal h,
facts of
o 356– 7 Discord can never establish the facts of h.
gateway to
g 537–16 Truth guards the gateway to h.
haste towards
gl 586–22 GAD (Jacob's son). . . . haste towards h.
health and
sp 72–31 the communicator of truth, health, and h
s 146– 9 health and h have been sacrificed.
p 412–27 normal conditions of health and h.
heaven-bestowed
f 253–10 your divine rights, and heaven-bestowed h,
heavenly
ap 560–11 interprets the Principle of heavenly h.
hour of
sp 96– 4 Love will finally mark the hour of h,
immutable
b 298– 6 silences for a while the voice of immutable h,

harmony

in man
b 276–14 H in man is as real and immortal as in music.
304–20 H in man is as beautiful as in music,
is the fact
p 412–23 insist that h is the fact,
is the real
ap 565– 2 h is the real and discord the unreal.
is the somethingness
b 276–27 H is the *somethingness* named Truth.
is universal
p 414–22 Even so, h is universal, and discord is unreal
keynote of
p 410–30 begins with Christ's keynote of h,
law of
s 134–22 natural law of h which overcomes discord,
light and
b 280– 4 the light and h which are the abode of Spirit,
g 501–12 which God illustrated by light and h,
503–28 God, Spirit, dwelling in infinite light and h
loss of
p 408– 2 sickness is loss of h.
man's
s 150–26 The doctrine that man's h is governed by
ph 170–10 present . . . the Principle of man's h.
f 232–22 He referred man's h to Mind, not to matter
normal as
p 368–12 beliefs . . . that discord is as normal as h,
obtained
p 427–12 understood and h obtained.
of all things
f 215– 2 Nothing can hide from them the h of all things
of being
pr 6–15 To reach heaven, the h of being,
sp 79–16 introduces the h of being.
s 123– 5 could not affect the h of being as does the
p 400–27 to bring out the h of being.
423–20 regarding the truth and h of being as
427–15 Nothing can interfere with the h of being
g 553– 6 an understanding of the h of being.
of health
p 400– 9 Mortals obtain the h of health, only as
of man
p 392–10 the health, holiness, and h of man,
423–13 and it restores the h of man.
of Science
sp 81–27 material sense hides the h of Science,
g 514–29 moving in the h of Science,
ap 562–15 divine Principle of man in the h of Science.
of Soul
p 390– 5 never deny the everlasting h of Soul,
or health
s 159–26 to ascertain how much h, or health,
origin of
f 217– 5 notion . . . tones are lost in the origin of h.
peace, and
p 417– 2 find health, peace, and h in God,
perfect
sp 76–22 the perfect h and immortality of Life,
g 130–10 reality is in perfect h with God,
g 511– 1 governing the universe, . . . in perfect h.
perpetual
p 381–28 abide by the rule of perpetual h,
perpetuates
sp 85– 8 whatever constitutes and perpetuates h,
primeval
ap 565–23 stars sang together and all was primeval h
produce
r 486–20 yet supposes Mind unable to produce h !
production of
ph 183–18 action of Truth is the production of h.
proof of
b 340– 2 make life its own proof of h and God.
realm of
s 138– 9 a firm foundation in the realm of h.
received the
a 54– 6 but earth received the h
recognition of
ap 576–24 man possesses this recognition of h
recognize
f 228–17 will recognize h as the spiritual reality
reign of
sp 93–32 the reign of h in the Science of being.
s 122– 7 the actual reign of h on earth.
gl 590– 1 The reign of h in divine Science ;
592–20 the kingdom of heaven, or reign of h.
represents
ap 560–10 Heaven represents h,
restores
p 390– 9 the right understanding of Him restores h
reverse of
t 447–17 When sin or sickness— the reverse of h
Science and
ph 192–19 this teaching accords with Science and h
scientific
r 486–12 will not establish his scientific h.

harmony

spiritual
f 248– 2 and glorious freedom of spiritual *h*·.
b 288–14 conflict . . . will cease, and spiritual *h*· reign.
g 503– 9 constitute spiritual *h*·,— heaven and eternity.
521– 3 to conscious spiritual *h*· and eternal being.

supreme
ap 573–15 even the declaration from heaven, supreme *h*·,

tones of
s 145– 2 natural musician catches the tones of *h*·,

true
m 57–10 their true *h*· is in spiritual oneness.

ultimate
b 324– 4 helps to precipitate the ultimate *h*·.

universal
f 208–23 the reign and rule of universal *h*·,
b 293–29 C. S. brings to light . . . universal *h*·,
r 483–19 and reveals the universal *h*·.

voice from
ap 559–16 Then will a voice from *h*· cry :

with God
s 130–10 reality is in perfect *h*· with God,
131– 1 in order to be in *h*· with God,

with the truth
sp 84– 8 to be in *h*· with the truth of being,

working out the
a 26–32 working out the *h*· of Life and Love.

would lose
b 304–23 they would lose *h*·, if time or accident

yield to the
pref viii– 6 must yield to the *h*· of spiritual sense,
s 162–11 it may yield to the *h*· of the divine Mind.

pr 2–16 but it tends to bring us into *h*· with it.
m 60–24 An ill-attuned ear calls discord *h*·,
65–12 To gain C. S. and its *h*·,
s 161–13 in *h*· with our Constitution and Bill of Rights,
ph 169–28 Truth, Life, and Love can give *h*·.
186–23 If we concede the same reality to discord as to *h*·,
186–24 as lasting a claim . . . as has *h*·.
186–27 and if so, *h*· cannot be the law of being.
f 219–10 and then expect that the result will be *h*·.
242– 9 There is but one way to heaven, *h*·,
253–30 law of Life instead of death, of *h*· instead of
b 304–16 *H*· is produced by its Principle,
304–23 If mortals caught *h*· through material sense,
o 352– 3 able . . . to make *h*· the reality
p 379–32 belief that . . . discord is as real as *h*·,
380–31 against Life, health, *h*·.
394–26 conquer discord of every kind with *h*·,
419–21 from immortal Mind, there is *h*· ;
t 454– 3 use of tobacco or . . . is not in *h*· with C. S.
r 471– 2 knows no lapse from nor return to *h*·,
481– 3 freedom, *h*·, and boundless bliss.
486–19 belief, which makes *h*· conditional upon death
492– 7 Being is holiness, *h*·, immortality.
495–24 and silence discord with *h*·.
g 537–14 Error excludes itself from *h*·.
553– 8 or . . . *h*· will never become the standard of
557–11 C. S. reveals *h*· as proportionately increasing
ap 564–29 serpent is perpetually close upon the heel of *h*·.
gl 587–25 HEAVEN. *H*· ; the reign of Spirit ;
592–19 spiritual facts and *h*· of the universe ;

harp
f 213–27 Mortal mind is the *h*· of many strings,

Harvard University
s 163– 4 Dr. Benjamin Waterhouse, Professor in *H*· *U*·,

harvest
sp 96– 9 summer and winter, seedtime and *h*·
f 207–19 separates the tares and wheat in time of *h*·.
238–18 to reap the *h*· we have not sown,
b 300–19 grow side by side until the *h*· ;
o 349– 1 what will the *h*· be, when this

hashish
sp 90–20 Opium and *h*· eaters mentally travel far

hast
pr 14–32 when thou *h*· shut thy door,— *Matt.* 6 : 6.
a 50– 8 why *h*· Thou forsaken me?"— *Matt.* 27 : 46.
sp 70– * *Now we know that thou h· a devil.— John* 8 : 52.

haste
m 68–12 Be not in *h*· to take the vow
gl 586–22 GAD (Jacob's son). . . . *h*· towards harmony.

hasten
sp 76–29 Death can never *h*· this state of

hastening
a 48–30 *h*· the final demonstration of what life is
sp 78– 7 belief that we are . . . *h*· to death,
82–31 *h*· to a greater development of power,
b 327–18 mortals are *h*· to learn that Life is God,
p 405–27 *h*· on to physical and moral doom.

hastens
ph 197– 5 Every one *h*· to get it.
f 251– 2 as it *h*· towards self-destruction.

hasty
a 22–20 Love is not *h*· to deliver us from temptation,

hatch
m 68–22 and the evil to *h*· their silly innuendoes

hatched
g 552– 4 That the earth was *h*· from the "egg of night"

hate

animality, and
ap 569–13 masters his mortal beliefs, animality, and *h*·,

called
gl 580–17 the opposite of Love, called *h*· ;

envy and
a 48–21 was silent before envy and *h*·.
t 462–27 wounds of selfishness, malice, envy, and *h*·.

evil, and
t 448–22 impossible for error, evil, and *h*· to

human
t 454– 9 Human *h*· has no legitimate mandate

Love destroys
b 339– 3 Truth destroys error, and Love destroys *h*·.

lust and
ap 565– 4 full of lust and *h*·, loathing the brightness of

malice, or
p 419– 2 error, lust, envy, revenge, malice, or *h*·

master of
a 44–10 He proved . . . Love to be the master of *h*·.

triumph over
a 43–32 Love must triumph over *h*·.

a 51–30 caused the selfish materialist to *h*· him ;
f 218–12 malice, lust, appetite, envy, *h*·."
241–10 envy, hypocrisy, malice, *h*·, revenge,
b 317–12 "If the world *h*· you,— *John* 15 : 18.
330–30 hypocrisy, slander, *h*·, theft, adultery,
p 420– 4 Love not *h*·, Spirit not matter, governs man.
ap 560–16 never reached while we *h*· our neighbor

hated
b 313–19 "loved righteousness and *h*· iniquity."— *Heb.* 1 : 9.
317–13 it *h*· me before it *h*· you ;"— *John* 15 : 18.
ap 564–28 "They *h*· me without a cause."— *John* 15 : 25.

hates
a 42– 3 priest and rabbi affirmed God . . . loves and *h*·.

hatred

and revenge
p 407– 7 selfishness, envy, *h*·, and revenge
t 445–22 *h*·, and revenge are cast out by the divine Mind
ap 564–25 envy, *h*·, and revenge,— all evil,

and torment
ap 574–21 which poured forth *h*· and torment,

astounded at
ap 563– 5 and still more astounded at *h*·,

error, and
g 522–30 Does Life, . . . produce death, error, and *h*·?

human
b 330– 5 and the human *h*· of Truth,
ap 571–19 Clad in the panoply of Love, human *h*· cannot

incur the
b 317–10 he will incur the *n*· of sinners, till

ingratitude and
a 47–11 The world's ingratitude and *h*· towards

no sense of
f 243–26 Love has no sense of *h*·.

pursues with
ap 564–30 pursues with *h*· the spiritual idea.

roused the
s 134– 9 roused the *h*· of the opponents of Christianity,

world's
a 50–31 the world's *h*· of Truth and Love.
52–11 the world's *h*· of the just and perfect Jesus,

an 106–22 *h*·, variance, emulations,— *Gal.* 5 : 20.
s 115–23 pride, envy, deceit, *h*·, revenge,
ph 188– 9 *h*·, revenge ripen into action, only to
f 201–10 *h*·, fear, all sensuality, yield to spirituality,
b 289–10 To suppose that sin, lust, *h*·, envy, hypocrisy,
p 374– 5 *H*· and its effects on the body
404–29 *H*·, envy, dishonesty, fear,
405– 2 *H*· inflames the brutal propensities.
405– 6 to hold *h*· in abeyance with kindness,
414–14 dementia, *h*·, or any other discord.
gl 586–13 FIRE. Fear ; remorse ; lust ; *h*· ;
588– 1 Mortal belief ; error ; lust ; remorse ; *h*· ;
589– 2 envy ; *h*· ; selfishness ; self-will ; lust.

haunt
b 317– 9 Resistance to Truth will *h*· his steps,

haunted
sp 86–17 *H*· houses, ghostly voices, unusual noises,
f 248–18 Then you are *h*· in your work
p 439–32 reported to be *h*· by Disease.

Hauser, Kaspar
ph 194–17 The authentic history of Kaspar H· is a

have
pref viii–16 On this basis C. S. will h· a fair fight.
pr 1– * he shall h· whatsoever he saith.— Mark 11 : 23.
1– * and ye shall h· them.— Mark 11 : 24.
1– * what things ye h· need of,— Matt. 6 : 8.
3– 9 we h· only to avail ourselves of
3–24 avail ourselves of the blessings we h·,
6– 9 supposition that we h· nothing to do but
8–27 than we are willing to h· our neighbors see?
9–24 and material sense and human will h· no place.
14– 6 to h·, not mere emotional ecstasy or
15–12 that man may h· audience with Spirit,
a 19–26 Those who cannot . . . h· no part in God.
19–29 "Thou shalt h· no other gods— Exod. 20 : 3.
19–31 Thou shalt h· no belief of Life as mortal ;
21–17 We h· separate time-tables to consult,
21–19 and we h· little opportunity to help each other.
21–21 we h· the same railroad guides,
23–22 faith and the words corresponding thereto h·
26– 7 h· the cup of sorrowful effort to drink
29– 5 If they keep the faith, they will h· the crown
31– 9 h· no record of his calling any man by the name
39– 8 We must h· trials and self-denials,
40– 6 when I h· a convenient season
41–11 hypocrite may h· a flowery pathway here, but
41–22 Jesus foresaw the reception C. S. would h·
45–27 flesh and bones, as ye see me h·."— Luke 24 : 39.
47–29 St. John, of whose death we h· no record.
m 61– 4 must h· ascendency over the evil
62– 3 h· the sanctity of virginity
66–14 higher joys of Spirit, which h· no taint of earth.
69–21 Do you h· one God and creator,
sp 70– * them that h· familiar spirits,— Isa. 8 : 19.
75– 5 to h· a material investiture,
76–19 they will h· no power over man,
76–28 those who h· the final understanding of Christ
79–18 bade men h· the Mind that was in the Christ.
79–25 says : . . You h· nervous prostration.
80– 1 We h· strength in proportion to our
81– 8 h· a continued existence after death
87–30 We h· but to close the eyes,
95–20 even human invention must h· its day,
an 101–17 and h· nothing in common with either
102–12 planets h· no more power over man than
105– 5 To say that these tribunals h· no
s 107–19 "I h· no pleasure in them."— Eccl. 12 : 1.
112–11 these opinions may h· occasional gleams of
121–13 So we h· goodness and beauty to gladden the
125–26 The mariner will h· dominion over the
127–21 h·— as matter— no intelligence, life, nor
130–14 good and its sweet concords h· all-power.
136–21 That a wicked king . . . should h· no
141–30 Let it h· fair representation by the press.
150–18 science (so-called) of physics would h·
151–19 brain, etc., h· nothing to do with Life,
151 ?? we h· overwhelming proof.
153–26 and we h· smallpox because others h· it ;
155–32 is it safe to say that the less in quantity you h·
160– 6 for they h· no innate power.
ph 167–17 To h· one God and avail yourself of the
169–29 Whatever teaches man to h· other laws
179–20 ailment, which a wild horse might never h·.
181–30 If you h· more faith in drugs
183– 6 discords h· no support from nature
185–13 They h· their birth in mortal mind,
185–18 Such theories h· no relationship to C. S.,
188–13 is like the dream we h· in sleep,
188–25 and you h· an abundant or scanty crop
188–29 physical senses h· no immediate evidence of
190– 1 Next we h· the formation of so-called
192–20 you can h· no power opposed to God,
196–17 They h· no relation to God
200–14 "Thou madest him to h· dominion— Psal. 8 : 6.
f 206– 1 we can h· no other Mind but His,
208– 6 and move, and h· our being."— Acts 17 : 28.
211–24 If it is true that nerves h· sensation,
212–16 and the nerves h· no sensation.
212–17 Mortals h· a modus of their own,
216–32 and h· but one Mind, even God ;
219–15 what we do not wish to h· manifested.
219–16 if we would h· it strong ;
220– 3 h· continual colds, catarrh, and cough."
228– 9 we shall h· no dangerous inheritances,
228–29 supposition that sin, . . . and death h· power.
231–17 discords h· only a fabulous existence,
238–10 said, "I h· nothing left but Christ."
238–27 h· no time for gossip about false law or
242–11 to h· no other consciousness of life
244– 9 goodness would h· no abiding-place
247–31 recipe for beauty is to h· less illusion
249– 3 and so let us h· one God, one Mind,
249–19 Organization and time h· nothing to do with
254–18 for we h· not the power to
c 255– * h· the firstfruits of the Spirit,— Rom. 8 : 23.

have
c 258–21 so-called senses h· no cognizance of either
258–25 Mortals h· a very imperfect sense
264– 2 They h· their day before the permanent facts
264–12 from Him in whom we h· our being.
267–14 they h· the same authority for the
b 268– * may h· fellowship with— I John 1 : 3.
269–18 and they h· this advantage over the
270–23 Meekness and charity h· divine authority.
271–27 h· the opportunity now, as aforetime,
276– 6 but all h· one Spirit, God,
278–11 Spirit can h· no opposite.
279–12 they h· the advantage of being eternal.
280–16 Through this error, human belief comes to h·
280–18 "Thou shalt h· no other gods— Exod. 20 : 3.
281–22 h· neither Principle nor permanency,
284– 8 Mind can h· no starting-point,
287– 1 They h· neither Principle nor permanence,
287–11 the infinite God can h· no unlikeness.
289–10 To suppose that sin, lust, . . . h· life
297–25 Human thoughts h· their degrees of
299–32 he would h· no eternal Principle
300–24 If . . . God would h· no representative,
301–22 Thou shalt h· one God, one Mind.
302–29 mortal sense would fain h· us so believe.
307–13 and matter shall seem to h· life
309–26 impossible . . . to h· an intelligence separate
310– 9 else the clay would h· power over the potter.
311–26 h· not the reality of substance.
320– 7 the Scriptures h· both a spiritual and
323–20 to realize their need of what they h· not,
329– 8 you h· no right to question the great might
339–30 never to admit that sin can h· intelligence
340–15 "Thou shalt h· no other gods— Exod. 20 : 3.
340–19 man shall h· no other spirit or mind but God,
340–20 all men shall h· one Mind.
o 348–17 I desire to h· no faith in evil or
349– 6 We h· the gospel, however,
358–25 effect Christian Scientists may h· on the sick,
358–28 belief that . . . these healers h· wonderful
358–29 Is it likely that church-members h·
358–32 than they h· in their own accredited and
359– 6 because the patients h· more faith in
359–30 says : "I h· spiritual ideals,
360– 5 replies : . . . I h· no mind-ideals except
360–11 replies : . . . I h· no notion of losing my
360–15 Both you cannot h·.
360–18 If you try to h· two models,
360–18 then you practically h· none.
361–19 and move, and h· our being."— Acts 17 : 28.
p 366–13 we h· the apostolic warrant for asking :
368–15 When we come to h· more faith in the truth
368–15 than we h· in error,
369–28 what h· they of the advantages of Mind
371– 5 Disquisitions on disease h· a mental effect
373– 3 then we must h· more faith in God
375–24 muscles h· no power to be lost,
376–30 after admitting that it must h· its course.
381–19 we live, move, and h· our being in the infinite
386– 6 says that you may catch cold and h· catarrh ;
387 15 If printers and authors h· the shortest span
388–25 we h· hope in immortality ;
390–23 You h· no law of His to support the
390–25 you h· divine authority for denying
393–18 H· no fear that matter can ache, swell,
393–20 self-evident that matter can h· no pain
394–30 the sick usually h· little faith in it till they
396–10 Never say . . . how much you h· to contend with
396–21 as if matter could h· sensation.
403–12 both h· their origin in the human mind,
409–27 We h· no right to say that life
413–31 A child may h· worms, if you say so,
415– 5 disease, and death h· no foundations in
417– 6 Never tell the sick that they h· more courage than
423–29 Bones h· only the substance of thought which
425– 1 His parents, . . . h· so believed.
425– 3 You will h· humors, just so long as
425–29 If you h· sound and capacious lungs
429–23 it must also h· an ending,
429–27 h· faith in all the sayings of our Master,
430–31 Although I h· the superintendence of
433–25 "May God h· mercy on your soul,"
438– 4 and let them h· dominion.— Gen. 1 : 26.
440–16 what greater justification can any deed h·,
441–33 We h· no trials for sickness before the
t 447– 2 We h· no authority in C. S. . . . . to attempt to
448–18 forsaketh them shall h· mercy."— Prov. 28 : 13
454–24 must "h· her perfect work."— Jas. 1 : 4.
454–26 feeling that you h· no more to do for them.
457– 9 never . . . fears to h· fairly understood.
458– 9 that error will finally h· the
459– 7 he will h· nothing in common with the
r 466– 6 manifestations of C. S. . . . . h· one Principle.
467– 4 "Thou shalt h· no other gods— Exod. 20 : 3.
467– 6 shalt h· no intelligence, . . . but that which
467– 9 all men h· one Mind, one God and Father,

have
r 469– 6   it would also *h·* an ending.
469–20   We can *h·* but one Mind, if that one is infinite.
469–23   for evil can *h·* no place, where all
470– 4   *h·* unity of Principle and spiritual power
470–16   The children of God *h·* but one Mind.
472–21   and we should *h·* a self-evident absurdity
475–24   *h·* dominion over the fish— *Gen.* 1 : 26.
478– 3   What evidence of Soul . . . *h·* you within
479– 2   the child must *h·* a material, not a
482– 9   you will *h·* the scientific signification.
486– 2   and you can *h·* no faith in falsehood
488– 9   they *h·* more the significance of
488–22   Nerves *h·* no more sensation, . . . than the
489–31   Mortal belief would *h·* the material senses
491–27   may *h·* an attractive personality.
496– 7   to *h·* one Mind, and to love another as
496–28   *H·* Christian Scientists any religious creed?
496–30   They *h·* not, if by that term is meant
497–26   as we would *h·* them do unto us ;
g 504–21   Here we *h·* the explanation of another
505– 3   sin, disease, and death *h·* no record in the
512–10   angels of His presence, which *h·* the holiest
515–12   *h·* dominion over the fish— *Gen.* 1 : 26.
515–21   "Let *them h·* dominion."— *Gen.* 1 : 26.
517–11   we *h·* not as much authority for considering
517–12   as we *h·* for considering Him feminine,
517–19   they all *h·* one Principle and parentage.
517–27   and *h·* dominion over the fish— *Gen.* 1 : 28.
529–23   We *h·* nothing in the animal kingdom which
529–28   we should *h·* faith to fight all claims of
530–21   saying, . . . Bow down to me and *h·* another
531–20   Who will say that . . . animals *h·* a
536–13   move, and *h·* our being,"— *Acts* 17 : 28.
538–17   Sin, sickness, and death *h·* no record in the
538–28   mortal man and sin *h·* a beginning,
538–29   they must consequently *h·* an end,
549–10   Creatures of lower forms . . . are supposed to *h·*,
553–10   *h·* no right to assume that individuals
555–11   Error would *h·* itself received as mind,
gl 583–23   matter and evil, which *h·* no Principle ;

having
pr 8–24   We confess to *h·* a very wicked heart
14–30   speak "as one *h·* authority."— *Matt.* 7 : 29.
a 21– 4   This is *h·* our part in the at-one-ment
23–17   as a pendulum swinging . . . *h·* no fixity.
24–13   This is *h·* part in the atonement ;
38–28   *H·* eyes ye see not,
38–29   and *h·* ears ye hear not ;
m 63–26   a race *h·* higher aims and motives.
sp 71–22   *h·* no scientific basis nor origin,
89– 5   *H·* more faith in others than in herself,
s 124– 7   *H·* neither moral might, spiritual basis, nor
ph 187– 1   *h·* other gods and believing in more than
f 215–30   *H·* sought man's spiritual state,
218–26   temptation to believe in matter as . . . *h·*
221–12   *h·* exhausted the skill of the doctors,
222–23   *h·* "dominion over the fish— *Gen.* 1 : 26.
231–30   governed by his Maker, *h·* no other Mind,
245–11   *H·* no consciousness of time, she literally
b 276– 1   *H·* one God, one Mind, unfolds the
291–17   man is found *h·* no righteousness of his own,
319– 7   *H·* faith in the divine Principle of
o 353– 7   *h·* the stronger evidence of Truth
p 366–16   Not *h·* this spiritual affection,
382– 3   *h·* only human approval for their sanction.
395– 7   speak to disease as one *h·* authority
t 458–15   *H·* seen so much suffering from quackery,
r 467–13   *H·* no other gods, turning to no other but
467–15   *h·* that Mind which was also in Christ.
486–31   "*h·* no hope, and without God— *Eph.* 2 : 12.
g 518–16   all *h·* the same Principle, or Father ;
522– 8   as *h·* broken away from Deity
531–32   *h·* dominion over all the earth.
536– 8   the sea, . . . is represented as *h·* passed away.
543– 1   *h·* no truth to support it,
ap 562–30   *h·* seven heads and ten horns,— *Rev.* 12 : 3.
568–22   *h·* great wrath, because he— *Rev.* 12 : 12.
gl 585– 3   "*H·* ears, hear ye not?"— *Mark* 8 : 18.
586– 5   "*H·* eyes, see ye not?"— *Mark* 8 : 18.

hay
ph 175–14   to fancy that . . . new-mown *h·* can cause

hay-fever
ph 175– 8   cerebro-spinal meningitis, *h·*, and rose-cold?

He
pr 2– 9   more than *H·* has already done,
2–10   since *H·* is unchanging wisdom and Love.
2–14   for *H·* already knows all.
2–25   of anything *H·* does not already
3– 1   *H·* who is immutably right will do right
6– 6   is not separate from the wisdom *H·* bestows.
6– 6   The talents *H·* gives we must improve.
15– 8   *H·* knows all things and rewards according to
a 26–17   prove what God is and what *H·* does for man.

He
m 67– 3   learn the lessons *H·* teaches?
sp 97–26   "*H·* uttered His voice, the earth— *Psal.* 46 : 6.
s 110– 6   in which all that *H·* has made is pronounced
142–29   God being All-in-all, *H·* made medicine ;
157–17   If drugs are part of God's creation, which . . . *H·*
157–18   If *H·* could create drugs intrinsically bad,
157–20   If *H·* creates drugs at all and designs them
ph 165– *   *H· sent His word, and healed— Psal.* 107 : 20.
166–21   *H·* can do all things for us in sickness as
f 206–21   Is God creating anew what *H·* has already
206–27   *H·* destroys them, and brings to light
208–13   not . . . that *H·* should make man sick,
212–23   this *H·* does by means of Mind,
223–32   "*H·* come whose right it is."— *Ezek.* 21 : 27.
226–15   and *H·* has built it on diviner claims.
229–24   all that *H·* makes is good and will stand
241– 1   "Whom the Lord loveth *H·*— *Heb.* 12 : 6.
244– 1   *H·* does not produce moral . . . deformity ;
254–11   When we wait patiently on God . . . *H·* directs
c 256–15   nor can *H·* be understood aright through
256–19   *H·* who, in the language of Scripture,
266–16   Thus *H·* teaches mortals to lay down their
b 275– 8   and therefore *H·* is divine Principle.
286–17   Scriptures declare all that *H·* made to be good,
286–20   is good, and reflects God as *H·* is.
287–14   how can *H·* be absent or suggest the absence of
295– ℓ   filled with spiritual ideas, which *H·* evolves,
303–26   *H·* would be without a witness
305–18   what things soever *H·* doeth,— *John* 5 : 19.
311– 5   and *H·* made all.
331– 6   If *H·* dwelt within what *H·* creates,
331–20   *H·* is all-inclusive, and is reflected by
331–22   *H·* fills all space,
o 341– *   *H· that raised up Christ— Rom.* 8 : 11.
354–22   out of the mouth of babes *H·* will perfect praise.
356–20   as incapable of producing sin, . . . as *H·* is of
357– 2   will not punish man for doing what *H·*
357–15   how dare we attempt to destroy what *H·* hath
360–26   *H·* putteth no trust in His— *see Job* 4 : 18.
360–27   His angels *H·* chargeth with— *see Job* 4 : 18.
p 381–16   *H·* is not the author of barbarous codes.
389–20   *H·* cannot annul these regulations by an
390–23   no more the author of sickness than *H·* is of sin.
414–21   "The Lord *H·* is God— *Deut.* 4 : 35.
t 455–24   When *H·* commissions a messenger, it is one who
r 471– 3   all that *H·* creates are perfect and eternal,
472–25   That which *H·* creates is good,
472–26   and *H·* makes all that is made.
k 499– *   *H· that is holy, H· that is true,— Rev.* 3 : 7.
499– *   *H· that hath the key of David,— Rev.* 3 : 7.
499– *   *H· that openeth, and no man— Rev.* 3 : 7.
g 504– 4   and the darkness *H·* called Night.— *Gen.* 1 : 5.
506–20   even as *H·* opens the petals of a
506–23   the waters called *H·* Seas :— *Gen.* 1 : 10.
510–15   *H·* made the stars also.— *Gen.* 1 : 16.
516–25   in the image of God created *H·* him ;— *Gen.* 1 : 27.
516–26   male and female created *H·* them.— *Gen.* 1 : 27.
518–24   saw everything that *H·* had made,— *Gen.* 1 : 31.
519– 4   How could *H·* be otherwise, since the
519–23   His work which *H·* had made ;— *Gen.* 2 : 2.
519–23   *H·* rested on the seventh day— *Gen.* 2 : 2.
519–24   all His work which *H·* had made.— *Gen.* 2 : 2.
524–17   that *H·* should now be called Jehovah?
525–15   after God's mind shaped *H·* him ;
525–15   and *H·* shaped them male and female.
525–21   Whatever is valueless or baneful, *H·* did not
525–23   we read that *H·* saw everything
525–23   everything which *H·* had made,
526–16   God pronounced good all that *H·* created,
526–17   the Scriptures declare that *H·* created all.
526–23   Did *H·* create this fruit-bearer of sin
527–13   neither tempteth *H·* any man."— *Jas.* 1 : 13.
528–11   and *H·* took one of his ribs,— *Gen.* 2 : 21.
528–13   the rib, . . . made *H·* a woman,— *Gen.* 2 : 22.
530–12   as able to feed and clothe man as *H·* doth the
532–24   God is all and *H·* is Mind
533– 5   And *H·* said, Who told thee— *Gen.* 3 : 11.
533–11   as if *H·* were the creator of evil.
535– 6   Unto the woman *H·* said,— *Gen.* 3 : 16.
535–19   And unto Adam *H·* said,— *Gen.* 3 : 17.
536– 1   the waters called *H·* Seas."— *Gen.* 1 : 10.
537– 5   So *H·* drove out the man :— *Gen.* 3 : 24.
537– 5   and *H·* placed at the east— *Gen.* 3 : 24.
541– 8   to his offering, *H·* had not respect.— *Gen.* 4 : 5.
541–27   And *H·* [Jehovah] said,— *Gen.* 4 : 10.
ap 576–19   *H·* must be worshipped in spirit and in love.
gl 579– *   *H· that is holy, H· that is true,— Rev.* 3 : 7.
579– *   *H· that hath the key of David,— Rev.* 3 : 7.
579– *   *H· that openeth, and no man— Rev.* 3 : 7.
580–26   supposition . . . creator entered what *H·* created,

head
and heart
f 213–26   Music is the rhythm of *h·* and **heart.**
and limbs
p 379–27   dry skin, pain in the *h·* and limbs,

head

anointeth my
ap 578–14　anointeth my *h·* with oil ;— *see Psal.* 23 : 5.
bruises the
f 216– 8　Truth bruises the *h·* of error
bruise the
g 534–29　woman, this idea, will bruise the *h·* of lust.
bruise thy
g 534–11　it shall bruise thy *h·*,— *Gen.* 3 : 15.
crowned
s 141–18　Its only crowned *h·* is immortal sovereignty.
his
m 66– 5　Wears yet a precious jewel in his *h·*.
p 362–14　with his *h·* towards the table
gl 598–11　"He bowed his *h·*, and— *John* 19 : 30.
hydra
ap 563– 6　hatred, which lifts its hydra *h·*,
of the corner
s 139–27　become "the *h·* of the corner."— *Matt.* 21 : 42.
upon her
ap 560– 8　and upon her *h·* a crown— *Rev.* 12 : 1.
upon his
ap 558– 4　and a rainbow was upon his *h·*,— *Rev.* 10 : 1.

———

s 140–13　of the heart and not of the *h·*.
ph 191–18　should no longer ask of the *h·*, heart, or
197–24　With rules of health in the *h·* and
f 243–16　The *h·*, heart, lungs, and limbs do not
b 308– 9　the *h·*, heart, stomach, blood, nerves,

headlong

ph 192–13　It is the *h·* cataract, the devouring flame,
f 244–28　Such admissions cast us *h·* into darkness and
r 490– 8　Will— blind, stubborn, and *h·*

heads

ph 165–17　distressed stomachs and aching *h·*.
ap 562–30　having seven *h·* and ten horns,— *Rev.* 12 : 3.
562–31　and seven crowns upon his *h·*.— *Rev.* 12 : 3.
569–18　not struggling to lift their *h·* above the

headstone

p 380– 5　Truth is the rock of ages, the *h·* of the corner,

heal

pref x–21　so little faith in His . . . power to *h·* disease.
a 38–30　converted, and I might *h·* you.
44–16　did not require the skill of a surgeon to *h·* the
sp 87–17　It enables one to *h·* through Mind,
95– 1　effect of his Mind was always to *h·*
s 110–26　the power of C. S. to *h·* mortal minds and
132– 3　this exhibition of the divine power to *h·*
136– 4　and *h·* both the sick and the sinning,
146–14　the power of God . . . to *h·* the body.
148– 1　never spoke of disease . . . as difficult to *h·*.
148– 2　a case they had failed to *h·*,
148– 4　requisite power to *h·* was in Mind.
152– 7　that it may give hope to the sick and *h·* them,
152–10　supposed this ceremony was intended to *h·* him,
155–21　in order to *h·* a single case of disease,
158–18　divine Mind and its efficacy to *h·*.
ph 168–12　and depend upon them to *h·* you,
179– 9　and to *h·* by the Truth-power,
f 202–29　yet we rely on a drug . . . to *h·* disease, as if
203– 6　shows that matter can neither *h·* nor make sick,
208–14　not . . . leave man to *h·* himself ;
218–18　without faith in God's . . . ability to *h·*
234– 1　Spiritual draughts *h·*,
b 272– 1　how shall they . . . *h·* multitudes, except
318– 9　saying that . . . Mind cannot or will not *h·* it.
318–25　and attempts to *h·* it with matter.
318–26　If disease is right it is wrong to *h·* it.
320–27　the divine power to *h·* the ills of the flesh,
o 350–23　and I should *h·* them."— *Matt.* 13 : 15.
351– 3　When we lose faith in God's power to *h·*,
351– 6　Neither can we *h·* through the help of Spirit, if
351–10　learned that her own prayers failed to *h·* her
352– 3　able to demonstrate His power to *h·*,
355– 8　which evince no spiritual power to *h·*.
359– 4　Will that faith *h·* them?
p 365– 8　benign thought of Jesus, . . . would *h·* the sick,
366– 7　but *h·* he cannot, while his own . . . barrenness
366–32　If we would *h·* by the Spirit, we must
380–11　and deny the power of Mind to *h·*.
382–20　is more difficult to *h·* through Mind than
395–15　Prayers, in which God is not asked to *h·*
399–32　How can I *h·* the body,
410–27　the power to *h·* mentally will
412–18　To *h·* by argument, find the type of
420– 5　If students do not readily *h·* themselves,
t 446–15　destroying his own power to *h·* and his own
449–17　than it does to *h·* the most difficult case.
452–24　Expect to *h·* simply by
459–12　Any attempt to *h·* mortals with erring
r 473–10　Truth, that comes to *h·* sickness and sin
482–29　It can *h·* in no other way, since the
483– 2　how do drugs, hygiene, and animal magnetism *h·*?
483– 3　It may be affirmed that they do not *h·*,
483– 6　which nothing but Truth or Mind can *h·*,

heal

r 483– 8　In order to *h·* by Science, you must
494–12　Jesus demonstrated the divine power to *h·*
ap 558–14　When you look it fairly in the face, you can *h·*
(*see also* **sick**)

healed

a 20–16　"with his stripes . . . we are *h·*."— *Isa.* 53 : 5.
sp 78–29　By it the sick are *h·*,
79–22　never described . . . but he *h·* disease.
94–21　Of the ten lepers whom Jesus *h·*,
94–23　to acknowledge the divine Principle which had *h·*
s 133–12　*h·* of the poisonous stings of vipers.
139–31　does not follow that the profane . . . cannot be *h·*
ph 165– *　He sent His word, and *h·* them,— *Psal.* 107 : 20.
168–21　He *h·* sickness in defiance of what is called
169– 7　said to the patient, "You are *h·*,"
169–26　sick are never really *h·* except by
185–32　is *h·* only by removing the influence
193–21　discharge . . . stopped, and the sore was *h·*.
193–28　God and that woman who *h·* him."
f 210–17　Jesus *h·* sickness and sin by
219–24　Those who are *h·* through metaphysical
230–23　the sick are never really *h·* by drugs,
230–27　We think that we are *h·* when a disease disappears,
230–29　never thoroughly *h·* until the liability to be
231– 9　If God heals not the sick, they are not *h·*,
o 346– 8　teaches how this . . . is to be saved and *h·*.
359– 7　I have *h·* infidels whose only objection to this
p 369–30　No man is physically *h·* in wilful error
386–12　*h·* disease through the action of Truth
403–13　can be *h·* only by the divine Mind.
406– 3　Sin and sickness are both *h·* by the same
412– 1　in wholly removing the fear, your patient is *h·*.
416–27　metaphysical method by which they can be *h·*.
428–30　The author has *h·* hopeless organic disease,
t 446–10　has generally completely *h·* such cases.
447–27　The sick are not *h·* merely by declaring
463–28　The sick are not *h·* by inanimate matter
r 493–10　Will you . . . show how it is to be *h·*?
(*see also* **sick**)

healer

and patient
t 457– 5　for teacher and student, for *h·* and patient,
Christian Science
p 417–20　To the C. S. *h·*, sickness is a dream
mental
p 401–31　while the mental *h·* confines himself chiefly
of mortal mind
b 326–15　*h·* of mortal mind is the healer of the body.
of sin
s 148–32　admits God to be the *h·* of sin but not of
f 251–24　the *h·* of sin, disease, death.
of the body
b 326–15　healer of mortal mind is the *h·* of the body.
of the sick
s 138– 7　Life, Truth, and Love, . . . was the *h·* of the sick
thoughts of the
t 446–16　Good must dominate in the thoughts of the *h·*,
would-be
p 365–27　through the would-be *h·*,

s 153–15　human faith or the divine Mind is the *h·*
p 394–32　faith is not the *h·* in such cases.
395– 6　the *h·* should speak to disease as one
401– 5　it is not a *h·*, but it engenders disease
t 459–31　more certain results than any other *h·*
r 482–31　human, mortal mind so-called is not a *h·*,
493–15　enables the *h·* to demonstrate and prove

healers

a 47– 6　became better *h·*, leaning no longer on matter
s 144–31　whether the ancient inspired *h·* understood the
146– 2　The ancient Christians were *h·*.
ph 179– 6　can heal the sick, who are absent from their *h·*,
180– 6　when he sees his would-be *h·* busy,
o 358–27　belief that . . . these *h·* have wonderful power,

healeth

b 276– 3　the Lord that *h·* thee,"— *Exod.* 15 : 26.
320–28　encourages mortals to hope in Him who *h·*

healing (noun)

adaptation to
s 116–12　view of C. S. and of its adaptation to *h·*
and teaching
o 349– 4　ask concerning our *h·* and teaching,
t 454–18　the true incentive in both *h·* and teaching.
455–32　the Science of mental *h·* and teaching,
458–28　through living as well as *h·* and teaching,
applicable to
t 463–27　There is a law of God applicable to *h·*,
branch of its
p 402– 2　surgery is the branch of its *h·* which will be
by the prophets
s 139–25　nor annul the *h·* by the prophets,
cases of
pref x–16　By thousands of well-authenticated cases of *h·*,

healing

Christian
pref viii–14   shows that Christian *h·* confers the
    ix–15   the Principle and practice of Christian *h·*,
a 40– 4   tendency of Christian *h·* and its Science,
    55– 4   the idea of Christian *h·* enjoined by Jesus ;
    55–26   the spirit and power of Christian *h·*.
s 109–19   cures were produced in primitive Christian *h·*
    134–18   Denial of the possibility of Christian *h·* robs
    144–31   understood the Science of Christian *h·*,
    145–21   If there is any mystery in Christian *h·*, it is the
    147–24   Our Master . . . practised Christian *h·*,
f 238–32   in the demonstration of Christian *h·*,
b 271–29   to learn and to practise Christian *h·*.
o 351–24   the Spirit-rule of Christian *h·*, which
    355–15   conflicting theories regarding Christian *h·*?
t 460–18   If Christian *h·* is abused by mere
g 515– 1   It supports Christian *h·*, and enables

Christian Science
t 456–14   the true conception of C. S. *h·*

demonstrated by
pref ix–23   this Science must be demonstrated by *h·*,
g 547– 2   statement of C. S., if demonstrated by *h·*,

demonstrate the
t 462–13   Whoever would demonstrate the *h·* of C. S.

demonstration of
a 41–17   this demonstration of *h·* was early lost,

divine
    (*see* **divine**)

divine law of
t 445–16   You render the divine law of *h·* obscure and

divine Principle of
pref x–22   The divine Principle of *h·* is proved
s 112–21   thus are the divine Principle of *h·* and
t 458–12   to think of aiding the divine Principle of *h·*

evoke
p 365–13   with which to evoke *h·* from the

gospel of
a 55– 9   the gospel of *h·* is again preached

in his
s 148– 7   would have . . . employed them in his *h·*.

is easier
p 373–12   *H·* is easier than teaching,

is instantaneous
p 411–12   and the *h·* is instantaneous.

Jesus'
s 147– 3   Principle, upon which Jesus' *h·* was based,

light and
t 446–12   through which Mind pours light and *h·*

living and
s 141– 6   Jesus' divine precepts for living and *h·*.

mental
pref x– 4   Various books on mental *h·* have since
s 107– 6   divine Principle of scientific mental *h·*.
t 455–32   the Science of mental *h·* and teaching,
    459–15   Committing the bare process of mental *h·* to

metaphysical
s 150–13   in the metaphysical *h·* of physical disease ;
ph 178–29   Ignorant of the . . . basis of metaphysical *h·*,
    178–31   none . . . mingled with metaphysical *h·*.
p 404–18   results from metaphysical *h·*, which
t 455–18   knowledge of C. S., or metaphysical *h·*,
r 484– 7   Does C. S., or metaphysical *h·*, include
    493–16   rule of C. S. or metaphysical *h·*.

methods of
s 143–31   Inferior and unspiritual methods of *h·* may
p 395–13   destroys all faith in . . . material methods of *h·*,

no
ph 169–20   There can be no *h·* except by this Mind,

physical
pref xi– 1   the phenomena of physical *h·* in C. S.
    xi– 9   The physical *h·* of C. S. results now, as in
s 150–12   is not primarily one of physical *h·*.
t 460–10   spiritual, though used for physical *h·*.

power of
b 271–12   the word indicates that the power of *h·* was not
t 452–29   destroys your power of *h·* from the

Principle of
s 157– 4   its one recognized Principle of *h·* is Mind,
o 343– 3   for teaching Truth as the Principle of *h·*,

proof of
ap 569–13   He . . . rejoices in the proof of *h·*,

purpose in
a 51–21   His purpose in *h·* was not alone to restore

recipe for all
p 406– 1   The Bible contains the recipe for all *h·*.

redemption and
s 151– 7   need of something . . . for its redemption and *h·*.

requisite for
t 448–21   spiritual qualifications requisite for *h·*,

rule of
r 496–17   enables you to demonstrate, . . . the rule of *h·*,

Science of
    (*see* **Science**)

Science of all
a 20–32   seek the divine Principle and Science of all *h·*.

healing

scientific
s 145–16   Scientific *h·* has this advantage over other
    147–18   demonstration of the rules of scientific *h·*

spiritual
p 367– 1   we must not hide the talent of spiritual *h·*

success in
sp 95–17   but it is important to success in *h·*,
t 448–28   he cannot fail of success in *h·*.

system of
s 132–17   Jesus' system of *h·* received no aid

theology, and
s 138–18   for all Christianity, theology, and *h·*.

true
ph 192–29   Christianity is the basis of true *h·*.

pref xii–25   consolation to the sorrowing and *h·* to the sick,
a 38–17   otherwise the *h·* could not have been done
       spiritually.
an 105–32   but to go in *h·* from the use of
s 109–20   but I must know the Science of this *h·*,
    146– 1   first article of faith . . . was *h·*,
    158– 9   to vegetable and mineral drugs for *h·*.
f 232–11   theories . . . make *h·* possible only through
t 445–13   by recourse to material means for *h·*.
r 483– 8   will ultimately supersede all other means in *h·*.

healing (adj.)

pref x– 7   They regard the human mind as a *h·* agent,
pr 12– 2   What is this *h·* prayer?
    12–12   the divine *h·* Principle as manifested in Jesus,
a 24– 9   *h·* currents of Truth are pointed out.
    55– 8   the *h·* Christ and spiritual idea of being.
sp 98–10   it is the *h·* influence of Spirit (not *spirits*)
s 141–14   *h·* effect followed the understanding of the
    147–11   lost none of its divine and *h·* efficacy,
    152– 9   Truth has a *h·* effect, even when not fully
    160– 5   drugs lose their *h·* force,
ph 166– 5   the *h·* effort is made on the wrong side,
    185–21   as a spiritual factor in the *h·* work.
f 217– 6   may inform us that the *h·* work of C. S
b 285–31   Truth, as the *h·* and saving power.
    312–29   the intelligent and divine *h·* Principle
    329– 2   the *h·* elements of pure Christianity
p 365–16   the *h·* work will be accomplished at one visit,
    398–25   a belief in the *h·* effects of time and
    410–28   until the practitioner's *h·* ability is
t 445–15   there will be no desire for other *h·* methods.
    449–12   registers his *h·* ability and fitness to teach.
    (*see also* **power**)

healing (ppr.)

pref viii–13   by *h·* both disease and sin ;
sp 95–10   for the purpose of *h·* them.
s 147–27   demonstrating this Principle of *h·*
    150– 3   this Christian system of *h·* disease.
f 227–32   by *h·* in direct opposition to them
o 343– 2   Shall I then be smitten for *h·*
    349– 7   annulled material law by *h·* contrary to it.
p 369–15   in order to discover some means of *h·* it.
    406– 2   for the *h·* of the nations."— *Rev.* 22 : 2.
    406– 9   demonstrated in the *h·* of mortals,
    419–28   To succeed in *h·*, you must conquer your
    430– 2   Jesus demonstrated this, *h·* the dying and
    (*see also* **sick, sickness**)

healing-power

sp 94–18   His *h·* evoked denial,

heals

s 135–11   same power which *h·* sin *h·* also sickness.
    137–15   Truth, Life, and Love, which *h·* mentally.
    155– 5   law of a general belief, . . . which *h·* ;
    158–11   truth which *h·* both mind and body.
    162–25   C. S. *h·* organic disease as surely as it
    162–26   as surely as it *h·* what is called functional,
ph 167– 3   the infinite divine Principle which *h·*
    179– 7   Immortal Mind *h·* what eye hath not seen ;
f 219–13   whereas divine Mind *h·*.
    231– 8   If God *h·* not the sick, they are not healed,
b 270–30   and that the divine Mind alone *h·*.
    318–23   The Science of Mind . . . *h·* with Truth.
    328– 7   the divine Principle which saves and *h·*,
o 344–11   more fully understood that Truth *h·*
p 375–12   demonstrates that divine Mind *h·*,
    386–20   despatch, correcting the mistake, *h·* your grief,
t 445–23   cast out by the divine Mind which *h·*
    450–23   he *h·* them both by understanding God's power
ap 559–22   sweet at its first taste, when it *h·* you ;
    (*see also* **sick, sickness**)

health

agrees only with
s 162– 3   the metaphysician agrees only with *h·*

and happiness
s 152–27   a spiritual source for *h·* and happiness.
c 261– 8   The effect of mortal mind on *h·* and happiness
p 442–12   his countenance beaming with *h·* and happiness

healthful
f 254–28 the ever-agitated but h· waters of truth,
o 344– 5 normal, h·, and sinless condition of man

health-giving
s 125– 6 will be found always harmonious and h·.

health-illusion
b 297– 7 It is as necessary for a h·, as for an

Health-laws
p 430–29 testifies thus :— I represent H·.
431–17 these assistants resigned to me, H·,
436– 1 principal witness (the officer of the H·)
439–25 You aided and abetted Fear and H·.
441–21 H·, Mesmerism, Hypnotism,

health-laws
p 413–27 illusions about disease, h·, and death,

Health-officer
p 439–13 the H· had Mortal Man in custody,

health-theories
p 388–18 ambiguous nature of all material h·.

healthy
m 62–22 if we would be wise and h·.
s 161– 1 supple and elastic condition of the h· limb,
162–22 bones have been restored to h· conditions.
162–24 and h· organizations have been established
ph 179–16 You can even educate a h· horse so far
197–22 helped to make them h·,
198–22 a picture of h· and harmonious formations.
f 232–20 never taught that drugs, . . . make a man h·,
b 276–21 is turned into new and h· channels,
p 373–26 disabled organ will resume its h· functions.
376–24 representing man as h· instead of diseased,
377–10 prove that they can be h· in all climates,
404–15 The h· sinner is the hardened sinner.
414–12 truth and love will establish a h· state,
420–18 It imparts a h· stimulus to the body,
431–28 testifies : . . . I have lost my h· hue

heap
b 339–14 h· up "wrath against the day of— Rom. 2 : 5.

hear
pr 2– 2 Do we pray . . . to benefit those who h· us,
a 27– 5 lepers are cleansed, the deaf h·,— Luke 7 : 22.
37–27 H· these imperative commands :
38–29 and having ears ye h· not ;
m 59–20 Husbands, h· this and remember
sp 75–32 the departing may h· the glad welcome of
s 132– 5 things which ye do h· and see :— Matt. 11 : 4.
132– 7 .he deaf h·, the dead are raised— Matt. 11 : 5.
f 211–26 If . . . causes the eyes to see and the ears to h·,
213–17 The ear does not really h·.
219–23 We may h· a sweet melody, and yet
220– 1 We h· it said : "I exercise daily
237–24 or to h· about the fallacy of matter
248–19 Do you not h· from all mankind of the imperfect
c 256–12 "H·, O Israel : the Lord our God— Deut. 6 : 4.
b 271–31 "How shall they h· without a— Rom. 10 : 14.
272– 2 how shall they preach, . . . except the people h·?
284–22 nor h· it through the ear,
292–21 because ye cannot h· my word.— John 8 : 43.
340– 7 "Let us h· the conclusion of— Eccl. 12 : 13.
340– 9 Let us h· the conclusion of the whole matter :
o 342–25 It causes the deaf to h·, the lame to walk,
350–21 h· with their ears, and should— Matt. 13 : 15.
354–24 spiritually to h· and to speak the new tongue.
360–22 H· the wisdom of Job, as given in the
p 397–26 when they act, walk, see, h·, enjoy,
r 479–11 Matter cannot see, feel, h·,
479–16 Does that which we call dead ever see, h·,
ap 558– * they that h· the words of this— Rev. 1 : 3.
gl 585– 4 "Having ears, h· ye not?"— Mark 8 : 18.

heard
iii– * Oh ! Thou hast h· my prayer ;
pr 2– 3 to enlighten the infinite or to be h· of men?
a 27– 4 things ye have seen and h· ;— Luke 7 : 22.
sp 89–21 God, is h· when the senses are silent.
s 117–14 Ear hath not h·, nor hath lip spoken,
ph 175– 7 In old times who ever h· of dyspepsia,
f 213–21 rapture of his grandest symphonies was never h·.
c 255–18 Eye hath not seen Spirit, nor hath ear h· His
262–17 "I have h· of Thee by the— Job 42 : 5.
b 268– * which we have h·, which we— I John 1 : 1.
268– * That which we have seen and h·— I John 1 : 3.
308–14 Soul-inspired patriarchs h· the voice of Truth,
o 352– 1 brought down no proof that it was h·,
355–12 discord of every name and nature be h· no more,
p 416–30 have already h· too much on that subject.
424–23 to make yourself h· mentally while
438–27 he disappeared and was never h· of more.
438–29 we have h· Materia Medica explain how
t 459– 3 "eye hath not seen nor ear h·."— I Cor. 2 : 9.
g 532–15 I h· Thy voice in the garden,— Gen. 3 : 10.
ap 559–12 h· in the desert and in dark places of fear.
568–13 And I h· a loud voice saying— Rev. 12 : 10.

hearers
a 54–17 His h· understood neither his words nor
f 235–30 They should so raise their h· spiritually,

hearest
s 134–26 "I knew that Thou h· me— John 11 : 42.

hearing
and sight
r 489–27 no organic construction can give it h· and sight
dull of
o 350–19 their ears are dull of h·,— Matt. 13 : 15.
material
g 526– 9 Belief involves theories of material h·,
medium of
f 214– 3 If the medium of h· is wholly spiritual,
of the ear
ph 192– 7 They come from the h· of the ear,
c 262–17 by the h· of the ear :— Job 42 : 5.
sight and
gl 582–22 physical sense put out of sight and h· ;
to the deaf
ph 183–28 sight to the blind, h· to the deaf,
f 210–13 gave sight to the blind, h· to the deaf,
r 487–11 gave . . . h· to the deaf centuries ago,

p 437–15 Spirit not allowed a h· ;
441–10 plea of False Belief we deem unworthy of a h·.
r 486–23 Sight, h· all the spiritual senses of man,
487– 7 more Christianity in seeing and h· spiritually
489–18 material means for knowing, h·, seeing?

hearken
b 321–28 neither h· to the voice of the— Exod. 4 : 8.

hearkened
g 535–20 thou hast h· unto the— Gen. 3 : 17.

hears
sp 86–30 It feels, h·, and sees its own thoughts.
ph 198– 3 A patient h· the doctor's verdict as a
198– 4 as a criminal h· his death-sentence.
r 467–28 Matter neither sees, h·, nor feels.
485– 5 Science declares that Mind, . . . sees, h·, feels,
gl 591–15 that which mortal mind sees, feels, h·,

heart (see also **heart's**)
all thy
pr 9–18 with all thy h·, and with all thy— Matt. 22 : 37.
and soul
s 113– 6 the h· and soul of C. S., is Love.
condemns
t 448– 6 Evil . . . which the h· condemns, has no
finds peace
m 59–15 in which the h· finds peace and home.
gladden the
s 121–13 goodness and beauty to gladden the h· ;
good
b 272– 6 "honest and good h·"— Luke 8 : 15.
head and
f 213–26 Music is the rhythm of head and h·.
his
pr 1– * and shall not doubt in his h·,— Mark 11 : 23.
a 32–26 to refresh his h· with brighter, . . . views.
sp 89–13 "As he thinketh in his h·,— Prov. 23 : 7.
f 213– 4 "As he thinketh in his h·,— Prov. 23 : 7.
p 383–28 "As he thinketh in his h·,— Prov. 23 : 7.
t 451–16 where his treasure is, there will his h· be also.
honest
pr 8– 3 We never need to despair of an honest h· ;
t 464–24 fall before an honest h·.
human
ph 190–27 When hope rose higher in the human h·,
hungering
r 482–25 to the hungering h· in every age.
many a
c 265–28 brightens the ascending path of many a h·.
meek in
a 33–26 preaches the gospel to the poor, the meek in h·.
nearer the
g 501– 7 are clearer and come nearer the h·.
of Christ
ap 568–28 and nearer to the great h· of Christ ;
of divinity
c 258–31 you can discern the h· of divinity,
of Love
t 448– 4 went out to the great h· of Love,
of prayer
pr 15–10 To enter into the h· of prayer,
or lungs
ph 191–18 no longer ask of the head, h·, or lungs :
overflows
a 26– 1 and the h· overflows with gratitude
pierces the
m 66– 7 a broken reed, which pierces the h·.
pure in
f 241–28 the pure in h· see God
b 324– 6 "Blessed are the pure in h· :— Matt. 5 : 8.
337–15 none but the pure in h· can see God,
o 341– 9 "Blessed are the pure in h· :— Matt. 5 : 8.

heart

purpose of the
pr 8–29   learn what is the affection and purpose of the *h·*,
receptive
a 46–11   It is revealed to the receptive *h·*,
reforms the
a 19–23   the practical repentance, which reforms the *h·*
rejoicing the
c 266– 2   are good, "rejoicing the *h·*." — *Psal.* 19 : 8.
struggling
m 57–28   for Love supports the struggling *h·*
suffering
p 365–32   poor suffering *h·* needs its rightful nutriment,
take
ap 573–29   Take *h·*, dear sufferer, for this reality of
this
pr 8–26   do we not already know more of this *h·*
this people's
o 350–18   "This people's *h·* is waxed gross, — *Matt.* 13 : 15.
valves of the
ph 187–13   valves of the *h·*, . . . obey the mandate of
while the
pr 3–32   While the *h·* is far from divine Truth
whole
f 219–12   "sick, and the whole *h·* faint ;" — *Isa.* 1 : 5.
wicked
pr 8–24   We confess to having a very wicked *h·*

an 100– *   *out of the h· proceed evil* — *Matt.* 15 : 19.
s 140–12   Religion will then be of the *h·*
151–19   The blood, *h·*, lungs, brain, etc.,
160–12   so-called mind quits the body, the *h·* becomes
ph 172–23   What is man? Brain, *h·*, blood,
172–32   When we admit that matter (*h·*, blood, brain,
181–29   there will your *h·* be also." — *Matt.* 6 : 21.
f 220–31   controls the stomach, bones, lungs, *h·*,
243–16   The head, *h·*, lungs, and limbs do not inform us
c 262–26   there will your *h·* be also." — *Matt.* 6 : 21.
b 308– 9   the admission from the head, *h·*, stomach,
o 350–22   should understand with their *h·*, — *Matt.* 13 : 15.
p 415–21   action . . . of the bowels, and of the *h·*.
425–27   will never believe that *h·* . . . can destroy you.
t 444–25   and say in thy *h·* :
g 521–16   engraved on the understanding and *h·*
ol 587–23   definition of

heartfelt
pr 4–10   not . . . sufficient to express loyal and *h·*

heart's
sp 88– 3   the poet Tennyson expressed the *h·* desire,

hearts

broken
p 364–27   by their broken *h·*, expressed by
chastened
a 35– 2   *h·* chastened and pride rebuked.
gross
b 272–14   not to impart to dull ears and gross *h·*
honest
pr 15–19   go forth with honest *h·* to work and watch
of men
s 131–25   until the *h·* of men are made ready for it.
our
s 116– 7   make this Scriptural testimony true in our *h·*,
struggling
a 45–16   and peace to the struggling *h·* !
their
a 46– 6   words, which made their *h·* burn within them,
b 312–16   with scarcely a spark of love in their *h·* ;
p 363–11   those around him were saying in their *h·*,
union of
m 64–17   Marriage should signify a union of *h·*.

f 233–24   including the *h·* which rejected him.

heat
and cold
p 374–26   *H·* and cold are products of mortal mind.
animal
p 374–30   Mortal mind produces animal *h·*,
chills and
p 375– 6   Chills and *h·* are often the form in which
cold and
s 125–22   cold and *h·*, latitude and longitude.
febrile
p 379–26   quickened pulse, coated tongue, febrile *h·*,
fervent
ap 565–21   with the fervent *h·* of Truth and Love,
light and
ph 189– 5   we still believe that there is solar light and *h·*.
g 538–11   The sun, giving light and *h·* to the earth,
light or
g 548– 9   How little light or *h·* reach our earth when
pain or
p 376–26   impossible for matter to suffer, to feel pain or *h·*,

heat
would pass
p 375– 1   *H·* would pass from the body as

ph 184–19   We say man suffers from the effects of cold, *h·*,
p 375– 5   the separation of *h·* from the body.
384– 9   though they expose him to fatigue, cold, *h·*,
gl 586–11   FEAR. *H·* ; inflammation ; anxiety ;

heathen
pr 13– 9   prayers . . . such as the *h·* use.
r 466–23   *H·* mythology and Jewish theology have
485–28   *h·* gods of mythology controlled war
g 552– 5   *H·* philosophy, modern geology,

Heaven
g 506– 8   God called the firmament *H·*. — *Gen.* 1 : 8.

heaven
and earth
sp 91– 2   Have you ever pictured this *h·* and earth,
s 131–19   O Father, Lord of *h·* and earth, — *Luke* 10 : 21.
b 334– 6   it illumines *h·* and earth ;
g 536– 5   *h·* and earth stand for spiritual ideas,
ap 576–20   John saw *h·* and earth
and eternity
g 503–10   constitute spiritual harmony, — *h·* and eternity.
army of
c 256–21   in the army of *h·*, and among the — *Dan.* 4 : 35.
banished from
s 158–14   Apollo, who was banished from *h·*
created the
r 479–18   created the *h·* and the earth. — *Gen.* 1 : 1.
g 502–22   created the *h·* and the earth. – *Gen.* 1 : 1.
declaration from
ap 573–14   even the declaration from *h·*, supreme harmony,
down from
a 33– 7   Their bread indeed came down from *h·*.
35–26   "which cometh down from *h·*," — *John* 6 : 33.
ap 558– 3   mighty angel come down from *h·*, — *Rev.* 10 : 1.
561–12   a bride coming down from *h·*, wedded to the
earth and
s 121–10   earth and *h·* were bright,
c 264–30   all the glories of earth and *h·* and man.
g 518– 3   lord of the belief in earth and *h·*,
earth to
a 48– 8   turned forever away from earth to *h·*,
firmament of
g 511–22   in the open firmament of *h·*. — *Gen.* 1 : 20.
512– 1   above the earth in the open firmament of *h·*,
firmament of the
g 509–10   lights in the firmament of the *h·*, — *Gen.* 1 : 14.
510– 7   lights in the firmament of the *h·*, — *Gen.* 1 : 15.
511– 8   in the firmament of the *h·*, — *Gen.* 1 : 17.
first
g 536– 3   the first *h·* and the first earth — *Rev.* 21 : 1.
ap 577–21   the first *h·* and the first earth — *Rev.* 21 : 1.
good man's
a 35–32   good man's *h·* would be a hell to the sinner
high
ap 568–27   sweeter than has ever before reached high *h·*,
his own
c 266–21   and the saint his own *h·* by doing right.
hosts of
ap 566–32   He leads the hosts of *h·* against the power of
impress of
g 511–12   the seal of Deity and has the impress of *h·*,
kingdom of
    (see **kingdom**)
new
sp 91– 1   "a new *h·* and a new earth." — *Rev.* 21 : 1.
g 536– 2   a new *h·* and a new earth — *Rev.* 21 : 1.
556– 8   Then will the new *h·* and new earth appear,
ap 572–20   a new *h·* and a new earth : — *Rev.* 21 : 1.
572–25   but he already saw a new *h·* and a new earth.
572–29   Were this new *h·* and new earth terrestrial
573–22   by which he could see the new *h·* and new earth,
of Soul
g 535–16   the open gate of C. S. into the *h·* of Soul,
order of
s 118–32   the natural order of *h·* comes down to earth.
our Father in
b 276–20   even as our Father in *h·* is perfect,
out of
ap 574–14   coming down from God, out of *h·*," — *Rev.* 21 : 2.
575– 9   "down from God, out of *h·*," — *Rev.* 21 : 2.
represents
ap 560–10   *H·* represents harmony, and divine Science
revealed from
m 56–13   its spiritual sense was revealed from *h·*,
stars of
ap 563–24   third part of the stars of *h·*, — *Rev.* 12 : 4.
thy home is
f 254–32   Pilgrim on earth, thy home is *h·* ;
to reach
pr 6–15   To reach *h·*, the harmony of being,
war in
ap 566–25   And there was war in *h·* : — *Rev.* 12 : 7.

heaven

which is in
a 31– 6 your Father, which is in *h*."— *Matt.* 23 : 9.
37–29 even as your Father which is in *h*·— *Matt.* 5 : 48.
s 137–24 my Father which is in *h*· ;"— *Matt.* 16 : 17.
c 259–20 even as your Father which is in *h*·— *Matt.* 5 : 48.
267–17 will of my Father which is in *h*·,— *Matt.* 12 : 50.
p 372–26 before my Father which is in *h*·."— *Matt.* 10 : 33.
r 485–23 even as the "Father which is in *h*·— *Matt.* 5 : 48.

wonder in
ap 560– 7 appeared a great wonder in *h*· ;— *Rev.* 12 : 1.
562–30 appeared another wonder in *h*· ;— *Rev.* 12 : 3.

pr 16–26 Our Father which art in *h*·,— *Matt.* 6 : 9.
17– 1 done in earth, as it is in *h*·.— *Matt.* 6 : 10.
17– 2 *Enable us to know,— as in h·, so on earth,*
a 36–26 suddenly pardoned and pushed into *h*·,
49–20 charged with the grandest trust of *h*·,
m 56– * *but are as the angels of God in h·.— Matt.* 22 : 30.
57–30 and begins to unfold its wings for *h*·.
ph 196–19 Sin makes its own hell, and goodness its own *h*·.
f 242– 9 There is but one way to *h*·, harmony,
c 263–10 cling to earth because he has not tasted *h*·.
266–26 infinite Mind enthroned is *h*·.
b 291–13 *H*· is not a locality, but a divine state
339–25 "in earth, as it is in *h*·."— *Matt.* 6 : 10.
p 372–17 Therefore he will be as the angels in *h*·.
g 506–16 Let the waters under the *h*· be— *Gen.* 1 : 9.
516–16 arbutus sends her sweet breath to *h*·.
ap 566–28 neither was. . .found any more in *h*·.— *Rev.* 12 : 8.
568–14 a loud voice saying in *h*·,— *Rev.* 12 : 10.
gl 587–25 definition of
589–15 JERUSALEM. . . . Home, *h*·.

heaven-bestowed
f 253–10 divine rights, your *h*· harmony,
ap 574–23 the four equal sides of which were *h*·

heaven-bestowing
ap 574–24 the four equal sides of which were . . . *h*·.

heaven-born
pr 16–21 the *h*· aspiration and spiritual

heavenly
pref ix–18 at the *h*· gate, waiting for the Mind of Christ.
a 33– 4 partook of the *h*· manna,
40–25 Our *h*· Father, divine Love, demands
s 108– 1 Whence came to me this *h*· conviction,
121– 5 the *h*· fields were incorrectly explored.
130–25 such as they belong to the *h*· kingdom.
c 265–25 aspiration after *h*· good comes
p 365– 2 pillow of the sick and the *h*· homesick
387–29 bestowed on man by his *h*· Father,
435– 1 court commended . . . to *h*· mercy,
t 447– 1 *h*· law is broken by trespassing upon
459– 6 gain *h*· riches by forsaking all worldliness.
r 480– 7 and not a trace of *h*· tints.
g 509–13 Spirit creates no other than *h*· . . . bodies,
535– 5 the other to be garnered into *h*· places.
ap 559–19 Mortals, obey the *h*· evangel.
560–11 interprets the Principle of *h*· harmony.
576– 3 This *h*· city, lighted by the Sun of
577–24 their honors within the *h*· city.
gl 592–25 gentleness ; prayer ; *h*· inspiration.

heavenly-minded
m 61–12 The offspring of *h*· parents

heavens

and earth
ap 573– 6 *h*· and earth to one human consciousness,
573–19 corporeal sense of the *h*· and earth
and the earth
g 519– 7 Thus the *h*· and the earth were— *Gen.* 2 : 1.
creates the
g 538–19 in which God creates the *h*·, earth, and
earth and the
g 520–18 made the earth and the *h*·,— *Gen.* 2 : 4.
543–32 made the earth and the *h*·,"— *Gen.* 2 : 4.
glorious
f 240– 5 festive flowers, and glorious *h*·,
in the
t 454– 9 "eternal in the *h*·."— *II Cor.* 5 : 1.
of astronomy
f 235–15 will reach higher than the *h*· of astronomy ;
rejoice, ye
ap 568–20 Therefore rejoice, ye *h*·,— *Rev.* 12 : 12.
spiritual
ap 562–17 lamps in the spiritual *h*· of the age,

g 520–16 the generations of the *h*·— *Gen.* 2 : 4.

heavenward
an 106– 5 to push vainly against the current running *h*·.

heavily
t 449– 7 wrong done another reacts most *h*·

heavy
p 431– 8 going to sleep immediately after a *h*· meal.
441– 8 to give *h*· bonds for good behavior.

heavy-laden
f 217–28 for matter cannot be weary and *h*·.

Hebrew
a 23–21 In *H*·, Greek, Latin, and English,
23–32 The *H*· verb *to believe* means also
sp 85–19 events . . . were foretold by the *H*· prophets.
s 112–31 divine commandment in the *H*· Decalogue,
161– 8 case of the three young *H*· captives,
ph 190–21 The *H*· bard, . . . thus swept his lyre
b 320–14 is quoted as follows, from the original *H*· :
333– 1 in common with other *H*· boys and men,
333– 7 the name Joshua, the renowned *H*· leader.
338–12 The word *Adam* is from the *H*· *adamah*,
r 488– 7 *H*· and Greek words often translated
g 523–32 the divine sovereign of the *H*· people,
525–11 in the *H*·, *image, similitude ;*
540–22 *H*· allegory, representing error as assuming
gl 590–15 LORD. In the *H*·, this term is sometimes
594– 1 (*ophis*, in Greek ; *nacash*, in *H*·).

Hebrew Lawgiver
b 321– 6 The *H· L·*, slow of speech,

Hebrews
s 112–22 characterized in the epistle to the *H*·.
133–14 attended the successes of the *H*· ;
b 313– 6 said of him in the first chapter of *H*· :
r 468–20 as the Scriptures use this word in *H*· :
ap 575–12 as we read in the book of *H*· ;

hecatombs
p 367– 6 better than *h*· of gushing theories,

hedge
g 536–23 *h*· about their achievements with thorns.

heed
s 159–11 to take no *h*· of mental conditions
f 232–27 voices of solemn import, but we *h*· them not.
b 299–16 By giving earnest *h*· to these spiritual guides
p 400–21 giving no *h*· to the body,
410– 1 If here we give no *h*· to C. S.,
t 462–14 abide strictly by its rules, *h*· every statement,
g 525–25 if we give the same *h*· to the history of

heeding
f 225–11 Science, *h*· not the pointed bayonet, marches on.

heedless
p 362– 7 *H*· of the fact that she was debarred

heel
f 216– 7 Error bites the *h*· of truth, but cannot kill
g 534–11 and thou shalt bruise his *h*·.— *Gen.* 3 : 15.
534–27 material sense, will bite the *h*· of the woman,
ap 563–20 untiring watch, that he may bite the *h*· of truth
564–29 is perpetually close upon the *h*· of harmony.

height
pref xii–14 in the *h*· of its prosperity.
f 237– 9 *h*· their little daughter so naturally attained.
241–25 We should strive to reach the Horeb *h*·
b 304– 7 nor *h*·, nor depth, nor any other— *Rom.* 8 : 39.
g 520– 4 *h*·, might, majesty, and glory of infinite Love

heightens
c 262– 3 does not lessen man's dependence on God, but
h· it.

heights
pref viii– 3 to reach the *h*· of C. S., man must
b 292– 5 Science alone can compass the *h*· and depths of
325–26 the divine *h*· of our Lord.
g 514– 8 In humility they climb the *h*· of holiness.
ap 560–11 moves before them, . . . leading to divine *h*·.

heir
s 107–10 from every ill "that flesh is *h*· to."

held
a 48– 6 *h*· uncomplaining guard over a world
sp 74–11 the error which has *h*· the belief dissolves
s 155–13 a belief *h*· by a minority,
159– 6 Her hands were *h*·, and she was forced into
p 379–28 The images, *h*· in this disturbed mind,
392–14 thought should be *h*· fast to this ideal.
400– 5 which must be *h*· in subjection before its
413–32 timorously *h*· in the beliefs
431–16 Materia Medica *h*· out the longest,
g 514–26 the control which Love *h*· over all,
ap 577– 4 His universal family, *h*· in the gospel of Love.

hell
a 35–32 good man's heaven would be a *h*· to the sinner.
s 137–32 and the gates of *h*·— *Matt.* 16 : 18.
ph 196–12 both soul and body in *h*·,"— *Matt.* 10 : 28.
196–19 Sin makes its own *h*·, and goodness its own
c 266–20 The sinner makes his own *h*· by doing evil,
266–27 beliefs which originate in mortals are *h*·.
b 330–31 dementia, insanity, inanity, devil, *h*·,
g 542–24 To envy's own *h*·, justice consigns the lie
gl 588– 1 definition of

helmsman
m 67– 7 We ask the *h*· : "Do you know your

help
divine
p 393– 3   through divine *h·* we can forbid this entrance.
t 453–17   Dishonesty . . . which forfeits divine *h·*.
effectual
p 372–29   acknowledgment . . . is an effectual *h·*.
ever-present
f 218–23   divine Love, who is an ever-present *h·*
finds
pr 12–23   common custom . . . finds *h·* in blind belief,
in time of
s 148–29   to render *h·* in time of physical need.
look for
sp 82–29   do we look for *h·* to the Esquimaux
needed no
r 494– 7   God, who needed no *h·* from Jesus' example
need of
b 308–27   perceiving his error and his need of *h·*,
obtaining
f 218–22   lead only into material ways of obtaining *h·*,
of Spirit
o 351– 6   Neither can we heal through the *h·* of Spirit, if
others'
t 455–14   little or no power for others' *h·*.
present
pr 13– 1   "a very present *h·* in trouble."— *Psal.* 46 : 1.
f 202–28   "a very present *h·* in trouble ;"— *Psal.* 46 : 1.
o 351–13   this spiritual sense was a *present h·*.
t 444–12   a very present *h·* in trouble."— *Psal.* 46 : 1.
receive no
t 444– 1   and they receive no *h·* from them,
should come
pr 12–23   *h·* should come from the enlightened

—

pr 12–28   and not *h·* another who offers the
a 19–18   will *h·* us to understand Jesus' atonement
  21–20   little opportunity to *h·* each other.
  21–23   if I take up their line of travel, they *h·* me on,
  23–27   *h·* thou mine unbelief !"— *Mark* 9 : 24.
sp 81–18   Man . . . cannot *h·* being immortal.
s 143– 9   if the sick cannot rely on God for *h·*
 160–31   a material fungus without Mind to *h·* him?
 163–23   we cannot *h·* being disgusted with the
ph 196–23   will *h·* to abate sickness and to destroy it.
f 222–11   Food had less power to *h·* or to hurt him
 234–13   and *h·* them on the basis of the
b 268– *   I can do no otherwise ; so h· me God !
p 404–31   neither . . . can *h·* him permanently, even in
r 494– 9   But mortals did need this *h·*,
g 518–15   The rich in spirit *h·* the poor
 527–28   asking a prospective sinner to *h·* Him.
ap 570–22   In this age the earth will *h·* the woman ;

helped
a 34–21   It *h·* them to raise themselves and others
ph 197–22   *h·* to make them healthy,
b 323– 7   *h·* onward in the march towards righteousness,
p 375–11   believes that matter, not mind, has *h·* him.
 435– 8   in obedience to higher law, *h·* his fellow-man,
ap 570–11   the earth *h·* the woman, — *Rev.* 12 : 16.

helpers
p 365– 5   and preparing their *h·* for the

helpful
ph 180– 7   is somewhat *h·* to them and to himself ;

helping
m 64–10   When a man lends a *h·* hand to
p 394–12   disarms man, prevents him from *h·* himself,
r 494–17   *h·* erring human sense to flee from its

helpless
m 61–19   reproduce in their own *h·* little ones
ph 191–19   Mind is not *h·*.
f 207–11   Evil is not supreme ; good is not *h·* ;
 230–14   to suppose Him capable of . . . punishing the *h·*
 231–13   If God makes sin, . . . Science and Christianity
         are *h·* ;
o 342–22   raises from the couch of pain the *h·* invalid.
 352–19   they may become its *h·* victims ;
p 377–28   a fear that Mind is *h·* to defend
 420–17   Instruct the sick that they are not *h·* victims,
 437–16   the *h·* innocent body tortured,
r 490–14   theories are *h·* to make man harmonious

helplessness
a 23–28   expresses the *h·* of a blind faith ;
f 235–19   Physicians, whom the sick employ in their *h·*,
 244–30   pictures age as infancy, as *h·* and
o 341– 3   raising up thousands from *h·* to strength

help meet
g 533–20   Is this an *h· m·* for man?

helps
b 324– 3   *h·* to precipitate the ultimate harmony.
p 374–20   this belief *h·* rather than hinders disease.
r 481– 7   Material sense never *h·* mortals to
g 548–14   Every agony of mortal error *h·* error to destroy

hem
ph 170–26   at least to touch the *h·* of Truth's garment.
ap 569–11   He that touches the *h·* of Christ's robe

hemisphere
sp 74–25   when we are in the opposite *h·*?

hemlock
f 215–28   feared not the *h·* poison.
ap 559–28   because you must share the *h·* cup

hemorrhage
p 425– 9   inflammation, tubercles, *h·*, and

hence
pr 13–27   *h·* men recognize themselves as merely
  14–18   *H·* the hope of the promise
a 25–19   *H·* the force of his admonition,
  30– 1   *H·* he could give a more spiritual idea
  52–10   *H·* the world's hatred of the just and
  53– 7   *h·* the cup he drank.
sp 80–32   *h·* that matter is intelligent.
s 131– 7   *H·* the opposition of sensuous man to the
 132– 4   *H·* his reply : "Go and show John— *Matt.* 11 : 4
 136–26   *H·* Herod's assertion : "John have I — *Luke* 9 : 9.
 143– 2   *H·* the fact that, to-day, as yesterday,
ph 176–29   *H·* decided types of acute disease
 198–27   *H·* the importance that doctors be
 199– 9   *H·* the great fact that Mind alone enlarges
f 213– 4   *h·* as a man spiritually *understandeth*,
 221–20   *H·* semi-starvation is not acceptable
 236–17   *H·* the importance of C. S.,
 251– 1   *h·* it is not more imperative
c 257–14   *H·* the Father Mind is not the
 258– 3   *H·* the unsatisfied human craving
 259–26   Vibration is not intelligence ; *h·* it is not a
 267–11   *H·* man and the spiritual universe
b 270– 6   *h·* both cannot be real.
 270–15   *h·* their foresight of the new dispensation
 270–29   *H·* the fact that the human mind alone
 271–16   *H·* the universal application of his saying :
 273–12   *H·* the enmity between Science and the senses,
 273–18   *H·* the importance of understanding the
 274–13   *H·* Christianity and the Science which
 275–24   *H·* all is reality the manifestation of Mind.
 278–14   *H·*, as we approach Spirit and Truth,
 290–12   *H·* Truth comes to destroy this error
 292–17   *H·* the so-called life of mortals is
 311– 6   *H·* evil is not made and is not real.
 316–12   *H·* the warfare between this spiritual idea and
 319–23   *H·* the misapprehension of the spiritual meaning
 331–24   *H·* all is Spirit and spiritual.
o 343–28   *H·* the mistake which allows words, rather than
 346–24   *h·* pain in matter is a false belief,
 347– 7   *h·* all is Life, and death has no dominion.
 350–27   *H·* its embodiment in the
 357–31   Can matter drive Life, Spirit, *h·*, and so defeat
 361–30   *h·* the many readings given the Scriptures,
p 374–32   *H·* it is mortal mind, not matter, which says,
 392– 1   *h·* it is through divine Mind that you overcome
 402–28   *H·* the proof that hypnotism is not scientific ;
t 455– 7   *H·* the necessity of being right yourself
 456–32   *H·* it gave the first rules for demonstrating
 461–25   error is not true, *h·* it is unreal.
r 466– 3   *H·* God combines all-power or potency,
 471–19   *H·* the spirituality of the universe is
 473–16   *h·* the duality of Jesus the Christ.
 474– 9   *h·* the misinterpretation and consequent
 476–10   *H·* man is not mortal nor material.
 480–22   *H·*, evil is but an illusion,
 481–29   *h·* the immortality of Soul.
 486–26   *h·* their permanence.
 488–11   *H·* the Scriptures often appear in our
 490– 6   *H·* it cannot govern man aright.
 492–26   *God is Mind, and God is infinite ; h· all is Mind.*
 495– 4   *h·* its healing power is not fully demonstrated.
g 503–15   *H·* the eternal wonder,
 525–22   He did not make, — *h·* its unreality.
 526–21   doctrine that . . . evil is as real, *h·* as
 532–25   there is but one God, *h·* one Mind
 533–31   *H·* she is first to abandon the belief in
 545–26   *H·* the seeming contradiction
 556–28   *h·* the author's experience ;
gl 584–11   Matter has no life, *h·* it has no real existence.
 597–25   *h·* it should not be confounded with the term.

henceforth
f 217–13   "*H·* know we no man after the — *II Cor.* 5 : 16.

Herald, Boston
an 102–24   following is an extract from the Boston *H·* :

herald
pref vii– 7   the human *h·* of Christ, Truth,
f 226– 6   the voice of the *h·* of this new crusade

heralds
sp 95–26   the light which *h·* Christ's eternal dawn

herb

g 507–12   the h· yielding seed,— Gen. 1 : 11.
  507–19   The tree and h· do not yield fruit because of
  508–10   h· yielding seed after his kind,— Gen. 1 : 12.
  518– 6   every h· bearing seed,— Gen. 1 : 29.
  518–11   every green h· for meat : — Gen. 1 : 30.
  520–20   h· of the field before it grew : — Gen. 2 : 5.
  535–25   shalt eat the h· of the field : — Gen. 3 : 18.

herbs

g 541–12   more spiritual type . . . than the h· of the
ap 559–28   share the hemlock cup and eat the bitter h· ;

herdmen

t 444–26, 27   between my h· and thy h· ; — Gen. 13 : 8.

herds

m 61–27   raising of stock to increase your flocks and h· ?

here

  iii– *   Thou h·, and everywhere.
pr 16–24   H· let me give what I understand to be the
a 35–31   If the sinner's punishment h· has been
  38–15   H· the word hands is used metaphorically,
  41–11   may have a flowery pathway h·, but he cannot
  42–29   He was h· to enable them to test his
sp 74–10   When h· or hereafter the belief of life
  77– 1   comes not suddenly h· or hereafter.
  77– 7   brings its own self-destruction both h· and
  83–12   h· Science takes issue with popular religions.
  91– 7   H· is the great point of departure for all true
  91–22   erroneous postulates should be h· considered
s 158– 7   It is h· noticeable that Apollo was
ph 168–30   H· let a word be noticed which will
  187– 6   H· you may see how so-called material sense
  196–13   h· the word soul means a false sense
f 216– 5   H· theories cease, and Science unveils the
b 268– *   H· I stand.   I can do no otherwise ;
  285– 4   not alone hereafter . . . but h· and now ;
  292– 4   H· prophecy pauses.
  296– 6   Either h· or hereafter, suffering or Science
  305–23   In the illusion of life that is h· to-day and
  308–10   is met by the admission . . . "Lo, h· I am,
  311–11   Sin exists h· or hereafter only so long as
  320–17   H· the original text declares plainly
  324–16   must conquer sin, . . . either h· or
  328–10   until, h· or hereafter, they gain the true
  338–21   H· a dam is not a mere play upon words ;
o 348– 8   H· is the difficulty :
  361– 2   H· C. S. intervenes, explains these
  361– 5   now and forever, h· and everywhere.
p 364–16   H· is suggested a solemn question,
  371– 9   Mortals are believed to be h· without their
  407–11   H· C. S. is the sovereign panacea.
  409–29   We cannot spend our days h· in ignorance
  410– 1   If h· we give no heed to C. S.,
  410–20   H· is a definite and inspired proclamation of
  427–30   must be mastered by Mind h· or hereafter.
  430–13   I h· present to my readers an allegory
  437–20   H· the opposing counsel, False Belief,
  440–33   H· the counsel for the defence closed,
t 463–20   By this we know that Truth is h·
r 465– *   h· a little, and there a little.— Isa. 28 : 10.
g 504–21   H· we have the explanation of another
  506–25   H· the human concept and divine idea seem
  520–23   H· is the emphatic declaration that
  521– 4   H· the inspired record closes its narrative
  523–14   It may be worth while h· to remark that,
  527–11   H· the metaphor represents God, Love, as
  527–26   H· the lie represents God as repeating creation,
  528–15   H· falsity, error, credits Truth, God, with
  533–10   H· there is an attempt to trace all human
  541–22   H· the serpentine lie invents new forms.
  547– 3   contains the proof of all h· said of C. S.
  549–20   H· these material researches culminate
  552– 2   But we cannot stop h·.
ap 564–12   the criminal instinct h· described.
  568–11   H·, also, the Revelator
  569– 4   Every moment at some period, h· or hereafter,
  569–24   H· the Scriptures declare that
  573–27   that we can become conscious, h· and now, of a
  576–22   is within reach of man's consciousness h·,
gl 598– 5   H· the original word is the same in both cases,

hereafter

a 41– 9   in the h· they will reap what they now sow.
sp 73–19   belief that . . . h· to rise up as
  74–10   When here or h· the belief of life
  77– 1   comes not suddenly here or h·.
  77– 7   its own self-destruction both here and h·,
ph 168–31   a word . . . which will be better understood h·,
b 285– 4   This Science of being obtains not alone h·
  296– 6   Either here or h·, suffering or Science must
  311–11   Sin exists here or h· only so long as
  324–11   we must conquer sin, . . . either here or h·,
  328–10   until, here or h·, they gain the true
p 410– 3   shall not be ready for spiritual Life h·.
  427–30   must be mastered by Mind here or h·.

hereafter

g 534– 2   This h· enabled woman to be the
  550–14   should appear now, even as it will h·.
ap 569– 4   here or h·, must grapple with and overcome

hereditary

p 392–18   If you think that consumption is h·
  412–32   Scientist knows there can be no h· disease,
  424–28   scrofula and other so-called h· diseases,

heredity

ph 178– 8   H· is not a law.
  178–24   we are freed from the belief of h·,
f 228– 7   H· is a prolific subject for mortal belief to
p 392–29   whether it be air, exercise, h·, contagion,
  425–32   the opposite belief in h·.

heresies

an 106–23   strife, seditions, h·,— Gal. 5 : 20.

heretic

o 343–32   is often accounted a h·.

heretofore

a 43 –6   H· they had only believed ;

heritage

f 228–12   when man enters into his h· of freedom,
b 315–19   when we subdue sin and prove man's h·,
g 535–17   the h· of the first born among men

hero

s 133–30   or only a mighty h· and king,

Herod

a 52–15   H· and Pilate laid aside old feuds
s 136–20   This ghostly fancy was repeated by H·
  136–25   But even H· doubted if Jesus was
  136–28   No wonder H· desired to see the new Teacher.
ap 565– 9   H· decreed the death of every male child
  565–13   and deprive H· of his crown.

Herod's

s 136–26   Hence H· assertion :

hesitate

f 229– 5   We should h· to say that Jehovah sins or

heterodoxy

c 257– 7   theory that Spirit is not . . . is pantheistic h·,

hew

pref vii–24   task of the sturdy pioneer to h· the tall oak

hewn

pr 6–28   "[It] is h· down."— Matt. 7 : 19.

hid

s 107– *   h· in three measures of meal,— Matt. 13 : 33.
  117–32   h· in three measures of meal,— Matt. 13 : 33.
  131–20   Thou hast h· these things from — Luke 10 : 21.
b 315–11   false views of the people h· from their sense
  325–17   "h· with Christ in God,"— Col. 3 : 3.
p 367–21   that is set on an hill cannot be h·."—Matt. 5 : 14.
  367–22   that this light be not h·, but radiate
t 445–14   "h· with Christ in God,"— Col. 3 : 3.
g 532–16   I was naked ; and I h· myself.— Gen. 3 : 10.
ap 560–22   h· from view the apostle's character,
  560–27   Because it has h· from them the true idea

Hiddekel

gl 588– 5   definition of

hidden

pr 15–25   h· from the world, but known to God.
a 44–29   while he was h· in the sepulchre,
an 102–18   looms of crime, h· in the dark recesses
s 118– 8   h· in sacred secrecy from the visible world?
f 205– 1   else God will continue to be h· from
o 343–12   and Truth will not be forever h·
p 376– 9   the most h·, undefined, and insidious beliefs.
t 453–20   H· sin is spiritual wickedness in high places.
ap 571– 2   expose evil's h· mental ways of
  576– 5   seems h· in the mist of remoteness,

hide

pr 8– 6   their wickedness and then seek to h· it.
a 45–14   had failed to h· immortal Truth
m 62–29   false views of life h· eternal harmony,
sp 95–11   Error . . . cannot h· from the law of God.
f 215– 1   Nothing can h· from them the harmony of
  242–32   We may h· spiritual ignorance from the world
b 299–26   Corporeal sense, or error, may seem to h· Truth,
  304– 4   which h· spiritual beauty and goodness.
  308– 7   and will h· from the demand,
  311– 1   clouds of mortal belief, which h· the truth of
p 366–32   we must not h· the talent of spiritual healing
r 480–32   One must h· the other.

hideous

f 248–19   by vicious sculptors and h· forms.
g 550–28   not so h· and absurd as the supposition that

hides

sp 81–26   inharmony . . . h· the harmony of Science,
  83–11   such a belief h· Truth and builds on error.
ph 183–20   that which h· the power of Spirit.
b 295–23   Then, . . . it no longer h· the sun.

hides

b 298– 4	**As a cloud** h· the sun it cannot extinguish,
326– 1	A false sense . . . h· the divine possibilities,
g 542– 5	Though error h· behind a lie
550–19	h· the true and spiritual Life,

hiding

b 294–30	the hypocrite that he is h· himself.
t 445–25	a lie, h· the divine Principle of harmony,
gl 596–28	Veil. A cover ; concealment ; h· ; hypocrisy.

hierarchies

a 24– 5	established by h·, and instigated . . . by the

hieroglyphs

f 240– 6	The floral apostles are h· of Deity.

high

iii– *	This is Thy h· behest :
s 136–22	no h· appreciation of divine Science
147–20	This proof lifts you h· above the perishing
153–20	administer . . . a h· signification of truth,
155–15	weighs against the h· and mighty truths of
156–10	h· attenuation of Sulphuris.
ph 168– 3	worldly, who think the standard of C. S. too h·
c 258–30	impossible . . . to fall from his h· estate.
p 426– 6	the h· goal always before her thoughts,
t 448–20	a h· sense of the moral . . . qualifications
453–20	Hidden sin is spiritual wickedness in h· places.
456– 8	alone entitles them to the h· standing which
r 469–25	the h· signification of omnipotence,
494–28	its lap piled h· with immortal fruits.
g 505–18	"The Lord on h· is mightier than — Psal. 93 : 4.
ap 563–30	"spiritual wickedness in h· places." — Eph. 6 : 12.
568 27	sweeter than has ever before reached h· heaven,
572– 1	lifts on h· only those who have

high-caste

p 362–10	the household of a h· Brahman,

higher

pr 6–18	h· we cannot look, farther we cannot go.
7–20	a h· experience and a better life
11–10	before mortals can "go up h·." — Luke 14 : 10.
u 18–16	Truth, which reaches no h· than itself.
18–17	fountain can rise no h· than its source.
43–21	Jesus rose h· in demonstration because of the
46–17	rose even h· in the understanding of Spirit,
m 57– 6	masculine mind reaches a h· tone through
60– 2	Science inevitably lifts one's being h·
60–21	education of the h· nature is neglected,
60–31	H· enjoyments alone can satisfy the
61– 8	and give h· aims to ambition.
61–31	If the propagation of a h· human species
62–19	understanding of man's h· nature.
62–27	h· nature of man is not governed by
63–26	a race having h· aims and motives.
65–18	will at length demand a h· affection.
66–13	Love propagates anew the h· joys of Spirit,
sp 97–23	the h· Truth lifts her voice, the louder
s 121– 8	Though no h· revelation than the horoscope was
128–17	giving mortals access to broader and h· realms.
128–25	destroys with the h· testimony of Spirit
150–15	attest the reality of the h· mission
151– 9	respect is due . . . the h· class of physicians.
158–26	letting in matter's h· stratum, mortal mind.
158–29	of a h· attenuation than the drug,
162–28	understanding . . . to demonstrate the h· rule.
ph 167– 3	If we rise no h· than blind faith,
169 15	find stronger supports and a h· home.
174– 4	Is civilization only a h· form of idolatry,
190–27	When hope rose h· in the human heart,
197–13	the h· will be the standard of living
198– 1	the h· stratum of mortal mind has
f 224–22	A h· and more practical Christianity,
226– 3	world-wide slavery, found on h· planes of
226–14	God has built a h· platform of human rights,
233– 2	makes its demands upon us for h· proofs
235–13	moral and spiritual culture, which lifts one h·.
235–15	will reach h· than the heavens of astronomy ;
246– 8	The stream rises no h· than its source.
247–17	reflecting those h· conceptions of loveliness
251–25	This process of h· spiritual understanding
c 255– 7	anciently classified as the h· criticism,
256– 2	Advancing to a h· plane of action,
258– 5	craving for something better, h·, holier,
258–14	rising h· and h· from a boundless basis.
259– 9	h· than their poor thought-models
260–16	and to bring out better and h· results,
262–14	clearer, h· views inspire the Godlike man
262–24	Starting from a h· standpoint, one rises
265–14	confers . . . a h· and more permanent peace.
266– 4	giving place to man's h· individuality
267–23	Thought is borrowed from a h· source
b 270–14	looked for something h· than the
290– 5	If . . . they will rise no h· spiritually
297–15	and the human consciousness rises h·.
297–20	Faith is h· and more spiritual than belief.
299–11	point upward to . . . h· ideals of life and
307–29	his province is . . . in the h· law of Mind.

higher

b 311–23	even the h· law of Soul, which prevails
313–14	Using this word in its h· meaning,
314–24	The h· his demonstration of divine Science
316–18	the Christ-man, rose h· to human view
323–32	listening to it and going up h·.
o 349–27	does not at once catch the h· meaning,
361–27	is the h· hope on earth,
p 364– 8	Which was the h· tribute to such ineffable
367–28	my hope, namely, the student's h· attainment
401–11	to the end of producing a h· manifestation.
416–31	away from their bodies to h· objects.
419–30	rise into h· and holier consciousness.
435– 8	Mortal Man, in obedience to h· law, helped
437–10	before the Judge of our h· tribunal.
439–27	Our h· statutes declare you all,
t 453– 9	and a h· basis is thus won ;
455–30	The h· your attainment in the Science
458–21	are summoned to give place to h· law,
r 473–27	his acts of h· importance than his words.
g 502–15	take on h· symbols and significations,
509–16	rarefaction of thought as it ascends h·.
518–14	the h· always protects the lower.
531– 9	represent the h· moral sentiments,
541– 5	instead of making his own gift a h· tribute
549– 7	give place to h· theories and demonstrations
553– 3	should awaken thought to a h· and purer
554–30	are less sickly than those possessing h·
ap 571–20	h· humanity will unite all interests in the
576–30	the word gradually approaches a h· meaning.
gl 581–19	The h· false knowledge builds
590–19	Its h· signification is Supreme Ruler.
593–10	a new and h· idea of immortality,
	(see also **sense, understanding**)

highest

pr 16– 2	The h· prayer . . . is demonstration.
a 43–11	Jesus' last proof was the h·,
49–14	the h· instructor and friend of man,
49–18	sentinel of God at the h· post of power,
49–27	those to whom he had given the h· proofs
50–15	in his h· demonstration?
52–23	The h· earthly representative of God,
54–16	the h· proof he could have offered
m 55– 2	should proceed from man's h· nature.
67–11	acting up to his h· understanding,
68– 8	which hinders our h· selfhood.
s 148–12	from the lowest, instead of from the h·,
153–11	The h· attenuation of homœopathy
163–16	medicine . . . in the h· degree uncertain ;
ph 182– 9	capable of producing the h· human good?
189–20	instead of from the h· mortal thought.
f 230–11	would be contrary to our h· ideas of God
c 265– 2	but of the h· qualities of Mind.
b 327– 9	Evil is sometimes a man's h· conception of
332–29	He expressed the h· type of divinity,
p 368– 2	a supposititious opposite of the h· right.
t 455–21	God selects for the h· service one who
455–23	does not bestow His h· trusts upon the un-worthy.
456– 2	adverse to its h· hope and achievement.
i 471 00	Since then her h· creed has been divine Science,
477–15	interwoven with matter's h· stratum,
482–19	Jesus was the h· human concept of the perfect
g 503– 4	the h· ideas are the sons and daughters of God,
514–18	and keep pace with h· purpose.
520– 1	h· and sweetest rest, . . . is in holy work.
ap 560–18	without a correct sense of its h· visible idea,
564–18	except the h· degree of human depravity.
gl 580–16	Jesus. The h· human corporeal concept of

high-handed

p 437–25	for such h· illegality.

highly

b 322– 9	It is h· important . . . to turn our thoughts

high-priest

gl 596–13	the stones in the breast-plate of the h·

highway

m 61–10	that the h· of our God may be prepared

hill

a 50–30	The real cross, which Jesus bore up the h·
b 326– 7	must not try to climb the h· of Science by
p 367–20	A city that is set on an h·.— Matt. 5 : 14.

hills

s 135– 4	and ye little h·, like lambs? — Psal. 114 : 6.
147–13	on the h· of Judæa and in the valleys of
f 240– 3	Arctic regions, sunny tropics, giant h·,
g 514–17	"the cattle upon a thousand h·." — Psal. 50 : 10.

Him

pref vii–19	apprehension of H· whom to know aright
pr 1– *	before ye ask H·.— Matt. 6 : 8.
1– 3	a spiritual understanding of H·,
2–23	God is Love. Can we ask H· to be more?
4–18	Simply asking . . . will never make us love H· ;
6– 7	Calling on H· to forgive our work

Him

pr 8–23 the reward of H· who blesses the poor.
    10– 4 leave our real desires to be rewarded by H·.
    13–15 God knows our need before we tell H·
a 19–27 If living in disobedience to H·, we ought
s 119–12 is not only to make H· responsible for
  119–13 but to announce H· as their source,
  119–14 thereby making H· guilty of maintaining
  140– 5 Bible represents H· as saying :
  140– 8 we know H· as divine Mind,
  140–10 love H· understandingly, warring no more
ph 166–18 Instead of thrusting H· aside in times of
  166–20 hour of strength in which to acknowledge H·,
f 208– 5 "In H· we live, and move, and — Acts 17 : 28.
  219–28 the honor due to H· alone.
  229–13 virtually declaring H· good in one instance
  230–12 to suppose H· capable of first arranging law
  231–32 "all things were made by H·— John 1 : 3.
  232– 1 without H· was not anything made — John 1 : 3.
c 256–22 none can stay His hand, or say unto H·, — Dan.
        4 : 35.
  262– 7 but it ascribes to H· the entire glory.
  264–11 act as possessing all power from H·
b 272–30 the divine Principle of all that represents H·
  273– 2 contrary to God, and cannot emanate from H·
  307–10 It says : . . . I aid H·.
  320–28 encourages mortals to hope in H· who healeth
  324–12 "acquaint now thyself with H·, — Job 22 : 21.
  328–12 which destroys human delusions about H·
  330–19 God is what the Scriptures declare H· to be,
  331–17 Everything in God's universe expresses H·.
  336–16 They are the emanations of H· who is Life,
o 341– * But if the Spirit of H· that raised up — Rom.
        8 : 11.
  348–15 when we ascribe to H· almighty Life
  351–21 if not superior to H·.
  356–21 is it possible for H· to create man subject to
  361–19 "For in H· we live, and move, — Acts 17 : 28.
p 362– * I shall yet praise H·, — Psal. 42 : 11.
  390– 9 right understanding of H· restores harmony.
  397–22 which the Scriptures declare H· to be.
  414–22 there is none else beside H·." — Deut. 4 : 35.
  421–18 and that there is none beside H·.
t 444–11 Step by step will those who trust H· find
r 473– 9 nothing apart from H· is present or has power.
  479–30 "For the invisible things of H·, — Rom. 1 : 20.
  480–26 "All things were made by H·— John 1 : 3.
  480–27 without H· was not anything made— John 1 : 3.
  483–28 does honor God as no other theory honors H·,
g 501– * made by H· ; and without H· was not — John 1 : 3.
  501– * In H· was life ; — John 1 : 4.
  503–16 reflecting H· in countless spiritual forms.
  504–19 indicate, . . . spiritually clearer views of H·,
  515–23 minds in accord with H·,
  517–13 as we have for considering H· feminine,
  519–12 How shall we declare H·, till, in the language of
  525–18 "and without H· . . . was not — John 1 : 3.
  527–28 asking a prospective sinner to help H·.
gl 581–13 all things are created by H·
  596– 5 makes H· better known as the All-in-all,
  596– 9 H· declare I unto you." — Acts 17 : 23.

Himself

a 18–15 how can God propitiate H·?
sp 94– 2 in the image and likeness of H·,
b 277– 7 As God H· is good and is Spirit,
  286–18 all that He made to be good, like H·,
  303–25 without the image and likeness of H·,
  335– 7 in and of H·.
o 356–24 Does God create a material man out of H·,
  357–29 Has the Father "Life in H·," — John 5 : 26.
p 380–31 against H·, against Life, health, harmony.
  395–16 besought to take the patient to H·,
  435– 2 Spirit which is God H·
t 455–25 one who is spiritually near H·.
g 518–13 God gives the lesser idea of H·
gl 583–25 could not create an atom . . . the opposite of H·.

hinder

a 28–19 did not h· men from saying :
s 145– 5 lack of the letter could not h· their work ;
f 209–12 Neither philosophy nor skepticism can h·
b 326–19 nothing but wrong intention can h· your
  326–21 "Who did h· you, — Gal. 5 : 7.
p 419– 1 A moral question may h· the recovery of
t 445– 7 to h· the demonstration of C. S.
  448–25 must always h· scientific demonstration.

hindered

a 28– 2 h· the success of Jesus' mission.
  41–23 but this foreknowledge h· him not.

hinders

pr 5– 1 Whatever . . . h· man's spiritual growth
m 68– 8 cherish nothing which h· our highest
f 205–24 h· man's normal drift towards the one Mind,
b 312–26 limits faith and h· spiritual understanding.
p 366– 9 h· him from reaching his patient's thought,

hinders

p 369– 2 and this h· his destroying them.
  374–21 this belief helps rather than h· disease.
  391–13 No law of God h· this result.
r 483–11 h· its approach to the standard in C. S.

Hindoo

p 362– 9 as positively as if she were a H· pariah
g 524– 4 in the H· Vishnu, in the Greek Aphrodite,

hindrance

f 253–23 without h· from the body.
p 372–31 this will be a h· to the recovery of the sick

hint

a 42– 4 theology gave no h· of the unchanging love of
m 58–25 This is a h· that a wife ought not to
sp 94–27 an infidel blasphemer who should h· that
ph 194–17 history of Kaspar Hauser is a useful h·
f 245–19 useful h·, upon which a Franklin might work
p 383–12 A h· may be taken from the emigrant,
g 528–30 may be a useful h· to the medical faculty.

hints

p 384–18 h· of inflammatory rheumatism,

hip

ph 193– 5 physician had just probed the ulcer on the h·,

hip-disease

ph 193– 1 confined to his bed six months with h·,

Hippocrates

s 158– 8 H· turned from image-gods to vegetable
  163– 1 impossible to calculate the mischief which H·

hireling

t 464–26, 27 h· fleeth, because he is an h·, — John 10 : 13.

His

pref x–21 there is so little faith in H· . . . power
  xi–22 called the author to proclaim H· Gospel
  xi–24 charge to plant and water H· vineyard.
pr 3– 2 without being reminded of H· province.
  3– 8 Shall we ask the divine Principle . . . to do H·
  3–10 in order to receive H· blessing,
  5–17 pours the riches of H· love into
  6–20 To suppose that God forgives. . .according as H·
a 23– 6 vented upon H· beloved Son is, . . . unnatural.
  42–22 which God bestowed on H· anointed,
  45–12 [seeming] death of H· Son, — Rom. 5 : 10.
m 56–10 and H· kingdom is come as in the vision
sp 97–26 "He uttered H· voice, the earth — Psal. 46 : 6.
  99– 8 to will and to do of H· good — Phil. 2 : 13.
s 109–29 "My doctrine is not mine, but H· — John 7 : 16.
  109–29 If any man will do H· will, he — John 7 : 17.
  110– 6 pronounced by H· wisdom good.
  114–11 noumenon and phenomena, God and H· thoughts.
  117– 9 to the Supreme Being or H· manifestation ;
  119–10 is to leave the creator out of H· own
  128– 5 refers only to the laws of God and to H·
  140–29 created man in H·, God's, image ;
ph 165– * sent H· word, and healed — Psal. 107 : 20.
  167– 2 out of H· personal volition,
  174–11 but the angels of H· presence
  183–17 supposed laws which result in. . .are not H· laws,
  187– 5 of the all-knowing Mind and of H· creations.
  192–18 holds the "wind in H· fists ;" — Prov. 30 : 4.
f 206– 1 we can have no other Mind but H·,
  222–28 had made him one, contrary to H· commands.
  224–14 and array H· vicegerent with pomp
  230–14 to suppose Him . . . punishing. . . of H· volition
  231–24 to doubt H· government
  231–25 and distrust H· omnipotent care.
  233–16 the shadow of H· right hand rests
  242–12 good, God and H· reflection,
  244–20 If man . . . God is without H· entire
  247–23 reflects the charms of H· goodness
  249– 4 producing H· own models of excellence.
c 255–18 hath not seen Spirit, nor hath ear heard H· voice.
  256–20 "doeth according to H· will — Dan. 4 : 35.
  256–22 none can stay H· hand. — Dan. 4 : 35.
  257–12 Mind creates H· own likeness in ideas,
  267– 6 The allness of Deity is H· oneness.
b 268– * and with H· Son Jesus Christ. — I John 1 : 3.
  270–18 divine Mind, in H· more infinite meanings,
  275–16 These are H· attributes,
  275–17 No wisdom is wise but H· wisdom ;
  280–28 being perpetual in H· own individuality,
  300– 4 of H· infinite image or reflection, man.
  303–27 without a witness or proof of H· own nature.
  306– 9 were parted for a moment from H· reflection,
  308– 4 and keeping H· commandment?"
  310–10 God is H· own infinite Mind, and expresses all.
  313–10 "the brightness of H· [God's] glory, — Heb. 1 : 3.
  313–11 the express [expressed] image of H· — Heb. 1 : 3.
  313–21 being a brightness from H· glory, — see Heb. 1 : 3.
  313–22 and an image of H·
  314– 7 inseparable as God and H· reflection
  318–30 are controlled and proved by H· laws.
  328–13 reveals the grand realities of H· allness.

His

b 331– 6   the creator reflected in *H·* creations.
331–13   the divine Mind and *H·* ideas.
332– 5   *H·* tender relationship to *H·* spiritual
332– 8   "For we are also *H·* offspring."— *Acts* 17 : 28.
339– 7   there is no room for *H·* unlikeness.
340– 8   and keep *H·* commandments :— *Eccl.* 12 : 13.
340–10   love God and keep *H·* commandments :
340–13   in and of God, and manifests *H·* love.
o 341– *   *by H· Spirit that dwelleth in you.* — *Rom.* 8 : 11.
345– 5   God cannot be in *H·* unlikeness
345– 7   When . . . *H·* absoluteness is set forth,
348–16   I deny *H·* cooperation with evil,
360–26   in *H·* ministering spirits,— *see Job* 4 : 18.
360–27   *H·* angels He chargeth with — *see Job* 4 : 18.
p 373– 5   and be more alive to *H·* promises.
390–24   no law of *H·* to support the necessity
419– 6   God and *H·* ideas alone are real and
439–27   and the righteous executor of *H·* laws.
t 455–23   All-wise does not bestow *H·* highest trusts upon
r 466– 1   *H·* reflection is man and the universe.
470–19   Has God taken down *H·* own standard,
472– 6   God has set *H·* signet upon Science,
472–10   nor belong to *H·* government.
472–10   *H·* law, rightly understood, destroys them.
478–29   and called me by *H·* grace,— *Gal.* 1 : 15.
483–29   does this in the way of *H·* appointing,
497– 6   We acknowledge *H·* Son, one Christ ;
g 508–13   God determines the gender of *H·* own ideas.
512–10   These angels of *H·* presence, which have
513–26   *H·* thoughts are spiritual realities.
516– 9   fashions all things, after *H·* own likeness.
517–17   *H·* personality can only be reflected,
519– 2   from all eternity knoweth *H·* own ideas.
519– 5   emanation, of *H·* infinite self-containment
522–31   Does the creator condemn *H·* own creation?
525–14   and God shaped man after *H·* mind ;
527–18   to be the tree of death to *H·* own creation?
529–11   are *H·* eternal children, belonging to
543–11   They cannot come into *H·* presence,
ap 558– *   *the mountain of H· holiness.*— *Psal.* 48 : 1.
560–17   whom God has appointed to voice *H·* Word.
561–15   God and *H·* Christ, bringing harmony to earth.
565– 8   unto God, and to *H·* throne.— *Rev.* 12 : 5.
567– 6   The Gabriel of *H·* presence has no contests.
568–15   and the power of *H·* Christ : — *Rev.* 12 : 10.
572–10   belongs not to *H·* children,
573–17   ever with men, and they are *H·* people.
577– 3   as one Father with *H·* universal family,
578– 9   for *H·* name's sake.— *Psal.* 23 : 3.
gl 580– 4   opposite of Spirit and *H·* creations ;
582–19   creates man as *H·* own spiritual idea,
599–11   and that man is His idea, the child of *H·* care.
    (*see also* **creation, idea, image, likeness, power, work**)

historian

g 537–25   the ordinary *h·* interprets it literally.

historic

u 27 23   only eleven left a desirable *h·* record.
an 105 10   these words . . . will become *h·*
g 523–30   In the *h·* parts of the Old Testament,

history

all
sp 93–22   The belief . . . has darkened all *h·*.
f 225–14   The history of our country, like all *h·*,
ancient
a 43–10   and is now repeating its ancient *h·*.
authentic
ph 194–17   The authentic *h·* of Kaspar Hauser is a
Bible
o 342– 9   presumptuously, in the face of Bible *h·*
brief
ap 565–14   a brief *h·* in the earthly life of our Master ;
central emblem of
f 238–31   The cross is the central emblem of *h·*.
Christian
b 328–16   has sadly disappeared from Christian *h·*.
ap 577–17   the Christ-idea in Christian *h·* ;
eternal
r 471– 4   remained unchanged in its eternal *h·*.
evil has no
g 538–21   evil has no *h·*,
false
g 522– 1   the false *h·* in contradistinction to the true.
glorious
g 521– 7   We leave this brief, glorious *h·*
has confirmed
a 54–27   and *h·* has confirmed the prediction.
her
f 245–16   those unacquainted with her *h·* conjectured
human
g 528–31   Later in human *h·*, when the forbidden fruit
Israelitish
o 351– 1   sprang from half-hidden Israelitish *h·*
Jesus'
a 20– 8   Jesus' *h·* made a new calendar,

history

material
f 204– 4   false conclusions . . . that material *h·* is as real
g 547–27   The true theory . . . is not in material *h·*
mortal
r 476–16   from the beginning of mortal *h·*,
natural
ph 195–17   Through astronomy, natural *h·*, chemistry,
b 277–13   Natural *h·* presents vegetables and animals
g 548–26   Natural *h·* is richly endowed by the
551– 7   In natural *h·*, the bird is not the product of
of Christianity
p 387–27   The *h·* of Christianity furnishes sublime
of error
g 521–29   The *h·* of error or matter, if veritable, would
522–12   unmistakably gives the *h·* of error
525–26   if we give the same heed to the *h·* of error as
530–26   The *h·* of error is a dream-narrative.
of Jesus
b 315–26   The *h·* of Jesus shows him to have been
of man
g 557–22   Popular theology takes up the *h·* of man as if
of mortality
g 547–15   In its *h·* of mortality, Darwin's theory of
of our country
f 225–14   The *h·* of our country, like all history,
of religion
a 37–10   one stage with another in the *h·* of religion.
of the errors
an 101– 5   in the *h·* of the errors of the human mind,
religious
a 36–30   Religious *h·* repeats itself in the
spiritual
f 204– 5   that material history is as . . . as spiritual *h·* ;
g 551– 8   In spiritual *h·*, matter is not the progenitor of
teaches
o 357–17   *H·* teaches that the popular and false notions

a 37– 5   *H·* is full of records of suffering.
s 158–12   The future *h·* of material medicine
f 245– 3   a sketch from the *h·* of an English woman,
g 501–17   than the *h·* of perpetual evil.
502– 9   *h·* of the untrue image of God,

History of Four Thousand Years of Medicine

s 158– 6   according to the "*H· of F· T· Y of M·*."

hit

t 457–22   and at the same time *h·* the mark.

hither

s 129–16   come *h·* to torment us before the— *Matt.* 8 : 29.
ap 574– 8   Come *h·*, I will show thee the bride, — *Rev.* 21 : 9.
575– 1   "Come *h·* ! Arise from your false consciousness

hitherto

sp 79–20   "My Father worketh *h·*, — *John* 5 : 17.
s 547–22   spiritual facts of being *h·* unattained

hobbled

c 261–16   he *h·* every day to the theatre,

hold

pr 8– 7   They *h·* secret fellowship with sin,
a 27–31   endeavored to *h·* him at the mercy of matter
28– 6   The determination to *h·* Spirit in the grasp of
28–12   we cannot *h·* to beliefs outgrown ;
30–27   to allow Soul to *h·* the control,
m 63–31   woman should be allowed to . . . *h·* real estate,
sp 97– 1   those who discern C. S. will *h·* crime in check.
an 105–12   over which courts *h·* jurisdiction?
s 127– 3   nor will Christianity lose its *h·* upon her.
143–29   you conclude that . . . nerves, bones, etc., *h·* the
158–25   Drug-systems are quitting their *h·* on matter
ph 177–22   nor can a lie *h·* the preponderance
181– 6   does it *h·* the issues of life?"
182–13   "*h·* to the one, and despise the— *Matt.* 6 : 24.
f 209–18   which constituent masses *h·* to each other,
226–29   *h·* the children of Israel in bondage.
231–20   To *h·* yourself superior to sin, because God
231–25   To *h·* yourself superior to sickness and
254– 5   who gain good rapidly and *h·* their position,
c 261– 4   *H·* thought steadfastly to the enduring,
b 308–27   did not loosen his *h·* upon this glorious light
p 395–22   mental quackery . . . to *h·* it as something seen
396– 1   never *h·* in mind the thought of disease,
405– 6   to *h·* hatred in abeyance with kindness,
412–15   adequate to unclasp the *h·* and to
414–25   *H·* these points strongly in view.
417–14   *h·* your ground with the unshaken understand-
    ing
426–26   *h·* the banner of Christianity aloft
428–23   We must *h·* forever the consciousness
t 444–15   to those who *h·* these differing opinions.
456– 9   high standing which most of them *h·*
464–20   *h·* fast that which is good."— *I Thess.* 5 : 21.
r 493–31   to *h·* man forever intact in his perfect state,
496–15   *H·* perpetually this thought.
ap 565–12   *h·* sway and deprive Herod of his crown.
gl 587–12   theories that *h·* mind to be a material sense,

holding

sp 87– 5 It is needless for the thought or for the person h·
s 124–10 thus limiting Life and h· fast to discord
ph 174–29 h· it before the thought of both
f 248–20 The world is h· it before your gaze
c 260– 5 while h· in thought the character of Judas.
p 422–26 h· that matter forms its own conditions
422–29 Not h· the reins of government
ap 563–19 h· untiring watch, that he may bite the heel of

holds

sp 71–16 images, which mortal mind h· and evolves
92– 3 fifth erroneous postulate is, that matter h·
ph 187–30 the human mind still h· in belief a body,
192–17 h· the "wind in His fists ;"— Prov. 30 : 4.
192–30 Whatever h· human thought in line with
f 209–11 intelligence which h· the winds in its grasp.
o 353–14 It still h· them more or less.
p 395–27 Mental practice, which h· disease as a
417–28 control which Mind h· over the body.
440–14 Even penal law h· homicide, . . . to be
441–16 h· him to be forever in the image and likeness
r 471– 2 h· the divine order or spiritual law,

holier

pr 4–19 but the longing to be better and h·,
c 258– 5 human craving for something better, higher, h·,
p 419–30 rise into higher and h· consciousness.

holiest

r 481– 6 man is free "to enter into the h·,"— Heb. 10 : 19.
g 512–10 angels of His presence, which have the h· charge,

holiness

and harmony
p 392–10 the health, h·, and harmony of man,
and immortality
f 230– 6 will bring us into health, h·, and immortality.
ap 563–22 prolific in health, h·, and immortality.
and life
a 52– 6 spiritual evidence of health, h·, and life ;
b 340–22 demonstrates health, h·, and life eternal.
and unholiness
f 229–10 sickness and health, h· and unholiness,
b 303–21 life and death, h· and unholiness,
beauty, and
f 246–26 unfolds wisdom, beauty, and h·.
beauty of
s 135–12 This is "the beauty of h·," that— Psal. 29 : 2.
f 253– 2 beauty of h·, the perfection of being,
being is
r 492– 7 Being is h·, harmony, immortality.
desire for
pr 11–22 We know that a desire for h· is requisite
fitness for
pr 15–32 Without a fitness for h·, we cannot
health and
a 37–25 by the demonstration of . . . health and h·.
f 236–25 the truths of health and h·.
241–24 the way to health and h·.
b 337–30 the rule of health and h· in C. S.,
heights of
g 514– 9 In humility they climb the heights of h·.
His
ap 558– * in the mountain of His h·.— Psal. 48 : 1.
if we desire
pr 11–24 if we desire h· above all else,
purity, and
g 509–26 beauty, sublimity, purity, and h·
receive
pr 15–32 Without . . . we cannot receive h·.
road to
pr 11–27 securely in the only practical road to h·.
sin to
b 339–24 sickness to health, sin to h·,
to gain
pr 11–23 requisite in order to gain h· ;

a 20–23 traversing anew the path from sin to h·.
s 116– 3 spiritual power, love, health, h·.
f 201–20 Grafting h· upon unholiness,
248–30 justice, health, h·, love
r 475–29 The real man cannot depart from h·,
g 518–22 expressions of God reflect health, h·,
gl 595–14 h· and purification of thought and deed,

holy

a 32–13 bowed in h· submission to the divine decree.
34– 4 "h·, acceptable unto God,"— Rom. 12 : 1.
48–10 sweat of agony which fell in h· benediction
sp 95– 3 His h· motives and aims were traduced
s 109–19 produced . . . by h·, uplifting faith ;
124– 8 spiritual basis, nor h· Principle of its own,
143–31 everlastingly due its h· name.
146–25 through the h· influence of Truth
161– 5 H· inspiration has created states of mind which
b 272–17 "Give not that which is h· unto— Matt. 7 : 6.
325–22 h·, acceptable unto God,— Rom. 12 : 1.
r 477– 5 Jesus taught that . . . man is pure and h·.

holy

k 499– * These things saith He that is h·,— Rev. 3 : 7.
g 506–20 even as He opens the petals of a h· purpose
510– 5 to be h·, thought must be purely spiritual.
512– 9 and also by h· thoughts, winged with Love.
520– 2 highest and sweetest rest, . . . is in h· work.
550–30 the pure and h·, the immutable and immortal
ap 567– 1 He leads the hosts . . . and fights the h· wars.
576– 8 further describing this h· city,
577–12 This spiritual, h· habitation has no
gl 579– * These things saith He that is h·,— Rev. 3 : 7.

Holy Comforter

b 331–31 divine Science or the H· C·.

Holy Ghost

a 23–13 said : "He . . . has the H· G· dwelling in him."
29–24 The H· G·, or divine Spirit, overshadowed
43– 8 what is meant by the descent of the H· G·,
46–30 His students then received the H· G·.
b 332–20 the H· G·, or Comforter, revealing the
o 358–28 wonderful power, derived from the H· G·."
p 365–28 convert . . . the temple of the H· G·,
r 496–16 the spiritual idea, the H· G· and Christ,
497– 7 the H· G· or divine Comforter ;
ap 558–17 It brings the baptism of the H· G·,
562– 2 the Messiah, who would baptize with the H· G·,
gl 588– 7 definition of

Holy One

s 135–18 danger of . . . limiting the H· O· of Israel

Holy Spirit

o 359– 9 I as a Christian Scientist believed in the H· S·,

Holy Writ

s 139–16 what should and should not be considered H· W·;
f 230–22 According to H· W·, the sick are never really
ap 573– 5 This testimony of H· W· sustains the fact

homage

a 18– 5 and for this we owe him endless h·.
20– 3 He at last paid no h· to forms of doctrine
42–10 Though entitled to the h· of the world
p 364–19 Do Christian Scientists seek . . . for personal h·?
g 541– 9 Had God more respect for the h·
gl 595–22 Contribution ; tenth part ; h· ; gratitude.

home

a 29– 2 must take up arms against error at h· and
m 58–20 desire for incessant amusement outside the h·
58–21 H· is the dearest spot on earth,
59–16 in which the heart finds peace and h·
65–17 powerlessness of vows to make h· happy,
s 121–16 "a weary searcher for a viewless h·."
124–30 restores them to their rightful h·
ph 169–16 find stronger supports and a higher h·.
f 254–31 Pilgrim on earth, thy h· is heaven ;
b 282–17 Truth has no h· in error,
p 363–21 and so brought h· the lesson to all,
gl 589–15 JERUSALEM. . . . H·, heaven.

Homer

sp 82– 7 discernment of the minds of H· and Virgil,
ph 199–32 When H· sang of the Grecian gods,

Homer's

s 164– 2 the groping of H· Cyclops around his cave."

homesick

p 365– 3 heavenly h· looking away from earth,

homicidal

p 433– 7 conclusion . . . laws of nature render disease h·.

homicide

p 433–24 which material laws condemn as h·.
439– 8 commanding him to take part in the h·.
440–13 disobedience to God, or an act of h·.
440–14 h·, under stress of circumstances,

homœopathic

ph 179–26 with h· pellet and powder in hand,
p 398–16 H· remedies, sometimes not containing a
416– 9 any physician — allopathic, h·, botanic, eclectic

homœopathy

allopathy and
o 344–30 Is it because allopathy and h· are
attenuation of
s 153–12 highest attenuation of h· and the most potent
experiments in
s 152–28 experiments in h· had made her skeptical
furnishes
p 370–10 H· furnishes the evidence to the senses,
step beyond
s 156–29 Metaphysics, . . . next stately step beyond h·.

s 155–25 H· diminishes the drug,
155–28 Vegetarianism, h·, and hydropathy
156–32 H· takes mental symptoms largely into
157– 3 It succeeds where h· fails,
157–10 H· mentalizes a drug with such repetition of
158–27 H·, a step in advance of allopathy,

honest

pref	xii–26	she commits these pages to h· seekers for Truth.
pr	8– 3	We never need to despair of an h· heart ;
	13– 6	beyond the h· standpoint of fervent desire.
	15–19	go forth with h· hearts to work and
a	21–12	If h·, he will be in earnest from the start,
ph	173–22	Phrenology makes man knavish or h· according
	197–19	more h· than our sleek politicians.
	199–21	devotion of thought to an h· achievement
b	272– 5	only as we are h·, unselfish, loving,
	272– 6	an "h· and good heart" — Luke 8 : 15.
	327–22	Fear of punishment never made man truly h·.
p	372–30	If . . . error prevents the h· recognition of
	384– 7	for h· labor, or for deeds of kindness,
	418– 7	Plead with an h· conviction of truth
t	446–19	it is imperative to be h·,
	458–26	h· and consistent in following the leadings of
	464–24	fall before an h· heart.
ap	570– 1	march of mind and of h· investigation

honestly

pref	x–12	bluntly and h· given the text of Truth.
pr	8–30	learn what we h· are.
	13–16	cherish the desire h· and silently
s	147– 8	and everywhere, when h· applied

honesty

m	64–29	H· and virtue ensure the stability of the
an	106– 4	the free course of h· and justice,
s	115–26	MORAL. Humanity, h·, affection,
f	239– 8	Break up cliques, level wealth with h·,
p	405 8	and to overcome deceit with h·.
t	449–14	in proportion to your h· and fidelity,
	453–16	H· is spiritual power.

honey

ap	559–19	shall be in thy mouth sweet as h·." — Rev. 10 : 9.

Honor

p	433– 7	his H·, Judge Medicine, urges the jury
	434–30	Your H·, the lower court has sentenced
	435–28	what jurisdiction had his H·, Judge Medicine,
	436–28	His H· sentenced Mortal Man to die

honor

s	143–30	the glory, h·, dominion, and power
ph	183–32	and the one Mind only is entitled to h·.
f	219–28	not rendering to God the h· due to Him
o	348– 1	which we desire neither to h· nor to fear.
	352–30	no longer seeming worthy of fear or h·.
r	483–27	And C. S. does h· God as no other theory

honored

a	28–27	because it is h· by sects and societies,
s	118–22	are h· with the name of laws.
o	359–18	Christianity is to be h· wherever found,
p	362– 2	Jesus was once the h· guest of a certain
	382–18	"more h· in the breach than the observance"?

honoring

ph	184 11	never h· erroneous belief with

honors

a	39– 4	He won eternal h·.
ph	183–30	it h· spiritual understanding ;
t	459– 5	achieves no worldly h· except by sacrifice,
r	483–25	if any system h· God, it ought to receive aid,
	483–28	honor God as no other theory h· Him,
ap	577–23	will lay down their h· within the

hope

anchor of

u	41– 1	the anchor of h· must be cast beyond the veil

and achievement

t	456– 2	adverse to its highest h· and achievement.

and faith

pr	9–16	enjoy the fruition of our h· and faith.
a	45–18	from the door of human h· and faith,
gl	581–15	ASHER (Jacob's son). H· and faith ;
	584–27	DOVE. . . . purity and peace ; h· and faith.

and fear

b	298–17	h· and fear, life and death,

and fruition

b	298– 7	Science armed with faith, h·, and fruition.

and triumph

p	434–18	solemn eyes, kindling with h· and triumph,

buoyant with

s	109–16	sweet, calm, and buoyant with h·,

depressed

p	420–18	The fact that . . . reassures depressed h·.

faith and

ap	559–31	into the El Dorado of faith and h·.

having no

r	446–31	"having no h·, and without God — Eph. 2 : 12.

health and

f	235–21	spiritual guides to health and h·.

human

a	45–18	from the door of human h·
b	319– 7	and misguide human h·.

in immortality

p	388–25	we have h· in immortality ;

hope

little

pr	8– 4	but there is little h· for those who come only

my weary

a	55–17	My weary h· tries to realize that happy day,

of forgiveness

a	22– 3	between sin and the h· of forgiveness,

of freedom

p	368–12	even the h· of freedom from the bondage of

of happiness

m	61–20	What h· of happiness, what noble ambition,

of the promise

pr	14–18	Hence the h· of the promise

on earth

o	361–27	is the higher h· on earth,

reason of its

r	487–23	from which to explain the reason of its h·.

rose higher

ph	190–7	When h· rose higher in the human heart,

strengthens

t	446–21	To understand God strengthens h·,

to the sick

s	152– 7	that it may give h· to the sick

turns

c	263–16	His "touch turns h· to dust,

without

g	536–11	The illusion of sin is without h· or God.

---

a	40–13	"While there 's life there 's h·,"
m	63–23	If . . . let us h· it will be granted.
	66–19	Amidst conjugal infelicity, it is well to h·,
s	115–27	h·, faith, meekness, temperance.
	125–14	changes . . . from fear to h·
f	206–12	exercise of the sentiments — h·, faith, love
	253– 9	I h·, dear reader, I am leading you into
	253–14	I h· that you are conquering this false sense.
b	298–14	involves intuition, h·, faith, understanding,
	298–20	joy is no longer a trembler, nor is h· a cheat.
	301–12	reflects the . . . Spirit, which mortals h· for.
	320–28	and encourages mortals to h· in Him who
p	362– *	H· thou in God ; for I shall yet — Psal. 42 : 11.
	367–28	I long to see the consummation of my h·,
	372–21	and h· to succeed with contraries?
	394– 8	we can accomplish the good we h· for,
g	531– 9	as if h· were ever prophesying thus :

hoped

b	279– 5	"the substance of things h· for." — Heb. 11 : 1.
r	468–20	"The substance of things h· for, — Heb. 11 : 1.

hopeful

s	149–19	remarked . . . advise our patients to be h·
p	304– 1	It is well to be calm . . . to be h· is still better ;

hopefulness

p	375–26	Consumptive patients always show great h·

hopeless

pref	x–18	abandoned as h· by regular medical attendants.
ph	196–25	Many a h· case of disease is induced by a
f	227– 9	and in subjection to h· slavery.
n	375–28	supposed to be in h· danger.
	376– 1	presents to mortal thought a h· state,
	382–30	more h· suffering and despair.
	394–23	Will you tell the sick that their condition is h·,
	405– 4	makes any man, . . . a h· sufferer.
	428–30	The author has healed h· organic disease,

hopelessly

f	213–24	Beethoven, who was so long h· deaf.

hopes

m	57–32	disappointments it involves or the h· it fulfils.
	66–12	not from seed sown in the soil of material h·,
c	265–27	The loss of earthly h· and pleasures
b	299– 9	human belief has buried its fondest earthly h·.
	330– 6	she cherished sanguine h· that C. S. would
t	451–16	If our h· and affections are spiritual,
ap	566– 5	through the great desert of human h·,

hopeth

pref	xii–23	"h· all things, endureth all — I Cor. 13 : 7.

hoping

m	67–14	H· and working, one should stick to the wreck.

Horeb

f	241–25	We should strive to reach the H· height

horizon

m	58–13	Never contract the h· of a worthy outlook
sp	98– 4	beholds in the mental h· the signs of

horn

s	119– 8	To seize the first h· of this dilemma
	119–11	while to grasp the other h· of the dilemma

horns

ap	562–31	having seven heads and ten h·, — Rev. 12 : 3.
	563– 6	showing its h· in the many inventions of evil.
	563–11	The ten h· of the dragon typify the belief

horoscope

s	121– 9	Though no higher revelation than the h· was

horse
- *s* 117– 3   as an individual man, an individual *h·* ;
- *ph* 179–16   You can even educate a healthy *h·* so far
-   179–19   ailment, which a wild *h·* might never have.

hospitably
- *o* 342–14   where they should be *h·* received.

hospitality
- *p* 364– 9   the *h·* of the Pharisee or the contrition of

host
- *p* 363–11   saying in their hearts, especially his *h·*,
- *g* 519– 8   finished, and all the *h·* of them.— *Gen. 2 : 1.*

hostility
- *f* 241– 3   He, who . . . obeys them, incurs the *h·* of envy ;

hosts
- *an* 102–15   has dominion over all the earth and its *h·*.
- *s* 150–31   The *h·* of Æsculapius are flooding the
- *ap* 566–32   He leads the *h·* of heaven against the

hot
- *p* 431–26   I am Sallow Skin. I have been dry, *h·*, and

hour
- **anticipating the**
  - *a* 33– 3   anticipating the *h·* of their Master's betrayal,
- **cometh**
  - *a* 31–26   "The *h·* cometh, and now is,— *John 4 : 23.*
  - *sp* 93– 5   "But the *h·* cometh, and *now is,— John 4 : 23.*
- **darkest**
  - *sp* 96–11   "The darkest *h·* precedes the dawn."
- **day and**
  - *b* 292– 3   "but of that day and *h·*,— *Matt. 24 : 36.*
- **every**
  - *an* 102–19   are every *h·* weaving webs more complicated
  - *c* 261–32   Good demands of man every *h·*, in which to
  - *p* 407– 9   Every *h·* of delay makes the struggle more
  - *r* 494–14   since to all mankind and in every *h·*,
- **has struck**
  - *o* 342– 2   *h·* has struck when proof and demonstration,
- **of development**
  - *c* 266–10   When this *h·* of development comes,
- **of harmony**
  - *sp* 96– 4   Love will finally mark the *h·* of harmony,
- **of strength**
  - *ph* 166–19   waiting for the *h·* of strength in which to
- **of woe**
  - *ap* 567– 4   Truth and Love come nearer in the *h·* of woe,
- **one**
  - *a* 48– 4   "Could ye not watch with me one *h·*?"— *Matt. 26 : 40.*
- **rests upon the**
  - *f* 233–17   shadow of His right hand rests upon the *h·*.
- **same**
  - *f* 245– 7   Believing that she was still living in the same *h·*
- **that**
  - *a* 50–17   or that *h·* would be shorn of its mighty blessing
  -   50–26   The burden of that *h·* was terrible
- **will bring the**
  - *ap* 570– 2   will bring the *h·* when the people will chain,

hourly
- *b* 291–29   the judgment-day of wisdom comes *h·*
- *g* 548–16   This is the new birth going on *h·*,

hours
- **few**
  - *g* 556–32   plunged his infant babe, only a few *h·* old,
- **morning**
  - *a* 34–31   in the bright morning *h·*
- **three**
  - *s* 153–10   administered at intervals of three *h·*,
  - *f* 221– 9   not wet his parched throat until three *h·*
- **twenty-four**
  - *f* 221– 7   partook of but one meal in twenty-four *h·*,
- **waking**
  - *p* 397–25   are no more material in their waking *h·*

- *sp* 95–29   cradle of infancy, dreaming away the *h·*.
- *f* 218– 7   rests us more than *h·* of repose

house
- *a* 33–11   They had borne this bread from *h·* to *h·*,
- *ph* 193– 3   On entering the *h·* I met his physician,
- *b* 269– 2   Pandemonium, a *h·* divided against itself.
- *p* 399–30   enter into a strong man's *h·*— *Matt. 12 : 29.*
- *t* 454– 8   leads to the *h·* built without hands
- *r* 478– 9   declaration that a *h·* was inhabited,
-   478–11   no such persons were seen to go into the *h·*
- *ap* 578–17   and I will dwell in the *h·*— *Psal. 23 : 6.*

household
- *ph* 179–30   her *h·* may erelong reap the effect
- *p* 362–10   Hindoo pariah intruding upon the *h·* of

households
- *a* 19–14   although his teaching set *h·* at variance,

houses
- *sp* 86–17   Haunted *h·*, ghostly voices, unusual noises,
- *b* 269–28   reeds shaken by the wind, not *h·* built on the

however
- *pref* ix–25   copies were, *h·*, in friendly circulation.
-   x– 9   A few books, *h·*, which are based on
- *pr* 12– 8   This, *h·*, is one belief casting out another,
- *a* 23– 3   One sacrifice, *h·* great, is insufficient to
- *m* 60–19   This, *h·*, in a majority of cases, is not its
- *sp* 88–23   These effects, *h·*, do not proceed from
- *an* 103– 9   As in the beginning, *h·*, this liberation
- *s* 109– 6   This great fact is not, *h·*, seen to be
-   127–14   It may be said, *h·*, that the term C. S.
- *ph* 169–21   *h·* much we trust a drug or any other means
-   183– 6   *h·* much is said to the contrary.
- *b* 320–19   (*h·* transcendental such a thought appears),
-   326–13   material systems, *h·* time-honored,
- *o* 349– 7   We have the gospel, *h·*,
-   361–24   *h·* limited, must be correct
- *p* 402– 3   *H·*, it is but just to say that the author has
-   414– 5   *H·* obstinate the case, it yields more readily
-   429– 4   We must begin, *h·*, with the more simple
-   436– 5   to reappear *h·* at the trial as a witness
- *r* 473–31   Few, *h·*, except his students understood
- *g* 549–27   At that point, *h·*, even this great observer

hue
- *s* 139–21   with its own *h·* darkening to some extent
- *ph* 193–11   its death-pallor gave place to a natural *h·*.
- *p* 379–15   invalid, inspecting the *h·* of her blood
-   431–28   I am Sallow Skin. . . . I have lost my healthy *h·*
- *t* 460–26   the *h·* of spiritual ideas from her own

hues
- *f* 247–25   which paints the petal with myriad *h·*,
- *r* 479–29   because it has none of the divine *h·*.
- *g* 513– 9   gray in the sombre *h·* of twilight ;

hug
- *f* 201–15   we shall not *h·* our tatters close about us.
-   237–31   they *h·* false beliefs and suffer the

human
- **ability**
  - *a* 52–24   speaking of *h·* ability to reflect divine power,
- **acts**
  - *gl* 595–18   limits, in which are summed up all *h·* acts,
- **affairs**
  - *p* 430–31   the superintendence of *h·* affairs,
- **affection**
  - *m* 57–22   *H·* affection is not poured forth vainly,
  -   65– 7   If the foundations of *h·* affection are
  - *p* 364–28   expressed by meekness and *h·* affection,
  -   366–13   is deficient in *h·* affection,
- **affections**
  - *m* 61– 4   good in *h·* affections must have ascendency
- **antipode**
  - *r* 484–23   it is the *h·* antipode of divine Science.
- **apprehension**
  - *r* 471–30   which, reduced to *h·* apprehension,
- **approval**
  - *p* 382– 3   having only *h·* approval for their sanction.
- **auxiliaries**
  - *t* 454–32   *h·* auxiliaries to aid in bringing thought into
- **being**
  - *pr* 2–20   as one pleads with a *h·* being,
  - *sp* 82–26   between a mole and a *h·* being.
- **beings**
  - *b* 298–25   Angels are not etherealized *h·* beings,
- **belief**
  - *sp* 80–26   movements arise from the volition of *h·* belief,
  -   84– 7   a groundwork of corporeality and *h·* belief.
  -   97– 8   According to *h·* belief, the lightning is fierce
  - *s* 124– 5   When this *h·* belief lacks organizations
  -   124–11   *h·* belief is a blind conclusion from material
  -   125–10   the prior states which *h·* belief created
  -   126– 9   *H·* belief has sought and interpreted
  -   143–11   required a material and *h·* belief before
  -   145–12   subdues the *h·* belief in disease.
  - *ph* 177–28   does *h·* belief, you ask, cause this death?
  -   178–15   When wrested from *h·* belief and based on
  -   183–30   If C. S. dishonors *h·* belief, it honors
  -   184–20   This is *h·* belief, not the truth of being,
  -   190– 8   This embryonic and materialistic *h·* belief
  -   194– 6   A change in *h·* belief changes all the
  - *f* 240– 2   but *h·* belief misinterprets nature.
  - *c* 261–32   which is only a form of *h·* belief,
  - *b* 273– 4   *H·* belief has sought out many inventions,
  -   280–16   Through this error, *h·* belief comes to have
  -   293– 7   are but different strata of *h·* belief.
  -   294– 2   These senses indicate the common *h·* belief,
  -   294–23   *h·* belief in them to be the father of mythology,
  -   297– 5   *H·* belief says to mortals, "You are sick !"
  -   298–16   This *h·* belief, alternating between a sense of
  -   299– 8   sepulchre, in which *h·* belief has buried its
  - *b* 310– 2   *h·* belief fancies that it delineates
  - *p* 374–11   originating in *h·* belief before it is
  -   377–30   Without this ignorant *h·* belief, any
  -   421– 6   the true definition of all *h·* belief in ill-health,
  - *r* 466– 8   To *h·* belief, they are personalities
  -   490–20   *H·* belief — or knowledge gained from the

human

belief
r 495–11   life-giving power of Truth acting on *h·* belief,
g 551–13   describes the gradations of *h·* belief,
553–24   If consentaneous *h·* belief agrees upon an
555– 3   *h·* belief, and not the divine arbitrament,
gl 585–20   *h·* belief before it accepts sin, sickness,

beliefs
a 24– 5   and willingness to give up *h·* beliefs
sp 79–11   Spiritualism relies upon *h·* beliefs
83–32   investigates and touches only *h·* beliefs.
98–15   Beyond the frail premises of *h·* beliefs,
s 164–19   caused by a majority of *h·* beliefs
ph 171– 7   gates of Paradise which *h·* beliefs have closed,
f 208–19   in the wilderness'' of *h·* beliefs — *Matt.* 3 : 3.
252– 7   When false *h·* beliefs learn even a little
c 260– 9   *h·* beliefs will be attaining diviner
r 471–27   This view rebuked *h·* beliefs,
478–25   is composed of material *h·* beliefs
g 505–30   The mortal, erring, and finite are *h·* beliefs,

birth
ph 190–14   *H·* birth, growth, maturity, and decay

blood
a 25– 5   by our sense of *h·* blood.

body
m 62–23   divine Mind, . . . will care for the *h·* body,
s 125– 3   organic and functional health in the *h·* body
t 458–13   or of trying to sustain the *h·* body

bondage
f 227– 8   The law of . . . must end *h·* bondage,

brutality
a 40–21   apostles of Truth may endure *h·* brutality

capacities
ph 200– 6   illustrated the grand *h·* capacities of being
c 258–22   *h·* capacities are enlarged and perfected

capacity
g 519–11   *H·* capacity is slow to discern and to grasp

changeableness
s 140–24   wrath, repentance, and *h·* changeableness.

character
ap 565–22   purifying even the gold of *h·* character.

codes
f 226–18   *H·* codes, scholastic theology,

concept
ph 177–14   body is a sensuous, *h·* concept.
c 259–25   Brain or matter never formed a *h·* concept.
b 277–26   not divine, — it is a *h·* concept.
277–31   a *h·* concept, sometimes beautiful,
o 359–13   you must change the *h·* concept of life,
r 469– 4   Matter is a *h·* concept.
482–19   the highest *h·* concept of the perfect man.
g 506–25   Here the *h·* concept and divine idea seem
541–12   even the *h·* concept of Love

conception
a 50–26   that hour was terrible beyond *h·* conception.
ph 185–14   puts forth a *h·* conception in the name of
g 505– 7   by which *h·* conception, material sense,

conceptions
c 255–12   to belittle Deity with *h·* conceptions.
257–16   material senses and *h·* conceptions would

concepts
m 62–26   thrusting in the laws of erring, *h·* concepts.
p 426–31   *h·* concepts named matter, death, disease,
g 516–31   genders are *h·* concepts.
531–12   exchanging *h·* concepts for the divine
536– 7   symbol of tempest-tossed *h·* concepts

conclusions
b 298– 1   the vague realities of *h·* conclusions.

conjecture
b 298–30   *H·* conjecture confers upon angels its own.
330–17   left either to *h·* conjecture or to the

consciousness
pref xi–12   lose their reality in *h·* consciousness
xi–17   influence ever present in *h·* consciousness
sp 95–31   lifts *h·* consciousness into eternal Truth.
b 297–14   and the *h·* consciousness rises higher.
327–27   Through *h·* consciousness, convince the mortal
332–11   speaking to the *h·* consciousness.
o 355–13   take possession of *h·* consciousness.
r 484–19   the false *h·* consciousness is educated to feel.
ap 573– 7   heavens and earth to one *h·* consciousness,

craving
c 258– 4   unsatisfied *h·* craving for something better,

creatures
b 298–32   making them *h·* creatures with suggestive

delusions
b 328–11   in the Science which destroys *h·* delusions

depravity
ap 564–18   the highest degree of *h·* depravity.

discord
b 306–32   parent of all *h·* discord was the Adam-dream.

displeasure
ap 571– 9   to tell a man his faults, and so risk *h·* displeasure

doctrine
b 286– 2   To seek Truth through belief in a *h·* doctrine

human

doctrines
s 117–31   which he defined as *h·* doctrines,
g 504–25   a thousand years of *h·* doctrines,
545–14   errors send falsity into all *h·* doctrines

doubts
pr 13–21   *h·* doubts and fears which attend such a belief,

duty
g 541–25   it repudiates even the *h·* duty of man towards

element
a 33–18   When the *h·* element in him struggled with

error
b 294– 1   the avenues and instruments of *h·* error,
p 401– 2   Any *h·* error is its own enemy,
ap 563–10   This dragon stands for the sum total of *h·* error.

errors
g 533–10   an attempt to trace all *h·* errors

existence
ph 190–22   with saddening strains on *h·* existence :
f 205–28   Selfishness tips the beam of *h·* existence

experience
sp 99–25   must deepen *h·* experience, until the
g 552–13   *H·* experience in mortal life, which
ap 572–24   stage in *h·* experience called death,

experiences
s 108– 7   *h·* experiences show the falsity of

eye
a 49–16   No *h·* eye was there to pity, no arm to save.
ph 188–30   The *h·* eye knows not where the orb of day is,

faculty
b 327–29   Reason is the most active *h·* faculty.

faith
pref xi– 6   the fruits of *h·* faith in matter,
pr 12–18   borrows its power from *h·* faith and belief.
sp 93–19   *h·* faith may clothe it with angelic vestments,
s 153–14   learned that either *h·* faith or the
ph 169–22   towards which *h·* faith or endeavor is directed.

family
an 103– 8   blesses the whole *h·* family.
ph 196–32   sorrows and diseases among the *h·* family.
f 202–11   but the whole *h·* family would be redeemed
234– 5   blesses the *h·* family with crumbs of comfort
g 532– 3   in order to create the rest of the *h·* family?

fear
ph 176–17   *H·* fear of miasma would load with disease
p 412– 3   to advance and destroy the *h·* fear of sickness.
ap 563– 4   We may well be perplexed at *h·* fear ;
566– 3   the dark ebbing and flowing tides of *h·* fear,

footsteps
f 254– 1   *h·* footsteps leading to perfection are

form
c 255–16   The *h·* form, or physical finiteness,
b 315–29   Wearing in part a *h·* form
g 554–31   especially those of the *h·* form.

forms
pr 4–32   and clothe religion in *h·* forms.

freedom
f 242– 7   towards *h·* freedom and the final triumph over

generation
m 68–30   Proportionately as *h·* generation ceases,

good
ph 182– 9   capable of producing the highest *h·* good ?

governments
p 378–32   usually find displayed in *h·* governments.

happiness
m 65– 1   and *h·* happiness should proceed from

hate
t 454– 9   *H·* hate has no legitimate mandate

hatred
b 330– 5   fixedness of mortal illusions, and the *h·* hatred
ap 571–19   *h·* hatred cannot reach you.

heart
ph 190–27   When hope rose higher in the *h·* heart,

herald
pref vii– 6   the Bethlehem babe, the *h·* herald of

history
g 528–31   Later in *h·* history, when the

hope
a 45–17   from the door of *h·* hope and faith,
b 319– 7   and misguide *h·* hope.

hopes
ap 566– 5   the great desert of *h·* hopes,

hypotheses
sp 98–12   Creeds, doctrines, and *h·* hypotheses do not
t 457– 2   Truth uncontaminated by *h·* hypotheses.
r 481–19   *H·* hypotheses first assume the reality of

ignorance
pr 13–25   Because of *h·* ignorance of the
t 252– 4   *H·* ignorance of Mind and of the

illusion
r 492–23   *h·* illusion as to sin, sickness, and death

illusions
c 259–23   and forms its offspring after *h·* illusions.
r 468– 2   and never can be coordinate with *h·* illusions.

image
s 140–31   and make God in their own *h·* image.

human

indignation
ap 570– 6 finally be shocked . . . into *h·* indignation ;
invention
  a 44–27 method infinitely above that of *h·* invention.
  sp 95–20 even *h·* invention must have its day,
  s 163–26 perhaps so ample an exhibition of *h·* invention
Jesus
  b 333–32 meant, not that the *h·* Jesus was or is eternal,
  334–20 even before the *h·* Jesus was incarnate to
joys
  m 66–18 well to remember how fleeting are *h·* joys.
justice
  g 542–20 and let *h·* justice pattern the divine.
kind
  m 56– 8 moral provision for generation among *h·* kind.
knowledge
  sp 92–19 an outgrowth of *h·* knowledge
  s 124– 3 Physical science (so-called) is *h·* knowledge,
  124–27 *H·* knowledge calls them forces of matter ;
  ph 197– 7 What a price for *h·* knowledge !
  f 213–30 Before *h·* knowledge dipped to its depths
  g 532– 5 All *h·* knowledge and material sense
  gl 582– 5 *h·* knowledge, or so-called mortal mind,
language
  g 520– 5 *H·* language can repeat only an infinitesimal
law
  a 43–22 *H·* law had condemned him,
  an 105– 8 to admit that the power of *h·* law is restricted
  105–14 and *h·* law rightly estimates crime,
life
  a 51– 3 loss of something more important than *h·* life
  54– 2 Through the magnitude of his *h·* life,
  m 65– 5 and give to *h·* life an inspiration by which
  ph 173–19 measuring . . . *h·* life by material law.
  f 225–32 and on the lowest plane of *h·* life,
  232–21 or that they could destroy *h·* life ;
  p 389–19 laws that food shall support *h·* life,
  t 451–32 to blast moral sense, health, and the *h·* life.
likeness
  b 301– 2 as the *h·* likeness thrown upon the mirror,
limb
  r 489– 6 Then the *h·* limb would be replaced as readily
links
  a 37– 9 Martyrs are the *h·* links which connect
logic
  b 300– 1 *H·* logic is awry when it attempts
man
  r 473–15 Jesus is the *h·* man, and Christ is the divine
memory
  p 378– 3 are reproduced in union by *h·* memory.
mind
  pref x– 7 They regard the *h·* mind as a healing agent,
  xi– 3 only a phase of the action of the *h·* mind,
  pr 12– 6 on the *h·* mind, making it act more powerfully
  m 58– 6 Tones of the *h·* mind may be different,
  65–18 *h·* mind will at length demand a higher
  sp 83– 1 the *h·* mind or the divine Mind which is
  85– 5 This Soul-sense comes to the *h·* mind
  85–10 when you are able to read the *h·* mind
  87–11 in the general atmosphere of *h·* mind.
  87–16 Science enables one to read the *h·* mind,
  an 101– 6 history of the errors of the *h·* mind,
  104–31 Is it not clear that the *h·* mind must
  s 111– 4 the will, or sensuous reason of the *h·* mind,
  114– 4 *h·* mind and evil in contradistinction to
  126–12 *h·* mind never produced a real tone
  128–11 The *h·* mind, imbued with this
  130–16 disabuse the *h·* mind of material beliefs
  143–13 *h·* mind uses one error to medicine another.
  143–15 *h·* mind takes the lesser to relieve the
  150–32 ignorant that the *h·* mind and body are myths.
  151– 5 *h·* mind has an absolute need of something
  151–21 *h·* mind has no power to kill
  151–24 The *h·* mind is opposed to God
  155–22 The *h·* mind acts more powerfully to offset
  157–13 becomes more like the *h·* mind than the
  162–10 stir the *h·* mind to a change of base,
  ph 166– 2 the *h·* mind is all that can produce pain.
  166–15 *h·* mind is inharmonious in itself.
  168–24 I have discerned disease in the *h·* mind,
  173–28 the error which the *h·* mind alone has created.
  174–31 cause of disease obtains in the mortal *h·* mind,
  176–14 mechanism of the *h·* mind gives place to
  176–28 The *h·* mind, not matter, is supposed to feel,
  177– 1 *H·* mind produces what is termed organic
  180–13 Ignorant that the *h·* mind governs the body,
  185–20 excludes the *h·* mind as a spiritual factor
  185–29 material stratum of the *h·* mind,
  186–32 The *h·* mind has been an idolater from the
  187–10 beliefs of the *h·* mind rob and enslave it,
  187–24 The *h·* mind tries to classify action as
  187–29 but the *h·* mind still holds in belief a body,
  187–31 which appears to the *h·* mind to live,
  189– 7 the cruder theories of the *h·* mind,
  f 214–10 is an object-lesson for the *h·* mind.

human

mind
  f 218– 5 If it were not for what the *h·* mind says
  218–13 the *h·* mind is the sinner, disinclined to
  219–17 must obtain in the *h·* mind before it can
  226–11 the fetters . . . be stricken from the *h·* mind
  234–30 laid great stress on the action of the *h·* mind,
  235– 2 cannot go forth, . . . from one *h·* mind to
  251–21 acts upon the so-called *h·* mind
  251–22 leads the *h·* mind to relinquish all error,
  c 264– 1 the fleeting concepts of the *h·* mind.
  b 270–29 the fact that the *h·* mind alone suffers,
  316–10 manifest by its effects upon the *h·* mind
  327– 7 and all the sinful appetites of the *h·* mind.
  o 357–19 have originated in the *h·* mind.
  p 378– 8 Without the so-called *h·* mind, there can be no
  396–31 sickness is formed by the *h·* mind,
  402–20 We say that one *h·* mind can
  403–10 The *h·* mind is employed to remove the
  403–12 both have their origin in the *h·* mind,
  403–27 The *h·* mind determines the nature of
  g 531–10 The *h·* mind will sometime rise above
  ap 559–11 inaudible voice of Truth is, to the *h·* mind,
  573– 9 while to another, the unillumined *h·* mind,
  573–10 what the *h·* mind terms matter
mind-forces
  ph 186– 7 Erring *h·* mind-forces can work only evil
minds
  f 210–15 action of the divine Mind on *h·* minds
misconceptions
  p 428–20 mental might to offset *h·* misconceptions
misery
  ap 574–17 the sum total of *h·* misery, represented by
mother
  b 315–30 being conceived by a *h·* mother,
motives
  f 239–23 the acknowledged seat of *h·* motives.
name
  b 333– 4 Jesus was a *h·* name, which belonged to him
nature
  b 272– 8 swinish element in *h·* nature uproots it.
need
  sp 95– 9 and in that ratio we know all *h·* need
  r 494–11 and always will meet every *h·* need.
needs
  pr 16–11 prayer which covers all *h·* needs.
  t 453–15 know others and minister to *h·* needs.
opinions
  s 112–10 some particular system of *h·* opinions.
  ph 192– 6 *H·* opinions are not spiritual.
  b 280–31 The only excuse for entertaining *h·* opinions
  o 360–12 replies: . . . my old doctrines or *h·* opinions."
  t 447– 6 must not forget that erring *h·* opinions,
origin
  b 305–29 These mortal dreams are of *h·* origin,
  g 553–21 theory . . . to account for *h·* origin,
parent
  a 50– 9 despairing appeal, if made to a *h·* parent,
peace
  c 265–23 Who that has felt the loss of *h·* peace
pen
  s 110–17 No *h·* pen nor tongue taught me the Science
perception
  s 119–28 As astronomy reverses the *h·* perception of
  o 361–23 A *h·* perception of divine Science,
  ap 561–18 reducing to *h·* perception and understanding
personality
  s 138– 7 Truth, and Love, and not a *h·* personality,
philosophy
  sp 99– 2 *H·* philosophy, ethics, and superstition
  s 144– 8 mortal beliefs formulated in *h·* philosophy,
  b 269– 9 *H·* philosophy has made God manlike.
  279–22 Every system of *h·* philosophy, doctrine,
platitudes
  t 446–25 Not *h·* platitudes, but the divine beatitudes,
power
  f 225–15 shows *h·* power to be proportionate to its
  g 539–27 gave him more than *h·* power to expound the
presence
  b 325–28 Science which ushered Jesus into *h·* presence,
probation
  a 35–16 its exemplification of *h·* probation,
progress
  ph 170–24 spiritual causation relates to *h·* progress.
propagation
  g 557– 9 *h·* propagation has its suffering because
race
  a 50–18 its mighty blessing for the *h·* race.
  s 111–25 a yearning of the *h·* race for spirituality.
  c 261–32 in remembering good and the *h·* race.
  g 548–25 he would have blessed the *h·* race more
  550– 4 whence cometh Life, . . . to the *h·* race?
  553–25 as the point of emergence for the *h·* race,
  gl 585–25 belief that the *h·* race originated materially

human

reason
s 117–25 relates solely to *h·* reason ;
117–26 *h·* reason dimly reflects and
ph 173–26 *H·* reason and religion come slowly to the

resistance
b 329–32 *H·* resistance to divine Science weakens

rights
a 48–29 decision against *h·* rights and divine Love,
s 134–12 and so it came about that *h·* rights were
f 226–14 God has built a higher platform of *h·* rights,

sacrifice
a 54–13 the inspiration of Jesus' intense *h·* sacrifice.

self
f 254–19 But the *h·* self must be evangelized.

sense
a 51– 7 He had power to lay down a *h·* sense of life
sp 99–16 the *h·* sense of things errs
b 325–19 where *h·* sense hath not seen man.
327–32 nothingness of the pleasures of *h·* sense
334–30 a reference to the *h·* sense of Jesus crucified.
p 369– 5 In proportion as matter loses to *h·* sense all
r 494–18 helping erring *h·* sense to flee from its
g 540–19 It saith to the *h·* sense of sin, sickness, and
ap 560–12 great miracle, to *h·* sense, is divine Love,
563– 1 *H·* sense may well marvel at discord,
573– 2 the *h·* sense of space is unable to
576–31 This *h·* sense of Deity yields to the divine sense

senses
s 116– 6 evidence before the corporeal *h·* senses,
r 461–10 from the standpoint of the *h·* senses.

shackles
c 256– 1 Progress takes off *h·* shackles.

society
ap 575–31 which binds *h·* society into solemn union ;

soul
ph 200–21 the so-called *h·* soul or spirit,
b 310–19 commonly taught that there is a *h·* soul

species
m 60–16 Marriage should improve the *h·* species,
61–24 Is not the propagation of the *h·* species a
61–31 If the propagation of a higher *h·* species
68–26 belief that agamogenesis applies to the *h·* species.
ph 172– 7 Materialism grades the *h·* species as

standpoint
g 520– 1 sweetest rest, even from a *h·* standpoint,

storehouses
a 54–12 into empty or sin-filled *h·* storehouses,

strength
ph 173–18 measuring *h·* strength by bones and sinews,

suffering
a 22–28 or that divinity is appeased by *h·* suffering,
f 227–19 of continued bondage and of *h·* suffering.

system
s 103–15 "The effects of medicine on the *h·* system
ph 170– 2 according to belief, poisons the *h·* system.
f 222– 7 nutriment and strength to the *h·* system.
p 385– 1 entire functions and organs of the *h·* system
415–23 organs of the *h·* system, including brain and
423–12 reaching to every part of the *h·* system.

systems
s 164–12 But all *h·* systems based on
ph 170–12 not only contradicts *h·* systems, but
f 234–21 present codes of *h·* systems disappoint

teacher
t 455–18 student, who receives . . . from a *h·* teacher,

testimony
sp 71–24 no proof nor power outside of *h·* testimony.

theories
s 117–19 *H·* theories are inadequate to interpret
149– 6 a bundle of speculative *h·* theories?
ph 170– 9 certainly present what *h·* theories exclude,
f 220–17 engendered solely by *h·* theories.
c 255– 6 The mythical *h·* theories of creation,
b 275–25 Our material *h·* theories are destitute of
p 381–22 understand your way out of *h·* theories
r 490–14 *H·* theories are helpless to make man harmonious
gl 590– 5 *h·* theories, doctrines, hypotheses ;

thought
pr 12–26 they are the merchandise of *h·* thought
s 125–12 As *h·* thought changes from one stage to
126– 8 *H·* thought never projected the least portion of
ph 189– 6 raises the *h·* thought above the cruder theories
191–10 divine Principle of man dawns upon *h·* thought,
191–16 The *h·* thought must free itself from
192–30 Whatever holds *h·* thought in line with
f 205–26 leads *h·* thought into opposite channels
206– 8 Material, erring, *h·* thought acts injuriously
210– 3 language which *h·* thought can comprehend.
234–23 the right education of *h·* thought.
b 297–21 It is a chrysalis state of *h·* thought,
297–30 *h·* thought has little relation to the actual
o 349–14 in conveying . . . accurately to *h·* thought
r 482– 3 *H·* thought has adulterated the meaning of
g 502–14 Even thus the crude forms of *h·* thought

human

thought
g 508–29 an important one to the *h·* thought,
ap 571– 1 not so willing to point out the evil in *h·* thought,

thoughts
b 297–24 *H·* thoughts have their degrees of comparison.
t 449–20 The inoculation of evil *h·* thoughts

understanding
pr 12–11 nor is it the *h·* understanding of the
sp 99–11 has opened the door of the *h·* understanding.

use
s 143– 6 God does not . . . provide them for *h·* use ;

verdicts
r 481–22 *h·* verdicts are the procurers of all discord.

view
s 150–22 This *h·* view infringes man's free moral agency ;
b 276–13 into *h·* view in their true light,
316–18 the Christ-man, rose higher to *h·* view

want
c 257–25 to meet the demands of *h·* want and woe,
g 501– 9 but richly recompensing *h·* want and woe

warfare
f 226–12 not through *h·* warfare, not with bayonet

weakness
t 453–17 Dishonesty is *h·* weakness, which forfeits

will
pr 9–24 and material sense and *h·* will have no place.
s 144–14 *H·* will belongs to the so-called material
ph 194– 2 with matter or with *h·* will.
f 206– 4 *h·* will should be exercised only in subordination
209– 4 in proportion as ignorance, *fear*, or *h·* will
b 329–22 You cannot mock it by *h·* will.
t 445–19 C. S. silences *h·* will, quiets fear with Truth
445–24 The *h·* will which maketh and worketh a lie,
451–20 knows that *h·* will is not C. S.,
451–23 defend himself from the influence of *h·* will.
r 490– 4 *H·* will is an animal propensity,

will-power
an 106– 1 the criminal misuse of *h·* will-power,
s 144–14 *H·* will-power is not Science.
144–18 *H·* will-power may infringe the

woe
f 238–20 until we seek this remedy for *h·* woe

wrath
a 49–23 but is above the reach of *h·* wrath,

yearning
a 48– 7 There was no response to that *h·* yearning,
49–13 O, why did they not gratify his last *h·* yearning

a 43–27 The divine must overcome the *h·*
sp 98–32 The way . . . not *h·* but divine,
99–15 that which is spiritual and divine, and not *h·*.
99–17 errs because it is *h·*.
an 102– 3 His power is neither animal nor *h·*.
s 112–11 wholly *h·* in their origin and tendency
114– 8 and calls *mind* both *h·* and divine
127–25 truth is not *h·*, and is not a law of matter,
ph 188–32 The *h·* or material senses yield to the
189–18 *h·* mortal mind, by an inevitable perversion,
f 213–29 as the hand, which sweeps over it, is *h·* or
c 263–27 The multiplication of a *h·* and mortal sense
b 282–24 all that is material is a . . . *h·*, mortal thought,
286–22 Material and temporal thoughts are *h·*,
286–31 are comprised in *h·* material belief,
327–20 in the *h·* or the divine economy.
329–23 Science is a divine demand, not a *h·*.
332–18 The corporeal man Jesus was *h·*.
334–16 when the *h·*, material concept, or Jesus,
o 345–28 This thought of *h·*, material nothingness,
353–27 and those limits are *h·*,
p 385– 7 the divine law, rising above the *h·*.
435–22 no demand, *h·* or divine, renders it just
440–22 beliefs of your *h·* mental legislators
t 445–16 when you weigh the *h·* in the scale with the
462–23 Are thoughts divine or *h·*?
r 472–28 seem real to *h·*, erring belief,
482–30 since the *h·*, mortal mind so-called is not
483– 6 and this Mind must be divine, not *h·*.
g 508– 1 fall to the level of a *h·* or material belief,
514–15 transmission from the divine thought to the *h·*,
525– 6 and is a *h·*, not a divine, creation.
549–20 including those which we call *h·*.
ap 561–16 John saw the *h·* and divine coincidence.
gl 586–23 the *h·* yielding to the divine ;
589–16 highest *h·* corporeal concept of the divine idea.

humane

ph 198– 9 The materialistic doctor, though *h·*, is an
p 385– 3 philanthropists engaged in *h·* labors

humanity (see also humanity's)

advances
sp 95–32 *H·* advances slowly out of sinning sense

and philanthropy
sp 80–12 no doubt of the *h·* and philanthropy

applied to
s 127–16 Science as applied to *h·*.

humanity
better views of
f 239–10 and we get better views of *h*·.
brought to
a 44–25 whereby divinity brought to *h*· the
common
p 365–12 if . . . common sense and common *h*· are disregarded,
Deity and
g 555–22 as if man were the offspring of . . . Deity and *h*·.
distinction from
s 116–27 divinity and its distinction from *h*·.
earth and
sp 72–32 communicator of truth, . . . to earth and *h*·.
emancipate
f 223–23 They will emancipate *h*·,
embracing
ap 561–17 shown . . . as divinity embracing *h*·
form of
b 332–25 appear to mortals in such a form of *h*· as
germ of
g 550– 1 he virtually affirms that the germ of *h*· is
great poet of
m 66– 2 Shakespeare, great poet of *h*· :
hidden from
f 205– 1 will continue to be hidden from *h*·,
higher
ap 571–20 The cement of a higher *h*· will unite
interests of
f 236– 5 in the interests of *h*·, not of sect.
lifting
p 407–14 lifting *h*· above itself into purer desires,
lifts
g 547–32 lifts *h*· out of disease and death
mortal
b 338–11 conclusions of material and mortal *h*·.
of Jesus
a 25–32 Christ was made manifest in the *h*· of Jesus.
permeate
a 37–12 and to permeate *h*· with purer ideals.
physical
c 256–14 within the narrow limits of physical *h*·,
poor
o 345–22 incongruity between God's idea and poor *h*·,
portal of
pref vii–15 Truth, . . . knocks at the portal of *h*·.
reaches
s 113– 4 The letter of Science plentifully reaches *h*·
rights of
a 54–32 Would they not deny him even the rights of *h*·,
sick
p 371–12 so sick *h*· sees danger in every direction,
sinful
s 114– 3 the author calls sick and sinful *h*· *mortal mind,*
spiritualizes
o 354–11 heals the sick and spiritualizes *h*·.
universal
b 328–31 and includes universal *h*·.

s 115–26 MORAL. *H*·, honesty, affection, compassion,
ph 173– 3 how . . . distinguish between *h*· and the brute,
c 258–23 in proportion as *h*· gains the true
b 311–22 When *h*· does understand this Science,
o 356–26 Does divine Love commit a fraud on *h*·
p 413–20 Water is not the natural habitat of *h*·.

humanity's
r 494– 4 and he did this for tired *h*· reassurance.

humanization
g 517– 3 anthropomorphism, or a *h*· of Deity.

humanly
pr 2–21 the belief in God as *h*· circumscribed,
a 53–14 Mortals believed in God as *h*· mighty,
s 147– 9 where demonstration was *h*· possible,
ph 179–19 The epizoötic is a *h*· evolved ailment,
f 247–20 its qualities before they are perceived *h*·.
gl 591–22 is divinely natural, but must be learned *h*· ;

humble
pr 2–12 We can do more for ourselves by *h*· fervent
12–13 whose *h*· prayers were deep and conscientious
s 119–32 is but the *h*· servant of the restful Mind,
f 228–27 The *h*· Nazarene overthrew the supposition
t 448– 5 it won his *h*· desire.

humbled
f 228–30 It should have *h*· the pride of the priests,
b 320–15 shall not forever rule [or be *h*·] in men,
320–21 avers that this fact is not forever to be *h*·

humblest
a 48–11 shall the *h*· or mightiest disciple murmur

humbly
pr 13–17 honestly and silently and *h*·,

humiliating
s 163–28 more than compensated by the *h*· view of

humility
pr 8–14 If we feel the aspiration, *h*·, gratitude,
8–20 Praying for *h*· with whatever fervency
s 142–19 *h*· and divine Science to be welcomed in.
b 326–29 in *h*· he took the new name of Paul.
g 514– 8 In *h*· they climb the heights of holiness.

humor
p 424–32 may tell you that he has a *h*· in the blood,

humors
s 162– 7 It changes the secretions, expels *h*·,
p 393–27 complex *h*·, lenses, muscles, the iris and pupil,
425– 3 You will have *h*·, just so long as you believe

hundred
a 27–24 two or three *h*· other disciples
s 111–19 prize of one *h*· pounds, offered in
122– 9 practically exposed nineteen *h*· years ago
139–19 and the three *h*· thousand in the New,
f 232–17 as it did over nineteen *h*· years ago,
o 344–29 while C. S. cures its *h*·

hundreds
b 328–19 *h*· . . . die there annually from serpent-bites

hung
p 363– 5 hair, which *h*· loosely about her shoulders,

hunger
f 221–10 He passed many weary years in *h*·
221–27 feeling childhood's *h*· and undisciplined by

hungering
pr 2– 5 the desire which goes forth *h*· after
r 482–25 to the *h*· heart in every age.

hungry
f 234– 7 feeding the *h*· and giving living waters to the

hurricane
ph 192–15 It is lightning and *h*·,

hurt
s 154–29 thinks she has *h*· her face by falling on the
154–31 and says, . . . "Mamma knows you are *h*·."
155– 1 You 're not *h*·, so don't think you are."
ph 165–19 in order to remember what has *h*· you,
f 222–11 Food had less power to help or to *h*· him
b 328–24 it shall not *h*· them.— *Mark* 16 : 18.
p 362– * *it shall not h· them ;— Mark* 16 : 18.
397–13 you think or exclaim, "I am *h*· !"
397–17 Declare that you are not *h*·
438– 6 nothing shall by any means *h*· you.— *Luke* 10 : 19.
r 491– 2 Needle-thrusts will not *h*· him.

husband
m 58–17 would confine a wife or a *h*· forever within
58–32 how she may please her *h*·,"— *I Cor.* 7 : 34.
60– 1 it never would, if both *h*· and wife were
63–28 If a dissolute *h*· deserts his wife,
66–24 than for a wife precipitately to leave her *h*·
66–24 or for a *h*· to leave his wife.
s 136–21 That a wicked king and debauched *h*· should
g 535– 9 thy desire shall be to thy *h*·,— *Gen.* 3 : 16.

husbandman
ph 180– 2 mortal mind is the *h*· of error,

husbands
m 59–20 *H*·, hear this and remember how slight a
66–21 *H*· and wives should never separate if there is

hushed
m 64–32 the voices of physical sense will be forever *h*·.

huts
sp 82–30 the Esquimaux in their snow *h*·?

hydra
ap 563– 6 hatred, which lifts its *h*· head,

hydropathy
s 155–28 Vegetarianism, homœopathy, and *h*·

hygiene
adherence to
f 222–19 the strictest adherence to *h*· and drugs,
p 382–31 Adherence to *h*· was useless.
diet and
t 457–25 some learners commend diet and *h*·.
drugs and
ph 167–12 Drugs and *h*· cannot successfully usurp the
r 484–16 Drugs and *h*· oppose the supremacy of the
drugs or
s 143– 5 God does not employ drugs or *h*·,
faith in
f 251–16 whether through faith in *h*·,
material
f 220– 5 open . . . to the inefficacy of material *h*·,
222–21 he dropped drugs and material *h*·,
t 453–31 never recommends material *h*·,
r 484– 7 medication, material *h*·, mesmerism,
matter and
p 430–15 the supposed laws oɪ matter and *h*·,
physiology and
ph 166–24 through adherence to physiology and *h*·,

hygiene

surgery, and
　　a 44–12　all the claims of medicine, surgery, and *h·*.
system of
　　ph 185– 6　No system of *h·* but C. S. is purely mental.
think about
　　p 389– 6　The less we know or think about *h·*,

　　s 138–12　neither . . . by *materia medica*, nor by *h·*,
　　144– 9　in human philosophy, physiology, *h·*,
　　145–14　whether faith in drugs, trust in *h·*,
　　f 222–27　fear, *h·*, physiology, and physics
　　226–19　material medicine and *h·*, fetter faith
　　230–23　the sick are never really healed by drugs, *h·*, or
　　p 382– 5　If half the attention given to *h·* were
　　r 483– 1　how do drugs, *h·*, and animal magnetism heal?

hygienic
　　p 370–25　*H·* treatment also loses its efficacy.
　　378–19　*h·* drilling and drugging, adopted to
　　382–13　He, who is ignorant of what is termed *h·* law,
　　382–15　the devotee of supposed *h·* law,
　　440– 2　on the ground of *h·* disobedience,

hymn
　　ap 566–20　prayer which concludes the same *h·*,

hypnotic
　　ph 181–32　Any *h·* power you may exercise will
　　p 402–31　pleasure or pain of the person under *h·* control
　　t 446–28　exercise of will brings on a *h·* state,
　　g 528–16　inducing a sleep or *h·* state in Adam

Hypnotism
　　p 430–23　Physiology, *H·*, Envy, Greed and
　　431–14　summoned Physiology, Materia Medica, and *H·*
　　439–18　the blind *H·*, and the masked Personal Sense,
　　441–22　*H·*, Oriental Witchcraft, and Esoteric Magic

hypnotism

and electricity
　　sp 78–26　*h·* and electricity are claimed to be the
called
　　an 101–30　effect of animal magnetism, recently called *h·*,
is not scientific
　　p 402–29　Hence the proof that *h·* is not scientific ;
magnetism nor
　　p 442–16　Neither animal magnetism nor *h·*
magnetism or
　　an 103–19　animal magnetism or *h·* is the specific term for
　　t 454– 1　nor . . . practise animal magnetism or *h·*.
　　gl 584–19　animal magnetism or *h·* ; the lust of the flesh,
mesmerism and
　　b 322–16　foreshadowed the mesmerism and *h·* of to-day.
mesmerism, or
　　an 102– 5　mesmerism, or *h·* is a mere negation,
　　p 402–23　The error, mesmerism— or *h·*, to use the
spiritualism, or
　　sp 99–19　theosophy, spiritualism, or *h·*,
without
　　ph 185–23　not only without drugs, but without *h·*,

　　an 103–24　The malicious form of *h·*
　　104–18　mesmerism, animal magnetism, *h·*.
　　s 129–17　Animal magnetism, *h·*, spiritualism,
　　ph 178–29　attempt to unite with it *h·*,
　　f 202–29　and yet we rely on a drug or *h·* . . . as if
　　p 378–19　whereas *h·* and hygienic drilling and
　　398–28　*h·* changes such ills into new and
　　r 484– 8　mesmerism, *h·*, theosophy, or spiritualism?

hypnotist
　　p 375–12　*h·* dispossesses the patient of his

hypnotized
　　p 431–23　Morbid Secretion *h·* the prisoner

hypnotizer
　　an 104–22　*h·* employs one error to destroy another.

hypochondria
　　ph 176–23　cases of hysteria, *h·*, and hallucination?

hypocrisy

folly of
　　p 426–15　and see the folly of *h·*,
ignorance or
　　f 243– 3　can never succeed . . . through ignorance or *h·*.

hypocrisy

is fatal
　　pr 7–32　*H·* is fatal to religion.
lust and
　　ap 567–28　beast and the false prophets are lust and *h·*.
　　571–31　outshining sin, sorcery, lust, and *h·*.
never spared
　　sp 85–28　never spared *h·* the sternest condemnation.
rebuked the
　　gl 597– 7　rebuked the *h·*, which offered long petitions

　　f 241–10　Falsehood, envy, *h·*, malice,
　　b 289–10　sin, lust, hatred, envy, *h·*,
　　329–21　There is no *h·* in Science.
　　330–30　*h·*, slander, hate, theft, adultery,
　　p 365–25　If *h·*, stolidity, inhumanity, or vice
　　gl 592–28　self-righteousness ; vanity ; *h·*.
　　596–28　VEIL. A cover ; concealment ; hiding ; *h·*.

hypocrite
　　pr 8– 2　though it makes the sinner a *h·*.
　　a 41–10　*h·* may have a flowery pathway here, but
　　52–31　The bigot, the debauchee, the *h·*,
　　c 263–12　They make man an involuntary *h·*,
　　b 294–30　the *h·* that he is hiding himself.

hypocrites
　　pr 3–30　sharp censure our Master pronounces on *h·*.
　　7–28　By it we may become involuntary *h·*,
　　sp 85–21　"O ye *h·* ! ye can discern the— *Matt.* 16 : 3.

hypocritical
　　a 20– 6　To the ritualistic priest and *h·* Pharisee

hypodermic
　　p 416– 6　A *h·* injection of morphine is
　　t 464–17　would give him a *h·* injection,

hypotheses

beliefs and
　　sp 79–11　Spiritualism relies upon human beliefs and *h·*.
　　79–13　C. S. removes these beliefs and *h·*
false
　　s 127–31　false *h·* that matter is its own lawgiver,
human
　　sp 98–12　Creeds, doctrines, and human *h·* do not
　　t 457– 2　Truth uncontaminated by human *h·*.
　　r 481–19　Human *h·* first assume the reality of
material
　　b 273– 7　Deductions from material *h·* are not scientific.
　　g 552– 6　geology, and all other material *h·*
materialistic
　　b 268–10　Materialistic *h·* challenge metaphysics
of mortals
　　ph 182–15　The *h·* of mortals are antagonistic to
physical
　　s 111–15　reverses perverted and physical *h·*
speculative
　　s 126–21　left to the mercy of speculative *h·*?
vague
　　s 110–32　No analogy exists between the vague *h·* of
　　g 549–21　in such vague *h·* as must necessarily

　　a 121–14　left to the *h·* of material sense
　　163–23　*h·* obtruded upon us at different times.
　　r 484–26　thus putting an end to the *h·*
　　g 504–25　a thousand years of human doctrines, *h·*,
　　gl 590– 6　human theories, doctrines, *h·* ;

hypothesis
　　f 209–27　based on the *h·* of material law or
　　244–16　*h·* that he returns eventually to his
　　b 270–10　Few deny the *h·* that intelligence,
　　p 388–12　Admit the common *h·* that food
　　t 445– 6　No *h·* as to the existence of another power
　　r 482– 4　*h·* that soul is both an evil and a good
　　489– 8　*h·* which supposes life to be in matter
　　g 522–28　based on some *h·* of error,

hypothetical
　　g 545–18　Outside of C. S. all is vague and *h·*,
　　551–32　ancient and *h·* question, Which is first,

hysteria
　　ph 176–23　cases of *h·*, hypochondria, and hallucination?
　　177– 2　as certainly as it produces *h·*,
　　f 217–11　even of catalepsy and *h·* ;

I

I
　　a 27–13　*I* [Spirit] will raise it up." — *John* 2 : 19.
　　27–14　The *I* — the Life, substance, and intelligence of
　　f 249–21　The *I* is Spirit. God never slumbers,
　　r 494– 3　*I* [Mind] will raise it up ;" — *John* 2 : 19.
　　g 501– *　*And I appeared unto Abraham,* — *Exod.* 6 : 3.
　　501– *　*was I not known to them.* — *Exod.* 6 : 3.

　　g 533– 6　whereof *I* commanded thee — *Gen.* 3 : 11.
　　535–21　of which *I* commanded thee, — *Gen.* 3 : 17.
　　540– 5　"*I* make peace, and create evil. — *Isa.* 45 : 7.
　　540– 5　*I* the Lord do all these things ;" — *Isa.* 45 : 7
　　gl 588– 9　definition of
　　588–11　There is but one *I*, or Us,
　　591–16　MIND. The only *I*, or Us ; the only Spirit,

I AM

f 253– 8	I am the substance of all, because *I A· THAT I A·*.
c 256–11	rather than the one ever-present *I A·*.
256–13	The everlasting *I A·* is not bounded nor
267–10	The great *I A·* made all
b 290– 1	the everlasting *I A·*, the Being who was and is
336– 1	Mind is the *I A·*, or infinity.
g 550–21	If . . . then the great *I A·* is a myth.
gl 587– 5	GOD. The great *I A·* ; the all-knowing,
588–20	definition of

ice

f 241–17	than can moonbeams to melt a river of *i·*.

Icelandic

g 525–11	the term *man* . . . in the *I·*, mind.
525–12	The following translation is from the *I·* :

idea

advanced
b 324– 2	renders thought receptive of the advanced *i·*.

can give no
ph 191– 1	The brain can give no *i·* of God's man.

clearest
g 517–13	Love imparts the clearest *i·* of Deity.

compound
r 468–24	a compound *i·*, reflecting the divine substance
475–14	He is the compound *i·* of God,
g 507–18	multiplication of the compound *i·* man.
gl 585– 8	to spiritual sense, it is a compound *i·*.
591– 5	The compound *i·* of infinite Spirit ;

divine
(see **divine**)

divine Mind and
s 109– 6	the only realities are the divine Mind and *i·*.

gives the
g 509–15	This text gives the *i·* of the rarefaction

God's
b 299–24	Truth never destroys God's *i·*.
o 345–22	incongruity between God's *i·* and
p 406–24	until we arrive at the fulness of God's *i·*,
ap 565–16	Christ, God's *i·*, will eventually rule all nations

great is the
ap 562–27	great is the *i·*, and the travail portentous.

highest visible
ap 560–18	without a correct sense of its highest visible *i·*,

His
sp 71– 2	nothing is Spirit,— but God and His *i·*.
an 103–16	good is the infinite God and His *i·*,
s 116– 9	so that God and His *i·* may be to us
ph 167–25	but one way — namely, God and His *i·*
b 284–32	is always from God to His *i·*,
o 344– 3	and man to be His *i·*,— that is, His image.
p 372– 9	divine Mind, or God and His *i·*,
r 495–15	cling steadfastly to God and His *i·*.
gl 589–10	and that man is His *i·*, the child of His care.

identity, or
sp 71– 5	The identity, or *i·*, of all reality continues

image or
c 257– 1	creation is the infinite image or *i·*
b 336– 9	was and is God's image or *i·*,

immaculate
ap 565–18	This immaculate *i·*, represented first by man

immortal
a 55–15	Truth's immortal *i·* is sweeping down the
c 262–14	above the mortal to the immortal *i·* of God.
b 325– 7	of Truth, unfolding its own immortal *i·*.
r 477–17	the immortal *i·* of being, indestructible

impelled the
ap 565–25	but this only impelled the *i·* to rise to the

individual
g 508–23	The intelligent individual *i·*, be it male or

infinite
sp 90–25	sets man free to master the infinite *i·*.
s 112–17	comes one Principle and its infinite *i·*,
c 258–13	God expresses in man the infinite *i·*
258–19	infinite Principle is reflected by the infinite *i·*
g 508– 4	Mind's infinite *i·*, man and the universe,
ap 577– 3	as the infinite Principle and infinite *i·*,
gl 582–11	gleam of the infinite *i·* of the infinite Principle ;

is clad
ap 561–26	*i·* is clad with the radiance of spiritual Truth,

lesser
g 518–13	God gives the lesser *i·* of Himself for a

Life's
b 289–12	Life and Life's *i·*, Truth and Truth's idea,

limitless
g 510–19	Love alone can impart the limitless *i·* of

man is
r 475–13	Man is *i·*, the image, of Love ;

mental
r 467–27	Spirit gives the true mental *i·*.

Mind's
r 492–20	All is Mind and Mind's *i·*.

new
b 281–31	cast out or the new *i·* will be spilled,
p 420–17	are ready to become receptive to the new *i·*.
t 463–14	The new *i·*, . . . is clad in white

idea

new-old
ph 191–12	even to the birth of a new-old *i·*,

not in its
r 467–22	leading point . . . that Principle is not in its *i·*.

of Christian healing
a 55– 4	the *i·* of Christian healing enjoined by Jesus ;

of divine power
g 534–15	the *i·* of divine power, which Jesus presented,

of God
(see **God**)

of good
b 325– 3	He who has the true *i·* of good loses all sense of
327–26	the man . . . who has not the true *i·* of good?
g 546–14	represents error as starting from an *i·* of good

of goodness
s 119–22	is represented only by the *i·* of goodness ;

of immortality
gl 593–10	a new and higher *i·* of immortality,

of Life
b 314–21	he presented to her, . . . the true *i·* of Life
325– 2	he who perceives the true *i·* of Life
gl 595– 7	the *i·* of Life, substance, and intelligence ;

of Love
b 326–31	He beheld for the first time the true *i·* of Love,
g 534–28	will struggle to destroy the spiritual *i·* of Love ;

of Spirit
a 29–30	Man as the offspring of God, as the *i·* of Spirit,
c 266–28	Man is the *i·* of Spirit ;

of the supremacy
b 324–28	if the *i·* of the supremacy of Spirit,

of Truth
c 263–22	the discovery of some distant *i·* of Truth ;
r 495– 6	If sickness is true or the *i·* of Truth,
g 526–18	stands for the *i·* of Truth,
543– 6	it is the *i·* of Truth and changes not,
555–32	Truth fosters the *i·* of Truth,
gl 595– 3	SWORD. The *i·* of Truth ; justice.

or intelligence
b 279–18	their only *i·* or intelligence is in God.

or reflection
r 470–22	*i·* or reflection, man, remains perfect.
gl 581– 8	ARK. Safety ; the *i·*, or reflection, of Truth,

presented the
ap 562– 4	Elias presented the *i·* of the fatherhood

presents the
g 503–20	divine Mind presents the *i·* of God :

present the
c 256–29	Finiteness cannot present the *i·* or the vastness

Principle and
c 259–13	includes a perfect Principle and *i·*,
b 285–22	Supreme Being, or divine Principle, and *i·*.
r 471– 1	God and man, divine Principle and *i·*,
476– 5	inseparable as divine Principle and *i·*.
g 503– 9	The divine Principle and *i·* constitute

Principle and its
r 465–17	Principle and its *i·* is one,
475– 4	all is Spirit, divine Principle and its *i·*.
g 520– 9	Principle and its *i·*, man, are coexistent

profound
b 320–26	gives a profound *i·* of the divine power to heal

pure
a 50–14	and to himself, Love's pure *i·*.

right
f 235–31	will love to grapple with a new, right *i·*

semblance of an
ph 195–15	Whatever furnishes the semblance of an *i·*

solitary
c 259– 4	nor is he an isolated, solitary *i·*,

Spirit as
sp 76–17	characterized by the divine Spirit as *i·*,

spiritual
(see **spiritual**)

substance of an
c 257–13	the substance of an *i·* is very far from

this
sp 88–19	but this *i·* can never be seen, . . . through the
t 463–10	this *i·* cannot injure its useful
g 534–29	this *i·*, will bruise the head of lust.
ap 562– 7	This *i·* reveals the universe as secondary

thought and
gl 597–17	Spontaneity of thought and *i·* ;

true
a 39–26	mortals must get the true *i·* and
43–15	true *i·* of God, which Jesus' persecutors had
47– 5	gaining the true *i·* of their glorified Master,
54–10	plant themselves in Christ, the true *i·* of God.
s 123– 3	The true *i·* and Principle of man will
132–25	Anticipating this rejection . . . of the true *i·* of
133–15	but when they departed from the true *i·*,
f 205–20	some word or deed which indicates the true *i·*,
235–26	Christ Jesus, the true *i·* of spiritual power.
c 255–17	cannot be made the basis of any true *i·* of
258– 7	insufficiency of this belief to supply the true *i·*
258–12	and this reflection is the true *i·* of God.
b 314–21	he presented to her, . . . the true *i·* of Life **and**

idea

true
- *b* 316–12   Jesus represented Christ, the true *i·* of God.
- 323–24   true *i·* of God gives the true understanding
- 324– 8   Unless . . . we are not gaining the true *i·* of
- 325– 2   he who perceives the true *i·* of Life
- 325– 3   He who has the true *i·* of good loses all sense of
- 325– 8   Jesus gave the true *i·* of being,
- 326–31   He beheld for the first time the true *i·* of Love,
- 327–26   the man . . . who has not the true *i·* of good?
- 332– 9   Christ is the true *i·* voicing good,
- 337–20   The true *i·* of man, as the reflection of the
- *o* 347–15   the spiritual or true *i·* of God, comes now
- 353–28   The true *i·* of being is spiritual and immortal,
- *r* 473–13   has presented Christ, the true *i·* of God,
- *g* 504– 1   from which emanates the true *i·*,
- 524– 9   the true *i·* of God seems almost lost.
- 536–25   the true *i·* is gained from the immortal side.
- *ap* 560–14   true *i·* of what constitutes the kingdom of
- 560–28   hid from them the true *i·* which has been pre-
-     sented.
- 562–13   man's divine origin and the true *i·*,
- *gl* 585–17   EUPHRATES (river). . . . the true *i·* of God ;

Truth's
- *b* 289–12   Life and Life's idea, Truth and Truth's *i·*,

unerring
- *r* 468– 2   evolves its own unerring *i·*

wise
- *g* 515– 7   a wise *i·*, charming in its adroitness,

- *a* 29–27   Christ dwelt forever an *i·* in the bosom of God,
- *s* 115–17   *I·* : An image in Mind ;
- 151–27   the divine Mind and its *i·*,
- *c* 258–21   no cognizance of either Principle or its *i·*.
- *b* 268– 8   is slowly yielding to the *i·* of a metaphysical
- 279–31   seeks cause in effect, Principle in its *i·*,
- 286–19   good in Principle and in *i·*.
- 301–24   man is "image" (*i·*).— *Gen.* 1 : 27.
- 303–29   an *i·* which cannot be lost nor separated from
- 320–19   harmonious existence as image, *i·*,
- 333–26   The divine image, *i·*, or Christ
- *r* 467–31   understood through the *i·* which expresses it
- *ap* 560–31   ignorance of the divine Principle of the *i·*

ideal

absolute
- *g* 520– 7   The absolute *i·*, man, is no more seen nor

Christ
- *p* 430– 5   immortal manhood, the Christ *i·*, will appear.

divine
- *s* 119–20   not the divine *i·* of omnipresent Love.

her
- *a* 29–18   gave to her *i·* the name of Jesus

infinite
- *g* 517–20   proper symbol . . . is Mind's infinite *i·*.

of God
- *a* 25–16   Jesus presented the *i·* of God better than
- *o* 361– 5   Christ, . . . is the *i·* of God now and forever,

of Truth
- *a* 30–19   As the individual *i·* of Truth, Christ Jesus
- *f* 207–29   is harmonious and is the *i·* of Truth.

spiritual
- *m* 67–29   presents the true likeness or spiritual *i·*.
- *b* 337–19   demonstrates Life in Christ, Life's spiritual *i·*.
- *ap* 561–11   the spiritual *i·* as a woman clothed in light,

this
- *a* 30–22   This *i·* was demonstrated throughout the
- *o* 360–16   This *i·* is either temporal or eternal,
- *p* 392–15   thought should be held fast to this *i·*.
- *g* 517–21   What is this *i·* ?
- 517–31   This *i·* is God's own image,

your own
- *o* 360–16   You are bringing out your own *i·*.

- *m* 69– 9   the real, *i·* man appears in proportion as
- *c* 260– 8   the *i·* of all that is perfect and eternal.
- *b* 317–24   Thomas, looking for the *i·* Saviour in matter
- 332–31   Into the real and *i·* man the fleshly element
-     cannot
- 338–30   Adam was not the *i·* man for whom the
- 338–31   The *i·* man was revealed in due time,
- *o* 346– 4   the *i·* man, reflecting God's likeness.
- *p* 442–24   material, transformed with the *i·*, disappears,
- *r* 473–10   Christ is the *i·* Truth, that comes to heal
- *g* 517– 8   The *i·* man corresponds to creation,
- 517–10   The *i·* woman corresponds to Life and to Love.

idealism

- *pref* xii–22   in order to elucidate her *i·*.
- *s* 132–24   Anticipating this rejection of *i·*,
- *ap* 571–23   immortal scribe of Spirit and of a true *i·*,

ideals

- *a* 37–12   and to permeate humanity with purer *i·*.
- *ph* 195–26   impossible *i·*, and specimens of depravity,
- *f* 249– 3   give up imperfect models and illusive *i·* ;
- *c* 260–19   Mortals must change their *i·*

ideals

- *b* 299–11   to higher *i·* of life and its joys.
- *o* 359–30   One says: "I have spiritual *i·*,
- 360– 1   these *i·* are real and eternal
- 360– 7   materiality renders these *i·* imperfect and

ideas

all
- *g* 515–22   Man is the family name for all *i·*,

are emanations
- *sp* 88–10   *I·* are emanations from the divine

are spiritual
- *sp* 88–14   *I·* are spiritual, harmonious, and eternal.

are tangible
- *b* 279–11   *I·* are tangible and real to immortal

became productive
- *g* 544– 4   In God's creation *i·* became productive,

Christian
- *ph* 170– 8   Christian *i·* certainly present . . . the Principle

countless
- *g* 517–18   God has countless *i·*, and they all have

creator of
- *f* 249–13   the creator of *i·* is not the creator of illusions.

dawn of
- *g* 506–13   Thus the dawn of *i·* goes on,

focus of
- *g* 504–24   when gathered into the focus of *i·*,

fragmentary
- *b* 302– 2   Principle is not to be found in fragmentary *i·*.

God and His
- *p* 419– 6   God and His *i·* alone are real and harmonious.

God's
- *g* 503 16   infinite space is peopled with God's *i·*,
- 504–16   The successive appearing of God's *i·*
- 505–28   God's *i·* reflect the immortal, unerring,
- 511– 4   God's *i·* "multiply and— *Gen.* 1 : 28.

grand
- *g* 511–25   and mountains stand for solid and grand *i·*.

highest
- *f* 230 11   would be contrary to our highest *i·* of God
- *g* 503– 4   highest *i·* are the sons and daughters of God.

His
- *h* 331–13   the divine Mind and His *i·*.

His own
- *g* 508–13   God determines the gender of His own *i·*.
- 519– 2   from all eternity knoweth His own *i·*.

immature
- *b* 313–27   To accommodate himself to immature *i·* of

immortal
- *c* 259–27   Immortal *i·*, pure, perfect, and enduring,

individual
- *b* 302–32   reproduction by Spirit's individual *i·*

infinite
- *g* 511–18   infinite *i·*, images, mark the periods of
- 514– 7   infinite *i·* run and disport themselves.

its
- *s* 110–21   Its *i·* may be temporarily abused
- *f* 210– 1   Its *i·* are expressed only in

its own
- *g* 517 00   Divine Love blesses its own *i·*, and causes them

Love's
- *g* 515– 8   Love's *i·* are subject to the Mind which

material
- *g* 507–30   inverts this appearing and calls *i·* material.

metaphysical
- *s* 115– 5   difficulty of so expressing metaphysical *i·*

Mind and its
- *g* 509 30   in which all is Mind and its *i·*,

Mind forms
- *g* 511– 1   This Mind forms *i·*, . . . subdivides and radiates

not
- *b* 283–11   They are not *i·*, but illusions.

of God
-     (*see* **God**)

of manhood
- *sp* 74–24   say that infancy can utter the *i·* of manhood,

of Mind
- *b* 280– 7   All things beautiful and harmless are *i·* of Mind.

of Soul
- *b* 269–16   exchanges the objects of sense for the *i·* of Soul.

of Spirit
- *g* 505–10   the *i·* of Spirit apparent only as Mind,

of Truth
- *g* 543–26   *I·* of Truth alone are reflected in the

perfect
- *g* 512–21   its own pure and perfect *i·*.

right
- *r* 475–15   compound idea of God, including all right *i·* ;

spiritual
-     (*see* **spiritual**)

systems of
- *f* 209– 6   the central sun of its own systems of *i·*,

these
- *b* 269–17   These *i·* are perfectly real and tangible to
- *g* 503– 3   These *i·* range from the infinitesimal to

ignorant

pr 13–28 *i·* of man as God's image or reflection
   13–30 The world of error is *i·* of the world of Truth,
a 48–28 Pilate was *i·* of the consequences
sp 79– 4 those who are *i·* of Life as God.
  86–14 may appear to the *i·* to be apparitions ;
  87–20 sea is *i·* of the gems within its caverns,
an 103–23 It is either *i·* or malicious.
s 150–32 *i·* that the human mind and body are myths.
  159–30 *I·* of the fact that a man's belief
ph 166– 4 *I·* of this, or shrinking from its implied
  178–28 *I·* of the methods and the basis of
  180–13 *I·* that the human mind governs the body,
  181–17 *i·* of the baneful effects of magnetism,
  186–28 Mortal mind is *i·* of self,
  187– 4 how *i·* must they be of the all-knowing Mind
  190– 3 matter is a belief, *i·* of itself,
  190– 3 *i·* of what it is supposed to produce.
f 225–30 *i·* how to obtain their freedom.
o 343– 6 Is not finite mind *i·* of God's method?
p 377–30 Without this *i·* human belief, any
  380–19 *i·* of the truth which chains disease.
  381– 2 *I·* of our God-given rights.
  382–13 He, who is *i·* of what is termed hygienic law,
  382–16 to teach the so-called *i·* one.
  393– 5 *i·* of itself, of its own actions,
  393– 6 *i·* that the predisposing, remote, and
  408–31 Mortal mind is *i·* of itself,
  408–32 *i·* of the errors it includes
  422–12 and *i·* that it is a favorable omen,
t 447– 7 *i·* attempts to do good may
r 474– 8 To the *i·* age in which it first appears,
  483– 9 must not be *i·* of the moral and spiritual
g 512–27 *I·* of the origin and operations of mortal mind,
  512–28 that is, *i·* of itself,
  512–30 *i·* of the existence of both
ap 560–29 *i·* of the divine idea he taught.

ignorantly

s 116–25 As the words . . . are commonly and *i·*
p 428–16 whom we "*i·* worship,"— *Acts* 17 : 23.
t 456–12 greatly errs, *i·* or intentionally,
gl 596– 9 "Whom therefore ye *i·* worship,— *Acts* 17 : 23.

ignore

ph 166–16 To *i·* God as of little use in sickness is a mistake.
p 275– 2 partnership of mind with matter would *i·*

ignores

s 148–28 it *i·* the divine Spirit as unable or

ill

sp 79–23 unscientific practitioner says: "You are *i·*.
s 107–10 delivering the children of men from every *i·*
f 218– 9 The body is supposed to say, "I am *i·*."
  222–19 and yet he continued *i·* all the while.
  227–31 disobedience to which would have made man *i·*,
  230–30 the liability to be *i·* is removed
  231– 3 Unless an *i·* is rightly met and fairly overcome
  231– 4 Unless . . . the *i·* is never conquered.
b 326– 7 find the divine remedy for every *i·*
p 430–19 The patient feels *i·*, ruminates, and
r 467–21 The belief that . . . is an error that works *i·*.

ill-arranged

m 58– 5 *I·* notes produce discord.

ill-attuned

m 60–24 An *i·* ear calls discord harmony,

ill-effects

ph 176–26 can carry its *i·* no farther than

illegal

p 434–23 His trial was a tragedy, and is morally *i·*.

illegality

p 437–25 expelling . . . for such high-handed *i·*.

illegitimate

f 203–27 The foam and fury of *i·* living
p 390–22 an abiding conviction that it is *i·*,

ill-health

p 377–28 mistaken belief . . . necessity and power of *i·* ;
  421– 6 true definition of all human belief in *i·*,

illimitable

s 127– 8 there can be nothing beyond *i·* divinity.

ill-nature

m 58–29 Wealth may obviate . . . the chance for *i·*

illness

p 396– 5 Avoid talking *i·* to the patient.
t 456–21 So long as matter is the basis . . . *i·* cannot

ills

destroy all
p 374–16 destroy all *i·* which proceed from mortal mind.
r 493–18 Mind must be found . . . able to destroy all *i·*.
fleshly
f 228–10 and fleshly *i·* will disappear.
of flesh
s 155–23 the discords of matter and the *i·* of flesh,
b 277–20 produces all the *i·* of flesh,

ills

of the flesh
ph 191–31 Truth is able to cast out the *i·* of the flesh.
b 320–27 the divine power to heal the *i·* of the flesh,
gl 581–16 ASHER . . . the *i·* of the flesh rebuked.
produce the
m 62–30 and produce the *i·* of which we complain.
such
r 398–29 hypnotism changes such *i·* into
  413–30 making it probable at any time that such *i·* may
these
p 395–26 to feel these *i·* in physical belief,
  424–29 you must destroy the belief in these *i·*
  425–13 Then these *i·* will disappear.

ph 170–31 from which all *i·* have gone forth,
p 405–28 penalties you incur and the *i·* they bring.
g 552–23 the redeeming power, from the *i·* they occasion,

ill-tempered

p 395–17 An *i·*, complaining, or deceitful person

illuminated

a 43– 9 that influx of divine Science which so *i·* the

illuminating

g 502–16 *i·* time with the glory of eternity.

illumination

a 29–20 The *i·* of Mary's spiritual sense
sp 85– 2 It is the *i·* of the spiritual understanding
t 461–11 Only by the *i·* of the spiritual sense,
q 510 10 and this *i·* is reflected spiritually by all who
gl 584– 5 the *i·* of spiritual understanding,
  596–13 believed that the stones . . . had supernatural *i·*,

illuminations

gl 596–15 The *i·* of Science give us a sense of the

illuminator

gl 596–15 reveals Spirit, not matter, as the *i·* of all.

illumine

gl 596–24 divine Life and Love *i·* it,

illumined

s 110–15 The Scriptures were *i·* ;
ap 571–29 and *i·* the night of paganism with the sublime

illumines

b 334– 6 from which it *i·* heaven and earth ;
t 454–19 inspires, *i·*, designates, and leads the way.
g 501– 7 Jesus *i·* them, showing the poverty of
  503–14 light of ever-present Love *i·* the universe.

illuming

c 266–28 *i·* the universe with light.

illusion

any
f 217–26 power of Mind over the body or any *i·* of
ceases to be even an
sp 97–16 boundary where, . . . it ceases to be even an *i·*,
death is the
p 428– 3 Life is real, and death is the *i·*.
destroying that
f 245– 2 benefits of destroying that *i·*, are illustrated in
dream, or
f 230– 5 the awakening from this mortal dream, or *i·*,
effect of
an 101–31 In no instance . . . other than the effect of *i·*.
effects of
p 408–12 baneful effects of *i·* on mortal minds
falsity and
g 554–28 and is simply a falsity and *i·*.
forged by the
f 223– 5 forged by the *i·* that he lives in body
human
r 492–23 human *i·* as to sin, sickness, and death
illustrate its
p 380–15 physical effects of fear illustrate its *i·*.
illustrates the
b 300– 7 The mirage, . . . illustrates the *i·* of
less
f 247–31 recipe for beauty is to have less *i·*
material
r 484–21 Mesmerism is mortal, material *i·*.
mental
p 403– 8 understood that the difficulty is a mental *i·*,
mortal
b 289–19 this shows that . . . death is but a mortal *i·*,
  302–16 always beyond and above the mortal *i·*
p 403–20 sweeps away the gossamer web of mortal *i·*.
of belief
r 490–31 Under the mesmeric *i·* of belief,
of death
f 251– 8 In the *i·* of death, mortals wake to the
r 493–28 awakened Lazarus from the dream, *i·*, of death,
of error
g 538–16 is significant of the *i·* of error,
of life
b 305–23 *i·* of life that is here to-day and gone to-morrow,

illusion

of material sense
sp 71– 3 simply a belief, an *i·* of material sense.
 s 122–15 another proof of the *i·* of material sense.
 f 227–26 The *i·* of material sense, not divine law,
of mind
 b 311–11 so long as the *i·* of mind in matter remains.
of mortal mind
ph 168–27 a latent *i·* of mortal mind,
 p 385–32 Any supposed . . . is an *i·* of mortal mind,
of Moses
 b 321–16 The *i·* of Moses lost its power to alarm
of pleasure
 p 398–21 destroy the *i·* of pleasure in intoxication,
of sickness
 b 297– 8 *i·* of sickness, to be instructed out of itself
 r 495–14 When the *i·* of sickness or sin tempts you,
of sin
 g 536–10 The *i·* of sin is without hope or God.
or dream
 r 490–30 oblivion, nothingness, or an *i·* or dream.
or error
 g 556– 1 and not the belief in *i·* or error.
point out the
 t 447–26 remove the mask, point out the *i·*,
prolong the
sp 77–20 so prolong the *i·* either of a soul inert or
remove the
 p 403–10 is employed to remove the *i·* in one case,
root of the
 b 303–16 Divine Science lays the axe at the root of the *i·*.
sensual
 f 221–32 another lesson,— that gluttony is a sensual *i·*,
springing from
 p 399–24 to make material beliefs, springing from *i·*.
suffer the
 p 381– 5 Be no more willing to suffer the *i·* that
this
 f 217–27 and so destroy this *i·*,
 b 303–18 will eventually destroy this *i·*

sp 92– 6 From the *i·* implied in this last postulate arises
 97–13 until matter reaches its mortal zenith in *i·*
 s 129–29 The very name, *i·*, points to nothingness.
 f 244– 3 is not real, but is *i·*, the mirage of error.
 245–31 decrepitude is . . . but an *i·*.
 b 271– 5 Neither emasculation, *i·*, nor
 287–22 it is *i·*, without spiritual identity or
 293–10 This so-called mind and body is the *i·*
 308–11 but finding only an *i·*,
 o 348– 7 appear to be— what it really is— an *i·*
 p 379–13 his sense of bleeding was an *i·*,
 r 473– 1 inharmony of mortal mind or body is *i·*,
 480–23 Hence, evil is but an *i·*,
 493–26 can only seem real and natural in *i·*.
 494–23 breaks their *i·* with the unbroken reality of
 g 540–12 when the symptoms of evil, *i·*, are aggravated,
 543–13 an *i·*, against which divine Science is
gl 582– 3 Believing. . . . Mortal thoughts, *i·*.
 582– 7 pride; envy; fame; *i·*; a false belief;
 584– 9 Death. An *i·*, the lie of life in matter;
 586–19 an *i·*; a belief that matter has sensation.
 587– 1 An *i·*; a belief that mind is outlined and limited;
 591– 9 another name for mortal mind; *i·*;

illusions

destroy all
 b 296– 7 suffering or Science must destroy all *i·*
dispelling the
 b 332–13 dispelling the *i·* of the senses;
disposal of
 b 305– 1 placed at the disposal of *i·*,
erring
 r 477–13 corporeal senses to be mortal and erring *i·*.
human
 c 259–23 and forms its offspring after human *i·*,
 r 468– 3 never can be coordinate with human *i·*.
laden with
 p 413–26 being laden with *i·* about disease,
leading
 s 129–27 quite as rational are some of the leading *i·*
mere
 g 556–20 In sleep, cause and effect are mere *i·*.
mortal
 f 214–23 for mortal *i·* would rob God, slay man,
 b 289–20 Matter and death are mortal *i·*.
 330– 4 learned . . . the fixedness of mortal *i·*,
not the creator of
 f 249–13 the creator of ideas is not the creator of *i·*.
of sin
ap 572–16 the myriad *i·* of sin, sickness, and death.
old
 f 223–17 but more are blinded by their old *i·*,
similar
 s 122–22 Experience is full of instances of similar *i·*,

illusions

stupefying
sp 95–28 Lulled by stupefying *i·*, the world is asleep
sp 88– 9 veritable ideas to be distinguished from *i·*
 f 230– 4 But if sickness and sin are *i·*,
 b 283–11 They are not ideas, but *i·*.
 p 368–26 its conditions are *i·*,

illusive
ph 187–11 to another *i·* personification, named Satan.
 191–28 The *i·* senses may fancy affinities with
 f 249– 2 give up imperfect models and *i·* ideals;
 b 293– 4 the least material form of *i·* consciousness,
 o 343–19 *i·* errors — which he could and did destroy.
 p 371–17 the *i·* sufferings which throng the gloaming.
 383–26 the *i·* physical effect of a false belief,

illustrate
 s 134–16 how can they *i·* the doctrines of Christ
 f 232–21 nor did he *i·* these errors by his practice.
 b 283–30 than we can teach and *i·* geometry by
 p 380–15 physical effects of fear *i·* its illusion.
ap 575–14 Did not Jesus *i·* the truths he taught

illustrated
sp 86– 8 His quick apprehension . . . *i·* his spirituality.
 s 123–26 they *i·* an ever-operative divine Principle.
 154– 9 This fact in metaphysics is *i·* by the
ph 171–14 Jesus *i·* the divine Principle
 200– 5 *i·* the grand human capacities of being
 f 245– 2 *i·* in a sketch from the history of
 b 285–12 *i·* by the opposite natures of
 333–11 the spirituality which is taught, *i·*, and
 o 358–16 uttered and *i·* by the prophets,
 p 410–22 Mental Treatment *I·*
 g 501–12 which God *i·* by light and harmony,
gl 579–12 This patriarch *i·* the purpose of Love to

illustrates
 s 152–20 Such a fact *i·* our theories.
 f 225–14 history of our country, . . . *i·* the might of
 b 300– 6 *i·* the illusion of material man,
 316–21 Christ *i·* that blending with God,
 332–32 *i·* the coincidence, or spiritual agreement,
 p 402–24 The error, mesmerism . . . *i·* the fact
 t 445–20 *i·* the unlabored motion of the divine energy
 454– 5 Truth, which *i·* the impotence of error.
 461– 6 that part *i·* and proves the entire Principle.
 g 507– 2 In metaphor, the *dry land i·* the
ap 561–23 *i·* the coincidence of God and man

illustrating
 s 117–17 *i·* and demonstrating Life and Truth

illustration
 s 118– 5 formal applications of the *i·*.
 f 245–29 the primary of that *i·* makes it plain that
 b 315–26 and presented an *i·* of creation.

illustrative
 p 430–13 allegory *i·* of the law of divine Mind

image

and likeness
pr 3–13 *i·* and likeness of the patient, tender, and true,
 a 19– 3 are not at war with God's *i·* and likeness.
sp 94– 3 who makes man in the *i·* and likeness of
 94– 5 implied by . . . "*i·*" and "likeness" — Gen. 1 : 26.
 s 151–24 maintains His own *i·* and likeness.
ph 172–19 man is the *i·* and likeness of Spirit,
 f 206–26 the spiritual *i·* and likeness of God?
 216–20 to suppose that man, God's *i·* and likeness,
 222–23 very far from being the *i·* and likeness of God,
 c 257–32 Finite man cannot be the *i·* and likeness of,
 258–17 as the true divine *i·* and likeness,
 265–20 not of a man in God's *i·* and likeness.
 b 281–12 the *i·* and likeness of perfect Mind,
 285– 8 not man, the *i·* and likeness of God,
 287–20 It saith, . . . I am not the *i·* and likeness of
 301–17 man is the divine *i·* and likeness,
 303–25 God, without the *i·* and likeness of Himself,
 330–13 neither seen God nor His *i·* and likeness,
 332–13 yea, the divine *i·* and likeness,
 340–12 man in His *i·* and likeness.
 p 414–27 man is the *i·* and likeness of God,
 441–17 forever in the *i·* and likeness of his Maker.
 r 468–14 Spirit is God, and man is His *i·* and likeness.
 475– 9 man is made in the *i·* and likeness of God.
 475–16 all that reflects God's *i·* and likeness;
 497– 8 and man in God's *i·* and likeness.
 g 519–16 and reach the spiritual *i·* and likeness.
 531–31 created by Mind in the *i·* and likeness of God
 544–26 nor the *i·* and likeness of the one God.
 548– 6 we discover man in the *i·* and likeness of God.
gl 580– 4 God's man, . . . is His own *i·* and likeness;
 580– 5 that which is not the *i·* and likeness of good,
 580–14 the *i·* and likeness of what God has not
 584–25 not after the *i·* and likeness of Spirit,
 591– 6 Man. . . . the spiritual *i·* and likeness of God

divine
 (see divine)

image

existence as
b 320–19 harmonious existence as *i·*, idea,
express
b 313–13 the phrase "express *i·*"— *Heb.* 1 : 3.
expressed
b 313–11 the express [expressed] *i·* of — *Heb.* 1 : 3.
God's
pr 13–28 ignorant of man as God's *i·* or reflection
a 19– 3 are not at war with God's *i·* and likeness.
s 116– 5 and man as God's *i·* appears.
120– 6 and reflects Soul, God, for man is God's *i·*.
140–29 God created man in His, God's, *i·* ;
f 204–25 notion that they can create . . . in God's *i·*,
216–20 to suppose that man, God's *i·* and likeness,
c 265–20 not of a man in God's *i·* and likeness.
b 284–11 Is God's *i·* or likeness matter,
305–13 The verity that God's *i·* is not a creator,
325–15 then shall man be found in God's *i·*.
336– 9 Immortal man was and is God's *i·* or idea,
o 346– 3 When man is spoken of as made in God's *i·*,
p 392–10 harmony of man, God's *i·*.
r 475–16 term for all that reflects God's *i·* and likeness ;
476–31 man in God's *i·* is unfallen
497– 8 and man in God's *i·* and likeness.
God's own
b 295–12 Mortals are not . . . created in God's own *i·* ;
g 517–22 This ideal is God's own *i·*, spiritual and infinite.
His
ph 188– 2 God, immortal Mind, and man is found in His *i·*.
b 330–12 neither seen God nor His *i·* and
333– 2 agreement, between God and man in His *i·*.
340–12 man in His *i·* and likeness.
o 344– 3 and man to be His idea,— that is, His *i·*.
345–24 God's man, made in His *i·*,
r 468–14 Spirit is God, and man is His *i·*
g 522–23 denunciations of man when not found in His *i·*,
His own
s 151–24 maintains His own *i·* and likeness.
o 344– 7 God has created man in His own *i·*
g 516–24 God created man in His own *i·*,— *Gen.* 1 : 27.
516–28 that God made man in His own *i·*,
gl 580– 4 God's man, . . . is His own *i·* and likeness ;
human
s 140–31 mortals would . . . make God in their own human *i·*.
infinite
c 257– 1 creation is the infinite *i·* or idea
b 300– 5 His infinite *i·* or reflection, man.
in Mind
s 115–17 IDEA : An *i·* in Mind ;
in mortal mind
s 116–19 matter is nothing beyond an *i·* in mortal mind.
inverted
s 111–17 optics rejects the incidental or inverted *i·*
111–17 what this inverted *i·* is meant to represent.
b 301–27 presents an inverted *i·* of Mind and substance
ap 572–11 materiality is the inverted *i·* of spirituality.
gl 580–13 ADAM. . . . an inverted *i·* of Spirit ;
lost
c 259–17 The *lost i·* is no image.
man is
sp 73–10 for man is *i·*.
b 301–24 while man is "*i·*"— *Gen.* 1 : 27.
mental
p 416– 4 unless the mental *i·* occasioning the pain
more terrifying
p 376– 1 *i·* more terrifying than that of most other
no
c 259–17 The *lost* image is no *i·*.
of disease
s 154– 7 the fear that creates the *i·* of disease
p 400–12 Eradicate the *i·* of disease from the
of God
(see God)
of His being
b 313–22 and an *i·* of His being."— see *Heb.* 1 : 3.
of his Maker
f 203–15 and so makes man the *i·* of his Maker
of Love
r 475–13 Man is idea, the *i·*, of Love ;
of mortal thought
r 479– 9 *i·* of mortal thought, reflected on the retina,
of Spirit
g 543– 5 The *i·* of Spirit cannot be effaced,
of the beast
b 327–14 Sin is the *i·* of the beast
of thought
p 411–23 Disease is an *i·* of thought externalized.
or idea
c 257– 1 creation is the infinite *i·* or idea
b 303–28 Spiritual man is the *i·* or idea of God,
336– 9 Immortal man was and is God's *i·* or idea,

image

or likeness
sp 71–19 neither . . . is the *i·* or likeness of God,
b 284–11 Is God's *i·* or likeness matter,
299–15 whither every . . . *i·*, or likeness of
g 515–25 mirrored reflection is your own *i·* or likeness.
or reflection
pr 13–28 ignorant of man as God's *i·* or reflection
f 204–26 without the nature of the *i·* or reflection
b 300– 5 His infinite *i·* or reflection, man.
our
p 438– 3 Let us make man in our *i·*,— *Gen.* 1 : 26.
r 475–23 "Let us make man in our *i·*,— *Gen.* 1 : 26.
g 515–12 Let us make man in our *i·*,— *Gen.* 1 : 26.
true
c 259– 6 man is the true *i·* of God.
b 285–12 claim that a mortal is the true *i·*
untrue
g 502–10 the history of the untrue *i·* of God,

———

ph 171–21 the spiritual,— yea, the *i·* of infinite Mind,
196–28 from the *i·* brought before the mind ;
200–18 for if man is the *i·*, reflection, of God,
p 400–25 the *i·* which becomes visible to the senses.
g 525–10 the primary sense being *i·*, *form* ;
525–11 in the Hebrew *i·*, *similitude* ;
ap 571–25 mirror in which mortals may see their own *i·*.
gl 584–25 but after its own *i·*."

imaged
p 370–30 *i·* on the body through the belief that
411–26 the physical condition is *i·* forth on the body.

image-gods
s 158– 9 Hippocrates turned from *i·* to

imagery
b 299– 6 artist's own observation and "chambers of *i·*."

images

and sounds
sp 86–19 *i·* and sounds evolved involuntarily by
beautiful
f 248– 9 supplying it with beautiful *i·* of thought
r 485–26 it cannot outline . . . beautiful *i·*, but it effaces
dark
p 418–31 dream-shadows, dark *i·* of mortal thought,
efface the
ph 196–21 efface the *i·* and thoughts of disease,
p 396–26 so efface the *i·* of sickness from mortal mind.
inverted
b 305–20 The inverted *i·* presented by the senses,
g 502– 7 inverted *i·* of the creator and His creation.
its own
c 259–22 Mortal thought transmits its own *i·*,
g 511– 2 Mind forms ideas, its own *i·*,
mental
p 413–28 these actions convey mental *i·* to
of disease
ph 175– 1 We should prevent the *i·* of disease from
197– 2 mirror *i·* of disease distinctly in thought.
of this mind
p 400–24 We see in the body the *i·* of this mind,
of thought
sp 86–13 Mortals evolve *i·* of thought.
f 208–29 the *i·* of thought impressed upon it.
248– 9 supplying it with beautiful *i·* of thought

———

sp 71–16 *i·*, which mortal mind holds and evolves
p 379–28 The *i·*, held in this disturbed mind,
391– 3 Blot out the *i·* of mortal thought
425–10 *i·* of mortal thought superimposed upon the
g 511–18 effulgence of God's infinite ideas, *i·*,

imaginary
sp 90– 6 the *i·* line called the equator
s 146–19 divests material drugs of their *i·* power,
ph 178–25 and we disarm sin of its *i·* power
f 241– 8 as *i·*, whimsical, and unreal as his pleasures.
b 274–28 Science and . . . destroy the *i·* copartnership,
340– 1 their *i·* power for good or evil,
o 352–13 child, who is frightened at *i·* ghosts
p 371–12 children look everywhere for the *i·* ghost,
403–19 error is deprived of its *i·* powers
t 460–14 Sickness is neither *i·* nor unreal,— that is,
r 479–24 Darkness and chaos are the *i·* opposites of

imagination
an 101– 3 or to the excitement of the *i·*
101– 7 experiment upon the power of the *i·*."
s 163–25 Nowhere is the *i·* displayed to a greater extent ;
ph 176–11 array of diseases was not paraded before the *i·*.

imagine
pref xi– 1 Many *i·* that the phenomena of physical healing
a 21–31 satisfied if he can only *i·* himself drifting
s 130–31 no longer *i·* evil to be ever-present
f 203–18 We *i·* that Mind can be imprisoned
r 494–11 It is not well to *i·* that Jesus

imagined
f 221–25 as he had i· he would

imbecility
ph 197–15 the farther mortals will be removed from i·

imbibe
r 495–27 Study thoroughly the letter and i· the spirit.

imbibes
t 462– 4 any student, who . . . i· the spirit of Christ,

imbued
s 128–12 The human mind, i· with this
145– 3 So divinely i· were they with the spirit of

imitate
a 37–17 and to i· his mighty works

imitates
s 121–28 astronomical order i· the action of

imitative
f 212–31 the unreal and i· movements of mortal belief,

imitators
a 25–28 will never alone make us i· of him.

immaculate
s 137– 5 when their i· Teacher stood before them,
ap 561–32 prophesied the coming of the i· Jesus,
564–15 he, the i·, met and conquered sin
565–18 This i· idea, represented first by man

immanent
s 150– 5 is widely demonstrated as an i·, eternal
f 209–13 i· sense of Mind-power enhances the glory of

Immanuel
pref xi–16 They are the sign of I·, or
a 34– 7 for demonstration is I·, or *God with us;*
s 107– 8 This . . . points to the revelation of I·,

immature
b 313–26 To accommodate himself to i· ideas of

immediate
s 115–17 IDEA : . . . the i· object of understanding.
ph 188–29 physical senses have no i· evidence of a sun.
b 328–29 Had it been given only to his i· disciples,
330– 7 would meet with i· and universal acceptance.
g 501– 5 often seems so smothered by the i· context
532–18 produced the i· fruits of fear and shame.

immediately
s 154–11 I· the symptoms of this disease appeared,
o 348–26 I have never supposed the world would i·
p 431– 7 going to sleep i· after a heavy meal.
r 486–15 his body was the same i· after death as before.
g 553–26 this potent belief will i· supersede the
557–23 as if he . . . i· fell into mental sin ;

immense
b 322–10 in view of the i· work to be accomplished

immensity
c 263–29 thrown into the face of spiritual i·,
g 504–13 Truth, Life, and Love fill i ·and are ever-present.
509–19 as nebulæ indicate the i· of space.

immoral
p 363–13 detect the woman's i· status
t 452–14 Never breathe an i· atmosphere, unless

immortal
and eternal
gl 588–10 incorporeal, unerring, i·, and eternal Mind.
and omnipotent
p 407–13 strength from the i· and omnipotent Mind,
and perfect
c 260–10 the i· and perfect model of God's creation
and spiritual
f 213– 7 I· and spiritual facts exist apart from
r 479– 7 it must be i· and spiritual.
g 544–23 antipodes of i· and spiritual being.
and unerring
f 243–20 Neither i· and unerring Mind nor matter,
beautiful and
b 276–14 and presents them as beautiful and i·.
being
ph 178–27 spiritual understanding of the status of i· being.
190–18 it never merges into i· being,
p 420–32 harmonious facts of Soul and i· being.
being is
g 554– 6 because being is i·, like Deity,
consciousness
b 279–11 tangible and real to i· consciousness,
r 486– 9 in order to possess i· consciousness.
cravings
s 108– 8 i· cravings, "the price of learning love,"
g 501–17 something more native to their i· cravings
evidence
a 29–31 i· evidence that Spirit is harmonious
existence
g 513–28 not within the range of i· existence
fact
b 327– 3 reveals the i· fact that neither pleasure nor

immortal
facts
b 279–17 the i· facts of being are seen,
p 428–28 the i· facts of being are admitted.
forms
g 503–22 i· forms of beauty and goodness.
fruit
o 361–29 That which when sown bears i· fruit,
fruits
r 494–28 its lap piled high with i· fruits.
good deeds are
p 435–12 but good deeds are i·, bringing joy
harmonious and
ph 166–32 man found to be harmonious and i·.
b 273–17 never made mortals whole, harmonious, and i·.
291–16 manifestations of Mind are harmonious and i·,
337–12 makes man harmonious and i·,
p 409–32 Death will not make us harmonious and i·
harmonious or
r 490–15 are helpless to make man harmonious or i·,
idea
a 55–15 Truth's i· idea is sweeping down the
c 262–13 above the mortal to the i· idea of God.
b 325– 7 Truth, unfolding its own i· idea.
r 477–17 i· idea of being, indestructible and eternal.
ideas
c 259–26 I· ideas, pure, perfect, and enduring,
immutable and
c 261–24 and the nature of the immutable and i·.
b 279– 3 the unerring, immutable, and i·?
286– 4 not seek the immutable and i· through the finite,
g 550–30 the pure and holy, the immutable and i·
keynotes
o 355–28 God's i· keynotes, proved to be such
law
a 36–20 i· law of justice as well as of mercy.
Life
r 496–22 mortal belief, at war with the facts of i· Life,
life
a 51–11 that he might furnish the proof of i· life.
Man
p 434–31 God made Man i· and amenable to Spirit
man
(see **man**)
man, being
f 209– 1 Man, being i·, has a perfect indestructible life.
manhood
p 430– 5 i· manhood, the Christ ideal,
man is
(see **man**)
men and women
f 247–15 I· men and women are models of
Mind
(see **Mind**)
Mind is
(see **Mind**)
Mind-reading
sp 83–26 mortal mind-reading and i· Mind-reading.
83–29 Mortal mind-reading and i· Mind-reading
modus
f 212–32 would reverse the i· modus and action,
nature
c 260–29 it must lose its i· nature.
perfect and
f 246– 5 The perfect and i· are the eternal likeness of
p 428–23 man *is*, not *shall be*, perfect and i·.
Principle
g 554– 4 God, who is its divine i· Principle.
proof
r 488–16 C. S. sustains with i· proof
real and
b 276–15 Harmony in man is as real and i· as in music.
reality
b 311–19 directly opposite to the i· reality of being.
Science is
sp 84– 1 Science is i· and coordinate neither with the
scribe
ap 571–22 the Revelator, i· scribe of Spirit
sense
sp 72– 3 Principle of man speaks through i· sense.
f 210–29 i· sense includes no evil nor
210–30 i· sense has no error of sense,
216–14 to supply the truth of i· sense.
sentences
f 225–17 i· sentences, breathing the omnipotence of
sentiment
s 161–15 they will do less violence to that i· sentiment
Shakespeare
m 66– 1 Thou art right, i· Shakespeare,
side
g 536–26 the true idea is gained from the i· side.
Soul
b 311–20 So long as we believe . . . that i· Soul is in

immortal

Soul is
- *b* 311– 7 Soul is *i·* because it is Spirit,
- 335–20 Because Soul is *i·*, it does not exist in mortality.
- *p* 381–13 destroyed by the understanding that Soul is *i·*,
- *r* 468– 6 Because Soul is *i·*, Soul cannot sin,

sovereignty
- *s* 141–18 Its only crowned head is *i·* sovereignty.

Spirit
- *s* 124–13 finite sense of things, which *i·* Spirit silences
- *p* 435– 1 court commended man's *i·* Spirit to

spiritual and
- *b* 289–24 God's universe is spiritual and *i·*.
- *o* 353–29 true idea of being is spiritual and *i·*,
- *p* 409–21 The real man is spiritual and *i·*,
- *g* 547–30 and adopts the spiritual and *i·*.

testimony
- *r* 490–25 destroy all material sense with *i·* testimony.
- 490–25 This *i·* testimony ushers in the

things
- *b* 276–22 towards the contemplation of things *i·*

Truth
   (see **Truth**)

truth
- *r* 493– 8 must yield to Science, to the *i·* truth of

Truth is
- *r* 466–13 Truth is *i·* ; error is mortal.
- 468– 4 If Truth is *i·*, error must be mortal,

wisdom
- *g* 519– 6 His infinite self-containment and *i·* wisdom

- *a* 42–28 is therefore not a mortal but an *i·*.
- *m* 60–10 purity and constancy, both of which are *i·*.
- *sp* 80– 8 as follows : . . . never will be, an *i·* spirit."
- 81–12 A man's assertion that he is *i·* no more proves
- 81–18 as revealed in Science cannot help being *i·*.
- *s* 152– 3 *i·* divine Mind takes away all its supposed
- *ph* 174–32 its cure comes from the *i·* divine Mind.
- 186–25 If evil is as real as good, evil is also as *i·*.
- 186–26 If pain is as real as the . . . both must be *i·* ;
- 189–22 all the formations of the *i·* divine Mind.
- 192– 9 from the mortal instead of from the *i·*.
- 192–13 of the mortal mind and not of the *i·*.
- 194–15 man, who is *i·* in spiritual understanding,
- *f* 211–31 these faculties be conceived of as *i·*.
- 229– 2 If Mind is not the master of . . . they are *i·*,
- 231– 7 seem to this so-called mind to be *i·*.
- 244–26 He does not pass . . . from the mortal to the *i·*,
- 246–28 Life and goodness are *i·*.
- *c* 256– 5 thought rises . . . from the mortal to the *i·*.
- 258–11 in order to be *i·*.
- 263– 5 *I·* spiritual man alone represents the truth of
- *b* 277– 6 The *i·* never produces the mortal.
- 277– 8 goodness and spirituality must be *i·*.
- 277–29 Nothing we can say . . . regarding matter is *i·*,
- 295–30 teaches that . . . his *i·* soul is resurrected
- 296– 6 the mortal is dropped for the *i·*.
- 296–10 Nothing sensual or sinful is *i·*.
- 297–16 and man found to be *i·*.
- 301–10 *i·*, spiritual man is really substantial,
- 306– 1 Pharisees, who believed error to be as *i·* as
- 310–20 taught . . . that soul may be lost, and yet be *i·*.
- 335–28 Reality is spiritual, . . . *i·*, divine, eternal.
- 336– 5 nor the *i·* into mortality.
- *p* 369–20 He understood man, whose Life is God, to be *i·*,
- 370– 2 To be *i·*, we must forsake the
- 427– 7 can no more die. . . than can Soul, for both are *i·*,
- 429–21 If we live after death and are *i·*, we must have
- 433–29 sense of Life, God, — which sense must be *i·*,
- *r* 474–25 must error still be *i·*?
- *g* 503–20 *I·* and divine Mind presents the idea of God :
- 505–28 God's ideas reflect the *i·*, unerring, and
- 520–27 the *i·* creating thought is from above,
- 530– 2 the *i·*, spiritual law of Truth is
- 536–29 material return to dust, and the *i·* is reached.
- *gl* 581– 9 proved to be as *i·* as its Principle ;

immortality

almightiness and
- *r* 487–29 reality of Life, its almightiness and *i·*.

and bliss
- *a* 39–12 out of mortality into *i·* and bliss.
- *f* 203–24 not a stepping-stone to Life, *i·*, and bliss.

and goodness
- *g* 518–20 Love giveth . . . might, *i·*, and goodness,

and life
- *sp* 98–31 way through which *i·* and life are learned

and Love
- *gl* 597–15 divine Science, — *i·* and Love.

and supremacy
- *gl* 589–20 showing the *i·* and supremacy of Truth ;

appears
- *sp* 76–31 overcome, not submitted to, before *i·* appears.

assurances of
- *p* 387–12 refreshed by the assurances of *i·*,

basis of
- *gl* 585–12 ELIAS. Prophecy ; . . . the basis of *i·*.

being and
- *f* 215– 4 If . . . then being and *i·* would be lost,

bring
- *r* 492–12 destroy all error, and bring *i·* to light.

brings
- *b* 305–26 destroys all error and brings *i·* to light.
- 336–28 and brings *i·* to light.

brings to light
- *sp* 72–13 destroys mortality, and brings to light *i·*.
- *f* 206–28 He destroys them, and brings to light *i·*.

brought to light
- *b* 335–24 Life as *i·* brought to light.
- *gl* 582–23 Submergence in Spirit ; *i·* brought to light.

communing with
- *sp* 78– 8 at the same time . . . communing with *i·* !

earnest of
- *b* 317–27 for an earnest of *i·*,

entity or
- *o* 356– 6 sickness, and death do not prove man's entity or *i·*.

eternity and
- *gl* 585– 5 A sphere ; a type of eternity and *i·*,

exempt from age
- *f* 247–13 *I·*, exempt from age or decay,

existence and
- *o* 356– 5 affords no evidence of spiritual existence and *i·*.

foundations of
- *g* 539– 5 sapping the foundations of *i·*,

harmony and
   (see **harmony**)

health and
- *f* 248– 7 ought to ripen into health and *i·*,

holiness, and
- *f* 230– 6 will bring us into health, holiness, and *i·*.
- *ap* 563–22 prolific in health, holiness, and *i·*.

hope in
- *p* 388–26 we have hope in *i·* ;

idea of
- *gl* 593–10 a new and higher idea of *i·*,

in deeds
- *o* 354–10 words of divine Science find their *i·* in deeds,

is not bounded
- *b* 301–32 *I·* is not bounded by mortality.

life and
- *p* 376–13 there is more life and *i·* in one good motive
- *g* 539– 5 as if life and *i·* were something which

man and
- *ph* 191–24 reveals man and *i·* as based on Spirit.

man's
- *sp* 81–28 man's *i·* depends upon that of God, good,
- *p* 395– 4 man's *i·* and eternal likeness to God.
- 428–27 The evidence of man's *i·* will become
- *gl* 589–18 destroying error and bringing to light man's *i·*.

matrix of
- *f* 250– 5 and suppose. . .mortality to be the matrix of *i·*.

Mind and
- *b* 318– 3 nothing can efface Mind and *i·*,
- *p* 369–29 of the advantages of Mind and *i·*?

of development
- *f* 244–31 everlasting grandeur and *i·* of development,

of good
- *sp* 81–30 necessary consequence of the *i·* of good.
- *f* 215–27 he understood the superiority and *i·* of good,

of man
   (see **man**)

of Soul
- *b* 306– 7 The *i·* of Soul makes man immortal.
- *r* 481–29 hence the *i·* of Soul.

prelude to
- *sp* 90–15 some insist that death is the . . . prelude to *i·*.

proof of
- *sp* 81–16 Life, Love, Truth, is the only proof of *i·*.
- *b* 306–18 If. . .we are left without a rational proof of *i·*.

purity, and
- *gl* 581– 6 the inspiration of goodness, purity, and *i·*,

put on
- *s* 164–27 mortal shall have put on *i·* — *I Cor.* 15 : 54.
- *c* 262– 8 mortals "put on *i·*." — *I Cor.* 15 : 54.
- *r* 496–25 mortal shall have put on *i·*, — *I Cor.* 15 : 54.

reality and
- *r* 486–24 Their reality and *i·* are in Spirit
- 488–21 no cognizance of spiritual reality and *i·*.

rejoice in
- *a* 22–24 whereby we rejoice in *i·*, boundless freedom,

revelation of
- *sp* 79–15 C. S., . . . in its revelation of *i·*,

Soul or of
- *r* 478– 3 What evidence of Soul or of *i·*

to man
- *f* 253– 4 saith : . . . I give *i·* to man, for I am Truth.

towards
- *sp* 90–27 and opens it wide towards *i·*.

- *sp* 78–13 why look to them . . . for proofs of *i·*,
- 80–11 assertion that . . . are our only proofs of *i·*.

immortality

sp 81–13 would prove *i·* a lie.
   81–15 Nor . . . when alleged spirits teach *i·*.
ph 186–25 If death is as real as Life, *i·* is a myth.
f 211–28 for their *i·* is not in Spirit ;
  215–24 mortality is lost, swallowed up in *i·*.
  230– 1 If sickness is real, it belongs to *i·* ;
b 275–14 *i·*, cause, and effect belong to God.
  283–32 Are mentality, *i·*, . . . resident in matter?
  312–17 without Love, God, *i·* cannot appear.
  339–26 The basis of all health, sinlessness, and *i·*
o 353–15 Time has not yet reached eternity, *i·*,
p 425–22 the more *i·* we possess.
r 476–18 Mortality is finally swallowed up in *i·*.
  492– 7 Being is holiness, harmony, *i·*.
  495–23 replace mortality with *i·*, and silence discord
g 518–22 reflect health, holiness, *i·*
  555–20 error would seek to unite . . . *i·* with mortality,
gl 592–23 the *i·* of all that is spiritual.
  593– 2 the good and beautiful, and their *i·*.
  598–28 man would be in the full consciousness of his *i·*

immortality's

gl 580–18 ADAM. . . . *i·* opposite, mortality ;

Immortal Mind

s 115–12 Scientific Translation of *I· M·*

immortals

b 295–11 Mortals are not like *i·*,
t 444–27 *I·*, or God's children in divine Science,
r 476– 1 Mortals are the counterfeits of *i·*.
  476–11 *i·*, or the children of God, will appear as the

immovable

s 160–17 when the cords contract and become *i·*?

immunity

f 219–29 Entire *i·* from the belief in sin, suffering,

immutable

s 134–25 because it is the *i·* law of God,
f 210–22 in obedience to the *i·* law of Spirit,
c 261–23 and the nature of the *i·* and immortal.
b 279– 2 or the unerring, *i·*, and immortal?
  286– 3 not seek the *i·* and immortal through the finite,
  298– 6 silences for a while the voice of *i·* harmony,
  300–14 The mutable and imperfect never touch the *i·*
  306–27 the *i·*, harmonious, divine Principle,
  335–27 Reality is spiritual, harmonious, *i·*,
t 446–20 victory rests on the side of *i·* right.
g 550–30 the pure and holy, the *i·* and immortal

immutably

pr 3– 1 He who is *i·* right will do right

impair

p 428–18 the Life which mortal sense cannot *i·*

impart

f 253– 5 saith : . . . I include and *i·* all bliss,
b 272–14 not to *i·* to dull ears and gross hearts
p 371–28 Mind can *i·* purity instead of impurity,
  401– 7 which you *i·* mentally while destroying error,
t 447–18 *i·* . . . the truth and spiritual understanding,
  452–19 He must live it and love it, or he cannot *i·* it
  460–25 she had to *i·*, while teaching its grand facts,
g 510–18 Love alone can *i·* the limitless idea of infinite
  516–11 which *i·* their own peace and permanence.
  539–11 God could never *i·* an element of evil,
ap 570–24 Those ready for the blessing you *i·* will give

impartation

m 68–29 *i·* of the divine Mind to man and the universe.
b 309– 3 incorporeal *i·* of divine Love to man,

imparted

f 235–15 pure and uplifting thoughts . . . *i·* to pupils,
g 514–19 Tenderness accompanies all the might *i·* by

impartial

pr 13– 2 Love is *i·* and universal in its adaptation
m 63–18 Our laws are not *i·*, to say the least,
o 355–27 Without this . . . no one is capable of *i·* or

imparting

sp 92– 6 but also capable of *i·* the sensations.
g 519–25 *I·* has not impoverished,
ap 567– 2 Gabriel has the more quiet task of *i·* a

imparts

sp 85–32 truth communicates itself but never *i·* error.
ph 194–22 manifests itself . . . by the false sense it *i·*.
b 271–30 spiritual import of the Word *i·* this power.
  280–29 *i·* and perpetuates these qualities
p 420–18 It *i·* a healthy stimulus to the body,
g 505–16 Spirit *i·* the understanding which uplifts
  515–23 All that God *i·* moves in
  517–13 for Love *i·* the clearest idea of Deity.

impassable

sp 83–24 as *i·* as that between Dives and Lazarus.

impatient

f 237–29 *I·* at your explanation,

impede

pr 5–23 Such an error would *i·* true religion.
ap 563–20 seemingly *i·* the offspring of

impedes

pr 2–21 an error which *i·* spiritual growth.
ph 166– 4 Mind is all that feels, acts, or *i·* action.
p 415– 6 belief quickens or *i·* the action of the system,

impediment

ap 577–10 no *i·* to eternal bliss,

impel

ap 563–31 which would *i·* them to devour each other

impelled

p 415–22 moving quickly or slowly and *i·* or palsied by
ap 565–25 *i·* the idea to rise to the zenith of

impels

s 118– 1 *i·* the inference that the spiritual leaven

imperative

a 37–27 Hear these *i·* commands :
m 56–19 The commandment, . . . is no less *i·* than
f 251– 1 hence it is not more *i·*
b 329–21 Principle is *i·*.
t 446–19 In the Science . . . it is *i·* to be honest,

imperatively

ap 565–17 God's idea, will eventually rule all . . . *i·*,

imperceptible

b 314–24 the spiritual Jesus was *i·* to them.
  334–10 invisible Christ was *i·* to the so-called

imperfect

s 114–20 must sometimes recur to the old and *i·*,
f 239–30 *I·* mortal mind sends forth its own
  246– 7 by no means a . . . germ rising from the *i·*
  248–20 Do you not hear from all mankind of the *i·* model?
  249– 2 give up *i·* models and illusive ideals ;
  254–12 *I·* mortals grasp the ultimate . . . slowly ;
c 258–25 Mortals have a very *i·* sense of
  260– 4 than the sculptor can . . . from an *i·* model,
b 300–14 The mutable and *i·* never touch the
o 360– 7 materiality renders these ideals *i·*
p 409–21 *i·* so-called "children of men" — *Psal.* 14 : 2.
r 477– 7 Soul, being Spirit, is seen in nothing *i·*
g 555–26 aught that can become *i·*,
gl 587–18 and cannot become finite and *i·*.

imperfection

sp 72–17 Perfection is not expressed through *i·*.
f 233– 8 In the midst of *i·*,
  243–32 Perfection does not animate *i·*.
  248–16 Is it *i·*, joy, sorrow, sin,
c 259–32 from *i·* instead of perfection, one can no more
p 414–29 whereas *i·* is blameworthy, unreal, and
  424–11 there is no room for *i·* in perfection.

imperfections

a 52– 9 Their *i·* and impurity felt the

imperfectly

pref ix– 9 voices the more definite thought, though still *i·*.
b 304–29 is, must be, *i·* expressed.
r 467–23 We reason *i·* from effect to cause,

imperial

b 324–25 Asia Minor, Greece, and even in *i·* Rome.

imperious

sp 98–18 It is *i·* throughout all ages

imperishable

a 21–11 looks towards the *i·* things of Spirit.
f 246–16 with bright and *i·* glories.
  253– 3 saith : . . . *i·* glory, — all are Mine,

impersonation

ap 565–13 *i·* of the spiritual idea had a brief history

impertinent

an 103–13 separate from any half-way *i·* knowledge,

impetuous

s 137–26 Before this the *i·* disciple had been called

impetuosity

s 137–16 With his usual *i·*, Simon replied

impious

s 139– 3 which the *i·* sought to destroy.

implacable

a 40–16 the crimes of his *i·* enemies

implant

ph 180–17 Doctors should not *i·* disease in the thoughts

implicit

a 25–26 *I·* faith in the Teacher and all the

implied

a 26–10 The Christ was the Spirit which Jesus *i·* in
sp 92– 7 the illusion *i·* in this last postulate
  94– 5 includes all that is *i·* by the terms
s 137–14 the narrow opinion *i·* in their citation
ph 166– 5 shrinking from its *i·* responsibility,
g 504–20 not *i·* by material darkness and dawn.

implies

```
  pr   6– 8  i· the vain supposition that we have
  a  20–25  to acknowledge what the spiritual fact i·.
 an 102–26  It i· the exercise of despotic control,
  s 114–14  the phrase mortal mind i· something untrue
  o 359–20  the goal which that word i·?
  p 421– 2  insanity i· belief in a diseased brain,
  g 507–21  A material world i· a mortal mind and
  547–20  Material evolution i· that the great
```

implore

```
  ph 167– 1  Should we i· a corporeal God to heal the
```

imply

```
  b 331–11  The Scriptures i· that God is All-in-all.
  336– 1  limits would i· and impose ignorance.
  g 515–18  does not i· more than one God,
  515–19  nor does it i· three persons in one.
  537–30  The literal meaning would i· that God
  550–22  If Life is God, as the Scriptures i·,
```

implying

```
  a  31– 7  i· that it is they who do the will of
  s 148– 3  i· that the requisite power to heal was in Mind.
```

import

```
  a  26–24  the precious i· of our Master's sinless career
  37–21  take up the more practical i· of that career!
  s 118–17  parable may i· that these spiritual laws,
  f 232–27  voices of solemn i·, but we heed them not.
  b 271–30  spiritual i· of the Word imparts this power.
  o 358–22  great i· to Christianity of those works
  p 411–18  Scripture seems to i· that Jesus
  r 471–27  gave the spiritual i·, expressed through
  g 501– 3  chiefly because the spiritual i· of the Word,
```

importance

```
  a  31–14  He attached no i· to dead ceremonies.
  ph 198–27  Hence the i· that doctors be Christian Scientists.
  199–18  of less i· than a knowledge of the fact,
  f 209–20  are of no real i·, when we remember
  236–17  Hence the i· of C. S.,
  c 256–17  The precise form of God must be of small i·
  b 273–19  Hence the i· of understanding the truth of
  r 473–27  making his acts of higher i· than his words.
```

important

```
  a  42–18  evidence so i· to mortals.
  51– 2  the possible loss of something more i· than
 sp  95–17  but it is i· to success in healing,
 an 101– 6  i· experiment upon the power of the
  105–20  no reason why metaphysics is not as i·
  b 320–24  The one i· interpretation of Scripture is
  322– 9  It is highly i· — in view of the
  o 350– 7  in the New Testament, sayings infinitely i·,
  p 387–17  it is not because they occupy the most i· posts
  404–21  one of the most i· points in the theology of
  424–15  equally i· in metaphysical practice
  t 462–24  That is the i· question.
  r 466–18  first and last it is the most i· to understand.
  481– 1  How i·, then, to choose good
  482–13  Is it i· to understand these explanations
  497– 1  brief exposition of the i· points,
  g 502– 9  third stage in the order of C. S. is an i· one
  548–28  discoveries have brought to light i· facts
  553– 2  accompany their descriptions with i· observa-
            tions,
  553–14  or i· to their origin and first introduction."
```

imported

```
  p 438–22  a foreign substance, i· by False Belief,
```

importer

```
  p 438–28  Morbid Secretion is not an i· or dealer
```

impose

```
  b 336– 1  limits would imply and i· ignorance.
  338–21  sin, would i· between man and his creator.
  p 381–31  Christ Jesus overruled the error which would i·
```

imposed

```
  ap 575– 5  physical plagues i· by material sense.
```

imposing

```
  p 440–34  with benign and i· presence,
```

imposition

```
  sp  99–26  are seen to be a bald i·,
```

impossibilities

```
  f 207–17  Science of being repudiates self-evident i·,
  245–27  I· never occur.
  g 550–32  C. S. repudiates self-evident i·,
```

impossibility

```
  s 116–31  Mind in a finite form is an absolute i·.
  b 273–13  i· of attaining perfect understanding till
  284– 1  would seem to spring from . . . but this is an i·.
  o 343–16  the i· of good evolving evil;
  p 409– 1  Intelligent matter is an i·.
  414– 9  i· that matter, brain, can control or derange
  t 455–22  renders any abuse of the mission an i·.
  r 488–17  the i· of any material sense,
```

impossible

```
  a  36–21  It is quite as i· for sinners to
  39–24  unreal, because i· in Science.
 sp  74– 6  would be as i· as would be the restoration
  74–20  Such a backward transformation is i· in Science.
  75–10  This gross materialism is scientifically i·,
  82–26  intercommunion is as i· as it would
  83–12  Miracles are i· in Science,
  s 120–18  i· for aught but Mind to testify truly
  153–16  You say a boil is painful; but that is i·,
  162–32  declared that "it is i· to calculate the
  ph 167–27  i· to gain control over the body in any other
            way.
  182–12  It is i· to work from two standpoints,
  195–26  i· ideals, and specimens of depravity,
  199–25  Had Blondin believed it i· to walk the rope
  f 211–23  The transfer of . . . Science renders i·.
  217– 2  The loss of man's identity . . . is i· ;
  228– 4  would be as i· if this great fact of being
  231–27  To fear them is i·, when you fully apprehend
  c 258–28  i· for man, . . . to fall from his high estate.
  b 302– 8  It is i· that man should lose aught
  309–24  i· for infinite Spirit or Soul to be in
  331–23  He fills all space, and it is i· to conceive of
  o 351–31  from a material standpoint, but this was i·.
  p 371–22  No i· thing do I ask
  376–25  showing that it is i· for matter to suffer,
  t 446–17  protracted, dangerous, and i· in
  448–22  i· for error, evil, and hate to accomplish the
  455–32  the more i· it will become for
  r 477–14  shows it to be i· that a material body,
  481–27  i·, since Truth cannot support error.
  492–30  theory, . . . uniting on some i· basis.
  g 506– 1  apportion to themselves a task i· for
  522–11  Existence, separate . . . Science explains as i·.
  550–23  An egg is an i· enclosure for Deity.
  551– 2  their reports are unnatural, i·, and unreal.
  551–15  material methods are i· in divine Science
```

impostor

```
  p 441–28  Your attorney, False Belief, is an i·,
```

impotence

```
  t 454– 5  Truth, which illustrates the i· of error.
```

impotent

```
  sp  97– 7  the more i· error becomes as a belief.
  s 160–18  or has it bidden them to be i·?
  g 555–18  Only i· error would seek to unite Spirit with
```

impoverish

```
  sp  79–31  Giving does not i· us in the service
  g 519–26  Imparting . . . can never i·, the divine Mind.
```

impoverished

```
  m  63–29  the wronged, and perchance i·, woman
  g 519–25  Imparting has not i·, can never impoverish,
```

impracticable

```
  s 163–30  as i· as to arrange the fleeting vapors
```

impress

```
  p 412–12  you are liable . . . to i· it upon the thought.
  t 448–20  to leave . . . the strong i· of divine Science,
  g 511–12  the seal of Deity and has the i· of heaven,
```

impressed

```
  f 208–29  the images of thought i· upon it.
```

impresses

```
  s 157–28  C. S. i· the entire corporeality,
  t 453–28  i· more deeply the wrong mind-picture.
```

impressing

```
  ph 196–22  i· them with forcible descriptions
```

impression

```
  s 115–10  great difficulty is to give the right i·,
  f 213–16  Sound is a mental i· made on mortal belief.
  t 449–22  The first i·, made on a mind which
  g 532–31  The first i· material man had of himself
```

impressions

```
  sp  87–26  The strong i· produced on mortal mind
  87–28  can perceive and reproduce these i·.
 an 101– 4  and the i· made upon the senses ;
  f 214– 1  i· from Truth were as distinct as sound,
  214–15  conveys the i· of Mind to man,
```

impressive

```
  pr   7– 8  Audible prayer is i· ;
```

imprison

```
  f 251–32  i· themselves in what they create.
```

imprisoned

```
  s 114–27  and sets free the i· thought.
  f 203–19  We imagine that Mind can be i·
```

improper

```
  s 114–13  involves an i· use of the word mind.
  r 466–19  The term souls or spirits is as i· as the
```

improve

```
  pr   6– 7  The talents He gives we must i·.
  m  60–16  Marriage should i· the human species,
  61– 7  would i· our progeny, diminish crime
```

improve

m	61–29	formation of mortals must greatly *i·*
sp	90–29	*i·* our time in solving the mysteries of being
ph	167–16	What can *i·* God's work?
	181–19	you must *i·* your mental condition
	197–28	never . . . until individual opinions *i·*
c	260–19	in order to *i·* their models.
p	370–28	and then they cease to *i·*.
	371–26	Mankind will *i·* through Science and
r	493–29	proved that the Christ could *i·* on a false sense.
g	523– 5	false claim, . . . that error can *i·* His creation.
	537–31	lest man should *i·* it and become better ;
	545– 8	mortals should so *i·* material belief by thought

improved

sp	81–14	Nor is the case *i·* when alleged spirits
s	156–10	She *i·* perceptibly.
b	296–28	An *i·* belief is one step out of error,
o	348–24	when by so doing our own condition can be *i·*
p	442–19	An *i·* belief cannot retrograde.
r	486–10	Earth's preparatory school must be *i·*
gl	582– 9	BENJAMIN . . . an *i·* state of mortal mind ;

improvement

m	63–24	rational means of *i·* at present
sp	77–30	the chances of the departed for *i·*
ph	195–31	for amusement instead of for *i·*.

improves

f	251–25	spiritual understanding *i·* mankind
p	370– 5	The body *i·* under the same regimen which
	403–28	*i·* or injures the case in proportion to
t	449–29	A proper teacher of C. S. *i·* the health

improving

a	25–29	else we are not *i·* the great blessings which

improvisation

sp	89–24	explains the phenomena of *i·*

impudently

g	545–20	yet this opposite, . . . *i·* demands a blessing.

impugn

a	50–10	would *i·* the justice and love of a father
b	273–23	and *i·* the wisdom of the creator.
o	343– 7	This makes it doubly unfair to *i·* and

impulse

sp	94–16	pattern of mortal personality, passion, and *i·*.
f	211–13	sensation of sickness and the *i·* to sin
c	261–11	strong *i·* of a desire to perform his part,
b	268– 5	those lower things which give *i·* to inquiry.
o	348–31	ethics and temperance have received an *i·*,

impulsion

sp	88–31	said to be a gift . . . received from the *i·*

impure

pr	8–11	If a man, . . . is *i·* and therefore insincere,
a	28–20	saying : He is a glutton and a friend of the *i·*,
ph	192–16	all that is selfish, wicked, dishonest, and *i·*.
t	449–27	The *i·* are at peace with the *i·*.
g	550–31	supposition that Spirit . . . can originate the *i·*
gl	595–24	UNCLEANLINESS. *I·* thoughts ; error ; sin ; dirt.

impurities

f	241–28	washing the body of all the *i·* of flesh,
p	401–19	forcing *i·* to pass away,

impurity

a	52– 9	Their imperfections and *i·* felt the
m	60–13	selfishness and *i·* alone are fleeting,
	65–22	*i·* and error are left among the lees.
b	272–23	earthward gravitation of sensualism and *i·*,
p	371–29	Mind can impart purity instead of *i·*,
	383–17	*i·* and uncleanliness, which do not trouble the

impute

ph	187–11	and then *i·* this result to another illusive
f	219–27	*i·* their recovery to change of air or diet,
g	554–17	to *i·* to God the creation of whatever is sinful

imputing

o	348–14	Are we . . . *i·* too much power to God,

in

sp	71– 6	Principle of all, is not *i·* Spirit's formations.
gl	588–22	definition of

inability

o	355–25	and to a consequent *i·* to demonstrate
r	494–16	Jesus demonstrated the *i·* of corporeality,

inaction

s	125– 6	Neither organic *i·* nor overaction is
p	428– 1	"There is no death, no *i·*,

inadequacy

s	115– 3	the *i·* of material terms for
ph	194–18	the frailty and *i·* of mortal mind.

inadequate

s	117–19	Human theories are *i·* to interpret
	125–32	belief, wholly *i·* to affect a man
o	349–15	English is *i·* to the expression of
p	438–19	Another witness, equally *i·*, said
ap	572–28	*i·* to take in so wonderful a scene.

inadmissible

a	22–32	Revenge is *i·*.
ph	167–30	timid conservatism is absolutely *i·*.

inalienable

an	106– 7	God has endowed man with *i·* rights,
s	161–17	*i·* rights, among which are life, liberty, and
f	227– 9	unaware of man's *i·* rights

inanimate

an	106– 1	to go in healing from the use of *i·* drugs
s	113– 8	letter is but the dead body . . . pulseless, cold, *i·*.
	155–11	When the general belief endorses the *i·* drug
	157– 7	never shares its rights with *i·* matter.
	160– 7	the *i·* drug becomes powerless.
ph	189–26	belief of *i·*, and then of animate matter.
	190– 4	mortal says that an *i·* unconscious seedling is
f	218– 6	body, like the *i·* wheel, would never be weary.
	243–21	matter, the *i·* substratum of mortal mind,
b	312–29	and so turns . . . to the *i·* drug.
t	463–29	The sick are not healed by *i·* matter

inanity

b	330–31	dementia, insanity, *i·*, devil,

inarticulate

sp	97–24	until its *i·* sound is forever silenced

inasmuch

s	127–23	*i·* as all truth proceeds from
f	243–32	*I·* as God is good and the fount of all
p	431– 9	*i·* as this offence is deemed punishable

inaudible

ap	559–10	The *i·* voice of Truth is, to the human mind,

inaugurated

b	288–13	foreshadowed by the prophets and *i·* by Jesus,

incantations

ph	174– 2	The Esquimaux restore health by *i·*

incapable

sp	89– 1	what the unaided medium is *i·* of knowing
	89–11	says, "I am *i·* of words that glow,
o	325– 6	the body *i·* of supporting life,
o	356–19	*i·* of producing sin, sickness, and death
t	447– 8	may render you *i·* of knowing or judging
r	468–17	eternal and *i·* of discord and decay.
	475–28	Man is *i·* of sin, sickness, and death.

incapacity

p	374–19	*i·* to preserve your own existence,

incarcerated

ph	194–22	*I·* in a dungeon, where neither sight nor

incarceration

ph	193–26	threatened with *i·* in an insane asylum

incarnate

b	332–28	*i·* in the good and pure Christ Jesus.
	334–20	before the human Jesus was *i·* to mortal eyes.
o	350–27	Hence its embodiment in the *i·* Jesus,
gl	583–11	comes to the flesh to destroy *i·* error.

incarnation

g	501–10	The *i·* of Truth, that amplification of wonder

incensed

sp	94– 9	*i·* the rabbis, and they said :

incentive

t	454–18	Love for God and man is the true *i·*

inception

sp	84–25	destroys . . . spiritualism at its very *i·*,

incessant

m	58–19	*i·* amusement outside the home circle is
	62– 8	If parents create . . . a desire for *i·* amusement,

inches

ph	193– 6	said the bone was carious for several *i·*.

incident

sp	89–30	This *i·* shows that the belief of
s	154–10	illustrated by the following *i·* :
ph	182–27	come from some sad *i·*, or else from
b	321–12	In this *i·* was seen the actuality of Science.
p	362– 5	While they were at meat, an unusual *i·* occurred,

incidental

s	111–16	optics rejects the *i·* or inverted image

incidents

s	111–24	one of many *i·* which show that C. S.

incipiency

t	459–23	latter is distrusted and thwarted in its *i·*.

incipient

m	68–18	was suffering from *i·* insanity,
p	390–29	Meet the *i·* stages of disease with
	391– 7	the *i·* or advanced stages of disease,

incisive

sp	94–27	hint that Jesus used his *i·* power injuriously ?

incisors

f	247– 6	*i·*, cuspids, bicuspids, and one molar.

incites
  f 203–12   This thought *i·* to a more exalted worship and
  ap 564– 5   *i·* mortals to kill morally and physically

inclination
  t 452–30   if you had the *i·* or power to

inclinations
  s 121– 3   favorite *i·* of a sensuous philosophy.

incline
  ph 181–31   will *i·* you to the side of matter and error.
  t 450–12   They do not *i·* longingly to error,

inclined
  f 214–19   Mortals are *i·* to fear and to
  o 356–26   by making man *i·* to sin,

include
  s 118–14   *i·* spiritual laws emanating from
  ph 191– 6   will *i·* in that likeness no material element.
  f 253– 5   saith : . . . I *i·* and impart all bliss,
  b 318–32   body does not *i·* soul, but manifests mortality,
  p 418–26   *I·* moral as well as physical belief in your
  r 484– 7   Does C. S., . . . *i·* medication, material hygiene,
  g 544–20   facts of creation, . . . *i·* nothing of the kind.
  552–12   *i·* no member of this dolorous and fatal triad.

included
  pr 5–32   all evil works, error and disease *i·*.
  s 120– 3   never . . . is *i·* in non-intelligence.
  f 209– 1   disease and sin and of other beliefs *i·* in matter.
  227– 3   I saw that the law of mortal belief *i·* all error,
  b 335–17   never *i·* in a limited mind or a
  o 344–20   not *i·* in the commonly accepted systems :
  p 399–28   All that is real is *i·* in this immortal Mind.
  425– 7   take up the leading points *i·*
  429–28   not *i·* in the teachings of the schools,
  r 484– 9   *Answer.—* Not one of them is *i·* in it.
  g 504– 8   not yet *i·* in the record of creation,

includes
  pr 9–19   This command *i·* much,
  a 23–30   *i·* spiritual understanding and confides all
  m 60– 9   the mother-love *i·* purity and constancy,
  sp 94– 5   *i·* all that is implied by the terms
  s 116–12   *i·* vastly more than is at first seen.
  145–31   The theology of C. S. *i·* healing the sick.
  ph 187–20   The divine Mind *i·* all action and volition,
  191–13   spiritual sense of being and of what Life *i·*.
  f 206–29   infinite Mind made all and *i·* all.
  210–30   immortal sense *i·* no evil nor pestilence.
  219–20   Science *i·* no rule of discord,
  249–16   and *i·* nothing unlike God.
  c 259–12   *i·* a perfect Principle and idea,
  b 288– 1   necessarily *i·* the correlated statement,
  328–31   and *i·* universal humanity.
  330–32   with all the etceteras that word *i·*.
  333–31   The one Spirit *i·* all identities.
  p 373– 3   physical exemption which Christianity *i·*,
  408–32   ignorant of the errors it *i·* and of their
  430– 1   *i·* all the phenomena of existence.
  r 469– 3   *i·* in itself all substance
  g 507–21   because they reflect the Mind which *i·* all.
  515–16   eternal Elohim *i·* the forever universe.

including
  sp 83–16   The belief that the universe, *i·* man,
  s 114–10   Mind is *one*, *i·* noumenon and phenomena,
  114–28   the universe, *i·* man, is spiritual,
  127– 5   creator of the spiritual universe, *i·* man,
  ph 171–10   Mind's control over the universe, *i·* man,
  f 233–23   *i·* the hearts which rejected him.
  c 256– 8   Father and Mother of the universe, *i·* man.
  b 276–23   Principle of the universe, *i·* harmonious man.
  295– 5   creates and governs the universe, *i·* man.
  330–12   only intelligence of the universe, *i·* man.
  p 415–24   organs of the human system, *i·* brain and
  r 468–23   The spiritual universe, *i·* individual man, is
  475–15   compound idea of God, *i·* all right ideas ;
  g 502–26   unity of God and man, *i·* the universe.
  510–30   governing the universe, *i·* man,
  547–19   theory, . . . to recreate the universe, *i·* man.
  547–26   The true theory of the universe, *i·* man,
  549–19   *i·* those which we call human.
  gl 584–24   to reproduce a mortal universe, *i·* man,

inclusive
  s 128– 6   His government of the universe, *i·* of man.
  g 554– 3   universe, *i·* of man, is as eternal as God,

incompatibility
  m 59–23   too late to grumble over *i·* of disposition.

incompetent
  m 57–15   *i·* to meet the demands of the affections,
  ph 200– 8   Whoever is *i·* to explain Soul
  p 377–29   a fear that Mind is . . . *i·* to control it.

incomprehensible
  b 304–32   thrusting aside his divine Principle as *i·*,
  337–21   is as *i·* to the limited senses as

inconceivable
  p 378–29   power, without the divine permission, is *i·* ;

inconceivably
  p 407– 2   a suffering *i·* terrible to man's self-respect.

incongruity
  o 345–21   Anybody, who is able to perceive the *i·*

inconsistency
  o 354–19   *I·* is shown by words without deeds,
  355– 3   charge of *i·* . . . is met by something practical,

inconsistent
  o 354–27   It is in itself *i·*, a divided kingdom.
  354–32   If the letter of C. S. appears *i·*,
  p 387–21   reading disquisitions on the *i·* supposition

incontrovertible
  ph 200–17   great truth in the Science of being, . . . is *i·* ;

incontrovertibly
  s 109– 4   C. S. reveals *i·* that Mind is All-in-all,

incorporeal
  pr 13–24   the wonders wrought by infinite, *i·* Love,
  13–29   ignorant . . . of man's eternal *i·* existence.
  sp 74–27   such opposite conditions as the . . . *i·*, and the
  84– 4   from a spiritual, *i·* standpoint,
  s 116–21   that God is not *corporeal*, but *i·*,
  116–23   Mortals are corporeal, but God is *i·*.
  c 258– 3   glories of limitless, *i·* Life and Love.
  b 309– 3   *i·* impartation of divine Love to man,
  331–18   God is individual, *i·*.
  332–12   The Christ is *i·*, spiritual,
  335–21   Soul must be *i·* to be Spirit,
  r 465– 9   God is *i·*, divine, supreme,
  g 512– 2   understanding of the *i·* and divine Principle,
  ap 577– 2   yields to the *i·* sense of God and man
  578– 2   the *i·* or spiritual sense of Deity :
  gl 588– 9   *i·*, unerring, immortal, and eternal Mind.
  588–20   I AM. God ; *i·* and eternal Mind ;

incorporeality
  ap 576–19   What further indication need we of the real man's *i·*

incorrect
  pref x– 5   most of them *i·* in theory
  sp 73–21   The belief that material bodies . . . is *i·*.
  73–21   Equally *i·* is the belief that spirit is confined
  ph 195–31   *I·* views lower the standard of truth.
  t 452– 4   *I·* reasoning leads to practical error.
  453– 2   to distinguish the correct from the *i·*

incorrectly
  s 121– 6   the heavenly fields were *i·* explored.

incorruption
  s 164–26   shall have put on *i·*,— *I Cor.* 15 : 54.
  r 496–25   shall have put on *i·*,— *I Cor.* 15 : 54.

increase
  pr 13–13   Can the . . . expression of our desires *i·* them?
  m 61–26   raising of stock to *i·* your flocks and herds?
  sp 95–19   We welcome the *i·* of knowledge
  s 145–26   and thus they *i·* the antagonism of
  159–32   ordinary physician is liable to *i·* disease
  f 220–23   adopted a diet of . . . to *i·* his spirituality.
  p 367–26   *i·* the beneficial effects of Christianity.
  397– 9   You cause bodily sufferings and *i·* them by
  t 443– *   *and he will i· in learning.— Prov.* 9 : 9.
  r 492–10   will *i·* longevity, will purify and elevate
  g 548–32   *i·* their numbers naturally and

increased
  pref viii–22   *i·* violence of diseases since the flood.
  s 157–15   power of action is proportionately *i·*.
  ph 198– 8   his fear, . . . is *i·* by the physician's words.
  199– 4   The trip-hammer is not *i·* in size by exercise,
  o 348–32   health has been restored, and longevity *i·*.
  r 465– 3   much labor and *i·* spiritual understanding,

increases
  sp 96–29   As . . . spiritual understanding *i·*,
  s 155–26   potency . . . *i·* as the drug disappears.
  p 374–31   or *i·* it to the point of self-destruction.
  404–25   *i·* his ability to master evil
  415–19   thought *i·* or diminishes the secretions,
  420–19   It *i·* or diminishes the action,
  423– 2   belief that he has met his master. . . *i·* his fear ;
  t 453–22   such a course *i·* fear, the foundation of
  g 530– 1   *i·* in falsehood and his days become shorter.
  ap 565– 2   when nearing its doom, this evil *i·*

increasing
  m 56–14   moral regulations as will secure *i·* virtue.
  69–12   sense of *i·* number in God's infinite plan.
  f 221– 4   His dyspepsia *i·*, he decided that
  224– 1   Longevity is *i·* and the power of
  o 352–20   instead of *i·* children's fears by
  p 375–19   *i·* his patient's spirituality while restoring him
  g 557–11   C. S. reveals harmony as proportionately *i·*
  fr 600– *   *i· in the knowledge of God.— Col.* 1 : 10.

incredible
  sp 83– 6   Science only can explain the *i·* good

incredulous
  ph 169– 8   sometimes to his discomfiture, when he was *i·*.

incubus
b 322–21   as the startled dreamer who wakens from an *i·*

inculcate
s 130–21   and to *i·* a grain of faith in God,

inculcates
s 112–30   it *i·* a breach of that divine commandment
b 340–17   It *i·* the tri-unity of God, Spirit, Mind ;
o 345–29   human, material nothingness, which Science *i·*,

incur
pr   3–29   *i·* the sharp censure our Master pronounces
   13–18   *i·* less risk of overwhelming our real wishes
m 68–23   salutary causes sometimes *i·* these effects.
f 238– 7   To obey the Scriptural command. . . . is to *i·*
b 317– 9   and he will *i·* the hatred of sinners,
p 384– 9   If man seems to *i·* the penalty through matter,
  405–28   conquered by the moral penalties you *i·*

incurred
b 322–21   *i·* through the pains of distorted sense.

incurs
a 40–10   first removing the sin which *i·* the penalty.
an 106–13   mental trespasser *i·* the divine penalty
f 241– 3   He, . . . *i·* the hostility of envy ;
g 542– 1   It *i·* divine displeasure,

indeed
pr 11–15   if *i·*, he has not already suffered sufficiently
   16–11   There is *i·* some doubt among Bible scholars.
a 33– 7   Their bread *i·* came down from heaven.
s 114–17   *I·*, if a better word or phrase could
  140–27   It is *i·* mournfully true that the older Scripture
  145–19   *I·*, its ethical and physical effects
  163–16   except, *i·*, that it has already destroyed more
  163–30   To harmonize the contrarieties . . . is *i·* a task
f 207– 8   *I·*, evil is not Mind.
  221–13   informed him that death was *i·* his only
c 257–31   *I·*, the phrase *infinite form* involves a
b 302–28   *I·*, the body presents no proper likeness of
o 345–12   It is *i·* no small matter to know one's self ;
  347–32   will then see that error is *i·* the nothingness,
p 364–30   that they *i·* love much,
  395–32   a moral offence is *i·* the worst of diseases.
  412–14   It is *i·* adequate to unclasp the hold
  415–29   *I·*, the whole frame will sink from
r 478–31   "neither *i·* can be ;"— *Rom.* 8 : 7.
g 521–19   *I·* there is, but the continued account is mortal
  534–20   neither *i·* can be.— *Rom.* 8 : 7.
  535–18   Truth is *i·* "the way."— *John* 14 : 6.
ap 559–21   It will be *i·* sweet at its first taste,
  573–28   This is *i·* a foretaste of absolute C. S.
  575–25   It is *i·* a city of the Spirit,
gl 598–15   What Jesus gave up was *i·* air,

indefinable
f 213–10   self-expressed, though *i·* as a whole.

indefinite
o 348–29   believed for an *i·* time ;

indefinitely
pr 12–25   Changes in belief may go on *i·*,

Independence, Declaration of
an 106– 7   C. S. has its Declaration of *I·*.

independence
ph 175–18   it would have been routed by their *i·*

independent
pref vii–13   Truth, *i·* of doctrines and time-honored systems
ph 200–10   Life is, always has been, and ever will be *i·* of
f 208– 6   What then is this seeming power, *i·* of God,
  247–19   Comeliness and grace are *i·* of matter.
c 263– 2   believe themselves to be *i·* workers,

independently
f 218–15   believing that the body can be sick *i·* of
p 388–11   thought that they could kill the body . . . *i·* of
  409–13   *i·* of this so-called conscious mind,

indestructible
a 51–14   his spiritual life, *i·* and eternal,
sp 76–25   constitutes the only veritable, *i·* man,
s 162–14   The *i·* faculties of Spirit exist
f 209– 2   Man, being immortal, has a perfect *i·* life.
  214– 4   wholly spiritual, it is normal and *i·*.
b 316–20   Christ presents the *i·* man,
  325–17   perfect as the Father, *i·* in Life,
o 359–31   One says: "I have spiritual ideals, *i·*
p 369–22   and the other to be made *i·*.
  402–12   Man is *i·* and eternal.
r 471– 1   divine Principle and idea, are *i·*
  477–17   the immortal idea of being, *i·* and eternal.
g 514–30   God's creatures, . . . are harmless, useful, *i·*.

indexes
pr 8– 6   Their prayers are *i·* which do not

India
b 328–18   Our missionaries carry the Bible to *I·*,

Indians
r 477–26   The *I·* caught some glimpses of the underlying

indicate
s 120–11   Is a man sick if the material senses *i·* that he
  136–17   this reply may *i·* that some of the people
ph 183–13   *i·* that obedience to God will remove this
b 294– 2   These senses *i·* the common human belief,
  332– 1   *i·* the divine Principle of scientific being,
t 455– 6   Such mental states *i·* weakness
r 466– 5   varied manifestations of C. S. *i·* Mind,
g 504–18   words which *i·*, in the absence of solar time,
  509–18   as nebulæ *i·* the immensity of space.
  554–32   This would *i·* that there is less disease
ap 575–21   This city is wholly spiritual, as its four sides *i·*.

indicated
pr 16–22   which is *i·* in the Lord's Prayer
s 121–28   thus *i·*, astronomical order imitates the
ph 177–19   *i·* matter's properties, qualities, and forms.
p 364–16   *i·* by one of the needs of this age.

indicates
sp 94–30   An approximation of this discernment *i·*
  97–27   Scripture *i·* that all matter will disappear
an 104–14   *i·* the rightness of all divine action,
s 123–28   The operation of this Principle *i·* the
  141– 1   *i·* the distance between the theological and
ph 188–18   The smile of the sleeper *i·* the sensation
f 205–20   in some word or deed which *i·* the true idea,
b 271–12   the word *i·* that the power of healing was
  282–28   Whatever *i·* the fall of man or the
  332– 4   *i·* His tender relationship to His
p 437– 6   It *i·* malice aforethought,
g 510–23   *i·* a supposed formation of matter
  532–11   this *i·* that the divine Spirit, or Father,
  538– 8   *i·* the infinite distance between Truth and
ap 573–11   *i·* states and stages of consciousness.
gl 581–13   The ark *i·* temptation overcome
  597–27   *i·* the might of omnipotence

indication
r 471– 8   afford no *i·* of the grand facts
ap 576–18   What further *i·* need we of the

indications
s 144–13   the weaker the *i·* of Soul.
f 217–10   *i·* of unnatural mental and bodily
p 422– 7   these *i·* are favorable.

indifference
m 59–20   more salutary . . . than stolid *i·* or jealousy.
f 216– 1   his faith in Soul and his *i·* to the body.

indigenous
b 270–32   but it was *i·* to his spirituality,

indigestion
ph 165–16   You say that *i·*, fatigue, sleeplessness,
p 389–28   A case of convulsions, produced by *i·*,

indignation
ap 570– 7   will finally be shocked . . . into human *i·* ;

indignities
a 39– 2   Such *i·* as he received, his followers will endur

indirectly
g 533–11   to trace all human errors . . . *i·* to God,

indiscriminately
t 445–27   danger in teaching Mind-healing *i·*,

indispensable
s 125– 4   may no longer be found *i·* to health.
f 254– 2   human footsteps leading to perfection are *i·*
o 359–12   you aver that the material senses are *i·*
t 462–24   This branch of study is *i·* to the

indissoluble
b 292–29   man's *i·* connection with his God,
r 491–15   and find the *i·* spiritual link which

indissolubly
m 60– 7   welding *i·* the links of affection.
s 145–20   ethical and physical effects are *i·* connected.

individual (*see also* **individual's**)
a 18– 5   His mission was both *i·* and collective.
  26– 5   Jesus spares us not one *i·* experience,
  30–19   As the *i·* ideal of Truth, Christ Jesus
  53–21   great distance between the *i·* and Truth.
m 68–16   I never knew more than one *i·* who
sp 72–23   In Science, *i·* good derived from God,
  76–16   but he will be an *i·* consciousness,
  88–21   and the *i·* manifests profound adoration.
  99–21   Therefore my contest is not with the *i·*,
an 102–28   employed, for the *i·* or society."
s 115–15   MAN : God's spiritual idea, *i·*, perfect,
  117– 2   because an *i·* may be one of a series,
  117– 3   one of many, as an *i·* man, an *i·* horse ;
  155– 4   a general belief, culminating in *i·* faith,
  155– 6   Even when you take away the *i·* confidence in
  155–12   *i·* dissent or faith, . . . is but a belief held by
ph 173–20   Man is spiritual, *i·*, and eternal ;
  174–24   Then, if an *i·* is sick,
  197–27   until *i·* opinions improve
f 217– 4   more absurd than to conclude that *i·*

individual
f 229–18 the *i·* who upholds it is mistaken
b 281–16 reality and divinity in *i·* spiritual man
302–32 reproduction by Spirit's *i·* ideas is but
331–18 God is *i* , incorporeal.
336–32 God is *i·* and personal in a scientific sense,
p 370–23 medical testimony and *i·* experience,
404–14 while its effects still remain on the *i·*,
408– 9 cannot, in a scientific diagnosis, shield the *i·* case
415– 8 when the *i·* looks upon some object which he
427– 5 Man's *i·* being can no more die . . . than can
t 447– 2 man's *i·* right of self-government.
449–24 a good detective of *i·* character.
r 468–23 spiritual universe, including *i·* man, is a
g 508–23 The intelligent *i·* idea, . . . unfolds the
512–13 Their *i·* forms we know not,
ap 577– 6 two *i·* natures in one ;
gl 588–13 unchanged forever in their *i·* characters,

individualism
b 298–29 no matter what their *i·* may be.

individualities
b 303– 8 The minutiæ of lesser *i·*
g 549–16 egg, from which one or more *i·*

individuality
and identity
g 550– 6 forms and preserves the *i·* and identity of
consciousness and
b 336–15 man's consciousness and *i·* are reflections of
divine
b 303– 9 reflect the one divine *i·*
enlarged
c 265–13 confers upon man enlarged *i·*,
eternal
sp 91–19 man's spiritual and eternal *i·*,
b 282– 9 the self-existent and eternal *i·* or Mind ;
false
f 242– 3 mortals put off their material beliefs and false *i·*.
his
c 259– 2 Man . . . cannot lose his *i·*,
b 337– 2 man, reflecting God, cannot lose his *i·* ;
p 375–13 hypnotist dispossesses the patient of his *i·*
His own
b 280–28 God, . . . being perpetual in His own *i·*,
infinite
b 281–15 infinite *i·*, which supplies all form and
man's
b 285– 2 Man's *i·* is not material.
man's higher
c 266– 4 giving place to man's higher *i·* and destiny.
of man
b 317–16 The *i·* of man is no less tangible
r 491–26 Personality is not the *i·* of man.
of Spirit
b 330–15 The *i·* of Spirit, . . . is unknown,
real
b 299–14 whither every real *i·*, image, or
spiritual
    (see spiritual)
the term
s 117– 1 The term *i·* is also open to objections,

sp 73– 9 both the *i·* and the Science of man,
b 331–18 to conceive of such omnipresence and *i·*
336– 6 The divine Ego, or *i·*, is reflected
g 513–20 existence, and continuity of all *i·* remain
514–19 The *i·* created by God is not carnivorous,

individualized
ph 173– 8 When the supposition, . . . is *i·*,
b 335– 4 The theory, that Spirit . . . to be *i·*,
p 424– 2 child becomes a separate, *i·* mortal mind,
r 477–23 Soul is the . . . intelligence of man, which is *i·*,
g 555–28 the *i·* manifestation of existence,

individualizes
g 513–17 Spirit diversifies, classifies, and *i·*

individually
m 58– 9 constitute *i·* and collectively true happiness,
sp 87– 6 to be *i·* and consciously present.

individual's
pr 11–19 not to annul the divine sentence for an *i·* sin,
s 150–20 and that, too, in spite of the *i·* protest

individuals
m 68–20 I have named her case to *i·*,
sp 81– 8 spiritualism can only prove that certain *i·*
87– 7 Though *i·* have passed away,
99–18 Those *i·*, who adopt theosophy, spiritualism,
f 236– 9 induce the infuriated attacks on *i·*,
254– 2 *I·* are consistent who, watching and
t 453–10 but with some *i·* the morbid moral or
462– 1 Some *i·* assimilate truth more readily than
g 549–15 *birth* of new *i·*, or personalities,
553–11 "We have no right to assume that *i·* have
ap 577– 6 as no longer two wedded *i·*.

indivisible
b 335–13 the only substance, the invisible and *i·*,
336–19 God is *i·*.

indolence
an 102–22 they ensnare the age into *i·*,

induce
pr 7–16 to *i·* or encourage Christian sentiment.
s 161–27 would naturally *i·* the very disease
f 220– 6 *i·* sufferers to look in other directions for
236– 8 Do not inferior motives *i·* the
p 370–21 A physical diagnosis . . . tends to *i·* disease.
417–29 Show them how mortal mind seems to *i·* disease

induced
s 121–21 deluded the judgment and *i·* false conclusions.
ph 196–25 Many a hopeless case of disease is *i·* by
p 403– 1 So the sick through their beliefs have *i·*
403– 4 voluntary mesmerism is *i·* consciously
403– 6 self-mesmerism is *i·* unconsciously
411–21 Disease is always *i·* by a false sense
421–21 excitement sometimes *i·* by chemicalization,

induces
p 371–14 Darkness *i·* fear.
374–21 Such a state of mind *i·* sickness.
381– 9 This fear . . . *i·* the physical effects.
392–28 When the condition is present which you say *i·*
413– 4 undue contemplation of physical wants . . . *i·*
425– 2 Mortal mind, not matter, *i·* this conclusion

inducing
p 415–12 They quiet the thought by *i·* stupefaction
g 528–15 falsity, error, credits Truth, God, with *i·*

induction
t 461– 5 C. S. must be accepted at this period by *i·*.

indulge
t 448– 1 to *i·* them, is a moral offence.

indulged
a 23– 1 is not destroyed, but partially *i·*.
ph 175–27 but they never *i·* in the refinement of

indulgence
p 405– 2 *i·* of evil motives and aims

indulging
p 380– 8 *i·* the demands of sin, disease, or death,

industry
ph 175–18 routed by their independence and *i·*.

indwelling
r 478– 7 What basis is there for the theory of *i·* spirit,

inebriate
b 294–28 The *i·* believes that there is pleasure in
322 18 cannot make the *i·* leave his besottedness, until
p 404– 3 If a man is an *i·*, a slave to tobacco,

ineffable
p 364– 8 the higher tribute to such *i·* affection,

inefficacy
f 220– 5 open people's eyes to the *i·* of material hygiene,

ineradicable
p 425 5 just so long as you believe them . . . *i·*.

inert
sp 77–20 and so prolong the illusion either of a soul *i·*
s 143–22 You lean on the *i·* and unintelligent,
f 253–21 can make no opposition . . . for matter is *i·*,
p 383–32 notion that health depends on *i·* matter
385–32 coming from the body or from *i·* matter
r 484–17 Drugs and *i·* matter are unconscious, mindless.

inertia
b 283– 5 there is no *i·* to retard or check its

inevitable
pr 11–20 sin brings *i·* suffering.
a 40–18 No ; but it was *i·*, for not otherwise could he
ph 189–19 human mortal mind, by an *i·* perversion,
f 216–25 health would seem the exception, death the *i·*,
b 310–26 the annihilation of Spirit would be *i·*.
312–19 Mortals claim that death is *i·* ;
314–32 in supposed accord with the *i·* law of life.

inevitably
m 60– 2 Science *i·* lifts one's being higher
s 120– 9 Then the question *i·* arises :
t 462–12 he will *i·* reap the error he sows.

inexhaustible
c 257–28 *i·* Love, eternal Life, omnipotent Truth.
g 507–29 from the nature of its *i·* source.

infallibility
b 330– 9 *i·* of divine metaphysics will be demonstrated.

infancy
sp 74–21 Darkness and light, *i·* and manhood,
74–23 Who will say that *i·* can utter the ideas of
95–29 the world is asleep in the cradle of *i·*,
f 244–29 Even Shakespeare's poetry pictures age as *i·*,
r 489– 9 In *i·* this belief is not equal to guiding

infant
ph 194–24   was still a mental *i·*, crying and chattering
194–27   An *i·* crying in the night,
194–28   An *i·* crying for the light,
p 371–20   I would not transform the *i·* at once into
412–28   If the case is that of a young child or an *i·*,
413–12   The daily ablutions of an *i·*
413–22   in caring for an *i·* one need not
t 463–17   the C. S. *i·* is born of the Spirit,
g 556–31   plunged his *i·* babe, only a few hours old,

infantile
pref ix– 2   but these jottings were only *i·* lispings
g 554–13   unconscious of his fœtal and *i·* existence ;

infants
p 413–24   Giving drugs to *i·*, noticing every symptom

infected
f 235– 4   Better suffer a doctor *i·* with smallpox to
b 279–23   medicine is more or less *i·* with the

infection
s 153–28   mortal mind, . . . contains and carries the *i·*.
154–16   If a child is exposed to contagion or *i·*,
ph 196–26   not from *i·* nor from contact with material virus,

infelicity
m 66–19   Amidst conjugal *i·*, it is well to hope, pray,

inference
s 118– 1   impels the *i·* that the spiritual leaven
118– 3   an *i·* far above the merely ecclesiastical

inferences
b 274–10   not mere *i·* drawn from material premises.

inferior
s 143–31   *I·* and unspiritual methods of healing
f 236– 8   Do not *i·* motives induce the
b 290–10   still seeking . . . from selfish and *i·* motives.
r 477–24   can never reflect anything *i·* to Spirit.
gl 590–16   has the *i·* sense of master, or ruler.

infers
ph 191–26   *i·* the mortality of the body.
b 282–31   rule of inversion *i·* from error its opposite,
o 347– 8   *i·* that if anything needs to be doctored,

infest
f 234–18   brood of evils which *i·* it would be cleared out.

infidel
sp 94–26   what would be said . . . of an *i·* blasphemer
o 342–22   C. S. awakens the sinner, reclaims the *i·*,
344–28   the physician may perchance be an *i·*

infidelity
m 56–15   *I·* to the marriage covenant is the
65–30   has brought conjugal *i·* to the surface,
s 129–18   pantheism, and *i·* are antagonistic to
f 229– 9   Not far removed from *i·* is the belief
r 494– 5   Is it not a species of *i·* to believe that

infidels
o 359– 7   *i·* whose only objection to this method was,

infinite (noun)
but one
b 334–32   for there can be but one *i·*
gleams of the
g 509–18   understanding gives gleams of the *i·* only,
God is the
f 249–15   God is the *i·*, and infinity never began,
nature of the
b 332– 1   the threefold, essential nature of the *i·*.
never began
f 245–32   The *i·* never began nor will it ever end.
reflection of the
b 313–17   the Son of God, the royal reflection of the *i·* ;
represents the
b 282– 6   The circle represents the *i·*
reveal the
b 292– 6   Science alone can . . . reveal the *i·*.
sustaining
pref vii– 1   To those leaning on the sustaining *i·*,
worship the
b 280–12   belief can neither apprehend nor worship the *i·* ;
yield to the
c 256– 2   The finite must yield to the *i·*.

pr 2– 3   to enlighten the *i·* or to be heard of men?
2– 9   nor can the *i·* do less than bestow all good,
sp 73–32   nor can the finite become the channel of the *i·*.
93–29   belief that the *i·* can be contained in the finite.
94–15   belief that the *i·* is formed after the pattern of
f 208– 4   Material sense . . . has a finite sense of the *i·*.
c 263–26   and attempts to pattern the *i·*.
265– 8   and gain some proper sense of the *i·*,
b 281–28   does not put . . . the *i·* into the finite.
284– 4   if the *i·* could be circumscribed within the
284–14   Can the *i·* dwell in the finite
284–15   or know aught unlike the *i·*?
285–18   for a finite conception of the *i·*
286– 3   is not to understand the *i·*.

infinite (noun)
b 312–28   between matter and Spirit, the finite and the *i·*,
330–16   The individuality of Spirit, or the *i·*,
336– 8   reflected . . . from the infinitesimal to the *i·*.
336–23   Allness is the measure of the *i·*,
339–23   until the finite gives place to the *i·*,
g 502–24   The *i·* has no beginning.
519–15   Mortals can never know the *i·*, until
gl 580–23   supposition . . . that the *i·* enters the finite,

infinite (adj.)
ability
r 494–17   as well as the *i·* ability of Spirit,
All
ap 576– 4   this *i·* All, which to us seems hidden in the
All-in-all
sp 72–24   derived from God, the *i·* All-in-all,
All-power
f 231– 9   no lesser power equals the *i·* All-power ;
being
ph 189–24   we constantly ascend in *i·* being.
blessings
pr 15–30   and they assuredly call down *i·* blessings.
b 325– 8   which results in *i·* blessings to mortals.
calculus
f 209–29   swallowed up in the *i·* calculus of Spirit.
g 520–15   and thought accepts the divine *i·* calculus.
capacities
sp 94–31   union with the *i·* capacities of the one Mind.
f 202–21   and the *i·* capacities of Truth,
character
c 257–28   or Mind would lose its *i·* character as
cycles
b 319–13   Throughout the *i·* cycles of eternal existence,
distance
a 47–16   *i·* distance between Judas and his Master.
g 538– 8   the *i·* distance between Truth and error,
elements
g 512–21   From the *i·* elements of the one Mind
expression
b 336–10   the *i·* expression of infinite Mind,
Father-Mother
g 516–23   reflect, . . . the *i·* Father-Mother
form
c 257–30   It would require an *i·* form to
257–31   phrase *i· form* involves a contradiction
God
(see **God**)
Godhead
c 255–17   any true idea of the *i·* Godhead.
God is
(see **God**)
good
sp 93–17   electricity is not the offspring of *i·* good.
idea
(see **idea**)
ideal
g 517–20   proper symbol . . . is Mind's *i·* ideal.
ideas
g 511–17   full effulgence of God's *i·* ideas,
514– 7   Mind's *i·* ideas run and disport themselves.
image
c 257– 1   creation is the *i·* image or idea
b 300– 4   His *i·* image or reflection, man.
individuality
b 281–15   Mind or Spirit called God, is *i·* individuality,
Life
o 347– 6   God, who is *i·* Life ;
p 381–17   In *i·* Life and Love there is no sickness,
g 518–23   varied expressions of God reflect . . . . *i·* Life,
light
g 503–28   God, Spirit, dwelling in *i·* light and harmony
511–12   God is revealed as *i·* light.
Love
(see **Love**)
manifestation
r 468–10   and its *i·* manifestation,
meanings
b 270–19   demonstration of God, . . . in His more *i·*
           meanings,
Mind
(see **Mind**)
One
s 112–16   From the *i·* One in C. S.
Person
s 116–29   then God *is i· Person*,—in the sense of
personality
s 116–28   If the term . . . means *i·* personality,
116–29   in the sense of *i·* personality,
plan
m 69–12   sense of increasing number in God's *i·* plan.
possibilities
a 34–23   into the perception of *i·* possibilities.
power
s 118–15   the invisible and *i·* power and grace.
Principle
(see **Principle**)

infinite (adj.)
range
  c 258–26 and of the i· range of his thought.
resources
  m 60–29 Soul has i· resources with which to bless
self-containment
  g 519– 5 the emanation, of His i· self-containment
space
  g 503–15 i· space is peopled with God's ideas,
Spirit
  (see **Spirit**)
tasks
  b 323– 9 Beholding the i· tasks of truth,
Truth
  (see **Truth**)
understanding
  f 253– 1 He reflects the i· understanding,

  pref x–14 or treat in full detail so i· a theme.
  pr 3–19 God is good, omnipotent, omnipresent, i·,
  13–23 wonders wrought by i·, incorporeal Love,
  m 69–25 or do you declare that Spirit is i·,
  sp 71–30 presupposes Spirit, which is ever i·, to be
  76– 7 as neither material nor finite, but as i·,
  84–19 To understand that Mind is i·,
  93–21 The belief that Spirit is finite as well as i·
  s 127–13 God, the i·, supreme, eternal Mind.
  ph 167– 3 the i· divine Principle which heals
  f 213–13 this attraction towards i· and eternal good
  c 267– 9 God is Father, eternal, self-created, i·.
  b 275–16 the i· divine Principle, Love.
  278–18 another admission, . . . that Spirit is not i·
  280– 3 not products of the i·, perfect, and eternal
  280–11 would compress Mind, which is i·, beneath a
  281– 3 and learn that Spirit is i· and supreme.
  284– 1 not rational to say that Mind is i·, but dwells in
  284– 3 or that matter is i· and the
  328–32 Its Principle is i·, reaching beyond the pale of
  340–12 Divine Love is i·.
  o 357–26 If . . . God is not supreme and i·.
  p 367–30 Because Truth is i·, error should
  399– 2 and therefore good is i·, is All.
  r 469– 1 Time is finite ; eternity is forever i·.
  469–21 We can have but one Mind, if that one is i·.
  g 505–29 God's ideas reflect the immortal, . . . and i·.
  517–22 This ideal is God's own image, spiritual and i·.
  550–23 Life is not embryonic, it is i·.
  ap 567– 7 To i·, ever-present Love, all is Love,
  gl 587–17 God is one God, i· and perfect,
  594–21 omnipresent, omnipotent, i·.
infinitely
  a 25– 4 i· greater than can be expressed by
  44–26 a method i· above that of human invention.
  b 334– 7 i· greater, than the fleshly Jesus,
  o 350– 7 in the New Testament, sayings i· important,
  g 533– 1 i· wise and altogether lovely,
infinitesimal
  ph 178– 6 not by the i· minority of opinions in the
  b 336– 7 from the i· to the infinite.
  g 503– 3 These ideas range from the i· to infinity,
  520– 6 can repeat only an i· part of what exists.
infinitude
  s 112–17 with this i· come spiritual rules,
  c 258–16 all that exists in the i· of Truth.
  b 280– 1 In the i· of Mind, matter must be unknown.
  302– 6 the conscious i· of existence and of all
  r 469–21 We bury the sense of i·, when we admit
  g 508–25 individual idea, . . . unfolds the i· of Love.
  511– 6 magnitude, and i· of spiritual creation.
  517–24 since there is no limit to i·
Infinity
  f 253– 2 saith : . . . for I am I·.
infinity
all-inclusive
  g 514– 5 nothing . . . beyond the range of all-inclusive i·,
God's being is
  r 481– 3 God's being is i·, freedom, harmony,
molecule to
  g 507–25 governs all, from the mental molecule to i·.
never began
  f 249–15 i· never began, will never end,
numerals of
  g 520–10 The numerals of i·, called *seven days,*
reflects
  c 258–11 Man reflects i·, and this reflection is the
Science reveals
  g 519–10 Science reveals i· and the fatherhood and
vastness of
  c 256–30 cannot present the idea or the vastness of i·.

  sp 76–32 The recognition of Spirit and of i· comes
  f 229– 8 Mind signifies God, — i·, not finity.
  b 336– 2 Mind is the I AM, or i·.
  r 469–23 when we admit that, . . . evil has a place in this i·,

infinity
  g 503– 4 from the infinitesimal to i·,
  513– 3 and is an attempted infringement on i·.
  519–17 What can fathom i· !
  544–30 It declares . . . i· to enter man's nostrils
  545–15 errors . . . do not accord i· to Deity.
  gl 581– 3 ALMIGHTY. All-power ; i· ; omnipotence.
  585–22 EUPHRATES . . . finity ; the opposite of i·.
  590–24 when the spiritual sense of God and of i· is
infirmities
  a 20–14 Jesus bore our i· ; he knew the error of
  53–28 at the time when Jesus felt our i·,
infirmity
  c 261–18 as oblivious of physical i· as if he had
  ap 564– 8 This last i· of sin will sink its perpetrator
inflamed
  a 47–20 this spiritual distance i· Judas' envy.
  ph 175–28 never indulged in the refinement of i·
  195– 1 His eyes were i· by the light.
  p 385–21 discolored, painful, swollen, and i·.
  392–15 If you believe in i· and weak nerves,
  393–19 Have no fear that matter can . . . be i·
  414–32 Matter cannot be i·.
  ap 565– 3 swollen with sin, i· with war against
inflames
  p 405– 2 Hatred i· the brutal propensities.
inflammation
and pain
  p 375– 3 belief that i· and pain must accompany
and swelling
  s 153–18 manifests, through i· and swelling,
destroy the so-called
  p 408–17 Can drugs . . . destroy the so-called i· of
glandular
  ph 175–14 glandular i·, sneezing, and nasal pangs.
never appears
  p 415– 9 I· never appears in a part which
pain nor
  p 393–21 self-evident that matter can have no pain nor i·.
prevention of
  p 401–32 confines himself . . . to the prevention of i·
relieve
  p 415–11 That is why opiates relieve i·.
to allay
  a 44–13 He took no drugs to allay i·.
to reduce
  ph 180–31 To reduce i·, dissolve a tumor,
will subside
  p 421–20 when the fear is destroyed, the i· will subside.

  p 373–24 The i·, . . . or deposit will abate,
  374– 3 Anodynes, . . . never reduce i· scientifically,
  414–32 I· is fear, an excited state of mortals
  415– 5 I· as a mortal belief quickens or impedes the
  416– 2 for the i· is not suppressed ;
  418–30 tubercles, i·, pain, deformed joints,
  425– 9 i·, tubercles, hemorrhage, . . . are beliefs,
  gl 586–11 FEAR. Heat ; i· ; anxiety ;
  593– 7 RED DRAGON. Error ; fear ; i· ; sensuality ;
inflammatory
  p 378– 9 Without . . . there can be no i· nor torpid action
  384–19 followed by . . . hints of i· rheumatism,
inflicted
  a 51–26 i· on the physical Jesus,
  p 381–30 a sentence never i· by divine authority.
inflictions
  p 388– 8 when dire i· failed to destroy his body.
influence
baneful
  p 400–30 the baneful i· of sinful thought on the body.
beneficent
  p 394–31 till they feel its beneficent i·.
divine
  pref xi–17 divine i· ever present in human consciousness
  f 236–16 or through divine i·,
exalting
  p 383– 6 the pure and exalting i· of the divine Mind
excel the
  f 228–31 excel the i· of their dead faith and ceremonies.
feel their
  sp 86–17 though we can always feel their i·.
hallowing
  r 474–24 Despite the hallowing i· of Truth in the
healing
  sp 98–10 for it is the healing i· of Spirit
holy
  s 146–25 demonstrated through the holy i· of Truth
losing its
  m 59–30 sacredness of this relationship is losing its i·,
manifested the
  f 245–24 manifested the i· of such a belief.

influence

mental
p 397– 6 We throw the mental *i·* on the

mutual
an 100– 8 as follows : "There exists a mutual *i·* between

of divine Love
ph 180–23 the *i·* of divine Love which casteth out fear.

of his career
a 51– 4 the sublimest *i·* of his career.

of human will
t 451–23 defend himself from the *i·* of human will.

of mortal mind
ph 185–32 A patient under the *i·* of mortal mind

of the belief
p 386–27 laboring under the *i·* of the belief of

of this agent
an 100–10 susceptible to the *i·* of this agent,

or action
sp 89–22 *i·* or action of Soul confers a freedom,

removing the
ph 186– 1 by removing the *i·* on him of this mind,

soporific
p 416–12 when the soporific *i·* of the opium is

stay his
a 43–19 slew him to stay his *i·*

strength and
ph 188– 5 has grown terrible in strength and *i·*,

sun's
ph 189– 3 explanation of the sun's *i·* over the earth.

supporting
p 387–28 supporting *i·* and protecting power

yield to this
p 402–27 If they yield to this *i·*, it is because

your
m 68–14 to your growth and to your *i·* on other lives.
ph 192–21 Your *i·* for good depends upon the
p 424–17 should not act against your *i·*
t 464– 1 it feels your *i·* without seeing you.

---

ph 168– 6 Whatever *i·* you cast on the side of matter,
    199–16 according as they *i·* them through
p 400– 5 before its *i·* upon health and morals can be
    402–20 We say that one human mind can *i·*
t 447– 4 to attempt to *i·* the thoughts of others,
    456– 1 to *i·* mankind adverse to its highest hope

influenced

pr 7–23 God is not *i·* by man.
p 440– 9 and were *i·* to give a verdict

influences

s 143–18 You admit that mind *i·* the body somewhat,
p 403–30 in proportion to the truth or error which *i·* his
t 462–29 It unfolds the hallowed *i·* of unselfishness,
    463– 3 *i·* not embraced in his diagnosis,

influencing

sp 83– 2 human mind or the divine Mind which is *i·* one.

influenza

p 384–17 followed by chills, dry cough, *i·*,

influx

a 43– 9 that *i·* of divine Science which so illuminated
    47– 7 The *i·* of light was sudden.

infolds

g 556–10 Mortal belief *i·* the conditions of sin.

inform

pr 2–24 Can we *i·* the infinite Mind
sp 70– 3 corporeal senses cannot *i·* us what is real
ph 183–11 and yet the Scriptures *i·* us that sin,
f 217– 6 Medical schools may *i·* us that the healing
    235–18 will degrade the characters it should *i·*
    243–17 The head, heart, lungs, and limbs do not *i·* us
c 265–25 The pains of sense quickly *i·* us that
b 276–29 Nature and revelation *i·* us that
    327–30 Let that *i·* the sentiments and awaken
p 389– 9 Matter does not *i·* you of bodily derangements ;
r 475– 8 The Scriptures *i·* us that man is made in the

information

pr 3–20 and then we try to give *i·* to
ph 188–32 Astronomy gives the desired *i·*
f 243–18 If this *i·* is conveyed, mortal mind conveys it.
p 385–31 Any supposed *i·*, coming from the body
g 548–21 will be changed with the progress of *i·*."

informed

s 156–21 she *i·* me that she could get along two days
ph 193–19 am *i·* that he went to work in two weeks.
    193–24 Since his recovery I have been *i·* that
f 221–13 the doctors, who kindly *i·* him

informer

ap 571–11 Is the *i·* one who sees the foe?

informs

pr 8–31 If a friend *i·* us of a fault,
f 232– 9 Scripture *i·* us that "with God — *Mark* 10 : 27.

infraction

s 134–24 nor because it is an *i·* of divine law,
p 389–23 belief in . . . penalties for their *i·*

infringe

s 144–18 will-power may *i·* the rights of man.
b 319– 6 would *i·* upon spiritual law and

infringement

p 435–22 is no *i·* of law,
g 513– 3 is an attempted *i·* on infinity.

infringes

s 150–22 This human view *i·* man's free moral agency ;

infringing

p 381– 8 When *i·* some supposed law, you say

infuriate

p 378–13 An animal may *i·* another by looking

infuriated

f 236– 8 inferior motives induce the *i·* attacks

ingenuously

f 237– 4 On being questioned about it she answered *i·*,

ingrafted

b 338– 9 proves that error has been *i·* into the premises

Ingratitude

p 430–24 Greed and *I·*, constitute the jury.

ingratitude

pr 4– 1 cannot conceal the *i·* of barren lives.
    5–16 *I·* and persecution filled it to the brim ;
a 47–10 The world's *i·* and hatred towards
    47–21 The greed for gold strengthened his *i·*,
sp 94–19 His healing-power evoked denial, *i·*,

inhabitant

sp 90–18 the supposed *i·* of that body carries it
b 317–31 so long as the Master remained an *i·* of the earth.

inhabitants

c 256–21 and among the *i·* of the earth ; — *Dan.* 4 : 35.

inhabited

sp 91– 3 *i·* by beings under the control of
r 478– 9 declaration that a house was *i·*, and by a

inhabiters

ap 568–21 Woe to the *i·* of the earth — *Rev.* 12 : 12.

inhabits

b 300–26 theory that soul, spirit, intelligence, *i·*

inhaled

c 261–19 as oblivious . . . as if he had *i·* chloroform,

inhaling

s 159– 4 protested against *i·* the ether
    159–10 not by the ether, but by fear of *i·* it.

inharmonies

f 243–31 They are *i·* which Truth destroys.

inharmonious

s 123– 9 the most absolutely weak and *i·*
ph 166–15 The erring human mind is *i·* in itself.
    166–16 From it arises the *i·* body.
f 228– 6 nothing *i·* can enter being, for Life *is* God.
    251–30 *I·* beliefs, which rob Mind,
b 300–15 The *i·* and self-destructive never touch the
o 347–30 harmonious will appear real, and the *i·* unreal.
r 472– 9 Sickness, sin, and death, being *i·*,

inharmony

sp 81–26 Though the *i·* resulting from material sense
    81–27 *i·* cannot destroy the divine Principle of
ph 183– 5 that God constitutes laws of *i·* is a mistake ;
f 233–32 sickness, which is solely the result of *i·*
b 271–10 Truth, casting out all *i·*
    276–12 The realization that all *i·* is unreal
p 406–25 *I·* of any kind involves weakness
r 473– 1 We learn in C. S. that all *i·* of mortal mind
    480–14 *I·* has no Principle ;
    480–16 *I·* would make matter the cause
    493–24 removes any other sense of moral or mental *i·*.

inherent

s 124–29 declares that they . . . are *i·* in this Mind,
f 225–26 The despotic tendencies, *i·* in mortal mind
b 282–23 There is no *i·* power in matter ;

inheres

s 107–16 false consciousness that life *i·* in the body,

inherit

m 61–12 *i·* more intellect, better balanced minds,
an 106–26 shall not *i·* the kingdom of God. — *Gal.* 5 : 21.
b 321– 4 cannot *i·* the kingdom of God." — *I Cor.* 15 : 50.
g 516–14 "The meek shall *i·* the earth." — *Psal.* 37 : 11.

inheritance

g 533– 2 Had he lost man's rich *i·* and God's behest,

inheritances

f 228– 9 we shall have no dangerous *i·*,

inherited

p 425– 8 Show that it is not *i·* ;
    425–32 Discard all notions about . . . *i·* consumption,

inherits
  m 61–21 child who *i·* propensities that must

inhuman
  p 390–32 employ to defeat the passage of an *i·* law.

inhumanity
  m 64– 2 caused by the selfishness and *i·* of man.
  p 365–25 If hypocrisy, stolidity, *i·*, or vice finds its way

inimical
  p 389–21 cannot . . . be *i·* to existence.

iniquity
  an 106– 3 is to drop . . . into the very mire of *i·*,
  b 313–19 "loved righteousness and hated *i·*."— *Heb.* 1 : 9.
  t 446–30 Covering *i·* will prevent prosperity
    448– 3 Blindness and . . . cling fast to *i·*.
  r 476–17 "conceived in sin and brought forth in *i·*."
    485– 9 because of their uselessness or their *i·*,
  g 540–29 and "shapen in *i·* ;"—*Psal.* 51 : 5.
  ap 571– 3 hidden mental ways of accomplishing *i·*.

initiate
  t 457–26 intending thereby to *i·* the cure

injected
  g 524–29 Is Spirit, God, *i·* into dust,

injection
  p 416– 6 A hypodermic *i·* of morphine is
  t 464–17 would give him a hypodermic *i·*,

injunction
  pr 15–23 The Master's *i·* is, that we pray in secret
  a 23–29 whereas the *i·*, "Believe — *Acts* 16 : 31.

injure
  sp 94–32 Jesus could *i·* no one by his Mind-reading.
    95–13 cannot *i·* others, and must do them good.
  t 453–18 You uncover sin, not in order to *i·*,
    463–11 this idea cannot *i·* its useful surroundings
  ap 567–20 claiming . . . either to benefit or to *i·* men

injured
  ph 194–13 it will be so without an *i·* nerve.
  r 488–28 If it were possible for . . . to be *i·*,

injures
  p 403–29 improves or *i·* the case in proportion to

injuries
  p 402–16 You say that accidents, *i·*, and disease kill

injuring
  c 263–14 *i·* those whom he would bless.
  p 397– 6 actually *i·* those whom we mean to bless.
    439–20 God will smite you, O whited walls, for *i·*
  t 449–11 than for you to benefit yourself by *i·* others.

injurious
  s 150– 4 what made them . . . beneficial or *i·*?
  ph 176– 2 was not so *i·* before inquisitive modern
  t 451–28 It is the *i·* action of one mortal mind

injuriously
  sp 94–28 used his incisive power *i·*?
  f 206– 8 acts *i·* both upon the body and through it.
  p 397– 3 acting beneficially or *i·* on the health,

injury
  ph 172–28 But the loss of a limb or *t·* to a tissue
    193–22 ever since the *i·* was received in boyhood.
  b 294–14 saying: . . . *I·* can cripple and matter can kill
  p 397–15 more powerful than . . . to make the *i·* real.
    422–28 doubts as to the ultimate outcome of the *i·*.
  t 464–13 If from an *i·* or from any cause,

injustice
  a 55 7 did Jesus no more *i·* than the
  m 63–14 C. S. furnishes no precedent for such *t·*,
  p 391–17 *I·* declares the absence of law.

inkling
  s 130–22 an *i·* of the ability of Spirit to make

innate
  s 160– 6 for they have no *i·* power.

innocence
  ap 564–14 the dragon as warring against *i·*.
    567–29 killed by *i·*, the Lamb of Love.
    568– 1 *I·* and Truth overcome guilt and error.
  gl 582–14 BRIDE. Purity and *i·*,
    590–10 self-immolation ; *i·* and purity ;
    594–12 SHEEP. *I·* ; inoffensiveness

innocent
  ph 175–29 They were as *i·* as Adam, before he
  p 437–16 the helpless *i·* body tortured,
    439–14 though Mortal Man was *i·*.
    439–24 an offence of which he was *i·*.
    442– 1 Man is adjudged *i·* of transgressing
  t 450– 6 so depraved that they appear to be *i·*.
  ap 564– 7 to charge the *i·* with the crime.

innuendoes
  m 68–22 to hatch their silly *i·* and lies,

innumerable
  r 479–23 the only facts are Spirit and its *i·* creations.

inoculation
  t 449–20 The *i·* of evil human thoughts ought to

inoffensiveness
  gl 594–12 SHEEP. . . . *i·* ; those who follow their leader.

inquire
  p 376–28 Some people, mistaught as to Mind-science, *i·*

inquirer
  g 555– 6 An *i·* once said to the discoverer of C. S. :

inquiries
  p 396– 6 Make no unnecessary *i·* relative to feelings

inquiring
  g 555–17 is like *i·* into the origin of God,

inquiry
  sp 86– 2 Supposing this *i·* to be occasioned by
    86– 6 Repeating his *i·*, he was answered by the
  s 131–31 to John's *i·*, "Art thou he — *Matt.* 11 : 3.
    133– 1 and sent the *i·* to Jesus,
    137– 9 This renewed *i·* meant : Who or what is it
  f 223–15 Many are ready to meet this *i·* with the
  b 268– 6 those lower things which give impulse to *i·*.

inquisitive
  ph 176– 3 not so injurious before *i·* modern Eves took

insane
  ph 193–26 threatened with incarceration in an *i·* asylum
  f 245– 6 she became *i·* and lost all account of time.
  p 408–11 people who are committed to *i·* asylums
    411–17 and the *i·* man was changed
    421– 1 he suffers only as the *i·* suffer,

insanity
  dementia or
    p 423 20 as directly . . . as is dementia or *i·*.
  implies
    p 421– 2 *i·* implies belief in a diseased brain,
  incipient
    m 68–18 was suffering from incipient *i·*,
  in curing
    p 414– 8 The arguments to be used in curing *i·* are
  sin is
    p 407–29 All sin is *i·* in different degrees.
  species of
    p 407–29 There are many species of *i·*.
    408–16 is in itself a mild species of *i·*.
  treatment of
    p 414– 4 treatment of *i·* is especially interesting.
  universal
    p 408– 6 There is a universal *i·* of so-called health,
  would produce
    p 408–23 would produce *i·* as perceptibly as
    b 330–31 dementia, *i·*, inanity, devil,
    p 408–10 from the special name of *i·*.
    408–14 The supposition that we can correct *i·* by

insect
  sp 74–17 caterpillar, transformed into a beautiful *i·*,
    74–18 nor does the *i·* return to fraternize with

insensible
  ph 173–10 is required to be made manifest through the *i·*.

insensibly
  p 383–30 sensibly well when it ought to be *i·* so

inseparable
  sp 70– 9 the Ego and the Father are *i·*.
  ph 184– 7 the penalties it affixes . . . are *i·* from it.
  b 314– 7 proved that he and the Father were *i·*
    333–27 *i·* from the divine Principle, God.
    336 26 are *i·*, harmonious, and eternal.
  p 404–28 require the same method and are *i·* in Truth.
  r 476– 5 God and the real man are *i·*
    482–20 He was *i·* from Christ, the Messiah,
    491–16 in the divine likeness, *i·* from his creator.
  g 554– 7 being and Deity are *i·*.

inside
  c 258– 9 more than a material form with a mind *i·*,

insidious
  p 376– 9 most hidden, undefined, and *i·* beliefs.

insight
  sp 94–25 this *i·* better enabled him to direct those
  s 128–18 into his native air of *i·* and perspicacity.
  p 363–25 did his *i·* detect this unspoken moral uprising?

insignificance
  b 317– 4 insisted on . . . the *i·* of spirit,

insincere
  pr 3–28 If we are ungrateful for . . . we are *i·*
    8–11 If a man, . . . is impure and therefore *i·*,

insist
  sp 90–14 some *i·* that death is the necessary prelude
  s 116–17 They never . . . *i·* upon the fact that God is all.
    122–31 They *i·* that soul is in body
    131–14 Must C.S. come through . . . as some persons *i·*?
  ph 168–15 Because man-made systems *i·* that man

insist
b 283–13   They *i·* that Life, or God, is one and the
p 409– 3   You may say : . . . why do you *i·* that disease
412–23   Mentally *i·* that harmony is the fact,
413–20   I *i·* on bodily cleanliness within and without.
421–15   *I·* vehemently on the great fact which

insisted
s 159– 1   her physicians *i·* that it would be unsafe to
b 317– 3   *i·* on the might of matter,

insists
b 307– 3   This pantheistic error, or so-called *serpent, i·*
p 368– 5   Divine Science *i·* that time will prove all this.

inspecting
p 379–15   invalid, *i·* the hue of her blood

inspection
p 438–25   without the *i·* of Soul's government officers.

inspiration
came through
b 319–22   original language of the Bible came through *i·*,
heavenly
gl 592–26   gentleness ; prayer ; heavenly *i·*.
holy
s 161– 5   Holy *i·* has created states of mind which
little
a 37–32   Why has this Christian demand so little *i·*
p 368–14   has little *i·* to nerve endeavor.
needs
b 319–22   and needs *i·* to be understood.
of a sermon
sp 80– 4   whether for the *i·* of a sermon or for
of goodness
gl 581– 5   the *i·* of goodness, purity, and immortality,
of Love
a 35–27   Our wine the *i·* of Love,
restores
f 242–28   while *i·* restores every part of the
spiritual
gl 596–17   they show the spiritual *i·* of Love and Truth
this
a 34– 2   Then why ascribe this *i·* to a dead rite,

a 54–12   the *i·* of Jesus' intense human sacrifice.
m 65– 5   and to give to human life an *i·*
sp 88–27   It is due to *i·* rather than to erudition.
b 281–31   the *i·*, which is to change our standpoint,
gl 589– 5   JACOB. . . . *I·* ; the revelation of Science,
598–17   WINE.   *I·* ; understanding.
599– 6   ZION. . . . *i·* ; spiritual strength.

inspirational
c 256– 4   from the scholastic to the *i·*,

inspirations
ph 184–30   The *i·* were deep and natural.

inspire
m 61–21   what noble ambition, can *i·* the child
ph 180–21   through the material faith which they *i·*.
c 262–14   These clearer, higher views *i·* the
p 370–27   Quackery likewise fails at length to *i·* the

inspired
a 46– 9   has spoken through the *i·* Word
49– 2   They knew what had *i·* their devotion,
51–23   He was *i·* by God, by Truth and Love,
53–17   not interpret aright the . . . which Jesus *i·*
sp 84–17   to be divinely *i·*, — yea, to reach the
s 107–12   *i·* with a diviner nature and essence :
133–26   who taught as he was *i·* by the Father
139–22   darkening to some extent the *i·* pages.
144–30   whether the ancient *i·* healers understood
b 319–27   wrote down what an *i·* teacher had said.
p 368– 3   The confidence *i·* by Science lies in the fact
410–20   Here is a definite and *i·* proclamation of C. S.
418–21   All metaphysical logic is *i·* by this simple
r 497– 3   we take the *i·* Word of the Bible as our
g 521– 4   Here the *i·* record closes its narrative
537–24   *I·* writers interpret the Word spiritually,
539–31   *i·* his wisest and least-understood sayings,
547–28   *I·* thought relinquishes a material,
ap 572– 8   and profound counsel of the *i·* writer.
gl 579– 3   elucidates the meaning of the *i·* writer.

inspires
f 234– 4   Whatever *i·* with wisdom, Truth, or Love
t 454–18   Love *i·*, illumines, designates, and leads the way.
g 547–32   lifts humanity out of disease and death and *i·*

instance
every
s 162–13   not in one instance, but in every *i·*.
familiar
sp 89–12   This familiar *i·* reaffirms the Scriptural word
first
f 234– 4   You must control evil thoughts in the first *i·*,
p 403– 7   In the first *i·* it is understood that
g 541–24   It is supposed to say in the first *i·*,

instance
for
b 319–29   for *i·*, to name Love as merely an attribute
no
an 101–29   In no *i·* is the effect of animal magnetism,
g 550–25   no *i·* of one species producing its opposite.
one
s 149– 7   The prescription which succeeds in one *i·*
152–11   in one *i·* and not in another.
160–20   Can . . . nerves rebel against mind in one *i·*
162–13   not in one *i·*, but in every instance.
f 229–13   declaring Him good in one *i·* and
245–27   One *i·* like the foregoing proves it possible
g 549–24   In one *i·* a celebrated naturalist, Agassiz,
this
ph 189– 5   Science (in this *i·* named natural)
f 245–18   This *i·* of youth preserved furnishes a
g 553–17   In this *i·*, it is seen that the maternal

instances
sp 79– 5   Thousands of *i·* could be cited of
s 122–21   Experience is full of *i·* of similar illusions,
b 319–26   misinterpretation of the Word in some *i·* by
p 383–25   Such *i·* only prove the illusive physical effect
386–12   in too many *i·* healed disease . . . not to know
398– 7   These *i·* show the concessions which
408–12   are only so many distinctly defined *i·* of the

instant
f 215–13   never for an *i·* deprived of the light and
244–20   If man flickers out in death . . . there must be an *i·*
b 290–23   The sin and error which possess us at the *i·* of
306–19   cannot be separated for an *i·* from God,
389–32   One *i·* she spoke despairingly of herself.
t 463– 2   among phenomena, which fluctuate every *i·*

instantaneous
p 377–16   has caused what is termed *i·* death.
411–12   and the healing is *i·*.

instantaneously
pr 16–23   spiritual consciousness, which . . . *i·* heals
g 504–24   gathered into the focus of ideas, bring light *i·*,

instead
a 34– 3   *i·* of showing, by casting out error
39–14   Jesus overcame death and the grave *i·* of
40–29   to mean public worship *i·* of daily deeds.
53–22   should weep over the warning, *i·* of
sp 87–14   when really it is first sight *i·* of second,
92–16   gained from matter, or evil, *i·* of
92–28   *i·* of urging the claims of Truth alone.
96–30   will be apprehended mentally *i·* of materially.
s 120–27   *i·* of reversing the testimony of the
121–18   *i·* of the earth from west to east.
129–23   *i·* of accepting only the outward sense of things.
132– 2   *i·* of referring to his doctrine,
146–16   *i·* of to the divine Principle, of the man Jesus ;
148–10   as created corporeally *i·* of spiritually
148–11   *i·* of from the highest, conception of being.
148–26   claims to rule man by material law, *i·* of
150– 5   eternal Science, *i·* of a phenomenal exhibition.
159–24   would learn . . . from matter *i·* of from Mind.
ph 165– 3   *I·* of so doing, it closed the eyes of mortals
166–18   *I·* of thrusting Him aside in times of
170– 6   faith in matter *i·* of in Spirit.
180–13   the ground that all causation is matter, *i·* of
180–21   *I·* of furnishing thought with fear,
181–22   are satisfied with good words *i·* of effects,
189–20   makes all things start from the lowest *i·* of
192– 8   from corporeality *i·* of from Principle,
192– 9   from the mortal *i·* of from the immortal.
195–30   demand for amusement *i·* of for improvement.
196–22   *i·* of impressing them with forcible
197–16   We should master fear, *i·* of cultivating it.
f 202–18   The days of our pilgrimage will multiply *i·* of
202–20   the true way leads to Life *i·* of to death,
203– 7   If God were understood *i·* of being merely believed,
206–14   governed by Science *i·* of the senses,
206–26   *I·* of God sending sickness and death,
212–15   take away this so-called mind *i·* of a piece of
216–16   bones, brain, etc., servants, *i·* of masters.
218–22   *i·* of turning in time of need to God,
223– 5   illusion that he lives in body *i·* of
223– 6   in matter *i·* of in Spirit.
224– 9   life and peace *i·* of discord and death.
242–32   the proof which he gave, *i·* of mere profession.
244–30   *i·* of assigning to man the everlasting grandeur
248– 7   *i·* of lapsing into darkness or gloom.
253–29   which is the law of Life *i·* of death,
253–30   of harmony *i·* of discord,
253–31   of Spirit *i·* of the flesh.
c 257–18   say that an anthropomorphic God, *i·* of
260– 1   from imperfection *i·* of perfection,
263–30   *i·* of a scientific eternal consciousness
b 274–20   which affirm that . . . are material, *i·* of spiritual
280–25   *i·* of possessing a sentient material form,

instead
- b 285–32 It is essential to understand, i· of believe,
- 286– 5 and so depend upon belief i· of demonstration,
- 290– 9 i· of through a spiritual sense of life,
- 301–31 and man to be material i· of spiritual.
- 302–23 this real man is governed by Soul i· of sense,
- 304–29 Controlled by belief, i· of understanding,
- 314–16 their material temple i· of his body.
- 315– 8 He knew that the Ego was Mind i· of body
- 315–15 i· of with God's spiritual idea as presented by
- 317–25 looking for the ideal Saviour in matter i· of in
- o 342– 3 proof and demonstration, i· of opinion and
- 348–21 I· of tenaciously defending the supposed
- 352–20 but i· of increasing children's fears
- p 371–29 Mind can impart purity i· of impurity,
- 371–29 strength i· of weakness,
- 371–30 and health i· of disease.
- 376–24 representing man as healthy i· of diseased,
- 384– 1 on inert matter i· of on Mind.
- 387–20 i· of reading disquisitions on the
- 391– 7 I· of blind and calm submission to
- 395– 1 The sick . . . argue for suffering, i· of against it.
- 407–25 perfect model . . . i· of its demoralized opposite.
- 415–13 by resorting to matter i· of to Mind.
- 419–17 Observe mind i· of body,
- 423–21 has rendered himself strong, i· of weak,
- 426–10 struggle for Truth makes one strong i· of weak,
- 426–11 resting i· of wearying one.
- 435–13 joy i· of grief, pleasure i· of pain,
- 435–14 and life i· of death.
- 438– 9 I· of being a ruler in the Province of Body,
- t 455– 6 indicate weakness i· of strength.
- 459–13 i· of resting on the omnipotence of the
- 460–20 I· of scientifically effecting a cure,
- 463–28 it is a spiritual law i· of material.
- r 495–21 Let C. S., i· of corporeal sense, support your
- g 504–14 a revelation i· of a creation
- 523–12 material myth, i· of the reflection of Spirit.
- 528–11 closed up the flesh i· thereof ;— Gen. 2 : 21.
- 528–19 Beginning creation with darkness i· of light,
- 531– 3 from dust i· of from Deity
- 536–15 by corporeality i· of divine Principle,
- 536 15 by body i· of by Soul,
- 536–17 Created by flesh i· of by Spirit,
- 541– 4 i· of making his own gift a higher tribute
- 544–32 Error begins with corporeality . . . i· of divine
- gl 585–26 materially i· of spiritually,
- (see also **matter, Spirit**)

instigated
- a 24– 6 i· sometimes by the worst passions of men
- ap 564–11 were i· by the criminal instinct

instinct
- m 63– 7 is not, like that of mortals, in brute i·,
- f 220– 8 I· is better than misguided reason,
- ap 563–31 It is the animal i· in mortals,
- 564– 4 This malicious animal i·, . . . incites mortals
- 564–12 were instigated by the criminal i·

instincts
- ph 170–18 whereas the wild animal, left to his i·,

instituted
- f 227–30 If God had i· material laws to govern
- p 380–19 If God has, . . . i· laws that food shall
- g 507– 2 the absolute formations i· by Mind,
- 526–22 Was evil i· through God, Love?

institutes
- g 531–25 Which i· Life,— matter or Mind?

Institutes and Practice of Physic
- s 163–19 Dr. Chapman, Professor of the I· and P· of P·

institution
- pref xi–31 enabled her to get this i· chartered
- gl 583–14 The Church is that i·, which affords proof

institutions
- pref xii– 2 No charters were granted to . . . such i· after 1883,
- s 141–31 Give to it the place in our i· of learning

instruct
- p 415–25 i· mortal mind with immortal Truth.
- 420–10 the sick that they are not helpless victims,
- t 451–32 I· him how to bar the door of his thought

instructed
- a 29–14 Those i· in C. S. have reached the glorious
- b 271– 7 Jesus i· his disciples whereby to heal the sick
- 297– 8 illusion of sickness, to be i· out of itself
- p 402–28 because their belief is not better i·
- 403– 7 and by his mistake a man is often i·.
- 426– 3 mortal mind, when i· by Truth, yields to
- g 552–20 but not yet i· by Science,

instructing
- r 485–11 Why malign C. S. for i· mortals

instruction
- a 27–27 never truly understood their Master's i·.
- o 358–20 more frequently cited for our i·
- t 443– * Give i· to a wise man, and he will— Prov. 9 : 9.

instructions
- t 448–24 reception or pursuit of i· opposite to
- r 488– 3 When, on the strength of these i·,

instructor
- a 49–14 the highest i· and friend of man,

instructors
- p 429–30 not understood generally by our ethical i·.

instruments
- b 293–32 the avenues and i· of human error,
- g 528–29 first performed mentally and without i· ;
- 529– 4 came about, also, that i· were needed

insubordinate
- p 438–11 Nerve was an i· citizen,

insubordination
- f 236–21 i· is an evil, blighting the
- b 271– 5 Neither emasculation, illusion, nor i·

insubstantial
- b 335–15 Things material and temporal are i·.

insufficiency
- c 258– 6 The i· of this belief to supply the

insufficient
- a 23– 3 One sacrifice, however great, is i· to
- 35–31 If the sinner's punishment here has been i· to

insure
- t 449–15 qualities which i· success in this Science ;

intact
- m 56– 9 Until the spiritual creation is discerned i·,
- 59–28 so long as its moral obligations are kept i· ;
- sp 76–27 This state of existence is scientific and i·,
- b 295–15 the real sense of being, perfect and forever i·,
- 306–20 Science proves man's existence to be i·.
- r 477– 5 the kingdom of God is i·, universal,
- 481–12 the unseen Truth, which remains forever i·.
- 492– 1 leaves mortal man i· in body and thought,
- 494– 1 to hold man forever i· in his perfect state,
- g 521–12 The harmony and immortality of man are i·.

intangible
- b 312– 5 That which material sense calls i ,
- o 352–10 to the rabbis the spiritual was the i·

integrity
- t 446 28 detrimental to health and i· of thought.
- 448–10 Evasion of Truth cripples i·,

intellect
- m 57–17 should never weigh against . . . claims of i·,
- 61–12 more i·, better balanced minds, and
- s 130– 1 petty i is alarmed by constant appeals to

intellectual
- pref x–30 No i· proficiency is requisite in the learner,
- ph 165– 6 To measure i· capacity by the size of
- 171–21 The i·, the moral, the spiritual,
- 195–29 Literary commercialism is lowering the i· standard
- p 397– 7 we conclude that i· labor
- t 452–16 Better is the frugal i· repast
- 460– 9 and its medicine is i· and spiritual,
- g 505–26 This understanding is not i·,

intelligence

and Life
- f 215–13 the light and might of i· and Life.

and life
- ph 171–26 beliefs that i· and life are present where
- 171–28 i· and life are spiritual, never material,
- b 269–31 possessing i· and life.

and non-intelligence
- sp 73–28 Spirit and matter, i· and non-intelligence,
- f 204–16 a supposed mixture of . . . i· and non-intelligence,

and sensation
- b 294–12 saying : "Matter has i· and sensation.

and sentiment
- p 408–21 a supposed effect on i· and sentiment.

and truth
- p 437–12 witness, Nerve, to be destitute of i· and truth

atmosphere of
- ph 192– 1 the aroma of Spirit, the atmosphere of i·.

disease has no
- p 378– 3 Disease has no i·.
- 391–25 Disease has no i· to declare itself something
- 419–12 Disease has no i· with which to move itself

divine
- ph 184–16 Controlled by the divine i·, man is

diviner sense of
- b 285–20 give place to a diviner sense of i·

existence and
- g 510–17 giving existence and i· to the universe.

fallacy that
- r 466–24 fallacy that i·, soul, and life can be in matter ;

intelligence

God is
pr 2–24   God is *i·*. Can we inform the infinite Mind

governing
ph 174– 1   less faith . . . in a supreme governing *i·*.

idea or
b 279–18   their only idea or *i·* is in God.

is not mute
ph 191–19   *I·* is not mute before non-intelligence.

is omniscience
r 469– 8   *Answer.— I·* is omniscience, omnipresence,

Life and
pr 14–13   Life and *i·* are purely spiritual,
b 310–15   reveals Soul . . . as the central Life and *i·*
r 477–22   Soul is the substance, Life, and *i·* of man,

life and
(see **life**)

Life, or
g 550– 5   God is the Life, or *i·*, which forms and

life or
r 485–32   The notion of any life or *i·* in matter
g 584–29   the absence of substance, life, or *i·*.

Life, substance, and
a 27–15   the Life, substance, and *i·* of the universe
ph 185–20   God as the only Life, substance, and *i·*,
gl 595– 7   the idea of Life, substance, and *i·* ;

life, substance, and
(see **life**)

material
a 48– 1   error of a belief in any possible material *i·*.
g 534–16   mythological material *i·* called *energy*

might of
f 215–13   the light and might of *i·* and Life.
p 378–17   latter occurrence represents . . . the might of *i·*

Mind or
f 204–22   realize only one God, one Mind or *i·*
216–12   there is but one Mind or *i·*,
g 508–21   The Mind or *i·* of production names the

mockery of
ph 192– 2   a mockery of *i·*, a mimicry of Mind.

more
m 62–20   must not attribute . . . more *i·* to matter,

never passes into
b 336– 2   *I·* never passes into non-intelligence, or matter.

no
pr 12–19   The drug does nothing, because it has no *i·*.
s 127–21   have— as matter— no *i·*, life, nor sensation.
136– 5   no *i·*, action, nor life separate from God.
p 399– 1   Evil has no power, no *i·*,
r 467– 6   have no *i·*, . . . but that which is spiritual.
g 530–27   The dream has no reality, no *i·*, no mind ;

nor power
t 454–11   evil or matter has neither *i·* nor power,

nor sensation
f 243–23   matter has neither *i·* nor sensation.

nor substance
s 133–27   no life, *i·*, nor substance outside of God.
r 468– 9   no life, truth, *i·*, nor substance in matter.

one
b 307– 8   affirms . . . that there is more than one *i·*

or power
b 339–30   never to admit that sin can have *i·* or power,

or reality
r 469–17   not Truth, but error, without *i·* or reality.

or substance
g 508– 5   The only *i·* or substance of a thought,

rights of
sp 79–27   contending for the rights of *i·*
p 384–31   at length quail before the divine rights of *i·*,

scale of
g 511–27   rising in the scale of *i·*,

separate
b 309–26   impossible . . . an *i·* separate from his Maker.

so-called
b 282–27   Error is the so-called *i·* of mortal mind.

Spirit, or
gl 591– 4   the one Spirit, or *i·*, named Elohim, or God.

spiritual
f 240– 6   all point to Mind, the spiritual *i·*

subjugate
ph 165– 8   to subjugate *i·*, to make mind mortal,

substance, life, and
sp 91–26   belief is, that substance, life, and *i·* are
ap 562–10   its reflected light, substance, life, and *i·*.
563– 9   belief that substance, life, and *i·* can

substance, or
p 418– 6   error that life, substance, or *i·* can be in matter.

the only
b 330–12   the only *i·* of the universe, including man.
g 508– 5   The only *i·* or substance of a thought,

Truth is the
b 282–26   Truth is the *i·* of immortal Mind.

Truth, or
r 468– 1   Thus we arrive at Truth, or *i·*, which

understanding and
g 557–13   towards enlarged understanding and *i·* ;

intelligence

unerring
g 546–12   is governed by unerring *i·*?

vibration is not
c 259–26   Vibration is not *i·* ; hence it is not a creator.

which holds
f 209–10   *i·* which holds the winds in its grasp.

m 63– 9   nor does he . . . prior to reaching *i·*.
an 102– 6   neither *i·*, power, nor reality,
s 129–11   a belief in the *i·* of matter,
ph 194–25   with no more *i·* than a babe,
f 204–12   is admitted to be good, an *i·* or Mind called God.
205–10   matter has neither *i·*, life, nor sensation,
211–25   If it is true . . . that matter has *i·*,
250– 4   and suppose . . . unintelligence to act like *i·*,
b 270–10   Few deny the hypothesis that *i·*, apart from
270–12   and it is generally admitted that this *i·* is
275–14   All substance, *i·*, wisdom, being,
276–31   *I·* never produces non-intelligence ;
277– 2   and therefore cannot spring from *i·*.
285–14   one is *i·* while the other is non-intelligence.
300–26   theory that soul, spirit, *i·*, inhabits
318–30   *I·* does not originate in numbers,
p 378–22   Disease is not an *i·* to dispute the
413– 1   and cannot transmit good or evil *i·* to man,
441–25   Supreme Bench decides in favor of *i·*,
r 469– 7   *Question.—* What is *i·*?
472–15   supposition that pleasure and pain, that *i·*,
475–21   possesses no life, *i·*, nor creative power of his own,
478–15   and is there *i·* in matter?
478–20   How can *i·* dwell in matter
480–17   would make matter the cause . . . of *i·*,
482– 5   hypothesis that soul is both an evil and a good *i·*,
g 511– 3   radiates their borrowed light, *i·*,
513–19   the *i·*, existence, and continuity of all
516– 4   The substance, Life, *i·*, Truth, and
517– 9   man corresponds to creation, to *i·*, and to
531– 6   error, . . . that non-intelligence becomes *i·*,
ap 567–19   claiming that there is *i·* in matter
gl 580–23   supposition that . . . *i·* passes into non-intelligence,
583–20   CREATOR. Spirit ; Mind ; *i·* ;
587– 8   Life ; Truth ; Love ; all substance ; *i·*.
588–24   definition of
591– 9   illusion ; *i·*, substance, and life in

intelligences
gl 591– 3   belief in many gods, or material *i·*,
594–23   evil minds ; supposed *i·*, or gods ;

intelligent
sp 73–27   the reality of *i·* existence,
80–32   belief . . . that matter is *i·*.
89–25   Matter is neither *i·* nor creative.
91–32   fourth erroneous postulate is, that matter is *i·*,
s 156– 1   If drugs possess . . . *i·* curative qualities,
f 205–16   error of believing that matter can be *i·*
211– 1   If brain, nerves, stomach, are *i·*,
218–26   Resist the temptation to believe in matter as *i·*,
b 275– 6   matter is neither substantial, living, nor *i·*.
276– 7   but all have . . . one *i·* source,
293–19   electricity is not *i·*,
294–24   matter is represented as divided into *i·* gods.
307–21   If we regard matter as *i·*,
312–29   away from the *i·* and divine healing Principle
332– 2   the *i·* relation of God to man
p 385–32   as if either were *i·*,
409– 1   *I·* matter is an impossibility.
412–32   since matter is not *i·* and cannot
r 466–14   Truth is *i·* ; error is non-intelligent.
487–24   belief that life is . . . *i·* matter is erroneous.
g 508–23   The *i·* individual idea, be it male or female,
526–12   a belief in *i·* matter.
531– 1   living, substantial, and *i·*.
556– 7   destroys forever all belief in *i·* matter.
gl 579–17   a curse ; a belief in *i·* matter,

intelligently
s 107–14   and thoughts acquaint themselves *i·* with God.

intended
a 27– 1   which was *i·* to prove beyond a question
38– 2   assured that this command was *i·* only for
s 152–18   supposed this ceremony was *i·* to heal him,
b 320–30   as if Job *i·* to declare that even if
r 465–13   They are also *i·* to express the nature,

intending
t 457–26   *i·* thereby to initiate the cure

intense
a 54–13   the inspiration of Jesus' *i·* human sacrifice.
sp 87–27   by friendship or by any *i·* feeling
ph 195– 1   gave him a belief of *i·* pain.
b 329–30   the more *i·* the opposition to spirituality,

intent
p 365–24   the result will correspond with the spiritual *i·*.
g 515– 5   tireless worm, . . . persevering in its *i·*,

intention
  b 326–19 nothing but wrong *i·* can hinder your

intentional
  f 251–28 Ignorance, like *i·* wrong, is not Science.

intentionally
  ph 177–29 as directly as if the poison had been *i·* taken.
  t 456– 1 impossible . . . for you *i·* to influence
  456–13 greatly errs, ignorantly or *i·*,

interchange
  m 58–18 the sweet *i·* of confidence and love ;

interchangeably
  s 127–11 The terms Divine Science, . . . she employs *i·*,

intercommunication
  sp 81– 1 not so much evidence to prove *i·*
  b 284–31 The *i·* is always from God to His idea, man.

intercommunion
  sp 72–30 Not personal *i·* but divine law is the
  82–25 so unlike, that *i·* is as impossible as

intercourse
  m 58– 1 by constant *i·* with those adapted to elevate it,
  sp 72–28 The joy of *i·* becomes the jest of sin, when

interest
  c 261–10 with such absorbed *i·* as to forget it,
  p 436– 6 and in the *i·* of Personal Sense,
  437– 8 to condemn Man in the *i·* of Personal Sense.

interested
  p 430–25 The court-room is filled with *i·* spectators,

interesting
  p 414– 4 treatment of insanity is especially *i·*.

interests
  a 21–22 and our mutual *i·* are identical ;
  m 59–15 thus hallowing the union of *i·* and affections,
  f 236– 5 Sacredly, in the *i·* of humanity, not of sect.
  p 414–18 lest you array the sick against their own *i·*
  t 462–10 dividing his *i·* between God and mammon
  ap 571–20 will unite all *i·* in the one divinity.

interfere
  m 62–24 let no mortal *i·* with God's government
  64–13 wife should not say, "It is never well to *i·*
  f 214–29 Neither age nor accident can *i·* with the
  234– 1 material lotions *i·* with truth,
  p 402–12 material beliefs will not *i·* with spiritual facts.
  427–14 Nothing can *i·* with the harmony of being

interfered
  an 106–12 invaded when the divine order is *i·* with,

interference
  m 63–32 and own her children free from *i·*.

interlaced
  s 114–26 disentangles the *i·* ambiguities of being,

intermixture
  g 552–27 The *i·* of different species,

interpose
  nr 12–27 Does Deity *i·* in behalf of one worshipper,
  t 445– 7 No hypothesis . . . should *i·* a doubt or fear

interpret
  a 53–16 The world could not *i·* aright the
  s 117–20 Human theories are inadequate to *i·* the
  127–27 Science . . . is alone able to *i·* God aright.
  b 272–28 divine Principle of the universe must *i·* the
  o 350–10 enables them to *i·* his spiritual meaning.
  r 467–27 We cannot *i·* Spirit, Mind, through matter.
  g 534– 6 enabled woman to be first to *i·* the Scriptures
  537–24 Inspired writers *i·* the Word spiritually,

interpretation
  meek
  a 54–19 They would not accept his meek *i·* of life
  metaphysical
  gl 579– 5 the metaphysical *i·* of Bible terms,
  of God
  t 461–14 furnishes the eternal *i·* of God and man.
  of Scripture
  b 320– 9 "The spiritual *i·* of Scripture
  320–24 The one important *i·* of Scripture
  g 547– 8 given you the correct *i·* of Scripture.
  scientific
  g 501– 1 Scientific *i·* of the Scriptures
  spiritual
  a 47– 1 even to the spiritual *i·* and discernment
  s 118– 3 Science of Christ and its spiritual *i·*,
  b 320– 9 "The spiritual *i·* of Scripture
  g 502–19 each text is followed by its spiritual *i·*

  b 321– 1 an *i·* which is just the opposite of the true,

interpretations
  c 265– 7 they must near the broader *i·* of being,

interpreted
  sp 83–31 standpoints, from which cause and effect are *i·*.
  s 124–14 universe, like man, is to be *i·* by Science
  126–10 Human belief has sought and *i·* in its own way
  f 210– 2 *i·* by the translation of the spiritual original
  g 511–24 Spiritually *i·*, rocks and mountains stand for
  546–20 cannot possibly be *i·* from a material standpoint.

interpreter
  ph 170–15 The best *i·* of man's needs said :
  g 513–13 until divine Science becomes the *i·*.
  ap 577–21 and divine Mind is its own *i·*.

interpreting
  b 285–23 By *i·* God as a corporeal Saviour

interprets
  r 471–25 that which *i·* God as above mortal sense.
  g 537–25 the ordinary historian *i·* it literally.
  ap 560–10 *i·* the Principle of heavenly harmony.
  569– 1 This rule clearly *i·* God as divine Principle,
  577–18 *i·* this great example and the great Exemplar.

interrupt
  p 362– 5 as if to *i·* the scene of Oriental festivity.

interruptions
  sp 96– 6 there will be *i·* of the general material routine.

intertwined
  g 523–28 become more and more closely *i·*

interval
  a 39–28 and the *i·* before its attainment is
  gl 598–27 would bridge over . . . the *i·* of death,

intervals
  s 153– 9 administered at *i·* of three hours,
  p 431– 7 partaking of food at irregular *i·*,

intervenes
  o 361– 2 Here C. S. *i·*, explains these

interwoven
  r 477–15 though *i·* with matter's highest stratum,

intimate
  p 437– 2 He also testified that he was on *i·* terms with

intimated
  g 554–25 Jesus never *i·* that God made a devil,

intimately
  p 408–25 tarsal joint is less *i·* connected with the
  432– 3 testifies : . . . I am *i·* acquainted with the

intimation
  p 391–21 therefore meet the *i·* with a protest.
  r 471–10 these so-called senses receive no *i·* of

intolerable
  r 491– 2 A delicious perfume will seem *i·*.

intolerance
  sp 94–14 Tyranny, *i·*, and bloodshed,

intoxicating
  s 158–20 to victimize the race with *i·* prescriptions
  t 454– 2 use of tobacco or *i·* drinks is not

intoxication
  b 294–28 inebriate believes that there is pleasure in *i·*,
  p 398–22 destroy the illusion of pleasure in *i·*,

intrinsic
  s 156– 1 If drugs possess *i·* virtues or

intrinsically
  s 157–19 If He could create drugs *i·* bad,

introduced
  pref xii– 5 the United States, where C. S. was first *i·*.
  a 51– 7 the harmony his glorified example *i·*.
  s 123–16 The term C. S. was *i·* by the author
  i 473–18 *i·* the teaching and practice of Christianity,
  gl 590–22 It is *i·* in the second and following chapters.

introduces
  pref vii–22 A book *i·* new thoughts,
  sp 79–15 *i·* the harmony of being,
  s 135– 7 The miracle *i·* no disorder,
  r 474– 5 Whoever *i·* the Science of Christianity
  g 543–32 *i·* the record of a material creation

introducing
  s 152–15 a thermometer into the patient's mouth.
  p 439– 1 and *i·* their goods into the market.

introduction
  g 538–18 have no record in the Elohistic *i·*
  553–14 or important to their origin and first *i·*.''
  gl 582–10 the *i·* of a more spiritual origin ;

intruding
  p 362–10 *i·* upon the household of a high-caste
  391–10 that you can possibly entertain a single *i·*
  393– 2 we admit the *i·* belief, forgetting that

intuition
  b 298–14 involves *i·*, hope, faith, understanding,

intuitions
sp 85– 7   Such *i·* reveal whatever constitutes and
ph 174–12   the angels of His presence — the spiritual *i·*
gl 581– 5   spiritual *i·*, pure and perfect ;

invaded
an 106–12   *i·* when the divine order is interfered with,

invalid
s 139–31   does not follow that the profane or atheistic *i·*
ph 166–24   the despairing *i·* often drops them,
180–14   the *i·* may unwittingly add more fear
o 342–23   raises from the couch of pain the helpless *i·*.
p 367– 4   Christian encouragement of an *i·*,
376–10   The pallid *i·*, . . . should be told that
379–14   Let the despairing *i·*, inspecting the hue of
t 460–22   starts a petty crossfire over every cripple and *i·*,

invalid's
ph 166–26   *i·* faith in the divine Mind is less than in
p 379–23   does not affect the *i·* health,

invalids
pref x–19   Few *i·* will turn to God till
s 145– 8   struggle for the recovery of *i·* goes on,
f 237–23   Some *i·* are unwilling to know the facts
b 318–19   *i·* grow more spiritual, as the
p 377– 6   *I·* flee to tropical climates
420–14   This fact of C. S. should be explained to *i·*
t 443–18   leave *i·* free to resort to whatever
443–20   such *i·* may learn the value of the

invariable
o 342–17   If . . . then there is no *i·* law,

invention
a 44–27   a method infinitely above that of human *i·*.
sp 95–20   even human *i·* must have its day,
s 163–26   so ample an exhibition of human *i·*
ph 195–20   Observation, *i·*, study, and original thought

inventions
ph 196– 2   Man has "sought out many *i·*," — *Eccl.* 7 : 29.
b 273– 5   Human belief has sought out many *i·*,
o 358–14   nor of the *i·* of those who scoff at God.
g 531–23   Has man sought out other creative *i·*,
ap 563– 6   showing its horns in the many *i·* of evil.

invents
g 541–22   Here the serpentine lie *i·* new forms.

inversion
s 113–27   divine metaphysics . . . proves the rule by *i·*.
f 207–32   The only evidence of this *i·* is
b 282–31   rule of *i·* infers from error its opposite,

invert
g 514– 2   could not . . . *i·* the divine creation,

inverted
s 111–16   rejects the incidental or *i·* image
111–17   what this *i·* image is meant to represent.
ph 200–19   he is neither *i·* nor subverted,
f 207–30   Spiritual facts are not *i·* ;
c 267–21   *i·* thoughts and erroneous beliefs
b 285– 9   man's counterfeit, the *i·* likeness,
301–27   presents an *i·* image of Mind and substance
305–20   The *i·* images presented by the senses,
g 502– 7   *i·* images of the creator and His creation.
ap 572–11   materiality is the *i·* image of spirituality.
gl 580–13   an *i·* image of Spirit ;

inverts
g 507–30   Mortal sense *i·* this appearing
512–25   Mortal mind *i·* the true likeness,

investigate
an 100–13   to *i·* Mesmer's theory and to report
f 237–30   unwilling to *i·* the Science of Mind
o 344–25   Why should one refuse to *i·* this method
g 550–10   Of what avail is it to *i·* what is miscalled

investigates
sp 83–32   *i·* and touches only human beliefs.

investigation
ap 570– 1   The march of mind and of honest *i·*

investiture
sp 75– 6   would need . . . to have a material *i·*,

invigorate
b 274– 2   and thus *i·* and sustain existence.

invigorates
s 162– 5   the sunlight of Truth, which *i·* and purifies.

invincible
a 55– 5   but this does not affect the *i·* facts.
t 453– 8   until victory rests on the side of *i·* truth.

inviolate
sp 98–20   remains *i·* for every man to understand and

invisible
a 55– 3   from a deadened sense of the *i·* God,
sp 78–31   the *i·* good dwelling in eternal Science.
s 118–15   the *i·* and infinite power and grace.
121–17   The earth's diurnal rotation is *i·*
c 264–15   objects of creation, which before were *i·*,

invisible
b 305– 8   the central light of being, the *i·* God.
334–10   The *i·* Christ was imperceptible
335–12   substance, the *i·* and indivisible infinite God.
337–21   man, as the reflection of the *i·* God,
337–24   poor counterfeits of the *i·* universe
r 479–30   "For the *i·* things of Him, — *Rom.* 1 : 20.
ap 573– 4   that which is *i·* to the uninspired thought.

invisibly
sp 80–31   both visibly and *i·*,

invites
p 422–32   This mental state *i·* defeat.

invoke
o 354– 6   Why do they *i·* the divine aid to enable them to
g 542–12   tend to perpetuate sin, *i·* crime,

involuntarily
sp 84– 9   men become seers and prophets *i·*,
86–20   images and sounds evolved *i·*
p 371–10   removed as *i·*, not knowing why nor when.
376– 2   patient turns *i·* from the contemplation of it,

involuntary
pr 7–28   By it we may become *i·* hypocrites,
ph 187–20   All voluntary, as well as miscalled *i·*, action
187–22   There is no *i·* action.
187–25   tries to classify action as voluntary and *i·*,
c 263–11   They make man an *i·* hypocrite,
p 402–30   The *i·* pleasure or pain of the person
403– 3   difference between voluntary and *i·* mesmerism
r 484–22   the voluntary or *i·* action of error
491– 7   Material man is made up of *i·* and voluntary
     error,

involve
sp 86–19   either *i·* feats by tricksters, or
f 212–28   and possibly that other methods *i·* so-called
b 339– 6   prophesy and *i·* the final destruction of all sin
ap 573–22   *i·* the spiritual idea and consciousness of

involved
a 26–22   Jesus' teaching . . . *i·* such a sacrifice
sp 82–11   because different states of consciousness are *i·*,
s 117–20   the divine Principle *i·* in the miracles
r 484–26   *i·* in all false theories and practices.

involves
pr 9–22   It *i·* the Science of Life,
m 57–32   the disappointments it *i·* or the hopes it fulfils.
s 114–12   *i·* an improper use of the word *mind*.
f 240–30   *i·* unwinding one's snarls,
c 257–31   the phrase *infinite form i·* a contradiction
b 298–13   Spiritual sense, . . . *i·* intuition, hope,
301– 8   but his sense of substance *i·* error
p 406–26   Inharmony of any kind *i·* weakness
429–27   why you . . . do not demonstrate the facts it *i·*.
t 446–18   A wrong motive *i·* defeat.
r 493–14   full answer to the above question *i·* teaching,
g 526– 9   Belief *i·* theories of material hearing, sight,

involving
b 286–23   temporal thoughts are human, *i·* error,

inward
s 139–14   sectarian bitterness, whenever it flows *i·*.
b 321–25   the *i·* voice became to him the voice of God,

iota
ph 186–20   It can never destroy one *i·* of good.

iris
p 393–27   complex humors, lenses, muscles, the *i·* and

iron
ph 199– 6   muscles are as material as wood and *i·*
f 225– 1   What is it that binds man with *i·* shackles
ap 565– 7   rule all nations with a rod of *i·* :— *Rev.* 12 : 5.

irradiance
gl 584– 1   DAY. The *i·* of Life ; light,

irrational
o 352–31   not *i·* to tell the truth about ghosts.
p 433– 9   urges the jury not . . . to be warped by the *i·*,

irreconcilable
a 19– 6   for Truth and error are *i·*.

irrefutably
b 315–22   to prove *i·* how spiritual Truth destroys

irregular
p 431– 6   partaking of food at *i·* intervals,

irresistible
m 67–15   until an *i·* propulsion precipitates his
c 265–21   senses represent . . . death as *i·*,

irrespective
p 423–19   Mind his basis of operation *i·* of matter

irreverent
o 348–14   Are we *i·* towards sin,

Isaac
g 501– *   *appeared unto Abraham, unto I·,* — *Exod.* 6 : 3.

Isaiah
s 109–25   Scripture of *I·* is renewedly fulfilled :
g 514–21   the millennial estate pictured by *I·* :
    540– 5   In *I·* we read: "I make peace, — *Isa.* 45 : 7.

Isaiah's
a 52–13   *I·* graphic word concerning the

isolated
c 259– 3   nor is he an *i·*, solitary idea,

Israel
s 133– 7   so great faith, no, not in *I·*."— *Matt.* 8 : 10.
    135–18   by limiting the Holy One of *I·*
f 211–19   It should no longer be said in *I·* that
    226–29   as of yore, hold the children of *I·* in bondage.
c 256–12   "Hear, O *I·* : the Lord our God — *Deut.* 6 : 4.
b 308–30   then his name was changed to *I·*,
    309–10   He was no longer called Jacob, but *I·*,
    309–16   were to be called the children of *I·*,
ap 562–12   The twelve tribes of *I·* with all mortals,
    566– 1   As the children of *I·* were guided
    566–15   When *I·*, of the Lord beloved,
gl 583– 5   definition of

Israelites
s 133– 8   In Egypt, it was Mind which saved the *I·*
    133–10   The *I·* looked upon the brazen serpent,
o 351–27   *I·* centred their thoughts on the material

Israelites
g 524– 6   It was also found among the *I·*,
ap 559–29   the *I·* of old at the Paschal meal

Israelitish
o 351– 1   sprang from half-hidden *I·* history

Issachar
gl 589– 1   definition of

issue
m 67–13   the mariner works on and awaits the *i·*.
sp 83–13   here Science takes *i·* with popular religions.
s 126–15   point at *i·* between C. S. on the one hand
r 483–17   has called the world to battle over this *i·*

issued
pref x– 5   books on mental healing have since been *i·*,
    xii–13   the first periodical *i·* by Christian Scientists.

issues
sp 92– 4   erroneous . . . that matter holds in itself the *i·*
ph 181– 9   Can matter . . . hold the *i·* of life?"
f 216– 5   What has touched Life, God, to such strange *i·* ?
p 392–32   *i·* of pain or pleasure must come through mind,
g 526– 6   this statement that life *i·* from matter,

Ivanhoe
ap 566–14   Rebecca the Jewess in the story of *I·*,

J

Jacob
s 135– 6   presence of the God of *J·*."— *Psal.* 114 : 7.
b 308–16   *J·* was *alone*, wrestling with error,
    308–28   When *J·* was asked, "What is thy name?"—
        Gen. 32 : 27.
    308–32   Then *J·* questioned his deliverer,
    309–10   He was no longer called *J·*, but Israel,
    333–23   Abraham, *J·*, Moses, and the prophets
g 501– *   *unto Isaac, and unto J·* — *Exod.* 6 : 3.
gl 589– 4   definition of

Jacob's
b 309– 7   result of *J·* struggle thus appeared.
gl 581–15   ASHER (*J·* son). Hope and faith ;
    582– 4   BENJAMIN (*J·* son). A physical belief as to life,
    583–26   DAN (*J·* son). Animal magnetism ;
    586–21   GAD (*J·* son). Science;
    589– 1   ISSACHAR (*J·* son). A corporeal belief ;
    590–11   LEVI (*J·* son). A corporeal and sensual belief ;
    593–12   REUBEN (*J·* son). Corporeality ; sensuality ;

Jahr
s 152–29   *J·*, from *Aconitum* to *Zincum oxydatum*,
ph 179–26   The sedulous matron— studying her *J·*

James (*see also* **Apostle James**)
o 343– 4   *J·* said : "Show me thy faith— *Jas.* 2 : 18.

Japhet
gl 589– 8   definition of

Jar
p 363– 1   She bore an alabaster *j·* containing costly and
    363– 4   Breaking the sealed *j·*, she perfumed Jesus' feet

jarring
b 306–25   Undisturbed amid the *j·* testimony of the

jaws
f 243– 6   from the fiery furnace, from the *j·* of the lion,

jealous
g 541– 3   *J·* of his brother's gift, Cain seeks

jealousy
m 58–16   The narrowness and *j·*, which would
    59–20   more salutary . . . than stolid indifference or *j·*.
    64– 8   Pride, envy, or *j·* seems on most occasions
    68– 9   *J·* is the grave of affection.

Jefferson's
t 445–29   Recalling *J·* words about slavery,

Jehovah (*see also* **Jehovah's**)
appeal to
o 351–32   They might appeal to *J·*, but their prayer
called
g 523–20   because Deity therein is always called *J·*,
    523–27   the creator is called *J·*, or the Lord.
    524–17   that He should now be called *J·*?
corporeal
b 312–15   over the sense of a corporeal *J·*,
declared
b 338–27   *J·* declared the ground was accursed ;
name of
g 524– 8   the Supreme Being by the national name of *J·*,
    524– 9   In that name of *J·*, the
prophets of
sp 83– 3   What the prophets of *J·* did,
ritualistic
s 135–28   nor a special gift from a ritualistic *J·* ;

Jehovah
said
b 320–14   "And *J·* said, My spirit shall not
synonymous with
ap 576–27   term Lord, . . . is often synonymous with *J·*,
tribal
s 140–23   Jewish tribal *J·* was a man-projected God,
went before
gl 595–14   on Aaron's breast when he went before *J·*,
       ——
s 133–29   Jewish conception of God, as Yawah, *J·*,
f 229– 5   We should hesitate to say that *J·* sins or suffers
g 501– *   *by My name J· was I not known*   *Exod.* 6 : 3.
    520– 4   in the day that the Lord God [*J·*] — *Gen.* 2 : 4.
    520–20   the Lord God [*J·*] had not caused — *Gen.* 2 : 5.
    523–31   In the historic parts . . . it is usually *J·*,
    524–13   the Lord God [*J·*] formed — *Gen.* 2 : 7.
    525–31   made the Lord God [*J·*] to grow — *Gen.* 2 : 9.
    526–26   the Lord God [*J·*] took the man, — *Gen.* 2 : 15.
    527– 6   the Lord God [*J·*] commanded — *Gen.* 2 : 16.
    527–22   the Lord God [*J·*] formed — *Gen.* 2 : 19.
    528– 9   and the Lord God [*J·*, Yawah] — *Gen.* 2 : 21.
    528–12   rib, which the Lord God [*J·*] had — *Gen.* 2 : 22.
    529–14   which the Lord God [*J·*] had made.— *Gen.* 3 : 1.
    532–13   And the Lord God [*J·*] called unto — *Gen.* 3 : 9.
    534– 8   And the Lord God [*J·*] said — *Gen.* 3 : 14.
    536–30   And the Lord God [*J·*] said, — *Gen.* 3 : 22.
    537– 3   the Lord God [*J·*] sent him   *Gen.* 3 : 23.
    538–25   gotten a man from the Lord [*J·*].— *Gen.* 4 : 1.
    540– 4   an offering unto the Lord [*J·*].— *Gen.* 4 : 3.
    541– 6   And the Lord [*J·*] had respect — *Gen.* 4 : 4.
    541–19   And the Lord [*J·*] said unto — *Gen.* 4 : 9.
    541–27   And He [*J·*] said, . . . The voice of — *Gen.* 4 : 10.
    542–14   And the Lord [*J·*] said unto him, — *Gen.* 4 : 15.
    542–16   And the Lord [*J·*] set a mark — *Gen.* 4 : 15.
    542–28   from the presence of the Lord [*J·*]. — *Gen.* 4 : 16.
    543–31   day that the Lord God [*J·* God] — *Gen.* 2 4.
gl 590–20   LORD GOD.   *J·*.
    (*see also* **Lord God**)

Jehovah's
b 280–17   Moses declared as *J·* first command of the Ten :

Jehovistic
g 523–19   The other document is called the *J·*,

jeopardize
g 542–12   *j·* self-control, and mock divine mercy.

Jeremias
s 136–16   *J·*, or one of the prophets."— *Matt.* 16 : 14.

Jerusalem
a 42–12   his brief triumphal entry into *J·*
gl 589–12   definition of

jest
sp 72–29   joy of intercourse becomes the *j·* of sin, when

Jesus (*see also* **Jesus'**)
acknowledged
a 31– 4   *J·* acknowledged no ties of the flesh.
acted boldly
a 18–10   *J·* acted boldly, against the accredited
also said
g 554–22   *J·* also said, "Have not I — *John* 6 : 70.
answered
b 305–16   "Then answered *J·* and said — *John* 5 : 19.
p 364–10   *J·* answered by rebuking self-righteousness

Jesus

appeal of
  a 50–12 The appeal of *J·* was made both to his

approached
  p 362–12 (Mary Magdalene, . . . approached *J·*.

approved
  p 363–20 *J·* approved the answer,

asked
  s 132–26 *J·* asked, "When the Son of man— *Luke* 18 : 8.
  p 411–13 once *J·* asked the name of a disease,

beheld
  r 476–32 *J·* beheld in Science the perfect man,

benign thought of
  p 365– 7 benign thought of *J·*, finding utterance

betrayal of
  a 47–24 he plotted the betrayal of *J·*

birth of
  g 539–31 Science of creation, so conspicuous in the birth
         of *J·*,

blood of
  a 25– 6 material blood of *J·* was no more efficacious

bore our infirmities
  a 20–14 *J·* bore our infirmities ; he knew the error

bore our sins
  a 53–25 *J·* bore our sins in his body.

brought to light
  b 292–30 connection with his God, which *J·* brought to
         light.

called himself
  r 482–16 *J·* called himself "the Son of— *Matt.* 9 : 6.

called the body
  b 313–29 *J·* called the body, which . . . he raised

came to destroy
  r 474–18 Now *J·* came to destroy sin, sickness, and

career of
  a 30–23 throughout the whole earthly career of *J·*,

cast out evil
  sp 79–17 *J·* cast out evil spirits, or false beliefs.
  ph 185–22 *J·* cast out evil and healed the sick,

command of
  o 342–10 and in defiance of the direct command of *J·*,

commemorated
  a 33–31 that you have commemorated *J·* in his cup?

conspired against
  a 47–10 Judas conspired against *J·*.

corporeal
  s 141–16 Christ-spirit which governed the corporeal *J·*.
  b 334– 3 not that the corporeal *J·* was one with the
    334–14 the eternal Christ and the corporeal *J·*

could restore
  g 555–28 Our great example, *J·*, could restore the

crucifixion of
  a 24–20 Does . . . theology regard the crucifixion of *J·*
  r 497–20 the crucifixion of *J·* and his resurrection

declaration of
  o 361–14 This declaration of *J·*, understood,

declared
  f 234–27 *J·* declared that to look with desire on

defined
  g 554–20 *J·* defined this opposite of God and His

demonstrated
  s 110–25 *J·* demonstrated the power of C. S. to heal
  f 244– 5 On their basis *J·* demonstrated Life,
  b 274–16 *J·* demonstrated this great verity.
    332–19 *J·* demonstrated Christ ;
  p 430– 2 *J·* demonstrated this, healing the dying and
  r 494–11 *J·* demonstrated the divine power to heal
    494–15 *J·* demonstrated the inability of corporeality,

demonstrated by
  f 230–10 divine Principle, Love, as demonstrated by *J·*.
  b 272–31 C. S., as demonstrated by *J·*, alone reveals the
    321–31 the Science of being was demonstrated by *J·*,

demonstrated through
  b 316– 8 Truth, was demonstrated through *J·*

demonstration of
  s 139–25 neither . . . mar the demonstration of *J·*, nor

demonstrations of
  s 122– 9 exposed . . . by the demonstrations of *J·* ;
  f 243– 9 It crowned the demonstrations of *J·* with

disciple of
  b 324–19 Paul was not at first a disciple of *J·*

disciples of
  a 29–13 disciples of *J·* believe him the Son of God."

elicited from
  s 137–22 elicited from *J·* the benediction,

enabled
  a 51–31 which enabled *J·* to heal the sick,
  r 482–12 enabled *J·* to demonstrate his

endured the
  a 36–10 *J·* endured the shame, that he might

enjoined by
  a 55– 4 the idea of Christian healing enjoined by *J·* ;

Jesus

established
  s 136– 1 *J·* established his church and maintained
    138–17 *J·* established in the Christian era
  o 348–11 for *J·* established this foundational fact,
  r 473–26 *J·* established what he said by demonstration,

exaltation of
  b 313–18 the cause given for the exaltation of *J·*,

example of
  g 515– 2 its possessor to emulate the example of *J·*.

experienced
  a 38–21 *J·* experienced few of the pleasures of the

forbade him
  a 48–22 *J·* forbade him, thus rebuking resentment

foresaw
  a 41–22 *J·* foresaw the reception C. S. would have

furnished proofs
  r 472–11 *J·* furnished proofs of these statements.

furnished the proof
  b 317–28 *J·* furnished the proof that he was unchanged

had taught
  a 42–28 *J·* had taught his disciples the Science of this

healed sickness
  f 210–16 *J·* healed sickness and sin by

history of
  b 315–26 history of *J·* shows him to have been more

human
  b 334– 1 not that the human *J·* was or is eternal,
    334–20 before the human *J·* was incarnate

humanity of
  a 25–32 was made manifest in the humanity of *J·*.

illumines
  g 501– 7 *J·* illumines them, showing the poverty of

illustrated
  ph 171–14 *J·* illustrated the divine Principle

immaculate
  ap 562– 1 prophesied the coming of the immaculate *J·*,

inaugurated by
  b 288–14 foreshadowed by the. . .and inaugurated by *J·*,

incarnate
  o 350–28 Hence its embodiment in the incarnate *J·*,

inspired
  a 53–17 could not interpret . . . the discomfort which
         J· inspired

instructed
  b 271– 7 *J·* instructed his disciples whereby to heal the

introduced
  r 473–18 *J·* introduced the teaching and practice of
         Christianity,

justification of
  f 203–11 was really the justification of *J·*,

life of
  b 317– 6 Whosoever lives most the life of *J·*

loved
  f 236–28 *J·* loved little children because of their

manger of
  ap 575–29 followed it to the manger of *J·* ;

manifested in
  pr 12–13 divine healing Principle as manifested in *J·*,

mapped out
  a 38–24 *J·* mapped out the path for others.

marked out
  f 227–23 *J·* marked out the way.

martyrdom of
  gl 597–10 martyrdom of *J·* was the culminating sin of

memory of
  a 33–32 Are all who eat bread . . . in memory of *J·*

mission of
  s 131–26 The mission of *J·* confirmed prophecy,

mother of
  g 534– 3 to be the mother of *J·* and to behold at the

name of
  a 29–18 and gave to her ideal the name of *J·*

never intimated
  g 554–24 *J·* never intimated that God made a devil,

never spoke of
  s 147–32 *J·* never spoke of disease as dangerous

never taught
  f 232–19 *J·* never taught that drugs, food, air,

no terror for
  a 42–23 sin, sickness, and death had no terror for *J·*.

of Nazareth
  a 18– 3 *J·* of Nazareth taught and demonstrated
  b 313–23 *J·* of Nazareth was the most scientific man
    333–16 The advent of *J·* of Nazareth marked
  ap 564–11 the accusations against *J·* of Nazareth

once asked
  sp 86– 1 *J·* once asked, "Who touched— *Luke* 8 : 45.

once said
  s 109–28 *J·* once said of his lessons :
    131–18 *J·* once said : "I thank Thee,— *Luke* 10 : 21.
  g 530– 7 Knowing this, *J·* once said,

origin of
  g 539–27 The divine origin of *J·* gave him more than

overcame death
  a 39–13 *J·* overcame death and the grave instead of

Jesus

overcome by
c 264–23   sickness and death were overcome by *J·*,
physical
a 51–26   vengeance, inflicted on the physical *J·*,
practice of
a 53–10   Because the divine Principle and practice of *J·*
practised
s 147–12   since *J·* practised these rules
prayed
a 32–22   yet *J·* prayed and gave them bread.
   32–25   *J·* prayed ; he withdrew from the
   38–18   *J·* prayed, not for the twelve only,
preached and
o 344–19   the C. S. which *J·* preached and practised
preached by
s 141– 3   and the truth preached by *J·*.
prepared by
p 388–21   If food was prepared by *J·* for his disciples,
presented
a 25–16   *J·* presented the ideal of God better than
g 534–15   the idea of divine power, which *J·* presented,
presented by
b 316–24   spiritual idea of God, as presented by *J·*,
proved
a 27–10   That Life is God, *J·* proved by his
ph 168–20   an authority which *J·* proved to be false
b 314–32   *J·* proved them wrong by his resurrection,
r 473–29   *J· proved* the Principle, which heals the sick
   486–14   *J·* proved by the prints of the nails, that
purposed
s 138– 2   *J·* purposed founding his society,
raised up
o 341– *   *that raised up J· from the dead—* Rom. 8 : 11.
realized
a 47–32   *J·* realized the utter error of a belief in
reappearing of
a 45–28   reappearing of *J·* was not the return of a spirit
rebuked
m 67–31   *J·* rebuked the suffering from any such cause
p 363–14   *J·* rebuked them with a short story or parable.
g 509–30   *J·* rebuked the material thought of his
record of
a 46–27   which closed the earthly record of *J·*,
referred
b 333–28   *J·* referred to this unity of his
represented
b 316–12   *J·* represented Christ, the true idea of
reputation of
a 53– 8   reputation of *J·* was the very opposite of his
restored Lazarus
ap 75 13   *J·* restored Lazarus by the understanding
rose higher
a 43–21   *J·* rose higher in demonstration because of
said
a 20– 7   *J·* said, "The publicans and the— *Matt.* 21 : 31.
   31–25   Referring to the materiality of the age, *J·* said :
   31–29   Again, foreseeing the persecution . . . . *J·* said :
   38–10   *J·* said : "These signs shall follow— *Mark* 16 : 17.
m 00 06   *J·* said, "The children of— *Luke* 20 ; 34.
sp 75 12   *J·* said of Lazarus : "Our friend— *John* 11 : 11.
s 134–26   *J·* said : "I knew that Thou— *John* 11 : 42.
ph 196–12   "Fear him which is able to . . . said *J·*.— Matt. 10 : 28.
f 201– 5   *J·* said, "No man can serve two— *Matt.* 6 : 24.
c 259–19   *J·* said : "Be ye therefore perfect,— *Matt.* 5 : 48.
   267–15   *J·* said : "For whosoever shall— *Matt.* 12 : 50.
b 273 8   *J·* said : "Ye do err, not knowing— *Matt.* 22 : 29.
   292–20   *J·* said : "Why do ye not understand— *John* 8 : 43
   324–32   *J·* said substantially, "He that— *see John* 11 : 26.
   326– 4   *J·* said, "He that believeth— *John* 14 : 12.
   328–22   knowing that there is no material law, *J·* said :
o 341– 8   *J·* said, "Blessed are the— *Matt.* 5 : 8.
   357– 7   *J·* said of personified evil, that it was
p 364–29   as *J·* said of the unwelcome truth,
   422– 2   Wiser than his persecutors, *J·* said :
   429–31   *J·* said . . . "If a man keep my— *John* 8 : 51.
   442–26   *J·* said, "Fear not,— *Luke* 12 : 32.
r 476–29   When speaking of God's children, . . . *J·* said,
   494– 2   *J·* said : "Destroy this temple— *John* 2 : 19.
g 539–23   *J·* said : "Do men gather— *Matt.* 7 : 16.
ap 564–26   *J·* said, quoting a line from the Psalms,
gl 580–30   *J·* said of the devil, "He was a— *John* 8 : 44.
   585– 3   *J·* said, referring to spiritual perception,
   586– 5   *J·* said, thinking of the outward vision,
says
p 410– 4   "This is life eternal," says *J·*,— *John* 17 : 3.
self-same
b 317–22   self-same *J·* whom they had loved before the
sent a message
a 27– 1   *J·* sent a message to John the Baptist,
sent forth
a 27–22   *J·* sent forth seventy students at one time,
   49– 7   Where were the seventy whom *J·* sent forth?

Jesus

spares us not
a 26– 5   *J·* spares us not one individual experience,
speaks of
ap 564–13   Revelator speaks of *J·* as the Lamb of God
spiritual
b 314–24   the spiritual *J·* was imperceptible to them.
spoke
p 367–18   of which *J·* spoke to his disciples, when he said :
ap 576–16   as when *J·* spoke of his material body
suffered
pr 11–18   *J·* suffered for our sins, not to annul the
a 24–15   the understanding, in which *J·* suffered and
sufferings of
a 34–11   commemorated the sufferings of *J·*
taught
a 25–13   *J·* taught the way of Life by demonstration,
   30–32   work out our salvation in the way *J·* taught.
   43–17   final demonstration of the truth which *J·* taught,
   43–28   The Science *J·* taught and lived
sp 94– 1   *J·* taught but one God, one Spirit,
s 135–26   Christianity as *J·* taught it was not a creed,
b 306– 5   *J·* taught them how death was to be overcome
r 477– 4   *J·* taught that the kingdom of God is intact,
taught by
a 41–28   The truth taught by *J·*, the elders scoffed at.
teachings of
b 269–23   on the teachings of *J·*, of his apostles,
   324–24   to follow the example and teachings of *J·*,
the anointed
b 313– 4   "*J·* the anointed," Jesus the God-crowned
the Christ
b 313– 2   The term Christ Jesus, or *J·* the Christ
   333 14   name of our Master . . . was *J·* the Christ :
r 473–16   hence the duality of *J·* the Christ.
the God-crowned
b 313– 4   "Jesus the anointed," *J·* the God-crowned
the man
a 26–13   This Christ, or divinity of the man *J·*,
   29–28   the divine Principle of the man *J·*,
s 116–17   the divine Principle, of the man *J·* :
r 473–24   rather than personality or the man *J·*,
ap 561–17   coincidence, shown in the man *J·*,
   565–11   in order that the man *J·*, . . . might never
theology of
s 138–30   It was this theology of *J·* which healed
p 369– 8   and comprehends the theology of *J·*
the true
b 314–20   This materialism lost sight of the true *J·* ;
time of
pr 6–30   magistrate, who lived in the time of *J·*,
title of
b 333– 9   Christ is . . . the divine title of *J·*.
told Simon
p 364–19   *J·* told Simon that such seekers as he
took bread
a 32–15   *J·* took bread, and blessed it— *Matt.* 26 : 26.
vanquished every
a 45– 1   *J·* vanquished every material obstacle,
walked on the
b 273–24   *J·* walked on the waves, fed the multitude,
was able
g 555–30   *J·* was able to present himself unchanged
was known
a 46– 5   In the walk to Emmaus, *J·* was known to
was the mediator
b 315–31   *J·* was the mediator between Spirit and the
was the offspring
a 29–32   *J·* was the offspring of Mary's self-conscious
was "the way"
a 46–25   *J·* was "the way ;"— *John* 14 : 6.
we adore
a 26– 1   While we adore *J·*, and the heart overflows
which identified
a 46– 8   The divine Spirit, which identified *J·* thus
wielded by
s 142–22   as twisted and wielded by *J·*,
words of
o 358–19   Why are the words of *J·* more frequently
g 539– 2   In the words of *J·*, it (evil, devil) is
work of
a 28–16   nor the work of *J·* was generally understood.

   pr 6–23   *J·* uncovered and rebuked sin before he
   8– 8   such externals are spoken of by *J·* as
   14–19   Hence the hope of the promise *J·* bestows :
   15– 3   So spake *J·*. The closet typifies the
a 19– 6   *J·* aided in reconciling man to God
   19–29   *J·* urged the commandment,
   24–25   presentation, after death, of the material *J·*,
   26–10   The Christ was the Spirit which *J·* implied
   26–15   Love gave *J·* authority over sin,
   30–12   *J·* would not have been appreciable to
   30–16   Not so did *J·*, the new executor for God,
   31–16   the practical Truth, which makes *J·*
   32–28   The Passover, which *J·* ate with his disciples

Jesus

a 40– 8 adjusts the balance as *J·* adjusted it.
40–17 Was it just for *J·* to suffer?
40–20 If a career so great and good as that of *J·*
41– 2 into the Shekinah into which *J·* has passed
41–14 The proofs . . . which *J·* gave by casting out
42–20 This error *J·* met with divine Science
43– 5 enabled the disciples to understand what *J·*
44– 5 precincts of the tomb gave *J·* a refuge
44–21 to sustain *J·* in his proof of man's . . . power?
44–28 His disciples believed *J·* to be dead
45–22 They who earliest saw *J·* after the
46–18 *J·* caused him to examine the nail-prints
47–19 placed a gulf between *J·* and his betrayer,
48– 8 *J·* turned forever away from earth
48–17 *J·* had not one of them,
49–32 esteemed *J·* as "stricken, smitten of— *Isa.* 53 : 4.
50–30 real cross, which *J·* bore up the hill
51– 6 *J·* could have withdrawn himself from his
51–12 *J·* could give his temporal life
51–28 *J·* was unselfish.
52–11 world's hatred of the just and perfect *J·*,
52–31 the hypocrite, called *J·* a glutton and a
53– 3 *J·* was no ascetic.
53–28 at the time when *J·* felt our infirmities,
55– 6 Christian era did *J·* no more injustice than
64–18 the time cometh of which *J·* spake,
m 56– 2 Reading his thoughts, *J·* added :
sp 75–17 Had *J·* believed that Lazarus had
79–19 *J·* did his own work by the one Spirit.
85–15 *J·*, as he once journeyed with his students,
85–24 *J·* knew the generation to be wicked
86– 4 *J·* knew, as others did not, that it was not
86– 9 *J·* possessed more spiritual susceptibility
93– 2 Remember *J·*, who nearly nineteen centuries ago
94–21 Of the ten lepers whom *J·* healed,
94–27 blasphemer who should hint that *J·* used
94–32 *J·* could injure no one by his Mind-reading.
95– 5 traduced . . . as they would be to-day if *J·*
s 107– * *by the revelation of J· Christ.— Gal.* 1 : 12.
117–21 the miracles (marvels) wrought by *J·*
117–29 *J·* bade his disciples beware of the leaven of
123–25 so-called miracles of *J·* did not specially
132– 1 *J·* returned an affirmative reply,
132–31 once pointed his disciples to *J·* as
133– 2 and sent the inquiry to *J·*,
133– 6 centurion of whose faith *J·* himself declared,
136– 9 How did *J·* heal the sick?
136–18 some of the people believed that *J·* was a
136–25 even Herod doubted if *J·* was controlled by
136–32 *J·* patiently persisted in teaching and
137–13 *J·* completely eschewed the narrow opinion
138–10 *J·* explained his cures, which appeared
138–15 was the foundation on which *J·* built.
141–14 *J·* elaborated the fact that the healing effect
143– 6 else *J·* would have recommended and
146–28 anterior to the period in which *J·* lived.
157–21 why did *J·* not employ them
ph 170– 7 Did *J·* understand the economy of man
170–19 *J·* healed the sick and cast out error,
200–26 *J·* Christ, and him crucified."— *I Cor.* 2 : 2.
200–28 *J·* Christ, and him glorified.
f 206–16 as *J·* showed with the loaves and the fishes,
227–31 *J·* would not have disregarded those laws
233– 5 by the power of Spirit, as *J·* destroyed them.
c 260– 5 can depict the form and face of *J·*,
b 268– * *and with His Son J· Christ.— I John* 1 : 3.
271–24 eternal life, not the death of *J·*, is its outcome.
286–13 was put aside . . . by this original man, *J·*.
292–31 *J·* showed that a mortal man is not the
314– 3 *J·* waited until the mortal or fleshly sense
314–12 When *J·* spoke of reproducing his body,
315–25 The divine conception of *J·* pointed to
317– 1 *J·* uttered things which had been
317–30 To this dull and doubting disciple *J·* remained
325– 7 *J·* gave the true idea of being, which results in
325–28 the divine Science which ushered *J·* into
328–19 can it be said that they explained it . . . as *J·* did,
329–10 Be thankful that *J·*, . . . did these things,
332– 9 *J·* was born of Mary.
332–18 The corporeal man *J·* was human.
332–23 *J·* was the son of a virgin.
333– 4 word *Christ* is not properly a synonym for *J·*,
333– 4 *J·* was a human name, which belonged to
333–32 By these sayings *J·* meant, not that
334– 8 greater, infinitely greater, than the fleshly *J·*,
334–11 *J·* appeared as a bodily existence.
334–16 material concept, or *J·*, disappeared,
334–30 a reference to the human sense of *J·* crucified.
o 343–14 *J·* strips all disguise from error, when
351–17 proof of Christianity, which *J·* required,
352– 8 To *J·*, not materiality, but spirituality,
356– 9 *J·* reasoned on this subject practically,
356–15 *J·* knew, "It is the spirit that— *John* 6 : 63.
358–17 illustrated by the prophets, by *J·*,
361–12 *J·* Christ is not God, as *J·* himself declared,

Jesus

p 362– 2 *J·* was once the honored guest of a
363– 8 Did *J·* spurn the woman?
365–21 commendation as the Magdalen gained from *J·*,
369–16 *J·* never asked if disease were acute
393–25 *J·* declares that "the light of— *Matt.* 6 : 22.
398– 1 Sometimes *J·* called a disease by name,
398– 8 concessions which *J·* was willing to make
410– 9 *J·* Christ, whom Thou hast sent."— *John* 17 : 3.
411–16 Thereupon *J·* cast out the evil,
411–18 *J·* caused the evil to be self-seen
r 473–12 *J·* is the name of the man who,
473–15 *J·* is the human man, and Christ is the divine
474–21 evils which *J·* lived to destroy
482–19 *J·* was the highest human concept of the
493–28 If *J·* awakened Lazarus from the
494– 9 *J·* pointed the way for them.
g 542– 2 would kill *J·* that it might be rid of
ap 562– 4 the fatherhood of God, which *J·*
564–14 Since *J·* must have been tempted in all points,
564–18 *J·* "opened not his mouth."— *Isa.* 53 : 7.
575–14 Did not *J·* illustrate the truths he taught
gl 589–16 definition of
598–15 What *J·* gave up was indeed air,
(*see also* **Christ Jesus, Galilean Prophet, Lamb, Master, Nazarene, Prince of Peace, Son, Teacher, Way-shower**)

Jesus'

pref xi–10 healing of C. S. results now, as in *J·* time,
pr 4–30 enable us to follow *J·* example.
7– 3 evidence that *J·* reproof was pointed
10– 6 If good enough to profit by *J·* cup of
11– 1 *J·* prayer, "Forgive us our debts,"— *Matt.* 6 : 12.
a 19– 8 the divine Principle of *J·* teachings,
19–19 will help us to understand *J·* atonement
20– 8 *J·* history made a new calendar,
24–23 Does spiritualism find *J·* death necessary
25– 4 The efficacy of *J·* spiritual offering is
26–21 *J·* teaching and practice of Truth involved
27–17 *J·* parables explain Life as never mingling with
27–29 *J·* persecutors made their strongest attack
28– 2 they only hindered the success of *J·* mission.
30– 5 *J·* advent in the flesh partook partly of
33– 1 this supper closed forever *J·* ritualism
37–16 When will *J·* professed followers learn
42– 1 *J·* life proved, . . . that God is Love,
43– 3 The magnitude of *J·* work,
43–11 *J·* last proof was the highest,
43–16 *J·* persecutors had mocked and
45– 7 *J·* deed was for the enlightenment of men
45–32 *J·* students, not sufficiently advanced
46–20 *J·* unchanged physical condition after
47– 2 discernment of *J·* teachings and
47–14 people were in doubt concerning *J·* teachings.
48–27 acquiescence with the demands of *J·* enemies.
50– 7 wrung from *J·* lips the awful cry,
50–22 Even what they did say,— that *J·* teachings
54–12 the inspiration of *J·* intense human sacrifice.
m 56– 4 *J·* concessions . . . to material methods
sp 75–22 you can then exercise *J·* spiritual power
s 117–27 feebly transmits *J·* works and words.
131–29 *J·* works established his claim
132–16 *J·* system of healing received no aid . . . from
141– 5 Few understand or adhere to *J·* divine precepts
142–18 As in *J·* time, so to-day, tyranny and pride
147– 3 divine Principle, upon which *J·* healing was
f 210– 6 are set forth in *J·* demonstrations,
c 266–24 Mortals must follow *J·* sayings
b 269– 5 *J·* demonstrations sift the chaff from the wheat,
272–13 *J·* parable of "the sower"— *Mark* 4 : 14.
312–31 *J·* spiritual origin and his demonstration
315–21 *J·* spiritual origin and understanding
317–12 blessed benedictions rest upon *J·* followers
324–20 but a persecutor of *J·* followers.
328–28 *J·* promise is perpetual.
o 343–25 those apostles who were *J·* students,
360–31 on the very basis of *J·* words and works.
p 363– 4 she perfumed *J·* feet with the oil,
369–11 All these deeds manifested *J·* control
382–10 receive a useful rebuke from *J·* precept,
428– 4 demonstration of the facts of Soul in *J·* way
t 446–22 enthrones faith in Truth, and verifies *J·* word :
r 494– 7 God, who needed no help from *J·* example
497–13 We acknowledge *J·* atonement
ap 573–32 When you read this, remember *J·* words.
576–16 Revelator was familiar with *J·* use of this word,
gl 598–10 In the record of *J·* supposed death, we read :

Jew

sp 85–23 Both *J·* and Gentile may have had acute
o 360–30 while to-day, *J·* and Christian can unite in
360–32 The *J·* believes that the Messiah or Christ
361– 6 The *J·* who believes in the First Commandment
361– 7 Thus the *J·* unites with the Christian's doctrine

jewel

m 66– 5 Wears yet a precious *j·* in his head.

Jewess
ap 566–13 Rebecca the *J·* in the story of Ivanhoe,

Jewish
a 32–11 used on convivial occasions and in *J·* rites,
42– 3 *J·* theology gave no hint of the unchanging love
s 133–25 one of the *J·* accusations against him who
133–29 The *J·* conception of God, as Yawah,
140–23 *J·* tribal Jehovah was a man-projected God,
o 350–31 In *J·* worship the Word was materially explained,
r 466–23 Heathen mythology and *J·* theology have
ap 576–28 expresses the *J·* concept, not yet elevated to
gl 596–29 *J·* women wore veils over their faces

Jew's
o 361–11 Thus he virtually unites with the *J·* belief

Jews
a 32– 7 Among the *J·* it was an ancient custom
sp 70– * *Then said the J· unto him,— John* 8 : 52.
s 135–18 danger of repeating the offence of the *J·*
b 314–10 The *J·*, who sought to kill this man of God,
o 352– 7 took a diametrically opposite view.
360–28 the *J·* put to death the Galilean Prophet,

Job (see also Job's)
s 115– 8 *J·* says : "The ear trieth words,— *Job* 34 : 3.
c 262–17 *J·* said : "I have heard of Thee— *Job* 42 : 5.
b 320–30 is continually quoted as if *J·* intended
321– 3 as may be seen by studying the book of *J·*.
o 360–22 Hear the wisdom of *J·*, as given in the
p 411– 1 Said *J·* : "The thing which I greatly— *Job* 3 : 25.
g 552–14 corresponds with that of *J·*, when he says,

Job's
c 262–19 Mortals will echo *J·* thought, when the

John (see also St. John and Apostle John)
a 36–12 He was forsaken by all save *J·*,
p 373–17 declare, through the exalted thought of *J·*,
t 459– 3 Paul and *J·* had a clear apprehension that,
g 625–17 In the Gospel of *J·*, it is declared that
ap 561–13 To *J·*, "the bride" and— *Rev.* 21 : 9.
561–10 *J·* saw the human and divine coincidence,
574–11 carried *J·* away in spirit
576–19 *J·* saw heaven and earth

John's
gl 598– 2 as in the passage in *J·* Gospel,

John
the Baptist
a 27– 1 Jesus sent a message to *J·* the Baptist,
s 132–28 Did the doctrines of *J·* the Baptist confer
136–15 "Some say that thou art *J·* the Baptist ;— *Matt.* 16 ; 14,
ap 558–19 prophetically described by *J·* the Baptist
561–32 the Baptist prophesied the coming of
562– 1 *J·* saw in those days the spiritual idea

a 27– 3 "Go your way, and tell *J·*— *Luke* 7 : 22.
27– 7 In other words : Tell *J·* what the
m 56– 2 came to him for baptism, *J·* was astounded.
s 132– 5 "Go and show *J·* again— *Matt.* 11 : 4.
136–19 believed that . . . the spirit of *J·* or of Elias.
136–27 "*J·* have I beheaded :— *Luke* 9 : 9.

John's
s 131–31 In reply to *J·* inquiry,
133– 3 Was *J·* faith greater than that of the

Johnson, Dr. James
s 163– 6 Dr. James *J·*, Surgeon to

join
s 122–17 sky and tree-tops apparently *j·* hands,

joined
m 56– * *What therefore God hath j·— Matt.* 19 : 6.
60–14 what she hath not *j·* together.

joining
b 339–15 He is *j·* in a conspiracy against himself,

joint
s 160–31 Is a stiff *j·* or a contracted muscle
p 408–22 A dislocation of the tarsal *j·* would produce
408–24 the tarsal *j·* is less intimately connected with

joints
s 162–21 ankylosed *j·* have been made supple,
p 402– 6 dislocated *j·*, and spinal vertebræ.
418–30 inflammation, pain, deformed *j·*,
423–13 searches "the *j·* and marrow,"— *Heb.* 4 : 12.

Jona
s 137–28 common names, Simon Bar-jona, or son of *J·* ;

Jordan
s 135– 2 Thou *J·*, that thou wast driven— *Psal.* 114 : 5.

Joseph
r 482–17 Son of man," but not the son of *J·*.— *Matt.* 9 : 6.
gl 589–19 definition of

Joshua
a 29–18 the name of Jesus— that is, *J·*, or Saviour.
s 139– 7 Moses proved the . . . so did *J·*, Elijah, and
b 333– 7 it is identical with the name *J·*,

jot
pref ix– 1 She also began to *j·* down her thoughts
f 239– 6 which weigh not one *j·* in the balance of God,

jottings
pref ix– 2 these *j·* were only infantile lispings

journeyed
sp 85–15 as he once *j·* with his students,

journeying
a 21–16 If . . . we are not *j·* together.
ap 574– 4 adapted to console the weary pilgrim, *j·*

joy (see also joy's)
affords us
ph 194–31 The light which affords us *j·* gave him a belief of
and sorrow
f 246– 2 *j·* and sorrow, sickness and health,
c 262–22 the false estimate of . . . *j·* and sorrow,
and strength
p 365–31 is not giving to mind or body the *j·* and strength
bringing
p 435–13 but good deeds are immortal, bringing *j·*
is spiritual
c 265–29 quickly inform us . . . that *j·* is spiritual.
life and
g 536–25 material conception of life and *j·*,
light or
g 548–12 Earth has little light or *j·* for mortals before
new pinions to
m 58– 3 Unity of spirit gives new pinions to *j·*,
not the master of
b 304–12 for sorrow is not the master of *j·* ;
of its presence
ph 175–10 The *j·* of its presence, its beauty and fragrance,
or grief
p 377–15 A sudden *j·* or grief has caused
promised
ap 566– 6 and anticipating the promised *j·*,
sinless
sp 76–22 The sinless *j·*,— tho perfect harmony
sorrow and
s 125–14 pain and painlessness, sorrow and *j·*,
source of
p 377– 4 affliction is often the source of *j·*,
spiritual
c 265–24 gained stronger desires for spiritual *j·*
sunshine of
m 66– 8 We do not half remember this in the sunshine of *j·*
turned into
pr 14–17 Sorrow is turned into *j·* when the body is
with
a 21–14 at last he finishes his course with *j·*.
o 359 23 In childhood, she often listened with *j·* to

sp 72–28 *j·* of intercourse becomes the jest of sin, when
an 106 27 fruit of the Spirit is love, *j·*,— *Gal.* 5 : 22.
f 248–16 Is it imperfection, *j·*, sorrow, sin, suffering?
b 298–20 *j·* is no longer a trembler, nor is hope a cheat.
304–11 *j·* cannot be turned into sorrow,
324– 3 and *j·* to see them disappear,
ap 562–26 remembering no more her sorrow for *j·* that the
575–23 the *j·* of the whole earth,— *Psal.* 48 : 2.

joyful
pref xii–24 *j·* to bear consolation to the sorrowing
a 34–31 *j·* meeting on the shore of the Galilean Sea !

joyfully
g 521–10 *j·* acknowledging now and forever

joyous
g 514– 6 Mind, *j·* in strength, dwells in the realm of

joy's
m 58– 3 or else *j·* drooping wings trail in dust.

joys
additional
m 58–15 With additional *j·*, benevolence should grow
and its
b 299–11 to higher ideals of life and its *j·*.
and sorrows
gl 587–23 motives, affections, *j·*, and sorrows.
and triumphs
a 41– 4 must come through the *j·* and triumphs of the
and victories
a 39– 9 trials and self-denials, as well as *j·* and victories,
fancied
f 252–28 says : . . . all my fancied *j·* are fatal.
fleeting
f 241– 7 Sin breaks in. . .and carries off their fleeting *j·*.
human
m 66–18 remember how fleeting are human *j·*.
of Soul
p 390–11 pleasures and pains of sense for the *j·* of Soul.

joys
  of Spirit
    m 66–14 Love propagates anew the higher *j·* of Spirit,
    f 242– 7 a great step towards the *j·* of Spirit,
  personal
    c 266–11 even if you cling to a sense of personal *j·*,
  supposed
    g 536–21 Their supposed *j·* are cheats.
  your
    p 397–11 as directly as you enhance your *j·*

Juda
  g 514–10 "the lion of the tribe of *J·*,"— *Rev. 5 : 5.*

Judæa
  s 147–13 practised these rules on the hills of *J·*

Judah
  gl 589–23 definition of

Judah's
  ap 566–21 And oh, when stoops on *J·* path

Judaic
  s 140–19 *J·* and other rituals are but types and
  gl 597– 3 *J·* religion consisted mostly of rites and

Judaism
  s 133–19 *J·* was the antithesis of Christianity,
    133–20 *J·* engendered the limited form of

Judas
  a 47–10 *J·* conspired against Jesus.
    47–17 distance between *J·* and his Master.
    48–17 *J·* had the world's weapons.
  c 260– 6 while holding in thought the character of *J·*.
  g 554–24 This he said of *J·*, one of Adam's race.

Judas Iscariot
  a 47–17 *J· I·* knew this.

Judas'
  a 47–20 this spiritual distance inflamed *J·* envy.

Judge (*see also* **Judge's**)
  p 432–16 The *J·* asked if by doing good to his neighbor,
    433–13 As the *J·* proceeds, the prisoner grows restless.
    437– 9 before the *J·* of our higher tribunal,
    442– 4 "Shall not the *J·* of all the earth— *Gen.* 18 : 25.

judge
  an 105– 3 Courts and juries *j·* and sentence mortals
  b 299–11 Ought we not then to *j·* the knowledge
  o 344–18 the Scriptural precept, "*J·* not."— *Matt.* 7 : 1.
  p 391– 5 delivered to the judgment of Truth, Christ, the
    j· will
    391–23 your adversary will deliver you to the *j·*
    391–24 and the *j·* will sentence you.
    404– 1 in order to *j·* the case according to C. S.
    405–12 They will deliver you to the *j·*, the arbiter of
    405–13 The *j·* will deliver you to justice,
    435–30 "Sittest thou to *j·*— *Acts* 23 : 3.
  t 443–12 "*J·* not, that ye be not judged."— *Matt.* 7 : 1.
    444–18 "*j·* righteous judgment,"— *John* 7 : 24.
    459– 8 *J·* not the future advancement of C. S. by the
  g 523– 1 might so *j·* from an unintelligent perusal of

judged
  f 239– 9 let worth be *j·* according to wisdom,
  t 443–13 "Judge not, that ye be not *j·*."— *Matt.* 7 : 1.

Judge Justice
  p 437–28 *J· J·* of the Supreme Court of Spirit

Judge Medicine
  p 430–25 and *J· M·* is on the bench.
    433– 2 *J· M·* arises, and with great solemnity
    433– 8 *J· M·*, urges the jury not to allow their
    433–18 *J· M·* then proceeds to pronounce the
    435–28 what jurisdiction had his Honor, *J· M·*,
    435–33 neither shall *J· M·* condemn him ;
    436–26 *J· M·* sat in judgment on the case,

Judge's
  p 433–26 "May God have mercy . . . the *J·* solemn

judges
  b 296–26 Mortal mind *j·* by the testimony of the
  p 434–11 Witnesses, *j·*, and jurors, who were
    439–28 witnesses, jurors, and *j·*, to be offenders,

judging
  s 157– 2 C. S. . . . in *j·* and destroying disease.
  f 204–19 *J·* them by their fruits, they are corrupt.
  t 447– 9 may render you incapable of knowing or *j·*

judgment
  by which
    b 291–30 the *j·* by which mortal man is divested of
  deluded the
    s 121–21 deluded the *j·* and induced false conclusions.
  misguide the
    f 206– 5 else it will misguide the *j·*
  mistaken in
    t 455–19 may be mistaken in *j·* and demonstration,
  no final
    b 291–28 No final *j·* awaits mortals,

judgment
  of Truth
    p 391– 5 when thou art delivered to the *j·* of Truth,
  pass
    o 345–17 well enough to pass *j·* upon them.
  righteous
    t 444–18 "judge righteous *j·*,"— *John* 7 : 24.
  sat in
    p 436–26 Judge Medicine sat in *j·* on the case,
  their
    p 433– 8 not to allow their *j·* to be warped

  an 106–15 Let this age, which sits in *j·* on C. S.,
  s 128–28 and not upon the *j·* of false sensation.

judgment-day
  b 291–28 the *j·* of wisdom comes hourly

judicial
  p 437–26 was overthrowing the *j·* proceedings of

jugular
  s 122–24 the severance of the *j·* vein

juices
  ph 175–24 was not so severe upon the gastric *j·*.

jungle
  p 378–12 sent it cowering back into the *j·*.

juries
  an 105– 3 Courts and *j·* judge and sentence mortals

jurisdiction
  an 105– 6 To say that these tribunals have no *j·*
    105–12 over which courts hold *j·*?
  f 218–16 believing . . . that the divine Mind has no *j·*
  p 379– 6 The real *j·* of the world is in Mind,
    435–28 what *j·* had his Honor, Judge Medicine,
    435–31 The only *j·* to which the prisoner can submit

Jurisprudence
  p 437–23 Physiology, Scholastic Theology, and *J·*

jurisprudence
  p 441–32 Our great Teacher of mental *j·* speaks of him

juror
  f 238–25 Society is a foolish *j·*, listening only to

jurors
  p 434–12 Witnesses, judges, and *j·*, who were at the
    437–11 and before its *j·*, the Spiritual Senses,
    439–28 witnesses, *j·*, and judges, to be offenders,
    441–27 personal *j·* in the Court of Error

Jury
  p 442– 5 The *J·* of Spiritual Senses agreed at once

jury
  p 430–24 Greed and Ingratitude, constitute the *j·*.
    433– 3 addresses the *j·* of Mortal Minds,
    433– 8 Judge Medicine, urges the *j·* not to allow
    433–10 The *j·* must regard in such cases only
    433–15 The case is given to the *j·*.
    433–16 and the *j·* returns a verdict of
    436–27 charged the *j·*, twelve Mortal Minds,

just
  a 36–31 in the suffering of the *j·* for the unjust.
    40–17 Was it *j·* for Jesus to suffer?
    47–11 ingratitude and hatred towards that *j·* man
    52–11 the world's hatred of the *j·* and perfect Jesus,
  s 126–23 *j·* as I have discovered them.
    164– 9 It is *j·* to say that generally the
  ph 168–14 through *j·* this false belief.
    193– 4 had *j·* probed the ulcer on the hip,
    193–30 the case, occurred *j·* as I have narrated.
  f 251–12 works out the nothingness of error in *j·* these
  b 321– 1 an interpretation which is *j·* the opposite of
  o 344–17 it would be *j·* to observe the
    348– 9 one disease can be *j·* as much a delusion as
    another.
    360–24 Shall mortal man be more *j·* than— *Job* 4 : 17.
  p 372–28 a *j·* acknowledgment of Truth
    376– 6 *J·* so is it with the greatest sin.
    391–27 be *j·* to yourself and to others.
    402– 3 However, it is but *j·* to say that
    402–24 illustrates the fact *j·* stated.
    411– 6 *j·* as a person replies more readily when
    425– 3 You will have humors, *j·* so long as
    435–23 no demand, . . . renders it *j·* to punish a man for
    440–30 I appeal to the *j·* and equitable decisions of
  t 443– * *teach a j· man, and he will—* *Prov.* 9 : 9.
    445–31 when I remember that God is *j·*,"
    453–24 treat sickness mentally *j·* as you would sin,
  r 493–23 *j·* as it removes any other sense of
    497–27 and to be merciful, *j·*, and pure.
  g 522–28 Scripture *j·* preceding declares God's work to

Justice
  p 434–13 before the bar of *J·* and eternal Truth.
    437– 9 in the presence of divine *J·*,
    440–34 the Chief *J·* of the Supreme Court,

justice

and affection
gl 592–13 the union of *j·* and affection,
and love
a 50–10 would impugn the *j·* and love of a father
approves
a 22–31 cancels the debt only when *j·* approves.
avoidance of
g 542–11 avoidance of *j·* and the denial of truth
common
o 357– 1 In common *j·*, we must admit that God
consigns the lie
g 542–24 To envy's own hell, *j·* consigns the lie
defies
an 105– 9 while mortal mind, . . . defies *j·* and is
demands
gl 592–14 *j·* demands penalties under the law.
demonstrating
f 224–23 demonstrating *j·* and meeting the needs of
denying
p 434–32 Denying *j·* to the body, that court
divine
a 105–10 Divine *j·* will manacle him.
f 225–18 breathing the omnipotence of divine *j·*,
b 293–25 The manifestations of evil, which counterfeit divine *j·*,
hands of
p 432–27 hands of *j·*, *alias* nature's so-called law ;
honesty and
an 106– 4 against the free course of honesty and *j·*,
human
g 542–20 let human *j·* pattern the divine.
law and
p 434– 5 Some exclaim, "It is contrary to law and *j·*."
law of
pr 5–10 there is no discount in the law of *j·*
a 36–20 the immortal law of *j·* as well as of mercy.
marks the sinner
g 542–22 *J·* marks the sinner, and teaches mortals
mercy and
g 538– 7 Radiant with mercy and *j·*, the sword of Truth

justice

outraged
p 440–17 Wherefore, then, in the name of outraged *j·*,
requires
a 22–30 *J·* requires reformation of the sinner.
sense of
p 390–14 Let your higher sense of *j·* destroy the false
timid
f 238–29 To reconstruct timid *j·* and place the fact
to Christian Science
s 141–29 Let our pulpits do *j·* to C. S.
to himself
a 18– 7 not only in *j·* to himself, but in mercy to
to Truth
b 280– 9 Finite belief can never do *j·* to Truth
uniform
m 64– 1 Want of uniform *j·* is a crying evil caused by

a 36– 9 since *j·* is the handmaid of mercy.
f 238–26 *J·* often comes too late to secure a verdict.
248–29 unselfishness, goodness, mercy, *j·*,
p 391–17 *J·* is the moral signification of law.
405–13 The judge will deliver you to *j·*,
440–11 but no warping of *j·* can render
r 465–14 The attributes of God are *j·*, mercy,
gl 595– 3 Sword. The idea of Truth ; *j·*.

justifiable
p 440–15 Even penal law holds homicide, . . . to be *j·*.

justification
f 203–10 was really the *j·* of Jesus,
p 436–13 Such acts bear their own *j·*,
440–15 Now what greater *j·* can any deed have,

justified
b 317–10 "wisdom is *j·* of her children." — *Matt.* 11 : 19.
t 456–10 a reputation experimentally *j·* by their

justly
p 435–23 to punish a man for acting *j·*.
436–24 from the penalty they considered *j·* due,

K

Kaspar
ph 194–17 The authentic history of *K·* Hauser
194–24 at the age of seventeen *K·* was still a

keep
pr 4– 5 To *k·* the commandments of our Master
4–11 *k·* my commandments." — *John* 14 : 15.
a 25–20 *k·* my commandments." — *John* 14 : 15.
29– 5 If they *k·* the faith, they will have the crown
m 64– 6 *k·* himself unspotted from the — *Jas.* 1 : 27.
69–20 "Do you *k·* the First Commandment?
sp 70– * *If a man k· my saying,* — *John* 8 : 51.
f 217–12 "If a man *k·* my saying, — *John* 8 : 51.
237–12 if mortals would *k·* proper ward over
237–19 *k·* out of the minds of your children
241–21 *k·* my commandments." — *John* 14 : 15.
b 340– 8 and *k·* His commandments : — *Eccl.* 12 : 13.
340 10 love God and *k·* His commandments :
o 360–10 replies : . . . and *k·* Soul well out of sight.
p 371–21 nor would I *k·* the suckling a lifelong babe.
383–19 to *k·* the body in proper condition.
396–26 *K·* distinctly in thought that man is the
413–23 to *k·* it sweet as the new-blown flower.
414 26 *K·* in mind the verity of being,
428– 8 "If a man *k·* my saying, — *John* 8 : 51.
429–31 "If a man *k·* my saying, — *John* 8 : 51.
438– 7 "If a man *k·* my saying, — *John* 8 : 51.
441– 7 but be enjoined to *k·* perpetual silence,
t 458–17 the author desires to *k·* it out of C. S.
r 492–31 theory would *k·* truth and error always at war.
g 514–18 and *k·* pace with highest purpose.
526–28 to dress it and to *k·* it. — *Gen.* 2 : 15.
527– 3 to dress it and *k·* it, — to make it beautiful
537– 7 to *k·* the way of the tree of life. — *Gen.* 3 : 24.
ap 558– * *k· those things which are written* — *Rev.* 1 : 3.

keeper
g 541–21 Am I my brother's *k·*? — *Gen.* 4 : 9.

keeping
m 60–31 more secure in our *k·*, if sought in Soul.
ph 189–30 *k·* always in the direct line of matter,
b 308– 4 God, and *k·* His commandment?"
p 413–17 only for the purpose of *k·* the body clean,
g 521– 9 in the *k·* of Spirit, not matter,

keeps
pr 5– 1 *k·* him from demonstrating his power
p 439– 4 He manufactures for it, *k·* a furnishing store,

kept
a 21– 3 I have *k·* the faith," — *II Tim.* 4 : 7.
m 59–28 so long as its moral obligations are *k·* intact ;

kept
m 62– 2 The foetus must be *k·* mentally pure
s 109–13 *k·* aloof from society, and devoted time and
f 222–18 he had been *k·* alive, as was believed, only by
237–16 *k·* from discussing or entertaining theories
p 387– 3 Because mortal mind is *k·* active, must it

key
sp 99–10 Truth has furnished the *k·* to the kingdom,
99–10 and with this *k·* C. S. has opened the door of the
ph 171– 6 man will reopen with the *k·* of divine Science
k 499 * *He that hath the k· of David,* — *Rev.* 3 : 7.
gl 579– * *He that hath the k· of David,* *Rev.* 3 : 7.

keynote
f 220 7 sounded the *k·* of universal freedom,
240–13 and you lose the *k·* of being,
p 410–30 begins with Christ's *k·* of harmony,

keynotes
o 355–29 are God's immortal *k·*,

KEY TO THE SCRIPTURES
o 361–32 Science and Health with *K· TO THE S·*.

kid
g 514–23 leopard shall lie down with the *k·* , — *Isa.* 11 : 6.

kill
a 27–32 endeavored . . . to *k·* him according to certain
51–11 Nothing could *k·* this Life of man.
m 56–20 "Thou shalt not *k·*." — *Exod.* 20 : 13.
s 151–22 The human mind has no power to *k·*
159– 4 protested . . . and said it would *k·* her,
f 203–26 and will continue to *k·* him so long as he sins
203–31 does not *k·* a man in order to give him
216– 7 Error bites the heel of truth, but cannot *k·* truth.
b 294–14 error, saying : . . . matter can *k·* man."
314–10 The Jews, who sought to *k·* this man of God,
p 388–10 thought that they could *k·* the body with matter,
389–15 and then discuss the certainty that food can *k·*
395–30 The knowledge that brain-lobes cannot *k·*
402–17 You say that accidents, . . . and disease *k·*
t 445– 5 who attempts to *k·* morally and
g 542– 2 incurs divine displeasure, and it would *k·* Jesus
542–11 lest any finding him should *k·* him. — *Gen.* 4 : 15.
ap 564– 6 incites mortals to *k·* morally and

killed
a 42–24 Let men think they had *k·* the body !
f 215–32 would have *k·* the venerable philosopher
b 316–16 belief, . . . that the spiritual idea could be *k·*
ap 567–10 dragon warreth not long, for he is *k·* by
567–29 detected and *k·* by innocence, the Lamb of Love.

killeth
   a 31–31   that whosoever *k·* you will think — *John* 16 : 2.

kills
   f 203–26   Sin *k·* the sinner and will continue to
   r 468– 4   sin is mortality's self, because it *k·* itself.

kind
after his
   g 507–13   yielding fruit after his *k·*, — *Gen.* 1 : 11.
   508–10   herb yielding seed after his *k·*, — *Gen.* 1 : 12.
   508–11   seed was in itself, after his *k·* : — *Gen.* 1 : 12.
   512– 7   every winged fowl after his *k·* : — *Gen.* 1 : 21.
   513–15   the living creature after his *k·*, — *Gen.* 1 : 24.
   513–16   beast of the earth after his *k·* : — *Gen.* 1 : 24.
   513–23   beast of the earth after his *k·*, — *Gen.* 1 : 25.
   513–24   upon the earth after his *k·* : — *Gen.* 1 : 25.
after its
   ph 180–10   seed within itself bearing fruit after its *k·*,
after their
   g 512– 6   abundantly, after their *k·*, — *Gen.* 1 : 21.
   513–23   and cattle after their *k·*, — *Gen.* 1 : 25.
another
   a 23–25   Another *k·* of faith understands divine Love
any
   sp 95–11   Error of any *k·* cannot hide from the law of
   p 393–20   as the result of a law of any *k·*,
   406–26   Inharmony of any *k·* involves
every
   a 23–19   Spirit, which rebukes sin of every *k·*
   s 143– 1   Truth is God's remedy for error of every *k·*,
   323– 4   in the endeavor to forsake error of every *k·*
   p 394–26   to conquer discord of every *k·* with harmony,
his own
   g 528–26   supposed to become the basis . . . of his own *k·*,
human
   m 56– 8   moral provision for generation among human *k·*.
one
   a 23–24   One *k·* of faith trusts one's welfare to others.
this
   sp 95–16   This *k·* of mind-reading is not clairvoyance,

   t 444–14   are advised . . . to be charitable and *k·*,
   g 508–17   *Gender* means simply *k·* or *sort*,
   528–27   calling them *mankind*, — that is, a *k·* of man.
   529– 1   bringing forth fruit of its own *k·*,
   544–20   facts of creation, . . . include nothing of the *k·*.

kinder
   f 220–14   *k·* than the atmosphere of mortal mind,

kindling
   p 434–18   earnest, solemn eyes, *k·* with hope

kindly
   s 162–29   I *k·* quote from Dr. Benjamin Rush,
   f 221–13   the doctors, who *k·* informed him that
   gl 594–14   *k·* affection ; love rebuking error ;

kindness
   pr 9–11   If selfishness has given place to *k·*,
   p 384– 8   for honest labor, or for deeds of *k·*,
   405– 6   to hold hatred in abeyance with *k·*,

kindred
   m 60– 4   *K·* tastes, motives, and aspirations are

King
   ap 575–24   the city of the great *K·*.'' — *Psal.* 48 : 2.

king
   s 133–30   Jehovah, or only a mighty hero and *k·*,
   136–21   That a wicked *k·* and debauched husband should
   144– 6   Naught is the squire, when the *k·* is nigh ;
   b 289–15   the "*k·* of terrors" to be but a — *Job* 18 : 14.
   g 514–11   Moral courage is . . . the *k·* of the mental realm.

kingdom
animal
   g 529–24   nothing in the animal *k·* which represents
divided
   o 354–27   It is in itself inconsistent, a divided *k·*.
   p 388–19   "*k·* divided against itself." — *Matt.* 12 : 25.
   389–17   and the *k·* divided against itself.
   gl 581–17   BABEL. . . . a *k·* divided against itself,
God's
   f 202–19   when God's *k·* comes on earth ;
   b 339–24   until . . . God's *k·* comes
heavenly
   s 130–25   such as they belong to the heavenly *k·*.
His
   m 56–10   Until . . . His *k·* is come as in the vision
his
   ap 565–15   "of his *k·* there shall be no end," — *Luke* 1 : 33.
key to the
   sp 99–10   Truth has furnished the key to the *k·*,
of God
   a 18– *   *until the k· of God shall come.* — *Luke* 22 : 18.
   20– 8   into the *k·* of God before you." — *Matt.* 21 : 31.
   an 106–26   shall not inherit the *k·* of God. — *Gal.* 5 : 21.
   b 321– 4   cannot inherit the *k·* of God." — *I Cor.* 15 : 50.
   p 382–22   receive the *k·* of God as a — *Luke* 18 : 17.
   r 476–29   "The *k·* of God is within you ;" — *Luke* 17 : 21.

kingdom
of God
   r 477– 4   Jesus taught that the *k·* of God is intact,
   ap 573–32   "The *k·* of God is within you." — *Luke* 17 : 21.
   576–21   This *k·* of God "is within — *Luke* 17 : 21.
of heaven
   sp 93–31   to becloud our apprehension of the *k·* of heaven
   s 107– *   *k· of heaven is like unto leaven*, — *Matt.* 13 : 33.
   110–11   establishment of the *k·* of heaven on earth.
   122– 6   and reveal the *k·* of heaven,
   ph 174–19   proclaiming the *k·* of heaven on earth.
   f 208–22   the reign of Spirit, the *k·* of heaven,
   241–32   to enter the *k·* of heaven,
   248–30   love — the *k·* of heaven
   o 361–26   though least in the *k·* of heaven,
   ap 560–14   constitutes the *k·* of heaven in man.
   gl 592–19   the *k·* of heaven, or reign of harmony.
of our God
   ap 568–15   and the *k·* of our God, — *Rev.* 12 : 10.
of Truth
   b 281– 2   we enter into the *k·* of Truth on earth
represent a
   s 118–27   represent a *k·* necessarily divided against itself,
that
   f 252– 2   that *k·* cannot stand." — *Mark* 3 : 24.
Thy
   pr 16–30   Thy *k·* come. — *Matt.* 6 : 10.
   16–31   *Thy k· is come ; Thou art ever-present.*

   pr 17–12   For thine is the *k·*, — *Matt.* 6 : 13.
   a 40–32   but in order to enter into the *k·*,
   m 66–10   Through great tribulation we enter the *k·*.
   an 102–32   C. S. despoils the *k·* of evil,
   f 252– 2   If a *k·* be divided against itself, — *Mark* 3 : 24.
   252–25   and says : . . . The world is my *k·*.
   p 442–28   to give you the *k·*." — *Luke* 12 : 32.
   t 454–10   hate has no legitimate mandate and no *k·*.

Kingdom of Heaven
   gl 590– 1   definition of

King of England
   s 163– 6   William IV, *K· of E·*,

kings
   s 141–12   as *k·* are crowned from a royal dynasty.
   141–20   "*k·* and priests unto God." — *Rev.* 1 : 6.

kings'
   s 133–18   in the fiery furnace and in *k·* palaces.

kinship
   b 319– 2   delusion . . . has no *k·* with the Life supernal.

kitten
   f 220–19   like a *k·* glancing into the mirror at itself
   220–21   thinking it sees another *k·*.

knavish
   ph 173–22   Phrenology makes man *k·* or honest according

knelt
   s 161–21   Madame Roland, as she *k·* before a statue of

knew
   a 20–10   He *k·* that men can be baptized, . . . and yet be
   20–14   he *k·* the error of mortal belief,
   47–18   Judas Iscariot *k·* this.
   47–18   He *k·* that the great goodness of that Master
   47–22   He *k·* that the world generally loves a
   49– 2   They *k·* what had inspired their devotion,
   51–15   He *k·* that matter had no life
   53–25   He *k·* the mortal errors which constitute the
   m 68–16   I never *k·* more than one individual who
   sp 85–16   Jesus, . . . "*k·* their thoughts," — *Matt.* 12 : 25.
   85–24   Jesus *k·* the generation to be wicked and
   85–30   The great Teacher *k·* both cause and effect,
   85–31   *k·* that truth communicates itself
   86– 4   Jesus *k·*, . . . that it was not matter,
   s 109–16   I *k·* the Principle . . . to be God,
   134–26   "I *k·* that Thou hearest me — *John* 11 : 42.
   ph 186–29   If mortal mind *k·* how to be better, it would be
   f 213–22   He was a musician beyond what the world *k·*.
   221– 1   I *k·* a person who when quite a child
   247– 4   A woman of eighty-five, whom I *k·*,
   b 270–17   But they *k·* not what would be the
   271– 8   He *k·* that the philosophy, Science, and proof of
   286–13   He *k·* that the divine Principle, Love, creates
   315– 6   He *k·* of but one Mind
   315– 7   He *k·* that the Ego was Mind
   o 356–15   Jesus *k·*, "It is the spirit — *John* 6 : 63.
   357– 3   and *k·* from the outset that man would do.
   p 364– 4   one who was soon, though they *k·* it not,
   369–21   *k·* that man has not two lives,
   374– 8   *k·* nothing about, until it appeared on my body
   377–19   author never *k·* a patient who did not
   432– 7   testifies : . . . I *k·* the prisoner would commit it,
   437– 3   testified that he . . . *k·* Personal Sense to be
   437– 4   testified . . . that he *k·* Man, and that Man was
   g 532–29   body had been naked, and Adam *k·* it not ;
   538–23   And Adam *k·* Eve his wife ; — *Gen.* 4 : 1.

knife

t	459–17	like putting a sharp k· into the hands of a

knights

t	457–14	led to a quarrel between two k·

knocking

f	224–24	stands at the door of this age, k· for admission.

knocks

pref	vii–14	Truth, . . . k· at the portal of humanity.

know

	iii–*	Ye shall k· the truth, — John 8 : 32.
pref	vii–10	Him whom to k· aright is Life eternal.
pr	8–26	do we not already k· more of this heart than
	11–22	We k· that a desire for holiness is requisite
	11–30	to k· and do the will of God,
	17– 2	Enable us to k·,— as in heaven, so on earth,
a	19–32	thou shalt not k· evil, for there is one Life,
	28– 1	The Pharisees claimed to k· and to teach the
	36– 1	They, who k· not purity and affection
m	67– 7	"Do you k· your course?
sp	70–*	Now we k· that thou hast a devil.— John 8 : 52.
	80–20	we already k· that it is mind-power which
	84–12	to k· the past, the present, and the future.
	84–28	All we correctly k· of Spirit comes from
	84–31	we can k· the truth more accurately than the
	90–31	At present we k· not what man is,
	90–31	certainly shall k· this when man reflects God.
	95– 8	in that ratio we k· all human need
s	109–19	I must k· the Science of this healing,
	109–30	he shall k· of the doctrine,— John 7 : 17.
	129– 7	If you wish to k· the spiritual fact,
	140– 8	we k· Him as divine Mind,
	149–18	"We k· that mind affects the body
	151– 9	We k· that if they understood the Science
	152– 8	although they k· not how the work is done.
ph	178– 1	though they k· nothing of this particular case
	181–27	they generally k· it and are satisfied.
	190–26	place thereof shall k· it no more.— Psal. 103 : 16.
	199–17	To k· whether this development is
	200–25	"For I determined not to k·— I Cor. 2 : 2.
	200–28	I am determined not to k·
f	217–13	k· we no man after the flesh !"— II Cor. 5 : 16.
	225– 5	You may k· when first Truth leads by the
	231–28	and k· that they are no part of His creation.
	237–23	Some invalids are unwilling to k· the facts
	238–15	"I k· you not."— Matt. 25 : 12.
	242– 4	"they shall all k· Me [God],— Jer. 31 : 34.
	242–10	It is to k· no other reality
	253–26	knowing (as you ought to k·)
c	255–*	we k· that the whole creation— Rom. 8 : 22.
	258–16	We k· no more of man as the true
	258–17	than we k· of God.
b	284–14	or k· aught unlike the infinite?
	291– 5	We k· that all will be changed
	317–12	"If the world hate you, ye k· that— John 15 : 18.
	318– 3	to k· that nothing can efface Mind
	323–14	must put into practice what we already k·.
o	342–28	"By their fruits ye shall k· them"— Matt. 7 : 20.
	345–13	It is indeed no small matter to k· one's self ;
	350–10	Then they k· how Truth casts out error
	352–14	Would a mother say . . . "I k· that ghosts are
	359–14	at length k· yourself spiritually
	360– 1	and k· that these ideals are real and eternal
p	365– 1	Did the careless doctor, . . . k· the thorns
	365– 4	Oh, did they k· !— this knowledge would
	360–19	never gave drugs, never prayed to k· if God
	376–29	K· in Science you cannot
	386–15	not to k· that this is so.
	387– 2	and k· that there is no death.
	389– 6	The less we k· or think about hygiene,
	390–22	illegitimate, because you k· that God is
	410– 8	that they might k· Thee, the only— John 17 : 3.
	416–24	The sick k· nothing of the mental process
	416–28	tell them only what is best for them to k·.
	419–31	k· that disease . . . cannot change forms,
	420– 8	to k· that error cannot produce
	425–19	and k· that there is nothing to consume,
	432– 4	and k· him to be truthful and upright,
	438–30	k· Morbid Secretion to be on friendly
t	447–31	but to k· it, he must demonstrate his
	448–15	or upon the good you k· and do not.
	449–13	You should practise well what you k·,
	452–18	The teacher must k· the truth himself.
	453–14	Teach your student that he must k· himself
	453–15	before he can k· others
	463–19	By this we k· that Truth is here
	464– 3	Could her friends k· how little time the author
r	476–27	shall k· it no more."— Psal. 103 : 16.
	490–17	Our only need is to k· this
	492–12	We k· that a statement proved to be good
k	499–*	I k· thy works :— Rev. 3 : 8.
g	512–13	Their individual forms we k· not,
	512–14	we do k· that their natures are allied to God's
	519–15	Mortals can never k· the infinite, until
	529–29	we k· that they are worthless and unreal.

know

g	530–14	God doth k· that in the day ye eat— Gen. 3 : 5.
	530–24	saying, . . . I shall k· you, and you will be
	536–31	to k· good and evil :— Gen. 3 : 22.
	540–14	but we ought to k· that God's law
	541–20	And he said, I k· not :— Gen. 4 : 9.
	553–30	before they think or k· aught of their origin,
ap	560–20	The botanist must k· the genus and species
	569–10	we k· that the nothingness of error is
	570–27	k· the great benefit which Mind has wrought.
	570–28	should also k· the great delusion of mortal
	571–16	K· thyself, and God will supply the
gl	579–*	I k· thy works :— Rev. 3 : 8.
fr	600–*	by their fruits ye shall k· them.— Matt. 7 : 20.

knoweth

pr	1–*	Your Father k· what things ye— Matt. 6 : 8.
sp	77–15	"k· no man . . . neither the Son,— Mark 13 : 32.
f	233–12	How long it must be . . . no man k·,
	252–18	says : I am wholly dishonest, and no man k· it.
b	292– 3	of that day and hour," no man."— Matt. 24 : 36.
g	519– 2	from all eternity k· His own ideas.
ap	568–23	k· that he hath but a short time.— Rev. 12 : 12.
	569–24	for the devil k· his time is short.

knowing

a	20–21	well k· that to obey the divine order
	48–29	k· not that he was hastening the
sp	89– 1	what the unaided medium is incapable of k·
f	201– 3	K· this and k· too that one affection
	205– 2	will sin without k· that they are sinning,
	210–11	K· that Soul and its attributes were
	253–15	K· the falsity of so-called material sense,
	253–26	k· (as you ought to know) that God never
b	272– 9	not k· the Scriptures."— Matt. 22 : 29.
	314–13	k·, as he did, that Mind was the builder,
	328–21	k· that there is no material law,
p	363–10	K· what those around him were saying
	363–14	k· this, Jesus rebuked them with a short story
	366–28	k·, as he does, that Life is God
	371–10	not k· why nor when.
	409–14	error which prevents mortals from k·
	417– 3	sometimes k· more than their doctors.
	419– 9	k· that there can be no reaction in Truth.
t	447– 8	incapable of k· or judging accurately the
	447–26	by k· that there is none.
	448–21	well k· it to be impossible for error,
	450–29	K· the claim of animal magnetism,
r	489–18	material means for k·, hearing, seeing?
g	509–29	K· the Science of creation,
	530– 7	K· this, Jesus once said,
	530–16	shall be as gods, k· good and evil.— Gen. 3 : 5.
	555–30	K· that God was the Life of man,

knowingly

f	253–18	If you believe in and practise wrong k·,

knowledge

according to

pr	7–12	"a zeal . . . not according to k·"— Rom. 10 : 2.

and pleasure

g	532–17	K· and pleasure, evolved through material sense,

belief and

gl	589–12	JERUSALEM. Mortal belief and k·

children in

m	62–17	should be allowed to remain children in k·,

comprised in a

s	127– 7	comprised in a k· or understanding of God,

departments of

ph	197–18	in the departments of k· now broadcast

destitute of any

g	554–10	destitute of any k· of the so-called
	554–12	destitute of any k· of its origin

dire effects of

ph	196– 4	from the dire effects of k·.

false

ph	175–30	Adam, before he ate the fruit of false k·,
gl	581–19	The higher false k· builds

fruit of

r	481–12	forbidden fruit of k·, . . . is the testimony of

gained

sp	91–20	destroys the erroneous k· gained from
	92–15	a k· gained from matter, or evil, instead of
b	269–27	k· gained through the material senses
	274– 3	k· gained from the five senses is only
	299–18	K· gained from material sense is
r	490–20	k· gained from the so-called material senses

hath no

g	540–21	a false sense which hath no k· of God."

human

(see **human**)

impertinent

an	103–13	separate from any half-way impertinent k·,

increase of

sp	95–19	We welcome the increase of k· . . . because

judge the

b	299–21	Ought we not then to judge the k·

knowledge

material
(*see* **material**)

materialistic
ph 196– 1 If materialistic *k·* is power, it is not wisdom.

mortal
g 527–17 constitutes evil and mortal *k·*.

obtained
b 296–22 The *k·* obtained from the
r 493– 7 *k·* obtained from physical sense
gl 589–12 Mortal belief and *k·* obtained from

of Christian Science
b 285–28 As mortals reach, through *k·* of C. S.,
t 455–17 receives his *k·* of C. S.,

of error
f 252– 8 A *k·* of error and of its operations must
g 533–26 cross-questioning man as to his *k·* of error,

of evil
g 526–21 erroneous doctrine that the *k·* of evil is as real,
527–14 It is true that a *k·* of evil would
537– 9 A *k·* of evil was never the essence of

of good
g 526–22 as the *k·* of good.

of good and evil
sp 92–14 commending . . . the *k·* of good and evil,
f 220–28 tree of the *k·* of good and evil,"— *Gen.* 2 : 17.
r 481–17 "tree of the *k·* of good and evil,"— *Gen.* 2 : 17.
g 526– 2 the tree of *k·* of good and evil.— *Gen.* 2 : 9.
527– 8 the tree of the *k·* of good and evil,— *Gen.* 2 : 17.

of Love
p 410– 6 the *k·* of Love, Truth, and Life.

of Science
b 286– 6 this is fatal to a *k·* of Science.

of the Science
s 128–14 A *k·* of the Science of being

of this
r 492– 8 It is already proved that a *k·* of this,
g 521– 1 *K·* of this lifts man above the sod,

of Truth
s 128–22 So it is with our *k·* of Truth.

physical
a 46–28 he rose above the physical *k·* of his disciples,

present
p 410– 5 a present *k·* of his Father and of himself,

slight
t 446– 1 teaching his slight *k·* of Mind-power,

so-called
b 312– 2 such so-called *k·* is reversed

this
p 365– 4 this *k·* would do much more
404–24 this *k·* strengthens his moral courage
g 532– 6 Is this *k·* safe, when eating its first fruits

tree of
sp 92–12 a serpent coiled around the tree of *k·*
ph 165– 2 one of the apples from "the tree of *k·*."— *Gen.* 2 : 9.
197– 8 God said of the tree of *k·*, which
f 214–22 like the original "tree of *k·*,"— *Gen.* 2 : 9.
g 526– 2 the tree of *k·* of good and evil.— *Gen.* 2 : 9.
526–30 The "tree of *k·*" stands for the — *Gen.* 2 : 9.
538–14 The "tree of *k·*" typifies — *Gen.* 2 : 9.

true
a 48–31 what the true *k·* of God can do for man.
s 133–31 has not quite given place to the true *k·* of God.
o 358–22 few who have gained a true *k·* of the
r 466– 4 all-science or true *k·*, all-presence.

knowledge

wake to the
f 251– 9 mortals wake to the *k·* of two facts :
___
sp 90–23 This shows what mortal mentality and *k·* are.
an 103–10 a *k·* of both good and evil,
ph 196– 3 not yet found it true that *k·* can
199–19 is of less importance than a *k·* of the fact.
b 279–27 the *k·* that there are not two bases of being,
330–17 a *k·* of it is left either to human conjecture or
p 394– 7 *K·* that we can accomplish the good
395–30 The *k·* that brain-lobes cannot kill
g 519–19 and of the *k·* of the Son of God,— *Eph.* 4 : 13.
gl 590– 4 definition of
592–22 *k·* of the nothingness of material things
595–19 human acts, thoughts, beliefs, opinions, *k·* ;
fr 600– * *increasing in the k· of God.— Col.* 1 : 10.

known

pr 7–26 to whom each need of man is always *k·*
15–26 hidden from the world, but *k·* to God.
a 32– 1 have not *k·* the Father nor me."— *John* 16 : 3.
46– 5 In the walk to Emmaus, Jesus was *k·* to
sp 73–13 belief, which ought to be *k·* by its fruit,
81–31 That somebody, somewhere, must have *k·*
an 106–17 and *k·* by their fruit,
f 227– 2 where . . . the rights of man are fully *k·*
b 284–15 Can Deity be *k·* through the material senses?
284–26 and are *k·* only by the effects
299–22 "the tree is *k·* by his fruit"— *Matt.* 12 : 33.
338–32 revealed in due time, and was *k·* as Christ Jesus.
o 350–25 Divine Truth must be *k·* by its effects
p 367–30 error should be *k·* as nothing.
379–13 Had he *k·* his sense of bleeding was an
398–17 are *k·* to relieve the symptoms of disease.
421– 8 afterwards make *k·* to the patient your motive
426–13 a "tree of life," *k·* by its fruits.— *Rev.* 22 : 2.
439– 2 be it *k·* that False Belief, the counsel for
t 456–31 it was the first book *k·*, containing
464– 3 Why do you not make yourself more widely *k·* ?"
464– 5 in which to make herself outwardly *k·*
g 501– * *by My name Jehovah was I not k·— Exod.* 6 : 3.
556–15 It is made *k·* most fully to him who
gl 596– 5 makes Him better *k·* as the All-in-all,

knows

pr 2–14 for He already *k·* all.
13–15 God *k·* our need before we tell Him
15– 8 He *k·* all things and rewards according to
sp 87–19 The mine *k·* naught of the emeralds within
s 154–30 and says, . . . "Mamma *k·* you are hurt."
ph 180–26 man *k·* that with God all things are possible.
188–30 The human eye *k·* not where the orb of day is,
f 241– 2 He, who *k·* God's will or the demands of
250–10 Ego . . . which never believes, but *k·* ;
b 307–17 Error . . . says : "The Lord *k·* it.
o 345–11 neither *k·* itself nor what it is saying.
p 380–13 defendant *k·* will be turned against himself.
388– 6 only because it *k·* less of material law.
412–31 Scientist *k·* that there can be no hereditary disease,
t 450–24 Scientist *k·* that they are errors of belief,
451–20 *k·* that human will is not C. S.
r 471– 1 *k·* no lapse from nor return to harmony,
g 523– 5 and finally declares that God *k·* error
557–14 the less a mortal *k·* of sin, disease, and

kurios

gl 590–17 In the Greek, the word *k·* almost always has

L

labor

pr 13–10 If our petitions are sincere, we *l·* for what we
a 21– 6 Christians do not continue to *l·* . . . because of
29– 9 because then our *l·* is more needed.
m 67–26 does not put to silence the *l·* of centuries.
sp 99–22 and shall continue to *l·* and to endure.
f 236– 1 should stimulate clerical *l·* and progress.
242–16 let us *l·* to dissolve with the universal solvent
p 384– 7 for honest *l·*, or for deeds of kindness,
387– 7 we conclude that intellectual *l·*
387–23 cannot suffer as the result of any *l·* of love,
t 457–11 since entering this field of *l·*,
457–20 no excellence without *l·* in a direct line.
r 465– 2 much *l·* and increased spiritual understanding,

labored

t 464–22 has *l·* to expound divine Principle,

laboring

s 130–20 *L·* long to shake the adult's faith in matter
p 386–26 *l·* under the influence of the belief of

laborious

t 464– 5 except through her *l·* publications,

labors

f 238–19 to enter unlawfully into the *l·* of others.
p 385– 3 and other philanthropists engaged in humane *l·*
431– 6 prisoner attended to his daily *l·*,
g 548–26 endowed by the *l·* and genius of great men.

lacerated

a 44–17 bind up the wounded side and *l·* feet,

lachrymal

f 211–15 the effect seen in the *l·* gland?

lack

m 65–16 Beholding the world's *l·* of Christianity
67–25 The *l·* of spiritual power in the
sp 85–20 Our Master rebuked the *l·* of this power
s 140–14 tyrannical and proscriptive from *l·* of love,
145– 5 *l·* of the letter could not hinder their work ;
f 243–14 not so much from *l·* of desire
243–15 as from *l·* of spiritual growth.
b 286–24 temporal thoughts . . . *l·* a divine cause.

lacking

p 365–11 but if the unselfish affections be *l·*,
382– 2 laws of matter, . . . *l·* divine authority
gl 592–14 there is something spiritually *l·*,

lacks
　a 19–22　he *l·* the practical repentance, which
　s 124– 5　When this human belief *l·* organizations to
　p 366–12　The physician who *l·* sympathy for his
　　366–17　physician *l·* faith in the divine Mind

ladder
　f 222– 2　and ascend the *l·* of life.

laden
　p 413–26　that mind being *l·* with illusions

laid
　pr 8–25　and ask that it may be *l·* bare before us,
　a 27–18　He *l·* the axe of Science at the root of
　　44– 2　before the thorns can be *l·* aside for a crown,
　　52–15　Herod and Pilate *l·* aside old feuds
　sp 92–26　The foundation of evil is *l·* on a belief in
　f 234–29　He *l·* great stress on the action of the
　　237– 8　would have *l·* aside their drugs,
　　241– 5　*l·* up "where moth and rust doth — *Matt.* 6 : 19.
　b 314–18　the body, which they *l·* in a sepulchre,
　　315– 6　He knew of but one Mind and *l·* no claim to
　o 353–30　from this it follows that whatever is *l·* off is
　p 390–17　nor *l·* upon a bed of suffering
　　409–23　to be *l·* aside for the pure reality.
　　414– 1　Thus are *l·* the foundations of the belief
　t 460– 1　rules . . . as *l·* down in this work,
　　462–15　and advance from the rudiments *l·* down.

lake
　r 477–28　when they called a certain beautiful *l·*

lama
　a 51– 1　"*Eloi, Eloi, l· sabachthani?*"—*Mark* 15 : 34.

Lamb (*see also* **Lamb's**)
of God
　s 132–32　"the *L·* of God ;"— *John* 1 : 29.
　ap 564–13　The Revelator speaks of Jesus as the *L·* of God
　gl 590– 9　definition of
of Love
　ap 561–12　bride . . . wedded to the *L·* of Love.
　　567–30　and killed by innocence, the *L·* of Love.

　b 334–21　*L·* slain from the foundation — *Rev.* 13 : 8.
　ap 561–13　"the bride" and "the *L·*"— *Rev.* 21 : 14.
　　567–31　Divine Science shows how the *L·* slays the wolf
　　568– 4　evil has tried to slay the *L·* ;
　　568–18　by the blood of the *L·*,— *Rev.* 12 : 11.
　　576–11　and the *L·* are the temple of it.— *Rev.* 21 : 22.

lamb
　a 50– 1　brought as a *l·* to the slaughter,— *Isa.* 53 : 7.
　g 514–22　wolf also shall dwell with the *l·*,— *Isa.* 11 : 6.
　　541– 1　A *l·* is a more animate form of existence,
　　541–11　No ; but the *l·* was a more spiritual type
　　550–27　nor does a lion bring forth a *l·*.

Lamb's
　ap 574– 9　show thee the bride, the *L·* wife.— *Rev.* 21 : 9.
　　575– 2　Arise . . . and behold the *L·* wife,
　　577– 4　The *L·* wife presents the unity of

lambs
　s 135– 5　and ye little hills, like *l·* ? — *Psal.* 114 : 6.

lame
　u 27– 4　how that the blind see, the *l·* walk, — *Luke* 7 : 22.
　s 132– 6　and the *l·* walk, — *Matt.* 11 : 5.
　　149–22　The logic is *l·*, and facts contradict it.
　ph 183–29　voice to the dumb, feet to the *l·*.
　f 210–14　hearing to the deaf, feet to the *l·*,
　　226–25　The *l·*, the deaf, the dumb, the blind, the sick,
　　243–18　dizzy, diseased, consumptive, or *l·*.
　c 201–10　This old man was so *l·* that he
　o 342–25　causes the deaf to hear, the *l·* to walk,

lameness
　f 205– 4　and mortals will . . .stumble with *l·*,

lament
　p 386–31　pass from our sight and we *l·*,

lamentation
　p 386–32　that *l·* is needless and causeless.

lamps
　ap 562–17　*l·* in the spiritual heavens of the age,

Lancet, The
　f 245– 4　the London medical magazine called The *L ·*.

land
dry
　r 491– 1　swimming when he is on dry *l·*.
　g 506–17　and let the dry *l·* appear : — *Gen.* 1 : 9.
　　506–22　And God called the dry *l·* Earth ; — *Gen.* 1 : 10.
　　507– 1　In metaphor, the *dry l·* illustrates
　　535–30　"And God called the dry *l·* Earth ; — *Gen.* 1 : 10.
　　557– 5　how to develop their children properly on dry *l·*.
of bondage
　ap 566–16　Out of the *l·* of bondage came,
of Christian Science
　f 226–32　the *l·* of C. S., where fetters fall

land
of Nod
　g 542–28　and dwelt in the *l·* of Nod.— *Gen.* 4 : 16.
our
　f 226– 1　when African slavery was abolished in our *l·*.
　　226– 6　was still echoing in our *l·*,
　p 404–17　The temperance reform, felt all over our *l·*,

landmarks
　b 323– 8　peace, and purity, which are the *l·* of
　　324– 2　Gladness to leave the false *l·*

landscape
　g 516–19　brightens the flower, beautifies the *l·*,

landscape-paintings
　sp 86–25　Portraits, *l·*, fac-similes of penmanship,

landscapes
　sp 71–14　and you may see *l·*, men, and women.

language
afforded by
　t 460–28　through the meagre channel afforded by *l·*
Bible
　c 263–17　He might say in Bible *l·* :
　p 435–29　To him I might say, in Bible *l·*,
essential
　s 117–10　God's essential *l·* is spoken of
human
　g 520– 5　Human *l·* can repeat only an infinitesimal **part**
of Scripture
　c 256–20　He who, in the *l·* of Scripture,
of Spirit
　s 117– 6　the *l·* of Spirit must be, and is, spiritual.
　　117–14　nor hath lip spoken, the pure *l·* of Spirit.
of the apostle
　g 519–18　till, in the *l·* of the apostle,
of the Master
　o 355–10　C. S. says, in the *l·* of the Master,
original
　b 319–21　taught in the original *l·* of the Bible
solecism in
　s 114–12　Mortal mind is a solecism in *l·*,
strong
　pr 6–31　The strong *l·* of our Master confirms **this**

　ph 194–29　And with no *l·* but a cry,
　f 210– 3　*l·* which human thought can comprehend.

languages
　o 349–15　like all other *l·*, English is inadequate
　g 510–31　In one of the ancient *l·* the word for *man*
　　525– 8　some of the equivalents . . . in different *l·*.

languidly
　p 373–28　*l·* creeps along its frozen channels,

languor
　p 373–31　producing the propulsion or the *l·*,

lap
　r 494–28　its *l·* piled high with immortal fruits.

lapse
　r 470–17　How can good *l·* into evil,
　　471– 2　knows no *l·* from nor return to harmony,

lapsing
　f 248– 7　instead of *l·* into darkness or gloom.
　g 540– 3　*l·* into sin, sickness, and death.

large
　p 363–16　He described two debtors, one for a *l·* sum and
　　394– 5　a *l·* majority of doctors depress mental energy,
　t 450– 1　There is a *l·* class of thinkers whose bigotry

largely
　sp 84–15　to commune more *l·* with the divine Mind,
　s 156–32　Homœopathy takes mental symptoms *l·* into
　p 439– 5　and advertises *l·* for his employers.

larger
　t 248– 6　Men and women of riper years and *l·* lessons

lasciviousness
　an 106–21　fornication, uncleanness, *l·*,— *Gal.* 5 : 19.

lash
　f 224–17　modern *l·* is less material than the Roman
　　239– 2　which endured the *l·* of their predecessors,

last
　pr 16–12　whether the *l·* line is not an addition
　a 34–29　a contrast between our Lord's *l·* supper and
　　34–30　his *l·* spiritual breakfast with his disciples
　　36–25　gloat over their offences to the *l·* moment
　　39– 3　endure until Christianity's *l·* triumph.
　　43–11　Jesus' *l·* proof was the highest,
　　47–27　desertion of their Master in his *l·* earthly
　　49–12　O, why did they not gratify his *l·* human
　　50– 5　supreme moment of mockery, desertion,
　m 63– 1　does not make . . . the superior law of Soul *l·*.
　sp 92– 7　From the illusion implied in this *l·* postulate
　s 116– 1　*l·* shall be first, and the first *l·*,"— *Matt.* 20 : **16.**
　　117–10　spoken of in the *l·* chapter of Mark's Gospel
　　153–11　sinking in the *l·* stage of typhoid fever.

last

ph 166–25   and in his extremity and only as a *l·* resort,
    177–13   but from first to *l·*, the body is a
    184– 7   the penalties it affixes *l·* so long as the
  f 207–15   Body is not first and Soul *l·*,
    210– 9   "the *l·* enemy that shall be — *I Cor.* 15 : 26.
    223–26   but the *l·* trump has not sounded,
    249–20   You say, "I dreamed *l·* night."
  b 269– 3   From first to *l·* the supposed coexistence
    272–11   referred to in the *l·* chapter of Mark's Gospel.
    286–13   was put aside from first to *l·*
    291– 6   when the *l·* trump shall sound ;
    291– 7   this *l·* call of wisdom cannot come till
    292– 1   When the *l·* mortal fault is destroyed,
    334–26   "I am the first and the *l·* : — *Rev.* 1 : 17.
  p 390–17   in payment of the *l·* farthing,
    390–18   the *l·* penalty demanded by error.
    402– 2   which will be *l·* acknowledged.
    405–15   will be manacled until the *l·* farthing is paid,
    427–19   "The *l·* enemy that shall be — *I Cor.* 15 : 26.
    427–28   Spirit is his *l·* resort, but it should have been
  r 466–16   This *l·* statement contains the point you will
    466–17   first and *l·* it is the most important to
  g 508–22   The Mind . . . names the female gender *l·*
  ap 564– 8   This *l·* infirmity of sin will sink its perpetrator
    565–19   represented first by man and, . . . *l·* by woman,
    572– 3   in both the first and *l·* books of the Bible,
    574– 7   full of the seven *l·* plagues, — *Rev.* 21 : 9.
  gl 585–24   mortality ; that which does not *l·* forever ;
    598–14   common statement, "He breathed his *l·*.''

last at —

a 20– 3   He at *l·* paid no homage to
    21–14   till at *l·* he finishes his course with joy.
    31–20   at *l·* we shall rest, sit down with him, in a
  m 65–21   until we get at *l·* the clear straining of truth,
  s 125–15   the visible manifestation will at *l·*
  ph 166–30   but when Mind at *l·* asserts its mastery
  b 295–13   will at *l·* yield to the scientific fact
  p 416– 1   At *l·* the agony also vanishes.
    431– 8   At *l·* he committed liver-complaint,
  g 556–12   only to go out at *l·* forever ;
  ap 569–23   comes back to him at *l·* with accelerated force,
    569–25   is at *l·* stung to death by his own malice ;
    574–22   at *l·* lifted the seer to behold the great city,

lasting

pr 7–10   But does it produce any *l·* benefit?
  sp 87–27   The strong impressions . . . are *l·*,
  ph 186–23   If we concede . . . discord has as *l·* a claim

lastly

an 104–11   *L·*, they say they have always believed it.''

lasts

r 497–12   punished so long as the belief *l·*.

late

m 59–23   After marriage, it is too *l·* to grumble
  sp 80– 6   purporting to come from the *l·* Theodore Parker
  s 147– 6   *L·* in the nineteenth century I demonstrated
  f 238–26   Justice often comes too *l·* to secure a verdict.
  b 313–20   in the translation of the *l·* George R. Noyes,
  o 360–23   the *l·* Rev. George R. Noyes, D.D.:
  g 547– 9   The *l·* Louis Agassiz, by his microscope

latent

s 128–15   the *l·* abilities and possibilities of man.
  ph 168–27   a *l·* illusion of mortal mind,
    199–20   *l·* mental fears are subdued by him.
  p 376– 4   the *l·* fear and the despair of recovery
    377–31   It is *l·* belief in disease,
  t 445– 8   Unfold the *l·* energies and capacities
  ap 559– 5   upon the sea, — upon elementary, *l·* error,
    559–13   stirs their *l·* forces to utter the
  gl 597– 8   but cloaked the crime, *l·* in thought,

later

pref ix– 8   *L·*, the tongue voices the more definite
  pr 7–32   or mean to ask forgiveness at some *l·* day.
    16–13   addition to the prayer by a *l·* copyist ;
  a 54– 9   must sooner or *l·* plant themselves in Christ,
    55– 7   no more injustice than the *l·* centuries have
  f 223– 3   Sooner or *l·* we shall learn that the
    240–24   Remember that mankind must sooner or *l·*,
  b 296–19   Whether mortals will learn this sooner or *l·*,
  o 351– 9   *L·* she learned that her own prayers
  p 428–25   sooner or *l·*, . . . we must master sin
  t 444– 3   In some way, sooner or *l·*, all must rise
    449– 8   Right adjusts the balance sooner or *l·*.
  g 528–31   *L·* in human history, when the forbidden fruit

Latin

a 23–21   In Hebrew, Greek, *L·*, and English,
    32– 4   The *L·* word for this oath was *sacramentum*,
  b 271–11   In *L·* the word rendered *disciple* signifies
  r 466– 2   *Omni* is adopted from the *L·* adjective

latitude

s 125–22   cold and heat, *l·* and longitude.

latter

a 53– 2   *l·* accusation was true, but not in their meaning.
  sp 81– 4   this *l·* evidence is destroyed by Mind-science.
    83– 8   to escape the error of these *l·* days.
    83–26   The *l·* is a revelation of divine purpose
    85– 5   when the *l·* yields to the divine Mind.
  an 103–11   for the *l·* is unreal.
  ph 187–17   allows the mental cause of the *l·* action,
  f 220–15   leaves catarrh to the *l·*.
    237–20   *l·* should be excluded on the same principle as
  b 269–10   The first is error ; the *l·* is truth.
    276–26   The *l·* destroys the former.
    320–31   as if Job intended to declare . . . in the *l·* days
    321–29   the voice of the *l·* sign.'' — *Exod.* 4 : 8.
  o 353– 9   How can a Christian, . . . think of the *l·* as real
  p 378–16   This *l·* occurrence represents the power of
  t 459–22   when the *l·* is distrusted and thwarted
  r 491– 8   the *l·* calling itself right.
  g 522–25   This *l·* part of the second chapter of
    544– 9   in the *l·* Life consisteth not of the things which

laughing

f 237– 5   Bounding off with *l·* eyes, she presently

launch

f 254–27   If you *l·* your bark upon the

launched

s 124–23   thought-force, which *l·* the earth in its orbit

lava

f 252–28   and says : . . . Like bursting *l·*, I expand

law

absence of
  p 391–18   Injustice declares the absence of *l·*.
all
  p 441– 1   comprehending and defining all *l·* and evidence.
and causation
  f 230–12   first arranging *l·* and causation so as to
and gospel
  p 441–29   a verdict contrary to *l·* and gospel.
and justice
  p 434– 5   "It is contrary to *l·* and justice.''
and order
  sp 97– 3   They will maintain *l·* and order,
and testimony
  p 436–10   Upon this statute hangs all the *l·* and testimony
breaking the
  o 349– 5   "Through breaking the *l·*, — *Rom.* 2 : 23.
broken
  pr 11–10   Broken *l·* brings penalty
broken no
  p 384–26   conviction abides that you have broken no *l·*,
by our
  sp 94–10   by our *l·* he ought to die, — *John* 19 : 7.
civil
  m 63–12   Civil *l·* establishes very unfair differences
disregard of
  m 64–28   Let not mortals permit a disregard of *l·*
divine
   (see **divine**)
eternal
  p 385–11   remember that the eternal *l·* of right,
explains the
  p 433– 5   explains the *l·* relating to liver-complaint.
false
  f 229–21   false *l·* should be trampled under foot.
    238–28   no time for gossip about false *l·* or testimony.
fulfils the
  ap 572–12   Love fulfils the *l·* of C. S.,
God's
  s 134–31   A miracle fulfils God's *l·*, but does not
  ph 168–22   in accordance with God's *l·*,
  f 229–20   If the transgression of God's *l·* produces
  p 381–28   the rule of perpetual harmony, — God's *l·*.
    404–14   remove this disorder as God's *l·* is fulfilled
  g 540–14   we ought to know that God's *l·* uncovers
heavenly
  t 447– 1   the heavenly *l·* is broken by trespassing upon
higher
  b 307–30   province is in . . . the higher *l·* of Mind.
    311–23   even the higher *l·* of Soul,
  p 435– 8   Mortal Man, in obedience to higher *l·*,
  t 458–22   summoned to give place to higher *l·*,
His
  r 472–11   His *l·*, rightly understood, destroys them.
human
  a 43–22   Human *l·* had condemned him,
  an 105– 8   the power of human *l·* is restricted to matter,
    105–14   and human *l·* rightly estimates crime,
hygienic
  p 382–13   ignorant of what is termed hygienic *l·*,
    382–16   the devotee of supposed hygienic *l·*,
immortal
  a 36–20   the immortal *l·* of justice as well as of mercy.
inhuman
  p 390–32   to defeat the passage of an inhuman *l·*.

law

material
(see **material**)

material sense of
s 118–18   perverted by a perverse material sense of *l·*,

moral
pr 11– 8   The moral *l·*, which has the right to acquit or
p 392– 4   broken moral *l·* should be taken into account
405–14   sentence of the moral *l·* will be executed upon
gl 592–12   type of moral *l·* and the demonstration

Mosaic
a 30–14   Rabbi and priest taught the Mosaic *l·*,

natural
s 119–16   under the name of natural *l·*.
134–22   natural *l·* of harmony which overcomes discord,

no
an 106–29   against such there is no *l·*.''— *Gal.* 5 : 23.
ph 196–17   No *l·* supports them.
p 390–24   no *l·* of His to support the necessity either of sin
391–13   No *l·* of God hinders this result.
441–26   no *l·* outside of divine Mind can punish

no infringement of
p 435–22   is no infringement of *l·*,

no such
f 253–28   for no such *l·* exists.

of a general belief
s 155– 3   it is the *l·* of a general belief,

of annihilation
f 243–27   Life, and Love are a *l·* of annihilation to

of any kind
p 393–19   inflamed as the result of a *l·* of any kind,

of being
ph 186–27   and if so, harmony cannot be the *l·* of being.

of cause
p 370– 8   This is the *l·* of cause and effect,

of Christ
ph 182–32   The *l·* of Christ, . . . makes all things possible
p 434– 6   Others say, ''The *l·* of Christ supersedes

of divine Love
a 19–10   the law of Spirit,— the *l·* of divine Love.
p 436–31   obedience to the *l·* of divine Love

of divine Mind
s 150–21   contrary to the *l·* of divine Mind.
f 216–17   If man is governed by the *l·* of divine Mind,
p 430–14   illustrative of the *l·* of divine Mind

of divorce
b 306–14   and then are separated as by a *l·* of divorce

of God
pr 14–10   to be in obedience to the *l·* of God,
sp 95–11   cannot hide from the *l·* of God.
s 134–25   because it is the immutable *l·* of God,
f 230–20   Does a *l·* of God produce sickness,
233– 6   and progress is the *l·* of God,
252–26   and says : . . . the *l·* of God, may
253–29   and death is destroyed by the *l·* of God,
p 372–16   nor disobey the *l·* of God.
391–13   No *l·* of God hinders this result.
t 463–27   There is a *l·* of God applicable to healing,
g 534–20   it is not subject to the *l·* of God,— *Rom.* 8 : 7.

of his being
m 63–11   and Life is the *l·* of his being.

of immortal Mind
f 229–21   made void by the *l·* of immortal Mind,

of justice
pr 5–10   there is no discount in the *l·* of justice
a 36–20   *l·* of justice as well as of mercy.

of Life
ph 180– 9   must understand the resuscitating *l·* of Life.
f 253–29   the *l·* of Life instead of death,
b 311–23   it will become the *l·* of Life to man,
p 381– 1   rendered null and void by the *l·* of Life,
436–32   construed . . . as disobedience to the *l·* of Life.

of life
b 314–32   supposed accord with the inevitable *l·* of life.
p 387–22   supposition that . . . in obedience to the *l·* of life,

of Love
a 30–17   the divine *l·* of Love, which blesses
s 118–30   and violate the *l·* of Love,
f 203– 2   as though evil could overbear the *l·* of Love,
p 384– 6   Let us reassure ourselves with the *l·* of Love.
ap 574–19   full compensation in the *l·* of Love.

of matter
a 19– 9   redeems man from the *l·* of matter,
45– 2   Jesus . . . overcame every *l·* of matter,
s 127–25   not a *l·* of matter, for matter is not a lawgiver.
ph 184–21   not because a *l·* of matter has been transgressed,
f 229–29   not of a *l·* of matter nor of
p 380–32   Every *l·* of matter or the body,
382–17   Must we not then consider the so-called *l·* of matter
385–26   for having broken a *l·* of matter,

of Mind
ph 168–23   in accordance with God's law, the *l·* of Mind.
b 307–30   province is in . . . the higher *l·* of Mind.
p 423–25   now at work . . . according to the *l·* of Mind,
r 484–11   supposed laws of matter yield to the *l·* of Mind.

law

of mortal belief
f 227– 3   the *l·* of mortal belief included all error,
r 496–21   *l·* of mortal belief, at war with the facts

of mortal mind
s 124– 4   a *l·* of mortal mind, a blind belief,
154– 4   Since it is a *l·* of mortal mind that
154–18   The *l·* of mortal mind and her own fears
f 208– 9   a *l·* of mortal mind, wrong in every sense,
229–19   *l·* of mortal mind, conjectural and
b 289–22   the universal *l·* of mortal mind,
p 385–26   a *l·* of mortal mind which you have disobeyed.

of righteousness
a 36–32   Can God . . . overlook the *l·* of righteousness

of sin
f 242–19   and is the *l·* of sin and death.
244–12   free from the *l·* of sin and death.''— *Rom.* 8 : 2.

of Sinai
ph 200– 3   the *l·* of Sinai lifted thought into

of Soul
m 63– 1   does not make . . . the superior *l·* of Soul last.
b 311–23   the higher *l·* of Soul, which prevails over
p 427– 3   Life is the *l·* of Soul,

of Spirit
a 19–10   the *l·* of Spirit,— the law of divine Love.
f 207–12   nor . . . the *l·* of Spirit secondary.
210–22   in obedience to the immutable *l·* of Spirit,
b 302–23   by the *l·* of Spirit, not by the so-called
p 435–27   punished, according to the *l·* of Spirit, God.

of the Spirit
f 244–11   ''The *l·* of the Spirit of life— *Rom.* 8 : 2.

of the spirit
p 427– 3   even the *l·* of the spirit of Truth,

of this action
p 422–13   explain to them the *l·* of this action.

of this so-called mind
ph 184–22   a *l·* of this so-called mind has been disobeyed.

of Truth
r 482–27   C. S. is the *l·* of Truth, which heals the sick

opposite
p 389–21   cannot annul these regulations by an opposite *l·*

our
p 441–15   Our *l·* refuses to recognize Man as sick

penal
p 440–14   Even penal *l·* holds homicide, under stress of

physical
ph 184–26   what is termed a fatally broken physical *l·*.

portray
s 118–28   these definitions portray *l·* as physical,

rabbinical
p 362– 9   under the stern rules of rabbinical *l·*,

recognize as
ph 183–20   mortals commonly recognize as *l·* that which

relative to colleges
pref xi–29   a *l·* relative to colleges having been passed,

signification of
p 391–17   Justice is the moral signification of *l·*.

so-called
f 229–19   The so-called *l·* of mortal mind,
p 382–17   Must we not then consider the so-called *l·* of
432–27   *alias* nature's so-called *l·* ;
441– 3   any so-called *l·*, which undertakes to punish

spiritual
(see **spiritual**)

supposed
p 381– 8   When infringing some supposed *l·*, you say

that
s 134–32   fulfils God's law, but does not violate that *l·*.
f 230–21   can man put that *l·* under his feet by healing

this
s 154– 5   this *l·* obtains credit through association,

title of
ph 184–11   never honoring . . . with the title of *l·*

tyrannical
s 161–12   put her foot on a proposed tyrannical *l·*,

unchangeable
s 135– 8   the Science of God's unchangeable *l·*.

vestments of
p 372–24   parading in the vestments of *l·*.

which gives
ph 183–27   the *l·* which gives sight to the blind,

which overcomes
ph 182–20   the *l·* which overcomes material conditions

your
p 436– 4   betraying him into the hands of your *l·*,
436–22   must obey your *l·*, fear its consequences,

---

s 127–32   false hypotheses . . . that *l·* is founded on
160–32   Is a stiff joint . . . as much a result of *l·*
ph 178– 8   Heredity is not a *l·*.
183–14   Truth never . . . devised a *l·* to perpetuate error.
f 221–19   never ordained a *l·* that fasting should be
227– 7   *l·* of the divine Mind must end human bondage,
229–16   mortal belief has constituted itself a *l·*
233– 6   whose *l·* demands of us only what we **can**
245–30   decrepitude is not according to *l·*,

law

b 273–28 the false claims of material sense or l·.
o 342–17 then there is no invariable l·,
p 369–28 Limited to matter by their own l·,
385–12 though it can never annul the l· which
385–23 You are a l· unto yourself.
387–24 It is a l· of so-called mortal mind,
390–16 process of mortal opinions which you name l·,
393– 8 a l· of so-called mortal mind,
435–11 The l· of our Supreme Court decrees
435–20 "is the fulfilling of the l·,"— Rom. 13 : 10.
435–30 to judge . . . after the l·,— Acts 23 : 3.
435–31 to be smitten contrary to the l· ?"— Acts 23 : 3.
442–30 Christian Scientists, be a l· to yourselves
t 458–24 thus becoming a l· unto himself.
r 496–21 the strength of sin is the l·,"— I Cor. 15 : 56.
gl 592–15 demands penalties under the l·.

Lawgiver

b 321– 6 The Hebrew L·, slow of speech,
p 440–25 In the presence of the Supreme L·,

lawgiver

s 119–18 The l·, whose lightning palsies . . . is not the
127–26 for matter is not a l·.
127–32 false hypotheses that matter is its own l·,
161– 2 and is God the l·?
f 250– 3 and suppose . . . matter to be a l·,
p 435– 2 Spirit which is God Himself and Man's only l· !

lawgivers

ph 184–14 they are spiritual l·, enforcing obedience

lawmaker

ph 183– 4 departing from the basis of one God, one l·.
p 381–16 God is the l· but He is not the author of

laws

agent of those
p 435–16 for the agent of those l· is an outlaw,
disregarded those
f 227–32 Jesus would not have disregarded those l·
divine
s 107– 2 the Christ Science or divine l· of Life,
eternal
g 542– 7 Truth, through her eternal l·, unveils error.
God's
f 236– 7 emolument rather than the dignity of God's l·,
His
ph 183–17 supposed laws which result in . . . are not His l·,
b 318–30 controlled and proved by His l·.
p 439–27 and the righteous executor of His l·.
ignorance of the
s 145–23 ignorance of the l· of eternal and unerring Mind.
its
p 425–22 the less we acknowledge matter or its l·,
material
(see material)
name of
s 118–23 are honored with the name of l·.
of God
s 128– 5 term Science, . . . refers only to the l· of God
ph 168–17 all in consonance with the l· of God,
of health
s 125–19 theories about l· of health to be valueless.
ph 165–12 Obedience to the so-called physical l· of health,
168–11 the material so-called l· of health,
182–27 l· of health come from some sad incident,
184– 1 The so-called l· of health are simply
p 369–18 never recommended attention to l· of health,
381–32 transgressions of the physical l· of health ;
of nature
ph 182– 6 what are termed l· of nature, appertain to
183–10 its germination according to the l· of nature ?
183–19 L· of nature are laws of Spirit ;
p 433– 6 conclusion is, that l· of nature render
t 463–25 never enjoined obedience to the l· of nature,
of Spirit
ph 183–19 Laws of nature are l· of Spirit ;
oppressive
f 227– 4 even as oppressive l· are disputed
other
ph 169–29 Whatever teaches man to have other l·
our
m 63–18 Our l· are not impartial, to say the least,
an 105–16 When our l· eventually take cognizance of
p 434– 6 "The law of Christ supersedes our l· ;
physical
m 62– 7 master the belief in so-called physical l·,
ph 165–12 Obedience to the so-called physical l· of health
p 381–32 transgressions of the physical l· of health ;
442– 2 innocent of transgressing physical l·,
reveals the
b 273–20 reveals the l· of spiritual existence.
sanitary
ph 175–23 nor referred to sanitary l·.

laws

so-called
sp 81–25 despite the so-called l· of matter,
ph 168–11 the material so-called l· of health,
171–25 so-called l· of matter are nothing but
177–22 create the so-called l· of the flesh,
182–19 supersede the so-called l· of matter.
183– 2 but the so-called l· of matter would render
184– 1 The so-called l· of health are simply
f 207–12 nor are the so-called l· of matter
210–10 his disregard of matter and its so-called l·.
223–24 supplant unscientific means and so-called l·.
b 273–16 so-called l· of matter and of medical science
274–16 supersede the so-called l· of matter.
302–24 not by the so-called l· of matter.
p 381–12 The so-called l· of mortal belief are
440–12 disobedience to the so-called l· of Matter
spiritual
s 118–15 include spiritual l· emanating from the
118–17 may import that these spiritual l·, perverted
state
f 224–20 opposition from church, state l·, and the press,
subject to
f 244–14 beasts and vegetables,— subject to l· of decay.
such
p 442– 3 because there are no such l·.
supposed
ph 183–16 The supposed l· which result in weariness
f 237–24 the fallacy of matter and its supposed l·.
p 382– 1 supposed l· of matter, opposed to the
430–14 and of the supposed l· of matter and hygiene,
r 484–10 supposed l· of matter yield to the law of
these
sp 83–18 belief that . . . Spirit sets aside these l·,
p 440–24 then render obedience to these l· punishable
transgress the
p 432–17 transgress the l·, and merit punishment,

---

m 62–25 the l· of erring, human concepts.
s 112–18 spiritual rules, l·, and their demonstration,
ph 183– 5 To suppose that God constitutes l· of
184– 1 laws of health are simply l· of mortal belief.
184– 3 Truth makes no l· to regulate sickness,
197–11 less that is said of physical structure and l·,
f 231–14 but there are no antagonistic powers nor l·.
p 384–22 but if you believe in l· of matter
389–19 If God has, . . . instituted l· that food shall
440–23 compel them to enact wicked l· of sickness
t 463–26 if by these are meant l· of matter,

Laws of Health

p 435–15 If . . . committed by trampling on L· of H·,
435–17 L· of H· should be sentenced to die.

lay

pref vii– 6 in cradled obscurity, l· the Bethlehem babe,
a 20–28 "Let us l· aside every weight,— Heb. 12 : 1.
24–27 efficacy of the crucifixion l· in the
38–11 they shall l· hands on the sick,— Mark 16 : 18.
51– 7 He had power to l· down a human sense
52– 2 His pursuits l· far apart from theirs.
s 138– 4 God-power which l· behind Peter's confession
156– 7 and yet, as she l· in her bed,
ph 181–15 but that you l· no stress on
193– 8 Mr. Clark l· with his eyes fixed
f 239– 3 l· it upon those who are in advance of
c 266–17 teaches mortals to l· down their fleshliness
b 311–30 as mortals l· off a false sense of life,
328–25 They shall l· hands on the sick,— Mark 16 : 18.
o 359–27 they shall l· hands on the sick,— Mark 16 : 18.
p 362– * *they shall l· hands on the sick,— Mark 16 : 18.*
364– 5 to l· down his mortal existence in behalf of
r 491–14 mortals can l· off mortality
ap 568–31 by which we l· down all for Truth,
577–23 dynasties will l· down their honors

layeth

a 55–23 whosoever l· his earthly all on the altar

laying

p 436–12 L· down his life for a good deed,
gl 593– 6 PURSE. L· up treasures in matter ; error.

lays

sp 75– 1 truth l· bare the mistaken assumption
f 216– 9 Spirituality l· open siege to materialism.
b 303–16 Divine Science l· the axe at the root

Lazarus

sp 75–12 Jesus said of L· :
75–12 "Our friend L· sleepeth ; — John 11 : 11.
75–14 Jesus restored L· by the understanding that
75–15 L· had never died,
75–17 Had Jesus believed that L· had
83–25 impassable as that between Dives and L·.
s 134–27 and he raised L· from the dead,
r 493–28 If Jesus awakened L· from the

lead

pr	7–27	it may *l·* us into temptation.
	17– 8	And *l·* us not into temptation.— *Matt.* 6 : 13.
m	64–28	might *l·* to a worse state of society
an	101–25	*l·* to moral and to physical death.
s	116–25	ignorantly employed, they often *l·*, . . . to
	119– 5	such theories *l·* to one of two things.
	158–18	It is pitiful to *l·* men into temptation through
f	201– 5	and take the *l·* in our lives,
	218–21	which *l·* only into material ways
	223–18	"If the blind *l·* the blind,— *Matt.* 15 : 14.
	227–20	but evil and error *l·* into captivity.
b	271–22	it will *l·* you into all truth.
	298–22	Spiritual ideas *l·* up to their divine origin,
	299–13	never *l·* towards self, sin, or materiality,
g	513– 7	*l·* on to spiritual spheres and exalted beings.
	514–25	And a little child shall *l·* them.— *Isa.* 11 : 6.

leaden

o	358– 2	Can a *l·* bullet deprive a man of Life,

leader

b	333– 7	Joshua, the renowned Hebrew *l·*.
gl	594–13	SHEEP. . . . those who follow their *l·*.

leaders

f	236– 7	emolument . . . which many *l·* seek?

leadeth

pr	17–10	*And God l· us not into temptation,*
s	127–29	the Comforter which *l·* into all truth.
t	451–13	the way, that *l·* to destruction,— *Matt.* 7 : 13.
ap	578– 7	*l·* me beside the still waters.— *Psal.* 23 : 2.
	578– 8	*l·* me in the paths of righteousness — *Psal.* 23 : 3.

leading

s	109– 2	the *l·* factor in Mind-science.
	129–26	quite as rational are some of the *l·* illusions
f	253– 9	I hope, dear reader, I am *l·* you into the
	254– 1	the human footsteps *l·* to perfection
b	332–22	and *l·* into all truth.
p	377–21	Remove the *l·* error or governing fear
	425– 7	take up the *l·* points included
r	467–21	This is a *l·* point in the Science of Soul,
g	536–19	The blind *l·* the blind, both would fall.
	549–25	Agassiz, discovers the pathway *l·* to
ap	566–11	*l·* to divine heights.

leadings

s	110–13	In following these *l·* of scientific revelation,
	151–30	and follow the *l·* of truth.
t	458–27	in following the *l·* of divine Mind.

leads

sp	92–30	*l·* to belief in the superiority of error.
s	120–29	and so *l·* to disease.
	153–13	This discovery *l·* to more light.
ph	167–26	but one way . . . which *l·* to spiritual being.
	191–11	dawns upon human thought, and *l·* it to
f	202–20	true way *l·* to Life instead of to death,
	205–26	*l·* human thought into opposite channels
	207– 7	Error of statement *l·* to error in action.
	225– 5	You may know when first Truth *l·*
	251–22	*l·* the human mind to relinquish all error,
c	256–26	material sense of God *l·* to formalism
b	277–21	error in the premise *l·* to errors in the
	278–24	*l·* to the conclusion that if a man is
	296–23	The knowledge . . . *l·* to sin and death,
	324–14	*l·* to the understanding that God is the
	338– 2	C. S., rightly understood, *l·* to eternal harmony.
o	346–16	and *l·* to the discernment of Truth.
t	452– 4	Incorrect reasoning *l·* to practical error.
	454– 8	*l·* to the house built without hands
	454–19	inspires, illumines, designates, and *l·* the way.
r	472– 5	The way which *l·* to C. S. is straight
g	505–17	uplifts consciousness and *l·* into all truth
ap	561– 4	*l·* to the discernment of the divine idea.
	566–30	He *l·* the hosts of heaven against the

leaf

ph	191–22	By its own volition, . . . not a *l·* unfolds
p	407– 4	a *l·* naturally attractive to no creature except
g	552–25	blending tints of *l·* and flower show the

leaflet

f	240– 8	*l·* turns naturally towards the light.

league

an	105–31	full many a *l·* in the line of light ;
c	255–12	In *l·* with material sense,

leagues

sp	87–10	Though bodies are *l·* apart

lean

m	66– 6	Trials teach mortals not to *l·* on a material
s	143–21	You *l·* on the inert and unintelligent,
f	205– 3	will *l·* on matter instead of Spirit,
b	321–16	this proof was a staff upon which to *l·*.

leaning

pref	vii– 1	To those *l·* on the sustaining infinite,
a	47– 6	*l·* no longer on matter, but on the

leaps

p	415– 7	thought moves quickly or slowly, *l·* or halts

learn

pr	5– 9	till we *l·* that there is no discount in
	8–28	*l·* what is the affection and purpose of the heart,
	8–30	for in this way only can we *l·*
a	37–16	When will Jesus' professed followers *l·* to
m	60–12	From the logic of events we *l·* that
	67– 2	shall we not drink it and *l·* the lessons
	68– 5	Sometime we shall *l·* how Spirit,
sp	71–11	Thus you *l·* that the flower is a product of the
	71–15	Thus you *l·* that these also are
	71–18	From dreams also you *l·* that
	96– 2	unwillingness to *l·* all things rightly,
an	102–30	Mankind must *l·* that evil is not power.
s	129–25	*l·* from discord the concord of being?
	153– 2	Thus we *l·* that it is not the drug which expels
	159–23	The medical schools should *l·* the state of
	160–27	Why then consult anatomy to *l·*
	160–28	if we are only to *l·* from anatomy that
ph	166–20	we should *l·* that He can do all things for us
	171–11	to *l·* how much of a man he is.
	186–15	must *l·* that there is neither power nor
f	207– 9	We must *l·* that evil is the awful deception
	208–20	Let us *l·* of the real and eternal,
	217–25	*l·* the power of Mind over the body
	223– 3	Sooner or later we shall *l·* that the fetters
	228– 8	if we *l·* that nothing is real but the right,
	236–18	from which we *l·* of the one Mind
	236–26	and *l·* more readily to love the simple verities
	239–16	we must *l·* where our affections are placed
	240–22	we must *l·* to loathe it.
	251–15	*l·* how mankind govern the body,
	251–17	We should *l·* whether they govern the
	252– 7	When false human beliefs *l·* even a little of
c	261–22	and you may *l·* the meaning of God,
	264–28	When we *l·* the way in C. S.
b	271–28	to *l·* and to practise Christian healing.
	276–19	When we *l·* in Science how to be perfect
	281– 3	*l·* that Spirit is infinite and supreme.
	281–22	we shall *l·* that sin and mortality are
	285–29	they will seek to *l·*, not from matter, but
	296–19	Whether mortals will *l·* this sooner or later,
	316– 3	mortals may *l·* how to escape from evil.
	322–29	Then we begin to *l·* Life in divine Science.
	327–19	hastening to *l·* that Life is God, good,
	327–32	by degrees he will *l·* the nothingness of
o	353–22	When we *l·* that error is not real,
p	366–31	first *l·* to bind up the broken-hearted.
	368–21	when we *l·* that life and man survive
	379–18	Then let her *l·* the opposite statement of Life
	386–21	you *l·* that your suffering was merely the
	386–23	You will *l·* at length that there is no
	388–23	self-evident, when we *l·* that God is our Life.
	407–17	Let the slave of wrong desire *l·* the
	430–33	they *l·* that Disease was never there,
t	443–20	may *l·* the value of the apostolic precept :
r	472–30	We *l·* in C. S. that all inharmony
	476–21	*L·* this, O mortal, and earnestly seek the
	481–29	we *l·* that it is material sense, not Soul, which
		sins,
	496– 1	You will also *l·* that in Science there is no
	496– 5	You will *l·* that in C. S. the first duty is
	496– 9	We all must *l·* that Life is God.
g	557– 4	*l·* how to develop their children properly
gl	579– 1	In C. S. we *l·* that the substitution of

learned

pref	ix–22	*l·* that this Science must be demonstrated
a	46– 3	Jesus' students, . . . *l·* that he had not died.
m	64–26	Until it is *l·* that God is the father of all,
sp	79–21	so far as can be *l·* from the Gospels,
	84–29	is *l·* through Christ and C. S.
	84–31	If this Science has been thoroughly *l·*
	98–31	through which immortality and life are *l·*
s	108–21	I *l·* these truths in divine Science :
	153–14	From it may be *l·* that either
	163– 5	declared himself "sick of quackery."
	163–13	Dr. Mason Good, a *l·* Professor in London,
ph	194–14	Every theory . . . (as I *l·* in metaphysics)
f	214–14	When it is *l·* that the spiritual sense,
	221–17	He *l·* that suffering and disease were
	222– 4	*l·* that food affects the body only as
	222– 7	He *l·* also that mortal mind makes a
	222–22	He *l·* that a dyspeptic was very far from
	228– 5	if this great fact of being were *l·*,
b	288–32	seem to have *l·* from error,
	308– 5	Until the lesson is *l·* that God is the
	312– 1	How true it is that whatever is *l·* through
	320–10	and in the *l·* article on Noah
	326–28	He *l·* the wrong that he had done
	326–31	and *l·* a lesson in divine Science.
	330– 3	author of this book *l·* the vastness of C. S.,
o	348–11	medical faculty and clergy have not *l·* this,
	351– 9	Later she *l·* that her own prayers
p	383– 1	wrote . . . I was cured when I *l·* my way in C. S."

learned

p 402–13   Sometime it will be *l·* that mortal mind
426–17   When it is *l·* that disease cannot destroy life,
r 467–32   and cannot be *l·* from its opposite, matter.
486– 2   when you have *l·* falsehood's true nature.
g 533–31   already *l·* that corporeal sense is the serpent.
548–13   before Life is spiritually *l·*.
552–29   Thus it is *l·* that matter is a
gl 591–22   divinely natural, but must be *l·* humanly ;

learner

pref x–31   No . . . is requisite in the *l·*,
a 26–20   to show the *l·* the way by practice
s 147– 2   This system enables the *l·* to demonstrate

learners

b 271–13   not a supernatural gift to those *l·*,
t 457–25   Departing from C. S., some *l·* commend diet

learning

sp 88–10   By *l·* the origin of each.
s 108– 9   immortal cravings, "the price of *l·* love,"
141–31   Give to it the place in our institutions of *l·*
156–12   *l·* that her former physician had prescribed
ph 195–23   tangled barbarisms of *l·* which we deplore,
f 235– 9   reference to their morals as to their *l·*
240–31   unwinding one's snarls, and *l·* from experience
b 274–24   permits no half-way position in *l·* its Principle
290–29   and *l·* that his cruel mind died not.
o 349–29   this is equally true of all *l·*,
p 426–15   *l·* the necessity of working out his
427– 8   *l·* that there is no reality in death,
t 443– *   *and he will increase in l·.— Prov.* 9 : 9.
452–17   luxury of *l·* with egotism and vice.

learns

b 289– 3   until he *l·* that God is the only Life.
p 425–16   when he *l·* that matter never sustained
g 554–15   he *l·* to say, "I am somebody ;

least

a 19–25   Those who cannot demonstrate, at *l·* in part,
m 63–18   Our laws are not impartial, to say the *l·*,
s 126– 9   Human thought never projected the *l·* portion
164–20   does not in the *l·* disprove C. S. ;
ph 170–26   and at *l·* to touch the hem of Truth's garment.
f 242– 5   *l·* of them unto the greatest."— Jer.* 31 : 34.
b 290– 4   If . . . not in the *l·* understood before
293– 3   *l·* material form of illusive consciousness,
o 345–15   at *l·* none which are apparent to those who
361–26   though *l·* in the kingdom of heaven,
p 407– 5   Puffing the obnoxious fumes . . . is at *l·* disgusting.
r 473–32   Few, however, . . . understood in the *l·*
478–20   discharge of the natural functions is *l·*
g 518–19   Love giveth to the *l·* spiritual idea

least-understood

g 539–32   inspired his wisest and *l·* sayings,

leave

pr 9–25   Are you willing to *l·* all for Christ,
10– 4   will *l·* our real desires to be rewarded by Him.
a 33–15   He must *l·* them.
34– 1   and *l·* all for the Christ-principle?
m 66–24   than for a wife precipitately to *l·* her husband
66–25   or for a husband to *l·* his wife.
sp 85–29   and not to *l·* the other undone."— Matt.* 23 : 23.
s 116–13   Works on metaphysics *l·* the grand point
119– 9   to *l·* the creator out of His own universe ;
141– 9   that is, . . . to *l·* all for Christ.
157–27   they *l·* both mind and body worse
ph 189– 2   they are willing to *l·* with astronomy the
192– 6   not Christian Scientists until we *l·* all for
f 208–13   not . . . *l·* man to heal himself ;
b 271–26   Those, who are willing to *l·* their nets
322–18   cannot make the inebriate *l·* his . . . until
324– 1   Willingness . . . to *l·* the old for the new,
324– 2   Gladness to *l·* the false landmarks
o 354– 6   to enable them to *l·* all for Christ,
p 401–28   better for Christian Scientists to *l·* surgery
419– 5   *l·* the field to God, Life, Truth, and Love,
424– 6   we must *l·* the mortal basis of belief
t 443–18   *l·* invalids free to resort to whatever
448–19   Try to *l·* on every student's mind the
g 521– 6   We *l·* this brief, glorious history
543–25   When Spirit made all, did it *l·* aught for

leaven

s 107– *   *l·, which a woman took, and hid— Matt.* 13 : 33.
117–29   *l·* of the Pharisees and of the Sadducees,
117–32   "*l·*, which a woman took, and hid— Matt.* 13 : 33.
118– 2   impels the inference that the spiritual *l·*
118–10   this *l·* of Truth is ever at work.
118–23   until the *l·* of Spirit changes the
b 329– 5   A little *l·* leavens the whole lump.
t 449– 3   A little *l·* causes the whole mass to ferment.

leavened

s 107– *   *till the whole was l·.— Matt.* 13 : 33.
118– 1   *till the whole was l·,"— Matt.* 13 : 33.

leavens

b 329– 5   A little leaven *l·* the whole lump.

leaves

pr 11–14   *l·* the offender free to repeat the offence,
m 66–30   It never *l·* us where it found us.
s 148–30   this ruling of the schools *l·* them to
f 208–16   or that Spirit, . . . *l·* the remedy to matter.
220–10   The *l·* clap their hands as nature's untired
220–15   *l·* catarrh to the latter.
238–23   He who *l·* all for Christ
b 340–28   and *l·* nothing that can sin, suffer,
p 383– 8   when he *l·* it most out of his thought,
406– 2   "The *l·* of the tree were— Rev.* 22 : 2.
r 492– 1   *l·* mortal man intact in body and thought,

leaving

an 104–27   *l·* the case worse than before it was grasped by
p 395– 7   *l·* Soul to master the false evidences of
415–31   *l·* the pain standing forth as distinctly as
r 478– 6   man has never beheld Spirit or Soul *l·* a body

led

pref vii–11   The Wisemen were *l·* to behold and to follow
viii–26   experiences which *l·* her, in the year 1866, to the
sp 95–23   *L·* by a solitary star amid the darkness,
s 109– 1   and *l·* up to my demonstration of the
f 215–15   We are sometimes *l·* to believe that darkness is
b 309–22   and *l·* to deny material sense,
316–15   which *l·* to the conclusion that the
321– 8   *l·* by wisdom to cast down his rod,
p 433–22   and this has *l·* him into the commission of
t 457–14   In the legend of the shield, which *l·* to a quarrel
ap 565– 9   *L·* on by the grossest element of mortal mind,
566– 3   as they were *l·* through the wilderness,

lees

m 65–23   impurity and error are left among the *l·*.

left

pr 6– 8   work badly done or *l·* undone,
6–30   a certain magistrate, . . . *l·* this record :
a 27–23   but only eleven *l·* a desirable historic record.
27–25   other disciples who have *l·* no name.
55–13   cannot be *l·* out of Christianity,
m 65–22   impurity and error are *l·* among the lees.
sp 74– 5   after having once *l·* it,
74–15   belief of having died and *l·* a material body
s 121–14   man, *l·* to the hypotheses of material sense
126–20   *l·* to the mercy of speculative hypotheses?
142–17   palsies the right hand, and causes the *l·* to
147–26   he *l·* no definite rule for demonstrating
149–10   *l·* without explanation except in C. S.
153– 7   not a single saline property *l·*.
ph 176– 8   *l·* the stomach and bowels free to act
179–17   the wild animal, *l·* to his instincts,
f 216–22   If the decision were *l·* to the corporeal senses,
238–10   said, "I have nothing *l·* but Christ."
251–26   nothing is *l·* which deserves to perish or
c 266– 8   solitary, *l·* without sympathy ;
b 304–26   *L·* to the decisions of material sense,
304–32   *l·* in the hands of ignorance,
306–17   If . . . *l·* without a rational proof of
329–11   Jesus, . . . *l·* his example for us.
330–17   *l·* either to human conjecture or to the
o 344–23   and *l·* to us as his rich legacy.
347–11   there is nothing *l·* to be doctored.
p 389– 2   If this decision be *l·* to C. S.,
436–21   You have *l·* Mortal Man no alternative.
g 520–29   nothing *l·* to be made by a lower power.
ap 558– 7   and his *l·* foot on the earth.— Rev.* 10 : 2.
559– 6   The angel's *l·* foot was upon the earth ;

legacy

o 344–24   and left to us as his rich *l·*.

legal

pr 11–12   Mere *l·* pardon . . . leaves the offender
m 56– 7   Marriage is the *l·* and moral provision for
an 105–17   and no longer apply *l·* rulings wholly to

legally

f 225–23   *L·* to abolish unpaid servitude in the

legend

t 457–13   In the *l·* of the shield, which led to a quarrel

legendary

g 526–14   in the *l·* Scriptural text

legerdemain

f 212–21   In *l·* and credulous frenzy, mortals believe

Legion

p 411–16   demon, or evil, replied that his name was *L·*.

legislate

p 381–14   mortal mind cannot *l·* the times, periods,

legislation

m 63–26   the achievement of a nobler race for *l·*,

legislator

p 390–31   as a *l·* would employ to defeat the

legislators
p 440–22 beliefs of your human mental *l·*

legitimate
s 120–28 confirms that testimony as *l·*
ph 182– 8 Which, then, are we to accept as *l·* and
183–17 the *l·* and only possible action of Truth
184–13 the only *l·* and eternal demands on man,
f 227–15 Slavery is not the *l·* state of man.
228–11 The enslavement of man is not *l·*.
254–10 To stop eating, drinking, . . . is not *l·*.
p 367– 8 are but so many parodies on *l·* C. S.,
t 454– 9 Human hate has no *l·* mandate

lending
an 102–25 a problem not *l·* itself to an easy explanation

lends
m 64–10 When a man *l·* a helping hand to some noble
f 209–15 Nearness, . . . *l·* enchantment to this view.

length
pref ix–31 she came at *l·* to its solution ;
a 42– 7 Death will be found at *l·* to be a
m 65–18 will at *l·* demand a higher affection.
s 134– 6 at *l·* the word *martyr* was narrowed in its
b 283–25 practically demonstrated in *l·* of days,
o 359–13 must at *l·* know yourself spiritually
p 370–27 Quackery likewise fails at *l·* to inspire the
380– 1 may rest at *l·* on some receptive thought,
384–30 Sickness, sin, and death must at *l·*
386–23 learn at *l·* that there is no cause for grief,
390–10 Truth will at *l·* compel us all to
431–16 but at *l·* all these assistants resigned to me,

lengthens
r 487–27 *l·* our days by strengthening our trust

lengthy
s 111–26 After a *l·* examination of my discovery

lens
f 214–27 may end the power of light and *l·* !

lenses
p 393–27 complex humors, *l·*, muscles, the iris

leopard
g 514–23 *l·* shall lie down with the kid ;—*Isa.* 11 : 6.

lepers
a 27– 5 *l·* are cleansed, the deaf hear,— *Luke* 7 : 22.
sp 94–21 Of the ten *l·* whom Jesus healed,
s 132– 6 *l·* are cleansed, and the deaf hear,— *Matt.* 11 : 5.

leprosy
b 321–19 scientifically demonstrated that *l·* was a

less
pref viii–18 Is there *l·* sickness because of these
pr 2– 9 nor can the infinite do *l·* than bestow all good,
13–18 *l·* risk of overwhelming our real wishes
a 25–17 any man whose origin was *l·* spiritual.
40–16 crimes of his implacable enemies *l·* criminal?
54– 1 he would have been *l·* sensitive to those beliefs.
m 56–19 is no *l·* imperative than the
62–13 Taking *l·* "thought for your— *Matt.* 6 : 25.
62–14 *l·* thought "for your body — *Matt.* 6 : 25.
62–21 but *l·* and *l·*, if we would be wise and healthy.
63–16 why usage should accord woman *l·* rights
sp 77–24 beautifully *l·* with every advanced stage
86–21 Seeing is no *l·* a quality of physical
98–13 much *l·* can they demonstrate it.
s 108–18 not a fraction more, not a unit *l·*.
123–31 but not on that account is it *l·* scientific.
128–14 and requires *l·* repose.
142– 1 in *l·* time than the old systems,
146– 5 governed more or *l·* by our systems of medicine.
155–23 puts *l·* weight into the material or fleshly scale
155–32 is it safe to say that the *l·* in quantity you have
161–15 they will do *l·* violence to that
163–12 there would be *l·* sickness and *l·* mortality."
ph 166–26 invalid's faith in the divine Mind is *l·* than
170– 7 Did Jesus understand . . . *l·* than Graham
173–32 call into action *l·* than Buddhism
175– 4 and *l·* thought is given to sanitary subjects,
175– 6 there will be better constitutions and *l·* disease.
175–19 Then people had *l·* time for selfishness,
176–30 *l·* distinct type and chronic form of disease.
197–11 The *l·* that is said of physical structure and
198–23 A patient's belief is more or *l·* moulded
198–32 or that a *l·* used arm must be weak.
199–18 of *l·* importance than a knowledge of the fact.
f 203–18 prone to believe . . . in some power *l·* than
217–20 the next toil will fatigue you *l·*,
222–11 Food had *l·* power to help or to hurt him
222–13 he also had *l·* faith in the so-called pleasures and
222–14 Taking *l·* thought about what he should eat
222–15 consulting the stomach *l·* about the
223–11 we cannot put the greater into the *l·*.
224–17 The modern lash is *l·* material than the
244–18 but man was never more nor *l·* than man.
247–31 recipe for beauty is to have *l·* illusion
248– 4 One marvels that a friend can ever seem *l·* than

less
f 249–28 night-dream has *l·* matter as its accompaniment.
b 279–23 medicine is more or *l·* infected with the
295–19 the glass is *l·* opaque than the walls.
314– 1 and no *l·* material until the ascension
317–16 no *l·* tangible because it is spiritual
336–23 else God would . . . become *l·* than God.
336–24 and nothing *l·* can express God.
o 343–24 Christendom generally demands so much *l·*.
344–31 are more fashionable and *l·* spiritual?
353–14 It still holds them more or *l·*.
360–10 They require *l·* self-abnegation,
p 374–24 your steps are *l·* firm because of your fear,
378– 7 Disease is *l·* than mind, and Mind can control
378–31 it would manifest *l·* wisdom than
381–20 Think *l·* of the enactments of mortal mind,
388– 6 Stolidity, which is a resisting state . . . suffers *l·*,
388– 6 only because it knows *l·* of material law.
389– 5 The *l·* we know or think about hygiene,
389– 6 the *l·* we are predisposed to sickness.
395–23 It is no *l·* erroneous to believe in the
397– 8 Suffering is no *l·* a mental condition than
405–29 The pains of sinful sense are *l·* harmful than
406–14 Sin and sickness will abate and seem *l·* real
408–25 tarsal joint is *l·* intimately connected with
415–15 only render mortal mind temporarily *l·* fearful,
419–18 Think *l·* of material conditions
421–12 If a crisis occurs . . . treat the patient *l·* for the
422–18 causing it to depend *l·* on material evidence.
425–15 Mortal man will be *l·* mortal, when he
425–21 and the *l·* we acknowledge matter or its laws,
426– 5 discoverer of C. S. finds the path *l·* difficult
t 449–19 baneful effect of evil associates is *l·* seen than
450–22 Sickness to him is no *l·* a temptation than sin,
461–22 to admit that . . . renders your case *l·* curable,
r 489– 1 The *l·* mind there is manifested in matter
490–13 mortals are more or *l·* deprived of Truth.
g 526– 8 Belief is *l·* than understanding.
542–29 misconception of Life as something *l·* than
554–29 belief that the lower animals are *l·* sickly
554–32 there is *l·* disease in proportion as
555– 1 as the force of mortal mind is *l·* pungent
556–25 Ontology receives *l·* attention than
557–14 the *l·* a mortal knows of sin, disease, and
557–15 the *l·* pain and sorrow are his

lessen
a 40–14 Another's suffering cannot *l·* our
s 155–30 if drugs are an antidote . . . why *l·* the
c 262– 2 does not *l·* man's dependence on God,
t 450–20 enlisted to *l·* evil, disease, and death ;

lessened
sp 80– 2 not *l·* by giving utterance to truth.
b 321–24 God had *l·* Moses' fear by this proof in

lessening
p 405–26 If sin is not regretted and is not *l·*,

lesser
a 40–21 *l·* apostles of Truth may endure
sp 95–14 The greater or *l·* ability of a
an 104–26 case of the greater error overcoming the *l·*.
s 108–14 the *l·* demonstration to prove the greater,
121–24 rule that the greater controls the *l·*.
143–15 takes the *l·* to relieve the greater.
ph 183–23 No reservation is made for any *l·* loyalty.
f 231– 9 no *l·* power equals the infinite All-power ;
b 291– 8 till mortals have already yielded to each *l·* call
303– 8 The minutiæ of *l·* individualities reflect
r 467–19 The greater cannot be in the *l·*.
467–20 belief that the greater can be in the *l·*
g 508–24 rising from the *l·* to the greater,
510–14 the *l·* light to rule the night :—*Gen.* 1 : 16.
518–13 God gives the *l·* idea of Himself for
529–11 belonging to no *l·* parent.
544–26 man, . . . is neither a *l·* god nor the

lesson
f 207–13 Without this *l·*, we lose sight of the
221–32 brings with it another *l·*,
c 226–14 until the *l·* is sufficient to exalt you ;
b 308– 5 Until the *l·* is learned that God is the
326–31 and learned a *l·* in divine Science.
p 363–21 and so brought home the *l·* to all,

lessons
m 67– 2 and learn the *l·* He teaches?
s 109–28 Jesus once said of his *l·* :
f 237–16 should be taught . . . C. S., among their first *l·*,
240– 7 Suns and planets teach grand *l·*.
248– 6 Men and women of riper years and larger *l·*
p 370–28 These *l·* are useful.
407–17 Let the slave of wrong desire learn the *l·* of

lest
pref x–29 *l·* their works be reproved.
a 38–29 *l·* ye should understand and be converted,
o 350–20 *l·* at any time they should see— *Matt.* 13 : 15.
p 366–22 The physician must also watch, *l·* he be
414–18 *l·* you array the sick against their

lest

p 419–17   *l·* aught unfit for development enter thought.
t 459–10   *l·* you yourself be condemned for failing to take
g 529–20   neither shall ye touch it, *l·* ye—*Gen.* 3 : 3.
537– 1   now, *l·* he put forth his hand,—*Gen.* 3 : 22.
537–31   *l·* man should improve it and become better ;
542–17   *l·* any finding him should kill him.—*Gen.* 4 : 15.

let

pr 15–24   and *l·* our lives attest our sincerity.
16–24   Here *l·* me give what I understand to be
a 20–27   "*L·* us lay aside every weight,—*Heb.* 12 : 1.
20–29   *l·* us run with patience the race—*Heb.* 12 : 1.
20–30   *l·* us put aside material self
33–20   *L·* not the flesh, but the Spirit, be represented
42–24   *L·* men think they had killed the body !
m 56– *   *l· not man put asunder.*—*Matt.* 19 : 6.
62–24   *l·* no mortal interfere with God's government
63–22   *l·* us hope it will be granted.
64–27   *L·* not mortals permit a disregard of law
sp 91– 5   *L·* us rid ourselves of the belief that man is
an 106–15   *L·* this age, which sits in judgment on C. S.,
s 141–28   *L·* our pulpits do justice to C. S.
141–29   *L·* it have fair representation by the
142–17   causes the left to *l·* go its grasp on the divine.
144– 3   *l·* us rely upon Mind, which needs no
ph 168–30   Here *l·* a word be noticed which will be
f 201–14   *L·* us disrobe error.
208–20   *L·* us learn of the real and eternal,
225– 9   and will command their sentinels not to *l·* truth
239– 8   *l·* worth be judged according to wisdom,
239–12   *L·* it be understood that success in error is
239–14   "*L·* the wicked forsake his way,—*Isa.* 55 : 7.
242–16   *l·* us labor to dissolve with the universal
246–29   *L·* us then shape our views of existence into
248–29   *L·* unselfishness, goodness, mercy,
249– 1   *L·* us accept Science, relinquish all theories
249– 3   *l·* us have one God, one Mind,
249– 5   *L·* the "male and female" of—*Gen.* 1 : 27.
249– 6   *L·* us feel the divine energy of Spirit,
249– 8   *L·* us rejoice that we are subject to
c 255– 3   "*L·* there be light,"—*Gen.* 1 : 3.
267–27   "*l·* thy garments be always white."—*Eccl.* 9 : 8.
b 276– 8   "*L·* this Mind be in you, which,—*Phil.* 2 : 5.
302–14   *l·* us remember that harmonious and
308–24   "*L·* me go. for the day breaketh ;"—*Gen.* 32 : 26.
327–29   *L·* that inform the sentiments
340– 6   "*L·* us hear the conclusion of—*Eccl.* 12 : 13.
340– 9   *L·* us hear the conclusion of the whole matter :
o 355–10   *l·* the dead bury their dead."—*Matt.* 8 : 22.
355–11   *L·* discord of every name and nature be heard no
355–12   *l·* the harmonious and true sense of Life
359– 3   *L·* any clergyman try to cure his friends by
p 367–21   *L·* us watch, work, and pray that this salt
368–32   Once *l·* the mental physician believe in the
379–14   *L·* the despairing invalid, inspecting the hue
379–18   *l·* her learn the opposite statement of Life
381–27   *L·* us banish sickness as an outlaw,
384– 5   *L·* us reassure ourselves with the
385–11   *L·* us remember that the eternal law of right,
390–13   *l·* your higher sense of justice
394–20   Will you bid a man *l·* evils overcome him,
407–17   *L·* the slave of wrong desire learn
407–24   *L·* the perfect model be present in your
422–22   *L·* us suppose two parallel cases of
434– 6   Others say, . . . *l·* us follow Christ."
436–25   but they were compelled to *l·* him be taken
438– 3   *L·* us make man in our image,—*Gen.* 1 : 26.
438– 4   and *l·* them have dominion.—*Gen.* 1 : 26.
441–11   *L·* what False Belief utters, now and forever,
t 444–16   *L·* us be faithful in pointing the way
444–18   but *l·* us also be careful always to
444–25   "*L·* there be no strife, I pray thee,—*Gen.* 13 : 8.
454–26   *L·* your loving care and counsel support all
457–30   *L·* this Principle be applied to the cure of
r 471–10   "*L·* God be true, but every—*Rom.* 3 : 4.
475–23   "*L·* us make man in our image,—*Gen.* 1 : 26.
475–24   and *l·* them have dominion—*Gen.* 1 : 26.
495–16   *L·* neither fear nor doubt overshadow your
495–20   *L·* C. S., instead of corporeal sense,
g 503–18   And God said, *L·* there be light :—*Gen.* 1 : 3.
505– 4   God said, *L·* there be a firmament—*Gen.* 1 : 6.
505– 5   and *l·* it divide the waters from—*Gen.* 1 : 6.
506–15   *L·* the waters under the heaven—*Gen.* 1 : 9.
506–16   and *l·* the dry land appear :—*Gen.* 1 : 9.
507–11   *L·* the earth bring forth grass,—*Gen.* 1 : 11.
509– 9   And God said, *L·* there be lights—*Gen.* 1 : 14.
509–11   and *l·* them be for signs, and for—*Gen.* 1 : 14.
510– 6   And *l·* them be for lights in the—*Gen.* 1 : 15.
511–19   *L·* the waters bring forth—*Gen.* 1 : 20.
512–18   *l·* fowl multiply in the earth.—*Gen.* 1 : 22.
513–14   *L·* the earth bring forth the—*Gen.* 1 : 24.
515–11   *L·* us make man in our image,—*Gen.* 1 : 26.
515–12   and *l·* them have dominion—*Gen.* 1 : 26.
515–21   "*L·* them have dominion."—*Gen.* 1 : 26.
525–13   Icelandic : . . . *L·* us make man after our mind
542–19   *L·* Truth uncover and destroy error

let

g 542–20   *l·* human justice pattern the divine.
548– 2   *l·* him take the water of life—*Rev.* 22 : 17.
556–19   "*L·* there be light."—*Gen.* 1 : 3.
fr 600– *   *L· us get up early to the vineyards ;*—*Song* 7 : 12.
600– *   *l· us see if the vine flourish,*—*Song* 7 : 12.

lethargy

a 38– 7   when the *l·* of mortals, produced by

lets

pr 15– 5   *l·* in Truth, Life, and Love.
p 407–26   spiritualization of thought *l·* in the light,

letter

absolute

r 483–21   revealed the spirit . . . if not the absolute *l·*.

and the spirit

b 330– 9   the *l·* and the spirit bear witness,

lack of the

s 145– 5   the lack of the *l·* could not hinder their work ;

of Christian Science

o 354–32   If the *l·* of C. S. appears inconsistent,

of Science

s 113– 3   The *l·* of Science plentifully reaches humanity
f 243–11   must always accompany the *l·* of Science

without the spirit

s 145– 6   *l·*, without the spirit, would have made void

s 113– 7   Without this, the *l·* is but the dead body of
114–22   has to be poured into the old bottles of the *l·*.
p 367– 3   nor bury the *morale* of C. S. in the . . . *l·*.
t 451– 8   Students of C. S., who start with its *l·*
454–31   Remember that the *l·* and mental argument are
r 495–27   Study thoroughly the *l·* and imbibe the spirit.

letting

s 158–26   *l·* in matter's higher stratum, mortal mind.
163– 2   and afterward *l·* her loose upon sick people."
g 508–29   *l·* in the light of spiritual understanding.

level

ph 173– 8   is reduced to the *l·* of error,
f 239– 8   Break up cliques, *l·* wealth with honesty,
p 369–27   Unscientific methods are finding their dead *l·*.
g 508– 1   the divine idea seems to fall to the *l·* of

lever

r 485–32   is like saying that the power is in the *l·*.

Levi

gl 590–11   definition of

liability

a 40–15   Another's suffering cannot lessen our own *l·*.
f 230–29   never thoroughly healed until the *l·*
p 377– 3   and that thought governs this *l·*.

liable

s 140–24   a man-projected God, *l·* to wrath, repentance,
159–32   physician is *l·* to increase disease
f 230–28   though it is *l·* to reappear ;
248–22   results is that you are *l·* to follow
b 304–27   *l·* to be misapprehended and lost in confusion.
p 369– 1   he is *l·* to admit also the reality of
392–16   If . . . you are *l·* to an attack from that source.
392–18   *l·* to the development of that thought
412–11   by naming it audibly, you are *l·*
419–22   mortal mind is *l·* to any phase of belief.

liar

he is a

b 292–25   he is a *l·*, and the father of it."—*John* 8 : 44.
g 554–21   "He is a *l·*, and the father of it."—*John* 8 : 44.
gl 580–31   he is a *l·* and the father of it."—*John* 8 : 44.

it was "a

o 357– 7   it was "a *l·*, and the father of it."—*John* 8 : 44.

s 113–25   "but every [mortal] man a *l·*."—*Rom.* 3 : 4.
b 296–31   Mortal belief is a *l·* from the beginning,
o 357– 9   Truth creates neither a lie, . . . nor a *l·*.
p 441–13   Material Law is a *l·* who cannot bear witness
441–31   Personal Sense, is recorded . . . as a *l·*.
r 441–14   but every [material] man a *l·*."—*Rom.* 3 : 4.
478–17   No, not if God is true and mortal man a *l·*.

liars

pr 16–19   the first lie and all *l·*.

liberal

pr 3–21   and for a *l·* outpouring of benefactions.

liberally

a 54–10   That he might *l·* pour his dear-bought treasures

liberation

an 103– 9   As in the beginning, however, this *l·* does not

liberator

f 225–22   Love is the *l·*.

Liberty

s 161–21   as she knelt before a statue of *L·*,
161–22   "*L·*, what crimes are committed in thy name !"
b 299– 3   when he carves his "Statue of *L·*,"

liberty

and life
p 434–26 conspiracy against the *l·* and life of Man.
and rights
p 435–17 a destroyer of Mortal Man's *l·* and rights.
elements of
f 224–28 Truth brings the elements of *l·*.
glorious
f 227–25 "glorious *l·* of the children of God,"—*Rom.* 8 : 21.
set at
pref xi–21 To set at *l·* them that are bruised.— *Luke* 4 : 18.
standard of
f 227–21 C. S. raises the standard of *l·*

s 161–17 life, *l·*, and the pursuit of happiness."
f 227–18 Spirit of the Lord is, there is *l·*."— *II Cor.* 3 : 17.
b 315–19 the *l·* of the sons of God.
p 435–35 *l·* of which he has been unjustly deprived.
r 481– 5 Spirit of the Lord is, there is *l·*."— *II Cor.* 3 : 17.

licentious

s 130– 2 The *l·* disposition is discouraged over its

lie (noun)

charges its
b 307–17 Error charges its *l·* to Truth and says :
claims to be
g 523– 7 the *l·* claims to be truth.
condemned this
g 539–16 Scriptures declare that God condemned this *l·*
consigns the
g 542–25 justice consigns the *l·* which,
destroys itself
b 286–30 error, the *l·*, destroys itself.
destroy this
ap 568– 5 Science is able to destroy this *l·*, called evil.
first
pr 16–19 is but another name for the first *l·*
gl 594–9 SERPENT . . . the first *l·* of limitation ;
first voluble
g 533–13 the snake-talker utters the first voluble *l·*,
from the beginning
ap 567–26 must be a *l·* from the beginning.
giving the
g 530–18 represents error as . . . giving the *l·* to
hides behind a
g 542– 6 Though error hides behind a *l·*
loves a
a 47–23 world generally loves a *l·* better than Truth ;
maketh a
ap 577–27 "defileth, . . . or maketh a *l·*."— *Rev.* 21 : 27.
gl 588– 4 "worketh . . . or maketh a *l·*."— *Rev.* 21 : 27.
material
ap 565–24 the material *l·* made war upon the
of false belief
p 370– 3 turn from the *l·* of false belief to Truth,
of material sense
b 318–12 We must silence this *l·* of material sense
rejecting a
o 357– 6 not by accepting, but by rejecting a *l·*.
serpentine
g 541–12 Here the serpentine *l·* invents new forms.
speaketh a
b 292–25 When he speaketh a *l·*, he— *John* 8 : 44.
suppositional
an 103–17 Evil is a suppositional *l·*.
symbolizes a
ap 563– 8 The great red dragon symbolizes a *l·*,
turns the
sp 92–21 Uncover error, and it turns the *l·* upon you.
worketh a
t 445–24 human will which maketh and worketh a *l·*,

sp 81–14 than the opposite . . . would prove immortality a *l·*.
ph 177–20 But a *l·*, the opposite of Truth, cannot
177–22 nor can a *l·* hold the preponderance of
b 330–28 manifested by mankind it stands for a *l·*,
o 357– 8 Truth creates neither a *l·*, . . . nor a liar.
t 448– 9 tell the truth concerning the *l·*.
r 480–25 The supposititious parent of evil is a *l·*.
g 524–25 or is it a *l·* concerning man and God?
524–27 It must be a *l·*, for God presently
527–20 Evil is unreal because it is a *l·*.
527–26 the *l·* represents God as repeating creation,
540–24 is to teach mortals never to believe a *l·*.
gl 584– 9 DEATH. An illusion, the *l·* of life in matter ;
584–17 DEVIL. Evil ; a *l·* ; error ;
594– 2 a *l·* ; the opposite of Truth, named error ;

lie (verb)

sp 87–23 the bodies which *l·* buried in its sands ;
f 252–19 says : . . . I can cheat, *l·*, commit adultery,
b 291–22 "As the tree falls, so it must *l·*."
o 357–20 Truth creates neither a lie, a capacity to *l·*, nor
g 514–23 shall *l·* down with the kid ;— *Isa.* 11 : 6.
ap 578– 6 to *l·* down in green pastures :— *Psal.* 23 : 2.

lies

pr 9– 3 The wrong *l·* in unmerited censure,
9– 5 *l·* in the answer to these questions :
m 68–22 to hatch their silly innuendoes and *l·*,
ph 165–19 your remedy *l·* in forgetting the whole thing ;
171–31 fundamental error *l·* in the supposition
f 250–20 To the observer, the body *l·* listless,
o 349–14 The chief difficulty . . . *l·* in this,
349–19 The elucidation of C. S. *l·* in its spiritual sense,
p 368– 3 confidence inspired by Science *l·* in the fact
385– 6 explanation *l·* in the support which they derived
427–22 difficulty *l·* in ignorance of what God is.
r 489–13 Corporeal sense defrauds and *l·* ;
g 514–12 Undisturbed it *l·* in the open field,

lieth

ap 574–16 the city which "*l·* foursquare."—*Rev.* 21 : 16.
575– 8 as one that "*l·* foursquare"— *Rev.* 21 : 16.

Life (*see also* Life's)

abideth in
b 325– 5 Such a one abideth in *L·*,
all
s 146–29 It lives through all *L·*,
g 526– 8 namely, that all *L·* is God.
all is
b 331–16 all is *L·*, and there is no death.
o 347– 7 all is *L* , and death has no dominion.
and goodness
f 246–28 *L·* and goodness are immortal.
and health
p 430–11 shut out the true sense of *L·* and health.
and intelligence
pr 14–12 *L·* and intelligence are purely spiritual,
b 310–15 Soul . . . as the central *L·* and intelligence
r 477–22 Soul is the substance, *L·*, and intelligence of
and its faculties
f 246– 4 *L·* and its faculties are not measured by
and Love
a 22–12 the demand of *L·* and Love,
26–32 working out the harmony of *L·* and Love.
sp 91– 6 obey only the divine Principle, *L·* and Love.
s 108– 5 It was the divine law of *L·* and Love,
c 258– 3 glories of limitless, incorporeal *L·* and Love.
h 323–25 gives the true understanding of *L·* and Love.
o 348–15 when we ascribe to Him almighty *L·* and Love
p 381–17 In infinite *L·* and Love there is no sickness,
430– 9 advance more rapidly towards God, *L·*, and Love.
g 538–12 a figure of divine *L·* and Love,
ap 561–10 Purity was the symbol of *L·* and Love.
gl 589– 7 yield to the spiritual sense of *L·* and Love.
596–23 divine *L·* and Love illumine it,
598–24 the spiritual understanding of *L·* and Love,
and Soul
o 344– 2 God as the only absolute *L·* and Soul,
and substance
b 314–22 the true idea of *L·* and substance.
and the universe
b 306–28 *L·* and the universe, ever present and eternal.
and Truth
s 117–18 illustrating and demonstrating *L·* and Truth
f 216–18 is in submission to everlasting *L·* and Truth
b 279–20 demonstration of eternal *L·* and Truth
304– 1 sweet sense and presence of *L·* and Truth.
as God
sp 79– 4 those who are ignorant of *L·* as God.
b 310–27 if Spirit should lose *L·* as God, good,
as Love
p 391–30 rise to the true consciousness of *L·* as Love,
as permanent
b 306–24 which cognizes *L·* as permanent.
bread of
f 222–10 and feeds thought with the bread of *L·*.
can be understood
p 427–11 before *L·* can be understood and harmony
corresponds to
g 517–10 ideal woman corresponds to *L·* and
demonstrates
b 306– 7 *L·* demonstrates *L·*.
337–18 which demonstrates *L·* in Christ,
divine
  (*see* **divine**)
eternal
pref vii–20 Him whom to know aright is *L·* eternal.
a 50–19 If his full recognition of eternal *L·* had
f 203–32 in order to give him eternal *L·*,
c 257–29 inexhaustible Love, eternal *L·*, omnipotent Truth.
258–27 To him belongs eternal *L·*.
259– 3 for he reflects eternal *L·* ;
b 279–20 demonstration of eternal *L·* and
p 380– 4 must be finally conquered by eternal *L·*.
426–27 with unflinching faith in God, in *L·* eternal.
429– 1 omnipotent and eternal *L·*.
r 469– 3 all substance and is *L·* eternal.
497– 4 the Bible as our sufficient guide to eternal *L·*.

Life

eternal
r 497–22 faith to understand eternal *L·*,
g 509– 8 the certain sense of eternal *L·*.
gl 584–15 until every belief . . . yields to eternal *L·*.
586– 9 FATHER. Eternal *L·* ; the one Mind ;
588– 8 development of eternal *L·*, Truth, and Love.
everlasting
f 216–18 his body is in submission to everlasting *L·*
r 489–12 yields to the reality of everlasting *L·*.
ever-present
b 312–20 man's eternal Principle is ever-present *L·*.
evidences of
b 289–17 with the spiritual evidences of *L·* ;
explain
a 27–17 Jesus' parables explain *L·* as never mingling
God is our
s 107–17 remembering that in reality God is our *L·*,
p 388–24 when we learn that God is our *L·*.
God, or
a 27–21 pantheism,— that God, or *L·*, is in or of matter.
sp 95– 7 We approach God, or *L·*. in proportion to
goes on unchanged
s 122–26 in Science, *L·* goes on unchanged
great facts of
s 122– 4 but the great facts of *L·*, rightly understood,
his
a 25–10 His true flesh and blood were his *L·* ;
immortal
r 496–22 at war with the facts of immortal *L·*,
immortality of
sp 76–23 perfect harmony and immortality of *L·*,
infinite
o 347– 7 God, who is infinite *L·*,
p 381–17 In infinite *L·* and Love there is no
g 518–23 varied expressions of God reflect . . . infinite *L·*,
in Himself
o 357–19 Has the Father "*L·* in Himself,"— *John* 5 : 26.
intelligence and
f 215–14 the light and might of intelligence and *L·*.
irradiance of
gl 584– 1 DAY. The irradiance of *L·* ;
is continuous
s 157–30 proof that *L·* is continuous and harmonious.
is deathless
r 487– 3 *L·* is deathless.
is divine Mind
r 469– 4 *L·* is divine Mind.
is divine Principle
r 468–26 *Answer.*— *L·* is divine Principle, Mind, Soul,
is eternal
f 246–27 *L·* is eternal.
is God
a 27–10 That *L·* is God, Jesus proved
51–16 He knew . . . that real *L·* is God ;
ph 193–32 demonstrated to me that *L·* is God
200–11 *L·* is God, and man is the idea of God,
f 228– 6 nothing . . . can enter being, for *L· is* God.
b 288–21 *L·* is God, good, and not evil ;
289–32 Because *L·* is God, Life must be eternal,
309–17 If these children . . . forget that *L·* is God,
327–19 mortals are hastening to learn that *L·* is God,
p 366–28 *L·* is God and God is All.
369–20 He understood man, whose *L·* is God,
394–28 We should remember that *L·* is God,
r 487–27 The understanding that *L·* is God, Spirit,
496– 9 We all must learn that *L·* is God.
g 526– 8 namely, that all *L·* is God.
550–21 If *L·* is God, as the Scriptures imply,
is Mind
b 331– 5 *L·* is Mind, the creator reflected
is not contingent
p 368–20 *L·* is not contingent on bodily conditions
is not embryonic
g 550–22 If Life is God, . . . then *L·* is not embryonic,
is not limited
r 469– 4 *L·* is not limited.
is real
p 428– 3 *L·* is real, and death is the illusion.
is reflected
g 516– 9 *L·* is reflected in existence,
is self-sustained
p 390– 4 We cannot deny that *L·* is self-sustained,
is Spirit
c 264–16 When we realize that *L·* is Spirit,
b 310–26 The only *L·* is Spirit,
p 376–12 that *L·* is Spirit, and that
is the law
m 63–10 and *L·* is the law of his being.
p 427– 2 *L·* is the law of Soul, even the law of
is the origin
r 487– 3 *L·* is the origin and ultimate of man,
is Truth
r 472– 1 and that this *L·* is Truth and Love ;
Jesus demonstrated
f 244– 5 On their basis Jesus demonstrated *L·*,

Life

law of
(*see* **law**)
laws of
s 107– 2 the Christ Science or divine laws of *L·*,
leads to
f 202–20 the true way leads to *L·* instead of to death,
life of
b 320– 2 of the truth of Truth and of the life of *L·*,
Love, and wisdom
b 283– 6 Mind is the same *L·*, Love, and wisdom
Love, Truth
sp 81–15 *L·*, Love, Truth, is the only proof of
manifestations of
g 543–27 reflected in the myriad manifestations of *L·*,
man's
o 358– 4 that is, of God, who is man's *L·*
p 425–17 can never destroy God, who is man's *L·*.
Mind and
b 276–17 admitted to be the only Mind and *L·*,
Mind or
b 291–26 No resurrection from the grave awaits Mind
or *L·*,
misconception of
g 542–29 The sinful misconception of *L·*
must be eternal
b 289–32 *L·* must be eternal, self-existent.
newness of
g 520–13 they will reveal eternity, newness of *L·*,
no matter in
s 113–31 no matter in *L·*, and no life in matter ;
not the fruits of
f 243–30 sin, and death are not the fruits of *L·*.
of all
g 509– 2 Spirit is discerned to be the *L·* of all,
of man
a 51–11 Nothing could kill this *L·* of man.
b 304–17 Divine Principle is the *L·* of man.
p 388–22 does not affect the absolute *L·* of man,
g 555–30 Knowing that God was the *L·* of man,
one
a 19–32 thou shalt not know evil, for there is one *L·*,
f 204– 4 false conclusions that there is more than one *L·* ;
b 283–19 deem this the manifestation of the one *L·*,
r 467–10 one God and Father, one *L·*, Truth, and Love.
or God
f 249–11 Any other theory of *L·*, or God, is delusive
b 283–14 They insist that *L·*, or God, is one . . . with
o 357–30 if so, can *L·*, or God, dwell in evil
g 543–29 belief . . . would make *L·*, or God, mortal.
or intelligence
g 550– 5 God is the *L·*, or intelligence, which
or Mind
sp 91–17 the substance of *L·* or Mind.
b 282– 3 The real *L·*, or Mind, and its opposite,
290–10 That *L·* or Mind is finite . . . is false.
g 509– 3 and the deathless *L·*, or Mind,
550– 3 If this be so, whence cometh *L·*, or Mind,
or Soul
b 306–13 If *L·* or Soul and its representative, man,
or Truth
a 42– 6 It cannot make *L·* or Truth apparent.
ph 196–16 are not concomitants of *L·* or Truth.
over death
p 406–22 the supremacy of . . . *L·* over death,
path of
t 451–12 strive, to enter the narrow path of *L·*,
Principle, or
b 283–24 The divine Principle, or *L·*, cannot be
g 507–16 creative power of the divine Principle, or *L·*,
real
a 51–16 He knew . . . that real *L·* is God ;
b 282– 3 The real *L·*, or Mind, and its opposite,
328– 5 God is good and the only real *L·*.
reality of
sp 72–27 earthly mortal is not the reality of *L·*
b 322– 5 we shall gain the reality of *L·*,
o 353–32 nor apprehend the reality of *L·*.
r 487–29 our trust in the deathless reality of *L·*,
reveals
f 250–30 Science reveals *L·* as not being at the mercy of
Science of
(*see* **Science**)
Soul, or
p 388–25 sin and sickness are not qualities of Soul, or *L·*,
Spirit, and
b 280–23 belief that . . . Spirit, and *L·*, is in finite forms.
spirit of
p 433–31 Ah ! but Christ, Truth, the spirit of *L·*
spiritual
(*see* **spiritual**)
statement of
p 379–19 let her learn the opposite statement of *L·*
substance and
b 286–22 God's thoughts . . . are substance and *L·*.

Life

substance, and intelligence
a 27–14 *L·*, substance, and intelligence of the universe
ph 185–19 God as the only *L·*, substance, and intelligence,
gl 595– 7 the idea of *L·*, substance, and intelligence ;
supernal
b 319– 2 has no kinship with the *L·* supernal.
that is Truth
sp 97–29 demonstrating the *L·* that is Truth,
the only
ph 185–19 God as the only *L·*, substance, and
b 289– 4 until he learns that God is the only *L·*.
307–13 as much as God, Spirit, who *is* the only *L·*.''
310–26 The only *L·* is Spirit,
324–15 the understanding that God is the only *L·*.
330–11 God is infinite, the only *L·*, substance,
p 428–32 the understanding of God as the only *L·*.
r 472– 1 Science teaches man that God is the only *L·*,
theory of
f 249–11 Any other theory of *L·*, or God, is delusive
true idea of
b 314–22 the true idea of *L·* and substance.
325– 2 he who perceives the true idea of *L·*
true sense of
o 355–13 the harmonious and true sense of *L·*
p 430–11 shut out the true sense of *L·* and health.
Truth and
    (see **Truth**)
Truth, and Love
pr 3–27 If we are ungrateful for *L·*, Truth, and Love,
14–18 controlled by spiritual *L·*, Truth, and Love.
a 50–14 Had *L·*, Truth, and Love forsaken him
54–14 proof that *L·*, Truth, and Love heal the sick
s 107– 2 divine laws of *L·*, Truth, and Love,
108–23 *L·*, Truth, and Love are all-powerful and
138– 6 evident to Peter that divine *L·*, Truth, and Love,
140– 8 as divine Mind, as *L·*, Truth, and Love.
164–24 *L·*, Truth, and Love save from sin,
b 298– 2 *L·*, Truth, and Love are the realities of
303–11 Whatever reflects Mind, *L·*, Truth, and Love, is
331–26 *L·*, Truth, and Love constitute the triune
336–16 emanations of Him who is *L·*, Truth, and Love.
p 419– 5 leave the field to God, *L·*, Truth, and Love,
427–22 God, *L·*, Truth, and Love make man undying.
r 467–10 one God and Father, one *L·*, Truth, and Love.
469–10 *L·*, Truth, and Love, — named God.
474– 1 *L·*, Truth, and Love . . . destroy all error,
474–16 If . . . are as real as *L·*, Truth, and Love,
g 502–27 The creative Principle — *L·*, Truth, and Love
505–23 unfolds Mind, — *L·*, Truth, and Love,
508– 7 *L·*, Truth, and Love which governs all.
510–27 a symbol of Mind, of *L·*, Truth, and Love,
515–20 the tri unity of *L·*, Truth, and Love.
518–23 reflect . . . infinite *L·*, Truth, and Love.
522–29 Does *L·*, Truth, and Love produce death,
ap 577–14 first, the Word of *L·*, Truth, and Love ;
gl 582–29 representatives of *L·*, Truth, and Love.
583–22 self-existent *L·*, Truth, and Love ;
588– 8 development of eternal *L·*, Truth, and Love.
592–16 eternal Principle ; *L·*, Truth, and Love.
593–20 *L·*, Truth, and Love understood and
599– 4 reflected animation of *L·*, Truth, and Love.
Truth, . . . and Love
    (see **Truth**)
Truth or
sp 91–14 is by no means the destruction of Truth or *L·*,
Truth, . . . or Love
f 207–26 presuppose the absence of Truth, *L·*, or Love.
Truth that is
sp 97–30 the Life that is Truth, and the Truth that is *L·*,
Truth which is
a 35–23 Life which is Truth and the Truth which is *L·*
f 235–23 who understand not the divine Truth which is *L·*
understanding of
    (see **understanding**)
unfolding of
b 335–23 can we gain the eternal unfolding of *L·*
unknown to
r 469– 5 Death and finiteness are unknown to *L·*.
vast forever of
c 266–31 into the vast forever of *L·*,
verities of
sp 75–32 when we awake . . . to the grand verities of *L·*,
vesture of
f 242–21 The vesture of *L·* is Truth.
way of
a 25–13 Jesus taught the way of *L·* by demonstration,
s 137–25 Love hath shown thee the way of *L·* !
we apprehend
ph 167– 6 We apprehend *L·* in divine Science
which is God
a 47– 3 a faint conception of the *L·* which is God.
ap 561–19 understanding the *L·* which is God.
which is Truth
a 35–22 as we reach the *L·* which is Truth

Life

will be recognized
sp 76– 6 *L·* will be recognized as neither material nor
Word of
ap 577–14 first, the Word of *L·*, Truth, and Love ;

———

pr 17–14 *L·*, Truth, Love, over all, and All.
a 19–31 Thou shalt have no belief of *L·* as mortal ;
44– 9 He proved *L·* to be deathless and Love to be
sp 72– 1 the *L·* of which corporeal sense can take no
98–19 Christ's revelation of Truth, of *L·*, and of Love.
s 113–19 *L·*, God, omnipotent good, deny death, evil,
113–21 evil, death, deny good, omnipotent God, *L·*.
115–13 GOD : Divine Principle, *L·*, Truth, Love, Soul,
124–10 thus limiting *L·* and holding fast to discord
151–20 lungs, brain, etc., have nothing to do with *L·*,
ph 172–20 belief that there is Soul in sense or *L·* in matter
186–25 If death is as real as *L·*, immortality is a
191–13 spiritual sense of being and of what *L·* includes.
200– 9 *L·* is, . . . and ever will be independent of
f 203–24 Death is not a stepping-stone to *L·*.
206– 2 no other Love, . . . no other sense of *L·*,
215–20 are the suppositional absence of *L·*, God,
216– 4 What has touched *L·*, God, to such strange
231–10 but God, Truth, *L·*, Love, does heal the
243–26 *L·* has no partnership with death.
249–18 *L·* is, like Christ, "the same — *Heb.* 13 : 8.
249–20 Organization and time have nothing to do with *L·*.
253– 7 without beginning and without end, for I am *L·*.
c 260–32 If we look to the body for. . .*L·*, we find death ;
b 275–12 Spirit, *L·*, Truth, Love, combine as one,
275–18 no life is *L·* but the divine ;
286–11 but by me,'' Christ, *L·*, — *John* 14 : 6.
288–24 that *L·* is not subject to death ;
289–11 *L·* and Life's idea, . . . never make men sick,
289–27 *L·* is not in matter.
289–32 not the offspring of flesh, but of Spirit, — of *L·*,
290– 1 *L·* is the everlasting I AM,
292–10 belief . . . and *L·* be controlled by death.
293–16 whose adhesion and cohesion are *L·*,
296–12 is what reveals man and *L·*, harmonious,
300–32 God is revealed only in that which reflects *L·*,
306– 8 if God, who is *L·*, were parted for a moment
307–15 is found to be not *L·*, but only a transient,
309–29 *L·* is never for a moment extinct.
322–29 Then we begin to learn *L·* in divine Science.
325–17 perfect as the Father, indestructible in *L·*,
330–20 Scriptures declare Him to be, — *L·*, Truth, Love.
331– 1 and *L·* is no more confined to
332–14 the Way, then the *L·*, and the *L·*,
335–19 Nothing but Spirit, Soul, can evolve *L·*,
o 347– 6 Nothing really has *L·* but God,
349–11 neither *L·* nor man dies,
357–31 Can matter drive *L·*, Spirit, hence,
358– 3 Can a leaden bullet deprive a man of *L·*,
p 378–27 never endowed matter with power to disable *L·*
380–31 opposing . . . against *L·*, health, harmony.
388–15 hypothesis . . . food has power to destroy *L·*,
406–20 Error is opposed to *L·*,
407–27 brings . . . *L·* not death, into your consciousness.
428–17 the *L·* which mortal sense cannot impair
429– 2 this *L·* must be brought to light
429–22 if *L·* ever had any beginning, it must also have
433–29 to prepare the frightened sense of *L·*,
r 465–10 Spirit, Soul, Principle, *L·*, Truth, Love.
468–25 *Question.* — What is *L·*?
468–27 *L·* is without beginning and without end.
468–29 Eternity, not time, expresses the thought of *L·*,
469– 1 *L·* is neither in nor of matter.
469– 6 If *L·* ever had a beginning, it would
470– 8 assumed . . . the loss of the spiritual presence of *L·*
486–18 If . . . a better friend than *L·*.
492– 5 *L·* cannot be united to its unlikeness,
495–19 life harmonious — as *L·* eternally is
495–20 belief in, that which *L·* is not.
g 516– 4 The substance, *L·*, intelligence, Truth, and
531–25 Which institutes *L·*, — matter or Mind?
531–25 Does *L·* begin with Mind or with matter?
531–26 Is *L·* sustained by matter or by Spirit?
539– 8 the standard of good, of Spirit, of *L·*,
544– 6 Mind, . . . the producer, *L·* was self-sustained.
544– 9 *L·* consisteth not of the things which
544–30 declares . . . so-called mortal life to be *L·*,
548–13 before *L·* is spiritually learned.
550–20 If *L·* has any starting-point whatsoever,
ap 561–17 in *L·* and its demonstration,
569– 1 as *L·*, represented by the Father ;
gl 580–22 false supposition that *L·* is not eternal,
584–10 the unreal and untrue ; the opposite of *L·*.
584–14 until every belief of life where *L·* is not
587– 7 *L·* ; Truth ; Love ; all substance ;
590–14 definition of
591–17 substance, *L·*, Truth, Love ; the one God ;

life (*see also* **life's**)

Abel's
  g 541– 4   Cain seeks Abel's *l·*, instead of making his

action, nor
  s 136– 6   claimed no...action, nor *l·* separate from God.

and being
  an 103–31   *L·* and being are of God.

and brotherhood
  g 541–17   ruptures the *l·* and brotherhood of man

and death
  sp 92– 4   the issues of *l·* and death,
  ph 190–10   thoughts of pain and pleasure, of *l·* and death,
  f 211– 4   good and evil, *l·* and death ;
  246– 3   sickness and health, *l·* and death.
  b 298–17   hope and fear, *l·* and death,
  303–21   belief that pain and pleasure, *l·* and death,
  r 466– 9   mind and matter, *l·* and death,

and happiness
  c 262–21   drop the false estimate of *l·* and happiness,
  g 536–28   their belief in perishable *l·* and happiness ;

and health
  ph 185–10   discussed . . . to regulate *l·* and health.
  p 428–31   and raised the dying to *l·* and health

and immortality
  p 376–13   more *l·* and immortality in one good motive
  g 539– 5   as if *l·* and immortality were something which

and intelligence
  a 52–20   the nothingness of material *l·* and intelligence
  sp 71–17   which simulate mind, *l·*, and intelligence.
  s 124– 9   seeks to find *l·* and intelligence in matter,
  ph 177–17   theory of *l·* and intelligence in matter,
  f 209–28   hypothesis of...*l·* and intelligence resident in
  222–32   the false belief that *l·* and intelligence are
  237–26   a belief in the *l·* and intelligence of matter,
  b 279–16   belief disappears that *l·* and intelligence are
  279–31   seeks . . . *l·* and intelligence in matter.
  294–21   the error that *l·* and intelligence are in matter,
  307– 1   delusion that *l·* and intelligence proceeded from
  319–16   presuppose *l·* and intelligence to exist in
  322– 3   changes the standpoints of *l·* and intelligence
  r 476– 7   claim . . . that *l·* and intelligence are in
  g 522–13   forms, called *l·* and intelligence in matter.
  533–23   belief in material *l·* and intelligence
  535–11   supposed material foundations of *l·* and intelligence.
  gl 584–20   saith : "I am *l·* and intelligence in matter.

and its joys
  b 299–11   higher ideals of *l·* and its joys.

and joy
  g 536–25   material conception of *l·* and joy,

and light
  f 209– 7   the *l·* and light of all its own vast creation ;

and man
  p 368–21   we learn that *l·* and man survive this body.

and mind
  b 296– 8   destroy all illusions regarding *l·* and mind,
  g 556– 5   are supposed to possess *l·* and mind.

and peace
  f 224– 9   painless progress, attended by *l·* and peace

and sensation
  b 278–12   That matter . . . has *l·* and sensation, is one of
  289– 4   belief that *l·* and sensation are in the body
  p 396–29   never giving the body *l·* and sensation.

and substance
  b 311–18   dream of *l·* and substance as existent in matter,

and truth
  c 262–12   efforts to find *l·* and truth in matter

appearance of
  ph 187–28   loses all appearance of *l·* or action,

arbiter of
  p 369–12   belief . . . that it can be the arbiter of *l·*

belief of
  (*see* **belief**)

belief that
  (*see* **belief**)

better
  pr 7–20   a higher experience and a better *l·*

breath of
  g 524–15   into his nostrils the breath of *l·* ;— *Gen.* 2 : 7.

cannot destroy
  p 388–21   prepared by Jesus . . . it cannot destroy *l·*.
  426–17   learned that disease cannot destroy *l·*,

chart of
  a 24– 8   and make the Bible the chart of *l·*,

consciousness of
  f 242–12   to have no other consciousness of *l·*

constitutes
  b 283–21   false belief as to what really constitutes *l·*

crown of
  c 267–30   he shall receive the crown of *l·*,— *Jas.* 1 : 12.

daily
  ph 179– 4   and following Christ in the daily *l·*,
  b 272–20   and Christianization of daily *l·*,
  283–28   We must receive . . . and live it in daily *l·* ;

days of my
  ap 578–17   all the days of my *l·* ;— *Psal.* 23 : 6.

life

demonstrated in the
  b 333–12   and demonstrated in the *l·* of which

demonstrated the
  s 149–13   have not demonstrated the *l·* of Christ,

demonstration of
  a 45–19   the revelation and demonstration of *l·* in God,
  f 214– 8   guided into the demonstration of *l·* eternal.
  b 278–24   contradicts the demonstration of *l·* as Spirit,

department of
  t 462–19   as they usually do in every department of *l·*.

earthly
  ap 565–14   a brief history in the earthly *l·* of our Master ;

embryonic
  g 547–14   the germinating speck of so-called embryonic *l·*
  548–29   facts in regard to so-called embryonic *l·*.
  ap 561– 6   at a point of so-called embryonic *l·*.

eternal
  a 54–26   and to share the glory of eternal *l·*.
  f 214– 8   guided into the demonstration of *l·* eternal.
  b 271–24   the essence of this Science, and the eternal *l·*,
  289– 2   Truth demonstrated is eternal *l·*.
  340–22   demonstrates health, holiness, and *l·* eternal.
  p 410– 4   "This is *l·* eternal," says Jesus,— *John* 17 : 3.
  410– 7   "This is *l·* eternal, that they— *John* 17 : 3.

everlasting
  sp 81–11   this fact affords no certainty of everlasting *l·*.
  p 410– 5   and then he defines everlasting *l·* as a
  g 556–12   *l·* everlasting is not to be gained by dying.

false views of
  m 62–29   false views of *l·* hide eternal harmony,

fountain of
  ph 190–30   with Thee is the fountain of *l·* ;— *Psal.* 36 : 9.

good
  ph 167–32   Substituting good words for a good *l·*,

had no
  a 51–16   He knew that matter had no *l·*

happiness and
  f 232– 5   beliefs . . . about happiness and *l·*
  b 308–11   looking for happiness and *l·* in the body,

health or
  s 148–27   When physiology fails to give health or *l·* by this

her
  pref xii–16   conviction that the next two years of her *l·*
  p 379–22   her belief that blood is destroying her *l·*.

his
  a 45–13   we shall be saved by his *l·*."— *Rom.* 5 : 10.
  ph 171–10   probabilities either of his *l·* or of
  b 317–17   his *l·* is not at the mercy of matter.
  326–27   and his *l·* became more spiritual.
  p 436–12   Laying down his *l·* for a good deed,

holiness, and
  a 52– 6   spiritual evidence of health, holiness, and *l·* ;
  b 340–22   demonstrates health, holiness, and *l·* eternal.

human
  (*see* **human**)

human concept of
  o 359–13   you must change the human concept of *l·*,

idea of
  a 30– 2   he could give a more spiritual idea of *l·*

illusion of
  b 305–23   In the illusion of *l·* that is here to-day and

immortal
  a 51–11   that he might furnish the proof of immortal *l·*.

immortality and
  sp 98–31   through which immortality and *l·* are learned

indestructible
  f 209– 2   Man, . . . has a perfect indestructible *l·*.

in God
  a 45–19   the revelation and demonstration of *l·* in God,
  b 324–18   the goal of Spirit, or *l·* in God.

in Soul
  pr 13–32   not cognizant of *l·* in Soul, not in body.

instead of
  p 435–13   pleasure instead of pain, and *l·* instead of

intelligence and
  ph 171–26   beliefs that intelligence and *l·* are present
  171–29   that intelligence and *l·* are spiritual,
  b 269–31   Mind, possessing intelligence and *l·*.

interpretation of
  a 54–19   would not accept his meek interpretation of *l·*

issues of
  sp 92– 4   the issues of *l·* and death,
  ph 181– 6   or does it hold the issues of *l·* ?"

its
  b 307–14   Its *l·* is found to be not Life, but only a

Jesus'
  a 42– 1   Jesus' *l·* proved, divinely and scientifically,

ladder of
  f 222– 3   and ascend the ladder of *l·*.

law of
  b 314–32   supposed accord with the inevitable law of *l·*.
  p 387–22   supposition that. . .in obedience to the law of *l·*,

man's
  ph 166–12   believes in his prescription, . . . to save a man's *l·*.
  f 203–32   for God alone is man's *l·*.

life

married
 m 59– 6 all the years of married *l·*.
material
 (*see* **material**)
matter has no
 b 275– 1 Matter has no *l·* to lose, and Spirit never dies.
 p 426–30 because matter has no *l·* to surrender.
 gl 584–11 Matter has no *l·*, hence it has no real
miscalled
 s 164–23 materiality miscalled *l·* in the body
misconception of
 g 554– 9 following from a misconception of *l·*,
mortal
 p 399–22 so-called mortal *l·* is mortal mind,
 g 503–25 God creates neither erring thought, mortal *l·*,
 544–30 declares . . . so-called mortal *l·* to be Life,
 552–13 Human experience in mortal *l·*, which starts
never gave
 p 376–12 should be told that blood never gave *l·*
newness of
 a 24–12 rise into newness of *l·* with regeneration.
 35– 9 rise . . . into newness of *l·* as Spirit.
 f 249– 7 bringing us into newness of *l·*
 p 426–19 will quicken into newness of *l·*.
no . . . in matter
 s 113–31 no matter in Life, and no *l·* in matter ;
nor sensation
 s 127–21 as matter— no intelligence, *l·*, nor sensation.
 f 205–10 matter has neither intelligence, *l·*, nor sensation,
of Christ Jesus
 b 270–31 The *l·* of Christ Jesus was not miraculous,
of Jesus
 b 317– 6 Whosoever lives most the *l·* of Jesus
of Life
 b 320– 2 of the truth of Truth and of the *l·* of Life,
of Man
 p 434–26 conspiracy against the liberty and *l·* of Man.
of man
 p 377–29 to defend the *l·* of man
 389–14 theories . . . that food sustains the *l·* of man,
 402–17 The *l·* of man is Mind.
 410–12 showing that Truth is the actual *l·* of man ;
 438–17 conspiracy against the rights and *l·* of man.
or existence
 b 311–29 all supposed . . . claim to *l·* or existence,
organic
 t 450–32 electricity, animal nature, and organic *l·*,
or intelligence
 r 485–32 The notion of any *l·* or intelligence in matter
 gl 584–28 the absence of substance, *l·*, or intelligence.
or love
 c 257–24 Who hath found finite *l·* or love sufficient to
or mind
 3p 76– 8 belief that *l·*, or mind, was ever in a finite form,
 b 303–17 illusion that *l·*, or mind, is formed by
or soul
 sp 70–15 Does *l·* or soul exist in the thing formed?
physical
 f 247– 1 The acute belief of physical *l·* comes on at
possesses no
 r 475–21 that which possesses no *l·*, . . . of his own,
queen of
 t 451– 7 Christianity, . . . must be their queen of *l·*.
reckoning
 g 539– 4 Error begins by reckoning *l·* as separate from
recognition of
 r 495 18 that the recognition of *l·* harmonious
recognize no
 s 133–27 would recognize no *l·*, . . . outside of God.
resurrection and the
 a 31–16 "the resurrection and the *l·*"— *John* 11 : 25.
 b 292– 7 "the resurrection and the *l·*"— *John* 11 : 25.
seem to have
 b 307–13 and matter shall seem to have *l·*
sensation nor
 s 108– 7 matter possesses neither sensation nor *l·* ;
sense of
 a 51– 7 He had power to lay down a human sense of *l·*
 sp 72–14 Mortal belief (the material sense of *l·*)
 b 290– 9 instead of through a spiritual sense of *l·*,
 308–17 struggling with a mortal sense of *l·*,
 311–30 as mortals lay off a false sense of *l·*,
 325–32 A false sense of *l·*, substance, and mind
 p 376–16 simulated a corporeal sense of *l·*.
 g 548– 5 spiritual sense of *l·*, substance, and intelligence.
so-called
 b 292–17 so-called *l·* of mortals is dependent on
 309–29 such so-called *l·* always ends in death.
 o 358– 2 axe, which destroys a tree's so-called *l·*,
soul, and
 r 466–25 fallacy that . . . soul, and *l·* can be in matter ;
span of
 f 252–23 says : . . . make my short span of *l·* one gala
spirit and in
 a 39–22 experience that salvation in spirit and in *l·*.

life

Spirit is the
 s 124–25 Spirit is the *l·*, substance, and continuity of
Spirit of
 f 244–11 law of the Spirit of *l·* in Christ— *Rom.* 8 : 2.
spiritual
 (*see* **spiritual**)
statement of
 g 554– 9 Any statement of *l·*, following from a
structural
 b 283–18 such as the structural *l·* of the tree
substance, and
 gl 591– 9 illusion ; intelligence, substance, and *l·* in
substance, and intelligence
 a 43–29 beliefs about *l·*, substance, and intelligence,
 f 249–24 dream that *l·*, substance, and intelligence are
 b 274–19 which affirm that *l·*, substance, and intelligence
 278–30 the opposite of *l·*, substance, and intelligence.
 287–24 supposition that *l·*, substance, and intelligence
 294– 2 belief, that *l·*, substance, and intelligence
 302–17 illusion of any *l·*, substance, and intelligence as
 308–17 a mortal sense of *l·*, substance, and intelligence
 311–30 a false sense of *l·*, substance, and intelligence.
 t 450–27 beliefs in *l·*, substance, and intelligence
 450–31 belief of *l·*, substance, and intelligence
 g 541–16 belief that *l·*, substance, and intelligence
 548– 5 spiritual sense of *l·*, substance, and intelligence.
 gl 583– 3 suppositions of *l·*, substance, and intelligence,
 585–24 concerning *l·*, substance, and intelligence
 586–19 that *l·*, substance, and intelligence are
 587– 9 a belief that *l·*, substance, and intelligence
 588–18 the belief that *l·*, substance, and intelligence
 592– 2 belief that *l·*, substance, and intelligence
substance, . . . and intelligence
 sp 91–26 belief is, that substance, *l·*, and intelligence
 ap 562–10 light, substance, *l·*, and intelligence.
 563– 9 belief that substance, *l·*, and intelligence
substance, and mind
 b 325–32 A false sense of *l·*, substance, and mind
 gl 582– 4 physical belief as to *l·*, substance, and mind ;
substance, or intelligence
 p 418– 6 error that *l·*, substance, or intelligence can
supposes
 r 489– 8 hypothesis which supposes *l·* to be in matter
supposititious
 b 322–26 belief in the supposititious *l·* of matter,
temporal
 a 51–12 Jesus could give his temporal *l·* into
 s 122–27 Temporal *l·* is a false sense of existence.
that approaches
 r 496–10 Am I living the *l·* that approaches the supreme
thought and in
 pr 11–32 It is best expressed in thought and in *l·*.
to suppose that
 sp 83–21 contrary to C. S. to suppose that *l·* is either
tree of
 p 426–13 this would be a "tree of *l·*," *Rev.* 22 : 2.
 t 458–19 to guard "the tree of *l·*."— *Gen.* 3 : 24.
 g 526– 1 tree of *l·* also, in the midst of the— *Gen.* 2 : 9.
 526–18 The "tree of *l·*" stands for the— *Gen.* 2 : 9.
 527–18 "the tree of *l·*" to be the— *Gen.* 2 : 9.
 537– 2 and take also of the tree of *l·*,— *Gen.* 3 : 22.
 537– 8 to keep the way of the tree of *l·*.— *Gen.* 3 : 24.
 538–13 The "tree of *l·*" is significant of— *Gen.* 2 : 9.
truth, and love
 b 284–18 testimony as to spiritual *l·*, truth, and love?
truth, and the
 a 26–11 the way, the truth, and the *l·* ;"— *John* 14 : 6.
 b 320– 3 the way, the truth, and the *l·*."— *John* 14 : 6.
 o 353–11 "the way, the truth, and the *l·*,"— *John* 14 : 6.
vegetable
 b 309–28 as organic animal or vegetable *l·*,
water of
 g 548– 2 take the water of *l·* freely."— *Rev.* 22 : 17.
Word of
 b 268– * handled, of the Word of *l·*,— *I John* 1 : 1.
your
 m 62–13 "thought for your *l·*, what ye— *Matt.* 6 : 25.
 ph 165– * Take no thought for your *l·*,— *Matt.* 6 : 25.
 170–16 "Take no thought for your *l·*,— *Matt.* 6 : 25.
 f 228–21 "Take no thought for your *l·*,"— *Matt.* 6 : 25.
 p 365– 8 "Take no thought for your *l·*,"— *Matt.* 6 : 25.
 g 530– 8 "Take no thought for your *l·*,— *Matt.* 6 : 25.
your own
 s 149–14 not demonstrated . . . more in your own *l·*,

 a 40–13 If the saying is true, "While there's *l·* there's
 48–31 hastening the final demonstration of what *l·* is
 m 65–12 *l·* should be more metaphysically regarded.
 sp 75– 2 assumption that man . . . comes to *l·* as spirit.
 78– 7 belief that we are wearing out *l·* and
 89–28 Cain . . . concluded that if *l·* was in the body,
 95– 6 "To be spiritually minded is *l·*."— *Rom.* 8 : 6.
 s 107–15 false consciousness that *l·* inheres in the body,
 122–25 To material sense, . . . takes away *l·* ;
 161–17 among which are *l·*, liberty, and the pursuit of

life

ph	165– *	*Is not the l· more than meat,*— *Matt.* 6 : 25.
	191–19	What are man's prospects for *l·*?
f	205– 7	error of believing that there is *l·* in matter,
	216–25	would seem the exception, . . . and *l·* a paradox.
	246–10	The measurement of *l·* by solar years robs
	247–21	Beauty is a thing of *l·*, which dwells
	253– 6	saith : . . . I give *l·*, without beginning
c	261–26	neither lose the solid objects and ends of *l·* nor
b	275–18	no *l·* is Life but the divine ;
	283–17	They claim that to be *l·* which is but the
	289–10	To suppose that sin, lust, hatred, . . . have *l·*
	289–21	The belief that matter has *l·* results, . . . in a
	300– 2	correct spiritual conclusions regarding *l·*
	304– 6	"Neither death, nor *l·*,— *Rom.* 8 : 38.
	304–14	nor *l·* result in death.
	306– 3	They would first make *l·* result in death, and
	318–11	They would put soul into soil, *l·* into limbo,
	319– 2	The delusion that there is *l·* in matter has no
	325– 6	*l·* obtained not of the body
	325– 6	the body incapable of supporting *l·*,
	325–11	"When Christ, who is our *l·*, shall— *Col.* 3 : 4.
	331– 3	If *l·* were in mortal man or
	340– 2	and make *l·* its own proof of harmony and God.
p	388–13	hypothesis that food is the nutriment of *l·*,
	409–10	no right to say that *l·* depends on matter now,
	428–21	the *l·* which is spiritual, not material.
t	445–13	*l·* "hid with Christ in God,"— *Col.* 3 : 3.
r	467– 6	no intelligence, no *l·*, . . . but that which is
	468– 9	There is no *l·*, truth, . . . in matter.
	472–15	Error . . . that intelligence, substance, *l·*,
g	501– *	*In Him was l· ; and the l· was*— *John* 1 : 4.
	511–20	the moving creature that hath *l·*,— *Gen.* 1 : 20.
	518–11	wherein there is *l·*,— *Gen.* 1 : 30.
	526– 6	this statement that *l·* issues from matter,
	535–23	eat of it all the days of thy *l·* :— *Gen.* 3 : 17.
	543–29	The belief that matter supports *l·*
	549– 4	supposition that *l·* germinates in eggs
	554–11	any knowledge of the so-called selfhood of *l·*,
gl	582– 8	error masquerading as the possessor of *l·*,
	584– 9	DEATH. An illusion, the lie of *l·* in matter ;
	591–10, 11	illusion;. . . *l·* resulting in death, and death in *l·*;
	594– 8	claim that . . . and death are the realities of *l·*.
	598–26	would bridge over with *l·* discerned spiritually

life-basis
| *ph* | 191– 8 | As a material, theoretical *l·* is found to be a |

life-giving
r	495–10	the *l·* power of Truth acting on human belief,
g	517– 7	The *l·* quality of Mind is Spirit.
	522–19	represented as the *l·* principle of the earth.

Life-laws
| *p* | 398– 9 | the popular ignorance of spiritual *L·*. |

life-link
| *o* | 350–28 | that *l·* forming the connection through which |

lifelong
| *a* | 53–23 | mocking the *l·* sacrifice which goodness makes |
| *p* | 371–21 | nor would I keep the suckling a *l·* babe. |

life-motives
| *m* | 58– 8 | Unselfish ambition, noble *l·*, and purity, |

life-practice
| *f* | 202– 4 | must be wrought out in *l·*, |

life-preserving
| *gl* | 579–13 | *l·* power of spiritual understanding. |

Life-principle
| *a* | 42–32 | They must understand more fully his *L·* |

Life-problem
| *pref* | ix–30 | comparative ignorance of the stupendous *L·* |

life-prospects
| *b* | 319– 5 | To calculate one's *l·* from a |

Life's
b	289–12	Life and *L·* idea, Truth and Truth's idea,
	337–18	Christ, *L·* spiritual ideal.
gl	580–16	*L·* counterfeit, which ultimates in death ;

life's
| *a* | 18– 6 | He did *l·* work aright |
| *m* | 60–28 | and teach us *l·* sweeter harmonies. |

life-work
a	48–16	until the consummation of a *l·*.
f	248–22	The result is that you . . . limit your *l·*,
b	328–30	The purpose of his great *l·* extends through

lift
m	67– 6	waves *l·* themselves into mountains.
ph	199– 2	could *l·* the hammer and strike the anvil,
p	373– 9	to *l·* a student out of a chronic sin.
g	515–26	If you *l·* a weight, your reflection does this also.
ap	569–18	not struggling to *l·* their heads above the
	574–25	it will *l·* the sackcloth from your eyes,

lifted
| *ph* | 200– 3 | *l·* thought into the song of David. |
| *c* | 259– 8 | *l·* their lives higher than their poor |

lifted
| *g* | 513–10 | anon the veil is *l·*, and the scene shifts |
| *ap* | 574–22 | *l·* the seer to behold the great city, |

lifting
| *p* | 400–18 | By *l·* thought above error, or disease, |
| | 407–14 | *l·* humanity above itself into purer desires, |

lifts
m	60– 2	Science inevitably *l·* one's being higher
sp	95–31	*l·* human consciousness into eternal Truth.
	97–24	the higher Truth *l·* her voice, the louder will
s	114–24	It *l·* the veil of mystery from Soul and body.
	147–20	This proof *l·* you high above the
f	220– 9	The violet *l·* her blue eye to greet the
	235–13	and spiritual culture, which *l·* one higher.
	252–16	Material sense *l·* its voice with the arrogance of
g	521– 1	Knowledge of this *l·* man above the sod,
	547–31	*l·* humanity out of disease and death
	557–20	and *l·* the curtain on man as never
ap	563– 5	hatred, which *l·* its hydra head,
	563–15	The Revelator *l·* the veil from this
	571–32	and *l·* on high only those who have

Light
| *ap* | 561–31 | to bear witness of that *L·*."— *John* 1 : 8. |

light (*see also* lights)

above the
| *ap* | 558–15 | it has for you a *l·* above the sun, |

absence of
| *f* | 215–17 | only a mortal sense of the absence of *l·*, |

according to their
| *t* | 443–11 | privileged to work . . . according to their *l·*, |

accustomed to the
| *t* | 452– 7 | we are accustomed to the *l·* |

all is
| *sp* | 72–11 | in the place of darkness all is *l·*, |

and darkness
ph	186– 9	*l·* and darkness, cannot mingle.
b	281– 5	no more commingle than *l·* and darkness.
r	474–31	for *l·* and darkness cannot dwell together.

and glory
| *ap* | 575– 9 | represents the *l·* and glory of divine Science. |
| | 577–24 | Its gates open towards *l·* and glory |

and harmony
b	280– 4	the *l·* and harmony which are the abode of
g	501–12	which God illustrated by *l·* and harmony,
	503–28	Spirit, dwelling in infinite *l·* and harmony

and healing
| *t* | 446–12 | through which Mind pours *l·* and healing |

and heat
| *ph* | 189– 4 | we still believe that there is solar *l·* and heat. |
| *g* | 538–11 | The sun, giving *l·* and heat to the earth, |

and might
| *f* | 215–13 | the *l·* and might of intelligence and Life. |
| *t* | 446–26 | the spiritual *l·* and might which heal the sick. |

and the glass
| *b* | 295–17 | The *l·* and the glass never mingle, |

beauty and
| *g* | 516–13 | bathes all in beauty and *l·*. |

beholds the
| *sp* | 95–26 | beholds the *l·* which heralds Christ's eternal |

borrowed
| *g* | 511– 2 | subdivides and radiates their borrowed *l·*, |

brave
| *s* | 144– 7 | when dawns the sun's brave *l·*. |

bring
| *g* | 504–24 | rays of infinite Truth, . . . bring *l·* |

bringing to
| *f* | 210–14 | thus bringing to *l·* the scientific action of |
| *gl* | 589–18 | bringing to *l·* man's immortality. |

brings to
sp	72–13	Truth . . . brings to *l·* immortality.
f	206–27	He destroys them, and brings to *l·* immortality.
b	293–29	C. S. brings to *l·* Truth and its supremacy,
	338– 2	brings to *l·* the only living and true God

bring to
| *b* | 300–10 | will bring to *l·* the true reflection of God |

brought to
s	110–10	The equipollence of God brought to *l·*
b	268– 1	brought to *l·* . . . many useful wonders.
	292–31	connection with his God, which Jesus brought to *l·*.
	335–24	Life as immortality brought to *l·*.
p	429– 2	this Life must be brought to *l·* by the
g	505–28	the reality of all things brought to *l·*.
	548–28	Modern discoveries have brought to *l·*
gl	582–23	immortality brought to *l·*.

central
| *b* | 305– 7 | Man, . . . reflects the central *l·* of being, |

clearer
| *a* | 55–12 | in a clearer *l·* than mere words can |

clothed in
| *ap* | 561–11 | the spiritual ideal as a woman clothed in *l·*, |

come not to the
| *pref* | x–29 | or discerning the truth, come not to the *l·* lest |

darkness and
| *sp* | 74–21 | Darkness and *l·*, infancy and manhood, |

light
depends upon Mind
p 393–26 certainly means that *l·* depends upon Mind,
destroys darkness
sp 72–10 As *l·* destroys darkness
divine
s 135–32 as must be the case in the cycles of divine *l·*.
t 457– 7 Since the divine *l·* of C. S. first dawned upon
emits
c 262–25 even as *l·* emits *l·* without effort ;
examined in the
c 267–1 examined in the *l·* of divine Science,
b 274–31 examined in the *l·* of divine metaphysics,
from darkness to
t 459– 1 as the flower turns from darkness to *l·*.
give
g 510– 7 to give *l·* upon the earth :— Gen. 1 : 15.
511– 8 to give *l·* upon the earth,— Gen. 1 : 17.
gives place to
pref xi–13 as necessarily as darkness gives place to *l·*
glorious
b 308–27 did not loosen his hold upon this glorious *l·*
God "is the
ap 558–16 for God "is the *l·* thereof."— Rev. 21 : 23.
God's
g 504–12 no place where God's *l·* is not seen,
God saw the
g 503–26 And God saw the *l·*,— Gen. 1 : 4.
greater
g 510–14 the greater *l·* to rule the day,— Gen. 1 : 16.
infinite
g 503–28 Spirit, dwelling in infinite *l·* and harmony
511–13 God is revealed as infinite *l·*.
influx of
a 47– 8 The influx of *l·* was sudden.
instead of
g 528–19 Beginning creation with darkness instead of *l·*,
in the line of
an 105–32 full many a league in the line of *l·* ;
is a symbol
g 510–27 L· is a symbol of Mind,
its own
g 510–30 one Mind, and this one shining by its own *l·*
lesser
g 510–14 the lesser *l·* to rule the night :— Gen. 1 : 16.
lets in the
p 407–26 This spiritualization of thought lets in the *l·*,
let there be
c 255– 3 "Let there be *l·*,"— Gen. 1 : 3.
g 503–18 God said, Let there be *l·* :— Gen. 1 : 3.
556–20 "Let there be *l·*."— Gen. 1 : 3.
life and
f 209– 7 life and *l·* of all its own vast creation ;
line of
an 105 32 full many a league in the line of *l·* ;
p 367–29 student's higher attainments in this line of *l·*
Love is the
ap 577–21 for Love is the *l·* of it,
manifesting the
an 562–29 and by manifesting the *l·* which shines
more
s 153–13 This discovery leads to more *l·*.
new
a 35–11 in the dawn of a new *l·*
obscured the
ap 560–26 not only obscured the *l·* of the ages, but
obscures
g 504–29 and darkness obscures *l·*.
of men
g 501– * the life was the *l·* of men.— John 1 : 4.
ap 561–29 which is "the *l·* of men."— John 1 : 4.
of the body
p 393–25 "the *l·* of the body is the eye,"— Matt. 6 : 22.
of Truth
b 308–36 the *l·* of Truth and Love dawns upon thee.
p 418–32 which flee before the *l·* of Truth.
g 557–19 rolls back the clouds of error with the *l·* of Truth,
of understanding
t 461–12 Only by . . . can the *l·* of understanding be
or heat
g 548– 9 How little *l·* or heat reach our earth when
or joy
g 548–12 little *l·* or joy for mortals before
pinions of
ph 191–14 transformed by Truth on its pinions of *l·*,
portrayed
ap 561–28 The *l·* portrayed is really neither solar nor
power of
f 214–27 may end the power of *l·* and lens !
ray of
f 250–12 like a ray of *l·* which comes from the sun,
b 300–31 the ray of *l·* which goes out from it.
o 361–17 a ray of *l·* one with the sun,
rays of
g 546–24 like rays of *l·*, shine in the darkness,
reflected
ap 562– 9 the universe borrows its reflected *l·*,

light
reflects no
r 479–28 not a color, because it reflects no *l·*.
shining
o 347–20 and is the *l·* shining in darkness,
ap 566–24 A burning and a shining *l·* !
solar
ph 189– 4 we still believe that there is solar *l·* and heat.
g 510–21 There is no Scriptural allusion to solar *l·* until
Spirit is
g 504–28 Spirit is *l·*, and the contradiction of Spirit is
spiritual
b 324–23 but spiritual *l·* soon enabled him to
t 446–26 the spiritual *l·* and might which heal the sick.
this
p 367–22 and that this *l·* be not hid,
g 504–10 This *l·* is not from the sun
ap 577–22 All who are saved must walk in this *l·*.
Thy
ph 190–31 In Thy *l·* shall we see light.— Psal. 36 : 9.
towards the
f 240– 9 leaflet turns naturally towards the *l·*.
true
s 117–26 and because of opacity to the true *l·*,
b 276–13 brings . . . into human view in their true *l·*,
o 359–32 in their true *l·* and loveliness,
Truth is the
b 282–32 but Truth is the *l·* which dispels error.
walking in the
t 452– 7 Walking in the *l·*, we are accustomed to the
walk in the
pr 10– 2 and will walk in the *l·* so far as we receive it,
g 510–11 reflected spiritually by all who walk in the *l·*
ye are the
p 367–19 "Ye are the *l·* of the world.— Matt. 5 : 14.

a 42– 8 comes in darkness and disappears with the *l·*.
sp 74–24 Who will say that . . . darkness can represent *l·*,
an 101–15 and as adapted to throw *l·* on physiological
ph 190–31 In Thy light shall we see *l·*.— Psal. 36 : 9.
194 28 An infant crying for the *l·*,
194–31 The *l·* which affords us joy gave him a
195– 2 His eyes were inflamed by the *l·*.
f 215–16 led to believe that darkness is as real as *l·* ;
c 266–29 beatific presence, illuming the universe with *l·*.
b 289– 1 man's real existence . . . comes to *l·*.
295–16 as *l·* passing through the window-pane.
305–27 destroys all error and brings immortality to *l·*.
325–30 When first spoken . . . Truth, like the *l·*,
336–28 and brings immortality to *l·*.
t 452– 9 are pained by the *l·*.
r 474–32 L· extinguishes the darkness,
470–24 the imaginary opposites of *l·*,
492–12 and bring immortality to *l·*.
g 502– 6 the *l·* over the dark,
503–14 the *l·* of ever-present Love illumines
503–19 and there was *l·*.— Gen. 1 : 3.
503–21 first, in *l·* ; second, in reflection ;
503– 27 divided the *l·* from the darkness.— Gen. 1 : 4.
504– 3 God called the *l·* Day,— Gen. 1 : 5.
504– 9 though solar beams are not . . . still there is *l·*.
504–27 Did Infinite Mind create matter, and call it *l·* ?
508–29 letting in the *l·* of spiritual understanding.
509–17 The *l·* of spiritual understanding gives
510–10 in whose "*l·* shall we see *l·* ;"— Psal. 36 : 9.
511– 9 to divide the *l·* from the darkness :— Gen. 1 : 18.
513–10 the veil is lifted, and the scene shifts into *l·*.
539–25 "What communion hath *l·*— II Cor. 6 : 14.
ap 578– 1 the *l·* which C. S. throws on the Scriptures
gl 584– 1 *l·*, the spiritual idea of Truth and Love.
591–23 MORNING. L· ; symbol of Truth ;
596–11 URIM. L·.

lighted
ap 576– 3 *l·* by the Sun of Righteousness,

lighting
pref vii–12 *l·* the way to eternal harmony.

lightning
sp 97– 8 According to human belief, the *l·* is fierce
s 119–19 lawgiver, whose *l·* palsies . . . is not the divine
ph 192–15 It is *l·* and hurricane, all that is
f 245–20 coaxed the enamoured *l·* from the clouds.
b 293–22 wind, wave, *l·*, fire, bestial ferocity
p 439–16 his words flashing as *l·* in the

lightnings
b 288–15 The *l·* and thunderbolts of error

lights
f 202–14 *l·* the torch of spiritual understanding.
g 509– 9 Let there be *l·* in the firmament— Gen. 1 : 14.
510– 6 And let them be for *l·*— Gen. 1 : 15.
510–13 And God made two great *l·* ;— Gen. 1 : 16.

like
pr 5–19 "*l·* a green bay tree ;"— Psal. 37 : 35.
8– 8 "*l·* unto whited sepulchres — Matt. 23 : 27.

like

pr	8–19	audible prayers are *l·* charity in one respect,
	12–16	Prayer to a corporeal God affects the sick *l·* a
a	21–27	He is *l·* a traveller going westward
	22– 3	Vibrating *l·* a pendulum between sin and the
	41– 6	*L·* our Master, we must depart from
	53–22	*L·* Peter, we should weep over the warning,
m	57–13	seasons of renewal *l·* the returning spring.
	61–16	droop and die, *i·* tropical flowers
	63– 7	His origin is not, *l·* that of mortals,
	66– 4	Which, *l·* the toad, ugly and venomous,
sp	78– 2	*l·* the discords of disease, sin, and death,
an	103–27	*l·* silly moths, singe their own wings
	105–22	*l·* an escaped felon
	106– 6	*L·* our nation, C. S. has its Declaration of
	106–24	revellings and such *l·* : — *Gal.* 5 : 21.
s	107– *	*kingdom of heaven is l· unto — Matt.* 13 : 33.
	112–19	spiritual rules, . . . which, *l·* the great Giver,
	113–26	*l·* the method in mathematics,
	124–14	The universe, *l·* man, is to be interpreted by
	124–18	the universe, *l·* man, is, and must
	135– 4	that ye skipped *l·* rams, — *Psal.* 114 : 6.
	135– 5	and ye little hills, *l·* lambs? — *Psal.* 114 : 6.
	154– 3	Disease arises, *l·* other mental conditions, from
	156– 8	and yet, . . . the patient looked *l·* a barrel.
	157–13	becomes more *l·* the human mind than
	164– 7	true, or anything *l·* the truth,
ph	187–32	a body *l·* the one it had before death.
	188–12	is *l·* the dream we have in sleep,
	193–14	and said : "I feel *l·* a new man.
	197– 3	*l·* a Parisian name for a novel garment.
f	214–11	The material senses, *l·* Adam, originate in
	214–19	*l·* the pagan idolater.
	214–22	*l·* the original "tree of — *Gen.* 2 : 9.
	218– 5	the body, *l·* the inanimate wheel,
	220–19	*l·* a kitten glancing into the mirror
	225–14	The history of our country, *l·* all history,
	235– 1	cannot go forth, *l·* wandering pollen,
	237–12	*l·* "the fowls of the air," — *Luke* 8 : 5.
	244–13	is *l·* the beasts and vegetables,
	245–27	One instance *l·* the foregoing
	249–18	*l·* Christ, "the same yesterday, — *Heb.* 13 : 8.
	250– 4	suppose. . .unintelligence to act *l·* intelligence,
	250–12	*l·* a ray of light which comes from the sun,
	250–29	chase one another *l·* snowflakes,
	251–28	Ignorance, *l·* intentional wrong, is not
	252–28	and says : . . . *L·* bursting lava, I expand
c	260– 3	and make himself *l·* it,
	263–28	A sensual thought, *l·* an atom of dust
	267–26	robes of Spirit . . . *l·* the raiment of Christ.
b	268– 3	With *l·* activity have thought's swift pinions
	268–11	*l·* the shepherd-boy with his sling,
	276–29, 30	inform us that *l·* produces *l·*.
	277–14	*l·* reproducing *l·*.
	286–18	all that He made to be good, *l·* Himself,
	295–11	Mortals are not *l·* immortals, created in
	295–23	Then, *l·* a cloud melting into thin vapor,
	298–21	Spiritual ideas, *l·* numbers and notes,
	305–10	so man, *l·* all things real, reflects God,
	322–28	turn us *l·* tired children to the arms of
	325–30	When first spoken in any age, Truth, *l·* the
o	349–14	*l·* all other languages, English is inadequate
	352–17	Children, *l·* adults, *ought* to fear a
	354–20	which are *l·* clouds without rain.
	359–29	Scientist and an opponent are *l·* two artists.
	360–19	*L·* a pendulum in a clock, you will be
p	364–22	If Christian Scientists are *l·* Simon, then
	365–18	*l·* dew before the morning sunshine.
	367–11	nor, *l·* the Pharisee, with the arrogance of
	367–13	but *l·* Mary Magdalene, from the summit of
	370– 9	cause and effect, or *l·* producing *l·*.
	374–22	*l·* walking in darkness on the edge of a
	383– 9	and, *l·* the Apostle Paul, is
	390– 2	I should *l·* something more to eat."
	393– 1	*l·* a watchman forsaking his post,
	395– 6	*L·* the great Exemplar, the healer should
	398–15	"was restored whole, *l·* as the — *Matt.* 12 : 13.
	421–30	The perversion of Mind-science is *l·*
t	459–17	*l·* putting a sharp knife into the hands of a
r	467– 8	The second is *l·* unto it,
	481– 5	*L·* the archpriests of yore, man is
	485–31	*l·* saying that the power is in the lever.
	486–31	in a terrible situation, where he would be *l·*
g	546–24	*l·* rays of light, shine in the darkness,
	551– 6	*L·* produces *l·*.
	554– 6	because being is immortal, *l·* Deity,
	555– 7	"I *l·* your explanations of truth,
	555–17	*l·* inquiring into the origin of God,
	557– 3	moving and playing without harm, *l·* a fish.
ap	571– 5	Because people *l·* you better when you
		(*see also* **manner**)

likely

an	102–27	much more *l·* to be abused by its
o	358–29	Is it *l·* that church-members have more
p	409– 7	the more prolific it is *l·* to become

likened

p	372– 5	*l·*, by Milton to "chaos and old night."
g	514–16	promptness, and perseverance are *l·* to

likeness

after our
p	438– 3	in our image, after our *l·* ; — *Gen.* 1 : 26.
r	475–24	in our image, after our *l·* ; — *Gen.* 1 : 26.
g	515–12	in our image, after our *l·* ; — *Gen.* 1 : 26.

divine
b	300–22	man as reflecting the divine *l·*.
o	356–23	man who is made in the divine *l·* ?
r	491–16	establishes man forever in the divine *l·*,

eternal
f	246– 6	the eternal *l·* of their Maker.
p	395– 5	man's immortality and eternal *l·* to God.

God's
sp	70– 8	spiritual man, made in God's *l·*,
ph	191– 5	man in God's *l·* will appear,
b	287–21	declare that man was made in God's *l·*.
	336–26	and man in God's *l·*
o	344– 9	God's *l·* is not found in matter, sin,
	346– 5	the ideal man, reflecting God's *l·*.

God's own
sp	90–24	man is God's own *l·*
r	477– 3	the Saviour saw God's own *l·*,

His
pr	4–22	until we awake in His *l·*.
sp	73– 7	God, and man is His *l·*.
s	148–24	unity of Spirit and His *l·*.
f	249–22	and His *l·* never dreams.
b	325–16	Then shall man be found, in His *l·*,
	338– 3	and man as made in His *l·* ;
o	344– 8	in His own image and after His *l·*.
r	495–16	Allow nothing but His *l·* to abide in your
g	516–20	Man, made in His *l·*, possesses and reflects

His own
c	257–12	Mind creates His own *l·* in ideas,
g	516– 9	God fashions . . . after His own *l·*.

human
b	301– 2	even as the human *l·*

image and
(*see* **image**)

image or
sp	71–19	neither . . . is the image or *l·* of God,
b	284–11	Is God's image or *l·* matter,
	299–15	whither every . . . image, or *l·* of
g	515–25	mirrored reflection is your own image or *l·*.

inverted
b	285–10	man's counterfeit, the inverted *l·*,

inverts the true
g	512–26	Mortal mind inverts the true *l·*,

its own
f	217– 1	this Mind forms its own *l·*.

man's
pr	12–14	of man's *l·* to God and of man's

no proper
b	302–28	the body presents no proper *l·* of divinity,

not that
r	475–10	Matter is not that *l·*.

of God
(*see* **God**)

of his Maker
f	252–13	recognized as the true *l·* of his Maker.
b	305– 7	Man, in the *l·* of his Maker,

of man's Maker
r	491–10	It is the *l·* of man's Maker.

of Spirit
(*see* **Spirit**)

of the divine
a	51– 8	spiritual identity in the *l·* of the divine ;

of this Ego
f	250–11	Spiritual man is the *l·* of this Ego.

our
g	525–14	after our mind and our *l·* ;

personal
b	302–27	not in any bodily or personal *l·* to

that
ph	191– 6	will include in that *l·* no material element.

this
b	315–18	and we realize this *l·* only when we
g	515–27	If you speak, the lips of this *l·* move
	544–25	a material personality is not this *l·*.

Thy
ph	190–29	when I awake, with Thy *l·*. — *Psal.* 17 : 15.

true
m	67–29	presents the true *l·* or spiritual ideal.
f	252–13	recognized as the true *l·* of his Maker.
c	259–18	The true *l·* cannot be lost in divine reflection.
p	406–16	all that is unlike the true *l·* disappears.
g	516– 8	we shall see this true *l·* and reflection

f	253– 1	saith : I am Spirit. Man, . . . is my *l·*.

likes
b	322–23	A man who *l·* to do wrong

likewise
a 25–29 We must go and do *l·*, else we are not
b 305–19 these also doeth the Son *l·*." — *John* 5 : 19.
320– 1 *L·* we can speak of the truth
p 370–27 Quackery *l·* fails at length to inspire the
gl 585– 6 which are *l·* without beginning or end.

lilies
f 212–23 makes and clothes the *l·* of the field,
g 530–12 to feed and clothe man as He doth the *l·*.

lily
m 62–24 even as it clothes the *l·* ;

limb
s 161– 1 elastic condition of the healthy *l·*,
ph 172–26 when you amputate a *l·* ;
172–27 But the loss of a *l·* or injury to a tissue
f 212– 4 A *l·* which has been amputated has continued
212– 6 If the sensation of pain in the *l·* can return,
212– 7 why cannot the *l·* reappear?
b 295– 1 The belief that a severed *l·* is aching
r 489– 6 Then the human *l·* would be replaced
489– 7 not with an artificial *l·*, but with the genuine

limbo
b 318–11 They would put soul into soil, life into *l·*,

limbs
s 120–32 and superstition chained the *l·*
162–20 shortened *l·* have been elongated,
f 227–27 entangled your free *l·*,
243–17 The head, heart, lungs, and *l·* do not inform us
p 379–27 pain in the head and *l·*,
415–28 the *l·* will vanish from consciousness.

limit
f 248–22 The result is that you . . . *l·* your life-work,
b 284– 9 and can return to no *l·*.
t 445–17 or *l·* in any direction of thought
g 517–23 since there is no *l·* to infinitude or to
ap 577–13 holy habitation has no boundary nor *l·*,

limitation
gl 585–22 mortal thought, the only error of which is *l·* ;
594– 5 the first lie of *l·* ; finity ;

limitations
c 256–28 limitless Mind cannot proceed from physical *l·*
b 331– 4 would be subject to their *l·* and would end in

limited
a 36–19 A selfish and *l·* mind may be unjust,
m 67–25 in the *l·* demonstration of popular Christianity
sp 71–29 *l·* and finite in character and quality.
s 133–20 *l·* form of a national or tribal religion.
c 255–13 mortals take *l·* views of all things.
256–31 A mind originating from a . . . must be *l·*
257–27 Infinite Mind cannot be *l·*
b 284– 4 If God were *l·* to man or matter,
284– 7 Mind would seem to spring from a *l·* body ;
309–31 never absorbed nor *l·* by its own formations.
313 28 was possessed only in a *l·* degree
329– 1 of a single period or of a *l·* following.
335–17, 18 never included in a *l·* mind or a *l·* body.
336– 5 never . . . the unlimited into the *l·*,
337–21 as incomprehensible to the *l·* senses as
o 361–24 however *l·*, must be correct in order to
p 369–27 *L·* to matter by their own law,
r 466–14 Truth is limitless ; error is *l·*.
469– 5 Life is divine Mind. Life is not *l·*.
494–13 a select number or for a *l·* period of time,
g 550– 8 and be *l·* within material bounds.
gl 587– 2 a belief that mind is outlined and *l·* ;
588–25 that which is never unconscious nor *l·*.

limiting
s 124–10 thus *l·* Life and holding fast to discord
135–18 repeating the offence of the Jews by *l·*
246–21 and *l·* all that is good and beautiful,

limitless
c 256–28 A *l·* Mind cannot proceed from
258– 3 glories of *l·*, incorporeal Life and Love.
b 335–32 The Ego is deathless and *l·*,
o 353–28 Mind is *l·*. It never was material.
r 466–14 Truth is *l·* ; error is limited.
g 510–18 Love alone can impart the *l·* idea of infinite

limits
final
r 476– 6 Error, urged to its final *l·*, is
former
sp 89–10 The former *l·* of her belief return.
narrow
c 256–14 nor compressed within the narrow *l·* of
g 536–22 Their narrow *l·* belittle their gratifications,
reach our
p 387– 6 When we reach our *l·* of
supposed
o 353–26 So long as there are supposed *l·* to Mind,
those
o 353–27 and those *l·* are human,

limits
utmost
g 552–28 urged to its utmost *l·*, results in a
within the
m 61– 2 within the *l·* of personal sense.
p 436– 9 acting within the *l·* of the divine law,
——
b 280–10 belief *l·* all things, and would compress
312–25 *l·* faith and hinders spiritual understanding.
335–32 *l·* would imply and impose ignorance.
gl 595–17 *l·*, in which are summed up all human acts.

line
along the
s 141–11 along the *l·* of scholarly . . . descent,
o 343–31 to press along the *l·* of gospel-healing,
direct
ph 189–31 always in the direct *l·* of matter,
t 457–21 no excellence without labor in a direct *l·*.
imaginary
sp 90– 6 the imaginary *l·* called the equator
last
pr 16–12 whether the last *l·* is not an addition
line upon
r 465– * *line upon l·, line upon l·; — Isa.* 28 : 10.
of creation
g 557–12 as the *l·* of creation rises towards
of demarcation
g 505–21 Understanding is the *l·* of demarcation
gl 586–16 *l·* of demarcation between Truth and error,
of light
an 105–32 full many a league in the *l·* of light ;
p 367–29 student's higher attainments in this *l·* of light.
of spiritual advancement
p 429 0 in the *l·* of spiritual advancement.
on this
r 492–19 "I propose to fight it out on this *l·*,
492–21 You must fight it out on this *l·*.
quoting a
ap 564–27 Jesus said, quoting a *l·* from the Psalms,
straight
b 282– 6 a circle or sphere and a straight *l·*.
282– 7 the straight *l·* represents the finite,
282–10 the straight *l·* represents evil,
282–14 straight *l·* finds no abiding-place in a curve,
282–15 curve finds no adjustment to a straight *l·*.
282–22 and the other a straight *l·*,
283–30 calling a curve a straight *l·*
283–31 or a straight *l·* a sphere.
g 502– 6 straight *l·* of Spirit over the mortal deviations
their
a 21–23 or, if I take up their *l·* of travel,
ph 192–30 Whatever holds human thought in *l·* with
g 507– 4 in the *l·* of spiritual creation,
557–13 in the *l·* of the corporeal senses,

lines
b 294–19 The *l·* of demarcation between immortal

link
sp 75–28 when the *l·* between their opposite beliefs is
ph 172–11 Spirit can form no real *l·* in this supposed
b 293– 5 forms no *l·* between matter and Mind,
r 491–15 and find the indissoluble spiritual *l·*
g 518–13 God gives the lesser idea of Himself for a *l·*

linked
b 316– 4 The real man being *l·* by Science to

links
a 37– 9 Martyrs are the human *l·* which
m 60– 7 welding indissolubly the *l·* of affection,
68–31 the unbroken *l·* of eternal, harmonious being

lion
f 243– 6 from the jaws of the *l·*,
p 380–16 Gazing at a chained *l·*, crouched for a spring,
g 514–10 "the *l·* of the tribe of Juda," — *Rev.* 5 : 5.
514–24 And the calf and the young *l·*, — *Isa.* 11 : 6.
549–26 beards the *l·* of materialism in its den.
550–27 nor does a *l·* bring forth a lamb.
ap 559–11 "as when a *l·* roareth." — *Rev.* 10 : 3.

lions'
g 514–27 Daniel felt safe in the *l·* den,

lip
s 117–14 Ear hath not heard, nor hath *l·* spoken,

lips
close the
pr 15–15 close the *l·* and silence the material senses.
faithful
a 51– 1 wrung from his faithful *l·* the plaintive cry,
or hands
f 212–26 we say the *l·* or hands must
untutored
sp 89–24 and the fervor of untutored *l·*.
——
pr 3–31 put the finger on the *l·* and remember our
9–31 why pray with the *l·* that you may

lips

pr	15–11	*L·* must be mute and materialism silent,
a	50– 7	wrung from Jesus' *l·* the awful cry,
o	359–23	from the *l·* of her saintly mother,
p	373–22	Disease is expressed not so much by the *l·* as
g	515–27	If you speak, the *l·* of this likeness move

lip-service

pr	2–13	does not grant them simply on the ground of *l·*,

liquid

f	213– 6	conceives of something as either *l·* or
g	511–23	To mortal mind, the universe is *l·*, solid, and

lisped

pref	ix–11	she "*l·* in numbers, for the numbers came."

lispings

pref	ix– 3	these jottings were only infantile *l·* of Truth.

list

a	31–12	First in the *l·* of Christian duties,

listen

pr	8–31	do we *l·* patiently to the rebuke
ap	571–12	If so, *l·* and be wise.

listened

f	237– 1	A little girl, who had occasionally *l·* to
o	359–22	In childhood, she often *l·* with joy to

listeners

f	235–30	their *l·* will love to grapple with a

listening

f	238–25	*l·* only to one side of the case.
b	323–31	or we are *l·* to it and going up higher.

listeth

gl	598– 4	bloweth where it *l·*.— *John* 3 : 8.

listless

f	250–20	To the observer, the body lies *l·*,

literal

a	32–24	This would have been foolish in a *l·* sense ;
b	320– 7	have both a spiritual and *l·* meaning.
	320–10	must rest upon both the *l·* and moral ;"
g	537–29	*l·* meaning would imply that God withheld

literally

f	218–30	applying it *l·* to moments of fatigue,
	245–11	she *l·* grew no older.
r	482–19	he was *l·* the Son of Man.
g	537–26	the ordinary historian interprets it *l·*.
	537–26	*L·* taken, the text is made to appear
ap	569– 7	is *l·* fulfilled, when we are conscious of the

literary

ph	195–28	*L·* commercialism is lowering the

little

pref	x–20	so *l·* faith in His disposition and power to
pr	8– 4	but there is *l·* hope for those who
	11–31	Such a desire has *l·* need of audible expression.
a	19–21	he has *l·* part in the atonement,
	21–13	gain a *l·* each day in the right direction,
	21–19	paths have diverged . . . *l·* opportunity to help
	37–32	Why has this Christian demand so *l·* inspiration
m	61–19	may reproduce in their own helpless *l·* ones
s	109–13	searched the Scriptures and read *l·* else,
	122–18	The barometer,— that *l·* prophet of
	130–24	our Master's love for *l·* children,
	135– 4	and ye *l·* hills, like lambs?— *Psal.* 114 : 6.
	149–20	remarked . . . take as *l·* medicine as possible ;
	154–28	Such a mother runs to her *l·* one,
ph	166–17	To ignore God as of *l·* use in sickness is a mis-
		take.
	196– 5	The power of . . . is *l·* understood.
f	236–28	Jesus loved *l·* children because of their
	237– 1	A *l·* girl, who had occasionally listened
	237– 9	their *l·* daughter so naturally attained.
	237–25	They devote themselves a *l·* longer to their
	252– 7	learn even a *l·* of their own falsity,
b	289– 8	He is *l·* else than the expression of error.
	297–30	has *l·* relation to the actual or divine.
	323–32	Willingness to become as a *l·* child
	328– 6	Understanding *l·* about the divine Principle
	329– 5	A *l·* leaven leavens the whole lump.
	329– 5	A *l·* understanding of C. S. proves the truth of
p	364–24	said of them also that they *love l·*.
	368–14	has *l·* inspiration to nerve endeavor.
	382–23	"Whosoever . . . as a *l·* child,— *Luke* 18 : 17.
	394–30	the sick usually have *l·* faith in it till they
	413–22	need not wash his *l·* body all over each day
	442–27	"Fear not, *l·* flock ;— *Luke* 12 : 32.
t	449– 2	A *l·* leaven causes the whole mass to
	455–13	if, . . . you can exercise *l·* or no power
	464– 3	Could her friends know how *l·* time
r	465– *	*here a l·, and there a l·*.— *Isa.* 28 : 10.
g	514–25	And a *l·* child shall lead them.— *Isa.* 11 : 6.
	548– 9	How *l·* light or heat reach our earth when
	548–12	Earth has *l·* light or joy for mortals before
ap	558– 6	in his hand a *l·* book open :— *Rev.* 10 : 2.
	559– 1	in his hand "a *l·* book,"— *Rev.* 10 : 2.

little

ap	559–17	"Go and take the *l·* book.— *Rev.* 10 : 8.
gl	597– 5	of *l·* value, if only he appeared unto men to fast.

live

pref	viii– 3	must *l·* in obedience to its divine Principle.
m	61–18	If perchance they *l·* to become parents
s	140– 7	shall no man see Me, and *l·*."— *Exod.* 33 : 20.
	147– 1	the thought of the age in which we *l·*,
ph	167– 7	only as we *l·* above corporeal sense
	187–32	which appears to the human mind to *l·*,
f	208– 5	Scriptures say, "In Him we *l·*,— *Acts* 17 : 28.
b	283–28	We must receive the . . . and *l·* it in daily life;
	326–16	The purpose and motive to *l·* aright can be
	328– 4	Mortals suppose that they can *l·* without
o	361–19	"For in Him we *l·*, and move,— *Acts* 17 : 28.
p	369–19	were willing that a man should *l·*.
	381–18	Scriptures declare that we *l·*, move, and
	388–10	neither eat to *l·* nor *l·* to eat.
	410–10	"Man shall not *l·* by bread *alone*,— *Matt.* 4 : 4.
	429–21	If we *l·* after death and are immortal,
t	448–31	To talk the right and *l·* the wrong is foolish
	451– 2	Christian Scientists must *l·* under the
	452–19	He must *l·* it and love it,
g	527– 4	or to cause it to *l·* and grow.
	536–13	"*l·*, and move, and have our— *Acts* 17 : 28.
	537– 2	and eat, and *l·* forever ;— *Gen.* 3 : 22.
	556–11	to *l·* again in renewed forms, only to

lived

pr	6–30	magistrate, who *l·* in the time of Jesus,
a	24–29	The truth had been *l·* among men ;
	43–28	The Science Jesus taught and *l·*
	53– 4	there never *l·* a man so far removed from
sp	75–16	not . . . died and then *l·* again.
	75–17	that Lazarus had *l·* or died in his body,
s	132–15	the spiritual idea and the man who *l·* it
	146–28	far anterior to the period in which Jesus *l·*.
p	429–22	If . . . we must have *l·* before birth,
r	474–22	the evils which Jesus *l·* to destroy
g	524–12	the divine Principle to be *l·* and loved.

liver

s	129–30	The generous *l·* may object to the author's

liver-attack

p	431–22	the night of the *l·*.
	431–27	since the night of the *l·*.

liver-complaint

chronic

p	389–30	In her belief the woman had chronic *l·*,

crime of

p	432– 6	witness to the crime of *l·*.

guilty of

p	433–17	"Guilty of *l·* in the first degree."

p	430–18	charged with having committed *l·*.
	431– 8	At last he committed *l·*,
	433– 5	He . . . explains the law relating to *l·*.
	433–23	*l·*, which material laws condemn as
	435–14	If *l·* was committed by trampling on
	436–17	to prevent his committing *l·*,
	439– 9	where the *l·* was in process,
	439–22	struggles against *l·* and Death.

lives

barren

pr	4– 2	cannot conceal the ingratitude of barren *l·*.
a	36–11	pour his dear-bought bounty into barren *l·*.

more

s	163–17	it has already destroyed more *l·* than war,

noble

f	248–29	in grand and noble *l·*.

other

m	68–15	and to your influence on other *l·*.

our

pr	15–24	and let our *l·* attest our sincerity.
s	131– 4	and our *l·* must be governed by reality
f	201– 5	supreme in us and take the lead in our *l·*,
	207– 4	until it disappears from our *l·*.
	232–29	pleasures and pains of sense pass away in our *l·*

their

c	259– 9	and lifted their *l·* higher than
p	377– 7	Invalids . . . in order to save their *l·*,
ap	568–19	and they loved not their *l·*— *Rev.* 12 : 11.

m	60–11	maternal affection *l·* on under whatever
sp	76–20	man is immortal and *l·* by divine authority.
	81–23	governing, divine Principle *l·* on,
s	126–28	and the *l·* of prophets and apostles.
	146–29	It *l·* through all Life,
f	203–23	escapes from matter and *l·* on ;
	204–30	belief that God *l·* in matter is pantheistic.
	223– 5	illusion that he *l·* in body instead of in Soul,
b	317– 6	Whosoever *l·* most the life of Jesus
p	369–21	and knew that man has not two *l·*,
	374–29	Nothing that *l·* ever dies, and *vice versa*.
	427– 1	If it is true that man *l·*, this fact can never
t	461– 3	but I do believe . . . that he *l·* in Spirit,

liveth

ph 170–11 "Whosoever *l·* and believeth— *John* 11 : 26.
b 315– 1 "Whosoever *l·* and believeth— *John* 11 : 26.
334–26 I am he that *l·*, and was dead— *Rev.* 1 : 18.

living

and healing
s 141– 5 divine precepts for *l·* and healing.
economy of
f 222–16 consulting . . . less about the economy of *l·*
faith in
p 368–17 more faith in *l·* than in dying,
illegitimate
f 203–28 foam and fury of illegitimate *l·*
in disobedience
a 19–27 If *l·* in disobedience to Him,
in this world
sp 73– 3 calls one person, *l·* in this world, *material*,
material
pr 14–26 the belief and dream of material *l·*,
only for pleasure
a 38–27 *l·* only for pleasure or the gratification of the
standard of
ph 197–14 the higher will be the standard of *l·*
the life
r 496–10 Am I *l·* the life that approaches the

---

pr 9–10 by *l·* consistently with our prayer?
a 31–15 It is the *l·* Christ, the practical Truth,
39–16 was not the threshold . . . into *l·* glory.
sp 74–15 belief of still *l·* in an organic, material body.
74–31 The so-called dead and *l·* cannot commune
75–25 when those *l·* on the earth and
81– 2 between the so-called dead and the *l·*,
an 100– 5 said could be exerted by one *l·* organism
s 137–18 the Son of the *l·* God !"— *Matt.* 16 : 16.
150– 1 *l·* witnesses and monuments to the
ph 180–28 The only way to this *l·* Truth,
f 204– 5 false . . . that material history is as real and *l·*
234– 7 giving *l·* waters to the thirsty.
237–28 the only *l·* and true God can do.
245– 7 Believing that she was still *l·* in the same hour
c 264–24 Spiritual *l·* and blessedness are the only
b 275– 5 Therefore matter is neither substantial, *l·*, nor
308– 3 or art thou in the *l·* faith that
325–22 your bodies a *l·* sacrifice,— *Rom.* 12 : 1.
333– 3 brings to light the only *l·* and true God
o 351–14 It was the *l·*, palpitating presence of
p 388–28 a clear comprehension of the *l·* Spirit.
t 458–28 He must prove, through *l·* as well as
r 477–21 in multifarious forms of *l·* Principle,
g 502– 2 the *l·* and real prelude of the older Scriptures
512– 5 and every *l·* creature that moveth,— *Gen.* 1 : 21.
513–15 the *l·* creature after his kind,— *Gen.* 1 : 24.
517–28 every *l·* thing that moveth *Gen.* 1 · 28.
524–15 and man became a *l·* soul.— *Gen.* 2 : 7.
527–24 whatsoever Adam called every *l·*— *Gen.* 2 : 19.
531– 1 it supposes that . . . matter becomes *l·*,

load

ph 176–17 Human fear of miasma would *l·* with disease

loaf

sp 90– 5 from which *l·* or fish could come?

loathe

a 30–28 we shall *l·* sin and rebuke it
f 240–22 we must learn to *l·* it.

loathing

pr 11–17 to make him turn from it with *l·*.
p 407– 1 in becoming a fool or an object of *l·* ;
ap 565– 4 hate, *l·* the brightness of divine glory.

loathsome

m 61–22 or reduce him to a *l·* wreck?
s 158–23 until . . . men and women become *l·* sots.
p 407– 5 attractive to no creature except a *l·* worm,

loaves

sp 90– 3 How were the *l·* and fishes multiplied
f 206–17 as Jesus showed with the *l·* and the fishes,
p 367–11 "for the *l·* and fishes,"— *see John* 6 : 26.

lobster

r 489– 2 When the unthinking *l·* loses its claw,

lobster's

r 489– 6 would be replaced as readily as the *l·* claw,

local

g 537–11 In the first chapter . . . evil has no *l·* habitation

localities

p 400–32 in certain *l·* he did not many

locality

sp 79– 1 its symptoms, *l·*, and fatality
b 291–13 Heaven is not a *l·*, but a divine state
p 439–31 send our best detectives to whatever *l·*

location

b 295– 1 that a severed limb is aching in the old *l·*,

lock

sp 99–12 None may pick the *l·* nor enter by some other

locomotion

sp 84–22 not dependent upon . . . bones for *l·*,

lodestar

f 238–32 It is the *l·* in the demonstration of

lodgment

f 235– 3 cannot go forth, . . . finding unsuspected *l·*,

loftiness

pr 8–13 If he reached the *l·* of his prayer,

lofty

g 515– 5 creeping over *l·* summits,

logic

divine
sp 72–22 it follows in divine *l·* that evil,
93–10 Divine *l·* and revelation coincide.
fair
r 490–21 would, by fair *l·*, annihilate man
human
b 300– 1 Human *l·* is awry when it attempts
materialistic
s 120–24 and refutes materialistic *l·*.
metaphysical
p 418–21 All metaphysical *l·* is inspired by this
of events
m 60–12 From the *l·* of events we learn that
66–23 It is better to await the *l·* of events

---

sp 93–12 otherwise, we may be sure that either our *l·* is
s 128–31 So is it with *l·*.
129– 2 its *l·* is as harmonious as the reasoning of
149–22 The *l·* is lame, and facts contradict it.
b 278–26 *l·* which would prove his annihilation.

logical

b 270– 9 are scientific and *l·* conclusions reached.
279–26 A *l·* and scientific conclusion is reached

logically

o 358–10 coincides with the Scriptures, and sustains *l·*

Logos

s 134–21 The true *L·* is demonstrably C. S.,
b 335–10 the *L·*, the Æon or Word of God,

logos

g 525–19 [the *l·*, or *word*]

London

s 163–13 a learned Professor in *L·*, said :
164– 4 the Royal College of Physicians, *L·*,
f 245– 4 published in the *L·* medical magazine

loneliness

gl 597–16 WILDERNESS. *L·* ; doubt ; darkness.

lonely

a 44– 5 The *l·* precincts of the tomb gave Jesus a

long

pr 4–30 *L·* prayers, superstition, and creeds
9–27 Then why make *l·* prayers about
a 90–19 men can . . . make *l·* prayers, and yet be
sp 87–29 Memory may reproduce voices *l·* ago silent,
s 130–20 Laboring *l·* to shake the adult's faith in matter
163– 8 founded on *l·* observation and reflection,
ph 174–10 and portend a *l·* night to the traveller ;
197– 1 and by printing *l·* descriptions
f 213–24 Beethoven, who was so *l·* hopelessly deaf.
233–10 How *l·* it must be before we arrive at
b 306–20 how *l·* they will suffer the pangs of
o 353–27 so *l·* will ghosts seem to continue
p 303– 5 wiping them with her *l·* hair,
367–27 I *l·* to see the consummation of my hope,
373– 8 she has struggled *l·*, and perhaps in vain ;
378–28 to chill harmony with a *l·* and cold night of
431–15 The struggle on their part was *l·*.
r 492–29 The conservative theory, *l·* believed,
ap 567– 9 Against Love, the dragon warreth not *l·*,
gl 597– 7 hypocrisy, which offered *l·* petitions

long so — as

a 39–31 so *l·* as he believes in the pleasures of sin?
m 59–27 so *l·* as its moral obligations are kept intact ;
ph 179–24 so *l·* as you read medical works
184– 7 penalties it affixes last so *l·* as the belief
f 203–27 so *l·* as he sins.
b 311–11 Sin exists here or hereafter only so *l·* as the
311–19 So *l·* as we believe that soul can sin
317–30 so *l·* as the Master remained an inhabitant of the
o 348–19 so *l·* as it remains in mortal mind,
353–26 So *l·* as there are supposed limits to Mind,
p 386– 8 So *l·* as mortals declare that
425– 4 so *l·* as you believe them to be safety-valves
t 456–20 So *l·* as matter is the basis of
r 486–20 So *l·* as this error of belief remains,
497–12 the belief in sin is punished so *l·* as the
g 551–25 so *l·* as it bases creation on materiality.

longer

sp 77–17 will be of *l·* or shorter duration
f 237–25 They devote themselves a little *l·* to their
o 346–25 how can he suffer *l·*?

longer no —

pref vii–17 Ignorance of God is no *l·* the stepping-stone
a 47– 4 They no *l·* measured man by material sense.
47– 6 leaning no *l·* on matter,
m 69–10 No *l·* to marry or to be "given in — *Matt.* 22 : 30.
sp 74–18 The caterpillar, . . . is no *l·* a worm,
76–13 can no *l·* commune with matter;
an 105–17 and no *l·* apply legal rulings wholly to
s 125– 4 may no *l·* be found indispensable to health.
125–28 astronomer will no *l·* look up to the stars,
126– 2 Error will be no *l·* used in stating truth.
130–30 no *l·* think it natural to love sin
130–31 no *l·* imagine evil to be ever-present
140–13 Mankind will no *l·* be tyrannical and
ph 171–13 no *l·* an open question, but is demonstrable
191–17 It should no *l·* ask of the head, heart, or
f 211–19 It should no *l·* be said in Israel that
c 263– 9 he will no *l·* grope in the dark and cling to earth
b 295– 3 nerves which are no *l·* there,
295–23 it no *l·* hides the sun.
298–20 joy is no *l·* a trembler, nor is hope a cheat.
309–10 He was no *l·* called Jacob, but Israel,
o 352–30 no *l·* seeming worthy of fear or honor.
p 416– 8 To him there is no *l·* any pain.
416–23 the body is no *l·* the parent,
442–13 Mortal Man, no *l·* sick and in prison,
t 460–32 shadow of old errors was no *l·* cast upon
ap 573–17 man was no *l·* regarded as a miserable sinner,
577– 5 as no *l·* two wedded individuals,

longest

p 431–16 Materia Medica held out the *l·*,

longevity

pref viii–21 the reputed *l·* of the Antediluvians,
s 126–25 the effects of Truth on the health, *l·*,
ph 167–10 our health, our *l·*, and our Christianity.
173–31 are far more fatal to health and *l·* than
f 223–32 *L·* is increasing
o 348–32 health has been restored, and *l·* increased.
r 492–10 will increase *l·*, will purify and elevate

longing

pr 4–18 the *l·* to be better and holier,

longingly

t 450–12 They do not incline *l·* to error,

longings

pr 15–17 In the quiet sanctuary of earnest *l·*,

longitude

s 125–22 cold and heat, latitude and *l·*.

longsuffering

an 106–27 *l·*, gentleness, goodness, faith, — *Gal.* 5 : 22.
t 443–21 with all *l·* and doctrine." — *II Tim.* 4 : 2.
ap 566–23 Be Thou, *l·*, slow to wrath,

look

pr 6–18 higher we cannot *l·*,
sp 78–12 Then why *l·* to them
82–29 do we *l·* for help to the Esquimaux
s 125–28 astronomer will no longer *l·* up to the stars,
125–29 he will *l·* out from them upon the universe;
129–22 We must *l·* deep into realism
154–26 says . . . "You *l·* sick," "You *l·* tired,"
ph 184–31 I then requested her to *l·* at the weather-vane.
f 219–30 we may *l·* for an abatement of these evils;
220– 6 to *l·* in other directions for cause and cure.
234–28 Jesus declared that to *l·* with desire on
248–27 and *l·* at them continually,
c 260–31 If we *l·* to the body for pleasure, we find pain;
261– 2 *L·* away from the body into Truth
264– 7 Mortals must *l·* beyond fading, finite forms,
264–10 We must *l·* where we would walk,
o 343–11 the blind *l·* up to C. S. with blessings,
p 371–11 children *l·* everywhere for the imaginary ghost,
429– 8 We *l·* before our feet,
429– 9 we *l·* beyond a single step
433–14 a *l·* of despair and death settles upon it.
434–18 earnest, solemn eyes, . . . *l·* upward.
g 521–13 We should *l·* away from the opposite
549–17 must therefore *l·* upon the simple ovum as
552–18 peck open their shells with C. S., and *l·* outward
ap 558–14 When you *l·* it fairly in the face,

looked

s 133–11 The Israelites *l·* upon the brazen serpent,
156– 8 the patient *l·* like a barrel.
161–30 if . . . philanthropists *l·* as deeply for
ph 184–32 She *l·* and saw that it pointed due east.
b 268– * *which we have l· upon,* — *I John* 1 : 1.
270–14 prophets of old *l·* for something higher

looker-on

sp 90–17 The *l·* sees the body in bed,

lookers-on

a 37–15 merit seen and appreciated by *l·*.

looking

pr 5–19 *l·* farther, the Psalmist could see their end,
7–10 *L·* deeply into these things, we find that
b 268– 8 *l·* away from matter to Mind as the cause of
308–10 *l·* for happiness and life in the body,
317–24 To the materialistic Thomas, *l·* for the
p 365– 3 the heavenly homesick *l·* away from earth,
378–11 By *l·* a tiger fearlessly in the eye,
378–13 may infuriate another by *l·* it in the eye,
t 450– 7 while *l·* you blandly in the face,

looks

a 21–11 and *l·* towards the imperishable things of Spirit.
p 271–13 *l·* for relief in all ways except the right
379– 5 where the ordinary physician *l·* for causes.
415– 9 *l·* upon some object which he dreads.
431–31 testifies: . . . I am robbed of my good *l·*.
t 451–15 walks in the direction towards which he *l·*,

looms

an 102–18 The *l·* of crime, hidden in the dark recesses

loose

s 163– 2 afterward letting her *l·* upon sick people."
t 459–18 turning him *l·* in the crowded streets of a city.

loosed

sp 89– 3 shows that the beliefs of mortal mind are *l·*.

loosely

p 363– 5 which hung *l·* about her shoulders,

loosen

b 308–27 did not *l·* his hold upon this glorious light

loosened

g 552–19 But thought, *l·* from a material basis

loosening

sp 98–16 above the *l·* grasp of creeds,

loquacious

s 153–30 avoid *l·* tattling about disease,

Lord (see also Lord's)

and Master
m 67–21 our *L·* and Master healed the sick,
b 317–20 Our *L·* and Master presented himself to

arm of the
a 24–11 "the arm of the *L·*" is revealed. — *Isa.* 53 : 1.

beloved
ap 566–15 When Israel, of the *L·* beloved,

cup of our
a 32–11 nor was the wine, used . . . the cup of our *L·*.

fear of the
p 373–15 "The fear of the *L·* is the — *Psal.* 111 : 10.

mind of the
b 291–18 "the mind of the *L·*," — *Rom.* 11 : 34.

of heaven
s 131–19 O Father, *L·* of heaven and earth, — *Luke* 10 : 21.

of Hosts
ap 568–25 and magnify the *L·* of Hosts.

on high
g 505–18 "The *L·* on high is mightier than — *Psal.* 93 : 4.

presence of the
s 135– 6 at the presence of the *L·*, — *Psal.* 114 : 7.
g 542–28 from the presence of the *L·* — *Gen.* 4 : 16.

present with the
pr 14– 4 "present with the *L·*" — *II Cor.* 5 : 8.
14– 6 "present with the *L·*" — *II Cor.* 5 : 8.
f 216–30 present with the *L·*." — *II Cor.* 5 : 8.
p 383–11 present with the *L·*." — *II Cor.* 5 : 8.
gl 581–26 present with the *L·*." — *II Cor.* 5 : 8.

shall reign
pref vii–20 "the *L·* shall reign forever." — *Exod.* 15 : 18.

Spirit of the
f 227–18 "Where the Spirit of the *L·* is, — *II Cor.* 3 : 17.
r 481– 4 "Where the Spirit of the *L·* is, — *II Cor.* 3 : 17.

thy God
pr 9–17 Dost thou "love the *L·* thy God — *Matt.* 22 : 37.

wait upon the
f 218– 27 "They that wait upon the *L·* — *Isa.* 40 : 31.

with our
a 35–10 This spiritual meeting with our *L·*

with the
pr 14– 9 To be "with the *L·*" is to be — *II Cor.* 5 : 8.
g 504–22 "one day is with the *L·* as a — *II Pet.* 3 : 8.
gl 598–21 "One day is with the *L·* as a — *II Pet.* 3 : 8.

---

pr 10– 3 and that waiting patiently on the *L·*,
a 23–27 "*L·*, I believe; help thou — *Mark* 9 : 24.
38–16 "The right hand of the *L·* is — *Psal.* 118 : 16.
f 201– * *Remember, L·, the reproach* — *Psal.* 89 : 50.
201– * *enemies have reproached, O L·;* — *Psal.* 89 : 51.
241– 1 "Whom the *L·* loveth He — *Heb.* 12 : 6.
c 256–12 the *L·* our God is one *L·*." — *Deut.* 6 : 4.
267–31 which the *L·* hath promised — *Jas.* 1 : 12.
b 276– 3 "I am the *L·* that healeth — *Exod.* 15 : 26.
b 293–26 "The anger of the *L·*." — *Deut.* 29 : 20.
307–17 and says: "The *L·* knows it.

Lord

  b 320–12 "And the *L·* said, — *Gen.* 6 : 3.
     325–26 the divine heights of our *L·*.
  p 365– 6 than all cries of "*L·*, *L·* !"
     414–21 "The *L·* He is God — *Deut.* 4 : 35.
  r 479– 5 "I have gotten a man from the *L·*" — *Gen.* 4 : 1.
  g 523–27 the creator is called Jehovah, or the *L·*.
     538–25 I have gotten a man from the *L·* — *Gen.* 4 : 1.
     538–31 "I have gotten a man from the *L·*," — *Gen.* 4 : 1.
     540– 6 I the *L·* do all these things ;" — *Isa.* 45 : 7.
     540–13 we may think in our ignorance that the *L·* hath
     540–26 an offering unto the *L·* — *Gen.* 4 : 3.
     541– 6 the *L·* [Jehovah] had respect unto — *Gen.* 4 : 4.
     541–19 the *L·* [Jehovah] said unto Cain, — *Gen.* 4 : 9.
     542–14 the *L·* [Jehovah] said unto him, — *Gen.* 4 : 15.
     542–16 the *L·* [Jehovah] set a mark upon — *Gen.* 4 : 15.
  ap 558– * *Great is the L·, and greatly* — *Psal.* 48 : 1.
     576–26 The term *L·*, as used in our version of
  gl 590–15 definition of
  fr 600– * *walk worthy of the L·* — *Col.* 1 : 10.

lord

  g 518– 2 He is *l·* of the belief in earth and heaven,

Lord God

  g 520–18 in the day that the *L· G·* — *Gen.* 2 : 4.
     520–20 the *L· G·* [Jehovah] had not caused — *Gen.* 2 : 5.
     523–20 is always called Jehovah, — or *L· G·*,
     524–13 the *L· G·* [Jehovah] formed man — *Gen.* 2 : 7.
     525–30 out of the ground made the *L· G·* — *Gen.* 2 : 9.
     526–26 the *L· G·* [Jehovah] took the — *Gen.* 2 : 15.
     527– 6 the *L· G·* [Jehovah] commanded — *Gen.* 2 : 16.
     527–21 out of the ground the *L· G·* — *Gen.* 2 : 19.
     528– 9 *L· G·* [Jehovah, Yawah] caused — *Gen.* 2 : 21.
     528–12 and the rib, which the *L· G·* — *Gen.* 2 : 22.
     529–14 the *L· G·* [Jehovah] had made. — *Gen.* 3 : 1.
     532–13 the *L· G·* [Jehovah] called unto — *Gen.* 3 : 9.
     534– 8 the *L· G·* [Jehovah] said — *Gen.* 3 : 14.
     536–30 the *L· G·* [Jehovah] said, — *Gen.* 3 : 22.
     537– 3 therefore the *L· G·* [Jehovah] — *Gen.* 3 : 23.
     543–31 "In the day that the *L· G·* — *Gen.* 2 : 4.
  ap 576–10 the *L· G·* Almighty and the Lamb — *Rev.* 21 : 22.
  gl 590–20 definition of
     (*see also* **Jehovah**)

lordly

  s 142–11 If the soft palm, upturned to a *l·* salary,

Lord of Hosts

  ap 568–25 we give thanks and magnify the *L·* of *H·*.

Lord's

  a 31–23 show the *L·* death till he come." — *I Cor.* 11 : 26.
     34–29 What a contrast between our *L·* last supper and
     35–15 They celebrate their *L·* victory over death,

lords

  b 280–17 "gods many and *l·* many." — *I Cor.* 8 : 5.
     307– 9 It says : "There shall be *l·* and gods many.
  gl 580– 8 "gods many and *l·* many " — *I Cor.* 8 : 5.

Lord's Prayer

  pr 14–23 The *L· P·* is the prayer of Soul,
     16– 8 which we name after him the *L· P·*,
     16–22 is indicated in the *L· P·*
     16–25 the spiritual sense of the *L· P·* :

lore

  a 23–12 Rabbinical *l·* said : "He that taketh
  s 134– 1 have not cleansed their hands of rabbinical *l·*.
  g 549–14 According to recent *l·*, successive generations

lose

  pref xi–11 before which sin and disease *l·* their reality
  m 65 26 must *l·* its present slippery footing,
     69– 5 only as they *l·* the sense of sin and disease.
  s 127– 2 she will not therefore *l·* faith in Christianity,
     127– 3 nor will Christianity *l·* its hold upon her.
     160– 5 drugs *l·* their healing force,
  ph 176–15 sin, disease and death, will *l·* their foothold.
  f 207–13 Without this lesson, we *l·* sight of the
     240–13 and you *l·* the keynote of being,
  c 257–28 or Mind would *l·* its infinite character
     259– 2 Man . . . cannot *l·* his individuality,
     260–29 If . . . it must *l·* its immortal nature.
     261–26 will neither *l·* the solid objects and ends of life
  b 265– 1 Matter has no life to *l·*, and Spirit never dies.
     278–15 we *l·* the consciousness of matter.
     296–16 must *l·* all satisfaction in error and sin
     302– 8 It is impossible that man should *l·* aught
     304–23 they would *l·* harmony, if time or
     310–27 if Spirit should *l·* Life as God, good,
     311– 9 he can only *l·* a sense material.
     311–28 sin, and mortality *l·* all supposed consciousness
     315–17 The likeness of God we *l·* sight of through sin,
     316– 5 and *l·* sight of mortal selfhood
     336–22 else God would . . . *l·* the deific character,
     337– 2 Therefore man, . . . cannot *l·* his individuality;
     337– 4 as material sensation, . . . mortals do *l·* sight of
     339–32 will never *l·* their imaginary power . . . until
     340– 1 until we *l·* our faith in them
  o 344–28 may *l·* ninety-and-nine patients, while

lose

  o 351– 2 When we *l·* faith in God's power to heal,
  p 367–22 that this salt *l·* not its saltness,
     370–24 a drug may eventually *l·* its supposed
  r 469–25 *l·* the high signification of omnipotence,
     472–22 Thus we should continue to *l·* the standard
     477–31 man, divorced from Spirit, would *l·* his entity.
  g 524–31 Does Spirit enter dust, and *l·* therein the
     555–23 We *l·* our standard of perfection . . . when

loses

  s 148–16 It *l·* Spirit, drops the true tone, and
  ph 187–28 *l·* all appearance of life or action,
     197–28 mortal belief *l·* some portion of its error.
  f 215–18 darkness *l·* the appearance of reality.
     248– 3 Love never *l·* sight of loveliness.
  b 325– 2 *l·* his belief in death.
     325– 3 *l·* all sense of evil, and by reason of this is
     327–11 Then he *l·* pleasure in wickedness,
  p 369– 5 In proportion as matter *l·* to human sense all
     370–26 Hygienic treatment also *l·* its efficacy.
  r 489– 2 When the unthinking lobster *l·* its claw,

losing

  m 59–30 sacredness of this relationship is *l·* its
  f 238– 9 *L·* her crucifix, the Roman Catholic girl said,
  b 309–19 thus *l·* the divine power which heals
     335–22 Only by *l·* the false sense of Soul can we
  o 360–11 replies : . . . I have no notion of *l·* my old

loss

no

  pr 1–11 no *l·* can occur from trusting God

of a limb

  ph 172–27 But the *l·* of a limb or injury to a tissue

of control

  p 406–20 a *l·* of control over the body.

of earthly hopes

  c 265–26 The *l·* of earthly hopes and pleasures

of harmony

  p 408– 2 sickness is *l·* of harmony.

of his identity

  c 265–12 by no means suggests . . . the *l·* of his identity,

of human peace

  c 265–23 Who that has felt the *l·* of human peace

of man's identity

  f 217– 1 The *l·* of man's identity . . . is impossible ;

of power

  ph 183–25 Submission to error superinduces *l·* of power.

possible

  a 51– 2 possible *l·* of something more important than

temporary

  b 311–16 belief strays into a sense of temporary *l·*

their

  r 487– 9 of the Mind-faculties than in their *l·*.

your

  p 386–19 You think that your anguish is occasioned by your *l·*.

            ———

  b 294– 6 If man is both mind and matter, the *l·* of one
  r 470– 7 assumed the *l·* of spiritual power,
     470– 7 assumed . . . the *l·* of the spiritual presence
     470– 9 assumed . . . the *l·* of Love as ever present

lost

  a 32–20 The true sense is spiritually *l·*, if the
     41–17 this demonstration of healing was early *l·*,
     49– 9 Had they so soon *l·* sight of his mighty works,
  sp 78–24 How can the majesty . . . of Spirit be *l·* ?
     87– 3 *l·* to the memory of the mind in which
     87–25 The true concept is never *l·*.
  s 110–26 But this power was *l·* sight of,
     143– 8 more deplorably *l·* than the sinning, if
     146– 3 Why has this element of Christianity been *l·*?
     147–10 Truth had *l·* none of its . . . efficacy,
     153– 7 The salt had "*l·* his savour ;" — *Matt.* 5 : 13.
     162–23 what is called the *l·* substance of lungs,
  ph 166– 7 thus the conscious control over the body is *l·*.
  f 208–23 cannot be *l·* nor remain forever unseen.
     211–27 If . . . these faculties must be *l·*,
     214–28 But the real sight or sense is not *l·*.
     215– 4 If Spirit, Soul, could sin or be *l·*,
     215– 5 then being and immortality would be *l·*,
     215– 6 being cannot be *l·* while God exists.
     215–24 Every quality and condition of mortality is *l·*,
     217– 4 more absurd than to conclude that . . . tones are *l·*
     245– 6 and *l·* all account of time.
     247– 3 age regain two of the elements it had *l·*,
  c 259–15 If man was once perfect but has now *l·* his
     259–17 The *l·* image is no image.
     259–18 true likeness cannot be *l·* in divine reflection.
  b 282– 1 and the inspiration, . . . will be *l·*.
     283–23 *l·* to all who cling to this falsity.
     295–21 that one which has *l·* much materiality
     302– 5 The identity of the real man is not *l·*,
     302–13 and this belief is all that will ever be *l·*.
     303–29 cannot be *l·* nor separated from its divine
     304–28 misapprehended *l·* in confusion.

lost
- *b* 310–19 human soul which sins and is spiritually *l*·,
- 310–20 commonly taught . . . that soul may be *l*·,
- 311– 8 Is man *l*· spiritually? No,
- 311–13 It is a sense of sin, . . . which is *l*·.
- 312– 2 must be *l*· because such so-called knowledge
- 314–19 This materialism *l*· sight of the true Jesus ;
- 321–16 The illusion of Moses *l*· its power to alarm him,
- 323–18 the one unused talent decays and is *l*·.
- 328–17 has been dormant, a *l*· element of Christianity.
- 331– 8 *l*· through a mortal sense, which
- *o* 360– 2 they will find that nothing is *l*·,
- *p* 375–24 muscles have no power to be *l*·,
- 407–21 If delusion says, "I have lost my memory,"
- 407–22 No faculty of Mind is *l*·.
- 410–29 until the . . . healing ability is wholly *l*·.
- 431–27 testifies : . . . I have *l*· my healthy hue
- *t* 455–11 If you are yourself *l*· in the belief and fear
- *r* 470–28 If man has *l*· perfection,
- 470–29 then he has *l*· his perfect Principle,
- 481–31 it is the sense of sin which is *l*·,
- 486–24 They cannot be *l*·.
- 487– 9 *L*· they cannot be, while Mind remains.
- 489– 5 the senses of Mind are never *l*·
- 491–24 In sleep, memory and consciousness are *l*·
- *g* 524–10 the true idea of God seems almost *l*·.
- 533– 1 Had he *l*· man's rich inheritance and
- 536–14 If man's spiritual gravitation . . . should be *l*·,
- 548– 7 man has never *l*· his spiritual estate

Lot
- *t* 444–25 as did Abraham when he parted from *L*·,

lotions
- *f* 234– 1 while material *l*· interfere with truth,

lots
- *f* 242–24 for my vesture they did cast *l*·."— *John* 19 : 24.

loud
- *ap* 568–13 And I heard a *l*· voice saying— *Rev.* 12 : 10.

louder
- *sp* 97–24 the *l*· will error scream, until its
- *ap* 568–26 A *l*· song, sweeter than has ever before

lovable
- *f* 232– 4 neither make man harmonious nor God *l*·.

Love (see also Love's)
abide in
- *b* 274–12 The senses of Spirit abide in *L*·,

all is
- *ap* 567– 8 all is *L*·, and there is no error, no sin,

alone can
- *g* 510–18 *L*· alone can impart the limitless idea of

and Truth
- *a* 19– 2 *L*· and Truth are not at war with God's image
- *f* 227–19 *L*· and Truth make free,
- *r* 470– 3 brotherhood of man would consist of *L*· and Truth,
- *gl* 596–17 the spiritual inspiration of *L*· and Truth

anointeth
- *ap* 578–14 [*L*·] anointeth my head with— *see Psal.* 23 : 5.

armed him with
- *a* 52–23 Mind-healing, or C. S., which armed him with *L*·.

chastened by
- *f* 241– 4 he who . . . is chastened by *L*·.

chastisements of
- *b* 323– 6 Through the wholesome chastisements of *L*·,

crown of
- *t* 451– 6 with the crown of *L*· upon her brow,

design of
- *a* 35–30 The design of *L*· is to reform the sinner.

destroys hate
- *b* 339– 3 Truth destroys error, and *L*· destroys hate.

Divine
- *p* 439–29 sentence which . . . Divine *L*· will pronounce.

divine
- (*see* divine)

divine Principle is
- *b* 330–21 and divine Principle is *L*·,

divine Principle or
- *pr* 12–20 It is a mortal belief, not divine Principle or *L*·,

efficacious
- *r* 497–14 evidence of divine, efficacious *L*·,

essence of
- *b* 333–26 in the divine nature, the essence of *L*·.

eternal
- *a* 19– 1 his own, derived from the eternal *L*·.

everlasting
- *a* 23–11 will fall at the feet of everlasting *L*·.

ever-present
- *p* 377– 5 should rejoice always in ever-present *L*·.
- *g* 501–13 is consonant with ever-present *L*·.
- 503–14 light of ever-present *L*· illumines the
- *ap* 567– 7 To infinite, ever-present *L*·, all is Love,

explained by that
- *g* 501–15 explained by that *L*· for whose rest the

flood-tides of
- *f* 201–18 to pour in truth through flood-tides of *L*·.

Love
fruits of
- *a* 35–24 by bringing forth the fruits of *L*·,

fulfils the law
- *ap* 572–12 *L*· fulfils the law of C. S.,

giveth
- *g* 518–19 *L*· giveth to the least spiritual idea might,

God is
- (*see* God)

Golden Shore of
- *ap* 576– 1 realization of the Golden Shore of *L*· and

gospel of
- *ap* 577– 4 held in the gospel of *L*·.

hand of
- *a* 36–27 or that the hand of *L*· is satisfied with

hath shown
- *s* 137–24 *L*· hath shown thee the way of Life !

heart of
- *t* 448– 4 went out to the great heart of *L*·,

he defined
- *a* 54– 4 Out of the amplitude of his . . . he defined *L*·.

held
- *g* 514–26 the control which *L*· held over all,

idea of
- *b* 326–31 He beheld for the first time the true idea of *L*·,
- *g* 534–29 will struggle to destroy the spiritual idea of *L*· ;
- *gl* 590– 9 LAMB OF GOD. The spiritual idea of *L*· ;

image, of
- *r* 475–14 Man is idea, the image, of *L*· ;

immortality and
- *gl* 597–15 divine Science,— immortality and *L*·.

imparts
- *g* 517–13 *L*· imparts the clearest idea of Deity.

incorporeal
- *pr* 13–24 wonders wrought by infinite, incorporeal *L*·,

inexhaustible
- *c* 257–29 inexhaustible *L*·, eternal Life,

infinite
- *pr* 10–30 In this case infinite *L*· will not grant the
- *a* 53–15 rather than as divine, infinite *L*·.
- *c* 256–25 No form . . . adequate to represent infinite *L*·.
- *b* 312–21 God is infinite *L*·, which must be
- *p* 366–18 recognition of infinite *L*· which alone confers
- *g* 520– 4 majesty, and glory of infinite *L*· fill all space.

infinitude of
- *g* 508–25 unfolds the infinitude of *L*·.

inspiration of
- *a* 35–28 Our wine the inspiration of *L*·,
- *gl* 596–17 the spiritual inspiration of *L*· and Truth

inspires
- *t* 454–18 *L*· inspires, illumines, designates, and

is enthroned
- *t* 454–10 *L*· is enthroned.

is impartial
- *pr* 13– 2 *L*· is impartial and universal

is Mind
- *b* 330–21 and *L*· is Mind,

is not hasty
- *a* 22–20 *L*· is not hasty to deliver us from temptation,

is reflected
- *pr* 17– 7 *And L*· *is reflected in love;*

is Spirit
- *sp* 96– 5 spiritualization will follow, for *L*· is Spirit.

is the light
- *ap* 577–20 no need of sun or satellite, for *L*· is the light

is with me
- *ap* 578–11 for [*L*·] is with me ;— *Psal.* 23 : 4.

Lamb of
- *ap* 561–13 wedded to the Lamb of *L*·.
- 567–30 killed by innocence, the Lamb of *L*·.

law of
- (*see* law)

leadeth me
- *ap* 578– 7 [*L*·] leadeth me beside the still— *Psal.* 23 : 2.
- 578– 8 [*L*·] leadeth me in the paths of— *Psal.* 23 : 3.

Life and
- (*see* Life)

Life, . . . and wisdom
- *b* 283– 6 Mind is the same Life, *L*·, and wisdom

Life as
- *p* 391–31 rise to the true consciousness of Life as *L*·,

Life, . . . Truth
- *sp* 81–15 Life, *L*·, Truth, is the only proof of

Life, Truth, and
- (*see* Life)

love of
- *b* 319–31 speak of the love of *L*·, meaning by that

maketh
- *ap* 578– 6 [*L*·] maketh me to lie down in— *Psal.* 23 : 2.

ministering
- *ap* 567– 3 a sense of the ever-presence of ministering *L*·.

misunderstand
- *pr* 6–21 is to misunderstand *L*· and to make prayer **the**

Love

mocking
g 528–21   mocking *L·* and declaring

motherhood of
g 519–11   the fatherhood and motherhood of *L·*.

must triumph
a 43–32   *L·* must triumph over hate.

no fear in
p 410–18   "There is no fear in *L·*, — *I John* 4 : 18.

no miracle to
r 494–15   miracle of grace is no miracle to *L·*.

no other
f 206– 1   no other *L·*, wisdom, or Truth,

not hate
p 420– 3   *L·* not hate, Spirit not matter, governs man.

not made perfect in
p 410–20   is not made perfect in *L·*." — *I John* 4 : 18.

omnipresent
s 119–21   is not the divine ideal of omnipresent *L·*.

opposite of
gl 580–17   the opposite of *L·*, called hate ;

panoply of
ap 571–12   Clad in the panoply of *L·*,

partakers of
pr 4–16   worthiness to be partakers of *L·*.

perfect
p 373–18   "perfect *L·* casteth out fear." — *I John* 4 : 18.
    406–10   "Perfect *L·* casteth out fear." — *I John* 4 : 18.
    410–18   perfect *L·* casteth out fear. — *I John* 4 : 18.

power of
f 231–22   is to misunderstand the power of *L·*

prepareth
ap 578–13   [*L·*] prepareth a table before — *see Psal.* 23 : 5.

propagates
m 66–13   *L·* propagates anew the higher joys

purpose of
gl 579–12   the purpose of *L·* to create trust in good,

realm of
a 20–27   commands sure entrance into the realm of *L·*.

redolent with
g 516–12   *L·*, redolent with unselfishness,

religion of
s 138–16   sublime summary points to the religion of *L·*.

removed by
p 374– 6   Hatred and its effects . . . are removed by *L·*.

restoreth
ap 578– 8   [*L·*] restoreth my soul — *Psal.* 23 : 3.

Science of
a 30– 3   and could demonstrate the Science of *L·*

sends forth
ap 568–29   *L·* sends forth her primal and everlasting strain.

shrine of
gl 595– 9   superstructure of Truth ; the shrine of *L·* ;

solvent of
f 242–17   to dissolve with the universal solvent of *L·*

spiritual
a 33–22   This is the new understanding of spiritual *L·*.
c 266–11   spiritual *L·* will force you to accept

supports
m 57–28   for *L·* supports the struggling heart

true sense of
ap 575– 2   Arise . . . into the true sense of *L·*,

truer sense of
a 19– 7   by giving man a truer sense of *L·*,
    19– 9   and this truer sense of *L·* redeems

Truth and
    (*see* **Truth**)

Truth, and Life
p 410– 7   the knowledge of *L·*, Truth, and Life.

Truth, Life, and
    (*see* **Truth**)

Truth, Life, or
f 207–26   presuppose the absence of Truth, Life, or *L·*.

Truth, or
f 234– 4   Whatever inspires with wisdom, Truth, or *L·*

universal
c 266–18   Universal *L·* is the divine way in C. S.

which paints
f 247–24   It is *L·* which paints the petal

will finally
sp 96– 4   *L·* will finally mark the hour of harmony,

winged with
g 512– 9   and also by holy thoughts, winged with *L·*.

wisdom and
pr 2–11   since He is unchanging wisdom and *L·*.
a 23– 1   Wisdom and *L·* may require many sacrifices
c 265–26   discover what belongs to wisdom and *L·*.

---

pr 13–26   human ignorance of the divine Principle, *L·*,
    15–13   divine Principle, *L·*, which destroys all error.
    17–14   Truth, *L·*, over all, and All.
a 22–21   *L·* means that we shall be tried and purified.
    26–23   makes us admit its Principle to be *L·*.
    35–14   commune with the divine Principle, *L·*.
    35–20   Our church is built on the divine Principle, *L·*.
    44– 9   He proved . . . *L·* to be the master of hate.

Love

a 45–21   man and his divine Principle, *L·*.
    50–13   to his divine Principle, the God who is *L·*,
    51–27   aimed at the divine Principle, *L·*,
sp 98–19   Christ's revelation of Truth, of Life, and of *L·*,
s 113– 6   the heart and soul of C. S., is *L·*.
    115–13   GOD : Divine Principle, Life, Truth, *L·*, Soul,
f 225–21   *L·* is the liberator.
    230–10   comes through God, the divine Principle, *L·*,
    231–10   but God, Truth, Life, *L·*, does heal the sick
    243–25   *L·* has no sense of hatred.
    248– 3   *L·* never loses sight of loveliness.
    253– 5   saith : . . . impart all bliss, for I am *L·*.
c 256– 7   *L·*, the divine Principle, is the Father and
b 270–13   eternal Mind or divine Principle, *L·*.
    275–12   Spirit, Life, Truth, *L·*, combine as one,
    275–17   the infinite divine Principle, *L·*.
    280– 4   From *L·* and from the light and harmony which
    286–11   Christ, Life, Truth, *L·* ;
    286–14   the divine Principle, *L·*, creates
    293–15   divine Mind, . . . whose attraction is *L·*,
    300–32   that which reflects Life, Truth, *L·*,
    305–25   were it not that *L·*, the divine Principle
    312–16   and without *L·*, God, . . . cannot appear.
    319–29   as, for instance, to name *L·* as merely an
    330–20   Scriptures declare Him to be, — Life, Truth, *L·*.
    331–19   He is divine Principle, *L·*,
    331–27   that is, the triply divine Principle, *L·*.
    332–22   revealing the divine Principle, *L·*,
    335–32   Mind is the divine Principle, *L·*,
r 465–10   Spirit, Soul, Principle, Life, Truth, *L·*.
    470– 9   assumed . . . the loss of *L·* as ever present
    473–24   God as divine Principle, *L·*,
    477–22   forms of the living Principle, *L·*.
    490–18   the real man's divine Principle, *L·*.
    496–18   based upon its divine Principle, *L·*.
g 512– 3   the incorporeal and divine Principle, *L·*.
    517–10   woman corresponds to Life and to *L·*.
    520– 9   no more . . . than is his infinite Principle, *L·*.
    524–11   *L·*, the divine Principle to be lived and loved.
    526–23   Was evil instituted through God, *L·* ?
    527–11   Here the metaphor represents God, *L·*, as
    537–32   this is not the nature of God, who is *L·*
    538– 1   *L·* infinitely wise and altogether lovely,
    541–12   the human concept of *L·*
ap 567– 9   Against *L·*, the dragon warreth not long,
    569– 2   as *L·*, represented by the Mother.
    574–29   The very circumstance, . . . *L·* can make an
    575– 3   *L·* wedded to its own spiritual idea."
    578–18   [the consciousness] of [*L·*] — *Psal.* 23 : 6.
gl 587– 7   Life ; Truth ; *L·* ; all substance ;
    591–17   divine Principle, substance, Life, Truth, *L·* ;

love (*see also* **love's**)

confidence and
m 58–18   the sweet interchange of confidence and *l·* ;

disappointed in
f 245– 5   Disappointed in *l·* in her early years,

emotional
a 25–27   and all the emotional *l·* we can bestow

enriches
m 57–23   *L·* enriches the nature, enlarging, purifying,

feminine
m 64–24   masculine wisdom and feminine *l·*,

for God
t 454–17   *L·* for God and man is the true incentive

God is
b 320– 1   "God is *l·*." — *I John* 4 : 8.

God's
b 326– 9   All nature teaches God's *l·* to man,

goodness and
m 66–16   unfolds new views of divine goodness and *l·*.

gratitude, and
pr 8–15   gratitude, and *l·* which our words express,

His
pr 5–17   God pours the riches of His *l·* into the
b 340–14   in and of God, and manifests His *l·*.

his
a 26– 8   in proportion to their demonstration of his *l·*,

is priestess
t 454–21   *L·* is priestess at the altar of Truth.

labor of
p 387–24   cannot suffer as the result of any labor of *l·*,

lack of
s 140–14   tyrannical and proscriptive from lack of *l·*,

life or
c 257–25   Who hath found finite life or *l·* sufficient

life, truth, and
b 284–18   testimony as to spiritual life, truth, and *l·* ?

Master's
s 130–24   our Master's *l·* for little children,

more expansive
c 265–14   confers upon man . . . a more expansive *l·*,

no
b 275–18   no *l·* is lovely, . . . but the divine ;
r 467– 7   no *l·*, but that which is spiritual.

of a father
a 50–10   would impugn the justice and *l·* of a father

love
of applause
pr 7–15   may embrace too much *l·* of applause
of Christianity
f 235–32   *L·* of Christianity, rather than love of
of God
a 42– 4   gave no hint of the unchanging *l·* of God.
b 304– 9   to separate us from the *l·* of God."— *Rom.* 8 : 39.
of Love
b 319–31   but we can . . . speak of the *l·* of Love,
of popularity
f 236– 1   rather than *l·* of popularity,
of sin
a 36– 6   sufficient suffering, . . . to quench the *l·* of sin.
p 373–14   The fear of disease and the *l·* of sin are the
of the good
gl 593– 1   The *l·* of the good and beautiful,
our
p 410–17   stronger should be our faith and the purer our *l·*.
pinions of
pr 4–31   creeds clip the strong pinions of *l·*,
power and
f 243– 9   with unsurpassed power and *l·*.
precious
a 22– 9   and through Christ's precious *l·* these efforts
rebuking error
gl 594–15   *l·* rebuking error ; reproof of sensualism.
reflected in
pr 17– 7   *And Love is reflected in l·;*
spiritual
c 264–27   comes from an all-absorbing spiritual *l·*.
t 462–30   unselfishness, philanthropy, spiritual *l·*.
truth and
a 50– 4   Who shall decide what truth and *l·* are?
f 215–21   phantoms of error before truth and *l·*.
p 414–11   truth and *l·* will establish a healthy state,
r 473–20   proof of Christianity's truth and *l·* ;
unselfed
pr 1– 4   understanding of Him, an unselfed *l·*.
ph 192–31   thought in line with unselfed *l·*,
variable
g 503–25   mutable truth, nor variable *l·*.

---

pr 4– 5   patience, meekness, *l·*, and good deeds.
an 106–27   the fruit of the Spirit is *l·*, joy,— *Gal.* 5 : 22.
s 108– 9   immortal cravings, "the price of learning *l·*,"
    116– 3   spiritual power, *l·*, health, holiness.
f 206–12   exercise of the sentiments— hope, faith, *l·*
    248–30   justice, health, holiness, *l·*
b 312–15   with scarcely a spark of *l·* in their hearts ;
p 435–20   in the exercise of a *l·* that
ap 576–14   worshipped in spirit and in *l·*.
gl 586–24, 25   *l·* meeting no response, but still remaining *l·*.

love (verb)
pr 4–11   "If ye *l·* me, keep my— *John* 14 : 15.
    4–17   Simply asking that we may *l·* God
    4–18   Simply asking . . . will never make us *l·* Him ;
    9– 6   Do we *l·* our neighbor better because of
    9–17   Dost thou "*l·* the Lord thy God— *Matt.* 22 : 37.
a 25–20   "If ye *l·* me, keep my— *John* 14 : 15.
    54–31   would not some, who now profess to *l·* him,
    55–18   and *l·* his neighbor as himself,
sp 88–18   To *l·* one's neighbor as one's self, is a
    99–22   I *l·* mankind, and shall continue to labor
s 130–31   and no longer think it natural to *l·* sin
    138–29   *L·* thy neighbor as thyself !"— *Matt.* 19 : 19.
    140–10   and *l·* Him understandingly,
ph 167–19   you must *l·* God supremely.
    181–21   If you are too material to *l·* the Science of
f 234–12   We should *l·* our enemies
    235–31   will *l·* to grapple with a new, right idea
    236–26   and learn more readily to *l·* the simple verities
    241–21   "If ye *l·* me, keep my— *John* 14 : 15.
c 267–31   promised to them that *l·* him."— *Jas.* 1 : 12.
b 326– 9   man cannot *l·* God supremely . . . while
    340–10   *l·* God and keep His commandments :
    340–25   "*L·* thy neighbor as thyself ;"— *Matt.* 19 : 19.
o 359– 2   whom they have seen and have been taught to *l·*
p 363–18   "Which of them will *l·* him most?"— *Luke* 7 : 42.
    364–23   said of them also that they *l·* little.
    364–30   that they indeed *l·* much,
    366–16   how can he *l·* God whom he— *I John* 4 : 20.
    404–25   to master evil and to *l·* good.
t 444– 5   to them that *l·* God,"— *Rom.* 8 : 28.
    452–19   He must live it and *l·* it,
r 467– 8   "Thou shalt *l·* thy neighbor as— *Matt.* 22 : 39.
    496– 7   to have one Mind, and to *l·* another as
ap 566– 9   up to the glory prepared for them who *l·* God.
    572– 6   *L·* one another"— *I John* 3 : 23.

loved
f 236–28   Jesus *l·* little children because of their
b 313–18   he "*l·* righteousness and— *Heb.* 1 : 9.
    317–23   self-same Jesus whom they had *l·* before the

loved
p 433–20   Because he has *l·* his neighbor
g 524–12   the divine Principle to be lived and *l·*.
ap 568–19   *l·* not their lives unto the death.— *Rev.* 12 : 11.
loveliness
f 246–30   shape our views of existence into *l·*,
    247–17   reflecting those higher conceptions of *l·*
    247–27   and covers earth with *l·*.
    248– 3   Love never loses sight of *l·*.
o 359–32   in their true light and *l·*,
lovely
pr 3–14   the One "altogether *l·* ;"— *Song* 5 : 16.
m 68–17   she was unmarried, a *l·* character,
b 275–18   no love is *l·*, . . . but the divine ;
g 538– 1   Love infinitely wise and altogether *l·*,
lover
m 58–24   Said the peasant bride to her *l·* :
f 245– 8   in the same hour which parted her from her *l·*,
lover's
f 245–10   watching for her *l·* coming.
Love's
a 50–14   and to himself, *L·* pure idea.
t 460– 8   on the divine Mind and *L·* essential qualities.
g 515– 8   *L·* ideas are subject to the Mind which
ap 578–11, 12   [*L·*] rod and [*L·*] staff— *Psal.* 23 : 4.
love's
m 68–11   and scatters *l·* petals to decay.
loves
a 42– 3   affirmed God to be a . . . who *l·* and hates.
    47–23   world generally *l·* a lie better than Truth ;
r 481– 9   Through spiritual sense only, man . . . *l·* Deity.
loveth
f 241– 1   "Whom the Lord *l·* He— *Heb.* 12 : 6.
p 366–14   "He that *l·* not his brother— *I John* 4 : 20.
loving
a 26– 3   treading alone his *l·* pathway
m 57–11   Both sexes should be *l·*, pure, tender, and strong.
f 205–23   the divine law of *l·* our neighbor
c 262–22   and attain the bliss of *l·* unselfishly,
b 272– 5   only as we are honest, unselfish, *l·*, and meek.
    326–10   cannot love God supremely . . . while *l·* the
t 454–27   Let your *l·* care and counsel support
loving-kindness
p 366– 2   a priceless sense of the dear Father's *l·*.
lovingly
f 254–20   This task God demands us to accept *l·*
p 412– 1   fact that God *l·* governs all,
low
m 61–10   every mountain of selfishness be brought *l·*,
lower
m 62–27   higher nature . . . is not governed by the *l·* ;
    67– 5   ocean is stirred by a storm, then the clouds *l·*,
s 116–30   but not in the *l·* sense.
    144– 4   needs no cooperation from *l·* powers,
ph 181– 1   divine Truth more potent than all *l·* remedies.
    189–29   in the *l·*, basal portion of the brain,
    195–31   Incorrect views *l·* the standard of truth.
f 206– 1   else it will . . . free the *l·* propensities.
    247– 8   his full set of upper and *l·* teeth
    248–22   are liable to follow those *l·* patterns,
b 268– 5   those *l·* things which give impulse to inquiry.
    319–10   *l·* appeal to the general faith in
p 377–21   governing fear of this *l·* so-called mind,
    434–30   the *l·* court has sentenced Mortal Man
    437–31   ranks above the *l·* Court of Error.
g 518–15   the higher always protects the *l·*.
    520–30   nothing left to be made by a *l·* power.
    549– 9   Creatures of *l·* forms of organism
    551–12   through all the *l·* grades of existence.
    554–29   It is the general belief that the *l·* animals are
    557– 6   the birth-throes in the *l·* realms of nature,
gl 590–18   almost always has this *l·* sense,
lowering
ph 195–28   Literary commercialism is *l·* the
lowest
s 148–11   and as emerging from the *l·*, instead of
ph 189–20   from the *l·* instead of from the highest
f 225–32   and on the *l·* plane of human life,
c 265– 2   Man is the offspring, not of the *l·*, but of the
p 405– 4   above the *l·* type of manhood,
loyal
pr 4–10   not of itself sufficient to express *l·* and
loyalty
ph 183–23   No reservation is made for any lesser *l·*.
lozenges
ph 175–31   tubercles and troches, lungs and *l·*.
lubricating
ph 199–29   the unscientific might attribute to a *l·* oil.

Luke
  p 369–14 We never read that *L·* or Paul made a
Luke's Gospel
  p 362– 1 in the seventh chapter of *L· G·*
lulled
  sp 95–28 *L·* by stupefying illusions, the world is asleep
  t 464–18 when the belief of pain was *l·*,
luminaries
  a 37–10 They are earth's *l·*, which serve to
lump
  b 329– 5 A little leaven leavens the whole *l·*.
lunar
  ap 561–28 light portrayed is really neither solar nor *l·*,
lungs
  action of the
    p 415–21 the action of the *l·*, of the bowels,
  and lozenges
    ph 175–31 tubercles and troches, *l·* and lozenges.
  capacious
    p 425–29 If you have sound and capacious *l·*
  heart, or
    ph 191–18 should no longer ask of the head, heart, or *l·* :
  notions about
    p 425–32 Discard all notions about *l·*, tubercles,
    ——
    s 127–20 nerves, brain, stomach, *l·*, and so forth,
    151–19 The blood, heart, *l·*, brain, etc.,
    159–25 They examine the *l·*, tongue, and pulse
    162–23 what is called the lost substance of *l·*,
    ph 185– 4 changed the action of her belief on the *l·*,
    f 220–31 and controls the stomach, bones, *l·*, heart,
    243–17 The head, heart, *l·*, and limbs do not inform us
    p 370–32 Physicians examine the pulse, tongue, *l·*,
    384–18 congestive symptoms in the *l·*,
    395–25 a tumor, a cancer, or decayed *l·*,
lurking
  p 419– 2 *L·* error, lust, envy, revenge, malice, or
lust
  and hate
    ap 565– 4 It is full of *l·* and hate,

lust
  and hypocrisy
    ap 567–28 beast and the . . . are *l·* and hypocrisy.
    571–31 outshining sin, sorcery, *l·*, and hypocrisy.
  head of
    g 534–30 this idea, will bruise the head of *l·*.
  of the flesh
    f 223– 3 shall not fulfil the *l·* of the flesh."— *Gal.* 5 : 16.
    gl 584–19 hypnotism ; the *l·* of the flesh,
  paganism and
    ph 171– 2 paganism and *l·* are so sanctioned by
    f 218–11 and say, "I am malice, *l·*, appetite,
    b 289–10 To suppose that sin, *l·*, hatred,
    330–29 *l·*, dishonesty, selfishness, envy,
    p 404–10 *L·*, malice, and all sorts of evil are
    405– 7 to conquer *l·* with chastity,
    419– 2 Lurking error, *l·*, envy, revenge,
    gl 586–13 FIRE. Fear ; remorse ; *l·* ; hatred ;
    588– 1 HELL. Mortal belief ; error ; *l·* ; remorse ;
    589– 3 envy ; hatred ; selfishness ; self-will ; *l·*.
lusteth
  ph 167–20 "flesh *l·* against the Spirit."— *Gal.* 5 : 17.
  o 347– 1 flesh *l·* against the Spirit,— *Gal.* 5 : 17.
lusts
  pr 10–28 may consume it upon your *l·*."— *Jas.* 4 : 3.
  a 18– * *the flesh with the affections and l·.*— *Gal.* 5 : 24.
  f 234–32 Evil thoughts, *l·*, and malicious purposes
  b 292–22 the *l·* of your father ye will do.— *John* 8 : 44.
Luther, Martin
  b 268– * quotation from
luxury
  t 452–17 Better . . . than the *l·* of learning with
lying
  g 529–21 Whence comes a talking, *l·* serpent
Lynn
  pref xi–27 with only one student in *L·*, Massachusetts,
  s 158–31 A woman in the city of *L·*, Massachusetts,
  159–20 The sequel proved that this *L·* woman died
  ph 192–32 I was called to visit Mr. Clark in *L·*,
lyre
  ph 190–22 thus swept his *l·* with saddening strains

M

machinations
  p 440– 3 the oleaginous *m·* of the counsel,
machine
  p 399–17 It constructs a *m·*, manages it,
mad
  an 105–29 "Whom the gods would destroy, they first make *m·*."
  t 462–28 It teaches the control of *m·* ambition.
made
  pref ix–27 she *m·* copious notes of Scriptural exposition,
    x 18 She has *m·* no effort to embellish,
  pr 4–13 Its motives are *m·* manifest in the blessings
    5–26 . . . that man is *m·* better merely by
  a 20– 8 Jesus' history *m·* a new calendar,
    25–31 The divinity of the Christ was *m·* manifest
    27–30 Jesus' persecutors *m·* their strongest attack
    41–32 never *m·* a disciple who could cast out evils
    46 6 words, which *m·* their hearts burn
    50– 9 This despairing appeal, if *m·* to a human parent,
    50–12 The appeal of Jesus was *m·* both to his
  sp 70– 8 man, *m·* in God's likeness, reflects God.
    72–18 Spirit is not *m·* manifest through matter,
    73–30 The sensual cannot be *m·* the mouthpiece of
    94–11 he *m·* himself the Son of God."— *John* 19 : 7.
  an 101– 4 the impressions *m·* upon the senses ;
    110– 6 in which all that He has *m·* is pronounced
  s 122–30 mistake . . . that Ptolemy *m·* regarding the
    131–25 until the hearts of men are *m·* ready for it.
    133–24 *m·* "himself equal with God,"— *John* 5 : 18.
    141–20 *m·* "kings and priests unto God."— *Rev.* 1 : 6.
    142–29 He *m·* medicine ; but that medicine was Mind.
    145– 6 would have *m·* void their practice.
    146–11 by which material sense is *m·* the servant
    151–23 The divine Mind that *m·* man maintains His
    152–28 Her experiments in homœopathy had *m·*
    154–10 A man was *m·* to believe that he
    156– 3 and what *m·* them good or bad
    162–21 ankylosed joints have been *m·* supple,
  ph 166– 5 the healing effort is *m·* on the wrong side,
    168–26 before the so-called disease *m·* its appearance
    173– 9 is required to be *m·* manifest through
    183–14 Truth never *m·* error necessary,
    183–22 No reservation is *m·* for any lesser loyalty.
    197–18 that *m·* them hardier than our trained
  f 203– 9 *m·* himself the Son of God,"— *John* 19 : 7.

made
  205–13 and *m·* all perfect and eternal.
  206–28 Omnipotent and infinite Mind *m·* all
  213 16 Sound is a mental impression *m·* on
  218– 2 that which affirms weariness, *m·* that
  219–18 before it can be *m·* manifest on the body,
  221 11 and finally *m·* up his mind to die,
  222–27 concluded that God never *m·* a dyspeptic,
  222–28 physiology, and physics had *m·* him one,
  226–16 These claims are not *m·* through code or creed,
  227–31 disobedience to which would have *m·* man ill,
  229– 7 God made all that was *m·*,
  229–29 is *m·* void by the law of immortal Mind,
  231–32 "all things were *m·* by Him— *John* 1 : 3.
  232– 1 anything *m·* that was *m·*."— *John* 1 : 3.
  233–27 tests I have *m·* of the effects of truth
  238–17 an experience we have not *m·* our own,
  243– 4 which *m·* harmless the poisonous viper,
  244–12 hath *m·* me free from the law of— *Rom.* 8 : 2.
  245–21 Years had not *m·* her old,
  c 255–11 Mortal man has *m·* a covenant with
  255–17 cannot be *m·* the basis of any true idea of
  261–18 a signal which *m·* him as oblivious of
  267–10, 11 I AM *m·* all "that was *m·*."— *John* 1 : 3.
  b 269– 9 Human philosophy has *m·* God manlike.
  273–17 have never *m·* mortals whole,
  286–18 The Scriptures declare all that He *m·* to be good,
  287–21 man was *m·* in God's likeness.
  288–29 *m·* him the Way-shower, Truth and Life.
  294–26 neither self-made nor *m·* by mortals.
  295–25 All that is called mortal thought is *m·* up of
  306–21 *m·* manifest as matter,
  307–18 and says : "The Lord knows it. He has *m·* man
  307–29 material laws which Spirit never *m·* ;
  310– 5 *m·* up of supposititious mortal mind-force ;
  311– 5 all that Mind, God, is, or hath *m·*,
  311– 6 and He *m·* all.
  311– 6 Hence evil is not *m·* and is not real.
  313–19 The passage is *m·* even clearer in the
  316– 9 *m·* manifest by its effects upon the human mind
  323–17 shall be *m·* rulers over many ;
  324–21 Paul was *m·* blind,
  327–22 Fear of punishment never *m·* man truly honest.
  335– 9 nothing in Spirit out of which matter could be *m·*,
  335–11, 12 anything *m·* that was *m·*."— *John* 1 : 3.
  338– 3 and man as *m·* in His likeness ;

made

o 344– 6   this claim is m· because the Scriptures say
  345–23   to discern the distinction (m· by C. S.)
  345–24   between God's man, m· in His image, and the
  346– 2   When man is spoken of as m· in God's image,
  346–26   when you believe that nitrous-oxide gas has m·
  350–24   "The Word was m· flesh."— John 1 : 14.
  356–22   man who is m· in the divine likeness
  357–15   dare we attempt to destroy what He hath m·,
  357–16   to deny that God m· man evil and m· evil good
  358–13   C. S. is neither m· up of contradictory
p 369–14   We never read that Luke or Paul m· a
  369–22   the other to be m· indestructible.
  370– 7   if health is not m· manifest under this regimen,
  380–22   years ago the author m· a spiritual discovery,
  393–13   God has m· man capable of this,
  410–19   He that feareth is not m· perfect— I John 4 : 18.
  437– 4   Man was m· in the image of God,
t 449–22   The first impression, m· on a mind which is
  450–18   but unless this admission is m·,
r 472–26   and He makes all that is m·.
  475– 6   Man is not matter ; he is not m· up of brain,
  475– 8   man is m· in the image and likeness of God.
  479–32   by the things that are m·."— Rom. 1 : 20.
  480–20   God, or good, never m· man capable of sin.
  480–26   "All things were m· by Him.— John 1 : 3.
  480–28   anything m· that was m·."— John 1 : 3.
  491– 7   Material man is m· up of involuntary and
  493–21   It is fear m· manifest on the body.
g 501– *   All things were m· by Him ;— John 1 : 3.
  501– *   anything m· that was m·.— John 1 : 3.
  509–23   Mind m· the "plant of the field— Gen. 2 : 5.
  510–15   He m· the stars also.— Gen. 1 : 16.
  516–20   Man, m· in His likeness, possesses
  517–31   Man is not m· to till the soil.
  518–25   saw everything that He had m·,— Gen. 1 : 31.
  519–23   ended His work which He had m· ;— Gen. 2 : 2.
  519–24   all His work which He had m·.— Gen. 2 : 2.
  520–18   m· the earth and the heavens,— Gen. 2 : 4.
  520–29   there is nothing left to be m· by a lower power.
  521– 5   All that is m· is the work of God,
  524–18   Mind had m· man, both male and female.
  525–18   all things were m· through the Word of God,
525–19, 20   anything m· that was m·."— John 1 : 3.
  525–23   He saw everything which He had m·,
  525–30   out of the ground m· the Lord God— Gen. 2 : 9.
  527–18   But is it true that God, good, m·
  528–13   from man, m· He a woman,— Gen. 2 : 22.
  529–15   the Lord God [Jehovah] had m·.— Gen. 3 : 1.
  530– 3   m· manifest as forever opposed to
  537–26   Literally taken, the text is m· to appear
  540–20   It saith . . . "God never m· you,
  543–25   When Spirit m· all, did it leave aught for
  543–32   m· the earth and the heavens,"— Gen. 2 : 4.
  545–32   shall all be m· alive."— I Cor. 15 : 22.
  553–12   formed under circumstances which m·
  554–16   to say, " I am somebody ; but who m· me?"
  554–16   Error replies, "God m· you."
  554–25   Jesus never intimated that God m· a devil,
  556–15   It is m· known most fully to him who
ap 559–15   m· manifest in the destruction of error.
  560–23   which m· him equal to his great mission.
  565–24   m· war upon the spiritual idea ;
  569–22   sin, which one has m· his bosom companion,
gl 583–24   God, who m· all that was m·
  (see also **God**)

madest

ph 200–14   "Thou m· him to have dominion— Psal. 8 : 6.

madly

p 373–27   When the blood rushes m· through the veins

madness

b 327–15   It is a moral m· which rushes forth
p 407–32   because its method of m· is in consonance with

magazine

f 245– 4   the London medical m· called The Lancet.

Magdalen

p 362–15   It was therefore easy for the M· to
  364–10   or the contrition of the M·?
  365–20   such commendation as the M· gained from

Magi

sp 95–24   M· of old foretold the Messiahship of Truth.

Magic

p 441–23   and Esoteric M· be publicly executed at the

magic

an 101–32   proportional to one's faith in esoteric m·.

magistrate

pr 6–29   It is believed by many that a certain m·,
  11– 5   A m· sometimes remits the penalty,

magnet

ap 575–27   the Word, the polar m· of Revelation ;

magnetic

an 100–20   no proof of the existence of the animal m· fluid ;
ph 185–10   which discussed . . . the earth's m· currents

magnetism

animal
an 100– 1   animal m· was first brought into notice
  100–18   "In regard to the . . . utility of animal m·,
  101–17   not conclusive in favor of the doctrine of animal m·,
  101–22   observations of the workings of animal m·
  101–26   If animal m· seems to alleviate
  101–30   In no instance is the effect of animal m·,
  102– 1   Animal m· has no scientific foundation,
  102– 5   in Science animal m·, . . . is a mere negation,
  102–16   The mild forms of animal m· are disappearing,
  102–21   So secret are the present methods of animal m·
  103–18   animal m· or hypnotism is the specific term for
  104– 3   When C. S. and animal m· are both comprehended,
  104–18   necromancy, mesmerism, animal m·,
s 129–17   Animal m·, hypnotism, spiritualism, theosophy,
  144–18   not . . . C. S., but is sheer animal m·.
ph 178–19   basis of sensation in matter, is animal m· ;
  178–25   freed from the belief of . . . animal m· ;
p 442–16   Neither animal m· nor hypnotism enters into
t 450–30   Knowing the claim of animal m·,
  454– 1   nor can he practise animal m· or hypnotism.
r 483– 2   how do drugs, hygiene, and animal m· heal?
  484–21   Animal m· is the . . . action of error in all its
  491– 3   Animal m· thus uncovers material sense,
gl 583–26   DAN (Jacob's son). Animal m· ;
  584–19   DEVIL. Evil ; a lie ; . . . animal m·
  593– 8   RED DRAGON. . . . animal m· ; envy ; revenge.
  594– 4   SERPENT . . . animal m· ; the first lie of
effects of
ph 181–17   ignorant of the baneful effects of m·,
electricity and
ph 181–10   When . . . you trust in electricity and m·
first record of
g 528–18   This is the first record of m·.
practice of
an 101– 2   observed in the public practice of m·,

magnetizer

an 101–14   promised by Monsieur Berna [the m·]

magnified

s 140–32   What is the god of a mortal, but a mortal m·?

magnify

ap 568–24   give thanks and m· the Lord of Hosts.

magnitude

a 43– 3   m· of Jesus' work, his material disappearance
  50– 6   an overwhelming sense of the m· of his work,
  54– 2   Through the m· of his human life,
m 63–22   without encouraging difficulties of greater m·,
g 511– 6   the sublimity, m·, and infinitude of

magnitudes

f 209–18   the m·, distances, and revolutions of

main

pref ix– 2   to jot down her thoughts on the m· subject,
o 345–30   the m· cause of the carnal mind's antagonism.

mainly

sp 71–22   spiritualism will be found m· erroneous,
s 144– 9   human philosophy, physiology, hygiene, are m·
p 412–29   m· through the parent's thought,

maintain

m 59– 7   Mutual compromises will often m· a
sp 81– 9   and m· their affiliation with
  97– 3   They will m· law and order,
f 246–23   still m· his vigor, freshness, and promise.
b 270–21   and m· the Science of Spirit.
p 389–19   If God has, as prevalent theories m·,
  395– 4   and m· man's immortality
  417–10   M· the facts of C. S.,
t 461– 1   I do not m· that anyone can

maintained

s 136– 1   m· his mission on a spiritual foundation
ph 172– 8   How then is the material species m·,
g 531– 3   m· in all the subsequent forms of belief.
  531–18   If, . . . why is not this divine order still m·

maintaining

s 119–14   making Him guilty of m· perpetual misrule
b 271– 3   m· its obvious correspondence with

maintains

sp 70–12   The divine Mind m· all identities,
s 151–24   m· His own image and likeness.
b 287– 7   contradicts this postulate and m· man's
  329–24   m· the claim of Truth by quenching error.

maintenance

g 553–13   to their m· and reproduction,

majesty
sp 78–23 the *m·* and omnipotence of Spirit be lost?
g 520– 4 The depth, breadth, height, might, *m·*,
ap 564–19 Until the *m·* of Truth should be demonstrated

major
s 128–31 If both the *m·* and the minor propositions of a

majority
m 60–19 This, however, in a *m·* of cases,
s 155–10 and the beliefs which are in the *m·* rule.
155–14 such a belief is governed by the *m·*.
164–18 caused by a *m·* of human beliefs
ph 177–32 but the vast *m·* of mankind, though they
178– 5 controlled by the *m·* of opinions,
p 394– 2 *m·* of doctors depress mental energy,
r 482– 2 gives the exact meaning in a *m·* of cases.

make
iii– * the truth shall *m·* you free.— *John* 8 : 32.
pref vii– 7 *m·* plain to benighted understanding the way
vii–22 but it cannot *m·* them speedily understood.
pr 2– 2 Do we pray to *m·* ourselves better
4–18 Simply asking . . . will never *m·* us love Him ;
6–21 is to misunderstand Love and to *m·* prayer the
9–27 Then why *m·* long prayers about
11–16 to *m·* him turn from it with loathing.
a 20–12 men can . . . *m·* long prayers, and yet be
22– 8 to *m·* vigorous efforts to save themselves ;
24– 8 and *m·* the Bible the chart of life,
25–28 will never alone *m·* us imitators of him.
40–15 Did the martyrdom of Savonarola *m·*
42– 6 It cannot *m·* Life or Truth apparent.
50–25 But this saying could not *m·* it so.
52–18 error and evil again *m·* common cause against
m 62–32 this does not *m·* materiality first
65–17 the powerlessness of vows to *m·* home happy,
sp 92–24 ability to *m·* nothing of error will be wanting.
an 105–29 "Whom the gods would destroy, they first *m·*
mad."
s 115– 5 as to *m·* them comprehensible to any reader,
116– 6 to *m·* this Scriptural testimony true
119–12 is not only to *m·* Him responsible for
120–12 matter can *m·* no conditions for man.
122–10 senses still *m·* mortal mind tributary
122–29 Our theories *m·* the same mistake regarding
130–18 denied and cast out to *m·* place for truth.
130–22 ability of Spirit to *m·* the body harmonious,
140–30 would . . . *m·* God in their own human image.
142–23 *m·* them meet dwelling-places for the
143–32 may try to *m·* Mind and drugs coalesce,
144– 1 Why should we wish to *m·* them do so,
148–22 Then theology tries to explain how to *m·*
152– 6 The author has endeavored to *m·* this book the
ph 165– 3 would open man's eyes and *m·* him as a god.
165– 8 is to subjugate intelligence, to *m·* mind mortal,
189–13 sins of others should not *m·* good men suffer.
197–22 helped to *m·* them healthy,
199–15 Mortals develop their own bodies or *m·*
f 203– 6 shows that matter can neither heal nor *m·* sick,
206–29 This Mind does not *m·* mistakes
208–13 not in accordance . . . that He should *m·* man sick,
210–28 appears to itself to *m·* good its claim.
221–31 neither food nor . . . can *m·* one suffer,
227–19 Love and Truth *m·* free,
230–19 Does wisdom *m·* blunders
232– 3 neither *m·* man harmonious nor God lovable.
232–11 theories . . . *m·* healing possible only through
232–20 never taught that . . . could *m·* a man healthy,
232–23 never tried to *m·* of none effect the sentence
236–27 the simple verities that will *m·* them happy
240– 8 The stars *m·* night beautiful,
252–22 says : . . . I mean to *m·* my short span of life
253–13 no cause (outside of . . . able to *m·* you sick
253–20 Matter can *m·* no opposition
c 260– 2 and *m·* himself like it,
263–11 They *m·* man an involuntary hypocrite,
b 289–12 Truth and Truth's idea, never *m·* men sick,
294–13 saying : . . . The stomach can *m·* a man cross.
303–15 can never *m·* both these contraries true.
306– 3 They would first *m·* life result in death,
307– 5 saying, . . . I will *m·* error as real and
317–32 Nothing but a display of matter could *m·*
322–18 cannot *m·* the inebriate leave his . . . until
339–13 the sinner would *m·* a reality of sin,
339–13 would *m·* that real which is unreal,
340– 2 and *m·* life its own proof of harmony
346–29 beliefs must be expelled to *m·* room for
o 351–18 while we *m·* a personal devil and
352– 3 to *m·* harmony the reality
p 371–31 can *m·* it "every whit whole."— *John* 7 : 23.
383–23 but does this *m·* it so?
383–30 pounding the poor body, to *m·* it sensibly well
391–27 Therefore *m·* your own terms with sickness,
395–21 It is mental quackery to *m·* disease a reality
396– 5 *M·* no unnecessary inquiries relative to

make
p 397–15 more powerful than the accident itself, to *m·*
398– 8 concessions which Jesus was willing to *m·*
399–24 there is no mortal mind out of which to *m·*
402–25 The operator would *m·* his subjects believe
404–30 envy, dishonesty, fear, . . . *m·* a man sick,
409–31 Death will not *m·* us harmonious
413–15 in order to *m·* it thrive more vigorously
417– 8 If you *m·* the sick realize this great truism,
417–24 is to *m·* disease unreal to him.
421– 8 *m·* known to the patient your motive
424–22 It is not more difficult to *m·* yourself heard
427–23 God, Life, Truth, and Love *m·* man undying.
438– 3 Let us *m·* man in our image,— *Gen.* 1 : 26.
440– 6 Morbid Secretion is taught how to *m·*
t 443– 6 those, who *m·* such a compromise,
444–31 The teacher must *m·* clear to students
451– 9 will either *m·* shipwreck of their faith or
464– 2 Why do you not *m·* yourself more widely
464– 4 in which to *m·* herself outwardly known
r 474–27 If evil is real, Truth must *m·* it so ;
475–23 "Let us *m·* man in our image,— *Gen.* 1 : 26.
480–16 Inharmony would *m·* matter the cause
480–22 evil— which seems to *m·* men capable of
485–12 how to *m·* sin, disease, and death . . . unreal
489–28 nor *m·* it the medium of Mind.
490–14 theories are helpless to *m·* man harmonious
g 515–11 Let us *m·* man in our image,— *Gen.* 1 : 26.
525–13 Icelandic : . . . Let us *m·* man after our mind
525–22 Whatever is valueless or baneful, He did not *m·*,
527– 3 to *m·* it beautiful or to cause it to live and grow.
527–15 knowledge of evil would *m·* man mortal.
533–19 aids man to *m·* sinners more rapidly than
540– 5 "I *m·* peace, and create evil.— *Isa.* 45 ; 7.
543–29 would *m·* Life, or God, mortal.
552–10 Mortal theories *m·* friends of sin, sickness,
ap 559–18 it shall *m·* thy belly bitter,— *Rev.* 10 : 9.
569– 7 I will *m·* thee ruler over many,"— *Matt.* 25 : 23.
574–29 Love can *m·* an angel entertained unawares.
gl 582–26 the error which would *m·* man mortal
582–26 and would *m·* mortal mind a slave to the body.

Maker
allegiance to his
f 226–21 man's birthright of sole allegiance to his *M·*
endowed by his
s 161–16 "Man is endowed by his *M·* with certain
governed by his
an 106–11 governed by his *M·*, divine Truth and Love.
f 231–30 Man, governed by his *M·*, having no other
his
an 102–13 no more power over man than over his *M·*,
b 309–26 to have an intelligence separate from his *M·*.
316– 4 being linked by Science to his *M·*,
o 360–25 more pure than his *M·*?— *Job* 4 : 17.
r 475–22 reflects spiritually all that belongs to his *M·*.
488–20 cannot be true either of man or of his *M·*.
g 518– 4 himself subordinate alone to his *M·*,
531–24 and so changed the method of his *M·*?
image of his
f 203–15 and so makes man the image of his *M·*
likeness of his
f 252–14 recognized as the true likeness of his *M·*.
b 305– 7 Man, in the likeness of his *M·*,
p 441–17 in the image and likeness of his *M·*.
likeness of their
f 246– 6 are the eternal likeness of their *M·*.
man and his
b 276– 9 Man and his *M·* are correlated in divine Science,
man's
p 437– 6 This is a foul aspersion on man's *M·*.
r 491–11 It is the likeness of man's *M·*.
reflection of his
b 305–28 Because man is the reflection of his *M·*,
service of our
sp 79–32 does not impoverish us in the service of our *M·*,
your
p 397–31 will understand yourself and your *M·* better

maker
p 428–14 "whose builder and *m·* is God."— *Heb.* 11 : 10.
ap 575–11 The builder and *m·* of this New Jerusalem

makes
pref viii–15 confers the most health and *m·* the best men.
pr 7–22 ventilation of fervent sentiments never *m·* a
8– 2 though it *m·* the sinner a hypocrite.
a 26–23 as *m·* us admit its Principle to be Love.
31–15 living Christ, the practical Truth, which *m·*
53–24 lifelong sacrifice which goodness *m·*
sp 78–25 where spiritism *m·* many gods,
s 114– 8 evidence of the . . . senses, which *m·* minds many
119–30 and *m·* body tributary to Mind.
153–23 this so-called mind *m·* its own pain
ph 183– 1 Truth, *m·* all things possible to Spirit ;
184– 3 Truth *m·* no laws to regulate sickness,
189–19 mortal mind, . . . *m·* all things start from

makes

ph 196–18	Sin *m·* its own hell, and goodness its own
199–21	*m·* the achievement possible.
f 201– 8	Truth *m·* a new creature.
208–27	*m·* it harmonious or discordant according to
209– 2	mortal belief which *m·* the body discordant
212–22	God alone *m·* and clothes the lilies
216–15	This understanding *m·* the body harmonious ;
216–15	it *m·* the nerves, bones, . . . servants,
219–11	*m·* the whole body "sick, — *Isa.* 1 : 5.
220–26	belief that either fasting or . . . *m·* men better
222– 8	mortal mind *m·* a mortal body,
229–25	all that He *m·* is good and will stand forever.
231–12	If God *m·* sin, if good produces evil,
233– 1	Every day *m·* its demands upon us
236–31	youth *m·* easy and rapid strides towards Truth.
237–22	This *m·* C. S. early available.
245–29	primary of that illustration *m·* it plain that
249–29	*m·* its mundane flights quite ethereal.
251–21	the divine Mind *m·* perfect,
c 266–20	The sinner *m·* his own hell by doing evil,
b 270–26	If sin *m·* sinners, Truth . . . can unmake them.
295– 8	they are obedient to the Mind that *m·* them.
300– 5	mirage, which *m·* trees and cities seem to be
307–10	It says : . . . God *m·* evil minds and evil spirits,
337–12	The truth of being *m·* man harmonious
o 343– 7	This *m·* it doubly unfair to impugn and
357–10	the belief that God *m·* sickness,
p 385–12	law which *m·* sin its own executioner,
404–32	unless it *m·* him better mentally,
405– 3	*m·* any man, . . . a hopeless sufferer.
407– 9	delay *m·* the struggle more severe.
410–14	Every trial of our faith in God *m·* us stronger.
415–17	Note how thought *m·* the face pallid.
426–10	The struggle for Truth *m·* one strong
t 456–18	Science *m·* no concessions to persons
458–30	Sin *m·* deadly thrusts at the Christian Scientist
464–25	Adulterating C. S., *m·* it void.
r 472–26	He *m·* all that is made.
486–18	Alas for the blindness of belief, which *m·*
487–31	This Principle *m·* whole the diseased,
g 505– 1	Mind *m·* its own record,
506– 6	and *m·* Truth final.
520–29	Because Mind *m·* all, there is
532– 3	God *m·* and governs all.
539–29	the one Mind which *m·* and governs man
ap 570–29	when it *m·* them sick or sinful.
gl 596– 5	*m·* Him better known as the All-in-all,
	(*see also* **man**)

maketh

t 445–24	The human will which *m·* and worketh a lie,
ap 577–27	"defileth, . . . or *m·* a lie." — *Rev.* 21 : 27.
578– 6	*m·* me to lie down in green — *Psal.* 23 : 2.
gl 588– 4	"worketh abomination or *m·* a — *Rev.* 21 : 27.
596–26	*m·* the valley to bud and blossom as the rose.

making

pr 12– 6	*m·* it act more powerfully on the body
a 34– 4	by casting out error and *m·*
m 66–28	*m·* his Xantippe a discipline for his
s 119–14	thereby *m·* Him guilty of maintaining
142–12	*m·* dome and spire tremulous with beauty,
b 298–32	*m·* them . . . with suggestive feathers ;
321– 7	despaired of *m·* the people understand
o 342– 4	"*m·* wise the simple." — *Psal.* 19 : 7.
348– 6	*m·* the disease appear to be . . . an illusion
356–26	by *m·* man inclined to sin, and then
p 375–22	*m·* certain portions of it motionless.
382–12	*m·* clean merely the outside of the platter.
410–13	mankind objects to *m·* this teaching practical.
413–29	*m·* it probable at any time that
423–18	*m·* Mind his basis of operation
431–24	took control of his mind, *m·* him despondent.
r 466–30	*m·* mankind better physically, morally, and
472– 6	*m·* it coordinate with all that is real
473–27	*m·* his acts of higher importance than his
g 520–31	but *m·* him superior to the soil.
541– 4	instead of *m·* his own gift a higher tribute
gl 580– 7	*m·* "gods many and lords many" — *I Cor.* 8 : 5.

malady

p 398– 6	clear evidence that the *m·* was not material.
413–32	or any other *m·*, timorously held in the
r 488– 4	When, . . . you are able to banish a severe *m·*,

male

f 249– 5	"*m·* and female" of God's creating — *Gen.* 1 : 27.
g 508–21	a neuter gender, neither *m·* nor female.
508–23	The intelligent individual idea, be it *m·* or
516–25	*m·* and female created He them. — *Gen.* 1 : 27.
524–19	Mind had made man, both *m·* and female.
525–15	and He shaped them *m·* and female.
528– 3	created man, both *m·* and female
ap 565–10	Herod decreed the death of every *m·* child
577– 5	the unity of *m·* and female

malevolent

o 357–11	on account of this *m·* triad.

malice

aforethought

p 437– 7	It indicates *m·* aforethought,
t 451–27	arises from ignorance or *m·* aforethought.

his own

ap 569–26	at last stung to death by his own *m·* ;

ignorance and

f 215–32	The ignorance and *m·* of the age

mortal

t 458–22	Science will ameliorate mortal *m·*.

or hate

p 419– 2	Lurking error, lust, envy, revenge, *m·*, or hate

or ignorance

t 459–20	Whether animated by *m·* or ignorance,

an 104–20	dishonesty, sensuality, falsehood, revenge, *m·*,
f 218–11	and say, "I am *m·*, lust, appetite,
241–10	Falsehood, envy, hypocrisy, *m·*, hate,
b 327– 8	What a pitiful sight is *m·*,
p 404–10	Lust, *m·*, and all sorts of evil are
t 462–27	selfishness, *m·*, envy, and hate.

malicious

an 103–23	It is either ignorant or *m·*.
103–24	The *m·* form of hypnotism
s 110–21	or by careless or *m·* students,
f 235– 1	Evil thoughts, lusts, and *m·* purposes
p 401– 5	cherishing evil passions and *m·* purposes,
t 446–14	from sinister or *m·* motives
ap 564– 4	This *m·* animal instinct,

malign

r 485–11	Why *m·* C. S. for instructing mortals

malignant

ph 176–31	Truth handles the most *m·* contagion
p 373– 6	easier to cure the most *m·* disease than

maligned

a 41–27	good deeds, for which they were *m·* and stoned.

malignity

a 43–12	The *m·* of brutal persecutors,

malpractice

p 375–15	any mental despotism or *m·*.
442–31	mental *m·* cannot harm you
t 451–27	*m·* arises from ignorance or malice
451–31	mental *m·* tends to blast moral sense,
457–17	to mental *m·*, . . . there is no good aspect,

malpractitioner

p 419–25	Never fear the mental *m·*,

maltreatment

r 474–10	consequent *m·* which it receives.

mamma

s 154–30	and says, . . . "*M·* knows you are hurt."
f 237– 5	"*M·*, my finger is not a bit sore."

mammon

a 52– 4	He served God ; they served *m·*.
o 346–31	We cannot serve both God and *m·*
t 462–11	dividing his interests between God and *m·*

Man (*see also* **Man's**)

p 434–27	conspiracy against the liberty and life of *M·*.
434–31	but God made *M·* immortal
437– 4	testified . . . that he knew *M·*,
437– 4	and that *M·* was made in the image of God,
437– 8	a determination to condemn *M·*
437–14	*M·* self-destroyed ; . . . Spirit not allowed a
438– 1	certain extracts on the Rights of *M·*,
438–12	bearing false witness against *M·*.
441–16	Our law refuses to recognize *M·* as sick
441–19	Spirit decides in favor of *M·*
442– 1	There, *M·* is adjudged innocent of transgressing
r 482–19	he was literally the Son of *M·*.
	(*see also* **Mortal Man**)

man (*see also* **man's**)

action of

f 207–28	spiritual fact, repeated in the action of *m·*

actuality of

g 502–13	and the spiritual actuality of *m·*,

affections of a

gl 597– 4	The motives and affections of a *m·* were

a man's a

ph 172–31	"a man's a *m·*, for a' that."

and creation

r 489–30	A wrong sense of God, *m·*, and creation is

and form

g 517– 5	from two Greek words, signifying *m·* and *form*,

and God

c 258–23	gains the true conception of *m·* and God.
g 524–25	or is it a lie concerning *m·* and God?

and his creator

b 338–24	would impose between *m·* and his creator.

and his Maker

b 276– 9	*M·* and his Maker are correlated in

man

and Mind
  b 281–20 false conception as to *m·* and Mind.
and the universe
  (*see* **universe**)
and woman
  a 37–23 privilege of every child, *m·*, and woman,
  g 516–21 *M·* and woman as coexistent and eternal with
  529–10 that both *m·* and woman proceed from God
  gl 588–12 *m·* and woman unchanged forever
another
  sp 73– 9 belief that one . . . can control another *m·*,
any
  a 25–17 any *m·* whose origin was less spiritual.
  31– 9 no record of his calling any *m·* by the name of
  s 109–29 If any *m·* will do His will,— *John* 7 : 17.
  p 405– 3 any *m·*, who is above the lowest type
  g 527–14 neither tempteth He any *m·*."— *James* 1 : 13.
apart from
  b 270–11 Few deny . . . that intelligence, apart from *m·*
appears
  r 477–10 *m·* appears to be matter and mind united ;
as created
  s 148– 7 Neither . . . has ever described *m·* as created
              by Spirit,
as God's image
  pr 13–28 ignorant of *m·* as God's image or reflection
  s 116– 4 and *m·* as God's image appears.
assigning to
  f 244–30 instead of assigning to *m·* the
as the offspring
  a 29–30 *M·* as the offspring of God, as the idea of Spirit,
author of
  a 29–16 God is the only author of *m·*.
beliefs that
  s 164–19 human beliefs that *m·* must die,
belief that
  (*see* **belief**)
belief that one
  sp 73– 8 belief that one *m·*, as spirit, can control another
believes
  ph 171–17 *m·* believes himself to be combined matter and
  p 427– 7 If *m·* believes in death now,
benefit to
  r 471–22 Are doctrines and creeds a benefit to *m·* ?
bestowed on
  p 387–29 protecting power bestowed on *m·* by
  393–15 ability and power divinely bestowed on *m·*.
better
  a 21– 4 because you are a better *m·*.
blesses
  sp 78–28 Spirit blesses *m·*,
blind
  t 459–18 a blind *m·* or a raging maniac,
brotherhood of
  b 340–24 constitutes the brotherhood of *m·* ;
  r 467–13 true brotherhood of *m·* will be established.
  470– 3 brotherhood of *m·* would consist of Love and
  g 541–18 ruptures the life and brotherhood of *m·*
called
  sp 81–22 give to the worms the body called *m·*,
  ph 190–13 bulk of a body, called *m·*,
  f 250–15 and that one is called *m·* ;
calling that
  s 148–20 calling that *m·* which is not the counterpart,
can do for
  a 48–32 what the true knowledge of God can do for *m·*.
can do no
  an 103–39 In C. S., *m·* can do no harm,
can no longer
  sp 76–13 When advanced . . . *m·* can no longer com-
                mune with
cannot exceed
  a 19– 4 *M·* cannot exceed divine Love,
cannot govern
  r 490– 6 Hence it cannot govern *m·* aright.
cannot kill a
  p 395–30 knowledge that brain-lobes cannot kill a *m·*
cannot lose
  c 259– 2 *m·* cannot lose his individuality,
changed the
  b 309– 9 This changed the *m·*.
chronicles
  g 522– 8 The second record chronicles *m·* as mutable
claims to rule
  s 148–26 Physiology . . . claims to rule *m·* by
clothe
  g 530–12 to feed and clothe *m·* as He doth the lilies.
coexists with
  s 120– 5 *m·* coexists with and reflects Soul, God,
commanded the
  g 527– 7 commanded the *m·*, saying,— *Gen.* 2 : 16.
commands
  p 405– 5 commands *m·* to master the propensities,
communicate with
  sp 78–22 How then can it communicate with *m·* through

man

compare
  g 515–28 Now compare *m·* before the mirror to his
compels
  p 436–30 which the divine law compels *m·* to commit.
comprehends
  r 481– 8 Through spiritual sense only, *m·* comprehends
conceptions of
  f 244– 7 to derive all our conceptions of *m·* from
concerning
  r 494–25 Which of these two theories concerning *m·*
  g 524–25 or is it a lie concerning *m·* and God?
concerning a
  sp 89–13 reaffirms the Scriptural word concerning a *m·*,
  p 383–28 the Scriptural conclusion concerning a *m·*,
conclusions as to
  c 259–32 Deducing one's conclusions as to *m·* from
condition of
  o 344– 5 sinless condition of *m·* in divine Science,
confers upon
  c 265–12 confers upon *m·* enlarged individuality,
corporeal
  b 332–18 The corporeal *m·* Jesus was human.
  t 453–19 but in order to bless the corporeal *m·* ;
correct view of
  r 477– 3 this correct view of *m·* healed the sick.
create
  o 356–21 is it possible for Him to create *m·* subject to
  g 522–21 represented as entering matter in order to create
              m·.
  528– 6 cannot be true that man was ordered to create
              m· anew
creates
  m 69–23 If the father replies, "God creates *m·* through
  gl 582–18 creates *m·* as His own spiritual idea,
creating
  b 338–20 was deemed the agent of Deity in creating *m·*,
creator of
  r 470–21 God is the creator of *m·*,
cross-questioning
  g 533–26 Truth, cross-questioning *m·* as to his
deathless
  m 69–16 and of *m·* deathless and perfect
  g 534– 5 to manifest the deathless *m·* of God's creating.
defile a
  an 100– * the things which defile a *m·*.— *Matt.* 15 : 20.
define
  s 148–13 define *m·* as both physical and mental,
definition of
  b 302–14 Continuing our definition of *m·*,
demands on
  ph 184–13 legitimate and eternal demands on *m·*,
demonstrates
  b 340–22 by which *m·* demonstrates health, holiness, and
  p 372–14 When *m·* demonstrates C. S. absolutely,
  405–20 Immortal *m·* demonstrates the government
demoralizes the
  g 533–14 beguiles the woman and demoralizes the *m·*.
denunciations of
  g 522–22 denunciations of *m·* when not found in His
              image,
deprive a
  o 358– 3 Can a leaden bullet deprive a *m·* of Life,
description of
  ph 170–28 The description of *m·* as purely physical,
disarms
  p 304–11 The admission that . . . disarms *m·*,
divinely royal
  b 313– 5 Jesus the God-crowned or the divinely royal *m·*,
divine Principle of (*see also* **Principle of**)
  sp 72– 3 divine Principle of *m·* speaks through
  ph 191–10 the spiritual and divine Principle of *m·*
  f 207–14 perfect Father, or the divine Principle of *m·*.
  b 336–25 God, the divine Principle of *m·*,
  r 470–22 the divine Principle of *m·* remaining perfect,
  481–28 Soul is the divine Principle of *m·*
  ap 562–15 the activities of the divine Principle of *m·*
divine Science of
  f 242–25 divine Science of *m·* is woven into one web
divorced from
  r 477–30 *m·*, divorced from Spirit, would lose his entity
does not pay the
  p 387–18 That *m·* does not pay the severest penalty
drove out the
  g 537– 5 So He drove out the *m·* :— *Gen.* 3 : 24.
duty of
  b 340– 9 for this is the whole duty of *m·*."— *Eccl.* 12 : 13.
  g 541–25 Now it repudiates even the human duty of *m·*
each need of
  pr 7–25 to whom each need of *m·* is always known
earth, and
  g 538–19 God creates the heavens, earth, and *m·*.
economy of
  ph 170– 7 Did Jesus understand the economy of *m·* less
              than

man

elevating
gl 586–14 affliction purifying and elevating *m·*.
empowers
ph 199–10 empowers *m··* through its mandate,
enables
a 19–24 enables *m·* to do the will of wisdom.
endows
g 522– 7 endows *m·* out of God's perfection and power.
enslavement of
f 228–11 The enslavement of *m·* is not legitimate.
enslaves
f 225– 3 Whatever enslaves *m·* is opposed to
error supposes
b 287– 6 Error supposes *m·* to be both mental and
establishes
r 491–15 establishes *m·* forever in the divine likeness,
eternal
a 29–32 Spirit is harmonious and *m·* eternal.
ph 191– 6 this eternal *m·* will include in that likeness
b 311–31 the spiritual, eternal *m·* is not touched by
every
sp 98–20 for every *m·* to understand and to practise.
s 144–28 every *m·* will be his own physician,
exempts
p 385–13 exempts *m·* from all penalties but those
existence of
p 427–16 Nothing can . . . end the existence of *m·*
exists
g 544–11 *m·* exists because God exists.
expresses in
c 258–13 God expresses in *m·* the infinite idea
false conception of
b 285–17 is a false conception of *m·*.
family of
r 470– 1 the whole family of *m·* would be brethren ;
finite
c 257–32 Finite *m·* cannot be the image and
forever intact
r 493–31 divine Mind to hold *m·* forever intact
formed
b 281–25 a *m·* formed from dust.
g 524–13 Lord God [Jehovah] formed *m·* — *Gen.* 2 : 7.
friend of
a 49–15 the highest instructor and friend of *m·*,
generic
ap 561–22 generic *m·*, the spiritual idea of God ;
generic term
c 259– 1 the generic term *m·*.
gives
ph 183–23 Obedience to Truth gives *m·* power and
f 202–22 God gives *m·* dominion over all the earth.
b 307–26 and gives *m·* dominion over all things.
316–22 which gives *m·* dominion over all the earth.
p 387–30 gives *m·* faith and understanding
430– 7 When *m·* gives up his belief in death,
giving
a 19– 7 by giving *m·* a truer sense of Love,
glorified
a 54–29 If that Godlike and glorified *m·* were
God and
  (*see* **God**)
God controls
sp 73–11 God controls *m·*, and God is the only Spirit.
God created
s 140–29 God created *m·* in His, God's, image ;
b 294–27 God created *m·*.
g 516–24 God created *m·* in His own image, — *Gen.* 1 : 27.
God has created
o 344– 7 God has created *m·* in His own image
God has endowed
an 106– 7 God has endowed *m·* with inalienable rights,
God has made
p 393–13 God has made *m·* capable of this,
God is not
r 480–19 Man is not God, and God is not *m·*.
Godlike
c 262–15 higher views inspire the Godlike *m·* to reach
God made
ph 167–15 If God made *m·* both good and evil,
f 227–16 God made *m·* free.
g 516–28 God made *m·* in His own image,
God's
sp 92–18 a burlesque of God's *m·* — is an outgrowth of
s 148– 8 man as created by Spirit, — as God's *m·*.
148–21 but the counterfeit, of God's *m·*.
151–23 it has no control over God's *m·*.
ph 191– 1 The brain can give no idea of God's *m·*.
b 306–30 God's *m·*, spiritually created, is not material
o 345–24 God's *m·*, made in His image,
r 476– 1 A mortal sinner is not God's *m·*.
gl 580– 3 the first god of mythology ; not God's *m·*,
God to
  (*see* **God**)
good
p 405–18 The good *m·* finally can overcome his fear of

man

good-will to
p 407–16 even into spiritual power and good-will to *m·*.
govern
f 206– 7 the province of spiritual sense to govern *m·*.
227–30 If God had instituted material laws to govern *m·*,
p 381– 1 law of matter . . . supposed to govern *m·*,
governed by
s 125–15 *m·* governed by Soul, not by material sense.
f 231–30 *M·*, governed by his Maker, having no other
246–23 *M·*, governed by immortal Mind, is
b 304–14 The perfect *m·* — governed by God,
governing
f 231–15 no antagonistic powers . . . governing *m·*
b 308– 6 God is the only Mind governing *m·*,
gl 595– 1 SUN. The symbol of Soul governing *m·*,
governs
pr 6– 3 Divine Love corrects and governs *m·*.
f 222–12 the fact that Mind governs *m·*,
231–21 God made you superior to it and governs *m·*,
p 420– 4 Spirit not matter, governs *m·*.
g 539–29 one Mind which makes and governs *m·*
harmonious
s 148–19 Principle which produces harmonious *m·*,
f 232– 4 neither make *m·* harmonious nor God lovable.
b 276–24 the universe, including harmonious *m·*.
337–12 The truth of being makes *m·* harmonious and
r 490–15 theories are helpless to make *m·* harmonious
harmony in
b 276–15 Harmony in *m·* is as real and immortal as in
304–20 Harmony in *m·* is as beautiful as in music,
harmony of
p 392–10 health, holiness, and harmony of *m·*,
423–14 and it restores the harmony of *m·*.
has never lost
g 548– 7 *m·* has never lost his spiritual estate
has "sought out"
ph 196– 2 *M·* has "sought out many inventions," — *Eccl.*
    7 : 29.
hath not seen
b 325–19 where human sense hath not seen *m·*.
help meet for
g 533–20 Is this an help meet for *m·*?
higher nature of
m 62–27 higher nature of *m·* is not governed by the
history of
g 557–22 theology takes up the history of *m·* as if
human
r 473–15 Jesus is the human *m·*, and Christ is the divine
ideal
m 69– 9 the real, ideal *m·* appears in proportion as
b 332–31 Into the real and ideal *m·* the
338–30 Adam was not the ideal *m·* for whom
338–31 The ideal *m·* was revealed in due time,
o 346– 4 the ideal *m·*, reflecting God's likeness.
g 517– 8 The ideal *m·* corresponds to creation,
idea of
a 45–21 spiritual idea of *m·* and his divine Principle,
ph 194– 4 coincidence of the spiritual idea of *m·* with
immortal
m 61– 1 can satisfy the cravings of immortal *m·*.
ph 173–25 the image of God, the real immortal *m·*.
190–19 immortal *m·*, spiritual and eternal,
f 202–16 but immortal *m·*, in accord with the
215–25 Mortal man is the antipode of immortal *m·*
b 288–28 glorious possibilities of immortal *m·*,
294–19 immortal *m·*, representing Spirit,
302–15 immortal *m·* has existed forever.
306– 8 The immortality of Soul makes *m·* immortal.
322– 8 before harmonious and immortal *m·* is
336– 9 Immortal *m·* was and is God's image
336–10 immortal *m·* is coexistent and coeternal with
336–17 Immortal *m·* is not and never was material,
p 405–20 Immortal *m·* demonstrates the government
417–19 is not the Science of immortal *m·*.
r 476–20 the facts which belong to immortal *m·*.
485–18 understanding of Life, makes *m·* immortal.
g 538–26 This account is given, not of immortal *m·*,
immortality of
f 215–31 he recognized the immortality of *m·*.
b 292– 9 Mind, the only immortality of *m·*,
324– 7 Unless the harmony and immortality of *m·* are
p 381–25 The harmony and immortality of *m·*
g 507–27 the immortality of *m·* and the universe.
521–12 The harmony and immortality of *m·* are intact.
including
sp 83–17 The belief that the universe, including *m·*,
s 114–28 the universe, including *m·*, is spiritual,
127– 5 the spiritual universe, including *m·*,
ph 171–12 control over the universe, including *m·*,
c 256– 8 Father and Mother of the universe, including *m·*.
b 295– 5 governs the universe, including *m·*.
330–12 intelligence of the universe, including *m·*.
g 511– 1 governing the universe, including *m·*,
547–19 to recreate the universe, including *m·*,
547–26 true theory of the universe, including *m·*,
gl 584–24 a mortal universe, including *m·*,

man

inclusive of
  s 128– 6   government of the universe, inclusive of *m·*.
  g 554– 3   the universe, inclusive of *m·*, is as eternal

indestructible
  sp 76–26   indestructible *m·*, whose being is spiritual.
  b 316–20   Christ presents the indestructible *m·*,

individual
  s 117– 3   an individual *m·*, an individual horse ;
  r 468–23   universe, including individual *m·*,

individuality of
  b 317–16   individuality of *m·* is no less tangible
  r 491–26   Personality is not the individuality of *m·*.

in God's image
  r 476–31   *m·* in God's image is unfallen and eternal.
    497– 7   and *m·* in God's image and likeness.

in God's likeness
  ph 191– 5   *m·* in God's likeness will appear,
  b 336–25   divine Principle of man, and *m·* in God's likeness

in His image
  b 340–11   for this is the whole of *m·* in His image

insane
  p 411–17   the insane *m·* was changed and straightway

in Science
  ph 187–23   *m·* in Science is governed by this Mind.
  f 244–23   *M·* in Science is neither young nor old.

intelligence of
  r 477–23   the substance, Life, and intelligence of *m·*,

in the idea
  gl 582–14   conceiving *m·* in the idea of God ;

in the image
  sp 94– 1   who makes *m·* in the image and likeness of
  g 548– 6   *m·* in the image and likeness of God.

in the likeness
  sp 81–17   *M·* in the likeness of God as revealed in
  b 305– 6   *M·*, in the likeness of his Maker, reflects

in this allegory
  g 544–25   *m·*, in this allegory, is neither a lesser god nor

is become
  g 536–31   the *m·* is become as one of us,— *Gen. 3 : 22.*
    545– 3   the *m·* is become as one of us."— *Gen. 3 : 22.*

is clothed
  p 442–24   and *m·* is clothed and fed spiritually.

is coexistent
  r 478– 1   for *m·* is coexistent with God.

is deathless
  c 266–29   *M·* is deathless, spiritual.

is endowed
  s 161–16   "*M·* is endowed by his Maker with certain

is found
  sp 97–19   *m·* is found in the likeness of Spirit.
  ph 179–10   is won only as *m·* is found, . . . reflecting
    188– 2   and *m·* is found in His image.
  b 291–16   *m·* is found having no righteousness of his own,

is free
  r 481– 5   *m·* is free "to enter into the— *Heb.* 10 : 19.

is God's image
  s 120– 5   reflects Soul, God, for *m·* is God's image.

is God's reflection
  y 527– 1   *M·* is God's reflection, needing no

is governed
  a 42–26   in C. S. the true *m·* is governed by God
  s 151–21   Every function of the real *m·* is governed by
  ph 180–25   When *m·* is governed by God,
  f 216–16   if *m·* is governed by the law of divine Mind,
  b 302–22   this real *m·* is governed by Soul
    318–29   In Science *m·* is governed by God,
  r 405– 1   whenever *m·* is governed by God.

is harmonious
  ph 184–10   *m·* is harmonious and eternal.
  b 273–18   *M·* is harmonious when governed by Soul.

is His image
  r 468–14   Spirit is God, and *m·* is His image and likeness.

is His likeness
  sp 73– 7   Spirit is God, and *m·* is His likeness.

is idea
  r 475–13   *M·* is idea, the image, of Love ;

is image
  sp 73–10   for *m·* is image.
  b 301–24   while *m·* is "image" (idea).— *Gen.* 1 : 27.

is immortal
  sp 76–20   *m·* is immortal and lives by divine authority.
  f 250–15   a mortal is not man, for *m·* is immortal.
    250–27   But the spiritual, real *m·* is immortal.
  p 426–29   *M·* is immortal, and the body cannot die,
  t 461– 3   but I do believe that the real *m·* is immortal
  r 478–31   man is not mortal . . . *m·* is immortal.
  g 546– 1   mortality of man is a myth, for *m·* is immortal.

is incapable of sin
  r 475–28   *M·* is incapable of sin, sickness, and death.

is indestructible
  p 402–12   *M·* is indestructible and eternal.

is never God
  sp 70– 7   *M·* is never God, but spiritual man, . . . reflects

is never sick
  p 393–29   *M·* is never sick, for Mind is not sick and

man

is not absorbed
  c 259– 1   *M·* is not absorbed in Deity,

is not God
  f 250–12   *M·* is not God, but like a ray of
  r 480–19   *M·* is not God, and God is not man.

is not material
  r 468–15   Therefore *m·* is not material ;

is not matter
  r 475– 6   *Answer.— M·* is not matter ;

is not mortal
  r 476–10   Hence *m·* is not mortal nor material.
    478–31   *m·* is not mortal, "neither indeed— *Rom.* 8 : 7.

is perfect
  r 485–23   in which *m·* is perfect, even as the

is pure
  r 477– 5   and that *m·* is pure and holy.

is self-governed
  s 125–17   Reflecting God's government, *m·* is self-governed.

is spiritual
  sp 93–26   *M·* is spiritual.
  ph 173–20   *M·* is spiritual, individual, and eternal ;
  b 302– 4   the real *m·* is spiritual and eternal.
  p 396–28   that *m·* is spiritual, not material ;
    409–20   The real *m·* is spiritual and immortal,
  r 475–11   *M·* is spiritual and perfect ;

is subject to
  p 429–12   Science declares that *m·* is subject to Mind.

is sustained
  g 530– 5   In divine Science, *m·* is sustained by God,

is the expression
  r 470–23   *M·* is the expression of God's being.
    477–26   *M·* is the expression of Soul.

is the idea
  ph 200–11   Life is God, and *m·* is the idea of God,
  c 266–27   *M·* is the idea of Spirit ;
  r 476–10   and *m·* is the idea of God.

is the image
  ph 172–18   *m·* is the image and likeness of Spirit ;
    200–18   *m·* is the image, reflection, of God,
  p 414–26   *m·* is the image and likeness of God,

is the likeness
  f 250–11   Spiritual *m·* is the likeness of this Ego.
  r 467–15   *m·* is the likeness of God,
  g 544–24   *M·* is the likeness of Spirit,

is the offspring
  m 63– 5   *m·* is the offspring of Spirit.
  c 265– 1   *M·* is the offspring, not of the lowest, but of
  p 396–27   *m·* is the offspring of God, not of man ;

is the reflection
  f 249–31   *M·* is the reflection of Soul.
  b 305–27   Because *m·* is the reflection of his Maker,
  r 475–17   *m·* is the reflection of God, or Mind,

is tributary
  f 209– 8   and *m·* is tributary to divine Mind.
  r 481– 2   *M·* is tributary to God, Spirit,

just
  a 47–11   ingratitude and hatred towards that just *m·*
  t 443– *   *teach a just m·, and he will— Prov.* 9 : 9.

let not
  m 56– *   *let not m· put asunder.— Matt.* 19 : 6.

let us make
  p 438– 3   Let us make *m·* in our image,— *Gen.* 1 : 26.
  r 475–23   "Let us make *m·* in our image,— *Gen.* 1 : 26.
  g 515–11   Let us make *m·* in our image,— *Gen.* 1 : 26.
    525–13   And God said, Let us make *m·*

life and
  p 368–21   life and *m·* survive this body.

Life of
  a 51–12   Nothing could kill this Life of *m·*.
  b 304–18   Divine Principle is the Life of *m·*.
  p 388–23   does not affect the absolute Life of *m·*
  g 555–30   Knowing that God was the Life of *m·*,

life of
  (see **life**)

makes
  sp 94– 1   makes *m·* in the image and likeness of
  ph 173–22   makes *m·* knavish or honest according to
  f 203–15   and so makes *m·* the image of his Maker
    225– 4   Truth makes *m·* free.
  b 269–10   C. S. makes *m·* Godlike.
    306– 8   immortality of Soul makes *m·* immortal.
    317–19   understanding . . . makes *m·* more real,
  o 357–10   belief that God . . . makes *m·* capable of
  t 453–30   the divine Truth that makes *m·* free.
  r 485–18   understanding of Life, makes *m·* immortal.

making
  o 356–26   by making *m·* inclined to sin,

manifested through
  f 210–12   forever manifested through *m·*,

many a
  ph 197– 6   costs many a *m·* his earthly days of comfort.

material
  (see **material**)

matter and
  b 294– 8   If . . . matter and *m·* would be one.

man
measured
   a 47– 4 They no longer measured *m·* by material sense.
Mind controls
   b 319–19 Mind controls *m·* and man has no Mind but God.
Mind of
   r 470–17 when God, the Mind of *m·*, never sins
Mind that made
   s 151–23 The divine Mind that made *m·* maintains His
Mind to
   f 214–16 conveys the impressions of Mind to *m·*,
misnamed
   b 294–11 mortal belief, misnamed *m·*, is error,
moral
   p 406–17 moral *m·* has no fear that he will commit a murder,
mortal
   (*see* **mortal**)
most scientific
   b 313–23 Jesus of Nazareth was the most scientific *m·*
motive-powers of
   r 490– 8 Truth and Love as the motive-powers of *m·*.
must be sinless
   b 290–16 To be wholly spiritual, *m·* must be sinless,
must find
   m 65–27 *m·* must find permanence and peace
must harmonize
   b 337– 8 *m·* must harmonize with his Principle,
must live
   pref viii– 3 *m·* must live in obedience to its divine
nature of
   sp 94– 4 The nature of *m·*, thus understood,
nearer to
   gl 596– 5 but C. S. brings God much nearer to *m·*,
never beheld in
   c 259–16 then mortals have never beheld in *m·* the
never causing
   g 520–31 never causing *m·* to till the ground,
never dies
   r 486–10 In reality *m·* never dies.
never punishes
   p 384– 7 God never punishes *m·* for doing right,
no
   a 31– 5 "Call no *m·* your father upon the— *Matt.* 23 : 9.
   sp 77–15 "knoweth no *m·*— *Mark* 13 : 32.
   s 140– 6 shall no *m·* see Me, and live."— *Exod.* 33 : 20.
   f 201– 5 "No *m·* can serve two masters."— *Matt.* 6 : 24.
   217–14 know we no *m·* after the flesh !"— *II Cor.* 5 : 16.
   233–12 no *m·* knoweth,— not even "the Son— *Mark* 13 : 32.
   252–18 wholly dishonest, and no *m·* knoweth it.
   c 255–14 That God is corporeal...no *m·* should affirm.
   b 286– 9 "No *m·* cometh unto the— *John* 14 : 6.
   292– 4 knoweth no *m·*."— *Matt.* 24 : 36.
   p 369–30 No *m·* is physically healed in wilful error
   t 458–25 He does violence to no *m·*.
   k 499– * *openeth, and no m· shutteth ;— Rev.* 3 : 7.
   499– * *shutteth, and no m· openeth ;— Rev.* 3 : 7.
   499– * *an open door, and no m· can shut it.— Rev.* 3 : 8.
   gl 579– * *openeth, and no m· shutteth ;— Rev.* 3 : 7.
   579– * *shutteth, and no m· openeth ;— Rev.* 3 : 7.
   579– * *an open door, and no m· can shut it.— Rev.* 3 : 8.
no power over
   sp 76–20 they will have no power over *m·*,
nor God
   g 533–30 as much as to say . . . "Neither *m·* nor God.
not influenced by
   pr 7–23 God is not influenced by *m·*.
of God
   b 314–10 The Jews, who sought to kill this *m·* of God,
of sorrows
   a 42– 9 The "*m·* of sorrows"— *Isa.* 53 : 3.
   52–19 The "*m·* of sorrows"— *Isa.* 53 : 3.
old
   ph 172–22 we must "put off the old *m·*."— *Col.* 3 : 9.
   c 261–15 This old *m·* was so lame that he
   262– 7 By putting "off the old *m·* — *Col.* 3 : 9.
   b 296– 9 The old *m·* with his deeds must be put off.
   g 519–15 until they throw off the old *m·*
origin of
   b 325–27 time cometh when the spiritual origin of *m·*,
   r 490–24 explanations of the nature and origin of *m·*
   g 529– 7 as to the nature and origin of *m·*,
   534– 2 the belief in the material origin of *m·*
   534– 7 which reveals the spiritual origin of *m·*.
   549–32 a belief in the material origin of *m·*,
   555–16 Searching for the origin of *m·*, who is the
or matter
   b 284– 4 If God were limited to *m·* or matter,
painless to
   p 401–13 but should be as painless to *m·* as to a fluid,
passing to
   gl 581– 4 ANGELS. God's thoughts passing to *m·* ;
perfect
   sp 99–29 and to God's spiritual, perfect *m·*.
   c 259–13 perfect God and perfect *m·*,— as the basis
   b 304–14 The perfect *m·*— governed by God,
   330–14 Neither God nor the perfect *m·* can be

man
perfect
   b 337–16 In proportion to his purity is *m·* perfect ;
   r 477– 1 Jesus beheld in Science the perfect *m·*,
   477– 2 In this perfect *m·* the Saviour saw
   477–16 the genuine and perfect *m·*,
   482–20 highest human concept of the perfect *m·*.
   g 519–20 unto a perfect *m·*,— *Eph.* 4 : 13.
place
   r 486–30 blindness, and deafness would place *m·* in
possesses
   g 539–11 *m·* possesses nothing which he has not
   ap 576–23 In divine Science, *m·* possesses this
possibilities of
   s 128–16 latent abilities and possibilities of *m·*
   t 445–10 Teach the great possibilities of *m·*
presupposes
   b 281– 7 Error presupposes *m·* to be both mind and
   r 480–15 and presupposes *m·* to be in matter.
Principle of (*see also* **divine Principle of**)
   s 123– 4 true idea and Principle of *m·* will then appear.
   r 476–10 God is the Principle of *m·*,
Principle of the
   a 29–28 the divine Principle of the *m·* Jesus,
   s 146–17 the divine Principle, of the *m·* Jesus ;
problem of
   f 216– 7 and solves the problem of *m·*.
produces in
   p 380–24 the divine Mind produces in *m·* health,
qualities in
   b 280–30 perpetuates these qualities in *m·*,
real
   s 151–21 Every function of the real *m·* is governed by
   ph 172–24 If the real *m·* is in the material body,
   190–20 immortal man, . . . is found to be the real *m·*.
   200–17 the real *m·* was, is, and ever shall be perfect,
   f 250–27 But the spiritual, real *m·* is immortal.
   b 288–25 the spiritual real *m·* has no birth,
   289–19 to the real *m·* and the real universe there is no
   300–11 the real *m·*, or the new man
   302– 4 the real *m·* is spiritual and eternal.
   302– 5 The identity of the real *m·* is not lost,
   302–22 this real *m·* is governed by Soul
   314–17 To such . . . the real *m·* seemed a spectre,
   316– 4 The real *m·* being linked by Science to
   316– 6 the real *m·* and his relation to God,
   p 409–20 The real *m·* is spiritual and immortal,
   409–24 and the new man or real *m·* is put on,
   t 461– 3 but I do believe that the real *m·* is immortal
   r 475–29 The real *m·* cannot depart from holiness,
   476– 4 In divine Science, God and the real *m·* are
   476–31 Truth and Love reign in the real *m·*,
   g 538–30 the sinless, real *m·* is eternal.
   543– 4 it is only mortal man and not the real *m·*,
reconcile
   a 19– 2 Christ's purpose to reconcile *m·* to God,
reconciles
   a 18–13 atonement of Christ reconciles *m·* to God,
reconciling
   a 19– 7 Jesus aided in reconciling *m·* to God
record of
   g 531–31 the scientifically Christian record of *m·*
redeems
   a 19– 9 redeems *m·* from the law of matter,
reflected by
   pr 3–12 The Divine Being must be reflected by *m·*,
   b 336–14 Mind can never be in man, but is reflected by *m·*.
   r 467–18 not in man but as reflected by *m·*.
   496– 5 omnipotent Mind is reflected by *m·*
reflects
   a 18– 2 whereby *m·* reflects divine Truth, Life, and
   sp 90–32 certainly shall know this when *m·* reflects God.
   94– 3 *M·* reflects infinite Truth, Life, and Love.
   c 258–11 *M·* reflects infinity,
   b 306–19 cannot be separated . . . if *m·* reflects God.
   p 393–17 in Science *m·* reflects God's government.
   g 525– 4 *M·* reflects God ;
reform of
   b 327–25 But how shall we reform the *m·* who
reign over
   g 529–31 He begins his reign over *m·* somewhat mildly,
relation of
   sp 94– 8 and of the relation of *m·* to God,
   s 114–25 It shows the scientific relation of *m·* to God,
representing
   p 376–24 representing *m·* as healthy instead of
reveals
   s 120–21 reveals *m·* as harmoniously existent
   ph 191–24 reveals *m·* and immortality as based on Spirit.
   b 296–12 reveals *m·* and Life, harmonious, real,
   302–19 The Science of being reveals *m·* as perfect,
   r 477–11 C. S. reveals *m·* as the idea of God,
righteous
   a 37–19 procured the martyrdom of that righteous *m·*
right of a
   a 49–31 turned "aside the right of a *m·* — *Lam.* 3 : 35.
rights of
   (*see* **rights**)

man

robs
ph 169–32 it robs *m·* of reliance on God,
said
f 239–32 of which the wise *m·* said,
g 533– 7 And the *m·* said, The woman whom — *Gen.* 3 : 12.
Science of
sp 73–10 the individuality and the Science of *m·*,
p 409–25 as mortals realize the Science of *m·*
Science teaches
r 472– 1 Science teaches *m·* that God is the only Life,
sees his reflection
s 126– 6 even as *m* sees his reflection in a glass.
senses of
b 284–29 the only real senses of *m·* are spiritual,
r 486–23 all the spiritual senses of *m·*, are eternal.
    488–28 If it were possible for the real senses of *m·* to be
    489–19 Who dares to say that the senses of *m·* can be
sensuous
s 131– 8 opposition of sensuous *m·* to the Science of Soul
sent from God
ap 561–30 "There was a *m·* sent from God — *John* 1 : 6.
separated from
r 477–29 Separated from *m·*, who expresses Soul,
shall recognize
a 55–17 when *m·* shall recognize the Science of Christ
shaped
g 525–14 and God shaped *m·* after His mind ;
should be
g 529– 3 that *m·* should be born of woman,
should be governed
g 536–14 if *m·* should be governed by corporeality
should lose aught
b 302– 8 It is impossible that *m·* should lose aught
should renew
p 426–14 M· should renew his energies and
should wish
b 301–18 *m·* should wish for, and in reality has,
sick
s 120–10 Is a *m·* sick if the material senses indicate
    152–18 the sick *m·* supposed this ceremony was
f 208–13 not . . . that He should make *m·* sick,
b 318–16 Is the sick *m·* sinful above all others? No !
p 404–30 envy, dishonesty, fear, . . . make a *m·* sick,
signifies that
b 340–18 it signifies that *m·* shall have no other spirit or
so-called
ph 188– 8 but afterwards it governs the so-called *m·*.
gl 580–11 a so-called *m·*, whose origin, substance, and
Son of
s 132–26 "When the Son of *m·* cometh, — *Luke* 18 : 8.
    136–12 say that I, the Son of *m·*, am?" — *Matt.* 16 : 13.
b 334–25 represents the Son of *m·* as saying
r 482–17 called himself "the Son of *m·*," — *Matt.* 9 : 6.
son of
gl 594–17 son of *m·*, the offspring of the flesh.
Soul of
b 280–27 God, the Soul of *m·* and of all existence,
    307–26 The divine Mind is the Soul of *m·*,
soweth
p 405–17 "Whatsoever a *m·* soweth, — *Gal.* 6 : 7.
g 537–13 "Whatsoever a *m·* soweth, — *Gal.* 6 : 7.
spiritual
    (see **spiritual**)
spiritualized
s 141–19 Its only priest is the spiritualized *m·*.
springs solely
g 543–28 *m·* springs solely from Mind.
standard of
g 553– 9 or . . . will never become the standard of *m·*.
state of
s 159–23 medical schools would learn the state of *m·* from
f 227–16 Slavery is not the legitimate state of *m·*.
status of
s 120–19 or to exhibit the real status of *m·*.
r 476–22 earnestly seek the spiritual status of *m·*,
strength to
m 60–18 a protection to woman, strength to *m·*,
strive with
b 320–13 shall not always strive with *m·*, — *Gen.* 6 : 3.
strong
p 399–31 first bind the strong *m·*?" — *Matt.* 12 : 29.
    400– 4 Mortal mind is "the strong *m·*," — *Matt.* 12 : 29.
    400– 7 we can despoil "the strong *m·*'" — *Matt.* 12 : 29.
such a
s 139–32 The moral condition of such a *m·* demands
supposition that
ph 171–31 supposition that *m·* is a material outgrowth
g 521–13 supposition that *m·* is created materially,
sustain
an 103–25 The truths of immortal Mind sustain *m·*,
sustains
b 319– 9 sustains *m·* under all circumstances ;
taken from
g 528–13 and the rib, . . . taken from *m·*, — *Gen.* 2 : 22.
    529– 4 not woman again taken from *m·*

man

talks with
b 308–15 as consciously as *m·* talks with *m·*.
tempting
g 527–12 represents God, Love, as tempting *m·*,
the best
a 52–16 the best *m·* that ever trod the globe.
the new
b 300–11 the real man, or the *new m·*
p 409–24 and the new *m·* or real man is put on,
the old
ph 172–22 we must "put off the old *m·*." — *Col.* 3 : 9.
c 262– 8 putting "off the old *m·* — *Col.* 3 : 9.
b 296– 9 The old *m·* with his deeds must be put off.
g 519–16 until they throw off the old *m·*
theories of
a 20– 4 to forms of doctrine or to theories of *m·*,
theory of
g 545–13 utterly opposed to the theory of *m·*
the term
g 525– 8 some of the equivalents of the term *m·*
this
s 148–22 tries to explain how to make this *m·* a Christian.
b 314–10 The Jews, who sought to kill this *m·* of God,
g 522–16 to be temporary and this *m·* to be mortal,
this original
b 286–13 from first to last by this original *m·*, Jesus.
through
r 495– 1 God will heal the sick through *m·*,
to become
ph 172–16 in order to become *m·*.
p 432–17 if . . . it is possible for *m·* to become diseased,
translation of
f 209–22 by the translation of *m·* and the universe
true
a 42–26 in C. S. the true *m·* is governed by God
true idea of
b 337–20 The true idea of *m·*, as the reflection of
truth-giver to
sp 72–12 God, is the only truth-giver to *m·*.
ultimate of
r 487– 4 Life is the origin and ultimate of *m·*,
understands
c 265– 3 M· understands . . . existence in proportion as
undying
p 427–23 Truth, and Love make *m·* undying,
unfashion
r 488–27 otherwise the very worms could unfashion *m·*.
universe and
gl 585–17 encompassing the universe and *m·* ;
unrighteous
s 139– 2 unrighteous *m·* his thoughts." — *Isa.* 55 : 7.
r 239–15 unrighteous *m·* his thoughts." — *Isa.* 55 : 7.
verities of
r 476–13 as the only and eternal verities of *m·*.
warns
r 481–13 against which wisdom warns *m·*,
was accounted
b 316–26 That *m·* was accounted a criminal who
was made
b 287–21 *m·* was made in God's likeness.
what constitutes
b 289– 0 the understanding of what constitutes *m·*
whatever teaches
ph 169–29 Whatever teaches *m·* to have other laws
what is
r 475– 5 *Question.* — What is *m·*?
which define
sp 81–25 which define *m·* as mortal.
wicked
f 239–11 The wicked *m·* is not the ruler of his
r 491–26 A wicked *m·* may have an attractive
will not punish
o 357– 2 must admit that God will not punish *m·* for
will recognize
g 531–13 Then *m·* will recognize his God-given dominion
will reopen
ph 171– 5 *m·* will reopen with the key of divine Science
wisdom of
pr 3– 2 The wisdom of *m·* is not sufficient to warrant
wise
sp 95–25 Is the wise *m·* of to-day believed, when he
f 239–32 of which the wise *m·* said,
t 443– * *Give instruction to a wise m·,* — *Prov.* 9 : 9.
worldly
a 21–25 worldly *m·* is at the beck and call of error,
would enjoy
f 246–21 *m·* would enjoy more than
would presuppose
ph 194–15 would presuppose *m·*, . . . a mortal in
would procreate
s 140–30 but mortals would procreate *m·*,

---

pr 3–13 else *m·* is not the image and likeness of the
    5–26 belief that sin is cancelled, and that *m·* is
    8–10 If a *m·*, though apparently fervent

man

pr 15–12   that *m·* may have audience with Spirit,
a   26–13   This Christ, or divinity of the *m·* Jesus,
    26–18   to prove what God is and what He does for *m·*.
    30–16   "Whoso sheddeth man's blood, by *m·* shall his
           — *Gen.* 9 : 6.
    43–15   glorification of the *m·* and of the true idea of
    53– 4   there never lived a *m·* so far removed from
m   59– 8   *M·* should not be required to participate
    64– 2   caused by the selfishness and inhumanity of *m·*.
    64–10   When a *m·* lends a helping hand
    64–21   but *m·* would be as the angels.
    67–28   *M·* delivered from sin, disease, and death
    68–32   and *m·*, not of the earth earthly
    69– 7   while believing that *m·* is a
    69– 8   only as *m·* finds the truth of
    69–22   or is *m·* a creator?''
    69–23   replies, "God creates man through *m·*,''
sp   70– *   *If a m· keep my saying,— John* 8 : 51.
    75– 2   mistaken assumption that *m·* dies as matter
    76–15   Neither will *m·* seem to be corporeal.
    78–28   *m·* cannot "tell whence it— *John* 3 : 8.
    81–23   in the case of *m·* as truly as
    83–28   by which *m·* gains the divine Principle and
    85–13   "Come, see a *m·*, which told me— *John* 4 : 29.
    89–27   *m·* is not the father of *m·*.
    89–29   if . . . *m·* gave it, *m·* had the right to take it
    90–24   admission to one's self that *m·* is God's own
    90–25   sets *m·* free to master the infinite idea.
    90–31   At present we know not what *m·* is,
    91–27   second erroneous postulate is, that *m·*
    92– 1   fourth erroneous postulate is, . . . that *m·* has
    93–27   If *m·* were Spirit, then men would be spirits,
an 102–12   planets have no more power over *m·* than
    102–13   *m·*, reflecting God's power, has dominion
    103– 7   Science, by which *m·* can escape from sin
    106– 9   *M·* is properly self-governed only when
s 107– *   *which was preached of me is not after m·.—*
           Gal. 1 : 11.
    107– *   *For I neither received it of m·,— Gal.* 1 : 12.
    115–15   *M·* : God's spiritual idea,
    119–31   Thus it is with *m·*, who is but the humble
    120– 3   and that *m·* is included in
    120–12   matter can make no conditions for *m·*.
    121–14   *m·*, left to the hypotheses of material sense
    123– 8   so that *m·* becomes the most absolutely
    124–14   The universe, like *m·*, is to be interpreted by
    124–18   the universe, like *m·*, is, . . . an enigma.
    125– 7   *m·* will be found normal and natural
    125–18   *m·* cannot be controlled by sin or death,
    1ɔ–32   mortal belief, wholly inadequate to affect a *m·*
    126– 5   mortality will cease when *m·* beholds
    132–15   thrust the spiritual idea and the *m·* who
    133–23   material system, . . . concerning God, *m·*,
    148–16   Anatomy takes up *m·* at all points materially.
    154–10   A *m·* was made to believe that he occupied
    154–13   and the *m·* died.
    160–30   Is *m·* a material fungus without Mind
ph 166– 3   As a *m·* thinketh, so is he.
    166–31   then is *m·* found to be harmonious
    167–15   If . . . *m·* must remain thus.
    168–15   Because man-made systems insist that *m·*
    171–11   to learn how much of a *m·* he is.
    172– 9   if *m·* passes through what we call death
    172–15   If *m·* was first a material being,
    172–17   If the material body is *m·*, he is a portion of
    172–23   What is *m·*?
    172–25   If . . . you take away a portion of the *m·* when
    173– 1   When we admit that . . . constitutes *m·*, we fail
    173– 4   or determine when *m·* is really *m·*
    173–17   Anatomy declares *m·* to be structural.
    174– 5   form of idolatry, that *m·* should bow down to
    174– 7   capable of doing so much for *m·* as
    174–24   Anatomy admits that mind is somewhere in *m·*,
    180–26   *m·* knows that with God all things are possible.
    183–12   error, first caused the condemnation of *m·*
    184–18   We say *m·* suffers from the effects of
    190–23   As for *m·*, his days are as— *Psal.* 103 : 15.
    193–14   and said : "I feel like a new *m·*,
    193–29   what I saw and did for that *m·*,
    198– 2   has in belief more power to harm *m·*
f 202–31   Common opinion admits that a *m·* may take
    203–31   God, divine good, does not kill a *m·*
    204–27   can never be said that *m·* has a
    206–25   Can there be any birth or death for *m·*,
    206–30   God does not cause *m·* to sin,
    208–13   then leave *m·* to heal himself ;
    209– 1   *M·*, being immortal, has a perfect . . . life.
    209– 9   mortal body or mind is not the *m·*.
    213– 3   Of a *m·* it has been said,
    213– 5   as a *m·* spiritually *understandeth*, so is he
    214–24   mortal illusions would rob God, slay *m·*,
    216– 3   Who shall say that *m·* is alive to-day, but
    216–19   mistake of mortals is to suppose that *m·*,
    217–12   "If a *m·* keep my saying,— *John* 8 : 51.
    225– 1   What is it that binds *m·* with iron shackles

man

f 227–31   disobedience to which would have made *m·* ill,
    228–12   when *m·* enters into his heritage of freedom,
    229–23   If God cause *m·* to be sick, sickness must
    230–20   which must afterwards be rectified by *m·*?
    230–21   can *m·* put that law under his feet
    231– 8   What God cannot do, *m·* need not attempt.
    232–20   never . . . could make a *m·* healthy,
    244– 9   would have no abiding-place in *m·*,
    244–13   *M·* undergoing birth, maturity, and decay
    244–15   If *m·* were dust in his earliest stage of
    244–18   but *m·* was never more nor less than *m·*.
    244–19   If *m·* flickers out in death or
    246– 1   *M·* is not a pendulum, swinging between
    246– 6   *M·* is by no means a material germ
    247– 7   One *m·* at sixty had retained his
    250–13   *m·*, the outcome of God, reflects God.
    250–15   but a mortal is not *m·*,
    250–26   matter has no more sense as a *m·* than
    252–12   *m·* created by and of Spirit,
    252–32   saith : . . . *M·*, whose senses are spiritual, is
    253– 4   saith : . . . I give immortality to *m·*,
c 258– 9   *M·* is more than a material form with
    258–16   We know no more of *m·* as the true divine image
    258–28   impossible for *m·*, under the government of
    259– 6   In divine Science, *m·* is the true image of God.
    259–10   thoughts which presented *m·* as fallen, sick,
    259–15   If *m·* was once perfect but has now lost
    260– 2   true conception or understanding of *m·*,
    261–32   Good demands of *m·* every hour,
    263–11   They make *m·* an involuntary hypocrite,
    264–31   all the glories of earth and heaven and *m·*.
    265–17   as if *m·* were a weed growing apace
    265–20   this is true only of a mortal, not of a *m·*
    267– 6   Generically *m·* is one,
    267– 7   specifically *m·* means all men.
    267–11   Hence *m·* and the spiritual universe
    267–28   "Blessed is the *m·* that— *Jas.* 1 : 12.
b 277–15   not produced by a vegetable nor the *m·* by the
    278–25   leads to the conclusion that if *m·* is material,
    280–26   *m·* has a sensationless body ;
    282–28   Whatever indicates the fall of *m·*
    282–30   Adam-dream, which is neither Mind nor *m·*,
    284–32   is always from God to His idea, *m·*.
    285– 8   It is not *m·*, the image and likeness of God,
    285–16   belief that a material body is *m·*
    287–19   It saith, "I am *m·*, but I am not the image
    289–22   So *m·*, tree, and flower are supposed to obe ;
    289–31   *M·* is not the offspring of flesh, but of Spirit,
    291–22   As *m·* falleth asleep, so shall he awake.
    292–28   *m·* would be annihilated, were it not for
    293–12   both strata, . . . are false representatives of *m·*.
    294– 6   If *m·* is both mind and matter,
    294– 7   some quality and quantity of the *m·*,
    294–14   saying : . . . stomach can make a *m·* cross.
    294–14   error, saying : . . . matter can kill *m·*.''
    294–26   *M·* is neither self-made nor made by mortals.
    295–30   It further teaches that when *m·* is dead,
    296– 1   theorizes that . . . *m·* has a resurrection from
    296– 2   *m·* is the spiritual, eternal reflection of God.
    297–16   and *m·* found to be immortal.
    299–31   If *m·* were solely a creature of the
    300– 5   His infinite image or reflection, *m·*.
    300– 9   So far as the scientific statement as to *m·*
    300–21   of *m·* as reflecting the divine likeness.
    301–10   *m·* is the divine image and likeness,
    301–31   presupposes . . . *m·* to be material
    303–12   statement that *m·* is conceived and evolved
    303–22   belief that . . . holiness and unholiness, mingle
           in *m·*,
    304–30   So *m·*, not understanding the Science of
    305– 3   discordant mortal is no more a *m·* than
    305–10   so *m·*, like all things real, reflects God.
    305–24   In the illusion . . . *m·* would be wholly mortal,
    306– 9   parted . . . from His reflection, *m·*,
    306–13   If Life or Soul and *m·* is representative, *m·*,
    306–18   But *m·* cannot be separated for an instant from
    307–18   says : "The Lord knows it. He has made *m·*
           mortal
    307–26   *M·* was not created from a material basis,
    309– 3   incorporeal impartation of divine Love to *m·*,
    309–25   or for *m·* to have an intelligence separate
    311– 8   Is *m·* lost spiritually? No,
    311–23   it will become the law of Life to *m·*,
    312– 8   The senses regard a corpse, not as *m·*,
    312– 9   People say, "*M·* is dead ;"
    319–14   Spirit and matter neither concur in *m·* nor in
    319–20   *m·* has no Mind but God.
    320–23   according to that error *m·* is mortal.
    322–22   A *m·* who likes to do wrong
    322–25   neither a temperate *m·* nor a reliable
    325–14   then shall *m·* be found in God's image.
    325–16   Then shall *m·* be found, in His likeness,
    326– 9   teaches God's love to *m·*, but *m·* cannot
    326–26   Then the *m·* was changed.
    327–22   Fear of punishment never made *m·* truly honest

mandate

t 454–10 Human hate has no legitimate *m·*
g 520–26 growth is the eternal *m·* of Mind.
556–19 Sleep is darkness, but God's creative *m·* was,

manger

s 142–15 In vain do the *m·* and the cross
ap 575–29 followed it to the *m·* of Jesus ;

manhood

common
an 106– 2 to drop from the platform of common *m·*
divinity or
g 537–10 was never the essence of divinity or *m·*.
essence of
b 292–24 mortal man is not the real essence of *m·*,
health, and
p 407–11 they crush out happiness, health, and *m·*.
ideas of
sp 74–24 Who will say that infancy can utter the ideas
  of *m·*,
immortal
p 430– 5 and immortal *m·*, the Christ ideal, will appear.
infancy and
sp 74–21 Darkness and light, infancy and *m·*,
lowest type of
p 405– 4 above the lowest type of *m·*,
mortal
g 543–21 thinking that apehood preceded mortal *m·*?
stature of
o 350– 9 must grow into that stature of *m·*

---

ph 172–27 If . . . the surgeon destroys *m·*,
f 246–12 *M·* is its eternal noon,
246–19 conspiracies against *m·* and womanhood.

maniac

t 459–18 into the hands of a blind man or a raging *m·*,

manifest

pr 4–13 made *m·* in the blessings they bring,
a 25–32 was made *m·* in the humanity of Jesus.
sp 72–18 Spirit is not made *m·* through matter,
an 106–20 works of the flesh are *m·*, — *Gal.* 5 : 19.
s 139–16 the *m·* mistakes in the ancient versions ;
ph 173– 9 sensible is required to be made *m·* through
f 219–18 before it can be made *m·* on the body,
239–21 objects we pursue and the spirit we *m·*
b 306–21 myriad forms of mortal thought, made *m·*
316–10 to show that Truth is made *m·*
334–14 the corporeal Jesus *m·* in flesh,
o 346–14 only as we cease to *m·* evil or the belief
p 370– 7 if health is not made *m·* under this
378–31 it would *m·* less wisdom than we
400–28 discord, *m·* as sin, sickness, and death.
t 452– 6 before it has a chance to *m·* itself.
r 493–21 It is fear made *m·* on the body.
g 517–31 causes them to multiply, — to *m·* His power.
530– 3 made *m·* as forever opposed to
534– 4 to *m·* the deathless man of God's creating.
ap 559–15 made *m·* in the destruction of error.

manifestation

and support
b 279–10 nor for the *m·* and support of Mind.
consequent
s 154– 7 and its consequent *m·* in the body.
higher
p 401–10 to the end of producing a higher *m·*.
His
s 117– 9 the Supreme Being or His *m·* ;
infinite
r 468–11 All is infinite Mind and its infinite *m·*,
mental
b 303– 2 The reflection, through mental *m·*,
of Christ
s 141–24 Neither can this *m·* of Christ be
of existence
g 555–29 the individualized *m·* of existence,
of God
b 295–16 The *m·* of God through mortals is as
gl 583–10 CHRIST. The divine *m·* of God,
of Mind
b 275–24 Hence all is in reality the *m·* of Mind.
of mortal mind
g 552–29 matter is a *m·* of mortal mind,
of Spirit
ph 173–12 Neither the substance nor the *m·* of Spirit
scientific
sp 83–13 The scientific *m·* of power is from
the first
g 532–26 Fear was the first *m·* of the error of
visible
s 125–15 the visible *m·* will at last be

---

s 148–15 for every function, formation, and *m·*.
f 244–21 If . . . God is without His entire *m·*,

manifestation

b 283–19 and deem this the *m·* of the one Life,
304–11 Love cannot be deprived of its *m·*,
311– 4 dependent on matter for *m·*,

manifestations

sp 99–24 the *m·* of which are health, purity,
s 125– 9 therefore more harmonious in his *m·*
144–12 the stronger are the *m·* of the corporeal senses,
b 275–16 *m·* of the infinite divine Principle,
285–20 a diviner sense of intelligence and its *m·*,
291–15 in which all the *m·* of Mind are harmonious
293–24 *m·* of evil, which counterfeit divine justice,
r 466– 4 The varied *m·* of C. S. indicate
g 543–27 reflected in the myriad *m·* of Life,

manifested

pr 12–12 the divine healing Principle as *m·* in Jesus,
f 210–12 forever *m·* through man,
219–15 what we do not wish to have *m·*.
234–26 must be thought before they can be *m·*.
245–24 *m·* the influence of such a belief.
b 274–18 are simply the *m·* beliefs of mortal mind.
284–10 It can never . . . be fully *m·* through
290–11 *m·* through brain and nerves,
318–31 but is *m·* through them.
325–11 Christ, . . . shall appear [be *m·*], — *Col.* 3 : 4.
325–12 then shall ye also appear [be *m·*] — *Col.* 3 : 4.
330–28 As *m·* by mankind it stands for
p 364– 3 and it was *m·* towards one who was soon,
369–10 All these deeds *m·* Jesus' control
404– 9 A corrupt mind is *m·* in a corrupt body.
t 463–22 whether error is *m·* in forms of sickness, sin,
r 489– 1 The less mind there is *m·* in matter
g 546–15 It supposes God and man to be *m·* only through
ap 562– 5 the idea . . . which Jesus afterwards *m·*,

manifesting

ap 562–19 and by *m·* the light which shines

manifestly

b 336–21 else God would be *m·* finite,

manifests

m 68–28 it *m·* no material growth from
sp 88–21 and the individual *m·* profound adoration.
s 153–18 The boil simply *m·*, . . . a belief in pain,
ph 173–11 What is termed matter *m·* nothing but a
194–21 mortal mind *m·* itself in the body
c 257–22 Finite mind *m·* all sorts of errors,
258–15 Mind *m·* all that exists in the
b 297– 6 this testimony *m·* itself on the body
301– 1 *m·* God's attributes and power,
318–32 body does not include soul, but *m·* mortality,
340–13 in and of God, and *m·* His love.
p 375– 6 often the form in which fever *m·* itself.
376–20 *m·* only what that so-called mind expresses.
402–18 body *m·* only what mortal mind believes,

manipulate

ph 181– 9 When you *m·* patients, you trust in electricity
181–14 foolish to declare that you *m·* patients but that
181–16 If this be so, why *m·*?
181–16 In reality you *m·* because you are ignorant of

manipulated

p 440– 3 was *m·* by the oleaginous machinations

manipulates

t 453–31 never recommends material hygiene, never *m·*.

manipulation

ph 181–15 but that you lay no stress on *m·*.

manipulations

an 101– 2 that the violent effects, . . . are due to *m·*,

mankind

all
m 57–20 but requires all *m·* to share it.
s 164–14 before all *m·* is saved
f 233–23 this truth was our Master's mission to all *m·*,
248–20 Do you not hear from all *m·* of the imperfect
r 494–13 since to all *m·* and in every hour,
deliver
s 151–14 would ultimately deliver *m·* from the
demonstrated for
a 24–28 goodness it demonstrated for *m·*.
dominion over
f 238–23 Attempts to . . . gain dominion over *m·*,
enriches
o 361–29 enriches *m·* only when it is understood,
health of
pr 1– 9 the Christianization and health of *m·*.
improves
f 251–25 spiritual understanding improves *m·*
majority of
ph 178– 1 but the vast majority of *m·*,
must learn
an 102–30 *M·* must learn that evil is not power.
objects
p 410–12 *m·* objects to making this teaching practical.

mankind

opinion of
b 306–17 this is the general religious opinion of *m·*,
redemption of
t 464–12 working for the redemption of *m·*.
represents
g 525– 5 *m·* represents the Adamic race,
thoughts of
sp 94–24 Our Master easily read the thoughts of *m·*,
to advance
m 61–30 must greatly improve to advance *m·*.
to bless
m 60–29 infinite resources with which to bless *m·*,
to rule
p 419–26 who, in attempting to rule *m·*,
to stir
a 38– 1 so little inspiration to stir *m·* to
weigh down
ph 176–18 and weigh down *m·* with superimposed
will become
r 467–11 *M·* will become perfect in proportion as
will improve
p 371–26 *M·* will improve through Science and

a 55–21 in what it has done and is doing for *m·*.
sp 99–22 I love *m·*, and shall continue
s 140–13 *M·* will no longer be tyrannical
157–31 *M·* is the better for this spiritual and profound
ph 171– 2 *m·* has caught their moral contagion.
f 240–24 Remember that *m·* must sooner or later,
251–15 learn how *m·* govern the body,
b 318–27 and are not adapted to elevate *m·*.
330–28 As manifested by *m·* it stands for
o 357– 9 If *m·* would relinquish the belief that
357–28 if another . . . exists and sways *m·*?
p 425–18 When this is understood, *m·* will be more
430–11 When will *m·* wake to this great fact
t 456– 1 to influence *m·* adverse to its highest
r 466–30 making *m·* better physically, morally, and
g 525– 8 In the Saxon, *m·*, a *woman, any one*;
528–27 calling them *m·*, — that is, a kind of man.
551–11 he adds that *m·* has ascended through
ap 571–10 Who is telling *m·* of the foe in ambush?

manlike

b 269– 9 Human philosophy has made God *m·*.

manliness

ph 172–28 is sometimes the quickener of *m·* ;

manly

p 397–30 and you will quickly become more *m·*

man-made

a 23– 7 Such a theory is *m·*.
38– 8 lethargy of mortals, produced by *m·* doctrines,
s 112–13 divine Science which coshows *m·* systems,
134–14 *M·* doctrines are waning.
ph 165–14 since *m·* material theories took the
168–15 Because *m·* systems insist that
o 352–25 traditional beliefs, erroneous and *m·*.
r 166–26 the outcome of all *m·* beliefs.

man-midwife

s 163–10 physician, surgeon, apothecary, *m·*,

manna

a 33– 4 partook of the heavenly *m·*,
s 133–10 and *m·* fell from the sky.

manner

after the
s 131–15 after the *m·* of God's appointing,
after this
pr 16– 9 "After this *m·* therefore pray ye," — *Matt.* 6 : 9.
sp 85–11 able to read the human mind after this *m·*
all
p 418–27 Cast out all *m·* of evil.
like
sp 82–18 In like *m·* it would follow,
85–17 In like *m·* he discerned disease
ph 189– 8 In like *m·* mortals should no more deny
p 398–21 In like *m·* destroy the illusion of
t 453– 4 In like *m·* it should be granted
most effectual
pr 11–18 but wipes it out in the most effectual *m·*.
unknown
b 306–16 at some uncertain future time and in a *m·* unknown,

f 224–15 this was not the *m·* of truth's appearing.
b 274–29 in a *m·* and at a period as yet unknown.

man-projected

s 140–23 Jewish tribal Jehovah was a *m·* God,

Man's

p 434–16 Mortal *M·* counsel regards the prisoner with
435– 2 Spirit which is . . . *M·* only lawgiver!
435–17 a destroyer of Mortal *M·* liberty

man's

pr 5– 1 hinders *m·* spiritual growth
12–14 of *m·* likeness to God
12–15 and of *m·* unity with Truth and Love.
13–29 *m·* eternal incorporeal existence.
14–27 the consciousness of *m·* dominion over the
a 18– 1 Atonement is the exemplification of *m·* unity
18– 4 and demonstrated *m·* oneness with the
30–15 "Whoso sheddeth *m·* blood, — *Gen.* 9 : 6.
35–32 good *m·* heaven would be a hell to the sinner.
44–21 in his proof of *m·* truly derived power?
m 62–19 in the understanding of *m·* higher nature.
65– 2 should proceed from *m·* highest nature.
65– 5 by which *m·* spiritual and eternal existence
69–11 neither closes *m·* continuity nor his sense of
sp 81–11 A *m·* assertion that he is immortal
81–28 *m·* immortality depends upon that of God,
84–23 by which we discern *m·* nature and existence.
91–12 the sooner *m·* great reality will appear
91–18 aids the discernment of *m·* spiritual and
an 106–12 *M·* rights are invaded when the
s 110–10 another glorious proposition, — *m·* perfectibility
118–12 eternally glorified in *m·* spiritual freedom.
150–22 human view infringes *m·* free moral agency ;
150–26 The doctrine that *m·* harmony is governed by
159–30 Ignorant of the fact that a *m·* belief produces
ph 165– 3 Evil declared . . . this fruit would open *m·* eyes
165– 4 it closed the eyes of mortals to *m·* God-given
166–11 believes in . . . drugs to save a *m·* life.
170–10 the Principle of *m·* harmony.
170–15 The best interpreter of *m·* needs said :
172– 3 Theorizing about *m·* development from
172–31 "a *m·* a man, for a' that."
175–23 A *m·* belief in those days was not so severe
182–25 denying *m·* God-given ability to demonstrate
183–21 rightly demands *m·* entire obedience, affection,
191–19 no longer ask . . . What are *m·* prospects for
f 203–32 for God alone is *m·* life.
205–25 hinders *m·* normal drift towards the one Mind,
215–30 Having sought *m·* spiritual state,
216–28 When you say, "*M·* body is material,"
217– 1 The loss of *m·* identity . . . is impossible ;
223– 4 the fetters of *m·* finite capacity are forged by
226–20 *m·* birthright of sole allegiance to his Maker
227– 9 unaware of *m·* inalienable rights
231–23 divine Science of being in *m·* relation to God,
232–22 He referred *m·* harmony to Mind,
c 262– 2 Consecration to good does not lessen *m·* dependence
262– 4 *m·* obligations to God,
262–28 a false sense of *m·* origin.
264–29 and recognize *m·* spiritual being,
265–11 by no means suggests *m·* absorption into
266– 4 materiality giving place to *m·* higher individuality
266–14 "*m·* extremity is God's opportunity."
b 285– 2 *M·* individuality is not material.
285– 9 *m·* counterfeit, the inverted likeness,
287– 8 and maintains *m·* spiritual identity.
288–32 *m·* real existence as a child of God
290– 3 rule, and demonstration of *m·* being
299–30 *m·* indissoluble connection with his God,
294–25 *M·* genuine selfhood is recognizable only in
295–10 and then recover *m·* original self
301–15 spiritual *m·* substantiality transcends
302–26 *M·* true consciousness is in the mental,
304–18 *M·* happiness is not, therefore, at the
312–19 *m·* eternal Principle is ever-present Life.
312–25 A personal sense of God and of *m·* capabilities
315–19 prove *m·* heritage, the liberty of the
320–18 even *m·* eternal and harmonious existence
322–14 *M·* wisdom finds no satisfaction in sin,
327– 9 Evil is sometimes a *m·* highest conception
327–30 the *m·* dormant sense of moral obligation,
328–14 This understanding of *m·* power,
336–14 *m·* consciousness and individuality are
337–22 as is *m·* infinite Principle.
338–29 blessed the earth "for *m·* sake." — *Gen.* 8 : 21.
o 356– 6 Sin, sickness, and death do not prove *m·* entity
358– 4 God, who is *m·* Life
p 373–15 are the sources of *m·* enslavement.
378–14 A *m·* gaze, fastened fearlessly on a ferocious
380–21 and prove *m·* dominion over error.
381–21 you will sooner grasp *m·* God-given dominion.
381–28 *m·* moral right to annul an unjust sentence,
395– 4 *m·* immortality and eternal likeness to God.
399–30 enter into a strong *m·* house — *Matt.* 12 : 29.
406– 4 The tree is typical of *m·* divine Principle,
407– 3 inconceivably terrible to *m·* self-respect.
407– 6 *M·* enslavement to the most relentless
414–28 *m·* perfection is real and unimpeachable,
425–17 can never destroy God, who is *m·* Life.
427– 5 *M·* individual being can no more
428– 6 *M·* privilege at this supreme moment
428–27 evidence of *m·* immortality will become
435– 1 commended *m·* immortal Spirit to

man's

p 437– 5 This is a foul aspersion on *m·* Maker.
t 447– 2 trespassing upon *m·* individual right of
449–11 *M·* moral mercury, rising or falling,
r 486– 6 What is *m·* remedy?
490–17 the real *m·* divine Principle, Love.
491– 9 *M·* spiritual individuality is never wrong.
491–10 It is the likeness of *m·* Maker.
494– 1 and to govern *m·* entire action
494–23 until the Science of *m·* eternal harmony
497–14 unfolding *m·* unity with God
g 530– 7 brings forth food for *m·* use.
531–15 If, in the beginning, *m·* body originated in
533– 2 Had he lost *m·* rich inheritance
536–11 If *m·* spiritual gravitation and attraction
539–17 God condemned this lie as to *m·* origin
544–30 infinity to enter *m·* nostrils
553– 4 higher and purer contemplation of *m·* origin.
ap 562–13 *m·* divine origin and the true idea,
576–19 of the real *m·* incorporeality
576–22 is within reach of *m·* consciousness here,
gl 589–18 and bringing to light *m·* immortality.
(see also **existence***)*

manufactured

p 438–30 heard Materia Medica explain how this fur is *m·*,

manufactures

p 439– 4 He *m·* for it,

manuscript

t 460–29 by her *m·* circulated among the students.

many

pref xi– 1 *M·* imagine that the phenomena of
pr 6–29 It is believed by *m·* that a certain magistrate,
a 23– 2 Wisdom and Love may require *m·* sacrifices
27–25 "*M·* are called, but few are—*Matt. 22 : 14.*
28– 3 Even *m·* of his students stood in his way.
38–19 not for the twelve only, but for as *m·* as should
46– 1 did not perform *m·* wonderful works, until
m 65–20 fermentation over this as over *m·* other
sp 71–28 Its spirits are so *m·* corporealities,
80–13 philanthropy of *m·* Spiritualists,
80–23 French toy which years ago pleased so *m·*
an 105–31 full *m·* a league in the line of light ;
s 110–30 apprehended by as *m·* as believe on Christ
111–24 one of *m·* incidents which show that C. S.
114– 8 evidence . . . which makes minds *m·*
117– 2 may be one of a series, one of *m·*,
ph 196– 2 Man has "sought out *m·* inventions,"—*Eccl. 7 : 29.*
196–25 *M·* a hopeless case of disease is induced
196–31 The press unwittingly sends forth *m·* sorrows
197– 6 costs *m·* a man his earthly days of comfort.
197–26 *M·* of the effeminate constitutions of our time
f 205–24 a belief in *m·* ruling minds hinders
213–27 Mortal mind is the harp of *m·* strings,
221–10 He passed *m·* weary years in hunger
223–15 *M·* are ready to meet this inquiry with
224–12 sects *m·* but not enough Christianity.
232– 3 *M·* theories relative to God and man
236– 7 emolument . . . which *m·* leaders seek?
246–19 are so *m·* conspiracies against manhood
c 260– 9 Through *m·* generations human beliefs will
265–28 brightens the ascending path of *m·* a heart.
b 268– 2 has brought to light . . . *m·* useful wonders.
273– 5 Human belief has sought out *m·* inventions,
280–17 "gods many and lords *m·*."—*I Cor. 8 : 5.*
280–20 the opposite error of *m·* minds.
319–16 are so *m·* ancient and modern mythologies.
323–18 shall be made rulers over *m·* ;
335– 1 There are neither spirits *m·* nor
o 361–30 hence the *m·* readings given the Scriptures,
p 367– 8 but so *m·* parodies on legitimate C. S.,
386–12 in too *m·* instances healed disease . . . not to know
400–32 in certain localities he did not *m·* mighty
407–29 There are *m·* species of insanity.
408– 4 nor discovered to be error by *m·*
408–11 so *m·* distinctly defined instances of the
t 450–16 *m·* are reluctant to acknowledge that they
451–14 *m·* there be which go in thereat."—*Matt. 7 : 13.*
r 474–14 misunderstood and misused by *m·*, until
483–29 by doing *m·* wonderful works through the
g 504–17 taking place on so *m· evenings* and *mornings,*
505–19 than the noise of *m·* waters,—*Psal. 93 : 4.*
517–15 The world believes in *m·* persons ;
548–19 "It is very possible that *m·* general statements
557– 8 *m·* animals suffer no pain in multiplying ;
ap 563– 6 showing its horns in the *m·* inventions of evil.
569– 7 I will make thee ruler over *m·*,—*Matt. 25 : 23.*
569–26 how *m·* periods of torture it may take
570–30 *M·* are willing to open the eyes of the people to
gl 580– 8 "gods many and lords *m·*"—*I Cor. 8 : 5.*
(see also **gods, years***)*

mapped

a 38–25 Jesus *m·* out the path for others.
s 121– 4 Copernicus *m·* out the stellar system,

maps

ph 176–27 no farther than mortal mind *m·* out the way.

mar

s 139–24 could neither . . . *m·* the demonstration of

marble

f 248–12 sculptor turns from the *m·* to his model

march

f 209–12 the *m·* of the Science which
225– 7 *m·* of time bears onward freedom's banner.
b 323– 7 in the *m·* towards righteousness,
ap 570– 1 The *m·* of mind and of honest investigation

marches

f 225–11 heeding not the pointed bayonet, *m·* on.

mariner

m 67–12 *m·* works on and awaits the issue.
s 125–25 The *m·* will have dominion over the

mark

sp 96– 4 Love will finally *m·* the hour of harmony,
t 446– 8 or it may *m·* the crisis of the disease.
457–22 and at the same time hit the *m·*.
g 511–18 *m·* the periods of progress.
542– 9 and sets upon error the *m·* of the beast.
542–16 [Jehovah] set a *m·* upon Cain,—*Gen. 4 : 15.*
555– 9 The *m·* of ignorance is on its forehead,

marked

a 46–25 that is, he *m·* the way for all men.
f 227–23 Jesus *m·* out the way.
b 298–31 *m·* with superstitious outlines,
333–16 *m·* the first century of the Christian era,
p 370–19 very direct and *m·* effects on the body.

market

f 225–19 abolish the whipping-post and slave *m·* ;
p 438–24 and smuggles Error's goods into *m·*
439– 2 introducing their goods into the *m·*.

marking

s 163– 1 first *m·* Nature with his name,
ph 174–15 *m·* out the path for generations yet unborn.

marks

g 542–22 Justice *m·* the sinner,

Mark's Gospel

s 117–11 in the last chapter of *M· G·*
b 272–11 referred to in the last chapter of *M· G·*.

marriage

after
m 59–23 After *m·*, it is too late to grumble
cares of
m 58–30 nothing can abolish the cares of *m·*.
given in
m 56– * *nor are given in* m·,—*Matt. 22 : 30.*
69–11 marry or to be "given in *m·*'"—*Matt. 22 : 30.*
69–27 and are given in *m· :*—*Luke 20 : 34.*
69–30 neither marry, nor are given in *m·*."—*Luke 20 : 35.*
giving in
m 64–20 no more marrying nor giving in *m·*,
scientific *morale* **of**
m 61–30 The scientific *morale* of *m·* is spiritual unity.
should improve
m 60–16 *M·* should improve the human species,
should signify
m 64–17 *M·* should signify a union of hearts.
will become
m 65–31 *m·* will become purer when the scum is gone.

m 56– 7 *M·* is the legal and moral provision for
56–13 *m·* will continue, subject to such moral
56–15 Infidelity to the *m·* covenant is the
57–31 *M·* is unblest or blest, according to
58–29 the chance for ill-nature in the *m·* relation,
64–26 Until . . . *m·* will continue.
64–30 ensure the stability of the *m·* covenant.
65–10 some fundamental error in the *m·* state.
ap 575– 4 Then cometh the *m·* feast,

married

m 58–31 "She that is *m·* careth—*I Cor. 7 : 34.*
59– 6 should wait on all the years of *m·* life.

marrow

p 423–13 it searches "the joints and *m·*,"—*Heb. 4 : 12.*

marry

m 56– * *In the resurrection they neither* m·,—*Matt. 22 : 30.*
69–10 *m·* or to be "given in marriage"—*Matt. 22 : 30.*
69–26 "The children of this world *m·*,—*Luke 20 : 34.*
69–29 neither *m·*, nor are given in—*Luke 20 : 35.*

marrying

m 64–20 in the resurrection . . . no more *m·*

martyr

a 28–22 Remember, thou Christian *m·*, it is enough if
s 134– 4 The word *m·*, from the Greek, means *witness;*
134– 6 at length the word *m·* was

martyrdom
a 37–18 procured the m· of that righteous man
40–15 Did the m· of Savonarola make the
gl 597–10 The m· of Jesus was the culminating sin
martyrs
a 37– 6 blood of the m· is the seed of the Church."
37– 9 M· are the human links which
p 388– 1 The Christian m· were prophets of C. S.
marvel
m 63–16 m· why usage should accord woman less rights
r 474–11 m· is the simple meaning of the Greek word
ap 563– 1 Human sense may well m· at discord,
marvellous
g 540– 1 was the basis of his m· demonstrations.
marvels
s 117–21 the miracles (m·) wrought by Jesus
f 223–28 M·, calamities, and sin will much more abound
248– 4 One m· that a friend can ever seem less than
r 474–11 Christian m· . . . will be misunderstood
474–14 until the glorious Principle of these m· is gained.
Mary (see also Mary's)
b 314–20 but the faithful M· saw him, and he presented
332– 9 Jesus was born of M·.
Mary Magdalene
p 362–11 (M· M·, as she has since been called)
367–13 nor, like the Pharisee, . . . but like M· M·,
Mary's
a 29–20 The illumination of M· spiritual sense
29–32 M· self-conscious communion with God.
30– 6 partook partly of M· earthly condition,
b 313–18 the exaltation of Jesus, M· son,
332–26 M· conception of him was spiritual,
masculine
m 57– 4 Union of the m· and feminine qualities
57– 5 The m· mind reaches a higher tone through
57– 8 courage and strength through m· qualities.
64–23 in one person m· wisdom and feminine love,
g 511–28 in m·, feminine, or neuter gender.
516–30 M·, feminine, and neuter genders are
517–12 not as much authority for considering God m·,
ap 565–11 the m· representative of the spiritual idea,
masculinity
g 508–18 does not necessarily refer either to m· or
mask
a 30–28 loathe sin and rebuke it under every m·.
t 447–25 remove the m·, point out the illusion,
masked
p 430–18 blind Hypnotism, and the m· Personal Sense,
masonry
t 450– 9 A third class of thinkers build with solid m·.
masquerader
t 453–21 The m· in this Science
masquerading
gl 582– 7 error m· as the possessor of life,
mass
s 118 11 It must destroy the entire m· of error,
t 449– 3 A little leaven causes the whole m· to ferment.
Massachusetts
pref xi–27 in Lynn, M·, about the year 1867.
s 158–31 A woman in the city of Lynn, M·,
161–11 In 1880, M· put her foot on a proposed . . . law,
Massachusetts Metaphysical College
pref xi–28 In 1881, she opened the M· M· C· in Boston,
masses
f 209–18 relations which constituent m· hold
Master (see also Master's)
dear
pr 9–30 to tread in the footsteps of our dear M·?
a 34–24 for soon their dear M· would rise again in the
enabled their
a 24–30 enabled their M· to triumph over the grave,
example of the
a 37–24 to follow . . . the example of the M·
forbore not
a 19–12 The M· forbore not to speak the whole truth,
gave him
s 137–28 but now the M· gave him a spiritual name
glorified
a 47– 5 After gaining the true idea of their glorified M·,
had taught
a 34–19 understood better what the M· had taught.
healed the sick
s 147–24 Our M· healed the sick, practised
f 210–12 the M· healed the sick, gave sight to the blind,
his
a 47–17 infinite distance between Judas and his M·.
48–22 would have smitten the enemies of his M·,
language of the
o 355–10 C. S. says, in the language of the M·,

Master
Lord and
m 67–21 our Lord and M· healed the sick,
b 317–21 Our Lord and M· presented himself to
often refused
o 350–16 The M· often refused to explain his words,
our
pr 3–29 censure our M· pronounces on hypocrites.
4– 6 To keep the commandments of our M·
6–31 The strong language of our M· confirms this
16– 7 Our M· taught his disciples one brief prayer,
16– 8 Our M· said, "After this manner— Matt. 6 : 9.
a 19–26 teachings and practice of our M·
25–30 our M· worked and suffered to bestow
26–28 Our M· taught no mere theory, doctrine, or
35–28 the draught our M· drank and commended
39– 1 Meekly our M· met the mockery of his
40–26 all men should follow the example of our M·
41– 6 Like our M·, we must depart from
45– 6 Our M· fully and finally demonstrated
sp 85–20 Our M· rebuked the lack of this power
94–18 our M· confirmed his words by his works.
94–24 Our M· easily read the thoughts of mankind,
94–28 Our M· read mortal mind on a scientific basis,
s 117–15 Our M· taught spirituality by similitudes
138–27 Our M· said to every follower :
147–24 Our M· healed the sick, practised
ph 192–28 following the example of our M·
f 228–20 If we follow the command of our M·,
241–21 Our M· said, "If ye love me,— John 14 : 15.
242–31 show the way our M· trod,
252– 1 our M· said, "If a kingdom be — Mark 3 : 24.
b 271–20 Our M· said, "But the Comforter— John 14 : 26.
272–14 shows the care our M· took not to impart to dull
314– 8 Our M· gained the solution of being,
315– 3 That saying of our M·, . . . separated him from
333–13 The proper name of our M· in the Greek
o 342–27 our M· says, "By their fruits— Matt. 7 : 20.
349– 7 our M· annulled material law
352– 5 Our M· declared that his material body
355–16 according to the commands of our M·,
355–29 proved to be such by our M·
p 382–21 This verifies the saying of our M· :
399–29 Our M· asked : "How can one— Matt. 12 : 29.
400–31 Even our M· felt this.
428– 7 to prove the words of our M· :
429–28 have faith in all the sayings of our M·,
t 463–24 Our M· treated error through Mind.
r 494–30 Our M· cast out devils (evils) and healed the
495– 8 classify sickness and error as our M· did,
g 509– 4 Our M· reappeared to his students,
539–21 this falsity is exposed by our M·
ap 565–15 brief history in the earthly life of our M· ;
gl 598 8 This shows how our M· had constantly to
our blessed
ap 571– 8 It requires the spirit of our blessed M·
our great
s 126–28 teachings and demonstrations of our great M·
149– 1 although our great M· demonstrated
promised by the
s 123–23 as promised by the M·.
150– 9 This coming, as was promised by the M·,
their
a 24–30 enabled their M· to triumph over the grave,
33– 9 Their M· had explained it all before,
33–13 their M· was about to suffer violence
47–27 The disciples' desertion of their M·
49– 5 caused the disciples to say to their M· :
s 136–29 apprehended their M· better than did others ;
b 271–15 divine Science, which their M· demonstrated
work of the
s 136 23 and the great work of the M·,

a 28– 4 If the M· had not taken a student
46–13 M· said plainly that physique was not Spirit,
47–19 He knew that the great goodness of that M·
sp 75–18 the M· would have stood on the same plane
s 137– 8 Yearning to be understood, the M· repeated,
b 286– 9 The M· said, "No man cometh— John 14 : 6.
317–31 so long as the M· remained an
master
as its
p 419–16 Meet every adverse circumstance as its m·.
Mind is the
p 393– 9 Mind is the m· of the corporeal senses,
not the
b 304–12 sorrow is not the m· of joy ;
of a feast
a 32– 7 an ancient custom for the m· of a feast
of ceremonies
m 64– 9 on most occasions to be the m· of ceremonies.
of chords
b 304–25 To be m· of chords and discords,
of death
b 316–19 thus proved that Truth was the m· of death.

master

of hate
　a 44– 9　He proved . . . Love to be the *m·* of hate.
of sin
　f 229– 1　If Mind is not the *m·* of sin, sickness,
or ruler
　gl 590–16　has the inferior sense of *m·*, or ruler.
our
　pr 9–23　divine control of Spirit, in which Soul is our *m·*,
their
　a 52– 3　their *m·* was matter.
unreal
　f 226–23　years of servitude to an unreal *m·*
was Spirit
　a 52– 2　His *m·* was Spirit ;

　m 62– 6　the child can meet and *m·* the belief in
　sp 90–25　sets man free to *m·* the infinite idea.
　ph 197–16　We should *m·* fear, instead of cultivating it.
　f 216–23　evil would appear to be the *m·* of good,
　p 369– 7　in that proportion does man become its *m·*.
　392– 1　you *m·* fear and sin through divine Mind ;
　392–22　Your decisions will *m·* you,
　395– 8　leaving Soul to *m·* the false evidences of
　404–25　increases his ability to *m·* evil
　405– 5　C. S. commands man to *m·* the propensities,
　415–15　till it can *m·* an erroneous belief.
　423– 1　The belief that he has met his *m·* in matter
　426–20　It will *m·* either a desire to die or a dread of
　428–26　through Christ and C. S., we must *m·* sin and death.

mastered

　a 44–10　He met and *m·* on the basis of C. S.,
　p 427–11　must be met and *m·* by Science,
　427–30　The dream of death must be *m·* by Mind

Master's

　pr 15–23　The *M·* injunction is, that we pray in secret
　a 26–24　precious import of our *M·* sinless career
　27–27　never truly understood their *M·* instruction.
　28–24　worthy to unloose the sandals of thy *M·* feet !
　33– 4　anticipating the hour of their *M·* betrayal,
　35– 4　wakened by their *M·* voice,
　46– 1　not . . . advanced fully to understand their *M·*
　s 130–23　our *M·* love for little children,
　139– 2　It was our *M·* theology which the
　145–32　Our *M·* first article of faith
　f 233–23　To reveal this truth was our *M·* mission
　b 317– 8　will drink of his *M·* cup.
　334–15　continued until the *M·* ascension,
　o 349– 8　We propose to follow the *M·* example.
　350– 6　To understand all our *M·* sayings
　354–14　proofs that their *M·* religion can
　p 363–19　the *M·* question to Simon the Pharisee ;
　t 443–12　our motto should be the *M·* counsel,

masters

　pr 14– 5　We cannot "serve two *m·*." — *Matt.* 6 : 24.
　ph 167–11　We cannot serve two *m·*
　f 201– 6　"No man can serve two *m·*." — *Matt.* 6 : 24.
　216–16　makes the nerves, . . . servants, instead of *m·*.
　228–22　but we shall be *m·* of the body,
　p 407– 6　Man's enslavement to the most relentless *m·*
　ap 569–12　*m·* his mortal beliefs, animality, and hate,

mastery

　ph 166–30　but when Mind at last asserts its *m·*
　198– 8　the disease that is gaining the *m·*,
　p 406–29　destroyed only by Mind's *m·* of the body.

match

　ph 185–15　to *m·* the divine Science of immortal Mind,

material

accompaniments
　sp 78–16　Spiritualism with its *m·* accompaniments
　b 310– 8　but without *m·* accompaniments.
age
　a 36–15　The earthly price of spirituality in a *m·* age
　sp 98– 9　Christianity is misinterpreted by a *m·* age,
　o 350–17　because it was difficult in a *m·* age to
　g 546–23　C. S. is dawning upon a *m·* age.
application
　p 421–29　or by employing a single *m·* application
art
　a 44–22　a method of surgery beyond *m·* art,
base
　p 422–16　and moral chemistry changes the *m·* base
basis
　b 268– 6　Belief in a *m·* basis, from which may be deduced
　307–27　Man was not created from a *m·* basis,
　319– 6　To calculate . . . from a *m·* basis,
　o 351– 7　if we plant ourselves on a *m·* basis.
　p 402– 9　its corporeal, structural, and *m·* basis,
　g 546–14　as starting from an idea of good on a *m·* basis.
　547–16　Darwin's theory of evolution from a *m·* basis
　552–19　thought, loosened from a *m·* basis

material

being
　ph 172–11　in this supposed chain of *m·* being.
　172–15　If man was first a *m·* being, he must
belief
　a 20–24　*M·* belief is slow to acknowledge what the
　ph 192–11　a *m·* belief, a blind miscalled force,
　194–16　would presuppose man, . . . a mortal in *m·* belief.
　f 216–31　Give up your *m·* belief of mind in matter,
　c 258– 6　*m·* belief in a physical God and man.
　258– 8　proves the falsity of *m·* belief.
　b 286–31　comprised in human *m·* belief,
　289–25　spiritual fact and the *m·* belief of things
　o 352– 6　a mortal and *m·* belief of flesh and bones,
　p 368–23　and the *m·* belief in them disappears
　425–24　Correct *m·* belief by spiritual understanding,
　r 481–18　this growth of *m·* belief, of which it is said :
　g 508– 1　to fall to the level of a human or *m·* belief,
　545– 8　should so improve *m·* belief by thought
　ap 568– 3　ever since error would establish *m·* belief,
　gl 580– 6　not the image and likeness of good, but a *m·* belief,
　589–23　JUDAH. A corporeal *m·* belief
　593–11　*m·* belief yielding to spiritual understanding.
beliefs
　a 19–15　brought to *m·* beliefs not peace, but a
　43–29　*m·* beliefs about life, substance, and
　sp 88–13　they are mortal *m·* beliefs.
　96–13　The breaking up of *m·* beliefs may seem to
　s 130–16　would disabuse the human mind of *m·* beliefs
　130–17　and these *m·* beliefs must be denied
　ph 186– 5　C. S. destroys *m·* beliefs through the
　f 242– 2　mortals put off their *m·* beliefs
　c 257–17　would translate spiritual ideas into *m·* beliefs,
　b 276–25　*M·* beliefs and spiritual understanding
　318–18　Weary of their *m·* beliefs,
　o 346–29　*M·* beliefs must be expelled to make room for
　p 399–24　*m·* beliefs, springing from illusion.
　400–11　and abandon their *m·* beliefs.
　402–11　*m·* beliefs will not interfere with spiritual
　428–27　more apparent, as *m·* beliefs are given up
　g 542– 3　*M·* beliefs would slay the spiritual idea
　gl 583–16　rousing the dormant understanding from *m·* beliefs
blood
　a 25– 6　The *m·* blood of Jesus was no more efficacious
bodies
　sp 73–19　The belief that *m·* bodies return to dust,
body
　a 53–26　mortal errors which constitute the *m·* body,
　sp 72– 4　If a *m·* body . . . were permeated by Spirit,
　73–22　confined in a finite, *m·* body,
　73–24　when it is freed from the *m·* body,
　74–15　belief of having died and left a *m·* body.
　74–16　belief of still living in an organic, *m·* body.
　92– 1　erroneous . . . that man has a *m·* body
　ph 172–17　If the *m·* body is man, he is a portion of
　172–24　If the real man is in the *m·* body,
　177–12　of which the *m·* body is the grosser portion ;
　187–27　mortal *m·* body loses all appearance of life
　189–15　We call the body *m·* ; but it is as
　f 203–20　When the *m·* body has gone to ruin,
　208–25　A *m·* body only expresses a
　214–20　obey what they consider a *m·* body more than
　b 284–31　but neither . . . goes from *m·* body to Mind.
　285–16　belief that a *m·* body is man
　285–18　finite conception . . . of a *m·* body as the
　302– 3　The *m·* body and mind are temporal,
　303–17　illusion that life, . . . is in the *m·* body,
　o 352– 5　declared that his *m·* body was not spirit,
　p 376–18　the so-called *m·* body is a mental concept
　399– 4　but if the *m·* body causes disease,
　402–18　The *m·* body manifests only what
　416–16　The *m·* body, . . . is mortal mind,
　r 477–14　shows it be impossible that a *m·* body,
　g 526–30　Eden stands for the mortal, *m·* body.
　ap 576–17　Jesus spoke of his *m·* body as the temple
bounds
　g 550– 8　God cannot . . . be limited within *m·* bounds.
brain
　ph 189–16　the *m·* brain which is supposed to
cause
　f 211–18　nature of all so-called *m·* cause and effect.
　p 416–11　will tell you that the troublesome *m·* cause is
combinations
　p 399– 3　You say that certain *m·* combinations
concept
　b 297–17　The only fact concerning any *m·* concept is,
　334–16　*m·* concept, or Jesus, disappeared,
conception
　f 213– 9　apart from this mortal and *m·* conception.
　g 536–24　erroneous, *m·* conception of life and joy,
conceptions
　sp 87– 1　So is it with all *m·* conceptions.
　t 463– 9　detach mortal thought from its *m·* conceptions,

material

concepts
f 239–24   It forms *m·* concepts and produces
g 556– 4   mortal and *m·* concepts classified,

condition
sp 74– 4   return to a *m·* condition, . . . impossible
p 389– 5   every erroneous belief, or *m·* condition.
   410–15   The more difficult seems the *m·* condition

conditions
a 46–21   his exaltation above all *m·* conditions ;
   49–22   the Christ is not subject to *m·* conditions,
m 61–32   If . . . then its *m·* conditions can only be
   63– 8   nor does he pass through *m·* conditions prior to
s 127–32   false . . . that law is founded on *m·* conditions,
ph 182–21   the law which overcomes *m·* conditions
f 228– 1   and in defiance of all *m·* conditions.
p 368–30   destroy the belief in *m·* conditions.
   419–18   Think less of *m·* conditions and more of
g 553–12   circumstances which made *m·* conditions

consciousness
ph 196–13   a false sense or *m·* consciousness.
b 295–26   matter, named *brain*, or *m· consciousness*,

conservatism
p 364–19   sought the Saviour, through *m·* conservatism

contact
s 154–14   had not caught the cholera by *m·* contact,

creation
ph 177–15   Scriptural allegory of the *m·* creation,
g 522–24   in declaring this *m·* creation false.
   544– 1   introduces the record of a *m·* creation

cross
a 50–32   Not the spear nor the *m·* cross

darkness
g 504–20   not implied by *m·* darkness and dawn.

declaration
p 427–31   will waken from its own *m·* declaration,

definition
gl 579– 2   substitution of the spiritual for the *m·* definition

dependence
s 152–23   Every *m·* dependence had failed her

disappearance
a 43– 3   his *m·* disappearance before their eyes

drugs
s 146 18   truth divests *m·* drugs of their

earth
c 263–32   the mortal body and *m·* earth, are the

ecstasy
pr 7–17   Physical sensation, . . . produces *m·* ecstasy

effect
p 403– 9   believed that the misfortune is a *m·* effect.

effects
sp 78–22   through electric, *m·* effects?

element
ph 191– 7   include in that likeness no *m·* element.

elements
b 284–24   the more subtle and misnamed *m·* elements
r 475– 7   blood, bones, and other *m·* elements.
g 551–19   composed of the simplest *m·* elements,

embryo
r 476– 3   declares that man begins in dust or as a *m·* embryo.

error
f 252–11   mortal, *m·* error finally disappears,
b 291–31   is divested of all *m·* error.
   309– 8   He had conquered *m·* error
   315–23   spiritual Truth destroys *m·* error,

evidence
a 52– 7   *m·* evidence of sin, sickness, and death.
p 422–18   causing it to depend less on *m·* evidence.
gl 584–15   Any *m·* evidence of death is false,

evidences
p 428– 9   false trusts and *m·* evidences

evolution
g 547–19   *M·* evolution implies that the

existence
sp 74– 1   between so-called *m·* existence and spiritual
   82–10   they cannot return to *m·* existence.
   99–26   beliefs of *m·* existence are seen to be a
s 162–16   false beliefs of a so-called *m·* existence.
b 272–21   the ghastly farce of *m·* existence ;
   282–11   a belief in a . . . temporary *m·* existence
   282–12   Eternal Mind and temporary *m·* existence never
o 356– 4   *m·* existence affords no evidence of
p 371– 8   By . . . nothing is really understood of *m·* existence.
r 467–26   *a priori* reasoning shows *m·* existence to be
g 552–32   the origin of mortal and *m·* existence

expedients
t 443–22   If the sick find these *m·* expedients

fable
s 129– 8   by reversing the *m·* fable,

faith
ph 180–20   through the *m·* faith which they inspire.

fetters
f 249–29   It throws off some *m·* fetters.

material

flesh
b 321– 1   still clad in *m·* flesh,

form
c 258– 9   Man is more than a *m·* form with a mind inside,
b 280–26   instead of possessing a sentient *m·* form,
   293– 3   the least *m·* form of illusive consciousness,

forms
b 301–31   an unsubstantial dweller in *m·* forms,

foundations
g 535–10   the supposed *m·* foundations of life

fungus
s 160–30   Is man a *m·* fungus without Mind

germ
f 246 6   Man is by no means a *m·* germ

god
s 158–13   may correspond with that of its *m·* god, Apollo,
ph 187– 9   With pagan blindness, it attributes to some *m·* god

gods
f 237–26   They devote themselves . . . to their *m·* gods,

growth
m 68–28   it manifests no *m·* growth from molecule to

habitation
r 477– 6   Man is not a *m·* habitation for Soul ;

health-theories
p 388–17   ambiguous nature of all *m·* health-theories.

hearing
g 526– 9   Belief involves theories of *m·* hearing,

history
f 204– 4   false . . . that *m·* history is as real
g 547–27   not in *m·* history but in spiritual development.

hopes
m 66–12   sown in the soil of *m·* hopes,

hygiene
f 220– 5   the inefficacy of *m·* hygiene,
   222–20   he dropped drugs and *m·* hygiene,
t 453–31   never recommends *m·* hygiene,
r 484– 7   medication, *m·* hygiene, mesmerism,

hypotheses
b 273– 7   Deductions from *m·* hypotheses are not
g 552– 6   and all other *m·* hypotheses

illusion
r 484–21   Mesmerism is mortal, *m·* illusion.

intelligence
a 48– 1   a belief in any possible *m·* intelligence
g 534–16   mythological *m·* intelligence called *energy*

intelligences
gl 591– 3   belief in many gods, or *m·* intelligences,

investiture
sp 75– 6   to have a *m·* investiture,

knowledge
a 27–19   axe of Science at the root of *m·* knowledge,
sp 96–27   As *m·* knowledge diminishes and
f 214–22   All *m·* knowledge, like the original
b 317– 2   since *m·* knowledge usurped the
gl 581–18   Self-destroying error ; . . . *m·* knowledge.

law
a 29–21   put to silence *m·* law and its order of
s 118–26   The definitions of *m·* law, as given by
   148–26   claims to rule man by *m·* law, instead of
ph 168 22   in defiance of what is called *m·* law,
   173–20   measuring . . . human life by *m·* law,
   179–22   sustained by what is termed *m·* law,
   182–19   Obedience to *m·* law prevents full obedience to
f 209–27   based on the hypothesis of *m·* law
   229–17   This customary belief is misnamed *m·* law,
   253–27   obedience to a so-called *m·* law,
b 273–21   God never ordained a *m·* law to annul
   273–22   If there were such a *m·* law,
   328–21   and knowing that there is no *m·* law,
o 340 7   and our Master annulled *m·* law
   349– 9   We should subordinate *m·* law to spiritual law.
p 384– 4   depressing thought that we have transgressed a *m·* law
   387–10   nor can so-called *m·* law trespass
   388– 6   only because it knows less of *m·* law.
g 549–29   great observer . . . allows matter and *m·* law to

laws
a 27–32   according to certain assumed *m·* laws.
m 62–31   Because mortals believe in *m·* laws
sp 83–17   governed in general by *m·* laws,
s 148– 5   urged no obedience to *m·* laws,
ph 170–18   If there are *m·* laws which prevent
f 227–30   If God had instituted *m·* laws to govern
b 273–26   raised the dead in direct opposition to *m·* laws.
   307–28   *m·* laws which Spirit never made ;
   314–29   depending on doctrines and *m·* laws
p 389–23   Their belief in *m·* laws and in
   433–23   liver-complaint, which *m·* laws condemn as
r 484–12   What are termed natural science and *m·* laws

lie
ap 565–24   the *m·* lie made war upon the spiritual idea ;

life
pr 6–14   until belief in *m·* life and sin is destroyed.
a 52–20   understood the nothingness of *m·* life

material

life

a	53–29	he had not conquered . . . his sense of *m·* life,
sp	77–13	required for this dream of *m·* life, . . . to vanish
b	282– 4	and its opposite, the so-called *m·* life
	283–14	They insist that . . . is one and the same with *m·* life
	288–25	has no birth, no *m·* life, and no death.
o	354– 2	notion that there can be *m·* life,
g	531–29	The mythologic theory of *m·* life
	533–23	The belief in *m·* life and intelligence
	543–12	*m·* life, with all its sin, sickness, and
	550–11	to investigate what is miscalled *m·* life,
	552–17	this notion of *m·* life as all-in-all.
	556–23	of which mortal and *m·* life is the dream.

living

pr	14–25	separate from the belief and dream of *m·* living,

lotions

f	234– 1	*m·* lotions interfere with truth,

man

b	283–18	the structural life of the tree and of *m·* man,
	292–19	Explaining the origin of *m·* man
	300– 7	illustrates the illusion of *m·* man,
	301– 7	To himself, . . . *m·* man seems to be substance,
	303–23	belief that . . . *m·* man is the likeness of God
	337–23	The visible universe and *m·* man are the
	338– 9	The mortality of *m·* man proves that error has
o	356–24	Does God create a *m·* man out of Himself,
r	471–21	but every [*m·*] man a liar.'' — *Rom.* 3 : 4.
	491– 7	*M·* man is made up of . . . error,
	491–21	Science reveals *m·* man as never the real
g	532–12	condemns *m·* man and remands him to dust.
	532–31	first impression *m·* man had of himself was
	540–28	Cain is the type of mortal and *m·* man,
	543– 8	*m·* man is shut out from the presence of
	545– 5	according to the record, *m·* man was

means

ph	169–17	we should put no faith in *m·* means.
	182–24	using *m·* means, thus working against
b	319–10	the general faith in *m·* means
	327–28	mistake in seeking *m·* means for
p	394–24	Are *m·* means the only refuge from fatal
t	445–12	by recourse to *m·* means for healing.
r	489–18	How can man, . . . be dependent on *m·* means

medicine

s	146–13	*M·* medicine substitutes drugs for the power of
	158–12	The future history of *m·* medicine
f	226–18	scholastic theology, *m·* medicine and
p	404–30	neither *m·* medicine nor Mind

mentality

ph	173–11	matter manifests nothing but a *m·* mentality.
	185–30	a mortal consolidation of *m·* mentality
b	292–27	*m·* mentality, misnamed *mind,*

method

sp	78–18	needs no *m·* method for the transmission of
s	145–13	matters not what *m·* method one may
f	230–24	by drugs, hygiene, or any *m·* method.

methods

m	56– 5	Jesus' concessions. . .to *m·* methods were for the
s	145– 9	not between *m·* methods, but between
ph	170– 4	The discord which calls for *m·* methods
f	222– 5	mortal mind has its *m·* methods of working,
b	318–26	*M·* methods are temporary,
p	395–13	faith in sin and in *m·* methods of healing,
g	551–14	*m·* methods are impossible in divine Science
gl	597– 8	petitions for blessings upon *m·* methods,

mind

c	257– 9	belief in a bodily soul and a *m·* mind,
g	529–31	Adam, . . . stands for a belief of *m·* mind.

mindlessness

b	293– 4	the *m·* mindlessness, which forms no link

modes

ph	170– 5	exercise of faith in *m·* modes,

mortality

b	293– 1	this unreal *m·* mortality disappears

motion

s	118–22	modes of *m·* motion are honored with the

myth

g	523–12	*m·* myth, instead of the reflection of Spirit.

mythology

g	524– 1	idolatry which followed this *m·* mythology

names

ph	187– 7	material sense . . . gives them *m·* names,

nature

g	551–17	"What can there be, of a *m·* nature,

nothingness

o	345–28	*m·* nothingness, which Science inculcates,

observations

r	483–24	schools, which wrestle with *m·* observations

obstacle

a	45– 2	but Jesus vanquished every *m·* obstacle,

offering

g	540–31	he brings a *m·* offering to God.

organism

f	211–25	that the *m·* organism causes the

material

organization

ph	165–10	*m·* organization and non-intelligent matter.
p	429–19	If man did not exist before the *m·* organization
g	509– 4	dependent upon no *m·* organization.
	524–20	How then could a *m·* organization become the

origin

s	127–28	It has a spiritual, and not a *m·* origin.
g	534– 1	belief in the *m·* origin of man
	549–32	a belief in the *m·* origin of man,

origins

f	213–31	knowledge dipped . . . into belief in *m·* origins

outgrowth

ph	171–32	supposition that man is a *m·* outgrowth

pain

b	307–22	every sin or supposed *m·* pain

pains

a	39– 23	so-called *m·* pains and material pleasures

perception

g	527–15	It is plain also that *m·* perception,

person

pr	14– 2	regard omnipotence as a . . . *m·* person,

personalities

sp	79–14	resting . . . not on *m·* personalities,
	84–26	*m·* personalities called spirits,

personality

b	285– 7	What, then, is the *m·* personality which
	337– 5	*M·* personality is not realism ;
g	544–25	a *m·* personality is not this likeness.

physician

t	463– 1	The *m·* physician gropes among phenomena,

pinions

b	298–27	flying on spiritual, not *m·*, pinions.

plane

o	349–25	dwelling on a *m·* plane, material terms must be

pleasure

p	418– 4	destroying all belief in *m·* pleasure or pain.

pleasures

a	39–23	so-called material pains and *m·* pleasures

premises

s	164–12	systems based on *m·* premises
b	274–11	not mere inferences drawn from *m·* premises.

power

f	249– 8	no mortal nor *m·* power as able to destroy.
p	378–25	Sickness is not a . . . self-constituted *m·* power,

reasoning

s	124–11	a blind conclusion from *m·* reasoning.

remedies

pref	viii–17	by doctors using *m·* remedies ;
t	453–13	effects from the use of *m·* remedies

remedy

p	427–26	Called to the bed of death, what *m·* remedy

researches

g	549–20	Here these *m·* researches culminate

resistance

s	134–30	spiritual power over *m·* resistance.

routine

sp	96– 7	interruptions of the general *m·* routine.

science

s	123–30	C. S. differs from *m·* science,

seed

g	551–29	declares that the *m·* seed must decay in order to

self

a	20–30	put aside *m·* self and sense,

selfhood

sp	91–16	Absorbed in *m·* selfhood we discern . . . faintly
	91–18	The denial of *m·* selfhood aids the
r	476–22	which is outside of all *m·* selfhood.

sensation

pr	9–20	even the surrender of all merely *m·* sensation,
f	249–32	He is the direct opposite of *m·* sensation,
b	303–10	formed by Spirit, not by *m·* sensation.
	337– 3	as *m·* sensation, or a soul in the body,
r	482–12	identical with sense, with *m·* sensation.

sensations

sp	73–20	with *m·* sensations and desires,

sense

pr	7– 7	relinquishment of error deprives *m·* sense of
	9–24	*m·* sense and human will have no place.
	14–23	prayer of Soul, not of *m·* sense.
a	21–10	He constantly turns away from *m·* sense,
	30–24	between the offspring of Soul and of *m·* sense,
	30–27	If we have triumphed . . . over the errors of *m·* sense
	34–27	he would disappear to *m·* sense
	37–12	rarefy the atmosphere of *m·* sense
	41– 6	we must depart from *m·* sense
	44–31	power of Spirit to overrule mortal, *m·* sense.
	47– 4	They no longer measured man by *m·* sense.
sp	71– 4	a belief, an illusion of *m·* sense.
	72– 4	in other words, mortal, *m·* sense
	72–14	Mortal belief (the *m·* sense of life)
	75– 9	from the spiritual . . . back into its *m·* sense.
	81–26	inharmony resulting from *m·* sense hides
	85– 4	capacity of Soul, not of *m·* sense.
	92–20	a mere offshoot of *m·* sense.

material
sense

sp	95–30	*M·* sense does not unfold the facts of existence ;
s	108–26	false testimony of false *m·* sense,
	118–18	perverted by a perverse *m·* sense of law,
	121–14	man, left to the hypotheses of *m·* sense,
	122–16	another proof of the illusion of *m·* sense.
	122–24	To *m·* sense, the severance of the jugular vein
	123–15	replaces the objects of *m·* sense with
	125–16	man governed by Soul, not by *m·* sense.
	139–20	*m·* sense stole into the divine record,
	146–10	by which *m·* sense is made the servant
ph	187– 6	Here you may see how so-called *m·* sense
	194–30	His case proves *m·* sense to be but a belief
f	202– 8	so-called pains and pleasures of *m·* sense,
	208– 2	*M·* sense defines all things materially,
	215–23	reverses the evidence of *m·* sense.
	225–30	in bondage to *m·* sense, ignorant how to
	227–26	The illusion of *m·* sense, . . . has bound you,
	247–18	loveliness which transcend all *m·* sense.
	252–15	The false evidence of *m·* sense contrasts
	252–16	*M·* sense lifts its voice with the arrogance of
	253–12	erring, mortal, *m·* sense.
	253–15	Knowing the falsity of so-called *m·* sense,
c	255–13	In league with *m·* sense, mortals take
	256– 3	thought rises from the *m·* sense to the spiritual,
	256–25	A finite and *m·* sense of God leads to
	266–22	opposite persecutions of *m·* sense,
b	269–19	advantage over the . . . thoughts of *m·* sense,
	273–28	the false claims of *m·* sense or law.
	279–30	Pantheism, starting from a *m·* sense of God,
	283–17	is but the objective state of *m·* sense,
	288–12	conflict between . . . Science and *m·* sense,
	296– 8	and regenerate *m·* sense and self.
	296–11	The death of a false *m·* sense and of sin,
	297–22	contradicting the testimony of *m·* sense,
	298– 8	What is termed *m·* sense can report only
	298–10	To *m·* sense, the unreal is the real until
	298–15	*M·* sense expresses the belief that mind is
	299–18	Knowledge gained from *m·* sense is
	301–25	from the false testimony of *m·* sense,
	304– 3	based on a *m·* sense of things,
	304–23	If mortals caught harmony through *m·* sense,
	304–24	if time or accident robbed them of *m·* sense.
	304–27	Left to the decisions of *m·* sense, music is
	305– 2	subjected to *m·* sense which is discord.
	309– 5	and rebuked his *m·* sense,
	309–22	led to deny *m·* sense, or mind in matter,
	310–22	belief of the flesh and of *m·* sense which sins.
	310–29	God is not seen by *m·* sense,
	310–30	Spirit, which *m·* sense cannot
	310–32	These changes are the mutations of *m·* sense,
	311– 9	he can only lose a sense *m·*.
	311–24	law of Soul, which prevails over *m·* sense
	312– 1	whatever is learned through *m·* sense
	312– 4	That which *m·* sense calls intangible,
	312– 5	what to *m·* sense seems substance,
	318–12	We must silence this lie of *m·* sense
	323–22	towards Soul and away from *m·* sense,
	330–26	a delusion of *m·* sense,
o	353– 2	whatever seems real to *m·* sense, is unreal in
p	396–14	refutation of the testimony of *m·* sense
	416–18	has originated from this *m·* sense
	428– 5	resolves the dark visions of *m·* sense into
t	444–29	"children of men" in *m·* sense,— *Psal.* 14 : 2.
	447–17	When sin or sickness. . .seems true to *m·* sense,
r	471–19	by evil, by matter, or by *m·* sense,
	480–12	*M·* sense has its realm apart from Science
	481– 7	*M·* sense never helps mortals to understand
	481–30	it is *m·* sense, not Soul, which sins ;
	484–25	Science must triumph over *m·* sense,
	484–29	is *m·* sense a necessary preliminary
	485– 2	*M· sense* is an absurd phrase,
	488–17	the impossibility of any *m·* sense,
	489–29	Outside the *m·* sense of things, all is harmony.
	490–24	destroy all *m·* sense with immortal testimony.
	490–29	the mythical nature of *m·* sense.
	490–29	Sleep shows *m·* sense as either oblivion,
	491– 3	Animal magnetism thus uncovers *m·* sense,
g	504–29	*M·* sense is nothing but a supposition of
	505– 8	*m·* sense, is separated from Truth,
	510–12	turn away from a false *m·* sense.
	513– 8	To *m·* sense, this divine universe is dim
	530– 4	forever opposed to mortal, *m·* sense.
	532– 5	All human knowledge and *m·* sense
	532–17	pleasure, evolved through *m·* sense,
	532–26	first manifestation of the error of *m·* sense.
	534–27	The serpent, *m·* sense, will bite the heel of
	544– 8	from the *m·* sense of things, not from the
	548–24	*m·* sense of animal growth and organization,
ap	566– 7	from a *m·* sense of existence to the spiritual,
	572– 9	but whatever is of *m·* sense, or mortal,
	575– 5	plagues imposed by *m·* sense.
	577– 1	the *m·* sense of personality yields to the
gl	580–24	supposition that . . . Soul dwells in *m·* sense ;
	582–25	the testimony of what is termed *m·* sense ;

material
sense

gl	585– 7	To *m·* sense, earth is matter ;
	585– 9	spiritual evidence opposed to *m·* sense ;
	587–13	theories that hold mind to be a *m·* sense,
	591–27	MORTAL MIND. . . . A suppositional *m·* sense,
	593– 4	disappearance of *m·* sense before the
	597–18	in which a *m·* sense of things disappears,

senses

pr	15–16	close the lips and silence the *m·* senses.
a	32–26	he withdrew from the *m·* senses to refresh
	38–31	He taught that the *m·* senses shut out Truth
	46–29	and the *m·* senses saw him no more.
sp	75– 6	or the *m·* senses could take no cognizance of
	88–15	Beliefs proceed from the so-called *m·* senses,
	91–21	or through what are termed the *m·* senses.
	98–10	which the *m·* senses cannot comprehend,
s	120–10	if the *m·* senses indicate that he
	120–16	nor can the *m·* senses bear reliable testimony
	126–19	beyond the cognizance of the *m·* senses
	144–15	belongs to the so-called *m·* senses,
ph	167–12	nor perceive divine Science with the *m·* senses.
	189– 1	human or *m·* senses yield to the authority of
	200–23	These so-called *m·* senses must yield to
f	214– 6	confined to the evidence before his *m·* senses,
	214–10	The *m·* senses, like Adam, originate in matter
	228–13	his God-given dominion over the *m·* senses.
c	257–15	The *m·* senses and human conceptions would
	262–13	and rise above the testimony of the *m·* senses,
b	268–17	based on the false testimony of the *m·* senses
	269–21	testimony of the *m·* senses is neither
	269–27	knowledge gained through the *m·* senses
	273–10	reverses the false testimony of the *m·* senses,
	274– 9	the evidence of the *m·* senses.
	278– 5	The *m·* senses oppose this,
	278– 6	there are no *m·* senses, for matter has no
	284–16	Can Deity be known through the *m·* senses?
	284–16	Can the *m·* senses, which receive no direct
	287–27	The five *m·* senses testify to truth and error
	288– 5	and the testimony of the *m·* senses,
	294–15	This verdict of the so-called *m·* senses
	296–27	judges by the testimony of the *m·* senses,
	298–13	Spiritual sense, contradicting the *m·* senses,
	299–31	If man were solely a creature of the *m·* senses,
	303–31	evidence before the *m·* senses yielded to
	300–22	not more distinct nor real to the *m·* senses than
	306–26	amid the jarring testimony of the *m·* senses,
	309–14	power of Spirit over the *m·* senses ;
	317–26	the testimony of the *m·* senses and the body,
	318– 9	*m·* senses originate and support all that
	330–15	Neither . . . can be discerned by the *m·* senses
o	359–11	Even though you aver that the *m·* senses are
	359–16	and is not apparent to the *m·* senses.
p	390–13	dispute the testimony of the *m·* senses
	408– 8	throughout the entire round of the *m·* senses,
	412–17	must break the dream of the *m·* senses.
t	461–13	reverses the evidence before the *m·* senses
r	481–10	various contradictions of . . . by the *m·* senses
	489–31	Mortal belief would have the *m·* senses
	490–21	knowledge gained from the so called *m·* senses
g	505–19	mindless matter nor the so-called *m·* senses.
	525–28	false conclusion of the *m·* senses,
	530–19	and saying, through the *m·* senses ;
	543–17	the evidence before the *m·* senses.
	546–16	*m·* senses can take no cognizance of Spirit
	550–32	the *m·* senses must father these absurdities,
	551– 1	*m·* senses and their reports are unnatural,
gl	585–11	spiritual fact of whatever the *m·* senses
	589– 6	*m·* senses yield to the spiritual sense
	592– 8	the subjective states of error ; *m·* senses ;
	596– 2	which is unknown to the *m·* senses

senses'

s	122– 7	*m·* senses' reversal of the Science of Soul

sensuousness

pr	16–20	Only as we rise above all *m·* sensuousness

sight

a	35–18	when he rose out of *m·* sight.

significance

gl	598– 9	to employ words of *m·* significance

source

c	256–31	A mind originating from a finite or *m·* source
g	552–22	From a *m·* source flows no remedy for sorrow,

species

ph	172– 8	How then is the *m·* species maintained,

spiritualism

sp	77–27	would outgrow their beliefs in *m·* spiritualism.

staff

m	66– 6	teach mortals not to lean on a *m·* staff,

standpoint

o	351–30	thought to worship Spirit from a *m·* standpoint,
t	458– 8	from both a mental and a *m·* standpoint.
g	546–20	cannot. . .be interpreted from a *m·* standpoint.
	551–26	From a *m·* standpoint, "Canst — *Job* 11 : 7.

standpoints

ph	174– 9	rising above *m·* standpoints,

material

state
sp 77–19 to prolong the m· state
p 411–24 The mental state is called a m· state.

stratum
ph 185–28 the m· stratum of the human mind,

structure
ph 172–24 Brain, heart, blood, . . . the m· structure?
173–21 m· structure is mortal.
g 509–21 no more contingent now on time or m· structure
ap 576–12 no m· structure in which to worship God,

substance
b 278–17 admission that there can be m· substance
301–23 seems to himself to be m· substance,

substances
f 209–25 M· substances or mundane formations,

suffering
p 405–30 Belief in m· suffering causes mortals to

superstructure
gl 595– 9 m· superstructure, where mortals congregate

suppositions
p 368–18 no m· suppositions can prevent us from healing
gl 583– 3 m· suppositions of life, substance, and

surface
b 313–24 He plunged beneath the m· surface of things,

symbols
a 34–14 his commemoration through m· symbols

system
s 133–21 It was a finite and m· system,

systems
b 326–12 must forsake the foundation of m· systems,
p 394–18 the fallacy of m· systems in general,

tangible and
sp 75– 5 would need to be tangible and m·,

temple
b 314–16 they thought that he meant their m· temple

terms
s 115– 3 the inadequacy of m· terms for
115–10 translating m· terms back into the original
o 349–17 one is obliged to use m· terms
349–25 m· terms must be generally employed.

theories
s 125–19 m· theories about laws of health
ph 165–14 m· theories took the place of
f 213–12 M· theories partially paralyze this
b 339–21 so will our m· theories yield to spiritual ideas,
o 355–32 Strangely enough, we ask for m· theories

theory
s 152–12 Such errors beset every m· theory,
c 257–23 the m· theory of mind in matter
g 545–16 Error tills the whole ground in this m· theory,

things
pr 16– 1 A great sacrifice of m· things must precede
a 35– 5 turned away from m· things,
s 108– 8 show the falsity of all m· things ;
f 247–11 the beauty of m· things passes away,
b 331– 3 If life were in mortal man or m· things,
335–14 Things m· and temporal are insubstantial.
o 356–12 Understanding the nothingness of m· things,
g 506–29 finding names for all m· things,
510–26 resolving of thoughts into m· things.
gl 592–23 knowledge of the nothingness of m· things

thought
c 267– 1 Every object in m· thought will be destroyed,
o 356– 2 the m· thought must become spiritualized
t 460–12 to the m· thought all is material,
g 509–30 the m· thought of his fellow-countrymen :

universe
f 238– 5 as well as in the m· universe.
g 545–12 notion of a m· universe is utterly opposed to

unreality
f 228–11 and discord as the m· unreality.

view
g 521–25 the opposite error, a m· view of creation,
521–27 this m· view of God and the universe,

views
b 314–11 showed plainly that their m· views were

virus
ph 196–27 not from infection nor from contact with m· virus,

ways
f 218–21 lead only into m· ways of obtaining help,

world
a 28–17 Not a single . . . part of his nature did the m· world
sp 96–12 This m· world is even now becoming the arena
b 268– 1 In the m· world, thought has brought to light
t 451– 4 to come out from the m· world and be separate.
g 507–21 A m· world implies a mortal mind

a 24–24 the presentation, after death, of the m· Jesus,
m 69–10 as the false and m· disappears.
sp 71–27 are alike m· and physical.
73– 3 Spiritualism calls one person, . . . m·, but
76– 7 Life will be recognized as neither m· nor
83–22 contrary to C. S. to suppose that life is either m·

material

sp 85–26 seeking the m· more than the spiritual.
91–28 erroneous . . . that man is both mental and m·.
97–17 The more m· the belief, the more obvious its
99– 1 not m· but scientifically spiritual.
99–13 The ordinary teachings are m·
s 132–23 a m· and a doctrinal theory.
143–11 matter required a m· and human belief
144–11 The more m· a belief, the more . . . tenacious
152–29 skeptical as to m· curative methods.
155–24 in proportion as it puts less weight into the m·
160– 4 When mortals forsake the m· for the spiritual
ph 168–11 the m· so-called laws of health,
169– 2 change of belief from a m· to a spiritual basis.
170–29 description of man as . . . both m· and
171–29 intelligence and life are spiritual, never m·,
177–18 had the naming of all that was m·.
181–21 If you are too m· to love the Science of Mind
185–12 as m· as the prevailing systems of medicine.
188–16 the dreamer thinks that his body is m·
191– 8 a m·, theoretical life-basis
199– 5 since muscles are as m· as wood and iron
f 206– 8 M·; erring, human thought acts injuriously
208–26 only expresses a m· and mortal mind.
209– 9 m· and mortal body or mind is not the man.
214–15 spiritual sense, and not the m·, conveys the
216–28 When you say, "Man's body is m·,"
218– 4 the body is as m· as the wheel.
224–18 less m· than the Roman scourge,
231–15 no antagonistic powers . . . spiritual or m·,
233–18 can discern the face of the sky,— the sign m·,
246–13 As the . . . m·, the transient sense of beauty fades,
249–25 the dream that life, substance, and . . . are m·.
254–21 to abandon so fast as practical the m·,
c 255–14 That God is corporeal or m·, no man should affirm.
258–20 but the m· so-called senses have no
263– 5 creations of mortal mind are m·.
b 270–29 disease is mental, not m·.
273– 3 There is no m· truth.
273–29 m·, conflicting mortal opinions
274–20 which affirm that life, substance, and. . . are m·,
275–25 Our m· human theories are destitute of
277–22 the order of m· so-called science.
278–25 leads to the conclusion that if man is m·,
282–24 all that is m· is a m·, human, mortal thought,
285– 3 Man's individuality is not m·.
286–22 M· and temporal thoughts are human,
286–25 temporal and m· are not then creations of Spirit.
287– 3 but belong, with all that is m· and temporal,
287– 6 Error supposes man to be both mental and m·.
289–27 and therefore the m· must be untrue.
290– 7 will remain as m· as before the transition,
290– 8 still seeking happiness through a m·,
290–31 His body is as m· as his mind, and vice versa.
292–16 The so-called senses of mortals are m·.
293–13 The m· so-called gases and forces are
295– 9 would transform the spiritual into the m·,
301– 8 and therefore is m·, temporal.
301–31 presupposes . . . man to be m· instead of
306– 2 thought that they could raise . . . from the m·.
306–30 God's man, spiritually created, is not m·
307–18 says : . . . He has made man mortal and m·,
314– 1 no less m· until the ascension
314–23 Because of mortals' m· and sinful belief,
318–10 all that is m·, untrue, selfish, or debased.
322– 4 from a m· to a spiritual basis,
326–16 while loving the m· or trusting in it
328– 2 a spiritual sense, which silences the m·
334–13 the unseen and the seen, the spiritual and m·,
336–17 Immortal man is not and never was m·,
338– 7 both good and evil, both spiritual and m·
338–10 and conclusions of m· and mortal humanity.
o 345– 5 the likeness of Spirit cannot be m·,
349–30 all learning, even that which is wholly m·.
351–27 Israelites centred their thoughts on the m·
353–28 Mind is limitless. It never was m·.
360– 6 those which are both mental and m·.
360–14 which . . . the m· or the spiritual?
p 372–13 and then call his bonds m·
376–17 If the body is m·, it cannot, . . . suffer with
378–20 represented by two m· erroneous bases.
385– 8 The spiritual demand, quelling the m·,
396–28 man is spiritual, not m·;
397–24 no more m· in their waking hours than
398– 7 clear evidence that the malady was not m·.
399–18 constructs a machine, . . . and then calls it m·.
416–17 this mind is m· in sensation,
416–19 even as the body, . . . is m·.
427–14 dream that existence can be m·.
428–21 the life which is spiritual, not m·.
442–21 until the m·, transformed with the ideal,
t 458– 5 one spiritual, the other m·,
460–12 to the material thought all is m·,
463–28 it is a spiritual law instead of m·.

material
r 468–15 Therefore man is not *m·* ;
476–11 Hence man is not mortal nor *m·.*
477– 8 is seen in nothing imperfect nor *m·.*
477– 9 Whatever is *m·* is mortal.
478–25 is composed of *m·* human beliefs
479– 2 must have a *m·,* not a spiritual origin.
479– 7 if aught comes from God, it cannot be…*m·* ;
493–24 That man is *m·,* and that matter suffers,
g 504– 7 both spiritual and *m·*
507–30 inverts this appearing and calls ideas *m·.*
508–14 Gender is mental not *m·.*
521–20 but the continued account is mortal and *m·.*
528– 5 is solely mythological and *m·.*
531–11 will sometime rise above all *m·* and
536–29 the mortal and *m·* return to dust,
538– 9 the *m·* and spiritual, — the unreal and the real.
540–30 *M·* in origin and sense,
541–17 belief that life, substance, and . . . can be *m·*
543–18 If man is *m·* and originates in an egg,
544–28 *M·,* erroneous belief reverses
547–21 implies that the great First Cause must become *m·,*
547–28 relinquishes a *m·,* sensual, and mortal theory
550–16 contemplation of existence as *m·* and
553–16 why are his deductions generally *m·* ?
ap 561–20 *m·* and corporeal selfhood disappear,
563– 9 belief that substance, life, and . . . can be *m·.*
572–27 Not through the *m·* visual organs for seeing,
572–29 terrestrial or celestial, *m·* or spiritual?
573– 9 while to another, . . . the vision is *m·.*
yl 580– 3 Spiritual discernment, — not *m·* but mental.
587–10 a belief that . . . are both mental and *m·* ;
588–19 the belief that . . . are both mental and *m·.*

Material Court of Errors
p 440– 1 Your *M· C· of E·,* when it condemned

materialism
and sensualism
m 65–14 in the *m·* and sensualism of the age,
gross
sp 75– 9 This gross *m·* is scientifically impossible,
lion of
g 549–26 and beards the lion of *m·* in its den.
silent
pr 15–11 Lips must be mute and *m·* silent,
wanes
ap 562–21 as the night of *m·* wanes.

pref vii–16 the cold conventionality of *m·*
sp 85–27 His thrusts at *m·* were sharp, but needed.
ph 172– 7 *M·* grades the human species as
f 216– 9 Spirituality lays open siege to *m·.*
b 314–19 This *m·* lost sight of the true Jesus ;
p 416–20 This *m·* of parent and child is only

materialist
a 51–29 caused the selfish *m·* to hate him ;

materialistic
s 120–24 overthrows false evidence, and refutes *m·* logic.
132–16 and retained their *m·* beliefs about God.
ph 183– 3 laws of matter . . . demand obedience to *m·*
183–26 Truth casts out all evils and *m·* methods
187–19 mortal mind, the cause of all *m·* action
190– 8 This embryonic and *m·* human belief
196– 1 If *m·* knowledge is power, it is not wisdom.
198– 9 The *m·* doctor, though humane, is an artist who
b 268– 9 *M·* hypotheses challenge metaphysics to
298–22 and admit no *m·* beliefs.
316–28 casting out evils, spiritualizing *m·* beliefs,
317–24 To the *m·* Thomas, looking for the
g 553–15 Why, then, is the naturalist's basis so *m·,*

materialists
b 314–17 To such *m·,* the real man seemed a spectre,
p 389–22 *M·* contradict their own statements.

materiality
departure from
f 213–11 Every step towards goodness is a departure from *m·,*
destroy
g 545–10 should so improve . . . as to destroy *m·.*
evil and
b 277–11 evil and *m·* are unreal
evolved from
g 544–22 but these gods must be evolved from *m·*
ghost of
o 353–25 The grave does not banish the ghost of *m·.*
ignorance and
sp 77–26 would gradually rise above ignorance and *m·,*
lost much
b 295–21 one which has lost much *m·*
night of
o 354–23 The night of *m·* is far spent,
of the age
a 31–25 Referring to the *m·* of the age. Jesus said :

materiality
opposite of
ph 171– 4 discernment of the spiritual opposite of *m·,*
rule the
s 164–22 rule the *m·* miscalled life
self-imposed
ph 191–17 must free itself from self-imposed *m·*
superior to
t 444– 3 all must rise superior to *m·,*

m 62–32 this does not make *m·* first
sp 86– 9 misconception of it uncovered their *m·.*
ph 169–25 whatever good they may seem to receive from *m·.*
c 266– 4 *m·* giving place to man's higher
b 276 23 away from *m·* to the Principle of the universe,
293–17 Electricity is the sharp surplus of *m·*
299–13 never lead towards self, sin, or *m·,*
o 352– 9 To Jesus, not *m·* but spirituality, was the
360– 6 It is true that *m·* renders these
r 484–28 *Question.* — Is *m·* the concomitant of
g 533–21 *M·,* so obnoxious to God, is already found in
551–26 so long as it bases creation on *m·.*
ap 572–10 *m·* is the inverted image of spirituality.

materialized
b 288–24 Spirit is not, and cannot be, *m·* ;

materializes
pr 4–32 Whatever *m·* worship hinders man's

Material Law
p 441–13 *M· L·* is a liar who cannot bear witness

materially
m 69–24 "Do you teach that Spirit creates *m·,*
sp 78–21 Spirit is not *m·* tangible.
96–30 will be apprehended mentally instead of *m·.*
s 126–12 seems to have reversed it and repeated it *m·* ;
140– 7 Not *m·* but spiritually we know Him
140–17 only as we cease to worship *m·.*
148–16 Anatomy takes up man at all points *m·.*
ph 200–12 not formed *m·* but spiritually,
f 208– 3 Material sense defines all things *m·,*
213– 7 and then classifies it *m·.*
254– 9 To stop eating, drinking, or being clothed *m·*
c 259–24 God, Spirit, works spiritually, not *m·.*
b 303–13 both spiritually and *m·,*
o 350–31 In Jewish worship the Word was *m·* explained
p 401–15 mortal mind only feels and sees *m·.*
r 487– 8 and hearing spiritually than *m·.*
g 521–14 supposition that man is created *m·,*
527–27 but doing so *m·,* not spiritually,
528–20 *m·* rather than spiritually,
531– 5 error, — that mortal man starts *m·,*
557–23 as if he began *m·* right,
yl 585–26 the belief that the human race originated *m·*

materials
p 402–15 constructs . . . with this mind's own mortal *m·.*

Materia Medica
p 430–22 *M· M·,* Anatomy, Physiology,
431–14 the prisoner summoned Physiology, *M· M·,* and
431–15 *M· M·* held out the longest,
432–25 One of the prisoner's friends, *M· M·,*
432–29 changed the purpose of *M· M·,*
436–16 professed friends, *M· M·* and Physiology,
437–22 *M· M·,* Anatomy, Physiology,
438–29 we have heard *M· M·* explain how
439–10 frightening away *M· M·,* who was then
439–12 *M· M·* was a misguided participant in the
439–17 Scholastic Theology, *M· M·,* Physiology,
441–20 We further recommend that *M· M·*

materia medica
a 41–19 No ancient school of philosophy, *m· m·,* or
s 138–12 cast out neither by corporeality, by *m· m·,* nor
149– 5 Is *m· m·* a science or a bundle of . . . theories?

maternal
m 60–10 Therefore *m·* affection lives on
g 553–18 the *m·* egg never brought forth Adam.

mathematical
s 108–13 to multiply with *m·* certainty

mathematically
s 113–13 showing *m·* their exact relation to Truth.

mathematician's
t 453– 1 You do not deny the *m·* right to

mathematics
pr 3– 5 Who would . . . pray the principle of *m·* to
an 105–21 important to medicine as to mechanics or *m·.*"
s 113–14 De Quincey says *m·* has not a
113–27 like the method in *m·,* proves the rule by
128–29 The addition of two sums in *m·* must always
ph 195–17 natural history, chemistry, music, *m·,*
f 219– 6 In *m·,* we do not multiply when we
p 422– 1 and then calling the process *m·.*
g 546–31 If *m·* should present a thousand different

matrimony
 m 59– 1 *M·* should never be entered into without
  65–25 *M·*, . . . must lose its present slippery footing,

matrix
 f 250– 5 and suppose . . . mortality to be the *m·* of

matron
 ph 179–26 The sedulous *m·*— studying her Jahr

Matter
 p 440–12 disobedience to the so-called laws of *M·*
  441–19 decrees of the Court of Error in favor of *M·*,
  441–20 Spirit decides in favor of Man and against *M·*.

matter (*see also* matter's)
admit that
 ph 172–32 When we admit that *m·* (heart, blood, brain,
always surrenders
 g 552–30 *m·* always surrenders its claims when the
and death
 b 289–29 *M·* and death are mortal illusions.
and error
 ph 181–31 will incline you to the side of *m·* and error.
 o 347–26 The dream that *m·* and error are something
and evil
 g 583–23 *m·* and evil, which have no Principle ;
and its claims
 b 273– 1 *M·* and its claims of sin, sickness, and death
and its effects
 b 283– 8 *M·* and its effects— sin, sickness, and death
and man
 b 294– 8 If . . . *m·* and man would be one.
and material law
 g 549–29 and allows *m·* and material law to usurp the
and Mind
 b 270– 5 *M·* and Mind are opposites.
  270– 9 but one power,— not two powers, *m·* and Mind,
  293– 5 which forms no link between *m·* and Mind,
and mind
 s 150–19 would have one believe that both *m·* and mind
 b 274–26 The conventional firm, called *m·* and mind,
  274–28 imaginary copartnership, *m·* and mind,
  279–28 not two bases of being, *m·* and mind, but one
 r 477–10 man appears to be *m·* and mind
  491–17 The belief that *m·* and mind are one,
  492–30 theory, . . . there are two factors, *m·* and mind,
and mortality
 a 43–25 in defiance of *m·* and mortality,
 f 215– 9 *m·* and mortality do not reflect the facts of
and mortal mind
 b 293– 6 *M·* and mortal mind are but different strata of
and Spirit
 ph 171–18 believes himself to be combined *m·* and Spirit.
 f 216–31 both *m·* and Spirit, both good and evil.
 b 312–27 *m·* and Spirit, the finite and the infinite,
appertain to
 ph 182– 7 what are termed laws of nature, appertain to *m·*.
approaches its
 p 409– 5 the nearer *m·* approaches its final statement,
ascension above
 a 35–17 his spiritual and final ascension above *m·*,
assigns to
 s 123– 7 reverses the order of Science and assigns to *m·*
assume that
 s 119– 7 they assume that *m·* is the product of Spirit.
atheism of
 gl 580–27 disappeared in the atheism of *m·*.
based on
 ph 191–26 defines mortal man as based on *m·*,
basis of
 ph 195–13 We should forsake the basis of *m·* for
 b 316–30 resting on the basis of *m·*,
belief in
 s 116–17 even to the extinction of all belief in *m·*,
 gl 581–10 understanding of Spirit, destroying belief in *m·*.
belief of life in
 sp 74–10 When . . . the belief of life in *m·* is extinct,
  89–30 This incident shows that the belief of life in *m·*
belief that
  (*see* belief)
believes that
 p 375–10 believes that *m·*, not mind, has helped him.
believing that
 f 205–15 error of believing that *m·* can be intelligent
body and
 a 42–17 his final triumph over body and *m·*,
body as
 f 214–31 the body as *m·* has no sensation of its own,
called
 sp 80–24 over its substratum, called *m·*.
 b 274–26 The conventional firm, called *m·* and mind,
 p 374–13 state of mortal mind, though it is called *m·*.
calling it
 f 251–31 beliefs, which rob Mind, calling it *m·*,
call upon
 ph 173–28 and so continue to call upon *m·*

matter
can have no pain
 p 393–20 *m·* can have no pain nor inflammation.
can make no
 s 120–11 *m·* can make no conditions for man.
 f 253–19 *M·* can make no opposition to right
can never produce
 b 304–13 *m·* can never produce mind nor
cannot be inflamed
 p 414–32 *M·* cannot be inflamed.
cannot believe
 r 487–16 *M·* cannot believe, and Mind understands.
cannot be sick
 p 372– 1 *M·* cannot be sick, and Mind is immortal.
cannot be weary
 f 217–27 *m·* cannot be weary and heavy-laden.
cannot connect
 r 491–11 *M·* cannot connect mortals with the true
cannot perform
 r 478–22 *M·* cannot perform the functions of Mind.
cannot suffer
 ph 184–20 This is human belief, . . . for *m·* cannot suffer.
cannot take cold
 p 377– 2 mentally convince him that *m·* cannot take cold,
cannot talk
 p 391–20 Since *m·* cannot talk, it must be mortal mind
claims of
 f 242– 6 Denial of the claims of *m·* is a great step
 r 491–14 Spirit, which annuls the claims of *m·*,
concessions to
 a 33– 2 closed forever Jesus' . . . concessions to *m·*.
conclude that
 r 467–25 when we conclude that *m·* is the
condition of
 p 371– 1 to discover the condition of *m·*,
conditions of
 s 162–15 without the conditions of *m·*
consider
 s 119– 9 and consider *m·* as a power
control over
 r 482–23 enabled Jesus to demonstrate his control over *m·*.
create
 b 278– 2 nothing in Spirit out of which to create *m·*.
 g 504–27 Did infinite Mind create *m·*,
creations of
 b 287– 5 creations of *m·* must return to dust.
 g 523– 8 The creations of *m·* arise from a mist
deals with
 p 423–15 The matter-physician deals with *m·*
death and
 r 486–19 conditional upon death and *m·*,
deflections of
 b 305–21 the deflections of *m·* as opposed to
demand of
 g 524–30 Is Spirit, . . . ejected at the demand of *m·*?
dependency on
 b 335– 5 would reduce God to dependency on *m·*,
dependent on
 b 292–18 so-called life of mortals is dependent on *m·*.
  311– 4 carnal mind, dependent on *m·*
devoted to
 gl 582– 6 so-called mortal mind, devoted to *m·* ;
did not originate
 b 275– 4 This shows that *m·* did not originate in God,
direct line of
 ph 189–31 always in the direct line of *m·*,
disappears
 s 156–30 In metaphysics, *m·* disappears from the remedy
 c 264–21 *M·* disappears under the microscope of Spirit.
discords of
 s 155–23 to offset the discords of *m·*
display of
 b 317–32 Nothing but a display of *m·* could make
disregard of
 f 210–10 his disregard of *m·* and its so-called laws.
distinct from
 f 217– 9 Mind to be scientifically distinct from *m·*,
 b 335– 3 Spirit is distinct from *m·*
does not appear
 f 211–11 *m·* does not appear in the spiritual
does not enter
 b 269–12 *m·* does not enter into metaphysical premises
does not express
 f 223– 7 *M·* does not express Spirit.
does not inform
 p 389– 9 *M·* does not inform you of bodily derangements ;
doom of
 b 279– 6 The doom of *m·* establishes the conclusion
dream of
 g 532–28 error began and will end the dream of *m·*.
elsewhere in
 ph 190– 7 neither . . . is found in brain or elsewhere in *m·*
emerge gently from
 r 485–14 Emerge gently from *m·* into Spirit.

matter

enthrones
ph 186–31 it enthrones *m·* as deity.
p 394–12 and enthrones *m·* through error.
error or
b 293–27 self-destruction of error or *m·*
g 521–30 The history of error or *m·*, if veritable, would
evidence of
s 128–26 the so-called evidence of *m·*.
evil and
b 277– 9 Their opposites, evil and *m·*, are mortal error,
evil or
t 454–11 evil or *m·* has neither intelligence nor power,
exalts
s 148–25 Physiology exalts *m·*, dethrones Mind,
examined
b 274–31 *m·*, examined in the light of . . . disappears.
excludes
s 123–13 excludes *m·*, resolves *things* into *thoughts*,
explains away
b 278– 3 Divine Metaphysics explains away *m·*.
faith in
(*see* faith)
fallacy of
f 237–24 the fallacy of *m·* and its supposed laws.
false sense of
p 399–26 It is only a false sense of *m·*,
false views of
b 281–29 Our false views of *m·* perish
fettered to
sp 77–21 a so-called mind fettered to *m·*.
flesh and
b 320–22 the belief that man is flesh and *m·*,
forces of
s 124–28 Human knowledge calls them forces of *m·* ;
formation of
g 510–24 indicates a supposed formation of *m·*
form of
sp 73–16 electricity or any other form of *m·*,
s 145–27 the antagonism of one form of *m·*
159–28 how much . . . one form of *m·* is
159–29 allowing another form of *m·*.
gl 598–10 was indeed air, an etherealized form of *m·*,
forms of
s 145–27 towards other forms of *m·* or error,
ph 172–16 through all the forms of *m·*
c 263–32 The fading forms of *m·*,
forsaking
c 265–10 forsaking *m·* for Spirit,
gained from
sp 91–20 erroneous knowledge gained from *m·*
92–15 a knowledge gained from *m·*, or evil,
gives to
sp 83–19 and gives to *m·* the precedence over Spirit.
gorgeousness of
f 252–26 says : . . . enthroned in the gorgeousness of *m·*.
grasp of
a 28– 7 determination to hold Spirit in the grasp of *m·*
ground, or
b 338–28 from this ground, or *m·*, sprang Adam,
had no life
a 51–15 He knew that *m·* had no life
has no
ph 166– 1 for *m·* has no sensation of its own,
f 211–10 and that *m·* has no sensation
250–26 *m·* has no more sense as a man than
b 275– 1 *M·* has no life to lose, and Spirit never dies.
279– 7 no material senses, for *m·* has no mind.
282–16 *m·* has no place in Spirit,
o 346–23 because *m·* has no sensation,
p 368–25 Because *m·* has no consciousness or Ego,
401–13 since *m·* has no sensation
426–30 because *m·* has no life to surrender.
r 485– 3 for *m·* has no sensation.
489– 5 and that *m·* has no sensation.
489–26 because *m·* has no sensation,
gl 584–11 *M·* has no life, hence it has no real existence.
holding that
p 422–26 holding that *m·* forms its own conditions
inanimate
s 157– 7 never shares its rights with inanimate *m·*.
t 463–29 The sick are not healed by inanimate *m·*
included in
f 209– 1 and of other beliefs included in *m·*.
independent of
ph 200–11 and ever will be independent of *m·* ;
f 247–19 Comeliness and grace are independent of *m·*.
inert
p 383–32 notion that health depends on inert *m·*
385–32 from the body or from inert *m·*
r 484–17 Drugs and inert *m·* are unconscious, mindless.
in proportion as
p 369– 5 In proportion as *m·* loses to human sense

matter

instead of
ph 200– 5 the worship of God in Spirit instead of *m·*,
f 223– 5 illusion that he lives . . . in *m·* instead of Spirit.
b 271– 8 to heal the sick through Mind instead of *m·*.
285–26 and resort to *m·* instead of Spirit for the
307–18 out of *m·* instead of Spirit."
320–19 harmonious existence as image, idea, instead of *m·*
p 415–13 resorting to *m·* instead of to Mind.
430– 7 by resting upon Spirit instead of *m·*.
g 536–17 starting from *m·* instead of from God,
544– 6 Mind, instead of *m·*, being the producer,
irrespective of
p 423–19 Mind his basis of operation irrespective of *m·*
is a belief
ph 190– 3 while *m·* is a belief, ignorant of itself,
is an error
b 277–26 *M·* is an error of statement.
is appealed to
p 403–11 but *m·* is appealed to in the other.
is devoid of
r 480– 9 whereas *m·* is devoid of sensation.
is inert
f 253–21 for *m·* is inert, mindless.
is mortal error
r 468–12 Spirit is immortal Truth ; *m·* is mortal error.
is naught
s 109– 2 Mind is All and *m·* is naught
is non-intelligent
f 217–32 *M·* is non-intelligent.
r 478–21 *m·* is non-intelligent and brain-lobes cannot
is not a lawgiver
s 127–25 for *m·* is not a lawgiver.
is nothing
s 116–18 *m·* is nothing beyond an image in mortal mind.
is not intelligent
p 412–32 since *m·* is not intelligent and cannot
is not self-sustaining
p 372–22 *M·* is not self-sustaining.
is not sensible
p 399–26 since *m·* is not sensible.
is not sentient
b 285– 1 *M·* is not sentient
is represented
b 294–24 *m·* is represented as divided into intelligent
g 522–19 *M·* is represented as the life-giving
is temporal
b 277–30 *m·* is temporal and is therefore
is the falsity
s 127–19 It teaches that *m·* is the falsity, not the fact,
is the unreal
r 468–13 *m·* is the unreal and temporal.
is unknown
r 469– 2 What is termed *m·* is unknown to Spirit,
g 503–11 In the universe of Truth, *m·* is unknown.
law of
(*see* law)
laws of (*see also* **so-called laws of** *and* **supposed laws of**)
p 384–22 but if you believe in laws of *m·*
t 463–26 if by these are meant laws of *m·*,
less
f 249–28 night-dream has less *m·* as its accompaniment.
limited to
p 369–28 Limited to *m·* by their own law.
man and
b 270–11 intelligence, apart from man and *m·*,
manifest as
b 306–22 forms of mortal thought, made manifest as *m·*,
manifested in
r 489– 1 The less mind there is manifested in *m·*
man is not
r 475– 6 Man is not *m·* ; he is not made up of
man or
b 284– 4 If God were limited to man or *m·*,
medium of
s 140–19 Worshipping through the medium of *m·* is
Mind and
b 260– 4 the supposed coexistence of Mind and *m·*
270– 1 as reasonable as the second, that Mind and *m·*
g 555–22 as if man were the offspring of both Mind and *m·*,
mind and
(*see* mind)
Mind is not in
sp 71–20 and that immortal Mind is not in *m·*.
p 381–26 understanding that Mind is not in *m·*,
mindless
s 159–13 as if she were so much mindless *m·*,
g 505–11 apparent only as Mind, never as mindless *m·*
mind nor
sp 71–19 neither mortal mind nor *m·* is the image
ph 188– 4 It is neither mind nor *m·*.
Mind, not
a 54–16 and triumph over death through Mind, not *m·*.
s 128–27 Science relates to Mind, not *m·*.
142–27 then Mind, not *m·*, must have been the first

matter

Mind, not
f 208–25 Mind, not *m·*, is causation.
212–24 this He does by means of Mind, not *m·*.
c 256– 6 Mind, not *m·*, is the creator.
b 280–30 perpetuates these . . . through Mind, not *m·*.
r 485– 5 Mind, not *m·*, sees, hears, feels, speaks.
g 505– 9 divine Mind, not *m·*, creates all identities,

mind, not
an 105–13 Mortal mind, not *m·*, is the criminal
s 153–27 mortal mind, not *m·*, contains and carries the
ph 169–23 It is mortal mind, not *m·*,
176–28 The human mind, not *m·*, is supposed to feel,
p 375– 1 Hence it is mortal mind, not *m·*, which says,
399–22 is mortal mind, not *m·*.
419–14 If disease moves, mind, not *m·*, moves it ;
425– 2 Mortal mind, not *m·*, induces this conclusion

Mind over
a 44–11 the power of Mind over *m·*,
45–31 the supremacy of Mind over *m·*,
s 139– 5 the triumph of Spirit, Mind, over *m·*.

misnamed
p 387–25 a law of so-called mortal mind, misnamed *m·*,

modes of
ph 170– 3 Modes of *m·* form neither a moral nor a

mortality, or
sp 78–10 If . . . in rapport with mortality, or *m·*,

must be unknown
b 280– 1 In the infinitude of Mind, *m·* must be unknown.

must disappear
ap 572–18 seen and acknowledged that *m·* must disappear.

never called
s 143–10 The divine Mind never called *m· medicine,*

never created
b 335– 8 Spirit never created *m·*.

never endowed
p 378–27 God never endowed *m·* with power to

never entered
sp 76–11 Spirit never entered *m·* and was therefore

never formed
c 259–24 Brain or *m·* never formed a human concept.

never produces
b 277– 5 *M·* never produces mind.

never sustained
p 425–16 he learns that *m·* never sustained existence

no
sp 75–11 to infinite Spirit there can be no *m·*.
s 113–30 no *m·* in Mind, and no mind in matter ;
113–31 no *m·* in Life, and no life in matter ;
113–31 no *m·* in good, and no good in matter.
b 278– 7 In Spirit there is no *m·*,
298–29 no *m·* what their individualism may be.
r 475– 3 To infinite Spirit there is no *m·*,

no affinity with
ph 191–30 Mind has no affinity with *m·*, and therefore

no cognizance of
r 479–15 matter can take no cognizance of *m·*.

no good in
s 113–32 no matter in good, and no good in *m·*.

no life in
s 113–31 no matter in Life, and no life in *m·* ;

no mind in
s 113–30 no matter in Mind, and no mind in *m·* :

non-intelligence and
b 282–19 Mind cannot pass into non-intelligence and *m·*,

non-intelligence, or
b 336– 3 never passes into non-intelligence, or *m·*.

non-intelligent
ph 165–11 material organization and non-intelligent *m·*.
c 257–14 the supposed substance of non-intelligent *m·*.

no place in
b 282–17 and Spirit has no place in *m·*.

no sensation in
f 237– 4 "There is no sensation in *m·*."

not a condition of
s 120–15 Health is not a condition of *m·*, but of Mind ;

not expressed in
s 119–18 spiritual and is not expressed in *m·*.

not found in
o 344– 9 God's likeness is not found in *m·*,

nothing is
s 113–18 God, Spirit, being all, nothing is *m·*.

nothingness of
r 480– 2 in C. S., the nothingness of *m·* is recognized.
497–23 and the nothingness of *m·*.

not the father of
c 257–20 the Father Mind is not the father of *m·*.

not through
g 520–24 God creates all through Mind, not through *m·*,

obtains in
p 409– 2 You may say : "But if disease obtains in *m·*,

of fact
r 486–32 as a *m·* of fact, these calamities often

on the side of
ph 168– 7 Whatever influence you cast on the side of *m·*,

matter

operation of
s 150–29 by the operation of *m·*,
ph 171–20 ejection by the operation of *m·*.

or body
ph 177–10 *M·*, or body, is but a false concept of

order of
g 552–26 order of *m·* to be the order of mortal mind.

or dust
b 338–18 *m·* or dust was deemed the agent of Deity

or error
s 145–27 towards other forms of *m·* or error,
f 206– 3 no consciousness of the existence of *m·* or error.

organic
b 296–12 not the death of organic *m·*,

or Mind
g 531–25 Which institutes Life,— *m·* or Mind?

possesses neither
s 108– 6 *m·* possesses neither sensation nor life ;

predicated of
s 144– 9 mortal beliefs . . . are mainly predicated of *m·*,

property of
g 510–28 and not a vitalizing property of *m·*.

proved that
f 229– 2 already proved that *m·* has not destroyed them,

regarding
b 277–29 Nothing we can say . . . regarding *m·* is immortal,

reliance on
ph 179–29 sowing the seeds of reliance on *m·*,

required
s 143–11 *m·* required a material and human belief

residence in
p 432– 8 messages from my residence in *m·*,

restricted to
an 105– 8 to admit that . . . law is restricted to *m·*,

rises above
s 153–12 the most potent rises above *m·* into mind.

sections of
s 122–11 sections of *m·*, such as brain and nerves,

seed of
g 535– 3 yea, the seed of Spirit and the seed of *m·*,

seems to be
s 123–12 *m·* seems to be, but is not.

senseless
f 202–29 as if senseless *m·* . . . had more power than

sifted through
ph 171–19 believes that Spirit is sifted through *m·*,

slave of
f 221–26 when, still the slave of *m·*, he thought

so-called
sp 97– 6 so-called *m·* resembles its essence, mortal mind,
f 217–23 control which Mind has over so-called *m·*,
c 257– 4 If *m·*, so-called, is substance,
gl 586–17 between Spirit and so-called *m·*.

so-called law of
p 382–18 Must we not then consider the so-called law of *m·* a

so-called laws of (see also **laws of**)
sp 81–25 despite the so-called laws of *m·*,
ph 171–25 The so-called laws of *m·* are nothing but
182–19 must supersede the so-called laws of *m·*.
183– 2 but the so-called laws of *m·* would render
f 207–12 nor are the so-called laws of *m·* primary,
b 273–16 The so-called laws of *m·* and of medical science
274–16 they supersede the so-called laws of *m·*.
302–24 not by the so-called laws of *m·*.

Soul and
f 215– 7 Soul and *m·* are at variance

Spirit and
(see **Spirit**)

Spirit or
b 324–11 understanding or belief, Spirit or *m·*.
o 360–17 Either Spirit or *m·* is your model.

standpoints of
sp 77–32 and they return to their old standpoints of *m·*.

striking the ribs of
o 360–20 striking the ribs of *m·*

supposed laws of (see also **laws of**)
p 382– 1 he annulled supposed laws of *m·*,
430–14 the supposed laws of *m·* and hygiene,
r 484–10 supposed laws of *m·* yield to the law of Mind.

sympathy with
a 21–25 Being in sympathy with *m·*, the worldly man is

termed
gl 584–23 the opposite of mind, termed *m·*,
594– 6 opposite of Spirit, or good, termed *m·*, or evil ;

terms
ap 573–11 what the human mind terms *m·*

testimony of
p 437–14 the testimony of *m·* respected ;

think of
o 350– 1 They think of *m·* as something

this
r 476– 9 will cease to claim . . . that this *m·* is man.

matter

through
sp 72–18   Spirit is not made manifest through *m*,
ph 171–19   believes that Spirit is sifted through *m*,
   173–13   Neither . . . is obtainable through *m*.
f 232–12   theories . . . healing possible only through *m*.
p 384–10   If man seems to incur the penalty through *m*,
   408–19   thus reaching mortal mind through *m*?
r 467–28   We cannot interpret Spirit, Mind, through *m*.
g 532–30   demands that *mind* shall see . . . through *m*,

to suppose that
sp 73–26   It is a grave mistake to suppose that *m* is
f 208–14   it is absurd to suppose that *m* can

tributary to
s 122–32   and mind therefore tributary to *m*.

trusting
s 146– 8   By trusting *m* to destroy its own discord,

veil of
a 41– 1   must be cast beyond the veil of *m*

versus Mind
b 319– 3   disease as error, as *m versus* Mind,

was shown
b 321–12   *M* was shown to be a belief only.

we define
b 278–29   We define *m* as error, because it is the

what is termed
s 114–29   Science shows that what is termed *m* is but the
ph 173–11   What is termed *m* manifests nothing but
   177–21   qualities and effects of what is termed *m*,
f 210–25   What is termed *m*, being unintelligent, cannot
p 384– 2   Can matter, or what is termed *m*, either feel or
   417–12   what is termed *m* cannot be sick ;
r 409– 2   What is termed *m* is unknown to Spirit,

where is
f 223– 9   what and where is *m*?

whole
b 340– 7   the conclusion of the whole *m* :— *Eccl.* 12 : 13.
   340–10   Let us hear the conclusion of the whole *m* :

will disappear
sp 97–27   indicates that all *m* will disappear before the

without mind
s 153–17   for *m* without mind is not painful.

would be identical
b 300–25   *m* would be identical with God.

you employ
ph 181–11   for that reason, you employ *m* rather than

---

pref viii–11   and *m* is Spirit's opposite.
pr 14–11   governed by divine Love,— by Spirit, not by *m*.
   14–14   neither in nor of *m*,
a 27–15   The I — the Life, . . . is not in *m*
   27–21   pantheism,— that God, or Life, is in or of *m*.
   27–31   endeavored to hold him at the mercy of *m*
   35– 8   sensuousness, or the burial of mind in *m*
   41– 3   this advance beyond *m* must come
   47– 6   leaning no longer on *m*, but on the
   52– 3   their master was *m*.
m 62 21   must not attribute more . . . intelligence to *m*,
   69–25   therefore *m* is out of the question
sp 71–14   a formation of thought rather than of *m*.
   73– 9   belief that . . . can control another man, as *m*,
   75– 2   mistaken assumption that man dies as *m*
   76–12   and was therefore never raised from *m*.
   76–14   no longer commune with *m* ; neither can he
   76–17   characterized by the divine Spirit . . . not *m*.
   78–25   not in the medley where *m* cares for *m*,
   80–25   which convulses its substratum, *m*.
   80–32   belief . . . that *m* is intelligent.
   81– 3   as there is to show the sick that *m* suffers
   86– 5   it was not *m*, but mortal mind, whose touch
   88–12   Thoughts, proceeding . . . from *m*,
   89–25   *M* is neither intelligent nor creative.
   90–10   the thought that there can be substance in *m*,
   91–32   erroneous postulate is, that *m* is intelligent,
   92– 3   erroneous postulate is, that *m* holds
   92– 4   postulate . . . that *m* is not only capable of
   94– 3   likeness of Himself, . . . not of *m*.
   97–11   The more destructive *m* becomes,
   97–12   until *m* reaches its mortal zenith
   97–19   divine Spirit, supreme in its domain, dominates all *m*,
an 103–20   false belief that mind is in *m*,
   105–10   Can *m* commit a crime?
   105–11   Can *m* be punished?
s 108–26   false material sense, of mind in *m* ;
   108–28   this same so-called mind names *m*,
   119– 1   When we endow *m* with vague
   119– 3   cannot really endow *m* with what it
   119– 7   presuppose the . . . self-government of *m*,
   119–12   and regard God as the creator of *m*,
   120– 3   never understand this while we admit . . . mind in *m*,
   120–26   deduced from supposed sensation in *m*
   122–13   seats of pain and pleasure, from which *m*
   124– 9   seeks to find life and intelligence in *m*,

matter

s 125–31   *m* will finally be proved nothing more than
   127–21   have — as *m* — no intelligence, life, nor
   127–31   false hypotheses that *m* is its own lawgiver,
   129–12   belief in the intelligence of *m*,
   142–30   It could not have been *m*,
   148–14   and place mind at the mercy of *m*
   148–20   deal . . . with *m*, calling that *man* which
   150–29   doctrine of the superiority of *m* over Mind,
   157–14   the substratum . . . which we call *m* ;
   157–23   *M* is not self-creative,
   158–26   Drug-systems are quitting their hold on *m*
   158–28   *M* is going out of medicine :
   159 13   as if *m* were the only factor to be consulted
   159–24   medical schools would learn . . . of man from *m*
159–26, 27   how much . . . health, *m* is permitting to *m*,
   161– 5   mortal mind, and not *m*, burns it.
   161–31   looked as deeply . . . into mind as into *m*.
   164–23   miscalled life in the body or in *m*.
ph 166–29   conceded to be with *m* by most
   170–32   *M*, which . . . claims to be a creator,
   172– 8   grades the human species as rising from *m*
   172–18   If the material body is man, he is a portion of *m*,
   172–20   the belief that there is . . . Life in *m*
   173–14   *M* is Spirit's contrary,
   177–17   erroneous theory of . . . intelligence in *m*,
   178–19   acting from the basis of sensation in *m*,
   178–24   the belief of heredity, of mind in *m*
   180–13   the ground that all causation is *m*,
   181– 3   Before deciding that the body, *m*, is
   181– 5   Can *m* speak for itself,
   181– 6   *M*, which can neither suffer nor enjoy,
   182–22   puts *m* under the feet of Mind.
   187–22   governed by this so-called mind, not by *m*.
   188–12   dream of pain and pleasure in *m*,
   189–27   belief of inanimate, and then of animate *m*.
   189–31   *m* is the subjective condition of mortal mind.
   191– 2   *M* is not the organ of infinite Mind.
   194– 2   Spirit shares not its strength with *m*
   198– 3   than the substratum, *m*.
   198–32   If *m* were the cause of action,
f 203– 5   shows that *m* can neither heal nor make sick,
   203–21   overtaxed the belief of life in *m*
   203–23   believe that . . . Soul, escapes from *m*
   204–30   belief that God lives in *m* is pantheistic.
   204–31   The error, which says . . . Mind is in *m*,
   205– 3   mortals . . . will lean on *m* instead of Spirit,
   205– 8   error of believing that there is life in *m*,
   205–10   *m* has neither intelligence, life, nor
   205–31   into the scale, not of Spirit, . . . but of *m*.
   206–17   Spirit, not *m*, being the source of supply.
   208–16   and leaves the remedy to *m*.
   209 28   hypothesis of . . . intelligence resident in *m*,
   211– 8   sensations of a so-called mortal mind or of *m*.
   211–24   If it is true . . . that *m* has intelligence,
   212 11   in the mortal mind, not in *m*.
   214–11   The material senses, . . . originate in *m*
   214–18   We bow down to *m*, . . . like the pagan
   216–31   Give up your material belief of mind in *m*,
   218–25   Resist the temptation to believe in *m* as
   219– 9   No more can we say . . . that *m* governs,
   222–14   so-called pleasures and pains of *m*.
   222–29   for dyspepsia consult *m* not at all,
   223– 1   belief that life and intelligence are in *m*,
   229–31   The remedy is Truth, not *m*,
   232–23   referred man's harmony to Mind, not to *m*,
   234– 3   If we trust *m*, we distrust Spirit.
   237–27   belief in the life and intelligence of *m*,
   239–19   *m* is then submitting to Spirit.
   240–13   suppose Mind to be governed by *m*
   243 20   Neither immortal and unerring Mind nor *m*,
   243–23   *m* has neither intelligence nor sensation.
   244–19   or springs from *m* into being,
   244–26   He does not pass from *m* to Mind,
   248–24   outline and deformity of *m* models.
   249–12   Mind is not the author of *m*,
   249–17   Whence then is soulless *m*?
   250– 3   suppose . . . mind to be in *m* and *m* to be a
c 257–10   governed by the body and a mind in *m*,
   257–23   theory of mind in *m* to be the antipode of
   261– 1   we find its opposite, *m*.
   261–21   Detach sense from the body, or *m*,
   262–12   efforts to find life and truth in *m*
   262–20   the supposed pain and pleasure of *m* cease
   262–31   Cause does not exist in *m*,
   264–17   Life is Spirit, never in nor of *m*,
   267– 3   start not from *m* or ephemeral dust.
   267–23   borrowed from a higher source than *m*,
b 268– 9   looking away from *m* to Mind as the cause
   269–29   theories I combat are these: (1) that all is *m* ;
   269–30   theories I combat . . . (2) that *m* originates in
   269–32   The first theory, that *m* is everything,
   270– 3   statements . . . (1) that everything is *m* ;
   275– 2   A partnership of mind with *m* would ignore
   275– 5   *m* is neither substantial, living, nor
   275–29   *m*, disease, sin, and death,

matter

b 276–32 but *m·* is ever non-intelligent
277–20 asserts that Spirit produces *m·* and *m·* produces
277–25 The unlikeness of Spirit is *m·*,
278– 1 Is Spirit the source or creator of *m·*?
278–12 That *m·* is substantial . . . is one of the false
278–16 we lose the consciousness of *m·*.
278–18 another admission, . . . that *m·* is self-creative,
278–23 belief of the eternity of *m·* contradicts the
278–25 if man is material, he originated in *m·*
278–30 *M·*, with its mortality, cannot be substantial
279– 7 *m·*, slime, or protoplasm never originated
279– 9 *M·* is neither created by Mind nor
279–17 that life and intelligence are in or of *m·*,
279–24 pantheistic belief that there is mind in *m·* ;
279–32 seeks . . . life and intelligence in *m·*.
281–18 mind supposed to exist in *m·* . . . is a myth,
281–28 Divine Science does not put . . . Soul into *m·*,
282–23 There is no inherent power in *m·* ;
284– 1 Are mentality, immortality, . . . resident in *m·* ?
284– 2 but dwells in finiteness, — in *m·*,
284– 2 that *m·* is infinite and the medium of
284–11 Is God's image or likeness *m·*,
284–12 Can *m·* recognize Mind?
284–13 Can infinite Mind recognize *m·* ?
285–29 seek to learn, not from *m·*, but from the divine
287–25 supposition that life, . . . and intelligence are in *m·*,
287–26 *M·* is neither a thing nor a person,
289–27 Life is not in *m·*.
289–28 it cannot be said to pass out of *m·*.
289–32 of Life, not of *m·*.
292–13 *M·* is the primitive belief of mortal mind,
292–15 To mortal mind, *m·* is substantial,
293– 8 The grosser substratum is named *m·*
293–10 is the illusion called a mortal, a mind in *m·*.
294– 4 human belief, . . . a unison of *m·* with Spirit.
294–12 error, saying : "*M·* has intelligence and
294–14 error, saying : . . . *m·* can kill man."
294–21 error that life and intelligence are in *m·*,
294–22 the pleasures and pains of *m·* to be myths,
295–18 but as *m·*, the glass is less opaque
295–26 The theoretical mind is *m·*, named *brain*, or
295–32 error theorizes that spirit is born of *m·*
295–32 error theorizes that spirit . . . returns to *m·*,
296–14 so-called pleasures and pains of *m·* perish,
298–16 the belief that mind is in *m·*.
300– 3 to draw . . . conclusions regarding life from *m·*.
300–23 therefore Soul is not in *m·*.
300–24 If Spirit were in *m·*,
300–27 theory that soul, spirit, intelligence, inhabits *m·*
301–20 the substance of Spirit, not *m·*.
302–10 The notion that mind is in *m·*,
302–12 sin, sickness, and death of *m·*,
302–18 illusion of any life, . . . as existent in *m·*.
303– 6 no power of propagation in *m·*,
307– 2 proceeded from and passed into *m·*.
307–12 says : . . . I will put spirit into what I call *m·*,
307–12 *m·* shall seem to have life
307–20 If we regard *m·* as intelligent,
308– 2 the belief that mind is in *m·*,
308–16 mortal sense of life, . . . as existent in *m·*
309–22 led to deny material sense, or mind in *m·*,
310– 3 fancies that it delineates thought on *m·*,
310– 4 but what is *m·* ?
310– 5 *M·* is made up of supposititious
311–12 so long as the illusion of mind in *m·*
311–15 false estimates of . . . mind as dwelling in *m·*,
311–18 dream of life and substance as existent in *m·*,
311–28 *M·*, sin, and mortality lose all supposed
312– 9 The senses regard a corpse, . . . simply as *m·*.
312–10 departure of a mortal's mind, not of *m·*.
312–11 The *m·* is still there.
312–13 yet you say that *m·* has caused his death.
312–24 premises, which cannot penetrate beyond *m·*.
315– 8 that *m·*, sin, and evil were not Mind ;
317– 4 knowledge . . . insisted on the might of *m·*,
317–18 his life is not at the mercy of *m·*.
317–25 Thomas, looking for the ideal Saviour in *m·*
318– 1 For him to believe in *m·* was no task,
318– 7 senses are saying that *m·* causes disease
318–20 the error — or belief that life is in *m·*
318–23 denies the error of sensation in *m·*,
318–25 and attempts to heal it, with *m·*.
319– 2 The delusion that there is life in *m·*
319–16 presuppose life and intelligence to exist in *m·*
321–20 and not a condition of *m·*,
322–27 belief in the supposititious life of *m·*,
327– 5 appetite nor passion, can exist in or of *m·*,
335– 9 nothing in Spirit out of which *m·* could be
338– 5 belief — that man originates in *m·*
338–20 when *m·*, . . . stood opposed to Spirit.
o 345–13 It is indeed no small *m·* to know one's self ;
346–24 pain in *m·* is a false belief,
350– 1 opponents of C. S. believe substance to be *m·*.
351–29 To them *m·* was substance,

matter

o 356– 8 *M·* is not the vestibule of Spirit.
357–31 Can *m·* drive Life, Spirit, hence,
358–4, 5 If God is at the mercy of *m·*, then *m·*
p 368–16 more faith in Spirit than in *m·*,
368–28 Admit the existence of *m·*, and you
368–30 Deny the existence of *m·*, and you can destroy
369– 1 Once let the mental physician believe in the reality of *m·*,
370–31 from error to Truth, from *m·* to Spirit.
372– 3 erroneous mortal belief of mind in *m·*.
372– 4 What you call *m·* was originally error in
372–16 He can neither . . . be subject to *m·*, nor
372–23 *M·* succeeds for a period only by
376–25 showing that it is impossible for *m·* to suffer,
378–20 drilling and drugging, adopted to cure *m·*,
379–31 the belief that mind is in *m·*,
384– 1 Can *m·*, . . . act without mind?
388–11 thought that they could kill the body with *m·*,
389– 7 not the nerves, not *m·*, but mortal mind,
391– 2 the plea of mortal mind, *alias m·*,
393– 8 a law of so-called mortal mind, not of *m·*.
393–18 Have no fear that *m·* can ache, swell,
393–29 Mind is not sick and *m·* cannot be.
396–21 as if *m·* could have sensation.
396–29 Soul is Spirit, outside of *m·*,
396–32 not by *m·* nor by the divine Mind.
398–24 reside in mortal mind, not in *m·*.
399– 5 can *m·* cure what *m·* has caused?
399–14 *m·* can return no answer to immortal Mind.
408–30 which we call sensation in *m·*
409– 1 Intelligent *m·* is an impossibility.
409– 4 formed by mortal mind and not by *m·*
409– 9 Unconscious mortal mind — *alias m·*, brain
409–17 its unconscious substratum, *m·*,
409–27 no right to say that life depends on *m·*
413– 2 Mind, does not produce pain in *m·*.
413– 8 Mind regulates . . . and *m·* does not.
414– 9 the impossibility that *m·*, brain, can control or
414–24 *m·* neither feels, suffers, nor enjoys.
417– 1 being is sustained by Spirit, not by *m·*,
418– 6 the error that life, . . . can be in *m·*.
420– 4 Love not hate, Spirit not *m·*, governs man.
422–31 he believes that . . . *m·* — governs the case.
423– 1 The belief that he has met his master in *m·*
423–18 the evidence which *m·* presents.
425–22 the less we acknowledge *m·* or its laws,
426–31 human concepts named *m·*, death, disease,
427–10 The belief that existence is contingent on *m·*
t 450–31 belief of life, . . . and intelligence in *m·*,
456–21 So long as *m·* is the basis of
458–32 causes men to turn naturally from *m·* to Spirit,
461– 4 and that he lives in Spirit, not *m·*.
r 466– 5 indicate Mind, never *m·*, and have one Principle.
466–25 fallacy that . . . soul, and life can be in *m·* ;
467–23 Soul, is not confined in man, and is never in *m·*.
467–28 *M·* neither sees, hears, nor feels.
467–32 cannot be learned from its opposite, *m·*.
468–10 no life, truth, intelligence, nor substance in *m·*.
469– 1 Life is neither in nor of *m·*.
469– 3 *M·* is a human concept.
471–15 is not supported by evil, by *m·*,
472–15 supposition that . . . are existent in *m·*.
475– 9 *M·* is not that likeness.
476– 8 claim . . . that life and intelligence are in *m·*,
477–24 individualized, but not in *m·*.
478–15 is there intelligence in *m·* ?
478–18 assertion that there can be pain . . . in *m·*
478–21 How can intelligence dwell in *m·*
479– 8 *M·* is neither self-existent nor a product of
479–10 *M·* cannot see, feel, hear, taste, nor
479–14 *m·* can take no cognizance of matter.
480– 9 belief that there is sensation in *m·*,
480–16 presupposes man to be in *m·*.
480–16 would make *m·* the cause as well as the effect
482– 5 hypothesis that soul is . . . resident in *m·*.
485–19 The belief that life can be in *m·*
485–31 To say that strength is in *m·*, is like saying
486– 1 The notion of any life or intelligence in *m·*
486–26 in Spirit and understanding, not in *m·*,
487–24 belief that life is . . . intelligent *m·*
488–31 they exist in immortal Mind, not in *m·*.
489– 8 hypothesis which supposes life to be in *m·*
491–17 belief . . . that *m·* is awake at one time and
491–29 we dream of the pains and pleasures of *m·*
492–15 theories — that *m·* is something, or that all is
492–21 *M·* can afford you no aid.
493–24 That man is material, and that *m·* suffers,
493–26 Any sense of soul in *m·* is not the reality
g 504–28 the contradiction of Spirit is *m·*,
506– 4 Therefore *m·*, not being the reflection of Spirit,
517– 8 The life-giving quality of Mind is Spirit, not *m·*.
521– 9 in the keeping of Spirit, not *m·*,
522–14 forms, called life and intelligence in *m·*.
522–18 In this erroneous theory, *m·* takes the place of
522–20 Spirit is represented as entering *m·*
522–26 Spirit as supposedly cooperating with *m·*

matter

g 524–22 M· is not the reflection of Spirit,
  524–28 Could Spirit evolve its opposite, m·,
  524–28 Could Spirit . . . give m· ability to sin and
  525– 1 Does Mind, God, enter m·
  525– 3 the validity of m· is opposed,
  526– 7 statement that life issues from m·, contradicts
  526–13 a belief in intelligent m·.
  527– 1 God could not put Mind into m·
  530–30 supposes . . . that m· precedes mind.
  530–31 Second, it supposes that mind enters m·,
  531– 1 Second, it supposes that . . . m· becomes living,
  531–21 Who dares to say either that God is in m·
  531–22 or that m· exists without God?
  531–26 Does Life begin with Mind or with m·?
  531–27 Is Life sustained by m· or by Spirit?
  532–22 Is Mind in m·?
  539– 6 as if life . . . were something which m· can
  539–10 such as evil, m·, error, and death?
  539–15 Has Spirit resigned to m· the government of
  542– 1 belief of life in m· sins at every step.
  543–23 the creations of erroneous thought, not of m·.
  543–26 When Spirit made all, did it leave aught for m·
  544–10 M· cannot change the eternal fact that
  544–13 In Science, Mind neither produces m· nor
  544–14 nor does m· produce mind.
  544–29 It declares mind to be in and of m·,
  544–31 It declares . . . that m· becomes spiritual.
  545–23 They believed in the existence of m·,
  546– 2 belief that spirit is now submerged in m·,
  546–11 while m· is governed by
  547–18 theory,— that Mind produces its opposite, m·,
  547–18 theory,— that Mind . . . endues m· with
  550– 4 M· surely does not possess Mind.
  550– 9 Spirit cannot become m·,
  551– 5 If Mind is first, it cannot produce . . . m·.
  551– 5 If m· is first, it cannot produce Mind.
  551– 8 m· is not the progenitor of Mind.
  551–23 How can m· originate or transmit mind?
  551–28 All must be Mind, or else all must be m·.
  552– 7 hypotheses deal with causation as contingent on m·
  552–29 m· is a manifestation of mortal mind,
  554–13 another false claim, that of self-conscious m·,
  554–27 mind in m· is the author of itself,
  555–19 error would seek to unite Spirit with m·,
  556– 7 destroys forever all belief in intelligent m·.
ap 561–27 and m· is put under her feet.
  563–13 by means of an evil mind in m·
  564–22 that the false claim of mind in m·
  567–20 claiming that there is intelligence in m·
gl 579–17 a belief in intelligent m·, finiteness,
  580–14 namely, m·, sin, sickness, and death;
  580–18 called self-creative m·;
  580–25 results in m·, and m· in mortal mind;
  584– 9 Death. An illusion, the lie of life in m·;
  584–21 saith: "I am life and intelligence in m·.
  585– 7 To material sense, earth is m·;
  585–25 belief concerning life, substance, and . . . in m·;
  586–19 supposition that life, substance, . . . are in m·;
  587–13 theories . . . sense, existing in brain, nerve, m·;
  587–14 going in and out of m·,
  591– 8 definition of
  591–12 mind originating in m·; the opposite of Truth;
  592– 1 the belief that sensation is in m·,
  592– 3 belief that . . . are in and of m·;
  593– 6 Purse. Laying up treasures in m·; error.
  595–19 opinions, knowledge; m·; error;
  596 14 reveals Spirit, not m·, as the illuminator of all.

matter-physician

s 162– 1 the m· agrees with the disease,
p 423–15 The m· deals with matter

matter's

s 120–26 m· supposed consciousness of health or disease,
 158–26 letting in m· higher stratum,
ph 177–19 These names indicated m· properties,
c 257– 4 then Spirit, m· unlikeness, must be shadow;
b 293–27 and point to m· opposite,
r 477–15 though interwoven with m· highest stratum,
 479–14 constitutes m· supposed selfhood,

matters

s 145–13 It m· not what material method

maturity

s 124–13 represented as subject to growth, m·, and
ph 190–14 Human birth, growth, m·, and decay
f 244–13 Man undergoing birth, m·, and decay is like the
b 305–28 not subject to birth, growth, m·, decay.
 310–31 neither growth, m·, nor decay in Soul.
t 463–16 its growth sturdy, and its m· undecaying.
g 549– 5 after it has grown to m·,
gl 583– 3 God's thoughts, not in embryo, but in m·;

maximum

an 103–15 The m· of good is the infinite God

mazes

sp 82–17 through different m· of consciousness.

Mazzaroth

c 257–20 M· in his season," — Job 38 : 32.

Me and me

a 19–30 no other gods before m·," — Exod. 20 : 3.
s 140– 6 no man see M·, and live." — Exod. 33 : 20.
f 242– 5 "they shall all know M· [God], — Jer. 31 : 34.
b 280–19 no other gods before m·!" — Exod. 20 : 3.
p 416–16 The material body, which you call m·,
r 467– 4 no other gods before m·." — Exod. 20 : 3.
 467– 4 This m· is Spirit.
g 541–28 crieth unto M· from the ground. — Gen. 4 : 10.

meagre

t 460–28 the m· channel afforded by language

meal

a 35–11 is the morning m· which Christian Scientists
sp 90– 4 and that, too, without m· or monad
s 107– * and hid in three measures of m·, — Matt. 13 : 33.
 118– 1 and hid in three measures of m·, — Matt. 13 : 33.
 118–19 presented as three measures of m·,
 118–25 as yeast changes the chemical properties of m·.
f 221– 6 partook of but one m· in twenty-four hours,
 221– 7 this m· consisting of only a thin slice of bread
p 431– 8 going to sleep immediately after a heavy m·.
ap 559–29 the Israelites of old at the Paschal m·

mean

pr 7–30 or m· to ask forgiveness at some later day.
 8–21 does not always m· one who
a 40–11 which I understand to m· God's method of
 40–29 has come so generally to m· public worship
g 134– 8 so has come always to m· one who
ph 168–32 By chemicalization I m· the process which
f 252–22 says: . . . I m· to make my short span of life
p 397– 7 those whom we m· to bless.
t 457–27 which they m· to complete with Mind,
r 488–13 they m· to enforce the necessity of

meaning

absolute
b 325–15 The absolute m· of the apostolic words
Christian
g 506–27 in the scientifically Christian m· of the text.
deific
r 482– 8 where the deific m· is required.
elucidates the
gl 579– 3 elucidates the m· of the inspired writer.
exact
r 482– 1 gives the exact m· in a majority of cases.
grasp the
o 349–20 in order to grasp the m· of this Science.
her
pref x–28 who do not understand her m·,
higher
b 313–14 Using this word in its higher m·,
o 349–27 does not at once catch the higher m·,
ap 576–31 the word gradually approaches a higher m·.
literal
b 320– 8 both a spiritual and literal m·.
g 537–29 The literal m· would imply that God
of God
c 261–22 you may learn the m· of God, or good,
of that passage
f 218–29 The m· of that passage is not perverted by
of that Scripture
o 359–25 she pondered the m· of that Scripture
of the Greek word
s 137–31 [the m· of the Greek word petros, or stone]
original
o 361–22 fuller expression of its original m·.
gl 579– 7 which is also their original m·.
profound
ap 575–17 description of the city . . . has a profound m·.
scientific
g 534–25 spiritual, scientific m· of the Scriptures
simple
r 474–12 marvel is the simple m· of the Greek word
spiritual
(see spiritual)
their
a 53– 3 accusation was true, but not in their m·.
whole
s 147–16 never believe that you can absorb the whole m· of

pr 16–14 does not affect the m· of the prayer itself.
a 39–19 m·, not that now men must prepare for a
s 114– 3 m· by this term the flesh opposed to Spirit,
b 319–31 m· by that what the beloved disciple meant
r 482– 3 Human thought has adulterated the m·
 488– 8 differ somewhat in m· from that

meanings

b 270–19 in His more infinite m·,

means (noun)
any
  p 438– 6 nothing shall by any *m·* hurt you.— *Luke* 10 : 19.
by no
  a 25–23 by no *m·* relieved others from giving the
  sp 91–14 The destruction of error is by no *m·* the
  an 104–21 and by no *m·* the mental qualities which heal
  f 246– 6 Man is by no *m·* a material germ
  c 265–11 by no *m·* suggests man's absorption into
corporeal
  t 443– 5 a resort to faith in corporeal *m·*
employ
  f 218–21 and employ *m·* which lead only into
eternal
  t 444–10 right use of temporary and eternal *m·*.
gracious
  pr 1– 7 God's gracious *m·* for accomplishing
material
  (*see* **material**)
mental
  p 373–31 when by mental *m·* the circulation is changed,
other
  m 67–24 potent beyond all other *m·* and methods.
  s 156–26 but employing no other *m·*,
  ph 169–22 however much we trust a drug or any other *m·*
  t 457–32 without exploiting other *m·*.
  r 483– 8 supersede all other *m·* in healing.
rational
  m 63–24 A feasible as well as rational *m·* of improvement
some
  p 369–15 in order to discover some *m·* of healing it.
source and
  pr 10–24 the source and *m·* of all goodness
spiritual
  ph 181–13 when you resort to any except spiritual *m·*.
unscientific
  f 223–24 supplant unscientific *m·* and so-called laws.
world's
  a 48–18 chose not the world's *m·* of defence.

  pr 6–11 is the *m·* of destroying sin.
  sp 96–32 wicked minds will endeavor to find *m·*
  an 100– 6 as a *m·* of alleviating disease.
  s 118–14 are *m·* of divine thought,
  152–25 the *m·* by which mortals are divinely driven to a
  ph 169–26 never . . . except by *m·* of the divine power.
  f 212–24 this He does by *m·* of Mind,
  221–20 never . . . that fasting should be a *m·* of health.
  p 428–11 the great attainment by *m·* of which
  ap 558–14 you can heal by its *m·*,
  563–12 and that by *m·* of an evil mind in matter

means (verb)
  pr 10– 1 Prayer *m·* that we desire to
  a 22–21 Love *m·* that we shall be tried and purified.
  23–32 Hebrew verb *to believe m·* also *to be firm*
  sp 93–24 It *m·* quantity and quality,
  s 116–28 If the term . . . *m·* infinite personality,
  134– 4 word *martyr*, from the Greek, *m· witness* ;
  ph 196–13 here the word *soul m·* a false sense
  c 267– 7 and specifically man *m·* all men.
  b 301– 6 what C. S. *m·* by the word *reflection.*
  p 393–26 he certainly *m·* that light depends upon Mind,
  r 466–22 Soul or Spirit *m·* only one Mind,
  467– 5 Therefore the command *m·* this :
  g 508–17 *Gender m·* simply *kind* or *sort,*
  526–29 name Eden, according to Cruden, *m· pleasure*,
  545– 7 condemnation of mortals to till the ground *m·*
  ap 576–15 The word *temple* also *m· body.*

meant
  a 43– 8 this understanding is what is *m·* by the
  46–31 By this is *m·*, that by all they had witnessed
  s 111–17 what this inverted image is *m·* to represent.
  112– 9 By this is *m·* that they adopt
  114–16 it is *m·* to designate that which has no
  137–10 renewed inquiry *m·* : Who or what is it that
  b 314–16 they thought that he *m·* their material
  319–31 what the beloved disciple *m·* in one of his
  333–32 By these sayings Jesus *m·*, not that the human
  p 367–10 This is what is *m·* by seeking Truth,
  t 463–26 if by these are *m·* laws of matter,
  r 496–30 if by that term is *m·* doctrinal beliefs.

meanwhile
  pref xii– 7 *M·* she was pastor of the first
  f 214–24 *m·* would spread their table with
  p 416–14 unless the belief . . . has *m·* been changed.
  439–25 *m·* declaring Disease to be God's servant

measure
of the infinite
  b 336–23 Allness is the *m·* of the infinite,
of the stature
  g 519–20 unto the *m·* of the stature of the— *Eph.* 4 : 13.
same
  pr 12–28 another who offers the same *m·* of prayer

measure
some
  m 63–15 civilization mitigates it in some *m·*.
  b 333–22 with some *m·* of power and grace
without
  a 30– 8 endowed with . . . the divine Spirit, without *m·*.

  pr 5–11 The *m·* ye mete
  a 28–18 Not a . . . did the material world *m·* aright.
  37– 3 "With what *m·* ye mete,— *Matt.* 7 : 2.
  ph 165– 6 To *m·* intellectual capacity by the size of
  190–12 which presently *m·* mind by the size of a
  r 485–30 as much as . . . muscles *m·* strength.

measured
  pr 5–12 "shall be *m·* to you again,"— *Luke* 6 : 38.
  a 37– 4 shall be *m·* to you again."— *Matt.* 7 : 2.
  47– 4 They no longer *m·* man by material sense.
  s 142– 4 *m·* Christianity by its power over sickness,
  f 246– 4 Life and its faculties are not *m·* by calendars.
  g 513–11 In the record, time is not yet *m·* by

measurement
  f 246–10 *m·* of life by solar years robs youth
  gl 598–19 YEAR. A solar *m·* of time ; mortality ;
  599– 1 Eternity is God's *m·* of Soul-filled years.

measurements
  gl 595–17 TIME. Mortal *m·* ; limits, in which

measures
  s 107– * and hid in three m· of meal,— *Matt.* 13 : 33.
  117–32 and hid in three *m·* of meal,— *Matt.* 13 : 33.
  118–19 presented as three *m·* of meal,
  gl 584– 6 *m·* time according to the good that is

measuring
  ph 173–18 Physiology . . . *m·* human strength
  f 246–20 the error of *m·* and limiting

meat
  s 115– 9 as the mouth tasteth *m·*."— *Job* 34 : 3.
  ph 165– * *Is not the life more than m·,— *Matt.* 6 : 25.
  p 362– 4 While they were at *m·*, an unusual incident
  g 518– 8 to you it shall be for *m·.*— *Gen.* 1 : 29.
  518–11 every green herb for *m·* :— *Gen.* 1 : 30.

Mecca
  ph 166– 8 Mohammedan believes in a pilgrimage to *M·*

mechanics
  an 105–21 as important to medicine as to *m·*

mechanism
  ph 176–13 When the *m·* of the human mind gives place
  p 399–16 If Mind is the only actor, how can *m·*

mediator
  a 30–10 this enabled him to be the *m·*,
  b 315–31 Jesus was the *m·* between Spirit and the flesh,
  332–16 "There is one God, and one *m·*— *I Tim.* 2 : 5.

medical
attendants
  pref x–18 abandoned as hopeless by regular *m·* attendants.
details
  ph 196–23 forcible descriptions and *m·* details,
doctrines
  s 163–29 the contrarieties of *m·* doctrines
effect
  t 463–30 Such seeming *m·* effect or action is
faculty
  an 100–12 French government ordered the *m·* faculty
  o 348–10 It is a pity that the *m·* faculty and clergy
  g 528–30 may be a useful hint to the *m·* faculty.
magazine
  f 245– 4 the London *m·* magazine called The Lancet.
method
  ph 179–12 Every *m·* method has its advocates.
mistake
  ph 166–13 the doctor's . . . is a *m·* mistake.
  p 383–31 another *m·* mistake, resulting from
practice
  an 105–30 from ordinary *m·* practice to C. S.
  s 112– 2 the most effective curative agent in *m·* practice.
  156–12 in the ordinary theories of *m·* practice,
  162–31 the famous Philadelphia teacher of *m·* practice.
  p 424–12 In *m·* practice objections would be raised if
practitioners
  s 164– 9 the cultured class of *m·* practitioners
purposes
  pref xi–31 to get this institution chartered for *m·* purposes.
researches
  s 152–21 The author's *m·* researches and experiments
results
  s 155–18 sustains medicine and produces all *m·* results,
schools
  s 159–23 *m·* schools would learn . . . of man from matter
  f 217– 6 *M·* schools may inform us that the
  t 444–22 If ecclesiastical sects or *m·* schools turn a deaf
science
  b 273–16 The so-called laws of matter and of *m·* science
  318–23 *M·* science treats disease as though

medical

study
t 443– 3 as to the . . .consistency of systematic m· study,
443– 8 While a course of m· study is
systems
ph 166–29 by most of the m· systems ;
testimony
p 370–23 According to both m· testimony and
theories
o 348– 3 M· theories virtually admit the
p 382–19 A patient thoroughly booked in m· theories
treatment
t 443–16 ordinary physical methods of m· treatment,
use
s 157–21 If He creates . . . and designs them for m· use,
works
ph 176– 4 modern Eves took up the study of m· works
179–24 so long as you read m· works

medication

p 398–26 belief in the healing effects of time and m·,
r 484– 7 Does C. S., or metaphysical healing, include m·,

Medicine

s 118–14 Science, Theology, and M· are
142–25 chapter sub-title

Medicine, Royal Academy of

an 101–20 adopted by the Royal Academy of M· in Paris.

medicine

claims of
a 44–12 all the claims of m·, surgery, and hygiene.
effects of
s 163–15 "The effects of m· on the human system are
equip the
s 155– 9 the doctor, and the nurse equip the m· with
first
s 142–28 Mind, not matter, must have been the first m·.
give up her
s 156–20 said that she would give up her m· for one day,
god of
s 158– 4 and designated Apollo as "the god of m·."
material
s 146–13 Material m· substitutes drugs for
158–12 The future history of material m·
f 226–18 scholastic theology, material m· and
p 404–30 neither material m· nor Mind can
mental
ph 185– 9 discussed "mental m·" and "mind-cure,"
Mind or
s 142–26 Which was first, Mind or m· ?
of Science
an 104–19 The m· of Science is divine Mind ;
potency of the
s 155–26 potency of the m· increases as the
practice of
s 161–12 law, restricting the practice of m·.
produced by
p 401–21 The only effect produced by m· is
profession of
s 158– 1 the profession of m· originated in idolatry
reform in
s 151–13 Even this one reform in m· would
religion and
m 67–30 Systems of religion and m· treat of
s 107–11 Through C. S., religion and m· are
t 444–15 towards differing forms of religion and m·,
same
p 370–17 but it uses the same m· in both cases.
statutes touching
s 161–19 state statutes touching m· remind one of
systems of
s 146– 5 are governed more or less by our systems of m·.
ph 185–13 as material as the prevailing systems of m·.
o 344–27 Why support the popular systems of m·,

an 105–20 as important to m· as to mechanics or
s 142–29 He made m· ; but that m· was Mind.
143–11 The divine Mind never called matter m·,
143–12 before it could be considered as m·.
143–13 human mind uses one error to m· another.
149–20 remarked . . . take as little m· as possible ;
154–27 says to her child : . . . "You need m·."
155–17 general belief, which sustains m·
156–16 she was unwilling to give up the m·
158–10 This was deemed progress in m· ;
158–29 Matter is going out of m· ;
ph 187– 9 it attributes to some material god or m· an
b 279–23 m· is more or less infected with the
p 398–17 sometimes not containing a particle of m·,
t 453–29 A Christian Scientist's m· is Mind,
460– 9 its m· is intellectual and spiritual,

medicines

p 382–29 wrote . . . treatises I had read and the m·

medium

of evil
sp 91–31 cannot be evil nor the m· of evil,
of hearing
f 214– 3 If the m· of hearing is wholly spiritual,
of matter
s 140–18 Worshipping through the m· of matter is
unaided
sp 89– 1 what the unaided m· is incapable of knowing

sp 72–27 nor the m· through which truth passes to earth.
s 136–18 some . . . believed that Jesus was a m·,
b 284– 3 or that matter is . . . the m· of Mind,
p 372–10 belief that matter is the m· of man,
r 486–28 If the five corporeal senses were the m·
489–20 at one time the m· for sinning
489–20 at another the m· for obeying
489–28 nor make it the m· of Mind.
g 524–21 How could the non-intelligent become the m· of

mediumship

sp 81– 6 their belief in m· would vanish.

medley

sp 78–24 God is not in the m· where

meek

a 33–25 preaches the gospel to the poor, the m· in heart.
49–14 The m· demonstrator of good,
54–19 would not accept his m· interpretation of life
b 272– 5 honest, unselfish, loving, and m·.
t 463–15 Its beginning will be m·, its growth sturdy,
g 516–14 m· shall inherit the earth." — Psal. 37 : 11.
533 20 as much as to say in m· penitence,
gl 597– 6 great Nazarene, as m· as he was mighty,

meekly

a 39– 1 M· our Master met the mockery of his
49–26 before whom he had m· walked,
o 343–30 Whoever is the first m· and conscientiously

meekness

pr 4– 4 in patience, m·, love, and good deeds.
a 30–32 In m· and might, he was found preaching
an 106–28 faith, m·, temperance : — Gal. 5 : 22, 23.
s 115–27 compassion, hope, faith, m·, temperance.
f 224–26 who cometh in the quiet of m·,
b 270–23 M· and charity have divine authority.
o 343–22 m· and spirituality are the conditions of
p 364–27 expressed by m· and human affection,
t 445–13 Teach the m· and might of life
gl 596–20 VALLEY. Depression ; m· ; darkness.

meet

pr 9–13 we shall never m· this great duty simply by
m 57–15 Beauty, wealth, or fame is incompetent to m·
57–23 though it m· no return.
62– 6 the child can m· and master the belief
sp 90–16 In dreams we fly to Europe and m· a
s 122–17 clouds and ocean m· and mingle.
142–23 m· dwelling-places for the Most High.
ph 195–30 to m· a frivolous demand for amusement
f 220–16 Many are ready to m· this inquiry with the
c 257–25 to m· the demands of human want and woe,
b 268–10 hypotheses challenge metaphysics to m· in
327–23 Moral courage is requisite to m· the wrong
330– 6 would m· with immediate . . . acceptance.
p 378– 6 and m· every circumstance with truth.
390–29 M· the incipient stages of disease with
391–21 therefore m· the intimation with a protest.
401 1 m· and destroy these errors with the truth
412– 5 to m· the peculiar or general symptoms
413– 0 to m· the simplest needs of the babe
419– 8 m· the cause mentally and courageously,
419–16 M· every adverse circumstance as its master.
420–25 they can m· disease fearlessly, if they only
422–15 As when an acid and alkali m· and
t 449–25 Certain minds m· only to separate
r 489–14 to m· its own demands.
494–10 and always will m· every human need.
ap 568– 8 fatal effects of trying to m· error with error.

meeting

a 34–32 joyful m· on the shore of the Galilean Sea !
35–10 This spiritual m· with our Lord
f 224–23 m· the needs of mortals in sickness and in health,
c 262– 5 shows the paramount necessity of m· them.
gl 586–24 love m· no response, but still remaining love.

meets

s 111–24 C. S. m· a yearning of the human race

melodies

f 213–25 Mental m· and strains of sweetest music

melody

f 219–23 We may hear a sweet m·, and yet

melt

f 205–18 or as they m· into such thinness that we
241–16 than can moonbeams to m· a river of ice.
b 299–29 sunshine of Truth, will m· away the shadow

melted
sp 97–26   uttered His voice, the earth *m·.*" — *Psal.* 46 : 6.
melting
b 295–23   Then, like a cloud *m·* into thin vapor,
ap 565–22   *m·* and purifying even the gold of . . . character.
melts
p 442–21   belief *m·* into spiritual understanding,
r 480–31   As vapor *m·* before the sun,
member
c 261–15   as actively as the youngest *m·* of the company.
o 351– 8   The author became a *m·* of the orthodox
p 416– 1   as if it were a separate bodily *m·.*
g 552–12   no *m·* of this dolorous and fatal triad.
memorials
pref x– 1   may treasure the *m·* of a child's growth,
a 34– 9   if . . . why need we *m·* of that friend?
memory
a 33–32   who eat bread and drink wine in *m·* of Jesus
sp 86–28   taken from pictorial thought and *m·*
     87– 3   even when they are lost to the *m·* of the
     87–29   *M·* may reproduce voices long ago silent.
f 212– 9   Because the *m·* of pain is more vivid
     212–10   than the *m·* of pleasure.
p 378– 3   reproduced in union by human *m·.*
     407–21   If delusion says, "I have lost my *m·*,"
r 491–23   In sleep, *m·* and consciousness are
men
all
a 40–26   all *m·* should follow the example of our Master
     46–26   that is, he marked the way for all *m·.*
s 130– 4   When all *m·* are bidden to the feast,
f 227–17   All *m·* should be free.
c 267– 7   and specifically man means all *m·.*
b 340–20   and that all *m·* shall have one Mind.
r 467– 9   understood that all *m·* have one Mind,
always guided
pr 7–19   If spiritual sense always guided *m·,*
among
a 24–29   The truth had been lived among *m·* ;
s 150–10   as a permanent dispensation among *m·* ;
g 535–17   the heritage of the first born among *m·*
and women
     (see **women**)
are assured
a 38– 1   Because *m·* are assured that this command
bade
sp 79–18   Apostle Paul bade *m·* have the Mind that was
become seers
sp 84– 8   When sufficiently advanced . . . *m·* become
         seers
beheld as
gl 583– 8   some of the ideas of God beheld as *m·,*
best
pref viii–15   confers the most health and makes the best *m·.*
boys and
b 333– 6   in common with other Hebrew boys and *m·,*
business
s 128– 7   From this it follows that business *m·* and
can be baptized
a 20–10   He knew that *m·* can be baptized, . . . and yet
causes
t 458–32   Christianity causes *m·* to turn naturally from
children and of
p 413– 8   the temperature of children and of *m·,*
children of
     (see **children**)
delivered
f 243– 5   which delivered *m·* from the boiling oil,
did not hinder
a 28–19   Even his . . . purity did not hinder *m·* from
doctrines of
s 131–24   the ceremonies and doctrines of *m·,*
drowning
a 22– 8   This causes them, even as drowning *m·,* to
enlightenment of
a 45– 8   Jesus' deed was for the enlightenment of *m·*
ever with
ap 573–16   the divine Principle of harmony, is ever with *m·,*
Father of
a 29–24   demonstrating God as the Father of *m·.*
fortunes of
s 121– 8   the fate of empires and the fortunes of *m·.*
God and
a 30–10   or *way-shower,* between God and *m·.*
b 332–17   mediator between God and *m·,* — *I Tim.* 2 : 5.
good
ph 189–14   should not make good *m·* suffer.
good-will toward
s 150– 8   good-will toward *m·.*" — *Luke* 2 : 14.
f 226–17   good-will toward *m·.*" — *Luke* 2 : 14.
great
g 548–27   by the labors and genius of great *m·.*
he allowed
a 51– 9   but he allowed *m·* to attempt the destruction of

men
heard of
pr 2– 4   to enlighten the infinite or to be heard of *m·*?
hearts of
s 131–25   until the hearts of *m·* are made ready for it.
light of
g 501– *   *and the life was the light of m·.* — *John* 1 : 4.
ap 561–29   which is "the light of *m·.*" — *John* 1 : 4.
men of
s 148– 9   The former explains the men of *m·,*
morals of
s 126–26   the health, longevity, and morals of *m·* ;
mortal
ph 190– 2   afterwards mortal *m·* or mortals,
other
pr 9– 1   "not as other *m·*"? — *Luke* 18 : 11.
a 30– 2   more spiritual idea of life than other *m·,*
r 473–13   Jesus . . . more than all other *m·,*
pitiful to lead
s 158–18   It is pitiful to lead *m·* into temptation
rejected of
a 20–16   "Despised and rejected of *m·,*" — *Isa.* 53 : 3.
     52–13   "Despised and rejected of *m·,*" — *Isa.* 53 : 3.
save
s 136– 8   he used his divine power to save *m·*
showing
pr 6–27   showing *m·* how to destroy sin,
status of
s 118–21   dignified as the natural status of *m·* and things,
unifies
b 340–23   One infinite God, good, unifies *m·* and nations ;
will teach
s 139–12   reform in religious faith will teach *m·*
worst passions of
a 24– 7   instigated sometimes by the worst passions of *m·*
would transfer
sp 75– 8   Spiritualism would transfer *m·* from the

         ——

pr 6– 3   *M·* may pardon, but this divine Principle
     13–27   hence *m·* recognize themselves as merely
a 39–20   meaning, not that now *m·* must prepare for a
     42–24   Let *m·* think they had killed the body !
sp 93–27   If man were Spirit, then *m·* would be spirits,
s 136–12   "Whom do *m·* say that I, — *Matt.* 16 : 13.
     139– 6   Moses proved . . . by what *m·* called miracles ,
ph 172– 4   and from monkeys into *m·*
f 202– 6   If *m·* would bring to bear upon the study of
     220–26   belief that either . . . makes *m·* better
b 285– 4   not alone hereafter in what *m·* call Paradise,
     289–12   Truth and Truth's idea, never make *m·* sick,
     308–32   "power with God and with *m·.*" — *Gen.* 32 : 28.
     320–16   forever rule [or be humbled] in *m·,* seeing that
         they
     329–27   If *m·* understood their real spiritual source
     332–10   the divine message from God to *m·*
o 354–24   Truth will waken *m* spiritually to hear
p 372–25   "Whosoever shall deny me before *m·,* — *Matt.*
         10 : 33.
r 480–22   which seems to make *m·* capable of wrong-doing.
g 539–23   "Do *m·* gather grapes of — *Matt.* 7 : 16.
     548–16   by which *m·* may entertain angels,
     550– 7   identity of animals as well as of *m·.*
ap 567–21   either to benefit or to injure *m·*
     573–25   is, and has been, possible to *m·*
gl 597– 5   if only he appeared unto *m·* to fast.
mend
p 423– 2   and may not be able to *m·* the bone,
meningitis
ph 175– 7   cerebro-spinal *m·,* hay-fever, and rose-cold
mental
action
an 104–13   C. S. goes to the bottom of *m·* action,
p 401–22   The only effect. . . is dependent upon *m·* action.
     404– 1   physician should be familiar with *m·* action
agencies
ap 570– 5   certain active yet unseen *m·* agencies
anatomy
t 462–32   Scientist, through understanding *m·* anatomy,
argument
t 454–31   the letter and *m·* argument are only
assassin
p 419–26   the *m·* assassin, who, in attempting to rule
t 445– 4   attacks of the would-be *m·* *assassin,*
assassins
s 164–19   or produced by *m·* assassins,
t 447–11   save the victims of the *m·* assassins.
attempt
g 517– 6   *m·* attempt to reduce Deity to corporeality.
call
sp 86– 8   His quick apprehension of this *m·* call
case
p 430–17   Suppose a *m·* case to be on trial,
causation
p 423– 9   Scientist, . . . commences with *m·* causation,

mental

cause
  s 157– 2 C. S. deals wholly with the *m·* cause
  ph 187–16 Anatomy allows the *m·* cause of the latter
  p 374–24 and ignorance of *m·* cause and effect.
chemicalization
  m 65–29 The *m·* chemicalization, which has
  ph 169– 4 occurred through *m·* chemicalization,
  p 401–18 *M·* chemicalization brings . . . to the surface,
  t 453– 8 *M·* chemicalization follows the explanation of
concept
  sp 87–24 Do not suppose that any *m·* concept is gone
  p 376–19 the so-called material body is a *m·* concept
conception
  p 403–30 *m·* conception and development of disease
condition
  ph 181–19 you must improve your *m·* condition
  p 397– 8 Suffering is no less a *m·* condition than
conditions
  s 153–29 we shall be more careful of our *m·* conditions,
  154– 3 Disease arises, like other *m·* conditions,
  159–11 Is it skilful . . . to take no heed of *m·* conditions
conflict
  b 288– 4 *m·* conflict between the evidence of the
contagion
  s 153–28 When this *m·* contagion is understood,
crime
  an 105–16 take cognizance of *m·* crime
despotism
  p 375–15 No person is benefited by . . . any *m·* despotism
direction
  s 160 23 never capable of acting contrary to *m·* direction.
disturbance
  p 421–12 treat . . . more for the *m·* disturbance
effect
  p 371– 5 Disquisitions on disease have a *m·* effect
element
  s 157– 5 whole force of the *m·* element is employed
endowments
  r 488–25 *m·* endowments are not at the mercy of
endurance
  p 387– 6 When we reach our limits of *m·* endurance,
energy
  p 394– 6 majority of doctors depress *m·* energy,
environment
  sp 87– 8 their *m·* environment remains
fears
  ph 199–20 latent *m·* fears are subdued by him.
fermentation
  sp 96–22 This *m·* fermentation has begun,
healer
  p 401–31 while the *m·* healer confines himself chiefly
healing
  pref x– 4 Various books on *m·* healing
  s 107– 6 divine Principle of scientific *m·* healing.
  t 455 31 the Science of *m·* healing and teaching,
  459–15 Committing the bare process of *m·* healing to
height
  f 237– 8 *m·* height their little daughter . . . attained.
horizon
  sp 98– 4 beholds in the *m·* horizon the signs
idea
  r 467–27 Spirit gives the true *m·* idea.
illusion
  p 403– 8 understood that the difficulty is a *m·* illusion,
image
  p 416– 4 unless the *m·* image occasioning the pain
images
  p 413–28 these actions convey *m·* images to
impression
  f 213–16 Sound is a *m·* impression
infant
  ph 194–24 Kaspar was still a *m·* infant,
influence
  p 397– 6 *m·* influence on the wrong side,
inharmony
  r 493–24 removes any other sense of moral or *m·* inharmony.
jurisprudence
  p 441–31 Our great Teacher of *m·* jurisprudence
legislators
  p 440–22 human *m·* legislators compel them to
malpractice
  p 442–30 *m·* malpractice cannot harm you
  t 451–26 All *m·* malpractice arises from ignorance or
  451–31 *m·* malpractice tends to blast moral sense,
  457–17 *m·* malpractice, prolific of evil,
malpractitioner
  p 419–25 Never fear the *m·* malpractitioner,
manifestation
  b 303– 2 The reflection, through *m·* manifestation,
means
  p 373–31 when by *m·* means the circulation is changed,
medicine
  ph 185– 8 discussed "*m·* medicine" and "mind-cure,"

mental

melodies
  f 213–24 *M·* melodies and strains of sweetest music
method
  sp 79– 7 A scientific *m·* method is more sanitary than
  79– 8 such a *m·* method produces permanent
miasma
  b 274– 2 Truth and Love antidote this *m·* miasma,
microbes
  s 164–15 all the *m·* microbes of sin
might
  p 428–19 We must realize the ability of *m·* might
molecule
  g 507–24 governs all, from the *m·* molecule to infinity.
negation
  p 392–12 should always be met with the *m·* negation.
opposition
  p 390–30 with as powerful *m·* opposition as a
  g 534–24 There will be greater *m·* opposition
origin
  p 374–18 is no argument against the *m·* origin of
penury
  p 366–10 while *m·* penury chills his faith and
physical and
  s 132–26 salvation from all error, physical and *m·*,
  148–14 Both . . . define man as both physical and *m·*,
physician
  p 368–32 Once let the *m·* physician believe in the
picture
  c 264– 6 when the *m·* picture is spiritual and eternal.
plea
  p 412–20 and array your *m·* plea against the physical.
power
  t 455–26 No person can misuse this *m·* power, if
powers
  an 105–22 Whoever uses his developed *m·* powers
  s 128– 9 C. S. enhances their endurance and *m·* powers,
practice
  ph 185–26 Erroneous *m·* practice may seem
  p 375–15 All unscientific *m·* practice is erroneous
  395–27 *M·* practice, which holds disease as a
  410–23 The Science of *m·* practice is susceptible of no
  410–25 If *m·* practice is abused or is
  t 447– 5 In *m·* practice you must not forget that
process
  p 416–24 The sick know nothing of the *m·* process
protest
  s 160–21 become cramped despite the *m·* protest?
  p 425–31 be always ready with the *m·* protest
quackery
  p 395–21 It is *m·* quackery to make disease a reality
  t 468– 1 *M·* quackery rests on the same platform as
qualities
  an 104–21 and by no means the *m·* qualities which heal
quality
  p 365–12 what *m·* quality remains, with which to
realm
  sp 82–22 the *m·* realm in which we dwell.
  g 514–11 the king of the *m·* realm.
reconstruction
  p 401–31 confines himself chiefly to *m·* reconstruction
reservoir
  ph 180–15 may . . . add more fear to the *m·* reservoir
self-knowledge
  t 462–20 Anatomy, . . . is *m·* self-knowledge,
sign
  f 233–19 how much more should ye discern the sign *m·*,
signs
  ph 169– 4 I have seen the *m·* signs, assuring me
sin
  g 557–23 as if he . . . fell into *m·* sin ;
slavery
  f 225–24 abolition of *m·* slavery is a more difficult task.
state
  (see **state**)
states
  sp 82–25 The *m·* states are so unlike,
  s 149– 9 the different *m·* states of the patient.
  t 455– 5 Such *m·* states indicate weakness
surgery
  p 402– 6 records of the cure, . . . through *m·* surgery
swaddling-clothes
  c 255– 2 drop off their *m·* swaddling-clothes,
symptoms
  s 156–32 Homœopathy takes *m·* symptoms largely into
trespasser
  an 106–13 the *m·* trespasser incurs the divine penalty
ways
  ap 571– 2 hidden *m·* ways of accomplishing iniquity.
work
  f 238–27 People with *m·* work before them

  pr 12–32 In divine Science, where prayers are *m·*,
  sp 91–28 erroneous . . . that man is both *m·* and
  s 114–23 C. S. explains all cause and effect as *m·*,

mental

s 156– 2 these qualities must be *m·*.
ph 169–10 disease has a *m·*, mortal origin,
169–19 origin of all disease as *m·*,
178–12 predisposing cause and the exciting cause are *m·*.
185– 7 No system of hygiene but C. S. is purely *m·*.
f 204– 6 is as conclusively *m·* as
217–10 unnatural *m·* and bodily conditions,
b 270–28 disease is *m·*, not material.
280– 8 and the product must be *m·*.
287– 6 Error supposes man to be both *m·* and material.
302–27 in the *m·*, not in any bodily or personal likeness
o 360– 5 those which are both *m·* and material.
p 375–18 adding to his patient's *m·* and moral power,
376–31 To fear . . . disease, is to paralyze *m·* and
377–26 The cause of all so-called disease is *m·*,
383– 1 The ailment was not bodily, but *m·*,
422–15 so *m·* and moral chemistry changes the
t 458– 7 from both a *m·* and a material standpoint.
g 508–14 Gender is *m·*, not material.
512–23 these are *m·*, both primarily and secondarily.
gl 586– 4 EYES. . . . not material but *m·*.
587–10 a belief that . . . are both *m·* and material ;
588–18 the belief that . . . are both *m·* and material.

mentality

sp 90–22 This shows what mortal *m·* and knowledge are.
an 105–11 Can you separate the *m·* from the body
ph 173–12 manifests nothing but a material *m·*.
185–30 a mortal consolidation of material *m·*
f 217–19 When *m·* gives rest to the body,
b 283–32 Are *m·*, immortality, consciousness,
292–27 material *m·*, misnamed *mind*,
p 375–14 yielding his *m·* to any mental despotism
g 513– 1 both this mortal *m·*, so-called, and its claim,

mentalizes

s 157–11 Homœopathy *m·* a drug with

mentally

m 62– 2 The fœtus must be kept *m·* pure
sp 86–31 Pictures are *m·* formed before the artist can
90–20 Opium and hashish eaters *m·* travel
96–29 will be apprehended *m·* instead of materially.
s 137–21 Christ, the spirit of God, . . . which heals *m·*.
153–20 Now administer *m·* to your patient a high
f 235– 5 than to be treated *m·* by one who does not obey
p 377– 1 *m·* convince him that matter cannot take cold,
391–20 *M·* contradict every complaint from the body,
392–13 must be expressed *m·*, and thought should be
401– 7 which you impart *m·*
404–32 unless it makes him better *m·*,
410–28 If . . . the power to heal *m·* will diminish,
411–22 induced by a false sense *m·* entertained,
412– 4 *M·* and silently plead the case
412–10 You may call the disease by name when you *m·*
412–20 Argue at first *m·*, not audibly, that the patient
412–23 *M·* insist that harmony is the fact,
418– 3 *m·* destroying all belief in material pleasure or
419– 9 meet the cause *m·* and courageously,
424–23 more difficult to make yourself heard *m·* while
425– 6 If the case to be *m·* treated is consumption,
t 447–15 when *m·* sustained by Truth,
453–24 You should treat sickness *m·* just as you would
461–29 you must *m·* unsee the disease ;
464–15 so violent that he could not treat himself *m·*,
464–19 he could handle his own case *m·*.
g 528–29 performed *m·* and without instruments ;

Mental Treatment Illustrated

p 410–22 chapter sub-title

mention

g 526–14 first *m·* of evil is in the legendary

merchandise

pr 12–25 they are the *m·* of human thought
s 130– 5 One has a farm, another has *m·*,

merciful

pr 10–31 Do you ask wisdom to be *m·*
r 497–27 and to be *m·*, just, and pure.

mercifully

o 344–13 would perhaps *m·* withhold their

merciless

o 352–21 declaring ghosts to be real, *m·*, and

mercury

t 449–11 Man's moral *m·*, rising or falling,

mercy

and justice
g 538– 7 Radiant with *m·* and justice,
at the
a 27–31 endeavored to hold him at the *m·* of matter
s 148–14 and place mind at the *m·* of matter
ph 165–10 to place this so-called mind at the *m·* of
f 250–31 not being at the *m·* of death,
b 317–17 his life is not at the *m·* of matter.
o 358– 4 If God is at the *m·* of matter,

mercy

at the
r 481–14 declaring existence to be at the *m·* of death,
488–25 not at the *m·* of organization and
cancels the
a 22–30 *M·* cancels the debt only when
divine
b 329–26 The pardon of divine *m·* is the
g 542–13 jeopardize self-control, and mock divine *m·*.
goodness and
ap 578–16 Surely goodness and *m·* shall — *Psal.* 23 : 6.
handmaid of
a 36– 9 since justice is the handmaid of *m·*.
heavenly
p 435– 1 commended man's immortal Spirit to heavenly *m·*,
His
pr 6–20 according as His *m·* is sought or unsought,
left to the
s 126–20 left to the *m·* of speculative hypotheses?
on your soul
p 433–25 "May God have *m·* on your soul,"
recommended to
an 105–10 defies justice and is recommended to *m·*.
p 437–16 Soul a criminal though recommended to *m·* ;
shall have
t 448–19 whoso confesseth . . . shall have *m·*." — *Prov.* 28 : 13.
to mortals
a 18– 7 did life's work aright . . . in *m·* to mortals,

---

a 36–21 the immortal law of justice as well as of *m·*.
f 248–29 goodness, *m·*, justice, health,
r 465–15 justice, *m·*, wisdom, goodness, and

mere

pr 2–18 The *m·* habit of pleading with
11–12 *M·* legal pardon . . . leaves the offender free
12– 2 A *m·* request that God will heal
13–12 Can the *m·* public expression of our desires
14– 7 is to have, not *m·* emotional ecstasy
a 23–16 Faith, if it be *m·* belief, is as a pendulum
26–28 Our Master taught no *m·* theory, doctrine,
55–12 in a clearer light than *m·* words can possibly do,
sp 92–19 a *m·* offshoot of material sense.
an 102– 6 mesmerism, or hypnotism is a *m·* negation,
ph 195–24 the *m·* dogma, the speculative theory,
f 242–26 *M·* speculation or superstition
242–32 proof which he gave, instead of *m·* profession.
b 274–10 not *m·* inferences drawn from material
330– 2 understanding of being supersedes *m·* belief.
338–21 Here a *dam* is not a *m·* play upon words ;
o 341–11 In C. S. *m·* opinion is valueless.
355– 7 proofs are better than *m·* verbal arguments
p 363–32 there was encouragement in the *m·* fact that
t 460–19 If Christian healing is abused by *m·* smatterers
r 487–21 *M·* belief is blindness
g 556–20 In sleep, cause and effect are *m·* illusions.

merely

pr 5–26 and that man is made better *m·* by
9–20 even the surrender of all *m·* material sensation,
13–27 hence men recognize themselves as *m·* physical,
16– 3 highest prayer is not one of faith *m·* ;
40–27 and not *m·* worship his personality.
sp 92–30 when it is *m·* the absence of truth,
s 118– 4 far above the *m·* ecclesiastical
135–30 not *m·* in the *name* of Christ, or Truth,
152–17 This he did *m·* to ascertain the temperature of
f 203– 7 If God were understood instead of being *m·* believed,
230–24 These *m·* evade the question.
b 287–26 Matter is neither a thing nor a person, but *m·*
319–29 for instance, to name Love as *m·* an attribute
339–27 must be not *m·* believed, but
p 382–12 beware of making clean *m·* the outside
386–21 your suffering was *m·* the result of your belief.
t 447–22 A sinner is not reformed *m·* by assuring him
447–27 The sick are not healed *m·* by declaring

merges

ph 190–18 it never *m·* into immortal being,

merit

a 37–14 is *m·* seen and appreciated by lookers-on.
p 432–18 transgress the laws, and *m·* punishment,
t 449–23 according to personal *m·* or demerit,

merited

pr 9– 3 has been most grateful for *m·* rebuke.

merits

f 202–12 redeemed through the *m·* of Christ,
o 344–16 rules which disclose its *m·* or demerits,

Mesmer (see also Mesmer's)

an 100– 2 brought into notice by *M·* in Germany in 1775.

mesmeric

r 490–31 Under the *m·* illusion of belief, a man will

Mesmerism
    p 441–22   Health-laws, M·, Hypnotism,

mesmerism
    an 100– 1   M· or animal magnetism was first brought into
        102– 5   animal magnetism, m·, or hypnotism
        102–25   "M· is a problem not lending itself to
        104–18   occultism, necromancy, m·,
    b 322–16   foreshadowed the m· and hypnotism of to-day.
    p 402–22   The error, m· — or hypnotism,
       403– 3   between voluntary and involuntary m·
       403– 4   voluntary m· is induced consciously
    r 484– 7   hygiene, m·, hypnotism, theosophy,
      484–21   M· is mortal, material illusion.
      490–28   Sleep and m· explain the mythical nature of

mesmerist
    sp 87–18   to heal through Mind, but not as a m·.

Mesmer's
    an 100–13   to investigate M· theory

message
    a 27– 1   Jesus sent a m· to John the Baptist,
    b 308–19   when an angel, a m· from Truth and Love,
      332–10   the divine m· from God to men
    p 399–13   both the service and m· of this telegraphy.
      432–28   with a m· from the Board of Health
      439– 7   when a m· came from False Belief,
    ap 558– 9   This angel or m· which comes from God,
      574–10   This ministry of Truth, this m· from
      574–20   the very m·, or swift-winged thought,

messages
    sp 78–19   for the transmission of m·.
    p 432– 7   testifies : . . . I convey m· from my
    ap 566–30   assigns to the angels, God's divine m·,
      567–26   His angels, or m·, are cast out with their

messenger (see also Eddy, Mrs. Mary Baker)
    b 309– 2   the m· was not a corporeal being,

Messiah (see also Messiah's)
    s 116–15   They never crown the power of Mind as the M·,
      137–19   The M· is what thou hast declared,
      138– 5   lay behind Peter's confession of the true M·.
    b 288–29   The Christ-element in the M·
      309–16   until the M· should rename them.
      333–10   The name is synonymous with M·,
      333–24   caught glorious glimpses of the M·,
    o 360–32   The Jew believes that the M· or Christ
    p 364–22   spiritual purgation which came through the M·,
    r 482–21   He was inseparable from Christ, the M·,
    ap 562– 2   the spiritual idea as the M·,
    gl 594–16   Son. The Son of God, the M· or Christ.

Messiah's
    r 494– 6   to believe that so great a work as the M·

Messiahship
    sp 95–24   the Magi of old foretold the M· of Truth.
    s 131–30   established his claim to the M·.

Messianic
    a 27– 9   God is the power in the M· work.
    s 133– 1   questioned the signs of the M· appearing,

met
    a 39– 1   Meekly our Master m· the mockery of
      42–20   This error Jesus m· with divine Science
      44–10   He m· and mastered on the basis of C. S.,
      49–15   m· his earthly fate alone with God.
    sp 92–23   Until . . . the moral demand will not be m·,
    s 130– 1   the demands of God must be m·.
    ph 168–29   if the error . . . was m· and destroyed by truth.
      193– 3   On entering the house I m· his physician,
    f 231– 3   Unless an ill is rightly m· and fairly overcome
    b 308– 9   is m· by the admission from the head, heart,
    o 355– 4   The charge . . . is m· by something practical,
    p 392–12   should always be m· with the mental negation.
      412–29   it needs to be m· mainly through the
      423– 1   The belief that he has m· his master
      427–10   must be m· and mastered by Science,
    r 483–25   this Science has m· with opposition ;
      494–10   Divine Love always has m·
    ap 564–16   he, . . . m· and conquered sin in every form.

metal
    m 66–32   that the precious m· may be graven with the

metaphor
    g 507– 1   In m·, the dry land illustrates the
      527–11   Here the m· represents God, Love, as
      529–23   enters into the m· only as evil.
    ap 571–22   Through trope and m·, the Revelator,

metaphoric
    ap 575–13   The description is m·.

metaphorical
    g 510–16   The sun is a m· representation of Soul

metaphorically
    a 38–15   is used m·, as in the text,
    g 511–26   Animals and mortals m· present the gradation

metaphors
    b 320– 4   M· abound in the Bible,
    p 389–16   the m· about the fount and stream,

metaphysical
    sp 99– 1   not physical but m·,
    s 111–30   I submitted my m· system of treating disease to
      113–15   not a foot to stand upon which is not purely m·,
      115– 4   inadequacy of material terms for m· statements,
      115– 5   difficulty of so expressing m· ideas
      144–17   is not the m· practice of C. S.,
    ph 185– 3   My m· treatment changed the action of
      195–13   m· Science and its divine Principle.
    f 210–17   by one and the same m· process.
      219–25   Those who are healed through m· Science,
    b 268– 8   is slowly yielding to the idea of a m· basis,
      269–12   matter does not enter into m· premises or
      338–26   aside from their m· derivation,
    p 397– 1   By not perceiving vital m· points,
      416–26   m· method by which they can be healed.
      418–21   All m· logic is inspired by this simple rule
      424–15   It is equally important in m· practice
    t 456–22   efficaciously treated by the m· process.
      460– 5   and it underlies all m· practice.
    gl 579– 5   the m· interpretation of Bible terms,
           (see also healing)

metaphysically
    m 65–12   should be more m· regarded.
    s 118–18   are m· presented as three measures of meal,

metaphysician
    s 162– 1   but upon different terms than does the m· ;
      162– 2   while the m· agrees only with health
    p 366– 3   In order to cure his patient, the m· must
      423–18   The m·, making Mind his basis of

metaphysics
act against
    s 160– 3   The systems of physics act against m·,
categories of
    b 269–13   The categories of m· rest on
challenge
    b 268–10   Materialistic hypotheses challenge m·
Christian
    s 155–16   the high and mighty truths of Christian m·.
devoid of
    g 549–23   which rely upon physics and are devoid of m·.
divine
           (see divine)
fact in
    s 154– 9   This fact in m· is illustrated by the following
of Christian Science
    s 152–22   prepared her thought for the m· of C. S.
Principle of
    p 419–27   the divine Principle of m·,
resolves things
    b 269–14   M· resolves things into thoughts,
scientific
    b 268–15   no substantial aid to scientific m·,
    r 465– 6   to elucidate scientific m·.
understood
    s 159–15   Had these unscientific surgeons understood m·,
works on
    s 116–13   Works on m· leave the grand point untouched.

    an 105–20   "I see no reason why m· is not
    s 156–28   M·, as taught in C. S., is the
      156–29   In m·, matter disappears from the remedy
    ph 194–14   (as I learned in m·)
    b 269–11   M· is above physics,
    t 460–11   Yet this most fundamental part of m· is
    gl 585–18   m· taking the place of physics ;

metastasis
    p 420– 2   There is no m·, no stoppage

mete
    pr 5–11   measure ye m· "shall be measured — Luke 6 : 38.
    a 37– 3   "With what measure ye m·, — Matt. 7 : 2.

method
but one
    s 112– 5   There can, therefore, be but one m·
changed the
    g 531–23   Has man . . . changed the m· of his Maker?
divine
    f 240–29   The divine m· of paying sin's wages
    b 339– 1   destruction of sin is the divine m· of pardon.
    ap 568– 6   the divine m· of warfare in Science,
false
    p 380–11   This false m· is as though the defendant
God's
    a 40–11   God's m· of destroying sin.
    o 343– 6   Is not finite mind ignorant of God's m·?
her
    pref x–28   Only those quarrel with her m· who
ignorance of the
    t 456–17   betrays a gross ignorance of the m·

method
material
  sp 78–18   it needs no material *m·* for the transmission of
  s 145–13   It matters not what material *m·*
  f 230–24   by drugs, hygiene, or any material *m·*.
medical
  ph 179–12   Every medical *m·* has its advocates.
mental
  sp 79– 7   A scientific mental *m·* is more sanitary than
     79– 8   such a mental *m·* produces permanent
metaphysical
  p 416–26   metaphysical *m·* by which they can be healed.
my
  f 219– 3   My *m·* of treating fatigue applies to all
of demonstrating
  t 456–11   *m·* of demonstrating C. S.
of divine Mind
  g 551–14   it does not acknowledge the *m·* of divine Mind,
of madness
  p 407–31   its *m·* of madness is in consonance with
of surgery
  a 44–22   It was a *m·* of surgery beyond material art,
revealed a
  a 44–26   revealed a *m·* infinitely above that of
same
  sp 85–18   After the same *m·*, events of great moment
  p 404–28   Both cures require the same *m·*
sanitary
  pref x–25   than that of any other sanitary *m·*.
scientific
  t 456– 6   divine Principle and rules of the scientific *m·*
successful
  s 154–31   The better and more successful *m·*
that
  ph 179–14   creates a demand for that *m·*,
this
  s 112– 6   Those who depart from this *m·*
  o 344–25   Why should one refuse to investigate this *m·*
     359– 8   infidels whose only objection to this *m·* was,
true
  ap 568–10   first the true *m·* of creation is set forth

  s 113–27   metaphysics of C. S., like the *m·* in
  ph 179–13   preference of mortal mind for a certain *m·*
  r 493–11   The *m·* of C. S. Mind-healing is touched upon
  g 553–23   appearance of its *m·* in finite forms

methods
changed their
  a 35– 4   they changed their *m·*,
conclusions and
  p 397– 5   in our conclusions and *m·*.
curative
  s 152–29   skeptical as to material curative *m·*.
different
  g 549–10   three different *m·* of reproduction
erroneous
  ph 185–28   because erroneous *m·* act on and through
healing
  t 445–15   there will be no desire for other healing *m·*.
ignorant of the
  ph 178–28   Ignorant of the *m·* and the basis of
material
  (*see* **material**)
materialistic
  ph 183–26   Truth casts out all evils and materialistic *m·*
means and
  m 67–24   potent beyond all other means and *m·*.
nature and
  t 451–25   may perceive the nature and *m·* of error
  ap 564– 4   with error's own nature and *m·*.
of Mind
  f 212–25   all the *m·* of Mind are not understood,
other
  s 145–16   has this advantage over other *m·*,
     145–25   Other *m·* undertake to oppose error with error,
  f 212–28   and possibly that other *m·* involve
pathological
  pref xi– 6   explains that all other pathological *m·* are the
physical
  t 443–16   ordinary physical *m·* of medical treatment,
present
  an 102–21   So secret are the present *m·* of
sanitary
  s 133–23   theories concerning God, man, sanitary *m·*,
scientific
  f 217–15   That scientific *m·* are superior to others,
  o 355– 4   in Christianly scientific *m·* of dealing with sin
studied
  ph 174– 3   civilized practitioners by their more studied *m·*.
such
  an 106–16   sanction only such *m·* as are demonstrable
these
  ph 178–30   but none of these *m·* can be mingled with
  o 355– 6   the proof of the utility of these *m·* ;

methods
unscientific
  p 369–27   Unscientific *m·* are finding their dead level.
unspiritual
  s 143–31   Inferior and unspiritual *m·* of healing
various
  o 344–19   There are various *m·* of treating disease,

Methods of Study in Natural History
  g 548–29   "*M· of S· in N· H·*,"

miasma
  ph 176–17   Human fear of *m·* would load with disease
  b 274– 2   Truth and Love antidote this mental *m·*,

Michael
  ap 566–26   *M·* and his angels fought — *Rev.* 12 : 7.

Michael's
  ap 566–30   *M·* characteristic is spiritual strength.

microbes
  s 164–15   and all the mental *m·* of sin

microscope
  c 264–21   Matter disappears under the *m·* of Spirit.
  ap 561– 5   Agassiz, through his *m·*, saw the sun in an egg

microscopic
  g 547– 9   Louis Agassiz, by his *m·* examination of

midnight
  sp 95–22   *M·* foretells the dawn.
  b 327–16   rushes forth to clamor with *m·* and tempest.
  p 365– 6   preparing their helpers for the "*m·* call,"

midst
  pr 7–30   and consoling ourselves in the *m·* of
  s 122–20   in the *m·* of murky clouds
  f 233– 8   In the *m·* of imperfection,
  b 291– 2   that happiness can be genuine in the *m·* of
  g 505– 5   firmament in the *m·* of the waters, — *Gen.* 1 : 6.
     526– 1   in the *m·* of the garden, — *Gen.* 2 : 9.
     529–19   in the *m·* of the garden, — *Gen.* 3 : 3.

might
all
  b 310– 6   but all *m·* is divine Mind.
  g 522– 6   assigns all *m·* and government to God,
and permanence
  f 215– 2   and the *m·* and permanence of Truth.
and wisdom
  gl 597–21   The *m·* and wisdom of God.
continuity, and
  b 325–14   in all its perfection, continuity, and *m·*,
full
  pref viii– 5   To develop the full *m·* of this Science,
great
  b 329– 9   no right to question the great *m·* of divine
imparted by
  g 514–19   accompanies all the *m·* imparted by Spirit.
light and
  f 215–13   the light and *m·* of intelligence and Life.
  t 446–26   the spiritual light and *m·* which heal the sick.
meekness and
  a 30–32   In meekness and *m·*, he was found preaching
  t 445–13   Teach the meekness and *m·* of
mental
  p 428–20   We must realize the ability of mental *m·*
moral
  s 124– 7   Having neither moral *m·*, spiritual basis, nor
  t 455– 9   You must utilize the moral *m·* of Mind
no other
  b 275– 8   there is no other *m·* nor Mind,
of divine Mind
  s 128– 1   the *m·* of divine Mind.
of intelligence
  f 215–13   the light and *m·* of intelligence and Life.
  p 378–17   the *m·* of intelligence exercised over mortal
of Mind
  s 146–14   even the *m·* of Mind
  f 225–15   all history, illustrates the *m·* of Mind,
  p 391–11   ruled out by the *m·* of Mind,
  t 455– 9   You must utilize the moral *m·* of Mind
of omnipotence
  gl 597–27   indicates the *m·* of omnipotence
of Truth
  pref vii–27   the author's discovery of the *m·* of Truth
spiritual
  ph 192–17   Moral and spiritual *m·* belong to Spirit,

  ph 194– 1   the *m·* of omnipotent Spirit shares not its
  b 317– 4   insisted on the *m·* of matter, the force of falsity,
  p 367–32   Truth's opposite, has no *m·*.
  g 518–20   Love giveth to the least spiritual idea *m·*,
     520– 4   The depth, breadth, height, *m·*, majesty, and
     544–14   No mortal mind has the *m·* or right or

mightier
  f 207–15   nor is evil *m·* than good.
  g 505–18   *m·* than the noise of many waters, — *Psal.* 93 : 4.

mightiest
a 48–12   shall the humblest or *m·* disciple murmur
mightily
s 155–20   *m·* outweigh the power of popular belief
mighty
pref xi–14   these *m·* works are not supernatural,
a 37–17   and to imitate his *m·* works?
42– 3   rabbi affirmed God to be a *m·* potentate,
49–10   Had they so soon lost sight of his *m·* works,
50–17   its *m·* blessing for the human race.
52–20   the *m·* actuality of all-inclusive God,
53–14   Mortals believed in God as humanly *m·*,
s 117–21   his *m·*, crowning, unparalleled, and
133–30   or only a *m·* hero and king,
155–16   high and *m·* truths of Christian metaphysics.
f 201– *   *reproach of all the m· people ;— Psal.* 89 : 50.
240– 4   winged winds, *m·* billows, verdant vales,
o 357–27   Can Deity be almighty, if another *m·* and
p 401– 1   in certain localities he did not many *m·* works
407– 8   is conquered only by a *m·* struggle.
g 505–19   yea, than the *m·* waves of the sea.”— *Psal.* 93 : 4.
ap 558– 3   And I saw another *m·* angel — *Rev.* 10 : 1.
568–25   What shall we say of the *m·* conquest over
577–22   *M·* potentates and dynasties will
gl 597– 6   The great Nazarene, as meek as he was *m·*,
migratory
f 244–25   not a beast, a vegetable, nor a *m·* mind.
mild
an 102–16   *m·* forms of animal magnetism
p 408–15   is in itself a *m·* species of insanity.
mildly
g 530– 1   He begins his reign over man somewhat *m·*.
miles
sp 87–31   which are thousands of *m·* away
militates
ph 168– 8   Your belief *m·* against your health,
mill
p 399–18   A *m·* at work or the action of a water-wheel
millenarianism
s 111– 2   theosophy, spiritualism, or *m·*
millennial
g 514–21   the *m·* estate pictured by Isaiah :
millennium
a 34–17   they will bring in the *m·*.
p 382– 7   this alone would usher in the *m·*.
million
a 50–28   a *m·* times sharper than the thorns which
millions
pr 10– 9   *m·* of vain repetitions will never
p 379–30   the fever-picture, drawn by *m·* of mortals
ap 570–14   *M·* of unprejudiced minds — simple seekers
millstones
an 105–26   His sins will be *m·* about his neck,
Milton
p 372– 5   likened by *M·* to “chaos and old night.”
mimicry
ph 192– 3   a mockery of intelligence, a *m·* of Mind.
gl 580– 9   product of nothing as the *m·* of something ;
Mind (*see also* **Mind’s**)
actual
p 387– 5   dares to say that actual *M·* can be overworked?
aid of
ph 182–24   forthwith shut out the aid of *M·*
all is
c 257– 2   If Mind is within and without . . . then all is *M·* ;
b 275–21   that all is *M·*, and that Mind is God,
p 371– 2   when in fact all is *M·*.
423– 9   understanding scientifically that all is *M·*,
t 444–32   teacher must make clear . . . that all is *M·*,
r 492–16   or that all is *M·*
492–20   Science says : All is *M·* and Mind’s idea.
492–26   *God is Mind, and . . . hence all is M·*
g 509–29   the Science of creation, in which all is *M·*
all-knowing
pr 7 –25   It is the all-hearing and all-knowing *M·*,
ph 187– 4   how ignorant must they be of the all-knowing *M·*
alone possesses
r 488–23   *M·* alone possesses all faculties,
and body
b 285–13   Spirit and matter, *M·* and body,
and drugs
s 143–32   to make *M·* and drugs coalesce,
and immortality
b 318– 3   nothing can efface *M·* and immortality,
p 369–29   the advantages of *M·* and immortality
and its formations
f 245–32   *M·* and its formations can never be annihilated.
p 402–10   when immortal *M·* and its formations will be

Mind
and matter
b 269– 3   the supposed coexistence of *M·* and matter
270– 1   as reasonable as the second, that *M·* and matter
g 555–22   as if man were the offspring of both *M·* and matter,
antipode of
c 257–24   mind in matter to be the antipode of *M·*.
apparent only as
g 505–11   the ideas of Spirit apparent only as *M·*,
appeals to
s 130– 2   is alarmed by constant appeals to *M·*.
atmosphere of
g 512–12   abound in the spiritual atmosphere of *M·*,
aught besides
ph 181–26   It is unnecessary to resort to aught besides *M·*
aught but
s 120–18   impossible for aught but *M·* to testify truly
belief that
b 292– 8   belief that *M·*, the only immortality of man,
called God
f 204–13   an intelligence or *M·* called God.
can control
p 378– 7   Disease is less than mind, and *M·* can control it.
can have no
b 284– 8   *M·* can have no starting-point,
can impart
p 371–28   *M·* can impart purity instead of impurity,
causation is
p 417–13   all causation is *M·*, acting through
character of
s 142–31   departs from the nature and character of *M·*,
controlled by
b 303– 4   controlled by *M·*, the Principle
controlling
m 63– 3   never . . . better . . . than the controlling *M·*,
control of
ph 169–16   If we understood the control of *M·* over body,
p 380–10   against the control of *M·* over body,
389– 4   it will be given in behalf of the control of *M·*
394–11   admission that . . . is beyond the control of *M·*
controls
sp 79–28   asserting that *M·* controls body and brain.
g 557– 6   *M·* controls the birth-throes in the
created by
g 531–31   record of man as created by *M·*
creates
c 257–12   *M·* creates His own likeness in ideas,
b 280– 7   *M·* creates and multiplies them,
g 507–24   Infinite *M·* creates and governs all,
deific
b 334–24   but undying in the deific *M·*.
derived from
s 143–27   except that which is derived from *M·*.
divine
(*see* **divine**)
divine state of
b 201–14   a divine state of *M·* in which
effect of his
sp 95– 1   effect of his *M·* was always to heal and to save,
Ego is
f 216–11   The understanding that the Ego is *M·*,
Ego was
b 315– 7   He knew that the Ego was *M·* instead of body
elements of
g 507– 3   while *water* symbolizes the elements of *M·*.
empire of
p 379–23   not an intelligence to dispute the empire of *M·*.
energies of
t 455–13   if, . . . you fail to use the energies of *M·*
eternal
s 127–14   the infinite, supreme, eternal *M·*.
f 247–22   which dwells forever in the eternal *M·*
b 270–13   this intelligence is the eternal *M·*
274–28   governed by the unerring and eternal *M·*,
277– 3   To all that is unlike unerring and eternal *M·*,
282–12   Eternal *M·* and temporary material
336–13   He has been forever in the eternal *M·*, God ;
g 511–13   In the eternal *M·*, no night is there.
519– 1   Nothing can be novel to eternal *M·*,
528– 2   all being is the reflection of the eternal *M·*,
552–31   when the perfect and eternal *M·* is understood.
gl 588–10   unerring, immortal, and eternal *M·*.
588–20   God ; incorporeal and eternal *M·* ;
588–25   self-existent and eternal *M·* ;
ever-present
ph 180–26   the ever-present *M·* who understands all things.
everything is
b 270– 4   that everything is *M·*.
evil is not
f 207– 9   Indeed, evil is not *M·*.
evolved from
g 545–13   the theory of man as evolved from *M·*.
facts of
b 268–18   as well as on the facts of *M·*.

Mind

faculties of
  f 215– 6   with all the faculties of *M·* ;
fetterless
  sp 84–18   yea, to reach the range of fetterless *M·*.
forms of
  b 303– 3   multitudinous forms of *M·* which people the
  g 505–10   and they are forms of *M·*,
  507–17   reproduces the multitudinous forms of *M·*
from material body to
  b 284–31   but neither . . . goes from material body to *M·*.
from matter to
  b 268– 9   looking away from matter to *M·*
functions of
  r 478–23   Matter cannot perform the functions of *M·*.
give to
  s 143–29   then give to *M·* the glory, honor, dominion,
glory of
  f 209–14   enhances the glory of *M·*.
God is
  f 239–30   Mind sends forth perfection, for God is *M·*.
  b 311– 4   God is *M·* : all that Mind, God, is,
  330–23   Mind is not both good and bad, for God is *M·* ;
  r 492–25   *God is M·, and God is infinite;*
God, or
  o 347– 9   it must be the one God, or *M·*.
  r 475–18   man is the reflection of God, or *M·*,
good is
  s 113–17   God is good. Good is *M·*.
governed by
  r 480–11   Consciousness, . . . is governed by *M·*,
governs man
  f 222–12   availed himself of the fact that *M·* governs man,
governs the body
  s 111–28   *M·* governs the body, not partially but wholly.
  162–12   the fact that *M·* governs the body,
had made man
  g 524–18   *M·* had made man, both male and female.
healing through
  t 456–30   C. S., or the Science of healing through *M·*.
heals sickness
  f 236–10   *M·* heals sickness as well as sin
heal through
  sp 87–17   It enables one to heal through *M·*,
  p 382–20   more difficult to heal through *M·* than one who
He is
  g 532–24   God is All and He is *M·* and there is but one
ideas of
  b 280– 7   All things beautiful and harmless are ideas of *M·*.
ignorance of
  f 252– 4   Human ignorance of *M·* and of the
image in
  s 115–17   IDEA : An image in *M·* ;
imagine that
  f 203–19   We imagine that *M·* can be imprisoned in
immortal
  sp 71–20   and that immortal *M·* is not in matter.
  an 103–25   The truths of immortal *M·* sustain man,
  s 115–12   Scientific Translation of Immortal *M·*
  145–10   between mortal minds and immortal *M·*.
  145–11   immortal *M·* through Christ, Truth, subdues
  ph 171–15   illustrated . . . the power of immortal *M·*
  177– 9   both must be destroyed by immortal *M·*.
  179– 7   Immortal *M·* heals what eye hath not seen ;
  185–16   to match the divine Science of immortal *M·*,
  188– 2   yields to God, immortal *M·*, and
  190– 7   neither a mortal mind nor the immortal *M·*
  195–12   whether it is mortal mind or immortal *M·*
  200– 7   capacities of being bestowed by immortal *M·*.
  f 208–11   It is the very antipode of immortal *M·*,
  229–21   made void by the law of immortal *M·*,
  246–24   Man, governed by immortal *M·*, is always
  248– 8   Immortal *M·* feeds the body with
  b 279– 8   never originated in the immortal *M·*,
  282–26   Truth is the intelligence of immortal *M·*.
  p 371– 4   yield to the mandate of immortal *M·*.
  374–15   Through immortal *M·*, or Truth, we can
  387– 8   when we realize that immortal *M·* is ever active,
  399–15   matter can return no answer to immortal *M·*.
  399–28   All that is real is included in this immortal *M·*.
  402–10   when immortal *M·* and its formations will be
  403–27   all that is unlike the immortal *M·*.
  415– 2   Immortal *M·* is the only cause ;
  419–21   from immortal *M·*, there is harmony ;
  424– 5   Accidents are unknown to God, or immortal *M·*,
  427–23   Immortal *M·*, governing all, must be
  r 487–20   Truth, flowing from immortal *M·*,
  488–30   since they exist in immortal *M·*, not in matter.
  g 505– 1   Immortal *M·* makes its own record,
  507–23   divine creation declares immortal *M·* and
  ap 564–23   its own crime of defying immortal *M·*.
  gl 580–25   supposition that . . . immortal *M·* results in
  591–14   of which immortal *M·* takes no cognizance ;
impressions of
  f 214–16   conveys the impressions of *M·* to man,
indicate
  r 466– 5   The varied manifestations of C. S. indicate *M·*,

Mind

infinite
  pr 2–24   Can we inform the infinite *M·*
  3–20   we try to give information to this infinite *M·*.
  s 116–30   infinite *M·* in a finite form is an
  151– 4   Infinite *M·* could not possibly create a
  ph 171–22   the spiritual, — yea, the image of infinite *M·*,
  191– 3   Matter is not the organ of infinite *M·*.
  f 206–28   infinite *M·* made all and includes all.
  244–22   If. . .there is no full reflection of the infinite *M·*.
  c 256–18   What is infinite *M·* or divine Love?
  256–32   Infinite *M·* is the creator,
  257–27   Infinite *M·* cannot be limited to a finite form,
  257–31   an infinite form to contain infinite *M·*.
  259– 4   infinite *M·*, the sum of all substance.
  266–26   Perfect and infinite *M·* enthroned is heaven.
  b 284– 8   Infinite *M·* can have no starting-point,
  284–13   Can infinite *M·* recognize matter?
  310–10   God is His own infinite *M·*, and expresses all.
  313–12   image of His person [infinite *M·*].” — *Heb.* 1 : 3.
  336–10   even the infinite expression of infinite *M·*,
  336–13   infinite *M·* can never be in man,
  r 465–10   infinite *M·*, Spirit, Soul, Principle,
  468–10   infinite *M·* and its infinite manifestation,
  469–10   quality of infinite *M·*, of the triune Principle,
  469–15   supposititious opposite of infinite *M·*
  g 503– 2   which are embraced in the infinite *M·*
  504–27   Did infinite *M·* create matter, and call it *light?*
  507–24   Infinite *M·* creates and governs all,
  510–19   the limitless idea of infinite *M·*.
  544–12   Nothing is new to the infinite *M·*.
  554–19   infinite *M·* sets at naught such a mistaken
  gl 587–11   the belief that infinite *M·* is in finite forms ;
infinitude of
  b 280– 1   In the infinitude of *M·*, matter must be un-known.
instead of
  ph 180–13   that all causation is matter, instead of *M·*.
  b 271– 8   to heal the sick through *M·* instead of matter.
  315– 7   He knew that the Ego was *M·* instead of body
  g 544– 6   *M·*, instead of matter, being the producer,
instead of to
  p 415–13   resorting to matter instead of to *M·*.
instituted by
  g 507– 2   the absolute formations instituted by *M·*,
inverted image of
  b 301–28   inverted image of *M·* and substance
is All
  s 109– 2   that *M·* is All and matter is naught
  g 508– 2   only as the divine *M·* is All and reproduces all
is All-in-all
  s 109– 4   reveals incontrovertibly that *M·* is All-in-all,
is first
  g 551– 3   If *M·* is first, it cannot produce its opposite
is foremost
  s 144– 3   If *M·* is foremost and superior, let us rely
is God
  sp 91–31   nor the medium of evil, for *M·* is God.
  b 275–21   that all is Mind, and that *M·* is God,
  310–29   *M·* is God, and God is not seen by
  r 469–13   *M·* is God. The exterminator of
is immortal
  s 114–13   As *M·* is immortal, the phrase *mortal mind*
  f 210–20   *M·* is immortal, and Truth pierces the error of
  p 372– 2   Matter cannot be sick, and *M·* is immortal.
  g 551–29   *M·* is immortal ; but error declares that the
  gl 584–11   Matter has no life, . . . *M·* is immortal.
  591–26   MORTAL MIND. Nothing . . . for *M·* is im-mortal ;
is infinite
  sp 84–19   To understand that *M·* is infinite,
  b 284– 1   not rational to say that *M·* is infinite, but dwells in
is Life
  g 508– 7   *M·* is Life, Truth, and Love
is limitless
  o 353–28   *M·* is limitless. It never was material.
is not in matter
  sp 71–19   and that immortal *M·* is not in matter.
  p 381–26   the understanding that *M·* is not in matter.
is not mortal
  f 211– 9   Is it not provable that *M·* is not *mortal*
is not sick
  p 393–29   *M·* is not sick and matter cannot be.
is one
  s 114–10   *M·* is *one*, including noumenon and
is Spirit
  b 310–30   *M·* is Spirit, which material sense cannot
  g 517– 8   The life-giving quality of *M·* is Spirit,
is substance
  p 414–24   C. S. declares that *M·* is substance,
is supreme
  p 375–24   for *M·* is supreme,
is the I AM
  b 336– 1   *M·* is the I AM, or infinity.

Mind

is the master
p 393– 8 M· is the master of the corporeal senses,
is the multiplier
g 508– 3 M· is the multiplier,
is the same
b 283– 6 M· is the same Life, Love, and wisdom
is the Soul
g 508– 6 M· is the Soul of all.
is the source
b 283– 4 M· is the source of all movement,
joyous in strength
g 514– 6 M·, joyous in strength, dwells in
law of
ph 168–23 in accordance with God's law, the law of M·.
b 307–30 in spiritual statutes, in the higher law of M·.
p 423–26 according to the law of M·, which ultimately
r 484–11 supposed laws of matter yield to the law of M·.
Life is
b 331– 5 Life is M·, the creator reflected
Life or
    (see **Life**)
light depends upon
p 393–26 he certainly means that light depends upon M·,
limitless
c 256–28 A limitless M· cannot proceed from
made the plant
g 509–23 M· made the "plant of the — Gen. 2:5.
makes all
g 520–29 Because M· makes all, there is
man and
b 281–20 false conception as to man and M·.
mandate of
g 520–26 because growth is the eternal mandate of M·.
manifestation of
b 275–24 all is in reality the manifestation of M·.
manifestations of
b 291–15 all the manifestations of M· are harmonious
manifests all
c 258–15 M· manifests all that exists
mastered by
p 427–30 The dream of death must be mastered by M·
matter and
b 270– 5 Matter and M· are opposites.
270– 9 not two powers, matter and M·,
293– 6 which forms no link between matter and M·
matter or
g 531–25 Which institutes Life, — matter or M·?
matter versus
b 319– 4 disease as error, as matter versus M·,
measures time
gl 584– 5 M· measures time according to the good
medicine nor
p 404–31 neither material medicine nor M· can
methods of
f 212–25 all the methods of M· are not understood,
might nor
b 275– 8 there is no other might nor M·,
might of
s 140–14 even the might of M· — to heal the body,
f 225–15 illustrates the might of M·, and shows
p 391–11 ruled out by the might of M·,
t 455– 9 You must utilize the moral might of M·
mimicry of
ph 192– 3 a mockery of intelligence, a mimicry of M·.
no matter in
s 113–30 no matter in M·, and no mind in matter;
no nerve in
s 113–29 no nerve in M·, and no mind in nerve;
no obstacle to
ph 179– 7 since space is no obstacle to M·.
no other
f 206– 1 we can have no other M· but His,
231–30 governed by his Maker, having no other M·,
r 469–19 if mortals claimed no other M·
not facts of
b 283–10 They are not facts of M·.
not matter
    (see **matter**)
obedient to
g 544– 4 ideas became productive, obedient to M·.
obedient to the
b 295– 7 they are obedient to the M· that makes them.
of man
r 470–17 God, the M· of man, never sins
omnipotent
pn 170– 1 reliance on God, omnipotent M·,
b 275– 3 would ignore omnipresent and omnipotent M·.
p 387–30 by his heavenly Father, omnipotent M·,
407–14 from the immortal and omnipotent M·
t 443– 7 from entire confidence in omnipotent M·
r 496– 4 omnipotent M· is reflected by man and governs
gl 590– 3 unerring, eternal, and omnipotent M·
omnipresence of
sp 94–29 scientific basis, that of the omnipresence of M·

Mind

one
sp 94–32 with the infinite capacities of the one M·.
ph 183–31 the one M· only is entitled to honor.
187– 2 believing in more than the one M·.
191– 5 delusion that there is more than one M·,
f 204–22 and realize only one God, one M· or intelligence
205–22 When we realize that there is one M·,
205–25 hinders man's normal drift towards the one M·,
213–32 belief in material origins which discard the one M·
216–12 The understanding . . . that there is but one M·
216–32 and have but one M·, even God ;
236–19 C. S., from which we learn of the one M·
249– 3 and so let us have one God, one M·,
c 267–24 serve as waymarks to the one M·, ,
b 276– 1 Having one God, one M·, unfolds the
281–14 The one Ego, the one M· or Spirit called God,
301–23 Thou shalt have one God, one M·.
314– 9 demonstrating the existence of but one M·
315– 6 He knew of but one M· and laid no claim to
330–23 there is in reality one M· only,
340–20 and that all men shall have one M·.
o 357–20 As there is in reality but one God, one M·,
p 399–27 The one M·, God, contains no mortal opinions.
419–25 for there is but one M·,
424– 7 and unite with the one M·,
r 466–22 Soul or Spirit means only one M·,
467–10 all men have one M·, one God and Father,
469–18 There can be but one M·,
469–20 We can have but one M·, if that one is infinite.
470– 2 with one M· and that God, or good,
470–12 statement that there is one M·
470–16 The children of God have but one M·
482–29 heals the sick on the basis of the one M·
496– 3 for there is but one M·, and this ever-present
496– 7 to have one M·, and to love another as
g 510–29 Science reveals only one M·,
512–22 From the infinite elements of the one M·
532–25 there is but one God, hence one M·
539–29 the one M· which makes and governs man
544–16 All is under the control of the one M·,
544–18 suggestion of more than the one M·, — is in the
gl 580– 6 a material belief, opposed to the one M·,
586– 9 FATHER. Eternal Life; the one M·,
588–16 All the objects of God's creation reflect one M·,
588–17 whatever reflects not this one M· is false
oneness of
f 205–30 Denial of the oneness of M·
or intelligence
f 204–22 and realize only one God, one M· or intelligence
216–12 there is but one M· or intelligence,
g 508–21 The M· or intelligence of production
or Life
b 291–26 No resurrection from the grave awaits M· or Life,
or medicine
s 142–26 Which was first, M· or medicine?
outcome of
g 555–15 error is neither mind nor the outcome of M·.
parent
b 336–31 God is the parent M·, and man is God's
g 507– 9 wanderers from the parent M·,
perfect
f 239–30 The perfect M· sends forth perfection.
247–16 models of spiritual sense, drawn by perfect M·
b 281–12 the image and likeness of perfect M·,
r 467–14 no other but the one perfect M·
point to
f 240– 5 all point to M·, the spiritual intelligence
pours light
t 446–12 through which M· pours light and healing
power of
    (see **power**)
produces
p 419–20 M· produces all action.
g 551– 3 Either M· produces, or it is produced.
properties of
s 124–21 cohesion, and attraction are properties of M·.
qualities of
c 265– 3 but of the highest qualities of M·.
quality of
g 517– 8 The life-giving quality of M· is Spirit,
rather than
ph 181–12 for that reason, you employ matter rather than M·.
f 226–24 belief that the body governed them, rather than M·.
real
sp 91–30 whereas the real M· cannot be evil
b 295–28 the exact opposite of real M·, or Spirit.
realities of
sp 78– 5 are not the eternal realities of M·.
realm of
c 264–10 in the unsearchable realm of M·?
g 514– 7 Mind, . . . dwells in the realm of M·.

Mind

recognize
  b 284–12   Can matter recognize *M·*?
reflects
  b 303–11   Whatever reflects *M·*, Life, Truth,
reflect the
  g 507–20   reflect the *M·* which includes all.
regulates
  p 413– 7   *M·* regulates the condition of the stomach,
rely upon
  s 144– 3   let us rely upon *M·*, which needs no
remains
  r 487–10   Lost they cannot be, while *M·* remains.
representation of
  gl 591– 7   MAN. . . . the full representation of *M·*.
resorted to
  ph 166–28   or he would have resorted to *M·* first.
restful
  s 119–32   the humble servant of the restful *M·*,
rests on
  s 157– 9   rests on *M·* alone as the curative Principle,
same
  f 243–10   same "*M·* . . . which was also in — *Phil.* 2 : 5.
Science of
  (see **Science**)
senses of
  r 489– 4   the senses of *M·* are never lost
signifies God
  f 229– 8   *M·* signifies God,— infinity, not finity.
solely from
  g 543–28   thus it is seen that man springs solely from *M·*.
Soul, or
  b 302–20   the Soul, or *M·*, of the spiritual man
spake
  g 557–26   *M·*, spake and it was done.
Spirit or
  b 331–24   except as infinite Spirit or *M·*.
subject to
  p 429–13   Science declares that man is subject to *M·*.
subject to the
  g 515– 8   are subject to the *M·* which forms them,
substance is in
  c 267– 2   the spiritual idea, whose substance is in *M·*,
substance or
  b 300–29   expresses the divine substance or *M·* ;
supposed limits to
  o 353–26   So long as there are supposed limits to *M·*,
supremacy of
  a 45–30   and so glorified the supremacy of *M·*
  f 209–13   Science which reveals the supremacy of *M·*.
  b 322– 2   cast out evils in proof of the supremacy of *M·*.
  p 401–28   admits the efficacy and supremacy of *M·*,
sustained by
  sp 90– 8   are sustained by *M·* alone.
symbol of
  g 510–27   Light is a symbol of *M·*,
synonym of
  r 468–22   Spirit, the synonym of *M·*, Soul, or God,
systems of
  b 310–17   all things in the systems of *M·*.
the all
  f 204–29   never . . . distinct from God, the *all M·*.
the only
  f 251–23   to find the divine Mind to be the only *M·*,
  b 276–17   If God is admitted to be the only *M·*
  308– 5   God is the only *M·* governing man,
  339–27   the great fact that God is the only *M·*;
  r 469–14   great truth that God, good, is the *only M·*,
this
  sp 84–12   thought which is in rapport with this *M·*,
  s 124–30   are inherent in this *M·*,
  151–27   in this *M·* the entire being is
  ph 169–21   There can be no healing except by this *M·*,
  187–24   man in Science is governed by this *M·*.
  f 206–29   This *M·* does not make mistakes
  216–32   this *M·* forms its own likeness.
  c 257– 1   image or idea emanating from this *M·*.
  b 276– 8   "Let this *M·* be in you,— *Phil.* 2 : 5.
  277– 3   this *M·* saith, "Thou shalt surely — *Gen.* 2 : 17.
  339–27   this *M·* must be not merely believed, but
  r 483– 6   this *M·* must be divine, not human.
  g 503–23   this *M·* creates no element nor symbol of discord
  511– 1   This *M·* forms ideas, . . . subdivides and radiates
  519–27   No exhaustion follows the action of this *M·*,
through (see *also* **healing through** *and* **heal through**)
  a 54–16   triumph over death through *M·*, not matter.
  sp 98– 8   Body cannot be saved except through *M·*.
  s 126–24   I have demonstrated through *M·* the effects of
  ph 170–15   and reach the body through *M·*.
  f 205–12   God created all through *M·*,
  217–18   When you have once conquered . . . through *M·*,
  b 271– 8   to heal the sick through *M·* instead of matter.
  280–30   perpetuates these qualities . . . through *M·*,
  p 395–23   and then to attempt its cure through *M·*.
  t 463–25   Our Master treated error through *M·*,
  g 520–24   declaration that God creates all through *M·*,

Mind

transcends all other
  r 483– 7   *M·* transcends all other power, and will
tributary to
  s 119–31   and makes body tributary to *M·*.
truth is
  b 293–20   while spiritual truth is *M·*.
Truth or
  r 483– 6   which nothing but Truth or *M·* can heal,
understands
  r 487–16   Matter cannot believe, and *M·* understands.
unerring
  s 145–24   the laws of eternal and unerring *M·*.
  f 243–20   Neither immortal and unerring *M·* nor
unfathomable
  g 520– 3   Unfathomable *M·* is expressed.
unfolds
  g 505–23   Spiritual understanding unfolds *M·*,
universe of
  f 240–16   revolutions of the universe of *M·* go on
  g 513– 7   in the teeming universe of *M·*
unlimited
  b 284– 6   If. . . unlimited *M·* would seem to spring from a
verity of
  s 123–11   The verity of *M·* shows conclusively
waiting for the
  pref ix–18   waiting for the *M·* of Christ.
was first
  s 142–26   If *M·* was first and self-existent, then Mind,
  143–27   If *M·* was first chronologically,
was the builder
  b 314–14   knowing, as he did, that *M·* was the builder,
we begin with
  r 467–30   we begin with *M·*, which must be understood
which saved
  s 133– 8   In Egypt, it was *M·* which saved the Israelites
would compress
  b 280–11   limits all things, and would compress *M·*,
would lose
  c 257–28   or *M·* would lose its infinite character

---

  sp 79–18   bade men have the *M·* that was in the Christ.
  89–18   *M·* is not necessarily dependent upon
  92– 9   *M·* is not an entity within the cranium
  s 115–14   GOD : Divine Principle, Life, . . . *M·*.
  120–15   Health is not a condition of matter, but of *M·* ;
  127–18   *M·*, exempt from all evil.
  139– 5   triumph of Spirit, *M·*, over matter.
  142–30   but that medicine was *M·*.
  143–26   *M·* is the grand creator,
  148– 4   the requisite power to heal was in *M·*.
  148–25   Physiology exalts matter, dethrones *M·*,
  149– 3   *M·* as far outweighs drugs in the cure of disease
  150–30   doctrine of the superiority of matter over *M·*,
  156–31   *M·* takes its rightful and supreme place.
  157– 5   its one recognized Principle of healing is *M·*,
  159–24   from matter instead of from *M·*.
  160–30   Is man a material fungus without *M·*
  ph 166–30   when *M·* at last asserts its mastery
  168– 7   on the side of matter, you take away from *M·*,
  171–26   false beliefs . . . where *M·* is not.
  180–11   deport themselves as if *M·* were non-existent,
  181– 1   since *M·*, God, is the source and
  182–22   puts matter under the feet of *M·*.
  191– 2   It can take no cognizance of *M·*.
  191–19   *M·* is not helpless.
  191–30   *M·* has no affinity with matter,
  191–32   *M·*, God, sends forth the aroma of Spirit,
  199–10   great fact that *M·* alone enlarges and
  f 203– 3   *M·* — omnipotence — has all-power,
  204–31   The error, which says . . . *M·* is in matter,
  209– 5   *M·*, supreme over all its formations
  209–10   The world would collapse without *M·*,
  217– 8   which prove *M·* to be scientifically distinct
  217–23   as you understand the control which *M·* has
  219– 4   *M·* should be, and is, supreme,
  221–22   in which being is sustained by God, *M·*.
  229– 1   If *M·* is not the master of sin, sickness,
  232–22   He referred man's harmony to *M·*,
  240–12   Change this statement, suppose *M·* to be
  240–14   *M·* is perpetual motion.
  244–26   He does not pass from matter to *M·*,
  249–12   *M·* is not the author of matter,
  250– 2   error when we . . . multiply *M·* into minds
  251–31   Inharmonious beliefs, which rob *M·*,
  253– 7   saith : . . . I am supreme and give all, for I am *M·*.
  c 257– 2   If *M·* is within and without all things,
  257–14   the Father *M·* is not the father of matter.
  b 269–30   theories I combat . . . matter originates in *M·*,
  269–31   *M·*, possessing intelligence and life.
  279– 9   Matter is neither created by *M·* nor
  279–10   nor for the manifestation and support of *M·*.
  279–29   but one alone,— *M·*.
  282–10   eternal individuality or *M·* ;

Mind

b 282–18 M· cannot pass into non-intelligence
282–30 which is neither M· nor man,
284– 3 or that matter is . . . the medium of M·.
285–19 finite conception of . . . body as the seat of M·
287–18 nor is error the offshoot of M·.
291–25 M· never becomes dust.
303–26 would be a nonentity, or M· unexpressed.
305–14 though he reflects the creation of M·,
307–21 If we regard . . . M· as both good and evil,
311– 4 What we term mortal mind . . . is not M·.
311– 5 all that M·, God, is, or hath made,
315– 9 matter, sin, and evil were not M· ;
319–20 man has no M· but God.
330–21 divine Principle is Love, and Love is M·,
330–22 M· is not both good and bad,
335–25 M· is the divine Principle, Love,
336– 2 M· never enters the finite.
336–12 coexistent and coeternal with that M·.
337–11 as perfect as the M· that forms him.
340–18 It inculcates the tri-unity of God, Spirit, M· ;
p 371–14 is father to the fact that M· can do it ;
377–28 mistaken belief . . . that M· is helpless
378–23 to dethrone M· and take the government
378–26 not a . . . power, which copes astutely with M·
379– 6 The real jurisdiction of the world is in M·,
383– 4 a body rendered pure by M·
384– 1 on inert matter instead of on M·.
394– 9 in the direction which M· points out.
399–15 If M· is the only actor,
402–18 The life of man is M·.
407–22 No faculty of M· is lost.
413– 2 M·, does not produce pain in matter.
415– 3 M· in every case is the eternal God, good.
417–28 control which M· holds over the body.
420–22 M· is the natural stimulus of the body,
422–30 he believes that something stronger than M·
423–19 making M· his basis of operation
t 453–29 A Christian Scientist's medicine is M·,
457–27 which they mean to complete with M·,
457–28 as if the non-intelligent could aid M· !
r 467–16 having that M· which was also in Christ.
467–27 cannot interpret Spirit, M·, through
468–26 Life is divine Principle, M·, Soul,
469–12 Question.— What is M· ?
469–16 evil — is not M·, is not Truth, but error,
470–31 If man ever existed without this . . . M·,
472–16 Error is neither M· nor one of Mind's faculties.
480–18 thus attempting to separate M· from God.
483–16 she affixed . . . the name "substance" to M·.
485– 4 declares that M·, not matter, sees,
486–20 supposes M· unable to produce harmony !
489–28 nor make it the medium of M·.
493–17 M· must be found superior to all the
494– 3 I [M·] will raise it up ;"— John 2: 19.
497–25 that M· to be in us which was also in Christ
g 513–19 as eternal as the M· conceiving them ;
524–21 How could . . . become the medium of M·,
525– 1 Is M· in matter
527– 1 God could not put M· into matter
531–26 Does Life begin with M· or with matter?
532–22 Is M· in matter?
532–22 Is M· capable of error as well as truth,
544–13 In Science, M· neither produces matter
546– 5 If M·, God, creates error, that error must
546–11 Has God no Science to declare M·,
547–18 theory,— that M· produces its opposite,
547–22 implies that . . . must either return to M· or
550– 4 Matter surely does not possess M·.
551– 6 If matter is first, it cannot produce M·.
551– 8 matter is not the progenitor of M·.
551–27 All must be M·, or else all must be matter.
ap 570–27 the great benefit which M· has wrought.
gl 583–20 CREATOR. Spirit ; M· ; intelligence ;
587– 7 Principle ; M· ; Soul ; Spirit ; Life ;
588–12 but one divine Principle, or M·,
591–16 definition of
594–19 SPIRIT. Divine substance ; M· ;
597–26 as applied to M· or to one of God's qualities.

mind (see also mind's)

absent
sp 82– 4 no more difficult to read the absent m· than
Æsculapius of
s 152– 6 to make this book the Æsculapius of m·
all thy
pr 9–18 all thy soul, and with all thy m·"— Matt. 22 : 37.
and body
(see body)
and matter
sp 80–31 the common conviction that m· and matter
b 281– 7 presupposes man to be both m· and matter.
294– 6 If man is both m· and matter,
p 397–27 can never treat mortal m· and matter separately,
r 466– 9 constituted of m· and matter,
492–22 The notion that m· and matter commingle

mind

and soul
g 531– 6 error, . . . that m· and soul are both right and
another
sp 89– 4 in the belief that another m· is speaking
attracting the
ph 169–12 fosters disease by attracting the m· to the
belief of
f 216–31 Give up your material belief of m· in matter,
p 372– 3 mortal belief of m· in matter.
belief that
(see belief)
body and
ph 190– 6 producing mortals, both body and m· ;
f 250–14 Mortal body and m· are one,
b 302– 3 The material body and m· are temporal,
body or
f 209– 9 mortal body or m· is not the man.
brain is not
p 372– 1 Remember, brain is not m·.
burial of
a 35– 8 sensuousness, or the burial of m· in matter,
can never produce
b 304–13 matter can never produce m· nor
carnal
s 131–10 "The carnal m· is enmity against — Rom. 8: 7.
b 311– 3 What we term mortal mind or carnal m·,
o 345–29 enrages the carnal m· and is the main cause of
p 395–12 overcomes faith in a carnal m·,
g 534–19 "The carnal m· is enmity against — Rom. 8: 7.
child's
s 154–19 more than the child's m· governs itself,
clean
p 383– 3 We need a clean body and a clean m·,
corrupt
p 404– 9 A corrupt m· is manifested in a corrupt body.
cruel
b 290–30 learning that his cruel m· died not.
directing the
p 413–25 and constantly directing the m· to such signs,
disturbed
p 379–29 The images, held in this disturbed m·,
400–21 by addressing the disturbed m·,
doctor's
ph 197–30 The doctor's m· reaches that of his patient.
erring
ph 187–27 If you take away this erring m·,
188– 1 only as the mortal, erring m· yields to God,
f 211–22 The transfer of the thoughts of one erring m· to
evil
f 207– 8 God is not the creator of an evil m·.
g 533–18 the rib . . . has grown into an evil m·,
ap 563–13 belief . . . that by means of an evil m· in matter
evil is not
p 398–32 fact remains that evil is not m·.
existence or
a 42–19 belief that man has existence or m· separate
false claim of
ap 504–22 the false claim of m· in matter
feminine
m 57– 7 the feminine m· gains courage and strength
finite
c 257–22 Finite m· manifests all sorts of errors,
o 343– 6 Is not finite m· ignorant of God's method?
gl 580– 7 so-called finite m·, producing other minds,
fleshly
pref xl– 8 not of Spirit, but of the fleshly m·
f 222– 9 whereas Truth regenerates this fleshly m·
functions of
p 395–31 cannot kill a man nor affect the functions of m·
God's
g 525–15 after God's m· shaped He him ;
His
g 525–14 and God shaped man after His m· ;
his
f 221–12 and finally made up his m· to die,
b 290–32 His body is as material as his m·, and vice versa.
p 431–23 hypnotized the prisoner and took control of his m·,
his own
s 159–32 liable to increase disease with his own m·,
hold
gl 587–12 theories that hold m· to be a material sense,
human
(see human)
less than
p 378– 7 Disease is less than m·, and Mind can control it.
life and
b 282– 4 material life and m·, are figured by
296– 8 must destroy all illusions regarding life and m·,
g 556– 5 and are supposed to possess life and m·.
life, or
sp 76– 9 belief that life, or m·, was ever in a finite form,
b 303–17 illusion that life, or m·, is formed by or is in

mind

limited
a 36–19   A selfish and limited *m·* may be unjust,
b 335–17   never included in a limited *m·*

mandate of
s 160–15   to convey the mandate of *m·* to muscle

march of
ap 570– 1   The march of *m·* and of honest investigation

masculine
m 57– 5   The masculine *m·* reaches a higher tone

material
c 257– 9   belief in a bodily soul and a material *m·*,
g 529–31   stands for a belief of material *m·*.

matter and
    (*see* matter)

migratory
f 244–25   not a beast, a vegetable, nor a migratory *m·*.

misnamed
s 108–31   My discovery, that erring, mortal, misnamed *m·*
b 292–27   material mentality, misnamed *m·*,
p 399–25   This misnamed *m·* is not an entity.
r 477–16   matter's highest stratum, misnamed *m·*,

mortal
    (*see* mortal)

mortal's
b 312–10   the departure of a mortal's *m·*,

must be clean
p 383–19   This shows that the *m·* must be clean

my
p 374– 7   the sick say : "How can my *m·* cause a

negative
s 143–25   not controlled scientifically by a negative *m·*.

no
s 113–30   no nerve in Mind, and no *m·* in nerve ;
    113–30   no matter in Mind, and no *m·* in matter ;
b 278– 7   for matter has no *m·*.
g 530–27   The dream has no reality, no intelligence, no *m·* ;

no separate
r 475–19   that which has no separate *m·* from God ;

not matter
    (*see* matter)

observe
p 419–17   Observe *m·* instead of body, lest aught unfit

of mortals
f 230–31   So-called mortal mind or the *m·* of mortals
    231– 6   not destroyed in the *m·* of mortals,
p 423–31   They are only phenomena of the *m·* of mortals.

of the Lord
b 291–18   "the *m·* of the Lord," — *Rom.* 11 : 34.

one
b 276– 6   in which one *m·* is not at war with another,
p 388– 9   Idolaters, believing in more than one *m·*,
r 469–29   belief that there is more than one *m·*
    470– 6   existence of more than one *m·* was the basic error
gl 584–21   which saith : . . . There is more than one *m·*,

opposite of
gl 584–23   the opposite of *m·*, termed matter,

or body
p 365–30   is not giving to *m·* or body the joy and strength
r 473– 1   all inharmony of mortal *m·* or body

our
g 525–13   Let us make man after our *m·*

parent's
p 424– 1   is formed first by the parent's *m·*,

popular
s 137–11   so mysterious to the popular *m·*

presently measure
ph 190–12   which presently measure *m·* by the size of a

quality of
b 279– 4   plainly describes faith, a quality of *m·*, as

rebel against
s 160–19   Can muscles, . . . and nerves rebel against *m·*

rights of
t 453–32   He does not trespass on the rights of *m·*

so-called
sp 71–13   the flower is a product of the so-called *m·*,
    77–21   a so-called *m·* fettered to matter.
s 108–28   which this same so-called *m·* names *matter*,
    122–13   reports to this so-called *m·* its status of
    152– 1   But this so-called *m·* is a myth,
    153–23   proof that this so-called *m·* makes its own pain
    157–14   substratum of this so-called *m·*,
    160–12   When this so-called *m·* quits the body,
ph 165– 9   and to place this so-called *m·* at the mercy of
    177–11   This so-called *m·* builds its own
    178–19   this so-called *m·*, from which comes all evil,
    184–23   a law of this so-called *m·* has been disobeyed.
    187–21   mortal body is governed by this so-called *m·*,
    187–29   and this so-called *m·* then calls itself dead ;
    194–20   education constitutes this so-called *m·*,
f 210–23   this so-called *m·* is self-destructive,
    211–15   does not this so-called *m·* produce the effect
    212–15   take away this so-called *m·* instead of
    231– 7   but seem to this so-called *m·* to be immortal.
    234–19   We must begin with this so-called *m·*
b 292–14   this so-called *m·* has no cognizance of Spirit.

mind

so-called
b 293– 9   This so-called *m·* and body is the
    293–23   and this so-called *m·* is self-destroyed.
p 371– 3   this so-called *m·* must finally yield to
    376–21   only what that so-called *m·* expresses.
    377–21   governing fear of this lower so-called *m·*,
    380–19   produced by a so-called *m·* ignorant of
    399–12   so-called *m·* is both the service and message
    400– 2   once destroyed in this so-called *m·*,
    401– 4   If so-called *m·* is cherishing evil passions
    403–26   so-called *m·* produces all that is unlike the
g 512–29   this so-called *m·* puts forth its own qualities,

spirit or
b 340–19   shall have no other spirit or *m·* but God,

state of
s 159–16   would have considered the woman's state of *m·*,
ph 188–15   to be wholly a state of *m·*.
p 374–21   Such a state of *m·* induces sickness.
    375–28   This state of *m·* seems anomalous

states of
s 161– 6   Holy inspiration has created states of *m·* which
p 377–12   Through different states of *m·*, the body

student's
t 448–19   Try to leave on every student's *m·* the

substance, and
b 325–32   A false sense of life, substance, and *m·*
gl 580–12   origin, substance, and *m·* are found to be
    582– 5   A physical belief as to life, substance, and *m·* ;

substance, or
b 301–21   belief that man has any other substance, or *m·*,
o 354– 2   material life, substance, or *m·*

such a
p 383–16   It is the native element of such a *m·*,

supposed
b 281–18   The *m·* supposed to exist in matter
    339–29   is to divest sin of any supposed *m·* or reality,

suppose error to be
f 250– 2   and suppose error to be *m·*,

supposes that
g 530–31   *Second,* it supposes that *m·* enters matter,

synonym of
g 517– 2   is used also as the synonym of *m·*.

theoretical
b 295–26   The theoretical *m·* is matter, named *brain,*

theory of
c 257–23   the material theory of *m·* in matter

this
pref x– 8   this *m·* is not a factor in the Principle of C. S.
ph 186– 1   by removing the influence on him of this *m·*,
p 400–24   We see in the body the images of this *m·*,
    416–17   this *m·* is material in sensation, even as the

tongue and
sp 89– 7   believing that . . . possesses her tongue and *m·*,

united in a
b 287–28   testify to truth and error as united in a *m·*

unscrupulous
f 235–16   while the debased and unscrupulous *m·*,

wicked
gl 584–22   a wicked *m·*, self-made or created by a

without
s 153–17   matter without *m·* is not painful.
f 217–31   Without *m·*, could the muscles be tired?
p 384– 2   Can matter, . . . act without *m·*?
    386– 7   but no such result occurs without *m·* to

your own
p 412– 7   be thoroughly persuaded in your own *m·*

---

m 68–28   no material growth from molecule to *m·*,
sp 71–17   which simulate *m·*, life, and intelligence.
    80–19   It should not seem mysterious that *m·*,
    87– 3   lost to the memory of the *m·* in which
    88– 6   *m·* may even be cognizant of a present flavor
    91–29   erroneous postulate is, that *m·* is both evil and
    93–15   Good does not create a *m·* susceptible of
s 108–26   false material sense, of *m·* in matter ;
    114– 1   Usage classes both evil and good together as *m·* ;
    114– 7   unscientific definition of *m·* is based on the
    114– 8   and calls *m·* both human and divine.
    114–13   involves an improper use of the word *m·*.
    120– 2   never . . . that soul is in body or *m·* in matter,
    122–31   and *m·* therefore tributary to matter.
    143–18   You admit that *m·* influences the body
    148–14   Both . . . place *m·* at the mercy of matter
    149–18   "We know that *m·* affects the body
    149–21   remarked . . . but *m·* can never cure organic
    151– 4   but this . . . they represent to be body, not *m·*.
    152–11   action as produced by *m·* in one instance
    153–13   rises above matter into *m·*.
    154–32   more successful method . . . . is to say : "Oh,
             never *m·* !
    161–31   looked as deeply for cause and effect into *m·*
ph 165– 8   to subjugate intelligence, to make *m·* mortal,
    166– 3   *M·* is all that feels, acts, or impedes action.
    174–23   Anatomy admits that *m·* is somewhere in man,
    174–26   why . . . administer a dose of despair to the *m·*?
    174–28   why . . . picture this disease to the *m·*,

mind

ph 178–24 the belief of heredity, of *m·* in matter or
188– 4 It is neither *m·* nor matter.
192– 2 belief that a pulpy substance . . . is *m·*
196–28 from the image brought before the *m·* ;
199– 6 nobody believes that *m·* is producing such a
199– 8 If *m·* does not move them, they are
f 204–14 It cannot therefore be *m·*,
204–28 can never be said that man has a *m·* of his own,
208–18 writes : "God is the father of *m·*,
211– 9 Nerves are not *m·*.
217–30 what is this *me ?* Is it muscle or *m·*?
250– 2 suppose . . . *m·* to be in matter
250–21 and the *m·* seems to be absent.
c 256–30 A *m·* originating from a finite or material
257–10 belief in . . . a *m·* in matter.
258– 9 more than a material form with a *m·* inside,
b 275– 2 partnership of *m·* with matter would ignore
277– 6 Matter never produces *m·*.
279–24 pantheistic belief that there is *m·* in matter ;
283–15 They speak of both Truth and error as *m·*,
293– 9 the more ethereal is called *m·*.
293–10 illusion called a mortal, a *m·* in matter.
302–10 The notion that *m·* is in matter,
307– 7 Evil still affirms itself to be *m·*, and declares
308– 2 dwelling in the belief . . . that evil is *m·*,
309–22 led to deny material sense, or *m·* in matter,
311–11 so long as the illusion of *m·* in matter remains.
311 15 false estimates of . . . *m·* as dwelling in matter,
330–27 Evil is nothing, no thing, *m·*, nor power.
o 345–11 It is sometimes said, . . . that the *m·* which
350–25 effects on the body as well as on the *m·*,
p 375–10 believes that matter, not *m·*, has helped him.
383–14 To the *m·* equally gross, dirt gives no
385–20 *M·* decides whether or not the flesh shall be
388–11 with matter, independently of *m·*.
393– 1 issues of pain or pleasure must come through *m·*,
396– 1 should never hold in *m·* the thought of disease,
401–22 If the *m·* were parted from the body,
408–25 less intimately connected with the *m·*
409– 6 animate error called nerves, brain, *m·*,
409–14 this so-called conscious *m·*,
413–26 that *m·* being laden with illusions about
414–10 impossibility that . . . can control or derange *m·*,
414–26 Keep in *m·* the verity of being,
416– 2 This process shows the pain to be in the *m·*,
429–13 affirms that *m·* is subordinate to the body,
t 449–22 The first impression, made on a *m·* which is
r 489– 1 The less *m·* there is manifested in matter
491–19 sometimes presenting no appearance of *m·*,
g 525 11 in the Icelandic, *m·*.
530–31 supposes . . . that matter precedes *m·*.
531–16 If, . . . *m·* was afterwards put into body
532 30 error demands that *m·* shall see and feel through
544–14 nor does matter produce *m·*.
544–29 It declares *m·* to be in and of matter,
551–24 How can matter originate or transmit *m·*?
554 27 *m·* in matter is the author of itself,
555–12 Error would have itself received as *m·*,
555–14 error is neither *m·* nor the outcome of Mind.
gl 584–18 neither corporeality nor *m·* ;
584–21 which saith : . . . for I am *m·*,
591–11 *m·* originating in matter ; the opposite of Truth ;

Mind-action

s 109–17 I knew the Principle of all harmonious *M·* to be

mind-cure

ph 185– 9 which discussed "mental medicine" and "*m·*,"
185–12 Such theories and such systems of so-called *m·*,

minded

sp 95– 6 "To be spiritually *m·* is life."— *Rom.* 8 : 6.

Mind-faculties

r 487– 9 in the perpetual exercise of the *M·*

mind-force

b 310– 5 Matter is made up of supposititious mortal *m·* ;

mind-forces

ph 186– 7 Erring human *m·* can work only evil

Mind-healing

Christian
sp 98–17 the demonstration of Christian *M·* stands a
Christian Science
pref xi–25 The first school of C. S. *M·*
r 493–11 The method of C. S. *M·* is touched upon in a
Principle of
t 454–15 He, who understands . . . the Principle of *M·*,
problem of
s 109–12 I sought the solution of this problem of *M·*,
Science of
(*see* **Science**)
scientific
o 342– 6 unqualified condemnations of scientific *M·*,
system of
t 460– 6 Our system of *M·* rests on the

Mind-healing

teaching
t 445–27 danger in teaching *M·* indiscriminately,

a 52–22 These were the two cardinal points of *M·*,

mind-ideals

o 360– 5 artist replies : . . . I have no *m·* except those

mindless

s 159–13 as if she were so much *m·* matter,
f 253–21 for matter is inert, *m·*.
r 484–17 Drugs and inert matter are unconscious, *m·*.
g 505–11 apparent only as Mind, never as *m·* matter

mindlessness

b 293– 4 the material *m·*, which forms no link

mind-offering

g 541– 3 more nearly resembles a *m·* than does Cain's

Mind-physician

t 443–17 *M·* should give up such cases,

mind-picture

o 360–13 which *m·* or externalized thought shall be real
t 453–28 and impresses more deeply the wrong *m·*.

Mind-power

f 209–14 immanent sense of *M·* enhances the glory of
t 446– 1 teaching his slight knowledge of *M·*,

mind-power

sp 80–21 it is *m·* which moves both table and hand.

mind-readers

sp 87– 1 *M·* perceive these pictures of thought.
87–27 *m·* can perceive and reproduce these impressions.

Mind-reading

sp 83–26 There is mortal mind-reading and immortal *M·*.
83–29 Mortal mind-reading and immortal *M·*
85– 1 This *M·* is the opposite of clairvoyance.
94–32 Jesus could injure no one by his *M·*.

mind-reading

sp 83–25 There is mortal *m·* and immortal Mind-reading.
83–29 Mortal *m·* and immortal Mind-reading
95–16 This kind of *m·* is not clairvoyance,

Mind-remedy

p 384–19 your *M·* is safe and sure.

Mind's

ph 171–12 *M·* control over the universe, including man,
177– 5 The evidence of divine *M·* healing power
182–18 *M·* government of the body must supersede the
182–26 ability to demonstrate *M·* sacred power.
p 389–11 better results of *M·* opposite evidence.
406–29 destroyed only by *M·* mastery of the body.
r 472–16 Error is neither Mind nor one of *M·* faculties.
492–20 Science says : All is Mind and *M·* idea.
g 508– 4 *M·* infinite idea, man and the universe, is the
509–25 the days and seasons of *M·* creation,
514– 7 *M·* infinite ideas run and
517 20 symbol of God as person is *M·* infinite ideal.

mind's

o 345–30 cause of the carnal *m·* antagonism.
p 402–14 with this *m·* own mortal materials.
490–16 mortal *m·* affirmation is not true.

minds

and bodies
s 110–26 the power of C. S. to heal mortal *m·* and bodies.
f 210–15 action of the divine Mind on human *m·* and
bodies
p 408–13 effects of illusion on mortal *m·* and bodies.
better balanced
m 61–13 better balanced *m·*, and sounder constitutions.
carnal
b 315–14 Their carnal *m·* were at enmity with it.
certain
t 449–25 Certain *m·* meet only to separate
discernment of the
sp 82– 7 discernment of the *m·* of Homer and Virgil,
evil
b 307–10 It says : . . . God makes evil *m·*
gl 594–22 evil *m·* ; supposed intelligences, or gods ;
many
s 114– 8 evidence of the . . . senses, which makes *m·* many
b 280–21 the opposite error of many *m·*.
mortal
(*see* **mortal**)
of mortals
ph 175– 3 formulated in the *m·* of mortals.
p 386–13 action of Truth on the *m·* of mortals,
of students
t 453– 7 will be at strife in the *m·* of students, until
of your children
f 237–19 keep out of the *m·* of your children
other
b 323–27 delusion that there are other *m·*,
gl 580– 7 a so-called finite mind, producing other *m·*,
relieve our
p 384– 3 relieve our *m·* from the depressing thought

minds
ruling
f 205–24 a belief in many ruling *m·* hinders
supposititious
gl 587–14 supposititious *m·*, or souls, going in and out
unprejudiced
ap 570–14 Millions of unprejudiced *m·*
which surround
p 424–16 the *m·* which surround your patient should not
wicked
sp 96–31 wicked *m·* will endeavor to find means

---

f 237–11 often choke the good seed in the *m·* of
250– 2 error when we . . . multiply Mind into *m·*
Mind-science
sp 79–29 *M·* teaches that mortals
81– 5 this latter evidence is destroyed by *M·*.
84–22 is a step towards the *M·*
an 103–12 On the other hand, *M·* is wholly separate from
103–13 because *M·* is of God
s 109– 3 as the leading factor in *M·*.
115– 2 through which the understanding of *M·* comes,
p 376–27 Some people, mistaught as to *M·*,
421–30 perversion of *M·* is like asserting that
Mine
f 253– 3 saith : . . . all are *M·*, for I am God.
mine
sp 87–19 The *m·* knows naught of the emeralds
mineral
s 158– 9 from image-gods to vegetable and *m·* drugs
b 277–15 A *m·* is not produced by a vegetable
g 509–20 So-called *m·*, vegetable, and animal substances
minerals
f 209–16 compounded *m·* or aggregated substances
g 531–19 Who will say that *m·*, vegetables, and animals
543–21 *M·* and vegetables are found, . . . to be the
557– 8 Vegetables, *m·*, and many animals suffer no
mingle
sp 72–32 As readily can you *m·* fire and frost
s 122–18 clouds and ocean meet and *m·*.
144– 1 but the two will not *m·* scientifically
ph 186–10 light and darkness, cannot *m·*.
f 239–29 Those two opposite sources never *m·* in fount or
b 276–26 beliefs and spiritual understanding never *m·*.
282–21 At no point can these opposites *m·* or unite.
295–18 The light and the glass never *m·*,
300–18 tares and wheat, which never really *m·*,
303–22 belief that . . . holiness and unholiness, *m·*
mingled
ph 178–31 none of these methods can be *m·* with
mingles
ph 191–29 in C. S., Truth never *m·* with error.
mingling
a 27–17 Life as never *m·* with sin and death.
m 58– 9 these constituents of thought, *m·*,
b 269– 4 the supposed . . . *m·* of good and evil
minister
t 453–15 and *m·* to human needs.
ministering
o 360–26 putteth no trust in His *m·* — see Job 4 : 18.
p 440–18 for *m·* to the wants of his fellow-man
ap 567– 2 a sense of the ever-presence of *m·* Love.
ministry
f 236– 4 A special privilege is vested in the *m·*.
ap 574–10 *m·* of Truth, this message from divine Love,
minor
s 128–31 If both the major and the *m·* propositions of a
145–15 or reliance on some other *m·* curative.
minority
s 155–13 is but a belief held by a *m·*,
ph 178– 6 *m·* of opinions in the sick-chamber.
minus
s 164–13 *m·* the unction of divine Science.
minute
p 390– 1 The next *m·* she said, "My food is all digested,
minutely
ph 197– 5 A *m·* described disease costs many a man his
minutes
ph 193–13 In about ten *m·* he opened his eyes and said :
p 389–32 I cured her in a few *m·*.
416– 7 in twenty *m·* the sufferer is quietly asleep.
g 556–32 plunged . . . into the water for several *m·*,
557– 2 the child could remain under water twenty *m·*,
minutiæ
b 303– 8 The *m·* of lesser individualities reflect

miracle
great
ap 560–12 The great *m·*, to human sense, is divine Love,
mystery and
g 501–14 So-called mystery and *m·*, which subserve the
of grace
r 494–15 The *m·* of grace is no miracle to Love.
word rendered
r 474–12 word rendered *m·* in the New Testament

---

s 134–31 A *m·* fulfils God's law, but does not violate
135– 1 seems more mysterious than the *m·* itself.
135– 6 The *m·* introduces no disorder, but unfolds
b 319–17 Mystery, *m·*, sin, and death will disappear
r 494–15 The miracle of grace is no *m·* to Love.
gl 591–21 definition of
miracles
attended the
s 133–13 *m·* attended the successes of the Hebrews ;
called
s 139– 7 Moses proved . . . by what men called *m·* ;
o 343–18 proving by what are wrongly called *m·*,
of grace
s 134–17 the doctrines of Christ or the *m·* of grace
so-called
s 123–25 the so-called *m·* of Jesus did not specially
131–27 explained the so-called *m·* of olden time
f 212–29 say . . . that other methods involve so-called *m·*.

---

sp 83–12 *M·* are impossible in Science,
s 117–20 Principle involved in the *m·* (marvels)
miraculous
s 128– 3 It is not *m·* to itself.
138–10 cures, which appeared *m·* to outsiders.
b 270–31 The life of Christ Jesus was not *m·*,
mirage
f 244– 3 but is illusion, the *m·* of error.
b 300– 5 The *m·*, which makes trees and cities seem to be
mire
an 106– 3 is to drop . . . into the very *m·* of iniquity,
mirror
ph 197– 2 descriptions which *m·* images of disease
f 220–20 like a kitten glancing into the *m·* at itself
b 301– 2 the *m·*, repeats the color, form, and
301– 4 the person in front of the *m·*,
305– 5 a face reflected in the *m·* is not the original,
g 515–29 Now compare man before the *m·* to his
515–29 Call the *m·* divine Science, and call man the
516– 3 As the reflection of yourself appears in the *m·*,
ap 571–24 *m·* in which mortals may see their own image.
mirrored
b 305– 9 As there is no corporeality in the *m·* form,
g 515–25 Your *m·* reflection is your own image
misapprehended
b 304–27 liable to be *m·* and lost in confusion.
misapprehension
pr 10–23 There is some *m·* of the source and means of
a 51– 3 the possible *m·* of the sublimest influence of
ph 191– 9 is found to be a *m·* of existence,
b 319–23 Hence the *m·* of the spiritual meaning
o 355–23 *m·* both of the divine Principle and practice of
miscalled
s 164–22 the materiality *m·* life in the body
ph 187–20 voluntary, as well as *m· involuntary*, action
192–11 a material belief, a blind *m·* force,
g 550–11 to investigate what is *m·* material life,
mischief
s 154–23 it is believed that exposure . . . wrought the *m·*.
162–32 "it is impossible to calculate the *m·* which
t 459–20 a false practitioner will work *m·*,
mischief-maker
t 460–20 abused . . . it becomes a tedious *m·*.
misconceived
b 281–19 *m·* sense and false conception as to man and
misconception
sp 86– 9 *m·* of it uncovered their materiality.
p 373–29 This is a *m·*.
g 542–29 *m·* of Life as something less than
554– 9 Any statement of life, following from a *m·*
misconceptions
sp 94–13 owe their false government to the *m·* of Deity
p 428–20 the ability of mental might to offset human *m·*
g 512–27 confers animal names and natures upon its own *m·*.
misconstrued
a 45–24 after the resurrection . . . *m·* that event.
f 242–22 the facts of being are commonly *m·*,
mis-creator
c 263–15 He becomes a general *m·*,

misdeed
  p 439–12 a misguided participant in the *m·*

misdirected
  b 274–18 five physical senses are *m·*,

miserable
  ap 573–17 man was no longer regarded as a *m·* sinner,

misery
  s 122–14 its status of happiness or *m·*.
  ph 172–2 constitutes his happiness or *m·*.
  b 327–12 way to escape the *m·* of sin is to cease sinning.
  ap 574–17 sum total of human *m·*, represented by

misfortune
  p 403–9 in the second it is believed that the *m·* is a

misfortunes
  p 394–21 assuring him that all *m·* are

misguide
  f 206–5 else it will *m·* the judgment and
  b 319–7 would infringe upon spiritual law and *m·*

misguided
  f 220–8 Instinct is better than *m·* reason,
  p 439–12 Materia Medica was a *m·* participant

misinterpretation
  b 319–25 the *m·* of the Word in some instances
  r 474–10 hence the *m·* and consequent maltreatment

misinterpreted
  sp 93–12 otherwise, we may be sure . . . that we have *m·*
  98–9 Science of Christianity is *m·* by a material age,
  g 507–31 *m·*, the divine idea seems to fall to the level of

misinterprets
  f 240–2 but human belief *m·* nature.

misleads
  b 275–27 It destroys the false evidence that *m·*

misled
  p 397–5 By not . . . we are *m·* in our conclusions

misnamed
  s 108–30 erring, mortal, *m· mind* produces all the
  f 229–17 This customary belief is *m·* material law,
  b 284–24 Even the more subtile and *m·* material elements
  292–27 material mentality, *m· mind*,
  294–11 This mortal belief, *m· man*, is
  p 387–25 so-called mortal mind, *m·* matter,
  399–25 This *m·* mind is not an entity.
  r 477–15 matter's highest stratum, *m·* mind,

misplaced
  b 319–27 A *m·* word changes the sense

misrepresent
  o 343–7 unfair to impugn and *m·* the facts,
  g 538–17 the false claims that *m·* God, good

misrepresentation
  o 341–18 *m·* and denunciation cannot overthrow it.

misrepresentations
  o 344–14 would perhaps mercifully withhold their *m·*,

misrepresented
  s 110–22 and its ideas may be temporarily abused and *m·*;

misrule
  s 119–15 maintaining perpetual *m·* in the form and

mission
  abuse of the
    t 455–22 renders any abuse of the *m·* an impossibility.
  curative
    a 55–11 that curative *m·*, which presents the Saviour
  earthly
    a 41–16 completed his earthly *m·*;
  fulfil one's
    r 483–31 One must fulfil one's *m·* without timidity
  higher
    s 150–16 to attest the reality of the higher *m·*
  his
    a 18–5 His *m·* was both individual and collective.
    26–16 His *m·* was to reveal the Science of
    50–28 disbelieving the purpose of his *m·*,
    s 136–1 established his church and maintained his *m·*
  his great
    ap 560–24 which made him equal to his great *m·*.
  Jesus'
    a 28–3 they only hindered the success of Jesus' *m·*.
  of Christ
    r 474–30 The apostle says that the *m·* of Christ is
  of Christian Science
    s 150–10 but the *m·* of C. S. now, as in the time of
  of Jesus
    s 131–26 The *m·* of Jesus confirmed prophecy,
  our Master's
    f 233–23 To reveal this truth was our Master's *m·*
  reformatory
    s 129–28 in its reformatory *m·* among mortals.

missionaries
  b 328–17 Our *m·* carry the Bible to India,

misstated
  g 546–10 Is the divine Principle of creation *m·*?

misstates
  b 319–28 and *m·* the Science of the Scriptures,

mist
  b 299–27 as the *m·* obscures the sun or the mountain ;
  g 521–21 went up a *m·* from the earth, — *Gen. 2 : 6.*
  523–3 the *m·* of obscurity evolved by error
  523–8 The creations of matter arise from a *m·*
  546–12 went up a *m·* from the earth.'' — *Gen. 2 : 6.*
  557–16 When the *m·* of mortal mind evaporates,
  ap 576–5 seems hidden in the *m·* of remoteness,

mistake
  correcting the
    p 386–20 Another despatch, correcting the *m·*,
  grave
    sp 73–26 It is a grave *m·* to suppose that matter is
  great
    f 216–19 The great *m·* of mortals is to suppose that
  his
    b 327–28 convince the mortal of his *m·* in
    p 403–6 by his *m·* a man is often instructed.
  medical
    ph 166–14 the doctor's . . . is a medical *m·*.
    p 383–31 another medical *m·* resulting from the
  only a
    sp 92–26 should blush to call that real which is only a *m·*;
  same
    s 122–29 Our theories make the same *m·* regarding
  terrible
    b 289–11 To suppose that . . . is a terrible *m·*.
  this
    ph 179–31 may erelong reap the effect of this *m·*.
  through
    ph 177–25 If a dose of poison is swallowed through *m·*,

    ———
  a 28–27 to *m·* the very nature of religion.
  sp 70–11 The supposition that . . . is a *m·*.
  92–29 The *m·* of thinking that error can be real,
  pn 166–17 To ignore God as of little use in sickness is a *m·*.
  183–5 To suppose that . . . is a *m·* ;
  197–22 but that is a *m·*.
  f 249–21 What a *m·* is that !
  o 343–28 Hence the *m·* which allows words, rather than
  t 455–20 but God cannot *m·*.
  r 474–9 To the ignorant age . . . Science seems to be a *m·*,
  g 549–6 shown by divine metaphysics to be a *m·*,

mistaken
  sp 75–1 This simple truth lays bare the *m·* assumption
  f 229–18 individual who upholds it is *m·* in theory
  p 377–27 a mortal fear, a *m·* belief or
  t 451–30 either with a *m·* or a wicked purpose
  455–19 may be *m·* in judgment and demonstration,
  g 554–19 infinite Mind sets at naught such a *m·* belief.

mistakenly
  p 386–16 despatch, *m·* announcing the death of a friend,

mistakes
  does not make
    f 206–29 This Mind does not make *m·*
  fatal
    m 59–31 fatal *m·* are undermining its foundations.
  grave
    b 201–5 those are grave *m·*.
  manifest
    s 139–17 the manifest *m·* in the ancient versions ;
  sins or
    pr 11–13 never pardons our sins or *m·* till they are
  such
    b 294–31 The Science of Mind corrects such *m·*,
  unconscious
    s 161–29 Such unconscious *m·* would not occur, if

    s 124–8 this belief *m·* effect for cause
    139–22 But *m·* could neither wholly obscure the
    p 408–7 universal insanity . . . which *m·* fable for fact
    g 549–27 even this great observer *m·* nature,

mistaking
  sp 84–5 not by . . . *m·* fact for fiction,
  ph 171–17 *M·* his origin and nature, man believes

mistaught
  p 376–27 Some people, *m·* as to Mind-science,

mistiness
  gl 586–1 EVENING. *M·* of mortal thought ;

mistrust
  m 68–10 The presence of *m·*, where confidence is due,

mists
  f 205–17 glimpses of God only as the *m·* disperse,

misunderstand
pr 6–21 is to *m·* Love and to make prayer the
f 219–23 and yet *m·* the science that governs it.
219–26 may *m·* it, and impute their recovery to
231–22 To fear sin is to *m·* the power of Love
ap 560–28 To *m·* Paul, was to be ignorant of the

misunderstood
a 53–10 divine Principle and practice of Jesus were *m·*.
r 474–13 will be *m·* and misused by many, until

misuse
an 106– 1 the criminal *m·* of human will-power,
p 410–24 The Science . . . is susceptible of no *m·*.
t 455–26 No person can *m·* this mental power, if

misused
r 474–13 will be misunderstood and *m·* by many, until

mitigates
m 63–15 civilization *m·* it in some measure.

mitre
ap 571–31 He takes away *m·* and sceptre.

mix
ph 182–16 antagonistic to Science and cannot *m·* with it.

mixture
f 204–16 supposed *m·* of the first and second

Moabitish
g 524– 2 in the *M·* god Chemosh,

moaning
s 154–29 *m·* more childishly than her child,

mock
b 329–22 You cannot *m·* it by human will.
g 542–12 jeopardize self-control, and *m·* divine mercy.

mocked
a 43–16 had *m·* and tried to slay.
49–28 *m·* him on the cross, saying derisively,

mockery
a 36–28 and *m·* of our motives
39– 1 Meekly our Master met the *m·* of
50– 5 The last supreme moment of *m·*, desertion,
ph 192– 2 a *m·* of intelligence, a mimicry of Mind.
192–25 It is a *m·* of strength, which erelong

mocking
a 53–23 *m·* the lifelong sacrifice which goodness makes
f 241–12 what a *m·* spectacle is sin !
g 528–21 simulates the work of Truth, *m·* Love

model
his
f 248–12 turns from the marble to his *m·*
imperfect
f 248–20 Do you not hear . . . of the imperfect *m·*?
c 260– 4 outlines from an imperfect *m·*,
mortal
f 248–17 Have you accepted the mortal *m·*?
perfect
c 260–11 the immortal and perfect *m·* of God's creation
p 407–24 Let the perfect *m·* be present in your thoughts
true
p 409–26 and seek the true *m·*.
your
o 360–17 Either Spirit or matter is your *m·*.

f 236–15 either after a *m·* odious to herself
248–15 What is the *m·* before mortal mind?

models
f 235–20 Physicians, . . . should be *m·* of virtue.
247–16 Immortal men and women are *m·* of
248–24 angular outline and deformity of matter *m·*.
248–27 We must form perfect *m·* in thought
249– 2 give up imperfect *m·* and illusive ideals ;
249– 4 producing His own *m·* of excellence.
c 260–20 in order to improve their *m·*.
o 360–18 If you try to have two *m·*, then you

modern
s 126–26 nothing in ancient or in *m·* systems on which to
142– 6 *m·* religions generally omit all but one of
ph 176– 3 *m·* Eves took up the study of medical works
f 224–17 The *m·* lash is less material than the
b 319–17 so many ancient and *m·* mythologies.
g 548–27 *M·* discoveries have brought to light
552– 6 Heathen philosophy, *m·* geology,

moderns
p 411–14 a disease which *m·* would call *dementia*.

modes
s 118–19 that is, three *m·* of mortal thought.
118–22 and *m·* of material motion are honored
ph 170– 3 *M·* of matter form neither a moral nor a
170– 6 exercise of faith in material *m·*,
p 373–10 Under all *m·* of pathological treatment,
406– 7 in place of *m·* and forms,

modest
g 516–15 The *m·* arbutus sends her sweet

modifying
sp 93–25 The *m·* derivatives of the word *spirit*

modus
f 212–17 Mortals have a *m·* of their own,
213– 1 would reverse the immortal *m·* and action,

modus operandi
g 529– 2 there came a suggestion of change in the *m· o·*,

Mohammedan
ph 166– 8 *M·* believes in a pilgrimage to Mecca

Mohammedan's
ph 166–12 The *M·* belief is a religious delusion ;

molar
f 247– 7 incisors, cuspids, bicuspids, and one *m·*.

mole
sp 82–26 as impossible as it would be between a *m·* and a

molecule
m 68–28 no material growth from *m·* to mind,
g 507–25 from the mental *m·* to infinity.

mollusca
g 556– 3 Vertebrata, articulata, *m·*, and radiata are

Moloch
g 524– 3 in the *M·* of the Amorites,

moment
any
f 252–27 says : . . . may at any *m·* annihilate my peace,
o 352–19 for at any *m·* they may become
at that
b 290–24 The sin and error . . . do not cease at that *m·*,
at the
b 290–17 would be won at the *m·* of dissolution,
during that
b 306–10 during that *m·* there would be no
for a
a 50–19 If his full recognition of eternal Life had for a *m·*
b 306– 9 If God, who is Life, were parted for a *m·* from
309–30 Life is never for a *m·* extinct.
great
sp 85–18 events of great *m·* were foretold by the
last
a 36–25 gloat over their offences to the last *m·*
one
gl 598–23 One *m·* of divine consciousness,
possible
sp 75–25 There is one possible *m·*, when those
single
pr 14–12 Become conscious for a single *m·* that
supreme
a 50– 5 The last supreme *m·* of mockery,
p 428– 7 Man's privilege at this supreme *m·* is to prove
when the link
sp 75–28 *m·* when the link between their opposite beliefs

sp 75–27 the *m·* previous to the transition,
r 470–24 If there ever was a *m·* when man
470–26 then there was a *m·* when man did not

momentary
pr 7– 8 gives *m·* solemnity and elevation to thought.

momentous
a 48–25 in the presence of his own *m·* question,
g 516–27 To emphasize this *m·* thought,

moments
pr 7–19 there would grow out of ecstatic *m·*
ph 184–29 I sat silently by her side a few *m·*.
193–10 In a few *m·* his face changed ;
f 218–30 applying it literally to *m·* of fatigue,

momentum
p 380–26 evidence will gather *m·* and clearness,

monad
sp 90– 4 and that, too, without meal or *m·*

monarch
s 152– 2 It would wield the sceptre of a *m·*,

money
t 445–32 for the petty consideration of *m·*,

monkeys
ph 172– 4 Theorizing . . . from mushrooms to *m·*
172– 4 and from *m·* into men

monopoly
s 141–18 no dynasty, no ecclesiastical *m·*.

monotheist
o 361– 7 The Jew . . . is a *m·* ;
361–10 The Christian . . . is a *m·*.

monstrous
g 550–28 Amalgamation is deemed *m·*

month
a 32–29 ate with his disciples in the *m·* Nisan

monthly
pref xii–10 Christian Scientist Association, convening *m·* ;

months
ph 168–25 *m·* before the so-called disease made its
193– 1 confined to his bed six *m·* with hip-disease.
f 212–12 a finger which had been cut off for *m·*.
237– 7 It might have been *m·* or years before

monuments
s 150– 1 *m·* to the virtue and power of Truth,

mood
p 420–15 when they are in a fit *m·* to receive it,
ap 570– 6 shocked into another extreme mortal *m·*,

moon
g 547–13 the gathering clouds, the *m·* and stars,
ap 560– 7 and the *m·* under her feet,— *Rev.* 12 : 1.
562– 7 The *m·* is under her feet.

moonbeams
f 241–16 than can *m·* to melt a river of ice.

moon-god
an 103– 5 Sin was the Assyrian *m·*.

moral
pr 11– 6 this may be no *m·* benefit to the criminal,
11– 8 The *m·* law, which has the right to acquit or
a 22– 5 Vibrating . . . our *m·* progress will be slow.
36–15 the great *m·* distance between Christianity and
m 56– 7 Marriage is the legal and *m·* provision for
56–13 subject to such *m·* regulations as will
58–12 There is *m·* freedom in Soul.
59–28 so long as its *m·* obligations are kept intact ;
62– 5 habits of obedience to the *m·* and spiritual law,
sp 92–23 the *m·* demand will not be met,
95–12 Whoever reaches this point of *m·* culture
96–21 will vanish in a *m·* chemicalization.
an 101–25 lead to *m·* and to physical death.
103–24 malicious form of . . . ultimates in *m·* idiocy.
s 115–26 definition of
118– 6 Did not this parable point a *m·*
119–13 all disasters, physical and *m·*,
124– 7 Having neither *m·* might, spiritual basis, nor
125– 5 *M·* conditions will be found always harmonious
139–32 The *m·* condition of such a man demands
140– 0 effectual in the treatment of *m·* ailments.
150–22 human view infringes man's free *m·* agency ;
ph 170– 3 neither a *m·* nor a spiritual system.
171– 3 mankind has caught their *m·* contagion.
171–21 The intellectual, the *m·*, the spiritual,
192–17 *M·* and spiritual might belong to Spirit,
197–12 the more . . . said about *m·* and spiritual law,
f 218–31 the *m·* and physical are as one in their results.
234–29 was to break a *m·* precept.
235–13 *m·* and spiritual culture, which lifts one higher.
244– 2 does not produce *m·* or physical deformity ;
c 260–23 evolves back physical and *m·* conditions.
b 288–10 When the final physical and *m·* effects of C. S.
320–10 must rest upon both the literal and *m·* ;"
327–15 It is a *m·* madness which rushes forth to
327–31 the man's dormant sense of *m·* obligation,
p 363–26 detect this unspoken *m·* uprising?
366– 4 must first cast *m·* evils out of himself
370–18 The *m·* and spiritual facts of health,
373– 1 If we are Christians on all *m·* questions, but
375–18 adding to his patient's mental and *m·* power,
381–11 except a *m·* or spiritual law.
381–29 man's *m·* right to annul an unjust sentence.
391–17 Justice is the *m·* signification of law.
392– 4 broken *m·* law should be taken into account
395–02 a *m·* offence is indeed the worst of diseases.
405–14 sentence of the *m·* law will be executed
405–27 hastening on to physical and *m·* doom.
405–28 conquered by the *m·* penalties you incur
406–16 *m·* man has no fear that he will commit a murder,
418–26 Include *m·* as well as physical belief in your
419– 1 A *m·* question may hinder the recovery of the
422– 6 *m·* and physical symptoms seem aggravated,
422–15 so mental and *m·* chemistry changes the
t 447– 3 no *m·* right to attempt to influence the
448– 2 to indulge them, is a *m·* offence.
448–20 the *m·* and spiritual qualifications requisite
449–11 Man's *m·* mercury, rising or falling,
451–32 malpractice tends to blast *m·* sense,
453–11 the morbid *m·* or physical symptoms
455– 8 You must utilize the *m·* might of Mind
460– 8 Its pharmacy is *m·*, and its medicine is
r 483– 9 you must not be ignorant of the *m·* and
483–10 *M·* ignorance or sin affects your
492– 9 will uplift the physical and *m·* standard of
493–23 any other sense of *m·* or mental inharmony.
g 531– 9 represent the higher *m·* sentiments,
540–11 In *m·* chemicalization, when the symptoms
gl 592–12 a type of *m·* law and the
(*see also* **courage**)

morale
m 61–30 The scientific *m·* of marriage is spiritual unity.
p 367– 2 nor bury the *m·* of C. S. in the grave-clothes of
t 456–19 One must abide in the *m·* of truth

morally
f 220–27 better *m·* or physically
p 369–31 any more than he is *m·* saved in or by sin.
434–23 His trial was a tragedy, and is *m·* illegal.
t 445– 5 who attempts to kill *m·* and physically.
451–23 He feels *m·* obligated to open the eyes of
461– 8 taught only by those who are *m·* advanced
r 466–31 better physically, *m·*, and spiritually.
495–13 and sets the captive free physically and *m·*.
ap 564– 6 incites mortals to kill *m·* and physically
gl 587– 4 acknowledged *m·*, civilly, and socially.

morals
and health
b 273–32 cannot be destructive to *m·* and health when
bad
t 446– 2 perhaps communicating his own bad *m·*,
health and
p 400– 6 its influence upon health and *m·*
426–25 would raise the standard of health and *m·*
r 485–17 through better health and *m·*
of men
s 126–25 the health, longevity, and *m·* of men ;
sound
pref x–31 but sound *m·* are most desirable.
———
f 235– 9 with as direct reference to their *m·* as to
p 397– 4 the *m·* and the happiness of mortals,
t 445–28 thus disregarding the *m·* of the student
449–29 improves the health and the *m·* of his student

morbid
p 377–22 the *m·* or excited action of any organ.
t 453–10 the *m·* moral or physical symptoms

Morbid Secretion
p 431–22 *M· S·* hypnotized the prisoner
438–21 foul fur was spread over him by *M· S·*,
438–28 *M· S·* is not an importer or dealer in fur,
438–30 we know *M· S·* to be on friendly terms with
440– 6 *M· S·* is taught how to make sleep befool

more
pref ix– 8 voices the *m·* definite thought,
x–24 its practice is safer and *m·* potent
pr 2– 8 *m·* than He has already done,
2–11 We can do *m·* for ourselves by humble fervent
2–23 God is Love. Can we ask Him to be *m·* ?
2–27 Shall we plead for *m·* at the open fount,
2–28 which is pouring forth *m·* than we accept
3–24 and thus be fitted to receive *m·*.
3–25 Gratitude is much *m·* than a verbal expression
3–26 Action expresses *m·* gratitude than speech.
4–20 to assimilate *m·* of the divine character,
6–13 will furnish *m·* than its equivalent of pain,
6–17 *M·* than this we cannot ask,
7–21 with *m·* devout self-abnegation and purity.
8–26 do we not already know *m·* of this heart than
11– 4 "Go, and sin no *m·*."—*John* 8 ; 11.
12– 4 to gain *m·* of the divine presence
12– 7 making it act *m·* powerfully on the body
a 25– 7 was no *m·* efficacious to cleanse from sin when
25–18 he demonstrated *m·* spiritually than
13–10 one's consecration to Christ is *m·* on the
29–13 by understanding *m·* of the divine Principle
29– 8 It bids us work the *m·* earnestly
29– 9 because then our labor is *m·* needed.
30– 2 *m·* spiritual idea of life than other men,
34–18 they became *m·* spiritual
35–13 to receive *m·* of his reappearing
37–21 the *m·* practical import of that career !
39– 4 even *m·* pernicious than the old doctrine of
41–29 demanded *m·* than they were willing to practise.
42–32 must understand *m·* fully his Life-principle
45–12 much *m·*, being reconciled,— *Rom.* 5 : 10.
46–29 and the material senses saw him no *m·*.
51– 2 something *m·* important than human life
51–17 he could no *m·* be separated from his
54–23 whose religion was something *m·* than a name.
55– 6 did Jesus no *m·* injustice than
m 57–27 serves to unite thought *m·* closely to God,
58–15 benevolence should grow *m·* diffusive.
58–24 " Two eat no *m·* together than they
59–18 will prove *m·* salutary in prolonging her health
60–30 happiness would be *m·* readily attained
60–31 would be *m·* secure in our keeping,
61–12 inherit *m·* intellect, better balanced minds,
61–25 a *m·* solemn charge, than the culture of
62–15 will do much *m·* for the health of the
62–20 We must not attribute *m·* and *m·* intelligence
64–20 no *m·* marrying nor giving in marriage,
65–12 life should be *m·* metaphysically regarded.
65–27 find permanence and peace in a *m·* spiritual
68–16 I never knew *m·* than one individual who
sp 76–14 neither can he return to it, any *m·* than
79– 7 A scientific mental method is *m·* sanitary than
81–12 no *m·* proves him to be so, than
82– 3 It is no *m·* difficult to read the absent mind
83– 9 Nothing is *m·* antagonistic to C. S. than

more

sp 84–15   to commune *m·* largely with the divine Mind,
84–32   we can know the truth *m·* accurately than
85–26   seeking the material *m·* than the spiritual.
86–10   Jesus possessed *m·* spiritual susceptibility
86–22   Then why is it *m·* difficult to see a thought
89–22   We are all capable of *m·* than we do.
96–32   means by which to accomplish *m·* evil ;
97– 5   In reality, the *m·* closely error simulates truth
97– 7   the *m·* impotent error becomes as a belief.
97–11   The *m·* destructive matter becomes,
97–12   the *m·* its nothingness will appear,
97–17   The *m·* material the belief, the *m·* obvious its
an 101– 5   that there is one *m·* fact to be recorded
102–12   The planets have no *m·* power over man than
102–20   weaving webs *m·* complicated and subtle.
102–27   much *m·* likely to be abused by its possessor,
103–22   belief . . . that evil is as real . . . and *m·* powerful.
s 108–18   not a fraction *m·*, not a unit less.
111– 7   Science of God and man is no *m·* supernatural
112– 3   Is there *m·* than one school of C. S. ?
116–12   includes vastly *m·* than is at first seen.
125– 9   *m·* harmonious in his manifestations than
125–31   be proved nothing *m·* than a mortal belief,
128–13   becomes *m·* elastic, is capable of greater
134–32   This fact at present seems *m·* mysterious than
138–23   the sick are *m·* willing to part with pain
140– 1   *m·* than it is needed in most cases ;
140– 2   Science is *m·* than usually effectual in
140–11   warring no *m·* over the corporeality,
141– 3   *M·* than profession is requisite for
143– 8   sick are *m·* deplorably lost than the sinning, if
144–11   The *m·* material a belief, the *m·* obstinately
146– 5   are governed *m·* or less by our systems of
149– 4   The *m·* excellent way is divine Science
149–14   Truth, *m·* in your own life,
153–13   This discovery leads to *m·* light.
153–29   *m·* careful of our mental conditions,
154–19   *m·* than the child's mind governs itself,
154–30   moaning *m·* childishly than her child,
154–31   The better and *m·* successful method
155–22   The human mind acts *m·* powerfully to offset
155–24   and *m·* weight into the spiritual scale.
157–13   drug becomes *m·* like the human mind than
160– 9   The motion of the arm is no *m·* dependent
161– 4   *m·* exact than you suppose ;
163–17   has already destroyed *m·* lives than war,
163–27   if it were not *m·* than compensated by the
164–11   they are *m·* scientific than are
ph 165– *   *Is not the life m· than meat, — Matt.* 6 : 25.
167–21   can no *m·* unite in action, than
170–23   for *m·* than all others spiritual causation
171–23   No *m·* sympathy exists between the flesh and
172–29   *m·* nobility than the statuesque athlete,
173–30   in *m·* fatal to health and longevity than
174– 3   by their *m·* studied methods.
176–12   *m·* "sermons in stones, and good in
176–25   One disease is no *m·* real than another.
180–15   the invalid may unwittingly add *m·* fear
180–32   I have found divine Truth *m·* potent than
181–10   electricity and magnetism *m·* than
187– 1   believing in *m·* than the one Mind.
189– 8   In like manner mortals should no *m·* deny the
190–26   place thereof shall know it no *m·*. — *Psal.* 103 : 16.
191– 4   delusion that there is *m·* than one Mind,
191– 5   delusion that there is . . . *m·* than one God,
194–25   with no *m·* intelligence than a babe,
197–12   the *m·* that is thought and said about
197–19   *m·* honest than our sleek politicians.
197–32   *m·* than his calomel and morphine,
198– 2   higher stratum of mortal mind has in belief *m·*
198–23   A patient's belief is *m·* or less moulded
f 202–26   Truth should "much *m·* abound." — *Rom.* 5 : 20.
202–30   as if senseless matter . . . had *m·* power than
203–12   incites to a *m·* exalted worship
203–17   We are prone to believe either in *m·* than
204– 4   false conclusions that there is *m·* than one
207– 2   evil becomes *m·* apparent and obnoxious
212– 9   the memory of pain is *m·* vivid
213–20   Mozart experienced *m·* than he expressed.
213–23   even *m·* strikingly true of Beethoven,
214–21   *m·* than they do a spiritual God.
217– 3   notion of such a possibility is *m·* absurd than
218– 7   rests us *m·* than hours of repose
219– 7   No *m·* can we say in Science that
220–13   procures a summer residence with *m·* ease than
221– 5   decided that his diet should be *m·* rigid,
222–16   consulting the stomach less . . . and God *m·*,
223–16   but *m·* are blinded by their old illusions,
223–29   will much *m·* abound as truth urges
224–22   A higher and *m·* practical Christianity,
225–25   abolition of mental slavery is a *m·* difficult
226– 4   under *m·* subtle and depraving forms.
230–17   God, good, can no *m·* produce sickness than
233–18   much *m·* should ye discern the sign mental,
233–26   is not *m·* unquestionable than the

more

f 234– 9   become *m·* familiar with good than with evil,
234–31   and do no *m·* harm than
236–25   children are *m·* tractable than adults,
236–26   and learn *m·* readily to love the simple verities
237–10   The *m·* stubborn beliefs and theories of
237–27   *m·* for them than they are willing to admit
238– 8   but this frown, *m·* than flatteries,
239–19   becoming nearer, dearer, and *m·* real to us,
241–16   that compilation can do no *m·* for
242–15   Self-love is *m·* opaque than a solid body.
243–13   That those wonders are not *m·* commonly
244–18   man was never *m·* nor less than man.
245–19   a Franklin might work with *m·* certainty
246–22   would enjoy *m·* than threescore years and ten
247–32   to have less illusion and *m·* Soul,
250–22   Is there any *m·* reality in the waking dream
250–26   matter has no *m·* sense as a man than
251– 1   hence it is not *m·* imperative
251– 4   an abscess should not grow *m·* painful
251– 5   neither should a fever become *m·* severe
c 258– 9   Man is *m·* than a material form with a
258–16   know no *m·* of man as the . . . than
260– 1   can no *m·* arrive at the true conception
264–13   As mortals gain *m·* correct views of God and
265–14   a *m·* expansive love,
265–14   a higher and *m·* permanent peace.
267–20   *m·* than is detected upon the surface,
b 270–19   divine Mind, in His *m·* infinite meanings,
279–14   one can no *m·* create the other than
279–23   *m·* or less infected with the pantheistic
281– 4   Spirit and matter no *m·* commingle than
283–29   and unless we so do, we can no *m·* demonstrate
284–24   Even the *m·* subtile and misnamed
287–16   How can there be *m·* than *all ?*
290–28   He is no *m·* spiritual for believing that
293– 8   the *m·* ethereal is called mind.
294– 9   not *m·* real than the belief that matter
297–20   Faith is higher and *m·* spiritual than belief.
299– 1   It has behind it no *m·* reality than has the
305– 3   discordant mortal is no *m·* a *man* than
306–22   not *m·* distinct nor real to the
307– 8   declares that there is *m·* than one intelligence
314– 1   and the body no *m·* perfect because of death
314–21   presented to her, *m·* than ever before,
314–26   the *m·* distinctly he uttered the demands
314–28   the *m·* odious he became to sinners
315–27   *m·* spiritual than all other earthly
317–19   *m·* real, *m·* formidable in truth,
317–27   to the testimony of . . . *m·* than to Soul,
318– 4   but for him to . . . was *m·* difficult.
318–19   invalids grow *m·* spiritual,
323–13   In order to apprehend *m·*, we must
324– 8   Unless the . . . are becoming *m·* apparent,
326–11   or trusting in it *m·* than in the spiritual.
326–27   and his life became *m·* spiritual.
327–25   the man who has *m·* animal than moral
329–30   the *m·* intense the opposition to spirituality,
331– 1   Life is no *m·* confined to the forms which
335–20   for Spirit is *m·* than all else.
339–21   has yielded to a *m·* spiritual idea of Deity,
o 344–11   Were it *m·* fully understood that Truth heals
344–30   *m·* fashionable and less spiritual?
349– 2   when this Science is *m·* generally understood
353–14   It still holds them *m·* or less.
354–18   seen in example *m·* than in precept.
355–12   Let discord . . . be heard no *m·*,
356–32   Then there must have been *m·* than one creator,
     m· than one God.
358–19   *m·* frequently cited for our instruction
360–24   Shall mortal man be *m·* just than — *Job* 4 : 17.
360–25   Shall man be *m·* pure than his — *see Job* 4 : 17.
p 365– 5   much *m·* towards healing the sick
369–31   any *m·* than he is morally saved in or by sin.
370–25   and do no *m·* for the patient.
371–15   no *m·* comprehends his real being than
372–19   How, then, in Christianity any *m·* than in C. S.,
373– 4   and be *m·* alive to His promises.
373–10   the sick recover *m·* rapidly from disease than
376– 1   an image *m·* terrifying than that of most
376–13   *m·* life and immortality in one good motive
380–28   Nothing is *m·* disheartening than
381– 4   Be no *m·* willing to suffer the illusion that
382–14   *m·* receptive of spiritual power
382–18   "*m·* honored in the breach than the
382–20   is *m·* difficult to heal through Mind than one
382–30   abandoned me to *m·* hopeless suffering
386– 3   any *m·* than it is in the case of sin.
388– 9   Idolaters, believing in *m·* than one mind,
390– 2   and I should like something *m·* to eat."
390–22   God is no *m·* the author of sickness than
393–22   Your body would suffer no *m·* from tension
395–29   may appear in a *m·* alarming form.
397–14   Your thought is *m·* powerful than your words,
397–14   *m·* powerful than the accident itself,
397–24   no *m·* material in their waking hours

more

p 397–30   you will quickly become *m·* manly or
398– 4   and enter no *m·* into him."— *Mark* 9 : 25.
398–29   changes such ills into new and *m·* difficult
406–25   no *m·* fear that we shall be sick
407– 9   delay makes the struggle *m·* severe.
409– 7   the *m·* prolific it is likely to become in sin and
410–15   The *m·* difficult seems the material condition
411– 6   the body would respond *m·* quickly,
411– 7   just as a person replies *m·* readily when
413–12   are no *m·* natural nor necessary than
413–15   in order to make it thrive *m·* vigorously
414– 5   it yields *m·* roadily than do most diseases
417– 3   sometimes knowing *m·* than their doctors.
417– 6   Never tell the sick that they have *m·* courage
     than
418–12   sickness is no *m·* the reality of being than
419–19   Think . . . *m·* of spiritual.
421–12   and *m·* for the mental disturbance
421–25   It is no *m·* Christianly scientific to see disease
422–17   giving *m·* spirituality to consciousness
423– 7   *m·* strongly than the expressed thought.
424– 2   It is not *m·* difficult to make yourself heard
425–18   mankind will be *m·* spiritual
425–21   God is *m·* to a man than his belief,
425–22   the *m·* immortality we possess.
427– 5   can no *m·* die . . . than can Soul,
428–27   immortality will become *m·* apparent,
429– 5   the *m·* simple demonstrations of control,
430– 8   he will advance *m·* rapidly towards God,
438–27   disappeared and was never heard of *m·*.
440–29   forbidden to enter . . . any *m·* suits
t 449– 5   but *m·* of C. S. must be gained
450– 5   Another class, still *m·* unfortunate,
453–28   impresses *m·* deeply the wrong mind-picture.
454–26   Do not dismiss . . . feeling that you have no *m·*
     to do
455–32   the *m·* impossible it will become
456–11   Whoever affirms that there is *m·* than one
457– 5   has done *m·* for teacher and student,
459–21   is *m·* harmful than wilful wickedness,
459–30   treats disease with *m·* certain results than
460 16   is *m·* than fancy ; it is solid conviction.
462– 2   assimilate truth *m·* readily than others,
463–19   and can cause the mother no *m·* suffering.
464– 2   Why do you not make yourself *m·* widely
r 465–16   *Question.—* Is there *m·* than one God
469–29   This belief that there is *m·* than one mind
470– 6   existence of *m·* than one mind was the basic
473–13   *m·* than all other men, has presented
476–27   shall know it no *m·*."— *Psal.* 103 : 16.
485–12   disease, and death appear *m·* and *m·* unreal
487– 6   *m·* Christianity in seeing . . . spiritually than
487– 8   There is *m·* Science in the perpetual exercise of
488– 9   they have *m·* the significance of faith,
488–22   Nerves have no *m·* sensation, apart from
490–13   are *m·* or less deprived of Truth.
g 501 16   *m·* native to their immortal cravings
509–14   but the stellar universe is no *m·* celestial than
509–21   are no *m·* contingent now on time or
510– 2   How much *m·* should we seek to apprehend the
515–18   does not imply *m·* than one God,
520– 7   no *m·* seen nor comprehended by mortals, than
521–18   will naturally ask if there is nothing *m·*
523–28   accounts become *m·* and *m·* closely intertwined
526– 3   *m·* scientific record of creation
529–13   the serpent was *m·* subtle than — *Gen.* 3 : 1.
530–22   *m·* pleasant to the eyes than
530–23   *m·* to be desired than
533–19   *m·* rapidly than he can alone.
536– 4   and there was no *m·* sea."— *Rev.* 21 : 1.
539–27   *m·* than human power to expound the facts
541– 2   A lamb is a *m·* animate form of existence,
541– 2   *m·* nearly resembles a mind-offering
541– 9   Had God *m·* respect for the homage
541–11   the lamb was a *m·* spiritual type
543– 6   *m·* beautifully apparent at error's demise.
544–18   first suggestion of *m·* than the one Mind,
546–18   seem *m·* obscure than other portions
547–16   *m·* consistent than most theories.
548–25   he would have blessed the human race *m·*
549–16   nucleus, or egg, from which one or *m·*
553–26   the *m·* ancient superstition about the creation
ap 561– 7   Because of his *m·* spiritual vision,
562–26   but remembering no *m·* her sorrow
563– 5   and still *m·* astounded at hatred,
564–32   "*m·* subtle than any beast of the— *Gen.* 3 : 1.
566–28   neither was their place found any *m·* — *Rev.*
     12 : 8.
567– 1   Gabriel has the *m·* quiet task
572–22   and there was no *m·* sea. — *Rev.* 21 : 1.
573–31   no *m·* pain, and all tears will be wiped away.
gl 581–20   the *m·* confusion ensues,
581–21   and the *m·* certain is the downfall
582–10   the introduction of a *m·* spiritual origin ;
584–21   which saith : . . . There is *m·* than one mind,

more

gl 592– 6   belief that there can be *m·* than one creator ;
594– 4   the belief in *m·* than one God ;
     (*see also* **faith**)

moreover

o 360–11   replies : . . . *M·*, I have no notion of losing
r 466–15   *M·*, Truth is real, and error is unreal.

morning

evening and
    g 510–22   already divided into evening and *m·* ;
evening and the
    (*see* **evening**)

     pref vii– 3   beholds the first faint *m·* beams,
     vii– 9   across a night of error should dawn the *m·*
     a 34–31   in the bright *m·* hours
     35–11   the *m·* meal which Christian Scientists com-
     memorate.
     p 365–18   like dew before the *m·* sunshine.
     g 509–22   when "the *m·* stars sang together."— *Job* 38 : 7.
     gl 591–23   definition of

mornings

g 504–17   taking place on so many *evenings* and *m·*,

morphine

ph 198– 1   more than his calomel and *m·*,
p 416– 6   A hypodermic injection of *m·* is

morsel

ph 174–28   rolling it under the tongue as a sweet *m·*

mortal (*see also* **mortal's**)

belief of that
    b 312–11   belief of that *m·* that he must die
convince the
    b 327–27   convince the *m·* of his mistake
corporeal
    gl 589– 4   A corporeal *m·* embracing duplicity,
    589–19   JOSEPH.   A corporeal *m·* ;   a higher sense of
    592–11   MOSES.   A corporeal *m·* ;   moral courage ;
    592–22   NOAH.   A corporeal *m·* ;
    594–14   SHEM (Noah's son).   A corporeal *m·* ;
disappears
    gl 595–20   until the *m·* disappears
discordant
    b 305– 3   discordant *m·* is no more a *man* than
dying
    b 292–11   dying *m·* is not the likeness of God,
earthly
    sp 72–26   A sinning, earthly *m·* is not the reality of
every
    ph 186–15   Every *m·* must learn that there is neither
    ap 569– 3   Every *m·* at some period, here or hereafter,
from one
    r 496– 3   from one *m·* to another,
from the
    f 244–26   does not pass . . . from the *m·* to the immortal,
let no
    m 62–24   let no *m·* interfere with God's government
never produces the
    b 277– 7   The immortal never produces the *m·*.
not a
    a 42–27   is therefore not a *m·* but an immortal.
says
    ph 190– 4   *m·* says that an inanimate unconscious seedling
sick
    p 431– 4   When the sick *m·* was thirsty,
this
    s 164–26   and this *m·* shall have put on— *I Cor.* 15 : 54.
    p 409–24   This *m·* is put off, . . . in proportion as
    r 496–25   and this *m·* shall have put on— *I Cor.* 15 : 54.
wicked
    b 289– 8   A wicked *m·* is not the idea of God.

     s 138– 3   not on the personal Peter as a *m·*, but on
     140–31   What is the god of a *m·*, but a *m·* magnified?
     ph 192– 9   from the *m·* instead of from the immortal.
     194–16   would presuppose man, . . . a *m·* in
     f 250–15   but a *m·* is not man,
     250–16   A *m·* may be weary or pained,
     250–18   When that dream vanishes, the *m·* finds
     c 265–20   this is true only of a *m·*,
     b 284–11   matter, or a *m·*, sin, sickness, and
     285–11   claim that a *m·* is the true image of
     293–10   the illusion called a *m·*,
     p 416–22   when the *m·* has resigned his body
     r 476–21   Learn this, O *m·*, and earnestly seek the
     g 502–10   untrue image of God, named a sinful *m·*.
     554–12   *m·* is unconscious of his fœtal . . . existence ;
     557–14   the less a *m·* knows of sin, disease,
     gl 599– 3   You. As applied to corporeality, a *m·* ;

mortal (adj.)

ailments
    ph 174–22   all that enables a drug to cure *m·* ailments.
basis
    p 424– 6   we must leave the *m·* basis of belief

mortal (adj.)

beings
g 554– 5   nor are there properly any m· beings,

belief
pr 12–19   It is a m· belief, . . . which causes a drug to be
a 20–14   he knew the error of m· belief.
sp 72–13   M· belief (the material sense of life)
73–12   attraction of so-called spirit is a m· belief,
88–25   for both arise from m· belief.
s 125–32   proved nothing more than a m· belief,
151–17   M· belief says that death has been occasioned
ph 174–22   M· belief is all that enables a drug to cure
181– 8   but m· belief has such a partnership.
184– 1   laws of health are simply laws of m· belief.
197–28   and m· belief loses some portion of its error.
f 209– 2   the m· belief which makes the body discordant
212–32   unreal and imitative movements of m· belief,
213–16   a mental impression made on m· belief.
227– 3   I saw that the law of m· belief included
228– 7   Heredity is a prolific subject for m· belief to
229–15   m· belief has constituted itself a law to bind
230–26   soothing syrups to . . . satisfy m· belief,
247–12   passes away, fading and fleeting as m· belief.
251– 7   Fright is so great at certain stages of m· belief
c 262–10   by diving into the shallows of m· belief.
b 278–28   and death is a m· belief.
281– 9   rebukes m· belief, and asks :
287–22   Error is false, m· belief ; it is illusion,
289–16   "king of terrors" to be but a m· belief, — Job 18 : 14.
294–11   This m· belief, misnamed man, is error,
296–16   M· belief must lose all satisfaction in error
296–31   M· belief is a liar from the beginning,
297– 2   M· belief says, "You are happy !"
297–32   A m· belief fulfils its own conditions.
302–12   that mind is in matter, . . . is a m· belief ;
308– 6   Until the lesson is learned . . . m· belief will be
311– 1   the varying clouds of m· belief, which hide the
311–27   They are only what m· belief calls them.
321–18   was really but a phase of m· belief.
p 372– 3   The mortal body is only an erroneous m· belief
381–12   so-called laws of m· belief are destroyed by the
401–17   is destroying erroneous m· belief.
407–32   in consonance with common m· belief.
415– 5   Inflammation as a m· belief quickens or
428–18   mortal sense cannot impair nor m· belief destroy.
r 478– 8   except the claim of m· belief?
489–31   M· belief would have the material senses
496–21   the law of m· belief, at war with the facts
g 556–10   M· belief infolds the conditions of sin.
556–10   M· belief dies to live again in renewed
ap 569– 5   the m· belief in a power opposed to God.
gl 588– 1   HELL. M· belief ; error ; lust ; remorse ;
589–12   JERUSALEM. M· belief and knowledge
589–20   higher sense of Truth rebuking m· belief,
597–20   WILL. The motive-power of error ; m· belief ;

beliefs
sp 84– 2   nor with the conclusions of m· beliefs.
s 144– 8   The various m· beliefs formulated in
f 231–18   m· beliefs which divine Truth and Love destroy.
o 353–31   M· beliefs can neither demonstrate
p 378–18   exercised over m· beliefs to destroy them ;
r 488–18   defines these so-called senses as m· beliefs,
ap 569–12   masters his m· beliefs, animality, and hate,
gl 583– 1   Sensual and m· beliefs ;
594–22   SPIRITS. M· beliefs ; corporeality ;

blindness
p 374–13   m· blindness and its sharp consequences

bodies
sp 92– 8   decomposition of m· bodies in what is termed
o 341– *   shall also quicken your m· bodies — Rom. 8 : 11.

body
a 51–10   to attempt the destruction of the m· body
s 108–32   the organism and action of the m· body,
122–11   senses . . . make mortal mind tributary to m· body,
151–32   claims to govern every organ of the m· body,
ph 187–21   action of the m· body is governed by this
f 209– 9   material and m· body or mind is not the man.
220–30   forms all conditions of the m· body.
222– 8   also that mortal mind makes a m· body,
250–14   M· body and mind are one,
c 263–32   The fading forms of matter, the m· body and
b 293–11   mortal mind and m· body, are false
305–11   divine Principle, not in a m· body,
311–21   or that immortal Soul is in m· body,
p 372– 2   The m· body is only an erroneous mortal belief
402–14   mortal mind constructs the m· body
403–17   producing on m· body the results of

concepts
c 256–15   nor can He be understood . . . through m· concepts.

consciousness
sp 77–22   Even if . . . to m· consciousness were possible,
b 278–14   in a supposititious m· consciousness.
295–13   m· consciousness will at last yield to

mortal (adj.)

consolidation
ph 185–30   a m· consolidation of material mentality

deviations
g 502– 7   the m· deviations and inverted images

discord
sp 98– 3   elevation of existence above m· discord
c 262–27   The foundation of m· discord is a false sense

discords
f 231–16   God is not the author of m· discords.

disorder
ph 184–10   belief which produces a m· disorder,

dream
a 42– 7   found at length to be a m· dream,
f 219– 2   and the m· dream will forever cease.
230– 5   the awakening from this m· dream,
250–25   whatever appears to be . . . is a m· dream.
b 311–17   This state of error is the m· dream
p 418–13   This m· dream of sickness, sin, and death

dreams
b 305–29   These m· dreams are of human origin,

elements
p 374–28   is resolved into its primitive m· elements.

error
sp 96–21   M· error will vanish in a moral chemicalization.
f 204– 5   that m· error is as conclusively mental
b 277– 9   Their opposites, evil and matter, are m· error,
315–15   Their thoughts were filled with m· error,
p 403–18   until m· error is deprived of its imaginary
r 468–12   Spirit is immortal Truth ; matter is m· error.
485–21   m· error which Christ, or Truth, destroys
g 533–15   Adam, alias m· error,
548–13   Every agony of m· error helps . . . destroy error,

errors
a 53–26   He knew the m· errors which constitute the

existence
sp 70– 1   M· existence is an enigma.
s 108–19   apparently near the confines of m· existence,
ph 187– 3   mortals do not comprehend even m· existence,
188–11   M· existence is a dream of pain and
f 250– 6   M· existence is a dream ;
250– 6   M existence has no real entity,
250–23   the waking dream of m· existence
p 364– 5   to lay down his m· existence in behalf of
403–15   m· existence is a state of self-deception
426–21   destroy the great fear that besets m· existence.
g 501– 8   showing the poverty of m· existence,

eyes
b 334–20   before the human Jesus was incarnate to m· eyes.

fault
b 292– 1   When the last m· fault is destroyed,

fear
p 377–26   cause of . . . disease is mental, a m· fear,

feelings
gl 587–23   HEART. M· feelings, motives, affections,

flesh
sp 81–10   their affiliation with m· flesh ;

forms
s 118–20   In all m· forms of thought, dust is

history
r 476–16   They were, from the beginning, of m· history,

humanity
b 338–10   conclusions of material and m· humanity.

ignorance
ph 188–22   springing from m· ignorance or fear.
b 280–32   The only excuse . . . is our m· ignorance

illusion
b 289–19   death is but a m· illusion,
302–16   is always beyond and above the m· illusion
p 403–20   sweeps away the gossamer web of m· illusion.

illusions
f 214–23   for m· illusions would rob God,
b 289–29   Matter and death are m· illusions.
330– 4   the fixedness of m· illusions,

knowledge
g 527–17   constitutes evil and m· knowledge.

life
p 399–22   so-called m· life is mortal mind,
g 503–25   m· life, mutable truth, nor variable love.
544–30   declares . . . so-called m· life to be Life,
552–13   Human experience in m· life,

malice
t 458–22   Science will ameliorate m· malice.

man
sp 92–17   for the common conception of m· man
s 113–24   "but every [m·] man a liar." — Rom. 3 : 4.
ph 190– 9   human belief called m· man
191–25   Physical sense defines m· man as based on
f 204– 9   (m· man) who carries out the delusions of sin,
204–15   m· man, is a supposed mixture of
208–26   m· man possesses this body,
215–24   M· man is the antipode of immortal man
250–24   whatever appears to be a m· man is a
c 255–11   M· man has made a covenant with his eyes
263– 7   When m· man blends his thoughts of
b 289– 2   M· man can never rise . . . until he learns

mortal (adj.)

man

b 291–23 As death findeth m· man, so shall he
291–30 the judgment by which m· man is divested of
292–32 a m· man is not the real essence of manhood,
294–20 m· man, representing the error that life and
296– 5 It is the ripening of m· man, through which
301–23 M· man seems to himself to be material
331– 3 If life were in m· man or material things,
o 346– 3 not sinful and sickly m· man who is
347–12 so-called m· man is not the reality of man.
360–24 Shall m· man be more just than —Job 4 : 17.
p 425–15 M· man will be less mortal.
t 459– 4 m· man achieves no worldly honors except by
r 476–23 Remember that the Scriptures say of m· man :
477– 1 where sinning m· man appears to mortals,
478–16 No, not if God is true and m· man a liar.
478–30 M· man is really a self-contradictory phrase,
491–32 that this dream . . . may not be m· man?
492– 1 leaves m· man intact in body and thought,
g 508– 1 human or material belief, called m· man.
531– 5 the error, — that m· man starts materially,
536–18 starting from matter . . . m· man would be
538–26 of m· man, and of sin which is temporal.
538–27 As both m· man and sin have a beginning,
540– 3 Spirit creates neither a wicked nor a m· man,
543– 4 but it is only m· man and not the real man,
gl 590–12 m· man ; denial of the fulness of God's creation ;

manhood

g 543–21 thinking that apehood preceded m· manhood?

materials

p 402–15 with this mind's own m· materials.

measurements

gl 595–17 TIME. M· measurements ;

men

ph 190– 2 afterwards m· men or mortals,

mentality

sp 90–22 shows what m· mentality and knowledge are.
g 513– 1 this m· mentality, so-called, and its claim,

mind

a 30–12 appreciable to m· mind as "the way." —John 14 : 6.
sp 71–16 images, which m· mind holds and evolves
71–18 neither m· mind nor matter is the image
77– 8 m· mind creates its own physical conditions.
78– 4 the changing deflections of m· mind ;
80–24 control of m· mind over its substratum,
80–25 It is m· mind which convulses its substratum,
80–27 M· mind produces table-tipping
83–32 act of reading m· mind investigates and
86– 5 m· mind, whose touch called for aid.
86–20 sounds evolved involuntarily by m· mind.
86–29 M· mind sees what it believes
87–15 it presents primal facts to m· mind.
87–26 strong impressions produced on m· mind
88–13 are offshoots of m· mind ;
89– 3 shows that the beliefs of m· mind are loosed.
90–11 transitions now possible for m· mind
94–28 Our Master read m· mind on a scientific basis,
95– 2 the only genuine Science of reading m· mind.
97– 6 resembles its essence, m· mind.
an 102– 8 unreal concept of the so-called m· mind.
103– 6 The destruction of the claims of m· mind
103–19 specific term for error, or m· mind,
103–26 they annihilate the fables of m· mind,
103–29 In reality there is no m· mind,
104–32 Is not m· mind the murderer?
105– 1 hands, without m· mind to direct them,
105– 6 jurisdiction over the carnal or m· mind,
105– 8 m· mind, evil, which is the real outlaw,
105–13 M· mind, not matter, is the criminal
s 108–10 the only sufferer is m· mind,
108–27 subjective state of m· mind which
114– 3 author calls sick and sinful humanity m· mind,
114–12 M· mind is a solecism in language,
114–14 m· mind implies something untrue
114–31 what is termed by the author m· mind.
115–19 Scientific Translation of M· Mind
116– 4 In the third degree m· mind disappears,
116–19 is nothing beyond an image in m· mind.
122–10 so-called senses still make m· mind tributary
124– 4 a law of m· mind, a blind belief,
125– 1 as m· mind changes its beliefs.
126– 4 m· mind will be without form and void,
138–13 casting out the errors of m· mind.
145–29 m· mind must continually weaken its own
151–31 m· mind claims to govern every organ of
152– 5 and saves m· mind from itself.
153–22 pain cannot exist where there is no m· mind
153–27 m· mind, not matter, contains and carries
154– 4 law of m· mind that certain diseases should be
154–18 law of m· mind and her own fears
157–24 m· mind confers the power which the drug
157–26 Narcotics quiet m· mind,
158–21 m· mind acquires an educated appetite
158–27 letting in matter's higher stratum, m· mind.
158–29 m· mind, of a higher attenuation than

mortal (adj.)

mind

s 159–21 from effects produced by m· mind,
160–10 no more dependent upon the direction of m· mind,
160–17 Has m· mind ceased speaking to them,
160–27 to learn how m· mind governs muscle,
161– 4 m· mind, and not matter, burns it.
161–28 if it were not already determined by m· mind.
ph 168–27 a latent illusion of m· mind,
168–32 process which m· mind and body undergo
169–23 It is m· mind, not matter, which brings
172–21 obtains in mortals, alias m· mind,
176– 2 action of m· mind on the body was not so
176–19 M· mind is the worst foe of the body,
176–27 no farther than m· mind maps out the way.
177– 8 M· mind and body are one.
177–10 body, is but a false concept of m· mind.
178– 4 it is set down as a poison by m· mind.
178–18 M· mind, acting from the basis of sensation
179–13 The preference of m· mind for a certain method
180– 2 As m· mind is the husbandman of error,
180–23 correct this turbulent element of m· mind
184–21 M· mind alone suffers,
185–14 They have their birth in m· mind,
185–32 A patient under the influence of m· mind
186–28 M· mind is ignorant of self,
186–29 If m· mind knew how to be better,
187–14 the mandate of m· mind
187–19 What is this my but m· mind,
188–24 The soil of disease is m· mind,
189–10 effect of m· mind on the body,
189–15 it is as truly m· mind, according to its
189–19 m· mind, by an inevitable perversion,
189–25 From m· mind comes the reproduction of
189–28 the development of embryonic m· mind
189–32 matter is the subjective condition of m· mind.
190– 2 so-called embryonic m· mind,
190– 6 neither a m· mind nor the immortal Mind
192–12 offspring . . . of the m· mind and not of the
194–12 if m· mind says, "I am deaf and blind,"
194–18 the frailty and inadequacy of m· mind.
194–21 and that, in turn, m· mind manifests itself
105–11 whether it is m· mind or immortal Mind
195–21 promote the growth of m· mind out of itself,
196– 5 The power of m· mind over its own body is
196– 6 Better the suffering which awakens m· mind
196–20 Such books as will rule disease out of m· mind,
198– 2 for the higher stratum of m· mind has
198–13 to prevent disease from forming in m· mind
199– 1 muscles, without volition of m· mind,
199–16 as they influence them through m· mind.
f 201–17 The way to extract error from m· mind is to
202–30 senseless matter or erring m· mind
208– 9 a law of m· mind, wrong in every sense,
208–26 only expresses a material and m· mind.
210–19 The expression m· mind is really a solecism,
210–27 It is the so-called m· mind which voices this
211– 8 the sensations of a so-called m· mind or
211–14 seem to obtain in m· mind.
211–16 Without m· mind, the tear could not
213–14 proves sensation to be in the m· mind,
213– 2 Whoever contradicts this m· mind supposition
213– 6 M· mind conceives of something as either
218– 1 M· mind does the false talking,
218–15 independently of m· mind
219–11 Not muscles, nerves, nor bones, but m· mind
220–15 kinder than the atmosphere of m· mind,
220–18 M· mind produces its own phenomena,
220–30 M· mind forms all conditions of the
221–30 without the consent of m· mind,
222– 1 this phantasm of m· mind disappears as we
222– 5 food affects the body only as m· mind has its
222– 8 He learned also that m· mind makes a
225–26 The despotic tendencies, inherent in m· mind
228– 4 or of certain idiosyncrasies of m· mind
229–20 The so-called law of m· mind, conjectural and
229–29 It is the transgression of a belief of m· mind,
230–30 So-called m· mind or the mind of mortals
234–17 If mortals would keep proper ward over m· mind,
236–14 form the embryo of another m· mind,
239–23 M· mind is the acknowledged seat of
239–27 If it comes from erring m· mind,
239–31 Imperfect m· mind sends forth its own
243–19 If this information is conveyed, m· mind
243–21 the inanimate substratum of m· mind,
248–15 What is the model before m· mind?
250–25 Take away the m· mind, and matter has no
250–28 Upon this stage . . . goes on the dance of m· mind.
251– 3 The so-called belief of m· mind apparent as
c 260–24 Selfishness and sensualism are educated in m· mind
261– 8 The effect of m· mind on health and
262–32 Cause does not exist in matter, in m· mind, or

mortal (adj.)
mind

c	263– 5	The creations of m· mind are material.
b	273–31	atmosphere of m· mind cannot be
	274– 5	the conception of m· mind, the offspring of
	274–19	simply the manifested beliefs of m· mind,
	282–27	Error is the so-called intelligence of m· mind.
	283– 9	states of m· mind which act, react, and
	289–22	results, by the universal law of m· mind, in
	292–13	Matter is the primitive belief of m· mind,
	292–15	To m· mind, matter is substantial,
	292–19	the origin of material man and m· mind,
	293– 7	Matter and m· mind are but different strata of human belief.
	293–11	m· mind and mortal body, are false
	293–21	There is no vapid fury of m· mind
	295– 8	M· mind would transform the spiritual into the
	295–19	The m· mind. . .which has lost much materiality
	296–26	M· mind judges by the testimony of the
	305–13	a characteristic of m· mind.
	311– 3	What we term m· mind or carnal mind,
	321–20	that leprosy was a creation of m· mind
	323–23	elevates even m· mind to the contemplation of
	326–15	great healer of m· mind is the healer of the
	329–29	the error into which m· mind is plunged,
	338–16	suggests the thought. . .of m· mind in solution.
o	348–19	Is it not well to eliminate from so-called m· mind
	348–20	so long as it remains in m· mind,
p	370–15	The effect, which m· mind produces through
	370–20	since m· mind must be the cause of disease
	371– 2	The body is the substratum of m· mind,
	372– 5	error in solution, elementary m· mind,
	372– 6	One theory about this m· mind is, that its
	373–30	M· mind is producing the propulsion or the
	374– 1	that standard which m· mind has decided upon
	374– 4	whispered into the ear of m· mind,
	374– 6	Because m· mind seems to be conscious,
	374–12	which is in fact the objective state of m· mind,
	374–16	can destroy all ills which proceed from m· mind.
	374–26	Heat and cold are products of m· mind.
	374–27	The body, when bereft of m· mind, at first cools,
	374–30	M· mind produces animal heat,
	375– 1	Hence it is m· mind, not matter, which says,
	375–23	show m· mind that muscles have no power
	376–19	a mental concept and governed by m· mind,
	377–13	showing m· mind to be the producer of
	379–28	are pictures drawn on the body by a m· mind.
	381–14	m· mind cannot legislate the times, periods,
	381–20	Think less of the enactments of m· mind,
	382–31	M· mind needed to be set right.
	384–10	this is but a belief of m· mind,
	385–26	it is a law of m· mind which you have disobeyed.
	386– 1	an illusion of m· mind,—one of its dreams.
	387– 3	Because m· mind is kept active, must it
	387–25	It is a law of so-called m· mind,
	388– 5	Stolidity, which is a resisting state of m· mind,
	389– 8	m· mind, which reports food as undigested.
	391– 1	to overthrow the plea of m· mind,
	391–20	it must be m· mind which speaks ;
	391–23	will deliver you to the judge (m· mind),
	391–26	M· mind alone sentences itself.
	392–31	Exclude from m· mind the offending errors ;
	393– 4	only because m· mind is ignorant of itself,
	393– 8	a law of so-called m· mind, not of matter.
	393–24	were it not for m· mind.
	396–26	so efface the images of sickness from m· mind.
	397– 2	not seeing how m· mind affects the body,
	397–27	can never treat m· mind and matter separately,
	398–23	Appetite and disease reside in m· mind, not in
	399– 5	M· mind prescribes the drug,
	399– 7	M· mind plans the exercise, and puts the
	399–10	mortal thought, alias m· mind.
	399–11	m· mind sends its despatches over its body,
	399–16	M· mind perpetuates its own thought.
	399–20	and continuation of, the primitive m· mind.
	399–22	so-called mortal life is m· mind,
	399–23	Scientifically speaking, there is no m· mind
	400– 1	m· mind, which directly controls the body
	400– 4	M· mind is "the strong man,"—Matt. 12 : 29.
	400–17	except what m· mind assigns to it.
	400–22	M· mind rules all that is mortal.
	400–26	action of so-called m· mind must be destroyed
	401–14	m· mind only feels and sees materially.
	402– 8	The time approaches when m· mind will forsake
	402–13	m· mind constructs the mortal body
	402–18	body manifests only what m· mind believes,
	403–16	M· mind is constantly producing on mortal body
	404–13	If the evil is over in the repentant m· mind,
	405– 1	The basic error is m· mind.
	405–14	will be executed upon m· mind and body.
	407–13	giving strength to the weakness of m· mind,
	408–18	thus reaching m· mind through matter?
	408–24	were it not that m· mind thinks that the
	408–31	M· mind is ignorant of itself,
	409– 3	formed by m· mind and not by matter?"
	409– 4	M· mind and body combine as one,

mortal (adj.)
mind

p	409– 9	Unconscious m· mind — alias matter,
	409–12	unconscious substratum of m· mind,
	409–16	so-called conscious m· mind is believed to be
	411–25	Whatever is cherished in m· mind
	414–12	love will . . . guide and govern m· mind
	415–15	They only render m· mind . . . less fearful,
	415–26	instruct m· mind with immortal Truth.
	416–16	material body, which you call me, is m· mind,
	416–21	This materialism . . . is only in m· mind,
	417–29	Show them how m· mind seems to induce
	419–21	m· mind is liable to any phase of belief.
	420–28	If it becomes necessary to startle m· mind
	421– 7	Should you thus startle m· mind
	421–19	When the supposed suffering is gone from m· mind,
	422–19	changes which go on in m· mind serve to
	423–28	as directly the action of m· mind as
	424– 2	a separate, individualized m· mind,
	425– 2	M· mind, not matter, induces this conclusion
	425–15	this is but one of the beliefs of m· mind,
	426– 2	m· mind, when instructed by Truth, yields to
	429–13	M· mind affirms that mind is subordinate
	430– 3	M· mind must part with error,
t	451–28	action of one m· mind controlling another
	454–23	to move upon the waters of m· mind,
	459–12	Any attempt to heal mortals with erring m· mind,
	463–31	action is that of so-called m· mind.
r	473– 1	all inharmony of m· mind or body is illusion,
	479–13	Take away so-called m· mind, which constitutes
	482–30	the human, m· mind so-called is not a healer,
	484–13	the objective states of m· mind.
	484–15	Physical force and m· mind are one.
	487–21	there is in reality no such thing as m· mind.
	493–21	Disease is an experience of so-called m· mind.
g	505– 2	but m· mind, . . . sin, disease, and death have no
	507–21	material world implies a m· mind
	511–23	To m· mind, the universe is liquid, solid, and
	512–25	M· mind inverts the true likeness,
	512–28	Ignorant of the origin . . . of m· mind,
	513–27	So-called m· mind — being non-existent
	536–24	M· mind accepts the erroneous,
	544–14	No m· mind has the might or right
	552–26	the order of matter to be the order of m· mind.
	552–29	matter is a manifestation of m· mind,
	555– 1	as the force of m· mind is less pungent
	555– 2	health attends the absence of m· mind.
	556–26	m· mind must waken to spiritual life
	557–16	When the mist of m· mind evaporates,
ap	564–21	before the tribunal of so-called m· mind,
	564–32	talking serpent typifies m· mind,
	565– 9	Led on by the grossest element of m· mind,
	570–28	should also know the great delusion of m· mind,
	571–26	the thoughts which he beholds in m· mind.
gl	580–25	and matter in m· mind ;
	582– 6	human knowledge, or so-called m· mind,
	582–10	self-offering ; an improved state of m· mind ;
	582–26	and would make m· mind a slave to the body.
	583–26, 27	so-called m· mind controlling m· mind ;
	586– 2	Evening. . . . weariness of m· mind ;
	591– 9	mortality ; another name for m· mind ;
	591–14	that which m· mind sees, feels, . . . only in belief.
	591–25	definition of
	597–24	Will, as a quality of so-called m· mind,
		(see also **Mortal Mind**)

mind-force

b	310– 5	made up of supposititious m· mind-force ;

mind-reading

sp	83–25	m· mind-reading and immortal Mind-reading.
	83–29	M· mind-reading and immortal Mind-reading

mind's

p	429–16	m· mind's affirmation is not true.

minds

a	50–27	The distrust of m· minds, disbelieving the
s	126–28	the power of C. S. to heal m· minds and bodies.
	145– 9	between m· minds and immortal Mind.
p	408–12	baneful effects of illusion on m· minds and
	419–24	in mortals or so-called m· minds,
		(see also **Mortal Minds**)

model

f	248–17	Have you accepted the m· model?

mood

ap	570– 6	shocked into another extreme m· mood,

night-dream

f	249–25	m· night-dream is sometimes nearer the fact

opinions

b	273–29	conflicting m· opinions and beliefs
p	390–15	false process of m· opinions which you name law,
	399–27	The one Mind, God, contains no m· opinions.

origin

ph	169–11	disease has a mental, m· origin,

passions

gl	597–29	Destruction ; anger ; m· passions.

mortal (adj.)
personality
  sp 94–16   *m·* personality, passion, and impulse.
phenomenon
  b 277–30   and is therefore a *m·* phenomenon,
seeming
  ph 190–17   This *m·* seeming is temporal ,
selfhood
  b 316– 5   and lose sight of *m·* selfhood
sense
  sp 72– 6   would disappear to *m·* sense,
  f 210–29   To *m·* sense, sin and suffering are real,
  212– 8   Why need pain, . . . come to this *m·* sense?
  212–31   realities of being, . . . are unseen to *m·* sense ;
  215–16   only a *m·* sense of the absence of light,
  216–13   to destroy the errors of *m·* sense
  c 263–27   a human and *m·* sense of persons and things
  b 301–14   seems to *m·* sense transcendental,
  302–29   *m·* sense would fain have us so believe.
  308–17   struggling with a *m·* sense of life,
  331– 8   *m·* sense, which falsely testifies to
  p 370– 1   we must forsake the *m·* sense of things,
  406–15   scientific period, in which *m·* sense is subdued
  428–18   the Life which *m·* sense cannot impair
  t 459–24   To *m·* sense C. S. seems abstract,
  r 471–26   that which interprets God as above *m·* sense.
  g 507–30   *M·* sense inverts this appearing
  558–10   To *m·* sense Science seems at first obscure,
  gl 596–23   Though the way is dark in *m·* sense,
senses
  b 288–28   unlimited by the *m·* senses.
  p 390– 6   to the *m·* senses, there is seeming discord.
sensuousness
  a 35– 7   to rise somewhat from *m·* sensuousness,
sight
  f 214–26   How transient a sense is *m·* sight,
  b 300–18   though (to *m·* sight) they grow side by side
sinner
  r 475–31   A *m·* sinner is not God's man,
  g 525– 2   to become there a *m·* sinner,
testimony
  b 297–27   no *m·* testimony is founded on the
  297–29   *M·* testimony can be shaken.
  r 494–26   One is the *m·* testimony, changing,
theories
  g 552–10   *M·* theories make friends of sin, sickness, and
theory
  g 547–29   sensual, and *m·* theory of the universe,
thought
  an 102–19   hidden in the dark recesses of *m·* thought,
  103–30   consequently no transference of *m·* thought
  s 118–20   that is, three modes of *m·* thought.
  118–24   changes the whole of *m·* thought,
  125– 8   normal and natural to changed *m·* thought,
  ph 189–18   the evidence of all *m·* thought or things.
  189–21   lowest instead of from the highest *m·* thought.
  189–27   According to *m·* thought, the development of
  198–20   until the elasticity of *m·* thought haply
  c 259–22   *M·* thought transmits its own images,
  263–23   multiplication or self-division of *m·* thought,
  264– 4   The crude creations of *m·* thought must
  b 282–24   is a material, human, *m·* thought,
  295–25   All that is called *m·* thought is made up of
  306–21   The myriad forms of *m·* thought,
  o 349–26   *M·* thought does not at once catch the
  p 375–32   belief in consumption presents to *m·* thought
  391– 3   Blot out the images of *m·* thought
  399–10   not . . . apart from the action of *m·* thought,
  415–10   in a part which *m·* thought does not reach.
  418–31   dark images of *m·* thought,
  425–10   beliefs, images of *m·* thought
  t 463– 8   detach *m·* thought from its material
  r 479– 9   image of *m·* thought, reflected on the retina,
  g 511–27   the gradation of *m·* thought,
  520–26   *M·* thought drops into the ground,
  553– 6   *M·* thought must obtain a better basis,
  553–21   theory . . . adopted by general *m·* thought
  gl 585–21   a state of *m·* thought, the only error of which
  586– 1   EVENING. Mistiness of *m·* thought ;
  596–23   Life and Love . . . destroy the unrest of *m·* thought,
  598–30   Time is a *m·* thought, the divisor of which
thoughts
  s 164–22   *m·* thoughts in belief rule the materiality
  ph 178–10   connection of past *m·* thoughts with present.
  190–21   Hebrew bard, swayed by *m·* thoughts,
  f 250–29   *M·* thoughts chase one another like snowflakes,
  gl 582– 3   BELIEVING. . . . *M·* thoughts, illusion.
universe
  gl 584–24   thence to reproduce a *m·* universe,
usage
  a 30–11   Had his . . . birth been wholly apart from *m·* usage,
veins
  p 376–15   which ever flowed through *m·* veins

---

mortal (adj.)
vestures
  c 260–29   If we array thought in *m·* vestures,
view
  b 315–30   (that is, as it seemed to *m·* view),
vision
  b 301–15   man's substantiality transcends *m·* vision
will
  gl 599– 5   Blind enthusiasm ; *m·* will.
zenith
  sp 97–13   until matter reaches its *m·* zenith in illusion

---

  a 19–32   Thou shalt have no belief of Life as *m·* ;
  44–31   power of Spirit to overrule *m·*, material sense.
  sp 72– 4   in other words, *m·*, material sense
  78–11   *m·*, sinning, suffering, and dying.
  81–13   the opposite assertion, that he is *m·*,
  81–25   so-called laws of matter, which define man as *m·*.
  88–13   they are *m·* material beliefs.
  93–28   Finite spirit would be *m·*,
  s 108–30   My discovery that erring, *m·*, . . . *mind*
  124–12   This is a *m·*, finite sense of things,
  139–20   these facts show how a *m·* and material sense
  ph 165– 8   to subjugate intelligence, to make mind *m·*,
  173–21   material structure is *m·*.
  174–31   cause of disease obtains in the *m·* human mind,
  184–18   governed by a false belief is discordant and *m·*.
  187–27   *m·* material body loses all appearance of life
  188– 1   only as the *m·*, erring mind yields to God,
  105–22   growth of mortal mind . . . out of all that is *m·*.
  f 210–23   I name it *m·*.
  211–10   Is it not provable that Mind is not *m·*
  213– 8   this *m·* and material conception.
  249– 7   no *m·* nor material power as able to destroy.
  252–11   until the entire *m·*, material error finally
  253–12   erring, *m·*, material sense
  c 256– 5   rises . . . from the *m·* to the immortal.
  258– 1   A *m·*, corporeal, or finite conception of God
  260– 7   The conceptions of *m·*, erring thought
  262–13   above the *m·* to the immortal idea of God.
  265–29   inform us that the pleasures of sense are *m·*
  b 276–16   Discord is unreal and *m·*.
  279– 2   changing, dying, the mutable and *m·*,
  286– 4   the finite, mutable, and *m·*,
  289–13   never make men sick, sinful, or *m·*.
  292–28   material mentality, . . . is *m·*.
  296– 5   the *m·* is dropped for the immortal.
  298– 8   a *m·* temporary sense of things,
  298–18   never reaches beyond the boundary of the *m·*
  300– 1   and would be mutable and *m·*.
  301– 6   *m·* and material man seems to be substance,
  303–23   belief . . . that *m·*, material man is the
  305–24   man would be wholly *m·*, were it not that
  306–31   God's man, . . . is not material and *m·*.
  307–18   says : . . . He has made man *m·*
  314– 3   Jesus waited until the *m·* or fleshly sense had
  320–23   for according to that error man is *m·*.
  337–13   while error is *m·* and discordant.
  o 347– 5   whatever is *m·* or discordant has no
  352– 6   a *m·* and material belief of flesh and bones,
  p 400–23   Mortal mind rules all that is *m·*.
  403–26   The *m·* so-called mind produces
  409–21   the *m·* and imperfect . . . are counterfeits
  425–15   Mortal man will be less *m·*, when he
  r 466–13   Truth is immortal ; error is *m·*.
  468– 3   If Soul sinned, it would be *m·*,
  468– 5   error must be *m·*, because error is unlike Truth.
  476–11   Hence man is not *m·* nor material.
  477– 9   Whatever is material is *m·*.
  477–13   corporeal senses to be *m·* and erring illusions
  478–24   this belief is *m·* and far from actual.
  478–25   whatever is *m·* is composed of
  478–31   for man is not *m·*,
  479– 6   it cannot be *m·* and material ;
  481–24   If Soul sins, it must be *m·*.
  484–21   Mesmerism is *m·*, material illusion.
  486–21   So long . . . mortals will continue *m·* in belief
  487–18   believer and belief are one and are *m·*.
  g 505–29   *m·*, erring, and finite are human beliefs,
  521–20   the continued account is *m·* and material.
  522– 8   chronicles man as mutable and *m·*,
  522–16   and this man to be *m·*,
  526–30   Eden stands for the *m·*, material body.
  527–15   a knowledge of evil would make man *m·*.
  530– 4   forever opposed to *m·*, material sense.
  536–28   the *m·* and material return to dust,
  540–28   Cain is the type of *m·* and material man,
  543–30   belief . . . would make Life, or God, *m·*.
  545– 1   Error . . . explains Deity through *m·* and finite
  546– 3   this belief alone is *m·*.
  550–31   originate the impure and the *m·*
  552–32   Naturalists describe the origin of *m·* and
  554–18   whatever is sinful and *m·* ;
  556– 3   are *m·* and material concepts
  556–23   *m·* and material life is the dream.

mortal (adj.)

ap 572– 9   whatever is of material sense, or *m*·,
gl 582–26   the error which would make man *m*·
587–15   supposititious minds, . . . erring and *m*· ;

Mortality

p 432–11   says :— I am *M*·, Governor of the Province of

mortality

and disease
p 395– 9   assert its claims over *m*· and disease.
claims of
ph 182– 6   the claims of *m*·, . . . appertain to
condition of
f 215–23   Every quality and condition of *m*· is lost,
death and
b 295–31   teaches that . . . is resurrected from death and *m*·.
destroys
sp 72–13   Truth destroys *m*·, and brings to light
b 323–27   The true idea of God . . . destroys *m*·.
disappears
b 293– 1   this unreal material *m*· disappears
g 520–12   These days will appear as *m*· disappears,
discord and
b 338– 7   belief . . . terminates in discord and *m*·,
disease, and
g 557–15   the less a mortal knows of sin, disease, and *m*·,
error and
b 292– 3   the battle of Truth with error and *m*· ;
error of
f 210–20   Truth pierces the error of *m*· as a sunbeam
escape from the
b 295–11   in order to escape from the *m*· of this error.
finiteness, and
gl 580– 1   a belief in intelligent matter, finiteness, and *m*· ;
history of
g 547–15   In its history of *m*·, Darwin's theory
infers the
ph 191–26   infers the *m*· of the body.
is finally
r 476–17   *M*· is finally swallowed up in immortality.
lay off
r 491–14   that mortals can lay off *m*·
less
s 163–12   there would be less sickness and less *m*·."
manifests
b 319– 1   body does not include soul, but manifests *m*·,
matter and
a 43–26   in defiance of matter and *m*·,
f 215–10   matter and *m*· do not reflect the facts of Spirit.
not bounded by
b 301–32   Immortality is not bounded by *m*·.
opposed to
p 387–12   the assurances of immortality, opposed to *m*·.
out of
a 39–12   out of *m*· into immortality and bliss.
phases of
b 311–32   is not touched by these phases of *m*·.
replace
r 495–23   replace *m*· with immortality,
sickness, and
b 335–30   Sin, sickness, and *m*· are the suppositional
sin and
  (see sin)
will cease
s 126– 5   *m*· will cease when man beholds

---

sp 78– 9   If the departed are in rapport with *m*·,
f 241– 6   *M*· is their doom.
250– 4   and suppose . . . *m*· to be the matrix of
b 278–31   Matter, with its *m*·, cannot be substantial
335–21   Soul . . . does not exist in *m*·.
336– 6   nor the immortal into *m*·.
338– 8   The *m*· of material man proves that
p 368–28   Admit the . . . and you admit that *m*·
r 478– 4   What evidence of Soul . . . have you within *m*·?
492– 6   Life cannot be united to its unlikeness, *m*·.
g 545–32   The *m*· of man is a myth,
554– 5   There is no such thing as *m*·,
555–20   would seek to unite . . . immortality with *m*·,
gl 580–19   immortality's opposite, *m*· ;
581– 7   counteracting all evil, sensuality, and *m*·.
585–20   *m*· ; that which does not last forever ;
590– 5   KNOWLEDGE. . . . *m*· ; beliefs and opinions ;
591– 8   MATTER. Mythology ; *m*· ;
591–10   MATTER. . . . life in non-intelligence and *m*· ;
593–13   sensuality ; delusion ; *m*· ; error.
595– 4   TARES. *M*· ; error ; sin ; sickness ;
598–19   A solar measurement of time ; *m*· ;

mortality's

468– 4   sin is *m*· self, because it kills itself.

mortally

g 517– 6   may be defined as a *m*· mental attempt to

Mortal Man

p 430–21   *M*· *M*· is the defendant.
431–10   Therefore I arrested *M*· *M*· in behalf of
431–18   getting *M*· *M*· into close confinement
432– 2   Commissioner for *M*· *M*·.
432– 5   whereas *M*· *M*·, the prisoner at the bar,
432–12   says : . . . Body, in which *M*· *M*· resides.
433–11   evidence of Personal Sense against *M*· *M*·.
433–20   *M*· *M*· has been guilty of benevolence
433–24   *M*· *M*· is sentenced to be tortured until
433–32   the spirit of Life and the friend of *M*· *M*·,
434–15   the case for *M*· *M*· *versus* Personal Sense
434–23   *M*· *M*· has had no proper counsel
434–30   lower court has sentenced *M*· *M*· to die,
435– 8   *M*· *M*·, in obedience to higher law,
435–25   *M*· *M*· can suffer only for his sin.
436– 3   for which *M*· *M*· is under sentence of death.
436– 6   as a witness against *M*· *M*·
436–12   *M*· *M*· should find it again.
436–20   It was Fear who handcuffed *M*· *M*·
436–21   You have left *M*· *M*· no alternative.
436–29   His Honor sentenced *M*· *M*· to die
436–32   Claiming to protect *M*· *M*· in right-doing,
437– 1   in which province *M*· *M*· resides.
438–10   in which *M*· *M*· was reported to reside,
439–13   Health-officer had *M*· *M*· in custody,
439–14   though *M*· *M*· was innocent.
439–21   unfortunate *M*· *M*· who sought your aid
439–25   You betrayed *M*· *M*·, meanwhile declaring
440– 2   when it condemned *M*· *M*·
440– 9   a verdict delivering *M*· *M*· to Death.
440–18   Wherefore, then, . . . do you sentence *M*· *M*·
440–20   *M*· *M*· has his appeal to Spirit,
440–28   forbidden to enter against *M*· *M*· any more
440–31   restore to *M*· *M*· the rights of which he
441–14   cannot bear witness against *M*· *M*·,
441–14   neither can Fear arrest *M*· *M*·
441–26   no law outside of . . . can punish or reward *M*· *M*·.
442–13   *M*· *M*·, no longer sick and in prison,

Mortal Man's

p 434–16   *M*· *M*· counsel regards the prisoner with
435–16   a destroyer of *M*· *M*· liberty

Mortal Mind

s 115–19   Scientific Translation of *M*· *M*·
p 435– 3   Has the body or has *M*· *M*· committed a
435– 6   *M*· *M*·, which alone is capable of sin

Mortal Minds

p 430–22   *M*· *M*·, Materia Medica, Anatomy,
433– 3   addresses the jury of *M*· *M*·.
436–28   charged the jury, twelve *M*· *M*·, to find the
440– 8   *M*· *M*· were deceived by your attorney,
441–29   persuading *M*· *M*· to return a verdict

mortal's

b 312–10   the departure of a *m*· mind,

mortals

all
ap 562–12   The twelve tribes of Israel with all *m*·,
alone
s 117– 9   *m*· alone do this.
among
s 129–28   in its reformatory mission among *m*·.
animals and
g 511–25   Animals and *m*· metaphorically present
appear to
b 332–24   and to appear to *m*· in such a form of humanity
apprehension of
p 368– 7   nearer . . . to the apprehension of *m*·,
are corporeal
s 116–22   *M*· are corporeal, but God is incorporeal.
are divinely driven
s 152–26   by which *m*· are divinely driven to a
are egotists
c 263– 1   *M*· are egotists.
are hastening
b 327–18   but *m*· are hastening to learn that Life is God,
are inclined
f 214–19   *M*· are inclined to fear and to
are not like
b 295–11   *M*· are not like immortals,
are taught
f 227– 4   *m*· are taught their right to freedom,
are unacquainted
f 215– 8   *M*· are unacquainted with the reality of
arrive at the
s 120– 8   by this reversal *m*· arrive at the
g 543–12   until *m*· arrive at the understanding that
assures
r 489–32   It assures *m*· that there is real pleasure in
attempt to heal
t 459–12   Any attempt to heal *m*· with
awaits
b 291–28   No final judgment awaits *m*·,

mortals

beliefs of
f 221–18 the self-imposed beliefs of m·,
b 278–13 is one of the false beliefs of m·,

believe
m 62–31 Because m· believe in material laws
f 203–22 then m· believe that the deathless Principle,
212–21 In legerdemain and credulous frenzy, m· believe
b 312–20 M· believe in a finite personal God ;

believed
a 53–13 M· believed in God as humanly mighty,

betrays
r 485– 7 betrays m· into sickness, sin, and death.

bind
f 229–16 a law to bind m· to sickness, sin, and death.

birth of
g 529– 5 were needed to assist the birth of m·.

blessings to
b 325– 9 which results in infinite blessings to m·.

blind
b 337– 4 blind m· do lose sight of spiritual

bring to
pr 11–21 Petitions bring to m· only the results of

can never know
g 519–14 M· can never know the infinite, until they

cannot connect
r 491–11 Matter cannot connect m· with the true

claim
b 312–19 M· claim that death is inevitable ;

claimed
r 469–19 if m· claimed no other Mind

cling to
b 328–10 must therefore cling to m· until,

commonly recognize
ph 183–19 m· commonly recognize as law that which

communed with
sp 73–15 If Spirit, or God, communed with m·

condemnation of
g 545– 7 The condemnation of m· to till the ground

congregate
gl 595– 9 where m· congregate for worship.

declare
p 386– 8 So long as m· declare that certain states of the

did need
r 494– 8 But m· did need this help,

does wonders for
t 449– 4 A grain of C. S. does wonders for m·,

drive
r 487– 1 these calamities often drive m· to seek and

encourages
b 320–28 and encourages m· to hope in Him

entreat the divine
ph 182–22 M· entreat the divine Mind to heal

experience
a 22– 6 Waking to Christ's demand, m· experience

eyes of
ph 165– 4 it closed the eyes of m·

formation of
m 61–29 The formation of m· must greatly improve

frail
o 346–32 is not this what frail m· are trying to do?
t 459–15 frail m·, untaught and unrestrained by C. S.,

gives
p 442–23 Truth, gives m· temporary food and clothing

give up
ph 191– 4 As m· give up the delusion that there is
b 330– 1 in proportion as m· give up error

giving
s 128–17 giving m· access to broader and higher realms.

governs
f 209– 4 as ignorance, . . . or human will governs m·.

happiness of
p 397– 4 on the morals and the happiness of m·,

healing of
p 406– 9 demonstrated in the healing of m·,

he taught
a 20–17 he taught m· the opposite of themselves,

He teaches
c 266–17 He teaches m· to lay down their fleshliness

hypotheses of
ph 182–15 The hypotheses of m· are antagonistic to

imperfect
f 254–12 Imperfect m· grasp the ultimate . . . slowly ;

important to
a 42–18 evidence so important to m·.

incites
ap 564– 5 incites m· to kill morally and physically

in mercy to
a 18– 8 not only in justice to himself, but in mercy to m·,

instructing
r 485–11 Why malign C. S. for instructing m·

lethargy of
a 38– 7 when the lethargy of m·, . . . is broken

may learn
b 316– 2 From him m· may learn how to

mortals

may see
ap 571–24 in which m· may see their own image.

may seek
b 322–32 M· may seek the understanding of C. S.,

millions of
p 379–30 the fever-picture, drawn by millions of m·

mind of
f 230–31 So-called mortal mind or the mind of m·
231– 6 If . . . they are not destroyed in the mind of m·,
p 423–31 They are only phenomena of the mind of m·.

minds of
ph 175– 3 formulated in the minds of m·.
p 386–13 the action of Truth on the minds of m·,

mistake of
f 216–19 The great mistake of m· is to suppose

move onward
f 240–18 M· move onward towards good or evil

must change
c 260–19 M· must change their ideals in order to

must emerge
g 552–16 M· must emerge from this notion of

must find
sp 83– 7 M· must find refuge in Truth

must follow
c 266–24 M· must follow Jesus' sayings

must get
a 39–25 To break this earthly spell, m· must get the

must look
c 204– 7 M· must look beyond fading, finite forms,

need
sp 85–24 but m· need spiritual sense.

need not
sp 79–29 m· need "not be weary in— Gal. 6 : 9.
b 291– 9 M· need not fancy that belief in the

need only
b 316– 5 m· need only turn from sin and lose sight of

needs of
f 224–23 meeting the needs of m· in sickness

never helps
r 481– 7 Material sense never helps m· to

obtains in
ph 172–20 obtains in m·, alias mortal mind,

obtain the harmony
p 400– 9 M· obtain the harmony of health, only as

offspring of
gl 592– 6 the belief that man is the offspring of m· ;

origin of
g 548–18 Speaking of the origin of m·,

other
sp 77– 3 Neither do other m· . . . at a single bound.

overtakes
b 290– 5 before what is termed death overtakes m·,

prevents
p 409–14 prevents m· from knowing how to govern

progress
m 68– 2 At present m· progress slowly

put off
f 242– 2 m· put off their material beliefs

put on
c 262– 8 m· "put on immortality."— I Cor. 15 : 54.

sacrificing
p 440– 7 before sacrificing m· to their false gods.

senses of
b 292–16 The so-called senses of m· are material.

sentence
an 105– 3 Courts and juries judge and sentence m·

sinful
f 204–25 notion that they can create . . . sinful m·

standard of
r 492–10 uplift the physical and moral standard of m·,

standards of
f 247–13 form the transient standards of m·.

suppose
b 328– 4 M· suppose that they can live without

tabernacled with
ap 576– 7 while yet he tabernacled with m·.

teach
m 66– 6 Trials teach m· not to lean on a material staff,
g 540–23 is to teach m· never to believe a lie.

teaches
c 266–17 He teaches m· to lay down their fleshliness
g 542–23 teaches m· not to remove the waymarks

thoughts of
f 249–27 than are the thoughts of m· when awake.
b 337–27 Temporal things are the thoughts of m·
r 484–14 conscious and unconscious thoughts of m·.

try in vain
a 37– 6 M· try in vain to slay Truth with the

try to believe
b 312–17 M· try to believe without understanding Truth ;

unfolding to
b 306–27 Science, still enthroned, is unfolding to m·

urges upon
f 223–29 truth urges upon m· its resisted claims ;

mortals

victimizes
b 294–16 victimizes *m·*, taught, as they are by physiology

wake
f 251– 9 *m·* wake to the knowledge of two facts :

waken
p 429–17 *M·* waken from the dream of death

will behold
o 347–27 Then *m·* will behold the nothingness of

will disappear
r 476–11 *M·* will disappear, and . . . will appear

will echo
c 262–18 *M·* will echo Job's thought,

will sin
f 205– 2 *m·* will sin without knowing that they are

would procreate
s 140–29 but *m·* would procreate man,

---

pr 11–10 always demands restitution before *m·* can
a 26– 2 gratitude for what he did for *m·*,
 39–11 belief that Soul is in the body causes *m·*
 39–32 When *m·* once admit that evil confers no
m 63– 7 His origin is not, like that of *m·*,
 64–27 Let not *m·* permit a disregard of law
 69– 4 *m·* gain the sense of health only as
 69– 6 *M·* can never understand God's creation while
sp 72–25 may flow from the departed to *m·* ;
 86–13 *M·* evolve images of thought.
 99– 4 divine Principle by which *m·* can escape
s 148–30 When *m·* sin, this ruling of the schools
 156– 3 what made them good or bad for *m·*,
 160– 4 When *m·* forsake the material for the
ph 187– 3 As *m·* do not comprehend even
 188–21 are traced upon *m·* by unmistakable signs.
 189– 8 *m·* should no more deny the power of C. S. to
 190– 2 afterwards mortal men or *m·*,
 190– 5 The mortal says . . . seedling is producing *m·*,
 190– 7 or elsewhere in matter or in *m·*.
 197–14 the farther *m·* will be removed from imbecility
 199–15 *M·* develop their own bodies
f 212–17 *M·* have a modus of their own,
 227– 8 or *m·* will continue unaware of
 228–14 *M·* will some day assert their freedom
 234–17 If *m·* would keep proper ward over mortal,
 240–19 If *m·* are not progressive,
 241–16 can do no more for *m·* than can moonbeams to
 249–22 *M·* are the Adam dreamers.
c 255– 1 As *m·* drop off their mental swaddling-clothes,
 255–13 *m·* take limited views of all things.
 258–25 *M·* have a very imperfect sense of
 259– 8 threw upon *m·* the truer reflection of God
 259–16 then *m·* have never beheld in man the reflex
 260–14 sets *m·* at work to discover what
 264–13 As *m·* gain more correct views of God and
 265– 5 *M·* must gravitate Godward,
 266–27 evil beliefs which originate in *m·* are hell.
 267–19 in the light of divine Science, *m·* present
b 270–24 *M·* think wickedly ; consequently they
 273–17 have never made *m·* whole, harmonious,
 283– 1 As *m·* begin to understand Spirit,
 285–27 As *m·* reach, . . . a higher sense,
 288–31 destroys what *m·* seem to have learned
 291– 8 till *m·* have already yielded to each lesser call
 292–17 so-called life of *m·* is dependent on
 294–27 neither self-made nor made by *m·*.
 295–16 The manifestation of God through *m·* is as
 295–29 Brainology teaches that *m·* are created to
 296–19 Whether *m·* will learn this sooner or later,
 296–32 It says to *m·*, "You are wretched !"
 297– 3 belief says, "You are happy !" and *m·* are so ;
 297– 5 Human belief says to *m·*, "You are sick !"
 301–12 substance, or Spirit, which *m·* hope for.
 304–22 If *m·* caught harmony through material sense,
 311–30 as *m·* lay off a false sense of life,
 325–21 the demands of Truth upon *m·*
 328– 7 *m·* get rid of sin, sickness, and death only in
o 357–13 if we theoretically endow *m·* with the
p 371– 9 *M·* are believed to be here without
 375–21 a belief that matter governs *m·*,
 379– 2 and control the body without the consent of *m·*,
 381–15 types of disease, with which *m·* die.
 388–31 If *m·* think that food disturbs the
 394–22 against whom *m·* should not contend?
 397–24 are no more material in their
 405–30 causes *m·* to retreat from their error,
 409–25 in proportion as *m·* realize
 415– 1 excited state of *m·* which is not normal.
 419–23 cannot in reality occur in *m·*
 426–18 *m·* are not saved . . . by death,
 435–23 If *m·* sin, our Supreme Judge in equity decides
t 444–29 *m·*, or the "children of men"— *Psal.* 14 : 2.
 458–30 by which *m·* are radically saved from sin and
r 476– 1 *M·* are the counterfeits of immortals.
 476–13 *M·* are not fallen children of God.
 477– 2 where sinning mortal man appears to *m·*.

mortals

r 486–21 So long . . . *m·* will continue mortal in belief
 490–13 *m·* are more or less deprived of Truth.
 491–14 It is only by . . . that *m·* can lay off mortality
g 520– 8 no more seen nor comprehended by *m·*, than
 536–27 Through toil, struggle, . . . what do *m·* attain?
 545– 8 *m·* should so improve material belief
 548–12 Earth has little light or joy for *m·* before
 551– 9 argues that *m·* spring from eggs
 553–29 You may say that *m·* are formed before they
ap 559–19 *M·*, obey the heavenly evangel.
 563–31 It is the animal instinct in *m·*,

mortals'

pr 11–21 only the results of *m·* own faith.
b 314–23 Because of *m·* material and sinful belief,

Mosaic Decalogue

r 489–14 it breaks all the commands of the *M· D·*

Mosaic law

a 30–14 Rabbi and priest taught the *M· l·*,

Moses

s 139– 6 *M·* proved the power of Mind by what men called
ph 185–17 strove to emulate the wonders wrought by *M·*.
 200– 4 *M·* advanced a nation to the worship of God in
b 280–17 *M·* declared as Jehovah's first command of the
 321– 9 When, . . . he saw it become a serpent, *M·* fled
 321–16 illusion of *M·* lost its power to alarm him,
 321–21 When *M·* first put his hand into his bosom
 333–23 Abraham, Jacob, *M·*, and the prophets
gl 592–11 definition of

Moses'

b 321–11 and then *M·* fear departed.
 321–25 God had lessened *M·* fear

most

pref viii–15 Christian healing confers the *m·* health
 x– 5 *m·* of them incorrect in theory
 x–17 These cases for the *m·* part have been
 x–31 but sound morals are *m·* desirable.
pr 4– 3 What we *m·* need is the prayer of
 9– 2 During many years the author has been *m·* grateful
 11–18 but wipes it out in the *m·* effectual manner.
a 43–11 Jesus' last proof was the . . . *m·* convincing,
 43–12 the *m·* profitable to his students.
m 59– 3 There should be the *m·* tender solicitude for
 64– 8 envy, or jealousy seems on *m·* occasions to
sp 97–21 The broadest facts array the *m·* falsities
s 112– 1 to be the *m·* effective curative agent
 123– 9 *m·* absolutely weak and inharmonious creature
 140– 1 more than it is needed in *m·* cases ;
 141– 8 even the *m·* cherished beliefs and practices,
 153–12 the *m·* potent rises above matter into mind.
ph 166–29 by *m·* of the medical systems :
 176–31 Truth handles the *m·* malignant contagion
 197–25 and the *m·* digestible food in the stomach,
b 286– 1 relates *m·* nearly to the happiness of being.
 295–20 through which Truth appears *m·* vividly
 313–23 Jesus of Nazareth was the *m·* scientific man
 317– 6 Whosoever lives *m·* the life of Jesus
 320– 5 The *m·* distinguished theologians in Europe
 327–29 Reason is the *m·* active human faculty.
o 355–21 and the *m·* egregious fallacies
p 363–18 "Which of them will love him *m·* ?"— *Luke* 7 : 42.
 363–20 "He to whom he forgave *m·*."— *Luke* 7 : 43.
 373– 5 easier to cure the *m·* malignant disease than
 376– 2 an image more terrifying than that of *m·* other
 376– 6 It is the *m·* subtle, and does its work
 376– 9 *m·* hidden, undefined, and insidious beliefs.
 383– 9 when he leaves it *m·* out of his thought,
 387–16 they occupy the *m·* important posts
 387–17 and perform the *m·* vital functions in society.
 387–19 That man . . . who does the *m·* good.
 402– 1 C. S. is always the *m·* skilful surgeon,
 403–21 The *m·* Christian state is one of rectitude
 404–21 is one of the *m·* important points in the
 407– 6 enslavement to the *m·* relentless masters
 414– 6 it yields more readily than do *m·* diseases
t 448–31 doing one's self the *m·* harm.
 449– 7 reacts *m·* heavily against one's self.
 449–18 than it does to heal the *m·* difficult case.
 456– 4 is *m·* dangerous quackery.
 456– 9 high standing which *m·* of them hold
 460–10 this *m·* fundamental part of metaphysics
 460–11 is the one *m·* difficult to understand
r 466–17 the point you will *m·* reluctantly admit,
 466–18 it is the *m·* important to understand.
 478–18 That body is *m·* harmonious in which
 495–25 *Question.*— How can I progress *m·* rapidly
g 547–17 is more consistent than *m·* theories.
 549–19 the *m·* complicated corporeal structures,
 556–16 It is made known *m·* fully to him who
 572– 7 is the *m·* simple and profound counsel

Most High

a	49– 31	before the face of the *M· H·*,'' — *Lam.* 3 : 35.
s	142– 24	make them meet dwelling-places for the *M· H·*.
p	436– 14	under the protection of the *M· H·*.
g	541– 5	a higher tribute to the *M· H·*.
gl	596– 19	presence and power of the *M· H·*.

mostly

gl 597– 3   The Judaic religion consisted *m·* of rites

mote

t 455– 16   the *m·* out of thy brother's eye.'' — *Matt.* 7 : 5.

moth

f 241– 5   "where *m·* and rust doth — *Matt.* 6 : 19.

Mother

c 256– 8   Father and *M·* of the universe, including man.
g 530– 11   recognizing God, the Father and *M·* of all,
ap 569– 3   as Love, represented by the *M·*.
gl 592– 16   definition of

mother (see also mother's)

any
s 154– 32   successful method for any *m·* to adopt
r 479– 4   could the Scriptural rejoicing be uttered by
         any *m·*,
of Jesus
g 534– 3   to be the *m·* of Jesus and to behold at the
saintly
o 359– 24   from the lips of her saintly *m·*,
such a
s 154– 28   Such a *m·* runs to her little one, who
who is my
a 31– 7   "Who is my *m·*, and who are my — *Matt.* 12 : 48.

s 154– 17   the *m·* is frightened and says,
154– 24   That *m·* is not a Christian Scientist,
ph 178– 14   produced, . . . by the fright of his *m·*.
193– 25   and that his *m·* has been threatened with
f 206– 19   giving the *m·* her child
236– 12   A *m·* is the strongest educator,
c 267– 15   the same authority for the appellative *m·*,
267– 18   my brother, and sister, and *m·*.'' — *Matt.* 12 : 50.
b 315– 30   being conceived by a human *m·*,
o 352– 12   Would a *m·* say to her child,
t 463– 19   and can cause the *m·* no more suffering

motherhood

g 507– 6   the fatherhood and *m·* of God.
519– 11   the fatherhood and *m·* of Love.
ap 562– 7   the spiritual idea of God's *m·*.

mother-love

m 60– 9   the *m·* includes purity and constancy,

mother's

m 60– 8   A *m·* affection cannot be weaned from
r 478– 28   separated me from my *m·* womb, — *Gal.* 1 : 15.

moths

an 103– 27   like silly *m·*, singe their own wings

motion

sp 90– 7   The earth's *m·* and position are sustained
s 118– 22   modes of material *m·* are honored with
119– 27   to believe that the earth is in *m·*
160– 9   *m·* of the arm is no more dependent upon
f 240– 15   Mind is perpetual *m·*.
t 445– 20   the unlabored *m·* of the divine energy

motionless

ph 190– 9   If mind does not move them, they are *m·*.
p 375– 23   making certain portions of it *m·*.

motions

p 399– 8   and puts the body through certain *m·*.
437– 29   overruled their *m·* on the ground that
r 471– 10   no intimation of the earth's *m·* or
g 513– 12   the *m·* and reflections of deific power

motive

good
p 376– 14   more life and immortality in one good *m·*
purpose and
b 326– 11   The purpose and *m·* to live aright can be
right
t 452– 29   destroys your power of healing from the right *m·*.
453– 19   a right *m·* has its reward.
without
ph 188– 7   an embryonic thought without *m·* ;
wrong
t 446– 18   A wrong *m·* involves defeat.
your
p 421– 9   afterwards make known to the patient your *m·*

m 58– 2   should be the *m·* of society.
an 104– 29   Our courts recognize evidence to prove the *m·*
105– 15   reasonably pass sentence, according to the *m·*.

motive-power

gl 597– 20   WILL. The *m·* of error ;

motive-powers

r 490– 8   reveals Truth and Love as the *m·* of man.

motives

abuse of the
ap 560– 22   Abuse of the *m·* and religion of St. Paul
according to
pr 15– 9   and rewards according to *m·*,
aims and
m 63– 27   a race having higher aims and *m·*.
and acts
f 238– 1   *M·* and acts are not rightly valued before
and affections
gl 597– 4   The *m·* and affections of a man
and aims
sp 95– 3   His holy *m·* and aims were traduced
p 405– 3   The indulgence of evil *m·* and aims
t 459– 8   the worldling's affections, *m·*, and aims.
and aspirations
m 60– 4   Kindred tastes, *m·*, and aspirations
and philanthropy
s 151– 8   the *m·* and philanthropy . . . of physicians.
for prayer
pr 2– 1   What are the *m·* for prayer?
for verbal prayer
pr 7– 14   *m·* for verbal prayer may embrace too much
human
f 239– 23   the acknowledged seat of human *m·*.
inferior
f 236– 8   Do not inferior *m·* induce the infuriated
b 290– 10   and from selfish and inferior *m·*.
its
pr 4– 13   Its *m·* are made manifest in the blessings
malicious
t 446– 11   from sinister or malicious *m·*
our
a 36– 29   and mockery of our *m·*
right
t 454– 19   Right *m·* give pinions to thought,
selfish
t 447– 7   erring human opinions, conflicting selfish *m·*,
sinful
t 452– 28   Acting from sinful *m·* destroys your
true
h 326– 20   Working and praying with true *m·*,
wicked
p 404– 12   the wicked *m·* which produce them.
wrong
t 451– 29   controlling another from wrong *m·*,

a 51– 24   The *m·* of his persecutors were pride, envy,
gl 587– 23   HEART. Mortal feelings, *m·*, affections,

motto

f 224– 29   On its banner is the Soul-inspired *m·*,
t 443– 11   our *m·* should be the Master's counsel,
458– 15   *Semper paratus* is Truth's *m·*.

mould

pr 4– 21   will *m·* and fashion us anew,
f 236– 14   Her thoughts . . . unconsciously *m·* it.

moulded

pr 1– 13   that they may be *m·* and exalted
ph 198– 23   *m·* and formed by his doctor's belief

moulding

f 248– 14   *m·* and chiseling thought.

mount

f 236– 17   pattern showed to thee in the *m·*.'' — *Heb.* 8 : 5.
ap 561– 9   beheld the spiritual idea from the *m·* of vision.
575– 23   joy of the whole earth, is *m·* Zion, — *Psal.* 48 : 2.

mountain

pr 1– *   whosoever shall say unto this *m·*, — *Mark* 11 : 23.
m 61– 10   and every *m·* of selfishness be brought low,
b 299– 28   as the mist obscures the sun or the *m·* ;
ap 558– *   in the *m·* of His holiness. — *Psal.* 48 : 1.

mountain-peak

p 415– 32   standing forth as distinctly as a *m·*,

mountains

m 67– 6   and the waves lift themselves into *m·*.
s 135– 3   Ye *m·*, that ye skipped like — *Psal.* 114 : 6.
p 442– 15   feet "beautiful upon the *m·*,'' — *Isa.* 52 : 7.
g 511– 24   rocks and *m·* stand for solid and grand ideas.

mournful

a 32– 30   was a *m·* occasion, a sad supper

mournfully

s 140– 27   *m·* true that the older Scripture is reversed.

mouth

cannon's
f 225– 21   nor did . . . freedom come from the cannon's *m·*.
cave's
a 45– 1   great stone must be rolled from the cave's *m·* :
her
ap 570– 11   and the earth opened her *m·*, — *Rev.* 12 : 16.

mouth

his
a	48–19	"He opened not his *m·*."— *Isa.* 53 : 7.
	50– 2	so he openeth not his *m·*."— *Isa.* 53 : 7.
ap	564–19	Jesus "*opened not his m·*."— *Isa.* 53 : 7.
	570– 9	serpent cast out of his *m·* water— *Rev.* 12 : 15.
	570–13	the dragon cast out of his *m·*.— *Rev.* 12 : 16.

of God
p	410–11	proceedeth out of the *m·* of God,"— *Matt.* 4 : 4.

patient's
s	152–16	introducing a thermometer into the patient's *m·*.

s	115– 9	as the *m·* tasteth meat."— *Job* 34 : 3.
o	354–22	and out of the *m·* of babes
r	489–10	not equal to guiding the hand to the *m·* ;
ap	559–19	in thy *m·* sweet as honey."— *Rev.* 10 : 9.
	566–13	into the *m·* of Rebecca the Jewess

mouthpiece
sp	73–30	sensual cannot be made the *m·* of the spiritual,

move
sp	80–20	should not seem mysterious that mind, . . . can
		m· a
an	104–31	clear that the human mind must *m·* the body
s	121–18	the sun seems to *m·* from east to west,
ph	179–28	to *m·* the bowels, or to produce sleep
	199– 8	If mind does not *m·* them,
f	208– 5	"In Him we live, and *m·*, and— *Acts* 17 : 28.
	212–26	we say the lips or hands must *m·* in order to
	240–18	Mortals *m·* onward towards good or evil
o	343–10	"None of these things *m·* me."— *Acts* 20 : 24.
	361–19	"For in Him we live, and *m·*,— *Acts* 17 : 28.
p	381–18	we live, *m·*, and have our being in the
	419–13	has no intelligence with which to *m·* itself
	419–15	therefore be sure that you *m·* it off.
t	454–22	Wait patiently for divine Love to *m·* upon the
g	515–27	If you speak, the lips of this likeness *m·*
	536–13	in whom we "live, and *m·*, and— *Acts* 17 : 28.

moved
pr	2– 8	God is not *m·* by the breath of praise
a	20– 4	*m·*, not by spirits but by Spirit.
	51– 3	It was the possible loss . . . which *m·* him,
ph	187–16	as does the hand, admittedly *m·* by the will.
g	503– 8	*m·* upon the face of the waters.— *Gen.* 1 : 2.
ap	565–17	Her fathers' God before her *m·*,

movement
s	119–29	the *m·* of the solar system,
b	283– 4	Mind is the source of all *m·*,

movement-cure
p	383–29	The *m·*— pinching and pounding the

movements
sp	80–26	These *m·* arise from the volition of
	90–10	the *m·* and transitions now possible
f	212–31	whereas the unreal and imitative *m·* of
gl	597–28	the *m·* of God's spiritual government,

moves
sp	80–21	mind-power which *m·* both table and hand.
f	220–32	as directly as the volition or will *m·* the hand.
b	329– 1	As time *m·* on, the healing elements
p	415– 7	because thought *m·* quickly or slowly,
	419–14, 15	If disease *m·*, mind, not matter, *m·* it ;
g	515–23	*m·* in accord with Him,
ap	566–10	but *m·* before them, a pillar of cloud by day

moveth
g	512– 5	every living creature that *m·*,— *Gen.* 1 : 21.
	517–29	over every living thing that *m·*— *Gen.* 1 : 28.

moving
p	415–22	The muscles, *m·* quickly or slowly
g	511–20	the *m·* creature that hath life,— *Gen.* 1 : 20.
	514–29	*m·* in the harmony of Science,
	557– 2	*m·* and playing without harm,

Mozart
f	213–20	*M·* experienced more than he expressed.

much
pr	3–25	Gratitude is *m·* more than a verbal expression
	7–15	may embrace too *m·* love of applause
	9–19	This command includes *m·*,
a	28–32	There is too *m·* animal courage in society
	37– 2	sin brings suffering as *m·* to-day as
	45–12	*m·* more, being reconciled,— *Rom.* 5 : 10.
m	62–15	will do *m·* more for the health of the
sp	81– 1	There is not so *m·* evidence to prove
	98–13	*m·* less can they demonstrate it.
an	102–27	*m·* more likely to be abused by its possessor,
s	159–13	as if she were so *m·* mindless matter,
	159–26	to ascertain how *m·* harmony, or health,
	159–27	how *m·* pain or pleasure, action or stagnation,
	160–32	Is a stiff joint . . . as *m·* a result of law
	163–28	humiliating view of so *m·* absurdity,
	164–13	*M·* yet remains to be said and done
ph	169–21	however *m·* we trust a drug
	171–11	to learn how *m·* of a man he is.
	172– 6	nothing in the right direction and very *m·* in

much
ph	174– 7	capable of doing so *m·* for man as
	183– 7	however *m·* is said to the contrary.
f	202–26	Truth should "*m·* more abound."— *Rom.* 5 : 20.
	223–28	calamities, and sin will *m·* more abound
	233–18	*m·* more should ye discern the sign mental,
	235–12	it is not so *m·* academic education,
	243–14	arises not so *m·* from lack of desire as from
	254–15	to *begin* aright and to continue . . . is doing *m·*.
b	271– 1	seed of Truth springs up and bears *m·* fruit.
	272– 7	else it beareth not *m·* fruit,
	295–21	one which has lost *m·* materiality— *m·* error
	307–13	shall seem to have life as *m·* as
	318–19	beliefs, from which comes so *m·* suffering,
	323–28	effects of C. S. are not so *m·* seen as felt.
	333– 8	not a name so *m·* as the divine title of Jesus.
o	343–24	Christendom generally demands so *m·* less.
	348– 9	one disease can be just as *m·* a delusion as another.
	348–14	Are we . . . imputing too *m·* power to God,
p	364–30	that they indeed love *m·*.
	364–31	because *m·* is forgiven them.
	373–22	Disease is expressed not so *m·* by the lips as
	394–14	as *m·* so as would be the advice to a man
	396–10	Never say . . . how *m·* you have to
	401– 3	nothing in the right direction and *m·* in
	416–29	they think too *m·* about their ailments,
	416–30	have already heard too *m·* on that subject.
	434– 8	After *m·* debate and opposition,
t	458–16	Having seen so *m·* suffering from quackery,
	464– 6	how *m·* time and toil are still required
r	465– 2	After *m·* labor . . . she revised that treatise
	485–29	controlled war and agriculture as *m·* as
g	510– 2	How *m·* more should we seek to apprehend the
	517–11	not as *m·* authority for considering
	533–29	as *m·* as to say in meek penitence,
ap	562–14	will through *m·* tribulation yield
gl	596– 5	C. S. brings God *m·* nearer to man,

muddy
g	540–10	The *m·* river-bed must be stirred in order to
gl	593–16	*m·*, foaming, and dashing, it is a type of error.

multifarious
r	477–21	in *m·* forms of the living Principle,

multiform
b	331–29	the same in essence, though *m·* in office :

multiplication
pref	viii–22	*m·* and increased violence of diseases
c	263–23	a new *m·* or self-division of mortal thought,
	263–27	The *m·* of a human and mortal sense
b	303– 5	*M·* of God's children comes from no power of
g	507–17	and governs the *m·* of the
	512–20	the *m·* of its own pure and perfect ideas.
	549– 2	shows that the *m·* of certain animals

multiplied
a	36–28	*m·* trials, and mockery of our motives
sp	90– 3	How were the loaves and fishes *m·*
s	108–15	the product of three *m·* by three,
ph	165–13	Diseases have *m·*, since
p	421–31	the products of eight *m·* by five,

multiplier
g	508– 3	Mind is the *m·*,

multiplies
f	214–23	All material knowledge, . . . *m·* their pains,
b	280– 7	Mind creates and *m·* them,
g	533–25	and *m·* until the end thereof.

multiply
pr	11– 1	Without punishment, sin would *m·*.
s	108–13	to *m·* with mathematical certainty
f	202–18	The days of our pilgrimage will *m·*
	219– 6	we do not *m·* when we should subtract,
	250– 1	We run into error when we . . . *m·* Mind into
g	511– 4	"*m·* and replenish the earth."— *Gen.* 1 : 28.
	512–18	Be fruitful, and *m·*,— *Gen.* 1 : 22.
	512–19	and let fowl *m·* in the earth.— *Gen.* 1 : 22.
	517–26	Be fruitful, and *m·*,— *Gen.* 1 : 28.
	517–31	causes them to *m·*,— to manifest His power.
	535– 7	I will greatly *m·* thy sorrow— *Gen.* 3 : 16.
	549–11	to *m·* their species sometimes through eggs,

multiplying
g	557– 9	many animals suffer no pain in *m·* ;

multitude
pr	8–20	they "cover the *m·* of sins."— *I Pet.* 4 : 8.
sp	86– 3	"The *m·* throng thee."— *Luke* 8 : 45.
s	163–29	the *m·* of hypotheses obtruded upon us
b	273–25	fed the *m·*, healed the sick,

multitudes
sp	98–24	*m·* consider that what they call *science*
s	151–16	theories, from which *m·* would gladly escape,
b	272– 2	how shall they preach. convert, and heal *m·*,

multitudinous
a 43–30 and the *m·* errors growing from
c 264–14 *m·* objects of creation, . . . will become visible.
b 303– 2 *m·* forms of Mind which people the realm of
g 507–16 reproduces the *m·* forms of Mind

mundane
f 209–25 Material substances or *m·* formations,
249–30 but makes its *m·* flights quite ethereal.

murder
an 105– 2 The hands, without . . . could not commit a *m·*.
f 252–19 says : . . . lie, commit adultery, rob, *m·*,
b 330–31 *m·*, dementia, insanity, inanity,
p 406–17 moral man has no fear that he will commit a *m·*,

murderer
sp 89–31 "a *m·* from the beginning."— *John* 8 : 44.
an 104–32 Is not mortal mind the *m·*?
b 290–27 The *m·*, though slain in the act, does not
292–23 a *m·* from the beginning,— *John* 8 : 44.
p 436– 7 in the interest of Personal Sense, a *m·*.
441–32 "a *m·* from the beginning."— *John* 8 : 44.
g 539– 3 "a *m·* from the beginning."— *John* 8 : 44.
gl 580–30 a *m·* from the beginning,— *John* 8 : 44.

murderers
f 234–12 against the approach of thieves and *m·*.

murders
an 100– * *evil thoughts, m·, adulteries,— Matt.* 15 : 19.
106–23 envyings, *m·*, drunkenness,— *Gal.* 5 : 21.

murky
s 122–20 in the midst of *m·* clouds and drenching rain.

murmur
a 48–12 shall the humblest or mightiest disciple *m·*
p 309–32 It is error even to *m·*
ap 559–22 *m·* not over Truth, if you find its digestion

murmuring
a 40–22 may endure human brutality without *m·*,

muscle
s 160–15 to convey the mandate of mind to *m·*
160–28 to learn how mortal mind governs *m·*,
160–29 only to learn from anatomy that *m·* is not
160–32 is a stiff joint or a contracted *m·*
ph 165– 7 To measure . . . strength by the exercise of *m·*,
f 217–30 But what is this *me?* Is it *m·* or mind?

muscles
and bones
sp 84–21 not dependent . . . upon *m·* and bones for
relaxes rigid
s 162– 8 dissolves tumors, relaxes rigid *m·*,
sprain the
p 385–19 If you sprain the *m·* or wound the flesh,

s 160–19 Can *m·*, bones, blood, and nerves rebel against
160–22 Unless *m·* are self-acting at all times,
160–24 If *m·* can cease to act . . . of their own preference,
ph 198–29 Because the *m·* of the blacksmith's arm are
199– 1 *m·*, without volition of mortal mind,
199– 4 thought . . . hammering would enlarge the *m·*,
199– 5 since *m·* are as material as wood and iron
199– 8 *M·* are not self-acting.
199–28 gave his thought-forces, called *m·*, their
f 217–31 Without mind, could the *m·* be tired?
217–32 Do the *m·* talk,
219– 8 No more can we say . . . that *m·* give strength,
219–11 Not *m·*, nerves, nor bones, but mortal mind
p 375–24 show . . . that *m·* have no power to be lost,
393–27 lenses, *m·*, the iris and pupil,
415–21 The *m·*, moving quickly or slowly
r 485–30 as much as . . . *m·* measure strength.

muscular
s 152–10 Anatomy describes *m·* action as
ph 199–12 Not because of *m·* exercise, but by reason of

muscularity
ph 200– 2 Pagan worship began with *m·*,

mushrooms
ph 172– 3 Theorizing about man's development from *m·*

music
poetry and
p 378– 2 even as poetry and *m·* are reproduced
science of
pref viii– 7 science of *m·* corrects false tones
b 304–22 The science of *m·* governs tones.
304–26 the science of *m·* must be understood.
sweetest
f 213–25 Mental melodies and strains of sweetest *m·*
tones of
sp 81–21 silence the tones of *m·*, . . . and yet the

a 26–19 A musician demonstrates the beauty of the *m·*
sp 81–24 in the case of numbers and of *m·*,
89–27 Sound is not the originator of *m·*,
ph 195–17 astronomy, natural history, chemistry, *m·*,

music
f 213–26 *M·* is the rhythm of head and heart.
c 255– 6 and discord into the *m·* of the spheres.
b 276–15 Harmony in man is as real . . . as in *m·*.
304–21 Harmony in man is as beautiful as in *m·*,
304–27 Left to the decisions of material sense, *m·* is
304–29 Controlled by belief, . . . *m·* is, must be,
305– 4 no more a *man* than discord is *m·*.

musical
f 217– 4 to conclude that individual *m·* tones are

musician
a 26–19 A *m·* demonstrates the beauty of the music
s 145– 2 caught its sweet tones, as the natural *m·*
f 213–22 He was a *m·* beyond what the world knew.
t 453– 3 You do not . . . disbelieve the *m·*

mustard-seed
ap 575–15 Did not Jesus illustrate . . . by the *m·*

mutable
f 202–15 Outside of this Science all is *m·* ;
b 279– 2 changing, and dying, the *m·* and mortal,
286– 4 through the finite, *m·*, and mortal,
299–32 and would be *m·* and mortal.
300–14 The *m·* and imperfect never touch the
g 503–25 mortal life, *m·* truth, nor variable love.
522– 8 second record chronicles man as *m·* and

mutations
c 261–25 Breaking away from the *m·* of time and sense,
b 310–32 These changes are the *m·* of material

mute
pr 15–11 Lips must be *m·* and materialism silent,
sp 89–16 tongue grows *m·* which before was eloquent.
ph 191–20 Intelligence is not *m·* before non-intelligence.

mutilated
a 37–20 into a *m·* doctrinal platform.

mutter
sp 70– * *wizards that peep and that m· ;— Isa.* 8 : 19.

mutual
a 21–22 our *m·* interests are identical ;
m 59– 4 *m·* attention and approbation should
59– 7 *M·* compromises will often maintain a
59–24 A *m·* understanding should exist
un 100– 8 as follows : "There exists a *m·* influence

My
s 140– 6 "Thou canst not see *M·* face ;— Exod.* 33 : 20.
g 501– * *but by M· name Jehovah— Exod.* 6 : 3.

my
ph 187–18 What is this *m·* but mortal mind,

myriad
f 247–25 Love which paints the petal with *m·* hues,
b 306–21 The *m·* forms of mortal thought,
p 404– 4 any one of the *m·* forms of sin,
g 543–27 reflected in the *m·* manifestations of Life,
ap 572–16 uncover the *m·* illusions of sin, sickness, and

mysteries
sp 90–20 improve our time in solving the *m·* of being

mysterious
sp 80–19 It should not seem *m·* that mind,
86–14 but they are *m·* only because
s 134–32 This fact at present seems more *m·* than
137–11 so *m·* to the popular mind
t 450– 3 teaches belief in a *m·*, supernatural God,

mystery
dispels
sp 80–15 Science dispels *m·* and explains
unveils the
f 216– 6 Science unveils the *m·* and solves the problem
veil of
s 114–24 It lifts the veil of *m·* from Soul and body.

sp 70– 2 Every day is a *m·*.
98–26 *M·* does not enshroud Christ's teachings,
s 145–20 If there is any *m·* in Christian healing,
145–21 *m·* which godliness always presents to the
145–22 the *m·* always arising from ignorance
b 319–17 *M·*, miracle, sin, and death will disappear
g 501–14 So-called *m·* and miracle, which subserve the

mystical
b 334–28 a *m·* statement of the eternity of the Christ,

mysticism
sp 80–14 It is *m·* which gives spiritualism its force.
80–18 from the domain of reason into the realm of *m·*

mystification
g 523– 9 arise from a mist or false claim, or from *m·*,

myth
s 152– 1 But this so-called mind is a *m·*,
ph 186–25 If death is as real as Life, immortality is a *m·*.
b 281–19 a *m·*, a misconceived sense and false
r 470–31 If . . . then man's existence was a *m·*.

myth

g 523–12 material *m*·, instead of the reflection of Spirit.
528– 8 this supposition was a dream, a *m*·.
530–17 This *m*· represents error as always asserting
546– 1 The mortality of man is a *m*·,
550–21 If . . . then the great I AM is a *m*·.

mythical

c 255– 6 The *m*· human theories of creation,
r 490–28 the *m*· nature of material sense.

mythologic

g 531–29 *m*· theory of material life at no point resembles

mythological

f 249–11 theory of Life, . . . is delusive and *m*·.
g 528– 5 is solely *m*· and material.
534–16 *m*· material intelligence called *energy*

mythologies

b 319–17 are so many ancient and modern *m*·.

mythology

ancient
r 469–30 as are ancient *m*· and pagan idolatry.

mythology

father of
b 294–23 and human belief in them to be the father of *m*·,
god of
gl 580– 2 nothingness ; the first god of *m*· ;
gods of
r 485–28 heathen gods of *m*· controlled war
heathen
r 466–23 Heathen *m*· and Jewish theology have

b 339–20 As the *m*· of pagan Rome has yielded to a
g 524– 1 idolatry which followed this material *m*·
gl 587– 9 GODS. *M*· ; a belief that life, substance, and
591– 2 From this follow idolatry and *m*·,
591– 8 MATTER. *M*· ; mortality ; another name for
591–26 *m*· ; error creating other errors ;
594– 3 the first statement of *m*· and idolatry ;

myths

s 151– 1 the human mind and body are *m*·.
b 294–22 show the pleasures and pains of matter to be *m*·,
p 441–28 Your personal jurors . . . are *m*·.

N

nabob

f 220–13 procures . . . with more ease than a *n*·.

nacash

gl 594– 1 (*ophis*, in Greek ; *n*·, in Hebrew).

nail-prints

a 46–18 Jesus caused him to examine the *n*· and

nails

r 486–14 Jesus proved by the prints of the *n*·,

naked

g 532–16 I was *n*· ; and I hid myself. — *Gen.* 3 : 10.
532–29 In the allegory the body had been *n*·,
533– 6 Who told thee that thou wast *n*·? — *Gen.* 3 : 11.

nakedness

g 533– 1 first impression . . . was one of *n*· and shame.

name (*see also* name's)

Adam
b 338–14 Divide the *n*· Adam into two syllables,
gl 580–21 The *n*· Adam represents the false
affixed the
r 483–14 she affixed the *n*· "Science" to Christianity,
and nature
o 355–11 Let discord of every *n*· and nature
r 483–30 through the divine *n*· and nature.
g 528– 4 That Adam gave the *n*· and nature of animals, is
announce its
p 391–26 has no intelligence to . . . announce its *n*·.
another
pr 16–19 is but another *n*· for the first lie
gl 591– 8 MATTER. . . . another *n*· for mortal mind ;
asked the
p 411–13 once Jesus asked the *n*· of a disease,
Christ's
p 436–11 Giving a cup of cold water in Christ's *n*·,
coupled with the
gl 590–19 unless specially coupled with the *n*· God.
Eden
g 526–29 *n*· Eden, according to Cruden, means *pleasure*,
family
g 515–21 Man is the family *n*· for all ideas,
gave no
p 398– 9 Often he gave no *n*· to the distemper he cured.
get its
p 412–19 get its *n*·, and array your mental plea
his
s 109–26 his *n*· shall be called Wonderful." — *Isa.* 9 : 6.
163– 2 by first marking Nature with his *n*·,
b 308–30 then his *n*· was changed to Israel,
p 411– 7 replies more readily when his *n*· is spoken ;
411–15 demon, or evil, replied that his *n*· was Legion.
holy
s 143–31 everlastingly due its holy *n*·.
human
b 333– 5 Jesus was a human *n*·, which belonged to
in Christ's
ap 570–17 Give them a cup of cold water in Christ's *n*·,
in my
p 362– * *In my n*· shall they cast out* — *Mark* 16 : 17.
in the
s 135–30 not merely in the *n*· of Christ, or Truth,
p 438–15 I ask your arrest in the *n*· of Almighty God
440–17 Wherefore, then, in the *n*· of outraged justice,
t 453–22 yet serves evil in the *n*· of good.
456– 3 Teaching or practising in the *n*· of Truth,
ap 563–28 but doing this in the *n*· of good.

name

Joshua
b 333– 7 it is identical with the *n*· Joshua,
left no
a 27–25 other disciples who have left no *n*·.
more than a
a 54–24 whose religion was something more than a *n*·.
My
g 501– * *by My n*· *Jehovah was I not known* — *Exod.* 6 : 3.
new
ph 197– 3 A new *n*· for an ailment affects people like a
b 326–30 in humility he took the new *n*· of Paul.
of father
a 31– 9 of his calling any man by the *n*· of *father*.
of God Almighty
g 501– * *by the n*· *of God Almighty* ; — *Exod.* 6 : 3.
of Jehovah
g 524– 8 by the national *n*· of Jehovah.
524– 9 In that *n*· of Jehovah,
of Jesus
a 29–18 gave to her ideal the *n*· of Jesus
of laws
s 118–22 are honored with the *n*· of *laws*.
of Science
s 111–11 some may deny its right to the *n*· of Science.
ph 185–15 a human conception in the *n*· of Science
of the disease
p 396– 9 avoid speaking aloud the *n*· of the disease.
Parisian
ph 197– 4 like a Parisian *n*· for a novel garment.
proper
b 333–13 The proper *n*· of our Master
special
p 408–10 from the special *n*· of insanity.
spiritual
s 137–29 but now the Master gave him a spiritual *n*·
the very
s 129–28 The very *n*·, *illusion*, points to nothingness.
Thy
pr 16–28 Hallowed be Thy *n*·. — *Matt.* 6 : 9.
thy
a 49– 6 subject unto us through thy *n*·." — *Luke* 10 : 17.
s 161–23 "Liberty, what crimes are committed in thy *n*· !"
b 308–29 "What is thy *n*·?" — *Gen.* 32 : 27.
309– 1 "Tell me, I pray thee, thy *n*· ;" — *Gen.* 32 : 29.
under the
s 119–15 in the form and under the *n*· of natural law.
usurping the
f 204–25 usurping the *n*· without the nature

pr 16– 8 which we *n*· after him the Lord's Prayer.
sp 76– 2 *n*· the face that smiles on them
93–23 Spirit, as a proper noun, is the *n*· of the
ph 169–10 I *n*· these facts to show that disease has a
177–20 the opposite of Truth, cannot *n*· the qualities
186– 8 under whatever *n*· or pretence they are
f 210–23 I *n*· it mortal.
228–15 their freedom in the *n*· of Almighty God.
b 319–29 for instance, to *n*· Love as merely an attribute
332– 4 Father-Mother is the *n*· for Deity,
333– 8 Christ is not a *n*· so much as the
333–10 The *n*· is synonymous with Messiah,
p 362– 3 a certain Pharisee, by *n*· Simon,
372–13 and *n*· them divine law.
390–15 mortal opinions which you *n*· law,
398– 1 Sometimes Jesus called a disease by *n*·,
411– 4 If the student silently called the disease by *n*·,
412–10 You may call the disease by *n*· when you

name

t 448–30	has any claim to the *n*.
449–32	is a Scientist only in *n*.
r 473–12	Jesus is the *n*. of the man who,
483–14	affixed . . . the *n*. "error" to corporeal sense,
483–15	affixed . . . the *n*. "substance" to Mind.
g 515–17	The *n*. Elohim is in the plural,
527–25	that was the *n*. thereof.— *Gen. 2: 19.*
537–11	has no local habitation nor *n*.
ap 563–19	that old serpent, whose *n*. is devil
567–19	that old serpent whose *n*. is devil
gl 581– 1	the *n*. often conferred upon him

named

m 68–19	I have *n*. her case to individuals,
an 103–18	As *n*. in C. S., animal magnetism
s 107– 3	and *n*. my discovery C. S.
156– 2	Who *n*. drugs, and what made them good or
ph 187–12	another illusive personification, *n*. Satan.
189– 5	Science (in this instance *n*. natural)
200–24	the infinite Spirit, *n*. God.
b 276–27	the *nothingness n*. error.
276–28	the *somethingness n*. Truth.
293– 8	The grosser substratum is *n*. matter
295–26	The theoretical mind is matter, *n*. brain,
p 426–31	human concepts *n*. matter, death, disease,
r 469–11	Life, Truth, and Love,— *n*. God.
469–28	still believe there is another power, *n*. evil.
471– 6	The unlikeness of Truth,— *n*. error,
471–31	which, . . . she has *n*. C. S.
g 502–10	untrue image of God, *n*. a sinful mortal.
533–18	the rib . . . grown into an evil mind, *n*. woman,
gl 591– 4	one Spirit, or intelligence, *n*. Elohim, or God.
594– 2	the opposite of Truth, *n*. error ;
594–10	claim . . . that there was another power, *n*. evil,

nameless

b 309– 2	a *n*., incorporeal impartation of divine Love
g 507– 9	*n*. offspring,— wanderers from the parent Mind,
550–12	which ends, . . . in *n*. nothingness

namely

pr 5– 6	the test of our sincerity,— *n*., reformation,
a 53–20	*n*., that this shock arises from the great
sp 92–22	fact concerning error— *n*., its nothingness
s 157–29	C. S. impresses the entire corporeality,— *n*.,
ph 167–25	There is but one way— *n*.,
f 204– 8	*n*., Spirit and matter,
204–24	notion . . . can create what God cannot,— *n*.,
228– 5	*n*., that nothing inharmonious can enter being,
b 278–18	requires another admission,— *n*.,
o 347–19	*n*., apostolic, divine healing
355– 5	*n*., the proof of the utility of these methods ;
p 367–28	*n*., the student's higher attainments
400– 7	his goods,— *n*., of sin and disease.
414– 9	*n*., the impossibility that matter, brain,
422–30	believes that something . . . *n*., matter
431–11	in behalf of the state (*n*., the body)
432–13	a statute regarding disease,— *n*.,
r 472–21	absurdity— *n*., erroneous truth.
474– 1	and their glorious proofs, — *n*.,
492– 4	but one fact before the thought, *n*.,
q 526– 8	*n*., that all Life is God.
gl 590–14	*n*., matter, sin, sickness, and death ;

name's

ap 578– 9	for his *n*. sake.— *Psal. 23 : 3.*

names

s 108–28	which this same so-called mind *n*. matter,
137–27	common *n*., Simon Bar-jona, or son of Jona ;
ph 177–18	These *n*. indicated matter's properties,
187– 7	gives them material *n*.,
197– 1	It does this by giving *n*. to diseases
b 275–13	and are the Scriptural *n*. for God.
320– 4	*n*. are often expressive of spiritual ideas.
t 453–26	nor are *n*. to diseases,
g 506–29	finding *n*. for all material things,
507– 6	Spirit *n*. and blesses all.
508–22	*n*. the female gender last
512–26	confers animal *n*. and natures upon its
528–24	Adam— *alias* error— gives them *n*.

naming

ph 177–18	had the *n*. of all that was material.
o 348– 1	which they chide us for *n*. nothing
p 412–11	by *n*. it audibly, you are liable

Napier, Sir Charles

p 378–12	Sir Charles *N*. sent it cowering back into the

napkin

a 44–18	to remove the *n*. and winding-sheet,
p 367– 1	under the *n*. of its form,

narcotics

s 157–26	*N*. quiet mortal mind, and so relieve the body ;
p 408–15	the use of purgatives and *n*. is in itself a

narrated

ph 193–31	occurred just as I have *n*.

narrating

pref viii–25	*n*. experiences which led her,

narrative

s 157–17	according to the *n*. in Genesis
g 502– 4	preponderance of unreality in the entire *n*.,
507– 1	Adam has not yet appeared in the *n*.
521– 4	closes its *n*. of being
525– 3	In this *n*., the validity of matter
528–28	according to this *n*., surgery was
530–29	*First*, this *n*. supposes that
ap 568– 9	The *n*. follows the order used in Genesis.

narratives

g 501– 6	whereas the New Testament *n*. are clearer

narrow

a 44–30	demonstrating within the *n*. tomb the
sp 77–30	where the chances . . . for improvement *n*. into
s 126–31	in "the straight and *n*. way"— *see Matt. 7 : 14.*
137–13	Jesus completely eschewed the *n*. opinion
151–28	The straight and *n*. way is to see and
c 256–14	within the *n*. limits of physical humanity,
b 324–1	The way is straight and *n*.,
t 451–12	strive, to enter the *n*. path of Life,
454–29	tread firmly in the straight and *n*. way.
r 472– 6	way which leads to C. S. is straight and *n*.
g 536–22	Their *n*. limits belittle their gratifications,

narrowed

s 134– 7	the word *martyr* was *n*. in its significance

narrowness

m 58–16	*n*. and jealousy, which would confine
c 256–26	material sense of God leads to formalism and *n*. ;

nasal

ph 175–15	glandular inflammation, sneezing, and *n*. pangs.

nation *(see also* nation's*)*

an 106– 6	Like our *n*., C. S. has its Declaration of
ph 200– 4	Moses advanced a *n*. to the worship of God

national

a 41–30	It was enough for them to believe in a *n*. Deity ;
s 133–13	In *n*. prosperity, miracles attended the
133–20	limited form of a *n*. or tribal religion.
g 524– 8	the Supreme Being by the *n*. name of Jehovah.

nation's

ph 200– 2	the gods became alive in a *n*. belief.

nations

ph 94–12	The eastern empires and *n*.
s 133–16	Even in captivity among foreign *n*.,
b 340–23	One infinite God, good, unifies men and *n*. ;
p 406– 2	were for the healing of the *n*."— *Rev. 22 : 2.*
ap 565– 7	to rule all *n*. with a rod of iron :— *Rev. 12 : 5.*
565–16	will eventually rule all *n*. and peoples

native

m 57–12	The attraction between *n*. qualities
sp 91–11	reduced to its *n*. nothingness,
s 128–18	It raises the thinker into his *n*. air of insight
ph 190–16	and return to its *n*. nothingness.
b 281–24	They are *n*. nothingness, out of which
p 365–17	will vanish into its *n*. nothingness
383–15	It is the *n*. element of such a mind,
g 501–16	something more *n*. to their immortal cravings
ap 544– 6	scientifically reduced to its *n*. nothingness

Natrum muriaticum

s 153– 5	The author has attenuated *N*. *m*.

natural

pref xi–15	not supernatural, but supremely *n*.
a 32–24	it was *n*. and beautiful.
44–24	On the contrary, it was a divinely *n*. act,
s 111– 6	C. S. is *n*., but not physical
118–21	as the *n*. status of men and things,
118–31	and the *n*. order of heaven comes down to earth.
119–15	under the name of *n*. law.
119–21	God is *n*. good, and is represented only by
125– 8	man will be found normal and *n*.
126–18	as being both *n*. and spiritual?
128– 2	Good is *n*. and primitive.
130–30	no longer think it *n*. to love sin
131–27	*n*. demonstrations of the divine power,
134–22	*n*. law of harmony which overcomes discord,
145– 1	as the *n*. musician catches the tones of
ph 175– 9	What an abuse of *n*. beauty to say that a rose,
184–30	The inspirations were deep and *n*.
189– 5	Science (in this instance named *n*.)
193–11	its death-pallor gave place to a *n*. hue.
193–12	and the breathing became *n*. ;
195–17	Through astronomy, *n*. history, chemistry,
f 240– 1	Nature voices *n*., spiritual law and
b 272–32	reveals the *n*., divine Principle of Science.
274– 8	is not really *n*. nor scientific, because it
277–13	*N*. history presents vegetables and animals as
321–23	presently restored his hand to its *n*. condition
p 387–14	faithfully perform the *n*. functions of being.
413–12	are no more *n*. nor necessary than
413–19	Water is not the *n*. habitat of humanity.

natural

p 420–22 Mind is the n· stimulus of the body,
t 450– 4 and in a n·, all-powerful devil.
463– 9 that the birth will be n· and safe.
r 478–19 in which the discharge of the n· functions
483–19 To those n· Christian Scientists,
493–26 seem real and n· in illusion.
g 501–14 which subserve the end of n· good,
548–26 N· history is richly endowed by the
551– 6 In n· history, the bird is not the product of
gl 591–21 MIRACLE. That which is divinely n·,
(see also science)

naturalist

an 104– 8 Agassiz, the celebrated n· and author,
g 548–18 a famous n· says : "It is very possible that
548–22 Had the n·, through his tireless researches,
549–24 In one instance a celebrated n·, Agassiz,
551– 9 One distinguished n· argues that
551–22 The question of the n· amounts to this :

naturalist's

g 553–15 Why, then, is the n· basis so materialistic,

naturalists

g 551–17 N· ask : "What can there be, of a material
552–32 N· describe the origin of mortal . . . existence
553–10 One of our ablest n· has said :

naturally

pref xi–12 disappear as n· and as necessarily
m 57– 9 These different elements conjoin n·
sp 89–28 Cain very n· concluded that if life was in the
s 161–26 would n· induce the very disease
ph 195–18 thought passes n· from effect back to cause.
f 237– 9 height their little daughter so n· attained.
240– 8 the leaflet turns n· towards the light.
p 376–29 should n· and genuinely change our basis
407– 4 n· attractive to no creature except
t 447–16 recuperative action . . . goes on n·.
458–32 Christianity causes men to turn n· from
r 485–16 but come n· into Spirit
g 521–18 The reader will n· ask if there is
548–32 increase their numbers n· and

Natural Science

s 111–20 for the best essay on N· S·,

Nature

s 163– 1 by first marking N· with his name,

nature (see also nature's)

ambiguous
p 388–17 a specimen of the ambiguous n· of
and character
s 142–31 departs from the n· and character of Mind,
and essence
s 107–12 inspired with a diviner n· and essence ;
b 270– 6 in its very n· and essence ;
t 460– 7 the n· and essence of all being,
and God
s 118–31 in which n· and God are one
and methods
t 451–25 the n· and methods of error of every sort,
ap 564– 4 with error's own n· and methods.
and operation
g 545–25 the n· and operation of Spirit.
and origin
r 490–24 explanations of the n· and origin of man
g 529– 7 as to the n· and origin of man,
and quality
c 262– 9 the n· and quality of God's creation
and revelation
b 276–29 N· and revelation inform us that
animal
t 450–32 electricity, animal n·, and organic life,
antipathies of
s 163–32 the fixed and repulsive antipathies of n·.
commonly called
b 319–11 material means (commonly called n·)
determines the
p 403–28 The human mind determines the n· of a case,
divine
(see divine)
enriches the
m 57–23 Love enriches the n·, enlarging, purifying,
entire round of
b 277–17 throughout the entire round of n·.
essential
b 332– 1 express . . . the threefold, essential n· of the
infinite.
eternal
b 333–10 Christ expresses God's spiritual, eternal n·.
explication of
sp 83–16 since Science is an explication of n·.
express the
r 465–13 intended to express the n·, essence, and
God of
a 44–20 Could it be called supernatural for the God of n·
God's
g 512–14 their natures are allied to God's n· ;

nature

higher
m 60–21 education of the higher n· is neglected,
62–19 in the understanding of man's higher n·.
62–27 The higher n· of man is not governed by
highest
m 65– 2 should proceed from man's highest n·.
his
pr 9–32 that you may be partakers of his n·
a 28–17 Not a single component part of his n·
b 308–28 until his n· was transformed.
His own
b 303–27 a witness or proof of His own n·.
human
b 272– 8 the swinish element in human n·
identical with
s 119–17 In one sense God is identical with n·,
immortal
c 260–30 it must lose its immortal n·.
laws of
(see laws)
lower realms of
g 557– 7 birth-throes in the lower realms of n·,
man's
sp 84–23 by which we discern man's n· and existence.
material
g 551–18 "What can there be, of a material n·,
misinterprets
f 240– 2 but human belief misinterprets n·.
mythical
r 490–28 the mythical n· of material sense.
name and
o 355–11 Let discord of every name and n·
r 483–30 through the divine name and n·.
g 528– 4 That Adam gave the name and n· of animals, is
no
a 18–18 could conciliate no n· above his own,
obedience to
ph 176– 9 free to act in obedience to n·,
of Christianity
a 40–31 n· of Christianity is peaceful and blessed,
of error
g 555– 9 This is the n· of error.
of God
a 20–18 even the n· of God ;
g 537–32 but this is not the n· of God, who is Love
of man
m 62–27 The higher n· of man is not governed by
sp 94– 4 The n· of man, thus understood,
of religion
a 28–28 is to mistake the very n· of religion.
of Spirit
s 119–23 it is opposed to the n· of Spirit, God.
origin and
ph 171–17 Mistaking his origin and n·, man believes
physical
s 117– 8 attaches no physical n· and significance to
precise
b 270–17 they knew not what would be the precise n· of
real
sp 93–18 Whatever contradicts the real n· of the
shows the
f 211–17 shows the n· of all so-called material cause
spiritual
g 512–24 Their spiritual n· is discerned only through the
teaches
b 326– 8 All n· teaches God's love to man,

s 119–17 but this n· is spiritual
ph 183– 6 discords have no support from n·
f 204–26 usurping the name without the n·
220– 8 as even n· declares.
240– 1 N· voices natural, spiritual law and
245–31 nor is it a necessity of n·, but an illusion.
c 261–23 the n· of the immutable and immortal.
b 283–22 from God's character and n·,
307–20 Thus error partakes of its own n·
r 486– 3 when you have learned falsehood's true n·.
g 507–29 from the n· of its inexhaustible source.
549–28 even this great observer mistakes n·,
ap 559–26 partaking of the n·, or primal elements, of

nature's

f 220–10 clap their hands as n· untired worshippers.
p 432–27 the hands of justice, alias n· so-called law ;

natures

m 67–18 The notion that animal n· can possibly
sp 99–19 may possess n· above some others who
f 215– 8 from the very necessity of their opposite n·.
b 285–12 is illustrated by the opposite n· of
g 507– 7 Without n· particularly defined,
512–14 their n· are allied to God's nature ;
512–26 confers animal names and n· upon its
ap 577– 6 but as two individual n· in one ;

naught
sp 87–19   The mine knows *n·* of the emeralds within
s 109– 2   Mind is All and matter is *n·*
144– 6   *N·* is the squire, when the king is nigh ;
c 262– 6   C. S. takes *n·* from the perfection of God,
p 435–26   For *n·* else can he be punished.
g 554–19   infinite Mind sets at *n·* such a mistaken belief.

nauseous
ph 195–25   the speculative theory, the *n·* fiction.

nautical
m 67–10   *n·* science is not equal to the Science of Mind.

navigator
s 120–32   chained the limbs of the brave old *n·*,

Nazarene
a 53– 5   so far removed from . . . passions as the *N·*.
54–25   it enabled them to understand the *N·*
f 228–27   The humble *N·* overthrew the supposition that
gl 597– 6   The great *N·*, as meek as he was mighty,

Nazareth
a 18– 3   Jesus of *N·* taught and demonstrated
b 313–23   Jesus of *N·* was the most scientific man
333–16   The advent of Jesus of *N·* marked the
ap 564–11   the accusations against Jesus of *N·*

near
sp 82– 1   as easy to read distant thoughts as *n·*.
82–19   even if our departed friends were *n·* us
s 108–19   When apparently *n·* the confines of
161–21   a statue . . . erected *n·* the guillotine :
c 265– 6   they must *n·* the broader interpretations
l 455–25   one who is spiritually *n·* Himself.
gl 506– 6   known as the All-in-all, forever *n·*.

nearer
pr 2–29   The unspoken desire does bring us *n·* the
sp 96–25   As this consummation draws *n·*,
97–14   The *n·* a false belief approaches truth
s 121–30   thus brought *n·* the spiritual fact,
f 239–19   If divine Love is becoming *n·*,
248–11   which each day brings to a *n·* tomb.
249–26   sometimes *n·* the fact of being than
p 368– 7   *n·* than ever before to the apprehension
409– 5   the *n·* matter approaches its final statement,
g 501– 7   are clearer and come *n·* the heart,
553– 7   get *n·* the truth of being,
ap 559–24   When you approach *n·* and *n·* to this
567– 4   Truth and Love come *n·* in the hour of woe,
568–28   *n·* to the great heart of Christ ;
gl 596– 5   but C. S. brings God much *n·* to man,

nearing
ap 565– 1   when *n·* its doom, this evil increases

nearly
sp 93– 2   Remember Jesus, who *n·* nineteen centuries ago
b 286– 1   what relates most *n·* to the happiness of being.
g 541– 2   more *n·* resembles a mind-offering than

nearness
f 209–15   *N·*, not distance, lends enchantment

nebulæ
g 509–18   as *n·* indicate the immensity of space,

necessarily
pref xi–13   as *n·* as darkness gives place to light
sp 89–18   not *n·* dependent upon educational processes.
s 118–27   a kingdom *n·* divided against itself;
b 288– 1   *n·* includes the correlated statement,
312–25   *n·* limits faith and hinders . . . understanding.
g 508–18   and does not *n·* refer either to
549–21   in such vague hypotheses as must *n·* attend
552– 8   as *n·* apparent to the corporeal senses,

necessary
a 24–23   Does spiritualism find Jesus' death *n·* only for
m 60– 4   Kindred tastes, motives, and aspirations are *n·*
sp 81–29   and follows as a *n·* consequence
89–32   If seed is *n·* to produce wheat,
90–14   some insist that death is the *n·* prelude
ph 183–14   Truth never made error *n·*,
194–11   are not *n·* to ensure deafness
b 297– 7   It is as *n·* for a health-illusion, as for
p 413– 5   A single requirement, beyond what is *n·*
413–13   no more natural nor *n·* than would be the
419–31   If it is found *n·* to treat against relapse,
420–28   If it becomes *n·* to startle mortal mind
t 460– 3   "the science of the *n·* constituents and
r 484–29   is material sense a *n·* preliminary
485– 1   *Answer.—* If error is *n·* to define
ap 571– 4   since exposure is *n·* to ensure

necessities
p 381– 7   the ground that sin has its *n·*.

necessity
and power
p 377–27   conviction of the *n·* and power of
assume the
r 481–21   hypotheses . . . assume the *n·* of these evils

necessity
belief in the
f 251–18   belief in the *n·* of sickness and death,
enforce the
r 488–13   when they mean to enforce the *n·* of
finds a
s 160–14   Anatomy finds a *n·* for nerves
for uplifting
p 371–27   *n·* for uplifting the race is father to the fact
learning the
p 426–16   while also learning the *n·* of
obviate the
m 58–28   Wealth may obviate the *n·* for toil
of being right
t 455– 7   Hence the *n·* of being right yourself
of existence
ap 560–13   and the grand *n·* of existence
paramount
c 262– 5   shows the paramount *n·* of meeting them.
remove this
ph 183–13   obedience to God will remove this *n·*.
reveals a
pr 10–12   C. S. reveals a *n·* for overcoming the world,
reveals the
a 36– 5   Divine Science reveals the *n·* of
second
g 502– 1   A second *n·* for beginning with Genesis is that
showing the
pr 7– 4   showing the *n·* for such forcible utterance,
sin's
p 405–19   This is sin's *n·*,— to destroy itself.
supposed
f 253–25   Do not believe in any supposed *n·* for sin,
p 365–10   to rise above the supposed *n·* for

s 116–10   is and must of *n·* be, — all-inclusive.
f 205–14   Where then is the *n·* for recreation or
215– 8   from the very *n·* of their opposite natures.
245–30   nor is it a *n·* of nature,
p 384– 5   and must of *n·* pay the penalty.
388–13   there follows the *n·* for another admission
390–24   You have no law of His to support the *n·*
390–25   you have divine authority for denying that *n·*

neck
an 105–26   His sins will be millstones about his *n·*,

necromancers
ph 185–16   as the *n·* of Egypt strove to emulate the

necromancy
an 104–18   evil, occultism, *n·*, mesmerism,
b 322–15   The *n·* of yesterday foreshadowed the

need (noun)
absolute
s 151– 6   erring, finite, human mind has an absolute *n·* of
brother's
g 518–18   that man who seeth his brother's *n·*
each
pr 7–25   to whom each *n·* of man is always known
has no
ap 577–20   has no *n·* of sun or satellite,
human
sp 95– 9   and in that ratio we know all human *n·*
r 494–11   and always will meet every human *n·*.
little
pr 11–31   Such a desire has little *n·* of audible expression.
our
pr 13–15   God knows our *n·* before we tell Him
p 371–25   we should not deny our *n·* of its spiritual
374–14   show our *n·* of divine metaphysics.
our only
r 490–16   Our only *n·* is to know this and reduce to practice
physical
s 148–29   to render help in time of physical *n·*.
precludes the
r 487–16   this precludes the *n·* of believing.
time of
f 218–22   turning in time of *n·* to God, divine Love,

---

pr 1– *   *knoweth what things ye have n· of, — Matt. 6 : 8.*
b 308–26   the patriarch, perceiving his error and his *n·*
323–19   awake to realize their *n·* of
t 447– 9   or judging accurately the *n·* of your

need (verb)
pr 4– 3   What we most *n·* is the prayer of fervent desire
pr 8– 3   We never *n·* to despair of an honest heart;
a 34– 8   if a friend be with us, why *n·* we memorials of
39– 7   We *n·* "Christ, and him crucified." — *I Cor. 2 : 2.*
sp 75– 5   would *n·* to be tangible and material,
79–29   Mind-science teaches that mortals *n·*
85–24   but mortals *n·* spiritual sense.
s 142–18   *n·* to be whipped out of the temple,
149–29   We *n·* to understand the affirmations of
154–25   her affections *n·* better guidance,

need (verb)

s	154–26	says to her child : . . . "You n· rest,"
	154–27	says to her child : . . . "You n· medicine."
	158–11	but what we n· is the truth
f	212– 8	Why n· pain, . . . come to this mortal sense?
	231– 8	What God cannot do, man n· not attempt.
b	291– 9	Mortals n· not fancy that belief in the
	316– 5	mortals n· only turn from sin and
o	346–10	we n· to understand that error
p	383– 3	We n· a clean body and a clean mind,
	413–22	but in caring for an infant one n· not
	420– 8	they n· only to know that error cannot produce
	424–21	still you n· the ear of your auditor.
t	454– 1	It n· not be added that the use of tobacco
r	494– 9	mortals did n· this help, and Jesus pointed the
ap	576–18	What further indication n· we of the real

needed

a	29–10	because then our labor is more n·.
	34–23	They n· this quickening,
m	67–28	Spiritual, not corporeal, consciousness is n·.
sp	85–27	His thrusts at materialism were sharp, but n·.
s	140– 1	more than it is n· in most cases ;
	142–22	are still n· to purge the temples of their
	159– 1	a n· surgical operation without the ether.
b	291–25	until . . . shall effect the n· change.
p	382–32	Mortal mind n· to be set right.
	411– 9	n· the arguments of truth for reminders.
t	448– 9	When n· tell the truth concerning the
r	494– 7	God, who n· no help from Jesus' example
g	529– 5	It came about, also, that instruments were n·

needing

ph	171– 9	not n· to consult almanacs for the
	171–10	not n· to study brainology
c	264–18	finding all in God, good, and n· no other
g	501–16	when n· something more native to their
	527– 4	God's reflection, n· no cultivation,

needle

an	102–10	The pointing of the n· to the pole symbolizes
f	241–32	to go through the eye of a n·,"— Matt. 19 : 24.
t	449–10	to go through the eye of a n·,"— Matt. 19 : 24.

needless

sp	87– 5	It is n· for the thought or for the person
p	386–32	that lamentation is n· and causeless.

needle-thrusts

r	491– 1	N· will not hurt him.

needs

pr	16–11	that prayer which covers all human n·.
m	66–26	the other pre-eminently n· good company.
sp	78–18	If Spirit pervades all space, it n· no
	78–19	Spirit n· no wires nor electricity
s	144– 4	Mind, which n· no cooperation from
	147–17	The book n· to be studied,
ph	170–15	The best interpreter of man's n· said :
	174–20	Truth is revealed. It n· only to be practised.
f	224–23	meeting the n· of mortals in sickness
b	319–22	and n· inspiration to be understood.
	339– 4	n· no other form of forgiveness.
o	347– 8	infers that if anything n· to be doctored,
p	364–17	indicated by one of the n· of this age.
	365–32	suffering heart n· its rightful nutriment,
	412–28	it n· to be met mainly through the
	413– 6	to meet the simplest n· of the babe
	417–21	from which the patient n· to be awakened.
t	453–15	before he can . . . minister to human n·.
r	490–12	The Science of Mind n· to be understood.

negation

an	102– 6	mesmerism, or hypnotism is a mere n·,
ph	186–11	Evil is a n·, because it is the
p	392–12	should always be met with the mental n·.
	418–18	the n· must extend to the supposed disease

negative

s	143–24	not controlled scientifically by a n· mind.
ph	173–15	to pass through a n· condition would be
b	284–20	The answer . . . must forever be in the n·.
r	491– 8	a n· right and a positive wrong,

neglect

a	48– 1	pangs of n· and the staves of

neglected

m	60–11	the education of the higher nature is n·,
p	364–13	what his rich entertainer had n· to do,

neighbor

loved his

p	433–20	Because he has loved his n· as himself,

love his

a	55–18	and love his n· as himself,

love thy

s	138–29	Love thy n· as thyself !"— Matt. 19 : 19.
	340–25	"Love thy n· as thyself ;"— Matt. 19 : 19.
r	467– 8	love thy n· as thyself."— Matt. 22 : 39.

one's

sp	88–18	To love one's n· as one's self,
p	440–16	than that it is for the good of one's n·?

neighbor

our

pr	8–27	than we are willing to have our n· see?
	9– 6	Do we love our n· better because of
	9–12	we shall regard our n· unselfishly,
f	205–23	the divine law of loving our n· as
ap	560–16	goal is never reached while we hate our n·

upright

f	239–12	is not the ruler of his upright n·.

p	432–16	Judge asks if by doing good to his n·,

neighbor's

m	64–13	never well to interfere with your n· business."

neither

pr	12–10	n· Science nor Truth which acts through
	14–13	purely spiritual,— n· in nor of matter,
a	28–15	N· the origin, the character, nor
	54–18	understood n· his words nor his works.
m	56– *	In the resurrection they n· marry, nor — Matt. 22 : 30.
	69–11	n· closes man's continuity nor his sense of
	69–29	n· marry, nor are given in — Luke 20 : 35.
sp	71– 2	It is n· person, place, nor thing,
	71–18	n· mortal mind nor matter is the image
	72–25	evil is n· communicable nor scientific.
	73– 6	n· the one nor the other is infinite
	76– 7	recognized as n· material nor finite,
	76–14	n· can he return to it, any more than
	76–15	N· will man seem to be corporeal,
	77– 2	N· do other mortals . . . at a single bound.
	77–16	n· the Son, but the Father."— Mark 13 : 32.
	79–32	n· does withholding enrich us.
	80–27	but they are n· scientific nor rational.
	84– 1	coordinate n· with the premises nor
	89–25	Matter is n· intelligent nor creative.
an	102– 3	His power is n· animal nor human.
	102– 6	possessing n· intelligence, power, nor reality,
s	107– *	n· received it of man, n· was I — Gal. 1 : 12.
	108– 6	matter possesses n· sensation nor life ;
	110–19	n· tongue nor pen can overthrow it.
	124– 7	Having n· moral might, spiritual basis, nor
	125– 6	N· organic inaction nor overaction
	135–23	but n· is unimportant or untrue,
	138–11	n· by corporeality, by materia medica, nor
	139–22	But mistakes could n· wholly obscure the
	141–24	N· can this manifestation of Christ be
	148– 7	N· anatomy nor theology has ever
	153–31	N· sympathy nor society should ever
ph	170– 3	Modes of matter form n· a moral nor a
	173–12	N· the substance nor the manifestation
	177– 8	N· exists without the other,
	181– 6	which can n· suffer nor enjoy,
	186–15	there is n· power nor reality in evil.
	188– 3	It is n· mind nor matter.
	190– 6	n· a mortal mind nor the immortal Mind
	194–23	n· sight nor sound could reach him,
	200–18	he is n· inverted nor subverted,
f	202–17	immortal man, . . . n· sins, suffers, nor
	203– 6	matter can n· heal nor make sick,
	205–10	matter has n· intelligence, life, nor
	209–11	N· philosophy nor skepticism can hinder
	214–28	N· age nor accident can interfere with
	221–29	This new-born understanding, that n· food nor
	225–20	oppression n· went down in blood, nor
	232– 3	n· make man harmonious nor God lovable.
	232–32	n· place nor opportunity in Science for error
	243–20	N· immortal and unerring Mind nor
	243–23	matter has n· intelligence nor sensation.
	244–23	Man in Science is n· young nor old.
	244–24	He has n· birth nor death.
	251– 5	n· should a fever become more severe
c	261–25	n· lose the solid objects and ends of life nor
	262– 3	N· does consecration diminish man's obligations
b	269–21	The testimony . . . is n· absolute nor divine.
	271– 5	N· emancipation, illusion, nor
	271–17	"N· pray I for these alone,— John 17 : 20.
	272–17	n· cast ye your pearls before— Matt. 7 : 6.
	275– 5	matter is n· substantial, living, nor intelligent.
	279– 9	Matter is n· created by Mind nor
	279–13	Spirit and matter can n· coexist nor
	280–12	Such belief can n· apprehend nor
	281–22	have n· Principle nor permanency,
	282–29	which is n· Mind nor man,
	284–22	They can n· see Spirit through the eye nor
	284–30	but n· sensation nor report goes from
	287– 1	They have n· Principle nor permanence,
	287–17	N· understanding nor truth accompanies error.
	287–26	Matter is n· a thing nor a person,
	294–26	Man is n· self-made nor
	297–17	it is n· scientific nor eternal,
	304– 5	"N· death, nor life,— Rom. 8 : 38.
	310–31	n· growth, maturity, nor decay in Soul.
	319–14	Spirit and matter n· concur in man nor in
	321–27	n· hearken to the voice of the— Exod. 4 : 8.
	322–24	n· a temperate man nor a

neither

b 327– 4   n· pleasure nor pain, appetite nor passion,
   327–20   evil has in reality n· place nor power
   330–13   Eye hath n· seen God nor His image
   330–14   N· God nor the perfect man can be
   335– 1   There are n· spirits many nor gods many.
   336–20   n· could God's fulness be reflected by a
o 345–11   n· knows itself nor what it is saying.
   348– 1   and which we desire n· to honor nor to fear.
   349–11   n· Life nor man dies,
   351– 5   N· can we heal through the help of Spirit, if we
   351–22   such starting-points are n· spiritual nor
   353–31   beliefs can n· demonstrate Christianity nor
   354–13   opponents of C. S. n· give nor offer any proofs
   356–17   n· a present nor an eternal copartnership
   357– 8   Truth creates n· a lie, a capacity to lie, nor
   358–13   C. S. is n· made up of contradictory
p 368–22   N· evil, disease, nor death can be
   372–15   He can n· sin, suffer, be subject to
   384–26   n· rheumatism, consumption, nor
   387– 9   spiritual energies can n· wear out nor
   388–30   we shall n· eat to live nor live to eat.
   404–30   n· material medicine nor Mind
   414–24   matter n· feels, suffers, nor enjoys.
   415– 2   disease is n· a cause nor an effect.
   419–10   N· disease itself, sin, nor fear has the power to
   435–33   n· shall Judge Medicine condemn him ;
   441–14   n· can Fear arrest Mortal Man
   442–16   N· animal magnetism nor hypnotism enters
t 454–11   evil or matter has n· intelligence nor power,
   458–25   N· is he a false accuser.
   460–14   Sickness is n· imaginary nor unreal,— that is,
   464–27   N· dishonesty nor ignorance ever
r 466–12   n· dwell together nor assimilate.
   467–28   Matter n· sees, hears, nor feels.
   469– 1   Life is n· in nor of matter.
   472–16   Error is n· Mind nor one of Mind's faculties.
   473– 2   illusion, possessing n· reality nor identity
   478–31   not mortal, ''n· indeed can be ;"— Rom. 8 : 7.
   479– 8   Matter is n· self-existent nor a product of
   484– 3   When this is accomplished, n· pride, prejudice,
   492–32   Victory would perch on n· banner.
   495–16   Let n· fear nor doubt overshadow your
g 503–24   God creates n· erring thought, mortal life,
   508–20   neuter gender, n· male nor female.
   515– 6   The serpent of God's creating is n· subtle nor
   527–13   n· tempteth He any man."— Jas. 1 : 13.
   529–20   n· shall ye touch it, lest ye die.— Gen. 3 : 3.
   529–27   has n· origin nor support in Truth
   530–28   the dreamer and dream are one, so far is it true
   533–30   as much as to say . . . "N· man nor God shall
   534–20   not subject to the law of God, n·— Rom. 8 : 7.
   540– 3   Spirit creates n· a wicked nor a mortal man,
   544–13   In Science, Mind n· produces matter nor
   544–26   Therefore man, in this allegory, is n· a
   551–28   N· can produce the other.
   555–10   it n· understands nor can be understood.
   555–13   C. S. attributes to error n· entity nor power,
   555–14   error is n· mind nor the outcome of Mind.
ap 561–28   light portrayed is really n· solar nor lunar,
   566–27   n· was their place found any more— Rev. 12 : 8.
   570–20   He can n· drown your voice with its roar, nor
gl 584–17   error ; n· corporeality nor mind ;
   592– 8   that which n· exists in Science nor

Nerve

p 432– 2   I am N·, the State Commissioner for
   436–35   N·, testified that he was a ruler of Body,
   437–12   I proclaim this witness, N·, to be destitute of
   438– 8   C. S. proved the witness, N·, to be a perjurer
   438–11   N· was an insubordinate citizen,

nerve

auditory
pr   7–24   The "divine ear" is not an auditory n·.
ph 194–10   Destruction of the auditory n· and
optic
ph 194–11   paralysis of the optic n·

s 113–29, 30   no n· in Mind, and no mind in n· ;
ph 171–19   carried on a n·, exposed to ejection
   194–13   if . . . it will be so without an injured n·.
f 212– 2   is not communicated through a n·.
   212–12   When the n· is gone, which we say was
p 368–14   has little inspiration to n· endeavor.
gl 587–13   theories . . . sense, existing in brain, n·,

nerves

are unable
p 399–13   N· are unable to talk,
blood, and
s 160–19   Can muscles, bones, blood, and n· rebel
brain and
s 122–12   certain sections of matter, such as brain and n·,
b 290–11   manifested through brain and n·,
have no sensation
f 212–16   and the n· have no sensation.

nerves

olfactory
f 212–20   bring the rose into contact with the olfactory n·
weak
p 392–15   If you believe in inflamed and weak n·,

an 100–11   through the substance of the n·."
s 127–20   n·, . . . have— as matter— no intelligence, life,
   143–19   you conclude that the stomach, blood, n·,
   160–14   Anatomy finds a necessity for n·
f 211– 1   If brain, n·, stomach, are intelligent,
   211– 8   N· are not mind.
   211–24   If it is true that n· have sensation,
   211–32   N· are not the source of pain or pleasure.
   216–15   it makes the n·, . . . servants, instead of
   219– 9   No more can we say . . . that n· give pain
   219–11   Not muscles, n·, nor bones, but
b 294–12   error, saying : . . . N· feel. Brain thinks and
   295– 2   seeming to be in n· which are no longer there,
   308–10   head, heart, stomach, blood, n·,
p 389– 7   Recollect that it is not the n·,
   409– 6   animate error called n·, brain, mind,
r 478–14   Question.— Does brain think, and do n· feel,
   480– 8   N· are an element of the belief that there is
   485–29   as much as n· control sensation
   488–21   N· have no more sensation,

nervous

sp 79–26   says : . . . You have n· prostration,

net

a 35– 5   and cast their n· on the right side.

nets

b 271–26   Those, who are willing to leave their n·

neuralgia

p 392–17   You will call it n·, but we call it a belief.

neuter

g 508–20   a n· gender, neither male nor female.
   511–28   in masculine, feminine, or n· gender.
   516–30   Masculine, feminine, and n· genders are

neutralizes

s 157–31   Science both n· error and destroys it.

neutralizing

s 162– 6   C. S. acts as an alterative, n· error

never

pref ix–28   notes . . . which have n· been published.
   xii–20   she had n· read this book throughout
   4–17   Simply asking . . . will n· make us love Him ;
   4–27   Audible prayer can n· do the works of
   7–22   ventilation of fervent sentiments n· makes a
   8– 3   We n· need to despair of an honest heart ;
   9–13   we shall n· meet this great duty simply by
   10–10   vain repetitions will n· pour into prayer the
   11–13   Principle n· pardons our sins . . . till they
a 24– 2   Firmness in error will n· save from sin,
   25–28   faith in the Teacher . . . will n· alone make
   27–17   parables explain Life as n· mingling with
   27–27   n· truly understood their Master's instruction.
   29–11   though we may n· receive it in this world.
   31– 2   God will n· place it in such hands.
   36– 2   They, . . . can n· find bliss in the
   38–24   his spiritual selfhood, n· suffered,
   41–31   belief, . . . n· made a disciple who could
   53– 4   n· lived a man so far removed from
m 57–16   should n· weigh against the better claims
   58–12   N· contract the horizon of a worthy outlook
   59– 1   Matrimony should n· be entered into without a
   59–27   nuptial vow should n· be annulled, so long as
   59–32   Separation n· should take place,
   59–32   it n· would, if both husband and wife were
   61– 6   or happiness will n· be won.
   63– 1   You would n· think that flannel was better
   64–12   n· well to interfere with your neighbor's
   65–24   transitional stage is n· desirable on its own
   66–21   Husbands and wives should n· separate if
   66–30   It n· leaves us where it found us.
   68–16   I n· knew more than one individual who
   69– 6   Mortals can n· understand God's creation while
sp 70– *   he shall n· see death.— John 8 : 51.
   70– 6   Whatever is false or sinful can n· enter
   70– 7   Man is n· God,
   71–25   I n· could believe in spiritualism.
   72–22   suppositional opposite of good, is n· present.
   74–12   n· returns to the old condition.
   74–23   different beliefs, which n· blend.
   74–29   In C. S. there is n· a retrograde step,
   74–30   n· a return to positions outgrown.
   75–15   the understanding that Lazarus had n· died,
   76–11   Spirit n· entered matter
   76–11   and was therefore n· raised from
   76–29   Death can n· hasten this state of
   79–20   He n· described disease,
   80–7, 8   "There n· was, and there n· will be, an
   80–16   Science n· removes phenomena from
   85–27   He n· spared hypocrisy the sternest

never

sp	85–31	truth communicates itself but *n·* imparts error.
	87–25	The true concept is *n·* lost.
	88–19	can *n·* be seen, . . . through the physical senses.
	93–13	Good *n·* causes evil,
an	105–24	Whoever uses . . . is *n·* safe.
s	110– 8	I beheld, as *n·* before, the awful unreality
	116–14	They *n·* crown the power of Mind as
	120– 1	shall *n·* understand this while we admit
	126– 8	Human thought *n·* projected the least portion of
	126–13	the human mind *n·* produced a real tone
	143–10	The divine Mind *n·* called matter *medicine,*
	143–22	*n·* discerning how this deprives you of the
	147–15	*n·* believe that you can absorb the whole
	147–32	Jesus *n·* spoke of disease as dangerous
	149–12	and its perfection of operation *n·* vary
	149–21	remarked . . . mind can *n·* cure organic
	151–18	Fear *n·* stopped being and its action.
	154–32	"Oh, *n·* mind ! You 're not hurt,"
	157– 6	*n·* shares its rights with inanimate matter.
	157–20	then they should *n·* be used.
	160–23	Unless . . . self-acting at all times, they are *n·*
	160–23	*n·* capable of acting contrary to
ph	169–25	the sick are *n·* really healed except by means of
	170–11	believeth in me shall *n·* die," — *John* 11 : 26.
	170–20	always in opposition, *n·* in obedience, to
	171–29	intelligence and life are spiritual, *n·* material,
	175–27	but they *n·* indulged in the refinement of
	179–20	epizoötic . . . which a wild horse might *n·* have.
	183–14	Truth *n·* made error necessary,
	184–10	*n·* honoring erroneous belief with the
	185– 4	and she *n·* suffered again from east winds,
	186–20	It can *n·* destroy one iota of good.
	186–28	ignorant of self, or it could *n·* be self-deceived.
	190–18	it *n·* merges into immortal being,
	191–29	Truth *n·* mingles with error.
	192–26	betrays its weakness and falls, *n·* to rise.
	195– 4	that he should *n·* be happy elsewhere.
	197–27	will *n·* grow robust until
	199–26	he could *n·* have done it.
f	204–18	They can *n·* stand the test of Science.
	204–27	in Science it can *n·* be said that man
	206–10	Will-power . . . can *n·* heal the sick,
	213–21	The rapture of . . . was *n·* heard.
	214– 6	he could *n·* have "walked with God," — *Gen.* 5 : 24.
	215–12	Whatever is governed by God, is *n·* . . . deprived
	217–13	he shall *n·* see death !" — *John* 8 : 51.
	217–18	once conquered . . . that condition *n·* recurs,
	218– 6	the body, . . . would *n·* be weary.
	219–14	When this is understood, we shall *n·* affirm
	220–24	and advised others *n·* to try dietetics for
	221–19	God *n·* decreed disease, — *n·* ordained a law that
	221–25	he *n·* enjoyed his food as he had
	222–27	concluded that God *n·* made a dyspeptic,
	228–21	we shall *n·* depend on bodily conditions,
	230–23	the sick are *n·* really healed by drugs,
	230–28	but we are *n·* thoroughly healed until
	231– 4	Unless . . . overcome by Truth, the ill is *n·*
	232–19	Jesus *n·* taught that drugs, food,
	232–23	and *n·* tried to make of none effect the
	234–21	empty it of . . . or sin and sickness will *n·* cease.
	236– 3	should emanate from the pulpit, but *n·* be
	238–13	To fall away . . . shows that we *n·* understood
	239–29	opposite sources *n·* mingle in fount or stream.
	243– 1	but we can *n·* succeed . . . through ignorance or
	244– 5	Jesus demonstrated Life, *n·* fearing nor
	244–18	but man was *n·* more nor less than man.
	245–27	Impossibilities *n·* occur.
	245–32	The infinite *n·* began nor will it ever end.
	246– 1	Mind and its formations can *n·* be annihilated.
	246–17	*N·* record ages.
	248– 3	Love *n·* loses sight of loveliness.
	248–28	look at them continually, or we shall *n·*
	249–15	infinity *n·* began, will *n·* end,
	249–22	God *n·* slumbers, and His likeness *n·* dreams.
	250– 8	Spirit is the Ego which *n·* dreams,
	250– 9	Spirit is the Ego . . . which *n·* errs,
	250–10	Spirit is the Ego . . . which *n·* believes, but
	250–10, 11	the Ego . . . which is *n·* born and *n·* dies.
	253–27	God *n·* requires obedience to a so-called
c	258–27, 28	*N·* born and *n·* dying, it were impossible for
	259–16	then mortals have *n·* beheld in man the
	259–25	Brain or matter *n·* formed a human concept.
	264–16	Life is Spirit, *n·* in nor of matter,
b	273–17	The so-called laws of matter . . . have *n·* made
	273–21	God *n·* ordained a material law to annul
	274–26	firm, called matter and mind, God *n·* formed.
	275– 1	Matter has no life to lose, and Spirit *n·* dies.
	276–25	beliefs and . . . understanding *n·* mingle.
	276–32	Intelligence *n·* produces non-intelligence ;
	277– 6	Matter *n·* produces mind.
	277– 6	The immortal *n·* produces the mortal.
	279– 7	protoplasm *n·* originated in the immortal Mind,
	280– 9	Finite belief can *n·* do justice to Truth
	282–12	*n·* unite in figure or in fact.

never

b	284– 9	It can *n·* be in bonds, nor be fully
	288– 9	Superstition and understanding can *n·*
	289– 2	Mortal man can *n·* rise . . . until he learns that
	289–12	Truth and Truth's idea, *n·* make men sick,
	291–25	Mind *n·* becomes dust.
	295–18	The light and the glass *n·* mingle,
	298–17	This human belief, . . . *n·* reaches beyond the
	299–13	These upward-soaring beings *n·* lead towards
	299–24	Truth *n·* destroys God's idea.
	300–13	The temporal and unreal *n·* touch the eternal
	300–14	The mutable and imperfect *n·* touch the
	300–16	The inharmonious and self-destructive *n·* touch
	300–18	tares and wheat, which *n·* really mingle,
	303–15	All the vanity of the ages can *n·* make
	304–13	good can *n·* produce evil ;
	304–13	matter can *n·* produce mind nor
	307–28	material laws which Spirit *n·* made ;
	309–30	Life is *n·* for a moment extinct.
	309–30	Therefore it is *n·* structural nor organic,
	309–31	Life is . . . *n·* absorbed nor limited by its
	311–21	So long as . . . we can *n·* understand the
	315– 2	and believeth in me shall *n·* die." — *John* 11 : 26.
	325–25	can *n·* reach in this world the divine heights of
	327–22	Fear of punishment *n·* made man truly
	329–24	its divine Principle *n·* repents,
	335– 8	Spirit *n·* created matter.
	335–17	*n·* included in a limited mind or a
	336– 2	Mind *n·* enters the finite.
	336– 3	Intelligence *n·* passes into non-intelligence,
	336– 4	Good *n·* enters into evil,
	336–13	but infinite Mind can *n·* be in man,
	336–17	Immortal man is not and *n·* was material,
	339–30	*n·* to admit that sin can have intelligence
	339–32	will *n·* lose their imaginary power . . . until
o	348–26	I have *n·* supposed the world would
	353–28	Mind is limitless. It *n·* was material.
	356– 7	Discord can *n·* establish the facts of harmony.
	358–31	whom they have perhaps *n·* seen
p	369–14	We *n·* read that Luke or Paul made a
	369–16	Jesus *n·* asked if disease were acute or chronic,
	369–17	*n·* recommended attention to laws of health,
	369–18	*n·* gave drugs, *n·* prayed to know if
	374– 2	Anodynes, counter-irritants, and depletion *n·*
	374– 8	"How can my mind cause a disease I *n·*
	376–12	blood *n·* gave life and can *n·* take it away,
	377–19	The author *n·* knew a patient who did not
	378–27	God *n·* endowed matter with power to
	381–23	or you will *n·* believe that you
	381–25	will *n·* be reached without the understanding
	381–29	a sentence *n·* inflicted by divine authority.
	384– 6	God *n·* punishes man for doing right,
	384–29	evidence before the senses can *n·* overrule.
	385–12	though it can *n·* annul the law which
	390– 5	*n·* deny the everlasting harmony of Soul,
	391–19	When the body is supposed to . . . *n·* plead guilty.
	393–29	Man is *n·* sick, for Mind is not sick
	396– 1	One should *n·* hold in mind the thought of disease,
	396– 6	*N·* startle with a discouraging remark
	396–10	*N·* say beforehand how much you have to
	396–29	outside of matter, *n·* in it, *n·* giving the
	397–27	can *n·* treat mortal mind and matter separately,
	403–23	*N·* conjure up some new discovery from
	409–18	*n·* yields to the weaker, except through fear or
	412– 2	governs all, *n·* punishing aught but sin,
	415–10	Inflammation *n·* appears in a part which
	417– 5	*N·* tell the sick that they have more courage than
	419–25	*N·* fear the mental malpractitioner,
	425–16	he learns that matter *n·* sustained existence
	425–17	can *n·* destroy God, who is man's Life.
	425–26	You will *n·* fear again except to offend God,
	425–27	will *n·* believe that heart . . . can destroy you.
	427– 1	can *n·* change in Science to the opposite belief
	427– 4	Soul is *n·* without its representative.
	427–18	If man is *n·* to overcome death, why do the
	428– 8	he shall *n·* see death." — *John* 8 : 51.
	429–12	is cold and decays, but it *n·* suffers.
	429–32	he shall *n·* see death." — *John* 8 : 51.
	434–28	alleged crime *n·* to have been committed.
	438– 7	he shall *n·* see death. — *John* 8 : 51.
	438–27	he disappeared and was *n·* heard of more.
	439–33	they learn that Disease was *n·* there,
t	444–19	and *n·* to condemn rashly.
	450– 7	*n·* fail to stab their benefactor in the back.
	452–14	*N·* breathe an immoral atmosphere, unless
	453–12	I have *n·* witnessed so decided effects from
	453–30, 31	*n·* recommends material hygiene, *n·* manipulates.
	457– 8	has *n·* used this newly discovered power in any
	463–25	He *n·* enjoined obedience to the laws of nature
r	466– 5	manifestations of . . . indicate Mind, *n·* matter,
	467–23	not confined in man, and is *n·* in matter.
	468– 2	*n·* can be coordinate with human illusions.
	470–18	when God, the Mind of man, *n·* sins
	476–14	They *n·* had a perfect state of being,
	477–24	can *n·* reflect anything inferior to Spirit.

never

r 478– 5	n· beheld Spirit or Soul leaving a body
480–20	good, n· made man capable of sin.
481– 7	Material sense n· helps mortals to understand
481–28	Soul is the divine Principle of man and n·
484– 1	will n· be based on a divine Principle . . . until
486–11	In reality man n· dies.
487– 4	n· attainable through death, but gained by
489– 5	found that the senses of Mind are n· lost
491–10	spiritual individuality is n· wrong.
491–21	reveals material man as n· the real being.
g 504– 1	is n· reflected by aught but the good.
505–11	apparent only as Mind, n· as mindless matter
509–28	in man and the universe n· to disappear.
510–19	Geology has n· explained the earth's
517–23	Even eternity can n· reveal the whole of God,
519–15	Mortals can n· know the infinite,
519–26	can n· impoverish, the divine Mind.
520–11	can n· be reckoned according to the calendar
520–31	n· causing man to till the ground,
533– 3	This had n· been bestowed on Adam.
537– 9	was n· the essence of divinity or manhood.
539–10	God could n· impart an element of evil,
540–20	It saith to the human sense . . . "God n· made
540–23	is to teach mortals n· to believe a lie.
543–16	verities of existence are n· excluded
545– 6	and n· had been divinely conceived.
546– 4	Spirit, God, n· germinates, but is
548– 7	man has n· lost his spiritual estate
550–26	A serpent n· begets a bird,
553– 8	or health will n· be universal,
553– 8	or . . . harmony will n· become the standard
553–18	the maternal egg n· brought forth Adam.
554–24	Jesus n· intimated that God made a devil,
557–20, 21	as n· born and as n· dying,
ap 560–15	This goal is n· reached while we hate our
560–19	without a correct sense of . . . we can n· understand
565–12	might n· hold sway and deprive Herod of his
570–18	and n· fear the consequences.
gl 588–14	as numbers which n· blend with each other,
588–25	that which is n· unconscious nor limited.
598–16	for n· did he give up Spirit, or Soul.

nevertheless

s 112–13	n· remain wholly human in their origin

New

s 139–19	and the three hundred thousand in the N·,

new

pref vii–22	A book introduces n· thoughts,
a 20– 9	Jesus' history made a n· calendar,
30–17	Jesus, the n· executor for God,
33–22	This is the n· understanding of spiritual Love.
33–29	which attend a n· and higher understanding
35–11	in the dawn of a n· light
43–18	opened a n· era for the world.
m 58– 3	Unity of spirit gives n· pinions to joy,
66–15	unfolds n· views of divine goodness
sp 74– 9	seed which has germinated has a n· form
96–17	sin, sickness, and death, which assume n· phases
98– 1	persecutions which attend a n· step
s 108–32	set my thoughts to work in n· channels,
109–24	When a n· spiritual idea is borne to earth,
112–27	If any so-called n· school claims to be C. S.,
114–19	in expressing the n· tongue we must
114–20	the n· wine of the Spirit has to be
114–32	opposition to everything n·,
117–11	spoken of . . . as the n· tongue,
134– 9	The n· faith in the Christ, Truth, so roused the
136–28	No wonder Herod desired to see the n· Teacher.
139–11	but the present n·, yet old, reform
ph 193–14	and said: "I feel like a n· man.
197– 3	A n· name for an ailment affects people
f 201– 8	Truth makes a n· creature,
201– 9	"all things are become n·."— II Cor. 5 : 17.
206–24	nothing is n· to God,
210– 1	expressed only in "n· tongues ;"— Mark 16 : 17.
225–27	always germinating in n· forms of tyranny,
226– 7	the voice of the herald of this n· crusade
235–31	will love to grapple with a n·, right idea
247– 6	Another woman at ninety had n· teeth,
251– 8	as to drive belief into n· paths.
251–11	they have but passed the portals of a n· belief.
c 263–21	Whatever seems to be a n· creation, is but
263–23	else it is a n· multiplication or self-division
b 270–16	their foresight of the n· dispensation
272–11	and is the n· tongue referred to in the
276–21	is turned into n· and healthy channels,
281–27	does not put n· wine into old bottles,
281–31	old belief must be cast out or the n· idea will
299–10	they point upward to a n· and glorified trust,
300–11	real man, or the n· man (as St. Paul has it).
324– 1	and to leave the old for the n·,
326–30	in humility he took the n· name of Paul.
o 349–23	shall speak with n· tongues."— Mark 16 : 17.
354–25	to hear and to speak the n· tongue.

new

p 362– *	shall speak with n· tongues ;— Mark 16 : 17.
398–20	and produces a n· effect upon the body.
398–20	changes such ills into n· and more difficult
403–23	Never conjure up some n· discovery from
404–22	Arouse the sinner to this n· and true view
409–24	and the n· or real man is put on,
420–17	ready to become receptive to the n· idea.
t 452–11	you should not fear to put on the n·.
463– 7	To attend properly the birth of the n· child,
463–10	Though gathering n· energy, this idea cannot
463–14	The n· idea, conceived and born of Truth
463–17	When this n· birth takes place,
r 492–13	N· thoughts are constantly obtaining the floor.
g 518–29	Nothing is n· to Spirit.
541–22	Here the serpentine lie invents n· forms.
544–11	Nothing is n· to the infinite Mind.
548–15	This is the n· birth going on hourly,
549–15	the birth of n· individuals, or personalities,
556–29	existence will be on a n· standpoint.
ap 560–25	spoken something n· and better of God
570–19	What if the old dragon should send forth a n·
gl 593– 9	a n· and higher idea of immortality,
	(see also earth, heaven)

new-blown

p 413–23	in order to keep it sweet as the n· flower.

new-born

a 33–28	can unite with this church only as we are n·
f 221–29	This n· understanding, that neither food nor

New Covenant

a 33–28	Have you shared the blood of the N· C·,

New Jerusalem

ap 574–13	"N· J·, coming down from God,— Rev. 21 : 2.
575–11	The builder and maker of this N· J· is God,
576– 4	this N· J·, this infinite All, which
gl 592–18	definition of

newly

pref viii–31	the first steps of a child in the n· discovered
t 457– 8	she has never used this n· discovered power in

new-mown

ph 175–14	perfume of clover and the breath of n· hay

newness

a 24–12	rise into n· of life with regeneration.
35– 8	from mortal sensuousness, . . . into n· of life
f 249– 7	bringing us into n· of life and recognizing
p 426–19	understanding will quicken into n· of life.
g 520–13	and they will reveal eternity, n· of Life,

new-old

ph 191–12	even to the birth of a n· idea,

New Testament

b 279– 3	A N· T· writer plainly describes faith,
o 350– 7	our Master's sayings as recorded in the N· T·,
r 474–13	Greek word rendered miracle in the N· T·
g 501– 6	whereas the N· T· narratives are clearer
gl 598– 7	and elsewhere in the N· T·.

next

pref xii–16	conviction that the n· two years of her life
pr 5– 4	The n· and great step required by wisdom is
sp 77– 9	on the n· plane of existence as on this, until
an 104–11	N·, they say it has been discovered before.
s 156–29	the n· stately step beyond homeopathy.
ph 190– 1	N· we have the formation of so-called
193–18	The n· day I saw him in the yard.
f 217–20	the n· toil will fatigue you less,
h 296–29	and aids in taking the n· step
o 350– 3	They think of . . . Spirit as n· to nothing,
p 390– 1	The n· minute she said, "My food is all digested,
413–16	"Cleanliness is n· to godliness,"
416–25	and n· to nothing of the metaphysical method
431–20	The n· witness is called:— I am Coated Tongue.
432– 1	The n· witness testifies :— I am Nerve,

Niagara

sp 76– 3	as one at N·, with eyes open only to that

Niagara's

ph 199–26	to walk the rope over N· abyss of waters,

nice

f 252–23	says : . . . What a n· thing is sin !

nigh

s 144– 6	Naught is the squire, when the king is n· ;

Night

g 504– 4	and the darkness He called N·.— Gen. 1 : 5.
gl 592–21	definition of

night

after

c 261–13	a noted actor was accustomed n· after n·

before his crucifixion

a 32–29	on the n· before his crucifixion,

blazons the

f 247–26	blazons the n· with starry gems,

cold

p 378–28	with a long and cold n· of discord.

night

day and
ap 568–17 before our God day and *n·.— Rev.* 12 : 10.
every
p 431– 4 watched with the sick every *n·* in the week.
frequent
ap 566–22 In shade and storm the frequent *n·*,
is far spent
ph 174–12 "the *n·* is far spent,— *Rom.* 13 : 12.
last
f 249–20 You say, "I dreamed last *n·*."
long
ph 174–10 and portend a long *n·* to the traveller ;
no
r 475– 2 there is "no *n·* there."— *Rev.* 22 : 5.
g 511–13 In the eternal Mind, no *n·* is there.
ap 575–20 for there shall be no *n·* there."— *Rev.* 21 : 25.
gl 584– 7 "there shall be no *n·* there."— *Rev.* 22 : 5.
of error
pref vii– 9 across a *n·* of error should dawn the morning
of gloom
a 47–31 During his *n·* of gloom and glory
of his arrest
p 436–15 Prior to the *n·* of his arrest, the prisoner
of materialism
ap 562–20 as the *n·* of materialism wanes.
of materiality
o 354–23 The *n·* of materiality is far spent,
of paganism
ap 571–29 and illumined the *n·* of paganism with the
old
p 372– 6 likened by Milton to "chaos and old *n·*."
ap 570–21 into the deep waters of chaos and old *n·*.
over the
g 511– 9 rule over the day and over the *n·*,— *Gen.* 1 : 18.
rule the
g 510–15 the lesser light to rule the *n·* :— *Gen.* 1 : 16.
traversed the
pref vii– 5 yet it traversed the *n·*, and came where,
without a star
ap 564– 8 will sink its perpetrator into a *n·* without a star.

ph 194–27 An infant crying in the *n·*,
f 240– 8 The stars make *n·* beautiful,
p 431–22 the *n·* of the liver-attack.
431–27 since the *n·* of the liver-attack.
436– 8 on the *n·* of the alleged offence
438–20 on the *n·* of the crime
g 509–10 to divide the day from the *n·* ;— *Gen.* 1 : 14.
552– 5 hatched from the "egg of *n·*"
ap 566–11 a pillar of cloud by day and of fire by *n·*,

night-dream

f 249–25 mortal *n·* is sometimes nearer the fact
249–27 The *n·* has less matter as its accompaniment.

Nightingale, Florence

p 385– 2 It is proverbial that Florence *N·*

nightmare

s 128–24 waking him from a cataleptic *n·*,

nights

p 430–29 testifies . . . I was present on certain *n·*

nine

an 101– 8 In 1837, a committee of *n·* persons was
s 108–16 three multiplied by three, equalling *n·*,
108–17 must be *n·* duodecillions,

nineteen

sp 93– 2 Remember Jesus, who nearly *n·* centuries ago
s 122– 8 *n·* hundred years ago
f 224–11 In the record of *n·* centuries, there are
232–17 as it did over *n·* hundred years ago,
r 495– 3 as surely as it did *n·* centuries ago.

nineteenth

s 147– 6 Late in the *n·* century I demonstrated the
ap 560– 2 in connection with the *n·* century.

ninety

f 247– 6 Another woman at *n·* had new teeth,

ninety-and-nine

o 344–28 may lose *n·* patients, while C. S. cures its

nipped

c 265–18 withered by the sun and *n·* by untimely frosts ;

Nisan

a 32–29 with his disciples in the month *N·*

nitrous-oxide

o 346–26 when you believe that *n·* gas has made

No

pref viii–20 A vigorous "*N·*" is the response

Noah

b 320–11 in the learned article on *N·*
gl 592–22 definition of

Noah's

gl 587–21 HAM (*N·* son). Corporeal belief ;
589– 8 JAPHET (*N·* son). A type of spiritual peace,
594–14 SHEM (*N·* son). A corporeal mortal ;

nobility

ph 172–29 may present more *n·* than the

noble

m 58– 8 Unselfish ambition, *n·* life-motives,
61–20 What hope of happiness, what *n·* ambition,
64–11 lends a helping hand to some *n·* woman,
f 248–29 carve them out in grand and *n·* lives.
t 450–10 They are sincere, generous, *n·*,

nobler

m 63–25 achievement of a *n·* race for legislation,
b 326–27 Thought assumed a *n·* outlook,

nobody

s 140– 4 That God is a corporeal creator, *n·* can truly affirm.
ph 199– 6 *n·* believes that mind is producing such a result

Nod

g 542–28 and dwelt in the land of *N·*.— *Gen.* 4 : 16.

noise

g 505–18 than the *n·* of many waters,— *Psal.* 93 : 4.

noises

sp 86–18 Haunted houses, ghostly voices, unusual *n·*,

none

sp 86–24 In reality there is *n·*.
99–12 *N·* may pick the lock nor enter by some other
s 147–11 had lost *n·* of its divine and healing efficacy,
164– 7 said : . . . *n·* can be adopted as a safe guidance
ph 178–30 *n·* of these methods can be mingled with
193–27 saying : "It was *n·* other than God and
f 232–23 never tried to make of *n·* effect the
250–19 experiencing *n·* of these dream-sensations.
c 256–22 and *n·* can stay His hand,— *Dan.* 4 : 35.
b 269–25 Other foundations there are *n·*.
291–32 As for spiritual error there is *n·*.
337–14 C. S. demonstrates that *n·* but the pure in heart
o 343–10 "*N·* of these things move me."— *Acts* 20 : 24.
345–15 *n·* which are apparent to those who understand
360–18 then you practically have *n·*.
p 414–22 there is *n·* else beside Him."— *Deut.* 4 : 35.
421–17 God, Spirit, is all, and that there is *n·* beside
t 447–29 by knowing that there is *n·*.
r 479–29 because it has *n·* of the divine hues.

nonentity

b 303–26 would be a *n·*, or Mind unexpressed.
r 477–30 Separated from . . . Spirit would be a *n·* ;

non-existent

ph 180–12 deport themselves as if Mind were *n·*,
g 513–27 mortal mind — being *n·* and consequently

non-intelligence

and matter
b 282–19 Mind cannot pass into *n·* and matter,
and mortality
gl 591–10 Mythology ; . . . life in *n·* and mortality ;
before
ph 191–20 Intelligence is not mute before *n·*.
intelligence and
sp 73–28 Spirit and matter, intelligence and *n·*,
f 204–17 intelligence and *n·*, of Spirit and matter.
never produces
b 276–12 Intelligence never produces *n·* ;
subject to
ph 171–22 infinite Mind,— subject to *n·* !

s 120– 3 and that man is included in *n·*.
b 282–19 nor can *n·* become Soul.
285–14 one is intelligence while the other is *n·*.
336– 3 Intelligence never passes into *n·*,
g 531– 5 the error, . . . that *n·* becomes intelligence,
gl 580–23 supposition . . . intelligence passes into *n·*,

non-intelligent

ph 165–10 material organization and *n·* matter.
f 214–12 material senses, . . . are proved *n·*.
217–32 Matter is *n·*.
c 257–14 the supposed substance of *n·* matter.
b 277– 1 but matter is ever *n·*
277– 5 The *n·* relapses into its own unreality.
t 457–28 as if the *n·* could aid Mind !
r 466–15 Truth is intelligent ; error is *n·*.
478–21 matter is *n·* and brain-lobes cannot think
g 524–21 How could the *n·* become the medium of Mind,
531–15 If, . . . man's body originated in *n·* dust,
550– 1 a circumscribed and *n·* egg.

non-sense

r 489–30 A wrong sense of God, man, and creation is *n·*,

noon

f 246–12 Manhood is its eternal *n·*, undimmed by a

noonday

m 56–17 destruction that wasteth at *n·*."— *Psal.* 91 : 6.
f 224–27 as he came of old to the patriarch at *n·*

noontide

p 367–23 but radiate and glow into n· glory.

normal

s 120–14 health is n· and disease is abnormal.
125– 8 n· and natural to changed mortal thought,
f 205–25 hinders man's n· drift towards the one Mind,
212–30 The realities of being, its n· action,
214– 4 it is n· and indestructible.
b 307–22 If . . . material pain and pleasure seems n·,
o 344– 5 the n·, healthful, and sinless condition of man
p 368–12 beliefs . . . that discord is as n· as harmony,
406–30 n· control is gained through divine strength
412–26 until the . . . corresponds with the n· conditions
415– 1 an excited state of mortals which is not n·.

north

ap 575–24 on the sides of the n·,— Psal. 48 : 2.

North Star

ap 575–26 Northward, its gates open to the N· S·,

northward

ap 575–26 N·, its gates open to the North Star,

nostrils

sp 88– 8 and no scent salutes the n·.
g 524–14 and breathed into his n·— Gen. 2 : 7.
544–30 to enter man's n· so that

notables

p 437–22 Various n·— Materia Medica, Anatomy,

note

f 245– 8 taking no n· of years,
p 415–17 N· how thought makes the face pallid.
g 515–30 Then n· how true, . . . is the reflection
538– 6 to n· the proper guests.
ap 574–19 N· this,— that the very message,

noted

c 261–12 a n· actor was accustomed night after night to

notes

pref ix–27 she made copious n· of Scriptural exposition,
m 58– 5 Ill-arranged n· produce discord.
b 298–21 Spiritual ideas, like numbers and n·, start from

noteworthy

b 313–12 n· that the phrase "express image"— Heb 1 : 3,

nothing

amounts to
ph 172– 5 amounts to n· in the right direction
and something
a 23–17 swinging between n· and something,
apart from
r 473– 9 n· apart from Him is present or has power.
but a display
b 317–31 N· but a display of matter
but a supposition
g 504–30 n· but a supposition of the absence of Spirit.
but false beliefs
ph 171–25 n· but false beliefs that intelligence
but His likeness
r 495–15 Allow n· but His likeness to abide in your
but Spirit
b 335–18 N· but Spirit, Soul, can evolve Life,
but Truth
r 483– 5 which n· but Truth or Mind can heal,
can abolish
m 58–29 but n· can abolish the cares of marriage.
can be novel
g 519– 1 N· can be novel to eternal Mind,
can change
b 297– 1 and n· can change this state, until
can efface
b 318– 3 n· can efface Mind and immortality,
can enter
ap 577–26 n· can enter that city, which
can erase
b 290– 2 was and is and shall be, whom n· can erase.
can hide
f 215– 1 N· can hide from them the harmony of
can interfere
p 427–14 N· can interfere with the harmony of being
can produce
b 335–26 and can produce n· unlike the eternal
can vitiate
p 393–13 n· can vitiate the ability and power
cherish
m 68– 7 cherish n· which hinders our highest
could alienate
b 303–32 declared that n· could alienate him from God,
could kill
a 51–11 N· could kill this Life of man.
covered
pr 8–17 "there is n· covered that shall not— Matt. 10 : 26.
difficult
t 462–16 There is n· difficult nor toilsome in this task,
drug does
pr 12–19 drug does n·, because it has no intelligence.

nothing

else
f 208–18 writes : "God is the father of mind, and of n· else."
b 331–22 reflected by all that is real . . . and by n· else
466–20 Soul or Spirit signifies Deity and n· else.
478–26 of material human beliefs and of n· else.
481– 2 tributary to God, Spirit, and to n· else.
error is
o 346–10 we need to understand that error is n·,
evil becomes
r 480– 4 Where the spirit of God is, . . . evil becomes n·,
evil is
b 330–27 Evil is n·, no thing, mind, nor power.
except God
f 243–29 because they declare n· except God.
imperfect
r 477– 7 Spirit, is seen in n· imperfect nor material.
in common
a 101–17 n· in common with either physiology or
t 459– 7 n· in common with the worldling's affections,
inharmonious
f 228– 5 namely, that n· inharmonious can enter being,
is left
f 251–26 n· is left which deserves to perish
is lost
o 360– 2 they will find that n· is lost, and all is won,
is matter
s 113–18 God, Spirit, being all, n· is matter.
is new
f 206–24 His work was finished, n· is new to God,
g 518–29 n· is new to Spirit.
544–11 N· is new to the infinite Mind.
leaves
b 340–29 and leaves n· that can sin, suffer,
less
b 336–24 and n· less can express God.
manifests
ph 173–11 What is termed matter manifests n· but
matter is
s 116–18 matter is n· beyond an image in mortal mind.
naming
o 348– 1 which they chide us for naming n·
narrow into
sp 77–31 the chances of . . . narrow into n·
next to
o 350– 3 They think of . . . Spirit as next to n·,
p 416–25 next to n· of the metaphysical method
nothingness of
o 346– 9 The nothingness of n· is plain ;
of the kind
g 544–20 facts of creation, . . . include n· of the kind.
product of
gl 580– 9 a product of n· as the mimicry of something ;
proved
s 125–31 matter will finally be proved n· more than a
reveals
b 278– 2 Science reveals n· in Spirit out of which
short of
t 448–20 n· short of right-doing has any claim to the
ap 572–12 n· short of this divine Principle, . . . can ever
that lives
p 374–29 N· that lives ever dies, and vice versa.
there can be
s 127– 8 there can be n· beyond illimitable divinity.
to consume
p 425–19 and know that there is n· to consume,
unlike God
f 249–16 and includes n· unlike God.
unspiritual
b 335–28 N· unspiritual can be real, harmonious,
when it is
b 287–19 Evil calls itself something, when it is n·.

pr 6– 9 vain supposition that we have n· to do but
m 61–27 N· unworthy of perpetuity should be
sp 71– 1 N· is real and eternal, . . . but God and His
71– 1 n· is Spirit,— but God and His idea.
83– 9 N· is more antagonistic to C. S. than
92–24 the ability to make n· of error
s 126–26 I have found n· in ancient or in modern
151–19 lungs, brain, etc., have n· to do with Life,
ph 174– 6 N· save divine power is capable of
178– 1 though they know n· of this particular case
186–12 It is n·, because it is the absence of
198–25 the doctor says n· to support his theory.
f 221– 3 and drank n· but water.
228– 8 if we learn that n· is real but the right,
238–10 Catholic girl said, " I have n· left but Christ."
249–19 Organization and time have n· to do with Life.
b 270–23 It has n· in Christ.
277–29 N· we can say or believe regarding matter is
296–10 N· sensual or sinful is immortal.
305–17 the Son can do n· of himself,— John 5 : 19.
326–19 n· but wrong intention can hinder
330–29 n· claiming to be something,

nothing

b 331–12 n· possesses reality . . . except the divine Mind
  335– 8 n· in Spirit out of which matter could be made,
o 345–27 to be something, when he is n·,— *Gal.* 6 : 3.
  347– 6 N· really has Life but God,
  347–10 there is n· left to be doctored.
  353–17 Without perfection, n· is wholly real.
  356–16 the flesh profiteth n·." — *John* 6 : 63.
p 367–31 error should be known as n·.
  371– 8 By those uninstructed . . . n· is really understood of
  374– 8 never thought of and knew n· about,
  378–14 and both will fight for n·.
  380–19 N· but the power of Truth can prevent the
  380–28 N· is more disheartening than to believe that
  401– 3 it does n· in the right direction
  416–24 sick know n· of the mental process by which
  431–28 testifies : . . . although n· on my part has
  438– 6 n· shall by any means hurt you.— *Luke* 10 : 19.
t 460–23 superficial and cold assertion, "N· ails you."
g 514– 3 n· exists beyond the range of
  520–29 n· left to be made by a lower power.
  521–18 will naturally ask if there is n· more about
  529–23 n· in the animal kingdom which
  530–30 supposes that something springs from n·,
  539–12 possesses n· which he has not derived from God.
gl 591–25 N· claiming to be something,

nothingness

aghast at
ap 563– 7 But why should we stand aghast at n·?
and unreality
f 205–21 the n· and unreality of evil.
counterpoise of
p 368– 1 Evil is but the counterpoise of n·.
discord is the
b 276–27 Discord is the n· named error.
dust and
g 547–22 or go down into dust and n·.
elements of
r 479–26 and they are the elements of n·.
exposes his
sp 91–10 because Science exposes his n· ;
its
sp 92–22 the fact concerning error— namely, its n·
  97–12 the more its n· will appear, until
o 346–11 its n· is not saved, but must be demonstrated
learn the
b 327–32 learn the n· of the pleasures of human sense
material
o 345–28 This thought of human, material n·,
nameless
g 550–12 material life, which ends, . . . in nameless n·
native
sp 91–11 the sooner error is reduced to its native n·,
ph 190–17 to wither and return to its native n·.
b 281–12 native n·, out of which error would simulate
p 365–18 the disease will vanish into its native n·
ap 572– 6 scientifically reduced to its native n·.
of error
f 251–12 Truth works out the n· of error
b 287– 3 the n· of error, which simulates the
o 351–24 which proves the n· of error, discord,
ap 569– 9 by which the n· of error is seen ;
  569–10 the n· of error is in proportion to its
gl 596–16 give us a sense of the n· of error,
of evil
b 269– 7 the unreality, the n·, of evil.
  293–30 the entireness of God, good, and the n· of evil.
ap 563–17 the n· of evil and the allness of God.
of hallucinations
o 348– 3 admit the n· of hallucinations,
of matter
r 480– 2 When . . . the n· of matter is recognized.
  497–22 and the n· of matter.
of nothing
o 346– 9 The n· of nothing is plain ;
of sickness
o 347–28 Then mortals will behold the n· of sickness and
phase of
an 102–31 Its so-called despotism is but a phase of n·.
points to
s 129–29 The very name, *illusion*, points to n·.
problem of
s 126– 3 The problem of n·, . . . will be solved,
proved its
a 42–21 This error Jesus met . . . and proved its n·.
prove its
t 446–24 Resisting evil, you overcome it and prove its n·.
proves their
o 347–25 destroys these evils, and so proves their n·.
proving their
a 39– 6 He overcame . . . thus proving their n·.
stand for
g 537–18 since ground and dust stand for n·.
teaches the
o 346– 7 It is sometimes said that C. S. teaches the n· of

nothingness

their
sp 96–18 until their n· appears.
t 450–21 will overcome them by understanding their n·
this
o 346– 8 said that C. S. . . . teaches how this n· is to be saved
understood as
r 480–31 If sin, sickness, and death were understood as n·,
understood the
a 52–19 understood the n· of material life
vanish into
o 352–29 The objects of alarm will then vanish into n·,

b 312– 6 What . . . seems substance, becomes n·,
  338–13 the *red color of the ground, dust,* n·.
o 347–32 will then see that error is indeed the n·,
  356–11 Understanding the n· of material things,
p 382–28 n· of the so-called pleasures and pains of sense.
r 490–30 shows material sense as either oblivion, n·,
g 540– 9 reducing it to its common denominator, n·.
  545–29 "Dust [n·] thou art,— *Gen.* 3 : 19.
  545–29 unto dust [n·] shalt thou return."— *Gen.* 3 : 19.
ap 567–24 show the dragon to be n·, dust to dust ;
gl 580– 2 "dust to dust ;" red sandstone ; n· ;
  584–28 DUST.   N· ; the absence of substance,
  592–22 knowledge of the n· of material things

notice

an 100– 2 was first brought into n· by Mesmer in Germany
f 237– 3 She seemed not to n· it.

noticeable

s 158– 7 It is here n· that Apollo was also regarded
r 478–20 discharge of the natural functions is least n·.

noticed

ph 168–30 Here let a word be n· . . . *chemicalization.*
p 442– 9 We n·, as he shook hands with his counsel,

noticing

p 413–24 n· every symptom of flatulency,

notion

against the
o 354– 1 against the n· that there can be material life,
common
p 383–32 common n· that health depends on inert matter
have no
o 360–11 replies : . . . I have no n· of losing my old
of any life
r 485–32 The n· of any life or intelligence in matter
of chance
p 424– 8 in order to change the n· of chance
that mind
b 302–10 The n· that mind is in matter,
r 492–22 The n· that mind and matter commingle
this
r 492–25 the Science of Mind, which denies this n·.
g 552–17 Mortals must emerge from this n· of

m 67–18 The n· that animal natures can possibly give
f 204–24 the n· that they can create
  217– 3 n· of such a possibility is more absurd than
b 278– 9 false supposition, the n· that there is
  330–25 The n· that both evil and good are real
g 545–11 n· of a material universe is utterly opposed to

notions

f 251–32 Inharmonious beliefs, . . . deify their own n·,
o 357–17 popular and false n· about the Divine Being
  357–20 wrong n· about God must have
p 425–32 Discard all n· about lungs, tubercles,
gl 597– 2 and in accordance with Pharisaical n·.

notwithstanding

b 338–28 n· God had blessed the earth
p 431– 2 N· . . . the prisoner watched with the sick

noumenon

s 114–10 including n· and phenomena,

noun

sp 93–23 Spirit, as a proper n·, is the name of the

nourishes

pr 5–25 If prayer n· the belief that

novel

ph 197– 4 like a Parisian name for a n· garment.
g 519– 1 Nothing can be n· to eternal Mind,

novels

ph 195–25 N·, remarkable only for their exaggerated

now

pref xl–10 healing of C. S. results n·, as in Jesus' time,
  xi–14 N·, as then, these mighty works are . . . natural.
  xi–18 coming n· as was promised aforetime,
a 31–26 "The hour cometh, and n· is,— *John* 4 : 23.
  33– 9 n· this bread was feeding and sustaining them.
  33–12 and n· it comforted themselves.
  39–18 "N·," cried the apostle, "is the— *II Cor.* 6 : 2.
  39–19 n· is the day of salvation,"— *II Cor.* 6 : 2.
  39–20 meaning, not that n· men must prepare for a

now

a	39–21	but that n· is the time in which to experience
	39–22	N· is the time for so-called . . . to pass away,
	41–10	in the hereafter they will reap what they n· sow.
	43– 7	they had only believed ; n· they understood.
	43–10	and is n· repeating its ancient history.
	54–30	would not some, who n· profess to love him,
	55– 8	N· that the gospel of healing is again
	55–25	drinketh of Christ's cup n·, and is endued with
m	56– 3	"Suffer it to be so n· :— Matt. 3 : 15.
	64–29	a worse state of society than n· exists.
sp	70– *	N· we know that thou hast a— John 8 : 52.
	83– 7	evil elements n· coming to the surface.
	90–10	movements and transitions n· possible for
	90–13	though n· some insist that death is the
	92–10	not . . . with the power of sinning n· and forever.
	93– 6	"But the hour cometh, and n· is,— John 4 : 23.
	93– 8	"Behold, n· is the accepted time ;— II Cor. 6 : 2.
	93– 8	n· is the day of salvation,"— II Cor. 6 : 2.
	96–12	This material world is even n· becoming the
	98–24	Even n· multitudes consider that which they call
an	106–20	" N· the works of the flesh are— Gal. 5 : 19.
s	123–26	did not . . . belong to a dispensation n· ended,
	125– 2	What is n· considered the best condition
	136– 9	The question then as n· was,
	137–28	but n· the Master gave him a spiritual name
	138– 6	It was n· evident to Peter
	138–19	under as direct orders n·, as they were then,
	141–22	did not then, and do not n·, understand
	141–31	Give to it the place . . . n· occupied by
	146–31	Divine metaphysics is n· reduced to a system,
	150–11	but the mission of C. S. n·, as in the time of
	150–12	N·, as then, signs and wonders are wrought
	151–15	bondage n· enforced by false theories,
	152–25	and she can n· understand why,
	153–20	N· administer mentally to your patient a
ph	197–18	departments of knowledge n· broadcast in the
f	221–15	and he is n· in perfect health
	222–20	N· he dropped drugs and material hygiene,
	250–22	N· I ask, Is there any more reality in
c	255– *	travaileth in pain together until n·.— Rom. 8 : 22.
	259–15	If man . . . has n· lost his perfection,
	261– 1	N· reverse this action.
	262–18	but n· mine eye seeth Thee."— Job 42 : 5.
b	271–28	the opportunity n·, as aforetime,
	282– 1	N·, as of old, Truth casts out evils
	285– 5	This Science of being obtains . . . here and n· ;
	324–12	"acquaint n· thyself with Him,— Job 22 : 21.
	326–17	purpose and motive . . . can be gained n·.
o	347–15	true idea of God, comes n· as of old,
	361– 5	the ideal of God n· and forever,
	361– 9	God is come and is present n· and forever.
p	409–28	to say that life depends on matter n·, but
	423–25	Both Science and consciousness are n· at work
	427– 7	If man believes in death n·, he must disbelieve
	434–13	n· summoned to appear before the bar of Justice
	436–20	Fear . . . would n· punish him.
	440–15	N· what greater justification can any deed have,
	441–11	Let what False Belief utters, n· and forever,
r	474 18	N· Jesus came to destroy sin, sickness, and
	495– 2	Truth casts out error n· as surely as
g	509–21	no more contingent n· on time or
	515–28	N· compare man before the mirror to his
	521–10	joyfully acknowledging n· and forever
	521–24	n· the opposite error, . . . is to be set forth.
	523– 2	Scriptural account n· under comment.
	524–17	that He should n· be called Jehovah?
	528–20	error n· simulates the work of Truth,
	529–13	N· the serpent was more subtle— Gen. 3 : 1.

now

g	532–29	but n· error demands that mind shall
	537– 1	and n·, lest he put forth his hand,— Gen. 3 : 22.
	541–25	N· it repudiates even the human duty of man
	541–29	And n· art thou cursed from the— Gen. 4 : 11.
	546– 2	belief that spirit is n· submerged in matter,
	548–20	many general statements n· current,
	550–13	perfection should appear n·, even as it will
ap	568–14	N· is come salvation, and strength,— Rev. 12 : 10.
	568–28	n· rises clearer and nearer to the great heart
	573–27	we can become conscious, here and n·, of a

nowhere

s	163–24	N· is the imagination displayed to a

Noyes, George R.

b	313–21	the late George R. N·, D.D. :
o	360–23	Rev. George R. N·, D.D. :

nucleus

g	549–16	the formation of the n·, or egg,

null

p	381– 1	rendered n· and void by the law of Life,
	441– 4	so-called law, which . . . is n· and void.

nullify

s	161– 6	able to n· the action of the flames,

number

a	38– 3	a select n· of followers.
m	69–12	sense of increasing n· in God's infinite plan.
sp	81–20	Erase the figures which express n·,
r	494–12	to imagine that Jesus . . . only for a select n·

numbered

p	367–16	and with those hairs all n· by the Father.

numbers

pref	ix–11	she "lisped in n·, for the n· came."
sp	81–24	as truly as in the case of n·
s	111– 8	no more supernatural than is the science of n·,
f	233–25	When n· have been divided according to
b	298–21	Spiritual ideas, like n· and notes, start from
	318–30	as n· are controlled and proved by
	318–31	Intelligence does not originate in n·,
g	548–32	increase their n· naturally and
gl	588–14	n· which never blend with each other,

numerals

g	520–10	The n· of infinity, called seven days,

numeration-table

b	326–18	You have begun at the n· of C. S.,

numerous

o	341–17	facts are so absolute and n· in support of

nuptial

m	59–27	The n· vow should never be annulled,

nurse

s	155– 9	the druggist, the doctor, and the n·
p	364–32	the careless doctor, the n·, the cook,
	395–18	complaining, . . . person should not be a n·.
	395 18	The n· should be cheerful, orderly,

nurseries

f	235–10	N· of character should be strongly garrisoned

nurtured

t	448– 7	if evil is uncondemned, it is undenied and n·.

nutriment

f	222– 6	to believe that proper food supplies n·
p	365–32	suffering heart needs its rightful n·,
	388–12	hypothesis that food is the n· of life,

O

oak

pref	vii–24	task of the sturdy pioneer to hew the tall o·
sp	78– 1	the gnarled o·, the ferocious beast,

oath

a	32– 4	The Latin word for this o· was sacramentum,
	32–10	does not commemorate a Roman soldier's o·,

obduracy

ap	569–28	must depend upon sin's o·.

obedience

and suffering
ap	572– 2	washed their robes white in o· and suffering.

demand
ph	183– 3	so-called laws of matter . . . demand o· to

demands our
c	256–19	Who is it that demands our o·?

devout
pr	4–29	silent prayer, watchfulness, and devout o·

enforcing
ph	184–14	enforcing o· through divine statutes.

entire
ph	183–21	man's entire o·, affection, and strength.

obedience

guarantee of
pref	vii–18	guarantee of o· is a right apprehension of

habits of
m	62– 5	habits of o· to the moral and spiritual law,

live in
pref	viii– 4	man must live in o· to its divine Principle.

patient
f	242–16	In patient o· to a patient God,

to divine law
p	440–19	in o· to divine law?

to God
a	25–18	By his o· to God, he demonstrated
ph	183–13	o· to God will remove this necessity.
f	241– 4	he who refuses o· to God, is chastened

to higher law
p	435– 8	in o· to higher law, helped his fellow-man,

to material law
ph	182–19	O· to material law prevents

to nature
ph	176– 8	free to act in o· to nature,

obedience

to spiritual law
ph 182–20 prevents full o· to spiritual law,
to the law
pr 14–10 is to be in o· to the law of God,
p 387–21 supposition that death comes in o· to the law of
436–31 construed o· to the law of divine Love as
to these laws
p 440–24 and then render o· to these laws punishable
to Truth
ph 183–23 O· to Truth gives man power and strength.
urged no
s 148– 5 urged no o· to material laws,
yielding
ph 184–12 nor yielding o· to it.

ph 165–12 O· to the so-called physical laws of health
170–21 always in opposition, never in o·, to physics.
f 210–22 in o· to the immutable law of Spirit,
253–27 never requires o· to a so-called material law,
p 436– 9 the divine law, and in o· thereto.
t 463–25 He never enjoined o· to the laws of nature,

obedient
b 295– 7 o· to the Mind that makes them.
g 544– 4 ideas became productive, o· to Mind.

obey
a 20–21 to o· the divine order and trust God,
m 67–23 commanded even the winds and waves to o·
sp 91– 6 and o· only the divine Principle, Life and Love.
s 140– 9 We shall o· and adore in proportion as we
ph 182– 9 We cannot o· both physiology and Spirit,
187–14 The valves of the heart, . . . o· the mandate of
f 214–20 to fear and to o· what they consider a
235– 5 one who does not o· the requirements of
236–21 Children should o· their parents ;
238– 6 To o· the Scriptural command,
239–18 whom we acknowledge and o· as God.
b 307–28 nor bidden to o· material laws
326–22 that ye should not o· the truth?"— Gal. 5 : 7.
o 354– 4 Why then dc Christians try to o· the
p 436–22 must o· your law, fear its consequences,
r 496– 6 in C. S. the first duty is to o· God,
ap 559–19 Mortals, o· the heavenly evangel.

obeyed
s 149–15 because you have not o· the rule
b 328–26 It were well had Christendom believed and o·

obeying
a 31–17 O· his precious precepts,
f 244– 6 never fearing nor o· error in any form.
r 489–21 the medium for o· God?

obeys
f 241– 3 He, who . . . o· them, incurs the hostility of

object
s 115–18 the immediate o· of understanding.
129–30 may o· to the author's small estimate of the
f 248– 4 Its halo rests upon its o·.
c 267– 1 Every o· in material thought will be destroyed,
b 304–11 cannot be deprived of its manifestation, or o· ;
p 407– 1 becoming a fool or an o· of loathing ;
415– 9 looks upon some o· which he dreads.
t 457–10 Her prime o·, since entering this field of labor,
g 507– 4 Spirit duly feeds and clothes every o·,

objected
o 344– 1 It is o· to C. S. that it claims

objectified
b 310– 2 picture is the artist's thought o·.

objection
o 359– 8 infidels whose only o· to this method was,

objections
s 117– 1 The term individuality is also open to o·,
p 424–12 In medical practice o· would be raised if

objective
b 283–17 the o· state of material sense,
287–27 the o· supposition of Spirit's opposite.
p 374–12 the o· state of mortal mind,
r 484–12 the o· states of mortal mind.

object-lesson
f 214–10 an o· for the human mind.

objects
all the
gl 588–15 All the o· of God's creation reflect one Mind,
and subjects
g 507– 7 o· and subjects would be obscure,
and thoughts
b 269–18 the o· and thoughts of material sense,
276–13 brings o· and thoughts into human view
cognized by
b 311–26 The o· cognized by the physical senses
forbidden
f 234–28 to look with desire on forbidden o· was to

objects
higher
p 416–31 away from their bodies to higher o·.
of alarm
o 352–29 The o· of alarm will then vanish into
of creation
c 264–14 o· of creation, which before were invisible,
of sense
b 269–15 exchanges the o· of sense for the ideas of Soul.
g 510– 3 to dwell on the o· of sense !
of time
gl 584– 4 The o· of time and sense disappear
real
sp 96–29 real o· will be apprehended mentally
solid
c 261–26 will neither lose the solid o· and ends of life
surrounding
p 415–31 will sink from sight along with surrounding o·,

sp 79–27 Science o· to all this, contending for
86–28 as readily as from o· cognizable by the senses.
s 123–14 replaces the o· of material sense with
f 239–20 The o· we pursue and the spirit we manifest
o 348– 5 and who o· to this?
p 410–13 mankind o· to making this teaching practical.
g 506– 2 O· utterly unlike the original do not

obligated
t 451–23 He feels morally o· to open the eyes of

obligation
b 327–31 the man's dormant sense of moral o·,

obligations
m 59– 2 recognition of its enduring o· on both sides.
59–28 so long as its moral o· are kept intact ;
68–13 Consider its o·, its responsibilities,
c 262– 4 Neither does . . . diminish man's o· to God,
p 363–17 who were released from their o· by

obliged
o 349–17 one is o· to use material terms

obliterated
f 231– 1 the cause of disease must be o· through Christ
p 426–12 If the belief in death were o·,
r 485–10 views of error ought to be o· by Truth.

obliterates
b 296–27 until Science o· this false testimony.

oblivion
sp 97–25 inarticulate sound is forever silenced in o·.
f 214–32 there is no o· for Soul and its faculties.
b 310–25 and spiritual death is o·.
o 341– 2 strictures on this volume would condemn to o·
p 382–24 One whom I rescued from seeming spiritual o·,
441–12 now and forever, fall into o·,
r 490–30 Sleep shows material sense as either o·,
g 556–21 O· and dreams, not realities, come with sleep.

oblivious
c 261–18 which made him as o· of physical infirmity

obnoxious
f 207– 3 evil becomes more apparent and o·
p 407– 3 Puffing the o· fumes of tobacco,
433–21 Materiality, so o· to God,

obscure
s 139–23 mistakes could neither wholly o· the
t 445–16 You render the divine law of healing o· and
g 507– 8 objects and subjects would be o·,
546–18 Genesis and the Apocalypse seem more o· than
ap 558–11 To mortal sense Science seems at first o·,

obscured
ap 560–26 not only o· the light of the ages, but
gl 586– 2 weariness of mortal mind ; o· views ;

obscures
b 299–27 as the mist o· the sun or the mountain ;
g 504–29 and darkness o· light.

obscurity
pref vii– 6 and came where, in cradled o·,
g 523– 3 the mist of o· evolved by error

observance
p 382–19 "more honored in the breach than the o·'"

observation
s 163– 9 founded on long o· and reflection,
ph 195–19 O·, invention, study, and original thought
b 299– 5 save in the artist's own o·
p 389–29 A case of convulsions, . . . came under my o·.

observations
an 101–31 The author's own o· of the workings of
r 483–24 schools, which wrestle with material o· alone,
g 553– 2 accompany their descriptions with important o·,

observe
a 20–12 support the clergy, o· the Sabbath,
o 344–17 it would be just to o· the
p 419–16 O· mind instead of body,

observed
an 101– 1　the violent effects, which are o· in the
observer
f 250–20　To the o·, the body lies listless,
g 549–27　even this great o· mistakes nature,
observes
p 422– 5　If the reader of this book o· a great stir
obsolete
sp 90–13　and death will be o·,
c 265–22　the error is unreal and o·.
b 274–31　This suppositional partnership is already o·,
gl 588–22　IN.　A term o· in Science if used with
obstacle
a 45– 2　Jesus vanquished every material o·,
s 115– 1　the one great o· to the reception of
ph 179– 6　since space is no o· to Mind.
b 338–23　the o· which the serpent, sin, would impose
p 424–21　certain that the divine Mind can remove any o·,
obstetrics
o 342–30　If . . . teaching or practising pharmacy or o·
t 463– 6　the o· taught by this Science.
g 529– 6　The first system of suggestive o· has changed.
obstinate
p 414– 5　However o· the case, it yields more readily
obstinately
s 144–11　the more o· tenacious its error ;
obstruction
b 338–15　and it reads, a dam, or o·.
338–22　It stands for o·, error,
obtain
m 69–28　worthy to o· that world, — Luke 20 : 35.
f 211–14　seem to o· in mortal mind.
219–17　must o· in the human mind before it
225–30　ignorant how to o· their freedom.
b 284–21　physical senses can o· no proof of God.
p 400– 9　Mortals o· the harmony of health, only as
427–20　shows that we shall o· the victory over
g 539–14　Whence does he o· the propensity or
553– 7　Mortal thought must o· a better basis,
obtainable
ph 173–13　Neither . . . is o· through matter.
192–24　gives you the only power o·.
obtained
sp 88–30　said to be a gift whose endowment is o· from
f 207–32　evidence of this inversion is o· from
b 296–22　knowledge o· from the corporeal senses
299–21　to judge the knowledge thus o· to be untrue
322– 8　before harmonious and immortal man is o·
325– 6　life o· not of the body incapable of
p 388– 3　they o· a victory over the corporeal senses,
426–12　and the understanding o· from
427–12　before Life can be understood and harmony o·.
434– 8　permission is o· for a trial in the Court of Spirit,
r 490–26　which can be o· in no other way
493– 7　all the knowledge o· from
gl 581–20　evidence o· from the five corporeal senses,
589–12　o· from the five corporeal senses ;
590– 4　Evidence o· from the five corporeal senses ;
598–25　This exalted view, o· and retained
obtaining
f 218–22　lead only into material ways of o· help,
r 492–14　New thoughts are constantly o· the floor.
obtains
s 154– 5　this law o· credit through association,
ph 172–20　and the belief that . . . o· in mortals,
174–31　the cause of disease o· in the
b 285– 3　Science of being o· not alone hereafter
305–25　the divine Principle that o· in divine Science,
p 409– 2　You may say : "But if disease o· in matter,
t 448– 5　Evil which o· in the bodily senses,
obtruded
s 163–24　hypotheses o· upon us at different times.
obviate
m 58–28　Wealth may o· the necessity for toil
obvious
sp 97–18　The more material the belief, the more o· its
b 271– 3　maintaining its o· correspondence with
occasion
pr 7–12　gives o· for reaction unfavorable to spiritual
8–14　there would be no o· for comment.
a 32–30　a mournful o·, a sad supper
f 212–13　When the nerve is gone, which we say was the o·
230–18　and health o· disease.
b 329–17　he should avoid their o·.
g 552–24　the redeeming power, from the ills they o·,
ap 571–17　and the o· for a victory over evil.
occasional
s 112–11　Although these opinions may have o· gleams of
156– 9　o· doses of a high attenuation of Sulphuris.
156–25　and receiving o· visits from me,

occasionally
sp 83–18　belief . . . that o· Spirit sets aside these laws,
f 237– 1　A little girl, who had o· listened to my
occasioned
m 62–12　which the parents themselves have o·.
sf 86– 2　Supposing this inquiry to be o· by
s 151–17　Mortal belief says that death has been o· by
159– 9　a verdict was returned that death was o·,
ph 199–23　failure is o· by a too feeble faith.
b 312–12　The belief of that mortal . . . o· his departure;
p 373–19　The fear o· by ignorance can be cured ;
386–19　You think that your anguish is o· by your loss,
431–29　testifies : . . . nothing on my part has o· this
occasioning
p 416– 4　unless the mental image o· the pain
occasions
a 32–10　nor was the wine, used on convivial o·
m 64– 8　Pride, envy, or jealousy seems on most o·
ph 182–32　presuppose that . . . is powerless on some o·,
f 252– 5　Human ignorance . . . o· the only skepticism
p 386–17　o· the same grief that the friend's
416–14　unless the belief which o· the pain has
430–32　testifies . . . was personally abused on those o·.
occultism
an 104–17　evil, o·, necromancy, mesmerism,
ap 570– 3　the growing o· of this period.
occupancy
c 261– 6　proportionally to their o· of your thoughts.
occupied
s 141–31　the place . . . now o· by scholastic theology and
154–10　was made to believe that he o· a bed where
occupies
an 104–26　This greater error thereafter o· the ground,
p 367–17　A Christian Scientist o· the place at this
occupy
a 22–13　"O· till I come !" — Luke 19 : 13.
m 60–23　Because . . . display, and pride, — o· thought.
p 387–16　it is not because they o· the most important posts
occupying
f 235–28　Clergymen, o· the watchtowers
occur
pt 1–11　no loss can o· from trusting God with
sp 77– 9　Death will o· on the next plane of
s 161–29　Such unconscious mistakes would not o·, if
f 245–27　Impossibilities never o·.
p 402–16　no breakage nor dislocation can really o·.
419–23　A relapse cannot in reality o· in
occurred
s 156–17　It then o· to me to give her
ph 160– 3　Whenever an aggravation of symptoms has o·
193–30　o· just as I have narrated.
p 362– 7　an unusual incident o·, as if to interrupt
occurrence
p 378–16　This latter o· represents the power of
occurs
an 105–23　to commit fresh atrocities as opportunity o·
p 386– 7　no such result o· without mind to demand it
421–11　If a crisis o· in your treatment, you must
ocean
m 67– 4　When the o· is stirred by a storm,
67–14　on the seething o· of sorrow.
sp 90–19　carries it through the air and over the o·,
s 122–17　On the eye's retina, . . . clouds and o· meet
o 361–17　As a drop of water is one with the o·,
ap 559– 9　thought reaches over continent and o·
o'clock
ph 193–15　between three and four o· in the afternoon
odds
a 22–15　If your endeavors are beset by fearful o·,
odious
f 236–15　either after a model o· to herself or
b 314–28　the more o· he became to sinners
odiousness
p 366–23　a sense of the o· of sin
odor
sp 88– 7　cognizant of a present flavor and o·,
s 128–20　An o· becomes beneficent and agreeable
offence
alleged
p 436– 8　on the night of the alleged o·
analyzes the
p 433– 4　He analyzes the o·, reviews the testimony
moral
p 395–32　a moral o· is indeed the worst of diseases
t 448– 2　and yet to indulge them, is a moral o·.
of the Jews
s 135–18　danger of repeating the o· of the Jews
preliminary
t 449–27　enemies without the preliminary o·

offence
repeat the
pr 5– 8   Temptation bids us repeat the *o·*,
    6–10   supposition . . . we shall be free to repeat the *o·*.
   11–15   leaves the offender free to repeat the *o·*,

pr 6–25   "Thou art an *o·* unto me." — *Matt.* 16 : 23.
p 431– 9   inasmuch as this *o·* is deemed punishable
  435– 7   The body committed no *o·*.
  439–23   an *o·* of which he was innocent.

offences
a 36–25   gloat over their *o·* to the last moment
an 105–18   no longer apply legal rulings wholly to physical *o·*,

offend
p 425–26   You will never fear again except to *o·* God,

offended
s 132– 9   whosoever shall not be *o·* in me." — *Matt.* 11 : 6.

offender
pr 11–14   leaves the *o·* free to repeat the offence,

offenders
p 439–28   *o·*, awaiting the sentence which

offending
p 392–31   Exclude from mortal mind the *o·* errors ;

offensive
t 463–13   truth removes properly whatever is *o·*.

offer
o 354–13   opponents of C. S. neither give nor *o·* any
ap 566–19   we may also *o·* the prayer which concludes the

offered
a 54–17   highest proof he could have *o·* of divine Love.
s 111–19   A prize of one hundred pounds, *o·* in Oxford
o 355–22   ever *o·* for acceptance,"
gl 597– 7   rebuked the hypocrisy, which *o·* long petitions

offering
a 25– 4   The efficacy of Jesus' spiritual *o·* is
p 406– 5   *o·* full salvation from sin, sickness, and death.
g 540–26   an *o·* unto the Lord — *Gen.* 4 : 3.
  540–31   he brings a material *o·* to God.
  541– 1   Abel takes his *o·* from the firstlings of the
  541– 7   unto Abel, and to his *o·* : — *Gen.* 4 : 4.
  541– 8   and to his *o·*, He had not respect. — *Gen.* 4 : 5.

offerings
b 286– 8   is better than all burnt *o·*.

offers
pr 12–28   another who *o·* the same measure of prayer

office
b 331–30   the same in essence, though multiform in *o·* :
p 392–29   then perform your *o·* as porter
  438–12   putting in false claims to *o·*
gl 595–16   can fit us for the *o·* of spiritual teaching.

officer
p 432–22   by the *o·* of the Board of Health,
  436– 1   (the *o·* of the Health-laws)

officers
p 438–25   without the inspection of Soul's government *o·*.

offices
ap 566–30   assigns to the angels, . . . different *o·*.

offset
s 111–21   essay calculated to *o·* the tendency of the age
  155–22   to *o·* the discords of matter
p 428–20   must realize the ability of mental might to *o·*

offshoot
sp 92–19   a mere *o·* of material sense.
b 287–18   nor is error the *o·* of Mind.

offshoots
sp 88–13   are *o·* of mortal mind ;

offspring
Christ's
gl 583– 9   CHILDREN OF ISRAEL. . . . Christ's *o·*.
fate of their
ph 176– 5   their own downfall and the fate of their *o·*
forms its
c 259–23   and forms its *o·* after human illusions.
His
b 332– 8   "For we are also His *o·*." — *Acts* 17 : 28.
man is the
m 63– 5   man is the *o·* of Spirit.
c 265– 1   Man is the *o·*, not of the lowest,
p 396–27   man is the *o·* of God, not of man ;
·*gl* 592– 5   the belief that man is the *o·* of mortals ;
nameless
g 507– 9   creation would be full of nameless *o·*,
not the
sp 93–17   electricity is not the *o·* of infinite good.
b 289–31   Man is not the *o·* of flesh, but of Spirit,
of error
gl 589– 2   A corporeal belief ; the *o·* of error ;

offspring
of God
a 29–30   Man as the *o·* of God, the idea of Spirit,
c 267– 3   The *o·* of God start not from matter
p 396–27   man is the *o·* of God, not of man
of mortals
gl 592– 5   the belief that man is the *o·* of mortals ;
of physical sense
r 479– 1   If a child is the *o·* of physical sense
of sense
b 274– 5   the *o·* of sense, not of Soul,
of Soul
a 30–24   the difference between the *o·* of Soul and
of Spirit
m 63– 5   man is the *o·* of Spirit.
g 540– 1   Christ is the *o·* of Spirit,
gl 583– 6   *o·* of Spirit, who, having wrestled with error,
of spirit
f 229–11   calls both the *o·* of spirit,
of the flesh
gl 594–17   The son of man, the *o·* of the flesh.
of will
ph 192–12   the *o·* of will and not of wisdom,
spiritual
b 336–31   and man is God's spiritual *o·*.
their
ph 176– 5   their own downfall and the fate of their *o·*
f 237–12   in the minds of themselves and their *o·*.
their own
m 69–17   educate their own *o·* spiritually,

a 29–32   *o·* of Mary's self-conscious communion with
m 61–11   The *o·* of heavenly-minded parents
sp 71–24   It is the *o·* of the physical senses.
o 350–12   His words were the *o·* of his deeds,
r 474–22   or the *o·* of the divine will?
g 555–21   as if man were the *o·* of both
ap 563–21   and seemingly impede the *o·* of the

oft
t 444– 4   suffering is *o·* the divine agent in this

often
pr 13– 5   In public prayer we *o·* go beyond our
a 31–22   "As *o·* as ye eat this bread, — *I Cor.* 11 : 26.
  53–19   the shock so *o·* produced by the truth,
m 59– 7   compromises will *o·* maintain a compact
  61–15   *o·* these beautiful children early droop
s 116–25   they *o·* lead, . . . to confused and erroneous
  121–22   Science shows appearances *o·* to be erroneous,
  122– 1   evidence of the physical senses *o·* reverses
  130–23   author has *o·* remembered our Master's love for
  134– 5   those who testified for Truth were so *o·* persecuted
  136–32   or they would not have questioned him so *o·*.
ph 166–24   the despairing invalid *o·* drops them,
f 206–32   There are evil beliefs, *o·* called evil spirits ;
  237–11   beliefs and theories of parents *o·* choke the
  238–19   Truth *o·* remains unsought, until we
  238–26   Justice *o·* comes too late to secure a verdict.
c 260–16   *o·* hampers the trial of one's wings
b 320– 4   names are *o·* expressive of spiritual ideas.
o 343–31   is *o·* accounted a heretic.
  350–16   The Master *o·* refused to explain his words,
  359–22   In childhood, she *o·* listened with joy to
  359–26   that Scripture she so *o·* quotes :
p 375– 6   Chills and heat are *o·* the form in which
  377– 4   affliction is *o·* the source of joy,
  378–15   *o·* causes the beast to retreat in terror.
  398– 9   *O·* he gave no name to the distemper he cured.
  403– 9   by his mistake a man is *o·* instructed.
  413–29   and *o·* stamp them there,
  422–10   the tremor which Truth *o·* brings to error
r 486–32   these calamities *o·* drive mortals to seek and
  488– 7   Hebrew and Greek words *o·* translated *belief*
  488–11   Hence the Scriptures *o·* appear . . . to
g 501– 4   *o·* seems so smothered by the immediate context
ap 576–27   term Lord, . . . is *o·* synonymous with Jehovah,
gl 579– 3   *o·* elucidates the meaning of the
  581– 1   the name *o·* conferred upon him in Scripture,

oftentimes
p 423– 6   Remember that the unexpressed belief *o·*
t 446–32   Ignorance of the error to be eradicated *o·*

ofttimes
t 444–30   are discordant and *o·* false brethren.

oil
boiling
f 243– 5   which delivered men from the boiling *o·*,
croton
ph 198–18   the application of caustic or croton *o·*,
fragrant
p 363– 2   jar containing costly and fragrant *o·*,
lubricating
ph 199–29   the unscientific might attribute to a lubricating *o·*.

oil

of gladness
  b 313– 8   o· of gladness above thy fellows.— *Heb.* 1 : 9.
  p 367–14   the o· of gladness and the perfume of *gratitude*,

sandal
  p 363– 2   sandal o· perhaps, which is in such common

  p 363– 4   she perfumed Jesus' feet with the o·,
     363–28   before she anointed them with the o·.
  ap 578–14   anointeth my head with o· ; — *see Psal.* 23 : 5.
  gl 592–25   definition of

old

  pr   9– 7   Do we pursue the o· selfishness, satisfied with
  a   38– 5   the o· doctrine of foreordination,
     52–15   Herod and Pilate laid aside o· feuds
  m   59–22   a word or deed may renew the o· trysting-times.
  sp   74–12   and never returns to the o· condition.
     77–31   they return to their o· standpoints of matter.
     92–11   In o· Scriptural pictures we see a
  s 114–20   must sometimes recur to the o· and imperfect,
     114–21   poured into the o· bottles of the letter.
     120–32   the limbs of the brave o· navigator,
     139–11   but the present new, yet o·, reform
     142– 1   in less time than the o· systems,
     143–21   you continue in the o· routine.
     144–24   the o· schools still oppose it.
     149–17   A physician of the o· school remarked
     161–30   if this o· class of philanthropists looked
  ph 172–22   we must "put off the o· man."— *Col.* 3 : 9.
     175– 6   In o· times who ever heard of dyspepsia,
  f 201– 8   in whom o· things pass away
     212– 4   and the pain seems to be in its o· place.
     221–16   without a vestige of the o· complaint.
     223–17   but more are blinded by their o· illusions,
     244–23   Man in Science is neither young nor o·.
     245– 1   error of thinking that we are growing o·,
     245–21   Years had not made her o·,
     245–23   nor thought of herself as growing o·.
  c 261–15   This o· man was so lame that he
     262– 7   By putting "off the o· man— *Col.* 3 : 9.
  b 281–27   does not put new wine into o· bottles,
     281–30   The o· belief must be cast out
     295– 1   belief that a . . . limb is aching in the o· location,
     296– 9   The o· man with his deeds must be put off.
     324– 1   Willingness . . . to leave the o· for the new,
  o 360–11   replies : . . . no notion of losing my o· doctrines
  p 372– 6   likened by Milton to "chaos and o· night."
  l 452–10   When outgrowing the o·, you should not fear
     460–31   until finally the shadow of o· errors
  g 519–15   until they throw off the o· man
     556–32   his infant babe, only a few hours o·,
  ap 563–18   The Revelator sees that o· serpent,
     567–15   that o· serpent, called the devil,— *Rev.* 12 : 9.
     567–18   that o· serpent whose name is devil (evil),
     570–18   What if the o· dragon should send forth a
     570–21   the deep waters of chaos and o· night.

old of —

  a   33– 5   manna, which of o· had fed in the wilderness
     52–17   To-day, as of o·, error and evil again
  sp   95–24   Magi of o· foretold the Messiahship of Truth.
  o 139 11   The Pharisees of o· thrust the spiritual idea and
  f 224–16   Of o· the cross was truth's central sign,
     224–27   as he came of o· to the patriarch at noonday
  c 255– *   Thy throne is *established of o·* : — *Psal.* 93 : 2.
  b 270–14   prophets of o· looked for something higher
     282– 1   Now, as of o·, Truth casts out evils
  o 347–16   true idea of God, comes now as of o·,
     360–28   Of o·, then to put to death the
  l 451–18   and they bear as of o· the fruits of the Spirit.
  r 482–24   Angels announced to the Wisemen of o·
  ap 559–29   for the Israelites of o· at the Paschal meal
     564– 3   As of o·, evil still charges the spiritual idea

olden

  s 131–27   explained the so-called miracles of o· time

older

  s 140–28   true that the o· Scripture is reversed.
  f 245–12   she literally grew no o·.
  g 502– 2   living and real prelude of the o· Scriptures

old-school

  p 375– 8   The o· physician proves this when

Old Testament

  s 139–18   thirty thousand different readings in the O· T·,
  g 501– 2   starts with the beginning of the O· T·,
     523–30   In the historic parts of the O· T·,
     557–26   the first chapter of the O· T·,
  ap 566–29   The O· T· assigns to the angels,
     576–26   as used in our version of the O· T·,

oleaginous

  p 440– 3   o· machinations of the counsel,

olfactory

  f 212–20   into contact with the o· nerves

ology

  f 223–21   efforts . . . to answer this question by some o·

Olympus

  ph 199–32   When Homer sang of the Grecian gods, O· was

omen

  p 422–12   and ignorant that it is a favorable o·,

omit

  s 142– 6   modern religions generally o· all but one of

omitted

  b 340– 6   when the word *duty*, . . . is o· :

omni

  r 466– 2   O· is adopted from the Latin adjective

omni-action

  gl 587–20   omniscience ; omnipresence ; o·.

omnipotence

divine nature and
  g 525– 1   Does . . . lose therein the divine nature and o· ?

escutcheon of
  p 437– 6   It blots the fair escutcheon of o·.

God's
  a   55–19   when he shall realize God's o·

might of
  gl 597–27   That which indicates the might of o·

of divine justice
  f 225–17   breathing the o· of divine justice,

of God
  o 345– 7   When the o· of God is preached
  t 445–18   the omnipresence and o· of God.

of Spirit
  sp 78–23   How can the majesty and o· of Spirit be lost?
  g 521–30   if veritable, would set aside the o· of Spirit ;

of the divine Mind
  t 459–13   instead of resting on the o· of the divine Mind,

of Truth
  l 454– 4   Teach your students the o· of Truth,

pure sense of
  b 318–15   would efface the pure sense of o·.

signification of
  r 469–25   We lose the high signification of o·, when

---

  pr 14– 1   If we are sensibly with the body and regard o·
     15–29   gain the ear and right hand of o·
  s 109–32   o·, omnipresence, omniscience,
  f 203– 4   Mind — o· — has all-power,
     228–25   O· has all-power,
     249–14   Either there is no o·, or o· is the only power.
  b 270–21   establish the definition of o·, and maintain
     275–22   o·, omnipresence, omniscience,
     287–15   or suggest the absence of . . . o· ?
  o 357–32   Can matter . . . and so defeat o· ?
     358– 2   Is the woodman's axe, . . . superior to o· ?
  r 469– 9   omniscience, omnipresence, and o·.
  g 521–11   supremacy, o·, and omnipresence.
     549–30   to usurp the prerogatives of o·.
  gl 581– 3   ALMIGHTY. All-power ; infinity ; o·.
     587–19   GOOD. God ; Spirit ; o· ; omniscience ;

omnipotent

  pr   3–18   o·, omnipresent, infinite,
     13–13   Do we gain the o· ear sooner by words than
     17– 3   *God is o·, supreme.*
  op 73 17   the Science of o·, omnipresent Spirit
     83–15   this belief belittles o· wisdom,
  s 113–19   Life, God, o· good, deny death, evil, sin,
     113–20   Disease, sin, evil, death, deny good, o· God,
     130–12   since you admit that God is o· ;
  ph 182–31   is to presuppose that o· power is
     186–14   God, the o· and omnipresent.
     194– 1   o· Spirit shares not its strength with matter
  f 202–30   as if . . . had more power than o· Spirit,
     206–28   O· and infinite Mind made all and includes all.
     231–25   To fear sin is to . . . distrust His o· care.
  c 257–29   inexhaustible Love, eternal Life, o· Truth.
  o 353–11   o· Truth certainly does destroy error.
     358– 5   If God is at the mercy of matter, then matter is o·.
  p 367–31   Because Truth is o· in goodness,
     394–29   that Life is God, and that God is o·.
     412–14   The power of C. S. and divine Love is o·.
     429– 1   sin to believe that aught can overpower o·
  t 449– 4   does wonders for mortals, so o· is Truth,
  r 465–18   this one is God, o·, omniscient, and omnipresent
     473– 8   The God-principle is omnipresent and o·.
  gl 594– 9   The first audible claim that God was not o·
     594–21   everlasting, omnipresent, o·,
     (see also **Mind**)

omnipresence

  sp   94–29   a scientific basis, that of the o· of Mind.
  s 109–32   omnipotence, o·, omniscience,
  b 275–22   omnipotence, o·, omniscience,
     287–15   how can He . . . suggest the absence of o·
     331–23   to conceive of such o· and individuality
  t 445–18   the o· and omnipotence of God.
  r 469– 8   Intelligence is omniscience, o·,
  g 521–11   supremacy, omnipotence, and o·.
  gl 587–19   omniscience ; o· ; omni-action.

omnipresent

pr	3–18	omnipotent, o·, infinite,
sp	73–17	the Science of omnipotent, o· Spirit
	78–20	Spirit needs no . . . in order to be o·.
s	119–21	not the divine ideal of o· Love.
ph	186–14	God, the omnipotent and o·.
f	223– 7	God is infinite o· Spirit.
b	275– 2	would ignore o· and omnipotent Mind.
o	361– 7	a monotheist ; he has one o· God.
r	465–18	omnipotent, omniscient, and o·
	469–26	admitting that God, or good, is o·
	473– 8	The God-principle is o· and omnipotent.
gl	594–21	SPIRIT. . . . o·, omnipotent,

omniscience

s	110– 1	omnipotence, omnipresence, o·,
b	275–22	omnipotence, omnipresence, o·,
r	469– 8	Intelligence is o·, omnipresence,
gl	587–19	o· ; omnipresence ; omni-action.

omniscient

r	465–18	omnipotent, o·, and omnipresent

once

a	39–32	o· admit that evil confers no pleasure,
m	65–25	which was o· a fixed fact among us,
sp	74– 5	after having o· left it,
	85–15	as he o· journeyed with his students,
	86– 1	o· asked, "Who touched me?"— Luke 8 : 45.
s	109– 9	This proof o· seen, no other conclusion can
	109–28	Jesus o· said of his lessons :
	121–26	the earth revolves about the sun o· a year,
	131– 6	When o· destroyed by divine Science,
	131–18	Jesus o· said : "I thank Thee,— Luke 10 : 21.
	132–31	o· pointed his disciples to Jesus
	152–14	o· apparently cured a case of paralysis
f	217–16	When you have o· conquered a diseased
	220–22	A clergyman o· adopted a diet of
	223–12	If Spirit were o· within the body,
c	259–15	If man was o· perfect but has now lost his
p	362– 2	Jesus was o· the honored guest of a certain
	368–32	O· let the mental physician believe in the
	400– 2	When disease is o· destroyed in this so-called
	411–13	o· Jesus asked the name of a disease,
g	530– 8	Knowing this, Jesus o· said,
	552– 5	was o· an accepted theory.
	555– 6	o· said to the discoverer of C. S. :

once at —

a	27– 8	he will at o· perceive that God is the
	77– 2	"I cannot turn at o· from good to evil."
f	204– 1	at o· the centre and circumference of being.
	216–12	begins at o· to destroy the errors of
	253–19	can at o· change your course and do right.
o	349–26	Mortal thought does not at o· catch the higher
p	363–13	why, . . . the exalted guest did not at o·
	371–20	I would not transform the infant at o· into
	432–30	he decided at o· that the prisoner should die.
	442– 5	The Jury of Spiritual Senses agreed at o·
ap	560–30	betrays at o· a greater ignorance

One

pr	3–14	the O· "altogether lovely ;"— Song 5 : 16.
	16–29	Adorable O·.
s	112–16	From the infinite O· in C. S. comes
	117– 4	whereas God is O·,
	135–18	danger of . . . limiting the Holy O·.

one (see also one's)

pref	xi–26	started by the author with only o· student
	xii–23	In the spirit of Christ's charity,— as o· who
pr	2–19	as o· pleads with a human being,
	5– 3	Sorrow for wrong-doing is but o· step
	8–19	audible prayers are like charity in o· respect,
	9– 4	the falsehood which does no o· any good.
	10–17	O· of the forms of worship in Thibet
	11– 7	only saves . . . from o· form of punishment.
	12– 8	This, however, is o· belief casting out another,
	12–27	Does Deity interpose in behalf of o· worshipper,
	13– 4	"Ho, every o· that thirsteth,— Isa. 55 : 1.
	14–30	"as o· having authority."— Matt. 7 : 29.
	16– 3	highest prayer is not o· of faith merely ;
	16– 7	taught his disciples o· brief prayer,
	16–19	"the evil one," or o· evil,
a	19–32	thou shalt not know evil, for there is o· Life,
	23– 3	O· sacrifice, however great, is insufficient
	23–12	taketh o· doctrine, firm in faith,
	23–23	O· kind of faith trusts one's welfare to others.
	26– 5	spares us not o· individual experience,
	26–12	"I and my Father are o·."— John 10 : 30.
	27–22	Jesus sent forth seventy students at o· time,
	31– 5	for o· is your Father,— Matt. 23 : 9.
	37– 9	human links which connect o· stage with
	47–28	each o· came to a violent death except St. John,
	48– 4	"Could ye not watch with me o· hour?"— Matt. 26 : 40.
	48–17	Jesus had not o· of them,
	49–13	why did they not gratify . . . with o· sign of

one

m	56–19	is no less imperative than the o·,
	57– 3	without it o· cannot attain the
	64–23	white robed purity will unite in o· person
	66–25	If o· is better than the other,
	67–15	o· should stick to the wreck,
	68–16	I never knew more than o· individual who
	69–14	to understand that there is but o· creator,
sp	72– 1	There is but o· spiritual existence,
	73– 1	In either case, o· does not support the other.
	73– 3	Spiritualism calls o· person, living in this
	73– 6	neither the o· nor the other is infinite
	73– 8	belief that o· man, as spirit, can control
	75–25	There is o· possible moment, when
	75–30	from o· dream to another dream,
	76– 3	as o· at Niagara, with eyes open only to
	78–31	These are the effects of o· universal God,
	82– 2	as easily as we do of o· present.
	82–11	o· person cannot exist in two different
	83– 2	or the divine Mind which is influencing o·.
	85– 8	enabling o· to do good, but not evil.
	86–22	to see a thought than to feel o· ?
	87–16	Science enables o· to read the human mind,
	87–17	It enables o· to heal through Mind,
	88–15	so-called material senses, which at o· time
	89–14	If o· believes that he cannot be an orator
	90– 1	if o· animal can originate another,
	90–22	yet their bodies stay in o· place.
	94–21	but o· returned to give God thanks,
	94–32	Jesus could injure no o· by his Mind-reading.
	95–17	and is o· of the special characteristics thereof.
	96–13	On o· side there will be discord and dismay ;
	97–10	the flight of o· and the blow of the other
an	100– 5	exerted by o· living organism over another,
	100–15	Benjamin Franklin was o· of the
	101– 4	and that there is o· more fact to be
	102– 9	There is but o· real attraction,
	103–22	This belief has not o· quality of Truth.
	104–23	The hypnotizer employs o· error to
s	111–19	A prize of o· hundred pounds, offered
	111–23	o· of many incidents which show that C. S.
	112– 3	Is there more than o· school of C. S.?
	112– 5	can, therefore, be but o· method in its teaching.
	113– 1	there can be but o· divine Principle
	114–10	In Science, Mind is o·,
	115– 1	the o· great obstacle to the reception of
	117– 2	an individual may be o· of a series, o· of many,
	117– 4	God is One,— not o· of a series, but o· alone
	118–31	in which nature and God are o·
	119– 5	such theories lead to o· of two things.
	119–17	In o· sense God is identical with nature,
	119–25	In viewing the sunrise, o· finds that it
	125–12	As human thought changes from o· stage to
	126–16	between C. S. on the o· hand and
	128–22	If o· would not quarrel with his fellow-man
	130– 5	O· has a farm, another has merchandise,
	132–10	to any o· who should not deny that
	133–24	was o· of the Jewish accusations
	134– 8	o· who suffers for his convictions.
	135–22	else o· or the other is false and useless ;
	135–25	This proves the o· to be identical with
	136–16	Jeremias, or o· of the prophets."— Matt. 16 : 14.
	142– 6	o· of these powers,— the power over sin.
	143–13	the human mind uses o· error to
	145–13	what material method o· may adopt,
	145–26	antagonism of o· form of matter towards
	148–19	the o· wholly, the other primarily
	150–12	not primarily o· of physical healing.
	150–18	physics would have o· believe that
	151– 2	as if there was but o· factor in the case ;
	151– 3	this o· factor they represent to be body,
	151–13	Even this o· reform in medicine would
	152–12	in which o· statement contradicts another
	153– 3	or changes o· of the symptoms of disease.
	153– 8	o· drop of that attenuation in a goblet of water,
	154–28	Such a mother runs to her little o·, who
	156–20	that she would give up her medicine for o· day,
	157– 4	its o· recognized Principle of healing is Mind,
	159–28	how much . . . o· form of matter is
	161–20	remind o· of the words of the famous
ph	165– 1	Physiology is o· of the apples from
	167–25	There is but o· way— namely,
	170–22	Spiritual causation is the o· question
	176–24	O· disease is no more real than another.
	177– 8	Mortal mind and matter are o·.
	180– 8	in Science o· must understand the
	181– 3	Before deciding . . . o· should ask,
	182–10	for o· absolutely destroys the other,
	182–11	and o· or the other must be supreme
	182–13	"hold to the o·, and despise the— Matt. 6 : 24.
	183– 4	departing from the basis of . . . o· lawmaker.
	186–20	It can never destroy o· iota of good.
	187–32	a body like the o· it had before death.
	188–13	in which every o· recognizes his condition
	195–11	The point for each o· to decide is,
	197– 4	Every o· hastens to get it.

one

ph	198–15	formed before *o·* sees a doctor
f	201– 4	knowing too that *o·* affection would be supreme
	203–17	We are prone to believe either in more than *o·*
	204– 4	conclusions that there is more than *o·* Life;
	205–22	When we realize that there is *o·* Mind,
	206–16	we find that whatever blesses *o·* blesses all,
	207–20	There is but *o·* primal cause.
	208–19	"the voice of *o·* crying in the — *Matt.* 3 : 3.
	210–17	by *o·* and the same metaphysical process.
	211–22	transfer of the thoughts of *o·* erring mind to
	218–31	moral and physical are as *o·* in their results.
	220–27	*o·* of the fruits of "the tree of — *Gen.* 2 : 17.
	221– 6	partook of but *o·* meal in twenty-four hours,
	221–31	neither food nor . . . can make *o·* suffer,
	222– 5	*o·* of which is to believe that proper food
	222–28	physiology, and physics had made him *o·*,
	235– 2	from *o·* human mind to another,
	235– 5	*o·* who does not obey the requirements of
	235–13	spiritual culture, which lifts *o·* higher.
	238– 8	enables *o·* to be Christian.
	238–25	listening only to *o·* side of the case.
	239– 6	which weigh not *o·* jot in the balance of God,
	240–11	In the order of . . . all is *o·* grand concord.
	240–27	*o·* must pay fully and fairly
	242– 9	but *o·* way to heaven, harmony,
	242–25	woven into *o·* web of consistency
	247– 7	cuspids, bicuspids, and *o·* molar.
	247– 7	*O·* man at sixty had retained his
	248– 4	*O·* marvels that a friend can ever seem less than
	249– 4	one Mind, and that *o·* perfect,
	249–32	and there is but *o·* Ego.
	250–14	Mortal body and mind are *o·*,
	250–14	and that *o·* is called man ;
	250–29	Mortal thoughts chase *o·* another like
	252–23	says : . . . make my short span of life *o·* gala
c	256–11	rather than the *o·* ever-present I AM.
	256–12	the Lord our God is *o·* Lord." — *Deut.* 6 : 4.
	260– 1	*o·* can no more arrive at the
	261– 9	If *o·* turns away from the body
	262–24	Starting from a higher standpoint, *o·* rises
	263–20	There can be but *o·* creator,
	267– 5	God is *o·*.
	267– 6	Generically man is *o·*,
b	269– 1	These . . . systems are *o·* and all pantheistic,
	269–14	The categories of metaphysics rest on *o·* basis,
	270– 2	*O·* only of the following statements can be true:
	270– 4	Which *o·* is it?
	270– 5	*O·* is contrary to the other
	270– 7	If *o·* is real, the other must be unreal.
	270– 8	there is but *o·* power, — not two powers,
	273– 5	not *o·* of them can solve the problem
	275–13	Spirit, Life, Truth, Love, combine as *o·*,
	276– 7	but all have . . . *o·* intelligent source,
	278–13	*o·* of the false beliefs of mortals,
	279–14	*o·* can no more create the other than
	279–28	not two bases of being, . . . but *o·* alone,
	281– 5	When *o·* appears, the other disappears.
	281–14	The *o·* Ego, the one Mind or Spirit called God,
	282–21	*o·* is still a curve and the other a straight line.
	283– 4	They insist that Life, or God, is *o·* and the
	283–19	and deem this the manifestation of the *o·* Life,
	285–13	for *o·* is intelligence while the other is
	294– 6	the loss of *o·* finger would take
	294– 8	If . . . matter and man would be *o·*.
	295–21	that *o·* which has lost much materiality
	296–28	An improved belief is *o·* step out of error,
	303– 8	reflect the *o·* divine individuality
	307– 8	affirms . . . there is more than *o·* intelligence
	315– 3	"I and my Father are *o·*," — *John* 10 : 30.
	319–32	beloved disciple meant in *o·* of his epistles.
	320–21	The *o·* important interpretation of Scripture
	323–18	the *o·* unused talent decays and is lost.
	325– 5	Such a *o·* abideth in Life,
	329–14	*O·* should not tarry in the storm if
	329–16	Until *o·* is able to prevent bad results,
	331–29	They represent a trinity in unity, three in *o·*,
	332–16	*o·* mediator between God and men,—*I Tim.* 2 : 5.
	333–30	"I and my Father are *o·* ;" — *John* 10 : 30.
	334– 3	not that the corporeal Jesus was *o·* with the
	334–32	for there can be but *o·* infinite
	335–16	Soul and Spirit being *o·*,
	335–17	God and Soul are *o·*,
	335–17	this *o·* never included in a limited mind
	339– 5	Does not God's pardon, destroying any *o·* sin,
	340–23	*O·* infinite God, good, unifies men and nations;
o	341– 7	grow in beauty and consistency from *o·* grand
	342– 6	*o·* may see with sorrow the sad effects
	343– 9	without this cross-bearing, *o·* might not
	343–26	Paul who was not *o·* of his students,
	344–21	there is only *o·* which should be presented
	344–25	Why should *o·* refuse to investigate this
	345–17	*O·* who understands C. S. can heal the sick
	345–20	evidence that *o·* does understand this Science.
	346– 1	as is alleged by *o·* critic.
	347– 3	It is said by *o·* critic, that to verify this

one

o	348– 9	*o·* disease can be just as much a delusion as
	349–17	*o·* is obliged to use material terms
	354–26	Sin should become unreal to every *o·*.
	355–15	*O·*, according to the commands of our Master, heals
	355–26	Without this understanding, no *o·* is
	356–27	Would any *o·* call it wise and good
	356–32	Then there must have been more than *o·* creator,
	358– 7	and *o·* is true, the other must be false.
	359–30	*O·* says : "I have spiritual ideals,
	361– 7	a monotheist ; he has *o·* omnipresent God.
	361–15	"I and my Father are *o·*," — *John* 10 : 30.
	361–15	that is, *o·* in quality, not in quantity.
	361–16	As a drop of water is *o·* with the ocean,
	361–17	a ray of light *o·* with the sun,
	361–18	Father and son, are *o·* in being.
p	363–16	*o·* for a large sum and *o·* for a smaller,
	364– 4	it was manifested towards *o·* who
	364–17	indicated by *o·* of the needs of this age.
	365–16	will be accomplished at *o·* visit,
	369–21	man has not two lives, *o·* to be destroyed
	370–16	effect, which . . . produces through *o·* belief,
	371–14	in all ways except the right *o·*.
	372– 6	*O·* theory about this mortal mind is, that
	372–18	C. S. and Christianity are *o·*.
	372–22	Its false supports fail *o·* after another.
	376–13	in *o·* good motive and act,
	382–17	to teach the so-called ignorant *o·*.
	382–21	more difficult to heal through Mind than *o·* who
	382–24	*O·* whom I rescued from seeming
	383– 5	*O·* says : "I take good care of my body."
	386– 1	illusion of mortal mind, — *o·* of its dreams.
	387–23	*o·* cannot suffer as the result of
	389–32	*O·* instant she spoke despairingly of herself.
	395– 7	as *o·* having authority over it,
	396– 1	*O·* should never hold in mind the thought of
	397–23	To heal the sick, *o·* must be familiar with the
	397–28	because they combine as *o·*.
	398– 6	and he was as *o·* dead," — *Mark* 9 : 26.
	399–29	"How can *o·* enter into a — *Matt.* 12 : 29.
	402–20	We say that *o·* human mind can influence
	403–11	to remove the illusion in *o·* case,
	403–21	The most Christian state is *o·* of rectitude
	404– 4	servant of any *o·* of the myriad forms of sin,
	404–21	*o·* of the most important points in the
	404–26	are *o·* and the same thing in C. S.
	409– 5	*Mortal mind* and body combine as *o·*,
	413–22	but in caring for an infant *o·* need not
	418–15	*o·* disease would be as readily destroyed as
	419–14	from *o·* form to another.
	420– 1	nor go from *o·* part to another,
	422–24	A surgeon is employed in *o·* case,
	424–12	if *o·* doctor should administer a drug
	425–14	this is but *o·* of the beliefs of mortal mind.
	426–10	struggle for Truth makes *o·* strong
	426–11	resting instead of wearying *o·*.
	432–24	*O·* of the prisoner's friends, Materia Medica,
	436–35	*O·* of the principal witnesses, Nerve,
	442–15	*o·* "that bringeth good tidings." — *Isa.* 52 : 7.
t	444–28	are *o·* harmonious family ;
	446–13	can practise on no *o·* from sinister
	451–28	It is the injurious action of *o·* mortal mind
	452– 2	when *o·* understands that evil has in reality no
	456–19	*O·* must abide in the *morale* of truth
	457–15	each of them could see but *o·* face of it,
	457–21	*O·* cannot scatter his fire, and at the same time
	458– 4	*o·* good and the other evil,
	458– 5	*o·* spiritual, the other material,
	458–29	the only *o·* by which mortals are
	460–11	the *o·* most difficult to understand
r	465–12	They refer to *o·* absolute God.
	465–17	Principle and its idea is *o·*,
	465–18	and this *o·* is God,
	467–10	*o·* Life, Truth, and Love.
	467–14	the *o·* perfect Mind to guide him,
	468–29	*O·* ceases in proportion as the other is
	469–21	but one Mind, if that *o·* is infinite.
	470– 1	With *o·* Father, even God,
	472–16	Error is neither Mind nor *o·* of Mind's faculties.
	476– 2	children of the wicked *o·*, or the *o·* evil,
	480–32	*O·* must hide the other.
	483– 4	exchanging *o·* disease for another.
	483–30	*O·* must fulfil one's mission without timidity
	484– 9	Not *o·* of them is included in it.
	484–15	Physical force and mortal mind are *o·*.
	486– 4	Suppose *o·* accident happens to the eye,
	486–13	*o·* error will not correct another.
	487–18	The believer and belief are *o·*
	489– 8	not with an artificial limb, but with the genuine *o·*
	489–19	at *o·* time the medium for
	491–17	The belief that matter and mind are *o·*,
	491–18	belief . . . that matter is awake at *o·* time and
	492– 3	but *o·* fact before the thought,
	492–16	until *o·* is acknowledged to be the victor.
	494–26	*O·* is the mortal testimony,

one

r	496– 3	no transfer . . . from o· mortal to another,
	497– 5	We acknowledge and adore o· supreme and
	497– 6	We acknowledge His Son, o· Christ ;
g	502–29	There is but o· creator and o· creation.
	504–22	"o· day is with the Lord as a— *II Pet.* 3 : 8.
	506–16	gathered together unto o· place,— *Gen.* 1 : 9.
	508–29	an important o· to the human thought,
	510–29	and this o· shining by its own light
	515–19	nor does it imply three persons in o·.
	516–31	In o· of the ancient languages the word
	517–16	but if God is personal, there is but o· person,
	518–16	in o· grand brotherhood,
	522– 4	If o· is true, the other is false,
	523– 1	o· might so judge from an unintelligent perusal
	523–17	O· is called the Elohistic,
	525– 9	In the Saxon, *mankind, a woman, any* o· ;
	528–11	and He took o· of his ribs,— *Gen.* 2 : 21.
	530–28	therefore the dreamer and dream are o·,
	532– 1	Did God at first create o· man unaided,
	533– 1	was o· of nakedness and shame.
	535– 4	o· to be burned, the other to be garnered
	536–12	gravitation and attraction to o· Father,
	536–31	the man is become as o· of us,— *Gen.* 3 : 22.
	537–19	No o· can reasonably doubt that the purpose
	545– 3	the man is become as o· of us."— *Gen.* 3 : 22.
	545–28	Truth has but o· reply to all error,
	546–32	a thousand different examples of o· rule,
	546–32	the proving of o· example would
	547– 4	If o· of the statements in this book is true,
	547– 5	every o· must be true,
	547– 5	for not o· departs from the stated system
	549–16	from which o· or more individualities
	550–25	no instance of o· species producing its opposite.
	551– 9	O· distinguished naturalist argues that
	553–10	O· of our ablest naturalists has said :
	554–23	and o· of you is a devil?"— *John* 6 : 70.
	554–24	This he said of Judas, o· of Adam's race.
ap	569–21	sin, which o· has made his bosom companion,
	570– 7	for o· extreme follows another.
	571–11	Is the informer o· who sees the foe?
	571–20	will unite all interests in the o· divinity.
	572– 6	"Love o· another"— *I John* 3 : 23.
	573– 7	heavens and earth to o· human consciousness,
	574– 6	o· of the seven angels— *Rev.* 21 : 9.
	575– 8	as o· that "lieth four-square"— *Rev.* 21 : 16.
	577– 3	as o· Father with His universal family,
	577– 7	two individual natures in o· ;
	577–32	In the following Psalm o· word shows,
gl	580–28	An adversary is o· who opposes,
	580–29	not o· who constructs and sustains reality
	583–28	o· belief preying upon another.
	584–13	frets itself free from o· belief only to be
	588–11	There is but o· I, or Us, but o· divine Principle,
	592– 7	belief that there can be more than o· creator ;
	597–26	as applied to Mind or to o· of God's qualities.
	598– 4	every o· that is born of the Spirit— *John* 3 : 8.
	598–21	"O· day is with the Lord as a— *II Pet.* 3 : 8.
	598–23	O· moment of divine consciousness,

(*see also* **God, instance, Mind, mind, Principle, Spirit**)

oneness

a	18– 4	demonstrated man's o· with the Father,
m	57–10	their true harmony is in spiritual o·.
f	205–29	Denial of the o· of Mind throws our weight into
c	267– 6	The allness of Deity is His o·.
p	424–25	the o· and the allness of divine Love ;
g	515–20	It relates to the o·, the tri-unity of

one's

a	22–26	pinning o· faith . . . to another's vicarious
	23–24	One kind of faith trusts o· welfare to others.
	23–26	work out o· "own salvation,— *Phil.* 2 : 12.
	28–10	o· consecration to Christ is more on the
m	60– 2	Science inevitably lifts o· being higher
sp	88–18	To love o· neighbor as o· self, is a
	90–24	The admission to o· self that man is
an	101–32	proportional to o· faith in esoteric magic.
ph	194– 8	When o· false belief is corrected,
f	234–32	no more harm than o· belief permits.
	240–30	involves unwinding o· snarls,
	241–23	O· aim, a point beyond faith,
c	259–32	Deducing o· conclusions as to man from
	260–15	but distrust of o· ability to gain
	260–17	often hampers the trial of o· wings
	260–25	by the thoughts ever recurring to o· self,
b	319– 5	To calculate o· life-prospects from a
	322–32	easier to desire Truth than to rid o· self of error.
o	345–13	no small matter to know o· self ;
p	368–24	in the ratio of o· spiritual growth.
	396– 4	both for o· own sake and for that of the patient.
	413– 3	The act of yielding o· thoughts to the
	440–16	that it is for the good of o· neighbor?
t	448–31	doing o· self the most harm.
	449– 8	reacts most heavily against o· self.
r	483–31	One must fulfil o· mission without timidity

ones

m	61–19	may reproduce in their own helpless little o·
sp	76– 1	The o· departing may whisper this vision,
g	501–16	that Love for whose rest the weary o· sigh

one-sided

f	235–12	School-examinations are o· ;

only

pref	vii–18	The o· guarantee of obedience is
	ix– 2	but these jottings were o·
	x–27	O· those quarrel with her method who
	xi– 2	o· a phase of the action of
	xi–26	was started by the author with o·
	xii– 3	hers was the o· College of this
pr	3– 9	we have o· to avail ourselves of
	3–30	In such a case, the o· acceptable prayer
	4– 7	o· worthy evidence of our gratitude
	5–24	o· as it is destroyed by Christ,
	7– 1	The o· civil sentence which he had for
	8– 4	those who come o· spasmodically
	8–30	in this way o· can we learn
	9–22	recognizes o· the divine control
	11– 7	it o· saves the criminal from
	11–21	Petitions bring to mortals o· the
	11–26	that we may walk securely in the o·
	12–30	o· petitioners (*per se* or by proxy)
	16–20	O· as we rise above all material
a	18– 7	not o· in justice to himself,
	21–31	satisfied if he can o· imagine himself
	22–31	Mercy cancels the debt o· when
	22–32	Wrath which is o· appeased is not
	24–24	o· for the presentation, after death,
	27–22	o· eleven left a desirable historic
	28– 2	but they o· hindered the success of
	29–16	God is the o· author of man.
	30–28	O· in this way can we bless
	31–10	recognized Spirit, God, as the o· creator,
	35–21	o· as we are new-born of Spirit,
	36–27	o· toil, sacrifice, cross-bearing,
	37– 8	error falls o· before the sword of Spirit.
	38– 2	assured that this command was intended o· for
	38–19	prayed, not for the twelve o·, but
	38–27	living o· for pleasure or the gratification of
	40– 9	Science removes the penalty o· by
	43– 6	Heretofore they had o· believed ;
	51–20	but o· through doing the works which
	52–26	speaking not for their day o· but
	54–22	o· a few unpretentious friends,
m	57–12	perpetual o· as it is pure and true,
	62– 1	can o· be permitted for the purpose of
	62–18	become men and women o· through
	69– 5	o· as they lose the sense of sin and disease.
	69– 8	o· as man finds the truth of being.
sp	71– 9	which forms o· reflect.
	72–12	God, is the o· truth-giver to man.
	73–11	and God is the o· Spirit.
	76– 4	with eyes open o· to that wonder,
	76–25	the o· veritable, indestructible man,
	76–27	a perfection discernible o· by those
	80–11	assertion that . . . are our o· proofs of
	81– 8	can o· prove that certain individuals
	81–15	Life, Love, Truth, is the o· proof
	83– 6	Science o· can explain the incredible good
	83–32	investigates and touches o· human beliefs.
	86–15	they are mysterious o· because
	89– 2	This phenomenon o· shows that the
	91– 6	and obey o· the divine Principle,
	92– 5	not o· capable of experiencing pleasure and
	92–26	to call that real which is o· a mistake.
	93–26	refer o· to quality, not to God.
	95– 2	and this is the o· genuine Science of
	98–11	which can o· be spiritually discerned.
	99–14	C. S. teaches o· that which is spiritual
an	103–15	working out the purposes of good o·.
	106–10	Man is properly self-governed o· when
	106–16	sanction o· such methods as
s	108–10	the o· sufferer is mortal mind,
	109– 5	the o· realities are the divine Mind and
	110–14	the Bible was my o· textbook.
	113– 5	but its spirit comes o· in small degrees.
	119–12	is not o· to make Him responsible for
	119–22	represented o· by the idea of goodness ;
	120–22	which is the o· basis of health ;
	126–29	The Bible has been my o· authority.
	128– 4	refers o· to the laws of God
	128–20	becomes beneficent and agreeable o· in
	129–23	o· the outward sense of things.
	133–30	Jehovah, or o· a mighty hero and king,
	137–27	called o· by his common names,
	140–16	We worship spiritually, o· as we
	141–18	Its o· crowned head is immortal
	141–19	Its o· priest is the spiritualized man.
	143– 2	destroys o· what is untrue.
	145–11	o· as immortal Mind . . . subdues the
	150–14	but these signs are o· to demonstrate
	159–14	as if matter were the o· factor

only

s	160–28	if we are o· to learn from
	162– 3	the metaphysician agrees o· with health
	162–27	o· a fuller understanding of the
ph	166–25	in his extremity and o· as a last resort,
	167– 6	o· as we live above corporeal sense
	167–30	O· through radical reliance on
	169–18	Science not o· reveals the origin of
	169–27	O· the action of Truth, Life, and
	170–11	not o· contradicts human systems, but
	172–14	yet this can be realized o· as the
	174– 4	Is civilization o· a higher form of
	174–20	It needs o· to be practised.
	176–23	o· in cases of hysteria,
	179– 2	but this can be done o· by
	179–10	o· as man is found, . . . reflecting the
	180–27	The o· way to this living Truth,
	182– 5	demands of God appeal to thought o· ;
	183–17	o· possible action of Truth
	183–31	the one Mind o· is entitled to honor.
	184–12	Truth, Life, and Love are the o·
	185–19	conception of God as the o· Life,
	185–22	not o· without drugs, but
	186– 1	o· by removing the influence on him
	186– 8	Erring human mind-forces can work o· evil
	186–19	The o· power of evil is to destroy itself.
	186–21	a failure, and o· aids in peremptorily
	188– 1	o· as the mortal, erring mind yields
	188– 9	ripen into action, o· to pass from
	192– 4	We are Christian Scientists, o· as we
	192–24	gives you the o· power obtainable.
	195–25	Novels, remarkable o· for their
	196– 9	sin is the o· element of destruction.
	199–22	Exceptions o· confirm this rule,
f	203–11	the o· true spirit is Godlike.
	204–21	and realize o· one God,
	205–17	o· as the mists disperse,
	206– 4	should be exercised o· in subordination to
	207–23	this great and o· cause.
	207–32	The o· evidence of this inversion is
	208–26	A material body o· expresses a
	210– 1	Its ideas are expressed o· in
	211 20	o· through dematerialization and
	215–16	o· a mortal sense of the absence of light,
	218–21	which lead o· into material ways
	221– 3	he ate o· bread and vegetables,
	221– 7	consisting of o· a thin slice of bread
	221–13	informed him that death was indeed his o·
	222– 4	food affects the body o· as
	222–18	o· by the strictest adherence to
	226– 1	o· prophetic of further steps towards
	231–18	discords have o· a fabulous existence,
	232– 8	eternal being is found o· in divine Science.
	232–12	and make healing possible o· through
	232–27	It is o· when the so-called pleasures and
	233– 7	o· what we can certainly fulfil.
	233– 9	acknowledged o· by degrees.
	237–28	the o· living mind God can do.
	238–25	listening o· to one side of the case.
	242– 0	It is o· a question of time when
	249 14	or omnipotence is the o· power.
	251–23	find the divine Mind to be the o· Mind,
	252– 5	the o· skepticism regarding the pathology
c	255– *	And not o· they, but— Rom. 8 : 23.
	257– 7	the o· substance and creator
	260–12	the o· true conception of being.
	261–21	which is o· a form of human belief,
	262 30	Divine Mind is the o· cause
	263– 8	and works o· as God works,
	264–20	are tho o· realities of being.
	264–25	the o· evidences, by which we can
	265–19	this is true o· of a mortal,
b	270– 2	One o· of the following statements can be true :
	270– 7	O· by understanding that there is
	272– 4	assimilated o· as we are honest,
	274– 4	knowledge gained from . . . is o· temporal,
	274–29	formed o· to be destroyed
	276–11	is cognizant o· of the things of God.
	276–17	If God is admitted to be the o· Mind
	278– 4	Spirit is the o· substance and
	278–13	exists o· in a supposititious
	279–18	their o· idea or intelligence is in God.
	279–19	Spirit is reached o· through the
	279–27	is reached o· through the knowledge that
	280– 5	o· reflections of good can come.
	280–30	o· excuse for entertaining human opinions
	281– 1	yields o· to the understanding of
	284–26	and are known o· by the effects
	284–28	the o· real senses of man are
	286–24	God, Spirit, is the o· cause,
	288– 4	o· the mental conflict between the
	289– 4	he learns that God is the o· Life.
	290–19	Perfection is gained o· by perfection.
	290–26	o· when he reaches perfection.
	292– 7	o· as it destroys all error
	292– 8	the o· immortality of man,

only

b	294–25	recognizable o· in what is good
	297–16	o· fact concerning any material concept
	298– 8	o· a mortal temporary sense of things,
	298–10	can bear witness o· to Truth.
	299– 1	but this is o· fancy.
	300–29	o· in the spiritual universe
	300–32	o· in that which reflects Life,
	301–13	the o· real and eternal entity.
	301–16	revealed o· through divine Science.
	301–18	o· the substance of good,
	307–13	God, Spirit, who is the o· Life."
	307–15	o· a transient, false sense of an
	308– 5	God is the o· Mind governing man,
	308–11	but finding o· an illusion,
	310–26	The o· Life is Spirit,
	311– 9	he can o· lose a sense material.
	311–11	o· so long as the illusion of mind in
	311–27	o· what mortal belief calls them.
	313–28	o· in a limited degree
	315–18	o· when we subdue sin
	316– 5	mortals need o· turn from sin and
	317–14	not o· in all time, but in all ways
	319–26	who o· wrote down what an
	321–13	was shown to be a belief o·.
	322–24	o· through fear of consequences
	324–15	understanding that God is the o· Life.
	326–14	the Christ as our o· Saviour.
	326–24	Saul of Tarsus beheld the way . . . o· when
	328– 2	he not o· will be saved, but is saved.
	328– 5	God is good and the o· real Life.
	328– 8	mortals get rid of sin, . . . o· in belief.
	328 28	Had it been given o· to his
	329–12	In Science we can use o· what we understand.
	330–11	God is infinite, the o· Life, substance,
	330–12	the o· intelligence of the universe,
	330–23	there is in reality one Mind o·,
	331–19	the universal cause, the o· creator,
	332–27	for o· purity could reflect Truth
	335–12	Spirit is the o· substance,
	335–22	O· by losing the false sense of Soul
	338– 3	the o· living and true God
	339–17	O· those, who repent of sin and forsake
	339–27	the great fact that God is the o· Mind ;
o	344– 2	the o· absolute Life and Soul,
	344–21	o· one which should be presented
	345–19	the o· feasible evidence that
	346–13	we are harmonious o as we cease to
	349–27	o· as thought is educated up to
	350– 2	as something and almost the o· thing,
	359– 8	whose o· objection to this method was,
	359–15	is palpable o· to spiritual sense,
	359–17	which cognize o· that which is the
	361–21	o· to give a clearer and fuller expression
	361–29	o· when it is understood,
p	371–19	the o· way out of this condition.
	372– 2	o· an erroneous mortal belief
	372–23	succeeds for a period o·
	376–20	o· what that so-called mind expresses.
	379– 4	finds o· effects, where the
	379–11	o· a stream of warm water was trickling
	380–17	The body is affected o· with the belief of
	382– 3	and having o· human approval for
	382–30	o· abandoned me to more hopeless suffering
	383–26	o· prove the illusive physical effect of
	384–11	and man has o· to enter his protest
	387–31	not o· from temptation, but
	388– 6	o· because it knows less of material law.
	389–11	destroyed o· by the better results of
	392– 3	O· while fear or sin remains can it
	392– 8	The o· course is to take antagonistic
	392–25	Admitting o· such conclusions as you
	393– 4	o· because mortal mind is ignorant of
	394– 6	the o· real recuperative power.
	394–25	the o· refuge from fatal chances?
	399–15	If Mind is the o· actor, how can mechanism be
	399–26	o· a false sense of matter.
	400– 9	o· as they forsake discord,
	401–14	o· feels and sees materially.
	401–21	The o· effect produced by medicine is
	402–18	The material body manifests o· what
	403–13	can be healed o· by the divine Mind.
	404–11	you can destroy them o· by
	406–29	destroyed o· by Mind's mastery of the body.
	407– 8	conquered o· by a mighty struggle.
	407–31	o· because its method of madness is
	408–11	o· so many distinctly defined
	410– 8	the o· true God,— John 17 : 3.
	413– 2	the o· Mind, does not produce pain
	413–17	o· for the purpose of keeping the
	415– 2	Immortal Mind is the o· cause ;
	415–14	They o· render mortal mind . . . less fearful,
	416–20	This materialism of parent and child is o·
	416–28	o· what is best for them to know.
	419–28	for God is the o· power.
	420– 8	they need o· to know that error cannot

only

p 420–11 for if they will *o·* accept Truth,
420–25 if they *o·* realize that divine Love gives
421– 1 *o·* as the insane suffer,
421– 1 The *o·* difference is, that insanity
423–30 *o·* the substance of thought which forms them.
423–31 They are *o·* phenomena of the mind of
427–29 should have been his first and *o·* resort.
428–32 understanding of God as the *o·* Life.
433–11 *o·* the evidence of Personal Sense
434–27 The *o·* valid testimony in the case
434–32 and amenable to Spirit *o·*.
435– 2 God Himself and Man's *o·* lawgiver!
435–25 Mortal Man can suffer *o·* for his sin.
435–31 The *o·* jurisdiction to which
439–23 *o·* to fasten upon him an offence
440–21 God, who sentences *o·* for sin.
t 444–14 not *o·* towards differing forms of religion
445–29 and caring *o·* for the fees.
449–25 meet *o·* to separate
449–28 *O·* virtue is a rebuke to vice.
449–31 is a Scientist *o·* in name.
451–11 They must not *o·* seek, but strive,
454–32 *o·* human auxiliaries to aid in bringing
456– 7 the *o·* success of the students of
458–29 that Christ's way is the *o·* one
461– 8 *o·* by those who are morally advanced
461–11 *O·* by the illumination of the
462–10 to practise Truth's teachings *o·* in part,
r 466–22 Soul or Spirit means *o·* one Mind,
468–22 God, is the *o·* real substance.
469–14 God, good, is the *o·* Mind,
470–15 evil can *o·* seem to be real
471–20 is the *o·* fact of creation.
472– 1 teaches man that God is the *o·* Life,
472– 7 *o·* with that which is harmonious
472–27 Therefore the *o·* reality of
476–12 the *o·* and eternal verities of man.
478–26 That *o·* is real which reflects God.
479–22 the *o·* facts are Spirit and its
480– 6 *o·* the darkness of vacuity
481– 8 Through spiritual sense *o·*,
483– 3 but *o·* relieve suffering temporarily,
485– 8 *o·* soon to disappear because of their
489–24 the *o·* source of evil or error.
490–16 Our *o·* need is to know this
491–12 *o·* by acknowledging the supremacy of
493–25 these propositions can *o·* seem real and
494–12 *o·* for a select number or for a
g 501–11 which angels could *o·* whisper
502–25 *beginning* is employed to signify *the o·*,
505–11 ideas of Spirit apparent *o·* as Mind,
508– 2 *o·* as the divine Mind is All
508– 5 The *o·* intelligence or substance of a
509–18 gives gleams of the infinite *o·*,
510–29 Science reveals *o·* one Mind,
512–24 *o·* through the spiritual senses.
517–11 His personality can *o·* be reflected,
517–19 The *o·* proper symbol of God as
520– 6 can repeat *o·* an infinitesimal part
529–23 enters into the metaphor *o·* as evil.
530–22 saying, . . . *O·* admit that I am real,
538–21 evil is brought into view *o·* as
540–15 *o·* that Truth may annihilate all
543– 4 *o·* mortal man and not the real man,
546–15 *o·* through the corporeal senses,
547–24 *o·* by this understanding can truth be
548–11 *o·* as the clouds of corporeal sense roll away.
554– 1 It can *o·* be replied, that
555–18 *O·* impotent error would seek to
556–11 *o·* to go out at last forever;
556–31 infant babe, *o·* a few hours old,
ap 560–26 not *o·* obscured the light of the ages, but
565–25 this *o·* impelled the idea to rise to
572– 1 *o·* those who have washed their robes
gl 582–19 God is the *o·* creative power.
584–13 *o·* to be fettered by another,
585–21 the *o·* error of which is limitation;
588–21 divine Principle; the *o·* Ego.
591–15 hears, tastes, and smells *o·* in belief.
591–16 MIND. The *o·* I, or Us; the *o·* Spirit,
594–20 that *o·* which is perfect,
596–17 the *o·* fit preparation for admission to
597– 5 if *o·* he appeared unto men to fast.

ontology

s 129–21 abandon pharmaceutics, and take up *o·*,
t 460– 3 *O·* is defined as "the science of the
g 556–25 *O·* receives less attention than physiology.

onward

f 225– 7 bears *o·* freedom's banner.
240–18 Mortals move *o·* towards good or evil
b 323– 7 we are helped *o·* in the march towards
323–10 Then we push *o·*, until boundless thought

opacity

s 117–25 because of *o·* to the true light,

opaque

f 242–15 Self-love is more *o·* than a solid body.
b 295–19 the glass is less *o·* than the walls.

open

pr 2–27 Shall we plead for more at the *o·* fount,
10–15 Spiritual attainments *o·* the door to
13– 3 It is the *o·* fount which cries,
15– 6 Closed to error, it is *o·* to Truth,
a 24– 7 *o·* the way for C. S. to be understood,
sp 76– 4 with eyes *o·* only to that wonder,
s 117– 1 term *individuality* is also *o·* to objections,
ph 165– 3 that eating this fruit would *o·* man's eyes
171–13 is no longer an *o·* question,
f 216– 9 Spirituality lays *o·* siege to materialism.
220– 1 We hear it said: "I exercise daily in the *o·* air.
220– 5 Such admissions ought to *o·* people's eyes to
224–25 Will you *o·* or close the door upon this angel
b 326–21 your Father will *o·* the way.
p 366–30 If we would *o·* their prison doors
433–30 can *o·* wide those prison doors
t 444– 2 these very failures may *o·* their blind eyes.
450–10 *o·* to the approach and recognition of Truth.
451–24 He feels morally obligated to *o·* the eyes of
r 491–23 goes on, whether our eyes are closed or *o·*.
k 499– * *I have set before thee an o· door,* — *Rev.* 3 : 8.
g 511–21 in the *o·* firmament of heaven. — *Gen.* 1 : 20.
511–29 which fly . . . in the *o·* firmament of heaven,
514–12 Undisturbed it lies in the *o·* field,
530–20 and saying, . . . "I can *o·* your eyes.
535–16 When will man pass through the *o·* gate of
552–18 They must peck *o·* their shells with C. S.,
ap 558– 6 had in his hand a little book *o·* : — *Rev.* 10 : 2.
559– 1 *o·* for all to read and understand.
570–30 Many are willing to *o·* the eyes of the
572–15 *o·* the seven seals of error with Truth,
575–26 Northward, its gates *o·* to the North Star,
577–24 Its gates *o·* towards light and glory
gl 579– * *I have set before thee an o· door,* — *Rev.* 3 : 8.

opened

pref xi–28 *o·* the Massachusetts Metaphysical College
a 43–18 *o·* a new era for the world.
48–19 "He *o·* not his mouth." — *Isa.* 53 : 7.
49– 3 *o·* the eyes of their understanding.
sp 99–11 *o·* the door of the human understanding.
ph 193–13 In about ten minutes he *o·* his eyes
p 434–16 When the case for Mortal Man . . . is *o·*,
g 530–15 then your eyes shall be *o·* : — *Gen.* 3 : 5.
ap 564–18 Jesus "*o· not his mouth.*" — *Isa.* 53 : 7.
570–11 and the earth *o·* her mouth, — *Rev.* 12 : 16.
571–28 he has *o·* wide the gates of glory,
gl 597–14 *o·* the sepulchre with divine Science,

openeth

a 50– 2 so he *o·* not his mouth." — *Isa.* 53 : 7.
k 499– * *He that o·, and no man shutteth* ; — *Rev.* 3 : 7.
499– * *and shutteth, and no man o·* ; — *Rev.* 3 : 7.
gl 579– * *He that o·, and no man shutteth* ; — *Rev.* 3 : 7.
579– * *and shutteth, and no man o·* ; — *Rev.* 3 : 7.

opening

ph 187–13 *o·* and closing for the passage of the blood,
f 221–23 These truths, *o·* his eyes,
ap 560– 2 In the *o·* of the sixth seal, typical of

openly

pr 13– 7 secretly yearning and *o·* striving
13–12 and our Father, . . . will reward us *o·*
15– 2 shall reward thee *o·*." — *Matt.* 6 : 6.

opens

sp 90–26 and *o·* it wide towards immortality.
ph 174–14 Whoever *o·* the way in C. S.
p 434–20 and *o·* the argument for the defence :
r 495–12 the prison doors to such as are bound,
g 506–20 even as He *o·* the petals of a holy purpose

operate

p 399– 9 not a secretion nor combination can *o·*, apart from

operating

ph 185– 9 *o·* through the power of the

operation

basis of
p 423–19 making Mind his basis of *o·*
from the
pref xi–10 from the *o·* of divine Principle,
of matter
s 150–28 by the *o·* of matter,
ph 171–20 ejection by the *o·* of matter.
perfection of
s 149–11 The rule and its perfection of *o·*
performed the
s 159–18 would have performed the *o·* without ether.

operation

surgical

s	159– 2	to perform a needed surgical o·
ph	198–18	caustic or croton oil, or by a surgical o·.
g	528–17	in order to perform a surgical o· on him

s	123–27	The o· of this Principle indicates
	159–22	and not from the disease or the o·.
b	272–24	attest the divine origin and o· of C. S.
o	346–27	the tooth, the o·, and the forceps are unchanged.
g	545–25	they could not apprehend the nature and o· of
	557– 1	and repeated this o· daily, until

operations

f	252– 9	A knowledge of error and of its o·
t	464– 7	to establish the stately o· of C. S.,
g	512–27	Ignorant of the origin and o· of mortal mind,
	553–23	appearance of its method in finite forms and o·.

operator

p	402–24	The o· would make his subjects believe that

ophis

gl	594– 1	(o·, in Greek ; *nacash*, in Hebrew).

opiates

p	415–11	That is why o· relieve inflammation.
	415–13	O· do not remove the pain in any scientific

opinion

s	137–14	Jesus completely eschewed the narrow o·
	163– 8	said : "I declare my conscientious o·,
f	202–31	Common o· admits that a man may
b	306–17	and this is the general religious o· of mankind,
o	341–11	In C. S. mere o· is valueless
	342– 3	proof and demonstration, instead of o· and
	355–23	an o· wholly due to a misapprehension

opinions

beliefs and

gl	590– 5	mortality ; beliefs and o· ;

differing

t	444–16	to those who hold these differing o·.

false

p	403–18	producing on mortal body the results of false o· ;

human

(*see* human)

individual

ph	197–27	until individual o· improve

majority of

ph	178– 6	controlled by the majority of o·,

minority of

ph	178– 6	minority of o· in the sick-chamber.

mortal

b	273–29	conflicting mortal o· and beliefs
p	390–15	destroy the false process of mortal o·
	399–27	The one Mind, God, contains no mortal o·.

persons or

t	456–18	Science makes no concessions to persons or o·.

popular

a	24–18	popular o· in regard to predestination and

such

p	424–18	such o· as may alarm or discourage,

these

s	112–11	these o· may have occasional gleams of

two

f	236–30	While age is halting between two o·

weight of

p	396–20	overwhelming weight of o· on the wrong side,

gl	595–18	thoughts, beliefs, o·, knowledge;

opium

sp	90–20	O· and hashish eaters mentally travel far
p	406–29	alcoholic drinks, tobacco, tea, coffee, o·,
	416–12	when the soporific influence of the o· is

opponent

o	359–29	A Christian Scientist and an o· are like

opponents

a	18–12	and he refuted all o· with his healing power.
s	134–10	the hatred of the o· of Christianity,
o	344–12	the o· of a demonstrable Science
	349–32	the o· of C. S. believe substance to be
	354–12	On the other hand, the Christian o· of C. S.
	354–30	The o· of divine Science must be charitable,
t	444–24	part from these o· as did Abraham

opportunities

f	238–15	Unimproved o· will rebuke us when we

opportunity

a	21–19	paths have diverged . . . and we have little o· to
an	105–23	to commit fresh atrocities as o· occurs
f	232–32	neither place nor o· in Science for error
c	266–15	for "man's extremity is God's o·."
b	271–27	o· now, as aforetime, to learn and to practise
	276–18	ceases to be any o· for sin and death.
g	537–30	would imply that God withheld from man the o·

oppose

s	144–25	the old schools still o· it.
	145–25	Other methods undertake to o· error with error,
b	273–22	it would o· the supremacy of Spirit,
	278– 6	The material senses o· this, but there are no
r	484–16	Drugs and hygiene o· the supremacy of the

opposed

s	111– 4	sensuous reason of the human mind, to be o· to
	114– 4	meaning by this term the flesh o· to Spirit,
	119–23	because it is o· to the nature of Spirit, God.
	134– 3	truth is still o· with sword and spear.
	139–29	theosophy, and agnosticism are o· to C. S.,
	151–25	The human mind is o· to God
ph	192–20	you can have no power o· to God,
	194–13	Every theory o· to this
f	225– 3	Whatever enslaves man is o· to the
b	273–32	when it is o· promptly and persistently by C. S.
	305–21	as o· to the Science of spiritual reflection,
	338–21	when matter, . . . stood o· to Spirit.
p	382– 1	o· to the harmonies of Spirit,
	387–12	assurances of immortality, o· to mortality.
	392– 9	o· to the health, holiness, and harmony of
	406–20	Error is o· to Life.
g	522–14	It records pantheism, o· to the
	525– 3	the validity of matter is o·,
	530– 4	forever o· to mortal, material sense.
	534–17	called *energy* and o· to Spirit.
	545–12	notion of a material universe is utterly o· to
ap	569– 5	overcome the mortal belief in a power o· to
gl	580– 6	a material belief, o· to the one Mind, or Spirit ;
	580–10	o· to the great reality of spiritual existence
	583– 4	suppositions . . . o· to the Science of being.
	585– 9	spiritual evidence o· to material sense ;

opposer

gl	580–15	the o· of Truth, termed error ;

opposes

f	224–32	supposed power, which o· itself to God
o	357–25	If what o· God is real,
gl	580–28	An adversary is one who o·, denies,

opposing

sp	93–16	evil is the o· error and not the truth of
p	380–30	to believe . . . that God endows this o· power
	437–20	Here the o· counsel, False Belief,

opposite (noun)

demoralized

p	407–25	instead of its demoralized o·.

direct

f	249–31	He is the direct o· of material sensation,

exact

b	295–27	the exact o· of real Mind, or Spirit.
g	521–28	which is the exact o· of scientific truth
	523– 7	presenting the exact o· of Truth,

immortality's

gl	580–19	ADAM. . . . immortality's o·, mortality ;

its

a	40–13	If the saying is true, . . . its o· is also true,
f	229–24	If . . . its o·, health, must be evil,
c	261– 1	we find its o·, matter.
b	282– 7	The real Life, or Mind, and its o·,
	282–32	inversion infers from error its o·, Truth,
r	467–32	cannot be learned from its o·, matter.
g	524–28	Could Spirit evolve its o·, matter,
	547–18	Darwin's theory,— that Mind produces its o·,
	550–10	nor can Spirit be developed through its o·.
	550–26	supplies no instance of one species producing its o·.
	551– 4	it cannot produce its o· in quality

just the

b	321– 1	an interpretation which is just the o· of the true,

matter's

b	293–27	and point to matter's o·,

of clairvoyance

sp	85– 2	This Mind-reading is the o· of clairvoyance.

of God

b	282–28	the fall of man or the o· of God
g	554–20	Jesus defined this o· of God and His
gl	591–13	the o· of God ;
	592– 3	and therefore the o· of God, or good ;

of good

sp	72–22	evil, the suppositional o· of good,
r	480–20	It is the o· of good
gl	579–16	o· of good,— of God and His creation ;

of Himself

gl	583–25	could not create. . . an element the o· of Himself.

of infinity

gl	585–22	limitation ; finity ; the o· of infinity.

of Life

gl	584–10	the unreal and untrue ; the o· of Life.

of life

b	278–29	error, because it is the o· of life,

of Love

gl	580–17	the o· of Love, called hate ;

of materiality

ph	171– 4	the spiritual o· of materiality,

opposite (noun)
of matter
gl 583–23　o· of matter and evil, which have no Principle ;
of mind
gl 584–19　the o· of mind, termed matter,
of Science
r 471– 6　o· of Science, and the evidence before the
of Spirit
b 278–10　the o· of Spirit.
o 359–17　that which is the o· of Spirit.
gl 580– 4　o· of Spirit and His creations ;
591–12　the o· of Spirit ;
592– 3　the o· of Spirit, and therefore the
594– 5　the first claim that there is an o· of Spirit,
of themselves
a 20–18　he taught mortals the o· of themselves,
of the real
b 277–25　and the o· of the real is not divine,
337–27　the o· of the real or the spiritual
of Truth
s 108–14　the o· of Truth, — called error,
ph 177–20　But a lie, the o· of Truth, cannot name the
b 307– 4　*serpent*, insists still upon the o· of Truth,
g 523– 7　presenting the exact o· of Truth,
545–19　vague and hypothetical, the o· of Truth ;
gl 584–18　the o· of Truth ; a belief in sin, sickness,
591–12　the o· of Truth ;
594– 2　a lie ; the o· of Truth, named error ;
supposititious
p 368– 2　a supposititious o· of the highest right.
r 469–15　the supposititious o· of infinite Mind
Truth's
p 367–32　Truth's o·, has no might.
very
a 53– 8　reputation of Jesus was the very o· of his

pref viii–11　and matter is Spirit's o·.
ph 168– 5　gives preponderance to the o·.
b 278–11　Spirit can have no o·.
287–27　the objective supposition of Spirit's o·.
r 480– 4　the o· of the something of Spirit.
g 545–19　yet this o·, in its false view of God and man,
gl 590– 7　the o· of spiritual Truth and understanding.
591– 3　as the o· of the one Spirit,

opposite (adj.)
sp 74–14　persons in such o· dreams
74–25　when we are in the o· hemisphere?
74–27　the gulf which divides two such o· conditions
75–28　the link between their o· beliefs
81–12　the o· assertion, that he is mortal,
83–30　are distinctly o· standpoints,
88–22　Excite the o· development, and he blasphemes.
92–28　This belief tends to support two o· powers,
an 104–17　wrongness of the o· so-called action,
s 154–21　prevented through the o· understanding.
161– 9　while an o· mental state might produce
ph 171–28　The o· truth, that intelligence and life are
195–10　those very senses, trained in an o· direction.
f 205–26　leads human thought into o· channels
207–30　the o· discord, which bears no
213–14　an o· attraction towards the finite,
215– 8　from the very necessity of their o· natures.
239–28　Those two o· sources never mingle
252–31　Spirit, bearing o· testimony, saith :
c 266–21　The o· persecutions of material sense,
b 280–26　the o· error of many minds.
285–12　the o· natures of Spirit and matter,
286–28　(by the supposition of o· qualities)
300–17　These o· qualities are the tares and wheat,
311–19　is directly o· to the immortal reality of being.
315–11　the o· and false views of the people
o 350– 5　C. S. takes exactly the o· view.
352– 8　whereas the Jews took a diametrically o· view.
b 379–18　Then let her learn the o· statement of Life
380–29　to believe that there is a power o· to God,
385–30　would produce the o· result.
388–14　another admission in the o· direction,
389–11　by the better results of Mind's o· evidence.
389–20　cannot annul these regulations by an o· law
417–31　how divine Mind can cure by o· thoughts.
t 448–24　pursuit of instructions o· to absolute C. S.
457–30　and there must and can be no o· rule.
g 521–13　should look away from the o· supposition
521–25　the o· error, a material view of creation,
526– 5　This o· declaration, . . . contradicts the
(see also **belief**)

oppositely
a 52– 7　their senses testified o·,

opposites
imaginary
r 479–24　the imaginary o· of light,
these
b 282–20　At no point can these o· mingle or unite.
two
o 356–13　he spoke of flesh and Spirit as the two o·,

opposites
unites such
f 229–10　belief which unites such o· as
――――
sp 74–22　sickness and health, are o·,
86–11　O· come from contrary directions,
ph 191–28　senses may fancy affinities with their o· ;
b 270– 5　Matter and Mind are o·.
277– 9　o·, evil and matter, are mortal error,
g 539– 9　if they produce their o·,
gl 594–23　the o· of God ; errors ;

opposition
debate and
p 434– 8　After much debate and o·,
direct
f 228– 1　healing in direct o· to them
b 273–26　in direct o· to material laws.
mental
p 390–30　Meet . . . disease with as powerful mental o·
g 534–24　There will be greater mental o·
met with
r 483–25　this Science has met with o· ;
no
f 253–20　Matter can make no o· to
usual
s 114–32　Apart from the usual o· to everything new,
――――
s 131– 8　Hence the o· of sensuous man to the Science of
ph 170–20　always in o·, never in obedience, to physics.
f 224–19　o· from church, state laws, and the press,
b 329–30　the more intense the o· to spirituality,
p 395– 3　They should plead in o· to the testimony of the
r 483–26　it ought to receive aid, not o·,
gl 595–25　Ungodliness. *O·* to the divine Principle and

oppressed
p 373–24　and you relieve the o· organ.

oppression
f 225–20　but o· neither went down in blood, nor
227–15　cannot fail to foresee the doom of all o·.
t 451– 5　must renounce aggression, o· and the pride of
gl 589–14　sensuality ; envy ; o· ; tyranny.

oppressive
s 151–14　from the awful and o· bondage
161–19　o· state statutes touching medicine
f 227– 4　even as o· laws are disputed

optic
ph 194–11　and paralysis of the o· nerve

optical
s 122–15　The o· focus is another proof of the

optics
s 111–16　even as the explanation of o· rejects
p 400–24　even as in o· we see painted on the retina
ap 572–27　o· are inadequate to take in so wonderful a

oracles
sp 78–13　and accept them as o·?

orally
t 460–27　and she had to do this o· through the

orator
sp 89–14　If one believes that he cannot be an o·

orb
ph 188–30　human eye knows not where the o· of day is,
189–12　when the o· of day disappears,

orbit
sp 90– 6　earth's o· and the imaginary line called the
s 124–23　launched the earth in its o·
g 522– 9　and as revolving in an o· of his own.

ordain
s 122–11　so-called senses . . . o· certain sections of

ordained
f 221–19　never o· a law that fasting should be a means
b 273–21　God never o· a material law

ordeal
a 48–14　the exalting o· of sin's revenge on its destroyer

order
astronomical
s 121–28　thus indicated, astronomical o· imitates the
disorder and
p 402–30　Science cannot produce both disorder and o·.
divine
(see **divine**)
follows the
ap 568– 9　The narrative follows the o· used in Genesis.
law and
sp 97– 3　They will maintain law and o·,
of being
b 275–10　To grasp the reality and o· of being
of celestial being
b 337–17　perfection is the o· of celestial being
of Christian Science
g 508–28　The third stage in the o· of C. S. is

order

of creation
  g 508–22   in the ascending *o·* of creation.
of divine Science
  b 334–18   exist in the eternal *o·* of divine Science,
  336–29   in the *o·* of divine Science, God and man
of generation
  a 29–21   material law and its *o·* of generation,
of genus
  b 277–16   the *o·* of genus and species is preserved
of heaven
  s 118–31   natural *o·* of heaven comes down to earth.
of matter
  g 552–26   the *o·* of matter to be the order of mortal mind.
of mortal mind
  g 552–26   the order of matter to be the *o·* of mortal mind.
of Science
  s 123– 7   which reverses the *o·* of Science
  f 240–10   In the *o·* of Science, in which the Principle is
of this allegory
  g 531– 2   The *o·* of this allegory —the belief that everything
of wisdom
  m 62–28   the *o·* of wisdom would be reversed.
primal
  s 135– 7   but unfolds the primal *o·*,
scientific
  s 123–28   the scientific *o·* and continuity of being.
this
  an 100–14   Under this *o·* a commission was appointed,
  b 277–19   Error relies upon a reversal of this *o·*,

  c 255– 5   changing chaos into *o·* and discord into the
  b 277–22   even the *o·* of material so-called science.
  p 437–21   False Belief, called C. S. to *o·*

order in — that

  a 51–10   in *o·* that he might furnish the proof of
  sp 91–23   in *o·* that the spiritual facts may be
  c 265– 8   in *o·* that sin and mortality may be put off.
  p 428– 9   in *o·* that the spiritual facts of being may
  g 506–21   in *o·* that the purpose may appear.
  ap 564–22   in *o·* that the false claim of
  565–10   in *o·* that the man Jesus, . . . might never

order in — to

  pref xii–21   in *o·* to elucidate her Idealism.
  pr 3–10   in *o·* to receive His blessing,
  11–11   in *o·* to compel this progress.
  11–23   in *o·* to gain holiness ;
  15–14   In *o·* to pray aright, we must
  a 26–20   in *o·* to show the learner the way by practice
  40–32   but in *o·* to enter into the kingdom,
  47–24   in *o·* to raise himself in popular estimation.
  52–15   in *o·* to unite in putting to shame and death
  m 58– 7   should be concordant in *o·* to blend properly.
  sp 75– 3   in *o·* to reappear
  78–19   in *o·* to be omnipresent.
  83– 8   in *o·* to escape the error of these latter days.
  an 105– 3   in *o·* to restrain crime,
  s 131– 4   in *o·* to be in harmony with God,
  155–21   in *o·* to heal a single case of disease.
  ph 165–18   in *o·* to remember what has hurt you,
  169–14   in *o·* to avoid it.
  172–16   in *o·* to become man.
  181–26   in *o·* to satisfy the sick
  f 203–31   does not kill a man in *o·* to give him
  212–26   in *o·* to convey thought,
  220– 2   said : . . . in *o·* to overcome a predisposition to
  243–11   in *o·* to confirm and repeat the
  248–11   in *o·* to perfect his conception.
  c 258–11   in *o·* to be immortal.
  260–19   in *o·* to improve their models.
  b 295–10   in *o·* to escape from the mortality of
  295–22   in *o·* to become a better transparency for Truth.
  296–17   in *o·* to part with them.
  323–13   In *o·* to apprehend more,
  o 346–12   in *o·* to prove the somethingness
  349–20   in *o·* to grasp the meaning of this Science.
  361–24   must be correct in *o·* to be Science
  p 366– 3   In *o·* to cure his patient, the metaphysician
  369–15   in *o·* to discover some means of healing it.
  375–13   hypnotist dispossesses . . . in *o·* to control
  377– 6   Invalids flee to tropical climates in *o·* to
  384–12   enter his protest . . . in *o·* to annul it.
  404– 1   in *o·* to judge the case according to C. S.
  413–15   in *o·* to make it thrive more vigorously
  413–23   in *o·* to keep it sweet as the new-blown flower.
  421– 8   in *o·* to remove its beliefs,
  424– 7   in *o·* to change the notion of chance
  t 449– 6   in *o·* to continue in well doing.
  451–22   in *o·* to defend himself from the influence of
  453–18   not in *o·* to injure, but in *o·* to bless
  455– 7   in *o·* to teach this Science of healing.
  455– 9   in *o·* to walk over the waves of error
  r 482–14   Is it important . . . in *o·* to heal the sick?
  483– 8   In *o·* to heal by Science, you must not
  486– 8   in *o·* to possess immortal consciousness.

order in — to

  g 522–21   in *o·* to create man.
  528–16   in *o·* to perform a surgical operation
  532– 2   in *o·* to create the rest of the human family?
  540–10   must be stirred in *o·* to purify the stream.
  551–30   in *o·* to propagate its species,
  ap 560–20   in *o·* to classify it correctly.
  gl 598– 9   in *o·* to unfold spiritual thoughts.

ordered

  an 100–12   In 1784, the French government *o·* the
  g 528– 6   It cannot be true that man was *o·* to

orderly

  p 395–19   The nurse should be cheerful, *o·*,

orders

  s 138–19   under as direct *o·* now, as they were then,

ordinary

  a 24–16   the *o·* theological views of atonement
  sp 99–13   The *o·* teachings are material
  an 105–30   from *o·* medical practice to C. S.
  s 128–11   ability to exceed their *o·* capacity.
  139–29   opposed to C. S., as they are to *o·* religion ;
  156–12   Believing then somewhat in the *o·* theories of
  159–31   the *o·* physician is liable to increase disease
  161–24   *o·* practitioner, examining bodily symptoms,
  p 379– 5   where the *o·* physician looks for causes.
  385– 5   exposures which *o·* people could not endure.
  t 443– 4   under *o·* circumstances a resort to
  443–16   *o·* physical methods of medical treatment,
  r 483–23   the *o·* scientific schools, which wrestle with
  g 537–25   the *o·* historian interprets it literally.
  548–31   besides the *o·* process of generation,

organ

  sp 88–20   Excite the *o·* of veneration or religious faith,
  s 151–31   claims to govern every *o·* of the mortal body,
  ph 191– 2   Matter is not the *o·* of infinite Mind.
  p 373–24   and you relieve the oppressed *o·*.
  373–25   disabled *o·* will resume its healthy functions.
  377–23   the morbid or excited action of any *o·*.

organic

  sp 74– 4   must be free from *o·* bodies ;
  74–16   belief of still living in an *o·*, material body.
  s 125– 3   now considered the best condition for *o·*
  125– 6   Neither *o·* inaction nor overaction is
  126– 1   its supposed *o·* action or supposed existence.
  149–21   remarked. . . mind can never cure *o·* difficulties."
  149–23   The author has cured what is termed *o·* disease
  160–10   *o·* action and secretion of the viscera.
  162–25   I have restored . . . where disease was *o·*.
  162–25   C. S. heals *o·* disease as surely as
  ph 176–21   Should all cases of *o·* disease be treated by a
  177– 1   Human mind produces what is termed *o·* disease
  180–31   dissolve a tumor, or cure *o·* disease,
  b 296–11   not the death of *o·* matter,
  309–28   *o·* animal or vegetable life,
  309–31   Therefore it is never structural nor *o·*,
  p 377–24   what are termed *o·* diseases
  428–30   author has healed hopeless *o·* disease,
  t 450–32   belief of . . . animal nature, and *o·* life,
  r 469–26   no *o·* construction can give it healing

organically

  sp 83–22   to suppose that life is . . . . *o·* spiritual.

organism

  an 100– 5   which he said could be exerted by one living *o·*
  s 108–31   all the *o·* and action of the mortal body,
  f 211–25   If it is true . . . that the material *o·*
  p 393–28   constituting the visual *o·*.
  g 549– 9   Creatures of lower forms of *o·*
  555– 5   brings the physical *o·* under the yoke of disease.

organization

and decomposition
  r 488–26   not at the mercy of *o·* and decomposition,
and time
  f 249–19   *O·* and time have nothing to do with Life.
growth and
  g 548–24   his material sense of animal growth and *o·*,
material
  ph 165–10   material *o·* and non-intelligent matter.
  p 429–19   If man did not exist before the material *o·*
  g 509– 4   dependent upon no material *o·*.
  524–20   How then could a material *o·* become the basis of
physical
  ph 170–30   in either case dependent upon his physical *o·*,

  p 401–25   Would the drug remove paralysis, affect *o·*,

organizations

  s 124– 5   When this human belief lacks *o·* to support it,
  162–24   and healthy *o·* have been established
  f 239– 5   Take away wealth, fame, and social *o·*,
  g 554–30   less sickly than those possessing higher *o·*,

organs

- p 384–32 the entire functions and o· of the
- 415–23 all the o· of the human system,
- ap 572–27 Not through the material visual o· for seeing,
- gl 585– 1 Not o· of the so-called corporeal senses,

Orient

- ap 575–28 star seen by the Wisemen of the O·,

Oriental

- p 362– 6 as if to interrupt the scene of O· festivity.
- 364–15 a special sign of O· courtesy.

Oriental Witchcraft

- p 441–22 Hypnotism, O· W·, and Esoteric Magic

origin

above his
- f 246– 8 by no means a material germ rising . . . above his o·.

and birth
- a 30–11 Had his o· and birth been wholly apart from

and enlightenment
- g 556–17 Did the o· and enlightenment of the race

and facts
- r 491–12 the true o· and facts of being,

and governor
- r 480–11 God, the o· and governor of all

and operations
- g 512–27 Ignorant of the o· and operations of mortal

and ultimate
- r 487– 3 Life is the o· and ultimate of man,

basis nor
- sp 71–28 having no scientific basis nor o·,

describe the
- g 552–32 Naturalists describe the o· of mortal and

divine
- (see **divine**)

explaining the
- b 292–19 Explaining the o· of material man

has no
- o 347– 5 whatever is mortal or discordant has no o·,

his
- a 30–11 Had his o· and birth been wholly apart from
- m 63– 6 His o· is not, like that of mortals,
- ph 171–17 Mistaking his o· and nature, man believes

human
- b 305–29 These mortal dreams are of human o·,
- g 553–21 to account for human o·,

learning the
- sp 88–10 By learning the o· of each.

man's
- c 262–28 a false sense of man's o·.
- g 539–17 God condemned this lie as to man's o·
- 553– 4 a higher and purer contemplation of man's o·.

material
- s 127–28 It has a spiritual, and not a material o·.
- g 534– 1 the belief in the material o· of man
- 549–32 a belief in the material o· of man,

material in
- g 540–30 Material in o· and sense, he brings a

mental
- p 374–18 no argument against the mental o· of

mortal
- ph 169–11 disease has a mental, mortal o·,

of all disease
- ph 169–18 Science not only reveals the o· of all disease

of all things
- f 212–30 its normal action, and the o· of all things

of man
- (see **man**)

of mortals
- g 548–18 Speaking of the o· of mortals,

of sin
- gl 590– 7 the o· of sin, sickness, and death ;

or existence
- b 287– 1 They are without a real o· or existence.
- g 554–12 any knowledge of its o· or existence.

primal
- sp 90– 2 how then can we account for their primal o·?

quantity, and
- t 462–22 to discover their quality, quantity, and o·.

spiritual
- (see **spiritual**)

their
- s 112–14 they . . . remain wholly human in their o·
- p 403–12 both have their o· in the human mind,
- g 553–14 their o· and first introduction."
- 553–30 before they think or know aught of their o·,

without actual
- b 281–23 sin and mortality are without actual o·

- a 25–17 any man whose o· was less spiritual.
- 28–15 Neither the o·, the character, nor the work
- f 215–25 in o·, in existence, and in his relation to God.
- 217– 5 in the o· of harmony.
- b 277–21 asserts . . . that good is the o· of evil.
- 281–10 What is the Ego, whence its o· and what its

origin

- g 529–27 and has neither o· nor support in Truth
- 555–17 is like inquiring into the o· of God,
- gl 580–11 a so-called man, whose o·, substance, and mind

original

- pr 16–15 the o· properly reads,
- a 24– 4 Acquaintance with the o· texts,
- sp 74– 7 the restoration to its o· condition
- 97–20 found in the likeness of Spirit, his o· being.
- s 115–11 into the o· spiritual tongue.
- ph 195–20 Observation, invention, study, and o· thought
- 197– 8 But the price does not exceed the o· cost.
- f 210– 3 the translation of the spiritual o· into the
- 214–22 like the o· "tree of knowledge," — Gen. 2 : 9.
- b 277–14 preserving their o· species,
- 286–13 from first to last by this o· man, Jesus.
- 295–10 and then recover man's o· self
- 305– 6 is not the o·, though resembling it.
- 319–21 taught in the o· language of the Bible
- 320–14 quoted as follows, from the o· Hebrew :
- 320–17 Here the o· text declares plainly the
- 340– 6 the word duty, which is not in the o·,
- o 356–31 Was there o· self-creative sin?
- 361–22 fuller expression of its o· meaning.
- g 506– 3 Objects . . . unlike the o· do not reflect that o·.
- 516– 2 how true, . . . is the reflection to its o·.
- 552–28 results in a return to the o· species.
- gl 579– 6 spiritual sense, which is also their o· meaning.
- 579–15 Error ; a falsity ; the belief in "o· sin,"
- 598– 5 Here the o· word is the same in both cases,

originally

- an 104–24 If . . . a belief o· caused the sickness,
- p 372– 4 What you call matter was o· error
- r 470–18 standard of perfection was o· God and man.

originals

- gl 583– 2 whose better o· are God's thoughts,

originate

- sp 90– 1 or if one animal can o· another,
- f 214–11 The material senses, like Adam, o· in matter
- c 266–27 The evil beliefs which o· in mortals are hell.
- b 275– 4 This shows that matter did not o· in God,
- 318– 9 senses o· and support all that is material,
- 318–31 Intelligence does not o· in numbers,
- r 472–10 Sickness, sin, and death, . . . do not o· in God
- g 543–24 Did man, whom God created . . . o· in an egg?
- 550–30 supposition that Spirit . . . can o· the impure
- 551–23 How can matter o· or transmit mind?

originated

- s 158– 1 profession of medicine o· in idolatry
- b 278–25 if man is material, he o· in matter
- 279– 7 protoplasm never o· in the immortal Mind,
- 307– 1 the deep sleep, in which o· the delusion
- o 357–18 notions about the Divine Being . . . have o· in
- 357–21 must have o· in a false supposition,
- p 416–18 body, which has o· from this material sense
- g 531–15 If, in the beginning, man's body o· in
- gl 585–26 belief that the human race o· materially

originates

- b 269–30 theories I combat. . . (2) that matter o· in Mind,
- 338– 4 opposite belief — that man o· in matter
- p 377–16 Because a belief o· unseen,
- g 543–18 If man is material and o· in an egg,

originating

- c 256–30 A mind o· from a finite or material source
- p 374–10 explanation of disease as o· in human belief
- gl 591–12 mind o· in matter ; the opposite of Truth ;

originator

- sp 89–26 Sound is not the o· of music,

originators

- c 263– 3 They believe themselves to be . . . o· of

origins

- f 213–31 belief in material o· which discard

orthodox

- o 351– 8 a member of the o· Congregational Church
- 358–32 their own accredited and o· pastors,
- r 471–23 subscribed to an o· creed in early youth,

ossification

- p 423–27 O· or any abnormal condition

other (see also other's)

- pref x–25 than that of any o· sanitary method.
- xi– 6 explains that all o· pathological methods are
- pr 9– 1 that we are "not as o· men" — Luke 18 : 11.
- 11–12 Mere legal pardon (and there is no o·,
- a 27– 6 In o· words : Tell John what the
- 27–24 two or three hundred o· disciples
- 30– 2 could give a more spiritual idea. . . than o· men,
- 34– 6 no o· commemoration is requisite,
- 38–22 the fruits of o· people's sins, not of his own.
- 46–16 in o· words, rose even higher in the
- 55– 1 if he entertained any o· sense of being
- m 58–19 on the o· hand, a wandering desire for

other

m 59–14   each partner sustaining the o·,
60–21   and o· considerations, — passion,
65–21   over this as over many o· reforms,
66–25   If one is better than the o·,
66–26   the o· pre-eminently needs good company.
67–23   potent beyond all o· means and methods.
68–14   and to your influence on o· lives.

sp 72– 4   in o· words, mortal, material sense
73– 2   In either case, one does not support the o·.
73– 6   neither the one nor the o· is infinite Spirit,
73–12   Any o· control or attraction of so-called spirit
73–16   electricity or any o· form of matter,
77– 3   Neither do o· mortals . . . at a single bound.
85–29   and not to leave the o· undone." — Matt. 23 : 23.
96–14   on the o· side there will be Science and peace.
97–10   the flight of one and the blow of the o·
98– 7   and no o· sign shall be given.
99–12   None may pick the lock nor enter by some o·

an 101–30   o· than the effect of illusion.
103–12   On the o· hand, Mind-science is wholly
s 109–10   once seen, no o· conclusion can be reached.
112– 9   the Spencerian, or some o· school.
119–10   while to grasp the o· horn of the dilemma
126–16   C. S. on the one hand . . . theology on the o·
126–30   I have had no o· guide
129–20   and so are some o· systems.
132–10   In o· words, he gave his benediction to
132–18   from o· sanitary or religious systems,
135–23   else one or the o· is false and useless ;
135–26   proves the one to be identical with the o·.
138– 2   In o· words, Jesus purposed founding his
140–19   Judaic and o· rituals are but types and
145–15   or reliance on some o· minor curative.
145–16   has this advantage over o· methods,
145–25   O· methods undertake to oppose error with
145–27   towards o· forms of matter or error,
148–19   the one wholly, the o· primarily
154– 3   Disease arises, like o· mental conditions,
156–26   employing no o· means, and she was cured.

ph 167–28   impossible to gain control . . . in any o· way.
160–22   however much we trust a drug or any o·
169–29   Whatever teaches man to have o· laws
169–30   Whatever teaches man to . . , acknowledge o·
177– 9   Neither exists without the o·,
182–10   for one absolutely destroys the o·,
182–11   one or the o· must be supreme
182–14   and despise the o·." — Matt. 6 : 24.
185– 7   o· books were in circulation, which
193–27   for saying : "It was none o· than God and
200–21   in o· words the five senses,

f 201–19   Christian perfection is won on no o· basis.
206– 1   we can have no o· Mind but His,
206– 1   no o· Love, wisdom, or Truth,
206– 2   no o· sense of Life,
207–21   there can be no effect from any o· cause,
208–32   and of o· beliefs included in matter.
212–28   and possibly that o· methods involve so-called
214–30   senses of Soul, and there are no o· real senses.
220– 6   to look in o· directions for cause and cure.
228–20   to acknowledge any o· power is to dishonor God
231–30   governed by his Maker, having no o· Mind,
242–11   It is to know no o· reality
242–11   to have no o· consciousness of life
249–10   Any o· theory of Life, or God, is delusive

c 257–18   infinite Principle, — in o· words, divine Love,
264–18   and needing no o· consciousness.

b 269–25   O· foundations there are none.
269–26   All o· systems . . . are roods shaken by the
270– 6   One is contrary to the o·
270– 7   If one is real, the o· must be unreal.
275– 7   there is no o· might nor Mind,
275–28   or so-called powers, such as matter,
279–14   and one can no more create the o· than
281– 5   When one appears, the o· disappears.
282–22   and the o· a straight line.
285–14   while the o· is non-intelligence.
286–16   In the Saxon and twenty o· tongues
301–10   On the o· hand, the immortal, spiritual man
301–20   belief that man has any o· substance,
304– 8   nor depth, nor any o· creature, — Rom. 8 : 39.
310–28   Spirit, which has no o· existence,
315– 7   and laid no claim to any o·.
315–27   more spiritual than all o· earthly personalities.
323– 5   and to possess no o· consciousness but good.
323–27   the delusion that there are o· minds,
326– 8   not try to climb the hill of Science by some o·
327–13   There is no o· way.
331–20   and there is no o· self-existence.
333– 6   in common with o· Hebrew boys and men,
333– 8   On the o· hand, Christ is not a name so much as
338– 1   heals the sick and sinning as no o· system can.
339– 4   Being destroyed, sin needs no o·
340– 9   In o· words : Let us hear the conclusion of
340–19   man shall have no o· spirit or mind but God,

other

o 348–25   and that of o· persons as well?
349–15   like all o· languages, English is inadequate
354–12   On the o· hand, the Christian opponents of C. S
355–16   The o·, popular religion, declines to admit
358– 7   If . . . one is true, the o· must be false.
360– 4   The o· artist replies :

p 363–28   In the absence of o· proofs,
364–25   On the o· hand, do they show their regard for
369–22   and the o· to be made indestructible.
376– 2   more terrifying than that of most o· diseases.
384–26   neither rheumatism, consumption, nor any o·
385– 2   Florence Nightingale and o· philanthropists
385– 9   energy and endurance surpassing all o· aids,
391–15   Truth, will destroy all o· supposed suffering,
398–15   restored whole, like as the o·." — Matt. 12 : 13.
399–31   In o· words : How can I heal the body, without
403–11   but matter is appealed to in the o·.
413– 9   views of parents and o· persons
413–32   or any o· malady, timorously held in the
414– 9   the same as in o· diseases :
414–14   dementia, hatred, or any o· discord.
421– 4   belief that o· portions of the body are
422–25   and a Christian Scientist in the o·.
424–28   scrofula and o· so-called hereditary diseases,
429– 3   as well as by o· graces of Spirit.

t 443–19   whatever o· systems they fancy will
444– 8   o· Scientists, — their brethren upon whom
444–20   turn to him the o· also." — Matt. 5 : 39.
445–15   will be no desire for o· healing methods.
452–29   On the o· hand, if you had the inclination
457– 2   O· works, which have borrowed from this
457– 6   more . . . than has been accomplished by o· books.
457 22   To pursue o· vocations and
457–31   without exploiting o· means.
458– 2   on the same platform as all o· quackery.
458– 4   one good and the o· evil,
458– 5   one spiritual, the o· material,
459–31   than any o· healer on the globe.

r 467–14   turning to no o· but the one perfect Mind
468–30   in proportion as the o· is recognized.
469–19   claimed no o· Mind and accepted no o·,
471–19   and there is no o· power nor presence.
473–13   who, more than all o· men, has presented
475– 7   blood, bones, and o· material elements.
481– 1   One must hide the o·.
482– 1   In o· cases, use the word sense,
482–30   It can heal in no o· way,
483– 7   Mind transcends all o· power,
483– 8   supersede all o· means in healing.
483–28   does honor God as no o· theory honors Him,
485–24   If thought yields its dominion to o· powers,
490–27   can be obtained in no o· way.
492– 5   In reality there is no o· existence,
493– 1   On the o· hand, C. S. speedily shows
493–23   just as it removes any o· sense of
494–27   The o· is the eternal and real evidence,

g 509 13   Spirit creates no o· than heavenly . . . bodies,
522– 4   If one is true, the o· is false,
523–18   The o· document is called the Jehovistic,
524– 5   and in a thousand o· so-called deities.
531–22   Has man sought out o· creative inventions,
535– 5   the o· to be garnered into heavenly places.
535–12   A belief in other gods, o· creators,
535–13   belief in . . . o· creations must go down
536– 9   there is no o· consciousness.
546–19   seem more obscure than o· portions of the
551–28   Neither can produce the o·.
552– 6   modern geology, and all o· material hypotheses

gl 580– 7   a so-called finite mind, producing o· minds,
591–26   mythology ; error creating o· errors ;
598– 6   as in o· passages in this same chapter
(see also **each, gods**)

other's

m 59– 4   tender solicitude for each o· happiness,
o 356–14   not contributing in any way to each o· happiness

others (see also **others'**)

all

a 25–19   demonstrated more spiritually than all o·
an 106–18   and classify all o· as did St. Paul
s 150–24   and will be to all o· at some future day,
ph 170–23   more than all o· spiritual causation relates
b 318–16   Is the sick man sinful above all o· ?

all the

g 547– 1   one example would authenticate all the o·.

beliefs of

a 53–32   Had he shared the sinful beliefs of o·,

cannot injure

sp 95–13   cannot injure o·, and must do them good.

doing "unto

p 435–21   doing "unto o· as ye would that they should do

faith in

sp 89– 6   Having more faith in o· than in herself,

others

injuring

   t 449–11 than for you to benefit yourself by injuring *o*·.

labors of

   f 238–19 to enter unlawfully into the labors of *o*·.

relieved

   a 25–23 by no means relieved *o*· from giving the

saved

   a 49–29 "He saved *o*· ; himself he cannot — *Matt.* 27 : 42.

say

   p 434– 5 *O*· say, "The law of Christ supersedes *our* laws ;

sins of

   ph 189–13 sins of *o*· should not make good men suffer.
   o 346–15 belief that we suffer from the sins of *o*·.

themselves and

   a 34–22 It helped them to raise themselves and *o*·
   r 494–32 cast fear . . . out of themselves and *o*·

---

   pr 8–17 wise not to try to deceive ourselves or *o*·,
   a 23–24 One kind of faith trusts one's welfare to *o*·.
   29– 3 must grapple with sin in themselves and in *o*·,
   33–12 *breaking* (explaining) it to *o*·,
   38–25 Jesus mapped out the path for *o*·.
   51–21 the works which he did and taught *o*· to do.
   m 69–18 they can educate *o*· spiritually
   sp 75–21 When you can waken yourself or *o*·
   86– 4 Jesus knew, as *o*· did not, that it was not
   99–19 may possess natures above some *o*·
   s 136–16 and *o*·, Jeremias, or one of the — *Matt.* 16 : 14.
   136–30 apprehended their Master better than did *o*· ;
   153–25 We weep because *o*· weep,
   153–26 and we have smallpox because *o*· have it ;
   f 217–15 That scientific methods are superior to *o*·,
   220–24 advised *o*· never to try dietetics for
   234–16 thereby robbing both themselves and *o*·.
   b 297–26 Some thoughts are better than *o*·.
   o 359–31 One says : . . . When *o*· see them as I do,
   p 391–28 be just to yourself and to *o*·.
   424–23 while *o*· are thinking about your patients
   435–10 should result in good to himself as well as to *o*·.
   t 447– 5 attempt to influence the thoughts of *o*·,
   452–20 live it and love it, or he cannot impart it to *o*·.
   453–15 must know himself before he can know *o*·
   461–18 if this be requisite to protect *o*·.
   462– 2 Some . . . assimilate truth more readily than *o*·,
   464– 9 *O*· could not take her place, even if willing
   r 497–26 to do unto *o*· as we would have

others'

   t 455–14 little or no power for *o*· help.

otherwise

   a 38–17 *o*· . . . could not have been done spiritually.
   40–18 for not *o*· could he show us the way
   m 59– 8 compact which might *o*· become unbearable.
   sp 75–24 you can then . . . but not *o*·.
   93–11 If we believe *o*·, we may be sure that
   an 102–28 more likely to be abused . . . than *o*· employed,
   s 120– 1 though it seems *o*· to finite sense.
   134–11 burned, crucified, and *o*· persecuted ;
   ph 168– 8 Mind, which would *o*· outweigh all else.
   b 268– * *Here I stand. I can do no o*· *; so help me God!*
   o 358–11 *O*· it would not be Science,
   p 392–21 unless Science shows you *o*·.
   423– 4 either verbally or *o*·,
   r 477–18 Were it *o*·, man would be annihilated.
   485– 2 If error is necessary to define . . . but not *o*·.
   488–26 *o*· the very worms could unfashion man.
   491–32 Who can rationally say *o*·,
   g 519– 4 How could He be *o*·, since the
   525–25 The corporeal senses declare *o*· ;

ought

   a 19–27 in disobedience to Him, we *o*· to feel no security,
   m 58–26 a wife *o*· not to court vulgar extravagance
   68– 6 We *o*· to weary of the fleeting and false
   sp 73–13 belief, which *o*· to be known by its fruit,
   85–29 "These *o*· ye to have done, — *Matt.* 23 : 23.
   94–10 by our law he *o*· to die, — *John* 19 : 7.
   s 130–28 *o*· we not, contrariwise, to be astounded
   ph 168– 9 when it *o*· to be enlisted on the side of health.
   f 220– 4 Such admissions *o*· to open people's eyes
   248– 6 *o*· to ripen into health and immortality,
   253–26 knowing (as you *o*· to know) that
   b 278–32 Which *o*· to be substance to us,
   299–20 *O*· we not then to judge the knowledge
   o 345–22 *o*· to be able to discern the distinction
   348– 5 *O*· we not, then, to approve
   352–17 *o*· to fear a reality which can harm them
   p 383–30 when it *o*· to be insensibly so
   t 449–20 *o*· to be understood and guarded against.
   r 483–26 it *o*· to receive aid, not opposition,
   485–10 views of error *o*· to be obliterated by Truth.
   g 540–13 but we *o*· to know that God's law

our

   p 438– 3 in *o*· image, after *o*· likeness ; — *Gen.* 1 : 26.
   r 475–23, 24 in *o*· image, after *o*· likeness ; — *Gen.* 1 : 26.
   g 515–11, 12 in *o*· image, after *o*· likeness ; — *Gen.* 1 : 26.
   525–13, 14 Let us make man after *o*· mind and *o*· likeness;

outcome

   f 250–13 man, the *o*· of God, reflects God.
   b 271–25 eternal life, not the death of Jesus, is its *o*·.
   277–12 and cannot be the *o*· of an infinite God,
   p 422–28 the ultimate *o*· of the injury.
   r 466–26 idolatry and ritualism are the *o*· of
   g 555–14 error is neither mind nor the *o*· of Mind.
   ap 577–16 third, Christianity, which is the *o*· of

outgrow

   sp 77–27 Spiritualists would *o*· their beliefs in

outgrowing

   t 452–10 *o*· the old, you should not fear to put on the new.

outgrown

   a 28–12 In conscience, we cannot hold to beliefs *o*· ;
   sp 74–30 never a return to positions *o*·.

outgrowth

   pr 12–26 and not the *o*· of divine Science.
   sp 92–18 is an *o*· of human knowledge
   ph 171–32 supposition that man is a material *o*·
   g 519– 5 the spiritual creation was the *o*·,

outlaw

   an 105– 9 while mortal mind, evil, which is the real *o*·,
   p 381–27 Let us banish sickness as an *o*·,
   435–16 for the agent of those laws is an *o*·,

outline

   f 247–24 in expression, form, *o*·, and color.
   248–23 angular *o*· and deformity of matter models.
   c 263–13 forming deformity when he would *o*· grace
   r 485–25 it cannot *o*· on the body its own

outlined

   ph 196–29 mental state, which is afterwards *o*· on the
   gl 587– 1 a belief that mind is *o*· and limited ;
   591–20 Deity, which outlines but is not *o*·.

outlines

   ph 175– 2 we should efface the *o*· of disease
   191–23 not a leaf unfolds its fair *o*·,
   198–10 *o*· his thought relative to disease,
   c 260– 3 than the sculptor can perfect his *o*· from
   b 298–31 marked with superstitious *o*·,
   gl 591–20 Deity, which *o*· but is not outlined.

outlived

   o 353–13 The age has not wholly *o*· the sense of

outlook

   m 58–13 Never contract the horizon of a worthy *o*·
   b 326–27 Thought assumed a nobler *o*·,

outpouring

   pr 3–21 and for a liberal *o*· of benefactions.
   ap 574–14 spiritual *o*· of bliss and glory,

outraged

   p 440–17 Wherefore, then, in the name of *o*· justice,

outset

   a 21–19 Our paths have diverged at the very *o*·,
   c 260–18 and ensures failure at the *o*·.
   o 357– 3 and knew from the *o*· that man would do.
   g 541–18 ruptures the life . . . of man at the very *o*·.

outshining

   ap 571–30 *o*· sin, sorcery, lust, and hypocrisy.

outside

   m 58–20 incessant amusement *o*· the home circle
   sp 71– 8 *o*· of finite form, which forms only reflect.
   71–23 no proof nor power *o*· of human testimony.
   89– 9 Destroy their belief in *o*· self,
   s 133–28 no life, intelligence, nor substance *o*· of God.
   151– 5 could not possibly create a remedy *o*· of itself,
   ph 195– 5 *O*· of dismal darkness and cold silence he
   f 202–15 *O*· of this Science all is mutable ;
   253–12 (*o*· of erring, mortal, material sense
   b 301–26 supposed standpoint *o*· the focal distance of
   p 382–12 making clean merely the *o*· of the platter.
   396–29 Spirit, *o*· of matter, never in it,
   405–32 and to appeal to divine sources *o*· of themselves.
   441–26 decides . . . that no law *o*· of divine Mind can
   r 476–22 which is *o*· of all material selfhood.
   482–21 the divine idea of God *o*· the flesh.
   489–28 *O*· the material sense of things, all is harmony.
   g 510–16 representation of Soul *o*· the body,
   545–17 *O*· of C. S. all is vague and hypothetical,

outsiders

   s 138–11 cures, which appeared miraculous to *o*·.
   141–21 The *o*· did not then, and do not now,

outstretched

    p 365–14 from the *o·* arm of righteousness?

outward

    pref ix– 3 drinks in the *o·* world through the eyes
    pr 4– 9 *O·* worship is not of itself sufficient to
    s 129–23 instead of accepting only the *o·* sense of things.
    f 254–22 which determines the *o·* and actual.
    g 552–18 peck open their shells with C. S., and look *o·*
    gl 586– 5 Jesus said, thinking of the *o·* vision,

outwardly

    t 464– 5 in which to make herself *o·* known

outweigh

    s 155–20 must mightily *o·* the power of popular belief
    ph 168– 8 which would otherwise *o·* all else.
    p 392– 8 enables truth to *o·* error.

outweighs

    s 149– 3 Mind as far *o·* drugs in the cure of disease

over

    pref xii– 6 During seven years *o·* four thousand students
    pr 5– 2 from demonstrating his power *o·* error.
    5–13 will be full "and running *o·*." — *Luke* 6 : 38.
    7–31 the recollection that we have prayed *o·* it
    14–28 man's dominion *o·* the whole earth.
    17–14 *Truth, Love, o· all, and All.*
    a 24–18 change . . . which has come *o·* popular opinions
    24–30 enabled their Master to triumph *o·* the grave,
    25 15 casts out error, and triumphs *o·* death.
    25–22 Though demonstrating his control *o·* sin and
    26–15 Love gave Jesus authority *o·* sin,
    26–25 his demonstration of power *o·* death.
    28–14 to heal the sick and to triumph *o·* sin.
    30–26 If we have triumphed . . . *o·* the errors of
    31–22 the divine Principle which triumphs *o·* death.
    35–15 They celebrate their Lord's victory *o·* death,
    36–25 gloat *o·* their offences to the last
    39–16 death was not the threshold *o·* which he
    42–16 his final triumph *o·* body and matter,
    43–28 must triumph *o·* all material beliefs
    43–32 Love must triumph *o·* hate.
    44– 1 seal the victory *o·* error and death,
    44–11 the power of Mind *o·* matter,
    45– 7 in his victory *o·* death and the grave.
    45–30 glorified the supremacy of Mind *o·* matter.
    48– 6 held uncomplaining guard *o·* a world
    49–24 to triumph *o·* sin, sickness, death,
    53–22 Like Peter, we should weep *o·* the warning,
    54–15 and triumph *o·* death through Mind,
    m 57–29 until it ceases to sigh *o·* the world
    59–23 After marriage, it is too late to grumble *o·*
    61– 5 The good . . . must have ascendency *o·* the evil
    61– 5 and the spiritual *o·* the animal,
    65–20 There will ensue a fermentation *o·* this
    65–20 as *o·* many other reforms,
    sp 76–20 they will have no power *o·* man,
    79– 9 Science must go *o·* the whole ground,
    80–24 *o·* its substratum, called matter.
    90–20 and gives to matter the precedence *o·* Spirit.
    90–10 through the air and *o·* the ocean.
    an 100– 5 said could be exerted by one . . . *o·* another,
    102–12 no more power *o·* man than *o·* his Maker,
    102–14 has dominion *o·* all the earth
    105– 6 To say . . . no jurisdiction *o·* the carnal or
    105–12 body *o·* which courts hold jurisdiction?
    s 111–13 utilization of the power of Truth *o·* error ;
    117–18 his power *o·* the sick and sinning.
    125–26 mariner will have dominion *o·* the atmosphere
    125–27 *o·* the fish of the sea and the fowls of the air.
    130– 3 discouraged *o·* its slight spiritual prospects.
    131–11 superiority of spiritual *o·* physical power.
    134–30 spiritual power *o·* material resistance.
    137– 6 the victor *o·* sickness, sin, disease, death, and
    139– 5 the triumph of Spirit, Mind, *o·* matter.
    140–11 warring no more *o·* the corporeality,
    142– 5 its power *o·* sickness, sin, and death ;
    142– 7 one of these powers, — the power *o·* sin.
    145–16 this advantage *o·* other methods,
    150–30 the superiority of matter *o·* Mind,
    151–23 it has no control *o·* God's man.
    152–13 one . . . contradicts another *o·* and *o·* again.
    ph 165– 5 man's God-given dominion *o·* the earth.
    166– 6 thus the conscious control *o·* the body is lost.
    166–30 its mastery *o·* sin, disease, and death,
    169– 5 assuring me that danger was *o·*,
    169–16 If we understood the control of Mind *o·* body,
    171–12 Mind's control *o·* the universe,
    175–17 If . . . had tried to tyrannize *o·* our forefathers,
    182–30 To admit that sickness is a condition *o·* which
    188–28 When darkness comes *o·* the earth,
    189– 3 the sun's influence *o·* the earth.
    190–25 wind passeth *o·* it, — *Psal.* 103 : 16.
    196– 5 The power of mortal mind *o·* its own body
    199–26 to walk the rope *o·* Niagara's abyss of waters,

over

    ph 200–14 *o·* the works of Thy hands. — *Psal.* 8 : 6.
    f 202–23 God gives man dominion *o·* all the earth.
    209– 5 Mind, supreme *o·* all its formations
    210– 1 superiority of faith by works *o·* faith in words.
    213–29 as the hand, which sweeps *o·* it, is human or
    217–23 understand the control which Mind has *o·* so-called
    222–24 "dominion *o·* the fish of the sea, — *Gen.* 1 : 26
    222–24 *o·* the fowl of the air, — *Gen.* 1 : 26.
    222–25 and *o·* the cattle," — *Gen.* 1 : 26.
    228–13 his God-given dominion *o·* the material senses.
    232– 2 can triumph *o·* sin, sickness, and death.
    232–17 as it did *o·* nineteen hundred years ago,
    232–18 healing the sick and triumphing *o·* death.
    234–17 If mortals would keep proper ward *o·* mortal
    238–22 Attempts to . . . gain dominion *o·* mankind,
    242– 8 and the final triumph *o·* the body.
    243– 8 and triumph *o·* sin and death.
    247–30 shining resplendent and eternal *o·* age
    b 269–18 *o·* the objects and thoughts of material sense,
    291–27 for the grave has no power *o·* either.
    307–26 gives man dominion *o·* all things.
    309–14 the power of Spirit *o·* the material senses ;
    310– 9 else the clay would have power *o·* the potter.
    311–24 which prevails *o·* material sense
    312–14 People go into ecstasies *o·* the sense of a
    316– 9 to prove the power of Spirit *o·* the flesh,
    316–23 which gives man dominion *o·* all the earth.
    322– 5 the control of Soul *o·* sense,
    323–17 "faithful *o·* a few things," — *Matt.* 25 : 21.
    323–18 shall be made rulers *o·* many ;
    o 346–21 If a dream ceases, . . . the terror is *o·*.
    p 369–10 raising the dead, and walking *o·* the wave.
    369–11 control *o·* the belief that matter is substance,
    369–32 or to be angry *o·* sin.
    378–17 represents the power of Truth *o·* error,
    378–18 might of intelligence . . . *o·* mortal beliefs
    379–12 stream of warm water was trickling *o·* his arm.
    380–10 the control of Mind *o·* body,
    380–21 and prove man's dominion *o·* error.
    384–32 the power of Mind *o·* the entire functions
    388– 3 obtained a victory *o·* the corporeal senses,
    389– 4 given in behalf of the control of Mind *o·*
    395– 7 as one having authority *o·* it,
    395– 9 assert its claims *o·* mortality and disease.
    396–23 power which their beliefs exercise *o·* their
    399–11 mortal mind sends its despatches *o·* its body,
    404–12 If the evil is *o·* in the repentant mortal mind,
    404–17 The temperance reform, felt all *o·* our land,
    406–22 the supremacy of Truth *o·* error,
    406–23 Life *o·* death, and good *o·* evil,
    406–27 involves . . . a loss of control *o·* the body.
    407–10 If man is not victorious *o·* the passions,
    413–22 need not wash his little body all *o·* each day
    418–2, 3 the conquest *o·* sickness, as well as *o·* sin,
    420–26 gives them all power *o·* every physical action
    427–21 obtain the victory *o·* death in proportion as
    438– 5 *o·* all the power of the enemy :— *Luke* 10 : 19.
    438–20 a garment of foul fur was spread *o·*
    t 447–26 and thus get the victory *o·* sin
    450–10 They do not . . . whine *o·* the demands of
    450–31 by understanding God's power *o·* them.
    454–30 superiority of spiritual power *o·* sensuous
    455– 9 in order to walk *o·* the waves of error
    460–21 it starts a petty crossfire *o·* every cripple
    r 475–24 let them have dominion *o·* the fish — *Gen.* 1 : 26.
    475–25 *o·* the fowl of the air, and *o·* the cattle, — *Gen.* 1 : 26.
    475–26 *o·* all the earth, and *o·* every creeping — *Gen.* 1 : 26.
    476–20 the wind passeth *o·* it, — *Psal.* 103 : 16.
    482–23 enabled Jesus to demonstrate his control *o·*
    483–17 Science has called the world to battle *o·* this
    484–17 Science must triumph *o·* material sense,
    484–25 and Truth *o·* error,
    g 502– 5 as if reality did not predominate *o·* unreality,
    502– 6 the light *o·* the dark,
    502– 6 straight line of Spirit *o·* the mortal deviations
    511–8, 9 to rule *o·* the day and *o·* the night, — *Gen.* 1 : 18.
    514–26 the control which Love held *o·* all,
    515– 5 creeping *o·* lofty summits,
    515–12 dominion *o·* the fish of the sea, — *Gen.* 1 : 26.
    515–13 *o·* the fowl of the air, and *o·* the cattle, — *Gen.* 1 : 26.
    515–14 *o·* all the earth, and *o·* every creeping — *Gen.* 1 : 26.
    516–21 reflects God's dominion *o·* all the earth.
    517–27 dominion *o·* the fish of the sea, — *Gen.* 1 : 28.
    517–28 *o·* the fowl of the air, and *o·* every — *Gen.* 1 : 28.
    529–31 He begins his reign *o·* man somewhat mildly,
    530–18 as always asserting its superiority *o·*
    531–32 and having dominion *o·* all the earth.
    533– 2 God's behest, dominion *o·* all the earth
    535– 9 and he shall rule *o·* thee. — *Gen.* 3 : 16.
    545–11 given dominion *o·* the whole earth.

over

  ap 559– 9   reaches *o·* continent and ocean
      559–23   murmur not *o·* Truth, if you find its
      568–24   For victory *o·* a single sin, we give thanks
      568–26   the mighty conquest *o·* all sin
      569– 6   faithful *o·* a few things,— *Matt.* 25 : 23.
      569– 7   I will make thee ruler *o·* many,"— *Matt.* 25 : 23.
      571–18   the occasion for a victory *o·* evil.
      578–15   my cup runneth *o·*.— *Psal.* 23 : 5.
  gl 593–21   and demonstrated as supreme *o·* all ;
      596–29   Jewish women wore veils *o·* their faces
      598–26   would bridge *o·* . . . the interval of death,
      (*see also* **body**)

overaction

  s 125– 7   Neither organic inaction nor *o·*
  p 428– 1   no inaction, diseased action, *o·*, nor

overbear

  f 203– 1   as though evil could *o·* the law of Love,

overcame

  a 39– 4   He *o·* the world, the flesh, and
     39–14   Jesus *o·* death and the grave
     45– 2   Jesus . . . *o·* every law of matter,
  b 289–14   Truth, *o·* and still overcomes death
  ap 568–17   *o·* him by the blood of the Lamb,— *Rev.* 12 : 11.

overcome

  a 43–27   The divine must *o·* the human at every point.
  m 61–22   propensities that must either be *o·* or
  sp 76–30   death must be *o·*, not submitted to,
  f 220– 2   said : . . . in order to *o·* a predisposition to
     231– 3   rightly met and fairly *o·* by Truth,
     240–26   convinced of the error that is to be *o·*.
     253–16   to *o·* the belief in sin, disease, or
  c 264–23   sickness and death were *o·* by Jesus,
  b 289– 5   should be *o·* by the understanding of
     289– 7   Then Spirit will have *o·* the flesh.
     306– 5   how death was to be *o·* by spiritual Life,
  p 392– 2   through divine Mind that you *o·* disease.
     394–21   Will you bid a man let evils *o·* him,
     405– 8   and to *o·* deceit with honesty.
     405–18   The good man finally can *o·* his fear of sin.
     410–16   material condition to be *o·* by Spirit,
     427–18   If man is never to *o·* death, why do the
     427–21   in proportion as we *o·* sin.
  t 446–24   Resisting evil, you *o·* it
     450–20   he will *o·* them by understanding their
  ap 568– 1   Innocence and Truth *o·* guilt and error.
     569– 4   must grapple with and *o·* the mortal belief in
     571–15   under all circumstances, *o·* evil with good.
  gl 581–14   temptation *o·* and followed by exaltation.

overcomes

  s 134–22   law of harmony which *o·* discord,
  ph 182–21   the law which *o·* material conditions
  b 289–15   Truth, overcame and still *o·* death
     315–24   Truth . . . heals sickness, and *o·* death.
  p 395–11   divine Science *o·* faith in a carnal mind,
     420–17   Truth *o·* both disease and sin

overcometh

  c 267–29   "Blessed is the man that endureth [*o·*]— *Jas.*
      1 : 12.

overcoming

  pr 10–12   C. S. reveals a necessity for *o·* the world,
  a 21– 1   If Truth is *o·* error in your daily walk
  an 104–25   a case of the greater error *o·* the lesser.
  f 233–20   *o·* the thoughts which produce them,
  b 273–27   Science, *o·* the false claims of
  r 497–18   and *o·* sin and death.

overeaten

  p 385–22   You say that you have not slept well or have *o·*.

over-exertion

  p 417–10   there will be no reaction from *o·*

overflowing

  ph 180–16   reservoir already *o·* with that emotion.

overflows

  a 26– 1   the heart *o·* with gratitude for what he

overlook

  a 36–32   Can God therefore *o·* the law of

overlooked

  t 455–29   This strong point in C. S. is not to be *o·*,

overlying

  r 496–18   *o·*, and encompassing all true being.

overmastering

  ph 186–17   It says : "I am a real entity, *o·* good."

overpower

  f 222–26   if eating a bit of animal flesh could *o·* him.
  p 429– 1   It is a sin to believe that aught can *o·*

overrule

  a 44–31   to *o·* mortal, material sense.
  s 128– 1   hypotheses . . . that these are final and *o·* the
  p 384–29   the evidence before the senses can never *o·*.

overruled

  a 43–14   were *o·* by divine Love
  v 381–31   Christ Jesus *o·* the error which would
     437–28   But Judge Justice . . . *o·* their motions

overshadow

  r 495–17   Let neither fear nor doubt *o·* your clear sense

overshadowed

  a 29–24   *o·* the pure sense of the Virgin-mother

overshadowing

  a 33–16   glory of an everlasting victory *o·* him,

overtake

  ph 174–18   are pursuing and will *o·* the ages,

overtakes

  b 290– 5   before what is termed death *o·* mortals,

overtaxed

  sp 79–24   says : . . . Your brain is *o·*,
  f 203–21   *o·* the belief of life in matter

overthrew

  f 228–27   The humble Nazarene *o·* the supposition

overthrow

  s 110–19   neither tongue nor pen can *o·* it.
  o 342– 1   denunciation cannot *o·* it.
  p 391– 1   to *o·* the plea of mortal mind,
  t 464–28   nor can they *o·* a scientific system

overthrowing

  p 437–26   C. S. was *o·* the judicial proceedings of a

overthrows

  s 120–23   heals the sick, *o·* false evidence,
     129–12   a belief which Science *o·*.

overturn

  f 223–31   God will *o·*, until

overwhelmed

  p 366–22   physician must also watch, lest he be *o·*

overwhelming

  pr 13–18   *o·* our real wishes with a torrent of words.
  a 47– 8   It was sometimes an *o·* power
     50– 6   added to an *o·* sense of the magnitude of
  s 151–32   That mortal mind claims . . . we have *o·* proof.
  p 396–19   the *o·* weight of opinions on the wrong side,

overworked

  p 387– 5   Who dares to say that actual Mind can be *o·*?

ovum

  g 547–10   microscopic examination of a vulture's *o·*,
     549–18   look upon the simple *o·* as the
     553–20   from Adam's rib, not from a fœtal *o·*.
     553–24   If . . . human belief agrees upon an *o·* as

owe

  a 18– 4   and for this we *o·* him endless homage.
  sp 94–12   The eastern empires and nations *o·* their

owing

  s 149– 8   *o·* to the different mental states of the patient.

own

  pref ix– 5   as sure of the world's existence as he is of his *o·* ;
     xii–11   she was . . . publisher of her *o·* works ;
  pr 3– 8   Shall we ask . . . to do His *o·* work?
     3–11   enables us to work out our *o·* salvation.
     7– 4   Still stronger evidence . . . found in his *o·* words,
     11–22   the results of mortals' *o·* faith.
     12–17   has no efficacy of its *o·*
  a 18–18   could conciliate no nature above his *o·*,
     22–11   "Work out your *o·* salvation,"— *Phil.* 2 : 12.
     23–26   work out one's "*o·* salvation,— *Phil.* 2 : 12.
     24–30   his *o·* disciples could not admit such
     25–24   the requisite proofs of their *o·* piety.
     26–11   which Jesus implied in his *o·* statements :
     37–13   right-doing brings its *o·* reward ;
     38–23   fruits of other people's sins, not of his *o·*.
     40–15   Another's suffering cannot lessen our *o·* liability.
     48–25   in the presence of his *o·* momentous question,
  m 61–19   may reproduce in their *o·* helpless little ones
     63–30   should be allowed to collect her *o·* wages,
     63–31   and *o·* her children free from interference.
     64–22   Then shall Soul rejoice in its *o·*,
     64–31   Spirit will ultimately claim its *o·*,
     65–25   is never desirable on its *o·* account.
     69–17   educate their *o·* offspring spiritually,
  sp 77– 7   Error brings its *o·* self-destruction
     77– 8   mortal mind creates its *o·* physical conditions.
     79–19   Jesus did his *o·* work by the one Spirit.

own

sp 81– 7   on its o· theories, spiritualism can only
86–31   It feels, hears, and sees its o· thoughts.
90–24   admission . . . that man is God's o· likeness
99– 6   "Work out your o· salvation— *Phil.* 2 : 12.
an 101–21   The author's o· observations of the workings
103–27   singe their o· wings and fall into dust.
s 119–10   to leave the creator out of His o· universe ;
121–27   besides turning daily on its o· axis.
124– 8   nor holy Principle of its o·,
126–10   interpreted in its o· way the echo of Spirit,
126–27   nothing . . . on which to found my o·, except
127–32   hypotheses that matter is its o· lawgiver,
131–18   "He came unto his o·,— *John* 1 : 11.
131–18   and his o· received him not."— *John* 1 : 11.
139–21   with its o· hue darkening to some extent
140–30   would . . . make God in their o· human image.
144–28   every man will be his o· physician,
145–30   must continually weaken its o· assumed power.
146– 8   By trusting matter to destroy its o· discord,
149–14   have not demonstrated . . . more in your o·
150–28   doctrine . . . that he is then thrust out of his o· body
151–24   maintains His o· image and likeness.
152– 1   and must by its o· consent yield to Truth.
153–24   this so-called mind makes its o· pain
153–24   that is, its o· *belief* in pain.
154–18   The law of mortal mind and her o· fears
159–32   is liable to increase disease with his o· mind,
160–25   If . . . become rigid of their o· preference,
ph 166– 1   matter has no sensation of its o·,
170–32   which takes divine power into its o· hands
176– 5   attributed their o· downfall and the fate of
177– 6   as certain as the evidence of my o· existence.
177–11   so-called mind builds its o· superstructure,
187– 7   creates its o· forms of thought,
191–21   By its o· volition, not a blade of grass springs
196– 5   The power of mortal mind over its o· body
196–18   Sin makes its o· hell,
196–19   and goodness its o· heaven.
199–15   Mortals develop their o· bodies or
f 204–28   never be said that man has a mind of his o·,
209– 6   the central sun of its o· systems of ideas,
209– 7   the life and light of all its o· vast creation ;
212–17   Mortals have a modus of their o·,
214–31   matter has no sensation of its o·,
217– 1   for this Mind forms its o· likeness.
220–18   Mortal mind produces its o· phenomena,
226–27   from the slavery of their o· beliefs
228–16   Then they will control their o· bodies
238–17   an experience we have not made our o·,
239–31   mortal mind sends forth its o· resemblances,
246–32   Acute and chronic beliefs reproduce their o· types.
247–15   a glory of its o·,— the radiance of Soul.
249– 4   producing His o· models of excellence.
251–32   and deify their o· notions,
252– 8   learn even a little of their o· falsity,
252–29   says : . . . I expand but to my o· despair,
c 257–12   Mind creates His o· likeness in ideas,
259–22   Mortal thought transmits its o· images,
261–28   nor your o· identity.
266–20   The sinner makes his o· hell
266–21   and the saint his o· heaven
b 277– 5   relapses into its o· unreality.
280–28   being perpetual in His o· individuality,
291–17   having no righteousness of his o·,
292–25   he speaketh of his o· :— *John* 8 : 44.
295–12   Mortals are not . . . created in God's o· image ;
297–32   A mortal belief fulfils its o· conditions.
298–31   confers upon angels its o· forms of thought,
299– 5   save in the artist's o· observation
303–27   witness or proof of His o· nature.
307–19   Thus error partakes of its o· nature
307–20   and utters its o· falsities.
309–32   never absorbed nor limited by its o· formations.
310–10   God is His o· infinite Mind, and expresses all.
325– 7   Truth, unfolding its o· immortal idea.
339–16   makes his o· awakening to the
340– 2   make life its o· proof of harmony and God.
o 344– 7   God has created man in His o· image
348–24   by so doing our o· condition can be improved
351–10   Later she learned that her o· prayers
358–32   their o· accredited and orthodox pastors,
360–16   You are bringing out your o· ideal.
p 365–20   enough Christly affection to win his o· pardon,
366– 7   his o· spiritual barrenness debars him
366–24   the unveiling of sin in his o· thoughts.
369–28   Limited to matter by their o· law,
372–11   or that man can enter his o· embodied thought,
372–12   bind himself with his o· beliefs,
374–20   incapacity to preserve your o· existence,
378–24   not . . . take the government into its o· hands.
380– 5   Sickness and sin fall by their o· weight.
384–23   if . . . you are not fit to conduct your o· case
385–13   law which makes sin its o· executioner,

own

p 389–22   Materialists contradict their o· statements.
391–14   It is error to suffer for aught but your o· sins.
391–16   real suffering for your o· sins
391–27   Therefore make your o· terms with sickness,
393– 5   ignorant of itself, of its o· actions,
396– 4   both for one's o· sake and for that of the patient.
399–17   Mortal mind perpetuates its o· thought.
401– 2   Any human error is its o· enemy,
402–14   this mind's o· mortal materials.
402–22   we govern our o· bodies.
403– 1   through their beliefs have induced their o· diseased
408–16   Can drugs go of their o· accord to the brain
412– 7   be thoroughly persuaded in your o· mind
413–16   to make it thrive . . . in its o· element.
414–18   lest you array the sick against their o· interests
418– 1   the baneful effects of their o· conclusions.
419–29   you must conquer your o· fears
422–26   holding that matter forms its o· conditions
422–29   Not holding the reins of government in his o·
424– 3   takes possession of itself and its o· thoughts
426–16   the necessity of working out his o· salvation.
427–31   waken from its o· material declaration,
436–13   Such acts bear their o· justification,
442–26   "Work out your o· salvation— *Phil.* 2 : 12.
t 443–11   privileged to work out their o· salvation
446– 2   perhaps communicating his o· bad morals,
446–15   destroying his o· power to heal and his o· health.
449– 1   With your o· wrists manacled,
455–13   energies of Mind in your o· behalf,
455–15   cast out the beam out of thine o· eye ;— *Matt.* 7 : 5.
460–26   to impart, . . . from her o· spiritual condition,
462–11   and substituting his o· views for Truth,
464–18   he could handle his o· case
r 468– 1   evolves its o· unerring idea
470–19   Has God taken down His o· standard,
475–22   no life, . . . nor creative power of his o·,
477– 3   the Saviour saw God's o· likeness,
485–25   If . . . it cannot outline on the body its o·
489–14   to meet its o· demands.
491–25   with their o· separate embodiment.
494–18   to flee from its o· convictions
g 505– 1   Mind makes its o· record,
507–20   not . . . any propagating power of their o·,
508–13   God determines the gender of His o· ideas.
510–30   one Mind, . . . shining by its o· light
511– 2   Mind forms ideas, its o· images,
512–12   reproduce their o· characteristics.
512–20   its o· pure and perfect ideas.
512–27   confers . . . upon its o· misconceptions.
512–29   this so-called mind puts forth its o· qualities,
514– 3   persons or things upon its o· plane,
515–25   Your mirrored reflection is your o· image
510– 9   after His o· likeness,
516–11   impart their o· peace and permanence.
516–24   created man in His o· image,— *Gen.* 1 : 27.
516–28   God made man in His o· image,
517–22   This ideal is God's o· image,
517–30   Divine Love blesses its o· ideas,
518–18   seeking his o· in another's good
519– 2   from all eternity knoweth His o· ideas.
522–10   and as revolving in an orbit of his o·.
522–31   Does the creator condemn His o· creation?
527–19   tree of death to His o· creation?
528–23   Beholding the creations of his o· dream
528–26   creation of woman and of his o· kind,
529– 1   bringing forth fruit of its o· kind,
531–20   a propagating property of their o·?
533–15   charges God and woman with his o· dereliction,
537–15   Sin is its o· punishment.
537–16   Error tills its o· barren soil
538– 2   "seeketh not her o·."— *I Cor.* 13 : 5.
541– 5   instead of making his o· gift a higher tribute
542–20   uncover and destroy error in God's o· way,
542–24   To envy's o· hell, justice consigns the lie
ap 563–12   belief that matter has power of its o·,
564– 4   error's o· nature and methods.
564–23   might uncover its o· crime of defying
569–26   at last stung to death by his o· malice ;
571–24   in which mortals may see their o· image.
575– 3   Love wedded to its o· spiritual idea."
577–21   divine Mind is its o· interpreter.
gl 580– 3   and is His o· image and likeness ;
582–19   man as His o· spiritual idea,
584–25   saith : . . . but after its o· image."

owner

f 212– 5   has continued in belief to pain the o·.

Oxford

p 379–16   the experiment of those O· boys,

Oxford University

s 111–19   offered in O· U·, England,

P

pace
g 514–18 and keep p· with highest purpose.

pacified
ap 570–24 The waters will be p·, and Christ will command

pagan
s 158– 2 p· priests, who besought the gods to heal
ph 187– 8 With p· blindness, it attributes to some
200– 2 P· worship began with muscularity,
f 214–19 finite thoughts of God like the p· idolater.
b 339–20 As the mythology of p· Rome has yielded to
340–26 annihilates p· and Christian idolatry,
r 469–30 ancient mythology and p· idolatry.

paganism
s 140–19 Worshipping through the medium of matter is p·.
ph 171– 1 p· and lust are so sanctioned by society
ap 571–29 illumined the night of p· with
gl 596– 3 P· and agnosticism may define Deity as

page
gl 585–15 ERROR. See . . . p· 472.
588–26 INTELLIGENCE. . . . p· 469.
590–14 LIFE. See . . . p· 468.
593– 3 PRINCIPLE. See . . . p· 465.
594–18 SOULS. See . . . p· 466.
594–24 SPIRITS. . . . (See p· 466.)
594–25 SUBSTANCE. See . . . p· 468.

pages
pref xii–26 she commits these p· to honest seekers for
s 139–22 darkening to some extent the inspired p·.
g 548– 4 and breathes through the sacred p· the

paid
pr 10–21 has p· for the privilege of prayer the price of
a 20– 3 He at last p· no homage to forms of doctrine
p 405–16 will be manacled until the last farthing is p·,

pain
absence of
ph 186–26 If pain is as real as the absence of p·, both must
and painlessness
s 125–13 p· and painlessness, sorrow and joy,
and pleasure
s 122–12 seats of p· and pleasure, from which
ph 181– 7 has no partnership with p· and pleasure,
188–11 dream of p· and pleasure in matter,
188–20 p· and pleasure, sickness and care,
190–10 fills itself with thoughts of p· and pleasure,
f 242–13 the so-called p· and pleasure of the senses.
c 262–19 when the supposed p· and pleasure of matter
b 303–21 The belief that p· and pleasure,
307–12 supposed material p· and pleasure
p 389–25 between p· and pleasure, good and evil,
and sorrow
g 557–15 the less p· and sorrow are his.
any
p 416– 9 To him there is no longer any p·.
belief in
s 153–19 The boil simply manifests, . . . a belief in p·,
153–24 its own pain—that is, its own belief in p·.
belief of
f 247–32 to retreat from the belief of p· or
o 346–23 that there is no reality in his belief of p·,
p 416– 3 the belief of p· will presently return, unless
t 464–18 when the belief of p· was lulled,
couch of
o 342–22 raises from the couch of p· the helpless invalid.
p 435–19 Watching beside the couch of p·
development of
p 391–12 can prevent the development of p·
does not produce
p 413– 2 Mind, does not produce p· in matter.
end in
g 536–20 Passions and appetites must end in p·.
equivalent of
pr 6–13 will furnish more than its equivalent of p·,
inflammation and
p 375– 4 the belief that inflammation and p· must
instead of
p 435–13 pleasure instead of p·, and life instead of death.
intense
ph 195– 1 gave him a belief of intense p·.
intruding
p 391–10 a single intruding p· which
makes its own
s 153–24 this so-called mind makes its own p·
memory of
f 212– 9 Because the memory of p· is more vivid
no
m 69–15 the sweet assurance of no parting, no p·,
s 113–28 no p· in Truth, and no truth in pain ;
c 261–11 the body experiences no p·.

pain
no
p 393–21 matter can have no p· nor inflammation.
421–19 gone from mortal mind, there can be no p· ;
g 557– 9 many animals suffer no p· in multiplying ;
no more
ap 573–31 no more p·, and all tears will be wiped away.
no truth in
s 113–29 no pain in Truth, and no truth in p· ;
occasion of
f 212–13 which we say was the occasion of p·,
occasions the
p 416–14 unless the belief which occasions the p· has
or fear
b 327– 6 the false beliefs of pleasure, p·, or fear
or heat
p 376–26 impossible for matter . . . to feel p· or heat,
or pleasure
s 159–27 p· or pleasure, action or stagnation,
f 211–32 Nerves are not the source of p· or pleasure.
212– 1 this p· or pleasure is not communicated through
219– 9 No more can we say . . . that nerves give p· or
pleasure,
247–32 to retreat from the belief of p· or pleasure
b 339–31 intelligence or power, p· or pleasure.
p 392–32 issues of p· or pleasure must come through mind,
r 478–17 assertion that there can be p· or pleasure in
part with
s 138–24 sick are more willing to part with p· than
pleasure and
sp 92– 5 experiencing pleasure and p·,
b 298–17 alternating between a sense of pleasure and p·,
r 472–15 Error is a supposition that pleasure and p·,
pleasure nor
b 327– 4 neither pleasure nor p·, appetite nor passion,
pleasure or
(see **pleasure**)
produce
ph 166– 2 the human mind is all that can produce p·.
quiets
s 143–17 and quiets p· with anodynes.
same
p 416–13 patient will find himself in the same p·, unless
seized with
t 464–14 seized with p· so violent
sensation of
f 212– 6 If the sensation of p· in the limb can return,
sorrow, and
ap 573–27 a cessation of death, sorrow, and p·.
suffer no
g 557– 9 many animals suffer no p· in multiplying ;
travaileth in
c 255– * travaileth in p· together until— Rom. 8 : 22.
where is the
p 416–15 Where is the p· while the patient sleeps?
without
f 215– 1 Spirit's senses are without p·,

s 153–22 p· cannot exist where there is no mortal mind
ph 186–26 If p· is as real as the absence of pain, both must
195– 9 gave him p· through those very senses,
f 212– 4 and the p· seems to be in its old place.
212– 5 has continued in belief to p· the owner.
212– 8 Why need p·, rather than pleasure, come
212–13 When . . . the p· still remains, it proves
219– 1 all disease, p·, weakness, . . . will be unknown,
c 260–31 If we look to the body for pleasure, we find p·;
b 285– 2 cannot be cognizant . . . of pleasure or of p·.
308–12 a blending of false claims, false pleasure, p·,
o 346–24 hence p· in matter is a false belief,
346–25 Do you feel the p· of tooth-pulling, when you
p 379–26 p· in the head and limbs,
415–14 Opiates do not remove the p· in any scientific
415–31 leaving the p· standing forth as distinctly as
416– 2 shows the p· to be in the mind,
416– 5 mental image occasioning the p·
418–30 Tumors, ulcers, tubercles, inflammation, p·,
421–15 belief that this chemicalization produces p·

pained
f 250–16 weary or p·, enjoy or suffer, according to
t 452– 9 eyes accustomed to darkness are p· by the light.
ap 562–23 and p· to be delivered.— Rev. 12 : 2.

painful
s 153–16 You say a boil is p· ;
153–17 for matter without mind is not p·.
f 251– 4 an abscess should not grow more p·
o 346–18 How then . . . "fraught with falsities p· to
p 385–21 discolored, p·, swollen, and inflamed.
r 495–19 can destroy any p· sense of, or belief in,

painless
f 224– 9 There should be p· progress,
p 401–13 but should be as p· to man as to a fluid,
414–28 in whom all being is p· and permanent.
painlessly
p 375– 2 as p· as gas dissipates into the air
painlessness
s 125–13 pain and p·, sorrow and joy,
pains
and pleasures
m 67–30 physical p· and pleasures,
f 202– 8 so-called p· and pleasures of material sense,
r 491–28 we dream of the p· and pleasures of matter.
material
a 39–23 material p· and material pleasures to pass away.
multiplies their
f 214–23 All material knowledge, . . . multiplies their p·,
of sense
f 232–28 so-called pleasures and p· of sense pass away
c 265–28 The p· of sense quickly inform us that
265–31 The p· of sense are salutary, if they
p 382–28 the so-called pleasures and p· of sense.
390–11 to exchange the pleasures and p· of sense for
of sinful sense
p 405–29 p· of sinful sense are less harmful than its
pleasures and
(see **pleasures**)

b 322–22 incurred through the p· of distorted sense.
painted
p 400–24 we see p· on the retina the image which
painter
c 260– 4 or the p· can depict the form and face of
painting
b 310– 1 The artist is not in his p·.
paints
f 247–24 It is Love which p· the petal with myriad hues,
pairs
r 466–11 but these contrasting p· of terms
palaces
s 133–18 in the fiery furnace and in kings' p·.
palate
sp 88– 7 when no viand touches the p·
pale
pref vii– 4 So shone the p· star to the prophet-shepherds ;
a 48–25 P· in the presence of his own momentous
b 328–32 reaching beyond the p· of a single period
p 415–18 causing a p· or flushed cheek.
pallid
p 376–10 p· invalid, whom you declare to be
415–17 Note how thought makes the face p·.
palm
s 142–11 If the soft p·, upturned to a lordly salary,
palms
a 44–16 to heal the torn p
48–15 Truth and Love bestow few p· until
palpable
o 359–15 p· only to spiritual sense,
palpitating
o 351–14 the living, p· presence of Christ,
palsied
p 415–22 impelled or p· by thought,
palsies
s 119–19 The lawgiver, whose lightning p· . . . is not
142–16 Sensuality p· the right hand,
palsy
p 375–21 P· is a belief that matter governs mortals,
375–25 and you cure the p·.
r 486–29 then p·, blindness, and deafness would
pampered
a 41–10 p· hypocrite may have a flowery pathway here,
pamphlet
pref ix–20 Her first p· on C. S. was copyrighted in 1870 ;
panacea
s 144–29 Truth will be the universal p·.
p 407–12 Here C. S. is the sovereign p·,
Pandemonium
b 269– 1 P·, a house divided against itself.
Pandora box
ph 170–30 the P· b·, from which all ills have
pang
a 19–17 Every p· of repentance and suffering,
pangs
a 48– 1 The p· of neglect and the staves of
ph 175–15 inflammation, sneezing, and nasal p·.
b 296–20 and how long they will suffer the p· of

panoply
ap 571–18 Clad in the p· of Love,
pantheism
a 27–20 to cut down the false doctrine of p·,
s 111– 1 agnosticism, p·; theosophy, spiritualism,
129–11 P· may be defined as a belief in the
129–18 p·, and infidelity are antagonistic to true
139–28 Atheism, p·, theosophy, and
c 257–11 This belief is shallow p·.
b 279–30 P·, starting from a material sense of
294– 4 This is p·, and carries within itself the
335– 6 would . . . establish a basis for p·.
g 522–14 It records p·, opposed to the
pantheistic
f 204–30 belief that God lives in matter is p·.
c 257– 7 theory that Spirit is not the . . . is p·
b 269– 1 These . . . systems are one and all p·,
279–23 p· belief that there is mind in matter ;
307– 3 This p· error, or so-called serpent,
parable
s 117–31 His p· of the "leaven, which a— Matt. 13 : 33.
118– 6 Did not this p· point a moral
118–16 The p· may import that these
b 272–13 Jesus' p· of "the sower"— Mark 4 : 14.
o 343–15 By p· and argument he explains the
p 363–15 Jesus rebuked them with a short story or p·.
g 539–20 In p· and argument, this falsity is
parables
a 27–17 Jesus' p· explain Life as never mingling with
s 117–16 taught spirituality by similitudes and p·.
paraded
ph 176–11 ghastly array of diseases was not p· before the
parading
p 372–24 only by falsely p· in the vestments of law.
Paradise
ph 171– 7 gates of P· which human beliefs have closed,
b 285– 4 not alone hereafter in what men call P·, but
paradox
f 216–25 would seem the exception, . . . and life a p·.
parallel
p 422–22 Let us suppose two p· cases of bone-disease,
paralysis
s 152–15 once apparently cured a case of p· simply by
ph 194–10 p· of the optic nerve
p 401–25 Would the drug remove p·,
420– 3 no stoppage of harmonious action, no p·.
paralyze
f 213–13 Material theories partially p· this attraction
p 375–22 belief that matter . . . can p· the body,
376–31 is to p· mental and scientific demonstration.
paramount
s 104–24 the forever fact remains p·
c 262– 5 shows the p· necessity of meeting them.
paraphernalia
f 209–26 all the p· of speculative theories,
paraphrased
g 532–21 Its summons may be thus p· :
parched
f 221– 9 that he should not wet his p· throat until
pardon
ask
pr   6– 9 supposition . . . nothing to do but to ask p·,
divine
a 40–11 This is my sense of divine p·,
God's
b 291– 4 suppositions . . . that God's p· is aught but
339– 5 Does not God's p·, destroying any one sin,
legal
pr 11–12 Mere legal p· (and there is no other,
no
pr 11–17 Truth bestows no p· upon error,
ready
a 24–21 chiefly as providing a ready p· for all sinners
sin and
f 251–19 sickness and death, sin and p·,
unmerited
pr   3–21 We plead for unmerited p·

pr   6– 4 Men may p·, but this divine Principle alone
a 36– 7 would be for Truth to p· error.
b 285–25 through p· and not through reform,
329–26 The p· of divine mercy is the
339– 2 destruction of sin is the divine method of p·.
p 365–20 enough Christly affection to win his own p·,
pardoned
a 36–26 suddenly p· and pushed into heaven,
b 291– 1 suppositions that sin is p· while unforsaken,
pardons
pr 11–13 never p· our sins or mistakes till

parent (*see also* **parent's**)
pref ix–32 as a *p·* may treasure the memorials of a
a 50– 9 despairing appeal, if made to a human *p·*,
m 69–20 Some day the child will ask his *p·* :
b 306–32 *p·* of all human discord was the
336–31 God is the *p·* Mind, and man is God's
p 416–20 This materialism of *p·* and child is only
416–23 is no longer the *p·*, even in appearance.
r 480–25 The supposititious *p·* of evil is a lie.
g 507– 9 wanderers from the *p·* Mind,
529–12 belonging to no lesser *p·*.
552– 2 is answered, if the egg produces the *p·*.
552– 3 Who or what produces the *p·* of the egg?

parentage
g 517–19 they all have one Principle and *p·*.

parental
m 63–19 person, property, and *p·* claims of the two sexes.

parent's
p 412–29 met mainly through the *p·* thought,
424– 1 formed first by the *p·* mind,

parents
devout
o 351–11 the prayers of her devout *p·*
gross
m 61–15 promising children in the arms of gross *p·*,
heavenly-minded
m 61–12 The offspring of heavenly-minded *p·*
her
f 237– 7 months or years before her *p·* would have
his
p 425– 1 His *p·* or some of his progenitors
obey their
f 236–21 Children should obey their *p·* ;
our first
sp 92–14 in the act of commending to our first *p·*
Puritan
o 359– 20 From Puritan *p·*, the discoverer of C. S.
those
m 62– 10 those *p·* should not, in after years, complain
views of
p 413– 9 views of *p·* and other persons on these subjects

m 61–18 If perchance they live to become *p·*
62– 8 If *p·* create in their babes a desire for
62–12 which the *p·* themselves have occasioned.
f 236–23 *P·* should teach their children at the earliest
237–11 stubborn beliefs and theories of *p·*
b 314–11 material views were the *p·* of their
g 557– 3 *P·* should remember this, and learn how to

pariah
p 362–10 as positively as if she were a Hindoo *p·*

Paris
an 100–13 ordered the medical faculty of *P·*
101–20 the Royal Academy of Medicine in *P·*.

Parisian
ph 197– 4 like a *P·* name for a novel garment.

Parker, Theodore
sp 80– 7 purporting to come from the late Theodore *P·*

Parmenter, Judge
an 105–18 these words of Judge *P·* of Boston will become

parodies
p 367– 8 but so many *p·* on legitimate C. S.,

parody
o 343–12 will not be forever hidden by unjust *p·*

part
any
sp 73–26 mistake to suppose that matter is any *p·* of
component
a 28–17 Not a single component *p·* of his nature
early
g 523–16 in the early *p·* of the book of Genesis.
every
f 242–28 restores every *p·* of the Christly garment
p 423–11 reaching to every *p·* of the human system.
from one
p 420– 1 nor go from one *p·* to another,
fundamental
t 460–10 this most fundamental *p·* of metaphysics
having
a 24–13 This is having *p·* in the atonement ;
his
c 261–12 strong impulse of a desire to perform his *p·*,
infinitesimal
g 520– 6 can repeat only an infinitesimal *p·* of what
is proved
t 461– 6 We admit the whole, because a *p·* is proved
latter
g 522–25 This latter *p·* of the second chapter
little
a 19–21 he has little *p·* in the atonement,
most
pref x–17 for the most *p·* have been abandoned

part
no
a 19–26 Those who cannot . . . have no *p·* in God.
m 64–22 in which passion has no *p·*.
f 231–28 and know that they are no *p·* of His creation.
242–27 appropriates no *p·* of the divine vesture,
246–17 Chronological data are no *p·* of the vast forever.
r 468–29 and time is no *p·* of eternity.
of himself
sp 92– 1 which is *p·* of himself.
of the error
r 482–26 Sickness is *p·* of the error which
only in
t 462–10 to practise Truth's teachings only in *p·*,
our
a 21– 5 This is having our *p·* in the at-one-ment
sinner's
a 23– 5 constant self-immolation on the sinner's *p·*.
tenth
gl 595–22 Tithe.   Contribution ; tenth *p·* ; homage ;
that
t 461– 6 that *p·* illustrates and proves the entire
their
p 431–15 The struggle on their *p·* was long.
third
ap 563–23 drew the third *p·* of the stars— *Rev.* 12 : 4.
vital
s 113– 5 The vital *p·*, the heart and soul of C. S.,

a 19–25 Those who cannot demonstrate, at least in *p·*,
m 68–12 "until death do us *p·*."
sp 98–23 has not been considered a *p·* of any religion,
s 138–23 the sick are more willing to *p·* with pain than
157–16 If drugs are *p·* of God's creation,
f 230– 2 if true, it is a *p·* of Truth.
b 296–17 in order to *p·* with them.
307–23 a *p·* of God's creation,
315–29 Wearing in *p·* a human form
p 415–10 Inflammation never appears in a *p·* which
430– 3 Mortal mind must *p·* with error,
431–29 testifies : . . . nothing on my *p·* has
439– 8 commanding him to take *p·* in the homicide.
t 444–23 then *p·* from these opponents as did Abraham

partake
a 20–11 can be baptized, *p·* of the Eucharist,
25–11 and they . . . who *p·* of that divine Life.
31–19 we drink of his cup, *p·* of his bread,

partaken
p 385–28 because you have *p·* of salt fish,

partakers
pr 4–16 attest our worthiness to be *p·* of Love.
9–31 that you may be *p·* of his nature?

partakes
b 307–19 Thus error *p·* of its own nature

partaking
p 431– 6 *p·* of food at irregular intervals,
ap 559–25 thus *p·* of the nature, or primal elements,

parted
f 242–23 "They *p·* my raiment— *John* 19 : 24.
245– 7 in the same hour which *p·* her from her lover,
b 306– 8 If God, who is Life, were *p·* for a moment from
p 401–22 If the mind were *p·* from the body,
t 444–24 as did Abraham when he *p·* from Lot,

partially
a 23– 1 is not destroyed, but *p·* indulged.
s 111–29 Mind governs the body, not *p·* but wholly.
149–26 divine Mind, governs all, not *p·* but
f 213–13 Material theories *p·* paralyze
223–26 Peals that should startle . . . are *p·* unheeded ;
b 326–14 Not *p·*, but fully, the great healer of

participant
p 439–12 a misguided *p·* in the misdeed

participate
m 59– 9 Man should not be required to *p·* in

participation
g 544– 3 so wholly apart . . . that Spirit had no *p·* in it.

particle
p 398–17 sometimes not containing a *p·* of medicine,

particular
a 38– 2 only for a *p·* period
s 112–10 some *p·* system of human opinions.
ph 178– 1 though they know nothing of this *p·* case

particularly
g 507– 7 Without natures *p·* defined,

parting
m 69–15 sweet assurance of no *p·*,

partly
a 30– 6 Jesus' advent in the flesh partook *p·* of
b 269–26 systems based wholly or *p·* on
p 373– 7 *p·* because they were willing to be restored,

partner
 m 59–14 each *p·* sustaining the other,

partners
 p 379– 3 announced as *p·* in the beginning.

partnership
 ph 181– 7 Matter, . . . has no *p·* with pain
 181– 8 but mortal belief has such a *p·*.
 f 243–26 Life has no *p·* with death.
 b 274–30 This suppositional *p·* is already obsolete,
 275– 2 A *p·* of mind with matter would
 p 438–23 who is in *p·* with Error
 t 458– 4 doctrine that Science has two principles in *p·*,
 g 528– 7 cannot be true that man was . . . in *p·* with God ;

partook
 a 30– 5 *p·* partly of Mary's earthly condition,
 33– 4 *p·* of the heavenly manna,
 34–10 If all who ever *p·* of the sacrament
 f 221– 6 *p·* of but one meal in twenty-four hours,

parts
 s 123–19 The revelation consists of two *p·* :
 g 523–30 In the historic *p·* of the Old Testament,

parturition
 g 557– 7 where *p·* is without suffering.

Paschal
 ap 559–29 the Israelites of old at the *P·* meal

pass
 pr 1– * *which he saith shall come to p·;— Mark* 11 : 23.
 a 32– 8 custom . . . to *p·* each guest a cup of wine.
 32–13 the cup which he prayed might *p·* from him,
 39–16 not the threshold over which he must *p·*
 39–24 and material pleasures to *p·* away,
 m 63– 8 nor does he *p·* through material conditions
 sp 75–30 In the vestibule through which we *p·*
 an 105–15 and courts reasonably *p·* sentence,
 s 118–10 Ages *p·*, but this leaven of Truth is ever
 135–16 "it came to *p·*, when the devil — *Luke* 11 : 14.
 164–27 then shall be brought to *p·* the — *I Cor.* 15 : 54.
 ph 173–15 For positive Spirit to *p·* through a
 188–10 only to *p·* from shame and woe to
 f 201– 8 new creature, in whom old things *p·* away
 225– 9 command their sentinels not to let truth *p·*
 232–28 so-called pleasures and pains of sense *p·* away
 244–25 He does not *p·* from matter to Mind,
 b 282–19 Mind cannot *p·* into non-intelligence,
 289–28 Therefore it cannot be said to *p·* out of
 321–27 "It shall come to *p·*, if they — *Exod.* 4 : 8.
 335– 4 theory, that Spirit . . . must *p·* through it, or
 o 345–16 well enough to *p·* judgment upon them.
 p 375– 2 Heat would *p·* from the body as painlessly
 386–31 So, when our friends *p·* from our sight
 401–19 forcing impurities to *p·* away,
 r 496–26 then shall be brought to *p·* the — *I Cor.* 15 : 54.
 g 535–15 When will man *p·* through the open gate of

passage
 another
  b 313– 9 With this agrees another *p·* in the same
  g 504–21 explanation of another *p·* of Scripture,
 defeat the
  p 390–31 to defeat the *p·* of an inhuman law.
 of the blood
  ph 187–13 opening and closing for the *p·* of the blood,
 perilous
  ap 559–30 prefigured this perilous *p·* out of bondage
 Scriptural
  b 328–29 the Scriptural *p·* would read *you*, not *they*.
 this
  b 320–29 whereas this *p·* is continually quoted as if
  g 504– 7 are answered in this *p·*,

 f 218–29 The meaning of that *p·* is not perverted
 b 313–19 The *p·* is made even clearer in the translation
 ap 566– 7 in their *p·* from sense to Soul,
 gl 598– 2 as in the *p·* in John's Gospel,

passages
 gl 598– 7 as in other *p·* in this same chapter

passed
 pref xi–30 a law relative to colleges having been *p·*,
 a 35– 1 His gloom had *p·* into glory,
 41– 2 into which Jesus has *p·* before us ;
 sp 87– 8 Though individuals have *p·* away,
 s 147–12 even though centuries had *p·* away since Jesus
 ph 172–15 he must have *p·* through all the forms of
 f 221–10 He *p·* many weary years in hunger
 251–11 they have but *p·* the portals of a new belief.
 b 307– 2 delusion that life . . . *p·* into matter.
 p 396–13 before a crisis is *p·*.
 g 536– 3 and the first earth were *p·* away ;— *Rev.* 21 : 1.
 536– 8 the sea, . . . is represented as having *p·* away.
 556– 9 for the former things will have *p·* away.
 ap 572–21 and the first earth were *p·* away ;— *Rev.* 21 : 1.
 572–23 The Revelator had not yet *p·* the

passes
 sp 72–28 nor the medium through which truth *p·* to
 ph 172– 9 if man *p·* through what we call death
 195–18 *p·* naturally from effect back to cause.
 f 247–11 the beauty of material things *p·* away,
 b 284–30 Thought *p·* from God to man,
 336– 3 Intelligence never *p·* into non-intelligence,
 gl 580–23 supposition that . . . intelligence *p·* into

passeth
 ph 190–25 the wind *p·* over it, — *Psal.* 103 : 16.
 r 476–26 the wind *p·* over it, — *Psal.* 103 : 16.

passing
 sp 97–14 approaches truth without *p·* the boundary
 an 104– 1 true thoughts, *p·* from God to man.
 f 245–22 she had taken no cognizance of *p·* time
 b 295–17 as light *p·* through the window-pane.
 gl 581– 4 ANGELS. God's thoughts *p·* to man ;

passion
 m 60–22 *p·*, frivolous amusements,
 64–22 in which *p·* has no part.
 sp 94–16 pattern of mortal personality, *p·*, and impulse.
 ph 188– 8 *P·*, depraved appetites, dishonesty,
 b 327– 4 neither pleasure nor pain, appetite nor *p·*,
 p 407– 7 relentless masters— *p·*, selfishness,
 t 445–22 Self-seeking, envy, *p·*, pride, hatred,
 r 490– 9 cooperates with appetite and *p·*.
 gl 598–18 Error ; fornication ; temptation ; *p·*.

passions
 a 24– 6 instigated sometimes by the worst *p·* of men
 53– 5 so far removed from appetites and *p·*
 s 115 21 Evil beliefs, *p·* and appetites, fear,
 f 201– 9 *P·*, selfishness, false appetites, hatred,
 p 401– 5 cherishing evil *p·* and malicious purposes,
 407–10 If man is not victorious over the *p·*,
 g 526–11 The appetites and *p·*, sin, sickness,
 536–20 *P·* and appetites must end in pain.
 gl 597–30 Destruction ; anger ; mortal *p·*.

Passover
 a 32–28 The *P·*, which Jesus ate with his disciples

passport
 a 22– 1 he would borrow the *p·* of some

past
 pref vii–15 Contentment with the *p·* and the
 a 28–25 To suppose that persecution . . . belongs to the *p·*,
 sp 84–13 to know the *p·*, the present, and the future.
 an 100–25 as I have also told you in time *p·*, — *Gal.* 5 : 21.
 ph 178–10 connection of *p·* mortal thoughts with present.
 f 224– 4 As the crude footprints of the *p·* disappear
 240–19 If mortals are not progressive, *p·* failures will

pastor (*see also* **Eddy, Mrs. Mary Baker**)
 o 359– 7 more faith in the Scientist than in their *p·*?

pastors
 o 359– 1 their own accredited and orthodox *p·*,

pastures
 g 514–13 or rests in "green *p·*, — *Psal.* 23 : 2.
 ap 578– 6 to lie down in green *p·* :— *Psal.* 23 : 2.

path
 along the
  s 129–27 along the *p·* which Science must tread
 ascending
  c 265–28 brightens the ascending *p·* of many a heart.
 Judah's
  ap 566–21 And oh, when stoops on Judah's *p·*
 narrow
  t 451–12 but strive, to enter the narrow *p·* of Life,
 our
  f 254–12 He directs our *p·*.
 true
  t 454– 7 and plants the feet in the true *p·*,

 a 20–22 traversing anew the *p·* from sin to holiness.
 38–25 Jesus mapped out the *p·* for others.
 m 66–20 wait patiently on divine wisdom to point out the *p·*.
 ph 174–15 marking out the *p·* for generations yet unborn.
 p 426– 5 finds the *p·* less difficult when she has
 t 454– 8 *p·* which leads to the house built without hands

pathological
 pref xi– 6 explains that all other *p·* methods are the
 ph 185–24 the reverse of ethical and *p·* Truth-power.
 p 373–10 Under all modes of *p·* treatment,
 t 464–21 In founding a *p·* system of Christianity,

pathology
 s 157–32 this spiritual and profound *p·*.
 f 252– 6 regarding the *p·* and theology of C. S.
 b 294–16 taught, as they are by physiology and *p·*,

paths

  a 21–18 Our *p·* have diverged at the very outset,
     22–25 is not reached through *p·* of flowers nor by
  f 224– 5 disappear from the dissolving *p·* of the
    251– 8 as to drive belief into new *p·*.
  ap 578– 9 in the *p·* of righteousness— *Psal.* 23 : 3.

pathway

  a 26– 3 treading alone his loving *p·*
    41–11 hypocrite may have a flowery *p·* here, but he
  r 487– 5 gained by walking in the *p·* of Truth
  g 549–25 the *p·* leading to divine Science,

patience

  pr 4– 4 expressed in *p·*, meekness, love, and good deeds
    4–25 and *p·* must bring experience.
  a 20–29 let us run with *p·* the race— *Heb.* 12 : 1.
    49–11 his divine *p·*, sublime courage,
  m 66–27 Socrates considered *p·* salutary under such
  p 366– 1 such as peace, *p·* in tribulation, and
    367– 4 pitiful *p·* with his fears
  t 454–24 *P·* must "have her perfect work."— *Jas.* 1 : 4.
  g 515– 4 *P·* is symbolized by the tireless worm,

patient (*see also* **patient's**)

cholera
  s 154–11 a bed where a cholera *p·* had died.
    154–14 no cholera *p·* had been in that bed.
cured a
  s 153–10 she has cured a *p·* sinking in the last stage of
cure his
  p 366– 3 In order to cure his *p·*, the metaphysician
cure the
  p 417–24 the way to cure the *p·* is to make
discouraging the
  t 447–18 without frightening or discouraging the *p·*
dispossesses the
  p 375–13 the hypnotist dispossesses the *p·* of his
healer and
  t 457– 6 for teacher and student, for healer and *p·*,
his
  ph 197–30 The doctor's mind reaches that of his *p·*.
  p 366– 7 to cast physical evils out of his *p·* ;
    375– 9 when his *p·* says, "I am better,"
needs to be
  p 417–21 from which the *p·* needs to be awakened.
physician and
  ph 174–29 the thought of both physician and *p·*?
    177–27 even though physician and *p·* are expecting
reaches his
  p 365–15 reaches his *p·* through divine Love,
sensitive
  p 423– 6 oftentimes affects a sensitive *p·*
strengthens his
  p 423–23 strengthens his *p·* with the stimulus of courage
telling the
  s 161–25 telling the *p·* that he is sick,
thought of the
  p 414–13 mortal mind or the thought of the *p·*,
treat the
  s 159–12 and to treat the *p·* as if she were
  p 421–12 treat the *p·* less for the disease and more for
while the
  p 416–15 Where is the pain while the *p·* sleeps?
will find
  p 416–12 the *p·* will find himself in the same pain, unless
your
  s 153–20 Now administer mentally to your *p·* a
  p 377– 1 If your *p·* believes in taking cold,
    395–26 than it is for your *p·* to feel these ills
    403–25 Never . . . and then acquaint your *p·* with it.
    412– 1 removing the fear, your *p·* is healed.
    419– 8 If your *p·* from any cause suffers a relapse,
    420–29 vehemently tell your *p·* that he must awake.
    424–16 the *minds* which surround your *p·* should not
    424–20 unspoken thoughts resting on your *p·*.

  s 149– 9 the different mental states of the *p·*.
    156– 8 the *p·* looked like a barrel.
    156–15 and told the *p·* so ;
  ph 169– 6 before the *p·* felt the change ;
    169– 7 and I have said to the *p·*, "You are healed,"
    177–26 swallowed through mistake, and the *p·* dies
    177–32 the potion swallowed by the *p·*
    185–32 A *p·* under the influence of mortal mind
    193– 4 said that the *p·* was dying.
    198– 3 A *p·* hears the doctor's verdict
    198– 5 The *p·* may seem calm under it,
  o 342–32 even if their treatment resulted in the death of
     a *p·*.
  p 370–25 and do no more for the *p·*.
    375–10 the *p·* believes that matter, not mind, has
    376– 2 The *p·* turns involuntarily from the
    377–19 The author never knew a *p·* who did not
    382–19 A *p·* thoroughly booked in medical theories
    395–16 besought to take the *p·* to Himself,
    395–28 fastens disease on the *p·*,
    396– 4 for one's own sake and for that of the *p·*.
    396– 5 Avoid talking illness to the *p·*.

patient

  p 398–19 faith of the doctor and the *p·*,
    403–32 are not understood by the *p·*,
    412–21 Argue . . . that the *p·* has no disease,
    416– 7 morphine is administered to a *p·*,
    421– 9 afterwards make known to the *p·* your motive
    421–24 sometimes explain the symptoms . . . to the *p·*.
    423– 3 belief should not be communicated to the *p·*,
    424–31 The *p·* may tell you that he
    430–19 The *p·* feels ill, ruminates, and
    430–30 when the prisoner, or *p·*, watched with a
  t 453–25 you must not tell the *p·* that he is sick
    460–15 to the frightened, false sense of the *p·*.

patient (adj.)

  pr 3–13 likeness of the *p·*, tender, and true,
  ph 180– 5 The *p·* sufferer tries to be satisfied when he
  f 242–15, 16 In *p·* obedience to a *p·* God,
  p 395–19 cheerful, orderly, punctual, *p·*,
    413–21 I am not *p·* with a speck of dirt ;
  gl 586–23 GETHSEMANE. *P·* woe ; the human yielding to

patiently

  pr 8–31 do we listen *p·* to the rebuke
    10– 3 and that waiting *p·* on the Lord,
  m 66–19 wait *p·* on divine wisdom to point out the path.
  s 136–32 Jesus *p·* persisted in teaching and
    139–12 *p·* and wisely to stem the
  f 254–11 When we wait *p·* on God and seek Truth
  c 262–23 the bliss of loving unselfishly, working *p·*,
  t 454–22 Wait *p·* for divine Love to move upon

patient's

  sp 79– 6 changing the *p·* thoughts regarding death.
  s 145–11 victory will be on the *p·* side only as
    152–16 introducing a thermometer into the *p·* mouth.
    152–17 to ascertain the temperature of the *p·* body ;
  ph 168–25 and recognized the *p·* fear of it,
    198–23 A *p·* belief is more or less moulded and
    198–26 His thoughts and his *p·* commingle,
  f 235–25 the *p·* feet may be planted on the rock
  p 365–29 the *p·* spiritual power to resuscitate himself.
    366– 9 hinders him from reaching his *p·* thought,
    375–18 adding to his *p·* mental and
    375–19 increasing his *p·* spirituality
    376–22 destroy the *p·* false belief
    396–11 nor encourage in the *p·* thought the

patients (*see also* **patients'**)

consumptive
  p 375–26 Consumptive *p·* always show great hopefulness
fear of
  p 411–28 by allaying the fear of *p·*.
his
  ph 197–32 will harm his *p·* even more than
  p 365–22 and deal with his *p·* compassionately ;
manipulate
  ph 181– 9 When you manipulate *p·*, you trust in
    181–14 to declare that you manipulate *p·* but that
ninety-and-nine
  o 344–28 may lose ninety-and-nine *p·*, while C. S. cures
our
  s 149–19 advise our *p·* to be hopeful
students and
  t 456–27 and so do all his students and *p·*.
your
  p 414–17 not until your *p·* are prepared for the
    417–27 Explain audibly to your *p·*,
    417–32 Give your *p·* an underlying understanding
    419–29 as well as those of your *p·*,
    424–24 while others are thinking about your *p·*

  ph 180–18 in the thoughts of their *p·*,
  o 359– 6 Is this because the *p·* have more faith in
    359–10 while they, the *p·*, did not.
  p 422–11 *P·*, unfamiliar with the cause of this
  t 443–14 If *p·* fail to experience the healing power
    446– 6 If *p·* sometimes seem worse while reading

patients'

  p 414–15 To fix truth steadfastly in your *p·* thoughts,

patriarch

  f 224–27 as he came of old to the *p·* at noonday?
  b 308–26 But the *p·*, perceiving his error and
  gl 579–12 This *p·* illustrated the purpose of Love

patriarchs

  b 283–26 in length of days, as it was by the *p·*,
    308–14 The Soul-inspired *p·* heard the voice

patron

  a 28–21 and Beelzebub is his *p·*.

pattern

  sp 94–16 *p·* of mortal personality, passion, and impulse.
  f 236–16 *p·* showed to thee in the mount."— *Heb.* 8 : 5.
  c 263–25 and attempts to *p·* the infinite.
  g 542–20 let human justice *p·* the divine.

patterns

  f 248–22 are liable to follow those lower *p·*,

Paul (*see also* **Paul's**)

alludes
  o 342– 1 *P·* alludes to "doubtful disputations."— *Rom.* 14 : 1.

asked
  f 216–25 *P·* asked : . . . "What concord hath— *II Cor.* 6 : 15.
  o 349– 3 As *P·* asked of the unfaithful in ancient days,
  g 539–24 *P·* asked : "What communion hath— *II Cor.* 6 : 14.

said
  sp 93– 9 the day of salvation," said *P·.*— *II Cor.* 6 : 2.
    95– 5 *P·* said, "To be spiritually minded— *Rom.* 8 : 6.
  f 223– 2 *P·* said, "Walk in the Spirit, and ye— *Gal.* 5 : 16.
    227–17 *P·* said, "I was free born."— *Acts* 22 : 28.
  b 304– 5 *P·* said : "Neither death, nor life,— *Rom.* 8 : 38.

saw
  gl 596– 7 *P·* saw in Athens an altar dedicated

says
  a 31–22 what says *P·*? "As often as ye— *I Cor.* 11 : 26.
  b 271–31 *P·* says, "How shall they hear— *Rom.* 10 : 14.
    321– 3 *P·* says, . . . "Flesh and blood cannot— *I Cor.* 15 : 50.
    332–16 *P·* says : "There is one God,— *I Tim.* 2 : 5.
  o 346–32 *P·* says : "The flesh lusteth against— *Gal.* 5 : 17.
  r 479–29 *P·* says : "For the invisible things of Him,— *Rom.* 1 : 20.
  g 534–18 *P·* says . . . "The carnal mind— *Rom.* 8 : 7.

to misunderstand
  ap 560–29 To misunderstand *P·*, was to be ignorant of

was not at first
  b 324–19 *P·* was not at first a disciple of Jesus

writes
  a 45–10 *P·* writes : "For if, when we were— *Rom.* 5 : 10.
  f 244–10 *P·* writes : "The law of the Spirit — *Rom.* 8 : 2.
  b 324–27 *P·* writes, "If Christ [Truth]— *I Cor.* 15 : 14.
    325–10 *P·* writes : "When Christ, who is— *Col.* 3 : 4.

  f 216–29 I say with *P·* : Be "willing rather— *II Cor.* 5 : 8.
  b 324–21 *P·* was made blind,
    325–20 *P·* had a clear sense of the demands of
    326–30 in humility he took the new name of *P·.*
  o 343–26 *P·* who was not one of his students,
  p 369–14 We never read that Luke or *P·* made a
  t 459– 3 *P·* and John had a clear apprehension
  g 514–27 *P·* proved the viper to be harmless.
  ap 563–29 Its sting is spoken of by *P·*,
    (*see also* **St. Paul** *and* **Apostle Paul**)

Paul's
  f 217– 7 *P·* peculiar Christian conversion and

pause
  f 223–18 and try to "give it *p·.*"
  b 323–10 Beholding the . . . we *p·,*— wait on God.

pauses
  b 292– 4 Here prophecy *p·.*
  ap 566– 9 Stately Science *p·* not, but moves before them,

pay
  pr 5–10 *p·* "the uttermost farthing."— *Matt.* 5 : 26.
  a 23– 4 insufficient to *p·* the debt of sin.
  f 240–27 one must *p·* fully and fairly
  p 384– 5 and must of necessity *p·* the penalty.
    387– 3 must it *p·* the penalty in a softened brain?
    387–18 That man does not *p·* the severest penalty who
    439– 1 receiving *p·* from them and introducing

paying
  f 240–30 The divine method of *p·* sin's wages

payment
  p 390–17 in *p·* of the last farthing,

peace

and harmony
  p 417– 1 find health, *p·,* and harmony in God,

and permanence
  g 516–11 which impart their own *p·* and permanence.

and purity
  b 323– 8 towards righteousness, *p·,* and purity,

and rest
  gl 586– 2 EVENING. . . . obscured views ; *p·* and rest.

annihilate my
  f 252–25 says : . . . may at any moment annihilate my *p·,*

be at
  b 324–12 "with Him, and be at *p·.*"— *Job* 22 : 21.
    329–29 to the spiritual and be at *p·* ;

brightness and
  s 139–11 even when the end has been brightness and *p·* ;

forever at
  f 215– 1 without pain, and they are forever at *p·.*

found no
  ph 195– 6 Outside of dismal darkness . . . he found no *p·.*

heart finds
  m 59–15 in which the heart finds *p·* and home.

human
  c 265–23 Who that has felt the loss of human *p·*

life and
  f 224– 9 life and *p·* instead of discord and death.

peace

make
  g 540– 5 "I make *p·,* and create evil.— *Isa.* 45 : 7.

not
  a 19–15 brought to material beliefs not *p·,* but

on earth
  s 150– 7 "on earth *p·,* good-will toward— *Luke* 2 : 14.
  f 226–17 "on earth *p·,* good-will toward— *Luke* 2 : 14.

permanence and
  m 65–27 man must find permanence and *p·*

perpetual
  m 64–25 spiritual understanding and perpetual *p·.*

purity and
  gl 584–20 purity and *p·* ; hope and faith.

Science and
  sp 96–15 on the other side there will be Science and *p·.*

spiritual
  gl 589– 8 JAPHET . . . A type of spiritual *p·,*

to the struggling
  a 45–16 and *p·* to the struggling hearts !

unspeakable
  c 264–26 and feel the unspeakable *p·* which

  a 28–26 To suppose . . . that Christianity to-day is at *p·*
  an 106–27 fruit of the Spirit is love, joy, *p·,*— *Gal.* 5 : 22.
  s 144–22 says to disease, "*P·,* be still."— *Mark* 4 : 39.
  c 265–15 a higher and more permanent *p·.*
  p 365–32 such as *p·,* patience in tribulation,
  t 449–27 The impure are at *p·* with the impure.
  g 506–12 The calm and exalted thought . . . is at *p·.*

peaceful
  a 40–31 nature of Christianity is *p·* and blessed,

Peaceful Sea
  ap 576– 1 and the *P· S·* of Harmony.

peaches
  s 129–24 Can we gather *p·* from a pine-tree,

peaks
  b 299–30 and reveal the celestial *p·.*

peals
  f 223–25 *P·* that should startle the slumbering thought

pearls
  f 204–14 avoid casting *p·* before those who trample them
  b 272–18 neither cast ye your *p·* before swine."— *Matt.* 7 : 6.

peasant
  m 58–24 Said the *p·* bride to her lover :

peck
  g 552–17 They must *p·* open their shells with C. S.,

peculiar
  f 217– 7 Paul's *p·* Christian conversion and experience,
  p 412– 6 to meet the *p·* or general symptoms

peculiarities
  sp 86–26 *p·* of expression, recollected sentences,
  g 551–20 by which all *p·* of ancestry,

peculiarly
  g 523–31 *p·* the divine sovereign of the Hebrew people,

pedantic
  o 351– 2 *p·* and void of healing power.

pedantry
  p 306–21 they swallow the camels of bigoted *p·.*

peep
  sp 70– * wizards that *p·* and that mutter ;— *Isa.* 8 : 19.

peers
  c 203–24 as when some finite sense *p·* from its cloister

pellet
  s 158–30 and mortal mind, . . . is governing the *p·.*
  ph 179–27 with homœopathic *p·* and powder in hand,

pellets
  s 156–18 to give her unmedicated *p·*
    156–25 in this way, taking the unmedicated *p·,*

pen
  s 110–17 No human *p·* nor tongue taught me the Science
    110–19 neither tongue nor *p·* can overthrow it.
  g 521–17 and the *p·* of an angel.

penal
  p 440–13 Even *p·* law holds homicide,

penalties
  ph 184– 6 the *p·* it affixes last so long as the belief
  p 381–32 would impose *p·* for transgressions of
    385–13 exempts man from all *p·* but those due for
    389–23 Their belief in material laws and in *p·* for
    405–28 conquered by the moral *p·* you incur
    440–11 into crimes, to which you attach *p·* ;
  gl 592–15 justice demands *p·* under the law.

penalty

brings
  pr 11–11 Broken law brings *p·* in order to

divine
  an 106–14 incurs the divine *p·* due this crime.

penalty
due for sin
pr 6– 1 We cannot escape the *p·* due for sin.
a 36– 6 To remit the *p·* due for sin, would be
escape the
pr 6– 1 We cannot escape the *p·* due for sin.
a 41–13 cannot forever . . . escape the *p·* due.
forestalls the
p 385–10 forestalls the *p·* which our beliefs would attach
full
g 542–21 Sin will receive its full *p·*,
incurs the
a 40–10 by first removing the sin which incurs the *p·*.
incur the
p 384– 9 If man seems to incur the *p·* through matter,
is coupled
p 389– 1 the *p·* is coupled with the belief.
last
p 390–18 the last *p·* demanded by error.
not the
p 385–25 Your sufferings are not the *p·* for
pay the
p 384– 5 and must of necessity pay the *p·*.
387– 4 must it pay the *p·* in a softened brain?
remits the
pr 11– 5 A magistrate sometimes remits the *p·*,
removes the
a 40– 9 Science removes the *p·* only by
severest
p 387–18 That man does not pay the severest *p·* who

p 435–24 decides what *p·* is due for the sin,
436–24 to rescue the prisoner from the *p·*

pendulum
a 22– 3 Vibrating like a *p·* between sin and
23–16 Faith, if it be mere belief, is as a *p·*
f 246– 2 Man is not a *p·*, swinging between evil and good,
o 360–19 Like a *p·* in a clock, you will be
penetrate
b 312–24 which cannot *p·* beyond matter.
penetrates
f 210–21 as a sunbeam *p·* the cloud.
Peniel
b 308–23 spiritual strength in this *P·* of divine Science.
penitence
g 533–29 as much as to say in meek *p·*,
penitent
p 364–12 and declaring the absolution of the *p·*.
penmanship
sp 86–25 landscape-paintings, fac-similes of *p·*,
penny
pr 10–19 and stop at the doors to earn a *p·* by
Pentecost, Day of
a 47– 9 overwhelming power as on the Day of *P·*.
Pentecostal Day
a 43– 9 which so illuminated the *P· D·*
penury
p 366–10 mental *p·* chills his faith and understanding.
people (*see also* **people's**)
affects
ph 197– 3 A new name for an ailment affects *p·* like a
are taught
o 342–32 The *p·* are taught in such cases to say, Amen.
go into ecstasies
b 312–14 *P·* go into ecstasies over the sense of
Hebrew
g 523–32 the divine sovereign of the Hebrew *p·*,
His
ap 573–17 ever with men, and they are His *p·*.
mighty
f 201– * *reproach of all the mighty p· ; — Psal.* 89 : 50.
of God
s 133–17 wrought wonders for the *p·* of God
b 288–19 a rest to the *p·* of God" — *Heb.* 4 : 9.
ordinary
p 385– 5 exposures which ordinary *p·* could not endure.
say
an 104–10 First, *p·* say it conflicts with the Bible.
b 312– 9 *P·* say, "Man is dead ;"
sick
s 163– 3 and afterward letting her loose upon sick *p·*."
p 417– 3 Give sick *p·* credit for sometimes knowing
so many
sp 80–23 French toy which years ago pleased so many *p·*
some
p 376–27 Some *p·*, mistaught as to Mind-science,
t 450–15 Some *p·* yield slowly to the touch of Truth.
unfortunate
p 408–10 Those unfortunate *p·* who are committed to
views of the
b 315–11 The opposite and false views of the *p·*

people
were in doubt
a 47–14 when the *p·* were in doubt concerning

sp 70– * *Should not a p· seek unto their God ? — Isa.* 8 : 19.
79– 2 Warning *p·* against death is an error that
s 136–18 may indicate that some of the *p·* believed
ph 175–19 Then *p·* had less time for selfishness,
f 238–27 *P·* with mental work before them
b 272– 2 how shall they preach, . . . except the *p·* hear?
272–16 Reading the thoughts of the *p·*,
303– 3 the multitudinous forms of Mind which *p·* the
321– 7 despaired of making the *p·* understand
o 343–13 from the quickened sense of the *p·*.
ap 570– 2 the hour when the *p·* will chain, with fetters
570–30 Many are willing to open the eyes of the *p·* to
571– 5 Because *p·* like you better when you tell them
peopled
c 264–32 The universe of Spirit is *p·* with
g 503–16 infinite space is *p·* with God's ideas,
people's
a 38–22 the fruits of other *p·* sins, not of his own.
f 220– 5 Such admissions ought to open *p·* eyes
o 350–18 "This *p·* heart is waxed gross, — *Matt.* 13 : 15.
peoples
g 509–17 God forms and *p·* the universe.
ap 565–17 will eventually rule all nations and *p·*
perceive
a 27– 8 he will at once *p·* that God is the power
sp 87– 1 Mind-readers *p·* these pictures of thought.
87–28 mind-readers can *p·* and reproduce these
ph 167–11 nor *p·* divine Science with the material
f 205–18 we *p·* the divine image in some word or
b 322– 6 and we shall *p·* Christianity, or Truth,
332–26 as they could understand as well as *p·*.
o 345–21 Anybody, who is able to *p·* the incongruity
p 387– 1 We shall *p·* this to be true
t 451–24 may *p·* the nature and methods of error
perceived
a 29–28 and woman *p·* this spiritual idea,
f 247–20 before they are *p·* humanly,
o 350–32 and the spiritual sense was scarcely *p·*.
perceives
b 325– 1 he who *p·* the true idea of Life
perceiving
a 40– 3 *p·* the scope and tendency of
b 308–26 the patriarch, *p·* his error and
p 397– 1 By not *p·* vital metaphysical points,
percentage
s 155–19 the *p·* of power on the side of this Science
perceptibly
s 156–11 She improved *p·*.
p 408–23 would produce insanity as *p·* as
408–26 and the results would be *p·* different.
perception
clear
p 418– 8 a clear *p·* of the unchanging, unerring,
Enoch's
f 214– 5 If Enoch's *p·* had been confined to the
glorious
a 29–16 the glorious *p·* that God is the only
human
s 119–28 As astronomy reverses the human *p·* of the
o 361–23 A human *p·* of divine Science,
ap 561–19 reducing to human *p·* and understanding
of character
s 128– 9 enlarges their *p·* of character,
spiritual
(*see* **spiritual**)
wholesome
pr 7–14 wholesome *p·* of God's requirements.

a 34–23 into the *p·* of infinite possibilities.
f 202–12 the *p·* and acceptance of Truth.
r 488–24 Mind alone possesses . . . *p·*, and
g 527–16 It is plain also that material *p·*,
gl 582– 2 the *p·* of spiritual Truth.
perch
r 492–32 Victory would *p·* on neither banner.
perchance
m 61–17 If *p·* they live to become parents
63–29 wronged, and *p·* impoverished, woman
o 344–27 the physician may *p·* be an infidel
peremptorily
ph 186–21 and only aids in *p·* punishing the evil-doer.
peremptory
b 327–18 the strict demands of C. S. seem *p·* ;
perennial
s 121–12 in God's *p·* and happy sunshine,
c 265–21 The truth of being is *p·*.

perfect (noun)

  g 555–25 when we admit that the *p·* is the author of

perfect (verb)

  f 248–13 in order to *p·* his conception.
  c 260– 3 than the sculptor can *p·* his outlines from
  o 354–22 out of the mouth of babes He will *p·* praise.

perfect (adj.)

  a 37–28 "Be ye therefore *p·*, — *Matt.* 5 ; 48.
     37–29 Father which is in heaven is *p·* !" — *Matt.* 5 : 48.
     52–11 the world's hatred of the just and *p·* Jesus,
  m 69–16 deathless and *p·* and eternal.
  sp 76–22 the *p·* harmony and immortality of Life,
     85– 9 You will reach the *p·* Science of healing when
  s 115–15 God's spiritual idea, individual, *p·*, eternal.
    130–10 reality is in *p·* harmony with God,
  ph 176–32 Truth handles . . . contagion with *p·* assurance.
    200–17 the real man was, is, and ever shall be *p·*,
  f 205–13 and made all *p·* and eternal.
    207–13 the *p·* Father, or the divine Principle of man.
    209– 1 Man, . . . has a *p·* indestructible life.
    221–15 and he is now in *p·* health
    223– 1 upon what is pure and *p·*.
    239–29 The *p·* Mind sends forth perfection,
    246– 5 *p·* and immortal are the eternal likeness of
    247–16 models of spiritual sense, drawn by *p·* Mind
    248–26 We must form *p·* models in thought
    249– 4 have one God, one Mind, and that one *p·*,
    251–21 understanding that the divine Mind makes *p·*,
    253–32 divine demand, "Be ye therefore *p·*," — *Matt.*
          5 : 48.
  c 259–12, 13 includes a *p·* Principle and idea, — *p·* God and
    259–15 If man was once *p·* but has now
    259–20 "Be ye therefore *p·*," — *Matt.* 5 : 48.
    259–21 Father which is in heaven is *p·*." — *Matt.* 5 : 48.
    259–27 Immortal ideas, pure, *p·*, and enduring,
    260– 8 the ideal of all that is *p·* and eternal.
    260–11 the immortal and *p·* model of God's creation
    266–25 *P·* and infinite Mind enthroned is heaven.
  b 273–14 impossibility of . . . *p·* understanding till
    276–19 When we learn in Science how to be *p·*
    276–20 even as our Father in heaven is *p·*,
    280– 3 not products of the infinite, *p·*, and eternal *All.*
    281–12 the image and likeness of *p·* Mind,
    286–21 God's thoughts are *p·* and eternal,
    292–12 not the likeness of God, the *p·* and eternal.
    295–14 and the real sense of being, *p·* and
    300–15 The . . . never touch the immutable and *p·*.
    302–19 The Science of being reveals man as *p·*,
    302–20 even as the Father is *p·*,
    304–15 governed by God, his *p·* Principle
    314– 1 and the body no more *p·* because of death
    325–17 *p·* as the Father, indestructible in Life,
    337– 6 it is not the . . . likeness of Spirit, the *p·* God.
    367–11 According to . . . man is in a degree as *p·* as
  p 372–15 When man demonstrates C. S. . . . he will be *p·*.
    373–18 "*p·* Love casteth out fear." *I John* 4 : 18.
    388–29 In that *p·* day of understanding,
    394– 4 is the universal and *p·* remedy.
    406– 9 "*P·* Love casteth out fear." — *I John* 4 : 18.
    407–23 spiritual, *p·*, harmonious in every action.
    407–24 Let the *p·* model be present in your thoughts
    410 18 but *p·* Love casteth out fear. — *I John* 4 : 18.
    410–19 He that feareth is not made *p·* — *I John* 4 : 18.
    428–23 man *is,* not *shall be, p·* and immortal.
  t 454–23 and form the *p·* concept.
    454–24 Patience must "have her *p·* work." — *Jas.* 1 : 4.
    463–20 is here and has fulfilled its *p·* work.
  r 467–11 Mankind will become *p·* in proportion as
    467–14 the one *p·* Mind to guide him,
    470–22 and, the divine Principle of man remaining *p·*,
    470–23 divine idea or reflection, man, remains *p·*.
    470–29 If . . . he has lost his *p·* Principle,
    470–30 If man ever existed without this *p·* Principle
    471– 4 all that He creates are *p·* and eternal,
    475–11 Man is spiritual and *p·*;
    475–12 and because he is spiritual and *p·*,
    476–14 They never had a *p·* state of being,
    476–32 Jesus beheld in Science the *p·*
    485–23 in which man is *p·*, even as the
    485–24 "Father which is in heaven is *p·*." — *Matt.* 5 : 48.
    494– 1 to hold man forever intact in his *p·* state,
    496–13 brighter "unto the *p·* day." — *Prov.* 4 : 18.
  g 511– 1 governing the universe, . . . in *p·* harmony.
    512–21 multiplication of its own pure and *p·* ideas.
    518–28 all must therefore be as *p·* as the
    518–29 as the divine Principle is *p·*.
    552–31 when the *p·* and eternal Mind is
  ap 562–20 which shines "unto the *p·* day" — *Prov.* 4 : 18.
  gl 581– 5 spiritual intuitions, pure and *p·* ;
    583–22 that which is *p·* and eternal ;
    587–17 God is one God, infinite and *p·*,
    591–19 of whom man is the full and *p·* expression ;
    594–20 that only which is *p·*, everlasting,
  (*see also* **man**)

perfected

  c 258–22 The human capacities are enlarged and *p·*

perfectibility

  s 110–10 glorious proposition, — man's *p·*
  ap 577–10 no impediment . . . to the *p·* of God's creation.

perfection

and power
  g 522– 7 endows man out of God's *p·* and power.
appears
  o 353–18 until *p·* appears and reality is reached.
celestial
  b 320–32 in celestial *p·* before Elohim,
Christian
  f 201–18 Christian *p·* is won on no other basis.
divine
  r 470–25 If . . . man did not express the divine *p·*,
eternal
  g 550–13 its eternal *p·* should appear now,
God requires
  f 254– 6 God requires *p·*, but not until the
health and
  ph 167–14 the divine source of all health and *p·*.
his
  a 52–10 the ever-present rebuke of his *p·* and purity.
  c 259–15 If man was once perfect but has now lost his *p·*,
in Spirit
  c 264– 3 permanent facts and their *p·* in Spirit
instead of
  c 260– 1 from imperfection instead of *p·*,
is gained
  b 290–19 *P·* is gained only by
is seen
  f 233– 8 *p·* is seen and acknowledged only by degrees.
leading to
  f 254– 1 human footsteps leading to *p·*
man's
  p 414–28 man's *p·* is real and unimpeachable,
of being
  f 253– 2 The beauty of holiness, the *p·* of being,
of Deity
  g 546– 7 assumption . . . would dethrone the *p·* of Deity.
of God
  c 262– 6 C. S. takes naught from the *p·* of God,
reaches
  b 290–27 becomes thus only when he reaches *p·*.
relating to
  ph 168–19 denies God's spiritual command relating to *p·*,
rule of
  b 336–27 The Science of being furnishes the rule of *p·*,
sends forth
  f 239–30 The perfect Mind sends forth *p·*,
spiritual
  f 254–13 mortals grasp . . . spiritual *p·* slowly ;
  gl 595–21 until . . . disappears and spiritual *p·* appears.
standard of
  r 470–18 standard of *p·* was originally God and man.
  g 555–24 We lose our standard of *p·* . . . when we
ultimate
  sp 97– 4 await the certainty of ultimate *p·*.
underlies
  o 353–16 *P·* underlies reality.
work up to
  f 233–10 ages must slowly work up to *p·*.

  pr 2–26 Do we expect to change *p·*?
  sp 72–17 *P·* is not expressed through imperfection.
    76–27 a *p·* discernible only by those who
  s 149–11 The rule and its *p·* of operation never vary
  f 243–31 *P·* does not animate imperfection.
  b 290–20 is gained only by *p·*,
    325–14 When spiritual being is understood in all its *p·*,
    337–17 *p·* is the order of celestial being
  o 353–17 Without *p·*, nothing is wholly real.
  p 388–28 foolish to stop eating until we gain *p·*
    424–11 since there is no room for imperfection in *p·*.
  r 470–28 If man has lost *p·*, then he has lost his
    488–29 Soul could reproduce them in all their *p·* ;
  gl 595–11 THUMMIM. *P·* ; the eternal demand of

perfectly

  b 269–17 These ideas are *p·* real and tangible to
  p 411– 8 the student was not *p·* attuned to

perform

  a 46– 1 did not *p·* many wonderful works, until
  s 159– 1 to *p·* a needed surgical operation
  ph 179– 1 will *p·* the sudden cures of which it is capable ;
  c 261–12 the strong impulse of a desire to *p·* his part,
  p 387–14 faithfully *p·* the natural functions of being.
    387–17 and *p·* the most vital functions in society.
    392–29 then *p·* your office as porter
    431–30 and *p·* my functions as usual,
  r 478–22 Matter cannot *p·* the functions of Mind.
  g 528–16 in order to *p·* a surgical operation on him

performed
s 159–18   would have p· the operation without ether.
g 528–28   according to . . . surgery was first p· mentally

perfume
ph 175–13   profane to fancy that the p· of clover
p 367–15   the oil of gladness and the p· of *gratitude*,
r 491– 2   A delicious p· will seem intolerable.

perfumed
p 363– 4   she p· Jesus' feet with the oil,

perfunctory
b 316–13   between this spiritual idea and p· religion,

perhaps
s 55– 6   P· the early Christian era did Jesus no more
s 163–25   p· so ample an exhibition of
ph 178–13   P· an adult has a deformity
198–17   by a counter-irritant,— p· by a blister,
o 344–13   would p· mercifully withhold their
358–30   whom they have p· never seen
p 363– 2   sandal oil p·, which is in such common use
373– 8   while she has struggled long, and p· in vain,
t 446– 1   p· communicating his own bad morals,

peril
a 42– 9   was in no p· from salary or popularity.

perilous
t 450–27   Who, that has felt the p· beliefs
ap 559–30   thus prefigured this p· passage

period
at some
ap 569– 3   at some p·, here or hereafter,
earliest possible
f 236–24   teach their children at the earliest possible p·
limited
r 494–13   a select number or for a limited p· of time,
of gestation
m 62– 3   p· of gestation have the sanctity of virginity.
particular
a 38– 3   for a particular p· and for a select number
remote
f 247– 2   comes on at a remote p·,
required
sp 77–13   p· required for this dream of material life,
revolutionary
b 268–11   In this revolutionary p·, . . . woman goes forth
scientific
p 406–15   as we approach the scientific p·, in which
single
b 329– 1   reaching beyond the pale of a single p·
that
sp 95– 4   traduced by the sinners of that p·,
this
sp 77–16   This p· will be of longer or
94–26   but what would be said at this p· of an
ph 197–24   Their diet would not cure dyspepsia at this p·.
f 219–30   may not be reached at this p·,
p 367–17   place at this p· of which Jesus
t 461– 5   must be accepted at this p· by induction.
g 509– 1   This p· corresponds to the resurrection,
ap 570– 3   the growing occultism of this p·.
was approaching
a 47–16   A p· was approaching which would reveal
s 146–27   far anterior to the p· in which Jesus lived.
b 274–30   in a manner and at a p· as yet unknown.
306–14   If Life or Soul and . . . man, unite for a p·
p 372–23   Matter succeeds for a p· only by falsely

periodical
pref xii–13   the first p· issued by Christian Scientists.
sp 80– 9   Yet the very p· containing this sentence

periods
b 271– 4   uniting all p· in the design of God.
p 381–14   the times, p·, and types of disease,
g 509–24   The p· of spiritual ascension are the
511–18   infinite ideas, images, mark the p· of progress.
ap 569–26   but how many p· of torture it may take

perish
f 251–27   nothing is left which deserves to p·
b 281–29   Our false views of matter p·
296–14   so-called pleasures and pains of matter p·,
g 542–18   shall p· with the sword."— *Matt.* 26 : 52.

perishable
b 274– 7   and symbolizes all that is evil and p·.
g 536–28   give up their belief in p· life

perishing
s 147–21   the p· fossils of theories already antiquated,

perjurer
p 438– 9   proved the witness, Nerve, to be a p·.

perjury
p 438–16   p·, treason, and conspiracy against the rights

permanence
m 58–11   true happiness, strength, and p·.
65–27   find p· and peace in a more spiritual **adherence.**
f 215– 3   and the might and p· of Truth.
b 287– 2   They have neither Principle nor p·,
r 486–26   hence their p·.
g 516–12   impart their own peace and p·.

permanency
b 281–22   have neither Principle nor p·,
293–28   opposite, the strength and p· of Spirit.

permanent
m 60– 5   a happy and p· companionship.
sp 79– 8   such a mental method produces p· health.
s 150– 9   its establishment as a p· dispensation
ph 185–27   but the recovery is not p·.
f 217–25   scientific and p· remedy for fatigue
232– 6   afford no scatheless and p· evidence of either.
c 264– 2   the p· facts and their perfection in Spirit
265–14   a higher and more p· peace.
b 290–18   happiness would be won . . . and be forever p· :
306–24   spiritual sense, which cognizes Life as p·.
p 414–28   in whom all being is painless and p·.

permanently
p 404–31   neither . . . can help him p·, even in body, unless

permeate
a 37–12   and to p· humanity with purer ideals.

permeated
sp 72– 5   p· by Spirit, that body would disappear

permission
p 378–29   power, without the divine p·, is inconceivable;
394–26   Is there no divine p· to conquer discord
434– 8   p· is obtained for a trial in the

permit
m 64–27   Let not mortals p· a disregard of law
f 227–10   some public teachers p· an ignorance of

permits
f 234–32   no more harm than one's belief p·.
b 274–23   Divine Science is absolute, and p· no

permitted
m 62– 1   only be p· for the purpose of generating.
p 441– 6   not p· to enter any suits at the bar of Soul,

permitting
s 159–26   how much harmony, or health, matter is p·

pernicious
a 38– 4   more p· than the old doctrine of
sp 78–14   Communications gathered from . . . are p·
p 394–19   their theories are sometimes p·,
r 469–29   is as p· to divine theology as

peroration
p 433–26   is the Judge's solemn p·.

perpetrator
p 403– 5   should and does cause the p· to suffer,
ap 564– 8   will sink its p· into a night without a star.

perpetual
m 57–12   will be p· only as it is pure and true,
64–24   spiritual understanding and p· peace.
s 119–14   making Him guilty of maintaining p· misrule
f 231–15   governing man through p· warfare.
240–15   Mind is p· motion.
c 255– 4   the p· demand of Truth and Love,
260–27   expectation of p· pleasure or pain
b 280–28   p· in His own individuality, harmony, **and**
283– 5   its p· and harmonious action.
328–28   Jesus' promise is p·.
p 381–28   and abide by the rule of p· harmony,
441– 7   but be enjoined to keep p· silence,
r 487– 8   the p· exercise of the Mind-faculties
g 501–17   than the history of p· evil.

perpetually
s 107–15   Feeling so p· the false consciousness
r 496–15   Hold p· this thought,— that it is the spiritual
ap 564–28   serpent is p· close upon the heel of harmony.

perpetuate
ph 183–15   nor devised a law to p· error.
196– 8   false pleasures which tend to p· this
p 419– 3   hate will p· or even create the belief in
g 542–11   and the denial of truth tend to p· sin,

perpetuated
a 43–19   p· and extended it.
r 466–24   mythology and Jewish theology have p· the

perpetuates
pr 2–20   p· the belief in God as humanly circumscribed,
sp 85– 7   whatever constitutes and p· harmony,
f 235–23   divine Truth which is Life and p· being,
b 280–29   and p· these qualities in man,
p 399–16   Mortal mind p· its own thought.

perpetuating
b 293–16   p· the eternal facts
g 531–18   maintained by God in p· the species?

perpetuation
m 68–23 The *p·* of the floral species by bud or

perpetuity
m 61–27 Nothing unworthy of *p·* should be transmitted

perplexed
s 164– 1 said : . . . Dark and *p·*, our devious career
ap 563– 4 We may well be *p·* at human fear ;

perplexing
p 414–19 by troubling and *p·* their thought.

per se
pr 12–31 only petitioners (*p· s·* or by proxy)

persecuted
a 33– 6 of old had fed . . . the *p·* followers of Truth.
41–26 *P·* from city to city, his apostles still
sp 98– 2 spiritual recompense of the *p·* is assured
an 104– 6 *p·* and belied by wolves in sheep's clothing.
s 134– 5 those who testified for Truth were so often *p·*
134–11 burned, crucified, and otherwise *p·* ;
ap 569–30 *p·* the woman which brought forth — *Rev.* 12 : 13.

persecuting
b 326–28 the wrong that he had done in *p·* Christians,

persecution
pr 5–16 Ingratitude and *p·* filled it to the brim ;
10–21 paid for the privilege of prayer the price of *p·*.
a 28–24 To suppose that *p·* for righteousness' sake
29– 9 bids us work the more earnestly in times of *p·*,
31–28 foreseeing the *p·* which would attend the
s 136– 7 Despite the *p·* this brought upon him,
139–10 been attended with bloodshed and *p·*,
f 238–12 To fall away from Truth in times of *p·*, shows
ap 560–24 *P·* of all who have spoken something new

persecutions
a 33–28 the *p·* which attend a new and higher
sp 97 32 Earth has no repayment for the *p·* which
c 266–21 The opposite *p·* of material sense,

persecutor
a 28– 7 determination to . . . is the *p·* of Truth and
b 324–19 not at first a disciple of Jesus but a *p·* of

persecutors
a 27–29 Jesus' *p·* made their strongest attack upon
43–13 The malignity of brutal *p·*,
43–16 Jesus' *p·* had mocked and
45–14 *p·* had failed to hide immortal Truth and Love
51–25 The motives of his *p·* were pride, envy,
p 422– 2 Wiser than his *p·*, Jesus said :
ap 560–27 but has been fatal to the *p·*.

perseverance
t 446– 9 *P·* in the perusal of the book has generally
q 514–16 diligence, promptness, and *p·* are likened to

persevering
q 515– 5 *p·* in its intent.

persisted
s 136–32 Jesus patiently *p·* in teaching and

persistence
t 462–18 sincerity, Christianity, and *p·* alone win

persistently
b 273–32 when it is opposed promptly and *p·* by C. S.
p 400–19 contending *p·* for truth, you destroy error.

Person
s 116–29 then God *is* infinite *P·*, — in the sense of
b 302–26 divine, infinite Principle, called *P·* or God.
331–26 Life, Truth, and Love constitute the triune *P·*

person
corporeal
pr 13–20 If we pray to God as a corporeal *p·*,
deceased
sp 81–32 deceased *p·*, supposed to be the communicator,
deceitful
p 395–18 deceitful *p·* should not be a nurse.
His
b 313–11 image of His *p·* [infinite Mind]." — *Heb.* 1 : 3.
material
pr 14– 2 as a corporeal, material *p·*,
no
p 375–14 No *p·* is benefited by yielding his
t 455–25 No *p·* can misuse this mental power, if
one
m 64–23 Then white-robed purity will unite in one *p·*
sp 73– 3 Spiritualism calls one *p·*, . . . *material*, but
82–12 one *p·* cannot exist in two different states of
q 517–16 if God is personal, there is but one *p·*,
scourged in
b 316–25 scourged in *p·*, and its Principle was rejected.
special
ph 178– 2 this particular case and this special *p·*,
third
f 204– 6 resulting in a third *p·* (mortal man)

m 63–19 *p·*, property, and mental claims of the
sp 71– 3 It is neither *p·*, place, nor thing,
87– 5 the *p·* holding the transferred picture

person
s 116–24 As the words *p·* and *personal* are commonly
146–15 clings for salvation to the *p·*, instead of
f 221– 1 I knew a *p·* who when quite a child
222– 4 This *p·* learned that food affects the
247–28 embellishments of the *p·* are poor substitutes
b 287–26 Matter is neither a thing nor a *p·*,
301– 3 the *p·* in front of the mirror.
p 402–31 The involuntary pleasure or pain of the *p·*
411– 6 just as a *p·* replies more readily when
432–13 namely, that he upon whose *p·* disease is found
q 517–20 symbol of God as *p·* is Mind's infinite ideal.

personal
pref x–23 proved in the *p·* experience of
m 60–22 passion, frivolous amusements, *p·* adornment,
61– 2 within the limits of *p·* sense.
sp 72–30 Not *p·* intercommunion but divine law is the
82– 7 of whose *p·* existence we may be in doubt?
s 116–24 As the words *person* and *p·* are commonly
138– 3 not on the *p·* Peter as a mortal,
ph 167– 2 to heal the sick out of His *p·* volition,
f 238– 4 Science is working changes in *p·* character
c 256– 9 (that is, a *p·* Trinity or Tri-unity)
263– 2 independent workers, *p·* authors,
266– 6 Would existence without *p·* friends
266–11 even if you cling to a sense of *p·* joys,
b 302–27 not in any bodily or *p·* likeness
312–21 Mortals believe in a finite *p·* God ;
312–24 A *p·* sense of God and of man's
334–11 imperceptible to the so-called *p·* senses,
336–32 God is individual and *p·* in a scientific sense,
o 351–18 a *p·* devil and an anthropomorphic God
360– 8 replies : . . . mine give me such *p·* pleasure,
p 364–19 material conservatism and for *p·* homage?
441–27 Your *p·* jurors in the Court of Error
t 449–23 according to *p·* merit or demerit,
q 517–15 but if God is *p·*, there is but one person,

personalities
sp 79–15 on divine Principle, not on material *p·*,
84–26 without the concession of material *p·*
b 315–28 more spiritual than all other earthly *p·*,
r 466– 8 *Answer.* — To human belief, they are *p·*
q 549–15 the *birth* of new individuals, or *p·*,

personality
attractive
r 491–27 wicked man may have an attractive *p·*.
dual
b 334–12 This dual *p·* of the unseen and the seen,
His
q 517–17 His *p·* can only be reflected, not transmitted.
his
a 40–27 and not merely worship his *p·*.
human
s 138– 7 Life, Truth, and Love, and not a human *p·*,
infinite
s 116–28 If the term . . as applied to God, means infinite *p·*,
116–29 in the sense of infinite *p·*, but not in
material
b 285– 7 What, then, is the material *p·*
337– 5 Material *p·* is not realism ;
q 544–25 but a material *p·* is not this likeness.
mortal
sp 94–16 pattern of mortal *p·*, passion, and impulse.
not to exalt
t 464–23 has labored . . . not to exalt *p·*.
physical
b 285–15 Is God a physical *p·*?
sense of
ap 577– 1 even as the material sense of *p·* yields to
statement of
sp 94– 7 Christian and scientific statement of *p·*

s 116–27 If the term *p·*, as applied to God, means
r 473–24 rather than *p·* or the man Jesus,
491–25 *P·* is not the individuality of man.

personally
sp 95– 5 if Jesus were *p·* present.
s 115– 6 any reader, who has not *p·* demonstrated C. S.
p 430–32 testifies . . . I was *p·* abused

Personal Sense
p 430–20 *P· S·* is the plaintiff.
430–22 False Belief is the attorney for *P· S·*.
432– 3 acquainted with the plaintiff, *P· S·*,
433– 1 The testimony for the plaintiff, *P· S·*,
433–11 evidence of *P· S·* against Mortal Man.
434–15 the case for Mortal Man *versus P· S·*
434–25 All the testimony has been on the side of *P· S·*,
436– 6 in the interest of *P· S·*
437– 3 testified that he . . . knew *P· S·* to be truthful ;
437– 8 in the interest of *P· S·*
438–13 Turning suddenly to *P· S·*, by this time silent,
438–23 False Belief, the attorney for *P· S·*,
438–31 the firm of *P· S·*, Error, & Co.,
439– 3 False Belief, the counsel for the plaintiff, *P· S·*,

Personal Sense

p 439–18   the blind Hypnotism, and the masked P· S·,
440–27   I repudiate the false testimony of P· S·.
441– 5   He also decided that the plaintiff, P· S·,
441–18   Reversing the testimony of P· S·
441–30   P· S·, is recorded in our Book of books as a liar.

personification

an 103– 3   The Apostle Paul refers to the p· of evil as
ph 187–12   another illusive p·, named Satan.

personified

o 357– 7   Jesus said of p· evil, that it was

persons

and souls
b 280–14   seeks to divide the one Spirit into p· and souls.
and things
c 263–27   a human and mortal sense of p· and things
certain class of
r 478–10   and by a certain class of p·,
few
ph 177–31   In such cases a few p· believe the
b 301– 5   Few p· comprehend what C. S. means by
many
g 517–15   The world believes in many p· ;
nine
an 101– 8   a committee of nine p· was appointed,
or things
g 514– 2   could not . . . recreate p· or things
other
o 348–25   and that of other p· as well?
p 413–10   views of parents and other p·
some
s 131–14   Must C. S. come . . . as some p· insist?
such
r 478–10   no such p· were ever seen to
three
c 256– 9   The theory of three p· in one God
g 515–19   nor does it imply three p· in one.

sp 74– 3   To be on communicable terms with Spirit, p· must
74–14   p· in such opposite dreams as the
b 328–20   hundreds of p· die there annually from
t 456–18   Science makes no concessions to p·
r 483–27   aid, not opposition, from all thinking p·.
ap 560–21   As it is with things, so is it with p·.

perspicacity

s 128–19   raises the thinker into his native air of . . . p·.

perspiration

p 384–17   while in a state of p·

persuaded

p 412– 7   be thoroughly p· in your own mind

persuading

p 441–28   p· Mortal Minds to return a verdict

pertain

o 350– 3   and of the things which p· to Spirit

perturbed

p 400–12   Eradicate the image . . . from the p· thought
439–16   in the p· faces of these worthies,

perusal

s 147–16   by a simple p· of this book.
t 446– 5   thorough p· of the author's publications
446– 9   Perseverance in the p· of the book has generally
g 523– 2   p· of the Scriptural account

pervades

sp 78–17   If Spirit p· all space,
r 465– 5   Absolute C. S. p· its statements,

perverse

s 118–18   perverted by a p· material sense of law,

perversion

ph 189–19   The human mortal mind, by an inevitable p·,
p 421–30   The p· of Mind-science is like

perverted

s 111–14   reverses p· and physical hypotheses
118–17   p· by a perverse material sense of law,
f 218–30   The meaning of that passage is not p· by

pestilence

m 56–16   "the p· that walketh in darkness,— Psal. 91 : 6.
sp 96–16   may seem to be famine and p·,
s 158– 8   the sender of disease, "the god of p·."
163–16   war, p·, and famine, all combined."
f 210–30   immortal sense includes no evil nor p·.

petal

f 247–24   It is Love which paints the p· with myriad hues,

petals

m 68–11   and scatters love's p· to decay.
g 506–20   even as He opens the p· of a holy purpose

Peter

pr 6–25   to P· he said, "Thou art an offence— Matt. 16 : 23.
a 48–21   P· would have smitten the enemies of his
53–22   Like P·, we should weep over the warning,
s 137–30   thou art P·; and upon this rock— Matt. 16 : 18.
138– 3   not on the personal P· as a mortal, but on
138– 6   It was now evident to P· that divine Life,

Peter's

s 138– 4   which lay behind P· confession

petition

pr 16–17   our scientific apprehension of the p·,

petitioners

pr 12–30   only p· (per se or by proxy)

petitions

pr 2–12   can do more for ourselves by humble fervent p·,
11–21   P· bring to mortals only the results of
13–10   If our p· are sincere, we labor for what we ask ;
gl 597– 7   hypocrisy, which offered long p· for

petros

s 137–31   [the meaning of the Greek word p·, or stone]

petty

s 130– 1   The p· intellect is alarmed by constant
t 445–32   for the p· consideration of money,
460–21   it starts a p· crossfire over every cripple

phantasm

f 222– 1   and that this p· of mortal mind disappears

phantoms

f 215–20   and flee as p· of error before truth and love.

Pharaohs

f 226–28   the educational systems of the P·, who to-day,

Pharisaical

a 18–11   against P· creeds and practices,
gl 597– 2   and in accordance with P· notions.

Pharisaism

gl 597–11   martyrdom of Jesus was the culminating sin of P·.

Pharisee

a 20– 6   To the ritualistic priest and hypocritical P·
p 362– 3   a certain P·, by name Simon,
363–19   the Master's question to Simon the P· ;
364– 9   the hospitality of the P· or the
367–11   nor, like the P·, with the arrogance of rank
gl 592–27   definition of

Pharisees

a 28– 1   The P· claimed to know and to teach the
47–13   thirty pieces of silver and the smiles of the P·.
52–29   The accusations of the P· were
s 117–30   leaven of the P· and of the Sadducees,
132–14   p· of old thrust the spiritual idea . . . out of
b 305–32   but not so blindly as the P·, who
306– 1   P· thought that they could raise the spiritual from
g 539–22   Disputing these points with the P·

pharmaceutics

s 129–21   We must abandon p·, and take up ontology,

pharmacist

ph 166–10   p· believes in the power of his drugs

pharmacist's

ph 166–13   the doctor's and the p· is a medical

pharmacy

o 342–30   teaching or practising p· or obstetrics
t 460– 8   Its p· is moral, and its medicine is intellectual

phase

pref xi– 2   only a p· of the action of the human mind,
an 102–31   Its so-called despotism is but a p· of
b 321–18   was really but a p· of mortal belief.
p 419–22   mortal mind is liable to any p· of belief.
427–13   Death is but another p· of the dream that

phases

sp 96–18   sin, sickness, and death, which assume new p·
f 249–24   Sleep and apathy are p· of the dream that
b 311–32   is not touched by these p· of mortality.
r 488– 1   enduring and harmonious p· of things.

phenomena

extraordinary
sp 80–16   Science . . . explains extraordinary p· ;
gropes among
t 463– 2   material physician gropes among p·, which
its own
f 220–18   Mortal mind produces its own p·,
noumenon and
s 114–10   including noumenon and p·,
of existence
p 430– 1   includes all the p· of existence.
of improvisation
sp 89–23   which explains the p· of improvisation

phenomena

spiritual
sp 88–24 nor are they spiritual *p·*,

pref xi– 1 Many imagine that the *p·* of physical healing
sp 80–17 Science never removes *p·* from the
an 101–11 the *p·* exhibited by a reputed clairvoyant.
p 423–31 They are only *p·* of the mind of mortals.

phenomenal
s 150– 6 eternal Science, instead of a *p·* exhibition.

phenomenon
sp 89– 2 This *p·* only shows that the beliefs of
ph 180–14 the human mind governs the body, its *p·*,
b 277–30 and is therefore a mortal *p·*,
gl 591–22 MIRACLE. . . . a *p·* of Science.

Philadelphia
s 162–31 the famous *P·* teacher of medical practice.

philanthropists
s 161–30 if this old class of *p·* looked as
p 385– 2 Florence Nightingale and other *p·*

philanthropy
sp 80–12 I entertain no doubt of the humanity and *p·*
s 151– 8 *p·* of the higher class of physicians.
t 462–29 hallowed influences of unselfishness, *p·*,

philosopher
f 216– 1 would have killed the venerable *p·*
g 556–14 may absorb the attention of sage and *p·*,

philosophy
heathen
g 552– 6 Heathen *p·*, modern geology, and
his
m 66–29 making his Xantippe a discipline for his *p·*.
f 215–29 faith of his *p·* spurned physical timidity.
human
sp 99– 2 Human *p·*, ethics, and superstition
s 144– 8 beliefs formulated in human *p·*,
b 269– 9 Human *p·* has made God manlike.
279–22 Every system of human *p·*, doctrine, and
school of
a 41–19 No ancient school of *p·*, . . . ever taught
sensuous
s 121– 3 the favorite inclinations of a sensuous *p·*.

f 209–12 Neither *p·* nor skepticism can hinder
b 269– 5 resulted from the *p·* of the serpent.
271– 8 He knew that the *p·*, Science, and proof of
o 347– 4 It is said . . . to verify this wonderful *p·*

Phoenician
g 524– 2 is seen in the *P·* worship of Baal,

phrase
absurd
r 485– 3 *Material sense* is an absurd *p·*,
divine service
a 40–20 It is said that the *p· divine service* has
"express image"
b 313–12 the *p·* "express image"— *Heb.* 1 : 3.
infinite form
c 257–31 *p· infinite form* involves a contradiction
mortal mind
s 114–14 the *p· mortal mind* implies something untrue
Scripture
g 511– 3 and so explains the Scripture *p·*,
self-contradictory
r 478–30 *Mortal man* is really a self-contradictory *p·*,
such a
g 517– 4 word *anthropomorphic*, in such a *p·* as
word or
s 114–18 if a better word or *p·* could be suggested,

pr 16–15 In the *p·*, "Deliver us from evil,"— *Matt.* 6 : 13.
s 114–15 as the *p·* is used in teaching C. S.
gl 598–13 the *p·* is equivalent to our common statement,

phraseology
o 354– 7 Why do they use this *p·*, and yet

phrenology
ph 173–22 *P·* makes man knavish or honest according
173–24 physiology, *p·*, do not define the image of God,

physical
action
p 420–26 gives them all power over every *p·* action
affirmation
p 392–11 The *p·* affirmation of disease
ailments
p 421– 3 *p·* ailments (so-called) arise from
belief
p 395–27 to feel these ills in *p·* belief.
418–26 Include moral as well as *p·* belief in your
gl 582– 4 A *p·* belief as to life, substance, and
586–18 FLESH. An error of *p·* belief ;
body
s 124–32 elements and functions of the *p·* body

physical
causation
b 286–12 *P·* causation was put aside
causes
s 111–22 to attribute physical effects to *p·* causes
combination
c 256–24 No form nor *p·* combination is adequate to
condition
a 46–20 Jesus' unchanged *p·* condition after what
b 297–11 change in either . . . affects the *p·* condition.
p 411–25 as the *p·* condition is imaged forth
conditions
sp 77– 8 mortal mind creates its own *p·* conditions.
s 150–27 *p·* conditions all his earthly days,
contact
sp 86– 2 to be occasioned by *p·* contact alone,
death
an 101–25 its effects . . . lead to moral and to *p·* death.
deformity
f 244– 2 He does not produce moral or *p·* deformity ;
diagnosis
s 161–26 according to his *p·* diagnosis . . . ,
p 370–20 A *p·* diagnosis of disease . . . tends to induce
disease
s 150–14 in the metaphysical healing of *p·* disease ;
effect
p 383–26 the illusive *p·* effect of a false belief,
effects
s 111–22 tendency of the age to attribute *p·* effects to
145–18 its ethical as well as its *p·* effects.
145–19 its ethical and *p·* effects are indissolubly
p 380–15 The *p·* effects of fear illustrate its
381–10 This fear . . . induces the *p·* effects.
enemies
s 116–16 nor do they carry the day against *p·* enemies,
evils
p 366– 6 to cast *p·* evils out of his patient ;
exemption
p 373– 2 in darkness as to the *p·* exemption which
eye
s 124–17 is invisible to the *p·* eye,
finiteness
c 255–16 The human form, or *p·* finiteness,
force
r 484–15 *P·* force and mortal mind are one.
forms
c 262–32 Cause does not exist . . . in *p·* forms.
healing
pref xi– 1 the phenomena of *p·* healing in C. S.
xi– 9 The *p·* healing of C. S. results now, as in
s 150–12 is not primarily one of *p·* healing.
t 460–10 though used for *p·* healing.
humanity
c 256–14 within the narrow limits of *p·* humanity,
hypotheses
s 111–15 reverses perverted and *p·* hypotheses
infirmity
c 261–18 made him as oblivious of *p·* infirmity
Jesus
a 51–26 inflicted on the *p·* Jesus,
knowledge
a 46–28 he rose above the *p·* knowledge of his disciples,
law
ph 184–25 what is termed a fatally broken *p·* law.
laws
m 62– 7 master the belief in so-called *p·* laws,
ph 165–12 Obedience to the so-called *p·* laws of health
p 381–32 transgressions of the *p·* laws of health ;
442– 2 adjudged innocent of transgressing *p·* laws,
life
f 247– 1 The acute belief of *p·* life comes on at a
limitations
c 256–28 Mind cannot proceed from *p·* limitations.
merely
pr 13–28 men recognize themselves as merely *p·*,
methods
t 443–16 ordinary *p·* methods of medical treatment,
nature
s 117– 7 C. S. attaches no *p·* nature and significance to
need
s 148–29 to render help in time of *p·* need.
offences
an 105–17 legal rulings wholly to *p·* offences,
organism
g 555– 5 which brings the *p·* organism under the
organization
ph 170–30 in either case dependent upon his *p·* organization,
pains
m 67–30 *p·* pains and pleasures,
personality
b 285–15 Is God a *p·* personality?
plagues
ap 575– 5 will destroy forever the *p·* plagues
power
s 131–11 the superiority of spiritual over *p·* power.

physical

proximity
  sp 82–15 despite his *p·* proximity,
realm
  p 427–25 acknowledged as supreme in the *p·* realm,
science
  s 124– 3 *P·* science (so-called) is human knowledge,
  127–23 There is no *p·* science, inasmuch as
  144–23 divine Science wars with so-called *p·* science,
sensation
  pr 7–17 *P·* sensation, . . . produces material ecstasy
sense
  m 60–25 *p·* sense, not discerning the true happiness
  64–31 voices of *p·* sense will be forever hushed.
  sp 86–21 no less a quality of *p·* sense than feeling.
  s 124–17 explained on the basis of *p·* sense
  ph 191–25 *P·* sense defines mortal man as based on
  b 304–19 not, therefore, at the disposal of *p·* sense.
  322–19 until his *p·* sense of pleasure yields to
  r 479– 1 If a child is the offspring of *p·* sense
  493– 6 All the evidence of *p·* sense and all the
  493– 7 knowledge obtained from *p·* sense must yield
  493–22 takes away this *p·* sense of discord,
  g 531–11 sometime rise above all material and *p·* sense,
  gl 582–21 *p·* sense put out of sight and hearing ;
  591– 1 through a *p·* sense of God as finite
senses
  pr 15– 7 The Father in secret is unseen to the *p·* senses,
  a 38–21 few of the pleasures of the *p·* senses.
  46–14 proved to the *p·* senses that his body
  sp 71–25 It is the offspring of the *p·* senses.
  75– 4 in the existence cognized by the *p·* senses,
  88–20 nor understood through the *p·* senses.
  s 108– 2 antagonistic to the testimony of the *p·* senses
  114– 7 is based on the evidence of the *p·* senses,
  117–24 Evidence drawn from the five *p·* senses
  120– 7 reverses the false testimony of the *p·* senses,
  120–21 reversing the testimony of the *p·* senses,
  120–28 instead of reversing the testimony of the *p·* senses,
  122– 1 The evidence of the *p·* senses often reverses
  ph 173– 1 acting through the five *p·* senses
  188–28 the *p·* senses have no immediate evidence of
  192–20 *p·* senses must give up their false testimony.
  f 231– 2 or the so-called *p·* senses will get the victory.
  b 273– 3 The *p·* senses can take no cognizance of God
  274–17 what we erroneously term the five *p·* senses
  284–21 The *p·* senses can obtain no proof of God.
  293–32 The five *p·* senses are the avenues and
  311–26 The objects cognized by the *p·* senses
  327–17 To the *p·* senses, the strict demands of
  o 353– 3 The *p·* senses and Science have ever
  353– 5 till the testimony of the *p·* senses yields
  r 479–16 hear, feel, or use any of the *p·* senses?
sight
  sp 87–32 or altogether gone from *p·* sight
structure
  ph 197–11 The less that is said of *p·* structure
supports
  pref x–20 till all *p·* supports have failed,
symptoms
  ph 194– 6 change in . . . changes all the *p·* symptoms,
  p 422– 6 and certain moral and *p·* symptoms seem
  t 453–11 the morbid moral or *p·* symptoms
testimony
  b 295– 4 proof of the unreliability of *p·* testimony.
theories
  s 123–13 Divine Science, rising above *p·* theories,
thought-taking
  p 365–10 the supposed necessity for *p·* thought-taking
timidity
  f 215–29 his philosophy spurned *p·* timidity.
universe
  r 484–13 *p·* universe expresses the . . . thoughts of
wants
  p 413– 4 the undue contemplation of *p·* wants
weariness
  f 217–26 or any illusion of *p·* weariness,
world
  s 125– 1 functions of the physical body and of the *p·* world

  sp 71–28 are alike material and *p·*.
  74–28 and the *p·*, or corporeal.
  99– 1 not *p·* but metaphysical,
  s 111– 6 C. S. is natural, but not *p·*.
  111– 9 departing from the realm of the *p·*,
  114–24 explains all cause and effect as mental, not *p·*.
  115–21 definition of
  118–29 these definitions portray law as *p·*,
  119–13 all disasters, *p·* and moral,
  132–25 salvation from all error, *p·* and mental,
  148–13 define man as both *p·* and mental,
  ph 170–28 The description of man as purely *p·*,
  f 218–31 the moral and *p·* are as one in their results.
  245–26 for the mental state governed the *p·*.
  246–13 As the *p·* and material, the transient sense

physical
  c 258– 6 material belief in a *p·* God and man.
  260–23 evolves bad *p·* and moral conditions.
  b 285–15 Spirit is not *p·*.
  288–10 When the final *p·* and moral effects of C. S. are
  290–11 That Life or Mind is finite and *p·* . . . is false.
  299– 5 which has no *p·* antecedent reality
  p 405–27 it is hastening on to *p·* and moral doom.
  412–20 and array your mental plea against the *p·*.
  r 492– 9 will uplift the *p·* and moral standard

physicality
  gl 587–11 a supposition of sentient *p·* ;

physically
  a 54–29 If that . . . glorified man were *p·* on earth
  s 151–12 to benefit the race *p·* and spiritually,
  ph 188–19 produced *p·* by the pleasure of a dream.
  f 220–27 better morally or *p·*
  b 325–21 demands of Truth upon mortals *p·* and
  p 369–30 No man is *p·* healed in wilful error
  370– 2 must be better spiritually as well as *p·*.
  375–20 while restoring him *p·* through divine Love.
  t 445– 5 who attempts to kill morally and *p·*.
  r 466–30 making mankind better *p·*, morally, and
  495–13 and sets the captive free *p·* and morally.
  ap 564– 6 incites mortals to kill morally and *p·*

physician (*see also* **physician's**)

alarm of the
  t 446– 8 either arise from the alarm of the *p·*, or
and patient
  ph 174–29 the thought of both *p·* and patient
  177–26 even though *p·* and patient are expecting
any
  p 416– 9 Yet any *p·* — allopathic, homœopathic, botanic,
her former
  s 156–13 her former *p·* had prescribed these remedies,
his
  ph 193– 3 On entering the house I met his *p·*,
  193–24 I have been informed that his *p·* claims to
  193–30 and what his *p·* said of the case,
  f 221– 8 His *p·* also recommended that he
his own
  s 144–28 every man will be his own *p·*,
material
  t 463– 1 The material *p·* gropes among phenomena,
mental
  p 368–32 Once let the mental *p·* believe in the
must understand
  p 417–25 To do this, the *p·* must understand
old-school
  p 375– 8 The old-school *p·* proves this when
ordinary
  s 159–31 the ordinary *p·* is liable to
  p 379– 5 where the ordinary *p·* looks for causes.
prescribes
  ph 198–19 the *p·* prescribes drugs,
who lacks
  p 366–12 The *p·* who lacks sympathy for his

  s 149–17 A *p·* of the old school remarked
  161–31 *p·* agrees with his "adversary — *Matt.* 5 : 25.
  163–10 if there were not a single *p·*, surgeon,
  ph 193– 4 The *p·* had just probed the ulcer
  344–27 when the *p·* may perchance be an infidel
  p 366–17 *p·* lacks faith in the divine Mind
  366–22 *p·* must also watch, lest he be overwhelmed
  403–32 *p·* should be familiar with mental action
  417–22 Disease should not appear real to the *p·*,
  422– 9 the book will become the *p·*,

physician's
  ph 198– 8 is increased by the *p·* words.

physicians
class of
  s 151– 9 philanthropy of the higher class of *p·*.
given by
  ph 179–32 Descriptions of disease given by *p·*
her
  s 158–32 her *p·* insisted that it would be unsafe
  159– 5 she was compelled by her *p·* to take it.

  ph 180–11 *P·* should not deport themselves as if
  235–19 *P·*, . . . should be models of virtue.
  235–24 *p·* should be able to teach it.
  p 370–32 *P·* examine the pulse, tongue, lungs,

physics
above
  b 269–11 Metaphysics is above *p·*,
belief in
  s 155–15 universal belief in *p·* weighs against the
disbelief in
  p 397–20 in exact proportion to your disbelief in *p·*,
doctrines of
  s 132–19 from doctrines of *p·* or of divinity ;
physiology, and
  f 222–28 physiology, and *p·* had made him one,

physics
place of
gl 585–19 metaphysics taking the place of p·;
rely upon
g 549–22 false systems, which rely upon p·
systems of
s 160– 3 systems of p· act against metaphysics,
theology and
pref viii– 9 Theology and p· teach that both

s 150–18 science (so-called) of p· would have one
ph 170–21 always in opposition, . . . to p·.

physiological
an 101–15 p· and therapeutical questions,

physiologists
ph 197–19 hardier than our trained p·,

Physiology
p 430–23 Materia Medica, Anatomy, P·, Hypnotism,
431–13 the prisoner summoned P·, Materia Medica,
436–16 professed friends, Materia Medica and P·,
437–22 Materia Medica, Anatomy, P·,
439–18 Scholastic Theology, Materia Medica, P·,

physiology
adherence to
ph 166–23 through adherence to p· and hygiene,
and health
ph 179–21 Treatises on anatomy, p·, and health,
and pathology
b 294–16 taught, as they are by p· and pathology,
and Spirit
ph 182– 9 We cannot obey both p· and Spirit,
exalts matter
s 148–25 P· exalts matter, dethrones Mind,
or therapeutics
an 101–18 nothing in common with either p· or therapeutics."
theology and
s 141–32 now occupied by scholastic theology and p·,

s 144– 9 in human philosophy, p·, hygiene,
148–27 When p· fails to give health
ph 165– 1 P· is one of the apples from
173–17 P· continues this explanation,
173–23 p·, phrenology, do not define the image of God,
179–16 can even educate a healthy horse so far in p·
f 222–27 fear, hygiene, p·, and physics
g 556–25 Ontology receives less attention than p·.

physique
a 46–13 Master said plainly that p· was not Spirit,
r 475–14 Man is idea, . . . he is not p·.

pick
sp 90–10 None may p· the lock nor enter by some other

pictorial
sp 86–27 can all be taken from p· thought and memory

picture
sp 87– 6 or for the person holding the transferred p·
ph 174–27 Why . . . p· this disease to the mind,
198–21 a p· of healthy and harmonious formations.
c 264– 6 when the mental p· is spiritual and eternal.
b 305– 5 A p· in the camera or a face reflected in the
310– 1 The p· is the artist's thought objectified,
g 526–25 second biblical account is a p· of error

pictured
sp 91– 2 Have you ever p· this heaven and earth,
g 514–21 the millennial estate p· by Isaiah :

pictures
sp 86–31 P· are mentally formed before the
87– 2 Mind-readers perceive these p· of thought.
92–11 In old Scriptural p· we see a serpent
ph 195–26 remarkable only for their exaggerated p·,
f 244–29 Even Shakespeare's poetry p· age as infancy,
p 379–27 p· drawn on the body by a mortal mind.

piece
f 212–16 this so-called mind instead of a p· of the flesh,

pieces
a 47–12 The traitor's price was thirty p· of silver

pierced
a 50–29 sharper than the thorns which p· his flesh.

pierces
m 66– 7 a broken reed, which p· the heart.
f 210–20 Truth p· the error of mortality

piety
a 25–24 requisite proofs of their own p·.
sp 98–26 connection with faith and p·.

Pilate
a 48–26 P· was drawn into acquiescence with the
48–27 P· was ignorant of the consequences of
52–15 Herod and P· laid aside old feuds

Pilate's
a 49– 1 women at the cross could have answered P·
question.

piled
r 494–28 its lap p· high with immortal fruits.

pilgrim
a 22– 1 borrow the passport of some wiser p·,
ph 174–15 Whoever opens the way in C. S. is a p· and
f 254–31 P· on earth, thy home is heaven ;
ap 574– 4 adapted to console the weary p·,

pilgrimage
ph 166– 8 Mohammedan believes in a p· to Mecca
f 202–18 The days of our p· will multiply

pillar
ap 566–10 a p· of cloud by day and of fire by night,

pillars
ap 558– 5 and his feet as p· of fire :— Rev. 10 : 1.
558–16 Its feet are p· of fire, foundations of Truth and

pillow
p 365– 2 the thorns they plant in the p· of the sick

pin
f 228– 7 subject for mortal belief to p· theories upon ;

pinching
p 383–29 p· and pounding the poor body,

pine-tree
s 129–25 Can we gather peaches from a p·,

pinions
pr 4–31 creeds clip the strong p· of love,
m 58– 3 Unity of spirit gives new p· to joy,
s 107–12 fresh p· are given to faith and understanding,
ph 191–14 transformed by Truth on its p· of light,
b 268– 3 With like activity have thought's swift p·
298–28 flying on spiritual, not material, p·.
t 454–20 Right motives give p· to thought,

pinnacle
t 448–11 casts thee down from the p·.

pinning
a 22–25 p· one's faith . . . to another's vicarious effort.

pioneer
pref vii–24 It is the task of the sturdy p· to hew the tall oak
vii–25 must declare what the p· has accomplished.
a 28–31 await, in some form, every p· of truth.

pious
sp 77– 1 The p· Polycarp said : "I cannot turn at once

Pison
gl 593– 1 definition of

pitiful
s 158–18 It is p· to lead men into temptation through the
b 327– 9 What a p· sight is malice, finding pleasure in
p 367– 4 p· patience with his fears and the removal

pitilessly
t 446– 3 dealing p· with a community unprepared for

pity
u 49–10 No human eye was there to p·, no arm to save,
o 348–10 It is a p· that the medical faculty and clergy

place
and power
ph 107–13 cannot successfully usurp the p· and power
t 450–14 nor play the traitor for p· and power.
everlasting
sp 99–27 everlasting p· to the scientific demonstration of
gave
ph 193–11 its death-pallor gave p· to a natural hue.
give
f 209–21 they all must give p· to the spiritual fact
c 264– 4 must finally give p· to the glorious forms which
b 285–19 to give p· to a diviner sense of intelligence
p 428–12 sweep away the false and give p· to the true.
t 458–21 summoned to give p· to higher law,
r 476–19 must disappear to give p· to the facts
g 549– 7 will finally give p· to higher theories and
given
pr 9–11 If selfishness has given p· to kindness,
s 133–31 not quite given p· to the true knowledge of God.
gives
pref xi–13 as necessarily as darkness gives p· to light
ph 176–14 mechanism of the human mind gives p· to
b 339–23 until the finite gives p· to the infinite,
giving
c 266– 4 giving p· to man's higher individuality
has no
b 282–16 matter has no p· in Spirit,
282–17 and Spirit has no p· in matter.
have no
pr 9–24 material sense and human will have no p·.
r 469–23 for evil can have no p·, where
her
t 464– 9 Others could not take her p·,

place

in its old
  f 212– 4   and the pain seems to be in its old *p*˙.

in our institutions
  s 141–31   Give to it the *p*˙ in our institutions of learning

in which
  a 44– 6   a *p*˙ in which to solve the great problem

is no
  r 480– 3   and there is no *p*˙ where God is not,
  g 504–12   there is no *p*˙ where God's light is not seen,

nor opportunity
  f 232–32   neither *p*˙ nor opportunity in Science for error

nor power
  b 327–20   evil has in reality neither *p*˙ nor power

nor thing
  sp 71– 3   It is neither person, *p*˙, nor thing,

occupies the
  p 367–17   A Christian Scientist occupies the *p*˙ at this

of modes
  p 406– 7   when, in *p*˙ of modes and forms,

of Spirit
  g 522–18   erroneous theory, matter takes the *p*˙ of Spirit.

one
  sp 90–22   yet their bodies stay in one *p*˙.
  g 506–16   gathered together unto one *p*˙,— *Gen.* 1 : 9

same
  b 287–13   fountain send forth at the same *p*˙— *Jas.* 3 : 11.

such a
  p 362– 8   she was debarred from such a *p*˙

supreme
  s 156–32   and Mind takes its rightful and supreme *p*˙.

take
  m 59–32   Separation never should take *p*˙,

takes
  t 463–17   When this new birth takes *p*˙, the C. S. infant
  g 549– 3   takes *p*˙ apart from sexual conditions.

taking
  g 504–17   represented as taking *p*˙ on so many *evenings*

taking the
  gl 585–19   metaphysics taking the *p*˙ of physics ;

their
  ap 566–28   neither was their *p*˙ found— *Rev.* 12 : 8.

thereof
  ph 190–26   the *p*˙ thereof shall know it no more.— *Psal.*
           103 : 16.
  r 476–26   the *p*˙ thereof shall know it no more."— *Psal.*
           103 : 16.

to make
  s 130–19   denied and cast out to make *p*˙ for truth.

took
  ph 193–16   in the afternoon when this took *p*˙.

took the
  ph 165–14   material theories took the *p*˙ of

---

  a 31– 2   God will never *p*˙ it in such hands.
  sp 72–10   in the *p*˙ of darkness all is light,
  s 148–14   Both . . . *p*˙ mind at the mercy of
  ph 165– 9   to *p*˙ this so-called mind at the mercy of
  167– 5   Soul-existence, in the *p*˙ of sense-existence,
  f 238–29   *p*˙ the fact above the falsehood,
  b 291–19   "In the *p*˙ where the tree falleth,— *Eccl.* 11 : 3.
  r 469–23   when we admit that, . . . evil has a *p*˙ in this
  486–30   would *p*˙ man in a terrible situation,
  ap 565–30   hath a *p*˙ prepared of God.— *Rev.* 12 : 6.
  573–20   in *p*˙ of this false sense was the

placed
  pr 5– 7   *p*˙ under the stress of circumstances.
  a 47–19   *p*˙ a gulf between Jesus and his betrayer,
  f 239–17   we must learn where our affections are *p*˙
  b 305– 1   *p*˙ at the disposal of illusions,
  p 431–22   covered with a foul fur, *p*˙ on me the night of
  g 537– 5   *p*˙ at the east of the garden— *Gen.* 3 : 24.

places
  m 60–26   So physical sense, . . . *p*˙ it on a false basis.
  61–14   If some fortuitous circumstance *p*˙ promising
  t 453–21   spiritual wickedness in high *p*˙.
  g 535– 5   the other to be garnered into heavenly *p*˙.
  537–27   text is made to appear contradictory in some *p*˙,
  538– 5   Truth *p*˙ the cherub wisdom at the gate
  ap 559–12   heard in the desert and in dark *p*˙ of fear.
  563–30   "spiritual wickedness in high *p*˙."— *Eph.* 6 : 12.

plagiarisms
  pref x– 6   and filled with *p*˙ from SCIENCE AND HEALTH.

plague
  p 405–22   better to be exposed to every *p*˙ on earth than

plagues
  s 133– 9   saved the Israelites from belief in the *p*˙.
  ap 574– 7   full of the seven last *p*˙,— *Rev.* 21 : 9.
  574–18   the seven angelic vials full of seven *p*˙,
  575– 5   the physical *p*˙ imposed by material sense.

plain

  pref vii– 7   make *p*˙ to benighted understanding the way of
  s 137–13   it is *p*˙ that Jesus completely eschewed the
  143– 5   It is *p*˙ that God does not employ drugs
  f 245–29   *p*˙ that decrepitude is not according to law,
  o 346– 9   The nothingness of nothing is *p*˙ ;
  g 527–15   It is *p*˙ also that material perception,

plainly
  a 46–13   Master said *p*˙ that physique was not Spirit,
  b 279– 3   New Testament writer *p*˙ describes faith,
  314–11   showed *p*˙ that their material views were
  320– 2   Christ *p*˙ declared, "I am the way,— *John* 14 : 6.
  320–17   text declares *p*˙ the spiritual fact of being,
  332–28   which were *p*˙ incarnate in the good and
  p 400–30   Scriptures *p*˙ declare the baneful influence of

plaintiff
  p 380–12   as though the defendant should argue for the *p*˙
  430–21   Personal Sense is the *p*˙.
  432– 3   acquainted with the *p*˙, Personal Sense,
  433– 1   The testimony for the *p*˙, Personal Sense,
  437– 3   he was on intimate terms with the *p*˙,
  439– 3   the *p*˙, Personal Sense, is a buyer for this firm.
  441– 5   He also decided that the *p*˙, Personal Sense,
  441–30   *p*˙, Personal Sense, is recorded in our

plaintive
  a 51– 1   the *p*˙ cry, "*Eloi, Eloi, lama*— *Mark* 15 : 34.

plan
  m 69–13   sense of increasing number in God's infinite *p*˙.
  r 493– 6   solar system as working on a different *p*˙.

planchette
  sp 80–22   Even *p*˙— the French toy which

plane
  sp 75–18   on the same *p*˙ of belief as those who
  77– 9   Death will occur on the next *p*˙ of existence
  f 225–32   on the lowest *p*˙ of human life,
  c 256– 2   Advancing to a higher *p*˙ of action,
  o 349–25   while dwelling on a material *p*˙,
  g 514– 3   recreate persons or things upon its own *p*˙,
  ap 573– 3   The Revelator was on our *p*˙ of existence,

planes
  f 226– 3   found on higher *p*˙ of existence

planet
  p 364– 3   the best man that ever trod this *p*˙.

planetary
  g 504–31   No . . . *p*˙ revolutions form the day of Spirit.

planets
  an 102–12   The *p*˙ have no more power over man than
  f 240– 7   Suns and *p*˙ teach grand lessons.

plank
  t 458– 2   The chief *p*˙ in this platform is the doctrine
  458– 8   Another *p*˙ in the platform is this,

plans
  p 399– 7   Mortal mind *p*˙ the exercise, and puts the

plant

every
  g 520–19   every *p*˙ of the field before it— *Gen.* 2 : 5.
  526– 4   "every *p*˙ of the field before it— *Gen.* 2 : 5.

fibres of a
  r 488–23   no more sensation, . . . than the fibres of a *p*˙.

grows
  g 520–24   the *p*˙ grows, not because of seed or soil,

Mind made the
  g 509–23   Mind made the "*p*˙ of the field— *Gen.* 2 : 5.

species of a
  ap 560–20   the genus and species of a *p*˙

---

  pref xi–23   the charge to *p*˙ and water His vineyard.
  a 54– 9   All must sooner or later *p*˙ themselves in Christ,
  s 147–19   *p*˙ you firmly on the spiritual groundwork of
  f 223– 1   *p*˙ ourselves upon what is pure and perfect.
  224– 6   shall *p*˙ our feet on firmer ground.
  b 269–22   I therefore *p*˙ myself unreservedly on the
  o 351– 6   if we *p*˙ ourselves on a material basis.
  p 365– 2   the thorns they *p*˙ in the pillow of the sick

planted
  s 133–25   him who *p*˙ Christianity on the foundation of
  f 231–31   *p*˙ on the Evangelist's statement that
  235–26   patient's feet may be *p*˙ on the rock

plants
  t 454– 7   and *p*˙ the feet in the true path,

platform
  a 37–20   into a mutilated doctrinal *p*˙.
  an 106– 2   to drop from the *p*˙ of common manhood
  f 226–14   God has built a higher *p*˙ of human rights,
  b 330– 8   When the following *p*˙ is understood
  t 458– 1   Mental quackery rests on the same *p*˙
  458– 2   The chief plank in this *p*˙ is the doctrine that
  458– 8   Another plank in the *p*˙ is this,

platitudes
  t 446–25   Not human *p*˙, but divine beatitudes,

Platonic
s 112– 8   adherents of the Socratic, the *P·*,

platter
p 382–12   merely the outside of the *p·*.

play
s 155– 2   Presently the child . . . is at *p·*.
b 338–21   Here *a dam* is not a mere *p·* upon words ;
t 450–14   nor *p·* the traitor for place and power.

playing
g 557– 2   moving and *p·* without harm, like a fish.

plea
p 391– 1   to overthrow the *p·* of mortal mind,
412–20   and array your mental *p·* against the physical.
417–17   When you silence the witness against your *p·*,
418–10   half equal to the truth of your *p·*,
430–15   in which the *p·* of C. S. heals the sick.
441–10   The *p·* of False Belief we deem unworthy of a

plead
pr   2–27   Shall we *p·* for more at the open fount,
3–20   We *p·* for unmerited pardon
15–18   we must deny sin and *p·* God's allness.
p 391–19   supposed to say, "I am sick," never *p·* guilty.
391–22   If you say, "I am sick," you *p·* guilty.
395– 3   should *p·* in opposition to the testimony of
412– 4   *p·* the case scientifically for Truth,
418– 7   *P·* with an honest conviction of truth

pleading
pr   2–19   The mere habit of *p·* with the divine Mind,

pleads
pr   2–19   as one *p·* with a human being,

pleas
ph 182–26   *P·* for drugs and laws of health come from

pleasant
m   65–24   fermentation even of fluids is not *p·*.
g 525–31   every tree that is *p·* to the sight, — *Gen.* 2 : 9.
530–23   more *p·* to the eyes than

pleasantest
m   58–32   and this is the *p·* thing to do.

please
m   58–31   how she may *p·* her husband," — *I Cor.* 7 : 34.
s 160–26   as they *p·* or as disease directs,
g 534–21   in the flesh cannot *p·* God. — *Rom.* 8 : 8.

pleased
sp   80–23   which years ago *p·* so many people
r 478–27   "But when it *p·* God, — *Gal.* 1 : 15.

pleasing
fr 600– *   *worthy of the Lord unto all p·,* — *Col.* 1 : 10.

pleasurable
c 265–32   if they wrench away false *p·* beliefs
g 506–28   Upon Adam devolved the *p·* task of

pleasure
  and pain
sp   92– 5   experiencing *p·* and pain,
b 298–17   alternating between a sense of *p·* and pain,
r 472–14   Error is a supposition that *p·* and pain,
  beliefs of
b 327– 6   destroy the false beliefs of *p·*, pain, or
  confers no
a   40– 1   once admit that evil confers no *p·*,
p 404–23   show him that sin confers no *p·*,
  false
b 308–12   false *p·*, pain, sin, sickness, and death."
  finding
b 322–13   finding *p·* in it and refraining . . . only through
327– 8   malice, finding *p·* in revenge !
  gives
ph 195– 8   All that gives *p·* to our educated senses
  good
p 442–28   it is your Father's good *p·* — *Luke* 12 : 32.
  have no
s 107–19   must say, "I have no *p·* in them." — *Eccl.* 12 : 1.
  His good
sp   99– 9   to will and to do of His good *p·*" — *Phil.* 2 : 13.
  illusion of
p 398–22   destroy the illusion of *p·* in intoxication,
  instead of
p 435–13   *p·* instead of pain, and life instead of death.
  knowledge and
g 532–17   Knowledge and *p·*, evolved through
  living only for
a   38–27   living only for *p·* or the gratification of the
  loses
b 327–11   Then he loses *p·* in wickedness,
  memory of
f 212–10   more vivid than the memory of *p·*.
  no abiding
b 327– 2   there is no abiding *p·* in evil,
  no real
p 404– 8   there is no real *p·* in false appetites.
404–20   that there is no real *p·* in sin, is one of the

pleasure
  nor pain
b 327– 4   neither *p·* nor pain, appetite nor passion,
  of a dream
ph 188–19   produced physically by the *p·* of a dream.
  or pain
sp   76–24   without a single bodily *p·* or pain,
f 224– 7   Every sensuous *p·* or pain is self-destroyed
c 260–27   the expectation of perpetual *p·* or pain
p 402–30   The involuntary *p·* or pain of the person
418– 4   destroying all belief in material *p·* or pain.
  pain and
    (*see* **pain**)
  pain or
    (*see* **pain**)
  personal
o 360– 9   replies : . . . mine give me such personal *p·*,
  rather than
f 212– 8   Why need pain, rather than *p·*, come to
  sense of
b 298–17   alternating between a sense of *p·* and pain,
322–19   until his physical sense of *p·* yields to a
  so-called
s 138–24   the sinful, so-called *p·* of the senses.
  supposed
pr   6–12   Every supposed *p·* in sin will furnish more than

c 260–31   If we look to the body for *p·*, we find pain ;
b 285– 2   cannot be cognizant . . . of *p·* or of pain.
294–28   The inebriate believes that there is *p·* in
r 490– 1   It assures mortals that there is real *p·* in sin ;
g 526–29   The name Eden, according to Cruden, means *p·*.

pleasures
  and pains
sp   77–14   embracing its so-called *p·* and pains,
f 222–13   less faith in the so-called *p·* and pains of matter.
232–28   so-called *p·* and pains of sense pass away
b 294–22   the *p·* and pains of matter to be myths,
296–14   so-called *p·* and pains of matter perish,
302–10   and that the so-called *p·* and pains,
308–18   matter with its false *p·* and pains,
p 382–28   nothingness of the so-called *p·* and pains of
390–10   to exchange the *p·* and pains of sense for the
  false
ph 196– 7   the false *p·* which tend to perpetuate
b 308–18   matter with its false *p·* and pains,
  few of the
a   38–21   Jesus experienced few of the *p·* of the
  hopes and
c 265–27   The loss of earthly hopes and *p·*
  material
a   39–23   material pains and material *p·* to pass away,
  of human sense
b 327–32   the nothingness of the *p·* of human sense
  of sense
c 265–29   quickly inform us that the *p·* of sense are
  of the table
s 129–31   author's small estimate of the *p·* of the table.
  pains and
m   67–31   physical pains and *p·*,
f 202– 8   so-called pains and *p·* of material sense,
r 491–28   awake, we dream of the pains and *p·* of matter.
  unreal as his
f 241– 9   sensualist's affections are . . . unreal as his *p·*.

a   21–29   The company is alluring and the *p·* exciting.
39–32   so long as he believes in the *p·* of sin?
p 405–30   pains of sinful sense are less harmful than its *p·*.

pleasure-trip
a   21–28   He is like a traveller going westward for a *p·*.

plentifully
s 113– 4   The letter of Science *p·* reaches humanity

plot
a   47–25   His dark *p·* fell to the ground,

plotted
a   47–23   he *p·* the betrayal of Jesus

pluck
s 141– 7   cut off the right hand and *p·* out the right eye,

plump
ph 175–27   empurpled the *p·* cheeks of our ancestors,

plunged
b 313–24   He *p·* beneath the material surface of things,
329–30   deeper the error into which mortal mind is *p·*,
g 556–31   *p·* his infant babe, . . . into the water

plural
r 466–23   Soul or . . . cannot be rendered in the *p·*.
g 515–17   The name Elohim is in the *p·*,

plurality
g 515–17   this *p·* of Spirit does not imply more than one

pneuma

gl 598– 1 The Greek word for *wind* (*p·*)
598– 3 "The wind [*p·*] bloweth where—*John* 3 : 8.
598– 5 is born of the Spirit [*p·*]."—*John* 3 : 8.
598–12 but this word *ghost* is *p·*.

poet

pref ix–10 As a certain *p·* says of himself,
m 66– 1 immortal Shakespeare, great *p·* of humanity :
sp 88– 2 which the *p·* Tennyson expressed
ph 176– 1 "Where ignorance is bliss, . . . says the English *p·*,
f 219–21 "The wish," says the *p·*, "is ever father to the
b 332– 7 quoted with approbation from a classic *p·* :

poetry

sp 89–19 It possesses of itself all beauty and *p·*,
f 244–29 Even Shakespeare's *p·* pictures age as
p 378– 2 even as *p·* and music are reproduced in union

point

at every
a 43–27 must overcome the human at every *p·*.
at issue
s 126–15 The *p·* at issue . . . is this :
at no
b 282–20 At no *p·* can these opposites mingle or unite.
g 531–30 theory of material life at no *p·* resembles
at that
g 549–27 At that *p·*, however, even this great observer
beyond faith
f 241–23 One's aim, a *p·* beyond faith, should be
central
t 454–30 the central *p·* of C. S.
contains the
r 466–16 contains the *p·* you will most reluctantly admit,
every
o 358–11 sustains logically . . . every *p·* it presents.
for each one
ph 195–11 The *p·* for each one to decide is,
fundamental
ph 167–29 On this fundamental *p·*, timid conservatism is
grand
s 116–13 Works on metaphysics leave the grand *p·*
great
sp 91– 7 Here is the great *p·* of departure for all true
leading
r 467–21 This is a leading *p·* in the Science of Soul,
of a diamond
g 521–16 the *p·* of a diamond" and the pen of an angel.
—*Jer.* 17 : 1.
of emergence
g 553–25 as the *p·* of emergence for the human race,
of self-destruction
p 374–32 or increases it to the *p·* of self-destruction.
strong
t 455–28 This strong *p·* in C. S. is not to be overlooked,
this
pr 9–27 Do you really desire to attain this *p·*?
sp 95–12 Whoever reaches this *p·* of moral culture
f 206–23 The Scriptures are definite on this *p·*,
221–14 At this *p·* C. S. saved him.
b 326–17 This *p·* won, you have started as you
this very
a 27–30 made their strongest attack upon this very *p·*.
won a
f 217–19 and you have won a *p·* in Science.

---

a 30–21 to *p·* out the way of Truth and Life.
m 66–20 wait patiently on divine wisdom to *p·* out the
s 118– 6 Did not this parable *p·* a moral
f 240– 5 all *p·* to Mind, the spiritual intelligence
b 293–27 and *p·* to matter's opposite, the strength and
299–10 they *p·* upward to a new and glorified trust,
t 447–25 remove the mask, *p·* out the illusion,
ap 561– 6 at a *p·* of so-called embryonic life.
571– 1 but they are not so willing to *p·* out the evil

pointed

pr 7– 3 Jesus' reproof was *p·* and pungent
a 24– 9 healing currents of Truth are *p·* out.
s 132–31 once *p·* his disciples to Jesus as
ph 184–32 She looked and saw that it *p·* due east.
f 225–11 but Science, heeding not the *p·* bayonet,
b 315–25 The divine conception of Jesus *p·* to this truth
t 462–17 nothing difficult . . . when the way is *p·* out ;
r 494– 9 Jesus *p·* the way for them.

pointedly

a 53– 6 He rebuked sinners *p·* and unflinchingly,

pointing

an 102–10 The *p·* of the needle to the pole symbolizes
t 444–16 Let us be faithful in *p·* the way through Christ,

points

all
s 148–16 Anatomy takes up man at all *p·* materially.
o 353–20 We must give up the spectral at all *p·*.
ap 564–15 Since Jesus must have been tempted in all *p·*,

points

cardinal
a 52–22 These were the two cardinal *p·* of Mind-healing,
ap 577–13 but its four cardinal *p·* are :
certain
p 422–27 and renders them fatal at certain *p·*,
doctrinal
o 361– 3 C. S. intervenes, explains these doctrinal *p·*,
hold these
p 414–25 Hold these *p·* strongly in view.
important
p 404–21 one of the most important *p·* in the theology of
r 497– 1 the important *p·*, or religious tenets, of C. S. :
leading
p 425– 7 take up the leading *p·* included
metaphysical
p 397– 1 By not perceiving vital metaphysical *p·*,
two essential
o 349–10 Two essential *p·* of C. S. are,

---

s 107– 7 apodictical Principle *p·* to the revelation of
122–20 *p·* to fair weather in the midst of
129–29 The very name, *illusion, p·* to nothingness.
138–15 His sublime summary *p·* to the religion of Love.
ph 170–12 *p·* to the self-sustaining and eternal Truth.
b 275–28 misleads thought and *p·* to other gods,
277–18 *p·* to the spiritual truth and Science of being.
p 394– 9 to act in the direction which Mind *p·* out.
t 454–15 *p·* out to his student error as well as truth,
g 539–22 Disputing these *p·* with the Pharisees

poison

ph 177–25 If a dose of *p·* is swallowed through mistake,
177–29 as if the *p·* had been intentionally taken.
178– 4 set down as a *p·* by mortal mind.
f 215–28 Socrates feared not the hemlock *p·*.
p 383–21 The tobacco-user, eating or smoking *p·*

poisonous

pr 12–21 to be apparently either *p·* or sanative.
s 133–12 healed of the *p·* stings of vipers.
157–18 If . . . then drugs cannot be *p·*.
ph 169–32 The good that a *p·* drug seems to do is evil,
178– 3 believe . . . the drug used, to be *p·*,
f 243– 4 divine Love, which made harmless the *p·* viper,
g 515– 7 serpent of God's creating is neither . . . nor *p·*,

poisons

ph 170– 2 and according to belief, *p·* the human system.

polar

ap 575–27 the Word, the *p·* magnet of Revelation ;

pole

an 102–10 The pointing of the needle to the *p·* symbolizes

policy

t 452–23 take no risks in the *p·* of error.

political

m 59–11 nor . . . be expected to understand *p·* economy.
b 340–27 civil, criminal, *p·*, and religious codes ;

politicians

ph 197–20 more honest than our sleek *p·*.

pollen

f 235– 1 cannot go forth, like wandering *p·*,

Polycarp

sp 77– 1 pious *P·* said : "I cannot turn at once from

polytheism

c 256–10 suggests *p·*, rather than the one ever-present

pomegranates

fr 600– * *and the p· bud forth.*— *Song* 7 : 12.

pomp

f 224–14 and array His vicegerent with *p·* and splendor ;

ponder

m 68–21 it may have caused the good to *p·*
ph 170–25 to *p·* somewhat the supremacy of Spirit,
ap 559–21 Read this book . . . Study it, *p·* it.

pondered

o 359–25 she *p·* the meaning of that Scripture

poor

pr 8–22 If we turn away from the *p·*, we are not
8–24 the reward of Him who blesses the *p·*.
a 27– 6 to the *p·* the gospel is preached."— *Luke* 7 : 22.
31– 1 he was found preaching the gospel to the *p·*.
33–25 preaches the gospel to the *p·*, the meek
34–16 and preach Christ, or Truth, to the *p·*,
m 58–20 a *p·* augury for the happiness of wedlock.
s 132– 8 the *p·* have the gospel preached— *Matt.* 11 : 5.
142–13 If the . . . turn the *p·* and the stranger from
ph 168– 1 is a *p·* shift for the weak and worldly,
f 247–28 are *p·* substitutes for the charms of being,
c 259– 9 higher than their *p·* thought-models
b 337–23 the *p·* counterfeits of the invisible universe
o 345–22 incongruity between God's idea and *p·* humanity,
347–16 preaching the gospel to the *p·*,

poor

p 364–13 He even said that this *p·* woman had
365–31 *p·* suffering heart needs its rightful nutriment,
383–29 pinching and pounding the *p·* body,
g 518–15 The rich in spirit help the *p·*

popular

a 24–18 *p·* opinions in regard to predestination
47–24 in order to raise himself in *p·* estimation.
m 67–26 the limited demonstration of *p·* Christianity
sp 83–13 and here Science takes issue with *p·* religions.
s 126–16 C. S. on the one hand and *p·* theology on the
137–11 the work, so mysterious to the *p·* mind?
141–10 All revelation (such is the *p·* thought !)
155–21 mightily outweigh the power of *p·* belief
ph 166– 9 *p·* doctor believes in his prescription,
b 291–21 has been transformed into the *p·* proverb,
316–15 and the blindness of *p·* belief,
o 344–26 Why support the *p·* systems of medicine, when
347–23 If C. S. takes away the *p·* gods,
355–17 *p·* religion, declines to admit that
357–17 *p·* and false notions about the Divine Being
p 398– 8 the *p·* ignorance of spiritual Life-laws.
g 557–22 *P·* theology takes up the history of man as if

popularity

a 42–10 was in no peril from salary or *p·*.
f 236– 1 Love of Christianity, rather than love of *p·*,
238–24 forsakes *p·* and gains Christianity.

pore

f 224– 3 feels the . . . effect of truth through every *p·*.

portal

pref vii–15 Truth, . . . knocks at the *p·* of humanity.

portals

p 251–11 they have but passed the *p·* of a new belief.

portend

ph 174–10 and *p·* a long night to the traveller ;

portentous

ap 562–28 great is the idea, and the travail *p·*.

porter

p 392–24 Stand *p·* at the door of thought,
392–30 then perform your office as *p·*

portion

basal
ph 189–29 in the lower, basal *p·* of the brain,
least
s 126– 9 Human thought never projected the least *p·* of
some
ph 197–28 and mortal belief loses some *p·* of its error.
pref xii–11 and (for a *p·* of this time) sole editor
ph 172–17 If the material body is man, he is a *p·* of
172–25 If . . . you take away a *p·* of the man when
177–13 of which the material body is the grosser *p·* ;
b 336–19 A *p·* of God could not enter man ;
p 425–27 will never believe that heart or any *p·* of the

portions

p 375–22 making certain *p·* of it motionless,
421– 4 belief that other *p·* of the body are
g 531– 8 It is well that the upper *p·* of the
546–19 seem more obscure than other *p·* of the

portraits

sp 86 25 *P·*, landscape-paintings, fac-similes of

portray

s 118–28 these definitions *p·* law as physical,

portrayal

sp 92–16 The *p·* is still graphically accurate,

portrayed

ap 561–28 The light *p·* is really neither solar nor

portrays

g 522–26 *p·* Spirit as supposedly cooperating

position

sp 90– 8 earth's motion and *p·* are sustained by Mind
ph 167–23 It is not wise to take a halting and half-way *p·*
182– 3 shows your *p·* as a Christian Scientist.
f 207– 5 This fact proves our *p·*,
254– 5 who gain good rapidly and hold their *p·*,
b 274–24 no half-way *p·* in learning its Principle
t 448–16 A dishonest *p·* is far from Christianly scientific.

positions

sp 74–30 never a return to *p·* outgrown.

positive

s 109–15 time and energies to discovering a *p·* rule.
126–13 human mind never . . . sent forth a *p·* sound.
ph 173–13 Spirit is *p·*.
173–15 For *p·* Spirit to pass through a
r 491– 8 a negative right and a *p·* wrong,

positively

p 362– 9 as *p·* as if she were a Hindoo pariah
420–12 as *p·* as they can the temptation to sin.

possess

sp 99–19 may *p·* natures above some others
s 119– 4 with what it does not and cannot *p·*,
138–20 to be Christlike, to *p·* the Christ-spirit,
156– 1 If drugs *p·* intrinsic virtues
157–25 confers the power which the drug seems to *p·*.
b 290–23 sin and error which *p·* us at the instant of
323– 4 and to *p·* no other consciousness but good.
p 425–23 the more immortality we *p·*.
r 486– 9 in order to *p·* immortal consciousness.
g 550– 4 Matter surely does not *p·* Mind.
556– 5 and are supposed to *p·* life and mind.

possessed

sp 86–10 Jesus *p·* more spiritual susceptibility than
b 313–27 was *p·* only in a limited degree

possesses

sp 89– 7 believing that somebody else *p·* her tongue
89–19 It *p·* of itself all beauty and poetry,
s 108– 6 matter *p·* neither sensation nor life ;
f 208–27 A mortal man *p·* this body,
247–20 Being *p·* its qualities before they
b 331–12 nothing *p·* reality nor existence except
r 475–21 *p·* no life, intelligence, nor . . . of his own,
488–24 Mind alone *p·* all faculties,
g 516–20 *p·* and reflects God's dominion
539–11 man *p·* nothing which he has not derived from
ap 576–23 In divine Science, man *p·* this recognition

possessing

sp 76–23 *p·* unlimited divine beauty and goodness
an 102– 6 *p·* neither intelligence, power, nor reality,
s 110– 1 Spirit *p·* all power, filling all space,
c 264–11 we must act as *p·* all power from Him
b 269–31 Mind, *p·* intelligence and life.
280–25 instead of *p·* a sentient material form,
t 443– 7 Mind as really *p·* all power.
r 473– 2 illusion, *p·* neither reality nor identity
g 554–30 less sickly than those *p·* higher organizations,

possession

s 151–11 if they . . . were in *p·* of the enlarged power
c 261–19 though he was in the full *p·* of his so-called
b 291–17 in *p·* of "the mind of the Lord,"— *Rom.* 11 : 34.
o 355–13 let the . . . , sense of Life and being take *p·*
p 393–11 Take *p·* of your body, and govern its feeling
402– 4 author has already in her *p·* well-authenticated
424– 3 takes *p·* of itself and its own thoughts
g 537–28 blessed the earth and gave it to man for a *p·*,

possessor

an 102–28 more likely to be abused by its *p·*, than
g 515– 1 enables its *p·* to emulate the example of Jesus.
gl 582– 7 error masquerading as the *p·* of life,

possibilities

divine
b 326– 1 A false sense of life, . . . hides the divine *p·*,
glorious
b 288–27 Science reveals the glorious *p·* of
infinite
a 34–23 into the perception of infinite *p·*.
of being
f 205–14 Spiritual perception brings out the *p·* of being,
of man
s 128–16 the latent abilities and *p·* of man.
t 445– 9 the great *p·* of man endued with divine Science.
of Spirit
b 316–31 the *p·* of Spirit and its correlative truth.
of thought
sp 90–20 This shows the *p·* of thought.
sp 88–28 the *p·* derived from divine Mind,

possibility

s 134–17 Denial of the *p·* of Christian healing robs
f 217– 3 the notion of such a *p·* is more absurd than
c 260–13 reveals the *p·* of achieving all good,
p 424–30 faith in the *p·* of their transmission.
t 445–11 Teach the dangerous *p·* of dwarfing
ap 574– 2 spiritual consciousness is . . . a present *p·*.

possible

pr 1– 3 all things are *p·* to God,
13–24 incorporeal Love, to whom all things are *p·*.
a 24–31 could not admit such an event to be *p·*.
37–22 It is *p·*,— yea, it is the duty and privilege
45–20 elevated them to *p·* at-one-ment with the
47–32 a belief in any *p·* material intelligence.
51– 2 the *p·* loss of something more important than
51– 3 *p·* misapprehension of the sublimest influence
sp 75–25 There is one *p·* moment, when those living
77–23 Even if communications . . . were *p·*,
78–12 even were communication *p·*
90–11 the movements and transitions now *p·*
90–12 will be found to be equally *p·* for the body.
s 147–10 where demonstration was humanly *p·*,
149–21 remarked . . . take as little medicine as *p·* ;
ph 178–16 the divine Mind, to which all things are *p·*,
180–27 man knows that with God all things are *p·*.

possible

ph 183– 1 Truth, makes all things *p·* to Spirit ;
183–17 the legitimate and only *p·* action of Truth
199–22 makes the achievement *p·*.
f 214– 1 it is *p·* that the impressions from Truth were
232–10 "with God all things are *p·*," — *Mark* 10 : 27.
232–10 all good is *p·* to Spirit ;
232–12 theories . . . make healing *p·* only through
236–24 teach their children at the earliest *p·* period
245–28 proves it *p·* to be young at seventy-four ;
o 356–21 is it *p·* for Him to create man subject to
p 365–27 it would, if it were *p·*, convert into a den of
432–17 The Judge asks if . . . it is *p·* for man to
t 456–15 and from its *p·* demonstration.
457–24 To pursue other vocations and . . . is not *p·*.
r 474–21 Is it *p·*, then, to believe that the evils
488–27 If it were *p·* for the real senses of man to
g 548–19 "It is very *p·* that many general statements
ap 573–25 *p·* to men in this present state of existence,

possibly

a 55–12 in a clearer light than mere words can *p·* do,
m 67–18 notion that animal natures can *p·* give force
s 151– 4 could not *p·* create a remedy outside of itself,
f 212–28 and *p·* that other methods involve
p 391– 9 Banish the belief that you can *p·* entertain a
440– 1 for he could not *p·* elude their search.
g 546–20 because they cannot *p·* be interpreted from a

post

a 49–19 faithful sentinel of God at the highest *p·*
m 67–12 firm at the post of duty, the mariner works on
p 393– 2 like a watchman forsaking his *p·*,
t 464–10 She therefore remains unseen at her *p·*,

post mortem

ph 196–26 induced by a single *p· m·* examination,

posts

p 387–17 not because they occupy the most important *p·*

postulate

erroneous
sp 91–25 The first erroneous *p·* of belief is,
91–27 The second erroneous *p·* is,
91–29 The third erroneous *p·* is,
91–32 The fourth erroneous *p·* is,
92– 3 The fifth erroneous *p·* is,
last
sp 92– 7 From the illusion implied in this last *p·* arises
this
b 287– 7 Divine Science contradicts this *p·*

postulates

sp 91–22 Certain erroneous *p·* should be here considered
b 288–21 are to be found in the following *p·* :

potency

s 155–26 *p·* of the medicine increases as the
158–17 the dignity and *p·* of divine Mind
b 293–14 whose *p·* is Truth, whose attraction is Love,
t 462– 7 understanding, *p·*, enlightenment, and success.
r 466– 3 Hence God combines all-power or *p·*,

potent

pref x–24 safer and more *p·* than that of any other
m 67–23 Grace and Truth are *p·* beyond all other means
s 153–12 and the most *p·* rises above matter into mind.
ph 180–32 I have found divine Truth more *p·* than
f 225–18 *p·* to break despotic fetters
o 351–17 cannot bring out . . . while error seems as *p·*
g 553–25 this *p·* belief will immediately supersede the

potentate

a 42– 3 rabbi affirmed God to be a mighty *p·*,

potentates

ap 577–23 *p·* and dynasties will lay down their honors

potentially

s 143–28 If Mind was first chronologically, is first *p·*,

potion

ph 177–31 a few persons believe the *p·* . . . to be harmless,

potter

ph 173– 7 supposition, that . . . the *p·* is subject to the
f 243–16 The clay cannot reply to the *p·*.
b 310– 8 The *p·* is not in the clay ;
310– 9 else the clay would have power over the *p·*.

pounding

p 383–29 pinching and *p·* the poor body,

pounds

s 111–19 A prize of one hundred *p·*,

pour

pr 10–10 vain repetitions will never *p·* into prayer the
a 36–10 that he might *p·* his dear-bought bounty into
54–10 liberally *p·* his dear-bought treasures into
f 201–17 to *p·* in truth through flood-tides of Love.

poured

m 57–22 Human affection is not *p·* forth vainly,
s 114–21 has to be *p·* into the old bottles of the letter.
ap 574–20 swift-winged thought, which *p·* forth hatred

pouring

pr 2–27 which is *p·* forth more than we accept

pours

pr 5–17 God *p·* the riches of His love into the
t 446–12 *p·* light and healing upon this generation,

poverty

g 501– 8 showing the *p·* of mortal existence,

powder

ph 179–27 homœopathic pellet and *p·* in hand,
p 380– 7 it will grind him to *p·*." — *Matt.* 21 : 44.

power

ability and
p 393–14 nothing can vitiate the ability and *p·*
admit that the
an 105– 8 to admit that the *p·* of human law is
against the
ap 566–32 He leads the hosts of heaven against the *p·* of
all
s 110– 1 Spirit possessing all *p·*, filling all space,
157–10 acknowledging that the divine Mind has all *p·*.
c 264–11 we must act as possessing all *p·* from Him
b 275–23 that is, all *p·*, all presence, all Science.
p 420–26 divine Love gives them all *p·* over every
t 443– 8 omnipotent Mind as really possessing all *p·*.
r 473–12 and attributes all *p·* to God.
490–11 since all *p·* belongs to God, good.
g 540–16 all sense of evil and all *p·* to sin.
all-embracing
an 102–11 symbolizes this all-embracing *p·*
all other
r 483– 7 Mind transcends all other *p·*,
almighty
f 202–27 We admit that God has almighty *p·*,
Almighty's
f 218–20 why do you substitute drugs for the Almighty's *p·*,
and grace
s 118–16 the invisible and infinite *p·* and grace.
b 333–22 has come with some measure of *p·* and grace
and prerogative
s 123– 8 the *p·* and prerogative of Spirit,
and prestige
f 244–32 of development, *p·*, and prestige.
and strength
ph 183–24 Obedience to Truth gives man *p·* and strength.
and willingness
r 493–31 the *p·* and willingness of divine Mind to
animal
gl 597–21 mortal belief ; animal *p·*.
another
t 445– 6 No hypothesis as to the existence of another *p·*
r 469–28 still believe there is another *p·*,
gl 594–10 claim . . . that there was another *p·*,
any
o 348–18 I desire to have no faith in . . . any *p·* but
any other
f 228–26 to acknowledge any other *p·* is to dishonor God.
assumed
s 145–30 must continually weaken its own assumed *p·*.
attributes and
b 301– 1 which manifests God's attributes and *p·*,
balance of
ph 166–28 The balance of *p·* is conceded to be with
belief in a
ap 569– 5 mortal belief in a *p·* opposed to God.
believes in the
ph 166–11 pharmacist believes in the *p·* of his drugs
bestows the
g 555–26 when we admit . . . that God bestows the *p·*
borrows its
pr 12–18 borrows its *p·* from human faith and belief.
Christian
f 233– 2 rather than professions of Christian *p·*.
coequal in
o 351–21 if we consider Satan as a being coequal in *p·*
conceding
p 394– 5 By conceding *p·* to discord,
conscious
p 423–24 with the stimulus of courage and conscious *p·*.
consecrating
p 388– 2 and consecrating *p·* of divine Truth,
creative
b 302–32 the reflection of the creative *p·* of
r 475–21 no life, intelligence, nor creative *p·* of his own,
g 507–15 creative *p·* of the divine Principle, or Life,
gl 582–20 God is the only creative *p·*.
deific
g 513–12 the motions and reflections of deific *p·*
514– 1 could not by simulating deific *p·* invert the
demonstrated the
sp 93– 3 demonstrated the *p·* of Spirit
s 110–25 Jesus demonstrated the *p·* of C. S. to heal

power

demonstration of
pr 10–11 in demonstration of p· and "with signs— *Mark* 16 : 20.
a 26–25 and of his demonstration of p· over death.
destroying the
r 473–15 and destroying the p· of death.
destroys your
t 452–28 Acting from sinful motives destroys your p·
destroy your
ph 181–12 You weaken or destroy your p· when you
development of
sp 82–32 hastening to a greater development of p·,
divine
(see **divine**)
dominant
ap 559– 4 dominant p· of which was upon the sea,
dominion, and
s 143–30 the glory, honor, dominion, and p·
enlarged
s 151–11 the enlarged p· it confers to benefit the race
entity nor
g 555–14 C. S. attributes to error neither entity nor p·,
erring
ph 192–11 Erring p· is a material belief,
evil is not
an 102–30 Mankind must learn that evil is not p·.
ph 192–24 Evil is not p·.
first
f 204–12 The first p· is admitted to be good,
flexibility and
ph 199–28 gave his . . . muscles, their flexibility and p·
God is the
a 27– 8 God is the p· in the Messianic work.
God's
a 42–16 the great demonstrator of God's p·
an 102–14 man, reflecting God's p·, has dominion
o 351– 3 When we lose faith in God's p· to heal,
t 450–24 by understanding God's p· over them.
goodness and
g 515–24 reflecting goodness and p·.
has no
pr 12– 4 A mere request . . . has no p· to gain more of
s 151–22 The human mind has no p· to kill
b 291–27 the grave has no p· over either.
p 399– 1 Evil has no p·, no intelligence,
hath no
sp 77–12 "the second death hath no p·."— *Rev.* 20 : 6.
b 290–15 the second death hath no p·."— *Rev.* 20 : 6.
healing
a 18–12 and he refuted all opponents with his healing p·.
31 13 the healing p· of Truth and Love.
38–32 shut out Truth and its healing p·.
55–20 and the healing p· of the divine Love
s 132–29 Did the doctrines . . . confer healing p·
141–23 they cannot demonstrate God's healing p·.
146–26 This healing p· of Truth must have been
150– 4 the healing p· of Truth is widely demonstrated
ph 167–31 Only through . . . can scientific healing p· be
177– 5 The evidence of divine Mind's healing p·
o 351– 2 pedantic and void of healing p·.
355–18 any systematic healing p· since the
p 366–19 infinite Love which alone confers the healing p·.
t 443–14 If patients fail to experience the healing p·
r 495– 4 hence its healing p· is not fully demonstrated.
496–11 demonstrating the healing p· of Truth and
he had
a 51– 7 He had p· to lay down a human sense of life
His
an 102– 3 and His p· is neither animal nor human.
s 108– 4 by the effectual working of His p·."— *Eph.* 3 : 7.
b 283–23 the true sense of His p· is lost to all who
o 352– 2 able to demonstrate His p· to heal,
g 517–31 causes them to multiply,— to manifest His p·.
his
pr 5– 2 and keeps him from demonstrating his p·
s 117–18 his p· over the sick and sinning.
ph 199–30 his p· of putting resolve into action
human
f 225–15 and shows human p· to be proportionate to
g 539–28 gave him more than human p· to expound the
identity or
r 479–28 So evil should be denied identity or p·,
imaginary
s 146–19 divests material drugs of their imaginary p·,
ph 178–25 disarm sin of its imaginary p· in proportion to
b 340– 1 will never lose their imaginary p· . . . until
incisive
sp 94–28 used his incisive p· injuriously?
inclination or
t 452–30 if you had the inclination or p·
intelligence nor
t 454–11 matter has neither intelligence nor p·,
intelligence or
b 339–31 never to admit that sin can have intelligence or p·,

power

less
f 222–11 Food had less p· to help or to hurt him
less than
f 203–18 prone to believe . . . in some p· less than God.
life-preserving
gl 579–13 life-preserving p· of spiritual understanding.
loss of
ph 183–25 Submission to error superinduces loss of p·.
lost its
b 321–16 The illusion of Moses lost its p· to alarm him,
lower
g 520–30 there is nothing left to be made by a lower p·.
manifestation of
sp 83–14 The scientific manifestation of p· is from the
man's
b 328–14 man's p·, when he is equipped by God,
material
f 249– 8 no mortal nor material p· as able to destroy.
p 378–25 Sickness is not a . . . material p·,
mental
t 455–26 No person can misuse this mental p·, if
moral
p 375–18 adding to his patient's mental and moral p·,
necessity and
p 377–28 conviction of the necessity and p· of
newly discovered
t 457– 9 has never used this newly discovered p· in any
no
sp 76–20 will have no p· over man, for man is immortal
s 143–26 no p· except that which is derived from Mind.
149–24 and with no p· but the divine Mind.
ph 192–20 you can have no p· opposed to God,
f 224–31 No p· can withstand divine Love.
228–25 There is no p· apart from God.
b 303– 6 no p· of propagation in matter,
p 375–24 show mortal mind that muscles have no p·
405–21 government of God, good, in which is no p· to sin.
t 452– 3 when one understands that evil has in reality no p·.
455–14 if, . . . you can exercise little or no p· for
no inherent
b 282–23 There is no inherent p· in matter ;
no innate
s 160– 6 for they have no innate p·.
no lesser
f 231– 9 no lesser p· equals the infinite All-power ;
no more
an 102–12 planets have no more p· over man than
no proof nor
sp 71–23 mainly erroneous, having . . . no proof nor p·
nor presence
i 471 10 there is no other p· nor presence.
nor reality
an 102– 6 possessing neither intelligence, p·, nor reality,
ph 186–16 there is neither p· nor reality in evil.
of action
a 157 14 p· of action is proportionately increased.
of Christian Science
s 110–25 Jesus demonstrated the p· of C. S. to heal
ph 189– 8 the p· of C. S. to establish harmony
b 317– 7 Whosoever . . . declares best the p· of C. S.,
p 412–13 The p· of C. S. and divine Love is omnipotent.
of divine Love
p 411–10 If Spirit or the p· of divine Love bear witness
of divine Principle
f 232–17 again demonstrating the p· of divine Principle,
of God
s 146–13 medicine substitutes drugs for the p· of God
f 224–30 p· of God brings deliverance to the captive.
p 406– 8 the p· of God is understood
of good
ap 570–31 the p· of good resident in divine Mind,
of healing
b 271–12 the p· of healing was not a supernatural gift
t 452–28 Acting from . . . destroys your p· of healing
of His Christ
ap 568–15 and the p· of His Christ :— *Rev.* 12 : 10.
of immortal Mind
ph 171–15 and the p· of immortal Mind
of its own
ap 563–12 the belief that matter has p· of its own,
of light
f 214–27 may end the p· of light and lens !
of Love
f 231–22 To fear sin is to misunderstand the p· of **Love**
of Mind
a 44–11 the p· of Mind over matter,
s 116–14 They never crown the p· of Mind as the
139– 6 Moses proved the p· of Mind
f 217–25 to learn the p· of Mind over the body
b 321–31 Jesus, who showed his students the p· of Mind
p 380–11 and deny the p· of Mind to heal.

power
of Mind
　p 382–27　　supporting the *p·* of Mind over the body
　384–31　　the *p·* of Mind over the entire functions
　417– 5　　their trust in the *p·* of Mind to sustain the
of pride
　gl 589–14　　the pride of power and the *p·* of pride ;
of Spirit
　a 44–30　　*p·* of Spirit to overrule mortal, material sense.
　sp 93– 3　　demonstrated the *p·* of Spirit
　ph 167–18　　and avail yourself of the *p·* of Spirit,
　183–20　　that which hides the *p·* of Spirit.
　f 233– 4　　the destruction of sin, . . . by the *p·* of Spirit,
　b 309–14　　the *p·* of Spirit over the material senses ;
　316– 8　　to prove the *p·* of Spirit over the flesh,
of the divine Mind
　s 160– 2　　destroying it through the *p·* of the divine Mind.
of their own
　g 507–20　　not . . . any propagating *p·* of their own,
of Truth
　　(*see* **Truth**)
omnipotent
　ph 182–31　　to presuppose that omnipotent *p·* is powerless
one
　b 270– 8　　there is but one *p·*, — not two powers,
opposing
　p 380–30　　to believe . . . that God endows this opposing *p·*
outweigh the
　s 155–20　　mightily outweigh the *p·* of popular belief
over all the
　p 438– 5　　over all the *p·* of the enemy :— *Luke* 10 : 19.
over sickness
　s 142– 5　　by its *p·* over sickness, sin, and death ;
over sin
　s 142– 7　　generally omit all but . . . the *p·* over sin.
overwhelming
　a 47– 9　　It was sometimes an overwhelming *p·*
percentage of
　s 155–19　　the percentage of *p·* on the side of this Science
perfection and
　g 522– 7　　endows man out of God's perfection and *p·*.
physical
　s 131–11　　the superiority of spiritual over physical *p·*.
place and
　ph 167–13　　cannot successfully usurp the place and *p·* of
　t 450–14　　nor play the traitor for place and *p·*.
place nor
　b 327–20　　evil has in reality neither place nor *p·*
post of
　a 49–19　　at the highest post of *p·*,
preponderance of
　s 143–20　　you conclude that . . . the preponderance of *p·*.
　ph 177–23　　the preponderance of *p·* in any direction
presence and
　g 512– 8　　symbolized by strength, presence, and *p·*,
　gl 596–18　　the presence and *p·* of the Most High.
pride of
　t 451– 5　　renounce . . . oppression and the pride of *p·*.
　gl 589–13　　the pride of *p·* and the power of pride ;
propagation and
　g 545–24　　They believed in . . . its propagation and *p·*.
propensity or
　g 539–14　　the propensity or *p·* to do evil?
protecting
　p 387–28　　the supporting influence and protecting *p·*
reality and
　p 372–20　　How, . . . can we believe in the reality and *p·* of
recuperative
　p 394– 7　　which is the only real recuperative *p·*.
redeeming
　g 552–23　　for the redeeming *p·*, . . . is not in egg nor in dust.
sacred
　ph 182–26　　ability to demonstrate Mind's sacred *p·*.
same
　s 135–11　　same *p·* which heals sin heals also sickness.
saving
　b 285–31　　the healing and saving *p·*.
second
　f 204–13　　so-called second *p·*, evil, is the unlikeness of
secondary
　ap 559– 7　　a secondary *p·* was exercised upon visible error
seeming
　s 122– 3　　assigning seeming *p·* to sin, sickness, and death ;
　f 208– 6　　What then is this seeming *p·*,
　t 452– 2　　bar the door of his thought against this seem-
　　　　　　　　ing *p·*,
sensation or
　f 218–26　　to believe in matter as . . . having sensation or *p·*.
spirit and
　a 55–25　　the spirit and *p·* of Christian healing.
spiritual
　　(*see* **spiritual**)
such a
　p 378–29　　Such a *p·*, . . . is inconceivable ;
　378–30　　if such a *p·* could be divinely directed,

power
supply of
　ph 199–12　　its demand for and supply of *p·*.
supposed
　f 224–32　　What is this supposed *p·*, which opposes
　370–24　　a drug may eventually lose its supposed *p·*
the only
　ph 186–19　　The only *p·* of evil is to destroy itself.
　192–24　　gives you the only *p·* obtainable.
　f 249–14　　omnipotence is the only *p·*.
　p 419–28　　for God is the only *p·*.
third
　f 204–15　　The third *p·*, mortal man, is a supposed
this
　a 25–25　　that they might demonstrate this *p·* as he did
　sp 85–20　　Our Master rebuked the lack of this *p·*
　s 110–26　　But this *p·* was lost sight of,
　151–29　　acknowledge this fact, yield to this *p·*,
　b 271–30　　spiritual import of the Word imparts this *p·*.
to act
　gl 582– 8　　strength, animation, and *p·* to act.
to demonstrate
　f 254–18　　not the *p·* to demonstrate what we do not
to heal
　pref x–21　　so little faith in His disposition and *p·* to heal
　s 148– 3　　implying that the requisite *p·* to heal was in
　o 351– 3　　When we lose faith in God's *p·* to heal,
　352– 2　　able to demonstrate His *p·* to heal,
　p 410–27　　If . . . the *p·* to heal mentally will diminish,
　t 446–15　　destroying his own *p·* to heal and his own
transcendent
　ph 182–29　　ignorance of C. S. and its transcendent *p·*.
truly derived
　a 44–21　　in his proof of man's truly derived *p·*?
unfolds the
　b 276– 1　　unfolds the *p·* that heals the sick,
unsurpassed
　f 243– 9　　with unsurpassed *p·* and love.
wrong
　t 452–32　　the wrong *p·* would be destroyed.

　pr 17–12　　Thine is the kingdom, and the *p·*, — *Matt.* 6 : 13.
　sp 89–20　　beauty and poetry, and the *p·* of expressing
　92– 9　　Mind is not an entity . . . with the *p·* of sinning
　an 101– 7　　upon the *p·* of the imagination."
　s 119– 9　　this dilemma and consider matter as a *p·*
　157–24　　confers the *p·* which the drug seems to
　ph 181–32　　Any hypnotic *p·* you may exercise will
　185–10　　discussed . . . "mind-cure," operating through
　　　　　　　　the *p·* of
　196– 1　　If materialistic knowledge is *p·*,
　196– 4　　The *p·* of mortal mind over its own body is
　196–18　　wherewith to establish their *p·*.
　198– 2　　has in belief more *p·* to harm
　f 202–30　　as if senseless matter . . . had more *p·* than
　206– 4　　The *p·* of the human will should be
　224– 1　　and the *p·* of sin diminishing,
　228–29　　supposition that sin, . . . and death have *p·*.
　253–13　　mortal, material sense which is not *p·*
　b 296–32　　a liar from the beginning, not deserving *p·*.
　308–31　　"*p·* with God and with men." — *Gen.* 32 : 28.
　310– 9　　else the clay would have *p·* over the potter.
　330–27　　Evil is nothing, no thing, mind, nor *p·*.
　o 348–15　　or imputing too much *p·* to God,
　358–28　　belief that . . . these healers have wonderful *p·*,
　p 368–11　　fatal beliefs . . . that evil is equal in *p·* to good
　376–31　　To fear and admit the *p·* of disease, is to
　378–27　　never endowed matter with *p·* to disable Life
　380–29　　to believe that there is a *p·* opposite to God,
　388–15　　another admission . . . that food has *p·*
　396–22　　At the right time explain to the sick the *p·*
　419–11　　Neither disease itself, sin, nor fear has the *p·* to
　438– 5　　Behold, I give unto you *p·* — *Luke* 10 : 19.
　r 473–10　　nothing apart from Him is present or has *p·*.
　485–32　　is like saying that the *p·* is in the lever.
　495–11　　a *p·* which opens the prison doors
　g 515– 9　　the *p·* which changeth the serpent into a staff.
　547–19　　theory, — that Mind . . . endues matter with *p·*

powerful
　an 103–22　　false belief . . . that evil is . . . more *p·*.
　o 352–21　　declaring ghosts to be real, merciless, and *p·*,
　p 390–30　　as *p·* mental opposition as a legislator
　397–14　　Your thought is more *p·* than your words,
　397–15　　more *p·* than the accident itself,

powerfully
　pr 12– 7　　making it act more *p·* on the body
　s 155–22　　The human mind acts more *p·* to offset

powerless
　s 152– 3　　would wield the sceptre of a monarch, but it is *p·*.
　160– 8　　the inanimate drug becomes *p·*.
　ph 182–32　　to presuppose that . . . is *p·* on some occasions.
　f 228–29　　He proved them *p·*.
　p 375–16　　All unscientific mental practice is . . . *p·*,
　377–31　　is of itself *p·* to produce suffering.
　ap 567–23　　and so proved to be *p·*.

powerlessness
  m 65–17 the *p·* of vows to make home happy,
  r 490–10 From this also comes its *p·*,

powers
broadcast
  m 65–13 broadcast *p·* of evil so conspicuous to-day
divine
  f 249– 9 the divine "*p·* that be."— *Rom.* 13 : 1.
God-given
  p 387–10 nor . . . trespass upon God-given *p·*
imaginary
  p 403–19 deprived of its imaginary *p·* by Truth,
lower
  s 144– 4 needs no cooperation from lower *p·*,
mental
  an 105–22 Whoever uses his developed mental *p·*
  s 128– 9 C. S. enhances their endurance and mental *p·*,
no antagonistic
  f 231–14 but there are no antagonistic *p·* nor laws,
not two
  b 270– 9 but one power,— not two *p·*,
of this world
  f 225– 8 The *p·* of this world will fight,
other
  ph 169–30 Whatever teaches man . . . to acknowledge
      other *p·*
  r 485–25 If thought yields its dominion to other *p·*,
so-called
  s 144– 5 even if these so-called *p·* are real.
  b 275–29 other gods, or other so-called *p·*,

  sp 92–28 This belief tends to support two opposite *p·*,
  s 142– 7 generally omit all but one of these *p·*,
  f 204– 8 false conclusions . . . two *p·*,— namely,
  204–16 the first and second antagonistic *p·*,
  o 357–26 If . . . there must be two *p·*,

practical
  pr 11–26 in the only *p·* road to holiness.
  a 19–23 the *p·* repentance, which reforms the heart
  24–27 the *p·* affection and goodness
  31–15 It is the living Christ, the *p·* Truth,
  37–21 the more *p·* import of that career !
  sp 98–17 a revealed and *p·* Science.
  98–28, 29 *p·* and complete, and being *p·* and complete,
  s 111–31 the broadest *p·* tests.
  147– 8 submitted to the broadest *p·* test,
  f 224–22 A higher and more *p·* Christianity,
  254–21 to abandon so fast as *p·* the material,
  o 341– 4 from a theoretical to a *p·* Christianity,
  345–19 and this *p·* proof is the only feasible evidence
  351–16 the *p·* proof of Christianity,
  355– 5 is met by something *p·*,
  p 410–13 mankind objects to making this teaching *p·*.
  t 452– 4 Incorrect reasoning leads to *p·* error.

practically
  s 122– 8 was *p·* exposed nineteen hundred years ago
  146–21 effects *p·* prove its divine origin and efficacy.
  150–24 the *p·* rejected doctrine of the predestination
  f 232–11 but our prevalent theories *p·* deny this,
  b 283–25 cannot be *p·* demonstrated . . . unless
  328–19 can it be said that they explain it *p·*,
  o 356– 9 Jesus reasoned on this subject *p·*,
  360–18 If you try to have two models, then you *p·* have
      none.

Practice, Christian Science
  r 493–13 a previous chapter entitled C. S. *P·*.

practice
basis of
  t 456–21 So long as matter is the basis of *p·*,
by his
  f 232–22 nor did he illustrate these errors by his *p·*.
Christian scientific
  p 410–29 Christian scientific *p·* begins with
contradict the
  f 202–25 beliefs . . . contradict the *p·* growing out of
experience in
  t 461–32 spiritual growth and experience in *p·*
guidance in
  s 164– 8 none can be adopted as a safe guidance in *p·*."
its
  pref x–24 its *p·* is safer and more potent than that of any
made void their
  s 145– 7 would have made void their *p·*.
medical
  (see **medical**)
mental
  (see **mental**)
metaphysical
  s 144–17 is not the metaphysical *p·* of C. S.,
  p 424–15 It is equally important in metaphysical *p·*
  t 460– 5 it underlies all metaphysical *p·*.

practice
of Christian Science
  s 144–17 is not the metaphysical *p·* of C. S.,
  o 355–24 the divine Principle and *p·* of C. S.
  p 442–17 Neither . . . enters into the *p·* of C. S.,
of divine metaphysics
  s 111–12 the *p·* of divine metaphysics is the
of magnetism
  an 101– 2 observed in the public *p·* of magnetism,
of medicine
  s 161–12 law, restricting the *p·* of medicine.
of sin
  a 39–31 Who will stop the *p·* of sin so long as
of Truth
  a 26–22 Jesus' teaching and *p·* of Truth
  p 410–24 does not appear in the *p·* of Truth
Principle and
  pref ix–14 the Principle and *p·* of Christian healing,
  a 53–10 the divine Principle and *p·* of Jesus
  o 355–24 the divine Principle and *p·* of C. S.
put into
  b 323–13 we must put into *p·* what we already know.
reduce to
  r 490–17 reduce to *p·* the real man's divine Principle,
right
  t 454–17 the wrong as well as the right *p·*.
Science in
  s 162–17 Working out the rules of Science in *p·*,
such a
  t 452–26 Such a *p·* does not demonstrate the
teaching and
  a 26–22 Jesus' teaching and *p·* of Truth
  r 473–19 the teaching and *p·* of Christianity,
teachings and
  a 19–26 the teachings and *p·* of our Master
theory and
  t 456–16 Any dishonesty in your theory and *p·*
theory and in
  f 229–19 mistaken in theory and in *p·*.
the student's
  p 411– 3 My first discovery in the student's *p·*
without
  f 241–18 The error of the ages is preaching without *p·*.

  pr 15–22 in so far as we put our desires into *p·*.
  15–28 *P·* not profession, understanding not belief,
  a 26–20 to show the learner the way by *p·* as well as
  t 458– 7 This theory is supposed to favor *p·* from
  ap 561– 3 destroys both faith in evil and the *p·* of

practices
  a 18–11 against Pharisaical creeds and *p·*,
  s 141– 9 even the most cherished beliefs and *p·*,
  r 484–27 involved in all false theories and *p·*.

practise
  a 41–30 demanded more than they were willing to *p·*.
  sp 98–21 for every man to understand and to *p·*.
  an 101–24 its effects upon those who *p·* it,
  f 253–18 If you believe in and *p·* wrong knowingly,
  b 271–28 to learn and to *p·* Christian healing,
  p 365–22 then he is Christian enough to *p·* scientifically
  431–29 testifies : . . . I *p·* daily ablutions
  t 446–13 can *p·* on no one from . . . motives without
  449–13 You should *p·* well what you know,
  452–30 the inclination or power to *p·* wrongly
  453–32 nor can he *p·* animal magnetism
  457–26 They even *p·* these, intending
  462– 9 to *p·* Truth's teachings only in part,

practised
  a 24– 2 Truth and Love understood and *p·*.
  26–30 which he taught and *p·*.
  s 147–12 Jesus *p·* these rules on the hills of Judæa
  147–24 healed the sick, *p·* Christian healing,
  ph 174–21 Truth is revealed. It needs only to be *p·*.
  f 201– 1 The best sermon ever preached is Truth *p·*
  o 344–23 the C. S. which Jesus preached and *p·*
  t 451–29 and it is *p·* either with a mistaken or a wicked

practises
  t 446–11 Whoever *p·* the Science the author teaches,
  449–30 if the student *p·* what he is taught,

practising
  o 342–29 If Christian Scientists were teaching or *p·*
  t 456– 3 Teaching or *p·* in the name of Truth,

practitioner
  sp 79–23 The unscientific *p·* says : "You are ill.
  s 161–24 ordinary *p·*, examining bodily symptoms,
  ph 176–22 Should . . . disease be treated by a regular *p·*,
  p 365–30 The unchristian *p·* is not giving
  403–28 *p·* improves or injures the case in proportion
  t 459–20 a false *p·* will work mischief,

practitioner's
  p 410–28 until the *p·* healing ability is

practitioners
pref viii–19 Is there less sickness because of these *p·*?
   s 164–10 the cultured class of medical *p·*
   ph 174– 3 as do civilized *p·* by their more studied methods.

praise
pr 2– 8 God is not moved by the breath of *p·* to do more
   o 354–23 out of the mouth of babes He will perfect *p·*.
   p 362– * *for I shall yet p· Him,— Psal.* 42 : 11.
   ap 558–13 When understood, it is Truth's prism and *p·*.

praised
ap 558– * *to be p· in the city of our God,— Psal.* 48 : 1.

pray
pr 1– * *when ye p·, believe that ye receive— Mark* 11 : 24.
   2– 1 Do we *p·* to make ourselves better or to
   3– 4 Who would . . . *p·* the principle of mathematics
   9–31 why *p·* with the lips that you may be
   12–30 If the sick recover because they *p·*
   13–20 If we *p·* to God as a corporeal person, this will
   14–32 *p·* to thy Father which is in— *Matt.* 6 : 6.
   15–14 In order to *p·* aright, we must enter into the
   15–21 We must "*p·* without ceasing."— *I Thess.* 5 : 17.
   15–23 The Master's injunction is, that we *p·* in secret
   16– 9 "After this manner therefore *p·*"— *Matt.* 6 : 9.
   a 19–20 if the sinner continues to *p·* and repent,
   21– 6 not . . . labor and *p·*, expecting because of
   m 66–19 it is well to hope, *p·*, and wait patiently
   f 218–17 Why *p·* for the recovery of the sick, if
   b 271–17 "Neither *p·* I for these alone,— *John* 17 : 20.
   309– 1 "Tell me, I *p·* thee, *thy* name ;"— *Gen.* 32 : 29.
   p 367–21 Let us watch, work, and *p·*
   t 444–26 "Let there be no strife, I *p·* thee,— *Gen.* 13 : 8.
   r 497–24 we solemnly promise to watch, and *p·*

prayed
pr 7–31 the recollection that we have *p·* over it
   9– 8 satisfied with having *p·* for something
   12–30 because they pray or are *p·* for audibly,
   a 32–12 the cup which he *p·* might pass from him,
   32–22 yet Jesus *p·* and gave them bread.
   32–25 Jesus *p·* ; he withdrew from the
   38–18 At another time Jesus *p·*, not for the twelve only,
   p 369–18 never gave drugs, never *p·* to know if

Prayer, the Lord's
pr 14–23 The Lord's *P·* is the prayer of Soul,
   16– 8 which we name after him the Lord's *P·*.
   16–23 which is indicated in the Lord's *P·*
   16–25 the spiritual sense of the Lord's *P·* :

prayer
acceptable
   pr 3–31 In such a case, the only acceptable *p·* is
audible
   pr 4–27 Audible *p·* can never do the works of
   7– 8 Audible *p·* is impressive ; it gives
child at
   s 119–20 palsies . . . the child at *p·*, is not the divine ideal
consistent
   pr 9–32 Consistent *p·* is the desire to do right.
desire is
   pr 1–11 Desire is *p·* ;
governed by Science
   f 206–13 This *p·*, governed by Science. . .heals the sick.
healing
   pr 12– 2 What is this healing *p·*?
heart of
   pr 15–10 To enter into the heart of *p·*,
highest
   pr 16– 2 The highest *p·* is not one of faith merely ;
Jesus'
   pr 11– 1 Jesus' *p·*, "Forgive us our debts,"— *Matt.* 6 · 12.
loftiness of his
   pr 8–13 If he reached the loftiness of his *p·*,
motives for
   pr 2– 1 What are the motives for *p·*?
of faith
   pr 12– 1 *p·* of faith shall save the sick,"— *Jas.* 5 : 15.
of fervent desire
   pr 4– 3 the *p·* of fervent desire for growth in grace,
of Soul
   pr 14–23 The Lord's Prayer is the *p·* of Soul,
of the righteous
   f 206–13 hope, faith, love— is the *p·* of the righteous.
   231–11 heal the sick through the *p·* of the righteous.
of the unrighteous
   f 206–11 Will-power . . . is the *p·* of the unrighteous ;
one brief
   pr 16– 7 Our Master taught his disciples one brief *p·*,
our
   pr 9–11 by living consistently with our *p·*?
public
   pr 13– 5 In public *p·* we often go beyond our
silent
   pr 4–28 silent *p·*, . . . and devout obedience enable us

prayer
such
   pr 12– 6 The beneficial effect of such *p·* for the sick
   15–21 Such *p·* is answered, in so far as we
   16– 4 Such *p·* heals sickness, and must destroy
test of all
   pr 9– 5 The test of all *p·* lies in the answer to these
their
   o 351–32 but their *p·* brought down no proof that it
unceasing
   pr 4–13 struggle to be always good is unceasing *p·*.
understanding of
   pr 10– 6 grow to the spiritual understanding of *p·*.
verbal
   pr 7–15 The motives for verbal *p·* may
wordy
   pr 8– 1 A wordy *p·* may afford a quiet sense of

   iii– * Oh ! Thou hast heard my *p·* ;
   pr 1– 1 The *p·* that reforms the sinner and heals
   1– 6 *P·*, watching, and working, combined with
   2–15 *P·* cannot change the Science of being,
   5–22 *P·* is not to be used as a confessional
   5–25 If *p·* nourishes the belief that sin is
   5–27 If . . . *p·* is an evil.
   6–21 is to misunderstand Love and to make *p·* the
   7–27 The danger from *p·* is that it may
   10– 1 *P·* means that we desire to walk and will
   10–10 vain repetitions will never pour into *p·* the
   10–20 to earn a penny by grinding out a *p·*.
   10–21 has paid for the privilege of *p·* the
   10–23 not always receive the blessings we ask for in *p·*.
   11–27 *P·* cannot change the unalterable Truth,
   11–28 nor can *p·* alone give us an understanding
   11–29 *p·*, coupled with a fervent habitual desire
   12–16 *P·* to a corporeal God affects the sick like a
   12–29 another who offers the same measure of *p·*?
   13–14 Even if *p·* is sincere, God knows our need
   16–10 that *p·* which covers all human needs.
   16–13 whether the last line is not an addition to the *p·*
   16–14 does not affect the meaning of the *p·* itself.
   ap 566–19 we may also offer the *p·* which concludes the
   gl 592–25 Consecration ; charity ; gentleness ; *p·* ;

prayerful
pr 8–10 If a man, though apparently fervent and *p·*,

prayers
are mental
   pr 12–32 In divine Science, where *p·* are mental,
audible
   pr 8–18 Professions and audible *p·* are like
constant
   pr 15–27 purity, and affection are constant *p·*.
her own
   o 351–10 her own *p·* failed to heal her
humble
   pr 12–13 Jesus, whose humble *p·* were
in which
   p 395–15 *P·*, in which God is not asked to heal
long
   pr 4–30 Long *p·*, superstition, and creeds
   9–28 Then why make long *p·* about it
   a 20–12 men can . . . make long *p·*, and yet
our
   pr 13– 9 If . . . our *p·* are "vain repetitions,"— *Matt.* 6 : 7.
their
   pr 8– 6 Their *p·* are indexes which do not
   ph 182–25 thus working against themselves and their *p·*

   o 351–10 the *p·* of her devout parents
   355– 7 *p·* which evince no spiritual power to heal.

prayest
pr 14–31 "When thou *p·*, enter into thy— *Matt.* 6 : 6.

praying
pr 2– 4 Are we benefited by *p·*? Yes,
   5–26 belief . . . that man is made better merely by *p·*,
   8–20 *P·* for humility with whatever fervency
   12–22 common custom of *p·* for the recovery of
   f 254– 3 are consistent who, watching and *p·*,
   b 326–20 Working and *p·* with true motives,
   t 464–11 *p·*, watching, and working for the

praying-machine
pr 10–18 to carry a *p·* through the streets,

preach
pref xi–19 To *p·* deliverance to the captives— *Luke* 4 : 18.
   a 18– * *not to baptize, but to p· the gospel.— I Cor.* 1 : 17.
   34–15 and *p·* Christ, or Truth, to the poor,
   37–30 *p·* the gospel to every creature !"— *Mark* 16 : 15.
   s 138–28 *p·* the gospel to every creature !— *Mark* 16 : 15.
   b 271–32 how shall they *p·*, except they be— *Rom.* 10 : 15.
   272– 1 how shall they *p·*, convert, and heal . . . except
   o 342–10 "Go ye into all the world, and *p·*— *Mark* 16 : 15.
   p 418–27 "*P·* the gospel to every creature."— *Mark* 16 : 15.

preached
a 27– 6 to the poor the gospel is *p*·."— *Luke* 7 : 22.
55– 9 Now that the gospel of healing is again *p*·
s 107– * *the gospel which was p· of me*— *Gal.* 1 : 11.
132– 8 the poor have the gospel *p*· to them.—*Matt.* 11 : 5.
141– 2 and the truth *p*· by Jesus.
f 201– 1 The best sermon ever *p*· is Truth practised
o 344–23 the C. S. which Jesus *p*· and practised
345– 7 When the omnipotence of God is *p*·

preacher
s 132–30 This righteous *p*· once pointed his disciples to
136–26 doubted if Jesus was controlled by the sainted *p*·.
b 271–32 "How shall they hear without a *p*·?— *Rom.* 10 : 14.

preaches
a 33–25 and *p*· the gospel to the poor,

preaching
a 23–14 This *p*· receives a strong rebuke in the
31– 1 In meekness and might, he was found *p*·
f 241–17 The error of the ages is *p*· without practice.
b 324–24 healing the sick and *p*· Christianity
324–28 "If . . . then is our *p*· vain."— *I Cor.* 15. 14.
o 347–16 *p*· the gospel to the poor, healing the sick,

precede
pr 16– 1 A great sacrifice of material things must *p*·
f 252– 9 must *p*· that understanding of Truth which
g 553– 5 must *p*· an understanding of the harmony of

preceded
g 543–21 thinking that apehood *p*· mortal manhood?

precedence
sp 83–20 and gives to matter the *p*· over Spirit.

precedent
m 63–14 C. S. furnishes no *p*· for such injustice,
sp 72– 7 A condition *p*· to communion with Spirit
an 105– 7 would be to contradict *p*· and to admit
s 138–17 Jesus established in the Christian era the *p*·

precedes
sp 96–11 "The darkest hour *p*· the dawn."
g 530–30 narrative supposes . . . that matter *p*· mind.
553–32 which *p*· the development of that belief.

preceding
g 522–28 for the Scripture just *p*· declares

precept
a 26–21 by practice as well as *p*·.
f 234–29 was to break a moral *p*·.
o 344–17 would be just to observe the Scriptural *p*·,
354–18 is seen in example more than in *p*·.
p 382–10 a useful rebuke from Jesus' *p*·,
t 443–21 may learn the value of the apostolic *p*· :
r 465– * *For p· must be upon p·, p· upon p·;— Isa.* 28 : 10.

precepts
a 31–17 Obeying his precious *p*·,
s 141– 5 Jesus' divine *p*· for living and healing.
141– 6 Because his *p*· require the disciple to
b 270– 4 When the divine *p*· are understood,

preclude
a 44– 5 The lonely *p*· of the tomb

precious
a 22– 9 through Christ's *p*· love these efforts are
26–24 *p*· import of our Master's sinless career
31–17 Obeying his *p*· precepts,
m 66– 5 Wears yet a *p*· jewel in his head.
66–32 that the *p*· metal may be graven with the

precipice
p 374–22 walking in darkness on the edge of a *p*·.

precipitate
b 324– 4 helps to *p*· the ultimate harmony.
p 436–19 Fear, the sheriff, to *p*· the result

precipitately
m 66–23 for a wife *p*· to leave her husband

precipitates
m 67–16 *p*· his doom or sunshine gladdens the

precise
c 256–16 *p*· form of God must be of small importance
b 270–17 knew not what would be the *p*· nature of

precisely
a 19–13 declaring *p*· what would destroy sickness,
o 354– 8 when it teaches *p*· this thought

preclude
a 36–16 *p*· C. S. from finding favor with the

precludes
r 487–15 this *p*· the need of believing.

preconceptions
s 129–10 be it in accord with your *p*· or

predecessors
f 239– 2 The sects, which endured the lash of their *p*·,

predestination
a 24–18 in regard to *p*· and future punishment.
s 150–25 the practically rejected doctrine of the *p*· of

predicated
s 144– 9 physiology, hygiene, are mainly *p*· of matter,

predicting
sp 84– 5 *p*· the future from a groundwork of
s 149–27 *p*· disease does not dignify therapeutics.

prediction
a 54–28 and history has confirmed the *p*·.
g 532– 9 the *p*· in the story under consideration.

predisposed
p 389– 6 the less we are *p*· to sickness.

predisposing
ph 178–11 *p*· cause and the exciting cause are mental.
f 230–31 remote, *p*·, and the exciting cause
p 393– 6 *p*·, remote, and exciting cause

predisposition
f 220– 2 in order to overcome a *p*· to take cold ;

predominate
c 262–20 supposed pain and pleasure of matter cease to *p*·.
g 502– 5 as if reality did not *p*· over unreality,

pre-eminently
a 42–11 endorsed *p*· by the approval of God,
m 66–26 the other *p*· needs good company.
an 102–32 *p*· promotes affection and virtue in families
s 123–32 On the contrary, C. S. is *p*· scientific,

preens
c 261–29 and *p*· its wings for a skyward flight.

preferable
an 101–29 Discomfort under error is *p*· to comfort.

preference
s 160–25 If muscles can . . . become rigid of their own *p*·.
ph 179–12 *p*· of mortal mind for a certain method

prefigured
ap 559–29 *p*· this perilous passage out of bondage

prefigures
ap 558–10 This angel . . . *p*· divine Science.

prejudice
s 144–25 Ignorance, pride, or *p*· closes the door to
r 484– 3 neither pride, *p*·, bigotry, nor envy can

preliminary
t 449–26 They are enemies without the *p*· offence.
r 484–29 is material sense a necessary *p*·

prelude
sp 90–14 some insist that death is the necessary *p*· to
g 502– 2 the living and real *p*· of the older Scriptures

premise
s 129– 6 can tolerate no error in *p*· or conclusion.
130–13 from this *p*· it follows that good and its
ph 107–17 an error in the *p*· must appear in the conclusion.
191–26 and from this *p*· infers the
b 277–27 error in the *p*· leads to errors in the conclusion

premises
sp 84– 2 coordinate neither with the *p*· nor
98–15 Beyond the frail *p*· of human beliefs,
s 164–13 human systems based on material *p*·
ph 184– 2 The *p*· being erroneous,
b 269–12 does not enter into metaphysical *p*· or
274–11 not mere inferences drawn from material *p*·.
312–23 theories are based on finite *p*·,
338–10 error has been engrafted into the *p*·

preparation
pref xii–16 given to the *p*· of the revision of
gl 596–18 the only fit *p*· for admission to the presence

preparatory
r 486– 9 Earth's *p*· school must be improved

prepare
a 39–20 not that now men must *p*· for a
f 208–21 and *p*· for the reign of Spirit,
p 433–28 is sent for to *p*· the frightened sense

prepared
m 61–11 that the highway of our God may be *p*·
s 152–22 *p*· her thought for the metaphysics of C. S.
b 322–12 finite belief may be *p*· to relinquish its error.
333–22 to all *p*· to receive Christ, Truth.
p 388–20 If food was *p*· by Jesus for his disciples,
414–17 not until your patients are *p*· for the
ap 565–30 where she hath a place *p*· of God.— *Rev.* 12 : 6.
566– 8 up to the glory *p*· for them who love God.

prepares
o 361–28 until God *p*· the soil for the seed.

prepareth
ap 578–13 [LOVE] *p*· a table before me— see *Psal.* 23 : 5.

preparing
s 107– 4 God had been graciously *p*· me
f 208–20 and *p*· the way of Science.
p 365– 5 and *p*· their helpers for the "midnight call,"

preponderance

s 143–20   you conclude that . . . hold the p· of power.
ph 168– 5   removal . . . from either scale gives p· to the
177–22   hold the p· of power in any direction
g 502– 4   the p· of unreality in the entire narrative,

prerogative

sp 84–11   the p· of the ever-present, divine Mind,
s 123– 8   the power and p· of Spirit,
f 253–16   your p· to overcome the belief in sin,
g 530–10   presuming not on the p· of his creator,

prerogatives

g 513– 2   for the claim usurps the deific p·
549–30   to usurp the p· of omnipotence.

prescribed

s 148– 4   He p· no drugs, urged no obedience to
156– 8   p· the fourth attenuation of *Argentum nitratum*
156–13   former physician had p· these remedies,
p 424–14   to counteract the working of a remedy p· by

prescribes

ph 198–19   p· drugs, until the elasticity of
p 399– 6   Mortal mind p· the drug,

prescription

s 149– 7   The p· which succeeds in one instance
158– 5   He was supposed to have dictated the first p·,
ph 166–10   The popular doctor believes in his p·,

prescriptions

s 158–21   to victimize the race with intoxicating p·
ph 175– 4   When there are fewer p·,

presence

all
b 275–23   all power, all p·, all Science.
and power
g 512– 8   symbolized by strength, p·, and power,
gl 596–18   the p· and power of the Most High.
beatific
c 266–28   he reflects the beatific p·, illuming the universe
calm in the
p 366–27   Christian Scientist will be calm in the p· of
divine
pr 12– 4   no power to gain more of the divine p· than
His
ph 174–11   but the angels of His p· . . . are our guardians
g 512–10   These angels of His p·, which have the
543–11   They cannot come into His p·,
ap 567– 6   The Gabriel of His p· has no contests.
human
b 325–28   which ushered Jesus into human p·,
imposing
p 441– 1   with benign and imposing p·,
joy of its
ph 175–11   The joy of its p·, its beauty and fragrance,
of Christ
o 351–14   the living, palpitating p· of Christ,
of divine Justice
p 437– 9   in the p· of divine Justice,
of God
g 543– 9   shut out from the p· of God.
of health
p 412–24   Realize the p· of health and
of his
a 50–11   withhold a clear token of his p·
of Life
b 304– 1   the sweet sense and p· of Life and Truth.
r 470– 8   assumed . . . the loss of the spiritual p· of Life
of mine enemies
ap 578–13   in the p· of mine enemies :— *Psal* 23 : 5.
of mistrust
m 68– 9   The p· of mistrust, where confidence is due,
of the Lord
s 135– 5   at the p· of the Lord,— *Psal.* 114 : 7.
g 542–27   went out from the p· of the Lord— *Gen.* 4 : 16.
of the reality
b 293– 1   mortality disappears in p· of the reality.
power and
g 519–13   the divine power and p· which go with it,
power nor
r 471–19   and there is no other power nor p·.
reproduce the
sp 75–23   to reproduce the p· of those who

a 48–25   Pale in the p· of his
s 135– 6   at the p· of the God of Jacob."— *Psal.* 114 : 7.
p 432–23   and that my p· was required to
440–25   In the p· of the Supreme Lawgiver,

present (noun)

sp 84–13   the past, the p·, and the future.
f 224– 5   disappear from the dissolving paths of the p·,

present (adj.)

pr 13– 1   "a very p· help in trouble."— *Psal.* 46 : 1.
14– 4   "p· with the Lord"— *II Cor.* 5 : 8.
14– 6   "p· with the Lord"— *II Cor.* 5 : 8.
14–22   and p· with Truth and Love.
a 22–16   If . . . you receive no p· reward, go not back to

present (adj.)

m 60–20   in a majority of cases, is not its p· tendency,
65– 3   May Christ, Truth, be p· at every bridal altar
65–26   must lose its p· slippery footing,
sp 72–23   suppositional opposite of good, is never p·.
82– 3   as easily as we do of one p·.
82– 4   no more difficult . . . than it is to read the p·.
87– 7   to be individually and consciously p·.
88– 6   may even be cognizant of a p· flavor
95– 5   would be to-day if Jesus were personally p·.
an 102–21   So secret are the p· methods of
s 123–24   The proof, by p· demonstration, that the
139–11   but the p· new, yet old, reform
147– 4   its p· application to the cure of disease.
ph 171–26   beliefs that intelligence and life are p·
178–10   connection of past mortal thoughts with p·.
179– 6   absent from their healers, as well as those p·,
f 202–28   "a very p· help in trouble ;"— *Psal.* 46 : 1.
216–30   and to be p· with the Lord."— *II Cor.* 5 : 8.
228–17   Dropping their p· beliefs, they will recognize
234–21   The p· codes of human systems disappoint the
b 304– 6   things p·, nor things to come,— *Rom.* 8 : 38.
o 348–32   If such are the p· fruits, what will the
349– 4   so the rabbis of the p· day ask concerning
351–13   this spiritual sense was a p· *help.*
356–17   neither a p· nor an eternal copartnership
361– 9   God is come and is p· now and forever.
p 383–10   p· with the Lord."— *II Cor.* 5 : 8.
388–27   foolish to venture beyond our p· understanding,
392–27   When the condition is p· which you say induces
407–25   Let the perfect model be p· in your thoughts
410– 5   a p· knowledge of his Father and of himself,
426–25   far beyond its p· elevation,
430–29   testifies . . . I was p· on certain nights when
432–25   Materia Medica, was p· when I arrived,
t 444–12   a very p· help in trouble."— *Psal.* 46 : 1.
r 473– 9   nothing apart from Him is p· or has power.
ap 560– 5   has reference to the p· age.
570– 4   The p· apathy as to the tendency of
573–25   in this p· state of existence,
574– 2   This . . . is therefore a p· possibility.
577–28   The writer's p· feeble sense of C. S.
gl 581–26   and to be p· with the Lord."— *II Cor.* 5 : 8.

present at —

m 63–24   rational means of improvement at p·
68– 2   At p· mortals progress slowly
sp 90–30   At p· we know not what man is,
s 134–32   This fact at p· seems more mysterious than
f 240–21   If at p· satisfied with wrong-doing,
240–22   If at p· content with idleness, we must

present ever —

pref xi–17   ever p· in human consciousness
sp 72–21   God, good, being ever p·, it follows
b 300–21   through the realization of God as ever p·
306–28   the universe, ever p· and eternal.
r 470– 9   assumed . . . the loss of Love as ever p·
471–18   God is infinite, therefore ever p·,

present (verb)

pref xi– 2   p· only a phase of the action of the
a 30–17   Not so did Jesus, . . . p· the divine law
ph 170– 8   Christian ideas certainly p· what human
172–29   unfortunate cripple may p· more nobility than
c 256–29   Finiteness cannot p· the idea or the vastness of
267–20   p· more than is detected upon the surface,
b 325–21   "P· your bodies a living sacrifice,— *Rom.* 12 : 1.
o 358–12   and could not p· its proofs.
p 430–13   I here p· to my readers an allegory
g 511–26   Animals and mortals metaphorically p· the
546–31   If mathematics should p· a thousand
555–31   Jesus was able to p· himself unchanged

presentation

a 24–24   only for the p·, after death, of

presented

a 25–16   Jesus p· the ideal of God better than
45–29   He p· the same body that he had before his
54–14   he p· the proof that Life, Truth, and Love heal
s 118–18   p· as three measures of meal,
c 259–10   thoughts which p· man as fallen,
b 305–20   The inverted images p· by the senses,
314–21   and he p· to her, . . . the true idea
315–16   God's spiritual idea as p· by Christ Jesus.
315–25   and p· an illustration of creation.
316–24   The spiritual idea of God, as p· by Jesus,
317–21   Our Lord and Master p· himself to his
o 344–21   only one which should be p· to the whole world,
r 473–13   has p· Christ, the true idea of God,
g 509– 7   p· to them the certain sense of eternal Life.
521–24   p· in the verses already considered,
529–26   evil, by whatever figure p·, contradicts itself
534–15   idea of divine power, which Jesus p·,
ap 560–28   hid from them the true idea which has been p·,
562– 3   Elias p· the idea of the fatherhood of

presenting
  r 491–19   sometimes *p*· no appearance of mind,
  g 523– 6   *p*· the exact opposite of Truth,

presently
  s 155– 1   *P*· the child forgets all about the accident,
  ph 182–13   If we attempt it, we shall *p*·
   190–11   so-called senses, which *p*· measure mind by
  f 237– 5   Bounding off . . . she *p*· added,
  b 321–23   *p*· restored his hand to its natural condition
  p 416– 4   the belief of pain will *p*· return, unless
  g 524–27   for God *p*· curses the ground.

presents
  a 55–11   *p*· the Saviour in a clearer light
  m 67–29   *p*· the true likeness or spiritual ideal.
   68–27   C. S. *p*· unfoldment, not accretion ;
  sp 87–14   for it *p*· primal facts to mortal mind.
  s 145–22   mystery which godliness always *p*· to the
  b 276–14   and *p*· them as beautiful and immortal.
   277–13   Natural history *p*· vegetables and
   301–27   *p*· an inverted image of Mind and substance
   302–28   body *p*· no proper likeness of divinity,
   316–20   Christ *p*· the indestructible man,
  o 358–11   and sustains logically . . . every point it *p*·.
   358–15   It *p*· the calm and clear verdict of Truth
  p 375–32   *p*· to mortal thought a hopeless state,
   423–18   according to the evidence which matter *p*·.
  g 503–20   Immortal and divine Mind *p*· the idea of God :
  ap 577– 5   The Lamb's wife *p*· the unity of

preserve
  p 374–19   incapacity to *p*· your own existence,
  r 494– 8   needed no help . . . to *p*· the eternal harmony

preserved
  f 245–18   This instance of youth *p*· furnishes a
  b 277–17   the order of genus and species is *p*·

preserves
  p 383–22   tells you that the weed *p*· his health,
  g 550– 6   which forms and *p*· the individuality

preserving
  b 277–14   as *p*· their original species,

President
  (see **Eddy, Mrs. Mary Baker**)

press
  s 141–30   Let it have fair representation by the *p*·.
  ph 196–31   The *p*· unwittingly sends forth many sorrows
  f 224–20   opposition from church, state laws, and the *p*·,
  o 343–30   to *p*· along the line of gospel-healing,

pressed
  f 226–31   but I *p*· on through faith in God,

pressure
  t 431– 3   constant *p*· of the apostolic command

prestige
  f 244–32   of development, power, and *p*·.

presuming
  g 530– 9   *p*· not on the prerogative of his creator,

presumptuously
  o 342– 8   He that decries this Science does it *p*·,

presuppose
  s 119– 6   They either *p*· the self-evolution and
  ph 182–31   is to *p*· that omnipotent power is powerless
   194–15   would *p*· man, . . . a mortal in material belief.
  f 207–25   which *p*· the absence of Truth,
  b 319–15   doctrines and theories which *p*·

presupposes
  sp 71–30   Spiritualism therefore *p*· Spirit, . . . to be
  ph 186–13   because it *p*· the absence of God,
  b 281– 7   Error *p*· man to be both mind and
   301–30   This falsity *p*· soul to be
  r 480–15   its action is erroneous and *p*· man to be

pretence
  ph 186– 8   under whatever name or *p*· they are employed ;
  ap 567–25   in his *p*· of being a talker,

pretensions
  an 103–27   mortal mind, whose flimsy and gaudy *p*·,
  ph 186–19   This falsehood should strip evil of all *p*·.

preternatural
  s 134–23   not because this Science is . . . *p*·,

prevail
  s 138– 1   shall not *p*· against it."— *Matt.* 16: 18.
  ap 567–10   Truth and Love *p*· against the dragon

prevailed
  b 308–31   "as a prince" had he *p*·— *Gen.* 32: 28.
  ap 566–27   dragon fought, . . . and *p*· not ;— *Rev.* 12: 7, 8.

prevailing
  ph 185–13   as material as the *p*· systems of medicine.

prevails
  b 311–24   law of Soul, which *p*· over material sense
  ap 567– 5   spiritual strength wrestles and *p*·

prevalent
  sp 94–13   the misconceptions of Deity there *p*·.
  f 232–10   our *p*· theories practically deny this,
   283–13   But what say *p*· theories?
  p 389–18   as *p*· theories maintain,

prevent
  pr 13–21   this will *p*· us from relinquishing the
  an 105– 4   to *p*· deeds of violence or to punish them.
  ph 170–18   If there are material laws which *p*· disease,
   174–32   We should *p*· the images of disease from
   198–12   to *p*· disease from forming in mortal mind
  f 237–18   To *p*· the experience of error and its sufferings,
  b 329–16   Until one is able to *p*· bad results, he should
  o 341–14   cannot *p*· that from being scientific which
  p 368–18   then no material suppositions can *p*· us from
   380–20   Nothing but the power of Truth can *p*· the
   391–12   you can *p*· the development of pain
   395–31   would *p*· the brain from becoming diseased,
   400–14   and you *p*· the development of disease.
   412–16   To *p*· disease or to cure it,
   424–28   To *p*· or to cure scrofula and other so-called
   431–14   summoned . . . Hypnotism to *p*· his punishment.
   436–17   to *p*· his committing liver-complaint,
   436–19   result which they were called to *p*·.
  t 446–30   Covering iniquity will *p*· prosperity
   457–11   to *p*· suffering, not to produce it.

prevented
  sp 82–24   Communion . . . would be *p*· by this difference.
  s 154–21   the very results which might have been *p*·

preventing
  s 147–28   he left no definite rule for . . . *p*· disease.

prevention
  p 401–32   reconstruction and to the *p*· of inflammation.

preventive
  p 309–23   (that is, the *p*· and curative) arts

prevents
  ph 182–19   Obedience to material law *p*· full obedience to
  p 372–30   *p*· the honest recognition of benefits received,
   394–11   *p*· him from helping himself,
  p 409–14   the error which *p*· mortals from

previous
  sp 75–27   that is the moment *p*· to the transition,
  p 434–12   were at the *p*· Court of Error,
  r 493–12   is touched upon in a *p*· chapter
  g 526– 3   The *p*· and more scientific record

previously
  g 544–19   The facts of creation, as *p*· recorded,

preying
  gl 583–28   one belief *p*· upon another.

price
  pr 10–21   has paid for . . . prayer the *p*· of persecution,
  a 36–15   The earthly *p*· of spirituality in a material age
   47–12   The traitor's *p*· was thirty pieces of silver
  s 108– 9   "the *p*· of learning love,"
  ph 197– 7   What a *p*· for human knowledge !
   197– 7   But the *p*· does not exceed the original cost.

priceless
  p 366– 1   a *p*· sense of the dear Father's loving-kindness.

pride
and fear
  a 31– 1   *P*· and fear are unfit to bear the standard of
and fustian
  s 142–16   tell their story to *p*· and fustian.
display, and
  m 60–23   personal adornment, display, and *p*·,
humbled the
  f 228–30   It should have humbled the *p*· of the priests,
of power
  t 451– 5   must renounce . . . oppression and the *p*· of power.
  gl 589–13   the *p*· of power and the power of pride ;
of priesthood
  b 270–22   The *p*· of priesthood is the prince of this world.
or prejudice
  s 144–25   Ignorance, *p*·, or prejudice closes the
power of
  gl 589–14   the pride of power and the power of *p*· ;
rebuked
  a 35– 2   hearts chastened and *p*· rebuked.
tyranny and
  s 142–18   tyranny and *p*· need to be whipped out of the

  a 51–25   *p*·, envy, cruelty, and vengeance,
  m 64– 8   *P*·, envy, or jealousy seems on most occasions
   68– 4   They are slaves to fashion, *p*·, and sense.
  s 115–22   *p*·, deceit, hatred, revenge,
  p 372–29   If *p*·, superstition, or any error prevents
  t 445–22   Self-seeking, envy, passion, *p*·, hatred,
  r 484– 3   When this is accomplished, neither *p*·, prejudice,
  gl 582– 6   *p*· ; envy ; fame ; illusion ; a false belief ;

priest
- *a* 20– 6 ritualistic *p·* and hypocritical Pharisee
- 30–14 Rabbi and *p·* taught the Mosaic law,
- 42– 2 *p·* and rabbi affirmed God to be a
- *s* 141–19 Its only *p·* is the spiritualized man.

priestess
- *t* 454–21 Love is *p·* at the altar of Truth.

priesthood
- *b* 270–22 The pride of *p·* is the prince of this world.

priests
- *a* 49–26 *p·* and rabbis, before whom he had
- *s* 141–21 "kings and *p·* unto God."— *Rev.* 1: 6.
- 158– 2 originated in idolatry with pagan *p·*,
- *f* 228–30 It should have humbled the pride of the *p·*,

primal
- *sp* 87–15 it presents *p·* facts to mortal mind.
- 90– 2 how then can we account for their *p·* origin?
- *s* 135– 7 unfolds the *p·* order,
- *f* 207–20 There is but one *p·* cause.
- *r* 469– 9 It is the *p·* and eternal quality of
- *ap* 559–26 *p·* elements, of Truth and Love,
- 568–30 Love sends forth her *p·* and everlasting strain.

primarily
- *s* 148–19 the one wholly, the other *p·*
- 150–12 is not *p·* one of physical healing.
- *g* 512–23 these are mental, both *p·* and secondarily.
- 543–19 who shall say that he is not *p·* dust?

primary
- *f* 207–12 nor are the so-called laws of matter *p·*,
- 245–29 the *p·* of that illustration makes it plain
- *g* 525–10 the *p·* sense being *image, form;*

prime
- *t* 457–10 Her *p·* object, since entering this field

primeval
- *s* 110– 4 These eternal verities reveal *p·* existence as
- *g* 553–28 from dust or from the rib of our *p·* father.
- *ap* 565–23 stars sang together and all was *p·* harmony,

primitive
- *m* 63– 9 Spirit is his *p·* and ultimate source of being ;
- 64– 9 ruling out *p·* Christianity.
- *s* 109–18 cures were produced in *p·* Christian healing
- 128– 2 Good is natural and *p·*.
- *ph* 176– 7 *p·* custom of taking no thought about food
- *f* 214– 3 they came as sound to the *p·* prophets.
- 244–17 that he returns eventually to his *p·* condition ;
- *b* 292–13 Matter is the *p·* belief of mortal mind,
- *o* 356–28 create the *p·*, and then punish its derivative?
- *p* 374–28 resolved into its *p·* mortal elements.
- 399–20 continuation of, the *p·* mortal mind.

prince
- *b* 270–22 The pride of priesthood is the *p·* of this world.
- 308–30 "as a *p·*" had he prevailed — *Gen.* 32 : 28.
- 309–11 Israel,— a *p·* of God, or a soldier of God,

Prince of Peace
- *a* 52–14 concerning the coming *P· of P·*.

principal
- *p* 436– 1 *p·* witness (the officer of the Health-laws)
- 436–35 One of the *p·* witnesses. Nerve, testified

Principle
- and idea
  - (see **idea**)
- and its idea
  - *r* 465–17 *P·* and its idea is one,
  - 475– 4 all is Spirit, divine *P·* and its idea.
  - *g* 520– 9 *P·* and its idea, man, are coexistent
- and practice
  - *pref* ix–14 the *P·* and practice of Christian healing,
  - *o* 355–24 misapprehension both of the divine *P·* and practice
- and proof
  - *f* 210– 5 *P·* and proof of Christianity are discerned
- and rule
  - *r* 493–15 prove for himself the *P·* and rule of C. S.
- an understood
  - *r* 487–30 This faith relies upon an understood *P·*.
- apodictical
  - *s* 107– 7 This apodictical *P·* points to the revelation of
- cause or
  - *c* 262–31 Divine Mind is the only cause or *P·* of existence.
- contradict its
  - *f* 232–14 religions which contradict its *P·* are false.
- creative
  - *g* 502–27 The creative *P·* — Life, Truth, and Love
  - 513–21 God who is the divinely creative *P·* thereof.
- curative
  - *s* 157– 9 rests on Mind alone as the curative *P·*,
- deathless
  - *f* 203–22 then mortals believe that the deathless *P·*,
- demonstrable
  - *g* 546–29 it cures on a divine demonstrable *P·*

Principle
- divine
  - (see **divine**)
- entire
  - *t* 461– 7 part illustrates and proves the entire *P·*.
- eternal
  - *b* 312–20 man's eternal *P·* is ever-present Life.
  - *gl* 579–11 faith in the divine Life and in the eternal *P·*
  - 592–16 divine and eternal *P·* ; Life, Truth, and **Love**.
- factor in the
  - *pref* x– 8 this mind is not a factor in the *P·* of C. S.
- fixed
  - *s* 128–28 It rests on fixed *P·* and not upon the
- glorious
  - *p* 382–26 but for the glorious *P·* you teach,
  - *r* 474–14 until the glorious *P·* of these marvels is gained.
- God is the
  - *s* 112–32 God is the *P·* of divine metaphysics.
  - *r* 476– 9 God is the *P·* of man, and man is the idea of
- good in
  - *b* 286–19 like Himself,— good in *P·* and in idea.
- governed by its
  - *ph* 195–16 semblance of an idea governed by its *P·*,
- healing
  - *pr* 12–12 the divine healing *P·* as manifested in Jesus,
  - *b* 312–29 away from the intelligent and divine healing *P·*
- heals the sick
  - *o* 354–10 *P·* heals the sick and spiritualizes humanity.
- holy
  - *s* 124– 8 nor holy *P·* of its own,
- immortal
  - *g* 554– 4 God, who is its divine immortal *P·*.
- infinite
  - *sp* 71– 8 the creative, governing, infinite *P·*
  - *c* 257–18 anthropomorphic God, instead of infinite *P·*,
  - 258–19 infinite *P·* is reflected by the infinite idea
  - *b* 300– 4 no true appreciation of infinite *P·*,
  - 302–25 infinite *P·*, called Person or God.
  - 337–22 as incomprehensible . . . as is man's infinite *P·*.
  - *g* 520– 8 no more seen . . . by mortals, than is his infinite *P·*.
  - 524–16 Did the divine and infinite *P·* become a
  - *ap* 577– 3 as the infinite *P·* and infinite idea,
  - *gl* 582–11 a gleam of the infinite idea of the infinite *P·* ;
- inharmony has no
  - *r* 480–15 Inharmony has no *P·* ;
- interprets the
  - *ap* 560–11 interprets the *P·* of heavenly harmony.
- is absolute
  - *b* 283–11 *P·* is absolute.
- is imperative
  - *b* 329–21 *P·* is imperative.
- is infinite
  - *b* 328–32 Its *P·* is infinite, reaching beyond the
- learning its
  - *b* 274–24 no half-way position in learning its *P·*
- living
  - *r* 477–21 in multifarious forms of the living *P·*;
- of all
  - *s* 109–17 *P·* of all harmonious Mind-action
- of all happiness
  - *c* 261– 3 Truth and Love, the *P·* of all happiness,
- of all science
  - *s* 124– 1 being based on Truth, the *P·* of all science.
- of being
  - *a* 25–19 more spiritually than all others the *P·* of being.
- of divine metaphysics
  - *s* 111–11 The *P·* of divine metaphysics is God ;
  - 112–32 God is the *P·* of divine metaphysics.
- of healing
  - *s* 147–27 demonstrating this *P·* of healing
  - *o* 343– 2 teaching Truth as the *P·* of healing,
- of man
  - *s* 123– 4 the true idea and *P·* of man will then appear.
  - *r* 476– 9 God is the *P·* of man, and man is the idea of
- of man's harmony
  - *ph* 170– 9 the *P·* of man's harmony.
- of Mind-healing
  - *t* 454–14 understands . . . the *P·* of Mind-healing,
- of the cure
  - *f* 219–26 not comprehending the *P·* of the cure,
- of the universe
  - *b* 272–28 divine *P·* of the universe must interpret
  - 276–23 from materiality to the *P·* of the universe,
- one
  - *s* 112–17 comes one *P·* and its infinite idea,
  - *t* 456–11 affirms that there is more than one *P·*
  - 457–29 The Scientist's demonstration rests on one *P·*,
  - *r* 466– 6 indicate Mind, never matter, and have one *P·*;
  - *g* 517–19 they all have one *P·* and parentage.
  - *gl* 588–15 though they are governed by one *P·*.
- or its idea
  - *c* 258–21 no cognizance of either *P·* or its idea.

Principle

perfect
- c 259–12   includes a perfect P· and idea,
- b 304–15   governed by God, his perfect P·
- r 470–29   his perfect P·, the divine Mind.
- 470–30   If man ever existed without this perfect P·

produced by its
- b 304–16   Harmony is produced by its P·,

proved the
- s 149–15   not . . . proved the P· of divine Science.
- r 473–30   Jesus proved the P·, which heals the

recognized
- s 157– 4   its one recognized P· of healing is Mind,

same
- p 395–10   The same P· cures both sin and sickness.
- 406– 4   Sin and sickness are both healed by the same P·.
- g 518–17   all having the same P·, or Father;

saving
- b 285–24   but not as the saving P·, or divine Love,

start from
- b 298–21   like numbers and notes, start from P·,

this
- s 123–28   The operation of this P· indicates
- 141–17   For this P· there is no dynasty,
- 147–27   demonstrating this P· of healing
- t 457–30   Let this P· be applied to the cure of disease
- r 487–31   This P· makes whole the diseased,
- ap 559–25   eat the divine body of this P·,

triune
- r 469–10   quality of infinite Mind, of the triune P·,

unerring
- g 522–32   Does the unerring P· of divine law change

unity of
- r 470– 4   and have unity of P· and spiritual power

views of
- f 239– 7   and we get clearer views of P·.

was rejected
- b 316–25   scourged in person, and its P· was rejected.

without
- r 487–22   Mere belief is blindness without P·

- a 26–23   makes us admit its P· to be Love.
- ph 192– 8   from corporeality instead of from P·,
- f 240–10   in which the P is above what it reflects,
- b 279–31   seeks cause in effect, P· in its idea,
- 281–22   and see that . . . have neither P· nor
- 287– 2   They have neither P· nor permanence,
- 290– 3   If the P·, rule, and demonstration of
- 299–32   If . . . he would have no eternal P·
- 302– 1   P· is not to be found in fragmentary ideas.
- 303– 4   the P· governing the reflection.
- 337– 8   man must harmonize with his P·,
- r 465–10   Spirit, Soul, P·, Life,
- 465–16   Is there more than one God or P·?
- 467–22   P· is not in its idea.
- 474– 1   (the P· of this unacknowledged Science)
- 492–27   the P· of this Science is divine,
- ap 561– 2   the P· which works out the ends of
- gl 581– 9   proved to be as immortal as its P·;
- 583–23   matter and evil, which have no P·;
- 587– 6   P·; Mind; Soul; Spirit; Life, Truth;
- 593– 3   definition of

principle
- pr 3– 5   Who would . . . pray the p· of mathematics to
- f 237–21   excluded on the same p· as the
- g 522–19   represented as the life-giving p· of the earth.

principles
- t 458– 3   doctrine that Science has two p·

print
- pref ix–21   it did not appear in p· until 1876,

printers
- p 387–14   If p· and authors have the shortest span of

printing
- ph 197– 1   by p· long descriptions which

prints
- r 486–14   Jesus proved by the p· of the nails, that

prior
- m 63– 8   nor does he pass through material conditions p· to
- s 125–10   the p· states which human belief created
- ph 178–13   deformity produced p· to his birth
- f 254–17   p· to the change called death,
- c 267–10   must have had children p· to Adam.
- b 310– 4   Did it exist p· to thought?
- p 436–15   P· to the night of his arrest, the prisoner

priority
- ph 178– 9   is not dangerous because of its p·

prism
- ap 558–13   When understood, it is Truth's p· and praise.

prison
- f 202–10   until disciplined by the p· and the scaffold;
- p 366–30   If we would open their p· doors for the sick,
- 431–12   arrested Mortal Man . . . and cast him into p·.
- 433–32   can open wide those p· doors
- 441–15   nor can Disease cast him into p·.
- 442–14   Mortal Man, no longer sick and in p·,
- r 495–12   opens the p· doors to such as are bound,

prison-cell
- g 516–18   glints from the church-dome, glances into the p·,

prisoner

assist the
- p 432–26   endeavoring to assist the p· to escape from

attended to
- p 431– 5   the p· attended to his daily labors,

at the bar
- p 432– 5   Mortal Man, the p· at the bar,
- 434–22   The p· at the bar has been unjustly sentenced.

grows restless
- p 433–13   As the Judge proceeds, the p· grows restless.

guilty
- p 436–28   twelve Mortal Minds, to find the p· guilty.

hypnotized the
- p 431–23   Morbid Secretion hypnotized the p·

is not guilty
- p 434– 3   "Delay the execution; the p· is not guilty."

is then remanded
- p 433–27   The p· is then remanded to his cell

manacling the
- p 439–11   who was then manacling the p·

regards the
- p 434–16   regards the p· with the utmost tenderness.

rescue the
- p 436–24   His friends struggled hard to rescue the p·

rose up
- p 442– 8   Then the p· rose up regenerated, strong, free.

should die
- p 432–30   he decided at once that the p· should die.

summoned
- p 431–13   the p· summoned Physiology, Materia Medica,
- 436–15   the p· summoned two professed friends,

unfortunate
- p 434–11   as counsel for the unfortunate p·.

watched with
- p 431– 3   the p· watched with the sick every night

would commit
- p 432– 7   testifies: . . . I knew the p· would commit it,

- p 430–30   the p·, or patient, watched with a sick friend.
- 431– 5   the p· gave him drink.
- 432–23   who protested that the p· had abused him,
- 433–19   solemn sentence of death upon the p·.
- 434–28   p· is not proved "worthy of death,— Acts 23:29.
- 435–32   The only jurisdiction to which the p· can submit
- 435–34   I ask that the p· be restored
- 436– 7   the p· on the night of the alleged offence

prisoner's
- p 432–25   One of the p· friends, Materia Medica,

prison-yard
- p 434– 4   Consternation fills the p·.

privations
- a 49–10   his mighty works, his toils, p·, sacrifices,

privilege
- pr 10–21   has paid for the p· of prayer
- a 37–23   duty and p· of every child, man, and woman,
- f 230– 3   A special p· is vested in the ministry.
- p 428– 6   Man's p· at this supreme moment is to prove

privileged
- c 263– 2   believe themselves to be . . . p· originators of
- t 443–10   p· to work out their own salvation

prize
- s 111–19   A p· of one hundred pounds, offered in
- t 462–18   self-denial, sincerity, . . . win the p·,

pro
- s 120–25   Any conclusion p· or con,
- 129– 9   be the fable p· or con,—

probabilities
- ph 171– 9   not needing to consult almanacs for the p·

probable
- p 413–29   making it p· at any time that such ills may

probation
- a 35–15   his p· in the flesh after death,
- 35–16   its exemplification of human p·,
- b 291–12   salvation rests on progression and p·,
- 291–24   until p· and growth shall effect the

probationary
- a 46–24   a p· and progressive state beyond the grave.

probe
- ph 193– 6   He even showed me the p·,
- t 462–26   to p· the self-inflicted wounds of selfishness,

probed
- ph 193– 5   had just p· the ulcer on the hip,

probing
- ph 184– 8   p· the trouble to the bottom,

problem

in theology
  a 23– 8 The atonement is a hard *p·* in theology,

mesmerism is a
  an 102–25 "Mesmerism is a *p·* not lending itself to an

of being
  a 44– 7 a place in which to solve the great *p·* of being.
  f 217–21 you are working out the *p·* of being
  254–14 demonstrating the great *p·* of being,
  c 262– 1 in which to work out the *p·* of being.
  b 273– 6 not one of them can solve the *p·* of being
  314–26 The higher his . . . carried the *p·* of being,
  g 556–27 before it cares to solve the *p·* of being,

of Euclid
  b 329–18 attempts to solve a *p·* of Euclid,

of man
  f 216– 6 unveils the mystery and solves the *p·* of man.

of Mind-healing
  s 109–12 I sought the solution of this *p·* of Mind-healing,

of nothingness
  s 126– 3 The *p·* of nothingness, or "dust to dust,"

rule of the
  b 329–19 and denies the rule of the *p·*

to solve the
  pr 3– 5 principle of mathematics to solve the *p·*?

proceed
  m 65– 2 should *p·* from man's highest nature.
  sp 88–15 Beliefs *p·* from the so-called material senses,
  88–23 These effects, . . . do not *p·* from Christianity,
  an 100– * *out of the heart p· evil thoughts,— Matt.* 15 : 19.
  ph 189–22 They *p·* from the divine source ;
  f 207–22 does not *p·* from this great and only cause.
  c 256–28 A limitless Mind cannot *p·* from
  260–22 Sickness, disease, and death *p·* from fear.
  o 356–25 Does evil *p·* from good?
  p 374–16 can destroy all ills which *p·* from mortal mind.
  r 484–18 Certain results, supposed to *p·* from drugs,
  g 529–10 both man and woman *p·* from God

proceeded
  b 307– 2 the delusion that life and intelligence *p·*

proceedeth
  p 410–11 every word that *p·* out of the— *Matt.* 4 : 4.

proceeding
  sp 88–12 Thoughts, *p·* from the brain or from matter,

proceedings
  p 437–26 *p·* of a regularly constituted court.

proceeds
  sp 88–31 When eloquence *p·* from the belief that a
  s 127–24 all truth *p·* from the divine Mind,
  f 239–25 If action *p·* from the divine Mind,
  p 419–20 If the action *p·* from Truth,
  433–13 As the Judge *p·*, the prisoner grows restless.
  433–18 Judge Medicine then *p·* to pronounce the
  r 471–28 all that *p·* from the divine Mind.
  480–14 Harmonious action *p·* from Spirit, God.
  g 543–17 All error *p·* from the evidence before the
  gl 583–13 rests upon and *p·* from divine Principle.

process

by this
  s 148–28 fails to give health or life by this *p·*,

calling the
  p 422– 1 and then calling the *p·* mathematics.

false
  p 390–15 false *p·* of mortal opinions which you name law,

is simple
  t 459–25 the *p·* is simple and the results are sure if

mental
  p 416–24 The sick know nothing of the mental *p·*

metaphysical
  f 210–18 by one and the same metaphysical *p·*.
  t 456–22 treated by the metaphysical *p·*.

of mental healing
  t 459–15 Committing the bare *p·* of mental healing to

of weaning
  b 322–30 Without this *p·* of weaning,

ordinary
  g 548–31 besides the ordinary *p·* of generation,

reverse the
  f 212–15 Reverse the *p·* ; take away this so-called mind
  p 397–17 Now reverse the *p·*.

simple
  b 321–24 restored his hand . . . by the same simple *p·*.

---

  ph 168–32 By chemicalization I mean the *p·* which
  f 251–24 This *p·* of higher spiritual understanding
  p 398–31 Then we understand the *p·*.
  413–13 the *p·* of taking a fish out of water every day
  416– 2 This *p·* shows the pain to be in the mind,
  439–10 where the liver-complaint was in *p·*,

processes
  sp 89–19 not necessarily dependent upon educational *p·*.

proclaim
  pref xi–22 When God called the author to *p·* His Gospel
  b 327–24 to meet the wrong and to *p·* the right.
  p 437–11 I *p·* this witness, Nerve, to be destitute of

proclaimed
  b 317– 5 and *p·* an anthropomorphic God.

proclaiming
  ph 174–19 *p·* the kingdom of heaven on earth.

proclaims
  g 557–24 revealed religion *p·* the Science of Mind

proclamation
  p 410–20 a definite and inspired *p·* of C. S.

procreate
  s 140–30 but mortals would *p·* man,

procreation
  f 205–14 the necessity for recreation or *p·*?

procured
  a 37–18 Those who *p·* the martyrdom of that righteous

procurers
  r 481–22 These human verdicts are the *p·* of all discord.

procures
  f 220–13 *p·* a summer residence with more ease than

procuring
  ph 171–27 the *p·* cause of all sin and disease.
  p 411–20 The *p·* cause and foundation of all sickness

prodigal
  ap 575–15 taught by the mustard-seed and the *p·*?

produce
  pr 7– 9 But does it *p·* any lasting benefit?
  m 58– 5 Ill-arranged notes *p·* discord.
  62–30 and *p·* the ills of which we complain.
  sp 86–11 Opposites . . . *p·* unlike results.
  89–32 If seed is necessary to *p·* wheat,
  90– 1 and wheat to *p·* flour,
  an 102–22 and *p·* the very apathy on the subject which
  s 148–23 to *p·* the concord and unity of Spirit
  154–20 and they *p·* the very results which
  161– 9 might *p·* spontaneous combustion.
  ph 166– 2 human mind is all that can *p·* pain.
  175–10 to say that a rose, . . . can *p·* suffering !
  179–28 to move the bowels, or to *p·* sleep
  183– 8 Can the agriculturist, . . . *p·* a crop without
  190– 4 ignorant of what it is supposed to *p·*.
  f 202–32 Common opinion . . . that this cold may *p·*
  211– 4 If . . . *p·* sickness and health, good and evil,
  211–15 does not this so-called mind *p·* the effect
  212–18 They *p·* a rose through seed and soil,
  212–22 mortals believe that unseen spirits *p·* the
  230–17 God, good, can no more *p·* sickness than
  230–20 Does a law of God *p·* sickness,
  233–21 by overcoming the thoughts which *p·* them,
  244– 1 He does not *p·* moral or physical deformity ;
  c 257– 5 and shadow cannot *p·* substance.
  259–30 that they may *p·* harmonious results.
  b 304–13 good can never *p·* evil ;
  304–13 matter can never *p·* mind nor
  335–25 can *p·* nothing unlike the eternal
  p 370–19 *p·* very direct and marked effects on the
  377–18 watched that it may not *p·* blindly its bad
  377–31 is of itself powerless to *p·* suffering.
  385–30 opposite belief would *p·* the opposite result.
  386– 8 to demand it and *p·* it.
  386– 9 mortals declare that . . . *p·* catarrh, fever,
  399– 3 You say that certain material combinations *p·*
  401–23 could you *p·* any effect upon the brain or body
  402–29 Science cannot *p·* both disorder and order.
  404–12 the wicked motives which *p·* them.
  408–22 would *p·* insanity as perceptibly as
  413– 2 Mind, does not *p·* pain in matter.
  413–10 *p·* good or bad effects on the
  420– 8 cannot *p·* this unnatural reluctance.
  t 457–12 to prevent suffering, not to *p·* it.
  461–21 because of the different effects they *p·*.
  r 486–20 yet supposes Mind unable to *p·* harmony !
  g 522–30 Does Life, Truth, and Love *p·* death,
  539– 9 if they *p·* their opposites,
  544–14 nor does matter *p·* mind.
  551– 4 If Mind is first, it cannot *p·* its opposite
  551– 5 If matter is first, it cannot *p·* Mind.
  551–28 Neither can *p·* the other.

produced
  a 38– 7 *p·* by man-made doctrines,
  53–19 the shock so often *p·* by the truth,
  sp 87–26 The strong impressions *p·* on mortal mind
  s 109–18 cures were *p·* in primitive Christian healing
  126–13 but the human mind never *p·* a real tone
  152–10 Anatomy describes muscular action as *p·* by
  159–21 this Lynn woman died from effects *p·* by
  164–19 or *p·* by mental assassins,

produced

ph	178–13	*p·* prior to his birth by the
	185– 2	The wind had not *p·* the difficulty.
	188–18	sensation *p·* physically by the
	195– 7	All that he ate, except his black crust, *p·*
	198–31	does not follow that exercise has *p·* this
	199–17	*p·* consciously or unconsciously,
b	277–15	A mineral is not *p·* by a vegetable
	304–16	Harmony is *p·* by its Principle,
p	370–11	symptoms, which might be *p·* by a
	371– 6	*p·* on children by telling ghost-stories
	373–20	the effects of fear *p·* by sin,
	380–18	belief of disease *p·* by a so-called
	389–28	A case of convulsions, *p·* by indigestion,
	392–12	Whatever benefit is *p·* on the body,
	401–16	*chemicalization* is the upheaval *p·* when
	401–21	The only effect *p·* by medicine is
	421–22	the alterative effect *p·* by Truth upon error,
	422–23	both similarly *p·* and attended by the same
g	532–18	*p·* the immediate fruits of fear and shame.
	551– 3	Either Mind produces, or it is *p·*.

producer

p	377–14	showing mortal mind to be the *p·* of
g	544– 6	Mind, instead of matter, being the *p·*,
	544–32	Error begins with corporeality as the *p·*

produces

pr	7–17	*p·* material ecstasy and emotion.
sp	79– 8	*p·* permanent health.
	80–28	Mortal mind *p·* table-tipping as certainly as
s	108–31	*p·* all the organism and action of the
	144–19	It *p·* evil continually, and is not a factor in
	148–18	the divine Principle which *p·* harmonious man,
	155–18	sustains medicine and *p·* all medical results,
	159–30	a man's belief *p·* disease and all its symptoms,
ph	177– 1	Human mind *p·* what is termed organic disease
	177– 2	as certainly as it *p·* hysteria.
	184– 6	Belief *p·* the results of belief,
	184–10	error of belief which *p·* a mortal disorder,
f	208–15	absurd to suppose that . . . God, *p·* disease
	220–18	Mortal mind *p·* its own phenomena,
	229–26	If the transgression of God's law *p·* sickness,
	231–12	If God makes sin, if good *p·* evil,
	239–24	It forms material concepts and *p·* every
b	270–27	If a sense of disease *p·* suffering
	276–29	inform us that like *p·* like.
	276–32	Intelligence never *p·* non-intelligence ;
	277– 6	Matter never *p·* mind.
	277– 6	The immortal never *p·* the mortal.
	277–20	Error . . . asserts that Spirit *p·* matter
	277–20	asserts that . . . matter *p·* all the
p	370–15	The effect, which mortal mind *p·* through one
	374–30	Mortal mind *p·* animal heat,
	379–23	her belief *p·* the very results she dreads.
	380–24	the divine Mind *p·* in man health,
	386–25	Error, not Truth, *p·* all the suffering on earth.
	390– 8	which *p·* apparent discord,
	398–18	What *p·* the change?
	398–20	and *p·* a new effect upon the body.
	403–28	The mortal so-called mind *p·* all
	408–29	The unconscious thought . . . *p·* no effect,
	419–20	Mind *p·* all action.
	421–15	belief that this chemicalization *p·* pain
t	459–27	The tree must be good, which *p·* good fruit.
g	544–13	In Science, Mind neither *p·* matter nor
	547–18	Darwin's theory,— that Mind *p·* its opposite,
	551– 6	Either Mind *p·*, or it is produced.
	551– 6	Like *p·* like.
	552– 1	if the egg *p·* the parent.
	552– 3	Who or what *p·* the parent of the egg?

producing

sp	81–22	the *p·*, governing, divine Principle lives on,
ph	182– 8	capable of *p·* the highest human good
	190– 5	The mortal says . . . seedling is *p·* mortals,
	199– 7	nobody believes that mind is *p·* such a result
f	249– 4	*p·* His own models of excellence.
c	263–12	*p·* evil when he would create good,
o	343–16	the impossibility of good *p·* evil ;
	356–19	incapable of *p·* sin, sickness, and death
p	370– 9	the law of cause and effect, or like *p·* like.
	373–30	Mortal mind is *p·* the propulsion or the
	401–11	to the end of *p·* a higher manifestation.
	403–17	*p·* on mortal body the results of false opinions ;
	415–25	To remove the error *p·* disorder,
g	550–25	no instance of one species *p·* its opposite.
gl	580– 7	a so-called finite mind, *p·* other minds,

product

cannot be the

b	339–10	and cannot be the *p·* of God.

flower is a

sp	71–12	the flower is a *p·* of the so-called mind,

not the

g	551– 7	the bird is not the *p·* of a beast.

of belief

r	490– 3	Will-power is but a *p·* of belief,

product

of nothing

gl	580– 9	a *p·* of nothing as the mimicry of something ;
s	108–15	as the *p·* of three multiplied by three,
	119– 7	they assume that matter is the *p·* of Spirit.
f	219– 7	and then say the *p·* is correct.
b	280– 8	and the *p·* must be mental.
r	479– 8	Matter is neither self-existent nor a *p·* of
g	508– 5	Mind's infinite idea, . . . is the *p·*.

production

ph	183–18	action of Truth is the *p·* of harmony.
g	508–21	The Mind or intelligence of *p·*

productive

g	544– 4	In God's creation ideas became *p·*,

products

b	274–21	These false beliefs and their *p·* constitute the flesh,
	280– 2	elements of discord and decay are not *p·* of
p	374–26	Heat and cold are *p·* of mortal mind.
	421–31	the *p·* of eight multiplied by five, and of

profane

s	139–30	the *p·* or atheistic invalid
ph	175–13	It is *p·* to fancy that the perfume of clover

profess

a	27–28	Why do those who *p·* to follow Christ reject the
	54–30	would not some, who now *p·* to love him, reject

professed

a	37–16	When will Jesus' *p·* followers learn to
p	436–16	the prisoner summoned two *p·* friends,

profession

pr	15–28	Practice not *p·*, understanding not belief,
a	28–11	more on the ground of demonstration than of *p·*.
s	141– 3	More than *p·* is requisite for
	158– 1	the *p·* of medicine originated in idolatry
f	242–32	the proof which he gave, instead of mere *p·*.

professional

f	236– 6	Is it not *p·* reputation and emolument

professions

pr	8–18	*P·* and audible prayers are like charity
f	233– 2	higher proofs rather than *p·* of Christian power.

Professor

s	163– 4	Dr. Benjamin Waterhouse, *P·* in Harvard
	163–13	Dr. Mason Good, a learned *P·* in London,
	163–19	*P·* of the Institutes and Practice of Physic

proficiency

pref	x–30	No intellectual *p·* is requisite in the learner,

profit

pr	10– 6	If good enough to *p·* by Jesus' cup

profitable

a	43–12	the most *p·* to his students.

profitably

pref	ix–24	before a work on the subject could be *p·* studied.

profiteth

o	356–16	the flesh *p·* nothing.''— *John* 6 : 63.

profound

sp	88–22	and the individual manifests *p·* adoration,
s	157–32	better for this spiritual and *p·* pathology.
b	320–26	a *p·* idea of the divine power to heal
ap	572– 7	the most simple and *p·* counsel of the
	575–17	description of the city . . . has a *p·* meaning.

progenitor

g	551– 8	matter is not the *p·* of Mind.

progenitors

ph	173– 5	progressed farther than his animal *p·*.
p	425– 1	or some of his *p·* farther back

progeny

m	61– 8	improve our *p·*, diminish crime,
g	532–10	Adam and his *p·* were cursed, not blessed ;
	539– 1	the author of sin and sin's *p·*.

Progress

p	441–24	executed at the hands of our sheriff, *P·*.

progress

civilization and

m	57– 1	the cement of civilization and *p·*.

consistent with

m	65– 8	If . . . consistent with *p·*, they will be strong

deemed

s	158–10	This was deemed *p·*

element of

f	233– 6	This is an element of *p·*,

evidences of

s	158–24	Evidences of *p·* and of spiritualization

human

ph	170–24	spiritual causation relates to human *p·*.

is born

b	296– 4	*P·* is born of experience.

is the law

f	233– 6	and *p·* is the law of God,

progress
labor and
   f 236– 2   should stimulate clerical labor and *p·*.
moral
   a 22– 5   Vibrating . . . our moral *p·* will be slow.
not united by
   sp 72–16   tares and the wheat, which are not united by *p·*,
of information
   g 548–21   changed with the *p·* of information.''
of truth
   sp 94–17   The *p·* of truth confirms its claims,
our
   f 239–16   To ascertain our *p·*, we must
   p 426– 9   expectation speeds our *p·*.
painless
   f 224– 9   There should be painless *p·*,
periods of
   g 511–18   infinite ideas, images, mark the periods of *p·*.
proof of
   b 324– 5   purification of sense and self is a proof of *p·*.
ready for
   o 353–23   When we learn that . . . we shall be ready for *p·*,
revelation and
   gl 591–24   symbol of Truth ; revelation and *p·*.
some
   pref ix–17   To-day, though rejoicing in some *p·*,
stage of
   g 506–14   forming each successive stage of *p·*.
takes off
   c 256– 1   *P·* takes off human shackles.
this
   pr 11–11   in order to compel this *p·*.
will finally destroy
   r 492–11   Thus *p·* will finally destroy all error,

   pr 10–20   the advance guard of *p·* has
   m 68– 2   At present mortals *p·* slowly
   s 142–15   they . . . shut the door on *p·*.
   r 495–25   How can I *p·* most rapidly in the

progressed
   ph 173– 4   *p·* farther than his animal progenitors.

progressing
   gl 589–23   material belief *p·* and disappearing ;

progression
   b 291–12   Universal salvation rests on *p·* and probation,

progressive
   a 46–24   probationary and *p·* state beyond the grave.
   f 240–19   If mortals are not *p·*,

projected
   s 126– 8   Human thought never *p·* the least portion of

prolific
   ph 180– 1   are both *p·* sources of sickness.
   f 205–11   the *p·* source of all suffering
   228– 7   Heredity is a *p·* subject for mortal belief to
   p 409– 7   the more *p·* it is likely to become in sin and
   t 457–17   mental malpractice, *p·* of evil,
   ap 563–21   *p·* in health, holiness, and immortality.

prolong
   sp 77–19   Of what advantage, . . . to *p·* the material
   77–20   and so *p·* the illusion

prolonged
   s 156–15   aggravation of symptoms from their *p·* use,
   f 212– 6   If the sensation . . . can return, can be *p·*,

prolonging
   m 59–19   in *p·* her health and smiles

promise
   pr 14–19   Hence the hope of the *p·* Jesus bestows :
   f 246–23   and still maintain his vigor, freshness, and *p·*.
   b 328–28   Jesus' *p·* is perpetual.
   o 342–11   the *p·* that his students should cast out evils
   r 497–24   we solemnly *p·* to watch, and pray
   ap 558–12   but a bright *p·* crowns its brow.
   562–25   waiting to be delivered of her sweet *p·*,

promised
   pref xi–18   coming now as was *p·* aforetime,
   an 101–13   *p·* by Monsieur Berna [the magnetizer]
   s 123–22   teachings of the Comforter, as *p·* by the Master.
   150– 8   This coming, as was *p·* by the Master,
   c 267–31   hath *p·* to them that love him.''— *Jas.* 1 : 12.
   g 566– 5   and anticipating the *p·* joy,

promises
   a 55–21   The *p·* will be fulfilled.
   p 373– 5   and be more alive to His *p·*.

promising
   m 61–14   places *p·* children in the arms of gross parents,

promote
   m 58–18   will not *p·* the sweet interchange of confidence
   ph 195–21   *p·* the growth of mortal mind out of itself,
   p 410–27   to *p·* right thinking and doing,

promoters
   ph 179–22   are the *p·* of sickness and disease.

promotes
   m 59–17   *p·* the welfare and happiness of your wife
   an 103– 1   *p·* affection and virtue in families
   c 266–12   to accept what best *p·* your growth.

promotive
   p 420–23   is not *p·* of health or happiness.

promptly
   b 273–32   when it is opposed *p·* and persistently by C. S.

promptness
   g 514–15   diligence, *p·*, and perseverance

promulgated
   s 164– 6   therapeutic agents, ever yet *p·*,

prone
   f 203–17   We are *p·* to believe either in more than

pronounce
   p 433–18   Judge Medicine then proceeds to *p·* the
   439–30   the sentence which . . . Divine Love will *p·*.

pronounced
   s 110– 6   is *p·* by His wisdom good.
   157–17   which . . . He *p·* *good,*
   p 436–33   that court *p·* a sentence of death for
   g 526–15   God *p·* good all that He created,

pronounces
   pr 3–29   sharp censure our Master *p·* on hypocrites.

proof
added
   b 295– 3   added *p·* of the unreliability of
affording the
   r 473–20   affording the *p·* of Christianity's truth
affords no
   f 208– 1   error, which affords no *p·* of God,
and demonstration
   o 342– 2   hour has struck when *p·* and demonstration,
another
   s 122–15   The optical focus is another *p·* of the
brings out the
   s 157–30   brings out the *p·* that Life is
contains the
   g 547– 3   contains the *p·* of all here said of C. S.
divine
   f 215–22   With its divine *p·*, Science reverses the
final
   a 45–23   beheld the final *p·* of all that he had taught,
furnished the
   b 317–28   to him Jesus furnished the *p·* that
furnish the
   a 51–11   that he might furnish the *p·* of immortal life.
great
   a 25– 1   the great *p·* of Truth and Love.
hence the
   p 402–28   Hence the *p·* that hypnotism is not scientific ;
highest
   a 54–17   This was the highest *p·* he could have offered
his
   a 26–30   His *p·* of Christianity was no form or
   44–21   in his *p·* of man's truly derived power
immortal
   r 488–17   C. S. sustains with immortal *p·*
is essential
   o 341–11   *P·* is essential to a due estimate of this subject.
Jesus' last
   a 43–11   Jesus' last *p·* was the highest,
no
   sp 71–23   no *p·* nor power outside of human testimony.
   an 100–20   no *p·* of the existence of the animal magnetic
   f 208– 1   error, which affords no *p·* of God,
   b 284–21   physical senses can obtain no *p·* of God.
   o 352– 1   but their prayer brought down no *p·* that
of Christianity
   a 26–30   His *p·* of Christianity was no form or
   s 142– 9   as our first *p·* of Christianity,
   f 210– 5   The Principle and *p·* of Christianity
   b 271– 9   the philosophy, Science, and *p·* of Christianity
   o 351–16   the practical *p·* of Christianity,
of harmony
   b 340– 2   make life its own *p·* of harmony and God.
of healing
   ap 569–13   rejoices in the *p·* of healing,
of immortality
   sp 81–15   Life, Love, Truth, is the only *p·* of immortality.
   b 306–18   a rational *p·* of immortality.
of its utility
   gl 583–14   institution, which affords *p·* of its utility
of progress
   b 324– 5   purification of sense and self is a *p·* of progress.
of the supremacy
   b 322– 2   in *p·* of the supremacy of Mind.
of the utility
   o 355– 5   the *p·* of the utility of these methods ;
once seen
   s 109– 9   *p·* once seen, no other conclusion can be reached.

proof

overwhelming
s 151–32   we have overwhelming p·.

practical
o 345–19   this practical p· is the only feasible evidence
351–16   the practical p· of Christianity,

presented the
a 54–14   he presented the p· that Life, Truth, and Love

requisite
g 552– 9   even where the p· requisite . . . is undiscovered.

spiritual
g 505–24   giving the spiritual p· of the universe

statement and
s 113–13   found to agree in statement and p·,
p 380–28   its culmination of scientific statement and p·.

subjected to
o 341–16   according to a divine given rule, and subjected to p·.

support of his
f 236–10   Christ's teachings in support of his p·

this
a 42–29   had taught his disciples the Science of this p·.
s 147–20   This p· lifts you high above the
b 321–15   this p· was a staff upon which to lean.
321–25   God had lessened Moses' fear by this p·

witness or
b 303–27   a witness or p· of His own nature.

a 24–25   as a p· that spirits can return to earth?
42–16   the p· of his final triumph over body
m 69– 4   as fixed in divine Science as is the p· that
s 123–24   The p·, by present demonstration, that
153–29   p· that this so-called mind makes its own pain
f 207– 6   every scientific statement . . . has its p·.
242–31   require of Christians the p· which he gave,
g 546–27   The p· that the system stated in this book
gl 592–12   the p· that, without the gospel,

proofs

any
o 354–13   neither give nor offer any p· that their

furnished
r 472–12   Jesus furnished p· of these statements.

glorious
r 474– 1   his teachings and their glorious p·,

higher
f 233– 2   makes its demands upon us for higher p·

highest
a 49–28   to whom he had given the highest p· of

of God's care
m 66–11   Trials are p· of God's care.

of immortality
sp 78–13   why look to them . . . for p· of immortality,
80–11   assertion that. . .are our only p· of immortality.

requisite
a 25–24   giving the requisite p· of their own piety.

sublime
p 387–27   history of Christianity furnishes sublime p·

these
f 233– 3   These p· consist solely in the destruction of

a 41–14   p· of Truth, Life, and Love, which Jesus gave
o 355– 6   p· are better than mere verbal arguments
358–13   Otherwise it . . . could not present its p·.
p 363–29   In the absence of other p·,

pro or con
s 120–25   Any conclusion p· or c· deduced from
129– 9   the material fable, be the fable p· or c·,

propagate
g 551–30   in order to p· its species,

propagated
b 272–27   from which are p· the dismal beliefs of

propagates
m 66–13   Love p· anew the higher joys of Spirit,

propagating
g 507–19   not . . . because of any p· power of their own,
531–20   a p· property of their own?

propagation
m 61–24   Is not the p· of the human species a
61–31   If the p· of a higher human species is requisite
s 142– 3   required for self-establishment and p·.
b 303– 6   from no power of p· in matter,
g 545–23   They believed in the existence of matter, its p·
557– 9   human p· has its suffering because it is a

propensities
m 61–21   p· that must either be overcome or
an 104–20   falsehood, revenge, malice, are animal p·
f 206– 6   and free the lower p·.
p 405– 2   Hatred inflames the brutal p·.
405– 5   C. S. commands man to master the p·,

propensity
f 252–21   Animal in p· deceitful in sentiment,
r 490– 5   Human will is an animal p·,
g 539–14   Whence does he obtain the p· or power to

proper
pr 4– 7   and follow his example, is our p· debt to him
sp 93–23   Spirit, as a p· noun, is the name of the
98–25   what they call science has no p· connection
s 112–29   without giving that author p· credit,
ph 179– 1   understanding of C. S. in its p· signification
f 222– 6   one of which is to believe that p· food supplies
234–17   If mortals would keep p· ward over mortal
c 265– 7   and gain some p· sense of the infinite,
b 302–28   body presents no p· likeness of divinity,
313– 3   the full and p· translation of the Greek),
319–30   but we can by special and p· capitalization
333–13   p· name of our Master in the Greek was
p 383–20   to keep the body in p· condition.
424– 8   the p· sense of God's unerring direction
434–24   Mortal Man has had no p· counsel in the case.
t 449–28   A p· teacher of C. S.
463–21   To decide quickly as to the p· treatment of
r 482– 6   The p· use of the word soul
g 502–12   serves to suggest the p· reflection of God
506–19   gathers unformed thoughts into their p· channels,
517–20   The only p· symbol of God as person is
538– 6   to note the p· guests.
555–24   and set aside the p· conception of Deity,

properly
pr 16–16   p· reads, "Deliver us from the— Matt. 6: 13.
m 58– 7   should be concordant in order to blend p·.
sp 84–31   If . . . thoroughly learned and p· digested,
an 106– 9   Man is p· self-governed only when he
s 128– 4   The term Science, p· understood,
128–32   conclusion, if p· drawn, cannot be false.
129– 4   a p· computed sum in arithmetic.
130–15   C. S., p· understood, would
b 333– 3   The word Christ is not p· a synonym for
t 449–17   to teach this subject p· and correctly
463– 6   To attend p· the birth of the new child,
463–13   truth removes p· whatever is offensive.
r 482–10   Soul is p· the synonym of Spirit, or God ;
g 501– 1   interpretation of the Scriptures p· starts with
554– 5   nor are there p· any mortal beings,
557– 4   how to develop their children p· on dry land.

properties
s 118–25   as yeast changes the chemical p· of meal.
124–20   cohesion, and attraction are p· of Mind.
ph 177–19   indicated matter's p·, qualities, and forms.

property
m 63–19   p·, and parental claims of the two sexes.
s 153– 6   until there was not a single saline p· left.
g 510–28   and not a vitalizing p· of matter.
531 20   a propagating p· of their own?

prophecy
s 118– 6   Did not this parable point a moral with a p·,
131–26   The mission of Jesus confirmed p·,
c 266–16   The author has experienced the foregoing p·
b 292– 4   Here p· pauses.
o 349–21   Out of this condition grew the p·
g 534–12   This p· has been fulfilled.
ap 559– ·   they that hear the words of this p·,— Rev. 1: 3.
gl 585– 9   ELIAS. P· ; spiritual evidence

prophesied
ap 561–32   John the Baptist p· the coming of

prophesy
b 330– 5   p· and involve the final destruction of all sin?

prophesying
g 531– 9   as if hope were ever p· thus :

prophesyings
r 490–19   Despise not p·."— I Thess. 5: 20.

Prophet
o 360–28   the Jews put to death the Galilean P·,
r 497–18   as demonstrated by the Galilean P·

prophet (see also **prophet's**)
a 28–29   trials encountered by p·, disciple, and apostle,
sp 98– 4   p· of to-day beholds in the mental horizon
122–19   The barometer,— that little p· of
p 363–12   they were wondering why, being a p·,
g 540– 6   but the p· referred to divine law
gl 593– 4   definition of

prophetic
s 109–25   p· Scripture of Isaiah is renewedly fulfilled :
f 226– 2   p· of further steps towards the banishment of

prophetically
a 52–25   p· said to his disciples,
ap 558–18   whose flames of Truth were p· described by

prophet's
a 52–12   p· foresight of the reception error would give

prophets

ancient
sp 84– 3   ancient p· gained their foresight from

prophets
and apostles
    s 126–29 and the lives of p· and apostles.
    f 243–12 the ancient demonstrations of p· and apostles.
false
    ap 567–28 The beast and the false p· are
healing by the
    s 139–25 nor annul the healing by the p·,
Hebrew
    sp 85–19 were foretold by the Hebrew p·.
of Christian Science
    p 388– 1 The Christian martyrs were p· of C. S.
of Jehovah
    sp 83– 2 What the p· of Jehovah did,
of old
    b 270–14 p· of old looked for something higher
primitive
    f 214– 3 and that they came as sound to the primitive p·.
seers and
    sp 84– 9 men become seers and p· involuntarily,

    s 136–16 Jeremias, or one of the p·." — Matt. 16 : 14.
    136–16 These p· were considered dead,
    b 269–24 teachings of Jesus, of his apostles, of the p·,
    288–13 foreshadowed by the p· and inaugurated by
    333–23 Abraham, Jacob, Moses, and the p·
    o 358–16 uttered and illustrated by the p·,

prophet-shepherds
    pref vii– 4 So shone the pale star to the p· ;

prophylactic
    p 369–23 The p· and therapeutic . . . arts

propitiate
    a 18–15 how can God p· Himself?

proportion
as humanity gains
    c 258–22 in p· as humanity gains the true conception
as ignorance
    f 209– 3 in p· as ignorance, fear, or
as matter
    p 369– 5 In p· as matter loses to human sense all
as mortals
    b 329–32 in p· as mortals give up error for Truth
    p 409–25 in p· as mortals realize the Science of man
as the belief
    b 279–16 In p· as the belief disappears that
as the false
    m 69– 9 in p· as the false and material disappears.
as the force
    g 554–32 in p· as the force of mortal mind is less pungent
as the sin
    p 391–16 will cease in p· as the sin ceases.
as this fact
    r 467–11 in p· as this fact becomes apparent,
as this is done
    f 209–23 In p· as this is done, man and the universe will
as we apprehend
    s 140– 9 in p· as we apprehend the divine nature
as we overcome
    p 427–21 in p· as we overcome sin.
as you understand
    f 217–22 in p· as you understand the control
to his purity
    b 337–16 In p· to his purity is man perfect ;
to his understanding
    ap 576–24 in p· to his understanding of God.
to its escape
    s 128–20 only in p· to its escape into the
to its wickedness
    ap 569–11 nothingness of error is in p· to its wickedness.
to our apprehension
    sp 80– 1 We have strength in p· to our apprehension of
to our spirituality
    sp 95– 7 in p· to our spirituality,
to our understanding
    ph 178–22 In p· to our understanding of C. S.,
to their courage
    p 417– 8 their strength is in p· to their courage.
to the truth
    p 403–29 in p· to the truth or error which influences
to your belief
    p 385–24 you will suffer in p· to your belief and fear.
to your disbelief
    p 397–19 in exact p· to your disbelief in physics,
to your honesty
    t 449–14 in p· to your honesty and fidelity,

    a 26– 7 in p· to their demonstration of his love,
    s 155–23 in p· as it puts less weight into the material
    ph 178–26 in p· to our spiritual understanding
    c 265– 4 Man understands spiritual existence in p· as
    p 369– 6 in that p· does man become its master.
    r 468–30 in p· as the other is recognized.

proportionably
    c 261– 6 p· to their occupancy of your thoughts.

proportional
    an 101–32 is p· to one's faith in esoteric magic.

proportionate
    s 167– 7 Our p· admission of the claims of
    f 225–15 p· to its embodiment of right thinking.

proportionately
    m 68–30 P· as human generation ceases,
    s 157–15 power of action is p· increased.
    f 207– 3 p· as we advance spiritually,
    p 423–22 and he p· strengthens his patient
    g 557–11 C. S. reveals harmony as p· increasing

propose
    o 349– 8 We p· to follow the Master's example.
    r 492–18 "I p· to fight it out on this line,

proposed
    s 161–11 Massachusetts put her foot on a p·

proposition
    s 109– 1 p· that Mind is All and matter is naught
    110–10 glorious p·, — man's perfectibility
    113–22 Which of the denials in p· four is true?
    164–21 the truth of its basic p·
    r 470–12 by the following self-evident p· :

propositions
    an 100– 6 His p· were as follows :
    s 113– 9 The fundamental p· of divine metaphysics
    113–11 the four following, to me, self-evident p·.
    113–11 Even if reversed, these p· will be
    128–31 If both the major and the minor p·
    o 345–16 to those who understand its p·
    349–17 the expression of spiritual conceptions and p·,
    r 471–12 yield assent to astronomical p·
    493–25 these p· can only seem real . . . in illusion.

propounded
    s 145–32 Our Master's first article of faith p· to

propriety
    t 443– 2 as to the p·, advantage, and consistency

propulsion
    m 67–16 until an irresistible p· precipitates his
    p 373–30 Mortal mind is producing the p·

proscriptive
    s 140–13 will no longer be tyrannical and p·

prosecution
    p 430–27 the evidence for the p· being called for,

prospect
    s 107–18 in the p· of those days in which we must say,

prospective
    g 527–28 lie . . . asking a p· sinner to help Him.

prospects
    s 130– 3 discouraged over its slight spiritual p·.
    ph 191–19 no longer ask . . . What are man's p·

prosper
    t 448–17 covereth his sins shall not p· : — Prov. 28 : 13.

prosperity
    pref xii–15 October 29, 1889, in the height of its p·
    m 66– 9 in the sunshine of joy and p·.
    s 133–13 In national p·, miracles attended the
    t 446–30 Covering iniquity will prevent p·

prostrates
    s 119–19 whose lightning palsies or p·

prostration
    sp 79–26 says : . . . You have nervous p·,

protect
    p 436–32 Claiming to p· Mortal Man in right-doing,
    t 461–18 if this be requisite to p· others.

protecting
    p 387–28 the supporting influence and p· power

protection
    m 60–17 a p· to woman, strength to man,
    p 436–14 and are under the p· of the Most High.

protects
    g 518–14 in return, the higher always p· the lower.

protest
    s 150–20 and that, too, in spite of the individual's p·
    160–21 and become cramped despite the mental p·?
    p 384–12 and man has only to enter his p· against
    391–21 therefore meet the intimation with a p·.
    425–31 be always ready with the mental p·

protested
    s 159– 3 p· against inhaling the ether
    p 432–22 p· that the prisoner had abused him,

protests
    pr 12–14 deep and conscientious p· of Truth,
    o 354– 1 Are the p· of C. S. against the

protoplasm
    b 279– 7 slime, or p· never originated in the

protracted
    t 446–17 or his demonstration is p·,

proud

s 124–24 and said to the *p*· wave,

provable

f 211– 9 Is it not *p*· that Mind is not *mortal*

prove

a 26–17 to *p*· what God is and what He does for man.
27– 2 intended to *p*· beyond a question that the
49–21 He was to *p*· that the Christ is not subject to
m 59–18 will *p*· more salutary in prolonging her
sp 81– 1 There is not so much evidence to *p*·
81– 8 on its own theories, spiritualism can only *p*·
81–13 than the opposite assertion, . . . would *p*·
an 104–29 courts recognize evidence to *p*· the motive
s 108–14 the lesser demonstration to *p*· the greater,
132–12 such effects, coming from divine Mind, *p*· the
138–25 The Christian can *p*· this to-day as readily as
146–22 practically *p*· its divine origin and efficacy.
ph 199–20 The feats of the gymnast *p*· that
f 217– 8 *p*· Mind to be scientifically distinct from
b 278–26 logic which would *p*· his annihilation.
315–19 subdue sin and *p*· man's heritage.
315–22 to *p*· irrefutably how spiritual Truth destroys
316– 8 to *p*· the power of Spirit over the flesh,
316–27 could *p*· God's divine power by healing the
329–13 We must *p*· our faith by demonstration.
o 346–12 in order to *p*· the somethingness
356– 6 Sin, sickness, and death do not *p*·
p 368– 6 Divine Science insists that time will *p*· all this.
373–31 we *p*· this to be so when by mental means the
377– 9 that they can be healthy in all climates,
380–21 and *p*· man's dominion over error.
380–24 to *p*· that the divine Mind produces
383–24 Does his assertion *p*· the use of tobacco to be
383–26 *p*· the illusive physical effect of a false belief,
384–14 will *p*· to himself, by small beginnings,
400–21 we *p*· that thought alone creates the suffering.
428– 7 Man's privilege . . . is to *p*· the words of
t 446–24 you overcome it and *p*· its nothingness.
447–26 get the victory over sin and so *p*· its unreality.
458–28 He must *p*·, through living as well as
459–14 Any attempt to . . . must *p*· abortive.
461–26 To *p*· . . . the error or unreality of sin,
461–28 to *p*· . . . the error or unreality of disease,
464–19 "*p*· all things ;— *I Thess.* 5 : 21.
r 493–15 and *p*· for himself the Principle and rule
496–14 will *p*· what the understanding of God
g 547– 6 You can *p*· for yourself, dear reader,

proved

pref x–16 have *p*· the worth of her teachings.
x–22 The divine Principle of healing is *p*· in the
a 26–25 He *p*· by his deeds that C. S. destroys sickness,
27–10 Jesus *p*· by his reappearance after the
42– 1 Jesus' life *p*·, divinely and scientifically,
42–21 and *p*· its nothingness.
44– 9 He *p*· Life to be deathless
46–14 he *p*· to the physical senses
s 109– 9 and thus *p*· absolute and divine.
111–32 *p*· itself, whenever scientifically employed,
112–24 already been stated and *p*· to be true,
125–31 matter will finally be *p*· nothing more than
138 26 as readily as it was *p*· centuries ago.
139– 6 Moses *p*· the power of Mind by what men called
146– 1 and he *p*· his faith by his works.
149–15 because you have not obeyed the rule and *p*·
159–20 The sequel *p*· that this Lynn woman
ph 168–20 an authority which Jesus *p*· to be false
f 214–12 material senses, . . . are *p*· non-intelligent.
228–29 He *p*· them powerless.
229– 2 *p*· that matter has not destroyed them,
c 264–23 who *p*· them to be forms of error.
267–30 when he is tried, [*p*· faithful],— *Jas.* 1 : 12.
b 300–10 So far as . . . is understood, it can be *p*·
307–14 This error has *p*· itself to be error.
314– 6 *p*· that he and the Father were inseparable
314–32 Jesus *p*· them wrong by his resurrection.
316–19 thus *p*· that Truth was the master of death.
318–30 as numbers are controlled and *p*· by
332–19 he *p*· that Christ is the divine idea
o 355–29 *p*· to be such by our Master
p 368–21 *p*·, when we learn that life and man survive this
386–30 might afterwards be *p*· to you.
394–17 Experience has *p*· to the author the fallacy of
402–31 *p*· to be a belief without a real cause.
434–20 not *p*· "worthy of death,— *Acts* 23 : 29.
438– 8 C. S. *p*· the witness, Nerve, to be a perjurer.
t 461– 6 We admit the whole, because a part is *p*·
r 473–28 He *p*· what he taught.
473–30 Jesus *p*· the Principle, . . . to be divine.
486–14 Jesus *p*· by the prints of the nails, that
492– 8 It is already *p*· that a knowledge of this,
492–13 a statement *p*· to be good must be correct.
493–29 *p*· that the Christ could improve on a false
g 514–27 Paul *p*· the viper to be harmless.
ap 567–23 and so *p*· to be powerless.
gl 581– 8 *p*· to be as immortal as its Principle ;

proverb

b 291–21 has been transformed into the popular *p*·,

proverbial

ph 179–24 It should not be *p*·, that so long as
p 385– 1 It is *p*· that Florence Nightingale

proves

ap 81–12 no more *p*· him to be so, than
s 108–16 *p*· conclusively that three times three
113–27 *p*· the rule by inversion.
135–25 This *p*· the one to be identical with the other.
ph 194–19 *p*· beyond a doubt that education constitutes
194–30 *p*· material sense to be but a belief
f 207– 5 This fact *p*· our position,
212–14 it *p*· sensation to be in the mortal mind,
245–28 *p*· it possible to be young at seventy-four ;
c 257–23 *p*· the material theory of mind in matter to be
258– 7 The insufficiency of this belief. . .*p*· the falsity of
b 289–15 *p*· the "king of terrors" to be but— *Job* 18 : 14.
306–20 Science *p*· man's existence to be intact.
329– 6 A little understanding of C. S. *p*· the truth of
338– 9 The mortality of material man *p*· that
o 347–25 and so *p*· their nothingness.
351–24 which *p*· the nothingness of error,
p 370– 8 this *p*· that fear is governing the body.
375– 9 The old-school physician *p*· this when
416–21 is only in mortal mind, as the dead body *p*· ;
t 461– 7 illustrates and *p*· the entire Principle.
g 522– 3 *p*· the falsity of the second.

provide

s 143– 6 nor *p*· them for human use ;

Providence

p 424–10 Under divine *P*· there can be no accidents,

providing

a 24–21 chiefly as *p*· a ready pardon for all sinners

Province

p 432–11 Governor of the *P*· of Body,
438– 9 Instead of being a ruler in the *P*· of Body,
439– 6 was absent from the *P*· of Body,

province

pr 3– 2 without being reminded of His *p*·.
f 206– 7 the *p*· of spiritual sense to govern man.
b 307–29 his *p*· is in spiritual statutes,
p 432–12 In this *p*· there is a statute regarding
437– 1 in which *p*· Mortal Man resides.

proving

a 39– 5 thus *p*· their nothingness.
s 125–19 *p*· our material theories . . . to be valueless.
ph 199–23 *p*· that failure is occasioned by
o 343– 3 and for *p*· my word by my deed
343–18 *p*· by what are wrongly called miracles,
g 546–32 the *p*· of one example would authenticate

provision

m 56– 7 the legal and moral *p*· for generation

provoke

t 452–11 Your advancing course may *p*· envy,

proximity

sp 82–15 dreamer by our side despite his physical *p*·,

proxy

pr 12–31 petitioners (*per se* or by *p*·)

prudent

s 131–21 from the wise and *p*·,— *Luke* 10 : 21.

Psalm

ap 577–32 In the following *P*· one word shows,
578– 4 chapter sub-title

Psalmist

pr 5–20 the *P*· could see their end,
s 135– 1 *P*· sang: "What ailed thee, O thou— *Psal.* 114 : 5.
ph 200–13 *P*· said: "Thou madest him to— *Psal.* 8 : 6.
b 309– 4 which, to use the word of the *P*·,
g 505–17 *P*· saith: "The Lord on high— *Psal.* 93 : 4.
ap 575–22 *P*· saith, "Beautiful for situation,— *Psal.* 48 : 2.

Psalms

ap 564–27 quoting a line from the *P*·,

pseudo-mental

p 389–10 This *p*· testimony can be destroyed only by

psychology

p 369–25 readily seen, if *p*·, . . . was understood.

Ptolemaic

s 123– 4 The *P*· blunder could not affect the

Ptolemy

s 122–30 mistake . . . that *P*· made regarding the

public

pr 13– 5 In *p*· prayer we often go beyond our
13–12 Can the mere *p*· expression of our desires
a 40–29 has come so generally to mean *p*· worship
an 101– 2 observed in the *p*· practice of magnetism,
227–10 some *p*· teachers permit an ignorance of

Publican's
  t 448– 3   When the *P·* wail went out to the
publicans
  a 20– 7   "The *p·* and the harlots— *Matt.* 21 : 31.
  53– 1   the "friend of *p·* and sinners." — *Luke* 7 : 34.
publications
  t 446– 5   A thorough perusal of the author's *p·*
  464– 6   except through her laborious *p·*,
publicly
  p 441–23   *p·* executed at the hands of our sheriff,
published
  pref ix–28   copious notes . . . which have never been *p·*.
  x– 3   SCIENCE AND HEALTH was *p·* in 1875.
  xii–18   which was *p·* in 1891.
  s 163–20   Dr. Chapman, . . . in a *p·* essay said :
  ph 185– 7   Before this book was *p·*,
  f 245– 3   *p·* in the London medical magazine
publisher
  (*see* **Eddy, Mrs. Mary Baker**)
Publius Lentulus
  a 29–12   There is a tradition that *P· L·* wrote to
puffing
  p 407– 3   *P·* the obnoxious fumes of tobacco,
pulmonary
  m 63– 2   for warding off *p·* disease
  f 203– 1   that this cold may produce fatal *p·* disease ;
  p 392–20   in the form of what is termed *p·* disease,
pulpit
  a 55–10   does not the *p·* sometimes scorn it?
  f 236– 2   Truth should emanate from the *p·*,
pulpits
  s 141–29   Let our *p·* do justice to C. S.
pulpy
  ph 192– 1   belief that a *p·* substance under the skull is
pulse
  s 159–25   They examine the lungs, tongue, and *p·*
  p 370–32   Physicians examine the *p·*, tongue, lungs,
  379–26   The quickened *p·*, coated tongue,
pulseless
  s 113– 8   letter is but the dead body of Science, — *p·*,
punctual
  p 395–19   cheerful, orderly, *p·*, patient,
pungent
  pr 7– 3   Jesus' reproof was pointed and *p·*
  g 555– 1   as the force of mortal mind is less *p·*
punish
  pr 10–32   Do you ask wisdom to be merciful and not to *p·* sin?
  an 105– 4   to prevent deeds of violence or to *p·* them.
  o 356–28   create the primitive, and then *p·* its derivative?
  357– 2   must admit that God will not *p·* man for
  p 435–23   to *p·* a man for acting justly.
  436–21   handcuffed Mortal Man and would now *p·* him.
  441– 4   which undertakes to *p·* aught but sin,
  441–26   no law outside of divine Mind can *p·*
  t 447–13   will in time disclose and *p·* itself.
punishable
  p 431–10   this offence is deemed *p·* with death.
  440–24   and then render obedience to these laws *p·*
punished
  a 47–28   The disciples' desertion . . . was *p·* ;
  an 105–11   Can matter be *p·*?
  f 251–27   nothing is left which deserves . . . to be *p·*.
  b 340–29   leaves nothing that can sin, suffer, be *p·* or
  p 432–15   treated as a criminal and *p·*
  435–26   For naught else can he be *p·*,
  436–22   fear its consequences, and be *p·* for his fear.
  r 497–11   But the belief in sin is *p·* so long as
  g 542–10   the disposition to excuse guilt . . . is *p·*.
punishes
  pr 6–19   To suppose that God forgives or *p·*
  p 384– 7   God never *p·* man for doing right,
  387–22   supposition. . .that God *p·* man for doing good,
punishing
  ph 186–12   only aids in peremptorily *p·* the evil-doer.
  f 230–14   and then *p·* the helpless victims
  o 356–27   and then *p·* him for it?
  p 412– 2   never *p·* aught but sin,
punishment
  escape from
  a 36– 8   Escape from *p·* is not in accordance with
  fear of
  b 327–22   Fear of *p·* never made man truly honest.
  final
  ph 188–10   from shame and woe to their final *p·*.
  full
  a 36–22   impossible . . . to receive their full *p·* this side
  future
  a 24–19   in regard to predestination and future *p·*.

punishment
  its own
  g 537–15   Sin is its own *p·*.
  merit
  p 432–18   transgress the laws, and merit *p·*,
  one form of
  pr 11– 8   only saves the criminal from one form of *p·*.
  prevent his
  p 431–14   summoned . . . to prevent his *p·*.
  the sinner's
  a 35–31   If the sinner's *p·* here has been insufficient
  without
  pr 11– 1   Without *p·*, sin would multiply.
pupil
  b 329–17   To be discouraged, is to resemble a *p·* in addition,
  p 393–28   lenses, muscles, the iris and *p·*,
  t 445– 9   capacities for good in your *p·*.
pupils
  pref ix–13   still in circulation among her first *p·* ;
  f 235–15   uplifting thoughts . . . imparted to *p·*,
pure
  a 29–25   the *p·* sense of the Virgin-mother
  44–14   He did not depend upon food or *p·* air
  50–14   and to himself, Love's *p·* idea.
  52– 5   His affections were *p·* ; theirs were carnal.
  54– 3   Out of the amplitude of his *p·* affection,
  m 57–11   Both sexes should be loving, *p·*,
  57–13   will be perpetual only as it is *p·* and true,
  62– 2   The fœtus must be kept mentally *p·*
  63– 6   The beautiful, good, and *p·* constitute his
  64– 4   "*P·* religion and undefiled— *Jas.* 1 : 27.
  s 117–14   the *p·* language of Spirit.
  147–29   A *p·* affection takes form in goodness,
  ph 171– 8   and will find himself unfallen, upright, *p·*,
  f 223– 1   and plant ourselves upon what is *p·* and perfect.
  235–14   The *p·* and uplifting thoughts of the teacher,
  241–28   the *p·* in heart see God
  c 259–27   Immortal ideas, *p·*, perfect, and enduring,
  b 298–28   Angels are *p·* thoughts from God,
  318–15   would efface the *p·* sense of omnipotence.
  324– 6   "Blessed are the *p·* in heart :— *Matt.* 5 : 8.
  329– 2   healing elements of *p·* Christianity will be
  332–29   incarnate in the good and *p·* Christ Jesus.
  337–15   none but the *p·* in heart can see God,
  o 341– 9   "Blessed are the *p·* in heart :— *Matt.* 5 : 8.
  360–25   Shall man be more *p·* than his— *see Job* 4 : 17.
  p 383– 4   a body rendered *p·* by Mind as well as
  383– 6   To do this, the *p·* and exalting influence of the
  391–31   as Love,— as all that is *p·*,
  409–23   to be laid aside for the *p·* reality.
  r 467–15   man is the likeness of God, *p·* and eternal,
  477– 5   and that man is *p·* and holy.
  497–27   and to be merciful, just, and *p·*.
  g 508–15   The seed within itself is the *p·* thought
  512–20   multiplication of its own *p·* and perfect ideas.
  550–29   the *p·* and holy, the immutable and immortal
  ap 567–21   That false claim . . . is *p·* delusion,
  571–32   He enthrones *p·* and undefiled religion,
  gl 581– 5   spiritual intuitions, *p·* and perfect ;
  582–17   the *p·* consciousness that God,
  589–21   *p·* affection blessing its enemies.
purely
  pr 14–13   Life and intelligence are *p·* spiritual,
  s 113–15   which is not *p·* metaphysical.
  149–24   as readily as she had cured *p·* functional disease,
  ph 170–28   The description of man as *p·* physical,
  185– 6   No system of hygiene but C. S. is *p·* mental.
  g 510– 5   to be holy, thought must be *p·* spiritual.
purer
  a 37–12   and to permeate humanity with *p·* ideals.
  m 65–31   marriage will become *p·* when the scum is gone.
  f 243–22   "of *p·* eyes than to behold evil," — *Hab.* 1 : 13.
  b 290–30   His thoughts are no *p·* until
  o 357– 4   "of *p·* eyes than to behold evil." — *Hab.* 1 : 13.
  p 407–15   lifting humanity above itself into *p·* desires,
  410–17   the stronger should be our faith and the *p·* our
  g 553– 4   a higher and *p·* contemplation of man's origin.
purgation
  p 364–21   in return for the spiritual *p·*
purgatives
  p 408–15   supposition that . . . by the use of *p·* and
purgatory
  sp 77–29   Spiritism consigns . . . to a wretched *p·*,
purge
  s 142–22   to *p·* the temples of their vain traffic
purification
  a 35–19   Our baptism is a *p·* from all error.
  b 324– 4   *p·* of sense and self is a proof of progress.
  gl 581–23   BAPTISM. *P·* by Spirit ;
  595–15   holiness and *p·* of thought and deed,
purified
  a 22–22   Love means that we shall be tried and *p·*.

purifies
s 162– 5 Truth, which invigorates and *p*.

purify
t 452–15 unless in the attempt to *p·* it.
r 492–10 will *p·* and elevate character.
g 540–10 river-bed must be stirred in order to *p·* the stream.

purifying
m 57–24 enlarging, *p·*, and elevating it.
ap 565–22 *p·* even the gold of human character.
gl 586–14 affliction *p·* and elevating man.

Puritan
o 359–20 From *P·* parents, the discoverer of C. S.

purity
and affection
pr 15–27 *p·*, and affection are constant prayers.
a 36– 1 They, who know not *p·* and affection
and constancy
m 60– 9 the mother-love includes *p·* and constancy,
and holiness
g 509–26 in which beauty, sublimity, *p·*, and holiness
and immortality
gl 581– 6 *p·*, and immortality, counteracting all evil,
and innocence
gl 582–14 BRIDE. *P·* and innocence,
and peace
gl 584–26 *p·* and peace ; hope and faith.
and self-immolation
sp 99–24 health, *p·*, and self-immolation,
chastity and
b 272–21 it is chastity and *p·* in contrast with the
goodness and
p 364– 1 a man of undoubted goodness and *p·*,
his
a 31–19 are baptized with his *p·* ;
b 337–16 In proportion to his *p·* is man perfect ;
impart
p 371–29 Mind can impart *p·* instead of impurity,
innocence and
gl 590–10 self-immolation ; innocence and *p·* ;
peace, and
b 323– 8 peace, and *p·*, which are the landmarks of
perfection and
a 52–10 ever-present rebuke of his perfection and *p·*.
righteousness and
a 28–19 Even his righteousness and *p·* did not
was the symbol
ap 561–17 *P·* was the symbol of Life and Love.
white-robed
m 64–23 white-robed *p·* will unite in one person

pr 7–21 with more devout self-abnegation and *p·*.
m 58– 8 Unselfish ambition, noble life-motives, and *p·*,
s 116– 2 Wisdom, *p·*, spiritual understanding,
f 241–27 the corner-stone of all spiritual building is *p·*.
b 332–27 only *p·* could reflect Truth and Love,

purporting
sp 80– 6 A communication *p·* to come from

purpose
affection and
pr 8–29 the affection and *p·* of the heart,
and motive
b 326–16 *p·* and motive to live aright can be gained
changed the
p 432–29 a message from the Board of Health changed the *p·*
Christ's
a 19– 1 Christ's *p·* to reconcile man to God,
divine
sp 83–27 The latter is a revelation of divine *p·*
fraudulent in
f 252–22 deceitful in sentiment, fraudulent in *p·*,
good
f 252–24 where the good *p·* waits!
highest
g 514–18 and keep pace with highest *p·*.
holy
g 506–20 He opens the petals of a holy *p·*
in healing
a 51–21 *p·* in healing was not alone to restore health,
its
pref x–24 Its *p·* is good, and its practice is safer
not the
o 345–31 not the *p·* of C. S. to "educate the idea of God,
of generating
m 62– 1 can only be permitted for the *p·* of generating.
of healing
sp 95–10 for the *p·* of healing them.
of his mission
a 50–28 disbelieving the *p·* of his mission,
of keeping
p 413–17 only for the *p·* of keeping the body clean,
of Love
gl 579–12 This patriarch illustrated the *p·* of Love

purpose
of this allegory
g 537–19 the *p·* of this allegory— this second account
wicked
t 451–30 either with a mistaken or a wicked *p·*.

b 328–30 *p·* of his great life-work extends through time
g 506–21 in order that the *p·* may appear.
540–21 The *p·* of the Hebrew allegory,

purposed
s 138– 2 Jesus *p·* founding his society, . . . on the God-power

purposes
pref xi–31 this institution chartered for medical *p·*.
an 103–15 working out the *p·* of good only.
f 235– 1 Evil thoughts, lusts, and malicious *p·*
p 401– 5 cherishing evil passions and malicious *p·*,

purse
ph 195–29 lowering the . . . standard to accommodate the *p·*
gl 593– 6 definition of

pursue
pr 9– 7 Do we *p·* the old selfishness,
a 21–18 different routes to *p·*.
21–21 On the contrary, if my friends *p·* my course,
f 239–20 The objects we *p·* and the spirit we manifest
t 457–22 To *p·* other vocations

pursues
ap 564–30 the serpent *p·* with hatred the spiritual idea.

pursuing
ph 174–18 are *p·* and will overtake the ages,

pursuit
s 161–18 life, liberty, and the *p·* of happiness."
t 448–24 The reception or *p·* of instructions opposite to

pursuits
a 52– 2 His *p·* lay far apart from theirs.

push
a 106– 4 and to *p·* vainly against the current
b 323–10 Then we *p·* onward,

pushed
a 36–26 suddenly pardoned and *p·* into heaven,

put
pr 3–31 to *p·* the finger on the lips and remember our
15–22 as we *p·* our desires into practice.
a 20–30 that is, let us *p·* aside material self and sense,
29–20 *p·* to silence material law and its order of
31–30 shall *p·* you out of the synagogues ; — John 16 : 2.
48–23 He said : "*P·* up thy sword." — John 18 : 11.
m 56– * let not man *p·* asunder. — Matt. 19 : 6.
60–14 wisdom will ultimately *p·* asunder what
62–15 your body what ye shall *p·* on," — Matt. 6 : 25.
67–26 does not *p·* to silence the labor of
s 151–25 The human mind . . . must be *p·* off,
161–11 In 1880, Massachusetts *p·* her foot on a
164–26 shall have *p·* on incorruption, — I Cor. 15 : 54.
164–26 shall have *p·* on immortality — I Cor. 15 : 54.
ph 165– * your body, what ye shall *p·* on. — Matt. 6 : 25.
169–17 we should *p·* no faith in material means,
172–22 we must "*p·* off the old man." — Col. 3 : 9.
179–27 ready to *p·* you into a sweat,
188– 1 This body is *p·* off only as the
200–15 hast *p·* all things under his feet." — Psal. 8 : 6.
f 223–10 and we cannot *p·* the greater into the less.
223–22 Spiritual rationality . . . cannot be *p·* down.
230–21 and can man *p·* that law under his feet
230–25 soothing syrups to *p·* children to sleep,
242– 2 mortals *p·* off their material beliefs
c 262– 8 mortals "*p·* on immortality." — I Cor. 15 : 54.
265– 9 in order that sin and mortality may be *p·* off.
b 281–20 When we *p·* off the false sense for the true,
281–27 does not *p·* new wine into old bottles,
286–12 Physical causation was *p·* aside
296– 9 The old man with his deeds must be *p·* off.
307–12 says : . . . I will *p·* spirit into what I call
318–11 They would *p·* soul into soil,
321–11 when Moses first *p·* his hand into his bosom
323–13 we must *p·* into practice what we already know.
o 360–28 the Jews *p·* to death the Galilean Prophet,
p 409–24 This mortal is *p·* off, . . . in proportion as
409–24 and the new man or real man is *p·* on,
425–12 treated as error and *p·* out of thought.
430– 4 Mortal mind . . . must *p·* off itself with its
t 447–24 To *p·* down the claim of sin, you must detect it,
452–11 you should not fear to *p·* on the new.
r 496–24 shall have *p·* on incorruption, — I Cor. 15 : 54.
496–25 shall have *p·* on immortality, — I Cor. 15 : 54.
g 509–24 *p·* him into the garden of Eden, — Gen. 2 : 15.
527– 1 God could not *p·* Mind into matter
531–16 If, . . . mind was afterwards *p·* into body
534– 9 I will *p·* enmity between thee and — Gen. 3 : 15.
537– 1 lest he *p·* forth his hand, — Gen. 3 : 22.
ap 561–27 and matter is *p·* under her feet.

put

gl	582–21	physical sense *p·* out of sight and hearing ;
	584–23	*p·* into the opposite of mind, termed matter,

puts

s	155–23	in proportion as it *p·* less weight into the
ph	182–21	and *p·* matter under the feet of Mind.
	185–14	which *p·* forth a human conception
p	399– 7	and *p·* the body through certain motions.
g	512–29	this so-called mind *p·* forth its own qualities,
ap	566–13	description which Sir Walter Scott *p·* into the

putteth

o	360–26	Behold, He *p·* no trust in— *see Job* 4 : 18.

putting

a	52–16	*p·* to shame and death the best man that ever
ph	199–30	his power of *p·* resolve into action
c	262– 7	By *p·* ''off the old man with his — *Col.* 3 : 9.
p	438–11	*p·* in false claims to office
t	459–17	like *p·* a sharp knife into the hands of a
r	484–25	thus *p·* an end to the hypotheses

Q

quackery

s	163– 5	declared himself "sick of learned *q·.*"
ph	180– 1	and advertisements of *q·* are
p	370–26	*Q·* likewise fails at length to inspire the
	395–21	It is mental *q·* to make disease a reality
t	456– 4	is most dangerous *q·*.
	458– 1	Mental *q·* rests on the same platform
	458– 2	on the same platform as all other *q·*.
	458–16	Having seen so much suffering from *q·*,

quail

p	384–30	Sickness, sin, and death must at length *q·*

qualifications

t	448–21	moral and spiritual *q·* requisite for healing,

qualified

pr	10– 8	Until we are thus divinely *q·*

qualities

and effects
ph	177–20	cannot name the *q·* and effects of what is

and forms
ph	177–19	indicated matter's properties, *q·*, and forms.

animal
b	298–26	not . . . evolving animal *q·* in their wings ;

curative
s	156– 1	If drugs possess . . . intelligent curative *q·*,

essential
t	460– 8	on the divine Mind and Love's essential *q·*.

feminine
m	57– 4	Union of the masculine and feminine *q·*

God's
gl	597–26	as applied to Mind or to one of God's *q·*.

its own
g	512–29	this so-called mind puts forth its own *q·*,

masculine
m	57– 8	courage and strength through masculine *q·*.

mental
an	104–21	by no means the mental *q·* which heal the sick.

native
m	57–12	The attraction between native *q·* will be

of Mind
c	265– 2	not of the lowest, but of the highest *q·* of Mind.

opposite
b	286–28	(by the supposition of opposite *q·*)
	300–17	These opposite *q·* are the tares and wheat,

possesses its
f	247–20	Being possesses its *q·* before they

these
s	156– 2	these *q·* must be mental.
b	280–29	perpetuates these *q·* in man,

which insure
t	449–15	*q·* which insure success in this Science ;

p	388–25	sin and sickness are not *q·* of Soul,

quality

and quantity
b	294– 7	would take away some *q·* and quantity of
g	512–22	all form, color, *q·*, and quantity,
	551– 4	cannot produce its opposite in *q·* and quantity,

character and
sp	71–29	limited and finite in character and *q·*.

discover their
t	462–22	to discover their *q·*, quantity, and

eternal
r	469– 9	It is the primal and eternal *q·* of

every
f	215–23	Every *q·* and condition of mortality is lost,

glorified
g	516–22	forever reflect, in glorified *q·*,

mental
p	365–13	what mental *q·* remains,

nature and
c	262– 9	We cannot fathom the nature and *q·* of

not a single
r	475–20	has not a single *q·* underived from Deity ;

not one
an	103–22	This belief has not one *q·* of Truth.

of God
g	506– 5	Understanding is a *q·* of God,

of Mind
g	517– 8	The life-giving *q·* of Mind is Spirit,

of mind
b	279– 4	plainly describes faith, a *q·* of mind, as

or a quantity
p	388–16	a deficiency or an excess, a *q·* or a quantity.

or condition
f	230– 3	to destroy a *q·* or condition of Truth?
b	299– 4	his conception of an unseen *q·* or condition,

quantity and
sp	93–24	It means quantity and *q·*,

refer only to
sp	93–26	modifying derivatives . . . refer only to *q·*,

third
p	422–15	meet and bring out a third *q·*,

sp	86–21	no less a *q·* of physical sense than feeling.
b	305–12	Gender also is a *q·*, . . . of mortal mind.
o	361–16	that is, one in *q·*, not in quantity.
g	506– 5	a *q·* which separates C. S. from supposition
gl	597–24	Will, as a *q·* of so-called mortal mind,

quantity

sp	93–24	It means *q·* and quality,
s	155–32	is it safe to say that the less in *q·* you have
b	294– 7	would take away some quality and *q·* of
o	361–16	that is, one in quality, not in *q·*.
p	388–16	a deficiency or an excess, a quality or a *q·*.
t	462–22	to discover their quality, *q·*, and
g	512–23	form, color, quality, and *q·*,
	551– 4	cannot produce its opposite in quality and *q·*,

quarrel

pref	x–27	Only those *q·* with her method who
s	128–23	If one would not *q·* with his fellow-man
t	457–14	In the legend of the shield, which led to a *q·*

queen

t	451– 7	Christianity, . . . must be their *q·* of life.

quelling

p	385– 8	the spiritual demand, *q·* the material,

quench

a	36– 6	sufficient suffering, . . . to *q·* the love of sin.
r	490–19	"*Q·* not the Spirit.— *I Thess.* 5 : 19.

quenched

b	314– 5	spiritual sense had *q·* all earthly yearnings.
r	486– 5	until every corporeal sense is *q·*.

quenching

b	329–25	maintains the claim of Truth by *q·* error.

query

p	364–10	This *q·* Jesus answered by

question

another
g	552– 2	Another *q·* follows : Who or what produces

answered this
p	374–10	The author has answered this *q·*

answer the
s	132– 4	would fully answer the *q·*.

answer this
f	223–20	The efforts of error to answer this *q·* by

arises
pref	viii–18	the *q·* arises, Is there less sickness because of

asking no
f	222–31	"asking no *q·* for conscience sake." — *I Cor.* 10 : 25.

beyond a
a	27– 4	intended to prove beyond a *q·* that the

evade the
f	230–24	These merely evade the *q·*.

hypothetical
g	551–32	The ancient and hypothetical *q·*,

important
t	462–24	That is the important *q·*.

Master's
p	363–19	the Master's *q·* to Simon the Pharisee ;

momentous
a	48–25	in the presence of his own momentous *q·*,

moral
p	419– 1	A moral *q·* may hinder the recovery of the sick.

question

of disease
p 406–18 and he should be as fearless on the *q·* of disease.

of time
f 242–'4 It is only a *q·* of time when

Pilate's
a 49– 2 could have answered Pilate's *q·*.

renewal of the
s 137–12 and his renewal of the *q·*,

rose to the
p 437–23 rose to the *q·* of expelling C. S. from

settles the
o 361– 4 cancels the disagreement, and settles the *q·*.

solemn
p 364–16 Here is suggested a solemn *q·*,

startling
a 50–16 This was a startling *q·*.

sublime
c 256–17 in comparison with the sublime *q·*,

then recurs
ph 181–24 the *q·* then recurs,

to be considered
ph 170–22 the one *q·* to be considered,

pref viii–12 The *q·*, What is Truth, is answered by
m 69–25 therefore matter is out of the *q·*
s 120– 9 Then the *q·* inevitably arises :
136– 9 *q·* then as now was, How did Jesus heal
136–10 His answer to this *q·* the world rejected.
144–30 It is a *q·* to-day, whether the ancient
ph 171–13 no longer an open *q·*, but is demonstrable
f 223–14 The *q·*, "What is Truth," — *John* 18 : 38.
b 329– 9 you have no right to *q·* the great might of
p 364–16 a *q·* indicated by one of the needs of
r 465– 8 Q·.— What is God?
465–11 Q·.— Are these terms synonymous?
465–16 Q·.— Is there more than one God or
466– 7 Q·.— What are spirits and souls?
467– 1 Q·.— What are the demands of the Science of
468– 8 Q·.— What is the scientific statement of being?
468–16 Q·.— What is substance?
468–25 Q·.— What is Life?
469– 7 Q·.— What is intelligence?
469–12 Q·.— What is Mind?
471–22 Q·.— Are doctrines and creeds a benefit to man?
472–13 Q·.— What is error?
472–23 Q·.— Is there no sin?
475– 5 Q·.— What is man?
477–19 Q·.— What are body and Soul?
478–14 Q·.— Does brain think, and do nerves feel,
482–13 Q·.— Is it important to understand these
483– 1 Q·.— Does he drug, hygiene,
484– 6 Q·.— Does C. S., or metaphysical healing, in- clude
484–28 Q·.— Is materiality the concomitant of
487–13 Q·.— You speak of belief. Who or what is
488–14 Q·.— Do the five corporeal senses constitute
493– 9 Q·.— Will you explain sickness
493–14 A full answer to the above *q·* involves
495–25 Q·.— How can I progress most rapidly in
496–28 Q·.— Have Christian Scientists any
g 551–22 The *q·* of the naturalist amounts to this :

questioned

s 132–33 yet afterwards he seriously *q·* the signs of
136–32 or they would not have *q·* him so often.
f 237– 3 On being *q·* about it she answered
b 308–32 Then Jacob *q·* his deliverer,

questions

pr 9– 6 test of all prayer lies in the answer to these *q·* :
sp 70–14 The *q·* are : What are God's identities?
an 101–15 physiological and therapeutical *q·*,
s 127– 1 or *q·* her use of the word Science,
b 284–19 The answer to all these *q·* must forever be
288– 7 will settle all *q·* through faith in
p 373– 1 If we are Christians on all moral *q·*, but
r 465– 7 chapter sub-title
g 504– 6 All *q·* as to the divine creation

quick

sp 86– 7 His *q·* apprehension of this mental call

quicken

o 341– * *shall also q· your mortal bodies* — *Rom.* 8 : 11.
p 367–26 *q·* and increase the beneficial effects of
426–19 will *q·* into newness of life.

quickened

o 343–13 not be forever hidden . . . from the *q·* sense of
p 379–25 The *q·* pulse, coated tongue, febrile heat,

quickener

ph 172–28 is sometimes the *q·* of manliness ;

quickeneth

o 356–15 "It is the spirit that *q· ;*" — *John* 6 : 63.

quickening

a 34–24 They needed this *q·*,

quickens

p 415– 6 *q·* or impedes the action of the system,
415–18 It either retards the circulation or *q·* it,

quickly

s 161–32 agrees with his "adversary *q·*," — *Matt.* 5 : 25.
c 265–28 *q·* inform us that the pleasures of sense are
p 390–19 "Agree with thine adversary *q·*, — *Matt.* 5 : 25.
397–30 will *q·* become more manly or womanly.
411– 6 the body would respond more *q·*,
415– 7 thought moves *q·* or slowly,
415–22 The muscles, moving *q·* or slowly
t 463–21 To decide *q·* as to the proper treatment of

quiet

pr 8– 1 A wordy prayer may afford a *q·* sense of
15–16 In the *q·* sanctuary of earnest longings,
s 157–26 Narcotics *q·* mortal mind,
f 224–20 angel visitant, who cometh in the *q·* of
230–26 satisfy mortal belief, and *q·* fear.
254–24 If you venture upon the *q·* surface of error
p 415–12 They *q·* the thought by inducing stupefaction
ap 567– 1 Gabriel has the more *q·* task of

quieted

a 47–22 and for a time *q·* his remorse.

quietly

p 416– 7 in twenty minutes the sufferer is *q·* asleep.

quiets

s 143–17 and *q·* pain with anodynes.
t 445–19 *q·* fear with Truth and Love,

quit

ph 192– 4 as we *q·* our reliance upon that which is false

quite

a 36–21 It is *q·* as impossible for sinners to
s 129–26 *q·* as rational are some of the leading illusions
133–30 has not *q·* given place to the true knowledge
ph 176–29 are *q·* as ready to yield to Truth as the
193– 2 a fall upon a wooden spike when *q·* a boy.
f 221– 1 I knew a person who when *q·* a child
249–30 but makes its mundane flights *q·* ethereal.
b 269–32 is *q·* as reasonable as the second.
p 362– 3 though he was *q·* unlike Simon the disciple.
381–24 that you are *q·* free from some ailment.

quits

s 160–12 When this so-called mind *q·* the body,

quitting

s 158–25 Drug-systems are *q·* their hold on matter

quote

s 162–30 I kindly *q·* from Dr. Benjamin Rush,

quoted

b 320–13 *q·* as follows, from the original Hebrew :
320–29 whereas this passage is continually *q·*
332– 7 *q·* with approbation from a classic poet :

quotes

o 359–26 that Scripture she so often *q·* :

quotient

f 233–26 the *q·* is not more unquestionable

quoting

ap 564–27 Jesus said, *q·* a line from the Psalms,

R

rabbi

a 30–14 R· and priest taught the Mosaic law,
42– 2 whereas priest and *r·* affirmed God to be

rabbinical

a 23–12 R· lore said : "He that taketh one doctrine,
30–20 Christ Jesus came to rebuke *r·* error
s 134– 1 have not cleansed their hands of *r·* lore.
p 362– 9 especially under the stern rules of *r·* law,

rabbins

gl 596–12 The *r·* believed that the stones in the

rabbis

a 49–26 priests and *r·*, before whom he had
sp 94– 9 incensed the *r·*, and they said :
f 203– 9 The accusation of the *r·*,
b 315– 4 the scholastic theology of the *r·*.
o 349– 4 *r·* of the present day ask concerning our
352–10 to the *r·* the spiritual was the intangible

race

Adamic
g 525– 5 *mankind* represents the Adamic *r·*,

race
Adam's
g 554–24   This he said of Judas, one of Adam's r·.
elevating the
gl 583–15   and is found elevating the r·,
human
  (see **human**)
nobler
m 63–26   achievement of a nobler r· for legislation,
our
ap 571–10   doing right and benefiting our r·.
sinning
o 345–25   and the sinning r· of Adam.

a 20–29   the r· that is set before us ;" — *Heb.* 12 : 1.
  22–17   nor become a sluggard in the r·.
m 63–26   a r· having higher aims and motives.
s 151–12   enlarged power it confers to benefit the r·
  158–20   to victimize the r· with intoxicating
p 371–27   The necessity for uplifting the r·
g 556–17   Did . . . the enlightenment of the r· come from
races
m 56–16   the social scourge of all r·,
f 225–29   Men and women of all climes and r·
g 551–10   argues that mortals spring from eggs and in r·.
radiance
pref vii– 3   ere cometh the full r· of a risen day.
f 246–14   the r· of Spirit should dawn upon the
  247–15   has a glory of its own, — the r· of Soul.
ap 561–26   The spiritual idea is clad with the r· of
radiant
s 110– 5   as the r· reality of God's creation,
f 246–11   r· sun of virtue and truth coexists with being.
g 538– 7   R· with mercy and justice, the sword of Truth
radiata
g 556– 3   Vertebrata, articulata, mollusca, and r·
radiate
p 367–23   but r· and glow into noontide glory.
radiates
g 511– 2   subdivides and r· their borrowed light,
radiation
g 556– 6   r· of Spirit destroys forever all belief in
radical
a 24–17   a change as r· as that which has come over
ph 167–30   Only through r· reliance on Truth can
p 398–31   come to the rescue, to work a r· cure.
t 452–18   Right is r·.
radically
t 458–30   by which mortals are r· saved from sin
raging
t 459–18   into the hands of a blind man or a r· maniac,
railroad
a 21–21   we have the same r· guides,
raiment
ph 165– *   *and the body than r·? — Matt.* 6 : 25.
f 242–23   "They parted my r· among them, — *John* 19 : 24.
c 267–26   like the r· of Christ.
t 461– 2   without food and r· ;
rain
s 122–21   in the midst of murky clouds and drenching r·.
c 257–19   divine Love, — is the father of the r·,
o 354–20   which are like clouds without r·.
g 520–21   had not caused it to r· upon the — *Gen.* 2 : 5.
  544– 5   There was no r· and "not a man to — *Gen.* 2 : 5.
rainbow
ap 558– 4   and a r· was upon his head, — *Rev.* 10 : 1.
raindrops
b 288–17   the r· of divinity refresh the earth.
raise
a 27–13   I [Spirit] will r· it up." — *John* 2 : 19.
  34–21   It helped them to r· themselves and others
  47–24   in order to r· himself in popular estimation.
  51–31   cast out evil, and r· the dead.
s 137– 3   heal the sick, cast out evil, r· the dead ;
f 235–29   They should so r· their hearers spiritually,
b 306– 2   The Pharisees thought that they could r· the
  314–15   and in three days I will r· it — *John* 2 : 19.
  329– 8   Because you cannot . . . r· the dead,
o 359–24   "God is able to r· you up from sickness ;"
p 426–24   would r· the standard of health and morals
r 494– 3   I [Mind] will r· it up ;" — *John* 2 : 19.
raised
a 27– 5   the deaf hear, the dead are r·, — *Luke* 7 : 22.
m 67–21   Lord and Master healed the sick, r· the dead,
sp 76–12   and was therefore never r· from matter.
s 132– 7   the deaf hear, the dead are r· up, — *Matt.* 11 : 5.
  134–27   he r· Lazarus from the dead,
b 273–25   healed the sick, and r· the dead
  313–30   which by spiritual power he r· from the grave,
o 341– *   *Him that r· up Jesus from the — Rom.* 8 : 11.

raised
o 341– *   *He that r· up Christ from the — Rom.* 8 : 11.
p 373– 7   The author has r· up the dying,
  424–12   In medical practice objections would be r·
  428–31   and r· the dying to life and health
raises
a 33–24   r· the dead from trespasses and sins,
s 128–18   It r· the thinker into his native air of insight
ph 189– 5   r· the human thought above the cruder theories
f 227–21   C. S. r· the standard of liberty
o 342–22   r· from the couch of pain the helpless invalid.
raising
a 43– 1   healing the sick, and r· the dead,
m 61–26   the r· of stock to increase your flocks and
b 316–29   casting out evils, . . . r· the dead,
o 341– 2   r· up thousands from helplessness to strength
p 369– 9   r· the dead, and walking over the wave.
  430– 3   healing the dying and r· the dead.
rallying
f 225–12   but there is a r· to truth's standard.
rams
s 135– 4   Ye mountains, that ye skipped like r·, — *Psal.* 114 : 6.
random
ph 175–16   If a r· thought, calling itself dyspepsia,
range
sp 84–17   yea, to reach the r· of fetterless Mind.
c 258–26   and of the infinite r· of his thought.
g 503– 3   These ideas r· from the infinitesimal to
  513–28   not within the r· of immortal existence
  514– 4   nothing exists beyond the r· of
rank
p 367–12   the arrogance of r· and display of scholarship,
ranks
p 437–30   r· above the lower Court of Error.
ransom
b 276– 4   "I have found a r·." — *Job* 33 : 24.
rapid
pref viii–22   r· multiplication and increased violence of
f 236–31   youth makes easy and r· strides towards Truth.
g 533–22   the r· deterioration of the bone and flesh
rapidity
b 268– 2   thought has brought to light with great r·
rapidly
f 222–17   he recovered strength and flesh r·.
  254– 4   who gain good r· and hold their position,
p 373–11   the sick recover more r· from disease than
  430– 8   he will advance more r· towards God,
t 457–23   and advance r· in the demonstration of
r 495–25   How can I progress most r· in the
g 533–19   more r· than he can alone.
rapport
sp 78– 9   If the departed are in r· with mortality,
  84–12   thought which is in r· with this Mind,
rapture
sp 76– 5   forgets all else and breathes aloud his r·.
f 213–21   r· of his grandest symphonies was never heard.
rarefaction
g 509–15   r· of thought as it ascends higher.
rarefy
a 37–11   and r· the atmosphere of material sense
rarely
p 402–21   we r· remember that we govern our own bodies.
rashly
t 444–19   and never to condemn r·.
rather
pr 9– 1   Do we not r· give thanks that we
a 53–14   as humanly mighty, r· than as divine,
sp 71–13   formation of thought r· than of matter.
  88–27   It is due to inspiration r· than to erudition.
s 111–23   physical causes r· than to a final spiritual
  146– 7   faith in drugs the fashion, r· than faith in Deity.
  164–21   r· does it evidence the truth of
ph 181–11   for that reason, you employ matter r· than Mind.
f 212– 8   Why need pain, r· than pleasure, come
  216–29   "willing r· to be absent from the — *II Cor.* 5 : 8.
  226–24   belief that the body governed them, r· than
  233– 2   higher proofs r· than professions
  235–32   Love of Christianity, r· than love of popularity,
  236– 6   emolument r· than the dignity of God's laws,
  246–30   freshness, and continuity, r· than into age
c 256–11   suggests polytheism, r· than the one
o 343–29   mistake which allows words, r· than works,
p 374–20   this belief helps r· than hinders disease.
  383–10   "willing r· to be absent from the — *II Cor.* 5 : 8.
  417– 7   Tell them r·, that their strength is in
t 445–26   human will . . . is the cause of disease r· than
r 473–24   Love, r· than personality or the man Jesus,
  491–31   this dream — r· than the dreamer

rather

g 524–11 a tribal god to be worshipped, r· than Love,
528–20 Beginning . . . materially r· than spiritually,
554– 6 or, r·, being and Deity are inseparable.
gl 581–25 "willing r· to be absent from the— *II Cor.* 5 : 8.

ratio

sp 95– 8 and in that r· we know all human need
p 368–24 in the r· of one's spiritual growth.

rational

m 63–23 A feasible as well as r· means of improvement
sp 80–27 but they are neither scientific nor r·.
s 129–26 quite as r· are some of the leading illusions
b 284– 1 It is not r· to say that Mind
306–18 If . . . we are left without a r· proof of

rationality

f 223–21 Spiritual r· and free thought accompany
b 268– 7 from which may be deduced all r·,

rationally

pref xi– 5 C. S. r· explains that all other
r 491–32 Who can r· say otherwise,

ray

f 250–12 like a r· of light which comes from the sun,
b 300–31 the r· of light which goes out from it.
o 361–17 a r· of light one with the sun,

rays

g 504–23 The r· of infinite Truth, . . . bring light
504–31 No solar r· nor planetary revolutions form the
546–24 spiritual facts of being, like r· of light,

reach

pref viii– 3 but to r· the heights of C. S.,
pr 4–22 We r· the Science of Christianity through
6–14 To r· heaven, the harmony of being, we must
16–21 r· the heaven-born aspiration and
a 21– 8 that they shall r· his harmony and reward.
35–22 as we r· the Life which is Truth
43–24 Out of r· of the barbarity of his enemies,
49–23 but is above the r· of human wrath,
m 61–32 If . . . is requisite to r· this goal,
sp 84–17 to r· the range of fetterless Mind.
85– 9 You will r· the perfect Science of healing when
ph 170–14 demands of Truth . . . r· the body through
194–23 where neither sight nor sound could r· him,
f 234–31 Evil thoughts and aims r· no farther
235–15 will r· higher than the heavens of astronomy ;
241–25 We should strive to r· the Horeb height
246– 7 and endeavoring to r· Spirit above his origin.
c 262–15 inspire the Godlike man to r· the
b 285–28 As mortals r·, . . . a higher sense,
323–12 is winged to r· the divine glory.
324–17 before we can r· the goal of Spirit,
325–25 can never r· in this world the divine heights of
326– 6 He, who would r· the source and find the
p 363– 1 to come behind the couch and r· his feet.
387– 5 When we r· our limits of
415–11 in a part which mortal thought does not r·.
426– 8 counts her footsteps in endeavoring to r· it.
r 473–21 to r· his example and to test its
g 519–16 and r· the spiritual image and likeness.
548– 9 How little light or heat r· our earth when
ap 571–19 human hatred cannot r· you.
576–22 is within r· of man's consciousness here,

reached

pr 8–12 If he r· the loftiness of his prayer,
a 22–25 is not r· through paths of flowers nor
20–15 Those instructed in C. S. have r· the
sp 77– 6 until the Science of being is r·.
77–11 until the spiritual understanding of Life is r·.
s 108–12 My conclusions were r· by allowing the
109–10 once seen, no other conclusion can be r·.
f 219–30 may not be r· at this period,
237– 8 or r· the mental height
b 270–10 are scientific and logical conclusions r·.
279–19 Spirit is r· only through the understanding
279–26 scientific conclusion is r· only through the
o 353–15 Time has not yet r· eternity,
353–19 until perfection appears and reality is r·.
p 381–25 will never be r· without the understanding
r 484– 2 until its absolute Science is r·.
g 536–29 and the immortal is r·.
ap 560–15 goal is never r· while we hate our neighbor
568–27 sweeter than has ever before r· high heaven,
576– 6 r· St. John's vision while yet he

reaches

a 18–16 Truth, which r· no higher than itself.
m 57– 5 The masculine mind r· a higher tone through
sp 95–12 Whoever r· this point of moral culture
97–12 until matter r· its mortal zenith in illusion
s 113– 4 letter of Science plentifully r· humanity
ph 178–32 Whoever r· the understanding of C. S.
197–30 doctor's mind r· that of his patient.
b 290–27 becomes thus only when he r· perfection.
298–18 never r· beyond the boundary of the mortal
o 350–29 through which the real r· the unreal,

reaches

p 365–15 If the Scientist r· his patient through
380–27 until it r· its culmination of scientific statement
406–12 spiritual perception, . . . r· Truth.
ap 559– 9 r· over continent and ocean

reaching

m 63– 9 prior to r· intelligence.
b 328–32 r· beyond the pale of a single period
p 366– 9 hinders him from r· his patient's thought,
408–18 thus r· mortal mind through matter?
423–11 r· to every part of the human system.
g 543– 2 This error, after r· the climax of

react

b 283– 9 act, r·, and then come to a stop.

reaction

pr 7–12 gives occasion for r· unfavorable to
ph 186– 3 the false stimulus and r· of will-power
198–21 haply causes a vigorous r· upon itself,
p 417– 9 there will be no r· from over-exertion
419–10 knowing that there can be no r· in Truth.
428– 2 no death, no inaction, . . . nor r·."

reacts

t 449– 7 The wrong done another r· most heavily

read

pref xii–21 she had never r· this book throughout
sp 82– 1 it is as easy to r· distant thoughts as
82– 3 It is no more difficult to r· the absent mind
82– 4 than it is to r· the present.
82– 5 yet we still r· his thought in his verse.
84–32 can r· the stars or calculate an eclipse.
85–10 to r· the human mind after this manner
85–16 r· them scientifically.
87–16 Science enables one to r· the human mind, but
94–24 Our Master easily r· the thoughts of mankind,
94–28 r· mortal mind on a scientific basis,
s 109–13 searched the Scriptures and r· little else,
121– 7 Chaldean Wisemen r· in the stars the fate of
ph 179–24 so long as you r· medical works
f 217 12 if we turn to the Scriptures, what do we r·?
253–11 I hope, . . . that, as you r·, you see there is no
b 291–20 So we r· in Ecclesiastes.
328–30 the Scriptural passage would r· *you,* not *they.*
p 369–14 We never r· that Luke or Paul made a
382–29 The treatises I had r·
422– 8 Continue to r·, and the book will become the
437–32 The attorney, C. S., then r· from the
g 525–23 In the Science of Genesis we r·
535–29 In the first chapter of Genesis we r· :
540– 5 In Isaiah we r· : "I make peace,— *Isa.* 45 : 7.
ap 559– 2 open for all to r· and understand.
559–20 R· this book from beginning to end.
572–19 In Revelation xxi. 1 we r· :
573–32 When you r· this, remember Jesus' words,
575–11 as we r· in the book of Hebrews ;
gl 598– 3 in John's Gospel, the third chapter, where we r· :
598–11 In the record of Jesus' supposed death, we r· :

reader

s 115– 6 to make them comprehensible to any r·,
f 253– 9 I hope, dear r·, I am leading you into the
o 360–13 Dear r·, which mind-picture or
p 422– 5 If the r· of this book observes a great stir
g 521–18 r· will naturally ask if there is nothing more
547– 6 You can prove for yourself, dear r·, the Science
ap 574–25 Think of this, dear r·, for it will lift the

readers

ph 195–27 specimens of depravity, fill our young r· with
f 235– 7 and the r· in churches
p 430–13 I here present to my r· an allegory

readeth

ap 558– * *Blessed is he that r·, and— Rev.* 1 : 3.

readily

m 60–30 happiness would be more r· attained
sp 72–32 As r· can you mingle fire and frost as Spirit and
86–28 as r· as from objects cognizable by the senses.
s 138–26 as r· as it was proved centuries ago.
149–23 as r· as she has cured purely functional disease,
f 236–26 and learn more r· to love the simple verities
p 369–25 as would be r· seen, if psychology,
377–24 as r· as functional difficulties.
411– 7 just as a person replies more r· when
414– 5 yields more r· than do most diseases
418–16 one disease would be as r· destroyed as
420– 5 If students do not r· heal themselves,
t 462– 2 Some . . . assimilate truth more r· than
489– 6 as r· as the lobster's claw,

reading

pr 16–17 This r· strengthens our
m 56– 2 R· his thoughts, Jesus added :
sp 83–31 r· mortal mind . . . touches only human beliefs
95– 2 the only genuine Science of r· mortal mind
f 235–10 their learning or their correct r·.
b 272–16 R· the thoughts of the people,

reading

  p 387–20 instead of *r·* disquisitions on the
  t 446– 6 If patients sometimes seem worse while *r·* this
  r 481–32 When *r·* the Scriptures,

readings

  s 139–18 different *r·* in the Old Testament,
  o 361–30 hence the many *r·* given the Scriptures,

readjust

  p 392– 7 to *r·* the balance for God.

reads

  pr 16–16 the original properly *r·*,
  sp 80– 7 communication purporting to come from . . . *r·*
  b 338–15 and it *r·*, *a dam*, or obstruction.
  o 361–19 Scripture *r·* : "For in Him we live,—*Acts* 17 : 28.

ready

  pr 8–23 If . . . we are not *r·* to receive the reward of
  a 24–21 chiefly as providing a *r·* pardon for all sinners
     27–19 to cut down the false doctrine of pantheism,
     49–20 was *r·* to be transformed by the renewing of the
     54– 8 Who is *r·* to follow his teaching and
  m 64–15 *r·* aid her sympathy and charity would afford.
  s 131–16 but the churches seem not *r·* to receive it,
    131–25 until the hearts of men are made *r·* for it.
  ph 170–24 The age seems *r·* to approach this subject,
    176–30 are quite as *r·* to yield to Truth as
    179–27 *r·* to put you into a sweat,
  f 223–15 Many are *r·* to meet this inquiry with the
    224–13 Centuries ago religionists were *r·* to hail an
    238– 3 wait till those whom you would benefit are *r·*
  o 347– 2 Who is *r·* to admit this?
    353–23 When we learn that . . . we shall be *r·* for
  p 410– 2 If . . . we shall not be *r·* for spiritual Life
    420–16 but are *r·* to become receptive to the new idea.
    425–30 be always *r·* with the mental protest
  t 458–14 the divine Mind is *r·* to take the case.
    458–15 Divinity is always *r·*.
  r 494–26 Which of these two . . . are you *r·* to accept?
  ap 563–25 which was *r·* to be delivered,— *Rev.* 12 : 4.
    570–23 Those *r·* for the blessing . . . will give thanks.
  gl 597– 9 which was *r·* to spring into action

reaffirms

  sp 89–12 *r·* the Scriptural word concerning a man,

real

  and continuous
  p 397–12 by believing them to be *r·* and continuous.
  and eternal
  sp 71– 1 Nothing is *r·* and eternal, . . . but God and
  f 208–21 Let us learn of the *r·* and eternal,
  b 289–30 things spiritual are the *r·* and eternal.
    296–12 reveals man . . . harmonious, *r·*, and eternal.
    301–13 which constitutes the only *r·* and eternal entity.
    307– 5 saying, . . . as *r·* and eternal as Truth.
    331–21 reflected by all that is *r·* and eternal
  o 360– 1 and know that these ideals are *r·* and eternal
  r 468–12 Spirit is the *r·* and eternal ;
  g 538–22 in contradistinction to the *r·* and eternal.
  gl 594–10 claim that . . . was as *r·* and eternal as God,
  and God-given
  g 528–23 and calling them *r·* and God-given,
  and good
  pref viii–10 physics teach that both . . . are *r·* and good,
  gl 583–21 divine Principle of all that is *r·* and good ;
  and harmonious
  p 419– 7 God and His ideas alone are *r·* and harmonious.
  and ideal
  b 332–31 Into the *r·* and ideal man the
  and immortal
  b 276–15 Harmony in man is as *r·* and immortal as in
  and tangible
  b 269–17 These ideas are perfectly *r·* and tangible to
  and the unreal
  o 360–21 swinging between the *r·* and the unreal.
  and unimpeachable
  p 414–29 perfection is *r·* and unimpeachable,
  and unreal
  g 505–22 demarcation between the *r·* and unreal.
  are styled the
  f 213– 1 movements of mortal belief, . . . are styled the *r·*.
  attraction
  an 102– 9 There is but one *r·* attraction,
  being
    (*see* **being**)
  cause
  p 402–32 a belief without a *r·* cause.
  t 463– 1 and deals with the *r·* cause of disease.
  Christianly scientific
  o 353– 1 The Christianly scientific *r·* is the
  cross
  a 50–30 The *r·* cross, . . . was the world's hatred of
  desires
  pr 10– 4 will leave our *r* desires to be rewarded by Him.
  error is not
  f 251– 1 Error is not *r·*, hence it is not
  o 353–23 When we learn that error is not *r·*,

real

  eternal and
  b 300–14 temporal and unreal never touch the eternal and *r·*.
  r 494–27 The other is the eternal and *r·* evidence,
  good and
  pref viii–11 whereas the fact is that Spirit is good and *r·*,
  harmony is the
  ap 563– 2 harmony is the *r·* and discord the unreal.
  individuality
  b 299–14 whither every *r·* individuality, image,
  is eternal
  o 353–16 All the *r·* is eternal.
  r 474–29 while all that is *r·* is eternal.
  jurisdiction
  p 379– 6 *r·* jurisdiction of the world is in Mind,
  Life
  a 51–16 He knew . . . that *r·* Life is God ;
  b 282– 3 The *r·* Life, or Mind, and its opposite,
    328– 5 God is good and the only *r·* Life.
  Life is
  p 428– 3 Life is *r·*, and death is the illusion.
  man
    (*see* **man**)
  Mind
  sp 91–30 whereas the *r·* Mind cannot be evil
  b 295–27 the exact opposite of *r·* Mind, or Spirit.
  nature
  sp 93–18 Whatever contradicts the *r·* nature of the
  objects
  sp 96–29 *r·* objects will be apprehended mentally
  opposite of the
  b 277–25 the opposite of the *r·* is not divine,
    337–28 the opposite of the *r·* or the spiritual and eternal.
  origin
  b 287– 1 They are without a *r·* origin or existence.
  or unreal
  g 524–24 Is this addition to His creation *r·* or unreal?
  outlaw
  an 105– 9 mortal mind, evil, which is the *r·* outlaw,
  prelude
  g 502– 2 living and *r·* prelude of the older Scriptures
  realm of the
  b 268– 4 rising towards the realm of the *r·*,
    277–24 The realm of the *r·* is Spirit.
    303– 4 which people the realm of the *r·*
    337–26 as they exist in the spiritual realm of the *r·*.
  Science
  s 122– 2 often reverses the *r·* Science of being,
  b 273– 8 They differ from *r·* Science because they
  sense
  b 295–14 the *r·* sense of being, perfect and forever intact,
  senses
  f 214–30 and there are no other *r·* senses.
  b 284–28 only *r·* senses of man are spiritual,
  r 488–28 If it were possible for the *r·* senses of man to
  sickness is not
  p 394– 2 to understand that sickness is not *r·*
  status
  s 120–19 or to exhibit the *r·* status of man.
  substance
  r 468–22 Spirit, . . . is the only *r·* substance.
  tangible and
  b 279–11 tangible and *r·* to immortal consciousness,
  tone
  s 126–13 the human mind never produced a *r·* tone
  Truth is
  b 288– 1 The statement that *Truth is r·*
  p 368– 4 the fact that Truth is *r·* and error is unreal.
  r 466–15 Moreover, Truth is *r·*, and error is unreal.
  universe
  b 289–19 to the . . . *r·* universe there is no death-process
  unreal and the
  g 538–10 the material and spiritual, — the unreal and the *r·*.
  unrealities seem
  r 472–28 that unrealities seem *r·* to human, erring belief.
  wishes
  pr 13–18 overwhelming our *r·* wishes with a torrent of

  pr 7–29 uttering desires which are not *r·*
  m 61– 2 The senses confer no *r·* enjoyment.
    69– 9 *r·*, ideal man appears in proportion as
  sp 70– 3 corporeal senses cannot inform us what is *r·*
    92–25 We should blush to call that *r·* which
    92–29 mistake of thinking that error can be *r·*,
  an 102– 2 God governs all that is *r·*,
    103–21 false belief . . . that evil is as *r·* as good
  s 114–17 to designate that which has no *r·* existence.
    131– 2 error should not seem so *r·* as truth.
    131– 3 Sickness should not seem so *r·* as health.
    144– 5 even if these so-called powers are *r·*.
  ph 172–11 Spirit can form no *r·* link in this supposed
    173–24 the image of God, the *r·* immortal man.
    176–25 One disease is no more *r·* than another.
    186–17 It says : "I am a *r·* entity,

real

ph	186–24	If evil is as *r·* as good,
	186–25	If death is as *r·* as Life,
	186–26	If pain is as *r·* as the absence of pain,
f	204– 5	false conclusions. . . that material history is as *r·*
	207–31	the opposite discord, . . . is not *r·*.
	209–20	are of no *r·* importance.
	210–29	To mortal sense, sin and suffering are *r·*,
	214–28	the *r·* sight or sense is not lost.
	215–15	led to believe that darkness is as *r·* as light ;
	228– 8	learn that nothing is *r·* but the right,
	230– 1	If sickness is *r·*, it belongs to immortality ;
	239–19	If divine Love is becoming . . . more *r·* to us,
	244– 3	therefore such deformity is not *r·*, but is illusion,
	250– 7	mortal existence has no *r·* entity,
b	269–31	I combat . . . that matter . . . is as *r·* as Mind,
	270– 7	hence both cannot be *r·*.
	270– 7	If one is *r·*, the other must be unreal.
	276–10	*r·* consciousness is cognizant only of
	277–11	If goodness and spirituality are *r·*,
	278– 9	the notion that there is *r·* substance-matter,
	286–15	and governs all that is *r·*.
	287–23	it is illusion, . . . and it has no *r·* existence.
	288–32	man's *r·* existence as a child of God
	292–16	To mortal mind, . . . evil is *r·*.
	292–29	the spiritual *r·* man's indissoluble
	292–32	mortal man is not the *r·* essence of manhood,
	294–10	is not more *r·* than the belief that
	297–13	that disappears which before seemed *r·*
	298–11	To material sense, the unreal is the *r·* until
	298– 9	When the *r·* is attained,
	302– 9	that man should lose aught that is *r·*,
	302–12	The notion that . . . are *r·*, is a mortal belief ;
	305–10	man, like all things *r·*, reflects God,
	306–22	not more distinct nor *r·* to the material senses
	311– 6	evil is not made and is not *r·*.
	317–19	makes man more *r·*, more formidable
	317–32	Nothing but . . . could make existence *r·* to Thomas.
	318–24	treats disease as though disease were *r·*,
	329–27	If men understood their *r·* spiritual source to be
	330–25	notion that both evil and good are *r·*
	335–29	Nothing unspiritual can be *r·*,
	339–13	would make that *r·* which is unreal,
o	347–30	The harmonious will appear *r·*,
	350–29	through which the *r·* reaches the unreal,
	351–18	while error seems as potent and *r·* to us as
	352–14	Would a mother say . . . ghosts are *r·*,
	353– 2	by declaring ghosts to be *r·*, merciless, and
	353– 2	whatever seems *r·* to material sense, is unreal in
	353– 9	How can a Christian,. . . think of the latter as *r·*
	353–18	Without perfection, nothing is wholly *r·*.
	357–25	If what opposes God is *r·*,
	360– 3	by a right estimate of what is *r·*."
	360–14	which mind-picture . . . shall be *r·* to you,
p	368–10	the fatal beliefs that error is as *r·* as Truth,
	379–32	the belief that . . . discord is as *r·* as harmony,
	386–18	the same grief that the friend's *r·* death would
	391–15	*r·* suffering for your own sins
	394– 6	which is the only *r·* recuperative power.
	395–24	to believe in the *r·* existence of a tumor,
	397–16	more powerful than . . . to make the injury *r·*.
	399–28	All that is *r·* is included in this
	404– 8	there is no *r·* pleasure in false appetites.
	404–20	there is no *r·* pleasure in sin,
	406–14	Sin and sickness will abate and seem less *r·* as
	417–22	Disease should not appear *r·* to the physician,
r	470–13	If God, or good, is *r·*,
	470–15	And evil can only seem to be *r·* by
	472– 7	making it coordinate with all that is *r·*
	473– 3	seeming to be *r·* and identical.
	474–16	If sin, sickness, and death are as *r·* as
	474–22	*r·* or the offspring of the divine will ?
	474–26	If evil is *r·*, Truth must make it so ;
	478–26	That only is *r·* which reflects God.
	480–23	and it has no *r·* basis.
	490– 1	It assures mortals that there is *r·* pleasure in
	490–17	the *r·* man's divine Principle, Love.
	493–25	seem *r·* and natural in illusion.
	494–21	sin, sickness, and death will seem *r·*
	494–22	the experiences of the sleeping dream seem *r·*
g	506– 4	matter, . . . has no *r·* entity.
	526–21	doctrine that the knowledge of evil is as *r·*,
	530–22	saying, . . . Only admit that I am *r·*,
	530–29	for neither is true nor *r·*.
	555–12	as if it were as *r·* and God-created as
	556– 1	That which is *r·*, is sustained by Spirit.
ap	576–19	the *r·* man's incorporeality
gl	584–11	hence it has no *r·* existence.

real estate

m	63–31	hold *r· e·*, deposit funds,

realism

s	129–23	We must look deep into *r·*
	144–20	and is not a factor in the *r·* of being.

realism

b	337– 5	Material personality is not *r·* ;
o	354–27	Its supposed *r·* has no divine authority,

realities

eternal

sp	78– 5	they are not the eternal *r·* of Mind.

ghosts are not

o	352–24	ghosts are not *r·*,

grand

b	328–12	reveals the grand *r·* of His allness.

of being

f	212–29	The *r·* of being, its normal action,
	229– 6	but if sin and suffering are *r·* of being,
c	264–20	Spirit and its formations are the only *r·* of being.

of divine Science

b	298– 2	the *r·* of divine Science.

of eternal existence

p	387–19	adhering to the *r·* of eternal existence,

of Spirit

b	325– 5	is being ushered into the undying *r·* of Spirit.

spiritual

g	513–27	His thoughts are spiritual *r·*.
gl	581–12	Science showing that the spiritual *r·*

supernal

c	261–27	Fixing your gaze on the *r·* supernal,

the only

s	109– 5	the only *r·* are the divine Mind and idea.
c	264–20	Spirit and its formations are the only *r·* of being.

the vague

b	298– 1	the vague *r·* of human conclusions.

b	318– 5	Corporeal senses define diseases as *r·* ;
y	550–22	Oblivion and dreams, not *r·*,
gl	594– 8	the first claim that . . . are the *r·* of life.

reality

admit its

p	395– 2	They admit its *r·*, whereas they should deny it.

all forms of

g	513–26	God creates all forms of *r·*.

and fatality

ph	197–32	his belief in its *r·* and fatality will

and immortality

r	486–24	Their *r·* and immortality are in Spirit

and in Science

b	293–10	In *r·* and in Science, both strata,

and power

p	372–20	can we believe in the *r·* and power of

and Truth

gl	580–29	not one who . . . sustains *r·* and Truth.

appearance of

f	215 18	darkness loses the appearance of *r·*.

appears

b	312– 7	as the sense-dream vanishes and *r·* appears.

assume the

r	481–20	Human hypotheses first assume the *r·* of

attest the

s	150–15	to attest the *r·* of the higher mission of

by giving

r	470 15	evil can only seem to be real by giving *r·* to the

cannot in

p	419–23	A relapse cannot in *r·* occur in mortals

complete

o	353–16	eternity, immortality, complete *r·*.

consciousness of

ap	573–23	the spiritual idea and consciousness of *r·*.

contradictions of

b	335–31	and must be contradictions of *r·*.

devoid of

g	525–20	as devoid of *r·* as they are of good,

divine

sp	95–22	succeeded by C. S., by divine *r·*.

eternal

g	538–14	significant of eternal *r·* or being.

fleshly

b	317–30	remained a fleshly *r·*, so long as

governed by

s	131– 4	our lives must be governed by *r·*

governs all

p	418–22	this simple rule of Truth, which governs all *r·*.

grasp the

b	275–10	To grasp the *r·* and order of being in its

great

sp	91–12	the sooner man's great *r·* will appear
gl	580–10	unreality as opposed to the great *r·* of

harmony the

o	352– 3	to make harmony the *r·*

idea, of all

sp	71– 5	idea, of all *r·* continues forever ;

is in God

r	472–24	All *r·* is in God and His creation,

is reached

o	353–19	until perfection appears and *r·* is reached.

is spiritual

b	335–27	*R·* is spiritual, harmonious, immutable,

reality

make a
b 339–13 the sinner would make a r· of sin,

no
sp 71– 2 Evil has no r·.
f 207–22 there can be no r· in aught which
o 346–22 there is no r· in his belief of pain,
p 427– 8 when learning that there is no r· in death,
t 447–22 but realize no r· in them.
g 530–27 The dream has no r·, no intelligence, no mind ;

no other
f 242–11 It is to know no other r·

nor existence
b 331–12 nothing possesses r· nor existence except

nor identity
r 473– 2 illusion, possessing neither r· nor identity

of being
b 297–15 Thus the r· of being is attained
311–19 opposite to the immortal r· of being.
p 418–13 no more the r· of being than is sin.
r 493–27 is not the r· of being.
ap 573–29 this r· of being will surely appear sometime

of existence
f 215– 9 unacquainted with the r· of existence,

of good
f 205–20 the supremacy and r· of good,
b 269– 7 and unfold the unity and the r· of good,
r 480–32 evil would vanish before the r· of good.
g 527–19 Has evil the r· of good?

of Life
sp 72–27 earthly mortal is not the r· of Life
b 322– 5 we shall gain the r· of Life,
o 353–32 nor apprehend the r· of Life,
r 487–29 our trust in the deathless r· of Life,

of man's existence
pr 13–31 blind to the r· of man's existence,
o 352– 9 spirituality, was the r· of man's existence,

of spiritual Life
b 318–21 yields to the r· of spiritual Life.

of substance
b 311–27 not the r· of substance.

power, nor
an 102– 7 possessing neither intelligence, power, nor r·,
ph 186–16 there is neither power nor r· in evil.

presence of the
b 293– 2 mortality disappears in presence of the r·.

pure
p 409–23 to be laid aside for the pure r·.

radiant
s 110– 5 the radiant r· of God's creation,

realm of
a 34–45 would rise again in the spiritual realm of r·,

reinstate
g 529– 9 destroy the *dream* of existence, reinstate r·,

same
ph 186–22 If we concede the same r· to discord as to

seeming
p 394– 3 Truth can destroy its seeming r·,

spiritual
f 207–27 The spiritual r· is the scientific fact
228–18 they will recognize harmony as the spiritual r·
r 488–21 senses can take no cognizance of spiritual r·

supposed
gl 596–25 and the supposed r· of error.

supposition of
f 213– 2 this mortal mind supposition of r·

their
pref xi–11 before which sin and disease lose their r·
o 352–17 If belief in their r· is destroyed,
p 395–26 while you argue against their r·,
397–10 by admitting their r· and continuance,
r 486–24 Their r· and immortality are in Spirit
g 546–26 though the darkness, . . . may deny their r·.

unbroken
r 494–24 breaks their illusion with the unbroken r· of

underlies
o 353–17 Perfection underlies r·.

underlying
b 305–15 the underlying r· of reflection.
r 477–27 caught some glimpses of the underlying r·,

without intelligence or
r 469–17 error, without intelligence or r·.

---

sp 73–27 mistake . . . that matter is any part of the r·
86–23 In r· there is none.
97– 5 In r·, the more closely error simulates truth
an 103–29 In r· there is no *mortal* mind,
s 107–17 remembering that in r· God is our Life,
130–10 It is unwise to doubt if r· is
ph 181–16 In r· you manipulate because you
184– 5 should not be recognized as r·.
f 250–22 Is there any more r· in the waking dream
252–17 lifts its voice with the arrogance of r·
b 275–24 all is in r· the manifestation of Mind.
281–16 which reflects r· and divinity

reality

b 293–26 In r·, they show the self-destruction of error
298–14 faith, understanding, fruition, r·.
299– 2 no more r· than has the sculptor's thought
299– 5 which has no physical antecedent r·
301–18 man should wish for, and in r· has,
309–28 error . . . that there can be such a r· as
327–20 evil has in r· neither place nor power
330–23 there is in r· one Mind only,
339–30 divest sin of any supposed mind or r·,
o 347–13 so-called mortal man is not the r· of man.
352–17 Children, like adults, *ought* to fear a r· which
357–19 As there is in r· but one God,
p 369– 1 Once let the mental physician believe in the r·
369– 1 he is liable to admit also the r· of
369–14 never . . . made a r· of disease
381–10 We cannot in r· suffer from
395–21 It is mental quackery to make disease a r·
395–28 mental practice, which holds disease as a r·,
403–11 In r·, both have their origin in the
t 452– 3 evil has in r· no power.
r 472–27 Therefore the only r· of
481– 2 How important, then, to choose good as the r· !
486–10 In r· man never dies.
487–21 there is in r· no such thing as
489–11 yields to the r· of everlasting Life.
492– 4 In r· there is no other existence,
g 502– 5 as if r· did not predominate over unreality,
505–27 the r· of all things brought to light.

realization

b 276–12 The r· that all inharmony is unreal
300–20 through the r· of God as ever present
g 514–30 A r· of this grand verity was a source of strength
ap 575–32 westward, to the grand r· of the

realize

a 55–17 My weary hope tries to r· that happy day,
55–19 when he shall r· God's omnipotence
f 204–21 and r· only one God,
205–22 When we r· that there is one Mind,
c 264–16 When we r· that Life is Spirit,
b 315–18 we r· this likeness only when we subdue sin
323–19 When the sick or the sinning awake to r·
p 386– 1 R· that the evidence of the senses is not
387– 8 when we r· that immortal Mind is ever active,
409–25 in proportion as mortals r· the Science of man
412–24 R· the presence of health and the fact of
417– 9 If you make the sick r· this great truism,
420–25 if they only r· that divine Love gives them
428–19 We must r· the ability of mental might
t 447–21 but r· no reality in them.

realized

a 47–32 Jesus r· the utter error of a belief in
ph 167–31 Only through . . . can scientific healing power
be r·.
172–14 yet this can be r· only as the
p 392–25 Admitting only such conclusions as you wish r·

realizing

ph 194–26 and r· Tennyson's description :

really

pr 3–22 Are we r· grateful for the good
9–26 Do you r· desire to attain this point?
a 34–10 r· commemorated the sufferings of Jesus
39–26 divine Principle of all that r· exists
m 64–31 Spirit will . . . claim its own, — all that r· is,
sp 87–14 when r· it is first sight instead of second,
s 116– 9 divinity r· is and must of necessity be,
119– 5 for of course we cannot r· endow matter with
151–26 All that r· exists is the divine Mind
ph 169–26 the sick are never r· healed except by means of
173– 4 or determine when man is r· *man*
f 203–10 was r· the justification of Jesus,
210–19 The expression *mortal mind* is r· a solecism,
213–17 The ear does not r· hear.
230–23 the sick are never r· healed by drugs,
b 272–24 which r· attest the divine origin and
272–30 the divine Principle . . . of all that r· exists.
274– 8 *Natural science*, . . . is not r· natural nor
275–12 the divine Principle of all that r· is.
283–21 belief as to what r· constitutes life
300–18 tares and wheat, which never r· mingle,
301–10 immortal, spiritual man is r· substantial,
321–17 was r· but a phase of mortal belief.
328– 9 These errors are not thus r· destroyed,
340–13 all that r· exists is in and of God,
o 347– 6 Nothing r· has Life but God,
348– 7 making the disease appear to be— what it r· is
p 371– 8 uninstructed in C. S., nothing is r· understood
402–16 no breakage nor dislocation can r· occur.
t 443– 7 omnipotent Mind as r· possessing all power.
r 478–30 *Mortal man* is a self-contradictory phrase,
484–18 are r· caused by the faith in them which
ap 561–28 is r· neither solar nor lunar,

realm
mental
sp 82–22 nor are they in the mental *r·* in which we dwell.
g 514–11 the king of the mental *r·*.
of God
r 481– 6 into the holiest," — the *r·* of God. — *Heb.* 10 : 19.
of harmony
s 138– 8 a firm foundation in the *r·* of harmony.
of Love
a 20–27 It commands sure entrance into the *r·* of Love.
of Mind
c 264– 9 in the unsearchable *r·* of Mind?
g 514– 7 Mind, . . . dwells in the *r·* of Mind.
of mysticism
sp 80–18 never . . . into the *r·* of mysticism.
of reality
a 34–25 rise again in the spiritual *r·* of reality,
of the physical
s 111– 9 though departing from the *r·* of the physical,
of the real
b 268– 4 rising towards the *r·* of the real,
277–24 The *r·* of the real is Spirit.
303– 3 which people the *r·* of the real
337–26 as they exist in the spiritual *r·* of the real.
physical
p 427–25 in the physical *r·*, so-called, as well as
unsearchable
c 264– 9 in the unsearchable *r·* of Mind?

r 480–13 Material sense has its *r·* apart from Science
gl 590– 2 *r·* of unerring, eternal, and omnipotent Mind ;
realms
s 128–18 giving mortals access to broader and higher *r·*.
g 557– 6 the birth-throes in the lower *r·* of nature,
realness
o 347– 5 has no origin, existence, nor *r·*.
reap
a 41– 9 in the hereafter they will *r·* what they now sow.
ph 179–30 may erelong *r·* the effect of this mistake.
f 238–18 when we . . . try to *r·* the harvest we have not
p 405–18 that shall he also *r·*." — *Gal.* 6 : 7.
t 462–12 he will inevitably *r·* the error he sows.
g 537–14 that shall he also *r·*." — *Gal.* 6 : 7.
reapeth
f 210–24 and *r·* the whirlwind.
reappear
sp 75– 3 The so-called dead, in order to *r·*
81–19 seemeth to wither and the flower to fade, they *r·*.
ph 139–13 or doubt that the sun will *r·*.
f 212– 7 why cannot the limb *r·*?
230–28 though it is liable to *r·* ;
p 436– 5 to *r·* however at the trial
t 453–11 but with some individuals . . . constantly *r·*.
reappearance
a 27–10 by his *r·* after the crucifixion
43– 4 his material disappearance . . . and his *r·*,
sp 98– 5 *r·* of the Christianity which heals the sick
reappeared
g 509– 5 Our Master *r·* to his students,
reappearing
a 35–13 to receive more of his *r·*
45–28 *r·* of Jesus was not the return of a spirit.
55–22 The time for the *r·* of the divine healing
s 132–21 unconscious of the *r·* of the spiritual idea,
b 271– 2 chain of scientific being *r·* in all ages,
reason
and conscience
an 106– 9 self-government, *r·*, and conscience.
and demonstration
s 109–21 divine revelation, *r·*, and demonstration.
and revelation
s 110–15 *r·* and revelation were reconciled,
o 347–27 must yield to *r·* and revelation.
befool
p 440– 6 how to make sleep befool *r·*
convince
g 522–23 convince *r·* and coincide with revelation
domain of
sp 80–17 from the domain of *r·* into the realm of
human
s 117–25 relates solely to human *r·* ;
117–26 human *r·* dimly reflects and
ph 173–26 Human *r·* and religion come slowly to the
misguided
f 220– 8 Instinct is better than misguided *r·*,
no
an 105–19 "I see no *r·* why metaphysics
of its hope
r 487–23 from which to explain the *r·* of its hope.
sensuous
s 111– 4 the will, or sensuous *r·* of the human mind,
that very
p 376–17 it cannot, for that very *r·*, suffer with a fever.

reason
understand the
p 397–18 Declare that you are not hurt and understand the *r·*

ph 181–11 for that *r·*, you employ matter rather than Mind.
199–11 by *r·* of its demand for and
199–12 by *r·* of the blacksmith's faith in
b 325– 4 by *r·* of this is being ushered into the
327–29 *R·* is the most active human faculty.
r 467–23 We *r·* imperfectly from effect to cause,
494–19 *R·*, rightly directed, serves to correct the
reasonable
b 270– 1 quite as *r·* as the second,
325–23 which is your *r·* service." — *Rom.* 12 : 1.
reasonably
an 105–14 courts *r·* pass sentence, according to the motive.
g 537–19 No one can *r·* doubt that the
reasoned
b 305–31 The Sadducees *r·* falsely
o 356– 9 Jesus *r·* on this subject practically,
reasoning
s 124–12 a blind conclusion from material *r·*.
129– 3 the *r·* of an accurately stated syllogism
b 279–26 belief contradicts alike revelation and right *r·*.
p 389–15 This false *r·* is rebuked in Scripture
t 452– 4 Incorrect *r·* leads to practical error.
r 467–25 *a priori r·* shows material existence to be
467–29 *R·* from cause to effect
492– 3 For right *r·* there should be but one fact
reassurance
r 494– 4 and he did this for tired humanity's *r·*.
reassure
p 384– 5 Let us *r·* ourselves with the law of Love.
411–28 Silently *r·* them as to their
reassures
p 420–18 The fact that . . . *r·* depressed hope.
Rebecca
ap 506–13 *R·* the Jewess in the story of Ivanhoe,
rebel
s 160–19 Can muscles, bones, blood, and nerves *r·*
rebellion
p 391– 8 rise in *r·* against them.
rebuilt
ap 576–17 as the temple to be temporarily *r·*
rebuke
ever-present
a 52–10 ever-present *r·* of his perfection and purity.
his
pr 6–31 left this record : "His *r·* is fearful."
merited
pr 9– 3 author has been most grateful for merited *r·*.
strong
a 23–14 receives a strong *r·* in the Scripture,
useful
p 382–10 receive a useful *r·* from Jesus' precept,
virtue is a
t 449–28 Only virtue is a *r·* to vice.

pr 8–32 do we listen patiently to the *r·*
a 30–20 Christ Jesus came to *r·* rabbinical error
30–28 loathe sin and *r·* it under every mask.
f 203 30 is designed to *r·* and destroy error
238–16 Unimproved opportunities will *r·* us when we
b 315– 5 His better understanding of God was a *r·*
t 443–21 "Reprove, *r·*, exhort" — *II Tim.* 4 : 2.
452–13 withhold not the *r·* or the explanation which
rebuked
pr 6–23 Jesus uncovered and *r·* sin before he cast it out.
a 35– 2 hearts chastened and pride *r·*.
51–27 Love, which *r·* their sensuality.
53– 6 He *r·* sinners pointedly and unflinchingly,
m 67–31 Jesus *r·* the suffering from any such cause
sp 85–20 Our Master *r·* the lack of this power
s 121–19 *r·* by clearer views of the everlasting facts,
b 309– 5 and *r·* his material sense.
p 363–14 Jesus *r·* them with a short story
389–15 This false reasoning is *r·* in Scripture
392– 5 be taken into account and the error be *r·*.
r 471–27 This view *r·* human beliefs,
g 509–30 Jesus *r·* the material thought of his
gl 581–16 spiritual compensation ; the ills of the flesh *r·*.
597– 6 *r·* the hypocrisy, which offered long petitions
rebukes
a 23–19 which *r·* sin of every kind
b 281– 8 *r·* mortal belief, and asks :
o 350–29 Soul *r·* sense, and Truth destroys **error.**
ap 571–27 Thus he *r·* the conceit of sin.

rebuking

a 48–22 thus r· resentment or animal courage.
ph 174–18 r· in their course all error
p 364–11 r· self-righteousness and declaring
gl 589–17 r· and destroying error,
589–20 a higher sense of Truth r· mortal belief,
594–15 love r· error ; reproof of sensualism.

recall

sp 88– 2 In our day-dreams we can r·
s 122–22 which every thinker can r· for himself.

recalling

t 445–29 R· Jefferson's words about slavery,

Recapitulation

gl 585–15 ERROR. See chapter on R·, page 472.
588–26 INTELLIGENCE, . . . See chapter on R·, page 469.
590–14 LIFE. See chapter on R·, page 468.
593– 3 PRINCIPLE. See chapter on R·, page 465.
594–18 SOULS. See chapter on R·, page 466.
594–25 SUBSTANCE. See chapter on R·, page 468.

receding

g 536– 7 human concepts advancing and r·,

receive

pr 1– * believe that ye r· them, — Mark 11 : 24.
3–10 in order to r· His blessing,
3–24 and thus be fitted to r· more.
8–23 If . . . we are not ready to r· the reward
10– 2 walk in the light so far as we r· it,
10–22 Experience teaches us that we do not always r·
10–26 or we should certainly r· that for which we ask.
10–27 "Ye ask, and r· not, because — Jas. 4 : 3.
10–30 it is not always best for us to r·.
15–32 Without a fitness for holiness, we cannot r·
a 22–15 and you r· no present reward,
22–19 and r· according to your deserving.
29–11 though we may never r· it in this world.
35–12 to r· more of his reappearing
36–22 impossible for sinners to r· their
s 131–16 but the churches seem not ready to r· it,
132– 6 the blind r· their sight — Matt. 11 : 5.
ph 169–25 whatever good they may seem to r· from
c 267–30 he shall r· the crown of life, — Jas. 1 : 12.
b 283–27 r· the divine Principle in the understanding,
284–16 which r· no direct evidence of Spirit,
333–22 to all prepared to r· Christ, Truth.
339–11 sinner can r· no encouragement from the
p 382–10 r· a useful rebuke from Jesus' precept,
382–22 "Whosoever shall not r· the — Luke 18 : 17.
420–15 when they are in a fit mood to r· it,
t 444– 1 and they r· no help from them,
444– 7 If Christian Scientists ever fail to r· aid
r 471–10 these so-called senses r· no intimation of
483–26 it ought to r· aid, not opposition,
488– 5 therefore you r· the blessing of Truth.
g 542–21 Sin will r· its full penalty,

received

pr 3–23 Are we really grateful for the good already r·?
a 39– 2 Such indignities as he r·, his followers
46–30 His students then r· the Holy Ghost.
54– 6 but earth r· the harmony
sp 88–30 r· from the impulsion of departed spirits.
s 107– * For I neither r· it of man, — Gal. 1 : 12.
131–18 his own r· him not." — John 1 : 11.
132–17 r· no aid nor approval from
ph 193–23 since the injury was r· in boyhood.
o 342–15 where they should be hospitably r·.
348–31 ethics and temperance have r· an impulse,
359–21 early r· her religious education.
p 372–31 prevents the honest recognition of benefits r·,
g 555–11 Error would have itself r· as mind,
gl 598– 6 yet it has r· different translations,

receives

a 23–14 This preaching r· a strong rebuke
ph 192–31 r· directly the divine power.
t 455–17 The student, who r· his knowledge of
r 474–11 consequent maltreatment which it r·.
g 556–25 Ontology r· less attention than physiology.

receiving

s 156–25 and r· occasional visits from me,
p 439– 1 r· pay from them

recent

p 402–23 mesmerism — or hypnotism, to use the r· term
g 549–13 According to r· lore,

recently

an 101–30 animal magnetism, r· called hypnotism,

reception

a 41–22 Jesus foresaw the r· C. S. would have
52–12 foresight of the r· error would give him.
s 107– 5 for the r· of this final revelation of
115– 1 the one great obstacle to the r· of
t 448–23 r· or pursuit of instructions opposite to
r 474– 4 The r· accorded to Truth in the

receptive

a 34–16 preach Christ, . . . to the poor, — the r· thought,
46–11 It is revealed to the r· heart,
b 323–20 they will be r· of divine Science,
324– 1 renders thought r· of the advanced idea.
p 380– 1 may rest at length on some r· thought,
382–14 is more r· of spiritual power
395–20 nurse should be . . . r· to Truth
420–16 are ready to become r· to the new idea.

receptiveness

f 236–29 their freedom from wrong and their r· of

recesses

an 102–18 hidden in the dark r· of mortal thought,

recipe

f 247–31 r· for beauty is to have less illusion
p 406– 1 The Bible contains the r· for all healing.

reckoned

g 520–11 can never be r· according to the

reckoning

b 275–11 begin by r· God as the divine Principle
g 539– 4 Error begins by r· life as separate from

reclaims

o 342–21 C. S. awakens the sinner, r· the infidel,

reclined

p 362–13 he r· on a couch

recognition

full
a 29–25 the full r· that being is Spirit.
50–19 If his full r· of eternal Life had
m 59– 2 without a full r· of its enduring obligations
honest
p 372–30 the honest r· of benefits received,
of being
ap 573–24 such a r· of being is, and has been, possible
of divine Science
b 322–10 before this r· of divine Science can come
of harmony
ap 576–24 possesses this r· of harmony consciously
of infinite Love
p 366–18 and has not that r· of infinite Love
of life
r 495–18 the r· of life harmonious — as Life eternally is
of Spirit
sp 76–32 r· of Spirit and of infinity comes not suddenly
90–28 understanding and r· of Spirit must finally come,
b 287–30 yield to Truth, — to the r· of Spirit
of Truth
t 450–11 open to the approach and r· of Truth.

ph 173–26 to the r· of spiritual facts,

recognizable

b 294–25 Man's genuine selfhood is r· only in

recognize

pr 13–27 hence men r· themselves as merely physical,
a 55–18 when man shall r· the Science of Christ
sp 93– 1 to r· Soul as substantial
an 104–29 courts r· evidence to prove the motive
s 133–27 r· no life, . . . nor substance outside of God.
ph 183–20 mortals commonly r· as law that which
f 228–17 they will r· harmony as the spiritual reality
c 264–26 evidences, by which we can r· true existence
264–28 When we . . . r· man's spiritual being,
b 284–12 Can matter r· Mind?
284–13 Can infinite Mind r· matter?
316– 7 and to r· the divine sonship.
p 441–16 Our law refuses to r· Man as sick or dying,
t 451–21 and he must r· this in order to defend himself
461–23 while to r· your sin, aids in destroying it.
g 508–20 and grammars always r· a neuter gender,
531–14 Then man will r· his God-given dominion

recognized

a 31–10 He r· Spirit, God, as the only creator,
sp 76– 6 When being is understood, Life will be r· as
90–12 Then being will be r· as spiritual,
s 157– 4 because its one r· Principle of healing is Mind.
ph 168–24 and r· the patient's fear of it,
184– 5 and should not be r· as reality.
f 215–31 he r· the immortality of man.
252–13 and r· as the true likeness of his Maker.
b 278– 5 the only substance and consciousness r· by
r 468–30 One ceases in proportion as the other is r·.
480– 2 the nothingness of matter is r·.
gl 592– 9 nor can be r· by the spiritual sense ;

recognizes

pr 9–22 and r· only the divine control of Spirit,
ph 188–14 in sleep, in which every one r· his
o 361–12 r· that Jesus Christ is not God,

recognizing

f 249– 7 r· no mortal nor material power as able to
p 379– 7 r· all causation as vested in divine Mind.
416– 5 removed by r· the truth of being.
g 530–10 r· God, the Father and Mother of all, as able

recollect
 b 323–14 We must *r·* that Truth is demonstrable when
 p 389– 7 *R·* that it is not the nerves, not matter,

recollected
 sp 86–26 peculiarities of expression, *r·* sentences,

recollection
 pr 7–30 with the *r·* that we have prayed over it

recommend
 s 157–22 why did Jesus not employ them and *r·*
 p 441–20 We further *r·* that Materia Medica

recommended
 an 105–10 defies justice and is *r·* to mercy.
 s 143– 7 else Jesus would have *r·* and employed
 f 221– 8 His physician also *r·* that he should not
 p 369–17 never *r·* attention to laws of health,
    437–16 though *r·* to mercy ;

recommends
 t 453–30 never *r·* material hygiene, never manipulates.

recompense
 sp 98– 1 spiritual *r·* of the persecuted is assured
 p 400–32 as a *r·* for ignorance.

recompensing
 g 501– 9 *r·* human want and woe with spiritual gain.

reconcile
 a 19– 2 to *r·* man to God, not God to man.
    19– 5 Even Christ cannot *r·* Truth to error,
 s 163–31 to *r·* the fixed and repulsive antipathies

reconciled
 a 45–11 we were *r·* to God by the— *Rom.* 5 : 10.
    45–12 being *r·*, we shall be saved by his— *Rom.* 5 : 10.
 s 110–15 reason and revelation were *r·*,

reconciles
 a 18–13 The atonement of Christ *r·* man to God,

reconciling
 a 19– 6 Jesus aided in *r·* man to God

reconstruct
 f 238–29 To *r·* timid justice and place the
 p 422–19 serve to *r·* the body.

reconstruction
 p 401–32 confines himself chiefly to mental *r·*

record
 according to the
   g 545– 5 for according to the *r·*, material man was
 divine
   s 139–21 and material sense stole into the divine *r·*,
 first
   g 522– 3 The Science of the first *r·* proves the
    522– 5 The first *r·* assigns all might and government to
    528–18 This is the first *r·* of magnetism.
 have no
   a 31– 9 We have no *r·* of his calling any man by the
    47–30 except St. John, of whose death we have no *r·*.
   g 505– 3 have no *r·* in the first chapter of Genesis.
    538–18 have no *r·* in the Elohistic introduction of
          Genesis,
 historic
   a 27–23 but only eleven left a desirable historic *r·*.
 inspired
   g 521– 4 Here the inspired *r·* closes its narrative
 introduces the
   g 544– 1 introduces the *r·* of a material creation
 its own
   g 505– 2 Mind makes its own *r·*,
 of creation
   g 504– 9 are not yet included in the *r·* of creation,
    521–15 turn our gaze to the spiritual *r·* of creation.
    526– 3 scientific *r·* of creation declares that God made
 of Jesus
   a 46–27 ascension, which closed the earthly *r·* of Jesus,
 of man
   g 531–31 the scientifically Christian *r·* of man
 of sin
   g 525–27 the Scriptural *r·* of sin and death
 of spiritual creation
   gl 590–22 the *r·* of spiritual creation.
 second
   g 522– 8 The second *r·* chronicles man as mutable
    522–12 second *r·* unmistakably gives the history of
 this
   pr 6–30 left this *r·* : "His rebuke is fearful."
   g 545–21 The translators of this *r·* of
 f 224–11 In the *r·* of nineteen centuries,
    246–17 Never *r·* ages.
 g 513–11 In the *r·*, time is not yet measured by
    528– 2 *r·* declares that God has already created
 gl 598–10 In the *r·* of Jesus' supposed death,

recorded
 sp 85–15 It is *r·* that Jesus, as he once journeyed
 an 101– 5 to be in the history of the errors of
 s 158– 1 It is *r·* that the profession of medicine
 b 272–25 triumphs of C. S. are *r·* in the destruction of error

recorded
 o 350– 6 as *r·* in the New Testament,
    358–17 as is *r·* throughout the Scriptures.
 p 400–32 *r·* that in certain localities he did not
    411–13 *r·* that once Jesus asked the name of
    441–30 *r·* in our Book of books as a liar.
 g 521–29 scientific truth as before *r·*.
    537–23 *r·* in the first chapter of Genesis.
    544–19 The facts of creation, as previously *r·*,
 ap 577–29 as *r·* by the great apostle,

recorder's
 gl 590–25 is disappearing from the *r·* thought,

records
 a 37– 5 History is full of *r·* of suffering.
 s 163–22 said : "Consulting the *r·* of our science,
 p 402– 5 well-authenticated *r·* of the cure,
    437–17 the terrible *r·* of your Court of Error,
 g 522–14 It *r·* pantheism, opposed to the
    525–26 as to the *r·* of truth,

recounting
 s 132– 1 *r·* his works instead of referring to

recourse
 b 329–28 they would struggle for *r·* to the spiritual
 t 445–12 by *r·* to material means for healing.

recover
 pr 12–29 If the sick *r·* because they pray
 a 38–12 and they shall *r·*."— *Mark* 16 : 18.
 s 144–16 Willing the sick to *r·* is not the
    155– 3 When the sick *r·* by the use of drugs, it is
 ph 166–23 Failing to *r·* health through adherence to
 b 205–10 and then *r·* man's original self
    328–25 and they shall *r·*."— *Mark* 16 : 18.
 o 359–28 and they shall *r·*."— *Mark* 16 : 18.
 p 362– * *and they shall r·*.— *Mark* 16 : 18.
    373–10 the sick *r·* more rapidly from disease than
    377–19 never knew a patient who did not *r·* when

recovered
 s 152–19 and he *r·* accordingly.
 f 222–16 he *r·* strength and flesh rapidly.

recovering
 pref xi–20 And *r·* of sight to the blind.— *Luke* 4 : 18.
 s 150–16 to give up the medicine while she was *r·*.

recovery
 facilitate
   p 421–10 showing him that it was to facilitate *r·*.
 impute their
   f 219–27 and impute their *r·* to change of air
 of invalids
   s 145– 4 The struggle for the *r·* of invalids goes on,
 of the sick
   pr 12–22 custom of praying for the *r·* of the sick
   f 218–17 Why pray for the *r·* of the sick, if
   p 372–31 this will be a hindrance to the *r·* of the sick
    419– 1 A moral question may hinder the *r·* of the sick.
 ph 185–27 but the *r·* is not permanent.
    193–24 Since his *r·* I have been informed that
 p 376– 4 the latent fear and the despair of *r·*
    396– 7 a discouraging remark about *r·*,

recreate
 g 514– 2 and afterwards *r·* persons or things
    547–19 theory, . . . endues matter with power to *r·*

recreation
 f 205–14 Where then is the necessity for *r·* or

rectified
 f 230–20 blunders which must afterwards be *r·* by man?
    240–21 until all wrong work is effaced or *r·*.
 t 460–13 is material, till such thought is *r·* by Spirit.

rectitude
 p 403–21 The most Christian state is one of *r·*

recuperative
 f 252– 4 and of the *r·* energies of Truth
 p 394– 7 is the only real *r·* power.
 t 447–14 The *r·* action of the system,

recur
 s 114–20 must sometimes *r·* to the old and imperfect,

recurring
 c 260–25 by the thoughts ever *r·* to one's self,

recurs
 ph 181–24 the question then *r·*,
 f 217–18 that condition never *r·*,

red
 b 338–13 signifying the *r· color of the ground*,
 ap 562–30 and behold a great *r·* dragon.— *Rev.* 12 : 3.
    563– 8 The great *r·* dragon symbolizes a lie,
    565– 2 and becomes the great *r·* dragon,
    567–21 is pure delusion, the *r·* dragon ;
 gl 580– 1 "dust to dust ;" *r·* sandstone ;

Red Dragon
 gl 593– 7 definition of

redeem
 o 354–21 God will *r·* that weakness,
redeemed
 a 26– 8 till all are *r·* through divine Love.
 f 202–11 *r·* through the merits of Christ,
 p 364– 7 they might be *r·* from sensuality and sin.
redeeming
 g 552–23 the *r·* power, from the ills they occasion,
redeems
 a 19– 9 *r·* man from the law of matter,
redemption
 s 151– 7 something beyond itself for its *r·* and healing,
 c 255– * *to wit, the r· of our body.— Rom.* 8 : 23.
 t 464–12 working for the *r·* of mankind.
redolent
 g 516–12 Love, *r·* with unselfishness,
Red Sea
 f 226–30 the *R· S·* and the wilderness ;
 ap 566– 2 were guided triumphantly through the *R· S·*,
reduce
 m 61–22 must either be overcome or *r·* him to a
 ph 180–31 To *r·* inflammation, dissolve a tumor,
 b 335– 5 would *r·* God to dependency on matter,
 p 374– 3 counter-irritants, and depletion never *r·*
 r 490–17 *r·* to practice the real man's divine Principle,
 g 517– 7 mental attempt to *r·* Deity to corporeality.
reduced
 sp 91–11 but the sooner error is *r·* to its
 s 146–31 Divine metaphysics is now *r·* to a system,
 ph 173– 9 supposition, . . . Truth is *r·* to the level of
 r 471–30 *r·* to human apprehension, she has named C. S.
 ap 572– 5 scientifically *r·* to its native nothingness.
reduces
 p 398–20 which *r·* self-inflicted sufferings
reducing
 g 540– 8 *r·* it to its common denominator,
 ap 561–18 *r·* to human perception and
re-echoes
 sp 88–26 Eloquence *r·* the strains of Truth and Love.
reed
 m 66– 7 a broken *r·*, which pierces the heart.
reeds
 b 269–27 *r·* shaken by the wind, not houses built on the
reefs
 sp 87–21 of the corals, of its sharp *r·*, of the tall ships
refer
 sp 93–26 *r·* only to quality, not to God.
 r 465–12 They *r·* to one absolute God.
 g 508–18 and does not necessarily *r·* either to
reference
 f 235– 8 as direct *r·* to their morals as to their learning
 b 334–29 a *r·* to the human sense of Jesus crucified.
 ap 560– 4 has *r·* to the present age.
 gl 588–22 if used with *r·* to Spirit, or Deity.
referred
 ph 175–22 nor *r·* to sanitary laws.
 f 232–22 He *r·* man's harmony to Mind,
 b 272–11 *r·* to in the last chapter of Mark's Gospel.
 333–28 Jesus *r·* to this unity of
 o 346– 4 not sinful and sickly mortal man who is *r·* to,
 g 523–32 it is usually Jehovah, . . . who is *r·* to.
 540– 6 *r·* to divine law as stirring up the belief in
referring
 a 31–25 *R·* to the materiality of the age,
 s 132– 2 instead of *r·* to his doctrine,
 gl 585– 3 Jesus said, *r·* to spiritual perception,
 596– 8 *R·* to it, he said to the Athenians :
refers
 an 103– 2 Paul *r·* to the personification of evil as
 s 128– 4 *r·* only to the laws of God
 ph 172–21 to which the apostle *r·* when he says
 b 313–10 passage in the same chapter, which *r·* to
 ap 563–29 Its sting is spoken of by Paul, when he *r·* to
refined
 p 383–18 could not be borne by the *r·*.
refinement
 ph 175–28 but they never indulged in the *r·* of
reflect
 a 52–25 speaking of human ability to *r·* divine power,
 sp 71– 9 outside of finite form, which forms only *r·*,
 91–16 Absorbed in . . . we discern and *r·* but faintly
 f 215–10 matter and mortality do not *r·* the facts of
 240– 6 the spiritual intelligence they *r·*.
 b 303– 8 *r·* the one divine individuality
 324– 9 and the body will *r·* what governs it,
 331– 2 no more confined to the forms which *r·* it
 332–27 only purity could *r·* Truth and Love,
 t 446–25 divine beatitudes, *r·* the spiritual light
 r 477–24 Soul can never *r·* anything inferior to

reflect
 g 505–28 God's ideas *r·* the immortal, unerring, and
 506– 3 Objects utterly unlike the original do not *r·*.
 507–20 they *r·* the Mind which includes all.
 516–22 forever *r·*, in glorified quality, the
 516–28 God made man . . . to *r·* the divine Spirit.
 518–22 the varied expressions of God *r·* health,
 gl 588–16 the objects of God's creation *r·* one Mind,
reflected
 pr 3–12 The Divine Being must be *r·* by man,
 17– 7 *And Love is r· in love ;*
 c 258–19 infinite Principle is *r·* by the infinite idea
 b 305– 5 a face *r·* in the mirror is not the original,
 306–10 If . . . there would be no divinity *r·*.
 331– 6 Mind, the creator *r·* in His creations.
 331– 7 God would not be *r·* but absorbed,
 331–21 *r·* by all that is real and eternal
 336– 7 is *r·* in all spiritual individuality
 336–14 but is *r·* by man.
 336–20 neither could God's fulness be *r·* by a single man,
 r 467–18 God as not in man but as *r·* by man.
 479– 9 An image of mortal thought, *r·* on the retina,
 496– 4 omnipotent Mind is *r·*
 g 503– 3 embraced in the infinite Mind and forever *r·*.
 504– 1 is never *r·* by aught but the good.
 510–10 *r·* spiritually by all who walk in the light
 516– 5 are *r·* by His creation ;
 516–10 Life is *r·* in existence, Truth in truthfulness,
 517–17 His personality can only be *r·*, not transmitted.
 524–23 yet God is *r·* in all His creation.
 543–26 *r·* in the myriad manifestations of Life,
 550–15 Error of thought is *r·* in error of action.
 ap 562– 9 the universe borrows its *r·* light,
 gl 599– 4 The *r·* animation of Life, Truth, and Love.
reflecting
 an 102–14 man, *r·* God's power, has dominion
 s 125–16 *R·* God's government, man is self-governed.
 ph 179–10 not in self-righteousness, but *r·* the
 f 247–17 *r·* those higher conceptions of loveliness
 b 300–21 man as *r·* the divine likeness.
 337– 2 man, *r·* God, cannot lose his individuality ;
 346– 4 the ideal man, *r·* God's likeness.
 r 468–24 *r·* the divine substance of Spirit.
 489–17 How can man, *r·* God, be dependent on
 g 503–16 *r·* Him in countless spiritual forms.
 515–23 *r·* goodness and power.
reflection
and demonstration
 f 241–19 the *r·* and demonstration of divine Love,
God's
 s 126– 6 when man beholds himself God's *r·*,
 r 471–17 Man is, and forever has been, God's *r·*.
 g 527– 4 Man is God's *r·*, needing no cultivation,
governing the
 b 303– 5 the Principle governing the *r·*.
His
 f 242–12 no other reality . . . than good, God and His *r·*,
 b 306– 9 If . . . parted for a moment from His *r·*,
 314– 7 inseparable as God and His *r·*
 r 466– 1 His *r·* is man and the universe.
idea or
 r 470–22 idea or *r·*, man, remains perfect.
 gl 581– 8 ARK. Safety ; the idea, or *r·*, of Truth,
image or
 pr 13–28 ignorant of man as God's image or *r·*
 f 204–26 without the nature of the image or *r·*
 b 300– 5 His infinite image or *r·*, man.
likeness and
 g 516– 8 we shall see this true likeness and *r·*
mirrored
 g 515–25 Your mirrored *r·* is your own image
observation and
 s 163– 9 founded on long observation and *r·*,
of God
 s 121–29 the *r·* of God, is thus brought nearer the
 ph 200–18 if man is the image, *r·*, of God,
 c 259– 8 threw upon mortals the truer *r·* of God
 b 296– 3 man is the spiritual, eternal *r·* of God.
 300–11 will bring to light the true *r·* of God
 333–21 the spiritual idea,— the *r·* of God,
 r 475–18 man is the *r·* of God, or Mind,
 g 502– 2 serves to suggest the proper *r·* of God
 516– 3 so you, being spiritual, are the *r·* of God.
 555–16 the origin of man, who is the *r·* of God,
of his Maker
 b 305–27 Because man is the *r·* of his Maker,
of Soul
 f 249–31 Man is the *r·* of Soul.
of Spirit
 b 303– 7 Multiplication . . . is the *r·* of Spirit.
 r 477–20 Identity is the *r·* of Spirit,
 g 506– 4 matter, not being the *r·* of Spirit,
 523–12 instead of the *r·* of Spirit.
 524–23 Matter is not the *r·* of Spirit,

reflection

of the Ego-God
b 281–11 The Ego-man is the r· of the Ego-God ;
of the infinite
b 313–17 the royal r· of the infinite ;
or likeness
b 337– 6 it is not the r· or likeness of Spirit,
scientific
sp 70– 9 In this scientific r· the Ego and the
spiritual
b 305–22 as opposed to the Science of spiritual r·,
r 480– 5 If there is no spiritual r·, then there remains
the right
b 299–25 which cannot destroy the right r·.
this
c 258–12 this r· is the true idea of God.
b 301–13 This r· seems to mortal sense transcendental,
your
g 515–26 If you lift a weight, your r· does this also.

s 126– 6 even as man sees his r· in a glass.
f 244–21 If . . . there is no full r· of the infinite Mind.
c 259–18 true likeness cannot be lost in divine r·.
b 301– 6 what C. S. means by the word r·.
302–32 is but the r· of the creative power of
303– 1 The r·, through mental manifestation,
305– 9 the mirrored form, which is but a r·,
305–15 constitutes the underlying reality of r·.
337–20 as the r· of the invisible God,
r 477–20 the r· in multifarious forms of
g 503–21 first, in light ; second, in r· ;
515–30 and call man the r·.
516– 1 how true, . . . is the r· to its original.
516– 2 As the r· of yourself appears in the mirror,
528– 2 all being is the r· of the eternal Mind,

reflections

b 280– 5 only r· of good can come.
336–15 man's consciousness and individuality are r· of
g 513–12 the motions and r· of deific power
517–24 there is no limit to infinitude or to its r·.

reflects

a 18– 2 whereby man r· divine Truth, Life, and Love.
sp 70 8 spiritual man, made in God's likeness, r· God.
90–32 we certainly shall know this when man r· God.
94– 3 Man r· infinite Truth, Life, and Love.
s 117–26 human reason dimly r· and
120– 5 man coexists with and r· Soul, God,
f 240–11 the Principle is above what it r·,
247–22 r· the charms of His goodness in expression,
250–13 man, the outcome of God, r· God.
253– 1 He r· the infinite understanding,
c 258–11 Man r· infinity, and this reflection is the
259– 2 for he r· eternal Life ;
266–28 he r· the beatific presence,
b 281–16 r· reality and divinity in individual . . . man
286–20 the spiritual universe is good, and r· God
300–28 r· and expresses the divine substance
300–32 God is revealed only in that which r· Life,
301–11 and r· the eternal substance, or Spirit,
301–21 He r· the divine, which constitutes the only
303–10 Whatever r· Mind, Life, Truth, and Love,
305– 7 r· the central light of being,
305–10 man, like all things real, r· God,
305–14 though he r· the creation of Mind,
306–19 cannot be separated . . . from God, if man r· God.
p 393–17 in Science man r· God's government.
t 458–23 Christianity scientific man r· the divine law,
r 475–16 term for all that r· God's image and likeness ;
475–22 but r· spiritually all that belongs to his Maker.
478–27 That only is real which r· God.
479–27 black is not a color, because it r· no light.
g 502–28 The universe r· God.
507–15 universe of Spirit r· the creative power
516–20 r· God's dominion over all the earth.
525– 4 Man r· God ; mankind represents
ap 577– 7 this compounded spiritual individuality r·
588–16 whatever r· not this one Mind, is false

reflex

c 259–16 mortals have never beheld in man the r· image

reform

pr 5– 3 is but one step towards r·
a 19–18 every effort for r·, every good thought
35–30 The design of Love is to r· the sinner.
35–31 If . . . insufficient to r· him,
s 139–11 but the present mere, yet old, r·
151–13 Even this one r· in medicine would
b 285–26 through pardon and not through r·,
327– 1 R· comes by understanding that there is no
327–24 But how shall we r· the man who
p 404–17 The temperance r·, felt all over our land,
g 537–31 the opportunity to r·,

reformation

pref xi–14 as darkness gives place to light and sin to r·.
pr 5– 6 the test of our sincerity, — namely, r·.
a 22–30 Justice requires r· of the sinner.
p 363–30 repentance, r·, and growth in wisdom?
404–15 God's law is fulfilled and r· cancels the crime.

reformatory

s 129–28 in its r· mission among mortals.

reformed

sp 78–30 sorrowing are comforted, and the sinning are r·.
o 343–27 healed the sick and r· the sinner
355–31 by the sinners who are r·.
p 363–25 Had she repented and r·,
t 447–22 A sinner is not r· merely by

reforming

p 404–26 Healing the sick and r· the sinner

reforms

pr 1– 1 The prayer that r· the sinner and heals
6– 4 this divine Principle alone r· the sinner.
a 19–23 the practical repentance, which r· the heart
m 65–21 over this as over many other r·,
s 139– 9 R· have commonly been attended with

refraining

b 322–23 r· from it only through fear of

refresh

a 32–26 he withdrew . . . to r· his heart with
b 288–17 the raindrops of divinity r· the earth.

refreshed

p 387–11 r· by the assurances of immortality,

refuge

a 44– 5 gave Jesus a r· from his foes,
sp 83– 8 Mortals must find r· in Truth in order to
p 394–25 Are material means the only r· from fatal
t 444–11 "God is our r· and strength, — Psal. 46 : 1.

refuse

o 344–25 Why should one r· to investigate this method

refused

o 350–16 The Master often r· to explain his words,

refuses

f 241– 4 he who r· obedience to God, is chastened
p 441–15 Our law r· to recognize Man as sick

refutation

p 396–14 r· of the testimony of material sense
396–16 The r· becomes arduous, not because

refuted

a 18–12 r· all opponents with his healing power.

refutes

s 120–24 and r· materialistic logic.

regain

f 247– 3 I have seen age r· two of the elements it had
r 486– 7 To die, that he may r· these senses?

regained

r 476–15 never had a . . . which may subsequently be r·.

regard

pref x– 7 They r· the human mind as a healing agent,
pr 9–12 we shall r· our neighbor unselfishly,
14– 1 If we are sensibly with the body and r·
a 24–18 in r· to predestination and future punishment.
24–20 Does erudite theology r· the crucifixion
39–11 causes mortals to r· death as a friend,
an 100–18 "In r· to the existence and utility of
s 119–11 and r· God as the creator of
b 307–20 If we r· matter as intelligent,
312– 8 The senses r· a corpse, not as man,
p 364–25 do they show their r· for Truth, or Christ,
376–23 true facts in r· to harmonious being,
433–10 jury must r· in such cases only the evidence
g 548–28 facts in r· to so-called embryonic life.

regarded

m 65–12 life should be more metaphysically r·.
an 100– 3 he r· this so-called force, which he said could be
s 119–23 evil should be r· as unnatural, because
154– 5 that certain diseases should be r· as
158– 7 Apollo was also r· as the sender of disease,
b 313–16 r· Christ as the Son of God,
o 345– 1 are often r· as synonymous terms ;
p 363– 9 He r· her compassionately.
364– 2 r· as the best man that ever trod this planet,
ap 573–17 no longer r· as a miserable sinner,

regarding

sp 79– 6 changing the patient's thoughts r· death.
s 122–29 the same mistake r· Soul and body
122–30 mistake . . . that Ptolemy made r· the
ph 188–32 the desired information r· the sun.
f 252– 5 r· the pathology and theology of C. S.
b 277–29 Nothing we can say . . . r· matter is immortal.
296– 8 must destroy all illusions r· life and mind,
300– 2 spiritual conclusions r· life
o 355–15 conflicting theories r· Christian healing?

regarding
p 403–24 Never conjure up some new discovery . . . r·
    disease
423–20 r· the truth and harmony of being
432–13 In this province there is a statute r· disease,
t 461–25 The truth r· error is, that error is not true,

regardless
pr 1– 4 R· of what another may say or think

regards
p 423–16 He r· the ailment as weakened or strengthened
434–16 r· the prisoner with the utmost tenderness.

regenerate
b 296– 8 and r· material sense and self.

regenerated
p 442– 8 Then the prisoner rose up r·, strong, free.

regenerates
pr 4–28 spiritual understanding, which r· ;
f 222– 8 whereas Truth r· this fleshly mind

regeneration
a 24–12 rise into newness of life with r·.
f 242– 2 Through repentance, spiritual baptism, and r·,

regimen
p 370– 6 The body improves under the same r·
370– 7 if health is not made manifest under this r·,

regions
f 240– 2 Arctic r·, sunny tropics, giant hills,

registered
t 457– 1 and r· the revealed Truth

registers
t 449–12 r· his healing ability and fitness to teach.

regret
o 346– 1 I r· that such criticism confounds man with

regretted
p 405–26 If sin is not r· and is not lessening, then

regular
pref x–18 abandoned as hopeless by r· medical
ph 176–22 treated by a r· practitioner,

regularly
p 437–26 proceedings of a r· constituted court.

regulate
ph 184– 3 Truth makes no laws to r· sickness,
185–10 discussed . . . to r· life and health.

regulates
p 413– 7 Mind r· the condition of the stomach,
420–19 It . . . r· the system.

regulations
m 56–14 subject to such moral r· as will
p 389–20 cannot annul these r· by an opposite law

rehearses
ph 188–23 Error r· error.

reign
and rule
f 208–22 the r· and rule of universal harmony,
of discord
s 122– 2 and so creates a r· of discord,
of harmony
sp 93–32 the r· of harmony in the Science of being.
s 122– 7 the actual r· of harmony on earth.
gl 590– 1 The r· of harmony in divine Science ;
592–20 the kingdom of heaven, or r· of harmony.
of righteousness
gl 585–19 EUPHRATES . . . the r· of righteousness.
of Spirit
f 208–21 the r· of Spirit, the kingdom of heaven,
gl 587–25 HEAVEN. Harmony ; the r· of Spirit ;
over man
g 529–31 He begins his r· over man somewhat mildly,

pref vii–21 "the Lord shall r· forever." — Exod. 15 : 18.
f 248–30 kingdom of heaven — r· within us,
b 288–14 will cease, and spiritual harmony r·.
r 476–30 Truth and Love r· in the real man,

reigns
f 205–27 into opposite channels where selfishness r·.
b 318– 4 Mind and immortality, in which Spirit r·
g 536– 8 The divine understanding r·, is all,

reins
p 422–29 Not holding the r· of government

reinstate
g 529– 9 r· reality, usher in Science and

reiterate
f 236– 9 who r· Christ's teachings

reject
a 27–28 Why do those who profess to follow Christ r·
54–31 would not some, who now profess to love him,
    r· him?
m 62–31 mortals believe in material laws and r· the
s 148–18 Anatomy and theology r· the divine Principle

rejected
a 20–16 "Despised and r· of men," — Isa. 53 : 3.
52–13 "Despised and r· of men," — Isa. 53 : 3.
s 136–10 His answer to this question the world r·.
139–26 "the stone which the builders r·" — Matt. 21 : 42.
150–24 as the practically r· doctrine of
f 233–24 including the hearts which r· him.
b 316–25 scourged in person, and its Principle was r·.
o 343–21 It would sometimes seem as if truth were r·
361–27 but it will be r· and reviled until

rejecting
b 280–31 and r· the Science of being
o 357– 6 not by accepting, but by r· a lie.

rejection
a 20–15 [the r· of error]
s 132–24 Anticipating this r· of idealism,
137–11 In his r· of the answer already given

rejects
s 111–16 r· the incidental or inverted image

rejoice
pr 15–25 Christians r· in secret beauty and bounty,
a 22–23 whereby we r· in immortality,
m 64–21 Then shall Soul r· in its own,
s 151–13 they would r· with us.
f 249– 8 Let us r· that we are subject to the
o 354–28 I r· in the apprehension of this grand verity.
p 377– 5 that he should r· always in ever-present Love.
g 529–25 should r· that evil, . . . contradicts itself
ap 568–20 Therefore r·, ye heavens, — Rev. 12 : 12.

rejoices
pref ix– 4 and r· in the draught.
ap 569–13 r· in the proof of healing,

rejoicing
pref ix–16 To-day, though r· in some progress,
a 29– 6 they will have the crown of r·.
40–22 r· to enter into fellowship with him
s 140–11 but r· in the affluence of our God.
c 266– 2 are good, "r· the heart." — Psal. 19 : 8.
o 342–24 and they answer with r·.
r 479– 4 could the Scriptural r· be uttered by any mother,
ap 562–17 These are the stars in the crown of r·.

relapse
p 419– 8 If your patient from any cause suffers a r·,
419–12 Neither . . . has the power to cause disease or
    a r·.
419–23 A r· cannot in reality occur in mortals
419–31 If it is found necessary to treat against r·,

relapses
b 277– 5 non-intelligent r· into its own unreality.

related
s 152–14 It is r· that Sir Humphry Davy once
p 362– 1 r· in the seventh chapter of Luke's Gospel
g 556–31 It is r· that a father plunged his

relates
s 117–24 r· solely to human reason ;
127–15 r· especially to Science as applied to
128–27 Science r· to Mind, not matter.
ph 170–23 spiritual causation r· to human progress.
b 286– 1 what r· most nearly to the happiness of being.
290–14 To the spiritual class, r· the Scripture :
g 515–19 r· to the oneness, the tri-unity of Life, Truth,

relating
s 123– 6 as does the error r· to soul and body,
127–13 stand for everything r· to God,
ph 168–19 God's spiritual command r· to perfection,
p 381–23 human theories r· to health,
433– 5 He . . . explains the law r· to liver-complaint.

relation
exact
s 113–13 showing mathematically their exact r· to
little
b 297–30 has little r· to the actual or divine.
marriage
m 58–29 the chance for ill-nature in the marriage r·,
of God
f 206–15 In the scientific r· of God to man,
b 332– 2 r· of God to man and the universe.
of man
sp 94– 7 and of the r· of man to God,
s 114–25 It shows the scientific r· of man to God,
seeming
s 119–30 C. S. reverses the seeming r· of Soul and body
to God
ph 196–17 They have no r· to God wherewith to
f 215–26 in origin, in existence, and in his r· to God
231–23 the divine Science of being in man's r· to God,
b 316– 6 to find Christ, the real man and his r· to God,

f 205–32 When we fully understand our r· to the Divine

relations

m 68–13	its r· to your growth and to your influence
s 123– 1	theory as to the r· of the celestial bodies,
f 209–17	the r· which constituent masses hold
t 460– 4	necessary constituents and r· of all beings,"
r 470–32	The r· of God and man,

relationship

m 59–29	sacredness of this r· is losing its influence
ph 185–18	Such theories have no r· to C. S.,
b 332– 5	His tender r· to His spiritual creation.

relative

pref xi–30	a law r· to colleges having been passed,
ph 198–10	outlines his thought r· to disease,
f 232– 3	Many theories r· to God and man
233–28	The counter fact r· to any disease
o 355–14	r· value of the two conflicting theories
p 396– 6	Make no unnecessary inquiries r· to feelings

relaxes

s 162– 8	dissolves tumors, r· rigid muscles,

release

p 431–19	into close confinement until I should r· him.

released

s 363–17	who were r· from their obligations

relentless

p 407– 6	Man's enslavement to the most r· masters

reliable

s 120–16	nor can the material senses bear r· testimony
b 322–25	nor a r· religionist.

reliance

s 145–14	or r· on some other minor curative.
ph 167–30	Only through radical r· on Truth
170– 1	it robs man of r· on God,
179–29	sowing the seeds of r· on matter,
192– 4	only as we quit our r· upon that which
f 203–14	destroys r· on aught but God,

relief

p 371–13	looks for r· in all ways except the right one.
374– 4	the truth of being, . . . will bring r·.
421–30	material application for its r·.
t 443–19	other systems they fancy will afford r·.

relies

sp 79–11	Spiritualism r· upon human beliefs
b 277–19	Error r· upon a reversal of this order,
r 487–30	This faith r· upon an understood Principle.

relieve

a 18– 9	but not to do it for them nor to r· them of a
s 143–15	takes the lesser to r· the greater.
157–26	quiet mortal mind, and so r· the body;
p 373–23	and you r· the oppressed organ.
384– 3	We should r· our minds from the
398–17	are known to r· the symptoms of disease.
415–11	That is why opiates r· inflammation.
t 464–16	and the Scientists had failed to r· him,
r 493– 3	but only r· suffering temporarily,

relieved

a 25–23	by no means r· others from giving the
s 156–23	and was r· by taking them,
f 221–23	r· his stomach, and he ate

religion

and medicine

m 67–30	Systems of r· and medicine treat of
s 107–11	Through C. S., r· and medicine are inspired with
t 444–14	towards differing forms of r· and medicine,

any

sp 98–23	has not been considered a part of any r·,

being and

a 55– 1	any other sense of being and r· than theirs?

Christ's

o 355–17	declines to admit that Christ's r· has

essential

a 27–29	the essential r· he came to establish

fatal to

pr 7–32	Hypocrisy is fatal to r·.

his

s 136– 3	He taught his followers that his r· had a

history of

a 37–10	one stage with another in the history of r·.

Judaic

gl 597– 3	The Judaic r· consisted mostly of rites

motives and

ap 560–22	Abuse of the motives and r· of St. Paul

nature of

a 28–28	is to mistake the very nature of r·.

of Love

s 138–15	His sublime summary points to the r· of Love.

ordinary

s 139–29	opposed to C. S., as they are to ordinary r· ;

perfunctory

b 316–14	this spiritual idea and perfunctory r·,

popular

o 355–17	The other, popular r·, declines to admit that

religion

pure

m 64– 4	"Pure r· and undefiled — Jas. 1 : 27.

reason and

ph 173–26	Human reason and r· come slowly to the

revealed

g 557–24	revealed r· proclaims the Science of Mind

ritualistic

s 141– 2	the theological and ritualistic r· of the ages

scientific

s 141–27	The adoption of scientific r· and

superficial

gl 597–13	false foundations . . . of superficial r·,

system of

a 26–31	proof of Christianity was no form or system of r·

systems of

m 67–30	Systems of r· and medicine treat of
s 146– 4	Because our systems of r· are governed

their

a 52–30	as self-contradictory as their r·.
o 343–28	and reformed the sinner by their r·.

tribal

s 133–21	the limited form of a national or tribal r·.

true

pr 5–23	Such an error would impede true r·.
m 68– 2	understanding . . . will be the basis of true r·.

undefiled

ap 571–32	He enthrones pure and undefiled r·,

pr 4–32	and clothe r· in human forms.
a 20–26	The truth is the centre of all r·.
54–23	whose r· was something more than a name.
s 140–12	R· will then be of the heart and not of the
146–11	and r· becomes Christlike.
b 326–29	whose r· he had not understood,
351– 1	r· which sprang from half-hidden Israelitish
354–14	proofs that their Master's r· can

religionist

b 322–25	neither a temperate man nor a reliable r·.

religionists

f 224–12	Centuries ago r· were ready to

religions

sp 83–13	and here Science takes issue with popular r·.
s 142– 6	but modern r· generally omit all but one of
f 232–14	r· which contradict its Principle are false.

religious

a 36–30	R· history repeats itself
53–13	above and contrary to the world's r· sense.
sp 88–21	Excite the organ of veneration or r· faith,
s 132–18	other sanitary or r· systems,
133–23	sanitary methods, and a r· cultus.
139–12	the present new, yet old, reform in r· faith
ph 166–12	Mohammedan's belief is a r· delusion ;
c 267–13	in a r· sense, they have the same authority
b 306–17	this is the general r· opinion of mankind,
340–27	civil, criminal, political, and r· codes ;
o 359–22	early received her r· education.
r 496–28	Have Christian Scientists any r· creed?
497– 1	the important points, or r· tenets, of C. S. :

relinquish

ph 177– 2	it must r· all its errors, sicknesses, and sins.
f 249– 1	r· all theories based on sense-testimony,
251–22	leads the human mind to r· all error,
b 322–13	that finite belief may be prepared to r· its
o 357– 9	If mankind would r· the belief that

relinquished

b 314– 3	had r· the belief of substance-matter,

relinquishes

g 547–28	r· a material, sensual, and mortal theory of

relinquishing

pr 13–21	this will prevent us from r· the

relinquishment

pr 7– 6	r· of error deprives material sense of its
p 426–23	The r· of all faith in death

reluctance

p 420– 9	cannot produce this unnatural r·.

reluctant

t 450–16	many are r· to acknowledge that they

reluctantly

r 466–17	the point you will most r· admit,

rely

s 143– 9	if the sick cannot r· on God for help
144– 3	let us r· upon Mind,
f 202–28	and yet we r· on a drug . . . as if
g 549–22	false systems, which r· upon physics

remain

m 62–17	should be allowed to r· children in knowledge,
s 110–23	the Science and truth therein will forever r·
112–13	they nevertheless r· wholly human
ph 167–15	If God made . . . man must r· thus.
f 208–23	which cannot be lost nor r· forever unseen.

remain

b 290– 7	will r· as material as before the transition,
329–15	nor should he r· in the devouring flames.
p 376– 4	fear and the despair of recovery r· in thought.
404–13	while its effects still r· on the individual,
425–30	capacious lungs and want them to r· so,
431– 1	must r· silent until called for at this trial,
g 513–20	r· in God, who is the divinely creative Principle
557– 1	until the child could r· under water

remained

s 147–28	This rule r· to be discovered in C. S.
f 245–10	In this mental state she r· young.
b 317–30	r· a fleshly reality, so long as
317–31	so long as the Master r· an inhabitant of
r 471– 4	r· unchanged in its eternal history.

remaineth

b 288–18	"There r· therefore a rest — Heb. 4: 9.

remaining

r 470–22	the divine Principle of man r· perfect,
gl 586–24	meeting no response, but still r· love.

remains

sp 87– 8	their mental environment r· to be discerned,
98–20	r· inviolate for every man to understand and
s 153– 2	to such a degree that not a vestige of it r·.
164–14	Much yet r· to be said and done
164–24	the forever fact r· paramount
f 212–13	When the nerve is gone, . . . and the pain still r·,
238–19	Truth often r· unsought, until we
b 289–23	the fact r·, that God's universe is spiritual
302– 7	is thereby discerned and r· unchanged.
311–12	so long as the illusion . . . r·.
o 348–19	so long as it r· in mortal mind,
p 365–13	what mental quality r·, with which to
392– 3	Only while fear or sin r· can it bring forth death.
398–32	fact r· that evil is not mind.
t 464–10	She therefore r· unseen at her post,
r 470–23	divine idea or reflection, man r· perfect.
480– 6	then there r· only the darkness of vacuity
481–11	the unseen Truth, which r· forever intact.
486–21	So long as this error of belief r·,
487–10	Lost they cannot be, while Mind r·.

remanded

p 433–27	The prisoner is then r· to his cell

remands

g 532–12	condemns material man and r· him to dust.

remark

p 396– 7	Never startle with a discouraging r· about
g 523–14	It may be worth while here to r· that,

remarkable

ph 195–25	Novels, r· only for their exaggerated
b 313–15	that the author of this r· epistle
o 358–20	more frequently cited . . . than are his r· works
p 363–22	following it with that r· declaration

remarked

s 149–17	A physician of the old school r·

remarking

p 438– 1	r· that the Bible was better authority than

remedial

an 101–23	convince her that it is not a r· agent,

remedies

pref viii–18	by doctors using material r· ;
s 152–32	which demand different r· ;
156–13	her former physician had prescribed these r·,
ph 181– 1	more potent than all lower r·.
p 398–16	r·, sometimes not containing a particle of
427–27	when all such r· have failed?
t 453–19	from the use of material r·

remedy

divine

b 326– 7	and find the divine r· for every ill,

efficient

p 376–21	the efficient r· is to destroy the

for every woe

f 236–19	availability of good as the r· for every woe.

God's

s 143– 1	Truth is God's r· for error of every kind,

knowing the

t 455–12	if, knowing the r·, you fail to use the

man's

r 486– 6	What is man's r·?

material

p 427–26	what material r· has man when

of Truth

s 140– 1	demands the r· of Truth more than

perfect

p 394– 4	the universal and perfect r·.

permanent

f 217–25	The scientific and permanent r· for fatigue is

m 63–21	If the elective franchise for women will r· the
s 151– 5	could not possibly create a r· outside of itself,
156–30	In metaphysics, matter disappears from the r·

remedy

ph 165–19	when your r· lies in forgetting the whole thing ;
184– 8	The r· consists in probing the trouble to the
f 208–16	or that Spirit, . . . leaves the r· to matter.
229–31	The r· is Truth, not matter,
238–20	until we seek this r· for human
248–25	To r· this, we must first turn our gaze
p 385–20	your r· is at hand.
423–16	deals with matter as both his foe and his r·.
424–14	to counteract the working of a r· prescribed by
t 461–24	and Truth is their r·.
g 534–13	unfolded the r· for Adam, or error ;
552–22	From a material source flows no r· for

remember

pr 3–32	put the finger on the lips and r· our blessings.
a 28–22	R·, thou Christian martyr, it is enough if
m 59–21	r· how slight a word or deed may
66– 8	We do not half r· this in the sunshine of
66–17	it is well to r· how fleeting are human joys.
67–20	when we r· that through spiritual ascendency
sp 93– 2	R· Jesus, who nearly nineteen centuries ago
ph 165–18	in order to r· what has hurt you,
f 201– *	R·, Lord, the reproach of Thy— Psal. 89 : 50.
209–20	when we r· that they all must give place to
223– 9	R· that truth is greater than error,
240–24	R· that mankind must sooner or later,
b 302–14	let us r· that harmonious and immortal man
p 372– 1	R·, brain is not mind.
385–11	Let us r· that the eternal law of right,
394–28	We should r· that Life is God,
402–21	we rarely r· that we govern our own bodies.
414–28	R· that man's perfection is real and
423– 5	R· that the unexpressed belief oftentimes
t 445–31	"I tremble, when I r· that God is just,"
454–31	R· that the letter and mental argument
r 476–23	R· that the Scriptures say of mortal man :
g 557– 3	Parents should r· this, and
ap 566–12	If we r· the beautiful description
573–32	When you read this, r· Jesus' words,

remembered

s 130–23	author has often r· our Master's love for
146–21	r· not, even when its elevating effects

remembering

a 48–10	R· the sweat of agony which
s 107–16	yet r· that in reality God is our Life,
c 261–31	We should forget our bodies in r· good
p 419– 6	r· that God and His ideas alone are real
ap 562–25	but r· no more her sorrow

remembrance

p 407– 2	but there is a very sharp r· of it,

remind

s 161–19	r· one of the words of the

reminded

pr 3– 2	without being r· of His province.

reminders

p 411–10	and needed the arguments of truth for r·.

remit

a 36– 6	To r· the penalty due for sin,

remits

pr 11– 5	A magistrate sometimes r· the penalty,

remorse

a 47–22	and for a time quieted his r·.
gl 586–13	FIRE. Fear ; r·; lust ; hatred ;
588– 1	HELL. Mortal belief ; error; lust ; r·;

remote

ph 178– 8	The r· cause or belief of disease
f 230–31	the r·, predisposing, and the exciting cause
247– 1	The acute belief of . . . comes on at a r· period,
p 393– 6	ignorant that the predisposing, r·, and

remoteness

ap 576– 5	which to us seems hidden in the mist of r·,

remotest

ap 559–10	to the globe's r· bound.

removal

ph 168– 4	the r· of a single weight from either scale
f 219–19	the destruction of the belief will be the r· of
o 358–20	in the r· of disease
p 367– 5	pitiful patience with his fears and the r·

remove

a 40– 1	R· error from thought, and it will not
44–17	to r· the napkin and winding-sheet,
an 101–28	since error cannot r· the effects of error.
ph 173–28	to r· the error which the human mind alone
183–20	obedience to God will r· this necessity.
p 373–20	but to r· the effects of fear
377–20	R· the leading error or governing fear
377–22	and you r· the cause of all disease
377–23	You also r· in this way what are termed
378– 9	R· the error, and you destroy its effects.
382– 9	to r· unhealthy exhalations from the cuticle
400–20	When we r· disease by addressing the

remove

p 401–25   Would the drug r· paralysis,
403–10   The human mind is employed to r· the
404–14   you can r· this disorder as
415–14   Opiates do not r· the pain in any scientific
415–24   To r· the error producing disorder, you must
421– 8   in order to r· its beliefs,
424–21   the divine Mind can r· any obstacle,
t 447–25   r· the mask, point out the illusion,
g 542–23   teaches mortals not to r· the waymarks of God.
ap 569–27   how many periods of torture it may take to r·

removed

pr 1– *   *Be thou r·, and be thou cast into— Mark* 11 : 23.
a 53– 5   yet there never lived a man so far r· from
ph 197–14   r· from imbecility or disease.
f 229– 9   Not far r· from infidelity is the belief which
230–30   until the liability to be ill is r·.
o 350– 4   or as very far r· from daily experience.
p 370–12   are r· by using the same drug
371–10   and to be r· as involuntarily,
374– 5   Hatred and its effects . . . are r· by Love.
400– 6   before its influence . . . can be r·.
416– 5   r· by recognizing the truth of being.
g 557–17   the curse will be r· which says to woman,

removes

a 40– 9   Science r· the penalty only by
sp 79–12   C. S. r· these beliefs and hypotheses
80–17   Science never r· phenomena from the
b 290–21   Christ, Truth, r· all ignorance and sin.
323–22   r· thought from the body,
p 370–16   it r· through an opposite belief,
398–28   blind faith r· bodily ailments for a season,
t 463 13   r· properly whatever is offensive.
r 493–23   r· any other sense of moral or mental inharmony.

removing

a 40– 9   only by first r· the sin
ph 186– 1   only by r· the influence on him of this mind,
p 411–32   If you succeed in wholly r· the fear,
421–14   by r· the belief that this chemicalization

rename

b 309–16   until the Messiah should r· them.

renamed

b 309–21   to be r· in C. S. and led to deny

render

s 148–29   to r· help in time of physical need.
ph 183– 2   but the so-called laws of matter would r·
p 415–14   only r· mortal mind temporarily less fearful,
433– 6   conclusion is, that laws of nature r·
440–12   but no warping of justice can r·
440–24   and then r· obedience to these laws
t 445 15   You r· the divine law of healing obscure
447– 8   ignorant attempts to do good may r· you

rendered

a 19–30   which may be r· : Thou shalt have no
20– 1   He r· "unto Cæsar the— Matt. 22 : 21.
s 146– 6   schools have r· faith in drugs the fashion,
b 271 11   In Latin the word r· *disciple* signifies
313– 3   may be r· "Jesus the anointed,"
p 375–17   should be understood and so r· fruitless,
381– 1   is r· null and void by the law of Life,
383– 4   a body r· pure by Mind as well as
423–21   has r· himself strong, instead of weak,
r 466 22   and cannot be r· in the plural,
474–12   meaning of the Greek word r· *miracle*

rendering

f 219–28   not r· to God the honor due to Him

renders

f 211–23   The transfer of . . . Science r· impossible.
218–12   What r· both sin and sickness difficult of cure
b 324– 1   r· thought receptive of the advanced idea.
o 360– 6   materiality r· these ideals imperfect
p 422–27   and r· them fatal at certain points,
435–23   for no demand, human or divine, r· it just
t 455–22   r· any abuse of the mission an impossibility.
461–22   r· your case less curable,
g 540–17   Science r· "unto Cæsar the— Matt. 22 : 21.

rends

f 226–20   Science r· asunder these fetters,

renew

m 59–21   may r· the old trysting-times.
p 426–14   Man should r· his energies and endeavors,

renewal

m 57–13   bringing sweet seasons of r·
s 137–12   and his r· of the question,
f 241–14   transformation of the body by the r· of Spirit.
gl 582– 9   R· of affections ; self-offering ;

renewed

s 137– 9   This r· inquiry meant :
162–20   the structure has been r·,
g 556–11   belief dies to live again in r· forms,

renewedly

s 109–25   Scripture of Isaiah is r· fulfilled :

renewing

a 49–20   transformed by the r· of the infinite Spirit.

renounce

t 451– 4   must r· aggression, oppression and the pride of

renowned

b 333– 7   Joshua, the r· Hebrew leader.

rent

f 242–26   one web of consistency without seam or r·.
p 398– 5   spirit [error] cried, and r· him— *Mark* 9 : 26.
gl 597–11   It r· the veil of the temple.

reopen

ph 171– 6   man will r· with the key of divine Science

reopened

pref xii–19   as its President, r· the College

repaired

p 439– 9   At this request Death r· to the spot

repast

t 452–16   Better is the frugal intellectual r·

repayment

sp 97–32   Earth has no r· for the persecutions

repeat

pr 5– 8   Temptation bids us r· the offence,
6–10   supposition . . . we shall be free to r· the offence.
11–14   leaves the offender free to r· the offence,
f 243–12   in order to confirm and r· the
r 487–12   and it will r· the wonder.
g 520– 6   can r· only an infinitesimal part of what exists.

repeated

s 126–12   seems to have reversed it and r· it materially ;
134– 1   To-day the cry of bygone ages is r·,
136–20   This ghostly fancy was r· by Herod
137– 8   Yearning to be understood, the Master r·,
f 207–28   The spiritual fact, r· in the action of man
240–20   past failures will be r· until
243–14   That those wonders are not more commonly r·
r 474– 5   reception accorded to Truth . . . is r·
g 516–27   To emphasize this momentous thought, it is r·
557– 1   r· this operation daily, until the child

repeating

pref xi–17   and r· itself, coming now
a 43–10   and is now r· its ancient history.
sp 86– 6   R· his inquiry, he was answered by the
s 135–17   There is to-day danger of r· the offence
t 452–24   simply by r· the author's words,
g 527–26   Here the lie represents God as r· creation,

repeats

a 28–28   Error r· itself.
36–30   Religious history r· itself in the suffering of
sp 80–10   r· weekly the assertion that
b 301– 2   r· the color, form, and action of the

repel

p 363– 8   Did he r· her adoration?

repelled

t 449–23   which is attracted or r· according to

repent

a 19–21   if the sinner continues to pray and r·,
b 309 18   Only those, who r· of sin and forsake the
g 522–32   Does the . . . Principle of divine law change
          or r·?

repentance

a 19–17   Every pang of r· and suffering,
19–23   the practical r·, which reforms the heart
35– 1   and his disciples' grief into r·,
s 140–24   a man-projected God, liable to wrath, r·,
f 242– 1   Through r·, spiritual baptism, and regeneration,
p 363–30   r·, reformation, and growth in wisdom?
364–26   by divine r·,
367–15   with . . . perfume of *gratitude*, with tears of r·
gl 584– 4   A corporeal mortal embracing duplicity, r·,
598–20   mortality ; space for r·.

repentant

p 404–13   If the evil is over in the r· mortal mind,

repented

p 363–25   Had she r· and reformed,

repents

b 329–24   Always right, its divine Principle never r·,

repetition

pr 2–31   Asking God to *be* God is a vain r·.
sp 73–13   its fruit,— the r· of evil.
s 157–11   with such r· of thought-attenuations,

repetitions

pr 10– 9   millions of vain r· will never
13– 9   "vain r·," such as the heathen— *Matt.* 6 : 7.

replace

p 428–20   r· them with the life which is spiritual,
r 495–23   r· mortality with immortality,

replaced

r 489– 6   would be r· as readily as the lobster's claw,

replaces
s 123–14 and r· the objects of material sense with

replenish
g 511– 4 "multiply and r· the earth."— *Gen.* 1 : 28.
517–26 multiply, and r· the earth,— *Gen.* 1 : 28.

replied
s 136–14 They r·, "Some say that thou art — *Matt.* 16 : 14.
137–16 Simon r· for his brethren,
p 363–19 Simon r·, "He to whom he— *Luke* 7 : 43.
411–15 r· that his name was Legion.
g 554– 1 It can only be r·, that C. S. reveals

replies
m 69–22 If the father r·, "God creates man through man,"
o 360– 4 other artist r· : "You wrong my experience.
p 411– 7 r· more readily when his name is spoken ;
432–18 and Governor Mortality r· in the affirmative.
g 554–16 Error r·, "God made you."

repliest
ph 181– 4 "Who art thou that r· to Spirit?

reply
a 45–26 His r· was : "Spirit hath not— *Luke* 24 : 39.
s 131–31 In r· to John's inquiry,
132– 1 Jesus returned an affirmative r·,
132– 4 his r· : "Go and show John— *Matt.* 11 : 4.
136–17 this r· may indicate that some of the people
137–17 and his r· set forth a great fact :
f 243–16 The clay cannot r· to the potter.
r 489–21 affirmative r· would contradict the Scripture,
g 545–28 Truth has but one r· to all error,

report
a 24–12 will believe our r·, and rise into
an 100–14 to investigate Mesmer's theory and to r·
101–12 Their r· stated the results as follows :
101–19 This r· was adopted by the
s 137–14 in their citation of the common r· about him.
ph 193–29 I cannot attest the truth of that r·,
194– 9 Truth sends a r· of health over the body.
f 211– 2 and r· how they feel,
b 284–31 but neither sensation nor r· goes from
298– 8 What is termed material sense can r· only a
p 432–21 shortly after the r· of the crime,

reported
an 100–16 r· to the government as follows :
p 438–10 in which Mortal Man was r· to reside,
439–31 to whatever locality is r· to be haunted by

reports
s 122–13 r· to this so-called mind its status
f 218– 9 The r· of sickness may form a
218–10 a coalition with the r· of sin,
p 389– 8 mortal mind, which r· food as undigested.
409–13 belief, that the . . . suffers and r· disease
g 551– 2 senses and their r· are unnatural,

repose
s 128–14 and requires less r·.
f 218– 8 more than hours of r· in unconsciousness.

reposed
s 160– 7 Unsupported by the faith r· in it,
ph 169–14 The faith r· in these things should find

represent
sp 74–24 Who will say . . . that darkness can r· light,
s 111–18 what this inverted image is meant to r·.
118–27 r· a kingdom necessarily divided against
151– 3 but this one factor they r· to be body,
c 256–24 No form . . . is adequate to r· infinite Love.
265–16 The senses r· birth as untimely
b 331–28 They r· a trinity in unity,
o 344– 4 this is claimed to r· the normal, healthful,
p 415–23 r· the action of all the organs of the
430–29 a witness testifies thus :— I r· Health-laws.
r 466–11 these contrasting pairs of terms r·
g 531– 8 r· the higher moral sentiments,

representation
s 141–30 Let it have fair r· by the press.
g 510–16 The sun is a metaphorical r· of Soul
gl 591– 6 MAN. . . . the full r· of Mind.

representative
a 52–24 The highest earthly r· of God,
b 300–24 If . . . God would have no r·,
306–13 If Life or Soul and its r·, man,
p 427– 4 Soul is never without its r·.
ap 565–11 the masculine r· of the spiritual idea,

representatives
b 293–12 both strata, . . . are false r· of man.
299–12 Angels are God's r·.
gl 582–28 The spiritual thoughts and r· of Life,
583– 5 The r· of Soul, not corporeal sense ;

represented
pr 13–26 is r· as a corporeal creator ;
a 33–21 Let not the flesh, but the Spirit, be r· in me.
s 119–21 is r· only by the idea of goodness ;
124–17 r· as subject to growth, maturity, and decay,

represented
f 214– 9 Adam, r· in the Scriptures as formed from
b 294–24 in which matter is r· as divided into
299–19 figuratively r· in Scripture as a tree,
316–12 Jesus r· Christ, the true idea
p 378–20 is r· by two material . . . bases.
g 504–16 is r· as taking place on so many *evenings* and
522–19 is r· as the life-giving principle of the earth.
522–20 Spirit is r· as entering matter
536– 7 the sea, . . . is r· as having passed away.
537–12 Creation is there r· as spiritual,
537–29 and divine Love, . . . is r· as changeable.
ap 561–13 r· the correlation of divine Principle and
565–18 immaculate idea, r· first by man
569– 1 as Life, r· by the Father ;
569– 2 as Truth, r· by the Son ;
569– 3 as Love, r· by the Mother.
574–17 r· by the seven angelic vials

representing
b 294–19 r· Spirit, and mortal man,
294–20 r· the error that life and intelligence are in
p 376–24 r· man as healthy instead of diseased,
g 540–22 r· error as assuming a divine character,

represents
sp 92–13 This r· the serpent in the act of commending
s 140– 5 The Bible r· Him as saying :
ph 177–16 which r· the erroneous theory of
c 259– 4 r· infinite Mind, the sum of all substance.
263– 6 Immortal spiritual man alone r· the
b 272–29 God is the divine Principle of all that r· Him
282– 6 The circle r· the infinite
282– 7 the straight line r· the finite,
282– 9 The sphere r· good, the self-existent and
282–10 the straight line r· evil,
334–24 The Revelator r· the Son of man as
p 378–16 r· the power of Truth over error,
g 525– 5 *mankind* r· the Adamic race,
527–11 Here the metaphor r· God, Love, as
527–26 Here the lie r· God as repeating creation,
529–24 nothing in the animal kingdom which r· the
530–17 This myth r· error as always asserting its
546–13 r· error as starting from an idea of good
ap 560–10 Heaven r· harmony, and divine Science
575– 9 r· the light and glory of divine Science.
gl 580– 3 not God's man, who r· the one God
580–21 The name Adam r· the false supposition

reproach
f 201– * *Remember, Lord, the r· of*— *Psal.* 89 : 50.
201– * *how I do bear in my bosom the r·*— *Psal.* 89 : 50.

reproached
f 201– * *wherewith Thine enemies have r·,*— *Psal.* 89 : 51.
201– * *wherewith they have r· the*— *Psal.* 89 : 51.

reproduce
m 61–18 may r· in their own helpless little ones
sp 75–23 to r· the presence of those who
87– 2 They copy or r· them, even when
87–28 can perceive and r· these impressions.
87–29 Memory may r· voices long ago silent.
f 246–32 Acute and chronic beliefs r· their own types.
b 306– 4 would . . . resort to death to r· spiritual life.
p 372– 7 that its sensations can r· man,
r 488–28 Soul could r· them in all their perfection ;
g 512–12 and consequently r· their own characteristics.
gl 584–24 thence to r· a mortal universe,

reproduced
p 378–22 even as poetry and music are r·
413–30 such ills may be r· in the very ailments feared.

reproduces
ph 198–21 and r· a picture of healthy and
g 507–16 which r· the multitudinous forms of Mind
508– 3 only as the divine Mind is All and r· all

reproducing
f 248–17 Are you r· it?
b 277–14 preserving their original species,— like r· like.
314–12 When Jesus spoke of r· his body,

reproduction
ph 189–25 From mortal mind comes the r· of the species,
b 277–16 In r·, the order of genus and species
302–31 r· by Spirit's individual ideas
g 549–10 three different methods of r·
553–13 to their maintenance and r·,

reproof
pr 7– 3 that Jesus' r· was pointed and pungent
gl 594–15 love rebuking error ; r· of sensualism.

reprove
t 443–21 "R·, rebuke, exhort— *II Tim.* 4 : 2.

reproved
pref x–30 lest their works be r·.

repudiate
p 440–27 r· the false testimony of Personal Sense.

repudiated
p 418–18 the belief must be r·,

repudiates
- *f* 207–16   *r·* self-evident impossibilities,
- *g* 541–25   Now it *r·* even the human duty of
-    550–32   As C. S. *r·* self-evident impossibilities,

repulsion
- *t* 449–26   only to separate through simultaneous *r·*.

repulsive
- *s* 163–32   or to reconcile the fixed and *r·* antipathies of

reputation
- *a* 53– 8   The *r·* of Jesus was the very opposite of
- *f* 236– 6   Is it not professional *r·* and emolument
- *t* 456– 9   a *r·* experimentally justified by their efforts.

reputed
- *pref* viii–21   the *r·* longevity of the Antediluvians,
- *an* 101–11   phenomena exhibited by a *r·* clairvoyant.

request
- *pr* 2–17   A *r·* that God will save us
-    10–31   In this case infinite Love will not grant the *r·*.
-    12– 2   A mere *r·* that God will heal the sick
- *p* 439– 8   At this *r·* Death repaired to the spot

requested
- *ph* 184–31   I then *r·* her to look at the weather-vane.

requests
- *pr* 9–10   though we give no evidence of the sincerity of our *r·*

require
- *a* 23– 2   Wisdom and Love may *r·* many sacrifices
-    44–15   He did not *r·* the skill of a surgeon
- *s* 141– 6   Why? Because his precepts *r·* the disciple to
- *ph* 179–14   and the body then seems to *r·* such treatment.
- *f* 242–31   and *r·* of Christians the proof which he gave,
- *c* 257–30   It would *r·* an infinite form to contain
- *o* 360–10   They *r·* less self-abnegation,
- *p* 404–27   Both cures *r·* the same method
-    420–20   or diminishes . . . as the case may *r·*,
- *t* 452– 8   Walking in the light, we . . . *r·* it ;
- *g* 501– 6   seems so smothered . . . . as to *r·* explication ;
-    532– 2   Did God at first create . . . but afterwards *r·*

required
- *pr* 2–18   is not all that is *r·*.
-    5– 4   The next and great step *r·* by wisdom is
- *a* 32– 3   In ancient Rome a soldier was *r·* to
- *m* 59– 9   Man should not be *r·* to participate in all the
- *sp* 77–13   The period *r·* for this dream of
- *s* 142– 2   *r·* for self-establishment and propagation.
-    143–11   matter *r·* a material and human belief
- *ph* 173– 9   is *r·* to be made manifest through
- *f* 239–29   The counter fact . . . is *r·* to cure it.
- *o* 351–17   proof of Christianity, which Jesus *r·*,
- *p* 432–24   was *r·* to confirm his testimony.
- *t* 464– 6   and how much time and toil are still *r·*
- *r* 473–25   a better understanding of God . . . is *r·*,
-    482– 8   where the deific meaning is *r·*.

requirement
- *p* 413– 5   A single *r·*, beyond what is necessary

requirements
- *pr* 7–14   wholesome perception of God's *r·*.
- *s* 127–11   according to the *r·* of the context.
- *f* 235– 6   one who does not obey the *r·* of
- *t* 445– 1   the Scientist must conform to God's *r·*.

requires
- *a* 22–30   Justice *r·* reformation of the sinner.
-    23– 4   The atonement *r·* constant self-immolation
- *m* 57–20   but *r·* all mankind to share it.
- *sp* 97–23   It *r·* courage to utter truth ;
- *s* 128–14   and *r·* less repose.
-    162–26   for it *r·* only a fuller understanding of
- *ph* 198–14   but to do this *r·* attention.
- *f* 253–27   God never *r·* obedience to a so-called
-    254– 6   God *r·* perfection, but not until
- *b* 278–17   another admission, — namely,
- *t* 449–16   it *r·* a higher understanding to teach this
-    456–25   A Christian Scientist *r·* my work
- *ap* 571– 7   It *r·* the spirit of our blessed Master

requisite
- *pref* x–30   No intellectual proficiency is *r·* in the learner,
- *pr* 11–23   We know that a desire for holiness is *r·*
- *a* 25–24   the *r·* proofs of their own piety.
-    34– 7   no other commemoration is *r·*,
- *m* 61–32   If the propagation of a higher human species is *r·*
- *s* 141– 3   More than profession is *r·*
-    148– 3   implying that the *r·* power to heal was in Mind.
- *ph* 195–19   Academics of the right sort are *r·*.
- *b* 327–23   Moral courage is *r·* to meet the wrong
- *o* 361–31   and the *r·* revisions of SCIENCE AND HEALTH
- *p* 383– 7   influence of the divine Mind on the body is *r·*,
- *t* 448–21   spiritual qualifications *r·* for healing,
-    461–18   if this be *r·* to protect others.
-    461–32   are *r·* for a thorough comprehension of C. S.
- *g* 527–30   Was it *r·* for the formation of man
-    552– 9   even where the proof *r·* to sustain this

rescue
- *p* 398–30   come to the *r·*, to work a radical cure.
-    436–23   struggled hard to *r·* the prisoner
-    439–23   You came to his *r·*, only to

rescued
- *p* 382–24   *r·* from seeming spiritual oblivion,

researches
- *s* 152–21   The author's medical *r·* and experiments
- *g* 548–22   Had the naturalist, through his tireless *r·*,
-    549–20   Here these material *r·* culminate

resemblance
- *f* 207–31   discord, which bears no *r·* to spirituality,

resemblances
- *f* 239–31   mortal mind sends forth its own *r·*,

resemble
- *b* 329–17   To be discouraged, is to *r·* a pupil in

resembles
- *sp* 97– 6   and so-called matter *r·* its essence,
- *s* 164– 1   *r·* the groping of Homer's Cyclops
- *g* 531–30   theory of material life at no point *r·*
-    541– 2   and more nearly *r·* a mind-offering

resembling
- *sp* 77–28   a state *r·* that of blighted buds,
- *b* 305– 6   is not the original, though *r·* it.

resentment
- *a* 48–22   thus rebuking *r·* or animal courage.

reservation
- *ph* 183–22   No *r·* is made for any lesser loyalty.

reservoir
- *ph* 180–15   mental *r·* already overflowing with that emotion

reside
- *p* 398–23   Appetite and disease *r·* in mortal mind,
-    438–10   in which Mortal Man was reported to *r·*,

residence
- *f* 220–13   and procures a summer *r·* with more ease than
- *p* 432– 8   testifies : . . . I convey messages from my *r·* in

resident
- *f* 209–28   hypothesis of . . . intelligence *r·* in matter,
- *b* 283–32   Are mentality, immortality, . . . *r·* in matter?
- *r* 482– 5   hypothesis that soul is . . . *r·* in matter.
- *ap* 570–31   the power of good *r·* in divine Mind.

resides
- *p* 432–12   says : . . . Body, in which Mortal Man *r·*.
-    437– 1   in which province Mortal Man *r·*.
- *g* 546–28   *r·* in the good this system accomplishes,

resigned
- *p* 416–22   when the mortal has *r·* his body
-    431–17   all these assistants *r·* to me,
- *g* 539–15   Has Spirit *r·* to matter the government of

resist
- *an* 101–25   and upon their subjects who do not *r·* it,
- *s* 128–24   he should not *r·* Truth, which banishes
- *f* 218–25   R· the temptation to believe in matter as
- *p* 393–12   to *r·* all that is unlike good.
-    406–19   R· evil — error of every sort
-    420–11   they can *r·* disease and ward it off,

resistance
- *s* 134–30   spiritual power over material *r·*.
- *f* 224–19   Cold disdain, stubborn *r·*,
- *b* 317– 8   R· to Truth will haunt his steps,
-    329–32   Human *r·* to divine Science weakens

resisted
- *f* 223–29   as truth urges upon mortals its *r·* claims ;

resisting
- *p* 388– 5   which is a *r·* state of mortal mind,
- *t* 446–24   R· evil, you overcome it

resists
- *s* 126–32   If Christendom *r·* the author's application of

resolve
- *pr* 7–13   unfavorable to spiritual growth, sober *r·*,
-    15–18   We must *r·* to take up the cross,
- *ph* 199–31   his power of putting *r·* into action
- *g* 514–17   They carry the baggage of stern *r·*,

resolved
- *p* 374–28   *r·* into its primitive mortal elements.

resolves
- *s* 123–14   excludes matter, *r·* *things* into *thoughts*,
- *b* 269–14   Metaphysics *r·* things into thoughts,
- *p* 428– 4   *r·* the dark visions of material sense

resolving
- *g* 510–24   by the *r·* of fluids into solids,
-    510–25   suppositional *r·* of thoughts into

resort
- *ph* 166–25   and only as a last *r·*, turns to God.
-    181–12   when you *r·* to any except spiritual means.
-    181–25   It is unnecessary to *r·* to aught besides Mind
- *b* 285–26   and *r·* to matter instead of Spirit for the
-    306– 4   They would . . . *r·* to death to reproduce

resort
p 427–28   Spirit is his last *r·*, but it should have been his
427–29   it should have been his first and only *r·*.
t 443– 5   a *r·* to faith in corporeal means
443–18   and leave invalids free to *r·* to whatever

resorted
ph 166–27   or he would have *r·* to Mind first.

resorting
p 415–13   by *r·* to matter instead of to Mind.

resounded
p 442– 6   *r·* throughout the vast audience-chamber

resources
m 60–29   Soul has infinite *r·* with which to bless
p 387–11   nor . . . trespass upon God-given powers and *r·*,

respect
pr 8–19   are like charity in one *r·*,
s 151– 8   Great *r·* is due the motives and
162–29   With due *r·* for the faculty,
t 452–12   may provoke envy, but it will also attract *r·*.
g 541– 6   Lord [Jehovah] had *r·* unto Abel,— *Gen. 4 : 4.*
541– 8   but unto Cain, . . . He had not *r·*.— *Gen. 4 : 5.*
541– 9   Had God more *r·* for the homage

respected
p 437–14   the testimony of matter *r·* ;

respecting
a 28– 9   While *r·* all that is good in the Church

resplendency
f 252–29   with the *r·* of consuming fire.

resplendent
f 247–29   shining *r·* and eternal over age and decay.

respond
p 411– 6   the body would *r·* more quickly,

responds
sp 89–15   the body *r·* to this belief,

response
pref viii–20   A vigorous "No" is the *r·*
a 48– 7   There was no *r·* to that human yearning,
gl 586–24   love meeting no *r·*, but remaining love.

responses
t 461–20   Your *r·* should differ because of the

responsibilities
m 68–13   Consider its obligations, its *r·*,

responsibility
a 18– 9   nor to relieve them of a single *r·*.
m 61–25   a greater *r·*, a more solemn charge,
ph 166– 5   or shrinking from its implied *r·*,

responsible
s 119–12   is not only to make Him *r·* for all disasters,
g 533–17   saying, "The woman, whom Thou gavest me, is
           r·."

rest
and drink
ap 570–16   are waiting and watching for *r·* and drink.
at
s 119–27   the earth is in motion and the sun at *r·*.
p 415–28   Before the thoughts are fully at *r·*,
create the
g 532– 3   in order to create the *r·* of the human family?
gives
f 217–20   When mentality gives *r·* to the body,
peace and
gl 586– 2   EVENING. . . . peace and *r·* .
sweetest
g 520– 1   The highest and sweetest *r·*, . . . is in holy work.

a 31–20   and at last we shall *r·*,
38– 6   doctrine . . . few to be saved, while the *r·* are
sp 79–24   says : . . . brain is overtaxed, and you must *r·*.
s 154–26   says . . . "You look tired," "You need *r·*,"
c 264– 9   Where shall the gaze *r·*
b 269–13   The categories of metaphysics *r·* on one basis,
288–19   a *r·* to the people of God"— *Heb. 4 : 9.*
317–11   These blessed benedictions *r·* upon
320– 9   must *r·* upon both the literal and moral ;"
o 358–24   Sometimes it is said : "*R·* assured that
p 380– 1   may *r·* at length on some receptive thought,
383–14   because mind and body *r·* on the same basis.
387–11   we are able to *r·* in Truth,
t 460– 1   and *r·* his demonstration on this sure basis.
g 501–15   Love for whose *r·* the weary ones sigh

rested
g 519–23   and He *r·* on the seventh day— *Gen. 2 : 2.*

restful
s 119–32   is but the humble servant of the *r·* Mind,

resting
sp 79–14   *r·* on divine Principle, not on
b 316–30   *r·* on the basis of matter,
p 424–20   through unspoken thoughts *r·* on your patient.

resting
p 426–11   *r·* instead of wearying one.
430– 7   and strengthen its base by *r·* upon Spirit
t 459–13   instead of *r·* on the omnipotence of the

resting-place
a 45– 3   and stepped forth from his gloomy *r·*,

restitution
pr 11– 9   always demands *r·* before

restless
p 433–13   the prisoner grows *r·*.

restoration
sp 74– 6   as impossible as would be the *r·* to its

restore
a 51–22   purpose in healing was not alone to *r·* health,
ph 174– 2   The Esquimaux *r·* health by incantations
p 401–25   Would the drug . . . *r·* will and action
440–31   to *r·* to Mortal Man the rights of which
g 555–28   Our great example, Jesus, could *r·* the
gl 585–13   first come and *r·* all things."— *Matt. 17 : 11.*

restored
sp 75–14   Jesus *r·* Lazarus by the understanding
79– 5   health *r·* by changing the patient's thoughts
s 162–17   the author has *r·* health in cases of
162–22   carious bones have been *r·* to healthy conditions.
162–23   I have *r·* what is called the lost substance of
ph 185– 5   but was *r·* to health.
b 309– 4   to use the word of the Psalmist, *r·* his Soul,
321–23   *r·* his hand to its natural condition
o 348–32   health has been *r·*, and longevity increased.
352–28   will depart and health be *r·*.
p 373– 8   partly because they were willing to be *r·*,
398–14   *r·* whole, like as the other."— *Matt. 12 : 13·*
435–34   be *r·* to the liberty of which

restores
s 124–30   and so *r·* them to their rightful home
162– 8   *r·* carious bones to soundness.
f 242–28   while inspiration *r·* every part of the
p 390– 9   the right understanding of Him *r·* harmony.
423–13   and it *r·* the harmony of man.
r 486–16   If death *r·* sight, sound,

restoreth
ap 578– 8   [LOVE] *r·* my soul— *Psal. 23 : 3.*

restoring
o 347–18   *r·* an essential element of Christianity,
347–20   Science of Christianity which is *r·* it,
p 375–19   while *r·* him physically through divine Love.

restrain
an 105– 4   in order to *r·* crime, to prevent deeds

restricted
an 105– 8   to admit that the power of human law is *r·* to

restricting
s 161–12   tyrannical law, *r·* the practice of medicine.

rests
sp 80–30   this belief *r·* on the common conviction that
s 128–27   It *r·* on fixed Principle
155–13   dissent or faith, unless it *r·* on Science, is
157– 8   C. S. exterminates the drug, and *r·* on Mind
ph 185–18   C. S., which *r·* on the conception of God as
f 218– 7   The consciousness of Truth *r·* us more than
233–16   shadow of His right hand *r·* upon the hour.
248– 3   Its halo *r·* upon its object.
b 283–12   admits of no error, but *r·* upon understanding.
291–12   Universal salvation *r·* on progression and
296–25   it *r·* upon foundations which time is
p 414–20   Christian Scientists' argument *r·* on the
t 446–20   for victory *r·* on the side of immutable right.
453– 7   until victory *r·* on the side of invincible truth.
457–29   demonstration *r·* on one Principle,
458– 1   Mental quackery *r·* on the
460– 6   Mind-healing *r·* on the apprehension of
r 492–26   On this statement *r·* the Science of being,
g 514–13   or *r·* in "green pastures,— *Psal. 23 : 2.*
519–25   God *r·* in action.
555–23   Creation *r·* on a spiritual basis.
gl 583–13   *r·* upon and proceeds from divine Principle.

result (noun)
affect a
g 553–31   how belief can affect a *r·* which
favorable
p 423– 5   diminishes the tendency towards a favorable *r·*.
glorious
f 202–13   For this glorious *r·* C. S. lights the
good
o 352–31   To accomplish a good *r·*, it is
of education
ph 176–26   All disease is the *r·* of education,
of inharmony
f 233–32   sickness, which is solely the *r·* of inharmony
of sin
pr 6–11   To cause suffering as the *r·* of sin,
of teaching
o 348–30   but this I do aver, that, as a *r·* of teaching C. S.,

result (noun)
  opposite
    p 385–30 opposite belief would produce the opposite *r·*.
  precipitate the
    p 436–19 to precipitate the *r·*
  same
    s 128–30 must always bring the same *r·*.
  this
    ph 187–11 and then impute this *r·* to another
    198–31 does not follow that . . . produced this *r·*
    p 391–13 No law of God hinders this *r·*.
    t 449–31 and unless this *r·* follows,
  watch the
    s 156–18 to give her unmedicated pellets and watch the *r·*,
    p 411–29 Watch the *r·* of this simple rule of C. S.,

    s 160–32 Is a stiff joint . . . as much a *r·* of law as the
    ph 170– 5 the *r·* of the exercise of faith in
    178– 5 the *r·* is controlled by the majority
    199– 7 nobody believes that mind is producing such a *r·*
    f 219–10 and then expect that the *r·* will be harmony.
    248–21 *r·* is that you are liable to follow those
    b 271–14 *r·* of their cultivated spiritual understanding
    309– 7 The *r·* of Jacob's struggle thus appeared.
    328– 6 What is the *r·*?
    o 342– 5 the *r·* of some unqualified condemnations
    p 365–23 *r·* will correspond with the spiritual intent.
    386– 7 no such *r·* occurs without mind to demand it
    386–21 suffering was merely the *r·* of your belief.
    387–23 cannot suffer as the *r·* of any labor of love,
    393–19 as the *r·* of a law of any kind,
    r 485–17 and as the *r·* of spiritual growth.
    485–21 *r·* of the mortal error which Christ, . . . destroys
    486–12 Death is not the *r·* of Truth
    488– 1 The *r·* of our teachings is
    g 505–26 This understanding . . . is not the *r·* of scholarly

result (verb)
  ph 183–16 The supposed laws which *r·* in weariness
  b 277– 7 good cannot *r·* in evil.
  304–14 can never produce mind nor life *r·* in death.
  306– 3 They would first make life *r·* in death,
  p 384–27 nor any other disease will over *r·* from
  435– 9 an act which should *r·* in good to himself

resulted
  b 269– 4 have *r·* from the philosophy of the serpent.
  o 342–32 even if their treatment *r·* in the death of

resulting
  sp 81–26 the inharmony *r·* from material sense
  f 204– 9 *r·* in a third person (mortal man)
  p 383–31 another medical mistake, *r·* from
  g 551–31 the *r·* germ is doomed to the same routine.
  gl 591–10 MATTER . . . life *r·* in death, and death in

results
  are sure
    t 459–25 the *r·* are sure if the Science is understood.
  bad
    b 329–16 Until one is able to prevent bad *r·*,
  better
    p 389–11 the better *r·* of Mind's opposite evidence.
  bodily
    f 245–23 The bodily *r·* of her belief that she was young
    p 392–26 conclusions as you wish realized in bodily *r·*,
  certain
    t 459–30 treats disease with more certain *r·* than
    r 484–18 Certain *r·*, supposed to proceed from drugs,
  evil
    f 230–13 so as to bring about certain evil *r·*,
  favorable
    ph 177–27 are expecting favorable *r·*,
  glorious
    ap 568– 7 warfare in Science, and the glorious *r·* of
  grand
    t 448–23 the grand *r·* of Truth and Love.
  harmonious
    c 259–31 that they may produce harmonious *r·*.
  higher
    c 260–16 and to bring out better and higher *r·*,
  its
    p 384–13 Through this action of thought and its *r·*
    425– 3 induces this conclusion and its *r·*.
  medical
    s 155–18 and produces all medical *r·*,
  of belief
    ph 184– 6 Belief produces the *r·* of belief,
  of false opinions
    p 403–17 producing on mortal body the *r·* of false opinions;
  of sin
    g 535–14 It unveils the *r·* of sin
  produces the very
    p 379–24 produces the very *r·* she dreads.
  produce the very
    s 154–20 and they produce the very *r·* which
  their
    f 218–31 the moral and physical are as one in their *r·*.
    p 393– 6 ignorant . . . of its own actions, and of their *r·*,

results
  unlike
    sp 86–12 Opposites . . . produce unlike *r·*.

  pref viii–29 give to friends the *r·* of her Scriptural study,
  xi– 4 which action in some unexplained way *r·* in
  xi– 9 *r·* now, as in Jesus' time,
  pr 11–21 only the *r·* of mortals' own faith.
  an 101–12 Their report stated the *r·* as follows :
  f 231–12 if truth *r·* in error, then
  b 272–20 the *r·* of the ghastly farce of
  289–21 belief that matter has life *r·*, . . . in a belief in
  325– 8 *r·* in infinite blessings to mortals.
  p 404–17 *r·* from metaphysical healing,
  408–26 and the *r·* would be perceptibly different.
  g 552–28 *r·* in a return to the original species.
  gl 580–25 supposition that . . . Mind *r·* in matter,

resume
  p 373–25 disabled organ will *r·* its healthy functions.

resurrected
  b 295–31 further teaches that . . . his immortal soul is *r·*

resurrection
  after his
    a 46–14 after his *r·* he proved to the physical senses
    b 317–22 after his *r·* from the grave,
  after the
    a 24–32 After the *r·*, even the unbelieving Thomas
    45–22 They who earliest saw Jesus after the *r·*
  and the life
    a 31–16 makes Jesus "the *r·* and the life"—*John* 11 : 25.
    b 292– 7 to us "the *r·* and the life"—*John* 11 : 25.
  his
    a 34–20 His *r·* was also their resurrection.
    b 292–31 In his *r·* and ascension, Jesus showed that
    315– 1 Jesus proved them wrong by his *r·*,
    r 497–21 the crucifixion of Jesus and his *r·*
  their
    a 34–20 His resurrection was also their *r·*.

    a 42–15 The *r·* of the great demonstrator of God's power
    m 56– * *In the r· they neither marry, nor*— *Matt.* 22 : 30.
    64–10 in the *r·* there should be no more marrying nor
    69–28 and the *r·* from the dead,— *Luke* 20 : 35.
    f 232–30 and the *r·* to spiritual life.
    b 291–25 No *r·* from the grave awaits Mind or Life,
    296– 1 error theorizes . . . man has a *r·* from dust ;
    305–31 Sadducees reasoned falsely about the *r·*,
    g 509– 2 This period corresponds to the *r·*,
    gl 593– 9 definition of

resuscitate
  a 44–14 to *r·* wasted energies.
  p 365–29 patient's spiritual power to *r·* himself.

resuscitated
  sp 75–20 and he could not have *r·* it.

resuscitating
  ph 180– 8 one must understand the *r·* law of Life.

retained
  pref xii–18 She *r·* her charter, and as its President,
  s 132–15 *r·* their materialistic beliefs about God,
  f 247– 8 One man at sixty had *r·* his full set of
  gl 598–25 *r·* when the Science of being is understood,

retains
  sp 73–24 belief that . . . spirit *r·* the sensations

retard
  b 283– 5 and there is no inertia to *r·* or check its

retards
  p 415–17 It either *r·* the circulation or quickens it,

retchings
  ph 195– 8 All that he ate, . . . produced violent *r·*.

retina
  s 122–16 On the eye's *r·*, sky and tree-tops apparently
  f 214–27 when a wound on the *r·* may
  p 400–25 in optics we see painted on the *r·* the image
  r 479– 9 An image of mortal thought, reflected on the *r·*,

retracing
  a 20–22 saves *r·* and traversing anew the path

retreat
  f 247–32 to *r·* from the belief of pain or pleasure
  p 378–16 often causes the beast to *r·* in terror.
  405–31 causes mortals to *r·* from their error,

retrograde
  sp 74–29 In C. S. there is never a *r·* step,
  p 442–19 An improved belief cannot *r·*.

retrograding
  g 527–29 Is the Supreme Being *r·*,

retrogression
  a 22– 5 selfishness and sensuality causing constant *r·*,

RETROSPECTION AND INTROSPECTION
  pref viii–24 In the author's work, *R· AND I·*,

return

in
    pr 5– 8   and woe comes in *r·* for what is done.
    a 36–29   in *r·* for our efforts at well doing.
    p 364–21   in *r·* for the spiritual purgation which
    g 518–14   in *r·*, the higher always protects the lower.
meet no
    m 57–23   even though it meet no *r·*.
never a
    sp 74–30   never a *r·* to positions outgrown.
not the
    a 45–28   reappearing of Jesus was not the *r·* of a spirit.
of sight
    f 247– 5   A woman of eighty-five, . . . had a *r·* of sight.
results in a
    g 552–28   results in a *r·* to the original species.
their
    sp 74– 4   and their *r·* to a material condition,

    pr 2– 6   and it does not *r·* unto us void.
        3–28   and yet *r·* thanks to God for all blessings,
    a 24–25   as a proof that spirits can *r·* to earth?
    sp 73– 5   and supposedly will *r·* to earth
        73–19   The belief that material bodies *r·* to dust,
        74–18   nor does the insect *r·* to fraternize with
        76–14   neither can he *r·* to it, any more than
        76–15   any more than a tree can *r·* to its seed.
        77–31   and they *r·* to their old standpoints of matter.
        82–10   they cannot *r·* to material existence,
        89–10   The former limits of her belief *r·*.
    ph 190–16   and *r·* to its native nothingness.
    f 212– 6   If the sensation of pain in the limb can *r·*,
        214–12   originate in matter and *r·* to dust,
    b 278–26   originated in matter and must *r·* to dust,
        284– 9   and can *r·* to no limit.
        287– 5   but creations of matter must *r·* to dust.
    p 399–14   and matter can *r·* no answer to
        416– 4   and the belief of pain will presently *r·*, unless
        441–29   to *r·* a verdict contrary to law and gospel.
    r 471– 2   knows no lapse from nor *r·* to harmony,
    g 535–26   till thou *r·* unto the ground ; — *Gen.* 3 : 19.
        535–28   and unto dust shalt thou *r·*.— *Gen.* 3 : 19.
        536–29   the mortal and material *r·* to dust,
        545–30   unto dust [nothingness] shalt thou *r·*." — *Gen.*
            3 : 19.
        547–21   and afterwards must either *r·* to Mind or

returned

    sp 94–21   but one *r·* to give God thanks,
    s 132– 1   Jesus *r·* an affirmative reply,
        159– 8   and a verdict was *r·* that

returning

    a 20–17   *r·* blessing for cursing,
    m 57–14   sweet seasons of renewal like the *r·* spring.
    g 522–17   dust *r·* to dust.

returns

    sp 74–12   and never *r·* to the old condition.
    f 244–17   hypothesis that he *r·* eventually to
    b 277– 4   Scripture says that dust *r·* to dust.
        295–32   error theorizes that spirit . . . *r·* to matter,
    p 373–32   and *r·* to that standard which
        433–16   and the jury *r·* a verdict of "Guilty
    g 543– 3   yields to Truth and *r·* to dust ;

Reuben

    gl 593–12   definition of

reveal

    a 26–16   His mission was to *r·* the Science of
        47–16   A period was approaching which would *r·*
    sp 85– 7   Such intuitions *r·* whatever constitutes
    s 110– 4   These eternal verities *r·* primeval existence
        122– 6   and *r·* the kingdom of heaven,
    f 233–22   To *r·* this truth was our Master's mission
        239–21   The objects we pursue . . . *r·* our standpoint,
    b 292– 5   Divine Science alone can . . . *r·* the infinite.
        299–29   and *r·* the celestial peaks.
    r 485– 1   If error is necessary to define or to *r·* Truth,
    g 517–23   Even eternity can never *r·* the whole of God,
        520–13   they will *r·* eternity, newness of Life,

revealed

    pr 8–18   nothing...that shall not be *r·*." — *Matt.* 10 : 26.
        14– 8   understanding of Life as *r·* in C. S.
    a 24–11   "the arm of the Lord" is *r·* — *Isa.* 53 : 1.
        44–26   *r·* a method infinitely above that of
        46–10   It is *r·* to the receptive heart,
        46–23   and *r·* unmistakably a . . . progressive state
    m 56–12   its spiritual sense was *r·* from heaven,
    sp 81–17   Man in the likeness of God as *r·* in Science
        98–17   stands a *r·* and practical Science.
    s 131–21   and hast *r·* them unto babes :— *Luke* 10 : 21.
        137–23   for flesh and blood hath not *r·* it — *Matt.* 16 : 17.
    ph 174–20   Truth is *r·*. It needs only to be practised.
    f 241–25   the Horeb height where God is *r·* ;
    b 275–20   Divine metaphysics, as *r·* to spiritual
        300–31   God is *r·* only in that which

revealed

    b 301–15   is *r·* only through divine Science.
        321– 7   what should be *r·* to him.
        322– 9   and his capabilities *r·*.
        338–32   The ideal man was *r·* in due time,
    t 457– 1   and registered the *r·* Truth
    r 483–20   God certainly *r·* the spirit of C. S.,
    g 511–12   God is *r·* as infinite light.
        557–24   *r·* religion proclaims the Science of Mind
    gl 593–23   SEAL. The signet of error *r·* by Truth.
        597–11   It *r·* the false foundations and superstructures

revealing

    pr 14–26   Life divine, *r·* spiritual understanding
    b 332–21   *r·* the divine Principle, Love,

reveals

    pr 10–12   C. S. *r·* a necessity for overcoming the world,
    a 36– 4   Divine Science *r·* the necessity of
    an 104–14   and *r·* the theodicy which indicates the
    s 109– 4   C. S. *r·* incontrovertibly that Mind is All-in-all,
        120–21   *r·* man as harmoniously existent in Truth,
        127–16   C. S. *r·* God, not as the author of sin,
        147–30   but Science alone *r·* the divine Principle
    ph 169–18   Science not only *r·* the origin of all disease
        172–12   Science *r·* the eternal chain of existence
        191–24   Science of being *r·* man and immortality as
    f 209–13   Science which *r·* the supremacy of Mind.
        213–17   Divine Science *r·* sound as
        244– 4   Divine Science *r·* these grand facts.
        250–30   Science *r·* Life as not being at the mercy of
    c 260–13   Science *r·* the possibility of achieving
    b 272–32   *r·* the natural, divine Principle of Science.
        273–20   *r·* the laws of spiritual existence.
        278– 1   Science *r·* nothing in Spirit out of which to
        288–27   Science *r·* the glorious possibilities of
        296–12   *r·* man and Life, harmonious, real,
        302–19   The Science of being *r·* man as perfect,
        310–14   So Science *r·* Soul as God,
        327– 3   Science, which *r·* the immortal fact that
        328–12   *r·* the grand realities of His allness.
    r 466–12   represent contraries, as C. S. *r·*,
        467–17   *r·* Spirit, Soul, as not in the body,
        477–11   C. S. *r·* man as the idea of God,
        480–12   the origin and governor of all that Science *r·*.
        483–18   and *r·* the universal harmony.
        490– 7   C. S. *r·* Truth and Love as the
        491–21   Science *r·* material man as never the real being.
    g 510–29   Science *r·* only one Mind,
        519–10   Science *r·* infinity and the fatherhood
        534– 7   *r·* the spiritual origin of man.
        554– 1   C. S. *r·* what "eye hath not seen," — *I Cor.* 2 : 9.
        557–11   C. S. *r·* harmony as proportionately increasing
    ap 562– 8   This idea *r·* the universe as secondary
        576–23   and the spiritual idea *r·* it.
        577–31   the acme of this Science as the Bible *r·* it.
    gl 596–14   C. S. *r·* Spirit, not matter, as the illuminator

Revelation

    s 139–24   seen from Genesis to *R·*,
    ap 558– 2   the tenth chapter of his book of *R·* :
        559–32   the Apocalypse, or *R·* of St. John,
        572–19   In *R·* xxi. 1 we read :
        574– 5   He writes, in *R·* xxi. 9 :
        575–27   the Word, the polar magnet of *R·* ;
        576– 8   In *R·* xxi. 22, further describing this
        577–29   St. John's *R·* as recorded by the great apostle,

revelation

all
    s 141–10   All *r·* (such is the popular thought !) must
and demonstration
    a 45–18   the *r·* and demonstration of life in God,
and progress
    gl 591–23   MORNING. . . . *r·* and progress.
another
    ap 573–14   another *r·*, even the declaration from heaven,
Bible
    g 537–22   Subsequent Bible *r·* is coordinate with
Christ's
    sp 98–19   Christ's *r·* of Truth, of Life, and of Love,
coincide with
    g 522–24   coincide with *r·* in declaring this
divine
    s 109–21   through divine *r·*, reason, and demonstration.
    ap 561–20   In divine *r·*, . . . the spiritual idea is
final
    s 107– 5   for the reception of this final *r·* of
fresh
    t 460–24   When the Science of Mind was a fresh *r·* to
logic and
    sp 93–10   Divine logic and *r·* coincide.
nature and
    b 276–29   Nature and *r·* inform us that
no higher
    s 121– 9   Though no higher *r·* than the horoscope was
of divine purpose
    sp 83–26   The latter is a *r·* of divine purpose

revelation

of divine Science
b 330–18   or to the r· of divine Science.
ap 559– 3   contain the r· of divine Science,

of Immanuel
s 107– 7   points to the r· of Immanuel,

of immortality
sp 79–15   in its r· of immortality,

of Jesus Christ
s 107– *   *by the r· of Jesus Christ.— Gal.* 1 : 12.

of Science
gl 589– 5   Inspiration ; the r· of Science,

of Truth
a 29–22   brought forth her child by the r· of Truth,
sp 98–19   Christ's r· of Truth, of Life, and of Love,
s 109–22   The r· of Truth in the understanding
g 504–11   it is the r· of Truth and of spiritual ideas.

reason and
s 110–15   reason and r· were reconciled,
o 347–27   must yield to reason and r·.

scientific
s 110–13   In following these leadings of scientific r·,

this
s 108–13   allowing the evidence of this r· to
g 529– 8   this r· will destroy the *dream* of
ap 575– 4   this r· will destroy forever the

Truth is a
s 117–28   Truth is a r·.

sp 93–13   or that we have misinterpreted r·.
s 123–19   The r· consists of two parts :
b 279–25   this belief contradicts alike r· and
g 504–14   Was not this a r· instead of

revelations
sp 70– 4   r· of C. S. unlock the treasures of Truth.

Revelator (*see also* **John** *and* **St. John**)

beheld
ap 561– 8   The R· beheld the spiritual idea

lifts the veil
ap 565–15   R· lifts the veil from this embodiment of

speaks of Jesus
ap 564–13   The R· speaks of Jesus as the Lamb of God

tells us
sp 91– 1   R· tells us of "a new heaven— *Rev.* 21 : 1.

was familiar
ap 576–15   R· was familiar with Jesus' use of this word,

b 334–24   R· represents the Son of man as saying
ap 561–10   The R· saw also the spiritual ideal
561–25   The R· symbolizes Spirit by the sun.
562– 5   R· completed this figure with woman,
563–18   The R· sees that old serpent,
565–19   according to the R·, . . . will baptize with fire
568–11   the R· first exhibits the true warfare
571–22   Through trope and metaphor, the R·,
572–23   R· had not yet passed the transitional stage
573– 3   The R· was on our plane of existence,
574– 3   The R· also takes in another view,

revellings
an 106–24   r· and such like :— *Gal.* 5 : 21.

revenge

conquer
p 405– 7   to conquer . . . r· with charity,

hatred, and
p 407– 7   selfishness, envy, hatred, and r·
t 445–32   hatred, and r· are cast out by the divine Mind
ap 564–25   sin, sickness, and death, envy, hatred, and r·,

is inadmissible
a 22–31   R· is inadmissible.

sin's
a 48–14   exalting ordeal of sin's r· on its destroyer?

an 104–20   sensuality, falsehood, r·, malice,
s 115–23   r·, sin, sickness, disease, death.
ph 188– 9   hatred, r· ripen into action, only to
f 241–10   Falsehood, envy, hypocrisy, malice, hate, r·,
b 289–10   To suppose that . . . hypocrisy, r·, have life
327– 8   malice, finding pleasure in r· !
p 419– 2   Lurking error, lust, envy, r·, malice, or hate
gl 588– 2   hatred ; r· ; sin ; sickness ; death ;
593– 8   animal magnetism ; envy ; r·.
595– 3   SWORD. The idea of Truth ; justice. R· ; anger.

revere
b 294–17   to r· false testimony,

reverence
p 364– 3   Her r· was unfeigned,
gl 597– 1   in token of r· and submission

Reverend Theology
p 435– 5   R· T· would console conscious Mortal Mind,

reversal
s 120– 8   by this r· mortals arrive at the fundamental
122– 7   The material senses' r· of the
c 267–24   by r·, errors serve as waymarks
b 277–19   Error relies upon a r· of this order,

reverse
ph 185–24   which is the r· of ethical and
189–21   The r· is the case with all the
f 212–15   R· the process ; take away this so-called mind
212–32   mortal belief, which would r· the
c 261– 1   Now r· this action.
262–11   We must r· our feeble flutterings
p 392–24   R· the case. Stand porter at the door of
397–17   Now r· the process.
408–26   R· the belief, and the results would be
437–18   Supreme Court of Spirit r· this decision.
442–18   but the r· of error is true.
t 447–17   sin or sickness— the r· of harmony

reversed
m 62–28   the order of wisdom would be r·.
s 113–11   Even if r·, these propositions will
126–12   and so seems to have r· it
140–28   mournfully true that the older Scripture is r·.
b 312– 3   r· by the spiritual facts of being
319– 4   error r· as subserving the facts
p 442–18   in which truth cannot be r·,

reverses
s 111–14   Divine metaphysics r· perverted and
116– 5   Science so r· the evidence before the
119–28   As astronomy r· the human perception
119–29   r· the seeming relation of Soul and body
120– 7   Science r· the false testimony of the
122– 1   often r· the real Science of being,
123– 7   which r· the order of Science
f 215–22   Science r· the evidence of material sense.
b 273–10   Divine Science r· the false testimony of
t 461–13   r· the evidence before the material senses
g 544–28   erroneous belief r· understanding and

reversing
s 120–20   r· the testimony of the physical senses,
120–27   instead of r· the testimony of the
129– 8   by r· the material fable,
p 441–17   R· the testimony of Personal Sense

reviewing
ph 194– 2   R· this brief experience, I cannot fail to

reviews
p 433– 4   He analyzes the offence, r· the testimony,

reviled
o 361–27   but it will be rejected and r· until

revised
o 361–21   I have r· SCIENCE AND HEALTH only to
r 465– 3   she r· that treatise for this volume in 1875.

revision
pref xii–17   should be given to the preparation of the r·

revisions
o 361–31   and the requisite r· of SCIENCE AND HEALTH

revolution
b 310–13   The sun is not affected by the r· of the earth.

revolutionary
b 268–11   In this r· period, . . . woman goes forth

revolutionized
a 34–12   they would have r· the world.

revolutions
f 209–19   distances, and r· of the celestial bodies,
240–16   The rotations and r· of the universe
g 504–31   No solar rays nor planetary r· form the
513–11   not yet measured by solar r·,

revolves
s 121–26   the earth r· about the sun once a year,

revolving
g 522– 9   and as r· in an orbit of his own.

reward

brings its own
a 37–13   Consciousness of right-doing brings its own r· ;

check the
f 203– 2   as though evil could . . . check the r· for

earthly
a 36–12   What was his earthly r·?

full
a 36–24   to bestow on the righteous their full r·.

harmony and
a 21– 8   that they shall reach his harmony and r·.

has its
t 453–20   a right motive has its r·.

of self-sacrifice
a 29–10   Great is the r· of self-sacrifice,

punish or
p 441–26   no law outside of divine Mind can punish or r·

receive the
pr 8–23   to receive the r· of Him who blesses the poor.

reward
small
 p 364–20 small *r·* in return for the spiritual purgation
your
 a 22–13 Wait for your *r·*,

 pr 13–11 our Father, who seeth in secret, will *r·*
  15– 2 shall *r·* thee openly.''—*Matt.* 6 : 6.
 a 22–16 If . . . you receive no present *r·*, go not back
  34–26 As the *r·* for his faithfulness, he would
 m 66–30 Sorrow has its *r·*.
 p 409–31 and expect to find beyond the grave a *r·* for this
rewarded
 pr 10– 4 will leave our real desires to be *r·* by Him.
rewards
 pr 15– 8 *r·* according to motives,
 f 203– 5 assigns sure *r·* to righteousness,
rheumatism
 p 384–19 or hints of inflammatory *r·*,
  384–26 neither *r·*, consumption, nor any other disease
  386–10 catarrh, fever, *r·*, or consumption,
rhythm
 f 213–26 Music is the *r·* of head and heart.
 g 510– 4 To discern the *r·* of Spirit
rib
 g 528–12 and the *r·*, which the Lord God—*Gen.* 2 : 22.
  533–17 the *r·* taken from Adam's side
  553–19 Eve was formed from Adam's *r·*,
  553–27 or from the *r·* of our primeval father.
 gl 585–27 first from dust, second from a *r·*,
ribs
 o 360–20 striking the *r·* of matter
 g 528–11 He took one of his *r·*, and—*Gen.* 2 : 21.
rich
 o 344–24 and left to us as his *r·* legacy.
 p 364–13 what his *r·* entertainer had neglected to do,
 g 518–15 The *r·* in spirit help the poor
  533– 2 Had he lost man's *r·* inheritance
riches
 pr 5–17 God pours the *r·* of His love into the
 t 459– 6 so he must gain heavenly *r·* by
richly
 b 312–32 Jesus' spiritual origin . . . *r·* endowed him
 g 501– 9 but *r·* recompensing human want and woe
  548–26 Natural history is *r·* endowed by the
rid
 sp 91– 5 Let us *r·* ourselves of the belief that man is
 f 237–30 would *r·* them of their complaints,
 b 322–32 easier to desire Truth than to *r·* one's self of
  328– 8 *r·* of sin, sickness, and death only in
  330–28 To get *r·* of sin through Science,
 p 371–17 before he can get *r·* of the illusive sufferings
 g 542– 3 that it might be *r·* of troublesome Truth.
ridiculous
 m 68– 3 for fear of being thought *r·*.
right (noun)
adjusts the
 t 449– 8 *R·* adjusts the balance sooner or later.
and wrong
 t 453– 6 *R·* and wrong, truth and error,
calling itself
 r 491– 9 the latter calling itself *r·*.
conception of
 b 327–10 sometimes a man's highest conception of *r·*,
divine
 f 227–26 This is your divine *r·*.
faith in the
 a 29– 7 Christian experience teaches faith in the *r·*
highest
 p 368– 2 a supposititious opposite of the highest *r·*.
immutable
 t 446–20 victory rests on the side of immutable *r·*.
individual
 t 447– 2 man's individual *r·* of self-government.
is radical
 t 452–18 *R·* is radical.
law of
 p 385–11 remember that the eternal law of *r·*,
man's moral
 p 381–29 man's moral *r·* to annul an unjust sentence,
negative
 r 491– 8 a negative *r·* and a positive wrong,
or wisdom
 g 544–15 No mortal mind has the might or *r·* or wisdom
proclaim the
 b 327–24 to meet the wrong and to proclaim the *r·*.
to acquit
 pr 11– 9 moral law, which has the *r·* to acquit or condemn,
to distinguish
 t 453– 1 mathematician's *r·* to distinguish the
to freedom
 f 227– 5 mortals are taught their *r·* to freedom,

right (noun)
to the name
 s 111–10 some may deny its *r·* to the name of Science.
uncertain sense of
 b 326–24 only when his uncertain sense of *r·* yielded to a

 pr 3– 1 He who is immutably right will do *r·*
  9–32 Consistent prayer is the desire to do *r·*.
 a 49–31 turned "aside the *r·* of a man—*Lam.* 3 : 35.
 sp 89–29 concluded . . . man had the *r·* to take it away.
 f 223–32 until "He come whose *r·* it is."—*Ezek.* 21 : 27.
  228– 9 learn that nothing is real but the *r·*,
  236–29 and their receptiveness of *r·*.
  253–19 can at once change your course and do *r·*.
 c 266–21 and the saint his own heaven by doing *r·*.
 b 329– 8 you have no *r·* to question the great might of
 p 384– 7 God never punishes man for doing *r·*,
  405–25 tends to destroy the ability to do *r·*.
  409–27 We have no *r·* to say that life depends on
  436–34 pronounced a sentence of death for doing *r·*.
  442– 4 "Shall not the Judge . . . do *r·*?"—*Gen.* 18 : 25.
 t 447– 4 and no moral *r·* to attempt to
  448–29 It is C. S. to do *r·*,
  448–30 To talk the *r·* and live the wrong is foolish
 g 553–11 "We have no *r·* to assume that individuals
 ap 571–10 for the sake of doing *r·* and benefiting our race.
right (adj., adv.)
 pref vii–19 a *r·* apprehension of Him whom to know **aright**
 pr 3– 1 He who is immutably *r·* will do right
 a 22– 2 to find and follow the *r·* road.
  35– 5 and cast their net on the *r·* side.
 m 66– 1 Thou art *r·*, immortal Shakespeare,
 s 115–10 The great difficulty is to give the *r·* impression,
  141– 7 and pluck out the *r·* eye,
 ph 192–23 the weight you throw into the *r·* scale.
  195–19 Academics of the *r·* sort are requisite.
 f 225–16 proportionate to its embodiment of *r·* thinking.
  229–27 If . . . produces sickness, it is *r·* to be sick ;
  234–23 the *r·* education of human thought.
  235–31 will love to grapple with a new, *r·* idea
  253–20 no opposition to *r·* endeavors
 b 271–27 or to cast them on the *r·* side for Truth,
  279–25 contradicts alike revelation and *r·* reasoning.
  299–25 which cannot destroy the *r·* reflection.
  318–24 as though disease were real, therefore *r·*,
  318–25 If disease is *r·* it is wrong to heal it.
  326–25 spiritual sense, which is always *r·*.
  329–23 Always *r·*, its divine Principle never repents,
  360– 3 all is won, by a *r·* estimate of what is real.''
 p 371–14 in all ways except the *r·* one.
  382–32 Mortal mind needed to be set *r·*.
  390– 9 *r·* understanding of Him restores harmony.
  396–22 At the *r·* time explain to the sick the
  410–27 to promote *r·* thinking and doing,
 t 444– 9 into the *r·* use of temporary and
  444–20 smite thee on thy *r·* cheek,—*Matt.* 5 : 39.
  452–25 by *r·* talking and wrong acting,
  452–29 destroys your power of healing from the *r·* motive.
  453–19 and a *r·* motive has its reward.
  454–16 the wrong as well as the *r·* practice.
  454–19 *R·* motives give pinions to thought,
  455– 7 Hence the necessity of being *r·* yourself
  460–17 through *r·* apprehension of the truth of being.
 r 475–15 compound idea of God, including all *r·* ideas ;
  492– 3 For *r·* reasoning there should be
 g 531– 7 error, . . . that mind and soul are both *r·* and
  543–20 May not Darwin be *r·* in thinking that apehood
  557–23 as if he began materially *r·*,
 ap 558– 7 and he set his *r·* foot upon the sea,—*Rev.* 10 : 2.
  559– 3 "*r·* foot" or dominant power—*Rev.* 10 : 2.
  566– 6 so shall the spiritual idea guide all *r·* desires
  (*see also* **direction, hand**)
right-doing
 a 37–13 Consciousness of *r·* brings its own reward ;
 p 436–33 Claiming to protect Mortal Man in *r·*,
 t 448–29 nothing short of *r·* has any claim to the name.
righteous
 a 22–27 Whosoever believeth that wrath is *r·*
  36–23 to bestow on the *r·* their full reward.
  37–19 procured the martyrdom of that *r·* man
  41– 4 through the joys and triumphs of the *r·*
 s 132–30 This *r·* preacher once pointed his disciples to
 f 206–13 the prayer of the *r·*.
  231–11 does heal the sick through the prayer of the *r·*.
 p 439–26 and the *r·* executor of His laws.
 t 444–18 "judge *r·* judgment,"—*John* 7 : 24.
righteously
 f 254–11 and seek Truth *r·*, He directs our path.
righteousness
and purity
 a 28–18 Even his *r·* and purity did not hinder men from
fulfil all
 m 56– 4 it becometh us to fulfil all *r·*.''—*Matt.* 3 : 15.

righteousness

garment of
f 242–29 every part of the Christly garment of *r·*.
hungering after
pr 2– 5 the desire which goes forth hungering after *r·*
law of
a 36–32 Can God therefore overlook the law of *r·*
loved
b 313–18 "loved *r·* and hated iniquity."— *Heb.* 1 : 9.
paths of
ap 578– 9 leadeth me in the paths of *r·* — *Psal.* 23 : 3.
reign of
gl 585–19 Euphrates . . . the reign of *r·*.

a 54– 5 The world acknowledged not his *r·*,
ph 190–28 I will behold Thy face in *r·* :— *Psal.* 17 : 15.
f 203– 5 assigns sure rewards to *r·*,
b 291–17 man is found having no *r·* of his own,
323– 7 helped onward in the march towards *r·*,
p 365–14 from the outstretched arm of *r·*

righteousness'

a 28–25 To suppose that persecution for *r·* sake

rightful

s 124–30 and so restores them to their *r·* home
156–31 and Mind takes its *r·* and supreme place.
b 281–23 without actual origin or *r·* existence.
p 365–32 The poor suffering heart needs its *r·* nutriment,

rightfully

p 364– 2 *r·* regarded as the best man that ever

rightly

sp 96– 2 unwillingness to learn all things *r·*,
an 105–14 human law *r·* estimates crime,
106–10 self-governed only when he is guided *r·*
s 122– 4 the great facts of Life, *r·* understood,
ph 183–21 *r·* demands man's entire obedience,
f 231– 3 Unless an ill is *r·* met and fairly overcome
238– 1 not *r·* valued before they are understood.
c 262–28 To begin *r·* is to end *r·*.
b 280–25 *R·* understood, . . . man has a sensationless
338– 1 C. S., *r·* understood, leads to eternal harmony.
r 472–11 His law, *r·* understood, destroys them.
494–19 Reason, *r·* directed, serves to correct the
g 502–11 This deflection of being, *r·* viewed,

rightness

an 104–14 which indicates the *r·* of all divine action,

rights

and life
p 438–17 against the *r·* and life of man.
divine
f 253–10 the understanding of your divine *r·*,
p 384–31 before the divine *r·* of intelligence,
God-given
p 381– 2 Ignorant of our God-given *r·*,
human
a 48–29 against human *r·* and divine Love,
s 134–19 and so it came about that human *r·*
f 226–14 God has built a higher platform of human *r·*,
inalienable
an 106– 8 God has endowed man with inalienable *r·*,
s 161–17 certain inalienable *r·*, among which are
f 227– 9 unaware of man's inalienable *r·*
less
m 60–16 marvel why usage should accord woman less *r·*
liberty and
p 435–17 Mortal Man's liberty and *r·*.
man's
an 106–12 Man's *r·* are invaded when the
of humanity
a 54–32 Would they not deny him even the *r·* of humanity,
of intelligence
sp 79–27 contending for the *r·* of intelligence
p 384–31 before the divine *r·* of intelligence,
of man
s 144–19 will-power may infringe the *r·* of man.
f 225–31 *r·* of man were vindicated in a single section
226– 9 a fuller acknowledgment of the *r·* of man
227– 1 and the *r·* of man are fully known and
227–14 Discerning the *r·* of man,
of mind
t 453–32 He does not trespass on the *r·* of mind
of woman
gl 587– 3 The *r·* of woman acknowledged
supposed
o 348–22 defending the supposed *r·* of disease,

m 63–13 unfair differences between the *r·* of the two
s 157– 7 never shares its *r·* with inanimate matter.
p 440–31 the *r·* of which he has been deprived.

Rights of Man

p 438– 1 certain extracts on the *R·* of *M·*,

rigid

s 160–24 If muscles can cease to act and become *r·*
162– 8 dissolves tumors, relaxes *r·* muscles,
f 221– 5 decided that his diet should be more *r·*,

ripe

ap 565– 3 the great red dragon, . . . *r·* for destruction

ripen

ph 188– 9 hatred, revenge *r·* into action,
f 248– 6 ought to *r·* into health and immortality,

ripening

b 296– 4 It is the *r·* of mortal man,

riper

sp 97–16 the *r·* it becomes for destruction.
f 248– 5 Men and women of *r·* years and larger lessons

rise

pr 16–20 Only as we *r·* above all material sensuousness
a 18–17 The fountain can *r·* no higher than its source.
24–12 and *r·* into newness of life
34–24 would *r·* again in the spiritual realm of reality,
35– 7 they were enabled to *r·* somewhat from
sp 73–20 belief that material bodies . . . *r·* up as
77–26 The departed would gradually *r·* above
87–30 close the eyes, and forms *r·* before us, which
ph 167– 3 If we *r·* no higher than blind faith,
192–26 betrays its weakness and falls, never to *r·*.
193–17 I told him to *r·*, dress himself, and take supper
f 242–13 and to *r·* superior to the so-called pain and
c 261–28 will *r·* to the spiritual consciousness of being,
262–12 *r·* above the testimony of the material senses,
b 289– 2 can never *r·* from the temporal *débris* of error,
290– 5 will *r·* no higher spiritually in the scale of
p 365– 9 and so enable them to *r·* above the supposed
373–21 you must *r·* above both fear and sin.
390–32 *R·* in the conscious strength of the spirit of
391– 8 *r·* in rebellion against them.
391–30 *r·* to the true consciousness of Life as Love,
393–12 *R·* in the strength of Spirit to resist
394–15 to *r·* above his difficulties.
406–21 We can, and ultimately shall, so *r·*
419–30 *r·* into higher and holier consciousness,
t 444– 3 all must *r·* superior to materiality,
r 493– 3 the sun appears to *r·* and set,
g 531–11 will sometime *r·* above all material
ap 565–25 to *r·* to the zenith of demonstration,

risen

pref vii– 4 ere cometh the full radiance of a *r·* day.
a 53–30 nor had he *r·* to his final demonstration
sp 74– 8 a sprout which has *r·* above the soil.
b 324–27 "If Christ [Truth] be not *r·*,— *I Cor.* 15 : 14.
p 379–14 he would have *r·* above the false belief.
t 448–13 if you have not *r·* above sin yourself,
g 534– 4 and to behold at the sepulchre the *r·* Saviour,

rises

s 153–12 *r·* above matter into mind.
f 246– 8 The stream *r·* no higher than its source.
c 256– 3 thought *r·* from the material sense to the
262–24 Starting from a higher standpoint, one *r·*
b 297–15 and the human consciousness *r·* higher.
t 448–12 *r·* above the evidence of the corporeal senses ;
g 525– 9 in the Welsh, *that which r·* up,
557–12 as the line of creation *r·* towards spiritual man,
ap 568–28 now *r·* clearer and nearer to the great heart of

rising

m 62–16 more for the health of the *r·* generation
s 123–13 Divine Science, *r·* above physical theories,
ph 172– 7 grades the human species as *r·* from
174– 9 *r·* above material standpoints,
f 246– 7 by no means a material germ *r·* from
c 258–14 broadening and *r·* higher and higher from a
b 268– 3 *r·* towards the realm of the real,
p 385– 7 the divine law, *r·* above the human.
t 449–11 Man's moral mercury, *r·* or falling,
g 508–24 *r·* from the lesser to the greater,
511–27 mortal thought, *r·* in the scale of intelligence,

risk

pr 13–18 incur less *r·* of overwhelming our real wishes
s 156–20 for one day, and *r·* the effects.
ap 571– 9 and so *r·* human displeasure for the sake of

risked

s 159–17 and not have *r·* such treatment.

risks

t 452–23 take no *r·* in the policy of error.

rite

a 34– 3 Then why ascribe this inspiration to a dead *r·*,

rites

a 32–11 used on convivial occasions and in Jewish *r·*,
gl 597– 3 consisted mostly of *r·* and ceremonies.

ritualism
  a 33– 1 closed forever Jesus' *r·*
  f 234– 2 even as *r·* and creed hamper spirituality.
  t 458–21 *r·* and creed are summoned to give place
  r 466–25 idolatry and *r·* are the outcome of

ritualistic
  a 20– 6 *r·* priest and hypocritical Pharisee
     20–10 but he established no *r·* worship.
  s 135–28 nor a special gift from a *r·* Jehovah ;
    141– 2 theological and *r·* religion of the ages

rituals
  s 133–32 Creeds and *r·* have not cleansed their hands of
    140–19 Judaic and other *r·* are but types and

river
  f 241–17 than can moonbeams to melt a *r·* of ice.
  gl 585–16 EUPHRATES (*r·*).   Divine Science
     587– 3 GIHON (*r·*).   The rights of woman
     588– 5 HIDDEKEL (*r·*).   Divine Science understood
     593– 1 PISON (*r·*).   The love of the good and
     593–14 definition of

river-bed
  g 540–10 The muddy *r·* must be stirred

road
  pr 11–26 in the only practical *r·* to holiness.
  a 22– 2 to find and follow the right *r·*.
  b 326– 8 must not try to climb . . . by some other *r·*.

roams
  g 514–11 Free and fearless it *r·* in the forest.

roar
  ap 570–20 He can neither drown your voice with its *r·*,

roareth
  ap 559–11 "as when a lion *r·*."— *Rev.* 10 : 3.

rob
  ph 187–10 beliefs of the human mind *r·* and enslave it,
  f 214–23 mortal illusions would *r·* God,
    244–10 and the worms would *r·* him of the flesh ;
    251–31 Inharmonious beliefs, which *r·* Mind,
    252–19 says : . . . I can cheat, lie, commit adultery. *r·*,

robbed
  b 304–24 if time or accident *r·* them of material
  p 431–30 testifies : . . . I am *r·* of my good looks.

robbing
  f 234–15 *r·* both themselves and others.

robe
  ap 569–12 He that touches the hem of Christ's *r·*

robes
  c 267–26 *r·* of Spirit are "white and— *Luke* 9 : 29.
  ap 572– 1 washed their *r·* white in obedience and

robs
  s 134–18 *r·* Christianity of the very element, which
  ph 169–32 for it *r·* man of reliance on God,
  f 246–10 *r·* youth and gives ugliness to age.
  b 275–26 It *r·* the grave of victory.
    323–25 *r·* the grave of victory,

robust
  ph 197–27 will never grow *r·* until

rock
  Christ Jesus
  f 235–26 may be planted on the *r·* Christ Jesus,
  divine
  b 297–28 no mortal testimony is founded on the divine *r·*.
  of ages
  p 380– 5 Truth is the *r·* of ages,
  upon the
  r 484– 5 for it is built upon the *r·*, Christ.
  upon this
  s 137–30 thou art Peter ; and upon this *r·*— *Matt.* 16 : 18.

  s 133–10 In the wilderness, streams flowed from the *r·*,
    138– 8 a *r·*, a firm foundation in the realm of
  b 269–28 shaken by the wind, not houses built on the *r·*.
  g 516–16 The great *r·* gives shadow and shelter.
  gl 593–18 definition of

rocked
  m 62– 9 fed, *r·*, tossed, or talked to,

rock-ribbed
  a 44–32 There were *r·* walls in the way,

rocks
  sp 87–20 the emeralds within its *r·* ;
  g 511–24 *r·* and mountains stand for solid and grand ideas.

rod
  b 321– 9 led by wisdom to cast down his *r·*,
  ap 565– 7 rule all nations with a *r·* of— *Rev.* 12 : 5.
    578–12 [LOVE'S] *r·* and [LOVE'S] staff— *Psal.* 23 : 4.

Roland, Madame
  s 161–20 the words of the famous Madame *R·*,

roll
  g 548–11 only as the clouds of corporeal sense *r·* away.

rolled
  a 45– 1 a great stone must be *r·* from the
     45–17 Christ hath *r·* away the stone from the

rolling
  ph 174–28 *r·* it under the tongue as a sweet morsel

rolls
  g 557–19 Divine Science *r·* back the clouds of error

Roman
  a 32– 9 does not commemorate a *R·* soldier's oath,
  f 224–18 less material than the *R·* scourge,
    238– 9 the *R·* Catholic girl said,

Romans
  g 534–18 Paul says in his epistle to the *R·* :

Rome
  a 29–13 wrote to the authorities at *R·* :
     32– 3 In ancient *R·* a soldier was required to
  ph 196–15 to beware, not of *R·*, Satan, nor of God, but of sin.
  c 255– 8 cultured scholars in *R·* and in Greece,
  b 324–26 and even in imperial *R·*.
    339–20 As the mythology of pagan *R·* has yielded to

room
  b 339– 7 there is no *r·* for His unlikeness.
  o 346–29 to make *r·* for spiritual understanding.
  p 424–11 there is no *r·* for imperfection in perfection.

root
  a 27–18 at the *r·* of material knowledge,
  *b·*303–16 at the *r·* of the illusion
  o 341– 7 Scriptures, which grow . . . from one grand *r·*,

rooted
  f 225–27 *r·* out through the action of the divine Mind.

roots
  o 352–22 thus watering the very *r·* of childish timidity,

rope
  ph 199–25 to walk the *r·* over Niagara's abyss

rose
  a 35–18 when he *r·* out of material sight.
     43–21 Jesus *r·* higher in demonstration
     46–16 *r·* even higher in the understanding of Spirit,
     46–27 he *r·* above the physical knowledge of
  ph 175– 9 to say that a *r·*, . . . can produce suffering !
    190–27 When hope *r·* higher in the human heart,
  f 212–18 They produce a *r·* through seed and soil,
    212–19 and bring the *r·* into contact with the
  b 316–18 The Christ-idea, . . . *r·* higher to human view
  p 437–23 *r·* to the question of expelling C. S.
    442– 8 Then the prisoner *r·* up regenerated, strong,
  g 509– 6 to their apprehension he *r·* from the grave,
    541–14 Cain *r·* up against Abel— *Gen.* 4 : 8.
  gl 596–27 to bud and blossom as the *r·*.

rose-cold
  ph 175– 8 cerebro-spinal meningitis, hay-fever, and *r·*?

rotation
  s 121–17 The earth's diurnal *r·* is invisible to the

rotations
  f 240–15 The *r·* and revolutions of the universe

rough
  pref vii–24 and to cut the *r·* granite.

round
  b 277–17 throughout the entire *r·* of nature.
  p 408– 7 the entire *r·* of the material senses,

roused
  a 46–32 they were *r·* to an enlarged understanding
  s 134– 9 so *r·* the hatred of the opponents of

rousing
  o 358–26 through *r·* within the sick a belief that
  gl 583–15 *r·* the dormant understanding from

routed
  ph 175–18 it would have been *r·* by their independence

routes
  a 21–18 We have . . . different *r·* to pursue.

routine
  sp 96– 7 interruptions of the general material *r·*.
  s 143–21 you continue in the old *r·*.
  g 551–31 the resulting germ is doomed to the same *r·*.

Roux
  an 101– 9 among whom were *R·*, Bouillaud, and Cloquet,

royal
  s 141–13 as kings are crowned from a *r·* dynasty.
  b 313– 5 the God-crowned or the divinely *r·* man,
    313–16 the *r·* reflection of the infinite ;
  ap 575–25 a city of the Spirit, fair, *r·*, and square.

Royal Academy of Medicine
  an 101–19 This report was adopted by the *R· A· of M·*

Royal College of Physicians
  s 164– 3 Fellow of the *R· C· of P·*, London,

rubbing

p 382– 8 bathing and *r·* to alter the secretions

Rubicon

ph 172–10 if . . . death is the *R·* of spirituality?

rudiments

t 462–15 and advance from the *r·* laid down.

ruin

f 203–20 When the material body has gone to *r·*,

rule (noun)

and demonstration
b 290– 3 If the Principle, *r·*, and demonstration of
clearly interprets
ap 568–32 *r·* clearly interprets God as divine Principle,
confirm this
ph 199–23 Exceptions only confirm this *r·*, proving that
definite
s 147–26 he left no definite *r·* for demonstrating this
denies the
b 329–19 denies the *r·* of the problem because he fails
fixed
f 233–26 divided according to a fixed *r·*,
furnishes the
b 336–27 Science of being furnishes the *r·* of perfection,
general
p 411– 5 as a general *r·* the body would respond more
t 457–20 C. S. is not an exception to the general *r·*,
given
o 341–16 demonstrated according to a divine given *r·*,
God's
pr 3–10 we have only to avail ourselves of God's *r·*
higher
s 162–28 to demonstrate the higher *r·*.
his
r 473–22 test its unerring Science according to his *r·*,
in Christian Science
ap 568–32 Self-abnegation . . . is a *r·* in C. S.
no opposite
t 457–30 and there must and can be no opposite *r·*.
not obeyed the
s 149–15 because you have not obeyed the *r·*
of Christian Science
p 411–30 the result of this simple *r·* of C. S.,
r 493–16 prove . . . the Principle and *r·* of C. S.
of discord
f 219–20 Science includes no *r·* of discord,
of divine Science
ph 184–24 demonstrated this as a *r·* of divine Science
of healing
r 496–17 to demonstrate, . . . the *r·* of healing,
of health
b 337–29 the *r·* of health and holiness in C. S.,
of inversion
b 282–31 The *r·* of inversion infers from error its
of perpetual harmony
p 381–28 and abide by the *r·* of perpetual harmony,
positive
s 109–15 to discovering a positive *r·*.
proves the
s 113–27 proves the *r·* by inversion.
reign and
f 208–22 the reign and *r·* of universal harmony,
simple
s 121–24 the simple *r·* that the greater controls the lesser.
p 411–30 the result of this simple *r·* of C. S.,
418–32 inspired by this simple *r·* of Truth,
system and
g 547– 6 not one departs from the stated system and *r·*.

pr 3– 6 The *r·* is already established,
s 147–28 This *r·* remained to be discovered in C. S.
149–11 The *r·* and its perfection of operation
f 216–24 would appear . . . to be the *r·* of existence,
b 274–24 in learning its Principle and *r·*
t 447–10 the *r·* is, heal the sick when called upon
g 546–32 a thousand different examples of one *r·*.

rule (verb)

s 148–26 and claims to *r·* man by material law,
155–11 and the beliefs which are in the majority *r·*.
164–22 *r·* the materiality miscalled life
ph 196–20 Such books as will *r·* disease out of mortal mind,
198–26 and the stronger thoughts *r·* the weaker.
320–15 Jehovah said, My spirit shall not forever *r·*
p 419–26 assassin, who, in attempting to *r·* mankind,
g 510–14 the greater light to *r·* the day,— *Gen.* 1 : 16.
510–14 and the lesser light to *r·* the night :— *Gen.* 1 : 16.
511– 8 to *r·* over the day— *Gen.* 1 : 18.
535– 9 and he shall *r·* over thee.— *Gen.* 3 : 16.
ap 565– 7 who was to *r·* all nations— *Rev.* 12 : 5.
565–16 Christ, God's idea, will eventually *r·* all

ruled

a 55–13 although it is again *r·* out of the synagogue.
p 391–11 *r·* out by the might of Mind,

Ruler

f 203–18 Supreme *R·* or in some power less
gl 590–19 Its higher signification is Supreme *R·*.

ruler

f 239–11 The wicked man is not the *r·* of
p 437– 1 Nerve, testified that he was a *r·* of Body,
438– 9 Instead of being a *r·* in the Province of Body,
ap 569– 7 I will make thee *r·* over many,"— *Matt.* 25 : 23.
gl 590–17 the inferior sense of master, or *r·*.

ruler's

p 398–10 To the synagogue *r·* daughter,

rulers

p 323–17 shall be made *r·* over many ;

rules

divine
s 147– 7 I demonstrated the divine *r·* of C. S.
t 462– 3 any student, who adheres to the divine *r·*
divine Principle and
t 456– 6 Strict adherence to the divine Principle and *r·*
first
t 456–32 it gave the first *r·* for demonstrating this
fixed
s 113– 2 there must be fixed *r·* for the demonstration of
of health
ph 169–11 faith in *r·* of health or in drugs begets
197–24 With *r·* of health in the head
of Science
s 162–17 Working out the *r·* of Science in practice,
sacred
s 147– 4 and the sacred *r·* for its present application
spiritual
s 112–18 and with this infinitude come spiritual *r·*,
stern
p 362– 9 under the stern *r·* of rabbinical law,
these
s 147–12 since Jesus practised these *r·*

s 111–13 its *r·* demonstrate its Science.
147–18 the demonstration of the *r·* of
147–31 but Science alone . . . demonstrates its *r·*.
o 344–16 according to the *r·* which disclose its merits or
p 400–23 Mortal mind *r·* all that is mortal.
431– 3 Notwithstanding my *r·* to the contrary,
t 448–27 ventures not to break its *r·*,
456– 4 but contrary to its spirit or *r·*,
459–32 adhere strictly to the *r·* of divine metaphysics
462–14 must abide strictly by its *r·*,

ruling

m 64– 9 ceremonies, *r·* out primitive Christianity.
s 141–22 did not . . . understand this *r·* of the Christ ;
148–30 this *r·* of the schools leaves them to
f 205–24 whereas a belief in many *r·* minds hinders

rulings

an 105–17 and no longer apply legal *r·* wholly to

ruminates

p 430–19 patient feels ill, *r·*, and the trial commences.

run

a 20–29 and let us *r·* with patience— *Heb.* 12 : 1.
f 218–28 shall *r·*, and not be weary ;— *Isa.* 40 : 31.
250– 1 We *r·* into error when we
254– 3 can "*r·*, and not be weary ; — *Isa.* 40 : 31.
g 514– 7 Mind's infinite ideas *r·* and disport themselves.

runneth

ap 578–15 my cup *r·* over.— *Psal.* 23 : 5.

running

pr 5–12 and it will be full "and *r·* over."— *Luke* 6 : 38.
an 106– 5 against the current *r·* heavenward.

runs

s 154–28 Such a mother *r·* to her little one,

ruptures

g 541–17 *r·* the life and brotherhood of man

Rush, Dr. Benjamin

s 162–30 I kindly quote from Dr. Benjamin *R·*,

rush

ph 168–10 When sick . . . you *r·* after drugs,

rushes

b 327–15 *r·* forth to clamor with midnight and tempest.
p 373–27 When the blood *r·* madly through the veins

rust

f 241– 5 moth and *r·* doth corrupt."— *Matt.* 6 : 19.

S

sabachthani
a 51– 1 *"Eloi, Eloi, lama s·?"*— *Mark* 15 : 34.

Sabbath
a 20–12 observe the *S·*, make long prayers, and yet

sackcloth
ap 574–25 for it will lift the *s·* from your eyes,

sacrament
a 32– 6 English word *s·* is derived from it.
32–20 if the *s·* is confined to the use of bread and
34–10 If all who ever partook of the *s·*

sacramentum
a 32– 5 The Latin word for this oath was *s·*,

sacred
a 37–20 would gladly have turned his *s·* career into a
s 118– 8 hidden in *s·* secrecy from the visible world?
147– 4 and the *s·* rules for its present application
ph 182–26 ability to demonstrate Mind's *s·* power.
f 232–26 In the *s·* sanctuary of Truth are voices of
b 328–27 believed and obeyed this *s·* saying.
r 483–13 After the author's *s·* discovery,
g 547–23 The Scriptures are very *s·*.
548– 4 breathes through the *s·* pages the
ap 575– 7 This *s·* city, described in the Apocalypse

sacredly
f 236– 4 *S·*, in the interests of humanity,

sacredness
m 59–29 divorce shows that the *s·* of this relationship is

sacrifice
great
   pr 16– 1 A great *s·* of material things
human
   a 54–13 the inspiration of Jesus' intense human *s·*.
lifelong
   a 53–23 the lifelong *s·* which goodness makes for
living
   b 325–22 "Present your bodies a living *s·*,— *Rom.* 12 : 1.
one
   a 23– 3 One *s·*, however great, is insufficient to

pr 11–24 we shall *s·* everything for it.
a 25– 3 The spiritual essence of blood is *s·*.
26–22 Jesus' teaching . . . involved such a *s·* as
36–28 toil, s·, cross-bearing, multiplied trials,
t 459– 5 achieves no worldly honors except by *s·*,
gl 590–10 self-immolation ; innocence and purity ; *s·*.
595–23 A *s·* to the gods.

sacrificed
s 146– 9 health and harmony have been *s·*.

sacrifices
a 23– 2 Wisdom and Love may require many *s·* of self
49–11 his mighty works, his toils, privations, *s·*,

sacrificing
p 440– 7 before *s·* mortals to their false gods.

sacrilegious
o 344– 8 Is it *s·* to assume that God's likeness is

sad
a 32–30 a *s·* supper taken at the close of day,
40–28 It is *s·* that the phrase *divine service*
ph 182–27 come from some *s·* incident, or else
o 342– 6 the *s·* effects on the sick of denying Truth.

saddening
ph 190–22 thus swept his lyre with *s·* strains

Sadducees
s 117–30 the leaven of the Pharisees and of the *S·*,
b 305–31 The *S·* reasoned falsely about the

sadly
a 42–14 who *s·* followed him to the foot of the cross.
b 328–15 has *s·* disappeared from Christian history.
t 451–10 or be turned *s·* awry.

safe
an 105–24 Whoever uses . . . is never *s·*.
s 155–31 is it *s·* to say that the less in quantity you have
164– 7 none can be adopted as a *s·* guidance
p 376–28 Some people, . . . inquire when it will be *s·* to
384–20 your Mind-remedy is *s·* and sure.
t 463–10 that the birth will be natural and *s·*.
g 514–27 Daniel felt *s·* in the lions' den,
532– 7 Is this knowledge *s·*,

safely
m 67– 8 Can you steer *s·* amid the storm?"
f 201– 7 We cannot build *s·* on false foundations.

safer
pref x–24 its practice is *s·* and more potent

safety
a 39–21 a future-world salvation, or *s·*,
m 67–10 the dauntless seaman is not sure of his *s·* ;
r 494–19 and seek *s·* in divine Science.
gl 581– 8 ARK. *S·* ; the idea, or reflection, of Truth,

safety-valve
pr 6–22 to misunderstand Love and to make prayer the *s·*

safety-valves
p 425– 4 so long as you believe them to be *s·* or

sage
g 556–14 C. S. may absorb the attention of *s·* and

said
pr 4–11 has *s·* : "If ye love me, keep— *John* 14 : 15.
6–24 he *s·* that Satan had bound her,
6–25 he *s·*, "Thou art an offence— *Matt.* 16 : 23.
6–28 He *s·* of the fruitless tree,
8–32 and credit what is *s·*?
11– 4 he *s·*, "Go, and sin no more."— *John* 8 : 11.
16– 9 Our Master *s·*, "After this manner— *Matt.* 6 : 9.
a 23–12 Rabbinical lore *s·* : "He that taketh
27–14 It is as if he had *s·* : The I — the Life,
30–14 taught the Mosaic law, which *s·* :
31– 4 He *s·* : "Call no man your father— *Matt.* 23 : 9.
32–16 and *s·*, Take, eat ; this is my— *Matt.* 26 : 26.
33–16 and *s·*, "Drink ye all of it."— *Matt.* 26 : 27.
33–19 great Teacher *s·* : "Not my will,— *Luke* 22 : 42.
38–28 he *s·* in substance : Having eyes ye see not,
43– 6 understand what Jesus had *s·*.
46–13 Master *s·* plainly that physique was not Spirit,
48– 3 *s·* unto them : "Could ye not— *Matt.* 26 : 40.
48–23 He *s·* : "Put up thy sword."— *John* 18 : 11.
50–21 what would his accusers have *s·*?
51–24 in all that he *s·* and did.
52–25 prophetically *s·* to his disciples,
52–32 They *s·* : "He casteth out devils— *Luke* 11 : 15.
54–26 He *s·* that those who followed him
m 58–24 *S·* the peasant bride to her lover :
64– 4 when he *s·* : "Pure religion and— *Jas.* 1 : 27.
sp 70– * *Then s· the Jews unto him,*— *John* 8 : 52.
77– 1 The pious Polycarp s· : "I cannot
79–19 He *s·* : "My Father worketh— *John* 5 : 17.
85–12 Samaritan woman *s·* : "Come, see a— *John* 4 : 29.
85–20 he *s·* : "O ye hypocrites !— *Matt.* 16 : 3.
85–28 He *s·* : "These ought ye to have— *Matt.* 23 : 23.
88–29 it is *s·* to be a gift whose endowment is
93– 3 *s·*, "He that believeth on me,— *John* 14 : 12.
93– 5 *s·*, "But the hour cometh,— *John* 4 : 23.
94– 9 *s·* : "Crucify him, crucify him— *John* 19 : 6.
94–26 but what would be *s·* at this period of
an 100– 4 which he *s·* could be exerted by one
104– 9 Agassiz, . . . has wisely *s·* : "Every great
s 109–28 *s·* of his lessons : "My doctrine— *John* 7 : 16.
124–23 and *s·* to the proud wave,
127–14 It may be *s·*, however, that the term C. S.
131–19 Jesus once *s·* : "I thank Thee,— *Luke* 10 : 21.
133– 4 who *s·*, "Is not this the Christ?"— *John* 4 : 29.
135–21 It has been *s·*, and truly, that Christianity
136–31 did not comprehend all that he *s·*
138–27 *s·* to every follower : "Go ye into— *Mark* 16 : 15.
148– 2 to them, "O faithless— *Mark* 9 : 19.
156–19 *s·* that she would give up her medicine
159– 4 and *s·* it would kill her,
163– 7 Dr. James Johnson, . . . of England, *s·* :
163–16 Dr. Mason Good, a learned Professor . . . *s·* :
163–21 Dr. Chapman, . . . in a published essay *s·* :
164– 4 Sir John Forbes, M.D., . . . *s·* :
164–14 Much yet remains to be *s·* and done
ph 169– 6 *s·* to the patient, "You are healed,"
170–16 *s·* : "Take no thought for your life,— *Matt.* 6 : 25.
183– 7 however much is *s·* to the contrary,
193– 3 I met his physician, who *s·* that the patient
193– 5 *s·* the bone was carious
193–14 opened his eyes and *s·* : "I feel like a new man.
193–30 what his physician *s·* of the case,
195– 4 *s·* that he should never be happy elsewhere.
197–11 The less that is *s·* of physical structure
197–12 the more that is thought and *s·* about moral
200–13 Psalmist *s·* : "Thou madest him to— *Psal.* 8 : 6.
200–25 St. Paul *s·* : "For I determined— *I Cor.* 2 : 2.
f 204–27 in Science it can never be *s·* that man
211–19 It should no longer be *s·* in Israel
213– 3 called a deceiver, and to be deceived.
213– 4 it has been *s·*, "As he thinketh— *Prov.* 23 : 7.
220– 1 We hear it *s·* : "I exercise daily
238–10 Losing her crucifix, the Roman Catholic girl *s·*,
239–32 the wise man *s·*, "All is vanity."— *Eccl.* 1 : 2.

said

f 241–21   Our Master s·, "If ye love me,— *John* 14 : 15.
252– 1   our Master s·, "If a kingdom be— *Mark* 3 : 24.
c 262–17   Job s·: "I have heard of Thee— *Job* 42 : 5.
b 271–20   Our Master s·,"But the Comforter— *John* 14 : 26.
272–16   s·: "Give not that which is holy— *Matt.* 7 : 6.
286– 9   s·, "No man cometh unto the— *John* 14 : 6.
289–28   Therefore it cannot be s· to pass out of
305–16   "Then answered Jesus and s·— *John* 5 : 19.
308–23   Then s· the spiritual evangel :
313– 5   as it is s· of him in the first chapter of Hebrews :
314–14   spoke of reproducing his body, . . . and s·,
315– 1   and s·: "Whosoever liveth— *John* 11 : 26.
319–27   wrote down what an inspired teacher had s·.
320– 1   he s·, "God is love."— *I John* 4 : 8.
320– 8   In Smith's Bible Dictionary it is s·:
320–12   "And the Lord s·, My spirit shall— *Gen.* 6 : 3.
320–15   "And Jehovah s·, My spirit shall not forever
321–26   became to him the voice of God, which s·:
325–21   when he s·: "Present your bodies— *Rom.* 12 : 1.
328–18   can it be s· that they explain it practically,
o 343– 4   James s·: "Show me thy faith— *Jas.* 2 : 18.
345–10   It is sometimes s·, in criticising C. S.
346– 6   It is sometimes s· that C. S. teaches the
347– 3   It is s· by one critic, that to verify this
350–18   He s·: "This people's heart is— *Matt.* 13 : 15.
358–24   Sometimes it is s·: "Rest assured that
p 364–12   He even s· that this poor woman had
364–23   then it must be s· of them also that they
364–29   If so, then it may be s· of them,
367–18   of which Jesus spoke to his disciples, when he s·:
386–26   If a Christian Scientist had s·, while you were
390– 1   she s·, "My food is all digested,
398– 2   as when he s· to the epileptic boy,
398–11   whom they called dead but of whom he s·,
398–12   s·, "Damsel, I say unto thee,— *Mark* 5 : 41.
398–14   To the sufferer with the withered hand he s·,
411– 1   S· Job: "The thing which I— *Job* 3 : 25.
438–19   Another witness, equally inadequate, s·
439–19   and s· :— God will smite you, O whited walls,
t 463–32   It has been s· to the author,
r 473–26   Jesus established what he s· by demonstration,
478–27   St. Paul s·, "But when it pleased— *Gal.* 1 : 15.
481–18   growth of material belief, of which it is s·:
487–25   James s·, "Show me thy faith— *Jas.* 2 : 18.
492–18   Discussing his campaign, General Grant s·:
494–31   it should he s· of his followers also,
g 529–15   And he s· unto the woman,— *Gen.* 3 : 1.
529–17   And the woman s· unto the serpent,— *Gen.* 3 : 2.
529–19   God hath s·, Ye shall not eat of it,— *Gen.* 3 : 3.
530– 8   s·, "Take no thought for your— *Matt.* 6 : 25.
530–13   the serpent s· unto the woman,— *Gen.* 3 : 4.
532–14   and s· unto him, Where art thou?— *Gen.* 3 : 9.
532–15   And he s·, I heard Thy voice— *Gen.* 3 : 10.
533– 5   He s·, Who told thee that thou— *Gen.* 3 : 11.
533– 8   the man s·, The woman whom— *Gen.* 3 : 12.
534– 8   And the Lord God [Jehovah] s·— *Gen.* 3 : 14.
535– 6   Unto the woman He s·, I will— *Gen.* 3 : 16.
535–19   And unto Adam He s·, because   *Gen.* 3 : 17.
536–30   And the Lord God [Jehovah] s·,— *Gen.* 3 : 22.
538–24   and s·, I have gotten a man from— *Gen.* 4 : 1.
541–19   the Lord [Jehovah] s· unto Cain,— *Gen.* 4 : 9.
541–20   And he s·, I know not :— *Gen.* 4 : 9.
541–27   s·, . . . The voice of thy brother's— *Gen.* 4 : 10.
542–14   the Lord [Jehovah] s· unto him,— *Gen.* 4 : 15.
547– 3   contains the proof of all here s· of C. S.
553–10   One of our ablest naturalists has s·:
554–21   Jesus defined this . . . when he s·,
554–22   s·, "Have not I chosen you—*John* 6 : 70,
554–24   This he s· of Judas, one of Adam's race.
555– 6   An inquirer once s· to the discoverer of C. S. :
gl 596– 8   Referring to it, he s· to the Athenians :
   (see also **God, Jesus, Paul**)

saint

c 266–21   and the s· his own heaven by doing right.

sainted

s 136–26   doubted if . . . controlled by the s· preacher.

saintly

o 359–24   from the lips of her s· mother,

saints

pr 5–14   S· and sinners get their full award,

saith

pr 1– *   *believe that those things which he s·— Mark* 11 : 23.
1– *   *he shall have whatsoever he s·.— Mark* 11 : 23.
f 250– 7   has no real entity, but s· "It is I."
252–31   Spirit, bearing opposite testimony, s· :
b 277– 3   s·, "Thou shalt surely die ;"— *Gen.* 2 : 17.
287–19   It s·, "I am man, but I am not the image and
k 499– *   *These things s· He that is holy,— Rev.* 3 : 7.
g 503–13   s· to the darkness upon the face of error,
505–17   Psalmist s·: "The Lord on high— *Psal.* 93 : 4.
540–19   It s· to the human sense of sin,
ap 575–22   s·, "Beautiful for situation,— *Psal.* 48 : 2.

saith

gl 579– *   *These things s· He that is holy,— Rev.* 3 : 7.
580–19   that of which wisdom s·,
584–20   the lust of the flesh, which s· :

sake

a 28–25   persecution for righteousness' s·
f 222–31   no question for conscience s·."— *I Cor.* 10 : 25.
b 338–29   blessed the earth "for man's s·."— *Gen.* 8 : 21.
p 396– 4   both for one's own s· and for that of the patient.
g 535–22   cursed is the ground for thy s· ;— *Gen.* 3 : 17.
ap 571– 9   for the s· of doing right and benefiting our
578– 9   for His name's s·.— *Psal.* 23 : 3.

salary

a 42– 9   was in no peril from s· or popularity.
s 142–11   If the soft palm, upturned to a lordly s·,

saline

s 153– 6   until there was not a single s· property left.

sallow

p 433–14   His s· face blanches with fear,

sallowness

p 442–10   all s· and debility had disappeared.

Sallow Skin

p 431–26   witness . . . testifies :— I am S· S·.

salt

s 153– 7   The s· had "lost his savour ;"— *Matt.* 5 : 13.
p 367–19   "Ye are the s· of the earth."— *Matt.* 5 : 13.
367–21   watch, work, and pray that this s· lose not its
385–28   because you have partaken of s· fish,

saltness

p 367–22   that this salt lose not its s·,

salubrious

p 383–24   Does his assertion prove the use . . . a s· habit,

salutary

m 59–18   more s· in prolonging her health
66– 9   Sorrow is s·.
66–27   Socrates considered patience s· under such
68–23   s· causes sometimes incur these effects.
c 265–31   The pains of sense are s·, if they
p 414– 6   to the s· action of truth,

salutes

sp 88– 8   and no scent s· the nostrils.

salvation

and strength
ap 568–14   Now is come s·, and strength,— *Rev.* 12 : 10.
day of
a 39–19   behold, *now* is the day of s·,"— *II Cor.* 6 : 2.
sp 93– 8   behold, *now* is the day of s·,"— *II Cor.* 6 : 2.
experience that
a 39–22   now is the time in which to experience that s·
from all error
s 132–25   this s· from all error, physical and mental,
full
a 59– 6   a full s· from sin, sickness, and death.
p 406– 6   offering full s· from sin, sickness, and death.
future-world
a 39–20   a future-world s·, or safety,
of us all
a 51–19   consummate example was for the s· of us all,
our
a 30–31   must work out our s· in the way Jesus taught.
own
pr 3–11   enables us to work out our own s·.
a 22–11   "Work out your own s·,"— *Phil.* 2 : 12.
23–26   how to work out one's "own s·,"— *Phil.* 2 : 12.
sp 99– 6   "Work out your own s·"— *Phil.* 2 : 12.
p 426–16   the necessity of working out his own s·.
442–26   "Work out your own s·"— *Phil.* 2 : 12.
t 443–11   to work out their own s· according to
seek
b 285–25   to seek s· through pardon
Soul and
f 210–16   a better understanding of Soul and s·.
universal
b 291–12   Universal s· rests on progression
way of
pref vii– 8   plain to benighted understanding the way of s·
b 316– 2   he became the way of s· to all who

a 45– 9   and for the s· of the whole world
s 146–15   Scholasticism clings for s· to the person,
150–26   predestination of souls to damnation or s·.
ph 166– 9   believes in a pilgrimage to Mecca for the s· of
f 230– 8   This is the s· which comes through God,
gl 593–20   definition of

Samaritan

sp 85–12   The S· woman said : "Come, see— *John* 4 : 29.
s 133– 3   that of the S· woman, who said.

same

pr	2–32	"the s· yesterday, and to-day,— *Heb.* 13 : 8.
	12–28	another who offers the s· measure of prayer?
a	21–21	we have the s· railroad guides,
	45–29	He presented the s· body that he had before his
	48–13	when he drinks from the s· cup,
	51–15	his spiritual life, . . . was found forever the s·.
sp	75–18	the s· plane of belief as those who
	78– 7	belief . . . that at the s· time we are communing with
	82–13	and one person cannot . . . at the s· time.
	85–18	After the s· method, events of great moment
s	108–28	which this s· so-called mind names *matter*,
	112–20	"the s· yesterday, and to-day,— *Heb.* 13 : 8.
	122–29	the s· mistake regarding Soul and body
	128–30	must always bring the s· result.
	135–11	The s· power which heals sin heals also
	142–14	they at the s· time shut the door on
ph	186–22	If we concede the s· reality to discord as to
	188–20	In the s· way pain and pleasure,
f	210–17	by one and the s· metaphysical process.
	229–12	and at the s· time admits that Spirit is God,
	237–21	The latter should be excluded on the s· principle
	243–10	the s· "Mind . . . which was also— *Phil.* 2 : 5.
	245– 7	Believing that she was still living in the s· hour
	249–18	"the s· yesterday, and to-day,— *Heb.* 13 : 8.
c	267–14	the s· authority for the appellative mother,
	267–17	s· is my brother, and sister,— *Matt.* 12 : 50.
b	283– 6	Mind is the s· Life, Love, and wisdom
	283–14	They insist that Life, . . . is one and the s· with
	287–13	at the s· place sweet water and— *Jas.* 3 : 11.
	313– 9	agrees another passage in the s· chapter,
	320–11	learned article on Noah in the s· work,
	321–24	restored his hand . . . by the s· simple process.
	331–29	the s· in essence, though multiform in office :
	336–29	God and man are not the s·,
o	346–31	cannot serve both God and mammon at the s· time ;
	359– 5	will take the s· cases, and cures will follow.
p	370– 6	s· regimen which spiritualizes the thought ;
	370–12	by using the s· drug which might cause the
	370–17	but it uses the s· medicine in both cases.
	379– 2	If . . . sin can do the s·,
	383–14	because mind and body rest on the s· basis.
	386–17	occasions the s· grief that the
	395–10	The s· Principle cures both sin and sickness.
	404–27	are one and the s· thing in C. S.
	404–28	Both cures require the s· method
	406– 3	Sin and sickness are both healed by the s· Principle.
	414– 8	are the s· as in other diseases :
	415–19	In the s· way thought increases or
	416–13	the patient will find himself in the s· pain,
	422–23	and attended by the s· symptoms.
	427–16	Man is the s· after as before a bone is broken
t	455–29	the s· fountain cannot send forth both
	457–22	One cannot scatter his fire, and at the s· time
	458– 1	Mental quackery rests on the s· platform as
	458– 9	the s· effect as truth.
r	474–17	If . . . then they must all be from the s· source ;
	486–15	was the s· immediately after death as before.
	489–22	for the s· fountain sendeth not forth
g	518–16	all having the s· Principle, or Father ;
	525–25	if we give the s· heed to the history of error
	546– 4	"the s· yesterday, and to-day,— *Heb.* 13 : 8.
	551–31	the resulting germ is doomed to the s· routine.
ap	559– 2	Did this s· book contain the revelation of
	566–19	the prayer which concludes the s· hymn,
gl	598– 5	Here the original word is the s· in both cases,
	598– 7	as in other passages in this s· chapter

Samson

s	124– 4	a blind belief, a *S·* shorn of his strength.

sanative

pr	12–21	apparently either poisonous or s·.

sanction

an	106–16	Let this age, . . . s· only such methods as are
s	146–23	Divine Science derives its s· from the Bible,
p	382– 4	having only human approval for their s·.

sanctioned

s	125–11	which human belief created and s·.
ph	171– 2	paganism and lust are so s· by society

sanctity

m	62– 3	the period of gestation have the s· of virginity.

sanctuary

pr	15– 3	The closet typifies the s· of Spirit,
	15–17	In the quiet s· of earnest longings,
f	232–26	In the sacred s· of Truth are voices of

sandal

p	363– 2	costly and fragrant oil,— s· oil perhaps,

sandals

a	28–23	to unloose the s· of thy Master's feet !

sands

sp	87–23	the bodies which lie buried in its s· :

sandstone

gl	580– 1	red s· ; nothingness ;

sang

s	135– 1	s· : "What ailed thee, O thou sea,— *Psal.* 114 : 5.
ph	190–27	When hope rose higher . . . he s· :
	199–32	When Homer s· of the Grecian gods,
g	509–23	"the morning stars s· together."— *Job* 38 : 7.
ap	565–23	After the stars s· together and all was

sanguine

b	330– 6	she cherished s· hopes that C. S.

sanitary

pref	x–25	than that of any other s· method.
sp	79– 7	A scientific mental method is more s· than
s	132–18	from other s· or religious systems,
	133–23	s· methods, and a religious cultus.
ph	175– 5	When . . . less thought is given to s· subjects,
	175–22	nor referred to s· laws.

sapped

o	357–12	the foundations of error would be s·

sapping

g	539– 4	thus s· the foundations of

sat

a	41–25	s· down at the right hand of the Father.
ph	184–29	I s· silently by her side a few moments.
f	245–15	youth s· gently on cheek and brow.
c	261–17	s· aching in his chair till his cue was spoken,
p	436–26	Judge Medicine s· in judgment on the case,

Satan

devil, and

ap	567–15	serpent, called the devil, and *S·*,— *Rev.* 12 : 9.

God and

p	389–26	good and evil, God and *S·*.

had bound her

pr	6–24	he said that *S·* had bound her,

hath bound

r	495– 9	"whom *S·* hath bound,"— *Luke* 13 : 16.

named

ph	187–12	another illusive personification, named *S·*.

this view of

gl	581– 1	This view of *S·* is confirmed by the name

pr	7– 2	"Get thee behind me, *S·*."— *Matt.* 16 : 23.
ph	196–15	not of Rome, *S·*, nor of God, but of sin.
o	351–20	if we consider *S·* as a being coequal in power
ap	566–32	the hosts of heaven against the power of sin, *S·*,

satellite

ap	577–20	no need of sun or s·,

satisfaction

b	296–17	must lose all s· in error and sin
	322–14	Man's wisdom finds no s· in sin,

satisfactory

pref	ix–15	not complete nor s· expositions of Truth.

satisfied

pr	9– 8	Do we pursue the old selfishness, s· with
a	21–30	s· if he can only imagine himself drifting
	36–27	or that the hand of Love is s· with
ph	180– 5	The patient sufferer tries to be s· when he
	181–22	and are s· with good words instead of effects,
	181–28	they generally know it and are s·.
	190–29	I shall be s·, when I awake,— *Psal.* 17 : 15.
f	240–21	If at present s· with wrong-doing,
b	316–30	those dead in trespasses and sins, s· with
g	519– 3	Deity was s· with His work.

satisfy

m	60–32	Higher enjoyments alone can s· the cravings
ph	181–26	in order to s· the sick that you are
f	230–25	soothing syrups to . . . s· mortal belief,
c	257–26	to still the desires, to s· the aspirations?

Saul

b	326–23	*S·* of Tarsus beheld the way— the Christ, or

save

pr	2–18	A request that God will s· us
	12– 1	prayer of faith shall s· the sick,"— *Jas.* 5 : 15.
a	22– 8	to make vigorous efforts to s· themselves ;
	23– 2	require many sacrifices of self to s· us from
	24– 3	Firmness in error will never s· from sin,
	36–12	He was forsaken by all s· John, . . . and a few women
	42–13	the desertion of all s· a few friends,
	49– 8	Were all conspirators s· eleven?
	49–17	No human eye was there to pity, no arm to s·.
	49–30	himself he cannot s·."— *Matt.* 27 : 42.
sp	95– 1	The effect of his Mind was always to heal and to s·
s	136– 8	to s· men both bodily and spiritually.
	149– 1	could s· from sickness as well as from sin.
	164–24	s· from sin, disease, and death.
ph	166–11	believes in the power of his drugs to s·

save

ph 174— 6 Nothing s· divine power is capable of
196— 4 not yet found it true that knowledge can s·
200—26 s· Jesus Christ, and him crucified."— *I Cor.*
2 : 2.
200—28 s· Jesus Christ, and him glorified.
f 226—26 to s· from the slavery of their own beliefs
b 299— 5 s· in the artist's own observation
314—30 depending on . . . . material laws to s· them
p 377— 6 in order to s· their lives,
436—17 and thus s· him from arrest.
439—11 in the attempt to s· him.
t 447 11 and s· the victims of the mental assassins.

saved

a 23—29 and thou shalt be s· !"— *Acts* 16 : 31.
38— 6 foreordination, — the election of a few to be s·,
45—12 we shall be s· by his life."— *Rom.* 5 : 10.
49—29 "He s· others ; himself he cannot— *Matt.* 27 : 42.
sp 98— 8 Body cannot be s· except through Mind.
s 133— 8 In Egypt, it was Mind which s· the Israelites
164—15 before all mankind is s·
f 221—14 At this point C. S. s· him,
b 328— 3 Then he not only will be s·, but *is* s·.
o 346— 8 then teaches how this . . . is to be s· and healed.
346—11 its nothingness is not s·,
p 369—31 any more than he is morally s· in or by sin.
426—18 are not s· from sin or sickness by death,
t 458—30 by which mortals are radically s· from sin
r 497—16 we acknowledge that man is s· through Christ,
ap 577—22 All who are s· must walk in this light.

saves

pr 11— 7 it only s· the criminal from one form of
a 20—22 s· retracing and traversing anew the path
s 143—16 On this basis it s· from starvation by
152— 5 takes away all its supposed sovereignty, and s·
b 328— 7 divine Principle which s· and heals,

saving

b 285—24 not as the s· Principle, or divine Love,
285—31 as the healing and s· power.

Saviour

a 29—19 that is, Joshua, or S·.
55—11 which presents the S· in a clearer light
b 285—24 By interpreting God as a corporeal S·
317—25 Thomas, looking for the ideal S· in matter
326—14 if we would gain the Christ as our only S·.
p 364—18 as Simon sought the S·,
r 477— 2 In this perfect man the S· saw
g 534— 4 and to behold at the sepulchre the risen S·,

Savonarola

a 40—15 Did the martyrdom of S· make the

savor

b 269— 1 pantheistic, and s· of Pandemonium,

savour

s 153— 7 The salt had "lost his s· ;"   *Matt.* 5 : 13.

saw

a 21 20 but until they s· that it enabled their Master
45—22 who earliest s· Jesus after the resurrection
46— 2 until they s· him after his crucifixion
46—29 and the material senses s· him no more.
s 137— 2 His students s· this power of Truth heal
ph 184—32 She looked and s· that it pointed due east.
193—18 The next day I s· him in the yard.
193—29 what I s· and did for that man,
f 226—22 I s· before me the task, wearing out years of
226—29 I s· before me the awful conflict,
227— 3 I s· that the law of mortal belief
228—30 when they s· the demonstration of Christianity
245—12 Some American travellers s· her when she
b 308—21 till he s· its unreality ;
314—20 but the faithful Mary s· him,
321— 9 he s· it become a serpent,
321—17 what he apparently s· was really but a
r 477— 3 In this perfect man the Saviour s·
g 503—26 And God s· the light, that it was — *Gen.* 1 : 4.
506—24 and God s· that it was good.— *Gen.* 1 : 10.
508—11 and God s· that it was good.— *Gen.* 1 : 12.
511—10 and God s· that it was good.— *Gen.* 1 : 18.
512— 7 and God s· that it was good.— *Gen.* 1 : 21.
513—24 and God s· that it was good.— *Gen.* 1 : 25.
515— 2 "And God s· that it was good."— *Gen.* 1 : 25.
518—24 And God s· everything that He— *Gen.* 1 : 31.
525—23 He s· everything which He had made,
536— 2 I s· a new heaven and a new earth :— *Rev.* 21 : 1.
ap 558— 3 And I s· another mighty angel— *Rev.* 10 : 1.
561— 5 through his microscope, s· the sun in an egg
561— 7 Because of his more spiritual vision, St. John s·
561—11 Revelator s· also the spiritual ideal
561—16 John s· the human and divine coincidence,
562— 1 John s· in those days the spiritual idea as
569—29 when the dragon s· that he— *Rev.* 12 : 13.
572—20 I s· a new heaven and a new earth :— *Rev.* 21 : 1.
572—25 but he already s· a new heaven and a new earth.

saw

ap 576—10 And I s· no temple therein :— *Rev.* 21 : 22.
576—19 John s· heaven and earth
gl 596— 7 Paul s· in Athens an altar dedicated

Saxon

b 286—16 In the *S·* and twenty other tongues
g 525— 8 In the *S·*, *mankind, a woman, any one ;*

say

pr 1— * *I s· unto you, That whosoever shall s·* — *Mark*
11 : 23.
1— * *I s· unto you, What things soever* — *Mark* 11 : 24.
1— 4 Regardless of what another may s·
a 18— * *I s· unto you, I will not drink of* — *Luke* 22 : 18.
21— 2 overcoming error . . . you can finally s·,
33—30 If not, can you then s· that you
38—13 was addressing his disciples, yet he did not s·,
40— 5 Another will s· : Go thy way— *Acts* 24 : 25.
49— 5 caused the disciples to s· to their Master :
50—22 Even what they did s·, — that Jesus' teachings
m 63—18 Our laws are not impartial, to s· the least,
64—12 his wife should not s·,
sp 70— * *And when they shall s· unto you,* — *Isa.* 8 : 19.
70— * *Verily, verily, I s· unto you,* — *John* 8 : 51.
74—23 Who will s· that infancy can utter the
92—32 Do you s· the time has not yet come
an 104—10 First, people s· it conflicts with the Bible.
104—11 Next, they s· it has been discovered before.
104—12 Lastly, they s· they have always believed it."
105— 5 To s· that these tribunals have no
s 107—18 the prospect of those days in which we must s·,
120—13 is he well if the senses s· he is sick?
136—12 "Whom do men s· that I, — *Matt.* 16 : 13.
136—15 "Some s· that thou art John— *Matt.* 16 : 14.
137— 9 "But whom s· ye that I am?"— *Matt.* 16 : 15.
137—29 "And I s· also unto thee,— *Matt.* 16 : 18.
153—16 You s· a boil is painful ;
154—32 to s· : "Oh, never mind !
155—31 is it safe to s· that the less in quantity
160—16 what does anatomy s· when the cords contract
161— 3 You s·, "I have burned my finger."
164— 9 It is just to s· that generally the
ph 165— * *Therefore I s· unto you,* — *Matt.* 6 : 25.
165 16 You s· that indigestion, fatigue,
175— 9 What an abuse of natural beauty to s·
184—18 We s· man suffers from the
187—18 We s·, "My hand hath done it."
f 210—25 matter, being unintelligent, cannot s·,
211— 5 and who shall s· whether Truth or error
212—12 When the nerve is gone, which we s· was the
212—26 we s· the lips or hands must move
216— 3 Who shall s· that man is alive to-day, but
216—28 When you s·, "Man's body is material,"
216—28 I s· with Paul : Be "willing— *II Cor.* 5 : 8.
217—29 You s·, "Toil fatigues me."
218— 3 You do not s· a wheel is fatigued ;
218— 9 The body is supposed to s·, "I am ill."
218—11 a coalition with the reports of sin, and s·,
219— 7 and then s· the product is correct.
219— 8 No more can we s· in Science that
229— 8 We should hesitate to s· that Jehovah sins
240—20 You s·, "I dreamed last night."
c 256—22 none can stay His hand, or s· unto— *Dan.* 4 : 35.
257—17 would s· that an anthropomorphic God,
263—17 He might s· in Bible language :
b 277—29 Nothing we can s· or believe regarding
278—21 we s· that Spirit is supreme and all-presence.
283—13 But what s· prevalent theories?
284— 1 It is not rational to s· that Mind is infinite, but
286—29 error must also s·, "I am true."
305—16 Verily, verily I s· unto you,— *John* 5 : 19.
312— 9 People s·, "Man is dead ;"
312—12 yet you s· that matter has caused his death.
324—31 if . . . you cannot be benefited by what I s·.
329— 7 proves the truth of all that I s· of it.
o 341— * *And if I s· the truth,* — *John* 8 : 46.
343— 1 people are taught in such cases to s·, Amen.
343— 9 one might not be able to s· with the apostle,
352—12 Would a mother s· to her child,
p 374— 7 the sick s· : "How can my mind cause a
381— 8 you s· that there is danger.
385—22 You s· that you have not slept well
385—27 You s· or think, because you have partaken of
387— 4 Who dares to s· that actual Mind can be overworked?
391— 5 when thou art delivered . . . the judge will s·,
391—19 When the body is supposed to s·, "I am sick,"
391—22 If you s·, "I am sick," you plead guilty.
392—28 When the condition is present which you s·
396—10 Never s· beforehand how much you
398—12 "Damsel, I s· unto thee, arise !"— *Mark* 5 : 41.
399— 3 You s· that certain material combinations
402— 3 it is but just to s· that the author has
402—16 You s· that accidents, injuries, and
402—20 We s· that one human mind can
409— 2 You may s· : "But if disease obtains in

say

p 409–10	cannot dictate terms . . . nor s·, "I am sick."
409–27	We have no right to s· that life depends on
413–31	A child may have worms, if you s· so,
434– 5	Others s·, "The law of Christ supersedes
435–29	To him I might s·, in Bible language,
t 444–25	s· in thy heart : "Let there be no— Gen. 13 : 8.
447–31	He may s·, as a subterfuge, that unreal is unreal,
448– 8	to s· that there is no evil,
450–28	Who, . . . can s· that there is no error of belief?
461–16	should you s·, "I am sick"? No.
r 485–30	To s· that strength is in matter,
489–19	Who dares to s· that the senses of man can
491–29	Who will s·, even though he does not understand C. S.,
491–32	Who can rationally s· otherwise,
g 531–19	Who will s· that minerals, vegetables, and
531–21	Who dares to s· either that God is in matter or
533–29	as much as to s· in meek penitence,
539–19	false to s· that Truth and error commingle
541–23	It is supposed to s· in the first instance,
543–19	who shall s· that he is not primarily dust?
544–21	The serpent is supposed to s·,
548– 1	Spirit and the bride s·, Come !— Rev. 22 : 17.
553–29	You may s· that mortals are formed before they
554–15	he learns to s·, "I am somebody ;
554–25	but he did s·, "Ye are of your father,—John 8 : 44.
555– 8	but I do not comprehend what you s· about
ap 568–25	What shall we s· of the mighty conquest over
gl 587–15	the serpents of error, which s·,

(see also **Scriptures**)

saying

his
b 271–17	Hence the universal application of his s· :

keep my
sp 70– *	If a man keep my s·,— John 8 : 51.
f 217–13	"If a man keep my s·,— John 8 : 51.
p 428– 8	"If a man keep my s·,— John 8 : 51.
429–31	"If a man keep my s·,— John 8 : 51.
438– 7	If a man keep my s·,— John 8 : 51.

of our Master
b 315– 3	That s· of our Master,
p 382–21	This verifies the s· of our Master :

Scriptural
s 131–17	according to the Scriptural s·,

this
a 50–24	But this s· could not make it so.
b 286–29	But by this s· error, the lie, destroys itself.

uncomprehended
a 42–30	to test his still uncomprehended s·,

a 28–11	did not hinder men from s· :
32–18	s·, Drink ye all of it."— Matt. 26 : 27.
40–12	If the s· is true, "While there's life there's
49–29	mocked him on the cross, s· derisively,
s 140– 5	The Bible represents Him as s· :
164–28	brought to pass the s·— I Cor. 15 : 54.
ph 193–27	threatened with incarceration . . . for s· :
b 294–11	mortal belief, misnamed man, is error, s· :
307– 4	insists still upon the opposite of Truth, s·,
318– 7	even while the corporeal senses are s· that
328–27	believed and obeyed this sacred s·.
334–25	Revelator represents the Son of man as s·
o 345–12	neither knows itself nor what it is s·.
p 363–11	Knowing what those around him were s·
385–23	S· this and believing it,
t 453–1	the author understands what she is s·.
r 485–31	is like s· that the power is in the lever.
496–26	brought to pass the s·— I Cor. 15 : 54.
g 512–17	And God blessed them, s·,— Gen. 1 : 22.
527– 7	commanded the man, s·,— Gen. 2 : 16.
530–19	and s·, through the material senses :
533–16	s·, "The woman, whom Thou gavest me,
535–21	of which I commanded thee, s·,— Gen. 3 : 17.
ap 568–13	And I heard a loud voice s·— Rev. 12 : 10.
574– 8	s·, Come hither, I will show thee— Rev. 21 : 9.

sayings

c 266–24	Mortals must follow Jesus' s·
b 276– 2	fulfils these s· of Scripture,
333–32	By these s· Jesus meant, not that the
o 350– 6	To understand all our Master's s·
350– 7	s· infinitely important,
361–15	conflicts not at all with another of his s· :
p 429–27	have faith in all the s· of our Master,
g 539–32	inspired his wisest and least-understood s·,
554–26	All these s· were to show that

says

pref ix–10	As a certain poet s· of himself,
pr 5–29	An apostle s· that the Son of God [Christ]
12– 1	shall save the sick," s· the Scripture.— Jas. 5 : 15.
m 58–32	"She that is married . . . s· the Bible ;—I Cor. 7 : 34.
sp 79–23	unscientific practitioner s· : "You are ill.
89–11	She s·, "I am incapable of words that glow,

says

sp 99– 6	"Work out your own . . . s· the apostle,— Phil. 2 : 12.
s 113–14	De Quincey s· mathematics has
115– 8	Job s· : "The ear trieth words,— Job 34 : 3.
144–21	the divine power which s· to disease,
151–17	Mortal belief s· that death has been
154–17	the mother is frightened and s·
154–25	That mother . . . who s· to her child :
154–29	s·, moaning more childishly than her child,
ph 172–21	to which the apostle refers when he s·
175–32	Where ignorance is bliss, . . . s· the
186–17	It s· : "I am a real entity,
190– 4	The mortal s· that an inanimate
194–12	for if mortal mind s·, "I am deaf
198–25	though the doctor s· nothing to support his
200–27	C. S. s· : I am determined not to
f 204–31	error, which s· that Soul is in body,
218– 5	If it were not for what the human mind s·
219–21	"The wish," s· the poet, "is ever father to the
252–17	with the arrogance of reality and s· :
b 277– 4	the Scripture s· that dust returns to
286–11	Christ s·, "I am the way."— John 14 : 6.
288–18	St. Paul s· : "There remaineth— Heb. 4 : 9.
291–18	as the Scripture s·.
296–22	It s· to mortals, "You are wretched !"
297– 2	Mortal belief s·, "You are happy !"
297– 5	Human belief s· to mortals, "You are sick !"
307– 8	It s· : "There shall be lords and gods many.
307–17	Error charges its lie to Truth and s· :
332–16	As Paul s· : "There is one God,— I Tim. 2 : 5.
o 342–27	our Master s·, "By their fruits— Matt. 7 : 20.
345–26	The apostle s· : "For if a man think— Gal. 6 : 3.
355– 9	C. S. s·, in the language of the Master,
359–30	One s· : "I have spiritual ideals,
p 375– 1	mortal mind, not matter, which s·, "I die."
375– 9	proves this when his patient s·, "I am better,"
383– 5	One s· : "I take good care of my body."
386– 6	belief s· that you may catch cold
407–21	If delusion s·, "I have lost my memory,"
410– 4	"This is life eternal," s· Jesus,— John 17 : 3.
410–18	John s· : "There is no fear in— I John 4 : 18.
432–10	Another witness is called . . . and s· :
442–25	St. Paul s·, "Work our your— Phil. 2 : 12.
r 474–29	The apostle s· that the mission of Christ
478–23	Error s·, "I am man ;" but this belief is mortal
492–19	Science s· : All is Mind and Mind's idea.
496–23	the spiritual law which s· to the grave,
g 527–12	s· : "God cannot be tempted— Jas. 1 : 13.
533–28	She s·, "The serpent beguiled me,— Gen. 3 : 13.
548–19	a famous naturalist s· : "It is very possible that
552–14	corresponds with that of Job, when he s·,
557–17	the curse will be removed which s· to woman,

(see also **Paul**)

scaffold

f 202–10	until disciplined by the prison and the s· ;

scale

ascending
ph 189–30	goes on in an ascending s· by evolution,

fleshly
s 155–24	puts less weight into the material or fleshly s·

of existence
b 290– 6	no higher spiritually in the s· of existence

of harmony
m 60– 2	in the s· of harmony and happiness.

of health
p 407–19	and ascend a degree in the s· of health,

of intelligence
g 511–27	rising in the s· of intelligence,

right
ph 192–23	the weight you throw into the right s·.

spiritual
s 155–25	and more weight into the spiritual s·.

ph 168– 5	the removal of a single weight from either s·
f 205–30	throws our weight into the s·, not of Spirit,
t 445–17	you weigh the human in the s· with the divine,

scales

ph 168– 4	If the s· are evenly adjusted,

scanty

ph 188–25	an abundant or s· crop of disease, according to

scarcely

b 312–15	though with s· a spark of love in their hearts ;
o 350–32	and the spiritual sense was s· perceived.

scatheless

f 232– 6	afford no s· and permanent evidence

scatter

m 57–26	and s· them to the winds ;
t 457–21	One cannot s· his fire, and at the same time

scatters

m 68–11	and s· love's petals to decay.

scene
p 362– 5 as if to interrupt the *s·* of Oriental festivity.
g 513–10 and the *s·* shifts into light.
ap 572–28 inadequate to take in so wonderful a *s·*.

scent
sp 88– 7 and no *s·* salutes the nostrils.

sceptre
s 152– 2 It would wield the *s·* of a monarch,
ap 571–31 He takes away mitre and *s·*.

scholarly
s 141–11 the line of *s·* and ecclesiastical descent.
f 235–17 though adorned with gems of *s·* attainment,
g 505–27 is not the result of *s·* attainments ;

scholars
pr 16–12 There is indeed some doubt among Bible *s·*,
s 128– 7 business men and cultured *s·*
c 255– 8 cultured *s·* in Rome and in Greece,
g 523–15 according to the best *s·*, there are

scholarship
p 367–12 arrogance of rank and display of *s·*,

scholastic
a 41–19 philosophy, *materia medica*, or *s·* theology
s 141–32 now occupied by *s·* theology and physiology,
f 226–18 Human codes, *s·* theology,
c 256– 4 from the *s·* to the inspirational,
b 315– 4 the *s·* theology of the rabbis.

scholasticism
s 146–15 *S·* clings for salvation to the person,

Scholastic Theology
p 433–28 and *S· T·* is sent for to prepare the
437–22 Materia Medica, Anatomy, Physiology, *S· T·*,
439–17 *S· T·*, Materia Medica, Physiology,

school
ancient
a 41–19 No ancient *s·* of philosophy, *materia medica*,
its
s 112– 7 forfeit their claims to belong to its *s·*,
new
s 112–27 Also, if any so-called new *s·* claims to be
of Christian Science
pref xi–25 The first *s·* of C. S. Mind-healing
s 112– 3 Is there more than one *s·* of C. S.?
of this Science
s 112–26 to establish a genuine *s·* of this Science.
of virtue
m 65– 1 Experience should be the *s·* of virtue,
old
s 149–17 A physician of the old *s·* remarked
preparatory
r 486–10 Earth's preparatory *s·* must be improved
some other
s 112– 0 the Spencerian, or some other *s·*
such a
s 112–29 such a *s·* is erroneous, for it

school-examinations
f 235–11 *S·* are one-sided ;

schools
have rendered
s 146– 6 The *s·* have rendered faith in drugs the fashion,
medical
s 159–23 The medical *s·* would learn the state of
f 217– 6 Medical *s·* may inform us that the
t 444–22 If ecclesiastical sects or medical *s·* turn a
old
s 144–24 the old *s·* still oppose it,
ruling of the
s 148–30 When mortals sin, this ruling of the *s·*
scientific
r 483–23 the ordinary scientific *s·*, which wrestle with
teachers of
f 235– 7 The teachers of *s·* and the readers in churches

s 141–11 from the *s·* and along the line of
b 300–27 theory that . . . is taught by the *s·*.
r 429–29 not included in the teachings of the *s·*,

Science
absolute
a 41–21 demonstrated the divine healing of absolute *S·*.
sp 72–11 so (in absolute *S·*) Soul, or God, is the only
s 484– 2 until its absolute *S·* is reached.
accept
f 249– 1 Let us accept *S·*, relinquish all theories
according to
b 327– 3 an affection for goodness according to *S·*,
actuality of
s 130– 9 can demonstrate the actuality of *S·*.
b 321–12 In this incident was seen the actuality of *S·*.
adulterated the
t 457– 4 Other works, . . . have adulterated the *S·*.
advanced in
sp 84– 8 When sufficiently advanced in *S·*
aided by
p 406–12 aided by *S·*, reaches Truth.

Science
all
s 110– 2 filling all space, constituting all *S·*,
113– 2 one divine Principle of all *S·* ;
126– 8 All *S·* is divine.
b 275–23 that is, all power, all presence, all *S·*.
g 551–16 all *S·* is of God, not of man.
and art
g 507–26 divine Principle of all expresses *S·* and art
and Christianity
f 231–13 If God makes sin, . . . then *S·* and Christianity
p 371–26 will improve through *S·* and Christianity.
and consciousness
p 123–24 Both *S·* and consciousness are now at work
and demonstration
f 243– 2 the *S·* and demonstration of spiritual good
and harmony
ph 192–19 and this teaching accords with *S·* and harmony.
and peace
sp 96–15 on the other side there will be *S·* and peace.
and the senses
b 273–13 Hence the enmity between *S·* and the senses,
and truth
s 110–23 the *S·* and truth therein will forever remain
r 479–22 In the vast forever, in the *S·* and truth of being,
g 521–23 The *S·* and truth of the divine creation
and understanding
b 274–27 *S·* and understanding, . . . destroy the imaginary
annihilates
b 330–26 a delusion . . . which *S·* annihilates.
announced by
b 298–19 real is attained, which is announced by *S·*,
antagonistic to
ph 182–15 hypotheses of mortals are antagonistic to *S·*
apart from
r 480–13 Material sense has its realm apart from *S·*
apprehended in
p 402–11 will be apprehended in *S·*,
approaching
f 223–22 accompany approaching *S·*, and cannot be put
axe of
a 27–18 He laid the axe of *S·* at the root of
basis of
ph 182–17 those who heal the sick on the basis of *S·*.
battle-axe of
p 389–27 falling before the battle-axe of *S·*.
beheld in
r 476–32 Jesus beheld in *S·* the perfect man,
can heal
ph 179– 5 *S·* can heal the sick, who are absent from
cannot destroy
b 298– 7 belief cannot destroy *S·* armed with faith,
cannot produce
p 402–29 *S·* cannot produce both disorder and order.
Christ
s 107– 1 In the year 1866, I discovered the Christ *S·*
127–10 The terms . . . Christ *S·* or C. S.,
Christian
pref viii– 3 to reach the heights of *C· S·*, man must
viii–16 On this basis *C· S·* will have a fair fight.
viii–28 the system that she denominated *C· S·*.
ix–20 Her first pamphlet on *C· S·* was copyrighted in
x– 9 is not a factor in the Principle of *C· S·*.
xi– 2 Many imagine that the phenomena . . . in *C· S·*
xi– 5 On the contrary, *C· S·* rationally explains that
xi– 9 The physical healing of *C· S·* results now,
xi–25 The first school of *C. S.* Mind-healing was
xii– 5 in the United States, where *C· S·* was first
pr 10–12 *C· S·* reveals a necessity for overcoming the
14– 9 understanding of Life as revealed in *C· S·*.
16–18 *C· S·* teaches us that "the evil one,"
a 24– 7 open the way for *C· S·* to be understood,
26–26 *C· S·* destroys sickness, sin, and death.
26–32 *C· S·*, working out the harmony of Life and
29–15 Those instructed in *C· S·* have reached the
36–17 preclude *C· S·* from finding favor with the
41–22 Jesus foresaw the reception *C· S·* would have
42–26 in *C· S·* the true man is governed by God
44–11 He met and mastered on the basis of *C· S·*,
52–23 two cardinal points of Mind-healing, or *C· S·*,
m 63–13 *C· S·* furnishes no precedent for such injustice,
63–17 less rights than does either *C· S·* or civilization.
65–11 To gain *C· S·* and its harmony,
68–27 *C· S·* presents unfoldment, not accretion ;
sp 70– 4 revelations of *C· S·* unlock the treasures of
71–32 a theory contrary to *C· S·*.
74–29 In *C· S·* there is never a retrograde step,
79–12 *C· S·* removes these beliefs and hypotheses
79–14 *C· S·*, . . . introduces the harmony of being.
83– 9 Nothing is more antagonistic to *C· S·* than
83–21 It is contrary to *C· S·* to suppose that
83–23 Between *C· S·* and all forms of superstition
84–30 is learned through Christ and *C· S·*.
93–22 In *C· S·*, Spirit, as a proper noun, is the
95–22 we want that day to be succeeded by *C· S·*,
97– 1 who discern *C· S·* will hold crime in check.
97– 9 in *C· S·* the flight of one and the blow of the

Science
Christian

sp 98–13	human hypotheses do not express *C· S·* ;
99–10	with this key *C· S·* has opened the door of
99–14	*C· S·* teaches only that which is spiritual
99–15	*C· S·* is unerring and Divine ;
an 102–32	*C· S·* despoils the kingdom of evil,
103–18	As named in *C· S·*, . . . hypnotism is the specific
103–32	In *C· S·*, man can do no harm,
104– 3	When *C· S·* and animal magnetism are
104–13	*C· S·* goes to the bottom of mental action,
105–31	from ordinary medical practice to *C· S·*
106– 6	*C· S·* has its Declaration of Independence.
106–16	Let this age, which sits in judgment on *C· S·*,
s 107– 3	and named my discovery *C· S·*.
107–11	Through *C· S·*, religion and medicine are
109– 4	*C· S·* reveals incontrovertibly that Mind is
110–17	the truth of *C· S·* was demonstrated.
110–25	Jesus demonstrated the power of *C· S·*
111– 3	the demonstrable truths of *C· S·* ;
111– 6	*C· S·* is natural, but not physical.
111–24	*C· S·* meets a yearning of the human race
112– 3	Is there more than one school of *C· S·*?
112– 4	*C· S·* is demonstrable.
112–16	From the infinite One in *C· S·* comes
112–23	Any theory of *C· S·*, which departs from
112–27	if any so-called new school claims to be *C· S·*,
113– 6	the heart and soul of *C· S·*, is Love.
113–26	The divine metaphysics of *C· S·*,
114–16	as the phrase is used in teaching *C· S·*,
114–23	*C· S·* explains all cause and effect as mental,
115– 7	who has not personally demonstrated *C· S·*
116–11	A correct view of *C· S·* and of its adaptation
116–20	*C· S·* strongly emphasizes the thought that God
117– 7	*C· S·* attaches no physical nature and
119–29	*C· S·* reverses the seeming relation of Soul and
123– 2	*C· S·* will surely destroy the greater error
123–16	The term *C· S·* was introduced by the author
123–30	*C· S·* differs from material science,
123–32	*C· S·* is pre-eminently scientific,
126–15	point at issue between *C· S·* on the one hand
126–22	I have set forth *C· S·* and its application
127–10	The terms . . . *C· S·*, or Science alone,
127–15	*C· S·* relates especially to Science as
127–16	*C. S.* reveals God, not as the author of sin,
127–30	*C· S·* eschews what is called natural science,
128– 8	have found that *C· S·* enhances their endurance
129– 1	in *C· S·* there are no discords nor contradictions,
130–15	*C· S·*, . . . would disabuse the human mind of
131–13	Must *C· S·* come through the Christian churches
134–21	The true Logos is demonstrably *C· S·*,
139–29	theosophy, and agnosticism are opposed to *C· S·*,
139–32	does not follow that the profane . . . cannot be
	healed by *C· S·*.
140–25	The *C· S·* God is universal, eternal,
141–29	Let our pulpits do justice to *C· S·*.
144–17	is not the metaphysical practice of *C· S·*,
145–31	The theology of *C· S·* includes healing the sick.
147– 7	I demonstrated the divine rules of *C· S·*.
147–20	on the spiritual groundwork of *C· S·*.
147–29	This rule remained to be discovered in *C· S·*.
149–11	without explanation except in *C· S·*.
150–11	mission of *C· S·* now, as in the time of
152–23	prepared her thought for the metaphysics of
	C· S·
155–19	general belief, . . . works against *C· S·* ;
156–28	Metaphysics, as taught in *C· S·*,
157– 2	*C· S·* deals wholly with the mental cause
157– 8	*C· S·* exterminates the drug,
157–28	*C· S·* impresses the entire corporeality,
162– 4	*C· S·* brings to the body the sunlight of Truth,
162– 5	*C· S·* acts as an alterative,
162–25	*C· S·* heals organic disease as surely as
162–28	the divine Principle of *C· S·*
164–12	false claimants to *C· S·*.
164–20	does not in the least disprove *C· S·* ;
ph 168– 2	who think the standard of *C· S·* too high
174–14	Whoever opens the way in *C· S·* is a pilgrim
178–23	In proportion to our understanding of *C· S·*,
178–32	reaches the understanding of *C· S·*
181–20	finally attain the understanding of *C· S·*.
182–28	or else from ignorance of *C· S·*
183–30	If *C· S·* dishonors human belief,
185– 6	No system of hygiene but *C· S·* is purely mental.
185–18	Such theories have no relationship to *C· S·*,
186– 5	*C· S·* destroys material beliefs
189– 9	should no more deny the power of *C· S·*
191–29	but in *C· S·*, Truth never mingles with error.
200–27	*C· S·* says : I am determined not to
f 202–14	*C· S·* lights the torch of
217– 7	inform us that the healing work of *C· S·*
221–14	At this point *C· S·* saved him,
227– 1	to guide me into the land of *C· S·*,
227–21	*C· S·* raises the standard of liberty
236–18	Hence the importance of *C· S·*,
237–16	should be taught the Truth-cure, *C· S·*,
237–22	This makes *C· S·* early available.

Science
Christian

f 239–13	The watchword of *C· S·* is Scriptural :
252– 6	regarding the pathology and theology of *C· S·*.
254–16	During the sensual ages, absolute *C· S·* may not
c 262– 6	*C· S·* takes naught from the perfection of God,
264–28	When we learn the way in *C· S·*
266–19	Universal Love is the divine way in *C· S·*.
b 269–10	*C· S·* makes man Godlike.
272–25	the divine origin and operation of *C· S·*.
272–25	The triumphs of *C· S·* are recorded in
272–31	*C· S·*, as demonstrated by Jesus,
274– 1	opposed promptly and persistently by *C· S·*.
284–28	According to *C· S·*, the only real senses of man
285–28	As mortals reach, through knowledge of *C· S·*,
288–11	the final physical and moral effects of *C· S·*
288–20	The chief stones in the temple of *C· S·*
293–28	*C· S·* brings to light Truth and its supremacy,
296–30	understanding the situation in *C· S·*.
298–12	until this sense is corrected by *C· S·*.
301– 5	Few persons comprehend what *C· S·* means by
	the
302–31	Even in *C· S·*, reproduction by
304–10	This is the doctrine of *C· S·* :
309–22	to be renamed in *C· S·* and led to deny
317– 7	declares best the power of *C· S·*,
323– 1	Mortals may seek the understanding of *C· S·*,
323– 2	to glean from *C· S·* the facts of being
323–28	effects of *C· S·* are not so much seen as felt.
326–19	have begun at the numeration-table of *C· S·*,
327–18	the strict demands of *C· S·* seem peremptory ;
329– 6	A little understanding of *C· S·* proves the
330– 4	learned the vastness of *C· S·*,
330– 6	she cherished sanguine hopes that *C· S·* would
337–14	*C· S·* demonstrates that none but the pure
337–30	the rule of health and holiness in *C· S·*,
338– 1	*C· S·*, rightly understood, leads to eternal
340– 5	This text . . . conveys the *C· S·* thought,
340–17	It demonstrates *C· S·*.
o 341–11	In *C· S·* mere opinion is valueless.
341–18	facts are so absolute . . . in support of *C· S·*,
342–21	*C· S·* awakens the sinner, reclaims the infidel,
343–11	the halt, and the blind look up to *C· S·*
344– 1	It is objected to *C· S·* that it claims
344–15	and until the enemies of *C· S·* test its
344–23	the *C· S·* which Jesus preached and practised
344–29	while *C· S·* cures its hundred
345– 3	uniformly used and understood in *C· S·*.
345–10	It is sometimes said, in criticizing *C· S·*,
345–18	One who understands *C· S·* can heal the
345–19	heal the sick on the divine Principle of *C· S·*,
345–23	able to discern the distinction (made by *C· S·*)
345–31	It is not the purpose of *C· S·* to
346– 6	It is sometimes said that *C· S·* teaches
347– 4	*C· S·* declares that whatever is mortal
347–23	If *C· S·* takes away the popular gods,
348–27	witness the full fruitage of *C· S·*,
348–30	as a result of teaching *C· S·*,
349–10	Two essential points of *C· S·* are,
349–19	The elucidation of *C· S·* lies in its
349–31	In *C· S·*, substance is understood to be
349–32	the opponents of *C· S·* believe substance to be
350– 5	*C· S·* takes exactly the opposite view.
351– 5	divine Principle which demonstrates *C· S·*,
353– 6	till the testimony . . . yields entirely to *C· S·*.
354– 1	Are the protests of *C· S·* against the
354– 8	and yet deny *C· S·*, when it teaches precisely this
354–13	opponents of *C· S·* neither give nor offer
354–32	If the letter of *C· S·* appears inconsistent,
355– 1	gain the spiritual meaning of *C· S·*,
355– 9	As for sin and disease, *C· S·* says,
355–20	The statement that the teachings of *C· S·*
355–25	wholly due to a misapprehension . . . of *C· S·*
358– 9	*C· S·*, understood, coincides with the
358–13	*C· S·* is neither made up of contradictory
359–21	the discoverer of *C· S·* early received
361– 2	Here *C· S·* intervenes, explains these
p 367– 2	nor bury the *morale* of *C· S·* in the
367– 8	are but so many parodies on legitimate *C· S·*,
369–25	preventive and curative) arts belong . . . to *C· S·*,
370–30	change our basis from sensation to *C· S·*,
371– 8	By those uninstructed in *C· S·*,
371–23	when urging the claims of *C· S·* ;
372–14	When man demonstrates *C· S·* absolutely,
372–18	*C· S·* and Christianity are one.
372–19	How, then, in Christianity any more than in
	C· S·,
372–27	In *C· S·*, a denial of Truth is fatal,
375–30	seems anomalous except to the expert in *C· S·*.
377– 9	Then is the time to cure them through *C· S·*,
379–19	opposite statement of Life as taught in *C· S·*,
382– 6	were given to the study of *C· S·* and to
383– 2	I was cured when I learned my way in *C· S·*."
384–15	prove to himself, . . . the grand verities of *C· S·*.
388– 2	Christian martyrs were prophets of *C· S·*.
388– 8	testified to the divine basis of *C· S·*,
389– 3	If this decision be left to *C· S·*, it will be

Science

dispels
sp 80–15 S· dispels mystery and explains

Divine
a 55–29 This Comforter I understand to be Divine S·.
s 127– 9 The terms Divine S·, Spiritual Science,

divine
pref vii–12 to behold and to follow this daystar of divine S·,
pr 12–26 not the outgrowth of divine S·.
12–32 In divine S·, where prayers are mental,
a 36– 4 Divine S· reveals the necessity of
38– 9 is broken by the demands of divine S·.
40– 8 Divine S· adjusts the balance
42–18 gave full evidence of divine S·,
42–21 This error Jesus met with divine S·
43– 9 that influx of divine S· which
43–23 he was demonstrating divine S·.
45– 6 demonstrated divine S· in his victory over
46–32 an enlarged understanding of divine S·,
53–11 He was at work in divine S·.
55–24 layeth his earthly all on the altar of divine S·,
m 69– 4 as fixed in divine S· as is the proof that
sp 76–19 When divine S· is universally understood,
76–29 final understanding of Christ in divine S·.
91– 9 difficult for the sinner to accept divine S·,
96–26 shaped his course in accordance with divine S·
s 108–21 I learned these truths in divine S· :
111– 5 divine Mind as expressed through divine S·.
112–12 divine S· which eschews man-made systems,
114–28 In divine S·, the universe, including man, is
121–31 is allied to divine S· as displayed in the
123–12 Divine S·, rising above physical theories,
123–20 discovery of this divine S· of Mind-healing,
124–28 divine S· declares that they belong wholly to
130– 7 vain to speak dishonestly of divine S·,
131– 6 When once destroyed by divine S·,
136–22 no high appreciation of divine S·
139–23 could neither wholly obscure the divine S· of
142–19 divine S· to be welcomed in.
144–23 divine S· wars with . . . physical science,
146–23 Divine S· derives its sanction from the Bible,
149– 5 more excellent way is divine S·
149–16 proved the Principle of divine S·.
149–30 to understand the affirmations of divine S·,
164–13 minus the unction of divine S·.
164–27 put on immortality [divine S·].— *I Cor.* 15 : 54.
ph 167– 6 We apprehend Life in divine S· only as we
167–11 nor perceive divine S· with the material
171– 6 will reopen with the key of divine S·
172–12 divine S· reveals the eternal chain
184–24 demonstrated this as a rule of divine S·
185–15 to match the divine S· of immortal Mind,
f 213–17 Divine S· reveals sound as communicated
221–28 undisciplined by self-denial and divine S·.
226–13 but through Christ's divine S·.
226–20 Divine S· rends asunder these fetters,
228–16 through the understanding of divine S·.
231– 1 obliterated through Christ in divine S·,
231–23 divine S· of being in man's relation to God,
231–27 is in accordance with divine S·.
232– 8 Security . . . is found only in divine S·.
235– 6 does not obey the requirements of divine S·.
241– 2 knows God's will or the demands of divine S·.
242–10 and Christ in divine S· shows us this way.
242–25 The divine S· of man is woven into
242–30 The finger-posts of divine S· show the way
244– 4 Divine S· reveals these grand facts.
c 259– 6 In divine S·, man is the true image of God.
259–28 through divine S·, which corrects error with
265– 1 and its government is divine S·.
267–19 examined in the light of divine S·,
b 271– 6 Neither . . . exists in divine S·.
271–15 divine S·, which their Master demonstrated
273– 7 without the divine Principle of divine S·.
273–10 Divine S· reverses the false testimony
274–23 Divine S· is absolute, and permits no
275– 6 The starting-point of divine S· is
276–10 Man and his Maker are correlated in divine S·,
276–30 Divine S· does not gather grapes from thorns
278– 5 the only substance . . . recognized by divine S·.
281– 1 yields only to the understanding of divine S·,
281– 8 Divine S· contradicts the corporeal senses,
281–27 Divine S· does not put new wine into old
287– 7 Divine S· contradicts this postulate
290–21 until in divine S· Christ, Truth, removes
292– 4 Divine S· alone can compass the heights
298– 3 Truth, and Love are the realities of divine S·.
301–16 and is revealed only through divine S·.
303–16 Divine S· lays the axe at the root of the
305–26 the divine Principle that obtains in divine S·
308–23 in this Peniel of divine S·.
314–25 The higher his demonstration of divine S·
315– 9 his understanding of this divine S· brought
316– 1 demonstrating the way of divine S·,
319–21 The divine S· taught in the original
321–15 destroyed through understanding divine S·,
321–25 by this proof in divine S·,

Science

divine
b 322–11 before this recognition of divine S· can come
322–30 Then we begin to learn Life in divine S·.
323–21 they will be receptive of divine S·,
325–27 the divine S· which ushered Jesus into
326–32 and learned a lesson in divine S·.
329– 9 to question the great might of divine S·
329–32 Human resistance to divine S· weakens
330–18 or to the revelation of divine S·.
331–31 divine S· or the Holy Comforter.
331–32 express in divine S· the threefold, essential
334–18 exist in the eternal order of divine S·,
336–29 in the order of divine S·, God and man coexist
337–10 According to divine S·, man is in a degree
o 344– 6 sinless condition of man in divine S·,
349–14 in conveying the teachings of divine S·
353– 3 real to material sense, is unreal in divine S·.
354– 9 The words of divine S· find their immortality in
354–30 opponents of divine S· must be charitable,
361–24 A human perception of divine S·,
p 368– 5 Divine S· insists that time will prove all this.
371–19 The way in divine S· is the only way out of
390–13 dispute the testimony of . . . with divine S·.
395–11 When divine S· overcomes faith in
411– 9 not perfectly attuned to divine S·.
418– 9 unerring, and certain effect of divine S·.
t 444–28 Immortals, or God's children in divine S·,
445–10 possibilities of man endued with divine S·.
448–20 the strong impress of divine S·,
460–32 was no longer cast upon divine S·.
r 470– 5 which constitute divine S·.
470–11 Divine S· explains the abstract statement
471–13 The facts of divine S· should be admitted,
471–30 her highest creed has been divine S·,
476– 4 In divine S·, God and the real man are
477–13 Divine S· shows it to be impossible that
480–29 This is the eternal verity of divine S·.
484–10 In divine S·, the supposed laws of matter
484–24 the human antipode of divine S·.
494–19 and seek safety in divine S·.
g 503–12 Divine S·, the Word of God, saith
506–10 Through divine S·, Spirit, God, unites
511–11 In divine S·, which is the seal of Deity
513–13 until divine S· becomes the interpreter.
515–30 Call the mirror divine S·,
517–11 In divine S·, we have not as much authority for
519–28 according to the apprehension of divine S·.
526–19 sword which guards it is the type of divine S·.
530– 5 In divine S·, man is sustained by God,
530–18 represents error . . . giving the lie to divine S·
535–10 Divine S· deals its chief blow at the
543– 8 In divine S·, the material man is shut out from
543–14 against which divine S· is engaged in a
543–22 are found, according to divine S·, to be
549–25 the pathway leading to divine S·
551–15 material methods are impossible in divine S·
557–19 Divine S· rolls back the clouds of error with
ap 558–10 This angel . . . prefigures divine S·.
559– 3 contain the revelation of divine S·,
559–20 Take divine S·.
560–10 divine S· interprets the Principle of
562– 3 baptize with the Holy Ghost,— divine S·.
564–20 should be demonstrated in divine S·,
565–18 will eventually rule . . . with divine S·.
567–31 Divine S· shows how the Lamb slays the wolf.
569–15 Alas for those who break faith with divine S·
571–30 with the sublime grandeur of divine S·,
575–10 represents the light and glory of divine S·.
575–19 the Word, Christ, Christianity, and divine S· ;
576–23 In divine S·, man possesses this recognition
gl 583– 8 are governed by divine S· ;
583–18 and the demonstration of divine S·,
584–26 DOVE. A symbol of divine S· ;
585–16 Divine S· encompassing the universe and man ;
588– 5 Divine S· understood and acknowledged.
588– 7 HOLY GHOST. Divine S·.
590– 2 The reign of harmony in divine S· ;
592–18 NEW JERUSALEM. Divine S· ;
595–12 the eternal demand of divine S·.
597–18 and opened the sepulchre with divine S·,

enables one
sp 87–15 S· enables one to read the human mind, but not

establishing the
s 135– 8 establishing the S· of God's . . . law.

eternal
sp 78–32 the invisible good dwelling in eternal S·.
s 150– 5 demonstrated as an immanent, eternal S·,
c 258–29 under the government of God in eternal S·,

explains
r 470–11 Divine S· explains the abstract statement
g 522–10 S· explains as impossible.

exposes
sp 91–10 because S· exposes his nothingness ;

expressed in
ph 178–22 Truth, or the divine Mind, expressed in S·.

Science

expressed through
r 471–28 the spiritual import, expressed through S·,
fact in
p 430–12 When will mankind wake to this great fact in S·?
ap 573– 6 Holy Writ sustains the fact in S·, that the
facts of
g 516– 7 subordinate the false . . . to the facts of S·,
founded on
r 487–19 Christian evidence is founded on S·
found in
r 475–17 conscious identity of being as found in S·,
genuine
sp 95– 2 the only genuine S· of reading mortal mind.
governed by
f 206–13 governed by S· instead of the senses,
harmony, and
b 299–27 seem to hide Truth, health, harmony, and S·,
harmony of
sp 81–27 hides the harmony of S·,
g 514–29 moving in the harmony of S·,
ap 562–16 divine Principle of man in the harmony of S·.
has called
r 483–16 S· has called the world to battle over this
has explained
b 334–28 [S· has explained me]."
heal by
r 483– 9 In order to heal by S·, you must not be
hill of
b 326– 8 must not try to climb the hill of S· by
illuminations of
gl 596–15 The illuminations of S· give us a sense of the
impossible in
a 39–25 both are unreal, because impossible in S·.
sp 74–21 backward transformation is impossible in S·.
83–12 Miracles are impossible in S·,
t 446–17 or his demonstration is . . . impossible in S·.
indestructible in
r 471– 1 are indestructible in S· ;
inevitably lifts
m 60– 2 S· inevitably lifts one's being higher in the
inspired by
p 368– 3 The confidence inspired by S· lies in the fact
instructed by
g 552–20 but not yet instructed by S·,
interpreted by
s 124–14 universe, like man, is to be interpreted by S·
is able
ap 568– 4 but S· is able to destroy this lie, called evil.
is divine
s 126– 8 All S· is divine.
r 492–27 the Principle of this S· is divine,
is immortal
vp 84– 1 S· is immortal and coordinate neither with the
knowledge of
b 286– 6 for this is fatal to a knowledge of S·.
knows no lapse
r 471– 1 S· knows no lapse from nor return to harmony,
landmarks of
b 320– 0 which are the landmarks of S·.
letter of
s 113– 4 The letter of S· plentifully reaches humanity
f 243–11 must always accompany the letter of S·
linked by
s 316– 4 The real man being linked by S· to his Maker,
mastered by
p 427–11 must be met and mastered by S·,
medicine of
an 104–19 The medicine of S· is divine Mind ;
metaphysical
ph 195–14 metaphysical S· and its divine Principle.
f 219–25 Those who are healed through metaphysical S·
more
r 487– 8 There is more S· in the perpetual exercise of
must be apprehended
s 110–30 Its S· must be apprehended by as many as
must be Christianity
s 135–22 and S· must be Christianity,
must triumph
r 484–24 S· must triumph over material sense,
Natural
s 111–20 A prize . . . for the best essay on Natural S·,
never change in
p 427– 2 this fact can never change in S· to the
never removes
sp 80–16 S· never removes phenomena from the
no error in
s 131– 3 There is no error in S·,
no hypocrisy in
b 329–21 There is no hypocrisy in S·.
obsolete in
gl 588–22 IN. A term obsolete in S· if
of being
pr 2–15 Prayer cannot change the S· of being,
m 63– 3 if you understood the S· of being.
sp 77– 6 until the S· of being is reached.
81– 6 If Spiritualists understood the S· of being,
84–14 Acquaintance with the S· of being enables

Science

of being
sp 93–32 of the reign of harmony in the S· of being.
s 122– 2 often reverses the real S· of being,
128–15 A knowledge of the S· of being
144–27 When the S· of being is . . . understood,
ph 191–24 The S· of being reveals man and immortality
200–16 The great truth in the S· of being.
f 207–16 The S· of being repudiates self-evident
207–24 belong not to the S· of being,
231–23 divine S· of being in man's relation to God,
249–10 Such is the true S· of being.
b 277–18 points to the spiritual truth and S· of being.
280–31 and rejecting the S· of being
285– 3 This S· of being obtains not alone hereafter
302–19 The S· of being reveals man as perfect,
304–30 man, not understanding the S· of being,
309–24 The S· of being shows it to be impossible
311–21 understand the S· of being.
321–30 the S· of being was demonstrated by Jesus,
331– 8 If . . . the S· of being would be forever lost
336–27 The S· of being furnishes the rule of perfection,
340–21 The divine Principle of . . . bases the S· of being,
o 350–26 before the S· of being can be demonstrated.
p 372– 8 The S· of being, in which all is divine Mind,
406–11 The S· of being unveils the errors of sense,
r 492–27 On this statement rests the S· of being,
g 518– 4 This is the S· of being.
gl 583– 4 suppositions . . . opposed to the S· of being.
598–25 retained when the S· of being is understood,
of celestial being
a 26–16 to reveal the S· of celestial being,
of Christ
a 55–18 when man shall recognize the S· of Christ
s 118– 2 spiritual leaven signifies the S· of Christ
of Christianity
pr 4–23 We reach the S· of Christianity
sp 98– 8 The S· of Christianity is misinterpreted by
f 203– 3 In the S· of Christianity, Mind . . . has
b 271–21 When the S· of Christianity appears, it will
o 347–19 it is the S· of Christianity which is restoring it,
351–12 discerned in the S· of Christianity,
r 466–26 S· of Christianity comes with fan in hand
473–29 This is the S· of Christianity.
474– 6 Whoever introduces the S· of Christianity
of creation
g 509–29 Knowing the S· of creation,
537–23 coordinate with the S· of creation
539–23 arguing for the S· of creation, Jesus said :
539–30 The S· of creation, so conspicuous in the
of divine Mind
ph 180–28 is found in the S· of divine Mind
of Genesis
g 525–22 In the S· of Genesis we read that
of God
s 111– 7 The S· of God and man is
111– 9 as the S· of God, Spirit, must,
of healing
sp 85– 9 You will reach the perfect S· of healing
ph 167– 4 If . . . the S· of healing is not attained,
t 444–31 make clear to students the S· of healing,
455– 8 in order to teach this S· of healing
456–29 C. S., or the S· of healing through Mind.
g 547– 7 prove for yourself, . . . the S· of healing,
of Life
pr 9–22 It involves the S· of Life,
m 57– 3 cannot attain the S· of Life.
b 303–20 beatified understanding of the S· of Life.
p 409–29 in ignorance of the S· of Life,
r 489– 3 if the S· of Life were understood,
of Love
a 30– 3 demonstrate the S· of Love —
of man
sp 73–10 the individuality and the S· of man,
f 242–25 The divine S· of man is woven into
p 409–25 as mortals realize the S· of man
of mental healing
t 455–31 in the S· of mental healing and teaching,
of mental practice
p 410–23 The S· of mental practice is
of Mind
m 62–32 Because mortals . . . reject the S· of Mind,
67–11 nautical science is not equal to the S· of Mind.
sp 71–21 When the S· of Mind is understood,
s 157– 6 is employed through the S· of Mind,
ph 181–21 If you are too material to love the S· of Mind
f 202– 7 bring to bear upon the study of the S· of Mind
237–30 unwilling to investigate the S· of Mind
b 269–25 on the testimony of the S· of Mind.
294–31 The S· of Mind corrects such mistakes,
318–22 The S· of Mind denies the error of
p 398–30 The S· of Mind must come to the rescue,
t 460–14 When the S· of Mind was a fresh revelation
r 467–29 in the S· of Mind, we begin with Mind,
473– 4 The S· of Mind disposes of all evil.
481–10 various contradictions of the S· of Mind by the
483–22 Because the S· of Mind seems to bring
490–12 The S· of Mind needs to be understood.

Science

of Mind
r 492–24   must eventually submit to the *S·* of Mind,
495–31   In the *S·* of Mind, you will soon ascertain
g 520–30   Spirit acts through the *S·* of Mind,
549– 1   This discovery is corroborative of the *S·* of Mind
557–24   revealed religion proclaims the *S·* of Mind

of Mind-healing
s 120–17   The *S·* of Mind-healing shows it to be
123–20   discovery of this divine *S·* of Mind-healing,
147–14   contains the complete *S·* of Mind-healing,
151–10   if they understood the *S·* of Mind-healing,
t 446–18   In the *S·* of Mind-healing, it is imperative
451–20   teacher of the *S·* of Mind-healing,

of Soul
s 122– 8   material senses' reversal of the *S·* of Soul
131– 8   opposition of sensuous man to the *S·* of Soul
r 467– 1   the demands of the *S·* of Soul?
467–21   This is a leading point in the *S·* of Soul,

of Spirit
a 31–29   which would attend the *S·* of Spirit,
b 270–21   and maintain the *S·* of Spirit.
p 369–26   psychology, or the *S·* of Spirit, God,

of spiritual reflection
b 305–21   opposed to the *S·* of spiritual reflection,

of the Scriptures
s 139–23   the divine *S·* of the Scriptures seen from
b 319–28   and misstates the *S·* of the Scriptures,

of this proof
a 42–29   taught his disciples the *S·* of this proof.

opposite of
r 471– 7   *error,* — the opposite of *S·,*

order of
s 123– 7   which reverses the order of *S·*
f 240–10   In the order of *S·,* in which the Principle is

phenomenon of
gl 591–22   MIRACLE. . . . a phenomenon of *S·.*

practical
sp 98–18   stands a revealed and practical *S·.*

practises the
t 446–11   Whoever practises the *S·* the author teaches,

prepared in
m 61–11   highway of our God may be prepared in *S·.*

Principle and
a 20–31   the divine Principle and *S·* of all healing.

Principle of
sp 81–28   cannot destroy the divine Principle of *S·.*
s 120–20   the divine Principle of *S·,* reversing the
b 272–32   reveals the natural, divine Principle of *S·.*

real
s 122– 2   often reverses the real *S·* of being,
b 273– 8   They differ from real *S·* because they

reality and in
b 293–11   In reality and in *S·,* both strata, . . . are false

removes
a 40– 9   *S·* removes the penalty only by

renders
g 540–17   *S·* renders "unto Cæsar the — *Matt.* 22 : 21.

rends asunder
f 226–20   *S·* rends asunder these fetters,

revealed in
sp 81–17   the likeness of God as revealed in *S·*

reveals
pr 10–12   C. *S·* reveals a necessity for overcoming the
a 36– 4   Divine *S·* reveals the necessity of
s 109– 4   C. *S·* reveals incontrovertibly that Mind is
127–16   C. *S·* reveals God, not as the author of sin,
ph 172–12   divine *S·* reveals the eternal chain
f 213–17   Divine *S·* reveals sound as communicated
244– 4   Divine *S·* reveals these grands facts.
250–30   *S·* reveals Life as not being at the mercy of
c 260–13   *S·* reveals the possibility of achieving
b 278– 1   *S·* reveals nothing in Spirit out of which to
288–27   *S·* reveals the glorious possibilities of
310–14   So *S·* reveals Soul as God, untouched by sin
r 466–12   represent contraries, as C. *S·* reveals,
467–17   *S·* reveals Spirit, Soul, as not in the body,
477–11   C. *S·* reveals man as the idea of God,
480–12   origin and governor of all that *S·* reveals.
490– 7   C. *S·* reveals Truth and Love as the
491–21   *S·* reveals material man as never the real
g 510–28   *S·* reveals only one Mind,
519–10   *S·* reveals infinity and the fatherhood
557–10   C. *S·* reveals harmony as
gl 596–14   but C. *S·* reveals Spirit, not matter,

revelation of
gl 589– 6   Inspiration; the revelation of *S·,* in which

reverses
s 120– 7   *S·* reverses the false testimony of the
f 215–22   *S·* reverses the evidence of
b 273–10   Divine *S·* reverses the false testimony
t 461–13   *S·* reverses the evidence before the material

rules of
s 162–17   Working out the rules of *S·* in practice,

separates the
f 207–18   *S·* separates the tares and wheat
b 300–19   *S·* separates the wheat from the tares,

servant of
s 146–11   material sense is made the servant of *S·*

Science

shows the cause
a 53–18   *S·* shows the cause of the

signet upon
r 472– 6   God has set His signet upon *S·,*

smatterers in
t 460–19   abused by mere smatterers in *S·,* it becomes a

spirit of
s 145– 4   So . . . imbued were they with the spirit of *S·,*

Spiritual
s 127– 9   The terms Divine Science, Spiritual *S·,*

spiritual sense and
b 294–18   destroyed . . . through spiritual sense and *S·.*

stately
ap 566– 9   Stately *S·* pauses not, but moves before them,

suffering or
b 296– 7   suffering or *S·* must destroy all illusions

sword of
c 266– 3   Such is the sword of *S·,* with which

test of
f 204–19   They can never stand the test of *S·.*

the word
s 127– 1   author's application of the word *S·*
127– 2   or questions her use of the word *S·,*
o 341–13   Sneers at the application of the word *S·*

this
pref viii– 5   To develop the full might of this *S·,*
ix–22   learned that this *S·* must be demonstrated
sp 84–30   If this *S·* has been thoroughly learned
s 112–26   to establish a genuine school of this *S·.*
131–14   This *S·* has come already,
134–23   not because this *S·* is supernatural
147–10   this *S·* showed that Truth had lost none of
155–20   percentage of power on the side of this *S·*
162– 9   effect of this *S·* is to stir the human mind
f 202–15   Outside of this *S·* all is mutable;
b 271–24   Sermon on the Mount is the essence of this *S·,*
285– 3   This *S·* of being obtains not alone hereafter
311–22   When humanity does understand this *S·,*
337–31   you ascertain that this *S·* is demonstrably true,
o 342– 8   He that decries this *S·* does it presumptuously,
345–20   evidence that one does understand this *S·.*
349– 1   when this *S·* is more generally understood?
349–21   in order to grasp the meaning of this *S·.*
355–26   inability to demonstrate this *S·.*
t 449–16   qualities which insure success in this *S·* ;
453–21   The masquerader in this *S·*
455– 8   in order to teach this *S·* of healing.
457– 1   gave the first rules for demonstrating this *S·,*
457–24   advance rapidly in the demonstration of this *S·,*
461–12   light of understanding be thrown upon this *S·,*
463– 6   familiar with the obstetrics taught by this *S·.*
r 467– 3   The first demand of this *S·* is,
471–31   This *S·* teaches that God is the only Life,
483–24   this *S·* has met with opposition ;
492–27   the Principle of this *S·* is divine,
g 548– 5   In this *S·,* we discover man in the image and
ap 577–30   for his vision is the acme of this *S·*

Truth or
g 545– 4   This could not be the utterance of Truth or *S·,*

truth, or
s 127– 6   entitled to a classification as truth, or *S·,*

unerring
r 473–21   and to test its unerring *S·* according to his rule,

unexplained by
s 121–15   man, . . . unexplained by *S·,* is as the

unfolds the
b 296– 2   whereas *S·* unfolds the eternal verity,

usher in
g 529– 9   usher in *S·* and the glorious fact of

warfare in
ap 568– 6   typifies the divine method of warfare in *S·,*

war with
f 252– 1   They are at war with *S·,*

which expounds
b 274–13   Christianity and the *S·* which expounds it

which governs
f 224– 6   the *S·* which governs these changes,

which reveals
f 209–13   the *S·* which reveals the supremacy of Mind.

will ameliorate
t 458–22   but *S·* will ameliorate mortal malice.

will correct
m 60–27   *S·* will correct the discord, and teach us

will declare
r 466–28   *S·* will declare God aright,

will destroy
sp 73–29   This error *S·* will destroy.

will eventually
b 303–18   *S·* will eventually destroy this illusion

yield to
pref xi– 8   the fleshly mind which must yield to *S·.*
r 493– 8   must yield to *S·,* to the immortal truth of all things.

———

pr 12–10   neither *S·* nor Truth which acts through
a 37– 1   Does not *S·* show that sin brings suffering

Science

 a 40– 5 tendency of Christian healing and its *S·*,
 43–28 *S·* Jesus taught and lived must triumph over
 63– 5 In *S·* man is the offspring of Spirit.
 68– 6 Spirit, . . . has created men and women in *S·*.
sp 72–23 In *S·*, individual good derived from God,
 73–17 the divine order and the *S·* of omnipotent,
 79– 9 *S·* must go over the whole ground,
 79–27 *S·* objects to all this, contending for the
 81–28 In *S·*, man's immortality depends upon that of
 83– 6 *S·* only can explain the incredible good
 83–12 *S·* takes issue with popular religions.
 83–15 since *S·* is an explication of nature.
an 102– 5 in *S·* . . . hypnotism is a mere negation,
 103– 7 The destruction of the claims of mortal mind
    through *S·*,
 s 109–20 I must know the *S·* of this healing,
 110–18 No human pen nor tongue taught me the *S·*
 111–11 some may deny its right to the name of *S·*.
 113– 7 letter is but the dead body of *S·*,
 114–10 In *S·*, Mind is *one*, including noumenon and
 114–29 *S·* shows that what is termed *matter* is but
 116– 5 *S·* so reverses the evidence before the
 118–13 *S·*, Theology, and Medicine are means of
 120–13 Yes, he is well in *S·* in which
 121–22 *S·* shows appearances often to be erroneous,
 122–26 in *S·*, Life goes on unchanged
 126–17 Shall *S·* explain cause and effect
 127–10 terms . . . Christ Science or C. S., or *S·* alone,
 127–16 relates especially to *S·* as applied to
 127–26 is an emanation of divine Mind,
 128– 4 term *S·*, properly understood, refers only to
 128–27 *S·* relates to Mind, not matter.
 129–12 a belief which *S·* overthrows.
 129–27 illusions along the path which *S·* must tread
 130–11 *S·*, when understood and demonstrated, will
 140– 2 and *S·* is more than usually effectual in the
 144–14 Human will-power is not *S·*.
 144–31 understood the *S·* of Christian healing,
 146–17 and his *S·*, the curative agent of God, is
 146–20 *S·* is the "stranger that is— *Exod.* 20 : 10.
 146–24 divine origin of *S·* is demonstrated
 147–16 the whole meaning of the *S·*
 147–30 *S·* alone reveals the divine Principle
 149–12 its perfection of operation never vary in *S·*.
 155–13 unless it rests on *S·*, is but a belief held by
 157–30 *S·* both neutralizes error and destroys it.
ph 169–18 *S·* not only reveals the origin of all disease
 178–15 based on *S·* or the divine Mind,
 180– 8 in *S·* one must understand the resuscitating
 185–15 a human conception in the name of *S·*
 187 23 man in *S·* is governed by His Mind.
 192–19 in *S·*, you can have no power opposed to God,
 f 204–27 in *S·* it can never be said that man
 208–20 and preparing the way of *S·*.
 211–23 transfer of the thoughts . . . *S·* renders impos-
    sible.
 215–16 *S·* affirms darkness to be only a
 216– 5 *S·* unveils the mystery and solves the problem
 217– ? through the understanding which *S·* confers
 217–19 and you have won a point in *S*.
 219– 8 No more can we say in *S·* that muscles
 219–20 *S·* includes no rule of discord.
 221–22 equally far from *S·*, in which being is
 225–10 *S·*, heeding not the pointed bayonet,
 232–32 neither place nor opportunity in *S·* for error
 234– 5 be it song, sermon, or *S·*
 238– 3 *S·* is working changes in personal character
 240–25 either by suffering or by *S·*, be convinced of
 241–23 Man in *S·* is neither young nor old.
 250–31 nor will *S·* admit that happiness is ever the
 251–28 Ignorance, like intentional wrong, is not *S·*.
 c 258–32 to comprehend in *S·* the generic term *man.*
 b 271– 9 He knew that the philosophy, *S·*, and proof of
 273–29 *S·* shows that material, conflicting
 275–10 grasp the reality and order of being in its *S·*,
 276–19 When we learn in *S·* how to be perfect
 283–26 unless its *S·* be accurately stated.
 283–29 unless we so do, we can no more demonstrate *S·*,
 285–21 to the better understanding that *S·* gives of the
 287–10 In *S·*, Truth is divine,
 288–12 the conflict between . . . *S·* and material sense,
 296–27 until *S·* obliterates this false testimony.
 299–28 *S·*, the sunshine of Truth, will melt away the
 305–21 as opposed to the *S·* of spiritual reflection,
 306–20 *S·* proves man's existence to be intact.
 306–26 *S·*, still enthroned, is unfolding to mortals the
 312– 4 the spiritual facts of being in *S·*.
 313– 1 entitled him to sonship in *S·*.
 318–29 In *S·* man is governed by God, divine Principle,
 319– 3 *S·* depicts disease as error,
 324–11 When the truth first appeared to him in *S·*,
 328–11 in the *S·* which destroys human delusions
 329–11 Jesus, who was the true demonstrator of *S·*,
 329–12 In *S·* we can use only what we understand.
 329–22 *S·* is a divine demand, not a human.
 339–29 To get rid of sin through *S·*, is to divest sin of

Science

 o 342–16 If . . . *S·* is not of God, then there is no
 345–28 material nothingness, which *S·* inculcates,
 353– 4 senses and *S·* have ever been antagonistic,
 358– 8 Is *S·* thus contradictory?
 358–12 Otherwise it would not be *S·*,
 361–25 must be correct in order to be *S·*
 p 376–29 in *S·* you cannot check a fever after admitting
 384–28 In *S·* this is an established fact
 388– 4 a victory which *S·* alone can explain.
 392–20 unless *S·* shows you otherwise.
 393–17 in *S·* man reflects God's government.
 402–15 In *S·*, no breakage nor dislocation can
 407 22 In *S·*, all being is eternal, spiritual,
 417–19 is not the *S·* of immortal man.
 417–26 understand the unreality of disease in *S·*.
 427–16 Nothing can . . . end the existence of man in *S·*.
 t 456–17 *S·* makes no concessions to persons or
 458– 3 the doctrine that *S·* has two principles
 459–25 the results are sure if the *S·* is understood.
 r 474– 2 (the Principle of this unacknowledged *S·*)
 474– 9 To the ignorant age . . . *S·* seems to be a mistake,
 481–29 In *S·* we learn that it is material sense,
 482–11 out of *S·*, soul is identical with sense,
 483–14 she affixed the name "*S·*" to Christianity,
 492–19 *S·* says : All is Mind and Mind's idea.
 494–22 until the *S·* of man's eternal harmony
 496– 2 in *S·* there is no transfer of evil suggestions
 g 522– 3 The *S·* of the first record proves the
 544–13 In *S·*, Mind neither produces matter nor
 546–10 Has God no *S·* to declare Mind,
 ap 558–11 To mortal sense *S·* seems at first obscure,
 572– 8 In *S·* we are children of God ;
 gl 581 11 *S·* showing that the spiritual realities
 586–21 *S·* ; spiritual being understood ;
 592– 8 that which neither exists in *S·* nor

science

all
 s 124– 2 being based on Truth, the Principle of all *s·*.
astronomical
 s 122–32 Astronomical *s·* has destroyed the false theory
 r 493– 4 but astronomical *s·* contradicts this,
material
 o 193 30 C. S. differs from material *s·*,
medical
 b 273–16 The so-called laws of matter and of medical *s·*
 318–23 Medical *s·* treats disease as though
natural
 sp 98–22 natural *s·* has not been considered a part of
 s 118–27 material law, as given by natural *s·*,
 127–30 C. S. eschews what is called natural *s·*,
 b 274– 7 *Natural s·*, as it is commonly called, is not
 p 429–24 according to the calculations of natural *s·*.
 r 471–12 yield assent . . . on the authority of natural *s·*.
 478– 5 Even according to the teachings of natural *s·*,
 484–12 What are termed natural *s·* and material laws
nautical
 m 67–10 nautical *s·* is not equal to the Science of Mind.
of astronomy
 r 471–11 earth's motions or of the *s·* of astronomy,
of music
 pref viii– 7 even as the *s·* of music corrects false tones
 b 304–22 The *s·* of music governs tones.
 304–25 To be master of chords . . . the *s·* of music must
    be
of numbers
 s 111– 8 no more supernatural than is the *s·* of numbers,
of real being
 s 190 22 ontology,— "the *s·* of real being."
physical
 s 124– 3 Physical *s·* (so-called) is human knowledge,
 127–23 There is no physical *s·*, inasmuch as all
 144–24 divine Science wars with so-called physical *s·*,
so-called
 s 124– 3 Physical *s·* (so-called) is human knowledge,
 150–18 The *s·* (so-called) of physics
 b 277–23 the order of material so-called *s·*.
this
 ph 189– 1 yield to the authority of this *s·*,
which they call
 sp 98–25 multitudes consider that which they call *s·*

 s 149– 6 Is *materia medica* a *s·* or a bundle of
 163–22 said : "Consulting the records of our *s·*,
 ph 189– 5 *S·* (in this instance named natural)
 f 219–24 and yet misunderstand the *s·* that governs it.
 t 460– 3 Ontology is defined as "the *s·* of

SCIENCE AND HEALTH

 pref ix–26 Before writing this work, *S· AND H·*,
 x– 3 first edition of *S· AND H·* was published in 1875.
 x– 6 filled with plagiarisms from *S· AND H·*.
 xii–17 the revision of *S· AND H·*,
 s 110–18 the Science contained in this book, *S· AND H·* ;
 o 361–21 I have revised *S· AND H·* only to
 361–31 *S· AND H· WITH KEY TO THE SCRIPTURES.*
 t 456–25 Scientist requires my work *S· AND H·*

scientific

pr	16–17	strengthens our s· apprehension of the
a	23– 8	but its s· explanation is, that
m	61–30	The s· *morale* of marriage is spiritual unity.
	69– 2	The s· fact that man and the universe
sp	70– 8	In this s· reflection the Ego and the Father are
	71–22	having no s· basis nor origin,
	72–26	but evil is neither communicable nor s·.
	76–27	This state of existence is s· and intact,
	79– 2	The act of describing disease . . . is not s·.
	79– 7	A s· mental method is more sanitary than
	80–27	are neither s· nor rational.
	83–13	s· manifestation of power is from the
	94–29	Our Master read mortal mind on a s· basis,
an	102– 1	Animal magnetism has no s· foundation,
	104– 1	s· thoughts are true thoughts,
	104– 9	"Every great s· truth goes through three stages.
s	107– 6	divine Principle of s· mental healing.
	110–13	In following these leadings of s· revelation,
	114–25	It shows the s· relation of man to God,
	123–17	the s· system of divine healing.
	123–28	the s· order and continuity of being.
	123–31	but not on that account is it less s·.
	124– 1	On the contrary, C. S. is pre-eminently s·,
	138– 9	On this spiritually s· basis Jesus explained his
	141–27	The adoption of s· religion and
	145–16	S· healing has this advantage
	147–18	demonstration of the rules of s· healing
	159–11	Is it skilful or s· surgery to take no heed of
	164–11	they are more s· than are false claimants
ph	167–26	The s· government of the body must be
	167–31	Only through . . . can s· healing power be
f	202– 3	The s· unity which exists between
	206–15	In the s· relation of God to man,
	207–27	spiritual reality is the s· fact in all things.
	210–14	thus bringing to light the s· action of
	217–15	That s· methods are superior to others,
	217–24	The s· and permanent remedy for fatigue
	219–31	this s· beginning is in the right direction.
	233–27	the s· tests I have made of the effects of truth
	253–32	The divine demand, . . . is s·,
c	257– 3	and this definition is s·.
	263–30	instead of a s· eternal consciousness of creation.
b	268–15	no substantial aid to s· metaphysics,
	270– 9	Only by . . . are s· and logical conclusions
	273– 8	Deductions from material hypotheses are not s·.
	274– 8	is not really natural nor s·,
	279–26	A logical and s· conclusion is reached
	295–13	will at last yield to the s· fact
	297–18	that it is neither s· nor eternal,
	313–23	the most s· man that ever trod the globe.
	338–26	definition of words, aside from . . . is not s·.
o	341–14	cannot prevent that from being s· which
	342– 6	condemnations of s· Mind-healing,
	342–16	If Christianity is not s·,
	351–23	are neither spiritual nor s·,
	353– 1	The Christianly s· real is the
	355– 3	Christianly s· methods of dealing with sin
p	380–23	s· evidence of which has accumulated
	402–29	Hence the proof that hypnotism is not s·;
	406–15	as we approach the s· period, in which
	408– 8	this general craze cannot, in a s· diagnosis,
	410–29	Christian s· practice begins with
	411–11	this is the ultimatum, the s· way,
	414–20	rests on the Christianly s· basis of being.
	421–25	It is no more Christianly s· to see disease
t	448–17	A dishonest position is far from Christianly s·.
	456– 6	divine Principle and rules of the s· method
	458–23	Christianly s· man reflects the divine law,
	459–29	the student — the Christian and s· expounder
	464–29	nor can they overthrow a s· system of ethics.
r	465– 5	to elucidate s· metaphysics.
	468– 8	What is the s· statement of being?
	482– 9	and you will have the s· signification.
	483–23	seems to bring into dishonor the ordinary s·
	486–12	belief . . . will not establish his s· harmony.
	496–17	to demonstrate, with s· certainty,
g	501– 1	S· interpretation of the Scriptures
	507–22	The s· divine creation declares
	521–29	which is the exact opposite of s· truth
	523–24	spiritually s· account of creation,
	526– 3	The previous and more s· record of
	534–25	spiritual, s· meaning of the Scriptures
	545–21	The translators of this record of s· creation
	546–28	system stated in this book is Christianly s·
	547–11	conclusions as to the s· theory of creation.
	552–11	whereas the spiritual s· facts of
ap	559– 9	"still, small voice" of s· thought — *I Kings* 19 : 12.
	573–13	Accompanying this s· consciousness was
gl	586–15	s· line of demarcation between Truth and
	590–25	when the true s· statements of the Scriptures

(*see also* **being, demonstration, sense, statement**)

scientifically

a	42– 1	Jesus' life proved, divinely and s·, that
sp	75–10	This gross materialism is s· impossible,
	85–16	"knew their thoughts," — read them s·. — *Matt.* 12 : 25.

scientifically

sp	95–15	ability . . . to discern thought s·, depends upon
	99– 1	not material but s· spiritual.
an	103–10	does not s· show itself in a knowledge of
s	111–32	and has proved itself, whenever s· employed,
	112–15	these opinions . . . are not s· Christian.
	141–25	until its divine Principle is s· understood.
	143–24	body is not controlled s· by a negative mind.
	144– 1	but the two will not mingle s·.
f	217– 9	which prove Mind to be s· distinct from matter,
b	275–31	Truth, spiritually discerned, is s· understood.
	321–19	It was s· demonstrated that leprosy was
o	343–17	he also s· demonstrates this great fact,
	359–14	at length know yourself spiritually and s·.
p	365–22	then he is Christian enough to practise s·
	374– 3	Anodynes, . . . never reduce inflammation s·,
	399–23	S· speaking, there is no mortal mind
	412– 4	plead the case s· for Truth.
	423– 8	understanding s· that all is Mind,
t	457–12	we cannot s· both cure and cause disease
	458–11	It is anything but s· Christian to
	460–20	Instead of s· effecting a cure, it starts a
	461–26	To prove s· the error or unreality of sin,
	461–28	to prove s· the . . . unreality of disease,
r	490–23	The s· Christian explanations of the nature and
g	502–15	s· Christian views of the universe
	506–26	not so in the s· Christian meaning of the text.
	531–30	at no point resembles the s· Christian record
ap	572– 5	s· reduced to its native nothingness.

Scientific Translation of Immortal Mind

s	115–12	chapter sub-title

Scientific Translation of Mortal Mind

s	115–19	chapter sub-title

Scientist (*see also* Scientist's)

become a

ph	182– 1	will diminish your ability to become a S·,

Christian

m	68–19	and a Christian S· cured her.
sp	95–14	ability of a Christian S· to discern thought
s	154–24	That mother is not a Christian S·, . . . who
ph	176–22	Should . . . the Christian S· try truth only in
	182– 4	shows your position as a Christian S·.
o	358–30	Christian S·, whom they have perhaps never
	359– 9	I as a Christian S· believed in the Holy Spirit,
	359–29	A Christian S· and an opponent are like
p	366–27	the Christian S· will be calm in the presence of
	367–17	A Christian S· occupies the place at this period
	375–11	The Christian S· demonstrates that
	375–18	The genuine Christian S· is adding to
	379– 4	The Christian S· finds only effects, where the
	383– 8	the Christian S· takes the best care of his
	384–20	If you are a Christian S·, such symptoms
	386–26	If a Christian S· had said, while you were
	420– 6	should early call an experienced Christian S·
	422–25	and a Christian S· in the other.
	423– 8	The Christian S·, understanding . . . that all is Mind,
t	450–19	Christian S· has enlisted to lessen evil,
	450–24	Christian S· knows that they are errors
	451–19	Christian S·, . . . knows that human will is not
	453–30	A Christian S· never recommends material
	456–25	A Christian S· requires my work SCIENCE AND HEALTH
	458–20	Sin makes deadly thrusts at the Christian S·
	458–26	The Christian S· wisely shapes his course,
	459–31	The Christian S· should understand and adhere
	462–31	The Christian S·, . . . deals with the real cause
	464–13	If . . . a Christian S· were seized with

must conform

t	445– 1	the S· must conform to God's requirements.

only in name

t	449–31	is a S· only in name.

reaches his patient

p	365–15	If the S· reaches his patient through

o	359– 6	more faith in the S· than in
p	365–19	If the S· has enough Christly affection to
	412–31	S· knows that there can be no hereditary disease,

Scientist's

p	414–19	The Christian S· argument rests on the
t	453–29	A Christian S· medicine is Mind,
	457–28	The S· demonstration rests on one Principle,

Scientists

Christian

pref	xii– 1	No charters were granted to Christian S· for
	xii–13	the first periodical issued by Christian S·.
a	35–11	morning meal which Christian S· commemorate.
m	60– 1	if both . . . were genuine Christian S·.
	69–17	If Christian S· educate their own offspring
ph	192– 4	We are Christian S·, only as we quit our
	192– 6	We are not Christian S· until we leave all for
	198–28	the importance that doctors be Christian S·.
c	267–13	Christian S· understand that, . . . they have
o	342–29	If Christian S· were teaching or
	358–25	it is said : . . . whatever effect Christian S·

Scientists
Christian
p 364–18 Do Christian S· seek Truth as Simon sought
364–22 If Christian S· are like Simon, then it must be
401–28 better for Christian S· to leave surgery
442–30 Christian S·, be a law to yourselves
t 444– 7 If Christian S· ever fail to receive aid from
451– 2 Christian S· must live under the constant
r 483–19 natural Christian S·, the ancient worthies,
496–28 Have Christian S· any religious creed?

o 359– 4 Yet S· will take the same cases,
p 366–19 Such so-called S· will strain out gnats,
t 443– 9 severely condemned by some S·,
444– 8 ever fail to receive aid from other S·,
464–15 and the S· had failed to relieve him,

scoff
o 358–14 nor of the inventions of those who s· at God.

scoffed
a 41–28 The truth taught by Jesus, the elders s· at.
r 474– 6 will be s· at and scourged

scoffers
a 49–30 s·, who turned "aside the right— Lam. 3 : 35.

scope
a 40– 4 perceiving the s· and tendency of

scorn
a 55–10 does not the pulpit sometimes s· it?

Scotch
sp 87–13 The S· call such vision "second sight,"

Scott, Sir Walter
ap 566–13 the beautiful description which Sir Walter S·

scourge
a 20–19 s· and the cross awaited the great Teacher.
m 56–15 the social s· of all races,
f 224–18 less material than the Roman s·,

scourged
b 316–25 s· in person, and its Principle was rejected.
r 474– 7 will be scoffed at and s· with worse cords than

scratch
f 212–11 unwitting attempt to s· the end of a finger

scream
sp 97–24 the louder will error s·,

scribe
ap 571–23 immortal s· of Spirit and of a true idealism,

Scriptural
pref viii–29 give to friends the results of her S· study,
ix–27 made copious notes of S· exposition,
sp 89–12 This familiar instance reaffirms the S· word
92–11 In old S· pictures we see a serpent
s 116– 7 as to make this S· testimony true
131–17 according to the S· saying,
ph 177–15 In the S· allegory of the material creation,
f 238– 6 To obey the S· command,
239–14 The watchword of C. S. is S· :
b 275–13 and are the S· names for God.
276– 8 in accordance with the S· command :
328–29 the S· passage would read you, not they.
o 342–20 Shall it be denied that . . . has S· authority?
344–17 it would be just to observe the S· precept,
p 383–27 confirming the S· conclusion concerning a
r 479– 4 With what truth, then, could the S· rejoicing
g 510–21 There is no S· allusion to solar light until
523– 2 the S· account now under comment.
525–26 the S· record of sin and death
526–14 in the legendary S· text
ap 573–23 This is S· authority for concluding that
gl 579– 2 the material definition of a S· word

Scripture
according to
p 423–12 According to S·, it searches
according to the
s 113–23 According to the S·, I find that
another passage of
g 504–22 the explanation of another passage of S·,
declares
p 414–21 S· declares, "The Lord He is God— Deut. 4 : 35.
r 475– 1 S· declares that there is "no night— Rev. 22 : 5.
dictum of
t 444– 6 is the dictum of S·.
fulfils the
b 340–25 fulfils the S·, "Love thy neighbor— Matt. 19 : 19.
informs
f 232– 9 S· informs us that "with God— Mark 10 : 27.
interpretation of
b 320– 9 "The spiritual interpretation of S·
320–24 The one important interpretation of S· is
g 547– 8 has given you the correct interpretation of S·.
is true
f 232–13 theories must be untrue, for the S· is true.
language of
c 256–20 He who, in the language of S·,

Scripture
older
s 140–28 true that the older S· is reversed.
perception of
g 547–31 It is this spiritual perception of S·, which
phrase
g 511– 3 and so explains the S· phrase,
portions of the
g 546–19 seem more obscure than other portions of the S·,
prophetic
s 109–25 prophetic S· of Isaiah is renewedly fulfilled :
rebuked in
p 389–16 This false reasoning is rebuked in S·
rebuke in the
a 23–15 receives a strong rebuke in the S·,
represented in
b 299–19 figuratively represented in S· as a tree,
sayings of
b 276– 2 and fulfils these sayings of S·,
says the
pr 12– 2 shall save the sick," says the S·.— Jas. 5 : 15.
seems to import
p 411–18 The S· seems to import that
significance of the
s 131– 9 and the significance of the S·,
r 481–16 This is the significance of the S·
this
sp 97–26 This S· indicates that all matter will
used in
sp 94– 6 and "likeness" as used in S·.— Gen. 1 : 26.

f 241–15 Take away the spiritual signification of S·, and
b 277– 4 the S· says that dust returns to dust.
290–14 To the spiritual class, relates the S· :
291–18 as the S· says.
o 359–25 that S· she so often quotes :
361–18 S· reads : "For in Him we live,— Acts 17 : 28.
r 489–22 affirmative reply would contradict the S·,
g 522–28 for the S· just preceding declares
545–26 Hence the seeming contradiction in that S·,
ap 569– 6 The S·, "Thou hast been faithful— Matt. 25 : 23.
gl 581– 2 the name often conferred upon him in S·,

Scriptures
according to the
o 342–19 a system which works according to the S·
also declare
b 331–14 The S· also declare that God is Spirit.
p 373–16 but the S· also declare,
are definite
f 206–22 The S· are definite on this point,
are very sacred
g 547–23 The S· are very sacred.
aver
r 474–20 S· aver, "I am not come to destroy,— Matt. 5 : 17.
confirms the
m 69–14 unfolds all creation, confirms the S·,
declare
b 286–17 The S· declare all that He made to be good,
287–20 S· declare that man was made in
318– 6 S· declare that God made all,
330–19 God is what the S· declare Him to be,
p 381–18 and the S· declare that we live, move, and
397–21 which the S· declare Him to be.
g 526–16 and the S· declare that He created all.
539–16 S· declare that God condemned this lie
ap 560–24 Here the S· declare that evil is temporal,
imply
b 331–11 The S· imply that God is All-in-all.
g 550–22 If Life is God, as the S· imply,
inform us
ph 183–11 S· inform us that sin, or error, first caused
r 475– 8 S· inform us that man is
interpret the
g 534– 6 enabled woman to be first to interpret the S·
KEY TO THE
o 361–32 SCIENCE AND HEALTH WITH KEY TO THE S·.
meaning of the
g 534–25 spiritual, scientific meaning of the S·
not knowing the
b 272– 9 "Ye do err, not knowing the S·."— Matt. 22 : 29.
obey the
o 354– 4 Why then do Christians try to obey the S·
often appear
r 488–11 Hence the S· often appear in our
older
g 502– 2 the living and real prelude of the older S·
plainly declare
p 400–30 The S· plainly declare the baneful influence of
reading the
r 481–32 When reading the S·, the substitution of the
say
pr 6– 1 The S· say, that if we deny Christ,
10–26 The S· say : "Ye ask, and receive not,— Jas. 4 : 3.
f 208– 5 The S· say, "In Him we live,— Acts 17 : 28.
218–27 S· say, "They that wait upon— Isa. 40 : 31.

Scriptures

say
- *o* 344– 6   *S·* say that God has created man in
- 357–29   "Life in Himself," as the *S·* say,— *John* 5 : 26.
- *p* 410– 9   *S·* say, "Man shall not live by— *Matt.* 4 : 4.
- 427–18   the *S·* say, "The last enemy that— *I Cor.* **15** : 26.
- *r* 476–23   Remember that the *S·* say of mortal man :

Science of the
- *s* 139–23   the divine Science of the *S·*
- *b* 319–29   and misstates the Science of the *S·*,

searched the
- *s* 109–12   searched the *S·* and read little else,

throughout the
- *o* 358–18   as is recorded throughout the *S·*.

turn to the
- *f* 217–11   yet if we turn to the *S·*, what do we read?

were illumined
- *s* 110–14   The *S·* were illumined ;

- *s* 123–21   through a spiritual sense of the *S·*
- 139– 4   the *S·* are full of accounts of the triumph of
- *f* 214– 9   represented in the *S·* as formed from dust,
- *b* 271– 4   its obvious correspondence with the *S·*
- 271–29   The *S·* contain it.
- 272–10   The spiritual sense of the *S·* brings out the
- 293–25   called in the *S·*, "The anger of— *Deut.* 29 : 20.
- 320– 7   the *S·* have both a spiritual and literal meaning.
- *o* 341– 6   Even the *S·*, . . . appear contradictory when
- 358–10   C. S., understood, coincides with the *S·*,
- 361–31   hence the many readings given the *S·*,
- *r* 468–19   as the *S·* use this word in Hebrews ;
- *g* 501– 1   Scientific interpretation of the *S·*
- *ap* 578– 1   the light which C. S. throws on the *S·*
- *gl* 590–26   *S·* become clouded through a physical sense of

scrofula
- *p* 424–28   To prevent or to cure *s·* and other so-called

scrofulous
- *p* 424–32   a humor in the blood, a *s·* diathesis.

scrubbing
- *p* 413–18   without *s·* the whole surface daily.

sculptor
- *f* 248–12   The *s·* turns from the marble to his model
- *c* 260– 3   no more . . . than the *s·* can perfect his out-
            lines from

sculptor's
- *b* 299– 2   *s·* thought when he carves his

sculptors
- *f* 248–13   We are all *s·*, working at various forms,
- 248–19   by vicious *s·* and hideous forms.

scum
- *m* 65–31   marriage will become purer when the *s·* is gone.

Sea
- *a* 34–32   joyful meeting on the shore of the Galilean *S·* !
- *f* 226–30   the Red *S·* and the wilderness ;
- *ap* 566– 2   were guided triumphantly through the Red *S·*,
- 576– 1   and the Peaceful *S·* of Harmony.

sea

cast into the
- *pr* 1– *   *and be thou cast into the s·;— Mark* 11 : 23.

fish of the
    (see **fish**)

no more
- *g* 536– 4   and there was no more *s·*."— *Rev.* 21 : 1.
- *ap* 572–22   and there was no more *s·*.— *Rev.* 21 : 1.

O thou
- *s* 135– 2   "What ailed thee, O thou *s·*,— *Psal.* 114 : 5.

surging
- *ap* 569–18   They are in the surging *s·* of error,

troubled
- *m* 67–17   or sunshine gladdens the troubled *s·*.

upon the
- *ap* 558– 7   and he set his right foot upon the *s·*,— *Rev.* 10 : 2.
- 559– 5   dominant power of which was upon the *s·*,

waves of the
- *g* 505–20   the mighty waves of the *s·*."— *Psal.* 93 : 4.

- *sp* 87–20   *s·* is ignorant of the gems within its caverns,
- *g* 536– 6   the *s·*, . . . is represented as having passed away.
- *ap* 568–21   of the earth and of the *s·* !— *Rev.* 12 : 12.

seal
- *pref* xi–29   under the *s·* of the Commonwealth,
- *a* 44– 1   must *s·* the victory over error and death,
- 44– 8   set the *s·* of eternity on time.
- *g* 511–11   In divine Science, which is the *s·* of Deity
- *ap* 560– 3   In the opening of the sixth *s·*,
- *gl* 593–23   definition of

sealed
- *f* 232–24   which *s·* God's condemnation of sin,
- *p* 363– 4   Breaking the *s·* jar, she perfumed Jesus' feet

seals
- *o* 354–17   who thereunto have set their *s·*.
- *ap* 572–15   open the seven *s·* of error with Truth,

seam
- *f* 242–26   one web of consistency without *s·* or rent.

seaman
- *m* 67– 9   the dauntless *s·* is not sure of his safety ;

seances
- *sp* 86–18   apparitions brought out in dark *s·*

search
- *s* 109–15   The *s·* was sweet, calm, and buoyant with hope,
- 152–24   in her *s·* for truth ;
- *ph* 168–11   rush after drugs, *s·* out the material so-called
- *p* 440– 1   he could not possibly elude their *s·*.

searched
- *s* 109–12   *s·* the Scriptures and read little else,

searcher
- *s* 121–16   "a weary *s·* for a viewless home."
- *f* 234–22   the weary *s·* after a divine theology,

searches
- *p* 423–12   it *s·* "the joints and marrow,"— *Heb.* 4 : 12.

searching
- *b* 322–31   "Canst thou by *s·* find out God?"— *Job* 11 : 7.
- *g* 551–27   "Canst thou by *s·* find out God?"— *Job* 11 : 7.
- 555–16   *S·* for the origin of man, who is the

Seas
- *g* 506–23   the waters called He *S·* :— *Gen.* 1 : 10.
- 536– 1   the waters called He *S·*."— *Gen.* 1 : 10.

seas
- *g* 512–18   and fill the waters in the *s·* ;— *Gen.* 1 : 22.

season
- *a* 40– 7   when I have a convenient *s·* I will— *Acts* 24 : 25.
- *c* 257–20   "forth Mazzaroth in his *s·*,"— *Job* 38 : 32.
- *p* 398–28   blind faith removes bodily ailments for a *s·*,

seasons
- *m* 57–13   bringing sweet *s·* of renewal like the
- *s* 125–21   The *s* will come and go with changes of
- *g* 509–11   let them be for signs, and for *s·*,— *Gen.* 1 : 14.
- 509–25   the days and *s·* of Mind's creation,

seat
- *f* 239–23   Mortal mind is the acknowledged *s·* of
- *b* 285–19   finite conception of . . . body as the *s·* of Mind

seats
- *s* 122–12   as the *s·* of pain and pleasure,

secluded
- *t* 464– 8   they would understand why she is so *s·*.

second
- *sp* 77–12   "the *s·* death hath no power."— *Rev.* 20 : 6.
- 87–13   The Scotch call such vision "*s·* sight,"
- 87–14   when really it is first sight instead of *s·*,
- 91–27   The *s·* erroneous postulate is,
- *s* 115–25   *S· Degree:* Evil beliefs disappearing.
- 118– 7   foretelling the *s·* appearing in the flesh
- *f* 204–13   The so-called *s·* power, evil, is the unlikeness
- 204–16   mixture of the first and *s·* antagonistic
- 234–27   or they will control you in the *s·*.
- *b* 270– 1   is quite as reasonable as the *s·*,
- 290–14   the *s·* death hath no power."— *Rev.* 20 : 6.
- 314– 9   but one Mind without a *s·* or equal.
- *p* 403– 9   in the *s·* it is believed that the
- 433–22   led him into the commission of the *s·* crime,
- *t* 456–30   *S·* : Because it was the first book
- *r* 467– 7   The *s·* is like unto it,
- *g* 502– 1   A *s·* necessity for beginning with Genesis
- 503–21   *first,* in light ; *s·*, in reflection ;
- 506– 9   and the morning were the *s·* day.— *Gen.* 1 : 8.
- 521–26   The *s·* chapter of Genesis contains a
- 522– 4   proves the falsity of the *s·*.
- 522– 7   The *s·* record chronicles man as mutable
- 522–12   This *s·* record unmistakably gives the
- 522–25   This latter part of the *s·* chapter of
- 523–23   and in three verses of the *s·*,
- 526–15   first mention of evil is in . . . the *s·* chapter
- 526–24   This *s·* biblical account is a picture of error
- 530–31   *S·*, it supposes that mind enters matter,
- 537–20   this *s·* account in Genesis
- *ap* 577–14   *s·*, the Christ, the spiritual idea of God ;
- *gl* 585–27   first from dust, *s·* from a rib,
- 590–23   in the *s·* and following chapters,

secondarily
- *g* 512–24   are mental, both primarily and *s·*.

secondary
- *f* 207–13   nor . . . the law of Spirit *s·*.
- *ap* 559– 7   a *s·* power was exercised upon visible error
- 562– 8   This idea reveals the universe as *s·*

secrecy
- *s* 118– 8   hidden in sacred *s·* from the visible world?

secret
- *pr* 8– 7   They hold *s·* fellowship with sin,
- 13–11   our Father, who seeth in *s·*, will reward us
- 15– 1   thy Father which is in *s·* ;— *Matt.* 6 : 6.
- 15– 2   thy Father, which seeth in *s·*,— *Matt.* 6 : 6.
- 15– 7   Father in *s·* is unseen to the physical senses

secret
pr 15–23 The Master's injunction is, that we pray in s·
15–25 Christians rejoice in s· beauty and bounty,
an 102–20 So s· are the present methods of
b 317– 1 "s· from the foundation of — *Matt.* 13 : 35.
ap 559–14 to utter the full diapason of s· tones.

secretion
s 160–11 the organic action and s· of the viscera.
p 399– 8 not a s· nor combination can operate, apart from

secretions
s 162– 7 It changes the s·, expels humors,
162–19 S· have been changed,
p 382– 9 Constant bathing and rubbing to alter the s·
415–20 the s·, the action of the lungs,

secretly
pr 13– 7 s· yearning and openly striving for the

sect
f 236– 5 in the interests of humanity, not of s·.

sectarian
s 139–13 wisely to stem the tide of s· bitterness,

section
f 225–32 rights of man were vindicated in a single s·

sections
s 122–11 certain s· of matter, such as brain and

sects
a 28–27 because it is honored by s· and societies,
f 224–11 s· many but not enough Christianity.
239– 2 The s·, which endured the lash of their
t 444–22 If ecclesiastical s· or medical schools

secure
m 56–14 such moral regulations as will s·
60–31 would be more s· in our keeping, if
f 238–26 Justice often comes too late to s· a verdict.

secured
t 456– 6 has s· the only success of the students of

securely
pr 11–26 that we may walk s· in the

security
a 19–27 in disobedience to Him, we ought to feel no s·,
f 232– 7 S· for the claims of harmonious and

seditions
an 106–23 wrath, strife, s·, heresies, — *Gal.* 5 : 20.

sedulous
ph 179–26 The s· matron — studying her Jahr

see
pr 5–20 the Psalmist could s· their end,
8–27 than we are willing to have our neighbor s·?
a 27– 4 how that the blind s·, — *Luke* 7 : 22,
38–29 Having eyes ye s· not,
45–27 as ye s· me have." — *Luke* 24 : 39.
sp 70– * he shall never s· death. — *John* 8 : 51.
71–10 you may dream that you s· a flower,
71–14 and you may s· landscapes, men,
85–12 "Come, s· a man, which — *John* 4 : 29.
86–15 only because it is unusual to s· thoughts,
86–22 why is it more difficult to s· a thought than
92–11 In old Scriptural pictures we s· a serpent
an 105–19 "I s· no reason why metaphysics is not
s 132– 5 things which we do hear and s· : — *Matt.* 11 : 4.
136–22 No wonder Herod desired to s· the new Teacher.
140– 6 "Thou canst not s· My face :— *Exod.* 33 : 20.
140– 6 shall no man s· Me, and live." — *Exod.* 33 : 20.
151–29 to s· and acknowledge this fact,
152–25 and can s· the means by which mortals
ph 173– 2 we fail to s· how anatomy can distinguish
187– 6 Here you may s· how so-called material sense
189– 3 If the eyes s· no sun for a week,
190–31 In Thy light shall we s· light. — *Psal.* 36 : 9.
211–26 If . . . organism causes the eyes to s·
f 217–13 he shall never s· death !" — *John* 8 : 51.
241–29 signifies that the pure in heart s· God
253–11 I hope, dear reader, . . . that, as you read, you s·
b 281–21 and s· that sin and mortality have neither
284–22 They can neither s· Spirit through the eye nor
320–26 "In my flesh shall I s· God," — *Job* 19 : 26.
324– 3 and joy to s· them disappear,
324– 6 for they shall s· God." — *Matt.* 5 : 8.
325– 1 shall not s· death." — *see John* 11 : 26.
337–15 none but the pure in heart can s· God,
o 341– 9 for they shall s· God" — *Matt.* 5 : 8.
342– 6 one may s· with sorrow the sad effects
342–26 the lame to walk, and the blind to s·,
347–31 These critics will then s· that error is indeed
350–20 lest at any time they should s· — *Matt.* 13 : 15.
359–31 When others s· them as I do,
p 367–27 I long to s· the consummation of my hope,
397–25 when they act, walk, s·, hear, enjoy,
400–23 We s· in the body the images of this mind,
400–24 we s· painted on the retina the image which
421–25 no more Christianly scientific to s· disease than
421–28 should not build it up by wishing to s· the forms

see
p 426–15 and s· the folly of hypocrisy,
428– 8 he shall never s· death." — *John* 8 : 51.
429–32 he shall never s· death." — *John* 8 : 51.
438– 7 he shall never s· death. — *John* 8 : 51.
t 452– 8 we cannot s· in darkness.
455–15 then shalt thou s· clearly to — *Matt.* 7 : 5.
457–15 because each of them could s· but one face of it,
461–27 you must first s· the claim of sin,
r 478–12 Who can s· a soul in the body?
479–10 Matter cannot s·, feel, hear, taste,
479–12 cannot feel itself, s· itself, nor understand itself.
479–16 Does that which we call dead ever s·, hear,
g 510–10 "light shall we s· light ;" — *Psal.* 36 : 9.
516– 7 we shall s· this true likeness and reflection
527–23 to s· what he would call them : — *Gen.* 2 : 19.
532–30 error demands that *mind* shall s· . . . through
matter,
547–12 was able to s· in the egg the earth's atmosphere,
548– 6 We s· that man has never lost his
551–14 nor s· that material methods are impossible in
ap 571–24 mirror in which mortals may s· their own image.
572– 3 Thus we s·, in both the first and last books
573– 4 while yet beholding what the eye cannot s·,
573–22 by which he could s· the new heaven and
gl 585–15 ERROR. S· chapter on Recapitulation, page 472.
586– 6 "Having eyes, s· ye not?" — *Mark* 8 : 18.
588–26 INTELLIGENCE. . . . S· chapter on Recapitulation, page 469.
590–14 LIFE. S· chapter on Recapitulation, page 468.
593– 3 PRINCIPLE. S· chapter on Recapitulation, page 465.
594–18 SOULS. S· chapter on Recapitulation, page 466.
594–24 SPIRITS. . . . (S· page 466.)
594–25 SUBSTANCE. S· chapter on Recapitulation, page 468.
fr 600– * let us s· if the vine flourish, — *Song* 7 : 12.

seed
and soil
f 212–18 They produce a rose through s· and soil,
bearing
g 518– 6 every herb bearing s·, — *Gen.* 1 : 29.
dig up every
sp 79–10 and dig up every s· of error's sowing.
good
f 237–11 theories of parents often choke the good s·
237–13 snatches away the good s· before it
is in itself
g 507–13 whose s· is in itself, — *Gen.* 1 : 11.
508– 2 But the s· is in itself, only as the
511– 4 "whose s· is in itself." — *Gen.* 1 : 11.
material
g 551–30 declares that the material s· must decay
of error
g 535– 2 The seed of Truth and the s· of error,
of matter
g 535– 3 the seed of Spirit and the s· of matter,
of Spirit
g 535– 3 the s· of Spirit and the seed of matter,
of the Church
a 37– 6 blood of the martyrs is the s· of the Church."
of Truth
b 271– 1 s· of Truth springs up and bears much fruit.
g 535– 1 The s· of Truth and the seed of error,
or soil
g 520–25 the plant grows, not because of s· or soil, but
sowing the
ph 183– 9 without sowing the s·
sown in the soil
m 66–12 not from s· sown in the soil of material hopes,
was in itself
g 508–11 whose s· was in itself, — *Gen.* 1 : 12.
within itself
ph 180– 9 This is the s· within itself
g 508–14 The s· within itself is the pure thought
yielding
g 507–12 the herb yielding s·, — *Gen.* 1 : 11.
508–10 and herb yielding s· after his kind, — *Gen.* 1 : 12.
518– 8 the fruit of a tree yielding s· ; — *Gen.* 1 : 29.

sp 74– 8 The s· which has germinated
76–15 any more than a tree can return to its s·.
89–32 If s· is necessary to produce wheat,
s 125–30 florist will find his flower before its s·.
b 272– 7 In . . . an "honest and good heart" the s· —
Luke 8 : 15.
o 361–28 until God prepares the soil for the s·.
g 508– 6 substance of a thought, a s·, or a flower
534–10 between thy s· and her s· ; — *Gen.* 3 : 15.

seedling
ph 190– 5 mortal says that an inanimate unconscious s· is

seedlings
ph 188–26 according to the s· of fear.

seeds
  ph 179–29 sowing the *s·* of reliance on matter,
   b 294– 5 carries within itself the *s·* of all error.

seedtime
  sp 96– 9 but summer and winter, *s·* and harvest

seeing
    a 54– 6 acknowledged not his righteousness, *s·* it not ;
  sp 86–20 *S·* is no less a quality of physical sense
   b 320–16 *s·* that they are [or, in their error they are]
   p 397– 1 not *s·* how mortal mind affects the body,
   t 464– 1 but it feels your influence without *s·* you.
   r 487– 7 more Christianity in *s·* and hearing spiritually
    489–18 material means for knowing, hearing, *s·*?
   g 529–27 *S·* this, we should have faith to
  ap 572–27 Not through the material visual organs for *s·*,

seek
  pr 5–31 and *s·* the destruction of all evil works,
    8– 5 their wickedness and then *s·* to hide it.
    a 20–31 and *s·* the divine Principle and Science
    34–13 If all who *s·* his commemoration
  sp 70– * *S· unto them that have familiar* — *Isa.* 8 : 19.
    70– * *Should not a people s· unto their* — *Isa.* 8 : 19.
   s 142– 8 We must *s·* the undivided garment,
   f 236– 7 reputation . . . which many leaders *s·*?
    238–20 until we *s·* this remedy for human woe
    254–11 *s·* Truth righteously, He directs our path.
   b 285–25 to *s·* salvation through pardon
    285–29 they will *s·* to learn, not from matter,
    286– 1 To *s·* Truth through belief in a human doctrine
    286– 3 We must not *s·* the immutable . . . through
    323– 1 Mortals may *s·* the understanding of C. S.,
   p 364–18 Do Christian Scientists *s·* Truth
    409–26 and *s·* the true model.
   t 451–11 They must not only *s·*, but strive,
   r 476–21 Learn this, O mortal, and earnestly *s·* the
    487– 1 to *s·* and to find a higher sense of happiness
    494–19 and *s·* safety in divine Science.
   g 510– 2 How much more should we *s·* to apprehend
    555–19 Only impotent error would *s·* to

seeker
  pref x–23 personal experience of any sincere *s·* of Truth.

seekers
  pref xii–26 she commits these pages to honest *s·* for Truth.
   p 364–20 Jesus told Simon that such *s·* as he
  ap 570–14 simple *s·* for Truth, weary wanderers,

seeketh
   g 538– 1 "*s·* not her own."— *I Cor.* 13 : 5.

seeking
  pr 10–14 *S·* is not sufficient.
  sp 85–25 *s·* the material more than the spiritual.
   f 222–29 In *s·* a cure for dyspepsia
   b 290– 8 still *s·* happiness through a material, . . . sense
    327–28 mistake in *s·* material means for
   p 367–10 This is what is meant by *s·* Truth, Christ,
   t 464–10 at her post, *s·* no self-aggrandizement
   g 518–18 *s·* his own in another's good.

seeks
   s 124– 9 *s·* to find life and intelligence in matter,
   b 279–31 Pantheism, . . . *s·* cause in effect,
    280–14 it *s·* to divide the one Spirit into persons
   g 541– 4 Cain *s·* Abel's life,

seem
  sp 76–15 Neither will man *s·* to be corporeal,
    80–19 It should not *s·* mysterious that mind,
    96–16 may *s·* to be famine and pestilence,
   s 131– 1 Truth should not *s·* so surprising
    131– 2 error should not *s·* so real as truth.
    131– 2 Sickness should not *s·* so real as
    131–16 but the churches *s·* not ready to receive it,
  ph 169–25 whatever good they may *s·* to receive from
    185–26 Erroneous mental practice may *s·*
    198– 5 may *s·* calm under it, but he is not.
   f 211–19 *s·* to obtain in mortal mind.
    216–24 while health would *s·* the exception,
    231– 6 but *s·* to this so-called mind to be immortal.
    248– 4 One marvels that a friend can ever *s·* less than
   b 282–21 though they *s·* to touch, one is still a curve
    284– 6 would *s·* to spring from a limited body ;
    288–31 what mortals *s·* to have learned
    299–26 error, may *s·* to hide Truth,
    300– 6 makes trees and cities *s·* to be where they
    307–12 matter shall *s·* to have life as much as
    327–18 the strict demands of C. S. *s·* peremptory ;
   o 343–21 It would sometimes *s·* as if
    353–27 so long will ghosts *s·* to continue.
   p 406–14 Sin and sickness will abate and *s·* less real
    422– 7 If . . . moral and physical symptoms *s·* aggravated,
   t 446– 6 If patients sometimes *s·* worse while
   r 470–14 can only *s·* to be real by giving reality to the
    472–28 unrealities *s·* real to human, erring belief,
    491– 2 A delicious perfume will *s·* intolerable.
    493–25 *s·* real and natural in illusion.

seem
   r 494–21 sin, sickness, and death will *s·* real . . . until
    494–22 experiences of the sleeping dream *s·* real
   g 502– 3 is so brief that it would almost *s·*,
    506–25 human concept and divine idea *s·* confused by
    546–18 Genesis and the Apocalypse *s·* more obscure
    556–21 They *s·* to be something, but are not.

seemed
    a 46–20 after what *s·* to be death
   s 131–22 so it *s·* good in Thy sight."— *Luke* 10 : 21.
   f 237– 2 She *s·* not to notice it.
   b 297–13 that disappears which before *s·* real
    314–17 To such . . . the real man *s·* a spectre,
    314–19 and the body, . . . *s·* to be substance.
    315–29 (that is, as it *s·* to mortal view),
   g 547–14 speck of so-called embryonic life *s·* a
    555–29 which *s·* to vanish in death.

seemeth
  sp 81–18 Though the grass *s·* to wither
   r 472–19 that which *s·* to be and is not.

seeming
    a 45–11 by the [*s·*] death of His Son,— *Rom.* 5 : 10.
  an 101–31 Any *s·* benefit derived from it is
   s 119–30 C. S. reverses the *s·* relation of Soul and body
    122– 3 assigning *s·* power to sin, sickness, and death ;
    164–18 The *s·* decease, caused by a
  ph 167–32 fair *s·* for straightforward character,
    190–17 This mortal *s·* is temporal ;
   f 208– 6 What then is this *s·* power,
   c 266– 9 this *s·* vacuum is already filled
   b 295– 2 sensation *s·* to be in nerves which
   o 352–30 no longer *s·* worthy of fear or honor.
   p 368–27 the source of all *s·* sickness.
    382–24 I rescued from *s·* spiritual oblivion,
    390– 6 simply because, . . . there is *s·* discord.
    394– 2 Truth can destroy its *s·* reality,
   t 452– 2 bar the door of his thought against this *s·* power
    463–30 Such *s·* medical effect or action is
   r 473– 2 though *s·* to be real and identical.
   g 545–26 the *s·* contradiction in that Scripture,

seemingly
   s 147–23 hitherto unattained and *s·* dim.
  ap 563–20 *s·* impede the offspring of the spiritual idea,

seems
  m 64– 8 Pride, envy, or jealousy *s·* on most occasions
  an 101–26 If animal magnetism *s·* to alleviate
   s 120– 1 though it *s·* otherwise to finite sense.
    121–18 and the sun *s·* to move from east to west,
    123–12 matter *s·* to be, but is not.
    126–11 and so *s·* to have reversed it
    134–32 This fact at present *s·* more mysterious than
    157–24 power which the drug *s·* to possess.
  ph 169–32 The good that a poisonous drug *s·* to do is evil,
    170–24 The age *s·* ready to approach this subject,
    179–14 the body then *s·* to require such treatment.
   f 212– 4 and the pain *s·* to be in its old place.
    250–21 and the mind *s·* to be absent.
   c 262–29 Every concept which *s·* to begin with the brain
    263–21 Whatever *s·* to be a new creation, is but the
   b 296–24 When the evidence of . . . *s·* to commingle,
    301– 7 To himself, mortal and material man *s·* to be
    301–14 *s·* to mortal sense transcendental,
    301–23 Mortal man *s·* to himself to be
    307–22 If . . . material pain and pleasure *s·* normal,
    312– 6 What to material sense *s·* substance,
    351–17 while error *s·* as potent and real
   o 353– 2 whatever *s·* real to material sense, is unreal in
   p 374– 6 Because mortal mind *s·* to be conscious,
    375–28 This state of mind *s·* anomalous except to the
    384– 9 If man *s·* to incur the penalty
    393– 4 The body *s·* to be self-acting,
    410–15 The more difficult *s·* the material condition
    411–18 The Scripture *s·* to import that Jesus caused
    417–29 Show them how mortal mind *s·* to induce
   t 447–17 When sin . . . *s·* true to material sense,
    459–24 To mortal sense C. S. *s·* abstract,
   r 474– 9 To the ignorant age . . . Science *s·* to be a mistake,
    480–21 which *s·* to make men capable of wrong-doing.
    483–22 Because the Science of Mind *s·* to bring into
   g 501– 5 often *s·* so smothered by the immediate context
    507–31 divine idea *s·* to fall to the level of
    524–10 the true idea of God *s·* almost lost.
  ap 558–11 To mortal sense Science *s·* at first obscure abstract,
    576– 5 which to us *s·* hidden in the mist of remoteness,

seen
    a 27– 4 things ye have *s·* and heard ;— *Luke* 7 : 22.
    37–14 but not amid the smoke of battle is merit *s·*
    46–11 again *s·* casting out evil and healing the sick.
  sp 88–19 can never be *s·*, felt, nor understood through
    99–26 are *s·* to be a bald imposition.
  an 104– 5 it will be *s·* why the author of this book
   s 109– 6 This great fact is not, however, *s·* to be

seen

s	109– 9	once s·, no other conclusion can be reached.
	116–12	includes vastly more than is at first s·.
	139–23	s· from Genesis to Revelation,
ph	169– 4	I have s· the mental signs, assuring me that
	176– 9	and gave the gospel a chance to be s· in its
	179– 8	Immortal Mind heals what eye hath not s· ;
	193–19	Since then I have not s· him,
f	211–15	the effect s· in the lachrymal gland?
	212–10	I have s· an unwitting attempt to
	217–16	is s· by their effects.
	233– 8	is s· and acknowledged only by degrees.
	244– 8	s· between the cradle and the grave,
	247– 3	I have s· age regain two of the elements
	251–29	Ignorance must be s· and corrected before we
c	255–18	Eye hath not s· Spirit, nor hath ear heard His
	260–11	s· as the only true conception of being.
	261– 9	The effect of mortal mind . . . is s· in this :
b	268– *	which we have s· with our eyes,— I John 1: 1.
	268– *	That which we have s· and heard— I John 1: 3.
	279–18	the immortal facts of being are s·,
	300–29	God is s· only in the spiritual universe
	300–30	as the sun is s· in the ray of light
	310– 7	and s· in all form, substance, and color,
	310–29	God is not s· by material sense,
	321– 2	as may be s· by studying the book of Job.
	321–12	In this incident was s· the actuality of Science.
	323–28	effects of C. S. are not so much s· as felt.
	325–19	where human sense hath not s· man.
	330–13	Eye hath neither s· God nor His image
	334–13	dual personality of the unseen and the s·,
o	354–18	Consistency is s· in example more than in
	358–31	whom they have perhaps never s·
	359– 1	orthodox pastors, whom they have s·
p	366–15	his brother whom he hath s·,— I John 4: 20.
	366–16	God whom he hath not s·?"— I John 4: 20.
	369–25	as would be readily s·, if psychology,
	395–22	mental quackery . . . to hold it as something s·
t	449–19	The baneful effect . . . is less s· than felt.
	458–15	Having s· so much suffering from quackery,
	459– 3	things which "eye hath not s·— I Cor. 2 : 9.
r	468–21	the evidence of things not s·,"— Heb. 11 : 1.
	477– 7	Soul, being Spirit, is s· in nothing imperfect
	478–10	no such persons were ever s· to go into the
	479 31	are clearly s·, being understood by— Rom. 1 : 20.
g	504– 3	no place where God's light is not s·,
	520– 7	is no more s· nor comprehended by mortals,
	524– 2	s· in the Phœnician worship of Baal,
	543–28	it is s· that man springs solely from Mind.
	548–10	So C. S. can be s· only as the
	553–18	it is s· that the maternal egg never
	554– 2	reveals what "eye hath not s·,"— I Cor. 2 : 9.
ap	569–10	by which the nothingness of error is s· ;
	571–13	unfaithful stewards who have s· the danger
	572–17	Under the supremacy of Spirit, it will be s·
	575–23	eastward, to the star s· by the Wisemen

seer

ap	574–22	lifted the s· to behold the great city,
gl	593– 4	PROPHET. A spiritual s· ;

seers

sp	84– 9	men become s· and prophets involuntarily,
b	333–25	which baptized these s· in the divine nature,

sees

sp	86 29	Mortal mind s· what it believes
	86–30	as certainly as it believes what it s·.
	86–31	It feels, hears, and s· its own thoughts.
	90–17	The looker-on s· the body in bed, but the
s	126– 6	as man s· his reflection in a glass.
	129–31	The sinner s·, in the system taught in
ph	180– 5	when he s· his would-be healers busy,
	198–15	formed before one s· a doctor
f	220–21	thinking it s· another kitten.
b	294– 9	The belief that matter thinks, s·, or feels
p	371–12	so sick humanity s· danger in every direction,
	401–14	and mortal mind only feels and s· materially,
t	445–32	whenever she s· a man, for the petty considera- tion
r	467–28	Matter neither s·, hears, nor feels.
	485– 5	Science declares that Mind, not matter, s·,
ap	563– 7	but he also s· the nothingness of evil
	563–18	The Revelator s· that old serpent.
	571–11	Is the informer one who s· the foe?
gl	591–14	that which mortal mind s·, feels, hears, tastes,

seeth

pr	13–11	our Father, who s· in secret, will reward us
	15– 1	thy Father, which s· in secret,— Matt. 6 : 6.
c	262–18	but now mine eye s· Thee."— Job 42 : 5.
b	305–18	what he s· the Father do :— John 5 : 19.
g	518–17	man who s· his brother's need and

seething

m	67–14	on the s· ocean of sorrow.

seize

s	119– 8	To s· the first horn of this dilemma

seized

t	464–14	s· with pain so violent

seldom

g	550–28	is deemed monstrous and is s· fruitful,

select

a	38– 3	and for a s· number of followers.
r	494–12	for a s· number or for a limited period

selected

f	235– 8	s· with as direct reference to their morals

selects

t	455–20	God s· for the highest service one who

self

and sense

a	20–30	put aside material s· and sense,

human

f	254–19	But the human s· must be evangelized.

ignorant of

ph	186–28	Mortal mind is ignorant of s·,

mortality's

r	468– 4	sin is mortality's s·, because it

one's

sp	88–18	To love one's neighbor as one's s·,
	90–24	The admission to one's s· that man is
c	260–25	by the thoughts ever recurring to one's s·,
b	322–32	easier . . . than to rid one's s· of error.
o	345–13	no small matter to know one's s· ;
t	448–31	doing one's s· the most harm.
	449– 8	reacts most heavily against one's s·.

original

b	295–10	and then recover man's original s·

sacrifices of

a	23– 2	and Love may require many sacrifices of s·

sense and

b	296– 9	and regenerate material sense and s·.
	324– 5	The purification of sense and s·

sin and

a	38–27	To those buried in the belief of sin and s·,

sin, or materiality

b	299–13	never lead towards s·, sin, or materiality,

spiritual

b	234–17	while the spiritual s·, or Christ,

self-abnegation

pr	7–21	with more devout o· and purity.
f	203–13	a more exalted worship and s·.
c	266–18	This is done through s·.
o	360 10	They require less s·,
ap	568–30	S·, . . . is a rule in C. S.

self-acting

s	160–22	Unless muscles are s· at all times,
ph	199– 8	Muscles are not s·.
p	393– 4	The body seems to be s·, only because

self-aggrandizement

t	464–10	remains unseen at her post, seeking no s·

self-assertive

ph	186–17	Evil is s·.
f	204–23	False and s· theories have

self-cognizant

r	479–11	It is not s·,— cannot feel itself,

self-completeness

c	264–17	this understanding will expand into s·,

self-condemnation

t	455– 3	A mental state of s· and

self-conscious

a	20–32	Mary's s· communion with God.
g	554–14	another false claim, that of s· matter,

self-constituted

p	378–25	Sickness is not a God-given, nor a s· material

self-containment

g	519– 5	His infinite s· and immortal wisdom

self-contradictory

a	52–29	as s· as their religion.
p	388–18	They are s· and self-destructive,
r	478–30	Mortal man is really a s· phrase,
g	552–21	may become wild with freedom and so be s·.

self-control

g	542–12	invoke crime, jeopardize s·,

self-correction

f	218–14	human mind is the sinner, disinclined to s·,

self-created

c	267– 8	God is Father, eternal, s·, infinite.

self-creative

s	157–23	Matter is not s·, for it is unintelligent.
b	278–18	another admission, . . . that matter is s·,
o	356–31	Was there original s· sin?
	357–28	if another mighty and s· cause exists
gl	580–18	usurper of Spirit's creation, called s· matter ;

self-deceived

ph	186–29	or it could never be s·.
p	376– 7	and does its work almost s·.

self-deception
p 403–15 mortal existence is a state of s·

self-defence
t 446– 3 a community unprepared for s·.

self-denial
f 221–28 undisciplined by s· and divine Science.
t 462–17 s·, sincerity, Christianity, and persistence

self-denials
a 39– 8 We must have trials and s·,

self-destroyed
f 224– 8 pain is s· through suffering.
b 293–23 and this so-called mind is s·.
o 346–21 If a dream ceases, it is s·,
p 368– 8 still clearer as error is s·.
437–14 Man s· ; the testimony of matter respected ;
r 476– 6 Error, urged to its final limits, is s·.

self-destroying
gl 581–17 BABEL. S· error ;

self-destruction
element of
b 310–24 Sin is the element of s·,
elements of
r 481–25 Sin has the elements of s·.
no element of
b 311– 8 which has no element of s·.
of all error
b 303–19 through the s· of all error
of error
b 293–26 In reality, they show the s· of error
point of
p 374–32 or increases it to the point of s·.
suffering and
gl 588– 2 suffering and s· ; self-imposed agony ;

sp 77– 7 Error brings its own s·
f 251– 2 as it hastens towards s·.

self-destructive
f 210–18 this so-called mind is s·,
b 300–16 The inharmonious and s· never touch the
p 388– 8 They are self-contradictory and s·,

self-directing
s 160–26 If muscles can cease to act . . . they must be s·.

self-division
c 263–23 a new multiplication or s· of mortal thought,
p 424– 1 by the parent's mind, through s·.
g 548–32 also increase their numbers . . . by s·."
549–13 and sometimes through s·.

self-establishment
s 142– 2 have required for s· and propagation.

self-evident
s 113–10 the four following, to me, s· propositions.
f 207–16 Science of being repudiates s· impossibilities,
b 309–27 It is a s· error to suppose that there can be
o 346–13 It is s· that we are harmonious only as we
p 388–23 and this becomes s·, when we learn that
393–30 when it is s· that matter can have no pain
t 457–13 cannot . . . both cure and cause disease is s·.
r 470–12 by the following s· proposition:
472–21 and we should have a s· absurdity
g 550–32 As C. S. repudiates s· impossibilities,

self-evidently
g 539–21 exposed by our Master as s· wrong.

self-evolution
s 119– 6 They either presuppose the s· . . . of matter,

self-existence
b 331–20 and there is no other s·.

self-existent
s 142–27 If Mind was first and s·,
r 213– 9 God, good, is s· and self-expressed,
b 278–19 admission, . . . that matter is self-creative, s·,
282– 9 The sphere represents good, the s·
290– 1 Because Life is God, Life must be eternal, s·.
300–17 The . . . never touch the harmonious and s·.
r 479– 8 Matter is neither s· nor a product of Spirit.
g 555–17 God, the s· and eternal.
gl 583–21 s· Life, Truth, and Love ;
588–24 Substance ; s· and eternal Mind ;

self-expressed
f 213–10 God, good, is self-existent and s·,

self-forgetfulness
pr 15–26 S·, purity, and affection are constant prayers.

self-governed
an 106– 9 Man is properly s· only when he
s 125–17 Reflecting God's government, man is s·.

self-government
an 106– 8 among which are s·, reason, and conscience.
s 119– 6 They either presuppose the . . . s· of matter,
f 236–22 blighting the buddings of s·.
t 447– 2 trespassing upon man's individual right of s·.

selfhood
a 38–24 Christ, his spiritual s·, never suffered.
m 68– 8 cherish nothing which hinders our highest s·.
sp 91–16 Absorbed in material s· we discern . . . faintly
91–18 The denial of material s· aids the
b 294–25 Man's genuine s· is recognizable only in
316– 6 and lose sight of mortal s·
r 476–22 outside of all material s·.
479–14 which constitutes matter's supposed s·,
g 538– 3 Truth . . . does, drive error out of all s·.
554–11 destitute of any knowledge of the so-called s·
ap 561–20 material and corporeal s· disappear,

self-immolation
pr 1– 6 watching, and working, combined with s·,
a 23– 5 The atonement requires constant s·
sp 99–24 health, purity, and s·,
gl 590– 9 LAMB OF GOD. The spiritual idea of Love ; s· ;

self-imposed
ph 191–16 must free itself from s· materiality
f 221–17 suffering and disease were the s· beliefs of
gl 588– 3 suffering and self-destruction ; s· agony ;

self-inflicted
p 398–20 which reduces s· sufferings
t 462–26 to probe the s· wounds of selfishness,

selfish
a 36–19 A s· and limited mind may be unjust,
51–29 and caused the s· materialist to hate him ;
m 58–13 the s· exaction of all another's time
s 109–16 buoyant with hope, not s· nor depressing.
ph 192–15 all that is s·, wicked, dishonest, and impure.
b 290–10 and from s· and inferior motives.
318–10 all that is material, untrue, s·, or debased.
t 447– 7 erring human opinions, conflicting s· motives,

selfishness
and impurity
m 60–12 s· and impurity alone are fleeting,
and sensualism
c 260–24 S· and sensualism are educated in
and sensuality
a 22– 4 s· and sensuality causing constant retrogression,
and sin
ph 176–14 s· and sin, disease and death, will lose their
mountain of
m 61–10 and every mountain of s· be brought low,
old
pr 9– 7 Do we pursue the old s·, satisfied with
tips the beam
f 205–28 S· tips the beam of human existence towards

pr 9–11 If s· has given place to kindness,
m 64– 2 caused by the s· and inhumanity of man.
ph 175–19 Then people had less time for s·, coddling, and
f 201– 9 Passions, s·, false appetites, hatred,
205–27 into opposite channels where s· reigns.
b 330–30 dishonesty, s·, envy, hypocrisy,
p 407– 7 passion, s·, envy, hatred,
410–24 S· does not appear in the practice of
t 462–27 the self-inflicted wounds of s·,
gl 589– 2 hatred ; s· ; self-will ; lust.

self-justification
pr 8– 1 may afford a quiet sense of s·,
s 115–22 depraved will, s·, pride, envy,
f 242–18 self-will, s·, and self-love,

self-knowledge
t 462–20 Anatomy, . . . is mental s·,

self-love
f 242–15 S· is more opaque than a solid body.
242–18 self-will, self-justification, and s·,

self-made
b 282–11 a belief in a s· and temporary
294–26 Man is neither s· nor made by mortals.
gl 584–22 saith : . . . a wicked mind, s· or

self-mesmerism
p 403– 5 while s· is induced unconsciously

self-offering
gl 579– 8 ABEL. Watchfulness ; s· ;
582– 9 Renewal of affections ; s· ;

self-reliant
a 23–30 demands s· trustworthiness,

self-respect
p 407– 3 inconceivably terrible to man's s·.

self-righteousness
ph 179–10 not in s·, but reflecting the divine
p 364–11 This query Jesus answered by rebuking s·
t 448– 2 Blindness and s· cling fast to
gl 592–27 PHARISEE. Corporeal and sensuous belief ; s· ;

self-sacrifice
a 29–10 Great is the reward of s·,

self-same
b 317–22 as the s· Jesus whom they had loved

self-satisfied
pr 7–21　A s· ventilation of fervent sentiments
self-seeking
t 445–21　S·, envy, passion, pride,
self-seen
p 411–19　Jesus caused the evil to be s·
self-sentence
p 378– 6　will enable you to commute this s·,
self-sustained
p 390– 4　We cannot deny that Life is s·,
g 544– 7　Mind, . . . being the producer, Life was s·.
self-sustaining
ph 170–12　points to the s· and eternal Truth.
p 372–22　Matter is not s·.
self-will
f 242–18　the adamant of error, — s·,
gl 589– 2　envy ; hatred ; selfishness ; s· ; lust.
semblance
ph 195–15　Whatever furnishes the s· of an idea
semi-god
c 263–16　mis-creator, who believes he is a s·.
semi-metaphysical
b 268–14　s· systems afford no substantial aid
268–18　These s· systems are one and all
semi-starvation
f 221–20　Hence s· is not acceptable to wisdom,
semper paratus
l 458–15　S· p· is Truth's motto.
send
f 206–19　Does God s· sickness,
o 287–12　"Doth a fountain s· forth — *Jas.* 3 : 11.
p 439–31　We s· our best detectives to
t 455–29　same fountain cannot s· forth both
g 545–14　errors s· falsity into all human doctrines
ap 570–19　What if the old dragon should s· forth a
sender
s 158– 7　Apollo was also regarded as the s· of disease,
sendeth
r 489–22　s· not forth sweet waters and bitter.
sending
f 206–26　Instead of God s· sickness and death,
sends
ph 191–32　Mind, God, s· forth the aroma of Spirit,
194– 9　Truth s· a report of health over the body.
196–31　The press unwittingly s· forth many sorrows
f 239–30　The perfect Mind s· forth perfection,
239–31　Imperfect mortal mind s· forth its own
p 399–11　mortal mind s· its despatches over its body,
g 516–15　arbutus s· her sweet breath to heaven.
ap 568–29　Love s· forth her primal and everlasting strain.
sensation
basis of
　ph 178–18　acting from the basis of s· in matter,
belief that
　gl 592– 1　*alias* the belief that s· is in matter,
changes
　r 491– 5　Change the belief, and the s· changes.
devoid of
　r 480– 9　whereas matter is devoid of s·.
disappears
　r 491– 6　Destroy the belief, and the s· disappears.
false
　s 128–28　and not upon the judgment of false s·,
has no
　ph 166– 1　matter has no s· of its own,
　f 211–10　Is it not provable . . . that matter has no s·?
　214–31　the body as matter has no s· of its own,
　o 346–23　because matter has no s·,
　p 401–14　since matter has no s·
　r 485– 4　for matter has no s·.
　489– 5　and that matter has no s·,
　489–26　because matter has no s·,
intelligence and
　b 294–12　error, saying : "Matter has intelligence and s·.
life and
　b 278–12　That matter . . . has life and s·, is one of the
　289– 4　The belief that life and s· are in the body
　p 396–30　never giving the body life and s·.
life, nor
　s 127–22　have — as matter — no intelligence, life, nor s·.
　f 205–11　matter has neither intelligence, life, nor s·,
material
　(see **material**)
material in
　p 416–17　and this mind is material in s·,
no
　f 212–16　and the nerves have no s·.
　237– 4　"There is no s· in matter."
　b 284–30　neither s· nor report goes from material body

sensation
nor life
　s 108– 6　matter possesses neither s· nor life ;
of pain
　f 212– 6　If the s· of pain in the limb can return,
of sickness
　f 211–13　The s· of sickness and the impulse to sin
physical
　pr 7–17　Physical s·, . . . produces material ecstasy
supposed
　s 120–25　deduced from supposed s· in matter
world of
　pr 13–31　the world of s· is not cognizant of
　　　　　——
　sp 81– 4　as there is to show the sick that matter . . . has
　　　　　s· ;
　ph 168–28　the s· would not appear if
　188–18　The smile of the sleeper indicates the s·
　f 211–24　If it is true that nerves have s·,
　212–14　it proves s· to be in the mortal mind,
　218–26　to believe in matter as . . . having s· or power.
　243–24　matter has neither intelligence nor s·.
　b 295– 2　the s· seeming to be in nerves
　318–22　denies the error of s· in matter,
　p 370–30　change our basis from s· to C. S.,
　396–21　as if matter could have s·.
　408–30　that condition of the body which we call s·
　r 480– 8　belief that there is s· in matter,
　485–29　as much as nerves control s·
　488–22　Nerves have no more s·, . . . than the
　gl 586–20　a belief that matter has s·.
　591–11　s· in the sensationless ;
sensationless
　f 250–20　the body lies listless, undisturbed, and s·,
　b 280–26　man has a s· body ;
　gl 591–11　MATTER. . . . sensation in the s· ;
　592–11　matter, which is s· ;
sensations
　sp 73–20　with material and desires,
　73–24　belief that . . . spirit retains the s·
　92– 6　but also capable of imparting these s·.
　f 211– 7　The s· of the body must either be the
　211– 7　the s· of a so-called mortal mind or of
　p 372– 7　theory . . . that its s· can reproduce man,
sense
allegorical
　ap 575–16　Taken in its allegorical s·,
and Soul
　f 240–31　how to divide between s· and Soul.
anthropomorphic
　b 337– 1　but not in any anthropomorphic s·.
captives [of
　pref xi–19　deliverance to the captives [of s·], — *Luke* 4 : 18.
certain
　g 509– 7　presented to them the certain s· of eternal Life.
　ap 569–14　in a sweet and certain s· that God is Love.
changes the
　b 319–28　A misplaced word changes the s·
clear
　b 325–20　Paul had a clear s· of the demands of Truth
　r 495–17　your clear s· and calm trust,
common
　p 365–12　and common s· and common humanity are
contradicting
　gl 596–26　C. S., contradicting s·, maketh the valley to bud
corporeal
　pref viii– 5　the discords of corporeal s· must yield to the
　m 56–11　where the corporeal s· of creation was cast out,
　sp 72– 2　of which corporeal s· can take no cognizance,
　77– 5　continues to be a belief of corporeal s· until the
　ph 167– 7　only as we live above corporeal s·
　b 299–26　Corporeal s·, or error, may seem to hide Truth,
　p 376–16　simulated a corporeal s· of life.
　r 483–15　the name "error" to corporeal s·,
　486– 5　until every corporeal s· is quenched.
　489–13　Corporeal s· defrauds and lies ;
　493– 2　To corporeal s·, the sun appears to rise and set,
　494–20　serves to correct the errors of corporeal s· ;
　495–21　Let C. S., instead of corporeal s·,
　g 533–31　learned that corporeal s· is the serpent.
　548–11　only as the clouds of corporeal s· roll away.
　ap 573–19　Because St. John's corporeal s· of the
　578– 2　substituting for the corporeal s·, the
　gl 583– 6　The representatives of Soul, not corporeal s ;
correct
　ap 560–18　without a correct s· of its highest visible idea,
deadened
　a 55– 2　from a deadened s· of the invisible God,
detach
　c 261–21　Detach s· from the body, or matter,
distorted
　b 322–22　incurred through the pains of distorted s·.
divine
　g 505–24　the divine s·, giving the spiritual proof
　ap 577– 1　human sense of Deity yields to the divine s·,

sense

diviner
b 285–20   to give place to a diviner *s·* of
p 369– 7   He enters into a diviner *s·* of the facts,
ap 563– 2   while, to a diviner *s·*, harmony is the real

dormant
b 327–31   awaken the man's dormant *s·* of

enraptured
f 246–15   should dawn upon the enraptured *s·*

erroneous
p 396–25   with which to combat their erroneous *s·*,

errors of
f 240–27   In trying to undo the errors of *s·*
b 273–14   till the errors of *s·* are eliminated.
p 406–11   The Science of being unveils the errors of *s·*,

every
f 208– 9   a law of mortal mind, wrong in every *s·*,

false
s 108–26   this false *s·* evolves, in belief, a
122–27   Temporal life is a false *s·* of existence.
ph 172–14   as the false *s·* of being disappears.
194–22   by the false *s·* it imparts.
196–13   here the word *soul* means a false *s·*
f 205– 5   their false *s·* concerning God and man.
213–31   dipped to its depths into a false *s·* of things,
253–14   I hope that you are conquering this false *s·*.
c 262–27   a false *s·* of man's origin.
b 281–21   When we put off the false *s·* for the true,
307–15   a transient, false *s·* of an existence which
311–30   as mortals lay off a false *s·* of life,
319– 1   manifests mortality, a false *s·* of soul.
325–32   A false *s·* of life, substance, and mind
335–23   Only by losing the false *s·* of Soul can we
p 399–26   It is only a false *s·* of matter,
411–22   induced by a false *s·* mentally entertained,
t 460–15   to the frightened, false *s·* of the patient.
r 485– 6   the false *s·*, which ever betrays mortals into
493–30   the Christ could improve on a false *s·*.
g 539– 1   This false *s·* of existence is fratricidal.
540–21   a false *s·* which hath no knowledge of God."
545–22   translators of this . . . entertained a false *s·* of
ap 573–20   and in place of this false *s·* was the

falsities of
sp 78– 4   They are the falsities of *s·*,

finite
s 120– 1   though it seems otherwise to finite *s·*.
124–12   This is a mortal, finite *s·* of things,
f 208– 3   and has a finite *s·* of the infinite.
c 263–24   as when some finite *s·* peers from its cloister
b 280–13   its finite *s·* of the divisibility of Soul
300– 3   Finite *s·* has no true appreciation of

fleshly
b 314– 3   waited until the mortal or fleshly *s·* had

for soul
r 482– 1   substitution of the word *s·* for *soul*

high
t 448–20   a high *s·* of the moral and

higher
b 285–29   As mortals reach, . . . a higher *s·*,
322–20   physical sense of pleasure yields to a higher *s·*.
p 390–14   Let your higher *s·* of justice destroy the
r 487– 1   to seek and to find a higher *s·* of happiness
gl 589–19   higher *s·* of Truth rebuking mortal belief,

human
    (*see* **human**)

identical with
r 482–12   out of Science, soul is identical with *s·*,

immanent
f 209–14   immanent *s·* of Mind-power enhances the glory of

immortal
sp 72– 3   Principle of man speaks through immortal *s·*.
f 210–30   immortal *s·* includes no evil nor pestilence.
210–31   immortal *s·* has no error of sense,
216–14   to supply the truth of immortal *s·*.

imparting a
ap 567– 2   imparting a *s·* of the ever-presence of

imperfect
c 258–25   Mortals have a very imperfect *s·* of the

incorporeal
ap 577– 2   yields to the incorporeal *s·* of God and man

inferior
gl 590–16   which has the inferior *s·* of master, or ruler.

instead of
b 302–23   this real man is governed by Soul instead of *s·*,

literal
a 32–24   This would have been foolish in a literal *s·*;

lower
s 116–30   but not in the lower *s·*.
gl 590–18   word *kurios* almost always has this lower *s·*,

material
    (*see* **material**)

misconceived
b 281–19   is a myth, a misconceived *s·*

moral
t 451–32   tends to blast moral *s·*, health, and

sense

mortal
    (*see* **mortal**)

must be immortal
p 433–29   sense of Life, God,— which *s·* must be immortal,

my
a 40–10   This is my *s·* of divine pardon,

no
f 210–31   it has no *s·* of error ; therefore it is
243–26   Love has no *s·* of hatred.

no error of
f 210–31   immortal sense has no error of *s·*,

no more
f 250–26   matter has no more *s·* as a man than

objects of
b 269–15   exchanges the objects of *s·* for the ideas of
g 510– 4   than to dwell on the objects of *s·* !

of being
    (*see* **being**)

of Christian Science
ap 577–28   The writer's present feeble *s·* of C. S.

of disease
b 270–27   If a *s·* of disease produces suffering
p 421–26   If you would destroy the *s·* of disease,

of ease
b 270–28   and a *s·* of ease antidotes suffering,

of error
f 210–31   it has no *s·* of error ; therefore it is
g 520–13   in which all *s·* of error forever disappears

of evil
b 325– 3   He who . . . loses all *s·* of evil,
g 540–15   that Truth may annihilate all *s·* of evil

offspring of
b 274– 5   the offspring of *s·*, not of Soul, Spirit,

of good
b 311–13   Evil is destroyed by the *s·* of good.

of health
m 69– 4   mortals gain the *s·* of health only as
p 373–23   Establish the scientific *s·* of health,

of infinitude
r 469–21   we bury the *s·* of infinitude, when we admit

of Life
f 206– 2   no other *s·* of Life, and no consciousness of the
o 355–12   let the harmonious and true *s·* of Life
p 430–11   shut out the true *s·* of Life and health.
433–29   *s·* of Life, God,— which sense must be

of life
    (*see* **life**)

of material life
a 53–29   beliefs of the flesh or his *s·* of material life,

of personal joys
c 266–11   even if you cling to a *s·* of personal joys,

of pleasure
b 208–16   alternating between a *s·* of pleasure and pain,
322–20   until his physical *s·* of pleasure yields to a

of sin
m 69– 5   only as they lose the *s·* of sin and disease.
b 311–12   It is a *s·* of sin, and not a sinful soul,
r 481–31   it is the *s·* of sin which is lost, and not

of Soul
b 335–23   Only by losing the false *s·* of Soul can we
gl 582–15   a *s·* of Soul, which has spiritual bliss

of soul
b 319– 1   manifests mortality, a false *s·* of soul.
r 493–26   Any *s·* of soul in matter is not the

of substance
b 301– 7   but his *s·* of substance involves error

one
s 119–17   In one *s·* God is identical with nature,

our
a 25– 5   expressed by our *s·* of human blood.

outward
s 129–24   instead of accepting only the outward *s·*

overwhelming
a 50– 6   overwhelming *s·* of the magnitude of his work,

painful
r 495–19   can destroy any painful *s·* of, or belief in, that

pains of
    (*see* **pains**)

personal
m 61– 2   within the limits of personal *s·*.
b 312–24   A personal *s·* of God and of

physical
    (*see* **physical**)

priceless
p 366– 1   priceless *s·* of the dear Father's loving-kindness.

primary
g 525–10   the primary *s·* being *image, form,*

proper
c 265– 8   gain some proper *s·* of the infinite,
424– 8   the proper *s·* of God's unerring direction

pure
a 29–25   overshadowed the pure *s·* of the Virgin-mother
b 318–15   would efface the pure *s·* of omnipotence.

purification of
b 324– 5   The purification of *s·* and self is a proof of

sense

quickened
o 343–13 from the quickened *s·* of the people.

quiet
pr 8– 1 A wordy prayer may afford a quiet *s·* of

real
b 295–14 the real *s·* of being, perfect and

rebukes
o 350–29 Soul rebukes *s·*, and Truth destroys error.

religious
a 53–13 contrary to the world's religious *s·*.
c 267–14 in a religious *s·*, they have the same authority

scientific
m 69–19 not conflict with the scientific *s·* of
c 265–10 This scientific *s·* of being, forsaking matter
b 272–10 brings out the scientific *s·*,
337– 1 in a scientific *s·*, but not in any anthropomorphic
p 373–23 Establish the scientific *s·* of health,
415–14 Opiates do not remove . . . in any scientific *s·*.

self and
a 20–31 put aside material self and *s·*, and seek the

sight and
sp 87–32 gone from physical sight and *s·*,

sight or
f 214–28 But the real sight or *s·* is not lost.

sin and
g 530–22 saying, . . . that sin and *s·* are more pleasant
gl 583– 7 who, having wrestled with error, sin, and *s·*,

sinful
pr 15– 4 the door of which shuts out sinful *s·*
16– 6 Truth that is sinless and the falsity of sinful *s·*.
a 23– 9 suffering is an error of sinful *s·*
p 405–29 pains of sinful *s·* are less harmful than

sinless
a 22–24 immortality, boundless freedom, and sinless *s·*,

sinning
sp 96– 1 Humanity advances slowly out of sinning *s·*

spiritual
(*see* **spiritual**)

suffering
sp 77–21 or of a sinning, suffering *s·*,
ap 574–28 which your suffering *s·* deems wrathful

sweet
b 304– 1 the sweet *s·* and presence of Life and Truth.

temporary
b 298– 9 a mortal temporary *s·* of things.

this
b 272– 4 This *s·* is assimilated only as we are honest,
298–11 until this *s·* is corrected by C. S.
o 349–19 this *s·* must be gained by its disciples
r 489–15 How then can this *s·* be the God-given channel

time and
c 261–25 the mutations of time and *s·*,
gl 584– 4 The objects of time and *s·* disappear in the

to Soul
a 48– 9 from earth to heaven, from *s·* to Soul.
c 266– 1 and transplant the affections from *s·* to Soul,
ap 566– 7 in their passage from *s·* to Soul,

transient
f 246–14 the transient *s·* of beauty fades,

true
a 32–20 The true *s·* is spiritually lost, if the
s 108–29 thereby shutting out the true *s·* of Spirit.
c 264– 8 if they would gain the true *s·* of things.
b 283–23 the true *s·* of His power is lost to all who
o 355–12 let the harmonious and true *s·* of Life
p 430–11 shut out the true *s·* of Life and health.
g 534– 7 to interpret the Scriptures in their true *s·*,
550–12 The true *s·* of being and its eternal perfection
ap 575– 2 Arise . . . into the true *s·* of Love,

truer
a 19– 7 by giving man a truer *s·* of Love,
19– 9 and this truer *s·* of Love redeems

uncertain
b 326–24 only when his uncertain *s·* of right yielded to

want of
r 489–30 A wrong sense . . . is *non-sense*, want of *s·*.

woes of
f 248–10 and destroying the woes of *s·*

wrong
r 489–29 A wrong *s·* of God, man, and creation is

---

m 68– 4 They are slaves to fashion, pride, and *s·*.
69–12 nor his *s·* of increasing number
an 102– 7 in *s·* it is an unreal concept of the
s 116–29 in the *s·* of infinite personality, but not
ph 172–20 belief that there is Soul in *s·* or Life in matter
175–12 and dissuade any *s·* of fear or fever.
f 214–26 How transient a *s·* is mortal sight,
c 265–29 inform us that the pleasures of *s·* are mortal
b 311–14 false estimates of soul as dwelling in *s·*
311–16 belief strays into a *s·* of temporary loss
312–14 the *s·* of a corporeal Jehovah,
315–12 hid from their *s·* Christ's sonship
322– 6 the reality of Life, the control of Soul over *s·*,
o 353–13 not wholly outlived the *s·* of ghostly beliefs.

sense

p 362– * *Why art thou cast down, O my soul* [*s·*]? — *Psal.* 42 : 11.
366–23 a *s·* of the odiousness of sin
379–13 Had he known his *s·* of bleeding was an
r 482– 8 use the word *s·*, and you will have the scientific
493–23 it removes any other *s·* of moral or mental
g 540–31 Material in origin and *s·*, he brings a
ap 572–26 Through what *s·* came this vision to St. John ?
gl 596–16 a *s·* of the nothingness of error,

sense-dream
b 312– 6 as the *s·* vanishes and reality appears.

sense-existence
ph 167– 5 Soul-existence, in the place of *s·*,

senseless
f 202–29 as if *s·* matter . . . had more power than

senses

are silent
sp 89–21 Spirit, God, is heard when the *s·* are silent.

are spiritual
f 252–32 Man, whose *s·* are spiritual, is

bodily
a 50–20 before the evidence of the bodily *s·*,
ph 172– 1 which he has through the bodily *s·*,
t 448– 5 Evil which obtains in the bodily *s·*,

cognizable by the
sp 86–29 as readily as from objects cognizable by the *s·*.

corporeal
sp 70– 2 corporeal *s·* cannot inform us what is real
85–24 Jew and Gentile may have had acute corporeal *s·*,
s 131– 7 the false evidence before the corporeal *s·*
144–13 the manifestations of the corporeal *s·*,
f 216–22 If the decision were left to the corporeal *s·*,
b 281– 8 Divine Science contradicts the corporeal *s·*,
296–22 knowledge obtained from the corporeal *s·*
318– 5 Corporeal *s·* define diseases as realities;
318– 7 even while the corporeal *s·* are saying that
334–23 according to the testimony of the corporeal *s·*,
p 388– 4 obtained a victory over the corporeal *s·*,
393– 9 Mind is the master of the corporeal *s·*,
305 0 master the false evidences of the corporeal *s·*
417–18 The evidence before the corporeal *s·*
t 448–13 rises above the evidence of the corporeal *s·* ;
r 471– 8 the evidence before the five corporeal *s·*,
477–10 To the five corporeal *s·*, man appears to be
477–12 declares the corporeal *s·* to be mortal and
486–28 If the five corporeal *s·* were the medium
488–14 Do the five corporeal *s·* constitute man?
488–20 corporeal *s·* can take no cognizance of
489–24 The corporeal *s·* are the only source of evil
493–18 the beliefs of the five corporeal *s·*,
g 516– 7 the false testimony of the corporeal *s·*
525–24 The corporeal *s·* declare otherwise ;
527–16 gathered from the corporeal *s·*,
531–28 corporeal *s·* can take no cognizance of Spirit.
532– 6 must be gained from the five corporeal *s·*.
532–21 calling out to the corporeal *s·*.
543– 9 five corporeal *s·* cannot take cognizance of
546–16 manifested only through the corporeal *s·*,
552– 8 necessarily apparent to the corporeal *s·* ,
557–14 but in the line of the corporeal *s·*,
gl 581–20 evidence obtained from the five corporeal *s·*,
585– 1 Not organs of the so-called corporeal *s·*,
589–13 knowledge obtained from the corporeal *s·* ;
590– 5 Evidence obtained from the five corporeal *s·* ;

deceitful
p 395– 4 the testimony of the deceitful *s·*,

educated
ph 195– 8 All that gives pleasure to our educated *s·*

enslaving
f 227– 6 claims of the enslaving *s·* must be denied

erring
pr 15–10 door of the erring *s·* must be closed.

evidence of the
a 18–11 against the accredited evidence of the *s·*,
p 386– 2 evidence of the *s·* is not to be accepted
420–31 Turn his gaze from the false evidence of the *s·*

evidence to the
p 370–10 furnishes the evidence to the *s·*,

five
ph 200–22 in other words the five *s·*,
b 274– 4 knowledge gained from the five *s·*
g 526–10 material hearing, sight, . . . termed the five *s·*
532–31 through matter, the five *s·*.

his
a 52– 5 His *s·* drank in the spiritual evidence of

human
s 116– 6 evidence before the corporeal human *s·*,
t 461–10 from the standpoint of the human *s·*.

illusions of the
b 332–13 dispelling the illusions of the *s·* ;

illusive
ph 191–28 The illusive *s·* may fancy affinities with

senses

limited
b 337–21 incomprehensible to the limited s·
material
  (*see* **material**)
mortal
b 288–28 unlimited by the mortal s·.
p 390– 6 to the mortal s·, there is seeming discord.
of man
b 284–28 the only real s· of man are spiritual,
r 486–23 all the spiritual s· of man, are eternal.
  488–28 If it were possible for the real s· of man to be
  489–19 Who dares to say that the s· of man can be
of Mind
r 489– 4 the s· of Mind are never lost
of Soul
f 213–18 communicated through the s· of Soul,
  214–29 Neither . . . can interfere with the s· of Soul,
of Spirit
b 274–12 The s· of Spirit abide in Love,
personal
b 334–11 imperceptible to the so-called personal s·,
physical
  (*see* **physical**)
real
f 214–30 and there are no other real s·.
b 284–28 the only real s· of man are spiritual,
r 488–28 If it were possible for the real s· of man to be
represent
c 265–16 The s· represent birth as untimely
Science and the
b 273–13 Hence the enmity between Science and the s·,
so-called
s 122–10 these so-called s· still make mortal
ph 190–11 arranges itself into five so-called s·,
c 258–20 material so-called s· have no cognizance
  261–20 he was in the full possession of his so-called s·.
b 292–16 The so-called s· of mortals are material.
r 471– 9 these so-called s· receive no intimation of
  488–18 defines these so-called s· as *mortal beliefs*,
Spirit's
f 214–32 Spirit's s· are without pain,
spiritual
b 288– 5 between the evidence of the spiritual s· and
r 486–23 all the spiritual s· of man, are eternal.
g 512–25 discerned only through the spiritual s·.
testimony of the
s 122–20 denying the testimony of the s·,
these
b 284–28 are beyond the cognizance of these s·,
  294– 2 These s· indicate the common human belief,
r 486– 7 To die, that he may regain these s·?
those very
ph 195– 9 gave him pain through those very s·,
unseen to the
f 234–30 action of the human mind, unseen to the s·.
visible to the
p 400–26 image which becomes visible to the s·.

a 38–28 living only for . . . the gratification of the s·,
  52– 7 their s· testified oppositely, and absorbed the
m 61– 2 The s· confer no real enjoyment.
an 101– 4 the impressions made upon the s· ;
s 119–26 contradicts the evidence before the s·
  120–13 is he well if the s· say he is sick?
  138–25 the sinful, so-called pleasure of the s·.
f 206–14 governed by Science instead of the s·,
  242–14 so-called pain and pleasure of the s·.
b 289–18 what appears to the s· to be death is but
  305–20 inverted images presented by the s·,
  312– 8 The s· regard a corpse, not as man,
p 382–25 oblivion, in which the s· had engulfed him,
  384–29 all the evidence before the s· can never

senses'
s 122– 7 The material s· reversal of the

sense-testimony
f 249– 2 relinquish all theories based on s·,

sensible
s 109– 7 not, . . . seen to be supported by s· evidence,
ph 173– 9 the s· is required to be made manifest through
p 399–27 since matter is not s·.

sensibly
pr 14– 1 If we are s· with the body and regard
p 383–30 pounding the poor body, to make it s· well

sensitive
a 54– 1 he would have been less s· to those beliefs.
p 423– 6 oftentimes affects a s· patient more
g 555– 1 mortal mind is less pungent or s·,

sensual
a 20–13 men can be baptized, . . . and yet be s· and
sp 73–30 The s· cannot be made the mouthpiece of
f 221–32 another lesson,— that gluttony is a s· illusion,
  226–26 the sick, the s·, the sinner, I wished to save
  241– 5 S· treasures are laid up "where moth —*Matt.* 6 : 19.

sensual
f 254–16 During the s· ages, absolute C. S. may not
c 263–28 A s· thought, like an atom of dust
b 296–10 Nothing s· or sinful is immortal.
g 547–28 s·, and mortal theory of the universe,
gl 583– 1 S· and mortal beliefs ;
  590–11 A corporeal and s· belief ; mortal man ;

sensualism
a 36–16 distance between Christianity and s·
m 65–14 in the materialism and s· of the age,
c 260–22 S· evolves bad physical and moral conditions.
  260–24 Selfishness and s· are educated in
b 272–23 earthward gravitation of s· and impurity,
  337– 6 S· is not bliss, but bondage.
gl 589– 5 mortal embracing duplicity, repentance, s·.
  594–15 love rebuking error ; reproof of s·.

sensualist's
f 241– 8 The s· affections are as imaginary, whimsical,

sensuality
all
f 201–10 false appetites, hatred, fear, all s·,
and sin
p 364– 7 might be redeemed from s· and sin.
arising from
sp 94–20 betrayal, arising from s·.
palsies
s 142–16 S· palsies the right hand, and causes the left to
rebuked their
a 51–27 divine Principle, Love, which rebuked their s·.
selfishness and
a 22– 4 selfishness and s· causing constant retrogression,
sin and
sp 82–31 In a world of sin and s· hastening to

sp 71–25 There is no s· in Spirit.
  92–19 an outgrowth of human knowledge or s·,
an 104–20 dishonesty, s·, falsehood, revenge,
gl 581– 6 counteracting all evil, s·, and mortality.
  587–21 Ham (Noah's son). Corporeal belief ; s· ;
  589–14 s· ; envy ; oppression ; tyranny.
  593– 7 Error ; fear ; inflammation ; s· ;
  593–12 Reuben (Jacob's son). Corporeality ; s· ;

sensuous
s 111– 3 the will, or s· reason of the human mind,
  121– 3 inclinations of a s· philosophy.
  131– 8 Hence the opposition of s· man
ph 177–14 the body is a s·, human concept.
f 203–19 imprisoned in a s· body.
  224– 7 s· pleasure or pain is self-destroyed
o 353– 1 scientific real is the s· unreal.
t 454–30 superiority of spiritual power over s·
gl 582–24 Canaan (the son of Ham). A s· belief ;
  592–27 Pharisee. Corporeal and s· belief ;

sensuousness
pr 16–20 Only as we rise above all material s· and
a 35– 8 enabled to rise somewhat from mortal s·,
  51–29 His spirituality separated him from s·,

sent
a 18– * *For Christ s· me not to baptize,*— *I Cor.* 1 : 17.
  27– 1 Jesus s· a message to John the Baptist,
  27–22 Jesus s· forth seventy students at one time,
  49– 7 Where were the seventy whom Jesus s· forth?
s 109–29 not mine, but His that s· me.— *John* 7 : 16.
  126–13 nor s· forth a positive sound,
  133– 1 and s· the inquiry to Jesus,
ph 165– * *He s· His word, and healed them,*— *Psal.* 107 : 20.
b 272– 1 except they be s·?"— *Rom.* 10 : 15.
  272– 1 If s·, how shall they preach, . . . except the
p 378–12 s· it cowering back into the jungle.
  410– 9 Jesus Christ, whom Thou hast s·."— *John* 17 : 3.
  433–28 and Scholastic Theology is s· for
g 537– 3 s· him forth from the garden— *Gen.* 3 : 23.
ap 561–30 "There was a man s· from God— *John* 1 : 6.

sentence
awaiting the
p 439–29 awaiting the s· which General Progress
civil
pr 7– 1 The only civil s· which he had for error
divine
pr 11–19 not to annul the divine s·
of death
p 433–19 proceeds to pronounce the solemn s· of death
  436– 3 for which Mortal Man is under s· of death.
  436–33 that court pronounced a s· of death for
of God
f 232–23 never tried to make of none effect the s· of God,
this
sp 80– 9 the very periodical containing this s·
unjust
p 381–29 man's moral right to annul an unjust s·,

an 105– 3 Courts and juries judge and s· mortals

sentence

an	105–15	courts reasonably pass *s·*, according to the mo-
		tive.
p	378– 4	Unwittingly you *s·* yourself to suffer.
	381–29	a *s·* never inflicted by divine authority.
	391–24	and the judge will *s·* you.
	405–13	*s·* of the moral law will be executed
	440–17	Wherefore, then, . . . do you *s·* Mortal Man

sentenced

b	322–15	since God has *s·* sin to suffer.
p	433–24	For this crime Mortal Man is *s·*
	434–22	The prisoner at the bar has been unjustly *s·*.
	434–30	the lower court has *s·* Mortal Man to die,
	435–17	Laws of Health should be *s·* to die.
	436–28	His Honor *s·* Mortal Man to die

sentences

sp	86–26	peculiarities of expression, recollected *s·*,
f	225–17	A few immortal *s·*, . . . have been potent
o	341– 5	are generally based on detached *s·*
p	391–26	Mortal mind alone *s·* itself.
	440–21	God, who *s·* only for sin.

sentient

b	280–25	instead of possessing a *s·* material form,
	285– 1	Matter is not *s·* and cannot
r	487–23	The belief that life is *s·* and intelligent
g	528– 1	Was it requisite . . . that dust should become *s·*,
gl	587–11	a supposition of *s·* physicality ;

sentiment

pr	7–16	to induce or encourage Christian *s·*.
s	161–15	that immortal *s·* of the Declaration,
ph	176– 1	and there is truth in his *s·*.
f	252–21	Animal in propensity, deceitful in *s·*,
p	408–21	a supposed effect on intelligence and *s·*.

sentiments

pr	7–22	A self-satisfied ventilation of fervent *s·*
ph	195–28	with wrong tastes and *s·*.
f	206–12	exercise of the *s·* — hope, faith, love
b	327–30	Let that inform the *s·* and awaken the
g	531– 9	represent the higher moral *s·*,

sentinel

a	49–18	faithful *s·* of God at the highest post of

sentinels

f	225– 9	and will command their *s·* not to let truth pass

separate

pr	6– 5	God is not *s·* from the wisdom He bestows.
	14–25	Entirely *s·* from the belief and dream of
a	21–13	We have *s·* time-tables to consult,
	42–19	belief that man has existence or mind *s·* from
m	66–21	Husbands and wives should never *s·* if
sp	74–32	in *s·* states of existence, or consciousness.
an	103–12	Mind-science is wholly *s·* from
	105–11	Can you *s·* the mentality from the body
s	136– 6	no intelligence, action, nor life *s·* from God.
ph	192–10	Spirit is not *s·* from God.
f	204– 7	false conclusions . . . that there are two *s·*,
	238– 7	and be ye *s·*," — *II Cor. 6 : 17.*
b	304– 8	to *s·* us from the love of God." — *Rom. 8 : 39.*
	309–26	impossible . . . for man to have an intelligence *s·*
p	415–32	as if it were a *s·* bodily member.
	424– 2	becomes a *s·*, individualized mortal mind,
t	449–25	only to *s·* through simultaneous repulsion.
	451– 4	to come out from the material world and be *s·*.
r	466–27	to *s·* the chaff from the wheat.
	475–19	that which has no *s·* mind from God ;
	480–18	thus attempting to *s·* Mind from God.
	491–25	apparently with their own *s·* embodiment.
g	522–10	Existence, *s·* . . . Science explains as impossible.
	535– 4	the wheat and tares which time will *s·*,
	539– 4	Error begins by reckoning life as *s·* from Spirit,

separated

a	51–17	therefore he could no more be *s·* from his
	51–28	His spirituality *s·* him from sensuousness,
sp	72–16	which are not united by progress, but *s·*.
	91– 5	the belief that man is *s·* from God,
b	303–29	nor *s·* from its divine Principle.
	306–14	and then are *s·* as by a law of divorce
	306–18	cannot be *s·* for an instant from God,
	315– 4	*s·* him from the scholastic theology of the
o	341– 5	or clauses *s·* from their context.
t	450–28	beliefs in . . . intelligence *s·* from God,
r	477–29	*S·* from man, who expresses Soul,
	478–28	God, who *s·* me from — *Gal. 1 : 15.*
g	505– 8	material sense, is *s·* from Truth,
ap	562–12	*s·* by belief from man's divine origin

separately

m	58–25	"Two eat no more together than they eat *s·*."
p	397–27	can never treat mortal mind and matter *s·*,

separates

m	66–31	furnace *s·* the gold from the dross
f	207–18	Science *s·* the tares and wheat in time of
b	300–20	Science *s·* the wheat from the tares,

separates

t	456–13	*s·* himself from the true conception of
g	506– 6	a quality which *s·* C. S. from supposition
	548– 3	C. S. *s·* error from truth,

separation

m	59–31	*S·* never should take place,
b	338–23	even the supposed *s·* of man from God,
p	375– 4	belief that . . . pain must accompany the *s·*

separator

gl	586– 7	FAN. *S·* of fable from fact ;

sepulchre

a	44– 8	His three days' work in the *s·*
	44–29	while he was hidden in the *s·*,
	45–15	failed to hide immortal Truth and Love in a *s·*.
b	299– 8	appearing at the door of some *s·*,
	314–18	the body, which they laid in a *s·*,
g	534– 4	and to behold at the *s·* the risen Saviour,
gl	597–14	opened the *s·* with divine Science,

sepulchres

pr	8– 9	"like unto whited *s·* — *Matt. 23 : 27.*

sequel

s	159–20	The *s·* proved that this Lynn woman

series

s	117– 2	because an individual may be one of a *s·*,
	117– 4	God is *One*, — not one of a *s·*, but

seriously

s	132–32	yet afterwards he *s·* questioned the signs of the

sermon

sp	80– 4	whether for the inspiration of a *s·* or
f	201– 1	best *s·* ever preached is Truth practised
	234– 5	be it song, *s·*, or Science

Sermon on the Mount

ph	174–17	The thunder of Sinai and the *S· on the M·*
b	271–23	The *S· on the M·* is the essence of

sermons

ph	176–12	"*s·* in stones, and good in everything."
o	345– 8	Christian *s·* will heal the sick.

serpent

argument of the

b	280–21	The argument of the *s·* in the allegory,

beguiled me

g	533–28	She says, "The *s·* beguiled me, — *Gen. 3 : 13.*

brazen

s	133–11	looked upon the brazen *s·*,

changeth the

g	515– 9	power which changeth the *s·* into a staff.

coiled around

sp	92–11	a *s·* coiled around the tree of knowledge

enters

g	529–22	*s·* enters into the metaphor only as

fable of the

g	544–19	first suggestion . . . is in the fable of the *s·*.

handle the

b	321–11	wisdom bade him come back and handle the *s·*,

is perpetually

ap	564–28	The *s·* is perpetually close upon the

is supposed

g	544–21	The *s·* is supposed to say,

lying

g	529–21	Whence comes a talking, lying *s·*

represents the

sp	92–13	This represents the *s·* in the act of

so-called

b	307– 3	This pantheistic error, or so-called *s·*,

strangle the

ap	569–16	and fail to strangle the *s·* of sin

talking

g	529–25	the species described, — a talking *s·*,
ap	564–31	allegorical, talking *s·* typifies mortal mind,

testimony of the

g	538–15	The testimony of the *s·* is significant of

typified by a

ap	564–26	are typified by a *s·*, or animal subtlety.

b	269– 5	resulted from the philosophy of the *s·*.
	321– 9	he saw it become a *s·*,
	321–13	*s·*, evil, under wisdom's bidding, was destroyed
	338–24	the obstacle which the *s·*, sin, would impose
g	515– 5	The *s·* of God's creating is neither subtle nor
	529–13	Now the *s·* was more subtle — *Gen. 3 : 1.*
	529–17	And the woman said unto the *s·*, — *Gen. 3 : 2.*
	530–13	the *s·* said unto the woman, — *Gen. 3 : 4.*
	533–31	learned that corporeal sense is the *s·*.
	534– 9	[Jehovah] said unto the *s·*, — *Gen. 3 : 14.*
	534–27	The *s·*, material sense, will bite the heel
	539–18	by condemning its symbol, the *s·*,
	550–26	A *s·* never begets a bird,
ap	563–18	that old *s·*, whose name is devil or evil,
	564–30	the *s·* pursues with hatred the
	567–15	that old *s·*, called the devil, — *Rev. 12 : 9.*
	567–18	that old *s·* whose name is devil (evil),
	570– 8	*s·* cast out of his mouth water — *Rev. 12 : 15.*
gl	594– 1	definition of

serpent-bites
b 328–20   hundreds . . . die there annually from *s·*

serpentine
g 541–22   Here the *s·* lie invents new forms.
ap 563–27   The *s·* form stands for subtlety,

serpents
b 322– 1   taught them how to handle *s·* unharmed,
328–23   they shall take up *s·*, — *Mark* 16 : 18.
p 362– *   *they shall take up s·*; — *Mark* 16 : 18.
gl 587–15   the *s·* of error, which say,

servant
a 44– 3   good and faithful *s·*," — *Matt.* 25 : 23.
s 119–32   is but the humble *s·* of the restful Mind,
146–11   by which material sense is made the *s·* of
p 404– 4   or the special *s·* of any one of the
439–26   declaring Disease to be God's *s·*

servants
f 201– *   *the reproach of Thy s·;* — *Psal.* 89 : 50.
216–16   it makes the nerves, . . . *s·*,

serve
pr 14– 5   We cannot "*s·* two masters." — *Matt.* 6 : 24.
a 37–11   *s·* to cleanse and rarefy the atmosphere of
ph 167–11   We cannot *s·* two masters
f 201– 5   "No man can *s·* two masters." — *Matt.* 6 : 24.
c 267–24   by reversal, errors *s·* as waymarks to the
o 346–30   We cannot *s·* both God and mammon
p 422–19   changes . . . in mortal mind *s·* to reconstruct

served
a 52– 4   He *s·* God ; they *s·* mammon.
r 497–21   his resurrection *s·* to uplift faith

serves
m 57–27   *s·* to unite thought more closely to God,
b 325–25   begotten of the beliefs of the flesh and *s·* them,
t 453–22   yet *s·* evil in the name of good.
r 494–20   *s·* to correct the errors of corporeal sense ;
g 502–11   *s·* to suggest the proper reflection of God

service
a 31–32   will think that he doeth God *s·* ; — *John* 16 : 2.
40–28   It is sad that the phrase *divine s·* has
sp 79–32   Giving does not impoverish us in the *s·* of our
b 325–24   which is your reasonable *s·*." — *Rom.* 12 : 1.
p 399–12   this so-called mind is both the *s·* and message
436–12   Giving a cup of cold water . . . is a Christian *s·*.
t 455–21   God selects for the highest *s·* one who

servitude
f 225–23   Legally to abolish unpaid *s·* in the
226–22   wearing out years of *s·* to an unreal master

sessions
an 101–10   which tested during several *s·* the phenomena

set
pref xi–21   To *s·* at liberty them that are — *Luke* 4 : 18.
a 19–14   although his teaching *s·* households at variance,
20–30   the race that is *s·* before us ;" — *Heb.* 12 : 1.
44– 8   His three days' work in the sepulchre *s·* the
s 108–32   *s·* my thoughts to work in new channels,
126–22   I have *s·* forth C. S. and its application to
137–17   his reply *s·* forth a great fact :
141– 8   to *s·* aside even the most cherished beliefs
ph 178– 4   it is *s·* down as a poison by mortal mind.
f 210– 6   are *s·* forth in Jesus' demonstrations,
211–20   children's teeth are *s·* on edge." — *Ezek.* 18 : 2.
222–30   and eat what is *s·* before you,
247– 8   retained his full *s·* of upper and lower teeth
b 326– 9   and *s·* his whole affections on spiritual things,
o 345– 8   When . . . His absoluteness is *s·* forth,
354–17   who thereunto have *s·* their seals.
p 367–20   A city that is *s·* on an hill — *Matt.* 5 : 14.
382–32   Mortal mind needed to be *s·* right.
434– 1   can open wide those prison doors and *s·* the
r 472– 6   God has *s·* his signet upon Science,
493– 3   the sun appears to rise and *s·*,
k 499– *   *I have s· before thee an open door,* — *Rev.* 3 : 8.
g 511– 7   And God *s·* them in the firmament — *Gen.* 1 : 17.
521–26   a material view of creation, is to be *s·* forth.
521–30   if veritable, would *s·* aside the omnipotence of
542–16   *s·* a mark upon Cain, lest any — *Gen.* 4 : 15.
555–24   and *s·* aside the proper conception of Deity,
ap 558– 7   he *s·* his right foot upon the sea, — *Rev.* 10 : 2.
568–10   first the true method of creation is *s·* forth
gl 579– *   *I have s· before thee an open door,* — *Rev.* 3 : 8.

sets
sp 83–18   belief that . . . Spirit *s·* aside these laws,
90–25   *s·* man free to master the infinite idea.
s 114–27   and *s·* free the imprisoned thought.
c 260–14   *s·* mortals at work to discover what
r 495–13   *s·* the captive free physically and morally.
g 542– 8   and *s·* upon error the mark of the beast.
554–19   infinite Mind *s·* at naught such a mistaken

settle
b 288– 7   will *s·* all questions through faith in

settles
o 361– 4   cancels the disagreement, and *s·* the question.
p 433–15   a look of despair and death *s·* upon it.

seven
pref xii– 6   During *s·* years over four thousand students
p 421–32   of eight multiplied by five, and of *s·* by ten,
g 520–10   The numerals of infinity, called *s·* *days*,
ap 559–13   It arouses the "*s·* thunders" — *Rev.* 10 : 3.
562–30   having *s·* heads and ten horns, — *Rev.* 12 : 3.
562–31   and *s·* crowns upon his heads. — *Rev.* 12 : 3.
572–15   open the *s·* seals of error with Truth,
574– 6   one of the *s·* angels which had — *Rev.* 21 : 9.
574– 7   the *s·* vials full of the *s·* last — *Rev.* 21 : 9.
574–18   the *s·* angelic vials full of *s·* plagues,

sevenfold
g 542–16   vengeance shall be taken on him *s·*. — *Gen.* 4 : 15.

seventeen
ph 194–24   at the age of *s·* Kaspar was still a

seventh
a 21–30   he turns east on the *s·*,
p 362– 1   in the *s·* chapter of Luke's Gospel
g 519–22   on the *s·* day God ended His work — *Gen.* 2 : 2.
519–23   and He rested on the *s·* day — *Gen.* 2 : 2.

seventy
a 27–22   Jesus sent forth *s·* students at one time,
49– 7   Where were the *s·* whom Jesus sent forth?
o 342–13   he bade the *s·* disciples, as well as the twelve,

seventy-four
f 245–13   saw her when she was *s·*,
245–28   proves it possible to be young at *s·* ;

several
an 101–10   which tested during *s·* sessions the phenomena
ph 193– 6   said the bone was carious for *s·* inches.
g 556–32   plunged . . . into the water for *s·* minutes,

severance
m 57–26   this *s·* of fleshly ties serves to
s 122–24   To material sense, the *s·* of the jugular vein

severe
ph 175–23   was not so *s·* upon the gastric juices
f 251– 5   neither should a fever become more *s·*
p 407– 9   Every hour of delay makes the struggle more *s·*.
r 488– 4   When, . . . you are able to banish a *s·* malady,

severed
b 295– 1   The belief that a *s·* limb is aching

severely
f 238–21   because we suffer *s·* from error.
t 443– 9   at times *s·* condemned by some

severest
s 162–19   in their *s·* forms.
p 387–18   That man does not pay the *s·* penalty who

sex
g 551–21   peculiarities of ancestry, belonging to either *s·*

sexes
m 57–10   Both *s·* should be loving, pure, tender, and
63–13   differences between the rights of the two *s·*.
63–20   property, and parental claims of the two *s·*.
65–10   The union of the *s·* suffers fearful discord.
b 340–28   equalizes the *s·* ; annuls the curse on man,
g 532– 2   the union of the two *s·*

sexual
g 549– 3   takes place apart from *s·* conditions.

sexuality
g 508–19   The word is not confined to *s·*,

shackles
f 225– 2   What is it that binds man with iron *s·*
c 256– 1   Progress takes off human *s·*.

shade
ap 566–22   In *s·* and storm the frequent night,

shadow
and shelter
g 516–16   The great rock gives *s·* and shelter.
beneath the
a 36–14   in silent woe beneath the *s·* of his cross.
of death
ap 578–10   valley of the *s·* of death, — *Psal.* 23 : 4.
gl 596–21   valley of the *s·* of death, — *Psal.* 23 : 4.
within the
s 108–20   within the *s·* of the death-valley,

f 233–16   Already the *s·* of His right hand
c 257– 5   If . . . then Spirit, matter's unlikeness, must be *s·* ;
257– 5   and *s·* cannot produce substance.
b 299–29   sunshine of Truth, will melt away the *s·*
331– 3   no more . . . than substance is in its *s·*.
o 351–29   To them . . . Spirit was *s·*.
t 460–31   the *s·* of old errors was no longer cast upon

shadows
  a 32-32 with *s·* fast falling around ;
  s 140-20 are but types and *s·* of true worship.
  b 310-11 Day may decline and *s·* fall,
shake
  s 130-20 Laboring long to *s·* the adult's faith in matter
shaken
  o 269-28 reeds *s·* by the wind, not houses built on the
  297-28 Mortal testimony can be *s·*.
Shakespeare
  m 66- 1 Thou art right, immortal *S·*,
Shakespeare's
  f 244-29 Even *S·* poetry pictures age as infancy,
shallow
  s 110-20 This book may be distorted by *s·* criticism
  c 257-11 This belief is *s·* pantheism.
shallows
  c 262-10 diving into the *s·* of mortal belief.
sham
  g 555-21 and call this *s·* unity *man*,
shame
  a 36-10 Jesus endured the *s·*,
  52-16 in order to unite in putting to *s·* and death
  ph 188-10 from *s·* and woe to their final punishment.
  g 532-18 produced the immediate fruits of fear and *s·*.
  533- 1 was one of nakedness and *s·*.
shape
  f 246-29 Let us then *s·* our views of existence
  p 400-14 before it has taken tangible *s·* in
shaped
  sp 96-26 *s·* his course in accordance with divine Science
  g 525-14 and God *s·* man after His mind ;
  525-15 after God's mind *s·* He him ;
  525-15 and He *s·* them male and female.
shapen
  g 540-29 and "*s·* in iniquity ;"—*Psal.* 51 : 5.
shapes
  t 458-26 The Christian Scientist wisely *s·* his course,
share
  a 54-25 and to *s·* the glory of eternal life.
  m 57-21 but requires all mankind to *s·* it.
  ap 559-28 because you must *s·* the hemlock cup
shared
  a 33-28 Have you *s·* the blood of the New Covenant,
  53-32 Had he *s·* the sinful beliefs of others,
shares
  s 157- 6 never *s·* its rights with inanimate matter.
  ph 194- 1 *s·* not its strength with matter
sharp
  pr 3-29 *s·* censure our Master pronounces on hypocrites.
  sp 85-27 His thrusts at materialism were *s·*, but needed.
  87-21 of the corals, of its *s·* reefs, of the tall ships
  322-20 The *s·* experiences of belief in the
  p 374-14 This mortal blindness and its *s·* consequences
  407- 1 but there is a very *s·* remembrance of it,
  t 459-17 is like putting a *s·* knife into the hands of
sharper
  a 50-29 *s·* than the thorns which pierced his flesh.
shearers
  a 50 2 as a sheep before her *s·* is dumb,—*Isa.* 53 : 7.
shed
  a 25- 7 *s·* upon "the accursed tree,"— see *Gal.* 3 : 13.
  30-16 by man shall his blood be *s·*."—*Gen.* 9 : 6.
  p 379-18 when not a drop of his blood was *s·*.
sheddeth
  a 30-15 "Whoso *s·* man's blood,—*Gen.* 9 : 6.
sheep
  a 50- 1 as a *s·* before her shearers is dumb,—*Isa.* 53 : 7.
  t 464-27 and careth not for the *s·*."—*John* 10 : 13.
  gl 594-12 definition of
sheep's
  an 104- 6 and belied by wolves in *s·* clothing.
  ap 567-29 These wolves in *s·* clothing are detected
sheer
  s 144-18 but is *s·* animal magnetism.
Shekinah
  a 41- 2 into the *S·* into which Jesus has passed
shells
  g 552-18 They must peck open their *s·* with C. S.,
shelter
  g 516-16 The great rock gives shadow and *s·*.
Shem
  gl 594-14 definition of
shepherd
  pref vii- 2 The wakeful *s·* beholds the first
  ap 578- 5 [DIVINE LOVE] is my *s·* ;—*Psal.* 23 : 1.

shepherd-boy
  b 268-11 like the *s·* with his sling,
sheriff
  p 436-18 But they brought with them Fear, the *s·*,
  441-23 executed at the hands of our *s·*, Progress.
shield
  p 408- 9 cannot, in a scientific diagnosis, *s·* the
  418- 1 to *s·* them from the baneful effects of
  t 457-14 In the legend of the *s·*, which led to a quarrel
shift
  ph 168- 1 a poor *s·* for the weak and worldly,
shifts
  g 513-10 and the scene *s·* into light.
shine
  pref vii-10 and *s·* the guiding star of being.
  f 252-29 and *s·* with the resplendency of
  g 518-20 immortality, and goodness, which *s·* through
  546-24 like rays of light, *s·* in the darkness,
shines
  g 518-21 as the blossom *s·* through the bud.
  ap 562-20 *s·* "unto the perfect day"—*Prov.* 4 : 18.
shineth
  b 325-31 like the light, "*s·* in darkness,—*John* 1 : 5.
shining
  f 247-29 *s·* resplendent and eternal over age and decay
  o 347-21 and is the light *s·* in darkness,
  g 510-29 and this one *s·* by its own light
  ap 566-24 A burning and a *s·* light !
ships
  sp 87-21 the tall *s·* that float on its bosom,
shipwreck
  t 451-10 will either make *s·* of their faith or
shock
  a 53-19 the *s·* so often produced by the truth,
  53-20 this *s·* arises from the great distance between
  p 421- 9 make known . . . your motive for this *s·*,
shocked
  ap 570- 6 *s·* into another extreme mortal mood,
shockingly
  o 360- 9 replies ; , , , they are not so *s·* transcendental.
shone
  pref vii- 4 So *s·* the pale star to the prophet-shepherds ;
shook
  p 442- 9 We noticed, as he *s·* hands with his counsel,
Shore
  ap 576- 1 of the Golden *S·* of Love
shore
  a 34-32 joyful meeting on the *s·* of the Galilean Sea !
  35- 6 Discerning Christ, Truth, anew on the *s·* of
  f 203-29 should disappear on the *s·* of time ;
shores
  sp 90- 3 loaves and fishes multiplied on the *s·* of
shorn
  a 50-17 that hour would be *s·* of its mighty blessing
  s 124- 4 a Samson *s·* of his strength,
short
  f 249-29 It falls *s·* of the skies, but
  252-22 says : . . . my *s·* span of life one gala day.
  o 352-26 In *s·*, children should be told not to
  p 363-15 Jesus rebuked them with a *s·* story or parable.
  t 448-29 nothing *s·* of right-doing has any claim to
  ap 568-23 that he hath but a *s·* time.—*Rev.* 12 : 12.
  569-24 for the devil knoweth his time is *s·*
  572-13 nothing *s·* of this divine Principle, understood
shortened
  s 162-20 *s·* limbs have been elongated,
shorter
  sp 77-17 will be of longer or *s·* duration
  g 530- 2 increases in falsehood and his days become *s·*.
shortest
  p 387-15 If printers and authors have the *s·* span of
shortly
  p 432-21 testifies : . . . I was called for, *s·* after the
shoulders
  p 363- 6 which hung loosely about her *s·*,
show
  pref ix-29 These efforts *s·* . . . the degrees by which
  a 18- 8 to *s·* them how to do theirs,
  26-20 to *s·* the learner the way by practice as well as
  31-23 *s·* the Lord's death till he come."—*I Cor.* 11 : 26.
  37- 1 Does not Science *s·* that sin brings suffering
  40-18 not otherwise could he *s·* us the way
  42-25 Afterwards he would *s·* it to them unchanged.
  m 65-14 *s·* themselves in the materialism and
  sp 81- 3 as there is to *s·* the sick that matter
  an 103-10 does not scientifically *s·* itself in a knowledge
  s 108- 7 human experiences *s·* the falsity of
  111-24 incidents which *s·* that C. S. meets a
  132- 4 "Go and *s·* John again those—*Matt.* 11 : 4.
  139-20 *s·* how a mortal and material sense stole into

show

ph	169–10	to s· that disease has a mental, mortal origin,
f	210– 7	set forth in Jesus' demonstrations, which s·
	239–21	and s· what we are winning.
	242–30	The finger-posts of divine Science s· the way
b	293–26	they s· the self-destruction of error
	294–21	s· the pleasures and pains of matter to be myths,
	313–30	To s· that the substance of himself was Spirit
	316– 9	to s· that Truth is made manifest by its effects
o	343– 4	"S· me thy faith without thy— Jas. 2 : 18.
	343– 5	I will s· thee my faith by my— Jas. 2 : 18.
	348–20	will s· itself in forms of sin, sickness, and
p	364–25	do they s· their regard for Truth, or Christ,
	374–14	s· our need of divine metaphysics.
	375–23	s· mortal mind that muscles have no power
	375–26	Consumptive patients always s· great hopefulness
	398– 7	These instances s· the concessions which
	404–23	s· him that sin confers no pleasure,
	417–29	S· them how mortal mind seems to induce
	418– 2	S· them that the conquest over sickness,
	425– 8	S· that it is not inherited ;
	438–21	while the facts in the case s· that this fur
t	443– 4	to s· them that under ordinary circumstances
	451–31	S· your student that mental malpractice
r	487–25	"S· me thy faith without thy— Jas. 2 : 18.
	487–26	I will s· thee my faith by my— Jas. 2 : 18.
	493– 9	Will you explain sickness and s· how
g	552–25	blending tints of leaf and flower s· the
	554–27	All these sayings were to s· that
ap	562–18	which s· the workings of the spiritual idea
	567–24	s· the dragon to be nothingness,
	574– 8	I will s· thee the bride,— Rev. 21 : 9.
gl	596–16	they s· the spiritual inspiration of Love

showed

s	138–11	He s· that diseases were cast out
	147–10	s· that Truth had lost none of its
ph	193– 6	He even s· me the probe,
f	206–16	as Jesus s· with the loaves and the fishes,
	236–17	the pattern s· to thee— Heb. 8 : 5.
b	292–19	In his resurrection and ascension, Jesus s·
	314–10	s· plainly that their material views were
	321–31	Jesus, who s· his students the power of Mind
gl	579–13	and s· the life-preserving power of

showing

pr	6–27	came teaching and s· men how to destroy sin,
	7– 4	s· the necessity for such forcible utterance,
a	30–23	s· the difference between the offspring of Soul
	34– 3	instead of s·, by casting out error
s	113–13	s· mathematically their exact relation
p	363–32	mere fact that she was s· her affection
	376–25	s· that it is impossible for matter to suffer,
	377–13	s· mortal mind to be the producer of
	382–27	s· me the nothingness of the so-called
	410–11	s· that Truth is the actual life of man ;
	421– 9	s· him that it was to facilitate recovery.
r	476–31	s· that man in God's image is unfallen
g	501– 8	s· the poverty of mortal existence,
ap	563– 6	s· its horns in the many inventions of evil.
gl	581–11	Science s· that the spiritual realities
	589–20	s· the immortality and supremacy of Truth ;

shown

s	137–25	Love hath s· thee the way of Life !
b	321–13	Matter was s· to be a belief only.
o	354–19	Inconsistency is s· by words without deeds,
g	535–14	the results of sin as s· in sickness and
	549– 6	s· by divine metaphysics to be a mistake,
ap	561–16	s· in the man Jesus,

shows

pref	viii–14	s· that Christian healing confers the
a	32–11	The cup s· forth his bitter experience,
	53–19	Science s· the cause of the shock
m	59–29	the frequency of divorce s· that the
sp	88–27	s· the possibilities derived from divine Mind,
	89– 2	s· that the beliefs of mortal mind are loosed,
	89–30	s· that the belief of life in matter was
	90–19	This s· the possibilities of thought.
	90–22	s· what mortal mentality and knowledge are.
s	111–17	s· what this inverted image is meant to
	114–25	s· the scientific relation of man to God,
	114–29	s· that what is termed matter is but the
	120–18	s· it to be impossible for aught but Mind to
	121–22	s· appearances often to be erroneous,
	123–11	s· conclusively how it is that matter seems
ph	182– 3	s· your position as a Christian Scientist.
	196–12	s· that here the word soul means a
f	203– 5	s· that matter can neither heal
	209–32	s· the superiority of faith by works
	211–17	s· the nature of all so-called material cause
	225–15	s· human power to be proportionate to its
	238–12	To fall away from Truth . . . s· that
	242–10	Christ in divine Science s· us this way.
c	262– 4	s· the paramount necessity of meeting them.
b	272–13	Jesus' parable of "the sower" s·— Mark 4 : 14.
	273–29	Science s· that material, conflicting

shows

b	275– 3	This s· that matter did not originate in God,
	275–21	s· clearly that all is Mind, and that Mind is
	289–18	s· that what appears to the senses to be death
	309–24	The Science of being s· it to be impossible
	315–27	The history of Jesus s· him to have been
p	383–19	This s· that the mind must be clean
	392–20	unless Science s· you otherwise.
	394–31	This s· that faith is not the healer in such cases.
	399–21	this deadness s· that so-called mortal life is
	416– 2	This process s· the pain to be in the mind,
	427–20	s· that we shall obtain the victory
	434–27	s· the alleged crime never to have been
r	467–26	s· material existence to be enigmatical.
	477–14	Divine Science s· it to be impossible
	488– 4	the cure s· that you understand this
	489–25	C. S. s· them to be false,
	490–29	Sleep s· material sense as either
	491– 4	uncovers material sense, and s· it to be a
	493– 1	C. S. speedily s· Truth to be triumphant.
g	504–12	This also s· that there is no place where
	533–12	The allegory s· that the snake-talker utters the
	540– 2	s· that Spirit creates neither a wicked nor a
	549– 2	for this discovery s· that the
ap	567–31	s· how the Lamb slays the wolf.
	573–10	This s· unmistakably that what the
	577–32	one word s·, though faintly, the light which C. S.
gl	598– 8	This s· how our Master had constantly

shrank

g	532–19	error s· abashed from the divine voice

shrieks

m	67– 5	s· through the tightened shrouds,

shrine

gl	595– 8	TEMPLE. . . . the s· of Love ;

shrinking

ph	166– 4	s· from its implied responsibility,

shrouds

m	67– 5	shrieks through the tightened s·,

shut

pr	14–32	when thou hast s· thy door, pray— Matt. 6 : 6.
	15–15	enter into the closet and s· the door.
a	38–31	the material senses s· out Truth
s	142–14	they at the same time s· the door on progress.
ph	182–23	and forthwith s· out the aid of Mind
p	392–30	s· out these unhealthy thoughts and fears.
k	499– *	open door, and no man can s· it.— Rev. 3 : 8.
g	543– 8	the material man is s· out from the
ap	575–19	"and the gates of it shall not be s·— Rev. 21 : 25.
gl	579– *	open door, and no man can s· it.— Rev. 3 : 8.

shuts

pr	15– 4	the door of which s· out sinful sense
sp	90–26	This conviction s· the door on death,
s	132–21	blind belief s· the door upon it,

shutteth

k	499– *	openeth, and no man s· ;— Rev. 3 : 7.
	499– *	s·, and no man openeth ;— Rev. 3 : 7.
gl	579– *	openeth, and no man s· ;— Rev. 3 : 7.
	579– *	s·, and no man openeth ;— Rev. 3 : 7.

shutting

s	108–28	thereby s· out the true sense of Spirit.

sick (noun)

affects the

pr	12–16	Prayer to a corporeal God affects the s· like a

and sinning

pr	7– 6	he cast out devils and healed the s· and sinning.
a	55–16	beneath its wings the s· and sinning.
s	117–19	by his power over the s· and sinning.
	132–22	condemns the cure of the s· and sinning
	141–13	In healing the s· and sinning, Jesus elaborated
b	271–16	by healing the s· and sinning.
	309–20	divine power which heals the s· and sinning,
	337–32	heals the s· and sinning as no other system can.

and the sinning

a	54–15	Truth, and Love heal the s· and the sinning,
sp	95–10	to discern the thought of the s· and the sinning
s	136– 5	and heal both the s· and the sinning.
	138–31	which healed the s· and the sinning.
r	473–14	healing the s· and the sinning
ap	562–19	by healing the s· and the sinning,

are healed

sp	78–29	the s· are healed, the sorrowing are comforted,

are terrified

p	366–25	The s· are terrified by their sick beliefs,

brings to the

ph	169–24	mortal mind, not matter, which brings to the s·

cure of the

s	132–22	and condemns the cure of the s· and sinning
b	285–27	and resort to matter . . . for the cure of the s·.

effects on the

o	342– 7	the sad effects on the s· of denying Truth.

evidenced by the

o	355–30	and evidenced by the s· who are cured

sick (noun)

explain to the
p 396–22 At the right time explain to the *s·* the power

healed the
pr 7– 6 when he cast out devils and healed the *s·*
a 49– 4 healed the *s·*, cast out evil,
m 67–21 our Lord and Master healed the *s·*,
sp 85–18 he discerned disease and healed the *s·*.
s 134–28 healed the *s·*, walked on the water.
138–31 theology of Jesus which healed the *s·*
147–24 Our Master healed the *s·*,
ph 170–20 Jesus healed the *s·* and cast out error,
185–22 healed the *s·*, not only without drugs, but
f 210–12 the Master healed the *s·*, gave sight to the
b 273–25 Jesus . . . healed the *s·*, and raised the dead
o 343–27 healed the *s·* and reformed the sinner
351–15 Christ, Truth, which healed the *s·*.
r 477– 4 this correct view of man healed the *s·*.
494–30 cast out devils (evils) and healed the *s·*.

healer of the
s 138– 8 Life, Truth, and . . . was the healer of the *s·*

healing the
a 33– 8 healing the *s·* and casting out error.
35–25 casting out error and healing the *s·*.
41–15 by casting out error and healing the *s·*,
43– 1 healing the *s·*, and raising the dead
46–12 again seen casting out evil and healing the *s·*.
sp 97–32 work of casting out error and healing the *s·*.
s 109– 8 is demonstrated by healing the *s·*
111–27 and its demonstration in healing the *s·*,
135–29 divine Love casting out error and healing the *s·*,
136–14 with casting out evils and healing the *s·* ?
141–13 In healing the *s·* and sinning, Jesus
145–32 The theology of C. S. includes healing the *s·*.
ph 182– 2 The act of healing the *s·* through divine Mind
f 210– 8 by his healing the *s·*, casting out evils,
232–18 by healing the *s·* and triumphing over death.
b 271–16 demonstrated by healing the *s·* and sinning.
316–28 prove God's divine power by healing the *s·*,
324–24 healing the *s·* and preaching Christianity
332–14 healing the *s·* and casting out evils,
o 347–17 preaching the gospel to the poor, healing the *s·*,
p 365– 5 would do much more towards healing the *s·*
366 19 no . . . can prevent us from healing the *s·*
369– 9 as demonstrated in healing the *s·*,
390–26 denying that necessity and healing the *s·*.
403–23 this is best adapted for healing the *s·*.
404 26 Healing the *s·* and reforming the sinner are
t 445–21 divine energy in healing the *s·*.
455– 5 unsuitable conditions for healing the *s·*.
r 473–14 healing the *s·* and the sinning
497–18 demonstrated . . . in healing the *s·*
ap 562–19 by healing the *s·* and the sinning,
gl 583– 9 casting out error and healing the *s·* ;
583–19 casting out devils, or error, and healing the *s·*.

healing to the
pref xii–25 and is joyful to bear . . . healing to the *s·*,

heals the
pr 1– 2 reforms the sinner and heals the *s·*
14–29 understanding casts out error and heals the *s·*,
16–23 and which instantaneously heals the *s·*.
a 25–15 how this divine Principle heals the *s·*,
33–24 It blesses its enemies, heals the *s·*,
sp 98– 6 Christianity which heals the *s·*
s 120–23 thus Science denies all disease, heals the *s·*,
135–13 when Truth heals the *s·*, it casts out evils,
135–15 casts out the evil called disease, it heals the *s·*.
139– 1 It is his theology . . . which heals the *s·*
143– 4 Christ casts out evils and heals the *s·*.
ph 180–28 way to this living Truth, which heals the *s·*,
f 206–14 prayer, governed by Science . . . heals the *s·*.
230– 8 which casts out error and heals the *s·*.
b 275–32 It casts out error and heals the *s·*.
276– 2 unfolds the power that heals the *s·*,
282– 2 Truth casts out evils and heals the *s·*.
309–20 thus losing the divine power which heals the *s·*
337–32 heals the *s·* and sinning as no other system can.
o 350–11 Truth casts out error and heals the *s·*.
354–10 heals the *s·* and spiritualizes humanity.
355–16 according to the commands of our Master, heals the *s·*.
p 430–16 in which the plea of C. S. heals the *s·*.
t 452–27 by which divine Mind heals the *s·*.
455– 2 heals the *s·* and the sinner.
r 472– 4 Truth casts out . . . error and heals the *s·*.
473–30 heals the *s·* and casts out error,
482–28 heals the *s·* on the basis of the one Mind
483–18 heals the *s·*, destroys error, and
ap 570–26 When God heals the *s·* or the sinning,

heal the
pr 12– 3 A mere request that God will heal the *s·*
a 28–14 enabled to heal the *s·* and to triumph over sin.
34–15 take up the cross, heal the *s·*, cast out evils,
37–11 "*Heal the s·!*"— *Matt.* 10 : 8.
41–32 cast out evils and heal the *s·*.
51–31 enabled Jesus to heal the *s·*, cast out evil,

sick (noun)

heal the
54–15 proof that Life, Truth, and Love heal the *s·*
an 104–22 by no means the mental qualities which heal the *s·*.
s 136–10 How did Jesus heal the *s·* ?
137– 2 students saw this power of Truth heal the *s·*,
138–21 to heal the *s·* as well as the sinning,
138–29 Heal the *s·* !— *Matt.* 10 : 8.
158– 3 priests, who besought the gods to heal the *s·*
ph 167– 1 Should we implore a corporeal God to heal the *s·*
179– 5 Science can heal the *s·*, who are absent
182–17 to those who heal the *s·* on the basis of Science.
182–23 Mortals entreat the divine Mind to heal the *s·*,
f 206–11 It can never heal the *s·*, for it is the
231–11 does heal the *s·* through the prayer of
243– 7 can heal the *s·* in every age
b 271– 7 instructed his disciples whereby to heal the *s·*
322– 1 taught them how to . . . heal the *s·*
o 342–12 students should cast out evils and heal the *s·*.
342–14 He bade the seventy disciples, . . . heal the *s·*
345– 6 cannot . . . work through drugs to heal the *s·*
345– 9 Christian sermons will heal the *s·*
345–18 One who understands C. S. can heal the *s·*
351– 5 When we lose faith . . . we cannot heal the *s·*.
354–14 nor offer any proofs that . . . can heal the *s·*.
365– 9 would heal the *s·*, and so enable them
p 397–23 To heal the *s·*, one must be familiar with
418–11 Then, . . . you will heal the *s·*.
418–25 by the spirit of . . . you will heal the *s·*.
t 446–27 spiritual light and might which heal the *s·*,
447 10 heal the *s·* when called upon for aid,
462– 6 cast out error, heal the *s·*.
r 482–14 Is it important . . . in order to heal the *s·* ?
494–32 out of themselves and others and heal the *s·*.
495– 1 God will heal the *s·* through man,

hope to the
s 152– 7 that it may give hope to the *s·* and heal them,

instruct the
p 420–10 Instruct the *s·* that they are not helpless

lay hands on the
a 38–11 they shall lay hands on the *s·*, — *Mark* 16 : 18.
b 328–25 They shall lay hands on the *s·*, — *Mark* 16 : 18.
o 359–27 they shall lay hands on the *s·*, — *Mark* 16 : 18.
p 302– * *they shall lay hands on the s·,* — *Mark* 16 : 18.

prayer for the
pr 12– 6 The beneficial effect of such prayer for the *s·*

recover
pr 12–29 If the *s·* recover because they pray
s 155– 3 When the *s·* recover by the use of drugs, it is
p 373–10 the *s·* recover more rapidly from disease than

recovery of the
pr 12–23 custom of praying for the recovery of the *s·*
f 218–17 Why pray for the recovery of the *s·*, if you
p 372–32 will be a hindrance to the recovery of the *s·*
419– 1 moral question may hinder the recovery of the *s·*.

save the
pr 12– 1 prayer of faith shall save the *s·*," — *Jas.* 5 : 15.

show the
sp 81– 3 as there is to show the *s·* that matter

treat the
s 151– 2 they sometimes treat the *s·* as if there was

willing the
s 144–16 Willing the *s·* to recover is not the

---

s 138 23 the *s·* are more willing to part with pain than
143– 8 *s·* are more deplorably lost than the sinning, if
143– 9 if the *s·* cannot rely on God for help
158–21 with intoxicating prescriptions for the *s·*,
ph 169–25 But the *s·* are never really healed except by
181–26 in order to satisfy the *s·* that you are
185–27 may seem for a time to benefit the *s·*,
f 226–22 I saw before me the *s·*, wearing out years of
226–25 The lame, the deaf, the dumb, the blind, the *s·*,
230–23 According to Holy Writ, the *s·* are never really
231– 8 If God heals not the *s·*, they are not healed,
233–28 tests . . . of the effects of truth upon the *s·*.
235–19 Physicians, whom the *s·* employ in their
b 323–19 When the *s·* or the sinning awake to realize their
o 343–10 The *s·*, the halt, and the blind look up to C. S.
344–14 misrepresentations, which harm the *s·* ;
358–25 effect Christian Scientists may have on the *s·*,
358–26 rousing within the *s·* a belief
p 365– 2 the thorns they plant in the pillow of the *s·*
366–30 If we would open their prison doors for the *s·*,
370–28 fails at length to inspire the credulity of the *s·*,
374– 7 the *s·* say : "How can my mind cause a disease
394–23 Will you tell the *s·* that their condition is
394–30 the *s·* usually have little faith in it till they
394–32 The *s·* unconsciously argue for suffering,
395–17 Prayers, in which . . . do not benefit the *s·*.
403– 1 So the *s·* through their beliefs have induced
414–18 lest you array the *s·* against their own interests
416–24 The *s·* know nothing of the mental process

sick (noun)

p	417– 6	Never tell the s· that they have more courage than
	417– 8	If you make the s· realize this great truism,
	420–24	Tell the s· that they can meet disease fearlessly,
	424–26	it is well to be alone with God and the s· when
	431– 3	the prisoner watched with the s· every night
t	443–22	If the s· find these . . . unsatisfactory,
	447–27	The s· are not healed merely by declaring
	458– 6	simultaneously at work on the s·.
	463–28	The s· are not healed by inanimate matter
r	495– 9	when he spoke of the s·,

sick (adj.)

pr	6–24	Of a s· woman he said that Satan had bound
sp	86– 7	he was answered by the faith of a s· woman.
s	114– 2	calls s· and sinful humanity mortal mind,
	120–13	And is he well if the senses say he is s·?
	154–17	is frightened and says, "My child will be s·."
	154–26	says to her child : "You look s·,"
	161–25	telling the patient that he is s·,
	163– 2	afterward letting her loose upon s· people."
	163– 5	declared himself "s· of learned quackery."
ph	168–10	When s· (according to belief) you rush after
	168–16	man-made systems insist that man becomes s·
	174–25	if an individual is s·, why treat the body alone
	179–25	so long as you read medical works you will be s·.
	199–15	develop their own bodies or make them s·,
f	203– 6	matter can neither heal nor make s·,
	206–31	God does not cause man to sin, to be s·, or to
	210–26	cannot say, "I suffer, I die, I am s·,
	218–15	believing that the body can be s·
	219–12	"s·, and the whole heart faint ;"— Isa. 1 : 5.
	229–23	If God causes man to be s·, sickness must be
	229–27	If . . . produces sickness, it is right to be s·
	253–13	no cause (outside of . . . able to make you s·
c	259–10	thoughts which presented man as fallen, s·,
	260–20, 21	A s· body is evolved from s· thoughts.
b	270–26	They think sickly thoughts, and so become s·.
	270–30	human mind alone suffers, is s·,
	289–13	Truth and Truth's idea, never make men s·,
	292–11	s·, and dying mortal is not the likeness of
	297– 6	Human belief says to mortals, "You are s· !"
o	352–13	and s· in consequence of the fear:
p	366–23	The sick are terrified by their s· beliefs,
	371–12	s· humanity sees danger in every direction,
	372– 1	Matter cannot be s·, and Mind is immortal.
	376–26	impossible for matter . . . to be thirsty or s·.
	381– 5	to suffer the illusion that you are s·
	391–19	When the body is supposed to say, "I am s·,"
	391–22	If you say, "I am s·," you plead guilty.
	393–29	Man is never s·, for Mind is not s·
	406–25	no more fear that we shall be s· and
	408– 5	nor discovered . . . by many who are s·.
	409–10	cannot dictate terms . . . nor say, "I am s·."
	417– 3	Give s· people credit for sometimes knowing
	417–12	Spirit is God, and therefore cannot be s· ;
	417–13	what is termed matter cannot be s· ;
	430–30	prisoner, or patient, watched with a s· friend.
	431– 4	When the s· mortal was thirsty,
	441–16	refuses to recognize Man as s· or dying,
	442–13	Mortal Man, no longer s· and in prison,
t	453–26	you must not tell the patient that he is s·
	461–16	If you believe that you are s·, should you say,
	461–17	should you say, "I am s· "? No,
	461–22	to admit that you are s·, renders your case
ap	570–29	delusion of mortal mind, when it makes them s·
		(see also man)

sick-bed

p	433–27	The prisoner is then remanded to his cell (s·),

sick-chamber

ph	178– 7	infinitesimal minority of opinions in the s·.
g	516–18	glances into the prison-cell, glides into the s·,

sickly

ph	175–20	selfishness, coddling, and s· after-dinner talk.
b	270–25	They think s· thoughts, and so become sick.
o	346– 3	it is not sinful and s· mortal man who
g	554–30	belief that the lower animals are less s· than

sickness

abate
ph	196–24	will help to abate s· and to destroy it.

and care
ph	188–20	s· and care, are traced upon mortals by

and death
f	206–27	Instead of God sending s· and death,
	231–26	To hold yourself superior to s· and death
	251–19	a belief in the necessity of s· and death,
c	264–22	s· and death were overcome by Jesus.
p	386–22	Thus it is with all sorrow, s·, and death.
	430– 9	Belief in s· and death, as certainly as
g	535–15	the results of sin as shown in s· and death.

and disease
ph	179–23	are the promoters of s· and disease.

and error
r	495– 8	Then classify s· and error as our Master did,

sickness

and health
sp	74–22	infancy and manhood, s· and health,
f	211– 4	s· and health, good and evil, life and death ;
	229–10	s· and health, holiness and unholiness,
	246– 3	joy and sorrow, s· and health,

and mortality
b	335–29	Sin, s·, and mortality are the suppositional

and sin
s	142– 1	it will eradicate s· and sin in less time than
	146–25	influence of Truth in healing s· and sin.
ph	171–15	healing s· and sin and destroying the
f	210–17	Jesus healed s· and sin by one and the same
	230– 4	But if s· and sin are illusions,
o	347–28	will behold the nothingness of s· and sin,
p	368–13	freedom from the bondage of s· and sin
	380– 4	S· and sin fall by their own weight.
	391– 4	mortal thought and its beliefs in s· and sin.
	426–32	matter, death, disease, s·, and sin
r	473–11	the ideal Truth, that comes to heal s· and sin

associates
p	377–32	associates s· with certain circumstances

banish
p	381–27	Let us banish s· as an outlaw, and abide by

belief in
		(see belief)

belief of
f	229–30	which causes the belief of s·.

calm in
p	393–32	It is well to be calm in s· ;

cast out
s	138–22	easier for Christianity to cast out s· than sin,

caused the
an	104–25	and a belief originally caused the s·,

conquest over
p	418– 2	the conquest over s·, as well as over sin,

disease, and death
c	260–21	S·, disease, and death proceed from fear.

efficient in
f	233–31	Why should truth not be efficient in s·,

every sort of
p	408– 1	Every sort of s· is error,

explain
r	493– 9	explain s· and show how it is to be healed?

fear of
p	412– 4	to advance and destroy the human fear of s·.

foundation of all
p	411–20	foundation of all s· is fear, ignorance, or sin.

fountain of
p	391–32	Fear is the fountain of s·,

has been combated
pref	viii–16	S· has been combated for centuries by doctors

has not checked
ph	165–13	Obedience to . . . has not checked s·.

healing
s	146–25	influence of Truth in healing s·
ph	171–15	by healing s· and sin
f	230–22	put that law under his feet by healing s·?
	241–20	healing s· and destroying sin.
b	316–11	healing s· and destroying sin.
r	473–22	healing s·, sin, and death,

heals
pr	16– 4	Such prayer heals s·, and must destroy sin
an	104–23	If he heals s· through a belief,
f	236–10	Mind heals s· as well as sin
b	315–24	heals s·, and overcomes death.
t	446– 6	perusal of the author's publications heals s·.

heals also
s	135–11	same power which heals sin heals also s·.

health and in
t	462–31	government of the body both in health and in s·.

he healed
ph	168–21	He healed s· in defiance of what is called

illusion of
b	297– 8	illusion of s·, to be instructed out of itself
r	495–14	When the illusion of s· or sin tempts you,

images of
p	396–26	efface the images of s· from

induces
p	374–21	Such a state of mind induces s·.

is a belief
r	493–18	S· is a belief, which must be annihilated

is a dream
p	417–20	To the C. S. healer, s· is a dream

is formed
p	396–31	understand that s· is formed by the human

is not real
p	394– 1	to understand that s· is not real

less
pref	viii–19	Is there less s· because of these practitioners?
s	163–12	there would be less s· and less mortality."

no trials for
p	441–33	We have no trials for s· before the tribunal of

or of sin
o	353– 9	either in the form of s· or of sin?

produces
f	229–26	If the transgression of God's law produces s·,

sickness

reports of
f 218–10   The reports of s· may form a coalition with

save from
s 149– 1   Truth could save from s· as well as from sin.

seeming
p 368–27   are the source of all seeming s·.

sensation of
f 211–13   sensation of s· and the impulse to sin

sin and
  (see sin)

sin, and death
a 19–13   what would destroy s·, sin, and death,
  26–26   C. S. destroys s·, sin, and death.
s 142– 5   by its power over s·, sin, and death;
ph 184– 3   makes no laws to regulate s·, sin, and death,
  196–15   S·, sin, and death are not concomitants of
f 227–22   Escape from the bondage of s·, sin, and death !''
  229–16   to bind mortals to s·, sin, and death.
  243–30   S·, sin, and death are not the fruits of Life.
c 257– 8   which ultimates in s·, sin, and death ;
b 290–13   error and its effects, — s·, sin, and death.
  297–32   S·, sin, and death are the vague
  337–29   Subject s·, sin, and death to the rule of
o 356–10   controlled s·, sin, and death on the basis of
  357–10   the belief that God makes s·, sin, and death,
p 384–30   S·, sin, and death must at length quail before
  393– 9   and can conquer s·, sin, and death.
  418–14   This mortal dream of s·, sin, and death
r 472– 9   S·, sin, and death, being inharmonious,
  473–22   healing s·, sin, and death,
  481–20   hypotheses first assume . . . s·, sin, and death,
  485– 7   betrays mortals into s·, sin, and death.

sin, . . . and death
  (see sin)

sin, nor death
p 381–17   In infinite Life . . . there is no s·, sin, nor death,

sin, . . . nor death
ap 567– 8   there is no error, no sin, s·, nor death.

sin or
f 253–21   right endeavors against sin or s·,
p 390–24   either of sin or s·,
  426–18   not saved from sin or s· by death,
t 447–16   When sin or s· . . . seems true

sin, or death
t 463–22   manifested in forms of s·, sin, or death

sin, . . . or death
r 472–27   the only reality of sin, s·, or death is the
gl 585–20   before it accepts sin, s·, or death ;

sources of
ph 180– 1   are both prolific sources of s·.

struggling with
p 394–13   To those struggling with s·, such admissions are

subject of
ph 169–13   by attracting the mind to the subject of s·,

terms with
p 391–27   Therefore make your own terms with s·,

thoughts about
f 237–18   theories or thoughts about s·.

treat
t 453–24   You should treat s· mentally just as you

victor over
s 137– 6   the victor over s·, sin, disease, death,

worse than
p 408– 3   sin is worse than s·,

a 49–24   to triumph over sin, s·, death, and the grave.
s 108–25   opposite of Truth, — called error, sin, s·, disease,
  115–23   revenge, sin, s·, disease, death.
  131– 2   S· should not seem so real as
  148–32   admits God to be the healer of sin but not of s·,
ph 166–17   To ignore God as of little use in s· is a mistake.
  166–21   He can do all things for us in s· as in health.
  182–30   To admit that s· is a condition over which God
  188–22   S· is a growth of error, springing from
f 206–19   Does God send s·,
  207–23   Sin, s·, disease, and death belong not to the
  208–31   delineate upon it thoughts of health, not of s·.
  216–23   and s· to be the rule of
  224–23   meeting the needs of mortals in s· and in health,
  229–23   If God causes man to be sick, s· must be good,
  230– 1   If s· is real, it belongs to immortality ;
  230–17   God, good, can no more produce s· than
  230–20   Does a law of God produce s·,
  239–28   it is discordant and ends in sin, s·, death.
  251–13   S·, as well as sin, is an error
b 297– 7   manifests itself on the body as s·.
  339–23   s· to health, sin to holiness,
o 349–12   God is not the author of s·.
  359–24   ''God is able to raise you up from s· ;''
p 378–24   S· is not a God-given, nor a
  386– 3   not to be accepted in the case of s·,
  389– 7   the less we are predisposed to s·.
  390–20   Suffer no claim of sin or of s· to grow
  390–23   is no more the author of s· than He is of sin.

sickness

p 408– 1   s· is loss of harmony.
  408– 3   s· is not . . . discovered to be error
  412–24   s· is a temporal dream.
  418–12   s· is no more the reality of being than is sin.
  440–23   compel them to enact wicked laws of s·
  442–20   Christ changes a belief of sin or of s· into a
t 447–28   by declaring there is no s·,
  450–22   S· to him is no less a temptation than is sin,
  460–14   S· is neither imaginary nor unreal, — that is,
  460–15   S· is more than fancy ;
r 482–26   S· is part of the error which Truth casts out.
  495– 6   If s· is true or the idea of Truth,
  495– 7   If . . . you cannot destroy s·,
ap 569–16   and fail to strangle . . . sin as well as of s· !
gl 588– 2   hatred ; revenge ; sin ; s· ; death ;
  592– 9   Mortal Mind. . . . sin ; s· ; death.
  595– 5   Tares. Mortality ; error ; sin ; s· ;

sicknesses

ph 177– 3   relinquish all its errors, s·, and sins.

sick-room

p 390–16   and then you will not be confined to a s·

side

Adam's
g 533–18   the rib taken from Adam's s·

by her
ph 184–29   I sat silently by her s· a few moments.

by our
sp 82–14   with the dreamer by our s·

diviner
g 548–23   gained the diviner s· in C. S.,

of error
f 205–29   tips the beam . . . towards the s· of error,

of God
f 201–11   superabundance of being is on the s· of God,

of health
ph 168–10   when it ought to be enlisted on the s· of health.

of immutable right
t 446–20   victory rests on the s· of immutable right.

of invincible truth
t 453– 7   victory rests on the s· of invincible truth.

of matter
ph 168– 6   Whatever influence you cast on the s· of matter,
  181–31   this faith will incline you to the s· of matter

of Personal Sense
p 434–25   has been on the s· of Personal Sense,

one
sp 96–13   On one s· there will be discord and dismay ;
f 238–25   listening only to one s· of the case.

on which
f 216–10   On which s· are we fighting?

other
sp 96–14   on the other s· there will be Science and peace.

right
g 35– 6   and cast their net on the right s·.
b 271–27   or to cast them on the right s· for Truth,

side by
b 300–19   (to mortal sight) they grow side by s· until the

this
a 36–23   this s· of the grave

wounded
a 44–16   bind up the wounded s· and lacerated feet,

wrong
ph 166– 6   healing effort is made on the wrong s·,
p 306–20   weight of opinions on the wrong s·,
  397– 6   mental influence on the wrong s·,

s 145–11   victory will be on the patient's s· only as
  155–20   percentage of power on the s· of this Science
g 536–26   the true idea is gained from the immortal s·.

sides

m 59– 3   its enduring obligations on both s·.
b 307–11   It says : . . . Truth shall change s·
t 457–16   both s· were beautiful according to their
ap 574–23   the four equal s· of which were heaven-bestowed
  575–18   The four s· of our city are
  575–21   This city is wholly spiritual, as its four s·
  575–23   mount Zion, on the s· of the north, — Psal. 48 : 2.

siege

f 216– 9   Spirituality lays open s· to materialism.

sieve

sp 72–19   Error is not a convenient s· through which

sift

b 269– 6   Jesus' demonstrations s· the chaff from the

sifted

ph 171–19   believes that Spirit is s· through matter,

sigh

m 57–29   until it ceases to s· over the world
g 501–16   that Love for whose rest the weary ones s·

sight

and teeth
f 247– 4　I have seen age regain . . . *s·* and teeth.

first
sp 87–14　when really it is first *s·* instead of second,

good in Thy
s 131–22　for so it seemed good in Thy *s·*."— *Luke* 10 : 21.

hearing and
r 489–27　no organic construction can give it hearing
　　　　　　and *s·*

lose
f 207–13　Without this lesson, we lose *s·* of the
b 315–17　The likeness of God we lose *s·* of through sin,
　　316– 5　and lose *s·* of mortal selfhood
　　337– 4　mortals do lose *s·* of spiritual individuality.

lost
a 49–10　Had they so soon lost *s·* of his mighty works,
s 110–27　But this power was lost *s·* of,
b 314–19　This materialism lost *s·* of the true Jesus ;

material
a 35–18　when he rose out of material *s·*.

mortal
f 214–26　How transient a sense is mortal *s·*,
b 300–19　though (to mortal *s·*) they grow side by side

never loses
f 248– 3　Love never loses *s·* of loveliness.

or sense
f 214–28　But the real *s·* or sense is not lost.

out of
ph 174–24　though out of *s·*.
o 360–11　replies : . . . and keep Soul well out of *s·*.
gl 582–22　physical sense put out of *s·* and hearing ;

pass from our
p 386–31　So, when our friends pass from our *s·*

physical
sp 87–32　or altogether gone from physical *s·*

pitiful
b 327– 8　What a pitiful *s·* is malice,

pleasant to the
g 525–31　every tree that is pleasant to the *s·*,— *Gen.* 2 : 9.

receive their
s 132– 6　the blind receive their *s·*— *Matt.* 11 : 5.

recovering of
pref xi–20　And recovering of *s·* to the blind,— *Luke* 4 : 18.

restores
r 486–16　If death restores *s·*, sound, and strength

return of
f 247– 5　A woman of eighty-five, . . . had a return of *s·*.

second
sp 87–13　The Scotch call such vision "second *s·*,"

sink from
p 415–30　Indeed, the whole frame will sink from *s·*

sound or
sp 84–21　not dependent upon the ear and eye for sound
　　　　　　or *s·*

to the blind
ph 183–28　the law which gives *s·* to the blind,
f 210–21　healed the sick, gave *s·* to the blind,
r 487–11　apprehension of this gave *s·* to the blind

ph 194–23　where neither *s·* nor sound could reach him,
r 486–23　*S·*, hearing, all the spiritual senses of man,
g 526–10　theories of material hearing, *s·*, touch, taste,

sightless
ph 193– 9　Mr. Clark lay with his eyes fixed and *s·*.

sign
pref xi–16　They are the *s·* of Immanuel,
a 49–13　with one *s·* of fidelity?
sp 98– 7　and no other *s·* shall be given.
f 224–17　Of old the cross was truth's central *s·*,
　　233–18　discern the face of the sky,— the *s·* material,
　　233–19　much more should ye discern the *s·* mental,
b 321–28　to the voice of the first *s·*,— *Exod.* 4 : 8.
　　321–29　the voice of the latter *s·*."— *Exod.* 4 : 8.
p 364–15　a special *s·* of Oriental courtesy.

signal
c 261–17　a *s·* which made him as oblivious of
g 553–22　the *s·* for the appearance of its method

signet
r 472– 6　God has set his *s·* upon Science,
　　494–28　eternal and real evidence, bearing Truth's *s·*,
gl 593–23　SEAL. The *s·* of error revealed by Truth.

significance
s 117– 8　C. S. attaches no physical nature and *s·* to the
　　118–13　In their spiritual *s·*, Science, Theology,
　　131– 9　and the *s·* of the Scripture,
　　134– 7　the word *martyr* was narrowed in its *s·*
r 481–16　This is the *s·* of the Scripture concerning this
　　488– 9　they have more the *s·* of faith,
gl 598– 9　to employ words of material *s·*

significant
g 538–13　*s·* of eternal reality or being.
　　538–16　The testimony of the serpent is *s·* of the
ap 571–25　In *s·* figures he depicts the thoughts

signification
a 32–24　in its spiritual *s·*, it was natural and beautiful.
ph 179– 1　the understanding of C. S. in its proper *s·*
f 241–14　Take away the spiritual *s·* of Scripture, and
p 391–17　Justice is the moral *s·* of law.
r 469–25　We lose the high *s·* of omnipotence, when
　　482– 9　and you will have the scientific *s·*.
g 545–27　Scripture, which is so glorious in its spiritual *s·*
gl 590–19　Its higher *s·* is Supreme Ruler.

significations
g 502–15　crude forms . . . take on higher symbols and *s·*,

signifies
s 118– 2　spiritual leaven *s·* the Science of Christ
f 229– 8　Mind *s·* God,— infinity,
　　241–28　*s·* that the pure in heart see God
b 271–11　the word rendered *disciple s·* student ;
　　333–14　but Christ Jesus better *s·* the Godlike.
　　340–18　it *s·* that man shall have no other
r 466–20　Soul or Spirit *s·* Deity and nothing else.

signify
m 64–17　Marriage should *s·* a union of hearts.
g 502–25　word *beginning* is employed to *s· the only*,

signifying
b 338–13　*s·* the *red color of the ground, dust,*
r 466– 2　is adopted from the Latin adjective *s· all.*
g 517– 5　two Greek words, *s· man* and *form,*

signs

and for seasons
g 509–11　let them be for *s·*, and for seasons,— *Gen.* 1 : 14.

and wonders
s 139– 8　Christian era was ushered in with *s·* and won-
　　　　　　ders.
　　150–13　Now, as then, *s·* and wonders are wrought

characteristic
s 152–32　the general symptoms, the characteristic *s·*,

following
pr 10–11　and "with *s·* following."— *Mark* 16 : 20.
s 110–29　with "*s·* following."— *Mark* 16 : 20.
　　117–12　attained through "*s·* following."— *Mark* 16 : 20.

mental
ph 169– 5　I have seen the mental *s·*, assuring me

of Christ's coming
o 347–14　would behold the *s·* of Christ's coming.

of these times
sp 98– 5　in the mental horizon the *s·* of these times,

of the times
sp 85–22　not discern the *s·* of the times?"— *Matt.* 16 : 3
g 510– 1　not discern the *s·* of the times?"— *Matt.* 16 : 3.

questioned the
s 133– 1　questioned the *s·* of the Messianic appearing,

such
p 413–26　constantly directing the mind to such *s·*,

these
a 38–10　"These *s·* shall follow them— *Mark* 16 : 17.
　　38–13　he did not say, "These *s·* shall follow *you*,"
　　52–28　"These *s·* shall follow them— *Mark* 16 : 17.
s 150–14　but these *s·* are only to demonstrate its
b 328–22　"These *s·* shall follow them— *Mark* 16 : 17.
o 359–26　these *s·* shall follow them— *Mark* 16 : 17.
p 362– *　these *s· shall follow them*— *Mark* 16 : 17.

unmistakable
ph 188–21　traced upon mortals by unmistakable *s·*,

unquestionable
f 232–30　unquestionable *s·* of the burial of error

silence
pr 15–16　close the lips and *s·* the material senses.
a 29–21　put to *s·* material law
m 67–26　does not put to *s·* the labor of centuries.
sp 81–20　*s·* the tones of music, give to the worms the
ph 195– 5　Outside of dismal darkness and cold *s·*
b 318–12　We must *s·* this lie of material sense
p 417–16　When you *s·* the witness against your plea,
　　441– 7　but be enjoined to keep perpetual *s·*,
r 495–23　and *s·* discord with harmony.

silenced
sp 97–25　until its inarticulate sound is forever *s·*
s 146–18　and his Science, the curative agent of God, is *s·*,

silences
s 124–13　finite sense . . . which immortal Spirit *s·*
b 298– 5　so false belief *s·* for a while the voice of
　　328– 2　*s·* the material or corporeal.
t 445–19　C. S. *s·* human will,

silent
pr 4–28　*s·* prayer, watchfulness, and devout obedience
　　15–11　Lips must be mute and materialism *s·*,
a 33– 3　His followers, sorrowful and *s·*,
　　36–14　in *s·* woe beneath the shadow of his cross.
　　48–20　great demonstrator of Truth and Love was *s·*
sp 87–29　Memory may reproduce voices long ago *s·*.
　　89–21　God, is heard when the senses are *s·*.
p 367–25　through *s·* utterances and divine anointing
　　431– 1　testifies . . . I was told that I must remain *s·*
　　438–13　Personal Sense, by this time *s·*,

silently
 pr 13–17 If we cherish the desire honestly and *s·*
 a 35–13 *s·* to commune with the divine Principle, Love.
 ph 184–29 I sat *s·* by her side a few moments.
 p 376–22 by both *s·* and audibly arguing
  411– 4 If the student *s·* called the disease by name,
  411–28 *S·* reassure them as to their exemption
  412– 4 Mentally and *s·* plead the case
  412–29 *s·* or audibly on the aforesaid basis of C. S.
 g 516–14 The grass beneath our feet *s·* exclaims,

silly
 m 68–22 to hatch their *s·* innuendoes and lies,
 an 103–27 flimsy and gaudy pretensions, like *s·* moths,

silver
 a 47–12 The traitor's price was thirty pieces of *s·*

silvern
 t 457–18 no good aspect, either *s·* or golden.

similar
 s 122–22 Experience is full of instances of *s·* illusions,
 p 371– 5 *s·* to that produced on children by telling

similarly
 b 282–15 *S·*, matter has no place in Spirit,
 p 422–23 cases of bone-disease, both *s·* produced

similitude
 g 525–11 in the Hebrew, *image*, *s·* ;

similitudes
 s 117–15 taught spirituality by *s·* and parables.

Simon (the disciple)
 g 137–16 *S·* replied for his brethren,
 p 362– 4 though he was quite unlike *S·* the disciple.

Simon Bar-jona
 s 137–22 "Blessed art thou, *S· B·* :— *Matt.* 16 : 17.
  137–27 his common names, *S· B·*, or son of Jona ;

Simon (the Pharisee)
 p 362– 3 guest of a certain Pharisee, by name *S·*,
  363–19 the Master's question to *S·* the Pharisee ;
  363–19 *S·* replied, "He to whom he forgave— *Luke* 7 : 43.
  364–18 as *S·* sought the Saviour,
  364–20 Jesus told *S·* that such seekers as he
  364–22 If Christian Scientists are like *S·*,

simple
 sp 75– 1 This *s·* truth lays bare the mistaken assumption
 s 121–23 the *s·* rule that the greater controls the lesser.
  147–16 a *s· perusal* of this book.
 ph 197–21 We are told that the *s·* food our forefathers ate
 f 236–26 and learn more readily to love the *s·* verities
 b 321–24 restored his hand . . . by the same *s·* process.
 o 342– 4 "making wise the *s·*."— *Psal.* 19 : 7.
 p 411–30 Watch the result of this *s·* rule of C. S.,
  418–21 this *s·* rule of Truth, which governs all reality.
  429– 5 with the more *s·* demonstrations of control,
 t 459–25 C. S. seems abstract, but the process is *s·*
 r 474–11 *marvel* is the *s·* meaning of the Greek word
 g 547– 1 A *s·* statement of C. S., if demonstrated by
  549–10 look upon the *s·* ovum as the germ,
 ap 570–14 *s·* seekers for Truth,
  572– 7 the most *s·* and profound counsel of the

simplest
 p 413– 6 to meet the *s·* needs of the babe
 g 551–19 composed of the *s·* material elements,

simply
 pr 9 13 does not grant them *s·* on the ground of
  4–17 *S·* asking that we may love God
  9–14 we shall never meet this great duty *s·* by
 a 36– 3 *s·* through translation into another sphere.
 sp 71– 3 *s·* a belief, an illusion of material sense.
 s 152–15 *s·* by introducing a thermometer into the
  153–17 The boil *s·* manifests, through inflammation
 ph 184– 1 are *s·* laws of mortal belief.
 b 274–18 *s·* the manifested beliefs of mortal mind,
  312– 8 The senses regard a corpse, . . . *s·* as matter.
 p 375–30 *s·* because it is a stage of fear so excessive
  390– 5 *s·* because, . . . there is seeming discord.
  398–12 he *s·* said, "Damsel, I say unto— *Mark* 5 : 41.
 t 452–24 *s·* by repeating the author's words,
 g 508–17 *Gender* means *s· kind* or *sort*,
  554–28 and is *s·* a falsity and illusion.

simulate
 sp 71–17 which *s·* mind, life, and intelligence.
 b 281–25 out of which error would *s·* creation

simulated
 p 376–15 and *s·* a corporeal sense of life.

simulates
 sp 97– 5 In reality, the more closely error *s·* truth
 b 287– 4 error, which *s·* the creations of Truth,
 g 528–20 error now *s·* the work of Truth,

simulating
 g 514– 1 could not by *s·* deific power invert the

simultaneous
 t 449–25 only to separate through *s·* repulsion.

simultaneously
 t 458– 6 *s·* at work on the sick.

sin (*see also* **sin's**)
 above
  c 266–30 He is above *s·* or frailty.
 all
  a 30–20 error and all *s·*, sickness, and death,
  ph 171–28 the procuring cause of all *s·* and
  b 311– 9 All *s·* is of the flesh.
   323–26 takes away all *s·* and the delusion that there are
   339– 6 and involve the final destruction of all *s·*?
  p 407–29 All *s·* is insanity in different degrees.
  ap 568–26 the mighty conquest over all *s·*?
   569–27 periods of torture it may take to remove all *s·*,
 and death
  pr 16– 5 heals sickness, and must destroy *s·* and death.
  a 19–10 the law of matter, *s·*, and death
   27–18 Life as never mingling with *s·* and death.
  f 242–19 and is the law of *s·* and death.
   243– 8 and triumph over *s·* and death.
   244–12 free from the law of *s·* and death."— *Rom.* 8 : 2.
   253–28 belief in *s·* and death is destroyed by the
  b 276–18 ceases to be any opportunity for *s·* and death.
   296–23 The knowledge . . . leads to *s·* and death.
   310–15 reveals Soul as God, untouched by *s·* and death,
   318–14 brought the belief of *s·* and death
   319–18 *s·*, and death will disappear when it
  p 422–20 Thus C. S., . . . destroys *s·* and death.
   428–26 we must master *s·* and death.
  r 497–19 and overcoming *s·* and death.
  g 525–27 the Scriptural record of *s·* and death favors the
   552–23 From . . . flows no remedy for sorrow, *s·*, and death,
 and disease
  pref xi–11 before which *s·* and disease lose their reality
  a 25–22 demonstrating his control over *s·* and disease,
  m 69– 5 only as they lose the sense of *s·* and disease.
  ph 171–28 the procuring cause of all *s·* and disease.
  f 234–25 *S·* and disease must be thought before
  o 355 4 scientific methods of dealing with *s·* and disease
   355– 9 As for *s·* and disease, C. S. says,
  p 366–28 calm in the presence of both *s·* and disease,
   400– 8 of his goods,— namely, of *s·* and disease.
 and error
  b 290–23 *s·* and error which possess us at the instant of
 and evil
  b 315– 8 He knew . . . that matter, *s·*, and evil were not
 and mortality
  an 103– 7 escape from *s·* and mortality,
  c 265– 8 in order that *s·* and mortality may be put off.
  b 281–21 *s·* and mortality have neither Principle nor
   281–23 *s·* and mortality are without actual origin
   311 28 Matter, *s·*, and mortality lose all supposed
 and pardon
  f 251–19 sickness and death, *s·* and pardon,
 and sense
  g 530–22 saying, . . . that *s·* and sense are more pleasant
  gl 583 7 who, having wrestled with error, *s·*, and sense,
 and sensuality
  sp 82–31 In a world of *s·* and sensuality
 and sickness
  f 218–12 What renders both *s·* and sickness difficult of
   233–20 compass the destruction of *s·* and sickness
   234–20 and empty it of *s·* and sickness,
   234–20 or *s·* and sickness will never cease.
   239– 1 by which *s·* and sickness are destroyed.
  b 314–30 to save them from *s·* and sickness,
  o 347–29 *s·* and sickness will disappear from
  p 388–24 *s·* and sickness are not qualities of Soul,
   395–10 The same Principle cures both *s·* and sickness.
   401–18 brings *s·* and sickness to the surface,
   406– 3 *S·* and sickness . . . healed by the same Principle.
   406–13 *S·* and sickness will abate and seem less real
  t 458–30 radically saved from *s·* and sickness.
   461–23 Both *s·* and sickness are error,
 and sorrow
  f 215–19 So *s·* and sorrow, disease and death, are the
 and suffering
  a 23–10 *s·* and suffering will fall at the feet of
  f 210–29 To mortal sense, *s·* and suffering are real,
   229– 6 but if *s·* and suffering are realities of being,
  p 435– 7 which alone is capable of *s·* and suffering.
 and the hope
  a 22– 3 Vibrating like a pendulum between *s·* and the hope of
 and the sinner
  p 393–31 the *s·* and the sinner, the disease and its cause.
 any one
  b 339– 5 Does not God's pardon, destroying any one *s·*,
 atonement for
  a 19–19 to understand Jesus' atonement for *s·*

sin

audible
  ap 559– 8   exercised upon visible error and audible *s*.
aught but
  p 441– 4   which undertakes to punish aught but *s*,
belief called
  a 37– 1   which destroys the belief called *s*
belief in
  (*see* **belief**)
belief of
  (*see* **belief**)
brought death
  p 426–28   *S* brought death, and death will disappear with
calamities, and
  f 223–28   calamities, and *s* will much more abound
ceases
  p 391–16   will cease in proportion as the *s* ceases.
chronic
  p 373– 9   to lift a student out of a chronic *s*.
claim of
  t 447–24   To put down the claim of *s*, you must detect it,
  461–27   first see the claim of *s*, and then destroy it.
cleanse from
  a 25– 7   no more efficacious to cleanse from *s* when
conceit of
  ap 571–27   Thus he rebukes the conceit of *s*,
conceived in
  r 476–16   "conceived in *s* and brought forth in iniquity."
  g 540–29   mortal and material man, conceived in *s*
conditions of
  g 556–10   Mortal belief infolds the conditions of *s*.
confers no pleasure
  p 404–23   show him that *s* confers no pleasure,
conquered
  ap 564–16   met and conquered *s* in every form.
continues in
  pr 5–27   He grows worse who continues in *s* because he
culminating
  gl 597–11   martyrdom of Jesus was the culminating *s* of
cure of
  s 149– 4   in the cure of disease as in the cure of *s*.
debt of
  a 23– 4   is insufficient to pay the debt of *s*.
deny
  pr 15–18   we must deny *s* and plead God's allness.
destroying
  pr 6–12   To cause suffering, . . . is the means of destroy-
      ing *s*.
  a 40–12   God's method of destroying *s*.
  f 241–21   healing sickness and destroying *s*.
  b 316–11   healing sickness and destroying *s*.
  332–15   Life, . . . destroying *s*, disease, and death.
  ap 565–26   destroying *s*, sickness, and death,
destruction of
  (*see* **destruction**)
disappearance of
  p 426–29   will disappear with the disappearance of *s*.
disarm
  ph 178–25   and we disarm *s* of its imaginary power
disease and
  pref viii–13   by healing both disease and *s* ;
  f 208–32   banish all thoughts of disease and *s*
  p 420–18   Truth overcomes both disease and *s*
  r 485–27   foreign agents, called disease and *s*.
disease, and death
  pr 17–11   *but delivereth us from s*, *disease, and death.*
  a 24– 3   error will never save from *s*, disease, and death.
  m 67–28   Man delivered from *s*, disease, and death
  sp 99–27   *s*, disease, and death give everlasting place
  s 164–25   save from *s*, disease, and death.
  ph 166–30   its mastery over *s*, disease, and death,
  197– 9   bears the fruit of *s*, disease, and death,
  f 248–31   *s*, disease, and death will diminish
  b 301–24   *s*, disease, and death arise from the
  317–20   to conquer *s*, disease, and death.
  332–15   Life, . . . destroying *s*, disease, and death.
  o 348–27   or that *s*, disease, and death would not be
  p 395–13   *s*, disease, and death will disappear.
  415– 4   *S*, disease, and death have no foundations in
  442–22   and *s*, disease, and death disappear.
  r 485–12   make *s*, disease, and death appear . . . unreal
  g 505– 2   *s*, disease, and death have no record in the
disease, . . . and death
  sp 78– 2   like the discords of disease, *s*, and death,
  b 275–29   such as matter, disease, *s*, and death,
  p 412–15   and to destroy disease, *s*, and death.
disease or
  b 323–24   something better than disease or *s*.
  p 402–19   whether it be a broken bone, disease, or *s*.
  t 455–11   lost in the belief and fear of disease or *s*,
disease, or death
  f 253–16   to overcome the belief in *s*, disease, or death.
  253–26   supposed necessity for *s*, disease, or death,
  p 380– 9   the demands of *s*, disease, or death,
divest
  b 339–29   to divest *s* of any supposed mind or reality,

sin

effects of
  gl 588– 3   self-imposed agony ; effects of *s* ;
error and
  b 296–17   lose all satisfaction in error and *s*
every
  b 307–21   every *s* or supposed material pain and
expiate their
  ap 569–21   They must eventually expiate their *s*
fear and
  p 373–21   you must rise above both fear and *s*.
  392– 1   you master fear and *s* through divine
fear of
  p 405–19   man finally can overcome his fear of *s*.
fellowship with
  pr 8– 8   They hold secret fellowship with *s*,
fettered by
  t 448–32   Fettered by *s* yourself, it is difficult to
forgiveness of
  r 497– 9   We acknowledge God's forgiveness of *s* in the
forms of
  p 404– 4   servant of any one of the myriad forms of *s*,
forsake
  b 290–28   The murderer, . . . does not thereby forsake *s*.
fruit-bearer of
  g 526–23   Did He create this fruit-bearer of *s*
grapple with
  a 29– 3   They must grapple with *s*
greatest
  p 376– 6   Just so is it with the greatest *s*.
has the elements
  r 481–24   *S* has the elements of self-destruction.
healer of
  s 148–32   a theology which admits God to be the healer of *s*
  f 251–24   the healer of *s*, disease, death.
heals
  s 135–11   same power which heals *s* heals also sickness.
hidden
  t 453–20   Hidden *s* is spiritual wickedness in high places.
if without
  p 385–16   all untoward conditions, *if without s*,
ignorance and
  b 290–22   Christ, Truth, removes all ignorance and *s*.
ignorance or
  p 411–21   foundation of . . . is fear, ignorance, or *s*.
  r 483–11   Moral ignorance or *s* affects your
illusion of
  g 536–11   The illusion of *s* is without hope or God.
infirmity of
  ap 564– 8   This last infirmity of *s* will
is destroyed
  pr 6–14   until belief in material life and *s* is destroyed.
is not there
  b 291–16   immortal, because *s* is not there
is the image
  b 327–13   *S* is the image of the beast
is unsustained
  c 264–21   *S* is unsustained by Truth,
jest of
  sp 72–29   joy of intercourse becomes the jest of *s*, when
love of
  a 36– 6   sufficient suffering, . . . to quench the love of *s*.
  p 373–14   The fear of disease and the love of *s* are the
mental
  g 557–24   but immediately fell into mental *s* ;
microbes of
  s 164–15   and all the mental microbes of *s*
midst of
  pr 7–30   in the midst of *s*
  b 291– 3   suppositions that . . . in the midst of *s*,
misery of
  b 327–13   The way to escape the misery of *s*
no
  t 447–24   not reformed merely by assuring him . . . there
      is no *s*.
  r 472–23   *Question.* — Is there no *s*?
  ap 567– 8   no error, no *s*, sickness, nor death.
no claim of
  p 390–20   Suffer no claim of *s* or of sickness to grow
no real pleasure in
  p 404–20   conviction, that there is no real pleasure in *s*,
no satisfaction in
  b 322–14   Man's wisdom finds no satisfaction in *s*,
odiousness of
  p 366–23   by a sense of the odiousness of *s*
or death
  s 125–18   man cannot be controlled by *s* or death,
or disease
  p 396–17   not because the testimony of *s* or disease is true,
or error
  ph 183–11   *s*, or error, first caused the condemnation of
or materiality
  b 299–13   never lead towards self, *s*, or materiality,
or sickness
  f 253–21   right endeavors against *s* or sickness,
  p 390–24   either of *s* or sickness,

sin

or sickness
p 426–18   are not saved from *s·* or sickness by death,
t 447–16   When *s·* or sickness . . . seems true
outshining
ap 571–30   outshining *s·*, sorcery, lust, and hypocrisy.
overcome
p 427–21   in proportion as we overcome *s·*.
path from
a 20–22   traversing anew the path from *s·* to holiness.
power over
s 142– 7   generally omit all but . . . the power over *s·*.
practice of
a 39–31   Who will stop the practice of *s·* so long as
produced by
p 373–20   the effects of fear produced by *s·*,
rebuked
pr 6–23   Jesus uncovered and rebuked *s·*
rebukes
a 23–19   Spirit, which rebukes *s·* of every kind
recognize your
t 461–23   to recognize your *s·*, aids in destroying it.
removing the
a 40–10   only by first removing the *s·*
repent of
b 339–18   Only those, who repent of *s·*
reports of
f 218–10   may form a coalition with the reports of *s·*,
result of
pr 6–11   To cause suffering as the result of *s·*,
results of
g 535–14   It unveils the results of *s·*
risen above
p 448–13   but if you have not risen above *s·* yourself,
save us from
a 23– 2   many sacrifices of self to save us from *s·*.
selfishness and
ph 176–15   selfishness and *s·*, disease and death, will lose
sense of
m 69– 5   only as they lose the sense of *s·*
b 311–12   It is a sense of *s·*, . . . which is lost.
r 481–31   it is the sense of *s·* which is lost,
g 540–19   the human sense of *s·*, sickness, and death,
sensuality and
p 364– 7   might be redeemed from sensuality and *s·*.
serpent of
ap 569–16   and fail to strangle the serpent of *s·*
show that
a 37– 2   Does not Science show that *s·* brings suffering
sickness and
(see sickness)
sickness, and death
pr 6–27   how to destroy *s·*, sickness, and death.
a 26–15   authority over *s·*, sickness, and death.
30–20   rebuke . . . error and all *s·*, sickness, and death,
39– 6   salvation from *s·*, sickness, and death.
42–23   *s·*, sickness, and death had no terror for
45– 9   the whole world from *s·*, sickness, and death.
52– 8   material evidence of *s·*, sickness, and death.
sp 96–17   *s·*, sickness, and death, which assume new phases
s 122– 3   seeming power to *s·*, sickness, and death ;
127–17   not as the author of *s·*, sickness, and death,
141–28   will ameliorate *s·*, sickness, and death.
ph 171–29   destroys *s·*, sickness, and death.
188–12   a dream of *s·*, sickness, and death ;
f 201– 9   the destruction of *s·*, sickness, and death.
204–10   the delusions of *s·*, sickness, and death,
205– 8   believing that . . . *s·*, sickness, and death are
208–10   embracing *s·*, sickness, and death?
225– 2   with iron shackles to *s·*, sickness, and death?
226–10   fetters of *s·*, sickness, and death be stricken
228–28   supposition that *s·*, sickness, and death have
229– 1   master of *s·*, sickness, and death,
231– 5   If God destroys not *s·*, sickness, and death,
232– 2   can triumph over *s·*, sickness, and death.
232–24   condemnation of *s·*, sickness, and death.
233– 4   destruction of *s·*, sickness, and death
b 270–20   destroy *s·*, sickness, and death,
272–27   the dismal beliefs of *s·*, sickness, and death.
273– 1   Matter and its claims of *s·*, sickness, and death
278–28   All that we term *s·*, sickness, and death,
283– 8   Matter and its effects — *s·*, sickness, and death
284–11   Is God's image . . . *s·*, sickness, and death?
285–10   called *s·*, sickness, and death.
286–31   *S·*, sickness, and death are comprised in
289– 3   belief in *s·*, sickness, and death,
290–16   belief in *s·*, sickness, and death,
299–20   bearing the fruits of *s·*, sickness, and death.
302–11   the birth, *s·*, sickness, and death of matter,
308–12   pleasure, pain, *s·*, sickness, and death."
324–16   we must conquer *s·*, sickness, and death,
328– 8   mortals get rid of *s·*, sickness, and death only in
o 343–19   *s·*, sickness, and death are beliefs
344– 9   not found in matter, *s·*, sickness, and death?
346– 7   the nothingness of *s·*, sickness, and death,
347–24   the popular gods, — *s·*, sickness, and death,

sin

sickness, and death
o 348–20   show itself in forms of *s·*, sickness, and death?
356– 5   *S·*, sickness, and death do not prove
356–19   incapable of producing *s·*, sickness, and death
p 400–29   manifest as *s·*, sickness, and death.
406– 6   full salvation from *s·*, sickness, and death.
r 473– 5   *S·*, sickness, and death are to be classified as
474–16   If *s·*, sickness, and death are as real as
474–19   Jesus came to destroy *s·*, sickness, and death ;
475–28   Man is incapable of *s·*, sickness, and death.
476–18   *S·*, sickness, and death must disappear
480–29   If *s·*, sickness, and death were understood
492–23   human illusion as to *s·*, sickness, and death
494–21   *s·*, sickness, and death will seem real
g 525–28   *S·*, sickness, and death must be deemed as
526–11   appetites and passions, *s·*, sickness, and death,
538–17   *S·*, sickness, and death have no record in the
540– 3   lapsing into *s·*, sickness, and death.
540–19   the human sense of *s·*, sickness, and death,
543–13   with all its *s·*, sickness, and death,
545–28   to all error, — to *s·*, sickness, and death :
552–10   friends of *s·*, sickness, and death ;
ap 563– 3   astonished at *s·*, sickness, and death.
564–24   *s·*, sickness, and death, envy, hatred,
565–26   destroying *s·*, sickness, and death,
572–16   myriad illusions of *s·*, sickness, and death.
gl 579–15   belief in "original *s·*," sickness, and death ;
580–15   namely, matter, *s·*, sickness, and death ;
584–18   a belief in *s·*, sickness, and death ;
590– 7   the origin of *s·*, sickness, and death ;
593–21   *s·*, sickness, and death destroyed.
594– 7   the first claim that *s·*, sickness, and death are
598–29   where *s·*, sickness, and death are unknown.
sickness, . . . and death
(see sickness)
sickness, nor death
ap 567– 8   no error, no *s·*, sickness, nor death.
sickness, . . . nor death
p 381–17   In . . . Love there is no sickness, *s·*, nor death,
sickness or
r 495–14   When the illusion of sickness or *s·* tempts you,
sickness, or death
r 472–27   the only reality of *s·*, sickness, or death is the
gl 585–20   before it accepts *s·*, sickness, or death ;
sickness or of
o 353–10   either in the form of sickness or of *s·*?
sickness, . . . or death
t 463–22   manifested in forms of sickness, *s·*, or death
single
ap 568–24   For victory over a single *s·*, we give thanks
so-called
g 540–14   uncovers so-called *s·* and its effects,
sorrow, and death
f 203–29   waves of *s·*, sorrow, and death beat in vain.
subdue
b 315–19   realize this likeness only when we subdue *s·*
swollen with
ap 565– 3   swollen with *s·*, inflamed with war against
to believe
p 420–32   It is a *s·* to believe that aught can overpower
to cure
p 373– 6   easier to cure . . . disease than it is to cure *s·*.
to fear
f 231–22   To fear *s·* is to misunderstand the power of
to holiness
b 339–24   sickness to health, *s·* to holiness,
to love
s 130–31   no longer think it natural to love *s·*
triumph over
a 28–14   enabled to heal the sick and to triumph over *s·*.
49–24   to triumph over *s·*, sickness, death,
f 232– 2   can triumph over *s·*, sickness, and death.
243– 8   and triumph over *s·* and death.
uncover
t 453–18   You uncover *s·*, . . . in order to bless
unreality of
t 461–26   To prove scientifically the . . . unreality of *s·*,
unveiling of
p 366–24   by the unveiling of *s·* in his own thoughts.
valley of
m 61– 9   Every valley of *s·* must be exalted, and
victory over
t 447–26   and thus get the victory over *s·*
view of
p 404–23   Arouse the sinner to this new and true view of *s·*,
will receive
g 542–21   *S·* will receive its full penalty,
will submit
p 406– 6   *S·* will submit to C. S. when, in place of modes
would be unknown
r 469–20   if mortals . . . *s·* would be unknown.
would multiply
pr 11– 1   Without punishment, *s·* would multiply.
pref viii– 1   treatment of disease as well as of *s·*,
xi–14   gives place to light and *s·* to reformation.

sin

pr 5–22 not to be used as a confessional to cancel s˙.
   5–23 S˙ is forgiven only as it is destroyed
   5–25 If prayer nourishes the belief that s˙ is
   6– 1 We cannot escape the penalty due for s˙.
   6–12 Every supposed pleasure in s˙ will
   6–19 To suppose that God . . . punishes s˙ according
  10–32 to be merciful and not to punish s˙?
  11–20 divine sentence for an individual's s˙,
  11–20 s˙ brings inevitable suffering.
  16–21 Only as we rise above all . . . s˙, can we
  a 20–28 s˙ which doth so easily beset us,— Heb. 12 : 1.
  30–28 we shall loathe s˙ and rebuke it
  36– 7 To remit the penalty due for s˙, would be
  39–32 so long as he believes in the pleasures of s˙?
  40–14 While there's s˙ there's doom.
  sp 99– 4 by which mortals can escape from s˙ ;
  99– 5 to escape from s˙, is what the Bible demands.
  an 103– 5 S˙ was the Assyrian moon-god.
  s 108–24 that the opposite of Truth,— called error, s˙,
  113–19 God, omnipotent good, deny death, evil, s˙,
  113–20 Disease, s˙, evil, death, deny good,
  115–23 hatred, revenge, s˙, sickness, disease,
  137– 6 the victor over sickness, s˙, disease,
  138–23 easier . . . to cast out sickness than s˙,
  149– 2 save from sickness as well as from s˙.
  ph 188–26 S˙ and the fear of disease must be
  196– 8 S˙ alone brings death,
  196– 9 s˙ is the only element of destruction,
  196–15 not of Rome, Satan, nor of God, but of s˙.
  196–18 S˙ makes its own hell,
  f 201–20 supposing that s˙ can be forgiven when
  203–26 S˙ kills the sinner and will continue to
  207–23 S˙, sickness, disease, and death belong not to
  218–24 Treat a belief in sickness as you would s˙,
  219– 1 sorrow, s˙, death, will be unknown,
  223–30 but the awful daring of s˙ destroys s˙,
  224– 1 the power of s˙ diminishing,
  231–12 If God makes s˙, if good produces evil,
  231–20 To hold yourself superior to s˙,
  236–11 Mind heals sickness as well as s˙
  239–28 it is discordant and ends in s˙, sickness,
  241– 6 S˙ breaks in upon them, and carries off their
  241:12 what a mocking spectacle is s˙ !
  248–16 Is it imperfection, joy, sorrow, s˙, suffering?
  251–13 Sickness, as well as s˙, is an error that
  252–23 and says : . . . What a nice thing is s˙ !
  252–24 and says : . . . How s˙ succeeds, where the
  b 270–26 If s˙ makes sinners, Truth . . . can unmake them.
  289– 9 To suppose that s˙, lust, hatred,
  291– 1 The suppositions that s˙ is pardoned while
  291– 3 that the so-called death of the body frees from s˙,
  296–11 The death of a false material sense and of s˙,
  310–24 S˙ is the element of self-destruction,
  310–25 If there was s˙ in Soul,
  311–10 S˙ exists here or hereafter only so long as
  315–17 likeness of God we lose sight of through s˙,
  316– 5 mortals need only turn from s˙
  322–15 God has sentenced s˙ to suffer.
  335–29 S˙, sickness, and mortality are the suppositional
  338–24 the obstacle which the serpent, s˙, would impose
  339– 4 Being destroyed, s˙ needs no other form of
  339–13 for the sinner would make a reality of s˙,
  339–28 To get rid of s˙ through Science, is to
  339–30 never to admit that s˙ can have intelligence
  o 341– * Which of you convinceth me of s˙?— John 8 : 46.
  348–16 Are we irreverent towards s˙, . . . when we
  353– 2 S˙, disease, whatever seems real to
  354–26 S˙ should become unreal to every one.
  356–31 Was there original self-creative s˙?
  p 369–31 any more than he is morally saved in or by s˙.
  369–32 to murmur or to be angry over s˙.
  373–11 more rapidly . . . than does the sinner from his s˙.
  379– 2 If . . . s˙ can do the same,
  381– 7 on the ground that s˙ has its necessities.
  385–12 the law which makes s˙ its own executioner,
  386– 4 any more than it is in the case of s˙.
  390–23 no more the author of sickness than He is of s˙.
  392– 3 Only while fear or s˙ remains can it bring forth
  395–12 faith in God destroys all faith in s˙
  405–26 If s˙ is not regretted and is not lessening,
  407–30 S˙ is spared from this classification, only because
  408– 3 s˙ is worse than sickness,
  409– 7 the more prolific it is likely to become in s˙
  412– 2 never punishing aught but s˙,
  418– 3 the conquest over sickness, as well as over s˙,
  418–13 is no more the reality of being than is s˙.
  419–11 Neither disease itself, s˙, nor fear
  435–25 decides what penalty is due for the s˙,
  435–26 and Mortal Man can suffer only for his s˙.
  440–21 God, who sentences only for s˙.
  t 445– 3 to defend themselves against s˙,
  445–12 by s˙, or by recourse to material means
  450–23 Sickness to him is no less a temptation than is s˙,
  453–25 treat sickness . . . as you would s˙, except that
  458–20 S˙ makes deadly thrusts at the

sin

r 468– 3 for s˙ is mortality's self,
  468– 7 s˙ is not the eternal verity of being.
  480–20 good, never made man capable of s˙.
  481–25 If s˙ is supported, God must uphold it,
  490– 1 assures mortals that there is real pleasure in s˙;
  496–20 "The sting of death is s˙ ;— I Cor. 15 : 56.
  496–20 the strength of s˙ is the law,"— I Cor. 15 : 56.
  g 537–14 S˙ is its own punishment.
  538–27 and of s˙ which is temporal.
  538–28 both mortal man and s˙ have a beginning,
  539– 1 supposes God to be the author of s˙
  542– 8 Truth causes s˙ to betray itself,
  542–11 and the denial of truth tend to perpetuate s˙,
  557–14 the less a mortal knows of s˙, disease, and
  ap 566–32 leads the hosts . . . against the power of s˙,
  569–21 s˙, which one has made his bosom companion,
  572– 4 s˙ is to be . . . reduced to its native nothingness.
  gl 588– 2 HELL. . . . revenge ; s˙ ; sickness ; death ;
  592– 9 MORTAL MIND. . . . s˙ ; sickness ; death.
  595– 5 TARES. Mortality ; error ; s˙ ; sickness ;
  595–24 UNCLEANLINESS. Impure thoughts ; error ; s˙ ;

sin (verb)

pr 11– 4 "Go, and s˙ no more."— John 8 : 11.
  a 19–21 if the sinner continues to . . . s˙ and be sorry,
  37– 3 They who s˙ must suffer.
  s 148–30 When mortals s˙, this ruling of the schools
  f 205– 2 and mortals will s˙ without knowing
  206–31 God does not cause man to s˙, to be sick, or to
  211–13 sensation of sickness and the impulse to s˙
  215– 4 If Spirit, Soul, could s˙ or be lost, then being
  b 310–21 If Soul could s˙, Spirit, Soul, would be flesh
  311–20 So long as we believe that soul can s˙
  340–29 and leaves nothing that can s˙, suffer,
  o 356–26 by making man inclined to s˙,
  p 372–15 He can neither s˙, suffer, be subject to
  405–21 good, in which is no power to s˙.
  420–13 as positively as they can the temptation to s˙.
  435–24 If mortals s˙, our Supreme Judge in equity
  r 468– 6 Because Soul is immortal, Soul cannot s˙,
  475–31 the capacity or freedom to s˙.
  g 524–29 Could Spirit . . . give matter ability to s˙
  540–16 all sense of evil and all power to s˙.
  555–27 when we admit . . . God bestows the power to s˙,

Sinai

ph 174–17 The thunder of S˙ and the Sermon on the Mount
  200– 3 the law of S˙ lifted thought into the

since

pref vii–27 S˙ the author's discovery of the
  viii–23 increased violence of diseases s˙ the flood.
  x– 5 books on mental healing have s˙ been issued,
  pr 2–10 s˙ He is unchanging wisdom and Love.
  4–10 s˙ he has said : "If ye love me,— John 14 : 15.
  9–29 s˙ you do not care to tread in the footsteps of our
  a 34–28 change which has s˙ been called the ascension.
  36– 9 s˙ justice is the handmaid of mercy.
  m 68–22 s˙ salutary causes sometimes incur these
  sp 75–10 s˙ to infinite Spirit there can be no matter.
  83–15 s˙ Science is an explication of nature.
  an 101–27 s˙ error cannot remove the effects of error.
  102–13 s˙ God governs the universe ;
  s 111–31 S˙ then this system has gradually gained
  129–14 s˙ the beginning of the world ;"— Matt. 24 : 21.
  130–12 s˙ you admit that God is omnipotent ;
  144– 2 s˙ no good can come of it?
  147–12 s˙ Jesus practised these rules
  149–26 S˙ God, divine Mind, governs all,
  154– 4 S˙ it is a law of mortal mind that certain
  ph 165–13 s˙ man-made material theories took the place
  179– 6 s˙ space is no obstacle to Mind.
  181– 1 s˙ Mind, God, is the source and condition of all
  186–30 S˙ it must believe in something besides itself,
  193–19 S˙ then I have not seen him, but am informed
  193–22 ever s˙ the injury was received in boyhood.
  193–24 S˙ his recovery I have been informed that
  199– 5 s˙ muscles are as material as wood and iron
  f 219– 4 s˙ Mind should be, and is, supreme,
  250–24 s˙ whatever appears to be a mortal man
  c 267–20 s˙ inverted thoughts and erroneous beliefs
  b 286–23 s˙ God, Spirit, is the only cause,
  299–22 s˙ "the tree is known by his— Matt. 12 : 33.
  317– 2 s˙ material knowledge usurped the throne of
  322–14 s˙ God has sentenced sin to suffer.
  339– 7 S˙ God is All, there is no room for
  o 355–18 systematic healing power s˙ the first century.
  p 362–12 Mary Magdalene, as she has s˙ been called
  364– 1 who has s˙ been rightfully regarded as
  370–20 s˙ mortal mind must be the cause of disease
  391–19 S˙ matter cannot talk, it must be mortal mind
  399–26 s˙ matter is not sensible.
  401–13 s˙ matter has no sensation
  412–32 s˙ matter is not intelligent
  417–23 s˙ it is demonstrable that the way to cure
  424–11 s˙ there is no room for imperfection in
  425–19 s˙ Spirit, God, is All-in-all.

since

p 427– 9   s· the truth of being is deathless.
   431–27   s· the night of the liver-attack.
t 457– 7   S· the divine light of C. S. first dawned upon
   457–10   s· entering this field of labor,
r 471–29   S· then her highest creed has been
   481–27   s· Truth cannot support error.
   482–15   s· Christ is "the way"— John 14 : 6.
   482–30   s· the human, mortal mind so-called is not
   488–30   s· they exist in immortal Mind, not in matter.
   490–11   s· all power belongs to God, good.
   490–15   s· he is so already, according to C. S.
   492– 5   s· Life cannot be united to its unlikeness,
   494–13   s· to all mankind and in every hour,
g 504–13   s· Truth, Life, and Love fill immensity
   514– 3   s· nothing exists beyond the range of
   517–23   s· there is no limit to infinitude
   519– 4   s· the spiritual creation was the outgrowth,
   531–27   s· flesh wars against Spirit
   534–26   s· the Christian era began.
   537–17   s· ground and dust stand for nothingness.
   543– 5   s· it is the idea of Truth and changes not,
ap 560– 3   typical of six thousand years s· Adam,
   564–14   S· Jesus must have been tempted in all points,
   568– 2   Ever s· the foundation of the world,
   568– 2   ever s· error would establish material belief,
   571– 4   s· exposure is necessary to ensure the
gl 592–14   s· justice demands penalties

sincere

pref   x–23   personal experience of any s· seeker of Truth.
pr 13–10   If our petitions are s·, we labor for what
   13–15   Even if prayer is s·, God knows our need
t 450– 9   They are s·, generous, noble, and

sincerity

pr   5– 5   the test of our s·,— namely, reformation.
   9– 9   no evidence of the s· of our requests
   15–24   and let our lives attest our s·.
t 462–17   self-denial, s·, Christianity, and persistence

sinew

b 308–20   smote the s·, or strength, of his error,

sinews

ph 173–19   measuring human strength by bones and s·,

sin-filled

a 54–11   empty or s· human storehouses,

sinful

pr 15– 4   the door of which shuts out s· sense
   16– 6   and the falsity of s· sense.
u 20–13   can be baptized, . . . and yet be sensual and s·.
   23– 9   suffering is an error of s· sense
   53–32   Had he shared the s· beliefs of others,
sp 70– 5   Whatever is false or s· can never enter
s 114– 2   author calls sick and s· humanity mortal mind,
   138–24   the s·, so-called pleasure of the senses.
f 204–26   notion that they can create . . . s· mortals
   237–20   either s· or diseased thoughts.
   241–32   than for s· beliefs to enter the kingdom
   253–14   to make you sick of s·
b 289–13   never make men sick, s·, or mortal.
   292–10   A s·, sick, and dying mortal is not the
   296–10   Nothing sensual or s· is immortal.
   311–12   It is a sense of sin, and not a s· soul,
   314–23   Because of mortals' material and s· belief,
   318–16   Is the sick man s· above all others?
   327– 7   and all the s· appetites of the human mind.
o 346– 3   it is not s· and sickly mortal man who
p 366–26   sinners should be affrighted by their s· beliefs ;
   381– 6   than you are to yield to a s· temptation
   400–31   the baneful influence of s· thought on the body.
   405–29   pains of s· sense are less harmful than
t 452–28   Acting from s· motives destroys your power of
r 481–32   the sense of sin which is lost, and not a s· soul.
g 502–10   untrue image of God, named a s· mortal.
   542–29   The s· misconception of Life as
   554–18   the creation of whatever is s· and mortal ;
ap 570–29   when it makes them sick or s·.

singe

an 103–27   s· their own wings and fall into dust.

single

pr 14–12   Become conscious for a s· moment that
a 18– 9   nor to relieve them of a s· responsibility.
   28–16   Not a s· component part of his nature
sp 76–24   without a s· bodily pleasure or pain,
   77– 4   Neither . . . from error to truth at a s· bound.
s 153– 6   until there was not a s· saline property left.
   155–21   in order to heal a s· case of disease.
   163– 9   if there were not a s· physician, surgeon,
ph 168– 4   the removal of a s· weight from either scale
   196–25   induced by a s· post mortem examination,
f 225–31   rights of man were vindicated in a s· section
b 290– 7   on account of that s· experience,
   329– 1   reaching beyond the pale of a s· period
   336–21   neither could . . . be reflected by a s· man,
p 391–10   that you can possibly entertain a s· intruding

single

p 413– 5   A s· requirement, beyond what is necessary
   421–29   or by employing a s· material application
   429– 9   we look beyond a s· step in the line of
t 463–12   spiritual idea has not a s· element of error,
r 475–20   has not a s· quality underived from Deity ;
g 524–18   With a s· command, Mind had made man,
ap 568–24   For victory over a s· sin, we give thanks

sings

f 220–11   The snowbird s· and soars amid the blasts ;

sinister

t 446–13   from s· or malicious motives

sink

p 415–30   the whole frame will s· from sight
ap 564– 8   s· its perpetrator into a night without a star.
   570–21   nor again s· the world into the deep waters of

sinking

s 153–10   patient s· in the last stage of typhoid fever.
p 385– 4   have been able to undergo without s·

sinless

pr 16– 6   Truth that is s· and the falsity of sinful sense.
a 22–24   boundless freedom, and s· sense,
   26–24   precious import of our Master's s· career
sp 76–22   The s· joy,— the perfect harmony and
b 288–22   Soul is s·, not to be found in the body ;
   290–26   To be wholly spiritual, man must be s·,
   304–15   The perfect man . . . is s· and eternal.
o 344– 5   normal, healthful, and s· condition of man
g 538–29   while the s·, real man is eternal.

sinlessness

b 339–25   basis of all health, s·, and immortality

sinned

b 310–23   If Soul s·, Soul would die.
p 435– 3   Who or what has s·?
r 468– 3   If Soul s·, it would be mortal,

sinner (see also sinner's)

a hypocrite
pr 8– 2   though it makes the s· a hypocrite.
arouse the
p 404 22   Arouse the s· to this new and true view of sin,
awakens the
o 342–21   C. S. awakens the s·,
is afraid
t 447–30   A s· is afraid to cast the first stone.
is a suicide
f 203–25   The so-called s· is a suicide.
miserable
ap 573–18   no longer regarded as a miserable s·,
mortal
r 475–31   A mortal s· is not God's man.
g 525– 2   to become there a mortal s·,
prospective
g 527–28   lie . . . asking a prospective s· to help Him.
reformed the
o 343–27   healed the sick and reformed the s·
reforming the
p 404–26   Healing the sick and reforming the s·
reforms the
pr 1– 1   The prayer that reforms the s·
   6– 5   divine Principle alone reforms the s·.
reform the
a 35–30   The design of Love is to reform the s·.
sin and the
p 393–31   the sin and the s·, the disease and its cause.
sin kills the
f 203–26   Sin kills the s· and will continue to kill him
such a
s 136–24   for how could such a s· comprehend

a 19–20   but if the s· continues to pray and repent,
   22–30   Justice requires reformation of the s·.
   36– 1   good man's heaven would be a hell to the s·.
sp 73– 4   another, who has died to-day a s·
   91– 9   difficult for the s· to accept divine Science,
s 129–31   The s· sees, in the system taught in this
f 218–14   the human mind is the s·,
   226–26   the sick, the sensual, the s·, I wished to save
c 266–20   The s· makes his own hell
b 339–11   A s· can receive no encouragement from
   339–12   for the s· would make a reality of sin,
p 373–11   sick recover more rapidly . . . than does the s·
   404–16   The healthy s· is the hardened s·.
t 447–22   A s· is not reformed merely by
   447–23   not . . . by assuring him that he cannot be a s·
   455– 2   Love, which heals the sick and the s·.
g 542–23   Justice marks the s·,

sinner's

a 23– 5   constant self-immolation on the s· part.
   35–31   If the s· punishment here has been

sinners

all
a 24–21   chiefly as providing a ready pardon for all s·
p 364– 6   in behalf of all s·,

sinners
counted among
  pr 9–26 and so be counted among *s·*?
flourish
  pr 5–18 *S·* flourish "like a green bay tree ;" — *Psal.* 37 : 35.
hatred of
  b 317–10 and he will incur the hatred of *s·*, till
he rebuked
  a 53– 6 He rebuked *s·* pointedly and unflinchingly,
saints and
  pr 5–14 Saints and *s·* get their full award,
traduced by the
  sp 95– 4 were traduced by the *s·* of that period,

  a 36–22 It is quite as impossible for *s·* to receive their
    53– 2 the "friend of publicans and *s·*." — *Luke* 7 : 34.
  s 138–24 than are *s·* to give up the sinful,
  f 204–23 theories have given *s·* the notion that
  b 270–26 If sin makes *s·*, Truth . . . can unmake them.
    314–28 the more odious he became to *s·*
  o 355–30 and by the *s·* who are reformed.
  p 366–26 *s·* should be affrighted by their sinful beliefs ;
  g 533–19 who aids man to make *s·*
sinneth
  p 435–12 decrees that whosoever *s·* shall die ;
sinning
  sp 72–26 A *s·*, earthly mortal is not the reality of
    76–18 Suffering, *s·*, dying beliefs are unreal.
    77–20 the illusion . . . of a *s·*, suffering sense,
    78–11 must still be mortal, *s·*, suffering,
    78–30 and the *s·* are reformed.
    92–10 with the power of *s·* now and forever.
    96– 1 Humanity advances slowly out of *s·* sense
  s 138–22 to heal the sick as well as the *s·*.
    143– 9 sick are more deplorably lost than the *s·*, if
    143–10 if the sick cannot rely on God . . . and the *s·* can.
  f 205– 3 will sin without knowing that they are *s·*,
  c 259–11 presented man as fallen, sick, *s·*, and dying.
  b 323–19 When the sick or the *s·* awake to realize
    327–13 way to escape the misery of sin is to cease *s·*.
  o 345–24 between God's man, . . . and the *s·* race of
  r 477– 1 where *s·* mortal man appears to mortals.
    489–20 the medium for *s·* against God,
  ap 570–26 When God heals the sick or the *s·*,
    (*see also* **sick**)

sin's
  a 48–14 exalting ordeal of *s·* revenge on its destroyer
  f 240–30 The divine method of paying *s·* wages
  p 405–19 This is *s·* necessity, — to destroy itself.
  g 539– 1 the author of sin and *s·* progeny.
  ap 569–28 must depend upon *s·* obduracy.

sins
bore our
  a 53–25 Jesus bore our *s·* in his body.
covereth his
  t 448–17 "He that covereth his *s·* shall not — *Prov.* 28 : 13.
experimental
  f 230–16 cannot be, the author of experimental *s·*.
his
  an 105–25 His *s·* will be millstones about his neck,
multitude of
  pr 8–20 they "cover the multitude of *s·*." — *I Pet* 4 : 8.
of others
  ph 189–13 *s·* of others should not make good men suffer.
  o 346–15 belief that we suffer from the *s·* of others.
of the world
  s 150–16 Christ-power to take away the *s·* of the world.
  b 334–18 taking away the *s·* of the world,
other people's
  a 38–23 the fruits of other people's *s·*, not of his own.
our
  pr 11–13 never pardons our *s·* or mistakes till
    11–19 Jesus suffered for our *s·*,
sicknesses, and
  ph 177– 3 relinquish all its errors, sicknesses, and *s·*.
thy
  p 363–23 "Thy *s·* are forgiven." — *Luke* 7 : 48.
trespasses and
  a 33–25 raises the dead from trespasses and *s·*,
  b 316–30 those dead in trespasses and *s·*,
your own
  p 391–14 It is error to suffer for aught but your own *s·*.
    391–16 and real suffering for your own *s·* will

  f 202–17 but immortal man, . . . neither *s·*, suffers, nor
    203–27 so long as he *s·*.
    229– 5 We should hesitate to say that Jehovah *s·* or
  b 285– 8 material personality which suffers, *s·*, and
    294–13 saying : . . . Nerves feel. Brain thinks and *s·*.
    310–19 taught that there is a human soul which *s·*
    310–23 It is the belief . . . of material sense which *s·*.
  r 470–18 God, the Mind of man, never *s·*
    481–24 If Soul *s·*, it must be mortal.

sins
  r 481–28 Soul is the divine Principle of man and never *s·*.
    481–30 it is material sense, not Soul, which *s·* ;
  g 542– 1 The belief of life in matter *s·* at every step.
sister
  s 159– 3 After the autopsy, her *s·* testified that the
    161–13 If her *s·* States follow this example
  c 267–15 as for that of brother and *s·*.
    267–17 my brother, and *s·*, and mother." — *Matt.* 12 : 50.
sit
  a 31–20 *s·* down with him, in a full understanding of
sits
  an 106–15 Let this age, which *s·* in judgment on C. S.,
sittest
  p 435–29 "*S·* thou to judge — *Acts* 23 : 3.
situation
  b 296–30 and in understanding the *s·* in C. S.
    297– 4 and no circumstance can alter the *s·*, until the
  p 403–14 You command the *s·* if you understand that
  r 486–30 would place man in a terrible *s·*,
  ap 575–22 Psalmist saith, "Beautiful for *s·*, — *Psal.* 48 : 2.
six
  a 21–30 After following the sun for *s·* days,
  ph 193– 1 confined to his bed *s·* months with
  ap 560– 3 typical of *s·* thousand years since Adam,
sixth
  g 518–26 and the morning were the *s·* day. — *Gen.* 1 : 31.
  ap 560– 3 In the opening of the *s·* seal,
sixty
  f 247– 7 One man at *s·* had retained
size
  ph 165– 6 To measure intellectual capacity by the *s·* of
    190–12 by the *s·* of a brain and the bulk of a body,
    199– 4 trip-hammer is not increased in *s·* by exercise.
skeptical
  s 152–28 experiments in homœopathy had made her *s·*
skepticism
  f 209–12 Neither philosophy nor *s·* can hinder the
    252– 5 occasions the only *s·* regarding the pathology
sketch
  pref viii–25 a biographical *s·*, narrating experiences
  f 245– 3 a *s·* from the history of an English woman,
sketches
  ph 198–11 fills in his delineations with *s·* from
skies
  f 249–29 It falls short of the *s·*, but makes its
  ap 575–30 with the Southern Cross in the *s·*,
skilful
  s 159–11 Is it *s·* or scientific surgery to take no
  p 402– 1 C. S. is always the most *s·* surgeon,
skill
  a 44–15 He did not require the *s·* of a surgeon
  s 142–12 architectural *s·*, making dome and spire
  f 221–12 having exhausted the *s·* of the doctors,
skin
  p 379–26 dry *s·*, pain in the head and limbs,
skipped
  s 135– 4 mountains, that ye *s·* like rams, — *Psal.* 114 : 6.
skull
  ph 192– 2 The belief that a pulpy substance under the *s·*
  b 280–11 would compress Mind, . . . beneath a *s·* bone.
    281–19 The mind supposed to exist . . . beneath a *s·* bone
  p 397–29 belief that mind is, . . . within the *s·*,
sky
  sp 85–21 discern the face of the *s·* ; — *Matt.* 16 : 3.
  s 122–16 *s·* and tree-tops apparently join hands,
    133–10 and manna fell from the *s·*.
  f 233–17 Ye who can discern the face of the *s·*,
  g 510– 1 discern the face of the *s·* ; — *Matt.* 16 : 3.
skyward
  c 261–30 and preens its wings for a *s·* flight.
slain
  b 290–27 The murderer, though *s·* in the act,
    334–21 This was "the Lamb *s·* from the — *Rev.* 13 : 8.
    334–22 *s·*, that is, according to the testimony of the
slander
  c 266–13 Friends will betray and enemies will *s·*,
  b 330–30 hypocrisy, *s·*, hate, theft, adultery,
slaughter
  a 50– 1 brought as a lamb to the *s·*, — *Isa.* 53 : 7.
slave
  f 221–26 when, still the *s·* of matter, he thought
    225–19 and abolish the whipping-post and *s·* market ;
    226– 5 The voice of God in behalf of the African *s·*
  p 404– 3 If a man is an inebriate, a *s·* to tobacco,
    407–17 Let the *s·* of wrong desire learn the
  gl 582–27 and would make mortal mind a *s·* to the body.

slavery

African
f 226– 1 when African s· was abolished in our land.
hopeless
f 227–10 and in subjection to hopeless s·,
mental
f 225–24 abolition of mental s· is a more difficult task.
world-wide
f 226– 3 banishment of a world-wide s·,

f 224–29 the Soul-inspired motto, "S· is abolished."
226–26 to save from the s· of their own beliefs
227–15 S· is not the legitimate state of man.
p 381– 4 the bias of education enforces this s·.
t 445–30 Recalling Jefferson's words about s·,
gl 587–22 Corporeal belief ; sensuality ; s· ; tyranny.

slaves
m 68– 4 They are s· to fashion, pride, and sense.

slay
a 37– 7 Mortals try in vain to s· Truth
43–16 had mocked and tried to s·.
f 214–24 mortal illusions would rob God, s· man,
g 542– 4 Material beliefs would s· the spiritual idea
ap 568– 3 evil has tried to s· the Lamb ;

slayeth
g 542–15 Therefore whosoever s· Cain.— Gen. 4 : 15.

slays
ap 567–31 Science shows how the Lamb s· the wolf.

sleek
ph 197–20 more honest than our s· politicians.

sleep

and apathy
f 249–24 S· and apathy are phases of the
and mesmerism
r 490–28 S· and mesmerism explain the mythical nature
deep
b 307– 1 the Adam-dream, the deep s·,
g 528–10 a deep s· to fall upon Adam,— Gen. 2 : 21.
556–18 the deep s· which fell upon Adam?
dreamy
sp 88– 1 and this not in dreamy s·.
earth's
sp 75–31 when we awake from earth's s· to the
is darkness
g 556–18 S· is darkness, but God's creative mandate

sp 75–13 that I may awake him out of s·."— John 11 : 11.
82–13 In s· we do not communicate with the
ph 179–28 to move the bowels, or to produce s·
188–13 is like the dream we have in s·,
f 230–25 They are soothing syrups to put children to s·,
250–17 according to the dream he entertains in s·.
p 431– 7 going to s· immediately after a heavy meal.
440– 6 is taught how to make s· befool reason
r 490–29 S· shows material sense as either
491–23 In s·, memory and consciousness are lost from
g 505– 2 mortal mind, s·, dreams, sin,
500–16 inducing a s· or hypnotic state in Adam
556–20 In s·, cause and effect are mere illusions.
556–22 and dreams, not realities, come with s·.

sleeper
ph 188–18 The smile of the s· indicates the

sleepeth
sp 75–12 "Our friend Lazarus s· ;— John 11 : 11.
p 398–12 "she is not dead, but s·,"— Luke 8 : 52.

sleeping
ph 188–15 In both the waking and the s· dream,
f 250–23 any more reality in . . . than in the s· dream?
r 494–22 experiences of the s· dream seem real

sleeplessness
ph 165–16 You say that indigestion, fatigue, s·, cause

sleeps
p 416–15 Where is the pain while the patient s·?

slept
a 48– 3 His students s·.
p 385–22 You say that you have not s· well
g 528–10 sleep to fall upon Adam, and he s· :— Gen. 2 : 21.

slew
a 43–19 Those who s· him to stay his influence
g 541–15 against Abel his brother, and s· him.— Gen. 4 : 8.

slice
f 221– 7 only a thin s· of bread without water.

slight
m 59–21 and remember how s· a word or deed
s 130– 3 discouraged over its s· spiritual prospects.
t 446– 1 teaching his s· knowledge of Mind-power,

slime
b 279– 7 s·, or protoplasm never originated in

sling
b 268–12 like the shepherd-boy with his s·,

slippery
m 65–26 must lose its present s· footing,

slough
ph 168–13 already brought yourself into the s· of disease

slow
a 20–24 Material belief is s· to acknowledge what the
22– 6 Vibrating . . . our moral progress will be s·.
ph 174–10 The footsteps of thought, . . . are s·,
b 321– 6 The Hebrew Lawgiver, s· of speech,
g 519–12 Human capacity is s· to discern and to grasp
ap 566–23 Be Thou, longsuffering, s· to wrath,

slowly
a 39–28 This thought is apprehended s·,
m 68– 2 At present mortals progress s·
sp 96– 1 Humanity advances s· out of sinning sense
ph 173–26 Human reason and religion come s· to the
f 233– 9 The ages must s· work up to perfection.
254– 5 or attain s· and yield not to discouragement.
254–13 mortals grasp the ultimate . . . s· ;
b 268– 7 is s· yielding to the idea of a
p 415– 7 because thought moves quickly or s·,
415–22 The muscles, moving quickly or s·
t 450–15 Some people yield s· to the touch of Truth.

sluggard
a 22–17 nor become a s· in the race.

slumbering
f 223–25 Peals that should startle the s· thought

slumbers
f 249–22 God never s·, and His likeness never

small
s 113– 5 but its spirit comes only in s· degrees.
129–30 the author's s· estimate of the pleasures of
c 256–17 precise form of God must be of s· importance
b 323–29 "still, s· voice" of Truth— I Kings 19 : 12.
o 345–13 It is indeed no s· matter to know one's self ;
p 364–20 such seekers as he gave s· reward
367–25 through a "still, s· voice,"— I Kings 19 : 12.
384–14 will prove to himself, by s· beginnings,
r 402– 8 a knowledge of this, even in s· degree,
g 547–15 speck of so-called embryonic life seemed a s· sun
ap 559– 8 The "still, s· voice" of— I Kings 19 : 12.

smaller
p 363–16 one for a large sum and one for a s·,

smallpox
s 153–26 and we have s· because others have it ;
f 235– 4 Better suffer a doctor infected with s· to
p 390–29 whether it is cancer, consumption, or s·.

smatterers
t 460–19 If Christian healing is abused by mere s·

smell
sp 71–11 that you see a flower,— that you touch and s·
f 212–20 and bring the rose . . . that they may s· it.
b 284–23 nor can they feel, taste, or s· Spirit.
r 479–11 cannot see, feel, hear, taste, nor s·.
g 526–10 material hearing, sight, touch, taste, and s·,

smells
gl 591–15 sees, feels, hears, tastes, and s· only in belief.

smile
ph 175–10 to say that a rose, the s· of God, can produce
188–18 The s· of the sleeper indicates the
r 477–28 "the s· of the Great Spirit."

smiles
a 47–13 thirty pieces of silver and the s· of the
m 59–19 in prolonging her health and s·
sp 76– 9 name the face that s· on them

smite
p 439–20 God will s· you, O whited walls,
t 444–20 "Whosoever shall s· thee on thy— Matt. 5 : 39.
444–21 Fear not that he will s· thee again

Smith's Bible Dictionary
b 320– 8 In S· B· D· it is said :

smitten
a 48–21 Peter would have s· the enemies of
49–32 "stricken, s· of God."— Isa. 53 : 4.
o 343– 2 Shall I then be s· for healing
p 435–31 and commandest . . . to be s·— Acts 23 : 3.

smoke
a 22–18 When the s· of battle clears away,
37–14 but not amid the s· of battle is merit seen
ap 566–18 An awful guide, in s· and flame,

smoking
p 383–21 The tobacco-user, eating or s· poison

smooth
gl 593–15 When s· and unobstructed, it typifies the

smooth-tongued
f 252–20 says : . . . and I elude detection by s· villainy.

smote
a 48– 2 bigoted ignorance s· him sorely.
b 308–20 and s· the sinew, or strength, of his error,

smothered
  g 501– 5 seems so *s·* by the immediate context
smuggles
  p 438–24 and *s·* Error's goods into market
snake-talker
  g 533–13 the *s·* utters the first voluble lie,
snarls
  s 240–30 involves unwinding one's *s·*,
snatches
  f 237–13 *s·* away the good seed before it has sprouted.
sneers
  o 341–12 *S·* at the application of the word *Science* to
sneezing
  ph 175–15 glandular inflammation, *s·*, and nasal pangs.
sniffs
  ph 179–18 the wild animal, . . . *s·* the wind with delight.
snow
  sp 82–30 to the Esquimaux in their *s·* huts?
  ph 175–26 Damp atmosphere and freezing *s·*
  b 321–22 white as *s·* with the dread disease,
snowbird
  f 220–11 The *s·* sings and soars amid the blasts;
snowflakes
  f 250–29 Mortal thoughts chase one another like *s·*,
snows
  m 61–17 like tropical flowers born amid Alpine *s·*.
soaring
  g 512– 1 *s·* beyond and above corporeality
soars
  f 220–11 The snowbird sings and *s·* amid the blasts;
sober
  pr 7–13 unfavorable to spiritual growth, *s·* resolve,
  b 324–13 Be watchful, *s·*, and vigilant.
so-called
  a 39–23 the time for *s·* material . . . to pass away,
  m 62– 6 and master the belief in *s·* physical laws,
  sp 72– 9 *S·* spirits are but corporeal communicators.
  73–12 Any other control or attraction of *s·* spirit
  73–32 between *s·* material existence and
  77–14 embracing its *s·* pleasures and pains,
  77–21 a *s·* mind fettered by matter.
  88–15 Beliefs proceed from the *s·* material senses,
  97– 6 and *s·* matter resembles its essence,
  an 100– 4 he regarded this *s·* force,
  102– 7 an unreal concept of the *s·* mortal mind.
  102–30 Its *s·* despotism is but a phase of
  104–17 wrongness of the opposite *s·* action,
  s 112–27 Also, if any *s·* new school claims to be C. S.,
  123–24 The proof, . . . that the *s·* miracles of Jesus
  124– 3 Physical science (*s·*) is human knowledge,
  128–26 forever destroys . . . the *s·* evidence of matter.
  131–27 the *s·* miracles of olden time
  138–24 the sinful, *s·* pleasure of the senses.
  144– 5 even if these *s·* powers are real.
  144–15 belongs to the *s·* material senses,
  144–23 divine Science wars with *s·* physical science,
  150–18 The science (*s·*) of physics would
  151–32 But this *s·* mind is a myth,
  162–16 false beliefs of a *s·* material existence.
  ph 165–12 Obedience to the *s·* physical laws of health
  168–25 before the *s·* disease made its appearance
  185–11 and such systems of *s·* mind-cure,
  187– 6 Here you may see how *s·* material sense
  188– 8 but afterwards it governs the *s·* man.
  190– 1 formation of *s·* embryonic mortal mind,
  200–21 the *s·* human soul or spirit,
  200–23 These *s·* material senses must yield to
  f 202– 7 the *s·* pains and pleasures of material sense,
  203–25 The *s·* sinner is a suicide.
  204–13 The *s·* second power, evil, is the unlikeness
  210–26 It is the *s·* mortal mind which voices this
  211– 8 sensations of a *s·* mortal mind
  211–17 the nature of all *s·* material cause and effect.
  212–29 possibly that other methods involve *s·* miracles.
  217–23 control which Mind has over *s·* matter,
  222–13 he also had less faith in the *s·* pleasures
  229–19 The *s·* law of mortal mind,
  230–30 *S·* mortal mind or the mind of mortals
  231– 2 or the *s·* physical senses will get the victory.
  232–28 the *s·* pleasures and pains of sense
  242–13 rise superior to the *s·* pain and pleasure of the
  251– 2 The *s·* belief of mortal mind
  251–21 acts upon the *s·* human mind
  253–15 the falsity of *s·* material sense,
  253–27 never requires obedience to a *s·* material law,
  c 257– 4 If matter, *s·*, is substance,
  258–20 material *s·* senses have no cognizance of
  b 275–28 other gods, or other *s·* powers,
  277–23 the order of material *s·* science.
  282– 3 and its opposite, the *s·* material life
  282–27 Error is the *s·* intelligence of mortal mind.
  283–14 with material life *s·*.

so-called
  291– 3 that the *s·* death of the body
  b 292–17 *s·* life of mortals is dependent on
  293–13 The material *s·* gases and forces are
  294–15 This verdict of the *s·* material senses
  296–14 *s·* pleasures and pains of matter perish,
  302–10 and that the *s·* pleasures and pains,
  307– 3 This pantheistic error, or *s·* *serpent*,
  309–29 such *s·* life always ends in death.
  312– 2 such *s·* knowledge is reversed
  334–11 imperceptible to the *s·* personal senses,
  o 347–12 the *s·* mortal man is not the reality of man.
  348–19 well to eliminate from *s·* mortal mind
  356– 4 *S·* material existence affords no
  358– 1 axe, which destroys a tree's *s·* life,
  p 366–19 Such *s·* Scientists will strain out gnats,
  376–18 *s·* material body is a mental concept
  377–26 cause of all *s·* disease is mental,
  378– 8 Without the *s·* human mind,
  379–22 The *s·* vital current does not affect the
  382–16 to teach the *s·* ignorant one.
  382–17 Must we not then consider the *s·* law of
  382–28 nothingness of the *s·* pleasures and
  387–10 nor can *s·* material law trespass
  387–24 It is a law of *s·* mortal mind,
  393– 8 a law of *s·* mortal mind,
  399–11 *S·* mortal mind sends its despatches
  399–22 *s·* mortal life is mortal mind,
  399–32 without beginning with *s·* mortal mind,
  400–26 The action of *s·* mortal mind
  408– 6 universal insanity of *s·* health,
  408–17 *s·* inflammation of disordered functions,
  409–13 independently of this *s·* conscious mind,
  409–16 *s·* conscious mortal mind is believed
  409–22 *s·* "children of men" — *Psal.* 14: 2.
  419–24 in mortals or *s·* mortal minds,
  421– 3 while physical ailments (*s·*) arise from
  423–32 The *s·* substance of bone is formed first
  424–28 scrofula and other *s·* hereditary diseases,
  427–25 in the physical realm, *s·*, as well as in the
  432–27 the hands of justice, *alias* nature's *s·* law;
  441– 3 any *s·* law, which undertakes to punish
  t 463–30 action is that of *s·* mortal mind.
  r 479–13 Take away *s·* mortal mind,
  482–30 mortal mind *s·* is not a healer,
  490–20 knowledge gained from the *s·* material senses
  492– 2 the *s·* dreamer is unconscious?
  493–21 Disease is an experience of *s·* mortal mind.
  g 501–13 *S·* mystery and miracle,
  505–12 mindless matter nor the *s·* material senses.
  509–20 *S·* mineral, vegetable, and
  513– 1 mortal mentality, *s·*, and its claim,
  513–27 *S·* mortal mind — being non-existent
  5?4– 5 and in a thousand other *s·* deities.
  540–14 uncovers *s·* sin and its effects,
  544–29 declares . . . *s·* mortal life to be Life,
  547–14 germinating speck of *s·* embryonic life
  548–28 important facts in regard to *s·* embryonic life.
  554–11 destitute of any knowledge of the *s·* selfhood
  ap 561– 6 at a point of *s·* embryonic life.
  564–21 before the tribunal of *s·* mortal mind,
  gl 580– 7 a *s·* finite mind, producing other minds,
  580–11 a *s·* man, whose origin, substance, and mind
  582– 5 human knowledge, or *s·* mortal mind,
  583–26 *s·* mortal mind controlling mortal mind;
  585– 1 Not organs of the *s·* corporeal senses,
  586–17 between Spirit and *s·* matter.
  589– 6 in which the *s·* material senses yield to
  597–24 Will, as a quality of *s·* mortal mind,
  (*see also* **dead, laws, mind, senses**)

social
  m 56–15 the *s·* scourge of all races,
  f 239– 5 wealth, fame, and *s·* organizations,
  b 340–27 whatever is wrong in *s·*, civil, criminal,
socially
  gl 587– 4 acknowledged morally, civilly, and *s·*.
societies
  a 28–27 because it is honored by sects and *s·*,
society
  aloof from
    s 109–13 kept aloof from *s·*,
  elevation of
    m 63–25 the elevation of *s·* in general
  founding his
    s 138– 2 Jesus purposed founding his *s·*,
  human
    ap 575–31 which binds human *s·* into solemn union;
  motive of
    m 58– 2 To happify existence . . . should be the motive
                  of *s·*.
  sanctioned by
    ph 171– 2 paganism and lust are so sanctioned by *s·*
  state of
    m 64–28 a worse state of *s·* than now exists.

society
sympathy nor
s 153–32 Neither sympathy nor s· should ever

a 28–32 There is too much animal courage in s·
m 57– 2 Without it there is no stability in s·,
an 102–29 employed, for the individual or s·."
f 238–21 Attempts to conciliate s· and so
238–25 S· is a foolish juror,
p 362– 8 debarred from such a place and such s·,
387–18 and perform the most vital functions in s·.

society's
f 238– 7 is to incur s· frown ;

Socrates
m 66–27 S· considered patience salutary
f 215–28 S· feared not the hemlock poison.

Socratic
s 112– 8 adherents of the S·, the Platonic,

sod
g 521– 2 Knowledge of this lifts man above the s·,

soever
pr 1– * *What things s· ye desire— Mark 11 : 24.*
b 305–18 for what things s· He doeth,— *John 5 : 19.*

soft
s 142–11 If the s· palm, upturned to a lordly salary,

softened
p 387– 4 must it pay the penalty in a s· brain?

soft-winged
ap 574–26 and you will behold the s· dove

soil
barren
g 537–16 Error tills its own barren s·
good
b 270–32 the good s· wherein the seed of Truth
of disease
ph 188–24 The s· of disease is mortal mind,
seed and
f 219 10 They produce a rose through seed and s·,
seed or
g 520–25 plant grows, not because of seed or s·,
sown in the
m 66–12 not from seed sown in the s· of material hopes,
till the
g 518– 1 Man is not made to till the s·.

sp 74– 8 a sprout which has risen above the s·.
ph 190–15 as the grass springing from the s·
b 272– 6 s· of an "honest and good heart"— *Luke 8 : 15.*
318–11 They would put soul into s·, life into limbo,
o 361–28 until God prepares the s· for the seed.
t 452–20 We s· our garments with conservatism,
g 521– 1 making him superior to the s·.

solar
g 110–29 perception of the movement of the s· system,
121–25 so far as our s· system is concerned,
122–30 mistake . . . regarding the s· system.
ph 189– 4 we still believe that there is s· light and heat.
f 246–10 The measurement of life by s· years
r 493– 5 and explains the s· system as
g 504– 8 though s· beams are not yet included in the
504–18 words which indicate, in the absence of s· time,
504–31 No s· rays nor planetary revolutions form the
510–21 There is no Scriptural allusion to s· light until
513–11 not yet measured by s· revolutions,
ap 561–28 light portrayed is really neither s· nor lunar,
gl 598–19 YEAR. A s· measurement of time ;
599– 1 the divisor of which is the s· year.

soldier
a 32– 3 In ancient Rome a s· was required to
b 309–11 a prince of God, or a s· of God,

soldier's
a 32– 9 does not commemorate a Roman s· oath,

sole
pref viii–30 for the Bible was her s· teacher ;
xii–11 s· editor and publisher of the C. S. Journal,
f 226–21 man's birthright of s· allegiance to his Maker
p 370–14 faith in the drug is the s· factor in the cure.
g 514– 6 of which God is the s· creator.

solecism
s 114–12 Mortal mind is a s· in language,
f 210–19 The expression *mortal mind* is really a s·,

solely
s 117–25 relates s· to human reason ;
157– 4 succeeds where homœopathy fails, s· because
f 220–16 engendered s· by human theories.
233– 3 proofs consist s· in the destruction of
233–31 sickness, which is s· the result of inharmony
b 299–31 If man were s· a creature of the
p 396–18 but s· on account of the tenacity of belief
g 528– 5 s· mythological and material.
543–28 it is seen that man springs s· from Mind.

solemn
m 61–25 more s· charge, than the culture of your garden
f 232–26 In the sacred sanctuary . . . are voices of s·
p 364–16 Here is suggested a s· question,
433–18 proceeds to pronounce the s· sentence
433–26 the Judge's s· peroration.
434–18 earnest, s· eyes, kindling with hope
ap 575–32 binds human society into s· union ;

solemnity
pr 7– 9 it gives momentary s· and elevation to
p 433– 2 and with great s· addresses the jury

solemnly
r 497–24 we s· promise to watch, and pray

solicitude
m 59– 4 There should be the most tender s·

solid
f 213– 7 conceives of something as either liquid or s·,
242–15 Self-love is more opaque than a s· body.
c 261–26 will neither lose the s· objects and ends of
t 450– 9 A third class of thinkers build with s· masonry.
460–16 Sickness is more than fancy ; it is s· conviction.
g 511–23 To mortal mind, the universe is liquid, s·, and
511–25 and mountains stand for s· and grand ideas.

solids
g 510–24 by the resolving of fluids into s·,

solitary
sp 95–23 Led by a s· star amid the darkness,
c 259– 3 nor is he an isolated, s· idea,
266– 8 Then the time will come when you will be s·,

solution
pref ix–32 degrees by which she came at length to its s· ;
pr 3– 7 and it is our task to work out the s·.
s 109–11 I sought the s· of this problem
b 314– 8 Our Master gained the s· of being,
338–17 of something fluid, of mortal mind in s·.
p 372– 4 matter was originally error in s·,

solve
pr 3– 5 to s· the problem?
a 44– 6 a place in which to s· the great problem
b 273– 6 not one of them can s· the problem of being
329–18 attempts to s· a problem of Euclid,
g 556–27 before it cares to s· the problem of being,

solved
s 126– 4 The problem of nothingness, . . . will be s·,

solvent
f 242–17 with the universal s· of Love

solves
f 216– 6 Science unveils the mystery and s· the problem

solving
sp 90–29 we may as well improve our time in s· the

sombre
g 513– 9 gray in the s· hues of twilight ;

some
pref ix–17 To-day, though rejoicing in s· progress,
xi 3 which action in s· unexplained way
pr 7–32 or mean to ask forgiveness at s· later day.
10–23 There is s· misapprehension of the
16–11 s· doubt among Bible scholars, whether
a 22– 1 would borrow the passport of s· wiser pilgrim,
28–30 await, in s· form, every pioneer of truth.
37–24 to follow in s· degree
54–30 would not s·, who now profess to love
m 61–14 If s· fortuitous circumstance
63–15 civilization mitigates it in s· measure.
64–11 When a man lends a helping hand to s·
65– 9 s· fundamental error in the marriage state.
69–19 S· day the child will ask his parent :
sp 90–14 s· insist that death is the necessary prelude
99–22 None may pick the lock nor enter by s· other
99–19 may possess natures above s· others
s 111–10 s· may deny its right to the name of
112– 8 the Spencerian, or s· other school.
112–10 s· particular system of human opinions.
129–19 and so are s· other systems.
129–26 s· of the leading illusions along the path
131–14 through the . . . churches as s· persons insist?
136–14 "S· say that thou art John— *Matt.* 16 : 14.
136–15 s·, Elias ; and others, Jeremias,— *Matt.* 16 : 14.
136–18 may indicate that s· of the people believed
139–21 darkening to s· extent the inspired pages.
145–15 or reliance on s· other minor curative.
150–24 and will be to all others at s· future day,
ph 182–27 come from s· sad incident, or else
182–32 presuppose that . . . is powerless on s· occasions
187– 9 it attributes to s· material god or medicine
197–28 mortal belief loses s· portion of its error.
f 203–18 or in s· power less than God.
205–19 we perceive the divine image in s· word
223–20 to answer this question by s· *ology*
225–12 There is always s· tumult,
227–10 s· public teachers permit an ignorance of

some

f	228–14	Mortals will s· day assert their freedom
	237–23	S· invalids are unwilling to know the facts
	245–12	S· American travellers saw her when she was
	249–28	It throws off s· material fetters.
c	263–22	the discovery of s· distant idea of Truth ;
	263–24	as when s· finite sense peers from its cloister
	265– 7	and gain s· proper sense of the infinite,
b	294– 7	would take away s· quality and
	297–25	S· thoughts are better than others.
	299– 8	appearing at the door of s· sepulchre,
	306–15	at s· uncertain future time
	319–26	misinterpretation of the Word in s· instances
	326– 8	must not try to climb . . . by s· other road.
	333–21	with s· measure of power and grace
o	342– 5	In the result of s· unqualified condemnations
	353–30	whatever is laid off is . . . s· unreal belief.
	354– 3	"utter falsities and absurdities," as s· aver?
	358–30	in s· Christian Scientist, whom they
p	369–15	in order to discover s· means of healing it.
	376–27	S· people, mistaught as to Mind-science,
	380– 1	may rest at length on s· receptive thought,
	381– 5	or that s· disease is developing
	381– 8	When infringing s· supposed law,
	381–24	quite free from s· ailment.
	403–23	Never conjure up s· new discovery from
	412–12	liable under s· circumstances to impress it
	415– 9	looks upon s· object which he dreads.
	425– 1	or s· of his progenitors farther back
	434– 4	S· exclaim, "It is contrary to law
t	443– 9	severely condemned by s· Scientists,
	444– 2	In s· way, sooner or later,
	450–15	S· people yield slowly to the touch of Truth.
	453–10	but with s· individuals the morbid moral or
	457–25	Departing from C. S., s· learners commend diet
	462– 1	S· individuals assimilate truth more readily
r	477–27	The Indians caught s· glimpses of the
	492–30	uniting on s· impossible basis.
g	522–27	is based on s· hypothesis of error,
	525– 7	s· of the equivalents of the term man
	537–27	is made to appear contradictory in s· places,
	546– 2	at s· future time to choose,
ap	569– 3	Every mortal at s· period, here or hereafter,
	570– 9	will chain, with fetters of s· sort,
	573–30	will surely appear sometime and in s· way.
gl	583– 8	s· of the ideas of God beheld as men,

somebody

sp	81–31	That s·, somewhere, must have known the
	89– 7	believing that s· else possesses her tongue
g	554–15	he learns to say, "I am s· ;

something

absence of
ph	186–12	It is nothing, because it is the absence of s·.

belief in
sp	92–27	laid on a belief in s· besides God.

calls itself
b	287–18	Evil calls itself s·, when it is nothing.

claiming to be
b	330–29	nothing claiming to be s·,
gl	591–25	MORTAL MIND. Nothing claiming to be s·,

conceives of
f	213– 6	Mortal mind conceives of s· as

gains
b	294–29	The thief believes that he gains s· by stealing,

looked for
b	270–14	looked for s· higher than the

mimicry of
gl	580– 9	product of nothing as the mimicry of s· ;

needing
g	501–16	when needing s· more native to their

need of
s	151– 6	an absolute need of s· beyond itself

new
ap	560–25	Persecution of all who have spoken s· new and

nothing and
a	23–17	swinging between nothing and s·,

possible loss of
a	51– 2	the possible loss of s· more important than

practical
o	355– 4	The charge . . . is met by s· practical,

prayed for
pr	9– 8	having prayed for s· better,

seen and felt
p	395–22	to hold it as s· seen and felt

supposes that
g	530–30	supposes that s· springs from nothing,

a	54–23	whose religion was s· more than a name.
sp	91–26	postulate of belief . . . s· apart from God.
s	114–14	the phrase mortal mind implies s· untrue
ph	181–26	to satisfy the sick that you are doing s·
	186–30	Since it must believe in s· besides itself,
f	220–19	and then charges them to s· else,
c	258– 4	human craving for s· better,
	263– 3	even privileged originators of s· which

something

b	323–23	contemplation of s· better than disease or sin.
	338–16	suggests the thought of s· fluid,
o	345–27	if a man think himself to be s·,— Gal. 6 : 3.
	347–26	The dream that matter and error are s·
	350– 1	They think of matter as s·
p	390– 2	and I should like s· more to eat."
	391–25	has no intelligence to declare itself s·
	422–30	he believes that s· stronger than Mind
r	480– 4	the opposite of the s· of Spirit.
	492–15	theories— that matter is s·, or that
g	539– 6	as if life and immortality were s· which
	542–29	misconception of Life as s· less than God,
	556–21	They seem to be s·, but are not.
gl	592–14	there is s· spiritually lacking,

somethingness

b	276–27	Harmony is the s· named Truth.
o	346–12	in order to prove the s·— yea, the allness
	353–21	not continue to admit the s· of superstition,

sometime

m	68– 4	S· we shall learn how Spirit,
p	402–13	S· it will be learned that mortal mind
g	531–10	The human mind will s· rise above
ap	573–30	will surely appear s· and in some way.

sometimes

pr	11– 5	A magistrate s· remits the penalty,
a	24– 6	s· by the worst passions of men),
	47– 8	It was s· an overwhelming power
	55–10	does not the pulpit s· scorn it?
m	64–14	A wife is s· debarred
	68–23	salutary causes s· incur these effects.
s	114–20	we must s· recur to the old and
	143–13	S· the human mind uses one error
	151– 1	To be sure, they s· treat the sick as if
ph	169– 7	s· to his discomfiture,
	172–28	is s· the quickener of manliness ;
f	212– 3	A tooth which has been extracted s· aches again
	215–15	We are s· led to believe that darkness is as
	249–26	mortal night-dream is s· nearer the fact
c	264– 5	the glorious forms which we s· behold in the
b	277–31	s· beautiful, always erroneous.
	327– 9	Evil is s· a man's highest conception of
o	343–21	It would s· seem as if truth were
	345–10	It is s· said, in criticising C. S.,
	346– 6	It is s· said that C. S. teaches the
	358–24	S· it is said : "Rest assured that
p	376– 8	diseases deemed dangerous s· come from
	383–22	s· tells you that the weed preserves his health,
	394–19	their theories are s· pernicious,
	398– 1	S· Jesus called a disease by name,
	398–16	remedies, s· not containing a
	417– 3	Give sick people credit for s· knowing
	421–21	Calm the excitement s· induced by
	421–23	s· explain the symptoms and their cause
	431– 7	s· going to sleep immediately after a
t	446– 6	If patients s· seem worse while
	461–17	you should tell your belief s·,
r	489–31, 32	would have the material senses s· good and s· bad.
	491–18	s· presenting no appearance of mind,
g	549–11, 12	s· through eggs, s· through buds,
	549–13	and s· through self-division.
gl	590–15	this term is s· employed as a title,

somewhat

a	35– 7	they were enabled to rise s· from
s	128–14	escapes s· from itself, and requires less repose.
	143–18	You admit that mind influences the body s·,
	149–18	remarked . . . mind affects the body s·,
	156–11	Believing then s· in the ordinary theories
ph	170–25	to ponder s· the supremacy of
	180– 7	his faith in their efforts is s· helpful
r	488– 8	differ s· in meaning from
g	529–31	He begins his reign over man s· mildly,

somewhere

sp	81–31	That somebody, s·, must have known the
ph	174–23	Anatomy admits that mind is s· in man,

Son

His
a	45–12	by the [seeming] death of His S·,— Rom. 5 : 10.
r	497– 6	We acknowledge His S·, one Christ :

His beloved
a	23– 6	vented upon His beloved S·,

of God
pr	5–29	An apostle says that the S· of God [Christ]
a	29–14	disciples of Jesus believe him the S· of God."
sp	94–11	he made himself the S· of God."— John 19 : 7.
f	203–10	"He made himself the S· of God,"— John 19 : 7.
	226– 9	rights of man as a S· of God,
b	313–16	regarded Christ as the S· of God,
o	361–13	Jesus Christ is not God, . . . but is the S· of God.
g	519–19	of the knowledge of the S· of God,— Eph. 4 : 13.
gl	594–16	The S· of God, the Messiah or Christ.

of Man
r	482–19	he was literally the S· of Man.

Son
of man
s 132–26   "When the *S·* of man cometh, — *Luke* 18 : 8.
136–12   that I, the *S·* of man, am?" — *Matt.* 16 : 13.
b 334–25   Revelator represents the *S·* of man as saying
r 482–17   called himself "the *S·* of man," — *Matt.* 9 : 6.
of the living God
s 137–18   Christ, the *S·* of the living God !" — *Matt.* 16 : 16.

sp 77–16   neither the *S·*, but the Father." — *Mark* 13 : 32.
f 233–13   not even "the *S·* but the Father ;" — *Mark* 13 : 32.
b 268– *   *and with his S· Jesus Christ. — I John* 1 : 3.
305–17   the *S·* can do nothing of himself, — *John* 5 : 19.
305–19   these also doeth the *S·* likewise." — *John* 5 : 19.
313–10   another passage . . . which refers to the *S·* as
337– 9   the *S·* must be in accord with the Father,
g 534–12   The *S·* of the Virgin-mother unfolded the
ap 569– 2   as Truth, represented by the *S·* ;
gl 594–16   definition of

son
Jacob's
gl 581–15   Asher (Jacob's *s·*). Hope and faith ;
582– 4   Benjamin (Jacob's *s·*). A physical belief as to
583–26   Dan (Jacob's *s·*). Animal magnetism ;
586–21   Gad (Jacob's *s·*). Science ;
589– 1   Issachar (Jacob's *s·*). A corporeal belief ;
590–11   Levi (Jacob's *s·*). A corporeal and sensual belief ;
593–12   Reuben (Jacob's *s·*). Corporeality ;
Mary's
b 313–18   the exaltation of Jesus, Mary's *s·*,
Noah's
gl 587–21   Ham (Noah's *s·*). Corporeal belief ;
589– 8   Japhet (Noah's *s·*). A type of spiritual peace,
594–14   Shem (Noah's *s·*). A corporeal mortal ;
of a virgin
b 313– 1   He was the *s·* of a virgin.
332–23   Jesus was the *s·* of a virgin.
of Ham
gl 582–24   Canaan (the *s·* of Ham). A sensuous belief ;
of Jona
s 137–27   Simon Bar-jona, or *s·* of Jona ;
of man
gl 594–17   The *s·* of man, the offspring of the flesh.

a 50–12   to sustain and bless so faithful a *s·*.
o 361–18   Father and *s·*, are one in being.
r 482–17   but not the *s·* of Joseph.
gl 594–17   "*S·* of a year."

song
ph 200– 4   lifted thought into the *s·* of David.
f 234– 5   be it *s·*, sermon, or Science
ap 568–26   A louder *s·*, sweeter than has ever before

Son of God
(see **Son**)

Son of man
(see **Son**)

Son of the living God
(see **Son**)

sons
c 257–21   guideth "Arcturus with his *s·*." — *Job* 38 : 32.
b 315–20   the liberty of the *s·* of God.
g 503– 4   highest ideas are the *s·* and daughters of God.
515–22   all ideas, — the *s·* and daughters of God.

sonship
b 312–32   and entitled him to *s·* in Science.
315–12   hid from their sense Christ's *s·* with God.
316– 7   and to recognize the divine *s·*.
331–31   Christ the spiritual idea of *s·* ;

soon
a 34–24   for *s·* their dear Master would rise again
49– 9   Had they so *s·* lost sight of his mighty works,
s 153–21   and it will *s·* cure the boil.
b 324–23   spiritual light *s·* enabled him to follow the
p 364– 4   manifested towards one who was *s·*,
414–16   explain C. S. to them, but not too *s·*,
417–27   as *s·* as they can bear it,
424– 1   *S·* the child becomes a separate, ... mortal mind,
r 485– 8   only *s·* to disappear because of their uselessness
495–31   *s·* ascertain that error cannot destroy error.
g 534– 4   *s·* to manifest the deathless man of
ap 563–26   to devour her child as *s·* as it — *Rev.* 12 : 4.

sooner
pr 13–14   Do we gain the omnipotent ear *s·* by words than
a 54– 9   must *s·* or later plant themselves in Christ,
sp 91–10   the *s·* error is reduced to its native nothingness,
91–12   the *s·* man's great reality will appear
f 223– 3   *S·* or later we shall learn that the fetters
240–24   Remember that mankind must *s·* or later,
b 296–19   Whether mortals will learn this *s·* or
p 381–21   and you will *s·* grasp man's God-given dominion.
428–25   *s·* or later, . . . we must master sin

sooner
p 429– 6   and the *s·* we begin the better.
t 444– 3   *s·* or later, all must rise superior to
449– 8   Right adjusts the balance *s·* or later.

soonest
pref x–26   The unbiased Christian thought is *s·* touched by

soothe
p 398–26   will *s·* fear and change the belief of disease to

soothing
f 230–25   They are *s·* syrups to put children to sleep,

soporific
p 416–12   when the *s·* influence of the opium is

sorcery
ap 571–30   outshining sin, *s·*, lust, and hypocrisy.

sore
ph 193–21   discharge from the *s·* stopped,
193–21   and the *s·* was healed.
f 237– 6   "Mamma, my finger is not a bit *s·*."
p 398– 5   rent him *s·* and came out of him, — *Mark* 9 : 26.

sorely
a 48– 2   the staves of bigoted ignorance smote him *s·*.

sorrow
and death
f 203–30   waves of sin, *s·*, and death beat in vain.
and joy
s 125–13   pain and painlessness, *s·* and joy,
and pain
ap 573–27   cessation of death, *s·*, and pain.
cup of
a 33–14   and drain to the dregs his cup of *s·*.
has its
m 66–30   *S·* has its reward.
her
ap 562–26   but remembering no more her *s·*
is salutary
m 66– 9   *S·* is salutary.
is turned
pr 14–16   *S·* is turned into joy when the
joy and
f 246– 3   swinging between evil and good, joy and *s·*,
c 262–22   false estimate . . . of joy and *s·*,
multiply thy
g 535– 7   will greatly multiply thy *s·* — *Gen.* 3 : 16.
ocean of
m 67–14   on the seething ocean of *s·*.
pain and
g 557–16   the less pain and *s·* are his.
sin and
f 215–19   So sin and *s·*, disease and death,
with
o 342– 6   one may see with *s·* the sad effects
your
p 386–27   "Your *s·* is without cause,"

pr 5– 3   *S·* for wrong-doing is but one step
f 219– 1   weakness, weariness, *s·*, sin, death,
248–10   Is it imperfection, joy, *s·*, sin, suffering?
b 304–12   joy cannot be turned into *s·*,
304–12   *s·* is not the master of joy ;
p 386–22   Thus it is with all *s·*, sickness, and death.
g 535– 7   in *s·* thou shalt bring forth — *Gen.* 3 : 16.
535–23   in *s·* shalt thou eat of it — *Gen.* 3 : 17.
536–26   Through toil, struggle, and *s·*,
552–22   From a material source flows no remedy for *s·*,
557–18   "In *s·* thou shalt bring forth — *Gen.* 3 : 16.

sorrowful
a 26– 7   all have the cup of *s·* effort to drink
33– 3   His followers, *s·* and silent,

sorrowing
pref xii–25   is joyful to bear consolation to the *s·*
sp 78–29   the sick are healed, the *s·* are comforted,

sorrows
pr 10– 7   to profit by Jesus' cup of earthly *s·*,
10– 7   God will sustain us under these *s·*.
a 41– 5   as well as through their *s·* and afflictions.
42– 9   "man of *s·*" was in no peril from — *Isa.* 53 : 3.
52–19   "man of *s·*" best understood the — *Isa.* 53 : 3.
ph 196–31   The press unwittingly sends forth many *s·*
gl 587–24   motives, affections, joys, and *s·*.

sorry
a 19–21   continues to pray and repent, sin and be *s·*,

sort
ph 195–19   Academics of the right *s·* are requisite.
f 233– 1   nor opportunity in Science for error of any *s·*.
p 406–19   Resist evil — error of every *s·*
408– 1   Every *s·* of sickness is error,
t 451–25   nature and methods of error of every *s·*,
g 508–17   *Gender* means simply *kind* or *s·*,
ap 570– 3   will chain, with fetters of some *s·*,

sorts
c 257–22 Finite mind manifests all *s·* of errors,
p 404–10 Lust, malice, and all *s·* of evil
   419– 4 Errors of all *s·* tend in this direction.

sots
s 158–23 and men and women become loathsome *s·*.

sought
pr 6–20 according as His mercy is *s·* or unsought,
m 60–31 more secure in our keeping, if *s·* in Soul.
s 109–11 I *s·* the solution of this problem
  126–10 has *s·* and interpreted in its own way
  139– 3 theology which the impious *s·* to destroy.
ph 196– 2 Man has "*s·* out many inventions," — *Eccl.* 7 : 29.
f 215–30 Having *s·* man's spiritual state,
b 273– 5 Human belief has *s·* out many inventions,
  314–10 The Jews, who *s·* to kill this man of God,
  329– 3 they will be *s·* and taught,
p 364–18 as Simon *s·* the Saviour,
  439–21 the unfortunate Mortal Man who *s·* your aid
g 531–22 Has man *s·* out other creative

Soul (*see also* **Soul's**)

action of
sp 89–23 The influence or action of *S·* confers a freedom,
allness of
r 497–22 even the allness of *S·*, Spirit,
and body
s 114–24 It lifts the veil of mystery from *S·* and body.
  119–30 reverses the seeming relation of *S·* and body
  122–29 the same mistake regarding *S·* and body
and its attributes
f 210–11 Knowing that *S·* and its attributes were
and matter
f 215– 7 *S·* and matter are at variance
and Spirit
b 335–16 *S·* and Spirit being one,
and substance
b 280–13 sense of the divisibility of *S·* and substance,
as God
b 310–14 Science reveals *S·* as God, untouched by
atmosphere of
gl 587–27 spirituality ; bliss ; the atmosphere of *S·*.
bar of
p 441– 6 not permitted to enter any suits at the bar of *S·*,
belief that
a 39–10 belief that *S·* is in the body causes mortals to
body and
r 477–19 *Question.* — What are body and *S·*?
body instead of by
g 536–16 governed . . . by body instead of by *S·*,
body instead of in
f 223– 5 the illusion that he lives in body instead of in *S·*,
cannot sin
r 468– 6 Because Soul is immortal, *S·* cannot sin,
capacity of
sp 85– 4 which demonstrates the capacity of *S·*,
changeth not
b 310–18 *S·* changeth not.
could reproduce
r 488–28 *S·* could reproduce them in all their perfection ;
explain
ph 200– 8 Whoever is incompetent to explain *S·*
expresses
r 477–30 Separated from man, who expresses *S·*,
facts of
p 420–32 harmonious facts of *S·* and immortal being.
  428– 4 A demonstration of the facts of *S·*
faith in
f 216– 1 his faith in *S·* and his indifference to the body.
false sense of
b 335–23 Only by losing the false sense of *S·* can we
freedom in
m 58–12 There is moral freedom in *S·*.
from sense to
a 48– 9 from earth to heaven, from sense to *S·*.
c 266– 1 and transplant the affections from sense to *S·*,
ap 566– 7 in their passage from sense to *S·*,
God and
b 335–16 God and *S·* are one,
governed by
s 125–16 man governed by *S·*, not by material sense.
b 273–18 Man is harmonious when governed by *S·*.
  302–22 this real man is governed by *S·*
gravitates towards
b 323–21 divine Science, which gravitates towards *S·*
harmony of
p 390– 5 never deny the everlasting harmony of *S·*.
has infinite
m 60–29 *S·* has infinite resources with which to bless
heaven of
g 535–16 into the heaven of *S·*, into the heritage of the
ideas of
b 269–16 exchanges the objects of sense for the ideas of *S·*.
immortal
b 311–20 or that immortal *S·* is in mortal body,

Soul

immortality of
b 306– 7 immortality of *S·* makes man immortal.
r 481–29 hence the immortality of *S·*.
indications of
s 144–13 the weaker the indications of *S·*.
intelligence, or
r 480–17 would make . . . the effect of intelligence, or *S·*,
is immortal
b 311– 7 *S·* is immortal because it is Spirit,
  335–20 *S·* is immortal, it does not exist in mortality.
p 381–13 by the understandng that *S·* is immortal,
r 468– 6 Because *S·* is immortal, Soul cannot sin,
is not in matter
b 300–23 therefore *S·* is not in matter.
is sinless
b 288–22 *S·* is sinless, not to be found in the body ;
is Spirit
f 223–11 *S·* is Spirit, and Spirit is greater than body.
p 396–28 *S·* is Spirit, outside of matter,
is supreme
gl 590– 3 the atmosphere of Spirit, where *S·* is supreme.
is synonymous
sp 71– 7 *S·* is synonymous with Spirit, God,
joys of
p 390–11 pleasures and pains of sense for the joys of *S·*.
law of
m 63– 1 does not make . . . the superior law of *S·* last.
b 311–24 even the higher law of *S·*,
p 427– 3 Life is the law of *S·*,
Life and
o 344– 2 it claims God as the only absolute Life and *S·*,
life in
pr 13–32 is not cognizant of life in *S·*, not in body.
Life or
b 306–13 If Life or *S·* and its representative, man,
Mind is the
b 307–25 divine Mind is the *S·* of man,
g 508– 7 Mind is the *S·* of all.
more
f 247–32 to have less illusion and more *S·*,
no oblivion for
f 214–32 there is no oblivion for *S·* and its faculties.
not qualities of
p 388–25 Because sin and sickness are not qualities of *S·*,
offspring of
a 30–24 the difference between the offspring of *S·* and of
of man
b 280–27 God, the *S·* of man and of all existence,
  307–25 divine Mind is the *S·* of man,
or God
sp 72–11 *S·*, or God, is the only truth-giver to man.
r 468–22 the synonym of Mind, *S·*, or God,
or Mind
b 302–20 *S·*, or Mind, of the spiritual man is God,
or Spirit
s 120– 4 *S·*, or Spirit, is God, unchangeable and
r 466–20 *S·* or Spirit signifies Deity and nothing else.
  466–21 *S·* or Spirit means only one Mind,
over sense
b 322– 5 the control of *S·* over sense,
prayer of
pr 14–23 The Lord's Prayer is the prayer of *S·*,
radiance of
f 247–15 has a glory of its own, — the radiance of *S·*.
rebukes sense
o 350–29 *S·* rebukes sense, and Truth destroys error.
recognize
sp 93– 1 to recognize *S·* as substantial and able to
reflection of
f 249–31 Man is the reflection of *S·*.
reflects
s 120– 5 and man coexists with and reflects *S·*, God,
rejoice in
m 64–21 Then shall *S·* rejoice in its own,
representation of
g 510–16 The sun is a metaphorical representation of *S·*
representatives of
gl 583– 5 representatives of *S·*, not corporeal sense ;
restored his
b 309– 4 to use the word of the Psalmist, *restored* his *S·*,
Science of
s 122– 8 material senses' reversal of the Science of *S·*
  131– 9 opposition of sensuous man to the Science of *S·*
r 467– 2 the demands of the Science of *S·*?
  467–21 This is a leading point in the Science of *S·*,
sense and
f 240–32 how to divide between sense and *S·*.
sense of
gl 582–15 a sense of *S·*, which has spiritual bliss
Spirit or
b 309–25 impossible for infinite Spirit or *S·* to be in a
  330–12 the only Life, substance, Spirit, or *S·*,
r 478– 6 has never beheld Spirit or *S·* leaving a body
gl 598–16 for never did he give up Spirit, or *S·*.

Soul

symbol of
g 595– 1　SUN. The symbol of *S·* governing man,
the senses of
f 213–18　as communicated through the senses of *S·*
　214–29　Neither . . . can interfere with the senses of *S·*,
understanding of
f 210–16　a better understanding of *S·* and salvation.

pr 7–17　Physical sensation, not *S·*, produces material
　9–23　control of Spirit, in which *S·* is our master,
a 30–27　to allow *S·* to hold the control,
m 60–31　more secure in our keeping, if sought in *S·*.
sp 70–15　What are God's identities? What is *S·*?
s 115–14　Life, Truth, Love, *S·*, Spirit, Mind.
ph 172–20　the belief that there is *S·* in sense
f 203–23　believe that the deathless Principle, or *S·*,
　204–31　The error, which says that *S·* is in body,
　207–15　Body is not first and *S·* last,
　215– 4　If Spirit, *S·*, could sin or be lost,
　240–13　to be governed by matter or *S·* in body,
　250– 1　We run into error when we divide *S·* into souls,
b 274– 6　the offspring of sense, not of *S·*, Spirit,
　280–23　the belief that *S·* is in body,
　281–28　Divine Science does not put . . . *S·* into matter,
　282–20　nor can non-intelligence become *S·*.
　300–23　Spirit is God, *S·* ;
　302– 1　*S·* is not compassed by finiteness.
　310–21　If *S·* could sin, Spirit, *S·*, would be flesh
　310–23　If *S·* sinned, *S·* would die.
　310–25　If there was sin in *S·*,
　310–32　neither growth, maturity, nor decay in *S·*.
　317–27　and to the testimony of . . . more than to *S·*,
　335–19　Nothing but Spirit, *S·*, can evolve Life,
　335–21　*S·* must be incorporeal to be Spirit,
o 359–15　evidence of the existence of Spirit, *S·*,
　360–10　replies : . . . and keep *S·* well out of sight.
p 395– 7　leaving *S·* to master the false evidences of the
　427– 4　*S·* is never without its representative.
　427– 6　can no more die . . . than can *S·*,
　407 15　*S·* a criminal though recommended to
r 465–10　God is . . . Mind, Spirit, *S·*,
　467–17　Science reveals Spirit, *S·*, as not in the body,
　467–22　Spirit, *S·*, is not confined in man,
　468– 3　If *S·* sinned, it would be mortal,
　468–26　Life is divine Principle, Mind, *S·*, Spirit.
　477– 6　Man is not a material habitation for *S·* ;
　477– 7　*S·*, being Spirit, is seen in nothing imperfect
　477–22　*S·* is the substance, Life, and
　477–24　*S·* can never reflect anything inferior
　477–26　Man is the expression of *S·*.
　478– 3　What evidence of *S·* or of immortality
　479– 2　offspring of physical sense and not of *S·*,
　481–24　If *S·* sins, it must be mortal.
　481–28　*S·* is the divine Principle of man
　481–30　it is material sense, not *S·*, which sins ;
　482–10　*S·* is properly the synonym of Spirit,
　480 5　Human will is . . . not a faculty of *S·*.
gl 580–24　supposition that . . . *S·* dwells in material
　587– 7　Principle ; Mind ; *S·* ; Life, Truth ;
　588– 9　I, or EGO. Divine Principle ; Spirit ; *S·* ;
　591–16　the only Spirit, *S·*, divine Principle, substance,

soul

absence of
b 311–16　sense of temporary loss or absence of *s·*,
and body
s 123– 6　the error relating to *s·* and body,
ph 196–11　able to destroy both *s·* and body — *Matt.* 10 : 28.
b 338– 6　belief . . . that he is both *s·* and body,
and life
r 466–25　fallacy that intelligence, *s·*, and life can be in
believe that
b 311–20　So long as we believe that *s·* can sin
bodily
c 257– 9　a bodily *s·* and a material mind,
false estimates of
b 311–14　Through false estimates of *s·* as dwelling in
false sense of
b 319– 1　manifests mortality, a false sense of *s·*.
his
ph 166– 9　pilgrimage to Mecca for the salvation of his *s·*.
human
ph 200–21　the so-called human *s·* or spirit,
b 310–19　are commonly taught that there is a human *s·*
hypothesis that
r 482– 4　hypothesis that *s·* is both an evil and a good
is identical
r 482–11　out of Science, *s·* is identical with sense,
is willing
f 235–24　Then when the *s·* is willing
life or
sp 70–15　Does life or *s·* exist in the thing formed?
living
g 524–15　and man became a living *s·*. — *Gen.* 2 : 7.
mind and
g 531– 6　error, . . . that mind and *s·* are both right and

soul

no finite
r 466–21　There is no finite *s·* nor spirit.
not a sinful
b 311–12　It is a sense of sin, and not a sinful *s·*,
r 481–32　sense of sin which is lost, and not a sinful *s·*.
of Christianity
s 140–17　Spiritual devoutness is the *s·* of Christianity.
of Christian Science
s 113– 6　the heart and *s·* of C. S., is Love.
sense for
r 482– 1　substitution of the word *sense* for *s·*
sense of
r 493–26　Any sense of *s·* in matter is not the
theory that
b 300–26　theory that *s·*, spirit, intelligence,
the word
ph 196–13　here the word *s·* means a false sense
r 482– 4　has adulterated the meaning of the word *s·*
　482– 6　The proper use of the word *s·* can always
with all thy
pr 9–18　and with all thy *s·*, — *Matt.* 22 : 37.
your
p 433–20　"May God have mercy on your *s·*,"

sp 77–20　and so prolong the illusion either of a *s·* inert
s 120– 2　never . . . while we admit that *s·* is in body
　122–31　They insist that *s·* is in body
c 257– 9　belief in . . . a *s·* governed by the body
b 295–30　teaches that . . . immortal *s·* is resurrected from
　301–30　This falsity presupposes *s·* to be an
　310–20　taught . . . that *s·* may be lost, and yet be
　318–11　They would put *s·* into soil,
　318–32　The body does not include *s·*, but
　337– 3　as material sensation, or a *s·* in the body,
p 362– *　*Why art thou cast down, O my s·* — *Psal.* 42 : 11.
r 476– 7　will cease to claim that *s·* is in body,
　478–12　Who can see a *s·* in the body?
　485–19　belief that life can be in matter or *s·* in body,
ap 578– 8　[LOVE] restoreth my *s·* — *Psal.* 23 : 3.

Soul-created
b 306–23　not more distinct . . . than are the *S·* forms

Soul-existence
ph 167– 5　*S·*, in the place of sense-existence,

Soul-filled
gl 599– 1　Eternity is God's measurement of *S·* years.

Soul-inspired
f 224–29　On its banner is the *S·* motto,
b 308–14　The *S·* patriarchs heard the voice of Truth,

soulless
f 249–16　Whence then is *s·* matter?

Soul's
p 438–25　without the inspection of *S·* government officers.

souls
s 150–25　doctrine of the predestination of *s·*
f 250– 1　We run into error when we divide Soul into *s·*,
b 280–15　seeks to divide . . . into persons and *s·*.
r 466– 7　*Question.* — What are spirits and *s·*?
　466–19　The term *s·* or *spirits* is as improper as the
gl 587–14　supposititious minds, or *s·*,
　594–18　definition of

Soul-sense
sp 85– 4　This *S·* comes to the human mind when the

sound
pref viii– 8　and gives sweet concord to *s·*.
　x –31　but *s·* morals are most desirable.
sp 84–21　not dependent upon the ear and eye for *s·* or
　88– 5　And the *s·* of a voice that is still.
　89–26　*S·* is not the originator of music,
　97–25　until its inarticulate *s·* is forever silenced
s 126–14　nor sent forth a positive *s·*.
ph 194–23　where neither sight nor *s·* could reach him,
　195– 6　Every *s·* convulsed him with anguish.
f 212–28　that the undulations of the air convey *s·*,
　213–16　*S·* is a mental impression
　213–18　reveals *s·* as communicated through the
　213–26　Mental melodies . . . supersede conscious *s·*.
　214– 2　impressions from Truth were as distinct as *s·*,
　214– 2　and that they came as *s·* to the
b 291– 7　when the last trump shall *s·* ;
　292– 2　then the final trump will *s·*
p 425–29　If you have *s·* and capacious lungs
r 486–16　If death restores sight, *s·*, and strength

sounded
f 223–27　but the last trump has not *s·*,
　226– 7　*s·* the keynote of universal freedom,

sounder
m 61–13　better balanced minds, and *s·* constitutions.

soundness
s 162– 9　restores carious bones to *s·*.

sounds
sp 86–20　or they are images and *s·* evolved

sour
  f 211–20 "the fathers have eaten *s·* grapes, — *Ezek.* 18 : 2.
source
  and condition
  ph 181– 2 God, is the *s·* and condition of all existence
  and means
  pr 10–24 misapprehension of the *s·* and means
  divine
  ph 167–14 the divine *s·* of all health and perfection.
  189–23 They proceed from the divine *s·* ;
  higher
  c 267–23 Thought is borrowed from a higher *s·*
  inexhaustible
  g 507–29 from the nature of its inexhaustible *s·*.
  intelligent
  b 276– 7 but all have . . . one intelligent *s·*,
  its
  a 18–17 The fountain can rise no higher than its *s·*.
  f 246– 9 The stream rises no higher than its *s·*.
  material
  c 256–31 A mind originating from a finite or material *s·*
  g 552–22 From a material *s·* flows no remedy for sorrow,
  not the
  f 211–32 Nerves are not the *s·* of pain or pleasure.
  of all movement
  b 283– 4 Mind is the *s·* of all movement,
  of being
  m 63–10 his primitive and ultimate *s·* of being ;
  f 213–32 discard the one Mind and true *s·* of being,
  of evil
  r 489–24 corporeal senses are the only *s·* of evil
  of joy
  p 377– 4 affliction is often the *s·* of joy,
  of strength
  g 514–31 realization of this . . . was a *s·* of strength
  of supply
  f 206–18 Spirit, not matter, being the *s·* of supply.
  or creator
  b 278– 1 Is Spirit the *s·* or creator of matter?
  prolific
  f 205–12 opposite belief is the prolific *s·* of all suffering
  reach the
  b 326– 6 He, who would reach the *s·*
  same
  r 474–17 then they must all be from the same *s·* ;
  spiritual
  s 152–26 divinely driven to a spiritual *s·*
  b 329–27 If men understood their real spiritual *s·*

  pr 2–29 nearer the *s·* of all existence and blessedness.
  s 119–14 to announce Him as their *s·*,
  p 368–27 the *s·* of all seeming sickness.
  392–16 liable to an attack from that *s·*.
  ap 559– 5 the *s·* of all error's visible forms
  564–17 could emanate from no *s·* except
sources
  ph 180– 1 both prolific *s·* of sickness.
  f 239–29 Those two opposite *s·* never mingle
  p 373–14 are the *s·* of man's enslavement.
  405–32 appeal to divine *s·* outside of themselves.
Southern Cross
  ap 575–30 with the *S· C·* in the skies,
southward
  ap 575–29 *s·*, to the genial tropics,
sovereign
  s 107– 8 the *s·* ever-presence,
  p 407–12 Here C. S. is the *s·* panacea,
  r 495–10 and find a *s·* antidote for error
  g 523–31 the divine *s·* of the Hebrew people,
sovereignty
  s 141–18 Its only crowned head is immortal *s·*.
  152– 4 takes away all its supposed *s·*,
sow
  a 41–10 in the hereafter they will reap what they now *s·*.
sower
  b 272–13 Jesus' parable of "the *s·*" shows — *Mark* 4 : 14.
soweth
  f 210–24 Error *s·* the wind and
  p 405–17 "Whatsoever a man *s·*, — *Gal.* 6 : 7.
  g 537–13 "Whatsoever a man *s·*, — *Gal.* 6 : 7.
sowing
  sp 79–10 and dig up every seed of error's *s·*.
  ph 179–29 *s·* the seeds of reliance on matter,
  180– 4 and to uproot its false *s·*.
  183– 9 without *s·* the seed
sown
  m 66–12 *s·* in the soil of material hopes,
  f 238–18 to reap the harvest we have not *s·*,
  b 272– 7 In the soil of . . . the seed must be *s·* ;
  o 361–29 That which when *s·* bears immortal fruit,
sows
  t 462–12 will inevitably reap the error he *s·*.

space
  all
  sp 78–18 If Spirit pervades all *s·*,
  s 110– 2 Spirit possessing all power, filling all *s·*,
  146–30 and extends throughout all *s·*.
  b 331–22 He fills all *s·*,
  r 469–24 where all *s·* is filled with God.
  g 520– 5 majesty, and glory of infinite Love fill all *s·*.
  brief
  f 206–20 for the brief *s·* of a few years
  immensity of
  g 509–19 as nebulæ indicate the immensity of *s·*.
  infinite
  g 503–16 infinite *s·* is peopled with God's ideas,

  ph 179– 6 since *s·* is no obstacle to Mind.
  ap 573– 2 human sense of *s·* is unable to
  gl 598–20 mortality ; *s·* for repentance.
spake
  pr 15– 3 So *s·* Jesus.
  a 20– 4 but acted and *s·* as he was moved,
  m 64–18 the time cometh of which Jesus *s·*,
  s 121– 5 before he *s·*, astrography was chaotic,
  135–17 "it came to pass, . . . the dumb *s·*." — *Luke* 11 : 14.
  o 348–13 delusions, were cast out and the dumb *s·*.
  g 557–27 when God, Mind, *s·* and it was done.
span
  f 252–22 says : . . . I mean to make my short *s·* of life
  p 387–15 If printers and authors have the shortest *s·* of
spared
  sp 85–28 never *s·* hypocrisy the sternest condemnation.
  p 407–30 Sin is *s·* from this classification, only because
spares
  a 26– 5 Jesus *s·* us not one individual experience,
  r 474–26 Truth *s·* all that is true.
spark
  b 312–15 with scarcely a *s·* of love in their hearts ;
spasmodically
  pr 8– 4 those who come only *s·* face to face with
speak
  pr 1– 5 I *s·* from experience.
  14–29 *s·* "as one having authority." — *Matt.* 7 : 29.
  a 19–12 forebore not to *s·* the whole truth,
  46– 9 has spoken . . . and will *s·* through it
  s 109–31 or whether I *s·* of myself." — *John* 7 : 17.
  130– 7 It is vain to *s·* dishonestly of
  ph 181– 5 Can matter *s·* for itself,
  195– 3 After the babbling boy had been taught to *s·*
  b 283–15 They *s·* of both Truth and error as *mind*,
  319–31 but we can . . . *s·* of the love of Love,
  320– 1 we can *s·* of the truth of Truth
  332–24 appointed to *s·* God's word and to
  o 349–22 shall *s·* with new tongues." — *Mark* 16 : 17.
  354–25 to hear and to *s·* the new tongue.
  p 362– * shall *s·* with new tongues ; — *Mark* 16 : 17.
  395– 6 the healer should *s·* to disease as one having
  412– 8 concerning the truth which you think or *s·*,
  418–28 *S·* the truth to every form of error.
  r 487–13 You *s·* of belief. Who or what is it that
  g 515–27 If you *s·*, the lips of this likeness move
speaketh
  b 292–25 When he *s·* a lie, — *John* 8 : 44.
  292–25 he *s·* of his own : — *John* 8 : 44.
speaking
  a 52–24 *s·* of human ability to reflect divine power,
  52–26 *s·* not for their day only but for all time :
  sp 88–32 the belief that a departed spirit is *s·*,
  89– 4 in the belief that another mind is *s·* through her,
  92–12 and *s·* to Adam and Eve.
  s 160–18 Has mortal mind ceased *s·* to them,
  b 332–10 *s·* to the human consciousness.
  o 349–24 *S·* of the things of Spirit
  p 396– 9 avoid *s·* aloud the name of the disease.
  399–23 Scientifically *s·*, there is no mortal mind
  r 476–28 When *s·* of God's children,
  g 548–18 *S·* of the origin of mortals,
speaks
  sp 72– 3 Principle of man *s·* through immortal sense.
  217–30 Which is tired and so *s·* ?
  o 342–23 It *s·* to the dumb the words of Truth,
  p 391–21 it must be mortal mind which *s·* ;
  441–32 great Teacher of mental jurisprudence *s·* of
  r 485 –5 Mind, not matter, sees, hears, feels, *s·*.
  ap 564–13 Revelator *s·* of Jesus as the Lamb of God
spear
  a 50–32 Not the *s·* nor the material cross
  s 134– 3 truth is still opposed with sword and *s·*.
spear-wound
  a 46–19 to examine the nail-prints and the *s·*.

special
sp 95–18 and is one of the s· characteristics thereof.
s 133–22 carried out in s· theories concerning God,
135–27 nor a s· gift from a ritualistic Jehovah ;
ph 178– 2 they know nothing of this . . . s· person,
f 236– 3 A s· privilege is vested in the ministry.
b 319–30 but we can by s· and proper capitalization
p 364–14 a s· sign of Oriental courtesy.
404– 3 a slave to tobacco, or the s· servant of
408– 9 from the s· name of insanity.
ap 560– 1 has a s· suggestiveness in connection with
specially
s 123–25 did not s· belong to a dispensation now ended,
gl 590–18 unless s· coupled with the name God.
species
  different
g 552–27 The intermixture of different s·,
  floral
m 68–24 perpetuation of the floral s· by bud or
  genus and
b 277–17 the order of genus and s· is preserved
ap 560–20 The botanist must know the genus and s·
  human
   (see **human**)
  many
p 407–29 There are many s· of insanity.
  material
ph 172– 8 How then is the material s· maintained,
  mild
p 408–15 is in itself a mild s· of insanity.
  original
b 277–14 as preserving their original s·,
g 552–28 results in a return to the original s·.
  their
g 549–11 to multiply their s· sometimes through eggs,

ph 189–26 From . . . comes the reproduction of the s·,
r 482–18 As woman is but a s· of the genera,
494– 5 Is it not a s· of infidelity to believe that
g 529–24 the s· described,— a talking serpent,
531–19 maintained by God in perpetuating the s·?
550–25 no instance of one s· producing its opposite.
551–30 in order to propagate its s·,
specific
an 103–19 animal magnetism or hypnotism is the s· term
specifically
c 267– 7 s· man means all men.
specified
pr 11– 2 s· also the terms of forgiveness.
specimen
p 388–17 a s· of the ambiguous nature of
specimens
ph 195–20 impossible ideals, and s· of depravity,
speck
p 413–21 I am not patient with a s· of dirt ;
g 517–14 germinating s· of so-called embryonic life
spectacle
f 241–12 what a mocking s· is sin !
spectators
p 430–25 court-room is filled with interested s·,
spectral
o 353–20 We must give up the s· at all points.
spectre
a 45–25 called him a spirit, ghost, or s·,
b 314–17 To such . . . the real man seemed a s·,
speculation
f 242–26 s· or superstition appropriates no part of
speculative
s 126–20 left to the mercy of s· hypotheses?
149– 6 or a bundle of s· human theories?
ph 195–24 the s· theory, the nauseous fiction.
f 209–26 and all the paraphernalia of s· theories,
229–20 law of mortal mind, conjectural and s·,
speech
pr 3–26 Action expresses more gratitude than s·.
15– 9 according to motives, not according to s·.
b 292–20 "Why do ye not understand my s·?— John 8 : 43.
321– 6 The Hebrew Lawgiver, slow of s·,
t 454–21 strength and freedom to s· and action.
speeches
p 367– 7 gushing theories, stereotyped borrowed s·,
speechless
a 26– 4 in s· agony exploring the way for us,
speedily
pref vii–23 but it cannot make them s· understood.
r 486–27 If this were not so, man would be s· annihilated.
493– 1 C. S. s· shows Truth to be triumphant.
speeds
p 426– 9 expectation s· our progress.

spell
a 39–25 To break this earthly s·, mortals must
Spencerian
s 112– 8 the Platonic, the S·, or some other school.
spend
p 409–29 We cannot s· our days here in ignorance of
spent
ph 174–13 "the night is far s·,— Rom. 13 : 12.
o 354–23 The night of materiality is far s·,
sphere
a 36– 4 simply through translation into another s·.
f 240–15 Its symbol is the s·.
c 265–13 enlarged individuality, a wider s· of thought
b 282– 5 a circle or s· and a straight line.
282– 8 The s· represents good, the self-existent
283–31 or a straight line a s·.
gl 585– 5 A s· ; a type of eternity and immortality,
spheres
m 59–12 the different demands of their united s·,
c 255– 6 changing . . . discord into the music of the s·.
g 513– 7 lead on to spiritual s· and exalted beings.
spike
ph 193– 2 caused by a fall upon a wooden s·
spilled
b 281–31 or the new idea will be s·,
spinal
p 402– 7 dislocated joints, and s· vertebræ.
spire
s 142–12 making dome and s· tremulous with beauty,
Spirit (see also **Spirit's**)
  ability of
s 130–22 the ability of S· to make the body harmonious,
r 494–17 as well as the infinite ability of S·,
  abode of
b 280– 5 light and harmony which are the abode of S·,
  acts
g 520–30 S· acts through the Science of Mind,
  alchemy of
p 422–20 C. S., by the alchemy of S·,
  all is
b 331–25 Hence all is S· and spiritual.
r 475– 3 all is S·, divine Principle and its idea.
  amenable to
p 434–32 immortal and amenable to S· only.
  and flesh
f 254– 7 until the battle between S· and flesh is fought
b 288– 6 this warfare between the S· and flesh
g 530–25 Thus S· and flesh war.
  and God
o 345– 1 S· and God are often regarded as
  and its formations
c 264–20 S· and its formations are the only
  and matter
pref viii– 9 physics teach that both S· and matter are real
sp 73– 1 As readily can you mingle . . . as S· and matter.
73–27 mistake to suppose . . . that S· and matter,
ph 167–31 with S· and matter, Truth and error.
186– 9 S· and matter, good and evil,
f 204– 9 namely, S· and matter,
204–17 a supposed mixture . . . of S· and matter.
211– 3 S· and matter, Truth and error,
b 279–13 S· and matter can neither coexist nor cooperate,
281– 4 S· and matter no more commingle than
285–13 the opposite natures of S· and matter,
296–23 When the evidence of S· and matter,
319–14 S· and matter neither concur in man nor in
p 372–21 Truth and error, S· and matter,
  and the bride
g 548– 1 "The S· and the bride say, Come !— Rev. 22 : 17.
  and the flesh
s 145–28 warfare between S· and the flesh goes on.
b 315–31 the mediator between S· and the flesh,
  and Truth
ph 177–23 against God, S· and Truth.
b 278–15 Hence, as we approach S· and Truth,
  and understanding
r 486–25 reality and . . . are in S· and understanding,
  antipode of
sp 72–19 matter, the antipode of S·.
  antipodes of
b 335–30 the suppositional antipodes of S·,
  appeal to
p 440–21 Mortal Man has his appeal to S·, God,
  aroma of
ph 191–32 Mind, God, sends forth the aroma of S·,
  atmosphere of
sp 70– 6 can never enter the atmosphere of S·.
gl 590– 9 the atmosphere of S·, where Soul is supreme.
  audience-chamber of
p 442– 7 the vast audience-chamber of S·
  audience with
pr 15–12 that man may have audience with S·,

Spirit

baptism of
f 241–27 The baptism of *S*·, washing the body of all the
bar of
p 440– 5 arraigns before the supreme bar of *S*·
based on
ph 191–25 reveals man and immortality as based on *S*·.
being is
a 29–26 with the full recognition that being is *S*·.
belief that
sp 93–21 The belief that *S*· is finite as well as infinite
belong to
ph 192–17 Moral and spiritual might belong to *S*·,
blesses
sp 78–28 *S*· blesses man,
g 512–20 *S*· blesses the multiplication of
born of
b 274–10 Ideas, on the contrary, are born of *S*·,
born of the
t 463–18 the C. S. infant is born of the *S*·,
gl 598– 4 every one that is born of the *S*·
cognizance of
g 543–10 corporeal senses cannot take cognizance of *S*·.
communion with
sp 72– 7 condition precedent to communion with *S*·
contradiction of
g 504–28 and the contradiction of *S*· is matter,
control of
pr 9–23 recognizes only the divine control of *S*·,
Court of
p 434– 9 a trial in the Court of *S*·,
437–10 our higher tribunal, the Supreme Court of *S*·,
437–18 I ask that the Supreme Court of *S*· reverse this
437–28 the Supreme Court of *S*· overruled their
created by
s 148– 8 described man as created by *S*·,
creates
m 69–24 "Do you teach that *S*· creates materially,
b 316–20 the indestructible man, whom *S*· creates,
g 509–13 *S*· creates no other than heavenly or
540– 2 *S*· creates neither a wicked nor a mortal man,
creations of
b 287– 4 All creations of *S*· are eternal ;
day of
g 505– 1 No...planetary revolutions form the day of *S*·.
demonstration of
pr 14– 5 in the demonstration of *S*·.
depend on
ph 181–18 not sufficiently spiritual to depend on *S*·.
diversifies
g 513–17 *S*· diversifies, classifies, and
divine
(*see* **divine**)
divorced from
r 477–31 man, divorced from *S*·, would lose his
duly feeds
g 507– 3 *S*· duly feeds and clothes every object,
echo of
s 126–11 interpreted in its own way the echo of *S*·,
energy of
f 249– 6 Let us feel the divine energy of *S*·,
evolved from
m 69– 3 man and the universe are evolved from *S*·,
existence of
o 359–15 The evidence of the existence of *S*·,
expression of
r 484–30 to the understanding and expression of *S*·?
facts of
f 215–10 matter and mortality do not reflect the facts of *S*·.
b 281–30 as we grasp the facts of *S*·.
faculties of
s 162–14 The indestructible faculties of *S*·
faith in
p 368–16 more faith in *S*· than in matter,
flesh and
(*see* **flesh**)
flesh opposed to
s 114– 4 meaning by this term the flesh opposed to *S*·,
formed by
b 303–10 formed by *S*·, not by material sensation.
forsakes
g 549–28 mistakes nature, forsakes *S*·
foundation of
s 133–26 planted Christianity on the foundation of *S*·,
from body to
p 405–31 to flee from body to *S*·,
from matter into
r 485–14 Emerge gently from matter into *S*·.
from matter to
p 370–31 from error to Truth, from matter to *S*·.
t 459– 1 turn naturally from matter to *S*·,
fruit of the
an 106–27 But the fruit of the *S*· is love, — *Gal.* 5 : 22.
fruits of
p 391–32 and bearing the fruits of *S*·.

Spirit

fruits of the
t 451–18 they bear as of old the fruits of the *S*·.
gained from
a 23–19 the evidence gained from *S*·,
gives the true
r 467–26 *S*· gives the true mental idea.
goal of
b 324–18 certainly before we can reach the goal of *S*·,
God is
s 117– 6 God is *S*· ; therefore the language of
f 207– 2 Because God is *S*·, evil becomes
b 331–14 Scriptures also declare that God is *S*·.
335– 2 There is no evil in Spirit, because God is *S*·.
God, or
gl 580–13 the antipode of God, or *S*· ;
graces of
p 429– 4 as well as by other graces of *S*·.
harmonies of
p 382– 2 opposed to the harmonies of *S*·,
hath not flesh
a 45–27 "*S*· hath not flesh and bones, — *Luke* 24 : 39.
hath not seen
c 255–18 Eye hath not seen *S*·, nor hath ear heard His voice.
heal by the
p 366–32 If we would heal by the *S*·, we must
help of
o 351– 6 Neither can we heal through the help of *S*·, if
he recognized
a 31–10 He recognized *S*·, God, as the only creator,
Holy
o 359– 9 I as a Christian Scientist believed in the Holy *S*·,
idea of
a 29–30 Man as the offspring of God, as the idea of *S*·,
c 266–28 Man is the idea of *S*· ;
ideas of
g 505–11 the ideas of *S*· apparent only as Mind,
if man were
sp 93–27 If man were *S*·, then men would be spirits,
ignorance of
b 280–32 only excuse . . . is our mortal ignorance of *S*·,
image of
g 543– 5 The image of *S*· cannot be effaced,
immortal
s 124–13 which immortal *S*· silences forever.
p 435– 1 commended man's immortal *S*· to heavenly
imparted by
g 514–19 accompanies all the might imparted by *S*·.
imparts
g 505–16 *S*· imparts the understanding which uplifts
individuality of
b 330–16 The individuality of *S*·, . . . is unknown,
infinite
a 49–21 by the renewing of the infinite *S*·.
sp 73– 7 neither the one nor . . . is infinite *S*·,
75–10 to infinite *S*· there can be no matter.
ph 200–20 suppositional antipode of divine infinite *S*·,
200–24 material senses must yield to the infinite *S*·,
b 280–23 belief . . . that infinite *S*·, and Life, is in
295–12 but infinite *S*· being all,
301–27 supposed standpoint outside . . . of infinite *S*·,
309–25 impossible for infinite *S*· or Soul to be in a
319–12 yield to the all-might of infinite *S*·.
331–24 except as infinite *S*· or Mind.
r 475– 3 To infinite *S*· there is no matter,
g 527– 2 God could not put . . . infinite *S*· into
gl 591– 5 MAN. The compound idea of infinite *S*· ;
infinite calculus of
f 209–30 swallowed up in the infinite calculus of *S*·.
influence of
sp 98–10 for it is the healing influence of *S*·
instead of
f 205– 3 will lean on matter instead of *S*·,
b 285–27 and resort to matter instead of *S*·
307–19 out of matter instead of *S*·."
310–22 Spirit, Soul, would be flesh instead of *S*·.
p 430– 7 by resting upon *S*· instead of matter.
instead of by
g 536–17 Created by flesh instead of by *S*·,
inverted image of
gl 580–13 an inverted image of *S*· ;
is all
f 223– 8 If *S*· is *all* and is everywhere,
p 421–17 God, *S*·, is all, and that there is none beside Him.
is all-knowing
r 487–15 *S*· is all-knowing ;
is eternal
b 335–18 *S*· is eternal, divine.
is God
sp 73– 7 *S*· is God, and man is His likeness.
s 120– 4 *S*·, is God, unchangeable and eternal ;
ph 192–10 Spirit is not separate from God. *S*· *is* God.
f 229–12 and at the same time admits that *S*· is God,
b 300–23 *S*· is God, Soul ;

Spirit

is God
p 417–11   S· is God, and therefore cannot be sick ;
r 468–13   S· is God, and man is His image and

is good
pref viii–11   the fact is that S· is good

is greater
f 223–11   Soul is Spirit, and S· is greater than body.

is harmonious
a 29–31   the immortal evidence that S· is harmonious

is immortal Truth
r 468–11   S· is immortal Truth ;

is infinite
m 69–25   or do you declare that S· is infinite,
b 281– 3   and learn that S· is infinite and supreme.

is light
g 504–28   S· is light, and the contradiction of

is more
b 335–19   for S· is more than all else.

is not finite
b 335–22   for S· is not finite.

is not physical
b 285–15   S· is not physical.

is reached
b 279–19   S· is reached only through the understanding

is represented
g 522–20   S· is represented as entering matter

is substantial
b 278–32   if S· is substantial and eternal.

is supreme
b 278–21   S· is supreme and all-presence.

is symbolized
g 512– 8   S· is symbolized by strength, presence, and

is the Ego
f 250– 7   S· is the Ego which never dreams,

is the life
s 124–25   S· is the life, substance, and continuity

is the real
r 468–12   S· is the real and eternal ;

it loses
s 148–16   It loses S·, drops the true tone,

joys of
m 66–14   Love propagates anew the higher joys of S·,
f 242– 7   a great step towards the joys of S·,

language of
s 117– 6   the language of S· must be, and is, spiritual.
117–15   the pure language of S·.

law of
(see law)

laws of
ph 183–19   Laws of nature are laws of S· ;

learn how
m 68– 5   we shall learn how S·, the great architect,

leaven of
s 118–23   until the leaven of S· changes the

life as
g 35– 9   into newness of life as S·.
b 278–24   contradicts the demonstration of life as S·,

Life is
c 264–16   When we realize that Life is S·,
b 310–26   The only Life is S·,
p 376–13   should be told . . . that Life is S·,

likeness of
sp 97–20   man is found in the likeness of S·.
ph 172–19   man is the image and likeness of S· :
b 337– 6   it is not the reflection or likeness of S·,
o 345– 4   the likeness of S· cannot be material,
r 475–10   The likeness of S· cannot be so unlike
g 522–23   in His image, the likeness of S·,
544–24   Man is the likeness of S·,
gl 584–25   not after the image and likeness of S·,

lives in
t 461– 4   and that he lives in S·, not matter.

living
p 388–29   a clear comprehension of the living S·.

Love is
sp 96– 5   spiritualization will follow, for Love is S·.

made all
g 543–25   When S· made all, did it leave aught

matter and
ph 171–18   believes himself to be combined matter and S·.
f 216–20   both matter and S·, both good and evil.
b 312–27   matter and S·, the finite and the infinite,

microscope of
c 264–21   Matter disappears under the microscope of S·.

Mind is
b 310–30   Mind is S·, which material sense cannot discern.
g 517– 8   The life-giving quality of Mind is S·,

Mind or
b 281–14   The one Ego, the one Mind or S· called God,
295–28   the exact opposite of real Mind, or S·,
gl 580– 6   belief, opposed to the one Mind, or S· ;

nature of
s 119–24   it is opposed to the nature of S·, God.

needs no wires
sp 78–19   S· needs no wires nor electricity

Spirit

never dies
b 275– 1   Matter has no life to lose, and S· never dies.

never entered
sp 76–11   understood that S· never entered matter

new-born of
a 35–22   only as we are new-born of S·,

new wine of the
s 114–21   and the new wine of the S· has to be

no cognizance of
b 292–14   this so-called mind has no cognizance of S·.
g 531–29   corporeal senses can take no cognizance of S·.
546–17   material senses can take no cognizance of S·

no evil in
f 207– 1   for there is no evil in S·.
b 335– 2   There is no evil in S·, because God is Spirit.

no sensuality in
sp 71–25   There is no sensuality in S·.

not the reflection of
g 524–23   Matter is not the reflection of S·,

not the vestibule of
o 356– 8   Matter is not the vestibule of S·.

offspring of
m 63– 5   man is the offspring of S·.
g 540– 2   Christ is the offspring of S·,
gl 583– 6   offspring of S·, who, having wrestled with

of life
f 244–11   "The law of the S· of life— Rom. 8 : 2.

of the Lord
f 227–18   "Where the S· of the Lord is,— II Cor. 3 : 17.
r 481– 4   "Where the S· of the Lord is,— II Cor. 3 : 17.

omnipotence of
sp 78–24   How can the . . . omnipotence of S· be lost?
g 522– 1   would set aside the omnipotence of S· ;

omnipotent
ph 194– 1   omnipotent S· shares not its strength with
f 202–30   as if . . . had more power than omnipotent S·.

omnipresent
sp 73–18   omnipresent S· would be destroyed.
f 223– 8   God is infinite omnipresent S·.

one
sp 70– 7   There is but one S·.
79–19   Jesus did his own work by the one S·.
84–10   controlled not by demons, . . . but by the
    one S·.
94– 1   Jesus taught but one God, one S·,
b 275–30   superior or contrary to the one S·.
276– 7   all have one S·, God,
280–14   it seeks to divide the one S· into persons
333–30   The one S· includes all identities.
334–31   but one S·, for there can be but one infinite
gl 591– 3   as the opposite of the one S·, or intelligence,

operation of
g 545–25   the nature and operation of S·.

opposed to
b 338–21   stood opposed to S·.
g 534–17   called energy and opposed to S·.

opposite of
(see opposite)

or Deity
gl 588–23   If used with reference to S·, or Deity.

or God
sp 73–15   If S·, or God, communed with mortals
r 482–11   Soul . . . the synonym of S·, or God ;

or matter
b 324–11   whether it be Truth or error, . . . S· or matter.
o 300–17   Either S· or matter is your model.

or Soul
b 309–25   impossible for infinite S· or Soul to be in
330–11   the only Life, substance, S·, or Soul,
r 478– 5   never beheld S· or Soul leaving a body
gl 598–16   for never did he give up S·, or Soul.

overcome by
p 410–16   the material condition to be overcome by S·,

perfection in
c 264– 3   and their perfection in S· appear.

permanency of
b 293–28   the strength and permanency of S·.

permeated by
sp 72– 5   If a material body . . . were permeated by S·,

pertain to
o 350– 3   and of the things which pertain to S·

physiology and
ph 182–10   We cannot obey both physiology and S·,

physique was not
a 46–13   Master said plainly that physique was not S·,

place of
g 522–18   In this . . . theory, matter takes the place of S·.

plurality of
g 515–18   this plurality of S· does not imply more than one

positive
ph 173–15   For positive S· to pass through a

possibilities of
b 316–31   the possibilities of S· and its correlative truth.

power of
(see power)

Spirit

prerogative of
s 123– 8   the power and prerogative of S·,

proceeds from
r 480–14   Harmonious action proceeds from S·, God.

purification by
gl 581–23   BAPTISM.   Purification by S· ;

quench not the
r 490–19   "Quench not the S·.— I Thess. 5 : 19.

radiance of
f 246–15   the radiance of S· should dawn upon the

radiation of
g 556– 6   radiation of S· destroys forever all belief in

realities of
b 325– 5   ushered into the undying realities of S·.

recognition of
sp 76–32   The recognition of S· and of infinity comes
   90–28   The understanding and recognition of S· must
b 287–30   to the recognition of S· and of the

rectified by
t 460–13   till such thought is rectified by S·.

reflection of
(see **reflection**)

reign of
f 208–22   and prepare for the reign of S·,
gl 587–25   HEAVEN.   Harmony ; the reign of S· ;

renewal of
f 241–14   transformation of the body by the renewal of S·.

representing
b 294–20   between immortal man, representing S·, and

reveals
r 467–17   Science reveals S·, Soul, as not in
gl 596–14   C. S. reveals S·, not matter, as the

rhythm of
g 510– 4   To discern the rhythm of S· and to be holy,

robes of
c 267–26   robes of S· are "white and— Luke 9 : 29.

sanctuary of
pr 15– 4   closet typifies the sanctuary of S·,

Science of
a 31–29   which would attend the Science of S·,
b 270–21   and maintain the Science of S·.
p 369–26   psychology, or the Science of S·, God,

scribe of
ap 571–23   the Revelator, immortal scribe of S·

seed of
g 535– 3   yea, the seed of S· and the seed of matter,

seek to unite
g 555–19   error would seek to unite S· with matter,

senses of
b 274–12   The senses of S· abide in Love,

Soul and
b 335–16   Soul and S· being one,

Soul is
f 223–11   Soul is S·, and Spirit is greater than body.
p 396–28   Soul is S·, outside of matter,

Soul or
r 466–20   Soul or S· signifies Deity and nothing else.
   466–22   Soul or S· means only one Mind,

straight line of
g 502– 6   the straight line of S· over the

strength of
p 393–12   Rise in the strength of S· to resist

submergence in
gl 581–24   BAPTISM. . . . submergence in S·,
   582–22   BURIAL. . . . Submergence in S· ;

submitting to
f 239–20   matter is then submitting to S·.

substance of
b 301–19   the substance of S·, not matter.
r 468–24   reflecting the divine substance of S·.
   480– 1   When the substance of S· appears

substance, or
b 301–11   reflects the eternal substance, or S·,

substantiality of
b 318– 2   to conceive of the substantiality of S·

supposition that
ph 173– 6   supposition, that S· is within what it
g 550–29   supposition that S· . . . can originate the

supremacy of
(see **supremacy**)

sustained by
p 417– 1   their being is sustained by S·,
g 556– 2   That which is real, is sustained by S·.

sword of
a 37– 8   error falls only before the sword of S·.

symbolizes
ap 561–25   The Revelator symbolizes S· by the sun.

synonym of
r 482–11   Soul is properly the synonym of S·,

synonymous with
sp 71– 7   Soul is synonymous with S·,

testimony of
s 128–26   destroys with the higher testimony of S·
f 252–16   contrasts strikingly with the testimony of S·.

Spirit

the only
sp 73–11   God is the only S·.
gl 591–16   the only S·, Soul, divine Principle,

things of
a 21–12   looks towards the imperishable things of S·.
o 349–24   Speaking of the things of S·

tributary to
ap 562– 8   reveals the universe as . . . tributary to S·,

triumph of
s 139– 5   accounts of the triumph of S·, Mind,

true sense of
s 108–29   thereby shutting out the true sense of S·.

unction of
pr 10–10   the unction of S· in demonstration of power

understand
b 283– 1   As mortals begin to understand S·,
r 481– 8   sense never helps mortals to understand S·,

understanding of
a 46–17   rose even higher in the understanding of S·,
ph 186– 6   through the understanding of S·,
b 309– 8   the understanding of S· and of spiritual power.
gl 581–10   the understanding of S·, destroying belief

unity of
s 148–24   to produce the concord and unity of S·

universe of
c 264–32   The universe of S· is peopled with
g 507–15   The universe of S· reflects the creative power

unknown to
r 469– 2   What is termed matter is unknown to S·,

unlike
b 305–22   The inverted images . . . are all unlike S·,
   307–11   shall change sides, not be unlike S·.
r 475–11   likeness of Spirit cannot be so unlike S·.

unlikeness of
b 277–24   The unlikeness of S· is matter,

validity of
g 525– 4   not the validity of S·

verities of
s 109–32   The three great verities of S·,

warreth against
ph 200–22   the flesh that warreth against S·.

warring against
gl 584–12   The flesh, warring against S· ;

wars against
b 274–22   and the flesh wars against S·.
g 531–28   since flesh wars against S·

will form
p 425–25   and S· will form you anew.

will ultimately
m 64–30   S· will ultimately claim its own,

world of
pref viii–32   in the newly discovered world of S·.

worship
o 351–30   They thought to worship S· from a material

would be finite
f 223–12   If . . . S· would be finite,

---

pref xi– 7   the workings, not of S·, but of the fleshly mind
pr 14–11   governed by divine Love,— by S·, not by
a 20– 5   as he was moved, not by spirits but by S·.
   26–10   The Christ was the S· which Jesus implied
   27–13   I [S·] will raise it up."— John 2 : 19.
   28– 6   determination to hold S· in the grasp of
   33–21   Let not the flesh, but the S·, be represented
   52– 3   His master was S· ; their master was matter.
m 63– 9   S· is his primitive and ultimate source
sp 71– 1   nothing is S·,— but God and His idea.
   71– 6   but S·, or the divine Principle of all,
   71–30   Spiritualism therefore presupposes S·, . . . to
   72–18   S· is not made manifest through matter,
   74– 3   To be on communicable terms with S·,
   78–17   If S· pervades all space, it needs no
   78–21   S· is not materially tangible,
   83–18   belief . . . that occasionally S· sets aside these
   83–20   gives to matter the precedence over S·.
   84–28   All we correctly know of S· comes from God,
   89–20   S·, God, is heard when the senses are silent.
   92–16   from matter, or evil, instead of from S·.
   93–22   S·, as a proper noun, is the name of the
   93–27   He is not God, S·.
   94– 2   image and likeness of Himself,— of S·,
an 102– 9   but one real attraction, that of S·.
s 110– 1   S· possessing all power, filling all space,
   111–10   as the Science of God, S·, must,
   113–18   God, S·, being all, nothing is matter.
   115–14   Life, Truth, Love, Soul, S·, Mind.
   119– 8   they assume that matter is the product of S·.
   146–19   and clothes S· with supremacy.
ph 167–20   "flesh lusteth against the S·."— Gal. 5 : 17.
   170– 6   faith in matter instead of in S·.
   171–18   believes that S· is sifted through matter,
   172–10   S· can form no real link in this
   173–13   nor the manifestation of S· is obtainable through
   173–13   S· is positive.
   173–14   Spirit's contrary, the absence of S·.

Spirit

ph 181– 5 "Who art thou that repliest to *S·*?
183– 1 Truth, makes all things possible to *S·*;
183– 2 so-called laws of matter would render *S·*
192– 9 *S·* is not separate from God.   Spirit *is* God.
200– 5 advanced . . . to the worship of God in *S·*
f 205–31 into the scale, not of *S·*, . . . but of matter.
206–17 *S·*, not matter, being the source of supply.
207– 1 but these evils are not *S·*,
208– 2 which affords no proof of God, *S·*,
208–15 to suppose that . . . . *S·*, God, produces disease
209–22 translation of man and the universe back into *S·*.
211–28 for their immortality is not in *S·*,
213–12 and is a tendency towards God, *S·*.
215– 4 If *S·*, Soul, could sin or be lost,
223– 2 "Walk in the *S·*, and ye shall not — *Gal.* 5: 16.
223– 6 in matter instead of in *S·*.
223– 7 Matter does not express *S·*.
223–12 If *S·* were once within the body,
223–13 and therefore could not be *S·*.
232–10 all good is possible to *S·*;
234– 3 If we trust matter, we distrust *S·*.
246– 8 endeavoring to reach *S·*
249–21 The I is *S·*.
252–12 man created by and of *S·*,
252–31, 32 *S·*, bearing opposite testimony, saith : I am *S·*.
253–30 the law of . . . *S·* instead of the flesh.
c 255– * *have the firstfruits of the S·,* – *Rom.* 8: 23.
257– 4 If matter, so-called, is substance, then *S·*,
257– 6 The theory that *S·* is not the only substance
259–23 God, *S·*, works spiritually, not materially.
260–32 If we look to the body . . . for *S·*, we find
265–11 forsaking matter for *S·*, by no means suggests
267– 4 They are in and of *S·*, divine Mind,
b 274– 6 the offspring of sense, not of Soul, *S·*,
275– 4 shows that matter did not originate in God, *S·*,
275– 7 *S·*, is All-in-all, and that there is no other might
275–12 *S·*, Life, Truth, Love, combine as one,
277– 8 As God Himself is good and is *S·*,
277–20 Error . . asserts that *S·* produces matter
277–24 The realm of the real is *S·*.
278– 1 Is *S·* the source or creator of matter?
278– 2 nothing in *S·* out of which to create matter.
278– 4 *S·* is the only substance and consciousness
278– 7 In *S·* there is no matter,
278–10 *S·*, God, is infinite, all.
278–11 *S·* can have no opposite.
278–18 another admission, — namely, that *S·* is not
281–12 the image and likeness of perfect Mind, *S·*,
282–16 matter has no place in *S·*,
282–16 and *S·* has no place in matter.
284–17 which receive no direct evidence of *S·*,
284–22 They can neither see *S·* through the eye nor
284 23 nor can they feel, taste, or smell *S·*.
286–23 since God, *S·*, is the only cause, they lack a
286–25 The temporal . . . are not then creations of *S·*.
288–19 people of God" (of *S·*). — *Heb.* 4: 9.
288–23 *S·* is not, and cannot be, materialized ;
289– 7 Then *S·* will have overcome the flesh.
289–29 *S·* and all things spiritual are the real
289–31 Man is not the offspring of flesh, but of *S·*,
294– 4 human belief, . . . a unison of matter with *S·*.
300–24 If *S·* were in matter,
302–28 not in any bodily . . . likeness to *S·*.
307–13 as much as God, *S·*, who *is* the only Life."
307–28 material laws which *S·* never made ;
310–21 If Soul could sin, *S·*, Soul, would be flesh
310–26 the annihilation of *S·* would be inevitable.
310–27 if *S·* should lose Life as God, good, then *S·*,
311– 7 Soul is immortal because it is *S·*,
313–31 To show that the substance of himself was *S·*
317–25 looking . . . in matter instead of in *S·*
318– 4 Mind and immortality, in which *S·* reigns
330–20 *S·* is divine Principle,
331–15 Therefore in *S·* all is harmony,
334– 7 not that the Father is greater than *S·*,
334–31 *S·* being God, there is but one Spirit,
335– 3 The theory, that *S·* is distinct from matter but
335– 7 *S·*, God, has created all in and of Himself.
335– 8 *S·* never created matter.
335– 8 nothing in *S·* out of which matter could be
335–12 *S·* is the only substance,
335–19 Nothing but *S·*, Soul, can evolve Life,
335–22 Soul must be incorporeal to be *S·*,
339– 8 God, *S·*, alone created all,
340–18 It inculcates the tri-unity of God, *S·*, Mind ;
o 344–32 the word *S·* is so commonly applied to Deity,
347– 1 flesh lusteth against the *S·*," — *Gal.* 5: 17.
347– 1 and the *S·* against the flesh." — *Gal.* 5: 17.
349–32 In C. S., substance is understood to be *S·*,
351–29 To them . . . *S·* was shadow.
356–24 Does God create a material man out of Himself, *S·*?
357–31 Can matter drive Life, *S·*, hence,
p 411–10 If *S·* . . . bear witness to the truth,

Spirit

p 420– 4 *S·* not matter, governs man.
425–19 since *S·*, God, is All-in-all.
427–27 *S·* is his last resort, but it should have
435– 1 *S·* which is God Himself
437–15 *S·* not allowed a hearing ;
441–19 *S·* decides in favor of Man
r 465–10 *S·*, Soul, Principle, Life, Truth, Love.
467– 4 This *me* is *S·*.
467–22 *S·*, Soul, is not confined in man,
467–25 when we conclude that matter is the effect of *S·* ;
467–27 We cannot interpret *S·*, Mind, through matter.
468–21 *S·*, the synonym of Mind, Soul, or God,
468–26 Life is divine Principle, Mind, Soul, *S·*.
477– 7 Soul, being *S·*, is seen in nothing imperfect
477–25 can never reflect anything inferior to *S·*.
477–30 *S·* would be a nonentity ;
479– 8 neither self-existent nor a product of *S·*.
479–22 the only facts are *S·* and its
480– 5 the opposite of the something of *S·*.
481– 2 Man is tributary to God, *S·*,
485–16 come naturally into *S·* through better health
487–27 The understanding that Life is God, *S·*,
497–22 even the allness of Soul, *S·*,
g 503–28 God, *S·*, dwelling in infinite light and
504–31 nothing but a supposition of the absence of *S·*.
506–10 *S·*, God, unites understanding to
506–18 *S·*, God, gathers unformed thoughts into their
507– 6 *S·* names and blesses all.
509– 2 when *S·* is discerned to be the Life of all,
518–27 divine Principle, or *S·*, comprehends and
518–29 Nothing is new to *S·*.
521– 9 in the keeping of *S·*, not matter,
522–26 *S·* as supposedly cooperating with matter
524–28 Could *S·* evolve its opposite, matter,
524–29 Is *S·*, God, injected into dust,
524–31 Does *S·* enter dust, and lose therein the
531–27 Is Life sustained by matter or by *S·*?
534–22 not in the flesh, but in the *S·*, — *Rom.* 8: 9.
539– 4 begins by reckoning life as separate from *S·*,
539– 8 What can be the standard of good, of *S·*,
539 14 Has *S·* resigned to matter the government
544– 2 *S·* had no participation in it.
546– 4 *S·*, God, never germinates,
550– 9 *S·* cannot become matter,
550– 9 nor can *S·* be developed through its opposite.
ap 575–25 It is indeed a city of the *S·*,
gl 583–20 CREATOR.   *S·* ; Mind ; intelligence ;
586–17 between *S·* and so-called matter.
587– 7 Principle ; Mind ; Soul ; *S·* ;
587–19 GOOD.   God ; *S·* ; omnipotence ; omniscience ;
588– 9 I, or EGO.   Divine Principle ; *S·* ; Soul ;
594–19 definition of

spirit

and in life
a 39–22 to experience that salvation in *s·* and in life.
and in truth
u 31 27 the Father in *s·* and in truth." — *John* 4 : 23.
sp 93– 7 the Father in *s·* and in truth." — *John* 4 : 23.
o 140–21 the Father in *s·* and in truth." — *John* 4 : 23.
and power
a 55–25 with the *o·* and power of Christian healing.
bear witness
b 330– 9 and the letter and the *s·* bear witness,
belief that
sp 73–22 the belief that *s·* is confined in a
chills the
c 256–26 it chills the *s·* of Christianity.
deaf
p 308– 2 "Thou dumb and deaf *s·*, I charge — *Mark* 9 : 25.
departed
sp 88–32 belief that a departed *s·* is speaking,
finite
sp 93–28 Finite *s·* would be mortal,
no other
b 340–19 shall have no other *s·* or mind but God,
of Christ
t 462– 4 and imbibes the *s·* of Christ,
offspring of
f 229–11 calls both the offspring of *s·*,
of God
s 137–20 the *s·* of God, of Truth, Life, and Love,
r 480– 3 Where the *s·* of God is,
g 503– 8 And the *s·* of God moved — *Gen.* 1 : 2.
534–22 if so be that the *s·* of God — *Rom.* 8 : 9.
of Life
p 433–31 Ah ! but Christ, Truth, the *s·* of Life
of Science
s 145– 4 So . . . imbued were they with the *s·* of Science,
of the Christ
s 131–23 As aforetime, the *s·* of the Christ,
of Truth
p 391– 1 in the conscious strength of the *s·* of Truth
418–24 and especially by the *s·* of Truth and Love
427– 3 law of Soul, even the law of the *s·* of Truth,
t 455– 1 into accord with the *s·* of Truth and Love,

spirit

requires the
ap 571– 8 It requires the *s·* of our blessed Master
revealed the
r 483–21 God certainly revealed the *s·* of C. S.,
rich in
g 518–15 The rich in *s·* help the poor
so-called
sp 73–12 Any other control or attraction of so-called *s·*
soul nor
r 466–21 There is no finite soul nor *s·*.
soul or
ph 200–21 the so-called human soul or *s·*,
supposition that
gl 587– 2 a supposition that *s·* is finite,
unity of
m 58– 3 Unity of *s·* gives new pinions to joy,
was not
o 352– 6 declared that his material body was not *s·*,
without the
s 145– 6 and that letter, without the *s·*, would have
t 451– 9 and think to succeed without the *s·*,
worshipped in
ap 576–14 He must be worshipped in *s·* and in love.

———

pref xii–23 In the *s·* of Christ's charity,
a 45–25 Even his disciples at first called him a *s·*,
45–28 reappearing of Jesus was not the return of a *s·*.
sp 73– 5 but another, . . . it terms a *s·*.
73– 8 The belief that one man, as *s·*, can control
73–24 belief that . . . *s·* retains the sensations
75– 2 assumption that man . . . comes to life as *s·*.
80– 8 as follows: "There never was, . . . an immortal *s·*."
93–26 The modifying derivatives of the word *s·*
s 113– 5 but its *s·* comes only in small degrees.
136–19 believed that Jesus was. . .controlled by the *s·* of
f 203–12 the only true *s·* is Godlike.
239–21 The objects we pursue and the *s·* we manifest
b 283–16 They speak of both . . . good and evil as *s·*.
295–32 Thus error theorizes that *s·* is born of matter
300–26 The theory that soul, *s·*, . . . inhabits matter
307–12 It says: . . . I will put *s·* into what I call
317– 5 insisted on . . . the insignificance of *s·*,
320–12 My *s·* shall not always strive— *Gen.* 6 : 3.
320–15 My *s·* shall not forever rule [or be humbled]
341– * *But if the s· of Him* — *Rom.* 8 : 11.
341– * *by His s· that dwelleth* — *Rom.* 8 : 11.
356–15 "It is the *s·* that quickeneth ;— *John* 6 : 63.
p 398– 4 *s·* [error] cried, and rent him— *Mark* 9 : 26.
t 456– 4 contrary to its *s·* or rules,
r 478– 7 the theory of indwelling *s·*,
495–28 Study . . . the letter and imbibe the *s·*.
g 546– 1 false belief that *s·* is now submerged in
ap 573–11 what the human mind terms matter and *s·*
574–11 carried John away in *s·*,
gl 598– 2 word for *wind (pneuma)* is used also for *s·*,

spirit-communications
sp 80–10 repeats weekly the assertion that *s·* are

spiritism
sp 77–28 *S·* consigns the so-called dead to a state
78–25 where *s·* makes many gods,

Spirit-rule
o 351–23 they cannot work out the *S·* of Christian

Spirit's
pref viii–11 and matter is *S·* opposite.
sp 71– 6 is not *in S·* formations.
ph 173–14 Matter is *S·* contrary,
173–16 would be *S·* destruction.
f 214–32 *S·* senses are without pain,
b 287–27 the objective supposition of *S·* opposite.
302–31 reproduction by *S·* individual ideas
g 525– 4 not the validity of Spirit or *S·* creations.
gl 580–18 the usurper of *S·* creation,

spirits (*see also* **spirits'**)
alleged
sp 81–14 Nor is the case improved when alleged *s·* teach
and electricity
sp 80–29 believes that . . . emanates from *s·* and electricity.
departed
sp 88–31 said to be . . . from the impulsion of departed *s·*.
evil
sp 70–11 supposition . . . that there are good and evil *s·*,
79–17 Jesus cast out evil *s·*, or false beliefs.
f 206–32 There are evil beliefs, often called evil *s·* ;
b 307–10 It says : . . . God makes evil minds and evil *s·*,
familiar
sp 70– * *them that have familiar s·,* — *Isa.* 8 : 19.
ministering
o 360–26 in His ministering *s·*, — see *Job* 4 : 18.
not by
a 20– 5 moved, not by *s·* but by Spirit.

spirits

so-called
sp 72– 9 So-called *s·* are but corporeal communicators.
unseen
f 212–22 mortals believe that unseen *s·* produce the

a 24–25 as a proof that *s·* can return to earth?
sp 70–10 supposition that corporeal beings are *s·*,
71–28 Its *s·* are so many corporealities,
77–22 Even if communications from *s·* to
84–10 controlled not by demons, *s·*, or demigods,
84–26 material personalities called *s·*,
88–17 and at another are called *s·*.
93–28 If man were Spirit, then men would be *s·*,
98–10 the healing influence of Spirit (not *s·*)
b 335– 1 There are neither *s·* many nor gods many.
r 466– 7 *Question.*— What are *s·* and souls?
466–19 The term *souls* or *s·* is as improper as the
gl 594–22 definition of

Spiritual
s 127– 9 The terms Divine Science, *S·* Science,

spiritual

actuality
g 502–13 and the *s·* actuality of man,
adherence
m 65–28 find . . . peace in a more *s·* adherence.
advancement
p 429–10 in the line of *s·* advancement.
affection
p 366–17 Not having this *s·* affection,
agreement
b 333– 1 *s·* agreement, between God and man in His
and eternal
 (*see* **eternal**)
apprehension
o 349–28 is educated up to *s·* apprehension.
g 506–12 calm and exalted thought or *s·* apprehension
ascendency
m 67–20 remember that through *s·* ascendency
ascension
g 509–25 The periods of *s·* ascension are the
atmosphere
g 512–11 abound in the *s·* atmosphere of Mind,
attainments
pr 10–15 *S·* attainments open the door to a
baptism
f 242– 1 repentance, *s·* baptism, and regeneration,
barrenness
p 366– 7 while his own *s·* barrenness debars him from
basis
s 124– 7 Having neither moral might, *s·* basis, nor
160– 5 forsake the material for the *s·* basis
ph 169– 2 change of belief from a material to a *s·* basis.
b 322– 4 standpoints . . . from a material to a *s·* basis,
g 555–23 Creation rests on a *s·* basis.
beauty
b 304– 4 which hide *s·* beauty and goodness.
being
a 33– 8 It was the great truth of *s·* being,
33–13 For this truth of *s·* being,
sp 76–12 *s·* being and the understanding of God,
ph 167–26 but one way . . . which leads to *s·* being.
c 264–29 and recognize man's *s·* being,
b 325–13 When *s·* being is understood in all its
g 544–23 the very antipodes of immortal and *s·* being.
gl 586–21 Science ; *s·* being understood ;
being is
sp 76–26 indestructible man, whose being is *s·*.
beings
c 264–32 universe of Spirit is peopled with *s·* beings,
birth
t 463–11 in the travail of *s·* birth.
blessings
a 53–17 *s·* blessings which might flow from
g 512–15 *s·* blessings, thus typified, are the
bliss
gl 582–15 a sense of Soul, which has *s·* bliss
bodies
sp 73–20 belief that . . . rise up as *s·* bodies
breakfast
a 34–30 his last *s·* breakfast with his disciples
building
f 241–26 the corner-stone of all *s·* building is purity.
capacity
ph 179– 8 the *s·* capacity to apprehend thought
causation
ph 170–22 *S·* causation is the one question to be
170–23 *s·* causation relates to human progress.
cause
s 111–23 rather than to a final *s·* cause,
b 268– 4 to the *s·* cause of those lower things
313–25 and found the *s·* cause.
class
b 290–13 To the *s·* class, relates the Scripture :

spiritual

clear-sightedness
  b 316–14 *s·* clear-sightedness and the blindness of
command
  ph 168–19 God's *s·* command relating to perfection,
communion
  a 35–25 Our Eucharist is *s·* communion with the
compensation
  gl 581–15 Hope and faith ; *s·* compensation ;
conceptions
  o 349–16 to the expression of *s·* conceptions
conclusions
  b 300– 2 when it attempts to draw correct *s·* conclusions
condition
  t 460–27 from her own *s·* condition,
consciousness
  pr 16–21 heaven-born aspiration and *s·* consciousness,
  c 261–28 you will rise to the *s·* consciousness of being,
  b 269–17 real and tangible to *s·* consciousness,
  ap 574– 1 This *s·* consciousness is therefore a
  577– 9 In this divinely united *s·* consciousness,
creation
  m 56– 8 Until the *s·* creation is discerned intact,
  f 208– 2 which affords no proof . . . of the *s·* creation.
  b 287–31 recognition of Spirit and of the *s·* creation.
  332– 5 His tender relationship to His *s·* creation.
  g 507– 5 as it appears in the line of *s·* creation,
  511– 6 magnitude, and infinitude of *s·* creation.
  519– 4 since the *s·* creation was the outgrowth,
  521– 7 this brief, glorious history of *s·* creation
  534– 2 Hence she is first . . . to discern *s·* creation.
  gl 590–22 the record of *s·* creation.
culture
  f 235–13 a moral and *s·* culture, which lifts one higher.
death
  b 310–24 and *s·* death is oblivion.
demand
  p 385– 7 The *s·* demand, quelling the material,
demands
  r 483– 9 must not be ignorant of the moral and *s·* demands
development
  m 66–11 *S·* development germinates not from
  g 547–27 not in material history but in *s·* development.
devoutness
  s 140–17 *S·* devoutness is the soul of Christianity.
discernment
  gl 586– 3 Eyes. *S·* discernment,
discovery
  p 380–22 Many years ago the author made a *s·* discovery,
distance
  a 47–20 this *s·* distance inflamed Judas' envy.
draughts
  f 234– 1 *S·* draughts heal,
dulness
  a 34–22 to raise themselves and others from *s·* dulness
energies
  p 387– 9 *s·* energies can neither wear out nor
era
  m 65–16 struggling against the advancing *s·* era.
essence
  a 25– 3 The *s·* essence of blood is sacrifice.
estate
  g 548– 7 man has never lost his *s·* estate
evangel
  b 308–24 Then said the *s·* evangel :
evidence
  a 52– 6 His senses drank in the *s·* evidence of
  b 297–21 *s·* evidence, contradicting the testimony of
  gl 585– 9 *s·* evidence opposed to material sense ;
evidences
  b 289–17 destroys with the *s·* evidences of Life ;
evolution
  s 135– 9 *S·* evolution alone is worthy of the
exaltation
  b 314– 2 (his further *s·* exaltation),
existence
  sp 72– 1 There is but one *s·* existence,
  f 222– 2 as we better apprehend our *s·* existence
  c 265– 3 Man understands *s·* existence in proportion as
  b 273–20 which reveals the laws of *s·* existence.
  315–13 They could not discern his *s·* existence.
  o 356– 5 affords no evidence of *s·* existence
  r 492– 4 fact before the thought, namely, *s·* existence.
  g 540– 2 *s·* existence shows that Spirit
  gl 580–10 the great reality of *s·* existence and creation
  593–10 higher idea of immortality, or *s·* existence ;
fact
  a 20–25 to acknowledge what the *s·* fact implies.
  s 121–30 thus brought nearer the *s·* fact,
  129– 7 If you wish to know the *s·* fact,
  f 207–28 The *s·* fact, repeated in the action of man
  209–11 they all must give place to the *s·* fact
  b 289–25 The *s·* fact and the material belief
  320–18 declares plainly the *s·* fact of being,
  o 356– 3 before the *s·* fact is attained.

spiritual

fact
  p 428–22 The great *s·* fact must be brought out
  gl 585–11 C. S., with which can be discerned the *s·* fact
factor
  ph 185–20 excludes the human mind as a *s·* factor
facts
  sp 91–23 that the *s·* facts may be better apprehended.
  s 130–17 beliefs which war against *s·* facts ;
  147–22 enables you to grasp the *s·* facts of being
  ph 173–27 to the recognition of *s·* facts,
  f 207–30 *S·* facts are not inverted ;
  213– 8 Immortal and *s·* facts exist apart from
  254– 9 before the *s·* facts of existence are gained
  b 312– 3 is reversed by the *s·* facts of being
  p 370–18 The moral and *s·* facts of health,
  402–12 material beliefs will not interfere with *s·* facts.
  428–10 that the *s·* facts of being may appear,
  g 546–24 The great *s·* facts of being,
  ap 574–12 till he became conscious of the *s·* facts of being
  gl 584–16 for it contradicts the *s·* facts of being.
  592–18 the *s·* facts and harmony of the universe ;
forces
  b 293–14 counterfeits of the *s·* forces of divine Mind,
forms
  g 503–17 reflecting Him in countless *s·* forms.
foundation
  s 136– 2 maintained his mission on a *s·* foundation
  gl 593–18 Rock. *S·* foundation ; Truth.
  599– 6 Zion. *S·* foundation and superstructure ;
freedom
  s 118–12 eternally glorified in man's *s·* freedom.
  p 366– 5 and thus attain the *s·* freedom which
gain
  g 501–10 richly recompensing human want and woe with *s·* gain.
God
  f 214–21 more than they do a *s·* God.
good
  m 56– 6 for the advancement of *s·* good.
  f 243– 2 the Science and demonstration of *s·* good
  g 505–20 Spiritual sense is the discernment of *s·* good.
government
  gl 597–28 the movements of God's *s·* government,
gravitation
  g 536–11 If man's *s·* gravitation and attraction to
groundwork
  s 147–19 will plant you firmly on the *s·* groundwork
growth
  pr 2–21 an error which impedes *s·* growth.
  5– 1 hinders man's *s·* growth
  7–13 reaction unfavorable to *s·* growth,
  sp 91 8 great point of departure for all true *s·* growth.
  94–30 indicates *s·* growth and union with the
  f 243–15 arises . . . from lack of *s·* growth.
  c 260 28 this education is at the expense of *s·* growth.
  p 368–24 disappears in the ratio of one's *s·* growth.
  t 461–31 Systematic teaching and the student's *s·* growth
  r 485–17 and as the result of *s·* growth.
guides
  f 205 20 They should be wise *s·* guides
  b 299–16 giving earnest heed to these *s·* guides
happiness is
  m 57–18 Happiness is *s·*, born of Truth and Love.
harmony
  f 248– 2 glorious freedom of *s·* harmony.
  b 288–14 will cease, and *s·* harmony reign.
  g 503– 9 divine Principle and idea constitute *s·* harmony,
  521 3 conscious *s·* harmony and eternal being.
healing
  p 367– 1 must not hide the talent of *s·* healing
heavens
  ap 562–17 They are the lamps in the *s·* heavens of the age,
history
  f 204– 5 that material history is as real . . . as *s·* history ;
  g 551– 7 In *s·* history, matter is not the
idea
  a 29–28 and woman perceived its *s·* idea,
  30– 2 Hence he could give a more *s·* idea of life
  38–26 the Christ, the *s·* idea of divine Love.
  45–20 possible at-one-ment with the *s·* idea of man
  55– 8 the healing Christ and *s·* idea of being.
  s 109–24 When a new *s·* idea is borne to earth,
  115–15 Man : God's *s·* idea,
  132–14 The Pharisees of old thrust the *s·* idea
  132–21 unconscious of the reappearing of the *s·* idea,
  ph 194– 4 coincidence of the *s·* idea of man with the
  f 233–21 and by understanding the *s·* idea
  c 267– 2 the *s·* idea, whose substance is in Mind,
  b 315–15 God's *s·* idea as presented by Christ Jesus.
  316–13 Hence the warfare between this *s·* idea and
  316–16 conclusion that the *s·* idea could be killed
  316–24 The *s·* idea of God, as presented by Jesus,
  331–30 Christ the *s·* idea of sonship ;
  333–20 the Christ, as the *s·* idea, — the reflection

spiritual

idea

b 334– 4 the s· idea, Christ, dwells forever in the
339–21 has yielded to a more s· idea of Deity,
o 361– 4 Christ, as the true s· idea, is the ideal of God
t 463–12 A s· idea has not a single element of
r 496–15 it is the s· idea, the Holy Ghost and Christ,
g 518–19 Love giveth to the least s· idea might,
534–28 will struggle to destroy the s· idea of Love ;
534–30 s· idea has given the understanding a foothold
542– 4 Material beliefs would slay the s· idea
546–17 can take no cognizance of Spirit or the s· idea.
ap 561– 9 The Revelator beheld the s· idea
561–14 the correlation of divine Principle and s· idea,
561–21 and the s· idea is understood.
561–23 generic man, the s· idea of God ;
561–26 The s· idea is clad with the radiance of
562– 1 John saw in those days the s· idea
562– 6 s· idea of God's motherhood.
562–11 The s· idea is crowned with twelve stars.
562–18 which show the workings of the s· idea
562–24 the s· idea is typified by a woman
563–21 seemingly impede the offspring of the s· idea,
564– 3 evil still charges the s· idea with
564–20 s· idea was arraigned before the tribunal of
564–30 pursues with hatred the s· idea.
565–12 the masculine representative of the s· idea,
565–14 The impersonation of the s· idea
565–24 the material lie made war upon the s· idea ;
566– 6 so shall the s· idea guide all right desires
567–22 cast out by Christ, Truth, the s· idea,
570–22 the s· idea will be understood.
573–23 which involve the s· idea and consciousness
575– 3 Love wedded to its own s· idea."
576–22 and the s· idea reveals it.
577–15 second, the Christ, the s· idea of God ;
gl 582–19 creates man as His own s· idea,
584– 1 light, the s· idea of Truth and Love.
590– 9 LAMB OF GOD. The s· idea of Love ;
595–26 the divine Principle and its s· idea.

ideal

m 67–29 presents the true likeness or s· ideal.
b 337–18 demonstrates Life in Christ, Life's s· ideal.
ap 561–11 saw also the s· ideal as a woman

ideals

o 359–30 One says : "I have s· ideals,

ideas

s 123–15 replaces the objects of . . . sense with s· ideas.
c 257–16 would translate s· ideas into material beliefs,
b 295– 6 The universe is filled with s· ideas,
298–20 S· ideas, like numbers and notes,
298–22 S· ideas lead up to their divine origin, God,
320– 5 and names are often expressive of s· ideas.
339–22 so will our material theories yield to s· ideas,
o 349–18 in dealing with s· ideas.
361–22 S· ideas unfold as we advance.
t 460–26 she had to impart, . . . the hue of s· ideas
g 503– 1 consists of the unfolding of s· ideas
504–11 but it is the revelation of Truth and of s· ideas.
510– 2 seek to apprehend the s· ideas of God,
536– 5 heaven and earth stand for s· ideas,
gl 583–17 to the apprehension of s· ideas

identity

a 51– 8 his s· identity in the likeness of the divine ;
b 287– 8 Divine Science . . . maintains man's s· identity.
287–22 it is illusion, without s· identity
333–28 this unity of his s· identity

ignorance

f 243– 1 We may hide s· ignorance from the world,

image

f 206–25 the s· image and likeness of God
g 519–16 until they . . . reach the s· image and likeness.
gl 591– 5 the s· image and likeness of God ;

immensity

c 263–29 thrown into the face of s· immensity,

import

b 271–30 The s· import of the Word imparts this power.
r 471–27 gave the s· import, expressed through
g 501– 3 chiefly because the s· import of the Word,

individuality

c 258–20 the infinite idea and s· individuality,
b 317–18 The understanding of his s· individuality
336– 7 is reflected in all s· individuality
337– 4 lose sight of s· individuality.
r 491– 9 Man's s· individuality is never wrong.
ap 577– 7 this compounded s· individuality reflects

inspiration

gl 596–17 they show the s· inspiration of Love and Truth

intelligence

f 240– 5 Mind, the s· intelligence they reflect.

intent

p 365–23 the result will correspond with the s· intent.

interpretation

a 47– 1 even to the s· interpretation and discernment of
s 118– 3 and its s· interpretation.

spiritual

interpretation

b 320– 9 "The s· interpretation of Scripture
g 502–19 each text is followed by its s· interpretation

intuitions

ph 174–11 the angels of His presence— the s· intuitions
gl 581– 4 s· intuitions, pure and perfect ;

Jesus

b 314–24 the s· Jesus was imperceptible to them.

joy

c 265–24 has not gained stronger desires for s· joy ?

law

a 43–25 he was acting under s· law
43–26 and that s· law sustained him.
m 62– 5 form habits of obedience to the moral and s· law,
ph 182–20 prevents full obedience to s· law,
183–27 casts out all evils . . . with the actual s· law,
197–13 and the more . . . about moral and s· law,
f 208–11 of immortal Mind, of Truth, and of s· law.
240– 1 Nature voices natural, s· law
b 273–21 never ordained a material law to annul the s· law.
319– 7 would infringe upon s· law
328–21 Understanding s· law . . . Jesus said :
o 349– 9 should subordinate material law to s· law.
p 381–12 except a moral or s· law.
417–14 causation is Mind, acting through s· law.
t 463–28 and it is a s· law instead of material.
r 471– 3 but holds the divine order or s· law,
485–22 by fulfilling the s· law of being,
496–22 the s· law which says to the grave,
g 530– 3 s· law of Truth is made manifest

lawgivers

ph 184–14 and they are s· lawgivers,

laws

s 118–14 which include s· laws emanating from the
118–17 may import that these s· laws, perverted

leaven

s 118– 2 the s· leaven signifies the Science of Christ

less

a 25–17 any man whose origin was less s·.

Life

pr 14–17 controlled by s· Life, Truth, and Love.
a 51–17 could no more be separated from his s· Life
f 241–29 see God and are approaching s· Life
b 306– 6 how death was to be overcome by s· Life,
318–21 yields to the reality of s· Life.
p 410– 2 shall not be ready for s· Life hereafter.
g 530–23 saying, . . . more pleasant to the eyes than s· Life,
550–19 hides the true and s· Life,
ap 561–28 The light portrayed is . . . s· Life,

life

a 51–14 his s· life, indestructible and eternal,
sp 72– 8 the gain of s· life.
74– 1 s· life which is not subject to death.
82– 9 If s· life has been won by the departed,
f 232–31 and the resurrection to s· life.
b 284–18 testimony as to s· life, truth, and love?
306– 4 would . . . resort to death to reproduce s· life.
p 430– 1 That statement is not confined to s· life,
g 556–26 Because mortal mind must waken to s· life

Life-laws

p 398– 9 the popular ignorance of s· Life-laws.

light

b 324–22 but s· light soon enabled him to follow the
t 446–26 reflect the s· light and might which heal

link

r 491–15 and find the indissoluble s· link

living

c 264–24 S· living and blessedness are the only

Love

a 33–22 This is the new understanding of s· Love.
c 266–11 s· Love will force you to accept what best

love

c 264–27 comes from an all-absorbing s· love.
t 462–29 unselfishness, philanthropy, s· love.

man

sp 70– 7 s· man, made in God's likeness, reflects God.
f 250–11 S· man is the likeness of this Ego.
c 258–25 a very imperfect sense of the s· man
263– 5 Immortal s· man alone represents the
b 281–17 in individual s· man and things.
300–30 the spiritual universe and s· man,
301–10 immortal, s· man is really substantial,
302–21 Mind, of the s· man is God,
303–28 S· man is the image or idea of God,
314– 7 God and His reflection or s· man.
337–24 the invisible universe and s· man.
g 557–12 as the line of creation rises towards s· man,

meaning

s 117–11 the s· meaning of which is attained through
138–32 his theology . . . and the s· meaning of this
b 319–24 misapprehension of the s· meaning of
o 350–10 enables them to interpret his s· meaning.
355– 1 they should gain the s· meaning of

spiritual

means
ph 181–13   when you resort to any except *s·* means.
meeting
a 35–10   This *s·* meeting with our Lord
might
ph 192–17   Moral and *s·* might belong to Spirit,
name
s 137–28   but now the Master gave him a *s·* name
nature
g 512–24   Their *s·* nature is discerned only through the
oblivion
p 382–24   rescued from seeming *s·* oblivion,
offering
a 25– 4   The efficacy of Jesus' *s·* offering is
offspring
b 336–31   man is God's *s·* offspring.
oneness
m 57–10   and their true harmony is in *s·* oneness.
opposite
ph 171– 4   Through discernment of the *s·* opposite
origin
b 312–31   Jesus' *s·* origin and his demonstration of
    315–21   Jesus' *s·* origin and understanding
    325–27   The time cometh when the *s·* origin of man,
r 479– 2   must have a material, not a *s·* origin.
g 519–14   demonstrating its *s·* origin.
    534– 7   which reveals the *s·* origin of man.
gl 582–10   the introduction of a more *s·* origin ;
original
f 210– 3   the translation of the *s·* original into the
outpouring
ap 574–14   the *s·* outpouring of bliss and glory,
peace
gl 589– 8   JAPHET (Noah's son). A type of *s·* peace,
perception
f 203–13   *S·* perception brings out the possibilities of
p 406–12   *s·* perception, aided by Science, reaches Truth.
g 531–12   exchanging it for *s·* perception,
    547–31   It is this *s·* perception of Scripture,
gl 585– 3   Jesus said, referring to *s·* perception,
perfection
f 254–12   grasp the ultimate of *s·* perfection slowly ;
gl 595–21   mortal disappears and *s·* perfection appears.
phenomena
sp 88–24   nor are they *s·* phenomena,
power
a 38–17   It expresses *s·* power ;
    53–31   his final demonstration of *s·* power.
m 67–25   The lack of *s·* power in the
sp 75–22   Jesus' *s·* power to reproduce the presence of
s 116– 3   *s·* power, love, health, holiness.
    119– 1   When we endow matter with vague *s·* power,
    134–30   believing in the superiority of *s·* power
    146–10   barren of the vitality of *s·* power,
f 235–26   Christ Jesus, the true idea of *s·* power.
b 309– 9   the understanding of Spirit and of *s·* power.
    313–27   to immature ideas of *s·* power,
    313–29   the body, which by *s·* power he raised
o 355– 5   prayers which evince no *s·* power to heal.
p 366–20   patient's *s·* power to resuscitate himself.
    382–14   receptive of *s·* power and of faith in one God,
    407–15   even into *s·* power and good-will to man.
t 453–16   Honesty is *s·* power.
    454–29   The superiority of *s·* power over sensuous
r 470– 4   unity of Principle and *s·* power
    470– 7   error assumed the loss of *s·* power,
presence
r 470– 8   the *s·* presence of Life as infinite Truth
proof
g 505–24   giving the *s·* proof of the universe
prospects
s 130– 3   discouraged over its slight *s·* prospects.
purgation
p 364–21   small reward in return for the *s·* purgation
qualifications
t 448–21   *s·* qualifications requisite for healing,
rationality
f 223–21   *S·* rationality and free thought accompany
realities
g 513–27   His thoughts are *s·* realities.
gl 581–12   *s·* realities of all things are created by Him
reality
f 207–27   The *s·* reality is the scientific fact
    228–18   will recognize harmony as the *s·* reality
r 488–21   senses can take no cognizance of *s·* reality
realm
a 34–25   would rise again in the *s·* realm of reality,
b 337–26   as they exist in the *s·* realm of the real.
recompense
sp 98– 1   the *s·* recompense of the persecuted
record
g 521–14   turn our gaze to the *s·* record of creation,
reflection
b 305–21   as opposed to the Science of *s·* reflection,
r 480– 5   If there is no *s·* reflection, then there remains

spiritual

rules
s 112–18   *s·* rules, laws, and their demonstration,
scale
s 155–25   and more weight into the *s·* scale.
seer
gl 593– 4   PROPHET. A *s·* seer ;
self
b 334–17   while the *s·* self, or Christ,
selfhood
a 38–24   his *s·* selfhood, never suffered.
sense
pref viii– 6   must yield to the harmony of *s·* sense,
pr 7–18   If *s·* sense always guided men,
    16–24   the *s·* sense of the Lord's Prayer :
a 29–20   The illumination of Mary's *s·* sense
    41– 7   from material sense into the *s·* sense of
m 56–12   and its *s·* sense was revealed from heaven,
sp 72–15   and immortal Truth (the *s·* sense)
    75– 8   would transfer men from the *s·* sense of
    85–24   but mortals need *s·* sense.
    95–31   *s·* sense lifts human consciousness into
s 122–25   to *s·* sense and in Science, Life goes on
    123–21   through a *s·* sense of the Scriptures
ph 191–12   the *s·* sense of being and of what Life includes
f 206– 7   the province of *s·* sense to govern man.
    209–31   *S·* sense is a conscious, constant capacity to
    210– 6   are discerned by *s·* sense.
    214–14   When it is learned that the *s·* sense,
    247–16   Immortal men and women are models of *s·* sense,
c 258–31   Through *s·* sense you can discern the
b 272– 3   The *s·* sense of truth must be gained
    272– 9   The *s·* sense of the Scriptures brings out the
    290– 9   instead of through a *s·* sense of life,
    294–18   destroyed by Truth through *s·* sense
    296–15   *s·* sense, and the actuality of being.
    298– 9   *s·* sense can bear witness only to Truth.
    298–13   *S·* sense, contradicting the material senses,
    298–23   and to the *s·* sense of being.
    303–31   before the material senses yielded to *s·* sense,
    306–24   *s·* sense, which cognizes Life as permanent.
    309– 5   gave him the *s·* sense of being
    314– 4   *s·* sense had quenched all earthly yearnings.
    015 17   which beclouds the *s·* sense of Truth ;
    318–13   silence this lie . . . with the truth of *s·* sense.
    326–25   yielded to a *s·* sense, which is always right.
    328– 1   the grandeur and bliss of a *s·* sense,
o 340–19   The elucidation of C. S. lies in its *s·* sense,
    350–32   and the *s·* sense was scarcely perceived.
    351–12   when the *s·* sense of the creed was discerned
    351–13   this *s·* sense was a *present help.*
    359–16   Soul, is palpable only to *s·* sense,
t 452–22   the *s·* sense of Truth unfolds its harmonies,
    461–11   Only by the illumination of the *s·* sense,
r 471–17   is fully sustained by *s·* sense,
    481– 8   Through *s·* sense only, man comprehends
    486– 8   gain spiritual understanding and *s·* sense
    490–26   ushers in the *s·* sense of being,
g 505–20   *S·* sense is the discernment of spiritual good.
    548– 4   *s·* sense of Life, substance, and intelligence.
    548–17   the true ideas of God, the *s·* sense of being.
ap 573–21   and in place of this . . . was the *s·* sense,
    578– 3   the incorporeal or *s·* sense of Deity :
    578– 8   restoreth my soul [*s·* sense] :— *Psal.* 23 : 3.
gl 579– 6   *s·* sense, which is also their original meaning.
    585– 7   to *s·* sense, it is a compound idea.
    589– 7   yield to the *s·* sense of Life and Love.
    590–24   when the *s·* sense of God and of infinity is
    592– 9   nor can be recognized by the *s·* sense ;
    596– 1   That which *s·* sense alone comprehends,
    597–18   *s·* sense unfolds the great facts of existence.
senses
b 288– 4   between the evidence of the *s·* senses and
r 486–23   all the *s·* senses of man,
g 512–25   is discerned only through the *s·* senses.
significance
s 118–13   In their *s·* significance, Science, Theology,
signification
a 32–24   in its *s·* signification, it was natural
f 241–14   Take away the *s·* signification of Scripture, and
g 545–27   which is so glorious in its *s·* signification.
source
s 152–26   divinely driven to a *s·* source for health
b 329–27   If men understood their real *s·* source
spheres
g 513– 7   lead on to *s·* spheres and exalted beings.
state
f 215–30   Having sought man's *s·* state,
status
r 476–21   and earnestly seek the *s·* status of man,
statutes
b 307–29   his province is in *s·* statutes,
steps
g 513– 6   Advancing *s·* steps in the teeming universe

spiritual

strength
- *b* 308–22   s· strength in this Peniel of divine Science.
- *ap* 566–31   Michael's characteristic is s· strength.
- 567– 5   s· strength wrestles and prevails
- 571–28   With his s· strength, he has opened wide the
- *gl* 599– 7   inspiration ; s· strength.

susceptibility
- *sp* 86–10   Jesus possessed more s· susceptibility than

system
- *ph* 170– 4   form neither a moral nor a s· system.

teaching
- *ap* 575–13   S· teaching must always be by symbols.
- *gl* 595–16   can fit us for the office of s· teaching.

teachings
- *b* 272–15   the s· teachings which dulness and

things
- *b* 326–10   and set his whole affections on s· things,
- 335–13   Things s· and eternal are substantial.

thoughts
- *c* 259–29   and demands s· thoughts, divine concepts,
- *gl* 582–28   The s· thoughts and representatives of
- 598–10   to unfold s· thoughts.

tongue
- *s* 115–11   back into the original s· tongue.

transfiguration
- *ap* 576–29   through s· transfiguration.

Truth
- *sp* 96–20   all discord will be swallowed up in s· Truth.
- *b* 273– 4   can take no cognizance of God and s· Truth.
- 315–23   how s· Truth destroys material error,
- *o* 350–17   in a material age to apprehend s· Truth.
- *ap* 561–27   idea is clad with the radiance of s· Truth,
- *gl* 582– 2   BELIEVING. . . . the perception of s· Truth.
- 590– 8   the opposite of s· Truth and understanding.
- 593– 5   before the conscious facts of s· Truth.

truth
- *ph* 165–14   theories took the place of s· truth.
- *b* 277–18   This points to the s· truth
- 293–20   while s· truth is Mind.
- 311–16   loss or absence of soul, s· truth.

type
- *g* 541–11   the lamb was a more s· type of
- *gl* 582–12   a s· type ; that which comforts, consoles,

ultimate
- *r* 485–15   Think not to thwart the s· ultimate of

understanding
- *pr* 1– 3   a s· understanding of Him, an unselfed love.
- 4–27   can never do the works of s· understanding,
- 10– 5   must grow to the s· understanding of prayer.
- 14–26   Life divine, revealing s· understanding
- 16– 2   must precede this advanced s· understanding.
- *a* 23–18   Faith, advanced to s· understanding,
- 23–30   which includes s· understanding and
- *m* 64–24   s· understanding and perpetual peace.
- *sp* 77–10   until the s· understanding of Life is
- 83–27   through s· understanding, by which man
- 85– 3   It is the illumination of the s· understanding
- 96– 1   advances slowly . . . into s· understanding ;
- 96–24   but s· understanding is changeless.
- 96–28   and s· understanding increases,
- *s* 116– 2   SPIRITUAL. Wisdom, purity, s· understanding,
- 128–12   imbued with this s· understanding,
- *ph* 178–26   in proportion to our s· understanding of
- 183–30   C. S. . . . honors s· understanding ;
- 194–15   man, who is immortal in s· understanding,
- *f* 202–14   lights the torch of s· understanding.
- 211–12   matter does not appear in the s· understanding
- 213–19   senses of Soul — through s· understanding.
- 226–19   fetter faith and s· understanding.
- 251–25   process of higher s· understanding
- *b* 271–14   the result of their cultivated s· understanding
- 274–14   are based on s· understanding,
- 275–20   metaphysics, as revealed to s· understanding,
- 276–25   beliefs and s· understanding never mingle.
- 286– 7   s· understanding is better than all burnt
- 297–29   and faith becomes s· understanding.
- 298– 4   and glow full-orbed in s· understanding.
- 312–26   limits faith and hinders s· understanding.
- *o* 346–30   expelled to make room for s· understanding.
- 355–28   demonstration and s· understanding are
- *p* 402–28   better instructed by s· understanding.
- 403–21   Christian state is one of . . . s· understanding,
- 425–25   Correct material belief by s· understanding,
- 442–21   then belief melts into s· understanding,
- *t* 445–11   dwarfing the s· understanding
- 447–19   impart . . . the truth and s· understanding,
- 462– 7   his store of s· understanding, potency,
- *r* 465– 3   much labor and increased s· understanding.
- 486– 8   must gain s· understanding and spiritual sense
- 497–10   s· understanding that casts out evil
- *g* 505– 7   S· understanding, . . . is the firmament.
- 505–22   S· understanding unfolds Mind,
- 509– 1   letting in the light of s· understanding.
- 509–17   The light of s· understanding gives gleams of
- 512–16   states of faith and s· understanding.

spiritual

understanding
- *gl* 579–14   the life-preserving power of s· understanding.
- 582–17   BRIDEGROOM. S· understanding ;
- 584– 5   in the illumination of s· understanding,
- 585– 2   EARS. . . . . s· understanding.
- 586–15   FIRMAMENT. S· understanding ;
- 589–24   the s· understanding of God and man
- 593–11   material belief yielding to s· understanding.
- 598–23   the s· understanding of Life and Love,

unfoldment
- *p* 371–25   our need of its s· unfoldment.

unity
- *m* 61–31   The scientific *morale* of marriage is s· unity.

universe
- *s* 127– 5   creator of the s· universe, including man,
- *c* 267–11   man and the s· universe coexist
- *b* 286–19   the s· universe is good, and reflects God
- 300–30   God is seen only in the s· universe
- *r* 468–23   s· universe, including individual man,

views
- *a* 32–27   refresh his heart with brighter, with s· views.

vision
- *f* 215–11   S· vision is not subordinate to
- *ap* 561– 7   Because of his more s· vision,

wickedness
- *t* 453–20   Hidden sin is s· wickedness in high places.
- *ap* 563–30   "s· wickedness in high places." — *Eph.* 6 : 12.

- *pr* 14–13   Life and intelligence are purely s·,
- *a* 34–19   they became more s· and understood better
- 35–17   his s· and final ascension above matter,
- *m* 61– 5   and the s· over the animal,
- 65– 5   s· and eternal existence may be discerned.
- 67–27   S·, . . . consciousness is needed.
- 69– 3   evolved from Spirit, and so are s·,
- *sp* 73–31   cannot be made the mouthpiece of the s·,
- 74–27   the s·, or incorporeal, and the physical,
- 78–10   If . . . they are not s·, but must still be mortal,
- 83–22   to suppose that life is . . . organically s·.
- 84– 4   foresight from a s·, incorporeal standpoint,
- 85–26   seeking the material more than the s·.
- 88–14   Ideas are s·, harmonious, and eternal.
- 90–13   Then being will be recognized as s·,
- 93–26   Man is s·.
- 99– 2   not material but scientifically s·.
- 99–13   ordinary teachings are material and not s·.
- 99–14   C. S. teaches only that which is s·
- 99–29   of divine Spirit and to God's s·, perfect man.
- *s* 114–28   the universe, including man, is s·.
- 116– 2   definition of
- 117– 7   the language of Spirit must be, and is, s·.
- 118–29   portray law as physical, not s·.
- 119–18   this nature is s· and is not expressed in matter.
- 126–18   as being both natural and s·?
- 127–28   It has a s·, and not a material origin.
- 131–11   the superiority of s· over physical power.
- 148–26   to rule man by material law, instead of s·.
- 157–32   better for this s· and profound pathology.
- *ph* 170–14   The demands of Truth are s·,
- 170–29   The description of man as . . . material and s·,
- 171–21   The intellectual, the moral, the s·,
- 171–29   intelligence and life are s·, never material,
- 172–13   eternal chain of existence as . . . wholly s· ;
- 173–20   Man is s·, individual, and eternal ;
- 181–18   are not sufficiently s· to depend on Spirit.
- 191– 9   the s· and divine Principle of man dawns
- 192– 7   Human opinions are not s·.
- *f* 214– 4   If the medium of hearing is wholly s·,
- 231–14   no antagonistic powers nor laws, s· or
- 250–27   But the s·, real man is immortal.
- 252–32   Man, whose senses are s·,
- 254–22   and to work out the s· which determines
- *c* 256– 4   rises from the material sense to the s·,
- 263– 8   blends his thoughts of existence with the s·
- 265– 6   their affections and aims grow s·,
- 265–30   and that joy is s·.
- 266–29   Man is deathless, s·.
- *b* 274–20   affirm that . . . are material, instead of s·.
- 275–26   The true understanding of God is s·.
- 284–29   the only real senses of man are s·,
- 288–25   the s· real man has no birth,
- 289–24   God's universe is s· and immortal.
- 289–26   but the s· is true, and therefore
- 289–30   Spirit and all things s· are the real and
- 290–25   To be wholly s·, man must be sinless,
- 290–29   no more s· for believing that his body died
- 291–31   As for s· error there is none.
- 292–29   s· real man's indissoluble connection with
- 295– 9   Mortal mind would transform the s· into the material,
- 296– 2   man is the s·, eternal reflection of God.
- 297–20   Faith is higher and more s· than belief.
- 298–27   flying on s·, not material, pinions.
- 299–24   Truth is s·, eternal substance, which cannot
- 301–14   the s· man's substantiality transcends

spiritual

```
  b 301–21  is not s· and breaks the First Commandment,
    301–32  presupposes . . . man to be material instead of s·.
    306– 2  thought that they could raise the s· from
    309–19  not in elements which are not s·,
    311–10  All sin is of the flesh.  It cannot be s·.
    311–31  But the s·, eternal man is not touched by
    315–27  more s· than all other earthly personalities.
    317–17  is no less tangible because it is s·
    318–20  invalids grow more s·, as the error
    320– 7  Scriptures have both a s· and literal meaning.
    320–25  important interpretation of Scripture is the s·.
    326–11  or trusting in it more than in the s·.
    326–27  and his life became more s·.
    329–28  they would struggle for recourse to the s·
    331–25  Hence all is Spirit and s·.
    332–12  The Christ is incorporeal, s·,
    332–27  Mary's conception of him was s·,
    333– 9  Christ expresses God's s·, eternal nature.
    334–13  the unseen and the seen, the s· and material,
    335–27  Reality is s·, harmonious, immutable,
    336–14  The s· man's consciousness and
    338– 6  both good and evil, both s· and material
  o 344–31  are more fashionable and less s·?
    347–14  Christ, as the s· or true idea of God,
    351–22  such starting-points are neither s· nor scientific,
    351–28  in their attempted worship of the s·.
    352–10  to the rabbis the s· was the intangible
    353–29  The true idea of being is s· and immortal,
    360–14  which . . . the material or the s·?
  p 368–23  Neither evil, disease, nor death can be s·,
    396–28  man is s·, not material;
    407–23  In Science, all being is eternal, s·, perfect,
    409–21  real man is s· and immortal,
    419–19  less of material conditions and more of s·.
    425–18  mankind will be more s·
    427–25  physical realm, so-called, as well as in the s·.
    428–21  to replace them with the life which is s·,
    442– 3  Our statute is s·,
  t 451–17  If our hopes and affections are s·,
    453–13  as from the use of s·.
    458– 5  one s·, the other material,
    460– 9  and its medicine is intellectual and s·,
  r 467– 7  no truth, no love, but that which is s·.
    468–15  man is not material ; he is s·
    475–11  Man is s· and perfect ;
    475–12  and because he is s· and perfect,
    477– 7  he is himself s·.
    479– 7  it must be immortal and s·.
  g 503–21  third, in s· and immortal forms
    504– 7  as to the divine creation being both s· and
    510– 5  to be holy, thought must be purely s·.
    516– 3  so you, being s·, are the reflection of God.
    517–22  This ideal is God's own image, s· and infinite.
    534–24  opposition to the s·, scientific meaning
    537–12  Creation is there represented as s·, entire,
    538– 7  distance . . . between the material and s·,
    544– 1  record of a material creation which followed
            the s·,
    544– 8  the material sense of things, not from the s·,
    544–31  declares . . . that matter becomes s·.
    547–20  and adopts the s· and immortal,
    552–11  whereas the s· scientific facts
 ap 566– 8  from a material sense of existence to the s·,
    573– 1  terrestrial or celestial, material or s·?
    573– 8  the heavens and earth to one . . . are s·,
    575–21  This city is wholly s·, as its four sides indicate.
    577–12  This s·, holy habitation has no boundary
 gl 579– 2  substitution of the s· for the material
    592–24  and of the immortality of all that is s·.
```

spiritualism

belief of
```
 sp 84–24  destroys the belief of s· at its very inception,
```
has no basis
```
 sp 84–26  s· has no basis upon which to build.
```
material
```
 sp 77–27  would outgrow their beliefs in material s·.
```
relies upon
```
 sp 79–11  S· relies upon human beliefs and hypotheses.
```
structure of
```
 sp 71–27  basis and structure of s· are alike material and
```
will be found
```
 sp 71–21  s· will be found mainly erroneous,
```
would transfer
```
 sp 75– 8  S· would transfer men from the
```

```
  a 24–23  Does s· find Jesus' death necessary only for the
 sp 71–26  I never could believe in s·.
    71–29  S· therefore presupposes Spirit, which is
    73– 3  S· calls one person, living in this world, material,
    78–16  S· . . . would destroy the supremacy of Spirit.
    80–14  It is mysticism which gives s· its force.
    81– 7  on its own theories, s· can only
    99–18  Those individuals, who adopt theosophy, s·,
  s 111– 1  agnosticism, pantheism, theosophy, s·,
```

spiritualism
```
  s 129–17  hypnotism, s·, theosophy, agnosticism,
 ph 178–30  may attempt to unite with it hypnotism, s·,
  r 484– 8  hypnotism, theosophy, or s·?
```

Spiritualists
```
 sp 77–26  and S· would outgrow their beliefs
    80–13  humanity and philanthropy of many S·,
    81– 5  If S· understood the Science of being,
```

spirituality

alludes to the
```
  b 333–11  alludes to the s· which is taught,
```
concomitant of
```
  r 484–28  Is materiality the concomitant of s·,
```
essence of
```
  b 293–18  counterfeits the true essence of s·
```
genuine
```
 sp 95–15  depends upon his genuine s·.
```
giving more
```
  p 422–17  giving more s· to consciousness
```
goodness and
```
  b 277– 8  goodness and s· must be immortal.
    277–10  If goodness and s· are real,
```
hamper
```
  f 234– 2  even as ritualism and creed hamper s·.
```
his
```
  a 51–28  His s· separated him from sensuousness,
 sp 86– 8  His quick apprehension . . . illustrated his s·.
  f 220–23  a diet of bread and water to increase his s·.
  b 270–32  but it was indigenous to his s·,
  o 356–10  on the basis of his s·.
```
his patient's
```
  p 375–19  increasing his patient's s· while restoring
```
in proportion to our
```
 sp 95– 7  approach God, or Life, in proportion to our s·,
```
lays open siege
```
  f 216– 9  S· lays open siege to materialism.
```
Master taught
```
  s 117–15  Our Master taught s· by similitudes
```
meekness and
```
  o 343–22  meekness and s· are the conditions of
```
no resemblance to
```
  f 207–31  which bears no resemblance to s·,
```
of the universe
```
  r 471–19  the s· of the universe is the only fact of
```
opposition to
```
  b 329–31  the more intense the opposition to s·,
```
price of
```
  a 36–15  The earthly price of s· in a material age
```
reception of that
```
  s 115– 1  obstacle to the reception of that s·,
```
Rubicon of
```
 ph 172–10  and death is the Rubicon of s·?
```
this
```
  a 51–30  this s· which enabled Jesus to heal the sick,
```
true
```
 sp 99–23  The calm, strong currents of true s·,
```
war against
```
 ap 565– 3  inflamed with war against s·,
```
wars against
```
  f 242–19  which wars against s·
```
yield to
```
  f 201–10  fear, all sensuality, yield to s·,
```

```
  s 111–25  meets a yearning of the human race for s·.
  c 266–17  lay down their fleshliness and gain s·.
  b 313–27  s· was possessed only in a limited degree
  o 352– 9  but s·, was the reality of man's existence,
 ap 572–11  materiality is the inverted image of s·.
 gl 587–26  s· ; bliss ; the atmosphere of Soul.
```

spiritualization
```
 sp 96– 4  s· will follow, for Love is Spirit.
    96–10  until the final s· of all things.
  s 158–24  Evidences of progress and of s· greet us
  f 211–29  through dematerialization and s· of thought
  b 272–19  It is the s· of thought and Christianization of
  p 382– 6  and to the s· of thought,
    407–10  This s· of thought lets in the light,
 gl 593– 9  RESURRECTION.  S· of thought ;
```

spiritualized
```
  s 141–19  Its only priest is the s· man.
  o 356– 2  the material thought must become s·
```

spiritualizes
```
  o 354–11  heals the sick and s· humanity.
  p 370– 6  the same regimen which s· the thought ;
```

spiritualizing
```
  b 316–28  s· materialistic beliefs,
```

spiritually
```
  a 21– 9  If the disciple is advancing s·,
    25–18  he demonstrated more s· than all others
    32–20  The true sense is s· lost,
    38–18  otherwise the healing could not have been done
            s·.
  m 68–32  the unbroken links . . . will be s· discerned ;
```

stages
an 104–10 scientific truth goes through three *s*·.
f 251– 7 Fright is so great at certain *s*· of
p 390–29 Meet the incipient *s*· of disease with
  391– 8 the incipient or advanced *s*· of disease,
  405– 9 Choke these errors in their early *s*·,
g 550–19 decay, and dissolution as its component *s*·
ap 573–11 indicate states and *s*· of consciousness.

stagnation
s 159–28 pain or pleasure, action or *s*·,

stake
a 37– 7 to slay Truth with the steel or the *s*·,

stammeringly
pref ix– 7 *s*· attempts to convey his feeling.

stamp
p 413–29 and often *s*· them there,

stand
pr 3– 4 Who would *s*· before a blackboard, and pray the
s 113–15 has not a foot to *s*· upon which is not
  127–13 These synonymous terms *s*· for
f 204–19 They can never *s*· the test of Science.
  229–25 all that He makes is good and will *s*· forever.
  252– 3 that kingdom cannot *s*·." — *Mark* 3: 24.
b 268– * *Here I s*·. I can do no otherwise*;
  320–32 *s*· in celestial perfection before Elohim,
p 392–24 S*· porter at the door of thought.
  431–25 Another witness takes the *s*· and testifies :
  432–20 Another witness takes the *s*· and testifies :
r 493– 3 appears to rise and set, and the earth to *s*· still ;
g 511–24 rocks and mountains *s*· for solid . . . ideas.
  536– 5 heaven and earth *s*· for spiritual ideas,
  537–17 since ground and dust *s*· for nothingness.
ap 563– 7 why should we *s*· aghast at nothingness?
gl 581–18 divided against itself, which cannot *s*· ;

standard
His own
r 470–19 Has God taken down His own *s*·,
in Christian Science
r 483–12 and hinders its approach to the *s*· in C. S.
intellectual
ph 195–29 lowering the intellectual *s*· to accommodate the
moral
r 492– 9 will uplift the physical and moral *s*· of mortals,
of Christian Science
ph 168– 2 worldly, who think the *s*· of C. S. too high
of good
g 539– 8 What can be the *s*· of good, of Spirit,
of man
g 553– 9 become the *s*· of man.
of perfection
r 470–18 The *s*· of perfection was originally God and man.
g 555–23 We lose our *s*· of perfection . . . when we
of Truth
a 31– 2 are unfit to bear the *s*· of Truth,
f 235–29 should uplift the *s*· of Truth.
r 472–22 Thus we should continue to lose the *s*· of Truth.
of truth
ph 195–31 Incorrect views lower the *s*· of truth.
our
g 550–20 and causes our *s*· to trail in the dust.
  555–23 We lose our *s*· of perfection . . . when we
raises the
f 227–21 C. S. raises the *s*· of liberty
raise the
p 426–24 would raise the *s*· of health and morals
truth's
f 225–13 but there is a rallying to truth's *s*·.

ph 197–13 the higher will be the *s*· of living
p 373–32 circulation is changed, and returns to that *s*·

standards
f 247–13 form the transient *s*· of mortals.

standing
s 108–20 *s*· already within the shadow of the
p 415–31 leaving the pain *s*· forth as distinctly as a
  440–25 *s*· at the bar of Truth,
t 456– 8 the high *s*· which most of them hold
ap 561– 8 an "angel *s*· in the sun." — *Rev.* 19: 17.

standpoint
higher
c 262–24 Starting from a higher *s*·,
honest
pr 13– 6 beyond the honest *s*· of fervent desire.
human
g 520– 1 sweetest rest, even from a human *s*·, is in
incorporeal
sp 84– 4 from a spiritual, incorporeal *s*·,
material
o 351–31 to worship Spirit from a material *s*·,
t 458– 8 from both a mental and a material *s*·.
g 546–20 cannot . . . be interpreted from a material *s*·.
  551–26 From a material *s*·, "Canst thou — *Job* 11: 7.

standpoint
new
g 556–29 existence will be on a new *s*·.
of error
g 545–24 From that *s*· of error, they could not apprehend
our
f 239–21 reveal our *s*·, and show what we
b 281–32 the inspiration, which is to change our *s*·,
supposed
b 301–26 from a supposed *s*· outside the
your
p 412– 2 that God lovingly governs all, . . . is your *s*·,

t 461–10 from the *s*· of the human senses.

standpoints
sp 77–31 and they return to their old *s*· of matter.
  83–30 are distinctly opposite *s*·,
ph 174– 9 rising above material *s*·,
  182–12 It is impossible to work from two *s*·.
b 322– 3 changes the *s*· of life and intelligence

stands
sp 98–17 *s*· a revealed and practical Science.
f 224–24 practical Christianity, . . . *s*· at the door of this
b 330–28 manifested by mankind it *s*· for a lie,
  338–22 it *s*· for obstruction, error,
g 526–18 *s*· for the idea of Truth,
  526–20 "tree of knowledge" *s*· for the — *Gen.* 2: 9.
  526–30 In this text Eden *s*· for the mortal, . . . body.
  529–30 Adam, . . . *s*· for a belief of material mind.
ap 563–10 This dragon *s*· for the sum total of human error.
  563–27 The serpentine form *s*· for subtlety,

star
pref vii– 1 So shone the pale *s*· to the prophet-shepherds ;
  vii–10 and shine the guiding *s*· of being.
sp 70–13 from a blade of grass to a *s*·,
  95–23 Led by a solitary *s*· amid the darkness,
s 115–16 is as the wandering comet or the desolate *s*·
  144– 7 Withdraws the *s*·, when dawns the
ap 564– 9 into a night without a *s*·.
  575–28 eastward, to the *s*· seen by the Wisemen

stared
s 121– 1 and starvation *s*· him in the face ;

starry
f 247–27 blazons the night with *s*· gems,

stars
moon and
g 547–13 the gathering clouds, the moon and *s*·,
morning
g 509–22 "the morning *s*· sang together." — *Job* 38: 7.
of heaven
ap 563–24 the third part of the *s*· of heaven, — *Rev.* 12: 4.
twelve
ap 560– 9 a crown of twelve *s*·. — *Rev.* 12: 1.
  562–11 The spiritual idea is crowned with twelve *s*·,

sp 85– 1 read the *s*· or calculate an eclipse.
s 121– 7 The Chaldean Wisemen read in the *s*·
  125–28 astronomer will no longer look up to the *s*·,
f 240– 8 The *s*· make night beautiful,
g 510–15 He made the *s*· also. — *Gen.* 1: 16.
ap 562–16 These are the *s*· in the crown of rejoicing.
  565–23 After the *s*· sang together

start
a 21–13 If honest, he will be in earnest from the *s*·,
ph 189–20 mortal mind, . . . makes all things *s*· from the
c 267– 3 offspring of God *s*· not from matter
b 298–21 Spiritual ideas, . . . *s*· from Principle,
t 451– 8 Students of C. S., who *s*· with its letter

started
pref xi–26 *s*· by the author with only one student
b 326–17 This point won, the battle *s*· as you should.
gl 585–27 the belief . . . that man *s*· first from dust,

starting
c 262–24 S*· from a higher standpoint, one rises
b 279–30 Pantheism, *s*· from a material sense of
g 536–17 *s*· from matter instead of from God,
  546–14 represents error as *s*· from an idea of good

starting-point
b 275– 6 *s*· of divine Science is that God, Spirit, is
  284– 8 Mind can have no *s*·,
g 549–18 the simple ovum as the germ, the *s*·,
  550–20 If Life has any *s*· whatsoever,

starting-points
o 351–20 and while we make . . . our *s*·,
  351–22 such *s*· are neither spiritual nor scientific,

startle
f 223–25 Peals that should *s*· the slumbering thought
p 396– 7 Never *s*· with a discouraging remark
  420–28 If it becomes necessary to *s*· mortal mind
  421– 7 Should you thus *s*· mortal mind

startled

s 130–26 If thought is *s·* at the strong claim of Science
b 322–21 as the *s·* dreamer who wakens from an incubus

startling

a 50–15 This was a *s·* question.

starts

ph 191–23 not a flower *s·* from its cloistered cell.
f 211–14 When a tear *s·*, does not this so-called mind
t 460–21 it *s·* a petty crossfire over every cripple and
g 501– 2 *s·* with the beginning of the Old Testament,
531– 5 error, — that mortal man *s·* materially,
552–13 mortal life, which *s·* from an egg,

starvation

s 120–32 and *s·* stared him in the face ;
143–16 On this basis it saves from *s·* by theft,
f 221–11 in hunger and weakness, almost in *s·*,

state

Christian

p 403–21 The most Christian *s·* is one of rectitude

chrysalis

b 297–21 It is a chrysalis *s·* of human thought,

excited

p 415– 1 an excited *s·* of mortals which is not normal.

healthy

p 414–12 truth and love will establish a healthy *s·*,

hopeless

p 376– 1 presents to mortal thought a hopeless *s·*,

hypnotic

t 446–28 exercise of will brings on a hypnotic *s·*,
g 528–16 inducing a sleep or hypnotic *s·* in Adam

improved

gl 582–10 an improved *s·* of mortal mind ;

marriage

m 65–10 some fundamental error in the marriage *s·*.

material

sp 77–19 to prolong the material *s·*
p 411–24 The mental state is called a material *s·*.

mental

s 161– 9 while an opposite mental *s·* might produce
ph 196–29 it is a mental *s·*, which is afterwards outlined
f 245–10 In this mental *s·* she remained young.
245–26 for the mental *s·* governed the physical.
p 375– 7 Change the mental *s·*, and the
375–30 This mental *s·* is not understood,
377–17 the mental *s·* should be continually watched
411–24 The mental *s·* is called a material state.
422–32 This mental *s·* invites defeat.
t 455– 3 A mental *s·* of self-condemnation and guilt

objective

b 283–17 is but the objective *s·* of material sense,
p 374–12 is in fact the objective *s·* of mortal mind,

of being

r 476–14 They never had a perfect *s·* of being,

of consciousness

sp 82–21 their *s·* of consciousness must be different from

of error

b 311–17 This *s·* of error is the mortal dream of life

of existence

sp 74– 9 a new form and *s·* of existence.
76–26 This *s·* of existence is scientific and intact,
76–29 Death can never hasten this *s·* of existence,
82–19 if . . . in as conscious a *s·* of existence as
ap 573–26 possible to men in this present *s·* of existence,

of her blood

p 379–20 not dying on account of the *s·* of her blood,

of man

s 159–23 medical schools would learn the *s·* of man from
f 227–16 Slavery is not the legitimate *s·* of man.

of Mind

b 291–14 not a locality, but a divine *s·* of Mind

of mind

s 159–16 considered the woman's *s·* of mind,
ph 188–14 to be wholly a *s·* of mind.
p 374–21 Such a *s·* of mind induces sickness.
375–28 This *s·* of mind seems anomalous

of mortal thought

gl 585–21 a *s·* of mortal thought, the only error of which

of perspiration

p 384–16 If exposure . . . while in a *s·* of perspiration

of self-deception

p 403–15 mortal existence is a *s·* of self-deception

of things

g 522–15 this *s·* of things is declared to be temporary

perfect

r 476–14 They never had a perfect *s·* of being,
494– 1 to hold man forever intact in his perfect *s·*,

progressive

a 46–24 a probationary and progressive *s·*

resembling

sp 77–28 a *s·* resembling that of blighted buds,

resisting

p 388– 5 Stolidity, which is a resisting *s·* of

spiritual

f 215–31 Having sought man's spiritual *s·*,

state

subjective

s 108–27 a subjective *s·* of mortal mind
114–30 subjective *s·* of what is termed by the
ap 573–21 the subjective *s·* by which he could see the

their

sp 82–21 their *s·* of consciousness must be different from
82–22 We are not in their *s·*, nor are they in the

worse

m 64–28 a worse *s·* of society than now exists.

pref ix–14 but they are feeble attempts to *s·* the
s 161–19 The oppressive *s·* statutes touching medicine
f 224–20 opposition from church, *s·* laws, and the press,
b 297– 1 nothing can change this *s·*, until the
p 431–11 arrested Mortal Man in behalf of the *s·*

State Commissioner

p 432– 2 I am Nerve, the *S· C·* for

stated

an 101–12 Their report *s·* the results as follows :
s 112–24 which departs from what has already been *s·*
129– 3 the reasoning of an accurately *s·* syllogism
b 283–27 unless its Science be accurately *s·*.
o 347– 9 Had he *s·* his syllogism correctly,
p 402–24 illustrates the fact just *s·*.
g 521– 8 (as *s·* in the first chapter of Genesis)
546–27 The proof that the system *s·* in this book
547– 5 not one departs from the *s·* system and

stately

s 156–29 Metaphysics, . . . is the next *s·* step beyond
t 464– 7 to establish the *s·* operations of C. S.,
ap 566– 9 *S·* Science pauses not, but moves before them

statement

abstract

r 470–11 Divine Science explains the abstract *s·*

agree in

s 113–12 found to agree in *s·* and proof,

any

g 554– 8 Any *s·* of life, following from a

change this

f 240–12 Change this *s·*, suppose Mind to be

common

gl 598–14 is equivalent to our common *s·*,

contains a

g 521–27 contains a *s·* of this material view

contradicts this

r 485– 6 Whatever contradicts this *s·* is the false sense,

correlated

b 288– 2 the correlated *s·*, that *error*, . . . *is unreal.*

demonstrate his

t 447–32 to know it, he must demonstrate his *s·*.

doubt the

p 429–26 This is why you doubt the *s·*

error of

f 207– 6 Error of *s·* leads to error in action.
b 277–26 Matter is an error of *s·*.

Evangelist's

f 231–31 planted on the Evangelist's *s·* that

every

b 277–28 in every *s·* into which it enters.
t 462–14 abide strictly by its rules, heed every *s·*,
g 527–20 a lie, — false in every *s·*.

exact

s 161– 4 This is an exact *s·*,

final

p 409– 5 the nearer matter approaches its final *s·*.

first

g 544–17 The first *s·* about evil,
gl 594– 3 the first *s·* of mythology and idolatry;

full

t 456–29 contains the full *s·* of C. S.,

mystical

b 334–28 a mystical *s·* of the eternity of the Christ,

of Christian Science

t 456–29 contains the full *s·* of C. S.,
456–31 first book known, containing a . . . *s·* of C. S.
g 547– 1 A simple *s·* of C. S., if demonstrated

one

152–13 theory, in which one *s·* contradicts another

opposite

p 379–18 Then let her learn the opposite *s·*

scientific

a 27–12 in strict accordance with his scientific *s·* :
sp 94– 7 Christian and scientific *s·* of personality
f 207– 5 every scientific *s·* in Christianity has its proof
b 300– 9 So far as the scientific *s·* as to man
p 380–27 culmination of scientific *s·* and proof.
r 468– 8 What is the scientific *s·* of being?

that

p 429–32 That *s·* is not confined to spiritual life,

this

b 302–18 This *s·* is based on fact, not fable.
r 492–26 On this *s·* rests the Science of being,
g 526– 6 this *s·* that life issues from matter,

statement

this last
r 466–16   This last *s·* contains the

b 287–32   The *s·* that *Truth is real*
303–12   but the *s·* that man is conceived and
o 355–20   The *s·* that the teachings of C. S.
r 492–13   a *s·* proved to be good
g 521–28   a *s·* which is the exact opposite of

statements

following
b 270– 2   One only of the following *s·* can be true :
general
g 548–19   "It is very possible that many general *s·*
his own
a 26–11   which Jesus implied in his own *s·* :
metaphysical
s 115– 4   material terms for metaphysical *s·*,
scientific
gl 590–26   when the true scientific *s·* of the
these
r 472–12   Jesus furnished proofs of these *s·*.
two
o 358– 6   If two *s·* directly contradict each other

o 345–15   in this volume . . . there are no contradictory *s·*,
p 389–22   Materialists contradict their own *s·*.
r 465– 5   Absolute C. S. pervades its *s·*,
q 547– 4   If one of the *s·* in this book is true,

States

s 161–13   If her sister *S·* follow this example

states

certain
p 386– 9   mortals declare that certain *s·* of the
different
sp 82–11   different *s·* of consciousness are involved,
82–12   cannot exist in two different *s·* . . . at the same time.
p 377–12   Through different *s·* of mind,
mental
sp 83–25   The mental *s·* are so unlike,
o 149– 9   the different mental *s·* of the patient.
t 455– 6   Such mental *s·* indicate weakness
objective
r 484–13   the objective *s·* of mortal mind.
of mind
s 161– 6   Holy inspiration has created *s·* of mind which
p 377–12   Through different *s·* of mind,
prior
s 125–10   the prior *s·* which human belief created
separate
sp 74–32   for they are in separate *s·* of existence,
subjective
g 512–16   subjective, *s·* of faith and
gl 592– 7   idolatry ; the subjective *s·* of error ;
these
o 149– 9   These *s·* are not comprehended,

b 283– 9   *s·* of mortal mind which act, react, and then
ap 573–11   indicates *s·* and stages of consciousness.

stating

s 126– 2   Error will be no longer used in *s·* truth.

Statue

b 299– 3   when he carves his "*S·* of Liberty,"

statue

s 161–21   knelt before a *s·* of Liberty,

statuesque

ph 172–30   may present more nobility than the *s·* athlete,

stature

o 350– 8   grow into that *s·* of manhood in Christ Jesus
g 519–20   unto the measure of the *s·* of— *Eph.* 4 : 13.

status

s 118–21   dignified as the natural *s·* of men
120–19   or to exhibit the real *s·* of man.
122–13   its *s·* of happiness or misery.
ph 178–26   the *s·* of immortal being.
p 363–14   detect the woman's immoral *s·*
r 476–22   and earnestly seek the spiritual *s·* of man,

statute

p 432–12   In this province there is a *s·* regarding
436–10   Upon this *s·* hangs all the law and
441–13   According to our *s·*, Material Law is a
442– 3   Our *s·* is spiritual,

statute-book

p 437–33   read from the supreme *s·*, the Bible,
441– 2   explained from his *s·*, the Bible,

statutes

s 161–19   oppressive state *s·* touching medicine
ph 184–15   enforcing obedience through divine *s·*.
b 307–29   his province is in spiritual *s·*,
p 439–27   Our higher *s·* declare you all,
440–27   and in accordance with the divine *s·*,

staves

a 48– 2   *s·* of bigoted ignorance smote him sorely.

stay

a 43–19   Those who slew him to *s·* his influence
sp 90–21   yet their bodies *s·* in one place.
c 256–22   and none can *s·* His hand,— *Dan.* 4 : 35.

steadfastly

c 261– 4   Hold thought *s·* to the enduring,
p 414–15   To fix truth *s·* in your patients' thoughts,
r 495–15   cling *s·* to God and His idea.
495–30   abiding *s·* in wisdom, Truth, and Love.

steal

s 112–31   "Thou shalt not *s·*."— *Exod.* 20 : 15.
f 241–10   hate, . . . *s·* away the treasures of Truth.

stealing

b 294–29   The thief believes that he gains something by *s·*,

steel

a 37– 7   Mortals try in vain to slay Truth with the *s·*

steer

m 67– 8   Can you *s·* safely amid the storm?"

steers

p 426– 3   divine power, which *s·* the body into health.

stellar

s 121– 4   Copernicus mapped out the *s·* system,
g 509–14   *s·* universe is no more celestial than our earth.

stem

s 139–13   to *s·* the tide of sectarian bitterness,

step

advancing
s 134– 2   At every advancing *s·*, truth is still opposed
easiest
pr 5– 4   and the very easiest *s·*.
every
f 213–11   Every *s·* towards goodness is a departure from
g 533–24   The belief . . . is growing worse at every *s·*,
542– 1   The belief of life in matter sins at every *s·*.
first
t 459–11   failing to take the first *s·*.
463–23   the first *s·* towards destroying error.
great
pr 5– 4   The next and great *s·* required by wisdom
f 242– 6   Denial of the claims of matter is a great *s·*
in advance
s 158–27   Homœopathy, a *s·* in advance of allopathy,
new
sp 98– 1   persecutions which attend a new *s·*
next
b 296–29   and aids in taking the next *s·*
one
pr 5– 3   Sorrow for wrong-doing is but one *s·*
b 296–28   An improved belief is one *s·* out of error,
retrograde
sp 74–29   In C. S. there is never a retrograde *s·*,
single
p 429– 9   we look beyond a single *s·*
stately
g 156–29   the next stately *s·* beyond homœopathy.
step by
f 254–10   facts of existence are gained step by *s·*,
t 444–11   Step by *s·* will those who trust Him find

sp 84–22   a *s·* towards the Mind-science by which

stepped

a 45– 3   and *s·* forth from his gloomy resting-place,

stepping-stone

pref vii–17   Ignorance of God is no longer the *s·* to faith.
a 39–11   causes mortals to regard death . . . as a *s·*
f 203–24   Death is not a *s·* to Life,

steps

pref viii–31   were crude,— the first *s·* of a child
f 226– 2   That was only prophetic of further *s·*,
b 317– 9   Resistance to Truth will haunt his *s·*,
p 374–23   your *s·* are less firm because of your fear,
t 459– 9   Judge not . . . by the *s·* already taken,
g 513– 6   Advancing spiritual *s·* in the teeming universe

stereotyped

s 144–26   to whatever is not *s·*.
p 367– 6   gushing theories, *s·* borrowed speeches,

stern

p 362– 8   under the *s·* rules of rabbinical law,
433– 7   In compliance with a *s·* duty, his Honor,
g 514–17   They carry the baggage of *s·* resolve,

sterner

s 121– 1   but *s·* still would have been his fate, if

sternest

sp 85–28   He never spared hypocrisy the *s·* condemnation.

stewards

ap 571–13   and designate those as unfaithful *s·*

stick
m 67–15 Hoping and working, one should *s·* to the wreck,
p 418– 5 *S·* to the truth of being

stiff
s 160–31 Is a *s·* joint or a contracted muscle as much a

still
pref ix– 9 voices the . . . thought, though *s·* imperfectly.
    ix–13 *s·* in circulation among her first pupils ;
    ix–17 *s·* finds herself a willing disciple at the
pr 7– 2 *S·* stronger evidence that Jesus' reproof was
a 41–26 *s·* went about doing good deeds,
    42–30 to test nis *s·* uncomprehended saying,
m 63–15 *S·*, it is a marvel why usage should accord
sp 74–15 and the belief of *s·* living in an
    75– 4 to those *s·* in the existence cognized by the
    78–10 they are not spiritual, but must *s·* be mortal,
    82– 5 yet we *s·* read his thought in his verse.
    88– 5 And the sound of a voice that is *s·*.
    92–16 The portrayal is *s·* graphically. accurate,
s 121– 1 but sterner *s·* would have been his fate, if
    122–10 so-called senses *s·* make mortal mind tributary
    134– 3 truth is *s·* opposed with sword and spear.
    142–22 are *s·* needed to purge the temples
    144–22 says to disease, "Peace, be *s·*."— *Mark* 4 : 39.
    144–25 the old schools *s·* oppose it.
ph 187–30 the human mind *s·* holds in belief a body,
    189– 4 we *s·* believe that there is solar light and heat.
    194–24 Kaspar was *s·* a mental infant,
    197–26 there would *s·* be dyspeptics.
f 212–13 When . . . the pain *s·* remains, it proves
    214–13 they are *s·* the error, not the truth of being.
    221–26 when, *s·* the slave of matter, he thought
    224–20 *s·* the harbingers of truth's full-orbed
    225–29 are *s·* in bondage to material sense,
    226– 6 voice of God . . . was *s·* echoing in our land,
    245– 7 Believing that she was *s·* living in the
    246–23 and *s·* maintain his vigor, freshness, and
c 257–26 to *s·* the desires, to satisfy the
b 282–22 one is *s·* a curve and the other a
    289–14 Truth, overcame and *s·* overcomes death
    290– 8 *s·* seeking happiness through a
    290–21 They . . . shall be unrighteous *s·*,
    306–26 Science, *s·* enthroned, is unfolding to mortals
    307– 4 insists *s·* upon the opposite of Truth,
    307– 7 Evil *s·* affirms itself to be mind,
    307–32 the voice of Truth *s·* calls :
    312–11 The matter is *s·* there.
    320–32 *s·* clad in material flesh,
    323–29 the "*s·*, small voice" of Truth— *I Kings* 19 : 12.
o 353–14 It *s·* holds them more or less.
p 367–25 through a "*s·*, small voice,"— *I Kings* 19 : 12.
    368– 8 truth will become *s·* clearer
    394– 1 to be hopeful is *s·* better ;
    404–13 while its effects *s·* remain on the individual,
    424–21 *s·* you need the ear of your auditor.
t 444– 9 God will *s·* guide them into the right use of
    450– 5 Another class, *s·* more unfortunate,
    464– 6 and how much time and toil are *s·* required
r 469–27 *s·* believe there is another
    474–25 must error *s·* be immortal?
    493– 4 appears to rise and set, and the earth to stand *s·* ;
g 504– 9 *s·* there is light.
    514–14 beside the *s·* waters."— *Psal.* 23 : 2.
    531–18 If, . . . why is not this divine order *s·* maintained
ap 559– 8 The "*s·*, small voice"— *I Kings* 19 : 12.
    563– 5 and *s·* more astounded at hatred,
    564– 3 evil *s·* charges the spiritual idea with
    564– 7 and worse *s·*, to charge the innocent with
    569–17 dwellers *s·* in the deep darkness of belief.
    578– 7 beside the *s·* waters.— *Psal.* 23 : 2.
gl 586–24 love meeting no response, but *s·* remaining love.

stilled
s 134–27 *s·* the tempest, healed the sick,

stillness
s 121–25 sun is the central *s·*, so far as our solar system is

stimulate
f 236– 1 should *s·* clerical labor and progress.

stimulates
p 394– 8 *s·* the system to act in the direction which

stimulus
ph 186– 2 by emptying his thought of the false *s·*
p 420–19 It imparts a healthy *s·* to the body,
    420–22 Mind is the natural *s·* of the body,
    423–23 the *s·* of courage and conscious power.

sting
p 426–24 and also of the fear of its *s·*
r 496–20 "The *s·* of death is sin ;— *I Cor.* 15 : 56.
ap 563–29 Its *s·* is spoken of by Paul,

stings
s 133–12 healed of the poisonous *s·* of vipers.

stir
a 38– 1 so little inspiration to *s·* mankind to
s 162–10 to *s·* the human mind to a change of base,
p 422– 5 If the reader of this book observes a great *s·*

stirred
m 67– 4 When the ocean is *s·* by a storm,
g 540–10 The muddy river-bed must be *s·*

stirring
g 540– 7 as *s·* up the belief in evil to its utmost,

stirs
ap 559–13 *s·* their latent forces to utter the

St. John (*see also* **John**)
a 47–29 except *St. J·*, of whose death we have no
    55–27 In the words of *St. J·* "He shall— *John* 14 : 16.
o 357–24 the vision of *St. J·* in the Apocalypse.
ap 558– 1 *St. J·* writes, in the tenth chapter of
    560– 1 the Apocalypse, or Revelation of *St. J·*,
    561– 7 *St. J·* saw an "angel standing in— *Rev.* 19 : 17.
    572–26 Through what sense came this vision to *St. J·* ?

St. John's
g 536– 4 In *St. J·* vision, heaven and earth stand for
ap 573–19 Because *St. J·* corporeal sense of the heavens
    576– 6 This heavenly city, . . . reached *St. J·* vision
    577–29 *St. J·* Revelation as recorded by the great

stock
m 61–26 culture of your garden or the raising of *s·*

stole
s 139–20 material sense *s·* into the divine record,

stolid
m 59–19 more salutary . . . than *s·* indifference

stolidity
p 365–25 If hypocrisy, *s·*, inhumanity, or
    388– 5 *S·*, which is a resisting state of mortal mind,

stomach
and bowels
ph 176– 8 left the *s·* and bowels free to act
consulting the
f 222–15 consulting the *s·* less about the
controls the
f 220–31 controls the *s·*, bones, lungs, heart,
food nor the
f 221–30 neither food nor the *s·*, . . . can make one
his
f 221–23 These truths, . . . relieved his *s·*,
——
s 127–20 nerves, brain, *s·*, lungs, and so forth,
    143–19 but you conclude that the *s·*, blood, nerves,
ph 175–21 The exact amount of food the *s·* could digest
    197–25 and the most digestible food in the *s·*,
f 211– 1 If brain, nerves, *s·*, are intelligent,
b 294–13 saying : . . . The *s·* can make a man cross.
    308– 9 the head, heart, *s·*, blood, nerves,
p 413– 7 Mind regulates the condition of the *s·*,

stomachs
ph 165–17 distressed *s·* and aching heads.

stone
a 45– 1 and a great *s·* must be rolled from the
    45–17 Christ hath rolled away the *s·* from the
s 137–31 [the meaning of the Greek word *petros*, or *s·*]
    139–26 *s·* which the builders rejected"— *Matt.* 21 : 42.
t 447–30 A sinner is afraid to cast the first *s·*.

stoned
a 41–28 for which they were maligned and *s·*.

stones
ph 176–13 "sermons in *s·*, and good in everything."
b 288–20 The chief *s·* in the temple of C. S.
gl 596–12 *s·* in the breast-plate of the high-priest

stood
a 28– 3 Even many of his students *s·* in his way.
sp 75–18 would have *s·* on the same plane of belief
s 137– 5 when their immaculate Teacher *s·* before them,
f 245– 9 she *s·* daily before the window watching
b 338–20 when matter, . . . *s·* opposed to Spirit.
ap 563–25 and the dragon *s·* before the woman— *Rev.* 12 : 4.

stoops
ap 566–21 And oh, when *s·* on Judah's path

stop
pr 10–18 and *s·* at the doors to earn a penny
a 39–31 Who will *s·* the practice of sin so long as
f 254– 8 To *s·* eating, drinking, or being clothed
b 283–10 which act, react, and then come to a *s·*.
p 388–27 foolish to *s·* eating until we gain perfection
g 552– 2 But we cannot *s·* here.

stoppage
p 420– 2 no *s·* of harmonious action,

stopped
s 151–18 Fear never *s·* being and its action.
ph 193–21 The discharge from the sore *s·*,

store
 p 439– 4   He manufactures for it, keeps a furnishing *s*˙,
 t 462– 6   his *s*˙ of spiritual understanding,
storehouses
 a 54–12   into empty or sin-filled human *s*˙,
storm
 m 67– 4   When the ocean is stirred by a *s*˙,
 67– 8   Can you steer safely amid the *s*˙?"
 s 122–19   that little prophet of *s*˙ and sunshine,
 b 329–14   One should not tarry in the *s*˙ if the
 ap 566–22   In shade and *s*˙ the frequent night,
storms
 f 254–28   you will encounter *s*˙.
story
 s 142–16   In vain do the manger and the cross tell their
      s˙ to
 p 363–15   Jesus rebuked them with a short *s*˙ or parable.
 g 532– 9   the prediction in the *s*˙ under consideration.
 ap 566–14   Sir Walter Scott . . . in the *s*˙ of Ivanhoe,
St. Paul (*see also* **Paul**)
 a 20–27   *St. P*˙ wrote, "Let us lay aside— *Heb.* 12 : 1.
 an 106–18   and classify all others as did *St. P*˙
 s 108– 3   According to *St. P*˙, it was "the gift of— *Eph.*
      3 : 7.
 151–25   must be put off, as *St. P*˙ declares.
 164–28   Death is swallowed up in victory"
      (*St. P*˙). — *I Cor.* 15 : 54.
 ph 200–25   *St. P*˙ said : "For I determined— *I Cor.* 2 : 2.
 b 288–18   *St. P*˙ says : "There remaineth— *Heb.* 4 : 9.
 300–12   the real man, or the *new* man (as *St. P*˙ has it).
 p 412–25   *St P*˙ says, "Work out your— *Phil.* 2 : 12.
 r 478–27   *St. P*˙ said, "But when it pleased— *Gal.* 1 ; 15.
 ap 560–22   Abuse of the motives and religion of *St. P*˙
straight
 s 126–30   "the *s*˙ and narrow way"— *see Matt.* 7 : 14.
 151–28   The *s*˙ and narrow way is to see and
 b 282– 5   a circle or sphere and a *s*˙ line.
 282– 7   the *s*˙ line represents the finite,
 282–10   the *s*˙ line represents evil,
 282–14   A *s*˙ line finds no abiding-place in a curve,
 282–15   a curve finds no adjustment to a *s*˙ line.
 282–22   and the other a *s*˙ line.
 283–30   by calling a curve a *s*˙ line
 283–31   or a *s*˙ line a sphere.
 324–13   The way is *s*˙ and narrow, which leads to the
 t 454–29   tread firmly in the *s*˙ and narrow way.
 r 472– 5   The way which leads to C. S. is *s*˙ and narrow.
 g 502– 6   the *s*˙ line of Spirit over the mortal deviations
straightforward
 ph 168– 1   fair seeming for *s*˙ character,
straightway
 sp 99– 7   he *s*˙ adds : "for it is God which— *Phil.* 2 : 13.
 s 133–11   and *s*˙ believed that they were healed
 b 308–29   he *s*˙ answered ; and then his name was changed
 p 411–17   man was changed and *s*˙ became whole.
strain
 p 366–20   Such so-called Scientists will *s*˙ out gnats,
 ap 568–30   Love sends forth her primal and everlasting *s*˙.
strained
 sp 72–20   not a . . . through which truth can be *s*˙
straining
 m 65–21   until we get at last the clear *s*˙ of truth,
 s 140–14   *s*˙ out gnats and swallowing camels.
 f 202– 2   foolish as *s*˙ out gnats and swallowing camels.
strains
 sp 88–26   Eloquence re-echoes the *s*˙ of Truth and Love,
 ph 190–22   thus swept his lyre with saddening *s*˙
 f 213–25   Mental melodies and *s*˙ of sweetest music
strange
 f 216– 5   What has touched Life, God, to such *s*˙ issues?
 p 362– 6   A "*s*˙ woman" came in.— *Prov.* 23 : 27.
 s 524– 7   constantly went after "*s*˙ gods."— *Jer.* 5 : 19.
strangely
 o 355–32   *S*˙ enough, we ask for material theories
stranger
 s 142–13   the poor and the *s*˙ from the gate,
 146–20   the "*s*˙ that is within thy— *Exod.* 20 : 10.
 ph 174–15   a pilgrim and *s*˙, marking out the path for
 f 254–32   *s*˙, thou art the guest of God.
strangers
 g 507–10   *s*˙ in a tangled wilderness.
strangle
 ap 569–15   and fail to *s*˙ the serpent of sin
strangled
 f 236– 3   but never be *s*˙ there.
strata
 b 293– 7   are but different *s*˙ of human belief.
 293–11   both *s*˙, mortal mind and mortal body,

stratum
 s 158–26   so letting in matter's higher *s*˙, mortal mind.
 ph 185–29   the material *s*˙ of the human mind,
 198– 1   for the higher *s*˙ of mortal mind has
 r 477–15   though interwoven with matter's highest *s*˙,
strays
 b 311–15   belief *s*˙ into a sense of temporary loss
stream
 f 239–29   opposite sources never mingle in fount or *s*˙.
 246– 8   The *s*˙ rises no higher than its source.
 p 379–11   only a *s*˙ of warm water was trickling over
 389–17   the metaphors about the fount and *s*˙,
 g 540–11   in order to purify the *s*˙.
streams
 s 133– 9   In the wilderness, *s*˙ flowed from the rock,
streets
 pr 10–18   to carry a praying-machine through the *s*˙,
 t 459–19   turning him loose in the crowded *s*˙ of a city.
strength
 affection, and
 ph 183–22   man's entire obedience, affection, and *s*˙.
 and freedom
 t 454–20   *s*˙ and freedom to speech and action.
 and influence
 ph 188– 5   has grown terrible in *s*˙ and influence,
 and permanence
 m 58–10   true happiness, *s*˙, and permanence.
 and permanency
 b 293–28   the *s*˙ and permanency of Spirit.
 conscious
 p 390–32   Rise in the conscious *s*˙ of the spirit of Truth
 courage and
 m 57– 8   feminine mind gains courage and *s*˙
 divine
 p 406–31   normal control is gained through divine *s*˙
 giving
 p 407–12   giving *s*˙ to the weakness of mortal mind,
 giving us
 pr 5–18   giving us *s*˙ according to our day.
 helplessness to
 o 341– 3   raising up thousands from helplessness to *s*˙
 hour of
 ph 166–20   Instead of . . . waiting for the hour of *s*˙
 human
 ph 173–19   measuring human *s*˙ by bones and sinews,
 in proportion
 sp 80– 1   We have *s*˙ in proportion to our
 instead of
 p 371–29   *s*˙ instead of weakness,
 t 455– 6   indicate weakness instead of *s*˙.
 joy and
 p 365–31   not giving to mind or body the joy and *s*˙ of
 joyous in
 g 514– 6   Mind, joyous in *s*˙, dwells in the realm of Mind.
 measure
 r 485–30   as much as . . . muscles measure *s*˙.
 mockery of
 ph 192–25   It is a mockery of *s*˙, which erelong betrays its
 nutriment and
 f 999– 7   nutriment and *s*˙ to the human system.
 of Spirit
 p 393–12   Rise in the *s*˙ of Spirit
 or weakness
 p 377–14   the producer of *s*˙ or weakness.
 our
 sp 80– 2   our *s*˙ is not lessened by giving
 power and
 ph 183–24   Obedience to Truth gives man power and *s*˙.
 recovered
 f 222–17   he recovered *s*˙ and flesh rapidly.
 refuge and
 t 444–12   "God is our refuge and *s*˙,— *Psal.* 46 : 1.
 salvation, and
 ap 568–14   Now is come salvation, and *s*˙,— *Rev.* 12 : 10.
 shares not its
 ph 194– 2   Spirit shares not its *s*˙ with matter
 shorn of his
 s 124– 5   a blind belief, a Samson shorn of his *s*˙.
 sound, and
 r 486–16   If death restores sight, sound, and *s*˙ to man,
 source of
 g 514–31   a source of *s*˙ to the ancient worthies.
 spiritual
    (*see* **spiritual**)
 symbolized by
 g 512– 8   Spirit is symbolized by *s*˙, presence, and
 their
 p 417– 7   their *s*˙ is in proportion to their courage.
 to man
 m 60–17   a protection to woman, *s*˙ to man,

    —————

 ph 165– 7   To measure . . . *s*˙ by the exercise of muscle,
 f 219– 8   No more can we say . . . that muscles give *s*˙,
 b 308–21   and smote the sinew, or *s*˙, of his error,

strength
p 380–30　this opposing power with s· to
407–13　s· from the immortal and omnipotent Mind,
417– 7　Never . . . that they have more courage than s·.
r 485–31　To say that s· is in matter,
488– 3　When, on the s· of these instructions,
496–20　the s· of sin is the law,"— I Cor. 15 : 56.
gl 582– 8　s·, animation, and power to act.

strengthen
p 430– 6　should enlarge its borders and s· its base

strengthened
a 47–21　greed for gold s· his ingratitude,
sp 79–25　says : . . . body is weak, and it must be s·.
p 423–17　He regards the ailment as weakened or s·

strengthening
r 487–28　s· our trust in the deathless reality of Life,

strengthens
pr 16–17　This reading s· our scientific apprehension
p 404–24　and this knowledge s· his moral courage
423–23　and he proportionately s· his patient with
t 446–21　To understand God s· hope,
g 547–10　s· the thinker's conclusions as to the

stress
pr 5– 7　placed under the s· of circumstances.
ph 181–15　but that you lay no s· on manipulation.
f 234–29　He laid great s· on the action of the
p 440–14　under s· of circumstances, to be justifiable.

stretch
p 393–23　or the electric wire which you s·,
398–14　"S· forth thine hand,"— Matt. 12 : 13.

stricken
a 49–32　"s·, smitten of God."— Isa. 53 : 4.
f 226–10　demanding that the fetters . . . be s· from the

strict
a 27–11　in s· accordance with his scientific statement :
b 327–17　the s· demands of C. S. seem peremptory ;
t 456– 5　S· adherence to the divine Principle and rules

strictest
f 222–18　only by the s· adherence to

strictly
t 448–26　If the student adheres s· to the teachings of
459–32　should understand and adhere s· to the
462–14　must abide s· by its rules,

strictures
o 341– 1　s· on this volume would condemn to oblivion

strides
f 236–31　youth makes easy and rapid s· towards Truth.

strife
an 106–23　wrath, s·, seditions, heresies,— Gal. 5 : 20.
f 254–14　but to begin aright and to continue the s·
b 323– 3　This s· consists in the endeavor to forsake error
t 444–25　"Let there be no s·,— Gen. 13 : 8.
453– 6　will be at s· in the minds of students,

strike
ph 199– 2　lift the hammer and s· the anvil,

striking
o 360–20　s· the ribs of matter

strikingly
f 213–23　This was even more s· true of Beethoven,
252–15　contrasts s· with the testimony of Spirit.

strings
f 213–27　Mortal mind is the harp of many s·,

strip
ph 186–18　This falsehood should s· evil of all pretensions.
f 254–26　What is there to s· off error's disguise?

stripes
a 20–15　and "with his s·— Isa. 53 : 5.

stripped
f 241–11　S· of its coverings,

strips
o 343–14　Jesus s· all disguise from error,
t 454–13　the great truth which s· all disguise from error.
r 472–29　until God s· off their disguise.

strive
f 241–25　We should s· to reach the Horeb height
b 320–13　My spirit shall not always s·— Gen. 6 : 3.
t 451–11　They must not only seek, but s·, to enter

striving
pr 4–20　s· to assimilate more of the divine character,
10–14　It is s· that enables us to enter.
13– 7　If we are not secretly yearning and openly s·
a 21– 9　he is s· to enter in.
b 309–13　through earnest s· followed his demonstration
323– 3　will not be able . . . without s· for them.

strong
pr 4–31　clip the s· pinions of love,
6–31　The s· language of our Master confirms this
a 23–14　This preaching receives a s· rebuke
m 57–11　Both sexes should be loving, pure, tender, and s·.
65– 8　they will be s· and enduring.
sp 87–26　The s· impressions produced on mortal mind
99–23　The calm, s· currents of true spirituality,
s 130–26　If thought is startled at the s· claim of
134–15　They have not waxed s· in times of trouble.
142–20　The s· cords of scientific demonstration.
158–22　acquires an educated appetite for s· drink,
f 219–16　if we would have it s· ;
226–32　trusting Truth, the s· deliverer, to guide me
235– 3　if virtue and truth build a s· defence.
c 261–11　Under the s· impulse of a desire to
p 377–13　suddenly weak or abnormally s·,
398–22　and the desire for s· drink is gone.
399–29　enter into a s· man's house— Matt. 12 : 29.
399–31　first bind the s· man?"— Matt. 12 : 29.
400– 4　Mortal mind is "the s· man,"— Matt. 12 : 29.
400– 7　we can despoil "the s· man"— Matt. 12 : 29.
423–21　has rendered himself s·, instead of weak,
426–10　The struggle for Truth makes one s·
442– 8　prisoner rose up regenerated, s·, free,
t 448–19　the s· impress of divine Science,
455–28　This s· point in C. S. is
ap 567– 4　when s· faith or spiritual strength wrestles

stronger
pr 7– 2　Still s· evidence that Jesus' reproof was
an 104–28　worse than before it was grasped by the s· error.
s 144–12　the s· are the manifestations of the
ph 169–15　should find s· supports and a higher home.
198–26　and the s· thoughts rule the weaker.
199–14　his arm becomes s·.
c 265–24　gained s· desires for spiritual joy
b 327–10　until his grasp on good grows s·.
o 353– 7　having the s· evidence of Truth
p 387–24　but grows s· because of it.
409–18　the s· never yields to the weaker, except
410–14　Every trial of our faith in God makes us s·.
410–16　the s· should be our faith and the purer our
422–30　he believes that something s· than

strongest
a 27–30　made their s· attack upon this very point.
f 236–12　A mother is the s· educator,

strongly
s 116–22　C. S. s· emphasizes the thought that
ph 198–30　muscles of the blacksmith's arm are s·
f 235–11　should be s· garrisoned with virtue.
p 414–25　Hold these points s· in view.
423– 7　more s· than the expressed thought.

strove
ph 185–16　s· to emulate the wonders wrought by Moses.

struck
o 342– 2　The hour has s· when proof and

structural
ph 173–17　Anatomy declares man to be s·.
b 283–18　such as the s· life of the tree
309–30　Therefore it is never s· nor organic,
p 402– 9　forsake its corporeal, s·, and material basis,

structure
sp 71–27　The basis and s· of spiritualism are
s 162–20　the s· has been renewed,
ph 172–24　Brain, heart, blood, . . . the material s·?
173–21　material s· is mortal.
197–11　The less that is said of physical s·
f 228–21　bodily conditions, s·, or economy,
g 509–21　no more contingent now on time or material s·
ap 576–12　no material s· in which to worship God,
gl 581–22　the more certain is the downfall of its s·.
583–12　CHURCH.　The s· of Truth and Love ;

structures
g 549–19　the most complicated corporeal s·,

struggle
earthly
a 47–28　desertion of their Master in his last earthly s·
final
b 268–14　In this final s· for supremacy,
for Truth
p 426–10　s· for Truth makes one strong
habitual
pr 4–12　The habitual s· to be always good
Jacob's
b 309– 7　The result of Jacob's s· thus appeared.
mighty
p 407– 8　is conquered only by a mighty s·.

s 145– 8　The s· for the recovery of invalids goes on,
b 329–28　they would s· for recourse to the spiritual
p 407– 9　Every hour of delay makes the s· more severe.
431–15　The s· on their part was long.

struggle
- *t* 450–16 Few yield without a *s·*,
- *g* 534–28 will *s·* to destroy the spiritual idea of Love ;
- 536–26 Through toil, *s·*, and sorrow,

struggled
- *a* 33–18 When the human element in him *s·* with the
- *p* 373– 8 *s·* long, and perhaps in vain, to
- 436–23 His friends *s·* hard to rescue the prisoner

struggles
- *a* 30– 8 This accounts for his *s·* in Gethsemane
- *p* 439–22 in his *s·* against liver-complaint

struggling
- *a* 45 16 and peace to the *s·* hearts !
- 48– 5 waiting and *s·* in voiceless agony,
- *m* 57–28 for Love supports the *s·* heart
- 64–11 some noble woman, *s·* alone with adversity,
- 65–15 *s·* against the advancing spiritual era.
- *b* 308–16 *s·* with a mortal sense of life,
- *p* 394–13 To those *s·* with sickness,
- *ap* 569–18 not *s·* to lift their heads above the

strychnine
- *ph* 178– 3 the *s·*, or whatever the drug used,

stubborn
- *f* 224–19 Cold disdain, *s·* resistance,
- 237–10 *s·* beliefs and theories of parents
- *r* 490– 8 Will — blind, *s·*, and headlong

stubbornness
- *gl* 593–19 ROCK. . . . Coldness and *s·*.

student (*see also* student's)
adheres
- *t* 448–26 If the *s·* adheres strictly to the teachings of

any
- *t* 462– 3 any *s·*, who adheres to the divine rules of C. S.

divine
- *s* 117–16 As a divine *s·* he unfolded God to man,

his
- *t* 449–30 improves the health and the morals of his *s·*
- 454–15 points out to his *s·* error as well as truth,

lift a
- *p* 373– 9 to lift a *s·* out of a chronic sin.

morals of the
- *t* 445 28 thus disregarding the morals of the *s·*

one
- *pref* xi–26 started by the author with only one *s·*

show your
- *t* 451 31 Show your *s·* that mental malpractice

signifies
- *b* 271–11 the word rendered *disciple* signifies *s·* ;

success of the
- *p* 372–21 will be a hindrance to the . . . success of the *s·*.

teacher and
- *t* 457– 5 has done more for teacher and *s·*,
- 463– 5 Teacher and *s·* should also be familiar with

teach your
- *t* 453–14 Teach your *s·* that he must know himself

will prove
- *p* 384 14 the *s·* will prove to himself, by

- *u* 28– 5 If the Master had not taken a *s·*
- *p* 411– 4 If the *s·* silently called the
- 411– 8 because the *s·* was not perfectly attuned to
- *t* 449–30 if the *s·* practises what he is taught,
- 455–17 The *s·*, who receives his knowledge of C. S.,
- 459–28 the *theologus* (that is, the *s·*
- 462– 9 If the *s·* goes away to practise

student's
- *p* 367–28 namely, the *s·* higher attainments
- 411– 3 My first discovery in the *s·* practice
- *t* 448–19 Try to leave on every *s·* mind
- 461–31 *s·* spiritual growth and experience

students
are advised
- *t* 444–13 *S·* are advised by the author

do not dismiss
- *t* 454–25 Do not dismiss *s·* at the close of a

English
- *p* 379– 9 on whom certain English *s·* experimented,

four thousand
- *pref* xii– 6 over four thousand *s·* were taught

her
- *pref* x–16 she and her *s·* have proved the worth of
- *p* 402– 5 records of the cure, by herself and her *s·*

his
- *a* 28– 3 Even many of his *s·* stood in his way.
- 43–12 the most profitable to his *s·*.
- 46–30 His *s·* then received the Holy Ghost.
- 48– 2 His *s·* slept.
- *sp* 85–16 Jesus, as he once journeyed with his *s·*,
- *s* 136–11 He appealed to his *s·* :
- 137– 1 His *s·* saw this power of Truth heal
- 146– 1 first article of faith propounded to his *s·*
- 147–26 and taught the generalities . . . to his *s·* ;
- 148– 1 When his *s·* brought to him a case

students
his
- *b* 321–31 Jesus, who showed his *s·* the power of Mind
- *o* 342–12 the promise that his *s·* should cast out evils
- 343–26 Paul who was not one of his *s·*,
- *t* 445– 2 teacher must thoroughly fit his *s·*
- 451–24 obligated to open the eyes of his *s·*
- 456–26 and so do all his *s·* and patients.
- *r* 473–31 Few, however, except his *s·* understood
- *g* 509– 5 Our Master reappeared to his *s·*,

Jesus'
- *a* 45–32 Jesus' *s·*, not sufficiently advanced
- *o* 343–25 those apostles who were Jesus' *s·*,

malicious
- *s* 110–21 or by careless or malicious *s·*,

minds of
- *t* 453– 7 will be at strife in the minds of *s·*,

of Christian Science
- *t* 451– 8 *S·* of C. S., who start with its letter
- 456– 7 secured the only success of the *s·* of C. S.

seventy
- *a* 27–22 Jesus sent forth seventy *s·* at one time,

your
- *t* 454– 4 Teach your *s·* the omnipotence of Truth,
- 454–28 until your *s·* tread firmly in the

- *p* 420– 5 If *s·* do not readily heal themselves,
- *t* 444–31 The teacher must make clear to *s·* the
- 460–29 by her manuscript circulated among the *s·*.

studied
- *pref* ix–24 before a work on the subject could be profitably *s·*,
- *s* 147–17 The book needs to be *s·*,
- *ph* 174 3 practitioners by their more *s·* methods.

study
branch of
- *t* 462–24 This branch of *s·* is indispensable to the

careful
- *ph* 196–12 A careful *s·* of this text shows that

classic
- *sp* 82– 6 What is classic *s·*, but discernment of the

medical
- *t* 443– 4 consistency of systematic medical *s·*,
- 443 8 While a course of medical *s·* is

Scriptural
- *pref* viii–29 give to friends the results of her Scriptural *s·*,

- *sp* 89–15 believes that he cannot be an orator without *s·*
- *ph* 171–10 not needing to *s·* brainology to learn
- 176– 4 modern Eves took up the *s·* of medical works
- 195–20 Observation, invention, *s·*, and
- *f* 202– 6 If men would bring to bear upon the *s·* of
- *p* 382– 6 given to the *s·* of C. S. and to the
- *r* 495–27 *S·* thoroughly the letter and imbibe the spirit.
- *ap* 559–21 *S·* it, ponder it,

studying
- *ph* 179 26 The sedulous matron — *s·* her Jahr
- *b* 321– 2 as may be seen by *s·* the book of Job.

stumble
- *f* 205 3 *s·* with lameness, drop with drunkenness.
- *t* 463– 4 and so he may *s·* and fall in the darkness.

stung
- *ap* 560–26 is at last *s·* to death by his own malice ;

stupefaction
- *p* 415–12 They quiet the thought by inducing *s·*

stupefying
- *sp* 95–28 Lulled by *s·* illusions, the world is asleep

stupendous
- *pref* ix–30 comparative ignorance of the *s·* Life-problem

stupid
- *m* 58–27 not to court vulgar extravagance or *s·* ease,
- *s* 158–16 cataplasms, and whiskey are *s·* substitutes

sturdy
- *pref* vii–23 the task of the *s·* pioneer to hew the tall oak
- *t* 463–16 Its beginning will be meek, its growth *s·*,

styled
- *f* 213– 1 movements of mortal belief, . . . are *s·* the real

subdivides
- *g* 511– 2 *s·* and radiates their borrowed light,

subdue
- *b* 315–19 we realize this likeness only when we *s·* sin
- *p* 421–13 and *s·* the symptoms by removing the
- *g* 517–27 replenish the earth, and *s·* it ; — *Gen.* 1 : 28.

subdued
- *ph* 199–20 latent mental fears are *s·* by him.
- *p* 406–15 period, in which mortal sense is *s·*

subdues
- *s* 145–12 Truth, *s·* the human belief in disease.

subduing
- *s* 142– 2 the old systems, devised for *s·* them,

subject
main
  pref ix– 2 began to jot down her thoughts on the main *s*·,
of sickness
  ph 169–13 by attracting the mind to the *s*· of sickness,
prolific
  f 228– 7 Heredity is a prolific *s*· for mortal belief to
that
  p 416–30 have already heard too much on that *s*·.
this
  pr 1– 5 what another may say or think on this *s*·,
  ph 170–25 The age seems ready to approach this *s*·,
  b 297– 4 until the belief on this *s*· changes.
  o 341–12 Proof is essential to a due estimate of this *s*·.
  356– 9 Jesus reasoned on this *s*· practically,
  p 373– 4 we must have more faith in God on this *s*·
  t 449–17 requires a higher understanding to teach this *s*·
work on the
  pref ix–23 before a work on the *s*· could

     —————

  a 49– 5 "Even the devils are *s*· unto us — *Luke* 10 : 17.
  49–22 the Christ is not *s*· to material conditions,
  m 56–13 *s*· to such moral regulations as will
  sp 74– 2 spiritual life which is not *s*· to death.
  an 102–23 produce the very apathy on the *s*· which
  s 120–16 nor . . . bear reliable testimony on the *s*·
  124–17 represented as *s*· to growth, maturity, and
  150–19 believe that both . . . are *s*· to disease,
  ph 171–22 infinite Mind,— *s*· to non-intelligence !
  173– 7 supposition, that . . . the potter is *s*· to the clay,
  200–13 and not *s*· to decay and dust.
  f 244–14 *s*· to laws of decay.
  249– 9 Let us rejoice that we are *s*· to the
  b 288–24 Life is not *s*· to death ;
  297–18 but *s*· to change and dissolution.
  305–28 not *s*· to birth, growth, maturity, decay.
  331– 4 it would be *s*· to their limitations
  337–29 *S*· sickness, sin, and death to the rule of
  o 356–22 How then is it possible for Him to create man *s*· to
  361–25 must be correct . . . and *s*· to demonstration.
  p 372–15 He can neither . . . be *s*· to matter, nor
  429–12 Science declares that man is *s*· to Mind.
  r 486–22 mortal in belief and *s*· to chance and change.
  g 515– 8 ideas are *s*· to the Mind which forms them,
  534–19 for it is not *s*· to the law of God, — *Rom.* 8 : 7.

subjected
  b 305– 2 *s*· to material sense which is discord.
  318–28 The governor is not *s*· to the governed.
  o 341– 8 appear contradictory when *s*· to such usage.
  341–16 according to a divine given rule, and *s*· to proof.

subjection
  f 227– 9 and in *s*· to hopeless slavery,
  240–29 is finally brought into *s*· to Truth.
  p 400– 5 which must be held in *s*· before its influence
  g 518– 1 His birthright is dominion, not *s*·.

subjective
  s 108–27 a *s*· state of mortal mind which
  114–30 what is termed *matter* is but the *s*· state of
  ph 189–31 for matter is the *s*· condition of mortal mind.
  g 512–16 externalized, yet *s*·, states of faith and
  ap 573–21 the *s*· state by which he could see the
  gl 592– 7 the *s*· states of error ; material senses ;

subjects
  a 55– 3 *s*· to unchristian comment and usage
  an 101–24 upon those who practise it, and upon their *s*·
  ph 175– 5 and less thought is given to sanitary *s*·,
  p 402–25 The operator would make his *s*· believe
  413–10 views of parents and other persons on these *s*·
  t 446–32 oftentimes *s*· you to its abuse.
  g 507– 8 objects and *s*· would be obscure,

subjugate
  ph 165– 8 to *s*· intelligence, to make mind mortal,

sublime
  a 45– 4 crowned with the glory of a *s*· success,
  49–11 sacrifices, his divine patience, *s*· courage,
  s 138–15 His *s*· summary points to the religion of Love.
  c 256–17 the *s*· question, What is infinite Mind ?
  p 387–27 history of Christianity furnishes *s*· proofs
  ap 571–30 the *s*· grandeur of divine Science,

sublimest
  a 51– 4 the *s*· influence of his career.

sublimity
  g 509–26 in which beauty, *s*·, purity, and holiness
  511– 5 the *s*·, magnitude, and infinitude

submerged
  g 546– 2 false belief that spirit is now *s*· in

submergence
  gl 581–23 Purification by Spirit ; *s*· in Spirit.
  582–22 *S*· in Spirit ; immortality brought to light.

submission
  a 32–13 he bowed in holy *s*· to the divine decree.
  s 157–27 both mind and body worse for this *s*·.
  159– 6 and she was forced into *s*·.
  ph 183–24 *S*· to error superinduces loss of power.
  f 216–17 his body is in *s*· to everlasting Life and
  p 391– 7 Instead of blind and calm *s*· to
  404– 7 suffering which his *s*· to such habits brings,
  gl 597– 1 in token of reverence and *s*·

submissive
  b 314–30 *s*· to death as being in supposed accord with

submit
  p 381– 2 Ignorant of . . . we *s*· to unjust decrees,
  406– 7 Sin will *s*· to C. S.
  435–32 only jurisdiction to which the prisoner can *s*·
  r 492–24 must eventually *s*· to the Science of Mind,

submitted
  sp 76–30 death must be overcome, not *s*· to,
  s 111–29 I *s*· my metaphysical system of
  147– 7 were *s*· to the broadest practical test,

submitting
  f 239–20 matter is then *s*· to Spirit.

subordinate
  s 125–17 When *s*· to the divine Spirit,
  f 215–11 Spiritual vision is not *s*· to
  o 349– 9 We should *s*· material law to spiritual law.
  p 429–14 affirms that mind is *s*· to the body,
  g 516– 6 when we *s*· the false testimony
  518– 3 himself *s*· alone to his Maker.

subordination
  f 206– 5 should be exercised only in *s*· to Truth ;

subscribed
  r 471–23 The author *s*· to an orthodox creed

subscribes
  f 225–10 until it *s*· to their systems ;

subsequent
  o 356–30 Does *s*· follow its antecedent ?
  g 531– 4 maintained in all the *s*· forms of belief.
  537–22 *S*· Bible revelation is coordinate with the

subsequently
  f 206–30 does not make mistakes and *s*· correct them.
  r 476–15 which may *s*· be regained.
  g 549–17 from which one or more individualities *s*·

subserve
  g 501–14 which *s*· the end of natural good,

subserving
  b 319– 4 error reversed as *s*· the facts

subside
  p 421–20 when the fear is destroyed, the inflammation will *s*·.

subsides
  p 384–25 When the fear *s*· and the conviction

substance
all
  c 259– 5 for he represents . . . the sum of all *s*·.
  b 275–14 All *s*·, intelligence, wisdom, being,
  r 469– 3 Spirit, which includes in itself all *s*·
  gl 587– 7 Truth ; Love ; all *s*· ; intelligence.
and color
  b 310– 7 seen in all form, *s*·, and color,
and continuity
  s 124–25 Spirit is the life, *s*·, and continuity
and creator
  c 257– 7 theory that Spirit is not the only *s*· and creator
and Life
  b 286–21 God's thoughts . . . are *s*· and Life.
and life
  gl 591– 9 intelligence, *s*·, and life
and mind
  b 325–32 A false sense of life, *s*·, and mind
  gl 580–12 *s*·, and mind are found to be the
any other
  b 301–21 The belief that man has any other *s*·,
are not
  sp 90– 7 The earth's orbit and . . . are not *s*·.
cannot produce
  c 257– 6 and shadow cannot produce *s*·.
divine
  b 300–29 universe reflects and expresses the divine *s*·
  r 468–24 reflecting the divine *s*· of Spirit.
  gl 594–19 SPIRIT. Divine *s*· ; Mind ;
eternal
  b 299–25 Truth is spiritual, eternal *s*·,
  301–11 and reflects the eternal *s*·, or Spirit,
foreign
  p 438–22 the facts . . . show that this fur is a foreign *s*·,
God is
  b 301–17 As God is *s*· and man is the
intelligence, nor
  s 133–28 no life, intelligence, nor *s*· outside of God.
  r 468– 9 no life, truth, intelligence, nor *s*· in matter.

substance

intelligence or
g 508– 5 The only intelligence or *s·* of a thought,
is in Mind
c 267– 2 the spiritual idea, whose *s·* is in Mind,
Life and
b 314–22 presented to her, . . . the true idea of Life and *s·*.
life and
b 311–18 dream of life and *s·* as existent in matter,
life, and intelligence
sp 91–25 postulate . . . that *s·*, life, and intelligence are
ap 562– 9 reflected light, *s·*, life, and intelligence.
 563– 9 belief that *s·*, life, and intelligence can be
Life, . . . and intelligence
a 27–14 Life, *s·*, and intelligence of the universe
ph 185–19 God as the only Life, *s·*, and intelligence,
gl 595– 7 the idea of Life, *s·*, and intelligence ;
life, . . . and intelligence
 (*see* life)
life, . . . and mind
gl 582– 5 belief as to life, *s·*, and mind ;
life, or
gl 584–28 the absence of *s·*, life, or intelligence.
material
b 278–17 The admission that there can be material *s·*
 301–23 seems to himself to be material *s·*,
Mind and
b 301–28 presents an inverted image of Mind and *s·*
Mind is
p 414–24 C. S. declares that Mind is *s·*,
of all
f 253– 8 the *s·* of all, because I AM THAT I AM.
of all devotion
f 241–19 *s·* of all devotion is the reflection and
of an idea
c 257–12 the *s·* of an idea is very far from
of good
b 301–19 and in reality has, only the *s·* of good,
of Life
sp 91–17 the *s·* of Life or Mind.
of Spirit
b 301–19 and in reality has, . . . the *s·* of Spirit,
r 468–24 reflecting the divine *s·* of Spirit.
 480– 1 When the *s·* of Spirit appears in C. S.,
of things
b 279– 4 "the *s·* of things hoped for."— *Heb.* 11 : 1.
r 468–20 "The *s·* of things hoped for,— *Heb* 11 : 1.
of thought
p 423–30 Bones have only the *s·* of thought
or intelligence
p 418– 6 error that life, *s·*, or intelligence can be in
or mind
o 351– 2 material life, *s·*, or mind
pulpy
ph 192– 2 The belief that a pulpy *s·* under the skull
real
r 468–22 Soul, or God, is the only real *s·*.
reality of
b 311–27 have not the reality of *s·*.
seemed to be
b 314–19 and the body, ... seemed to be *s·*.
seems
b 312– 6 What to material sense seems *s·*,
seems to be
b 301– 7 To himself, . . . material man seems to be *s·*,
sense of
b 301– 8 his sense of *s·* involves error
so-called
p 423–32 The so-called *s·* of bone is
Soul and
b 280–14 finite sense of the divisibility of Soul and *s·*,
supposed
c 257–13 the supposed *s·* of non-intelligent matter.
the only
c 257– 7 theory that Spirit is not the only *s·*
b 278– 4 Spirit is the only *s·* and consciousness
 335–12 Spirit is the only *s·*,

a 38–28 he said in *s·* : Having eyes ye see not,
sp 90– 9 the thought that there can be *s·* in matter,
an 100–11 through the *s·* of the nerves."
s 162–23 what is called the lost *s·* of lungs,
ph 173–12 Neither the *s·* nor the manifestation
c 257– 4 If matter, so-called, is *s·*,
b 279– 1 Which ought to be *s·* to us,
 312– 5 is found to be *s·*.
 313–31 To show that the *s·* of himself was Spirit
 330–11 God is infinite, the only Life, *s·*, Spirit,
 331– 2 no more . . . than *s·* is in its shadow.
o 349–11 In C. S., *s·* is understood to be Spirit,
 350– 1 opponents of C. S. believe *s·* to be matter.
 351–21 To them matter was *s·*,
 369–11 the belief that matter is *s·*,
r 467– 6 no *s·*, no truth, no love, but that which
 468–16 *Question.*— What is *s·* ?

substance

r 468–17 *S·* is that which is eternal
 468–19 Truth, Life, and Love are *s·*,
 472–15 that intelligence, *s·*, life,
 477–22 Soul is the *s·*, Life, and
 483–15 she affixed . . . the name "*s·*" to Mind.
g 516– 4 The *s·*, Life, intelligence, Truth, and
gl 588–24 *S·* ; self-existent and eternal Mind ;
 591–17 divine Principle, *s·*, Life, Truth, Love ;
 594–25 definition of

substance-matter
sp 88–16 at one time are supposed to be *s·*
b 278– 9 the notion that there is real *s·*,
 314– 4 relinquished the belief of *s·*,

substances
f 209–16 compounded minerals or aggregated *s·*
 209–25 Material *s·* or mundane formations,
g 509–20 So-called mineral, vegetable, and animal *s·*

substantial
sp 93– 1 as *s·* and able to control the body
b 268–15 semi-metaphysical systems afford no *s·* aid
 275– 5 matter is neither *s·*, living, nor
 278–12 That matter is *s·* or has life and
 278–31, 32 cannot be *s·* if Spirit is *s·*
 292–15 To mortal mind, matter is *s·*,
 301–11 immortal, spiritual man is really *s·*,
 335–14 Things spiritual and eternal are *s·*.
g 531– 1 living, *s·*, and intelligent.

substantiality
b 301–15 spiritual man's *s·* transcends mortal vision
 318– 2 but for him to conceive of the *s·* of Spirit

substantially
b 324–32 said *s·*, "He that believeth— *see John* 11 : 26.
p 436–27 *s·* charged the jury, twelve Mortal Minds,

substitute
f 218–19 why do you *s·* drugs for the

substitutes
s 146–13 Material medicine *s·* drugs for the
 158–16 Drugs, cataplasms, and whiskey are stupid *s·*
f 247–28 embellishments of the person are poor *s·*

substituting
ph 167–32 *S·* good words for a good life,
t 462–11 and *s·* his own views for Truth,
r 482– 7 can always be gained by *s·* the word *God*,
ap 578– 2 by *s·* for the corporeal sense, the incorporeal

substitution
r 481–32 *s·* of the word *sense* for *soul*
gl 579– 1 the *s·* of the spiritual for the material

substratum

corporeal
p 408–28 in the corporeal *s·* of brain
grosser
b 293– 8 The grosser *s·* is named matter
inanimate
f 243–21 the inanimate *s·* of mortal mind,
its
sp 80–24 control of mortal mind over its *s·*,
 80–25 mortal mind which convulses its *s·*.
unconscious
p 409–11 the unconscious *s·* of mortal mind,
 400–17 superior to its unconscious *s·*, matter,

s 157–13 more like the human mind than the *s·* of
ph 198– 3 more power . . . than the *s·*, matter.
p 371– 2 body is the *s·* of mortal mind,

subterfuge
t 447–31 He may say, as a *s·*, that evil is unreal,

subtile
b 284–24 the more *s·* and misnamed material elements

subtle
an 102–20 weaving webs more complicated and *s·*.
f 226– 4 under more *s·* and depraving forms.
p 376– 6 It is the most *s·*,
t 451–26 especially any *s·* degree of evil,
g 515– 6 serpent of God's creating is neither *s·* nor
 529–13 Now the serpent was more *s·*— *Gen.* 3 : 1.
ap 564–32 "more *s·* than any beast of the— *Gen.* 3 : 1.

subtlety
t 447–12 Ignorance, *s·*, or false charity does not
ap 563–27 The serpentine form stands for *s·*,
 564–26 are typified by a serpent, or animal *s·*.
gl 593– 8 sensuality ; *s·* ; animal magnetism;
 594– 2 *S·* ; a lie ; the opposite of Truth,

subtract
f 219– 7 we do not multiply when we should *s·*,

subverted
ph 200–19 he is neither inverted nor *s·*,

succeed

s 149–12	If you fail to s· in any case,
f 243– 2	but we can never s· . . . through ignorance
p 372–21	and hope to s· with contraries?
411–32	If you s· in wholly removing the fear,
419–28	To s· in healing, you must conquer your
t 451– 9	and think to s· without the spirit,

succeeded

sp 95–21	and we want that day to be s· by C. S.,
p 431–17	s· in getting Mortal Man into

succeeding

f 246–25	Each s· year unfolds wisdom,

succeeds

s 149– 7	The prescription which s· in one instance
157– 3	It s· where homœopathy fails,
f 252–24	says : . . . How sin s·,
p 372–23	Matter s· for a period only by falsely parading

success

crowned with

a 22–10	these efforts are crowned with s·.

enlightenment, and

t 462– 8	potency, enlightenment, and s·.

happiness, and

p 405–11	conspirators against health, happiness, and s·.

in error is defeat

f 239–12	s· in error is defeat in Truth.

in healing

sp 95–17	but it is important to s· in healing,
t 448–28	he cannot fail of s· in healing.

insure

t 449–15	qualities which insure s· in this Science ;

of Jesus' mission

a 28– 2	they only hindered the s· of Jesus' mission.

of the student

p 372–32	recovery of the sick and the s· of the student.

of the students

t 456– 7	has secured the only s· of the students

sublime

a 45– 4	crowned with the glory of a sublime s·,

unequalled

s 134–20	and unequalled s· in the first century.

successes

s 133–13	miracles attended the s· of the Hebrews ;

successful

s 154–31	The better and more s· method
p 369– 3	unfitted for the s· treatment of disease.

successfully

pr 1– 8	whatever has been s· done for the
ph 167–13	Drugs and hygiene cannot s· usurp the

successive

m 66–14	Each s· stage of experience
g 504–16	The s· appearing of God's ideas
506–14	forming each s· stage of progress.
549–14	s· generations do not begin with the

such

pref xii– 2	for s· institutions after 1883,
pr 3–30	In s· a case, the only acceptable prayer is to
5–23	S· an error would impede true religion.
7– 4	showing the necessity for s· forcible utterance,
8– 8	s· externals are spoken of by Jesus
11–31	S· a desire has little need of
12– 6	The beneficial effect of s· prayer for the sick is
13– 9	s· as the heathen use.
13–22	doubts and fears which attend s· a belief,
15–21	S· prayer is answered, in so far as we
16– 4	S· prayer heals sickness,
a 23– 7	S· a theory is man-made.
24–31	could not admit s· an event to be possible.
26–22	involved s· a sacrifice as makes us admit
31– 3	and God will never place it in s· hands.
39– 2	S· indignities as he received,
43–30	errors growing from s· beliefs.
53–18	which might flow from s· discomfort.
m 56–13	s· moral regulations as will secure increasing
62– 4	education of children should be s· as to
63–14	C. S. furnishes no precedent for s· injustice,
66–28	salutary under s· circumstances,
67–32	rebuked the suffering from any s· cause
sp 74–14	persons in s· opposite dreams
74–19	S· a backward transformation is impossible
74–27	two s· opposite conditions as the
77–23	s· communications would grow beautifully less
79– 8	s· a mental method produces permanent
83–10	for s· a belief hides Truth
85– 7	S· intuitions reveal whatever constitutes
87–13	Scotch call s· vision "second sight,"
an 106–16	sanction only s· methods as are
106–24	revellings and s· like : — Gal. 5 : 21.
106–26	they which do s· things — Gal. 5 : 21.
106–29	against s· there is no law." — Gal. 5 : 23.
s 112–29	s· a school is erroneous, for it
119– 5	s· theories lead to one of two things.
122–11	s· as brain and nerves,

such

s 129–14	tribulation s· as was not since — Matt. 24 : 21.
130–24	s· as they belong to the heavenly kingdom.
132–11	s· effects, coming from divine Mind,
136–23	for how could s· a sinner comprehend
139–32	The moral condition of s· a man demands
141–10	All revelation (s· is the popular thought !)
146– 9	S· systems are barren of the vitality of
152–11	S· errors beset every material theory,
152–19	S· a fact illustrates our theories.
153– 1	is frequently attenuated to s· a degree
154–28	S· a mother runs to her little one,
155–14	s· a belief is governed by the majority.
157–11	s· repetition of thought-attenuations,
159–17	and not have risked s· treatment.
161–29	S· unconscious mistakes would not occur, if
ph 177–31	In s· cases a few persons believe the
179–15	body then seems to require s· treatment.
181– 8	but mortal belief has s· a partnership.
185–11	S· theories and s· systems of so-called
185–17	S· theories have no relationship to C. S.,
196–20	S· books as will rule disease out of
199– 7	producing s· a result on the hammer.
f 204–18	S· theories are evidently erroneous.
204–32	must unsay it and cease from s· utterances ;
205–18	or as they melt into s· thinness that
207–17	s· as the amalgamation of Truth and error
208–18	S· an utterance is "the voice of — Matt. 3 : 3.
216– 4	What has touched Life, God, to s· strange issues?
217– 3	and the notion of s· a possibility is
220– 4	S· admissions ought to open people's eyes
229–10	the belief which unites s· opposites
243–22	Neither . . . can carry on s· telegraphy ;
244– 2	therefore s· deformity is not real,
244–27	S· admissions cast us headlong
245–24	manifested the influence of s· a belief.
249–10	S· is the true Science of being.
253–28	for no s· law exists.
c 261– 9	with s· absorbed interest as to forget it,
266– 2	S· is the sword of Science,
b 273–22	If there were s· a material law, it would
275–29	s· as matter, disease, sin, and death,
280–11	S· belief can neither apprehend nor
283–18	s· as the structural life of the tree
290–14	"On s· the second death hath no — Rev. 20 : 6.
294–31	The Science of Mind corrects s· mistakes,
309–28	to suppose that there can be s· a reality as
309–29	s· so-called life always ends in death.
312– 2	s· so-called knowledge is reversed
314–16	To s· materialists, the real man seemed a
320–20	however transcendental s· a thought
325– 5	S· a one abideth in Life,
331–25	S· omnipresence and individuality
332–24	in s· a form of humanity as they
o 341– 8	when subjected to s· usage.
343– 1	are taught in s· cases to say, Amen.
343–29	to follow s· examples !
346– 1	S· criticism confounds man with Adam.
348–32	If s· are the present fruits,
351–22	Because s· starting-points are neither
352–27	because there are no s· things.
355–29	proved to be s· by our Master
358– 5	S· doctrines are "confusion
360– 8	for mine give me s· personal pleasure,
p 362– 8	debarred from s· a place and s· society,
363– 3	sandal oil perhaps, which is in s· common use
364– 8	tribute to s· ineffable affection,
364–20	Jesus told Simon that s· seekers as he
365– 7	finding utterance in s· words as
365–20	s· commendation as the Magdalen gained
365–32	s· as peace, patience in tribulation,
366–19	S· so-called Scientists will strain out gnats.
374–21	S· a state of mind induces sickness.
378–29	S· a power, . . . is inconceivable;
378–30	and if s· a power could be divinely directed,
383–15	It is the native element of s· a mind,
383–25	S· instances only prove the illusive
384–20	s· symptoms are not apt to follow
386– 7	no s· result occurs without mind
392–25	Admitting only s· conclusions as you
394–13	s· admissions are discouraging,
394–32	faith is not the healer in s· cases.
398–29	changes s· ills into new and more difficult
404– 7	suffering which his submission to s· habits
413–25	directing the mind to s· signs,
413–30	probable at any time that s· ills may
422–13	If s· be the case, explain to them the
424–18	s· opinions as may alarm or discourage,
427–27	when all s· remedies have failed
433–10	The jury must regard in s· cases only the
436–13	S· acts bear their own justification,
437–24	for s· high-handed illegality.
442– 2	because there are no s· laws.
t 443– 6	those, who make s· a compromise,
443–18	give up s· cases, and leave invalids free
443–20	s· invalids may learn the value of

such

```
    t 446–10  has generally completely healed s· cases.
      448– 8  Under s· circumstances, to say that there is no
      450–12  To teach C. S. to s· as these is no task.
      452–26  S· a practice does not demonstrate the
      453–26  for s· a course increases fear,
      455– 5  S· mental states indicate weakness
      455–21  one who has grown into s· a fitness for it
      460–13  till s· thought is rectified by Spirit
      463–30  S· seeming medical effect or action is that of
    r 478– 1  But there is, there can be, no s· division,
      478–10  when no s· persons were ever seen to go into
      487–21  there is in reality no s· thing as mortal mind.
      495–12  opens the prison doors to s· as are bound,
    g 504–26  vague conjectures emit no s· effulgence.
      517– 4  in s· a phrase as "an anthropomorphic God,"
      539– 9  s· as evil, matter, error, and death?
      545–13  S· fundamental errors send falsity into
      549–21  culminate in s· vague hypotheses
      554– 4  There is no s· thing as mortality,
      554–19  Mind sets at naught s· a mistaken belief.
   ap 573– 2  is unable to grasp s· a view.
      573–24  s· a recognition of being is, . . . possible
```

suckling
```
    p 371–21  nor would I keep the s· a lifelong babe.
```

sudden
```
    a  47– 8  The influx of light was s·.
   ph 179– 1  the s· cures of which it is capable ;
    f 218–24  Treat a belief in sickness . . . with s· dismissal.
    p 377–15  A s· joy or grief has caused what is termed
```

suddenly
```
   pr  14–16  you will find yourself s· well.
    a  36–30  s· pardoned and pushed into heaven,
   sp  77– 1  recognition of Spirit and of infinity comes not s·
    p 377–13  becomes s· weak or abnormally strong,
      434–19  Then C. S. turns s· to the supreme tribunal,
      438–13  Turning s· to Personal Sense.
```

suffer
```
    a  33–14  their Master was about to s· violence
      37– 3  They who sin must s·.
      40–17  Was it just for Jesus to s·?
    m  56– 3  "S· it to be so now.— Matt. 3 : 15.
    s 108–11  for the divine Mind cannot s·.
   ph 176–28  human mind, . . . is supposed to feel, s·, enjoy.
      181– 7  which can neither s· nor enjoy,
      184–21  for matter cannot s·.
      189–14  sins of others should not make good men s·.
    f 210–26  matter, being unintelligent, cannot say, "I s·,
      212– 1  We s· or enjoy in our dreams,
      221–31  neither food nor . . . can make one s·,
      235– 4  Better s· a doctor infected with smallpox to
      237–31  they hug false beliefs and s· the delusive
      238–21  because we s· severely from error.
      250–16  weary or pained, enjoy or s·, according to
    b 295–29  teaches that mortals are created to s· and die.
      296–20  will s· the pangs of destruction,
      322–15  since God has sentenced sin to s·.
      340–29  leaves nothing that can sin, s·, be punished or
    o 346–14  belief that we s· from the sins of others.
      346–24  how can he s· longer?
    p 372–15  He can neither sin, s·, be subject to
      376–18  it cannot, for that very reason, s· with a fever.
      376–25  showing that it is impossible for matter to s·,
      378– 4  Unwittingly you sentence yourself to s·.
      381– 4  Be no more willing to s· the illusion that you
      381–10  cannot in reality s· from breaking anything
              except
      385–24  will s· in proportion to your belief and fear.
      387–23  one cannot s· as the result of any labor of love,
      390–20  S· no claim of sin or of sickness to grow
      391–13  It is error to s· for aught but your own sins.
      392–32  then the body cannot s· from them.
      393–31  Your body would s· no more from tension
      397–26  walk, see, hear, enjoy, or s·
      403– 5  should and does cause the perpetrator to s·,
      414–10  impossibility that matter, brain, . . . can s·
      421– 1  he suffers only as the insane s·,
      435–25  and Mortal Man can s· only for his sin.
    g 524–29  Could Spirit . . . give matter ability to sin and s·?
      557– 8  many animals s· no pain in multiplying ;
   gl 582–16  has spiritual bliss and enjoys but cannot s·.
```

suffered
```
   pr  11–16  if indeed, he has not already s· sufficiently
      11–18  Jesus s· for our sins,
    a  24–15  in which Jesus s· and triumphed,
      25–30  worked and s· to bestow upon us.
      38–24  his spiritual selfhood, never s·.
      46–31  by all they had witnessed and s·,
    s 156–23  but on the third day she again s·,
   ph 185– 4  and she never s· again from east winds,
```

sufferer
```
    s 108–10  the truism that the only s· is mortal mind,
   ph 180– 5  The patient s· tries to be satisfied when he sees
    o 346–22  When a s· is convinced that there is no
```

sufferer
```
    p 377– 4  convince the s· that affliction is often the
      398–13  To the s· with the withered hand
      405– 4  makes any man, . . . a hopeless s·.
      416– 7  and in twenty minutes the s· is quietly asleep.
    t 464–16  the s· could call a surgeon,
   ap 573–29  Take heart, dear s·, for this reality
```

sufferers
```
    f 220– 6  and induce s· to look in other directions
```

suffering
```
all the
    p 386–25  Error, not Truth, produces all the s· on earth.
and death
    f 219–29  the belief in sin, s·, and death
and despair
    p 382–30  to more hopeless s· and despair.
and disease
    f 221–17  He learned that s· and disease were the
and triumph
    a  21– 7  another's goodness, s·, and triumph,
another's
    a  40–14  Another's s· cannot lessen our own liability.
antidotes
    b 270–28  and a sense of ease antidotes s·,
bed of
    p 390–17  nor laid upon a bed of s·
bodily
    p 387–32  not only from temptation, but from bodily s·.
capable of
    o 357–11  belief that God . . . makes man capable of s·
cause
    p 414–11  that matter, . . . can suffer or cause s· ;
cause of all
    f 230–32  predisposing, and the exciting cause of all s·,
causes
    p 377– 3  If grief causes s·, convince the
climax of
    g 543– 2  This error, after reaching the climax of s·,
creates the
    p 400–22  we prove that thought alone creates the s·.
delusion of
   ph 184–25  by destroying the delusion of s·
dream of
    p 420–29  to break its dream of s·,
evil and
   sp  72–29  when evil and s· are communicable.
experience
    a  22– 7  Waking to Christ's demand, mortals experience
              s·.
from quackery
    t 458–16  Having seen so much s· from quackery,
human
    a  22–28  or that divinity is appeased by human s·,
    f 227–13  of continued bondage and of human s·
inevitable
   pr  11–20  sin brings inevitable s·.
is an error
    a  23– 9  s· is an error of sinful sense
material
    p 405–30  Belief in material s· causes mortals to
no more
    t 463–19  and can cause the mother no more s·.
obedience and
   ap 572– 2  washed their robes white in obedience and s·.
of the just
    a  36–30  the s· of the just for the unjust.
or Science
    b 296– 6  Either here or hereafter, s· or Science
prevent
    t 457–11  Her prime object, . . . has been to prevent s·,
produces
    b 270–27  If a sense of disease produces s·
real
    p 391–15  and real s· for your own sins will
rebuked the
    m  67–31  Jesus rebuked the s· from any such cause
records of
    a  37– 5  History is full of records of s·.
relieve
    r 483– 3  they do not heal, but only relieve s· temporarily
repentance and
    a  19–17  Every pang of repentance and s·,
sin and
    a  23–10  and that eventually both sin and s· will
    f 210–29  To mortal sense, sin and s· are real,
      229– 6  but if sin and s· are realities of being,
    p 435– 7  which alone is capable of sin and s·.
sin brings
    a  37– 2  sin brings s· as much to-day as yesterday
source of all
    f 205–12  the prolific source of all s·
sufficient
    a  36– 5  sufficient s·, . . . to quench the love of sin.
supposed
    p 391–15  Truth, will destroy all other supposed s·,
      421–18  When the supposed s· is gone from
```

suffering

through
  pr 5–21 the destruction of sin through s·.
  f 224– 8 is self-destroyed through s·.
  ap 569–21 eventually expiate their sin through s·.
to cause
  pr 6–11 To cause s· as the result of sin,
weakness and
  p 406–26 Inharmony . . . involves weakness and s·,
which awakens
  ph 196– 6 Better the s· which awakens mortal mind
without
  f 221–24 and he ate without s·,
  p 385–17 can be experienced without s·.
  g 557– 7 where parturition is without s·.
your
  p 386–21 you learn that your s· was merely the

  pr 14–15 If s· from a belief in sickness,
  m 68–18 was s· from incipient insanity,
  sp 76–18 S·, sinning, dying beliefs are unreal.
     77–21 or of a sinning, s· sense,
     78–11 must still be mortal, sinning, s·, and dying.
  ph 175–10 to say that a rose, . . . can produce s· !
     188–16 thinks that . . . the s· is in that body.
     193–14 My s· is all gone.''
  f 240–25 must sooner or later, either by s· or by Science,
     248–16 Is it imperfection, joy, sorrow, sin, s·?
  b 318–19 beliefs, from which comes so much s·,
  o 348–22 while complaining of the s· disease brings,
  p 365–31 The poor s· heart needs its
     377–31 is of itself powerless to produce s·.
     379–21 but is s· from her belief that blood is
     389–30 was then s· from a complication of symptoms
     395– 1 The sick unconsciously argue for s·,
     397– 8 S· is no less a mental condition than
     404– 6 s· which his submission to such habits brings,
     407– 2 a s· inconceivably terrible to
  t 444– 4 s· is oft the divine agent in this elevation.
  g 557–10 has its s· because it is a false belief.
  ap 574–28 which your s· sense deems wrathful
  gl 588– 2 death ; s· and self-destruction ;

sufferings

bodily
  p 397– 9 You cause bodily s· and increase them by
error and its
  f 237–19 To prevent the experience of error and its s·,
great
  s 158–14 and endured great s· upon earth.
his
  a 38–22 his s· were the fruits of other people's sins,
illusive
  p 371–17 before he can get rid of the illusive s·
of Jesus
  a 34–11 had really commemorated the s· of Jesus
self-inflicted
  p 398–20 which reduces self-inflicted s·
your
  p 385–25 Your s· are not the penalty for

suffers

  m 65–11 The union of the sexes s· fearful discord.
  sp 81– 3 to show the sick that matter s·
  s 134– 8 one who s· for his convictions.
  ph 168–16 sick and useless, s· and dies,
     184–18 We say man s· from the effects of
     184–21 Mortal mind alone s·,
     187–25 and s· from the attempt.
  f 202–17 but immortal man, . . . neither sins, s·, nor
     229– 5 should hesitate to say that Jehovah sins or s· ;
  b 270–30 Hence the fact that the human mind alone s·,
     285– 7 the material personality which s·,
     294–10 that matter enjoys and s·.
  p 388– 5 s· less, only because it knows less of
     396–21 all teaching that the body s·,
     409–12 belief, that . . . the body, s· and reports disease
     414–25 matter neither feels, s·, nor enjoys.
     419– 8 If your patient from any cause s· a relapse,
     420–32 Tell him that he s· only as the insane suffer,
     429–12 is cold and decays, but it never s·.
  r 493–25 That man is material, and that matter s·,

sufficient

  pr 3– 3 is not s· to warrant him in advising God.
      4– 9 Outward worship is not of itself s· to
     10–14 Seeking is not s·.
  a 29– 1 and not s· moral courage.
     36– 5 reveals the necessity of s· suffering,
  c 257–25 Who hath found finite life or love s·
     266–14 until the lesson is s· to exalt you ;
  p 363–29 was her grief s· evidence to warrant the
  t 454–14 He, who understands in a s· degree the Principle
  r 488– 2 result of our teachings is their s· confirmation.
     497– 4 the Bible as our s· guide to eternal Life.

sufficiently

  pr 11–16 if indeed, he has not already suffered s·
  a 30–26 If we have triumphed s· over the errors
     45–32 Jesus' students, not s· advanced
  sp 84– 7 When s· advanced in Science
  ph 181–18 or are not s· spiritual to depend on Spirit.
  o 352– 1 because they did not s· understand God
  p 387– 7 we conclude that . . . has been carried s· far ;

suggest

  b 287–15 how can He be absent or s· the absence of
  g 502–12 serves to s· the proper reflection of God

suggested

  a 114–18 if a better word or phrase could be s·,
  p 364–16 Here is s· a solemn question,

suggestion

  g 529– 2 a s· of change in the *modus operandi*,
     544–18 the first s· of more than the one Mind,

suggestions

  p 433– 9 warped by the irrational, unchristian s·
  r 496– 2 in Science there is no transfer of evil s·

suggestive

  b 298–32 making them human creatures with s· feathers ;
  g 529– 6 The first system of s· obstetrics has changed.

suggestiveness

  ap 560– 1 a special s· in connection with the

suggests

  c 256–10 s· polytheism, rather than the one
     265–11 by no means s· man's absorption
  b 338–16 This s· the thought of something fluid,
     338–17 It further s· the thought of

suicide

  a 43–13 the treason and s· of his betrayer,
  f 203–25 The so-called sinner is a s·.

suit

  pref x–11 to s· the general drift of thought,
  t 450– 2 twist every fact to s· themselves.

suits

  p 440–29 forbidden to enter . . . any more s·
     441– 6 not permitted to enter any s· at the bar of

Sulphuris

  s 156–10 occasional doses of a high attenuation of S·.

sum

  s 129– 4 a properly computed s· in arithmetic.
  c 259– 4 he represents infinite Mind, the s· of all
  p 363–16 one for a large s· and one for a smaller,
     422– 1 and that their combined s· is
  ap 563–10 dragon stands for the s· total of human error.
     574–17 the s· total of human misery,

summarize

  p 363–24 Why did he thus s· her debt to

summarized

  s 113–10 propositions of divine metaphysics are s· in the

summary

  s 138–15 His sublime s· points to the religion of Love.

summed

  gl 595–18 limits, in which are s· up all human acts,

summer

  sp 96– 8 s· and winter, seedtime and harvest
  f 220–13 procures a s· residence with more ease than
  r 492–19 fight it out on this line, if it takes all s·.''

summit

  p 367–13 from the s· of devout consecration,
  g 549–31 He absolutely drops from his s·,

summits

  g 515– 5 creeping over lofty s·,

summoned

  o 342– 3 are s· to the support of Christianity,
  p 431–13 the prisoner s· Physiology,
     434–13 s· to appear before the bar of Justice
     436–15 the prisoner s· two professed friends,
     438–26 Court of Truth s· Furred Tongue
  t 458–21 as ritualism and creed are s· to give place to

summons

  g 532–21 Its s· may be thus paraphrased :

sums

  s 128–29 The addition of two s· in mathematics

sun (see also **sun's**)

appears to rise
  r 493– 2 To corporeal sense, the s· appears to rise and set,
a small
  g 547–15 germinating speck . . . seemed a small s·.
at rest
  s 119–27 the earth is in motion and the s· at rest.
central
  f 209– 6 is the central s· of its own systems
clothed with the
  ap 560– 7 a woman clothed with the s·,— *Rev.* 12 : 1.

sun

declining
f 246–13   undimmed by a declining *s*.
following the
  a 21–29   After following the *s*· for six days,
hides the
  b 298– 4   As a cloud hides the *s*· it cannot extinguish,
melts before the
  r 480–31   As vapor melts before the *s*·,
obscures the
  b 299–28   as the mist obscures the *s*· or the mountain ;
of virtue
  f 246–11   The radiant *s*· of virtue and truth
or satellite
  ap 577–20   has no need of *s*· or satellite,
seems to move
  s 121–18   and the *s*· seems to move from east to west,
standing in the
  ap 561– 8   an "angel standing in the *s*·."— *Rev.* 19 : 17.

    s 121–24   The *s*· is the central stillness,
       121–26   earth revolves about the *s*· once a year,
  ph 188–29   senses have no immediate evidence of a *s*·.
     188–32   desired information regarding the *s*·.
     189– 3   If the eyes see no *s*· for a week,
     189–12   or doubt that the *s*· will reappear.
    f 250–13   like a ray of light which comes from the *s*·,
  c 265–18   or a flower withered by the *s*·
  b 295–24   it no longer hides the *s*·.
     300–30   the *s*· is seen in the ray of light which
     310–12   The *s*· is not affected by the revolution of the
  o 361–17   a ray of light one with the *s*·,
  g 504–10   This light is not from the *s*·
     510–16   The *s*· is a metaphorical representation of
     538–11   The *s*·, giving light and heat to the earth,
  ap 558– 5   his face was as it were the *s*·,— *Rev.* 10 : 1.
     558–15   it has for you a light above the *s*·,
     561– 5   Agassiz, . . . saw the *s*· in an egg
     561–26   The Revelator symbolizes Spirit by the *s*·.
  gl 595– 1   definition of

sunbeam

  f 210–21   as a *s*· penetrates the cloud.
     247–25   glances in the warm *s*·,

sundered

  sp 75–29   the moment when the link . . . is being *s*·.

sunlight

  s 162– 4   C. S. brings to the body the *s*· of Truth,
  ph 189–11   the existence of the *s*·
  g 516–17   *s*· glints from the church-dome,

sunny

  f 240– 3   Arctic regions, *s*· tropics, giant hills,

Sun of Righteousness

  ap 576– 3   lighted by the *S*· *of R*·,

sunrise

  s 119–25   In viewing the *s*·, one finds that it

sun's

  f 144– 7   when dawns the *s*· brave light.
  ph 189– 3   the *s*· influence over the earth.
  g 548–10   when clouds cover the *s*· face !

suns

  f 240– 7   *S*· and planets teach grand lessons.

sunshine

  m 66– 8   in the *s*· of joy and prosperity.
     67–16   or *s*· gladdens the troubled sea.
  s 121–12   in God's perennial and happy *s*·,
     122–19   that little prophet of storm and *s*·,
  b 299–28   *s*· of Truth, will melt away the shadow
  p 365–18   like dew before the morning *s*·.

superabundance

  f 201–11   *s*· of being is on the side of God, good.

superficial

  t 460–22   the *s*· and cold assertion, "Nothing ails you."
     461– 9   for it is not *s*·, nor is it
  gl 597–12   the false foundations . . . of *s*· religion,

superimposed

  ph 176–18   with *s*· and conjectural evils.
  p 425–10   images of mortal thought *s*· upon the body ;

superinduced

  sp 89–15   without study or a *s*· condition,

superinduces

  ph 183–24   Submission to error *s*· loss of power.

superintendence

  p 430–31   Although I have the *s*· of human affairs.

superior

  m 63– 1   and the *s*· law of Soul last.
  s 144– 3   If Mind is foremost and *s*·,
  f 217–15   That scientific methods are *s*· to others,
     231–20   To hold yourself *s*· to sin,
     231–21   because God made you *s*· to it
     231–25   To hold yourself *s*· to sickness and death
     242–13   and to rise *s*· to the so-called pain and

superior

  b 275–29   *s*· or contrary to the one Spirit.
  o 351–21   if not *s*· to Him.
     358– 2   Is the woodman's axe, . . . *s*· to omnipotence?
  p 368–11   beliefs . . . that evil is equal . . . if not *s*·,
     409–17   conscious mortal mind is believed to be *s*· to
     423–20   as *s*· to error and discord,
  t 444– 3   all must rise *s*· to materiality,
  r 493–17   Mind must be found *s*· to all the beliefs of the
  g 521– 1   but making him *s*· to the soil.

superiority

  sp 92–31   leads to belief in the *s*· of error.
  s 131–11   the *s*· of spiritual over physical power.
     134–29   *s*· of spiritual power over material resistance.
     143–23   deprives you of the available *s*· of
     150–29   even the doctrine of the *s*· of matter over
  f 209–32   It shows the *s*· of faith by works
     215–27   understood the *s*· and immortality of good,
  t 454–29   The *s*· of spiritual power over sensuous
  g 530–17   as always asserting its *s*·

supernal

  f 248– 8   feeds the body with *s*· freshness
  c 261–27   Fixing your gaze on the realities *s*·,
  b 319– 2   has no kinship with the Life *s*·.

supernatural

  pref xi–15   these mighty works are not *s*·,
  a 44–20   Could it be called *s*· for the God of nature to
     44–23   but it was not a *s*· act.
  sp 83–15   is not *s*·, since Science is an explication
  s 111– 7   no more *s*· than is the science of numbers,
     126–20   Or shall all that . . . be called *s*·,
     134–23   not because this Science is *s*· or preternatural,
  b 271–13   was not a *s*· gift to those learners,
  t 450– 3   teaches belief in a mysterious, *s*· God,
  gl 596–13   believed that the stones . . . had *s*· illumination,

supersede

  ph 182–18   must *s*· the so-called laws of matter.
  f 213–25   strains of sweetest music *s*· conscious sound.
  b 274–15   and they *s*· the so-called laws of matter,
  r 483– 7   will ultimately *s*· all other means in healing.
  g 553–26   this potent belief will immediately *s*· the

superseded

  f 227– 7   must be denied and *s*·.

supersedes

  b 330– 2   understanding of being *s*· mere belief.
  p 434– 6   law of Christ *s*· our laws ; let us follow Christ."

superstition

  pr 4–31   Long prayers, *s*·, and creeds
  sp 83–23   Between C. S. and all forms of *s*·
     90– 2   Human philosophy, ethics, and *s*· afford no
  s 120–31   ignorance and *s*· chained the limbs
     149–30   dismiss *s*·, and demonstrate truth
  f 237–12   *S*·, . . . snatches away the good seed
     242–27   Mere speculation or *s*· appropriates no part of
  b 288– 9   *S*· and understanding can never combine.
  o 353–21   not continue to admit the somethingness of *s*·,
  p 372–29   If pride, *s*·, or any error prevents
  g 555–26   unfolds *s*· about the creation from dust
  gl 597–13   tore from bigotry and *s*· their coverings,

superstitious

  b 298–31   forms of thought, marked with *s*· outlines,

superstructure

  ph 177–12   so-called mind builds its own *s*·,
  gl 595– 8   *s*· of Truth ; the shrine of Love ;
     595– 9   a material *s*·, where mortals congregate
     599– 6   ZION. Spiritual foundation and *s*· ;

superstructures

  gl 597–12   false foundations and *s*· of

supper

  a 32–30   a sad *s*· taken at the close of day,
     33– 1   and this *s*· closed forever Jesus' ritualism
     34–29   contrast between our Lord's last *s*· and
  ph 193–17   I told him to rise, dress himself, and take *s*·

supplant

  f 223–23   *s*· unscientific means and so-called laws.
  r 495–22   understanding will *s*· error with Truth,

supple

  s 160–32   the *s*· and elastic condition of the healthy limb,
     162–21   ankylosed joints have been made *s*·,

supplied

  pr 7–26   and by whom it will be *s*·.

supplies

  m 58–27   because another *s*· her wants.
  f 222– 6   to believe that proper food *s*· nutriment
  b 281–15   *s*· all form and comeliness
  p 385– 8   *s*· energy and endurance surpassing all other
  r 494–14   and in every hour, divine Love *s*· all good.
  g 550–25   Embryology *s*· no instance of

supplieth

  g 518–18   seeth his brother's need and *s*· it,

supply
ph 199–11 by reason of its demand for and *s·* of power.
f 206–18 Spirit, not matter, being the source of *s·*.
216–13 to *s·* the truth of immortal sense.
c 258– 7 insufficiency of this belief to *s·* the true idea
ap 571–16 Know thyself, and God will *s·* the wisdom

supplying
f 248– 9 *s·* it with beautiful images of thought

support
basis and
f 229– 4 but is their basis and *s·*.
discords have no
ph 183– 6 discords have no *s·* from nature or
manifestation and
b 279–10 nor for the manifestation and *s·* of Mind.
of bodily endurance
sp 80– 5 or for the *s·* of bodily endurance.
of Christian Science
o 341–17 so absolute and numerous in *s·* of C. S.,
of his proof
f 236– 9 in *s·* of his proof by example that the divine
origin nor
g 529–27 and has neither origin nor *s·* in Truth
summoned to the
o 342– 4 are summoned to the *s·* of Christianity,
theories in
o 355–32 material theories in *s·* of
which they derived
p 385– 6 explanation lies in the *s·* which they derived from

---

a 20–11 partake of the Eucharist, *s·* the clergy,
40– 5 The advanced thinker . . . will *s·* them.
sp 73– 1 one does not *s·* the other.
92–27 This belief tends to *s·* two opposite powers,
s 124– 6 When this . . . lacks organizations to *s·* it,
124–21 and *s·* the equipoise of that thought-force,
ph 198–25 says nothing to *s·* his theory.
f 204– 3 All forms of error *s·* the false conclusions
b 318–10 The material senses originate and *s·*
o 344–26 Why *s·* the popular systems of
p 389–19 If God has,. . .instituted laws that food shall *s·*
390–24 You have no law of His to *s·* the
417– 4 Always *s·* their trust in the power of Mind
417–32 an underlying understanding to *s·* them
t 454–27 *s·* all their feeble footsteps, until
455–10 and *s·* your claims by demonstration.
r 481–27 since Truth cannot *s·* error.
495–21 Let C. S., . . . *s·* your understanding
g 543– 1 having no truth to *s·* it,

supported
s 109– 7 is not, . . . *s·* by sensible evidence, until
r 471–14 the evidence . . . is not *s·* by evil,
481–26 If sin is *s·*, God must uphold it,

supporting
b 325– 6 not of the body incapable of *s·* life,
p 382–27 *s·* the power of Mind over the body
387–28 sublime proofs of the *s·* influence and

supports
pref x–20 till all physical *s·* have failed,
m 57–28 for Love *s·* the struggling heart
ph 169–15 should find stronger *s·* and a higher home.
196–17 No law *s·* them.
p 372–22 Its false *s·* fail one after another.
g 511– 5 The divine Mind *s·* the sublimity,
515– 1 It *s·* Christian healing, and
543–29 The belief that matter *s·* life
gl 582–13 that which comforts, consoles, and *s·*.

suppose
pr 6–19 To *s·* that God forgives or punishes sin according
a 28–24 To *s·* that persecution for righteousness' sake
36–24 It is useless to *s·* that the wicked can
sp 73–26 It is a grave mistake to *s·* that matter is
83–21 It is contrary to C. S. to *s·* that life
87–24 Do not *s·* that any mental concept is
s 161– 4 more exact than you *s·* ;
ph 183– 4 To *s·* that God constitutes laws of
f 208–14 it is absurd to *s·* that matter can
216–19 The great mistake of mortals is to *s·* that man
230–12 to *s·* Him capable of first arranging law and
240–12 *s·* Mind to be governed by matter
f 250– 2 and *s·* error to be mind,
b 289– 9 To *s·* that sin, lust, hatred, envy, hypocrisy,
309–27 It is a self-evident error to *s·* that
328– 4 Mortals *s·* that they can live without goodness,
p 422–22 Let us *s·* two parallel cases of bone-disease,
430–17 *S·* a mental case to be on trial,
r 486– 4 *S·* one accident happens to the eye,

supposed
pr 6–12 Every *s·* pleasure in sin
sp 81–32 deceased person, *s·* to be the communicator,
88–16 at one time are *s·* to be substance-matter
90–17 but the *s·* inhabitant of that body

supposed
s 120–25 deduced from *s·* sensation in matter
120–26 or from matter's *s·* consciousness of
126– 1 its *s·* organic action or *s·* existence.
152– 4 takes away all its *s·* sovereignty,
152–18 sick man *s·* this ceremony was intended to
158– 4 was *s·* to have dictated the first prescription,
ph 172–11 Spirit can form no real link in this *s·* chain
176–28 The human mind, not matter, is *s·* to feel,
189–17 brain which is *s·* to furnish the evidence
190– 4 ignorant of what it is *s·* to produce.
f 204–15 The third power, mortal man, is a *s·* mixture
218– 9 The body is *s·* to say, "I am ill."
224–32 What is this *s·* power, which opposes
245–13 and *s·* her to be a young woman.
253–25 Do not believe in any *s·* necessity for sin,
c 257–13 the *s·* substance of non-intelligent matter.
262–19 when the *s·* pain and pleasure of matter
b 269– 3 the *s·* coexistence of Mind and matter
281–18 The mind *s·* to exist in matter
289–23 So man, tree, and flower are *s·* to die ;
301–26 *s·* standpoint outside the focal distance of
307–22 every sin or *s·* material pain and
311–29 Matter, sin, and mortality lose all *s·*
314–31 in *s·* accord with the inevitable law of life.
338–22 even the *s·* separation of man from
339–29 is to divest sin of any *s·* mind or reality,
o 348–21 defending the *s·* rights of disease,
348–26 I have never *s·* the world would immediately
353–26 So long as there are *s·* limits to Mind,
354–27 Its *s·* realism has no divine authority,
p 365– 9 *s·* necessity for physical thought-taking
370–24 a drug may eventually lose its *s·* power
375–27 even when they are *s·* to be in hopeless danger.
380–32 Every law of matter or the body, *s·* to govern
381– 8 When infringing some *s·* law,
382–15 the devotee of *s·* hygienic law,
385–31 Any *s·* information, coming from the body
389–10 Matter does not . . . it is *s·* to do so.
391–15 will destroy all other *s·* suffering,
391–18 When the body is *s·* to say,
408–21 a *s·* effect on intelligence and
418–19 negation must extend to the *s·* disease
421–18 When the *s·* suffering is gone from
t 458– 7 This theory is *s·* to favor
r 470– 5 *s·* existence of more than one mind
479–14 constitutes matter's *s·* selfhood,
484–18 Certain results, *s·* to proceed from
g 510–23 indicates a *s·* formation of matter
528–25 Afterwards he is *s·* to become the basis of
535–10 *s·* material foundations of life and intelligence.
536–21 Their *s·* joys are cheats.
541–23 It is *s·* to say in the first instance,
544–21 The serpent is *s·* to say,
549– 9 are *s·* to have, as classes, three different
556– 4 classified, and a *s·* to possess life and mind.
gl 594–23 evil minds ; *s·* intelligences, or gods ;
596–25 fear of death, and the *s·* reality of error.
598–10 In the record of Jesus' *s·* death, we read :
(see also **laws**)

supposedly
sp 73– 4 and *s·* will return to earth to-morrow,
g 522–26 portrays Spirit as *s·* cooperating with matter

supposes
b 287– 6 Error *s·* man to be both mental and material.
r 486–20 yet *s·* Mind unable to produce harmony !
489– 8 hypothesis which *s·* life to be in matter
g 530–29 *s·* that something springs from nothing,
530–31 it *s·* that mind enters matter,
538–31 *s·* God to be the author of sin
546–15 *s·* God and man to be manifested only through

supposing
sp 86– 1 *S·* this inquiry to be occasioned by
f 201–20 *s·* that sin can be forgiven when it

supposition
error is a
r 472–14 Error is a *s·* that pleasure and pain,
false
b 278– 9 It is a false *s·*, the notion that there is
o 357–21 must have originated in a false *s·*,
gl 580–21 the false *s·* that Life is not eternal,
inconsistent
p 387–21 inconsistent *s·* that death comes in obedience to
no
g 503–11 No *s·* of error enters there.
objective
b 287–27 objective *s·* of Spirit's opposite.
of opposite qualities
b 286–28 (by the *s·* of opposite qualities)
of reality
f 213– 2 contradicts this mortal mind *s·* of reality
opposite
g 521–13 We should look away from the opposite *s·*
overthrew the
f 228–28 The humble Nazarene overthrew the *s·*

supposition

that man is
ph 171-31   the s· that man is a material outgrowth

that Spirit is
ph 173- 6   the s·, that Spirit is within what it creates

that spirit is
gl 587- 2   a s· that spirit is finite.

vain
pr   6- 8   the vain s· that we have nothing to do but

sp 70-10   The s· that corporeal beings are spirits,
b 287-24   The s· that life, substance, and intelligence
p 408-14   The s· that we can correct insanity by
g 504-30   a s· of the absence of Spirit.
506- 6   a quality which separates C. S. from s·
528- 7   this s· was a dream, a myth.
549- 4   The s· that life germinates in eggs
550-29   not so hideous and absurd as the s· that Spirit
gl 586-18   a s· that life, substance, and intelligence
587-10   a s· of sentient physicality ;

suppositional

sp 72-22   evil, the s· opposite of good,
an 103-17   Evil is a s· lie.
ph 185-31   material mentality and its s· activities.
200-20   The s· antipode of divine infinite Spirit,
f 208- 1   s· error, which affords no proof of God,
215-19   the s· absence of Life, God,
b 274-30   This s· partnership is already obsolete,
288- 3   The s· warfare between truth and error
335-30   the s· antipodes of Spirit,
r 472- 3   Truth casts out s· error and heals
g 510-25   analogous to the s· resolving of thoughts
533-25   but error has its s· day
gl 591-27   a s· material sense, alias the belief that

suppositions

b 277-22   These s· contradict even the order of
291- 1   s· that sin is pardoned while unforsaken,
p 368-18   no material s· can prevent us from
gl 583- 3   material s· of life, substance, and intelligence,

supposititious

b 278-14   in a s· mortal consciousness.
310- 5   Matter is made up of s· mortal mind-force ;
322-26   belief in the s· life of matter,
p 368- 2   a s· opposite of the highest right.
r 469-15   the s· opposite of infinite Mind
480-24   The s· parent of evil is a lie.
gl 587-13   s· minds, or souls, going in and out of matter,

suppress

ph 197-31   The doctor should s· his fear of disease,

suppressed

p 416- 3   for the inflammation is not s· ;

suppurates

f 251- 4   should not grow more painful before it s·,

supremacy

absolute
p 423-26   which ultimately asserts its absolute s·.

and reality
f 205-20   the s· and reality of good,

God's
g 521-10   God's s·, omnipotence, and omnipresence.

its
b 293-29   C. S. brings to light Truth and its s·,

of divine Mind
p 400-24   acknowledge the s· of divine Mind,

of divine Spirit
g 522-15   opposed to the s· of divine Spirit ;

of God
s 130-27   strong claim of Science for the s· of God,

of good
s 130-27   and doubts the s· of good,

of Mind
a 45-30   glorified the s· of Mind over matter.
f 209-13   the Science which reveals the s· of Mind.
b 322- 2   cast out evils in proof of the s· of Mind.
p 401-27   admits the efficacy and s· of Mind,

of Spirit
a 44- 3   and the s· of Spirit be demonstrated.
sp 78-17   would destroy the s· of Spirit.
97-28   will disappear before the s· of Spirit.
s 138-14   The s· of Spirit was the foundation on which
ph 170-26   to ponder somewhat the s· of Spirit,
b 273-23   it would oppose the s· of Spirit, God,
324-28   if the idea of the s· of Spirit,
p 391- 2   matter, arrayed against the s· of Spirit.
r 491-13   It is only by acknowledging the s· of Spirit,
ap 572-17   Under the s· of Spirit, it will be seen

of the divine Mind
r 484-16   Drugs and...oppose the s· of the divine Mind.

of Truth
p 406-22   the s· of Truth over error,
ap 569- 8   when we are conscious of the s· of Truth,
gl 589-21   showing the immortality and s· of Truth ;

supremacy

struggle for
b 268-14   In this final struggle for s·,

s 146-19   and clothes Spirit with s·.

supreme

pr 17- 3   *Enable us to know, . . . God is omnipotent,* s·.
a 50- 5   The last s· moment of mockery, desertion,
sp 91- 3   by beings under the control of s· wisdom?
97-18   until divine Spirit, s· in its domain,
s 127-14   God, the infinite, s·, eternal Mind.
156-31   and Mind takes its rightful and s· place.
ph 174- 1   in a s· governing intelligence.
182-11   one or the other must be s·
f 201- 4   knowing too that one affection would be s·
207-11   Evil is not s· ; good is not helpless ;
209- 5   Mind, s· over all its formations
219- 4   Mind should be, and is, s·, absolute, and final.
253- 7   saith : . . . I am s· and give all, for I am Mind.
b 278-21   and yet we say that Spirit is s·
281- 4   and learn that Spirit is infinite and s·.
o 357-26   If . . . and God is not s·
p 375-25   no power to be lost, for Mind is s·,
427-24   acknowledged as s· in the physical realm,
428- 6   Man's privilege at this s· moment
434-20   Then C. S. turns suddenly to the s· tribunal,
437-33   read from the s· statute-book, the Bible,
440- 5   whom Truth arraigns before the s· bar of
r 465- 9   God is incorporeal, divine, s·,
496-10   the life that approaches the s· good?
497- 5   one s· and infinite God.
ap 573-14   the declaration from heaven, s· harmony,
gl 590- 3   atmosphere of Spirit, where Soul is s·,
593-21   understood and demonstrated as s· over all ;

Supreme Being

93-23   Spirit, as a proper noun, is the name of the S· B·.
s 117- 8   the S· B· or His manifestation ;
127-18   as divine Principle, S· B·, Mind,
f 202-24   Our beliefs about a S· B· contradict
b 285-22   the S· B·, or divine Principle, and idea.
g 523-18   the S· B· is therein called Elohim.
524- 7   They called the S· B· by the national name of
527-20   Is the S· B· retrograding,

Supreme Bench

p 440-20   cannot trample upon the decree of the S· B·.
441-25   S· B· decides in favor of intelligence,

Supreme Court

p 435-11   The law of our S· C· decrees that whosoever
436- 7   Your S· C· must find the prisoner on the night of
437-10   the Judge of our higher tribunal, the S· C·
437-18   I ask that the S· C· of Spirit reverse this
437-28   Judge Justice of the S· C· of Spirit
440-34   the Chief Justice of the S· C·,

Supreme Judge

p 435-24   If mortals sin, our S· J· in equity decides

Supreme Lawgiver

p 440-25   In the presence of the S· L·,

supremely

pref xi-15   not supernatural, but s· natural.
s 149-27   divine Mind, governs all, not partially but s·,
ph 167-19   you must love God s·.
b 326- 9   cannot love God s·...while loving the material

Supreme Ruler

f 203-17   prone to believe either in more than one S· R·
gl 500-10   Its higher signification is S· R·.

sure

pref ix- 5   He is as s· of the world's existence as he is
a 20-26   It commands s· entrance into the realm of Love.
m 67-10   dauntless seaman is not s· of his safety ;
sp 93-11   otherwise, we may be s· that either our logic is
s 151- 1   To be s·, they sometimes treat the sick as if
f 203- 4   assigns s· rewards to righteousness,
p 384-20   your Mind-remedy is safe and s·
419-15   therefore be s· that you move it off.
t 459-25   the results are s· if the Science is understood.
460- 2   and rest his demonstration on this s· basis.
g 553-22   that theory is s· to become the signal for the

surely

s 123- 2   will s· destroy the greater error
162-26   as s· as it heals what is called functional,
ph 197-10   thou shalt s· die." — *Gen.* 2 : 17.
b 277- 3   "Thou shalt s· die ;" — *Gen.* 2 : 17.
o 354-14   S· it is not enough to cleave to
r 481-19   thou shalt s· die." — *Gen.* 2 : 17.
495- 3   as s· as it did nineteen centuries ago.
g 527-10   thou shalt s· die. — *Gen.* 2 : 17.
530-14   Ye shall not s· die." — *Gen.* 3 : 4.
532- 9   thou shalt s· die," — *Gen.* 2 : 17.
550- 4   Matter s· does not possess Mind.
ap 573-30   will s· appear sometime and in some way.
578-16   S· goodness and mercy shall — *Psal.* 23 : 6.
gl 580-20   "Thou shalt s· die." — *Gen.* 2 : 17.

surface

m	65–30	has brought conjugal infidelity to the s·,
sp	83– 7	elements now coming to the s·.
f	254–24	If you venture upon the quiet s· of error
c	267–20	more than is detected upon the s·,
b	313–25	He plunged beneath the material s·
p	401–19	brings sin and sickness to the s·,
	413–19	without scrubbing the whole s· daily.
g	540– 8	when bringing it to the s· and

Surgeon

s	163– 6	Dr. James Johnson, S· to William IV,

surgeon

a	44–15	He did not require the skill of a s·
s	163–10	physician, s·, apothecary, man-midwife,
ph	172–26	If . . . the s· destroys manhood,
p	401–30	leave . . . to the fingers of a s·,
	402– 1	C. S. is always the most skilful s·,
	422–24	A s· is employed in one case,
	422–25	The s·, holding that matter forms its
t	464–16	the sufferer could call a s·,

surgeons

s	159–15	Had these unscientific s· understood

surgery

a	44–12	the claims of medicine, s·, and hygiene.
	44–22	It was a method of s· beyond material art,
s	159–11	Is it skilful or scientific s· to take no heed of
p	401–29	to leave s· and the adjustment of
	402– 2	but s· is the branch of its healing which
	402– 6	the cure, . . . through mental s· alone,
g	528–28	s· was first performed mentally

surgical

s	159– 2	to perform a needed s· operation
ph	198–18	perhaps by a blister, . . . or by a s· operation.
g	528–17	in order to perform a s· operation on him

surging

ap	569–17	They are in the s· sea of error,

surpassing

p	385– 9	energy and endurance s· all other aids,

surplus

b	293–17	Electricity is the sharp s· of materiality

surprised

ap	559–27	do not be s· nor discontented

surprising

s	131– 1	Truth should not seem so s· and
	136–23	That a wicked king . . . was not s· ;

surrender

pr	9–19	s· of all merely material sensation,
p	426–30	because matter has no life to s·.

surrendering

gl	579– 8	s· to the creator the early fruits of

surrenders

g	552–30	and that matter always s· its claims

surround

p	424–16	the minds which s· your patient should not

surrounding

s	128–21	its escape into the s· atmosphere.
p	415–31	will sink from sight along with s· objects,

surroundings

p	383–16	symbolized, and not chafed, by its s· ;
t	463–11	cannot injure its useful s·

survive

p	368–21	when we learn that life and man s· this body.

susceptibility

sp	86–10	possessed more spiritual s· than the disciples.

susceptible

sp	93–15	Good does not create a mind s· of
an	100–10	as follows : . . . Animal bodies are s· to the
p	410–23	Science of mental practice is s· of no misuse.

sustain

pr	10– 7	God will s· us under these sorrows.
a	44–21	to s· Jesus in his proof of
	50–11	to s· and bless so faithful a son.
an	103–25	The truths of immortal Mind s· man,
ph	198– 6	His fortitude may s· him,
c	261–14	and s· his appointed task,
b	274– 2	and thus invigorate and s· existence.
o	357– 5	We s· Truth, . . . by rejecting a lie.
p	417– 5	the power of Mind to s· the body.
t	458–12	or of trying to s· the human body
r	481–25	It cannot s· itself.
g	552– 9	even where the proof requisite to s· this

sustained

a	43–26	and that spiritual law s· him.
sp	90– 8	earth's motion and position are s· by Mind
ph	179–21	s· by what is termed material law,
f	221–22	in which being is s· by God,
p	416–32	Teach them that their being is s· by Spirit,
	425–16	learns that matter never s· existence
t	447–15	when mentally s· by Truth,

sustained

r	471–16	is fully s· by spiritual sense.
g	530– 5	In divine Science, man is s· by God,
	531–26	Is Life s· by matter or by Spirit?
	556– 1	That which is real, is s· by Spirit.

sustaining

pref	vii– 1	To those leaning on the s· infinite,
a	33–10	now this bread was feeding and s· them.
m	59–14	each partner s· the other,
g	538–12	enlightening and s· the universe.

sustains

s	155–17	erroneous general belief, which s· medicine
b	319– 9	s· man under all circumstances ;
o	358–10	and s· logically and demonstratively
p	389–13	theories first admit that food s· the life of
r	488–16	C. S. s· with immortal proof
ap	573– 6	This testimony of Holy Writ s· the fact
gl	580–29	not one who constructs and s· reality

swaddling-clothes

c	255– 2	As mortals drop off their mental s·,

swallow

p	366–20	while they s· the camels of bigoted pedantry.

swallowed

sp	96–20	all discord will be s· up in spiritual Truth.
s	164–28	Death is s· up in victory."— I Cor. 15 : 54.
ph	177–25	If a dose of poison is s· through mistake,
	177–31	a few persons believe the potion s· by the
f	209–29	s· up in the infinite calculus of Spirit.
	215–24	s· up in immortality.
r	476–17	Mortality is finally s· up in immortality.
	496–27	Death is s· up in victory."— I Cor. 15 : 54.
ap	570–12	and s· up the flood— Rev. 12 : 16.

swallowing

s	140–15	straining out gnats and s· camels.
f	202– 2	straining out gnats and s· camels.

sway

ap	565–12	that the man Jesus, . . . might never hold s·

swayed

ph	190–21	The Hebrew bard, s· by mortal thoughts,

sways

o	357–28	if another . . . cause exists and s· mankind?

swear

a	32– 3	was required to s· allegiance to his general.

sweat

a	48–10	the s· of agony which fell in holy benediction
ph	179–28	ready to put you into a s·,
b	327–14	to be effaced by the s· of agony.
g	535–25	in the s· of thy face shalt thou— Gen. 3 : 19.

sweep

p	428–11	we shall s· away the false

sweeping

a	55–15	Truth's immortal idea is s· down the centuries,

sweeps

f	213–29	as the hand, which s· over it, is human or divine.
p	403–20	s· away the gossamer web of mortal illusion.

sweet

pref	viii– 7	and gives s· concord to sound.
m	57–13	bringing s· seasons of renewal
	58–18	the s· interchange of confidence and love ;
	59–13	should blend in s· confidence and cheer,
	66– 3	S· are the uses of adversity ;
	69–15	brings the s· assurance of no parting,
s	109–15	The search was s·, calm, and buoyant with hope,
	130–14	good and its s· concords have all-power.
	145– 1	whether they caught its s· tones, as the
ph	174–28	rolling it under the tongue as a s· morsel
f	219–23	We may hear a s· melody, and yet
b	287–13	same place s· water and bitter?"— Jas. 3 : 11.
	304– 1	the s· sense and presence of Life and Truth.
p	413–23	in order to keep it s· as the new-blown flower.
t	455–30	cannot send forth both s· waters and bitter.
r	489–23	sendeth not forth s· waters and bitter.
g	516–15	The modest arbutus sends her s· breath to
ap	559–19	shall be in thy mouth s· as honey."— Rev. 10 : 9.
	559–22	s· at its first taste, when it heals you ;
	562–25	waiting to be delivered of her s· promise,
	569–13	in a s· and certain sense that God is Love.

sweeter

m	60–28	and teach us life's s· harmonies.
ap	568–26	s· than has ever before reached high heaven,

sweetest

f	213–25	Mental melodies and strains of s· music
g	520– 1	s· rest, even from a human standpoint,

swell

p	393–19	Have no fear that matter can ache, s·,

swelling

s	153–18	through inflammation and s·,

swept

ph	190–22	thus s· his lyre with saddening strains

swerved
a 20–20 Yet he *s·* not, well knowing that to obey
swift
sp 97– 9 and the electric current *s·*,
b 268– 3 With like activity have thought's *s·* pinions
p 434– 1 *S·* on the wings of divine Love,
swift-winged
ap 574–20 the very message, or *s·* thought,
swimming
r 491– 1 and that he is *s·* when he is on dry land.
swine
b 272–18 neither cast ye your pearls before *s·*."—*Matt.* 7 : 6.
swinging
a 23–16 pendulum *s·* between nothing and something,
f 246– 2 is not a pendulum, *s·* between evil and good,
o 360–20 *s·* between the real and the unreal.
swinish
b 272– 8 *s·* element in human nature uproots it.
swollen
p 385–21 discolored, painful, *s·*, and inflamed.
ap 565– 2 the great red dragon, *s·* with sin,
sword
and spear
s 134– 3 truth is still opposed with *s·* and spear.
flaming
g 537– 6 Cherubims, and a flaming *s·*— *Gen.* 3 : 24.
of Science
c 266– 2 Such is the *s·* of Science,
of Spirit
a 37– 8 but error falls only before the *s·* of Spirit.
of Truth
t 458–17 The two-edged *s·* of Truth must turn
g 538– 7 the *s·* of Truth gleams afar and indicates
put up thy
a 48–24 He said : "Put up thy *s·*."— *John* 18 : 11.
two-edged
t 458–17 The two-edged *s·* of Truth must turn
g 538– 4 Truth is a two-edged *s·*, guarding and
which guards
g 526–18 the *s·* which guards it is the type of

a 19–16 to material beliefs not peace, but a *s·*.
g 542–11 "They that take the *s·*— *Matt.* 26 : 52.
542–19 shall perish with the *s·*."— *Matt.* 26 : 52.
gl 595– 3 definition of
syllables
b 338–14 Divide the name Adam into two *s·*,
syllogism
s 128–32 the major and the minor propositions of a *s·*
129– 3 the reasoning of an accurately stated *s·*
o 347– 9 Had he stated his *s·* correctly,
symbol
condemning its
g 539–17 by condemning its *s·*, the serpent, to grovel
of God
g 517–20 The only proper *s·* of God as person
of Life
ap 561–10 Purity was the *s·* of Life and Love.
of Mind
g 510–27 Light is a *s·* of Mind, of Life, Truth, and
of Soul
gl 595– 1 Sun. The *s·* of Soul governing man,
of Truth
gl 591–23 Morning. Light, *s·* of Truth ;

f 240–15 Its *s·* is the sphere.
g 503–23 creates no element nor *s·* of discord and decay.
536– 6 as a *s·* of tempest-tossed human concepts
gl 584–26 Dove. A *s·* of divine Science ;
symbolized
p 383–16 *s·*, and not chafed, by its surroundings ;
g 512– 8 Spirit is *s·* by strength, presence, and
515– 4 Patience is *s·* by the tireless worm,
symbolizes
an 102–10 The pointing of the needle to the pole *s·* this
b 274– 6 and *s·* all that is evil and perishable.
g 507– 3 while *water s·* the elements of Mind.
ap 561–22 woman in the Apocalypse *s·* generic
561–25 The Revelator *s·* Spirit by the sun.
563– 8 The great red dragon *s·* a lie,
symbols
a 34–14 If all who seek . . . . through material *s·*
b 280– 2 *S·* and elements of discord and decay are
282– 5 are figured by two geometrical *s·*,
g 502–15 take on higher *s·* and significations,
ap 575–14 Spiritual teaching must always be by *s·*.
symmetrical
s 160–25 If muscles can . . . be deformed or *s·*,
sympathetically
p 365– 1 *s·* know the thorns they plant in the

sympathies
m 59–12 their *s·* should blend in sweet confidence
sympathy
a 21–25 Being in *s·* with matter,
m 64–15 the ready aid her *s·* and charity would afford.
s 153–32 Neither *s·* nor society should ever tempt us to
ph 171–23 No more *s·* exists between the flesh and
f 211–21 *S·* with error should disappear.
254–25 and are in *s·* with error,
c 266– 8 solitary, left without *s·* ;
p 366–12 The physician who lacks *s·* for his
symphonies
f 213–21 rapture of his grandest *s·* was never heard.
symptom
p 413–24 noticing every *s·* of flatulency,
symptoms
aggravation of
s 156–14 to fear an aggravation of *s·* from
ph 169– 3 Whenever an aggravation of *s·* has occurred
alleviates the
p 411–31 it alleviates the *s·* of every disease.
all its
s 159–31 belief produces disease and all its *s·*,
approaching
p 390–27 approaching *s·* of chronic or acute disease,
bodily
s 161–24 ordinary practitioner, examining bodily *s·*,
certain
p 396– 8 nor draw attention to certain *s·*
complication of
p 389–31 complication of *s·* connected with this belief.
congestive
p 384–18 congestive *s·* in the lungs, or hints of
disease or its
p 419–32 disease or its *s·* cannot change forms,
general
s 152–31 the general *s·*, the characteristic signs,
p 412– 6 to meet the peculiar or general *s·* of the case
mental
s 156–32 Homœopathy takes mental *s·* largely into
of disease
s 153– 3 or changes one of the *s·* of disease.
p 390–12 When the first *s·* of disease appear,
398–17 are known to relieve the *s·* of disease.
of evil
g 540–11 when the *s·* of evil, illusion, are aggravated,
of this disease
s 154–12 Immediately the *s·* of this disease appeared,
physical
ph 194– 6 changes all the physical *s·*,
p 422– 7 and certain moral and physical *s·* seem
t 453–11 morbid moral or physical *s·*
same
p 429–23 and attended by the same *s·*.
subdue the
p 421–14 subdue the *s·* by removing the belief that
such
p 384–21 such *s·* are not apt to follow exposure ;
type and
p 418–20 and to whatever decides its type and *s·*.

sp 79– 1 The act of describing disease— its *s·*,
p 370–11 *s·*, which might be produced by
370–13 drug which might cause the *s·*.
421–23 and sometimes explain the *s·* and their cause
synagogue
a 55–14 although it is again ruled out of the *s·*.
p 398–10 To the *s·* ruler's daughter, whom they
synagogues
a 31–30 "They shall put you out of the *s·* ;— *John* 16 : 2.
s 132–15 thrust . . . the man who lived it out of their *s·*,
synonym
b 333– 3 word *Christ* is not properly a *s·* for Jesus,
r 468–21 Spirit, the *s·* of Mind, Soul, or God,
482–10 Soul is properly the *s·* of Spirit,
g 517– 1 word for *man* is used also as the *s·* of
529–30 Adam, the *s·* for error,
synonymous
sp 71– 7 Soul is *s·* with Spirit, God,
s 127–12 These *s·* terms stand for
b 333–10 The name is *s·* with Messiah,
o 345– 1 Spirit and God are often regarded as *s·* terms ;
r 465–11 *Question.* — Are these terms *s·*?
ap 576–27 The term Lord, . . . is often *s·* with Jehovah,
syrups
f 230–25 They are soothing *s·* to put children to sleep,
system
action of the
p 378– 9 no inflammatory nor torpid action of the *s·*.
415– 6 quickens or impedes the action of the *s·*,
t 447–15 The recuperative action of the *s·*,
and rule
g 547– 5 not one departs from the stated *s·* and rule.

system

any
r 483–25 but if any *s·* honors God,

Christian
s 150– 3 this Christian *s·* of healing disease.

developing in the
p 381– 6 or that some disease is developing in the *s·*,

discovery of the
pref viii–27 led her, . . . to the discovery of the *s·*

entire
p 371–31 Truth is an alterative in the entire *s·*,

every
b 279–22 Every *s·* of human philosophy, doctrine,

false
sp 99–21 not with the individual, but with the false *s·*.

first
g 529– 6 The first *s·* of suggestive obstetrics has

Graham
f 221– 2 adopted the Graham *s·* to cure dyspepsia.

her
pref viii– 1 her *s·* has been fully tested

human
(*see* **human**)

Jesus'
s 132–17 Jesus' *s·* of healing received no aid nor

material
s 133–22 It was a finite and material *s·*,

metaphysical
s 111–30 my metaphysical *s·* of treating disease

no other
b 338– 1 heals the sick and sinning as no other *s·* can.

of ceremonies
s 135–27 was not a creed, nor a *s·* of ceremonies,

of hygiene
ph 185– 6 No *s·* of hygiene but C. S. is purely mental.

of Mind-healing
t 460– 5 Our *s·* of Mind-healing rests on the

of religion
a 26–31 Christianity was no form or *s·* of religion

particular
s 112–10 some particular *s·* of human opinions.

pathological
t 464–21 In founding a pathological *s·* of Christianity,

reduced to a
s 146–31 Divine metaphysics is now reduced to a *s·*,

regulates the
p 420–19 and regulates the *s·*.

scientific
s 123–17 the scientific *s·* of divine healing.
t 464–29 a scientific *s·* of ethics.

solar
s 119–29 the movement of the solar *s·*,
  121–25 so far as our solar *s·* is concerned,
  122–30 mistake . . . regarding the solar *s·*.
r 493– 5 science . . . explains the solar *s·*

spiritual
ph 170– 4 neither a moral nor a spiritual *s·*.

stellar
s 121– 4 Copernicus mapped out the stellar *s·*,

stimulates the
p 394– 9 stimulates the *s·* to act in the direction which

this
s 111–31 Since then this *s·* has gradually gained ground,
  147– 1 This *s·* enables the learner to demonstrate
g 546–28 resides in the good this *s·* accomplishes,

system

whole
p 422– 6 a great stir throughout his whole *s·*,
s 129–32 The sinner sees, in the *s·* taught in this
o 342–18 Shall it be denied that a *s·* which
g 546–27 The proof that the *s·* stated in this book

systematic
s 164– 5 "No *s·* or theoretical classification of
o 355–18 any *s·* healing power since the
t 443– 3 consistency of *s·* medical study,
  461–31 *S·* teaching and the student's spiritual growth

systems

accepted
o 344–20 not included in the commonly accepted *s·* ;

educational
f 226–28 and from the educational *s·* of the Pharaohs,

false
g 549–22 false *s·*, which rely upon physics

human
s 164–12 But all human *s·* based on
ph 170–12 not only contradicts human *s·*, but
f 234–22 present codes of human *s·* disappoint

man-made
s 112–13 divine Science which eschews man-made *s·*,
ph 168–15 Because man-made *s·* insist that man

material
b 326–12 forsake the foundation of material *s·*,
p 394–18 fallacy of material *s·* in general,

medical
ph 166–29 conceded . . . by most of the medical *s·* ;

modern
s 126–27 nothing in ancient or in modern *s·* on which to

of ideas
f 209– 6 the central sun of its own *s·* of ideas,

of medicine
s 146– 5 governed more or less by our *s·* of medicine.
ph 185–13 as material as the prevailing *s·* of medicine.
o 344–26 Why support the popular *s·* of medicine,

of Mind
b 310–16 all things in the *s·* of Mind.

of physics
s 160– 3 *s·* of physics act against metaphysics,

of religion
m 67–30 *S·* of religion and medicine treat of
s 146– 4 Because our *s·* of religion are

old
s 142– 1 in less time than the old *s·*, . . . have required

other
s 129–20 and so are some other *s·*.
b 269–26 All other *s·* — systems based wholly or partly on
t 443–19 whatever other *s·* they fancy will afford relief.

religious
s 132–18 from other sanitary or religious *s·*,

semi-metaphysical
b 268–15 semi-metaphysical *s·* afford no substantial
  269– 1 semi-metaphysical *s·* are one and all

such
s 146– 9 Such *s·* are barren of the vitality of
ph 185–11 Such theories and such *s·* of so-called mind-cure,

time-honored
pref vii–14 independent of doctrines and time-honored *s·*,

their
f 225–10 until it subscribes to their *s·* ;

b 269–26 *s·* based wholly or partly on knowledge gained
  270–15 higher than the *s·* of their times ;

T

tabernacled
ap 576– 6 while yet he *t·* with mortals.

table
sp 80–20 not seem mysterious that mind, . . . can move a *t·*,
  80–21 mind-power which moves both *t·* and hand.
s 129–31 small estimate of the pleasures of the *t·*.
  135–19 "Can God furnish a *t·* in the— *Psal.* 78 : 19.
f 214–24 would spread their *t·* with cannibal tidbits
  234– 6 with crumbs of comfort from Christ's *t·*,
p 362–14 on a couch with his head towards the *t·*
ap 578–13 prepareth a *t·* before me in the— *see Psal.* 23 : 5.

table-salt
s 153– 6 *Natrum muriaticum* (common *t·*)

table-setting
sp 80–28 table-tipping as certainly as *t·*,

tablet
f 227–29 and defaced the *t·* of your being.

table-tipping
sp 80–28 Mortal mind produces *t·* as certainly as

tail
ap 563–23 his *t·* drew the third part of the— *Rev.* 12 : 4.

taint
m 66–14 joys of Spirit, which have no *t·* of earth.

take
pr 1–13 before they *t·* form in words
  15–19 We must resolve to *t·* up the cross,
a 21–23 if I *t·* up their line of travel,
  29– 1 Christians must *t·* up arms against error
  32–17 *T·*, eat ; this is my body.— *Matt.* 26 : 26.
  34– 1 *t·* his cross, and leave all
  34–14 *t·* up the cross, heal the sick,
  37–21 May the Christians of to-day *t·* up the more
m 59–32 Separation never should *t·* place,
  68–12 Be not in haste to *t·* the vow
sp 72– 2 of which corporeal sense can *t·* no cognizance.
  75– 6 material senses could *t·* no cognizance of the
  89–29 concluded . . . man had the right to *t·* it away.
an 105–16 When our laws eventually *t·* cognizance of
s 129–21 abandon pharmaceutics, and *t·* up ontology,
  149–20 remarked . . . . *t·* as little medicine as possible ;
  150–16 to *t·* away the sins of the world.

take

- s 155– 6   *t·* away the individual confidence in the drug,
- 159– 5   compelled by her physicians to *t·* it.
- 159–11   Is it skilful or scientific surgery to *t·* no heed
- ph 165– *   *T· no thought for your life,— Matt.* 6 : 25.
- 167–22   not wise to *t·* a halting and half-way position
- 168– 7   you *t·* away from Mind,
- 170–16   "*t·* no thought for your life,— *Matt.* 6 : 25.
- 172–25   If . . . you *t·* away a portion of the man when
- 179–16   he will *t·* cold without his blanket,
- 180–12   nor *t·* the ground that all causation
- 187–27   If you *t·* away this erring mind,
- 191– 1   It can *t·* no cognizance of Mind.
- 193–17   I told him to rise, dress himself, and *t·* supper
- f 201– 5   would be supreme in us and *t·* the lead in our
- 202–31   Common opinion admits that a man may *t·* cold
- 212–15   *t·* away this so-called mind instead of a piece of
- 220– 2   We hear it said : . . . I *t·* cold baths, in order to
- 220– 3   to overcome a predisposition to *t·* cold ;
- 228–20   "*T·* no thought for your life,"— *Matt.* 6 : 25.
- 239– 5   *T·* away wealth, fame, and social
- 241–14   *T·* away the spiritual signification of Scripture,
- 250–25   *T·* away the mortal mind, and matter has no
- 254–30   *T·* it up and bear it, for through it you win
- c 255–13   mortals *t·* limited views of all things.
- b 273– 3   The physical senses can *t·* no cognizance of God
- 294– 7   would *t·* away some quality and quantity of
- 328–23   they shall *t·* up serpents,— *Mark* 16 : 18.
- o 355–13   true sense of Life and being *t·* possession
- 359– 5   will *t·* the same cases, and cures will follow.
- p 362– *   *they shall t· up serpents ;— Mark* 16 : 18.
- 365– 8   "*T·* no thought for your life,"— *Matt.* 6 : 25.
- 376–12   never gave life and can never *t·* it away,
- 377– 2   convince him that matter cannot *t·* cold,
- 378–23   and *t·* the government into its own hands.
- 382–11   "*T·* no thought . . . for the— *Luke* 12 : 22.
- 383– 5   One says : "I *t·* good care of my body."
- 392– 9   is to *t·* antagonistic grounds against all that
- 392–22   will master you, whichever direction they *t·*.
- 393–10   *T·* possession of your body, and govern its
- 395–16   but is besought to *t·* the patient to Himself,
- 425– 6   *t·* up the leading points included
- 439– 8   commanding him to *t·* part in the homicide.
- t 452–23   *t·* no risks in the policy of error.
- 458–14   the divine Mind is ready to *t·* the case.
- 459–11   for failing to *t·* the first step.
- 464– 9   could not *t·* her place, even if willing so to do.
- r 479–13   *T·* away so-called mortal mind, which constitutes
- 479–15   matter can *t·* no cognizance of matter.
- 488–20   The corporeal senses can *t·* no cognizance of
- 497– 3   As adherents of Truth, we *t·* the inspired
- g 502–15   the crude forms of human thought *t·*
- 530– 8   "*T·* no thought for your life,— *Matt.* 6 : 25.
- 531–28   corporeal senses can *t·* no cognizance of Spirit.
- 537– 1   lest he put forth his hand, and *t·*— *Gen.* 3 : 22.
- 539– 0   as if . . . matter can both give and *t·* away.
- 542–18   "They that *t·* the sword— *Matt.* 26 : 52.
- 543 19   corporeal senses cannot *t·* cognizance of Spirit.
- 546–17   material senses can *t·* no cognizance of Spirit
- 548– 2   let him *t·* the water of life freely."— *Rev.* 22 : 17.
- ap 559–17   "Go and *t·* the little book.— *Rev.* 10 : 8.
- 559–17   *T·* it, and eat it up ;— *Rev.* 10 : 9.
- 559–20   *T·* divine Science.
- 569–27   but how many periods of torture it may *t·*
- 572–28   are inadequate to *t·* in so wonderful a scene.
- 573–29   *T·* heart, dear sufferer, for this reality

taken

- pr 9–15   There is a cross to be *t·* up before we
- a 28– 4   If the Master had not *t·* a student
- 32–30   a sad supper *t·* at the close of day,
- sp 86–27   can all be *t·* from pictorial thought and
- ph 177–30   as if the poison had been intentionally *t·*.
- 195– 3   he asked to be *t·* back to his dungeon,
- f 245–22   she had *t·* no cognizance of passing time
- p 371–16   adult must be *t·* out of his darkness,
- 382–30   the medicines I had *t·* only abandoned me to
- 383–12   A hint may be *t·* from the emigrant,
- 392– 5   broken moral law should be *t·* into account
- 400–13   before it has *t·* tangible shape in
- 420–23   erroneous belief, *t·* at its best, is not
- 436–25   compelled to let him be *t·* into custody,
- t 459–10   Judge not . . . by the steps already *t·*,
- r 470–19   Has God *t·* down His own standard,
- g 528–13   and the rib, . . . *t·* from man,— *Gen.* 2 : 22.
- 529– 4   not woman again *t·* from man.
- 533–17   According to this belief, the rib *t·* from
- 535–27   out of it wast thou *t·* :— *Gen.* 3 : 19.
- 537– 4   the ground from whence he was *t·*.— *Gen.* 3 : 23.
- 537–26   Literally *t·*, the text is made to
- 542–15   vengeance shall be *t·* on him— *Gen.* 4 : 15.
- ap 575–16   *T·* in its allegorical sense,

takes

- sp 83–13   here Science *t·* issue with popular religions.
- s 122–25   To . . . sense, the severance of the jugular vein *t·*

takes

- s 143–15   *t·* the lesser to relieve the greater.
- 147–29   A pure affection *t·* form in goodness,
- 148–15   Anatomy *t·* up man at all points materially.
- 152– 4   Mind *t·* away all its supposed sovereignty,
- 156–31   Mind *t·* its rightful and supreme place.
- 156–32   Homœopathy *t·* mental symptoms largely into
- ph 170–32   which *t·* divine power into its own hands
- c 256– 1   Progress *t·* off human shackles.
- 262– 6   C. S. *t·* naught from the perfection of
- b 323–26   *t·* away all sin and the delusion that
- o 347–23   If C. S. *t·* away the popular gods,
- 350– 5   C. S. *t·* exactly the opposite view.
- p 383– 8   *t·* the best care of his body when he
- 424– 3   *t·* possession of itself and its own thoughts
- 429– 7   The final demonstration *t·* time
- 431–25   Another witness *t·* the stand and testifies :
- 432–20   Another witness *t·* the stand and testifies :
- t 463–17   When this new birth *t·* place,
- r 492–19   if it *t·* all summer."
- 493–22   *t·* away this physical sense of discord,
- g 522–18   In this erroneous theory, matter *t·* the
- 541– 1   Abel *t·* his offering from the firstlings of the
- 549– 3   *t·* place apart from sexual conditions.
- 557–22   Popular theology *t·* up the history of man
- ap 571–31   He *t·* away mitre and sceptre.
- 574– 3   The Revelator also *t·* in another view,
- gl 591–14   that of which immortal Mind *t·* no cognizance ;

taketh

- a 23–12   "He that *t·* one doctrine, firm in faith,
- s 131–23   which *t·* away the ceremonies and doctrines

taking

- m 62–13   *T·* less "thought for your life,— *Matt.* 6 : 25.
- s 156–24   was relieved by *t·* them.
- 156–24   *t·* the unmedicated pellets,
- ph 175– 1   prevent the images of disease from *t·* form
- 176– 7   primitive custom of *t·* no thought about food
- 179– 3   this can be done only by *t·* up the cross
- f 206–20   and then *t·* it away by death?
- 222–14   *T·* less thought about what he should eat
- 245– 8   *t·* no note of years,
- b 296–29   and aids in *t·* the next step
- 334–18   *t·* away the sins of the world,
- p 377– 1   If your patient believes in *t·* cold,
- 413–13   *t·* a fish out of water every day
- g 504–17   *t·* place on so many *evenings* and *mornings,*
- 511–27   *t·* form in masculine, feminine, or
- gl 585–18   metaphysics *t·* the place of physics ;

talent

- b 323–18   but the one unused *t·* decays and is lost.
- p 366–32   we must not hide the *t·* of spiritual healing

talents

- pr 6– 6   The *t·* He gives we must improve.

talk

- ph 175–20   coddling, and sickly after-dinner *t·*.
- f 211– 1   If they *t·* to us, tell us their condition,
- 217–32   Do the muscles *t·*, or do you *t·* for them?
- p 391 20   Since matter cannnot *t·*, it must be mortal mind
- 399–14   Nerves are unable to *t·*,
- t 448–30   To *t·* the right and live the wrong is foolish

talked

- a 45–13   Three days after his bodily burial he *t·* with
- m 62– 9   fed, rocked, tossed, or *t·* to,
- b 308–15   heard the voice of Truth, and *t·* with God
- ap 574– 7   *t·* with me, saying, Come hither,— *Rev.* 21 : 9.

talker

- ap 507–25   and therefore, in his pretence of being a *t·*,

talking

- f 218– 1   Mortal mind does the false *t·*,
- p 396– 5   Avoid *t·* illness to the patient.
- t 452–25   by right *t·* and wrong acting,
- g 529–21   Whence comes a *t·*, lying serpent
- 529–25   the species described,— a *t·* serpent,
- ap 564–31   this allegorical, *t·* serpent typifies

talks

- sp 89– 8   believing that . . . she *t·* freely.
- b 308–15   as consciously as man *t·* with man.

tall

- pref vii–24   task of the sturdy pioneer to hew the *t·* oak
- sp 87–21   of the *t·* ships that float on its bosom,

tangible

- sp 75– 5   would need to be *t·* and material,
- 78–21   Spirit is not materially *t·*.
- b 269–17   These ideas are perfectly real and *t·*
- 279–11   Ideas are *t·* and real to
- 317–16   is no less *t·* because it is spiritual
- p 400–13   before it has taken *t·* shape in

tangled

- ph 195–23   It is the *t·* barbarisms of learning which
- g 507–10   strangers in a *t·* wilderness.

tapping
s 156– 6 *T·* had been employed,
tares
sp 72–15 the *t·* and the wheat, which are not united
f 207–19 separates the *t·* and wheat in time of harvest.
b 300–17 These opposite qualities are the *t·* and wheat,
300–20 Science separates the wheat from the *t·*,
g 535– 4 the wheat and *t·* which time will separate,
gl 595– 5 definition of
tarry
b 299–16 they *t·* with us, and we entertain
329–14 One should not *t·* in the storm if the body is
tarsal
p 408–22 A dislocation of the *t·* joint would produce
408–24 mortal mind thinks that the *t·* joint is
Tarsus
b 326–23 Saul of *T·* beheld the way — the Christ,
task
appointed
c 261–14 go upon the stage and sustain his appointed *t·*,
difficult
f 225–25 abolition of mental slavery is a more difficult *t·*.
no
b 318– 1 For him to believe in matter was no *t·*,
t 450–12 To teach C. S. to such as these is no *t·*.
not a difficult
p 396–15 is not a difficult *t·* in view of the conceded
our
pr 3– 7 and it is our *t·* to work out the solution.
pleasurable
g 506–28 Upon Adam devolved the pleasurable *t·* of
quiet
ap 567– 1 Gabriel has the more quiet *t·* of
this
f 254–20 This *t·* God demands us to accept lovingly
p 400–15 This *t·* becomes easy, if you understand that
t 462–16 There is nothing difficult nor toilsome in this *t·*,

pref vii–23 It is the *t·* of the sturdy pioneer to hew the
s 163–30 is indeed a *t·* as impracticable as to arrange
t 452– 2 a *t·* not difficult, when one understands
g 506– 1 apportion to themselves a *t·* impossible
tasks
b 323– 9 Beholding the infinite *t·* of truth,
taste
b 284–23 nor can they feel, *t·*, or smell Spirit.
r 479–11 Matter cannot see, feel, hear, *t·*,
g 526–10 material hearing, sight, touch, *t·*, and smell,
ap 559–22 It will be indeed sweet at its first *t·*,
tasted
c 263–10 and cling to earth because he has not *t·* heaven.
tastes
m 60– 4 Kindred *t·*, motives, and aspirations are
ph 195–27 fill our young readers with wrong *t·* and
gl 591–15 feels, hears, *t·*, and smells only in belief.
tasteth
s 115– 9 as the mouth *t·* meat." — *Job* 34 : 3.
tatters
f 201–16 we shall not hug our *t·* close about us.
tattling
s 153–30 and we shall avoid loquacious *t·*
taught
pref xii– 7 were *t·* by the author in this College.
pr 16– 7 Our Master *t·* his disciples one brief prayer,
a 18– 3 Jesus of Nazareth *t·* and demonstrated man's
20–17 he *t·* mortals the opposite of themselves,
25–13 Jesus *t·* the way of Life by demonstration,
26–28 Our Master *t·* no mere theory, doctrine,
26–30 the divine Principle of all real being which he *t·*
28– 5 and *t·* the unseen verities of God,
30–14 Rabbi and priest *t·* the Mosaic law,
30–32 must work out our salvation in the way Jesus *t·*.
31–12 he *t·* his followers the healing power
34–20 understood better what the Master had *t·*.
38–31 He *t·* that the material senses shut out Truth
41–20 ever *t·* or demonstrated the divine healing
41–28 The truth *t·* by Jesus, the elders scoffed at.
42–28 Jesus had *t·* his disciples the Science of this
43–17 final demonstration of the truth which Jesus *t·*,
43–28 The Science Jesus *t·* and lived must triumph
45–23 and beheld the final proof of all that he had *t·*,
46– 4 the truthfulness of all that he had *t·*.
51–21 the works which he did and *t·* others to do.
m 64– 3 in the direction *t·* by the Apostle James,
sp 94– 1 Jesus *t·* but one God, one Spirit,
s 107– * *neither was I t· it,* — *Gal.* 1 : 12.
110–18 No human pen nor tongue *t·* me the Science
110–28 spiritually discerned, *t·*, and demonstrated
117–15 Our Master *t·* spirituality by similitudes
129–32 The sinner sees, in the system *t·* in this book,
133–26 who *t·* as he was inspired by the Father
135–26 Christianity as Jesus *t·* it was not a creed,

taught
s 136– 2 He *t·* his followers that his religion
147–25 and *t·* the generalities of its divine Principle
156–28 Metaphysics, as *t·* in C. S., is the next
ph 180– 3 it should be *t·* to do the body no harm
180–29 as *t·* and demonstrated by Christ Jesus.
195– 2 After the babbling boy had been *t·* to speak
f 227– 5 and mortals are *t·* their right to freedom,
232–19 Jesus never *t·* that drugs,
237–15 Children should be *t·* the Truth-cure,
b 294–16 *t·*, as they are by physiology and pathology,
300–27 is *t·* by the schools.
306– 5 Jesus *t·* them how death was to be overcome
310–18 We are commonly *t·* that there is a
319–21 *t·* in the original language of the Bible
321–32 *t·* them how to handle serpents unharmed,
329– 3 they will be sought and *t·*,
333–11 which is *t·*, illustrated, and demonstrated
o 343– 1 The people are *t·* in such cases to say, Amen.
359– 1 whom they have seen and have been *t·* to love
p 379–19 the opposite statement of Life as *t·* in C. S.,
440– 6 is *t·* how to make sleep befool reason
t 449–30 if the student practises what he is *t·*,
455–26 if he is *t·* of God to discern it.
461– 8 C. S. can be *t·* only by those who are
463– 6 familiar with the obstetrics *t·* by this Science.
r 473–28 He proved what he *t·*.
477– 4 Jesus *t·* that the kingdom of God is intact,
ap 560–30 was to be ignorant of the divine idea he *t·*.
575–15 Did not Jesus illustrate the truths he *t·*
tea
sp 80– 3 A cup of coffee or *t·* is not the equal of truth,
p 406–29 alcoholic drinks, tobacco, *t·*, coffee, opium,
teach
pref viii– 9 Theology and physics *t·* that both Spirit and
a 28– 1 The Pharisees claimed to know and to *t·* the
m 60–27 and *t·* us life's sweeter harmonies.
66– 6 Trials *t·* mortals not to lean on a material
69–23 the child may ask, "Do you *t·* that
sp 81–15 when alleged spirits *t·* immortality.
s 139–12 will *t·* men patiently and wisely to stem the
f 235–24 physicians should be able to *t·* it.
236–23 Parents should *t·* their children at the earliest
240– 7 Suns and planets *t·* grand lessons.
b 271–21 shall *t·* you all things." — *John* 14 : 26.
283–29 than we can *t·* and illustrate geometry by
p 382–16 than is the devotee . . . who comes to *t·* the
382–26 but for the glorious Principle you *t·*,
416–32 *T·* them that their being is sustained by Spirit,
t 443– * *t· a just man, and he will* — *Prov.* 9 : 9.
445– 9 *T·* the great possibilities of man endued with
445–10 *T·* the dangerous possibility of
445–13 *T·* the meekness and might of life
449–13 registers his healing ability and fitness to *t·*.
449–16 to *t·* this subject properly and correctly
450–11 To *t·* C. S. to such as these is no task.
453–14 *T·* your student that he must know himself
454– 4 *T·* your students the omnipotence of Truth,
455– 8 in order to *t·* this Science of healing.
g 540–23 is to *t·* mortals never to believe a lie.
Teacher
faith in the
a 25–27 faith in the *T·* and all the emotional love
great
a 20–20 the scourge and the cross awaited the great *T·*
25–23 the great *T·* by no means relieved others from
33–19 our great *T·* said : "Not my will, — *Luke* 22 : 42
m 56– 1 When our great *T·* came to him for baptism,
sp 85–30 The great *T·* knew both cause and effect,
p 441–31 Our great *T·* of mental jurisprudence
immaculate
s 137– 5 when their immaculate *T·* stood before them,
new
s 136–28 No wonder Herod desired to see the new *T·*.
teacher
and student
t 457– 5 this book has done more for *t·* and student,
463– 5 *T·* and student should also be familiar with
human
t 455–18 student, who receives . . . from a human *t·*,
inspired
b 319–27 wrote down what an inspired *t·* had said.
of Christian Science
t 449–28 A proper *t·* of C. S. improves the health and
sole
pref viii–30 for the Bible was her sole *t·* ;
thoughts of the
f 235–14 The pure and uplifting thoughts of the *t·*,

s 162–31 the famous Philadelphia *t·* of medical practice.
t 444–31 The *t·* must make clear to students the
445– 2 *t·* must thoroughly fit his students
449–31 the *t·* is a Scientist only in name.
451–19 every conscientious *t·* of the Science of
452–18 The *t·* must know the truth himself.

teachers
f 227–10 some public *t'* permit an ignorance of
235– 7 The *t'* of schools and the

teaches
pr 10–22 Experience *t'* us that we do not always
16–18 C. S. *t'* us that "the evil one,"
a 26–20 demonstrates the beauty of the music he *t'*
29– 7 Christian experience *t'* faith in the right
m 67– 3 and learn the lessons He *t'*?
sp 79–29 Mind-science *t'* that mortals
99–14 C. S. *t'* only that which is spiritual
s 127–19 It *t'* that matter is the falsity,
ph 169–29 Whatever *t'* man to have other laws
f 241–13 Bible *t'* transformation of the body by the
c 266–16 Thus He *t'* mortals to lay down their
b 295–28 Brainology *t'* that mortals are created to suffer
295–30 It further *t'* that when man is dead,
309–23 led to deny material sense, . . . as the gospel *t'*.
326– 8 All nature *t'* God's love to man,
337–16 pure in heart can see God, as the gospel *t'*.
o 346– 6 It is sometimes said that C. S. *t'*
346– 7 and then *t'* how this nothingness is to be
354– 8 it *t'* precisely this thought
357–17 History *t'* that the popular and
t 446–11 Whoever practises the Science the author *t'*,
450– 3 Their creed *t'* belief in a mysterious,
462–26 The anatomy of C. S. *t'* when and how to probe
462–28 It *t'* the control of mad ambition.
r 472– 1 This Science *t'* man that God is the only Life,
g 542–23 *t'* mortals not to remove the waymarks of God.

teaching
and demonstration
b 270–18 nature of the *t'* and demonstration of God,
and practice
a 26–21 Jesus' *t'* and practice of Truth involved
r 473–19 Jesus introduced the *t'* and practice of
became clearer
t 460–31 the *t'* became clearer, until finally
contradicts the
g 526– 7 contradicts the *t'* of the first chapter,
easier than
p 373–12 Healing is easier than *t'*, if the
healing and
o 349– 5 ask concerning our healing and *t'*,
t 454–18 the true incentive in both healing and *t'*.
455–32 in the Science of mental healing and *t'*,
458–29 through living as well as healing and *t'*,
his
a 19–14 although his *t'* set households at variance,
54– 8 Who is ready to follow his *t'*
in its
s 112– 5 can, therefore, be but one method in its *t'*.
involves
r 493–14 full answer to the above question involves *t'*,
or practising
o 342–29 If Christian Scientists were *t'* or practising
t 456– 3 *T'* or practising in the name of Truth,
spiritual
ap 575–13 Spiritual *t'* must always be by symbols.
gl 595–16 alone can fit us for the office of spiritual *t'*.
systematic
t 461–31 Systematic *t'* and the student's spiritual
this
a 38– 4 This *t'* is even more pernicious
ph 192–18 this *t'* accords with Science and harmony.
p 371–24 because this *t'* is in advance of the age,
410–13 mankind objects to making this *t'* practical.
r 488– 5 the cure shows that you understand this *t'*,

pr 6–26 He came *t'* and showing men how to
s 114–16 as the phrase is used in *t'* C. S.,
137– 1 and demonstrating the truth of being.
ph 172–30 *t'* us by his very deprivations, that
o 343– 2 for *t'* Truth as the Principle of healing,
348–30 this I do aver, that, as a result of *t'* C. S.,
p 373–12 If the *t'* is faithfully done.
396–20 all *t'* that the body suffers,
t 445–27 danger in *t'* Mind-healing indiscriminately,
446– 1 *t'* his slight knowledge of Mind-power,
460–25 while *t'* its grand facts,

teachings
and demonstrations
a 47– 2 discernment of Jesus' *t'* and demonstrations,
s 126–27 except the *t'* and demonstrations of
and practice
a 19–25 of the *t'* and practice of our Master
Christ's
sp 98–27 Mystery does not enshroud Christ's *t'*,
f 236– 9 individuals, who reiterate Christ's *t'*
her
pref x–17 have proved the worth of her *t'*.
his
o 343–14 when his *t'* are fully understood.
r 473–32 his *t'* and their glorious proofs,

teachings
Jesus'
a 19– 8 the divine Principle of Jesus' *t'*,
47– 2 discernment of Jesus' *t'* and demonstrations,
47–15 the people were in doubt concerning Jesus' *t'*.
50–22 Even what they did say, — that Jesus' *t'* were
of Christian Science
o 355–20 The statement that the *t'* of C. S.
t 444–23 medical schools turn a deaf ear to the *t'* of C. S.,
448–26 adheres strictly to the *t'* of C. S.
g 502–19 according to the *t'* of C. S.
of divine Science
o 349–13 in conveying the *t'* of divine Science
of Jesus
b 269–23 plant myself unreservedly on the *t'* of Jesus,
324–23 to follow the example and *t'* of Jesus,
of natural science
r 478– 4 Even according to the *t'* of natural science,
of the Comforter
s 123–22 and through the *t'* of the Comforter,
of the schools
p 429–29 not included in the *t'* of the schools,
ordinary
sp 99–13 The ordinary *t'* are material
result of our
r 488– 2 result of our *t'* is their sufficient confirmation.
spiritual
b 272–15 the spiritual *t'* which dulness and
Truth's
t 462– 9 goes away to practise Truth's *t'* only in part,

tear
f 211–14 When a *t'* starts, does not this so-called mind
211–16 Without mortal mind, the *t'* could not appear:

tears (noun)
p 363–27 She bathed his feet with her *t'*
367–15 with *t'* of repentance and with
ap 573–31 no more pain, and all *t'* will be wiped away.

tears (verb)
b 273–11 thus *t'* away the foundations of error.

teaspoonful
s 153– 9 and a *t'* of the water administered at

tedious
t 460–20 it becomes a *t'* mischief-maker.

teeming
g 513– 6 in the *t'* universe of Mind

teeth
f 211–20 children's *t'* are set on edge." — *Ezek.* 18: 2.
247– 4 two of the elements it had lost, sight and *t'*.
247– 6 Another woman at ninety had new *t'*,
247– 8 his full set of upper and lower *t'*

telegraphy
f 243–22 Neither . . . can carry on such *t'*;
p 399–13 both the service and message of this *t'*.

tell
pr 13–15 God knows our need before we *t'* Him
a 27– 3 *t'* John what things ye have seen — *Luke* 7: 22.
27– 7 *T'* John what the demonstration of divine
sp 78–28 cannot "*t'* whence it cometh." — *John* 3: 8.
89– 1 who can *t'* what the unaided medium
an 106–24 of the which I *t'* you before, — *Gal.* 5: 21.
s 142–15 In vain do the manger and the cross *t'* their
ph 174–12 the spiritual intuitions that *t'* us when
f 211– 2 if they talk to us, *t'* us their condition,
b 308–32 "*T'* me, I pray thee, thy name;" — *Gen.* 32: 29.
o 341– * *And because I t' you the truth,* — *John* 8: 45.
352–32 not irrational to *t'* the truth about ghosts.
p 394–23 Will you *t'* the sick that their condition is
416–10 will *t'* you that the troublesome material cause
416–27 *t'* them only what is best for them to know.
417– 6 Never *t'* the sick that they have more courage than
417– 7 *T'* them rather, that their strength is
420–24 *T'* the sick that they can meet disease
420–29 vehemently *t'* your patient that he must awake.
420–32 *T'* him that he suffers only as the insane suffer,
424–31 The patient may *t'* you that he has a humor in
t 448– 9 When needed *t'* the truth concerning
453–25 you must not *t'* the patient that he is sick
461–17 you should *t'* your belief sometimes,
ap 571– 6 people like you better when you *t'* them their
571– 7 than when you *t'* them their vices.
571– 8 to *t'* a man his faults, and so risk

telling
s 161–25 examining bodily symptoms, *t'* the patient that
p 371– 6 by *t'* ghost-stories in the dark.
ap 571–10 Who is *t'* mankind of the foe in ambush?

tells
sp 91– 1 *t'* us of "a new heaven — *Rev.* 21: 1.
p 383–22 sometimes *t'* you that the weed preserves his

temperance
an 106–28   goodness, faith, meekness, *t·* :— *Gal.* 5 : 22, 23.
s 115–27   compassion, hope, faith, meekness, *t·*.
o 348–31   ethics and *t·* have received an impulse,
p 404–17   The *t·* reform, felt all over our land,

temperate
b 322–25   is neither a *t·* man nor a reliable religionist.

temperature
s 152–17   to ascertain the *t·* of the patient's body ;
p 413– 8   the *t·* of children and of men,

temperatures
p 386– 5   Expose the body to certain *t·*,

tempest
s 134–28   stilled the *t·*, healed the sick,
b 327–16   to clamor with midnight and *t·*.

tempest's
ph 192–14   the devouring flame, the *t·* breath.

tempest-tossed
g 536– 6   as a symbol of *t·* human concepts

temple
also means body
   ap 576–14   The word *t·* also means *body*.
destroy this
   a 27–12   "Destroy this *t·* — *John* 2 : 19.
   b 314–14   "Destroy this *t·*, — *John* 2 : 19.
   r 494– 2   "Destroy this *t·* — *John* 2 : 19.
material
   b 314–16   their material *t·* instead of his body.
no
   ap 576–10   And I saw no *t·* therein :— *Rev.* 21 : 22.
   576–12   There was no *t·*, — that is, no material
   576–20   with "no *t·* [body] therein" — *Rev.* 21 : 22.
of Christian Science
   b 288–20   The chief stones in the *t·* of C. S.
of the Holy Ghost
   p 365–28   *t·* of the Holy Ghost, — the patient's spiritual
or body
   p 428–13   Thus we may establish in truth the *t·*, or body,
veil of the
   gl 597–11   It rent the veil of the *t·*.

   s 142–19   need to be whipped out of the *t·*,
   ap 576–11   and the Lamb are the *t·* of it. — *Rev.* 21 : 22.
   576–17   spoke of his material body as the *t·*
   gl 595– 7   definition of

temples
s 142–22   to purge the *t·* of their vain traffic

temporal
a 51–12   Jesus could give his *t·* life into his
s 122–27   *T·* life is a false sense of existence.
ph 190–17   This mortal seeming is *t·* ;
b 274– 4   knowledge gained from the five senses is only *t·*,
   277–30   for matter is *t·* and is therefore a
   286–22   Material and *t·* thoughts are human,
   286–25   The *t·* and material are not then creations of
   287– 3   but belong, with all that is material and *t·*,
   289– 2   the *t· débris* of error, belief in sin,
   300–13   The *t·* and unreal never touch the
   301– 9   involves error and therefore is material, *t·*.
   302– 3   The material body and mind are *t·*,
   335–14   Things material and *t·* are insubstantial.
   336– 5   never . . . the eternal into the *t·*,
   337–26   *T·* things are the thoughts of mortals
o 360–16   This ideal is either *t·* or eternal.
p 412–24   and that sickness is a *t·* dream.
r 468–13   matter is the unreal and *t·*.
g 538–27   This account is . . . of sin which is *t·*.
ap 569–25   Scriptures declare that evil is *t·*,

temporarily
s 110–22   and its ideas may be *t·* abused
p 397–29   the belief that mind is, even *t·*, compressed
   415–15   They only render mortal mind *t·* less fearful,
r 483– 3   they do not heal, but only relieve suffering *t·*,
ap 576–11   the temple to be *t·* rebuilt

temporary
f 213–15   towards the finite, *t·*, and discordant.
b 282–11   a belief in a . . . *t·* material existence
   282–12   Eternal Mind and *t·* material existence
   298– 9   a mortal *t·* sense of things,
   311–16   a sense of *t·* loss or absence of soul,
   318–26   Material methods are *t·*.
p 442–23   Christ, Truth, gives mortals *t·* food
t 444–10   right use of *t·* and eternal means.
g 522–16   this state of things is declared to be *t·*

tempt
s 153–32   Neither sympathy nor society should ever *t·*
g 529–21   Whence comes a talking, lying serpent to *t·*

temptation
bids us repeat
   pr 5– 7   *T·* bids us repeat the offence,
deliver us from
   a 22–21   Love is not hasty to deliver us from *t·*,

temptation
may lead us into
   pr 7–27   danger . . . that it may lead us into *t·*.
not into
   pr 17– 8   And lead us not into *t·*, — *Matt.* 6 : 13.
   17–10   *And God leadeth us not into t·*,
resist the
   f 218–25   Resist the *t·* to believe in
sinful
   p 381– 6   than you are to yield to a sinful *t·*
to sin
   p 420–13   as positively as they can the *t·* to sin.

   a 42–22   *t·*, sin, sickness, and death had no terror
   s 158–19   It is pitiful to lead men into *t·*
   c 267–31   the man that endureth . . . *t·* :— *Jas.* 1 : 12
   p 387–31   not only from *t·*, but from bodily suffering.
   441– 8   to keep perpetual silence, and in case of *t·*,
   t 450–22   Sickness to him is no less a *t·* than is sin.
   gl 581–13   The ark indicates *t·* overcome
   598–18   Error ; fornication ; *t·* ; passion.

tempted
p 393–31   false belief is both the tempter and the *t·*,
g 527–13   "God cannot be *t·* with evil, — *Jas.* 1 : 13.
ap 564–15   Since Jesus must have been *t·* in all points,

tempter
p 393–30   false belief is both the *t·* and the tempted,

tempteth
g 527–13   neither *t·* He any man." — *Jas.* 1 : 13.

tempting
g 527–11   represents God, Love, as *t·* man,

tempts
r 495–14   When the illusion of sickness or sin *t·* you,

Ten
b 280–18   declared as Jehovah's first command of the *T·* :
ap 563–31   belief that . . . the *T·* Commandments can be

ten
sp 94–20   Of the *t·* lepers whom Jesus healed,
ph 193–13   In about *t·* minutes he opened his eyes
f 246–22   would enjoy more than threescore years and *t·*
p 421–32   of eight multiplied by five, and of seven by *t·*,
ap 562–31   having seven heads and *t·* horns, — *Rev.* 12 : 3.
   563–11   The *t·* horns of the dragon typify the

tenacious
s 144–12   the more obstinately *t·* its error ;

tenaciously
o 348–21   Instead of *t·* defending the supposed

tenacity
sp 77–18   according to the *t·* of error.
b 296–21   depends upon the *t·* of error.
p 396–18   on account of the *t·* of belief in its truth,

tend
ph 196– 8   false pleasures which *t·* to perpetuate this
p 419– 4   Errors of all sorts *t·* in this direction.
g 542–11   avoidance of justice and the denial of truth *t·* to

tendencies
f 225–25   despotic *t·*, inherent in mortal mind
b 272–22   in contrast with the downward *t·* and

tendency
a 40– 4   devout Christian, perceiving the scope and *t·* of
m 60–20   is not its present *t·*, and why?
sp 78–15   gathered from ignorance are pernicious in *t·*.
s 111–21   an essay calculated to offset the *t·* of the·
   112–14   wholly human in their origin and *t·*
f 213–12   and is a *t·* towards God, Spirit.
p 423– 5   the *t·* towards a favorable result.
ap 570– 4   The present apathy as to the *t·* of

tender
pr 3–14   is not the image and likeness of the patient, *t·*,
m 57–11   should be loving, pure, *t·*, and strong.
   59– 3   There should be the most *t·* solicitude for
   59–17   *T·* words and unselfish care in what
b 332– 5   His *t·* relationship to His spiritual creation.
p 367– 3   The *t·* word and Christian encouragement of
fr 600– *   *whether the t· grape appear*, — *Song* 7 : 12.

tenderly
g 507– 5   *t·* expressing the fatherhood and

tenderness
p 434–17   regards the prisoner with the utmost *t·*.
g 514–18   *T·* accompanies all the might imparted by

tending
g 545– 9   by thought *t·* spiritually upward

tends
pr 2–16   but it *t·* to bring us into harmony
sp 79– 3   *t·* to frighten into death those who are ignorant
   92–27   This belief *t·* to support two opposite powers,
   93–30   This belief *t·* to becloud our apprehension of
p 370–21   physical diagnosis . . . *t·* to induce disease.
   405–25   *t·* to destroy the ability to do right.

tends

p 430–10 *t·* to shut out the true sense of Life
t 443– 6 *t·* to deter those, who make such a
451–31 *t·* to blast moral sense, health, and

tenets

r 497– 1 important points, or religious *t·*, of C. S. :

Tennyson

sp 88– 2 the poet *T·* expressed the heart's desire,

Tennyson's

ph 194–26 and realizing *T·* description :

tenor

p 427–20 The *t·* of the Word shows that we shall obtain

tension

p 393–22 Your body would suffer no more from *t·*

tentative

p 422–32 His treatment is therefore *t·*.

tenth

ap 558– 1 in the *t·* chapter of his book of Revelation :
gl 595–22 Tithe. Contribution ; *t·* part ; homage ;

term

class
t 454–25 at the close of a class *t·*,
double
gl 590–21 This double *t·* is not used in the first chapter
for God
b 286–16 In the Saxon . . . *good* is the *t·* for God.
generic
c 259– 1 to comprehend in Science the generic *t· man.*
r 475–15 the generic *t·* for all that reflects God's
g 516–30 It follows that *man* is a generic *t·*.
gods
r 466–19 is as improper as the *t·* gods.
Lord
ap 576–26 The *t·* Lord, as used in our version
man
g 525– 7 some of the equivalents of the *t· man*
obsolete
gl 588–22 A *t·* obsolete in Science if used with
recent
p 402–23 mesmerism — or hypnotism, to use the recent *t·*
souls
r 466–19 The *t· souls* or *spirits* is as improper as
specific
an 103–19 the specific *t·* for error, or mortal mind.
this
s 114 4 meaning by this *t·* the flesh opposed to Spirit,
gl 590–15 this *t·* is sometimes employed as a title,

s 116–27 If the *t·* personality, as applied to God,
117– 1 The *t· individuality* is also open to objections,
120–16 The *t·* C. S. was introduced by the author
127–15 the *t·* C. S. relates especially to
129– 4 The *t·* Science, properly understood,
b 274–17 what we erroneously *t·* the five physical senses
278–28 All that we *t·* sin, sickness, and death
311– 3 What we *t·* mortal mind or
313– 1 The *t·* Christ Jesus, or Jesus the Christ
p 401–16 What I *t· chemicalization* is the upheaval
r 496–30 if by that *t·* is meant doctrinal beliefs.
gl 597–25 the *t·* as applied to Mind or to one of God's

termed

sp 91–20 or through what are *t·* the material senses.
92– 8 decomposition of mortal bodies in what is *t·* death.
s 114–29 what is *t· matter* is but the subjective state
114–30 of what is *t·* by the author *mortal mind.*
149–23 has cured what is *t·* organic disease
ph 173–11 What is *t·* matter manifests nothing but
177– 1 produces what is *t·* organic disease
177–21 qualities and effects of what is *t·* matter,
179–22 sustained by what is *t·* material law,
182– 6 what are *t·* laws of nature, appertain to matter.
184–25 what is *t·* a fatally broken physical law.
188– 3 What is *t·* disease does not exist.
f 210–25 What is *t·* matter, being unintelligent,
b 290– 4 before what is *t·* death overtakes mortals,
298– 8 What is *t·* material sense can report only a
p 377–16 caused what is *t·* instantaneous death.
377–24 what are *t·* organic diseases as readily as
382–13 He, who is ignorant of what is *t·* hygienic law,
384– 1 Can matter, or what is *t·* matter, either feel or
392–20 in the form of what is *t·* pulmonary disease,
409–12 substratum of mortal mind, *t·* the body,
417–10 what is *t·* matter cannot be sick ;
r 469– 2 What is *t·* matter is unknown to Spirit,
484–11 What are *t·* natural science and material laws
g 526–10 material hearing, sight, . . . *t·* the five senses.
gl 580–16 the opposer of Truth, *t·* error ;
582–25 the testimony of what is *t·* material sense ;
gl 584–23 the opposite of mind, *t·* matter,
594– 6 opposite of Spirit, or good, *t·* matter, or evil ;
595–20 continues after, what is *t·* death, until

terminates

b 338– 7 *t·* in discord and mortality,

terms

Bible
gl 579– 5 the metaphysical interpretation of Bible *t·*,
communicable
sp 74– 3 To be on communicable *t·* with Spirit,
contradiction of
c 257–32 *infinite form* involves a contradiction of *t·*.
dictate
p 409–10 cannot dictate *t·* to consciousness
dictate its
f 228–23 dictate its *t·*, and form and control it with
different
s 161–32 different *t·* than does the metaphysician ;
friendly
p 438–31 to be on friendly *t·* with the firm of
implied by the
sp 94– 5 includes all that is implied by the *t·*
intimate
p 437– 2 he was on intimate *t·* with the plaintiff,
material
s 115– 3 the inadequacy of material *t·*
115–10 when translating material *t·* back into
o 349–17 one is obliged to use material *t·*
349–25 material *t·* must be generally employed.
of forgiveness
pr 11– 2 specified also the *t·* of forgiveness.
pairs of
r 466–11 but these contrasting pairs of *t·*
synonymous
s 127–13 These synonymous *t·* stand for
o 345– 2 are often regarded as synonymous *t·* ;
r 465–11 *Question.*— Are these *t·* synonymous?
your own
p 391–27 Therefore make your own *t·* with sickness,

sp 73– 5 but another, . . . it *t·* a *spirit*
s 127– 9 The *t·* Divine Science, Spiritual Science,
ap 573–10 what the human mind *t·* matter

terrestrial

s 123– 3 the greater error as to our *t·* bodies.
ap 572–29 Were this new heaven and new earth *t·* or

terrible

a 50–26 The burden of that hour was *t·*
s 156– 6 It was a *t·* case.
ph 188– 5 belief of sin, which has grown *t·* in strength
b 289–11 To suppose that . . . is a *t·* mistake.
p 407– 2 inconceivably *t·* to man's self-respect,
437–17 the *t·* records of your Court of Error,
r 486–30 would place man in a *t·* situation.

terrified

p 366–25 The sick are *t·* by their sick beliefs,

terrify

p 380–17 Gazing at a chained lion, . . . should not *t·* a

terrifying

p 376– 1 more *t·* than that of most other diseases.

terror

a 42–23 sin, sickness, and death had no *t·* for Jesus.
o 346–21 If a dream ceases, . . . the *t·* is over.
352–28 *t·* of ghosts will depart
p 378–16 often causes the beast to retreat in *t·*.

terrors

b 289–15 proves the "king of *t·*" to be but a — *Job.* 18 : 14.

test

pr 5– 5 the *t·* of our sincerity,— namely, reformation.
9– 5 The *t·* of all prayer lies in the answer to
a 42–30 to *t·* his still uncomprehended saying,
s 147– 8 submitted to the broadest practical *t·*,
f 204–19 They can never stand the *t·* of Science.
o 344–15 until the enemies of C. S. *t·* its efficacy
r 473–21 and to *t·* its unerring Science according to his
493–30 Who dares to doubt this consummate *t·*

Testament (*see also* Old *and* New Testament)

b 313–14 is, in the Greek *T·*, *character.*

tested

pref viii– 2 her system has been fully *t·*
an 101–10 which *t·* during several sessions the

testified

a 52– 7 their senses *t·* oppositely,
s 134– 5 those who *t·* for Truth were so often persecuted
159– 3 her sister *t·* that the deceased protested
p 388– 7 Apostle John *t·* to the divine basis of C. S.,
436–35 *t·* that he was a ruler of Body,
437– 2 He also *t·* that he was on intimate terms with
439– 6 Death *t·* that he was absent from the

testifies

b 331– 9 falsely *t·* to a beginning and an
p 430–28 being called for, a witness *t·* thus :
431–25 Another witness takes the stand and *t·* :
432– 1 The next witness *t·* :
432–20 Another witness takes the stand and *t·* :

testify
s 120–19   impossible for aught but Mind to *t·* truly
b 287–28   five material senses *t·* to truth and error
p 431– 2   would be allowed to *t·* in the case.

testimony
according to the
  b 334–22   according to the *t·* of the corporeal senses,
all the
  p 434–24   All the *t·* has been on the side of
confirm his
  p 432–24   my presence was required to confirm his *t·*.
confirms that
  s 120–28   confirms that *t·* as legitimate
correct
  b 284–17   Can the material . . . give correct *t·*
denying the
  s 122–19   denying the *t·* of the senses,
dispute the
  p 390–13   dispute the *t·* of the material senses
false
  s 108–25   is the false *t·* of false material sense,
  120– 7   Science reverses the false *t·* of the
  121–21   false *t·* of the eye deluded the
  ph 192–21   senses must give up their false *t·*.
  b 268–17   based on the false *t·* of the material
  273–10   Divine Science reverses the false *t·*
  294–17   taught, . . . to revere false *t·*,
  296–28   until Science obliterates this false *t·*.
  301–25   arise from the false *t·* of material sense,
  p 440–27   repudiate the false *t·* of Personal Sense.
  g 516– 6   when we subordinate the false *t·* of
for the plaintiff
  p 433– 1   The *t·* for the plaintiff, Personal Sense,
human
  sp 71–24   no proof nor power outside of human *t·*.
immortal
  r 490–10   destroy all material sense with immortal *t·*.
  490–25   This immortal *t·* ushers in the
jarring
  b 306–25   Undisturbed amid the jarring *t·* of the
law and
  p 436–10   Upon this statute hangs all the law and *t·*.
law or
  f 238–28   no time for gossip about false law or *t·*.
medical
  p 370–23   According to both medical *t·* and
mortal
  b 297–27   no mortal *t·* is founded on the
  297–28   Mortal *t·* can be shaken.
  r 494–26   One is the mortal *t·*, changing,
of error
  r 481–13   the *t·* of error, declaring existence to be
of material sense
  b 297–22   contradicting the *t·* of material sense,
  301–25   arise from the false *t·* of material sense,
  p 396–14   refutation of the *t·* of material sense
of matter
  p 437–14   the *t·* of matter respected ;
of sin
  p 396–17   not because the *t·* of sin or disease is true,
of Spirit
  s 128–25   forever destroys with the higher *t·* of Spirit
  f 252–16   contrasts strikingly with the *t·* of Spirit.
of the Science
  b 269–24   and on the *t·* of the Science of Mind.
of the serpent
  g 538–15   The *t·* of the serpent is significant of the
opposite
  f 252–31   Spirit, bearing opposite *t·*, saith :
opposition to the
  p 395– 3   in opposition to the *t·* of the deceitful senses,
physical
  b 295– 4   proof of the unreliability of physical *t·*.
pseudo-mental
  p 389–10   This pseudo-mental *t·* can be destroyed
reversing the
  s 120–20   reversing the *t·* of the physical senses,
  120–27   instead of reversing the *t·* of the physical
  p 441–18   Reversing the *t·* of Personal Sense
reviews the
  p 433– 4   He analyzes the offence, reviews the *t·*,
rise above the
  c 262–12   rise above the *t·* of the material senses,
Scriptural
  s 116– 7   as to make this Scriptural *t·* true
their
  ap 568–18   by the word of their *t·* ;— *Rev.* 12 : 11.
this
  b 297– 6   this *t·* manifests itself on the body
  p 396–16   the conceded falsity of this *t·*.
  ap 573– 5   This *t·* of Holy Writ sustains the
valid
  p 434–27   The only valid *t·* in the case shows

  sp 70– 2   *t·* of the corporeal senses cannot inform us
  s 108– 2   a conviction antagonistic to the *t·* of

testimony
s 120–16   nor can the material senses bear reliable *t·*
b 269–21   *t·* of the material senses is neither
288– 5   and the *t·* of the material senses,
296–26   Mortal mind judges by the *t·* of the
317–25   the *t·* of the material senses
o 353– 5   till the *t·* of the physical senses yields
r 488–19   *beliefs*, the *t·* of which cannot be true
gl 582–25   the *t·* of what is termed material sense ;

tests
s 111–31   to the broadest practical *t·*.
f 233–27   not more unquestionable than the scientific *t·*

text
each
  g 502–18   each *t·* is followed by its
familiar
  b 320–11   in the same work, the familiar *t·*, Genesis vi. 3,
favorite
  b 340–16   The First Commandment is my favorite *t·*.
of Truth
  pref x–13   but has bluntly and honestly given the *t·* of Truth.
original
  b 320–17   original *t·* declares plainly the spiritual fact
this
  ph 196–12   A careful study of this *t·* shows that
  b 291–20   This *t·* has been transformed into the
  340– 4   This *t·* in the book of Ecclesiastes
  g 509–15   This *t·* gives the idea of the rarefaction
  526–30   In this *t·* Eden stands for the mortal,
  ap 574–16   The beauty of this *t·* is, that the sum total of

  a 38–15   in the *t·*, "The right hand of — *Psal.* 118 : 16.
  ph 170–10   The *t·*, "Whosoever liveth and— *John* 11 : 26.
  b 320–25   the *t·*, "In my flesh shall I— *Job* 19 : 26.
  g 506–27   in the scientifically Christian meaning of the *t·*.
  508–17   feminine gender is not yet expressed in the *t·*.
  526–15   in the legendary Scriptural *t·*
  537–26   the *t·* is made to appear contradictory
  543–31   The *t·* "In the day that the Lord— *Gen.* 2 : 4.

textbook
s 110–14   the Bible was my only *t·*.
t 456–26   Science and Health for his *t·*,

textbooks
ph 198–11   fills in his delineations with sketches from *t·*.

texts
a 24– 4   Acquaintance with the original *t·*,

thank
s 131–19   "I *t·* Thee, O Father,— *Luke* 10 : 21.

thankful
b 329–10   *t·* that Jesus, who was the true demonstrator of

thanks
expression of
  pr 3–26   more than a verbal expression of *t·*.
gave
  a 32–18   he took the cup, and gave *t·*,— *Matt.* 26 : 27.
  33–16   he gave *t·* and said,
give
  pr 9– 1   Do we not rather give *t·* that we
  f 214–25   with cannibal tidbits and give *t·*.
  ap 568–24   For victory over a single sin, we give *t·*
  570–24   Those ready for the blessing you impart will give *t·*.
to God
  pr 3–28   and yet return *t·* to God for all blessings,

  sp 94–22   but one returned to give God *t·*,
  f 221–24   "giving God *t·* ;"— *see Eph.* 5 : 20.
  t 453–21   masquerader in this Science *t·* God that there is

theatre
c 261–16   so lame that he hobbled every day to the *t·*,

Thee
s 131–19   "I thank *T·*, O Father,— *Luke* 10 : 21.
ph 190–30   For with *T·* is the fountain of life ;— *Psal.* 36 : 9.
c 262–17   "I have heard of *T·* by the— *Job* 42 : 5.
262–18   but now mine eye seeth *T·*."— *Job* 42 : 5.
p 410– 8   that they might know *T·*,— *John* 17 : 3.

theft
s 143–17   it saves from starvation by *t·*,
b 330–30   hypocrisy, slander, hate, *t·*, adultery,

thefts
an 100– *   *t·*, *false witness, blasphemies* :— *Matt.* 15 : 19.

The Lancet
f 245– 4   medical magazine called *T·. L·*.

theme
pref x–15   or treat in full detail so infinite a *t·*.

theodicy
an 104–14   and reveals the *t·* which indicates

theogony
ph 170– 3   Truth is not the basis of *t·*.

theologians
b 320– 6   The most distinguished *t·* in Europe

theological
a   24–16   the ordinary *t·* views of atonement
s   141– 1   indicates the distance between the *t·* and

theologus
t   459–28   the *t·* (that is, the student

Theology
s   118–13   Science, *T·*, and Medicine are means of
131–12   chapter sub-title

theology
anatomy and
    s   148–13   anatomy and *t·* define man as
    148–17   Anatomy and *t·* reject the divine Principle
anatomy nor
    s   148– 7   Neither anatomy nor *t·* has ever described
and healing
    s   138–18   precedent for all Christianity, *t·*, and healing.
and physics
    pref viii– 9   *T·* and physics teach that both
divine
    f   234–23   the weary searcher after a divine *t·*,
    r   469–29   is as pernicious to divine *t·* as are
erudite
    a   24–20   Does erudite *t·* regard the crucifixion of
guidance of a
    s   148–31   leaves them to the guidance of a *t·* which
his
    s   138–31   It is his *t·* in this book and the
Jewish
    a   42– 3   The Jewish *t·* gave no hint of the
    r   466–24   Heathen mythology and Jewish *t·* have
of Christian Science
    s   145–31   The *t·* of C. S. includes healing
    f   252– 6   regarding the pathology and *t·* of C. S.
    p   404–21   most important points in the *t·* of C. S.
of Jesus
    s   138–30   It was this *t·* of Jesus which healed
    p   369– 8   and comprehends the *t·* of Jesus
our Master's
    o   139– 3   It was our Master's *t·* which the impious
popular
    s   126–16   C. S. on the one hand and popular *t·* on the
    g   557–22   Popular *t·* takes up the history of man
problem in
    a   23– 8   The atonement is a hard problem in *t·*,
scholastic
    a   41–19   philosophy, *materia medica*, or scholastic *t·*
    s   141–32   now occupied by scholastic *t·* and physiology,
    f   220–18   scholastic *t·*, material medicine
    b   315– 4   the scholastic *t·* of the rabbis.
tries to explain
    s   148–21   Then *t·* tries to explain how to make this

    s   138–32   spiritual meaning of this *t·*,

theoretical
op   98–27   and they are not *t·* and fragmentary,
s   164– 5   "No systematic or *t·* classification of
ph   191– 8   As a material, *t·* life-basis is found to be a
b   295–26   The *t·* mind is matter, named *brain*, or
o   341– 4   from a *t·* to a practical Christianity.

theoretically
pr   3–18   We admit *t·* that God is good, . . . and then
o   357–13   but if we *t·* endow mortals with the

theories
are sometimes pernicious
    p   394–18   that their *t·* are sometimes pernicious,
cease
    f   216– 5   Here *t·* cease, and Science unveils the mystery
common
    o   342–30   according to the common *t·*,
conflicting
    o   355–14   the relative value of the two conflicting *t·*
contradictory
    r   492–15   These two contradictory *t·* . . . will dispute
cruder
    ph   189– 6   raises the human thought above the cruder *t·*
dietetic
    p   389–13   Our dietetic *t·* first admit that food
doctrines and
    b   319–15   The varied doctrines and *t·* which
false
    s   151–15   false *t·*, from which multitudes would gladly
    r   484–26   involved in all false *t·* and practices.
fossils of
    s   147–21   perishing fossils of *t·* already antiquated,
gushing
    p   367– 6   better than hecatombs of gushing *t·*,
higher
    g   549– 7   give place to higher *t·* and demonstrations.
human
    (*see* human)
its own
    sp   81– 7   At the very best and on its own *t·*, spiritualism
many
    f   232– 3   Many *t·* relative to God and man

theories
material
    (*see* material)
medical
    o   348– 3   Medical *t·* virtually admit the nothingness or
    p   382–20   A patient thoroughly booked in medical *t·*
mortal
    g   552–10   Mortal *t·* make friends of sin,
most
    g   547–17   is more consistent than most *t·*.
of man
    a   20– 4   to forms of doctrine or to *t·* of man,
of parents
    f   237–10   The more stubborn beliefs and *t·* of parents
ordinary
    s   156–12   Believing then somewhat in the ordinary *t·*
or thoughts
    f   237–17   discussing or entertaining *t·* or thoughts
our
    s   119– 2   that is, when we do so in our *t·*,
    122–29   Our *t·* make the same mistake regarding
    152–20   Such a fact illustrates our *t·*.
    b   312–23   Our *t·* are based on finite premises,
physical
    s   123–13   Divine Science, rising above physical *t·*,
prevalent
    f   232–11   but our prevalent *t·* practically deny this,
    b   283–13   But what say prevalent *t·*?
    p   389–18   If God has, as prevalent *t·* maintain,
relinquish all
    f   249– 1   Let us accept Science, relinquish all *t·*
self-assertive
    f   204–23   False and self-assertive *t·* have given
special
    s   133–22   carried out in special *t·* concerning God,
speculative
    f   209–27   the paraphernalia of speculative *t·*,
such
    s   119– 5   such *t·* lead to one of two things.
    ph   185–11   Such *t·* and such systems of so-called mind-cure,
    185–17   Such *t·* have no relationship to C. S.,
    f   204–18   Such *t·* are evidently erroneous.
these
    f   232–12   These *t·* must be untrue,
two
    r   494–25   Which of these two *t·* concerning
various
    b   339–32   Our various *t·* will never lose their imaginary
    gl   587–12   the various *t·* that hold mind to be a

    f   228– 7   prolific subject for mortal belief to pin *t·* upon;
    b   269–29   The *t·* I combat are these:
    g   526– 9   Belief involves *t·* of material hearing,

theorizes
b   295–31   error *t·* that spirit is born of matter

theorizing
ph   172– 3   *T·* about man's development from

theory
accepted
    g   552– 5   was once an accepted *t·*.
any other
    f   249–10   Any other *t·* of Life, or God, is delusive
confirms my
    p   370–14   This confirms my *t·* that faith in the drug
conservative
    r   492–29   The conservative *t·*, long believed, is
contrary to Christian Science
    sp   71–31   a *t·* contrary to C. S.
Darwin's
    g   547–15   Darwin's *t·* of evolution from a material basis
    547–17   Darwin's *t·*,— that Mind produces its opposite,
doctrinal
    s   132–24   on any but a material and a doctrinal *t·*.
erroneous
    ph   177–16   erroneous *t·* of life and intelligence in matter,
    g   522–18   In this erroneous *t·*, matter takes the place
every
    ph   194–13   Every *t·* opposed to this fact
false
    s   123– 1   false *t·* as to the relations of the celestial
first
    b   269–32   The first *t·*, that matter is everything,
incorrect in
    pref   x– 5   incorrect in *t·* and filled with plagiarisms
material
    s   152–12   Such errors beset every material *t·*,
    c   257–23   the material *t·* of mind in matter
    g   545–16   Error tills the whole ground in this material *t·*.
mere
    a   26–28   Our Master taught no mere *t·*, doctrine, or
Mesmer's
    an   100–13   to investigate Mesmer's *t·* and to report
mistaken in
    f   229–19   mistaken in *t·* and in practice.

theory

mortal
g 547–29 sensual, and mortal *t·* of the universe,
mythologic
g 531–29 The mythologic *t·* of material life
no other
r 483–28 does honor God as no other *t·* honors Him,
of Christian Science
s 112–23 Any *t·* of C. S., which departs from
one
p 372– 6 One *t·* about this mortal mind is,
opposed to the
g 545–12 opposed to the *t·* of man as evolved from
scientific
g 547–11 conclusions as to the scientific *t·* of creation.
speculative
ph 195–24 the speculative *t·*, the nauseous fiction.
such a
a 23– 7 Such a *t·* is man-made.
support his
ph 198–25 though the doctor says nothing to support his *t·*.
this
b 300–27 This *t·* is unscientific.
t 458– 7 This *t·* is supposed to favor practice from
r 492–31 This *t·* would keep truth and error always at war.
true
g 547–25 The true *t·* of the universe, including man,
whatever
g 553–20 Whatever *t·* may be adopted by
your
t 456–16 Any dishonesty in your *t·* and practice

c 256– 9 The *t·* of three persons in one God
257– 6 The *t·* that Spirit is not the only substance
b 300–26 The *t·* that soul, spirit, intelligence,
335– 2 The *t·*, that Spirit is distinct from matter
r 478– 7 What basis is there for the *t·* of
g 553–22 that *t·* is sure to become the signal for

theosophy

sp 99–18 Those individuals, who adopt *t·*,
s 111– 1 hypotheses of agnosticism, pantheism, *t·*,
129–17 spiritualism, *t·*, . . . are antagonistic to
139–28 *t·*, and agnosticism are opposed to C. S.,
r 484– 8 mesmerism, hypnotism, *t·*, or spiritualism?

therapeutic

s 164– 6 "No . . . classification of diseases or of *t·* agents,
p 369–23 The prophylactic and *t·* . . . arts

therapeutical

an 101–15 physiological and *t·* questions,

therapeutics

an 101–18 nothing in common with either physiology or *t·*."
s 149–27 predicting disease does not dignify *t·*.

thereafter

an 104–26 This greater error *t·* occupies the ground,
f 221– 6 *t·* he partook of but one meal in

thereat

t 451–14 many there be which go in *t·*."— *Matt.* 7 : 13.

thereby

s 108–28 *t·* shutting out the true sense of Spirit.
119–14 *t·* making Him guilty of maintaining
f 234–15 *t·* robbing both themselves and others.
b 290–28 The murderer, . . . does not *t·* forsake sin.
302– 7 is *t·* discerned and remains unchanged.
308–22 and Truth, being *t·* understood,
p 397– 6 *t·* actually injuring those whom we
t 457–26 intending *t·* to initiate the cure which they
g 528–17 and *t·* create woman.
gl 583–18 *t·* casting out devils, or error,

therefore

pr 1– * *T· I say unto you,* — *Mark* 11 : 24.
8–11 and *t·* insincere, what must be the comment
16– 9 "After this manner *t·* pray ye,"— *Matt.* 6 : 9.
a 19– 1 It was *t·* Christ's purpose to reconcile man to
31–11 the only creator, and *t·* as the Father of all.
36–32 Can God *t·* overlook the law
37–28 "Be ye *t·* perfect, even as— *Matt.* 5 : 48.
39–15 To him, *t·*, death was not the threshold
42–27 and is *t·* not a mortal but an immortal.
51–16 *t·* he could no more be separated from
m 56– * *What t· God hath joined*— *Matt.* 19 : 6.
57–19 It is unselfish ; *t·* it cannot exist alone,
60–10 *T·* maternal affection lives on
69–25 *t·* matter is out of the question
sp 71–30 Spiritualism *t·* presupposes Spirit, . . . to be
76–11 Spirit never entered matter and was *t·*
99–20 *T·* my contest is not with the individual,
an 103– 1 virtue in families and *t·* in the community.
s 112– 4 can, *t·*, be but one method in its teaching.
114– 2 *t·*, to be understood, the author
114–15 implies something untrue and *t·* unreal ;
116–18 *t·* that matter is nothing beyond an image in
117– 6 *t·* the language of Spirit must be,
118–29 *T·* they contradict the divine decrees

therefore

s 120–19 *T·* the divine Principle of Science, reversing
122–31 and mind *t·* tributary to matter.
125– 9 *t·* more harmonious in his manifestations
127– 2 she will not *t·* lose faith in Christianity,
127–24 *T·* truth is not human, and is not a law of matter
130– 6 and *t·* they cannot accept.
141–22 *t·* they cannot demonstrate God's healing
ph 164–10 *t·* they are more scientific than are
165– * *T· I say unto you,* — *Matt.* 6 : 25.
191–31 *t·* Truth is able to cast out the ills of the
f 204–14 It cannot *t·* be mind, though so called.
207–20 *T·* there can be no effect from any other cause,
210–31 *t·* it is without a destructive element.
223–13 and *t·* could not be Spirit.
231–17 *T·* we accept the conclusion that
244– 2 *t·* such deformity is not real,
253–32 "Be ye *t·* perfect,"— *Matt.* 5 : 48.
c 259–19 "Be ye *t·* perfect,— *Matt.* 5 : 48.
267–27 Even in this world, *t·*,
b 269–22 I *t·* plant myself unreservedly on the
275– 5 *T·* matter is neither substantial, living, nor
275– 8 and *t·* He is divine Principle.
277– 1 and *t·* cannot spring from intelligence.
277–21 and *t·* that good is the origin of
277–30 for matter is temporal and is *t·* a
279– 8 and is *t·* not eternal.
286–19 *T·* the spiritual universe is good,
288–18 "There remaineth *t·* a rest— *Heb.* 4 : 9.
289–26 and *t·* the material must be untrue.
289–28 *T·* it cannot be said to pass out of matter.
292–28 *T·* man would be annihilated,
300–23 *t·* Soul is not in matter.
300–29 *t·* God is seen only in the spiritual
301– 8 involves error and *t·* is material,
302–25 He is *t·* the divine, infinite Principle,
304–18 Man's happiness is not, *t·*, at the disposal of
309–30 *T·* it is never structural nor organic,
313– 7 *T·* God, even thy God,— *Heb.* 1 : 9.
318–24 as though disease were real, *t·* right,
324–11 *T·* "acquaint now thyself with— *Job* 22 : 21.
328– 9 and must *t·* cling to mortals until,
330–23 *t·* there is in reality one Mind only,
331–15 *T·* in Spirit all is harmony, and there can be
334– 2 and *t·* antedated Abraham ;
334–32 and *t·* one God.
337– 1 *T·* man, reflecting God, cannot lose his
339– 9 *T·* evil, being contrary to good,
340–12 *T·* all that really exists is in and of God,
p 362–15 It was *t·* easy for the Magdalen to
368–28 that mortality (and *t·* disease) has a
372–16 *T·* he will be as the angels in heaven.
376–21 *T·* the efficient remedy is to destroy the
391–21 *t·* meet the intimation with a protest.
391–26 *T·* make your own terms with sickness,
399– 1 and *t·* good is infinite, is All.
400– 3 and *t·* the disease is thoroughly cured.
415– 2 *t·* disease is neither a cause nor an effect.
417–12 Spirit is God, and *t·* cannot be sick ;
419–15 *t·* be sure that you move it off.
422–31 His treatment is *t·* tentative.
431–10 *T·* I arrested Mortal Man in behalf of
t 446–29 This must *t·* be watched and guarded against.
447– 9 *T·* the rule is, heal the sick when called upon
450–10 and are *t·* open to the approach and
460–17 It is *t·* to be dealt with through
464–10 She *t·* remains unseen at her post,
r 467– 5 *T·* the command means this :
468–14 *T·* man is not material ; he is spiritual.
471–18 God is infinite, *t·* ever present,
472–26 *T·* the only reality of sin, sickness, or death
475–18 reflection of God, or Mind, and *t·* is eternal ;
488– 5 *t·* you receive the blessing of Truth.
488–25 *T·* mental endowments are not at the mercy of
g 506– 3 *T·* matter, not being the reflection of Spirit,
518–28 and all must *t·* be as perfect as the
530–27 *t·* the dreamer and dream are one,
537– 2 *t·* the Lord God [Jehovah] sent— *Gen.* 3 : 23.
542–15 *T·* whosoever slayeth Cain,— *Gen.* 4 : 15.
544–25 *T·* man, in this allegory, is neither a
549–10 we must *t·* look upon the simple ovum as
ap 567–25 and *t·*, in his pretence of being a talker,
568–19 *T·* rejoice, ye heavens,— *Rev.* 12 : 12.
574– 2 This spiritual consciousness is *t·* a
gl 592– 3 and *t·* the opposite of God, or good;
592– 5 belief that life has a beginning and *t·*
596– 9 "Whom *t·* ye ignorantly worship,— *Acts* 17 : 23.

therein

s 110–23 the Science and truth *t·* will forever remain
p 382–23 shall in no wise enter *t·*."— *Luke* 18 : 17.
g 523–18 the Supreme Being is *t·* called Elohim.
523–19 Deity *t·* is always called Jehovah,
524–31 Does Spirit enter dust, and lose *t·* the
ap 558– * *those things which are written t· :* — *Rev.* 1 : 3.
576–10 And I saw no temple *t·* :— *Rev.* 21 : 22.
576–20 with "no temple [body] *t·*"— *Rev.* 21 : 22.

thereof

sp 95–18 one of the special characteristics t·.
ph 190–26 place t· shall know it no more.— *Psal.* 103 : 16.
197–10 "In the day that thou eatest t·— *Gen.* 2 : 17.
f 246–28 find this out, and begin the demonstration t·.
r 476–26 place t· shall know it no more."— *Psal.* 103 : 16.
481–19 "In the day that thou eatest t·— *Gen.* 2 : 17.
g 513–21 God, who is the divinely creative Principle t·.
527–10 in the day that thou eatest t·— *Gen.* 2 : 17.
527–25 that was the name t·.— *Gen.* 2 : 19.
528–12 closed up the flesh instead t· ;— *Gen.* 2 : 21.
530–15 in the day ye eat t·,— *Gen.* 3 : 5.
532– 8 "In the day that thou eatest t·— *Gen.* 2 : 17.
533–25 and multiplies until the end t·.
540–27 his flock, and of the fat t·.— *Gen.* 4 : 4.
ap 558–16 for God "is the light t·."— *Rev.* 21 : 23.
gl 592–12 a type of moral law and the demonstration t· ;

thereto

a 23–22 *faith and the words corresponding t·*
p 436–10 the divine law, and in obedience t·.

thereunto

o 354–17 who t· have set their seals.

thereupon

p 411–16 T· Jesus cast out the evil,
436–26 T· Judge Medicine sat in judgment on the case,

thermometer

s 152–16 introducing a t· into the patient's mouth.

Thibet

pr 10–17 One of the forms of worship in T·

thief

b 294–29 t· believes that he gains something by stealing,

thieves

f 234–11 against the approach of t· and murderers.
p 365–28 convert into a den of t· the temple

thin

f 221– 7 only a t· slice of bread without water.
b 295–23 like a cloud melting into t· vapor,

Thine

pr 17–12 For T· is the kingdom, and the— *Matt.* 6 : 13.
a 33–20 "Not my will, but T·, be done !"— *Luke* 22 : 42.
f 201– * T· enemies have reproached,— *Psal.* 89 : 51.
201– * *the footsteps of T· anointed.*— *Psal.* 89 : 51.

thing

creeping
r 475–26 and over every creeping t·— *Gen.* 1 : 26.
g 513–15 cattle, and creeping t·,— *Gen.* 1 : 24.
515–15 and over every creeping t·— *Gen.* 1 : 26.
deadly
b 328–24 and if they drink any deadly t·,— *Mark* 16 : 18.
p 362– * *and if they drink any deadly t·,*— *Mark* 16 : 18.
every living
g 517–28 and over every living t·— *Gen.* 1 : 28.
no
b 330–27 Evil is nothing, no t·, mind, nor power.
g 554– 8 Error is always error. It is *no t·.*
no impossible
p 371–22 No impossible t· do I ask when urging the
nor a person
b 287–26 Matter is neither a t· nor a person,
no such
r 487–21 there is in reality no such t· as *mortal* mind.
g 554– 4 There is no such t· as mortality,
of life
f 247–21 Beauty is a t· of life, which dwells forever
place, nor
sp 71– 3 It is neither person, place, nor t·,
pleasantest
m 59– 1 and this is the pleasantest t· to do.
same
p 404–27 are one and the same t· in C. S.
whole
ph 166– 1 your remedy lies in forgetting the whole t· ;

sp 70–15 Does life or soul exist in the t· formed?
f 252–23 says : . . . What a nice t· is sin !
o 350– 2 as something and almost the only t·,
p 411– 1 "The t· which I greatly feared— *Job* 3 : 25.

things

all
pref xii–24 "hopeth all t·, endureth all t·,"— *I Cor.* 13 : 7.
pr 1– 2 faith that all t· are possible to God,
13–24 Love, to whom all t· are possible.
15– 8 but He knows all t·
sp 83–29 the divine Principle and explanation of all t·.
85–13 told me all t· that ever I did :— *John* 4 : 29.
96– 2 unwillingness to learn all t· rightly,
96–11 until the final spiritualization of all t·.
s 124–26 life, substance, and continuity of all t·.
ph 166–21 He can do all t· for us in sickness
178–16 divine Mind, to which all t· are possible,
180–26 ever-present Mind who understands all t·,
180–27 man knows that with God all t· are possible.

things

all
ph 183– 1 makes all t· possible to Spirit ;
189–20 makes all t· start from the lowest instead of
200–15 hast put all t· under his feet."— *Psal.* 8 : 6.
f 201– 9 and "all t· are become new."— *II Cor.* 5 : 17.
207–27 spiritual reality is the scientific fact in all t·.
208– 3 Material sense defines all t· materially,
212–30 its normal action, and the origin of all t·
215– 2 Nothing can hide from them the harmony of
all t·
231–31 "all t· were made by Him— *John* 1 : 3.
232– 9 "with God all t· are possible,"— *Mark* 10 : 27.
250– 8 which never dreams, but understands all t· ;
c 255–14 mortals take limited views of all t·.
256– 6 All t· are created spiritually.
257– 2 If Mind is within and without all t·,
b 271–21 shall teach you all t·."— *John* 14 : 26.
280– 6 All t· beautiful and harmless are ideas of Mind.
280–10 Finite belief limits all t·, and would compress
289–30 Spirit and all t· spiritual are the real
305–10 so man, like all t· real, reflects God,
307–26 and gives man dominion over all t·.
310–16 around which circle harmoniously all t·
318–12 and doom all t· to decay.
o 353–18 All t· will continue to disappear, until
p 387–26 which causes all t· discordant.
t 444– 5 "All t· work together for good— *Rom.* 8 : 28.
464–19 "prove all t· ;— *I Thess.* 5 : 21.
r 480–26 "All t· were made by Him— *John* 1 : 3.
485–15 Think not to thwart the spiritual ultimate of
all t·,
493– 8 to the immortal truth of all t·.
g 501– * All t· were made by Him ;— *John* 1 : 3.
505–27 it is the reality of all t·
516– 9 God fashions all t·, after His own likeness.
519– 2 eternal Mind, the author of all t·,
525–17 all t· were made through the Word of God,
gl 581–12 the spiritual realities of all t· are
585–13 shall first come and restore all t·."— *Matt.* 17 : 11.
597–29 spiritual government, encompassing all t·.
animated
an 100– 9 the celestial bodies, the earth, and animated t·,
belief of
b 289–25 The spiritual fact and the material belief of t·
eternal
b 337–25 Eternal t· (verities) are God's thoughts
evidence of
r 468–21 the evidence of t· not seen."— *Heb.* 11 : 1.
false sense of
f 213–31 dipped to its depths into a false sense of t·,
few
b 323–17 "faithful over a few t·,"— *Matt.* 25 : 21.
ap 569– 7 faithful over a few t·,— *Matt.* 25 : 23.
finite sense of
s 124–12 This is a mortal, finite sense of t·,
forgetting those
o 353–24 "forgetting those t· which— *Phil.* 3 : 13.
former
g 556– 9 for the former t· will have passed away.
good
s 155–31 If drugs are good t·, is it safe to say
great
g 528–22 and declaring what great t· error has done.
human sense of
sp 99–16 the human sense of t· errs
immortal
b 276–22 towards the contemplation of t· immortal
imperishable
a 21–11 looks towards the imperishable t· of Spirit.
invisible
r 479–30 "For the invisible t· of Him,— *Rom.* 1 : 20.
lower
b 268– 5 to the spiritual cause of those lower t·
man and
b 281–17 reflects reality and divinity in . . . man and t·.
material
(*see* material)
material sense of
b 304– 4 based on a material sense of t·,
r 489–30 Outside the material sense of t·, all is harmony.
g 544– 8 arise from the material sense of t·,
gl 597–18 in which a material sense of t· disappears,
men and
s 118–21 as the natural status of men and t·,
mortal sense of
p 370– 3 we must forsake the mortal sense of t·,
no such
o 352–27 because there are no such t·.
of God
b 276–11 is cognizant only of the t· of God.
of Spirit
a 21–11 looks towards the imperishable t· of Spirit.
o 349–24 Speaking of the t· of Spirit
old
f 201– 8 a new creature, in whom old t· pass away

things

persons and
c 263–28   mortal sense of persons and t· is not creation.
persons or
g 514– 3   could not . . . recreate persons or t·
phases of
r 488– 1   enduring and harmonious phases of t·.
present
b 304– 6   nor t· present, nor things to come,— *Rom.* 8 : 38.
resolves
s 123–14   excludes matter, resolves t· into *thoughts,*
b 269–15   Metaphysics resolves t· into thoughts,
spiritual
b 289–30   Spirit and all t· spiritual are the real
326–10   and set his whole affections on spiritual t·,
335–13   T· spiritual and eternal are substantial.
state of
g 522–15   this state of t· is declared to be temporary
substance of
b 279– 4   "the *substance* of t· hoped for."— *Heb.* 11 : 1.
r 468–20   "The substance of t· hoped for,— *Heb.* 11 : 1.
such
an 106–26   they which do such t·— *Gal.* 5 : 21.
surface of
b 313–25   He plunged beneath the material surface of t·,
temporal
b 337–26   Temporal t· are the thoughts of mortals
temporary sense of
b 298– 9   a mortal temporary sense of t·,
these
pr 7–11   Looking deeply into these t·, we find
a 31–32   and these t· will they do unto you,— *John* 16 : 3.
s 131–20   hast hid these t· from the wise— *Luke* 10 : 21.
ph 169–15   The faith reposed in these t· should
b 329–11   Be thankful that Jesus, . . . did these t·,
o 343–10   "None of these t· move me."— *Acts* 20 : 24.
k 499– *   *These t· saith He that is holy,— Rev.* 3 : 7.
g 540– 6   I the Lord do all these t· ;"— *Isa.* 45 : 7.
gl 579– *   *These t· saith He that is holy,— Rev.* 3 : 7.
those
pr 1– *   *shall believe that those t· which*— *Mark* 11 : 23.
s 132– 5   those t· which ye do hear and see— *Matt.* 11 : 4.
t 459– 2   Man then appropriates those t· which
ap 558– *   *keep those t· which are written*— *Rev.* 1 : 3.
to come
b 304– 7   nor things present, nor t· to come,— *Rom.* 8 : 38.
true sense of
c 264– 8   if they would gain the true sense of t·.
unpleasant
p 415– 8   when it contemplates unpleasant t·,
uttered
b 317– 1   Jesus uttered t· which had been
which pertain
o 350– 2   and of the t· which pertain to Spirit

---

pr 1– *   *What t· soever ye desire*— *Mark* 11 : 24.
 1– *   *knoweth what t· ye have need of,*— *Matt.* 6 : 8.
a 20– 1   the t· which are Cæsar's ;— *Matt.* 22 : 21.
 20– 2   the t· that are God's."— *Matt.* 22 : 21.
 27– 3   what t· ye have seen and heard ;— *Luke* 7 : 22.
an 100– *   *the t· which defile a man.*— *Matt.* 15 : 20.
s 119– 5   such theories lead to one of two t·.
129–24   accepting only the outward sense of t·.
ph 189–18   evidence of all mortal thought or t·.
b 305–18   for what t· soever He doeth,— *John* 5 : 19.
r 479–32   by the t· that are made."— *Rom.* 1 : 20.
g 540–17   the t· which are Cæsar's ;— *Matt.* 22 : 21.
540–18   the t· that are God's.— *Matt.* 22 : 21.
544– 9   consisteth not of the t· which a man eateth.
ap 560–21   As it is with t·, so is it with persons.

think

pr 1– 5   Regardless of what another may say or t·
a 31–31   whosoever killeth you will t·— *John* 16 : 2.
 42–24   Let men t· they had killed the body !
 48–13   and t·, or even wish, to escape the
m 63– 1   You would never t· that flannel was better for
sp 82– 2   We t· of an absent friend as easily as we
 87–25   because you do not t· of it.
s 130–30   no longer t· it natural to love sin and
155– 1   You're not hurt, so don't t· you are."
ph 168– 2   who t· the standard of C. S. too high for them.
f 230–27   We t· that we are healed when a disease
b 270–24   Mortals t· wickedly ; consequently they
270–25   They t· sickly thoughts, and so become sick.
297– 1   and they t· they are so ;
o 345–26   if a man t· himself to be something,— *Gal.* 6 : 3.
350– 1   They t· of matter as something
353– 8   How can a Christian, . . . t· of the latter as real
p 379–16   t· of the experiment of those Oxford boys,
381–20   T· less of the enactments of mortal mind,
385–27   You say or t·, because you have partaken of
386–18   You t· that your anguish is occasioned by your
        loss.
388–31   If mortals t· that food disturbs the
389– 6   The less we know or t· about hygiene,

think

p 392–17   If you t· that consumption is hereditary
397–13   When an accident happens, you t·
412– 8   concerning the truth which you t· or speak,
416–29   they t· too much about their ailments,
419–18   T· less of material conditions
429–18   unseen by those who t· that they bury the body.
t 443–15   and t· they can be benefited by
449– 9   T· it "easier for a camel— *Matt.* 19 : 24
451– 9   and t· to succeed without the spirit,
458–11   to t· of aiding the divine Principle of healing
r 478–14   *Question.* — Does brain t·, and do nerves feel,
478–22   and brain-lobes cannot t·
485–14   T· not to thwart the spiritual ultimate
490–32   will t· that he is freezing when he is warm,
g 540–12   we may t· in our ignorance that the
553–30   before they t· or know aught of their origin,
ap 574–25   T· of this, dear reader, for it will lift the

thinker

a 40– 3   The advanced t· and devout Christian,
s 122–22   which every t· can recall for himself.
128–18   It raises the t· into his native air of insight

thinker's

g 547–10   strengthens the t· conclusions

thinkers

pref vii–13   The time for t· has come.
p 387–13   Our t· do not die early because they
t 450– 1   There is a large class of t· whose bigotry
450– 9   A third class of t· build with solid masonry.

thinketh

sp 89–13   "As he t· in his heart,— *Prov.* 23 : 7.
ph 166– 3   As a man t·, so is he.
f 213– 4   "As he t· in his heart,— *Prov.* 23 : 7.
p 383–28   "As he t· in his heart,— *Prov.* 23 : 7.

thinking

a 22– 1   t· . . . to find and follow the right road.
sp 92–29   The mistake of t· that error can be real,
f 220–20   and t· it sees another kitten.
225–16   proportionate to its embodiment of right t·.
245– 1   The error of t· that we are growing old,
p 410–27   to promote right t· and doing,
424–23   while others are t· about your patients
r 483–26   it ought to receive aid, . . . from all t· persons.
g 543–20   May not Darwin be right in t· that
gl 586– 5   Jesus said, t· of the outward vision,

thinks

s 154–28   who t· she has hurt her face by falling on the
ph 188–16   the dreamer t· that his body is material
b 294– 9   The belief that matter t·, sees, or feels
294–13   saying : . . . Nerves feel. Brain t· and sins.
322–17   The drunkard t· he enjoys drunkenness,
p 408–24   were it not that mortal mind t· that the

thinness

f 205–18   or as they melt into such t· that we

third

sp 91–29   The t· erroneous postulate is,
s 116– 1   T· Degree: Understanding.
116– 4   In the t· degree mortal mind disappears,
156–23   but on the t· day she again suffered,
f 204– 9   Spirit and matter,— resulting in a t· person
204–15   The t· power, mortal man, is
p 422–15   meet and bring out a t· quality,
t 450– 8   A t· class of thinkers build with solid masonry.
457– 4   T· : Because this book has done more for
g 503–21   t·, in spiritual and immortal forms of beauty
508–27   and the morning were the t· day. — *Gen.* 1 : 13.
508–28   The t· stage in the order of C. S.
509– 6   he rose from the grave,— on the t· day of his
ap 563–23   And his tail drew the t· part— *Rev.* 12 : 4.
577–15   t·, Christianity, is the outcome of the
gl 585–28   second from a rib, and t· from an egg.
598– 2   John's Gospel, the t· chapter, where we read :

thirsteth

pr 13– 4   "Ho, every one that t·,— *Isa.* 55 : 1.

thirsty

f 234– 8   and giving living waters to the t·.
p 366– 8   debars him from giving drink to the t·
376–26   to feel pain or heat, to be t· or sick,
385–29   must be t·, and you are t· accordingly,
431– 4   When the sick mortal was t·,

thirty

a 47 –12   The traitor's price was t· pieces of silver
s 139–18   the t· thousand different readings in the

thistles

b 276–31   not . . . grapes from thorns nor figs from t·.
g 535–24   thorns also and t· shall it— *Gen.* 3 : 18.

thitherward

a 21–26   and will be attracted t·.

Thomas
a 24–32   unbelieving *T·* was forced to acknowledge
46–18   To convince *T·* of this, Jesus caused him to
b 317–24   To the materialistic *T·*, looking for
318– 1   Nothing but . . . could make existence real to *T·*.

thorns
a 44– 1   before the *t·* can be laid aside for
50–29   was a million times sharper than the *t·*
b 276–31   Divine Science does not gather grapes from *t·*
p 365– 1   the *t·* they plant in the pillow of the sick
g 535–23   *t·* also and thistles shall it — *Gen.* 3 : 18.
536–23   and hedge about their achievements with *t·*.
539–24   "Do men gather grapes of *t·* ?" — *Matt.* 7 : 16.

thorough
t 446– 5   A *t·* perusal of the author's publications
456–31   containing a *t·* statement of C. S.
461–32   requisite for a *t·* comprehension of C. S.

thoroughly
sp 84–30   If this Science has been *t·* learned
f 230–29   we are never *t·* healed until
p 382–19   A patient *t·* booked in medical theories
400– 3   and therefore the disease is *t·* cured.
412– 7   be *t·* persuaded in your own mind
t 445– 2   teacher must *t·* fit his students
r 467– 9   It should be *t·* understood that
495–27   Study *t·* the letter and imbibe the spirit.

thoroughness
ph 186– 6   and the *t·* of this work determines health.

Thou
iii– *   Oh ! *T·* hast heard my prayer ;
iii– *   *T·* here, and *everywhere.*
pr 16–31   Thy kingdom is come ; *T·* art ever-present.
a 50– 8   why hast *T·* forsaken me?" — *Mark* 15 : 34.
s 125–24   "As a vesture shalt *T·* change — *Psal.* 102 : 26.
131–20   *T·* hast hid these things from the— *Luke* 10 : 21.
134–26   "I knew that *T·* hearest me— *John* 11 : 42.
ph 200–13   "*T·* madest him to have dominion— *Psal.* 8 : 6.
200–15   *T·* hast put all things under his— *Psal.* 8 : 6.
c 255– *   *T·* art from everlasting.— *Psal.* 93 : 2.
256–23   or say unto Him, What doest *T·* ?" — *Dan.* 4 : 35.
p 410– 9   Jesus Christ, whom *T·* hast sent." — *John* 17 : 3.
g 533– 8   The woman whom *T·* gavest — *Gen.* 3 : 12,
533–16   woman, whom *T·* gavest me, is responsible."
ap 566–23   Be *T·*, longsuffering, slow to wrath,

thought *(see also* **thought's***)*
accepts
g 520–14   and *t·* accepts the divine infinite calculus.
action of
p 384–13   Through this action of *t·* and its results
aid in bringing
t 455– 1   auxiliaries to aid in bringing *t·* into accord
and action
c 265–13   a wider sphere of *t·* and action,
and deed
a 19–18   every effort for reform, every good *t·* and deed,
gl 595–15   purification of *t·* and deed,
and demonstration
c 260 11   as the basis of *t·* and demonstration.
appeal to
ph 182– 5   The demands of God appeal to *t·* only ;
apprehend
ph 179– 9   the spiritual capacity to apprehend *t·*
array
c 260–29   If we array *t·* in mortal vestures,
artist's
b 010– 2   picture is the artist's *t·* objectified.
ascending
g 509– 7   on the third day of his ascending *t·*,
assumed
b 326–26   *T·* assumed a nobler outlook,
atmosphere of
s 128–17   It extends the atmosphere of *t·*,
awaken
g 553– 3   should awaken *t·* to a higher and purer
benign
p 365– 7   The benign *t·* of Jesus,
body and
r 492– 2   leaves mortal man intact in body and *t·*,
boundless
b 323–11   until boundless *t·* walks enraptured,
channel of
gl 593–14   RIVER.   Channel of *t·*.
chiseling
f 248–15   moulding and chiseling *t·*.
Christian
pref x–26   unbiased Christian *t·* is soonest touched by
Christian Science
b 340– 5   conveys the C. S. *t·*,
conscious
p 379–29   The images, held in . . . mind, frighten conscious *t·*.
400–14   before it has taken tangible shape in conscious *t·*,
consecration of
pr 3–16   absolute consecration of *t·*, energy, and

thought
constituents of
m 58– 9   these constituents of *t·*, mingling,
convey
f 212–27   in order to convey *t·*,
creating
g 520–28   but the immortal creating *t·* is from above,
definite
pref ix– 9   the tongue voices the more definite *t·*,
delineates
b 310– 3   belief fancies that it delineates *t·* on matter,
depressing
p 384– 3   relieve our minds from the depressing *t·*
deserted by
p 429–11   The corpse, deserted by *t·*, is cold
discern the
sp 95– 9   are able to discern the *t·* of the sick and the
divest
p 428– 9   To divest *t·* of false trusts
divine
s 118–14   Theology, and Medicine are means of divine *t·*,
g 514–15   transmission from the divine *t·* to the
door of
p 392–24   Stand porter at the door of *t·*.
drift of
pref x–12   to suit the general drift of *t·*,
efface from
p 396– 3   efface from *t·* all forms and
elevation to
pr 7– 9   momentary solemnity and elevation to *t·*.
embodied
p 372–11   belief . . . that man can enter his own embodied *t·*,
embryonic
ph 188– 7   an embryonic *t·* without motive ;
emphasizes the
s 116–20   C. S. strongly emphasizes the *t·* that
encompass
g 551–25   Darkness and doubt encompass *t·*,
erring
c 260– 7   The conceptions of mortal, erring *t·*
g 503–24   God creates neither erring *t·*, mortal life.
erroneous
g 513 23   to be the creations of erroneous *t·*,
error of
g 550–15   Error of *t·* is reflected in error of action.
exalted
p 373–17   through the exalted *t·* of John,
g 506–12   exalted *t·* or spiritual apprehension
expands
c 255– 2   *t·* expands into expression.
expressed
p 423– 7   more strongly than the expressed *t·*.
expressed in
pr 11–32   It is best expressed in *t·* and in life.
expresses the
r 468–28   Eternity, not time, expresses the *t·* of Life,
externalized
o 360 13   which mind-picture or externalized *t·*
father to the
f 219–22   "is ever father to the *t·*."
feeds
f 222– 9   and feeds *t·* with the bread of Life.
food for
ph 195–16   furnishes food for *t·*.
footsteps of
ph 174– 9   The footsteps of *t·*, rising above
formation of
sp 71–13   a formation of *t·* rather than of matter.
forms of
s 118–20   In all mortal forms of *t·*, dust is dignified
ph 187– 7   material sense creates its own forms of *t·*,
b 298–31   confers upon angels its own forms of *t·*,
free
f 223–21   Spiritual rationality and free *t·* accompany
gently whispers
ap 574–30   Then *t·* gently whispers : "Come hither !
gives action to
gl 586– 8   that which gives action to *t·*.
guides
s 149–28   Whatever guides *t·* spiritually benefits
her
s 152–22   and experiments had prepared her *t·*
ph 185– 1   but her *t·* of it had
t 460–30   beliefs were gradually expelled from her *t·*,
his
sp 82– 5   we still read his *t·* in his verse.
ph 186– 2   by emptying his *t·* of the false stimulus
198–10   outlines his *t·* relative to disease,
c 258–26   and of the infinite range of his *t·*.
p 383– 9   when he leaves it most out of his *t·*,
t 452– 1   how to bar the door of his *t·*
hold
c 261– 4   Hold *t·* steadfastly to the enduring,
human
(see **human**)

thought

image of
p 411–23   an image of *t·* externalized.
images of
sp 86–13   Mortals evolve images of *t·.*
f 208–29   according to the images of *t·* impressed upon it.
248–10   supplying it with beautiful images of *t·*
imprisoned
s 114–27   and sets free the imprisoned *t·.*
increases or diminishes
p 415–19   *t·* increases or diminishes the
inspired
g 547–28   Inspired *t·* relinquishes a material, . . . theory
integrity of
t 446–29   detrimental to health and integrity of *t·.*
is borrowed
c 267–22   *T·* is borrowed from a higher source
its own
p 399–17   Mortal mind perpetuates its own *t·.*
Job's
c 262–19   Mortals will echo Job's *t·,*
latent in
gl 597– 8   but cloaked the crime, latent in *t·,*
less
m 62–13   Taking less "*t·* for your life,— *Matt.* 6 : 25.
62–14   less *t·* "for your body — *Matt.* 6 : 25.
ph 175– 4   and less *t·* is given to sanitary subjects,
f 222–14   Taking less *t·* about what he should eat
lifted
ph 200– 3   lifted *t·* into the song of David.
lifting
p 400–18   By lifting *t·* above error, or disease,
material
c 267– 1   Every object in material *t·* will be destroyed,
o 356– 2   the material *t·* must become spiritualized
460–12   for to the material *t·* all is material,
g 509–30   Jesus rebuked the material *t·* of his
misleads
b 275–28   misleads *t·* and points to other gods,
models in
f 248–27   We must form perfect models in *t·*
momentous
g 516–27   To emphasize this momentous *t·,*
mortal
(*see* **mortal**)
note how
p 415–17   Note how *t·* makes the face pallid.
occupy
m 60–23   and other considerations, . . . occupy *t·.*
of disease
ph 198–14   *t·* of disease is formed before one
p 396– 2   One should never hold in mind the *t·* of disease,
of the age
s 146–32   and adapted to the *t·* of the age
of the patient
p 414–13   mortal mind or the *t·* of the patient,
original
ph 195–20   invention, study, and original *t·* are
palsied by
p 415–23   quickly or slowly and impelled or palsied by *t·,*
parent's
p 412–29   met mainly through the parent's *t·,*
patient's
p 366– 9   hinders him from reaching his patient's *t·,*
396–12   nor encourage in the patient's *t·* the
perturbed
p 400–13   Eradicate the image . . . from the perturbed *t·*
pictorial
sp 86–27   can all be taken from pictorial *t·*
pictures of
sp 87– 2   Mind-readers perceive these pictures of *t·.*
pinions to
t 454–20   Right motives give pinions to *t·,*
popular
s 141–10   All revelation (such is the popular *t·* !)
possibilities of
sp 90–20   This shows the possibilities of *t·.*
prior to
b 310– 4   Did it exist prior to *t·* ?
pure
g 508–15   seed within itself is the pure *t·*
put out of
p 425–13   treated as error and put out of *t·.*
quiet the
p 415–12   They quiet the *t·* by inducing stupefaction
random
ph 175–16   If a random *t·,* calling itself dyspepsia,
rarefaction of
g 509–16   gives the idea of the rarefaction of *t·*
receptive
a 34–16   to the poor,— the receptive *t·,*
p 380– 1   may rest at length on some receptive *t·,*
recorder's
gl 590–25   disappearing from the recorder's *t·,*
remain in
p 376– 5   fear and the despair of recovery remain in *t·.*

thought

remove error from
a 40– 2   Remove error from *t·,* and it will not appear
removes
b 323–22   removes *t·* from the body,
rises
c 256– 3   *t·* rises from the material sense to the spiritual,
scientific
ap 559– 9   scientific *t·* reaches over continent and ocean
sculptor's
b 299– 2   no more reality than has the sculptor's *t·*
sensual
c 263–28   A sensual *t·,* like an atom of dust
sinful
p 400–31   the baneful influence of sinful *t·* on the body.
slumbering
f 223–25   Peals that should startle the slumbering *t·*
spiritualization of
f 211–30   dematerialization and spiritualization of *t·*
b 272–19   It is the spiritualization of *t·* and
p 382– 7   and to the spiritualization of *t·,*
407–26   This spiritualization of *t·* lets in the light,
gl 593– 9   Resurrection. Spiritualization of *t·* ;
spiritualizes the
p 370– 6   regimen which spiritualizes the *t·* ;
spontaneity of
gl 597–17   Spontaneity of *t·* and idea ;
substance of
p 423–30   Bones have only the substance of *t·*
substance of a
g 508– 5   The only intelligence or substance of a *t·,*
such
t 460–13   till such *t·* is rectified by Spirit.
such a
b 320–20   (however transcendental such a *t·* appears),
suggests the
b 338–16   This suggests the *t·* of something fluid,
338–17   It further suggests the *t·* of that
swift-winged
ap 574–20   the very message, or swift-winged *t·,*
take no
ph 165– *   *Take no t· for your life,— Matt.* 6 : 25.
170–16   "Take no *t·* for your life,— *Matt.* 6 : 25.
f 228–21   "Take no *t·* for your life,"— *Matt.* 6 : 25.
p 365– 8   "Take no *t·* for your life,"— *Matt.* 6 : 25.
382–11   "Take no *t· . . .* for the body."— *Luke* 12 : 22.
g 530– 8   "Take no *t·* for your life,— *Matt.* 6 : 25.
taking form in
ph 175– 1   prevent the images . . . from taking form in *t·,*
taking no
ph 176– 7   custom of taking no *t·* about food
that
p 392–19   liable to the development of that *t·*
this
a 39–27   This *t·* is apprehended slowly,
f 203–12   This *t·* incites to a more exalted worship
o 345–28   This *t·* of human, material nothingness,
354– 9   when it teaches precisely this *t·* ?
p 388–32   the food or this *t·* must be dispensed with,
r 496–15   Hold perpetually this *t·,*— that it is the
to discern
sp 95–15   to discern *t·* scientifically, depends upon
unconscious
p 408–28   unconscious *t·* in the corporeal substratum
uninspired
ap 573– 5   that which is invisible to the uninspired *t·.*
uplift the
ph 175–12   its beauty and fragrance, should uplift the *t·,*
whispered into
p 370–19   spiritual facts of health, whispered into *t·,*
will waken
p 427–30   *T·* will waken from its own material
wrong
t 452– 5   The wrong *t·* should be arrested before it
your
f 208–30   You embrace your body in your *t·,*
b 324–30   if the idea . . . come not to your *t·,*
p 397–14   Your *t·* is more powerful than your words,
r 495–16   nothing but His likeness to abide in your *t·.*

m 57–27   serves to unite *t·* more closely to God,
sp 84–12   *t·* which is in rapport with this Mind,
86–22   Then why is it more difficult to see a *t·* than
87– 5   It is needless for the *t·* or for the person
90– 9   Divest yourself of the *t·* that there can be
s 130–26   If *t·* is startled at the strong claim of
ph 174–29   and holding it before the *t·* of both
180–22   Instead of furnishing *t·* with fear,
195–18   *t·* passes naturally from effect back to cause.
197– 2   which mirror images of disease distinctly in *t·.*
199–21   The devotion of *t·* to an honest achievement
c 260– 5   while holding in *t·* the character of Judas.
b 268– 1   In the material world, *t·* has brought to light
276–21   *t·* is turned into new and healthy channels,
284–30   *T·* passes from God to man,
310– 6   *T·* will finally be understood and seen

thought

b	324– 1	renders *t·* receptive of the advanced idea.
o	349–27	as *t·* is educated up to spiritual apprehension.
p	377– 2	and that *t·* governs this liability.
	390–21	Suffer no claim . . . to grow upon the *t·*.
	392–14	*t·* should be held fast to this ideal.
	396–27	Keep distinctly in *t·* that man is the
	400–21	*t·* alone creates the suffering.
	412–13	you are liable . . . to impress it upon the *t·*.
	414–19	by troubling and perplexing their *t·*.
	415– 7	*t·* moves quickly or slowly,
	419–18	lest aught unfit for development enter *t·*.
	422–16	changes the material base of *t·*,
t	445–18	or limit in any direction of *t·*
r	485–24	If *t·* yields its dominion to other powers,
	492– 4	should be but one fact before the *t·*,
g	510– 5	to be holy, *t·* must be purely spiritual.
	545– 9	by *t·* tending spiritually upward
	552–19	*t·*, loosened from a material basis

thought (verb)

m	68– 3	for fear of being *t·* ridiculous.
sp	75–23	those who have *t·* they died,
ph	197–12	and the more that is *t·* and said about
	199– 3	might be *t·* true that hammering would
f	221–26	he *t·* of the flesh-pots of Egypt,
	234–25	Sin and disease must be *t·* before they
	245–22	nor *t·* of herself as growing old.
b	306– 1	Pharisees *t·* that they could raise the spiritual
	314–15	they *t·* that he meant their material temple
o	351–30	They *t·* to worship Spirit from a
	374– 8	I never *t·* and knew nothing about,
	388–10	*t·* that they could kill the body with matter,
r	478– 8	What would be *t·* of the declaration that

thought-attenuations

s	157–12	with such repetition of *t·*,

thought-force

s	124–22	support the equipoise of that *t·*,

thought-forces

ph	199–27	His belief . . . gave his *t·*, called muscles,

thought-germs

s	164–16	mental microbes of sin and all diseased *t·*

thought-models

c	259– 9	higher than their poor *t·* would allow,

thought's

b	268– 3	With like activity have *t·* swift pinions

thoughts

about sickness

f	237–17	entertaining theories or *t·* about sickness.

all

f	208–32	You should banish all *t·* of disease and sin
g	513–18	classifies, and individualizes all *t·*,

budding

p	413–29	mental images to children's budding *t·*,

centred their

o	351–27	The Israelites centred their *t·* on the

depicts the

ap	571–26	depicts the *t·* which he beholds in mortal mind.

direct those

sp	94–25	better enabled him to direct those *t·* aright ;

diseased

f	237–20	keep out . . . either sinful or diseased *t·*.

disease in the

ph	180–17	should not implant disease in the *t·*

dissection of

t	462–21	and consists in the dissection of *t·*

distant

sp	82– 1	it is as easy to read distant *t·* as near.

ever recurring

c	260–25	by the *t·* ever recurring to one's self,

evil

an	100– *	*out of the heart proceed evil t·,*— Matt. 15 : 19.
f	234–26	must control evil *t·* in the first instance,
	234–31	Evil *t·* and aims reach no farther
	234–32	Evil *t·*, lusts, and malicious purposes

exalted

b	299– 7	My angels are exalted *t·*, appearing at the

finite

f	214–18	and entertain finite *t·* of God

God's

b	286–21	God's *t·* are perfect and eternal,
	337–25	Eternal things (verities) are God's *t·*
gl	581– 4	ANGELS. God's *t·* passing to man ;
	583– 2	whose better originals are God's *t·*,

her

pref	ix– 1	She also began to jot down her *t·*
f	236–13	Her *t·* form the embryo of another
p	426– 7	the high goal always before her *t·*,

His

s	114–11	noumenon and phenomena, God and His *t·*.
g	513–26	His *t·* are spiritual realities.

thoughts

his

m	56– 2	Reading his *t·*, Jesus added :
s	139– 2	the unrighteous man his *t·*."— Isa. 55 : 7.
ph	198–25	His *t·* and his patient's commingle,
	239–15	and the unrighteous man his *t·*."— Isa. 55 : 7.
c	263– 7	blends his *t·* of existence with the
b	290–30	His *t·* are no purer until evil is disarmed by

his own

p	366–24	by the unveiling of sin in his own *t·*.

holy

g	512– 9	and also by holy *t·*, winged with Love.

human

b	297–24	Human *t·* have their degrees of comparison.
t	449–20	The inoculation of evil human *t·*

impure

gl	595–24	UNCLEANLINESS. Impure *t·* ; error ; sin ; dirt.

influence the

t	447– 4	to attempt to influence the *t·* of others,

inverted

c	267–21	inverted *t·* and erroneous beliefs

its own

sp	86–31	It feels, hears, and sees its own *t·*.
p	424– 3	takes possession of itself and its own *t·*

knew their

sp	85–16	Jesus, . . . "knew their *t·*,"— Matt. 12 : 25.

mortal

(see **mortal**)

my

s	108–32	set my *t·* to work in new channels,

new

pref	vii–22	A book introduces new *t·*,
r	492–14	New *t·* are constantly obtaining the floor.

objects and

b	269–19	the objects and *t·* of material sense,
	276–13	brings objects and *t·* into human view

of disease

ph	196–21	so efface the images and *t·* of disease,
f	208–32	You should banish all *t·* of disease and sin

of health

f	208–31	should delineate upon it *t·* of health,

of mankind

sp	94–24	Our Master easily read the *t·* of mankind,

of mortals

f	249–27	than are the *t·* of mortals when awake.
b	337–27	Temporal things are the *t·* of mortals
r	484–14	the conscious and unconscious *t·* of mortals.

of pain

ph	190– 9	fills itself with *t·* of pain and pleasure,

of the healer

t	446–16	Good must dominate in the *t·* of the healer,

opposite

p	417–31	and how divine Mind can cure by opposite *t·*.

our

b	322–11	to turn our *t·* towards divine Principle,

overcoming the

f	233–20	by overcoming the *t·* which produce them,

patient's

sp	79– 6	by changing the patient's *t·* regarding death.

patients'

p	414–15	To fix truth steadfastly in your patients' *t·*,

pure

b	298–28	Angels are pure *t·* from God, winged with

reading the

b	272–16	Reading the *t·* of the people,

resolving of

g	510–25	suppositional resolving of *t·* into

scientific

an	104– 1	for scientific *t·* are true thoughts,

sick

c	260–21	A sick body is evolved from sick *t·*.

sickly

b	270–25	They think sickly *t·*,

some

b	297–25	Some *t·* are better than others.

spiritual

c	259–29	and demands spiritual *t·*,
gl	582–28	The spiritual *t·* and representatives of
	598–10	to unfold spiritual *t·*.

stronger

ph	198–26	and the stronger *t·* rule the weaker.

temporal

b	286–22	Material and temporal *t·* are human,

these

g	506–19	and unfolds these *t·*, even as

things into

s	123–14	excludes matter, resolves *things* into *t·*,
b	269–15	Metaphysics resolves things into *t·*,

time and

m	58–14	selfish exaction of all another's time and *t·*.

transfer of the

f	211–22	transfer of the *t·* of one erring mind

transitory

b	286–27	Transitory *t·* are the antipodes of

true

an	104– 1	scientific thoughts are true *t·*,

thoughts

turn their
p 416–31 Turn their *t·* away from their bodies
unformed
g 506–18 God, gathers unformed *t·* into their
unhealthy
p 392–30 and shut out these unhealthy *t·*
unspoken
pr 1–10 *T·* unspoken are not unknown to the
p 424–19 unspoken *t·* resting on your patient.
uplifting
f 235–14 The pure and uplifting *t·* of the teacher,
yielding one's
p 413– 3 The act of yielding one's *t·* to the
your
c 261– 7 proportionably to their occupancy of your *t·*.
p 407–25 Let the perfect model be present in your *t·*

pr 13–14 sooner by words than by *t·*?
sp 86–16 only because it is unusual to see *t·*,
88–11 *T·*, proceeding from the brain
s 107–13 *t·* acquaint themselves intelligently with God.
c 259–10 *t·* which presented man as fallen,
b 315–14 Their *t·* were filled with mortal error,
p 415–28 Before the *t·* are fully at rest,
t 462–23 Are *t·* divine or human?
gl 595–18 *t·*, beliefs, opinions, knowledge ; matter ;

thought-taking
p 365–10 supposed necessity for physical *t·*

thousand
pref xii– 6 During seven years over four *t·* students
s 139–18 thirty *t·* different readings in the Old
139–19 and the three hundred *t·* in the New,
g 504–22 is with the Lord as a *t·* years."— *II Pet.* 3 : 8.
504–25 whereas a *t·* years of human doctrines,
514–16 "the cattle upon a *t·* hills."— *Psal.* 50 : 10.
524– 5 and in a *t·* other so-called deities.
546–31 a *t·* different examples of one rule,
ap 560– 3 typical of six *t·* years since Adam,
gl 598–21 is with the Lord as a *t·* years."— *II Pet.* 3 : 8.

thousands
pref x–15 By *t·* of well-authenticated cases of healing,
sp 79– 5 *T·* of instances could be cited of health restored
87–31 which are *t·* of miles away
o 341– 2 raising up *t·* from helplessness to strength

threatened
ph 193–26 *t·* with incarceration in an insane asylum

three
a 27–13 in *t·* days I [Spirit] will raise— *John* 2 : 19.
27–24 credits him with two or *t·* hundred other
41–18 about *t·* centuries after the crucifixion.
44– 7 His *t·* days' work in the sepulchre
45–13 *T·* days after his bodily burial he talked with
an 104–10 scientific truth goes through *t·* stages.
s 107– * *and hid in t· measures of meal,— Matt.* 13 : 33.
108–15, 16 the product of *t·* multiplied by *t·*,
108–16, 17 *t·* times *t·* duodecillions must be
109–11 For *t·* years after my discovery, I sought
109–32 The *t·* great verities of Spirit,
117–32 and hid in *t·* measures of meal,— *Matt.* 13 : 33.
118–19 presented as *t·* measures of meal,
118–19 that is, *t·* modes of mortal thought.
139–19 and the *t·* hundred thousand in the New,
153–10 administered at intervals of *t·* hours,
161– 7 the *t·* young Hebrew captives, cast into the
ph 193–15 It was between *t·* and four o'clock
f 221– 9 until *t·* hours after eating.
c 256– 9 The theory of *t·* persons in one God
b 314–15 in *t·* days I will raise it up,"— *John* 2 : 19.
331–28 a trinity in unity, *t·* in one,
331–32 These *t·* express in divine Science
p 438–15 on *t·* distinct charges of crime, to wit :
r 494– 3 and in *t·* days I [Mind] will— *John* 2 : 19.
g 515–19 nor does it imply *t·* persons in one.
523–22 and in *t·* verses of the second,
549–10 *t·* different methods of reproduction

threefold
b 331–32 the *t·*, essential nature of the infinite.

threescore
f 246–22 would enjoy more than *t·* years and ten

threshold
a 39–16 To him, therefore, death was not the *t·*

threw
c 259– 8 *t·* upon mortals the truer reflection of God

thrive
p 413–15 in order to make it *t·* more vigorously

throat
f 221– 9 that he should not wet his parched *t·*

throne
a 26– 3 pathway up to the *t·* of glory,
c 255– * *Thy t· is established of old :— Psal.* 93 : 2.
b 317– 3 the *t·* of the creative divine Principle,
ap 565– 8 caught up unto God, and to His *t·*.— *Rev.* 12 : 5.

throng
sp 86– 3 "The multitude *t·* thee."— *Luke* 8 : 45.
p 371–18 the illusive sufferings which *t·* the gloaming.

throughout
pref xii–21 she had never read this book *t·*
a 30–22 *t·* the whole earthly career of Jesus,
55–23 reappearing of the divine healing is *t·* all time ;
sp 98–18 It is imperious *t·* all ages
s 146–29 and extends *t·* all space.
b 277–17 *t·* the entire round of nature.
319–13 *T·* the infinite cycles of eternal existence,
324–25 *t·* Asia Minor, Greece, and even in
333–19 *T·* all generations both before and after the
o 358–17 as is recorded *t·* the Scriptures.
p 408– 7 *t·* the entire round of the material senses,
422– 5 a great stir *t·* his whole system,
442– 6 *t·* the vast audience-chamber of Spirit
g 507–26 expresses Science and art *t·* His creation,
523–22 *T·* the first chapter of Genesis
526–25 This second . . . is a picture of error *t·*.

throw
m 65–30 will assuredly *t·* off this evil,
an 101–15 to *t·* light on physiological and
ph 192–22 the weight you *t·* into the right scale.
p 397– 5 We *t·* the mental influence on the
g 519–15 until they *t·* off the old man and reach the

thrown
c 263–29 *t·* into the face of spiritual immensity,
b 301– 2 as the human likeness *t·* upon the mirror,
o 360–19 Like a pendulum . . . you will be *t·* back and
t 461–12 light of understanding be *t·* upon this Science,

throws
f 205–30 *t·* our weight into the scale, . . . of matter.
249–28 It *t·* off some material fetters.
ap 578– 1 the light which C. S. *t·* on the Scriptures

thrust
s 132–14 The Pharisees of old *t·* the spiritual idea
150–28 and that he is then *t·* out of

thrusting
m 62–25 by *t·* in the laws of erring, human concepts.
ph 166–18 Instead of *t·* Him aside in times of
b 304–31 *t·* aside his divine Principle as

thrusts
sp 85–27 His *t·* at materialism were sharp, but needed.
t 458–20 Sin makes deadly *t·* at the Christian Scientist

Thummim
gl 595–11 definition of
595–13 The Urim and *T·*, which were

thunder
ph 174–17 The *t·* of Sinai and the Sermon on the Mount

thunderbolts
b 288–15 lightnings and *t·* of error may burst and flash

thunders
ap 559–13 It arouses the "seven *t·*" of evil,— *Rev.* 10 : 3.

thwart
r 485–15 Think not to *t·* the spiritual ultimate

thwarted
t 459–22 distrusted and *t·* in its incipiency.

Thy
iii– * This is *T·* high behest :
pr 16–28 Hallowed be *T·* name— *Matt.* 6 : 9.
16–30 *T·* kingdom come.— *Matt.* 6 : 10.
16–31 *T· kingdom is come ;*
17– 1 *T·* will be done in earth,— *Matt.* 6 : 10.
s 131–22 so it seemed good in *T·* sight."— *Luke* 10 : 21.
ph 190–28 As for me, I will behold *T·* face— *Psal.* 17 : 15.
190–29 when I awake, with *T·* likeness.— *Psal.* 17 : 15.
190–31 In *T·* light shall we see light.— *Psal.* 36 : 9.
200–14 over the works of *T·* hands.— *Psal.* 8 : 6.
f 201– * *the reproach of T· servants ;— Psal.* 89 : 50.
c 255– * *T· throne is established— Psal.* 93 : 2.
g 532–15 I heard *T·* voice in the garden,— *Gen.* 3 : 10.

tidbits
f 214–25 would spread their table with cannibal *t·*

tide
s 125–22 with changes of time and *t·*, cold and heat,
139–13 wisely to stem the *t·* of sectarian bitterness,

tides
ap 566– 2 the dark ebbing and flowing *t·* of human fear,

tidings
p 442–15 as of one "that bringeth good *t·*."— *Isa.* 52 : 7.

ties
a 31– 4 Jesus acknowledged no *t·* of the flesh.
m 57–27 but this severance of fleshly *t·*

tiger
p 378–11 By looking a *t·* fearlessly in the eye,

tightened
m 67– 5 the wind shrieks through the *t·* shrouds,

till

ph	183–12	the condemnation of man to *t·* the ground,
g	518– 1	Man is not made to *t·* the soil.
	520–22	was not a man to *t·* the ground. — *Gen.* 2 : 5.
	520–31	never causing man to *t·* the ground,
	537– 4	to *t·* the ground from whence he — *Gen.* 3 : 23.
	544– 5	"not a man to *t·* the ground." — *Gen.* 2 : 5.
	545– 7	The condemnation of mortals to *t·* the ground

tills

g	537–16	Error *t·* its own barren soil
	545–15	Error *t·* the whole ground in this material

time

accepted
a	39–18	"*Now*," . . . "is the accepted *t·* ; — *II Cor.* 6 : 2.
sp	93– 8	*now* is the accepted *t·* ; — *II Cor.* 6 : 2.

all
a	38–14	in all *t·* to come.
	52–26	not for their day only but for all *t·* :
	55–23	divine healing is throughout all *t·* ;
b	317–14	not only in all *t·*, but in *all ways*

all account of
f	245– 6	she became insane and lost all account of *t·*.

and energies
s	109–14	and devoted *t·* and energies to discovering a

and eternity
b	285– 5	the great fact of being for *t·* and eternity.

and medication
p	398–26	belief in the healing effects of *t·* and medication,

and tide
s	125–21	will come and go with changes of *t·* and tide,

and toil
t	464– 6	and how much *t·* and toil are still required

another
a	38–18	another *t·* Jesus prayed, not for the twelve only,

another's
m	58–14	the selfish exaction of all another's *t·* and

any
o	350–20	lest at any *t·* they should see — *Matt.* 13 : 15.
p	413–30	making it probable at any *t·* that such ills

approaches
p	402– 8	The *t·* approaches when mortal mind will

at one
u	27–22	Jesus sent forth seventy students at one *t·*,
sp	88–16	at one *t·* are supposed to be substance-matter
r	489–19	at one *t·* the medium for
	491–18	that matter is awake at one *t·* and

at the
a	53–27	but at the *t·* when Jesus felt our infirmities,
p	431–13	At the *t·* of the arrest the prisoner

barriers of
c	266–31	He does not cross the barriers of *t·*

before the
s	129–16	to torment us before the *t·* ?" — *Matt.* 8 : 29.

calendar of
g	520–11	according to the calendar of *t·*.

cometh
a	31–31	yea, the *t·* cometh, that — *John* 16 : 2.
m	64–18	the *t·* cometh of which Jesus spake,
b	325–26	The *t·* cometh when the spiritual origin of man,

extends through
b	328–31	his great life-work extends through *t·*

first
b	326–31	He beheld for the first *t·* the true idea

for thinkers
pref	vii–13	The *t·* for thinkers has come.

future
b	306–15	at some uncertain future *t·*
g	546– 2	at some future *t·* to be emancipated from it,

glides on
f	240–18	Mortals move onward . . . as *t·* glides on.

has come
b	285–17	The *t·* has come for a finite . . . to give place

help in
s	148–29	to render help in *t·* of physical need.

his
a	47–14	He chose his *t·*, when the people were in doubt
ap	569–24	for the devil knoweth his *t·* is short.

illuminating
g	502–17	illuminating *t·* with the glory of eternity.

indefinite
o	348–29	believed for an indefinite *t·* ;

is at hand
ap	558– *	for the *t·* is at hand. — *Rev.* 1 : 3.

is finite
r	468–30	*T·* is finite ; eternity is forever

is not distant
a	24–15	The *t·* is not distant when the

Jesus'
pref	xi–10	results now, as in Jesus' *t·*,
s	142–18	As in Jesus' *t·*, so to-day, tyranny and pride

less
s	142– 1	in less *t·* than the old systems,
ph	175–19	Then people had less *t·* for selfishness,

little
t	464– 4	Could her friends know how little *t·* the author

time

march of
f	225– 7	march of *t·* bears onward freedom's

measurement of
gl	598–19	YEAR. A solar measurement of *t·* ;

measures
gl	584– 6	measures *t·* according to the good that is

moves on
b	329– 1	As *t·* moves on, the healing elements of

mutations of
c	261–25	Breaking away from the mutations of *t·*

no
f	238–28	no *t·* for gossip about false law or testimony.

objects of
gl	584– 4	The objects of *t·* and sense disappear

of harvest
f	207–19	separates the tares and wheat in *t·* of harvest.

of Jesus
pr	6–30	a certain magistrate, who lived in the *t·* of Jesus,

of need
f	218–22	turning in *t·* of need to God, divine Love,

olden
s	131–27	explained the so-called miracles of olden *t·*

or accident
b	304–24	if *t·* or accident robbed them of

organization and
f	249–19	Organization and *t·* have nothing to do with Life.

our
sp	90–29	may as well improve our *t·* in solving the
ph	197–27	the effeminate constitutions of our *t·*

passing
f	245–22	she had taken no cognizance of passing *t·*

past
an	106–25	as I have also told you in *t·* past, — *Gal.* 5 : 21.

period of
r	494–13	or for a limited period of *t·*,

question of
f	242– 4	It is only a question of *t·* when

right
p	396–22	At the right *t·* explain to the sick the

same
sp	78– 8	and that at the same *t·* we are
	82–13	different states of consciousness at the same *t·*.
s	142–14	they at the same *t·* shut the door on
f	229–12	and at the same *t·* admits that Spirit is
o	346–31	cannot serve both God and mammon at the same *t·* ;
t	457–22	One cannot scatter his fire, and at the same *t·*

shore of
a	35– 7	Discerning Christ, . . . anew on the shore of *t·*,
f	203–29	should disappear on the shore of *t·* ;

short
ap	568–23	he hath but a short *t·*. — *Rev.* 12 : 12.

solar
g	504–19	words which indicate, in the absence of solar *t·*,

takes
p	429– 7	The final demonstration takes *t·*

their
a	41–31	but that belief, from their *t·* to ours,

this
pref	xII–11	and (for a portion of this *t·*) sole editor
a	40– 6	"Go thy way for this *t·* ; — *Acts* 24 : 25.
p	431– 5	During all this *t·* the prisoner attended to his
	438–13	Personal Sense, by this *t·* silent,

will come
c	266– 7	the *t·* will come when you will be solitary,

will prove
p	368– 6	Divine Science insists that *t·* will prove all this.

will separate
g	535– 4	the wheat and tares which *t·* will separate,

work of
f	238–30	place the fact above the falsehood, is the work of *t·*.

---

pref	ix–31	her comparative ignorance . . . up to that *t·*,
a	39–21	now is the *t·* in which to experience that
	39–23	Now is the *t·* for so-called
	44– 8	set the seal of eternity on *t·*.
	47–21	and for a *t·* quieted his remorse.
	55–22	The *t·* for the reappearing of the
sp	92–32	Do you say the *t·* has not yet come
s	150–11	now, as in the *t·* of its earlier demonstration,
ph	185–26	may seem for a *t·* to benefit the sick,
f	245–11	Having no consciousness of *t·*,
b	296–25	foundations which *t·* is wearing away.
	338–32	The ideal man was revealed in due *t·*,
o	353–14	*T·* has not yet reached eternity.
p	377– 8	Then is the *t·* to cure them through C. S.,
t	447–13	evil will in *t·* disclose and punish itself.
r	468–28	Eternity, not *t·*, expresses the thought of **Life,**
	468–29	and *t·* is no part of eternity.
	470–27	and consequently a *t·* when Deity was
g	509–21	are no more contingent now on *t·* or
	510–21	until *t·* has been already divided into

time

g 513–11   t· is not yet measured by solar revolutions,
gl 595–17 definition of
598–30   T· is a mortal thought,

time-honored

pref vii–14 independent of doctrines and t· systems,
b 326–13   the foundation of material systems, however t·,

times

all
s 160–22   Unless muscles are self-acting at all t·,
b 273–30   beliefs emit the effects of error at all t·,
ap 571–15 At all t· and under all circumstances,
a million
a 50–29   a million t· sharper than the thorns
different
s 163–24   hypotheses obtruded upon us at different t·.
of persecution
a 29– 9   work the more earnestly in t· of persecution,
f 238–12   To fall away from Truth in t· of persecution,
of trouble
s 134–15   They have not waxed strong in t· of trouble.
old
ph 175– 6 In old t· who ever heard of dyspepsia,
signs of the
sp 85–22   discern the signs of the t·?" — Matt. 16 : 3.
g 510– 1   discern the signs of the t·?" — Matt. 16 : 3.
signs of these
sp 98– 5   in the mental horizon the signs of these t·,
their
b 270–15   higher than the systems of their t· ;
three
s 108–16   three t· three duodecillions must be

ph 166–18 Instead of thrusting Him aside in t· of
p 381–14   mortal mind cannot legislate the t·, periods,
t 443– 8   at t· severely condemned by some Scientists,

time-tables

a 21–17   We have separate t· to consult,
f 246–18   T· of birth and death are

timid

ph 167–29 On this fundamental point, t· conservatism is
f 238–29   To reconstruct t· justice and place the fact

timidity

f 215–30   his philosophy spurned physical t·,
o 352–22   thus watering the very roots of childish t·,
r 483–31   One must fulfil one's mission without t·

timorously

p 413–32   or any other malady, t· held in the beliefs

tints

r 480– 7   and not a trace of heavenly t·.
g 552–25   The blending t· of leaf and flower

tips

f 205–28   Selfishness t· the beam of human existence

tired

s 154–26   says . . . "You look sick," "You look t·,"
f 217–30   Which is t· and so speaks?
217–31   Without mind, could the muscles be t·?
b 322–28   turn us like t· children to the arms of
r 494– 4   and he did this for t· humanity's reassurance.

tireless

g 515– 4   Patience is symbolized by the t· worm,
548–22   Had the naturalist, through his t· researches,

tissue

ph 172–28 But the loss of a limb or injury to a t·

tithe

gl 595–22 definition of

title

ph 184–11 never honoring erroneous belief with the t· of
b 333– 9   not a name so much as the divine t· of
gl 590–16 this term is sometimes employed as a t·,

toad

m 66– 4   Which, like the t·, ugly and venomous,

tobacco

p 383–24   Does his assertion prove the use of t· to be
404– 3   If a man is an inebriate, a slave to t·,
406–28   depraved appetite for alcoholic drinks, t·,
407– 3   Puffing the obnoxious fumes of t·,
t 454– 2   the use of t· or intoxicating drinks

tobacco-user

p 383–21   The t·, eating or smoking poison

to-day

alive
f 216– 3   Who shall say that man is alive t·, but may
and forever
pr 2–32   yesterday, and t·, and forever ;" — Heb. 13 : 8.
s 112–20   yesterday, and t·, and forever ;" — Heb. 13 : 8.
f 249–18   yesterday, and t·, and forever." — Heb. 13 : 8.
b 283– 7   "yesterday, and t·, and forever." — Heb. 13 : 8.
g 546– 5   yesterday, and t·, and forever." — Heb. 13 : 8.
ap 577–18 which t· and forever interprets this great

to-day

Christianity
a 28–26   and that Christianity t· is at peace with
Christians of
a 37–21   May the Christians of t· take up the
conspicuous
m 65–13   broadcast powers of evil so conspicuous t·
grace for
pr 17– 5   Give us grace for t· ;
prophet of
sp 98– 4   The prophet of t· beholds in the mental horizon
repeated
f 243–14   are not more commonly repeated t·,
r 474– 5   reception accorded to Truth . . . is repeated t·.
wise man of
sp 95–25   Is the wise man of t· believed, when he

pref vii– 1 To those . . . t· is big with blessings.
ix–16   T·, though rejoicing in some progress,
a 37– 2   sin brings suffering as much t· as yesterday
52–17   T·, as of old, error and evil again make
54–30   glorified man were physically on earth t·,
55– 3   t· subjects to unchristian comment
sp 73– 4   but another, who has died t·
95– 5   as they would be t· if Jesus were
s 113– 4   plentifully reaches humanity t·,
132–20   T·, as of yore, unconscious of the reappearing
134– 1   T· the cry of bygone ages is repeated,
135–17   There is t· danger of repeating
138–25   The Christian can prove this t· as readily as
142–18   As in Jesus' time, so t·, tyranny and pride
143– 2   t·, as yesterday, Christ casts out evils
144–30   It is a question t·, whether the ancient
149–31   T· there is hardly a city, village, or hamlet, in
150– 4   T· the healing power of Truth is widely
f 224–17   cross was truth's central sign, and it is t·.
226–28   the Pharaohs, who t·, as of yore,
254–21   demands us to accept lovingly t·,
b 305–23   illusion of life that is here t· and gone to-morrow,
322–17   foreshadowed the . . . hypnotism of t·.
o 360–30   while t·, Jew and Christian can unite in

together

a 21–16   we are not journeying t·.
m 56– *   What therefore God hath joined t·, — Matt. 19 : 6.
58–25   "Two eat no more t· than they eat separately.
60–15   put asunder what she hath not joined t·.
sp 73–29   mistake to suppose that . . . can commune t·.
74–31   so-called dead and living cannot commune t·,
75–26   can commune t·, and that is the moment
s 114– 1   classes both evil and good t· as mind ;
f 215– 5   t· with all the faculties of Mind ;
c 255– *   travaileth in pain t· until now. — Rom. 8 : 22.
b 306–15   to be brought t· again
t 444– 5   "All things work t· for good — Rom. 8 : 28.
r 466–12   neither dwell t· nor assimilate.
474–32   for light and darkness cannot dwell t·.
g 506–16   be gathered t· unto one place, — Gen. 1 : 9.
506–23   the gathering t· of the waters — Gen. 1 : 10.
509–23   "the morning stars sang t·. — Job 38 : 7.
514–24   young lion, and the fatling t· ; — Isa. 11 : 6.
535–30   the gathering t· of the waters — Gen. 1 : 10.
ap 565–23 After the stars sang t·

toil

a 35– 3   the fruitlessness of their t· in the dark
36–28   t·, sacrifice, cross-bearing, multiplied trials,
m 58–28   Wealth may obviate the necessity for t·
f 217–20   the next t· will fatigue you less,
217–29   You say, " T· fatigues me."
p 385–15   Constant t·, deprivations, exposures,
t 464– 6   and how much time and t· are still required
g 536–26   Through t·, struggle, and sorrow,

toils

a 49–10   his t·, privations, sacrifices, his divine patience,

toilsome

t 462–16   There is nothing difficult or t· in this task,

token

a 50–11   who could withhold a clear t· of his presence
gl 596–29 in t· of reverence and submission

told

sp 85–13   t· me all things that ever I did : — John 4 : 29.
an 106–25 as I have also t· you in time past, — Gal. 5 : 21.
s 156–15   and t· the patient so ;
ph 193–17 I t· him to rise, dress himself,
197–21   t· that the simple food our forefathers ate
o 352–26   children should be t· not to believe in ghosts,
p 364–20   Jesus t· Simon that such seekers as he
376–11   should be t· that blood never gave life
430–32   I was t· that I must remain silent until
g 533– 5   Who t· thee that thou wast naked? — Gen. 3 : 11.

tolerate

s 129– 5   and can t· no error in premise or conclusion.

tomb
a 44– 5   the *t·* gave Jesus a refuge from his foes,
   44–30   demonstrating within the narrow *t·* the
f 248–11   which each day brings to a nearer *t·*.

to-morrow
sp 73– 5   supposedly will return to earth *t·*,
f 216– 4   alive to-day, but may be dead *t·*?
b 305–24   illusion of life that is here to-day and gone *t·*,

tone
m 57– 6   The masculine mind reaches a higher *t·*
s 126–13   the human mind never produced a real *t·*
  148–17   It loses Spirit, drops the true *t·*, and

tones
pref viii– 7   even as the science of music corrects false *t·*
m 58– 5   *T·* of the human mind may be different,
sp 81–21   silence the *t·* of music, . . . and yet the
s 145– 1   or whether they caught its sweet *t·*,
  145– 2   musician catches the *t·* of harmony,
f 217– 4   to conclude that individual musical *t·*
b 304–22   The science of music governs *t·*.
ap 559–14   to utter the full diapason of secret *t·*.

Tongue
p 431–21   The next witness is called :— I am Coated *T·*.

tongue
and pulse
s 159–25   They examine the lungs, *t·*, and pulse
coated
p 379–26   coated *t·*, febrile heat, dry skin,
grows mute
sp 89–16   the *t·* grows mute which before was eloquent.
new
s 114–19   in expressing the new *t·* we must sometimes
  117–11   the new *t·*, the spiritual meaning of which
b 272–11   and is the new *t·* referred to in the
o 354–25   to hear and to speak the new *t·*.
nor pen
s 110–19   neither *t·* nor pen can overthrow it.
pen nor
s 110–17   No human pen nor *t* taught me the Science
possesses her
sp 89– 7   believing that somebody else possesses her *t·*
spiritual
s 115–11   back into the original spiritual *t·*.
under the
ph 174–28   rolling it under the *t·* as a sweet morsel
voices
pref ix– 8   the *t·* voices the more definite thought,

p 370–32   Physicians examine the pulse, *t·*, lungs,

tongues
f 210– 2   expressed only in "new *t·* ;" — *Mark* 16 : 17.
h 286–16   In the Saxon and twenty other *t·*
o 349–23   "They shall speak with new *t·*" — *Mark* 16 : 17.
p 362– *   *they shall speak with new t· ;* — *Mark* 16 : 17.

tonic
p 420–21   better than any drug, alterative, or *t·*.

took
a 32–15   Jesus *t·* bread, and blessed it — *Matt.* 26 : 26.
  32–17   he *t·* the cup, and gave thanks, — *Matt.* 26 : 27.
  44–13   He *t·* no drugs to allay inflammation.
s 107– *   *leaven, which a woman t·,* — *Matt.* 13 : 33.
  117–32   "leaven, which a woman *t·*, — *Matt.* 13 : 33.
ph 165–14   *t·* the place of spiritual truth.
  176– 3   Eves *t·* up the study of medical works
  193–16   in the afternoon when this *t·* place.
b 272–14   shows the care our Master *t·*
  336–30   and in humility he *t·* the new name of Paul.
o 352– 7   the Jews *t·* a diametrically opposite view.
p 431–23   hypnotized the prisoner and *t·* control of
g 526–26   *t·* the man, and put him into the— *Gen.* 2 : 15.
  528–11   *t·* one of his ribs, and closed up— *Gen.* 2 : 21.

tooth
f 212– 2   A *t·* which has been extracted
o 346–27   the *t·*, the operation, and the forceps

tooth-pulling
o 346–25   Do you feel the pain of *t·*, when you

torch
f 202–14   lights the *t·* of spiritual understanding.

tore
gl 597–13   *t·* from bigotry and superstition their coverings,

torment
s 129–16   to *t·* us before the time?" — *Matt.* 8 : 29.
b 327–12   and it becomes his *t·*.
ap 574–21   which poured forth hatred and *t·*,

torn
a 44–16   to heal the *t·* palms and bind up the

torpid
s 160–12   the heart becomes as *t·* as the hand.
p 378– 9   Without . . . there can be no inflammatory nor *t·*

torrent
pr 13–19   overwhelming our real wishes with a *t·* of words.

torture
a 50– 5   moment of mockery, desertion, *t·*,
ap 569–27   but how many periods of *t·* it may take

tortured
p 433–25   sentenced to be *t·* until he is dead.
  437–16   the helpless innocent body *t·*,

tossed
m 62– 9   fed, rocked, *t·*, or talked to,

total
ap 563–10   dragon stands for the sum *t·* of human error.
  574–17   that the sum *t·* of human misery,

totters
p 389–26   This belief *t·* to its falling

touch
sp 71–11   that you *t·* and smell it.
  86– 5   mortal mind, whose *t·* called for aid.
  88– 4   the *t·* of a vanished hand,
ph 170–26   and at least to *t·* the hem of Truth's garment.
f 252–26   says : . . . But a *t·*, an accident, the law of God,
c 263–16   His "*t·* turns hope to dust,
b 282–21   Even though they seem to *t·*,
  300–13   temporal and unreal never *t·* the eternal and
  300–14   mutable and imperfect never *t·* the immutable
  300–16   inharmonious and self-destructive never *t·* the
t 450–15   Some people yield slowly to the *t·* of Truth.
g 526–10   material hearing, sight, *t·*, taste, and smell,
  529–20   neither shall ye *t·* it, lest ye die.— *Gen.* 3 : 3.

touched
pref x–26   unbiased Christian thought is soonest *t·*
sp 86– 1   Jesus once asked, "Who *t·* me?" — *Luke* 8 : 45.
f 216– 4   What has *t·* Life, God, to such strange issues?
b 311–31   But the spiritual, eternal man is not *t·*
r 493–12   is *t·* upon in a previous chapter

touches
sp 83–32   investigates and *t·* only human beliefs.
  88– 7   when no viand *t·* the palate
ap 569–11   He that *t·* the hem of Christ's robe

touching
s 161–19   The oppressive state statutes *t·* medicine

toward
s 150– 8   peace, good-will *t·* men." — *Luke* 2 : 14.
f 226–17   peace, good-will *t·* men." — *Luke* 2 : 14.

towards
pr 5– 3   one step *t·* reform and the very easiest step.
a 21–11   looks *t·* the imperishable things of Spirit.
  47–11   The world's ingratitude and hatred *t·*
sp 84–22   is a step *t·* the Mind-science by which
  90–27   and opens it wide *t·* immortality.
s 145–27   *t·* other forms of matter or error,
ph 169–22   or any other means *t·* which
f 205–25   hinders man's normal drift *t·* the one Mind,
  205–28, 29   the side of error, not *t·* Truth.
  213–11   Every step *t·* goodness is a departure from
  213–12   and is a tendency *t·* God, Spirit.
  213–13   this attraction *t·* infinite and eternal good
  213–14   by an opposite attraction *t·* the finite,
  226– 9   further steps *t·* the banishment of a
  236–31   youth makes easy and rapid strides *t·* Truth.
  240– 9   and the leaflet turns naturally *t·* the light.
  240–18   Mortals move onward *t·* good or evil
  242– 6   *t·* the joys of Spirit,
  242– 7   *t·* human freedom and the final
  251– 2   as it hastens *t·* self-destruction.
b 269– 4   rising *t·* the realm of the real,
  276–22   *t·* the contemplation of things immortal
  299–13   never lead *t·* self, sin, or materiality,
  322–12   turn our thoughts *t·* divine Principle,
  323– 7   helped onward in the march *t·* righteousness,
  323–21   gravitates *t·* Soul and away from
o 348–14   Are we irreverent *t·* sin, or
p 362–14   with his head *t·* the table
  364– 4   and it was manifested *t·* one who was
  365– 5   would do much more *t·* healing the sick
  423– 5   diminishes the tendency *t·* a favorable result.
  430– 9   he will advance more rapidly *t·* God,
t 444–14   not only *t·* differing forms of religion and
  451–15   walks in the direction *t·* which he looks,
  463–31   is the first step *t·* destroying error.
g 541–25   even the human duty of man *t·* his brother.
  557–12   as the line of creation rises *t·* spiritual man,
  557–12   *t·* enlarged understanding and intelligence ;
ap 577–24   Its gates open *t·* light and glory
gl 586–22   spiritual being understood ; haste *t·* harmony.

town
o 342–14   heal the sick in any *t·* where they should

toy
sp 80–22   Even planchette— the French *t·* which

trace
r 480– 6   and not a *t·* of heavenly tints.
g 533–10   an attempt to *t·* all human errors

traceable
  g 523–29   after which the distinction is not definitely *t·*.
traced
  ph 188–21   are *t·* upon mortals by unmistakable signs.
tracing
  ph 189–23   in *t·* them, we constantly ascend
tractable
  f 236–25   Children are more *t·* than adults,
tradition
  a 27–23   *T·* credits him with two or three hundred
  29–12   There is a *t·* that Publius Lentulus wrote
traditional
  o 352–24   *t·* beliefs, erroneous and man-made.
traditions
  o 354–16   derived from the *t·* of the elders
traduced
  sp 95– 3   His holy motives and aims were *t·* by
traffic
  s 142–23   to purge the temples of their vain *t·*
tragedy
  b 317–23   whom they had loved before the *t·* on Calvary.
  p 434–23   His trial was a *t·*, and is morally illegal.
trail
  m 58– 4   or else joy's drooping wings *t·* in dust.
  g 550–20   and causes our standard to *t·* in the dust.
train
  g 526–12   sickness, and death, follow in the *t·* of this error
trained
  ph 195– 9   those very senses, *t·* in an opposite direction.
  197–19   hardier than our *t·* physiologists,
traitor
  a 47–26   fell to the ground, and the *t·* fell with it.
  t 450–14   nor play the *t·* for place and power.
traitor's
  a 47–12   The *t·* price was thirty pieces of silver
traits
  m 61–19   the grosser *t·* of their ancestors.
trample
  f 234–14   pearls before those who *t·* them
  p 440–19   You cannot *t·* upon the decree of the
trampled
  f 229–22   false law should be *t·* under foot.
tramples
  p 419–27   *t·* upon the divine Principle
trampling
  p 435–15   If liver-complaint was committed by *t·* on
transcend
  f 247–18   which *t·* all material sense.
transcendent
  ph 182–28   from ignorance of C. S. and its *t·* power.
transcendental
  b 301–14   This reflection seems to mortal sense *t·*,
  320–20   (however *t·* such a thought appears),
  o 360– 9   replies : . . . they are not so shockingly *t·*.
transcends
  b 301–15   the spiritual man's substantiality *t·*
  r 483– 7   Mind *t·* all other power,
transfer
  sp 75– 8   Spiritualism would *t·* men from the
  f 211–22   The *t·* of the thoughts of one erring mind
  r 496– 2   there is no *t·* of evil suggestions
transference
  an 103–30   and consequently no *t·* of
transferred
  sp 87– 6   or for the person holding the *t·* picture
transfiguration
  ap 576–29   to deific apprehension through spiritual *t·*.
transform
  b 295– 8   Mortal mind would *t·* the spiritual
  p 371–20   I would not *t·* the infant at once into a man,
  401–10   truth of being must *t·* the error
transformation
  sp 74–20   Such a backward *t·* is impossible in Science.
  f 241–13   *t·* of the body by the renewal of Spirit.
transformed
  a 49–20   *t·* by the renewing of the infinite Spirit.
  sp 74–17   The caterpillar *t·* into a beautiful insect,
  ph 191–14   Thus the whole earth will be *t·* by Truth
  b 291–21   has been *t·* into the popular proverb,
  308–28   until his nature was *t·*.
  p 440–10   Good deeds are *t·* into crimes,
  442–24   until the material, *t·* with the ideal,
transgress
  p 432–17   *t·* the laws, and merit punishment,

transgressed
  ph 184–22   not because a law of matter has been *t·*,
  p 384– 4   the depressing thought that we have *t·* a
  384–23   and their fatal effects when *t·*,
transgressing
  p 442– 2   adjudged innocent of *t·* physical laws,
transgression
  f 229–26   If the *t·* of God's law produces
  229–29   It is the *t·* of a belief of mortal mind,
transgressions
  p 381–32   for *t·* of the physical laws of health;
transient
  f 214–26   How *t·* a sense is mortal sight, when a
  246–14   As the . . . material, the *t·* sense of beauty fades,
  247–13   form the *t·* standards of mortals.
  b 307–15   but only a *t·*, false sense of an existence
transition
  sp 75–27   and that is the moment previous to the *t·*,
  b 290– 8   but will remain as material as before the *t·*,
transitional
  m 65–24   *t·* stage is never desirable on its own account.
  ap 572–23   The Revelator had not yet passed the *t·*
transitions
  sp 90–10   *t·* now possible for mortal mind
transitory
  b 286–27   *T·* thoughts are the antipodes of
translate
  c 257–16   would *t·* spiritual ideas into material beliefs,
translated
  r 488– 7   Hebrew and Greek words often *t· belief*
  gl 598–12   It might be *t· wind* or *air*,
translates
  g 523–21   as our common version *t·* it.
translating
  s 115–10   when *t·* material terms back into the
translation
  a 36– 3   simply through *t·* into another sphere.
  f 209–22   by the *t·* of man and the universe back into
  210– 2   the *t·* of the spiritual original into the
  b 313– 3   (to give the full and proper *t·* of the Greek),
  313–20   is made even clearer in the *t·* of the
  o 360–22   as given in the excellent *t·* of the
  g 525–12   The following *t·* is from the Icelandic:
Translation
  s 115–12   Scientific *T·* of Immortal Mind
  115–19   Scientific *T·* of Mortal Mind
translations
  gl 598– 6   yet it has received different *t·*,
translator
  g 506–26   seem confused by the *t·*,
translators
  g 545–21   *t·* of this record of scientific creation
transmission
  sp 78–18   needs no material method for the *t·* of
  f 228– 3   The *t·* of disease or of
  p 424–30   belief . . . in the possibility of their *t·*.
  g 514–14   In the figurative *t·* from the divine thought
transmit
  p 413– 1   cannot *t·* good or evil intelligence
  g 551–23   How can matter originate or *t·* mind?
transmits
  s 117–27   dimly reflects and feebly *t·* Jesus' works
  c 259–22   Mortal thought *t·* its own images,
transmitted
  m 61–28   Nothing unworthy . . . should be *t·* to children.
  sp 87– 9   to be discerned, described, and *t·*.
  c 259–27   *t·* by the divine Mind through divine Science,
  g 517–18   His personality can only be reflected, not *t·*.
  551–18   *t·* through these bodies called eggs,
transparency
  b 295–22   in order to become a better *t·* for Truth.
transparent
  g 546–21   To the author, they are *t·*,
transplant
  c 265–32   and *t·* the affections from sense to Soul,
travail
  t 463–11   in the *t·* of spiritual birth.
  ap 562–24   the spiritual idea is typified by a woman in *t·*,
  562–28   for great is the idea, and the *t·* portentous.
travaileth
  c 255– *   *t· in pain together until now. — Rom. 8 : 22.*
travailing
  ap 562–22   she being with child cried, *t· — Rev. 12 : 2.*
travel
  a 21–23   or, if I take up their line of *t·*,
  sp 90–21   hashish eaters mentally *t·* far and
traveller
  a 21–27   He is like a *t·* going westward for a
  ph 174–10   and portend a long night to the *t·* ;

travellers
  f 245–12 Some American *t·* saw her when she was
traversed
  pref vii– 5 yet it *t·* the night, and came where,
traversing
  a 20–22 *t·* anew the path from sin to holiness.
tread
  pr 9–29 since you do not care to *t·* in the footsteps of
  s 124–26 We *t·* on forces.
  129–27 along the path which Science must *t·* in its
  t 454–28 until your students *t·* firmly in the straight and
treading
  a 26– 2 *t·* alone his loving pathway up to the throne
treason
  a 43–13 the *t·* and suicide of his betrayer,
  p 438–16 perjury, *t·*, and conspiracy against the rights
treasure
  pref x– 1 may *t·* the memorials of a child's growth,
  ph 181–29 "Where your *t·* is, there will— *Matt.* 6 : 21.
  c 262–26 "where your *t·* is, there will— *Matt.* 6 : 21.
  t 451–15 where his *t·* is, there will his heart be also.
treasures
  a 54–11 That he might liberally pour his dear-bought *t·*
  sp 70– 4 revelations of C. S. unlock the *t·* of Truth.
  f 241– 5 Sensual *t·* are laid up "where moth— *Matt.* 6 : 19.
  241–11 hate, revenge, . . . steal away the *t·* of Truth.
  c 265– 4 as his *t·* of Truth and Love are enlarged.
  gl 593– 6 PURSE. Laying up *t·* in matter ; error.
treat
  pref x–14 or *t·* in full detail so infinite a theme.
  m 67–30 Systems of religion and medicine *t·* of
  s 151– 1 To be sure, they sometimes *t·* the sick as if
  159–12 and to *t·* the patient as if she were
  ph 174–25 if an individual is sick, why *t·* the body alone
  f 218–24 T· a belief in sickness as you would sin,
  o 345–32 or *t·* it for disease,"
  340–19 We *t·* error through the understanding of
  p 397–27 can never *t·* mortal mind and matter separately,
  412– 6 symptoms of the case you *t·*,
  419–31 If it is found necessary to *t·* against relapse,
  421–11 you must *t·* the patient less for the
  t 453–24 You should *t·* sickness mentally just as you
  464–15 so violent that he could not *t·* himself
treated
  sp 79–26 says : . . . and must be *t·* for it."
  ph 176–21 Should all cases of organic disease be *t·* by a
  f 235– 5 than to be *t·* mentally by one who does not obey
  p 425– 6 If the case to be mentally *t·* is consumption,
  425–12 *t·* as error and put out of thought.
  432–14 *t·* as a criminal and punished with death.
  t 456–22 cannot be efficaciously *t·* by the
  463–24 Our Master *t·* error through Mind.
treating
  s 111–30 my metaphysical system of *t·* disease
  161–25 *t·* the case according to his physical diagnosis,
  f 219– 0 My method of *t·* fatigue applies to
  o 344–19 There are various methods of *t·* disease,
  344–26 to investigate this method of *t·* disease?
  348– 4 even while *t·* them as disease ;
  p 424–27 well to be alone . . . when *t·* disease.
treatise
  r 465– 4 she revised that *t·* for this volume in 1875.
treatises
  ph 179–21 T· on anatomy, physiology, and health,
  p 382–29 wrote . . . The *t·* I had read
treatment
  begin your
  p 411–27 Always begin your *t·* by allaying the fear
  his
  p 422–31 His *t·* is therefore tentative.
  hygienic
  p 370–26 Hygienic *t·* also loses its efficacy.
  medical
  t 443–17 certain ordinary physical methods of medical *t·*,
  mental
  p 410–22 chapter sub-title
  metaphysical
  ph 185– 3 My metaphysical *t·* changed the action of
  occurs in your
  p 421–11 If a crisis occurs in your *t·*, you must
  of disease
  pref viii– 1 the *t·* of disease as well as of sin,
  s 126–23 and its application to the *t·* of disease
  157–22 and recommend them for the *t·* of disease?
  p 369– 4 unfitted for the successful *t·* of disease.
  of insanity
  p 414– 4 *t·* of insanity is especially interesting.
  of moral ailments
  s 140– 3 effectual in the *t·* of moral ailments.
  pathological
  p 373–10 Under all modes of pathological *t·*,

treatment
  proper
  t 463–21 To decide quickly as to the proper *t·* of error
  such
  s 159–17 and not have risked such *t·*.
  ph 179–15 the body then seems to require such *t·*.
  their
  o 342–32 even if their *t·* resulted in the death of
treats
  b 318–23 Medical science *t·* disease as though
  t 459–30 *t·* disease with more certain results than
tree (*see also* **tree's**)
  accursed
  a 25– 8 shed upon "the accursed *t·*,"— see *Gal.* 3 : 13.
  and flower
  b 289–22 So man, *t·*, and flower are supposed to die ;
  and herb
  g 507–19 The *t·* and herb do not yield fruit because of
  and its fruit
  p 389–17 the fount and stream, the *t·* and its fruit,
  every
  p 404–18 cuts down every *t·* that brings not forth
  g 518– 7 and every *t·*, in the which is the— *Gen.* 1 : 29.
  525–31 every *t·* that is pleasant to the— *Gen.* 2 : 9.
  527– 7 Of every *t·* of the garden— *Gen.* 2 : 16.
  529–16 Ye shall not eat of every *t·*— *Gen.* 3 : 1.
  falleth
  b 291–19 "In the place where the *t·* falleth,— *Eccl.* 11 : 3.
  fruitless
  pr 6–28 He said of the fruitless *t·*,
  fruit of the
  g 529–18 but of the fruit of the *t·* which is— *Gen.* 3 : 3.
  is known
  b 299–22 "the *t·* is known by his fruit"— *Matt.* 12 : 33.
  is typical
  p 406– 4 The *t·* is typical of man's divine Principle,
  leaves of the
  p 406– 2 leaves of the *t·* were for the— *Rev.* 22 : 2.
  life of the
  b 283–18 such as the structural life of the *t·*
  of death
  g 527–18 the *t·* of death to His own creation?
  of knowledge
  (*see* **knowledge**)
  of life
  (*see* **life**)
  trunk of a
  p 393–22 the trunk of a *t·* which you gash
  yielding fruit
  g 507–12 the fruit *t·* yielding fruit— *Gen.* 1 : 11.
  508–10 the *t·* yielding fruit, whose seed— *Gen.* 1 : 12.
  yielding seed
  g 518– 7 the fruit of a *t·* yielding seed ;— *Gen.* 1 : 29.

  pr 5–19 flourish "like a green bay *t·* ;"— *Psal.* 37 : 35.
  sp 76–15 any more than a *t·* can return to its seed.
  89–25 The *t·* is not the author of itself.
  f 220–28 "the *t·* of the knowledge of— *Gen.* 2 : 17.
  250–27 no more sense as a man than it has as a *t·*.
  b 291–21 "As the *t·* falls, so it must lie."
  299–19 figuratively represented in Scripture as a *t·*,
  t 459–26 The *t·* must be good, which produces good fruit.
  r 481–16 this "*t·* of the knowledge of— *Gen.* 2 : 17.
  g 527– 8 the *t·* of the knowledge of— *Gen.* 2 : 17.
  533– 6 Hast thou eaten of the *t·*,— *Gen.* 3 : 11.
  533– 9 she gave me of the *t·*,— *Gen.* 3 : 12.
  535–21 and hast eaten of the *t·*— *Gen.* 3 : 17.
tree's
  o 358– 1 which destroys a *t·* so-called life,
trees
  b 300– 6 The mirage, which makes *t·* and cities seem
  g 529–18 the fruit of the *t·* of the garden :— *Gen.* 3 : 2.
tree-tops
  s 122–16 sky and *t·* apparently join hands,
tremble
  s 107–17 we may well *t·* in the prospect of
  135– 5 T·, thou earth, at the presence— *Psal.* 114 : 7.
  t 445–30 "I *t·*, when I remember that God is just,"
trembler
  b 298–20 joy is no longer a *t·*, nor is hope a cheat.
tremblers
  f 235–21 To the *t·* on the brink of death,
trembles
  t 445–31 the author *t·* whenever she
trembling
  a 23–26 with fear and *t·*."— *Phil.* 2 : 12.
  sp 99– 6 with fear and *t·*,"— *Phil.* 2 : 12.
  p 442–26 with fear and *t·* :"— *Phil.* 2 : 12.
tremor
  p 422– 9 will become the physician, allaying the *t·*
tremulous
  s 142–12 making dome and spire *t·* with beauty,

trespass

p 387–10 nor . . . *t·* upon God-given powers and resources,
t 453–32 He does not *t·* on the rights of mind

trespasser

an 106–13 the mental *t·* incurs the divine penalty

trespasses

a 33–24 raises the dead from *t·* and sins,
b 316–29 those dead in *t·* and sins,

trespassing

t 447– 1 The heavenly law is broken by *t·* upon

triad

s 122– 5 facts of Life, . . . defeat this *t·* of errors,
o 356–22 How then . . . subject to this *t·* of errors,
357–11 on account of this malevolent *t·*,
g 552–12 include no member of this dolorous and fatal *t·*.

trial

brought to
s 159– 7 The case was brought to *t·*.
commences
p 430–20 The patient feels ill, . . . and the *t·* commences.
hampers the
c 260–17 often hampers the *t·* of one's wings
in the Court
p 434– 9 permission is obtained for a *t·* in the Court of
Spirit,
of our faith
p 410–14 Every *t·* of our faith in God makes us stronger.

p 430–17 Suppose a mental case to be on *t·*,
431– 1 must remain silent until called for at this *t·*,
434–23 His *t·* was a tragedy, and is morally illegal.
436– 5 to reappear however at the *t·*

trials

a 28–29 The *t·* encountered by prophet, disciple,
36–28 toil, sacrifice, cross-bearing, multiplied *t·*,
39– 8 We must have *t·* and self-denials,
m 66– 6 *T·* teach mortals not to lean on a
66–10 *T·* are proofs of God's care.
p 441–33 We have no *t·* for sickness before the

tribal

s 133–21 limited form of a national or *t·* religion.
140–23 The Jewish *t·* Jehovah was a man-projected God,
g 524–11 God becomes . . . a *t·* god to be worshipped,
gl 584–22 self-made or created by a *t·* god

tribe

g 514–10 "the lion of the *t·* of Juda,"— *Rev.* 5: 5.

tribes

ap 562–12 The twelve *t·* of Israel with all mortals,

tribulation

m 66–10 Through great *t·* we enter the kingdom.
s 129–13 there will be "great *t·* — *Matt.* 24: 21.
b 309–21 to be brought back through great *t·*,
p 366– 1 such as peace, patience in *t·*,
ap 562–14 will through much *t·* yield to the

tribunal

p 434–20 C. S. turns suddenly to the supreme *t·*,
437–10 before the Judge of our higher *t·*,
441–33 before the *t·* of divine Spirit.
ap 564–21 before the *t·* of so-called mortal mind,

tribunals

an 105– 5 To say that these *t·* have no jurisdiction

tributary

s 119–31 and makes body *t·* to Mind.
122–10 make mortal mind *t·* to mortal body,
122–31 They insist . . . mind therefore *t·* to matter.
f 209– 8 and man is *t·* to divine Mind.
r 481– 2 Man is *t·* to God, Spirit, and to nothing else.
ap 562– 8 reveals the universe as secondary and *t·* to

tribute

p 364– 8 Which was the higher *t·*
g 541– 5 instead of making his own gift a higher *t·*

trickling

p 379–12 only a stream of warm water was *t·* over his arm.

tricksters

sp 86–19 either involve feats by *t·*, or

tried

a 22–21 Love means that we shall be *t·* and purified.
43–16 persecutors had mocked and *t·* to slay.
ph 175–17 had *t·* to tyrannize over our forefathers,
f 232–23 and never *t·* to make of none effect the
c 267–29 for when he is *t·*,— *Jas.* 1: 12.
p 430–17 as cases are *t·* in court.
436–25 taken into custody, *t·*, and condemned.
440–29 to be *t·* at the Court of Material Error.
r 471–24 and *t·* to adhere to it until she
ap 568– 3 evil has *t·* to slay the Lamb ;

tries

a 55–17 My weary hope *t·* to realize that happy day,
s 148–22 Then theology *t·* to explain how to make
ph 180– 5 The patient sufferer *t·* to be satisfied
187–24 The human mind *t·* to classify action as
t 443– 4 she *t·* to show them that under ordinary

trieth

s 115– 8 Job says: "The ear *t·* words,— *Job* 34: 3.

Trinity

c 256–10 (that is, a personal *T·* or Tri-unity)

trinity

b 331–28 They represent a *t·* in unity,

trip-hammer

ph 199– 4 The *t·* is not increased in size by exercise.

triply

b 331–27 that is, the *t·* divine Principle, Love.

triumph

hope and
p 434–18 solemn eyes, kindling with hope and *t·*,
last
a 39– 4 until Christianity's last *t·*.
Master's
a 46– 1 fully to understand their Master's *t·*,
of Spirit
s 139– 5 are full of accounts of the *t·* of Spirit,
of truth
f 223–31 and foreshadows the *t·* of truth.
over body
a 42–16 his final *t·* over body and matter,
over the body
f 242– 8 and the final *t·* over the body.
suffering, and
a 21– 7 another's goodness, suffering, and *t·*,
ultimate
t 446–31 and the ultimate *t·* of any cause.

a 24–30 it enabled their Master to *t·* over the grave,
28–14 are enabled to heal the sick and to *t·* over sin.
43–28 must *t·* over all material beliefs
43–32 Love must *t·* over hate.
49–24 to *t·* over sin, sickness, death,
54–15 and *t·* over death through Mind, not matter.
f 232– 2 can *t·* over sin, sickness, and death.
243– 7 and *t·* over sin and death.
r 484–24 Science must *t·* over material sense,

triumphal

a 40–23 through the *t·* arch of Truth and Love.
42–12 his brief *t·* entry into Jerusalem

triumphant

s 117–22 and *t·* exit from the flesh.
r 493– 2 speedily shows Truth to be *t·*.

triumphantly

ap 566– 1 were guided *t·* through the Red Sea,

triumphed

a 24–15 in which Jesus suffered and *t·*.
30–26 If we have *t·* sufficiently over the errors

triumphing

f 232–18 by healing the sick and *t·* over death.

triumphs

a 25–15 casts out error, and *t·* over death.
31–21 the divine Principle which *t·* over death.
39–30 attended with doubts and defeats as well as *t·*.
41– 4 the joys and *t·* of the righteous
b 272–25 The *t·* of C. S. are recorded in the destruction of

triune

b 331–26 Life, Truth, and Love constitute the *t·* Person
r 469–10 quality of infinite Mind, of the *t·* Principle,

Tri-unity

c 256–10 (that is, a personal Trinity or *T·*)

tri-unity

b 340–17 It inculcates the *t·* of God, Spirit, Mind ;
g 515–20 It relates to the . . . *t·* of Life, Truth, and Love.

troches

ph 175–31 tubercles and *t·*, lungs and lozenges.

trod

a 52–17 the best man that ever *t·* the globe.
f 242–31 show the way our Master *t·*,
c 263–17 the dust we all have *t·*."
b 313–24 most scientific man that ever *t·* the globe.
p 364– 2 the best man that ever *t·* this planet.

trope

ap 571–22 Through *t·* and metaphor, the Revelator,

tropical

m 61–16 like *t·* flowers born amid Alpine snows.
p 377– 6 Invalids flee to *t·* climates

tropics

f 240– 3 Arctic regions, sunny *t·*, giant hills,
ap 575–30 southward, to the genial *t·*,

trouble

pr 13– 1   "a very present help in *t·*." — *Psal.* 46 : 1.
s 134–15   They have not waxed strong in times of *t·*.
ph 166–19   thrusting Him aside in times of bodily *t·*,
   184– 8   remedy consists in probing the *t·* to the bottom,
f 202–28   "a very present help in *t·* ;" — *Psal.* 46 : 1.
p 383–18   which do not *t·* the gross,
t 444–12   a very present help in *t·*." — *Psal.* 46 : 1.
g 536–21   "of few days, and full of *t·*." — *Job.* 14 : 1.
   552–16   of few days, and full of *t·*." — *Job* 14 : 1.

troubled

m 67–17   or sunshine gladdens the *t·* sea.

troublesome

p 416–10   will tell you that the *t·* material cause
g 542– 3   that it might be rid of *t·* Truth.

troubling

p 414–18   by *t·* and perplexing their thought.

true

pr 3–14   likeness of the patient, tender, and *t·*,
   5–23   Such an error would impede *t·* religion.
a 25–10   His *t·* flesh and blood were his Life ;
   31–26   the *t·* worshippers shall — *John* 4 : 23.
   40–12   If the saying is *t·*, "While there 's life there 's
   40–13   its opposite is also *t·*, While there 's sin there 's
   42–26   in C. S. the *t·* man is governed by God
   48–31   and of what the *t·* knowledge of God can do
   53– 2   The latter accusation was *t·*, but not in
m 57–10   their *t·* harmony is in spiritual oneness.
   57–13   perpetual only as it is pure and *t·*,
   58–10   *t·* happiness, strength, and permanence.
   60–25   not discerning the *t·* happiness of being,
   68– 2   understanding . . . will be the basis of *t·* religion.
sp 87–25   The *t·* concept is never lost.
   91– 7   point of departure for all *t·* spiritual growth.
   93– 6   when the *t·* worshippers shall — *John* 4 : 23.
   99–23   The calm, strong currents of *t·* spirituality,
an 104– 1   for scientific thoughts are *t·* thoughts,
s 112–24   has already been stated and proved to be *t·*,
   113–22   Which of the denials in proposition four is *t·*?
   113–23   Both are not, cannot be, *t·*.
   113–24   According to the Scripture, I find that God is *t·*,
   116– 7   to make this Scriptural testimony *t·* in our
   117–26   and because of opacity to the *t·* light,
   126– 9   never projected the least portion of *t·* being.
   129–18   are antagonistic to *t·* being and fatal to its
   133–31   given place to the *t·* knowledge of God.
   134–21   The *t·* Logos is demonstrably C. S.,
   138– 4   behind Peter's confession of the *t·* Messiah.
   140–20   rituals are but types and shadows of *t·* worship.
   140–20   "The *t·* worshippers shall worship — *John* 4 : 23.
   140–28   mournfully *t·* that the older Scripture
   148–17   It loses Spirit, drops the *t·* tone,
   164– 6   "No . . . classification of diseases . . . is *t·*,
ph 192– 5   quit our reliance upon . . . and grasp the *t·*.
   192–29   Christianity is the basis of *t·* healing.
   198– 3   but he has not yet found it *t·* that knowledge
   199– 3   it might be thought *t·* that hammering would
f 202–20   for the *t·* way leads to Life instead of to death,
   203–11   to the Christian the only *t·* spirit is Godlike.
   203–24   but this is not *t·*.
   211–11   Is it not equally *t·* that matter does not
   211–24   If it is *t·* that nerves have sensation,
   213–23   This was even more strikingly *t·* of Beethoven,
   213–32   discard the one Mind and *t·* source of being,
   230– 1   If *t·*, it is a part of Truth.
   231–21   To hold yourself superior to sin, . . . is *t·* wisdom.
   232–13   theories must be untrue, for the Scripture is *t·*.
   237–29   the only living and *t·* God can do.
   249–10   Such is the *t·* Science of being.
c 258–17   as the *t·* divine image and likeness.
   259– 6   In divine Science, man is the *t·* image of God.
   261– 5   the enduring, the good, and the *t·*,
   264–26   by which we can recognize *t·* existence
   265–19   but this is *t·* only of a mortal, not of a man
b 270– 3   One only of the following statements can be *t·* :
   275–18   no truth is *t·*, . . . but the divine;
   275–26   *t·* understanding of God is spiritual.
   276–13   into human view in their *t·* light,
   281–21   When we put off the false sense for the *t·*,
   283– 2   belief that there is any *t·* existence apart from
   285–12   claim that a mortal is the *t·* image of
   286–29   error must also say, "I am *t·*."
   289–26   but the spiritual is *t·*,
   293–18   counterfeits the *t·* essence of spirituality
   294–29   recognizable only in what is good and *t·*.
   300– 3   Finite sense has no *t·* appreciation of
   300–10   will bring to light the *t·* reflection of God
   302–26   Man's *t·* consciousness is in the mental,
   303–16   can never make both these contraries *t·*.
   312– 1   How *t·* it is that whatever is learned through
   314–20   This materialism lost sight of the *t·* Jesus ;
   321– 2   which is just the opposite of the *t·*,
   323–25   the *t·* understanding of Life and Love,
   326–20   Working and praying with *t·* motives,
   328–10   they gain the *t·* understanding of God

true

b 329–10   Jesus, who was the *t·* demonstrator of
   337– 7   For *t·* happiness, man must harmonize with
   337–32   this Science is demonstrably *t·*, for it heals
   338– 3   brings to light the only living and *t·* God
o 349–29   this is equally *t·* of all learning,
   353– 9   How can a Christian, . . . think of the latter as real or *t·*,
   358– 7   If . . . one is *t·*, the other must be false.
   358–21   a *t·* knowledge of the great import
   359–18   *T·* Christianity is to be honored wherever
   359–32   in their *t·* light and loveliness,
   360– 6   It is *t·* that materiality renders these
   361– 4   Christ, as the *t·* spiritual idea, is the ideal of
p 376–23   audibly arguing the *t·* facts
   387– 1   We shall perceive this to be *t·* when we
   391–30   rise to the *t·* consciousness of Life as Love,
   396–18   not because the testimony of sin or disease is *t·*,
   402–17   but this is not *t·*.
   404–23   Arouse the sinner to this new and *t·* view of sin,
   409–26   and seek the *t·* model.
   410– 8   might know Thee, the only *t·* God, — *John* 17 : 3.
   419– 4   Your *t·* course is to destroy the foe,
   421– 6   a word which conveys the *t·* definition of
   427– 1   If it is *t·* that man lives, this fact can never
   428–12   sweep away the false and give place to the *t·*.
   429–16   mortal mind's affirmation is not *t·*.
   439–11   *T·*, Materia Medica was a misguided
   442–18   but the reverse of error is *t·*.
t 447–17   When sin or sickness . . . seems *t·* to material
   454– 7   and plants the feet in the *t·* path,
   454 17   Love for God and man is the *t·* incentive
   461–25   error is not *t·*, hence it is unreal.
r 466– 4   all-science or *t·* knowledge, all-presence.
   467–12   the *t·* brotherhood of man will be
   467–27   Spirit gives the *t·* mental idea.
   471–21   "Let God be *t·*," but every — *Rom.* 3 : 4.
   472–20   If error were *t·*, its truth would be error,
   472–30   They are not *t·*, because they are not of God.
   474–26   Truth spares all that is *t·*.
   478–16   No, not if God is *t·* and mortal man a liar.
   486– 3   when you have learned falsehood's *t·* nature.
   488–19   testimony of which cannot be *t·* either of man or
   491–11   the *t·* origin and facts of being,
   495– 6   If sickness is *t·* or the idea of Truth,
   496–19   overlying, and encompassing all *t·* being.
k 499– *   *He that is holy, He that is t·*, — *Rev.* 3 : 7.
g 506– 2   distinguishing between the false and the *t·*.
   512–25   Mortal mind inverts the *t·* likeness,
   516– 1   Then note how *t·*, according to C. S.,
   522– 2   false history in contradistinction to the *t·*.
   522– 4   If one is *t·*, the other is false,
   523–10   which God erects between the *t·* and false.
   527–14   It is *t·* that a knowledge of evil would
   527–17   But is it *t·* that God, good,
   528– 6   It cannot be *t·* that man was ordered to
   530–29   dreamer and dream are one, for neither is *t·*
   547– 4   If one of the statements in this book is *t·*,
   547– 5   every one must be *t·*,
   547–25   The *t·* theory of the universe, including man,
   548–16   may entertain angels, the *t·* ideas of God,
   550–19   hides the *t·* and spiritual Life, and causes our
ap 568–10   first the *t·* method of creation is set forth
   568–12   first exhibits the *t·* warfare and then the false.
   571–23   immortal scribe of Spirit and of a *t·* idealism,
gl 579– *   *He that is holy, He that is t·*, — *Rev.* 3 : 7.
   590–25   *t·* scientific statements of the Scriptures
     (*see also* **conception, idea, likeness, sense**)

truer

a 19– 7   by giving man a *t·* sense of Love,
   19– 8   and this *t·* sense of Love redeems
c 259– 8   threw upon mortals the *t·* reflection of God

truest

s 132–29   with the *t·* conception of the Christ?

truism

s 108– 9   the *t·* that the only sufferer is mortal mind,
p 417– 9   make the sick realize this great *t·*,

truly

a 25–10   and they *t·* eat his flesh and drink his blood,
   27–27   never *t·* understood their Master's instruction.
   34– 1   willing *t·* to drink his cup,
   44–21   in his proof of man's *t·* derived power
sp 81–23   in the case of man as *t·* as in the case of
   94– 6   The *t·* Christian and scientific statement of
s 112–12   borrowed from that *t·* divine Science which
   120–19   impossible for aught but Mind to testify *t·*
   130–24   and understood how *t·* such as they belong to
   135–21   It has been said, and *t·*, that Christianity
   140– 4   That God is a corporeal being, nobody can *t·*
ph 189–15   it is as *t·* mortal mind, according to its degree,
b 268– *   *and t· our fellowship is with* — *I John* 1 : 3.
   327–22   Fear of punishment never made man *t·* honest.
gl 585–13   "Elias *t·* shall first come — *Matt.* 17 : 11.

trump
f 223–27   but the last *t·* has not sounded, or this would
b 291– 7   when the last *t·* shall sound ;
   292– 2   then the final *t·* will sound which will end the

trumpet-word
p 427–32   to catch this *t·* of Truth,

trunk
p 393–22   the *t·* of a tree which you gash

trust
calm
   r 495–18   your clear sense and calm *t·*,
doubting
   t 455– 4   or a faltering and doubting *t·* in Truth
glorified
   b 299–11   they point upward to a new and glorified *t·*,
grandest
   a 49–19   charged with the grandest *t·* of heaven,
in good
   gl 579–13   the purpose of Love to create *t·* in good,
in hygiene
   s 145–14   whether faith in drugs, *t·* in hygiene,
our
   r 487–28   lengthens our days by strengthening our *t·*
support their
   p 417– 4   Always support their *t·* in the power of Mind

   a 20–21   to obey the divine order and *t·* God, saves
   ph 169–21   however much we *t·* a drug
   181– 9   When you manipulate patients, you *t·* in
   181–23   if you adhere to error and are afraid to *t·*
   f 234– 3   If we *t·* matter, we distrust Spirit.
   o 359– 2   have seen and have been taught to love and to *t·*
   360–26   Behold, He putteth no *t·* in His— *see Job* 4 : 18.
   t 444–11   Step by step will those who *t·* Him
   r 488–10   faith, understanding, *t·*, constancy,

trustfulness
   a 23–23   these two definitions, *t·* and *trustworthiness*.

trusting
   pr 1–12   and no loss can occur from *t·* God
   s 146– 8   By *t·* matter to destroy its own discord,
   f 226–31   *t·* Truth, the strong deliverer,
   b 326–11   or *t·* in it more than in the spiritual.

trusts
   a 23–24   One kind of faith *t·* one's welfare to others.
   p 428– 9   To divest thought of false *t·*
   t 455–24   does not bestow His highest *t·* upon the

trustworthiness
   pr 15–30   *T·* is the foundation of enlightened faith.
   a 23–23   these two definitions, *trustfulness* and *t·*.
   23–30   demands self-reliant *t·*, which includes

Truth (*see also* **Truth's**)
accept
   p 420–11   for if they will only accept *T·*,
acceptance of
   f 202–13   the perception and acceptance of *T·*.
acknowledgment of
   p 372–28   a just acknowledgment of *T·*
action of
   ph 169–27   Only the action of *T·*, Life, and Love can
   183–18   legitimate and only possible action of *T·*
   p 386–13   through the action of *T·* on the minds of
adherents of
   r 497– 3   As adherents of *T·*, we take the inspired Word
affluence of
   a 54– 4   With the affluence of *T·*, he vanquished error.
afraid to trust
   ph 181–23   if you adhere to error and are afraid to trust *T·*,
all
   pr 11–31   will bring us into all *T·*.
all is
   r 475– 2   To Truth there is no error,— all is *T·*.
allness— of
   o 346–13   the somethingness— yea, the allness— of *T·*.
all of
   r 495– 4   All of *T·* is not understood ;
altar of
   t 454–22   Love is priestess at the altar of *T·*.
and error
   a 19– 6   for *T·* and error are irreconcilable.
   ph 167–24   with Spirit and matter, *T·* and error.
   f 207–18   such as the amalgamation of *T·* and error
   211– 3   Spirit and matter, *T·* and error,
   b 283–15   They speak of both *T·* and error as *mind*,
   287– 9   *T·* and error are unlike.
   296–24   When the evidence of . . . *T·* and error, seems
   315–32   Spirit and the flesh, between *T·* and error.
   p 372–20   can we believe in . . . both *T·* and error,
   g 538– 9   the infinite distance between *T·* and error,
   539–19   It is false to say that *T·* and error commingle
   gl 586–16   line of demarcation between *T·* and error,
and good
   s 114– 6   the divine Mind, or *T·* and good.
   g 529–27   neither origin nor support in *T·* and good.

Truth
and Life
   pr 5–24   as it is destroyed by Christ,— *T·* and Life.
   a 30–21   to point out the way of *T·* and Life.
   37–25   by the demonstration of *T·* and Life,
   43–32   *T·* and Life must seal the victory over error and
   b 274–13   and they demonstrate *T·* and Life.
   288–30   made him the Way-shower, *T·* and Life.
   p 410– 7   the knowledge of Love, *T·*, and Life.
and Love
   pr 4– 1   While the heart is far from divine *T·* and Love,
   12–15   man's unity with *T·* and Love.
   14–22   and present with *T·* and Love.
   15–20   to work and watch for wisdom, *T·*, and Love.
   a 21– 5   our part in the at-one-ment with *T·* and Love.
   24– 1   *T·* and Love understood and practised.
   25– 2   the great proof of *T·* and Love.
   28– 7   is the persecutor of *T·* and Love.
   31–13   the healing power of *T·* and Love.
   36– 3   in the blessed company of *T·* and Love
   40–24   through the triumphal arch of *T·* and Love.
   45–15   failed to hide immortal *T·* and Love in a
   48–14   *T·* and Love bestow few palms until the
   48–20   The great demonstrator of *T·* and Love
   50–31   the world's hatred of *T·* and Love.
   51–24   He was inspired by God, by *T·* and Love,
   m 57–19   Happiness is spiritual, born of *T·* and Love.
   sp 88–26   Eloquence re-echoes the strains of *T·* and Love.
   95– 8   our fidelity to *T·* and Love ;
   an 106–11   governed by his Maker, divine *T·* and Love.
   ph 192–27   We walk in the footsteps of *T·* and Love
   f 216–18   submission to everlasting Life and *T·* and Love.
   231–19   beliefs which divine *T·* and Love destroy.
   c 255– 4   the perpetual demand of *T·* and Love,
   261– 2   Look away from the body into *T·* and Love,
   265– 4   as his treasures of *T·* and Love are enlarged.
   b 270–26   *T·* and Love alone can unmake them.
   274– 1   *T·* and Love antidote this mental miasma,
   279–20   demonstration of eternal Life and *T·* and Love.
   298–29   pure thoughts . . . winged with *T·* and Love,
   308–20   a message from *T·* and Love, appeared to him
   308–25   the light of *T·* and Love dawns upon thee.
   314–28   demands of its divine Principle, *T·* and Love,
   332–27   only purity could reflect *T·* and Love,
   p 394–27   to conquer discord . . . with *T·* and Love
   395–20   nurse should be . . . receptive to *T·* and Love.
   417–15   unshaken understanding of *T·* and Love,
   418–24   and especially by the spirit of *T·* and Love,
   t 445–20   quiets fear with *T·* and Love,
   448–23   the grand results of *T·* and Love.
   455– 1   into accord with the spirit of *T·* and Love,
   463–14   conceived and born of *T·* and Love,
   r 472– 2   and that this Life is *T·* and Love ;
   476–30   that is, *T·* and Love reign in the real man,
   490– 7   C. S. reveals *T·* and Love as the
   495–30   abiding steadfastly in wisdom, *T·*, and Love.
   496–12   the healing power of *T·* and Love
   g 510– 9   *T·* and Love enlighten the understanding,
   516– 4   substance, Life, intelligence, *T·*, and Love,
   540–30   he is not the type of *T·* and Love.
   ap 558–17   pillars of fire, foundations of *T·* and Love.
   559–26   the nature, or primal elements, of *T·* and Love,
   561– 1   ignorance of *T·* and Love.
   561– 1   The understanding of *T·* and Love,
   565–21   with the fervent heat of *T·* and Love,
   567– 3   *T·* and Love come nearer in the hour of woe,
   567–10   *T·* and Love prevail against the dragon
   gl 583–12   CHURCH. The structure of *T·* and Love ;
   584– 2   light, the spiritual idea of *T·* and Love.
apostles of
   a 40–21   apostles of *T·* may endure human brutality
appearing of
   f 230– 7   the advanced appearing of *T·*,
arraigns
   p 440– 4   *T·* arraigns before the supreme bar of Spirit
arrive at
   r 468– 1   Thus we arrive at *T·*, or intelligence,
ashamed before
   g 532–19   Ashamed before *T·*, error shrank abashed
bar of
   p 437– 8   At the bar of *T·*, in the presence of
   437–30   unjust usages were not allowed at the bar of *T·*,
   440–26   standing at the bar of *T·*,
based on
   s 124– 1   based on *T·*, the Principle of all science.
battle of
   b 292– 2   will end the battle of *T·* with error
belief in
   b 297–26   belief in *T·* is better than a belief in error,
blaze of
   b 296–15   and they must go out under the blaze of *T·*,
blessing of
   r 488– 6   receive the blessing of *T·*.
capacities of
   f 202–22   and the infinite capacities of *T·*,

Truth

casts out
  s 135–13   when *T·* casts out the evil called disease,
  ph 183–26   *T·* casts out all evils
  b 282– 1   Now, as of old, *T·* casts out evils
  o 350–11   Then they know how *T·* casts out error
  r 482–26   Sickness is part of the error which *T·* casts out.
  495– 2   *T·* casts out error now as surely as
celestial
  c 267–25   in which all error disappears in celestial *T·*.
Christ is
  a 18–16   Christ is *T·*, which reaches
Christ, or
  (see **Christ**)
claim of
  b 329–25   maintains the claim of *T·* by quenching error.
claims of
  sp 92–28   instead of urging the claims of *T·* alone.
comes
  b 290–12   Hence *T·* comes to destroy this error
condition of
  f 230– 7   to destroy a quality or condition of *T·* ?
consciousness of
  f 218– 7   The consciousness of *T·* rests us
contradiction of
  r 472–17   Error is the contradiction of *T·*.
controls error
  s 145–17   this advantage . . . that in it *T·* controls error.
counterfeits of
  c 267–22   erroneous beliefs must be counterfeits of *T·*.
course of
  gl 593–16   unobstructed, it typifies the course of *T·* ;
coward before
  p 368– 5   Error is a coward before *T·*.
creations of
  b 287– 4   which simulates the creations of *T·*.
creative
  g 549–29   Spirit as the divine origin of creative *T·*,
currents of
  a 24– 9   the buoys and healing currents of *T·*
decapitates error
  c 266– 3   Science, with which *T·* decapitates error,
defeat in
  f 239–13   success in error is defeat in *T·*.
demands of
  ph 170–14   The demands of *T·* are spiritual,
  b 325–20   Paul had a clear sense of the demands of *T·*
  t 450–13   They do not . . . whine over the demands of *T·*,
demonstrable
  r 487–10   founded on Science or demonstrable *T·*,
demonstrable in
  an 100–17   such methods as are demonstrable in *T·*
demonstrated
  b 280– 1   *T·* demonstrated is eternal life.
  ap 559–15   Then is the power of *T·* demonstrated,
demonstrates
  b 294–31   for *T·* demonstrates the falsity of error.
demonstration of
  pr 2–17   Goodness attains the demonstration of *T·*.
  a 37–25   by the demonstration of *T·* and Life,
  s 135–31   in demonstration of *T·*, as must be the case
  t 445–12   understanding and demonstration of *T·*
denial of
  p 372–27   In C. S., a denial of *T·* is fatal,
denying
  o 342– 7   the sad effects on the sick of denying *T·*.
deprived of
  r 490–14   mortals are more or less deprived of *T·*.
destroyed by
  b 294–18   destroyed by *T·* through spiritual sense
  338– 8   the error which must be destroyed by *T·*.
destroys
  a 23–10   an error of sinful sense which *T·* destroys,
  sp 72–12   *T·* destroys mortality,
  s 143– 1   and *T·* destroys only what is untrue.
  f 243–31   They are inharmonies which *T·* destroys.
  b 288–31   The eternal *T·* destroys what mortals seem
  289–16   a mortal belief, or error, which *T·* destroys
  p 420– 1   nor go from one part to another, for *T·* destroys
  r 474–31   *T·* destroys falsity and error,
destroys error
  b 339– 2   *T·* destroys error, and Love destroys hate.
  o 350–30   Soul rebukes sense, and *T·* destroys error.
discernment of
  o 346–16   and leads to the discernment of *T·*.
dispensation of
  b 270–16   the new dispensation of *T·*.
divine
  (see **divine**)
does not distribute
  p 408–20   *T·* does not distribute drugs through the blood,
does the work
  t 456–22   *T·* does the work, and you must both
drawn from
  o 360– 2   real and eternal because drawn from *T·*,

Truth

easier to desire
  b 322–32   It is easier to desire *T·* than to
effects of
  s 126–25   the effects of *T·* on the health, longevity,
  p 386–14   corresponding effects of *T·* on the body,
energies of
  ph 186– 4   and filling it with the divine energies of *T·*.
  f 252– 5   and of the recuperative energies of *T·*
error and
  o 356–13   as the two opposites, — as error and *T·*,
  356–18   nor an eternal copartnership between error and *T·*,
error, credits
  g 528–15   error, credits *T·*, God, with inducing a
error, not
  p 386–25   Error, not *T·*, produces all the suffering
  r 474–27   error, not *T·*, is the author of the unreal,
eternal
  sp 95–32   lifts human consciousness into eternal *T·*.
  ph 170–13   points to the self-sustaining and eternal *T·*.
  178–21   must finally yield to the eternal *T·*,
  c 255– 1   Eternal *T·* is changing the universe.
  b 288–31   The eternal *T·* destroys what mortals seem
  p 434–14   the bar of Justice and eternal *T·*.
evasion of
  t 448–10   Evasion of *T·* cripples integrity,
everlasting
  b 286–28   are the antipodes of everlasting *T·*,
evidence of
  o 353– 8   having the stronger evidence of *T·*
existent in
  s 120–22   reveals man as harmoniously existent in *T·*,
explanation of
  t 453– 9   chemicalization follows the explanation of *T·*,
expositions of
  pref ix–16   not complete nor satisfactory expositions of *T·*.
faith in
  b 286– 7   gives full faith in *T·*,
  t 446–21   strengthens hope, enthrones faith in *T·*,
find refuge in
  sp 83– 8   Mortals must find refuge in *T·*
flames of
  ap 558–18   flames of *T·* were prophetically described
followers of
  a 33– 6   the persecuted followers of *T·*.
footsteps of
  ph 192–27   We walk in the footsteps of *T·* and Love
  f 241–24   the footsteps of *T·*, the way to health
for teaching
  o 343– 2   smitten for healing and for teaching *T·*
fosters the idea
  g 555–32   *T·* fosters the idea of Truth,
from error to
  p 370–31   from error to *T·*, from matter to Spirit.
God is
  b 312–19   yet God *is* *T·*.
God, or
  s 130–27   the supremacy of God, or *T·*,
  144–10   afford faint gleams of God, or *T·*.
golden with
  s 121–12   happy sunshine, golden with *T·*.
grace and
  m 67–23   Grace and *T·* are potent beyond all other
harmonious
  o 351–26   the all-inclusiveness of harmonious *T·*.
has come
  a 34– 5   instead of showing, . . . that *T·* has come to the
has no beginning
  b 307–25   *T·* has no beginning.
hatred of
  b 330– 5   and the human hatred of *T·*,
heals
  s 135–12   when *T·* heals the sick, it casts out evils,
  o 344–11   Were it more fully understood that *T·* heals
heals with
  b 318–23   Science of Mind . . . heals with *T·*.
higher sense of
  gl 589–19   higher sense of *T·* rebuking mortal belief,
ideal
  r 473–10   Christ is the ideal *T·*, that comes to heal
ideal of
  a 30–19   As the individual ideal of *T·*, Christ Jesus
  f 207–29   is harmonious and is the ideal of *T·*.
idea of
  (see **idea**)
ideas of
  g 543–26   Ideas of *T·* alone are reflected in the
immortal
  a 45–15   had failed to hide immortal *T·* and Love in a
  sp 72–14   and immortal *T·* (the spiritual sense)
  f 204– 7   conclusively mental as immortal *T·* ;
  o 357–22   in a false supposition, not in immortal *T·*,
  p 401–17   when immortal *T·* is destroying erroneous

Truth

immortal
p 415–26   instruct mortal mind with immortal *T*·.
r 468–12   Spirit is immortal *T*· ;
g 548–15   and so aids the apprehension of immortal *T*·.

impressions from
f 214– 1   impressions from *T*· were as distinct as sound,

incarnation of
g 501–10   The incarnation of *T*·, that amplification of

infinite
sp 94– 3   Man reflects infinite *T*·, Life, and Love.
o 361–26   A germ of infinite *T*·, . . . is the
p 367–24   The infinite *T*· of the Christ-cure has come
r 470– 8   spiritual presence of Life as infinite *T*·
g 504–23   The rays of infinite *T*·, when gathered into

infinitude of
c 258–16   all that exists in the infinitude of *T*·.

influence of
s 146–25   through the holy influence of *T*·
r 474–24   Despite the hallowing influence of *T*·

innocence and
ap 568– 1   Innocence and *T*· overcome guilt and error.

inseparable in
p 404–28   Both cures . . . are inseparable in *T*·.

instructed by
p 426– 3   mortal mind, when instructed by *T*·, yields

intelligence, and to
g 517– 9   corresponds to creation, to intelligence, and to *T*·.

is able
ph 191–31   *T*· is able to cast out the ills of the flesh.

is affirmative
p 418–20   *T*· is affirmative, and confers harmony.

is an alterative
p 371–30   *T*· is an alterative in the entire system,

is a revelation
s 117–27   *T*· is a revelation.

is demonstrable
b 323–15   We must recollect that *T*· is demonstrable

is divine
b 287–10   In Science, *T*· is divine,

is ever truthful
s 129– 5   *T*· is ever truthful, and can tolerate no error

is God's remedy
s 142–31   *T*· is God's remedy for error of every kind,

is immortal
r 466–13   *T*· is immortal ; error is mortal.
468– 4   If *T*· is immortal, error must be mortal,

is infinite
p 367–30   Because *T*· is infinite, error should be known as

is intelligent
r 466–14   *T*· is intelligent ;

is limitless
r 466–13   *T*· is limitless ; error is limited.

is made manifest
b 316– 9   to show that *T*· is made manifest by its effects

is omnipotent
p 367–31   Because *T*· is omnipotent in goodness,

is overcoming
a 21– 1   If *T*· is overcoming error in your daily walk

is real
b 288– 1   The statement that *T*· *is real*
p 368– 4   *T*· is real and error is unreal.
r 466–15   *T*· is real, and error is unreal.

is the intelligence
b 282–26   *T*· is the intelligence of immortal Mind.

is their remedy
t 461–24   and *T*· is their remedy.

is the light
b 282–32   but *T*· is the light which dispels error.

is the rock
p 380– 5   *T*· is the rock of ages, the headstone of the

its opposite
b 282–32   infers from error its opposite, *T*· ;

judgment of
p 391– 5   delivered to the judgment of *T*·,

kingdom of
b 281– 3   into the kingdom of *T*· on earth

knowledge of
s 128–22   So it is with our knowledge of *T*·.

law of
r 482–28   C. S. is the law of *T*·, which heals the sick
g 530– 3   spiritual law of *T*· is made manifest

leaven of
s 118–10   but this leaven of *T*· is ever at work.

Life and
s 117–18   illustrating and demonstrating Life and *T*·
f 216–18   is in submission to everlasting Life and *T*·
b 279–20   demonstration of eternal Life and *T*·
304– 2   sweet sense and presence of Life and *T*·.

Life, and Love
pr 15– 5   but lets in *T*·, Life, and Love.
a 18– 2   whereby man reflects divine *T*·, Life, and Love.
26–14   *T*·, Life, and Love gave Jesus authority
41–14   proofs of *T*·, Life, and Love, which Jesus gave
49–23   able, through *T*·, Life, and Love, to triumph

Truth

Life, and Love
sp 94– 3   Man reflects infinite *T*·, Life, and Love.
s 137–20   *T*·, Life, and Love, which heals mentally.
ph 169–27   Only the action of *T*·, Life, and Love can
184–12   *T*·, Life, and Love are the only legitimate
f 243–27   *T*·, Life, and Love are a law of annihilation to
p 435–32   jurisdiction . . . of *T*·, Life, and Love.
r 468–18   *T*·, Life, and Love are substance,
497–17   *T*·, Life, and Love as demonstrated
g 504–13   since *T*·, Life, and Love fill immensity
gl 595– 2   symbol of Soul . . . of *T*·, Life, and Love.

Life, . . . and Love
(see **Life**)

Life, Love
sp 81–15   Life, Love, *T*·, is the only proof of

Life or
a 42– 6   It cannot make Life or *T*· apparent.
ph 196–16   are not concomitants of Life or *T*·.

Life, or Love
f 207–25   presuppose the absence of *T*·, Life, or Love.

Life that is
sp 97–30   demonstrating the Life that is *T*·,

Life which is
a 35–23   as we reach the Life which is *T*·

lifts her voice
sp 97–23   for the higher *T*· lifts her voice,

light of
p 418–32   which flee before the light of *T*·.
g 557–20   rolls back the clouds of error with the light of *T*·,

lispings of
pref ix– 3   were only infantile lispings of *T*·.

Love and
a 19– 3   Love and *T*· are not at war with God's image
f 227–19   Love and *T*· make free,
r 470– 3   brotherhood of man would consist of Love and *T*·,
gl 596–17   the spiritual inspiration of Love and *T*·

majesty of
ap 564–19   Until the majesty of *T*· should be demonstrated

may annihilate
g 540–15   that *T*· may annihilate all sense of evil

Messiahship of
sp 95–25   Magi of old foretold the Messiahship of *T*·.

might of
pref vii–27   author's discovery of the might of *T*·

ministry of
ap 574–10   This ministry of *T*·, this message from

murmur not over
ap 559–23   but murmur not over *T*·, if you find

name of
t 456– 3   Teaching or practising in the name of *T*·,

never mingles
ph 191–29   in C. S., *T*· never mingles with error.

no pain in
s 113–28   There is no pain in *T*·, and no truth in pain ;

no reaction in
p 419–10   knowing that there can be no reaction in *T*·.

not resist
s 128–24   he should not resist *T*·, which banishes

not the result of
r 486–12   Death is not the result of *T*·

not towards
f 205–29   towards the side of error, not towards *T*·.

obedience to
ph 183–23   Obedience to *T*· gives man power

obliterated by
r 485–10   views of error ought to be obliterated by *T*·.

omnipotence of
t 454– 4   Teach your students the omnipotence of *T*·,

omnipotent
c 257–29   inexhaustible Love, eternal Life, omnipotent *T*·.
o 353–11   omnipotent *T*· certainly does destroy error.

opposer of
gl 580–15   the opposer of *T*·, termed error ;

opposite of
(see **opposite**)

or error
f 211– 5   and who shall say whether *T*· or error
b 324–10   whether it be *T*· or error,

or Life
sp 91–14   is by no means the destruction of *T*· or Life,

or Love
f 234– 4   Whatever inspires with wisdom, *T*·, or Love

or Mind
r 483– 5   which nothing but *T*· or Mind can heal,

overcome by
f 231– 4   rightly met and fairly overcome by *T*·,

overcomes
p 420–17   *T*· overcomes both disease and sin

pathway of
r 487– 5   gained by walking in the pathway of *T*·

permanence of
f 215– 3   and the might and permanence of *T*·.

Truth

pierces the error
   f 210–20   and *T·* pierces the error of mortality
places
   g 538– 5   *T·* places the cherub wisdom at the gate
potency is
   b 293–15   whose potency is *T·*, whose attraction is Love,
power of
   a 20–19   and when error felt the power of *T·*,
      31–13   the healing power of *T·* and Love.
      40–19   show us the way and the power of *T·*.
   s 111–13   utilization of the power of *T·* over error ;
     137– 2   His students saw this power of *T·*
     146–26   This healing power of *T·* must
     150– 2   monuments to the virtue and power of *T·*,
     150– 4   To-day the healing power of *T·* is
   p 378–17   represents the power of *T·* over error,
     380–20   Nothing but the power of *T·* can prevent the
     412–16   the power of *T·*, ... must break the dream
   r 495–11   in the life-giving power of *T·* acting on
     496–12   the healing power of *T·* and Love
   ap 559–15   Then is the power of *T·* demonstrated,
practical
   a 31–15   It is the living Christ, the practical *T·*,
practice of
   a 26–22   Jesus' teaching and practice of *T·*
   p 410–25   does not appear in the practice of *T·*
practised
   f 201– 1   best sermon ever preached is *T·* practised
proceeds from
   p 419–21   If the action proceeds from *T·*,
produced by
   p 421–23   the alterative effect produced by *T·*
protests of
   pr 12–14   deep and conscientious protests of *T·*,
reality and
   gl 580–30   not one who . . . sustains reality and *T·*.
recognition of
   t 450–11   open to the approach and recognition of *T·*.
reflection, of
   gl 581– 8   ARK. Safety ; the idea, or reflection, of *T·*,
regard for
   p 364–26   do they show their regard for *T·*, or Christ,
regenerates
   f 222– 8   whereas *T·* regenerates this fleshly mind
relation to
   s 113–14   showing . . . their exact relation to *T·*.
reliance on
   ph 167–31   Only through radical reliance on *T·*
remedy of
   s 140– 1   demands the remedy of *T·* more than
resistance to
   b 317– 9   Resistance to *T·* will haunt his steps,
rest in
   p 387–11   we are able to rest in *T·*, refreshed by the
reveal
   r 485– 2   If error is necessary to define or to reveal *T·*,
revealed
   t 457– 1   and registered the revealed *T·*
revealed by
   gl 593–29   FINAL. The signet of error revealed by *T·*.
revelation of
   a 29–23   brought forth her child by the revelation of *T·*,
   sp 98–19   Christ's revelation of *T·*, of Life, and of Love,
   s 109–22   The revelation of *T·* in the understanding
   g 504–11   it is the revelation of *T·* and of spiritual ideas.
rule of
   p 418–22   simple rule of *T·*, which governs all reality.
sanctuary of
   f 232–26   In the sacred sanctuary of *T·* are voices of
seed of
   b 271– 1   seed of *T·* springs up and bears much fruit.
   g 535– 1   The seed of *T·* and the seed of error,
seek
   f 254–11   When we wait patiently on God and seek *T·*
   b 286– 2   To seek *T·* through belief in a human doctrine
   p 364–18   Do Christian Scientists seek *T·* as Simon sought
seeker of
   pref x–23   personal experience of any sincere seeker of *T·*.
seekers for
   pref xii–26   commits these pages to honest seekers for *T·*.
   ap 570–15   simple seekers for *T·*, weary wanderers,
seeking
   p 367–10   This is what is meant by seeking *T·*, Christ,
sends a report
   ph 194– 9   *T·* sends a report of health over the body.
separated from
   g 505– 8   material sense, is separated from *T·*,
somethingness named
   b 276–28   Harmony is the *somethingness* named *T·*.
Spirit and
   ph 177–24   nor can a lie . . . against God, Spirit and *T·*.
   b 278–15   as we approach Spirit and *T·*, we lose the
spirit of
   p 391– 1   in the conscious strength of the spirit of *T·*
     418–24   especially by the spirit of *T·* and Love

Truth

spirit of
   p 427– 4   even the law of the spirit of *T·*,
   t 455– 1   into accord with the spirit of *T·* and Love,
spiritual
   (see **spiritual**)
spiritual sense of
   b 315–18   which beclouds the spiritual sense of *T·* ;
   t 452–22   When the spiritual sense of *T·* unfolds its
standard of
   a 31– 2   are unfit to bear the standard of *T·*,
   f 235–29   should uplift the standard of *T·*.
   r 472–22   should continue to lose the standard of *T·*.
strength of
   p 365–31   not giving . . . the joy and strength of *T·*.
struggle for
   p 426–10   The struggle for *T·* makes one strong
subjection to
   f 240–29   is finally brought into subjection to *T·*.
subordination to
   f 206– 5   exercised only in subordination to *T·* ;
sunlight of
   s 162– 5   C. S. brings to the body the sunlight of *T·*,
sunshine of
   b 299–28   the sunshine of *T·*, will melt away the
superstructure of
   gl 595– 8   superstructure of *T·* ; the shrine of Love ;
supremacy of
   p 406–22   to avail ourselves . . . of the supremacy of *T·*
   ap 569– 9   when we are conscious of the supremacy of *T·*,
   gl 589–21   the immortality and supremacy of *T·* ;
sustained by
   t 447–15   when mentally sustained by *T·*,
sword of
   t 458–18   two-edged sword of *T·* must turn in every
   g 538– 7   the sword of *T·* gleams afar
symbol of
   gl 591–23   MORNING. Light ; symbol of *T·* ;
testified for
   s 134– 5   who testified for *T·* were so often persecuted
text of
   pref x–13   but has bluntly and honestly given the text of
           T·.
that is Life
   sp 07 30   again demonstrating . . . the *T·* that is Life,
the ever-present
   b 297–23   *T·*, the ever-present, is becoming understood.
this living
   ph 180–28   The only way to this living *T·*,
touched by
   pref x–26   unbiased Christian thought is soonest touched by *T·*.
touch of
   t 450–15   Some people yield slowly to the touch of *T·*.
transformed by
   ph 191–14   transformed by *T·* on its pinions of light,
transparency for
   b 295–22   in order to become a better transparency for *T·*.
treasures of
   sp 70– 5   revelations of C. S. unlock the treasures of *T·*,
   f 241–11   hate, revenge, . . . steal away the treasures of *T·*.
   c 265– 4   as the treasures of *T·* and Love are enlarged,
trumpet-word of
   p 427–32   to catch this trumpet-word of *T·*,
trusting
   f 226–32   trusting *T·*, the strong deliverer, to guide me
truth of
   b 320– 2   Likewise we can speak of the truth of *T·*
unalterable
   pr 11–28   Prayer cannot change the unalterable *T·*,
unbelief" in
   p 401– 1   "because of their unbelief" in *T·*.— *Matt.* 13 : 58.
understand
   s 110–31   believe on Christ and . . . understand *T·*.
understanding of
   (see **understanding**)
universe of
   g 503–10   In the universe of *T·*, matter is unknown.
unknown to
   ph 184– 4   for these are unknown to *T·*
unlike
   r 468– 6   because error is unlike *T·*.
unlikeness of
   r 471– 6   The unlikeness of *T·*,— named *error,*
unseen
   r 481–11   do not change the unseen *T·*,
unsustained by
   c 264–22   Sin is unsustained by *T·*,
utterance of
   g 545– 4   This could not be the utterance of *T·* or Science,
verdict of
   o 358–15   It presents the calm and clear verdict of *T·*
voice of
   (see **voice**)

Truth

what is
pref viii–12   The question, What is *T·*, is answered by
   a 48–26   question, "What is *T·*," — *John* 18 : 38.
   f 223–14   The question, "What is *T·*," — *John* 18 : 38.
wisdom, or
   f 206– 9   no other Love, wisdom, or *T·*,
words of
   o 342–24   It speaks to the dumb the words of *T·*,
work of
   g 528–21   error now simulates the work of *T·*,
world of
   pr 13–30   The world of error is ignorant of the world of *T·*,
yields to
   b 329–31   opposition to spirituality, till error yields to *T·*.
   g 543– 3   This error,. . . yields to *T·* and returns to dust ;
yield to
   s 152– 2   and must by its own consent yield to *T·*.
   ph 176–30   are quite as ready to yield to *T·* as the
   b 287–30   Their false evidence will finally yield to *T·*,

      —

pref vii– 7   the human herald of Christ, *T·*,
    vii–13   *T·*, . . . knocks at the portal of humanity.
  pr   9–25   Are you willing to leave all for Christ, for *T·*,
    11–17   *T·* bestows no pardon upon error,
    12–10   neither Science nor *T·* which acts through
    15– 6   Closed to error, it is open to *T·*,
    16– 5   between *T·* that is sinless and the
    17–14   *all Life, T·, Love, over all,*
    18–18   *T·*, could conciliate no nature above his own,
  a   19– 5   Even Christ cannot reconcile *T·* to error,
    30–24   between the offspring . . . of *T·* and of error.
    34– 6   If Christ, *T·*, has come to us in demonstration,
    35– 6   Discerning Christ, *T·*, anew on the shore of
    35–12   They bow before Christ, *T·*,
    35–23   the Life which is Truth and the *T·* which is Life
    35–27   Our bread, . . . from heaven," is *T·*. —*John* 6 : 33.
    36– 7   would be for *T·* to pardon error.
    37– 7   Mortals try in vain to slay *T·*
    38–31   He taught that the material senses shut out *T·*
    47–23   the world generally loves a lie better than *T·* ;
    53–21   distance between the individual and *T·*.
  m   65– 3   May Christ, *T·*, be present at every bridal altar
  sp   83–11   belief hides *T·* and builds on error.
    99– 9   *T·* has furnished the key to the kingdom,
  an 103–23   This belief has not one quality of *T·*.
  s 115–13   God : Divine Principle, Life, *T·*, Love,
    118– 8   second appearing in the flesh of the Christ, *T·*,
    126–31   straight and narrow way" of *T·*. —*see Matt.* 7 : 14.
    129–15   "Art thou [*T·*] come hither to— *Matt.* 8 : 29.
    134– 9   The new faith in the Christ, *T·*, so roused the
    142– 9   for Christ, *T·*, alone can furnish
    144–20   *T·*, and not corporeal will, is the divine power
    144–24   even as *T·* wars with error,
    144–28   *T·* will be the universal panacea.
    145–12   *T·*, subdues the human belief in disease.
    147–10   *T·* has lost none of its divine and
    149– 1   *T·* could save from sickness as well as from
    149–14   have not demonstrated the life of Christ, *T·*,
    152– 8   *T·* has a healing effect, even when
    162– 7   neutralizing error with *T·*.
  ph 170– 2   *T·* is not the basis of theogony.
    171– 5   through Christ, *T·*, man will reopen
    173– 8   supposition, . . . *T·* is reduced to the level of
    174–20   *T·* is revealed.
    176–31   *T·* handles the most malignant contagion
    181–10   in electricity and magnetism more than in *T·*,
    181–30   If you have more faith in drugs than in *T·*,
    182– 3   casting out error with *T·*, shows your position
    183–14   *T·* never made error necessary,
    184– 3   *T·* makes no laws to regulate sickness,
  f 201– 7   *T·* makes a new creature,
    202–26   *T·* should "much more abound." — *Rom.* 5 : 20.
    208–11   antipode of immortal Mind, of *T·*,
    216– 8   *T·* bruises the head of error
    224–28   *T·* brings the elements of liberty.
    225– 3   *T·* makes man free.
    225– 5   You may know when first *T·* leads
    228–24   and form and control it with *T·*.
    229–31   The remedy is *T·*, not matter,
    230– 2   if true, it is a part of *T·*.
    231–10   but God, *T·*, Life, Love, does heal
    236–32   makes easy and rapid strides towards *T·*.
    238–12   To fall away from *T·* in times of persecution,
    238–13   shows that we never understood *T·*.
    238–19   *T·* often remains unsought, until we
    242–21   The vesture of Life is *T·*.
    243–25   *T·* has no consciousness of error.
    251–11   *T·* works out the nothingness of error
    251–13   an error that Christ, *T·*, alone can destroy.
    253– 5   saith: . . . I give immortality to man, for I
            am *T·*.
  c 260–32   If we look to the body . . . for *T·*, we find error ;
  b 271– 9   in *T·*, casting out all inharmony,
    271–27   to cast them on the right side for *T·*,

Truth

  b 272– 4   must be gained before *T·* can be understood.
    275–12   Spirit, Life, *T·*, Love, combine as one,
    275–31   *T·*, spiritually discerned, is scientifically
    278– 8   even as in *T·* there is no error,
    279–15   no more . . . than *T·* can create error, or
    280– 9   Finite belief can never do justice to *T·*
    282–17   *T·* has no home in error,
    282–18   and error has no foothold in *T·*.
    285–31   Christ, *T·*, as the healing and saving power.
    286–11   Christ, Life, *T·*, Love ;
    287– 9   We call the absence of *T·*, error.
    287–11   Did God, *T·*, create error?
    287–32   *T·* cannot be contaminated by error.
    289–12   Life and Life's idea, *T·* and Truth's idea,
    290–21   Christ, *T·*, removes all ignorance and sin.
    292– 7   *T·* will be to us "the resurrection— *John* 11 : 25.
    293–29   C. S. brings to light *T·* and its supremacy,
    295–20   through which *T·* appears most vividly
    298–10   spiritual sense can bear witness only to *T·*.
    299–24   *T·* never destroys God's idea.
    299–24   *T·* is spiritual, eternal substance,
    299–26   error, may seem to hide *T·*,
    300–32   in that which reflects Life, *T·*, Love,
    304–19   *T·* is not contaminated by error.
    306– 1   who believed error to be as immortal as *T·*.
    307– 6   as real and eternal as *T·*.
    307–17   It says : . . . *T·* shall change sides
    307–17   Error charges its lie to *T·*
    308–22   *T·*, being thereby understood, gave him
    312–18   Mortals try to believe without understanding
            T· ;
    316– 7   Christ, *T·*, was demonstrated through
    316–19   thus proved that *T·* was the master of death.
    322– 7   Christianity, or *T·*, in its divine Principle.
    324–27   "If Christ [*T·*] be not risen,— *I Cor.* 15 : 14.
    325– 7   *T·*, unfolding its own immortal idea.
    325–18   with *T·* in divine Love,
    325–30   When first spoken in any age, *T·*,
    326– 3   If we wish to follow Christ, *T·*,
    330– 1   as mortals give up error for *T·*
    330–20   Scriptures declare Him to be,— Life, *T·*, Love.
    332–14   the Way, the *T·*, and the Life,
    333–23   to all prepared to receive Christ, *T·*.
  o 341–10   for they shall see God" [*T·*]. — *Matt.* 5 : 8.
    343–12   and *T·* will not be forever hidden
    346–20   because *T·* is error's antidote.
    347–24   it is Christ, *T·*, who destroys these evils,
    351–14   presence of Christ, *T·*, which healed the sick.
    351–18   while error seems as potent and real to us as *T·*,
    354– 7   to enable them to leave all for Christ, *T·*?
    354–24   and with the dawn *T·* will waken men
    357– 5   We sustain *T·*, . . . by rejecting a lie.
    357– 8   *T·* creates neither a lie, a capacity to lie,
  p 368–10   fatal beliefs that error is as real as *T·*,
    370– 4   turn from the lie of false belief to *T·*,
    374–15   Through immortal Mind, or *T·*,
    380– 4   *T·* is always the victor.
    390– 9   *T·* will at length compel us all
    394– 2   *T·* can destroy its seeming reality,
    403–19   deprived of its imaginary powers by *T·*,
    406–12   and spiritual perception, . . . reaches *T·*.
    410–12   showing that *T·* is the actual life of man ;
    412– 5   plead the case scientifically for *T·*.
    415– 5   disease, and death have no foundations in *T·*.
    420– 3   *T·* not error, Love not hate,
    422–10   the tremor which *T·* often brings to error
    433–31   Ah ! but Christ, *T·*, the spirit of Life
    442–22   Christ, *T·*, gives mortals temporary food and
  t 449– 5   does wonders for mortals, so omnipotent is *T·*,
    450–25   errors of belief, which *T·* can and will destroy.
    451– 1   the errors which *T·* must and will annihilate
    455– 4   or a faltering and doubting trust in *T·*
    462–12   and substituting his own views for *T·*,
    463–19   *T·* is here and has fulfilled its perfect work.
  r 465–10   Spirit, Soul, Principle, Life, *T·*, Love.
    469–17   evil— is not Mind, is not *T·*,
    473– 4   *T·*, God, is not the father of error.
    474– 4   The reception accorded to *T·* in the
    474–25   *T·* spares all that is true.
    474–26   If evil is real, *T·* must make it so ;
    475– 2   To *T·* there is no error,— in *T·* is Truth.
    481–27   impossible, since *T·* cannot support error.
    484–25   and *T·* over error,
    493– 2   C. S. speedily shows *T·* to be triumphant.
    495–23   this understanding will supplant error with *T·*,
  g 506– 7   and makes *T·* final.
    516–10   Life is reflected in existence, *T·* in truthfulness,
    524–22   How could . . . error be the enunciator of *T·*?
    530–24   saying, . . . more to be desired than *T·*,
    533–26   *T·*, cross-questioning man as to his
    535–17   *T·* is indeed "the way." — *John* 14 : 6.
    537–15   *T·* guards the gateway to harmony.
    538– 3   *T·* should, and does, drive error out of
    538– 4   *T·* is a two-edged sword,
    539– 9   the standard of good, of Spirit, of Life, or of *T·*,

Truth

g 542– 3 that it might be rid of troublesome *T·*.
542– 7 *T·*, through her eternal laws, unveils error.
542– 8 *T·* causes sin to betray itself,
542–19 Let *T·* uncover and destroy error in
545–27 *T·* has but one reply to all error,
545–31 even so in Christ [*T·*] — *I Cor.* 15 : 22.
555–27 or that *T·* confers the ability to
ap 567–22 cast out by Christ, *T·*, the spiritual idea,
568–31 by which we lay down all for *T·*, or Christ,
569– 2 as *T·*, represented by the Son ;
572–16 open the seven seals of error with *T·*,
gl 587– 7 Mind ; Soul ; Spirit ; Life ; *T·* ; Love ;
591–17 divine Principle, substance, Life, *T·*, Love ;
593–18 Rock. Spiritual foundation ; *T·*.

truth

about ghosts
o 352–32 not irrational to tell the *t·* about ghosts.
absence of
sp 92–30 when it is merely the absence of *t·*,
ph 186–11 because it is the absence of *t·*.
action of
p 414– 7 yields . . . to the salutary action of *t·*,
all
s 127–23 all *t·* proceeds from the divine Mind.
127–29 the Comforter which leadeth into all *t·*.
b 271–22 it will lead you into all *t·*.
332–22 and leading into all *t·*.
g 505–17 the understanding which . . . leads into all *t·*.
and error
b 287–28 five material senses testify to *t·* and error
288– 3 suppositional warfare between *t·* and error
288–11 the conflict between *t·* and error,
p 368– 6 Both *t·* and error have come nearer than
t 453– 6 *t·* and error, will be at strife
r 466– 9 life and death, *t·* and error,
492–31 would keep *t·* and error always at war.
and harmony
p 423–20 regarding the *t·* and harmony of being
and love
a 50– 4 Who shall decide what *t·* and love are?
f 215–21 phantoms of error before *t·* and love.
p 414–11 *t·* and love will establish a healthy state,
r 473–20 proof of Christianity's *t·* and love ;
and the life
a 26–11 the way, the *t·*, and the life ;" — *John* 14 : 6.
b 320– 3 the way, the *t·*, and the life." — *John* 14 : 6.
o 353–11 "the way, the *t·*, and the life," — *John* 14 : 6.
apprehension of the
sp 80– 2 in proportion to our apprehension of the *t·*,
t 460–18 right apprehension of the *t·* of being.
approaches
sp 97–14 The nearer a false belief approaches *t·*
arbiter of
p 405–12 the arbiter of *t·* against error.
arguments of
p 411– 9 and needed the arguments of *t·* for reminders.
assimilate
t 402– 2 Some individuals assimilate *t·* more readily
attenuation of
s 153–21 a high attenuation of *t·*,
beauty, as well as
f 247–10 Beauty, as well as *t·*, is eternal ;
belief in its
p 300–10 an account of the tenacity of belief in its *t·*,
bites the heel of
f 216– 7 Error bites the heel of *t·*,
bite the heel of
ap 563–20 that he may bite the heel of *t·*
communicates itself
sp 85–31 *t·* communicates itself but never imparts error.
concerning the
p 412– 8 persuaded in your own mind concerning the *t·*
conviction of
p 418– 7 Plead with an honest conviction of *t·*
correlative
b 316–21 the possibilities of Spirit and its correlative *t·*.
demonstrate
s 149–31 dismiss superstition, and demonstrate *t·*
denial of
g 542–11 avoidance of justice and the denial of *t·*
denying the
a 53–23 Instead of denying the *t·*
destroyed by
ph 168–29 if the error . . . was met and destroyed by *t·*.
b 297–12 Erroneous belief is destroyed by *t·*.
discerning the
pref x–29 or discerning the *t·*, come not to the light
effect of
f 224– 2 world feels the alterative effect of *t·*
effects of
f 233–28 tests I have made of the effects of *t·*
enables
p 392– 8 enables *t·* to outweigh error.
erroneous
r 472–21 absurdity — namely, *erroneous t·*.

truth

error simulates
sp 97– 5 the more closely error simulates *t·*
establish in
p 428–13 Thus we may establish in *t·* the temple,
eternal
b 303–14 statement . . . contradicts this eternal *t·*.
explanations of
g 555– 7 said . . . "I like your explanations of *t·*,
exponents of
a 52–18 common cause against the exponents of *t·*.
first appeared
b 324–20 When the *t·* first appeared to him in Science,
formidable in
b 317–19 makes man . . . more formidable in *t·*,
giving utterance to
sp 80– 3 is not lessened by giving utterance to *t·*.
great
a 33– 7 It was the great *t·* of spiritual being,
ph 200–16 The great *t·* in the Science of being.
t 454–13 the great *t·* which strips all disguise from error.
r 469–14 exterminator of error is the great *t·* that
health, and harmony
sp 72–31 the communicator of *t·*, health, and harmony
ignorant of the
p 380–19 a so-called mind ignorant of the *t·*
immortal
r 493– 8 to the immortal *t·* of all things.
infinite tasks of
b 323–10 Beholding the infinite tasks of *t·*,
in his sentiment
ph 176– 1 and there is *t·* in his sentiment.
intelligence and
p 437–12 to be destitute of intelligence and *t·*
interfere with
f 234– 2 material lotions interfere with *t·*,
invincible
t 453– 8 until victory rests on the side of invincible *t·*.
is greater
f 223– 9 Remember that *t·* is greater than error,
is not human
s 127–24 Therefore *t·* is not human,
know the
ap 81–32 we can know the *t·* more accurately than the
t 452–18 teacher must know the *t·* himself.
leadings of
s 151–30 and follow the leadings of *t·*.
life and
c 262–12 reverse . . . our efforts to find life and *t·* in
life, . . . and love
b 284–18 testimony as to spiritual life, *t·*, and love?
***morale* of**
t 456–19 One must abide in the *morale* of *t·*
mutable
g 503–25 mortal life, mutable *t·*, nor variable love.
no
s 113–29 no pain in Truth, and no *t·* in pain ;
b 275–18 no *t·* is true, . . . but the divine ;
302–24 because there is no *t·* in him. — *John* 8 : 44.
r 467– 7 no *t·*, no love, but that which is spiritual.
g 543– 1 having no *t·* to support it,
not the
p 425–11 that they are not the *t·* of man ;
not the equal of
ap 80– 4 A cup of coffee or tea is not the equal of *t·*,
obey the
b 326–22 that ye should not obey the *t·*?" — *Gal.* 5 : 7.
of being
m 68– 1 *t·* of being will be the basis of
69– 8 as man finds the *t·* of being.
sp 84– 8 to be in harmony with the *t·* of being,
s 137– 1 teaching and demonstrating the *t·* of being.
ph 184–20 This is human belief, not the *t·* of being,
f 214–14 still the error, not the *t·* of being.
218–32 When we wake to the *t·* of being,
c 265–21 The *t·* of being is perennial,
b 273–19 importance of understanding the *t·* of being,
311– 1 clouds . . . which hide the *t·* of being.
337–11 The *t·* of being makes man harmonious
p 368–15 to have more faith in the *t·* of being
374– 3 the *t·* of being, whispered into the ear of
401– 7 If faith in the *t·* of being, . . . causes
401–10 *t·* of being must transform the error
403–16 mortal existence is . . . not the *t·* of being.
404– 5 destroy these errors with the *t·* of being,
416– 5 removed by recognizing the *t·* of being.
418– 5 Stick to the *t·* of being
423–10 mental causation, not the *t·* of being,
427– 9 since the *t·* of being is deathless.
t 460–18 right apprehension of the *t·* of being.
r 479–22 in the Science and *t·* of being,
g 538– 2 Until that which contradicts the *t·* of being
553– 7 obtain a better basis, get nearer the *t·* of being,
of Christian Science
s 110–16 afterwards the *t·* of C. S. was demonstrated.

truth
of creation
  sp 93–16 and not the *t·* of creation.
  c 263– 6 spiritual man alone represents the *t·* of creation.
of spiritual sense
  b 318–13 silence this lie . . . with the *t·* of spiritual sense.
of that report
  ph 193–28 I cannot attest the *t·* of that report,
of Truth
  b 320– 2 we can speak of the *t·* of Truth
of your plea
  p 418–10 half equal to the *t·* of your plea,
opposite
  ph 171–28 The opposite *t·*, . . . destroys sin, sickness, and
or error
  p 403–29 in proportion to the *t·* or error which
or Science
  s 127– 6 entitled to a classification as *t·*, or Science,
pioneer of
  a 28–31 await, in some form, every pioneer of *t·*.
pour in
  f 201–18 pour in *t·* through flood-tides of Love.
preached by
  s 141– 2 and the *t·* preached by Jesus.
progress of
  sp 94–17 The progress of *t·* confirms its claims,
proves the
  b 329– 6 proves the *t·* of all that I say of it.
records of
  g 525–26 as to the records of *t·*,
regarding error
  t 461–24 *t·* regarding error is, that error is not true,
Science and
  s 110–23 the Science and *t·* therein will
  r 479–22 in the Science and *t·* of being,
  g 521–23 The Science and *t·* of the divine creation
scientific
  an 104– 9 scientific *t·* goes through three stages.
  g 521–29 the exact opposite of scientific *t·*
search for
  s 152–24 in her search for *t·* ;
should emanate
  f 236– 2 *T·* should emanate from the pulpit,
simple
  sp 75– 1 This simple *t·* lays bare the
speak the
  p 418–29 Speak the *t·* to every form of error.
spirit and in
  a 31–28 in spirit and in *t·*.”— *John* 4 : 23.
  sp 93– 7 in spirit and in *t·*.”— *John* 4 : 23.
  s 140–22 in spirit and in *t·*.”— *John* 4 : 23.
spiritual
  ph 165–15 theories took the place of spiritual *t·*.
  b 277–18 This points to the spiritual *t·*
  293–20 while spiritual *t·* is Mind.
  311–17 loss or absence of soul, spiritual *t·*.
spirituality or
  b 293–18 the true essence of spirituality or *t·*,
spiritual sense of
  b 272– 3 spiritual sense of *t·* must be gained
standard of
  ph 195–32 Incorrect views lower the standard of *t·*.
stating
  s 126– 2 Error will be no longer used in stating *t·*.
supply the
  f 216–14 to supply the *t·* of immortal sense.
that disease
  f 229–31 the *t·* that disease is *unreal*.
to utter
  sp 97–23 It requires courage to utter *t·* ;
triumph of
  f 223–31 and foreshadows the triumph of *t·*.
understanding and
  g 544–29 belief reverses understanding and *t·*.
understanding nor
  b 287–17 Neither understanding nor *t·* accompanies
utterance of
  f 233–30 utterance of *t·* is designed to rebuke
virtue and
  f 235– 1 if virtue and *t·* build a strong defence.
  246–11 The radiant sun of virtue and *t·*
waters of
  f 254–28 the ever-agitated but healthful waters of *t·*,
which heals
  s 158–11 *t·* which heals both mind and body.
whole
  a 19–12 The Master forbore not to speak the whole *t·*,
would be error
  r 472–20 If error were true, its *t·* would be error,

  iii– * Ye shall know the *t·*,— *John* 8 : 32.
  iii– * the *t·* shall make you free.— *John* 8 : 32.
 a 20–25 The *t·* is the centre of all religion.
  24–29 The *t·* had been lived among men ;
  33–13 For this *t·* of spiritual being,
  41–28 *t·* taught by Jesus, the elders scoffed at.

truth
 a 43–17 demonstration of the *t·* which Jesus taught,
  53–20 the shock so often produced by the *t·*,
 m 65–22 until we get at last the clear straining of *t·*,
 sp 72–20 not a . . . sieve through which *t·* can be strained.
  72–28 nor the medium through which *t·* passes to
  77– 3 accomplish the change from error to *t·*
 s 130–19 to make place for *t·*.
  130–32 *T·* should not seem so surprising . . . as error,
  131– 2 error should not seem so real as *t·*.
  134– 2 *t·* is still opposed with sword and spear.
  146–18 *t·* divests material drugs of their
  164– 7 true, or anything like the *t·*,
  164–21 rather does it evidence the *t·* of
 ph 176–23 and the Christian Scientist try *t·* only in
 f 203–18 the image of his Maker in deed and in *t·*.
  213– 5 as a man . . . *understandeth*, so is he in *t·*.
  216– 8 Error . . . cannot kill *t·*.
  223–29 as *t·* urges mortals its
  225– 9 command their sentinels not to let *t·* pass
  231–12 if *t·* results in error,
  233–23 To reveal this *t·* was our Master's
  233–31 Why should *t·* not be efficient
  251–22 acts upon the so-called human mind through *t·*,
 c 259–29 which corrects error with *t·*
 b 269–11 The first is error ; the latter is *t·*.
  273– 3 There is no *material t·*.
  292–24 and abode not in the *t·*,— *John* 8 : 44.
  315–25 conception of Jesus pointed to this *t·*
 o 341– * *And because I tell you the t·*,— *John* 8: 45.
  341– * *And if I say the t·*,— *John* 8: 46.
  341– 2 the *t·*, which is raising up thousands
  342–17 If . . . *t·* becomes an accident.
  343–21 It would sometimes seem as if *t·* were
  360–29 put to death . . . for the *t·* he spoke
 p 368– 8 and *t·* will become still clearer
  378– 6 and meet every circumstance with *t·*.
  400–19 and contending persistently for *t·*,
  411–11 If Spirit . . . bear witness to the *t·*,
  414–15 To fix *t·* steadfastly in your
  442–17 in which *t·* cannot be reversed,
  442–28 This *t·* is C. S.
 t 447–19 impart . . . the *t·* and spiritual understanding,
  448– 9 tell the *t·* concerning the lie.
  454–16 points out . . . error as well as *t·*,
  458–10 the same effect as *t·*.
  463–13 this *t·* removes properly whatever is
 r 468– 9 no life, *t·*, intelligence, nor substance in
  479– 3 With what *t·*, then, could the Scriptural
  482–16 the *t·* casting out all error.
 g 523– 7 the lie claims to be *t·*.
  524–25 Is it the *t·*, or is it a lie
  530–18 error . . . asserting its superiority over *t·*,
  532–23 Is Mind capable of error as well as of *t·*,
  547–25 only by this understanding can *t·* be gained.
  548– 3 C. S. separates error from *t·*,
  555–12 as if it were as real and God-created as *t·* ;

Truth-cure
 f 237–15 Children should be taught the *T·*,
truthful
 s 129– 5 Truth is ever *t·*, and can tolerate no error
 p 418–23 By the *t·* arguments you employ,
  432– 4 and know him to be *t·* and upright,
  437– 3 testified that he. . .knew Personal Sense to be *t·* ;
truthfulness
 a 46– 4 This convinced them of the *t·* of
 g 516–10 Truth in *t·*, God in goodness,
truth-giver
 sp 72–12 Soul, or God, is the only *t·* to man.
Truth-power
 ph 179– 9 and to heal by the *T·*,
  185–24 reverse of ethical and pathological *T·*.
Truth's
 a 55–15 *T·* immortal idea is sweeping down the
 ph 170–27 to touch the hem of *T·* garment.
 b 288– 2 error, *T· unlikeness, is unreal*.
  289–12 Life and Life's idea, Truth and *T·* idea,
 p 367–32 *T·* opposite, has no might.
 t 458–15 *Semper paratus* is *T·* motto.
  462– 9 to practise *T·* teachings only in part,
 r 494–28 eternal and real evidence, bearing *T·* signet,
 ap 558–13 When understood, it is *T·* prism and praise.
truth's
 f 224–16 this was not the manner of *t·* appearing.
  224–16 Of old the cross was *t·* central sign,
  224–21 the harbingers of *t·* full-orbed appearing.
  225–12 there is a rallying to *t·* standard.
truths
 an 103–25 The *t·* of immortal Mind sustain man,
 s 108–21 I learned these *t·* in divine Science :
  111– 2 and the demonstrable *t·* of C. S. ;
  155–16 high and mighty *t·* of Christian metaphysics.
 f 221–23 These *t·*, opening his eyes,
  236–24 the *t·* of health and holiness.

truths

o	356– 1	in support of spiritual and eternal *t*,
r	490– 1	the grand *t·* of C. S. dispute this error.
ap	575–15	Did not Jesus illustrate the *t·* he taught

try

pr	3–19	and then we *t·* to give information to this
	8–16	wise not to *t·* to deceive ourselves or others,
a	37– 6	Mortals *t·* in vain to slay Truth with the steel
s	143–32	may *t·* to make Mind and drugs coalesce,
ph	176–22	and the Christian Scientist *t·* truth only in
	180–22	they should *t·* to correct this turbulent element
f	220–25	never to *t·* dietetics for growth in grace.
	223–17	and *t·* to "give it pause."
	238–17	will rebuke us when we . . . *t·* to reap the
b	312–17	Mortals *t·* to believe without understanding
	326– 7	must not *t·* to climb the hill of Science by
o	354– 4	Why then do Christians *t·* to obey the
	359– 3	Let any clergyman *t·* to cure his friends by
	360–18	If you *t·* to have two models, then you
p	394–15	that he should not *t·* to rise above his
t	448–19	*T·* to leave on every student's mind the
r	495–1	and it would be absurd to *t·*.

trying

s	156–21	After *t·* this, she informed me that she could
	161–27	the very disease he is *t·* to cure,
f	240–27	In *t·* to undo the errors of sense one must
o	346–32	is not this what frail mortals are *t·* to do?
t	453–12	or of *t·* to sustain the human body
ap	568– 8	of *t·* to meet error with error.

trysting-times

m	59–22	a word or deed may renew the old *t·*.

tubercles

ph	175–30	*t·* and troches, lungs and lozenges.
p	418–30	Tumors, ulcers, *t·*, inflammation,
	425– 9	*t·*, hemorrhage, and decomposition are beliefs,
	425–32	Discard all notions about lungs, *t·*,

tubes

ph	175–28	never indulged in . . . inflamed bronchial *t·*.

tumor

ph	180–31	To reduce inflammation, dissolve a *t·*,
p	395–24	erroneous to believe in the real existence of a *t·*,

tumors

s	162– 8	dissolves *t·*, relaxes rigid muscles,
p	418–29	*T·*, ulcers, tubercles, inflammation,

tumult

f	225–12	There is always some *t·*,
b	288–16	the *t·* dies away in the distance.

turbulent

ph	180–22	to correct this *t·* element of mortal mind

turn

pref	x–19	Few invalids will *t·* to God till
pr	8–22	If we *t·* away from the poor,
	11–16	to make him *t·* from it with loathing.
a	40– 1	evil confers no pleasure, they *t·* from it.
m	61–18	live to become parents in their *t·*,
	65– 4	at every bridal altar to *t·* the water into wine
sp	77– 2	Polycarp said : "I cannot *t·* at once
s	142–13	If the . . . *t·* the poor and the stranger from
ph	190– 9	belief . . . in *t·* fills itself with thoughts of
	194–20	in *t·*, mortal mind manifests itself in the body
f	217–11	if we *t·* to the Scriptures, what do we read?
	239– 3	in their *t·* lay it upon those who
	243–16	must first *t·* our gaze in the right direction,
b	316– 5	mortals need only *t·* from sin
	322–11	to *t·* our thoughts towards
	322–28	*t·* us like tired children to the arms of divine
p	370– 3	*t·* from the lie of false belief to Truth,
	416–30	*T·* their thoughts away from their bodies
	420–30	*T·* his gaze from the false evidence of the
t	444–20	*t·* to him the other also." — *Matt.* 5 : 39.
	444–22	If ecclesiastical sects . . . *t·* a deaf ear to the
	458–18	sword of Truth must *t·* in every direction
	458–32	Christianity causes men to *t·* naturally from
g	510–11	and *t·* away from a false material sense.
	521–14	*t·* our gaze to the spiritual record of creation,

turned

pr	14–17	Sorrow is *t·* into joy when the body
a	35– 4	*t·* away from material things,
	37–19	would gladly have *t·* his sacred career into a
	48– 8	*t·* forever away from earth to heaven,
	49–30	*t·* "aside the right of a man — *Lam.* 3 : 35.
s	158– 8	Hippocrates *t·* from image-gods to vegetable
b	276–21	is *t·* into new and healthy channels,
	301–28	with everything *t·* upside down.
	304–11	joy cannot be *t·* into sorrow,
	310–12	when the earth has again *t·* upon its axis.
p	380–14	knows will be *t·* against himself.
	439–15	C. S. *t·* from the abashed witnesses,
t	451–10	or be *t·* sadly awry.
g	537– 7	flaming sword which *t·* every way, — *Gen.* 3 : 24.

turning

s	121–27	besides *t·* daily on its own axis.
f	218–22	instead of *t·* in time of need to God,
b	323–30	We are either *t·* away from this utterance, or
p	438–13	*T·* suddenly to Personal Sense,
t	459–18	*t·* him loose in the crowded streets
r	467–14	Having no other gods, *t·* to no other but the

turns

a	21–10	He constantly *t·* away from material sense,
	21–30	he *t·* east on the seventh, satisfied if he
sp	92–21	Uncover error, and it *t·* the lie upon you.
ph	166–25	and only as a last resort, *t·* to God.
f	240– 8	the leaflet *t·* naturally towards the light.
	248 –12	The sculptor *t·* from the marble to his model
c	261– 9	If one *t·* away from the body with such
	263–16	His "touch *t·* hope to dust,
b	312–28	and so *t·* away from the intelligent
	322–20	he *t·* from his cups, as the startled dreamer
p	376– 2	The patient *t·* involuntarily from the
	431–27	dry, hot, and chilled by *t·*
	434–19	Then C. S. *t·* suddenly to the supreme tribunal,
t	459– 1	as the flower *t·* from darkness to light.

twelfth

ap	559–32	The *t·* chapter of the Apocalypse, . . . has a
	568– 5	The *t·* chapter of the Apocalypse typifies

twelve

a	38–19	not for the *t·* only, but for as many
o	342–13	He bade the seventy disciples, as well as the *t·*,
p	436–27	charged the jury, *t·* Mortal Minds,
g	523–29	closely intertwined to the end of chapter *t·*,
	554–23	"Have not I chosen you *t·*, — *John* 6 : 70.
ap	560– 8	upon her head a crown of *t·* stars. — *Rev.* 12 : 1.
	562–11	The spiritual idea is crowned with *t·* stars.
	562–12	The *t·* tribes of Israel with all mortals,

twenty

f	245–17	conjectured that she must be under *t·*.
b	286–16	In the Saxon and *t·* other tongues
p	416– 7	in *t·* minutes the sufferer is quietly asleep.
g	557– 2	child could remain under water *t·* minutes,

twenty-four

f	221– 6	partook of but one meal in *t·* hours,

twilight

a	32–01	in the *t·* of a glorious career
g	513– 9	gray in the sombre hues of *t·* ;

twinkling

b	291– 6	"in the *t·* of an eye," — *I Cor.* 15 : 52.

twist

t	450– 2	*t·* every fact to suit themselves.

twisted

s	142–21	as *t·* and wielded by Jesus,

two

pref	viii–20	deducible from *t·* connate facts,
	xii–16	conviction that the next *t·* years of her life
pr	14– 5	We cannot "serve *t·* masters." — *Matt.* 6 : 24.
a	23–22	*t·* definitions, *trustfulness* and *trustworthiness.*
	27–24	*t·* or three hundred other disciples
	52–22	These were the *t·* cardinal points of
m	58–24	"*T·* eat no more together than they
	63–13	differences between the rights of the *t·* sexes.
	63–20	property, and parental claims of the *t·* sexes.
sp	74–27	gulf which divides *t·* such opposite conditions
	82–12	cannot exist in *t·* different states of
	92–28	belief tends to support *t·* opposite powers,
s	119– 5	for such theories lead to one of *t·* things.
	123–19	The revelation consists of *t·* parts :
	128–29	The addition of *t·* sums in mathematics
	143–14	Driven to choose between *t·* difficulties,
	143–32	but the *t·* will not mingle scientifically,
	156–22	could get along in *t·* days without globules ;
ph	167–11	We cannot serve *t·* masters
	182–12	It is impossible to work from *t·* standpoints.
	193–20	informed that he went to work in *t·* weeks.
f	201– 6	"No man can serve *t·* masters." — *Matt.* 6 : 24.
	204– 7	and that there are *t·* separate, antagonistic
	204– 8	antagonistic entities and beings, *t·* powers,
	236–30	While age is halting between *t·* opinions
	239–28	Those *t·* opposite sources never mingle
	247– 3	*t·* of the elements it had lost, sight and teeth.
	251– 9	mortals wake to the knowledge of *t·* facts :
b	270– 8	not *t·* powers, matter and Mind,
	278–20	From this it would follow that there are *t·*
	279–27	knowledge that there are not *t·* bases of being,
	282– 4	are figured by *t·* geometrical symbols,
	338–14	Divide the name Adam into *t·* syllables,
o	349–10	*T·* essential points of C. S. are,
	355–14	*t·* conflicting theories regarding Christian
	356– 1	when the *t·* are so antagonistic that
	356–13	he spoke of flesh and Spirit as the *t·* opposites,
	357–25	If what opposes God is real, there must be *t·*
	358– 1	If *t·* statements directly contradict each other
	359–29	A Christian Scientist and an opponent are like *t·*
	360–18	If you try to have *t·* models, then you
p	363–15	He described *t·* debtors, one for a large sum

two

p 369–21 He . . . knew that man has not t· lives,
378– 1 and causes the t· to appear conjoined,
378–20 represented by t· material erroneous bases.
422–22 Let us suppose t· parallel cases of
436–16 the prisoner summoned t· professed friends,
t 457–14 which led to a quarrel between t· knights
458– 3 the doctrine that Science has t· principles
458– 5 and that these t· may be simultaneously
r 492–14 These t· contradictory theories
492–30 theory, . . . is that there are t· factors,
494–25 Which of these t· theories concerning man
g 510–13 And God made t· great lights ; — Gen. 1 : 16.
517– 5 is derived from t· Greek words,
523–15 clear evidences of t· distinct documents
523–26 From the fourth verse of chapter t· to chapter
532– 2 the union of the t· sexes
ap 577– 6 as no longer t· wedded individuals,
577– 6 but as t· individual natures in one ;

two-edged

t 458–17 t· sword of Truth must turn in every direction
g 538– 4 Truth is a t· sword, guarding and guiding.

type

and symptoms
p 418–20 and to whatever decides its t· and symptoms.
Cain is the
g 540–28 Cain is the t· of mortal and material man,
dragon is the
ap 564– 5 animal instinct, of which the dragon is the t·,
find the
p 412–18 find the t· of the ailment,
highest
b 332–29 He expressed the highest t· of divinity,
lowest
p 405– 4 above the lowest t· of manhood,
no character nor
p 400–17 and has no character nor t·, except
of divine Science
g 526–19 sword which guards it is the t· of divine Science.
of error
gl 593–16 foaming, and dashing, it is a t· of error.
of eternity
gl 585– 5 A sphere ; a t· of eternity and immortality,
of moral law
gl 592–11 t· of moral law and the demonstration thereof ;
of spiritual peace
gl 589– 8 JAPHET . . . A t· of spiritual peace,
of the glory
gl 585–17 a t· of the glory which is to come ;

type

spiritual
g 541–11 No ; but the lamb was a more spiritual t·
gl 582–12 a spiritual t· ; that which comforts,

———

ph 176–30 the less distinct t· and chronic form of disease.
g 540–30 he is not the t· of Truth and Love.

types

s 140–20 rituals are but t· and shadows of true worship.
ph 176–29 Hence decided t· of acute disease
f 246–32 Acute and chronic beliefs reproduce their own t·.
p 379–25 Fevers are errors of various t·.
381–15 cannot legislate the times, . . . and t· of disease,
396– 3 efface from thought all forms and t· of

typhoid

s 153–11 sinking in the last stage of t· fever.

typical

p 406– 4 The tree is t· of man's divine Principle,
ap 560– 3 t· of six thousand years since Adam,

typified

g 512–15 spiritual blessings, thus t·, are the
ap 562–24 the spiritual idea is t· by a woman
564–25 t· by a serpent, or animal subtlety.

typifies

pr 15– 3 The closet t· the sanctuary of Spirit,
g 538–15 "tree of knowledge" t· unreality. — Gen. 2 : 9.
ap 564–31 talking serpent t· mortal mind,
568– 6 t· the divine method of warfare in Science,
gl 593–15 unobstructed, it t· the course of Truth ;

typify

ap 563–11 ten horns of the dragon t· the belief that

typifying

ap 562– 6 t· the spiritual idea of God's motherhood.

tyrannical

s 140–13 Mankind will no longer be t·
161–12 t· law, restricting the practice of

tyrannize

ph 175–17 If a random thought, . . . had tried to t· over

tyranny

sp 94–14 T·, intolerance, and bloodshed, wherever found,
s 142–18 t· and pride need to be whipped out of the
f 225–27 always germinating in new forms of t·,
gl 587–22 Corporeal belief ; sensuality ; slavery ; t·.
589–14 sensuality ; envy ; oppression ; t·.

tyrant

m 64–14 sometimes debarred by a covetous domestic t·

U

ugliness

f 246–11 robs youth and gives u· to age.

ugly

m 66– 4 Which, like the toad, u· and venomous,

ulcer

ph 193– 5 had just probed the u· on the hip,

ulcers

p 418–29 Tumors, u·, tubercles, inflammation, pain,

ultimate

m 63– 9 Spirit is his primitive and u· source
sp 97– 4 await the certainty of u· perfection.
s 137– 3 the u· of this wonderful work
f 254–12 Imperfect mortals grasp the u· . . . slowly ;
b 324– 4 helps to precipitate the u· harmony.
p 422–28 the u· outcome of the injury.
t 446–31 and the u· triumph of any cause.
r 485–15 Think not to thwart the spiritual u·
487– 3 Life is the origin and u· of man,

ultimately

m 60–14 wisdom will u· put asunder
64–30 Spirit will u· claim its own,
s 151–14 would u· deliver mankind from the awful
f 209–28 will u· vanish, swallowed up in the
p 406–20 We can, and u· shall, so rise as to
423–26 Mind, which u· asserts its absolute supremacy.
r 483– 7 will u· supersede all other means in healing.

ultimates

an 103–24 malicious form of hypnotism u· in
c 257– 8 which u· in sickness, sin, and death ;
gl 580–16 Life's counterfeit, which u· in death ;

ultimatum

p 411–11 this is the u·, the scientific way,

unable

s 148–28 it ignores the divine Spirit as u· or unwilling
p 399–13 Nerves are u· to talk,
r 486–20 yet supposes Mind u· to produce harmony !
ap 573– 2 human sense of space is u· to grasp such a view.

unacknowledged

p 376– 3 but though u·, the latent fear and the despair
r 474– 2 (the Principle of this u· Science)

unacquainted

f 215– 9 u· with the reality of existence,
245–16 those u· with her history conjectured

unaided

sp 89– 1 what the u· medium is incapable of
g 532– 1 Did God at first create one man u·,

unalterable

pr 11–27 Prayer cannot change the u· Truth,

unanimous

an 100–19 we have come to the u· conclusions that

unattainable

b 291–13 and is u· without them.

unattained

s 147–23 hitherto u· and seemingly dim.

unaware

f 227– 8 or mortals will continue u· of

unawares

b 299–17 we entertain "angels u·." — Heb. 13 : 2.
ap 574–30 Love can make an angel entertained u·.

unbearable

m 59– 8 which might otherwise become u·.

unbelief

a 23–27 help thou mine u· !" — Mark 9 : 24.
p 401– 1 "because of their u·" in Truth. — Matt. 13 : 58.

unbelieving

a 24–32 After the resurrection, even the u· Thomas

unbiased

pref x–25 The u· Christian thought is soonest touched

unblest

m 57–31 Marriage is u· or blest, according to the

unborn

ph 174–16 marking out the path for generations yet u·.

unbroken

m 68–31 the u· links of eternal, harmonious being
r 494–24 breaks their illusion with the u· reality of

unceasing

pr 4–12 struggle to be always good is u· prayer.

uncertain

s 163–16 are in the highest degree u· ;
b 306–15 at some u· future time
326–24 only when his u· sense of right yielded
o 352–11 the spiritual was the intangible and u·,

unchangeable

s 120– 4 Soul, or Spirit, is God, u· and eternal ;
135– 8 establishing the Science of God's u· law.

unchanged

a 42–25 Afterwards he would show it to them u·.
46–20 Jesus' u· physical condition after what seemed
s 122–26 Life goes on u· and being is eternal.
b 302– 8 is thereby discerned and remains u·.
317–29 proof that he was u· by the crucifixion.
o 346–28 the operation, and the forceps are u·.
r 471– 4 remained u· in its eternal history.
g 555–31 Jesus was able to present himself u·
gl 588–12 man and woman u· forever in their

unchanging

pr 2–10 since He is u· wisdom and Love.
a 42– 4 gave no hint of the u· love of God.
f 248– 1 the u· calm and glorious freedom of
p 418– 8 the u·, unerring, and certain effect of

unchristian

a 55– 3 u· comment and usage
p 365–30 u· practitioner is not giving to mind or body
433– 9 warped by the irrational, u· suggestions

unclasp

p 412–14 adequate to u· the hold and to destroy

uncleanliness

p 383–17 impurity and u·, which do not trouble the gross,
gl 595–24 definition of

uncleanness

pr 8– 9 sepulchres . . . full , of all u·."—Matt. 23 : 27.
an 106–21 fornication, u·, lasciviousness,—Gal. 5 · 19.

uncoffined

p 441–12 "unknelled, u·, and unknown."

uncomplaining

a 48– 6 held u· guard over a world

uncomprehended

a 42–30 to test his still u· saying,

uncondemned

t 448– 7 but if evil is u·, it is undenied

unconfined

b 323–12 conception u· is winged to reach the divine

unconscious

sp 82–15 because both of us are either u· or
s 132–20 u· of the reappearing of the spiritual idea,
161–29 Such u· mistakes would not occur, if
ph 188– 5 is an u· error in the beginning,
190– 5 The mortal says that an inanimate u· seedling
o 346–26 believe that nitrous-oxide gas has made you u·
p 408–28 The u· thought in the corporeal substratum
400– 9 U· mortal mind—alias matter,
409–11 belief, that the u· substratum of mortal mind,
409–17 believed to be superior to its u· substratum,
r 484–14 conscious and u· thoughts of mortals,
484–17 Drugs and inert matter are u·, mindless.
492– 2 although the so-called dreamer is u·
g 554–13 The mortal is u· of his fœtal and
gl 588–25 that which is never u· nor limited.

unconsciously

ph 199–18 is produced consciously or u·,
f 236–14 Her thoughts . . . u· mould it,
p 395– 1 The sick u· argue for suffering,
403– 6 self-mesmerism is induced u·

unconsciousness

f 218– 8 rests us more than hours of repose in u·.
p 427– 6 can no more die nor disappear in u· than

uncontaminated

t 457– 1 Truth u· by human hypotheses.

uncover

sp 92–21 U· error, and it turns the lie upon you.
t 453–18 You u· sin, not in order to injure, but
g 542–19 Let Truth u· and destroy error
ap 564–23 might u· its own crime of defying
572–16 u· the myriad illusions of sin, sickness, and

uncovered

pr 6–23 Jesus u· and rebuked sin
sp 86– 9 misconception of it u· their materiality.

uncovers

r 491– 3 Animal magnetism thus u· material sense,
g 540–14 u· so-called sin and its effects,

unction

pr 10–10 will never pour into prayer the u· of Spirit
s 164–13 minus the u· of divine Science.

undecaying

t 463–16 its growth sturdy, and its maturity u·.

undefiled

m 64– 4 "Pure religion and u·—Jas. 1 : 27.
ap 571–32 He enthrones pure and u· religion,

undefined

p 376– 9 the most hidden, u·, and insidious beliefs.

undenied

t 448– 7 but if evil is uncondemned, it is u·

under

pref xi–29 u· the seal of the Commonwealth,
pr 5– 7 placed u· the stress of circumstances.
10– 7 God will sustain us u· these sorrows.
a 30–28 loathe sin and rebuke it u· every mask.
43–25 he was acting u· spiritual law
m 60–11 affection lives on u· whatever difficulties.
66–27 considered patience salutary u· such
sp 91– 3 inhabited by beings u· the control of
97–22 for they bring error from u· cover.
an 100–14 U· this order a commission was appointed,
101–28 Discomfort u· error is preferable to
s 119–15 u· the name of natural law.
138–19 Christians are u· as direct orders now,
147– 9 applied u· circumstances where
ph 174–28 rolling it u· the tongue as a
182–22 puts matter u· the feet of Mind.
185–32 A patient u· the influence of mortal mind
186– 8 u· whatever name or pretence
102– 2 a pulpy substance u· the skull
198– 5 The patient may seem calm u· it, but
200–15 all things u· his feet."—Psal. 8 : 6.
f 226– 4 u· more subtle and depraving forms.
229–22 should be trampled u· foot.
230–21 can man put that law u· his feet
234–15 trample them u· foot,
245–17 conjectured that she must be u· twenty.
c 258–28 man, u· the government of God
261–11 U· the strong impulse of a desire to
264–21 Matter disappears u· the microscope of
b 296–15 must go out u· the blaze of Truth,
319– 9 sustains man u· all circumstances ;
321–13 The serpent, evil, u· wisdom's bidding,
p 362– 8 especially u· the stern rules of
367– 1 u· the napkin of its form,
370– 5 The body improves u· the same regimen
370– 7 made manifest u· this regimen,
373– 9 U· all modes of . . . treatment,
386–27 u· the influence of the belief of grief,
389–29 came u· my observation.
402–31 the person u· hypnotic control
412–11 you are liable u· some circumstances
424–10 U· divine Providence there can be no
436– 3 for which Mortal Man is u· sentence
436–14 u· the protection of the Most High.
440–14 u· stress of circumstances,
t 443– 4 u· ordinary circumstances a resort to
448– 7 u· all circumstances, to say that
451– 2 Christian Scientists must live u· the
463– 3 u· influences not embraced in his
r 490–31 U· the mesmeric illusion of belief,
g 505–14 waters which were u· the—Gen. 1 : 7.
506–15 Let the waters u· the—Gen. 1 : 9.
523– 2 the Scriptural account now u· comment.
532– 9 prediction in the story u· consideration.
544–16 u· the control of the one Mind,
553–12 been formed u· circumstances which
555– 5 physical organism u· the yoke of disease.
557– 2 could remain u· water twenty minutes,
ap 560– 8 the moon u· her feet,—Rev. 12 : 1.
561–27 matter is put u· her feet.
562– 7 The moon is u· her feet.
571–15 At all times and u· all circumstances,
572–17 U· the supremacy of Spirit, it will
gl 592–15 justice demands penalties u· the law.

undergo

a 24–17 views of atonement will u· a great change,
ph 169– 1 the process which mortal mind and body u·
p 385– 4 have been able to u· without sinking

undergoing

f 244–13 Man u· birth, maturity, and decay

underived

r 475–20 has not a single quality u· from Deity ;

underlies

o 353–17 Perfection u· reality.
t 460– 4 and it u· all metaphysical practice.

underlying

b 305–15 constitutes the u· reality of reflection.
p 417–32 Give your patients an u· understanding to
r 477–27 caught some glimpses of the u· reality,
496–18 u·, overlying, and encompassing all true being.

undermined
s 121– 2 if his discovery had *u·* the

undermining
m 59–31 fatal mistakes are *u·* its foundations.

understand
pref x–28 Only those . . . who do not *u·*
pr 3–15 but to *u·* God is the work of eternity,
6–15 we must *u·* the divine Principle of being.
16–24 Here let me give what I *u·* to be the
a 19–19 will help us to *u·* Jesus' atonement
22–29 Whosoever believeth that . . . does not *u·* God.
25–14 may *u·* how this divine Principle heals
25–26 and *u·* its divine Principle.
38–29 lest ye should *u·* and be converted,
40–11 divine pardon, which I *u·* to mean
42–32 They must *u·* more fully his Life-principle
43– 2 even as they did *u·* it after his
43– 5 enabled the disciples to *u·*
45–32 not sufficiently advanced fully to *u·*
54–25 it enabled them to *u·* the Nazarene
55–29 This Comforter I *u·* to be Divine Science.
m 59–11 nor . . . be expected to *u·* political economy.
69– 6 Mortals can never *u·* God's creation while
69–13 Spiritually to *u·* that there is but one creator,
sp 84–19 To *u·* that Mind is infinite,
98–20 remains inviolate for every man to *u·*
s 110–31 and spiritually *u·* Truth.
120– 1 But we shall never *u·* this while we
136–25 what the disciples did not fully *u·*
141– 4 Few *u·* or adhere to Jesus' divine precepts
141–22 did not then, and do not now, *u·* this
149–29 We need to *u·* the affirmations of
152–25 and she can now *u·* why,
ph 167– 2 or should we *u·* the infinite divine Principle
170– 7 Did Jesus *u·* the economy of man less than
174–30 We should *u·* that the cause of disease
180– 8 must *u·* the resuscitating of Life.
f 204–20 When will the ages *u·* the Ego,
205–32 When we fully *u·* our relation to the Divine,
209–31 a conscious, constant capacity to *u·* God.
217–22 and in proportion as you *u·* the
224– 5 we shall better *u·* the Science
235–22 To the tremblers . . . who *u·* not the
254–19 not the power to demonstrate what we do not *u·*.
c 264–29 we shall behold and *u·* God's creation,
267–13 Christian Scientists *u·* that, . . . they have the
b 271–18 which shall believe on me [*u·* me] — *John* 17 : 20.
283– 1 As mortals begin to *u·* Spirit,
285–32 It is essential to *u·*, instead of believe,
286– 2 is not to *u·* the infinite.
292–20 "Why do ye not *u·* my speech? — *John* 8 : 43.
311–21 So long as . . . we can never *u·* the Science of
311–32 When humanity does *u·* this Science,
321– 7 despaired of making the people *u·* what should
329–12 In Science we can use only what we *u·*.
332–25 in such a form of humanity as they could *u·*
339–18 Only those, . . . can fully *u·* the unreality of evil.
o 345–16 none which are apparent to those who *u·*·
345–20 evidence that one does *u·* this Science.
346–10 we need to *u·* that error *is* nothing,
350– 6 To *u·* all our Master's sayings as recorded
350–21 and should *u·* with their heart, — *Matt.* 13 : 15.
352– 2 because they did not sufficiently *u·* God
352–18 which can harm them and which they do not *u·*,
p 379–20 will *u·* that she is not dying on account of
381–22 You must *u·* your way out of human theories
394– 1 to *u·* that sickness is not real
396–30 *u·* that sickness is formed by the human mind,
397–18 Declare that you are not hurt and *u·* the reason
397–31 will *u·* yourself and your Maker
398–31 Then we *u·* the process.
400–16 if you *u·* that every disease is an error,
403–14 You command the situation if you *u·* that
417–25 *u·* the unreality of disease in Science.
424–24 if you *u·* C. S.
429–25 Do you *u·* it?   No!
t 444–17 pointing the way through Christ, as we *u·* it,
446–20 To *u·* God strengthens hope, enthrones faith
456–23 must both *u·* and abide by the divine Principle
459–32 should *u·* and adhere strictly to the rules
460–11 the one most difficult to *u·* and demonstrate,
464– 8 they would *u·* why she is so secluded.
r 466–18 it is the most important to *u·*.
479–13 cannot feel itself, see itself, nor *u·* itself.
481– 7 Material sense never helps mortals to *u·*
482–13 Is it important to *u·* these explanations
486–29 If . . . the medium through which to *u·* God,
488– 5 the cure shows that you *u·* this teaching,
491–30 even though he does not *u·* C. S.,
497–21 faith to *u·* eternal Life,
g 523–23 in what we *u·* to be the spiritually scientific
546–30 demonstrable Principle which all may *u·*.
ap 559– 2 open for all to read and *u·*.
560–19 without . . . we can never *u·* the divine

understandeth
f 213– 5 as a man spiritually *u·*, so is he in truth.

understanding (noun)
and affections
pr 5–17 riches of His love into the *u·* and affections,
and belief
b 288–12 between truth and error, *u·* and belief,
and demonstration
b 279–19 through the *u·* and demonstration of
and expression
r 484–30 to the *u·* and expression of Spirit?
and heart
g 521–16 should be engraved on the *u·* and heart
and intelligence
g 557–13 towards enlarged *u·* and intelligence;
and recognition
sp 90–27 The *u·* and recognition of Spirit
and truth
g 544–28 belief reverses *u·* and truth.
arrive at the
g 543–12 until mortals arrive at the *u·* that
beatified
b 303–20 beatified *u·* of the Science of Life.
belief without
sp 83–10 a blind belief without *u·*,
r 472–18 Error is a belief without *u·*.
benighted
pref. vii– 8 would make plain to benighted *u·*
better
f 210–16 a better *u·* of Soul and salvation.
b 285–21 to the better *u·* that Science gives of the
315– 5 His better *u·* of God was a rebuke to them.
r 473–23 a better *u·* of God as divine Principle,
Christlike
c 259–11 The Christlike *u·* of scientific being
demonstration and
pr 14– 8 the actual demonstration and *u·*
destroyed by the
p 381–13 laws of mortal belief are destroyed by the *u·*
divine
g 536– 8 The divine *u·* reigns, is *all,*
divine strength and
p 406–31 gained through divine strength and *u·*.
dormant
gl 583–16 rousing the dormant *u·* from material beliefs
enlightened
pr 12–24 help should come from the enlightened *u·*.
enlighten the
g 510– 9 Truth and Love enlighten the *u·*,
eyes of their
a 49– 3 winged their faith, opened the eyes of their *u·*,
faith and
s 107–13 fresh pinions are given to faith and *u·*,
b 312–27 It divides faith and *u·* between matter and
p 366–10 mental penury chills his faith and *u·*.
387–30 gives man faith and *u·* whereby to
final
sp 76–28 the final *u·* of Christ in divine Science.
firm in your
p 393–16 Be firm in your *u·* that the divine Mind
flowing from the
gl 589– 9 flowing from the *u·* that God is the
followed the
s 141–15 followed the *u·* of the divine Principle
full
a 31–21 in a full *u·* of the divine Principle
fuller
s 162–27 requires only a fuller *u·* of the divine Principle
gate of
g 538– 6 places the cherub wisdom at the gate of *u·*
growth in the
m 62–19 growth in the *u·* of man's higher nature.
higher
pr 10–16 to a higher *u·* of the divine Life.
a 33–29 which attend a new and higher *u·* of God?
sp 79–13 through the higher *u·* of God,
f 251–20 or govern it from the higher *u·*
t 449–16 but it requires a higher *u·* to teach this
highest
m 67–11 Yet, acting up to his highest *u·*,
his
b 315– 9 his *u·* of this divine Science
human
pr 12–11 nor is it the human *u·* of the divine
sp 99–11 C. S. has opened the door of the human *u·*.
imparts the
g 505–16 Spirit imparts the *u·* which uplifts
infinite
f 253– 1 He reflects the infinite *u·*,
instead of
b 304–29 Controlled by belief, instead of *u·*,
leads to the
b 324–14 leads to the *u·* that God is the only Life.

understanding (noun)
  light of
    t 461–12   light of *u·* be thrown upon this Science,
  mutual
    m 59–24   A mutual *u·* should exist before this union
  necessity of
    r 488–13   when they mean to enforce the necessity of *u·*.
  new
    a 33–22   This is the new *u·* of spiritual Love.
  new-born
    f 221–29   This new-born *u·*, that neither food nor
  nor truth
    b 287–17   Neither *u·* nor truth accompanies error,
  object of
    s 115–18   the immediate object of *u·*.
  of being
    b 330– 1   *u·* of being supersedes mere belief.
    r 495–21   Let C. S., . . . support your *u·* of being,
  of Christian Science
    ph 178–23   In proportion to our *u·* of C. S.,
    178–32   Whoever reaches the *u·* of C. S.
    181–20   till you finally attain the *u·* of C. S.
    b 323– 1   Mortals may seek the *u·* of C. S.,
    329– 5   A little *u·* of C. S. proves the truth of
    r 495–26   How can I progress most rapidly in the *u·* of C. S.?
  of divine Love
    b 288– 7   through faith in and the *u·* of divine Love,
  of divine metaphysics
    ph 192–28   our Master in the *u·* of divine metaphysics.
  of divine Science
    a 46–32   roused to an enlarged *u·* of divine Science,
    f 228–16   through the *u·* of divine Science.
    b 281– 1   yields only to the *u·* of divine Science,
  of God
    (*see* God)
  of Life
    pr 14– 8   *u·* of Life as revealed in C. S.
    sp 77–10   until the spiritual *u·* of Life is reached.
    b 323–25   God gives the true *u·* of Life and Love,
    p 287– 1   when we grow into the *u·* of Life,
    r 485–18   the *u·* of Life, makes man immortal.
  of man
    c 260– 2   the true conception or *u·* of man,
  of Mind-science
    s 115– 2   through which the *u·* of Mind-science comes,
  of Spirit
    a 46–17   rose even higher in the *u·* of Spirit,
    ph 186– 6   through the *u·* of Spirit,
    b 309– 8   the *u·* of Spirit and of spiritual power.
    gl 581– 9   the *u·* of Spirit, destroying belief in matter.
  of Truth
    pr 11–28   nor can prayer alone give us an *u·* of Truth ;
    f 252–10   that *u·* of Truth which destroys error,
    b 286– 6   The *u·* of Truth gives full faith in
    o 346–19   We treat error through the *u·* of Truth,
    p 417–15   the unshaken *u·* of Truth and Love,
    up 561 1   The *u·* of Truth and Love,
  opposite
    s 154–21   prevented through the opposite *u·*,
  or belief
    b 324–11   whether it be Truth or error, *u·* or belief,
  perception and
    ap 561–19   reducing to human perception and *u·* the Life
  perfect
    b 273–14   impossibility of attaining perfect *u·* till
  perfect day of
    p 388–20   In that perfect day of *u·*, we shall
  precede an
    g 553– 5   clearer consciousness must precede an *u·* of
  present
    p 388–27   foolish to venture beyond our present *u·*,
  rests upon
    b 283–12   It admits of no error, but rests upon *u·*.
  right
    p 390– 9   the right *u·* of Him restores harmony.
  Science and
    b 274–27   Science and *u·*, governed by the
  Spirit and
    r 486–25   reality and immortality are in Spirit and *u·*,
  spiritual
    (*see* spiritual)
  superstition and
    b 288– 9   Superstition and *u·* can never combine.
  that Life is God
    r 487–27   The *u·* that Life is God, Spirit,
  this
    pr 14–28   This *u·* casts out error and heals
    a 43– 7   this *u·* is what is meant by the descent of the
    f 203– 8   this *u·* would establish health.
    216–14   This *u·* makes the body harmonious ;
    c 264–17   this *u·* will expand into self-completeness,
    328–14   This *u·* of man's power, when he
    o 355–26   Without this *u·*, no one is capable of
    p 394– 3   this *u·* is the universal and perfect remedy.
    426–19   this *u·* will quicken into newness of life.

understanding (noun)
  this
    r 495–22   and this *u·* will supplant error with Truth,
    g 505–26   This *u·* is not intellectual,
    547–24   only by this *u·* can truth be gained.
  through the
    f 217– 2   through the *u·* which Science confers
    228–16   through the *u·* of divine Science.
    b 279–19   through the *u·* and demonstration of
    o 346–19   We treat error through the *u·* of Truth,
  Truth and
    gl 590– 8   the opposite of spiritual Truth and *u·*.
  Truth in the
    s 100–22   The revelation of Truth in the *u·*
  underlying
    p 417–32   Give your patients an underlying *u·* to support
  wholesome
    p 396–24   Give them divine and wholesome *u·*,
  without the
    p 381–26   without the *u·* that Mind is not in matter.
  yield to
    sp 96–23   until all errors of belief yield to *u·*.

    pr 15–28   Practice not profession, *u·* not belief,
    a 24–14   the *u·*, in which Jesus suffered and triumphed.
    34– 5   showing, . . . that Truth has come to the *u·*
    44–25   divinity brought to humanity the *u·* of
    m 68– 1   epoch approaches when the *u·* of the truth
    sp 75–14   restored Lazarus by the *u·* that
    s 116– 1   *Third Degree: U·.*
    125–14   from fear to hope and from faith to *u·*,
    f 216–11   The *u·* that the Ego is Mind,
    223–16   the assurance which comes of *u·*;
    253– 9   into the *u·* of your divine rights,
    b 281– 2   the *u·* by which we enter into the
    283–27   receive the divine Principle in the *u·*,
    289– 5   by the *u·* of what constitutes man
    297– 9   into the *u·* of what constitutes health ;
    298–14   intuition, hope, faith, *u·*, fruition,
    315–21   Jesus' spiritual origin and *u·* enabled him
    317–18   The *u·* of his spiritual individuality
    322– 3   When *u·* changes the standpoints of life
    p 378– 5   The *u·* of this will enable you to
    420 12   and the *u·* obtained that there is no death,
    429– 2   by the *u·* that there is no death,
    t 454– 5   The *u·*, even in a degree, of the
    r 479–24   imaginary opposites of light, *u·*, and
    488–10   *u·*, trust, constancy, firmness.
    489–17   channel to man of divine blessings or *u·*
    g 505–21   *U·* is the line of demarcation between
    506– 5   *U·* is a quality of God,
    506–10   God, unites *u·* to eternal harmony.
    512– 2   the *u·* of the incorporeal and divine
    523– 9   and not from the firmament, or *u·*,
    526– 9   Belief is less than *u·*.
    534–30   The spiritual idea has given the *u·* a foothold
    535– 2   The seed . . . of belief and of *u·*,
    gl 598–17   WINE. Inspiration ; *u·*.

understanding (ppr.)
    a 28–12   by *u·* more of the divine Principle
    f 233–21   by *u·* the spiritual idea which corrects and
    c 259–19   *U·* this, Jesus said :
    b 270– 8   Only by *u·* that there is but one power,
    273–19   importance of *u·* the truth of being,
    296–29   and in *u·* the situation in C. S.
    304– 5   *U·* this, Paul said :
    304–30   So man, not *u·* the Science of
    312–18   Mortals try to believe without *u·* Truth ;
    319– 8   spiritually *u·* God, sustains man
    321–14   was destroyed through *u·* divine Science,
    327– 1   Reform comes by *u·* that there is no
    328– 6   *U·* little about the divine Principle
    328–20   *U·* spiritual law and knowing that
    o 356–11   *U·* the nothingness of material things,
    p 394–29   Not *u·* C. S., the sick usually
    423– 8   *u·* scientifically that all is Mind,
    t 450–21   will overcome them by *u·* their nothingness
    450–23   by *u·* God's power over them.
    462–32   through *u·* mental anatomy,
    g 514–26   *U·* the control which Love held over all,

understandingly
    s 140–10   love Him *u·*, warring no more over

understands
    a 23–25   Another kind of faith *u·* divine Love
    ph 180–26   the ever-present Mind who *u·* all things,
    f 250– 8   which never dreams, but *u·* all things ;
    c 265– 3   Man *u·* spiritual existence in proportion
    o 345–17   One who *u·* C. S. can heal the sick
    t 452– 2   when one *u·* that evil has in reality no power.
    453– 5   The author *u·* what she is saying.
    454–14   He, who *u·* in a sufficient degree the
    r 487–17   Matter cannot believe, and Mind *u·*.
    g 555–10   for it neither *u·* nor can be understood.
    556–16   to him who *u·* best the divine Life.

understood

pref vii–23	but it cannot make them speedily *u*·.
a 24– 2	applies to Truth and Love *u*· and practised.
24– 8	open the way for C. S. to be *u*·,
27–27	they never truly *u*· their Master's instruction.
28–16	nor the work of Jesus was generally *u*·.
34–19	and *u*· better what the Master had taught.
41–23	reception C. S. would have before it was *u*·,
43– 7	they had only believed ; now they *u*·.
52–19	best *u*· the nothingness of material life
54–18	hearers *u*· neither his words nor his works.
m 56– 9	discerned intact, is apprehended and *u*·,
63– 3	if you *u*· the Science of being.
sp 71–21	When the Science of Mind is *u*·,
76– 6	When being is *u*·, Life will be recognized as
76–10	will be *u*· that Spirit never entered matter
76–19	When divine Science is universally *u*·,
81– 5	If Spiritualists *u*· the Science of being,
88–19	nor *u*· through the physical senses.
91–13	and his genuine being will be *u*·.
94– 4	The nature of man, thus *u*·, includes
s 114– 2	therefore, to be *u*·, the author
122– 4	but the great facts of Life, rightly *u*·,
124–15	and then it can be *u*· ;
128– 4	The term Science, properly *u*·,
130–11	Science, when *u*· and demonstrated,
130–15	C. S., properly *u*·, would disabuse the
130–24	and *u*· how truly such as they belong to
131–29	demonstrations which were not *u*·.
137– 8	Yearning to be *u*·, the Master repeated,
141–26	until its divine Principle is scientifically *u*·.
144–27	When the Science of being is universally *u*·,
144–31	*u*· the Science of Christian healing,
151– 9	if they *u*· the Science of Mind-healing,
152– 9	has a healing effect, even when not fully *u*·.
153–29	When this mental contagion is *u*·,
159–15	Had these unscientific surgeons *u*·
ph 168–31	a word . . . which will be better *u*· hereafter,
169–16	If we *u*· the control of Mind over body,
196– 5	The power of . . . is little *u*·.
f 203– 7	If God were *u*· instead of being merely
205– 9	When will it be *u*· that matter has neither
212–25	Because all the methods of Mind are not *u*·,
214–16	being will be *u*· and found to be harmonious.
215–27	Because he *u*· the superiority and
219–14	When this is *u*·, we shall never
238– 2	are not rightly valued before they are *u*·.
238–13	shows that we never *u*· Truth.
239–12	Let it be *u*· that success in error is defeat
252–13	*u*· and recognized as the true likeness
c 256–15	nor can He be *u*· aright through
b 272– 4	must be gained before Truth can be *u*·.
275–31	spiritually discerned, is scientifically *u*·.
276– 5	When the divine precepts are *u*·,
280–25	Rightly *u*·, . . . man has a sensationless body ;
290– 4	if . . . not in the least *u*·
297–24	Truth, the ever-present, is becoming *u*·.
300– 9	So far as the scientific statement as to man is *u*·,
304–26	the science of music must be *u*·.
308–22	Truth, being thereby *u*·, gave him
310– 7	Thought will finally be *u*· and seen
319–19	when it becomes fairly *u*· that the
319–23	and needs inspiration to be *u*·.
323–15	Truth is demonstrable when *u*·,
323–16	and that good is not *u*· until demonstrated.
325–13	When spiritual being is *u*· in all its perfection,
325–28	will be *u*· and demonstrated.
326–29	Christians, whose religion he had not *u*·,
329–27	If men *u*· their real spiritual source
330– 8	When the following platform is *u*·
334–27	liveth, and was dead [not *u*·] ; — *Rev.* 1 : 18.
338– 1	C. S., rightly *u*·, leads to
339–28	not merely believed, but it must be *u*·.
o 343–15	when his teachings are fully *u*·.
344–11	Were it more fully *u*· that Truth heals
345– 3	thus they are uniformly used and *u*· in C. S.
348– 8	it is not generally *u*· how
349– 2	when this Science is more generally *u*·
349–15	In C. S., substance is *u*· to be Spirit,
350–13	both of which must be *u*·.
358– 9	C. S., *u*· coincides with the Scriptures,
361–14	This declaration of Jesus, *u*·, conflicts not
361–30	enriches mankind only when it is *u*·,
p 369–20	He *u*· man, whose Life is God, to be immortal,
369–26	readily seen, if psychology, . . . was *u*·.
371– 8	By . . . nothing is really *u*· of material
375–16	should be *u*· and so rendered fruitless.
375–30	This mental state is not *u*·, simply because
386–24	divine wisdom will then be *u*·.
386–29	you would not have *u*· him,
403– 7	In the first instance it is *u*· that the
403–31	are not *u*· by the patient,
406– 8	power of God is *u*· and demonstrated
425–18	When this is *u*·, mankind will be
427–11	before Life can be *u*· and harmony obtained.
429–29	not *u*· generally by our ethical instructors.

understood

t 449–21	ought to be *u*· and guarded against.
457–10	never . . . fears to have fairly *u*·.
459–26	the results are sure if the Science is *u*·.
r 467– 9	should be . . . *u*· that all men have one Mind,
467–30	*u*· through the idea which expresses it
472– 2	God is to be *u*·, adored, and demonstrated ;
472–11	His law, rightly *u*·, destroys them.
473–31	Few, however, except his students *u*·
475–12	he must be so *u*· in C. S.
479–31	being *u*· by the things that — *Rom.* 1 : 20.
480–30	If sin, sickness, and death were *u*· as nothingness,
487–30	This faith relies upon an *u*· Principle.
489– 3	If the Science of Life were *u*·,
490–12	The Science of Mind needs to be *u*·.
490–13	Until it is *u*·, mortals are more or less
495– 4	All of Truth is not *u*· ;
g 547–24	Our aim must be to have them *u*· spiritually,
552–31	perfect and eternal Mind is *u*·.
555–11	it neither understands nor can be *u*·.
ap 558–13	When *u*·, it is Truth's prism and praise.
561–21	and the spiritual idea is *u*·.
570–23	the spiritual idea will be *u*·.
572–13	this divine Principle, *u*· and demonstrated,
gl 586–21	spiritual being *u*· ; haste towards harmony.
588– 5	Divine Science *u*· and acknowledged.
593–20	Life, Truth, and Love *u*· and demonstrated
598–26	when the Science of being is *u*·,

undertake

s 145–25	Other methods *u*· to oppose error with error,
ph 200– 9	not to *u*· the explanation of body.

undertakes

ph 198–16	and before the doctor *u*· to dispel it
p 441– 3	which *u*· to punish aught but sin,

under-world

s 137–32	[*hades*, the *u*·, or the *grave*]

undigested

p 389– 8	mortal mind, which reports food as *u*·.

undimmed

f 246–12	Manhood is its eternal noon, *u*· by a declining

undirected

f 212–17	Mortals have a modus of their own, *u*· and

undisciplined

f 221–27	*u*· by self-denial and divine Science.

undiscovered

g 552– 9	proof requisite to sustain this assumption is *u*·

undisturbed

f 250–20	To the observer, the body lies listless, *u*·,
b 306–25	*U*· amid the jarring testimony of the
g 514–12	*U*· it lies in the open field,

undivided

s 142– 8	We must seek the *u*· garment,

undo

f 240–27	In trying to *u*· the errors of sense

undone

pr 6– 8	work badly done or left *u*·,
sp 85–30	and not to leave the other *u*·." — *Matt.* 23 : 23.

undoubted

p 364– 1	a man of *u*· goodness and purity,

undue

p 413– 3	*u*· contemplation of physical wants

undulations

f 212–27	that the *u*· of the air convey sound,

undying

b 325– 5	being ushered into the *u*· realities of Spirit.
334–23	but *u*· in the deific Mind.
p 427–23	God, Life, Truth, and Love make man *u*·.

unearth

p 434–26	and we shall *u*· this foul conspiracy

uneasiness

p 383–15	To the mind equally gross, dirt gives no *u*·.

uneducated

sp 89–11	She says, . . . I am *u*·."

unequalled

s 134–20	its astonishing and *u*· success in the first

unerring

sp 99–15	C. S. is *u*· and Divine ;
s 145–23	ignorance of the laws of eternal and *u*· Mind.
f 243–20	Neither immortal and *u*· Mind nor matter,
b 274–27	governed by the *u*· and eternal Mind,
277– 2	To all that is unlike *u*· and eternal Mind,
279– 2	the *u*·, immutable, and immortal
p 418– 8	*u*·, and certain effect of divine Science.
424– 9	the proper sense of God's *u*· direction
r 468– 2	which evolves its own *u*· idea
473–21	and to test its *u*· Science according to his rule,
484– 2	on a divine Principle and so found to be *u*·,
g 505–29	God's ideas reflect the immortal, *u*·, and
522–31	Does the *u*· Principle of divine law change

unerring
g 546–11 is governed by *u·* intelligence?
gl 588–10 incorporeal, *u·*, immortal and eternal Mind.
590– 2 realm of *u·*, eternal, and omnipotent Mind ;

unexplained
pref xi– 3 which action in some *u·* way results in the
s 121–14 the hypotheses of material sense *u·* by Science,

unexpressed
b 303–26 would be a nonentity, or Mind *u·*.
306–11 The Ego would be *u·*,
p 423– 6 Remember that the *u·* belief oftentimes
r 470–27 consequently a time when Deity was *u·*

unfair
m 63–12 Civil law establishes very *u·* differences
o 343– 7 This makes it doubly *u·* to impugn and

unfaithful
o 349– 3 As Paul asked of the *u·* in ancient days,
ap 571–13 *u·* stewards who have seen the danger

unfaithfulness
gl 509– 7 Emptiness ; *u·* ; desolation.

unfallen
ph 171– 8 and will find himself *u·*, upright, pure,
r 476–32 man in God's image is *u·* and eternal.

unfamiliar
b 314–18 seemed a spectre, unseen and *u·*,
p 422–11 Patients, *u·* with the cause of this commotion

unfashion
r 488–27 otherwise the very worms could *u·* man.

unfathomable
g 520– 3 *U·* Mind is expressed.

unfavorable
pr 7–13 reaction *u·* to spiritual growth,
p 396– 9 nor draw attention to certain symptoms as *u·*,

unfeigned
p 364– 3 Her reverence was *u·*,

unfit
a 31– 1 Pride and fear are *u·* to bear the standard of
p 419–17 lost aught *u·* for development enter

unfitted
p 369– 3 Thus he is *u·* for the successful

unflinching
p 426–27 with *u·* faith in God, in Life eternal.

unflinchingly
a 53– 6 He rebuked sinners pointedly and *u·*,

unfold
m 57–29 and begins to *u·* its wings for heaven.
sp 95 30 Material sense does not *u·* the facts of existence ;
b 269– 6 and *u·* the unity and the reality of good,
276– 5 they *u·* the foundation of fellowship,
o 361–23 Spiritual ideas *u·* as we advance.
t 445– 8 *U·* the latent energies and capacities
gl 598– 9 to employ words . . . to *u·* spiritual thoughts.

unfolded
s 117–17 As a divine student he *u·* God to man,
f 205–23 law of loving our neighbor as ourselves is *u·* ;
g 534–13 *u·* the remedy for Adam, or error ;
gl 584– 6 according to the good that is *u·*.

unfolding
s 108– 5 *u·* to me the demonstrable fact that
b 306–26 Science, still enthroned, is *u·* to mortals
306–28 is *u·* Life and the universe,
325– 7 *u·* its own immortal idea.
335–23 gain the eternal *u·* of Life
r 497–14 *u·* man's unity with God
g 503– 1 consists of the *u·* of spiritual ideas
gl 584– 7 This *u·* is God's day,

unfoldment
m 68–27 C. S. presents *u·*, not accretion ;
p 371–25 our need of its spiritual *u·*.

unfolds
m 66–15 Each successive stage of experience *u·* new
69–14 *u·* all creation, confirms the Scriptures,
s 135– 7 introduces no disorder, but *u·* the primal order,
ph 191–22 not a leaf *u·* its fair outlines,
f 246–25 Each succeeding year *u·* wisdom,
b 276– 1 *u·* the power that heals the sick,
296– 2 whereas Science *u·* the eternal verity,
t 452–22 When the spiritual sense of Truth *u·*
462–28 It *u·* the hallowed influences of unselfishness,
g 505–22 Spiritual understanding *u·* Mind,
506–19 Spirit, . . . *u·* these thoughts,
508–24 *u·* the infinitude of Love.
gl 597–19 spiritual sense *u·* the great facts of existence.

unformed
g 506–18 Spirit, God, gathers *u·* thoughts into their

unforsaken
b 291– 1 suppositions that sin is pardoned while *u·*,

unfortunate
ph 172–29 the *u·* cripple may present more nobility than
p 408–10 Those *u·* people who are committed to
434–11 to appear as counsel for the *u·* prisoner.
439–21 the *u·* Mortal Man who sought your aid
t 450– 5 Another class, still more *u·*, are so depraved

ungodliness
gl 595–25 definition of

ungodly
s 145–22 mystery which godliness always presents to the *u·*,

ungrateful
pr 3–27 If we are *u·* for Life, Truth, and Love,

unharmed
b 322– 1 and taught them how to handle serpents *u·*,

unhealthy
p 382– 9 or to remove *u·* exhalations
392–22 If you decide that climate or atmosphere is *u·*,
392–30 shut out these *u·* thoughts and fears.

unheeded
f 223–26 Peals that should startle . . . are partially *u·* ;

unholiness
f 201–20 Grafting holiness upon *u·*,
229–11 sickness and health, holiness and *u·*,
b 303–22 life and death, holiness and *u·*,

unifies
b 340–23 One infinite God, good, *u·* men and nations ;

uniform
m 64– 1 Want of *u·* justice is a crying evil

uniformly
o 345– 2 thus they are *u·* used and understood in C. S.

unillumined
ap 573– 9 while to another, the *u·* human mind,

unimpeachable
p 414–29 man's perfection is real and *u·*,

unimportant
s 135–23 but neither is *u·* or untrue,
r 485– 7 If the *u·* and evil appear, only soon to

unimproved
f 238–15 *U·* opportunities will rebuke us when we

uninspired
b 319–26 misinterpretation of the Word . . . by *u·* writers,
ap 573– 5 that which is invisible to the *u·* thought.

uninstructed
p 371– 7 By those *u·* in C. S., nothing is really

unintelligence
f 250– 4 and suppose . . . *u·* to act like intelligence,

unintelligent
s 143–22 You lean on the inert and *u·*, never discerning
157 23 Matter is not self-creative, for it is *u·*.
f 210–25 What is termed matter, being *u·*, cannot say,
g 523– 1 Yet one might so judge from an *u·* perusal of

uninterrupted
ph 172–13 reveals the eternal chain of existence as *u·*

union
hallowing the
m 59–14 hallowing the *u·* of interests and affections,
of hearts
m 64–17 Marriage should signify a *u·* of hearts.
solemn
ap 575–32 which binds human society into solemn *u·* ;

———

m 57– 4 *U·* of the masculine and feminine qualities
59–25 should exist before this *u·* and continue
65–10 The *u·* of the sexes suffers fearful discord.
sp 94–31 *u·* with the infinite capacities of the one Mind.
p 378– 3 are reproduced in *u·* by human memory.
g 532– 2 the *u·* of the two sexes in order to
gl 592–13 the *u·* of justice and affection,

unison
b 294– 3 human belief, . . . a *u·* of matter with Spirit.

unit
s 108–18 not a fraction more, not a *u·* less.

unite
a 35–21 We can *u·* with this church only as we
52–15 in order to *u·* in putting to shame and death
m 57–27 *u·* thought more closely to God,
64–23 will *u·* in one person masculine wisdom and
ph 167–21 can no more *u·* in action, than
178–29 you may attempt to *u·* with it hypnotism,
b 282–12 never *u·* in figure or in fact.
282–21 At no point can these opposites mingle or *u·*.
306–13 If Life or Soul and . . . man, *u·* for a
o 360–30 Jew and Christian can *u·* in doctrine
p 424– 7 and *u·* with the one Mind, in order to
g 555–19 error would seek to *u·* Spirit with matter,
ap 571–20 will *u·* all interests in the one divinity.

united
m 59–12 different demands of their u· spheres,
sp 72–16 which are not u· by progress, but separated.
b 287–28 material senses testify to truth and error as u·
r 477–10 man appears to be matter and mind u· ;
  492– 5 since Life cannot be u· to its unlikeness,
ap 577– 9 In this divinely u· spiritual consciousness,

United States
pref xii– 4 which had been established in the U· S·,
f 225–23 Legally to abolish unpaid servitude in the 'U· S·

unites
f 229–10 the belief which u· such opposites as
o 361– 8 Thus the Jew u· with the Christian's doctrine
  361–11 he virtually u· with the Jew's belief in one God,
g 506–10 God, u· understanding to eternal harmony.

uniting
b 271– 4 u· all periods in the design of God.
r 492–30 u· on some impossible basis.

unity
man's
pr 12–15 and of man's u· with Truth and Love.
a 18– 1 the exemplification of man's u· with God,
r 497–14 unfolding man's u· with God
of God
s 132–12 such effects, . . . prove the u· of God,
g 502–26 the eternal verity and u· of God and man,
of Principle
r 470– 4 and have u· of Principle and spiritual power
of Spirit
s 148–24 the concord and u· of Spirit and His likeness.
of spirit
m 58– 2 U· of spirit gives new pinions to joy,
of the faith
g 519–18 "we all come in the u· of the faith, — Eph. 4 : 13.
presents the
ap 577– 5 The Lamb's wife presents the u· of
scientific
f 202– 3 scientific u· which exists between God and man
sham
g 555–21 error would . . . call this sham u· man,
spiritual
m 61–31 The scientific morale of marriage is spiritual u·.
this
b 333–28 Jesus referred to this u· of
trinity in
b 331–28 They represent a trinity in u·,
unfold the
b 269– 7 and unfold the u· and the reality of good,

universal
pr 13– 2 Love is impartial and u· in its adaptation
a 42– 5 The u· belief in death is of no advantage.
sp 76– 8 but as infinite, — as God, u· good ;
  78–31 These are the effects of one u· God,
  84–16 events which concern the u· welfare,
s 140–25 The C. S. God is u·, eternal, divine Love,
  144–29 and Truth will be the u· panacea.
  155–15 The u· belief in physics weighs against
f 208–23 the reign and rule of u· harmony,
  226– 7 sounded the keynote of u· freedom,
  229–15 By u· consent, mortal belief has
  242–17 to dissolve with the u· solvent of Love
c 266–18 U· Love is the divine way in C. S.
b 271–16 Hence the u· application of his saying :
  289–21 results, by the u· law of mortal mind, in a
  291–12 U· salvation rests on progression and
  293–29 Truth and its supremacy, u· harmony,
  328–31 extends through time and includes u· humanity.
  329– 4 in all the grandeur of u· goodness.
  330– 7 would meet with immediate and u· acceptance.
  331–19 divine Principle, Love, the u· cause,
p 394– 3 the u· and perfect remedy.
  408– 6 There is a u· insanity of so-called health,
  414–23 Even so, harmony is u·, and discord is unreal.
r 470–10 Love as ever present and u·.
  477– 5 taught that the kingdom of God is intact, u·,
  483–18 and reveals the u· harmony.
g 519– 9 the ideas of God in u· being are complete
  553– 8 nearer the truth . . . or health will never be u·,
  577– 3 as one Father with His u· family,

universally
sp 76–19 When divine Science is u· understood,
s 144–27 When the Science of being is u· understood,
f 202– 5 and God's will must be u· done.

universe
and man
gl 585–17 Divine Science encompassing the u· and man ;
changing the
c 255– 1 Eternal Truth is changing the u·.
constructing the
g 522–27 supposedly . . . in constructing the u·,
control over the
ph 171–12 Mind's control over the u·, including man,
divine
g 513– 8 To material sense, this divine u· is dim

universe
God and the
c 266–32 but he coexists with God and the u·.
g 521–28 this material view of God and the u·,
God's
b 289–24 God's u· is spiritual and immortal.
  331–17 Everything in God's u· expresses Him.
governing the
g 510–30 governing the u·, including man,
government of the
s 121–32 in the everlasting government of the u·.
  128– 5 His government of the u·, inclusive of man.
g 539–15 resigned to matter the government of the u·?
governs the
a 39–27 and governs the u· harmoniously.
an 102–13 since God governs the u· ;
b 270–11 intelligence, . . . governs the u· ;
  295– 5 God creates and governs the u·, including man.
harmony of the
gl 592–19 the spiritual facts and harmony of the u· ;
His own
s 119–10 to leave the creator out of His own u· ;
illumines the
g 503–15 light of ever-present Love illumines the u·.
illuming the
c 266–29 the beatific presence, illuming the u· with light.
intelligence of the
a 27–15 the Life, substance, and intelligence of the u·
b 330–12 the only intelligence of the u·,
invisible
b 337–24 the invisible u· and spiritual man.
is filled
b 295– 6 The u· is filled with spiritual ideas,
Life and the
b 306–28 Life and the u·, ever present and eternal.
man and the
m 68–30 an impartation . . . to man and the u·.
  69– 2 man and the u· are evolved from Spirit,
f 209–22 translation of man and the u· back into Spirit.
  209–23 man and the u· will be found harmonious
b 332– 3 relation of God to man and the u·.
r 466– 1 His reflection is man and the u·.
g 507–28 immortality of man and the u·.
  508– 4 man and the u·, is the product.
  509–27 appear in man and the u· never to disappear.
  539–30 makes and governs man and the u·.
material
f 238– 5 in personal character as well as in the mate-rial u·.
g 545–12 notion of a material u· is utterly opposed to
Mind and the
g 507–23 Mind and the u· created by God.
mortal
gl 584–24 thence to reproduce a mortal u·,
of Mind
f 240–16 rotations and revolutions of the u· of Mind
g 513– 6 spiritual steps in the teeming u· of Mind
of Spirit
c 264–32 u· of Spirit is peopled with spiritual beings,
g 507–15 The u· of Spirit reflects the creative power of
of Truth
g 503–10 In the u· of Truth, matter is unknown.
peoples the
g 509–17 God forms and peoples the u·.
physical
r 484–13 The physical u· expresses the conscious and
Principle of the
b 272–28 The divine Principle of the u· must
  276–23 Principle of the u·, including . . . man.
real
b 289–19 for to the real man and the real u·
recreate the
g 547–19 to recreate the u·, including man.
reflects
b 300–28 The u· reflects and expresses the divine
g 502–28 The u· reflects God.
reveals the
ap 562– 8 This idea reveals the u· as secondary
spiritual
  (see **spiritual**)
stellar
g 509–14 but the stellar u· is no more celestial than
sustaining the
g 538–13 enlightening and sustaining the u·.
theory of the
g 547–26 The true theory of the u·, including man, is
  547–29 sensual, and mortal theory of the u·,
views of the
g 502–16 Christian views of the u· appear,
visible
b 337–22 The visible u· and material man are the
whole
f 207–29 repeated in the action of man and the whole u·,

sp 83–16 The belief that the u·, including man,
s 114–28 the u·, including man, is spiritual,

universe
- *s* 121–29 the *u·*, the reflection of God,
- 123–10 the most . . . inharmonious creature in the *u·*.
- 124–14 The *u·*, like man, is to be interpreted by
- 124–18 the *u·*, like man, is, and must continue to be, an
- 125–29 will look out from them upon the *u·* ;
- *c* 256– 8 Father and Mother of the *u·*, including man.
- *b* 272–29 must interpret the *u·*.
- 319–11 neither concur in man nor in the *u·*.
- *r* 471–20 the spirituality of the *u·* is the only fact
- 496– 5 and governs the entire *u·*.
- *g* 502–27 unity of God and man, including the *u·*.
- 505–24 giving the spiritual proof of the *u·*
- 510 18 giving existence and intelligence to the *u·*.
- 511–23 To mortal mind, the *u·* is liquid, solid, and
- 515–16 eternal Elohim includes the forever *u·*.
- 554– 3 the *u·*, inclusive of man, is as eternal as God,
- *ap* 562– 9 from which the *u·* borrows its

University of Pennsylvania
- *s* 163–20 Dr. Chapman, Professor . . . in the *U· of P·*,

unjust
- *a* 36–19 A selfish and limited mind may be *u·*,
- 36–31 in the suffering of the just for the *u·*.
- *o* 343–12 will not be forever hidden by *u·* parody
- *p* 381– 2 Ignorant of . . . we submit to *u·* decrees,
- 381–29 man's moral right to annul an *u·* sentence,
- 437–29 *u·* usages were not allowed at the bar of Truth,
- 440–22 The false and *u·* beliefs of your

unjustly
- *an* 104– 6 *u·* persecuted and belied by wolves in
- *p* 434–22 prisoner at the bar has been *u·* sentenced,
- 435–35 the liberty of which he has been *u·* deprived.

unknelled
- *p* 441–12 "*u·*, uncoffined, and unknown."

unknowable
- *gl* 596– 4 may define Deity as "the great *u·* ;"

unknown
- *pr* 1–10 Thoughts unspoken are not *u·* to the
- 12– 9 a belief in the *u·* casting out a belief in
- *a* 53–12 His words and works were *u·* to the world
- *ph* 184– 4 for these are *u·* to Truth
- *f* 210– 2 sorrow, sin, death, will be *u·*,
- *b* 274–30 in a manner and at a period as yet *u·*.
- 280– 1 In . . . Mind, matter must be *u·*.
- 306–16 and in a manner *u·*,
- 330–16 The individuality of Spirit, . . . is *u·*,
- *p* 424– 5 Accidents are *u·* to God,
- 428–15 not "to the *u·* God" — *Acts* 17 : 23.
- 441–12 "unknelled, uncoffined, and *u·*."
- *r* 469– 2 What is termed matter is *u·* to Spirit,
- 469– 5 Death and finiteness are *u·* to Life.
- 469–20 if mortals claimed no other . . . sin would be *u·*.
- *q* 503–11 In the universe of Truth, matter is *u·*.
- *gl* 596– 1 definition of
- 596– 2 and which is *u·* to the material senses.
- 596– 7 dedicated "to the *u·* God." — *Acts* 17 : 23.
- 598–29 where sin, sickness, and death are *u·*.

unlabored
- *t* 445–20 illustrates the *u·* motion of the divine energy

unlawfully
- *f* 238–19 to enter *u·* into the labors of others.

unless
- *s* 155–12 dissent or faith, *u·* it rests on Science,
- 160–22 *U·* muscles are self-acting at all times,
- *f* 231– 3 *U·* an ill is rightly met and fairly overcome
- *b* 283–26 *u·* its Science be accurately stated.
- 283–28 *u·* we so do, we can no more demonstrate
- 324– 7 *U·* the harmony and immortality of man are
- *o* 350–13 *U·* the works are comprehended
- *p* 379–29 *U·* the fever-picture, drawn by
- 392–20 *u·* Science shows you otherwise.
- 394–23 *u·* it can be aided by a drug
- 404–32 *u·* it makes him better mentally,
- 416– 4 *u·* the mental image occasioning the pain
- 416–13 *u·* the belief which occasions the pain has
- *t* 449–31 and *u·* this result follows,
- 450–17 but *u·* this admission is made,
- 452–15 Never breathe an immoral atmosphere, *u·*
- *gl* 590–18 *u·* specially coupled with the name God.

unlike
- *sp* 82–25 The mental states are so *u·*,
- 86–12 and produce *u·* results.
- *f* 243–28 a law of annihilation to everything *u·*
- 249–16 and includes nothing *u·* God.
- *c* 262–23 and conquering all that is *u·* God.
- *b* 277– 2 To all that is *u·* unerring and eternal Mind,
- 284–14 or know aught *u·* the infinite?
- 287–10 Truth and error are *u·*.
- 305–22 the deflections of matter . . . are all *u·* Spirit,
- 307–11 shall change sides and be *u·* Spirit.
- 335–26 and can produce nothing *u·* the eternal
- *p* 362– 3 though he was quite *u·* Simon the disciple.
- **393–12** to resist all that is *u·* good.

unlike
- *p* 403–26 so-called mind produces all that is *u·* the
- 406–16 all that is *u·* the true likeness disappears.
- *r* 468– 5 because error is *u·* Truth.
- 475–11 The likeness of Spirit cannot be so *u·* Spirit.
- *g* 506– 2 Objects utterly *u·* the original do not

unlikeness
- *f* 204–14 evil, is the *u·* of good.
- *c* 257– 5 then Spirit, matter's *u·*, must be
- *b* 277–24 The *u·* of Spirit is matter,
- 285–10 the *u·* called sin, sickness, and **death**.
- 287–11 the *infinite* God can have no *u·*.
- 288– 2 *error, Truth's u·, is unreal.*
- 339– 8 there is no room for His *u·*.
- *o* 345– 6 God cannot be in His *u·*.
- *r* 470– 9 infinite Truth without an *u·*,
- 470–14 *u·* of God, is unreal.
- 471– 6 The *u·* of Truth, — named *error*,
- 492– 6 Life cannot be united to its *u·*,

unlimited
- *a* 36–19 *u·* and divine Mind is the immortal law
- *sp* 76–23 possessing *u·* divine beauty and goodness
- *b* 284– 6 and *u·* Mind would seem to spring from a
- 288–28 *u·* by the mortal senses.
- 312–22 God is infinite Love, which must be *u·*.
- 336– 4 never . . . the *u·* into the limited,

unlock
- *sp* 70– 4 revelations of C. S. *u·* the treasures of

unloose
- *a* 28–23 if thou art found worthy to *u·* the sandals of

unloosed
- *ap* 564–22 *u·* in order that the false claim

unmake
- *b* 270–27 If sin makes sinners, Truth . . . can *u·* them.

unmanly
- *ph* 176– 4 and *u·* Adams attributed their own downfall

unmarried
- *m* 68–17 she was *u·*, a lovely character,

unmasked
- *f* 205– 9 When will the error . . . be *u·*?

unmedicated
- *s* 156–17 to give her *u·* pellets
- 156–25 She went on in this way, taking the *u·* pellets,

unmerited
- *pr* 3–21 We plead for *u·* pardon
- 9– 3 The wrong lies in *u·* censure,

unmistakable
- *ph* 188–21 are traced upon mortals by *u·* signs.

unmistakably
- *a* 46–23 and revealed *u·* a probationary
- *g* 522–12 This second record *u·* gives the
- *ap* 573–10 This shows *u·* that what the human mind

unnatural
- *a* 23– 7 divinely *u·*. Such a theory is man-made.
- *sp* 78– 3 discords of disease, sin, and death, — are *u·*.
- *s* 119–23 while evil should be regarded as *u·*,
- 130–31 no longer think it . . . *u·* to forsake it,
- 131– 1 should not seem so surprising and *u·* as error,
- *f* 217–10 *u·* mental and bodily conditions,
- *b* 304–21 and discord is *u·*, unreal.
- *p* 420– 9 cannot produce this *u·* reluctance.
- *g* 551– 2 material senses and their reports are *u·*,

unnecessary
- *ph* 181–25 It is *u·* to resort to aught besides Mind
- *b* 274– 3 *U·* knowledge gained from the
- *p* 396– 5 Make no *u·* inquiries relative to feelings

unobstructed
- *gl* 593–15 When smooth and *u·*, it typifies the

unpaid
- *f* 225–23 Legally to abolish *u·* servitude in the

unparalleled
- *s* 117–22 his mighty, crowning, *u·*, and

unpleasant
- *p* 415– 8 when it contemplates *u·* things,

unprejudiced
- *ap* 570–14 Millions of *u·* minds — simple seekers

unprepared
- *t* 446– 3 with a community *u·* for self-defence.

unpretentious
- *a* 54–22 There adhered to him only a few *u·* friends,

unqualified
- *o* 342– 5 In the result of some *u·* condemnations

unquestionable
- *f* 232–29 *u·* signs of the burial of error
- 233–26 is not more *u·* than the scientific tests

unreal
and the real
  g 538–10 the material and spiritual,— the *u·* and the real.
and untrue
  gl 584– 9 the *u·* and untrue ; the opposite of Life.
author of the
  r 474–28 error, not Truth, is the author of the *u·*,
both are
  a 39–24 both are *u·*, because impossible in Science.
concept
  an 102– 7 it is an *u·* concept of the so-called
discord is
  b 276–16 Discord is *u·* and mortal.
  p 414–23 harmony is universal, and discord is *u·*.
discord the
  ap 563– 2 harmony is the real and discord the *u·*.
disease is
  f 229–32 the truth that disease is *u·*.
error is
  c 265–21 the error is *u·* and obsolete.
  b 288– 2 correlated statement, that *error.* . . . *is u·*.
  p 368– 4 Truth is real and error is *u·*.
  r 466–16 Moreover, Truth is real, and error is *u·*.
  472–18 Error is *u·* because untrue.
evil is
  t 447–31 He may say, as a subterfuge, that evil is *u·*,
  g 527–19 Evil is *u·* because it is a lie,
forsake the
  b 339–18 repent of sin and forsake the *u·*,
in divine Science
  o 353– 2 real to material sense, is *u·* in divine Science.
inharmony is
  b 276–12 The realization that all inharmony is *u·*
master
  f 226–23 years of servitude to an *u·* master
matter is the
  r 468–13 matter is the *u·* and temporal.
real and
  g 505–22 line of demarcation between the real and *u·*.
real and the
  o 360–21 swinging between the real and the *u·*.
real or
  g 524–24 Is this addition to His creation real or *u·* ?
sensuous
  o 353– 1 scientific real is the sensuous *u·*.
temporal and
  b 300–13 temporal and *u·* never touch the eternal and
vanishes
  r 474–28 the *u·* vanishes, while all that is real is eternal.

  sp 76–18 Suffering, sinning, dying beliefs are *u·*.
  an 103–11 for the latter is *u·*.
  s 114–15 implies something untrue and therefore *u·* ;
  ph 186–13 It is *u·*, because it presupposes the
  f 212–31 *u·* and imitative movements of mortal belief,
  241– 9 as imaginary, whimsical, and *u·* as his
  b 270– 7 If one is real, the other must be *u·*.
  277–11 evil and materiality are *u·*
  293– 1 this *u·* material mortality disappears
  298–11 To material sense, the *u·* is the real
  298–18 the boundary of the mortal or the *u·*.
  304–21 and discord is unnatural, *u·*.
  337–27 Temporal things . . . are the *u·*,
  339–10 evil, being contrary to good, is *u·*,
  339–14 would make that real which is *u·*,
  o 347–31 and the inharmonious *u·*.
  350–29 through which the real reaches the *u·*,
  352–11 the intangible and uncertain, if not the *u·*.
  353–30 the ghost, some *u·* belief.
  354–26 Sin should become *u·* to every one.
  p 408–31 sensation in matter is *u·*.
  414–30 whereas imperfection is blameworthy, *u·*,
  417–24 to cure the patient is to make disease *u·*
  t 460–14 Sickness is neither imaginary nor *u·*,— that is,
  461–25 error is not true, hence it is *u·*.
  r 470–14 then evil, the unlikeness of God, is *u·*.
  470–16 seem to be real by giving reality to the *u·*.
  480–13 has its realm apart from Science in the *u·*.
  485–13 sin, disease, and death appear more and more *u·*
  494–27 mortal testimony, changing, dying, *u·*.
  497–11 casts out evil as *u·*.
  g 529–29 we know that they are worthless and *u·*.
  538–22 and evil is brought into view only as the *u·*
  551– 2 their reports are unnatural, impossible, and *u·*.
unrealities
  r 472–28 *u·* seem real to human, erring belief,
unreality
awful
  s 110– 9 I beheld, as never before, the awful *u·* called
  b 339–16 against his own awakening to the awful *u·*
deception and
  f 207–10 evil is the awful deception and *u·* of existence.
discord the
  o 352– 4 and discord the *u·*.

unreality
material
  f 228–19 and discord as the material *u·*.
of disease
  p 417–25 must understand the *u·* of disease in Science.
  t 461–28 the error or *u·* of disease,
of evil
  f 205–21 the nothingness and *u·* of evil.
  b 339–12 Science demonstrates the *u·* of evil,
  339–19 fully understand the *u·* of evil.
of sin
  t 461–26 To prove scientifically the error or *u·* of sin,
prove its
  t 447–27 get the victory over sin and so prove its *u·*.
relapses into its own
  b 277– 5 The non-intelligent relapses into its own *u·*.
saw its
  b 308–21 till he saw its *u·* ;
typifies
  g 538–15 "tree of knowledge" typifies *u·*.— *Gen. 2 : 9.*

  b 269– 7 the *u·*, the nothingness, of evil.
  285–11 The *u·* of the claim that a mortal
  g 502– 4 preponderance of *u·* in the entire narrative,
  502– 5 as if reality did not predominate over *u·*,
  525–22 valueless or baneful, . . . hence its *u·*.
  gl 580–10 an *u·* as opposed to the great reality of
unreasonable
  sp 78– 6 How *u·* is the belief that we are
unrecognized
  a 39– 1 met the mockery of his *u·* grandeur.
unreliability
  b 295– 3 proof of the *u·* of physical testimony.
unremoved
  p 416–11 will tell you that the . . . material cause is *u·*
unrequited
  a 49–11 sublime courage, and *u·* affection
unreservedly
  b 269–22 I therefore plant myself *u·* on the
unrest
  gl 596–24 illumine it, destroy the *u·* of mortal thought,
unrestrained
  t 459–16 untaught and *u·* by C. S.,
unrighteous
  s 139– 2 the *u·* man his thoughts."— *Isa. 55 : 7.*
  f 206–11 for it is the prayer of the *u·* ;
  239–15 the *u·* man his thoughts."— *Isa. 55 : 7.*
  b 290–20 They who are *u·* shall be *u·* still,
unsafe
  s 159– 1 her physicians insisted that it would be *u·*
unsatisfactory
  t 444– 1 If the sick find these material expedients *u·*,
unsatisfied
  c 258– 4 Hence the *u·* human craving for
unsay
  f 204–32 must *u·* it and cease from such utterances ;
unscientific
  sp 79–23 The *u·* practitioner says : "You are ill.
  s 114– 6 The spiritually *u·* definition of mind
  159–15 Had these *u·* surgeons understood metaphysics,
  ph 199–29 the *u·* might attribute to a lubricating oil.
  f 223–23 and supplant *u·* means and so-called laws.
  b 300–28 This theory is *u·*.
  375–15 All *u·* mental practice is erroneous
  p 369–22 *U·* methods are finding their dead level.
unscrupulous
  f 235–16 while the debased and *u·* mind,
unsearchable
  c 264– 9 Where . . . but in the *u·* realm of Mind?
unsee
  t 461–29 you must mentally *u·* the disease ;
unseen
  pr 15– 7 The Father in secret is *u·* to the physical
  a 28– 5 taught the *u·* verities of God,
  ph 189–11 though the cause be *u·*,
  f 208–24 cannot be lost nor remain forever *u·*.
  212–22 mortals believe that *u·* spirits produce the
  212–30 origin of all things are *u·* to mortal sense ;
  234–30 action of the human mind, *u·* to the senses.
  b 299– 4 which embodies his conception of an *u·* quality
  314–17 seemed a spectre, *u·* and unfamiliar,
  334–13 This dual personality of the *u·* and the seen,
  p 377–17 Because a belief originates *u·*,
  429–17 bodies *u·* by those who think that they bury the
          body.
  t 464–10 She therefore remains *u·* at her post,
  r 481–11 contradictions . . . do not change the *u·* Truth,
  ap 570– 5 certain active yet *u·* mental agencies

unselfed
  pr 1– 4 a spiritual understanding of Him, an u· love.
  ph 192–30 thought in line with u· love,
unselfish
  a 51–28 Jesus was u·.
  m 57–19 It is u· ; therefore it cannot exist alone,
      58– 7 U· ambition, noble life-motives, and purity,
      59–17 Tender words and u· care in what promotes
  b 272– 5 only as we are honest, u·, loving,
  p 365–11 but if the u· affections be lacking,
unselfishly
  pr 9–12 we shall regard our neighbor u·,
  c 262–22 and attain the bliss of loving u·,
  r 483–32 to be well done, the work must be done u·.
unselfishness
  f 248–29 Let u·, goodness, mercy, justice,
  t 462–29 It unfolds the hallowed influences of u·,
  g 516–12 Love, redolent with u·,
unsettled
  m 65–24 An u·, transitional stage is never
unshaken
  p 417–15 hold your ground with the u· understanding of
unsightly
  p 431–28 lost my healthy hue and become u·,
unsought
  pr 6–20 according as His mercy is sought or u·,
  f 238–20 Truth often remains u·, until we
unspeakable
  c 264–26 and feel the u· peace which comes from an
unspiritual
  s 143–31 Inferior and u· methods of healing
  b 335–28 Nothing u· can be real, harmonious, or
unspoken
  pr 1–10 Thoughts u· are not unknown to the
      2–28 The u· desire does bring us nearer the
  p 363–26 did his insight detect this u· moral uprising?
    424–19 through u· thoughts resting on your patient.
unspotted
  m 04– 0 keep himself u· from the world."— Jas. 1 : 27.
unsubstantial
  b 301–30 presupposes soul to be an u· dweller in
unsuitable
  t 455– 4 u· conditions for healing the sick.
unsupported
  s 160– 6 U· by the faith reposed in it,
unsurpassed
  f 243– 9 u· power and love.
unsuspected
  f 235– 2 cannot go forth, . . . finding u· lodgment.
unsustained
  f 212–17 modus of their own, undirected and u·
  c 264–22 Sin is u· by Truth.
untaught
  t 450–16 u· and unrestrained by C. S.,
unthinking
  r 489– 2 When the u· lobster loses its claw,
until
  pref ix–21 did not appear in print u· 1876,
      ix–24 From 1807 u· 1875,
      xii–20 U· June 10, 1907, she had never
  pr 4–22 u· we awake in His likeness.
      6–13 u· belief in material life and sin is
     10– 8 U· we are thus divinely qualified
  a 18– * u· the kingdom of God— Luke 22 : 18.
     24–29 u· they saw that it enabled their Master to
     29– 4 continue this warfare u· they have
     39– 3 will endure u· Christianity's last
     39– 9 u· all error is destroyed.
     46– 2 u· they saw him after his crucifixion
     46–15 his body was not changed u· he himself
     48–15 Truth and Love bestow few palms u· the
  m 56– 8 U· the spiritual creation is discerned
     57–28 u· it ceases to sigh over the world
     64–26 U· it is learned that God is the Father
     65–21 u· we get at last the clear straining of
     67–15 one should stick to the wreck, u·
     68–12 "u· death do us part."
  sp 77– 6 u· the Science of being is reached.
     77–10 u· the spiritual understanding of Life is
     77–11 Then, and not u· then, will it be
     92–21 U· they cast concerning error
     96–10 u· the final spiritualization of
     96–18 u· their nothingness appears.
     96–19 will continue u· the end of error,
     96–23 u· all errors of belief yield to
     97–12 u· matter reaches its mortal zenith
     97–18 the more obvious its error, u·
     97–24 the louder will error scream, u·

until
  sp 99–25 u· the beliefs of material existence are
  s 109– 7 u· its divine Principle is demonstrated
    118–23 This continues u· the leaven of Spirit
    121–19 U· rebuked by clearer views of the
    131–24 u· the hearts of men are made ready
    137– 4 u· after the crucifixion, when their
    141–25 u· its divine Principle is scientifically
    153– 6 u· there was not a single saline property
    158–21 u· mortal mind acquires an
  ph 192– 6 we leave all for Christ.
    197–27 will never grow robust u·
    198–20 u· the elasticity of mortal thought
  f 202–10 u· disciplined by the prison and the
    207– 4 u· it disappears from our lives.
    221– 9 should not wet his parched throat u·
    223–32 God will overturn, u·
    225–10 u· it subscribes to their systems ;
    230–29 u· the liability to be ill is removed.
    233–14 error continues its delusions u·
    238–20 we seek this remedy for human woe
    240–20 will be repeated u· all wrong work is
    240–28 u· all error is finally brought into
    248–31 will diminish u· they finally disappear.
    251–25 improves mankind u· error disappears,
    252–11 u· the entire mortal, material error finally
    254– 7 u· the battle between Spirit and flesh is
  c 255– * in pain together u· now.— Rom. 8 : 22.
    266–13 u· the lesson is sufficient to
  b 289– 3 u· he learns that God is the only
    290–21 u· in divine Science Christ, Truth,
    290 24 u· the death of these errors.
    290–30 u· evil is disarmed by good.
    291–24 u· probation and growth shall
    296–27 u· Science obliterates this false testimony.
    297– 1 and nothing can change this state, u·
    297– 4 u· the belief on this subject changes.
    297–28 U· belief becomes faith,
    298–11 u· this sense is corrected
    300–19 they grow side by side u· the harvest ;
    308– 5 U· the lesson is learned that
    308–20 u· his nature was transformed.
    309–16 u· the Messiah should rename them.
    314– 2 no less material u· the ascension
    014 3 u· the mortal or fleshly sense had
    322–19 u· his physical sense of pleasure yields
    323–11 u· boundless thought walks enraptured,
    323–16 good is not understood u· demonstrated.
    327–10 u· his grasp on good grows stronger.
    328–10 must therefore cling to mortals u·,
    329–15 U· one is able to prevent bad results,
    330– 2 U· the author of this book learned the
    334–15 continued u· the Master's ascension,
    339–22 u· the finite gives place to the infinite,
    340– 1 u· we lose our faith in them
  o 344–15 u· the enemies of C. S. test its
    353–18 u· perfection appears and reality is reached.
    361–28 u· God prepares the soil for the seed.
  p 374– 9 u· it appeared on my body?"
    380 27 u· it reaches its culmination of
    388–27 u· we gain perfection
    401 27 U· the advancing age admits the
    403–18 u· mortal error is deprived of its
    405–15 u· the last farthing is paid,
    405–16 u· you have balanced your account
    406–24 u· we arrive at the fullness of
    410–28 u· the practitioner's healing ability is
    412–25 u· the body corresponds with the
    414–17 not u· your patients are prepared for
    431– 1 u· called for at this trial,
    431–18 u· I should release him.
    433–25 sentenced to be tortured u· he
    442–23 gives mortals temporary food and clothing u·
  t 453– 7 u· victory rests on the side of
    454–28 u· your students tread firmly in the
    458–13 trying to sustain the human body u·
    460–31 u· finally the shadow of old errors was
  r 471–24 and tried to adhere to it u· she
    472–29 u· God strips off their disguise
    474–14 u· the glorious Principle of these marvels is
              gained.
    484– 2 u· its absolute Science is reached.
    486– 5 u· every corporeal sense is quenched.
    490–12 U· it is understood, mortals are
    492–16 u· one is acknowledged to be the
    494–22 u· the Science of man's eternal harmony
  g 510–21 u· time has been already divided
    513–13 u· divine Science becomes the
    519–15 u· they throw off the old man and
    533–25 and multiplies u· the end thereof.
    538–19 U· that which contradicts the truth of
    543–12 u· mortals arrive at the understanding
    557– 1 repeated this operation daily, u· the
  ap 564–19 U· the majesty of Truth should be
  gl 584–14 u· every belief of life where Life is not
    595–20 u· the mortal disappears

untimely
 c 265–16 The senses represent birth as *u·*
  265–19 withered by the sun and nipped by *u·* frosts ;

untired
 f 220–11 leaves clap their hands as nature's *u·*

untiring
 ap 563–19 devil or evil, holding *u·* watch,

unto
 pr   1– * *verily I say u· you,* — *Mark* 11 : 23.
      1– * *whosoever shall say u·* — *Mark* 11 : 23.
      1– * *Therefore I say u· you,* — *Mark* 11 : 24.
      2– 7 and it does not return *u·* us void.
      6–26 "Thou art an offence *u·* me." — *Matt.* 16 : 23.
      8– 9 "like *u·* whited sepulchres — *Matt.* 23 : 27.
     14–21 I go *u·* my Father," — *John* 14 : 12.
  a 18– * *I say u· you, I will not* — *Luke* 22 : 18.
     20– 1 "*u·* Cæsar the things which — *Matt.* 22 : 21.
     20– 2 *u·* God the things that — *Matt.* 22 : 21.
     32– 1 will they do *u·* you, — *John* 16 : 3.
     34– 4 acceptable *u·* God," — *Rom.* 12 : 1.
     48– 3 He said *u·* them :
     49– 6 devils are subject *u·* us — *Luke* 10 : 17.
 sp 70– * *they shall say u· you,* — *Isa.* 8 : 19.
     70– * *Seek u· them that have* — *Isa.* 8 : 19.
     70– * *u· wizards that peep* — *Isa.* 8 : 19.
     70– * *Should not a people seek u·* — *Isa.* 8 : 19.
     70– * *verily, I say u· you,* — *John* 8 : 51.
     70– * *Then said the Jews u· him,* — *John* 8 : 52.
     96–10 will continue *u·* the end,
  s 107– * *is like u· leaven,* — *Matt.* 13 : 33.
    108– 4 given *u·* me by the — *Eph.* 3 : 7.
    109–26 " *U·* us a child is born, — *Isa.* 9 : 6.
    131–18 "He came *u·* his own, — *John* 1 : 11.
    131–21 hast revealed them *u·* babes : — *Luke* 10 : 21.
    134– 6 so often persecuted *u·* death,
    137–23 hath nor revealed it *u·* — *Matt.* 16 : 17.
    137–30 I say also *u·* thee, — *Matt.* 16 : 18.
    141–21 "kings and priests *u·* God." — *Rev.* 1 : 6.
 ph 165– * *Therefore I say u· you,* — *Matt.* 6 : 25.
  f 242– 5 from the least of them *u·* — *Jer.* 31 : 34.
  c 256–22 or say *u·* Him, What does Thou?" — *Dan.* 4 : 35.
  b 268– * *declare we u· you,* — *I John* 1 : 3.
    272–17 "Give not that which is holy *u·* — *Matt.* 7 : 6.
    286– 9 cometh *u·* the Father — *John* 14 : 6.
    305–16 and said *u·* them : — *John* 5 : 19.
    305–17 verily I say *u·* you, — *John* 5 : 19.
    325–23 acceptable *u·* God, — *Rom.* 12 : 1.
  p 385–23 You are a law *u·* yourself.
    398–12 I say *u·* thee, arise !" — *Mark* 5 : 41.
    435–20 "*u·* others as ye would
    435–21 that they should do *u·* you,"
    438– 5 I give *u·* you power — *Luke* 10 : 19.
  t 446–23 *u·* the end of the world." — *Matt.* 28 : 20.
    458–24 becoming a law *u·* himself.
  r 467– 8 The second is like *u·* it,
    496–13 "*u·* the perfect day." — *Prov.* 4 : 18.
    497–26 do *u·* others as we would have them do *u·* us ;
  g 501– * *u· Abraham, u· Isaac, and u· Jacob* — *Exod.* 6 : 3.
    506–16 gathered together *u·* — *Gen.* 1 : 9.
    517–25 and God said *u·* them, — *Gen.* 1 : 28.
    519–19 *u·* a perfect man, — *Eph.* 4 : 13.
    519–20 *u·* the measure of the — *Eph.* 4 : 13.
    527–23 brought them *u·* Adam — *Gen.* 2 : 19.
    528–13 brought her *u·* the man. — *Gen.* 2 : 22.
    529–15 said *u·* the woman, — *Gen.* 3 : 1.
    529–17 said *u·* the serpent, — *Gen.* 3 : 2.
    530–13 said *u·* the woman, — *Gen.* 3 : 4.
    532–14 called *u·* Adam, and said *u·* him, — *Gen.* 3 : 9.
    534– 9 said *u·* the serpent, — *Gen.* 3 : 14.
    535– 6 *U·* the woman He said, — *Gen.* 3 : 16.
    535–19 And *u·* Adam He said, — *Gen.* 3 : 17.
    535–20 *u·* the voice of thy wife, — *Gen.* 3 : 17.
    535–26 return *u·* the ground ; — *Gen.* 3 : 19.
    535–27 *u·* dust shalt thou return. — *Gen.* 3 : 19.
    540–17 "*u·* Cæsar the things which — *Matt.* 22 : 21.
    540–18 *u·* God the things that are — *Matt.* 22 : 21.
    540–26 an offering *u·* the Lord — *Gen.* 4 : 3.
    541– 7 had respect *u·* Abel, — *Gen.* 4 : 4.
    541– 7 but *u·* Cain, and to his — *Gen.* 4 : 5.
    541–19 Lord . . . said *u·* Cain, — *Gen.* 4 : 9.
    541–28 crieth *u·* Me from the ground. — *Gen.* 4 : 10.
    542–14 Lord . . . said *u·* him, — *Gen.* 4 : 15.
    545–29 *u·* dust . . . shalt thou — *Gen.* 3 : 19.
 ap 562–20 "*u·* the perfect day" — *Prov.* 4 : 18.
    565– 8 caught up *u·* God, — *Rev.* 12 : 5.
    565–27 and to be caught up *u·* God,
    567–24 "cast *u·* the earth" — *Rev.* 12 : 9.
    568–19 loved not their lives *u·* the — *Rev.* 12 : 11.
    568–22 is come down *u·* you, — *Rev.* 12 : 12.
    569–30 was cast *u·* the earth, — *Rev.* 12 : 13.
    574– 6 there came *u·* me one of — *Rev.* 21 : 9.
 gl 596– 9 Him declare I *u·* you." — *Acts* 17 : 23.
    597– 5 if only he appeared *u·* men to fast.
 fr 600– * *u· all pleasing,* — *Col.* 1 : 10.

untouched
  s 116–14 Works on metaphysics leave the grand point *u·*
  b 310–14 Soul as God, *u·* by sin and death,

untoward
  p 385–15 deprivations, exposures, and all *u·* conditions.

untrue
  s 114–14 implies something *u·* and therefore unreal ;
    135–24 neither is unimportant or *u·*,
    143– 2 and Truth destroys only what is *u·*.
  f 232–13 These theories must be *u·*,
  b 289–27 and therefore the material must be *u·*.
    299–22 judge the knowledge thus obtained to be *u·*
    318–10 all that is material, *u·*, selfish, or debased.
  r 472–19 Error is unreal because *u·*.
  g 502–10 the history of the *u·* image of God,
 gl 584–10 the unreal and *u·* ; the opposite of Life.

untutored
 sp 89–24 and the fervor of *u·* lips.

unused
  b 323–18 but the one *u·* talent decays and is lost.

unusual
 sp 86–15 only because it is *u·* to see thoughts,
    86–17 Haunted houses, ghostly voices, *u·* noises,
  p 362– 4 While they were at meat, an *u·* incident

unveiled
  a 38–25 He *u·* the Christ, the spiritual idea of

unveiling
  p 366–24 and by the *u·* of sin in his own thoughts.

unveils
  f 216– 6 Science *u·* the mystery and solves the problem
  p 406–11 The Science of being *u·* the errors of sense,
  g 535–14 It *u·* the results of sin as shown in
    542– 7 Truth, through her eternal laws, *u·* error.

unwelcome
  p 364–30 as Jesus said of the *u·* visitor,

unwilling
 pr 9–30 If *u·* to follow his example, why
  s 148–29 it ignores the divine Spirit as unable or *u·*
    156–16 she was *u·* to give up the medicine
  f 237–23 Some invalids are *u·* to know the facts
    237–29 *u·* to investigate the Science of Mind
  p 420– 7 If they are *u·* to do this for themselves,

unwillingness
 sp 96– 2 *u·* to learn all things rightly,

unwinding
  f 240–30 involves *u·* one's snarls,

unwise
  s 130– 9 It is *u·* to doubt if reality is
  p 413– 9 The wise or *u·* views of parents

unwitting
  f 212–10 an *u·* attempt to scratch the end of a finger

unwittingly
 ph 179–29 *u·* sowing the seeds of reliance on matter,
    180–15 the invalid may *u·* add more fear
    196–31 The press *u·* sends forth many sorrows
  p 378– 4 *U·* you sentence yourself to suffer.

unwontedly
 sp 89– 5 the devotee may become *u·* eloquent.

unworthy
  m 61–27 Nothing *u·* of perpetuity should be
  p 441–10 The plea of False Belief we deem *u·* of
  t 455–24 does not bestow His highest trusts upon the *u·*.

upheaval
  p 401–16 *chemicalization* is the *u·* produced when

uphill
 ap 574– 4 journeying "*u·* all the way."

uphold
  r 481–26 If sin is supported, God must *u·* it,

upholds
  f 229–18 the individual who *u·* it is mistaken in

uplift
 ph 175–11 its beauty and fragrance, should *u·* the thought,
  f 235–29 should *u·* the standard of Truth.
  r 492– 9 will *u·* the physical and moral standard
    497–21 his resurrection served to *u·* faith

uplifting
  s 109–19 cures were produced . . . by holy, *u·* faith ;
  f 235–14 The pure and *u·* thoughts of the teacher,
  p 371–27 The necessity for *u·* the race is father to
    388– 2 Through the *u·* and consecrating power of

uplifts
  g 505–16 Spirit imparts the understanding which *u·*

upper
  f 247– 8 retained his full set of *u·* and lower teeth
  g 531– 8 It is well that the *u·* portions of the brain

upright
ph 171– 8 and will find himself unfallen, *u·*, pure,
200–19 neither inverted nor subverted, but *u·* and
f 239–11 is not the ruler of his *u·* neighbor.
p 432– 4 and know him to be truthful and *u·*,

uprising
p 363–26 did his insight detect this unspoken moral *u·*?

uproot
m 57–25 may *u·* the flowers of affection,
ph 180– 3 and to *u·* its false sowing.

uprooted
ph 188–27 disease must be *u·* and cast out.

uproots
b 272– 8 the swinish element in human nature *u·* it.

upsets
sp 73– 9 The belief . . . *u·* both the individuality and

upside
b 301–28 with everything turned *u·* down.

upturned
s 142–11 If the soft palm, *u·* to a lordly salary,

upward
ph 172– 8 as rising from matter *u·*.
b 299–10 they point *u·* to a new and glorified trust,
p 434–18 earnest, solemn eyes, . . . look *u·*.
g 545– 9 by thought tending spiritually *u·*
552–19 open their shells . . . and look outward and *u·*.

upward-soaring
b 299–12 These *u·* beings never lead towards self,

urged
a 19–29 Jesus *u·* the commandment,
s 148– 5 He prescribed no drugs, *u·* no obedience to
r 476– 6 *u·* to its final limits, is self-destroyed.
g 552–27 *u·* to its utmost limits, results in a return to

urges
f 223–29 as truth *u·* upon mortals its resisted claims ;
b 280–22 *u·* through every avenue the belief that
p 433– 8 Judge Medicine, *u·* the jury not to allow
t 402–00 It *u·* the government of the body

urging
sp 92–28 instead of *u·* the claims of Truth alone.
p 371–22 No impossible thing do I ask when *u·* the

Urim
gl 595–13 The *U·* and Thummim, which were to be
596–11 definition of

Us
gl 588–11 but one I, or *U·*, but one divine Principle,
591–16 MIND. The only I, or *U·* ; the only Spirit,

usage
a 30–12 wholly apart from mortal *u·*,
55– 4 to unchristian comment and *u·*
m 63–16 marvel why *u·* should accord woman less
s 114– 1 *U·* classes both evil and good together
o 341– 8 appear contradictory when subjected to such *u·*.

usages
p 437–29 on the ground that unjust *u·* were not allowed

use
common
p 363– 3 which is in such common *u·* in the East.
human
s 143– 6 nor provide them for human *u·* ;
its
s 141 15 and its *u·* is to be condemned.
Jesus'
ap 576–16 was familiar with Jesus' *u·* of this word,
little
ph 166–17 To ignore God as of little *u·* in sickness is a
man's
g 530– 7 brings forth food for man's *u·*.
medical
s 157–21 If He . . . designs them for medical *u·*,
of drugs
sp 79– 8 is more sanitary than the *u·* of drugs,
s 155– 3 When the sick recover by the *u·* of drugs,
of inanimate drugs
an 105–32 from the *u·* of inanimate drugs to the
of material remedies
t 453–12 never . . . from the *u·* of material remedies
of purgatives
p 408–14 by the *u·* of purgatives and narcotics
of the word
s 114–13 involves an improper *u·* of the word *mind.*
127– 1 or questions her *u·* of the word
r 482– 6 The proper *u·* of the word *soul* can always
of tobacco
p 383–24 Does his assertion prove the *u·* of tobacco
t 454– 2 the *u·* of tobacco or intoxicating drinks
prolonged
s 156–15 from their prolonged *u·*,

use
right
t 444–10 guide them into the right *u·* of
———
pr 13–10 such as the heathen *u·*.
a 32–21 confined to the *u·* of bread and wine.
44–17 that he might *u·* those hands to remove **the**
b 309– 4 which, to *u·* the word of the Psalmist,
329–12 we can *u·* only what we understand.
o 349–17 one is obliged to *u·* material terms
354– 7 Why do they *u·* this phraseology, and yet
p 402–22 or hypnotism, to *u·* the recent term
t 453–13 as from the *u·* of spiritual.
455–12 if, knowing the remedy, you fail to *u·* the
463–26 nor did he *u·* drugs.
r 468–19 as the Scriptures *u·* this word in Hebrews :
479–16 or *u·* any of the physical senses?
482– 8 In other cases, *u·* the word *sense,*

used
pr 5–22 Prayer is not to be *u·* as a confessional
a 32–10 nor was the wine, *u·* on convivial occasions
38–15 Here the word *hands* is *u·* metaphorically,
sp 94– 6 implied by the terms . . . as *u·* in Scripture.
94–27 blasphemer who should hint that Jesus *u·* his
s 114–16 and as the phrase is *u·* in teaching C. S.,
114–19 if . . . could be suggested, it would be *u·* ;
126– 2 Error will be no longer *u·* in stating truth.
136– 7 he *u·* his divine power to save men
157–20 then they should never be *u·*.
ph 178– 3 the strychnine, or whatever the drug *u·*,
198–32 or that a less *u·* arm must be weak.
f 236– 4 How shall it be *u·*?
b 333– 4 though it is commonly so *u·*.
o 345– 2 thus they are uniformly *u·* and understood in
p 380–30 with strength to be *u·* against
410–26 if mental practice is abused or is *u·*
414– 8 The arguments to be *u·* in curing insanity
418–17 if arguments are *u·* to destroy it,
t 457– 8 has never *u·* this newly discovered power in
460– 9 though *u·* for physical healing.
r 482– 9 As *u·* in C. S., Soul is properly the
g 517– 1 word for *man* is *u·* also as the synonym of *mind.*
ap 568– 9 The narrative follows the order *u·* in Genesis.
576–26 as *u·* in our version of the Old Testament,
gl 588–22 obsolete in Science if *u·* with reference to Spirit,
590–21 This double term is not *u·* in the first chapter of
598– 1 word for *wind (pneuma)* is *u·* also for *spirit,*

useful
pref x–10 A few books, however, . . . are *u·*.
ph 194–17 history of Kaspar Hauser is a *u·* hint
f 245–18 instance of youth preserved furnishes a *u·* hint,
b 268– 2 has brought to light . . . many *u·* wonders.
p 370–29 These lessons are *u·*.
382–10 receive a *u·* rebuke from Jesus' precept,
t 463–11 this idea cannot injure its *u·*
g 514–30 All of God's creatures, . . . are harmless, *u·*,
528–30 may be a *u·* hint to the medical faculty.

useless
a 36–24 It is *u·* to suppose that the wicked can
s 135–23 else one or the other is false and *u·* ;
ph 168–16 systems insist that man becomes sick and *u·*,
p 382–31 Adherence to hygiene was *u·*.

uselessness
r 485– 9 because of their *u·* or their iniquity,

uses
m 66– 3 Sweet are the *u·* of adversity ;
an 105–22 Whoever *u·* his developed mental powers like
s 112–28 and yet *u·* another author's discoveries
143–13 the human mind *u·* one error to
p 370–17 but it *u·* the same medicine in both cases.

usher
p 382– 7 this alone would *u·* in the millennium.
g 529– 9 *u·* in Science and the glorious fact of creation,

ushered
s 130– 8 The Christian era was *u·* in with signs and
b 325– 4 *u·* into the undying realities of Spirit.
325–28 which *u·* Jesus into human presence,

ushers
r 490–25 immortal testimony *u·* in the

using
pref viii–17 by doctors *u·* material remedies ;
ph 182–24 and forthwith shut out the aid of Mind by *u·*
b 313–14 *U·* this word in its higher meaning,
p 370–12 *u·* the same drug which might cause the

usual
s 114–32 the *u·* opposition to everything new,
137–16 With his *u·* impetuosity, Simon replied
p 431–30 and perform my functions as *u·*,

usually
s 140– 2 Science is more than *u·* effectual in
p 378–31 we *u·* find displayed in human governments.
394–30 the sick *u·* have little faith in it till they

usually

t 461–21   *U·* to admit that you are sick,
462–18   as they *u·* do in every department
g 523–31   it is *u·* Jehovah, . . . who is referred to.

usurp

ph 167–13   cannot successfully *u·* the place and power of
g 549–30   to *u·* the prerogatives of omnipotence.

usurped

b 317– 3   since material knowledge *u·* the throne of

usurper

gl 580–17   the *u·* of Spirit's creation,

usurping

f 204–25   thus *u·* the name without the nature

usurps

g 513– 2   for the claim *u·* the deific prerogatives
541–23   At first it *u·* divine power.

utility

an 100–18   "In regard to the existence and *u·* of
o 355– 6   the proof of the *u·* of these methods ;
gl 583–15   that institution, which affords proof of its *u·*

utilization

s 111–12   *u·* of the power of Truth over error ;

utilize

t 455– 8   You must *u·* the moral might of Mind

utmost

f 240–28   must pay fully and fairly the *u·* farthing,
p 434–17   regards the prisoner with the *u·* tenderness.
r 486–10   preparatory school must be improved to the *u·*.
g 540– 8   stirring up the belief in evil to its *u·*,
552–27   intermixture . . . urged to its *u·* limits,

utter

pr 14–14   and the body will then *u·* no complaints.
a 47–32   Jesus realized the *u·* error of a belief in
sp 74–23   Who will say that infancy can *u·* the ideas of
97–23   It requires courage to *u·* truth ;

utter

o 354– 2   "*u·* falsities and absurdities,"
t 450– 6   They *u·* a falsehood, while
ap 559–14   to *u·* the full diapason of secret tones.

utterance

pr 7– 5   showing the necessity for such forcible *u·*,
sp 80– 3   is not lessened by giving *u·* to truth.
s 127–29   It is a divine *u·*, — the Comforter
f 208–18   Such an *u·* is "the voice of— *Matt.* 3 : 3.
233–29   The *u·* of truth is designed to rebuke
b 323–31   We are either turning away from this *u·*,
p 365– 7   The benign thought of Jesus, finding *u·*
g 545– 4   This could not be the *u·* of Truth or Science,

utterances

f 205– 1   must unsay it and cease from such *u·* ;
p 367–25   through silent *u·* and divine anointing

uttered

sp 97–26   *u·* His voice, the earth melted."— *Psal.* 46 : 6.
b 314–27   the more distinctly he *u·* the demands of
317– 1   Jesus *u·* things which had been
o 358–16   *u·* and illustrated by the prophets,
r 479– 4   could the Scriptural rejoicing be *u·* by any

uttering

pr 7–28   *u·* desires which are not real
sp 89– 2   is incapable of knowing or *u·*
b 323–30   "still, small voice" of Truth *u·*— *I Kings* 19 : 12.

utterly

s 129–10   your preconceptions or *u·* contrary to them.
g 506– 2   Objects *u·* unlike the original do not
545–12   is *u·* opposed to the theory of

uttermost

pr 5–11   we must pay "the *u·* farthing."— *Matt.* 5 : 26.

utters

b 307–20   partakes of its own nature and *u·* its own falsities.
p 441–11   Let what False Belief *u·*, now and forever,
g 533–13   the snake-talker *u·* the first voluble lie,

V

vacuity

r 480– 6   then there remains only the darkness of *v·*

vacuum

c 266– 9   this seeming *v·* is already filled with

vacuums

o 346–17   There are no *v·*.

vague

s 110–32   No analogy exists between the *v·* hypotheses
119– 1   When we endow matter with *v·* spiritual power,
b 298– 1   the *v·* realities of human conclusions.
g 504–26   hypotheses, and *v·* conjectures emit no such
545–18   Outside of C. S. all is *v·* and hypothetical,
549–21   in such *v·* hypotheses as must necessarily

vain

pr 2–31   Asking God to *be* God is a *v·* repetition.
6– 8   implies the *v·* supposition that we
10– 9   millions of *v·* repetitions will never
13– 9   "*v·* repetitions," such as the— *Matt.* 6 : 7.
a 37– 7   Mortals try in *v·* to slay Truth with the steel
s 130– 7   *v·* to speak dishonestly of divine Science,
142–15   In *v·* do the manger and the cross tell their
142–23   to purge the temples of their *v·* traffic
f 203–30   waves of sin, sorrow, and death beat in *v·*.
223–21   efforts of error to answer . . . by some *ology* are *v·*.
b 324–28   then is our preaching *v·*."— *I Cor.* 15 : 14.
p 373– 9   has struggled long, and perhaps in *v·*, to lift a

vainly

m 57–22   Human affection is not poured forth *v·*,
an 106– 4   and to push *v·* against the current

vale

ph 191–22   not a spray buds within the *v·*,

vales

f 240– 4   mighty billows, verdant *v·*, festive flowers,

valid

p 434–27   The only *v·* testimony in the case shows

validity

r 491– 4   without actual foundation or *v·*.
g 525– 3   the *v·* of matter is opposed,
525– 4   not the *v·* of Spirit or Spirit's creations.

valley

m 61– 9   Every *v·* of sin must be exalted,
ap 578–10   the *v·* of the shadow of death,— *Psal.* 23 : 4.
gl 596–20   definition of
596–21   the *v·* of the shadow of death,— *Psal.* 23 : 4.
596–26   maketh the *v·* to bud and blossom as the rose.

valleys

s 147–13   and in the *v·* of Galilee.

value

o 355–14   What is the relative *v·* of the two
t 443–20   may learn the *v·* of the apostolic precept :
gl 597– 5   were of little *v·*, if only he

valued

f 238– 1   are not rightly *v·* before they are understood.

valueless

s 125–20   theories about laws of health to be *v·*.
o 341–11   In C. S. mere opinion is *v·*.
g 525–21   Whatever is *v·* or baneful, He did not make,

values

pref ix–32   but she *v·* them as a parent may

valves

ph 187–13   The *v·* of the heart, opening and closing

vanish

sp 77–14   period required for this dream . . . to *v·* from
81– 6   their belief in mediumship would *v·*.
96–21   error will *v·* in a moral chemicalization.
f 209–29   will ultimately *v·*, swallowed up in the
o 352–29   objects of alarm will then *v·* into nothingness,
355– 2   and then the ambiguity will *v·*.
p 365–17   will *v·* into its native nothingness
415–29   the limbs will *v·* from consciousness.
r 480–32   evil would *v·* before the reality of good.
g 555–29   which seemed to *v·* in death.

vanished

sp 88– 4   the touch of a *v·* hand,
ap 573–20   the heavens and earth had *v·*,

vanishes

f 250–18   When that dream *v·*, the mortal finds
b 312– 7   as the sense-dream *v·* and reality appears.
p 416– 1   At last the agony also *v·*.
r 474–28   the unreal *v·*, while all that is real is eternal.

vanity

s 163–27   might gratify our *v·*, if it were not
f 239–32   the wise man said, "All is *v·*."— *Eccl.* 1 : 2.
b 303–15   All the *v·* of the ages can never make
gl 592–28   self-righteousness ; *v·* ; hypocrisy.

vanquished

a 45– 2   Jesus *v·* every material obstacle,
54– 4   With the affluence of Truth, he *v·* error.

vapid

b 293–21   There is no *v·* fury of mortal mind

vapor

b 295–23   Then, like a cloud melting into thin *v·*,
r 480–31   As *v·* melts before the sun,

vapors

s 163–31   to arrange the fleeting *v·* around us,

variable
g 503–25   mortal life, mutable truth, nor *v·* love.

variance
a 19–14   his teaching set households at *v·*,
an 106–22   hatred, *v·*, emulations, wrath, strife, — *Gal.* 5 : 20.
f 215– 7   Soul and matter are at *v·*

varied
b 319–15   The *v·* doctrines and theories which
r 466– 4   The *v·* manifestations of C. S. indicate Mind,
g 518–21   *v·* expressions of God reflect health,

various
pref x– 4   V· books on mental healing have since
s 144– 8   The *v·* mortal beliefs formulated in the
f 248–14   We are all sculptors, working at *v·* forms,
b 339–32   Our *v·* theories will never
o 344–19   There are *v·* methods of treating disease,
p 379–25   Fevers are errors of *v·* types.
437–21   V· notables — Materia Medica, Anatomy,
r 481– 9   The *v·* contradictions of the Science of Mind
g 553– 1   in the *v·* forms of embryology,
gl 587–12   the *v·* theories that hold mind to be

vary
s 149–12   its perfection of operation never *v·* in Science.
p 412– 5   You may *v·* the arguments to meet the

varying
b 311– 1   the *v·* clouds of mortal belief, which hide

vast
ph 177–32   but the *v·* majority of mankind,
f 209– 7   the life and light of all its own *v·* creation ;
246–18   Chronological data are no part of the *v·* forever.
c 266–31   into the *v·* forever of Life,
p 442– 6   throughout the *v·* audience-chamber of Spirit
r 479–21   In the *v·* forever, in the Science and truth of

vastly
s 116–12   includes *v·* more than is at first seen.

vastness
c 256–29   Finiteness cannot present the idea or the *v·* of
b 330– 3   learned the *v·* of C. S.,

vegetable
s 158– 9   from image-gods to *v·* and mineral drugs
f 244–24   He is not a beast, a *v·*, nor a migratory mind.
b 277–15   A mineral is not produced by a *v·*
309–28   error to suppose that there can be . . . *v·* life,
g 509–20   So-called mineral, *v·*, and animal substances

vegetables
f 221– 3   he ate only bread and *v·*,
244–14   like the beasts and *v·*, — subject to
b 277–13   Natural history presents *v·* and animals
g 531–19   Who will say that minerals, *v·*, and animals
543–22   Minerals and *v·* are found, according to
557– 7   V·, minerals, and many animals

vegetarianism
s 155–28   V·, homœopathy, and hydropathy

vehemently
p 420–29   *v·* tell your patient that he must awake.
421–15   Insist *v·* on the great fact

veil
a 41– 1   must be cast beyond the *v·* of matter
s 114–24   It lifts the *v·* of mystery from Soul and body.
g 513–10   but anon the *v·* is lifted, and the scene shifts
ap 563–15   Revelator lifts the *v·* from this embodiment of
gl 596–28   definition of
597–11   It rent the *v·* of the temple.

veils
gl 596–29   Jewish women wore *v·* over their faces

vein
s 122–24   the severance of the jugular *v·*

veins
a 25– 9   than when it was flowing in his *v·*
p 373–27   When the blood rushes madly through the *v·*
376–15   all the blood which ever flowed through mortal *v·*

venerable
f 215–32   would have killed the *v·* philosopher

veneration
sp 88–20   Excite the organ of *v·* or religious faith,

vengeance
a 51–25   pride, envy, cruelty, and *v·*,
g 542–15   *v·* shall be taken on him — *Gen.* 4 : 15.

venomous
m 66– 4   Which, like the toad, ugly and *v·*,

vented
a 23– 6   That God's wrath should be *v·* upon His

ventilation
pr 7–22   A self-satisfied *v·* of fervent sentiments

venture
f 254–24   If you *v·* upon the quiet surface of error
p 388–26   foolish to *v·* beyond our present understanding,

ventures
t 448–27   and *v·* not to break its rules,

verb
a 23–32   The Hebrew *v· to believe* means also *to be firm*
r 488– 9   from that conveyed by the English *v· believe;*

verbal
pr 3–25   Gratitude is much more than a *v·* expression
7–15   The motives for *v·* prayer may embrace
o 355– 7   and proofs are better than mere *v·* arguments

verbally
p 423– 3   either *v·* or otherwise,

verdant
f 240– 4   winged winds, mighty billows, *v·* vales,

verdict
s 159– 8   and a *v·* was returned that
ph 198– 4   A patient hears the doctor's *v·* as a
f 238–26   Justice often comes too late to secure a *v·*.
b 294–15   This *v·* of the so-called material senses
o 358–15   It presents the calm and clear *v·* of Truth
p 433–16   and the jury returns a *v·* of "Guilty of
440– 9   to give a *v·* delivering Mortal Man to Death.
441–29   to return a *v·* contrary to law and gospel.
442– 6   Spiritual Senses agreed at once upon a *v·*,

verdicts
r 481–22   human *v·* are the procurers of all discord.

verifies
p 382–21   This *v·* the saying of our Master :
t 446–22   enthrones faith in Truth, and *v·* Jesus' word :

verify
o 347– 3   It is said by one critic, that to *v·* this

verily
pr 1– *   *v·* I say unto you, — *Mark* 11 : 23.
sp 70– *   V·, *v·*, I say unto you, — *John* 8 : 51.
b 305–16   V·, *v·* I say unto you, — *John* 5 : 19.

veritable
sp 76–25   constitutes the only *v·*, indestructible man,
88– 9   How are *v·* ideas to be distinguished from
g 521–30   The history of error or matter, if *v·*, would

verities
eternal
s 110– 4   These eternal *v·* reveal primeval existence as
r 476–13   as the only and eternal *v·* of man.
grand
sp 75–31   from earth's sleep to the grand *v·* of Life,
p 384–15   will prove to himself, . . . the grand *v·* of C. S,
great
s 109–32   The three great *v·* of Spirit,
p 397–24   one must be familiar with the great *v·* of
g 543–15   The great *v·* of existence are never
simple
f 226–20   the simple *v·* that will make them happy
unseen
a 28– 5   and taught the unseen *v·* of God,
b 337–25   Eternal things (*v·*) are God's thoughts

verity
s 123–11   The *v·* of Mind shows conclusively
f 252–12   and the eternal *v·*, man created by
b 274–17   Jesus demonstrated this great *v·*.
296– 2   whereas Science unfolds the eternal *v·*,
305–13   that God's image is not a creator
339–32   You conquer error by denying its *v·*.
o 354–29   I rejoice in the apprehension of this grand *v·*.
p 114–26   Keep in mind the *v·* of being,
r 468– 7   for sin is not the eternal *v·* of being.
480–29   This is the eternal *v·* of divine Science.
g 502–25   the eternal *v·* and unity of God and man,
514–31   A realization of this grand *v·* was a

verse
sp 82– 6   yet we still read his thought in his *v·*.
ph 200– 1   through his *v·* the gods became alive in a
g 523–26   From the fourth *v·* of chapter two

verses
g 521–24   presented in the *v·* already considered,
523–23   and in three *v·* of the second,

version
r 488–12   often appear in our common *v·*
g 523–21   Lord God, as our common *v·* translates it.
ap 576–26   as used in our *v·* of the Old Testament,

versions
s 139–17   manifest mistakes in the ancient *v·* ;

versus
b 319– 3   disease as error, as matter *v·* Mind,
p 434–15   the case for Mortal Man *v·* Personal Sense

vertebræ
p 402– 7   dislocated joints, and spinal *v·*.

vertebrata
g 556– 3   V·, articulata, mollusca, and radiata are

very
pr	5– 4	one step towards reform and the *v·* easiest step.
	8–24	We confess to having a *v·* wicked heart
	13– 1	"a *v·* present help in trouble."— *Psal.* 46 : 1.
a	21–19	Our paths have diverged at the *v·* outset,
	27–30	made their strongest attack upon this *v·* point.
	28–28	is to mistake the *v·* nature of religion.
	53– 8	The reputation of Jesus was the *v·* opposite of
m	63–12	Civil law establishes *v·* unfair differences
sp	80– 9	Yet the *v·* periodical containing this sentence
	81– 7	At the *v·* best and on its own theories,
	84–25	destroys the belief of spiritualism at its *v·*
	89–28	Cain *v·* naturally concluded that if
an	102–22	produce the *v·* apathy on the subject which
	106– 3	is to drop . . . into the *v·* mire of iniquity,
s	129–28	The *v·* name, *illusion*, points to nothingness.
	134–18	robs Christianity of the *v·* element, which
	154–20	and they produce the *v·* results which
	161–27	would naturally induce the *v·* disease
ph	172– 6	nothing in the right direction and *v·* much in
	172–31	teaching us by his *v·* deprivations,
	195– 9	gave him pain through those *v·* senses,
f	202–28	"a *v·* present help in trouble ;"— *Psal.* 46 : 1.
	208–10	It is the *v·* antipode of immortal Mind,
	215– 8	from the *v·* necessity of their opposite
	222–22	He learned that a dyspeptic was *v·* far from
c	257–13	*v·* far from being the supposed substance of
	258–25	Mortals have a *v·* imperfect sense of
	266–23	would deceive the *v·* elect.
b	270– 6	in its *v·* nature and essence ;
o	350– 3	or as *v·* far removed from daily experience.
	352–22	thus watering the *v·* roots of childish timidity,
	360–31	on the *v·* basis of Jesus' words and works.
p	370–19	*v·* direct and marked effects on the body.
	376–17	it cannot, for that *v·* reason, suffer with a fever.
	379–24	her belief produces the *v·* results she dreads.
	407– 1	but there is a *v·* sharp remembrance of it,
	413– 4	induces those *v·* conditions.
	413–30	may be reproduced in the *v·* ailments feared.
	436–29	sentenced Mortal Man to die for the *v·* deeds
t	444– 2	these *v·* failures may open their blind eyes.
	444–12	a *v·* present help in trouble."— *Psal.* 46 : 1.
r	488–26	otherwise the *v·* worms could unfashion man.
g	518–25	"and, behold, it was *v·* good.— *Gen.* 1 : 31.
	525–24	"and, behold, it was *v·* good."— *Gen.* 1 : 31.
	541–18	ruptures the . . . brotherhood of man at the *v·*
	544–23	*v·* antipodes of immortal and spiritual being.
	547–23	The Scriptures are *v·* sacred.
	548–19	"It is *v·* possible that many general statements
ap	574–20	the *v·* message, or swift-winged thought,
	574–27	The *v·* circumstance, which your

vessel
s	130–20	cannot add to the contents of a *v·* already full.

vessels
f	201–13	We cannot fill *v·* already full.

vested
f	236– 3	A special privilege is *v·* in the ministry.
p	379– 7	recognizing all causation as *v·* in divine Mind.

vestibule
sp	75–29	In the *v·* through which we pass
o	356– 8	Matter is not the *v·* of Spirit.
gl	597–17	the *v·* in which a material sense of things

vestige
s	153– 1	that not a *v·* of it remains.
f	221–15	without a *v·* of the old complaint.

vestments
sp	93–20	human faith may clothe it with angelic *v·*,
p	372–24	parading in the *v·* of law.

vesture
s	125–24	"As a *v·* shalt Thou— *Psal.* 102 : 26.
f	242–21	The *v·* of Life is Truth.
	242–24	and for my *v·* they did cast lots."— *John* 19 : 24.
	242–27	appropriates no part of the divine *v·*,

vestures
c	260–29	If we array thought in mortal *v·*,

vials
ap	574– 7	which had the seven *v·* full of the— *Rev.* 21 : 9.
	574–18	the seven angelic *v·* full of seven plagues,

viand
sp	88– 7	when no *v·* touches the palate

vibrating
a	22– 3	*V·* like a pendulum between sin and the

vibration
c	259–25	*V·* is not intelligence ; hence it is not a creator.

vicarious
a	22–26	pinning one's faith . . . to another's *v·* effort.

vice
pr	11–16	suffered sufficiently from *v·* to make him
m	60–17	becoming a barrier against *v·*,
p	365–25	hypocrisy, stolidity, inhumanity, or *v·*
t	449–28	Only virtue is a rebuke to *v·*.
	452–17	the luxury of learning with egotism and *v·*.

vicegerent
f	224–14	and array His *v·* with pomp and splendor ;

vices
ap	571– 7	than when you tell them their *v·*.

vice versa
pr	15– 6	Closed to error, it is open to Truth, and *v· v·*.
s	160– 4	physics act against metaphysics, and *v· v·*.
ph	182– 1	will diminish your ability to become a Scientist, and *v· v·*.
b	279–15	no more. . .than Truth can create error, or *v· v·*.
	290–32	His body is as material as his mind, and *v· v·*.
p	374–30	Nothing that lives ever dies, and *v· v·*.

vicious
f	248–18	by *v·* sculptors and hideous forms?

victimize
s	158–20	to *v·* the race with intoxicating

victimizes
b	294–15	verdict of the so-called material senses *v·*

victims
f	230–14	and then punishing the helpless *v·*
o	352–19	at any moment they may become its helpless *v·* ;
p	420–10	that they are not helpless *v·*,
	447–11	and save the *v·* of the mental assassins.

victor
s	137– 6	the *v·* over sickness, sin, disease, and the
p	380– 4	Truth is always the *v·*.
	412– 9	and you will be the *v·*.
r	492–17	until one is acknowledged to be the *v·*.

victories
a	39– 9	trials and self-denials, as well as joys and *v·*,

victorious
p	407–10	If man is not *v·* over the

victory

everlasting
a	33–16	With the great glory of an everlasting *v·*
	45– 5	a sublime success, an everlasting *v·*.

get the
f	231– 2	so-called physical senses will get the *v·*.

obtained a
p	388– 3	obtained a *v·* over the corporeal senses,

over a single sin
ap	568–24	For *v·* over a single sin, we give thanks

over death
a	35–15	They celebrate their Lord's *v·* over death,
	45– 7	in his *v·* over death and the grave.
p	427–20	obtain the *v·* over death in proportion as

over evil
ap	571–17	the wisdom and the occasion for a *v·* over evil.

over sin
t	447–26	get the *v·* over sin and so prove its unreality.

seal the
a	44– 1	must seal the *v·* over error and death,
s	145–10	*v·* will be on the patient's side only as
	164–29	Death is swallowed up in *v·*"— *I Cor.* 15 : 54.
f	254– 8	until the battle . . . is fought and the *v·* won.
b	275–27	It robs the grave of *v·*.
	323–26	robs the grave of *v·*, takes away all sin
p	388– 4	a *v·* which Science alone can explain.
t	446–19	for *v·* rests on the side of immutable right.
	453– 7	until *v·* rests on the side of invincible truth.
r	492–32	*V·* would perch on neither banner.
	496–24	"Where is thy *v·* ?"— *I Cor.* 15 : 55.
	496–27	Death is swallowed up in *v·*."— *I Cor.* 15 : 54.

view

another
ap	574– 3	The Revelator also takes in another *v·*,

brought into
g	538–21	is brought into *v·* only as the unreal

correct
s	116–11	A correct *v·* of C. S. and of its adaptation to
r	477– 3	and this correct *v·* of man healed the sick.

exalted
gl	598–25	This exalted *v·*, obtained and retained when

false
g	545–17	a false *v·*, destructive to existence
	545–19	in its false *v·* of God and man,

hid from
ap	560–23	hid from *v·* the apostle's character,

human
s	150–22	human *v·* infringes man's free moral agency ;
b	276–13	brings objects and thoughts into human *v·*
	316–18	rose higher to human *v·* because of the

humiliating
s	163–28	more than compensated by the humiliating *v·*

material
g	521–25	a material *v·* of creation,
	521–27	this material *v·* of God and the universe,

mortal
b	315–30	(that is, as it seemed to mortal *v·*),

view

of sin
p 404–23 Arouse the sinner to this new and true v˙ of sin,

opposite
o 350– 5 C. S. takes exactly the opposite v˙.
352– 8 the Jews took a diametrically opposite v˙.

strongly in
p 414–26 Hold these points strongly in v˙.

such a
ap 573– 2 is unable to grasp such a v˙.

this
f 209–15 Nearness, . . . lends enchantment to this v˙.
p 408– 2 This v˙ is not altered by the fact that
r 471–27 This v˙ rebuked human beliefs,
gl 581– 1 This v˙ of Satan is confirmed by the name
b 322– 9 in v˙ of the immense work to be accomplished
p 396–15 in v˙ of the conceded falsity of

viewed
g 502–11 This deflection of being, rightly v˙,

viewing
s 119–25 In v˙ the sunrise, one finds that it

viewless
s 121–16 "a weary searcher for a v˙ home."

views

accurate
c 255– 9 afforded no foundation for accurate v˙ of

better
f 239– 9 and we get better v˙ of humanity.

clearer
s 121–20 rebuked by clearer v˙ of the everlasting facts,
f 239– 7 and we get clearer v˙
g 504–19 spiritually clearer v˙ of Him,

correct
c 264–13 As mortals gain more correct v˙ of God and

false
m 62–29 Our false v˙ of life hide eternal harmony,
b 281–29 Our false v˙ of matter perish
315–11 The opposite and false v˙ of the people

higher
c 262–14 These clearer, higher v˙ inspire the

his own
t 462–11 and substituting his own v˙ for Truth,

incorrect
ph 195–31 Incorrect v˙ lower the standard of truth.

limited
c 255–13 mortals take limited v˙ of all things.

material
b 314–11 showed plainly that their material v˙ were

new
m 66–15 unfolds new v˙ of divine goodness and love.

obscured
gl 586– 2 weariness of mortal mind ; obscured v˙ ;

of error
r 485–10 v˙ of error ought to be obliterated by Truth.

of parents
p 413– 9 v˙ of parents and other persons

of the universe
g 503–10 scientifically Christian v˙ of the universe

shape our
f 246–29 Let us then shape our v˙ of existence into

spiritual
a 32–27 refresh his heart with brighter, with spiritual v˙.

theological
a 24–16 the ordinary theological v˙ of atonement
sp 80–14 but I cannot coincide with their v˙.
g 504–19 v˙ which are not implied by

vigilant
b 324–13 Be watchful, sober, and v˙.

vigor
f 246–23 still maintain his v˙, freshness, and promise.

vigorous
pref viii–19 A v˙ "No" is the response
a 22– 8 to make v˙ efforts to save themselves ;
s 130–29 astounded at the v˙ claims of evil
ph 198–21 haply causes a v˙ reaction upon itself,

vigorously
p 413–15 in order to make it thrive more v˙

village
s 149–32 there is hardly a city, v˙, or hamlet, in which

villainy
f 252–20 says :. . .elude detection by smooth-tongued v˙.

vindicated
f 225–31 The rights of man were v˙ in a single section

vine
a 18– * not drink of the fruit of the v˙, — Luke 22 : 18.
fr 600– * let us see if the v˙ flourish, — Song 7 : 12.

vineyard
pref xi–24 also the charge to plant and water His v˙.

vineyards
fr 600– * Let us get up early to the v˙ ; — Song 7 : 12.

violate
s 118–30 and v˙ the law of Love, in which
134–31 A miracle fulfils God's law, but does not v˙ that

violence
pref viii–22 increased v˙ of diseases since the flood.
a 33–14 their Master was about to suffer v˙
an 105– 4 to prevent deeds of v˙ or to punish them.
s 161–15 less v˙ to that immortal sentiment
t 458–25 He does v˙ to no man.

violent
a 47–28 each one came to a v˙ death except St. John,
an 101– 1 that the v˙ effects, which are observed
ph 195– 7 All . . . except his black crust, produced v˙
t 464–14 seized with pain so v˙

violet
f 220– 9 The v˙ lifts her blue eye to greet the

viper
f 243– 5 made harmless the poisonous v˙,
g 514–28 Paul proved the v˙ to be harmless.

vipers
s 133–12 healed of the poisonous stings of v˙.

Virgil
sp 82– 7 discernment of the minds of Homer and V˙,

virgin
b 313– 1 He was the son of a v˙.
332–23 Jesus was the son of a v˙.

virginity
m 62– 3 period of gestation have the sanctity of v˙.

Virgin-mother
a 29–17 The V˙ conceived this idea of God,
29–25 overshadowed the pure sense of the V˙
g 534–12 The Son of the V˙ unfolded the remedy

virtually
f 229–12 v˙ declaring Him good in one instance
o 348– 3 Medical theories v˙ admit the
361–11 Thus he v˙ unites with the Jew's belief
p 380– 9 we v˙ contend against the control of
g 549–32 for he v˙ affirms that the germ of humanity

virtue

affection and
an 103– 1 promotes affection and v˙ in families

and power
s 150– 1 monuments to the v˙ and power of Truth,

and truth
f 235– 3 if v˙ and truth build a strong defence.
246–11 radiant sun of v˙ and truth coexists with being.

contentment and
t 452–16 intellectual repast with contentment and v˙,

garrisoned with
f 235–11 should be strongly garrisoned with v˙

goodness, and
m 57–18 the better claims of intellect, goodness, and v˙.

honesty and
m 64–20 Honesty and v˙ ensure the stability of the

increasing
m 86–14 moral regulations as will secure increasing v˙.

is a rebuke
t 449–28 Only v˙ is a rebuke to vice.

models of
f 235–20 Physicians, . . . should be models of v˙.

school of
m 65– 1 Experience should be the school of v˙,

virtues
s 156– 1 If drugs possess intrinsic v˙
ap 571– 6 like you better when you tell them their v˙

virus
ph 196–27 not from infection nor from contact with material v˙,

viscera
s 160–11 the organic action and secretion of the v˙.
p 415–24 all the organs . . . including brain and v˙.

Vishnu
g 524– 4 in the Hindoo V˙, in the Greek Aphrodite,

visible
s 118– 8 hidden in sacred secrecy from the v˙ world
125–15 the v˙ manifestation will at last be
c 264–15 multitudinous objects . . . will become v˙.
b 337–22 The v˙ universe and material man are the
p 400–25 the image which becomes v˙ to the senses.
r 478–12 nor were they even v˙ through the windows?
ap 559– 6 the source of all error's v˙ forms?
559– 8 exercised upon v˙ error and audible sin.
560–18 without a correct sense of its highest v˙ idea,

visibly
sp 80–31 both v˙ and invisibly,

vision

mortal
b 301–15 man's substantiality transcends mortal v˙

vision

mount of
ap 561– 9 beheld the spiritual idea from the mount of *v*·.

of St. John
o 357–24 the *v*· of St. John in the Apocalypse.

of the Apocalypse
m 56–10 as in the *v*· of the Apocalypse,
ap 572–14 can ever furnish the *v*· of the Apocalypse,

outward
gl 586– 5 Jesus said, thinking of the outward *v*·,

spiritual
f 215–11 Spiritual *v*· is not subordinate to
ap 561– 7 Because of his more spiritual *v*·,

St. John's
g 536– 5 In St. John's *v*·, heaven and earth stand for
ap 576– 6 reached St. John's *v*· while yet he

such
sp 87–13 The Scotch call such *v*· "second sight,"

whisper this
sp 76– 2 The ones departing may whisper this *v*·,

ap 572–26 Through what sense came this *v*· to St. John?
573– 9 while to another, . . . the *v*· is material.
577–30 his *v*· is the acme of this Science

visions
p 428– 5 resolves the dark *v*· of material sense

visit
m 64– 5 To *v*· the fatherless and widows— *Jas.* 1 : 27.
ph 192–32 I was called to *v*· Mr. Clark in Lynn,
p 365–17 healing work will be accomplished at one *v*·,

visitant
f 224–26 open or close the door upon this angel *v*·,

visitants
b 298–27 celestial *v*·, flying on spiritual, . . . pinions.

visiting
p 439–32 but on *v*· the spot, they learn that

visitor
p 364–30 as Jesus said of the unwelcome *v*·,
365– 1 the nurse, the cook, and the brusque business *v*·

visits
s 156–25 and receiving occasional *v*· from me,

visual
p 393–28 constituting the *v*· organism.
ap 572–27 Not through the material *v*· organs for seeing,

vital
a 54–24 It was so *v*·, that it enabled them to
s 113– 5 The *v*· part, the heart and soul of C. S.,
b 293– 3 Electricity is not a *v*· fluid,
p 379–22 The so-called *v*· current does not affect the
387–17 and perform the most *v*· functions in society.
397– 1 By not perceiving *v*· metaphysical points,

vitality
sp 98–30 they are not deprived of their essential *v*·.
s 146–10 barren of the *v*· of spiritual power,

vitalizing
g 510–28 and not a *v*· property of matter.

vitiate
p 393–14 and nothing can *v*· the ability and power

vivid
f 212– 9 Because the memory of pain is more *v*·

vividly
b 295–20 through which Truth appears most *v*·

vocations
t 457–23 To pursue other *v*· and

voice

divine
g 532–20 error shrank abashed from the divine *v*·

from harmony
ap 559–16 Then will a *v*· from harmony cry :

His
sp 97–26 "He uttered His *v*·,— *Psal.* 46 : 6.
c 255–18 Eye hath not seen Spirit, nor hath ear heard
His *v*·.

inward
b 321–26 the inward *v*· became to him the

lifts her
sp 97–24 for the higher Truth lifts her *v*·,

lifts its
f 252–16 Material sense lifts its *v*· with the arrogance of

loud
ap 568–13 And I heard a loud *v*·— *Rev.* 12 : 10.

Master's
a 35– 4 and wakened by their Master's *v*·,

of God
f 226– 5 The *v*· of God in behalf of the African slave
b 321–26 became to him the *v*· of God, which said :

of one
f 208–19 "the *v*· of one crying in the — *Matt.* 3 : 3.

of the first sign
b 321–28 to the *v*· of the first sign,— *Exod.* 4 : 8.

voice

of the herald
f 226– 6 the *v*· of the herald of this new crusade

of the latter sign
b 321–29 the *v*· of the latter sign."— *Exod.* 4 : 8.

of thy wife
g 535–20 hearkened unto the *v*· of thy wife,— *Gen.* 3 : 17.

of Truth
b 307–31 the *v*· of Truth still calls :
308–14 Soul-inspired patriarchs heard the *v*· of Truth,
323–29 the "still, small *v*·" of Truth— *I Kings* 19 : 12.
t 456–27 Because it is the *v*· of Truth to this age,
ap 559–10 inaudible *v*· of Truth is, to the human mind,

still, small
b 323–29 the "still, small *v*·" of Truth— *I Kings* 19 : 12.
p 367–25 through a "still, small *v*·,"— *I Kings* 19 : 12.
ap 559– 8 "still, small *v*·" of scientific— *I Kings* 19 : 12.

Thy
g 532–15 I heard Thy *v*· in the garden,— *Gen.* 3 : 10.

to the dumb
ph 183–28 hearing to the deaf, *v*· to the dumb,

your
ap 570–20 He can neither drown your *v*· with its roar,

sp 88– 5 And the sound of a *v*· that is still.
b 298– 6 silences for a while the *v*· of immutable
g 541–28 The *v*· of thy brother's blood— *Gen.* 4 : 10.
ap 560–17 whom God has appointed to *v*· His Word.

voiceless
a 48– 5 waiting and struggling in *v*· agony,

voices
pref ix– 8 the tongue *v*· the more definite thought,
m 64–31 and the *v*· of physical sense will be forever
hushed.
sp 86–17 Haunted houses, ghostly *v*·, unusual noises,
87–29 may reproduce *v*· long ago silent.
f 210–27 so-called mortal mind which *v*· this
232–26 In the sacred sanctuary of Truth are *v*· of
240– 1 Nature *v*· natural, spiritual law and

voicing
b 332–10 Christ is the true idea *v*· good,

void
pr 2– 7 and it does not return unto us *v*·.
s 126– 5 mortal mind will be without form and *v*·,
145– 6 would have made *v*· their practice.
f 229–20 made *v*· by the law of immortal Mind,
o 351– 2 was pedantic and *v*· of healing power.
p 381– 1 is rendered null and *v*· by the law of Life,
441– 4 so-called law, which . . . is null and *v*·.
t 445–16 You render the divine law . . . obscure and *v*·,
464–25 Adulterating C. S., makes it *v*·.
r 479–19 earth was without form, and *v*· ;— *Gen.* 1 : 2.
g 503– 6 earth was without form, and *v*· ;— *Gen.* 1 : 2.

volcanic
g 504–10 not from the sun nor from *v*· flames,

volition
sp 80–26 These movements arise from the *v*· of
ph 167– 2 to heal the sick out of His personal *v*·,
187–23 The divine Mind includes all action and *v*·,
191–21 By its own *v*·, not a blade of grass
199– 1 without *v*· of mortal mind,
f 220–32 as directly as the *v*· or will moves the hand.
230–14 to suppose Him . . . punishing . . . of His *v*·

voluble
g 533–13 the snake-talker utters the first *v*· lie,

volume
s 147–14 Although this *v*· contains the complete Science
o 341– 1 The strictures on this *v*· would condemn
345–14 but in this *v*· of mine there are no
r 465– 4 she revised that treatise for this *v*· in 1875.

voluntarily
p 402–25 his subjects believe that they cannot act *v*·

voluntary
ph 187–20 *v*·, as well as miscalled *involuntary*, action
187–25 tries to classify action as *v*· and
p 403– 2 great difference between *v*· and involuntary
403– 3 *v*· mesmerism is induced consciously
r 484–22 the *v*· or involuntary action of error
491– 7 made up of involuntary and *v*· error,

vote
s 139–15 The decisions by *v*· of Church Councils

vow
m 59–27 The nuptial *v*· should never be annulled,
68–12 Be not in haste to take the *v*·

vows
m 65–17 the powerlessness of *v*· to make home happy,

vulgar
m 58–26 a wife ought not to court *v*· extravagance

vulture's
g 547–10 microscopic examination of a *v*· ovum,

W

wages
m 63–30 woman should be allowed to collect her own *w*,
f 240–30 The divine method of paying sin's *w*

wail
t 448– 3 When the Publican's *w* went out to the

wait
a 22–13 *W* for your reward,
m 59– 5 should *w* on all the years of married life.
66–19 *w* patiently on divine wisdom to point out the
f 218–27 "They that *w* upon the Lord — *Isa.* 40 : 31.
238– 2 well to *w* till those whom you would benefit
254–10 When we *w* patiently on God and seek Truth
b 323–10 we pause, — *w* on God.
t 454–22 *W* patiently for divine Love to move upon the

waited
b 314– 3 *w* until the mortal or fleshly sense had

waiting
pref ix–18 at the heavenly gate, *w* for the Mind of Christ.
pr 10– 3 and that *w* patiently on the Lord,
a 48– 5 *w* and struggling in voiceless agony,
ph 166–19 *w* for the hour of strength in which
c 255– * *w* for the adoption, to wit, — Rom.* 8 : 23.
ap 562–25 *w* to be delivered of her sweet promise,
570–15 *w* and watching for rest and drink.

waits
f 252–24 where the good purpose *w* !

wake
f 218–32 When we *w* to the truth of being,
251– 9 mortals *w* to the knowledge of two facts :
p 430–11 When will mankind *w* to this great fact in

wakeful
pref vii– 2 The *w* shepherd beholds the

waken
sp 75–21 When you can *w* yourself or others out of
o 354–24 Truth will *w* men spiritually
p 427–31 Thought will *w* from its own material
429–17 Mortals *w* from the dream of death
g 556–26 Because mortal mind must *w* to spiritual life

wakened
a 35– 3 *w* by their Master's voice, they changed

wakens
b 322–21 as the startled dreamer who *w* from an

waking
a 22– 6 *W* to Christ's demand, mortals experience
s 128–23 for *w* him from a cataleptic nightmare,
ph 188–15 In both the *w* and the sleeping dream,
f 250–22 the *w* dream of mortal existence
p 397–25 Mortals are no more material in their *w*
418–30 *w* dream-shadows, dark images of

walk
pr 10– 1 desire to *w* and will *w* in the light
11 26 that we may *w* securely in the only
a 21– 1 If Truth is overcoming error in your daily *w*
27– 4 the blind see, the lame *w*, — *Luke* 7 : 22.
41– 8 The God-inspired *w* calmly on
46– 5 In the *w* to Emmaus, Jesus was known to
s 132– 6 the blind receive their sight and the lame *w*, —
Matt.* 11 : 5.
ph 192–27 We *w* in the footsteps of Truth and Love
199–25 Had Blondin believed it impossible to *w* the
f 218–29 they shall *w*, and not faint." — *Isa.* 40 : 31.
223– 2 Paul said, "*W* in the Spirit, — *Gal.* 5 : 16.
248–26 in the right direction, and then *w* that way.
254– 4 *w*, and not faint," — *Isa.* 40 : 31.
c 264–10 We must look where we would *w*,
b 329– 7 Because you cannot *w* on the water
o 342–25 It causes the deaf to hear, the lame to *w*,
p 397–25 when they act, *w*, see, hear, enjoy,
t 455– 9 in order to *w* over the waves of error
g 510–11 reflected spiritually by all who *w* in the light
ap 577–22 All who are saved must *w* in this light.
578–10 though I *w* through the valley — *Psal.* 23 : 4.
gl 596–21 "Though I *w* through the valley — *Psal.* 23 : 4.
fr 600– * *That ye might w worthy — Col.* 1 : 10.

walked
a 49–27 rabbis, before whom he had meekly *w*,
s 134–28 healed the sick, *w* on the water.
f 214– 6 he could never have "*w* with God," — *Gen.* 5 : 24.
b 273–24 Jesus *w* on the waves, fed the multitude,
p 442–14 no longer sick and in prison, *w* forth,

walketh
m 56–16 pestilence that *w* in darkness, — *Psal.* 91 : 6.

walking
c 261–14 *w* about as actively as the youngest member
p 369–10 raising the dead, and *w* over the wave.
374–22 *w* in darkness on the edge of a precipice.

walking
p 429– 7 When *w*, we are guided by the eye.
t 452– 7 *W* in the light, we are accustomed to the
r 487– 4 gained by *w* in the pathway of Truth
ap 566– 4 *w* wearily through the great desert of

walks
b 323–11 until boundless thought *w* enraptured,
t 451–14 *w* in the direction towards which he looks,

walls
a 44–32 There were rock-ribbed *w* in the way,
m 58–17 would confine . . . forever within four *w*,
b 295–19 the glass is less opaque than the *w*.
p 439–20 God will smite you, O whited *w*,

wander
r 491–24 and they *w* whither they will

wanderers
g 507– 9 nameless offspring, — *w* from the parent Mind,
ap 570–15 weary *w*, athirst in the desert

wandering
m 58–19 a *w* desire for incessant amusement
sp 82–16 *w* . . . through different mazes of consciousness
82–28 When *w* in Australia, do we look for
s 121–15 is as the *w* comet or the desolate star
f 235– 1 cannot go forth, like *w* pollen,

wanes
ap 562–21 as the night of materialism *w*.

waning
s 134–14 Man-made doctrines are *w*.

want
m 64– 1 *W* of uniform justice is a crying evil
sp 95–21 and we *w* that day to be succeeded by C. S.,
96–16 *w* and woe, sin, sickness, and death,
c 257–26 to meet the demands of human *w* and woe,
p 425–29 capacious lungs and *w* them to remain so,
r 489–30 A wrong sense . . . is *non-sense*, *w* of sense.
g 501 0 richly recompensing human *w* and woe
ap 578– 5 I shall not *w*. — *Psal.* 23 : 1.

wanting
pref viii– 2 and has not been found *w* ;
sp 92–25 Until . . . ability to make nothing of error will
be *w*.

wants
m 58–28 because another supplies her *w*.
p 413– 4 the undue contemplation of physical *w*
440–18 ministering to the *w* of his fellow-man

war
always at
r 492–32 would keep truth and error always at *w*.
and agriculture
r 485–28 gods of mythology controlled *w* and agriculture
inflamed with
ap 565– 3 inflamed with *w* against spirituality.
in heaven
ap 566–25 And there was *w* in heaven :— *Rev.* 12 : 7.
made
ap 565–24 material lie made *w* upon the spiritual idea ;
man of
g 524–10 God becomes "a man of *w*," — *Exod.* 15 : 3.
not at
a 19– 3 Love and Truth are not at *w* with
b 276– 6 in which one mind is not at *w* with another,
will cease
r 467–12 as this fact becomes apparent, *w* will cease
with Science
f 252– 1 They are at *w* with Science,
with the facts
r 496–21 the law of mortal belief, at *w* with the facts of

s 130–16 beliefs which *w* against spiritual facts ;
163–17 *w*, pestilence, and famine, all combined."
o 354– 5 and *w* against "the world, the flesh, and the
g 530–25 Thus Spirit and flesh *w*.
ap 567–11 the dragon cannot *w* with them.

ward
f 234–17 If mortals would keep proper *w* over
p 420–12 they can resist disease and *w* it off,

warding
m 63– 2 for *w* off pulmonary disease

warfare
human
f 226–12 freedom be won, not through human *w*,
in Science
ap 568– 6 typifies the divine method of *w* in Science,

warfare
of extermination
  g 543–14   is engaged in a *w·* of extermination.
our
  ap 568–31   we lay down all for Truth, or Christ, in our *w·*
perpetual
  f 231–16   governing man through perpetual *w·*.
suppositional
  b 288– 3   The suppositional *w·* between truth and error
this
  a 29– 4   and continue this *w·* until they have
  b 288– 6   this *w·* between the Spirit and flesh
  g 534–14   the Apostle Paul explains this *w·* between
  ap 568– 7   the glorious results of this *w·*.
true
  ap 568–12   first exhibits the true *w·* and then the false.
with the flesh
  b 324–15   It is a *w·* with the flesh, in which we must

  s 145–28   the *w·* between Spirit and the flesh goes on.
  b 316–13   Hence the *w·* between this spiritual idea and

warm
  f 247–25   glances in the *w·* sunbeam, arches the cloud
  p 379–12   a stream of *w·* water was trickling over his arm.
  r 190–32   will think that he is freezing when he is *w·*,

warn
  m 65– 9   Divorces should *w·* the age of some

warned
  o 358–31   against whom they have been *w·*,

warning
  a 53–22   Like Peter, we should weep over the *w·*,
  sp 79– 2   W· people against death is an error
  ph 196–14   The command was a *w·* to beware,
  f 238–14   the *w·*, "I know you not."— *Matt.* 25 : 12.
  ap 571–14   have seen the danger and yet have given no *w·*.

warns
  r 481–13   against which wisdom *w·* man,

warped
  p 433– 9   not to allow their judgment to be *w·* by

warping
  p 440–11   but no *w·* of justice can render

warrant
  pr 3– 3   is not sufficient to *w·* him in advising God.
  p 363–29   was her grief sufficient evidence to *w·* the
  366–14   we have the apostolic *w·* for asking :

warreth
  ph 200–22   the flesh that *w·* against Spirit.
  ap 567– 9   Against Love, the dragon *w·* not long,

warring
  s 140–10   *w·* no more over the corporeality,
  b 278–20   *w·* forever with each other ;
  ap 564–14   the dragon as *w·* against innocence.
  gl 584–12   The flesh, *w·* against Spirit ;

wars
  s 144–23   Science *w·* with so-called physical science,
  144–24   even as Truth *w·* with error,
  f 242–19   which *w·* against spirituality
  b 274–22   and the flesh *w·* against Spirit.
  340–24   ends *w·* ; fulfils the Scripture,
  g 531–28   since flesh *w·* against Spirit
  ap 567– 1   He leads the hosts . . . and fights the holy *w·*.

wash
  p 364–14   *w·* and anoint his guest's feet,
  413–22   need not *w·* his little body all over each day
  t 452–21   and afterwards we must *w·* them clean.
  r 484– 4   neither . . . can *w·* away its foundation,

washed
  p 383– 4   rendered pure by Mind as well as *w·* by water.
  ap 572– 1   *w·* their robes white in obedience and

washing
  f 241–27   *w·* the body of all the impurities of flesh,
  p 413–17   *w·* should be only for the purpose of

wasted
  a 44–14   to resuscitate *w·* energies.

wasteth
  m 56–17   destruction that *w·* at noonday."— *Psal.* 91 : 6.

wasting
  p 376–10   whom you declare to be *w·* away

watch
  pr 15–20   to work and *w·* for wisdom, Truth, and Love.
  a 48– 4   not *w·* with me one hour?"— *Matt.* 26 : 40.
  48– 5   Could they not *w·* with him who,
  s 156–18   to give her unmedicated pellets and *w·* the
  p 366–22   The physician must also *w·*, lest he be
  367–21   Let us *w·*, work, and pray that this
  411–29   W· the result of this simple rule
  r 497–24   we solemnly promise to *w·*, and pray
  ap 563–19   holding untiring *w·*, that he may bite the heel

watched
  p 377–18   the mental state should be continually *w·*
  430–30   the prisoner, or patient, *w·* with a sick friend.
  431– 3   *w·* with the sick every night in the week.
  t 446–29   This must therefore be *w·* and guarded against.

watchful
  b 324–13   Be *w·*, sober, and vigilant.

watchfully
  f 234–10   as *w·* as we bar our doors against the

watchfulness
  pr 4–19   expressed in daily *w·* and in striving
  4–29   silent prayer, *w·*, and devout obedience
  gl 579– 8   ABEL.   W· ; self-offering ;

watching
  pr 1– 6   Prayer, *w·*, and working, combined with
  f 245– 9   she stood daily before the window *w·*
  254– 2   Individuals are consistent who, *w·*
  p 435–19   W· beside the couch of pain
  t 464–11   praying, *w·*, and working for
  ap 570–16   waiting and *w·* for rest and drink.

watchman
  p 393– 1   like a *w·* forsaking his post,

watchtowers
  f 235–28   Clergymen, occupying the *w·* of the world,

watchword
  f 239–13   The *w·* of C. S. is Scriptural :

water
as a flood
  ap 570– 9   out of his mouth *w·* as a flood, — *Rev.* 12 : 15.
bread and
  f 220–22   once adopted a diet of bread and *w·*
cold
  p 436–11   Giving a cup of cold *w·* in Christ's name,
  ap 570–17   Give them a cup of cold *w·* in Christ's name,
goblet of
  s 153– 9   one drop of that attenuation in a goblet of *w·*,
nothing but
  f 221– 4   and drank nothing but *w·*.
of life
  g 548– 2   take the *w·* of life freely."— *Rev.* 22 : 17.
out of
  p 413–14   taking a fish out of *w·* every day
sweet
  b 287–13   at the same place sweet *w·* and— *Jas.* 3 : 11.
symbolizes
  g 507– 3   while *w·* symbolizes the elements of
turn the
  m 65– 4   be present . . . to turn the *w·* into wine
under
  g 557– 2   child could remain under *w·* twenty minutes,
walked on the
  s 134–28   healed the sick, walked on the *w·*,
warm
  p 379–12   stream of warm *w·* was trickling over his arm.
washed by
  p 383– 4   rendered pure by Mind as well as washed by *w·*
without
  f 221– 8   only a thin slice of bread without *w·*.

  pref xi-24   also the charge to plant and *w·* His vineyard.
  s 153– 9   a teaspoonful of the *w·* administered
  b 321–32   by changing *w·* into wine,
  329– 8   Because you cannot walk on the *w·*
  o 361–16   As a drop of *w·* is one with the ocean,
  p 413–19   W· is not the natural habitat of humanity.
  g 556–32   plunged . . . into the *w·* for several minutes,

watered
  g 521–22   *w·* the whole face of the ground.— *Gen.* 2 : 6.

Waterhouse, Dr. Benjamin
  s 163– 4   Dr. Benjamin *W·*, Professor in Harvard

watering
  o 352–21   thus *w·* the very roots of childish timidity,

waters
abyss of
  ph 199–26   to walk the rope over Niagara's abyss of *w·*,
come ye to the
  pr 13– 4   come ye to the *w·*."— *Isa.* 55 : 1.
deep
  ap 570–21   the deep *w·* of chaos and old night.
disturb the
  f 254–25   what is there to disturb the *w·* ?
divided the
  g 505–14   and divided the *w·* which were— *Gen.* 1 : 7.
divide the
  g 505– 5   and let it divide the *w·* from— *Gen.* 1 : 6.
face of the
  g 503– 8   moved upon the face of the *w·*.— *Gen.* 1 : 2.
fill the
  g 512–18   and fill the *w·* in the seas ;— *Gen.* 1 : 22.
healthful
  f 254–28   the ever-agitated but healthful *w·* of truth,

waters

living
f 234– 7   and giving living *w·* to the thirsty.
many
g 505–19   than the noise of many *w·*,— *Psal.* 93 : 4.
midst of the
g 505– 5   in the midst of the *w·*,— *Gen.* 1 : 6.
move upon the
t 454–23   for divine Love to move upon the *w·*
still
g 514–14   beside the still *w·*."— *Psal.* 23 : 2.
ap 578– 7   beside the still *w·*.— *Psal.* 23 : 2.
sweet
t 455–30   cannot send forth both sweet *w·* and bitter.
r 489–23   sendeth not forth sweet *w·* and bitter.
upon the
m 68–21   when casting my bread upon the *w·*,
will be pacified
ap 570–24   The *w·* will be pacified,

g 505– 6   divide the waters from the *w·*.— *Gen.* 1 : 6.
505–14   from the *w·* which were above the— *Gen.* 1 : 7.
506–15   And God said, Let the *w·*— *Gen.* 1 : 9.
506–23   gathering together of the *w·*— *Gen.* 1 : 10.
511–19   And God said, Let the *w·*— *Gen.* 1 : 20.
512– 5   which the *w·* brought forth— *Gen.* 1 : 21.
536– 1   gathering together of the *w·*— *Gen.* 1 : 10.

water-wheel
p 399–19   A mill at work or the action of a *w·*

wave
s 124–24   and said to the proud *w·*,
b 293–22   wind, *w·*, lightning, fire, bestial ferocity
p 369–10   raising the dead, and walking over the *w·*.
ap 569–19   to lift their heads above the drowning *w·*.
570–25   and Christ will command the *w·*.

waves
m 67– 6   and the *w·* lift themselves into mountains.
67–22   and commanded even the winds and *w·*
f 203–29   the *w·* of sin, sorrow, and death beat in vain.
b 273 25   Jesus walked on the *w·*, fed the multitude,
t 455– 9   in order to walk over the *w·* of error
g 505–19   than the mighty *w·* of the sea."— *Psal.* 93 : 4.

waxed
s 134–14   They have not *w·* strong in times of trouble.
o 350–18   "This people's heart is *w·* gross,— *Matt.* 13 : 15.

Way
b 332–14   the *W·*, the Truth, and the Life,

way
all the
ap 574– 4   journeying "uphill all the *w·*."
beheld the
b 326–23   Saul of Tarsus beheld the *w·*— the Christ,
broad is the
t 451–13   broad is the *w·*, that leadeth to— *Matt.* 7 : 13.
Christ's
t 458–29   Christ's *w·* is the only one by which mortals
divine
c 266–19   Universal Love is the divine *w·* in C. S.
every
g 537– 7   sword which turned every *w·*,— *Gen.* 3 : 24.
exploring the
a 26– 4   in speechless agony exploring the *w·* for us,
finds its
p 365–26   finds its *w·* into the chambers of disease
forsake his
s 139– 1   the wicked to "forsake his *w·*,— *Isa.* 55 : 7.
f 239–14   the wicked forsake his *w·*,— *Isa.* 55 : 7.
give
c 260– 8   erring thought must give *w·* to the ideal
given
a 50–20   had for a moment given *w·* before the
God's own
g 542–20   Let Truth . . . destroy error in God's own *w·*,
go thy
a 40– 6   "Go thy *w·* for this time ;— *Acts* 24 : 25.
go your
a 27– 3   "Go your *w·*, and tell John— *Luke* 7 : 22.
in any
o 356–14   not contributing in any *w·* to each other's
p 410–26   or is used in any *w·* except to
in some
t 444– 2   In some *w·*, sooner or later, all must rise
ap 573–30   will surely appear sometime and in some *w·*.
in the
a 30–31   work out our salvation in the *w·* Jesus taught.
37–27   do they follow him in the *w·* that he
44–32   There were rock-ribbed walls in the *w·*,
b 326– 4   it must be in the *w·* of God's appointing.
p 390–19   whiles thou art in the *w·* with— *Matt.* 5 : 25.
r 483–28   and it does this in the *w·* of His appointing,
in the same
ph 188–20   In the same *w·* pain and pleasure,
p 415–19   In the same *w·* thought increases or

way
is dark
gl 596–23   Though the *w·* is dark in mortal sense,
is pointed out
t 462–16   when the *w·* is pointed out ;
is straight
b 324–13   The *w·* is straight and narrow,
its own
s 126–10   has sought and interpreted in its own *w·*
Jesus'
p 428– 4   demonstration of the facts of Soul in Jesus' *w·*
keep the
g 537– 7   to keep the *w·* of the tree of life.— *Gen.* 3 : 24.
leads the
t 454–19   inspires, illumines, designates, and leads the *w·*.
learned my
p 383– 1   was cured when I learned my *w·* in C. S."
learn the
c 264–28   When we learn the *w·* in C. S.
lighting the
pref vii–12   lighting the *w·* to eternal harmony.
maps out the
ph 176–27   no farther than mortal mind maps out the *w·*.
marked out the
f 227–24   Jesus marked out the *w·*.
marked the
a 46–25   that is, he marked the *w·* for all men.
more excellent
s 149– 4   The more excellent *w·* is divine Science
my
s 109–20   and I won my *w·* to absolute conclusions
narrow
s 126–31   "the straight and narrow *w·*"— see *Matt.* 7 : 14.
151 28   The straight and narrow *w·* is to see and
t 454–29   tread firmly in the straight and narrow *w·*.
no other
b 327–13   There is no other *w·*.
r 482–30   It can heal in no other *w·*,
490–27   can be obtained in no other *w·*.
of divine Science
b 316– 1   demonstrating the *w·* of divine Science,
of error
g 536–10   The *w·* of error is awful to contemplate.
of Life
a 25–13   Jesus taught the *w·* of Life by demonstration,
s 137–25   Love hath shown thee the *w·* of Life !
of salvation
pref vii– 8   would make plain . . . the *w·* of salvation
b 316– 1   he became the *w·* of salvation to all who
one
ph 167–25   There is but one *w·* — namely, God and His idea
f 242– 9   There is but one *w·* to heaven, harmony,
only
ph 180–27   The only *w·* to this living Truth,
p 371–19   the only *w·* out of this condition.
opens the
ph 174–14   Whoever opens the *w·* in C. S. is a pilgrim
open the
a 24– 7   open the *w·* for C. S. to be understood,
b 326–21   your Father will open the *w·*.
other
ph 167–28   impossible to gain control . . . in any other *w·*.
pointed the
r 494– 9   and Jesus pointed the *w·* for them.
pointing the
t 444–17   Let us be faithful in pointing the *w·*
point out the
a 30–21   to point out the *w·* of Truth and Life.
preparing the
f 208–20   and preparing the *w·* of Science.
scientific
p 411–12   this is the ultimatum, the scientific *w·*,
show the
f 242–30   The finger-posts of divine Science show the *w·*
show us the
a 40–18   for not otherwise could he show us the *w·*
stood in his
a 28– 4   Even many of his students stood in his *w·*.
this
pr 8–29   for in this *w·* only can we learn
a 30–29   Only in this *w·* can we bless our enemies,
s 156–24   She went on in this *w·*, taking the
f 242–10   and Christ in divine Science shows us this *w·*.
p 377–24   You also remove in this *w·* what are termed
391–11   and in this *w·* you can prevent the
402–21   and in this *w·* affect the body,
t 446– 2   and in this *w·* dealing pitilessly with a
through Christ
ph 171– 5   even the *w·* through Christ, Truth,
to cure
p 417–23   since it is demonstrable that the *w·* to cure the
to escape
b 327–12   The *w·* to escape the misery of sin is to cease
to extract
f 201–17   The *w·* to extract error from mortal mind is to

way
to health
  f 241–24 the *w*· to health and holiness.
true
  f 202–20 the true *w*· leads to Life instead of to death,
unexplained
  pref xi– 4 which action in some unexplained *w*· results in
walk that
  f 248–26 in the right direction, and then walk that *w*·.
which leads
  r 472– 5 *w*· which leads to C. S. is straight and narrow.
will grow
  r 496–12 the *w*· will grow brighter
winding its
  ap 563–28 winding its *w*· amidst all evil,
your
  p 381–22 understand your *w*· out of human theories

  a 26–11 "I am the *w*·, the truth,— *John* 14 : 6.
    26–20 in order to show the learner the *w*·
    30–13 to mortal mind as "the *w*·."— *John* 14 : 6.
    39–15 He was "the *w*·."— *John* 14 : 6.
    46–25 Jesus was "the *w*· ;"— *John* 14 : 6.
  sp 98–31 The *w*· through which immortality and life
  b 286–11 "I am the *w*·."— *John* 14 : 6.
    320– 3 "I am the *w*·,— *John* 14 : 6.
  o 353–10 Christ is "the *w*·,— *John* 14 : 6.
  p 371–18 The *w*· in divine Science is the only way out of
  r 482–15 since Christ is "the *w*·"— *John* 14 : 6.
  g 535–18 Truth is indeed "the *w*·."— *John* 14 : 6.

waymarks
  c 267–24 by reversal, errors serve as *w*· to
  g 542–24 not to remove the *w*· of God.

ways
  a 37–17 learn to emulate him in *all* his *w*·
  f 218–21 lead only into material *w*· of obtaining help,
    251–12 Truth works . . . in just these *w*·.
  b 317–14 not only in all time, but in *all w*· and
  p 371–13 looks for relief in all *w*· except the right one.
  ap 571– 2 hidden mental *w*· of accomplishing iniquity,

Way-shower and **way-shower**
  a 30–10 enabled him to be the mediator, or *w*·,
  b 288–30 made him the *W*·, Truth and Life.
  r 497–15 unity with God through Christ Jesus the *W*· ;

wayside
  a 55–10 gospel of healing is again preached by the *w*·,

weak
  sp 79–25 says : . . . Your body is *w*·,
  s 123– 9 becomes the most absolutely *w*· and
  ph 168– 1 a poor shift for the *w*· and worldly,
    198–32 or that a less used arm must be *w*·.
  f 219–16 We shall not call the body *w*·, if we
    235–25 when the soul is willing and the flesh *w*·,
  p 377–13 becomes suddenly *w*· or abnormally strong,
    392–15 If you believe in inflamed and *w*· nerves,
    423–24 has rendered himself strong, instead of *w*·,
    426–10 struggle for Truth makes one strong instead of *w*·,

weaken
  s 145–30 must continually *w*· its own assumed power.
  ph 181–12 You *w*· or destroy your power

weakened
  p 423–16 He regards the ailment as *w*· or strengthened
  g 517– 2 This definition has been *w*· by

weakens
  b 329–32 Human resistance to divine Science *w*·

weaker
  s 144–13 the *w*· the indications of Soul.
  ph 198–27 and the stronger thoughts rule the *w*·.
  p 409–18 the stronger never yields to the *w*·, except

weakness
betrays its
  ph 192–25 which erelong betrays its *w*·
human
  t 453–17 Dishonesty is human *w*·, which forfeits
indicate
  t 455– 6 Such mental states indicate *w*· instead of
involves
  p 406–26 Inharmony of any kind involves *w*·
strength or
  p 377–14 the producer of strength or *w*·.
worldly
  f 238–23 Attempts to . . . arise from worldly *w*·.

  ph 176– 6 to the *w*· of their wives.
  f 219– 1 all disease, pain, *w*·, weariness, sorrow,
    221–11 passed many weary years in hunger and *w*·,
  o 354–22 God will redeem that *w*·,
  p 371–29 strength instead of *w*·,
    407–13 giving strength to the *w*· of mortal mind,

wealth
  m 57–15 Beauty, *w*·, or fame is incompetent
    58–28 *W*· may obviate the necessity for toil
  f 239– 5 Take away *w*·, fame, and
    239– 8 Break up cliques, level *w*· with honesty,

weaned
  m 60– 8 mother's affection cannot be *w*· from her child,

weaning
  b 322–30 Without this process of *w*·,

weapons
  a 48–17 Judas had the world's *w*·.
  t 464–23 The *w*· of bigotry, ignorance, envy,

wear
  f 254–31 for through it you win and *w*· the crown.
  p 387– 9 spiritual energies can neither *w*· out nor

wearily
  ap 566– 4 walking *w*· through the great desert of

weariness
  ph 183–16 *w*· and disease are not His laws,
  f 217–26 or any illusion of physical *w*·,
    218– 2 that which affirms *w*·, made that *w*·.
    219– 1 all disease, pain, weakness, *w*·, sorrow,
  gl 586– 1 *w*· of mortal mind ; obscured views ;

wearing
  sp 78– 6 the belief that we are *w*· out life
  f 226–22 *w*· out years of servitude to an
  b 296–26 foundations which time is *w*· away.
    315–29 *W*· in part a human form

wears
  m 66– 5 *W*· yet a precious jewel in his head.

weary
  a 22–14 "be not *w*· in well doing."— *II Thess.* 3 : 13.
    55–17 My *w*· hope tries to realize that happy day,
  m 68– 6 We ought to *w*· of the fleeting and false
  sp 79–29 need "not be *w*· in well doing."— *Gal.* 6 : 9.
  s 121–16 "a *w*· searcher for a viewless home."
  f 217–27 for matter cannot be *w*· and heavy-laden.
    218– 6 the body, . . . would never be *w*·.
    218–28 shall run, and not be *w*· ;— *Isa.* 40 : 31.
    221–10 He passed many *w*· years in hunger
    234–22 human systems disappoint the *w*· searcher
    250–16 A mortal may be *w*· or pained, enjoy or suffer,
    254– 3 "run, and not be *w*· ;— *Isa.* 40 : 31.
  b 318–14 *W*· of their material beliefs,
  g 501–16 that Love for whose rest the *w*· ones sigh
  ap 570–15 *w*· wanderers, athirst in the desert
    574– 4 adapted to console the *w*· pilgrim,

wearying
  p 426–11 instead of weak, resting instead of *w*· one.

weather
  s 122–20 points to fair *w*· in the midst of murky clouds
  ph 171–10 either of his life or of the *w*·,
  p 384–27 neither . . . will ever result from exposure to the *w*·.

weather-vane
  ph 184–31 I then requested her to look at the *w*·.

weaving
  an 102–19 *w*· webs more complicated and subtle.

web
  f 242–25 The divine Science of man is woven into one *w*·
  p 403–20 the gossamer *w*· of mortal illusion.

webs
  an 102–20 weaving *w*· more complicated and subtle.

Webster
  s 115–18 definition from

wedded
  ap 561–12 *w*· to the Lamb of Love.
    575– 3 Love *w*· to its own spiritual idea."
    577– 6 as no longer two *w*· individuals,

wedlock
  m 58–21 a poor augury for the happiness of *w*·.

weed
  c 265–17 as if man were a *w*· growing apace
  p 383–22 sometimes tells you that the *w*· preserves his

week
  ph 189– 4 If the eyes see no sun for a *w*·,
  p 431– 4 watched with the sick every night in the *w*·.

weekly
  sp 80–10 repeats *w*· the assertion that

weeks
  ph 193–20 am informed that he went to work in two *w*·.

weep
  a 53–22 Like Peter, we should *w*· over the warning,
  s 153–25 We *w*· because others *w*·, we yawn because

weigh
m 57–16	should never *w·* against the better claims of
ph 176–18	and *w·* down mankind with superimposed
f 239– 6	which *w·* not one jot in the balance of God,
t 445–16	when you *w·* the human in the scale with

weighing
an 105–26	*w·* him down to the depths of ignominy

weighs
s 155–15	The universal belief in physics *w·* against
b 307–23	and so *w·* against our course Spiritward.

weight
a 20–28	"Let us lay aside every *w·*,— *Heb.* 12 : 1.
s 155–21	in proportion as it puts less *w·* into
155–24	and more *w·* into the spiritual scale.
ph 168– 5	removal of a single *w·* from either scale
192–22	the *w·* you throw into the right scale.
f 205–30	Denial of the oneness of Mind throws our *w·*
p 380– 5	Sickness and sin fall by their own *w·*.
396–20	and the overwhelming *w·* of opinions
g 515–26	If you lift a *w·*, your reflection does this also.

welcome
sp 75–32	the departing may hear the glad *w·*
95–19	We *w·* the increase of knowledge

welcomed
s 142–20	humility and divine Science to be *w·* in.

welding
m 60– 7	*w·* indissolubly the links of affection.

welfare
a 23–24	One kind of faith trusts one's *w·* to others.
m 59–18	promotes the *w·* and happiness of your wife
sp 84–16	foretell events which concern the universal *w·*,

well
pref viii– 1	in the treatment of disease as *w·* as of sin,
pr 12–31	If . . . only petitioners . . . should get *w·*.
14–16	you will find yourself suddenly *w·*.
a 20–21	Yet he swerved not, *w·* knowing that
22–14	"be not weary in *w·* doing."— *II Thess.* 3 : 13.
26–21	by practice as *w·* as precept.
36–21	law of justice as *w·* as of mercy.
36–29	in return for our efforts at *w·* doing.
39– 8	trials and self-denials, as *w·* as joys and
39–29	attended with doubts and defeats as *w·* as triumphs.
41– 5	as *w·* as through their sorrows and afflictions.
44– 3	"*W·* done, good and faithful— *Matt.* 25 : 23.
m 63–23	A feasible as *w·* as rational means of
64–12	"It is never *w·* to interfere with your
66–17	it is *w·* to remember how fleeting are
66–19	it is *w·* to hope, pray, and wait patiently
sp 79–30	need "not be weary in *w·* doing."— *Gal.* 6 : 9.
90–29	we may as *w·* improve our time in solving the
93–21	belief that Spirit is finite as *w·* as infinite
an 101 30	to prove the motive as *w·* as the commission of
s 107–17	we may *w·* tremble in the prospect of
120–12	And is he *w·* if the senses say he is sick?
120–13	Yes, he is *w·* in Science in which health is
138–21	and to heal the sick as *w·* as the sinning.
145–18	its ethical as *w·* as its physical effects.
149– 2	could save from sickness as *w·* as from sin.
152– 6	Æsculapius of mind as *w·* as of body,
ph 179– 6	as *w·* as those present,
187–20	as *w·* as miscalled *involuntary,* action
f 210–26	cannot say, . . . I am sick, or I am *w·*."
222–21	he dropped drugs and . . . hygiene, and was *w·*.
236–11	Mind heals sickness as *w·* as sin
238– 2	*w·* to wait till those whom you would benefit
238– 5	as *w·* as in the material universe.
247–10	Beauty, as *w·* as truth, is eternal ;
251–15	Sickness, as *w·* as sin, is an error
b 268–18	as *w·* as on the facts of Mind.
322–27	as *w·* as our disappointments and ceaseless
328–26	It were *w·* had Christendom believed
332–26	as they could understand as *w·* as perceive.
o 342–13	He bade the seventy disciples, as *w·* as the
343–26	as *w·* as Paul who was not one of his students,
345–16	who understand its propositions *w·* enough to
348–18	Is it not *w·* to eliminate from so-called mortal
348–23	would it not be *w·* to abandon the defence,
348–25	improved and that of other persons as *w·*
350–25	its effects on the body as *w·* as on the
360–10	They . . . keep Soul *w·* out of sight.
p 370– 1	better spiritually as *w·* as physically.
377–22	remove the cause of all disease as *w·* as
377–32	as *w·* as the fear of disease,
383– 4	rendered pure by Mind as *w·* as washed by
383–30	pounding the poor body, to make it sensibly *w·*
385–22	You say that you have not slept *w·*
393–32	It is *w·* to be calm in sickness ;
397– 3	as *w·* as on the morals and the happiness of
418– 3	the conquest over sickness, as *w·* as over sin,
418–26	Include moral as *w·* as physical belief
419–29	as *w·* as those of your patients,
424–26	it is *w·* to be alone with God and the

well
p 427–25	physical realm, so-called, as *w·* as in the
429– 3	as *w·* as by other graces of Spirit.
435– 9	result in good to himself as *w·* as to others.
t 448–21	*w·* knowing it to be impossible for error,
449– 6	in order to continue in *w·* doing.
449–13	You should practise *w·* what you know,
454–16	points out to his student error as *w·* as truth,
454–16	the wrong as *w·* as the right practice.
458–28	through living as *w·* as healing and
r 480–10	Consciousness, as *w·* as action,
480–17	would make matter the cause as *w·* as
483–32	to be *w·* done, the work must be done unselfishly.
494–11	It is not *w·* to imagine that Jesus
494–16	as *w·* as the infinite ability of Spirit,
g 531– 8	It is *w·* that the upper portions of the brain
532–23	Is Mind capable of error as *w·* as of truth,
532–23	Is Mind capable . . . of evil as *w·* as of good,
550– 7	identity of animals as *w·* as of man
ap 563– 1	Human sense may *w·* marvel at discord,
563– 3	We may *w·* be astonished at sin,
563– 4	We may *w·* be perplexed at human fear ;
569–16	the serpent of sin as *w·* as of sickness !

well-authenticated
pref x–15	By thousands of *w·* cases of healing,
p 402– 4	already in her possession *w·* records

Welsh
g 525– 9	in the *W·*, that which rises up,

went
a 25– 9	as he *w·* daily about his Father's business.
41 26	still *w·* about doing good deeds,
s 156–24	She *w·* on in this way, taking the
ph 193– 8	The doctor *w·* out.
193– 9	I *w·* to his bedside.
193–20	am informed that he *w·* to work in two weeks.
f 225–20	oppression neither *w·* down in blood, nor
p 377– 7	they come back no better than when they *w·*
t 448– 4	When the Publican's wail *w·* out to the
g 521–21	there *w·* up a mist from the earth,— *Gen.* 2 : 6.
524– 7	*w·* after "strange gods."— *Jer.* 5 : 19.
542–27	Cain *w·* out from the presence of— *Gen.* 4 : 16.
546–12	"There *w·* up a mist— *Gen.* 2 : 6.
gl 595–14	on Aaron's breast when he *w·* before Jehovah,

west
s 121–18	sun seems to move from east to *w·*,
121–19	instead of the earth from *w·* to east.

westward
a 21–27	like a traveller going *w·*
ap 575–32	*w·*, to the grand realization of the

wet
f 220–12	he has no catarrh from *w·* feet,
221– 9	should not *w·* his parched throat until

whales
g 512– 4	And God created great *w·*.— *Gen.* 1 : 21.

whatever
pr 1– 8	*w·* has been successfully done for the
4–32	*W·* materializes worship hinders
8–20	Praying for humility with *w·* fervency of
m 60 11	maternal affection lives on under *w·*
op 70– 5	*W·* is false or sinful can never enter
85– 7	*w·* constitutes and perpetuates harmony,
93–18	*W·* contradicts the real nature of the
s 144–26	pride, or prejudice closes the door to *w·*
149–28	*W·* guides thought spiritually benefits
ph 168– 6	*W·* influence you cast on the side of matter,
169–24	*w·* good they may seem to receive from
160 20	*W·* teaches man to have other laws
178– 3	arsenic, the strychnine, or *w·* the drug used,
184–17	*W·* is governed by a false belief
186– 8	under *w·* name or pretence they are employed ;
192–30	*W·* holds human thought in line with
195–15	*W·* furnishes the semblance of an idea
f 206–16	we find that *w·* blesses one blessses all,
215–12	*W·* is governed by God, is never
225– 2	*W·* enslaves man is opposed to
234– 4	*W·* inspires with wisdom, Truth, or
250–24	*w·* appears to be a mortal man is a
c 263–21	*W·* seems to be a new creation, is but
b 282–28	*W·* indicates the fall of man
303–10	*W·* reflects Mind, Life, Truth, and Love,
312– 1	*w·* is learned through material sense
340–26	*w·* is wrong in social, civil, criminal,
o 347– 4	C. S. declares that *w·* is mortal
353– 2	*w·* seems real to material sense,
353–30	from this it follows that *w·* is laid off
358–24	it is said : "Rest assured that *w·* effect
p 385–17	*W·* it is your duty to do, you can do
392–12	*W·* benefit is produced on the
411–24	*W·* is cherished in mortal mind as the
418–16	*W·* the belief is, if arguments are used
418–19	and to *w·* decides its type and symptoms.
439–31	*w·* locality is reported to be haunted by Disease,
t 443–19	*w·* other systems they fancy will afford relief.

whatever

t	463–13	truth removes properly *w·* is offensive.
r	477– 9	*W·* is material is mortal.
	478–25	From beginning to end, *w·* is mortal is
	485– 5	*W·* contradicts this statement is the
g	525–21	*W·* is valueless or baneful, He did not make,
	529–26	evil, by *w·* figure presented,
	553–20	*W·* theory may be adopted by
	554–18	the creation of *w·* is sinful and mortal ;
ap	572– 9	but *w·* is of material sense, or mortal,
gl	583–12	*w·* rests upon and proceeds from
	585–11	*w·* the material senses behold ;
	588–16	*w·* reflects not this one Mind,

whatsoever

pr	1– *	*he shall have w· he saith.— Mark* 11 : 23.
p	405–17	"*W·* a man soweth,— *Gal.* 6 : 7.
g	527–24	and *w·* Adam called every living— *Gen.* 2 : 19.
	537–13	"*W·* a man soweth,— *Gal.* 6 : 7.
	550–21	If Life has any starting-point *w·*,

wheat

sp	72–15	tares and the *w·*, which are not united
	89–32	If seed is necessary to produce *w·*,
	89–32	and *w·* to produce flour,
f	207–19	separates the tares and *w·* in time of harvest.
b	269– 6	Jesus' demonstrations sift the chaff from the *w·*,
	300–18	These opposite qualities are the tares and *w·*,
	300–20	Science separates the *w·* from the tares,
r	466–28	to separate the chaff from the *w·*.
g	535– 3	the *w·* and tares which time will separate,

wheel

f	218– 3	You do not say a *w·* is fatigued ;
	218– 4	yet the body is as material as the *w·*.
	218– 6	the body, like the inanimate *w·*,

whence

sp	78–28	cannot "tell *w·* it cometh."— *John* 3 : 8.
s	108– 1	*W·* came to me this heavenly conviction,
f	225– 1	*W·* cometh it?
	229– 6	*w·* did they emanate?
	249–16	*W·* then is soulless matter?
b	281–10	*w·* its origin and what its destiny?
g	529–21	*W·* comes a talking, lying serpent
	537– 4	the ground from *w·* he was taken.— *Gen.* 3 : 23.
	539–13	*W·* does he obtain the propensity or power
	550– 3	If this be so, *w·* cometh Life, or Mind,

whenever

s	111–32	proved itself, *w·* scientifically employed,
	139–13	stem the tide . . . *w·* it flows inward.
ph	169– 3	*W·* an aggravation of symptoms has
t	445–31	*w·* she sees a man, for the petty consideration
r	495– 1	*w·* man is governed by God.
g	542– 4	*w·* and wherever it appears.

whereas

pref	viii–10	*w·* the fact is that Spirit is good and real,
	x– 8	*w·* this mind is not a factor in the
pr	12–23	*w·* help should come from the enlightened
a	23–28	*w·* the injunction, "Believe— *Acts* 16 : 31.
	42– 2	*w·* priest and rabbi affirmed God to be a
	44–29	*w·* he was alive, demonstrating within the
sp	91–30	*w·* the real Mind cannot be evil
s	117– 3	*w·* God is One,
ph	179–17	*w·* the wild animal, left to his instincts,
f	205–24	*w·* a belief in many ruling minds
	211–28	*w·* the fact is that only through
	212–31	*w·* the unreal and imitative movements
	219–12	*w·* divine Mind heals.
	222– 8	*w·* Truth regenerates this fleshly mind
b	287–20	*w·* the Scriptures declare that
	296– 1	*w·* Science unfolds the eternal verity,
	298– 9	*w·* spiritual sense can bear witness only to
	319–10	*w·* the lower appeal to the general faith in
	320–29	*w·* this passage is continually quoted as if
	334–11	*w·* Jesus appeared as a bodily existence.
	338– 4	*w·* the opposite belief— that man
o	352– 7	*w·* the Jews took a diametrically opposite view.
p	378–18	*w·* hypnotism and hygienic drilling
	395– 2	They admit its reality, *w·* they should deny it.
	414–29	*w·* imperfection is blameworthy,
	432– 4	*w·* Mortal Man, the prisoner at the bar,
t	461–28	*W·*, to prove scientifically the error
r	480– 9	*w·* matter is devoid of sensation.
g	501– 6	*w·* the New Testament narratives are clearer
	504–24	*w·* a thousand years of human doctrines,
	552–11	*w·* the spiritual scientific facts of existence
	557–24	*w·* revealed religion proclaims the Science or

whereby

a	18– 2	*w·* man reflects divine Truth, Life, and
	22–23	*w·* we rejoice in immortality,
	44–24	*w·* divinity brought to humanity the
b	271– 7	*w·* to heal the sick through Mind
p	387–31	faith and understanding *w·* to defend himself,

wherefore

p	440–16	*W·*, then, in the name of outraged justice,
fr	600– *	*W· by their fruits— Matt.* 7 : 20.

wherein

b	270–32	the good soil *w·* the seed of Truth
g	518–10	*w·* there is life,— *Gen.* 1 : 30.

whereof

g	533– 6	Hast thou eaten of the tree, *w·*— *Gen.* 3 : 11.

wherever

sp	94–14	intolerance, and bloodshed, *w·* found,
o	359–18	True Christianity is to be honored *w·*
g	542– 5	would slay . . . whenever and *w·* it appears.

wherewith

ph	196–18	They have no relation to God *w·* to establish
f	201– *	*w· Thine enemies have reproached,— Psal.* 89 : 51.
	201– *	*w· they have reproached the— Psal.* 89 : 51.

whether

pr	16–12	*w·* the last line is not an
sp	80– 4	*w·* for the inspiration of a sermon or
	83– 1	*w·* it is the human mind or
s	109–30	*w·* it be of God,— *John* 7 : 17.
	109–31	*w·* I speak of myself."— *John* 7 : 17.
	144–30	*w·* the ancient inspired healers
	145– 1	*w·* they caught its sweet tones,
	145–14	*w·* faith in drugs, trust in hygiene,
ph	195–11	*w·* it is mortal mind or
	199–17	To know *w·* this development is produced
f	211– 5	*w·* Truth or error is the greater?
	251–16	*w·* through faith in hygiene, in drugs, or
	251–17	We should learn *w·* they govern the
b	296–19	*W·* mortals will learn this sooner or later,
	324–10	*w·* it be Truth or error,
p	385–20	Mind decides *w·* or not the
	390–28	*w·* it is cancer, consumption, or
	392–28	*w·* it be air, exercise, heredity,
	402–19	*w·* it be a broken bone, disease, or sin.
	414–13	*w·* it is called dementia, hatred, or
t	459–19	*W·* animated by malice or
	463–22	*w·* error is manifested in forms of
r	491–22	*w·* our eyes are closed or open.
fr	600– *	*w· the tender grape appear,— Song* 7 : 12.

whichever

p	392–23	Your decisions will master you, *w·* direction

whimsical

f	241– 9	as imaginary, *w·*, and unreal as his pleasures.

whine

t	450–13	They do not . . . *w·* over the demands of Truth,

whipped

s	142–19	tyranny and pride need to be *w·* out of the

whipping-post

f	225–19	abolish the *w·* and slave market ;

whirlwind

f	210–24	and reapeth the *w·*.

whiskey

s	158–16	cataplasms, and *w·* are stupid substitutes

whisper

sp	76– 1	The ones departing may *w·* this vision,
r	482–24	and angels *w·* it, through faith, to the
g	501–12	glory which angels could only *w·*

whispered

p	370–18	spiritual facts of health, *w·* into thought,
	374– 4	truth of being, *w·* into the ear of

whispers

ap	574–30	Then thought gently *w·* : "Come hither !

whit

p	370– 1	To be every *w·* whole, man must be
	371–31	can make it "every *w·* whole."— *John* 7 : 23.

white

c	267–26	are "*w·* and glistering,"— *Luke* 9 : 29.
	267–28	"let thy garments be always *w·*."— *Eccl.* 9 : 8.
b	299– 9	With *w·* fingers they point upward to a
	321–22	*w·* as snow with the dread disease,
t	463–15	The new idea, . . . is clad in *w·* garments.
ap	572– 1	washed their robes *w·* in obedience

whited

pr	8– 9	"like unto *w·* sepulchres— *Matt.* 23 : 27.
p	439–20	God will smite you, O *w·* walls,

white-robed

m	64–23	Then *w·* purity will unite in one person

whither

b	299–14	*w·* every real individuality, image, or
r	491–24	and they wander *w·* they will

whoever

sp	95–12	*W·* reaches this point of moral culture
an	105–22	*W·* uses his developed mental powers
ph	174–14	*W·* opens the way in C. S.
	178–32	*W·* reaches the understanding of C. S.
	200– 8	*W·* is incompetent to explain Soul
f	213– 1	*W·* contradicts this mortal mind supposition

whoever

   o 343–30 *W·* is the first meekly and conscientiously to
   t 446–11 *W·* practises the Science the author teaches,
   456–10 *W·* affirms that there is more than one
   462–13 *W·* would demonstrate the healing of C. S.
   r 474– 5 *W·* introduces the Science of Christianity

whole

   pr 14–28 man's dominion over the *w·* earth.
   a 19–12 The Master forbore not to speak the *w·* truth,
   30–22 throughout the *w·* earthly career of Jesus,
   45– 9 for the salvation of the *w·* world from sin,
   sp 79– 9 Science must go over the *w·* ground,
   an 103– 8 blesses the *w·* human family.
   s 107– * *measures of meal, till the w· was* — *Matt.* 13 : 33.
   118– 1 measures of meal, till the *w·* was — *Matt.* 13 : 33.
   118–24 changes the *w·* of mortal thought,
   142– 8 must seek the undivided garment, the *w·* Christ,
   147–15 never . . . can absorb the *w·* meaning of
   157– 5 the *w·* force of the mental element is
   ph 160– 1 remedy lies in forgetting the *w·* thing ;
   191–13 Thus the *w·* earth will be transformed by
   f 202–11 but the *w·* human family would be redeemed
   207–29 in the action of man and the *w·* universe,
   213–10 self-expressed, though indefinable as a *w·*.
   219–12 makes the *w·* body "sick, — *Isa.* 1 : 5.
   219–12 and the *w·* heart faint ;" — *Isa.* 1 : 5.
   c 255– * * the w· creation groaneth* — *Rom.* 8 : 22.
   b 273–17 never made mortals *w·*, harmonious, and
   326–10 and set his *w·* affections on spiritual things,
   329– 5 A little leaven leavens the *w·* lump.
   340– 7 the conclusion of the *w·* matter : — *Eccl.* 12 : 13.
   340– 8 for this is the *w·* duty of man." — *Eccl.* 12 : 13.
   340–10 Let us hear the conclusion of the *w·* matter :
   340–11 for this is the *w·* of man in His image
   o 344–22 should be presented to the *w·* world,
   p 370– 1 To be every whit *w·*, man must be better
   371–32 can make it "every whit *w·*." — *John* 7 · 23.
   391– 6 "Thou art *w·* !" — *see John* 5 : 14.
   398–15 *w·*, like as the other." — *Matt.* 12 : 13.
   411–18 was changed and straightway became *w·*.
   413–19 without scrubbing the *w·* surface daily.
   415–30 the *w·* frame will sink from sight
   421–16 the great fact which covers the *w·* ground,
   422– 6 a great stir throughout his *w·* system,
   t 449 3 A little leaven causes the *w·* mass to ferment.
   461– 6 We admit the *w·*, because a part is proved
   r 470– 1 the *w·* family of man would be brethren ;
   487–31 This Principle makes *w·* the diseased,
   g 517–23 Even eternity can never reveal the *w·* of God,
   521–22 watered the *w·* face of the ground. — *Gen.* 2 : 6.
   545–11 was given dominion over the *w·* earth.
   545–16 Error tills the *w·* ground in this
   ap 567–16 which deceiveth the *w·* world : — *Rev.* 12 : 9.
   575–23 the joy of the *w·* earth, — *Psal.* 48 : 2.

wholeness

   r 465–14 the nature, essence, and *w·* of Deity.

wholesome

   pr 7–14 *w·* perception of God's requirements.
   b 323– 6 Through the *w·* chastisements of Love,
   p 396–24 Give them divine and *w·* understanding.

wholly

   a 30–11 Had his origin and birth been *w·* apart from
   sp 96– 6 Before error is *w·* destroyed,
   an 103–12 Mind-science is *w·* separate from any
   105–17 no longer apply legal rulings *w·* to
   s 111–29 Mind governs the body, not partially but *w·*.
   112–14 *w·* human in their origin and tendency
   124–29 they belong *w·* to divine Mind,
   125–32 mortal belief, *w·* inadequate to affect a man
   139–23 But mistakes could neither *w·* obscure the
   148–19 and deal — the one *w·*, the other primarily
   157– 2 C. S. deals *w·* with the mental cause
   ph 172–13 as uninterrupted and *w·* spiritual ;
   188–14 recognizes his condition to be *w·* a state of
   f 214– 3 If the medium of hearing is *w·* spiritual,
   252–18 says : I am *w·* dishonest,
   b 269–26 systems based *w·* or partly on
   290–25 To be *w·* spiritual, man must be sinless,
   305–24 man would be *w·* mortal, were it not that
   o 349–30 all learning, even that which is *w·* material.
   353–13 The age has not *w·* outlived the sense of
   353–17 Without perfection, nothing is *w·* real.
   355–23 an opinion *w·* due to a misapprehension
   p 410–29 until the practitioner's healing ability is *w·* lost.
   411–32 If you succeed in *w·* removing the fear,
   g 544– 2 a creation so *w·* apart from God's,
   ap 575–21 This city is *w·* spiritual,

whomsoever

   p 380– 6 "but on *w·* it shall fall, — *Matt.* 21 : 44.

whoso

   a 30–15 "*W·* sheddeth man's blood, — *Gen.* 9 : 6.
   t 448–18 but *w·* confesseth and — *Prov.* 28 : 13.

whosoever

   pr 1– * *w· shall say unto this mountain,* — *Mark* 11 : 23.
   a 22–27 *W·* believeth that wrath is righteous
   31–31 *w·* killeth you will think that he — *John* 16 : 2.
   55–23 and *w·* layeth his earthly all on the altar of
   s 132– 9 *w·* shall not be offended in me." — *Matt.* 11 : 6.
   ph 170–10 "*W·* liveth and believeth in me — *John* 11 : 26.
   c 267–16 *w·* shall do the will of my Father — *Matt.* 12 : 50.
   b 315– 1 "*W·* liveth and believeth in me — *John* 11 : 26.
   317– 6 *W·* lives most the life of Jesus in this
   p 372–25 "*W·* shall deny me before men, — *Matt.* 10 : 33.
   382–22 "*W·* shall not receive the — *Luke* 18 : 17.
   435–11 our Supreme Court decrees that *w· sinneth*
   t 444–19 "*W·* shall smite thee on thy — *Matt.* 5 : 39.
   g 542–15 Therefore *w·* slayeth Cain, — *Gen.* 4 : 15.
   548– 1 and *w·* will, let him take the — *Rev.* 22 : 17.

wicked

   pr 4–24 but in this *w·* world goodness will
   8–24 We confess to having a very *w·* heart
   a 36–25 to suppose that the *w·* can gloat over their
   sp 85–25 Jesus knew the generation to be *w·*
   96–31 During this final conflict, *w·* minds will
   an 104–32 must move the body to a *w·* act?
   s 136–21 That a *w·* king and debauched husband should
   139– 1 causes the *w·* to "forsake his way, — *Isa.* 55 : 7.
   ph 192–16 all that is selfish, *w·*, dishonest,
   f 239–11 The *w·* man is not the ruler of his
   239–14 "Let the *w·* forsake his way, — *Isa.* 55 : 7.
   b 270–25 consequently they are *w·*.
   289– 8 A *w·* mortal is not the idea of God.
   314–12 were the parents of their *w·* deeds.
   p 404–11 destroying the *w·* motives which produce them.
   440–23 compel them to enact *w·* laws
   t 451–30 either with a mistaken or a *w·* purpose.
   r 491–26 A *w·* man may have an attractive
   g 540– 3 Spirit creates neither a *w·* nor a mortal man,
   gl 584–22 saith : . . . I am mind, — a *w·* mind, self-made

wickedly

   b 270–24 Mortals think *w·* ; consequently they

wickedness

   pr 8– 5 face to face with their *w·*
   b 327–11 Then he loses pleasure in *w·*,
   t 453–20 Hidden sin is spiritual *w·* in high places.
   459–21 is more harmful than wilful *w·*,
   ap 563–30 "spiritual *w·* in high places." — *Eph.* 6 : 12.
   569–11 nothingness of error is in proportion to its *w·*.

wicked one

   r 476– 2 They are the children of the *w· o·*,

wide

   sp 90–27 shuts the door on death, and opens it *w·* towards
   p 433–32 can open *w·* those prison doors and set the
   t 451–12 "*w·* is the gate, and broad is the — *Matt.* 7 : 13.
   ap 571–28 he has opened *w·* the gates of glory,

widely

   s 150– 4 healing power of Truth is *w·* demonstrated
   t 464– 2 Why do you not make yourself more *w·* known?"

wider

   c 265–13 a *w·* sphere of thought and action,

widows

   m 64– 6 To visit the fatherless and *w·* — *Jas.* 1 : 27.

wield

   s 152– 2 It would *w·* the sceptre of a monarch,

wielded

   s 142–21 as twisted and *w·* by Jesus,

wife (*see also* wives)

deserts his
   m 63–28 If a dissolute husband deserts his *w·*,
husband and
   m 60– 1 it never would, if both husband and *w·* were
Lamb's
   ap 574– 9 the bride, the Lamb's *w·*. — *Rev.* 21 : 9.
   575– 3 behold the Lamb's *w·*, — Love wedded to its
   577– 5 The Lamb's *w·* presents the unity of
your
   m 59–18 the welfare and happiness of your *w·*

   m 58–17 a *w·* or a husband forever within four walls,
   58–26 a *w·* ought not to court vulgar extravagance
   64–12 his *w·* should not say, "It is never well to
   64–13 A *w·* is sometimes debarred by a
   66–23 for a *w·* precipitately to leave her husband
   66–25 or for a husband to leave his *w·*.
   g 535–20 unto the voice of thy *w·*, — *Gen.* 3 : 17.
   538–23 And Adam knew Eve his *w·* ; — *Gen.* 4 : 1.

wild

   ph 179–17 whereas the *w·* animal, left to his instincts,
   179–19 ailment, which a *w·* horse might never have.
   g 552–20 may become *w·* with freedom

wilderness

a 33– 5 manna, which of old had fed in the w·
s 133– 9 In the w·, streams flowed from the rock,
135–19 furnish a table in the w·?"— *Psal.* 78 : 19.
158–19 the byways of this w· world,
f 208–19 voice of one crying in the w·"— *Matt.* 3 : 3.
226–30 the awful conflict, the Red Sea and the w· ;
g 507–10 strangers in a tangled w·.
ap 565–29 And the woman fled into the w·,— *Rev.* 12 : 6.
566– 4 as they were led through the w·,
gl 597–16 definition of

wilful

p 369–30 No man is physically healed in w· error
t 459–21 is more harmful than w· wickedness,

will

and action
p 401–26 Would the drug . . . restore w· and action
corporeal
s 144–21 Truth, and not corporeal w·, is the divine power
depraved
s 115–22 depraved w·, self-justification, pride,
divine
a 28– 2 claimed to know and to teach the divine w·,
r 474–23 or the offspring of the divine w·?
exercise of
t 446–27 The exercise of w· brings on a
God's
f 202– 4 and God's w· must be universally done.
241– 2 He, who knows God's w· or the demands of
His
s 109–29 If any man will do His w·,— *John* 7 : 17.
c 256–20 "doeth according to His w·— *Dan.* 4 : 35.
human
(see **human**)
mortal
gl 599– 5 ZEAL. . . . Blind enthusiasm ; mortal w·.
not my
a 33–19 "Not my w·, but Thine, be done !"— *Luke* 22 : 42.
offspring of
ph 192–12 the offspring of w· and not of wisdom,
of God
pr 11–30 habitual desire to know and do the w· of God,
gl 597–22 "For this is the w· of God."— *I Thess.* 4 : 3.
of his Father
a 31– 8 they who do the w· of his Father.
of my Father
c 267–16 shall do the w· of my Father— *Matt.* 12 : 50.
of the Father
ph 168–20 He did the w· of the Father.
of wisdom
a 19–24 and enables man to do the w· of wisdom.
Thy
pr 17– 1 Thy w· be done in earth,— *Matt.* 6 : 10.
volition or
f 220–32 as directly as the volition or w· moves the

sp 99– 8 to w· and to do of His good pleasure"— *Phil.* 2 : 13.
s 111– 3 the w·, or sensuous reason of the human mind,
ph 187–16 the hand, admittedly moved by the w·.
r 490– 8 W·— blind, stubborn, and headlong
gl 597–20 definition of
597–24 W·, as a quality of so-called mortal mind, is a

William IV

s 163– 6 W· IV, King of England,

willing

pref ix–17 a w· disciple at the heavenly gate,
pr 8–27 than we are w· to have our neighbor see?
9–25 Are you w· to leave all for Christ, for Truth,
10– 9 Until we are . . . w· to drink his cup,
11–25 We must be w· to do this, that we may
a 24–22 and are w· to be forgiven?
33–32 w· truly to drink his cup, take his cross,
41–29 more than they were w· to practise.
s 138–23 the sick are more w· to part with pain than
144–16 W· the sick to recover is not the
ph 189– 2 w· to leave with astronomy the explanation of
f 216–29 "w· rather to be absent from the— *II Cor.* 5 : 8.
235–25 when the soul is w· and the flesh weak,
237–28 more . . . than they are w· to admit
b 271–26 Those, who are w· to leave their nets
p 369–19 were w· that a man should live.
373– 7 partly because they were w· to be restored,
381– 4 Be no more w· to suffer the illusion that you
383–10 "w· rather to be absent from the— *II Cor.* 5 : 8.
398– 8 the concessions which Jesus was w· to make
t 464– 9 could not take her place, even if w· so to do.
ap 570–30 Many are w· to open the eyes of the people
571– 1 not so w· to point out the evil in human thought,
gl 581–25 "w· rather to be absent from the— *II Cor.* 5 : 8.

willingness

a 24– 4 and w· to give up human beliefs
f 218–18 if you are without faith in God's w·
b 323–32 W· to become as a little child
r 493–31 this consummate test of the power and w· of

will-power

an 103–31 no transference of mortal thought and w·.
106– 1 to the criminal misuse of human w·,
s 144–14 Human w· is not Science.
144–18 Human w· may infringe the rights of man.
ph 186– 3 the false stimulus and reaction of w·
f 206–10 W· is capable of all evil.
251–16 in hygiene, in drugs, or in w·.
r 490– 3 W· is but a product of belief,

win

f 254–31 for through it you w· and wear the crown.
p 365–20 enough Christly affection to w· his own pardon,
417–16 hold your ground . . . and you will w·.
t 462–18 Christianity, and persistence alone w· the

wind

holds the
ph 192–18 holds the "w· in His fists ;"— *Prov.* 30 : 4.
shrieks
m 67– 5 the w· shrieks through the tightened shrouds,
sniffs the
ph 179–18 left to his instincts, sniffs the w· with delight.
soweth the
f 210–24 soweth the w· and reapeth the

ph 184–28 when the w· was from the east.
184–32 w· had not changed, but her thought of it had
185– 2 The w· had not produced the difficulty.
190–25 For the w· passeth over it,— *Psal.* 103 : 16.
b 269–28 are reeds shaken by the w·,
293–22 w·, wave, lightning, fire, bestial ferocity
r 476–25 For the w· passeth over it,— *Psal.* 103 : 16.
gl 597–27 definition of
598– 1 Greek word for w· (*pneuma*) is used also for
598– 3 w· [*pneuma*] bloweth where it— *John* 3 : 8.
598–13 It might be translated w· or *air*,

winding

ap 563–27 w· its way amidst all evil,

winding-sheet

a 44–18 to remove the napkin and w·,

window

f 245– 9 she stood daily before the w· watching for

window-pane

b 295–17 is as light passing through the w·.

windows

r 478–12 nor were they even visible through the w·?

winds

m 57–26 may uproot . . . and scatter them to the w· ;
67–22 even the w· and waves to obey him.
ph 185– 5 and she never suffered again from east w·,
f 201–15 Then, when the w· of God blow,
209–11 which holds the w· in its grasp.
240– 3 giant hills, winged w·, mighty billows,

wine

bread and
a 32–21 confined to the use of bread and w·.
cup of
a 32– 8 to pass each guest a cup of w·.
new
s 114–21 the new w· of the Spirit has to be poured into
b 281–27 does not put new w· into old bottles,
our
a 35–27 Our w· the inspiration of Love,

a 32–10 the w·, used on convivial occasions
33–32 Are all who eat bread and drink w· in memory of
m 65– 4 at every bridal altar to turn the water into w·
b 321–32 by changing water into w·,
gl 598–17 definition of

wine-bibber

a 52–32 the hypocrite, called Jesus a glutton and a w·.

winged

a 49– 3 inspired their devotion, w· their faith,
f 240– 3 giant hills, w· winds, mighty billows,
b 298–29 pure thoughts from God, w· with Truth and
323–12 and conception unconfined is w· to reach the
g 512– 6 and every w· fowl after his kind :— *Gen.* 1 : 21.
512– 9 and also by holy thoughts, w· with Love.

wings

drooping
m 58– 4 or else joy's drooping w· trail in dust.
its
a 55–16 gathering beneath its w· the sick and sinning.
m 57–29 and begins to unfold its w· for heaven.
c 261–29 and preens its w· for a skyward flight.
one's
c 260–17 often hampers the trial of one's w·
their
b 298–26 evolving animal qualities in their w· ;
their own
an 103–27 singe their own w· and fall into dust.

p 434– 1 Swift on the w· of divine Love, there comes

winning
f 239–22 and show what we are *w·*.

winter
sp 96– 8 summer and *w·*, seedtime and harvest

wintry
m 57–24 The *w·* blasts of earth may uproot the flowers of

wiped
ap 573–31 no more pain, and all tears will be *w·* away.

wipes
pr 11–18 but *w·* it out in the most effectual manner.

wiping
p 363– 5 *w·* them with her long hair, which hung loosely

wire
p 393–23 or the electric *w·* which you stretch,

wires
sp 78–19 Spirit needs no *w·* nor electricity in order to

wisdom (*see also* wisdom's)
according to
  f 239– 9 let worth be judged according to *w·*,
and Love
  pr 2–11 since He is unchanging *w·* and Love.
  a 23– 1 *W·* and Love may require many sacrifices
  c 265–26 before we discover what belongs to *w·* and Love.
bade him
  b 321–10 but *w·* bade him come back and handle the
beginning of
  p 373–16 is the beginning of *w·*," — *Psal.* 111 : 10.
bridal chamber of
  f 238–14 From out the bridal chamber of *w·* there will
decrees of
  f 229–28 should not if we could, annul the decrees of *w·*.
divine
  m 66–20 wait patiently on divine *w·* to point out the
  p 386–24 and divine *w·* will then be understood.
growth in
  p 363–31 repentance, reformation, and growth in *w·*
He bestows
  pr 6– 5 God is not separate from the *w·* He bestows.
His
  s 110– 6 is pronounced by His *w·* good.
  b 275–18 No wisdom is wise but His *w·* ;
immortal
  g 519– 6 His infinite self-containment and immortal *w·* ?
inspires with
  f 234– 4 Whatever inspires with *w·*, Truth, or Love
is justified
  b 317–10 "*w·* is justified of her children." — *Matt.* 11 : 19.
judgment-day of
  b 291–29 the judgment-day of *w·* comes hourly
last call of
  b 291– 7 but this last call of *w·* cannot come till
led by
  b 321– 8 When, led by *w·* to cast down his rod,
less
  p 378–31 it would manifest less *w·* than
Life, Love, and
  b 283– 6 Mind is the same Life, Love, and *w·*
Man's
  b 322–14 Man's *w·* finds no satisfaction in sin,
masculine
  m 64–23 masculine *w·* and feminine love,
of God
  gl 597–21 The might and *w·* of God.
of Job
  o 360–22 Hear the *w·* of Job, as given in the
of man
  pr 3– 2 The *w·* of man is not sufficient to
of the creator
  b 273–24 and impugn the *w·* of the creator.
omnipotent
  sp 83–19 this belief belittles omnipotent *w·*,
or Truth
  f 206– 2 no other Love, *w·*, or Truth,
required by
  pr 5– 5 The next and great step required by *w·*
saith
  gl 580–19 that of which *w·* saith,
supply the
  ap 571–17 Know thyself, and God will supply the *w·* and
supreme
  sp 91– 4 under the control of supreme *w·* ?
true
  f 231–21 To hold yourself superior to sin, . . . is true *w·*,
Truth, and Love
  pr 15–20 to work and watch for *w·*, Truth, and Love.
  r 495–30 abiding steadfastly in *w·*, Truth, and Love.
unchanging
  pr 2–11 since He is unchanging *w·* and Love.
warns man
  r 481–13 against which *w·* warns man,
will of
  a 19–24 and enables man to do the will of *w·*.

wisdom
work of
  sp 83– 5 claimed that they could equal the work of *w·*.

  pr 10–31 Do you ask *w·* to be merciful and not to punish
  m 60–13 *w·* will ultimately put asunder what she
  62–28 the order of *w·* would be reversed.
  s 116– 2 *W·*, purity, spiritual understanding,
  ph 192–12 the offspring of will and not of *w·*,
  196– 1 If materialistic knowledge is power, it is not *w·*.
  f 221–21 semi-starvation is not acceptable to *w·*,
  230–19 Does *w·* make blunders
  246–25 unfolds *w·*, beauty, and holiness.
  b 275–14 All substance, intelligence, *w·*, being,
  275–17 No *w·* is wise but His wisdom ;
  p 384–11 a belief of mortal mind, not an enactment of *w·*,
  r 465–15 justice, mercy, *w·*, goodness, and so on.
  g 538– 5 the cherub *w·* at the gate of understanding
  544–15 the might or right or *w·*

wisdom's
  b 321–14 evil, under *w·* bidding, was destroyed

wise
  pr 8–16 and it is *w·* not to try to deceive ourselves
  m 62–21 if we would be *w·* and healthy.
  sp 82–32 it is *w·* earnestly to consider whether it is the
  95–25 Is the *w·* man of to-day believed,
  s 131–20 hast hid these things from the *w·* — *Luke* 10 : 21.
  ph 167–22 It is not *w·* to take a halting and half-way
  175–32 "Where ignorance is bliss, 't is folly to be *w·*,"
  200– 8 would be *w·* not to undertake the
  f 231–26 To hold yourself superior to . . . is equally *w·*,
  235–20 They should be *w·* spiritual guides
  239–32 the *w·* man said, "All is vanity." — *Eccl.* 1 : 2.
  b 275–17 No wisdom is *w·* but His wisdom ;
  o 342– 4 "making *w·* the simple." — *Psal.* 19 : 7.
  353–22 we must yield up all belief in it and be *w·*.
  356–28 Would any one call it *w·* and good to
  p 382–23 shall in no *w·* enter therein." — *Luke* 18 : 17.
  413– 9 The *w·* or unwise views of parents
  429– 9 and if we are *w·*, we look beyond a
  t 443– * *Give instruction to a w· man, — Prov.* 9 : 9.
  g 515– 7 a *w·* idea, charming in its adroitness,
  538– 1 infinitely *w·* and altogether lovely,
  ap 571–12 If so, listen and be *w·*.

wisely
  an 104– 9 the celebrated naturalist and author, has *w·* said:
  s 139–12 will teach men patiently and *w·* to
  t 458–26 The Christian Scientist *w·* shapes his course,

Wisemen
  pref vii–10 The *W·* were led to behold and to follow
  s 121– 7 The Chaldean *W·* read in the stars the fate
  r 482–23 Angels announced to the *W·* of old
  ap 575–28 the star seen by the *W·* of the Orient,

wiser
  u 22– 1 would borrow the passport of some *w·* pilgrim,
  p 422– 2 *W·* than his persecutors, Jesus said :
  t 443– * *and he will be yet w· : — Prov.* 9 : 9.

wisest
  g 539–31 inspired his *w·* and least-understood sayings,

wish
  a 48–13 and think, or even *w·*, to escape the exalting
  s 129– 7 If you *w·* to know the spiritual fact,
  144– 1 Why should we *w·* to make them do so,
  f 219–15 what we do not *w·* to have manifested.
  219–21 "The *w·*," . . . "is ever father to the thought."
  238–18 *w·* to enter unlawfully into the labors of others.
  b 301–18 man should *w·* for, and in reality has,
  326– 3 If we *w·* to follow Christ, Truth, it must be
  p 392–25 only such conclusions as you *w·* realized

wished
  f 226–26 I *w·* to save from the slavery of their

wishes
  pr 13–19 less risk of overwhelming our real *w·*

wishing
  p 421–28 *w·* to see the forms it assumes

wit
  c 255– * *to w·, the redemption of our — Rom.* 8 : 23.
  p 438–16 three distinct charges of crime, to *w·* :

Witchcraft
  p 441–22 Mesmerism, Hypnotism, Oriental *W·*,

witchcraft
  an 106–22 idolatry, *w·*, hatred, variance, — *Gal.* 5 : 20.

withdraw
  s 124–26 *W·* them, and creation must collapse.

withdrawn
  a 51– 6 Jesus could have *w·* himself

withdraws
  s 144– 7 *W·* the star, when dawns the

withdrew
  a 32–25 he *w·* from the material senses

wither

sp 81–19 Though the grass seemeth to w·
ph 190–16 to w· and return to its native nothingness.

withered

c 265–18 or a flower w· by the sun
p 398–13 To the sufferer with the w· hand

withers

m 68–10 mistrust, . . . w· the flowers of Eden

withheld

b 309– 1 but this appellation was w·,
g 537–30 would imply that God w· from man the

withhold

a 50–10 who could w· a clear token of his presence
o 344–13 mercifully w· their misrepresentations,
t 452–13 w· not the rebuke or the explanation

withholding

sp 79–32 neither does w· enrich us.

within

a 44–30 demonstrating w· the narrow tomb
46– 6 made their hearts burn w· them,
m 58–17 would confine . . . forever w· four walls,
61– 1 cannot circumscribe happiness w· the
sp 87–19 the emeralds w· its rocks ;
87–20 the gems w· its caverns,
92– 9 Mind is not an entity w· the cranium
s 108–20 w· the shadow of the death-valley,
146–20 that is w· thy gates,'' — *Exod.* 20 : 10.
ph 173– 6 supposition, that Spirit is w· what it
180– 9 This is the seed w· itself
191–22 not a spray buds w· the vale,
f 223–12 If Spirit were once w· the body,
248–31 Let unselfishness, . . . reign w· us,
c 255– * *groan w· ourselves,* — *Rom.* 8 : 23.
256–14 nor compressed w· the narrow limits
257– 2 If Mind is w· and without all things,
b 284– 5 if the infinite could be . . . w· the finite,
294– 5 carries w· itself the seeds of all error.
331– 6 If He dwelt w· what He creates,
o 358–26 through rousing w· the sick a
p 362– * *disquieted w· me ?* — *Psal.* 42 : 11.
397–29 compressed w· the skull,
413–20 bodily cleanliness w· and without.
436– 9 w· the limits of the divine law,
r 476–29 kingdom of God is w· you ;'' — *Luke* 17 : 21.
478– 4 What evidence of Soul . . . w· mortality?
g 508–14 The seed w· itself is the pure
513–28 consequently not w· the range of
550– 8 and be limited w· material bounds.
ap 574– 1 kingdom of God is w· you.'' — *Luke* 17 : 21.
576–21 ''is w· you,'' — *Luke* 17 : 21.
576–21 is w· reach of man's consciousness
577–24 honors w· the heavenly city.
577–25 Its gates open towards light . . . w· and

without

pr 3– 1 w· being reminded of His province.
11– 1 W· punishment, sin would multiply.
15–21 We must ''pray w· ceasing.'' — *I Thess.* 5 : 17.
15–31 W· a fitness for holiness, we cannot
a 22–26 pinning one's faith w· works to
23–15 ''Faith w· works is dead.'' — *Jas.* 2 : 26.
30– 7 the divine Spirit, w· measure.
40–22 endure human brutality w· murmuring,
m 57– 2 W· it there is no stability in society,
57– 2 w· it one cannot attain the
59– 2 w· a full recognition of its
63–21 w· encouraging difficulties
sp 76–24 w· a single bodily pleasure or pain,
80–19 w· the aid of hands,
83–10 a blind belief w· understanding,
84–25 w· the concession of material personalities
89–14 w· study or a superinduced condition,
90– 4 and that, too, w· meal or monad
93–20 Whatever contradicts . . . is w· foundation.
97–14 w· passing the boundary where,
an 105– 1 w· mortal mind to direct them,
s 112–28 w· giving that author proper credit,
113– 6 W· this, the letter is but the
117– 4 one alone and w· an equal.
126– 4 mortal mind will be w· form and
145– 2 w· being able to explain them.
145– 6 letter, w· the spirit, would have
149–10 left w· explanation except in C. S.
153–17 matter w· mind is not painful.
156–22 could get along two days w· globules ;
159– 2 surgical operation w· the ether.
159–19 performed the operation w· ether.
160–30 Is man a material fungus w· Mind
162–14 w· the conditions of matter
162–15 w· the false beliefs of a so-called
ph 177– 8 Neither exists w· the other,
179–17 will take cold w· his blanket,
183– 9 produce a crop w· sowing the seed
185–22, 23 not only w· drugs, but w· hypnotism,

without

ph 188– 7 an embryonic thought w· motive ;
194–13 it will be so w· an injured nerve.
199– 1 w· volition of mortal mind,
f 204–26 usurping the name w· the nature
205– 2 w· knowing that they are sinning,
207–13 W· this lesson, we lose sight of
209–10 w· Mind. w· the intelligence which holds the
210–32 it is w· a destructive element.
211–16 W· mortal mind, the tear could not
214–32 Spirit's senses are w· pain,
217–31 W· mind, could the muscles be tired?
218–17 w· faith in God's willingness
221– 8 a thin slice of bread w· water.
221–15 w· a vestige of the old complaint.
221–24 and he ate w· suffering,
221–30 w· the consent of mortal mind,
230– 3 Would you attempt with drugs, or w·,
231–32 w· Him was not anything made — *John* 1 : 3.
241–17 error of the ages is preaching w· practice.
242–26 one web of consistency w· seam
244–20 w· His entire manifestation,
247– 8 w· a decaying cavity.
253– 6 without beginning and w· end,
253–23 w· hindrance from the body.
c 257– 2 If Mind is within and w· all things,
262–25 even as light emits light w· effort ;
266– 6 Would existence w· personal friends be
266– 8 solitary, left w· sympathy ;
b 271–31 ''How shall they hear w· a— *Rom.* 10 : 14.
273– 6 w· the divine Principle of
281–23 sin and mortality are w· actual origin
287– 1 are w· a real origin or existence.
287–22 w· spiritual identity or
291–13 is unattainable w· them.
303–25 w· the image and likeness of
303–27 w· a witness or proof of His
306–17 w· a rational proof of immortality.
310– 8 w· material accompaniments.
312–16 w· Love, . . . immortality cannot appear.
312–18 w· understanding Truth ;
314– 9 one Mind w· a second or equal.
322–30 W· this process of weaning,
323– 3 w· striving for them.
328– 4 that they can live w· goodness,
335–10 w· the Logos, the Æon
o 343– 4 thy faith w· thy works, — *Jas.* 2 : 18.
343– 8 w· this cross-bearing,
353–17 W· perfection, nothing is wholly real.
354–19 shown by words w· deeds,
354–20 are like clouds w· rain.
355–26 W· this understanding, no one
p 371– 9 believed to be here w· their consent
377–29 W· this ignorant human belief,
378– 8 W· the so-called human mind,
378–29 w· the divine permission,
379– 1 w· the consent of mortals,
381–26 will never be reached w· the
384– 2 Can matter, . . . act w· mind?
385– 4 undergo w· sinking fatigues and
385–16 *if w· sin,* can be experienced w·
385–18 can do w· harm to yourself.
386– 7 w· mind to demand it
386–28 ''Your sorrow is w· cause,''
399–20 W· this force the body is
400–28 W· divine control there is discord,
402–32 a belief w· a real cause.
413–18 w· scrubbing the whole surface daily.
413–20 bodily cleanliness within and w·.
427– 4 never w· its representative.
438–24 w· the inspection of
t 446–14 w· destroying his own power to heal
447–18 w· frightening or discouraging
449–26 w· the preliminary offence.
450–16 Few yield w· a struggle,
451– 9 and think to succeed w· the spirit,
454– 8 leads to the house built w· hands
457– 3 w· giving it credit,
457–20 there is no excellence w· labor in a
457–31 w· exploiting other means.
461– 2 w· food and raiment ;
464– 1 feels your influence w· seeing you.
r 468–27 Life is without beginning and w· end.
469–17 error, w· intelligence or reality.
470– 8 infinite Truth w· an unlikeness,
470–28 unexpressed — that is, w· entity.
470–30 If man ever existed w· this perfect
472–18 Error is a belief w· understanding.
479–19 w· form, and void ; — *Gen.* 1 : 2.
480–27 and w· Him was not — *John* 1 : 3.
483–31 w· timidity or dissimulation,
486– 1 is w· foundation in fact,
486–31 w· God in the world ;'' — *Eph.* 2 : 12.
487–22 belief is blindness w· Principle
487–25 ''Show me thy faith w·— *Jas.* 2 : 18.
491– 4 a belief w· actual foundation

without

g 501– * *and w· Him was not*— *John* 1 : 3.
503– 6 w· form, and void ;— *Gen.* 1 : 2.
507– 7 W· natures particularly defined,
525–18 "and w· Him . . . was not — *John* 1 : 3.
528–29 performed mentally and w· instruments ;
531–22 or that matter exists w· God?
536–11 The illusion of sin is w· hope
557– 2 moving and playing w· harm,
557– 7 where parturition is w· suffering.
ap 560–18 w· a correct sense of its highest
564– 9 into a night w· a star.
564–28 hated me w· a cause." — *John* 15 : 25.
577–25 both within and w·,
gl 592–13 the proof that, w· the gospel,
(see also **beginning**)

withstand

f 224–31 No power can w· divine Love.

witness

another
p 431–25 Another w· takes the stand and testifies :
432– 9 Another w· is called for by the
432–20 Another w· takes the stand and testifies :
438–19 Another w·, equally inadequate, said
bear
b 298–10 spiritual sense can bear w· only to Truth.
330– 9 and the letter and the spirit bear w·,
411–11 bear w· to the truth,
441–14 Material Law is a liar who cannot bear w·
ap 561–31 to bear w· of that Light." — *John* 1 : 8.
false
an 100– * *thefts, false w·, blasphemies :* — *Matt.* 15 : 19.
p 437–13 Nerve, . . . to be a false w·.
438–12 and bearing false w· against Man.
next
p 431–20 The next w· is called :
432– 1 The next w· testifies :
principal
p 436– 1 The principal w· (the officer of the
proved the
p 430– 8 proved the w·, Nerve, to be a perjurer.
silence the
p 417–16 When you silence the w· against your plea,
testifies
p 430–28 a w· testifies thus : — I represent Health-laws.
without a
b 303–27 would be without a w· or proof of

a 54–13 In w· of his divine commission, he presented
s 134– 4 word *martyr,* from the Greek, means w· ;
o 348–27 would immediately w· the full fruitage of
p 432– 6 w· to the crime of liver-complaint.
436– 5 to reappear however at the trial as a w· against
437–11 I proclaim this w·, Nerve, to be destitute of
s 514–20 as w· the millennial estate pictured by

witnessed

a 46–31 that by all they had w· and suffered,
t 453–12 I have never w· so decided effects from

witnesses

s 122– 6 contradict their false w·, and reveal the
150– 1 w· and monuments to the virtue and power of
p 434–11 W·, judges, and jurors, who were at the
436–35 One of the principal w·, Nerve, testified
439–15 C. S. turned from the abashed w·,
439–28 w·, jurors, and judges, to be offenders,

wives

m 66–21 Husbands and w· should never separate if
ph 176– 6 attributed . . . to the weakness of their w·.

wizards

sp 70– * w· that peep and that mutter; — *Isa.* 8 : 19.

woe

comes
pr 5– 8 and w· comes in return for what is done.
every
f 236–20 good as the remedy for every w·.
hour of
ap 567– 4 Truth and Love come nearer in the hour of w·,
human
f 238–20 until we seek this remedy for human w·
patient
gl 586–23 GETHSEMANE. Patient w· ; the human yielding
shame and
ph 188–10 from shame and w· to their final punishment.
silent
a 36–14 a few women who bowed in silent w· beneath the
want and
sp 96–17 want and w·, sin, sickness, and death,
c 257–26 to meet the demands of human want and w·,
g 501– 9 but richly recompensing human want and w·

ap 568–20 W· to the inhabiters of the earth — *Rev.* 12 : 12.

woes

f 248–10 and destroying the w· of sense
b 322–28 as well as our disappointments and ceaseless w·,

wolf

g 514–22 w· also shall dwell with the lamb, — *Isa.* 11 : 6.
ap 567–31 shows how the Lamb slays the w·.

wolves

an 104– 6 and belied by w· in sheep's clothing.
ap 567–28 These w· in sheep's clothing are detected

woman (see also **woman's**)

accord
m 63–16 a marvel why usage should accord w· less
adulterous
pr 11– 3 When forgiving the adulterous w· he said,
another
f 247– 5 Another w· at ninety had new teeth,
beguiles the
g 533–14 beguiles the w· and demoralizes the man.
born of
g 529– 3 that man should be born of w·,
born of a
a 30– 5 Born of a w·, Jesus' advent in the flesh
g 552–15 "Man that is born of a w· — *Job* 14 : 1.
clothed in light
ap 561–11 as a w· clothed in light,
clothed with
ap 560– 7 a w· clothed with the sun, — *Rev.* 12 : 1.
create
g 528–18 and thereby create w·.
creation of
g 528–26 supposed . . . basis of the creation of w·
enabled
g 534– 3 This hereafter enabled w· to be the
534– 6 This enabled w· to be first to interpret the
English
f 245– 3 sketch from the history of an English w·,
fled
ap 565–29 the w· fled into the wilderness, — *Rev.* 12 : 6.
God and
g 533–15 *mortal error,* charges God and w· with his own
goes forth
b 268–12 w· goes forth to battle with Goliath.
helped the
ap 570–11 And the earth helped the w·, — *Rev.* 12 : 16.
help the
ap 570–22 In this age the earth will help the w· ;
ideal
g 517–10 The ideal w· corresponds to Life and to Love.
impoverished
m 63–29 the wronged, and perchance impoverished, w·
man and
a 37–23 duty and privilege of every child, man, and w·
g 516–21 Man and w· as coexistent and eternal
529–10 both man and w· proceed from God
gl 588–12 man and w· unchanged forever in their
noble
m 64–11 lends a helping hand to some noble w·,
perceived
a 20–28 and w· perceived this spiritual idea,
persecuted the
ap 569–30 he persecuted the w· which — *Rev.* 12 : 13
protection to
m 60–17 a barrier against vice, a protection to w·,
rights of
gl 587– 3 The rights of w· acknowledged morally,
Samaritan
sp 85–12 The Samaritan w· said :
s 133 1 than that of the Samaritan w·, who said,
sick
pr 6–24 Of a sick w· he said that Satan had
sp 86– 7 he was answered by the faith of a sick w·.
stood before the
ap 563–25 and the dragon stood before the w· — *Rev.* 12 : 4.
strange
p 362– 6 A "strange w·" came in. — *Prov.* 23 : 27.
that
ph 193–27 "It was none other than God and that w·
this
p 362–11 this w· (Mary Magdalene, . . . approached Jesus.
364–28 do they show their regard . . . as did this w·?
this poor
p 364–13 He even said that this poor w· had
young
f 245–13 and supposed her to be a young w·.

m 59–10 nor should w· be expected to
s 107– * *leaven, which a w· took, and hid* — *Matt.* 13 : 33.
117–32 "leaven, which a w· took, and hid — *Matt.* 13 : 33.
158–31 A w· in the city of Lynn,
159–20 sequel proved that this Lynn w·
ph 184–27 A w·, whom I cured of consumption,
f 247– 4 A w· of eighty-five, whom I knew,
p 363– 8 Did Jesus spurn the w·?
363–22 that remarkable declaration to the w·,
389–29 In her belief the w· had chronic liver-complaint

woman

r	482–18	As *w·* is but a species of the genera,
g	525– 9	In the Saxon, *mankind, a w·, any one*;
	528–13	and the rib, . . . made He a *w·*,— *Gen.* 2 : 22.
	529– 3	not *w·* again taken from man.
	529–15	And he said unto the *w·*,— *Gen.* 3 : 1.
	529–17	And the *w·* said unto the serpent,— *Gen.* 3 : 2.
	530–13	And the serpent said unto the *w·*,— *Gen.* 3 : 4.
	533– 8	The *w·* whom Thou gavest — *Gen.* 3 : 12.
	533–16	"The *w·*, whom Thou gavest me, is responsible."
	533–19	has grown into an evil mind, named *w·*,
	533–27	finds *w·* the first to confess her fault.
	534–10	enmity between thee and the *w·*,— *Gen.* 3 : 15.
	534–28	material sense, will bite the heel of the *w·*,
	534–29	and the *w·*, this idea, will bruise the head of
	535– 6	Unto the *w·* He said,— *Gen.* 3 : 16.
	557–17	the curse will be removed which says to *w·*,
ap	561–22	The *w·* in the Apocalypse symbolizes
	562– 6	*w·*, typifying the spiritual idea of
	562–24	spiritual idea is typified by a *w·* in travail,
	565–19	represented first by man and, . . . last by *w·*,
	570– 9	water as a flood, after the *w·*,— *Rev.* 12 : 15.

womanhood

f	246–20	conspiracies against manhood and *w·*.

womanly

p	397–30	will quickly become more manly or *w·*.

woman's

s	159–16	would have considered the *w·* state of mind,
p	363–13	detect the *w·* immoral status

womb

r	478–28	separated me from my mother's *w·*,— *Gal.* 1 : 15.

women

at the cross

a	49– 1	The *w·* at the cross could have answered

few

a	36–13	a few *w·* who bowed in silent woe

franchise for

m	63–21	If the elective franchise for *w·* will remedy

Jewish

gl	596–29	The Jewish *w·* wore veils over their faces

men and

m	62–18	should become men and *w·* only through
	68– 6	has created men and *w·* in Science.
sp	71–15	and you may see landscapes, men, and *w·*.
s	158–22	and men and *w·* become loathsome sots.
	164–10	generally . . . are grand men and *w·*,
f	225–29	Men and *w·* of all climes and races
	247–15	Immortal men and *w·* are models of
	248– 5	Men and *w·* of riper years and larger lessons

p	363– 6	as was customary with *w·* of her grade.

won

a	39– 4	He *w·* eternal honors.
m	61– 6	or happiness will never be *w·*.
sp	82– 9	If spiritual life has been *w·* by the departed,
s	109–20	and I *w·* my way to absolute conclusions
ph	179– 9	*w·* only as man is found, not in
f	201–19	Christian perfection is *w·* on no other basis.
	217–19	and you have *w·* a point in Science.
	226–11	and that its freedom be *w·*,
	233–15	until the goal . . . is assiduously earned and *w·*.
	254– 8	is fought and the victory *w·*.
b	290–17	happiness would be *w·* at the
	326–17	This point *w·*, you have started as you should.
o	360– 3	nothing is lost, and all is *w·*,
t	448– 4	it *w·* his humble desire.
	453–10	and a higher basis is thus *w·* ;

wonder

sp	76– 4	with eyes open only to that *w·*,
	80–29	and believes that this *w·* emanates from
s	136–28	No *w·* Herod desired to see the new Teacher.
r	487–12	centuries ago, and it will repeat the *w·*.
g	501–11	that amplification of *w·* and glory
	503–15	Hence the eternal *w·*,
ap	560– 6	And there appeared a great *w·* — *Rev.* 12 : 1.
	562–29	And there appeared another *w·* — *Rev.* 12 : 3.

Wonderful

s	109–27	and his name shall be called *W·*." — *Isa.* 9 : 6.

wonderful

a	46– 2	did not perform many *w·* works, until
s	137– 3	but the ultimate of this *w·* work was not
o	347– 3	to verify this *w·* philosophy
	358–26	a belief that . . . these healers have *w·* power,
r	483–29	by doing many *w·* works through the
ap	572–28	are inadequate to take in so *w·* a scene.

wondering

p	363–12	they were *w·* why, being a prophet,

wonders

pr	13–23	the *w·* wrought by infinite, incorporeal Love,
sp	90–21	hashish eaters mentally travel far and work *w·*,
s	133–17	the divine Principle wrought *w·* for the
	139– 9	was ushered in with signs and *w·*.

wonders

s	150–13	Now, as then, signs and *w·* are wrought in the
ph	185–17	strove to emulate the *w·* wrought by Moses.
f	243–13	That those *w·* are not more commonly repeated
b	268– 2	has brought to light . . . many useful *w·*.
t	449– 4	A grain of C. S. does *w·* for mortals,

wondrous

a	42–21	the *w·* glory which God bestowed on His

wood

ph	199– 6	since muscles are as material as *w·* and iron

wooden

ph	193– 2	caused by a fall upon a *w·* spike

woodman's

o	358– 1	Is the *w·* axe, which destroys a

Word

His

ap	560–17	whom God has appointed to voice His *W·*.

inspired

a	46– 9	has spoken through the inspired *W·*
r	497– 3	As adherents of Truth, we take the inspired *W·*

interpret the

g	537–25	Inspired writers interpret the *W·* spiritually,

of God

f	231–32	made by Him [the *W·* of God] ; — *John* 1 : 3.
b	335–11	the Logos, the Æon or *W·* of God,
g	503–12	the *W·* of God, saith to the darkness upon the
	525–18	were made through the *W·* of God,

of Life

ap	577–14	first, the *W·* of Life, Truth, and Love ;

of life

b	268– *	*have handled, of the W· of life,*— *I John* 1 : 1.

spiritual import of the

b	271–30	spiritual import of the *W·* imparts this power.
g	501– 4	chiefly because the spiritual import of the *W·*,

tenor of the

p	427–20	The tenor of the *W·* shows that we shall

the divine

r	480–27	made by Him [the divine *W·*] ; — *John* 1 : 3.

was made flesh

o	350–24	"The *W·* was made flesh." — *John* 1 : 14.

b	319–25	and the misinterpretation of the *W·*
o	350–31	the *W·* was materially explained,
ap	575–18	the *W·*, Christ, Christianity, and divine Science ;
	575–27	the *W·*, the polar magnet of Revelation ;

word

accepted his

b	316– 2	salvation to all who accepted his *w·*.

Adam

b	338–12	The *w· Adam* is from the Hebrew *adamah*,

anthropomorphic

g	517– 3	The *w· anthropomorphic*, in such a phrase as

cannot hear my

b	292–10	because ye cannot hear my *w·*. — *John* 8 : 43.

Christ

b	333– 3	The *w· Christ* is not properly a synonym for

created with a

g	543–24	Did man, whom God created with a *w·*,

duty

b	340– 5	when the *w· duty*, which is not in the original,

English

a	32– 5	our English *w· sacrament* is derived from it.

every

p	410–11	every *w·* that proceedeth out of— *Matt.* 4 : 4.

for man

g	517– 1	*w·* for *man* is used also as the synonym of *mind*

God

r	482– 7	gained by substituting the *w· God*,

God's

b	332–24	appointed to speak God's *w·* and to

graphic

a	52–14	Isaiah's graphic *w·* concerning the coming

Greek

s	137–31	[the meaning of the Greek *w· petros*, or *stone*]
r	474–12	the Greek *w·* rendered *miracle* in the
gl	598– 1	The Greek *w·* for *wind* (*pneuma*) is used also

hands

a	38–15	Here the *w· hands* is used metaphorically,

indicates

b	271–12	and the *w·* indicates that the power of healing

Jesus'

t	446–22	enthrones faith in Truth, and verifies Jesus' *w·* :

kurios

gl	590–17	In the Greek, the *w· kurios* almost always has

Latin

a	32– 4	The Latin *w·* for this oath was *sacramentum*,

logos, or

g	525–19	without Him [the *logos*, or *w·*] — *John* 1 : 3.

martyr

s	134– 4	*w· martyr*, from the Greek, means *witness* ;
	134– 6	*w· martyr* was narrowed in its significance

misplaced

b	319–28	A misplaced *w·* changes the sense

word

or deed
m 59–21   remember how slight a *w·* or deed may renew
f 205–19   perceive the divine image in some *w·* or deed
original
gl 598– 5   Here the original *w·* is the same in both cases
or phrase
s 114–18   if a better *w·* or phrase could be suggested,
proving my
o 343– 5   for proving my *w·* by my deed
reflection
b 301– 6   what C. S. means by the *w·* *reflection.*
rendered
b 271–11   the *w·* rendered *disciple* signifies student ;
Science
s 127– 1   author's application of the *w·* Science
127– 2   or questions her use of the *w·* Science,
o 341–13   the application of the *w· Science* to Christianity
Scriptural
sp 89–13   reaffirms the Scriptural *w·* concerning a man,
gl 579– 3   the material definition of a Scriptural *w·*
sense
r 482– 1   substitution of the *w· sense* for *soul* gives the
482– 8   In other cases, use the *w· sense,*
sent His
ph 165– *   *He sent His w·, and healed them,— Psal.* 107 : 20.
soul
ph 196–13   shows that here the *w· soul* means a false sense
r 482– 4   has adulterated the meaning of the *w· soul*
482– 6   The proper use of the *w· soul* can always
Spirit
o 344–32   the *w· Spirit* is so commonly applied to Deity,
spirit
sp 93–25   The modifying derivatives of the *w· spirit*
temple
ap 576–14   The *w· temple* also means *body.*
tender
p 367– 3   The tender *w·* and Christian encouragement
this
b 313–14   Using this *w·* in its higher meaning, we may
r 468–19   as the Scriptures use this *w·* in Hebrews :
g 502–21   This *w· beginning* is employed to signify
ap 576–16   was familiar with Jesus' use of this *w·*,
gl 598–12   but this *w· ghost* is pneuma.
through his
p 304– 6   that through his *w·* and works they might
through their
a 38–20   believe "through their *w·.*"— *John* 17 : 20.
b 271–19   believe . . . through their *w·.*"— *John* 17 : 20.

s 114–13   involves an improper use of the *w· mind.*
124–11   In a *w·* human belief is a blind conclusion
ph 168–30   Here let a *w·* be noticed which will be
b 309– 4   which, to use the *w·* of the Psalmist,
330–32   with all the etceteras that *w·* includes.
o 359–19   the goal which that *w·* implies
p 421– 5   Derangement, or *disarrangement,* is a *w·* which
g 508–19   The *w·* is not confined to sexuality,
ap 568–18   and by the *w·* of their testimony :— *Rev.* 12 : 11.
576–30   the *w·* gradually approaches a higher meaning.
577–32   In the following Psalm one *w·* shows,

words

about slavery
t 445–30   Recalling Jefferson's *w·* about slavery,
apostolic
b 325–16   The absolute meaning of the apostolic *w·*
are blind
o 350–14   Unless the works are comprehended . . . the *w·* are blind.
audible
pr 4–15   which, even if not acknowledged in audible *w·*,
definition of
b 338–25   The dissection and definition of *w·*,
ear trieth
s 115– 8   "The ear trieth *w·*, as the— *Job* 34 : 3.
employ
gl 598– 9   to employ *w·* of material significance
faith in
f 210– 1   superiority of faith by works over faith in *w·*.
few
pref ix– 6   He finds a few *w·*, and with these he
ph 195– 3   taught to speak a few *w·*,
good
ph 167–32   Substituting good *w·* for a good life,
181–22   satisfied with good *w·* instead of effects,
Greek
r 488– 7   The Hebrew and Greek *w·* often translated
g 517– 5   two Greek *w·*, signifying *man* and *form,*
his
a 53–11   His *w·* and works were unknown to the
54–18   understood neither his *w·* nor his works.
sp 94–18   our Master confirmed his *w·* by his works.
o 350–12   His *w·* were the offspring of his deeds,
350–14   Unless the works are comprehended which his *w·*
350–16   The Master often refused to explain his *w·*.

words

his
p 439–16   his *w·* flashing as lightning in the
r 473–28   his acts of higher importance than his *w·*.
his own
pr 7– 4   stronger evidence . . . is found in his own *w·*,
in other
a 27– 6   In other *w·* : "Tell John what the demonstration
46–16   in other *w·*, rose even higher in the
sp 72– 4   in other *w·*, mortal, material sense
s 132–10   In other *w·*, he gave his benediction to
138– 2   In other *w·*, Jesus purposed founding his
200–21   in other *w·* the five senses,
c 257–18   in other *w·*, divine Love,— is the father of the
b 340– 9   In other *w·* : Let us hear the conclusion of the
p 399–31   In other *w·* : How can I heal the body, without
Jesus'
b 360–32   the very basis of Jesus' *w·* and
ap 573–32   When you read this, remember Jesus' *w·*,
mere
a 55–12   clearer light than mere *w·* can possibly do,
of divine Science
o 354– 9   The *w·* of divine Science find their immortality
of Jesus
b 358–19   Why are the *w·* of Jesus more frequently
g 539– 2   In the *w·* of Jesus, it (evil, devil)
of our Master
p 428– 7   is to prove the *w·* of our Master :
of St. John
a 55–27   *w·* of St. John : "He shall give— *John* 14 : 16.
of this prophecy
ap 558– *   *that hear the w· of this prophecy,— Rev.* 1 : 3.
of Truth
o 342–23   It speaks to the dumb the *w·* of Truth,
our
pr 8–15   gratitude, and love which our *w·* express,
a 30–30   though they may not so construe our *w·*.
o 354–20   If our *w·* fail to express our deeds,
physician's
ph 198– 8   is increased by the physician's *w·*.
tender
m 59–17   Tender *w·* and unselfish care in what
the author's
t 452–24   simply by repeating the author's *w·*,
these
an 105–18   these *w·* of Judge Parmenter of Boston
s 137–29   gave him a spiritual name in these *w·* :
o 359–23   she often listened with joy to these *w·*,
torrent of
pr 13–19   overwhelming our real wishes with a torrent of *w·*.
which indicate
g 504–18   *w·* which indicate, in the absence of solar
without deeds
o 354–19   Inconsistency is shown by *w·* without deeds,
works and
s 117–27   feebly transmits Jesus' works and *w·*.
your
p 397–14   Your thought is more powerful than your *w·*,

pr 1–13   take form in *w·* and in deeds.
13–14   Do we gain the omnipotent ear sooner by *w·*
a 23–22   *faith* and the *w·* corresponding thereto
46– 6   by the *w·*, which made their hearts burn
sp 89–11   incapable of *w·* that glow,
s 116–24   As the *w· person* and *personal* are commonly
161–20   the *w·* of the famous Madame Roland,
b 332– 6   in *w·* which he quoted with approbation
338–22   Here *a dam* is not a mere play upon *w·* ;
o 343–20   Hence the mistake which allows *w·*, rather than
p 365– 8   finding utterance in such *w·* as
ap 567–23   The *w·* "cast unto the earth"— *Rev.* 12 : 13.

wordy
pr 8– 1   A *w·* prayer may afford a quiet sense of

wore
gl 596–29   The Jewish women *w·* veils over their faces

work (noun)

apostolic
sp 97–31   the apostolic *w·* of casting out error and
author's
pref viii–24   In the author's *w·*, RETROSPECTION AND
ever at
s 118–10   but this leaven of Truth is ever at *w·*.
God's
ph 167–16   What can improve God's *w·*?
g 522–29   Scripture . . . declares God's *w·* to be finished.
healing
ph 185–21   as a spiritual factor in the healing *w·*.
f 217– 6   may inform us that the healing *w·* of C. S.
p 365–16   the healing *w·* will be accomplished
His
pr 3– 9   His *w·* is done, and we have only to
f 206–23   declaring that His *w·* was *finished,*
g 519– 3   Deity was satisfied with His *w·*.

work (noun)

His
g 519–23   God ended His *w·* — *Gen.* 2 : 2.
   519–24   all His *w·* which He had made. — *Gen.* 2 : 2.
His own
pr 3– 9   Shall we ask the divine . . . to do His own *w·* ?
his own
sp 79–19   Jesus did his own *w·* by the one Spirit.
holy
g 520– 2   highest and sweetest rest, . . . is in holy *w·*.
immense
b 322–10   in view of the immense *w·* to be accomplished
Jesus'
a 43– 3   The magnitude of Jesus' *w·*,
life's
a 18– 6   He did life's *w·* aright
magnitude of his
a 50– 7   overwhelming sense of the magnitude of his *w·*,
mental
f 238–27   People with mental *w·* before them
Messianic
a 27– 9   God is the power in the Messianic *w·*.
my
t 456–25   my *w·* Science and Health for his textbook,
of eternity
pr 3–15   to understand God is the *w·* of eternity,
of God
g 521– 6   All that is made is the *w·* of God,
of the Master
s 136–22   and the great *w·* of the Master,
of time
f 238–30   To reconstruct timid justice. . . is the *w·* of time.
of Truth
g 528–21   error now simulates the *w·* of Truth,
of wisdom
sp 83– 5   claimed that they could equal the *w·* of wisdom.
on the subject
pref ix–23   before a *w·* on the subject could be
our
pr 6– 7   Calling on Him to forgive our *w·*
perfect
t 454–24   must "have her perfect *w·*." — *Jas.* 1 : 4.
   463–20   Truth . . . has fulfilled its perfect *w·*.
same
b 320–11   in the same *w·*, the familiar text, Genesis vi. 3,
so great a
r 494– 6   so great a *w·* as the Messiah's
their
a 47– 7   but on the divine Principle of their *w·*.
s 145– 5   the lack of the letter could not hinder their *w·* ;
this
pref ix–26   Before writing this *w·*, Science and Health,
ph 186– 6   thoroughness of this *w·* determines health.
o 355–21   statement that the teachings of C. S. in this *w·*
t 460– 1   divine metaphysics as laid down in this *w·*,
three days'
a 44– 7   His three days' *w·* in the sepulchre
Truth does the
t 456–23   Truth does the *w·*, and you must both understand and
wonderful
s 137– 3   but the ultimate of this wonderful *w·*
wrong
f 240–20   until all wrong *w·* is effaced or rectified.
your
f 248–18   Then you are haunted in your *w·* by

a 28–15   Neither the origin, the character, nor the *w·*
s 53–11   He was at *w·* in divine Science.
s 137–10   Who or what is it that is able to do the *w·*,
  152– 8   although they know not how the *w·* is done.
  160– 1   should address himself to the *w·* of
c 260–14   and sets mortals at *w·* to discover
p 376– 7   and does its *w·* almost self-deceived.
  399–18   A mill at *w·* or the action of a water-wheel
  423–25   are now at *w·* in the economy of being
t 458– 6   simultaneously at *w·* on the sick.
r 483–32   the *w·* must be done unselfishly.
fr 600– *   *being fruitful in every good w·,* — *Col.* 1 : 10.

work (verb)

pr 3– 7   it is our task to *w·* out the solution.
  3–11   enables us to *w·* out our own salvation.
  15–20   to *w·* and watch for wisdom, Truth, and Love.
a 22–11   "*W·* out your own salvation," — *Phil.* 2 : 12.
  23–26   *w·* out one's "own salvation, — *Phil.* 2 : 12.
  29– 8   It bids us *w·* the more earnestly in times of
  30–31   *w·* out our salvation in the way Jesus taught.
sp 79–20   worketh hitherto, and I *w·*." — *John* 5 : 17.
  90–21   mentally travel far and *w·* wonders,
  99– 5   "*W·* out your own salvation — *Phil.* 2 : 12.
an 106– 3   to *w·* against the free course of honesty
s 108–32   set my thoughts to *w·* in new channels,
ph 167–23   or to expect to *w·* equally with
  180–20   even before they go to *w·* to eradicate the
  182–12   It is impossible to *w·* from two standpoints.
  186– 7   Erring human mind-forces can *w·* only evil

work (verb)

ph 193–20   informed that he went to *w·* in two weeks.
f 233–10   The ages must slowly *w·* up to perfection.
  245–19   a useful hint, upon which a Franklin might *w·*
  254–22   and to *w·* out the spiritual which determines
c 262– 1   in which to *w·* out the problem of being.
o 345– 6   and *w·* through drugs to heal the sick?
  351–23   they cannot *w·* out the Spirit-rule of
p 367–21   watch, *w·*, and pray that this salt lose not
  398–31   must come to the rescue, to *w·* a radical cure.
  442–25   "*W·* out your own salvation — *Phil.* 2 : 12.
t 443–10   privileged to *w·* out their own salvation
  444– 5   "All things *w·* together for good — *Rom.* 8 : 28.
  459–20   false practitioner will *w·* mischief,

worked
a 25–24   He *w·* for their guidance,
  25–30   our Master *w·* and suffered to bestow

workers
c 263– 2   They believe themselves to be independent *w·*,

worketh
a 22–12   for to this end God *w·* with you.
sp 79–20   "My Father *w·* hitherto, — *John* 5 : 17.
  99– 8   "for it is God which *w·* in you — *Phil.* 2 : 13.
t 445–24   The human will which maketh and *w·* a lie,
gl 588– 4   that which "*w·* abomination — *Rev.* 21 : 27.

working
pr 1– 6   Prayer, watching, and *w·*, combined with
a 26–32   *w·* out the harmony of Life and Love.
m 67–14   Hoping and *w·*, one should stick to the wreck,
an 103–15   *w·* out the purposes of good only.
s 108– 8   by the effectual *w·* of His power." — *Eph.* 3 : 7.
  162–16   *W·* out the rules of Science in practice,
ph 182–24   thus *w·* against themselves and their prayers
f 217–21   for you are *w·* out the problem of being
  222– 5   has its material methods of *w·*,
  238– 4   Science is *w·* changes in personal character
  248–14   We are all sculptors, *w·* at various forms,
c 262–23   the bliss of loving unselfishly, *w·* patiently,
b 326–20   *W·* and praying with true motives,
p 424–13   to counteract the *w·* of a remedy
  426–16   the necessity of *w·* out his own salvation.
t 464–11   *w·* for the redemption of mankind.
r 493– 5   solar system as *w·* on a different plan.
gl 583–27   error, *w·* out the designs of error ;

workings
pref xi– 7   in the *w·*, not of Spirit, but of the
an 101–21   The author's own observations of the *w·* of
ap 562–18   which show the *w·* of the spiritual idea

works (noun)

by his
sp 94–18   our Master confirmed his words by his *w·*.
s 146– 2   and he proved his faith by his *w·*.
by my
o 343– 5   will show thee my faith by my *w·*." — *Jas.* 2 : 18.
r 487–26   will show thee my faith by my *w·*." — *Jas.* 2 : 18.
doing the
a 51–20   but only through doing the *w·* which he did
evil
pr 5–32   and seek the destruction of all evil *w·*,
faith by
f 209–32   It shows the superiority of faith by *w·*
faith without
a 23–15   "Faith without *w·* is dead." — *Jas.* 2 : 26.
good
o 342–27   to disown the Christliness of good *w·*,
her own
pref xii–11   publisher of her own *w·* ;
his
a 54–18   understood neither his words nor his *w·*.
Jesus'
s 117–27   feebly transmits Jesus' *w·* and words.
  131–29   Jesus' *w·* established his claim
medical
ph 176– 4   took up the study of medical *w·*
  179–24   so long as you read medical *w·*
mighty
pref xi–14   these mighty *w·* are not supernatural,
a 37–17   in *all* his ways and to imitate his mighty *w·* ?
  49–10   Had they so soon lost sight of his mighty *w·*,
p 401– 1   in certain localities he did not many mighty *w·*
of the devil
pr 5–30   "destroy the *w·* of the devil." — *I John* 3 : 8.
r 474–30   "destroy the *w·* of the devil." — *I John* 3 : 8.
of the flesh
an 106–20   "Now the *w·* of the flesh are — *Gal.* 5 : 19.
of Thy hands
ph 200–14   dominion over the *w·* of Thy hands. — *Psal.* 8 : 6.
on metaphysics
s 116–13   *W·* on metaphysics leave the grand point untouched.
other
t 457– 2   Other *w·*, which have borrowed from this book
rather than
o 343–29   mistake which allows words, rather than *w·*,

works (noun)
  recounting his
    s 132– 1   recounting his *w·* instead of referring to his
  remarkable
    o 358–20   than are his remarkable *w·*?
  that I do
    pr 14–20   the *w·* that I do shall he do also ; — *John* 14 : 12.
    a 42–31   the *w·* that I do shall he do also." — *John* 14 : 12.
    52–27   the *w·* that I do shall he do also;" — *John* 14 : 12.
    sp 93– 4   the *w·* that I do shall he do also," — *John* 14 : 12.
    b 326– 5   the *w·* that I do shall he do also." — *John* 14 : 12.
  their
    pref x–30   lest their *w·* be reproved.
  without
    a 22–26   nor by pinning one's faith without *w·*
  without thy
    o 343– 4   thy faith without thy *w·*, — *Jas.* 2 : 18.
    r 487–26   thy faith without thy *w·*, — *Jas.* 2 : 18.
  wonderful
    a 46– 2   did not perform many wonderful *w·*, until
    r 483–29   by doing many wonderful *w·* through the
  word and
    p 364– 6   that through his word and *w·* they might
  words and
    a 53–12   His words and *w·* were unknown to the
    o 360–32   on the very basis of Jesus' words and *w·*.

    pr 4–27   Audible prayer can never do the *w·* of
    o 350–13   Unless the *w·* are comprehended which
    358–23   great import to Christianity of those *w·*
    k 499– *   *I know thy w· :* — *Rev.* 3 : 8.
    gl 579– *   *I know thy w· :* — *Rev.* 3 : 8.

works (verb)
    m 67–12   the mariner *w·* on and awaits the issue.
    s 155–18   general belief, . . . *w·* against C. S. ;
    f 251–12   Truth *w·* out the nothingness of error
    c 259–23   God, Spirit, *w·* spiritually, not materially.
    263– 8   and *w·* only as God *w·*,
    o 342–19   which *w·* according to the Scriptures
    p 401– 2   its own enemy, and *w·* against itself ;
    r 467–21   The belief that . . . is an error that *w·* ill.
    ap 501– 2   *w·* out the ends of eternal good

world (*see also* **world's**)
  acknowledged not
    a 54– 5   The *w·* acknowledged not his righteousness,
  all the
    a 37–29   "Go ye into all the *w·*, and preach — *Mark* 16 : 15.
    s 138–28   "Go ye into all the *w·*, and preach — *Mark* 16 : 15.
    o 342–10   "Go ye into all the *w·*, and preach — *Mark* 16 : 15.
  beginning of the
    s 129–18   not since the beginning of the *w·* ;" — *Matt.* 24 : 21.
  believes in
    g 517–15   The *w·* believes in many persons ;
  citizens of the
    f 227–24   Citizens of the *w·*, accept the
  convulses the
    f 223–14   The question, . . . convulses the *w·*.
  could not
    a 53–16   The *w·* could not interpret aright the
  creation of the
    r 470–31   from the creation of the *w·*. — *Rom.* 1 : 20.
  describe the
    pref ix– 9   yet he cannot describe the *w·*.
  end of the
    t 446–23   even unto the end of the *w·*." — *Matt.* 28 : 20.
  feels the
    f 224– 2   for the *w·* feels the alterative effect of truth
  flooding the
    s 150–31   The hosts of Æsculapius are flooding the *w·*
  foundation of the
    b 317– 2   from the foundation of the *w·*,   *Matt.* 13 : 35.
    334–22   from the foundation of the *w·*." — *Rev.* 13 : 8.
    ap 568– 2   Ever since the foundation of the *w·*,
  from the
    pr 15–26   hidden from the *w·*, but known to God.
    m 64– 7   unspotted from the *w·*." — *Jas.* 1 : 27.
    f 243– 1   We may hide spiritual ignorance from the *w·*,
  guard over a
    a 48– 6   held uncomplaining guard over a *w·*
  homage of the
    a 42–10   Though entitled to the homage of the *w·*
  is asleep
    sp 95–28   the *w·* is asleep in the cradle of infancy,
  is benefited by
    t 463–32   said to the author, "The *w·* is benefited by
  light of the
    p 367–20   "Ye are the light of the *w·*. — *Matt.* 5 : 14.
  material
    (*see* **material**)
  must grow
    pr 10– 5   *w·* must grow to the spiritual understanding of
  new era for the
    a 43–19   opened a new era for the *w·*.
  newly discovered
    pref viii–32   in the newly discovered *w·* of Spirit.

world
  of error
    pr 13–30   *w·* of error is ignorant of the world of Truth,
  of sensation
    pr 13–31   *w·* of sensation is not cognizant of
  of sin
    sp 82–31   In a *w·* of sin and sensuality
  of Truth
    pr 13–30   world of error is ignorant of the *w·* of Truth,
  outward
    pref ix– 3   A child drinks in the outward *w·*
  overcame the
    a 39– 5   He overcame the *w·*, the flesh, and
  overcoming the
    pr 10–13   overcoming the *w·*, the flesh, and evil,
  physical
    s 125– 1   of the physical body and of the physical *w·*
  revolutionized the
    a 34–13   they would have revolutionized the *w·*.
  sigh over the
    m 57–29   until it ceases to sigh over the *w·*
  sink the
    ap 570–21   nor again sink the *w·* into the deep waters
  sins of the
    s 150–17   to take away the sins of the *w·*.
    b 334–19   taking away the sins of the *w·*,
  this
    pr 5–15   full award, but not always in this *w·*.
    a 29–11   though we may never receive it in this *w·*.
    36–23   impossible . . . for this *w·* to bestow
    m 69–26   "The children of this *w·* marry, — *Luke* 20 : 34.
    sp 73– 3   one person, living in this *w·*,
    an 103– 4   "the god of this *w·*," — *II Cor.* 4 : 4.
    f 225– 8   The powers of this *w·* will fight,
    c 267–27   Even in this *w·*, therefore,
    b 270–22   The pride of priesthood is the prince of this *w·*,
    325–25   can never reach in this *w·* the divine heights of
  to battle
    r 483–16   Science has called the *w·* to battle over this
  unknown to the
    a 53–12   His words and works were unknown to the *w·*
  visible
    s 118– 9   hidden in sacred secrecy from the visible *w·*
  was not worthy
    a 28–30   "of whom the *w·* was not worthy," — *Heb.* 11 : 38.
  whole
    a 45– 9   for the salvation of the whole *w·* from sin,
    o 344–22   one which should be presented to the whole *w·*,
    ap 567–16   which deceiveth the whole *w·* : — *Rev.* 12 : 9.
  wicked
    pr 4–24   but in this wicked *w·* goodness will
  with the
    a 28–26   Christianity to-day is at peace with the *w·*

    a 47–22   the *w·* generally loves a lie better than Truth ;
    m 69–28   worthy to obtain that *w·*, — *Luke* 20 : 35.
    s 136–10   His answer to this question the *w·* rejected.
    158–20   the byways of this wilderness *w·*,
    f 200–10   The *w·* would collapse without Mind.
    213–22   He was a musician beyond what the *w·* knew.
    235–28   occupying the watchtowers of the *w·*,
    248–20   The *w·* is holding it before your gaze
    252–24   says : . . . The *w·* is my kingdom.
    b 317–12   "If the *w·* hate you, ye know that — *John* 15 : 18.
    o 348–26   never supposed the *w·* would immediately
    354– 5   against "the *w·*, the flesh, and the devil"?
    p 379– 6   The real jurisdiction of the *w·* is in Mind,
    394–15   advice to a man who is down in the *w·*,
    r 486–32   and without God in the *w·* ;" — *Eph.* 2 : 12.

worldliness
    t 459– 6   gain heavenly riches by forsaking all *w·*.

worldling's
    t 459– 8   nothing in common with the *w·* affections,

worldly
    a 21–25   the *w·* man is at the beck and call of error,
    s 142–23   purge the temples of their vain traffic in *w·*
    ph 168– 2   is a poor shift for the weak and *w·*,
    f 238–23   arise from *w·* weakness.
    t 459– 5   achieves no *w·* honors except by sacrifice,

worldly-minded
    a 36–17   preclude C. S. from finding favor with the *w·*.

world's
    pref ix– 5   He is as sure of the *w·* existence as he is of his own ;
    a 47–10   The *w·* ingratitude and hatred towards
    48–17   Judas had the *w·* weapons.
    48–18   and chose not the *w·* means of defence.
    50–31   the *w·* hatred of Truth and Love.
    52–10   the *w·* hatred of the just and perfect Jesus,
    53–13   and contrary to the *w·* religious sense.
    m 65–16   Beholding the *w·* lack of Christianity

world-wide
    f 226– 3   the banishment of a *w·* slavery,

worm

sp 74–18	caterpillar, transformed . . . is no longer a w·,
74–19	to fraternize with or control the w·.
p 407– 5	attractive to no creature except a loathsome w·,
g 515– 4	Patience is symbolized by the tireless w·,

worms

sp 81–21	give to the w· the body called man,
ph 172–27	and w· annihilate it.
f 244–10	and the w· would rob him of the flesh ;
b 320–31	if disease and w· destroyed his body,
p 413–31	A child may have w·, if you say so,
r 488–27	otherwise the very w· could unfashion man.

worse

pr 5–27	He grows w· who continues in sin
m 64–28	a w· state of society than now exists.
an 104–27	leaving the case w· than before
s 157–27	but they leave both mind and body w·
ph 194– 8	and determines a case for better or for w·.
f 202– 9	they would not go on from bad to w·,
o 358– 6	Such doctrines are "confusion w· confounded."
p 396–12	nor encourage . . . the expectation of growing w·
408– 3	sin is w· than sickness,
t 446– 6	If patients sometimes seem w· while reading
r 474– 7	with w· cords than those which cut the flesh.
g 533–24	The belief . . . is growing w· at every step,
ap 564– 7	and w· still, to charge the innocent

worship

affection, and

pr 9–21	merely material sensation, affection, and w·.

attempted

o 351–28	in their attempted w· of the spiritual.

congregate for

gl 595–10	where mortals congregate for w·.

expressed by

g 541–10	than for the w· expressed by Cain's fruit?

forms of

pr 10–17	One of the forms of w· in Thibet is

Jewish

o 350–31	In Jewish w· the Word was materially

materializes

pr 5– 1	materializes w· hinders man's

more exalted

f 203–13	a more exalted w· and self-abnegation.

no ritualistic

a 20–10	but he established no ritualistic w·.

of God

ph 200– 5	Moses advanced a nation to the w· of God

outward

pr 4– 9	Outward w· is not of itself sufficient

pagan

ph 200– 2	Pagan w· began with muscularity,

Phoenician

g 524– 2	is seen in the Phoenician w· of Baal,

public

a 40–29	has come so generally to mean public w·

religion and

a 26–31	no form or system of religion and w·,

true

s 140–20	are but types and shadows of true w·.

worldly

s 142–23	their vain traffic in worldly w·

a 31–27	shall w· the Father in spirit— John 4 : 23.
40–27	and not merely w· his personality.
sp 93– 7	shall w· the Father in spirit— John 4 : 23.
s 140–16	We w· spiritually, only as we
140–16	only as we cease to w· materially.
140–21	shall w· the Father in spirit— John 4 : 23.
b 280–12	can neither apprehend nor w· the infinite ;
o 351–30	They thought to w· Spirit from a
p 428–16	whom we "ignorantly w·,"— Acts 17 : 23.
ap 576–13	no material structure in which to w· God,
gl 596– 9	"Whom therefore ye ignorantly w·,— Acts 17 : 23.

worshipped

g 524–11	"a man of war," a tribal god to be w·,— Exod. 15 : 3.
ap 576–13	for He must be w· in spirit and in love.

worshipper

pr 12–27	Does Deity interpose in behalf of one w·,

worshippers

a 31–26	when the true w· shall worship the— John 4 : 23.
sp 83– 3	the w· of Baal failed to do ;
93– 6	when the true w· shall worship the— John 4 : 23.
s 140–21	"The true w· shall worship the— John 4 : 23.
f 220–11	leaves clap their hands as nature's untired w·.

worshipping

s 140–18	W· through the medium of matter is paganism.

worships

ph 187– 8	and then w· and fears them.

worst

a 24– 6	instigated sometimes by the w· passions
ph 176–19	Mortal mind is the w· foe of the body,
p 396– 1	a moral offence is indeed the w· of diseases.

worth

pref x–17	have proved the w· of her teachings.
f 239– 8	let w· be judged according to wisdom,
g 523–14	It may be w· while here to remark that,

worthies

p 439–17	in the perturbed faces of these w·,
r 483–20	To those . . . ancient w·, and to Christ Jesus,
g 514–31	a source of strength to the ancient w·.

worthiness

pr 4–15	attest our w· to be partakers of Love.

worthless

g 529–29	we know that they are w· and unreal.

worthy

pr 4– 8	the only w· evidence of our gratitude
a 28–23	if thou art found w· to unloose the
28–30	"of whom the world was not w·,"— Heb. 11 : 38.
m 58–13	Never contract the horizon of a w· outlook
69–28	they which shall be accounted w·— Luke 20 : 35.
s 135– 9	Spiritual evolution alone is w· of
o 352–30	no longer seeming w· of fear or honor.
p 434–29	"w· of death, or of bonds."— Acts 23 : 29.
g 525–20	Everything good or w·, God made.
fr 600– *	That ye might walk w·— Col. 1 : 10.

would-be

ph 180– 6	when he sees his w· healers busy,
p 365–26	through the w· healer,
t 445– 4	attacks of the w· mental assassin,

wound

f 214–26	when a w· on the retina may end the
p 385–19	If you sprain the muscles or w· the flesh,

wounded

a 44–16	bind up the w· side and lacerated feet,
f 237– 2	A little girl, . . . badly w· her finger.

wounds

p 393–22	would suffer no more from tension or w·
t 462–27	when and how to probe the self-inflicted w·

woven

f 242–25	The divine Science of man is w· into

wrath

a 22–27	Whosoever believeth that w· is righteous
22–32	W· which is only appeased is not destroyed,
23– 6	That God's w· should be vented upon His
49–23	but is above the reach of human w·,
an 106–22	emulations, w·, strife, seditions,— Gal. 5 : 20.
s 140–24	w·, repentance, and human changeableness.
b 339–14, 15	"w· against the day of w·."— Rom. 2 : 5.
ap 566–23	Be Thou, longsuffering, slow to w·,
568–22	having great w·, because he— Rev. 12 : 12.

wrathful

ap 574–29	suffering sense deems w· and afflictive,

wreck

m 61–23	or reduce him to a loathsome w·?
67–15	Hoping and working, one should stick to the w·

wrench

c 265–31	if they w· away false pleasurable beliefs

wrested

ph 178–14	When w· from human belief and

wrestle

r 483–23	which w· with material observations alone,

wrestled

gl 583– 7	who, having w· with error, sin, and sense,

wrestles

ap 567– 5	spiritual strength w· and prevails

wrestling

b 308–16	Jacob was alone, w· with error,

wretched

sp 77–29	consigns the . . . to a w· purgatory,
b 296–32	It says to mortals, "You are w· !"

wrinkles

f 245–14	no care-lined face, no w· nor gray hair,

wrists

t 449– 1	With your own w· manacled,

write

pref viii–28	As early as 1862 she began to w· down

writer

b 279– 3	A New Testament w· plainly describes
o 347– 8	This w· infers that if anything needs to
ap 572– 8	profound counsel of the inspired w·.
gl 579– 4	elucidates the meaning of the inspired w·

writer's

(see **Eddy, Mrs. Mary Baker**)

writers
b 319–26 uninspired w·, who only wrote
g 537–24 Inspired w· interpret the Word spiritually,

writes
a 45–10 Paul w· : "For if, when we — Rom. 5 : 10.
f 208–17 John Young of Edinburgh w· :
244–11 Paul w· : "The law of the — Rom. 8 : 2.
b 324–27 Paul w·, "If Christ [Truth] — I Cor. 15 : 14.
325–10 Paul w· : "When Christ, who is — Col. 3 : 4.
ap 558– 1 St. John w·, in the tenth chapter of his
574– 5 He w·, in Revelation xxi. 9 :
576– 9 Revelation xxi. 22, . . . the beloved Disciple w· :

writing
pref ix–26 Before w· this work, SCIENCE AND HEALTH,

written
pref ix–12 Certain essays w· at that early date
s 164–28 the saying that is w·,— I Cor. 15 : 54.
f 242–23 for it is w· : "They parted my — John 19 : 24.
r 496–27 the saying that is w·,— I Cor. 15 : 54.
g 536– 2 In the Apocalypse it is w· :
ap 558– * *those things which are w· therein : — Rev. 1 : 3.*
561–30 it is w·, "There was a man sent — John 1 : 6.

wrong
disbelief in the
a 29– 8 and disbelief in the w·.
done another
t 449– 7 The w· done another reacts most heavily
freedom from
f 236–29 because of their freedom from w·
greatest
p 368– 1 The greatest w· is but a supposititious
intentional
f 251–28 Ignorance, like intentional w·, is not
learned the
b 326–28 He learned the w· that he had done
meet the
b 327–23 Moral courage is requisite to meet the w·
positive
r 491– 8 a negative right and a positive w·,
practise
f 253–18 If you believe in and practise w· knowingly,
right and
t 453– 6 Right and w·, truth and error,
g 531– 7 error, . . . that mind and soul are both right and w·.
self-evidently
g 539–22 exposed by our Master as self-evidently w·.

pr 9– 3 The w· lies in unmerited censure,
ph 166– 6 the healing effect is made on the w· side,
172– 6 and very much in the w·.
184– 3 the conclusions are w·.
195–27 Novels, . . . fill our young readers with w·
f 208– 9 a law of mortal mind, w· in every sense,
240–20 until all w· work is effaced
253–23 you can alter this w· belief and action
b 314–32 Jesus proved them w· by his resurrection,
318–26 If disease is right it is w· to heal it.
322–23 A man who likes to do w·
326–19 nothing but w· intention can hinder your

wrong
b 340–26 whatever is w· in social, civil, criminal,
o 357–20 w· notions about God must have
360– 4 replies : "You w· my experience.
p 396–20 weight of opinions on the w· side,
397– 6 mental influence on the w· side,
401– 4 nothing in the right . . . and much in the w·.
407–17 Let the slave of w· desire learn the
t 446–18 A w· motive involves defeat.
448–31 To talk the right and live the w·
451–29 controlling another from w· motives,
452– 5 The w· thought should be arrested
452–25 by right talking and w· acting,
452–32 the w· power would be destroyed.
453–28 impresses more deeply the w· mind-picture.
454–16 the w· as well as the right practice.
r 489–29 A w· sense of God, man, and creation
491–10 spiritual individuality is never w·.

wrong-doer
p 404– 6 by exhibiting to the w· the suffering which
gl 597–24 Will, as a quality of so-called mortal mind, is a w· ;

wrong-doing
pr 5– 3 Sorrow for w· is but one step towards
6–22 the safety-valve for w·.
f 240–22 If at present satisfied with w·,
p 385–14 from all penalties but those due for w·.
405–24 The abiding consciousness of w· tends to
r 480–22 which seems to make men capable of w·.
g 539–13 How then has man a basis for w· ?

wronged
m 63–29 the w·, and perchance impoverished, woman

wrongly
o 343–18 proving by what are w· called miracles,
t 452–31 the inclination or power to practise w·

wrongness
an 104–16 and the consequent w· of the opposite

wrote
a 20–27 St. Paul w·, "Let us lay aside — Heb. 12 : 1.
29–12 w· to the authorities at Rome :
sp 82– 5 Chaucer w· centuries ago, yet we still read his
an 106–19 in his great epistle to the Galatians, when he w·
b 319–26 who only w· down what an inspired
p 382–25 One whom I rescued . . . w· to me :

wrought
pr 13–23 and so we cannot grasp the wonders w· by
a 39– 6 He w· a full salvation from sin, sickness, and
s 117–21 in the miracles (marvels) w· by Jesus
132–23 if it is w· on any but a material and
133–16 w· wonders for the people of God
150–13 Now, as then, signs and wonders are w·
154–22 believed that exposure . . . w· the mischief.
ph 185–17 strove to emulate the wonders w· by Moses.
f 202– 4 must be w· out in life-practice,
g 540–13 may think . . . that the Lord hath w· an evil ;
ap 570–27 know the great benefit which Mind has w·.

wrung
a 50– 7 w· from Jesus' lips the awful cry,
50–32 w· from his faithful lips the plaintive cry,

X, Y

Xantippe
m 66–28 making his X· a discipline for his

yard
ph 193–19 The next day I saw him in the y·.

Yawah
s 133–29 The Jewish conception, of God, as Y·,
g 528– 9 And the Lord God [Jehovah, Y·] — Gen. 2 : 21.

yawn
s 153–25, 26 we y· because they y·,

yea
a 31–30 y·, the time cometh, that — John 16 : 2.
37–22 It is possible,— y·, it is the duty and privilege
sp 84–17 y·, to reach the range of fetterless Mind.
98–22 For centuries — y·, always — natural science
s 128–25 y·, forever destroys with the higher testimony
ph 171–22 the spiritual, — y·, the image of infinite Mind,
b 301– 1 y·, which manifests God's attributes
332–12 y·, the divine image and likeness,
o 346–12 to prove the somethingness — y·, the allness
p 366–10 y·, while mental penury chills his faith
g 505–19 y·, than the mighty waves of — Psal. 93 : 4.
509–27 purity, and holiness — y·, the divine nature
529–15 Y·, hath God said, Ye shall not — Gen. 3 : 1.
535– 2 y·, the seed of Spirit and the seed of matter,
ap 578–10 Y·, though I walk through the — Psal. 23 : 4.

year
pref viii–20 experiences which led her, in the y· 1866,
xi–27 was started by the author . . . about the y· 1867.
s 107– 1 In the y· 1866, I discovered the Christ Science
121–26 earth revolves about the sun once a y·,
f 246–25 Each succeeding y· unfolds wisdom,
gl 594–17 "Son of a y·."
598–19 definition of
599– 1 mortal thought, the divisor of which is the solar y·.

yearning
pr 13– 7 If we are not secretly y· and openly striving
a 48– 7 There was no response to that human y·,
49–13 O, why did they not gratify his last human y·
s 111–25 C. S. meets a y· of the human race
137– 8 Y· to be understood, the Master repeated,

yearnings
b 314– 5 had quenched all earthly y·.

years
all the
m 59– 5 should wait on all the y· of married life.
days, and
g 509–12 and for days, and y·.— Gen. 1 : 14.
during the
pref ix–28 This was during the y· 1867 and 1868.
early
f 245– 5 Disappointed in love in her early y·,
o 351– 9 became a member . . in early y·.

years

few
f 206–20 for the brief space of a few y·

in after
m 62–10 those parents should not, in after y·, complain

many
pr 9– 2 During many y· the author has been most grateful
s 107– 5 graciously preparing me during many y· for the
f 221– 2 For many y·, he ate only bread and
222–17 For many y· he had been kept alive,
p 380–22 Many y· ago the author made a . . . discovery,

months or
f 237– 7 It might have been months or y· before

nineteen hundred
s 122– 9 exposed nineteen hundred y· ago
f 232–18 as it did over nineteen hundred y· ago,

of servitude
f 226–22 wearing out y· of servitude to an

riper
f 248– 6 Men and women of riper y· and larger lessons

seven
pref xii– 6 During seven y· over four thousand students

six thousand
ap 560– 3 typical of six thousand y· since Adam,

solar
f 246–10 The measurement of life by solar y· robs youth

Soul-filled
gl 599– 2 Eternity is God's measurement of Soul-filied y·.

thousand
g 504–23 with the Lord as a thousand y·."— II Pet. 3 : 8.
504–25 whereas a thousand y· of human doctrines,
gl 598–21 with the Lord as a thousand y·."— II Pet. 3 : 8.

three
s 109–11 For three y· after my discovery, I sought

threescore
f 246–22 would enjoy more than threescore y· and ten

two
pref xii–16 conviction that the next two y· of her life

weary
f 221–10 He passed many weary y· in hunger and

sp 80–23 French toy which y· ago pleased so many people
f 245– 8 taking no note of y·, she stood daily
245–21 Y· had not made her old,
b 333–18 without beginning of y· or end of days.

yeast
s 118–24 as y· changes the chemical properties of meal.

yesterday
pr 2–32 "the same y·, and to-day, — Heb. 13 : 8.
a 37– 2 brings suffering as much to-day as y·
s 112–20 "the same y·, and to-day, — Heb. 13 : 8.
143– 3 to-day, as y·, Christ casts out evils
f 249–18 "the same y·, and to-day, — Heb. 13 : 8.
b 283– 7 "y·, and to-day, and forever." — Heb. 13 : 8.
322–15 The necromancy of y· foreshadowed the
g 546– 5 "the same y·, and to-day, — Heb. 13 : 8.

yet
pref vii– 5 y· it traversed the night, and came
ix– 5 y· he cannot describe the world.
pr 3–28 y· return thanks to God for all blessings,
a 20–12 and y· be sensual and sinful.
20–20 Y· he swerved not, well knowing that
26– 5 y· Jesus spares us not one individual
32–22 y· Jesus prayed and gave them bread.
38–13 addressing his disciples, y· he did not say,
53– 4 y· there never lived a man so far removed
m 66– 5 Wears y· a precious jewel in his head.
67–11 Y·, acting up to his highest understanding,
sp 80– 9 Y· the very periodical containing this
81– 4 y· this latter evidence is destroyed by
81–22 and y· the producing, governing, divine
82– 5 y· we still read his thought in his verse.
83– 3 y· artifice and delusion claimed
87–23 y· these are all there.
90–21 y· their bodies stay in one place.
92–32 Do you say the time has not y· come
97– 9 the electric current swift, y· in C. S.
99– 4 y· to escape from sin, is what the
3 107–16 y· remembering that in reality
112–28 y· uses another author's discoveries
122–10 y· these so-called senses still make
129–26 Y· quite as rational are some of the
132–19 has not y· been generally accepted.
132–32 y· afterwards he seriously questioned
139–11 but the present new, y· old, reform
153– 7 and y·, with one drop of that attenuation
155– 7 have not y· divorced the drug from the
156– 7 y· all, as she lay in her bed,
164– 6 or of therapeutic agents, ever y· promulgated,
164–14 Much y· remains to be said
ph 165– * nor y· for your body, — Matt. 6 : 25.
172–13 y· this can be realized only as
174–16 the path for generations y· unborn.
183–11 and y· the Scriptures inform us that

yet
ph 190– 6 and y· neither a mortal mind nor the
196– 3 has not y· found it true that knowledge can
f 202–28 and y· we rely on a drug . . . as if
217–11 y· if we turn to the Scriptures,
218– 3 y· the body is as material as the wheel.
219–23 and y· misunderstand the science that
220– 3 said : . . . and y· I have continual colds,
222–19 and y· he continued ill
b 274–30 at a period as y· unknown.
278–21 and y· we say that Spirit is supreme
310–20 and y· be immortal.
312–12 y· you say that matter has caused his death.
312–16 y· God is Love,
312–18 y· God is Truth.
320–31 y· in the latter days he should stand
346–27 Y·, in your concept, the tooth,
o 353–15 Time has not y· reached eternity,
354– 8 and y· deny C. S., when it teaches
359– 4 Y· Scientists will take the same cases,
360– 7 y· I would not exchange mine for
361– 1 Jew believes that . . . Christ has not y· come ;
p 362– * I shall y· praise Him, — Psal. 42 : 11.
416– 9 Y· any physician . . . will tell you
423– 2 y· this belief should not be
t 443– * and he will be y· wiser : — Prov. 9 : 9.
448– 1 and y· to indulge them, is a moral offense.
453–22 y· serves evil in the name of good.
460–10 Y· this most fundamental part of
r 474–19 y· the Scriptures aver,
486–19 and y· supposes Mind unable to
g 504– 8 though solar beams are not y· included
506–29 Adam has not y· appeared in the narrative.
508–16 The feminine gender is not y· expressed in
512–15 the externalized, y· subjective, states
513–11 time is not y· measured by solar revolutions,
523– 1 Y· one might so judge from an
524–23 y· God is reflected in all His creation.
545–19 y· this opposite, in its false view
552–20 but not y· instructed by Science,
ap 570– 5 certain active y· unseen mental agencies
571–14 and y· have given no warning.
572–23 The Revelator had not y· passed the
573– 3 while y· beholding what the
576– 6 while y· he tabernacled with mortals.
576–28 not y· elevated to deific apprehension
576–30 Y· the word gradually approaches a
gl 598– 6 y· it has received different translations,

yield
pref viii– 6 must y· to the harmony of spiritual sense,
xi– 8 the fleshly mind which must y· to Science.
sp 96–23 until all errors of belief y· to understanding.
s 151–29 y· to this power, and follow the leadings of
152– 1 and must by its own consent y· to Truth,
162–11 it may y· to the harmony of the divine Mind.
ph 176–30 are quite as ready to y· to Truth as
178–21 must finally y· to the eternal Truth,
189– 1 human or material senses y· to the authority of
200–23 material senses must y· to the infinite Spirit,
f 201–10 fear, all sensuality, y· to spirituality,
254– 6 or attain slowly and y· not to discouragement.
c 256– 2 The finite must y· to the infinite.
b 287–30 Their false evidence will finally y· to Truth,
295–13 will at last y· to the scientific fact
319–11 must y· to the all-might of
339–22 so will our material theories y· to spiritual
o 347–27 must y· to reason and revelation.
353–21 we must y· up all belief in it and be wise.
p 371– 3 this so-called mind must finally y· to
381– 6 than you are to y· to a sinful temptation
402–26 If they y· to this influence, it is because
t 450–15 Some people y· slowly to the touch of Truth.
450–16 Few y· without a struggle,
r 471–11 y· assent to astronomical propositions
484–10 supposed laws of matter y· to the law of Mind.
493– 7 All the evidence of physical sense . . . must y·
g 507–19 tree and herb do not y· fruit because of
ap 562–14 y· to the activities of the divine Principle
gl 589– 6 y· to the spiritual sense of Life and Love.

yielded
b 291– 8 cannot come till mortals have already y· to
303–31 When the evidence before the material senses y·
326–24 only when his uncertain sense of right y·
339–20 As the mythology of pagan Rome has y· to a
t 450–17 reluctant to acknowledge that they have y· ;

yielding
a 39–14 overcame death and the grave instead of y·
ph 184–11 nor y· obedience to it.
b 268– 7 Belief in a material basis, . . . is slowly y· to the
p 375–14 No person is benefited by y· his mentality to
413– 3 The act of y· one's thoughts to
g 507–12 the herb y· seed, — Gen. 1 : 11.
507–12 and the fruit tree y· fruit — Gen. 1 : 11.
508–10 herb y· seed after his kind, — Gen. 1 : 12.
508–10 and the tree y· fruit, — Gen. 1 : 12.

yielding

g 518– 8 the fruit of a tree y· seed ;— *Gen.* 1 : 29.
gl 586–23 the human y· to the divine ;
593–11 material belief y· to spiritual understanding.

yields

sp 85– 5 when the latter y· to the divine Mind.
ph 188– 1 only as the mortal, erring mind y· to God,
b 281– 1 ignorance which y· only to the understanding
318–21 y· to the reality of spiritual Life.
322–19 his physical sense of pleasure y· to a higher
329–31 till error y· to Truth.
o 353– 6 till the testimony of the physical senses y·
p 409–18 the stronger never y· to the weaker, except
414– 5 it y· more readily than do most diseases
426– 3 when instructed by Truth, y· to divine power,
r 485–24 If thought y· its dominion to other powers,
489–11 y· to the reality of everlasting Life.
g 543– 3 This error, . . . y· to Truth and returns to dust ;
ap 576–31 human sense of Deity y· to the divine sense,
577– 1 y· to the incorporeal sense of God and man
gl 584–15 until every belief . . . y· to eternal Life.

yoke

g 555– 5 the physical organism under the y· of disease.

yore

s 132–20 To-day, as of y·, unconscious of the reappearing
f 226–29 the Pharaohs, who to-day, as of y·,
r 481– 5 Like the archpriests of y·, man is free

you

gl 599– 3 definition of

young

s 161– 8 the Bible case of the three y· Hebrew captives,
ph 191–11 "where the y· child was,"— *Matt.* 2 : 9.
195–27 Novels, . . . fill our y· readers with wrong
f 244–23 Man in Science is neither y· nor old.
245–10 In this mental state she remained y·.
245–13 and supposed her to be a y· woman.
245–24 The bodily results of her belief that she was y·
245–25 She could not age while believing herself y·,
245–28 proves it possible to be y· at seventy-four ;
p 412–28 If the case is that of a y· child
g 514–24 And the calf and the y· lion,— *Isa.* 11 : 6.

Young, John

f 208–17 John Y· of Edinburgh writes :

youngest

c 261–15 as actively as the y· member of the company.

youth

f 236–31 y· makes easy and rapid strides towards Truth·
245–15 y· sat gently on cheek and brow.
245–18 This instance of y· preserved furnishes a
246–10 robs y· and gives ugliness to age.
r 471–24 subscribed to an orthodox creed in early y·,

Z

zeal

pr 7–11 "a z· . . . not according to— *Rom.* 10 : 2.
b 280–20 But behold the z· of belief to establish
gl 599– 4 definition of

zenith

sp 97–13 until matter reaches its mortal z· in illusion
ap 565–25 to rise to the z· of demonstration,

zigzag

a 21–32 By-and-by, ashamed of his z· course,

Zincum oxydatum

s 152–30 Jahr, from *Aconitum* to Z· o·,

Zion

ap 575–23 joy of the whole earth, is mount Z·,—*Psal.* 48 : 2.
gl 599– 6 definition of

Appendix A
Comprehensive Index to the
Marginal Headings in
Science and Health with Key to the Scriptures

Comprehensive Index to the Marginal Headings in Science and Health with Key to the Scriptures

Beginning, scientific, 219.
Begin rightly, 382.
Beguiling first lie, the, 533.
Behest of the cross, 20.
Being, and seeming, 123.
  deflection of, 502.
  figures of, 282.
  indestructible, 325.
  is immortal, 553.
  man's genuine, 91.
  real, never lost, 215.
Belief an autocrat, 297.
  and climate, 386.
  and firm trust, 488.
  and practice, 202.
  and understanding, 183.
  and understanding, our, 203.
  change of, 194.
  faith higher than, 297.
  in death, a, 42.
  in many gods, 280.
  in physics, 155.
  laws of human, 184.
  on the wrong side, 168.
  physical science a blind, 124.
  suicidal, a, 39.
  understanding *versus*, 487.
Beliefs and fears, conquer, 419.
  illusive, 383.
  material, 485.
Benefactor, death no, 409.
Beneficence, trustworthy, 15.
Benefit of philanthropy, 385.
Benefits of metaphysics, 380.
  recognition of, 372.
Benevolence hindered, 64.
Be not afraid, 410.
Better basis than embryology, 553.
Biblical basis, 126.
  facts, scientific and, 358.
  foundations, 269.
Biological inventions, 531.
Birth and death, mortal, 265.
  and death unreal, 206.
  the immortal, 191.
Birthright, immortal, 479.
  of man, 518.
Blessing of Christ, 65.
Blessings from pain, 265.
Blight of avarice, 445.
Blind belief, physical science a, 124.
  force, human power a, 192.
Blissful ignorance, 382.
Blood, mind circulates, 373.
  true flesh and, 25.
Blunders and blunderers, 149.
  philosophical, 250.
Bodily presence, 14.
  resurrection, the, 314.
Body, a clean mind and, 383.
  material, never God's idea, 477.
  mind governs, 377.
  sensationless, 280.
  Soul greater than, 223.
  Soul not confined in, 467.
  the, death and, 187.
Bondage, higher law ends, 227.
  house of, 226.
Bone-healing by surgery, 422.
Book, effect of this, 422.
Both words and works, 350.
Brain, medicine and, 401.

Brain not intelligent, 372.
Brain-disease, Mind heals, 387.
Brain-lobes, drugs and, 408.
Brainology a myth, 295.
Breakfast, the last, 34.
Bridgeless division, 74.
Bright outlook, a, 323.
Brotherhood, assistance in, 518.
  repudiated, 541.
  universal, 276.
Bruising sin's head, 534.
Buried secrets, 87.
Business, Master's, 52.

C

Calmness, source of, 366.
Camera, Mind's true, 264.
Cancellation of human sin, 5.
Career, Jesus' sinless, 19.
Careful guidance, 429.
Carnality, the error of, 131.
Case, a mental court, 430.
Cast out, moral evils to be, 366.
Causation considered, 170.
  mental, 114.
  not in matter, 552.
Cause, Mind the only, 262.
  one primal, 207.
  supreme, one, 278.
  the universal, 331.
Causes of sickness, 165.
Celestial evidence, 471.
Central intelligence, the, 310.
Centre for affections, 60.
Certain contradictions, 118.
Certainty of results, 459.
Chalice sacrificial, the, 9.
Challenge, materialistic, 268.
Change demanded, a, 141.
  of belief, 194.
  requisite, of our ideals, 260.
Changed mentality, 168.
Changes, corporeal, 125.
  radical, 24.
Chaos and darkness, 479.
Character, and reputation, 53.
Charge of the Chief Justice, 441.
Charity to those opposed, 444.
Charlatanism, mental, 458.
Chicanery impossible, 456.
Chief Justice, charge of the, 441.
  stones in the temple, the, 288.
Childless, divinity not, 306.
Childlike receptivity, 323.
Children and adults, 130.
  teaching, 237.
Children's ailments, 154.
  tractability, 236.
Cholera, imaginary, 154.
Choose ye to-day, 360.
Chord and discord, 58.
Christ, blessing of, 65.
  eternity of the, 334.
  fellowship with, 34.
  Jesus, 332.
  Messiah or, 333.
  rejected, 132.
  the great physician, 442.
  the ideal Truth, 473.
  treatment, the, 369.
Christ's demonstration, 26.

Christ's mission, 233.
  reappearance, 95.
Christ-element, the, 288.
Christ-mission, the, 136.
Christ-power, absence of, 134.
Christian history, 387.
  pleading, 418.
  standard, 426.
  warfare, 29, 354.
Christian Science as old as God, 146.
  discovered, 107.
  mission of, 107.
Christian's privilege, the, 556.
Christianity, and Science, 127.
  essential element of, 347.
  scientific, 342.
  still rejected, 97.
  the unity of Science and, 135.
Christly warning, 571.
Churchly neglect, 131.
City foursquare, the, 575.
  of our God, the, 577.
Claim, false, or mist, 523.
Claims, false, annihilated, 450.
  two, omitted, 142.
Clairvoyance, magnetism, 101.
Classes, three, of neophytes, 450.
Classified, diseases not to be, 176.
Clay replying to the potter, 429.
Cleanliness, ablutions for, 413.
Clean mind and body, a, 383.
Cleansing the mind, 234.
  upheaval, 540.
Clergymen's duty, 235.
Climate and belief, 386.
  harmless, 377.
Climax of suffering, 543.
Closed question, a, 171.
Clouds dissolving, the, 548.
Coalescence, impossible, 143.
Coalition of sin and sickness, 218.
Combinations, corporeal, 399.
Comfort, crumbs of, 234.
Comforter, Holy Ghost or, 332.
Commands of Jesus, 342.
  two chief, 467.
Compassion requisite, 365.
Complete emulation, 37.
Completeness, the divine, 275.
Conception, erroneous, 538.
  immaculate, 315.
  spiritual, 29.
Conceptions, misleading, 28.
Concepts, insidious, 376.
Concessions, no dishonest, 456.
Conclusions, personal, 101.
Concord, spiritual, 60.
Condition of progress, 496.
Conditions, mental, to be heeded, 159.
  of criticism, 355.
  opposing, 74.
Confidence, and self-reliance, 23.
  personal, 358.
Confirmation by healing, 488.
  in a parable, 399.
Confirmatory tests, 111.
Conflict, the great, 288.
  with purity, the, 565.
Conflicting standpoints, 83.
Conforming to explicit rules, 445.
Confusion, ancient, 389.
  confounded, 268.

ំ

Conquer beliefs and fears, 419.
Conscious development, our, 554.
Consciousness, spiritualized, 14.
Consecration, intelligent, 428.
  required, 325.
Conservative antagonism, 144.
Consistency, scientific, 354.
Consolation, vials of wrath and, 574.
Conspiracy, the traitor's, 47.
Conspirators, mental, 405.
Construction, organic, valueless, 489.
Consume, nothing to, 425.
Contact, mental, 86.
Contagion, source of, 153.
Contention, misdirected, 380.
Contest, arena of, 96.
Continuity of existence, 429.
  of interest, 454.
  of thoughts, 513.
Contradict error, 391.
Contradicting first creation, 526.
Contradictions, certain, 118.
  not found, 345.
Contrasted testimony, 538.
Contrasts, unspiritual, 272.
Contumely, cruel, 49.
Conversion of Saul, 326.
Convincing evidence, 43.
Copartnership impossible, 356.
Coping with difficulties, 423.
Corporeal changes, 125.
  combinations, 399.
  ignorance, 13.
  penalties, 384.
Corporeality and Spirit, 46.
  no divine, 256.
Corrective, scientific, 423.
Counsel for defence, 434.
Counterfeit, and real, 368.
  creation's, 527.
  forces, the, 293.
  the human, 285.
Courage, moral, 327.
Course, zigzag, 21.
Court case, a mental, 430.
Cramping systems, 226.
Cravings, morbid, 406.
Creation, ever-appearing, 507.
  first, contradicting, 526.
  God's, intact, 68.
  inadequate theories of, 255.
  no baneful, 525.
  no material, 256.
  no new, 263.
  perfect, 205.
  perfection of, 519.
  reversed, 524.
Creation's counterfeit, 527.
Creator, Life the, 331.
Creators, two infinite, absurd, 357.
Creatures of God useful, 514.
Creditor, parable of the, 363.
Crimes, mental, 105.
Crisis, how to treat a, 421.
Criticism, conditions of, 355.
Cross and crown, the, 254.
  behest of the, 20.
Crown, and cross, the, 254.
Crucifixion, purpose of, 24.
Cruel contumely, 49.
  desertion, 42.
Crumbs of comfort, 234.

Crusade, liberty's, 226.
Cry of despair, a, 50.
Cumulative repentance, 405.
Cup of Jesus, the, 317.
Curative, error not, 143.
Cure for palsy, 375.
  of infants, the, 412.
  of insanity, 414.
Currents, Life's healing, 24.
Curse, murder brings its, 542.
  removed, the, 557.

D

Danger from audible prayer, 7.
Dangerous knowledge, 459.
  resemblances, 97.
  shoals avoided, 196.
Darkest hours of all, the, 96.
Darkness, and light, 215.
  and chaos, 479.
  egotistic, 452.
  light shining in, 108.
  scattered, 511.
  Spirit versus, 504.
Dawning of spiritual facts, 546.
Day of judgment, 291.
  tests in our, 149.
Dead, raising the, 75.
Deadness in sin, 316.
Death, a belief in, 42.
  and birth unreal, 206.
  and the body, 187.
  an error, 486.
  but an illusion, 289.
  illusion of, 251.
  mortal birth and, 265.
  no advantage, 290.
  no, nor inaction, 427.
  no benefactor, 409.
  outdone, 42.
  second, 77.
  thought regarding, 79.
  triumph over, 496.
Decalogue disregarded, 489.
Decapitation of error, 266.
Decision, important, 105.
  the important, 181.
  unhesitating, 463.
Deeds, not words but, 181.
Deep-reaching interrogations, 550.
Defamatory accusations, 52.
Defence, counsel for, 434.
  indispensable, 452.
Defensive weapons, 48.
Deference to material law, 549.
Definite rule discovered, a, 147.
Definition of man, 302.
  of mortal mind, 114.
Definitions of man, 525.
  the deific, 330.
Deflection of being, 502.
Deflections, unnatural, 78.
Deformity and perfection, 244.
Degrees, advancing, 158.
  of development, 172.
Deific definitions, the, 330.
  naturalism, the, 44.
  supremacy, the, 330.
Deity, divine sense of, 576.
  finite views of, 255.
  nearness of, 573.

Deity, tribal, Jehovah a, 524.
  unchangeable, 2.
Deliverance not vicarious, 22.
Deluded invalids, 237.
Delusion, all disease a, 348.
Delusions, mortal, 90.
  pagan and medical, 166.
Demands, affection's, 57.
  peremptory, 327.
Demonstrable evidence, 108.
Demonstration, Christ's, 26.
  lost and found, the, 110.
Denial, and ingratitude, 94.
  of immortality, a, 80.
Denials of divine power, 232.
Derivatives of spirit, 93.
Desertion, cruel, 42.
Desire for holiness, 11.
Despair, a cry of, 50.
Despatch, erroneous, 386.
Despotism, mental, 103.
Destroy all ills, Mind can, 374.
Destruction, final, of error, 328.
  of all evil, 231, 495.
Dethroned, mortal mind, 152.
Development, degrees of, 172.
  our conscious, 554.
  progressive, 64.
Devotion, veritable, 4.
Diabolism destroyed, 5.
Diagnosis of matter, 371.
Dictation of error, 409.
Diet and digestion, 389.
  and dyspepsia, 107.
Differences, irreconcilable, 356.
Differing duties, 59.
Difficulties, coping with, 423.
Digestion, and diet, 389.
Dilemma, unescapable, 119.
Disappearance, mortal mind's, 251.
Disciples, doubting, 136.
  example of the, 343.
  recreant, 27.
  studious, 271.
Discipline, and help, 57.
Discontent, inspiring, 53.
  with life, 107.
Discord, chord and, 58.
  sickness as, 318.
Discovery, a higher, 380.
  spiritual, 260.
Discrimination, unfair, 63.
Disease, a delusion, all, 348.
  a dream, 188.
  avoid talking, 396.
  depicted, 198.
  far more docile than iniquity, 373.
  foreseen, 168.
  images of, effacing, 396.
  mental, 151.
  neutralized, 422.
  no real, 393.
  powerless, 378.
  to be made unreal, 417.
  treatment of, 390.
Disease-production, 403.
Diseases, naming, 411.
  not to be classified, 176.
  novel, 175.
Dishonest concessions, no, 456.
Disregard of matter, Jesus', 210.
Distinct documents, 523.

Evil obsolete, 330.
of mesmerism, the, 402.
subordination of, 207.
thought depletes, 416.
Evils cast out, 411.
moral, to be cast out, 366.
Evolution, embryonic, 547.
godless, 172.
Exaggerations, public, 13.
Exalted thought, 506.
Example for our salvation, 51.
of the disciples, 343.
perfect, 20.
Exclusion of malpractice, 446.
Excuses for ignorance, 130.
Exercise of Mind-faculties, 487.
Existence, mortal, a dream, 250.
continuity of, 429.
spiritual proofs of, 264.
spiritual, the one fact, 491.
stages of, 550.
Expectations, unwarranted, 452.
Experience, individual, 26.
Paul's, 217.
personal, 343.
the test of, 471.
Experiments, the author's, in med-
icine, 152.
Expiation by suffering, 569.
Explanation, healthful, 396.
Exploded doctrine, 150.
Expose sin without believing in it, 447
Eyes and teeth renewed, 247.

F

Fact, spiritual existence the one, 491.
Factors, fleshly, unreal, 475.
Facts, Biblical, and scientific, 358.
spiritual, dawning of, 546.
supported by, 341.
Faculties, all, from Mind, 488.
Failure, geology a, 510.
Failure's lessons, 443.
Faith according to works, 133.
and doctrines, 23.
higher than belief, 297.
of Socrates, 215.
results of, in Truth, 368.
the action of, 398.
Fallacious hypotheses, 79.
Fall of error, the, 536.
False claim, or mist, 523.
claims annihilated, 450.
source of knowledge, 159.
stimulus, 186.
testimony refuted, 396.
womanhood, 533.
Falsehood, a type of, 539.
Falsities, human, 212.
physical, 80.
Falsity, Truth destroys, 474.
Fatal premises, 351.
Fatherhood of God, the, 29.
Father-Mother, 332.
Fatigue is mental, 217.
Fear and sickness identical, 135.
as the foundation, 411.
comes of error, 532.
effects of, 159.
fevers the effect of, 379.
ghost-stories inducing, 371.

Fear, latent, diagnosed, 375.
latent, subdued, 199.
Love casteth out, 410.
Love frees from, 373.
of the serpent overcome, 321.
or sin, the root of sickness, 404.
Fears, conquer beliefs and, 419.
Fellowship with Christ, 34.
Fever, remedy for, 376.
Fevers the effect of fear, 379.
Fidelity required, 56.
Field, winning the, 453.
Figures of being, 282.
Final destruction of error, 328.
perfection, and patience, 254.
purpose, 36.
Finalities, scientific, 90.
Finite views of Deity, 255.
Firmament, spiritual, 505.
First evil suggestion, 544.
Five senses deceptive, 274.
Flesh, and Spirit, 534.
sin only of the, 311.
true, and blood, 25.
Fleshly factors unreal, 475.
heredity, no, 228.
ties temporal, 31.
Flowers, the thorns and, 41.
Followers of Jesus, 495.
Food, and sleep, our, 385.
Footsteps heavenward, our, 426.
to intemperance, 158.
Force, all, mental, 124.
blind, human power a, 192.
Forces, the counterfeit, 293.
Foreknowing, scientific, 84.
Foreseeing, scientific, 84.
Foreshadowings, spiritual, 98.
Foresight, scientific, 169.
Forgetfulness of self, 262.
Formation from thought, 423.
Form of insanity, sin a, 407.
Foundation, fear as the, 411.
Foundations, Biblical, 269.
on sandy, 112.
righteous, 65.
Scriptural, 110.
Found wanting, 71.
Frailty, human, 190.
Freedom, mutual, 58.
native, 227.
spiritual, 191.
Friends, recollected, 87.
Friendship, spiritual, 54.
Fruit forbidden, the, 481.
Fruitage, full, yet to come, 348.
Fruitless worship, 351.
Fulfilment, divine, 474.
of the Law, 572.
Full fruitage yet to come, 348.
Functions, harmonious, 478.
teachers', 235.
Future purification, 290.

G

Garden of Eden, 527.
Gates, the royally divine, 575.
Gateway, spiritual, 538.
Genera classified, 556.
Genuine being, man's, 91.
healing, 367.

Genuine repentance, 364.
Genus of error, the, 103.
Geology a failure, 510.
Gethsemane glorified, 48.
Ghost, Holy, or Comforter, 332.
Ghosts not realities, 352.
Ghost-stories inducing fear, 371.
Glory, millennial, 34, 96.
God, accidents unknown to, 424.
and His image, 281.
and nature, 119.
Christian Science as old as, 146.
creatures of, useful, 514.
evil not produced by, 339.
goodness a portion of, 286.
invisible to the senses, 140.
Jesus not, 473.
loving, supremely, 326.
man reflects, 246.
man reflects the perfect, 337.
never inconsistent, 230.
no temptation from, 527.
real Life is, 76.
sustains man, 388.
the city of our, 577.
the Fatherhood of, 29.
the infinitude of, 267.
the only Mind, 319.
the parent Mind, 336.
the Principle of all, 272.
the Son of, 332.
the things of, are beautiful, 280.
God's allness learned, 110.
creation intact, 68.
idea, material body never, 477.
idea the ideal man, 346.
law destroys evil, 472.
man discerned, 259.
messenger, true estimate of, 560.
standard, 2.
thoughts are spiritual realities,
514.
God-given dominion, 228, 381.
Godless evolution, 172.
Godliness, mystery of, 145.
Gods, belief in many, 280.
of the heathen, 524.
Godward gravitation, 265.
Gold and dross, the, 66.
Good and evil, knowledge of, 92.
ascendency of, 61.
hospitality to health and, 234.
indefinable, 213.
Goodness a portion of God, 286.
transparent, 295.
Gospel, and law, 349.
narrative, a, 362.
Government, one, 73.
perfection of divine, 104.
spiritual, 316.
true, of man, 420.
Governor, the sole, 469.
Gratitude and humility, 367.
Grave, victory over the, 45.
Gravitation, Godward, 265.
Great conflict, the, 288.
question, the, 308.
Growth is from Mind, 520.
rudiments and, 495.
Guarding the door, 392.
Guests, reluctant, 130.
Guidance, careful, 429.

Inebriate, saving the, 322.
Inexhaustible divine Love, 257, 494.
Infants, the cure of, 412.
Infinite, indivisibility of the, 336.
  one Spirit, the, 70.
  physique impossible, 258.
  Spirit, 335.
Infinitude of God, the, 267.
  true sense of, 469.
Infinity measureless, 519.
Infinity's reflection, 258.
Ingratitude and denial, 94.
  prayerful, 3.
  students', 49.
Inharmonious travellers, 21.
Inheritance heeded, 62.
Iniquity, disease far more docile than, 373.
  hidden ways of, 570.
  overcome, 446.
Injustice to the Saviour, 54.
Inoculation of thought, 449.
Insanity and agamogenesis, 68.
  cure of, 414.
  sin a form of, 407.
Insensibility to Spirit, our physical, 284.
Insidious concepts, 376.
Insight, divine, 363.
  spiritual, 95.
Insistence requisite, 412.
Inspiration of sacrifice, 54.
Inspired interpretation, 537.
Inspiring discontent, 53.
Instructions, author's early, 460.
Instruments of error, 294.
Integrity assured, 455.
Intelligence and substance, Spirit the only, 204.
  the central, 310.
Intelligent, brain not, 372.
  consecration, 428.
Intemperance, footsteps to, 158.
Intentions respected, 151.
Intercommunion, impossible, 82.
Interest, continuity of, 454.
Interior meaning, 320.
Interpretation, inspired, 537.
  right, 124.
  spiritual, 46, 501.
Interrogations, deep-reaching, 550.
Intolerance, and society, 238.
Introspection, unscientific, 319
Intuition, value of, 85.
Invalid's outlook, the, 180.
Invalids, deluded, 237.
Inventions, biological, 531.
Inversion, truth by, 129.
Inversions, metaphysical, 113.
Inverted images, 305.
  images and ideas, 301.
Investigations, earliest, 100.
Investiture, unscientific, 75.
Invocation, effectual, 15.
Irreconcilable differences, 356.
Israel the new name, 309.

J

Jacob, wrestling of, 308.
Jehovah a tribal deity, 524.
  or Elohim, 523.

Jesus and hypnotism, 185.
  as mediator, 316.
  commands of, 342.
  followers of, 495.
  imitation of, 329.
  in the tomb, 44.
  new era in, 138.
  not God, 473.
  not understood, 473.
  sonship of, 482.
  the cup of, 317.
  the miracles of, 117.
  the Scientist, 313.
  the way-shower, 30.
Jesus' disregard of matter, 210.
  own practice, 148.
  sad repast, 32.
  sinless career, 19.
  teaching belittled, 38.
Jesus Christ, the prayer of, 16.
Jewish traditions, 306.
Job, on the resurrection, 320.
John's misgivings, 132.
John the Baptist, and the Messiah, 131.
Joy, and travail, 562.
Jubilee, pæan of, 568.
Judaism antipathetic, 133.
Judge Medicine charges the jury, 433.
Judgment, day of, 291.
  on error, 535.
Jurisdiction of Mind, 379.
Jury, Judge Medicine charges the, 433.
Justice and recompense, 537.
  and substitution, 23.
Juvenile ailments, 413.

K

Key to the kingdom, 99.
Kingdom, key to the, 99.
  within, the, 476.
Knowledge and honesty, 453.
  and Truth, 290.
  dangerous, 459.
  false source of, 159.
  material, illusive, 274.
  of good and evil, 92.
  useful, 195.

L

Lack of originality, a, 126.
Language inadequate, 349.
  spiritual, 117.
Last breakfast, the, 34.
Latent fear diagnosed, 375.
  fear subdued, 199.
  power, 378.
Law and gospel, 349.
  fulfilment of the, 572.
  God's, destroys evil, 472.
  higher, ends bondage, 227.
  material, deference to, 549.
  no material, 182.
  self-constituted, 229.
  spiritual, the only law, 273.
  superior, of Soul, 62.
Lawful wonders, 135.
Laws of human belief, 184.
  of matter, no, 381.
  of nature spiritual, 183.

Learning, priestly, 133.
Leaven of Truth, 117.
Leaves of healing, the, 406.
Leprosy healed, 321.
Lesson, to-day's, 560.
Lessons, failure's, 443.
  some, from nature, 240.
Liberation of mental powers, 103.
Liberty, standard of, 227.
Liberty's crusade, 226.
Lie, the beguiling first, 533.
Life, abiding in, 325.
  all-inclusive, 430.
  and action, source of all, 283.
  discontent with, 107.
  eternal and present, 410.
  eternity of, 468.
  independent of matter, 368.
  never structural, 309.
  not contingent on matter, 427.
  of man, indestructible, 402.
  only in Spirit, 222.
  possibilities of, 489.
  real, is God, 76.
  spiritual sense of, 122.
  the creator, 331.
  true, eternal, 246.
Life's healing currents, 24.
Life-link, the divine, 350.
Life-power indestructible, 51.
Life-work, harmonious, 202.
Light and darkness, 215.
  preceding the sun, 504.
  rising to the, 509.
  shining in darkness, 108.
Like curing like, 370.
  evolving like, 276.
Likeness, reflected, 515.
Limitless Mind, 256.
Lines, new, of thought, 108.
Living temple, 27.
Loftiest adoration, 16.
Logic and revelation, 93.
  scientific, and mathematics, 128.
Loss, and selfishness, 142.
Love, and aspiration, 8.
  and man coexistent, 520.
  casteth out fear, 410.
  divine, inexhaustible, 257, 494.
  frees from fear, 373.
  impartial and universal, 12.
  imparts beauty, 516.
  man inseparable from, 304.
  the incentive, 454.
Love's endowment, 248.
Loveliness, the divine, 247.
Loving God supremely, 326.
Loyalty, divided, 462.
Lungs re-formed, the, 425.

M

Magnetism, animal, destroyed, 178.
  animal, error, 484.
  clairvoyance, 101.
Main purpose, the, 150.
Maladies, naming, 398.
Malicious barbarity, 564.
Malpractice, exclusion of, 446.
Man, Adam not ideal, 338.
  a mortal not, 200.
  and Love, coexistent, 520.

Man, birthright of, 518.
definition of, 302.
definitions of, 525.
eternal, recognized, 252.
God sustains, 388.
God's, discerned, 259.
governed by Mind, 151.
ideal, and woman, 516.
ideal, God's idea the, 346.
immortal, 292.
immutable identity of, 261.
indestructible life of, 402.
inseparable from Love, 304.
inseparable from Spirit, 477.
linked with Spirit, 491.
mortal, a mis-creator, 263.
Mortal, sentenced, 433.
never less than man, 244.
not evolved, 244.
not structural, 165, 173.
of anatomy and of theology, the, 148.
old and new, 300.
reflects God, 246.
reflects the perfect God, 337.
scientific, 94.
springs from Mind, 543.
true government of, 420.
true idea of, 337.
unfallen, 475.
wickedness is not, 289.
Man's entity, 369.
entity spiritual, 303.
genuine being, 91.
present possibilities, 572.
Manhood, the real, 336.
Manifestations, Mind's, immortal, 81.
Manipulation unscientific, 181.
Mankind redeemed, 466.
Man-made theories, 312.
Marriage temporal, 56.
Martyrs inevitable, 37.
testimony of, 134.
Marvels and reformations, 139.
Master's business, 52.
Masters, and servants, 216.
serving two, 346.
the two, 167.
Materia medica, and mythology, 158.
Material, and spiritual, 540.
basis, no truth from a, 546.
beliefs, 485.
creation, no, 256.
body never God's idea, 477.
error, 277.
inception, 544.
knowledge illusive, 274.
law, deference to, 549.
law, no, 182.
man as a dream, 491.
misconceptions, 285.
mortality, 279.
personality, 544.
pleasures, 38.
recognition impossible, 284.
skepticism, 317.
Materialistic challenge, 268.
Materialists, opposition of, 314.
Materiality, evanescent, 472.
Mathematics and scientific logic, 128.
the spiritual, 3.
Matter and animate error, 408.

Matter, causation not in, 552.
diagnosis of, 371.
impotent, 358.
is not inflamed, 415.
is not substance, 257.
Jesus' disregard of, 210.
life independent of, 368.
life not contingent on, 427.
mindless, 210.
Mind over, 160, 198.
modes of, 169.
no laws of, 381.
no pain in, 393.
not, but Mind, 384.
not medicine, 369.
sensationless, 211.
versus matter, 145.
versus Spirit, 171.
Matter's supposed selfhood, 479.
Meaning, interior, 320.
spiritual, 354.
Mechanism, automatic, 399.
Mediator, Jesus as, 316.
Medica, materia, and mythology, 158.
Medical and pagan delusions, 166.
errors, 174.
works objectionable, 179.
Medicine and brain, 401.
Judge, charges the jury, 433.
matter not, 369.
study of, 443.
the author's experiments in, 152.
Mediumship, no, 73.
Members, severed, 295.
Memory, immortal, 407.
Mendacity of error, 554.
Mental and physical oneness, 177.
causation, 114.
charlatanism, 458.
conditions to be heeded, 159.
conspirators, 405.
contact, 86.
court case, a, 430.
crimes, 105.
despotism, 103.
elements, 57.
emancipation, 224.
environment, 87.
midwifery, 528.
narcotics, 230.
powers, liberation of, 103.
preparation, 493.
propagation, 303.
quackery, 395.
sculpture, 248.
strength, 399.
telegraphy, 243.
tillage, 545.
Mentality, changed, 168.
independent, 397.
opposing, 424.
Mercy without partiality, 6.
Mere negation, 102.
Mesmerism, the evil of, 402.
Messenger, true estimate of God's, 560.
Messengers, our angelic, 299.
Messiah, John the Baptist, and the, 131.
or Christ, 333.
Metaphysical inversions, 113.
treatment, 453.

Metaphysics, benefits of, 380.
challenges physics, 161.
divine, 269.
Method, the one divine, 344.
Methods, mindless, 484.
misleading, 397.
mistaken, 79.
of reproduction, 548.
rejected, 143.
right, 106.
Midwifery, mental, 528.
Millennial glory, 34, 96.
Mind, all faculties from, 488.
anatomy and, 160.
and body, a clean, 383.
and stomach, 221.
can destroy all ills, 374.
circulates blood, 373.
cleansing the, 234.
creative, the, 62.
cures hip-disease, 193.
destroys all ills, 493.
God the only, 319.
governs body, 377.
growth is from, 520.
heals brain-disease, 387.
imparts purity, health, and beauty, 371.
is substance, 90.
jurisdiction of, 379.
limitless, 256.
man governed by, 151.
man springs from, 543.
mortal, action of, 187.
mortal, controlled, 400.
mortal, definition of, 114.
mortal, dethroned, 152.
mortal, not a healer, 401.
never limited, 284.
never weary, 218.
not matter, but, 384.
not mortal, 210.
one and all, 492.
over matter, 160, 198.
parent, God the, 336.
removes scrofula, 424.
sickness from mortal, 229.
sinlessness of, Soul, 467.
the one divine, 335.
the only cause, 262.
the only healer, 169.
unbounded, the, 84.
Mind's idea faultless, 503.
manifestations immortal, 81.
mortal, disappearance, 251.
pure thought, 508.
true camera, 264.
Mind-cure, a so-called, 185.
Mind-faculties, exercise of, 487.
Mindless methods, 484.
Mind-methods, no miracles in, 212.
Mind-science, no perversion of, 421.
Miracles, ancient and modern, 243.
basis of, 134.
in Mind-methods, no, 212.
of Jesus, the, 117.
proof from, 343.
rejected, 474.
Misbeliefs, pulmonary, 175.
Mischievous imagination, 460.
Misconceptions, material, 285.
Mis-creator, mortal man a, 263.

Pain, origin of, 153.
  unreality of, 261.
Painful prospect, 31.
Palsy, cure for, 375.
Panacea, universal, 407.
Pangs caused by the press, 197.
Panoply of wisdom, the, 458.
Pantheistic tendencies, 279.
Parable, confirmation in a, 399.
  of the creditor, 363.
Paradise regained, 171.
Pardon and amendment, 6.
  divine, 339.
Parentage, author's, 359.
Parent Mind, God the, 336.
Partiality, mercy without, 6.
Partnership, impossible, 274.
Path to perfection, purity the, 337.
Pathway, narrow, 324.
Patience and final perfection, 254.
  is wisdom, 66.
Patient, awaken the, 420.
  waiting, 238.
Patients, absent, 179.
Paul's enlightenment, 324.
  experience, 217.
Peculiarities, transmitted, 551.
Penalties, corporeal, 384.
Penalty, and sin, 40.
  honest toil has no, 385.
  remission of, 11.
Penitence or hospitality, 364.
Pentecostal power, 47.
Pentecost repeated, 43.
Perceiving the divine image, 205.
Perception, Scriptural, 548.
Peremptory demands, 327.
Perennial beauty, 121.
Perfect example, 20.
  God, man reflects the, 337.
  models, 248.
Perfection, and deformity, 244.
  final, and patience, 254.
  gained slowly, 233.
  of creation, 519.
  of divine government, 104.
  purity the path to, 337.
  requisite, 276.
  the divine standard of, 470.
Perfunctory prayers, 10.
Permanency, individual, 258.
Permanent affection, 60.
  obligation, 59.
  sensibility, 486.
Perpetual motion, 240.
  youth, 245.
Persecution harmful, 560.
  prolonged, 28.
Persistence of species, 552.
Personal conclusions, 101.
  confidence, 358.
  experience, 343.
  identity, 216.
Personality, divine, 116, 517.
  material, 544.
Pertinent proposal, 111.
Perusal and practice, 147.
Perversion of Mind-science, no, 421.
Petitions, efficacious, 4.
Phenomena explained, 86.
  scientific, 72.
  the reflex, 220.

Philanthropy, benefit of, 385.
Philological inadequacy, 115.
Philosophical blunders, 250.
Physical affinity, no, 191.
  falsities, 80.
  insensibility to Spirit, our, 284.
  oneness, mental and, 177.
  science a blind belief, 124.
  science, no, 127.
Physician, Christ the great, 442.
  old-school, 149.
  the true, 366.
Physicians, harm done by, 198.
Physicians' privilege, 235.
Physics, belief in, 155.
  metaphysics challenges, 161.
Physiology deficient, 148.
  or Spirit, 182.
  unscientific, 170.
  versus ontology, 556.
Physique, infinite, impossible, 258.
Pilate's question, 48.
Pillory, the real, 50.
Pleading, Christian, 418.
  unspoken, 411.
Pleasure, immaterial, 76.
  mythical, 294.
Pleasures, material, 38.
Plurality, Elohistic, 515.
Poison defined mentally, 177.
Poor post-mortem evidence, 81.
Position, strong, 344.
Positive reassurance, 420.
Possibilities, man's present, 572.
  of Life, 489.
Post-mortem evidence, poor, 81.
Postulates, erroneous, 91.
Potency, transient, of drugs, 370.
Potter, clay replying to the, 429.
Power, divine, denials of, 232.
  error's, imaginary, 403.
  human, a blind force, 192.
  latent, 378.
  mental, the misuse of, 105.
  of habit, 194.
  of imagination, 379.
  opposing, 92.
  Pentecostal, 47.
  spiritual, 67.
  the one real, 192.
Powerless promises, 65.
Powers, mental, liberation of, 103
Practical arguments, 355.
  preaching, 201.
  religion, 9.
  Science, 128.
  success, 162.
Practice, and perusal, 147.
  and Principle, 113.
  belief and, 202.
  Jesus' own, 148.
  proof in, 26.
Prayer, audible, danger from, 7.
  for the sick, 12.
  of Jesus Christ, the, 16.
Prayerful ingratitude, 3.
Prayers, perfunctory, 10.
Praying, audible, 7.
Preaching, practical, 201.
Precedence, question of, 142.
Prediction of a naturalist, 548.
  Saviour's, 52.

Premises, fatal, 351.
Preparation, mental, 493.
Prerogative, heaven-bestowed, 253.
Presence, beatific, 266.
  bodily, 14.
Present immortality, the, 428.
  Life eternal and, 410.
  salvation, 39.
Press, pangs caused by the, 197.
Pride, priestly, humbled, 228.
Priestly learning, 133.
  pride humbled, 228.
Primitive error, 292.
Principle and practice, 113.
  of all, God the, 272.
  the divine, and idea, 333.
  unchanging, 112.
Privilege, physicians', 235.
  the age's, 93.
  the Christian's, 556.
Probation, and salvation, 291.
Processes, the three, 549.
Producer, the real, 551.
Profession, more than, required,
  141.
  and proof, 233.
Progeny cursed, 532.
Progress and purgatory, 77.
  condition of, 496.
  demanded, 240.
Progressive development, 64.
Promise perpetual, 328.
Promises, powerless, 65.
Proof, and profession, 233.
  by induction, 461.
  from miracles, 343.
  given in healing, 547.
  in practice, 26.
  of immortality, no, 81.
Proofs, spiritual, of existence, 264.
Propensities inherited, 61.
Propensity, will-power an animal,
  490.
Propagation, divine, 507.
  mental, 303.
Proper self-government, 106.
  stimulus, 420.
Prophetic ignorance, 270.
Proposal, pertinent, 111.
Propositions, reversible, 113.
Prospect, painful, 31.
Prostration, unnecessary, 390.
Providence, divine, 530.
Psychical, and Ptolemaic error, 123.
Ptolemaic and psychical error,
  123.
Public exaggerations, 13.
Pulmonary misbeliefs, 175.
Pure ideas, multiplication of, 512.
  religion enthroned, 571.
Purgation, scientific, 296.
Purgatory, and progress, 77.
Purification, future, 290.
Purity, health, and beauty, Mind
  imparts, 371.
  of science, 457.
  the conflict with, 565.
  the path to perfection, 337.
Purity's rebuke, 52.
Purpose, final, 36.
  of crucifixion, 24.
  the main, 150.

Scriptures misinterpreted, 319.
Scrofula, Mind removes, 424.
Sculpture, mental, 248.
Sea, new earth and no more, 536.
Searching the heart, 8.
Seclusion of the author, 464.
Second death, 77.
 sight, 87.
Secrets, buried, 87.
Sectarianism and opposition, 224.
Sedatives valueless, 416.
Seed, and soil, 237.
Seeming and being, 123.
Seemingly independent authority, 208.
Self, forgetfulness of, 262.
Self-completeness, 264.
Self-constituted law, 229.
Self-government, proper, 106.
Selfhood, matter's supposed, 479.
 renewed, 249.
Self-improvement, 297.
Selfishness, redemption from, 205.
 and loss, 142.
Self-reliance and confidence, 23.
Sensationless body, 280.
Sense and pure Soul, 481.
Sense, Soul and, 144.
 of Deity, divine, 576.
 Science versus, 273.
 spiritual, of life, 122.
 testimony of, 252.
 the true, 262.
 true, of infinitude, 469.
 yields to understanding, 188.
 versus Soul, 486.
Sense-dreams, 312.
Senses, five, deceptive, 274.
 God invisible to the, 140.
 of Soul, the, 214.
 opacity of the, 117.
 testimony of the, 122.
 the, Adam and, 214.
 the, and health, 120.
 what the, originate, 318.
Sensibility, permanent, 486.
Sentences, immortal, 225.
Sentinel, heaven's, 49.
Seraphic symbols, 512.
Serpent, fear of the, overcome, 321.
 harmless, the, 515.
 mythical, 529.
 of error, the, 216.
 the sting of the, 563.
Serpent's whisper, the, 307.
Servants and masters, 216.
Service and worship, 40.
Serving two masters, 346.
Severed members, 295.
Severity, divine, 6.
Shame the effect of sin, 532.
Shoals, dangerous, avoided, 196.
Shrine celestial, the, 576.
Sick, prayer for the, 12.
Sickness, aids in, 395.
 akin to sin, 218.
 and fear, identical, 135.
 and sin, superiority to, 231.
 as discord, 318.
 as only thought, 208.
 causes of, 165.
 coalition of sin and, 218.

Sickness, elimination of, 348.
 erroneous, 482.
 from mortal mind, 229.
 one basis for all, 177.
 sin or fear the root of, 404.
 will abate, 406.
Side, wrong, belief on the, 168.
Sight, second, 87.
Sign of error, ignorance the, 555.
Signs following, 232.
Silence, eloquent, 412.
Sin a form of insanity, 407.
 and penalty, 40.
 and sickness, superiority to, 231.
 and suicide, 203.
 coalition of sickness and, 218.
 deadness in, 316.
 destroyed through suffering, 196.
 expose, without believing in it, 447.
 human, cancellation of, 5.
 is punished, 290.
 native nothingness of, 572.
 no healing in, 370.
 only of the flesh, 311.
 or fear the root of sickness, 404.
 shame the effect of, 532.
 sickness akin to, 218.
 the doom of, 241.
 to be overcome, 391.
Sin's head, bruising, 534.
Sinless career, Jesus', 19.
Sinlessness of Mind, Soul, 467.
Sins, bearing our, 53.
Skepticism, material, 317.
Skilful surgery, 401.
Slavery abolished, 225.
Sleep and food, our, 385.
 an illusion, 490.
Soaring aspirations, 511.
So-called mind-cure, a, 185.
 physical ego, the, 416.
 superiority, 409.
Society and intolerance, 238.
Socrates, faith of, 215.
Soil and seed, 237.
Sole governor, the, 469.
Solitary research, 109.
Some lessons from nature, 240.
Son of God, the, 332.
Son's duality, the, 334.
Sonship of Jesus, 482.
 the true, 315.
Sorrow and reformation, 5.
 salutary, 66.
Soul and sense, 144.
 and Spirit one, 335.
 defined, 482.
 greater than body, 223.
 impeccable, 311.
 imperishable, 310.
 not confined in body, 467.
 sense and pure, 481.
 sense versus, 486.
 sinlessness of Mind, 467.
 superior law of, 62.
 testimony of, 253.
 the senses of, 214.
 the sun and, 119.
Soundness maintained, 425.
Source, false, of knowledge, 159.
 of all life and action, 283.
 of calmness, 366.

Source of contagion, 153.
Sources, antagonistic, 239.
Species, persistence of, 552.
 the ascent of, 551.
Speedy healing, 365.
Spheres, spiritual, 513.
Spirit, allegiance to, 540.
 allness of, 331.
 and corporeality, 46.
 and flesh, 534.
 and Soul, one, 335.
 derivatives of, 93.
 harmony from, 480.
 infinite, 335.
 intangible, 78.
 life only in, 222.
 man inseparable from, 477.
 man linked with, 491.
 matter versus, 171.
 names and blesses, 506.
 no evil in, 207.
 our physical insensibility to, 284.
 physiology or, 182.
 reflection of, 477.
 substance is, 278.
 the infinite one, 70.
 the one Ego, 250.
 the only intelligence and substance, 204.
 the starting-point, 275.
 the strength of, 393.
 the tangible, 352.
 transforms, 241.
 versus darkness, 504.
Spirits obsolete, 72.
Spiritual and material, 540.
 ascension, 46.
 awakening, 95.
 baptism, 242.
 conception, 29.
 concord, 60.
 discovery, 260.
 Eucharist, 35.
 existence the one fact, 491.
 facts, dawning of, 546.
 firmament, 505.
 foreshadowings, 98.
 freedom, 191.
 friendship, 54.
 gateway, 538.
 government, 316.
 guidance, 566.
 harmony, 503.
 idea crowned, 562.
 idea revealed, 562.
 ideas apprehended, 510.
 ignorance, 251.
 insight, 95.
 interpretation, 46, 501.
 language, 117.
 law the only law, 273.
 laws of nature, 183.
 mathematics, the, 3.
 meaning, 354.
 narrative, 521.
 offspring, 289.
 oneness, 334.
 origin, 63.
 overture, 502.
 power, 67.
 proofs of existence, 264.
 realities, God's thoughts are, 514

Treatment of disease, 390.
the Christ, 369.
Trespass on human rights, no, **447.**
Tribal deity, Jehovah a, 524.
Tribunal, appeal to a higher, 434.
Trinity, divine, 331.
Tritheism impossible, 256.
Triumph, effective, 25.
over death, 496.
True and living rock, the, 137.
attainment, 536.
estimate of God's messenger, 560.
flesh and blood, 25.
government of man, 420.
healing, the, 230.
healing transcendent, 483.
idea of man, 337.
life eternal, 246.
nature and origin, 490.
new idea, the, 281.
physician, the, 366.
sense, the, 262.
sense of infinitude, 469.
sonship, the, 315.
theory of the universe, **547.**
worship, the, 140.
Trust, firm, and belief, 488.
of the All-wise, the, 455.
steadfast and calm, 495.
Trustworthy beneficence, 15.
Truth, adulteration of, 104.
allness of, 209.
an alterative, 162.
and knowledge, 299.
annihilates error, 11.
antidotes error, 346.
a present help, 351.
by inversion, 129.
calms the thought, 415.
Christ the ideal, 473.
demonstrated, 337.
desecrated, 365.
destroys falsity, 474.
efficacy of, 233.
from a material basis, no, 546.
is not inverted, 282.
leaven of, 117.
mockery of, 39.
one school of, 112.
results of faith in, 368.
the uses of, 201.
victory for, 493.
waymarks to eternal, 267.
Truth's grand results, 448.
ordeal, 225.
volume, 559.
witness, 298.
Truthful arguments, 418.
Trysting renewed, 59.
Two chief commands, 467.
claims omitted, 142.
different artists, 359.
infinite creators absurd, 357.
masters, the, 167.
records, the, 522.
Type of falsehood, a, 539.
the dragon as a, 563.

U

Ultimate harmony, 390.
Ultimatum, scientific, 492.
Unchanging Principle, 112.
Unchristian, drugging, 157.
Understanding, belief and, **183.**
imparted, 505.
our belief and, 203.
sense yields to, 188.
versus belief, 487.
Undesirable records, 246.
Unescapable dilemma, 119.
Unfair discrimination, 63.
Unfolding of thoughts, 506.
Unfoldings, astronomic, 121.
Unhesitating decision, 463.
Unimproved opportunities, 238.
Union of opposites, no, 229.
Unity of Science and Christianity, the, 135.
Universal brotherhood, 276.
cause, the, 331.
panacea, 407.
Universe, spiritual, 116.
true theory of the, 547.
Unnatural deflections, 78.
Unnecessary prostration, 390.
Unreal, and the real, the, 353.
disease to be made, 417.
versus real, 466.
Unrealities that seem real, 472.
Unreality, 115.
of pain, 261.
Unscientific introspection, **319.**
investiture, 75.
theories, 204.
Unspiritual contrasts, 272.
Unspoken pleading, 411.
Unwarranted expectations, 452.
Upheaval, cleansing, 540.
Useful knowledge, 195.
suggestion, a, 58.
Uses of adversity, 266.
of suffering, 322.
of truth, the, 201.
Utterances, emotional, **7.**

V

Vacant domicile, a, **478.**
Vain ecstasies, 312.
Value of intuition, 85.
Vanishing, a dream, 77.
Vapor and nothingness, 480.
Veil, within the, 41.
Verdict, divine, 442.
mortal, 294.
Veritable devotion, 4.
success, 372.
Vestments, divided, 242.
Vials of wrath and consolation, 574.
Vicarious, deliverance not, 22.
suffering, 36.
Victory, divine, 43.
for Truth, 493.
moral, 21.
over the grave, 45.
the struggle and, **145.**

Views, finite, of Deity, 255.
right, of humanity, 239.
Vision of the dying, 75.
Vision opening, 428.
Volition far-reaching, 220.
Volume, this, indispensable, **456.**
Truth's, 559.

W

Wait for reward, 22.
Waiting, patient, 238.
Warfare, Christian, 29, **354.**
with error, 568.
Warning, Christly, 571.
Watchfulness requisite, 4.
Water, and salt, only, 153.
Way, Science the, 483.
the one only, 242.
wrong and right, 180.
Waymarks to eternal Truth, **267.**
Way-shower, Jesus the, 30.
Ways of iniquity, hidden, 570.
Weakness and guilt, 455.
of material theories, 356.
Weapons, defensive, 48.
Weathering the storm, 67.
Wedlock, spiritual, 574.
What the senses originate, 318.
Wheat, the tares and, 300.
When man is man, 173.
Whisper, the serpent's, 307.
Wicked evasions, 448.
Wickedness is not man, 289.
Will-power an animal propensity, **490.**
detrimental, 144.
unrighteous, 206.
Winning the field, 453.
Wisdom, patience is, 66.
the panoply of, 458.
Within the veil, 41.
Witness, Truth's, 298.
Woman, ideal man and, **516.**
the rights of, 63.
Womanhood, false, 533.
Wonders, lawful, 135.
natural, 83.
Words, not, but deeds, 181.
Work, holy, resting in, 519.
Works, argument of good, 342.
both words and, 350.
faith according to, 133.
medical, objectionable, 179.
Worship, and service, 40.
fruitless, 351.
the true, 140.
Wrath, vials of, and consolation, 574.
Wrestling of Jacob, 308.
Wrong and right way, 180.
Wrong-doer should suffer, 403.

Y

Youth perpetual, 245.

Z

Zenith, revelation's pure, **576.**
Zigzag course, 21.

Appendix B
List of the
Scriptural Quotations
in
Science and Health with Key to the Scriptures

List of the
Scriptural Quotations
in
Science and Health with Key to the Scriptures

OLD TESTAMENT

Genesis

1: 1 In the beginning God created the heaven and the earth. — *g* 502–22.
1: 1, 2 "In the beginning God created the heaven and the earth. And the earth was without form, and void; and darkness was upon the face of the deep." — *r* 479–18.
1: 2 And the earth was without form, and void; and darkness was upon the face of the deep. And the spirit of God moved upon the face of the waters. — *g* 503–6.
1: 2 "darkness...upon the face of the deep," — *b* 338–18.
1: 3 And God said, Let there be light: and there was light. — *g* 503–18.
1: 3 "Let there be light," — *c* 255–3; *g* 556–19.
1: 4 And God saw the light, that it was good: and God divided the light from the darkness. — *g* 503–26.
1: 5 And God called the light Day, and the darkness He called Night. And the evening and the morning were the first day. — *g* 504–3.
1: 5 "And the evening and the morning were the first day." — *gl* 584–3.
1: 6 And God said, Let there be a firmament in the midst of the waters, and let it divide the waters from the waters. — *g* 505–4.
1: 7 And God made the firmament, and divided the waters which were under the firmament from the waters which were above the firmament: and it was so. — *g* 505–13.
1: 8 And God called the firmament Heaven. And the evening and the morning were the second day, — *g* 506–8.
1: 9 And God said, Let the waters under the heaven be gathered together unto one place, and let the dry land appear: and it was so. — *g* 506–15.
1: 10 And God called the dry land Earth; and the gathering together of the waters called He Seas: and God saw that it was good. — *g* 506–22.
1: 10 "And God called the dry land Earth; and the gathering together of the waters called He Seas." — *g* 535–29.
1: 11 And God said, Let the earth bring forth grass, the herb yielding seed, and the fruit tree yielding fruit after his kind, whose seed is in itself, upon the earth: and it was so. — *g* 507–11.
1: 11 "whose seed is in itself." — *g* 511–3.
1: 12 And the earth brought forth grass, and herb yielding seed after his kind, and the tree yielding fruit, whose seed was in itself, after his kind: and God saw that it was good. — *g* 508–9.
1: 13 And the evening and the morning were the third day. — *g* 508–26.
1: 14 And God said, Let there be lights in the firmament of the heaven, to divide the day from the night; and let them be for signs, and for seasons, and for days, and years. — *g* 509–9.
1: 15 And let them be for lights in the firmament of the heaven, to give light upon the earth: and it was so. — *g* 510–6.
1: 16 And God made two great lights; the greater light to rule the day, and the lesser light to rule the night: He made the stars also. — *g* 510–13.
1: 17, 18 And God set them in the firmament of the heaven, to give light upon the earth, and to rule over the day and over the night, and to divide the light from the darkness: and God saw that it was good. — *g* 511–7.

Genesis

1: 19 And the evening and the morning were the fourth day. — *g* 511–15.
1: 20 And God said, Let the waters bring forth abundantly the moving creature that hath life, and fowl that may fly above the earth in the open firmament of heaven. — *g* 511–19.
1: 21 And God created great whales, and every living creature that moveth, which the waters brought forth abundantly, after their kind, and every winged fowl after his kind: and God saw that it was good. — *g* 512–4.
1: 22 And God blessed them, saying, Be fruitful, and multiply, and fill the waters in the seas; and let fowl multiply in the earth. — *g* 512–17.
1: 23 And the evening and the morning were the fifth day. — *g* 513–4.
1: 24 And God said, Let the earth bring forth the living creature after his kind, cattle, and creeping thing, and beast of the earth after his kind: and it was so. — *g* 513–14.
1: 25 And God made the beast of the earth after his kind, and cattle after their kind, and everything that creepeth upon the earth after his kind: and God saw that it was good. — *g* 515–2.
1: 25 "And God saw that it was good." — *g* 515–2.
1: 26 And God said, Let us make man in our image, after our likeness; and let them have dominion over the fish of the sea, and over the fowl of the air, and over the cattle, and over all the earth, and over every creeping thing that creepeth upon the earth. — *r* 475–23; *g* 515–11.
1: 26 Let us make man in our image, after our likeness; and let them have dominion. — *p* 438–0.
1: 26 "image" "likeness" — *sp* 94–5, 6.
1: 26 "Let *them* have dominion." — *g* 515–21.
1: 26 "dominion over the fish of the sea, and over the fowl of the air, and over the cattle," — *f* 222–23.
1: 27 So God created man in His own image, in the image of God created He him; male and female created He them. — *g* 516–24.
1: 27 "image" — *b* 301–24.
1: 27 "male and female" — *f* 249–5
1: 28 And God blessed them, and God said unto them, Be fruitful, and multiply, and replenish the earth, and subdue it; and have dominion over the fish of the sea, and over the fowl of the air, and over every living thing that moveth upon the earth. — *g* 517–25.
1: 28 "multiply and replenish the earth." — *g* 511–4.
1: 29, 30 And God said, Behold, I have given you every herb bearing seed, which is upon the face of all the earth, and every tree, in the which is the fruit of a tree yielding seed; to you it shall be for meat. And to every beast of the earth, and to every fowl of the air, and to everything that creepeth upon the earth, wherein there is life, I have given every green herb for meat: and it was so. — *g* 518–5.
1: 31 And God saw everything that He had made, and, behold, it was very good. And the evening and the morning were the sixth day. — *g* 518–24.
1: 31 "and, behold, it was very good." — *g* 525–24.
2: 1 Thus the heavens and the earth were finished, and all the host of them. — *g* 519–7.
2: 2 And on the seventh day God ended His work which He had made; and He rested on the seventh day from all His work which He had made. — *g* 519–22.

Genesis

2: 4 "In the day that the Lord God [Jehovah God] made the earth and the heavens,"— *g* 543–31.

2: 4, 5 These are the generations of the heavens and of the earth when they were created, in the day that the Lord God [Jehovah] made the earth and the heavens, and every plant of the field before it was in the earth, and every herb of the field before it grew : for the Lord God [Jehovah] had not caused it to rain upon the earth, and there was not a man to till the ground.— *g* 520–16.

2: 5 "plant of the field before it was in the earth."— *g* 509–23.

2: 5 "every plant of the field before it was in the earth."— *g* 526–4.

2: 5 "not a man to till the ground."— *g* 544–5.

2: 6 But there went up a mist from the earth, and watered the whole face of the ground.— *g* 521–21.

2: 6 "There went up a mist from the earth."— *g* 546–12.

2: 7 And the Lord God [Jehovah] formed man of the dust of the ground, and breathed into his nostrils the breath of life ; and man became a living soul. — *g* 524–13.

2: 9 And out of the ground made the Lord God [Jehovah] to grow every tree that is pleasant to the sight, and good for food ; the tree of life also, in the midst of the garden, and the tree of knowledge of good and evil.— *g* 525–30.

2: 9 "the tree of life"— *g* 527–18.

2: 9 "tree of life,"— *p* 426–13 ; *g* 526–17 ; 538–13.

2: 9 "the tree of knowledge."— *ph* 165–1.

2: 9 "tree of knowledge,"— *f* 214–22 ; *g* 526–19 ; 538–14.

2: 15 And the Lord God [Jehovah] took the man, and put him into the garden of Eden, to dress it and to keep it.— *g* 526–26.

2: 16, 17 And the Lord God [Jehovah] commanded the man, saying, Of every tree of the garden thou mayest freely eat : but of the tree of the knowledge of good and evil, thou shalt not eat of it : for in the day that thou eatest thereof thou shalt surely die. — *g* 527–6.

2: 17 "the tree of the knowledge of good and evil,"— *f* 220–27.

2: 17 "tree of the knowledge of good and evil,"— *r* 481–16.

2: 17 "Thou shalt not eat of it."— *f* 220–29.

2: 17 "In the day that thou eatest thereof thou shalt surely die."— *ph* 197–9 ; *r* 481–18 ; *g* 532–8.

2: 17 "Thou shalt surely die ;"— *b* 277–3 ; *gl* 580–20.

2: 19 And out of the ground the Lord God [Jehovah] formed every beast of the field, and every fowl of the air ; and brought them unto Adam to see what he would call them : and whatsoever Adam called every living creature, that was the name thereof.— *g* 527–21.

2: 21, 22 And the Lord God [Jehovah, Yawah] caused a deep sleep to fall upon Adam, and he slept: and He took one of his ribs, and closed up the flesh instead thereof ; and the rib, which the Lord God [Jehovah] had taken from man, made He a woman, and brought her unto the man.— *g* 528–9.

3: 1–3 Now the serpent was more subtle than any beast of the field which the Lord God [Jehovah] had made. And he said unto the woman, Yea, hath God said, Ye shall not eat of every tree of the garden? And the woman said unto the serpent, We may eat of the fruit of the trees of the garden : but of the fruit of the tree which is in the midst of the garden, God hath said, Ye shall not eat of it, neither shall ye touch it, lest ye die.— *g* 529–13.

3: 1 "more subtle than any beast of the field."— *ap* 564–32.

3: 4, 5 And the serpent said unto the woman, Ye shall not surely die : for God doth know that in the day ye eat thereof, then your eyes shall be opened ; and ye shall be as gods, knowing good and evil.— *g* 530–13.

3: 5 "Ye shall be as gods."— *b* 280–21 ; 307–5 ; *g* 541–24 ; 544–21 ; *gl* 587–15.

3: 9, 10 And the Lord God [Jehovah] called unto Adam, and said unto him, Where art thou? And he said, I heard Thy voice in the garden, and I was afraid, because I was naked ; and I hid myself.— *g* 532–13.

3: 9 "Adam, where art thou?"— *ph* 181–24 ; *b* 308–8.

3: 9 "Where art thou?"— *b* 308–7.

3: 11, 12 And He said, Who told thee that thou wast naked? Hast thou eaten of the tree, whereof I commanded thee that thou shouldst not eat? And the man said, The woman whom Thou gavest to be with me, she gave me of the tree, and I did eat.— *g* 533–5.

3: 13 "The serpent beguiled me, and I did eat ;"— *g* 533–28.

3: 14, 15 And the Lord God [Jehovah] said unto the serpent, . . . I will put enmity between thee and the woman, and between thy seed and her seed ; it shall bruise thy head, and thou shalt bruise his heel.— *g* 534–8.

3: 16 Unto the woman He said, I will greatly multiply thy

Genesis

sorrow and thy conception : in sorrow thou shalt bring forth children ; and thy desire shall be to thy husband, and he shall rule over thee.— *g* 535–6.

3: 16 "In sorrow thou shalt bring forth children."— *g* 557–18.

3: 17–19 And unto Adam He said, Because thou hast hearkened unto the voice of thy wife, and hast eaten of the tree of which I commanded thee, saying, Thou shalt not eat of it : cursed is the ground for thy sake ; in sorrow shalt thou eat of it all the days of thy life : thorns also and thistles shall it bring forth to thee ; and thou shalt eat the herb of the field : in the sweat of thy face shalt thou eat bread, till thou return unto the ground ; for out of it wast thou taken : for dust thou art, and unto dust shalt thou return.— *g* 535–19.

3: 19 "Dust [nothingness] thou art, and unto dust [nothingness] shalt thou return."— *g* 545–29.

3: 22–24 And the Lord God [Jehovah] said, Behold, the man is become as one of us, to know good and evil : and now, lest he put forth his hand, and take also of the tree of life, and eat, and live forever ; therefore the Lord God [Jehovah] sent him forth from the garden of Eden, to till the ground from whence he was taken. So He drove out the man : and He placed at the east of the garden of Eden Cherubims, and a flaming sword which turned every way, to keep the way of the tree of life.— *g* 536–30.

3: 22 "Behold, the man is become as one of us."— *g* 545–3.

3: 24 "the tree of life."— *t* 458–18.

4: 1 And Adam knew Eve his wife ; and she conceived, and bare Cain, and said, I have gotten a man from the Lord [Jehovah].— *g* 538–23.

4: 1 "I have gotten a man from the Lord,"— *r* 479–4 ; *g* 538–30.

4: 3, 4 Cain brought of the fruit of the ground an offering unto the Lord [Jehovah]. And Abel, he also brought of the firstlings of his flock, and of the fat thereof.— *g* 540–25.

4: 4, 5 And the Lord [Jehovah] had respect unto Abel, and to his offering : but unto Cain, and to his offering, He had not respect.— *g* 541–6.

4: 8 Cain rose up against Abel his brother, and slew him. — *g* 541–14.

4: 9 And the Lord [Jehovah] said unto Cain, Where is Abel thy brother? And he said, I know not : Am I my brother's keeper?— *g* 541–19.

4: 10, 11 And He [Jehovah] said, . . . The voice of thy brother's blood crieth unto Me from the ground. And now art thou cursed from the earth.— *g* 541–27.

4: 15 And the Lord [Jehovah] said unto him, Therefore whosoever slayeth Cain, vengeance shall be taken on him sevenfold. And the Lord [Jehovah] set a mark upon Cain, lest any finding him should kill him.— *g* 542–14.

4: 16 And Cain went out from the presence of the Lord [Jehovah], and dwelt in the land of Nod.— *g* 542–27.

5: 24 "walked with God,"— *f* 214–6.

6: 3 "And the Lord said, My spirit shall not always strive with man, for that he also is flesh,"— *b* 320–12.

8: 21 "for man's sake."— *b* 338–29.

9: 6 "Whoso sheddeth man's blood, by man shall his blood be shed."— *a* 30–15.

13: 8 "Let there be no strife, I pray thee, between me and thee, and between my herdmen and thy herdmen ; for we be brethren."— *t* 444–25.

18: 25 "Shall not the Judge of all the earth do right?"— *t* 442–4.

32: 26 "Let me go, for the day breaketh ;"— *b* 308–24.

32: 27 "What is thy name?"— *b* 308–29.

32: 28 "as a prince"— *b* 308–30.

32: 28 "power with God and with men."— *b* 308–31.

32: 29 "Tell me, I pray thee, *thy* name ;"— *b* 308–32.

Exodus

4: 8 "It shall come to pass, if they will not believe thee, neither hearken to the voice of the first sign, that they will believe the voice of the latter sign."— *b* 321–27.

6: 3 *And I appeared unto Abraham, unto Isaac, and unto Jacob by the name of God Almighty ; but by My name Jehovah was I not known to them.*— *g* 501–*.

15: 3 "a man of war,"— *g* 524–10.

15: 18 "the Lord shall reign forever."— *pref* vii–20.

15: 26 "I am the Lord that healeth thee,"— *b* 276–2.

20: 3 "Thou shalt have no other gods before me."— *a* 19–29 ; *b* 280–18 ; 340–15 ; *r* 467–3.

20: 10 "stranger that is within thy gates,"— *s* 146–20.

20: 13 "Thou shalt not kill."— *m* 56–19.

20: 14 "Thou shalt not commit adultery,"— *m* 56–18.

20: 15 "Thou shalt not steal,"— *s* 112–31.

33: 20 "Thou canst not see My face ; for there shall no man see Me, and live."— *s* 140–5.

Deuteronomy

4 : 35 "The Lord He is God [good] ; there is none else beside Him." — *p* 414–21.

6 : 4 "Hear, O Israel : the Lord our God is one Lord." — *c* 256–12.

29 : 20 "The anger of the Lord." — *b* 293–25.

I Kings

19 : 12 "still, small voice" — *b* 323–29 ; *p* 367–25 ; *ap* 559–8.

Job

3 : 25 "The thing which I greatly feared is come upon me." — *p* 411–1.

4 : 17, 18 Shall mortal man be more just than God?
Shall man be more pure than his Maker?
Behold, He putteth no trust in His ministering spirits,
And His angels He chargeth with frailty. — *o* 360–24.
(The above reference is from the translation of the late Rev. George R. Noyes, D.D.)

11 : 7 "Canst thou by searching find out God?" — *b* 322–31 ; *g* 551–26.

14 : 1 "Man that is born of a woman is of few days, and full of trouble." — *g* 552–14.

14 : 1 "of few days, and full of trouble." — *g* 536–21.

18 : 14 "king of terrors" — *b* 289–15.

19 : 26 "In my flesh shall I see God," — *b* 320–25.

22 : 21 "acquaint now thyself with Him, and be at peace." — *b* 324–12.

33 : 24 "I have found a ransom." — *b* 276–3.

34 : 3 "The ear trieth words, as the mouth tasteth meat." — *s* 115–8.

38 : 7 "the morning stars sang together." — *g* 509–22.

38 : 28 "who hath begotten the drops of dew," — *c* 257–19.

38 : 32 "forth Mazzaroth in his season," — *c* 257–20.

38 : 32 "Arcturus with his sons." — *c* 257–21.

42 : 5 "I have heard of Thee by the hearing of the ear : but now mine eye seeth Thee." — *c* 262–17.

Psalms

8 : 6 "Thou madest him to have dominion over the works of Thy hands. Thou hast put all things under his feet." — *ph* 200–13.

14 : 2 "children of men," — *s* 148–9 ; *p* 409–22 ; *l* 444–29.

17 : 15 As for me, I will behold Thy face in righteousness : I shall be satisfied, when I awake, with Thy likeness. — *ph* 190–28.

19 : 7 "making wise the simple." — *o* 342–4.

19 : 8 "rejoicing the heart." — *c* 266–2.

23 : 1– 6 [Divine love] is my shepherd ; I shall not want.
[Love] maketh me to lie down in green pastures :
[Love] leadeth me beside the still waters.
[Love] restoreth my soul [spiritual sense] : [Love] leadeth me in the paths of righteousness for His name's sake.
Yea, though I walk through the valley of the shadow of death, I will fear no evil : for [Love] is with me ; [Love's] rod and [Love's] staff they comfort me.
[Love] prepareth a table before me in the presence of mine enemies : [Love] anointeth my head with oil ; my cup runneth over.
Surely goodness and mercy shall follow me all the days of my life ; and I will dwell in the house [the consciousness] of [Love] for ever. — *ap* 578–5.

23 : 2 "green pastures, . . . beside the still waters." — *g* 514–13.

23 : 4 "Though I walk through the valley of the shadow of death, I will fear no evil." — *gl* 590–21.

29 : 2 "the beauty of holiness," — *o* 135–12.

36 : 9 For with Thee is the fountain of life ;
In Thy light shall we see light. — *ph* 190–30.

36 : 9 "light shall we see light ;" — *g* 510–10.

37 : 11 "The meek shall inherit the earth." — *g* 516–14.

37 : 35 "like a green bay tree ;" — *pr* 5–19.

42 : 11 Why art thou cast down, O my soul [sense] ?
And why art thou disquieted within me ?
Hope thou in God ; for I shall yet praise Him,
Who is the health of my countenance and my God. — *p* 362–*.

46 : 1 "God is our refuge and strength, a very present help in trouble." — *t* 444–11.

46 : 1 "a very present help in trouble." — *pr* 13–1 ; *f* 202–27.

46 : 6 "He uttered His voice, the earth melted." — *sp* 97–26.

48 : 1 Great is the Lord, and greatly to be praised in the city of our God, in the mountain of His holiness. — *ap* 558–*.

48 : 2 "Beautiful for situation, the joy of the whole earth, is mount Zion, on the sides of the north, the city of the great King." — *ap* 575–22.

50 : 10 "the cattle upon a thousand hills." — *g* 514–16.

51 : 5 "shapen in iniquity ;" — *g* 540–29.

78 : 19 "Can God furnish a table in the wilderness?" — *s* 135–19.

89 : 50, 51 Remember, Lord, the reproach of Thy servants;
how I do bear in my bosom the reproach of all the mighty people; wherewith Thine enemies

Psalms

have reproached, O Lord; wherewith they have reproached the footsteps of Thine anointed. — *f* 201–*.

91 : 6 "the pestilence that walketh in darkness, . . . the destruction that wasteth at noonday." — *m* 56–16.

93 : 2 Thy throne is established of old :
Thou art from everlasting. — *c* 255–*.

93 : 4 "The Lord on high is mightier than the noise of many waters, yea, than the mighty waves of the sea." — *g* 505–18.

102 : 26 "As a vesture shalt Thou change them and they shall be changed." — *s* 125–24.

103 : 15, 16 "As for man, his days are as grass : as a flower of the field, so he flourisheth. For the wind passeth over it, and it is gone ; and the place thereof shall know it no more." — *ph* 190–23 ; *r* 476–24.

107 : 20 He sent His word, and healed them, and delivered them from their destructions. — *ph* 165–*.

111 : 10 "The fear of the Lord is the beginning of wisdom," — *p* 373–15.

114 : 5– 7 "What ailed thee, O thou sea, that thou fleddest? Thou Jordan, that thou wast driven back? Ye mountains, that ye skipped like rams, and ye little hills, like lambs? Tremble, thou earth, at the presence of the Lord, at the presence of the God of Jacob." — *s* 135–1.

118 : 16 "The right hand of the Lord is exalted." — *a* 38–16.

146 : 10 "the Lord shall reign forever." — *pref* vii–20.

Proverbs

4 : 18 "unto the perfect day." — *r* 496–13 ; *ap* 562–20.

9 : 9 Give instruction to a wise man, and he will be yet wiser : teach a just man, and he will increase in learning. — *t* 443–*.

23 : 7 "As he thinketh in his heart, so is he." — *sp* 80–13 ; *f* 213–4 ; *p* 383–28.

23 : 27 "strange woman" — *p* 362–6.

28 : 13 "He that covereth his sins shall not prosper : but whoso confesseth and forsaketh them shall have mercy." — *t* 448–17.

30 : 4 "wind in His fists ;" — *ph* 192–18.

Ecclesiastes

1 : 2 "All is vanity." — *f* 239–32.

7 : 29 "sought out many inventions," — *ph* 196–2.

9 : 8 "let thy garments be always white." — *c* 267–27.

11 : 3 "In the place where the tree falleth, there it shall be." — *b* 291–19.

12 : 1 "I have no pleasure in them." — *s* 107–18.

12 : 13 "Let us hear the conclusion of the whole matter : Fear God, and keep His commandments : for this is the whole duty of man." — *b* 340–6.

Song of Solomon

5 : 16 "altogether lovely ;" — *pr* 3–14.

7 : 12 Let us get up early to the vineyards; let us see if the vine flourish, whether the tender grape appear, and the pomegranates bud forth. — *fr* 600–*.

Isaiah

1 : 5 "sick, and the whole heart faint ;" — *f* 219–12.

8 : 19 And when they shall say unto you,
Seek unto them that have familiar spirits,
And unto wizards that peep and that mutter;
Should not a people seek unto their God? — *sp* 70–*.

9 : 6 "Unto us a child is born, . . . and his name shall be called Wonderful." — *s* 109–26.

11 : 6 The wolf also shall dwell with the lamb,
And the leopard shall lie down with the kid ;
And the calf and the young lion and the fatling together ;
And a little child shall lead them. — *g* 514–22.

28 : 10 For precept must be upon precept, precept upon precept; line upon line, line upon line; here a little, and there a little. — *r* 465–*.

40 : 31 "They that wait upon the Lord . . . shall run, and not be weary ; and they shall walk, and not faint." — *f* 218–27.

40 : 31 "run, and not be weary ; . . . walk, and not faint," — *f* 254–3.

45 : 7 "I make peace, and create evil. I the Lord do all these things ;" — *g* 540–5.

52 : 7 "beautiful upon the mountains," — *p* 442–14.

52 : 7 "that bringeth good tidings." — *p* 442–15.

53 : 1 "the arm of the Lord" — *a* 24–11.

53 : 3 "Despised and rejected of men," — *a* 20–16 ; 52–13.

53 : 3 "man of sorrows" — *a* 42–9 ; 52–19.

53 : 4 "stricken, smitten of God." — *a* 49–32.

53 : 5 "with his stripes [the rejection of error] we are healed." — *a* 20–15.

53 : 7 "He opened not his mouth." — *a* 48–19.

53 : 7 "opened not his mouth." — *ap* 564–18.

53 : 7 "He is brought as a lamb to the slaughter, and as a sheep before her shearers is dumb, so he openeth not his mouth." — *a* 50–1.

53 : 8 "Who shall declare his generation?" — *a* 50–3.

55 : 1 "Ho, every one that thirsteth, come ye to the waters." — *pr* 13–3.

Isaiah

55: 7 "Let the wicked forsake his way, and the unrighteous man his thoughts."—*f* 239–14.

55: 7 "forsake his way, and the unrighteous man his thoughts."—*s* 139–1.

Jeremiah

5: 19 "strange gods."—*g* 524–7.

17: 1 "with the point of a diamond"—*g* 521–16.

31: 34 "they shall all know Me [God], from the least of them unto the greatest."—*f* 242–4.

Lamentations

3: 35 "aside the right of a man before the face of the Most High,"—*a* 49–31.

Ezekiel

18: 2 "the fathers have eaten sour grapes, and the children's teeth are set on edge."—*f* 211–19.

21: 27 "He come whose right it is."—*f* 223–32.

Daniel

4: 35 "doeth according to His will in the army of heaven, and among the inhabitants of the earth ; and none can stay His hand, or say unto Him, What doest Thou?"—*c* 256–20.

7: 9 "the Ancient of days."—*s* 146–28.

Habakkuk

1: 13 "of purer eyes than to behold evil,"—*f* 243–22 ; *o* 357–4.

NEW TESTAMENT

Matthew

1: 23 "God with us,"—*pref* xi–16 ; *s* 107–8.

2: 9 "where the young child was,"—*ph* 191–11.

3: 3 "the voice of one crying in the wilderness"—*f* 208–19.

3: 15 "Suffer it to be so now : for thus it becometh us to fulfil all righteousness."—*m* 56–3.

4: 4 "Man shall not live by bread *alone*, but by every word that proceedeth out of the mouth of God,"—*p* 410–10.

5: 8 "Blessed are the pure in heart : for they shall see God."—*b* 324–5; *o* 341–9.

5: 13 "Ye are the salt of the earth."—*p* 367–18.

5: 13 "lost his savour ;"—*s* 153–7.

5: 14 "Ye are the light of the world. A city that is set on an hill cannot be hid."—*p* 367–19.

5: 17 "I am not come to destroy, but to fulfil."—*r* 474–20.

5: 25 "Agree with thine adversary quickly, whiles thou art in the way with him."—*p* 390–18.

5: 25 "adversary quickly,"—*s* 161–32.

5: 26 "the uttermost farthing."—*pr* 5–11.

5: 38 "An eye for an eye,"—*a* 30–15.

5: 39 "Whosoever shall smite thee on thy right cheek, turn to him the other also."—*t* 444–19.

5: 48 "Be ye therefore perfect, even as your Father which is in heaven is perfect !"—*a* 37–28 ; *c* 259–19.

5: 48 "Be ye therefore perfect,"—*f* 253–32.

5: 48 "Father which is in heaven is perfect."—*r* 485–23.

6: 6 "When thou prayest, enter into thy closet, and, when thou hast shut thy door, pray to thy Father which is in secret ; and thy Father, which seeth in secret, shall reward thee openly."—*pr* 14–31.

6: 7 "vain repetitions,"—*pr* 13–9.

6: 8 *Your Father knoweth what things ye have need of, before ye ask Him.*—*pr* 1–*.

6: 9 "After this manner therefore pray ye,"—*pr* 16–9.

6: 9 Our Father which art in heaven, Hallowed be Thy name.—*pr* 16–26.

6: 10 Thy kingdom come.—*pr* 16–30.

6: 10 Thy will be done in earth, as it is in heaven.—*pr* 17–1.

6: 10 "in earth, as it is in heaven."—*b* 339–24.

6: 11 Give us this day our daily bread ;—*pr* 17–4.

6: 12 And forgive us our debts, as we forgive our debtors.—*pr* 17–6.

6: 12 "Forgive us our debts,"—*pr* 11–2.

6: 13 And lead us not into temptation, but deliver us from evil ;—*pr* 17–8.

6: 13 For Thine is the kingdom, and the power, and the glory, forever.—*pr* 17–12.

6: 13 "Deliver us from evil,"—*pr* 16–15.

6: 19 "where moth and rust doth corrupt."—*f* 241–5.

6: 21 "Where your treasure is, there will your heart be also."—*ph* 181–29 ; *c* 262–25.

6: 22 "the light of the body is the eye,"—*p* 393–25.

6: 24 "No man can serve two masters."—*f* 201–5.

6: 24 "serve two masters."—*pr* 14–5.

6: 24 "hold to the one, and despise the other."—*ph* 182–13.

6: 25 *Therefore I say unto you, Take no thought for your life, what ye shall eat, or what ye shall drink ; nor yet for your body, what ye shall put on. Is not the life more than meat, and the body than raiment ?*—*ph* 165–*.

6: 25 "thought for your life, what ye shall eat, or what ye shall drink" ;—*m* 62–13.

6: 25 "for your body what ye shall put on,"—*m* 62–14.

6: 25 "Take no thought for your life, what ye shall eat, or what ye shall drink."—*ph* 170–16 ; *g* 530–8.

6: 25 "Take no thought for your life,"—*f* 228–20 ; *p* 365–8.

7: 1 "Judge not."—*o* 344–18.

7: 1 "Judge not, that ye be not judged."—*t* 443–12.

7: 2 "With what measure ye mete, it shall be measured to you again."—*t* 455–14.

7: 5 "First cast out the beam out of thine own eye ; and then shalt thou see clearly to cast out the mote out of thy brother's eye."—*t* 455–14.

7: 6 "Give not that which is holy unto the dogs, neither cast ye your pearls before swine."—*b* 272–17.

Matthew

7: 13 "wide is the gate, and broad is the way, that leadeth to destruction, and many there be which go in thereat."—*t* 451–12.

7: 16 "Do men gather grapes of thorns?"—*g* 539–23.

7: 19 "[It] is hewn down."—*pr* 6–28.

7: 20 *Wherefore by their fruits ye shall know them.*—*fr* 600–*.

7: 20 "By their fruits ye shall know them"—*o* 342–27.

7: 29 "as one having authority."—*pr* 14–30.

8: 10 "I have not found so great faith, no, not in Israel."—*s* 133–6.

8: 22 "Follow me ; and let the dead bury their dead."—*o* 355–10.

8: 29 "Art thou [Truth] come hither to torment us before the time?"—*s* 129–15.

9: 6 "the Son of man,"—*r* 482–16.

10: 8 Heal the sick !—*a* 37–30 ; *s* 138–29.

10: 26 "there is nothing covered that shall not be revealed."—*pr* 8–17.

10: 28 "Fear him which is able to destroy both soul and body in hell,"—*ph* 196–11.

10: 33 "Whosoever shall deny me before men, him will I also deny before my Father which is in heaven."—*p* 372–25.

11: 3 "Art thou he that should come?"—*s* 131–31 ; 133–2.

11: 4–6 "Go and show John again those things which ye do hear and see : the blind receive their sight and the lame walk, the lepers are cleansed, and the deaf hear, the dead are raised up, and the poor have the gospel preached to them. And blessed is he, whosoever shall not be offended in me."—*s* 132–4.

11: 19 "friend of publicans and sinners."—*a* 53–1.

11: 19 "wisdom is justified of her children."—*b* 317–10.

12: 13 "Stretch forth thine hand,"—*p* 398–14.

12: 13 "was restored whole, like as the other."—*p* 398–14.

12: 25 "knew their thoughts,"—*sp* 85–16.

12: 25 "kingdom divided against itself,"—*p* 388–19.

12: 25 "brought to desolation."—*p* 388–20.

12: 27 "If I by Beelzebub cast out devils, by whom do your children cast them out?"—*p* 422–3.

12: 29 "How can one enter into a strong man's house and spoil his goods, except he first bind the strong man?"—*p* 399–29.

12: 29 "the strong man,"—*p* 400–4 ; 400–7.

12: 33 "the tree is known by his fruit"—*b* 299–22.

12: 48 "Who is my mother, and who are my brethren,"—*a* 31–6.

12: 50 "For whosoever shall do the will of my Father which is in heaven, the same is my brother, and sister, and mother."—*c* 267–16.

13: 15 "This people's heart is waxed gross, and their ears are dull of hearing, and their eyes they have closed ; lest at any time they should see with their eyes, and hear with their ears, and should understand with their heart, and should be converted, and I should heal them."—*o* 350–18.

13: 33 *The kingdom of heaven is like unto leaven, which a woman took, and hid in three measures of meal, till the whole was leavened.*—*s* 107–*.

13: 33 "leaven, which a woman took, and hid in three measures of meal, till the whole was leavened,"—*s* 117–32.

13: 35 "secret from the foundation of the world,"—*b* 317–1.

13: 58 "because of their unbelief"—*p* 401–1.

15: 14 "If the blind lead the blind, both shall fall into the ditch."—*f* 223–18.

15: 19, 20 *For out of the heart proceed evil thoughts, murders, adulteries, fornications, thefts, false witness, blasphemies : these are the things which defile a man.*—*an* 100–*.

16: 3 "O ye hypocrites ! ye can discern the face of the sky ; but can ye not discern the signs of the times?"—*sp* 85–21.

16: 3 "Ye can discern the face of the sky ; but can ye not discern the signs of the times?"—*g* 509–31.

16: 13 "Whom do men say that I, the Son of man, am?"—*s* 136–11.

16: 14 "Some say that thou art John the Baptist ; some,

Matthew

Elias; and others, Jeremias, or one of the prophets." — s 136–14.
16 : 15 "But whom say ye that I am?" — s 137–9.
16 : 16 "Thou art the Christ, the Son of the living God !" — s 137–17.
16 : 17 "Blessed art thou, Simon Bar-jona : for flesh and blood hath not revealed it unto thee, but my Father which is in heaven ; " — s 137–22.
16 : 18 "And I say also unto thee, That thou art Peter ; and upon this rock [the meaning of the Greek word petros, or stone] I will build my church ; and the gates of hell [hades, the under-world, or the grave] shall not prevail against it." — s 137–29.
16 : 23 "Get thee behind me, Satan." — pr 7–2.
16 : 23 "Thou art an offence unto me." — pr 6–25.
17 : 11 "Elias truly shall first come and restore all things." — gl 585–13.
19 : 6 What therefore God hath joined together, let not man put asunder. — m 56–*.
19 : 19 "Love thy neighbor as thyself ;" — s 138–29 ; b 340–25.
19 : 24 "easier for a camel to go through the eye of a needle," — f 241–31 ; t 449–9.
20 : 16 "The last shall be first, and the first last," — s 116–8.
21 : 31 "The publicans and the harlots go into the kingdom of God before you." — a 20–7.
21 : 42 "the stone which the builders rejected" — s 139–26.
21 : 42 "the head of the corner." — s 139–27.
21 : 44 "but on whomsoever it shall fall, it will grind him to powder." — p 380–6.
22 : 14 "Many are called, but few are chosen." — a 27–25.
22 : 21 "unto Cæsar the things which are Cæsar's ; and unto God the things that are God's." — a 20–1 ; g 540–17.
22 : 29 "Ye do err, not knowing the Scriptures." — b 272–9.
22 : 30 In the resurrection they neither marry, nor are given in marriage, but are as the angels of God in heaven. — m 56–*.
22 : 30 "given in marriage" — m 69–11.
22 : 37 "love the Lord thy God with all thy heart, and with all thy soul, and with all thy mind" — pr 9–17.
22 : 39 "Thou shalt love thy neighbor as thyself." — r 467–8.
23 : 9 "Call no man your father upon the earth : for one is your Father, which is in heaven." — a 31–4.
23 : 23 "These ought ye to have done, and not to leave the other undone." — sp 85–29.
23 : 27 "like unto whited sepulchres . . . full . . . of all uncleanness." — pr 8–8.
24 : 21 "great tribulation such as was not since the beginning of the world ;" — s 129–13.
24 : 36 "but of that day and hour, knoweth no man." — b 292–3.
25 : 12 "I know you not." — f 238–15.
25 : 21 "faithful over a few things," — b 323–17.
25 : 23 "Well done, good and faithful servant," — a 44–3.
25 : 23 "Thou hast been faithful over a few things, I will make thee ruler over many," — ap 569–6.
26 : 26, 27 "As they were eating, Jesus took bread, and blessed it and brake it, and gave it to the disciples, and said, Take, eat ; this is my body. And he took the cup, and gave thanks, and gave it to them saying, Drink ye all of it." — a 32–15.
26 : 27 "Drink ye all of it." — a 33–17.
26 : 40 "Could ye not watch with me one hour?" — a 48–3.
26 : 52 "They that take the sword shall perish with the sword." — g 542–18.
27 : 42 "He saved others ; himself he cannot save." — a 49–29.
27 : 46 "My God, why hast thou forsaken me?" — a 50–8.
28 : 20 "Lo, I am with you alway, even unto the end of the world." — t 446 22.
28 : 20 "Lo, I am with you alway," — b 317–13.

Mark

3 : 24 "If a kingdom be divided against itself, that kingdom cannot stand." — f 252–2.
4 : 14 "the sower" — b 272–13.
4 : 39 "Peace, be still." — s 144–22.
5 : 41 "Damsel, I say unto thee, arise !" — p 398–12.
6 : 50 "Be not afraid !" — p 410–30.
8 : 18 "Having eyes, see ye not?" — gl 586–5.
8 : 18 "Having ears, hear ye not?" — gl 585–3.
9 : 19 "O faithless generation," — s 148–2.
9 : 24 "Lord, I believe ; help thou mine unbelief !" — a 23–27.
9 : 25 "Thou dumb and deaf spirit, I charge thee, come out of him, and enter no more into him." — p 398–2.
9 : 26 "the spirit [error] cried, and rent him sore and came out of him, and he was as one dead," — p 398–4.
10 : 27 "with God all things are possible," — f 232–9.
11 : 23, 24 For verily I say unto you, That whosoever shall say unto this mountain, Be thou removed, and be thou cast into the sea ; and shall not doubt in his heart, but shall believe that those things which he saith

Mark

shall come to pass ; he shall have whatsoever he saith. Therefore I say unto you, What things soever ye desire when ye pray, believe that ye receive them, and ye shall have them. — pr 1–*.
12 : 30 "love the Lord thy God with all thy heart, and with all thy soul, and with all thy mind" — pr 9–17.
13 : 32 "knoweth no man . . . neither the Son, but the Father." — sp 77–15.
13 : 32 "the Son but the Father ;" — f 233–12.
15 : 34 "Eloi, Eloi, lama sabachthani ?" — a 51–1.
15 : 34 "My God, why hast Thou forsaken me?" — a 50–8.
16 : 15 "Go ye into all the world, and preach the gospel to every creature !" — a 37–29 ; s 138–27.
16 : 15 "Go ye into all the world, and preach the gospel," — o 342–10.
16 : 15 "Preach the gospel to every creature." — p 418–27.
16 : 17, 18 And these signs shall follow them that believe : In my name shall they cast out devils : they shall speak with new tongues ; they shall take up serpents ; and if they drink any deadly thing, it shall not hurt them ; they shall lay hands on the sick, and they shall recover. — p 362–*.
16 : 17, 18 "These signs shall follow them that believe , . . . they shall take up serpents, and if they drink any deadly thing, it shall not hurt them. They shall lay hands on the sick, and they shall recover." — b 328–22.
16 : 17, 18 "These signs shall follow them that believe ; . . . they shall lay hands on the sick, and they shall recover." — a 38–10 ; o 359–26.
16 : 17 "These signs shall follow them that believe." — a 52–28.
16 : 17 "them that believe" — a 38–14.
16 : 17 "They shall speak with new tongues." — o 349–22.
16 : 17 "new tongues ;" — f 210–1.
16 : 20 "with signs following." — pr 10–11.
16 : 20 "signs following." — s 110–29 ; 117–12.

Luke

1 : 33 "of his kingdom there shall be no end," — ap 565–15.
2 : 14 "on earth peace, good-will toward men." — s 150–7 ; f 226–17.
2 : 49 "Father's business." — a 52–1.
4 : 18 To preach deliverance to the captives [of sense], And recovering of sight to the blind, To set at liberty them that are bruised. — pref xi–19.
6 : 38 "shall be measured to you again," — pr 5–11.
6 : 38 "and running over." — pr 5–12.
7 : 22 "Go your way, and tell John what things ye have seen and heard ; how that the blind see, the lame walk, the lepers are cleansed, the deaf hear, the dead are raised, to the poor the gospel is preached." — a 27–3.
7 : 34 "friend of publicans and sinners." — a 53 1.
7 : 42 "Which of them will love him most?" — p 363–18.
7 : 43 "He to whom he forgave most." — p 363–20.
7 : 48 "Thy sins are forgiven." — p 363–23.
8 : 5 "the fowls of the air." — f 237–12.
8 : 15 "honest and good heart" — b 272–6.
8 : 45 "Who touched me?" — sp 86–1.
8 : 45 "The multitude throng thee." — sp 86–3.
8 : 52 "she is not dead, but sleepeth." — p 308 11.
9 : 9 "John have I beheaded : but who is this?" — s 136–27.
9 : 29 "white and glistering." — c 267–26.
10 : 17 "Even the devils are subject unto us through thy name." — a 49–5.
10 : 19 Behold, I give unto you power . . . over all the power of the enemy : and nothing shall by any means hurt you. — p 438–5.
10 : 21 "I thank Thee, O Father, Lord of heaven and earth, that Thou hast hid these things from the wise and prudent, and hast revealed them unto babes : even so, Father, for so it seemed good in Thy sight." — s 131–19.
11 : 14 "it came to pass, when the devil was gone out, the dumb spake." — s 135–16.
11 : 15 "He casteth out devils through Beelzebub," — a 52–32.
12 : 22 "Take no thought . . . for the body." — p 382–11.
12 : 32 "Fear not, little flock ; for it is your Father's good pleasure to give you the kingdom." — p 442–27.
13 : 16 "whom Satan hath bound," — r 495–9.
14 : 10 "go up higher." — pr 11–10.
17 : 21 "The kingdom of God is within you ;" — r 476–29 ; ap 573–32.
17 : 21 "is within you," — ap 576–21.
18 : 8 "When the Son of man cometh, shall he find faith on the earth?" — s 132–26.
18 : 11 "not as other men" — pr 9–1.
18 : 17 "Whosoever shall not receive the kingdom of God as a little child, shall in no wise enter therein." — p 382–22.
19 : 13 "Occupy till I come !" — a 22–13.
20 : 34, 35 "The children of this world marry, and are given in marriage : But they which shall be accounted worthy to obtain that world, and the resurrection

Luke

from the dead, neither marry, nor are given in marriage."— *m* 69–26.

20 : 35　"given in marriage"— *m* 69–11.

22 : 18　*For I say unto you, I will not drink of the fruit of the vine, until the kingdom of God shall come.—* *a* 18–*.

22 : 42　"Not my will, but Thine, be done !"— *a* 33–19.

24 : 39　"Spirit hath not flesh and bones, as ye see me have."— *a* 45–27.

24 : 39　"flesh and bones."— *b* 313–30.

John

1 : 3　*All things were made by Him; and without Him was not anything made that was made.—* *f* 231–31 ; *r* 480–26 ; *g* 501–*.

1 : 3　"and without Him [the *logos,* or *word*] was not anything made that was made."— *g* 525–18.

1 : 3　"was not anything made that was made."— *b* 335–11.

1 : 3　"that was made."— *c* 267–11.

1 : 4　*In Him was life ; and the life was the light of men.*— *g* 501–*.

1 : 4　"the light of men."— *ap* 561–29.

1 : 5　"shineth in darkness, and the darkness comprehended it not."— *b* 325–31.

1 : 6, 8　"There was a man sent from God . . . to bear witness to that Light."— *ap* 561–30.

1 : 11　"He came unto his own, and his own received him not."— *s* 131–17.

1 : 14　"The Word was made flesh."— *o* 350–24.

1 : 29　"the Lamb of God ;"— *s* 132–31.

2 : 19　"Destroy this temple, and in three days I will raise it up."— *a* 27–12 ; *b* 314–14 ; *r* 494–2.

3 : 8　"The wind [*pneuma*] bloweth where it listeth. . . . So is every one that is born of the Spirit [*pneuma*]."— *gl* 598–3.

3 : 8　"tell whence it cometh."— *sp* 78–28.

4 : 23　"The hour cometh, and now is, when the true worshippers shall worship the Father in spirit and in truth."— *a* 31–26 ; *sp* 93–5.

4 : 23　"The true worshippers shall worship the Father in spirit and in truth."— *s* 140–20.

4 : 29　"Come, see a man, which told me all things that ever I did : is not this the Christ ?"— *sp* 85–12.

4 : 29　"Is not this the Christ ?"— *s* 133–4.

5 : 14　"Thou art whole !"— *p* 391–5.

5 : 17　"My Father worketh hitherto, and I work."— *sp* 79–19.

5 : 18　"himself equal with God,"— *s* 133–24.

5 : 19　"Then answered Jesus and said unto them : Verily, verily I say unto you, the Son can do nothing of himself, but what he seeth the Father do : for what things soever He doeth, these also doeth the Son likewise."— *b* 305–15.

5 : 26　"Life in Himself,"— *o* 357–29.

6 : 33 }
6 : 50 }　"which cometh down from heaven,"— *a* 35–26.

6 : 63　"It is the spirit that quickeneth ; the flesh profiteth nothing."— *o* 356–15.

6 : 70　"Have not I chosen you twelve, and one of you is a devil?"— *g* 554–**22.**

7 : 16, 17　"My doctrine is not mine, but His that sent me. If any man will do His will, he shall know of the doctrine, whether it be of God, or whether I speak of myself."— *s* 109–28.

7 : 23　"every whit whole."— *p* 371–31.

7 : 24　"judge righteous judgment,"— *t* 444–18.

8 : 11　"Go, and sin no more."— *pr* 11–4.

8 : 32　Ye shall know the truth, and the truth shall make you free.— iii–*.

8 : 43, 44　"Why do ye not understand my speech? Even because ye cannot hear my word. Ye are of your father, the devil [evil], and the lusts of your father ye will do. He was a murderer from the beginning, and abode not in the truth, because there is no truth in him. When he speaketh a lie, he speaketh of his own : for he is a liar, and the father of it."— *b* 292–20.

8 : 44　"He was a murderer from the beginning,…he is a liar and the father of it."— *ap* 580–30.

8 : 44　"a murderer from the beginning."— *sp* 89–31 ; *p* 441–32 ; *g* 539–3.

8 : 44　"Ye are of your father, the devil."— *g* 554–25.

8 : 44　"He is a liar, and the father of it."— *g* 554–21.

8 : 44　"a liar, and the father of it."— *o* 357–7.

8 : 45, 46　*And because I tell you the truth, ye believe me not. Which of you convinceth me of sin? And if I say the truth, why do ye not believe me?*— *o* 341–*.

8 : 51, 52　*Verily, verily, I say unto you, If a man keep my saying, he shall never see death. Then said the Jews unto him, Now we know that thou hast a devil.*— *sp* 70–*.

8 : 51　"If a man keep my saying, he shall never see death !"— *f* 217–12 ; *p* 428–7 ; 429–31 ; 438–7.

8 : 58　"Before Abraham was, I am ;"— *b* 333–29.

John

10 : 13　"The hireling fleeth, because he is an hireling, and careth not for the sheep."— *t* 464–26.

10 : 30　"I and my Father are one."— *a* 26–12 ; *b* 315–3 ; 333–29 ; *o* 361–15.

11 : 11　"Our friend Lazarus sleepeth ; but I go, that I may awake him out of sleep."— *sp* 75–12.

11 : 25　"the resurrection and the life"— *a* 31–16 ; *b* 292–7.

11 : 26　"Whosoever liveth and believeth in me shall never die,"— *ph* 170–10 ; *b* 315–1 ; (*see also b* 324–32).

11 : 42　"I knew that Thou hearest me always ;"— *s* 134–26.

12 : 38　"the arm of the Lord"— *a* 24–11.

14 : 6　"I am the way, the truth, and the life."— 26–11 ; *b* 320–3.

14 : 6　"the way, the truth, and the life,"— *o* 353–10.

14 : 6　"I am the way."— *b* 286–11.

14 : 6　"the way."— *a* 30–13 ; 39–15 ; 46–25 ; *r* 482–15 ; *g* 535–18.

14 : 6　"No man cometh unto the Father [the divine Principle of being] but by me,"— *b* 286–9.

14 : 12　"He that believeth on me, the works that I do shall he do also; . . . because I go unto my Father,"— *pr* 14–19.

14 : 12　"He that believeth on me, the works that I do shall he do also."— *a* 42–30 ; 52–27 ; *sp* 93–4 ; *b* 326–4.

14 : 15　"If ye love me, keep my commandments."— *pr* 4–11 ; *a* 25–20 ; *f* 241–21.

14 : 16　"He shall give you another Comforter, that he may abide with you *forever*."— *a* 55–27.

14 : 26　"But the Comforter…shall teach you all things." — *c* 271–20.

14 : 28　"My Father is greater than I."— *b* 333–30.

15 : 18　"If the world hate you, ye know that it hated me before it hated you ;"— *b* 317–12.

15 : 25　"They hated me without a cause."— *ap* 564–27.

16 : 2, 3　"They shall put you out of the synagogues ; yea, the time cometh, that whosoever killeth you will think that he doeth God service ; and these things will they do unto you, because they have not known the Father nor me."— *a* 31–30.

17 : 3　"This is life eternal, that they might know Thee, the only true God, and Jesus Christ, whom Thou hast sent."— *p* 410–7.

17 : 3　"This is life eternal,"— *p* 410–4.

17 : 20　"Neither pray I for these alone, but for them also which shall believe on me [understand me] through their word."— *b* 271–17.

17 : 20　"through their word."— *a* 38–20.

18 : 11　"Put up thy sword."— *a* 48–23.

18 : 38　"What is Truth,"— *a* 48–26 ; *f* 223–14.

19 : 6, 7　"Crucify him, crucify him . . . by our law he ought to die, because he made himself the Son of God." — *sp* 94–9.

19 : 6　"Crucify him !"— *s* 134–2.

19 : 7　"He made himself the Son of God,"— *f* 203–9.

19 : 24　"They parted my raiment among them, and for my vesture they did cast lots."— *f* 242–23.

19 : 30　"He bowed his head, and gave up the ghost ;"— *gl* 598–11.

Acts

16 : 31　"Believe . . . and thou shalt be saved !"— *a* 23–29.

17 : 23　"to the unknown God"— *p* 428–15 ; *gl* 596–7.

17 : 23　"Whom therefore ye ignorantly worship, Him declare I unto you."— *gl* 596–8.

17 : 23　"ignorantly worship,"— *p* 428–16.

17 : 28　"For in Him we live, and move, and have our being."— *o* 361–19 ; *f* 208–5.

17 : 28　"live, and move, and have our being,"— *g* 536–13.

17 : 28　"For we are also His offspring."— *b* 332–8.

20 : 24　"None of these things move me."— *o* 343–10.

22 : 28　"I was free born."— *f* 227–17.

23 : 3　"Sittest thou to judge . . . after the law, and commandest . . . to be smitten contrary to the law ?"— *p* 435–29.

23 : 29　"worthy of death, or of bonds."— *p* 434–29.

24 : 25　"Go thy way for this time ; when I have a convenient season I will call for thee."— *a* 40–6.

26 : 31　"worthy of death, or of bonds."— *p* 434–29.

Romans

1 : 20　"For the invisible things of Him, from the creation of the world, are clearly seen, being understood by the things that are made."— *r* 479–30.

2 : 5　"wrath against the day of wrath."— *b* 339–14.

2 : 23　"Through breaking the law, dishonorest thou God ?" — *o* 349–5.

3 : 4　"Let God be true, but every [material] man a liar." — *r* 471–20.

3 : 4　"but every [mortal] man a liar."— *s* 113–24.

5 : 10　"For if, when we were enemies, we were reconciled to God by the [seeming] death of His Son, much more, being reconciled, we shall be saved by his life."— *a* 45–10.

5 : 20　"much more abound."— *f* 202–26.

7 : 19　"The good that I would, I do not : but the evil which I would not, *that I do*."— *c* 263–17.

Romans

8 : 2 "The law of the Spirit of life in Christ Jesus hath made me free from the law of sin and death."— *f* 244–11.

8 : 6 "To be spiritually minded is life."— *sp* 95–6.

8 : 7–9 "The carnal mind is enmity against God ; for it is not subject to the law of God, neither indeed can be. So then they that are in the flesh cannot please God. But ye are not in the flesh, but in the Spirit, if so be that the spirit of God dwell in you."— *g* 534–18.

8 : 7 "The carnal mind is enmity against God."— *s* 131–9.

8 : 7 "neither indeed can be ;"— *r* 478–31.

8 : 11 *But if the spirit of Him that raised up Jesus from the dead dwell in you, He that raised up Christ from the dead shall also quicken your mortal bodies by His spirit that dwelleth in you.*— *o* 341–*.

8 : 21 "glorious liberty of the children of God,"— *f* 227–24.

8 : 22, 23 *For we know that the whole creation groaneth and travaileth in pain together until now. And not only they, but ourselves also, which have the firstfruits of the Spirit, even we ourselves groan within ourselves, waiting for the adoption, to wit, the redemption of our body.*— *c* 255–*.

8 : 28 "All things work together for good to them that love God,"— *t* 444–4.

8 : 31 "If God be for us, who can be against us?"— *f* 238–10.

8 : 38, 39 "Neither death, nor life, . . . nor things present, nor things to come, nor height, nor depth, nor any other creature, shall be able to separate us from the love of God."— *b* 304–5.

10 : 2 "a zeal . . . not according to knowledge"— *pr* 7–11.

10 : 14, 15 "How shall they hear without a preacher? and how shall they preach, except they be sent?"— *c* 271–31.

11 : 34 "the mind of the Lord,"— *b* 291–18.

12 : 1 "Present your bodies a living sacrifice, holy, acceptable unto God, which is your reasonable service."— *b* 325–21.

12 : 1 "holy, acceptable unto God,"— *a* 34–4.

13 : 1 "powers that be."— *f* 249–9.

13 : 10 "is the fulfilling of the law,"— *p* 435–20.

13 : 12 "the night is far spent, the day is at hand"— *ph* 174–12.

14 : 1 "doubtful disputations."— *o* 342–1.

14 : 16 "be evil spoken of,"— *pr* 4–25.

I Corinthians

1 : 17 *For Christ sent me not to baptize, but to preach the gospel.*— *a* 18–*.

2 : 2 "For I determined not to know anything among you, save Jesus Christ, and him crucified."— *ph* 200–25.

2 : 2 "Christ, and him crucified."— *a* 39–7.

2 : 9 "eye hath not seen nor ear heard."— *t* 459–2.

2 : 9 "eye hath not seen,"— *g* 554–1.

7 : 34 "She that is married careth . . . how she may please her husband,"— *m* 58–31.

8 : 5 "gods many and lords many."— *b* 280–16 ; *yl* 580–8.

8 : 5 "gods many,"— *n* 388–10.

10 : 25 "asking no question for conscience sake."— *r* 222–30.

11 : 26 "As often as ye eat this bread, and drink this cup, ye do show the Lord's death till he come."— *a* 31–22.

13 : 5 "seeketh not her own."— *g* 538–11.

13 : 7 "hopeth all things, endureth all things,"— *pref* xii–23.

15 : 14 "If Christ [Truth] be not risen, then is our preaching vain." — *b* 324–27.

15 : 22 "As in Adam [error] all die, even so in Christ [Truth] shall all be made alive."— *g* 545–31.

15 : 26 "The last enemy that shall be destroyed is death"— *p* 427–19.

15 : 26 "the last enemy that shall be destroyed,"— *f* 210–9.

15 : 50 "Flesh and blood cannot inherit the kingdom of God."— *b* 321–4.

15 : 52 "in the twinkling of an eye,"— *b* 291–6.

15 : 54 "when this corruptible shall have put on incorruption, and this mortal shall have put on immortality, then shall be brought to pass the saying that is written, Death is swallowed up in victory."— *s* 164–25 ; *r* 496–24.

15 : 54 "put on immortality."— *c* 262–8.

15 : 55 "Where is thy victory?"— *r* 496–23.

15 : 56 "The sting of death is sin ; and the strength of sin is the law,"— *r* 496–20.

II Corinthians

3 : 17 "Where the Spirit of the Lord is, there is liberty."— *f* 227–18 ; *r* 481–4.

4 : 4 "the god of this world,"— *an* 103–3.

5 : 1 "eternal in the heavens."— *t* 454–9.

5 : 8 "willing rather to be absent from the body, and to be present with the Lord."— *f* 216–29 ; *p* 383–10 ; *gl* 581–25.

II Corinthians

5 : 8 "absent from the body"— *pr* 14–3.

5 : 8 "present with the Lord"— *pr* 14–4, 6.

5 : 8 "with the Lord"— *pr* 14–9.

5 : 16 "Henceforth know we no man after the flesh !"— *f* 217–13.

5 : 17 "all things are become new."— *f* 201–9.

6 : 2 "Behold, *now* is the accepted time ; behold, *now* is the day of salvation,"— *sp* 93–7.

6 : 2 "*Now*," cried the apostle, "is the accepted time ; behold, *now* is the day of salvation,"— *a* 39–18.

6 : 14 "What communion hath light with darkness?— *g* 539–24.

6 : 15 And what concord hath Christ with Belial?"— *f* 216–26 ; *g* 539–25.

6 : 17 "Come out from among them, and be ye separate,"— *f* 238–6.

Galatians

1 : 11, 12 *But I certify you, brethren, that the gospel which was preached of me is not after man. For I neither received it of man, neither was I taught it, but by the revelation of Jesus Christ.*— *s* 107–*.

1 : 15, 16 "But when it pleased God, who separated me from my mother's womb, and called me by His grace, . . . I conferred not with flesh and blood."— *r* 478–27.

5 : 7 "Who did hinder you, that ye should not obey the truth?"— *b* 326–21.

5 : 16 "Walk in the Spirit, and ye shall not fulfil the lust of the flesh."— *f* 223–2.

5 : 17 "The flesh lusteth against the Spirit, and the Spirit against the flesh."— *o* 347–1.

5 : 17 "flesh lusteth against the Spirit."— *ph* 167–20.

5 : 19 "Now the works of the flesh are manifest, which are these ; Adultery, fornication, uncleanness, lasciviousness,— *an* 106–20.

5 : 20, 21 idolatry, *witchcraft*, hatred, variance, emulations, wrath, strife, seditions, heresies, envyings, murders, drunkenness, revellings and such like : of the which I tell you before, as I have also told you in time past, that they which do such things shall not inherit the kingdom of God. *an* 106–22.

5 : 22, 23 But the fruit of the Spirit is love, joy, peace, longsuffering, gentleness, goodness, faith, meekness, temperance : against such there is no law,"— *an* 106–26.

5 : 24 *And they that are Christ's have crucified the flesh with the affections and lusts.*— *a* 18–*.

6 : 3 "For if a man think himself to be something, when he is nothing, he deceiveth himself."— *o* 345–26.

6 : 7 "Whatsoever a man soweth, that shall he also reap." *p* 405–17 ; *g* 537–13.

6 : 9 "not be weary in well doing."— *sp* 79–29.

Ephesians

2 : 12 "having no hope, and without God in the world ;"— *r* 480–31.

3 : 7 "the gift of the grace of God given unto me by the effectual working of His power."— *s* 108–3.

4 : 13 "we all come in the unity of the faith, and of the knowledge of the Son of God, unto a perfect man, unto the measure of the stature of the fulness of Christ."— *g* 519–13.

6 : 12 "spiritual wickedness in high places."— *ap* 563–30.

Philippians

2 : 5 "Let this Mind be in you, which was also in Christ Jesus."— *b* 276–8.

2 : 5 "Mind . . . which was also in Christ Jesus"— *f* 243–10.

2 : 12 "Work out your own salvation with fear and trembling."— *sp* 99–5 ; *p* 442–25.

2 : 12 "Work out your own salvation,"— *a* 22–11.

2 : 12 "own salvation, with fear and trembling."— *a* 23–26.

2 : 13 "for it is God which worketh in you both to will and to do of His good pleasure."— *sp* 99–7.

3 : 13 "forgetting those things which are behind."— *o* 353–23.

Colossians

1 : 10 *That ye might walk worthy of the Lord unto all pleasing, being fruitful in every good work, and increasing in the knowledge of God.*— *fr* 600–*.

3 : 3 "hid with Christ in God,"— *b* 325–17 ; *t* 445–14.

3 : 4 "When Christ, who is our life, shall appear [be manifested], then shall ye also appear [be manifested] with him in glory."— *b* 325–10.

3 : 9 "put off the old man."— *ph* 172–22.

3 : 9 "off the old man with his deeds,"— *c* 262–7.

I Thessalonians

4 : 3 "For this is the will of God."— *gl* 597–22.

5 : 17 "pray without ceasing."— *pr* 15–21.

5 : 19, 20 "Quench not the Spirit. Despise not prophesyings."— *r* 490–19.

5 : 21 "prove all things ; [and] hold fast that which is good."— *t* 464–19.

II Thessalonians
3 : 13   "be not weary in well doing." — *a* 22–14.

I Timothy
2 : 5   "There is one God, and one mediator between God and men, the man Christ Jesus." — *b* 332–16.

II Timothy
2 : 12   "he also will deny us." — *pr* 6–2.
4 : 2   "Reprove, rebuke, exhort with all longsuffering and doctrine." — *t* 443–21.
4 : 7   "I have fought a good fight . . . I have kept the faith," — *a* 21–2.

Hebrews
1 : 3   "the brightness of His [God's] glory, and the express [expressed] image of His person [infinite Mind]." — *b* 313–10.
1 : 3   "Who, being a brightness from His glory, and an image of His being." — *b* 313–21.
    (The above reference is from the translation of the late Rev. George R. Noyes, D.D.)
1 : 3   "express image" — *b* 313–12.
1 : 9   "loved righteousness and hated iniquity." — *b* 313–18.
1 : 9   Therefore God, even thy God, hath anointed thee With the oil of gladness above thy fellows. —*b* 313–7.
4 : 9   "There remaineth therefore a rest to the people of God" — *b* 288–18.
4 : 12   "the joints and marrow," — *p* 423–13.
8 : 5   "according to the pattern showed to thee in the mount." — *f* 236–16.
10 : 19   "to enter into the holiest," — *r* 481–6.
11 : 1   "The substance of things hoped for, the evidence of things not seen." — *r* 468–20.
11 : 1   "the *substance* of things hoped for." — *b* 279–4.
11 : 10   "a city which hath foundations." — *ap* 575–12.
11 : 10   "whose builder and maker is God." — *p* 428–13.
11 : 38   "of whom the world was not worthy." — *a* 28–30.
12 : 1   "Let us lay aside every weight, and the sin which doth so easily beset us, and let us run with patience the race that is set before us ;" — *a* 20–27.
12 : 6   "Whom the Lord loveth He chasteneth." — *f* 241–1.
13 : 2   "angels unawares." — *b* 299–17.
13 : 8   "the same yesterday, and to-day, and forever ;" — *pr* 2–32 ; *s* 112–19 ; *f* 249–18 ; *b* 283–7 ; *g* 546–4.

James
1 : 4   "have her perfect work." — *t* 454–24.
1 : 12   "Blessed is the man that endureth [overcometh] temptation : for when he is tried, [proved faithful], he shall receive the crown of life, which the Lord hath promised to them that love him." — *c* 267–28.
1 : 13   "God cannot be tempted with evil, neither tempteth He any man." — *g* 527–12.
1 : 27   "Pure religion and undefiled before God and the Father, is this, To visit the fatherless and widows in their affliction, and to keep himself unspotted from the world." — *m* 64–4.
2 : 18   "Show me thy faith without thy works, and I will show thee my faith by my works." — *o* 343–4 ; *r* 487–25.
2 : 26   "Faith without works is dead." — *a* 23–15.
3 : 11   "Doth a fountain send forth at the same place sweet water and bitter?" — *b* 287–12.
4 : 3   "Ye ask, and receive not, because ye ask amiss, that ye may consume it upon your lusts." — *pr* 10–27.
4 : 3   "ye ask amiss." — *pr* 10–32.
5 : 15   "The prayer of faith shall save the sick," — *pr* 12–1.

I Peter
4 : 8   "cover the multitude of sins." — *pr* 8–19.
5 : 8   "adversary." — *gl* 581–2.

II Peter
3 : 8   "one day is with the Lord as a thousand years." — *g* 504–22 ; *gl* 598–21.

I John
1 : 1, 3   *That which was from the beginning, which we have heard, which we have seen with our eyes, which we have looked upon, and our hands have handled, of the Word of life, . . . That which we have seen and heard declare we unto you, that ye also may have fellowship with us : and truly our fellowship is with the Father, and with His Son Jesus Christ.* — *b* 268–*.
3 : 8   "destroy the *works* of the devil." — *pr* 5–30 ; *r* 474–30.
3 : 23   "Love one another" — *ap* 572–6.
4 : 8   "God is love." — *pr* 6–17 ; *b* 320–1.
4 : 18   "There is no fear in Love ; but perfect Love casteth out fear. . . . He that feareth is not made perfect in Love." — *p* 410–18.
4 : 18   "perfect Love casteth out fear." — *p* 373–18 ; 406–9.
4 : 20   "He that loveth not his brother whom he hath seen, how can he love God whom he hath not seen?" — *p* 366–14.

Revelation
1 : 3   *Blessed is he that readeth, and they that hear the words of this prophecy, and keep those things which are written therein : for the time is at hand.* — *ap* 558–*.
1 : 6   "kings and priests unto God." — *s* 141–20.
1 : 17, 18   "I am the first and the last : I am he that liveth, and was dead [not understood] ; and, behold, I am alive for evermore, — *b* 334–25.
3 : 7, 8   *These things saith He that is holy, He that is true, He that hath the key of David, He that openeth, and no man shutteth ; and shutteth, and no man openeth ; I know thy works : behold, I have set before thee an open door, and no man can shut it.* — *k* 499–* ; *gl* 579–*.
5 : 5   "the lion of the tribe of Juda," — *g* 514–10.
10 : 1, 2   And I saw another mighty angel come down from heaven, clothed with a cloud : and a rainbow was upon his head, and his face was as it were the sun, and his feet as pillars of fire : and he had in his hand a little book open : and he set his right foot upon the sea, and his left foot on the earth. — *ap* 558–3.
10 : 2   "a little book," — *ap* 559–1.
10 : 2   "right foot" — *ap* 559–3.
10 : 3   "as when a lion roareth." *ap* 559–11.
10 : 3   "seven thunders" — *ap* 559–13.
10 : 8, 9   "Go and take the little book. . . . Take it, and eat it up ; and it shall make thy belly bitter, but it shall be in thy mouth sweet as honey." — *ap* 559–17.
12 : 1   And there appeared a great wonder in heaven ; a woman clothed with the sun, and the moon under her feet, and upon her head a crown of twelve stars. — *ap* 560–6.
12 : 2   And she being with child cried, travailing in birth, and pained to be delivered. — *ap* 562–22.
12 : 3   And there appeared another wonder in heaven ; and behold a great red dragon, having seven heads and ten horns, and seven crowns upon his heads. — *ap* 562–29.
12 : 4   And his tail drew the third part of the stars of heaven, and did cast them to the earth : and the dragon stood before the woman which was ready to be delivered, for to devour her child as soon as it was born. — *ap* 563–23.
12 : 5   And she brought forth a man child, who was to rule all nations with a rod of iron : and her child was caught up unto God, and to His throne. — *ap* 565–6.
12 : 6   And the woman fled into the wilderness, where she hath a place prepared of God. — *ap* 565–29.
12 : 7, 8   And there was war in heaven : Michael and his angels fought against the dragon ; and the dragon fought, and his angels, and prevailed not ; neither was their place found any more in heaven. —*ap* 566–25.
12 : 9   And the great dragon was cast out, that old serpent, called the devil, and Satan, which deceiveth the whole world : he was cast out into the earth, and his angels were cast out with him. — *ap* 567–14.
12 : 10–12   And I heard a loud voice saying in heaven, Now is come salvation, and strength, and the kingdom of our God, and the power of His Christ : for the accuser of our brethren is cast down, which accused them before our God day and night. And they overcame him by the blood of the Lamb, and by the word of their testimony ; and they loved not their lives unto the death. Therefore rejoice, ye heavens, and ye that dwell in them. Woe to the inhabiters of the earth and of the sea! for the devil is come down unto you, having great wrath, because he knoweth that he hath but a short time. — *ap* 568–13.
12 : 13   And when the dragon saw that he was cast unto the earth, he persecuted the woman which brought forth the man child. — *ap* 569–29.
12 : 13   "cast unto the earth" — *ap* 567–23.
12 : 15, 16   And the serpent cast out of his mouth water as a flood, after the woman, that he might cause her to be carried away of the flood. And the earth helped the woman, and the earth opened her mouth, and swallowed up the flood which the dragon cast out of his mouth. — *ap* 570–8.
13 : 8   "the Lamb slain from the foundation of the world," — *b* 334–21.
19 : 17   "angel standing in the sun." — *ap* 561–8.
20 : 6   "On such the second death hath no power." — *b* 290–14.
20 : 6   "the second death hath no power." — *sp* 77–12.
21 : 1   "And I saw a new heaven and a new earth : for the first heaven and the first earth were passed away ; and there was no more sea." — *g* 536–2 ; *ap* 572–20.
21 : 1   "a new heaven and a new earth." — *sp* 91–1.
21 : 2   "New Jerusalem, coming down from God, out of heaven," — *ap* 574–13.

Revelation

21 : 2   "down from God, out of heaven," — *ap* 575–8.
21 : 9   And there came unto me one of the seven angels which had the seven vials full of the seven last plagues, and talked with me, saying, Come hither, I will show thee the bride, the Lamb's wife. — *ap* 574–6.
21 : 9   "the bride" — *ap* 561–13.
21 : 14   "the Lamb" — *ap* 561–13.
21 : 16   "lieth foursquare." — *ap* 574–16 ; 575–8.
21 : 22   And I saw no temple therein : for the Lord God Almighty and the Lamb are the temple of it. — *ap* 576–10.
21 : 22   "no temple [body] therein" — *ap* 576–20.

Revelation

21 : 23   "is the light thereof." — *ap* 558–15.
21 : 25   "and the gates of it shall not be shut at all by day : for there shall be no night there." — *ap* 575–19.
21 : 27   "defileth, . . . or maketh a lie." — *ap* 577–26.
21 : 27   "worketh abomination or maketh a lie." — *gl* 588–4.
22 : 2   "tree of life," — *p* 426–13.
22 : 2   "The leaves of the tree were for the healing of the nations." — *p* 406–1.
22 : 5   "there shall be no night there." — *gl* 584–7.
22 : 5   "no night there." — *r* 475–1.
22 : 17   "The Spirit and the bride say, Come ! . . . and whosoever will, let him take the water of life freely." — *g* 548–1.

A Complete
CONCORDANCE
to the Writings of
MARY BAKER EDDY
other than Science and Health with Key to the Scriptures

A Complete
CONCORDANCE

to the Writings of

MARY BAKER EDDY

other than Science and Health with Key to the Scriptures

Together with an Index to the Chapter Sub-titles, Headings,
and Titles of the Poems, and an Index to the Scriptural Quotations
contained in these Writings as finally revised
and arranged by their author

MARY BAKER EDDY

Discoverer and Founder of Christian Science

Marcas Registradas

Published by

THE FIRST CHURCH OF CHRIST, SCIENTIST

in Boston, Massachusetts, U.S.A.

Important Notice

If the user of this book does not readily find the
reference desired, the Compiler's Preface and List
of Abbreviations should be consulted.

The method employed in the Compilation of this
Concordance is carefully set forth in the Preface,
and instructions are given as to where certain
references may be found.

Compiler's Preface

The plan of this Concordance to the WRITINGS OF MARY BAKER EDDY, other than SCIENCE AND HEALTH, follows in every detail the plan of the Concordance to SCIENCE AND HEALTH, which was compiled in 1902 under the personal direction and supervision of MRS. EDDY. It therefore (with the exceptions noted below) contains every noun, verb, adjective, and adverb in the above-mentioned books, together with such pronouns, prepositions, and conjunctions as were deemed of sufficient importance to be introduced.

The books are indexed in the order in which they stand in the list of abbreviations on page viii.

The words are indexed in each book by page and line numbers. The titles of the poems in "Poems," and the titles of the chapters in the other books are not numbered; but all other lines including chapter sub-titles, headings and Scriptural quotations are numbered.

The numbers indicating page and line refer to the word under consideration and not necessarily to the beginning of the line quoted. The letters preceding some of the numbers are abbreviations of the titles of the books indexed, and indicate the books in which these references are to be found. Vacant spaces below the abbreviations indicate that the references are from the same book until a different abbreviation appears.

A special feature of the work is to be found in the fact that every noun of frequent occurrence is provided with sub-titles. These sub-titles are arranged in alphabetical order, under their respective nouns, and consist of adjectives or other qualifying words or phrases, preserving in every case the exact phraseology of the books from which they are taken. By this method all that is said on any given subject will be found grouped in one place.

For example: Man is often referred to as the "image and likeness" of God. More than fifty references to this subject will be found in the sub-title "and likeness" under the principal title "image." The sub-titles also enable those who are familiar with the text to look up passages by means of such words as God, Life, Truth, Love, Mind, matter, error, etc., without searching through several hundred references.

A few adjectives also, such as human, material, mortal, spiritual, etc., are furnished with sub-titles.

Certain words occurring in some places as nouns, are used in other places as verbs or adjectives. For example: the word "healing" is used as a noun, an adjective, and a participle. All such words appearing more than fifty times are classified and grouped under their respective parts of speech. If used less than fifty times in all, these words are not so separated.

The capitalization used in the sixteen books indexed presented many puzzling problems. Where a word referred to Deity when capitalized, and to humanity when not capitalized, it has been indexed under both headings, as for example: Life, life; Truth, truth; Love, love. The two headings have also been retained where the capitalization gave the word a different signification, as in such cases as Master, master; Physician, physician, where the capital referred to Christ Jesus. But where the word began a sentence, or was capitalized simply for emphasis, as in the headings in the Manual, or in the chapter sub-titles in the other books, and the capital did not change the meaning, the word has been indexed under the lower case heading only. For example: "Editor" and "editor" both appear under "editor." In some cases dual headings have been employed, as for example: "Masonic and masonic"; "Massachusetts and Mass."

All references to the Discoverer and Founder of Christian Science are arranged as sub-titles under the title "Eddy." Mrs. Eddy's signatures to various documents and communications will be found under "Eddy-signatures." A few references concerning Mrs. Eddy's childhood and the members of her family are indexed under "Baker" and "Glover."

For all Chapter Sub-titles, Headings, and Titles of the Poems in their entirety see Appendix "A." For individual words in same, consult the main body of the book.

Every Scriptural quotation is indexed under every important word in it, in the same manner as other words, and is followed by the book, chapter, and verse where it may be found in the Bible. A separate index of all the books, chapters, and verses of the Bible from which passages in quotation marks have been taken for use in the Writings of Mary Baker Eddy other than Science and Health will be found in Appendix "B."

All passages quoted by Mrs. Eddy from other authors, and also reports of church officials, letters, editorials, and other newspaper articles, etc., not written by Mrs. Eddy, are indexed in the usual way; but all such references may be identified by the * which precedes the lines taken from these sources. All signatures to documents not written by Mrs. Eddy will be found under the title "signatures."

The list of "Church Officers" on page 21, and also the "Application Forms," "Orders of Services," and "Deeds of Trusts" in the Appendix to the Church Manual, and the article entitled "Concord, N.H., to Mrs. Eddy and Mrs. Eddy's Reply" are indexed under their headings only. In indexing the Manual, the 1914 edition was used, and attention is called to the fact that the first three lines on page 85, are to be found at the bottom of page 84 in earlier editions. To find the name of any "Article" in the Manual consult the title "Church Manual." In these references the number of the line corresponds with the beginning of the line quoted. The names of the "Sections" will be found under the titles "Section I," "Sect. II," "Sect. III," etc.

Proper names are indexed under the surnames.

All dates containing years are indexed under "dates," and arranged chronologically; all dates containing months, but not years, are arranged chronologically under "months."

All values given in dollars and cents are indexed under "values."

All numbers consisting of one word, as "one, two, twenty, thirty, etc.," are indexed in their alphabetical places: all numbers consisting of more than one word, as "two thousand, one million, etc.," are indexed under "numbers."

Hours of the day are indicated by sub-titles under the title "time."

For the passages read from the BIBLE and SCIENCE AND HEALTH at the dedication of the extension to The Mother Church, consult "Lesson Sermon on Dedication Sunday."

Page numbers referring to SCIENCE AND HEALTH are indexed as sub-titles under "SCIENCE AND HEALTH."

All words used in the description of the organ in the original Mother Church are indexed as sub-titles under the word "organ."

Titles of more than one word, as "Falmouth and Norway Streets" are indexed in the place indicated by the first important word in the title. The above title is therefore to be found in the "F's."

The complete Concordance to all the writings of our beloved Leader and Teacher, published in book form, is embodied in the Concordance to SCIENCE AND HEALTH WITH KEY TO THE SCRIPTURES and the present volume.

ALBERT F. CONANT
Compiler

List of Abbreviations

The abbreviations made use of in this Concordance are as follows:—

BOOKS INDEXED

Mis...Miscellaneous Writings
Man...Manual of The Mother Church
Chr....Christ and Christmas
Ret....Retrospection and Introspection
Un....Unity of Good
Pul....Pulpit and Press
Rud..Rudimental Divine Science
No....No and Yes
Pan..Christian Science versus Pantheism
'00....Message to The Mother Church, June 1900
'01....Message to The Mother Church, June 1901
'02....Message to The Mother Church, June 1902

Hea...Christian Healing
Peo....The People's Idea of God
Po...:Poems
My....The First Church of Christ, Scientist, and Miscellany

These abbreviations appear at the left of the references and indicate the book in which the reference is found. Vacant space in this column following the abbreviation indicates that the references are from the same book until another abbreviation appears.

The words "Christian Science" and "Science and Health" have been abbreviated in the lines to C.S., and S. and H. respectively.

BOOKS OF THE BIBLE

Gen..........Genesis
Exod..........Exodus
Lev..........Leviticus
Deut..........Deuteronomy
Josh..........Joshua
Judg..........Judges
Ruth ....Ruth
I Sam. ......I Samuel
II Sam. .....II Samuel
I Kings......I Kings
II Kings.....II Kings
I Chron. .....I Chronicles
II Chron. .....II Chronicles
Job ....Job
Psal..........Psalms
Prov. ....Proverbs
Eccl..........Ecclesiastes

Song.........Song of Solomon
Isa. ....Isaiah
Jer. ....Jeremiah
Lam. ....Lamentations
Ezek.........Ezekiel
Dan. ....Daniel
Mic..........Micah
Hab. ....Habakkuk
Zech.........Zechariah
Mal. ....Malachi
Matt. ....Matthew
Mark........Mark
Luke ....Luke
John ....John
Acts ....Acts
Rom.........Romans

I Cor. ....I Corinthians
II Cor.......II Corinthians
Gal..........Galatians
Eph.........Ephesians
Phil.........Philippians
Col..........Colossians
I Thess. .....I Thessalonians
I Tim. ......I Timothy
II Tim. .....II Timothy
Heb. ....Hebrews
Jas. ....James
I Pet.........I Peter
II Pet.........II Peter
I John ......I John
II John .....II John
Rev. ....Revelation

A Complete

CONCORDANCE

to the Writings of

MARY BAKER EDDY

other than Science and Health

A

Aaron's
My. 127–15   even as *A·* rod swallowed up the
Abaddon
Mis. 190–28   In the Hebrew, "devil" is . . . *A·* ;
abandon
Mis. 27– 9   other systems . . . *a·* their own logic.
250–12   which in their human *a·* become
261–29   one will either *a·* his claim
My. 40–13   * *a·* their strongholds of rivalry.
249– 9   moral *a·* of hating even one's
abandoned
Mis. 393–11   Soon *a·* when the Master
Po. 51–16   Soon *a·* when the Master
My. 140–22   *a·* so soon as God's Way-shower,
abandonment
Mis. 205–25   *a·* of sin finally dissolves all
abased
My. 140–24   This instructs us how to be *a·*
abashed
Ret. 31–23   I gazed, and stood *a·*.
abate
Mis. 324– 9   footfalls *a·*, the laughter ceases
366–27   *a·* dishonesty, self-will, envy, and
Un. 54– 8   is to *a·* the fear of it ;
abated
Mis. 366–26   never have *a·* . . . self-will, envy, and
abating
Mis. 8– 2   we can aid in *a·* suffering
Abba
Mis. 184–28   saith *A·*, Father, and *is* born of
abbess
Pul. 32–13   * like any *a·* of old.
Abbott, D. D., Lyman
Pan. 12– 4   Lyman *A·*, D.D., writes,
Abel
No. 34–19   better things than that of *A·*.
Abercrombie, Dr.
Peo. 6– 3   Dr. *A·*, . . . writes : "Medicine is the
ab extra
My. 348– 6   not within but *a· e·*,
abhor
Mis. 147–21   *a·* whatever is base or unworthy ;
Po. 27– 4   I, dying, dare *a·* !"
abhors
Mis. 317–29   My soul *a·* injustice,
abide
Mis. 11– 4   to *a·* by our State statutes ;
135– 6   and if we *a·* in these,
149–30   shall *a·* steadfastly in the faith
153–30   be and *a·* with this church.
154–19   *A·* in His word,
154–20   and it shall *a·* in you ;
215–13   To *a·* by these we must first
227–21   thoughts *a·* in tabernacles of
265–24   Those who *a·* by them do well.
270–19   the Word must *a·* in us,
298–20   *A·* by the *morale* of absolute C. S.,
Man. 60–16   love should *a·* in every heart

abide
Ret. 56– 4   and that we must *a·* by them.
04–24   It is scientific to *a·* in conscious
82–16   and therein *a·*.
88–26   *a·* in such a spiritual attitude
92– 8   "If ye *a·* in me,— *John* 15 : 7.
92– 9   my words *a·* in you,— *John* 15 : 7.
Pul. 21–25   there *a·* in confidence and hope.
'01. 34–22   be steadfast, *a·* and abound in
'02. 9–20   should *a·* forever in man.
Hea. 16–10   *a·* by your statements, and abound in
Po. 43– 5   You in Him *a·*.
My. 6– 6   To *a·* in our unselfed better self
31– 5   * "*A·* with me ,"
33–15   who shall *a·* in thy — *Psal.* 15 : 1.
63–14   * to *a·* with us and enable us
107–23   *a·* under the shadow of — *Psal.* 91 : 1.
112– 7   those who *a·* in its teachings
128–19   Christian Scientists *a·* by the laws of
148– 7   be and *a·* with you henceforth.
150–23   "If ye *a·* in me,— *John* 15 : 7.
150–24   my words *a·* in you,— *John* 15 : 7.
187–16   love of God be and *a·* with you
192–14   be and *a·* with you.
227 28   I *a·* by this rule and triumph by
360–20   *A·* in fellowship with and obedience
abides
Mis. 19–21   one who *a·* by his statements
Un. 40–16   Hence Life *a·* in man,
40–17   if man *a·* in good.
'02. 9–17   and *a·* in Christlikeness.
My. 124–16   *a·* in the hearts of these hearers
160– 2   he *a·* in a right purpose,
210–15   *a·* under the shadow of the Almighty.
358– 1   C. S. *a·* by the definite rules
abideth
Mis. 111–22   but the Word of God *a·*.
367–32   and *a·* in Himself,
abiding
Mis. 26– 2   hath life *a·* in it,
100–29   *a·* faith, and affection,
135– 7   *A·* in Love, not one of you can
311–16   *a·* consciousness of health,
331– 8   Thus *a·* in Truth,
Ret. 23– 3   could be a real and *a·* rest.
My. 140– 1   *a·* spiritual understanding
abilities
Mis. 185– 7   *a·* or disabilities, pains or
ability
  and popularity
Mis. 295–19   whose *a·* and popularity
  his
No. 22–26   indicated his *a·* to cast it out.
  man's
Mis. 16–12   man's *a·* to meet them is from **God** ;
192–20   man's *a·* to prove the truth of
199– 5   thence comes man's *a·* to
  might and
Un. 42–17   might and *a·* to subdue material
  Mrs. Eddy's
My. 273– 3   * proof of Mrs. Eddy's *a·*

ability

my
| *My.* | 42–19 | * to the best of my *a*. |
| | 304–20 | he knew my *a*· as an editor. |

natural
| *Mis.* | 183–18 | but by the natural *a*·, that |

of Christians
| *Hea.* | 7–27 | *a*· of Christians to heal the sick ; |

one's
| *Ret.* | 72– 5 | it deteriorates one's *a*· to do good, |
| *No.* | 2–24 | destroys one's *a*· to heal mentally. |

our
| *Mis.* | 236–18 | to the best of our *a*·, |

student of
| *My.* | 320–10 | * and as a student of *a*·. |

their
Mis.	351– 1	called on students to test their *a*·
No.	40–19	forfeit their *a*· to heal
My.	227–16	their *a*· to cope with the claim,

this
| *My.* | 82–18 | * would seem that this *a*· |

to comply
| *Mis.* | 286– 8 | *a*· to comply with absolute Science, |

to demonstrate
Mis.	55– 5	*a*· to demonstrate to the extent
'01.	4– 9	*a*· to demonstrate Love according to
My.	242–13	forfeit your *a*· to demonstrate it.

to gain
| *Mis.* | 38– 3 | *a*· to gain and maintain health, |

to grasp
| *Man.* | 62–21 | *a*· to grasp the simpler meanings of |

to rise
| *Mis.* | 97– 2 | gives man *a*· to rise above the |

to teach
| *Hea.* | 14–23 | to reach the *a*· to teach ; |

will give the
| *Mis.* | 115–26 | God will give the *a*· to overcome |

your
| *My.* | 242–13 | or you forfeit your *a*· to |
| | 320–23 | * spoke of your *a*· without any |

| *Mis.* | 335–16 | the *a*·, in belief, of evil |

abject
| *My.* | 110–29 | made his life an *a*· failure. |

abjure
| *Mis.* | 197–29 | Let man *a*· a theory that is |
| *My.* | 97– 7 | * of the sick who *a*· medicine |

abjured
| *My.* | 139–14 | Justice, honesty, cannot be *a*· ; |

ablaze
| *My.* | 150–17 | moon *a*· with her mild glory. |

able
Mis.	5– 8	*a*· to produce perfect health
	7–23	*a*· to reach many homes
	26–17	Matter is not intelligent, and thus *a*·
	42–16	*a*· to communicate with and to
	45– 6	is *a*· to do more than to heal a
	54–25	*Because none of your students have been a· to*
	93– 1	and by reason thereof is *a*· to
	114–32	and to be *a*·, through Christ,
	126–18	*a*· editors of *The C. S. Journal*,
	133–28	It affords me great joy to be *a*· to attest
	153–21	May you be *a*· to say,
	185– 2	*a*· to discern fully and
	200–20	Christians to-day should be *a*· to say,
	260– 4	and found *a*· to heal them.
	300–30	pays whatever he is *a*· to pay
	338– 4	to be *a*· to lift others
	342–32	*a*· to make us wise unto salvation!
	352– 6	it is *a*· for the first time to discern
	352– 8	*a*· to behold the facts of Truth
	359–16	insomuch as he was *a*· to do this ;
Ret.	7–15	* As a lawyer he was *a*· and learned,
	44–14	*a*· to maintain the church
	84–20	and by reason thereof is *a*· to
	90–12	they were *a*· to fulfil his behest
Un.	1–17	practically *a*· to testify, by their lives,
	7–13	I have been *a*· to replace
	24–24	*a*· to see, taste, hear, feel, smell.
	48–20	faintly *a*· to demonstrate Truth
Pul.	29–24	* The discourse was *a*·,
	47– 2	* *a*· lectures upon Scriptural topics.
Rud.	14–15	only from those who were *a*· to pay.
'01.	4–23	should be *a*· to explain
Po.	79– 7	God *a*· is To raise up seed
My.	15–15	all that you are *a*· to bear now,
	28– 1	* *a*· to make this announcement
	29–12	* will ever be *a*· to forget.
	29–29	* *a*· to wait patiently for the
	40– 3	* church *a*· to give more adequate
	51–14	* who is so *a*· as she to lead us
	99– 3	* faith which is *a*· to raise its
	99– 7	* cult *a*· to promote its faith with
	121–10	*a*· to carry navies,

able
My.	137–30	*a*· to select the Trustees I need
	145–12	* I do not feel *a*· to keep about.
	147–20	*a*· to heal both sin and disease.
	156– 5	persuaded that He is *a*·'' — *II Tim.* 1 : 12.
	156– 5	''*a*· to do exceeding — *Eph.* 3 : 20.
	156– 6	''*a*· to make all grace — *II Cor.* 9 : 8.
	156– 9	''*a*· to keep that which — *II Tim.* 1 : 12.
	162–17	was not *a*· to finish.'' — *Luke* 14 : 30.
	165–20	*a*· to impart truth, health, and
	177– 9	I am quite *a*· to take the trip
	196–13	*a*· also to bridle the — *Jas.* 3 : 2.
	228–29	*a*· to keep that which — *II Tim.* 1 : 12.
	273– 6	* fortunate in being *a*· to point to
	296– 2	The *a*· discourse of our ''learned
	316–22	under Mr. Flower's *a*· guardianship
	323–27	* not have been *a*· to appreciate

ablution
| *Peo.* | 9– 3 | not an *a*· of the body, |

ably
Man.	44–21	these periodicals are *a*· edited
Ret.	42– 9	lectured so *a*· on Scriptural topics
No.	45–18	these rights are *a*· vindicated
My.	125–14	Principle they so *a*· vindicate,

abnegation
| *My.* | 134– 1 | *a*·, constant battle against the |

abnormal
Mis.	17–25	normal or *a*· material conditions
	32–10	The query is *a*·, when
	200– 4	and evil as the *a*· ;
Man.	41– 4	is *a*· in a Christian Scientist,

abode
Mis.	174–16	*a*· of Spirit, the realm of the real.
Un.	32–22	truth *a*· not in you. — *see John* 8 : 44.
Rud.	7–17	truth *a*· not in him.'' — *see John* 8 : 44.
No.	24–23	truth *a*· not in him.'' — *see John* 8 : 44.
	36– 7	It *a*· forever above,
Pan.	5–14	*a*· not in the truth — *John* 8 : 44.

abolish
| *Mis.* | 286–15 | To *a*· marriage at this period, |
| *My.* | 141–16 | * *a*· its famous communion seasons. |

abolished
Mis.	258– 4	*a*· this unrelenting false claim
Peo.	10–28	when African slavery was *a*·
My.	141– 2	* chapter sub-title
	141– 5	* has been *a*· by order of
	142– 4	* *a*· the disappointment of
	241– 2	* Class teaching will not be *a*·

abolishing
| *My.* | 140–11 | * chapter sub-title |
| | 142–11 | *a*· the communion season |

abolition
| *Ret.* | 6–29 | *a*· of imprisonment for debt. |

abolitionist
| *Peo.* | 11– 4 | a new *a*· struck the keynote |

abomination
| *My.* | 229– 6 | an *a*· unto the Lord :— *Deut.* 18 : 12. |

abominations
| *My.* | 229– 7 | because of these *a*· — *Deut.* 18 : 12. |

abortive
| *Un.* | 11–10 | this mind and its *a*· laws. |
| | 44–13 | This *a*· ego, this fable of error, |

abound
Mis.	135– 6	they will *a*· in us,
'01.	33– 7	* ''Quackery and dupery do *a*·
	34–22	be steadfast, abide and *a*· in faith,
Hea.	16–10	*a*· in Love and Truth,
Po.	77– 5	Plenty and peace *a*· at Thy behest,
My.	140–24	how to be abased and how to *a*·.
	156– 7	all grace *a*· toward you ;— *II Cor.* 9 : 8.
	156– 8	*a*· to every good work,'' — *II Cor.* 9 : 8.
	182–30	*a*· in the righteousness of Love,

abounded
| *'01.* | 33– 9 | * they have fearfully *a*· ; |

abounding
My.	139– 7	its *a*·, increasing, advancing
	140– 1	this *a*· and abiding spiritual
	155– 5	*a*· in love and good works,

abounds
| *My.* | 88–15 | * its dedication *a*· in remarkable |
| | 124–15 | What more *a*· and abides in |

about
Mis.	29–17	ranks of my *a*· five thousand students.
	32– 4	*what a· that clergyman's remarks*
	47– 2	*carry a· this weight daily?*
	69–28	for information *a*· his case.
	122–12	were hanged *a*· his neck, — *Matt.* 18 : 6.
	130–10	talking *a*· it, thinking it over,
	141–17	parties concerned *a*· the legal quibble,
	143–22	within *a*· three months, donated

about

Mis.	154– 7	He will dig *a·* this little church,
	158– 6	the changes *a·* to be made.
	163– 8	Three years he went *a·* doing good.
	163–30	forever *a·* the Father's business ;
	177–13	What will you do *a·* it?
	178–15	"I think it was *a·* a year ago
	225–28	In *a·* one hour he awoke, and was hungry.
	239– 5	*a·* to commence a large class
	248–11	simple falsehoods uttered *a·* me
	266–18	assertion that I have said hard things *a·*
	271–20	Much is said at this date, 1889, *a·*
	276–10	*a·* one thousand Christian Scientists,
	277–25	Though clouds are round *a·* Him,
	281– 2	*a·* to chant hymns of victory for triumphs.
	348–18	once in *a·* seven years
	349– 4	instructions included *a·* twelve lessons,
	349–31	no pay from my church for *a·*
	349–32	put into the church-fund *a·*
	350–14	second P. M. convened in *a·* one week
	353–26	at *a·* three years of scientific age,
	370–16	twines its loving arms *a·* the
	371– 4	wandering *a·* without a leader,
	375–10	* *a·* the wonderful new book
Man.	61–24	*a·* eight or nine minutes
	104– 9	and hedge it *a·* with divine Love.
Ret.	2–28	grandmother's stories *a·* General Knox,
	4– 4	farm of *a·* five hundred acres,
	8– 3	when I was *a·* eight years old,
	9– 4	Mother told Mehitable all *a·* this
	19–21	directions to his brother masons *a·*
	20– 8	my little son, *a·* four years of age,
	24–22	withdrew from society *a·* three years,
	40–10	stood by her side *a·* fifteen minutes
	48– 6	conscientious scruples *a·* diplomas,
	51– 3	*a·* twenty thousand dollars,
	52– 4	to build a hedge round *a·* it
	89– 9	scattered *a·* in cities and villages,
	93– 1	Jesus went *a·* doing good.
	93– 3	evangelists of those days wandered *a·*.
Un.	6–16	leading questions *a·* God and sin,
	6–21	*a·* the problems of Euclid.
	6–24	our declarations *a·* sin and Deity
	28–13	The common hypotheses *a·* souls
Pul.	47–26	* so picturesque all *a·* Concord
	54–28	NOTE :— *A·* 1868, the author
	58– 4	* Coming to Boston *a·* 1880,
	68–16	* organized in this city *a·* a year ago.
	69– 1	* came to Baltimore *a·* three years ago
	69– 3	* *a·* eighteen months ago.
	69–17	* to explain fully all *a·* it,
	71–12	* THE NEWS *A·* MRS. MARY BAKER EDDY,
	72–27	* going *a·* doing good and healing
	73– 2	* why should we worry ourselves *a·*
	86– 2	* *a·* six inches in each dimension,
Rud.	7–25	bring *a·* alteration of opinion
	8–20	also uttering falsehood *a·* good.
	11–28	He never talks *a·* the
No.	22– 1	"driven *a·* by every— *see Eph.* 4 : 14.
	26– 5	infantile talk *a·* Mind-healing
'01.	10 20	one hundred falsehoods told *a·* it
	21– 9	* ideas *a·* the spiritual world
	32– 9	busy *a·* their Master's business,
	33–12	* that they were *a·* to die."
'02.	13– 7	*a·* one hundred and twenty thousand
	13–14	*a·* one half the price paid,
	14– 1	*A·* five thousand dollars
Hea.	0– 2	We should have no anxiety *a·*
	14– 3	in fine, much ado *a·* nothing.
	16–16	A word *a·* the five personal senses,
My.	vi– 7	* knows anything *a·* C. S. except
	24–18	* inquired *a·* the progress of the work
	27– 5	*a·* the time of our annual meeting
	29–28	* began to congregate *a·* the church
	38–12	* in *a·* twenty minutes,
	53–14	* *a·* two hundred and twenty-five.
	54–14	* were present *a·* eight hundred
	60– 2	* *a·* the early history of C. S.
	61–21	* One feature *a·* the work
	68– 6	* *a·* one mile and a half of pews.
	71– 8	* no need of fussing *a·* the underlying
	74– 7	* arrive in this city just *a·* in time
	83– 2	* of never going *a·* labelled
	87–26	* There is one thing *a·* it :
	89– 9	* needs only an open space *a·* it,
	91–13	* and shed sunshine *a·* them
	95–13	* cost them *a·* two million dollars,
	95–20	* They go *a·* telling of miracles
	98–18	* This structure cost *a·* two million
	100– 5	* cost *a·* two million dollars
	114–16	read no other book . . . for *a·* three years.
	123–18	now *a·* twenty thousand dollars.
	135–18	*a·* forty thousand members,
	137–25	before . . . I knew aught *a·* them,
	137–26	consulted Lawyer Streeter *a·* the
	145–12	* I do not feel able to keep *a·*.

about

My.	162–13	*a·* eighty thousand dollars,
	169–18	call of *a·* three thousand believers
	173–19	number of visitors, *a·* four thousand,
	223–13	questions *a·* secular affairs,
	225–11	used in writing *a·* C. S.
	241–25	* beliefs I entertained *a·* it ;
	242– 2	in your statement *a·* yourself.
	308–22	as they were *a·* to start for church.
	312–21	and died in *a·* nine days.
	313– 8	stories told . . . *a·* my father
	313–10	and *a·* persons being hired to
	314–19	*a·* to have Dr. Patterson arrested
	315– 5	* conversation with him *a·* his wife,
	319–22	* *a·* the preparation of a theme,
	319–25	* which I did *a·* the twentieth of
	320– 6	* converse *a·* you and your work,
	322–10	* *a·* the Rev. James H. Wiggin's work
	323–10	* not going to lie *a·* anything
	324– 2	* *a·* you and your work,
	328–16	* how this came *a·* in Kinston
	331– 1	*a·* accompanying her on her sad
	344–19	If I harbored that idea *a·* a
	344–21	* heading
	345–24	*a·* advice on surgical cases."
	346–12	* several turns *a·* the court-house
		(*see also* **year**)

above

Mis.	ix–17	requires strength from *a·*,
	xii– 7	lift my readers *a·* the smoke of conflict
	12– 9	*a·* all, do not fancy that
	28–18	he arose *a·* the illusion of
	34– 3	metaphysics is *a·* physics.
	53–18	*a·* the standard of metaphysics ;
	67– 2	*A·* physical wants, lie the
	68–18	Does the gentleman *a·* mentioned
	87– 1	soar *a·*, as the bird
	97– 2	gives man ability to rise *a·* the
	102–18	in modes *a·* the human.
	106–13	On to the blest *a·*,
	106–25	*a·*, beyond, methinks I hear
	107– 8	As we rise *a·* the seeming mists
	120–17	heard *a·* the din of battle,
	139–16	with a portion of the *a·* Scripture
	143– 6	*a·* the plane of matter.
	155–27	Experience and, *a·* all, *obedience,*
	158– 4	the heavens *a·* the earth
	158– 4	is His wisdom *a·* ours.
	174–12	*A·* Arcturus and his sons,
	178–12	those things which are *a·*,— *Col. 3: 1.*
	187– 5	*a·* every sense of matter,
	192–23	as the *a·* Scripture plainly declares,
	206– 5	*A·* the waves of Jordan,
	216–13	might add to the *a·* definition
	234– 4	attempt to mount *a·* error by
	242– 2	article . . . having the *a·* caption,
	255–27	metaphysics is *a·* physics.
	267– 1	to make itself heard *a·* Truth's voice.
	277– 4	but Truth will soar *a·* it,
	277– 6	trying to be heard *a·* Truth,
	279– 7	but over and *a·* it all
	282–20	the *a·* rule of mental practice.
	286– 1	The *a·* prophecy, written years ago,
	291– 7	*a·* personal motives, unworthy aims
	306–18	* a member of the *a·* organization,
	307–17	and *a·* all, God's love
	309–22	infinitely *a·* a bodily form of
	312–21	this man must have risen *a·*
	317–19	my answers to the *a·* questions.
	323– 4	celestial city *a·* all clouds,
	331–22	*a·* the frozen crust of creed
	355–18	but to lift your head *a·* it,
	357– 9	*a·* the present status of religion
	368– 9	* keeping watch *a·* His own."
	374–11	*A·* the fogs of sense and
	376–19	*a·* the horizon, in the east,
	385– 2	* *A·* the sod Find peace in God,
	391– 4	For things *a·* the floor,
	392–17	As grandly rising to the heavens *a·*.
	394–12	God-given mandate that speaks from *a·*,
	395–19	May rest *a·* my head.
	395–23	Is registered *a·*.
Man.	40–17	a Church Rule shall be read
	85–20	since receiving instruction as *a·*,
Ret.	18–17	May soar *a·* matter.
	67–13	rising *a·* corporeal personality,
	69–25	" *A·* error's awful din, blackness,
	73–14	lift thought *a·* physical personality,
	81–24	* *a·* all : To thine own self be true ;
	89–26	*A·* all, trespass not intentionally
Un.	18–16	from outside and *a·* ourselves?
	38–13	*a·* the living and true God.
	61– 1	*a·* the false, to the true evidence
Pul.	13–18	their heads *a·* the drowning wave.
	28– 4	* star of Bethlehem shines down from *a·*.

above

Pul.	28– 5	* A· this is a panel containing the
	41–24	* one hundred and twenty-six feet a· the
	42–20	* the choir gallery a· the platform,
	53–19	* a· the level of the brute,
	86–28	* Bible and the book alluded to a·,
Rud.	12– 3	A· all, he keeps unbroken the
No.	14–17	chapter sub-title
	14–26	Are frozen dogmas, . . . from a·?
	36– 7	It abode forever a·,
Pan.	2– 7	looms a· the mists of pantheism
	2– 8	higher than Mt. Ararat a· the deluge.
	6– 8	but lifteth his head a· it
	12–13	high a· the so-called laws of matter,
	13–23	who is a· all, — Eph. 4 : 6.
	14– 4	Set your affections on things a·;
'00.	5– 1	who is a· all, — Eph. 4 : 6.
	15– 4	are distinguished a· human title
'01.	18–20	teaches that . . . is a· a demonstration
	18–21	a· the grandeur of our great master
	33– 7	* a· all, in the more advanced
'02.	10–12	a· itself towards the Divine,
Hea.	11–28	excellence a· other systems.
Peo.	5–17	has risen a· the sod
	9–23	is seen to rise a· physics,
	11– 9	A· the platform of human rights
	12–16	a· the demands of matter.
Po.	9–10	wishing this earth more gifts from a·,
	10–13	Betokened from a·.
	16– 5	it blossoms a·;
	20–21	rising to the heavens a·.
	22– 4	and, beckoning from a·,
	23–10	A· the world's control?
	24–19	And from a·, Dear heart of Love,
	25–13	And breath of the living a·.
	28–11	A· the tempest's glee ;
	29–17	so far a· All mortal strife,
	30–17	a patient love a· earth's ire,
	34–20	in azure bright soar far a·;
	37– 2	* A· the sod Find peace in God,
	38– 3	For things a· the floor,
	45–16	mandate that speaks from a·,
	47– 7	Ever the gross world a·;
	58– 4	May rest a· my head.
	58– 8	Is registered a·.
	64– 8	May soar a· matter,
	67–21	flowers of feeling may blossom a·,
My.	6–24	a· the work of men's hands,
	14– 4	a· the song of angels,
	15–19	* Of unseen things a·,
	32–10	* a· the usual platform tone.
	38– 3	* every perfect gift cometh from a·,
	40–19	* wisdom that is from a· — Jas. 3 : 17.
	59– 7	* It was a· conception
	66– 3	* gives to the a· society the ownership
	66– 9	* by the a· society,
	67– 1	* raises its dome a· the city
	68–11	* two hundred and twenty-four feet a·
	68–22	* a· the Readers' special rooms.
	88– 7	* a· the average in intelligence.
	94–27	high a· the work of men's hands,
	99– 4	* a· the suffering of petty ills ;
	106– 8	I name those mentioned a· simply to
	106–10	over and a· matter in every mode
	114–24	Truth and Love, infinitely a· me,
	131–14	a· the symbol seize the spirit,
	143–14	A· all this fustian of either denying or
	156– 6	a· all that we ask or think," — Eph. 3 : 20.
	165–19	rise a· the oft-repeated inquiry,
	182–21	Love that reigns a· the shadow,
	186–10	point the path a· the valley,
	190–20	a· matter in healing disease,
	202– 2	soar a· it, pointing the path
	215– 2	I was a· begging
	217–15	complied with my request as a·
	227–21	The a· quotation by the editor-in-chief
	235–25	adopt as truth the a· statements?
	238–17	man rises a· the letter, law, or
	245– 1	a· the approved schools of
	245–17	a· the dire din of mortal
	248–16	rising a· theorems into the
	249– 5	When error strives to be heard a·
	250–26	impulsion of this action . . . from a·.
	252–29	the impetus comes from a·
	320–21	* at the time a· referred to,
	337–14	Betokened from a·.
	350–19	Thou infinite — dost doom a·.
	351–12	morale of Free Masonry is a· ethics
	354–26	* The a· lines were written
	360–30	God is a· your teacher, your healer,

above-ground
My.	110– 4	a· in material sense.

above-mentioned
My.	315–13	* was the a· woman.
	323– 2	* so well written in the a· letter.

above-named
Mis.	32–16	My sympathies extend to the a· class
	92–23	own a copy of the a· book
	301– 5	author of the a· book
	301–10	instances of the a· law-breaking
	349–11	student had taken the a· course
'00.	2– 3	springing up in the a· cities,
My.	238– 6	by reading the a· books
	319–26	* twentieth of the a· month.

Abraham
Mis.	189–14	"Before A· was, I am." — John 8 : 58.
	360–29	"Before A· was, I am," — John 8 : 58.
Chr.	55–15	Before A· was, I am. — John 8 : 58.
Ret.	26–19	He who antedated A·,
Pul.	82–16	* never called A· "Father,"
'01.	8–25	"Before A· was, I am." — John 8 : 58.
My.	161–11	when ye shall see A·, — Luke 13 : 28.

abreast
Man.	44–21	kept a· of the times.

abridge
Mis.	266– 5	to a· a single human right or

abroad
Mis.	39– 7	There are a· at this early date
	159–30	and some from a·,
	266–28	The spirit of lies is a·.
	370– 6	antagonistic spirit of evil is still a·;
	370– 7	greater spirit of Christ is also a·,
Ret.	85–24	and scatter the sheep a·;
Pul.	46– 1	* story has been a· that Judge Hanna
No.	2–28	not spread a· patchwork ideas
Po.	33–16	faith spreads her pinions a·,
	77– 9	blessings spreadst a·,
My.	3–11	scattered a· in Zion's waste places,
	74– 1	* from a· and from the far West

abrogate
No.	44–15	a· the rights of conscience

abrogated
Mis.	244–15	* "Has the law been a· that
'02.	4–20	a law never to be a·

absence
Mis.	27–21	for evil signifies the a· of good,
	65–28	for the a· of the other,
	289– 7	It is suppositional a· of good.
	353–15	in the overseer's a·,
	363– 6	supposition that the a· of good is
Ret.	58– 5	trying to compensate for the a· of
	60–12	It declares that evil is the a· of
Un.	4–12	destroys our sense . . . of His a·,
No.	17– 4	evil, is the a· of Spirit
My.	94–12	* a· of dissent among them
	193– 5	that you will not feel my a·.
	220–14	Injustice denotes the a· of law.
	312– 3	during her temporary a·.

absent
Mis.	78– 8	taught to those who are a·?
	116–26	Never a· from your post,
	278–19	students, who are a· from me,
	322–19	though I be present or a·,
	344–22	a· from the body, — II Cor. 5 : 8.
Man.	36–15	deceased, a·, or disloyal,
	111–17	deceased, a·, or disloyal,
Ret.	89–16	when he had been some time a·
Un.	59– 7	never a· from the earth and heaven ;
	60–21	He is neither a· from Himself
	62– 9	God, good, is never a·,
	63– 4	never a· for a moment.
No.	20–18	Love must seem ever a· to
'00.	1– 5	we may be a· from the body
	7–19	this Christ is never a·.
Po.	page 23	poem
My.	118–14	"a· from the body," — II Cor. 5 : 8.
	301–29	If mind be a· from the body,

absentness
Mis.	206–14	no illusive vision, no dreamy a·,

absolute
Mis.	99– 1	Science is a· and final.
	108– 7	attested the a· powerlessness
	136–17	the a· demonstration of C. S.
	148–20	a· doctrines destined for future
	156–17	Science is a·,
	177– 3	an a· consecration to the
	205–25	repentance and a· abandonment
	234–29	God is regarded more as a·,
	260–23	pure Mind as a· and entire,
	286– 8	ability to comply with a· Science,
	286–28	Until this a· Science of being
	288–15	and thence achieves the a·.
	298–20	the morale of a· C. S.,
	299–16	is the only a· good;
	299–17	is the only a· evil.
	307–20	this a· basis of C. S.;
	311–24	The works . . . contain a· Truth,

absolute
Mis.	318– 2	obsolete terms in *a·* C. S.,
	355– 9	This *a·* demonstration of Science
	359–23	The *way* is *a·* divine Science:
	364–28	If . . . there is no *a·* good.
Man.	3–17	*a·* doctrines destined for future
	63–10	must not deviate from the *a·*
Ret.	27– 7	the *a·* Science of Mind-healing,
	31– 5	The *a·* proof . . . of Truth
	83–30	deviating from *a·* C. S.
Un.	8–10	for this evidence is not *a·*,
	58–18	Thus the *a·* unreality of sin,
Pul.	vii–20	*a·* power of Truth
	75– 9	the *a·* antipode of C. S.,
Rud.	6–25	definite and *a·* form of healing,
	11–15	*a·* consciousness of harmony
No.	27–23	Who can say what the *a·* personality
Pan.	7–16	*a·* oneness and infinity of God,
'00.	4–22	found final, *a·*, and eternal.
'01.	1–24	gain the *a·* and supreme certainty
	2–13	*A·* certainty in the practice of divine
	22–30	its *a·* simple statement as to Spirit
'02.	5–18	This *a·* definition of Deity
My.	22–13	* shown the *a·* necessity of giving.
	79– 3	* kneeling . . . in *a·* stillness,
	146–19	the *a·* truth of his sayings
	241–15	* should be *a·* and correct teaching.
	242– 5	C. S. is *a·*;
	246–14	*a·* scientific unity which must exist
	260–10	the real, the *a·* and eternal,
	293–14	lack of the *a·* understanding
	293–16	the power of *a·* Truth
	349–23	God of nature in *a·* Science.
	357– 7	*a·* opposite of spiritual means,

absolutely
Mis.	22–12	*a·* refutes the amalgamation,
	50–13	*a·* no additional secret
	91– 5	not *a·* necessary to ordain
	92– 6	understood to be *a·* demonstrated.
	288–12	conclusion . . . is not *a·* right.
	317–12	not *a·* requisite for some people
Ret.	26–28	*a·* reduce the demonstration of
Un.	15– 6	*a·* cognizant of sin?
	29–13	*a·* immutable and eternal,
No.	6–24	is *a·* unreal.
'01.	3–10	loyal Christian Scientists *a·* adopt
My.	vi– 4	* to state truth *a·*
	77–27	* open its doors *a·* free of debt,
	85–27	* this structure, which is *a·* unique
	91–30	* is *a·* free from debt.
	98–20	* dedicated *a·* free of debt,
	104–23	of which a man knows *a·* nothing
	224–29	which is not *a·* genuine.
	284–24	*a·* and religiously opposed to war,
	338–28	Board of Lectureship is *a·*
	348– 1	*a·* healed of so-called disease

absolve
My.	274– 5	Death alone does not *a·* man from

absolved
My.	119– 8	but is *a·* by it.
	218–14	*a·* from death and the grave.

absorb
Ret.	80–18	will so *a·* it that this warning will be
Pul.	51–26	* C. S. cannot *a·* the world's

absorbed
Mis.	333– 5	could be *a·* in error!
Pul.	72–11	* very much *a·* in the work
No.	25–19	Man is not *a·* in Deity ;
My.	119– 7	man is not *a·* in the divine nature,

absorbing
My.	234– 3	*a·* one's time writing or reading
	336–19	* of *a·* interest to Christian Scientists

absorbs
Mis.	333– 8	it *a·* all the rays of light.

absorption
Mis.	22–13	*a·*, or annihilation of
	195– 2	*a·* of all action, motive, and

abstain
My.	114– 4	*a·* from alcohol and tobacco;
	339–26	Merely to *a·* from eating was not

abstinence
Mis.	288–31	*a·* from intoxicating beverages.
	289– 4	only temperance is total *a·*.

abstract
Mis.	38–15	such a dry and *a·* subject?
	38–17	is far from dry and *a·*.
	53–27	*a·* or difficult to perceive.
	82–21	comprehend only as *a·* glory.
	200–32	*a·* statement that all is Mind,
	222–25	Error is more *a·* than Truth.
	264–16	assimilate pure and *a·* Science
Ret.	67– 6	Sin is both concrete and *a·*.

abstract
Hea.	16–17	leave our *a·* subjects for this time.
My.	249– 1	You may condemn evil in the *a·*

abstraction
Mis.	53–28	Its seeming *a·* is the mystery of
	250–20	Love cannot be a mere *a·*,
My.	113–23	is C. S. a cold, dull *a·*,

abstractions
Mis.	174– 6	Let us have a clearing up of *a·*.
	195–27	were spiritual *a·*,
My.	218–16	introduction of pure *a·* into

abstruse
Ret.	7–10	* *a·* and metaphysical principles,
'02.	4–25	*a·* problems of Scripture,

absurd
Mis.	171– 7	is as *a·* as to think,
My.	111–20	be *a·* and unscientific?
	111–23	Were the apostles *a·* and
	111–29	they may pronounce it *a·*,
	344–12	*a·* to say that when a man dies,

absurdities
Un.	16– 3	unheard-of contradictions,— *a·*;

absurdly
Un.	17–23	Would it not *a·* follow

abundance
My.	36–19	* *a·* of salvation through His divine
	274–22	an *a·* of material presents ;
	340–29	are succeeded by our time of *a·*,

abundant
My.	198– 8	but their *a·* and ripened fruit.

abundantly
Pul.	1– 1	*They shall be a· satisfied — Psal. 36 : 8.*
	2–13	"they shall be *a·* satisfied,"— *Psal.* 36 : 8.
	3–16	"They shall be *a·* satisfied — *Psal.* 36 : 8.
	4–26	"They shall be *a·* satisfied — *Psal.* 36 : 8.
	7–29	"They shall be *a·* satisfied — *Psal.* 36 : 8.
My.	156– 5	"able to do exceeding *a·* — *Eph.* 3 : 20.
	194–26	May divine Love *a·* bless you,
	209– 3	God will *a·* bless this willing

abuse
Mis.	31– 8	the *a·* of mental treatment,
	78–20	this *a·*, has become too common :
	282–29	The *a·* which I call attention to,
	289– 3	its slightest use is *a·*;
Pan.	4–13	will is capable of use and of *a·*,
'02.	9–28	bitter comment and personal *a·*
	11–10	*a·* of him who, having a new idea
My.	219–10	otherwise its use is *a·*.
	343–18	shower of *a·* upon my head,

abused
Mis.	238–12	unmentioned, save when he is *a·*
	250– 4	is the best become the most *a·*,
Hea.	6– 0	The spiritualists *a·* me for it

abuses
Mis.	284– 5	C. S., . . . is subject to *a·*,
	338–16	uses of good, to *a·* from evil ;
Ret.	45–15	uses and *a·* of organization.
	76–24	never *a·* the corporeal personality,

abusing
Ret.	85–20	of *a·* the practice of Mind-healing

abyss
Un.	60– 9	the dark *a·* of nothingness,
My.	200–24	bottomless *a·* of self-damnation,
	291–18	fathomed the *a·* of difficulties

academic
My.	310– 2	were given an *a·* education,
	310– 5	In addition to my *a·* training,

academics
Pan.	4–12	In *a·* and in religion it is patent
My.	217– 2	You will want it for *a·*,

academies
My.	175–14	up-to-date *a·*, humane institutions,

Academy of Greece
Pul.	5–27	in the *A· o· G·*,

accelerated
Pul.	13–22	comes back . . . with *a·* force,
My.	239–29	*a·* by the advent of C. S.,

accent
Mis.	116–15	As *crescendo* and . . . *a·* music,

accented
Pul.	24–11	* *a·* by stone porticos and turreted

accents
Mis.	107– 3	are earth's *a·*,
Ret.	17– 8	tremble with *a·* of bliss.
Po.	62– 8	tremble with *a·* of bliss.

accentuating
Mis.	206–20	*a·* harmony in word and deed,

accept

Mis.	27–13	Mortals *a·* natural science, wherein
	27–14	why not *a·* divine Science
	76–18	and *a·* it on other topics
	83–12	No person can *a·* another's belief,
	83–16	to reject or to *a·* this error ;
	132–21	inconvenient to *a·* your invitation
	137– 2	*A·* my thanks for your card of
	142–11	*A·* my thanks for the beautiful
	146– 9	I cannot *a·* hearsay,
	185–17	as *a·* the truth of being,
	189– 4	willing to *a·* the divine Principle
	191–32	*a·* the Scriptures in their broader,
	194–23	*how to a·* God's power and guidance,
	218–11	It is erroneous to *a·* the evidence
	242–10	Will the gentleman *a·* my thanks
	242–11	if I should *a·* his bid on Christianity,
	244–17	Will he *a·* my reply
	319–18	Will all the dear Christian Scientists *a·*
	349–24	before I would *a·* the slightest
Man.	51– 3	and if he neglect to *a·*
Ret.	50– 9	was finally led, . . . to *a·* this fee.
Un.	5– 9	not to *a·* any personal opinion
	43–20	I exhort them to *a·* Christ's promise,
Pul.	38–17	* Scientists do not *a·* the belief
	44–28	* refused to *a·* any further checks
	54–12	* We *a·* the statement of Hudson :
	76–27	* to *a·* the magnificent new edifice
	77–15	* invited to visit and formally *a·*
	78–14	* formally *a·* this testimonial
	87– 4	* to *a·* this offering,
	87–13	*a·* my profound thanks.
	87–19	*a·* your grand church edifice.
'00.	6–26	in the degree that you *a·* it,
'01.	3–13	we *a·* God, emphatically,
Hea.	18–13	the world would *a·* our sentiments ;
My.	24– 4	* all who *a·* its divine ministry.
	25–16	my dear correspondents *a·* this,
	51–20	* *a·* the pastorate for the ensuing
	85–11	* One does not need to *a·* the
	93–17	* who do not *a·* the doctrine of
	120– 7	*A·* my gratitude for the chance
	129–29	*A·* my counsel and teachings only as
	142–10	*A·* my thanks for your approval
	156– 2	*a·* my gratitude for your dear letter,
	160–11	*a·* dead truisms which can be
	167– 1	*A·* my deep thanks therefor,
	172–18	*a·* my thanks for your kind,
	172–21	* "I *a·* this gift in behalf of
	172–27	*a·* from me the accompanying gift
	175– 6	Please *a·* the enclosed check
	186–25	*A·* my thanks for your cordial card
	190–13	*a·* our Master as authority,
	191–30	*A·* my thanks.
	194–23	gratefully *a·* the spirit of it ;
	196– 6	*a·* my tender counsel in these words
	199–11	*a·* my grateful acknowledgment of
	201–27	Please *a·* a line from me in lieu of
	208– 3	*A·* my deep thanks for your
	215–14	begging me to *a·* it,
	224–24	not safe to *a·* the latter as standards.
	229–22	*a·* profound thanks for their swift
	231–28	*a·* my thanks for your interesting
	236– 2	*a·* my full heart's love for them
	237–10	wise to *a·* only my teachings
	253–15	*A·* my love and these words of
	253–21	*a·* my profound thanks
	273–13	I for one *a·* his wise deduction,
	274–20	*a·* my thanks for their magnificent
	285– 2	*a·* my thanks for your kind
	285– 5	*a·* my hearty congratulations.
	308–24	but declined to *a·* the stick,
	332– 8	* *a·* it as a tribute of grateful hearts
	341–10	*a·* your Leader's Spring greeting,
	347– 8	*a·* my heartfelt acknowledgment of
	352–27	*A·* my thanks for your

acceptable

Mis.	184–11	presenting our bodies holy and *a·*,
	262–11	*a·* to those who have hearts.
No.	28–10	*a·* time for beginning the lesson.
	41– 7	that is most *a·* to God
My.	17–12	*a·* to God by Jesus Christ. — *I Pet.* 2 : 5.
	36–12	* service that shall be *a·* unto God.
	167–17	be one *a·* in His sight,
	184–22	service *a·* in God's sight.
	250– 9	*a·* service as church Readers,

acceptably

Man.	89–14	practised C. S. healing *a·*
My.	37– 6	* can *a·* ascend heavenward
	310– 3	taught school *a·* at various times

acceptance

Mis.	110–23	obvious that the world's *a·*
	181–23	urges upon our *a·* this great fact :
	196–31	*a·* of the truths they present ;
Pul.	87–14	permit me, . . . to decline their *a·*,

acceptance

'01.	1– 9	nearer the whole world's *a·*.
My.	99–29	* no choice but the *a·* of them
	123– 8	urge the perfect model for your *a·*
	184–29	*a·* throughout the earth,

accepted

Mis.	5–28	is something not easily *a·*,
	19–13	*a·* the divine claims of Truth
	75–29	and the commonly *a·* view is
	81–10	*in the commonly a· teachings*
	132– 3	substance whereof you had already *a·*
	187–11	This rule of harmony must be *a·*
	237– 6	*a·* as the penalty for sin.
	247–23	is not so easily *a·*.
	297–19	and *a·* the claims of the marriage
	349–27	I *a·*, for a time, fifteen dollars
	349–30	I have *a·* no pay from my
Man.	18– 6	She *a·* the call, and was ordained
	81– 6	not *a·* by the Pastor Emeritus
Ret.	15–15	I *a·* the invitation and commenced
	16–19	She *a·* the call,
	44– 7	I *a·* the call, and was ordained
Un.	9–17	They have not *a·* the simple teaching
	55– 1	*a·* the one fact whereby
Rud.	6–16	* fact "almost universally *a·*,
No.	23–10	after the *a·* definition.
	31–24	forgiven in the generally *a·* sense,
My.	12–18	now is the *a·* time." — *II Cor.* 6 : 2.
	49–32	* Mrs. Eddy *a·* the call.
	53–18	* which invitation she *a·*.
	59–11	* tenets be *a·* wholly or in part by
	145– 6	showed it to me, and I *a·* it.
	236–16	uniformity with which they *a·* the
	324–26	* why he *a·* your invitation

accepting

Mis.	ix– 3	* prevent a man from *a·* charity ;
	101– 5	and *a·* spiritual truth,
	347–17	*a·* the premonition of one of them,
Rud.	5–24	*A·* the verdict of these material

accepts

Mis.	13–20	frail human reason *a·*.
	47–29	depends upon what one *a·* as
'00.	6–15	child not only *a·* C. S. more readily

access

Mis.	155– 9	find *a·* to the heart of humanity.

accessible

Mis.	x– 8	*a·* as reference,

accession

Mis.	204–28	Through the *a·* of spirituality,

accessions

Mis.	149–12	full of *a·* to your love,
My.	9– 1	* large *a·* to their membership.

accessories

My.	149–23	the Principle in its *a·*,

accessory

Mis.	119– 7	punish the dupe as *a·* to the fact.
Ret.	63–19	becomes *a·* to it.

accident

Mis.	24– 9	an injury caused by an *a·*,
	282–27	*a·*, when there is no time for
	380–13	an *a·*, called fatal to life,
Ret.	24–13	an injury caused by an *a·*,
Pul.	34– 6	* met with a severe *a·*,

accidental

Mis.	224–23	no . . . *a·* disturbance shall agitate or

accommodate

Mis.	66–31	I endeavor to *a·* my instructions to
'01.	22–17	nor say this to *a·* popular opinion
My.	22– 5	* *a·* the constantly increasing
	39– 1	* in order to *a·* those who
	80–25	* to *a·* the great throngs who
	82–12	* wagons enough to *a·* the demand.
	86–28	* *a·* the throng of participants.

accommodated

Mis.	136–26	will be *a·* by this arrangement.
My.	75– 6	* chapter sub-title

accommodation

My.	8–16	* to make reasonable *a·* for

accommodations

My.	75–15	* in the matter of securing *a·*.
	88–14	* its *a·* are so wide,
	123–20	my outdoor *a·* at Pleasant View

accompanied

Mis.	51– 5	*a·* by great mental depression,
	143–28	always *a·* with a touching letter
	177–24	* *a·* by Rev. D. A. Easton,
My.	31–23	* *a·* by the Second Reader,
	313–18	always *a·* by some responsible
	331– 7	* who *a·* her to the train

accompanies
Mis. 47–15　a· thought with less impediment

accompaniment
My. 23–26　* with its inseparable a·,

accompany
Mis. 306– 3　* book which will a· the bell
Un. 64–14　forever a· our being.
My. 74–13　* a· them in their triumph of mind
332–10　* to a· her only to New York,

accompanying
Mis. 189–23　a· consciousness of spiritual power
Ret. 19–22　a· her on her sad journey
58– 8　an a· sense of power
Un. 37–18　The evil a· physical personality
Pul. 86–13　* A· the stone testimonial
My. 172–28　accept from me the a· gift
331– 1　a· her on her sad journey

accomplish
Mis. 41– 4　to a· an evil purpose.
69–23　in their effort to a· this result,
137–23　To a· this, you must give much time
148–21　absolute doctrines . . . might not a·.
273–31　more than one person can well a·,
Man. 3–18　absolute doctrines . . . might not a·.
No. 2– 9　to a· this, you cannot begin by
Hea. 13– 3　and a· less on either side.
My. 150–12　can a· the full scale ;
308– 1　divine Love will a· what

accomplished
Mis. 8– 3　we shall have a· much ;
130–19　that they could have a·,
130 21　such Herculean tasks as they have a·.
171–16　the basis upon which are a·
172–13　until the three measures be a·,
238–10　All that ever was a·,
273–18　have not yet a· all the good
297– 6　more than has been a· by legally
302–14　Much good has been a·
Ret. 45– 9　and fellowship has a· its end,
49– 7　having a· the worthy purpose for which
86–21　If . . . the duty will not be a·.
Pul. 21–11　faithfully struggle till it be a·
44– 4　* The 'prayer in stone' is a·
54–17　greatest good could be a·.''
Pan. 10–23　a· by the grace of God,
'02. 11–15　how much more is a· when
14–12　a· on this solid basis.
My. 45–14　* prophetically seen has been a·.
59–30　* has a· such a work or
61–16　* that the work would be a·
78–19　* The seating is a· in a
126–23　saw in spiritual vision will be a·.
203–29　if you have not a· all you
241– 0　* until it has a· that for which it
247–28　The little that I have a·
278– 6　this means and end will be a·
280–10　* a· through the righteous prayer
283–22　a· when self is lost in Love
292– 2　All that can be a·, and more
298– 6　already reported of the good a·
308– 2　can never prevent being a·
321– 4　* had a· this great work.

accomplishing
Mis. 122– 8　this holy (?) alliance for a· such a
214–15　a· its purpose of Love,
230–12　is no proof of a· much.
273–19　good they are capable of a· ;
292–25　C. S., . . . is a· great good,
358–25　a· the greatest work of the ages,
Ret. 83– 2　is a· the divine purpose
Pul. 15– 4　mental ways of a· iniquity.

accomplishment
Man. 52–24　a· of what she understands is

accord
Mis. 143–27　"with one a· — Acts 2 : 1.
238–29　I a· these evil-mongers due credit
354–19　body and soul in a· with God.
372–19　in a· with the ancient . . . artists.
Man. 42–14　in a· with all of Mrs. Eddy's
Ret. 24–21　in perfect scientific a· with divine law.
45–15　in a· with my special request,
76–22　when the disciples were of one a·.
81– 6　keeping them in a· with Christ,
Pul. 34–23　perfect scientific a· with the divine law.''
Peo. 7 32　to a· with our thoughts.
My. 3– 6　not alone in a· with human desire
36–18　* with blessed a· we are come,
157–16　* in a· with the expressed wish of
212–19　"with one a· — Acts 2 : 1.
232–28　does that watch a· with Jesus' saying?
362–15　* gathered in one place with one a·,

accordance
Mis. 11–16　in a· with common law,

accordance
Mis. 266–25　in a· with my students' desires,
272–13　* In a· with Statutes of 1883,
Man. 42–11　In a· with the C. S. textbooks,
66– 5　then act in a· therewith.
68–25　calls a student in a· with
69– 7　to serve our Leader in a· with
72–13　proper application, made in a· with
80–10　in a· with the By-Laws
100–15　in a· with said By-Laws.
Un. 38– 5　not in a· with His law,
Pul. 85–18　* in a· with the prayer and
My. 78–17　* in a· with the custom of the
112–23　not in a· with the Scriptures.
212–16　they do not practise in strict a·
323– 1　* in a· with what Mr. Bates has
361–21　* in a· with your desire for a

accorded
Ret. 6– 8　a· special household privileges.
My. 284– 4　you may have a· me more than

according
Mis. 17–24　a· to the timely or
22–23　a· to the rules of its
23–30　a· to natural science,
27–20　A· to reason and revelation,
30– 3　a· to Jesus' example
44– 1　"a· to the pattern — Heb. 8 : 5.
61–21　A· to the Word, man is the
66–10　a· to divine decree.
68–21　A· to Webster, metaphysics is
69–24　A· to their diagnosis,
72– 7　A· to the beliefs of the flesh,
76–11　A· to human belief the bodies
91–26　answer them a· to it,
104–12　A· to C. S., perfection is normal,
114–16　enunciation of these a· to Christ.
117–22　A· to my calendar, God's time
147–15　a· as Truth and the voice of
165–32　origin of man a· to divine Science,
171– 7　a· to the report of some,
191–10　A· to the Scripture,
215–17　not a· to the infantile conception
217–25　A· to Holy Writ, it is a kingdom
219– 1　A· to lexicography, teleology is
220–30　it would be a· to the woman's belief ;
223– 4　a· to God's command.
247–27　reflects harmony or discord a· to
257–32　a· to this lawless law which
261– 6　A· to divine law, sin and suffering
265–13　demonstrates its Principle a· to rule,
289–16　a· to the divine precept,
309– 4　A· to C. S., material personality is
331– 1　doeth a· to His will — Dan. 4 : 35.
337–25　such as lived a· to his precepts,
347– 1　a· to his folly, — Prov. 26 : 4.
348–15　a· to his folly, — Prov. 26 : 5.
360–21　"the Israel a· to Spirit"
360–28　a· to His mode of C. S. ;
370–13　a· to humanity's needs.
376–19　A· to terrestrial calculations,
Man. 28–12　neither did a· to his will, — Luke 12 : 47.
34– 8　a· to the platform and teaching
39– 2　to live a· to its requirements
39– 2　application for membership a· to
42–22　practised a· to the Golden Rule :
46– 5　a· to the laws of our land.
48–19　A· to the Scripture they shall
56– 3　a· to Article XI, Sect. 4.
62–20　a· to their understanding or ability
81–17　a· to the provisions in the
98 13　published a· to copy ;
100– 8　carried out a· to her directions.
100–11　a· to these By-Laws,
112–10　a· to the form on page 114.
Ret. 1– 1　My ancestors, a· to the flesh,
14– 9　a· to his views,
28–20　a· to the law of God.
36– 3　would not expound the gospel a· to
71–20　a· to pure and undefiled religion.
83–23　and be answered a· to it,
89–20　even a· to his promise,
Un. 2–20　A· to this same rule,
6–13　Until the heavenly law of health, a· to
11–21　a· to the ruder sort then prevalent,
30– 9　suffers, a· to material belief,
31–11　A· to C. S., the first idolatrous claim
31–23　evil does, a· to belief,
36–11　solved by C. S. a· to Scripture.
36–16　demonstration, a· to C. S.,
44–11　a· to Biblical history.
Rud. 7–12　A· to the evidence of the so-called
7–23　A· to divine Science,
13–21　a· to their own belief
No. v– 2　a· to the apostle's admonition,
9–26　and a· to Webster, it is

according

No.	23–12	*A·* to Crabtre, these devils were
	24– 3	*A·* to Spinoza's philosophy
	24– 6	*a·* to Spinoza, man is an
	24–10	*A·* to false philosophy and
	25–13	*a·* to a law of "the survival
Pan.	2–10	*A·* to Webster the word
	13– 6	demonstrated *a·* to Christ,
'01.	4– 9	demonstrate Love *a·* to Christ,
	8–13	man, *a·* to C. S.,
	8–18	*a·* to Holy Writ
	10–28	faith *a·* to works.
	11–27	*a·* to his folly,— *Prov.* 26 : 4.
	16–17	*a·* to Holy Writ these qualities
	23–15	*a·* to the Master's teaching and proof.
'02.	3–29	*A·* to Holy Writ, the first lie
Hea.	10–24	win or lose *a·* to your plea.
	19–22	*a·* to the model on the mount,
Peo.	10–22	*a·* to the images that thought
My.	5– 2	*a·* to the Scriptural allegory,
	13–12	*A·* to his description,
	34–29	* are *a·* to the 1913 edition.
	75–25	* *A·* to the custom of the
	79–17	* *A·* to the despatches,
	93–10	* *a·* to the pledges which it
	126–17	*a·* to her works : — *Rev.* 18 : 6.
	127– 5	to be judged *a·* to their works,
	128–15	*a·* to the dictates of his own
	128–29	God will reward your enemies *a·* to
	141–20	*A·* to the following statement,
	143–27	*a·* to His purpose.— *Rom.* 8 : 28.
	167–16	*a·* to time-tables,
	168– 2	worship God *a·* to the dictates of
	186–15	all your needs *a·* to His riches
	194–26	reward you *a·* to your works,
	222– 1	Gospel *a·* to St. Matthew,
	229–16	*a·* to this saying of Christ Jesus :
	240–18	*a·* to the word of God.
	241–24	* *a·* to the beliefs I entertained
	243– 2	*A·* to reports, the belief is
	247– 7	are *a·* to Christ Jesus ;
	254–28	are *a·* to Christ Jesus ;
	261– 6	*a·* to the custom of the age
	268–11	*a·* to the Principle of law
	277–13	shall be *a·* to His laws.
	291–10	zeal *a·* to wisdom,
	300– 4	overcome sin *a·* to the Scripture,
	300–24	*a·* to Christ's command,
	302– 3	*a·* to a man's belief,
		(*see also* **Scriptures**)

accordingly

Mis.	165–25	*a·* as this account is settled
	381–13	*A·*, her counsel asked the
Ret.	9– 1	*A·* she returned with me to
	38–10	*A·*, I set to work,
'00.	14–30	you prepare *a·* for the festivity.
Peo.	1–17	*a·* as the understanding that we
My.	180–24	what we know is right, and act *a·*,
	329– 2	* license was *a·* taken out.

accords

Ret.	65–20	It *a·* with the trend and tenor of
'01.	3–15	this *a·* with the literal sense of
'02.	7– 3	It *a·* all to God, Spirit,
My.	294–12	whatever *a·* not with a full faith

account

Mis.	65–25	balancing man's *a·* with his Maker.
	115– 7	can *a·* for this state of mind
	165–25	as this *a·* is settled with divine Love,
	297– 1	Taking into *a·* the short time that
Ret.	2–24	full *a·* of the death and burial of
	36– 8	This will *a·* for certain published
No.	41– 9	on *a·* of persecution,
My.	79– 8	* to read the *a·* of the dedication
	81–26	* any *a·* of the marvellous cures
	161– 7	balancing his *a·* with divine Love,
	179– 4	an *a·* of the spiritual creation,
	334–10	* *a·* of her husband's demise
	351– 5	* on *a·* of its beautiful tribute to

accountant

Man.	77– 3	by an honest, competent *a·*.

accounted

Un.	17– 2	to be *a·* true.
My.	269– 6	which shall be *a·* worthy — *Luke* 20 : 35.

accounts

Mis.	131–24	opportunity to cancel *a·*.
	131–30	to itemize or audit their *a·*,
	221–16	This *a·* for many helpless
Pul.	54–18	* A careful reading of the *a·* of his
'02.	17–19	to square *a·* with each passing hour.
My.	9–27	what my heart gives to balance *a·*.

accredited

Pul.	73–25	* has been *a·* as having been deified.

accretion

Mis.	206–12	gained through growth, not *a·*.

accrue

Mis.	350–25	benefit that would otherwise *a·*.

accrues

Un.	2–11	pain which *a·* to him from it.

accumulates

Mis.	348–14	Error, left to itself, *a·*.

accumulating

Mis.	17–30	*a·* pains of sense,
Ret.	44–13	*a·* work in the College,
My.	276– 7	When *a·* work requires it,

accumulation

Ret.	82–19	an *a·* of power on his side
My.	12– 8	* *a·* of a sum sufficient to

accumulative

Mis.	316–18	Imperative, *a·*, sweet demands
My.	291– 2	Imperative, *a·*, holy demands

accurate

Pul.	67– 9	* *a·* census of the religious faiths

accurately

Un.	31– 1	or, more *a·* translated,

accuse

Ret.	73–22	or *a·* people of being unduly personal,
My.	285–24	whereof they now *a·* me. — *Acts* 24 : 13.

accused

Man.	52–12	guilty of that whereof he is *a·*
Pul.	12– 8	*a·* them before our God — *Rev.* 12 : 10.
My.	138–13	cruelly, unjustly, and wrongfully *a·*.

accuser

Mis.	191–26	define him as an "*a·*," — *Rev.* 12 : 10.
Pul.	12– 7	*a·* of our brethren — *Rev.* 12 : 10.
	12–20	for the *a·* is not there,
'01.	16–16	defines *devil* as *a·*, *calumniator*;
	33– 4	"*a·*" or "calumniator" — *Rev.* 12 : 10.

accusing

Un.	21– 3	*a·* or else excusing — *Rom.* 2 : 15.

accustomed

Mis.	135–29	in my *a·* place with you,
	256–22	*a·* to think and to speak of

achieve

'02.	1– 4	no special effort to *a·* this result,
My.	89–10	* to *a·* its extreme of beauty.
	292– 1	What cannot love . . . *a·* for the race?

achieved

Mis.	xi– 7	by what they have hitherto *a·*
	67–22	right practice of Mind-healing *a·*,
	120–12	*a·* great guerdons in the vineyard
	238–10	unselfed love *a·* for the race
	297– 5	*a·* far more than has been
	316–25	had my students *a·* the point
Ret.	78– 4	student has not yet *a·* the entire
	88–16	*a·*, both by example and precept.
Pul.	32–29	* *a·* eminence as a lawyer.
'02.	14–12	the only success I have ever *a·*
Peo.	11– 7	this victory is *a·*, not with bayonet

achievement

Mis.	185– 9	*a·* of his spiritual identity
	319–25	opportunity for the grandest *a·*
	340–22	they work on to the *a·* of good ;
Un.	43– 9	*a·* of this ultimatum of Science,
Pul.	33–26	* to more than ordinary *a·*,
	84–17	* Of the significance of this *a·*
	84–26	* This *a·* is the result of long years of
'02.	14–20	*a·* after *a·* has been blazoned on
My.	37–16	* By reason of your spiritual *a·*
	43–29	* with wonder upon this grand *a·*,
	86–18	* regarded as an extraordinary *a·*,
	98–30	* has been a wonderful *a·*,
	124– 8	growth, grandeur, and *a·*,
	234–13	from faith to *a·*,
	253– 5	What nobler *a·*, what greater glory
	357–18	their success and glory of *a·*

achievements

Mis.	v– 5	*a·* WHICH CONSTITUTE THE SUCCESS
	10– 1	purposes and *a·* wherewith to
	125–29	remarkable *a·* that have been
	250–18	noble sacrifices and grand *a·*
My.	6–26	beauty, and *a·* of goodness.
	10– 4	* *a·* of its followers.
	64– 2	* *a·* of our beloved Leader
	74–15	* one of the finest architectural *a·*
	94–30	beauty, and *a·* of goodness."
	134–11	Joy over good *a·*
	256–14	pleasures, *a·*, and *aid*.
	287–20	new possibilities, *a·*, and

achieves

Mis.	288–14	and thence *a·* the absolute.
My.	274–14	one *a·* the Science of Life,

achieving
Mis. 230–24 * Still a·, still pursuing,
266–22 who are toiling and a· success
My. 185– 6 * Still a·, still pursuing,
268– 9 affections are enduring and a·.

aching
Mis. 275– 9 bendeth his a· head ;
Po. 35–10 An a·, voiceless void,

acknowledge
Mis. 5–24 They a· an erring or mortal mind,
35– 8 a· and attest the blessings
77– 9 not only a· the incarnation,
98–25 to a· its divine Principle.
247–20 They a· the existence of mortal mind,
Man. 15– 6 We a· and adore one supreme
15– 7 We a· His Son, one Christ ;
15–10 We a· God's forgiveness of sin in
15–14 We a· Jesus' atonement as the
16– 1 we a· that man is saved through
16– 5 We a· that the crucifixion of Jesus
74–17 societies are required to a·
Un. 64– 3 God can no more behold it, or a· it,
Pul. 85– 8 * will, in . . . time, see and a· it.
Rud. 10–26 learn to a· God in all His ways.
Pan. 1–19 shall know and a· one God
'01. 35– 1 all thy ways a· Him, — Prov. 3 : 6.
Peo. 12–12 a· only God in all thy ways,
My. 52– 8 * a· our indebtedness to her,
62–26 * We a· with many thanks
133– 5 at last come to a· God,
180–20 refuses to see . . . or to a· it,
280– 3 * We a· with rejoicing
352– 8 * a· our debt of gratitude to you

acknowledged
Mis. 49–12 a· and notable cases of
164– 8 until it be a·, understood,
166–27 even if not a·, has come to be
183– 4 must be a· and demonstrated.
340–21 students have openly a· this.
Man. 72–11 This church shall be a· publicly as
Pul. 71–10 * the a· C, S. Leader,
82–17 * a· woman as man's proper helpmeet.
No. 18– 3 a· God in all His ways.
My. 103– 2 reluctantly seen and a·.
146– 7 not been a· since the third century.
240– 3 a· throughout the earth.
307–12 He even a· this himself,

acknowledges
Mis. 62–21 a· this fact in her work

acknowledging
Mis. 53–15 which is virtually a· that
256– 7 a· the public confidence
260–23 a· pure Mind as absolute
Ret. 94– 7 though a· the true way,
My. 195– 4 a· your card of invitation
357–20 I thank you for a· me as

acknowledgment
Mis. 185– 9 a· and achievement of his
221–20 and a· of it in another
Ret. 41– 6 without even an a· of the benefit.
Un. 7–20 an a· of the perfection of
Pul. 60–21 * a· of certain Christian and
Po. vii–10 * grateful a·, . . . of this permission,
My. 19–26 with a· of exemplary giving,
75– 2 * respectful a· of its enthusiasm,
164– 6 chapter sub-title
184–13 I omitted to wire an a·
199–12 my grateful a· of the receipt of
283– 1 chapter sub-title
336–10 * She makes grateful a· of this
347– 8 a· of their beautiful gift

acknowledgments
Mis. 274–12 with grateful a· to the public
Man. 75– 9 she, with grateful a· thereof,

acme
Mis. 100–22 the a· of C. S.
122–14 The divine order is the a· of mercy :
176–28 act up to the a· of divine energy
252–17 C. S. is not only the a· of Science
355– 6 good healing is to-day the a· of
Un. 61–20 earthly a· of human sense.
My. 208–26 reaching the very a· of C. S.

aconite
Ret. 26– 6 preparation of poppy, or a·,
Hea. 13–11 We have attenuated a grain of a·
13–11 until it was no longer a·,

acoustic
My. 32– 7 * a· properties of the new structure
72– 1 * nicely adjusted a· properties
78–22 * The a· properties of the temple,

acoustics
No. 6–25 optics, a·, and hydraulics are

acquaint
Mis. 328–11 a· sensual mortals with the
342–30 a· themselves with the etiquette of
Ret. 28– 3 one must a· himself with God,
'02. 12–23 a privilege to a· communicants with
Peo. 6–24 "a· now thyself with Him — Job 22 : 21.
My. 7– 6 a privilege to a· communicants with
239– 6 a· the student with God.

acquaintance
Mis. 151–12 make Him thy first a·.
216–15 an a· with the author justifies
Un. 4–21 forbid man's a· with evil.
54–17 then a· with that claimant becomes
54–26 and disowned its a·,
'01. 31–12 long a· with the communicants of my
Po. v–18 * and who made her a·,
My. 223–12 with whom I have no a·
320–27 * proud of his a· with you.
322–29 * told me of his a· with you

acquaintances
Mis. 249–14 as well as my intimate a·.
Ret. 19–14 large circle of friends and a·,
My. 87–15 * congratulate these comfortable a·
330–26 large circle of friends and a·,

acquainted
Mis. 43– 4 a· with the mental condition of
151–19 art thou a· with God?
Un. 55– 5 and a· with grief," — Isa. 53 : 3.
56–25 become a· with that Love which is
My. 42– 9 * no doubt already a· with him
145– 2 You are by this time a· with
226–28 becomes better a· with C. S.,

acquaints
Mis. 175–25 healing which a· us with God

acquiescence
Mis. 213– 8 a· in the methods of divine Love.
291–10 A tacit a· with others' views
Un. 36–18 instead of a· therein
Rud. 3– 2 Hence their comparative a· in
My. 170– 3 simply my a· in the request of
292– 7 joy of a· consummated.
293– 7 in his loving a·, believed that

acquire
My. 229–11 a· in one year the Science that

acquired
Mis. ix– 9 a· by healing mankind morally,
Ret. 87– 8 more thoroughly and readily a· by
'00. 13–18 There Æsculapius, . . . a· fame ;
'01. 26–27 a· taste for what was problematic
My. 273–15 sense of rightness a· by experience

acquirements
Ret. 7–21 * from his talents and a·.

acquiring
Mis. 156–26 no aid to students in a· solid C. S.
'01. 2– 4 indispensable to the a· of greater

acquisition
My. 87–18 * a· of an edifice so handsome

acquitted
My. 125–21 have a· themselves nobly.

acre
Mis. 376–21 an a· of eldritch ebony.

acres
Mis. 140–26 Our title to God's a· will be safe
Ret. 4– 5 of about five hundred a·,
4– 7 One hundred a· of the old farm
4–21 covered areas of rich a·,

across
Mis. 71–29 shadows flitting a· the dial of time.
143– 7 A· lakes, into a kingdom,
Ret. 5– 1 just a· the bridge,
Pul. 44– 5 * A· two thousand miles of space,
48–10 * a· the farm, which stretches
My. 59–14 * gazing a· that sea of heads,
124–12 a· continents and oceans,
183–11 Beloved Brethren a· the Sea :
200–12 stretches a· the sea and rises
259–12 To this church a· the sea
342–17 * smaller parlor a· the hall,

Act
Mis. 272– 4 * under A· of 1874, Chapter 375,
272– 5 * "This A· was repealed from
272– 9 * till the repealing of said A·
272–11 * substance of this A· is at present

act
Mis. 32– 7 in what manner they should a·
43– 2 the capabilities of Mind to a·
85– 9 every thought and a· leading to good.
90–11 It is always right to a· rightly ;
108–25 Remember, and a· on, Jesus' definition
112–18 regarded his a· as one of simple

act

Mis.	117– 6	motive, and *a·* superinduced by the
	124–24	The last *a·* of the tragedy
	124–26	This grand *a·* crowned . . . Christianity :
	131–18	did not *a·* under that By-law ;
	134– 4	contrition for an *a·* which you
	139–27	it will be found that this *a·* was
	146–24	you will *a·*, relative to this matter,
	173–18	space to occupy, power to *a·*,
	176–28	*a·* up to the acme of divine energy
	197– 3	the motive-power of every *a·*.
	205–15	omnipotent *a·* drops the curtain on
	219–12	mortals think . . . and *a·* wickedly :
	272–29	I have endeavored to *a·* toward
	289–14	to *a·* as a whole and per agreement.
	300–17	When I consent to this *a·*,
	305–32	* we ask every one . . . *to a· at once.*
	352–17	enables the practitioner to *a·*
Man.	53– 1	or shall influence others thus to *a·*,
	66– 5	then *a·* in accordance therewith.
	98–22	*a·* under the direction of this
	99–22	*a·* as District Manager of the
	100–14	*a·* upon this important matter
Pul.	3– 8	power to think and *a·* rightly,
Hea.	7–11	begins with motive, instead of *a·*,
	7–12	it corrects the *a·* that results from
	7–16	begins in motive to correct the *a·*,
	7–20	regardless of any outward *a·*,
Peo.	10– 2	Thought is the essence of an *a·*,
My.	12–27	* "*a·* in the living present."
	13– 3	*a·* in God's time.
	108– 6	I challenge matter to *a·* apart from
	108– 8	as it is seen to *a·* apart from matter.
	180–24	and *a·* accordingly,
	250–23	wait for the favored moment to *a·*
	293– 4	*a·* as the different properties of
	293– 5	*a·* — one against the other
	327–20	* section of an *a·* in the Legislature
	328–23	* machinery *a·* of the Legislature
	345–15	could be made to *a·* on me.
	359– 2	Directors do not *a·* contrary to
	362–18	* as their first *a·* send you their

acted

'01.	13– 6	ought not to be seen, felt, or *a·* :
	14–24	Wrong is thought before it is *a·* ;
Po.	33–15	If these resolutions are *a·* up to,
My.	345–17	they *a·* just the same

acting

Mis.	96–28	not one mind *a·* upon another mind ;
	117–15	basis of all right thinking and *a·* ;
	119– 3	this were no apology for *a·* evilly.
	130–13	*a·* thus regarding disease
	204–32	evil speaking and *a·* ;
	365–13	right thinking and right *a·*,
Ret.	31–14	Truth and Love, *a·* through C. S.
	81–11	false thinking, feeling, and *a·* ;
No.	12– 4	right thinking and right *a·*
	18– 9	Right thinking and right *a·*,
'00.	9– 9	right thinking and *a·* is open to
Hea.	3– 7	foundation of . . . right *a·*,
	15–19	*a·* oppositely to your prayer,
My.	7–18	* *a·* in behalf of ourselves
	12–22	lost in speaking or in *a·*,
	139– 3	living, loving, *a·*, enjoying.
	209– 6	in right thinking and right *a·*,
	254–12	reward of right thinking and *a·*,
	273–14	of thinking, feeling, and *a·*,
	274–11	right feeling, and right *a·*
	309– 5	even *a·* as counsel in a lawsuit

action

all

Mis.	195– 2	follow the absorption of all *a·*,
Hea.	12– 8	mind, the basis of all *a·*,

and effects

Mis.	12–21	*a·* and effects of this so-called

any

Ret.	89–28	to any *a·* not first made known

atomic

Mis.	23–21	is not a result of atomic *a·*,
	190– 1	Atomic *a·* is Mind, not matter.

before

Man.	66–10	before *a·* is taken

ceaseless

Mis.	224–16	the ceaseless *a·* and reaction

element of

Peo.	10– 2	the stronger element of *a·* ;

every

'01.	32–30	governing impulse of every *a·* ;
Peo.	8–18	governs every *a·* of the body

excess of

Mis.	353– 4	is either an excess of *a·* or

fading warmth of

Mis.	342– 6	their fading warmth of *a·* ;

form of

Man.	28– 7	form of *a·*, nations, individuals,

action

God's

Mis.	354–22	pride would regulate God's *a·*.

governed the

Ret.	33– 3	governed the *a·* of material medicine.

harmonious

No.	11– 6	their intelligent and harmonious *a·*,

human

Mis.	268– 3	queries give point to human *a·* :
	288–13	Wisdom in human *a·* begins with
Ret.	93–16	it becomes the model for human *a·*.
'00.	11–28	highest criticism on all human *a·*,

immediate

Man.	51–19	provides for immediate *a·*.

impulse, and

Rud.	3–20	all true volition, impulse, and *a·* ;

incentive for

My.	217– 5	generous incentive for *a·*,

independent

Mis.	289–14	surrenders independent *a·*

internal

Mis.	347– 4	foretell the internal *a·* of

is Science

Mis.	58–25	the *a·* is Science.

its

Mis.	222–16	mental argument and its *a·* on

legal

Man.	67–10	Unauthorized Legal *A·*.
	67–12	nor take legal *a·* on a case

legitimate

No.	9–10	to prevent their legitimate *a·*

liberal

My.	11–17	* because of prompt and liberal *a·*,

misguide

'00.	9–13	bias human judgment and misguide *a·*,

motives for

Mis.	51–17	the right motives for *a·*,

normal

Mis.	350–24	Hence it prevents the normal *a·*,
My.	218– 1	to its normal *a·*, functions, and

of fear

Mis.	41–22	through the *a·* of fear,

of God

Hea.	4– 7	we limit the *a·* of God to the

of man

Mis.	58–24	If God does not govern the *a·* of man,

of Mind

Mis.	70– 6	healing *a·* of Mind upon the body

of mind

Mis.	48–17	through the *a·* of mind alone.
	197–15	such an *a·* of mind would be of no
	220–28	in this *a·* of mind over mind,
	244–14	which are the *a·* of mind
	341– 1	right *a·* of mind or body.

of sickness

Mis.	353– 4	like the *a·* of sickness,

of the body

Peo.	8–18	governs every *a·* of the body

of the church

Mis.	310–23	will determine the *a·* of the church

of the churches

Man.	70–19	*a·* of the churches in said State.

of the divine Mind

Mis.	62–28	based on the *a·* of the divine Mind
My.	108– 7	*a·* of the divine Mind is salutary

of the divine Spirit

Mis.	40–16	namely, the *a·* of the divine Spirit,

organizing

Mis.	177– 9	in organizing *a·* against us.

origin and

Un.	32–10	cannot be separated in origin and *a·*.

points of

Hea.	13– 1	so weaken both points of *a·* ;

put into

Mis.	288– 8	before being put into *a·*.

right

Mis.	171–12	our right *a·* is not to condemn
	341– 1	right *a·* of mind or body.
	354–17	right *a·* of the mental mechanism,

rule of

My.	43– 6	* definite rule of *a·* whereby to

special

Man.	27– 6	shall order no special *a·* to be taken

sphere of

Ret.	89–25	to enlarge their sphere of *a·*.

stage of

'01.	17–22	next more difficult stage of *a·*

such

My.	362–22	* such *a·* as will unite the churches

systematizes

Mis.	235–16	systematizes *a·*, gives a keener sense
My.	287–23	systematizes *a·*, and insures

tending the

Mis.	353–20	tending the *a·* that He adjusts.

their

Man.	94– 5	the churches shall decide their *a·*.

action

their
  My. 250–13   please send . . . notice of their a˙.
this
  Mis. 166–26   This a˙ of the divine energy,
      214–11   This a˙ of Jesus was stimulated by
      220–28   in this a˙ of mind over mind,
  Pul. 45–27   * This a˙, it appears, was the result
  My. 250–26   the impulsion of this a˙ in
      252–27   You are not aroused to this a˙ by
thought and
  (*see* **thought**)
thought or
  Mis. 3–16   this line of thought or a˙.
     260– 8   line of Jesus' thought or a˙.
  My. 278–30   brings into human thought or a˙
     308– 7   aroused to thought or a˙ only by
unchristian
  Mis. 81– 4   all unpleasant and unchristian a˙
unity of
  My. 212–18   there would be unity of a˙.
unprecedented
  Ret. 45–17   noble, unprecedented a˙ of
without
  Mis. 269–21   without Mind the body is without a˙ ;
wrong
  Mis. 279– 4   prevent the wrong a˙
  Pan. 4–14   of right and wrong a˙,
your
  Mis. 146– 7   to direct your a˙ on receiving or

  Mis. 267–27   a˙, in obedience to God,
     353– 5   excess of action or not a˙ enough ;
  Man. 90– 7   a˙ OF THE BOARD.
  My. 278– 2   proper incentive to the a˙ of all
     361–20   * by a˙ at its annual meeting

actions

  Mis. 23–29   mirror repeats . . . the looks and a˙
     220–10   sick man's thoughts, words, and a˙,
     237– 7   wrought a change in the a˙ of men.
     280– 5   weigh the thoughts and a˙ of men ;
     291 10   other people's thoughts and a˙.
  My. 203–16   Our thoughts beget our a˙ ;
     276–20   * seek to dictate the a˙ of others.

active

  Mis. 206–17   by the a˙, all-wise, law-creating,
     250–16   call for a˙ witnesses to prove it,
     276–11   Scientists, a˙, earnest, and loyal,
     278–30   withdrawing from a˙ membership in
     340–23   Be a˙, and, however slow, thy
  Man. 73– 4   at least one a˙ practitioner
     73–17   unanimous vote of, the a˙ members
     85–19   a˙ and loyal Christian Scientists
  Ret. 33–22   is found to be even more a˙.
  Pul. 14– 4   a˙ yet unseen mental agencies
     36– 6   * from a˙ contact with the world.
     68–10   * from a˙ contact with the world.
  '00. 3– 2   his thoughts are right, a˙, and
  '02. 8–22   it makes man a˙,
  My. 165–16   an a˙ portion of one stupendous
     230– 4   amid ministries aggressive and a˙,

actively

  My. 272– 2   a˙ strives for perfection,

activities

  Mis. 204–19   increases the intellectual a˙,
     362–32   or lessens the a˙ of virtue.
  My. 37–20   * supreme cause of all the a˙ of
     362–16   * enlarging the a˙ of the Cause

activity

  Mis. 250–21   or goodness without a˙ and power.
     329–21   challenging . . . shadows to a˙,
     339–11   because of the supposed a˙ of evil.
  No. 39–15   purifies, and quickens a˙,
  '00. 8–19   a percentage due to our a˙
  My. 8–28   * religious denomination and its a˙.
     37–24   * unbroken a˙ of your labors,
     66– 5   * considerable a˙ has been going on
     159–17   this is the only right a˙,
     213– 3   spiritual growth and a˙.
     213– 5   and give a˙ to evil.
     213– 6   a˙ is by no means a right of evil
     259–25   give the a˙ of man infinite scope ;
     353–14   a˙ and availability of Truth ;

Act of 1874, Chapter 375, Section 4.

  Mis. 272– 4   * under A˙ of 1874, C˙ 375, S˙ 4.

actor

  Mis. 199–24   but the a˙ was human.

actors

  Mis. 275– 1   chief a˙ in scenes like these,
  '02. 17–13   Earth's a˙ change earth's scenes ;

acts

  Mis. 46–18   weight of his thoughts and a˙
     51–16   Motives govern a˙,

acts

  Mis. 119– 4   responsible for our thoughts and a˙ ;
     130–23   and the majority of one's a˙ are right,
     147–26   for he a˙ no studied part ;
     204–30   ambition, and a˙ of the Scientist.
     216– 2   inference from his a˙,
     219–27   feels wickedly and a˙ wickedly,
     264–19   it a˙ for a season.
     278–12   when my motives and a˙ are
  Man. 40– 4   A Rule for Motives and A˙
     40– 6   the motives or a˙ of the members
  Ret. 78– 1   a˙ like a diseased physique,
     79–10   in unselfish motives and a˙,
  Hea. 5–22   of our own thoughts and a˙ ;
  Peo. 11–19   as directly as men pass legislative a˙
  My. 3–17   for it a˙ and a˙ wisely,
     211–16   committal of a˙ foreign to the
     240–13   for it a˙ and a˙ wisely,
     352–13   reflect in our thoughts and a˙ the

actual

  Mis. 71–14   All a˙ causation must interpret
     103–22   hides the a˙ power,
     129– 8   an imaginary or an a˙ wrong,
     164–23   in the a˙ likeness of his Maker.
     182– 6   perceive man's a˙ existence
     188–27   not . . . an a˙ change in the realities
     269–15   the a˙ Science of Mind-healing
  Un. 25–22   it is not individual, not a˙.
     56–11   the a˙ understanding of C. S.
  Pul. vii–21   the a˙ bliss of man's existence
     55–29   * a˙ members of different congregations
  Rud. 13– 8   body is not the a˙ individuality
  No. 24–10   denies the a˙ existence of both
     31– 9   never a˙ persons or real facts.
  Hea. 16– 7   hath the most a˙ substance,
  My. 86–14   * before the a˙ work was completed,
     160–17   for a˙ being, health, holiness, and
     348–22   an a˙, unfailing causation,

actuality

  Un. 19–16   without any a˙ which Truth can know.

actually

  Mis. 171– 6   To suppose that Jesus did a˙ anoint
  Ret. 61– 8   a˙ conscious of the truth of C. S.,
  My. 72–26   * before the work was a˙ completed.

actuate

  '01. 33–28   motives which a˙ one sect to

actuated

  '02. 8–11   unless he is a˙ by love

actuating

  Mis. 141–17   spirit of Christ a˙ all the parties

acute

  Mis. 6– 9   majority of the a˙ cases
     20–22   a˙ diseases that had defied medical
     41–23   a belief of chronic or a˙ disease,
     44– 6   Can C. S. cure a˙ cases
     204– 7   sometimes chronic, but oftener a˙.
  Pan. 10–19   organic, chronic, and a˙ diseases

Adam (*see also* Adam's)

  Mis. 2–11   this A˙ legacy must first be seen,
     79–24   "As in A˙ all die,— *I Cor.* 15 : 22.
     100–19   allegory of A˙ and Eve
     179–10   "A˙, where art thou?"— *see Gen.* 3 : 9.
     182–19   man was never lost in A˙,
     185–27   The first man A˙— *I Cor.* 15 : 45.
     185–28   last A˙ was made— *I Cor.* 15 : 45.
     186– 3   In the creation of A˙ from dust,
     186–29   last A˙ represented by the Messias,
     188–29   she know that the last A˙,
     244– 1   from the side of A˙,— *see Gen.* 2 : 21.
     258–19   Error, or A˙, might give names
  Chr. 53–22   By A˙ bid,
  Ret. 55– 8   improves the race of A˙.
     69–26   'A˙, where art thou?
  Un. 30–14   "The first man A˙— *I Cor.* 15 : 45.
     30–15   last A˙ was made— *I Cor.* 15 : 45.
     30–16   refers to the second A˙ as
     30–23   I discerned the last A˙ as a
     51–17   but not one . . . is an Eve or an A˙.
  '01. 5–17   the material race of A˙,
  '02. 8–28   of man not as the offspring of A˙,
  Hea. 2–12   * "Old A˙ is too strong for
     17–14   The allegory of A˙
     17–16   sleep" that fell upon A˙— *Gen.* 2 : 21.
  My. 33– 8   "A˙, Where Art Thou?"— *see Gen.* 3 : 9.

Adam-dream

  Ret. 69– 5   was the A˙, the deep sleep,
  My. 5– 1   A˙ . . . in which man is supposed to
     109– 4   A˙ of mind in matter,
     296–18   the waking out of his A˙ of evil

Adam-race

  '00. 3–16   A˙ are not apt to worship the pioneer

Adam's
Ret. 67–22 in no way contingent on A· thought,
No. 20–23 A· mistiness and Satan's reasoning,

adaptability
Mis. 192–19 learned its a· to human needs,
210–15 woman's special a· to lead on C. S.,
My. 250–21 discriminate as regards its a· to

adapted
Mis. 46– 7 a· to destroy the appearance of evil
138–22 not so a· to the members of
313–13 jewels of thought, so a· to the hour,
314–31 such as is a· to that service.
315– 3 especially a· to the occasion,
Man. 63– 6 a· to a juvenile class,
104– 6 a· to The Mother Church only.
104– 8 a· to form the budding thought
Ret. 49–10 S. and H. is a· to work this result ;
82–30 better a· to spiritualize thought
Pul. 59–17 * was well a· for its purpose,
My. 127–31 a defence a· to all men,
216–21 a· to your present unfolding
233–12 better a· to deliver mortals from
237–11 a· to the present demand.
256– 4 a· to the key of my feeling

add
Mis. 135–19 A· one more noble offering to the
216–13 might a· to the above definition
306–17 * We would a·, as being of interest,
314–25 and a· to this announcement,
Ret. 40–17 It is sufficient to a· her babe was
Pul. 39– 9 a· . . . a little poem that I consider
45– 6 * but a· that they can get their
50– 7 * thus a· her influence toward the
No. 8– 4 a· one more privilege
'00. 2–22 Here we a· : The doom of such
'01. 1–13 a· to your treasures of thought the
26–26 allow me to a· I have read little of their
My. 20–14 please a· to your givings
122–10 and, you may a·, with tedious prosaics.
134–15 And here let me a· :
163–22 Here let me a· that,

added
Mis. 178–26 * pastor again came forward, and a·
270–15 shall be a· unto you."— Matt. 6 : 33.
339–19 a· one furrow to the brow of care?
Chr. 55–11 shall be a· unto you.— Matt. 6 : 33.
Pul. 69–14 * and a· : "This C. S. really is a
72–25 * a· the speaker,
81–11 * the woman of the past with an a· grace
No. 45– 4 a· : "Charity suffereth long,— I Cor. 13 : 4.
'00. 10–18 wisdom of our forefathers is not a·
'01. 2–30 been a· since last November
22–16 I do not say that one a· to one is
'02. 1– 7 a· to our church during the year
Hea. 2–15 a· his testimony :
My. 8–30 * congregations have been a·,
50–25 * members were a· to the church."
69–14 * a· magnificent carvings to the
130–22 must have the author's name a·
210– 5 plain that nothing can be a· to
222–12 Also he a· : "This kind — Matt. 17 : 21.
307– 2 a· to his copy when I corrected it.
318– 2 where Mr. Wiggin a· words,

addenda
'01. 21– 3 They are not the a·,

addendum
Mis. 57–14 That this a· was untrue, is seen

addicted
Mis. 242–30 a· to the use of opium

adding
Ret. 44–29 A· to its ranks and influence,
My. 195–18 our only means of a· to that talent

addition
Mis. 30– 4 Should we adopt the "simple a·"
60–15 to say that a· is not subtraction
106–19 In a·, I can only bring
234–23 in a· to this, she has
Man. 68–12 in a· to rent and board.
99–21 he shall, in a· to his other duties,
Ret. 59– 8 It is like saying that a· means
59– 9 and a· in another,
Un. 53–18 assertion that the rule of a· is
54–22 distinct a· to human wisdom,
My. 16–13 * In a· to the members of
67–19 * a· to The First Church of Christ,
75–26 * big a· to The Mother Church
299–13 In a· to this, C. S. presents
310– 5 In a· to my academic training,

additional
Mis. 50–14 There is absolutely no a· secret
Un. 35–27 which can gather a· evidence of
Pul. 50–14 * no a· sums outside of the
My. 335–11 * A· facts regarding Major Glover,

Address
Mis. 98– 7 my A· at the National Convention
106–15 chapter sub-title
110–13 chapter sub-title
116– 7 chapter sub-title
120–26 chapter sub-title
143–13 chapter sub-title
251– 1 chapter sub-title
My. 131–17 chapter sub-title
148– 9 chapter sub-title
170–11 chapter sub-title

address
Mis. 63–13 a· himself to the healing of
69–27 I will send his a· to any one
144– 9 laid away a copy of this a·,
155–25 when they a· me I shall be apt to
253– 8 speakers should will now a· you
280–23 brief a· by Mr. D. A. Easton,
315–24 shall not . . . mentally a· the thought,
322– 9 present to a· this congregation,
368–19 silent a· of a mental malpractitioner
Man. 52– 9 shall a· a letter of inquiry
Pul. 5– 4 a· on C. S. from my pen,
60– 4 * There was no a· of any sort,
86–14 * a· from the Board of Directors :
My. 53–31 * so many different ones a· them
64–22 * a· ourselves with renewed faith
299– 4 kindly referring to my a·
363–21 a· before the Christian Scientist

addressed
Mis. 60– 3 the Bible is a· to sinners
Man. 36–24 A· to Clerk.
36–25 a· to the Clerk of the Church.
Ret. 90–10 St. John a· one of his epistles
Pul. 74–11 * a· to the editor of the Herald :
Rud. 15–23 who cannot be a· individually,
My. 140–12 * letter a· to Christian Scientists
223–23 a· to the C. S. Board of Directors
271–20 * a· this question, requesting the
351– 3 * her letter of recent date, a· to

addresses
Ret. 15–22 made memorable by eloquent a·
My. 74–19 * not only evident from their a·

addressing
Mis. 320–21 a· to dull ears and undisciplined
My. 318–24 and, a· me, burst out with :

adds
Ret. 60– 9 Material sense a· that the
Un. 36– 1 only as it a· lie to lie.
Pul. 68–21 * a· interest to the Baltimore
Rud. 2– 4 He a·, that among Trinitarian
6–15 he a· that this is not
Hea. 11–19 metaphysics a·, "until you arrive at
My. 121–22 C. S., however, a· to these graces,
310–25 and a· that these "fits" were

adequacy
'02. 4– 6 their a· and correct analysis of

adequate
Mis. 4–18 a· to meet the requirement.
43–11 trifling sense of it as being a· to
341–31 neither . . . are a· to plead for
Man. 101– 6 who shall receive an a· salary
My. 22– 8 * sum of money a· to
40– 4 * able to give more a· reception to
56– 2 * be a· for years to come.
243–14 who are a· to take charge of
248–12 a· for the emancipation of the race.

adhere
Mis. 92–16 teacher should strictly a· to the
233–28 they only who a· to that standard.
284–10 Students who strictly a· to the right,
307–27 a· to the divine Principle
309–29 a· to the Bible and S. and H.,
Ret. 82–12 a· to the orderly methods
'01. 2–17 these are they who will a· to it.
22–19 I a· to my text, that one and one
Hea. 8–26 a· to the rule of this Principle
My. 111–18 Can Scientists a· to it,
182–30 May this beloved church a· to
251–29 A· to the teachings of the Bible,

adhered
Mis. 172–29 must be understood and a· to ;

adherence
Mis. 65–27 proves that strict a· to one is
140– 9 their a· to the superiority of
198–23 suffering is the fruit of . . . a· to
Man. 44– 2 show strict a· to the Golden Rule,
Ret. 50–21 a· to divine Truth and Love.
87–13 implicit a· to fixed rules,
My. 84–19 * in numbers, . . . and faithful a·.
94–11 * a· of its converts to the faith,

ADHERENT 13 ADMITTING

adherent
Mis. 62–20 An a· to this method honestly
Pul. 59–18 * not an a· of the order,

adherents
Mis. 213–18 a· of Truth have gone on rejoicing.
Man. 15– 3 As a· of Truth, we take the
Pul. 30–10 * is not limited to the Boston a·,
57–16 * a· of this church have proved
60–14 * thousands of a· who had come
79–11 * a· in every part of the civilized
My. 45– 4 * ultimate regeneration of its a·
59– 9 * should number its a· by
85– 7 * a· number probably a million,
93–31 * a· number hundreds of thousands,
96–17 * generosity of its a· towards

adheres
Ret. 84– 9 he strictly a· to the teachings in

adhering
Mis. 108–28 believing in, or a· to,
Man. 70– 6 a· strictly to her advice thereon.
My. 111–23 in a· to his premise
235– 7 a· to the imperative rules of

adieu
My. 347–13 * nor ever bid the Spring a·!

ad infinitum
Mis. 364–30 reality and power to evil a· i·.
Un. 41–27 phenomena appear to go on a· i·;
No. 21–19 perpetuate the supposed power. . . . a· i·.
My. 245–19 majestic march of C. S. go on a· i·,

adipose
Mis. 47– 5 a· belief of yourself as substance;

adjoining
Ret. 4– 5 a· towns of Concord and Bow,
9– 2 led my cousin into an a· apartment.
Pul. 34–15 * she walked into the a· room,
58–23 * A· the chancel is a pastor's
My. 12– 7 * land a· The Mother Church,
69–21 * A· this foyer are the

adjourn
Mis. 139– 1 recommend this honorable body to a·,

adjourned
Mis. 156–13 proposed to merge the a· meeting in

adjudged
Man. 44– 4 shall not be a· C. S.

adjust
Mis. 283– 5 upset, and a· his thoughts
317–20 Human desire is inadequate to a·

adjusted
Mis. 321– 9 balance a· more on the side of God,
My. 72– 1 * nicely a· acoustic properties

adjusting
Mis. 379–30 a· in the scale of Science

adjustment
My. 277–13 its a· shall be according to

adjusts
Mis. 353–20 the action that He a·.

ad libitum
Mis. 285–23 new-style conjugality, which, a· l·,
318– 9 affection for goodness must go on a· l·

administer
Mis. 90–22 a· the communion,
241–18 a· this alterative Truth:
Peo. 9–19 and then a· drugs
My. 129–21 Then will angels a· grace,

administered
Mis. 90–25 a· to his disciples the Passover,
'01. 18–11 who a· no remedy apart from Mind,
My. 247– 3 its government is a· by
254–24 its government is a· by

administering
Hea. 13–13 a· one teaspoonful of this water

administers
My. 107–15 homœopathist a· half a dozen or

administration
My. 69–22 * and the a· offices,

admirable
Pul. 29–19 * In his a· discourse Judge Hanna

admirably
My. 256– 4 a· adapted to the key of my feeling

Admiral
Mis. 281–12 A· Coligny, in the time of the

admiration
Mis. 167–22 in a· of his origin, he exclaims,
Pul. 61–21 * Much a· was expressed by all
My. 25–24 a· for and faith in the
31–16 * expressions of surprise and of a·
70–14 * stood in silent a· while

admire
My. 85–22 * to reverence and a·!
282– 4 I a· the faith and friendship of

admired
Po. 2–12 A· by all, still art thou drear

admirer
Mis. 294–26 an a· of Edgar L. Wakeman's

admirers
Pul. 47– 4 * her circle of pupils and a·

admires
My. 41–19 * affection which a· friends and hates

admiring
My. 86– 1 * the greeting of a· eyes,

admissible
Mis. 32–15 love alone is a· towards friend and
Ret. 21–28 may be a· and advisable;

admission
Mis. 46– 1 The a· of the reality of evil
196–30 require more than a simple a·
346–16 mortal a· of the reality of evil
Man. 67– 3 candidates for a· to this Church,
88–18 applying for a· to this Board
91–14 President gives free a· to classes.
Pul. 60– 2 * waiting for a·.
No. 2–14 through such an a·,
My. 30– 2 * or awaiting a· to one.
30–29 * for a· at the ten o'clock service,
57–20 * more than the hitherto largest a·,
79–12 * to gain a· to the temple

admissions
Mis. 42–31 our own false a· prevent us

admit
Mis. 2– 9 a· the total depravity of mortals,
14–11 to a· this vague proposition,
57– 4 which you a· cannot discern
58–29 you a· that there is more than
59–15 to a· that it has been lost
74–30 If you will a·, with me,
76–25 You will a· that Soul is the
81– 3 scholarly physicians openly a·.
100– 9 how much of this claim you a·
193–22 to a· that all Christians are
Man. 36–23 may a· said applicant to membership.
Ret. 54– 6 to a· the claims of the
Un. 22– 9 Thou shalt not a· that error
22–11 To a· the existence of error
22–12 would be to a· the truth of a lie.
36–22 yet a· the reality of moral
54– 3 is to a· all there is of sickness;
54–11 To a· that sin has any claim
54–12 is to a· a dangerous fact.
Pul 56–10 * Space does not a· of an elaborate
No. 2–12 healers who a· that disease is real
31– 2 if you a· that God sends it
41–18 never a· such as come to steal
'01. 23– 4 a· that God is Spirit and infinite,
33–18 a· that they do not kill people with
'02. 10–17 Religions in general a· that man
Hea. 12–25 a· the higher attenuations are
18–25 You must a· that what is termed
My. 61–22 * as the workmen began to a· that
97– 1 * almost every one is inclined to a·.
97– 2 * a· the power of mind over matter.
315–27 which they a· has snatched me from

admits
Mis. 102–13 His character a· of no degrees
209–13 physics a· the so-called pains of
Ret. 54–14 when it a· Truth without
Un. 34– 4 Mortal mind a· that it sees only
Hea. 15–17 a· in statement what he denies in
My. 211–31 which a· of no intellectual culture

admittance
My. 39– 2 * those who could not gain a·
188–31 When divine Love gains a· to
265– 5 and that it finds a

admitted
Mis. 219–12 a· that mortals think wickedly
Man. 35– 6 may be a· to membership
Ret. 6–22 a· to the bar in two States,
13– 1 a· to the Congregational . . . Church,
54–17 if Truth is a·, but not understood,
Un. 23–16 evidence of . . . is not to be a·,
54–24 both knew and a· the dignity of
'01. 33– 5 must not be a· to the vineyard
My. 38–11 * no more were a· until the next
57–18 * number of candidates a·
57–21 * number a· during the last year
311– 5 knocked at the door and was a·.

admitting
Mis. 18–24 Only by a· evil as a
27–31 first a· that it is substantial.

admitting
 Mis. 109–21 *a·* the existence of both, mortals
 No. 2–10 you cannot begin by *a·* its reality.
   46–13 begin by *a·* individual rights.
 Pan. 4–28 By *a·* self-evident affirmations
 Hea. 5– 2 While *a·* that God is omnipotent,
 My. 222–14 *a·* the claims of the senses
  329–23 * *a·* its interest in the movement,

admixtures
 Pan. 8–25 are *a·* of matter and Spirit,

admonish
 Mis. 107– 7 to *a·* them,
  141–25 I *a·* you : Delay not longer
 Man. 56– 2 to *a·* that member according to
 My. 106– 2 I *a·* Christian Scientists either to

admonished
 Mis. 361–17 To this great end, Paul *a·*,
  366–20 even as Jesus *a·*.
 Man. 51– 1 shall be *a·* in consonance with

admonishes
 Mis. 339–15 The past *a·* us :
 Peo. 10–25 and, as St. Paul *a·*,

admonition
 Mis. 292–23 Charity thus serves as *a·* and
  328–27 observe the apostle's *a·*,
 Man. 51– 4 if he neglect to accept such *a·*,
  78– 3 fails to heed this *a·*,
 No. v– 3 according to the apostle's *a·*,
 My. 37–29 * its wise counsel and *a·*.
  287– 8 serving as *a·*, instruction, and

admonitions
 My. 46–26 * *a·* of our Church Manual

ado
 Hea. 14– 3 in fine, much *a·* about nothing.

adopt
 Mis. 19–11 to *a·* them and bring them out in
  30– 4 Should we *a·* the "simple addition"
  215–28 nor *a·* the words, that Jesus used
 Man. 59–11 to *a·* the aforenamed method for
  72– 2 Branch churches shall not *a·*,
 Ret. 88–25 we should *a·* the spirit of
 Un. 50–25 *A·* this rule of Science,
 '01. 3–10 *a·* Webster's definition of God,
  30–28 and to *a·* Pope's axiom :
 Hea. 18–14 would willingly *a·* the new idea,
 My. 128–14 man's right to *a·* a religion,
  224–30 let us *a·* the classic saying,
  235–24 *a·* as truth the above statements?
  236– 9 please *a·* generally for your name,
  250– 7 *a·* this By-law in their churches,
  250–12 churches who *a·* this By-law

adopted
 Mis. x–26 *a·* that form of signature,
  111– 2 to demonstrate what you have *a·*
  111–32 or is a spiritually *a·* child,
  140–18 *a·* and urged only the
  359– 4 Christly method . . . must be *a·*.
 Man. 18–23 The Church Tenets, . . . were *a·*.
  18–24 By-Law *a·* March 17, 1903,
  46– 3 who claims a spiritually *a·* child
  46– 3 or a spiritually *a·* husband or wife.
  105– 2 No new Tenet or By-Law shall be *a·*,
 Ret. 43–10 my *a·* son, Ebenezer J. Foster-Eddy,
  44–25 proper measures were *a·* to
 Hea. 2– 8 afterwards pardoned and *a·*,
 My. 266–28 more spiritual modes . . . are *a·*.
  282– 9 Douma recently *a·* in Russia
  313–28 wounded her pride when I *a·* C. S.,

adopting
 Mis. 77–20 In *a·* all this vast idea of
  193–21 a word which the people are now *a·*.
 My. 250–20 churches *a·* this By-law will

adoption
 Mis. 15– 6 "waiting for the *a·*,— *Rom.* 8: 23.
  15–15 joyful *a·* of good ;
  95–22 "waiting for the *a·*,— *Rom.* 8: 23.
  101– 6 that which blesses its *a·* by
  182–10 find their *a·* with the Father ;
  184–25 as the seal of man's *a·*.
 Man. 46– 1 Illegal *A·*.
  46– 4 There must be legal *a·* and
 Ret. 78–16 the *a·* of a worldly policy
 Peo. 10–25 "waiting for the *a·*,— *Rom.* 8: 23.

adopts
 Man. 71–17 or *a·* The Mother Church's form of

adorable
 Mis. 106–23 the most *a·*, but most unadored,
  331–30 this *a·*, all-inclusive God,

adoration
 Pul. 5– 3 offered his audible *a·* in the words
 No. 35– 6 through deep humility and *a·*

adore
 Mis. 96–20 I reverence and *a·* Christ
  124–22 *a·* the white Christ,
 Man. 15– 6 *a·* one supreme and infinite God.
 Ret. 18–18 freely *a·* all His spirit hath made,
 Un. 4– 1 He is near to them who *a·* Him.
 Po. 64– 9 *a·* all His spirit hath made,

adoring
 Pan. 14– 6 if daily *a·*, imploring, and

adoringly
 Ret. 26– 3 *A·* I discerned the Principle of

adorn
 Mis. 392– 3 Clouds to *a·* thy brow,
 Po. 20– 3 Clouds to *a·* thy brow,
 My. 121–16 gems that *a·* the Christmas ring
  195–30 continue to build, rebuild, *a·*, and

adorned
 Pul. 48–20 * *a·* the mantel.
 My. 125–26 the bride (Word) is *a·*,

adornment
 Pul. 42–19 * was rich with the *a·* of flowers.
 My. 71–11 * great *a·* to the city.

adorns
 Pul. 76–14 * superb mantel . . . *a·* the south wall.
 My. 285– 8 Whatever *a·* Christianity crowns the

adown
 '02. 4–16 *a·* the corridors of time,

adulation
 My. 302–24 and I refuse *a·*.

adult
 Mis. 34–19 or the *a·* can return to his
  159–20 risen Christ, and the *a·* Jesus.
  241– 2 faith of both youth and *a·* should
 Pul. 1– 8 An old year is time's *a·*,
 No. 26– 7 identical with the *a·*,
 '00. 6–16 more readily than the *a·*,
  6–19 sense which the *a·* entertains of it.

adulterate
 Mis. 67– 6 thou shalt not *a·* Life, Truth, or
  268–25 let us not *a·* His preparations

adulterated
 Man. 43–20 prevent C. S. from being *a·*.
 Ret. 61–30 let not the milk be *a·*.

adulterating
 Man. 43–13 No *A·* C. S.

adulterer
 My. 106–25 a profane swearer, an *a·*,

adulterers
 Mis. 324–13 Within this mortal mansion are *a·*,

adulteries
 '01. 20–27 will handle its thefts, *a·*, and

adultery
 Mis. 67– 5 shalt not commit *a·*;"— *Exod.* 20: 14.
  335–18 murder, steal, commit *a·*,
 Hea. 7–22 Jesus knew that *a·* is a crime,
 My. 268–16 shalt not commit *a·*"— *Exod.* 20: 14.
  314–16 cause nevertheless was *a·*.

advance
 Mis. xi– 6 are still in *a·* of their time ;
  6–15 will rank far in *a·* of allopathy
  21–12 As the ages *a·* in spirituality,
  22– 8 far in *a·* of human knowledge
  29–26 nor *a·* health and length of days.
  50–26 *a·* Christianity a hundredfold.
  108–16 and *a·* the second stage of
  118–14 *a·* individual growth,
  139–28 in *a·* of the erring mind's
  199–25 as we *a·* in the spiritual
  274– 9 more than my teaching would *a·* it :
  359–21 were in *a·* of the period
  366– 3 they would *a·* the world.
 Ret. 54–21 is far in *a·* of their theory.
  70–12 or *a·* speculative theories
  94– 2 Having perceived, in *a·* of others,
 '01. 33–28 persecute another in *a·* of it.
 '02. 10– 7 call them false or in *a·* of the
 Peo. 12–17 As our ideas of Deity *a·*
 My. 20–11 name your gifts to her, in *a·*?
  21– 9 * *a·* the erection of many branch
  148–28 scourging the sect in *a·* of it.
  216–26 *a·* in the knowledge of self-support,
  252–25 was a step in *a·*.
  342–32 will *a·* nearer perfection."

advanced
 Mis. 52–28 before solving the *a·* problem.
  234–16 never has *a·* man a single step
  295–24 The most *a·* ideas are
  308–12 *A·* scientific students are ready
  311–12 not quite ready to take this *a·* step
  345–21 against an *a·* form of religion,

advanced

Mis.	379–16	He certainly had *a·* views
Ret.	34–18	he is *a·* morally and spiritually.
Pul.	vii–12	telescope of that *a·* age,
'01.	33–8	* in the more *a·* decaying stages
Hea.	1–11	to wait until the age *a·*
My.	22–24	* *a·* position taken by our
	44–15	* *a·* to the front of the platform,
	80–5	* of consumption in its *a·* stages,
	95–21	* when "*a·*'" clergymen of other
	139–23	you have *a·* from the audible to
	140–23	Christ, points the *a·* step.
	160–28	*a·* psychist knows that this hell is
	310–2	sufficiently *a·* so that they

advancement

Mis.	6–7	needed for the *a·* of the age.
Ret.	49–2	for the *a·* of the world in Truth
	81–30	requisite at every stage of *a·*.
Pul.	50–7	* toward the *a·* of better home life
Hea.	8–12	slow to perceive individual *a·* ;
My.	113–30	steady *a·* of this Science
	239–28	state and stage of mental *a·*,
	241–8	* prevent their *a·* in this direction.
	281–25	* *a·* of the cause of arbitration."
	339–13	New Hampshire's *a·* is marked.

advances

Mis.	309–11	He *a·* most in divine Science who
My.	140–20	*a·* it spiritually.

advancing

Mis.	2–1	the evolutions of *a·* thought,
	42–19	our joys and means of *a·*
	200–11	The *a·* stages of C. S.
	222–5	to believe that he is *a·* while
	246–31	The *a·* faith and hope
	247–3	*proofs* of *a·* truth
	360–32	No *a·* modes of human mind
	363–30	every *a·* epoch of Truth
Ret.	70–21	the *a·* idea of God,
Un.	61–12	Human perception, *a·* toward the
	61–15	neither *a·*, retreating, nor
No.	19–8	second thought of *a·* humanity.
	33–7	by *a·* the kingdom of Christ.
	39–24	*A·* in this light, we reflect it ;
	46–6	The *a·* hope of the race,
'01.	1–7	more extended, more rapidly *a·*,
	29–5	mortals in the *a·* stages of their
'02.	10–12	*a·* above itself towards the Divine,
	11–20	Therefore it is thine, *a·* Christian,
Hea.	2–7	condemned at every *a·* footstep,
My.	45–26	* each *a·* step has logically
	135–12	more peace in my *a·* years,
	135–27	cheer my *a·* years.
	139–7	*a·* footsteps of progress,
	200–2	rapidly *a·*, . . . the genius of C. S.
	242–6	nor *a·* towards it ;
	322–25	* *a·* many good points in the Science,

advantage

Mis.	35–25	it is greatly to your *a·*
	150–14	no *a·*, but great disadvantage,
	255–17	chapter sub-title
	283–2	one can to *a·* speak the
Pul.	62–7	* *a·* of great economy of space,
No.	2–25	Taking *a·* of the present ignorance
	41–10	to the best *a·* for mankind
My.	37–11	* everlasting *a·* of this race.
	97–13	* Scientists have a little the *a·*

advantageous

Mis.	43–14	far more *a·* to the sick
Man.	52–25	of what she understands is *a·*
My.	244–5	if a larger class were *a·* to

advantageously

Rud.	15–19	can *a·* enter a class,

advantages

Mis.	33–21	*What are the a· of your system*
	33–23	C. S. has the following *a·*:
	255–18	What are the *a·* of your system
	255–21	I claim . . . the following *a·*:
Ret.	34–10	following *a·*: . . . It does away with

advent

Mis.	10–26	this is the *a·* of spiritualization.
	162–5	*a·* of a higher Christianity.
	320–5	its earthly *a·* and nativity,
Ret.	70–21	spiritual *a·* of the advancing idea
	81–15	supreme *a·* of Truth in the heart,
Pul.	55–8	* is the *a·* of C. S.
'01.	24–19	its earthly *a·* is called
My.	239–30	accelerated by the *a·* of C. S.,
	256–19	earthly *a·* and nativity of our Lord
	308–3	*a·* of divine healing

adventure

My.	158–9	in an age of Love's divine *a·*

adversary

'00.	2–24	than the *a·* can hope.

adverse

No.	6–22	more apparent than the *a·* but true
'01.	29–19	and *a·* winds are blowing,
'02.	11–4	to and fro by *a·* circumstances,
My.	41–9	* thoughts *a·* to the law of love.
	195–5	*A·* circumstances, loss of help,
	213–25	*a·* influence of animal magnetism.

adversity

Mis.	8–22	* "Sweet are the uses of *a·*."
My.	139–10	Christian Scientist thrives in *a·*;

advertise

Man.	46–10	which *a·* his business or profession,
	82–18	shall not *a·* as healers.
My.	191–5	Your enemies will *a·* for you.

advertised

Man.	72–15	may be *a·* in *The C. S. Journal*.
	74–19	churches and . . . *a·* in said *Journal*,
My	57–23	* *a·* in *The C. S. Journal*
	57–25	* number of societies *a·*
	306–24	I *a·* that I would pay
	334–8	* *a·* in every weekly issue of

Advertiser

Pul.	88–12	* *A·*, Calais, Me.
	88–13	* *A·*, Boston, Mass.
	88–25	* *A·*, New York City.

advertiser

Man.	82–12	without the request of the *a·*,

advertising

'02.	13–21	*a·* the property in the

advice

Mis.	137–18	dear ones, if you take my *a·*
	226–8	giving *a·* on personal topics.
	236–16	to give, to one or the other, *a·*
	243–23	alludes to Paul's *a·* to Timothy.
	298–24	chapter sub-title
	350–5	By and with *a·* of the very student
	350–10	There was no *a·* given,
Man.	70–6	adhering strictly to her *a·*
'00.	9–4	I sometimes withdraw that *a·*
My.	122–1	*a·* that one gratuitously bestows
	313–24	nor did . . . seek my *a·*.
	345–24	about *a·* on surgical cases."

advisable

Mis.	53–11	*Do you sometimes find it a· to*
	89–10	*a·* in most cases that Scientists
Ret.	21–28	may be admissible and *a·*;
	85–3	Teachers of C. S. will find it *a·*

advise

Mis.	308–32	I earnestly *a·* all Christian Scientists
	347–15	Two individuals, . . . *a·* me.
Man.	87–12	No member . . . shall *a·* against class
No.	8–10	*A·* students to rebuke
'00.	8–30	I sometimes *a·* students not to
My.	360–17	I *a·* you with all my soul to

advised

'02.	15–26	*a·* me to drop both the book and the
My.	319–20	* may interest you to be *a·* that

advisors

Hea.	9–11	their moral *a·* talk for them

advises

My.	226–27	"Mrs. Eddy *a·*, until the public

advising

Rud.	15–12	*a·* diseased people not to enter a

advisory

My.	63–4	* *a·* capacity in the later days ;

advocacy

Ret.	7–18	* *a·* of the side he deemed right.

advocate

Ret.	78–12	which *a·* materialistic systems ;

Æolian

Pul.	26–13	* with *Æ·* attachment,
	60–21	* having an *Æ·* attachment.

aerial

Ret.	11–5	If fancy plumes *a·* flight,
Po.	60–1	If fancy plumes *a·* flight,

Æsculapius (*see also* Esculapius)

'00.	13–18	*Æ·*, the god of medicine,
	13–19	serpent was the emblem of *Æ·*.
	13–23	school of Balaam and *Æ·*,
My.	105–4	This *Æ·*, defined Christianly
	205–17	spiritual *Æ·* and Hygeia, saith,

æsthetic

My.	88–28	* *æ·* debt to that great and growing

afar

Mis.	174–19	Is this kingdom *a·* off?
	342–20	fables flee, and heaven is *a·*
	393–16	From the shores *a·*, complete.
	397–13	From tired joy and grief *a·*,
Chr.	53–2	Bright, blest, *a·*,

afar
Pul. 18–22 From tired joy and grief *a·*,
Po. 13– 1 From tired joy and grief *a·*,
     51–21 From the shores *a·*,
     68–23 whether near or *a·*.
     73–17 *a·* from life's turmoil its goal.
My. 183–25 Not *a·* off I am
     290– 4 near seems *a·*, the distant nigh,
     290–18 when all earthly joys seem most *a·*.

affair
Mis. 52–13 occasionally a love *a·*.

affairs
Mis. 204–25 all the minutiæ of human *a·*.
     267–23 human *a·* should be governed by
     297–12 reports of American *a·*
     312–14 * of divine Providence in human *a·*
Man. 69–24 or attend to other *a·* outside
     74– 9 interfere with its *a·*.
Pul. 55–28 * in the management of its own *a·*.
My. 43– 6 * order aright the *a·* of daily life.
     135– 9 attended to my secular *a·*,
     137–12 to my secular *a·*,
     137–19 *a·* carefully taken care of for
     216– 1 wisdom should temper human *a·*,
     223–13 questions about secular *a·*,
     340–25 rule righteously the *a·* of state.
     359– 9 involved in the *a·* of the church

affect
Mis. 31– 5 disastrously *a·* the happiness of
Pul. 51–16 * *a·* the well-established methods.
My. 179–25 in no wise *o·* C. S.
     301–25 or *a·* cerebral conditions in any

affected
Ret. 33–17 patients not *a·* by a larger dose.

affecting
Ret. 71–13 know not what is *a·* them,
My. 328–11 * the law *a·* them passed by the

affection (*see also* **affection's**)
distinguishing
Ret. 94–26 distinguishing *a·* illustrated in
faith, and
Mis. 100–29 forgiveness, abiding faith, and *a·*,
faithful
Mis. 110– 6 innocence, unselfishness, faithful *a·*,
fervid
My. 248–12 honest, fervid *a·* for the race
gratitude and
Mis. 203– 5 mine through gratitude and *a·*.
growing
Mis. 337–18 unless it produces a growing *a·*
higher
Mis. 276–23 a purer, higher *a·* and ideal.
human
Mis. 287–20 foundations of human *a·*
My. 234–12 human *a·* to spiritual understanding,
     268– 8 If the motives of human *a·* are right,
its
Mis. 351–28 chastens its *a·*, purifies it,
just
Ret. 76–19 This just *a·* serves to
large
Mis. 318– 5 I have a large *a·*,
legitimate
Mis. 287– 9 discerning not the legitimate *a·*
may dwell
Ret. 18–20 the spot where *a·* may dwell
Po. 64–12 the spot where *a·* may dwell
miscall
Mis. 250– 5 Mortals misrepresent and miscall *a·*;
natural
Mis. 318– 9 natural *a·* for goodness
objects of
Ret. 31– 1 material objects of *a·*
of nations
My. 290– 7 live on in the *a·* of nations.
one
No. 39–18 include all mankind in one *a·*.
or love
Ret. 80– 1 an unselfish *a·* or love,
our
Ret. 80–28 in proportion to our *a·*.
My. 9–12 * declare the depth of our *a·*
permanence of
Mis. 160– 1 power and permanence of *a·*
preserve
Mis. 287–30 preserve *a·* on both sides.
pride and
Mis. 295–13 Scotchman's national pride and *a·*,
protection and
Mis. 263–12 divine protection and *a·*.
pure
Mis. 107–11 A pure *a·*, concentric,
are in
Mis. 152–19 made ready for the pure in *a·*,

affection
real
Mis. 91–16 real *a·* for Jesus' character
reason and
Mis. 363–23 misguides reason and *a·*,
respect and
My. 37– 9 * gratitude, respect, and *a·*
     88–25 * turn with respect and *a·*.
same
No. 12–13 The same *a·*, desire, and
sentimental
My. 41–19 * rise from sentimental *a·* which
significance of
Mis. 250–22 the glorious significance of *a·*
so-called
Mis. 250– 6 so-called *a·* pursuing its
tender
My. 36–27 * tender *a·* for the cause of
this
Ret. 76–15 This *a·*, so far from being
true
Mis. 142–18 varying types of true *a·*,
undivided
Mis. 341– 3 undivided *a·* that leaves the
wealth of
My. 291–14 enfolded a wealth of *a·*,
zealous
Mis. 322–26 zealous *a·* for seeking good,

Mis. 154–29 Have no ambition, *a·*, nor

affectional
Ret. 81–12 spiritual sense, *a·* consciousness,

affectionate
Mis. 147–22 the trusty friend, the *a·* relative,
     240–21 *a·*, and generally brave.
Un. 48–13 the *a·* Father and Mother
Pul. 86– 6 * from her *a·* Students,
My. 322– 6 * Your *a·* student,

affectionately
Mis. 132– 6 *A·* yours,
     136–28 Yours *a·*,
     146–26 *A·* yours,
     151–29 *A·* yours in Christ,
     153–31 *A·* yours,

affection's
Mis. 388–17 *A·* wreath, a happy home;
Po. 21– 6 *A·* wreath, a happy home;
My. 258–10 bowed in strong *a·* anguish,

affections
aims and
Mis. 266– 3 unselfish and pure aims and *a·*.
alone in the
Mis. 145– 4 shall exist alone in the *a·*,
and desires
Ret. 79–12 purification of the *a·* and desires.
and lives
My. 156–22 receive into their *a·* and lives
and motives
Mis. 19–10 the *a·* and motives of men
and understanding
Un. 2–26 through their *a·* and understanding.
are enduring
My. 268– 8 *a·* are enduring and achieving.
changing the
Mis. 268–20 changing the *a·*, enlightening the
chastened
Mis. 356–10 chastened *a·*, and costly hopes,
chasten the
Ret. 21–18 to chasten the *a·*, to rebuke human
educate the
Mis. 235–23 educate the *a·* to higher resources,
enrich the
Man. 41–24 enrich the *a·* of all mankind,
false
My. 125– 2 false *a·*, motives, and aims,
foundation for the
Mis. 74– 7 spiritual foundation for the *a·*
human
    (*see* human)
hypocrite's
Un. 56–22 The hypocrite's *a·* must first be
increased
Mis. 289–25 exalted and increased *a·*,
interests and
Mis. 289–29 Mutual interests and *a·* are the
my
Mis. 290–20 my *a·* involuntarily flow out
     310–13 While my *a·* plead for all
Ret. 23–18 my *a·* had diligently sought
new
Mis. 204–14 new purposes, new *a·*,
our
Mis. 174–10 Let us open our *a·* to the
Ret. 28–16 must be supreme in our *a·*,

affections
our
Pul. 35—20 must be supreme in our *a*,
permeate the
Mis. 223—20 so permeate the *a* of all
purifies the
My. 131— 1 that which purifies the *a*
union of the
Mis. 52—16 it must be a union of the *a*
your
Pan. 14— 4 Set your *a* on things above ;
Hea. 16—13 Life and Love will occupy your *a*,

Mis. 147—17 not guided merely by *a*
172—21 received through the *a*,

affects
Mis. 5—31 believe that the body *a* the mind,
5—32 than that the mind *a* the body.
247—26 believe that the body *a* mind,

affidavit
My. 137— 1 chapter sub-title
137— 2 * *a*, in the form of a letter
314—31 *a* by R. D. Rounsevel

affiliate
Mis. 80—14 to *a* with a wrong class

affinities
Mis. 291— 4 personal channels, *a*, self-interests,

affinity
Mis. 296—24 *a* for the worst forms of vice?
Un. 57—16 neither held her error by *a* nor

affirm
Mis. 293—24 To *a* mentally and audibly
298— 5 as some *a* that we say,
374—24 frantically *a* what is what :
Man. 92— 5 demonstrates what we *a* of C. S.,
Un. 2—15 *a* that the Mind which is good,
49—25 than to *a* it to be something which
Peo. 3—11 would *a* that these are natural,
My. 217—23 all that the material senses *a*.

affirmation
Ret. 9— 7 and emphasized her *a*.
My. 22—18 * put its seal of *a* upon

affirmations
Mis. 65— 8 why not submit to the *a*
Pan. 4—28 By admitting self-evident *a*

affirmative
Mis. 67—29 I modify my *a* answer.
193— 3 we reply in the *a*
337— 5 certain of so momentous an *a*?
Un. 45—17 *a* to Truth's negative.
My. 61— 1 * I gladly answered in the *a*,

affirmed
Mis. 169—14 She *a* that the Scriptures
345—22 pagan slanderers *a* that
My. 84—10 * has *a* its wisdom.

affirming
Un. 38—16 thus *a* the existence and
Pul. 31— 5 * in *a* the present application of

affirms
Un. 24—25 Whatever matter thus *a*
Pul. 30—18 * It *a* the atonement;
30—20 * *a* the power of Truth

affixed
Mis. x—13 To some articles are *a* data,

afflatus
Mis. 166— 7 in our midst a divine *a*.
Ret. 31—30 a present spiritual *a*.

afflict
Mis. 73— 6 doth not *a* willingly."— Lam. 3 : 33.

afflicted
Mis. 168— 8 hear not, and are *a* with
208—22 "Before I was *a*—Psal. 119 : 67.
My. 96— 6 * and none of them *a* with

afflicteth
Ret. 74— 8 *a* me not wittingly :
Rud. 10—20 know that He *a* not willingly

affliction
Mis. 9— 2 *a* rightly understood,
66—16 suffering is the lighter *a*.
151— 8 the furnace of *a*.
276—20 Love is found in *a*.
My. 303—32 molten in the furnace of *a*.

afflictions
Mis. 327—25 consoling their *a*, and helping

afford
Mis. 13—26 to *a* opportunity for proof
35—11 *a* the most concise, yet complete,
64—19 philosophy and religion that *a*
120—24 as often as they can *a* to

afford
Mis. 136—19 You can well *a* to give me up,
224— 5 can hardly *a* to be miserable for
338— 6 not by "words,"— these *a* no proof,
338—13 *a* the only rule I have found
Man. 44—18 every member, who can *a* it,
Ret. 6—14 more space than this little book can *a*.
Un. 34—18 What evidence does mortal mind *a*
Rud. 5— 1 spiritual senses *a* no such evidence,
7—14 they *a* the only true evidence
'02. 14—28 and *a* an open field and fair play.
Hea. 16—20 senses *a* no evidence of Truth
My. 151— 8 these attacks *a* opportunity for
161—25 do not *a* a sufficient defence
179—30 They *a* such expositions of
219— 1 that which my books *a*,
224—28 cannot *a* to recommend
262—19 *a* little divine effulgence,
349—10 *a* little aid in understanding

afforded
Mis. 275—21 satisfaction that you *a* me
Ret. 83—11 *a* by the Bible and my books,
'02. 14—23 *a* me neither favor nor

affords
Mis. 72—31 passage quoted *a* no evidence of
106—29 *a* the only strains that thrill
133—28 It *a* me great joy to be able
164—31 Science *a* the evidence that God is
186—22 *a* self-evident proof of immortality ;
319—24 *a* ample opportunity for
Rud. 1—11 word *person* *a* a large margin for
No. 34—14 Physical torture *a* but a slight
'00. 7—27 Christ is found near, *a* help,
Hea. 19—18 *a* him fresh opportunities
My. 42—20 * It *a* me great pleasure to
91— 4 It *a* refutation of the notion
189— 6 it *a* even me a perquisite of joy.

aflame
Po. 22— 5 One hundred years, *a* with Love,

afloat
My. 144— 5 lies *a* that I am sick,

aforenamed
Man. 59—11 to adopt the *a* method

aforesaid
Mis. 302—24 copying of my writings as *a*.
371— 1 If, as the gentleman *a* states,
378—10 *en route* for the *a* doctor
Man. 43— 2 a second offense as *a* shall
75—18 own the *a* premises
My. 135—19 of this, the *a* transaction.
136—24 To my *a* Trustees I have
144— 7 either of the *a* conditions
284—18 the *a* Memorial service

aforethought
Mis. 227— 9 yet with malice *a*
248—15 malice *a* of sinners."

aforetime
Un. 10— 9 intended it, or ordered it *a*,
'01. 9—30 now, as *a* they cast out evils
My. 185—30 Christ, as *a*, heals the sick,
204—29 based as *a* on this divine Principle,
219—17 healing, as *a*, of all manner of
239— 8 mankind will, as *a*,

afraid
Mis. 39—17 not *a* to take their own medicine,
109—29 "Be not *a*!"— Mark 6 : 50.
211—19 Or, are you *a* to do this
324—23 he is *a* to go on
335—20 *a* of its supposed power,
Ret. 9—12 I was *a*, and did not answer.
Un. 20— 9 *Third:* I am *a* of it.
Pul. 3—27 so small that I am *a*.
4— 2 "Be not *a* "— Mark 6 : 50.
33— 9 * was *a* and did not reply.
'02. 20— 3 be not *a*."— Mark 6 : 50.
My. 165—26 He who is *a* of being too generous
336— 4 * was *a* to have her brother,

Africa
My. 147—28 From the interior of *A* to

African
Mis. 88—25 * miraculous to the equatorial *A*,
Peo. 10—27 *A* slavery was abolished on this

after
Mis. x—20 *A* my first marriage,
24—13 ever *a* was in better health
32—20 seekers *a* Truth whose teacher
34— 1 none of the harmful "*a* effects"
42— 1 *A* the change called death
42— 5 *A* the momentary belief of
43— 4 *a* having been made acquainted
54—18 *a* one month's treatment
57—12 *a* the truth of man had been demonstrated,

after

Mis.
60– 9   a· all other means have failed.
67–30   a· all the footsteps requisite
69–11   a· our likeness :— Gen. 1 : 26.
82–13   a· the destruction of mortal mind
87–17   to look a· the students;
87–20   A· class teaching, he does best in
88–18   like a benediction a· prayer,
89–22   I am a seeker a· Truth.
90–28   a· his resurrection,
90–29   a· his disciples had left their
105–10   to all seekers a· Truth.
114– 2   to all seekers a· Truth.
131–28   A· this financial year,
149– 7   a· presenting the various offerings,
149– 8   one a· another has opened his lips
156– 4   readers, and seekers a· Truth.
158– 9   a· His messenger has obeyed the
162–23   a· the similitude of the Father,
163–25   A· his brief brave struggle,
186– 5   the embryo-man a· his birth,
188–14   walk not a· the flesh,— Rom. 8 : 1.
188–14   but a· the Spirit." — Rom. 8 : 1.
197– 6   and to strive a· holiness
197–20   compel us to pattern a· both ;
201– 9   reproduced his body a· its burial,
201–25   more securely a· a robbery,
201–26   a· losing those jewels of character,
205–16   A· this, man's identity or
216–22   * some time a· the rest of it had gone."
219–14   think also a· a sickly fashion.
225–13   Soon a· this conversation,
226– 5   a· eating several ice-creams,
235–18   and thirsting a· a better life,
246–32   earnest seeking a· practical truth
261–25   a kind of men a· man's own making.
265–21   A· . . . explaining spiritual Truth
272– 5   * repealed from and a· January 31,
295–27   an institution which names itself a·
302–22   at once a· said service.
304– 7   * A· the close of the Exhibition
315–16   look a· the welfare of his students,
315–17   not only through . . . but a· it ;
341– 7   a· much slipping and clambering,
358–25   a· accomplishing the greatest work
360–19   "Israel a· the flesh," — I Cor. 10 : 18.
364–13   is not a search a· wisdom,
378– 8   A· much consultation among
379– 1   A· treating his patients, Mr. Quimby
379–27   It was a· Mr. Quimby's death

Man.
17– 2   earnest seekers a· Truth
26–22   a· the candidate is approved by
36–21   a· which, the unanimous vote
37– 4   a· the blank has been properly filled
46– 9   a· his name on circulars,
55–16   a· three years of exemplary character.
62–14   a· reaching the age of twenty.
64–22   nineteen hundred and three and a·,
75–19   A· the first church was built,
76– 1   a· the debts are paid,
83–16   not only during the class . . . but a·
84–10   A· 1907, the Board of Education
86– 3   A· a student's pupil has been
94– 7   no receptions nor festivities a· a
109–12   a· being filled out by the

Ret.
7– 3   age of thirty-one, a· a short illness,
10–11   A· my discovery of C. S.,
14–30   A· the meeting was over
19– 5   A· parting with the dear home circle
20– 1   A· returning to the paternal roof
20– 3   until a· my mother's decease.
20–16   written a· this separation :
20–25   a· our marriage his stepfather
21– 1   A· his removal a letter was read
24– 1   a· the death of the magnetic doctor,
27– 7   a· my discovery of the
31–10   hunger and thirst a· divine things,
36– 5   Five years a· taking out my
38– 7   A· months had passed,
43– 6   No charter was granted . . . a· 1883.
43–10   A· I gave up teaching,
43–18   a· which I judged it best
45– 8   A· this material form of cohesion
47–18   A· having received instructions in
49– 6   a· having accomplished the worthy
49–27   A· due deliberation and earnest
81–15   A· the supreme advent of Truth
92– 6   a· that the full corn — Mark 4 : 28.

Un.
6– 3   fruit a· its kind." — Gen. 1 : 11.
14– 5   long a· God made the universe,
22– 2   made a· God's eternal likeness,
60–14   who are made a· — see Jas. 3 : 9.

Pul.
5– 6   one friendship a· another
5–13   A· the publication of "S. and H.
9–16   A· the loss of our late lamented
14– 9   a· the woman, — Rev. 12 : 15.

after

Pul.
33–13   * and a· that it ceased.
36– 1   * a year a· her founding of the
41– 4   * a· the full amount needed
43–13   * A· an organ voluntary,
50–25   * a· a little skirmishing,
51–10   * are searching a· religious truth.
57–27   * who, a· many vicissitudes,
64–19   * A· careful study she became
69– 8   * a· several doctors had pronounced
72–13   * a· she had practically been given up
73– 6   * an ardent follower a· God.
82–14   * because she was created a· man,

No.
12– 9   A· a lifetime of orthodoxy
13–10   centuries passed a· those words were
21– 7   It was not a search a· wisdom;
23–10   a· the accepted definition.
27–27   a· the change called death,
28– 2   a· the transition called death,
39– 6   a· the fashion of Baal's prophets,

Pan.
7– 8   belief, that a· God, Spirit, had
10–13   a· graduation, the best students
11– 5   a· the image of Him — Col. 3 : 10.

'00.
7–12   a· reading "S. and H.
10– 4   that a· a fight vanisheth
13–13   a· a series of wars
15–10   a· this Passover cometh victory,

'01.
6–17   a· this model of personality?
10–24   a· the pattern of the mount.
10–30   A· Jesus had fulfilled his mission
21–14   a· Mrs. Eddy has gone.
28–29   A· a hard and successful career
29– 2   Have we looked a· or even known
31–12   A· a long acquaintance with the

'02.
13–19   A· the mortgage had expired
14–20   achievement a· achievement has
16– 1   a· the earthquake and the fire.

Hea.
4–15   a· infinite Spirit is
4–18   a· a temporary lapse,
13–18   A· these experiments you cannot

Peo.
9–14   a· the model of our Father,

My.
v–19   * a· nine years of arduous
4– 8   followeth a· me, — Matt. 10 : 38.
13–30   returns it unto them a· many days,
16– 7   * a· paying out the sum of
17–27   * a· which the following extracts
20–20   * were returned a· having been
32– 3   * a· five minutes of silent communion
32–29   * A· the reading of the
38–24   * Scientists said a· the service
40– 5   * thirst a· practical righteousness ;
47–10   * A· a work has been established,
50–32   * committee met a· the services
52–32   * "Day a· day flew by,
53–18   * A· establishing itself as a church
54–25   * Sunday a· Sunday."
61–13   * but a· a while, in the night,
91–30   * A· but a few years,
105– 7   * A· my discovery of C. S.,
113–12   not a· the flesh, but a· — Rom. 8 : 1.
114–19   I could not write . . . a· sunset.
173– 3   * a· the visit of the Christian Scientists
173– 9   A· the C. S. periodicals
178– 2   do not mislead the seeker a· Truth.
205– 3   not a· the flesh, but a· — Rom. 8 : 1.
214–19   Four years a· my discovery of C. S.,
229–18   and come a· me, — Luke 14 : 27.
233–25   followeth a· me, — Matt. 10 : 38.
241–25   * a· coming to the light of Truth,
246– 1   a· receiving the first degree,
247–26   a· many or a few days
250– 9   a· three years of acceptable service
251–12   if, a· examination in the Board of
251–19   a· three years of good practice,
285–25   a· the way which they call heresy,
302–25   a· it was built and dedicated
307–10   A· this I noticed he used that word,
309–10   A· it was decided,
309–24   a· the prevailing style of
311– 7   Shortly a·, ... my good housekeeper
312– 7   * six months a· his marriage,
313–30   a· my father's second marriage
314– 3   says that a· my marriage
314–18   A· the evidence had been
320–28   * several times a· the class closed,
327–19   * A· the amendment had been passed,
328–26   * a· enumerating the different
331–25   * bereaved widow a· his decease.
331–31   * extended to her a· his death,
332–24   * A· frequent searchings
335–15   * for many years a· his death.
336– 5   * a· her husband's death,
336–12   "A· returning to the paternal roof
336–14   a· my mother's decease."
338–13   till a· the lecture was delivered
342– 5   * and a· a kindly greeting

after

My.	342–25	* a· all now concerned in its
	343– 5	* a· a prolonged exordium.
	346–10	* a· I reached Concord
		(see also **death, manner**)

Afterglow

My.	250–14	chapter sub-title

afternoon

Mis.	168–27	* on the a· of October 26,
Ret.	16– 1	One memorable Sunday a·,
	38–15	The a· that he left Boston
Pul.	37– 9	* and drives in the a·.
My.	39– 3	* at two o'clock in the a·.
	56– 5	* were held, morning and a·,
	65– 7	* voted yesterday a· to raise.
	78– 4	* morning, a·, and evening
	80–29	* as early as three o'clock in the a·
	147– 5	morning and a· services
	171–13	at two o'clock in the a·,
	171–20	* on her regular a· drive

afterpiece

Mis.	xii– 5	this a· of battle.

aftersmile

Mis.	389–24	heaven's a· earth's tear-drops gain,
Po.	5– 4	heaven's a· earth's tear-drops gain,

afterward

Mis.	373– 7	A few days a·,
Man.	39– 9	a·, when sufficient time
	64–19	a· consented on the ground that
Ret.	9–12	A· I wept, and prayed that
Pul.	55–17	* A· she selected the name C. S.
	65–26	* exemplar a· became a saint.
Po.	v–23	* for years a·,

afterwards

Mis.	11– 8	a· assisting them pecuniarily,
	81–16	a· to go up into the wilderness,
	248–25	A·, the glorious revelations of
	285– 5	A·, by a blunder of the gentleman
	318–16	and a· studied thoroughly
	325–11	and a· try to kill him.
	332–19	a· to have formed an evil sense
	348–31	and a· denied this and objected
Ret.	6–19	a· President of the United States ;
	24– 6	which I a· named C. S.
	38–12	As it a· appeared,
	40–12	A· they showed me the clothes
	40–18	The mother a· wrote to me,
	47–20	and a· studied thoroughly
'00.	3–23	Yahwah, a· transcribed Jehovah ;
'01.	13–24	as it is destroyed, and never a· ;
'02.	13–28	I a· gave to my church
Hea.	2– 8	a· pardoned and adopted,
My.	213–10	A·, with touching tenderness,
	307–18	a· I concluded that he only
	309– 7	Franklin Pierce, a· President
	311–20	a· Mrs. Judge Potter,
	319– 6	a· he wrote a kind

again

Mis.	10–12	if they fall they shall rise a·,
	50– 1	that God made all . . . is a· Scriptural ;
	54–22	But not to be subject a· to
	57– 1	created man over a·
	61–26	A· : mortals are the embodiments
	73– 5	and a· "He doth not — Lam. 3 : 33.
	99–29	is a· casting out evils
	126– 4	I half wish for society a· ;
	127– 7	and a· earnestly request,
	135– 2	A· I repeat, person is not
	137–18	if you take my advice a·,
	139– 3	meet a· in three years.
	150–29	A·, this infinite Principle, with its
	154–21	a· be made manifest in the flesh
	178–24	* a· to preach, here or elsewhere.
	178–25	* the pastor a· came forward,
	180– 8	* Has Christ come a· on earth?"
	191–22	A·, our text refers to the devil as
	217–21	A·, that matter is both cause and
	221–18	A· : If error is the cause of disease,
	243–31	A·, the Professor quotes,
	246–27	a· deluge the earth in blood?
	261– 1	A· : evil, as mind, is doomed,
	261–13	is measured to him a·,
	298– 9	measured to you a·— Matt. 7 : 2.
	302– 5	seeks a· to "cast lots — Matt. 27 : 35.
	317–12	A·, it is not absolutely requisite
	324–26	rushes a· into the lonely streets,
	327–21	only to take them up a·,
	337–30	is a· reproduced in the character
	369–25	would find our Father's house a·
	370–10	Let the sentinels . . . shout once a·,
	380–15	I a·, in faith, turned to divine help,
	392–23	Scenes that I would see a·.
	394– 9	bless, and make joyful a·.

again

Man.	39–18	he shall not a· be received
Ret.	8–15	the call a· came,
	8–19	till a· the same call was
	9–10	when the voice called a·,
	9–15	When the call came a·
	9–16	never a· to the material senses
	20–24	dominant thought in marrying a·
	21– 6	We never met a· until he had
	62– 1	Unless . . . healing will a· be lost,
	89–17	once a· entered the synagogue
Un.	14– 3	do His work over a·,
	23– 6	God has no bastards to turn a· and
	34–18	A· I ask : What evidence
	61–14	retreats, and a· goes forward ;
Pul.	14–20	nor a· sink the world into the
	33– 8	* if she heard the voice a· to reply
	33–12	* reply if the call came a·
	54– 1	* A·, in a poem entitled "The Master,"
	54– 5	* And we are whole a·.
	60–13	* The place was a· crowded,
No.	31–25	returned, to be a· forgiven ;
	44–21	or rule of error will a· unite
Pan.	6–18	A· : Did one Mind, or two
	7–26	A· : The hypothesis of mind in
	11–19	falls physically needs to rise a·
'00.	6–25	A·, that C. S. is the Science of
'01.	7– 8	A·, God being infinite Mind,
	8– 2	A· I reiterate this cardinal point :
	8–13	A· : Is man, according to C. S.,
	14– 2	A· : To assume there is no reality in
	22–28	A· : Even the numeration table of
	24– 9	A·, while descanting on the virtues of
	34–16	Give us, dear God, a· on earth
'02.	2–29	we shall meet a·, never to part.
	4– 3	I a· repeat, Follow your
	19– 4	A· : True to his divine nature,
Hea.	2–23	A·, they knew it was not
	3– 9	must a· become the head of
	4–17	to show itself infinite a·.
	7–19	A·, he charged home a crime
	16–23	A·, shall we say that God hath
Peo.	8–21	shall a· be swept by the divine
	8–23	Then shall C. S. a· appear,
	14–17	and behold once a· the power of
Po.	vi– 4	* and a· in Boston, in 1856.
	22– 6	A· shall bid old earth good-by
	41–20	just breaking, reecho a·
	45–12	bless, and make joyful a·.
	47– 1	Are the dear days ever coming a·,
	51– 5	Scenes that I would see a·.
	72– 3	ne'er a· Quench liberty that's just.
My.	12–22	it comes not back a·.
	18– 1	and a· earnestly request,
	36–10	* a· to consecrate all that we are
	37– 9	* declare a· our high appreciation
	54–22	* Hawthorne Rooms were a· secured.
	59–15	* listening a· to your words
	62–22	* we a· express our thankful
	104–13	A·, what shall be said of him who
	122–29	Christ, Truth, a· healing the sick
	128– 4	not laying a· the — Heb. 6 : 1.
	174– 7	in a· opening their spacious
	185–19	"was dead, and is alive a· ;— Luke 15 : 32.
	196–18	reviled not a· ; —I Pet. 2 : 23.
	214– 8	Christianity is a· demonstrating
	215–13	it was a· mailed to me in letters
	227–25	turn a· and rend you."— Matt. 7 : 6.
	256–17	A· loved Christmas is here,
	259– 1	look a· at your gift,
	280– 4	* which a· gives assurance of
	290–24	where the high and holy call you a·
	343–30	all back to union and love a·.

against (see also 'gainst)

Mis.	2–29	beliefs that war a· Spirit,
	8–24	a· you falsely, for my sake ;— Matt. 5 : 11.
	25– 1	a· his holiness and health.
	31–18	argue a· his own convictions
	36–25	mortal mind] is enmity a· God ;— Rom. 8 : 7
	55–13	are using that power a·
	55–14	the sin a· the Holy Ghost
	56–17	a kingdom divided a· itself,
	61– 5	a· the material symbolic counterfeit
	68– 8	* Christian would protest a·
	89– 3	kingdom divided a· itself — Matt. 12 : 25.
	114–19	a· original sin,
	114–31	how to guard a· evil
	115– 2	an offense a· God and humanity.
	115–23	a· the subtler forms of evil,
	119–14	strives to tip the beam a· the
	119–15	the flesh strives a· Spirit,
	119–15	a· whatever or whoever opposes
	119–17	a· man's high destiny.
	121– 9	human struggles a· the divine,
	124– 8	warreth a· Spirit,

against

Mis.	130–25	sin that one can commit a·
	139–12	*exalteth itself a· the — II Cor.* 10 : 5.
	140–24	would not be found fighting a· God.
	141– 8	and a· this church temple
	144–20	shall not prevail a· it." — *Matt.* 16 : 18.
	148– 2	meditates evil a· us in his heart.
	150–21	who can be a· us?" — *Rom.* 8 : 31.
	152–23	beat a· this sure foundation,
	174– 3	to talk and disclaim a· Truth ;
	174–20	to declare a· this kingdom is
	177– 6	conspiracy a· the Lord
	177– 7	and a· His Christ,
	177–10	in organizing action a· us.
	177–11	sworn enmity a· the lives of
	197–26	that is divided a· itself,
	201–28	bar his door a· further robberies.
	206– 5	dashing a· the receding shore,
	212–18	currents of human nature rush in a·
	213–12	a· the evil which, if seen,
	214– 7	at variance a· his father, — *Matt.* 10 : 35.
	214– 7	the daughter a· her· *Matt.* 10 : 35.
	214– 8	the daughter-in-law a· — *Matt.* 10 : 35.
	216–17	a big protest a· injustice ;
	217–24	and man a rebel a· his Maker.
	217–26	kingdom divided a· itself,
	221–25	a· both evil and disease,
	222–19	This sin a· divine Science
	224–27	unless the offense be a· God.
	234–21	That one should . . . a· such odds,
	246–26	intolerance, arrayed a· the
	247–12	charges a· my views are false,
	254–11	whose children rise up a· her ;
	256– 8	in daily letters that protest a·
	281– 5	will-power that you must guard a·.
	284–19	a· human error and hate.
	293–13	a· the opposite claims of error.
	307–29	must guard a· the deification of
	309–18	a· falling into the error of
	312– 2	to guard a· that temptation.
	316– 1	to defend themselves a·
	319–12	protest a· the reality of sin,
	325–27	a· sensualism in its myriad forms.
	328–14	and closed it a· Truth,
	345– 4	a· the charge of atheism ;
	345–21	a· an advanced form of religion,
	355–17	To strike out . . . a· the mist,
	367–22	It was not a· evil,
	367–22	but a· *knowing* evil,
	383–11	beat in vain a· the immortal parapets
Man.	42– 6	a· aggressive mental suggestion,
	51–26	complaints a· church members ;
	52– 4	A complaint a· a member of
	52–20	Working A· the Cause.
	52–22	working a· the interests of
	77– 5	Prior to paying bills a· the
	84– 1	Defense a· Malpractice.
	84– 3	how to defend themselves a·
	87–13	No member . . . shall advise a·
Ret.	22–10	a· himself." — *Heb.* 12 : 3.
	63–16	is nothing but a conspiracy a·
	67–10	self-arrayed a· the infinite,
	67–11	the mortal a· immortality,
	78–23	is to conspire a· the blessings
	78–23	a· your own success
	78–24	a· the progress of the human race
	79– 1	a· *honest* metaphysical theory
	85–13	Guard yourselves a· the subtly
	85–24	who can be a· us?" — *Rom.* 8 : 31.
Un.	17– 6	fought a· Sisera. — *Judg.* 5 : 20.
	26–20	protest a· this stanza of Bowring's,
	36– 4	this lie was the false witness a·
	46–17	incensed the rabbins a· Jesus,
	60– 4	a kingdom divided a· itself.
Pul.	12–23	in our warfare a· error,
	50–23	* The opposition a· it from the
Rud.	8–20	falsity shuts a· him the Truth
	9–18	weighs a· his healing power ;
	9–28	that whatever militates a· health,
No.	2– 7	leaves you to work a· that which
	5–19	and yet is arrayed a· being,
	5–22	divided a· itself — *Luke* 11 : 17.
	9–15	a· too great leniency, on my part,
	18–25	This demand militates a· the
	23–22	can have no such warfare a· Himself.
	38–11	a· which the gates of hell cannot
'00.	9–23	no one can fight a· God, and win.
	11–16	measures himself a· deeper grief.
	12–18	somewhat a· thee, — *Rev.* 2 : 4.
'01.	3– 5	all manner of evil a· you — *Matt.* 5 : 11.
	14–23	a· the approach of thieves.
	15–17	measure of wickedness a· all light.
	18– 9	Those who laugh at or pray a·
	24–14	when the storms of disease beat a·
	25–29	kingdom divided a· itself,
	26–10	In one sentence he declaims a·

against

'02.	11–23	all manner of evil a· you — *Matt.* 5 : 11.
	14– 7	shield a· the powers of darkness,
	16–22	in self-defense a· false witnesses,
	19–12	no person can commit an offense a·
Hea.	2– 4	prejudices arrayed a· it,
	11–16	before lifting its foot a· its neighbor,
Peo.	11–28	a· the liberty and lives of men.
My.	v–12	* a· the mesmerism of personal pride
	6– 2	knows will be turned a· himself.
	10–21	* to contribute money a· their will
	11– 6	* storms that have surged a· her
	33–20	reproach a his neighbor. — *Psal.* 15 : 3.
	33–26	reward a· the innocent. — *Psal.* 15 : 5.
	40–29	* Human sense often rebels a· law,
	50–11	* a· the currents of dogma,
	64–20	* warn all her followers a· the
	104–31	all manner of evil a· you — *Matt.* 5 : 11.
	130– 3	a· evil suggestions and a· malicious
	134– 2	battle a· the world,
	143–28	who can be a· us?" — *Rom.* 8 : 31.
	150–31	the disclaimer a· God
	151–16	who can be a· us?" — *Rom.* 8 : 31.
	156–10	unto Him a· that day." — *II Tim.* 1 : 12.
	161–26	a sufficient defence a· it.
	162–30	rock of ages a· which the waves
	164–28	a· which envy, enmity, or malice
	193–18	Protesting a· error, you unite with
	196–21	contradiction . . . a· himself, — *Heb.* 12 : 3.
	199– 7	I have naught a· thee.
	213–19	Be ever on guard a· this enemy.
	219–27	precautions a· the spread of
	224–26	"He that is not a· us — *Mark* 9 : 40.
	228–30	unto him a· that day" — *II Tim.* 1 : 12.
	229–31	measures the infinite a· the finite.
	232–31	watching a· a negative watch,
	233–23	should one watch a· such a result?
	234–29	and when the laws are a· it,
	292–18	a· the *modus operandi* of another,
	293– 5	one a· the other
	316– 8	all manner of evil a· you — *Matt.* 5 : 11.
	339–28	and all that wars a· Spirit
	358– 8	whereby the conflict a· Truth is

Agassiz

Professor

'01.	27–27	Professor A· said : "Every great
My.	304–24	A·, the celebrated naturalist

Age

Mis.	231– 1	A·, on whose hoary head

age (*see also* age's)

advanced

Pul.	vii–12	telescope of that advanced a·,
Hea.	1–10	until the a· advanced to a more

advancement of the

Mis.	6– 8	needed for the advancement of the a·.

and Christianity

'01.	16–24	to handle . . . a· and Christianity!

and manhood

Mis.	257–24	childhood, a·, and manhood go

any

Pul.	75– 1	Whoever in any a· expresses most of

apostolic

'00.	12–27	in the apostolic a·

apprehension of the

Ret.	26–30	to the apprehension of the a·.

commercial

My.	91– 6	* in this so-called commercial a·.

custom of the

My.	261– 6	according to the custom of the a·

demand of the

Ret.	48–23	demand of the a· for something higher

early

Pul.	34– 1	* At an early a· Miss Baker was

eight years of

Pul.	33– 3	* When eight years of a· she began,

every

Mis.	213–17	In every a·, the pioneer reformer
	374–23	Extremists in every a· either
No.	44–26	In every a· and clime,
Peo.	2–21	people's belief of God, in every a·,
Po.	28– 1	Father of every a·,
My.	103–10	In every a· and at its every

four years of

Ret.	20– 8	my little son, about four years of a·,

his

'01.	28–26	among the worldlings in his a·,

legal

My.	217–13	shall have arrived at legal a·,

manhood, and

Mis.	324– 6	youth, manhood, and a· gayly tread

marvel of the

My.	85– 4	* this cult is the marvel of the a·.

material

My.	221– 2	earthly price . . . in a material a·

age
middle
Mis. 231– 2   middle *a·*, in . . . full fruition of
of miracles
My. 80– 2   * back to the *a·* of miracles.
of seventeen
My. 311–13   I joined the . . . at the *a·* of seventeen
of thirty-four
Ret. 21– 7   reached the *a·* of thirty-four,
of thirty-one
Ret. 7– 3   passed away at the *a·* of thirty-one,
of twelve
Man. 35– 2   arrived at the *a·* of twelve years,
Ret. 13– 1   At the *a·* of twelve I was admitted
of twenty
Man. 62–10   up to the *a·* of twenty years,
  62–15   after reaching the *a·* of twenty.
old
Mis. ix–19   There is an old *a·* of the heart,
My. 135– 6   may be applied to old *a·*,
  273– 3   * proof of Mrs. Eddy's ability in old *a·*
origin and
Mis. 185–23   by which to learn his origin and *a·*,
our
Chr. 53–50   So in our *a·*,
present
My. 63–24   * which has come to the present *a·*.
scientific
Mis. 353–27   about three years of scientific *a·*,
scoff of the
My. 204–22   which was then the scoff of the *a·*.
ten years of
Ret. 10– 4   At ten years of *a·* I was as
that
Mis. 21– 5   and in that *a·* culminates in
  161–21   or preach in public under that *a·*.
  187–17   writers and translators in that *a·*
Man. 62–12   may be received . . . up to that *a·*,
No. 14–22   to Jesus' students in that *a·*,
  38– 2   could be done in that *a·*,
this
Mis. 1–13   seer of this *a·* should be a sage.
  159– 2   God has given to this *a·* ''S. and H.
  167– 1   The material questions at this *a·*
  222–29   cost of investigating, for this *a·*,
  232– 6   This *a·* is reaching out towards
  310– 6   Truth, amplified in this *a·* by
  370–13   In this *a·* it assumes,
  382–14   healed in this *a·* by C. S.
Pul. 14–21   In this *a·* the earth will help the
  77–14   * through you to this *a·*.
  78–13   * through you to this *a·*.
No. 14–23   but they extend to this *a·*,
'01. 28–27   not popular with them in this *a·* ;
My. vii– 8   * as the revelator to this *a·*
  40–16   * demand of this *a·* is for
  113–32   great men and women of this *a·*.
  146–22   not been demonstrated in this *a·*,
  213– 8   this *a·* is cursed with one rancorous
  323–21   * giving this *a·* such a Leader
twelve years of
My. 169– 6   Busy Bees, under twelve years of *a·*,
  311–15   culminate at twelve years of *a·*.
yellow with
Ret. 2–22   some newspapers, yellow with *a·*.

Mis. 4–17   is necessary for the *a·*,
  159–27   been unveiled to us, and to the *a·*!''
  161–20   when he was thirty years of *a·* ;
  171–10   When one comes to the *a·* with
  234–26   midst of an *a·* so sunken in sin
Un. 6–12   as the *a·* has strength to bear.
Pul. 32–20   * some sixty years of *a·*,
  73–12   * Biblical scholars of the *a·*.
Hea. 7–23   I wish the *a·* was up to his
  11–11   though it may seem to the *a·* like
My. 158– 9   *a·* of Love's divine adventure
  190– 7   The *a·* is fast answering this question :
  271–14   * at eighty-six years of *a·* the most
  272–25   * nearly eighty-seven years of *a·*,
  304–10   At sixteen years of *a·*,
  306–15   *A·*, with . . . patience and unselfed
  318–14   spiritual effect upon the *a·* of

aged
Mis. 226– 4   unbiased youth and the *a·* Christian
'01. 29– 7   The *a·* reformer should not be
My. 153–11   *a·* gentleman healed from the day
  271–19   * this *a·* woman of world-wide renown

agencies
Mis. 95–20   no human *a·* were employed,
  244–16   * visible *a·* for specific ends?''
Pul. 14– 5   active yet unseen mental *a·*
agency
Mis. 113– 7   free moral *a·* is lost ;
  119–19   a plea for free moral *a·*,

agency
Rud. 12–11   then restored through its *a·*.
No. 46–12   upon free moral *a·* ;
My. 14– 9   Godlike *a·* of man.
  91–12   * debased through its *a·*.
agent
Mis. 4– 3   remedial *a·* on the earth.
  83–15   you are a free moral *a·*
  272–14   * officer, *a·*, or servant of any
Rud. 2– 2   a self-conscious being ; a moral *a·* ;
agents
Un. 60–18   Mortals are free moral *a·*,
Rud. 2– 6   one of the three subjects, or *a·*,
age's
'02. 9–25   Did the *a·* thinkers laugh long over
ages
Mis. 21–11   As the *a·* advance in spirituality,
  112– 5   The *a·* are burdened with
  140–29   our church will stand the storms of *a·* :
  176– 7   has been exemplified in all *a·*,
  192–27   that extends to all *a·*
  194– 9   to heal in all *a·*,
  205–23   order of Science is the chain of *a·*,
  235–22   must push on the *a·*,
  319– 1   are in the darkness of all the *a·*,
  320–27   is the light of all *a·* ;
  346– 7   The origin of evil is the problem of *a·*.
  358–26   the greatest work of the *a·*,
  370–12   In different *a·* the divine idea
  374–19   brought a great light to all *a·*,
  383–13   it will go on with the *a·*,
Ret. 33–17   mixed with the faith of *a·*,
Un. 9–23   spiritual thinkers in all *a·*.
  26–14   * Man decays and *a·* move ;
Pul. 72–25   * dormant in mankind for *a·*,''
No. 12–14   true Christianity in all *a·*,
  31– 3   has for *a·* been a pretender,
  41–19   Through long *a·* people have
'00. 3– 5   does the thinking for the *a·*.
'01. 12–16   Christ's command to heal in all *a·*,
  21– 5   Science leading the *a·*.
Hea. 3–14   engrossed the attention of the *a·*.
My. 37–19   * philosophy of the *a·* transformed.
  103– 3   severest conflicts of the *a·*
  116–24   Had the *a·* helped their leaders
  129–19   ye who leap . . . from this rock of *a·*,
  152–20   even as the *a·* have shown.
  162–30   may it build upon the rock of *a·*
  180– 8   which applies to all *a·*,
  188–25   As you work, the *a·* win ;
  190–24   all peoples, in all *a·*,
  279– 9   Reappearing in all *a·*,
  285–11   belong to the darker *a·*,
  288– 2   unselfish men and pushes on the *a·*.
aggregate
Mis. 62–12   making the *a·* positive,
My. 100– 3   * as remarkable in their *a·*
aggregates
No. 10– 9   it *a·*, amplifies, unfolds, and
aggregating
Pul. 40–17   * *a·* nearly six thousand persons,
aggregation
My. 99– 8   * *a·* of good and beneficial works,
aggressive
Mis. 284–26   Evil let alone grows more real, *a·*,
Man. 42– 6   against *a·* mental suggestion,
'01. 20– 2   yielding to its *a·* features
My. 230– 3   amid ministries *a·* and active,
aggrieve
Man. 51– 8   *a·* or vilify the Pastor Emeritus
agitate
Mis. 224–23   no passing breath . . . shall *a·* or
Un. 5– 1   rudely or prematurely *a·* a theme
agitated
My. 266–26   are now *a·*, modified, and
agitation
Pul. 31–19   * central figure in all this *a·*
  51–11   * is more or less in a state of *a·*.
My. 318–22   manifested more and more *a·*,
aglow
Mis. 276–17   The wise will have their lamps *a·*,
  341–32   tended to keep *a·* the flame
'00. 1– 3   glad faces, *a·* with gratitude,
agnosticism
Mis. 56– 1   theories of *a·* and pantheism,
Ret. 23–21   *A·*, pantheism, and theosophy
My. 318–21   until I began my attack on *a·*.
ago
Mis. 165– 2   more than eighteen centuries *a·*,
  178–15   * it was about a year *a·* that I

ago

Mis.	182–32	more than eighteen centuries *a·*.
	242–15	difficult tasks fifteen years *a·*.
	248–24	Many years *a·* my regular
	281– 7	I learned long *a·* that the world could
	286– 1	prophecy, written years *a·*,
	321– 4	less of a miracle than eighteen centuries *a·* ;
	375–11	* Years *a·*, while in Italy,
Ret.	1– 7	English authoress of a century *a·*.
	16– 9	entered this church one hour *a·*
	41– 2	encountered a quarter-century *a·*,
Un.	6–22	Not much more than a half-century *a·*
Pul.	6–13	* "Six months *a·* your book,
	35– 9	* nineteen hundred years *a·*.
	36–20	* Several years *a·* Mrs. Eddy removed
	45–23	* A week *a·* Judge Hanna withdrew from
	53– 3	* nineteen hundred years *a·*,
	66– 5	* was founded fifteen years *a·*
	67–15	* Founded twenty-five years *a·*.
	68–16	* in this city about a year *a·*,
	69– 2	* came to Baltimore about three years *a·*
	69– 3	* about eighteen months *a·*.
	69– 8	* some twelve years *a·*,
	72–13	* healed a number of years *a·*
	79–10	* starting fifteen years *a·*, has already
	85– 1	* nearly thirty years *a·*
Rud.	8– 5	the lion of six thousand years *a·* ;
'01.	18– 6	the sneers forty years *a·*
	27–17	if . . . could start thirty years *a·*
Po.	3–15	Written many years *a·*.
	35–15	Written more than sixty years *a·*
My.	10– 6	* externalized itself, ten years *a·*,
	11–14	* A year *a·* she quietly alluded to
	14–11	* A few days *a·* we received a letter
	22–14	* almost forty years *a·*,
	43–21	* Forty years *a·* the Science of
	50–30	* more than twenty-six years *a·*,
	52–20	* Eighteen years *a·*, the Rev. . . . Wiggin,
	55–31	* Twelve years *a·* . . . the corner-stone
	59– 3	* nearly forty years *a·*
	67–25	* temple, begun nearly two years *a·*,
	68–15	* old church . . . built twelve years *a·*,
	70– 5	* its first church . . . twelve years *a·*,
	72–29	* in Boston twelve years *a·*
	76–28	* twenty-seven years *a·* was founded
	85– 5	* it is but a few years *a·* that
	92–14	* few years *a·*, men there were who
	99–22	* Less than a generation *a·*
	104–28	to learn of her who, thirty years *a·*,
	109–10	If nineteen hundred years *a·*
	147– 4	Over a half century *a·*,
	176– 5	Long *a·* you of the dear South
	181–21	Thirty years *a·* (1866) C. S. was
	181–25	thirty years *a·* the death-rate was
	182– 1	Thirty years *a·* Chicago had few
	182– 4	Thirty years *a·* at my request
	237– 3	in the *Sentinel* a few weeks *a·*,
	237– 6	some twenty-five years *a·*
	297–21	as when he visited me a year *a·*.
	313– 2	a silly song of years *a·*
	322–15	* Thanksgiving Day twenty years *a·*,
	325–12	* Years *a·* I offered my services
	342– 9	* to the portraits of twenty years *a·*,

agonies

Mis.	253–24	*a·* that gave that child birth
Rud.	17–11	of friendlessness, toil, *a·*, and
Pan.	12–19	*a·* whereby the way-seeker gains and

agony

Mis.	69–17	barely alive, and in terrible *a·*.
	70–12	Paradisaical rest from physical *a·*
	204– 1	*a·* struggles, pride rebels, and
	222–20	cancelled only through human *a·* :
Un.	58–11	what is humanly called *a·*.
No.	33–15	the brief *a·* of the cross ;
'01.	20–20	*a·* and death that it must sooner or
	35–12	From the human *a·*!
'02.	16–17	*a·* in the life of our Lord ;
My.	105–22	breathing at intervals in *a·*.
	132–15	no longer . . . to strive with *a·* ;
	335–29	* these nine days and nights of *a·*

agree

Mis.	58–29	if you *a·* that God is Mind,
	81– 7	let each society . . . *a·* to
	117–10	I *a·* with Rev. Dr. Talmage,
	243–13	I *a·* with the Professor, that every
	309– 6	All will *a·* with me that material
	365–23	Even doctors *a·* that infidelity,
No.	19– 5	doctors will *a·* that infidelity
	45–21	we should *a·* to disagree ;
Pan.	4– 7	may *a·* with physics and anatomy
'02.	2–25	or at least *a·* to disagree, in love,
My.	7–19	* we *a·* to contribute any portion of
	71–10	* all *a·* that it is a stunning
	154–22	I *a·* with him ; and in our era

agree

My.	273–24	*a·* with me that the material body is

agreeable

Pul.	72–10	* a very pleasant and *a·* lady,
'00.	4–13	ought not this to be an *a·* surprise,
My.	74–10	* chapter sub-title
	74–12	* very interesting and *a·* visitors,
	342– 2	* warmth within . . . was *a·*.

agreeably

Ret.	15–28	*a·* informed the congregation that

agreed

My.	9– 4	* we have *a·* to contribute
	138– 3	*a·* . . . to take care of my property
	318–19	I *a·* not to question him
	320– 7	* *a·* with what you had told me.

agreement

Mis.	289–14	to act as a whole and per *a·*.
Man.	68–23	A· Required.
	69– 2	shall come under a signed *a·* to
My.	vi–22	* under *a·* to pay all future profits
	138– 5	I consider this *a·* a great benefit
	168– 3	practical religion in *a·* with
	318–31	"you have broken our *a·*.

agreements

Mis.	289–12	partnerships are formed on *a·*

agrees

Un.	23– 9	*a·* with the word of Scripture,
Pan.	4– 1	*a·* with certain forms of pantheism

agriculture

Mis.	340–13	*a·* instead of litigation,
My.	216– 7	manufacture, *a·*, tariff, and
	265–28	*a·*, manufacture, commerce,

agriculturist

Mis.	26– 9	*a·* ponders the history of a seed,

aid

apply for

Man.	98–10	apply for *a·* to the Committee

best

Pul.	38–30	* their best *a·* and guidance,

different

Ret.	87–30	and different *a·* is sought.

divine

Peo.	9–18	invoke the divine *a·* of Spirit to heal
My.	166–20	divine *a·* is near.

his

Mis.	89–18	to some who sought his *a·* ;

juvenile

Pul.	8–30	By juvenile *a·*, . . . have come $4,460.

little

My.	349–10	afford little *a·* in understanding

material

Mis.	225–23	Looking away from all material *a·*,
My.	105–25	restored by me without material *a·*,

no

Mis.	31–13	no place in, and receives no *a·* from,
	156–25	is no *a·* to students in acquiring

no other

Mis.	270–17	Then you will need no other *a·*,
	282–28	and no other *a·* is near.

no personal

Mis.	283–26	he needs no personal *a·*.

no real

Mis.	267–25	is no real *a·* to being.

of mind

My.	301–28	without the *a·* of mind.

Mis.	3–17	never are needed to *a·*
	8– 2	If we can *a·* in abating suffering
	52– 2	such as seek . . . to *a·* the spiritual,
	57– 1	by the *a·* of mankind,
	58–19	*Does the theology of C. S. a·*
	62– 6	*a·* an artist in painting a landscape.
	80– 8	and possibly to *a·* individual rights
	98–11	mutually to *a·* one another
	143–25	in *a·* of our Church Building Fund,
	149–21	to send him to *a·* me.
	262– 5	you will *a·* our prospect
	263–23	lacks the *a·* and protection of
	264–27	to *a·* the mental development of
	266–26	thus we mutually *a·* each other,
	282–26	which may call for *a·* unsought,
	291–29	*a·* the solution of this problem,
	333–19	to *a·* in understanding and securing
	372–25	Not by *a·* of foreign device
Ret.	94–27	*a·* the establishment of Christ's
Un.	17– 5	and all that is good will *a·*
'01.	29–26	To *a·* my students in starting
Po.	28–10	A· our poor soul to sing
My.	21–13	* *a·* the progress of our Cause
	155– 2	a mutual *a·* society,
	175– 7	to *a·* in repairing your church
	222–30	will *a·* the ejection of error,
	236–29	and it will greatly *a·* the students

aid

My.	256–15	pleasures, achievements, and *a*.
	283– 9	To *a·* in this holy purpose is

aided

Ret.	33– 1	*a·* by hints from homœopathy,
Rud.	12–13	*a·* in this mistaken fashion,
Pan.	9–18	ought to be *a·*, not hindered,
My.	181– 5	*a·* only at long intervals with

aiding

Mis.	79–27	*a· persons brought before the courts*
	119– 4	*a·* other people's devices

aids

Mis.	64–23	*a·* to a student of the Bible
	156–27	are the *a·* and tests of growth
'01.	25–11	call *a·* to divine metaphysics,
Hea.	14–15	are miserable medical *a·*.
My.	217–25	*a·* in taking the next step
	261–13	*a·* in perpetuating purity and

ailing

Rud.	12– 3	of the body supposed to be *a·*.

ailment

Mis.	66–25	like the more physical *a·*.
	241– 9	the other having a physical *a·*.
	241–28	easier to heal . . . than the moral *a·*.
Pul.	6–17	* of an *a·* of seven years' standing.
	69– 7	* cured . . . of a physical *a·*
My.	145–13	* an old *a·* my mother had."

ailments

Mis.	6–28	confined to the *a·* of the body,
	45–17	effectual in treating moral *a·*.
	168–10	buried in dogmas and physical *a·*,
	268–24	antidotes for the *a·* of mortal mind
Ret.	57–13	causes all bodily *a·*,
Rud.	12–13	their *a·* will return,

aim

Mis.	11– 5	*a·* a ball at my heart,
	67–11	shalt not strike . . . with a malicious *a·*,
	154–30	Have no . . . *a·* apart from holiness.
	220– 9	*a·* to refute the sick man's thoughts,
	267– 7	whose chief *a·* is to injure me,
	277– 9	archers *a·* at Truth's mouthpiece ;
	348– 1	But the Scientists *a·* highest.
Ret.	22–17	He alone is our origin, *a·*, and
Pul.	37–14	* it is her most earnest *a·* to
My.	71–28	* *a·* and object of the architect :
	213– 3	*a·* of perverted mind-power,
	257–13	Christ's heavenly origin and *a·*.

aimed

Mis.	372–24	I *a·* to reproduce.
Ret.	48– 4	was *a·* at its vital purpose,
'01.	32–14	they armed quickly, *a·* deadly,
My.	128–28	shaft *a·* at you or your practice

aiming

My.	126– 5	strong swimmer . . . *a·* for Truth,

aims

Mis.	9–24	unworthy of human *a·*.
	50–21	human affections, desires, and *a·*,
	204–29	governs the *a·*, ambition, and acts
	214–23	their motives, *a·*, and tendency.
	227–17	wider *a·* of a life made honest :
	266– 3	summit of unselfish and pure *a·*
	291– 7	demonstrates above . . . unworthy *a·*
	330–22	higher joys, holier *a·*,
'02.	17–26	take its answer as to thy *a·*,
My.	125– 2	false affections, motives, and *a·*,

air

Mis.	7– 2	nor to breathe the cold *a·*,
	7–19	so loaded with . . . seems the very *a·*.
	69–13	over the fowl of the *a·*." — *Gen.* 1 : 26.
	102–29	as one that beateth the *a·*,
	240– 3	through the cold *a·* the little one
	291–20	will at length dissolve into thin *a·*.
	347– 7	hanging like a horoscope in the *a·*,
	356– 8	from lack of *a·* and freedom.
	356–18	and the birds of the *a·*,
	357–15	The fowls of the *a·* pick them up.
Ret.	2–15	comes that heart-stirring *a·*,
	11–22	Free as the generous *a·*,
Pul.	32–10	* wonderful tumult in the *a·*
	49– 4	* *a·* of hospitality that marks its
Po.	24– 2	Breathe through the summer *a·*
	60–20	Free as the generous *a·*,
	65– 8	And left but a parting in *a·*.
My.	81– 2	* struck with the *a·* of well-being
	110–14	navigation of the *a·* ;
	341–27	* change from the misty *a·* outside

air-castles

Mis.	230–18	in building *a·* or floating off on

airy

Po.	34– 7	Bird of the *a·* wing,
My.	110–16	early dreams of flying in *a·* space,

aisles

Ret.	15–19	and benches were used in the *a·*.
My.	56– 4	* many stood in the *a·*,
	71–21	* neither nave, *a·*, nor transept
	151–18	vaulted *a·* by flaunting folly trod,

ajar

Mis.	394–19	* I fain would keep the gates *a·*,
Ret.	9– 3	The door was *a·*,
Po.	57– 5	* I fain would keep the gates *a·*,

akin

Mis.	372–29	is *a·* to its *Science :*
Un.	9–22	because ideas *a·* to mine have been

alabaster

My.	258–31	beautiful statuette in *a·*

alacrity

My.	236–15	with the sweet *a·* and uniformity

alarm

Un.	40–20	Death can never *a·* or even

alarmed

'02.	4–25	Alternately transported and *a·* by

alarming

No.	43–15	*a·* the hypocrite, and

alas

Mis.	223–15	But, *a·*! for the mistake of
	231–29	But, *a·*! for the desolate home ;
	344–13	*A·* for such a material science
Pul.	13–14	*A·* for those who break faith with
'01.	16–22	*A·*! if now it is permitted
Po.	65–13	*A·*! that from dreams so boundless
My.	257– 1	*a·* for the broken household band!

Albany, N. Y.

Pul.	89– 3	* *Knickerbocker, A·, N.Y.*
	89– 8	* *Press, A·, N.Y.*

Albany (N. Y.) Knickerbocker (see also **Knicker-bocker**)

My.	94–15	* [*A· (N. Y.) K·*]

Albert (Baker)

(see **Baker**)

Albion's

Mis.	295–24	resound from *A·* shores.

album

Mis.	280–20	elegant *a·* costing fifty dollars,

alchemy

Mis.	78–13	occultism, magic, *a·*, or

alcohol

Mis.	37–22	appetite for *a·* yields to Science
	48–16	produce the effect of *a·*,
Ret.	65– 9	odors of persecution, tobacco, and *a·*
My.	106–24	not a brawler, an *a·* drinker,
	114– 4	abstain from *a·* and tobacco ;
	212–10	the evil effects of *a·*.

alcoholic

Mis.	71– 4	an appetite for *a·* drink
	243–27	tell you that *a·* drinks cause
	297– 9	destroys the appetite for *a·* drinks.
My.	212–10	The *a·* habit is the use of

Alcott, A. Bronson

Pul.	5–12	the late A. Bronson *A·*.

alcoves

Pul.	76– 9	* *a·* are separated from the
	76–18	* One of the two *a·* is a

alder

Ret.	18– 6	nestling is whispering low,
	18–26	*a·* growing from the bent branch
Po.	63–15	nestling *a·* is whispering low,
	63–24	*a·* growing from the bent branch

alders

Mis.	330–14	*a·* bend over the streams to

alehouses

Mis.	296–10	barmaids of English *a·*

alert

Mis.	374– 7	Keen and *a·* was their indignation
My.	226–26	told by the *a·* editor-in-chief of

alertness

Man.	42– 4	*A·* to Duty.

Alexander the Great

'00.	12–16	night that *A· the G·* was born.
	13–12	*A· the G·* founded the city of

Alger, Rev. William R.

Pul.	6–24	the Rev. William R. *A·* of Boston,

alias

Mis.	2–10	mortals, *a·* mortal mind,
	41–25	for health, *a·* harmony,
	75–28	mortal man (*a·* material sense)
	257–11	*a·* the minds of mortals.
Ret.	36– 6	Science of Mind-healing, *a·* C. S.,
	43– 8	*a·* the Science of Mind-healing.

alias

Ret.	63– 8	pleasure of sin, *a·* the reality of sin,
	64– 6	to efface sin, *a·* the sinner,
	67–13	Silencing self, *a·* rising above
	67–24	the "devil" (*a·* evil), — *John* 8 : 44.
	68– 5	*a·* an evil offspring.
Un.	22–21	*will-power,* — *a·* intelligent matter.
No.	26– 5	spirits, or souls, — *a·* gods.
	32–17	A lie is negation, — *a·* nothing,
'01.	13–13	evil, *a·* devil, sin, is a lie
Peo.	11–17	Mortals, *a·* mortal minds,
My.	232–31	negative watch, *a·*, no watch,

alien

My.	260– 3	would make matter an *a·*

alight

Mis.	239–13	*a·* and take from his carriage
My.	160– 5	is seldom *a·* with love.

alighting

Po.	v–16	* *a· from her carriage,*

alike

Mis.	200–29	were *a·* unreal to Jesus ;
	268–21	curing *a·* the sin and the
Ret.	64–13	are *a·* simply nothingness ;
	85–20	Christian Scientist is incapable *a·* of
Pul.	45–15	* of workman and onlooker *a·*
My.	220–31	should share *a·* liberty of conscience,
	324– 7	* were too much *a·* for the book to

alive

Mis.	69–17	I found him barely *a·*,
	79–25	shall all be made *a·*." — *I Cor.* 15 : 22.
Pul.	34–10	* no probability that she would be *a·*
'02.	18–30	made him keenly *a·* to the injustice,
My.	139– 4	*a·* to the reality of living,
	185–19	"was dead, and is *a·* again ; — *Luke* 15 : 32.
	275–15	*a·* to the truth of being

All

Mis.	16–21	God is a divine *Whole,* and *A·*,
	24–24	when good is God, and God is *A·*
	26–22	God is *A·*, in all.
	26–22	What can be more than *A·*?
	27–23	when God is really *A·*.
	101–26	If God is *A·*, and God is good,
	108– 5	that good is infinite, *A·*.
	125–19	*A·* that is real is divine,
	151–23	God is — what? Even *A.*
	173–17	preexisted in the *A·* and Only
	174–21	the *A·* of God, and His omnipresence
	208– 5	God is *A·*, and by virtue of this
	250– 1	the infinite *A·* of good,
	258– 9	the great truth that God is *A·*,
	258–14	God is One and *A·*;
	260–18	opposite to Him who is *A·*.
	293–24	God is *A·* and there is no sickness
	350–16	"God is *A·*";
Ret.	60– 6	Science reveals Spirit as *A·*,
	60–11	God and His idea as the *A·*
	63– 5	recognition that God *is A·*,
Un.	3–24	If He is *A·*, He can have no
	4– 6	Truth is *A·*, and there is no error.
	5– 2	involving the *A·* of infinity.
	7–23	because God is *A·*,
	18–25	I am *A·*.
	24– 2	I am the infinite *A·*.
	25–24	elements which belong to the eternal *A·*,
	31– 5	If God is Spirit, and God is *A·*,
	31– 6	for the divine *A·* must be Spirit.
	34–11	God is *A·*, and God is Spirit ;
	36– 5	the fact that Spirit is *A·*,
	48–12	To me God is *A·*.
	60– 6	God is *A·*, and there is none beside
Rud.	9–26	that He is *A·*.
	11– 8	Therefore good is one and *A·*.
No.	16–18	Mortals do not understand the *A·* ;
	16–20	He who is *A·*, understands all.
	17– 6	God is good, ever-present, and *A·*.
	24– 9	rests on God as One and *A·*,
	25– 2	God becomes the *A·* and Only
	30–11	God's law is . . . "I am *A·*,"
	38– 7	God is *A·*, and He is good,
Pan.	13–21	life in Life, all in *A·*.
'00.	4–24	God is One and *A·*
'02.	7–16	*A·*, than which there is naught else.
Hea.	10–13	God is *A·*, and in all :
Po.	79–17	And God is *A·*.
My.	108–16	omnipotent, infinite, *A·*.
	109–19	God is one because God is *A·*.
	178–13	Scripture declares that God is *A·*.
	225–12	all belongs to God, for God is *A·* ;
	299–19	and that God is *A·*

all *(see also* **all's***)*

Mis.	xi–18	to suit and savor *a·* literature.
	1– 6	the scoffed of *a·* scoffers,

all

Mis.	3–10	applicable to *a·* the needs of
	3–19	The Principle of *a·* cure is God,
	5–16	I have done *a·* that can be done.
	6–18	Mind governs *a·*.
	6–30	*a·* that she can attend to in
	7–15	if you cannot bring peace to *a·*,
	8–16	that blesses infinitely one and *a·*?
	9– 6	passes *a·* His flock under His rod
	9–32	*a·* that an enemy or enmity can **obtrude**
	11–18	in *a·* the manifestations wherein
	11–22	not leaving *a·* retribution to
	11–31	taking by the hand *a·* who
	12– 9	above *a·*, do not fancy that you
	12–30	doing good to *a·* ;
	12–32	to *a·* within the radius of our
	13– 3	so far as one and *a·* permit me
	13–10	consideration of *a·* Christian Scientists.
	19–14	*a·* the wicked endeavors of
	20– 4	*a·* ye that labor — *Matt.* 11 : 28.
	21–11	*a·* his words and works.
	21–17	*A·* is infinite Mind and its
	22–16	*a·* true thoughts revolve in
	23–27	manifests *a·* His attributes
	23–30	*A·* must be Mind and Mind's ideas ;
	24–30	put down *a·* subtle falsities
	25–13	rejects *a·* other theories of causation,
	25–23	the Latin word meaning *a·*,
	26–22	God is All, in *a·*.
	27–11	(including *a·* inharmony,
	27–25	and *a·* that really is,
	30– 7	demonstrate *a·* the possibilities
	32–17	If I had the time to talk with *a·*
	32–22	to give to my own flock *a·* the
	32–27	*a·* people can and should be just,
	33– 5	*a·* ministers and ministries of Christ,
	33– 7	*A·* clergymen may not understand
	33–25	It does away with *a·* material
	33–27	*a·* "the ills that flesh is heir to,"
	34–23	*A·* that are called "communications
	36–22	*a·* beliefs relative to the so-called
	36–23	and *a·* material objects,
	37– 5	in *a·* thoughts and desires
	37–18	Its antidote for *a·* ills is God,
	38– 2	*a· the good we can do*
	39–12	*a·* her years in giving it birth.
	40–14	*A·* true healing is governed **by,**
	41–20	and produces *a·* harmony
	41–28	sufficient for *a·* emergencies.
	43– 6	*Do a· who at present claim to*
	44–23	is but a dream at *a·* times.
	45–21	*If God made a· that was made,*
	48– 2	and avoid *a·* that works ill.
	49–15	*If a· that is mortal is a dream*
	49–19	spirit of Truth leads into *a·* truth,
	50– 1	God made *a·* that was made,
	51– 7	*A·* mesmerism is of one of three **kinds ;**
	52– 9	beyond *a·* human means
	53–22	*so that a· can readily understand it?*
	54–12	power of C. S. over *a·* obstacles
	54–17	*to keep well a· my life?*
	55– 4	prove *a·* its possibilities.
	55–22	*a·* that is unlike Spirit.
	57– 1	*a·* was later made which *He*
	57– 6	The creative "Us" made *a·*,
	57–29	But *a·* that really is, always was
	59–18	*Is not a· argument mind over mind?*
	60– 9	after *a·* other means have failed.
	61– 1	belief, in *a·* its manifestations,
	61– 6	*A·* the knowledge and vain strivings
	63– 8	Principle of *a·* pure theology;
	66–11	is verified in *a·* directions
	67–30	after *a·* the footsteps requisite
	71–14	*A·* actual causation must interpret
	72–21	*need of a· these things,"* — *Matt.* 6 : 32.
	73–20	*a·* subjective states of false sensation
	74– 9	*a·* human systems of etiology
	74–31	you may have *a·* that is left of it ;
	77–20	In adopting *a·* this vast idea
	78–22	*a·* the clearer for the purification
	79– 1	*A·* these mortal beliefs will be
	79– 8	reflects *a·* whereby we can know God.
	79–24	"As in Adam *a·* die, — *I Cor.* 15 : 22.
	79–24	shall *a·* be made alive." — *I Cor.* 15 : 22.
	80–19	promotes and impels *a·* true reform ;
	81– 4	*a·* unpleasant and unchristian action
	81–17	*shall go forth into a· the cities*
	81–19	*if a· this be a fair or correct view*
	82–11	grasp and gather — in *a·* glory
	83– 1	Principle, of *a·* real being ;
	85– 6	*a·* that he knows of Life,
	87– 3	To take *a·* earth's beauty into
	89– 7	*be right to treat this patient at a· ;*
	89–15	*to do him a· the good you can ;*
	90– 4	*you remove a· reality from its power.*
	90– 6	will save *a·* who understand it.

all

Mis.	91–13	It is imperative, at *a·* times
	91–17	Be it remembered, that *a·* types
	93–18	*a·* cause and effect are in God.
	96– 4	an ever-present help in *a·* times of trouble,
	96–21	*a·* who entertain this understanding
	97–12	*A·* human control is animal magnetism,
	97–14	more despicable than *a·* other methods
	97–25	we have not seen *a·* of man ;
	98–23	The lives of *a·* reformers attest
	99– 2	it upsets *a·* that is not upright.
	101–26	it follows that *a·* must be good ;
	101–32	elements of *a·* forms and individualities,
	102–21	which blots out *a·* our iniquities
	102–21	and heals *a·* our diseases.
	107– 9	*a·* the heart's homage belongs to God.
	108–23	the conception of it at *a·* as
	111– 4	as meekly, you have toiled *a·* night ;
	113– 6	*a·* that is real and eternal,
	113–19	so that *a·* are without excuse.
	114– 2	value to *a·* seekers after Truth.
	114–20	*a·* the *et cetera* of evil.
	114–27	will test *a·* mankind on *a·* questions ;
	116– 3	The God of *a·* grace be with you,
	117–14	the basis of *a·* right thinking
	118–24	they will uproot *a·* happiness.
	119–20	full exemption from *a·* necessity to
	119–25	demands of *a·* trespassers
	122–28	He made *a·* that was made.
	125– 6	since *a·* that is *real* is *right.*
	125–14	that passeth *a·* understanding ;
	131–19	not in existence *a·* of the year.
	131–22	May God give unto us *a·* that
	132–18	inquiries from *a·* quarters,
	133–29	Love makes *a·* burdens light,
	135– 1	Christians, and *a· true* Scientists,
	135–10	conquers *a·* opposition,
	135–11	surmounts *a·* obstacles,
	136–17	*A·* our thoughts should be given to
	137– 4	*a·* of which are complete.
	137–27	give to the world the benefit of *a·* this,
	138–26	to *a·* His soldiers of the cross
	138–28	we *a·* shall take step and march on
	139–25	like *a·* true wisdom,
	139–29	As with *a·* former efforts in the
	140– 7	*a·* spiritual good comes to
	141–10	*A·* loyal Christian Scientists hail with
	141–17	*a·* the parties concerned
	141–19	to the satisfaction of *a·*.
	143–26	quiet call . . . found you *a·*
	147–22	at *a·* times the trusty friend,
	147–28	In *a·* his pursuits, he knows
	149– 4	Invite *a·* cordially and freely
	149–22	*a·* the rich graces of the Spirit.
	150–11	with *a·* who are with Truth,
	150–27	Not more to one than to *a·*,
	150–30	is *a·* that really is or can be ;
	155–17	*a·* of her interesting correspondence,
	155–23	give to us *a·* the pleasure of
	156– 8	*A·* is well at headquarters,
	156–23	the basis of *a·* true thought
	156–27	and, above *a·, obedience,*
	157–10	*a·* questions important for your case,
	157–11	they furnish *a·* information
	158–13	The meaning of it *a·,*
	158–19	*A·* God's servants are minute men
	159– 7	God of *a·* grace give you peace,
	159–29	*a·* gifts of Christian Scientists
	159–29	from *a·* parts of our nation,
	163–27	idea which leadeth into *a·* Truth
	164–32	*a·* that is real and eternal.
	166– 4	but this is not *a·* of the
	166–26	and *a·* materialism disappear.
	167– 9	*a·* that resembles God.
	169– 1	I found *a·* the divine Science
	169– 2	*a·* along the way of her researches
	169–25	health and peace and hope for *a·*.
	170–15	interpreted *a·* spiritually :
	170–18	we also may *a·* partake of.
	171–29	*a·* clad in the shining mail
	172–10	charity, brooding over *a·,*
	173– 6	who healeth *a·* our sickness
	174– 7	removeth *a·* iniquities
	174– 8	and healeth *a·* our diseases.
	174–11	moves *a·* in harmony,
	174–32	that leadeth into *a·* Truth ;
	175–32	remember God in *a·* thy ways,
	176– 7	been exemplified in *a·* ages,
	177– 2	God makes to us *a·,* right here,
	177– 4	greatest and holiest of *a·* causes.
	179–24	God does *a·* this through
	182–24	possibility of *a·* finding their place
	184–13	healeth *a·* thy diseases." — *Psal.* 103 : 3.
	184–26	which casteth out *a·* fear,
	185– 6	strips matter of *a·* claims,
	185– 8	renunciation of *a·* that

all

Mis.	185–13	cleansing mortals of *a·* uncleanness,
	186–14	that God made *a·* ;
	189– 6	that leadeth into *a·* truth.
	191– 5	*a·* the beasts of the field." — *see Gen.* 3 : 1.
	191–21	*a·* consistent supposition
	192– 8	disease and death, in *a·* their forms,
	192–27	extends to *a·* ages
	192–27	and throughout *a·* Christendom.
	193– 4	Jesus did mean *a·,* and even more
	193– 8	practicality of *a·* Christ's teachings
	193–23	*a·* Christians are properly called
	194– 9	command to heal in *a·* ages,
	194–25	Love that casts out *a·* fear.
	195– 2	the absorption of *a·* action,
	198–25	*a·* of which is corrected
	199–26	understanding that *a·* substance,
	202– 1	basis of *a·* supposed miracles ;
	204–14	*a·* pointing upward.
	204–24	*a·* the minutiæ of human affairs.
	204–31	it banishes forever *a·* envy,
	205–24	and unites *a·* periods in the
	205–26	dissolves *a·* supposed material life
	206– 1	have turned *a·* revolutions,
	206–25	and good is the reward of *a·* who
	208–17	*A·* states and stages of human
	211–29	"Drink ye *a·* of it," — *Matt.* 26 : 27.
	211–29, 30	drink it *a·,* and let *a·* drink
	213– 3	*A·* that I have written,
	215– 5	I do it *a·* in love ;
	217– 4	*a·* should conceive and understand
	218– 9	*a·* its conceptions of life,
	223– 3	I was saying *a·* the time,
	223–20	*a·* those who have named
	224–14	character, from *a·* the rest ;
	225–23	away from *a·* material aid,
	226– 3	* Father of *a·* will care for him.
	228–14	momentary success of *a·* villanies,
	229–14	*a·* other influences governing
	230–14	*A·* successful individuals have
	230–19	*a·* of which drop human life into
	232– 1	God comfort them *a·* !
	232–20	that most important of *a·* arts,
	209–25	fixed Principle of *a·* healing
	235–13	cut down *a·* that bringeth not
	236–12	yield obedience to them in *a·*
	236–13	rights of conscience, as we *a·* have,
	236–13	follow God in *a·* your ways.
	236–24	remedy for *a·* human discord.
	236–27	blamed for *a·* that is not right :
	237–13	*A·* the different phases of error
	238– 5	for *a·* who dare to be true,
	238–10	*A·* that ever was accomplished,
	238–16	but what of *a·* that?
	240–11	*A·* education should contribute
	240–16	to the satisfaction of *a·*.
	244–27	The teachings . . . were for *a·* peoples
	245–19	in *a·* the good tendencies,
	246– 3	*a·* unmitigated systems of crime ;
	246– 5	blot out *a·* inhuman codes.
	253– 1	and selleth *a·* that he hath
	254– 5	*a·* that love which brooded
	254– 5	for *a·* that love that hath fed them
	258–12	*a·* law was vested in the
	258–25	*a·* law, Life, Truth, and Love.
	259–21	the sons of God shouted
	259–29	applicable to *a·* the needs of man.
	260–12	annulled *a·* other laws.
	262– 2	happiness to *a·* households
	262–24	*a·* the homage beneath the skies,
	263–13	meet *a·* human needs
	263–14	and reflect *a·* bliss.
	265– 9	*A·* must have *one* Principle
	265–10	*a· who follow the Principle*
	267–16	Through *a·* human history,
	267–26	exciting cause of *a·* defeat
	270–15	*a·* these things shall be added — *Matt.* 6 : 33.
	271–11	should eschew *a·* magazines . . . which
	272– 2	* with *a·* the rights and privileges
	272–19	* *A·* the mind-healing colleges
	272–29	endeavored to act toward *a·* students
	273–13	and gather *a·* my students, in the
	273–18	not yet accomplished *a·* the good
	274–10	therefore I leave *a·* for Christ.
	275–16	and bless *a·* who mourn.
	276– 4	like *a·* else, was purely Western
	276– 5	I did not hold interviews with *a·*
	276–24	I pray that *a·* my students shall
	278–14	Job sinned not in *a·* he said,
	279– 7	but over and above it *a·* are
	279–21	evil is naught and good is *a·*.
	279–24	they had *a·* to shout *together*
	280–11	Because God does *a·,*
	280–14	we imagine *a·* is well if we
	284–32	thus it is with *a·* moral obligations.
	284–32	I am opposed to *a·* personal attacks.

all

Mis. 289–12	A· partnerships are formed on
290– 7	a· bonds that hinder progress.
290–20	involuntarily flow out towards a·.
290–29	a· who are receptive share this
291–13	growth and prosperity of a·
291–24	on the hearts and lives of a·
292–18	to shut out a· opposite sense.
293– 3	a· the claims and modes of evil ;
293–15	will not understand a· your instructions ;
294–18	from . . . a· ravening beasts.
296–18	to intemperance, to a· immorality,
297– 3	has distanced a· other religious
297–21	a· the claims growing out of this
297–28	a· that belongs to the rights of freedom.
298– 1	with a· thine heart ; — *Prov.* 3 : 5.
298–19	a· the claims of sensuality.
302–21	a· destroyed the copies at once
203–10	will rest upon us a·.
307– 5	you will have a· you need
307– 9	assurance . . . to a· human fears,
307–17	and above a·, God's love
307–22	easily-besetting sin of a· peoples.
308–19	I thank you, each and a·,
308–32	I earnestly advise a·
309– 6	A· will agree with me that
309–21	include a· obstacles to health,
309–30	which contain a· and much more than
310–14	plead for a· and every one,
310–15	a· shall be redeemed,
310–19	A· who desire its fellowship,
310–27	cordially invite a· persons who
311– 1	a· who love God and keep His
311–16	would help a· to gain the abiding
311–28	take the cup, drink a· of it,
312– 1	sorry that I spoke at a·,
312– 6	lays a· upon the altar,
312– 7	and alone, bears a· burdens,
312– 7	suffers a· inflictions,
312– 8	endures a· piercing for the sake
314–18	shall read a· the selections
315– 9	a· over the world,
317– 4	we are a· of one kindred.
318–23	demands on a· those who
319– 1	the darkness of a· the ages,
319–18	a· the dear Christian Scientists
320–18	"healeth a· our — see *Psal.* 103 : 3.
320–27	is the light of a· ages ;
321–24	In reply to a· invitations
321–30	infinitely beyond a· earthly
323– 3	city above a· clouds,
324–25	find the lights a· wasted
325– 7	a· "drunken without wine." —see *Isa.* 29 : 9.
326–16	Thus are a· mortals, . . driven out
327–13	insisted upon taking a· of it
327–23	A· this time the Stranger is
329– 2	nature in a· her moods
329–16	rippling a· nature in
329–17	* "breath a· odor and cheek a· bloom."
331– 7	over a· the earth" — *Gen.* 1 : 26.
331–30	a· earth's hieroglyphics
333– 8	it absorbs a· the rays
334–11	a· its supposed power
335– 1	Love that casteth out a· fear,
336–22	cognomen of a· true religion,
338– 7	A· must go and do likewise.
339–21	venturing its a· of happiness
339–24	Remember, that for a· this
341–19	find Life eternal : you gain a·.
342–27	you shall receive a·.
343– 4	a· that we have to sacrifice,
346–21	a· its divine requirements.
347–14	with a· the goodness of
349–19	My counsel to a· of them
354–20	the Principle of a· that
354–24	wherein a· is controlled,
356–17	least of a· seeds," — *Matt.* 13 : 32.
357– 2	and a· the et cetera of the
357–20	the greatest of a· stages
358–30	fulfilled a· the good ends
361–12	overshadowed a· human philosophy,
361–25	a· eternal individuality.
362– 6	and reflects a· real mode,
362–12	that God, having made a·,
362–12	a· that He made was good.
362–25	We a· must find shelter
364–16	governing a· identity,
364–18	He made a· that was made,
365–29	and more than a· else,
366–23	a· mortal conclusions start from
368–12	a· are not metaphysicians,
369– 9	which governs a· effects,
370–25	would gather a· sorts into a
370–27	the good shepherd cares for a·
370–28	Shepherd does care for a·,
371–15	mixing a· grades of persons

all

Mis. 374– 9	justified of a· — *Luke* 7 : 35.
374–19	brought a great light to a· ages,
375–10	* I did not utter a· I felt
375–32	* A· that I can say to you,
379– 9	it was not at a· metaphysical
379–15	Principle of a· healing.
384– 5	And a· is morn and May.
386–29	a· the crowned and blest,
389–13	me, and mine, and a·.
393– 7	Science, a· unweary,
398– 4	A· the rugged way.
399– 2	Love wipes your tears a· away,
399–10	A· thy sorrow and sickness
Man. 27–16	a· other C. S. literature
28–18	If an officer fails to fulfil a· the
31– 5	and of a· its branch churches
32–22	read a· notices and remarks
32–24	in a· the branch churches.
36–24	A· applications for membership
42–14	and in accord with a· of
45– 3	occupation for a· its members.
46–14	a· private communications
47–17	a· thy diseases" — *Psal.* 103 : 3.
47–24	Charity to A·.
49– 4	a· who understand the teachings
59–17	a· sects and denominations
60–17	each day of a· the years.
66–19	if a· of the letter has been read,
66–20	require a· of it to be read ;
74–18	a· other C. S. churches
77– 6	submit them a· to said committee
77–20	a· the proceedings of the members
90– 1	A· members of this class must
91– 6	on a· certificates issued.
92–10	be a· that we claim for it.
99–15	By-Law applies to a· States except
102–10	A· deeds of further purchases
102–13	a· the trusts mentioned
102–18	in a· such deeds
110–10	A· names, whether of applicants,
110–16	A· names must be written
110–16	written the same in a· places
Chr. 53–12	That stills a· strife.
55–10	a· these things shall — *Matt.* 6 : 33.
Ret. 5–19	in a· the walks of life.
5–25	* was felt by a· around her.
9– 4	told Mehitable a· about this
18–18	a· His spirit hath made,
19–20	remarked by a· observers.
20– 1	lost a· my husband's property,
20–19	life is dead, bereft of a·,
22–17	God is over a·.
22–20	a· the children of one parent,
24– 8	to trace a· physical effects to
24–10	a· causation was Mind,
27– 8	like a· great truths,
29– 3	I esteem a· honest people,
30– 9	a· moral and religious reform.
31–21	he is guilty of a·." — *Jas.* 2 : 10.
34–11	a· material medicines,
34–12	antidote for a· sickness,
34–14	a· the ills which befall mortals.
38– 5	A· efforts to persuade him
38–19	printed a· the copy on hand,
42– 6	He forsook a· to follow
46–10	A· the rugged way.
47– 5	a· over our continent,
47–12	In view of a· this,
48– 4	a· that was aimed at its
48– 9	a· these considerations moved me
48–21	sent to a· parts of our country,
49– 2	willing to sacrifice a·
49–17	a· that is unlike Christ
49–28	a· debts of the corporation
57–13	causes a· bodily ailments,
57–20	sufficient to supply a·
57–22	A· must be of God,
58– 4	a· this is like trying to
59–19	and a· that is made by Him,
60–14	good is a· that is real.
61–13	the cause of a· sickness ;
64–10	good is equally one and a·,
64–24	they are no claims at a·.
64–26	to a· the illusive forms,
69– 5	The parent of a· human discord
69–22	God created a· through Mind,
69–22	and made a· perfect and eternal.
70–28	virtually stands at the head of a·
80–11	* With exactness grinds He a·.
81–24	* This above a· :
89–26	Above a·, trespass not intentionally
90–23	give a· her hours to those
91–18	spiritual needs of a· who
94–14	When a· fleshly belief is
Un. 3–22	He is a· the Life and Mind there is

all

Un.
4–12 diviner sense that God is a·
8–11 A· that is beautiful and good
8–17 A· forms of error are uprooted
9– 9 that a· are without excuse who
9–23 few spiritual thinkers in a· ages.
10– 2 separates my system from a· others.
11– 6 a· in direct opposition to
14–21 a· cannot be good therein.
15– 2 * death into the world, and a· our woe.
17– 5 and a· that is good will aid
17– 9 predestined from a· eternity ;
19– 7 If God knows evil at a·,
20–17 a· hate and the sense of evil.
23–13 a· are partakers, — Heb. 12 : 8.
24– 3 all consciousness, a· individuality
24–17 Spirit is a· that endureth,
24–20 constitute a· that exists.
26– 7 a· responsibility for myself
26–24 A· is real, a· is serious.
27– 9 doubts a· existence except its own.
29– 4 as does a· criminal law,
29–13 a· that is absolutely immutable
31–19 a· that denies and defies Spirit,
35–16 immortal Mind, the Parent of a·.
37–13 a· Life is eternal.
38– 9 a· is real which proceeds from
38–18 false sense of life is a· that dies,
39–28 Science and . . . conflict at a· points,
41–12 come to a· sooner or later ;
41–22 A· Life is Spirit,
42–14 a· the sons of God — Job. 38 : 7.
43–16 till a· be fulfilled." — Matt. 5 : 18.
45– 8 need most of a· to be rid of
46– 3 A· Truth is from inspiration
47– 5 A· that can exist is God and
48– 9 He heals a· my ills,
48–14 Father and Mother of a· He creates ;
51–11 generic term for a· humanity.
51–16 the generic term for a· women ;
51–16 of a· these individualities
53– 2 a· its forms are inverted good.
54– 4 a· there is of sickness ;
57–27 Science wipes away a· tears.
58–14 over a· mortal mentality
58–16 "in a· points tempted — Heb. 4 : 15.
60– 2 mortal inventions, one and a·
62–25 is a· that can be buried
64– 1 A· that is, God created.

Pul.
3–13 assurance ends a· warfare,
3–23 a· human desires are quenched,
4–20 lives in a· Life,
4–29 used, in a· its public sessions,
5–20 with a beauty a· its own
8– 1 A· praise to the press of
8–11 the donors a· touchingly told their
10– 6 a· thine iniquities ;— Psal. 103 : 3.
10– 7 a· thy diseases," — Psal. 103 : 3.
11– 6 May a· whose means, energies, and
12–22 by which we lay down a· for Truth,
15–16 At a· times and under a· circumstances,
15–20 will unite a· interests in the
17– 9 A· the rugged way.
21– 6 This we a· must do to be
21–15 doing good in a· denominations
22– 3 A· Christian churches have one bond
25–12 The girders are a· of iron,
29–20 * Judge Hanna said that while a· these
30–10 * includes those a· over the country.
31–19 * the central figure in a· this
33–20 * A· inquiry in the neighborhood
37– 3 * its attitude toward a· questions.
38–26 * each and a· these movements,
38–29 * good that each and a· shall prosper.
39– 1 * that a· meet on common ground
39– 5 * A· teach that one great truth,
39–25 * 'mid them a· I only see one face,
41–10 * a· the territory that lies between,
41–13 * From a· New England the members
41–20 * a· who wished had heard and seen ;
41–27 * A· hail the power of Jesus' name,
42– 2 * a· filled with a waiting multitude.
43– 3 * numbering thirty-five singers in a·
44–11 * While we a· rejoice, yet the mother
44–12 * the mother in Israel, alone of us a·,
44–18 * chapter sub-title
44–25 * has flowed in from a· parts of the
47–26 * picturesque a· about Concord
49–11 * has come forth a· this beauty!
51– 1 * C. S. does not strike a· as a system of
51– 3 * the same impressions upon a·.
52–23 * obliterated a· vital belief in his
54–23 * "put them a· out," — Luke 8 : 54.
55–19 * a· causation is of Mind,
55–26 * a· others being branches,
57–12 * and, indeed, in a· New England.

all

Pul.
58–18 * The floors are a· mosaic,
58–20 * a· the windows are of colored glass.
58–28 * furnished with a· conveniences
60–15 * from a· parts of the country.
61–21 * admiration was expressed by a·
62–13 * and call forth a· the purity
62–17 * They have a· the beauties of a
62–22 * as they range in a· sizes,
63–25 * Scientists a· over the country,
64– 8 * Money came freely from a·
68– 7 * from a· parts of the world,
69–17 * to explain fully a· about it,
70–16 * Scientists a· over the country.
70–18 * causation was Mind,
71–13 * in fact a· over the country,
73–21 * versed in a· their beliefs
73–23 * but that a· comes from God.
74–22 not at a· as I have heard her talk.
75–21 * a· over North America
76–19 * a· heavily plated with gold.
79– 6 * the money was a· paid in
80–29 * a· these ideas are Christian.
81– 2 * A· hail the power of Jesus' name,
81–10 * We a· know her — she is simply the
81–15 * of a· those who scorn self
81–16 * of a· those who seek the brightness
81–21 * a· the harmonies of the universe
81–25 * a· that the twelve have left undone.
81–26 * of missions — the highest of a·
84– 7 * a· that is worth living for,
84–15 * a· predictions and prognostications
84–19 * A· who are awake thereto have some
84–23 * a· obstacles to its completion
85–15 * gratitude and love of a·
86–20 * students and a· contributors

Rud.
v– 4 RESPECTFULLY DEDICATED TO a·
3– 4 obstinate resistance to a· efforts
3–19 which gives a· true volition,
4– 6 Principle of a· science,
4–10 A· true Science represents a
4–21 a· is God, and there is naught beside
5– 5 then a· must be Mind,
6– 6 A· beauty and goodness are
7– 1 Not that a· healing is Science,
8–15 In a· moral revolutions,
9–20 lust, and a· fleshly vices.
10–26 acknowledge God in a· His ways.
12– 3 Above a·, he keeps unbroken the
12–20 a· the conditions requisite for
13–26 give a· their time to C. S. work,
14– 3 must give Him a· their services,
15–17 should be fortified on a· sides

No.
v– 7 transparent to the hearts of a·
2– 9 rob disease of a· reality ;
5– 1 A· true Christian Scientists are
6–11 as a· understand who practise
6–26 a· at war with the testimony of
8– 4 faithful, and charitable with a·
8– 8 passeth a· understanding, — Phil. 4 : 7.
9–24 and includes a· Truth.
10–11 postulate of a· that I teach,
10–12 Principle for a· scientific truth,
10–25 turns . . . a· hope and faith to God,
12–14 true Christianity in a· ages,
12–27 removes a· limits from divine power.
12–28 a· instead of a part of being,
13– 5 the Principle of a· harmony,
14– 6 a· sensible phenomena are merely
15– 5 would convince a· that their purpose is
16–20 He who is All, understands a·.
16–22 can take in no more than a·.
17–21 these two words a· and nothing,
18– 3 acknowledged God in a· His ways.
18– 5 a· presence, power, and glory,
20–25 a· human philosophy.
21–10 the Principle of a· phenomena,
24– 2 loses a· place, person, and power.
24– 8 A· these vagaries are at variance
26–13 A· real being represents God,
33–25 Jesus suffered for a· mortals
34– 1 the delusion of a· human error,
38–25 A· prayer that is desire is
39–23 most of a·, it shows us what God is.
41–12 sinners in a· societies,
42– 8 supplies a· human needs.
42–10 a· "the ills that flesh is heir to."
42–11 a· the vain power of dogma
43– 4 a· ye that labor — Matt. 11 : 28.
45–19 with a· its sweet amenities

Pan.
1–18 even the day when a· people
2–11 Greek words meaning "a·"
3– 2 pantheism suits not at a· the
4– 4 who possesses a· wisdom,
4–25 a· thine iniquities ;— Psal. 103 : 3.
4–25 healeth a· thy diseases. — Psal. 103 : 3.

all

Pan.	6– 2	more effectual than a· other
	6–17	made a· that was made,
	10–22	A· this is accomplished by
	12–14	it showeth to a· peoples
	12–25	a· that the term implies,
	12–25	a· that is real and eternal.
	13–13	Love a· Christian churches
	13–18	a· shall know Him,
	13–21	life in Life, a· in All.
	13–23	Father of a·,— *Eph.* 4 : 6.
	13–23	above a·, and through a·,— *Eph.* 4 : 6.
	13–24	and in you a·.'' — *Eph.* 4 : 6.
'00.	2–27	Well, a· that is good.
	4–28	reflects a· that really is,
	4–29	a· personality and individuality.
	5– 1	Father of a·, who is above a·,— *Eph.* 4 : 6.
	5– 1	through a·, and in you a·.'' — *Eph.* 4 : 6.
	5–25	a· systems of religion.
	7– 8	more Bibles sold than in a· the
	7–11	those in a· the walks of life,
	9–16	must be a hero at a· points,
	10– 2	A· that worketh good is
	11–28	criticism on a· human action,
	14–24	At a· times respect the character
	15–10	which of a· human experience is
	15–16	a· this time divine Love has been
'01.	1–18	A· that is true is a sort of
	2–24	a· their returning footsteps.
	5– 9	possesses the nature of a·,
	5–13	the divine Principle of a·.
	6–27	a· conceivable idea of Him
	7–23	The God whom a· Christians
	10– 3	For a· these things they will — *see Matt.* 10:17.
	12–16	command to heal in a· ages,
	14–26	To overcome a· wrong, it must
	15–17	wickedness against a· light.
	23– 6	If . . . the infinite is not a· ;
	24– 7	a· the ills of mortals
	24–11	* greatest of a· temporal blessings,
	25–15	matter minus, and God a·,
	25–17	a· such gilded sepulchres
	27– 2	independent of a· other authors
	27–24	taken out of its metaphysics a· matter
	28–22	a· that worketh or maketh a lie.
	29–10	a· the best of his earthly years.
	29–22	A· honor and success to those
	30– 1	a· other religious denominations
	30–13	birth to nothing and death to a·,
	30–19	destroying a· lower considerations.
	30–27	under a· circumstances to obey the
	32–12	to renounce a· for Him.
	33– 7	* above a·, in the more advanced
	33–18	judged (if at a·) by their works.
	34–29	with a· thine heart ;— *Prov.* 3 : 5.
	35– 1	In · thy ways— *Prov.* 3 : 6.
'02.	2–10	It is purifying a· peoples,
	4– 7	Let us a· pray . . . for more grace,
	4–23	applicable to a· periods
	5– 6	C. S. stills a· distress
	5–30	silences a· questions on this subject,
	6–13	Here a· human woe is seen to
	6–17	a· it includes is obliterated,
	6–20	A· Christian faith, hope, and
	6–20	a· devout desire, virtually petition,
	7– 3	It accords a· to God, Spirit,
	7–11	*omni*, which signifies a·,
	9– 4	a· law and gospel.
	12–15	conflicts not at a· with another
	14–27	silence a· private criticisms,
	14–28	a· unjust public aspersions,
	16–20	no darkness, but a· is light,
	17– 6	a· are ready to seek and obey
	17–27	will put to flight a· care
	18–28	death of a· his disciples
	19– 9	a· the malice of his foes.
	19–23	of a· these things.'' — *Matt.* 6 : 32.
	20–22	but in this, as a· else,
	20–24	meeting you a· *occasionally*
Hea.	2–18	a· ye that labor— *Matt.* 11 : 28.
	4–23	Principle of a· that is right,
	7–19	more than they a·.'' — *see Mark* 12 : 43.
	9–23	God made a· that was made,
	10–13	God is All, and in a· :
	11–23	Metaphysics places a· cause
	12– 8	mind, the basis of a· action,
	12–10	a· physical effects originate in
	14–27	in sympathy with a· that is right
	14–28	opposed to a· that is wrong,
	15– 5	understood, to heal a· ills
	15–14	why should man deny a· might to
	16– 3	for the benefit of a· who,
	17– 8	God made a· that was made ;
	17–10	with a· their evidences of sin,
	17–12	we shall a· learn this as we awake
	17–23	but a· appeared through the

all

Hea.	19–11	origin of a· mortal things.
Peo.	4– 1	a· systems of *materia medica*
	6– 1	* a· the better for mankind
	6– 1	* a· the worse for the fishes.
	6–26	for which we are to leave a·
	7– 2	We are a· sculptors,
	9–24	a· evidence of any other power
	11–23	a· the woes of mankind
	12–12	acknowledge only God in a· thy ways,
	12–13	a· thine iniquities ;— *Psal.* 103 : 3.
	12–13	healeth a· thy diseases.'' — *Psal.* 103 : 3.
Po.	vi–22	* A· of the author's best-known hymns
	2–10	With a· the strength of weakness
	2–12	Admired by a·, still art thou drear
	4–12	encircles me, and mine, and a·.
	9– 9	leaves a· faded, the fruitage shed,
	9–11	reason made right and hearts a· love.
	11– 3	Victorious, a· who live it,
	14– 8	A· the rugged way.
	16–19	when the winds are a· still.
	24–14	Is a· I need to comfort mine.
	29–18	so far above A· mortal strife,
	29–21	Fill us today With a· thou art
	32–20	comfort my soul a· the wearisome day,
	33– 8	vanity, folly, and a· that is wrong
	36– 4	And a· is morn and May.
	39– 1	Author of a· divine
	39–18	''Temples of Honor,'' a·,
	40– 1	''Good Templars'' one and a·,
	41–18	didst call them to banish a· pain,
	46–16	Be a· thy life in music given,
	50–16	with a· the crowned and blest,
	51–12	Art and Science, a· unweary,
	53–19	dead are a· The vernal songs
	64– 9	a· His spirit hath made
	75– 9	Love wipes your tears a· away,
	75–17	A· thy sorrow and sickness and sin.''
My.	vi–22	* to pay a· future profits to
	vii–14	* a· Christian Scientists can render
	4–15	loves a· who love God, good ;
	5–10	God giving a· and man having a·
	6–10	overcome sin in a· its forms,
	8–21	* if they are a· to get in.''
	11– 5	* constantly at her post during a·
	11–11	* we know that in a· this time
	13–20	a· thine iniquities ;— *Psal.* 103 : 3.
	13–20	*healeth a· thy diseases;* — *Psal.* 103 : 3.
	13–26	reverberating through a· cycles of
	15–15	a· that you are able to bear now,
	17– 4	a· malice, and a· guile,— *I Pet.* 2 : 1.
	17– 5	a· evil speakings,— *I Pet.* 2 : 1.
	18–21	Love a· Christian churches for the
	18–30	* a· other published writings of
	19–11	be with you a·.— *II Cor.* 13 : 14.
	20–13	Bring a· your tithes into
	21– 3	* We a· know of the loving
	21–10	* a· Christian Scientists will gladly
	21–26	* a· will rejoice in the glad reunion
	22– 6	* attendance at a· the services,
	22–27	* Is it not therefore the duty of a·
	24– 4	* is ready to heal a· who accept its
	25–16	Will one and a· of my dear
	25–25	a· vanity of victory disappears
	25–27	divinity appears in a· its promise.
	27–25	* pay a· bills in connection with
	30– 3	* a· the services were precisely
	30– 7	* Scientists from a· over the world,
	30– 7	* nearly a· the local Scientists,
	32– 5	* they began a· together,
	36–11	* a· that we are or hope to be
	36–26	* a· the beauty of color and design,
	37– 1	* natural healer of a· our diseases
	37–10	* appreciation of a· that you have
	37–20	* supreme cause of a· the activities
	38– 3	* in God is a· consolation
	38– 5	* our love for you and for a· that
	38– 6	* a· that you have done for us.
	38–10	* a· seating space had been filled
	38–18	* a· the seats in the body of the
	38–22	* their service was the same as a·
	39–12	* Lord's Prayer, in which a· joined.
	41–21	* love which is just and kind to a·
	47– 5	* from a· parts of the world,
	47–16	* victories . . . precious each and a·.
	48–25	* are a· forces that make for
	48–31	* to say, in a· fairness,
	50–24	* a very inspiring season to us a·,
	51– 5	* a· others now interested in
	51–30	* thanks and gratitude shared by a·
	52– 9	* a·, will make greater efforts
	59–32	* marvellous beyond a· imagining
	60–10	* expressed the thought of a·
	60–19	* ''With a· thy getting get — *Prov.* 4 : 7.
	64– 7	* for a· that she has done.
	64–15	* In a· her writings, through a· the

all

My. 64–20 * Fearlessly does she warn *a·* her
64–24 * overcoming *a·* that is unlike God,
68–18 * color scheme for *a·* the auditorium
70– 7 * and they are *a·* paid for.
70–12 * The effect on *a·* within earshot
71– 9 * *a·* agree that it is a stunning
71–19 * In fact, nearly *a·* the traditions of
72– 9 * From *a·* the centres of Europe
72–14 * chapter sub-title
72–22 * members of the church *a·* over the
73– 4 * churches *a·* over this country
73–13 * flocking from *a·* over the world
73–21 * here the visitors will receive *a·*
73–23 * to which *a·* mail may be directed,
75–12 * *a·* the preliminary arrangements
75–17 * take it *a·* very good-naturedly.
76– 3 * the largest of them *a·*.
76–14 * *a·* of which goes to show the
76–21 * *a·* contributions have been voluntary.
77– 1 * the cynosure of *a·* eyes
77– 9 * From *a·* over the world
77–23 * Scientists from *a·* quarters
78– 2 * in order that *a·* might participate
78–31 * apparently understanding *a·* they
80–27 * when these places had *a·* been filled,
82– 1 * they *a·* have the same stories
82– 6 * this morning it looked as though *a·*
84– 3 * practically *a·* the resources
84–12 * Scientists *a·* over the world.
88– 7 * It shows strength in *a·* parts,
88–22 * *a·* that increasing host
89– 4 * *a·* facts inhospitable to it
89– 5 * deemed . . . not to exist at *a·*.
89–18 * different from almost *a·* other
89–29 * greatest religious phenomenon of *a·*
90– 4 * *a·* these things are new,
90–10 * *A·* the passionate love for life
90–25 * from *a·* over the civilized world,
96– 2 * from *a·* parts of the world
96–29 * from *a·* parts of the United States.
98–19 * *a·* of the funds required
99–18 * from *a·* parts of the world,
100–8, 9 * coming from *a·*, or nearly *a·*,
104– 5 *a·* sorts of institutions flourish
106–27 the very antipode of *a·* these?
107–24 God made *a·* that was made,
110–14 *a·* the *et cetera* of mortal mind
113–24 *a·* around us is demonstrated
114–19 *A·* thoughts in the line of Scriptural
117–25 May *a·* Christian Scientists ponder
117–31 is *a·* that I ask of mankind.
119–17 "healeth *a·* thy diseases"— *Psal.* 103 : 3.
121–24 is not only polite to *a·* but is
125–11 *A·* honor to the members of our
127–11 than *a·* other religions since then
127–32 *a·* times, climes, and
129– 6 *a·* concomitants of C. S.
130–21 *A·* published quotations from
130–28 in *a·* your public ministrations,
131–24 "Bring ye *a·* the tithes – *Mal.* 3 : 10.
132–21 God *a·*, one, — one Mind
133– 5 So shall *a·* earth's children
133–27 my book is not *a·* you know of me.
134–17 Life lessens *a·* pride
137–14 selected *a·* my investments,
138–18 except I leave *a·* for Christ.
141–19 * from *a·* parts of the world.
143–10 one and *a·* of my beloved friends
143–14 *a·* this fustian of either denying or
146– 2 understood by *a·* Christians that
146–17 if they are true at *a·*,
148– 4 *A·* that we ask of any people
148– 7 God of *a·* grace, truth, and love
148–13 *a·* unthought of till the day had
151–26 discovery of *a·* cause and effect.
152–16 Principle of *a·* that really is,
152–18 there is none else and in whom is *a·*
152–25 God demands *a·* our faith and love ;
152–29 cause of *a·* that is rightly done.
153–28 to *a·* human thought and action,
154– 1 *a·* salvation from sin, disease,
154– 2 Science of *a·* healing is based on
156– 6 above *a·* that we ask— *Eph.* 3 : 20.
156– 7 *a·* grace abound— *II Cor.* 9 : 8.
156– 8 having *a·* sufficiency— *II Cor.* 9 : 8.
158–28 and *a·* who worship therein
159–29 *A·* rights reserved.
160–20 a hell for *a·* who persist in
161– 9 *a·* ye workers of— *Luke* 13 : 27.
161–12 and *a·* the prophets,— *Luke* 13 : 28.
162– 4 fulfil *a·* righteousness."— *Matt.* 3 : 15.
162–11 Scientists *a·* over the field,
163– 9 Not having the time to receive *a·*
163–25 *a·* and more than I anticipated.
164–12 *a·* within the human heart

all

My. 164–26 the sum of *a·* reality and good.
165– 1 promote and pervade *a·* his success.
166– 1 infinite source where is *a·*,
166–20 If *a·* our years were holidays,
167–19 Give to *a·* the dear ones
169– 2 I invite you, one and *a·*,
170–10 in the minds of *a·* present
171–11 invite *a·* my church communicants
173–21 my heart welcomed each and *a·*.
178–10 and prepared for *a·* peoples.
178–13 Then *a·* is Spirit and spiritual.
178–15 pronounces *a·* that God made
178–18 for He made *a·*
178–31 *a·* else reported as his sayings
179–11 *a·* of which divine Science shows
180– 8 which applies to *a·* ages,
181– 2 settle *a·* points beyond cavil,
183– 2 with *a·* thy heart,— *Luke* 10 : 27.
183– 2 with *a·* thy soul,— *Luke* 10 : 27.
183– 3 with *a·* thy strength,— *Luke* 10 : 27.
183– 3 with *a·* thy mind ;— *Luke* 10 : 27.
186–13 o'er *a·* victorious!
186–14 in whom dwelleth *a·* life, health,
186–15 will supply *a·* your needs
187– 8 exclude *a·* darkness or doubt,
187–17 be and abide with you *a·*.
188–27 convey *a·* impressions to man,
190–23, 24 *a·* peoples, in *a·* ages,
191–17 Love, which wipes away *a·* tears.
193– 6 mine to watch and work for *a·*,
193–18 unite with *a·* who believe in Truth.
195–16 To do good to *a·* because we love *a·*,
195–17 the one talent that we *a·* have,
199–16 *a·* loyal lovers of God and man.
201–24 *A·* the rugged way.
202– 8 "Render therefore to *a·* — *Rom.* 13 : 7.
203– 4 *a·* is in your textbooks.
203–10 *A·* that is worth reckoning
203–26 safe from *a·* chance of being
203–29 if you have not accomplished *a·* you
205–23 shorn of *a·* personality,
210–10 *a·* whom your thoughts rest upon
211– 9 *A·* that error asks is to
214–27 cast my *a·* into the treasury
216– 2 give *a·* their time to spiritual
216– 4 *A·* systems of religion stand on this
217–18 * "If *a·* matter is unreal, why do we
217–22 *a·* that the material senses affirm.
218– 4 fulfil *a·* righteousness."— *Matt.* 3 : 15.
219– 6 have *a·* the honor of their success
220–15 I pray for the pacification of *a·*
221–24 *A·* issues of morality,
223–17 *A·* such questions are superinduced
223–20 *A·* inquiries, coming directly or
223–29 Do *a·* Christian Scientists see or
225–12 In divine Science *a·* belongs to God,
225–15 distinguishes it from *a·* other names,
225–22 In this, as in *a·* that is right,
226–20 divine Principle includes them *a·*.
226–13 governs *a·* from the infinitesimal to
229– 5 *a·* that do these things
229–14 and thus lose *a·* selfishness,
230–10 but to one and *a·* equally.
230–27 *a·* taught of God."— *John* 6 : 45.
232– 7 whereby *a·* our debts are paid,
232–14 I say unto *a·*, Watch"— *Mark* 13 : 37.
234–21 *a·* our great Master's sayings
235–16 Did God make *a·* that was made?
237–23 I recommend its careful study to *a·*
239–14 and *a·* are taught of God
239–18 and so includes *a·* in one.
239–22 is the reflection of *a·* that is real
239–27 Spirit, who made *a·* that was made.
240–17 *a·* that is unlike God, good
241–29 * so that *a·* may know it."
242–17 *a·* inquiries . . . relating to C. S.
243–17 give *a·* possible time and attention
244– 9 any or *a·* of you who are ready
244–21 *a·* loyal students of my books
245–24 of *a·* who claim to teach C. S.
247–28 has *a·* been done through love,
249–14 *a·* this only to satiate its loathing
251–24 for *a·* is thine and mine.
252–29 *A·* hail to this higher hope
256– 9 I beg to send to you *a·* a
257–16 healing *a·* sorrow, sickness, and sin.
257–20 *a·* human hate, pride, greed,
258– 8 to *a·* of holiest worth.
258–24 sounded *a·* depths of love, grief,
259–13 *A·* our dear churches' Christmas
260–26 appeals to *a·* conditions,
263– 6 wishes you *a·* a *happy Christmas*,
265–30 reaching out to *a·* classes
266–17 *a·* codes, modes, hypotheses,
266–19 origin of *a·* that really is,
266–21 by the spiritualization of *a·*

all

My. 267– 6 the originator of *a·* that really is.
267–30 *a·* the divine modes, means, forms,
269–12 * *A·* are but parts of one stupendous
271– 5 little understood *a·* that I indited ;
271–23 * will be read with deep interest by *a·*
273– 7 * emerging . . . from *a·* attacks
275–20 is *a·* that prevents my daily drive.
275–27 charity brooding over *a·*,
276–12 to *a·* her dear friends and enemies.
277–20 can settle *a·* questions amicably
279– 9 reappearing in *a·* ages,
279–10 *a·* periods in the design of God.
279–13 is sufficient to still *a·* strife.
279–14 Had *a·* peoples one Mind,
280– 8 * reminder from you that *a·* the things
280–19 He will bless *a·* the inhabitants
280–22 bless *a·* with His own truth
281–10 brotherhood of *a·* peoples
282– 7 *a·* the ends of the earth.'' — *Isa.* 45 : 22.
283–15 remedies for *a·* earth's woe.
284–26 *a·* quarrels between nations
285– 7 in *a·* your wise endeavors for
286– 5 prayed that *a·* the peoples on earth
287– 9 governing *a·* that really is.
288–11 and He is the Father of *a·*.
288–31 because God made *a·*,
289– 1 *A·* education is work.
290–17 never so near as when *a·* earthly joys
291–11 the interests of *a·* peoples ;
292– 2 *A·* that can be accomplished,
294– 6 omnipresent, supreme over *a·*.
294–14 control *a·* the conditions of man
297– 4 *a·* that Miss Barton really is,
298– 7 distinguished *a·* my working years.
302– 1 *a·* modes of healing disease
302– 8 mind is the cause of *a·* effect
303–21 what feeds a few feeds *a·*.
303–25 pith and finale of them *a·*.
305–21 *A·* that I am in reality,
307– 5 word science was not used at *a·*,
308– 1 *a·* the powers of earth combined
309–31 * practically *a·* the intellectual life.
310– 1 *A·* my father's daughters were given
310– 3 they *a·* taught school acceptably
310–17 allegation . . . that *a·* the family,
315–30 *a·* this because the truth
316–25 and of *a·* that is right.
320–15 * the author of *a·* your works.
320–18 * did not endorse *a·* the statements
323–18 * *a·* that your wonderful life and
323–19 * Neither do I now feel at *a·* equal
325– 2 * when amidst *a·* your duties you
327–12 * it has made glad the hearts of *a·*
327–25 * ''*A·* other professionals who
328–28 * ''and *a·* other professionals who
330–11 * are appreciated by *a·*,
330–31 was remarked by *a·* observers.
332– 7 * yet it is *a·* we can award :
336–12 I lost *a·* my husband's property,
338– 3 Victorious, *a·* who live it,
338–23 But *a·* Christian Scientists deeply
338–29 charitable towards *a·*,
339–14 *a·* that it formerly signified,
339–28 and *a·* that wars against Spirit
340–26 Jesus' example in this, as in *a·* else,
341– 9 Beloved brethren *a·* over our land
341–14 A love for *a·*
341–26 * It had been raining *a·* day
342–25 * after *a·* now concerned in its
343–29 brought *a·* back to union and love
344– 3 then *a·* his rays collectively
345–26 They *a·* tend to newer, finer,
346–29 ''S. and H. makes it plain to *a·*
347–19 in exchange for *a·* else.
347–20 with *a·* its sweet associations.
348– 4 *a·* effect must be the offspring of
348– 8 the greatest of *a·* questions
349–30 including *a·* law and supplying *a·* the
350–19 Thou *a·*, Thou infinite
351–20 divine Science is *a·* they need,
353– 9 I have given the name to *a·* the
353–26 the spiritual have *a·* place and
357–22 therefore *Spirit is a·*.
358–13 however much I desire to read *a·*
358–21 through whom *a·* my business is
359–11 *a·* of which can be read by the
360–17 I advise you with *a·* my soul to
361– 5 *A·* I say is stated in C. S.
362–13 Trustees and Readers of *a·* the
(*see also* **being, churches, consciousness, disease,
earth, error, evil, faith, good, mankind, manner,
men, Mind, minds, nations, power, Science,
sense, sin, space, suffering, things, time, way,
world**)

all-absorbing

Un. 6–17 such a grand and *a·* verity

allay

Mis. 45– 7 although its power to *a·* fear,
Ret. 26– 6 to *a·* the tortures of crucifixion.

allaying

My. 335–19 * in the hope of *a·* the excitement

all-conquering

My. 258–11 with Christ's *a·* love.

allegation

My. 310–17 the *a·* by *McClure's Magazine*
334– 5 * *a·* that copies of Mrs. Eddy's book,

allegations

My. 317– 4 * *a·* in the public press

allege

Mis. 199– 3 to *a·* that only mortal, erring mind

alleged

Mis. 48–13 It is *a·* that at one of his
248–20 is *a·* to have reported my demise,
My. 136–16 for which it is *a·* he was
315–24 her *a·* double or dummy
354– 2 because of *a·* misrepresentations

allegement

Mis. 238–25 public *a·* that I am ''sick,

allegiance

Mis. 134–18 Firm in your *a·* to the reign of
276–32 firmer than ever in their *a·* to God.
Ret. 50–19 I mean this, — *a·* to God,
My. 42–27 * how faithful is her *a·* to God,
299– 9 * claim the *a·* of mankind.''

allegiant

My. 189–17 for love is *a·*,

alleging

Mis. 380–32 *a·* that the copyrighted works of

allegorical

My. 179– 7 In this *a·* document

allegories

'00. 11–27 His *a·* are the highest criticism

allegory

Mis. 24–28 or rather the *a·* describing it.
109–19 *a·* of Adam and Eve
323– 1 chapter sub-title
332–13 In the *a·* of Genesis,
Pan. 6–19 enter into the Scriptural *a·*,
Hea. 17–14 The *a·* of Adam,
17–24 Sin was first in the *a·*,
My. 5– 2 according to the Scriptural *a·*,
179– 6 second was an opposite story, or *a·*,

alleviate

Mis. 89–12 save him or *a·* his sufferings,

All-Father

Ret. 91–25 holy messages from the *A·*.

All-Father-Mother

Mis. 77–24 learn, . . . somewhat of the *A·* God.

All-God

No. 10–10 and expresses the *A·*.

all-harmonious

Mis. 18–16 the *a·* ''male and female,'' — *Gen.* 1 : 27.

alliance

Mis. 122– 8 instrument in this holy (?) *a·*

allied

Mis. 97–12 It is in no way *a·* to divine power.
Un. 17– 5 Be *a·* to the deific power,
Pul. 83–18 * our own *a·* armies of evil
No. 14–12 is no more *a·* to C. S. than
Po. 10–17 *A·* by nations' grace,
My. 177–17 genesis of C. S. was *a·* to
337–18 *A·* by nations' grace,

allies

Mis. 288–28 temperance and truth are *a·*,
My. 129–22 and be thy dearest *a·*.

all-important

'01. 33– 1 *a·* consideration of their being,
Peo. 13– 8 This *a·* understanding is gained in

All-in-all

God is
    (*see* **God**)

———

Mis. 25– 9 God is Truth, and *A·*.
45–25 imply Him to be, *A·*,
49–27 This belief . . . that God is not *A·*,
55–26 If God is Spirit, . . . and *A·*,
64– 1 Spirit might be found ''*A·*.''
115–20 since God, good, is *A·*.
183– 8 it will be found that Mind is *A·*,
200– 7 Spirit was to him *A·*,
366–12 because He is *A·*,

All-in-all
Ret. 34– 3 the *A·* of Spirit,
Un. 20–18 perception of God as *A·*.
37–15 God is Life and *A·*.
60–20 He will be unto them *A·*.
No. 18– 4 lie that denies Him as *A·*,
36– 4 and therefore as the *A·* ;
My. 158–10 Love's divine adventure to be *A·*.

all-in-all
My. 5–15 are the *a·* of C. S.
64–14 are the *a·* of C. S."

all-inclusive
Mis. 331–30 this adorable, *a·* God,
My. 46–26 * *a·* instructions and admonitions

all-in-one
My. 247– 1 *a·* and one-in-all.
254–22 *a·* and one-in-all.

all-just
Mis. 124–13 unchangeable, all-wise, *a·*,

all-knowing
Mis. 71–15 omnipotence, the *a·* Mind.
71–26 God, good, the *a·* Mind.
'01. 7– 8 *a·*, all-loving Father-Mother,

all-knowledge
Un. 27–15 His own all-presence, *a·*,

all-loving
'01. 7– 9 all-wise, all-knowing, *a·*

all-merciful
Mis. 124–14 all-wise, all-just, *a·* ;
Po. 28–14 *A·* and good, Hover the homeless

All-Mind
Un. 7–25 highest phenomena of the *A·*.

allness
Mis. 90 8 declare the *a·* and oneness of God
109– 2 the unity of Truth, and its *a·*
188–24 up to its infinite meaning, its *a·*.
206– 9 eternal existence, God's *a·*, and
208– 6 by virtue of this nature and *a·*
253–11 make amends . . . with the *a·* of Mind.
Man. 16– 7 even the *a·* of Soul, Spirit, and
Ret. 26–28 know yet more of . . . the *a·* of Spirit,
Un. 10– 1 you demonstrate the *a·* of God,
Rud. 10–27 understanding of the *a·* of God,
No. 30– 8 by virtue of the *a·* of God,
35–12 *a·* of Love and the nothingness of
'01. 12–23 we then see the *a·* of Spirit,
'02. 16–15 the divine presence and *a·*.
My. 280–21 Out of His *a·* He must bless all
349–15 he is conscious of the *a·* of God
364–15 supremacy and *a·* of good.

allopath
My. 108– 3 the *a·* who depends upon drugs.

allopathic
Ret. 43–13 from Dr. W. W. Keen's (*a·*)
'01. 17–28 where the *a·* doses would not.

allopathy
Mis. 6–15 will rank far in advance of *a·*
252– 4 medical systems of *a·* and
Ret. 33– 8 *a·*, homœopathy, hydropathy,
Pul. 47–12 * schools of *a·*, homœopathy, and
64–17 * She investigated *a·*,
Hea. 11–16 recover from the heel of *a·*

allotted
Mis. 95–11 time so kindly *a·* me
My. 273– 6 * beyond the *a·* years of man,

allow
Mis. 108– 4 To *a·* sin of any sort is
118– 9 then *a·* one numeral to make
303–14 *a·* to each and every one the same
315–25 nor *a·* their students to do thus,
Man. 91– 2 shall not *a·* it or a copy of it
Ret. 82– 5 my students should not *a·* their
No. 7– 5 No personal considerations should *a·*
Pan. 11–12 When will the schools *a·* mortals
'01. 17–19 when the public sentiment would *a·*
26–26 *a·* me to add I have read little of
'02. 12–21 *a·* me to interpolate some matters of
Po. vii– 8 * *to a· a popular edition to be*
My. 7– 4 *a·* me to interpolate some matters of
39–19 * You will *a·* me, however,
41–12 * will *a·* no one to escape that
53– 5 * would she *a·* printer and binder
156– 3 *a·* me to reply in words of the
163–11 must not *a·* myself the pleasure
167–23 *A·* me to send forth a pæan of
173– 5 *A·* me through your paper
175–11 *A·* me to say to the good folk of
213–18 *a·* himself to drift in the wrong
256– 2 *a·* me to improvise some new notes,

allow
My. 274–21 *a·* me to say that I am not fond of
315–25 *a·* me to thank the enterprising
324–18 * too honorable to *a·* the thought

allowable
Mis. 297–10 Smart journalism is *a·*, . . . but

allowed
Mis. 7– 1 These children must not be *a·* to
95– 5 * *a·* ten minutes in which to reply
247– 4 be *a·* due consideration,
289–31 *a·* to rise to the spiritual altitude
296– 2 *a·* myself to be elected an associate
302–18 I *a·*, till this permission was
315– 6 No copies from my books are *a·*
353– 1 the consciousness be *a·* to rejoice
Man. 60–23 No large gathering . . . shall be *a·*
71–19 specially *a·* and named in this Manual.
81–24 no evil speaking shall be *a·*.
93–19 The Board of Lectureship is not *a·*
Ret. 88–28 Itinerancy should not be *a·* to
Un. 54–14 for if sin's claim be *a·*
'01. 29–27 I *a·* them for several years
33–15 to be *a·* the rights of conscience
My. 311– 5 She begged to be *a·* to remain
338–16 not *a·* to consult me relative to

alloweth
Ret. 94–19 that thing which he *a·*.— *Rom.* 14 : 22.

allowing
My. 173–26 *a·* the visitors to assemble on the
211– 7 *a·* it first to smoulder,
359–29 *a·* your students to deify you

allows
Mis. 245–24 but, if the pulpit *a·* the people
Man. 68–18 calls to her home or *a·* to visit

all-pervading
Mis. 16–21 an *a·* intelligence and Love,
Un. 45–15 its *a·* presence in certain forms of

All-power
Mis. 200– 7 understood omnipotence to be *A·* :
'02. 9– 3 the *A·* — giving life, health,
Peo. 9–26 omnipotence is the *A·*.

all-power
Mis. 14– 4 the ever-presence and *a·* of good ;
25–24 this medicine is *a·* ;
101–21 Science saith to man, "God hath *a·*."
141– 5 revealed to you God's *a·*,
173–21 Mind, God, is *a·* and all-presence,
197–30 God as omnipotent, having *a·* ;
332–29 The supposition is, that . . . are not *a·* ;
Ret. 60–19 God is *a·* and all-presence,
Un. 27–15 all-presence, all-knowledge, *a·*.
Rud. 11–23 *a·* and ever-presence of good,
'02. 7–12 signifies *a·*, all-presence,
Peo. 13– 9 the one God and His *a·*
My. 152–11 conception of Spirit and its *a·*.
226–22 even as you value His *a·*,
274– 9 its *a·*, all-presence, all-Science.

All-presence
'02. 9– 2 Then God becomes to him the *A·*

all-presence
Mis. 141– 5 God's all-power, *a·*, and all-science.
173–22 Mind, God, is all-power and *a·*,
Ret. 60–19 God is all-power, and *a·*,
Un. 27–15 *a·*, all-knowledge, all-power.
'02. 7–13 signifies all-power *a·*,
My. 226–22 His all-power, *a·*, all-Science,
274– 9 its all-power, *a·*, all-Science.

all's
My. 40–27 * "*A·* love, but *a·* law."

All-science
'02. 9– 4 *A·* — all law and gospel.

all-Science and **all-science**
Mis. 25–25 omniscience means as well, *a·*.
141– 6 all-power, all-presence, and *a·*.
'02. 7–13 all-power, all-presence, *a·*,
My. 226–22 His all-power, all-presence, *a·*,
274– 9 its all-power, all-presence, *a·*.

allude
Mis. 280–27 *a·* briefly to a topic of great import
379–15 *a·* to God as the divine Principle

alluded
Mis. 57– 9 its spiritual Science is *a·* to
301–31 to whom Isaiah *a·* thus :
Pul. 86–28 * Bible and the book *a·* to
'01. 25–14 *a·* to or required in such
My. 11–14 * she quietly *a·* to the need of

alludes
Mis. 243–23 *a·* to Paul's advice to Timothy.
Hea. 3–17 Josephus *a·* to several individuals

alluding
My. 103–15 *A·* to this divine method,

all-unbeguiled
Mis. 386– 9 Truth's new birth *A·*
Po. 49–14 Truth's new birth *A·*

allurements
My. 211–14 silent *a·* to health and holiness,
  252–27 *a·* of wealth, pride, or power ;

allusion
Mis. 88–14 His *a·* to C. S. in the
  193–17 thankful even for his *a·* to

all-wise
Mis. 124–13 unchangeable, *a·*, all-just,
  206–18 by the active, *a·*, law-creating,
'01. 7– 8 He is the *a·*, all-knowing,
Po. 28– 7 To Thy *a·* behest

Alma Mater
Mis. 359– 1 follow the example of the *A· M·*.
Ret. 49– 6 follow the example of the *A· M·*

Almighty
Un. 57– 8 shadow of the *A·*."— *Psal.* 91 : 1.
My. 107–23 shadow of the *A·*"— *Psal.* 91 : 1.
  210–16 abides under the shadow of the *A·*.

almighty
Mis. 227–32 is the command of *a·* wisdom ;
Hea. 15–16 he calls God *a·* and admits

Almighty God
My. 147–19 will, in the name of *A· G·*,
  200– 6 our trust is in the *A· G·*,

almond-blossom
Mis. 231– 1 *a·* formed a crown of glory ;

almost
Mis. 159–30 *a·* marvel at the power and
  375–21 * an *a·* identical resemblance,
Ret. 7– 9 * by intense and *a·* incessant study
Pul. 29–27 * *a·* the entire congregation was
  49–16 *a·* as big as they are now,
  63–13 *a·* as big as they are now,
Rud. 6–16 * fact "*a·* universally accepted,
No. 41–22 Church seems *a·* chagrined that
'01. 28–11 into *a·* every Christian tongue,
'02. 5– 9 this *a·* unconceived light of
Hea. 20– 7 * In notes *a·* divine."
My. 22–14 * Since 1866, *a·* forty years ago,
  22–14 * *a·* forty years in the wilderness,
  38–21 * in *a·* perfect time.
  43–13 * was *a·* as marvellous as
  89–18 * different from *a·* all other
  89–19 * *a·* as constant as petitions for
  97– 1 * *a·* every one is inclined to admit.
  106– 7 organic diseases of *a·* every kind.
  225–20 Mankind *a·* universally gives
  248– 3 its grandeur *a·* surprises me.
  306–13 *a·* unutterable truths to translate,
  318– 2 In *a·* every case where Mr. Wiggin
  347–14 would *a·* suggest that nature had

alms
Mis. ix– 4 * best *a·* are to show and to enable
  ix– 5 * enable a man to dispense with *a·*."

aloft
Ret. 53– 5 designed to bear *a·* the standard of

alone
Mis. 2–18 will be found *a·* the remedy for sin,
  4–18 *a·* adequate to meet the requirement.
  4–29 It is not *a·* the mission of C. S.
  28–16 he demonstrated that divine Science *a·*
  32–15 love *a·* is admissible
  48–17 through the action of mind *a·*.
  66– 9 for the offender *a·* suffers,
  97–15 C. S. is not a remedy of faith *a·*,
  101– 3 He *a·* knows these wonders who
  104–31 This *a·* gives me the forces of God
  118–18 willing to work *a·* with God
  126– 8 *a·* he has his own thoughts to guard,
  137–21 to work out individually and *a·*,
  138–11 student should seek *a·* the guidance of
  142–16 Why the letter *a·* ?
  145– 4 shall exist *a·* in the affections,
  166– 1 *a·* demonstrates the divine Principle
  198–26 all of which is corrected *a·* by
  236–22 but be guided by God *a·* ; "
  243–19 their works *a·* should declare them,
  244– 5 Mind *a·* constructing the human system,
  245–28 can walk *a·* the straight and
  250– 2 the *a·* God, is Love.
  266–13 dashing through space, headlong and *a·*.
  268–27 Right *a·* is irresistible,
  275–10 bereft wife or husband, silent and *a·*,
  284–26 Evil let *a·* grows more real,
  290– 2 Let other people's marriage relations *a·* :
  293– 5 leave . . . *a·*, and to the special care of

alone
Mis. 301–32 trodden the winepress *a·* ;— *Isa.* 63 : 3.
  303– 8 governed by divine Love *a·*
  312– 7 speechless and *a·*, bears all burdens,
  318– 5 not *a·* for my students,
  319–26 feel themselves *a·* among the stars.
  324–16 he *a·* who looks from that dwelling,
  328– 2 "Let them *a·* ; they must learn
  328–21 He *a·* ascends the hill of C. S.
  339–24 thou *a·* canst and must atone.
  352–23 Through the divine energies *a·*
  353–27 set up housekeeping *a·*.
  358–10 God *a·* is his help,
  359– 7 instantaneously, and through Spirit *a·*.
  365– 1 This philosophy *a·* will bear the strain
  365–11 for it rests *a·* on demonstration.
  365–19 for what immortal Mind *a·* can supply.
  373–31 it presents not words *a·*, but works,
  380– 2 if a divine Principle *a·* heals,
  388–10 For Love *a·* is Life ;
Man. 40– 8 divine Love *a·* governs man ;
  51–26 and they *a·* shall vote on cases
  61–23 Music from the organ *a·* should
  71–12 The Mother Church stands *a·* ;
  95–22 The duties *a·* of a Reader are ample.
  104– 7 It stands *a·*, uniquely adapted
  111– 4 Initials *a·* will not be received.
Ret. 22–17 He *a·* is our origin, aim, and being.
  25–15 because Soul *a·* is truly substantial.
  28– 1 became evident that the divine Mind *a·*
  30– 1 As the pioneer of C. S. I stood *a·*
Un. 18–19 which *a·* enable Me to rebuke,
  31–23 God, or good, is Spirit *a·* ;
  35–24 Spirit is *spiritual* consciousness *a·*.
  38– 3 To God *a·* belong the indisputable realities
  38–15 by declaring that not He *a·* is Life,
  55– 1 Jesus accepted the one fact whereby *a·* the
  58– 6 "the winepress *a·*."— *Isa.* 63 : 3.
Pul. 32–16 experiences which *a·* are significant.
  44–12 * mother in Israel, *a·* of us all,
  52–18 * The name C. S. *a·* is new.
Rud. 6–25 can *a·* answer this question
  10– 5 know that God *a·* governs man ;
No. 5– 7 As Truth *a·* is real, then it follows
  9– 9 let your opponents *a·*,
  18– 7 it rests *a·* on the demonstration of
  18–25 asks for what Mind *a·* can supply.
  25–23 immortal man *a·* is God's likeness,
'01. 9–20 "Let us *a·* ;— *Mark* 1 : 24.
  19–19 through spiritual ascendency *a·*.
  20– 8 The Christian Scientist is *a·* with his
  30–24 working *a·* with God,
'02. 10– 8 and reiterate, Let me *a·*.
Hea. 18–26 death has been produced by a belief *a·*.
Peo. 10–15 Mental Science *a·* grasps the standard
  10–19 they *a·* have fettered free limbs,
Po. 7–10 For Love *a·* is Life ;
  page 8 poem
  8– 1 sitting *a·* where the shadows fall
  8– 7 I'm waiting *a·* for the bridal hour
  8–11 watching *a·* o'er the starlit glow,
  8–16 I'm dreaming *a·* of its changeful sky
  8–20 I'm thinking *a·* of a fair young bride,
  9– 3 picturing *a·* a glad young face,
  9– 8 weeping *a·* that the vision is fled,
  19– 3 God's eye is upon me — I am not *a·*
  66–12 'Tis breaking *a·*, but a young heart
My. 3– 6 this not *a·* in accord with
  89–24 * not . . . of interest to that city *a·*,
  89–25 * not to the nation *a·*,
  89–25 * not to this time *a·*,
  92– 7 * brushed aside by ridicule *a·*.
  109–25 not *a·* by miracle and parable,
  116–24 let them *a·* in, God's glory,
  148–19 I, as usual at home and *a·*,
  148–24 Christianity is not *a·* a gift,
  180–13 It appeals *a·* to God,
  189–32 Am I not *a·* in soul?
  211– 9 All that error asks is to be let *a·* ;
  211–11 "Let us *a·* ;— *Mark* 1 : 24.
  247–22 it is Love *a·* that feeds them.
  249–20 I *a·* know what that means.
  263– 2 leaving one *a·* and without
  273–30 death *a·* does not awaken man
  273–31 *a·* gives the true sense of life
  274– 5 Death *a·* does not absolve man from
  277–20 words and deeds of men *a·*
  302–28 went *a·* . . . to the church,
  306–18 Divinity *a·* solves the problem
  309–26 * states: "*A·* of the Bakers, he
  332– 4 * silent gush of grateful tears *a·* can
  338–24 he stands *a·* in word and deed,
  342–22 in it *a·* is the simplicity of the

along
Mis. 169– 2 all *a·* the way of her researches

along

Mis. 214–26   cannot . . . take error a· with Truth,
     250–26   little feet tripping a· the
     265–19   extends a· the whole line of
     274–29   rolls a· the streets besmeared with
     291–28   sentinels a· the lines of thought,
     295– 6   * "a· a gamut of isms and ists,
     339–26   sent a· the ocean of events
Ret.   15– 3   and my protest a· with me.
Pul.   66–18   * the mystical which, a· many lines,
No.   2–20   a· the shores of erudition ;
'01.   25–22   a· with this the
Hea.   19–24   a· the rugged way,
My.   308–17   * a· the highway,
     339–12   A· the lines of progressive

alongside

Pul.   51–28   * a· other great demonstrations

aloud

Mis. 266–29   Because Truth has spoken a·,
     388– 5   Love whose finger traced a·
Ret.   83–24   occasionally reading a· from the book
'02.   20–14   Love whose finger traced a·
Po.   7– 5   Love whose finger traced a·
     71–22   "Cry a·!" — Isa. 58 : 1.
My.   61–17   * I said a·, "Why, there is no fear ;

Alpha

Mis. 333–10   "A· and Omega" of C. S.— Rev. 1 : 8.
Un.   10–19   whereof God is the A· and Omega,
'02.   2–22   wherein Christ is A· and Omega.
My.   267– 9   not the A· and Omega of man
     267–12   no end, no A· and no Omega.

alphabet

Mis.   67– 2   beyond the mere a· of Mind-healing.
Ret.   11– 4   poem
Po.   vi–28   * poem
     page 60   poem

Alphabet and Bayonet

Po.   vi–28   * poem
     (see also **Appendix A**)

Alpine

My.   257–29   monarch's palace, the A· hamlet,

Alps

Po.   65–20   O'er ocean or A·, the stranger

already

Mis.   7–25   A great work a· has been done,
     65–19   must be, and a· is, apprehended
     70–19   and had a· begun to die,
     98–13   interest a· felt in a higher mode
     101– 9   We a· have had two in this nation ;
     110–23   a· obvious that the world's acceptance
     113–21   A· I clearly recognize that mental
     131–30   these will be found a· itemized,
     132– 2   had a· accepted as a By-law,
     136– 8   a· brought to your earnest consideration,
     150– 3   a· you have the great Shepherd
     150–15   We have a· seen the salvation
     154–12   have a· proof of the prosperity of
     154–18   the reign of harmony a· within us.
     183–18   ability, that reflection a· has
     238–20   and it a· hath a benediction :
     261– 1   evil, as mind, is doomed, a·
     261–26   a· saved with an everlasting salvation.
     286– 1   above prophecy, . . . has a· been fulfilled.
     307–12   the rapid sale a· of two editions
     317–25   having a· seen in many instances
     335–27   I would have you a· out,
     362–18   evil mind a· doomed,
     379–20   I had a· experimented in medicine
Man.   65– 2   a· used in our periodicals.
Ret.   35–19   it a· was and is demonstrated
     38– 3   I had a· paid him
     38– 9   what I had a· observed
     40–12   a· prepared for her burial ;
     83– 2   a· been proven that this volume
     83– 9   are a· laid in their minds
     87–28   It is a· understood that
Un.   5– 4   a· gained of the wholeness of Deity,
     7– 2   as a· He is glorified
     12– 1   fields are a· white for the harvest ;
     48– 3   a· told a hundred times,
     52– 7   reign of harmony, a· with us.
Pul.   30– 5   * unite with churches a· established
     52– 3   * no sums except those a· subscribed
     79–10   * a· gained to itself adherents
     86–29   * a· ordained as our pastor.
     87–18   I a· speak to you each Sunday.
No.   39–23   what we a· have and are ;
Pan.   15– 1   a· murdering her peaceful seamen
'00.   1–16   C. S. a· has a hearing
     2– 1   are a· interested in C. S. ;
Peo.   3–14   a· spans the moral heavens
     8–25   a· charred, are fast fading into
My.   15–14   A· I have said to you

already

My.   22– 9   * Scientists have contributed a·
     42– 9   * You are no doubt a· acquainted
     48–32   * a· manifest in their faces,
     57–30   * no sums except those a· subscribed
     74– 2   * are a· in Boston.
     75–12   * not a· been provided for.
     91– 3   * most of whom were a·
     106–17   It is a· proved that C. S.
     124–13   the "well done" a· yours, — Matt. 25 : 21.
     133–12   in sundries a· given out.
     135– 8   Perhaps you a· know that I have
     138– 5   a great benefit to me a·.
     139–23   A· you have advanced from
     147–23   a· dedicated to Christ's service,
     170–15   only that this gift is a· yours.
     177–11   (a· imputed to me),
     210– 5   added to the mind a· full.
     252–21   and are a· rich rays from
     253–25   you have His rich blessing a·
     282–14   we must practise what we a· know
     298– 5   a· reported of the good
     307–31   had a· dawned on me.
     339–13   A· Massachusetts has exchanged
     347– 1   a· been revealed in a degree

also

Mis.   11– 7   I thought, a·, that if I taught
     13–12   for sinners a· love — Luke 6 : 32.
     21–10   shall ye do a· ;" — see John 14 : 12.
     26–29   Saxon term for God is a· good.
     27– 9   Here a· is found the pith of
     28–15   A·, he demonstrated that
     29– 8   "for them a· which shall — John 17 : 20.
     36–22   a·, all beliefs relative to the
     50–22   a·, that there must be a change from
     63– 8   a·, that this divine trinity is
     66– 7   that shall he a· reap." — Gal. 6 : 7.
     68– 5   include a· man's changed appearance
     68– 9   * He a· maintained that pain and
     73–25   ye a· shall sit upon — Matt. 19 : 28.
     76–28   then shall ye a· appear — Col. 3 : 4.
     79–18   cause is perfect, its effect is perfect a· ;
     83–25   a· may glorify Thee." — John 17 : 1.
     87–17   a·, that no one there was working
     91–30   a· to require their pupils to study the
     105–30   that shall he a· reap." — Gal. 6 : 7.
     110– 7   You need a· to watch, and pray
     121–27   if I a· ask you, — Luke 22 : 68.
     124– 4   It is a· plain, that we should not
     125– 4   Then shall he a· reign with him :
     126–10   We a· have gained higher heights ;
     132–15   * and, by the way, from Mrs. Eddy, a·."
     136–23   a·, that hereafter you hold
     145–22   "The wolf a· shall dwell — Isa. 11 : 6.
     152– 5   includes a· His presence
     157– 4   shall a· reign with him." – II Tim. 2 : 12.
     157–22   trust a· in Him ; — Psal. 37 : 5.
     161–21   A·, it is natural to conclude
     170–12   So, a·, she spoke of the hades,
     170–18   we a· may all partake of.
     186–23   a·, that the Principle of man cannot
     191–26   A·, the original texts define him as
     192–10   shall he do a·; — John 14 : 12.
     192–24   A·, the last chapter of Mark
     193–18   and a· of what had been said when
     195–19   shall he do a·." — John 14 : 12.
     196–15   a·, the character of the votaries
     197–21   a· in Christ Jesus. — Phil. 2 : 5.
     198–18   disease a· is treated and healed.
     201–12   he a· showed forth the error
     209–11   a· demonstrates this Principle
     219–14   think a· after a sickly fashion.
     221–24   a· contradicts the doctrine that we
     228–15   This will bring us a· to look on a
     234–14   a· his effort to steal from others
     242–26   A·, Mr. C. M. H——, of Boston,
     256–12   a·, that this must prevent
     260–16   a·, that pure Mind is the truth
     264–26   status of thought must be right a·.
     265– 7   a· predisposes his students to make
     269– 1   trust a· in Him ; — Psal. 37 : 5.
     281– 6   I find a· another mental condition
     284–21   It must a· be remembered that
     298– 7   causing others to go astray, we a·
     305–26   * She is a· asked to collect two dollars
     306– 7   * a· welcome suggestions of events
     311– 6   A·, I would extend a tender invitation
     314–10   A·, this First Reader shall
     314–18   a·, shall read all the selections from
     314–27   This form shall a· be observed at
     335–28   a·, to remember the Scripture
     347– 2   lest thou a· be like — Prov. 26 : 4.
     370– 7   spirit of Christ is a· abroad,
     382–26   a· the constitution and by-laws
Man.   16–10   which was a· in Christ Jesus ;

also

Man.	26– 1	a· for the editors and the manager
	27–18	It shall a· be the duty of the
	43–26	A· the spirit in which the writer
	46–15	a· such information as may come to
	46–24	A· he shall reasonably reduce his
	59–10	Members shall a· instruct their pupils
	64– 8	a· the literature published or sold by
	64–25	See a· Article XXV, Sect. 7.
	66–20	a· to have any authority supposed to
	73–13	A· members in good standing with
	78–11	A· important movements of the manager
	98–16	It shall a· be the duty of the
	102–17	A· there shall be incorporated in
Ret.	2–17	My childhood was a· gladdened by
	15– 2	the good clergyman's heart a· melted,
	27– 1	I wrote a·, at this period,
	38–28	must a· gain its spiritual significance,
	42– 9	a· taught a special Bible-class ;
	43–12	and who a· received a certificate from
	45–21	turn to him the other a·." — Matt. 5 : 39.
	45–23	I a· saw that Christianity has
	76–17	was a· in Christ Jesus," — Phil. 2 : 5.
	80– 3	This a· is proverbial,
	83–10	A·, they are prepared to receive
	83–25	It is a· highly important that
	85– 9	Of this a· rest assured,
Un.	2– 2	they a· declare that God pitieth
	4–19	was a· in Christ Jesus," — Phil. 2 : 5.
	7– 8	to make a· the following statement :
	14– 7	"the stars a·," — Gen. 1 : 16.
	26–18	how can it be a· true that
	37– 2	but a· "the life." — John 14 : 6.
	38–16	but that something else a· is life,
	43–25	in the third chapter of Philippians, we are a·
	53–15	it is a· self-destructive.
	56–14	He a· suffereth in the flesh,
Pul.	vii– 9	but a· a registry of the rise of
	3– 6	He a· said : "The kingdom of — Luke 17 : 21.
	4–20	Who lives in good, lives a· in God,
	5–23	a· the same in Great Britain,
	6–29	A· that renowned apostle of anti-slavery,
	7– 9	remember a· that God is just,
	9–10	warmed a· our perishless hope,
	14–28	should a· know the great delusion of
	47–16	* And she a· defines carefully the
	67–19	* In Canada, a·, there is a large number of
	73–17	* is a· a very prominent member
Rud.	8–19	is a· uttering falsehood about good.
	12–24	The practitioner should a· endeavor
No.	5–15	a· avers that Spirit, or Truth,
	6–21	a· that the error of the revolution of
	24– 5	A·, according to Spinoza, man is
	31–26	said a· : "If a man keep — John 8 : 51.
	32– 9	that shall he a· reap." — Gal. 6 : 7.
	35–10	conquered a· the drear subtlety of
	35–13	He lived that we a· might live.
	37–28	What God knows, He a· predestinates ;
	40– 5	they expect a· what is impossible,
Pan.	4– 9	a·, that the functions of
	4–16	but that man a· is a creator,
	6–22	if . . . evil a· is mind,
	12– 2	Then a· will it be learned that
'00.	3–23	a· that women's names contained this
	8– 5	the evil man a· exhales consciously
	9–27	A· that I strove earnestly to
	12–26	and a· in private houses.
	13– 5	which I a· hate." — Rev. 2 : 6.
'01.	3–13	a·, we accept God, emphatically,
	9–11	a· the mysticism complained of
	11–27	lest thou a· be like — Prov. 26 : 4.
	27– 3	My critic a· writes :
	27–19	a· sinners reformed and
Hea.	5–28	that shall he a· reap." — Gal. 6 : 7.
My.	6– 6	that shall he a· reap." — Gal. 6 : 7.
	11–20	* we have a· made good the pledge.
	16–28	"Judgment a· will I lay — Isa. 28 : 17.
	17– 3	* A·, 1 Peter 2 : 1–6,
	17–11	"Ye a·, as lively stones, — I Pet. 2 : 5.
	17–14	"Wherefore a· it is — I Pet. 2 : 6.
	20– 1	this a· that she hath done — Mark 14 : 9.
	21– 9	* a· advance the erection of many
	23–24	* not only to faith but a· to sight ;
	24– 7	* and a· to symbolize your
	37–21	* we a· recognize that He has
	40– 6	* will a· enlarge their hospitality,
	49–14	* a· the tenets and church covenant.
	52–16	* a· realize we must use more energy
	62–29	* a· the services of other members
	66– 2	* a· in the shape of a triangle,
	69–11	* a· placed on the two sides of
	71– 4	* There is a· a solo organ
	72–21	* a· through the C. S. Sentinel
	73–23	* There is here a· a post-office
	94–14	* a· much to convince the skeptic.
	131– 1	that which purifies . . . a· strengthens

also

My.	132–10	he a· knows they embark for
	132–24	Divine Love will a· rebuke and
	135–29	a· you spiritually and scientifically
	136–21	a· in Canada, Australia, etc.
	144– 1	* Mrs. Eddy a· sent the following
	152–24	It will a· be seen that this God
	153– 1	A· I hear that the loving hearts
	162–18	the love that rebukes praises a·,
	163–24	a· received from the leading people of
	164–17	that faith a· possesses them.
	170–22	Delight thyself a· in — Psal. 37 : 4.
	170–23	trust a· in Him ; — Psal. 37 : 5.
	173–28	a· to Mr. George D. Waldron,
	174– 2	a· for throwing open their doors for
	190–28	them a· which shall believe — John 17 : 20.
	196–13	able a· to bridle the — Jas. 3 : 2.
	196–16	"Christ a· suffered for us, — I Pet. 2 : 21.
	220–18	I a· have faith that my prayer
	221–23	shall he do a·." — John 14 : 12.
	222–12	A· he added : "This kind — Matt. 17 : 21.
	223– 4	A· that I neither listen to
	224–14	A· be sure that you are not
	224–27	a· speak in loving terms of their
	224–31	* "They a· serve who only stand and
	227–28	turn to him the other a·." — Matt. 5 : 39.
	231– 7	a· from the undeserving poor
	233–16	"They have healed a· — Jer. 6 : 14.
	256– 9	A· I beg to send to you all
	273–25	a· that the five personal senses
	276–18	* she has a· believed that in such
	280– 7	* We rejoice a· in this new reminder
	295–13	is a· the gift of gifts ;
	299–12	as a· whatever portions of truth
	308–29	McClure's Magazine a· declares
	312–11	* a· paid Mrs. Glover's fare
	314–25	I was a· the means of
	319–14	* and a· indicate what he
	319–28	* I a· recall very plainly the
	320– 5	* He a· seemed very much pleased
	320– 8	* He a· expressed himself freely
	321– 8	* a· your position as regards
	321–30	* I am a· pleased to have had
	322–12	* a· Mr. Edward P. Bates' letter
	328–12	* apt a· to be pleased with the fact
	336–11	* In this book (p. 20) she a· states,

altar

Mis.	87–31	imagine they can . . . steady God's a·
	149–24	whose a· is a loving heart,
	162–16	lay himself as a lamb upon the a·
	312– 6	which lays all upon the a·,
	343– 4	have laid upon the a·
	394– 6	at the a· or bower,
Ret.	86–16	when we offer our gift upon the a·.
Pul.	9– 7	May the a· you have built
'00.	15–19	and you kneel at its a·.
'01.	35– 6	and lay ourselves upon the a·
Hea.	2–27	and sprinkled the a· of Love
Po.	26–10	on her a· our loved Lincoln's own
	32–18	To kneel at the a· of mercy and pray
	39– 8	from its a· to Thy throne
	45– 8	at the a· or bower,
My.	36–21	* At this a·, dedicated to the only
	302–30	upon the steps of its a·.

altars

Mis.	120– 2	take off their shoes at our a· ;
	287–32	attempts to steady other people's a·,
	326–14	wrapping their a· in ruins.
	360–20	who partaketh of its own a·,
Hea.	11–13	burn upon the a· of to-day ;
My.	125– 1	kindle a· for human sacrifice.
	126–30	at our fire-sides, on our a·,
	184–21	lay upon its a· a sacrifice

alter

My.	41– 5	* nor in any wise a· its effects.

alteration

Rud.	7–25	bring about a· of species

alterative

Mis.	241– 9	the great a·, Truth :
	241–19	administer this a· Truth :
Pan.	12–19	without the a· agonies whereby

alternately

Mis.	314–16	a· in response to the congregation,
Man.	99– 1	a· appoint a Committee on
	99– 9	shall annually and a· appoint a
Pul.	28–20	* The reading is from the two a· ;
'02.	4–25	A· transported and alarmed by

alternative

Mis.	31–17	leaves the individual no a·

although

Mis.	xi– 5	a· a reproduction of what
	7–10	a· skepticism and incredulity
	45– 7	a· its power to allay fear,

although

Mis.	89–13	a· the medical attendant and friends
	243– 6	a· students treat sprains,
	260–24	evil is naught, a· it seems
	273– 3	a· it will cost him much,
	286–18	a· it is to-day problematic.
	371–16	a· he who has self-interest
	374– 3	A· clad in panoply of power,
	380–18	A· I could heal mentally,
Man.	18– 7	A· walking through deep waters,
	55–14	A· repentant and forgiven by the
Ret.	38–12	a· I had not thought of such a result,
	68– 1	a· as a serpent it claimed to
Pul.	37– 7	* and a· her hair is white,
'01.	6–15	must be One a· He is three.
	24–19	a· its earthly advent is called
Hea.	5–15	a· we have no evidence of the fact
	11–17	a· homœopathy has laid the
Po.	vi–13	a· Boston has since been the pioneer
My.	11– 3	* a· we may falter or stumble
	55– 7	* a· given up for a time,
	82–27	* A· the Scientists came to Boston
	89–13	* a· it cost two million dollars,
	94–24	* A· Mrs. Eddy, the Founder of C. S.,
	146–21	a· it has not been demonstrated
	281–29	a· its purpose is good will towards
	308–26	A· McClure's Magazine attributes
	314–13	A·, as McClure's Magazine claims,
	320–17	* a· he did not endorse all the
	336– 6	* A· he desired to go to her

altitude

Mis.	16–28	this new-born spiritual a· ;
	67– 1	until its a· reaches beyond the
	255–11	that a· of Mind which was in
	289–31	a· whence they can choose only good.
Ret.	76–12	to the a· which perceived a light
Pan.	6–26	tho a· of mind gives it power,
	12–12	The a· of Christianity openeth,
My.	68–11	* reaches an a· twenty-nine feet
	110–24	mount higher in the a· of being.
	146–14	a· of its highest propositions
	272–10	is not the a· of the infinite.

altogether

Mis.	167– 6	the one a· lovely.
	342–12	"a· lovely." — Song 5 : 16.
Ret.	23–19	"a· lovely." — Song 5 : 16.
Pul.	66–17	* A· the belief and service are
'01.	6–30	"a· lovely." — Song 5 : 16.
Hea.	13–19	resigned the imaginary medicine a·,
Peo.	6–17	because He is found a· lovely.
My.	29–23	* assuming an a· different status
	154–25	A· it makes the church militant,

Alumni

Mis.	110–13	chapter sub-title

alway

Mis.	39–15	"Lo, I am with you a·" — Matt. 28 : 20.
	389–21	"Lo, I am with you a·," — Matt. 28 : 20.
Ret.	89–21	"Lo, I am with you a·!" — Matt. 28 : 20.
Pul.	10–30	God within you, — with you a·,
No.	46– 1	"Lo, I am with you a·," — Matt. 28 : 20.
'01.	35–10	Love is the way a·.
Po.	4–20	"Lo, I am with you a·," — Matt. 28 : 20.
	29–22	be thou our saint, Our stay, a·
	65–16	moments most sweet are fleetest a·,
My.	44–12	* "Lo, I am with you a·, — Matt. 28 : 20.
	58–24	* "Lo, I am with you a·." — Matt. 28 : 20.
	159– 5	"Lo, I am with you a·, — Matt. 28 : 20.
	190–32	"Lo, I am with you a·" — Matt. 28 : 20.

always

Mis.	5–26	a· perfect in God,
	19– 3	lust, hatred, malice, are a· wrong,
	32–29	a· should try to bless their
	41–29	may not a· prove equal to
	57–30	a· was and forever is ;
	64–16	and are a· materialistic.
	66–10	a· according to divine decree.
	73–12	it is a· mental and moral,
	78–30	hypotheses are a· human vagaries,
	88–20	* have a· insisted that this Science
	90–11	It is a· right to act rightly ;
	95–17	have a· attended my life phenomena
	114–17	They must a· have on armor,
	117– 9	We a· know where to look
	117–10	and a· find him there.
	119–12	will a· be found arguing for itself,
	126–26	honesty a· defeats dishonesty.
	129–18	will a· find somebody in his way,
	138– 9	is not a· to cooperate,
	143–28	a· accompanied with a touching letter
	180–10	Truth is a· here,
	203– 8	it will a· mirror their love,
	236–18	a· with the purpose to restore
	237–24	is delayed, and a· has been ;
	260–26	Words are not a· the auxiliaries of

always

Mis.	261–23	spirit of sacrifice a· has saved,
	262–11	its language is a· acceptable
	263–12	A· bear in mind that His
	276–15	will a· be the bridal hour,
	278–16	is a· a blessing to the human race.
	281–22	a· as debtors to Christ, Truth.
	304–28	* It will a· ring at nine o'clock
	330–11	in the Lord a·." — see Phil. 4 : 4.
	343–20	are not a· destroyed by the
	345–19	* a· assured and reassured me
	347– 9	cannot a· discern the mental signs
	347–22	it is a· straight and narrow ;
	353– 8	human concept is a· imperfect ;
	371–22	error a· strives to unite,
	374– 6	a· the opposite of what it was.
Ret.	8– 8	Her answer was a·, " Nothing,
	8–23	She answered as a· before.
	44–22	danger to its members which must a·
	49–12	spiritual formation first, last, and a·,
	82– 9	have a· been attained by
	85–18	a· wait for God's finger to point the
	91–19	a· leading them into the divine
Un.	18–15	Is not our comforter a·
	59–18	the divine idea is a· present.
Pul.	26–28	* a· burning day and night.
	33–23	* and Mr. Parker a· believed,
	36–18	* and a· with this experience repeated.
No.	8–10	rebuke each other a· in love,
'00.	8–17	apathy is a· egotism and animality.
'01.	1–20	must a· characterize heroic hearts ;
	27–30	* they say they had a· believed it."
	31– 1	a· stung by a clear elucidation of
'02.	1–17	has a· met with opposition and
	2–29	I have a· taught the student
My.	vi–14	* a· has been and is now its guide,
	3–18	a· unfolding the highway of hope,
	21–21	* a· experienced much pleasure in
	28– 4	"Divine Love a· has met and a· will
	52–26	* has a· filled her coffers anew.
	73–9, 10	"Divine Love a· has met and a· will
	112– 2	Science has a· been first met with
	121–13	reliable, helpful, and a· at hand.
	121–18	a· a diamond of the first water ;
	125–17	which a· thrills the soul.
	148–24	Bear in mind a· that Christianity
	155– 5	a· abounding in love
	155–26	a· be gathering Easter lilies
	156– 7	a· having all sufficiency
	163–12	I a· try to be just,
	214– 5	Divine Love a· has met and a· will
	228– 6	a· saying the unexpected to them.
	240–13	a· unfolding the highway of hope,
	248– 4	Let your watchword a· be :
	252– 4	a· distributing sweet things
	276–17	* has a· believed that those who
	283–18	It is a· safe to be just.
	290–25	Thou hearest me a·," — John 11 . 42.
	304–28	* say they have a· believed it."
	305– 6	"I have a· known it."
	313–18	a· accompanied by some responsible
	313–20	I have a· consistently declared
	320–14	* He a· spoke of you as the author
	320–22	* he a· referred to you as the author
	321– 3	* a· referred to you as the one who
	321– 9	* and he a· gave you that position
	324–21	* we a· thought that Mr. Wiggin
	342–14	* and which are a· bright.
	345–32	* a· from the standpoint of C. S.,

amalgamation

Mis.	22–13	It absolutely refutes the a·,
'00.	13–25	* a· of different pagan religions
'01.	23–18	all error, a·, and compounds.

amaranth

Peo.	14– 4	a· blossoms, evergreen leaves,

amateur

My.	313–23	* never was "an a· clairvoyant,"

amazed

Mis.	325–20	a· beyond measure that anybody

amazement

Mis.	325–19	porter starts up in blank a·
	375–20	* to my a· and delight I find

Amazons

Pul.	83–16	* In olden times it was the A· who

ambassador

Mis.	141–25	As the a· of Christ's teachings,
Ret.	3– 3	held the position of a· to Persia.

ambiguous

My.	111–29	pronounce it absurd, a·,
	113– 6	Can such a book be a·,
	317–14	points that might seem a· to

ambition

Mis.	110– 9	What grander a· is there than to

ambition
Mis.	154–29	Have no *a·*, . . . apart from
	204–29	governs the aims, *a·*, and
	228–14	mad *a·* and low revenge.
	254–13	The victim of mad *a·*
	263–27	mad *a·* drives them to
	281– 1	and with laudable *a·* are about to
	281– 9	and I have now one *a·*
	281–10	But if one cherishes *a·* unwisely,
	296–21	or foster a feminine *a·*
	351–16	repeated attempts of mad *a·*
Ret.	79–13	Dishonesty, envy, and mad *a·*
Pul.	10–13	No dream of avarice or *a·*
'00.	15– 7	start forward with true *a·*.
'02.	3–28	the only true *a·* is to serve God
Po.	16– 7	*A·*, come hither!
	33– 9	*a·* that binds us to earth ;
My.	129– 9	counteract the trend of mad *a·*.
	202– 3	from human *a·*, fear, or distrust
	250– 5	promotes wisdom, quiets mad *a·*,
	262–23	mad *a·*, rivalry, and ritual of our

ambitions
Mis.	224–13	human wills, opinions, *a·*,
	291– 8	unworthy aims and *a·*.

ambitious
Po.	2– 7	who can fathom thee! *A·* man,

ambler
Mis.	183–11	silly *a·* to the so-called pleasures

Ambrose
Abigail Barnard
Ret.	4–23	Abigail Barnard *A·*, daughter of

Deacon
Pul.	32–25	* Deacon *A·*, her maternal grandfather,

Deacon Nathaniel
Ret.	4–24	Deacon Nathaniel *A·* of Pembroke,

Grandfather
Ret.	5– 3	Grandfather *A·* was a very religious

ambush
Mis.	126–25	strong race to run, and foes in *a·* ;
Pul.	15–11	telling mankind of the foe in *a·*?

amelioration
No.	8–22	pray for the *a·* of sin,

ameliorative
Mis.	235– 9	This Science is *a·* and regenerative,
My.	287–19	Philanthropy is loving, *a·*,

Amen
My.	19–11	be with you all. *A·*.'' — *II Cor.* 13 : 14.
	297– 6	I will say, *A·*, so be it.

amenable
Mis.	199– 7	*a·* only to moral and spiritual law,
Man.	67–23	break a rule . . . and are *a·* therefor.

amended
Man.	105– 3	nor any Tenet or By-Law *a·*
My.	15– 4	* has been *a·* to read as follows :

amende honorable
My.	236– 8	permit me to make the *a· h·*

amendment
Mis.	318–12	is an *a·* of the paragraph
Man.	105– 1	*A·* of By-Laws.
My.	15– 2	chapter sub-title
	327–17	* An *a·* was obtained by
	327–19	* After the *a·* had been passed,

amendments
My.	230–19	your approval of the *a·*

amends
Mis.	253–10	*a·* for the nothingness of matter

amenities
Man.	40– 9	reflects the sweet *a·* of Love,
No.	45–20	woman's hour, with all its sweet *a·*

America (*see also* **America's**)
Mis.	170–21	history of Europe and *A·* ;
	295– 6	same power which in *A·* leads women
Ret.	2– 8	came to *A·* seeking ''freedom to
Pul.	5–23	colleges, and universities of *A·* ;
	70–11	* most remarkable women in *A·*.
No.	23–14	eminent divines, in Europe and *A·*,
Po.	11– 1	Brave Britain, blest *A·*!
My.	79–11	* seat of learning of *A·* ;
	89– 2	* one of the largest . . . in *A·*,
	181–22	C. S. was discovered in *A·*.
	338– 1	Brave Britain, blest *A·*!

American
Mis.	295– 1	certain references to *A·* women
	295–14	has our *A·* correspondent lost
	296– 6	Was it ignorance of *A·* society
	296– 8	work and career of *A·* women,
	297–11	reports of *A·* affairs from
Ret.	2–24	for they were *A·* newspapers,
Pul.	67– 6	* said by a great *A·* writer.
Rud.	6–13	the young *A·* astronomer

American
My.	85–31	* sky-lines in an *A·* city,

American, The
Pul.	68–12	* *The A·*, Baltimore, Md.,

American Art Journal
Pul.	57–18	* *A· A· J·*, New York,

Americans
My.	271–24	* read with deep interest by all *A·*,

American Secretary
My.	282–18	Mr. Hayne Davis, *A· S·*,

America's
Pul.	8– 1	the press of *A·* Athens,

Amesbury
Pul.	54–29	at his home in *A·*,

amiable
My.	333–27	* He has left an *a·* wife,

amicable
My.	279–24	for the *a·* settlement of the war

amicably
Mis.	156–25	listening to each other *a·*,
My.	277–21	can settle all questions *a·*
	360–13	settle this church difficulty *a·*

amid (*see also* **'mid**)
Mis.	ix–16	*a·* the uniform darkness of storm
	228– 7	is to be calm *a·* excitement,
	228– 7	just *a·* lawlessness,
	228– 7	pure *a·* corruption,
	277–28	one can be just *a·* lawlessness,
Hea.	2– 9	never seen *a·* the smoke of battle,
Po.	30–21	*a·* the hymning spheres of light,
My.	150–15	sleeping *a·* willowy banks
	182–27	*a·* the fair foliage of this vine
	230– 3	*a·* ministries aggressive and active,

amidst
No.	33–22	*a·* physical suffering and
Peo.	3– 6	eternal roasting *a·* noxious vapors ;
My.	262– 8	born in a manger *a·* the flocks and
	325– 2	* when *a·* all your duties you

Amiens
Pul.	65–18	* the story of the cathedral of *A·*,

amiss
Mis.	51–31	because ye ask *a·*, — *Jas.* 4 : 3.
No.	20–19	Hence this asking *a·*
	40– 2	because ye ask *a·*, — *Jas.* 4 : 3.
Hea.	15–24	because ye ask *a·* ;'' — *Jas.* 4 : 3.
	15–24	is it not asking *a·* to pray for
Peo.	9–17	because we ''ask *a·* ;'' — *Jas.* 4 : 3.

among
Mis.	ix– 6	*a·* my thousands of students
	117–12	* enduring vivacity *a·* God's people.''
	136–15	come out from *a·* them, — *II Cor.* 6 : 17.
	142– 9	*a·* other beautiful decorations,
	184– 6	made flesh and dwell *a·* mortals,
	203–11	waters that run *a·* the valleys,
	225– 6	*A·* the guests, were an
	270–29	*A·* the foremost virtues of
	281–23	*A·* the gifts of my students,
	296– 4	*a·* its constituents and managers
	319–27	feel themselves alone *a·* the stars.
	323–12	Venomous serpents hide *a·* the rocks,
	334– 2	and *a·* the inhabitants — *Dan.* 4 : 35.
	343–26	*A·* the manifold soft chimes
	371– 1	*a·* the first lessons on healing
	378– 8	After much consultation *a·* ourselves,
Man.	66– 8	If . . . . shall arise *a·* the members
Ret.	2– 1	*a·* the Scotch Covenanters,
	2–21	*A·* grandmother's treasures were
	6– 9	*A·* the treasured reminiscences of
	6–27	*A·* other important bills which
	13– 8	*a·* those who were doomed
	15–23	*A·* other diseases cured
	23–20	''*a·* ten thousand.'' — *Song* 5 : 10.
	70–27	Preeminent *a·* men, he virtually
Un.	15– 9	Was evil *a·* these good things?
	39– 1	''made flesh'' *a·* mortals, — *John* 1 : 14.
	62–23	*a·* the dead? — *Luke* 24 : 5.
Pul.	38–27	* they may differ *a·* themselves,
	43–27	* to discourage *a·* her followers
	46–17	* *A·* the many souvenirs that Mrs. Eddy
	51– 9	* numbered *a·* the many pioneers
	56– 6	* *a·* the members of all the churches
	60–14	* *a·* the thousands of adherents
	63–17	* people *a·* her devoted followers.
Rud.	2– 5	*a·* Trinitarian Christians the word
	16–24	springing up *a·* unchristian students,
No.	9– 3	which have sprung up *a·* Scientists
	9– 6	or established *a·* another class
	23–11	not one person was named *a·* them.
	42– 3	* will . . . God's power increase *a·* us.''
	46–14	were *a·* the first settlers of
Pan.	13– 4	Chief *a·* the questions herein,

among

'00.
2– 5   *a·* the best people on earth
5–15   way under heaven and *a·* men
11– 7   jarring elements *a·* musicians
14–18   Let no . . . bitterness spring up *a·* you,
'01.
27– 6   * arise *a·* the Christian Scientists
28–25   *a·* the worldlings in his age,
31–20   *A·* the list of blessings infinite
31–28   *a·* whom were the Rev. . . . . Burnham
'02.
3– 4   *a·* the educated classes
Po.
vi–26   * *A· her earliest poems*
My.
40– 9   * subsidence of criticism *a·* workers.
40–14   * Through rivalries *a·* leaders
53–23   * *a·* whom was the Rev. A. J. Peabody,
53–27   * statements, *a·* which is this :
53–29   * interest in C. S. *a·* the people,
85–17   * *a·* the architectural beauties of
87–10   * *a·* them visitors of title
88– 7   * *a·* classes above the average
90–30   * Prominent *a·* these is the
94–13   * absence of dissent *a·* them
95– 1   * soon be included *a·* the cults which
97– 8   * than *a·* those who were
100–13   * *a·* religious bodies,
113–31   *a·* the scholarly and the titled,
164–19   wrought a resurrection *a·* you,
177–23   prophecy . . . is fulfilled *a·* you :
182–14   seemed the least *a·* seeds,
197–19   else C. S. will disappear from *a·*
212–15   dissension *a·* mental practitioners?
243– 3   belief is springing up *a·* you
244– 3   *a·* those who wish to share this
274–24   unity *a·* brethren, and love to God
274–28   health *a·* all nations."— *Psal.* 67 : 2.
286–12   preserving peace *a·* nations.
304– 6   *A·* my early studies were
321–26   * I was *a·* your early students
324–23   * *a·* his literary friends.
331– 5   * *a·* whom she remembers the

amount

Mis.
43–22   rivalry does a vast *a·* of injury
227–29   *a·* of happiness it has bestowed
230– 4   great *a·* of time is consumed in
305–27   * send with the *a·* the name of
349–30   contributions, . . . doubled that *a·*.
Man.
76–11   *a·* of funds which the Church has
76–12   the *a·* of its indebtedness
76–23   *a·* of funds received by the
Ret.
50– 7   This *a·* greatly troubled me.
Pul.
41– 4   * full *a·* needed was received.
64–10   * When the necessary *a·* was raised,
No.
23–24   *a·* of good or evil he possesses.
'02.
13–24   *a·* due on the mortgage.
My.
9–26   draw on God for the *a·* I owe you,
10–15   * as to *a·* and date of payment.
11–28   * the *a·* to be expended
12–11   * *a·* to be expended
14–14   * entire *a·* . . . had been paid in ;
20–26   * expenditure of a large *a*
21– 1   * *a·* which they would have expended
23– 4   * *a·* each shall send the Treasurer.
23–10   * *A·* on hand June 1, 1905,
23–14   * *A·* necessary to complete the sum
123–18   *a·* is now about twenty thousand
312–22   took with him the usual *a·* of money

amphitheatre

My.
59–19   * couple of pews in this grand *a·* ;

ample

Mis.
319–24   affords *a·* opportunity for
Man.
44–23   Church Organizations *A·*.
82–20   *a·* time for faithful practice.
95–23   duties alone of a Reader are *a·*.
Ret.
82–17   is *a·* to supply many practitioners,
'02.
15–14   income from literary sources was *a·*,
My.
10– 9   * in a beautiful *a·* building,
13–19   * with which to build an *a·* temple
24– 5   * express in its *a·* auditorium
56–15   * *a·* room for growth of attendance
312–29   My salary . . . gave me *a·* support.
318–28   *a·* fund of historical knowledge,
342– 1   *a·*, richly furnished house

amplification

Mis.
261–11   every effect and *a·* of wrong will
No.
24– 3   According to . . . God is *a·*.
My.
288–24   *a·* of wrong will revert to the
336–20   * as *a·* of the facts given by Mrs. Eddy

amplified

Mis.
310– 6   Truth, *a·* in this age by

amplifies

No.
10– 9   it aggregates, *a·*, unfolds, and

amplitude

Mis.
249–24   in the *a·* of His love ;
322–24   shown you the *a·* of His mercy,
My.
236–18   opens wide on the *a·* of liberty

amply

My.
261– 5   seems to have *a·* provided for this,

amputation

My.
105–14   ready for their *a·*.

amuse

My.
325– 5   * that I think will *a·* you :

amusement

Mis.
230–11   or planning for some *a·*,
Man.
60– 9   *A·* or idleness is weariness.
'00.
2–13   He takes no time for *a·*,

amusements

Mis.
357– 2   no time for idle words, vain *a·*,

amusing

Mis.
62–25   which is *a·* to astute readers,
Peo.
6–12   * *a·* the patient while nature

analogy

Mis.
29–12   no *a·* between C. S. and

analysis

Pan.
2– 9   chapter sub-title
'02.
4– 7   correct *a·* of C. S.

analyzing

Ret.
30–11   *a·*, uncovering, and annihilating the
My.
319–24   * in *a·* and arranging the topics,

anarchy

My.
166– 2   will never end in *a·*

anathema

Mis.
105– 6   *a·* of priesthood and the senses ;
My.
104–29   *a·* spoken of in Scripture :

anatomical

Rud.
15–26   laid bare for *a·* examination.

anatomically

Un.
57– 3   *A·* considered, the design of

anatomy

Man.
47– 7   on the *a·* involved.
Un.
28– 4   *A·* has not descried nor described
45–17   *A·* and physiology make mind-matter
Rud.
11–26   the subject of human *a·* ;
Pan.
4– 8   belief may agree with physics and *a·*

ancestors

Ret.
1– 1   My *a·*, according to the flesh,
Pul.
48–27   * She had a long list of worthy *a·*
No.
46–14   The author's *a·* were among the
My.
163–28   thank their *a·* for helping to

ancestral

Pul.
46–13   * in going back to the *a·* tree
My.
309–28   * at the *a·* home at Bow.

ancestry

Ret.
68–29   good, and pure constitute his *a·*.
Pul.
32–24   * from Scotch and English *a·*,
My.
270–10   records of my *a·* attest honesty and
311–25   which is of my mother's *a·*.

anchor

No.
45–22   *a·* the Church in more spiritual
My.
132–11   and *a·* in omnipotence.

anchorage

Un.
43– 7   too finite for *a·* in infinite good,

anchored

My.
152– 3   *a·* its faith in troubled waters.

anchors

'00.
10–21   our hope *a·* in God who reigns,

ancient

Mis.
1– 2   *a·* Greek looked longingly for
40–14   equal the *a·* prophets as healers.
148–10   solemn conclave as in *a·* Sanhedrim.
169– 4   bypaths of *a·* philosophies
173– 1   *A·* and modern philosophy
333–30   The *a·* Chaldee hung his destiny
333–31   but *a·* or modern Christians,
344–16   *A·* and modern philosophies
372–20   *a·* and most distinguished artists.
Man.
3– 6   solemn conclave as in *a·* Sanhedrim.
Ret.
2–23   were not very *a·*,
10– 9   I received lessons in the *a·* tongues,
34– 7   Neither *a·* nor modern philosophy
57– 4   Neither *a·* nor modern philosophy
Pul.
8– 4   through the leaves of an *a·* oak,
46–26   * looking into the *a·* languages,
47–13   * No *a·* or modern philosophy
52–14   * reviver of the *a·* faith
No.
11–23   *A·* and modern human philosophy
'01.
9– 6   *a·* worthies caught glorious glimpses
28– 8   *a·* writers since the first century
Hea.
11–13   fires of *a·* proscription burn upon the
19–12   *a·* question, Which is first,
Po.
10– 7   Thy palm, in *a·* day,
My.
70–21   * of both *a·* and modern masters,
103–22   in *a·* or in modern systems
178–32   *a· Logia*, or imputed sayings of
337– 8   Thy palm, in *a·* day,

anciently
Mis. 121–11 A·, the blood of martyrs was
Pul. 20–21 a· one of the many dates selected
'01. 12–10 was a· an opprobrium ;

ancients
Mis. 191–6 a· changed the meaning of the term,

Andover Seminary
Un. 7– 4 by the changes at A· S·

Andover Theological School
Mis. 178– 3 a graduate . . . of A· T· S·.

Andrew, Governor
Po. vi–19 To-day, by order of Governor A·,

anew
Mis. 109–27 and consecrate one's life a·.
125– 9 Then shall he drink a· Christ's cup,
246–16 to forge a· the old fetters ;
343–17 burnishing a· the . . . gems of Love,
346– 8 It confronts each generation a·.
384– 6 Come Thou! and now, a·,
Rud. 15–28 fill a· the individual mind.
'00. 10– 9 unconquerable right is begun a·,
Hea. 4–19 to begin a· as infinite Life,
Po. 36– 5 Come Thou! and now, a·,
My. 46–18 * pledge ourselves a· to this demand,
52–26 * has always filled her coffers a·.
97–21 * opened the eyes of the country a·
307–19 referred to the coming a· of Truth,

angel (see also **angel's**)
Mis. 141–31 O recording a·! write :
275– 6 Who — but God's avenging a·!
374–31 my ideal of an a· is
396–22 wake a white-winged a· throng
Pul. 18– 6 wake a white-winged a· throng
'00. 13–29 a· of the church in Philadelphia
14–20 a· that spake unto the churches
15–22 may the a· of The Mother Church
'02. 16–18 enigmatical seals of the a·,
Peo. 5–15 in a· form, saying unto us,
5–22 not entertain the a· unawares.
7–11 * As an a· dream passed o'er him.
Po. 12– 6 wake a white-winged a· throng
My. 126– 3 purpose of the destroying a·,
126– 7 recording a·, standing with
148–23 as with the pen of an a·
153– 8 a· of the church in — Rev. 3 : 7.

angelic
Ret. 85–11 upon which a· thoughts ascend
My. 163– 3 a· song chiming chaste challenge

Angelico's
Mis. 375–25 * hands and feet in A· 'Jesus,'

angel's
Mis. 388–22 To fold an a· wings below ;
'00. 11–23 * Like the close of an a· psalm,
Po. 21–11 To fold an a· wings below ;

angels (see also **angels'**)
Mis. 78– 3 and the overture of the a·.
106–26 the soft, sweet sigh of a· answering,
111– 3 work, well done, would dignify a·.
145–29 and echo the song of a· :
149–26 fellowship with saints and a·.
152–27 no element of earth to cast out a·,
166–14 for the overture of a·
204–11 sings to the heart a song of a·.
251–21 where a· are as men,
251–21 and men as a·
280– 4 one of the a· presented himself
280– 6 not a· with wings, but messengers
286–15 but are as the a·.
306–22 chapter sub-title
306–23 When a· visit us, we do not hear the
306–29 shall give His a· — Psal. 91 : 11.
374–14 A·, with overtures, hold charge
375– 3 are not my concepts of a·.
386–20 a· beckoned me to this bright land,
389–20 Seeking and finding, with the a· sing :
391–21 When a· shall repeat it,
Ret. 10–17 Prosody, the song of a·,
Un. 28–10 peopled with demons or a·,
Pul. 11– 6 mingle with the joy of a·
39–21 * sculptured a·, on the gray church
No. 46–11 for joining the overture of a·.
'00. 8– 2 and with saints and a· shall be
'01. 26–22 of men and of a·, — I Cor. 13 : 1.
34–17 solace us with the song of a·
'02. 3–25 and the lay of a·
19–14 He entertains a· who listens to
Peo. 1–11 are the a· of His presence,
Po. 4–19 with the a· sing :
10–14 List, brother! a· whisper
38–20 When a· shall repeat it,
50– 5 a· beckoned me to this bright land,
My. 14– 4 blessing above the song of a·,

angels
My. 46–29 * company of a·, — Heb. 12 : 22.
122–23 Can we say with the a· to-day :
129–21 Then will a· administer grace,
148–20 What are the a· saying or singing
155–24 sing as the a· heaven's symphonies
189– 1 warmest wish of men and a·.
269– 9 equal unto the a· ; — Luke 20 : 36.
337–15 List, brother! a· whisper
354–23 The tongue of a·

angels'
Po. 30–22 and a· loving lays,
My. 354–21 Give us not only a· songs,

Angelus
My. 70–16 * "A·" had living reproductions

angel-vision
Peo. 7–15 * He had caught the a·.
7–23 * Our lives that a·."

anger
Mis. 36–13 Appetites, passions, a·, revenge,
123–13 to appease the a· of a so-called god
223–26 "He that is slow to a· — Prov. 16 : 32.
My. 196–10 "He that is slow to a· — Prov. 16 : 32.

angles
Pul. 47–30 * a· and pitch of the roof,
My. 69– 6 * no sharp a· are visible,

Anglican
Pul. 65– 5 * Eastern churches and the A· fold

Anglo-Israel
Po. 10–19 A·, lo ! Is marching under orders ;
My. 337–20 A·, lo ! Is marching under orders ;

Anglo-Saxon
Mis. 13–28 Seek the A· term for God,
216–12 given to the A· tongue,
Pul. 6– 7 Good, the A· term for God,

angry
Mis. 162– 9 stem these rising a· elements,
397– 5 o'er earth's troubled, a· sea
Pul. 18–14 o'er earth's troubled, a· sea
Po. 12–14 o'er earth's troubled, a· sea
46– 4 blasts of winter's a· storm,
My. 310–29 * "When do you ever see Mary a·?"

anguish
Mis. 104– 1 was on earth and in a·,
237– 5 mental a· is generally accepted as
253–25 Can that child conceive of the a·,
Un. 57–25 Mortal throes of a·
Peo. 14–15 ye may go to the bed of a·,
My. 258–10 bowed in strong affection's a·,
350–16 This weight of a· which they

animal
Mis. 23– 6 * or dream in the a·,
36–14 a· qualities of sinning mortals ;
36–16 qualities of the so-called a· man ;
37–13 leave the a· for the spiritual,
156–22 through which the a· magnetizer preys,
184–31 mortal mind purged of the a·
217–14 vegetable, and a· kingdoms,
257– 4 dreams in the a·,
281– 3 this a· element flings open
287–15 the spiritual over the a·,
294–13 but he is a small a· :
297–24 If the man is dominant over the a·,
Ret. 70– 2 confers a· names and natures
Un. 38–24 mineral, vegetable, or a· kingdoms.
No. 24– 6 according to . . . . man is an a· vegetable,
Pan. 3– 4 horned and hoofed a·,
9– 2 * dreams in the a·,
'01. 19–14 That a· natures give force to
Hea. 14– 2 the bigger a· beats the lesser ;
My. 245–14 a· elements manifested in ignorance,

animality
Mis. 277–32 drunkenness produced by a·.
375– 2 personality blind with a·,
Pul. 13–12 mortal beliefs, a·, and hate,
'00. 8–17 apathy is always egotism and a·.

Animal Magnetism
Mis. 350– 9 "There is no A· M·."
Ret. 37–22 the chapter on A· M·,
Pul. 38–12 "Marriage," "A· M·,"

animal magnetism
(see **magnetism**)

animals
Mis. 36– 6 Do a· and beasts have a mind?
Un. 14– 6 earth, man, a·, plants,
Rud. 7–27 transforming . . . plants into a·,

animate
My. 206– 2 would unite dead matter with a·,

animated
Mis. 325–21 that anybody is a· with a purpose,

animated
Peo. 5–23 not self-existent matter a· by mind,
My. 294–26 have a· the Church of Rome
    320–32 * he spoke in a very a· manner
animosities
Mis. 284–29 I deprecate personal a·
animosity
Man. 40– 5 Neither a· nor mere personal
My. 40–13 * forsake a·, and abandon their
animus
Mis. 38–18 Science that has the a· of Truth.
    48–18 as to the a· of animal magnetism
  113–32 spiritual a· is felt throughout the
  290– 4 so long as the a· of the contract is
Man. 31–13 spiritual a· so universally needed.
Pul.   3–30 unfitness for such a spiritual a·
    32– 9 * but a spiritual a·.
Pan. 11– 9 gauge the a· of man?
'00. 3–29 a· of heathen religion was not
My. 3–16 persuasive a·, an unerring impetus,
  26–24 to give the true a· of our church
  45–12 * a· and spirit of our movement.
  277–11 The mental a· goes on,
  339–27 The a· of his saying was :
annals
My. 45– 8 * in the a· of our history.
  98– 9 * such as religious a· hardly parallel
  148–10 In the a· of our denomination
annexed
My. 138–28 * contained in the a· letter
annihilate
Mis. 3–32 thus to a· hallucination.
  56– 6 would destroy Spirit and a man.
Ret. 64– 6 This, however, does not a· man,
My. 226–16 a· matter, and man . . . would remain
annihilated
Mis. 10–26 material tendencies . . . are thus a· ;
  42– 4 Man is not a·, nor does he lose
Ret. 94–14 When all fleshly belief is a·,
Un. 31–10 as emphatically as they a· sin.
  58– 4 before error is a·.
No. 26–18 If . . . he would be a·,
annihilates
Mis. 14–29 Science of Truth a· error,
Un. 39– 7 omnipotent Love which a· hate,
'01. 13– 3 a· its own embodiment :
annihilating
Mis. 141–14 even the a· law of Love.
Ret. 30–11 a· the false testimony of
My. 110–13 forces a· time and space,
annihilation
Mis. 22–14 or a· of individuality.
'01. 13– 4 this is the only a·.
anniversaries
Mis. 304–24 * a· of the days on which
  304–27 * on the a· of their death.
anniversary
Mis. 305–29 * the a· of the inauguration of
My. 174–19 one hundred and seventy-fifth a· of
  175– 2 this deeply interesting a·,
  270– 8 its one hundred and seventy-fifth a· ;
Anno Domini
Mis. 131–21 encountered in A· D· 1894,
Pul. 24–14 * erected A· D· 1894.
  84–14 * close of the year, A· D· 1894,
announce
Mis. 374–15 a· their Principle and idea.
Man. 32–13 a· the full title of the book
  59– 9 a· the name of the author.
Ret. 42– 5 to a· himself a Christian Scientist,
Pul. 86–17 * We are happy to a· to you
My. 242–16 I hereby a· to the C. S. field
announced
Mis. 114–11 a· in the Bible and their textbook,
  177–25 * who was a· to preach the sermon,
  256–13 as was a· in the October number of
Pul. 55–15 * the ninety-first edition is a·.
My. 31–28 * a· simply that they would sing
  81–11 * a· at the main meeting that
  91–20 * since C. S. was a·
  132– 3 We begin with the law as just a·,
  157–18 * first a· in the Concord Monitor
  237– 2 a· in the Sentinel a few weeks ago,
announcement
Mis. 168–25 * a· that the Rev. Mary B. G. Eddy
  314–25 this a·, "the C. S. textbook."
Man. 32–15 Such a· shall be made but once
My. 26– 2 * chapter sub-title
  27–22 * a· made by Mr. Chase
  28– 1 * make this a· coincident with
  61– 9 * a· that the services would be

announcement
My. 76– 8 * formal a· was made that no more
  83–23 * a·, which has just been made,
  98–15 * remarkable a· to the effect
  141–12 * a· in regard to the services
  163– 8 chapter sub-title
  281–18 * a· of peace between Russia and
  294–23 a· of the decease of Pope Leo XIII,
announcements
Mis. 84– 4 to receive startling a·.
Pul. 71–15 * a· in New York papers
announcing
Mis. 300– 5 a· the author's name,
  314–24 a· the full title of this book,
Man. 58–20 A· Author's Name.
No. 35–24 Jesus came a· Truth.
My. 26– 4 * takes pleasure in a· that
  134–24 * In a· this letter, he said :
  204–14 A LETTER A· THE PURPOSE OF
annoy
Po. 31– 6 Sad sense, a· No more the peace of
annual
Mis. 134–11 at the a· session of the
Man. 56–10 A· Meetings.
  76–11 report at the a· Church meeting
  95–16 A· Lectures.
  97–13 shall receive an a· salary,
'00. 7– 3 show the a· death-rate to have
'02. 20–17 our a· gathering at Pleasant View,
My. 8–25 * convened in a· business meeting
  23–19 * in a· business meeting assembled,
  25–19 at our a· communion
  26– 5 * on the date of the a· communion,
  32–26 * Reading of a· Message from
  37–27 * We have read your a· Message
  53–25 * a· report of the business committee
  57– 1 * a· meetings were overcrowded
  63–11 * Our a· communion and
  76–20 * assembled in their a· church meeting
  124– 6 Looking on this a· assemblage of
  133–11 my a· Message is swallowed up in
  140–13 * dropping the a· communion service
  141–17 * the a· communion season of
  170– 7 in my a· Message to the church
  207– 8 * in a· conference assembled,
  (see also **meeting**)
annually
Mis. 136–24 hold three sessions a·,
  315–11 can teach a· three classes only.
Man. 29–17 salary . . . shall be at present . . . a·.
  44–13 pay a· a per capita tax
  56–12 shall be held a·, on Monday
  76–18 Its members shall be appointed a·
  77– 2 audited a· by an honest,
  79– 3 elect a· a Committee on Business,
  84–17 The associations . . . shall convene a·.
  88–11 vice-president shall be elected a·
  91–17 shall be paid over a· to
  93– 0 shall be elected a·
  95–18 branch churches shall call . . . a·
  97–10 He shall be elected a·
  98–26 shall a· and alternately appoint
  99– 8 shall a· and alternately appoint
'02. 12–27 who a· favor us with their presence
My. 7–10 who a· favor us with their presence
  141– 4 * held a· in The First Church
  284–19 has been held a· in some church
  328–14 * This license of five dollars a·,
Annual Meeting
Mis. 125–21 chapter sub-title
Man. 93– 7 on Monday preceding the A· M·,
My. 7–12 chapter sub-title
  22– 1 * chapter sub-title
  23–16 * Greeting to Mrs. Eddy from the A· M·
  38–27 * chapter sub-title
  131–17 chapter sub-title
  154–14 chapter sub-title
  156– 1 chapter sub-title
annuity
Ret. 40– 3 living on a small a·.
annul
Mis. 199– 6 to a· his own erring mental law,
My. 219–22 cannot a· nor make void the laws
annulled
Mis. 28–29 a· the claims of physique
  244–18 who a· the so-called laws of matter
  260–12 these laws a· all other laws
  290– 4 nuptial vow is never a· so long as
Man. 28–20 nor any Tenet or By-Law . . . a·,
Un. 11– 8 He a· the laws of matter,
  31– 8 a· the claims of matter,
Pan. 8–15 a· the so-called laws of matter,
My. 268– 3 should never be a· so long as

annulling
Man. 28– 6   *a·* its Tenets and By-Laws.
My. 340–17   immediately *a·* such bills

annuls
Mis.   99– 3   It *a·* false evidence,
  103– 1   *a·* the testimony of the senses,
My. 234– 6   personal worship which C. S. *a·*.

anoint
Mis. 171– 6   *a·* the blind man's eyes

anointed
Mis. 161–13   Christ-Jesus, the Godlike, the *a·*.
  347–26   those whom He has *a·*.
  355–22   is unlike "the *a·*," — see Acts 10 : 38.
Ret. 28–30   character and practice of the *a·* ;

anointing
Mis. 258– 8   *a·* the wounded spirit with
Pul. 27–21   * Mary *a·* the head of Jesus,

anointings
Pul. 9–26   prayers, prophecies, and *a·*.

anoints
Mis. 130–30   the meek and loving, God *a·*
Chr. 53– 9   The Christ-idea, God *a·*
Ret. 91– 1   He *a·* His Truth-bearers,
My. 270–26   or by C. S., which *a·* with Truth,

anomalous
Mis.   63– 2   and *a·* in the other.
  92– 1   To omit these important points is *a·*,
  108– 4   To allow sin of any sort is *a·*
  256–26   The assertion that . . . is *a·*.
Ret. 83–27   is *a·*, when we consider the
Pan.   2– 3   that C. S. is pantheism is *a·*

anonymous
Mis. 295– 8   This *a·* talker further declares,
'02. 15– 1   *a·* letters mailed to me

another (see also another's)
Mis.   1–20   reveals *a·* scene and *a·* self
  22–16   from one individual to *a·* ;
  29– 7   At *a·* time he prayed, not for
  37– 2   if there were in reality *a·* mind
  40–32   unintentionally harms himself or *a·*.
  43–21   If one student tries to undermine *a·*,
  58–28   even one human mind governing *a·* ;
  59–23   speaking often one to *a·*,
  59–24   one individual has with *a·*
  60–20   with *a·* who is awake.
  63– 4   claim that one erring mind cures *a·*
  67–27   by equivalent words in *a·*,
  71– 7   and *a·* that he had sore eyes ;
  91–11   love for one *a·*.
  96–28   not one mind acting upon *a·*
  98–11   to aid one *a·* in finding ways
  104–30   I will love, if *a·* hates.
  111–31   or is *a·* Christ,
  129–16   an atom of *a·* man's indiscretion,
  147– 3   *A·* year has rolled on,
  147– 4   *a·* annual meeting has convened,
  147– 4   *a·* space of time has been given us,
  147– 5   has *a·* duty been done
  147– 6   *a·* victory won for time and
  147– 7   in unity, preferring one *a·*,
  148– 3   never . . . at variance with *a·*
  148–12   one person might impose on *a·*.
  149– 8   one after *a·* has opened his lips
  155– 6   Sacrifice self to bless one *a·*,
  158– 8   *a·* change in your pulpit
  173–22   man is not met by *a·* power
  175–23   supposition . . . one mind controls *a·* ;
  175–24   one belief takes the place of *a·*.
  183–25   for it claims *a·* father.
  191– 3   embodies . . . in *a·* term, serpent,
  191–19   cast out of *a·* individual
  197–24   He believes there is *a·* power
  198–27   supposition of *a·* intelligence
  212–29   before letting *a·* know it.
  215– 3   to go from one extreme to *a·* :
  219–15   one person feels sick, *a·* feels
  219–27   *a·* knows that if he can change
  220– 4   whom *a·* would heal mentally.
  221–20   acknowledgment of it in *a·*
  221–30   Who would tell *a·* of a crime that
  224–29   wilfully attempt to injure *a·*,
  236–26   in one's efforts to help *a·*,
  238–27   *a·* evidence of the falsehoods
  242–15   I am in *a·* department of
  246–14   from *a·* direction there comes
  246–15   *a·* sharp cry of oppression.
  246–15   *A·* form of inhumanity
  248– 6   as, in *a·* Scripture.
  273–27   *a·* and a larger number would
  281– 6   But I find also *a·* mental condition
  283– 8   management of *a·* man's property.
  283–15   to treat *a·* student without his
  292– 5   That ye love one *a·*." — John 13 : 34.

another
Mis. 311– 9   so, loving one *a·*, go forth
  311–20   as soon harm myself as *a·* ;
  325–13   patiently seeks *a·* dwelling,
  336–21   What is it but *a·* name for C. S.,
  395–18   Ere autumn blanch *a·* year,
Man.   3– 8   one person might impose on *a·*.
  34–18   a member of *a·* Church of Christ,
  37–18   cannot recommend the pupil of *a·*
  45– 4   Joining *A·* Society.
  62–11   transfer from *a·* Church of Christ,
  84–24   shall not teach *a·* loyal
  99–14   with *a·* Church of Christ, Scientist.
  100–18   *a·* Committee to fill the vacancy ;
Ret. 40–16   to be delivered of *a·* child.
  59– 9   and addition in *a·*,
  86–19   and *a·* one undertakes to carry his
  88– 3   professional intercourse . . . with one *a·*.
  88– 4   *A·* command of the Christ,
  88–17   *a·* part of C. S. work,
  89–23   employing *a·* student to take charge
  90– 6   while he is serving *a·* fold?
Un.   3– 4   they awake only to *a·* sphere of
  3– 5   must pass through *a·* probationary
  6–28   and in less than *a·* fifty years
  8– 1   Let *a·* query now be considered,
  21– 3   excusing one *a·*." — Rom. 2 : 15.
  21– 7   good and evil talk to one *a·* ;
  26–22   *a·* line of this hymn,
  34–14   Take *a·* train of reasoning.
  38–13   must enthrone *a·* power,
  39–15   claims *a·* father, and denies
Pul.   5– 6   light of one friendship after *a·*
  6–23   *A·* brilliant enunciator, seeker,
  14– 5   *a·* extreme mortal mood,
  14– 7   for one extreme follows *a·*.
  21– 2   inevitably love one *a·*
  27–20   * *A·* great window tells its
  33–24   * believed, . . . form from *a·* world.
  38–30   * one form of belief or *a·*
  42– 3   * At 10 : 30 o'clock *a·* service began,
  42– 4   * and at noon still *a·*.
  48–19   * *a·* distinguished relative,
  48–26   * many *a·* well-born woman's.
No.   7–22   between one person and *a·*,
  9– 6   *a·* class who are clearer
  24–26   *a·* and more glorious truth,
  30–13   rebuke any claim of *a·* law.
  40–21   for one mind to meddle with *a·*
Pan. 11– 3   "Lie not one to *a·*, — Col. 3 : 9.
  13–13   rebuke and exhort one *a·*.
  14– 5   Once more I write, . . . love one *a·* ;
'00.   5–16   loving *a·* as himself.
  8–20   work that belongs to *a·*.
'01.   5–14   This suggests *a·* query :
  13– 2   *a·* nonentity that belittles
  33–28   to persecute *a·* in advance of it.
'02.   1– 1   *a·* year of God's loving providence
  7–22   chapter sub-title
  7–23   proceed to *a·* Scriptural passage
  7–26   love one *a·* ; — John 13 : 34.
  12–15   with *a·* of his sayings:
  12–25   *a·* united effort to purchase
  18–16   "Love one *a·*, — John 13 : 34.
Hea.   2–14   And still *a·* Christian hero,
  4–26   and the opposite of it at *a·*,
  5–20   covered, in one way or *a·*,
  13–27   while it is supposed to cure *a·*,
  13–28   one lie getting the better of *a·*,
  15–15   *a·* mind perpetually at war
Peo.   2– 8   gives *a·* letter to the word
  8– 5   prayer of one and not of *a·* ;
  11– 9   *a·* staging for diviner claims,
Po.   43– 4   Loving God and one *a·*,
  58– 3   Ere autumn blanch *a·* year,
My.   7– 8   before making *a·* united effort,
  14–12   * letter from a friend in *a·* city,
  18–21   rebuke and exhort one *a·*.
  69–20   * *A·* unusual feature is the foyer,
  81– 9   * laughingly give precedence to *a·*
  84–17   * *a·* great demonstration of
  85–20   * *A·* glory for Boston, *a·* "landmark"
  94– 1   * through *a·* decade
  113–19   Neither is it presumptuous . . . for *a·*,
  122–16   *a·* Christmas has come and gone.
  152– 1   turned to *a·* form of idolatry,
  167– 6   and unites us to one *a·*,
  187–15   we should love one *a·*." — I John 3 : 11.
  187–28   "that ye love one *a·*." — John 15 : 12.
  189–12   vibrating from one pulpit to *a·*
  189–12   from one heart to *a·*,
  202–11   but to love one *a·* : — Rom. 13 : 8.
  202–11   he that loveth *a·* hath — Rom. 13 : 8.
  216–19   indicates *a·* field of work
  218–28   to one no more than to *a·*.
  221–12   Earth has not known *a·* so great

another

My. 224–19	same time giving full credit to *a·*
227– 6	minifying of his own goodness by *a·*.
234–20	gives the subject quite *a·* aspect.
240–15	I now repeat *a·* proof,
267–21	*a·* with that of relief from fear
267–22	still *a·* with a bitter sense of
292–18	against the *modus operandi* of *a·*,
292–21	belief unwittingly neutralizing *a·*,
306–11	I have quite *a·* purpose in life
311–24	I have *a·* coat-of-arms,
346– 5	* *a·* opportunity for presenting *a·*
	(*see also* **member, person**)

another's

Mis. 11–16	could save it . . . by taking *a·*,
39–23	"one *a·* burdens, — *Gal.* 6 : 2.
83–10	*your own thought or a·.*"
83–12	No person can accept *a·* belief,
83–15	originated in *a·* mind,
97– 6	transmitted to *a·* thought
98–28	* *a·* heart would'st reach."
127–19	finds one's own in *a·* good.
184–27	not her own, but *a·* good ;
213–16	chastened and illumined *a·* way
223–30	arrow shot from *a·* bow
224– 2	makes *a·* criticism rankle,
224– 3	makes *a·* deed offensive,
224– 4	feels hurt by *a·* self-assertion.
338–23	* *A·* soul wouldst reach ;
Ret. 72– 2	that hazards *a·* happiness,
88–23	to enter unasked *a·* pulpit,
No. 3–23	not so much thine own as *a·* good,
29– 2	for his own sin, but not for *a·*.
43–20	their own on *a·* foundation.
'00. 14–19	not only her own, but *a·* good.
'01. 34–19	seeketh another her own but *a·* good,
My. 18–16	finds one's own in *a·* good."
19–23	not her own" but *a·* good, — *1 Cor.* 13 : 5.
188–24	one man's head lies at *a·* feet.
227– 5	because of *a·* wickedness

answer (noun)

Mis. 4–16	has been devoted to their *a·*.
23–11	The *a·* is self-evident,
50– 2	therefore your *a·* is, that error
55– 1	failed to get the right *a·*,
67–29	I modify my affirmative *a·*.
89–23	the proper *a·* to this question
93–21	Your *a·* is, that neither fear nor
96–25	This *a·* includes too much
121–25	this *a·* to the questions of the
127–16	fitness to receive the *a·* to its desire ;
130– 4	She readily leaves the *a·* to
310–11	My *a·* to manifold letters
349–22	In *a·* to a question on the
380–09	*A·* was filed by the defendant,
Man. 41– 9	"A soft *a·* turneth away — *Prov.* 15 : 1.
Ret. 8– 7	Her *a·* was always, "Nothing,
30–17	The *a·* is plain.
34– 5	If I sought an *a·* from the
Pul. 74–10	* preferred to prepare a written *a·*
Rud. 9–15	and an *a·* of the lips
Pan. 5–11	gave the proper *a·* for all time
'02. 17 26	take its *a·* as to thy aims,
Hea. 1–13	our *a·* was, "Then there were no
9–21	only correct *a·* to the question,
My. 18–13	to receive the *a·* to its desire ;
25–17	my *a·* to their fervid question :
43–32	* The *a·* is, The way out of
51–22	* "she gave no definite *a·*,
59–26	* My *a·* has invariably been,
107– 5	and you have the correct *a·*.
113–29	emphasize the *a·* to this
124–22	what shall the *a·* be?
149–16	Epictetus made *a·*,
271–17	heading
277–12	*a·* to the sublime question as to
292–13	My *a·* to the inquiry,
323– 5	* written in *a·* to an unfair criticism
343– 4	* in her own way, reaching an *a·*

answer (verb)

Mis. 41–19	We *a·*, Yes.
51–11	cannot *a·* your question
91–26	*a·* them according to it,
92–14	students will *a·* them from the same
121–27	ye will not *a·* me, — *Luke* 22 : 68.
132–21	to accept your invitation to *a·*
142–24	*a·* in a commonplace letter.
145–10	*a·* to his name in this corner-stone
155–18	and less wherein to *a·* it
177–19	*A·* at once and practically,
177–20	and *a·* aright!
238–20	Let one's life *a·* well
280–26	I met the class to *a·* some
299– 9	simply *a·* the following question
300– 7	We *a·*, It is a mistake ;

answer (verb)

Mis. 301–21	I *a·* : It is not right to copy my
347– 1	"*A·* not a fool — *Prov.* 26 : 4.
348–15	"*A·* a fool according — *Prov.* 26 : 5.
Ret. 9–12	I was afraid, and did not *a·*.
9–15	*a·*, in the words of Samuel,
14–24	I replied that I could only *a·*
28– 2	the divine Mind alone must *a·*,
68–20	We *a·* that it cannot.
Un. 6–15	not prepared to *a·* intelligently
45– 7	We should *a·* : "Yes!
48– 4	yet ask, and I will *a·*.
Pul. 74–14	to *a·* for myself,
Rud. 6–25	can alone *a·* this question
No. 46– 9	must *a·* the constant inquiry :
'00. 2–19	is supposed to *a·* smilingly :
'01. 11–26	"*A·* not a fool — *Prov.* 26 : 4.
14– 7	We *a·*, Yes and No!
My. 83–15	* questions as to locality to *a·*,
120– 8	*a·* your excellent letter.
186–22	I will *a·* ; — *Isa.* 65 : 24.
212–15	We *a·*, Because they do not
223–14	about secular affairs, I do not *a·*.
343– 8	I can *a·* that. It will be a man."
343–10	"I cannot *a·* that now."
351– 9	in which to *a·* it.
360– 1	*A·* this letter immediately.

answered

Mis. 4–26	When it is *a·* that there is no
218–28	echo *a·*, "Pretty well,
249– 9	met and *a·* *legally.*
281–17	She *a·* him, "It is wiser
326–32	He *a·*, "The sight of thee
327– 7	He *a·*, "I will."
378–16	He *a·* kindly and squarely,
Ret. 8–18	I *a·* not, till again the same
8–23	She *a·* as always before.
9– 6	My cousin *a·* quickly,
14–11	I *a·* without a tremor,
25– 3	It *a·* my questions as to how I
83 23	and be *a·* according to it,
Pul. 33–12	* as her mother had bidden her,
34–27	It *a·* my questions as to
'00. 11–12	human sigh for peace and love is *a·*
'02. 5–15	can never be *a·* satisfactorily by
5–17	*a·* this great question forever
14–27	This pregnant question, *a·* frankly
Hea. 19–13	is *a·* by the Scripture,
My. 61– 1	* I gladly *a·* in the affirmative,
105–26	When *a·* in the negative,
133– 9	chapter sub title
190–16	He *a·*, "This kind — *Matt.* 17 : 21.
218–21	chapter sub-title
222– 8	the master Metaphysician, *a·*,
339–20	he *a·* them in substance :

answereth

Mis. 152– 4	in water face *a·* to face," — *Prov.* 27 : 19.
203– 9	in water face *a·* to face, — *Prov.* 27 : 19.

answering

Mis. 106 26	soft, sweet sigh of angels *a·*,
132–17	or *a·* personally manifold letters
'00. 1– 7	I am with thee, heart *a·* to heart,
My. 190– 7	The age is fast *a·* this question :
192–28	*a·* your prayers, crowning your

answers

Mis. 23– 6	Christianity *a·* this question.
81–26	*a·* the human call for help ;
92–16	questions and *a·* contained in
95–13	confine myself to questions and *a·*
132–17	dictating *a·* through my secretary,
167– 3	though their *a·* pertain to
317–19	prompt my *a·* to the above
Man. 63– 5	questions and *a·* as are adapted to
Un. 8– 3	before Science *a·* it.
'00. 2–29	he *a·* : "I am not so successful
'01. 19– 1	God *a·* their prayers,
Peo. 8– 5	or that *a·* the prayer of one
My. 238– 1	chapter sub-title
343– 1	* plain that the *a·* to questions

antagonism

Mis. 200–19	spiritual law and its *a·* to
320–21	It doth meet the *a·* of error ;
My. 11– 8	* encountered the full force of *a·*.

antagonist

Ret. 7– 4	His noble political *a·*,
Un. 41–22	can never dwell in its *a·*, matter.

antagonistic

Mis. 78–30	views *a·* to the divine order
217–22	but that the effect is *a·* to its
296–17	C. S., *a·* to intemperance,
370– 6	*a·* spirit of evil is still abroad ;
Ret. 78–12	works, *a·* to C. S.,
Un. 38– 5	not in accordance . . . but *a·* thereto.

antagonistic
No. 20–27 mortal hypotheses, *a·* to Revelation
My. 87–28 * nothing *a·* to it in this doctrine
antagonize
Mis. 85–21 Spirit and flesh *a·*.
Un. 21–13 This would *a·* individual
antagonized
Ret. 56– 1 *a·* by finite theories,
My. 306– 9 false should be *a·* only for
antagonizes
Mis. 309–23 human concept *a·* the divine.
antecedent
Mis. 26–24 Spirit, God, has no *a·* ;
No. 17– 1 consequent of an *a·* false assumption
17– 2 If God knows the *a·*,
My. 303–27 her duplicate, *a·*, or subsequent.
antedated
Mis. 182– 1 he *a·* his own existence,
Ret. 26–19 He who *a·* Abraham,
anteroom
Mis. 379– 2 Mr. Quimby would retire to an *a·*
anthem
Mis. 330– 3 What is the *a·* of human life?
My. 186–12 *a·* of one Father-Mother God,
anthems
Pul. 81–23 * the unwritten *a·* of love.
Anthony, Susan
Mis. 248–22 my property to Susan *A·*.
anthropomorphic
'01. 4–18 is not corporeal nor *a·*.
6–23 in the corporeal or *a·* sense.
anti-Christ
Mis. 111–30 The belief in *a·* :
309–18 falling into the error of *a·*.
anti-Christian
Un. 53–11 Matter and evil are *a·*,
anticipate
My. 219– 2 Nor should patients *a·* being
anticipated
My. 21–18 * forego their *a·* visit this year
21–22 * who have *a·* much joy in meeting
163–25 all and more than I *a·*.
anticipating
My. 346– 7 * Those who have been *a·* nature
anticipation
My. 219– 4 such an *a·* on the part of
anticipations
Ret. 81–28 the frailty of mortal *a·*,
antics
Mis. 369–15 indulge in mad *a·*.
antidote
Mis. 33–27 *a·* for sickness, as well as for sin,
37–18 Its *a·* for all ills is God,
44–29 applying this mental remedy or *a·*
255–23 fact that the *a·* for sickness,
255–26 because it is this divine *a·*,
334–24 Then it cannot *a·* error.
Ret. 34–12 recognizes the *a·* for all sickness,
antidotes
Mis. 3–23 *a·* and destroys these material
189–11 Love *a·* and destroys the errors of
195– 1 Truth that *a·* all error.
209– 1 penalties as its *a·* and remedies.
268–23 *a·* for the ailments of mortal mind
antiphonal
Pul. 59–15 * *A·* paragraphs were read from
antipode
Mis. 31– 3 and is the *a·* of C. S.
217–12 is the *a·* of Spirit,
267–24 *a·* of Spirit, which we name
308–30 human likeness is the *a·* of man
332–26 the *a·* of immortal man.
351–26 declares itself the *a·* of Love ;
351–30 Material life is the *a·* of
Ret. 29– 2 spiritualism is the *a·* of C. S.
60– 8 says that matter, His *a·*,
67–12 a sinner was the *a·* of God.
Un. 31–18 matter, the *a·* of Spirit,
Pul. 75– 9 the absolute *a·* of C. S.,
No. 5– 5 *a·*, — the reality of error ;
27–17 Mortal man is the *a·* of
35–19 matter, — which is the *a·* of God,
'02. 5–28 an *a·* of *infinite* Love
Hea. 13–25 is the *a·* of mesmerism,
My. 106–27 he is the very *a·* of all these
181–30 material earth or *a·* of heaven.
301– 1 a peaceable party quite their *a·*

antipodes
Mis. 34–25 are the *a·* of C. S. ;
55–20 these facts are the direct *a·* of
56– 1 the very *a·* of C. S.
Ret. 25–17 and its *a·*, or the temporal,
59–15 is the *a·* of Life, or God,
Un. 53–11 are anti-Christian, the *a·* of Science.
My. 85– 9 * meet in Europe and in the *a·*,
antique
Pul. 24–27 * with doors of *a·* oak richly carved.
59– 1 * behind an *a·* lamp,
anti-slavery
Pul. 6–29 that renowned apostle of *a·*,
Po. vi–14 *has since been the pioneer of a·*
antithesis
Pul. 6– 3 continue till the *a·* of Christianity,
Peo. 8–12 not more the *a·* of Christianity than
anxiety
Hea. 9– 2 We should have no *a·* about
anxious
Man. 39– 1 *a·* to live according to its
Ret. 8–12 my mother was perplexed and *a·*.
anxiously
Mis. 324–11 *a·* surveying him who waiteth
any
Mis. 5–17 There is no longer *a·* reason for
7–30 naturally without *a·* assistance.
8–14 or *a·* other creature separate you
17– 5 *a·* supposititious law of sin,
24–31 and thus destroy *a·* supposed effect
28–32 drink *a·* deadly thing, — *Mark* 16 : 18.
29–13 and *a·* speculative theory.
30–26 for *a·* seeming mysticism
46– 8 *a·* doctrine previously entertained.
48–16 effect of alcohol, or of *a·* drug,
53–15 by *a·* compromise with matter ;
54–23 to *a·* disease whatsoever,
57– 5 of *a·* other creation?
58– 2 *does that disease have a· more power*
59–21 *A·* copartnership with that Mind
60– 2 *God does not recognize a·*,
69–27 I will send his address to *a·* one
72–16 not have occasion *a·* more — *Ezek.* 18 : 3.
74–23 *a·* supposition that matter is
78–10 than can science in *a·* other direction.
78–28 *a·* more than goodness,
79–29 Beware of joining *a·* medical league
87–19 I never commission *a·* one to
96–25 to give you *a·* conclusive give
98– 1 making this question . . . of *a·* importance,
103–21 *A·* inference of the divine
108– 4 To allow sin of *a·* sort is
113–15 refuses to be influenced by *a·*
128–10 if there be *a·* virtue, — *Phil.* 4 : 8.
128–10 if there be *a·* praise, — *Phil.* 4 : 8.
137–10 if you had *a·* questions to propose,
144–32 more than *a·* other institution,
170–28 as having *a·* power to see.
178–17 * If *a·* one had said to me
179– 9 *a·* other consciousness than
194–32 to exclude all faith in *a·* other
197–16 *a·* historical event or person.
229– 1 *a·* one is liable to have them
229– 3 prepares one to have *a·* disease
229–18 neither shall *a·* plague — *Psal.* 91 : 10.
229–26 *a·* other possible sanative method ;
230– 3 more than upon *a·* other one thing.
230–23 * With a heart for *a·* fate ;
241–21 *a·* man's bondage to sin and
249– 6 drink *a·* deadly thing, — *Mark* 16 : 18.
256–10 from *a·* other than Mrs. Eddy,
259– 2 was not *a·* thing made.'' — *John* 1 : 3.
260–17 destroys *a·* suppositional
263– 6 to be found in *a·* language
266–19 New York, or *a·* other place,
272–14 * *a·* officer, agent, or servant
272–14 * of *a·* corporation or
272–16 * *a·* diploma or degree,
272–21 * such as *a·* stock company
272–22 * for *a·* secular purposes ;
283–13 *A·* exception to the old wholesome rule,
284– 4 more than *a·* other system
288–12 *a·* conclusion drawn therefrom
291–16 If *a·* are not partakers thereof,
304–13 * *a·* great patriotic celebration
306– 5 * *a·* ideas on that subject
308– 6 love or hatred or *a·* other cause
309– 1 the personal sense of *a·* one,
314–11 give out *a·* notices from the pulpit,
318–14 *A·* student, having received instructions
322–15 By *a·* personal presence, or word
337–32 Sin of *a·* sort tends to hide from
349–17 I claim no jurisdiction over *a·*

any

Mis.	351– 9	and would not if I could, harm *a·* one
	351–10	method of Mind-healing, or in *a·* manner.
	353– 9	concept of me, or of *a·* one,
	371–21	To sympathize in *a·* degree with
	380–25	*a·* outward form of practice.
Man.	28–25	It is the duty of *a·* member
	29– 3	or of *a·* other officer in this
	45–16	shall not be a member of *a·* church whose
	49– 3	in *a·* church or locality,
	50–23	violating *a·* of the By-Laws
	51– 8	*A·* member who shall unjustly aggrieve
	62– 4	*a·* special hymn selected
	62– 9	Sunday School classes of *a·*
	62–14	Sunday School of *a·* Church of
	65–16	comply with *a·* written order,
	66–20	*a·* authority supposed to come
	73–10	students in *a·* university
	74– 5	or control over *a·* other church.
	77–24	*a·* possible future deviation from
	78– 2	If *a·* Director fails to heed
	78–19	not exceeding $200 for *a·* one
	91–15	*A·* surplus funds left in the
	92–17	in *a·* class in the
	95– 6	*a·* member of this Board
	97–20	or circulated literature of *a·* sort.
	100– 6	to *a·* Committee on Publication,
	100–17	*a·* Church of Christ, Scientist,
	100–23	and *a·* Committee so named
	102–16	land purchased for *a·* purpose
	104–17	if a discrepancy appears in *a·*
	105– 2	nor *a·* Tenet or By-Law
Ret.	14–17	*a·* profession of religion,
	14–21	not designate *a·* precise time.
	14–27	*a·* wicked way in me, — *Psal.* 139 : 24.
	25–26	to form *a·* proper conception
	27– 6	never been read by *a·* one but myself,
	40– 2	refusing to take *a·* pay
	50–13	*a·* real equivalent for my instruction
	60–29	*A·* attempt to divide these
	61–12	fear or suffering of *a·* sort.
	64– 9	Need it be said that *a·* opposite
	78–18	or *a·* name given to it other than
	82–29	clearer than *a·* previous edition,
	85– 6	*a·* other organic operative method
	85–15	*a·* deviation from the order
	89–22	*a·* precedent for employing
	89–27	*a·* action not first made known
Un.	5– 9	not to accept *a·* personal opinion
	5–13	frightened sense of *a·* need
	10– 6	*a·* previous teachers, save Jesus
	10– 8	If there be *a· monopoly* in my
	13–10	in ethics *a·* more than in music.
	13–15	If God has *a·* real knowledge of
	14– 5	Can it be seriously held, by *a·*
	19–16	without *a·* actuality which
	29–16	*a·* standpoint of their own.
	43– 3	for *a·* strong demonstration over
	48– 7	no faith in *a·* other thing or being.
	54– 7	becomes as tangible as *a·* reality.
	54–12	To admit that sin has *a·* claim
	54–14	if sin's claim be allowed in *a·* degree,
	64– 1	If sin has *a·* pretense of existence,
Pul.	21–20	the welfare of *a·* one.
	21–28	cannot come from *a·* other source.
	21–29	aught that can darken in *a·* degree
	23– 5	* Most Unique Structure in *A·* City
	24– 6	* most unique structure in *a·* city.
	28–16	* not differ widely from that of *a·* other
	32– 8	* not by *a·* crude self-assertion,
	32–13	* like *a·* abbess of old.
	36–17	* walked *a·* conceivable distance.
	37– 1	* *a·* information for *The Inter-Ocean,*"
	37–22	* depending on *a·* one personality.
	42– 8	* at *a·* one of these services.
	44–26	* without *a·* special appeal,
	44–28	* refused to accept *a·* further checks
	47–13	* without receiving *a·* real satisfaction.
	47–14	* *a·* distinct statement of the Science
	50–19	* *A·* new movement will awaken some
	50–28	* live down *a·* attempted repression.
	53–16	* "That word, more than *a·* other,
	58–17	* Scarcely *a·* wood-work is to be found.
	60– 4	* There was no address of *a·* sort,
	72–17	* "I have not taken *a·* medicine
	72–17	* or drugs of *a·* kind,
	72–22	* *a·* power other than that which
	75– 1	Whoever in *a·* age expresses
	75– 8	to think or speak of me in *a·* manner as
	87– 2	* *a·* services that may be held therein.
Rud.	5–14	If there is *a·* such thing as matter,
	6–15	* "*a·* metaphysical subtlety,"
	7– 2	Not . . . is Science, by *a·* means ;
	12–25	from *a·* sense of subordination
	16– 7	in *a·* branch of education.
	16–16	*A·* departure from Science is

any

No.	5–26	*A·* contradictory fusion of Truth with
	7– 5	*a·* root of bitterness to spring up
	7– 6	nor cause *a·* misapprehension
	10– 4	*a·* proof that can be given
	14–20	more than *a·* other religious sect,
	15– 6	would enable *a·* one to prove
	17–15	or *a·* mode of mortal mind,
	30– 9	*a·* more than the legislator need
	30–12	to rebuke *a·* claim of another law.
	30–17	if He possessed *a·* knowledge of
	32–10	chapter sub-title
	38 23	*a·* other state or stage of being.
Pan.	6– 4	will never disappear in *a·* other way.
'00.	6– 9	*A·* mystery in C. S. departs when
'01.	7–26	nor can they gain *a·* evidence of
	19–23	to *a·* susceptible misuse of
	27–13	If *a·* one as yet has healed
'02.	3– 8	to *a·* lingering sense of the
	6– 1	the thought of *a·* other reality,
	14–11	success possible for *a·* Christian
	14–15	on *a·* other foundation,
	20 -18	breaking *a·* seeming connection
Hea.	1– 3	drink *a· deadly thing,— Mark* 16 : 18.
	5–14	Does *a·* one think the departed
	7–20	regardless of *a·* outward act,
	7–25	drink *a· deadly thing,— Mark* 16 : 18.
	9–15	a duty for *a·* one to believe that
	15–11	drink *a· deadly thing,— Mark* 16 : 18.
	15–12	to *a·* one's perfect satisfaction
Peo.	9–24	all evidence of *a·* other power
	12– 3	drink *a· deadly thing,— Mark* 16 : 18.
My.	8– 1	* *a·* portion of two million dollars
	9– 5	* *a·* portion of two million dollars
	10–18	* in *a·* particular,
	11–30	* "*a·* portion of two million dollars
	33–11	*a·* wicked way in me, — *Psal.* 139 : 24.
	41– 5	* nor in *a·* wise alter its effects.
	41–21	* unable to cherish *a·* enmity.
	41–25	* Why should *a·* one postpone his
	42–10	* so that *a·* further words
	48– 1	* drink *a· deadly thing,— Mark* 16 : 18.
	61–20	* never more did I have *a·* doubt.
	67–26	* surpass *a·* church edifice erected
	69–19	* view of the platform from *a·* seat.
	70– 7	* than *a·* other denomination
	71–18	* different from *a·* other church
	72–15	* do not send us *a·* more money
	74–15	* in this or *a·* other city,
	79–14	* in the world on *a·* occasion;
	81–26	* to give *a·* account of the
	83– 9	* or insignia of *a·* kind.
	91–18	* this country or *a·* other country
	93– 8	* to attract *a·* class save the
	98–12	* if they would deal . . . with *a·* effect.
	98–24	* to *a·* of the latter-day methods of
	98–25	* record is one of which *a·* church
	104 26	in this or *a·* other country.
	106– 1	than *a·* material method.
	118– 5	*a·* imaginary benefit they receive
	119–11	Buddhism or *a·* other "ism."
	146– 4	drink *a· deadly thing, — Mark* 16 : 18.
	148– 5	All that we ask of *a·* people is to
	103–11	pleasure of receiving *a·* of them.
	182- 3	*a·* other city in the United States.
	185– 5	* With a heart for *a·* fate ;
	202–10	Owe no man *a·* thing,
	220– 2	to this century or to *a·* epoch,
	223– 7	or to *a·* class of individual discords.
	223–22	which relate in *a·* manner to
	224–24	cannot afford to recommend *a·*
	242–23	nor to reply to *a·* received,
	244– 9	*a·* or all of you who are ready for it,
	249– 2	without harming *a·* one
	267– 8	*a·* thing made that was— *John* 1 : 3.
	269– 9	can they die *a·* more :— *Luke* 20 : 36.
	272–28	* for *a·* publications outside of
	299– 6	* "If they . . . have *a·* truth to reveal
	301–26	in *a·* manner whatever.
	303– 8	Catholics, or *a·* other sect.
	305–21	claim no special merit of *a·* kind.
	306– 5	or to dissever *a·* unity that may
	313–11	Nor do I remember *a·* such stuff
	318–18	not ask him *a·* questions.
	320–24	* without *a·* hesitation or restriction.
	321–10	* without *a·* restriction.
	323–11	* nor willingly leave *a·* false
	324– 5	* *a·* idea for your book,
	324– 7	* book to have come from *a·* one but
	324–16	* had *a·* other thought but that you
	324–31	* could have done so *a·* better.
	325–12	* in *a·* capacity in which I could
	333–16	* nor by *a·* Christian Scientists
	344–27	Were vaccination of *a·* avail,
	344–29	more dangerous than *a·* material
	345–17	pellets without *a·* medication

any

My. 346– 4   * puzzled by *a·* question,
346–23   * had in mind *a·* particular person
351–25   *a·* assertions to the contrary are
353–24   of *a·* special interest.
359–10   in *a·* other way than through
360–30   your healer, or *a·* earthly friend.
363–26   *a·* other individual but the
363–28   *A·* deviation from this direct
364– 5   *A·* departure from this golden rule
364–12   *a·* other cause or effect
    (*see also* **man, part, time, way**)

anybody

Mis. 80–10   *A·* and everybody, who
87–30   imagine they can help *a·*
325–21   that *a·* is animated with a purpose,

anything

Mis. 45–29   without Him was not *a·* made— *John* 1: 3.
61–24   A culprit, a sinner,— *a·* but a man !
68–13   that pain and sickness are *a·*
236–23   by *a·* that is said to you,
281– 8   nor give me *a·*,
367–15   to claim that He is ignorant of *a·* ;
379– 3   if he indited *a·* pathological
Un. 3–24   of *a·* unlike Himself ;
8– 4   *Is a· real of which the physical*
23–21   *a·* so wholly unlike Himself
'01. 5–24   *a·* that is real, good, or true ;
'02. 5–27   on the existence of *a·* which is
Hea. 18–18   never did *a·* for sickness
My. vi– 7   * knows *a·* about C. S. except
98– 6   * *a·* that its foes try to prove
321–13   * that he has ever said *a·* whatever of
323–10   * not going to lie about *a·*

anywhere

My. 69–18   * *a·* in the vast space
79–14   * seldom witnessed *a·* in the world
98–21   * no member of the church *a·*,
129– 1   see if there be found *a·* a

anywise

Man. 93–19   not allowed in *a·* to meddle with

apace

My. 224–32   Our Cause is growing *a·*

apart

Mis. 34–12   They are wholly *a·* from it.
57– 3   *a·* from the evidence of that
71–26   nothing can be formed *a·* from God,
123–31   far *a·* from physical sensation
125–24   *A·* from the common walks of
154–30   Have no . . . aim *a·* from holiness.
183–24   Asserting a selfhood *a·* from God,
186–21   *a·* from its fundamental basis.
196– 3   claim no mind *a·* from God.
200–24   *a·* from the personal senses.
333– 2   sin— yea, selfhood— is *a·* from God,
364–20   nothing *a·* from this Mind,
Ret. 20–27   A plot . . . for keeping us *a·*.
31–11   better than matter, and *a·* from it,
60– 1   as something *a·* from God,
95– 7   * may'st consecrated be And set *a·*
Pul. 59–28   * seats were especially set *a·* for
Rud. 5–10   considered *a·* from Mind.
No. 35–16   a supposed existence *a·* from God.
'01. 18–12   no remedy *a·* from Mind,
24– 1   * Matter *a·* from conscious mind is an
'02. 6– 3   law, *a·* or other than God
7– 2   no origin or causation *a·* from God.
Hea. 11– 5   man is seen wholly *a·* from
My. 3–13   C. S. is not a dweller *a·*
5– 7   Wholly *a·* from this mortal dream,
108– 6   I challenge matter to act *a·* from
108– 8   as it is seen to act *a·* from matter.
115– 6   were I, *a·* from God, its author.
118–29   entirely *a·* from limitations,
133–25   and we live *a·*.
166–15   we will live on and never drift *a·*.
167– 6   which is *a·* from matter,
189–17   there is no loyalty *a·* from love.
205–24   *a·* from human hypotheses,
225–19   sacredly holding His name *a·* from
273–19   utterly *a·* from a material or
274– 3   *a·* from the so-called life of matter
357– 2   materiality is wholly *a·* from C. S.,

apartment

Ret. 9– 2   led my cousin into an adjoining *a·*.
Pul. 29– 9   * The spacious *a·* was thronged
42–13   * a superb *a·* intended for
76– 3   * *a·* known as the "Mother's Room,"
76– 9   * alcoves are separated from the *a·*
My. 231–23   not an empty *a·* in his house,

apartments

Mis. 275–29   floral offerings sent to my *a·*
329– 8   various *a·* are dismally dirty.
Pul. 27– 1   * *a·*, with full-length French mirrors

apathy

Mis. 115– 4   astounded at the *a·* of some students
Pul. 14– 4   present *a·* as to the tendency of
'00. 8–17   mental idleness or *a·* is always
My. 233–20   for *a·*, dishonesty, sin, follow

ape

Ret. 63–22   * "The devil is but the *a·* of God."
No. 42–18   said that the devil is the *a·* of God.

apes

Mis. 294–18   thy offerings from asps and *a·*,

aphorisms

Mis. 316–21   tired *a·* and disappointed ethics ;
My. 291– 5   than a mere rehearsal of *a·*,

aping

Mis. 61– 7   *a·* the wisdom and magnitude of
No. 42–21   false claimants, *a·* its virtues,

Apocalypse

Un. 3– 9   of which we read in the *A·*
Pul. 27–23   * woman spoken of in the *A·*,
38–16   Genesis, *A·*, and Glossary.
No. 21– 2   the vision of the *A·*.

Apocalyptic

No. 27– 8   similitude of the *A·* pictures.

Apocryphal New Testament

Ret. 22– 6   essayed in the *A· N· T·*

Apollo

'00. 13–24   in the city of Thyatira was *A·*.
Peo. 4–23   pagan priests appointed *A·*

Apollyon

Mis. 190–29   in the Greek, *A·*, serpent, liar,

apologist

Mis. 227– 5   without friend and without *a·*.

apology

Mis. 119– 2   this were no *a·* for acting evilly.
134– 6   To reiterate such words of *a·*
Pan. 7–21   or a vague *a·* for contradictions.
'01. 28–18   my only *a·* for trying to follow it
My. 288– 5   incentive and sacrifice need no *a·*.

apostate

My. 131–13   *a·* praise return to its first love,

apostle (*see also* **apostle's**)

Mis. 46–21   what the *a·* meant by the
51–30   The *a·* James said,
77– 8   in those few words of the *a·*.
96–14   to the *a·* who declared it,
180–25   Here, the *a·* assures us that
181–23   The *a·* urges upon our acceptance
182–22   The *a·* indicates no personal plan
185–30   the *a·* first spake from their
186–28   As the *a·* proceeds in this line
188–12   but the *a·* says,
190–30   The *a·* Paul refers to this
200–11   *a·* Paul insists on the rare rule
200–21   the sweet sincerity of the *a·*,
255–13   recognition of what the *a·* meant
307–23   The *a·* saith, "Little— *I John* 5: 21.
368–20   in these words of the *a·*,
Ret. 54–16   belief cannot say with the *a·*,
Un. 1– 5   as the *a·* Peter declared
30–15   *a·* refers to the second Adam as
Pul. 6–29   renowned *a·* of anti-slavery,
81–24   * She is the *a·* of the true,
No. 39–10   Prophet and *a·* have glorified God
40– 1   The *a·* James said :
Pan. 10– 2   But what saith the *a·* ?
'00. 13–10   the *a·* justly regards as heathen,
Peo. 5– 1   the *a·* devoutly recommends

apostle's

Mis. 128– 6   with the *a·* injunction :
328–27   observe the *a·* admonition,
Un. 21– 1   *a·* description of mental processes
No. v– 2   according to the *a·* admonition,
'02. 8– 1   it emphasizes the *a·* declaration,
9–11   and fulfilling the *a·* saying :
Hea. 5–24   but on the *a·* rule,

apostles

Mis. 23– 7   the *a·*, demonstrated a divine
40–10   same method . . . Jesus and the *a·* used,
179–24   These flowers are floral *a·*.
Ret. 22– 6   Writers less wise than the *a·*
Un. 10– 6   Jesus and his *a·*, who have thus
56–18   *a·* suffered from the thoughts of
Pul. 65– 2   * is not confined to its original *a·*
85–14   * of Jesus and the *a·*,
Peo. 5– 4   prophets and *a·*, whose lives are
Po. 25–10   Fair floral *a·* of love,
My. 103–25   and the lives of prophets and *a·*.
106–32   prophets and *a·* and the Christians
111–23   Were the *a·* absurd and
153–31   flowers should be to us His *a·*,

apostleship
My. 191–14   will seal your a·.

apostolic
Mis. 245–26   and rejects a· Christianity,
Ret. 43– 2   since the a· days.
Pul. 54–11   * as were necessary in a· times.
'00. 12–27   Revelation of St. John in the a· age

apothecary
Peo. 6– 8   * physician, surgeon, a·,

apothegm
Mis. ix– 1   a· of a Talmudical philosopher

apparel
Mis. 373–17   soft raiment or gorgeous a· ;

apparent
Mis. 48– 6   One thing is quite a· ;
     60–11   make the unreality of both a·
     191–17   evils, a· wrong traits,
     239–21   Her a· pride at sharing in
Man. 95– 4   When the need is a·,
     100–12   becomes a· to the C. S. Board
Ret. 64– 7   makes a·, the real man,
     81–13   genuine goodness become so a·
Un. 63– 5   kingdom, not a· to material sense,
No. 6–22   is more a· than the adverse
'02. 3– 4   in the Orient are a·.
My. 87– 6   * a· to the most casual observer.
     94–16   * the a· permanency of C. S.
     222–26   as God's government becomes a·,
     239–14   and see their a· identity as
     265– 7   more a· to reason ;
     266–16   This flux . . . so generally a·,
     306–10   purpose of making the true a·.

apparently
Mis. 3–27   in a· deluding reason,
     241–13   big enough a· to neutralize
     378– 5   returned a· well,
Ret. 14– 6   He was a· as eager to
Hea. 19–23   divide one's faith a· between
My. 50–18   * over the a· discouraging outlook
     78–30   * a· understanding all they heard,
     92–28   * due a· to nothing save the

apparition
Pul. 34–16   and that it was my a·,"

appeal
Mis. 179– 6   This a· resolves itself into
     253–23   should it not a· to human sympathy?
Man. 60–19   a· to daily Christian endeavors
Ret. 54– 7   and a· to God for relief through
Un. 49– 5   simple a· to human consciousness.
Pul. 41– 2   * an a·, not for more money, but
     44–26   * without any special a·,
     83– 7   * courage to prosecute the a·.
Peo. 7–25   a· to mind to improve its subjects
My. 2–11   a· to reformers,
     10–15   * No a· has ever been made in
     32– 6   * in a heartfelt a· to the creator,
     90–14   * it is not the only source of a·.
     108–17   divine Mind is the sovereign a·,
     132–14   no longer to a· to human strength,
     219–31   a· to the gospel to save him from
     270–22   a· to Him as my witness to the truth
     316–17   dignified, eloquent a· to the press

appealed
My. 29–15   * that a· more to the eye,
     29–21   * a· to and fired the imagination.
     86–16   * a· to his brethren to give no more
     288–19   He never a· to matter

appeals
Mis. 63–25   a· to its hope and faith,
     105– 2   C. S., which a· intelligently to
     252–18   It a· to man as man ;
Pul. 83– 5   * and a· from Philip drunk to
'01. 35– 7   a· loudly to those asleep
My. 153–20   a· to an unknown power
     180–13   It a· alone to God,
     260–26   a· to all conditions,

appear
Mis. 56–19   will a· at the full revelation
     57–13   the postulate of error must a·.
     76–28   "When Christ, . . . shall a·,— Col. 3 : 4.
     76–29   shall ye also a· — Col. 3 : 4.
     78–22   C. S. will some time a·
     86– 5   but it doth not yet a·.
     97–31   hence, it doth not a·
     144– 9   subscription list on which a·
     175–11   and when this shall a·,
     196–21   Life that is God, good, shall a·,
     213–29   God's universal kingdom will a·,
     217–30   must disappear, for Spirit to a·.
     229– 3   whenever there a· the
     232–13   next to a· as its divine origin.
     236–29   whatever else may a·,

appear
Mis. 250–18   Unless these a·, I cast aside the
     252–12   and they should a· thus.
     285–28   may a· in the rôle of a superfine
     340–32   sickness, sin, and death still a·
     343–18   their pure perfection shall a·
     386– 2   Beyond the shadow, infinite a·
Man. 47–21   testimonials which a· in the
     98– 9   desirable that this correction shall a·,
Un. 40–21   Death can never alarm or even a·
     41–19   and when this Life shall a·
     41–27   these phenomena a· to go on
     49–18   One should a· real to us,
     49–20   * we make "the worse a· the better
     51– 1   everlasting facts of being a·,
     62–12   Then shall it a· that the true ideal
No. 31– 6   a· to-day in subtler forms
'00. 8–13   takes it off for his poverty to a·.
Peo. 8–23   Then shall C. S. again a·,
Po. 49– 4   Beyond the shadow, infinite a·
My. 22–26   * a· in their proper perspective.
     92– 6   * makes it a· that Science
     110–10   and the daystar will a·,
     154–17   the new-old vesture in which to a·
     227– 7   but when charity does a·,
     265–15   a· full-orbed in millennial glory ;
     329–16   * as they a· in that paper

appearance
Mis. 46– 7   adapted to destroy the a· of evil
     68– 5   include also man's changed a·
     147–25   He assumes no borrowed a·.
     379– 8   descriptive of the general a·,
Pul. 58–12   * Its a· is shown in the pictures
Rud. 1–17   in distinction from one's a·
My. 69– 7   * presenting an oval and dome a·
     100–12   * since the C. S. sect made its a·
     195–12   under an a· of indifference.
     234– 5   they give the a· of personal worship

appeared
Mis. 123–21   at-one-ment with Christ has a·
     164– 6   has a· in the ripeness of time,
     164–12   spiritual idea . . . a· as a star.
     214– 3   it a· hate to the carnal mind,
     216– 8   there a· a review of,
     239–17   sweet face a· in the vestibule,
     280– 2   Mind spake and form a·.
     359–22   period in which he personally a· ;
Ret. 25– 6   Their spiritual signification a· ;
     38–12   As it afterwards a·,
     93– 3   Christ, or the spiritual idea, a·
Un. 59–14   Jesus a· as a child,
     61– 5   Jesus first a· as a helpless
Pul. 33–19   * suddenly a· at his side,
     83–27   * there a· a great wonder— Rev. 12 : 1.
No. 36–20   in which he a· at his birth.
'01. 27–10   nothing has since a· that is
Hea. 17–23   a· through the false supposition of
Po. vi– 8   * a· in a Lynn, Mass., newspaper,
     vi–25   * which a· in various publications
My. 49–15   * a· in the Methodist Review
     138–26   * personally a· Mary Baker Eddy
     173– 2   * following letter a· in the
     232–10   A· IN THE C. S. SENTINEL,
     246–21   of the spirit and the Word a·,
     315–16   * personally a· R. D. Rounsevel
     319–19   * questions which have recently a·,
     329–11   * which a· in the Wilmington
     334–27   * obituary which a· in 1845
     346–19   * recent interview which a· in
     350–17   * a· under the heading "None good but

appearing
Mis. 1– 3   Chaldee watched the a· of a star ;
     17–22   human birth is the a· of a mortal,
     33–10   a· in the womanhood as well as
     73–28   It is the a· of divine law
     76–30   Science of Soul, Spirit, involves this a·,
     114–19   sin, in its myriad forms;
     161–15   the a· of this dual nature,
     165– 7   The last a· of Truth will be a
     165–10   The daystar of this a· is the
     168–19   "We behold the a· of the star!"
     320– 7   Christ's a· in a fuller sense
     320–18   shall be the sign of his a·
     338– 1   a· of good in an individual
     373–15   delineates Christ's a· in the flesh,
Ret. 70–20   The second a· of Jesus is,
Un. 63– 2   interpreted this a· as a risen
     63– 7   so-called a·, disappearing, and
Pan. 1–16   waiteth patiently the a·
'00. 7–18   and hath Christ a second a· ?
     7–29   wait for the full a· of Christ
Po. vi– 1   * a·, . . . in a book "Gems for You,"
My. 74–21   * intelligent and a happy a· body,
     103–11   In every age and at its every a·,
     185– 2   waited patiently for the a· of

appearing

My. 262–30 my conception of Truth's *a*.

appears

Mis. 14–21 What *a*. to mortals from their
15–25 the stature of man in Christ *a*.
41–20 produces all harmony that *a*.
77–30 where the miracle of grace *a*.,
105–24 Nothing *a*. to the physical senses but
147–27 is indeed what he *a*. to be,
165–16 perfect and eternal, *a*.
188– 7 that which *a*. second, material, and
259– 3 Whatever *a*. to be law,
276–22 and the bridegroom *a*.
291–12 at least it so *a*. in results.
371–14 he who deprecates their condition *a*. to,
Man. 104–17 if a discrepancy *a*. in any
Un. 25–10 and hence, whatever it *a*. to say
32–23 Here it *a*. that a *liar* was
38–18 is all that dies, or *a*. to die.
41–26 *a*. to both live and die,
Pul. 45–27 * This action, it *a*., was
No. 6–24 has shown that what *a*. real,
24–20 Then *a*. the grand verity of C. S. :
Po. 16– 3 hopeful though winter *a*.
My. 25–27 divinity *a*. in all its promise.
94– 5 * evidence *a*. in the concrete

appease

Mis. 123–12 to *a*. the anger of a so-called god
No. 35–11 It was not to *a*. the wrath of God,

appeased

Peo. 3– 8 to be *a*. by the sacrifice and

appeases

Un. 15–26 as a criminal *a*., with a money-bag,

appellative

Man. 64–20 this *a*. in the Church meant
'*00.* 3–24 contained this divine *a*.
My. 236–17 this *a*. seals the question of
302–15 the endearing *a*. "Mother,"

append

Pul. 88– 8 can *a*. only a few of the names

appendages

Mis. 17– 9 lay aside your material *a*.,

appended

Mis. x–13 a few articles are herein *a*.

appetite

Mis. 37–22 *a*. for alcohol yields to Science
71– 4 an *a*. for alcoholic drink
71– 5 saved many . . . from this fatal *a*.
137–24 control *a*., passion, pride, envy,
209–19 tend to rebuke *a*. and
297– 8 destroys the *a*. for alcoholic drinks.
Ret. 65–11 gratification of *a*. and passion,
Po. 32–16 As reason with *a*., pleasures deny,

appetites

Mis. 36–13 *A*., passions, anger, revenge,
114–20 passion, *a*., hatred, revenge,
231– 7 rich viands made busy many *a*. ;
240–22 Passions, *a*., pride, selfishness,
296–28 and the bad *a*. of men
324–15 *A*. and passions have
Pan. 10–29 Sin, sickness, *a*., and passions,
'*00.* 6–21 which destroys his false *a*.
'*01.* 27–19 habits and *a*. of mankind corrected,
30–22 or by the stress of the *a*.
Hea. 18–22 Pride, *a*., passions, envy, and
My. 339–28 Silence *a*., passion, and all that

appetizing

Mis. 275–29 and the fare is *a*.

applause

Mis. 325– 9 puffed up with the *a*. of the world :

apple

Mis. 22–28 A falling *a*. suggested to Newton
Ret. 24–14 was the falling *a*. that led me to
Rud. 8– 1 No rock brings forth an *a*. ;

apples

Mis. 346–23 like *a*. of gold — *Prov.* 25 : 11.
Ret. 4–15 orchards of *a*., peaches, pears,

appliances

Mis. 243–10 removed these *a*. the same day
Pul. 9– 9 whose *a*. warm this house,

applicable

Mis. 3– 9 *a*. to all the needs of man.
29– 4 Had it been *a*. only to his
138–20 My counsel is *a*. to the
200–13 *a*. to every stage and state of
259–29 *a*. to all the needs of man.
'*02.* 4–23 *a*. to all periods — past, present,
My. 19–30 These are *a*. words :
238–21 and *a*. to every human need.
302–18 name is not *a*. to me.

applicant

Mis. 256–18 send to each *a*. a notice
Man. 34– 7 *a*. must be a believer in the
36–23 admit said *a*. to membership.
37– 5 properly filled out by an *a*.
37–10 shall send to the *a*. a notice of
109–17 the *a*. will be notified,
111– 5 If the *a*. is a married woman
112– 8 If the *a*. is not a member of a

applicants

Man. 35–16 evidence of the loyalty of the *a*.
35–17 *A*. for membership who have not
38– 9 *A*. for membership in this Church,
89–10 *a*. AND GRADUATES.
109–11 Those who approve *a*. should
109–13 after being filled out by the *a*.,
110–10 All names, whether of *a*., . . . or
111– 1 heading
111–14 *A*. will find the chief points of
Ret. 47– 8 *a*. were rapidly increasing.

application

Mis. 25–10 in its direct *a*. to human needs.
38–19 *a*. to benefit the race,
44– 9 and its *a*. direct.
170–21 the spiritual *a*. bears upon
216– 1 in your *a*. of his words
289–10 at present the *a*. of scientific rules
298–13 special *a*. to Christian Scientists ;
375–18 * conscientious *a*. to detail,
Man. 37– 3 nor countersign an *a*. for membership
37– 7 If an *a*. for membership with
38– 7 the *a*. must be countersigned by
39– 2 and make *a*. for membership
72–12 proper *a*. made in accordance with
73–16 may become members . . . by *a*. to,
111– 2 In filling out the *a*. blank,
111– 9 two regular forms of *a*.
111–21 furnished special forms on *a*. to
112– 9 fill out his *a*. . . . according to
113– 1 heading
Ret. 36– 1 its *a*. in all time to those who
Pul. 31– 5 * present *a*. of the principles
'*01.* 27–12 The *a*. of C. S. is healing and
Peo. 12–22 *a*. of its Principle
My. 41–22 * brings into present and hourly *a*.
103–18 C. S. and its *a*. to the treatment of
146–20 their present *a*. to mankind,
328–24 * *a*. for license was made

applications

Mis. 273–23 one hundred and sixty *a*.
Man. 35– 3 whose *a*. are countersigned by
35– 9 *a*. FOR MEMBERSHIP.
35–10 *A*. for membership with
36– 4 *A*. for membership with
36–17 refuse to endorse their *a*.
36–24 All *a*. for membership must be
37– 1 Endorsing *A*.
38–10 whose *a*. are correctly prepared,
39– 6 their *a*. shall be void.
71– 7 nor written on *a*. for membership
109– 2 *A*. for Church Membership.
109– 6 eligible to countersign *a*.
109–12 should have *a*. returned to them
109–18 new *a*. will be required,
110– 3 prevent *a*. being duplicated
111–19 whose teachers refuse, . . . to sign *a*.
Ret. 47– 7 *a*. from persons desiring to

applied

Mis. 180–28 This term, as *a*. to man,
353–14 a man who *a*. for work,
Pul. 46–23 * *a*. herself, like other girls,
54–17 * *a*. it where the greatest good could
'*00.* 5–10 *A*. to Deity, Father and Mother are
My. 30–29 * *a*. for admission at the ten o'clock
135– 6 declaration may be *a*. to old age,
162–13 *a*. to building, embellishing, and

applies

Mis. 203–14 medicine *a*. it physically,
Man. 32–24 This By-Law *a*. to Readers in all
47–21 This By-Law *a*. to testimonials which
65–17 *a*. to their official functions.
99–15 By-Law *a*. to all States except
Rud. 1–16 Blackstone the word *personal* to
My. 180– 8 healing Christianity which *a*. to all
250–18 By-law *a*. only to C. S. churches in

apply

Mis. 39– 1 Many who *a*. for help are
69–28 *a*. to him for information about
Man. 36–19 *a*. to the Clerk of this Church,
89–19 may *a*. to the Board of Education
95–10 may *a*. through their clerks
98–10 *a*. for aid to the Committee
102–16 this rule shall not *a*. to

apply

Ret.	59–11	even as mortals *a·* finite terms to God,
Un.	12– 4	*a·* to the waiting grain the
Pul.	51– 5	* *a·* themselves to a matter like
'01.	27– 7	* *a·* them more rationally to human
My.	220– 6	as to *a·*, on the basis of C. S.,
	230– 9	rules *a·* not to one member only,

applying

Mis.	44–28	*a·* this mental remedy or antidote
Man.	88–18	*a·* for admission to this Board
Ret.	59–10	then *a·* this rule to a
Un.	27–12	*A·* these distinctions to evil and
'01.	1–23	by feeling and *a·* the nature and

appoint

Mis.	335–10	*a·* him his portion — *Matt.* 24 : 51.
Man.	29–13	shall *a·* five suitable members
	69–16	*a·* a proper member of this Church
	94–16	shall *a·* a Circuit Lecturer.
	96– 2	not *a·* a lecture for Wednesday
	99– 1	*a·* a Committee on Publication
	99– 9	*a·* a Committee on Publication
	99–12	can *a·* a Committee on Publication
	100– 5	Readers shall *a·* said candidate.
	100–18	*a·* another Committee to fill the
	101– 5	*a·* an assistant manager,
My.	339–25	but he did not *a·* a fast.

appointed

Man.	17–14	Mrs. Eddy was *a·* on the committee
	76–18	Its members shall be *a·* annually
	97– 4	shall be *a·* by The Mother Church
	99–20	*a·* by the C. S. Board of Directors,
	99–26	*a·* by the First and Second Readers
Ret.	21– 3	a guardian was *a·* him,
	21–11	was *a·* United States Marshal
	32– 1	its divinely *a·* human mission,
Pul.	29–12	* Before the *a·* hour every seat in
No.	7–18	God has *a·* for Christian Scientists
'01.	19– 2	prayer is a divinely *a·* means of
Peo.	3–28	way that our Lord has *a·* ;
	4–23	pagan priests *a·* Apollo
My.	49–13	* Mrs. Eddy was *a·* on the committee
	340– 2	no record of his observing *a·* fasts.

appointee

Man.	69–17	*a·* shall go immediately

appointing

Mis.	208–19	in the way of God's *a·*.

appointment

Mis.	215–16	in the way of His *a·*,
Man.	80–19	the right to fill the same by *a·* ;
	99–24	*A·*.
My.	223– 3	without previous *a·* by letter.
	283– 1	chapter sub-title
	283– 6	Your *a·* of me as *Fondateur*
	310–23	*a·* on the staff of the Governor of

appointments

My.	140–17	by those with whom I have *a·*.

appoints

Mis.	130–30	God anoints and *a·* to
Chr.	53–11	The Way in Science He *a·*,
Ret.	90–30	He *a·* and He anoints His

appreciable

My.	107–14	without harm and without *a·* effect.

appreciate

Mis.	165–20	can neither *a·* nor appropriate his
	317– 6	to *a·* the signs of the times ;
Ret.	73–13	fall to *a·* individual character.
Pul.	87–15	I fully *a·* your kind intentions.
'00.	3–12	workers who *a·* a life,
My.	149–21	to *a·* or to demonstrate Christian
	174– 5	I greatly *a·* the courtesy
	194–22	I deeply *a·* it,
	323–27	* may not have been able to *a·*

appreciated

Mis.	88–11	whose thought is *a·* by many
	305–20	* will be particularly *a·*
	365–31	To be *a·*, it must be . . . understood
Pul.	10–21	If you are less *a·* to-day
No.	11–14	To be *a·*, Science must be understood
'00.	7–12	loved the Bible and *a·* its worth
'01.	1– 8	better *a·*, than ever before,
My.	26–14	unexpected . . . but not the less *a·*.
	61–31	* I *a·* as never before the faithful,
	330–11	* are *a·* by all,

appreciating

'02.	20–23	while gratefully *a·* the privilege

appreciation

Mis.	224–19	*a·* of everything beautiful,
	263–28	without credit, *a·*, or
Pul.	85–26	* the *a·* of her labors
My.	37– 9	* *a·* of all that you have done
	48–15	* splendid *a·* of her efforts
	51–26	* *a·* of Mrs. Eddy's tireless labors,

appreciation

My.	51–31	* *a·* of her earnest endeavors,
	62–23	* thankful *a·* of your wise counsel,
	176– 3	IN *A·* OF A GIFT OF FIFTY DOLLARS
	197–11	*a·* of your labor and success
	316–24	sound *a·* of the rights of

apprehend

Ret.	28–10	in order to *a·* Spirit.
	88–12	*a·* the living beauty of Love,
Un.	43–23	enable us to *a·*, or lay hold upon,
Pul.	35–14	in order to *a·* Spirit.
Rud.	6–24	The proof of what you *a·*,
No.	v–13	*a·* the pure spirituality of Truth.
Peo.	3–21	begins wrongly to *a·* the infinite,
My.	282–13	to *a·* more, we must practise

apprehended

Mis.	65–20	*a·* by those who understand my
Ret.	25– 6	and I *a·* for the first time,
Un.	1–12	so little *a·* and demonstrated by
	43–25	"*a·* of . . . Christ Jesus," — *Phil.* 3 : 12.
Pul.	35– 1	I *a·* the spiritual meaning
No.	20– 9	may seem distant . . . until better *a·*.
'00.	6– 5	not myself to have *a·* : — *Phil.* 3 : 13.
'01.	7–25	He cannot be *a·* through
My.	90–29	* can be readily *a·*.

apprehending

Mis.	261–27	*a·* the moral law so clearly

apprehends

Un.	40–27	A sense material *a·* nothing
	58–13	*a·* Christ as "the way." — *John* 14 : 6.

apprehensible

Ret.	26–13	divinely natural and *a·* ;

apprehension

Mis.	74– 6	a new *a·* of the true basis
	139–28	in advance of the erring mind's *a·*.
	201–22	beyond the common *a·* of sinners ;
	363–31	a more spiritual *a·* of the
Ret.	26–30	to the *a·* of the age.
	30–13	necessary to the right *a·* of
	32– 2	bearing . . . to my *a·*,
	47– 1	The *a·* of what has been,
	79– 4	nor cometh this *a·* from the
	81–17	blunders which arise from wrong *a·*.
Un.	5– 6	will increase their *a·* of God,
	7– 1	will be magnified in the *a·* of
	17–15	A right *a·* of the wonderful
	61–13	toward the *a·* of its nothingness,
'01.	11– 5	has risen to human *a·*,
	14–28	scientific *a·* of this grand verity.
My.	183–12	Spiritual *a·* unfolds, transfigures,

approach

Mis.	30–29	as we *a·* spirituality,
	180–13	shuddered at her material *a·* ;
	233–20	some fall short, others will *a·* it ;
	352–12	lengthen as they *a·* the light,
Un.	4– 3	*a·* Him and become like Him.
	13– 5	Men must *a·* God reverently,
	57– 4	warn mortals of the *a·* of danger
No.	16–24	in proportion as mortals *a·* Spirit,
'00.	4– 9	neither *a·* to monotheism
'01.	14–23	against the *a·* of thieves.
Hea.	16–25	through which it is impossible to *a·*
Peo.	7–31	must spiritualize to *a·* Him,
My.	93–18	* prone to *a·* it in a spirit of
	178–29	nearest *a·* to the sayings of

approached

Pul.	26–20	* The "Mother's Room" is *a·* by
	76– 4	* *a·* through a superb archway of
'02.	15–13	*a·* the mythical.

approaches

Mis.	2–17	time *a·* when divine Life,
	363– 1	an erring so-called mind *a·*
Pul.	25–15	* and marble *a·*.
	27– 3	* in marble *a·* and rich carving,
	49–28	* the visitor as he *a·* Pleasant View.
My.	344–15	gradual *a·* to Soul's perfection."

approaching

Mis.	321–28	offered upon this *a·* occasion.
'01.	28– 2	*a·* the last stage of the

approbation

Mis.	214–27	in the recognition or *a·* of it.
My.	166– 3	will continue with divine *a·*.

appropriate

Mis.	165–20	can neither appreciate nor *a·* his
	263–28	*a·* my ideas and discovery,
	280–23	who in *a·* language and metaphor
	304– 6	* the most *a·* place
	358– 6	the only *a·* seals for C. S.
Man.	61–20	of an *a·* religious character
Pul.	28–10	* in *a·* decorative effect.
My.	24–31	* could be no more *a·* time for
	80–17	* an *a·* reading from the Bible,

appropriate
My. 85–28   * in its symmetrical and *a·* design.
    169–19   I was rejoiced at the *a·* beauty of
    259–27   most *a·* and proper exercise.
    281–19   * seems to offer an *a·* occasion for

appropriated
Mis. 150–26   God is universal ; . . . *a·* by no sect.
    249– 8   false report that I have *a·* other
Ret. 51– 4   to be *a·* for the erection,
My. 158– 1   to be *a·* in building a granite

appropriates
Mis. 203–15   metaphysics *a·* it topically as

appropriating
Mis. 299–32   does it justify you in *a·* them,
Ret. 75– 7   *a·* my language and ideas,

approval
Mis. 262–27   little need of words of *a·*
    383– 4   met with the universal *a·*
Man. 25– 9   *a·* of the Pastor Emeritus.
    28– 2   the *a·* of the Pastor Emeritus.
    35–20   only by *a·* from students of
    36–11   shall have the *a·* and signature of
    63–22   the *a·* of Mary Baker Eddy.
    65–24   the *a·* of Mary Baker Eddy.
    78–14   the *a·* of Mary Baker Eddy.
    78–26   shall be reported, . . . for their *a·*.
    79–14   to Mrs. Eddy for her written *a·*.
    80–21   subject to her *a·*,
    85–21   *a·* of The C. S. Board of Directors.
    88–15   *a·* of the Pastor Emeritus.
    89– 8   on receiving her *a·* shall be elected
    93– 7   subject to the *a·* of the
    101– 4   with the *a·* of the Pastor Emeritus.
No. 40– 5   receive, a material sense of *a·* ;
'00. 13–30   being bidden to write the *a·* of
My. 36– 5   * rose as one to indicate their *a·*
    142–11   Accept my thanks for your *a·* of
    230–18   I read with pleasure your *a·*
    359–25   * with the latter's unqualified *a·*.

approve
Man. 38– 1   qualified to *a·* for membership
    109– 4   are eligible to *a·* candidates
    109–11   Those who *a·* applicants should
My. 240–24   * Does Mrs. Eddy *a·* of class teaching :
    358–30   *a·* the By-laws of The Mother Church,

approved
Man. 26–22   after the candidate is *a·* by
    35– 3   who are *a·*, and whose applications
    94–17   His term of office, if *a·*,
My. 49–22   * minutes . . . were read and *a·*.
    245– 1   over and above the *a·* schools of

approver
Man. 38– 5   If the *a·* is not a loyal student

approvers
Man. 110–10   applicants, *a·*, or countersigners,

approves
Man. 82– 1   *a·*, and publishes the books and
My. 240–18   *a·* or disapproves according to

approximate
Un. 64–10   The nearer we *a·* to such a Mind,
Pul. 22–12   *a·* the understanding of C. S.
    52– 6   * a faith *a·* to that of these
No. 38–17   as mortals *a·* the understanding of
My. 58– 1   * a faith *a·* to that of these

approximately
My. 96–19   * cost *a·* two million dollars.

approximates
Mis. 374–12   the one illustrating my poem *a·* it.
My. 31–11   * which *a·* two millions of dollars,

approximation
Mis. 161–12   Jesus' *a·* to this state of being

A Priest of the Church
My. 299– 3   signature "A *P·* of the *C·*,"

April
    (see **months**)

April's
    (see **months**)

apt
Mis. 155–25   I shall be *a·* to forward their letters
    279– 6   too *a·* to weep with those who weep,
    287–29   and he will be *a·* to please you ;
    300–31   more *a·* to recover than he who
    371–17   self-interest in this mixing is *a·* to
'00. 3–16   Adam-race are not *a·* to worship the
'01. 25– 6   is *a·* to be the cross,
My. 224– 9   not *a·* to be correctly drawn.
    328–12   * *a·* also to be pleased with the fact

aptness
Mis. 264–16   *a·* to assimilate pure and abstract

Araby
Mis. 110– 2   The costly balm of *A·*,

Arbiter
Un. 30–27   reflect the Life of the divine *A·*.

arbiter
Mis. 83–16   you are the *a·* of your own fate,
    152–12   as a dictator, *a·*, or ruler,

arbitrary
Mis. 148–11   not *a·* opinions nor dictatorial
Man. 3– 7   not *a·* opinions nor dictatorial
My. 49– 6   * and control, in no *a·* sense,

arbitrated
My. 286– 8   should be, *a·* wisely, fairly ;

arbitration
My. 281–25   * advancement of the cause of *a·*."
    284–26   to conciliate by *a·* all quarrels

arbutus
Mis. 329–23   paint in pink the petals of *a·*,

archers
Mis. 277– 9   *a·* aim at Truth's mouthpiece ;

arches
My. 46– 1   * in symmetrical *a·*,
    68– 5   * supported on four *a·*
    68–26   * plaster work for the great *a·*
    78– 9   * *a·* in the several facades.

archipelago
Mis. 368–16   upas-tree in the eastern *a·*.

architect
Mis. 4¹–19   Mind is the *a·* that builds its own
My. 16–19   * *a·* and the builder of the new
    71–28   * aim and object of the *a·* :
    89– 8   * *a·* has joined lightness and grace

architectural
Pul. 9–13   quibbled over an *a·* exigency,
    65–19   * whose *a·* construction and
My. 67–21   * marvel of *a·* beauty.
    68–22   * It has an *a·* stone screen
    74–15   * one of the finest *a·* achievements
    84–14   * crown for the other *a·* efforts
    85–17   * among the *a·* beauties of
    86– 2   * unaccustomed to fine *a·* effects,
    88–13   * *a·* symbolisms of aspiration

architecturally
My. 87–18   * an edifice so handsome *a·*.

architecture
Pul. 24–24   * The *a·* is Romanesque throughout.
My. 31–17   * beauty and the grace of the *a·*.
    71– 7   * chapter sub-title
    71–10   * a stunning piece of *a·*
    71–18   * For in its interior *a·* it is
    71–20   * traditions of church interior *a·*
    72– 3   * traditions of interior church *a·*.
    77– 2   * its great size, beautiful *a·*,
    309–23   * building of rudimentary *a·*."
    309–25   style of *a·* at that date.

archway
Pul. 76– 4   * superb *a·* of Italian marble

Arctic
Pul. 76–16   * brought from the *A·* regions.

Arcturus
Mis. 174–12   Above *A·* and his sons,

ardent
Ret. 90–19   like the *a·* mother
Pul. 73– 5   * an *a·* follower after God.

ardently
My. 50– 5   * labored faithfully and *a·*,

arduous
Hea. 14–18   most *a·* task I ever performed.
My.   v–19   * years of *a·* preliminary labor,
    51–31   * earnest endeavors, her *a·* labors,

area
My. 67– 9   * *A·* of site . . . 40,000 sq. ft.

areas
Ret. 4–21   covered *a·* of rich acres,

argue
Mis. 31– 4   To mentally *a·* in a manner that
    31–18   *a·* against his own convictions of
Hea. 10–20   *a·* with yourself on the side of
    10–23   or to *a·* stronger for sorrow than

argued
My. 160–22   Physical science has sometimes *a·*

argues
'01. 24– 3   *a·* that matter is not *without* the

arguing
Mis. 119–12   always be found *a·* for itself,
Un. 21– 5   perpetually *a·* with ourselves ;
Hea. 1–12   before *a·* with the world
My.   6– 1   *a·* for the plaintiff in favor of

argument

Mis.	32– 1	with his wrong a·,
	59–18	*Is not all a· mind over mind?*
	116–21	The ultimate . . . is not an a· :
	119–18	not an a· either for pessimism or
	220– 6	The healer begins by mental a·.
	221– 3	by a false mental a· ;
	222–15	The malicious mental a·
	319– 5	closes the a· of aught besides Him,
	350–23	soundness of the a· used.
	352–25	or he must, through a· and
	359– 5	you continue the mental a· in
Ret.	21–30	a·, with its rightful conclusions,
Un.	20–10	By a reverse process of a·
Rud.	9–22	an audible or even a mental a·,
'01.	3–20	* but this is no a· that Love is
Hea.	7–28	it contains no a· for a creed
My.	318–27	continued with a long a·,

arguments

Mis.	12–22	human mind in its silent a·,
	220– 9	His mental and oral a· aim to
	350–26	I issue no a·,
	350–29	such a· only as promote health
	351– 6	a· which, perverted, are
Un.	9–14	their a· and conclusions as to
	33– 1	lesser a· which prove matter to be
My.	211–13	by unseen, silent a·.

aright

Mis.	51–18	they will lead him a· :
	84–28	and teaches Life's lessons a·.
	108–12	hence the utility of knowing evil a·,
	116–13	filling the measures of life's music a·,
	125–15	"to know a· is Life eternal,"
	177–20	and answer a· !
	235–20	learn God a·, and know
	235–23	must start the wheels of reason a·,
	299– 4	The error that is seen a· as error,
	352– 3	quickened to behold a· the error,
Un.	14– 4	it was not at first done a·.
Pul.	69–23	* must understand these laws a·.
No.	40–22	and control a· the thought
'02.	17– 7	When mortals learn to love a· ,
Peo.	6–16	when we learn God a·,
My.	43– 6	* to order a· the affairs of daily life.
	193– 2	Him whom to know a· is life
	203– 4	Pray a· and demonstrate your prayer ;
	248–22	to conceive God a· you must be good.
	261–12	mould a· the first impressions

arise

Mis.	196–26	a· to spiritual recognition of being,
	245– 7	*A·, let us go hence :— John* 14 : 31.
	303–12	therefore no queries should a·
Man.	60– 8	a· among the members
Ret.	11–15	Hero and sage a· to show
	81–17	which a· from wrong apprehension.
Un.	52–18	From this falsehood a· the
Pul.	53–13	* "A·, go thy way :— Luke 17 : 19.
Rud.	10– 9	These beliefs a· from the subjective
No.	4–21	they do not a· from the
	45–11	a· from a spiritual lack,
'01.	27– 6	* I look to see some St. Paul a·
'02.	9– 9	Truth will a· in human thought
Peo.	8–22	I say unto thee, a·."— Mark 5 : 41.
Po.	60–12	Hero and sage a· to show
	79–10	darkling sense, a·, go hence !
My.	183–26	"A·, shine ; for thy light — Isa. 60 : 1.
	359–27	Awake and a· from this temptation

arisen

My.	321–18	* circumstances which have a·
	346–23	* Various conjectures having a· as to

arises

Mis.	59–23	a· from the success that one
Ret.	60–30	a· from the fallibility of sense,
Un.	8–15	a· from their deleterious effects,
No.	5– 9	Disease a· from a false and material

arising

Mis.	24–32	supposed effect a· from false claims
Ret.	47– 9	had shown the dangers a· from
My.	335–20	* excitement which was fast a·,

aristocracy

My.	72– 8	* members of the titled a·

aristocratic

Pul.	46–12	* A· to the backbone,

Aristotle

Mis.	226–18	A· was asked what a person could

arithmetic

My.	8–18	* my faint knowledge of a·
	311–31	* reached long division in a·,"

ark

Mis.	92–28	attempting to steady the a· of Truth,
Ret.	84–16	attempting to steady the a· of Truth,
No.	20–25	emerged from the a·,

ark

My.	188– 9	your a· of the covenant will

Arlington, Massachusetts

Mis.	225– 2	Mr. Rawson, of A·, M·,

arm

Mis.	114–18	They cannot a· too thoroughly
	183–21	He to whom the a· of the Lord is
	389–13	His a· encircles me, and mine,
Un.	39–10	He to whom the a· of the Lord is
Pul.	7–15	with His outstretched a·.
No.	32–13	Mind-healing lifts with a steady a·,
	44–22	through the civil a· of government,
Pan.	14–17	right a· of His righteousness.
'01.	1– 5	never lack God's outstretched a·
'02.	14–26	outstretched a· of infinite Love
Peo.	8–20	controls the muscles of the a·.
Po.	4–12	His a· encircles me, and mine,
My.	42–30	* with an outstretched a·" — Deut. 26 : 8.
	355–11	strong supporting a· to religion

Armageddon

Mis.	177– 5	The great battle of A· is upon us.

armament

Un.	6–27	manual of their spiritual a·.
My.	127–25	Unlike Russia's a·, ours is
	286–11	a· of navies is necessary,
	355–14	the untiring spiritual a·.

armaments

Mis.	xii– 2	privileged a· of peace.

armed

Mis.	5–18	a· with the power of Spirit,
	10– 9	He has called His own, a· them,
'01.	32–14	they a· quickly, aimed deadly,
My.	277–23	a· with power girt for the hour.
	278–11	faith a· with the understanding

Armenians

Mis.	123– 2	butchers the helpless A·,

armies

Mis.	338–19	a· of earth press hard upon you.
Pul.	83–18	* overcome our own allied a· of evil

armor

Mis.	xii– 3	With a· on, I continue the march,
	114–17	They must always have on a·,
	120–15	with a· on, not laid down
	171–30	keep bright their invincible a· ;
'02.	19–12	Meekness is the a· of a Christian,
Peo.	14–14	put on the whole a· of Truth ;
My.	189– 2	Clad in invincible a·,
	210– 8	Good thoughts are an impervious a· ;

armored

Mis.	176–29	divine energy wherewith we are a·

armors

My.	351–25	God gives, elucidates, a·, and tests

arms

Mis.	120–15	Christian success is under a· ,
	124–23	stretch out our a· to God.
	140–23	put back into the a· of Love,
	270–16	babe that twines its loving a· about
	398–16	Take them in Thine a· ;
Ret.	46–22	Take them in Thine a· ;
	80–23	carries his lambs in his a·
Pul.	17–21	Take them in Thine a· ;
	48–21	* her family coat of a·
No.	15–10	have the civil and religious a·
Pan.	14–12	for her victory under a·,
Po.	14–20	Take them in Thine a· ;
My.	113–19	in the a· of divine Love,
	124–11	world's a· outstretched to us,

Armstrong, Joseph

Pul.	43– 8	* Joseph A·, Stephen A. Chase, and
	59–21	* on the platform sat Joseph A·,
	86–10	* William B. Johnson, Joseph A·,
	87– 7	* signature
My.	21–29	* signature

Armstrong, C. S. D., Joseph

My.	296–11	Joseph A·, C.S.D., is not dead,

army

Mis.	334– 2	in the a· of heaven, — Dan. 4 : 35.
Pul.	63–19	* great hold she has upon this a·
	80–21	* an a· of well-meaning people
	83–13	* as an a· with banners?" — Song 6 : 10.
My.	98– 3	* a twentieth of the C. S. a·
	175–15	provisions for the a·,

Arnold, Sir Edwin

Mis.	153–23	Sir Edwin A·, to whom I presented

aroma

Mis.	20– 3	a· of Jesus' own words,

arose

Mis.	28–18	he a· above the illusion of matter.
	164–30	a· from the testimony of the senses.
	249–20	The report that I was dead a·

arose

Mis.	345–28	thence *a·* the rumor that it was
	351–11	*a·* solely from mental malicious
Ret.	50–28	the blessings which *a·* therefrom.
Pul.	79–26	* But when C. S. *a·*,
Po.	68–19	When the star of our friendship *a·*

around

Mis.	54– 5	the planets to revolve *a·* it
	210– 8	post *a·* it placards warning people
	230–12	Rushing *a·* smartly is no proof of
	279–17	went seven times *a·* these walls,
Ret.	5–25	* was felt by all *a·* her.
Pul.	37–23	* not to centre too closely *a·*
	39– 6	* flows *a·* our incompleteness,
	42– 2	* sidewalks *a·* the church were
No.	6–18	revolves *a·* our planet,
	6–21	error of the revolution of the sun *a·*
Po.	25– 7	*A·* you in memory rise !
My.	13–11	* planets, revolving *a·* it.
	99–20	* baskets when passed *a·* were
	113–24	all *a·* us is demonstrated
	161– 1	hung *a·* the necks of the wicked.
	186– 5	cluster *a·* this rock-ribbed church
	192–15	My heart hovers *a·* your churches
	343– 3	* and works *a·* a question

arouse

Un.	6–25	declarations about sin . . . must *a·*,

aroused

Mis.	352–30	moral sense be *a·* to reject the
Ret.	13–10	*a·* by this erroneous doctrine,
No.	1–11	when public sentiment is *a·*,
'01.	26–16	land is reached and the world *a·*,
My.	252–27	You are not *a·* to this action by
	308– 7	man is *a·* to thought or action

arranged

No.	9–27	* it is "knowledge, duly *a·* and

arrangement

Mis.	136–27	will be accommodated by this *a·*.
	283– 8	and suit one's self in the *a·*
Ret.	82–28	*a·* of my last revision, in 1890,
Pul.	65–19	* *a·* of statuary and paintings
My.	83– 6	* members of the local *a·* committee

arrangements

Pul.	49–19	* something of her domestic *a·*,
My.	75–13	* all the preliminary *a·* for

arranging

Mis.	330–17	*a·* in the beauty of holiness
My.	173–26	for *a·* the details and allowing
	319–24	* in analyzing and *a·* the topics,

arrant

Mis.	163–10	*a·* hypocrite and to dull disciples

array

Mis.	299–19	*a·* myself in them, and
Po.	15–10	enchantment in beauty's *a·*,

arrayed

Mis.	246–26	*a·* against the rights of man,
No.	5–19	If disease . . . is *a·* against being,
Hea.	2– 4	prejudices *a·* against it,

arrest

Mis.	79–31	because they chance to be under *a·*
	117– 7	*a·* the former, and obey the latter.
	121–21	*a·*, trial, and crucifixion of
	231–18	to *a·* the peel !
	300–10	liable to *a·* for infringement of
My.	88–16	* which must *a·* public attention.
	314–22	prevented Dr. Patterson's *a·*

arrested

Mis.	40– 3	its power would be *a·* if one
'01.	17–13	would not have *a·* public attention
My.	13– 9	my attention was *a·* by
	222–15	Jesus was not *a·* . . . because of
	222–18	but he was *a·* because,
	227–10	*a·* for manslaughter because
	314–20	about to have Dr. Patterson *a·*

arrival

Mis.	69–16	Upon my *a·* I found him barely alive,
Ret.	40– 5	On my *a·* my hostess told me
My.	54– 9	* before the *a·* of the pastor,
	244– 1	I have awaited your *a·* before

arrive

Mis.	183–30	will *a·* at the true status of man
	198– 4	To *a·* at this point of unity
	341–11	to *a·* at the results of Science :
Hea.	4–21	*a·* at a proper conception of
	11–20	"until you *a·* at no medicine."
	14– 3	Medicine will not *a·* at the science of
My.	73–28	* due to *a·* in Boston to-night,
	74– 7	* who will *a·* in this city just about
	357– 3	*a·* at the spiritual fulness of God,

arrived

Mis.	142–13	Each day since they *a·* I have

arrived

Man.	35– 2	who have *a·* at the age of twelve
Ret.	23–13	when the moment *a·* of the heart's
My.	96–22	* day set for the dedication *a·*
	217–12	shall have *a·* at legal age,

arrives

Mis.	172–13	and he *a·* at fulness of stature ;

arrogance

My.	41– 9	* Pride, *a·*, and self-will are

arrogant

Mis.	92–27	in times past, *a·* ignorance and
Ret.	84–15	In times past, *a·* pride,
Un.	17–13	taught the *a·* Pharisees that,

arrogated

My.	340–14	has *a·* to itself the prerogative of

arrow

Mis.	223–30	mental *a·* shot from another's bow
	330– 6	wherein no *a·* wounds the dove
	387–12	*a·* that doth wound the dove
No.	3– 3	shoot its *a·* at the idea which
Po.	6– 7	*a·* that doth wound the dove
My.	290–22	where no *a·* wounds the eagle

art

Mis.	107– 4	*A·* must not prevail over Science.
	232– 7	is pushing towards perfection in *a·*,
	365– 7	what a child's love of pictures is to *a·*.
	372–17	* are truly a work of *a·*,
	372–26	Not by aid of . . . could I copy *a·*,
	372–27	but the *a·* of C. S.,
	373– 2	illustrate the simple nature of *a·*.
	374–12	and its *a·* will rise triumphant ;
	375– 5	The truest *a·* of C. S.
	375– 7	to delineate *this a·*.
	375–13	* and their great works of *a·*
	375–14	* an idea of what constitutes true *a·*.
	375–16	* the study of music and *a·*.
	375–19	* which is the foundation of true *a·*.
	375–22	* In other words, the *a·* is perfect.
	375–28	* to see produced to-day that *a·*
	375–29	* the only true *a·*
	376– 1	* the *a·* is perfect.
	376– 2	* It is the true *a·* of the oldest,
	393– 7	*A·* and Science, all unweary,
	393–17	*A·* hath bathed this isthmus-lordling
Ret.	95– 5	* skill in comfort's *a·* :
Pul.	65–24	* and so was memorialized in *a·*
	66– 1	* what they term the divine *a·* of healing,
	78– 3	* examples of the goldsmith's *a·*
No.	18–16	what a child's love of pictures is to *a·*.
'00.	11–16	his composition is the triumph of *a·*,
Peo.	6–11	* "The *a·* of medicine consists in
Po.	2– 4	chisel of the sculptor's *a·*
	51–12	*A·* and Science, all unweary,
	52– 1	*A·* hath bathed this isthmus-lordling
My.	70–20	* is replete with rare bits of *a·*,
	124–18	reflects man and *a·* pencils him,
	270–29	than I would because of his *a·*.
	270–31	control both religion and *a·*
	327–25	* who practise the *a·* of healing,"
	328–29	* practise the *a·* of healing for pay,

Article

Man.	36–13	provided for in Sect. 4 of this *A·*.
	72– 8	conformity with Sect. 7 of this *A·*,
	(see also **Church Manual**)	

article

Mis.	88–10	the author of the *a·* in question
	132–26	I read in your *a·* these words :
	133– 2	at the close of your *a·*,
	242– 2	The *a·* of Professor T——,
Man.	48– 8	an *a·* that is uncharitable
	53–25	an *a·* that is false or unjust,
	71– 5	*a·* "The" must not be used
	82– 6	A book or an *a·* of which
	98– 3	corrected a false newspaper *a·*
	98–13	*last proof sheet* of such an *a·*
	98–15	papers containing such an *a·*
	112– 4	The *a·* "the" . . . must not be
Pul.	29– 7	* speak, a little later, in this *a·*.
	55– 5	* In a previous *a·* we have referred
	74– 4	* *a·* published in the *Herald*
	84–18	* not undertake to speak in this *a·*.
'01.	21– 7	*a·* published in the *New York Journal,*
My.	237–21	The *a·* on the Church Manual by
	254–19	* following extract from your *a·*
	266–12	*a·* on the decrease of students in
	272–21	* an *a·* sent to us by Mrs. Eddy,
	303–12	his *a·*, of which I have seen only
	316–11	The *a·* in the January number of
	327–11	* I know the enclosed *a·* will
	328– 7	* The following *a·*, copied from

articles

Mis.	x–10	most of these *a·* were
	x–12	a few *a·* are herein appended.

articles
Mis.   x–13   To some *a·* are affixed data,
     305–20   * *a·* of historic interest
     313–15   I was impressed by the *a·*
Pul. 88– 1   chapter sub-title
     88– 5   uniformly kind and interesting *a·*
     88– 9   whose *a·* are reluctantly omitted.
My. 18–29   It contained the following *a·* :
     82–10   * trunks and smaller *a·* of baggage

articulate
Ret. 27–25   experience and confidence to *a·* it.
'01. 30– 9   struggles to *a·* itself.
My. 133–26   this inmost something becomes *a·*,

articulated
Mis. 100– 2   were *a·* in a decaying language,
     163–14   His words were *a·* in the language of

articulates
Un. 60– 5   With the same breath he *a·* truth and

artisans
Pul. 41– 1   * forth from the hands of the *a·*
My. 66–19   * *A·* and artists are working

artist (see also artist's)
Mis. 62– 6   an *a·* in painting a landscape.
     230–28   needing but . . . the touch of an *a·*
     270– 5   What *a·* would question the skill of
     372–17   * the *a·* seems quite familiar with
     373– 4   My *a·* at the easel objected,

artistic
Mis. 308–20   scholarly, *a·*, and scientific notices
     374–32   is it less *a·* or less natural?
My. 67–24   * never was a more *a·* effect reached.

artist's
Mis. 393– 4   Gives the *a·* fancy wings.
Po. 51– 9   Gives the *a·* fancy wings.

artists
Mis. 372–10   from *a·* and poets.
     372–20   and most distinguished *a·*.
Rud. 9 13   what the models . . . are to *a·*.
My. 66–19   * Artisans and *a·* are working

artless
Mis. 100– 1   to *a·* listeners and dull disciples.
     357–13   by the wayside, on *a·* listeners.
Ret. 35–22   beneath the stroke of *a·* workmen.

arts
Mis. 232–20   most important of all *a·*,— healing.
Pul. 47–20   * definitions of these two healing *a·*.
'00. 12–16   Magical *a·* prevailed at Ephesus ;

Asa
Mis. 245– 5   *A* . . . sought not to— *II Chron.* 16 : 12.
     245– 6   *A·* slept with his— *II Chron,* 16 : 13.

ascend
Mis. 232–16   meekly to *a·* the hill of Science,
     323–18   Would ye *a·* the mountain,
     327–17   *a·* faster than themselves,
     356–13   songs should *a·* from the mount of
Ret. 85–11   upon which angelic thoughts *a·*
My. 34– 1   Who shall *a·* into the hill— *Psal.* 24 : 3.
     37– 6   * *a·* heavenward from this house of God.

ascended
My. 119–16   to the *a·* Christ,

ascendency
'01. 19–19   through spiritual *a·* alone.

ascending
Mis. 57–28   *a·* the scale of being up to man.
     151–27   on the *a·* scale of everlasting Life
     292–10   a new tone on the scale *a·*,
Ret.   8– 5   three times, in an *a·* scale.
My. 211–12   in its *a·* steps of evil,

ascends
Mis. 96–12   as thought *a·* the scale of being
     328–21   He alone *a·* the hill of C. S. who
My. 188–32   *a·* the scale of miracles
     268–27   harmoniously *a·* the scale of life.

ascension
Mis. 28–18   great truth was shown by his *a·*
     165– 3   because of the *a·* of Jesus,
'02. 19– 5   rebuked them on the eye of his *a·*,
My. 131– 7   sacrament, sacrifice, and *a·*,
     218–12   incorporeal idea, came with the *a·*.

ascent
Mis. 206–29   scaled the steep *a·* of C. S.,
     265–31   must stop at the foot of the grand *a·*,
     323–10   descent and *a·* are beset with peril,
     327–14   which must greatly hinder their *a·*.
     347–23   *a·* is easy and the summit can be
'01. 19–22   From . . . to C. S. is a long *a·*,
Hea. 19–25   up the steep *a·*, on to heaven,
My. 117– 9   to pursue the infinite *a·*,
     189– 3   you have started in this sublime *a·*,
     229–21   steep *a·* of Christ's Sermon on the

ascertain
My. 53–16   * to *a·* if she would preach

ascribe
No. 18– 5   nor does it *a·* to Him all presence,

ascribed
Mis. 191–28   opposite characters *a·* to him

ashes
Mis. 1–17   fire from the *a·* of dissolving self,
     285–26   from the *a·* of free-love,
Peo. 8–26   are fast fading into *a·* ;
My. 178–27   If the world were in *a·*,
     306– 4   Far be it from me to tread on the *a·*
     308–11   tread not ruthlessly on their *a·*.

Asheville, N. C.
My. 326–14   Elizabeth Earl Jones of *A·*, *N.C.*,
     328– 5   * 105 Bailey St., *A·*, *N.C.*,

Asia Minor
'00. 12– 8   the capital of *A· M·*.

Asiatics
Pul. 66–26   * pre-Christian ideas of the *A·*

aside
Mis. 9–23   we voluntarily set it *a·*
     15– 8   Nothing *a·* from the spiritualization
     17– 8   lay *a·* your material appendages,
     71–11   Does *C. S.* set *a·* the law of
     72– 4   Science sets *a·* man as a creator,
     129–19   and try to push him *a·* ;
     136–10   in turning *a·* for one hour
     137– 8   speaking a few words *a·* to your
     179–28   must lay *a·* material consciousness,
     250–19   I cast *a·* the word as a sham
     335–31   seeking power or good *a·* from
     361–17   "Let us lay *a·* —*Heb.* 12 : 1.
Ret. 81–18   loathes error, and casts it *a·* ;
     90– 2   most careful not to thrust *a·* Science,
Pul. 21–30   aught that can darken . . . must be set *a·*.
'00. 9–26   years I have desired to step *a·*
     15– 1   Putting *a·* the old garment,
'01. 6–20   which is set *a·* to some degree,
My. vi– 6   * no one on earth . . . *a·* from Mrs. Eddy,
     17– 4   laying *a·* all malice,— *I Pet.* 2 : 1.
     67–18   * was set *a·* for the building of this
     71–20   * have been set *a·* in this temple,
     72– 2   * set *a·* the traditions of
     85–29   * *A·* from every other consideration,
     92– 7   * cannot be brushed *a·* by ridicule
     191–17   With grave-clothes laid *a·*, Christ,
     256–21   springs *a·* at the touch of Love.

ask
Mis. 51–30   "Ye *a·*, and receive not,— *Jas.* 4 : 3.
     51–31   because ye *a·* amiss,— *Jas.* 4 : 3.
     54–29   You would not *a·* the pupil in
     89–21   I *a·* for information, *not for*
     91–26   *a·* questions from it,
     121–27   if I also *a·* you,— *Luke* 22 : 68.
     145– 9   let him *a·* himself,
     149– 5   *A·* them to bring what they possess of
     157 10   *a·* them all questions important.
     195 15   We *a·* what is the authority
     244– 9   But, we *a·*, have those conditions
     298– 9   *A·* yourself : Under the same
     299–24   The spectators may *a·*,
     305–31   * we *a·* every one receiving this
     307– 2   Never *a·* for to-morrow :
     307– 7   More we cannot *a·*:
     317– 1   students whom I have not seen that *a·*,
     359–29   To *a·* wisdom of God, is the
     378–15   but she did *a·* him how
     390–20   *A·* of its June, the long-hushed heart,
Ret. 20–22   compelled to *a·* for a bill of divorce,
     50–12   *a·* my loyal students if they consider
     71–15   *A·* the unbridled mind-manipulator
     83–22   they should *a·* questions from it,
     91–29   *A·*, rather, what has he *not* done.
     92– 9   shall *a·* what ye will,— *John* 15 : 7.
     95– 4   * *A·* God to give thee skill
Un. 34–18   Again I *a·* : What evidence does
     35–14   I *a·*, Which was first,
     48– 1   to *a·* of every one a reason
     48– 3   *a·* *a·* and I will answer.
Pul. 87–18   You *a·* too much when asking
Rud. 14– 4   *a·* a suitable price for
No. 40– 1   "Ye *a·*, and receive not,— *Jas.* 4 : 3.
     40– 2   because ye *a·* amiss,— *Jas.* 4 : 3.
     41– 6   as much as to *a·*,
     42–28   Here a skeptic might well *a·*
Pan. 12– 6   we naturally *a·*, how can Spirit
'00. 2–17   *A·* how he gets his money,
     14–28   invited to a feast you naturally *a·*
'01. 19– 8   "*A·*, and ye shall receive ; '"— *John* 16 : 24.
     19– 9   continue to *a·*, and because of
     33–13   Scientists . . . *a·* not to be judged on a
     33–15   *a·* to be allowed the rights of

ask

'01.   33-17   they *a·* to be known by their works,
'02.   14-24   I *a·* : What has shielded and
Hea.   4- 9   even as we *a·* a person with
        4-10   *a·* infinite wisdom to possess our
       15-23   "Ye *a·*, and receive not, — *Jas. 4 : 3.*
       15-24   because ye *a·* amiss ; " — *Jas. 4 : 3.*
Peo.   9-17   We *a·* and receive not,
        9-17   because we "*a·* amiss ; " — *Jas. 4 : 3.*
Po.   34-15   Yet wherefore *a·* thy doom?
       55-21   *A·* of its June, the long-hushed
My.   19-19   but I *a·* for more, even this :
       20-30   *a·* the members to contribute
       24- 1   * those who pass by are impelled to *a·*,
       60-27   * may I *a·* a little of your time
       73- 7   * If you *a·* a Christian Scientist
      117-31   is all that I *a·* of mankind.
      127- 4   who *a·* only to be judged according to
      130-15   Therefore I *a·* the help of others
      130-16   I *a·* that according to the Scriptures
      133-23   and a question to *a·*.
      138-14   *a·* me to receive persons whom I
      148- 5   All that we *a·* of any people is to
      149-31   while those . . . *a·* no praising.
      150-18   *a·* God to enable you to reflect God,
      150-24   ye shall *a·* what ye will, — *John* 15 : 7.
      152-14   *A·* thyself, Do I enter by the door
      156- 6   above all that we *a·* — *Eph.* 3 : 20.
      175-18   May I *a·* in behalf of the public
      221-31   earnestly *a·* : Shall we not believe
      232-18   Here we *a·* : Are Christ's teachings
      318-18   not *a·* him any questions.
      329-25   * we *a·* you to give your readers the
      343- 7   You would *a·*, perhaps,

asked

Mis.   33-14   question that is being *a·* every day.
        40- 9   It is often *a·*, "If C. S.
       137- 9   when, having *a·* in general assembly
       180- 7   A dear old lady *a·* me,
       226-18   When Aristotle was *a·* what a
       255-18   sometimes *a·*, What are the advantages
       287-22   When *a·* by a wife or a husband
       299-26   have you *a·* yourself this question
       305-16   * many persons are to be *a·*
       305-24   * is *a·* to contribute one cent
       305-26   * She is also *a·* to collect two dollars
       316- 7   When will you . . . is often *a·*,
       333-22   *a·* : "What communion — *II Cor.* 6 : 14.
       346- 9   The question is often *a·*,
       379- 4   *a·* if I could see his pennings
       381-13   her counsel *a·* the defendant's
Ret.   8-22   *a·* her if she had summoned me
         9- 5   *a·* if she really did hear Mary's
        14-23   *a·* me to say how I felt when
        30-10   often *a·* why C. S. was revealed to
        40- 7   I *a·* permission to see her.
        54- 1   *a·*, Why are faith-cures sometimes
        82-27   often *a·* which revision of S. and H.
        89-16   as Jesus was once *a·* to exhort,
Pul.   50-15   * no additional sums . . . are *a·* for.
Hea.   1-10   We have *a·*, in our selfishness,
Po.   v-19   * *a· her what she was writing,*
My.   43-18   * it was *a·*, "What mean ye — *Josh.* 4 : 6.
        59-24   * In years gone by I have been *a·*,
        60-29   * I was *a·* by one of the Directors
        96-23   * members were *a·* to quit giving.
        98-22   * no member . . . was *a·* to contribute
       105-25   he *a·* earnestly if I had a work
       139-17   When I *a·* you to dispense with
       160-19   I am *a·*, "Is there a hell?"
       190-15   *a·* their great Teacher,
       212-14   The question is often *a·*,
       222- 7   When his disciples *a·* him why they
       276-23   I am *a·*, "What are your politics?"
       324-29   * When we *a·* him if he found you could

asking

Mis.   27-16   *a·*, "Do men gather — *Matt.* 7 : 16.
       305-12   * *a·* for her personal cooperation
Ret.   50- 8   I shrank from *a·* it,
Pul.   87-19   *a·* me to accept your grand church
No.   20-19   Hence this *a·* amiss
        39-17   True prayer is not *a·* God for love ;
Hea.   15-24   is it not *a·* amiss to pray for
My.   43-31   * many are *a·*, "What mean ye — *Josh.* 4 : 6.
       148-20   and my heart is *a·* :
       240- 6   * "Would it be *a·* too much of you
       280-30   And why this *a·* ?

asks

Mis.   26-13   *a·*, Whence came the first seed,
       127-14   faithfully *a·* divine Love to feed it
       244-15   He *a·*, "Has the law been abrogated
       315-26   *a·* for mental treatment.
       353- 7   If one *a·* me, Is my concept of you
Ret.   60-16   Material sense *a·*, in its ignorance
Un.   15- 3   *a·* the poet-patriarch.

asks

No.   18-24   *a·* for what Mind alone can supply.
Pan.   6-15   and *a·*, If God is *infinite* good,
My.   18-11   *a·* divine Love to feed it with the
       211- 9   All that error *a·* is to be let alone ;
       235- 8   *a·* herself : Can I teach my child

asleep

Mis.   44-21   when awake, or when *a·* in a dream.
       108- 2   or the so-called Christian *a·*,
       325-14   only to find its inmates *a·*
       392- 7   *a·* in night's embrace,
Ret.   61- 8   fall *a·*, actually conscious of
'01.   35- 7   appeals loudly to those *a·*
Po.   20- 9   *a·* in night's embrace,

aspect

My.   28-31   * changed the whole *a·* of medicine
        89- 2   * in its size, if not in its *a·*,
       234-20   gives the subject quite another *a·*.

aspects

Mis.   355- 3   presents two opposite *a·*,
Pul.   23-12   * under several different *a·*
My.   86-24   * in some of its *a·* the most notable

aspersion

Mis.   255- 4   no fairness or propriety in the *a·*.

aspersions

'02.   14-28   all unjust public *a·*,

aspirants

Mis.   351-14   of *a·* for place and power.
Rud.   16-25   class of *a·* which snatch at

aspiration

Pul.   23-21   * manifested in unrest or in *a·*,
My.   88-13   * symbolisms of *a·* and faith,
       303-26   not the inspiration nor the *a·*

aspirations

My.   91-10   * no person's spiritual *a·*

aspire

Pul.   51-28   * *a·* to take its place alongside
My.   113-15   to *a·* to this knowledge of Christ

asps

Mis.   294-17   keep back thy offerings from *a·*
       368-21   "the poison of *a·* — *Rom.* 3 : 13.

assail

'00.   10-15   *a·* even the new-old doctrines of

assailable

Mis.   122-15   it is neither questionable nor *a·* :

assailant

My.   331-15   * would have punished the *a·* of

assailed

'01.   32-12   When infidels *a·* them,
Po.   vi-15   and *a·* . . . *William Lloyd Garrison*
My.   138-11   My personal reputation is *a·*

assails

Mis.   335-12   One mercilessly *a·* me for

assassin

Mis.   112-16   the *a·* of President Garfield,
       226-29   red-tongued *a·* of radical worth ;

assemblage

Mis.   276-12   *a·* for the third convention of our
       276-13   an *a·* found waiting and watching
My.   124- 6   annual *a·* of human consciousness,

assemble

Man.   84-21   or *a·* a selected number of them,
My.   27- 4   *A·* not at the residence of your
       147- 9   a modest hall, in which to *a·*
       173-27   allowing the visitors to *a·* on
       284-21   desire to *a·* in my church building,

assembled

Mis.   279-11   *A·* FEB. 25, 1889,
Man.   98-20   in annual meeting *a·*.
Ret.   89- 7   Men *a·* in the one temple
My.   23-20   * in annual business meeting *a·*,
        36- 9   * *a·* at this sacred time to commune
        44-25   * in annual meeting *a·*,
        46-22   * in the presence of this *a·* host,
        65- 3   * *A·* in the largest church . . . meeting
        76-20   * in their annual church meeting
        88- 3   * *a·* at Boston to attend the
        96- 2   * *a·* to participate in
       171-24   * who were *a·* on the lawn of the
       207- 9   * in annual conference *a·*,
       352- 4   * Informally *a·*, we, the ushers

assemblies

Mis.   315- 8   either in private or in public *a·*,
Man.   50- 9   in public debating *a·*,
        56-14   These *a·* shall be for listening to
Rud.   15-23   to promiscuous and large *a·*,

assembling

Mis.   144-22   *a·* of His people in this temple,
       156-24   *A·* themselves together,

assembling
My. 79–12   * thirty thousand people *a·*
    85– 1   * character of the *a·* membership,

assembly
Mis. 137–10   having asked in general *a·* if you
Pul.   5– 5   in that unique *a·*.
    22– 6   with every praying *a·* on earth,
My. 46–30   * to the general *a·* — Heb. 12 : 23.
    79 17   * that *a·* was not a gathering of
    95–15   * During the great *a·* of

assent
Mis. 109– 3   *a·* where they should dissent ;
    240–13   without the *a·* of mind,
Ret. 14–13   if *a·* to this doctrine was essential
My. 291– 6   a quiet *a·* or dissent.

assented
Po. vii– 9   * to which she *a·*.

assert
Mis. 55–21   verities of Spirit *a·* themselves
Un. 40– 4   is to *a·* what we have not proved ;
Pul. 23–22   * *a·* that the end of a cycle,
Hea. 18–23   will cease to *a·* their Cæsar sway
My. 106–13   C. S. has healed cases that I *a·*

asserted
Mis. 77– 6   great truths *a·* of the Messiah :
Pul. 31– 6   * the principles *a·* by Jesus,

asserting
Mis. 183–24   *A·* a selfhood apart from God,
    335–21   by *a·* its nothingness,
'00. 10– 3   *a·* and developing good.
'01. 34– 4   Bible is our authority for *a·* this,
My. 143–14   this fustian of either denying or *a·*

assertion
Mis. 191–14   *a·* indicating the existence of
    256–25   The *a·* that matter is a law,
    266–18   *a·* that I have said hard things
Ret 14–22   he persisted in the *a·* that I *had* been
Un.   6–22   tho *a·* of universal salvation
    53–17   than would be the *a·* that the
My. 84– 1   * speak more plainly than mere *a·*

assertions
Un. 44– 5   The foundations of these *a·*,
My. 351–25   any *a·* to the contrary are false.

asserts
Mis. 59–26   who *a·* himself the least,
Pul. 70–17   * Mrs. Eddy *a·* that in 1866

assets
My. vi 21   * *a·* valued at forty-five thousand

asseverated
Pul. 45–18   * repeatedly *a·* to the contrary.

assiduously
Mis. 262–14   at work conscientiously and *a·*,
    263–17   working *a·* for our common Cause,
    379–24   *a·* pondering the solution of

assigned
Man. 79–10   the business *a·* to them
    95–13   one shall be *a·* them by the Board.
Rud.   2–20   takes away the trammels *a·* to
My. 75–11   * where they were *a·* rooms

assigns
Peo. 3–24   and *a·* them mortal fetters

assimilate
Mis. 264–16   to *a·* pure and abstract Science
Ret. 28–29   *a·* the character and practice of
    84–12   *a·* this inexhaustible subject — C. S.
Un.   6–17   world is far from ready to *a·* such a
Rud. 15–21   *a·* what has been taught them.

assimilated
Mis. 213– 6   in the proportion that . . . are *a·*,
    317–16   Scarcely a moiety, . . . is yet *a·*
My. 292– 6   the right government is *a·*,

assimilation
Mis. 317–17   yet this *a·* is indispensable to
My. 230– 7   during the senses' *a·* thereof,

assist
Mis. 53–12   *a·* in producing a cure,
    79–30   which in any way obligates you to *a·*
My. 62–28   * ready to *a·* us in every way
    222–29   *a·* in the holding of crime in check,
    319–24   * to *a·* me in analyzing and
    320– 4   * he readily consented to *a·* me,

assistance
Mis.   7–30   naturally without any *a·*.
    349– 2   even the offer of pecuniary *a·*
My. 331–31   * the *a·* volunteered to
    336– 6   * he desired to go to her *a·*,

assistant
Man. 101– 3   If . . . the manager . . . needs an *a·*,
    101– 5   appoint an *a·* manager,

assistant
Ret. 43–20   the only *a·* teachers in the College.

assisted
My. 130–10   whom I have *a·* pecuniarily
    330–11   * *a·* by a Mason of good standing

assisting
Mis. 11– 9   afterwards *a·* them pecuniarily,

assists
Mis. 75–20   *a·* one to understand C. S.

associate
Mis. 296– 2   elected an *a·* life-member of
Ret. 24– 3   spiritualists would *a·* therewith,

associated
Mis. 296–19   is by no means *a·* therewith.
Pan. 14–15   those *a·* with his executive trust,
My. 45– 7   * significant events *a·* with this,
    153–14   imbued and *a·* with no intrinsic

Associated Press
My. 346–25   * gave the following to the *A· P·*,

Association
Mis. 111–28   call the attention of this *A·* to
    120–20   *A·* hereafter meet triennially :
    134– 9   chapter sub-title
    135–23   chapter sub-title
    137– 1   chapter sub-title
Pul. 37–25   * heading
My. 251–23   chapter sub-title
    252–18   chapter sub-title
    253–10   chapter sub-title
    283–12   fruits of said grand *A·*,

association
Mis. 272–15   * of any corporation or *a·*,
Man. 85– 6   may teach and receive into his *a·*
    86–12   who is not in charge of an *a·*
    86–14   conduct the meetings of their *a·*.
Pul. 58– 5   * gathered an *a·* of students,
'01. 23–29   * phenomena connected by *a·*
    31–24   my early *a·* with
'02. 19–28   and crowns the *a·* with

Association for International Conciliation
My. 282–22   in the success of the *A· for I· C·*
    283– 2   chapter sub-title
    283– 7   *Fondateur* of the *A· for I· C·*
    285–15   embodied in the *A· for I· C·*

associations
Mis. 137–29   organize their students into *a·*,
    315–22   shall form *a·* for this purpose ;
    358–22   organizing churches and *a·*.
Man. 84–16   *A·*.
    84–16   *a·* of the pupils of loyal teachers
    85– 3   attend each other's *a·*.
Ret. 50–25   organize churches, schools, and *a·*
    52–16   branch *a·* in other States,
    85– 4   band together their students into *a·*,
No. 41–13   for perfection in churches or *a·*.
My. 347–21   loving-cup with all its sweet *a·*.

assume
Mis. x–19   to *a·* various *noms de plume*
    2– 3   those *a·* most who have the least
    281–27   realized what a responsibility you *a·*
Man. 70–11   shall *a·* no general official control of
    71–14   branch church to *a·* such position
    83–12   shall not *a·* personal control of,
Pul. 65– 9   * whatever attitude Rome may *a·*
'01. 14– 2   To *a·* there is no reality in sin,
My. 334–20   "To *a·* there is no reality in sin,

assumed
Mis. 44–25   your belief *a·* a new form,
    63–30   Jesus *a·* for mortals the weakness of
Un. 45–11   evil ego, and his *a·* power,
    46–28   Jesus *a·* the burden of disproof
Pul. 68– 1   * Mrs. Eddy *a·* the pastorship of
My. 111– 9   now *a·* by many doctors

assumes
Mis. 39–28   Scientist, *a·* no more when claiming
    147–25   He *a·* no borrowed appearance.
    274–18   when the press *a·* the liberty to
    370–12   divine idea *a·* different forms,
    370–14   In this age it *a·*,

assuming
Un. 33–14   Brain, thus *a·* to testify,
Rud.   6– 3   *a· manifold forms and colors,*
My. 29–23   * *a·* an altogether different status
    42–12   * Mr. Gross, on *a·* office, said :

assumption
No. 17– 1   false *a·* of the realness of
'01. 13– 8   an *a·* that nothing is something.

assumptions
Un. 24– 6   Your *a·* insist that there is more than

assurance

Mis.	307– 8	*a·* is the "Peace, be still " — *Mark* 4 : 39.
	373–25	this *a·* is followed by
Un.	44–20	thus carrying out the serpent's *a·* :
	55–17	Job's faith . . . gained him the *a·*
Pul.	3–13	heavenly *a·* ends all warfare,
	9–21	O glorious hope and blessed *a·*,
	83–10	* With the *a·* of faith she prays,
My.	38– 4	* we rest in this satisfying *a·*,
	44–30	* and their confident *a·*
	65–11	* with both unanimity and *a·*.
	280– 4	* gives *a·* of your watchful care
	295– 3	blessed *a·* that life is not lost ;
	333–24	* *a·* of his willingness to die,
	356–15	I have given no *a·*,

assure

Ret.	24–19	could only *a·* him that the divine
My.	80– 4	* earnestly *a·* thousands of auditors
	362–21	* *a·* you that it is our intention to

assured

Mis.	10–16	more *a·* to press on safely.
	114–26	Rest *a·* that God in His wisdom
	160–13	Of this we rest *a·*, that every trial
	276– 8	rest *a·* my heart's desire met
	303–25	I feel *a·* that many Christian Scientists
	345–19	* has always *a·* and reassured me
Ret.	85– 9	Of this also rest *a·*,
'01.	1– 4	rest *a·* you can never lack
Peo.	13–27	* "My heart has *a·* and reassured me
My.	139– 2	Rest *a·* that your Leader is living,
	151–12	Rest *a·* that the injustice done
	162– 1	God's mercy . . . is *a·* ;
	186–13	Rest *a·* that He in whom dwelleth all
	230–20	Be *a·* that fitness and fidelity
	252– 8	Rest *a·* that the good you do
	333–31	* "We are *a·* that reports of
	342–20	continuity of The . . . "is *a·*.

assuredly

My.	240–26	* She most *a·* does,

assures

Mis.	180–25	apostle *a·* us that man has power to
'01.	21–24	My faith *a·* me that God knows
Peo.	10–17	It *a·* us, of a verity, that

Assyrian Merodach

Mis.	123–14	The *A· M·*, or the god of sin,

astonished

Mis.	189–27	were *a·* at his doctrine : — *Matt.* 7 : 28.
Ret.	58–10	"were *a·* at his doctrine : — *Matt.* 7 : 28.
Un.	42–18	were *a·* at his doctrine ; — *Matt.* 7 : 28.

astonishing

My.	65– 2	* chapter sub-title
	65–10	* This *a·* motion was passed
	92–15	* *a·* revelation was made

astonishment

Ret.	15– 1	To the *a·* of many,

astounded

Mis.	115– 3	*a·* at the apathy of some students

astray

Mis.	208–22	I went *a·* : — *Psal.* 119 : 67.
	298– 7	causing others to go *a·*,

astrology

Mis.	334– 5	*A·* is well in its place,

astronomer

Mis.	363–26	confutes the *a·*,
Rud.	6–13	Langley, the young American *a·*

astronomy

Mis.	344– 5	have you studied music, *a·*, and
	344–27	Not through *a·* did he point out
Ret.	87– 6	in religion and scholarship as in *a·*
Un.	13– 2	same principle that it does in *a·*.
No.	6–25	*A·*, optics, acoustics, and

astute

Mis.	62–26	which is amusing to *a·* readers,

astutely

Mis.	71–23	St. Paul declares *a·*,

asunder

Mis.	335–10	"And shall cut him *a·*, — *Matt.* 24 : 51.

asylums

My.	301–21	are committed to insane *a·*

ate

Mis.	170–17	The bread he *a·*,

atheism

Mis.	345– 4	against the charge of *a·* ;
Pan.	3–22	It is opposed to *a·* and monotheism,
My.	90–15	* which teaches that hate is *a·*,

atheist

Mis.	45–12	*Can an a· or a profane man be cured*

Athenian

Pul.	26–27	* *A·* lamp over two hundred years old,

Athenians

Ret.	93–17	St. Paul said to the *A·*,

Athens

Mis.	344–30	when he stood on Mars' hill at *A·*,
Pul.	8– 1	the press of America's *A·*,
'02.	10–11	* not *A·*, but Calvary."

athirst

Mis.	324–28	Naked, hungry, *a·*, this time he
Pul.	14–15	weary wanderers, *a·* in the desert
No.	v– 9	*a·* for the life-giving waters of

athletic

Pul.	5–14	his *a·* mind, scholarly and serene,

Athol (Mass.) *Transcript*

My.	97–24	* [*A· (M·.) T·*]

athwart

Po.	43–16	Beacon beams— *a·* the weakly,

Atlanta

Ga.

Pul.	89–18	* *Journal, A·*, Ga.

Georgia

My.	187–21	chapter sub-title

Pul.	56– 4	* Scranton, Peoria, *A·*, Toronto, and
'00.	1–20	*A·*, New Orleans, Chicago,

Atlantic

Mis.	251– 5	from the Pacific to the *A·* shore,
	359–17	to step upon the *A·*
Ret.	2– 9	crossed the *A·* more than a score of
Pul.	88– 3	from the *A·* to the Pacific ocean,
My.	85– 9	* as from the *A·* to the Pacific

atmosphere

Mis.	12–32	the radius of our *a·* of thought.
	86–26	The *a·* of mortal mind
	129–17	send it into the *a·* of mortal mind
	174–13	higher than the *a·* of our planet,
	260–25	Pure Mind gives out an *a·* that heals
	355–28	from thine own mental *a·*.
	356– 3	illumine its own *a·* with spiritual
Man.	31–11	mental *a·* they exhale shall
Pul.	31–17	* Boston *a·* was largely thrilled
No.	9–26	Science is the *a·* of God ;
'00.	9–15	till the mental *a·* is clear.
'02.	3–29	Envy is the *a·* of hell.
My.	57– 6	* sacred *a·* of a church home.
	197–17	translucent *a·* of the former must
	265–24	the *a·* of the human mind,

atmospheres

Mis.	267–21	for rarefied *a·* and upward flight.

atom

Mis.	129–16	an *a·* of another man's indiscretion,
	173–28	Whence, then, is the *a·* or molecule
Un.	35–26	material *a·* is an outlined falsity of
My.	162– 7	unity and power are not in *a·* or in
	349–32	from *a·* and dust draws its conclusions

atomic

Mis.	23–20	is not a result of *a·* action,
	190– 1	*A·* action is Mind, not matter.

atoms

Mis.	26–14	Was it molecules, or material *a·*?
	224–17	of these different *a·*.

atone

Mis.	118–14	sympathy can neither *a·* for error,
	330–25	thou alone canst and must *a·*,
My.	104–22	but what can *a·* for the vulgar

atoned

No.	35–15	He *a·* for the terrible unreality of

atonement

Mis.	96–17	Do I believe in the *a·* of Christ?
	96–18	this *a·* becomes more to me
	123–20	majestic *a·* of divine Love,
	125– 3	then hath he part in Love's *a·*,
	261–16	the *a·* of Christ loses no efficacy.
Man.	15–14	We acknowledge Jesus' *a·* as the
Pul.	30–18	* It affirms the *a·* ;
No.	33–12	chapter sub-title
	34–19	The real *a·* — so infinitely beyond
	37–11	the vicarious *a·* of Jesus,
	37–18	would make the *a·* to be less than
	42–28	ask if the *a·* had lost its
'01.	10–22	*a·* of Christ, whereby good
Hea.	18–11	The doctrine of *a·* never

at-one-ment

Mis.	123–21	*a·* with Christ has appeared
Un.	54–15	*a·*, or oneness with God
No.	33–19	sustains man's *a·* with God ;
	37–19	would make . . . less than the *a·*,

Atonement and Eucharist

Pul.	38–13	"Prayer," "*A· and E·*,"
My.	136– 6	depicted in the chapter *A· and E·*,

atones
  My. 288–27 Love *a·* for sin through love

attach
  Mis. 174– 8 Let us *a·* our sense of Science to

attached
  Mis. 291– 9 Too much and too little is *a·* to me
  Pul. 77– 6 * *A·* to the scroll is a golden key
      78–21 * *A·* by a white ribbon to the scroll
  My. 70–30 * *A·* to the organ is a set of
      71– 5 * There is also a solo organ *a·*.
    335– 7 * He was devotedly *a·* to Masonry,

attaches
  Mis. 209– 1 *a·* to sin due penalties

attaching
  My. 93–21 * *a·* meanwhile no importance to

attachment
  Man. 40– 5 nor mere personal *a·* should impel
  Pul. 26–13 * with Æolian *a·*,
     60–21 * having an Æolian *a·*.

attack
  Mis. 90–12 it is inexpedient to *a·*
    316–2 never to *a·* the malpractitioner,
  Ret. 63– 7 We *a·* the sinner's belief in
    63–10 we *a·* the belief of the sick in
  My. 127–22 culminating in fierce *a·*,
    143–12 I do not regard this *a·* upon me as
    213–24 wiser and better through every *a·*
    304–29 The first *a·* upon me was :
    308–11 The *a·* on me and my late father
    318–21 began my *a·* on agnosticism.

attacked
  Mis. 11–15 If one's life were *a·*,
    193–19 when critics *a·* me for
  Ret. 19– 9 *a·* by this insidious disease,
  My. 335–16 * Mr. Glover was *a·* with yellow fever

attacking
  My. 300–32 or are they *a·* a peaceable party

attacks
  Mis. 285– 1 I am opposed to all personal *a·*,
    323–14 masters their secret and open *a·*
  No. 5–23 *a·* a normal and real condition
  My. 151– 2 present schoolboy epithets and *a·*
    151– 8 these *a·* afford opportunity for
    210– 9 shielded from the *a·* of error
    273– 7 * emerging triumphantly from all *a·*
    316–13 *A·* on C. S. and its Founder,

attain
  Mis. 80– 4 the Christian will, must, *a·* it ;
    147–30 rather fall of success than *a·* it by
  Ret. 49–15 *a·* the bliss of loving unselfishly,
  '01. 2–16 others will *a·* it,
    24–30 I relinquished the form to *a·* the
  '02. 16–13 To *a·* peace and holiness is
  Hea. 14–26 to *a·* a mind in harmony with God,
  My. 123–27 Seeing that we have to *a·* to the
    149– 1 To *a·* to these works, men must

attained
  Mis. 42–11 not *a·* by the death of the body,
    46–28 thought has not yet wholly *a·* unto
    86– 5 Until this be *a·*, the Christian
    220–14 The end is *a·*, and the patient says
  Ret. 82–10 *a·* by those loyal students who
  No. 31–18 until a perfect consciousness is *a·*.
    32–19 When this sense is *a·*, we shall no longer
  Hea. 13–15 highest attenuation we ever *a·*
  My. 237– 8 not *a·* the full understanding of
    345–22 or rather *a·* by us,

attaining
  My. 93–13 * or *a·* dominion over others,

attainment
  Mis. 101–13 holiness, and the *a·* of heaven.
    116–20 research and *a·* in divine Science
  Un. 4– 9 but the *a·* of the understanding of
  Pan. 9–15 *a·* of scientific Christianity
  My. 131– 5 courage, devotion, and *a·*.

attainments
  Mis. 345–32 directed them to spiritual *a·*.
  '00. 1–14 rich spiritual *a·*,
  My. 64– 5 * to us through her spiritual *a·*
    244–12 fresh impulse to our spiritual *a·*,
    251– 1 duties and *a·* beckoning them.

attains
  My. 103–13 *a·* the stature of man in Christ
    228–27 He who strives, and *a·* ;

attempt
  Mis. 18–27 *a·* to separate Life from God.
    52–24 should *a·* to work out a rule
    118–28 Every *a·* of evil to harm good
    171– 5 with the second *a·*,
    175–28 The *a·* to mix matter and Mind.

attempt
  Mis. 216–27 * *a·* of phenomenism to conceive
    216–29 * it is an *a·* to conceive a grin
    224–29 He who can wilfully *a·* to injure
    234– 4 *a·* to mount above error
    234– 8 *a·* to seem what we have not
    268– 5 but not vain enough to *a·*
  Man. 83–13 *a·* to dominate his pupils,
  Ret. 60–29 Any *a·* to divide these
    71–28 one who is unaware of this *a·*,
    78–19 an *a·* to demonstrate the facts of
  Un. 10–21 To *a·* the calculation of His mighty
  Rud. 16–10 None . . . should *a·* overmuch in their
  No. 6– 3 to *a·* to destroy the realities of Mind
    45–10 Such an *a·* indicates weakness,
  '00. 7–25 ofttimes this *a·* measurably fails,
  '01. 2– 8 To *a·* to twist . . . into harmony with
    29–18 if they *a·* to help their parents,
  My. 42–22 * I shall not *a·* to speak of the
    74–24 * it would be idle to *a·* to deny them
    81–26 * If an *a·* were made to give
    110–28 Robert Ingersoll's *a·* to convict the
    197– 4 *A·* nothing without God's help.
    332– 3 * an *a·* at expressing the feelings of
    340–16 this *a·* is shorn of some of its

attempted
  Ret. 70– 6 is an *a·* infringement on infinity"
  Pul. 50–28 * and live down any *a·* repression.

attempting
  Mis. 92–27 *a·* to steady the ark of Truth,
    277–15 the present mode of *a·* this
  Ret. 84–15 *a·* to steady the ark of Truth,
  Un. 5–13 *a·* to solve every Life-problem in

attempts
  Mis. 62–23 *a·* to solve its divine Principle by
    217– 4 neither philosophy nor reason *a·* to
    233–11 and so strangled in its *a·*.
    287–31 *a·* to steady other people's altars,
    351–15 These repeated *a·* of mad ambition
  '00. 9–22 Whosoever *a·* to ostracize C. S.
  My. 59–22 * feeble *a·* to lead the singing.
    305– 3 Failing in these *a·*,
    306– 2 *a·* to narrow my life into

attend
  Mis. 6–30 has all that she can *a·* to
    209–25 happiness should still *a·* it.
  Man. 30–18 the Board shall *a·* to the insurance
    59–23 come to *a·* the morning services.
    62–16 *a·* the Sunday School exercises.
    69–23 or *a·* to other affairs outside
    85– 3 *a·* each other's associations.
  Pul. 40–12 * TO *A·* THE EXERCISES
    91– 3 * We did not *a·*,
  '00. 5–30 might and majesty *a·* every
  '01. 7–22 *a·* their petitions to divine Love.
  My. 25– 7 * children who *a·* the Sunday School
    72–11 * who come to *a·* the dedication
    72–20 * to *a·* the dedication exercises,
    73–15 * *a·* the June meetings of The
    88– 4 * *a·* the opening of their great new
    105–19 I was wired to *a·* the patient of a
    141– 9 * to *a·* the communion seasons
    142–28 I will *a·* the meeting,
    171–12 communicants who *a·* this communion,
    173–16 Why not invite those who *a·* the
    174–18 your kind invitation to *a·*
    285– 4 *a·* the Industrial Peace Conference,
    289–23 It being inconvenient for me to *a·*

attendance
  Mis. 279–12 WITH AN *A·* OF SIXTY-FIVE STUDENTS.
  Man. 94– 3 unite in their *a·* on his lecture,
  '01. 34– 5 d tains the patient from the *a·* of
  My. 20–23 * a general *a·* of the members
    22– 5 * increasing *a·* at all the services,
    30–11 * the character of the *a·*.
    55– 9 * not only was the *a·* rapidly
    55–30 * a steady increase in *a·*.
    56– 2 * *A·* at the Sunday service
    56–16 * growth of *a·* in The Mother Church,
    56–21 * *a·* at them and at The Mother Church
    86–26 * The *a·* at the ceremonies
    87– 1 * *a·* was greater than the
    94–23 * many . . . were in *a·*.
    94–25 * Mrs. Eddy, . . . was not in *a·*,

attendant
  Mis. 89–13 the medical *a·* and friends
  Un. 37–19 good *a·* upon spiritual individuality

attendants
  Pul. 59– 7 * so long as there were *a·* ;
  My. 53–19 * number of *a·* steadily increased.
    56–18 * the number of *a·* increased
    56–23 * *a·* at The Mother Church.

attended

Mis.	69–18	next day he *a·* to his business.
	95–17	There have always *a·* my life
	204– 7	*a·* throughout with doubt, hope,
Ret.	24–17	homœopathic physician who *a·* me,
My.	30– 4	* nobody *a·* more than one,
	51–30	* all who have *a·* the services,
	58–29	* *a·* the dedicatory services
	96–28	* *a·* by people from all parts of
	99–18	* *a·* the dedicatory exercises,
	135– 9	*a·* to my secular affairs,
	137–12	*a·* personally to my secular affairs,
	141– 6	* services *a·* last Sunday
	331–23	* *a·* him during his last sickness,
	333–23	* friends who *a·* him during his illness
	335–25	* *a·* cases of this terrible disease
	340– 1	Jesus *a·* feasts,

attending

Mis.	17–26	material conditions *a·* it.
Pul.	29– 8	* *a·* the service held in Copley Hall.
'01.	15–29	* of *a·* His solemn worship.
My.	140–15	* *a·* occasionally The Mother Church.
	140–27	occasionally *a·* this church.
	145–19	at home *a·* to the machinery

attends

Mis.	123–32	such as *a·* eating and drinking
Pul.	37–10	* *a·* to a vast correspondence ;

attent

My.	188– 6	*a·* unto the prayer— *II Chron.* 7: 15.

attention

call

Mis.	282–29	The abuse which I call *a·* to,
My.	91–17	* serves to call *a·* to one of the most
	110–32	serve to call *a·* to that book,

call the

Mis.	111–27	Let me specially call the *a·* of

close

Mis.	127–31	need close *a·* and examination.
Pul.	12– 4	stillness . . . indicated close *a·*.

constant

My.	175– 5	requires my constant *a·* and time,

daily

My.	237–14	give daily *a·* thereto.

definite

Pul.	24– 2	* a keynote of definite *a·*.

direct

Mis.	319–26	Christian Scientists can direct *a·*,

directed

Ret.	5–27	* directed *a·* to themes at once pleasing

her

Pul.	72–12	* given so much of her *a·*.
Po.	v– 8	* *that claimed her a·*.

immediate

Mis.	146–16	but will give them immediate *a·*,

kind

My.	331–29	* recounting the kind *a·* paid to
	332–11	* or remit his kind *a·* until he

less

My.	259–15	they require less *a·* than packages

much

Mis.	353–11	People give me too much *a·*

my

Mis.	276– 7	circumstances demanded my *a·*
My.	13– 8	my *a·* was arrested by

no mean

Mis.	376– 1	* as one who gives no mean *a·* to

our

My.	27– 7	should engage our *a·* at this sacred

present

Mis.	299– 8	which demands our present *a·*.

profound

My.	250– 4	has received profound *a·*.

public

Mis.	171–28	obtruding upon the public *a·*
	221–31	or call public *a·* to that crime?
'01.	17–13	would not have arrested public *a·*
My.	88–17	* which must arrest public *a·*,
	316–18	appeal . . . demands public *a·*.

require

My.	177– 7	daily duties require *a·* elsewhere,

serious

Man.	43–18	not only calls more serious *a·* to

share of

Pul.	51–27	* the share of *a·* it deserves,

special

Rud.	13–20	then give special *a·* to
'02.	7–27	special *a·* to his *new commandment.*

their

Man.	67–18	who turn their *a·* from the

time and

(*see* **time**)

time or

Mis.	366–	time or *a·* that human hypotheses

attention

your

Mis.	121– 6	cup to which I call your *a·*,
	133– 8	I call your *a·* and
'00.	14–14	I call your *a·* to this to remind you
My.	224– 5	call your *a·* to this demand,
Pul.	2–11	Turning the *a·* from sublunary views,
	36–10	* such earnestness of *a·* as
	47– 1	* the *a·* of many clergymen
	65–13	* *A·* is directed to the progress
'02.	1–21	C. S., engaging the *a·* of
Hea.	3–14	engrossed the *a·* of the ages.
My.	v– 5	* *a·* of . . . world is fixed on C. S.,
	295–19	engages the *a·* and enriches the

attentive

My.	185–23	spoke to an *a·* audience

attenuate

My.	108–18	nothing in the divine Mind to *a·*.

attenuated

Un.	61–24	how *a·* are our demonstration and
Pul.	35–25	* the more *a·* the drug,
'01.	18– 2	*a·* one thousand degrees less
Hea.	13–10	We have *a·* a grain of aconite until

attenuation

Mis.	252– 5	gains no potency by *a·*,
	260–32	is the highest *a·* of evil.
	271– 2	*a·* of a drug up to the point of
	379–21	up to the highest *a·* in homœopathy,
Ret.	33–15	One drop of the thirtieth *a·* of
No.	16–26	its highest *a·* is mortal mind ;
'01.	17–27	and this *a·* in some cases
Hea.	13– 6	thirty times at every *a·*.
	13–15	highest *a·* we ever attained

attenuations

Ret.	33–18	drug disappears in the higher *a·*
'01.	17–25	In the highest *a·* of homœopathy
Hea.	11–28	higher *a·* of homœopathy
	12–23	higher *a·* prove that the power was
	12–26	higher *a·* are the most powerful.
	13– 8	reached soonest by the higher *a·*,
My.	107–10	the one thousandth *a·*
	107–12	the lower *a·* have so little

attest

Mis.	35– 8	acknowledge and *a·* the blessings
	98–24	lives of all reformers *a·* the
	106–27	"So live, that your lives *a·* your
	133–28	*a·* to the truth of Jesus' words.
Pul.	22– 9	If the lives of Christian Scientists *a·*
Pan.	10– 8	will *a·* its uplifting power,
Po.	31–16	but Truth and Love *a·*
My.	111–31	thousands upon thousands *a·*
	270–10	*a·* honesty and valor.

attestation

Mis.	220– 8	by audible explanation, *a·*, and

attested

Mis.	108– 7	*a·* the absolute powerlessness
	121–11	omnipotence of good, as divinely *a·*.
Man.	66–22	come from her satisfactorily *a·*.
My.	194–16	It stands . . . for Truth as *a·* by

attesting

Man.	66–14	Reading and *A·* Letters.
My.	96–12	* joy in *a·* their faith in the creed

attitude

Mis.	214–24	*a·* of mortal mind in being healed
	214–25	is the same as its *a·* physically.
	215–27	cannot in the beginning take the *a·*,
Man.	74–20	an *a·* of Christian fellowship.
Ret.	88–26	abide in such a spiritual *a·* as will
Pul.	37– 3	* in its *a·* toward all questions."
	65– 9	* whatever *a·* Rome may assume
My.	199–14	show explicitly the *a·* of this
	290–26	Hold this *a·* of mind,
	322–11	* work for and *a·* towards you ;
	329–24	* fair *a·* of the press everywhere,
	345– 7	* "What is your *a·* to science

Attleboro, Mass.

Pul.	88–23	* *Sun, A·, M·.*

attorney

Man.	67–11	shall not employ an *a·*,
Hea.	10–23	You are the *a·* for the case,

attract

My.	93– 8	* to *a·* any class save the

attracted

Pul.	47– 1	* *a·* the attention of many clergymen
	61–25	* *a·* quite a throng of people,

attracting

Pul.	46– 2	* that he was *a·* listeners

attraction

Mis.	173–29	Have *a·* and cohesion formed it?

attraction
Un. 36– 2   This process it names material a`,
My. 49– 5   * as by an irresistible a`.
    85–23   * become the great centre of a`,
    159–18   tend to check spiritual a`
    159–20   a` towards the temporary and

attribute
Mis. 2–12   justice, the eternal a` of Truth,
Pul. 53–18   * It is that a` of mind which

attributed
Mis. 48– 3   If mesmerism has the power a` to it
My. 312–32   rhyme a` to me by McClure's

attributes
Mis. 1–18   Meekness heightens immortal a`
    23–27   manifests all His a` and power,
    69– 2   His essence, relations, and a`.
    69– 6   Mind, or God, and His a`.
No. 10–15   or relates to its so-called a`,
My. 308–26   McClure's Magazine a` to my father

attune
My. 158– 8   in a` with faith's fond trust.

attuned
Mis. 151– 2   their ears are a` to His call.

Auburn, N. Y.
Pul. 88–26   * Bulletin, A`, N. Y.

audacious
My. 97–16   * speaks of "the a`, stupendous,

audacity
Un. 54–27   a` of diabolical and sinuous logic

audible
Mis. 220– 8   by a` explanation, attestation, and
    222–13   listen complacently to a` falsehoods
    267– 2   a` and inaudible wail of evil
    319–11   mental and a` protest against the
    351–12   the a` falsehood designed to
Ret. 9– 6   Mary's name pronounced in a` tones.
Pul. 5– 3   offered his a` adoration in
Rud. 9–22   an a` or even a mental argument,
No. 39– 4   The a` prayer may be offered
    40–12   a` prayer of the right kind ;
My. 17–25   * a` repetition of the Lord's Prayer
    32–17   * a` repetition of the Lord's Prayer
    32–30   * a` repetition of the Lord's Prayer.
    39–11   * a` repetition of the Lord's Prayer,
    78–20   * a` repetition of the Lord's Prayer.
    139–23   from the a` to the inaudible prayer ;

audibly
Mis. 67–14   a lie, either mentally or a`,
    283– 3   speak the truth a` ;
    293–24   affirm mentally and a` that God is
Ret. 38–22   Not a word . . . a` or mentally,
No. 2–14   by healing one case a`,
My. 146–26   Scientist never mentally or a`

audience
Mis. 48–15   informed his a` that he could
    95– 5   * was presented to Mr. Cook's a`,
    168–27   * drew a large a`.
Ret. 15–18   not sufficient to seat the a`
Pul. 12– 3   impressive stillness of the a`
Hea. 17–18   claimed a` with a serpent.
Po. vi– 7   * and was sung by the a`
My. 81–17   * No more cosmopolitan a` ever
    185–23   spoke to an attentive a`

audience-room
My. 9– 3   * a` in The Mother Church which will

audiences
My. 68– 3   * impressing the a` with the beauty and

audit
Mis. 131–30   to itemize or a` their accounts,

audited
Man. 76–10   have the books . . . a` semi-annually,
    77– 2   books of the Church Treasurer a`
    77– 3   books are to be a` on May first.

Auditorium
My. 77– 5   * In this respect it leads the A` of

auditorium
Pul. 25– 8   * a`, seating eleven hundred people
    25–19   * entrances leading to the a`,
    25–21   * a` is seated with pews of
    27–12   * In the a` are two rose windows
    27–25   * One more window in the a`
    41–16   * The large a`, with its capacity for
    42–18   * pulpit end of the a` was rich with
    57– 5   * The a` is said to seat
    58–16   * main a` has wide galleries,
My. 7–16   * a` for The Mother Church that will
    16–11   * The corner-stone of the new a`
    24– 5   * to express in its ample a`
    46– 2   * in exquisite and expansive a`,
    57– 4   * need was felt of an a` that would

auditorium
My. 68– 4   * a`, with its high-domed ceiling,
    68–18   * color scheme for all the a` is
    69–16   * The a` contains seven galleries,
    71–21   * just one vast a` which will seat
    71–25   * every person seated in the a`,
    71–29   * a` that would seat five thousand
    80–11   * old a` of The Mother Church,
    80–21   * into the a` of the extension of
    80–31   * a` was comfortably filled.
    86–28   * Not even the great size of the a`

auditors
Pul. 59–29   * the a` left by the rear doors,
My. 80– 4   * earnestly assure thousands of a`

aught
Mis. 10–31   that a` but good exists in Science.
    12–26   Whatever manifests a` else
    18–31   but to believe that a`
    27– 4   or a` that can result in evil,
    72–29   cannot cognize a` material,
    124– 1   It is plain that a` unspiritual,
    171–26   Few people at present know a` of
    319– 5   This closes the argument of a`
    319– 5   a` else than good.
    344– 7   a` of that which leads to bliss,
    358–11   He that seeketh a` besides
    367–19   if He did know a` else,
    390– 9   Too pure for a` so mute.
Un. 10–14   toward a` but infinite Deity.
    18–26   of a` beside Myself is impossible.
    38–21   in a` which is unlike God,
Pul. 21–29   a` that can darken in any degree our
    74–21   If she said a` with intention to be
No. 17–10   to be conscious of a` but good.
    27– 4   Matter is not Mind, to claim a` ;
Pan. 9– 4   no reality in a` else.
'00. 5– 5   idolatry or a` besides God, good.
'02. 6– 2   to have a` unlike the infinite.
Po. 55–10   Too pure for a` so mute.
My. 137–25   before . . . I knew a` about them,
    153–19   Faith in a` else misguides the
    261– 9   that Santa Claus has a` to do with
    300– 2   belief in sin or in a` besides God,

augment
My. 10– 4   * and a` the achievements of its

augmented
Mis. 289–30   they should be consulted, a`, and

August
    (see **months**)

august
My. 294–27   The a` ruler . . . has now passed

Augusta, Me.
Pul. 88–16   * Kennebec Journal, A`, M`.

Augustus, Emperor
'00. 12–10   in the time of the Roman Emperor A .

auspices
Man. 88– 5   under the a` of Mary Baker Eddy,
    90–15   under the a` of this Board.
Pul. 6–20   * He went out under the a` of
My. 125–20   a` of the Massachusetts Metaphysical
    246– 6   examined under its a` by the Board

auspicious
Pul. 44–10   * a` hour in your eventful career.
    60–15   * come to Boston for this a` occasion
My. 201–16   on the a` occasion of the opening
    257–17   To this a` Christmastide,

Australia
'00. 1–17   in A`, the Philippine Islands,
My. 30–15   * from A`, from India, from England,
    136–21   also in Canada, A`, etc.
    208– 2   chapter sub-title

authentic
Mis. 376– 2   * most a` Italian school, revived.
    376– 3   * I use the words most a`
    376– 7   * said to have been a` ;

authentically
My. 181–27   a` said that one expositor of

authenticate
My. 179–20   a` Christ's Christianity as the

authenticated
Mis. 347–30   only a` organ of C. S.

authenticity
Mis. 98–24   attest the a` of their mission,
    193–10   the a` of the Gospels,
Ret. 35–18   no authority for querying the a` of
    70– 8   We do not question the a` of

author (see also **author's**)
Mis. 50– 3   God is not its a`,
    62–23   In that work the a` grapples with
    83– 6   "Every sin is the a` of itself,

author

Mis.	83–17	sin is the *a·* of sin.
	88– 7	*a· of that genuine critique in the*
	88– 9	*a·* of the article in question is
	196–13	God was not the *a·* of it ;
	216–15	an acquaintance with the *a·*
	296– 8	unknown *a·* cited by Mr. Wakeman
	361–20	Jesus the *a·* and finisher— *Heb.* 12 : 2.
	381–12	claim that Dr. Quimby was the *a·*
Ret.	70– 5	and claims God as their *a·* ;
Un.	26– 5	God is my *a·*, authority,
	26–10	Neither is He the *a·* of the material
Pul.	6–11	The *a·* of "Marriage of the Lamb,"
	39–11	*a·* of "The World Beautiful."
No.	42–24	would make a lie the *a·* of Truth,
'01.	4–12	God is the *a·* of Science
	17– 5	the *a·* and finisher of our faith,
Hea.	9–22	"Who is the *a·* of evil?"
Po.	39– 1	*A·* of all divine Gifts,
My.	258–13	Jesus the *a·* and finisher— *Heb.* 12 : 2.
	304– 6	*a·* of Sanborn's Grammar.
	304–24	the celebrated naturalist and *a·*,
	338–19	talented *a·* of this lecture has
	347–26	man is not the *a·* of Science,
	349–16	Jesus the *a·* and finisher— *Heb.* 12 : 2.
		(*see also* **Eddy**)

authoress

Ret.	1– 6	the pious and popular English *a·*
		(*see also* **Eddy**)

authoritative

My.	326– 6	* in an official and *a·* manner.

authoritatively

My.	346– 8	* may learn *a·* from the *Herald* that

authorities

Rud.	2– 9	word is used by the best *a·*,
'00.	13–27	* *a·* of the Judæo-Christian church."
Po.	vi–17	*a· could protect him nowhere but in*
My.	220– 7	reporting . . . to the proper *a·*
	332–25	* much interviewing with Masonic *a·*,
	335–20	* *a·* gave the cause of death as

authority

and law
Un.	26– 9	is not your *a·* and law.

and power
Mis.	333–25	God had *a·* and power,

any
Man.	66–21	any *a·* supposed to come from her

Biblical
Hea.	5–18	Such hypotheses ignore Biblical *a·*,

book as
Mis.	91–27	read from the book as *a·* for

brief
No.	22– 5	* clothed with a " brief *a·* ;"
My.	340–14	clad in a little brief *a·*,

cited as
Man.	104–18	these editions shall be cited as *a·*.

comes into
Un.	20– 6	Through these . . . evil comes into *a·* :

divine
Mis.	93–16	fear, . . . is without divine *a·*.
Un.	33– 7	we have it on divine *a·* ;
'01.	14–27	wrong has no divine *a·* ;

for Christian Science
My.	305– 4	as the *a·* for C. S. !
	318–31	not find my *a·* for C. S. in history,

good
My.	14–13	* claimed to have good *a·* for

having
Mis.	189–28	as one having *a·*,— *Matt.* 7 : 29.
Ret.	58–11	as one having *a·*,— *Matt.* 7 : 29.
Un.	42–19	as one having *a·*,— *Matt.* 7 : 29.

his
Mis.	76–18	no man can rationally reject his *a·*

no
Ret.	35–18	There is no *a·* for querying the
'01.	20– 3	no *a·* in C. S. for

no Biblical
Mis.	274– 2	we have no Biblical *a·* for a

no legal
Mis.	141–28	had no legal *a·* for obtaining,

of God
Un.	31–17	usurps the *a·* of God, Spirit ;

of Jesus
'01.	8–11	we have the *a·* of Jesus for
Peo.	9–20	despite the *a·* of Jesus

of sin
Ret.	63–11	When we deny the *a·* of sin,

of their Church
Man.	87– 5	consent of the *a·* of their Church.

only
My.	104– 1	The Bible has been my only *a·*.

our
'01.	25–20	What, then, is our *a·* in
	34– 4	Bible is our *a·* for asserting **this,**

authority

position of
My.	343–22	"A position of *a·*," she went on,

recognized
Pul.	55–29	* Truth is the sole recognized *a·*.

Scriptural
'02.	7–17	Scriptural *a·* for divine metaphysics

true
My.	232–18	Are Christ's teachings the true *a·*

Mis.	109– 4	or who take me as *a·* for
	195–15	We ask what is the *a·* for
	265– 1	and gives me as *a·* for it ;
	291– 9	as *a·* for other people's thoughts
Man.	51–20	*A·*.
	66–17	or she is referred to as *a·* for
	66–24	shall not report on *a·* an order
	104–12	Seventy-third Edition the *A·*.
Un.	26– 5	God is my author, *a·*, governor,
My.	190–13	accept our Master as *a·*,

authorize

Mis.	195–13	does not *a·* us to expect the

authorized

Man.	49–22	a clergyman who is legally *a·*.
	80– 9	is *a·* to order its disposition
	86– 3	*A·* to Teach.
	86– 4	*a·* to be a teacher of C. S.,
	87– 9	*a·* by its By-Laws to teach C. S.,
	111–11	studied C. S. with an *a·* teacher ;
My.	vi–29	* and *a· Der Herold der C. S.*,

Authorized Version

'02.	16– 5	which is rendered in the *A·V·*

authorizes

Mis.	93–10	C. S. *a·* the logical conclusion
	272–15	* who confers, or *a·* to be conferred,

author's

Mis.	216–23	to illustrate the *a·* following point
Ret.	75–17	embraced in the *a·* own mental mood,
	76– 1	plagiarizing an *a·* ideas
My.	224–15	not caught in some *a·* net,
		(*see also* **Eddy**)

authors

Mis.	80– 1	*a·* of spurious works on
	264– 1	while they quote from other *a·*
	301– 7	Those *a·* and editors of pamphlets
Man.	59– 3	writings of *a·* who think at random
Ret.	75– 9	citing from the works of other *a·*
	91–10	or by the Scripture *a·*.
'01.	27– 2	of all other *a·* except the Bible.
My.	52–28	* sacrifices from which most *a·* would
	114–15	I consulted no other *a·*
	224–15	would not deny their *a·* a hearing,
	305–20	* of the foremost living *a·*."

authorship

Mis.	301–11	gospel-opposing system of *a·*,
No.	42–22	Denial of the *a·* of "S. and H.
'01.	21–13	improved in its teaching and *a·*
My.	306– 2	my character, education, and *a·*,
	317– 6	* in the *a·* of "S. and H.
	321–25	* knowledge of the *a·* of your works

autographs

Mis.	280–22	on each page, with their *a·*.

autopsy

Man.	50– 1	an *a·* shall be made by qualified

Autumn

Mis.	395–14	poem
Po.	vi–28	* poem
	page 58	poem

autumn

Mis.	142–18	shaded as *a·* leaves with bright hues
	332– 9	may its sober-suited *a·* follow
	395–18	Ere *a·* blanch another year,
Ret.	4–16	shone richly in the mellow hues of *a·*,
Po.	58– 3	Ere *a·* blanch another year,

autumnal

Mis.	355–30	at the close of a balmy *a·* day,

autumn's

Mis.	395–27	Enhancing *a·* gloom.
Po.	58–12	Enhancing *a·* gloom.

auxiliaries

Mis.	260–26	not always the *a·* of Truth.
Man.	43– 7	as *a·* to teaching C. S.

auxiliary

My.	246–22	is an *a·* to the College called
	288–18	matter was not the *a·* of Spirit.

avail

Mis.	7–13	of what can mortal opinion *a·*?
	89–30	*a·* himself of the efficacy of Truth,
	165–26	is the sinner ready to *a·* himself of
	181–12	What *a·*, then, to quarrel over
	344–14	Of what *a·* would geometry be to

avail
My. 317–11   so as to a· myself of
344–27   Were vaccination of any a·,

availability
My. 353–15   universal activity and a· of Truth ;

available
Mis. 62–13   by that much, less a·.
359–23   and is a· at the right time.
My. 54–18   * could be found that was a·,

availed
My. 318–10   I a· myself of the name of

availeth
My. 220–19   I also have faith that my prayer a·,
280–11   * righteous prayer which a· much.

avails
Mis. 33– 2   It is the righteous prayer that a·

avarice
Pul. 10–13   No dream of a· or ambition

ave
My. 204–10   sacred a· and essence of Soul

avenge
Mis. 129– 8   To a· an imaginary or an actual
227–31   Not to a· one's self upon one's
228– 5   and yet not to a· thyself,

avenging
Mis. 275– 6   Who — but God's a· angel !
My. 161–27   When evil was a· itself on its

Aventine
Pul. 10– 8   Rome's fallen fanes and silent A·

avenue
Mis. 185–12   good flows into every a· of being,

avenues
'01.   1– 3   through the mental a· of mankind

aver
Mis. 49–30   God is Truth, the Scriptures a· ;
Rud. 13–19   To a· that harmony is the real
No.   2– 5   To a· that disease is normal,
My. 193–23   Here I a· that you have
300–14   or a· that there is no death,

average
Mis. 131– 7   of more than a· avoirdupois
Pan. 10–12   were the a· man and woman.
My. 88– 7   * above the a· in intelligence.
106–24   more than does the a· man,

averred
Pan. 10–13   best students in the class a·

averring
Ret. 60– 6   a· that there is nothing beside God ;

avers
Mis. 253– 3   not merely a gift, as St. Paul a·,
295– 4   a· that the "cursed barmaid system"
No.   5–15   Material sense also a· that Spirit,

avert
Un. 19– 6   yet which He cannot a·.
No.   2–25   Conceit cannot a· the effects of deceit.

averts
Mis. 71–14   Science never a· law,
Po. 10–21   His hand a· the blow."
My. 337–22   His hand a· the blow."

avoid
Mis. 39– 4   To a· being *subject* to disease,
48– 2   and a· all that works ill,
127–25   cannot a· wielding it if we reflect
130–23   a· referring to past mistakes.
234–14   his effort to . . . a· hard work ;
322– 7   To a· this, I may hereafter
347– 4   To a· danger from this source
363–22   a· the shoals of a sensual religion
Ret. 65–18   it will continue to a· whatever
84–29   a· leaving his own regular institute
No.   8– 6   A· voicing error ;
35–15   and how to a· paying it.
My. 160–15   most men a· until compelled to
224–13   A· . . . public debating clubs.
226– 1   To a· using this word incorrectly,
244– 2   in order to a· the stir that might be
363–25   a· naming, in his mental treatment,

avoidance
Mis. 257–19   reliance where there should be a·,
Pul. 15– 6   to ensure the a· of the evil?
My. 211–23   reliance where there should be a·,

avoided
Mis. 80–10   A league which . . . should be a·.
240– 3   squills and bills would have been a· ;

avoiding
Mis. 45– 8   a· the fatal results that frequently
300– 1   a· the cost of hiring or purchasing?

avoirdupois
Mis. 131– 7   man of more than average a·

avowal
Mis. 83–26   for the a· of this great truth,

avowals
No. 42– 4   Such sentiments are wholesome a· of

avowed
'01. 25–26   since been a· to be as real,

avowing
My. 95–22   * a· their disbelief in the miraculous.
200– 2   a· and consolidating the genius of

await
Mis. 241–14   else he will doubtingly a· the result ;
Man. 66–12   to a· her explanation thereof.
My. 222–31   a· the end — justice and judgment.

awaited
My. 244– 1   I have a· your arrival before
244–13   I have a· the right hour,
318–13   confidently a· the years to declare

awaiting
Mis. 358–28   a·, with staff in hand, God's
360– 4   a· the hammering, chiselling, and
Ret. 85–22   a· only an opportunity
'00. 15– 3   for many years has been a· you.
My. 20– 9   a· on behalf of your Leader
30– 2   * or a· admission to one.
150– 2   and where its tender lesson is not a·

awaits
Mis. 246–21   a· the crouching wrong that
'02. 11– 7   a· with warrant and welcome,
19–24   a spiritual behest, in reversion, a·
My. 177–22   joy of many generations a· it,
230– 2   eternity a· our Church Manual,
290–21   He a· to welcome you where no arrow

awake
Mis. 15–21   and man a· in His likeness.
30–31   and a· in His likeness.
44–21   when a·, or when asleep in a dream.
47–17   with less impediment than when a·,
60–20   with another who is a·.
205–12   a·, and caught napping?
299– 1   a· to their cause and character.
331–29   As mortals a· from their dream
358–12   "a· in His likeness," — see *Psal.* 17 : 15.
400– 3   Slumbers not in God's embrace ; Be a· ;
Ret. 61–11   you cannot a· in fear or
Un. 2–21   a· from a sense of death
3– 4   they a· only to another sphere of
20–18   You will a· to the perception of
50–21   and a· from the troubled dream,
Pul. 84–19   * All who are a· thereto have
Rud. 11–16   a· from a night-dream ;
11–17   just so you can a· from the dream of
No. 36– 5   when we a· in the divine likeness.
'00. 3–13   a· the slumbering capability of man.
8– 3   till we a· in his likeness.
'01. 15– 2   must a· from his belief in this awful
'02. 17–12   who should keep themselves a·
Hea. 17–12   we shall all learn this as we a· to
Peo. 14–12   a· to a higher and holier love for
Po. 76–14   Slumbers not in God's embrace ; Be a· ;
My. 356– 1   When will mankind a· to know their
350–27   A· and arise from this temptation

awaken
Mis. 42– 9   to a· with thoughts, and being,
100– 5   was to a· the dull senses,
106–30   and a· the heart's harpstrings.
Ret. 61– 6   as when you a· from sleep
Pul. 50–20   * will a· some sort of interest.
'01. 17– 2   a· the sufferer from the mortal
My. 204– 5   which storms a· to vigor and to
230–14   and to a· the sinner.
267–20   a· from his dream of life in matter
273–30   death alone does not a· man in God's
297–21   If we would a· to this recognition,

awakened
Mis. 4–19   Much interest is a· and expressed
16–24   This newly a· consciousness is wholly
123–19   there has risen to the a· thought
201–28   is a· to bar his door against
347–19   A true sense . . . has been a·.
No. 39–20   an a· desire to be and do good.
40– 9   pure pearls of a· consciousness,
'00. 15–13   a· to see through sin's disguise
15–18   a feast for this a· consciousness.
My. 155–20   an a· sense of the risen Christ.
257– 7   To the a· consciousness,
281– 2   and a· a wiser want,

awakening
Mis. 16–16   a· from the dream of life in matter,
Ret. 21–21   The a· from a false sense of life,
Pul. 23– 9   * The "great a·" of the time of

awakening
My. 316- 5　song of the Redeemer *a·* the nations,

awakes
Mis. 15- 3　until he *a·* from it.
222-18　the subject scarcely *a·* in time,
Un. 56-21　Until he *a·* from his delusion,
My. 273-28　"Man *a·* from the dream of death

award
My. 332- 7　* yet it is all we can *a·* :

aware
Mis. 148-23　not *a·* that the contribution box was
176-26　Are we duly *a·* of our own great
227-13　ere that one himself become *a·*,
335- 9　hour that he is not *a·* of, — Matt. 24 : 50.
Pul. 31-15　* in the early '80's that I became *a·*
34-11　* became *a·* of a divine illumination
My. 342- 2　* I became *a·* of a white-haired lady
358- 6　You are *a·* that animal magnetism is

away
Mis. 10-24　wherein old things pass *a·*
17- 7　before the flames have died *a·*
27-32　Take *a·* the mortal sense of
33-25　It does *a·* with all material
48-27　That persons have gone *a·* from
53-27　the thought educated *a·* from it
58-25　Take *a·* the theology of
58-26　and you take *a·* its science,
59-25　leading his thoughts *a·* from
74-19　rolled *a·* the stone from the door
77-26　belief that man has fallen *a·* from
84-27　takes them *a·*, and teaches
90- 3　Take *a·* this pleasure, and you
98- 4　should turn *a·* from inharmony,
99-21　earth shall pass *a·*, — Matt. 24 : 35.
99-22　shall not pass *a·* ; " — Matt. 24 : 35.
111-17　earth shall pass *a·*, — Matt. 24 : 35.
111-18　shall not pass *a·* ; " — Matt. 24 : 35.
120-25　*a·* from their own fields of labor.
121- 2　his words can never pass *a·* :
121-16　put *a·* the guilt — Deut. 19 : 13.
123-18　Divine Science has rolled *a·* the stone
144- 8　there are laid *a·* a copy of
144-14　laid *a·* as a sacred secret
156- 9　when the mist shall melt *a·*
163-19　earth shall pass *a·*, — Matt. 24 : 35.
163-19　shall not pass *a·* ! " — Matt. 24 : 35.
168-29　* and many had to go *a·*
176-22　melted *a·* in the fire of love
179- 2　roll *a·* the stone? " — see Mark 16 : 3.
179- 3　The stone has been rolled *a·* by
189-18　quickening spirit takes it *a·*
198- 5　turning *a·* from material gods ;
205- 5　and melting *a·* the shadows
210-14　and takes *a·* its sting.
212-14　One step *a·* from the direct line
222- 1　It takes *a·* a man's proper sense of
225-23　Looking *a·* from all material aid,
246-11　washed it divinely *a·* in C. S. !
254-19　take *a·* a third part of the stars
255-22　It does *a·* with material medicine,
275- 3　would you take *a·* even woman's
275- 4　Who can roll *a·* the stone
285- 4　I ordered to be laid *a·*
289-21　Rights that are bargained *a·*
292-15　*a·* from the open sepulchres of sin,
324-22　Stealing cautiously *a·* from his comrades,
325-11　seize his pearls, throw them *a·*,
325-17　dreaming *a·* the hours.
325-24　*A·* from this charnel-house
327-32　wipes *a·* the blood stains,
328-18　stumbled, and wandered *a·*?
333-15　*a·* from the only living and
333-17　*a·* from the divine source of being,
334-11　*a·* goes all its supposed power
335- 1　*a·* from this divine Principle
336-28　only to take *a·* its frailty.
343-12　*a·* from the sordid soil of self
343-15　picking *a·* the cold, hard pebbles
343-23　and tear them *a·* from their
345-31　turned men *a·* from the thought
357-16　what has been sown has withered *a·*,
359-10　I put *a·* childish things. — I Cor. 13 : 11.
360-16　When C. S. has melted *a·* the
370- 5　they went *a·* and took counsel
381-23　publishing, selling, giving *a·*,
385-24　and doomed To pass *a·*.
388- 4　What chased the clouds *a·*?
399- 2　Love wipes your tears all *a·*,
399-19　Rolled *a·* from loving heart
Man. 41- 9　turneth *a·* wrath." — Prov. 15 : 1.
48-20　*a·* from personality and numbering
94-10　should go *a·* contemplating truth ;
Chr. 53-53　To-day, as oft, *a·* from sin
Ret. 7- 3　passed *a·* at the age of thirty-one,
18-10　and perfume from buds burst *a·*,

away
Ret. 18-25　This life is a shadow, and hastens *a·*.
20- 8　was sent *a·* from me,
34-11　does *a·* with all material medicines,
42-13　In 1882 he passed *a·*.
80-25　sees the door and turns *a·* from it,
89-15　had been *a·* from the neighborhood ;
Un. 2- 9　takes *a·* man's fondness for sin
11-18　taking *a·* the material evidence.
14-23　infinite model would be taken *a·*.
25-25　evil can never take *a·*.
30-10　takes *a·* this belief and restores
34-19　Take *a·* mortal mind,
34-21　Take *a·* matter, and mortal mind
43-16　never "pass *a·* — see Matt. 5 : 18.
57-27　Science wipes *a·* all tears.
Pul. 7-16　and with power to wash *a·*,
14-10　carried *a·* of the — Rev. 12 : 15.
16- 4　Rolled *a·* from loving heart
36-16　* I came *a·* in a state of
49-20　* to get *a·* from her busy career
50-22　* thoroughly carried *a·* with
54-23　* He kept the unbelievers *a·*,
Rud. 2-20　takes *a·* the trammels assigned to
11-21　takes *a·* every human belief,
No. 1-16　flames die *a·* on the mount
7-12　*a·* from the enemy of sinning sense,
36-24　rolled *a·* the stone from the
40-17　never to take *a·* the rights,
43-23　which they go *a·* to disgrace.
Pan. 10- 1　it takes *a·* man's personality
'00. 11- 9　turns mortals *a·* from earth
'01. 7-20　have not taken *a·* their Lord,
9-17　taketh *a·* the sin of — John 1 : 29.
16-26　and go *a·* to pray?
26-12　*a·* from Christ's purely spiritual
31-27　yielded up . . . what He took *a·*.
'02. 19-20　troubled sea foams itself *a·*,
19-22　treasures, taken *a·* from you?
20-13　That swept the clouds *a·* ;
Hea. 10- 1　he saw it pass *a·*, — an illusion.
Peo. 1- 5　crumbling *a·* of material elements
5- 5　have not taken *a·* our Lord,
5-18　points *a·* from matter and
9- 5　washing *a·* the motives for sin ;
11-13　gnawing *a·* life and hope ;
Po. 2-16　On wings of morning gladly flit *a·*,
7- 4　What chased the clouds *a·*?
15-11　whispering voices are calling *a·*
22-10　wipes the tears of time *A·*,
23-22　Bid error melt *a·* !
31-21　That wipes *a·* the sting of death
33-19　That waft me *a·* to my God.
41-14　sunny slopes of the woodland *a·* ;
48-20　and doomed To pass *a·*.
63-21　and perfume from buds burst *a·*,
64-22　This life is a shadow, and hastens *a·*.
65-18　and death like mist melt *a·*,
70- 1　*a·* In the dim distance,
70-14　*A·*, then, mortal sense !
75- 9　Love wipes your tears all *a·*,
76- 3　Rolled *a·* from loving heart
78-12　When to be wiped *a·*, Thou knowest
My. 4-21　the iron in human nature rusts *a·* ;
16-29　the hail shall sweep *a·* — Isa. 28 : 17.
24-26　* they have gone *a·* with the conviction
30-28　* hundreds had to be turned *a·*,
44- 4　* tears are being wiped *a·*,
45-25　* "He took not *a·* the — Exod. 13 : 22.
54- 2　* hundreds going *a·* who could not
69-31　* in Cambridge, some four miles *a·*.
82- 8　* trying to get *a·* at the same time.
82-19　* seem that this ability to get *a·*
83-10　* but this is usually hidden *a·*
92-22　* but one cannot sneer *a·* the
94- 6　* "One cannot sneer *a·* the
111-10　swept *a·* their illogical syllogisms
119-16　*a·* from the supposedly crucified
119-30　spirit of Truth that leadeth *a·* from
120-11　God's spiritual idea that takes *a·* all sin,
132-31　wipes *a·* the unavailing, tired tear,
135- 5　I put *a·* childish things." — I Cor. 13 : 11.
153-31　pointing *a·* from matter and man
166- 6　Religions may waste *a·*,
171- 7　sighing shall flee *a·*." — Isa. 35 : 10.
191-16　Love, which wipes *a·* all tears.
191-23　The stone is rolled *a·*.
193-16　Love gives nothing to take *a·*.
247-22　*persuasion* that takes *a·* their fear,
252-13　and run *a·* in the storm,
261-17　I put *a·* childish things." — I Cor. 13 : 11.
297-14　blows *a·* the baubles of belief,
313-25　to describe scenes far *a·*,
335-18　* at the end of nine days he passed *a·*.

awe
Mis. 249-28　I am in *a·* before it.

awe
Ret. 25–29 I beheld with ineffable *a·*
My. 63–21 * *a·* and of reverence beyond words,
awed
My. 78–28 * the little children, *a·* by the grandeur of
awe-filled
No. 10– 2 I employ this *a·* word in both a
awestruck
Po. 71–10 Righteousness ne'er — *a·* or dumb
awful
Mis. 14–18 This *a·* deception is evil's umpire
17– 1 *a·* detonations of Sinai.
99– 8 cost Galileo, what? This *a·* price :
238– 1 *a·* story that "he helped 'niggers'
Ret. 69–25 "Above error's *a·* din,
No. 35–14 the *a·* price paid by sin,
'01. 15– 2 must awake from his belief in this *a·*
Po. 27– 3 Bloated oppression in its *a·* hour,
awhile
Po. 33–11 (And mem'ry but part us *a·*),
awoke
Mis. 180– 1 I *a·* from the dream of
225–28 In about one hour he *a·*,
Ret. 20–18 *A·* new beauty in the surge's roll !
axe
Mis. 37–17 C. S. lays the *a·* at the root of
235–12 It lays the *a·* at the root of
285–19 laying the *a·* at the root of error.

axe
'01. 13–15 C. S. lays the *a·* at the root of sin,
23–17 he laid the *a·* at the root of
My. 268–25 lays the *a·* at the root of all evil,
287–21 it lays the *a·* at the root of the
296– 3 lays the *a·* "unto the root — *Matt. 3 : 10.*
axiom
'01. 30–28 and to adopt Pope's *a·* :
Hea. 11–18 it has established this *a·*,
My. 58– 6 * proves the truth of the *a·*,
177–17 was allied to that olden *a·* :
236–10 An old *a·* says :
357–23 the *a·* of true C. S.,
axiomatic
Mis. 271–16 take in this *a·* truism :
Ret. 87– 4 is so eternally true, so *a·*,
axioms
'01. 25–13 No Christly *a·*, practices, or
axis
Ret. 88–30 Mind revolves on a spiritual *a·*,
Ayer, D. D., Rev. Franklin D.
My. 174–13 To the Rev. Franklin D. *A·*, *D.D.*,
ayont
Po. 79–15 and lifteth me, *A·* hate's thrall :
azure
Mis. 323– 3 city above all clouds, in serene *a·*
Po. 18– 1 in the *a·* the eagle's proud wing,
34–20 in *a·* bright soar far above ;

B

Baal (*see also* **Baal's**)
Mis. 333–24 worshippers of *B·* worshipped the sun.
Baalites
My. 151–24 the *B·* or sun-worshippers failed to
Baal's
No. 39– 6 after the fashion of *B·* prophets,
babbling
No. 1– 8 *b·* brooks fill the rivers till they
babe
Mis. 72– 2 For the innocent *b·* to be born
111–32 or is an incarnated *b·*,
159–19 not so much the Bethlehem *b·*,
164–13 *b·* Jesus seemed small to mortals ;
167– 7 Is the *b·* a son, or daughter?
370–15 This is the *b·* we are to cherish.
370–16 *b·* that twines its loving arms
300–24 nurse the Bethlehem *b·* so sweet,
Chr. 53–24 O'er *b·* and crib.
Ret. 19–18 my *b·* was born.
20–20 *b·* of my soul.
31–28 as by the tearful lips of a *b·*.
40–15 at the birth of her last *b·*,
40–17 her *b·* was safely born,
70– 9 Virgin-mother and Bethlehem *b·*,
90–19 comprehend the needs of her *b·*
Un. 6–21 talk to her *b·* about the problems of
61– 6 appeared as a helpless human *b·* ;
Pul. 1– 4 a *b·* of time, a prophecy
No. 26– 7 than the *b·* is identical with
36–27 was a *b·* born in a manger,
Po. 21–13 the Bethlehem *b·* so sweet,
29–12 The Bethlehem *b·* — Beloved,
70–20 As when this *b·* was born,
My. 257– 7 the Bethlehem *b·* has left his
258–17 The memory of the Bethlehem *b·*
262– 7 mortal *b·* — a *b·* born in a manger
262–10 This homely origin of the *b·* Jesus
330–30 my *b·* was born.
Babel
My. 245–15 and to their *B·* of confusion
babes
Mis. 167–26 revealed them unto *b·* !" — *Luke 10 : 21.*
Ret. 61–29 Let there be milk for *b·*,
Pul. 8–18 and *b·* gave kisses to
8–22 "Out of the mouths of *b·* — *Matt. 21 : 16.*
Rud. 8– 3 or provides breast-milk for *b·*.
No. v–11 if you are *b·* in Christ,
45– 2 revealed them unto *b·*." — *Luke 10 : 21.*
My. 6–21 evidencing the praise of *b·*
17– 6 "As newborn *b·*, — *I Pet. 2 : 2.*
baby
Mis. 231–16 And the *b·* !
231–21 Now ! *b·* has tumbled,
231–26 That was a scientific *b·* ;
Babylon
'00. 3–22 Israelites in *B·* hesitated not

Babylonian
Pan. 8– 3 *B·* sun god, moon god,
'00. 4– 8 *B·* and Neoplatonic religion,
Babylonian Yawa
Mis. 123–15 *B· Y·*, or Jehovah,
Babylonish
My. 125–29 The doom of the *B·* woman,
120–24 The *B·* woman is fallen,
Bachelor
My. 245–29 degrees of *B·* and Doctor of C. S.,
back
Mis. xi–20 to fling it *b·* and forth.
23– 3 the power *b·* of gravitation,
50– 7 *is there a secret b· of what*
52–27 would be obliged to turn *b·*
93– 6 *bring b· old beliefs of disease*
93–22 bring on disease or bring *b·* disease,
99–15 take not *b·* the words of Truth.
112–20 he sank *b·* in his chair,
140–23 and now it must be put *b·* into
169– 6 *b·* to the inspired pages.
184–24 The Science of being gives *b·* the
184–32 giving *b·* the lost sense of
195– 8 is held *b·* by reason of the lack of
211–18 to be pitied and brought *b·*
294–17 keep *b·* thy offerings from asps
324–23 he departs ; then turns *b·*,
327– 1 When I went *b·* into the house
327–27 Obstinately holding themselves *b·*,
327–31 goes *b·* and kindly binds up their
328– 4 will call thee *b·* to the path
328–17 turned *b·*, stumbled, and wandered
329–27 calling the feathered tribe *b·* to
365–28 held *b·* by the common ignorance
376–14 * You have given us *b·* our Jesus,
390– 8 Gives *b·* some maiden melody,
Ret. 20–25 to get *b·* my child,
Un. 64–17 can never turn *b·* what Deity knoweth,
Pul. 13–21 comes *b·* to him at last
20– 5 gave *b·* the land to the church.
46–13 * in going *b·* to the ancestral tree
No. 11–11 this system is held *b·* by
Hea. 6– 3 and so come *b·* to the world?
6–24 lying *b·* in the unconscious thought,
Peo. 1– 6 translation of law *b·* to its
Po. 23– 7 Or give . . . *b·* An image of the soul.
55– 9 Gives *b·* some maiden melody,
71– 7 Corruption's band is driven *b·* ;
My. 12–22 it comes not *b·* again.
47–13 * look *b·* to the picturesque,
47–16 * To-day we look *b·* over the years
59–16 * my mind was carried *b·* to
68–21 * great organ is placed *b·* of the
69–17 * and three at the *b·*,
80– 1 * *b·* to the age of miracles.
84– 6 * retards and holds *b·* work
132–32 brings *b·* the wanderer to
184–18 brought *b·* to me the odor of

back

My.	307– 5	*b·* of his magnetic treatment
	316–20	turn *b·* the foaming torrents of
	336– 5	* to take her *b·* to the North.
	342–18	* Mrs. Eddy sat *b·* to be questioned.
	343–29	brought all *b·* to union and love

Back Bay

Pul.	24– 3	* church is in the fashionable *B· B·*,
	57–23	* this new edifice on *B· B·*,
My.	77–29	* edifice in the *B· B·* district
	84–15	* in that section of the *B· B·*.
	86–23	* edifice of the . . . on the *B· B·*
	325– 7	* very sure *B· B·* property would never
	325–11	* greater future than the new *B· B·*.

Back Bay Park

Mis.	139–19	near the beautiful *B· B· P·*,
Pul.	36–22	* at the entrance to the *B· B· P·*,

backbiteth

My.	33–19	He that *b·* not — *Psal.* 15 : 3.

backbone

Pul.	46–12	* Aristocratic to the *b·*,

background

Mis.	266–10	Stationary in the *b·*,
	376–25	on a *b·* of cerulean hue ;

backs

Mis.	325–17	or, flat on their *b·*,

back-to-back

Mis.	171– 8	*b·* seances with their patients,

backward

Mis.	340– 1	One *b·* step, one relinquishment of
Pul.	vii–11	instructive to turn *b·* the

backwardness

Pul.	15– 5	Why this *b·*, since exposure is

bacteria

My.	344–16	* reject utterly the *b·* theory

bad

Mis.	25–29	then they are *b·* and unfit for man ;
	69–20	neutralized the *b·* effects of
	71–12	*good or b· influences on the unborn*
	72– 8	good and *b·* traits of the parents
	198–24	belief, fear, theory, or *b·* deed,
	243– 3	with no *b·* results,
	296–28	and the *b·* appetites of men
	345–10	* I cannot change from good to *b·*.''
	362–31	the influence of *b·* inclinations
Man.	63–24	shall have no *b·* habits,
Un.	15–23	*b·* deity, who seeks to do
Pul.	69–13	* leave no room there for the *b·*,
Hea.	10–14	question of a good and a *b·* side to
Peo.	13–20	* cannot change . . . from good to *b·*.''
My.	87–24	* not be a *b·* thing if all the world
	205–18	* as the thing made is good or *b·*,
	220– 1	save him from *b·* physical results.
	310–26	* mingled with *b·* temper.''

bade

Mis.	197–10	and *b·* his followers pursue.
Ret.	9– 9	*b·* me, when the voice called again,
	13–18	*b·* me lean on God's love,
Pul.	33– 7	* and *b·* her, if she heard the voice
My.	149– 3	by doing as he *b·* :
	156–13	he *b·* them say to the good man
	215– 5	He it was that *b·* me do what I did,
	215–24	he *b·* them take no scrip
	215–26	Next, . . . he *b·* them take scrip.

badge

Mis.	137– 3	your card of invitation, your *b·*,
Pul.	42–15	* each of them wore a white satin *b·*

badges

My.	83– 8	* has been no flaunting of *b·*

badly

Mis.	12– 5	If you have been *b·* wronged, forgive

badness

My.	123–29	small things in goodness or in *b·*,

baffle

Mis.	125–26	the controversies which *b·* it,

baffles

Mis.	221–22	*b·* the student of Mind-healing,

baggage

Mis.	327–12	These had heavy *b·* of their own,
	327–17	those who, having less *b·*,
	327–22	determined not to part with their *b·*.
	327–31	Then he who has no *b·* goes
'02.	10–21	discharges burdensome *b·*,
My.	82–10	* trunks and smaller articles of *b·*

Bailey St., 105

My.	328– 5	* 105 *B· S·*, Asheville, N. C.,

Baker

Abigail (Ambrose)

Pul.	32–18	* Mark and Abigail (Ambrose) *B·*,

Albert

Ret.	6–11	my second brother, Albert *B·*,
	6–15	My brother Albert was graduated at
	6–20	Albert spent a year in the office of
	7– 7	* Albert *B·* was a young man of
	10– 8	From my brother Albert I received
Pul.	32–28	* Albert *B·*, graduated at Dartmouth
My.	309–27	*[Albert] received a liberal education.
	310– 4	Albert was a distinguished lawyer.
	310–18	* all the family, ''excepting Albert,

Congressman

Pul.	48–17	* Congressman *B·* from New Hampshire,

George

My.	312–13	taken to . . . by her brother George.

George S.

My.	332–14	* signature
	336– 4	* her brother, George S. *B·*,

George Sullivan

My.	310– 9	youngest brother, George Sullivan *B·*,

Grandfather

Ret.	2–26	A relative of my Grandfather *B·*

Hon. Henry M.

My.	135–15	namely, the Hon. Henry M. *B·*,
	136–15	Hon. Henry M. *B·*, who won a suit
	137–22	namely, the Hon. Henry M. *B·*,

Hon. Henry Moore

Ret.	4– 9	brother of the Hon. Henry Moore *B·*

James

Ret.	4– 4	and with his brother, James *B·*,

Joseph

Ret.	1–18	an Englishman, named Joseph *B·*,
	2– 7	Joseph *B·* and his wife,

Mark (*see also* Baker's)

Ret.	4– 2	was my father, Mark *B·*,
	4–23	The wife of Mark *B·* was
Pul.	32–17	* daughter of Mark and Abigail . . . *B·*,
My.	172– 6	* grown on the farm of Mark *B·*,
	309– 9	and Mark *B·* for Bow.
	309–17	Mark *B·* was the youngest of

Mary (*see also* Eddy)

Ret.	8–10	I heard somebody call Mary,
Pul.	32–17	* Mary *B·* was the daughter of
	33– 2	* As a child Mary *B·* saw visions
My.	309–27	* Mary *B·* passed her first fifteen years at
	310–23	* Mary, a child ten years old,
	310–29	* ''When do you ever see Mary angry?''
	311–30	* ''Mary *B·* completed her education

Mary Morse

Mis.	x–18	my Christian name, Mary Morse *B·*.

Mary's

Ret.	9– 5	if she really did hear Mary's name

Miss

Pul.	34– 1	* At an early age Miss *B·* was married

Mrs. Abigail Ambrose

Ret.	5–21	* character of Mrs. Abigail Ambrose *B·*

Mrs. Marion McNeil

Ret.	2– 1	Mrs. Marion McNeil *B·* was reared

Samuel D.

My.	310–15	My oldest brother, Samuel D. *B·*,

Uncle James (*see* Baker's)

Ret.	5– 6	In the *B·* homestead at Bow
My.	309–21	describing the *B·* homestead at Bow :
	313–28	to a *B·* that was a sorry offence.

Baker's

Grandmother

Ret.	2–18	one of my Grandmother *B·* books,
	2–30	line of my Grandmother *B·* family

Mark

My.	309–20	Mark *B·* father paid the largest tax

Uncle James

Ret.	4– 8	owned by Uncle James *B·* grandson,

Bakers

My.	309–26	* ''Alone of the *B·*, he [Albert]

Balaam

'00.	12–29	It refers to the Hebrew *B·* as the
	13–23	school of *B·* and Æsculapius,

balance

Mis.	104–30	gain a *b·* on the side of good,
	263–21	poise the wavering *b·* on the right
	317–21	is inadequate to adjust the *b·*
	321– 9	*b·* adjusted more on the side of God,
	350– 2	the *b·* was never receipted for.
Man.	75–20	the *b·* of the building funds,
	75–23	*b·* of the church building funds,
No.	18–13	when weighed in the *b·*,
My.	9–27	what my heart gives to *b·* accounts.
	16– 6	* there was a *b·* of $226,285.73

balances
  Mis. 280– 5 with *b·* to weigh the thoughts and
  288– 7 should be dropped into the *b·* of God
  365– 5 weighed in the *b·* of God
balancing
  Mis. 65–25 *b·* man's account with his Maker.
  325–18 *B·* on one foot, with eyes half open,
  My. 161– 7 thus *b·* his account with divine Love,
bald
  Pan. 12–27 unpierced . . . by *b·* philosophy,
ball
  Mis. 11– 5 if a man should aim a *b·* at my heart,
Ballard, William P.
  My. 174–16 John C. Thorne, William P. *B·*,
balloon
  Mis. 129–16 will seek occasion to *b·* an atom of
balm
  Mis. 110– 1 The costly *b·* of Araby,
  No. 44–19 healing *b·* of Truth and Love
  Po. vii–14 * a *b·* to the weary heart.
  22–16 probe the wound, then pour the *b·*
  24– 3 A *b·* — the long-lost leaven
  My. 38– 1 * the *b·* of heavenly joy,
  129–12 brook, blossom, breeze, and *b·*
  175–22 Sweeter than the *b·* of Gilead,
balmy
  Mis. 355–30 at the close of a *b·* autumnal day,
Baltimore
  Md
  Pul. 68–12 * *The American, B·,* Md.,

  Pul. 68–21 * adds interest to the *B·* organization.
  68–24 * The *B·* congregation was organized
  69– 1 * the pastor, came to *B·*
  '00. 1–20 *B·,* Charleston, S. C., Atlanta,
Bancroft, S. P.
  My. 60–21 * signature
band
  Mis. 144– 6 a little *b·* called Busy Bees,
  279–16 Joshua and his *b·* before the walls
  279–24 in the case of Joshua and his *b·*
  386–19 o'er thy broken household *b·*,
  Man. 17– 1 little *b·* of earnest seekers
  Ret. 85– 4 to *b·* together their students
  Po. 50– 4 o'er thy broken household *b·*,
  71– 6 Corruption's *b·* Is driven back ;
  My. 50– 6 * little *b·* of prayerful workers.
  50– 9 * so this little *b·* of pioneers,
  50–21 * fresh courage to the earnest *b·*,
  158–24 will bless this dear *b·* of brethren.
  257– 2 alas for the broken household *b·* !
bandage
  Hea. 19– 9 removed the *b·* from his eyes,
bandages
  Mis. 243– 9 doctor had put on splints and *b·*
bands
  Un. 12– 5 bind it with *b·* of Soul.
  Rud. 4–13 "loose the *b·* of Orion." — *Job.* 38 : 31.
bane
  '00. 8– 9 comes forth a blessing or a *b·*
  '01. 20–15 This mental *b·* could not bewilder,
  My. 224– 7 *b·* which follows disobedience,
baneful
  Mis. 115–29 *b·* effects of sin on yourself,
  My. 301–22 *b·* effects of illusion on mortal
banish
  Po. 41–17 didst call them to *b·* all pain,
  My. 95–24 * *b·* faith in the supernatural,
banished
  Ret. 31–15 *b·* at once and forever the
  Po. 70–24 sin, and death are *b·* hence.
banishes
  Mis. 204–31 *b·* forever all envy, rivalry,
banishment
  Ret. 13– 9 doomed to perpetual *b·*
bank
  Ret. 5– 2 left *b·* of the Merrimac River.
bank-notes
  My. 78–15 * every basket piled high with *b·*,
bankrupt
  Mis. 374–20 homage is indeed due, — but is *b·*.
  My. 9–19 I am *b·* in thanks to you,
bankruptcy
  Mis. 122–24 Neither spiritual *b·* nor a
banks
  My. 150–15 willowy *b·* dyed with emerald.

banner
  Mis. 138–27 under the *b·* of His love,
  285–11 hold high the *b·* of Truth
  Po. 10– 1 fling thy *b·* To the billows
  My. 232– 2 unfurling your *b·* to the breeze
  291–21 bear its *b·* into the vast forever.
  337– 3 fling thy *b·* To the billows
banners
  Pul. 83–13 * as an army with *b·*." — *Song* 6 : 10.
banquet
  Mis. 149– 4 to this *b·* of C. S.,
  Ret. 18–13 Oft plucked for the *b·*,
  Po. 64– 3 Oft plucked for the *b·*,
banquet-rooms
  Mis. 324– 8 parlors, dancing-halls, and *b·*.
bans
  Mis. 172– 8 regardless of the *b·* or clans
banter
  My. 322–23 * seemed inclined to *b·* me
baptism
  Mis. 30–31 bathe in the *b·* of Spirit,
  82– 8 out of the *b·* of Spirit,
  125– 2 be baptized with his *b·* !
  131–12 one faith, one God, one *b·*.
  203–17 *b·* serves to rebuke the senses
  203–19 *First :* The *b·* of repentance
  204–12 *Second :* The *b·* of the Holy Ghost
  205–13 *Third :* The *b·* of Spirit,
  213–18 must pass through a *b·* of fire.
  298–16 the material rite of water *b·*,
  328–20 wakened through the *b·* of fire
  345–12 through the *b·* of flame.
  345–24 a *b·* not of water but of
  Ret. 48–26 like the *b·* of Jesus,
  54–10 being baptized with his *b·*,
  94– 9 so Christ's *b·* of fire,
  Pul. 20–23 *b·* of our master Metaphysician,
  No. 34– 2 through the *b·* of suffering,
  '01. 1–15 The *b·* of the Spirit,
  '02. 5– 8 with the *b·* of Jesus.
  Hea. 10–27 for the true fount and Soul's *b·*.
  Peo. 1– 1 one faith, one *b·*. — *Eph.* 4 : 5.
  5– 3 one faith, one *b·*." — *Eph.* 4 : 5.
  9– 1 one faith, one Lord, one *b·* ;
  9– 2 this *b·* is the purification of mind,
  9– 9 *b·* of Spirit that washes our robes
  13–22 went up through the *b·* of fire
  14–19 one faith, one *b·*." — *Eph.* 4 : 5.
  My. 161–20 with the *b·* that I — *Matt.* 20 : 23.
  174–21 offered me to Christ in infant *b·*.
baptismal
  Mis. 206–31 *b·* font of eternal Love.
  292– 3 and its spirit is *b·* ;
baptismals
  Mis. 18– 1 *b·* that come from Spirit,
Baptist
  No. 41–24 a Boston *B·* clergyman,
  '01. 32– 3 Rev. Mr. Boswell, of Bow, N. H., *B·* ;
  My. 331– 6 * Mr. Reperton, a *B·* clergyman,
  339–18 disciples of St. John the *B·*
  (*see also* **John the Baptist**)
Baptist Tabernacle
  Ret. 15–14 *B· T·* of Rev. Daniel C. Eddy, D. D.,
baptized
  Mis. 81–13 *footsteps of Truth being b· of John,*
  125– 1 be *b·* with his baptism !
  194–25 Then are you *b·* in the Truth
  206– 7 saying forever to the *b·* of Spirit :
  Ret. 54–10 being *b·* with his baptism,
  No. 34–12 *b·* in the purification of persecution
  Pan. 14– 9 and be *b·* in Spirit.
  '01. 9– 7 truer sense of Christ *b·* them
  12– 5 he *b·* with the Holy Ghost
  My. 161–20 be *b·* with the baptism — *Matt.* 20 : 23.
  161–21 that I am *b·* with." — *Matt.* 20 : 23.
baptizing
  Mis. 184–29 John came *b·* with water.
bar
  Mis. 114–22 or *b·* their doors too closely,
  201–28 *b·* his door against further robberies.
  Ret. 6–22 admitted to the *b·* in two States,
  '00. 7–10 members of the *b·* and bench.
  Po. 46–17 While beauty fills each *b·*.
barbarisms
  Mis. 29–25 esoteric magic and Oriental *b·*
  Peo. 5–12 the *b·* of spiritless codes.
barbarous
  My. 278–26 War is in itself an evil, *b·*,
  286– 4 *b·* slaughtering of our fellow-beings ;
barbs
  Mis. 224– 1 unless our own thought *b·* it.

bard
Mis. 126–30   Hebrew b· spake after this manner :
142–23   spiritual strains of the Hebrew b·.
192–14   The Hebrew b· saith,
297–29   The Hebrew b· wrote,
My. 273–10   King David, the Hebrew b·,

bare
Mis. 335–16   I lay b· the ability, in belief,
348– 9   one should lay it b· ;
391–16   With b· feet soiled or sore,
Un. 44–13   is laid b· in C. S.
Rud. 15–25   laid b· for anatomical examination.
'01. 35– 5   willing to b· our bosom to the blade
Po. 38–15   With b· feet soiled or sore,
My. 322–21   * in Boston on the b· hope of

barefaced
Mis. 43–28   the b· errors that are taught

barely
Mis. 69–17   I found him b· alive,
Ret. 50– 7   for tuition lasting b· three weeks.

bares
Ret. 17–16   b· a brave breast to the lightning
Po. 62–20   b· a brave breast to the lightning

bargained
Mis. 289–21   Rights that are b· away

bark
Mis. 385–10   thy b· is past The dangerous sea,
Pul. 6–25   as my lone b· rose and fell
No. 43–27   envy and hatred b· and bite at its
Po. 48– 1   thy b· is past The dangerous sea,
My. 184–15   birch b· on which it was written

barmaid
Mis. 295– 5   * "cursed b· system" in England
296–29   b· and Christian Scientist

barmaids
Mis. 294–24   chapter sub-title
296– 4   not b·, but bishops
296–10   b· of English alehouses
296–25   And the b· !

barren
Mis. 151–11   He saith of the b· fig-tree,
228–12   seeking to raise those b· natures
398– 9   Strangers on a b· shore,
Ret. 46–15   Strangers on a b· shore,
Pul. 17–14   Strangers on a b· shore,
49–10   * yet from a b· waste
Po. 14–13   Strangers on a b· shore,
24–17   The b· brood, O call With song of

barricaded
Pul. 2–17   in a poorly b· fort,

barriers
Mis. 269– 4   He cannot escape from b·
Pul. 22–16   doctrinal b· between the churches
No. 28– 5   will burst the b· of sense,

barrister
Mis. 340–12   b· who never brings out a brief.

barter
Mis. 270– 4   such as b· integrity and peace for

Bartimeus
Mis. 241–24   Then, like blind B·,

Barton
Miss
My. 297– 1   Now if Miss B· were not a
297– 4   all that Miss B· really is,
Miss Clara
My. 296–24   chapter sub-title
296–26   Miss Clara B· dipped her pen in

basal
Mis. 27–10   the pith of the b· statement,

base
Mis. 147–21   abhor whatever is b· or unworthy ;
228– 2   a deception dark as it is b·
Pul. 25–24   * The b· and cap are of . . . marble.
Rud. 9–13   your practice on immortal Mind,
No. 40– 8   wise to hide from dull and b· ears

based
Mis. 34–13   C. S. is b· on divine Principle ;
55–16   Is C. S. b· on the facts of
55–18   C. S. is b· on the facts of Spirit
62–28   The theology of C. S. is b· on
71–18   b· on a mortal or material formation ;
198–24   b· on physical material law,
Ret. 93– 5   human concept of Christ is b· on
Un. 9–13   have not b· upon revelation their
46– 8   not b· on a human conception
Pul. 55–18   * It is b· upon what is held to be
Rud. 11–20   b· on a true understanding of God
No. 10–25   b· as it is on His omnipotence
'01. 25–20   metaphysics b· on materialism?
Peo. 2– 5   b· on material conceptions of

based
Peo. 2–14   b· on the evidences gained from
3–20   A personal God is b· on finite
My. 96–13   * It is a faith b· upon reason,
108–14   is b· on the law of divine Mind.
116–17   b· upon personal sight or sense.
119– 5   b· on one infinite God, and man,
154– 2   Science of all healing is b· on Mind
179–26   b· on the divine Principle of being,
204–29   b· as aforetime on this divine
205–27   it is forever b· on Love,
283–27   b· on the enlightened sense of God's
348–14   was b· upon her discovery

baseless
Mis. 48–29   is a b· fabrication
No. 43–19   build a b· fabric of their own

basement
Pul. 25– 4   * two large boilers in the b·
58–14   * Inside is a b· room,
My. 69–23   * in the b· is a cloak-room

bases
Mis. 101–19   b· his conclusions on mortality,
297– 7   b· its work on ethical conditions
Ret. 68–21   so long as it b· creation on

basic
Mis. 6–20   with that b· truth we conquer
Un. 49–19   Standing in no b· Truth,
My. 348–29   b· Principle of all Science,

basis
absolute
Mis. 307–20   on this absolute b· of C. S. ;
and support
No. 38–15   the b· and support of creation,
Biblical
My. 181– 2   Biblical b· that God is All-in-all ;
broad
Mis. 143– 2   broad b· and sure foundation of
Christian
Man. 80– 2   on a strictly Christian b·,
false
Mis. 209–24   on the false b· that evil should
287–10   may place love on a false b·
firm
Mis. 232–24   its infinite value and firm b·.
former
Hea. 3– 8   reestablished on its former b·.
for others
Mis. 156–16   becoming the b· for others :
for teaching
Man. 86–16   B· for Teaching.
founded upon the
Mis. 13–18   founded upon the b· of material
fundamental
Mis. 186–21   torn apart from its fundamental b·.
heathen
My. 118–25   rests on a heathen b· for its Nirvana,
immortal
Hea. 1– 9   builds on less than an immortal b·,
its
My. 111–19   healing on its b·,
less
Un. 28–15   and have less b· ;
liberal
My. 245– 7   on a broad and liberal b·.
material
Mis. 254–22   mental healing on a material b·
341– 4   unreal material b· of things,
Ret. 85–21   or of healing on a material b·.
No. 6–16   trying to heal on a material b·.
of a lie
'02. 6– 8   into the world on the b· of a lie,
of all action
Hea. 12– 8   mind, the b· of all action,
of Christian Science
Mis. 307–20   absolute b· of C. S. ;
Ret. 15– 5   built on the b· of C. S.,
Rud. 13– 5   Whatever saps, . . . this b· of C. S.,
My. 220– 6   as to apply, on the b· of C. S.,
of Christmas
My. 260–17   The b· of Christmas is the rock,
260–22   b· of Christmas is love loving its
of divine liberty
Mis. 163–20   are the b· of divine liberty,
of fixed Principle
My. 106–17   rests on the b· of fixed Principle,
of harmony
Ret. 60–24   the only sure b· of harmony.
of his words
'02. 11–30   very b· of his words and works.
of hypnotism
Mis. 4– 5   healing on the b· of hypnotism,
of its demonstration
Mis. 357–32   the b· of its demonstration,

basis
  of its unreality
    Mis. 63–14 on the *b·* of its unreality
  of justice
    My. 283–21 unite . . . on the *b·* of justice,
  of malpractice
    Rud. 9–10 The *b·* of malpractice is in
  of *materia medica*
    Mis. 81– 2 not the *b·* of *materia medica*,
    379–21 beyond the *b·* of *materia medica*,
  of matter
    Mis. 243–21 who practise on the *b·* of matter,
  of Mind-healing
    Rud. 6–18 *Is not the b· of Mind-healing a*
  of nothingness
    '01. 13–16 destroys it on the very *b·* of nothingness.
  of Science
    My. 357– 1 He is the only *b·* of Science ;
  of the sentiments
    Chr. 55– 1 *b·* of the sentiments in the verses,
  only
    My. 357– 1 He is the only *b·* of Science ;
    357–24 only *b·* upon which this Science
  practical
    Ret. 48–19 healing on a purely practical *b·*,
  same
    Mis. 54–28 *they do not heal on the same b·*
    Un. 8–18 same *b·* whereby sickness is healed,
  scientific
    Mis. 148–18 hence their simple, scientific *b·*,
    267–27 rests on this scientific *b·* :
    269–17 Christian, mental, scientific *b·* ;
    Man. 3–15 hence their simple, scientific *b·*,
    Ret. 37–17 interpretation of the scientific *b·* for
    57– 5 furnishes a scientific *b·* for
  Scriptural
    My. 240–18 on a Scriptural *b·*,
  solid
    '02. 14–13 accomplished on this solid *b·*.
  sound
    My. v–15 * established the Cause on a sound *b·*
  spiritual
    Un. 25–19 material, not a spiritual *b·*.
    Hea. 1–21 more spiritual *b·* and tendency
  spirituality is the
    Mis. 156–23 Spirituality is the *b·* of all true
  such a
    My. 119– 3 or on such a *b·* to demonstrate
  that
    '01. 7–25 cannot be conceived of on that *b·* ;
  that Christ
    '02. 12– 5 on the *b·* that Christ is the Messiah,
    Hea. 18–21 on the *b·* that Christ, Truth, heals
  their
    Mis. 200–17 for the sole reason that it is their *b·*.
  this
    Mis. 289–11 human life seems to rest on this *b·*.
    Rud. 13– 5 Whatever sups, . . . this *b·* of C. S.,
    No. 5– 1 can only be — healed on this *b·*.
    37–22 on this *b·* Messiah and prophet
    My. 4– 0 On this *b·*, how many are following
    216– 5 systems of religion stand on this *b·*.
    281–10 On this *b·* the brotherhood of all
    300– 1 On this *b·* they endeavor to
  true
    Mis. 74– 6 apprehension of the true *b·* of being,

    Mis. 19–22 as high a *b·* as he understands,
    117–14 the *b·* of all right thinking
    171–16 seeking out of the *b·* upon which
    188–16 St. Paul first reasons upon the *b·*
    202– 1 *b·* of all supposed miracles.
    289–27 on the *b·* of a bill of rights.
    333– 7 on the *b·* that black is not
    Ret. 35– 5 *b·* it laid down for physical and
    56–16 on the *b·* of the omnipotence
    No. 10–17 on the *b·* that all consciousness is
    38– 6 on the *b·* that God is All,
    Pan. 8–22 on the *b·* of the First Commandment
    '01. 27–11 the *b·* whereof cannot be traced
    My. 10–19 * on the *b·* of fretful or
    281–12 the *b·* on which and by which
    294– 4 on the *b·* that God has all power,

bask
  Po. 22–11 And *b·* in one eternal day.

basket
  Pul. 42–28 * large *b·* of white carnations
  My. 78–15 * *b·* piled high with bank-notes,

baskets
  Mis. 149–11 *b·* full of accessions to your love,
  My. 99–20 * *b·* when passed around

bastard
  Un. 23– 2 from his *b·* son Edmund

bastards
  Un. 23– 6 God has no *b·* to turn again and
    23–14 *b·*, and not sons." — *Heb.* 12 : 8.

bat
  Peo. 14– 8 * "*b·* and owl on the bending stones,

bated
  Ret. 9– 3 I listened with *b·* breath.

Bates
  Caroline S.
    Pul. 77–20 * signature
    78–18 * signature
  Edward P. (*see also* **Bates'**)
    Pul. 59–25 * Edward P. *B·*, Stephen A. Chase,
    77–19 * signature
    78–17 * signature
    My. 322– 7 * signature
  Gen. Erastus N.
    Ret. 43–17 Gen. Erastus N. *B·* taught one Primary
  Mr.
    My. 172–20 * In reply Mr. *B·* said,
    323– 1 * what Mr. *B·* has so well written
  Mr. E. P.
    My. 171–25 * by the President, Mr. E. P. *B·*,
  President
    My. 172– 8 * this gavel to President *B·*,

Bates'
  Mr. Edward P.
    My. 322–12 * Mr. Edward P. *B·* letter to you

bath
  Hea. 5– 5 the neglect of a *b·*, and so on.
  Peo. 9– 6 The cool *b·* may refresh the body,

bathe
  Mis. 30–31 *b·* in the baptism of Spirit,
    323–20 and *b·* in its streams,

bathed
  Mis. 393–17 Art hath *b·* this isthmus-lordling
  Ret. 13–18 as she *b·* my burning temples,
  Po. 52– 1 Art hath *b·* this isthmus-lordling

bathes
  Mis. 203–14 Theology religiously *b·* in water,
    206–30 *b·* in the baptismal font of eternal
    097 27 *b·* it in the cool waters of peace
  Peo. 9–10 *b·* us in the life of Truth

bathing
  My. 228–19 *b·* the human understanding with

battle (*see also* **battle's**)
  Mis. xii– 5 this afterpiece of *b·*.
    99–18 and be in the *b·* every day
    105–19 follow this line of light and *b·*.
    120–17 be heard above the din of *b·*,
    136– 5 still with you on the field of *b·*,
    177– 5 *b·* of Armageddon is upon us.
    246–20 conflict more terrible than the *b·* of
    339–10 In the *b·* of life,
    348–13 and show the plan of *b·*.
    Ret. 3–11 neighboring *b·* of Chippewa.
    30– 4 they have won fields of *b·* from which
    Pan. 14–20 whether in camp or in *b·*.
    '02. 14–18 From the beginning of the great *b·*
    Hea. 2– 9 never seen amid the smoke of *b·*.
    My. 62– 2 * stood at the breastworks in the *b·*,
    134– 2 constant *b·* against the world,
    268–22 lively *b·* with "the world, the flesh

battle-axe
  No. 32–14 cleaves sin with a broad *b·*.

Battle-Axe Plug
  Mis. 240–29 "*B· P·*" takes off men's heads ;

battledores
  Mis. xi–20 no *b·* to fling it back and forth.

battle-field
  Mis. 304–12 * the *b·* of New Orleans (1812),
    383–14 and on every *b·* rise higher

battle-ground
  Un. 46–27 It furnished the *b·* of the past,

battle-grounds
  Mis. xi–25 to old *b·*, there sadly to survey

battle-plan
  Po. 11– 2 Unite your *b·* ;
  My. 338– 2 Unite your *b·* ;

battle's
  My. 278– 3 to be subserved by the *b·* plan

battles
  Mis. xi–22 preliminary *b·* that purchased it.
  No. 7–21 students must now fight their own *b·*.
  Peo. 10–16 *b·* for man's whole rights,
    11– 3 scarcely done with their *b·* before

battle-worn
  Mis. 85– 1 To the *b·* and weary

battling
Mis. 321–22 And b· for a brighter crown.
baubles
My. 297–14 blows away the b· of belief,
bay
Ret. 17–17 While palm, b·, and laurel,
Pul. 26–26 * Before the great b· window
27–30 * A large b· window,
Po. 63– 1 While palm, b·, and laurel,
bayonet
Ret. 11– 4 poem
Peo. 11– 7 not with b· and blood,
Po. vi–29 * poem
page 60 poem
Bay State (*see also* **Massachusetts**)
Mis. 211–10 people in the old B· S·.
Po. 39–14 Sons of the old B· S·,
bay-tree
My. 95– 2 * like a green b·,
B. C.
Pul. 82–28 * The date is no longer B. C.
beach
Po. 73–11 Laving with surges thy silv'ry b·!
beacon
Po. 43–16 B· beams — athwart the weakly,
beacon-lights
No. 2–20 such teachers are becoming b·
Beacon St., No. 5
Mis. 242–27 Mr. C. M. H——, of Boston,... No. 5 B· S·,
beam
Mis. 119–14 nature strives to tip the b· against
212–27 cast the b· out of his own eye,
336–14 b· in your own eye that hinders
355–21 "Cast the b· out — see Matt. 7 : 5.
398–18 Till the morning's b· ;
Ret. 46–24 Till the morning's b· ;
Pul. 17–23 Till the morning's b· ;
Po. 14–22 Till the morning's b· ;
29–15 Thou gentle b· of living Love,
My. 277–19 mercy tips the b· on the right side,
beams
Ret. 87–26 Truth b· with such efficacy as to
Un. 58–19 revelation that b· on mortal sense
Po. 43–16 Beacon b· — athwart the weakly,
My. 62–12 * brightest b· on your pathway,
190– 5 morning b· and noonday glory of
269–21 b· of right have healing in their
bear
Mis. 39–23 b· "one another's — Gal. 6 : 2.
54–10 they b· witness to this fact.
67–13 not b· false witness ;" — Exod. 20 : 16.
93–24 B· in mind, however,
99–24 never b· into oblivion his words.
126–25 b· in mind that, in the long race,
144–27 so may our earthly sowing b· fruit
151– 8 Those who b· fruit He purgeth,
151– 9 that they may b· more fruit.
196–11 b· in mind that a serpent said that ;
211–32 refuses to b· the cross and
228–10 b· with patience the buffetings
263–12 b· in mind that His presence,
328–31 b· thy cross up to the throne
330–20 learn what report they b·,
365– 1 will b· the strain of time
382–10 b· witness to this gift of God
Man. 48– 3 calls a member to b· testimony
53–20 shall b· witness to the offense
93–13 b· testimony to the facts
Ret. 22– 3 b· brief testimony even to the
25–27 "If I b· witness — John 5 : 31.
53– 5 to b· aloft the standard of
87–24 b· the weight of others' burdens,
Un. 6–13 as the age has strength to b·.
7–15 can b· witness to these cures.
33– 8 "If I b· witness — John 5 : 31.
Pul. 11– 1 b· you outward, upward,
'00. 9–29 "b· the burden — see Matt. 20 : 12.
'01. 15–25 * He is of purer eyes than to b· to
31–17 would b· loving testimony.
'02. 3– 2 b· testimony to this fact.
20–22 I can b· the cross,
Hea. 12–18 power of thought brought to b· on
Po. 15– 6 unless thou canst b· A message
26–17 "This record I will b·
35–13 Bird, b· me through the sky!
My. 15–15 all that you are able to b· now,
36–19 * b· witness to the abundance of
83–30 * to b· each his or her share of
120– 9 B· with me the burden of discovery
128–32 take no root . . . nor b· fruit.
148–24 B· in mind always that Christianity
202–29 that ye b· much fruit." — John 15 : 8.

bear
My. 229–17 doth not b· his cross, — Luke 14 : 27.
291–21 b· its banner into the vast forever.
297– 5 knowing that she can b· the blows
beard
Un. 11– 4 b· the lions in their dens.
Pul. 33–18 * an old man with a snowy b·
bearer
Man. 91– 9 b· of a card of free scholarship
bearest
Mis. 386– 7 "B· thou no tidings from
Po. 49–11 "B· thou no tidings from
beareth
Mis. 46–22 Spirit itself b· witness — Rom. 8 : 16.
218–19 b· witness of things spiritual,
255–14 Spirit itself b· witness — Rom. 8 : 16.
Man. 42–18 whereof the Scripture b· testimony.
bearing
Mis. 158–18 obedience in b· this cross.
357–17 and is b· fruit.
Ret. 32– 2 b· on its white wings,
54–12 without b· the fruits of goodness,
85–11 b· on their pinions of light
Un. 6– 3 "b· fruit after its kind." — see Gen. 1 : 11.
Pul. 26–11 * b· six . . . silver lamps,
26–24 * with sprays of fig leaves b· fruit.
27–17 * two small windows b· palms
31–26 * winning in b· and manner,
32–21 * elastic b· of a woman of thirty,
Hea. 19–23 b· the cross meekly
Po. 34–18 B· no bitter memory at heart ;
My. 49– 1 * their conversation, and their b·,
73–28 * b· the first instalments of
170–30 b· your sheaves with you.
bears
Mis. 21– 8 whereof C. S. now b· testimony.
170–21 b· upon our eternal life.
220–21 has power and b· fruit,
312– 7 b· all burdens, suffers all
320–14 calms man's fears, b· his burdens,
Ret. 11–10 No despot b· misrule,
Un. 40– 8 and b· the fruits of Love,
55–15 and the wounds it b·.
Pul. 78– 6 * It b· upon its face the following
No. 21–22 b· the strain of time,
Po. 60– 7 No despot b· misrule,
77–19 B· hence its sunlit glow
My. 258–17 b· to mortals gifts greater than
beast
Mis. 18– 3 efface the mark of the b·.
36–10 ferocious mind seen in the b·
36–12 for His b· is the lion that
113–10 name of the b·, — Rev. 13 : 17.
269–32 name of the b·, — Rev. 13 : 17.
'01. 20– 8 to harm either man or b·.
Hea. 10– 5 b· bowed before the Lamb :
beasts
Mis. 36– 6 Do animals and b· have a mind?
36– 7 B·, as well as men, express Mind
36–15 b· that have these propensities
191– 5 b· of the field." — see Gen. 3 : 1.
294–19 and all ravening b·.
323–12 b· of prey prowl in the path,
323–20 taming the b· of prey,
345– 8 * "I will set the b· upon you,
Ret. 64–17 like the b· that perish." — Psal. 49 : 20.
Un. 52–21 rabid b·, fatal reptiles, and
Hea. 14– 2 it is the fight of b·,
Peo. 13–18 let loose the wild b· upon him,
My. 245–13 poisonous reptiles and devouring b·,
beat
Mis. 152–23 b· against this sure foundation,
383–11 b· in vain against the immortal
'01. 24–13 storms of disease b· against
My. 162–31 waves and winds b· in vain.
164–29 enmity, or malice b· in vain.
beaten
Man. 28–13 b· with many stripes." — Luke 12 : 47.
'00. 4–18 b· path of human doctrines
Hea. 5– 4 saying He is b· by certain kinds of
beateth
Mis. 102–29 as one that b· the air,
Pan. 6– 7 not as one that b· the mist,
beating
'01. 1– 3 b· through the mental avenues of
My. 308–17 * regularly b· the ground with
341–13 And in her heart is b· A love for all
beatings
Peo. 1–14 b· of our heart can be heard ;
beatitude
My. 227–29 The sinner may sneer at this b·,

Beatitudes
Mis. 303–19 imbibe the spirit of Christ's B·.
My. 129–31 Ten Commandments, the B·,
beatitudes
Mis. 82–17 unfolding the endless b· of Being ;
My. 200–13 glorious b· of divine Love.
beats
Mis. 267–19 while the left b· its way downward,
Hea. 14– 2 the bigger animal b· the lesser;
My. 160– 4 The heart that b· mostly for self
beauties
Mis. 87– 7 let us say of the b· of
Pul. 62–17 * b· of a great cathedral chime,
My. 85–17 * among the architectural b· of
88–19 * striking as are its b·,
beautifies
Mis. 390–18 When sunshine b· the shower,
Po. 55–19 When sunshine b· the shower,
Beautiful
My. 132–19 Divine Love hath opened the gate B·
beautiful
Mis. 86–16 Earth is more spiritually b·
139–19 near the b· Back Bay Park,
141–32 how b· are her feet!
142– 1 how b· are her garments !
142– 7 a b· boat presented by
142– 9 among other b· decorations,
142–12 b· boat and presentation poem.
160–29 * how b· and inspiring are the
224–19 appreciation of everything b·,
230–27 It was a b· group!
280–21 b· hand-painted flowers
281–24 one of the most b·
321–25 hospitality of their b· homes
355–29 more b· than the rainbow
356– 1 radiant sunset, b· as blessings
Ret. 4–20 singing brooklets, b· wild flowers,
5–13 Park Cemetery of that b· village.
6–13 To speak of his b· character
17– 1 in the b· suburbs of Boston.
23–22 Being was b·,
27–26 natural manifestation is b·
45– 2 more b· became the garments
68–28 The b·, good, and pure constitute
Un. 8–11 All that is b· and good
52–24 b· blossom is often poisonous,
52–25 b· mansion is sometimes the home of
52–27 form the condition of b· evil,
53– 1 which make a b· lie.
Pul. 22–20 her most b· garments,
23– 5 * A B· Temple and Its Furnishings
24– 5 * It is one of the most b·,
27– 3 * directors' room is very b·
32– 5 * her b· complexion and
36–23 * one of the most b· residences
37– 0 * where she has a b· residence,
37–17 * sat in the b· drawing-room,
39–11 * author of "The World B·,"
40–14 * B· Room Which the Children Built
41– 7 * to help erect this b· structure,
42–30 * filled with b· pink roses.
48–11 * b· meadows and pastures
57–12 * b· buildings in Boston,
58– 7 * b· estate called Pleasant View ;
58–22 * a b· sunburst window.
61–15 * B· suggestions greet you
65–16 * b· structure of gray granite,
68–11 * lives in a b· country residence
75–16 * B· Church at Boston
76– 3 * b· apartment known as
76– 6 * described as "particularly b·,
81–20 * full of b· possibilities as a
81–24 * apostle of the true, the b·,
85–25 * a b· and unique testimonial
86–11 * The b· souvenir is encased in
Peo. 14– 2 we express them by objects more b·.
Po. vii– 1 * in the b· suburbs of Boston);
9– 6 birth of that b· boy.
My. 10– 9 * in a b·, ample building,
66–24 * from her b· home, Pleasant View,
66–29 * many b· houses of worship
68–17 * platform is of a b· foreign marble,
70–24 * more b·, more musical,
71– 3 * b· effects by means of the bells.
77– 2 * its great size, b· architecture,
84–27 * dedication of the b· structure
87–24 * gives such serene, b· expressions,
88–18 * and this b· temple,
121–15 plain dealing is a jewel as b· as
125–25 Zion must put on her b· garments
155–29 sweet scents and b· blossoms
157– 7 * to build a b· church edifice
157–11 * commodious and b· church home
157–14 * of the same b· Concord granite

beautiful
My. 166–28 your gift to me of a b· cabinet,
171–13 and view this b· structure,
174– 1 b· lawn surrounding their church
182–19 this b· house of worship
184–15 The b· birch bark on which
184–26 "How b· upon the mountains — Isa. 52 : 7.
187–23 to consecrate your b· temple
202–14 on the builders of this b· temple,
258–23 b· are the Christmas memories of him
258–30 b· statuette in alabaster
347– 9 b· gift to me, a loving-cup,
347–16 b· pearls that crown this cup
351– 5 * b· tribute to Free Masonry.
beautifully
Mis. 229–21 would thus become b· less ;
231–12 mammoth turkey grew b· less.
Ret. 73–10 human concept grew b· less
'00. 4–29 St. Paul b· enunciates this
My. 171–27 * b· bound with burnished brass.
322–30 * spoke earnestly and b· of you
beautify
Mis. 394– 9 b·, bless, and make joyful again.
Peo. 7– 7 to b· and exalt our lives.
Po. 45–12 b·, bless, and make joyful again.
My. 134–19 b·, bless, and inspire man's power.
173–15 b· our new church building in
beautifying
Mis. 143– 5 participants in b· this boat
beauty (see also **beauty's**)
and bounty
My. 260– 1 b· and bounty of Life everlasting,
and goodness
Rud. 6– 6 b· and goodness are in and of Mind,
6– 8 the nature of b· and goodness
and perfume
Ret. 18–10 b· and perfume from buds burst away,
Po. 46–12 yield its b· and perfume
63–20 b· and perfume from buds burst away,
and strength
My. 68– 3 * b· and strength of the design.
and the grace
My. 31–16 * b· and the grace of the architecture.
and use
My. 256–11 for those things of b· and use
appropriate
My. 169–19 appropriate b· of time and place
architectural
My. 67–21 * marvel of architectural b·.
bowers of
Ret. 17– 4 zephyrs at play In bowers of b·,
Po. 62– 3 zephyrs at play In bowers of b·,
burdened with
My. 162–32 its goodly temple — burdened with b·,
composite
Pul. 81–14 * She represents the composite b·,
conception of
Mis. 86–23 Even the human conception of b·,
divine
Mis. 86–24 It is next to divine b·
earth's
Mis. 87– 3 To take all earth's b· into
Ret. 18–14 Earth's b· and glory delude
Po. 64– 5 Earth's b· and glory delude
evidence of that
My. 88–20 * evidence of that b· and serenity of
extreme of
My. 89–11 * to achieve its extreme of b·.
fled
Mis. 306– 8 It voices b· fled.
Po. 58–20 It voices b· fled.
Helen's
Mis. 374–26 * "Helen's b· in a brow of Egypt."
isle of
Mis. 392–20 Isle of b·, thou art singing
393–21 Isle of b·, thou art teaching
Po. 51– 2 Isle of b·, thou art singing
52– 5 Isle of b·, thou art teaching
is marred
Rud. 6– 9 the b· is marred, through a false
label
Mis. 87– 4 and label b· nothing,
new
Ret. 20–18 Awoke new b· in the surge's roll !
new-born
Po. 30– 3 new-born b· in the emerald sky,
My. 158–15 lends a new-born b· to holiness,
of color
My. 36–26 * all the b· of color and design,
of holiness
Mis. 197–18 understand the b· of holiness,
330–18 arranging in the b· of holiness
363–17 declare the b· of holiness,
Ret. 32– 3 "the b· of holiness," — Psal. 29 : 2.
No. 8– 7 the b· of holiness, the joy of Love

beauty

'01.	33– 2	the original *b·* of holiness
'02.	17–21	to show man the *b·* of holiness
My.	41–32	* "*b·* of holiness," — *Psal.* 29 : 2.
	114–12	the *b·* of holiness is not yet won.
	196–29	The *b·* of holiness comes with
	197– 5	May the *b·* of holiness be upon this

of Love
Ret. 88–13 to apprehend the living *b·* of Love,
of the building
My. 24–23 * The *b·* of the building,
of the universe
Mis. 86–14 My sense of the *b·* of the universe is,
personal
Pul. 31–27 * with great claim to personal *b·*.
ravished with
Po. 8–10 Ravished with *b·* the eye of day.
rich
My. 69–15 * the rich *b·* of the interior.
spirit of
Pul. 2– 6 spirit of *b·* dominates The
spiritual
My. 141–29 has blossomed into spiritual *b·*,
strength and
My. 39–29 * strength and *b·* of her character.
strong
Mis. 393–18 In a *b·* strong and meek
Po. 52– 2 In a *b·* strong and meek
sweetness and
Mis. 107– 2 even the sweetness and *b·* in
this
Pul. 49–12 * has come forth all this *b·*!"
typifies holiness
Mis. 86–15 *b·* typifies holiness,

Mis.	87–13	*b·*, grandeur, and glory of the
Un.	52–22	elaborate in *b·*, color, and form,
Pul.	5–19	with a *b·* all its own
Peo.	7–22	* Its heavenly *b·* shall be our own,
Po.	46–17	While *b·* fills each bar.
My.	6–26	*b·*, and achievements of goodness.
	94–30	*b·*, and achievements of goodness."

beauty's

Po. 15– 9 enchantment in *b·* array,
46– 8 A gem in *b·* diadem,

became

Mis.	153– 9	the rock *b·* a fountain ;
	162–11	Here the cross *b·* the emblem
	191– 7	serpent *b·* a symbol of wisdom.
	326–11	until they *b·* unmanageable ;
	359–10	when I *b·* a man, — *I Cor.* 13 : 11.
Ret.	1–18	*b·* my paternal grandmother,
	23– 6	As these pungent lessons *b·* clearer,
	28– 1	It *b·* evident that the divine Mind
	45– 2	more beautiful *b·* the garments
	73–12	corporeality *b·* less to me than
	91–24	a fishing-boat *b·* a sanctuary,
	91–25	The grove *b·* his class-room,
Pul.	31–14	* in the early '80's that I *b·* aware
	34–11	* she suddenly *b·* aware of a
	35–23	* Mrs. Eddy *b·* convinced of the
	46–28	* *b·* the wife of Asa Gilbert Eddy.
	64–20	* she *b·* convinced that
	65–26	* afterward *b·* a saint.
	70–17	* *b·* certain that "all causation was
No.	12 –11	it *b·* a sacred duty for her to
'01.	32– 5	I *b·* early a child of the Church,
'02.	13–20	the note therewith *b·* due,
	15–15	I *b·* poor for Christ's sake.
Hea.	18–17	until it *b·* popular.
Peo.	4– 7	belief that . . . infinity *b·* finity,
Po.	vii– 7	* *When this b· known to her friends,*
My.	40–15	* *b·* divided into warring sects ;
	43–11	* finally by *b·* willingly obedient to
	76– 6	* *b·* evident to the Board
	135– 4	when I *b·* a man, — *I Cor.* 13 : 11.
	165– 4	in doing this the Master *b·*
	238–15	*b·* requisite in the divine order.
	245– 2	they *b·* deeply interested in it.
	261–17	when I *b·* a man, — *I Cor.* 13 : 11.
	304–18	Judge S. J. Hanna *b·* editor
	342– 2	* *b·* aware of a white-haired lady
	343–22	position of . . . "*b·* necessary.

because

Mis.	2– 5	*b·* they have so little of their own.
	3–25	*B·* God is supreme and
	7– 2	*b·* there is danger in it ;
	7–27	*b·* people do not understand
	9–29	*B·* it is the great and only danger
	10– 9	*B·* He has called His own,
	11–26	*B·* I can do much general good
	12– 1	*B·* I thus feel, I say to others :
	31–20	*b·* he has no faith in the
	35–21	Only *b·* both are important.
	51–31	*b·* ye ask amiss, — *Jas.* 4 : 3.

because

Mis.	52–26	*b·* the first rule was not easily
	53–24	*b·* of their great lack of spirituality.
	54–25	*B· none of your students have been*
	54–30	*b·* he failed to get the right answer,
	65– 7	this is *b·* Science is true,
	72– 3	*b·* of his parents' mistakes
	75– 9	*b·* it includes a rule that must
	75–15	*B·* Soul is a term for Deity,
	79–30	*b·* they chance to be under arrest
	93–27	*b·* it cannot go unpunished
	100–26	*b·* he loves God most.
	103–15	*b·* eternally conscious.
	105–31	*B·* God is Mind,
	122– 3	*b·* of offenses! — *Matt.* 18 : 7.
	132–16	*B·* of the great demand upon
	133–19	*b·* of my desire to set you right
	138–23	*B·* the growth of these
	142–16	*B·* your dear hearts expressed
	155–16	*B·* Mother has not the time
	156–14	*b·* I saw no advantage,
	165– 3	*b·* of the ascension of Jesus,
	165– 5	*b·* of the corruption of the Church.
	178– 5	*b·* he was not satisfied with a
	179–32	"*B·* he lives, — *see John* 14 : 19.
	183–31	arrive at the true status of man *b·*
	184–22	good *b·* it is of God,
	187–14	*b·* their transcribing thoughts
	188– 8	*B·* of human misstatement
	192– 2	*b·* the Hebrew term for Deity
	192– 4	*b·* the original text defines devil
	192–11	*b·* *I go unto my Father.* — *John* 14 : 12.
	194–20	"*b·* I go unto my Father." — *John* 14 : 12.
	194–20	"*B·*" in following him, you — *John* 14 : 12.
	196–25	*b·* the "I" does go unto the Father,
	199– 2	*b·* of this, we have the right to
	200– 7	*b·* Spirit was to him All-in-all,
	200–23	*b·* it compels me to seek the
	201– 2	*b·* it meets the immortal demands
	201–20	*b·* they were so many proofs
	201–32	*b·* it illustrates through the flesh
	210– 9	*b·* they have stings?
	211–16	*B·* you wish to save him from
	215–19	*b·* he is a somnambulist,
	222–14	*b·* the false seems true.
	229–16	"*B·* thou hast made — *Psal.* 91 : 9.
	233–24	*b·* unwilling to work hard
	242–14	*B·* I performed more difficult tasks
	244–31	*b·* of their medical discoveries?
	247–19	*b·* they do not understand that
	255–26	*b·* it is this divine antidote,
	262–29	*b·* I take so much pleasure
	266–28	*B·* Truth has spoken aloud,
	276– 6	solely *b·* so many people and
	280–10	*B·* God does all,
	281–24	*b·* you have signed your names.
	285– 4	*b·* I had been personal
	290–29	emits light *b·* it reflects ;
	297– 7	*b·* this Science bases its work on
	299–30	*b·* you have confessed that they are
	333– 8	*b·* it absorbs all the rays of light.
	334–15	*b·* it is a lie, without one word of
	334–28	*B·* I have uncovered evil,
	339–11	*b·* of the supposed activity of evil.
	340–12	*B·* he followed agriculture
	350–19	*b·* of the misconception of
	353–22	and *b·* it *is* thus governed,
	360– 6	good, *b·* fashioned divinely,
	366– 6	*b·* they contain and offer Science,
	366–12	And *b·* He is All-in-all,
	374–31	*B·* my ideal of an angel is a
	378–17	"*B·* it conveys *electricity* to them."
Chr.	55–16	dead *b·* of sin ; — *Rom.* 8 : 10.
	55–17	*b·* of righteousness. — *Rom.* 8 : 10.
Ret.	1–11	*b·* my great-grandmother wrote a
	25–10	*Christian, b·* it is compassionate.
	25–14	*b·* Soul alone is truly substantial.
	44–13	*b·* of accumulating work in the
	54– 3	*B·* faith is belief, and not
	63– 3	*B·* C. S. heals sin
	78–13	*b·* such works and words becloud the
	87–12	*b·* their religion demands implicit
	89–12	*b·* he was bidden to this privileged
Un.	2–23	*b·* their lives have grown so far
	3–25	*b·*, if He is omnipresent,
	4–21	*B·* evil is no part of the
	5– 7	*b·* their mental struggles and pride
	7–23	*b·* God is All,
	9–21	*b·* ideas akin to mine
	10– 3	*b·* they are not to be found in God,
	10–17	They live, *b·* He lives ;
	10–17	perfect, *b·* He is perfect,
	14– 3	*b·* it was not at first done aright.
	14–16	*b·* His created children proved sinful ;
	17–20	*b·* He knows all things ;
	21–16	*b·* there is nothing beside Him

because

Un.	22– 2	B· man is made after God's eternal
	24–18	no evil mind, *b·* Mind is God.
	28–15	*b·* material theories are built on the
	29– 6	Spirit never sins, *b·* Spirit is God.
	37–11	B· God is ever present,
	37–13	*b·* God is Life, all Life is eternal.
	41– 5	*b·* sin shuts out the real sense of
	41–23	*b·* God cannot be the opposite of
	42– 2	*b·* there is no place left for it.
	42– 7	*b·* it is not a living . . . reality.
	43– 7	*b·* mortals now believe in the
	43–18	B· of these profound reasons
	46–17	*b·* it was an indignity to
	48– 9	B· He lives, I live.
	54–22	*b·* the knowledge of evil would
	57–24	*b·* to suffer with him is to
	59–15	*b·* he could reach and teach mankind
	59–18	*b·* the divine idea is always present.
Pul.	3–29	B· of my own unfitness for
	12–14	*b·* he knoweth that he — *Rev.* 12 : 12.
	15– 6	B· people like you better
	21– 4	*b·* it *is* Love.
	43–26	* *b·*, as heretofore stated in
	56–17	* *b·* dogma and truth could not unite,
	81–12	* *b·* she thinks so much of herself
	82–14	* *b·* she was created after man,
Rud.	3– 1	*b·*, while mortals love to sin,
	3–11	more *b·* of his spiritual than his
	7–18	*b·* there is no material sense.
	10–21	punished *b·* of disobedience to His
	12–14	*b·* the relief is unchristian
	12–17	belief that they live in or *b·* of
	14–19	*b·* their first classes furnished students
	15– 5	B· the glad surprise
No.	4–19	*b·* they embody not the idea of
	11–21	*b·* they teach divine Science,
	16–16	*b·* it has no darkness to emit.
	21–18	*b·* by it we lose God's ways
	24–17	*b·* the evil that is hidden by
	24–18	*b·* evil, being thus uncovered,
	32– 5	*b·* forgiveness, in the popular sense
	33–10	*b·* they involve divine Science,
	35–17	*b·* of the shocking human idolatry
	40– 2	*b·* ye ask amiss, — *Jas.* 4 : 3.
	40– 3	B· of vanity and self-righteousness,
	40–24	mankind are better *b·* of this.
Pan.	5–14	*b·* there is no truth — *John* 8 : 44.
	6– 2	*b·* it was more effectual than
	6– 3	*b·* evil and disease will never
	8–27	suffering *b·* of it,
	11–30	And *b·* Christ's dear demand,
'00.	9– 5	not *b·* it is the best thing to do,
	9– 6	*b·* the student is not willing
	12–18	*b·* thou hast left thy — *Rev.* 2 : 4.
'01.	3– 9	*b·* their God is not a person.
	3–28	*b·* God is Love, Love is divine
	4–21	*b·* we understand that God is
	4–25	*b·* He is infinite ;
	4–25	*b·* He is Life, Truth, Love,
	6–16	*b·* He is not after this model
	7–18	B· Christian Scientists call their
	7–27	thou hast seen — *John* 20 : 29.
	11– 3	*b·* of Jesus' great work on earth,
	13– 6	*b·* it ought not, we must know
	13–17	*b·* he fears it or loves it.
	18–14	*b·* the substance of Truth transcends
	19– 9	*b·* of your often coming
	25–12	*b·* of their more spiritual import
	29–11	not *b·* reformers are not loved,
	29–11	*b·* well-meaning people
	34– 1	B· the effect of prayer,
'02.	7–28	B· it emphasizes the apostle's
Hea.	3–21	B· God is the Principle of
	6–23	*b·* it is lying back in the
	15–23	*b·* ye ask amiss ;" — *Jas.* 4 : 3.
	15–26	*b·* you do not understand God,
Peo.	4–11	*b·* a serpent said it.
	6–17	*b·* He is found altogether lovely.
	6–21	*b·* the grand realities of Life
	7–30	B· God is Spirit, our thoughts
	9–17	*b·* we "ask amiss ;" — *Jas.* 4 : 3.
	10– 3	simply *b·* it is more ethereal.
My.	10–24	* *b·* they recognize the importance
	11–17	* *b·* of prompt and liberal action,
	13–28	B· Christian Scientists virtually
	15–23	* B· I know 'tis true ;
	19–28	*b·* of that gift which you
	36–13	* Most of us are here *b·* we have
	39–28	* B· our own growth in love
	40–25	* *b·* she is an exact metaphysician.
	41– 8	* *b·* they have thoughts adverse to
	64– 9	* it is *b·* our Leader has
	77– 1	* *b·* of its great size,
	103– 2	B· Science is unimpeachable,
	104– 8	B· they could find no fault in him,

because

My.	105–10	declared incurable *b·* the lungs
	106–23	Is it *b·* he minds his own business
	106–27	*b·* he is the very antipode of
	106–28	Is it *b·* he heals the sick
	109–19	God is one *b·* God is All.
	112–21	*b·* of their uniformly pure morals
	113–16	*b·* he was not a disciple of
	114–10	Simply *b·* the treasures of
	116–10	B· it would dethrone the
	119–13	Mary of old wept *b·* she
	127–30	B· it is "on earth peace, — *Luke* 2 : 14.
	135–28	"Fret not thyself *b·* of — *Psal.* 37 : 1.
	137–27	*b·* I had implicit confidence in
	138– 2	*b·* I wanted it protected
	138–16	solely *b·* I find that I cannot
	146– 6	*b·* I understand it,
	151– 4	(1) B· I sympathize with their
	151– 6	(2) B· I know that no Christian can
	151– 8	(3) B· these attacks afford
	151–10	(4) B· it is written :
	161–25	*b·* one's thought and conduct
	178–10	*b·* Science is naturally divine,
	195–16	To do good to all *b·* we love all,
	212–16	B· they do not practise in strict
	213– 8	B· this age is cursed with
	217–21	*b·* we can meet this negation
	222– 4	*b·* of this Jesus rebuked them,
	222– 9	"B· of your unbelief" — *Matt.* 17 : 20.
	222–16	*b·* of his faith and his great
	222–18	he was arrested *b·*, as was said,
	223–14	*b·* I have not sufficient time to
	223–15	*b·* I do not consider myself
	227– 5	*b·* of another's wickedness
	227– 5	or *b·* of the minifying of his
	227–10	*b·* one out of three of their
	229– 6	*b·* of these abominations — *Deut.* 18 : 12.
	235–21	B· Spirit is God and *infinite;*
	236– 5	B· I suggested the name
	240–16	higher criticism *b·* it criticizes evil,
	241–20	* *b·* I referred to myself as an
	241–22	* *b·* I still lived in my flesh
	260–19	not *b·* of tradition, usage, or
	260–20	but *b·* of fundamental and
	260 21	*b·* of the heaven within us.
	270– 4	B· of the magnitude of their
	270–28	quarrel with a man *b·* of his religion
	270–29	than I would *b·* of his art.
	273–20	*b·* death alone does not awaken man
	276– 7	or *b·* of a preference to remain
	280–18	*b·* of oft speaking,
	280–30	B· a spiritual foresight of
	284– 1	B· of my rediscovery of C. S.,
	288–31	all is good *b·* God made all,
	290–15	*b·* he trusteth in Thee." — *Isa.* 26 : 3.
	294– 8	*b·* of their unbelief," — *Matt.* 13 : 58.
	294– 8	*b·* of the mental . . . elements,
	302–23	B· C. S. is not yet popular,
	313–30	*b·* after my father's second marriage
	316– 1	*b·* the truth I have promulgated
	316– 4	*b·* I still hear the harvest song
	316– 6	*b·* "blessed are ye, — *Matt.* 5 : 11.
	318– 8	*b·* at that date some critics
	326– 5	* not *b·* a favor has been extended,
	326– 5	* but *b·* their inherent rights are
	327–21	* *b·* the representative men of
	334– 7	* *b·* she has contradicted
	342–22	*b·* in it alone is the simplicity of
	349–15	*b·* he is conscious of the allness of
	349 22	*b·* they are spiritual,
	354– 2	*b·* of alleged misrepresentations
	355–27	Mrs. Eddy is happier *b·* of them;
	357– 6	*b·* matter is the absolute opposite

beck

My.	350– 2	at the *b·* of material phenomena,

beckoned

Mis.	386–20	angels *b·* me to this bright land,
Po.	50– 5	angels *b·* me to this bright land,

beckonest

Po.	30– 1	thou *b·* from the giant hills

beckoning

Po.	22– 3	and, *b·* from above,
My.	46– 4	* *b·* us on towards a higher
	251– 1	duties and attainments *b·* them.

beckons

Mis.	320–14	*b·* him on to Truth and Love

becloud

Ret.	78–13	*b·* the right sense of metaphysical
	78–21	To *b·* mortals, . . . is to conspire
Hea.	8–17	*b·* the light of revelation,
My.	161–23	Lest human reason *b·* spiritual

beclouds

Un.	40–20	A sense of death . . . *b·* it.

become

Mis.	xi–16	*b·* footsteps to joys eternal.
	4–13	a newspaper . . . has *b·* a necessity.
	7– 4	until their bodies *b·* dry,
	9–20	having tasted . . . we *b·* intoxicated ;
	9–20	*b·* lethargic, dreamy objects of
	9–27	*b·* educated to gratification
	10–24	and all things *b·* new.
	16– 8	requisite to *b·* wholly Christlike,
	35–17	*is one obliged to b· a student*
Mis.	78–20	this abuse, has *b·* too common :
	92– 5	*b·* sufficiently understood to be
	107–24	may *b·* morally blind,
	127–21	condition whereby to *b·* blessed,
	134– 2	have *b·* "wise— *II Tim.* 3 : 15.
	164–22	as it shall *b·* understood,
	164–26	*b·* so magnified to human sense,
	177–15	*b·* real and consecrated warriors
	178– 6	wanted to *b·* a God-like man.
	179–14	Truth has *b·* more to us,
	187–24	*b·* a clod, in order to
	188–31	This knowledge did *b·* to her
	189– 3	*b·* willing to accept the divine
	194–24	*b·* imbued with divine Love
	196–10	and thus *b·* material, sensual, evil.
	196–24	is *b·* the head stone— *Psal.* 118 : 22.
	197– 2	*b·* the motive-power of every act.
	217– 5	cannot *b·* less than Spirit ;
	217–28	must change in order to *b·*
	217–29	or to *b·* both finite and infinite ;
	227–13	ere that one himself *b·* aware,
	229–21	would thus *b·* beautifully less ;
	229–24	*b·* healthier, holier, happier,
	230–14	*b·* such by hard work ;
	235–19	and *b·* Christian Scientists ;
	236– 7	and *b·* weary with study to
	250– 3	the best *b·* the most abused,
	250–12	*b·* jealousy and hate.
	253–26	until she herself is *b·* a mother?
	289–23	the right to *b·* a mother ;
	294–23	*b·* an admirer of Edgar L. Wakeman's
	310–20	and to *b·* members of it,
	316–12	Until minds *b·* less worldly-minded,
	318–24	all those who *b·* teachers.
	344– 3	to *b·* one of his disciples.
	368–27	may *b·* the worst,
Man.	18– 2	is *b·* the head— *Matt.* 21 : 42.
	18– 6	to *b·* their pastor.
	34– 5	To *b·* a member of The Mother Church,
	45– 8	shall not hereafter *b·* members of
	73–15	may *b·* members of the
	110– 8	and *b·* a part thereof.
Ret.	16–19	to *b·* their pastor.
	28–10	It must *b·* honest,
	28–12	The first must *b·* last.
	38–24	grown disgusted . . . and *b·* silent.
	44– 7	call to me to *b·* their pastor.
	64–29	will *b·* the victims of error.
	76–29	I *b·* responsible, as a teacher,
	81–13	genuine goodness *b·* so apparent
	87– 4	that it has *b·* a truism ;
	87–22	*b·* a law unto themselves.
Un.	4– 3	approach Him and *b·* like Him.
	14–27	never said that man would *b·* better by
	15–19	*b·* only an echo of the divine?
	40–14	than they can *b·* perfect by
	52– 8	consciousness should *b·* divine,
	56–25	*b·* acquainted with that Love
	58– 3	and must *b·* *dis-eased,*
	64–12	mind-pictures would *b·* to us ;
Pul.	10–20	is *b·* the head— *Matt.* 21 : 42.
	35–14	It must *b·* honest,
	35–16	The first must *b·* last.
	73– 3	* If we *b·* sick, God will care for us,
	79–27	* *b·* materialistically "lopsided,"
	86–27	* to *b·* the permanent pastor of
Rud.	3– 6	and *b·* their Saviour,
	5–27	must either *b·* non-existent, or
No.	24–15	claims of evil *b·* both less and more
	38–14	is *b·* the head— *Matt.* 21 : 42.
'00.	5–24	it will *b·* the head of the corner,
'01.	5– 6	*b·* less coherent than the
	14–26	it must *b·* unreal to us ;
	26–23	*b·* as sounding brass,— *I Cor.* 13 : 1.
Hea.	3– 9	again *b·* the head of the corner.
	4–15	and *b·* finite for a season ;
	4–18	*b·* finite, and have an end ;
	5–28	The more spiritual we *b·*
	8–25	If we work to *b·* Christians
	12–11	before they can *b·* manifest
Peo.	2–22	has their Deity *b·* good ;
	4–10	*b·* intelligent of good and evil,
	7–29	*b·* more or less perfect
	10– 6	matter will *b·* vague,
	14– 1	ideas of Deity *b·* more spiritual,
My.	4–26	*b·* as little children,— *Matt.* 18 : 3.

become

My.	41– 1	* to *b·* gladly obedient to law,
	49–11	* to Mrs. Eddy to *b·* its pastor.
	49–19	* to *b·* pastor of the church.
	60–13	* has *b·* the corner-stone of
	63–13	* has *b·* a part of our expanding
	85–22	* *b·* the great centre of attraction,
	107– 9	the old school has *b·* reconciled.
	111–19	*b·* successful healers and models of
	123– 2	they have *b·* a wonder !
	126–25	"is *b·* the habitation of— *Rev.* 18 : 2.
	150–19	to *b·* His own image and likeness,
	190–25	*b·* students of the Christ, Truth,
	190–25	thus *b·* God-endued with power
	236–12	may *b·* equivalent to no centre.
	251– 9	* to *b·* teachers of Primary classes
	253–28	*b·* one with his creator,
	267– 1	*b·* the one and the only religion
		(see also **power**)

becomes

Mis.	59–27	and thus *b·* a transparency
	96–13	God *b·* to me,
	96–18	this atonement *b·* more to me
	101– 2	how healing *b·* spontaneous,
	115–24	*b·* a means of grace.
	156–22	and in turn *b·* a prey.
	203– 5	*b·* mine through gratitude
	216–25	* "When philosophy *b·* fairy-land,
	218– 1	in which nature *b·* Spirit ;
	222–10	he *b·* morally paralyzed
	235– 6	*b·* the partaker of that Mind
	277– 8	*b·* the mark for error's shafts.
	284–25	not something . . . that *b·* more real
	293–23	*b·* the creator of the claim
	346–25	*b·* requisite to bring out Truth.
	351–25	joy that *b·* sorrow.
	363– 2	more conscious it *b·* of its
	391–13	And Love *b·* the substance,
Man.	100–12	*b·* apparent to the C. S. Board
Ret.	21–30	*b·* correspondingly obscure.
	63–19	*b·* accessory to it.
	80–14	heart *b·* obediently receptive
	93–16	*b·* the model for human action.
Un.	24–24	In my mortal mind, matter *b·*
	45–16	where it *b·* error's affirmative
	45–26	until it *b·* non-existent.
	54– 6	then disease *b·* as tangible as
	54–18	*b·* legitimate to mortals,
Pul.	79– 9	* it *b·* us as students of
No.	4–13	*b·* fable instead of fact.
	5–20	Disease *b·* indeed a stubborn
	25– 2	the All and Only of our being.
Pan.	6–21	what *b·* of theism in Christianity?
'01.	16–10	hatred gone mad *b·* imbecile
	25– 2	*b·* clear to the godly.
'02.	6–25	In the degree that man *b·*
	6–26	he *b·* Godlike.
	9– 2	God *b·* to him the All-presence
	10–17	man *b·* finally spiritual.
Po.	38–12	And Love *b·* the substance,
My.	133–26	this inmost something *b·* articulate,
	148–11	this church *b·* historic,
	165–23	Human reason *b·* tired and calls for
	179– 9	man *b·* both good and evil,
	183–19	when the forest *b·* a fruitful field,
	222–26	as God's government *b·* apparent,
	226–28	*b·* better acquainted with C. S.,
	308–10	It *b·* my duty to be just to the

becometh

My.	162– 4	thus it *b·* us to— *Matt.* 3 : 15.
	218– 3	thus it *b·* us to— *Matt.* 3 : 15.

becoming

Mis.	156–16	*b·* the basis for others :
	281–16	* wise to count the cost of *b·* a
	281–18	* cost of *not b·* a true Christian."
Pul.	83–12	* *b·* "as fair as the morn,— *see Song* 6 : 10.
No.	2–20	such teachers are *b·* beacon-lights
	3–25	*b·* odious to honest people ;
	30–14	not by *b·* human, and knowing sin,
My.	197– 2	but *b·* slaves to pleasure is.

bed

Mis.	127–32	human heart. like a feather *b·*,
	376–19	for me, on my *b·*
Ret.	17–12	heart of the pink— in its odorous *b·*;
	40–11	the sick woman rose from her *b·*,
Peo.	14–15	ye may go to the *b·* of anguish,
Po.	62–15	heart of the pink— in its odorous *b·* ;

bedew

Pul.	5–15	was the first to *b·* my hope with a

bedewing

Po.	67– 7	*b·* these fresh-smiling flowers !

Bedford

My.	45–29	* granite and *B·* stone,

Bedford

My. 68–19	* to harmonize with the *B·* stone
68–25	* *B·* stone and marble form the
68–30	* bronze, marble, and *B·* stone.

bedridden

Mis. 241–18	to the *b·* sufferer administer

beds

Pul. 48– 3	* dotted with *b·* of flowering shrubs,
54– 3	* Is by our *b·* of pain ;
My. 36–14	* delivered from *b·* of sickness
188–24	like *b·* in hospitals,

bedside

Mis. 63–13	go to the *b·* and address himself to
201–30	Go to the *b·* of pain,
My. 105–23	Her physician, who stood by her *b·*,
153–12	my flowers visited his *b·* :

Bee

Pul. 89–24	* *B·*, Omaha, Neb.

bee

Mis. 294–13	a hived *b·*, with sting ready
My. 252– 4	Then you will be toilers like the *b·*,

beefsteak

No. 42–27	* eat *b·* and drink strong coffee

beehive

Pul. 42–16	* golden *b·* stamped upon it,
42–16	* and beneath the *b·* the words,

Beelzebub

Mis. 63– 3	healed through *B·* ;
97–10	casting out devils through *B·*.
'01. 10– 5	"If they have called . . . *B·*, — *Matt.* 10 : 25.
Hea. 13–26	antipode of mesmerism, *B·*.

beest

Hea. 8–16	* "What thou seest, that thou *b·*."

Beethoven

'00. 11–14	*B·* besieges you with tones

befall

Mis. 229–18	there shall no evil *b·* thee, — *Psal.* 91 : 10.
Ret. 34–14	all the ills which *b·* mortals.

befogs

Mis. 121–18	whatever belittles, *b·*, or

befools

Mis. 173–24	pains, fetters, and *b·* him.

before

Mis. 7–14	Cast not your pearls *b·* swine
8–25	which were *b·* you." — *Matt.* 5 : 12.
9–19	to fall in fragments *b·* our eyes.
10–12	stronger than *b·* the stumble.
14–15	from evidences *b·* him
16–32	You stand *b·* the awful detonations
17– 6	And, *b·* the flames have died away
17–13	meekly bow *b·* the Christ,
18–10	no other gods *b·* me ;" — *Exod.* 20 : 3.
21– 3	no other gods *b·* me." — *Exod.* 20 : 3.
23–13	no other gods *b·* me." — *Exod.* 20 : 3.
21–14	better health than I had *b·* enjoyed.
26–12	*b·* it was in the earth." — *Gen.* 2 : 5.
28–21	no other gods *b·* me," — *Exod.* 20 : 3.
29–10	even *b·* the Christian era ;
30– 2	*b·* we prove it,
34– 7	*b·* the body is renewed
34–16	as they were *b·* death,
42– 2	*do we meet those gone b·?*
42–10	and being, as material as *b·*.
42–15	with those gone *b·*,
42 17	*b·* the change whereby we meet
45–27	having "other gods *b·* me." — *Exod.* 20 : 3.
49– 3	to withdraw *b·* its close.
49– 4	*b·* entering the College,
52–28	*b·* solving the advanced problem.
53– 3	*b·* this false claim can be
79–27	*persons brought b· the courts*
81–17	*b· it shall go forth into all the cities*
89–17	"pearls *b·* swine" — *Matt.* 7 : 6.
91–31	study the lessons *b·* recitations.
92– 4	Centuries will intervene *b·* the
92–20	to study it *b·* the recitations ;
96–20	I reverence and adore Christ as never *b·*.
96–30	the evidence *b·* the personal senses,
99–10	courage of his convictions fell *b·* it.
107–14	*b·* poor humanity is regenerated
107–20	pass through . . . *b·* yielding error.
109–14	*b·* they can be reduced to
110–13	chapter sub-title
112– 4	*b·* they know it,
116– 7	chapter sub-title
117–29	make their moves *b·* God makes His,
123– 4	no other gods *b·* me :" — *Exod.* 20 : 3.
132– 5	are opening, even wider than *b·*,
134–14	such as you never *b·* received.
151–24	May mercy and truth go *b·* you :
153– 6	God went forth *b·* His people,

before

Mis. 161– 3	SUNDAY *b·* CHRISTMAS, 1888.
162– 7	stepped suddenly *b·* the people
165–30	*b·* man can truthfully conclude
166–31	*b·* it could make him the glorified.
168–26	* speak *b·* the Scientist denomination
169– 9	*b·* Truth dawned upon her
169–16	*b·* their message can be borne fully to
172– 7	a higher sense than ever *b·*,
178–18	* that to-day I should stand *b·* you
178–22	* I should not be standing *b·* you :
179–26	*b·* it sprang from the earth :
187–28	*b·* he can be good ;
187–29	dying, *b·* deathless ;
187–29	material, *b·* spiritual ;
189–14	"*B·* Abraham was, — *John* 8 : 58.
204– 3	humble *b·* God, he cries,
206–28	going *b·* you, has scaled the steep
208–21	"*B·* I was afflicted — *Psal.* 119 : 67.
209–22	having "other gods *b·* me,"— *Exod.* 20 : 3.
209–23	but are punished *b·* extinguished.
210–31	Charity never flees *b·* error,
212–28	*b·* letting another know it.
214–17	*b·* it could be returned
214–29	*b·* they can be burned,
216–29	* the attempt . . . may succeed, but not *b·* ;
218–10	*b·* it can reach the immortality of
230–15	improving moments *b·* they pass
238–28	kept constantly *b·* the public.
239–12	draw up *b·* a stately mansion ;
242–29	*b·* leaving the class he took a patient
244– 6	*b·* surgical instruments were invented,
249–28	What a word ! I am in awe *b·* it.
251– 2	chapter sub-title
251–27	will fall *b·* Truth demonstrated,
251–29	*b·* the evangel of Truth
251–30	as the mountain mists *b·* the sun.
264–20	*b·* they are quite free from the
271–15	*B·* considering a subject that is
273–24	lying on the desk *b·* me,
274–26	are held up *b·* the rabble
277–19	Benjamin Franklin's report *b·* the
277–23	No evidence *b·* the material senses
278– 1	vision of the Revelator is *b·* me.
279 10	*b·* the walls of Jericho.
280–27	some questions *b·* their dismissal,
284–24	not something to fear and flee *b·*,
287– 3	will go out *b·* the forever fact
288– 5	*b·* you are sure of being a
288– 8	*b·* being put into action.
288–19	*b·* it is understood
307–21	Cast not pearls *b·* the unprepared
312–12	in his remarks *b·* that body,
316–24	*B·* entering the . . . College,
318–19	*B·* entering this sacred field of labor,
328–29	which are *b·*." — *Phil.* 3 : 13.
330–15	let mortals bow *b·* the creator,
330–31	stoops meekly *b·* the blast ;
343– 3	others *b·* us have laid upon the
345– 3	had stood four hundred years *b·*,
347–20	guardians of His presence go *b·* me.
349–24	*b·* I would accept the slightest
352 29	uncovered *b·* it can be destroyed,
360–29	"*B·* Abraham was, — *John* 8 : 58.
361–19	race that is set *b·* us, — *Heb.* 12 : 1.
370–14	more intelligently than ever *b·*,
373– 9	I had never *b·* seen it :
382– 4	*B·* the publication of my first work
391–20	Some good ne'er told *b·*,
Man. 26–16	*b·* they are elected ;
30–19	attend to the insurance *b·* it expires,
32–12	*b·* commencing to read from this book,
52– 7	shall be laid *b·* this Board,
57– 3	may properly come *b·* these meetings,
57– 8	*B·* calling a meeting of the members
57–16	*b·* he can call said meeting.
66– 3	*b·* presenting it to the Church
66–10	*b·* action is taken it shall be the duty
66–16	brought *b·* a meeting of this Church,
69– 8	*b·* the expiration of the time
71– 6	*b·* titles of branch churches,
79–12	*B·* being eligible for office
93–17	copies of his lectures *b·* delivering them.
109–16	*b·* sending them to the Clerk
110–15	sign "Miss" or "Mrs." *b·* their names
112– 6	*b·* titles of branch churches.
Chr. 55–15	*B·* Abraham was, — *John* 8 : 58.
Ret. 7– 4	after a short illness, *b·* his election.
8–23	answered as always *b·*.
9– 8	That night, *b·* going to rest,
13– 5	*B·* this step was taken,
16– 7	she has not sung *b·* since she
20– 5	*b·* my father's second marriage,
20–12	The night *b·* my child was taken
22–11	joy that was set *b·* him — *Heb.* 12 : 2.
26–12	had *b·* seemed to me supernatural,

before

Ret.	26–18	b· the material world saw him.
	27–23	b· the mind can duly express it
	27–25	b· gathering experience and
	31–24	bent low b· the omnipotence of Spirit,
	35– 9	b· a work on this subject
	40– 4	called to speak b· the Lyceum Club,
	40–19	"I never b· suffered so little
	44– 9	five years b· being ordained.
	47–23	b· entering this field of labor
	55– 1	true sense of the great work b· them,
	67– 1	b· the human concept of sin
	71–25	b· the wheat can be garnered
	80–14	b· this heart becomes obediently
	83–26	study each lesson b· the recitation.
	84– 1	Centuries will intervene b· the
Un.	2–23	beyond what they possessed b· ;
	3– 6	b· it can be truly said of them :
	8– 2	b· Science answers it.
	10–22	evidence b· the material senses,
	42– 9	b· he can be virtuous,
	42–10	dying b· he can be deathless,
	42–10	material b· he can be spiritual,
	54–21	Satan held it up b· man
	58– 4	b· error is annihilated.
	58–13	b· he apprehends Christ as
	59–15	to suffer b· Pilate and on Calvary,
Pul.	6–15	* I had not read three pages b· I
	8–17	Little hands, never b· devoted to
	12– 8	accused them b· our — Rev. 12 : 10.
	12–19	than has ever b· reached high heaven,
	26–26	* B· the great bay window
	29–12	* B· the appointed hour every seat
	31–24	* b· Mrs. Eddy entered the room.
	34– 9	* b· proceeding to his morning service,
	38– 3	* b· being ordained in this church,
	39–24	* hurrying throng b· me pass,
	41–30	* B· this service had closed
	43–29	* B· presenting the sermon,
	45–11	* b· the close of the year
	45–16	* b· April or May of 1895.
	46–16	* not long b· the Revolution.
	54–15	* as no one b· him understood it ;
	59–29	* B· one service was over
	60– 6	* b· coming into this work,
	63–24	* paid for b· it was begun,
	65– 8	* and may have a future b· it.
	76–14	* b· the hearth is a large rug
	80–23	* did not believe in them b·.
Rud.	12– 9	until they hold stronger than b·
No.	8–24	b· this state of mortal mind,
	13–10	b· this reappearing of Truth,
	13–12	b· that saying is demonstrated
	39–22	more clearly than we saw b·,
	42– 6	to have other gods b· Him,
Pan.	9–10	no other gods b· me ;" — Exod. 20 : 3.
	10–14	stronger and better than b· it.
	10–16	broadened and brightened b· them,
'00.	5–20	no other gods b· me ;" — Exod. 20 : 3.
	6– 7	those things which are b·, — Phil. 3 : 13.
	8–22	b· we can successfully war with
	9–12	b· the time?" — Matt. 8 : 29.
	9–17	b· he can conquer others.
'01.	1– 8	better appreciated, than ever b·,
	8–25	"B· Abraham was," — John 8 : 58.
	14–24	thought b· it is acted ;
	22–22	rules, are b· the people,
	22–24	b· they have learned its numeration
	26–25	B· leaving this subject of the
	27–29	* say it has been discovered b·.
'02.	4–20	no other gods b· me," — Exod. 20 : 3.
	5–30	no other gods b· me," — Exod. 20 : 3.
	6–20	no other gods b· me." — Exod. 20 : 3.
	10– 6	b· the time?" — Matt. 8 : 29.
	11–26	which were b· you." — Matt. 5 : 12.
	12–25	b· making another united effort
	15–13	B· entering upon my great life-work,
Hea.	1–11	b· arguing with the world
	4– 4	b· calculating the results of an
	10– 5	But the beast bowed b· the Lamb :
	10– 7	fell b· the womanhood of God,
	11–16	b· lifting its foot against its neighbor,
	12–11	b· they can become manifest
	17–17	material sense that b· had claimed
	19–14	b· it was in the earth." — Gen. 2 : 5.
Peo.	2–26	constantly b· the people's mind,
	5–26	lecture b· the Harvard Medical
	7– 9	* With his marble block b· him ;
	7–17	* With our lives uncarved b· us,
	11– 3	scarcely done with their battles b·
Po.	38–19	Some good ne'er told b·,
My.	5–14	no other gods b· me," — Exod. 20 : 3.
	7– 8	b· making another united effort
	9–24	I never b· felt poor in thanks,
	29–24	* different status b· the world !
	30–32	* B· half past seven the chimes

before

My.	37–15	* b· the gaze of universal humanity.
	43– 3	* wilderness was b· them.
	43–15	* Red Sea forty years b·.
	45–19	* Him who went b· you
	50– 1	* deliberation b· a Communion Sabbath
	50– 9	* knew not the trials b· them,
	50–14	* for deliberation b· Communion
	54– 8	* b· the service commenced,
	54– 9	* b· the arrival of the pastor,
	57–27	* Shortly b· the dedication of The
	59–27	* b· it was ever written.
	59–28	* b· it was ever printed."
	61– 8	* completed b· the end of summer,
	61–18	* I bowed my head b· the might of
	61–31	* I appreciated as never b· the
	64–10	* name an honored one b· the world.
	64–13	no other gods b· me,' — Exod. 20 : 3.
	64–19	* standing of C. S. b· the world.
	64–27	* members of The Mother Church b· men.
	66–30	* never b· has such a grand church
	72– 7	* Never b· has the city been
	72–26	* b· the work was actually completed.
	74–17	* paying for their church b·
	79– 2	* kneeling . . . b· the pews,
	79–22	* than it ever occupied b·.
	80–31	* b· seven the auditorium was
	81–14	* told to name, b· beginning,
	83–25	* even b· the building itself has
	86–14	* b· the actual work was completed,
	88– 5	* as now b· this continent,
	91– 9	* paid for b· they are dedicated.
	95–11	* b· the press gallery of
	96–21	* b· the day set for the dedication
	137–24	b· the present proceedings were
	138–30	* B· me : ALLEN HOLLIS,
	140– 5	darkness light b· them, — Isa. 42 : 16.
	149–18	emptied b· it can be refilled.
	150– 1	where Love has not been b· thee
	153–17	no other gods b· me" — Exod. 20 : 3.
	155–14	run in joy, . . . the race set b· it,
	186–21	"B· they call, — Isa. 65 : 24.
	197–20	hope set b· us in the Word
	221–18	no other gods b· me." — Exod. 20 : 3.
	227–24	your pearls b· swine, — Matt. 7 : 6.
	229– 8	from b· thee." — Deut. 18 : 12.
	234–28	b· the minds of the people are
	244– 1	b· informing you of my
	256– 2	B· the Christmas bells shall ring,
	257–14	Christ is, more than ever b·,
	258–14	joy that was set b· him — Heb. 12 : 2.
	260– 5	withdraw itself b· Mind.
	260– 6	would flee b· such reality,
	265– 4	knocks more loudly than ever b·
	270– 2	prophets which were b· — Matt. 5 : 12.
	270–11	nearer my consciousness than b·,
	273– 2	* to put b· its readers.
	278– 9	no other gods b· me," — Exod. 20 : 3.
	279–12	no other gods b· me" — Exod. 20 : 3.
	298– 9	placing this book b· the public,
	299– 8	* b· they claim the allegiance of
	302–22	am less lauded, . . . than others b· me
	304–27	* say it has been discovered b·.
	306–25	B· his decease, in January, 1866,
	310– 8	died b· the election.
	315–19	* B· me, (Signed) H. M. MORSE,
	321–31	* knew you years b· I did,
	322–17	* I had seen you the day b· at
	323– 2	* B· we left that evening,
	323– 8	* How long must it be b· the
	329– 7	* b· a board of medical examiners.
	329–26	* It will put b· them some
	344–14	better than he was b· death.
	346–12	* drove into town . . . before returning.
	363–21	address the Christian Scientist
	364– 8	no other gods b· me." — Exod. 20 : 3.

beforehand

Mis.	338– 4	gained its height b·,

befriended

Pul.	7– 6	her laws have b· progress.

beg

Ret.	50–11	I b· disinterested people to
My.	118– 9	I b· to thank you for your
	165–12	I b· to thank the dear brethren
	256– 9	I b· to send to you all a

began

Mis.	33–16	when they b· treatment,
	101–10	b· and ended in a contest for
	168–30	* speaker b· by saying :
	182– 1	b· spiritually instead of
	237–17	as when this nation b·,
	345–17	* since the reign of Christianity b·
Ret.	43– 2	I b· by teaching one student
Pul.	33– 3	* she b·, like Jeanne d'Arc,

began

Pul.	42– 4	* At 10 : 30 o'clock another service *b*.,
	58– 4	* about 1880, she *b*. teaching,
	80– 6	* *b*. in the most intellectual city
	85– 1	* *b*. to lay the foundation of
'02.	2–27	I but *b*. where the Church left off.
	3–30	leap into perdition *b*. with
Po.	v–15	* *b*. to take form in her thought,
	v–17	* seated herself . . . and *b*. to write.
	1– 8	when first creation vast *b*.,
	70–16	discord ne'er in harmony *b*.!
My.	6–18	*b*. with the cross ;
	29–27	* *b*. to congregate about the church
	31– 1	* chimes . . . *b*. to play,
	32– 4	* *b*. to repeat the Lord's Prayer,
	32– 5	* they *b*. all together,
	61–22	* as soon as the workmen *b*. to admit
	72–28	* the way the Christian Scientists *b*.
	77–18	* *b*. to gather at daybreak
	114–14	*b*. with notes on the Scriptures.
	116–23	Every loss in . . . since time *b*.
	162–16	"This man *b*. to build, — Luke 14 : 30.
	291– 7	His work *b*. with heavy strokes,
	291– 9	*b*. by warming the marble of
	304–10	I *b*. writing for the leading
	318–21	*b*. my attack on agnosticism.

begat

My.	132–15	"Of His own will *b*. He us— Jas. 1 : 18.

beget

Ret.	68– 4	it claimed to *b*. the offspring of
My.	203–16	Our thoughts *b*. our actions ;

begets

Mis.	210–19	Intemperance *b*. a belief of
Ret.	74– 1	and *b*. a fear of the senses
No.	39–20	Prayer *b*. an awakened desire to
Hea.	3–13	divine Principle that *b*. the quality,

beggar

Pul.	65–24	* half of the garment to a naked *b*. ;

beggared

My.	332– 3	* language would be but *b*. by

begged

My.	302–14	I *b*. the students who first
	311– 5	She *b*. to be allowed to remain

begging

Pul.	8–13	no urging, *b*., or borrowing;
	31–20	* *b*. the favor of an interview
My.	215– 2	I was above *b*.
	215–13	in letters *b*. me to accept it,
	273–12	nor his seed *b*. bread." — Psal. 37 : 25.

begin

Mis.	14–13	we *b*. with the correct statement,
	32–24	and charity must *b*. at home.
	98–22	must *b*. with individual growth,
	106–24	and where shall *b*. that praise
	218–21	To *b*. with, the notion of
	335– 5	shall *b*. to smite — Matt. 24 : 49.
	380–11	call for help impelled me to *b*.
Mun.	90– 9	The lecture year shall *b*. July 1
Ret.	63–12	we *b*. to sap it ;
Pul.	31– 7	* tempted to "*b*. at the beginning"
	44– 3	* At last you *b*. to see the fruition
	83–26	* *b*. to know what John on Patmos meant
No.	2–10	cannot *b*. by admitting its reality.
	37– 7	to *b*. and end, to know both
	46–13	*b*. by admitting individual rights.
'01.	22–15	I *b*. at the feet of Christ
'02.	4– 2	dishonesty in trusts, *b*. with
	20–17	*b*. omitting our annual gathering
Hea.	4–19	to *b*. anew as infinite Life,
My.	41–30	* and we *b*. to understand how
	41–32	* we *b*. to comprehend the
	42–25	* *b*. to comprehend, even in small degree,
	132– 2	*b*. with the law as just announced,
	203– 9	*b*. with work and never stop
	204– 8	can *b*. and never end.
	216–31	*b*. now to earn for a purpose
	274–13	To *b*. rightly enables one
	350– 3	*b*. with the divine noumenon, Mind,
	357–15	*b*. on a wholly spiritual foundation,

beginner

Mis.	66–25	*b*. in sin-healing must know this,

beginning

at the

Mis.	215–23	My students are at the *b*. of their
Pul.	31– 8	* tempted to "begin at the *b*."
	52–18	* At the *b*. of Christianity it was
My.	78–14	* The offertory taken at the *b*. of
	107– 4	at the *b*. of the Christian era,

end for the

Mis.	215–11	if we take the end for the *b*.

from the

Mis.	56–27	have existed from the *b*.,
	108– 7	of Satan as a liar from the *b*.,

beginning

from the

Mis.	164–15	prophet beheld it from the *b*. as the
	208–23	He who knows the end from the *b*.,
	257–21	"a murderer from the *b*.." — John 8 : 44.
	363–14	Truth said, and said from the *b*.,
Un.	17–14	that, from the *b*., their father,
	32–21	a murderer from the *b*.— John 8 : 44.
	36– 4	From the *b*. this lie was the false
No.	24–23	"a murderer from the *b*., — John 8 : 44.
Pan.	5–14	a murderer from the *b*., — John 8 : 44.
'01.	13– 7	sin is a lie from the *b*.,
'02.	14–18	From the *b*. of the great battle
My.	187–15	ye heard from the *b*., — I John 3 : 11.

in the

Mis.	60–26	Evil in the *b*. claimed the power,
	186–24	than it produced in the *b*.
	196– 7	saying as in the *b*.,
	215–27	cannot in the *b*. take the attitude,
	258–32	as harmonious to-day as in the *b*.,
	359– 2	is requisite in the *b*. ;
Ret.	48–25	in the *b*. in this institution.
	50–30	in the *b*. of pioneer work.
'01.	18– 2	less than in the *b*.,
	25–25	which Satan demanded in the *b*.,
My.	117–18	"In the *b*. was the Word, — John 1 : 1.

its

My.	92– 4	* its *b*. has been impressive,

no

Mis.	167–13	Of his days there is no *b*.
Ret.	58–12	Life, as defined by Jesus, had no *b*. ;
Un.	42–21	Life had no *b*. ;
My.	267–11	eternal Mind that hath no *b*.

of Christian Science

My.	164–14	*b*. of C. S. in Chicago

of days

Chr.	55–20	neither *b*. of days, — Heb. 7 : 3.

of war

'02.	3–20	at the close than the *b*. of war.

of wisdom

Mis.	359–29	To ask wisdom . . . is the *b*. of wisdom.

or end

Mis.	189–31	Life without *b*. or end.
No.	37– 9	He cannot know *b*. or end.
My.	119–24	Life without *b*. or end of days.

the very

Un.	54–20	to know evil at the very *b*.,

without

Mis.	189–31	Life without *b*. or end.
Ret.	59– 6	eternal, without *b*. or ending.
Un.	13–17	"without *b*. of years — see Heb. 7 : 3.
	40–23	without *b*. and without end,
'02.	7–15	Love, without *b*. and without end,
Hea.	4– 19	Life, without *b*. and without end.
Peo.	2–24	Life without *b*. or ending,
My.	119–24	Life without *b*. or end of days.

Mis.	47– 5	a *b*. must have an ending.
	57–28	*b*. with the lowest form
	216–20	* *b*. with the end of the tail,
	219–13	it is *b*. to be seen by thinkers,
Mun.	66–99	*b*. on page 330 of the revised
	88–12	*B*. with 1907, the teacher shall be
	91–24	once in three years *b*. A.D. 1907.
Ret.	60– 1	apart from God, *b*. and ending,
No.	28–11	acceptable time for *b*. the lesson.
My.	6–20	remains in the *b*. of this edifice,
	56–28	* Therefore, *b*. October 1, 1905,
	81–14	* been told to name, before *b*.,
	170– 1	the *b*. of the gospel writings,
	236–25	paragraph *b*. at line 30 of page 442

beginnings

My.	123–26	ofttimes small *b*. have large endings.
	303– 1	foresplendor of the *b*. of truth

begins

Mis.	15–13	*b*. with moments, and goes on with
	21– 1	C. S. *b*. with the First Commandment
	220– 5	The healer *b*. by mental argument.
	288–13	Wisdom in human action *b*. with
	347–11	Where my vision *b*. and is clear,
'00.	8–20	man *b*. to quarrel with himself
'01.	21–19	*b*. his calculation erroneously ;
Hea.	7–10	It *b*. with motive, instead of act,
	7–15	*b*. in mind to heal the body,
	7–15	*b*. in motive to correct the act.
Peo.	3–20	*b*. wrongly to apprehend the infinite,
My.	82– 5	* chapter sub-title
	216–28	that charity *b*. at home,
	225–17	*b*. in the minds of men
	253–26	that which *b*. in ourselves

begirt

Mis.	194– 7	*b*. with the Urim and Thummim of
	392– 5	With peaceful presence hath *b*. thee
'01.	12–13	Though a man were *b*. with
Po.	20– 6	With peaceful presence hath *b*. thee

begotten

Mis.	164–25	the only *b·* of the Father,
Ret.	26–24	It must be *b·* of spirituality,
Pul.	35– 9	"Divine Science is *b·* of

begs

Mis.	330–26	mere mendicant that boasts and *b·*,
My.	276– 4	she *b·* to say, in her own behalf,

beguile

Po.	33–14	Whose mercies my sorrows *b·*,
	35– 2	*B·* the lagging hours of weariness

begun

Mis.	16–25	is the new birth *b·* in C. S.
	70–19	and had already *b·* to die,
	141– 6	This building *b·*, will go up,
	302– 2	purpose to kill the reformation *b·*
	354–27	for a flight well *b·*,
	384–12	The reign of heaven *b·*,
Pul.	63–24	* was paid for before it was *b·*,
'00.	10– 9	unconquerable right is *b·* anew,
	15–29	The reign of heaven *b·*,
Po.	36–11	The reign of heaven *b·*,
My.	57–12	* was *b·* in October, 1903,
	67–25	* *b·* nearly two years ago,
	254– 2	have *b·* to be a Christian Scientist.

behalf

Mis.	23–17	Satan, the first talker in its *b·*,
	156– 1	in *b·* of a suffering race,
	292–20	what he is doing in their *b·*,
Man.	75– 5	in *b·* of The First Church of Christ,
Pul.	86–20	* In *b·* of your loving students
My.	7–18	* acting in *b·* of ourselves and
	10–16	* has ever been made in this *b·*,
	20– 9	awaiting on *b·* of your Leader
	99–12	* it must be said in their *b·*
	171–24	* greeted in *b·* of the church
	172–21	* "I accept this gift in *b·* of
	175–18	May I ask in *b·* of the public
	190–21	a divine decision in *b·* of Mind.
	216–16	on *b·* of the room of
	265–12	in *b·* of the sacred rights of
	276– 4	she begs to say, in her own *b·*,
	280– 5	* care and guidance in our *b·*
	285– 3	on *b·* of the Civic League of
	312–24	their provisions in my *b·*
	316–17	in *b·* of common justice and truth
	331–19	* in *b·* of the relatives and friends
	332– 6	* in *b·* of the unfortunate,

behave

No.	45– 5	not *b·* itself unseemly, — *I Cor.* 13 : 5.

beheld

Mis.	21– 7	*b·* "a new heaven — *Rev.* 21 : 1.
	82– 7	*b·* the forthcoming Truth,
	164–14	prophet *b·* it from the beginning
	188–32	for she *b·* the meaning of
	269–29	The Revelator *b·* the opening of
Ret.	25–29	I *b·* with ineffable awe our great
My.	148–14	Then we *b·* the omen,
	290–21	Through a . . . mist he *b·* the dawn.

behest

Mis.	385– 7	This is Thy high *b·* :
Ret.	90–12	until they were able to fulfil his *b·*
'02.	19–24	a spiritual *b·*, in reversion,
Po.	28– 7	To Thy all-wise *b·*
	31–18	The ever Christ, and glorified *b·*,
	37– 7	This is Thy high *b·* :
	77– 5	Plenty and peace abound at Thy *b·*,

behind

Mis.	141– 8	the power that is *b·* it ;
	160– 5	But a mother's love *b·* words
	170–11	This is the reality *b·* the symbol.
	232–10	never do to be *b·* the times
	302– 1	*B·* the scenes lurks an evil
	327–28	they fall *b·* and lose sight of
	328–28	things which are *b·*, — *Phil.* 3 : 13.
	368– 8	* and, *b·* the dim unknown,
	373– 3	placing the serpent *b·* the woman
	373–10	out of his mouth, *b·* the woman,
	374–28	Looking *b·* the veil,
Pul.	1–15	path *b·* thee is with glory crowned ;
	48– 1	* terrace that slopes *b·* the
	59– 1	* electric light, *b·* an antique lamp,
	60–19	* recess *b·* the spacious platform,
No.	23– 7	"Get thee *b·* me, Satan ;" — *Matt.* 16 : 23.
'00.	6– 6	things which are *b·*, — *Phil.* 3 : 13.
Po.	26– 2	track *b·* thee is with glory crowned ;
My.	38–19	* not a whit *b·* their elders,
	92–18	* would soon be left *b·*.
	94– 2	* every other sect will be left *b·*
	155–11	leave *b·* those things that are *b·*,
	242– 6	neither *b·* the point of perfection
	355–19	* "*B·* a frowning providence

behold

Mis.	vii– 6	* Then do I love thee, and *b·* thy ends

behold

Mis.	2–14	we *b·* but the first faint view
	16–31	and *b·* for the first time
	17–15	you *b·* for the first time
	107– 9	we *b·* more clearly that all the
	123–17	too pure to *b·* iniquity,
	133–32	*b·* the sick who are healed,
	134–23	Like Elisha, look up, and *b·* :
	159–25	Thy children grown to *b· Thee !*
	168–19	*b·* the appearing of the star !"
	210– 2	*b·* the result : evil, uncovered,
	213– 1	could not *b·* his immortal being
	322– 3	invite you . . . to preparation to *b·* it.
	323– 7	*b·* a Stranger wending his way
	326–27	*B·*, your house — *Matt.* 23 : 38.
	330–16	*b·* man in God's own image
	336–25	*b·* a better man, woman, or child.
	342–12	to *b·* the bridegroom,
	342–18	But how could they *b·* him?
	352– 3	to *b·* aright the error,
	352– 8	able to *b·* the facts of Truth
	367–30	too pure to *b·* iniquity ;
	371– 6	and *b·* the remedy,
	389–11	Can I *b·* the snare, the pit, the fall :
Chr.	55–26	*B·*, I stand at the— *Rev.* 3 : 20.
Ret.	42–15	and *b·* the upright :— *Psal.* 37 : 37.
	86–10	*B·* its vileness, and remember
	86–13	may *b·* the real man,
Un.	1–11	*Does God know or b· sin,*
	2– 1	too pure to *b·* iniquity — *see Hab.* 1 : 13.
	18– 8	too pure to *b·* iniquity,
	29–28	to *b·* Spirit as the sole origin
	55–20	and *b·* the truth of being,
	55–22	Now and here shall I *b·* God,
	64– 3	for God can no more *b·* it,
Pul.	2– 4	"*B·*, the half was not — *I Kings* 10 : 7.
Rud.	10– 7	too pure to *b·* iniquity,
No.	22–17	greater than the corporeality we *b·*.
	24–22	for *b·* evil (or devil) is,
Pan.	13– 7	*b·*, the kingdom of God — *Luke* 17 : 21.
'00.	7–21	we *b·* the Christ
	8– 1	*b·* more nearly the embodied Christ,
	14– 3	*B·*, I will make them — *Rev.* 3 : 9.
'02.	19– 2	Yet *b·* his love !
Hea.	17–12	as we awake to *b·* His likeness.
Peo.	14–17	*b·* once again the power of divine
Po.	4–10	Can I *b·* the snare, the pit,
My.	12–17	"*B·*, now is the accepted — *II Cor.* 6 : 2.
	16–24	saith the Lord God, *B·*, — *Isa.* 28 : 16.
	17–15	*B·*, I lay in Sion — *I Pet.* 2 : 6.
	122–24	*b·* the place where they — *Mark* 16 : 6.
	122–28	spiritualized to *b·* this Christ,
	191–20	*B·* the place where they laid me ;
	267–28	"*B·*, the kingdom of God — *Luke* 17 : 21.
	300– 1	than to *b·* evil." — *Hab.* 1 : 13.

beholding

Mis.	68– 6	visible to those *b·* him here.
	180– 6	*b·* me restored to health.
	182–18	*b·* the truth of being ;
	324–19	Startled beyond measure at *b·* him,
	342– 9	*b·* the bridal of Life and Love,
My.	274–23	blessed when *b·* Christian healing,

beholds

Un.	41– 1	and *b·* nothing but mortality,

behooves

Mis.	171–29	it *b·* all clad in the shining mail
Pul.	2–26	it *b·* us to defend our heritage.

Being

Mis.	82–18	endless beatitudes of *B·* ;
Ret.	56– 7	*B·* into beings, — is a misstatement
Un.	19– 3	must be one, in an infinite *B·*.
No.	26–20	reflect the supreme individual *B·*,
Pan.	4– 4	will of a self-existent divine *B·*,
'00.	12– 5	the radiance of glorified *B·*.
'01.	3–11	* definition of God, "A Supreme *B·*,"
	3–12	* Supreme *B·*, self-existent and
	3–19	fundamental, intelligent, divine *B·*,
Hea.	15– 4	omnipotence of the Supreme *B·*
	19–18	Tireless *B·*, patient of man's
Peo.	2– 5	people's . . . views of the Supreme *B·*.
	4–27	false ideals of the Supreme *B·*
	13– 5	Divine *B·* is more than a person,

(*see also* **Supreme Being**)

being (noun)

actual

My.	160–17	for actual *b·*, health, holiness,

aid to

Mis.	267–25	is no real aid to *b·*.

aim, and

Ret.	22–17	He alone is our origin, aim, and *b·*.

all

Mis.	78– 6	His glory encompasseth all *b·* ;
	104– 9	In Science all *b·* is individual ;
	399–12	Life of all *b·* divine :
Ret.	28– 2	Life, or Principle, of all *b·* ;

being (noun)

all
Un. 24– 4 all individuality, all b·.
29–10 Soul of all b·, the only Mind
Rud. 3–27 divine Principle of all b·,
Po. 75–19 Life of all, b· divine :

altitude of
My. 110–24 higher in the altitude of b·.

arrayed against
No. 5–19 and yet is arrayed against b·,

avenue of
Mis. 185–12 good flows into every avenue of b·,

basis of
Mis. 74– 6 of the true basis of b·,

chain of
My. 202–18 onward and upward chain of b·.
339– 4 leads upward in the chain of b·.

cognizes
Rud. 5–19 consciousness which cognizes b·.

concrete
Mis. 82–20 Infinite progression is concrete b·,

conscious
Un. 56–19 Their conscious b· was not fully
No. 36– 6 Jesus' true and conscious b·

constituency of
No. 4–23 and true constituency of b·.

deathless
My. 195–24 lives, moves, and has deathless b·.

demonstration of
Ret. 26–29 demonstration of b·, in Science,

dome of
Mis. 1– 5 dawned on the dome of b·

dynamics of
Mis. 258–31 the eternal dynamics of b·,

enriches the
My. 295–20 enriches the b· of all men.

eternal
Un. 43– 1 eternal b· and its perfections,
No. 11– 4 Principle, and an eternal b·.

exhaustless
My. 149–12 mysteries of exhaustless b·.

fact of
Mis. 180–20 is not the scientific fact of b· ;
My. 109– 6 is not the spiritual fact of b·.

facts of
Mis. 37– 7 spiritual facts of b·.
187–26 primal facts of b· are eternal ;
234–24 into the spiritual facts of b·
Un. 51– 1 everlasting facts of b· appear,

fate to
No. 42–18 determine the fact and fate to b·.

finite
Mis. 102– 4 is only an infinite finite b·,

fragrance of
Mis. 330–23 freshen the fragrance of b·.

good in
My. 196–25 good in b·, . . . is your daily bread.

grounds of
Mis. 68–28 * the ultimate grounds of b·,

harmonious
Mis. 77–17 one eternal round of harmonious b·.
188– 5 grand chorus of harmonious b·.

harmony of
(see **harmony**)

her
Mis. 160– 7 paramount portion of her b·.

His
Mis. 102–11 His b· is individual,
Un. 13–17 in the very fibre of His b·,
32–14 the eternal qualities of His b·.

his
Mis. 85– 8 the divine Principle of his b·,
181– 4 reality of his b·, in divine Science
Ret. 69– 4 and Life is the law of his b·"
No. 36–17 reality and royalty of his b·,
Pan. 11–11 the divine Principle of his b·,
My. 164–29 lives, moves, and has his b· in God,

his own
'01. 20– 9 Scientist is alone with his own b·

human
(see **human**)

idea of
Mis. 166– 2 Principle and spiritual idea of b·.
188–10 divine Principle and idea of b·,

immortal
Mis. 213– 1 could not behold his immortal b·
Un. 57–26 forward the birth of immortal b· ;
No. 27–28 learn the definition of immortal b· ;
'02. 16–20 and man's immortal b·.

individual
Mis. 104– 2 his individual b·, the Christ,
No. 17– 9 is a spiritual and individual b·,
26–19 Man's individual b· must reflect the

infinite
My. 262–17 with the glory of infinite b·.

being (noun)

is God
Mis. 72–28 B· is God, infinite Spirit ;

is understood
Mis. 361–13 and b· is understood in startling

justice and
'02. 15–12 connection between justice and b·

knowledge, and
Ret. 32– 4 spiritual insight, knowledge, and b·.

law of
Mis. 181– 9 blind obedience to the law of b·,
259–18 the only law of b·.
No. 2– 8 is natural and a law of b·.
My. 217–31 not to destroy the law of b·,

laws of
Mis. 31– 7 subverts the scientific laws of b·.

Life and
Ret. 68–25 Life and b· are of God.

man's
Mis. 202– 4 lift man's b· into the sunlight of
Un. 53–15 harmony of man's b· is not built on
Rud. 9–14 divine Principle of man's b· ;
My. 4– 7 C. S., the truth of man's b·.
155– 1 Such communing uplifts man's b· ;
246–17 divine Mind or Principle of man's b·
257–22 make man's b· pure and blest.
274– 7 consummate man's b· with the

misapprehension of
Un. 53–13 is a misapprehension of b·,

my
My. 189–27 song and the dirge, surging my b·,
241–27 * and moved and had my b· in God,

of God
Un. 47– 4 with good, the b· of God,
Rud. 7–15 evidence of the b· of God and man,

one in
'02. 12–19 Father and son, are one in b·.

or consciousness
Un. 3–21 is perfect b·, or consciousness.

order of
Mis. 104–23 the divine law and order of b·.
Un. 40–11 imperative in the divine order of b·.

our
Mis. 8– 6 and have our b·," — Acts 17 : 28.
32–30 and have our b·." — Acts 17 : 28.
Ret. 93–18 and have our b·." — Acts 17 : 28.
Un. 64–14 forever accompany our b·.
Pul. 2–23 and have our b·" — Acts 17 : 28.
No. 17– 7 and have our b· ;" — Acts 17 : 28.
25– 3 becomes the All and Only of our b·.
Pan. 13–20 and have our b·" — Acts 17 : 28.
'02. 12–20 and have our b·." — Acts 17 : 28.
My. 109–23 and have our b·." — Acts 17 : 28.

part of
No. 12–28 all instead of a part of b·,

personal
Ret. 25–21 personal b·, like unto man ;

phenomena of
No. 10–28 constitute the phenomena of b·,

power of
Pul. 4–25 with it cometh the full power of b·.

predicate of
Mis. 103– 6 ultimate and predicate of b·.

present
Un. 41–16 illumine our present b· with

Principle of
Mis. 93–17 by the unerring Principle of b·.
269–11 elucidate the Principle of b·,
Man. 67–19 from the divine Principle of b· to
My. 170–27 based on the divine Principle of b·,

problem of
(see **problem**)

problems of
Mis. 125–25 hitherto untouched problems of b·,

real
Mis. 83– 1 Principle, of all real b· ;
No. 26–13 All real b· represents God,

realities of
(see **realities**)

reality of
Mis. 367–11 reality of b· — goodness and harmony
Un. 38–27 reality of b·, whose Principle is
51– 5 reality of b· is neither seen, felt,
No. 10–25 Spirit, which is the reality of b·.

recognition of
Mis. 196–26 arise to spiritual recognition of b·,

regard
My. 178–14 those who regard b· as material.

resources of
Un. 9–15 as to the source and resources of b·,

right
'01. 2–11 a fair seeming for right b·,

rule of
Mis. 189– 4 divine Principle and rule of b·,

scale of
(see **scale**)

being (noun)
  Science of
    (see **Science**)
  scientific
    Mis. 288–18   consciousness of scientific *b·*
    My. 272– 8   ultimate of scientific *b·* presents,
        279– 8   is the chain of scientific *b·*
  self-conscious
    Rud. 2– 2   *"a living soul; a self-conscious *b·* ;
  sense of
    (see **sense**)
  source of
    Mis. 333–18   away from the divine source of *b·*,
    Ret. 69– 3   primitive and ultimate source of *b·* ;
    Un. 46–12   spiritual sense and source of *b·*.
  spiritual
    Mis. 105–10   his individual spiritual *b·*,
        113–13   scale of moral and spiritual *b·*,
        352– 1   it mocks the bliss of spiritual *b·* ;
    Peo. 2– 6   material conceptions of spiritual *b·*,
  stage of
    Mis. 288–22   in every state and stage of *b·*.
    No. 38–23   any other state or stage of *b·*.
  statement of
    Ret. 94– 1   this scientific statement of *b·*.
    My. 19– 7   * scientific statement of *b·*,"
        33– 4   "the scientific statement of *b·*"
      111–26   "The scientific statement of *b·*"
  state of
    Mis. 161–12   approximation to this state of *b·*
    No. 5–19   and is itself a state of *b·*,
      17–17   there is no fallen state of *b·* ;
  states of
    Mis. 357–20   of all stages and states of *b·* ;
  statuesque
    Pan. 10–28   promotes statuesque *b·*, health, and
  substance of
    Un. 49–10   reality and substance of *b·* are *good*,
  sum of
    Mis. 52–29   have the sum of *b·* to work out,
  their
    '01. 33– 1   consideration of their *b·*,
    My. 200–28   save sinners and fit their *b·* to
  to be eternal
    No. 4–25   *b·*, to be eternal, must be
  true
    Mis. 104–31   on the side of good, my true *b·*.
  true estimate of
    Ret. 21–20   joy and true estimate of *b·*.
  truth of
    (see **truth**)
  unrealities of
    Mis. 60– 7   as the woeful unrealities of *b·*,
  upholds
    Mis. 105–15   It upholds *b·*, and destroys the
  verities of
    (see **verities**)
  verity of
    Mis. 261– 8   demonstrates this verity of *b·* ;
      286–27   should recognize this verity of *b·*,
  visible
    Mis. 205–18   whose visible *b·* is invisible to
  was beautiful
    Ret. 23–22   *B·* was beautiful, its substance,
  wonder of
    Un. 37–10   would reveal this wonder of *b·*.
  your
    My. 139–28   redeem . . . your *b·* from sensuality ;

    Mis. 42– 9   awaken with thoughts, and *b·*, as
      50–25   live thereby, and have *b·*.
      79– 9   we live, move, and have *b·*.
    Un. 48– 7   no faith in any other thing or *b·*.

being (ppr.)
    Mis. 14– 1   it fills all space, *b·* omnipresent ;
      16–12   *b·* His likeness and image,
      24–17   this Life *b·* the sole reality of
      27–24   *b·* in and of Spirit,
      39– 4   To avoid *b·* *subject* to disease,
      42–29   *Can I be treated without b· present*
      43–11   as *b·* adequate to make safe
      46– 5   *b·* real, evil, good's opposite, is
      67–30   I believe in this removal *b·* possible
      79–10   origin and existence *b·* in Him,
      93–15   This *b·* true, sin has no power ;
     108– 8   a lie, *b·* without foundation in fact,
     115– 9   and fear of *b·* found out.
     116–28   *b·* "faithful over a — *Matt.* 25 : 21.
     133– 8   As to *b·* "prayerless,"
     188– 6   presents as *b·* first that which
     193–17   *b·* a modification of silence
     206– 2   the former *b·* servant to the latter,
     209– 8   the Principle of divine Science *b·* Love,
     220–26   and speak of him as *b·* sick,
     221–18   Truth *b·* the cure,

being (ppr.)
    Mis. 259–12   to conceive of good as *b·* unlike
      271–21   *b·* the only chartered College of
     288– 5   *b·* a fit counsellor.
     300–30   pays . . . for *b·* healed,
     306–17   * We would add, as *b·* of interest,
     346–20   good *b·* real, its opposite is
     367– 7   fact of there *b·* no mortal mind,
     381– 6   the defendant *b·* present personally
    Man. 99– 5   dividing line *b·* the 36th parallel
    Ret. 1– 3   *b·* John McNeil of Edinburgh.
      15– 6   *b·* the chief corner-stone." — *Eph.* 2 : 20.
      19–11   *b·* a member in Saint Andrew's Lodge,
      34–19   body *b·* but the objective state of
      64–23   error *b·* a false claim,
      73– 1   The immortal man *b·* spiritual,
      73–22   or accuse people of *b·* unduly personal,
      76–15   so far from *b·* personal worship,
      78– 2   *b·* too fast or too slow.
      86– 6   There is but one way of *b·* good,
    Un. 29–28   Virgin-mother's sense *b·* uplifted
      30– 7   *b·* spiritual Life, never sins.
      31–14   *fourth*, that matter, *b·* so endowed,
      33– 6   Now these senses, *b·* material,
      42– 1   Life, God, *b·* everywhere,
      46–23   as *b·* equally identical and
      49– 4   as *b·* the eternally divine idea.
      49–22   *B·* destitute of Principle,
      53– 5   *B·* a lie, it would be truthful to
      53–14   *b·* self-contradictory, it is also
      58–16   *b·* "in all points tempted — *Heb.* 4 : 15.
    Pul. 1–18   To-day, *b·* with you in spirit,
      3– 1   Such *b·* its nature,
      4–13   in *b·* and doing right,
      26– 3   * the centre *b·* of pure white light,
      55–26   * all others *b·* branches,
      58–11   * every bill *b·* paid.
      59–10   * certain hymns and psalms *b·* omitted.
      62–15   * superb, *b·* rich and mellow.
      68– 2   * *b·* now known as the Rev. . . . . Eddy.
      69– 7   * *b·* cured by Mrs. Eddy of a
      73–19   * *b·* of the same theory as Mrs. Copeland.
      76– 1   * *b·* that used in the doors and pews.
      86– 1   * *b·* of granite, about six inches in
    Rud. 5– 7   *b·* made in the image of Spirit,
      7–16   material evidence *b·* wholly false.
      14–25   People are *b·* healed by means of
    No. 13–17   not susceptible of *b·* held as
      24–18   evil, *b·* thus uncovered, is found out,
      25– 5   that *b·* dead wherein — *Rom.* 7 : 6.
      27– 3   and the claim, *b·* worthless,
    Pan. 4–26   This *b·* the case, what need have we
    '00. 4–20   *b·* demonstrable, they are undeniable ;
      5–17   This *b·* the divine Science of
    '01. 3–25   light, *b·* matter, loses the nature of
      6–18   The logic of divine Science *b·* faultless,
      7– 5   The trinity . . . *b·* Life, Truth, Love,
      7– 8   Again, God *b·* infinite Mind,
      9–24   and these things *b·* spiritual,
      10– 8   Christ *b·* the Son of God,
      23–30   * nature *b·* nothing more than
      27–15   rejoice in *b·* informed thereof.
      31– 6   *b·* neither personal nor human,
    '02. 8–18   evidence of *b·* Christian Scientists
      17–22   in *b·* and in doing good ;
    Po. v– 5   * *b·* *the spontaneous outpouring of*
      34– 2   soul of melody by *b·* blest
    My. 56–30   * second and third *b·* repetitions of
      66–15   * *b·* in a fine part of the city.
     165–27   power of *b·* magnanimous.
     179–14   *b·* translations, the Scriptures are
     179–26   *b·* contingent on nothing written
     212–18   *B·* like the disciples of old,
     238– 9   God *b·* Spirit, His language and
     273– 6   * in *b·* able to point to a Leader
     289–23   It *b·* inconvenient for me to
     315– 6   * *b·* a pure and Christian woman,
     315– 8   * separation *b·* wholly on his part ;
     320–12   * *b·* a very unique book,
     330–23   *b·* a member in St. Andrew's Lodge,
     356–28   God *b·* infinite, He is the only basis

beings
    Ret. 56– 7   Being into *b·*, — is a misstatement
    Un. 37–17   Human *b·* are physically mortal,
    Pul. 51– 7   * their inherent right as human *b·*,
    Rud. 4– 3   peopled with perfect *b·*,
    Peo. 1–18   that we are spiritual *b·* here
    Po. 17– 1   Blest *b·* departed!
    My. 294–28   The august ruler of . . . human *b·*
     303–14   divine rights in human *b·*.

belated
    My. 74– 6   * numbers of *b·* church members
belay
    Mis. 327–16   They stoutly *b·* those who,

belch
  Mis. 237– 9   *b·* forth their latent fires.
beleaguered
  Mis. 326–18   wanderers in a *b·* city,
belfry
  Pul. 58–13   * In the *b·* is a set of tubular
  Po. 71–14   Joy is in every *b·* bell
Belial
  Mis. 333–23   hath Christ with *B·*?" — *II Cor.* 6: 15.
belial
  Hea. 6–28   in Hebrew it is *b·*,
belie
  No. 32–23   to *b·* and belittle C. S.,
  40–10   Words may *b·* desire,
belied
  Mis. 337–23   life of Jesus was belittled and *b·* by
  My. 139–13   when misrepresented, *b·*, and
belief
according to
  Un. 32– 1   according to *b·*, obtain in matter ;
adipose
  Mis. 47– 5   adipose *b·* of yourself as substance ;
alone
  Hea. 18–26   produced by a *b·* alone.
and service
  Pul. 66–17   * *b·* and service are well suited to
and understanding
  Pul. 47–19   * the terms *b·* and understanding,
another's
  Mis. 83–12   No person can accept another's *b·*,
baubles of
  My. 297–14   blows away the baubles of *b·*,
begets a
  Mis. 210–19   Intemperance begets a *b·* of
blind
  Ret. 54–15   Blind *b·* cannot say with the apostle,
bodily
  Mis. 352–16   supposed bodily *b·* of the patient
called
  Ret. 54–17   in this mental state called *b·* ;
called death
  Mis. 42– 5   passing through the *b·* called death.
changed
  Mis. 237–6   This changed *b·* has wrought a change
common
  Mis. 49–21   common *b·* in the opposite of
concerning Deity
  Pan. 2–25   *b·* concerning Deity in theology.
conditions of a
  Mis. 73–16   Belief fulfils the conditions of a *b·*,
conscientious
  Peo. 6– 7   * "I declare my conscientious *b·*,
darkness of
  Pul. 13–10   in the deep darkness of *b·*.
desire or
  My. 292–21   effect of one human desire or *b·*
destroy belief
  Mis. 334–21   Can *b·* destroy belief?
destroy the
  Mis. 28– 6   Destroy the *b·* that you can walk,
  73–17   these conditions destroy the *b·*.
  Un. 35– 6   Destroy the *b·*, and . . . disappears.
  My. 132–25   destroy the *b·* of life in
entertain a
  Man. 42–16   shall neither entertain a *b·* nor
erring
  Mis. 186 0   this erring *b·* even separates its
erroneous
  Mis. 10–30   erroneous *b·* that you have enemies ;
error of
  Mis. 45–27   This error of *b·* is idolatry,
  220–32   error of *b·* has not the power of
  No. 4–10   error of *b·*, named disease,
even in
  Mis. 10–29   Even in *b·* you have but one
evil
  Mis. 247–30   only an evil *b·* of mortal mind,
  Un. 53–10   evil *b·* that renders them obscure.
except in
  Un. 51– 7   hair white or black, except in *b·* ;
extension of
  Un. 7– 3   in the wide extension of *b·*
fad of
  My. 218–22   fad of *b·* is the fool of mesmerism.
faith is
  Ret. 54– 3   Because faith is *b·*, and not
false
  Mis. 45–24   It is but a false *b·* ;
  48– 2   its demonstrations as a false *b·*,
  56–19   final destruction of this false *b·*
  63–16   to save them from *this* false *b·*;
  198–14   false *b·* of the personal senses ;
  233–30   must be understood as a false *b·*

belief
false
  Mis. 332–23   second, a false *b·* ;
  Un. 50–21   which are but states of false *b·*,
felon's
  Hea. 19– 8   Had they changed the felon's *b·*
fervor of
  My. 81–30   * fervor of *b·* with which each
finite
  No. 25–12   is beyond a finite *b·*.
fleshly
  Ret. 94–14   When all fleshly *b·* is annihilated,
fulfils
  Mis. 73–16   *B·* fulfils the conditions of a belief,
her
  Pul. 73–28   * concise idea of her *b·*
his
  '01. 15– 2   awake from his *b·* in this awful
his own
  Mis. 83–13   with the consent of his own *b·*.
human
  (*see* **human**)
ignorant
  Ret. 54–19   same channel of ignorant *b·*.
improved
  My. 217–25   "An improved *b·* is one step out
in anti-Christ
  Mis. 111–30   The *b·* in anti-Christ :
in Christian Science
  Pul. 57–22   * how extensive is the *b·* in C. S.
in death
  Un. 40– 9   subordinates the *b·* in death,
  41–11   (that is, from the *b·* in death)
in disease
  Mis. 256– 2   cured of their *b·* in disease,
in evil
  Mis. 221–32   *b·* in evil and in the process of
in God
  Pul. 79–25   * breath of his soul is a *b·* in God.
  Rud. 11– 4   *b·* in God as omnipotent ;
in material origin
  Mis. 361– 3   *b·* in material origin, mortal mind,
in material sense
  Mis. 37–10   we oppose the *b·* in material sense,
in matter
  Mis. 56–19   this false *b·* in matter
  Un. 50– 8   pantheistic *b·* in matter
in one God
  Pan. 3–21   In religion, it is a *b·* in one God,
  '02. 12–12   unites with the Jew's *b·* in one God,
in safety
  Mis. 257–19   It fosters . . . a *b·* in safety
  My. 211–23   fosters . . . a *b·* in safety
in sin
  Mis. 319– 8   not seeing their own *b·* in sin,
  Man. 15–12   *b·* in sin is punished so long as
  No. 32– 7   *b·* in sin — its pleasure, pain, or
  My. 233–13   from the effects of *b·* in sin
  300– 2   *b·* in sin or in aught besides God,
in their reality
  Ret. 62– 6   than a *b·* in their reality has
in the personality
  Pan. 3–18   Theism is the *b·* in the personality
is strong
  Hea. 6–17   if the *b·* is strong enough to
lasts
  Man. 15–13   punished so long as the *b·* lasts.
law of
  Mis. 209–10   human belief fulfils the law of *b·*.
  Peo. 11–21   ignorant of the law of *b·*,
man's
  My. 302 3   according to a man's *b·*,
material
  Mis. 60–28   material *b·* hints the existence of
  61– 1   it will be seen that material *b·*,
  186– 7   material *b·* has fallen far below
  Un. 30– 9   suffers, according to material's *b·*,
matter
  Mis. 60–28   its counterfeit in some matter *b·*.
may attend
  '01. 7–22   in order that *b·* may attend their
mere
  Pul. 9–27   spiritual understanding, not mere *b·*,
mistaken
  Rud. 12–17   C. S. erases . . . their mistaken *b·*
momentary
  Mis. 42– 6   After the momentary *b·* of dying
mortal
  (*see* **mortal**)
of chronic
  Mis. 41–23   *b·* of chronic or acute disease,
of death
  Mis. 170– 1   salvation from the *b·* of death,
of disease
  Mis. 198–20   a *b·* of disease is as much the
of error
  Rud. 12– 8   encouraging them in the *b·* of error

belief

of eyesight
  Mis. 58–17 through a *b·* of eyesight ;
of life
  Un. 40– 6 *b·* of life in matter, must perish,
  My. 132–25 destroy the *b·* of life in matter.
of material existence
  Mis. 42–21 a *b·* of material existence
of material eyes
  Mis. 170–28 contempt for the *b·* of material eyes
of mind
  Mis. 26–19 *b·* of mind in matter is pantheism.
  179–21 It is the *b·* of mind in matter.
of nervousness
  Mis. 51– 5 *b· of nervousness, accompanied by*
of our brethren
  '01. 8– 5 than the *b·* of our brethren,
of pain
  Mis. 44–18 could only have been a *b·* of pain
of pantheism
  Pan. 9– 1 reiterate the *b·* of pantheism,
of sensation
  Mis. 93–19 Fear is a *b·* of sensation in matter :
of the sick
  Ret. 63–10 *b·* of the sick in the reality of
old
  Hea. 18–15 if . . . reconciled with the old *b·* ;
one
  Mis. 175–23 one *b·* takes the place of another.
one form of
  Pul. 38–30 * in one form of *b·* or another
one's
  Peo. 9– 7 religious rite may declare one's *b·* ;
opposite
  Ret. 69–21 opposite *b·* is the prolific source of
our
  Mis. 234– 1 only by reason of our *b·* in it :
pantheistic
  Un. 50– 8 pantheistic *b·* in matter
people's
  Peo. 2–20 people's *b·* of God, in every age,
perpetuates the
  Mis. 46– 1 perpetuates the *b·* or faith in evil.
reason, or
  Un. 28–21 human reflection, reason, or *b·*
religious
  Pul. 50–16 * phase of religious *b·*
  51–21 * new project in religious *b·*
  51–29 * demonstrations of religious *b·*
  63–16 * new phase of religious *b·*,
revived
  Pul. 52–25 * revived *b·* in what he taught
self-constituted
  Mis. 186– 6 self-constituted *b·* of the Jews
sickness is a
  Ret. 61– 3 declares that sickness is a *b·*,
signify a
  Man. 42–16 nor signify a *b·* in more than one
sinner's
  Ret. 63– 7 sinner's *b·* in the pleasure of sin,
some
  Mis. 198–23 some *b·*, fear, theory, or bad deed,
stubborn
  My. 233–20 most stubborn *b·* to overcome,
that God
  Mis. 45–24 *b·* that God is not what the
  Un. 14– 2 *b·* that God must one day
  Peo. 4– 4 sprang from the *b·* that God is a form,
that intelligence
  Mis. 36–28 *b·* that intelligence, Truth, and
that it has
  Mis. 334– 7 *b·* that it has, deceives itself.
that Jesus
  Pan. 8– 6 *b·* that Jesus, . . . is God,
that Life
  Mis. 77–32 resurrecting . . . to the *b·* that Life,
that man
  Mis. 77–26 *b·* that man has fallen away from
that Mary
  Pan. 8– 8 *b·* that Mary was the mother of God
that matter
  Rud. 10–23 *b·* that matter can master Mind,
  No. 5–10 *b·* that matter has sensation.
that Mind
  Mis. 49–25 *b·*, that Mind is in matter,
that mind
  Ret. 69–27 *b·* that mind is in matter,
that produces
  Hea. 6–22 *b·* that produces this result may
that sees
  Mis. 58–16 as mortal mind, it is a *b·* that sees.
that Spirit
  Peo. 4– 6 *b·* that Spirit materialized into a
that the man
  My. 348–12 *b·* that the man Jesus, rather than

belief

their
  Mis. 256– 2 cured of their *b·* in disease,
  My. 273– 5 * enthusiastic in their *b·*,
their own
  Mis. 319– 8 not seeing their own *b·* in sin,
  Rud. 13–21 according to their own *b·*
theological
  Pan. 4– 7 theological *b·* may agree with physics
  My. 307–17 my theological *b·* was offended
this
  Mis. 49–26 This *b·* presupposes not only a
  72–10 this *b·* is as false as it is
  93–19 this *b·* is neither maintained by
  197–27 This *b·* breaks the First Commandment
  210–20 this *b·* serves to uncover and
  346–13 This *b·* is a species of idolatry,
  352–18 in destroying this *b·*.
  Ret. 63– 9 in order to destroy this *b·*
  Un. 30–10 understanding takes away this *b·*
  Rud. 5–21 this *b·* of seeing with the eye,
thought, or
  Mis. 70– 8 thought, or *b·*, was removed,
unreal
  No. 5–13 substitutes for Truth an unreal *b·*,
vital
  Pul. 52–23 * all vital *b·* in his teachings.
we call spiritualism
  Pul. 38–17 * the *b·* we call spiritualism.
woman's
  Mis. 220–30 according to the woman's *b·* ;
your
  Mis. 44–25 your *b·* assumed a new form,
  44–27 When your *b·* in pain ceases,
  44–29 antidote directly to your *b·*,
  59– 4 practise your *b·* of it in

  Mis. 18–26 can we in *b·* separate one man's
  45– 4 matter is but a *b·*,
  50–22 *b·* that the heart is matter
  58– 8 *b·* in the power of disease
  60–14 *dead only in b·?*
  182– 3 putting him to death, only in *b·*,
  193–32 condition insisted upon is, first, "*b·*;"
  197–16 a *b·* in any historical event or person.
  198–28 a *b·* in self-existent evil,
  210–24 *b·* in venereal diseases tears the
  293–23 Truth perverted, in *b·*, becomes the
  335–16 *b·*, of evil to break the Decalogue,
  346–12 It is but a *b·* that there is an
  Ret. 13–13 *b·* in a final judgment-day,
  54–14 *B·* is virtually blindness,
  64–20 in *b·* an illusion termed sin,
  Un. 26–11 *b·* in which leads to such teaching
  40–26 mortals die, in *b·*,
  41– 7 Knowledge of evil, or *b·* in it,
  Pul. 65– 1 * *b·* in that curious creed is
  80–26 * The *b·* that "thoughts are things,"
  Rud. 12– 9 *b·* that they are first made sick by
  Pan. 6–27 the *b·* in more than one spirit,
  7– 8 *b·*, that after God, Spirit, had
  My. 74–25 * a *b·* in such emancipation.
  218–22 The *b·* that an individual can
  243– 3 *b·* is springing up among you that

beliefs

all
  Mis. 36–22 all *b·* relative to the so-called
and doctrines
  Pul. 73–21 * versed in all their *b·* and doctrines.
evil
  Mis. 191–29 could only be possible as evil *b·*,
false
  Mis. 111–28 false *b·* inclining mortal mind
  Peo. 3–10 false *b·* that have produced sin,
human
  Mis. 320–25 long night of human *b·*,
  Rud. 10– 8 material laws are only human *b·*,
  My. 44– 1 * the wilderness of human *b·*
  206– 8 human *b·* are not parts of C. S. ;
I entertained
  My. 241–24 * according to the *b·* I entertained
its own
  Mis. 47–15 when let loose from its own *b·*.
material
  Mis. 2–29 material *b·* that war against Spirit,
  5–29 mortal thought with material *b·*.
  334–27 remedies the ills of material *b·*.
mortal
  (*see* **mortal**)
of mortals
  My. 146–23 *b·* of mortals tip the scale of being,
of Scientists
  Pul. 73–20 * in the *b·* of Scientists,
of the flesh
  Mis. 28–14 destroy the *b·* of the flesh,

beliefs

of the flesh
  Mis. 72– 7   According to the *b·* of the flesh,
old
  Mis. 93– 6   *Can fear or sin bring back old b·*
producing the
  Rud. 10–10   producing the *b·* of a mortal
religious
  '02.   1–16   systems of religious *b·*
  My. 163–27   I respect their religious *b·*,
      271–24   * whatever their religious *b·*,
these
  Rud. 10– 9   These *b·* arise from the subjective
undisciplined
  Mis. 320–22   to dull ears and undisciplined *b·*

  Mis. 28– 5   *b·* that mortals entertain
  Peo.   4–22   out of *b·* that are as material as
  My. 241–28   * the *b·* of an earthly mortal.

belies

  Mis. 121–18   whatever belittles, befogs, or *b·*

believe

  Mis.   5–25   but *b·* it to be brain matter.
      5–31   to *b·* that the body affects the
    13–15   to *b·* in the reality of evil
    18–30   to *b·* that aught that God sends is
    22– 1   *b·* in one God, one Christ
    24–27   God warned man not to *b·*
    28–31   them that *b·* ;— *Mark* 16 : 17.
    29– 3   Do you *b·* his words?
    29– 8   which shall *b·* on me— *John* 17 : 20.
    47– 1   *How can I b· that there is no*
    50–18   *Do you b· in change of heart?*
    50–19   We do *b·*, and understand
    60– 1   *How can you b· there is no sin,*
    60– 4   *How can you b· there is no sickness,*
    63–15   to save such as *b·* in the
    67–24   *Do you b· in translation?*
    67–29   I *b·* in this removal being possible
    68–11   * *to b· they are illusions.*
    68–12   It is unchristian to *b·* that pain
    70– 2   That the Bible is true I *b·*,
    77– 4   verb *b·* took its original meaning,
    77–20   To *b·* is to be firm.
    77–22   To *b·* thus was to enter the
    96– 7   Do I *b·* in a personal God?
    96– 8   I *b·* in God as the Supreme Being.
    96–17   Do I *b·* in the atonement of Christ?
  121–26   ye will not *b·* ;— *Luke* 22 : 67.
  132–23   as to what I *b·* and teach,
  141–16   I *b·*, yea, I understand,
  170– 5   may still *b·* in death
  180–22   even to them that *b·*— *John* 1 : 12.
  192–29   follow them that *b·* ;— *Mark* 16 : 17,
  194– 1   *b·* that the power of God equals
  194–31   set forth in the text, namely, *b·* ;
  196– 7   *"B·* in me, and I will make
  196–28   *B· on the Lord Jesus*— *Acts* 16 : 31.
  197–10   let us see what it is to *b·*.
  220–16   people *b·* that a man is sick
  220–29   he will *b·* that he is sick,
  222– 5   causes the victim to *b·* that
  225–19   * I may be led to *b·*."
  228–27   *b·* what others *b·*,
  228–30   People *b·* in infectious and
  229– 9   If only the people would *b·* that
  230– 3   sometimes made to *b·* a lie,
  244–28   as many as should *b·* in him.
  247–21   but *b·* it to reside in matter
  247–25   to *b·* that the body affects mind,
  282–22   and they *b·* in the efficacy of
  313–25   Humbly, and, as I *b·*, divinely
  349–31   *b·* that I have put into the
  Man. 34– 4   *B·* in C. S.
    47–25   do not *b·* in the doctrines of
    48– 1   those who do *b·* in such doctrines,
  Ret. 10– 1   taught to *b·* that my brain was
    16–15   follow them that *b·*."— *Mark* 16 : 17.
    28–28   I *b·* in no *ism.*
    49–23   which we *b·* will prove a healing
    54– 4   easier to *b·*, than to understand
    59– 2   to *b·* man has a finite and
    90–26   * "I *b·* the proper thing for us to do
  Un.   3– 2   and still *b·* in matter's reality,
    19–11   But this we cannot *b·* of God ;
    20–21   and that He can see
    24– 5   To *b·* in minds many is to
    37–14   Is it unchristian to *b·* there is no
    37–15   unless it be a sin to *b·* that
    38–11   It is unchristian to *b·* in the
    38–21   no divine fiat commands us to *b·* in
    40–12   Jesus declares that they who *b·*
    41– 8   to know death, or to *b·* in it,
    43– 8   now *b·* in the possibility that
    45– 1   says . . . you shall *b·* a lie,

believe

  Un. 48– 5   *Do you b· in God?*
    48– 6   I *b·* more in Him than do most
    48–19   I *b·* that of which I am conscious
    49– 1   *Do you b· in man?*
    49 –2   I *b·* in the individual man,
    49– 7   But I *b·* less in the sinner,
    50– 3   *Do you b· in matter?*
    50– 4   I *b·* in matter only as I *b·* in evil,
  Pul. 38–18   * They *b·* those who have passed the
    38–25   * what they *b·* to be the literal
    51– 4   * Freedom to *b·* or to dissent
    65–27   * expresses the faith of those who *b·*
    71–10   * chapter sub-title
    72–21   * nor did she *b·* that Mrs. Lathrop had,
    73– 4   * *b·* in His unlimited and divine power.
    79–16   * We *b·* there are two reasons for
    80–22   * people to *b·* in God
    80–23   * did not *b·* in them before.
    85–16   * and who *b·* it to be possible to
  Rud.   5–25   *b·* man and the universe to be the
    10–28   to *b·* in the existence of matter,
  No. 14–23   to as many as shall *b·* on him.
    15–14   It is no easy matter to *b·* there are
    26– 1   mind-quacks *b·* that mortal man is
    29– 8   they *b·* . . . sinning sense to be
    42– 2   * to *b·* all things written in the
  Pan.   5–20   we should neither *b·* the lie,
    5–20   nor *b·* that it hath embodiment
    5–22   we should not *b·* that a lie,
    9–23   (though they *b·* it not),
    11–21   may *b·* that evil develops good,
  '00.   2–27   however, I *b·* in working
    4–24   Do religionists *b·* that God is *One*
    7–23   we *b·* in the second coming,
  '01.   5–14   Do Christian Scientists *b·* in
    5–19   We *b·*, according to the Scriptures,
    6–26   We *b·* in God as the infinite Person ;
    7–21   They do not *b·* there must be
    7–24   Christians now claim to *b·* in
    12– 7   too transcendental for me to *b·*,
    13–30   or *b·* in the power of sin,
    14– 6   Do Christian Scientists *b·* that
    18–30   they *b·* that God answers their prayers,
    19– 2   They *b·* that divine power, besought,
    22– 8   I do not *b·* in such a compound.
    32–26   I *b·*, if those venerable Christians
  '02.   3–30   began with *"B·* in me."
    15–19   for I could never *b·* that a
  Hea.   1– 1   *follow them that b·*;— *Mark* 16 : 17.
    6–26   follow them that *b·*;— *Mark* 16 : 17.
    7– 5   "Them that *b·*"— *Mark* 16 : 17.
    9–15   Is it a duty for any one to *b·* that
    15–20   and *b·* that sickness is something
    18–28   *b·* he was bleeding to death.
    19–27   follow them that *b·* ;— *Mark* 16 : 17,
  Peo.   5–27   I firmly *b·* that if the whole
    13– 3   *b·* that God is a personal Spirit.
  My.   8–17   * I *b·* really, with my
    47–30   * follow them that *b·* ;— *Mark* 16 : 17.
    74–22   * if those outside are unable to *b·*
    90– 6   * Thousands upon thousands *b·*
    97– 3   * They *b·* that firm faith
  107–16   he tells you, and you *b·* him,
  119– 3   impossible in Science to *b·* this,
  146– 5   I *b·* this saying because I
  146–12   Few *b·* this saying.
  146–12   Few *b·* that C. S. contains
  190–20   them also which shall *b·*— *John* 17 : 20.
  193–18   unite with all who *b·* in Truth.
  212– 2   is led to *b·* and do what he
  219–13   not be more preposterous than to *b·*
  220–12   I *b·* in obeying the laws of the land.
  221–31   Shall we not *b·* the Scripture,
  234–20   I *b·* that all our great Master's
  261– 8   not be taught to *b·* that Santa Claus
  278–18   Japanese may *b·* in a heaven for
  282– 3   *b·* strictly in the Monroe doctrine,
  284–25   I do *b·* implicitly in the
  293–31   *b·* that ye receive them,— *Mark* 11 : 24.
  299–17   Do Christians, who *b·* in sin,
  299–18   *b·* that God is good,
  300–10   not *b·* in the reality of disease,
  303– 2   I *b·* in one Christ,
  303– 3   I *b·* in but one incarnation,
  321–10   * I *b·* that Mr. Wiggin
  321–13   * cannot *b·* that he has ever
  345–18   *b·* in a science of drugs?"

believed

  Mis. 44–23   *b·* that if the tooth were extracted,
    77–21   to *know* in whom he *b·*.
  108–29   who *b·* in the use of drugs,
  121–12   was *b·* to be the seed of the Church.
  183–20   "Who hath *b·* our— *Isa.* 53 : 1.
  195–25   I once *b·* that the practice and

believed

Mis.	229– 4	If he b· as sincerely that health is
	333–24	They b· that something besides
Ret.	54–16	whom I have b·." — II Tim. 1 : 12.
	57– 6	Plato b· he had a soul,
Un.	3–14	Him in whom they have b·.
	33–15	and is b· to be mind
	35– 3	If every mortal mind b·
	39– 9	"Who hath b· our — Isa. 53 : 1.
	46–22	This evil ego they b· must
Pul.	33–23	* and Mr. Parker always b·,
	75–25	* b· to be the most nearly fire-proof
No.	36– 8	even while mortals b· it was here.
'01.	7–28	thou hast b· : — John 20 : 29.
	7–29	and yet have b·." — John 20 : 29.
	27–30	* say they had always b· it."
My.	79–27	* conviction that they would be b·,
	80– 9	* yet they were b·.
	118–17	and yet have b·." — John 20 : 29.
	156– 4	"I know whom I have b·, — II Tim. 1 : 12.
	228–28	I know whom I have b·, — II Tim. 1 : 12.
	276–17	* has always b· that those who
	276–19	* also b· that in such matters
	293– 8	b· that his martyrdom was
	293– 9	thousands of others b· the same,
	304–28	* say they have always b· it."

believer

Mis.	332–25	Is man the supposer, false b·,
Man.	34– 7	b· in the doctrines of C. S.,
Ret	28–28	Am I a b· in spiritualism?
My.	309–15	strong b· in States' rights,

believers

Mis.	325– 5	are b· of different sects,
Ret.	14– 8	elect b· converted and rescued
Pul.	40–11	* Enabling Six Thousand B· to
	41–19	* nearly a thousand local b·.
	44–17	* chapter sub-title
	52–15	* b· receive light, health, and
	58– 8	* b· throughout this country
	66– 6	* the number of b· has grown
	67–17	* quarter of a million of b·,
	67–22	* single b· or little knots of them
	71– 8	* money comes from C. S. b·
My.	77–25	* nearly forty thousand b·
	95–11	* prosperous body of b·
	99– 4	* able to raise its b· above the
	169–18	three thousand b· of my faith,
	271–18	* beloved of thousands of b·

believes

Mis.	26–10	b· that his crops come from the
	197–23	Mortal man b· in, but does not
	197–24	He b· there is another power
	221–12	unless he b· that sin has produced
	223–12	to discern what it b·,
	229– 4	which he b· produce it.
Pul.	50– 3	* b· that "the laborer — Luke 10 : 7.
No.	29– 5	He b· that Spirit, or Soul,
Pan.	11–17	If . . . it matters not what he b· ;
'01.	5– 1	b· that three persons are defined
	5– 3	he b· three persons constitute the
'02.	12– 1	The Jew b· that the Messiah
	12– 2	Christian b· that Christ is come
	12– 7	The Jew who b· in the
	12–10	who b· in the First Commandment
My.	97–11	* b· that if the figures could be
	271– 9	what a man thinks or b· he knows ;
	297–16	Scientist who b· that he dies,
	300– 8	Does he who b· in sickness know
	300–13	Does he who b· in death understand

believeth

Mis.	192–10	He that b· on me, — John 14 : 12.
	193–27	"He that b· on me, — John 14 : 12.
	195–18	"He that b· on me, — John 14 : 12.
Chr.	55–28	liveth and b· in me — John 11 : 26.
No.	13– 8	liveth and b· in me — John 11 : 26.
Pan.	9–13	liveth and b· in me — John 11 : 26.
My.	16–26	he that b· shall — Isa. 28 : 16.
	17–16	he that b· on him shall — I Pet. 2 : 6.
	221–22	"He that b· on me, — John 14 : 12.

believing

Mis.	62– 9	B· a lie veils the truth from our
	68–14	penalty for b· in their reality
	77– 2	depend merely on his b· that
	77– 3	this b· was more than faith in
	93–25	by b· that sin is pardoned without
	108–12	is to be in danger of b· it ;
	108–27	b· in, or adhering to,
	108–32	an individual b· in that
	179– 5	b· we have lost sight of Truth,
	184–18	persisting in b· that he is sick
	223–15	But, alas! for the mistake of b·
	239–29	saying even more bravely, and b· it,
	288–20	b· otherwise would prevent
	832–27	false b·, suffering are not

believing

Mis.	362–11	make the mortal mistake of b· that
Ret.	54–12	Millions are b· in God, or good,
	69–17	b· that there is life in matter,
Un.	40–14	can no more receive . . . life by b·
	40–15	than they can become perfect by b·
Pul.	34–13	* b· her delirious.
	59–26	* The children of b· families
	69–10	* b· that disease comes from evil
'01.	14–20	from b· in what is unreal,
Peo.	6–14	B· that man is the victim of his
My.	51–22	* b· that it was for the interest of
	106– 8	to show the folly of b· that
	206–13	b· that you see an individual who
	285–27	b· all things which — Acts 24 : 14.

belittle

No.	32–23	great evil to belie and b· C. S.,

belittled

Mis.	337–22	Even the life of Jesus was b·

belittles

Mis.	121–18	whatever b·, befogs, or belies
Pan.	11–22	b· man's personality.
'01.	13– 3	another nonentity that b· itself

bell

Mis.	304– 8	* b· will pass from place to place
	304–22	* is the proposed use of the b· :
	305–14	* In creating the b· it is
	305–19	* can be made a part of the b· ;
	305–23	* with which to pay for the b·.
	305–25	* to be fused into the b·,
	305–28	* In order that the b· shall be
	306– 1	* material to be melted into the b·,
	306– 3	* book which will accompany the b·
Pul.	31–23	* rang the b· at a spacious house
Po.	71–14	Joy is in every belfry b·
My.	189–30	Wherefore, pray, the b· did toll?

bells

Mis.	120–18	sound of vintage b· to villagers
	356–15	sweeter than the sound of vintage b·.
Pul.	26–17	* chime of b· includes fifteen,
	62– 6	* cast b· of old-fashioned chimes.
	62– 8	* a chime of fifteen b·
	62–20	* to which these b· may be put.
	62–23	* down to little sets of silver b·
Po.	vi– 8	* poem
	vi–19	b· are ringing to celebrate the
	page 71	poem
My.	31– 7	* "Oh, the clanging b· of time ;"
	71– 4	* by means of the b·.
	89– 7	* a chime of b·,
	185– 3	harvest b· are ringing.
	256– 2	Christmas b· shall ring,
	302–28	with escort and the ringing of b·,

belly

'01.	11–28	him whose god is his b· :

belong

Mis.	22–18	untruths b· not to His creation,
	112–12	seem to b· to the latter days,
	228–23	b· to mind and not to matter.
Un.	10– 9	to whom b· all things.
	25–24	The elements which b· to
	38– 3	To God alone b· the
	61– 3	b· to mortal consciousness.
Pul.	8–29	They b· to the twentieth century.
Po.	29–10	No natal hour . . . To thee b·.
My.	242–24	leave these duties . . . to whom they b·.
	285–11	war, and . . . b· to the darker ages,

belonged

Man.	75–22	building funds, . . . b· to the Church,

belonging

Mis.	375–30	* b· to them exclusively,
Ret.	53– 2	and the funds b· thereto.
Un.	21–20	b· to true individuality.
	40–28	b· to the nature and office of Life.
Pul.	46–18	* b· to her grandparents
My.	100– 2	* facts and figures b· to it,
	340– 6	b· not to the Christian era,

belongs

Mis.	51–15	that sensation b· to matter.
	107–10	the heart's homage b· to God.
	190–25	b· to Mind instead of matter,
	192–23	b· to every period ;
	240–31	something which b· to nature,
	259–27	b· not to nature nor to God.
	297–29	b· to the rights of freedom.
Man.	52– 5	if said member b· to no branch
Pul.	57–26	* site . . . b· to the followers of
No.	42–11	All power b· to God ;
'00.	8–19	the work that b· to another.
My.	110– 1	b· not to a dispensation now ended,
	225–12	all b· to God, for God is All ;
	260–13	Nothing conditional . . . b· to it.
	340–24	which virtually b· to the past,

belongs
  My. 354–22 But Science vast, to which *b·*

Beloved
  Chr. 53–13 What the *B·* knew and taught,

beloved
  Mis. 110– 4 *B·* children, the world has need of
    121–22 crucifixion of His *b·* Son,
    149–20 your *b·* pastor, Rev. Mr. Norcross,
    151–18 Brother, sister, *b·* in the Lord,
    152– 3 *B· Pastor and Brethren:*
    156– 7 *B· Christian Scientists:*
    157– 5 Reign then, my *b·* in the Lord.
    170– 5 over the graves of their *b·* :
    206– 7 "This is my *b·* — *Matt.* 3 : 17.
    322–18 Therefore, *b·*, my often-coming
  Man. 60–18 sacred words of our *b·* Master,
  Pul. 10–29 this is His redeemed ; this, His *b·*.
    24–15 * A testimonial to our *b·* teacher,
    48– 5 * straight to her *b·* "lookout"
    63–27 * "a testimonial to our *b·* teacher,
    84–27 * our *b·* teacher and Leader,
    86– 4 * "To our *B·* Teacher,
    86–16 * our *B· Teacher and Leader :*
    87–11 *B· Directors and Brethren :*
  '00. 14– 9 *B·*, let him that hath an ear
  '02. 18–20 *B·*, how much of what he did are we
  Po. 29–13 *B·*, replete, by flesh embound
  My. 5–23 *B·*, I am not with you
    22–15 * our *b·* Leader and teacher,
    23–17 * *B· Teacher and Leader :*
    27– 2 *To the B· Members of my Church,*
    36– 8 * *B· Teacher and Leader :*
    42–13 * *B· Friends :* — Most unexpectedly
    42–26 * inaugurated by our *b·* Leader,
    43–22 * was revealed to our *b·* Leader,
    44–23 * *B· Teacher and Leader :*
    51–29 * to our *b·* pastor, Mrs. Eddy,
    62–19 * *B· Leader and Teacher :*
    64– 2 * achievements of our *b·* Leader
    118– 1 *b·* members of my church who
    129– 8 throughout our *b·* country
    131– 1 *B·*, that which purifies the
    134–26 * been secured from our *b·* Leader
    135–26 My *B· Church:* — Your love
    140–18 *B· Christian Scientists :* Take
    142–10 *B· Christian Scientist :* — Accept my
    143–10 my *b·* friends and followers
    150–26 *B·* in Christ, what our Master said
    157– 3 * *B· Teacher and Leader :*
    162–10 such as my *b·* Christian Scientists
    163– 9 *b·* ones who have so kindly come
    170–27 *B·*, some of you have come long
    193–15 *B· :* — The spiritual dominates the
    207– 7 * *B· Leader:* — The representatives of
    208–12 *B· Christian Scientists :* — Like the
    210– 2 *B· Christian Scientists,* keep your
    216–15 *My B· Children :* — Tenderly thanking
    236– 5 *B· Christian Scientists :* — Because I
    243–20 *B· Christian Scientists :* — Your prompt
    254– 5 *B· :* — I am glad you enjoy the dawn
    256– 7 This year, my *b·* Christian Scientists,
    263– 5 *B· :* — A word to the wise
    271–17 * *b·* of thousands of believers
    279–22 *Dearly B· :* — I request that every
    280– 3 * *B· Leader:* — We acknowledge
    289–16 long honored, revered, *b·*.
    290– 9 *b·* as this noble woman,
    291– 3 *b·* President, William McKinley.
    297–18 My *b·* Edward A. Kimball,
    312–26 the remains of my *b·* one
    315–29 and made me the *b·* Leader of
    322– 9 * *My B· Teacher :* — I have just read
    323–17 * *B· Teacher :* — My heart has
    325–14 * in any way, *b·* Leader.
    327–11 * *B· Leader:* — I know the enclosed
    335– 9 * *b·* by his brothers and companions,
    352– 4 * *B· Leader:* — Informally assembled,
    352–19 *B· Ushers of The Mother Church*
    352–27 *B· Christian Scientists :* — Accept my
    358– 9 *B· !* you need to watch and pray
    361–19 * *B· Leader:* — We rejoice that our
    (*see also* **brethren, church, student, students**)

below
  Mis. 53–18 seeks what is *b·* instead of above
    95– 9 * and is transcribed *b·*.
    186– 7 material belief has fallen far *b·*
    388–22 To fold an angel's wings *b·* ;
  Pul. 39–22 * Gaze on the world *b·*.
    48–10 * whole landscape that lies *b·*,
  No. 26–16 into something *b·* infinitude.
  '00. 7–28 Thus it is we walk here *b·*,
  Po. 21–11 To fold an angel's wings *b·* ;

Beman, Mr.
  My. 63– 4 * of Mr. *B·* in an advisory capacity

Bemis
  Mrs.
  Pul. 43–24 * was then read by Mrs. *B·*.
    43–29 * Mrs. *B·* read the following letter
    57– 9 * sermon, . . . was read by Mrs. *B·*.
  Mrs. Henrietta Clark
  Pul. 43–10 * and Mrs. Henrietta Clark *B·*,
    59–19 * read by . . . Mrs. Henrietta Clark *B·*,

bench
  '00. 7–10 members of the bar and *b·*,

benches
  Ret. 15–18 and *b·* were used in the aisles.

bend
  Mis. 134–17 *b·* or outweigh your purpose
    330–14 alders *b·* over the streams
    387–11 And on the same branch *b·*.
  Ret. 17– 4 In bowers of beauty, — I *b·* to thy lay,
  No. 3– 2 sad it is that envy will *b·* its bow
  Po. 6– 6 And on the same branch *b·*.
    62– 3 In bowers of beauty, — I *b·* to thy lay,
  My. 125– 6 to *b·* upward the tendrils

bended
  Mis. 127–10 not verbally, nor on *b·* knee,
    204– 3 falling on the *b·* knee of prayer,
  My. 18– 7 not verbally, nor on *b·* knee,

bendeth
  Mis. 275– 9 *b·* his aching head ;

bending
  Mis. 387–14 If thou the *b·* reed wouldst break
  Ret. 4–14 broad fields of *b·* grain
  Hea. 2–19 *b·* beneath the malice of the world.
  Peo. 14– 9 * "bat and owl on the *b·* stones,
  Po. 6– 9 If thou the *b·* reed wouldst break

bends
  Mis. 240–17 The sapling *b·* to the breeze,

beneath (*see also* **'neath**)
  Mis. 55–29 in matter and *b·* a skull bone,
    106–25 *B·*, above, beyond, methinks I hear
    154–13 *b·* your own vine and fig-tree
    195–21 cannot fall to the ground *b·* the
    262–24 With all the homage *b·* the skies,
    263– 9 "*b·* the shadow of — see *Isa.* 32 : 2.
    389–18 *B·* the shadow of His mighty wing ;
    396–16 *B·* the maple's shade.
  Ret. 35–21 fall to the ground *b·* the stroke
    79– 8 the material pigment *b·*
  Pul. 27–14 * with six small windows *b·*,
    27–17 * *B·* are two small windows
    42–16 * and *b·* the beehive the words,
  No. 14–16 chapter sub-title
    14–24 were not from *b·*.
    15– 2 Are the dews of . . . from *b·* ?
  '02. 17–29 like the sun *b·* the horizon,
  Hea. 2–19 bending *b·* the malice of the world.
  Po. 4–17 *B·* the shadow of His mighty wing ;
    59– 8 *B·* the maple's shade.
  My. 78– 9 * entrances *b·* a series of arches
    350–23 foundations . . . Sunk from *b·* man,

benediction
  Mis. 8–29 fulfilled through the gospel's *b·*.
    81–15 *b·* of an honored Father,
    81–29 This *is* the Father's *b·*.
    86–17 like a *b·* after prayer,
    143– 8 with this silent *b·* :
    152– 8 silent *b·* over all the earth,
    238–21 and it already hath a *b·* .
    314–14 shall pronounce the *b·*.
    320– 2 God will give the *b·*.
  Pul. 87– 5 * with our humble *b·*.
  No. 8–25 quietly, with *b·* and hope,
  '01. 3– 3 *b·* of our Father-Mother God
  '02. 11–21 this is thy Lord's *b·* upon it :
  Po. 78–16 In that *b·* which knoweth best !
  My. 19– 8 * and the *b·*, 2 Corinthians 13 : 14 :
    33– 7 * The *b·*.
    132–13 may there come this *b·* :
    188–18 breathing a *b·* for God's largess.
    202–13 *b·* of "Well done, — *Matt.* 25 : 23.
    295–21 chapter sub-title

benedictions
  Mis. 213–17 perfect their own lives by gentle *b·*
    320– 8 with divine *b·* for mankind.
  My. 167–13 their loving *b·* upon your lives.
    256–17 Christmas . . . full of divine *b·*

benefactor
  Mis. 161–18 of our Master as a public *b·*,

benefactors
  My. 200–22 by pulling down its *b·*,

benefice
My. 245- 3 demand for this universal b· is
beneficence
Ret. 81- 2 threaten to paralyze its b·.
My. 340-30 b· of the laws of the universe
beneficent
My. 26-12 Your b· gift is the largest sum
beneficial
Mis. 348-27 drugs have no b· effect
Ret. 85- 7 useful to the Cause and b· to
My. 99- 8 * aggregation of good and b· works,
beneficially
Man 75-19 own the aforesaid premises . . . b·.
benefit
brought a
Pul. 51-20 * on the other hand, have brought a b·.
great
Pul. 14-27 great b· which Mind has wrought.
My. 138- 5 a great b· to me already.
imaginary
My. 118- 5 any imaginary b· they receive is
most
Mis. 316-26 derived most b· from their pupilage,
my
My. 138- 8 not for my b· in any way,
no personal
'02. 13-11 I receive no personal b·
of all
Hea. 16- 3 b· of all who, having ears, hear
of our Cause
Man. 59-11 for the b· of our Cause.
of our race
Un. 13-20 for the b· of our race.
of this Church
Man. 76- 3 used for the b· of this Church,
only
Mis. 59-22 only b· in speaking often
share the
Mis. 290-26 share the b· of that radiation.

Mis. 11-25 general effort to b· the race.
35-19 of what b· is your book?
38-19 application to b· the race,
64-17 ethics . . . must b· every one ;
137-27 give to the world the b· of
227-20 odor they send forth to b· mankind ;
241- 2 to b· the body,
241- 3 as to b· the mind.
271-26 * "To b· the community,
290-24 one must b· those who
302-25 b· which the student derived
350-24 the b· that would otherwise accrue.
351-17 nor b· mankind by such endeavors.
378-16 how manipulation could b· the sick.
Ret. 41- 6 an acknowledgment of the b·.
72- 5 to b· himself and mankind.
No. v- 2 to b· no favored class,
'01. 20- 4 to serve God and b· mankind.
21-23 whereby to b· the race
My. 24-17 * state, for the b· of those who
203-28 doing so much to b· mankind
231- 7 whom she has labored much to b·
benefited
Mis. 35-24 You are b· by reading S. and H.,
273- 3 neophyte will be b· by experience,
291-15 has equal opportunity to be b·
Ret. 83- 7 seldom b· by the teachings of other
85-14 b·, by any deviation from
My. 210-11 but all . . . are thereby b·.
benefiting
Mis. 130- 1 of thereby b· him
Pul. 15-10 doing right and b· our race.
My. 136-26 b· the human race ;
benefits
Pan. 9-23 this love b· its enemies
'00. 2-12 b· society by his example
'02. 1-19 honors God and b· mankind
My. 81- 7 * b· and the healing power of
benevolence
Mis. 50-28 b· and love for God and man ;
199- 1 God does not reward b· . . . with penalties;
My. 165-24 Goodness and b· never tire.
262-28 in quietude, humility, b·, charity,
benevolent
Man. 47- 1 he is b·, forgiving,
benighted
My. 234-17 success of C. S. in b· China,
benign
Mis. 63- 5 to hinder his b· influence
Peo. 2-27 a b· and elevating influence
My. 128- 8 less than God's b· government,

benison
My. 257-25 I group you in one b·
bent
Mis. 264-18 * "As the twig is b·,
Ret. 18-26 b· branch of a pear-tree.
31-24 My heart b· low before the
Po. 63-24 b· branch of a pear-tree.
bequeathed
Mis. 248-21 and b· my property to
bequeathing
'01. 30- 5 is only the b· of itself to
bequests
Ret. 30- 3 The rare b· of C. S. are costly,
bereaved
My. 289-13 sympathy with the b· nation,
331-20 * in behalf of . . . his b· lady,
331-25 * b· widow after his decease.
bereavement
Ret. 19-16 in this terrible b·.
My. 290- 3 this sudden international b·,
330-28 * in this terrible b·.
bereft (see also **'reft**)
Mis. 275-10 b· wife or husband,
352- 1 b· of permanence and peace.
Ret. 20-19 life is dead, b· of all,
Un. 51-10 In pantheism the world is b· of
'01. 34-15 wantonly b· of the Word of God.
Berkeley (see also **Berkeley's**)
Bishop
Ret. 37-12 now declare Bishop B·, David Hume,
No. 22- 5 Hegel, Spinoza, Bishop B·,
'01. 21- 8 * Bishop B· of the Church of England
23-23 Bishop B· published a book

Mis. 361-15 Plato, Kant, Locke, B·,
No. 22- 6 B· ended his metaphysical theory
'01. 24-18 B·, Darwin, or Huxley.
My. 349- 9 B·, Tyndall, and Spencer
Berkeley's
Bishop
'01. 24-14 Bishop B· metaphysics and

'01. 24-21 I had not read one line of B·
Berlin
'00. 1-23 Dublin, Paris, B·, Rome,
berries
Ret. 4-19 green pastures bright with b·,
beseeching
Ret. 8- 6 b· her to tell me what she wanted.
beset
Mis. 318-26 Two points of danger b· mankind ;
319- 9 b· with egotism and hypocrisy.
323-10 descent and ascent are b· with
361-18 doth so easily b· us,— Heb. 12 : 1.
Ret. 71- 7 temptations b· an ignorant or an
79-17 If b· with misguided emotions,
No. 42-20 C. S. is b· with false claimants,
'01. 2-24 b· all their returning footsteps.
besetments
Mis. 10-18 with fear and the b· of evil ;
besets
'02. 19-24 A danger b· thy path?
beside
Mis. 63-20 none else b· Him,"— Deut. 4 : 35.
97-19 no God b· me."— Isa. 45 : 5.
151-17 that I desire b· thee."— Psal. 73 : 25.
206-32 b· the still waters,"— Psal. 23 : 2.
225-21 and sat down b· the sofa
227-24 b· the still waters, on isles of
322-15 b· the still waters."— Psal. 23 : 2.
350-16 none b· Him."— see Deut. 4 : 35.
357- 8 and rest b· still waters.
366-12 none b· Him."— see Deut. 4 : 35.
Ret. 60- 7 that there is nothing b· God ;
60-19 and there is nothing b· Him ;"
63- 5 and there is none b· Him,
Un. 18-26 A knowledge of aught b· Myself
21-16 there is nothing b· Him
25-12 claiming to be something b· God,
36- 5 b· which there is no other
60- 6 and there is none b· Him,
62- 9 there is none b· good.
Rud. 4-11 and there is naught b· Him.
9-26 and that there can be none b· Him ;
13-15 none else b· Him."— Deut. 4 : 35.
No. 16-13 for there is none b· God
16-18 inference of some other existence b·
17-20 "none b· Him."— see Deut. 4 : 35.
24-28 As there is none b· Him,
37-22 God, and none b· Him ;

beside

Peo.	5–15	it sitteth *b·* the sepulchre
Po.	67–13	*B·* you they walk while you weep,
My.	77– 5	* *B·* it the dome of the
	112–32	a book which lies *b·* the Bible
	129–26	green pastures *b·* still waters,
	162–26	*b·* the still waters.'' — *Psal.* 23 : 2.
	247–15	when I stood silently *b·* it,

besides

Mis.	22–20	it dwelleth in Him *b·* whom
	27– 1	What can there be *b·* infinity?
	27–23	matter claims something *b·* God,
	37– 1	and no power *b·* God, good.
	93–12	there is in reality none *b·*
	173–25	whence, then, is something *b·* Him
	319– 5	the argument of aught *b·* Him,
	332–30	that there is something *b·* Him ;
	333–25	believed that something *b·* God had
	358–11	He that seeketh aught *b·* God,
Ret.	1– 9	*b·* other verses and enigmas
	60– 8	is something *b·* God.
	60–22	something *b·* Him, which
Un.	22–13	But there is something *b·*
Pul.	5– 3	*b·* listening to an address on C. S.
	47–21	* *B·* her Boston home, Mrs. Eddy has
	56– 5	* *b·* a large and growing number of
Rud.	14–21	doing charity work *b·*.
	15–13	Few were taken *b·* invalids
'00.	5– 5	or aught *b·* God, good.
'02.	6– 7	of something *b·* God, good,
Hea.	15–20	trying everything else *b·* God,
My.	300– 3	belief in sin or in aught *b·* God,

besieged

Mis.	274–17	press is gagged, liberty is *b·* ; .
Pul.	2–17	fiercely *b·* by the enemy.
My.	54–24	* crowds had *b·* the doors

besieges

'00.	11–14	Beethoven *b·* you with tones

besmear

Mis.	337–31	sensualism, . . . would hide or *b·*.

besmeared

Mis.	274–29	the streets *b·* with blood.

besought

'01.	19– 3	They believe that divine power, *b·*,

bespeaks

My.	133–29	The spiritual *b·* our temporal

best

Mis.	ix– 4	* *b·* aims are to show and to enable
	2–32	decided views as to the *b·* method
	5– 2	devote our *b·* energies to the work.
	9–12	are virtually thy *b·* friends
	10–17	*b·* lesson of their lives is gained by
	32–19	I would gladly do my *b·* towards
	43–10	who understands it *b·*,
	59–26	That individual is the *b·* healer who
	80–20	at the *b·* time, will redress wrongs
	87–20	he does *b·* in the investigation of
	156–17	*b·* understood through the study of
	210–17	but, the *b·* may be mistaken.
	233– 3	malpractice of the *b·* system
	236–17	and the *b·* way to overcome them,
	236–18	to the *b·* of our ability,
	236–21	though it be your *b·* friend ;
	250– 3	the *b·* become the most abused,
	257–14	repays our *b·* deeds with sacrifice
	267– 5	are the *b·* friends to our growth.
	268– 4	Who shall be *b·*?
	271–12	books which are less than the *b·*.
	273–25	I cannot do my *b·* work for a
	288– 2	convictions regarding what is *b·*
	293– 4	*b·* to leave the righteous unfolding
	295–28	unquestionably the *b·* queen on earth ;
	298–11	having my *b·* friend break troth
	307–14	thought *b·* to stop its publication.
	316–12	the hour *b·* for the student.
	349–17	should do as he deemed *b·*,
	368–26	But while the *b·*, perverted,
Ret.	43–19	judged it *b·* to close the institution.
	49–29	*b·* to dissolve this corporation,
	82–28	which revision . . . is the *b·*.
	83–12	and are their *b·* guides.
	93–13	*b·* spiritual type of Christly method
Un.	48–12	He is *b·* understood as Supreme
	50–11	At *b·*, matter is only a phenomenon
Pul.	38–30	* their *b·* aid and guidance,
	82–23	* sing *b·* by singing most for their
Rud.	2– 8	used by the *b·* authorities,
	6–23	Mind-healing is *b·* understood in
	15–15	to fill in the *b·* possible manner
No.	41–10	repeat his work to the *b·* advantage
	44– 6	having its *b·* interpretation in the
Pan.	9–27	the *b·* of people sometimes object to
	10–13	*b·* students in the class averred

best

Pan.	11–14	superior to the *b·* church-member
'00.	2– 5	among the *b·* people on earth
	3– 5	right thinker and worker does his *b·*,
	3–14	what the *b·* thinker and worker has said
	7– 9	*b·* and most scholarly men and
	9– 1	which I know it were *b·* not to do,
	9– 5	not because it is the *b·* thing
	9–22	challenge . . . workers to do their *b·*.
	10– 5	new birth of the greatest and *b·*.
'01.	17–15	the respect of our *b·* thinkers.
	27– 3	* ''The *b·* contributions that
	29–10	all the *b·* of his earthly years.
'02.	10 25	martyrdom of God's *b·* witnesses
	11–28	the *b·* Christian on earth,
Po.	28– 9	Knowing Thou knowest *b·*.
	77– 7	Thou knowest *b·* !
	77–13	of Thee, who knowest *b·* !
	77–20	Thou knowest *b·* !
	78– 7	Thou knowest *b·* !
	78–12	Thou knowest *b·* !
	78–16	that benediction which knoweth *b·* !
My.	8– 9	* the *b·* church in the world,
	8 10	* *b·* expression of the religion of
	8–11	* let us have the *b·* material symbol of
	8–12	* in the *b·* city in the world.
	10– 9	* *b·* of design, material, and
	12–12	* *b·* evidenced by the liberality and
	15–27	* For those who know it *b·*
	42–19	* to the *b·* of my ability.
	46– 8	* In the *b·* sense it stands in
	60–16	* as a reward for the *b·* paper on
	69–29	* *b·* point of view is on top of the
	97– 2	* *b·* physicians now admit the power of
	108–23	Master designated as his *b·* work,
	108–25	*b·* work of a Christian Scientist.
	112–31	chief cities and the *b·* families
	136– 5	it is *b·* explained by its fruits,
	145– 4	one of Concord's *b·* builders
	165– 3	namely, of choosing the *b·*,
	165– 8	The *b·* help the worst ;
	165–28	The *b·* man or woman is the most
	178–20	and this is the *b·* of it.
	180–26	misconstrues our *b·* motives,
	195–18	*b·* way to silence a deep discontent
	203–10	*b·* of everything is not too good,
	205–22	theology at its *b·* touches but the
	229–28	Thou knowest *b·* what we need most,
	237– 7	The *b·* mathematician has not
	249–25	individual *b·* fitted to perform this
	250– 7	The *b·* Christian Scientists will be
	253–26	We understand *b·* that which
	285–13	*b·*, bravest, most cultured men and
	288–30	can make the *b·* of what God has made.
	304–11	I wrote for the *b·* magazines
	305 10	*b·* and most distinguished men
	331– 5	* of Wilmington's *b·* citizens,
	331 13	* by Wilmington's *b·* men,
	332–30	* giving *b·* praises to his honorable
	358–11	your Leader and *b·* earthly friend.
	358–23	Give my *b·* wishes and love to

best-known

Po.	vi–22	* *All of the author's b· hymns*

bestow

Mis.	272–23	* *b·* no rights to *confer degrees*.
	291–20	to *b·* it upon others,
My.	38– 1	* *b·* upon you the balm of heavenly
	231– 2	*b·* her charities for such purposes

bestowal

My.	247–21	to receive your *b·*,

bestowed

Mis.	77–16	Love that He hath *b·* upon us,
	127– 5	hath His love been *b·* upon her ;
	183–18	reflection already has *b·* on him,
	227–29	happiness it has *b·* upon others.
	289–23	has *b·* on a wife the right to
Ret.	2–14	*b·* by Sir William Wallace,
Pul.	46–21	* sword had been *b·* by
Po.	74– 3	moments to memory *b·*
My.	18– 2	hath His love been *b·* upon her ;
	19–29	gift which you so sacredly *b·*
	157–12	* church home you have so freely *b·*.
	215– 3	*b·* without money or price.

bestows

Mis.	345– 1	The Spirit *b·* spiritual gifts,
Rud.	10– 3	you forfeit the power that Truth *b·*,
'01.	15–15	blessings that divine Love *b·*
Peo.	12–27	our Father *b·* heaven
My.	122– 1	advice that one gratuitously *b·*

Bethany

Ret.	31–26	Bethlehem and *B·*, Gethsemane and

Bethel

Un.	57–18	This is earth's *B·* in stone,

Bethlehem
Mis. 159–19   not so much the *B·* babe,
320–23   star of *B·* is the star of Boston,
320–27   star of *B·* is the light of all ages ;
388–24   To nurse the *B·* babe so sweet,
Ret. 31–26   *B·* and Bethany, Gethsemane and
70– 9   Virgin-mother and *B·* babe,
Pul. 28– 4   * star of *B·* shines down from above.
Po. 21–13   To nurse the *B·* babe so sweet,
29–12   The *B·* babe— Beloved,
My. 110– 5   At the present time this *B·* star
257– 7   the *B·* babe has left his
258–17   The memory of the *B·* babe

betide
Po. 79– 5   pure peace is thine, Whate'er *b·*.

betimes
Mis. 206–32   As you journey, and *b·* sigh for rest
327–18   and *b·* burden them with their own.

betokened
Po. 10–13   bless a bridal *B·* from above.
My. 337–14   bless a bridal *B·* from above.

betokens
My. 290– 1   It *b·* a love and a loss felt by

betray
Po. 2– 1   no soul those looks *b·* ;

betrayed
Ret. 90–14   *b·* him, and others forsook him.
My. 283–16   even though it be *b·*.

betrays
Mis. 212– 3   a caressing Judas that *b·* you,
Ret. 73–24   *b·* a violent and egotistical
My. 128–24   A lack of wisdom *b·* Truth

better
Mis. 24–14   ever after was in *b·* health
42–27   a *b·* state of existence.
45–20   *b·* both morally and physically.
59– 8   without this Science there had *b·*
80–12   It is *b·* to be friendly
88– 4   the *b·* it is for that student.
110– 1   Repentance is *b·* than sacrifice.
122–11   "It were *b·* for him— *Matt.* 18 *:* 6.
130– 6   understand how much *b·* it is to
175– 9   giving *b·* views of Life ;
194– 6   know Him *b·*, and love Him more.
200– 5   the *b·* representatives of God
218–27   *b·* than Pat's echo, when he said
223–26   *b·* than the mighty." *Prov.* 16 *:* 32.
229– 7   quite as surely and with *b·* effect
229–25   a *b·* preventive of contagion
235–18   and thirsting after a *b·* life,
239– 4   I never was in *b·* health.
252– 6   the more the *b·* in every case.
268–12   in pursuit of *b·* means for healing
269–10   who can *b·* define ethics,
269–10   *b·* elucidate the Principle
273–12   as well as the *b·* part of mankind,
278–28   sooner this lesson is gained the *b·*.
318– 7   *b·* than some of mine
333–32   the prophet *b·* understood Him
336–26   behold a *b·* man, woman, or child.
343– 7   Thought must be made *b·*,
365–14, 15   *b·* health and *b·* men.
371– 8   guide Christian Scientists *b·* than
371–16   not productive of the *b·* sort,
376–14   * and in a much *b·* form.
396–14   I hope it's *b·* made,
Man. 87–20   the *b·* it will be for both
92– 3   Healing *B·* than Teaching.
Ret. 11– 2   suited my emotions *b·* than prose.
31–11   higher and *b·* than matter,
33–13   the *b·* the work is done ;
47–17   a *b·* healer and teacher than
62– 5   bring forth *b·* fruits of health,
82–30   and it is therefore *b·* adapted to
84–26   the *b·* it will be for both teacher and
Un. 1–15   had *b·* leave the subject untouched,
14–27   never said that man would become *b·* by
45–21   finally dies in order to *b·* itself.
49–20   * "the worse appear the *b·* reason,"
Pul. 9–19   who, with his *b·* half, is a very
15– 7   Because people like you *b·* when
50– 8   * *b·* home life and citizenship.
56–16   * It makes people *b·* and happier.
69–24   * may gain a *b·* understanding than the
82–11   * far *b·* than her teachers.
83– 4   * our *b·* self is shamed and
84–18   * It can be *b·* felt than expressed.
85–10   * *b·* and higher conception of God
85–16   * a *b·* and grander humanity,
Rud. 14–16   must of necessity do *b·* than
No. 3– 6   *b·* to fall into the hands of God,
4– 4   had *b·* be undertaken in health
18–11   need of *b·* health and morals.

better
No. 20– 9   distant or cold, until *b·* apprehended.
29–16   *B·* far that we impute such doctrines
34–18   The blood of Christ speaketh *b·* things
40–24   mankind are *b·* because of this.
40–27   made *b·* only by divine influence.
Pan. 10–14   stronger and *b·* than before it.
10–20   *b·* still, they reform desperate cases
'00. 6–27   you are made *b·* physically,
14–25   philanthropy of the *b·* class of M.D.'s
'01. 1– 8   *b·* appreciated, than ever before,
1–21   the *b·* side of man's nature
15–20   dis-ease in sin is *b·* than ease.
17– 7   departed from his *b·* self
21–23   Does this critic know of a *b·* way
'02. 9– 9   we shall have *b·* practitioners,
11– 3   mortals who seek for a *b·* country
Hea. 3– 4   to make men *b·*, to cast out error,
8–15   Plato did *b·* ; he said,
9– 4   if we understood the Principle *b·*
9– 7   the *b·* for mankind, morally
11–19   "The less medicine the *b·*,"
13–28   one lie getting the *b·* of another,
15–28   as we understand God *b·*.
Peo. 6– 1   * all the *b·* for mankind
7–26   and give to the body those *b·*
Po. 59– 6   I hope it's *b·* made,
My. 5–22   to love more and to serve *b·*.
6– 7   To abide in our unselfed *b·* self
26–16   I thought it *b·* to be brief
39–29   * comprehend *b·* the strength and
63–14   * enable us *b·* to work out the
108–19   The more of this Mind the *b·*
112–22   *b·* representatives of C. S.
150– 8   * rendering the world happier and *b·*
162– 8   is *b·* than a wilderness of dullards
164–25   into the greater and *b·*,
174–28   humbly pray to serve Him *b·*.
196–10   *b·* than the mighty ;— *Prov.* 16 *:* 32.
213–23   Thus you will grow wiser and *b·*
215–26   Can we find a *b·* example
221–13   can we find a *b·* moral philosophy,
221–14   or a *b·* religion than his?
226–28   becomes *b·* acquainted with C. S.,
229–13   *B·* far that Christian Scientists
233–10   are you not made *b·* by watching?
233–12   *b·* adapted to deliver mortals from
236–20   the more the *b·*.
264–16   signifies . . . the Bible *b·* understood
307–21   understood what I said *b·* than
324–31   * no man could have done so any *b·*.
329–21   * At no *b·* time than now,
334–16   * no *b·* terms than to quote her own
344–13   *b·* than he was before
352–11   * is proved in *b·* lives.
355–25   world is *b·* for this happy group

better-tended
Mis. 342– 8   *b·* lamps of the faithful.

between
Mis. x–15   difference *b·* then and now,
16–32   conflict *b·* the flesh and Spirit.
19–25   *B·* the centripetal and centrifugal
29–12   no analogy *b·* C. S. and
29–13   *b·* it and any speculative theory.
36–19   *distinction b· mortal mind and*
42–21   The difference *b·* a belief of
49–20   *b·* the real and the unreal.
52– 4   divided *b·* catnip and Christ ;
60–24   *b· them and real identity,*
65–10   Every question *b·* Truth and error,
95–16   *b·* the so-called dead and living.
102–27   conflict *b·* sense and Soul.
110–20   while leagues have lain *b·* us.
111–23   *b·* his doctrines and those of Jesus,
111–25   *b·* the Catholic and Protestant sects.
117– 5   *b·* the thought, motive, and
119–23   *b·* the real and the unreal
124– 1   intervening *b·* God and man,
168– 5   those halting *b·* two opinions
178–29   wall *b·* the old and the new ;
178–30   *b·* the old religion in which we
179–19   *b·* us and the resurrection morning?
188–11   a war *b·* the flesh and Spirit,
188–12   a contest *b·* Truth and error ;
203– 3   *b·* my students and your students ;
256–17   intervals *b·* my class terms,
257– 6   distinction *b·* that which is and
269–18   his choice *b·* matter and Mind,
271–27   * *b·* true and false teachers
289– 9   mortals must first choose *b·*
302–11   discriminate *b·* error and Truth,
312–17   * *b·* religion and Science,
319–28   *b·* the promise and event ;
329– 7   *b·* taking up the white carpets and
347–16   *B·* the two I stand still ;

between

Mis.	351–13	designed to stir up strife b· brethren,
	352–28	b· the healing of sin and the
	374–29	b· the thinker and his thought
Man.	41– 6	gulf b· C. S. and theosophy,
	75–12	b· the C. S. Board of Directors and
Ret.	38–22	Not a word had passed b· us,
	56–12	War is waged b· the evidences
	68– 9	great difference b· these opposites is,
Un.	5–22	spring up b· C. S. students and
	27– 4	have a shade of difference b· them.
	29–18	b· the true Science of Soul and
Pul.	2–16	the war b· China and Japan.
	20–15	warfare b· the flesh and Spirit,
	21–20	b· our denomination and other sects,
	22–16	doctrinal barriers b· the churches
	24– 3	* b· Commonwealth and Huntington
	38–20	* b· the embodied and disembodied
	41–10	* and all the territory that lies b·,
	47–17	* b· faith-cure and C. S.,
	55–30	* b· one hundred thousand and
	57– 6	* b· fourteen and fifteen hundred,
No.	7– 5	to spring up b· Christian Scientists,
	7–22	b· one person and another,
	14– 4	he would know that b· those who
	31–17	b· what is and is not,
Pan.	6–20	colloquy b· good and evil,
	13–15	the war b· flesh and Spirit,
	14–28	b· United States and Spain
'01.	5–12	metaphysics discriminates b·
	23–28	* "only the constant relation b·
'02.	4–10	peace b· Soul and sense
	8–12	b· the law and the gospel,
	8–13	b· the old and the new commandment,
	15–12	the connection b· justice and
	20–19	breaking any seeming connection b·
Hea.	1–20	The difference b· religions is,
	5–11	* "b· Christianity and spiritualism,
	6–12	b· the so-called dead and the
	12–28	b· matter and mind,
	18– 8	no connection b· Spirit and matter.
Peo.	1– 7	final unity b· man and God.
	9–13	b· matter and Spirit ;
My.	18–23	war b· flesh and Spirit,
	65– 9	* b· four and five thousand persons.
	108–10	difference b· metaphysics in
	124–19	b· these lines of thought
	147– 5	b· the morning and afternoon services
	180–30	b· divine theology and C. S.,
	181–18	line of justice b· the classes
	199–20	fourfold unity b· the churches
	200–25	gap b· this course and C. S.
	221– 3	moral distance b· Christianity and
	238– 5	degree of comparison b· the effects
	246–15	exist b· the teaching and letter of
	259– 3	on its pedestal b· my bow windows,
	265–10	peace b· nations,
	277– 3	b· the United States and Spain
	277– 7	difficulties b· individuals
	279–24	war b· Russia and Japan ;
	281–18	* peace b· Russia and Japan
	284–26	quarrels b· nations and peoples.
	306– 5	unity that may exist b· C. S. and
	309– 6	b· the towns of Loudon and Bow,
	310–22	* b· Mary, a child ten years old, and
	316– 3	Truth divides b· sect and Science

beverages

Mis.	288–32	abstinence from intoxicating b·.

beware

Mis.	39–10	false teachers . . . of such b·.
	79–29	B· of joining any medical league
	109– 2	B· of those who misrepresent facts ;
	307–27	should b· of unseen snares,
	366–18	"b· of the leaven of — Matt. 16 : 6.
No.	41– 1	chapter sub-title
	41– 4	warned the people to b· of Jesus,
My.	241– 7	* b· the net that is craftily laid

bewilder

'01.	20–15	This mental bane could not b·,

bewilderment

Pul.	34–14	* to their b· and fright,

beyond

Mis.	9–14	far b· the present sense
	12– 5	throughout time and b· the grave.
	46– 8	b· the power of any doctrine
	52– 9	b· all human means and methods.
	67– 1	until its altitude reaches b· the
	68–30	* soars b· the bounds of experience,"
	81–18	many of the people from b· Jordan?
	106–25	above, b·, methinks I hear
	111– 7	extended it b· safe expansion ;
	165– 4	grown b· the human sense of him,
	201–22	b· the common apprehension of sinners;
	202– 6	* b· the walks of common life,

beyond

Mis.	223– 9	Science proves, b· cavil, that
	228–17	and honest b· reproach,
	321–30	b· all earthly expositions
	324–19	Startled b· measure at beholding
	325–20	amazed b· measure that anybody
	339– 8	and is one day b· it,
	357– 9	b· the walks of common life,
	367–20	knows nothing b· Himself
	379–20	b· the basis of materia medica,
	385–12	moored at last — B· rough foam.
	386– 2	B· the shadow, infinite appear
Ret.	71– 1	exalts a mortal b· human praise,
	76–12	a light b· what others saw.
	89– 3	is proven b· a doubt
Un.	2–23	b· what they possessed before ;
Pul.	26– 6	* b· the power of words to depict.
	36–21	* just b· Massachusetts Avenue,
	40– 4	* B· the sapphire sea?
No.	4–17	b· other systems of medicine,
	12–21	b· doctrine and ritual ;
	25–11	the infinite idea of Truth is b· a
	34–19	b· the heathen conception
'00.	12– 1	b· the power of the pen.
'01.	24–18	It dates b· Socrates,
	28–21	proven to me b· a doubt
'02.	4–27	b· the ken of mortals,
Hea.	8– 1	it implies no necessity b· the
Po.	1– 5	B· the ken of mortal e'er to tell
	48– 5	moored at last — B· rough foam.
	49– 4	B· the shadow, infinite appear
	70– 1	B· the clouds, away
My.	8– 6	* necessity here indicated is b·
	8– 7	* b· resistance in your thought."
	14– 4	b· the ken of mortals
	45–22	* marvellous b· human ken.
	59– 7	* b· our mortal vision.
	59–32	* marvellous b· all imagining
	63–21	* awe and of reverence b· words,
	65–12	* b· two brief explanations
	77–11	* From b· the Rockies,
	91– 1	* established b· cavil.
	96–26	* b· the sneering point.
	97– 1	* C. S. just goes a little b·
	107–27	nothing b· illimitable divinity,
	108– 6	I have proved b· cavil that
	123– 2	gifts to me are b· comparison
	127–26	but it is rich b· price,
	180– 3	knows b· a doubt that its life-giving
	181– 2	settle all points b· cavil,
	190–20	remains b· questioning a divine
	250–29	have b· it duties and attainments
	273– 6	* b· the allotted years of man,
	349–20	b· the so-called natural sciences

bias

Mis.	264–21	b· of their first impressions,
'00.	9–13	Strong desires b· human judgment
Hea.	5– 7	b· a man's character.

biased

Mis.	240–20	than the b· mind.

Bible (see also Holy Bible)

Mis.	24–11	I called for my B·,
	35–20	Why do we read the B·, and then go
	60– 3	and the B· is addressed to sinners
	64–14	the B·, and "S. and H.
	64–24	a student of the B· and of C. S.
	70– 2	That the B· is true I believe,
	111–12	in the B· and their textbook,
	130– 8	the B·, and in the C. S. textbook,
	160– 1	Within B· pages she had found all
	169–28	* Taking several B· passages, Mrs. Eddy
	170–19	The material record of the B·,
	170–32	"Hand," in B· usage, — Isa. 59 : 1.
	180–20	chapter sub-title
	279–13	three picture-stories from the B·
	284–11	make the B· and S. and H. a study,
	300–27	the spiritual meaning of B· texts ;
	309–29	soberly adhere to the B· and
	313–26	I hereby ordain the B·, and
	314– 9	the chapter) in the B·,
	314–29	both the B· and the C. S. textbook
	318–21	a good B· scholar and a devout,
	322–11	the B·, and "S. and H.
	363–27	B· is the learned man's masterpiece,
	366– 1	the B· and "S. and H.
	382–32	I ordained that the B·, and
	383– 7	its pastor is the B· and my book.
Man.	15– 4	the B· as our sufficient guide
	29–22	one to read the B·,
	32– 5	shall read the B· texts.
	34–12	The B·, together with S. and H.
	42–12	the B·, and S. and H.
	58– 5	ordain the B·, and S. and H.
	84–18	shall be guided by the B·, and
Ret.	25– 3	The B· was my textbook.

Bible

Ret.	26–12	The miracles recorded in the *B·*,
	27– 3	the Science of the *B·*,
	47–25	*B·* scholar and a consecrated Christian.
	76– 7	The *B·* is not stolen,
	83–11	afforded by the *B·* and my books,
	91– 9	compilers and translators of the *B·*,
Pul.	7–24	I have ordained the *B·* and
	25–27	* illuminated texts from the *B·* and
	28–19	* equal measure to its use of the *B·*.
	29–15	* selections from the *B·* and
	34–27	"the *B·* was my only textbook.
	45–26	* the *B·* and "S. and H.
	52–24	* The *B·* was a sealed book.
	58–25	* only pastor shall be the *B·*,
	60– 5	* no explanation of *B·* or
	65–20	* called the *B·* of that city.
	66–15	* the literal teachings of the *B·*
	69–20	* We find in this view of the *B·*
	70–19	* Taking her text from the *B·*,
	86–28	* the *B·* and the book alluded to
Rud.	5– 3	*B·* says: "Let God— *Rom.* 3 : 4.
	16– 9	the spiritual signification of the *B·*,
No.	11–15	If the *B·* and S. and H.
	15– 8	Fatiguing *B·* translations and
	33– 5	If the *B·* and my work
'00.	7–12	they never loved the *B·* and
'01.	3–14	definition derived from the *B·*,
	5– 8	named in the *B·* Life, Truth, Love
	8–23	follow the teachings of the *B·*.
	11–13	True, . . . the *B·*, and "S. and H.
	27– 2	all other authors except the *B·*,
	27–29	* people say it conflicts with the *B·*.
	31–22	daily *B·* reading and family prayer ;
	32–22	Such churchmen and the *B·*,
	34– 4	The *B·* is our authority
	34–12	or must we have a new *B·*
	34–23	study the *B·* and the textbook
'02.	4–28	thoughts of the *B·* utter our lives.
	5– 7	doubtful interpretations of the *B·* ;
Hea.	15–14	miracles recorded in the *B·*.
My.	34–15	* citations from the *B·* and "S. and H.
	39– 5	* read from the *B·* and S. and H.
	46–25	* sacred teachings of the *B·*
	48–12	* a prayerful study of the *B·*,
	48–19	* daily reading of the *B·*
	60–15	* little *B·* which you gave me
	80–18	* an appropriate reading from the *B·*,
	103– 6	our textbooks, the *B·* and "S. and H.
	103–25	The *B·* has been my only authority.
	112–27	S. and H. in connection with the *B·*.
	112–32	a book which lies beside the *B·*
	114–16	read no other book but the *B·*
	130–28	used as a companion to the *B·*
	147–15	*B·* and the C. S. textbook
	178– 1	Your *B·* and your textbook,
	190–23	*B·* was written in order that all
	219–19	*B·* record of our great Master's life
	238– 2	*B·*, *if read and practised*,
	238–19	When the *B·* is thus read
	251–29	Adhere to the teachings of the *B·*,
	264–16	the *B·* better understood
	295– 8	chapter sub-title
	295–10	*B·*, PRINTED IN NUREMBERG IN 1733
	295–13	time-worn *B·* in German.
	295–17	The *B·* is our sea-beaten rock.
	299– 7	* by the church or the *B·*,
	299–15	Principle and rules of the *B·*,
	299–16	in the translations of the *B·*
	304–26	* say it conflicts with the *B·*.
	308–29	*B·* was the only book in his

Bible-class

Ret.	42– 9	He also taught a special *B·* ;

Bible Lesson

Pul.	60– 8	* the *Quarterly B· L·*,

Bible Lessons

Mis.	180–20	chapter sub-title
Man.	104–13	the Committee on *B· L·*.

Bibles

'00.	7– 8	more *B·* sold than in all the
My.	354– 3	offering *B·* and other books

Biblical

Mis.	120–27	*B·* record of the great Nazarene,
	169–18	dual meaning to every *B·* passage,
	274– 2	we have no *B·* authority for
Man.	58–15	*B·* texts in the Lesson-Sermon
Un.	44–11	according to *B·* history.
Pul.	73–10	* delved deep into the *B·* passages,
	73–11	* one of the greatest *B·* scholars of
Hea.	5–18	Such hypotheses ignore *B·* authority,
My.	181– 2	*B·* basis that God is All-in-all ;

bid

Mis.	242–11	his *b·* on Christianity,
Chr.	53–22	earthly Eves, By Adam *b·*,

bid

Pul.	34– 8	* her pastor came to *b·* her good-by
Po.	22– 6	Again shall *b·* old earth good-by
	23–22	*B·* error melt away !
	53–13	*B·* faithful swallows come
My.	347–13	* nor ever *b·* the Spring adieu !

bidden

Mis.	158–14	when you were *b·* to be ordained,
Ret.	9–14	as my mother had *b·* me.
	89–12	*b·* to this privileged duty
Un.	16– 1	perfection which he is *b·* to imitate.
Pul.	33–13	* answered as her mother had *b·* her,
'00.	13–30	*b·* to write the approval of
My.	99– 9	* and *b·* Godspeed."

bidding

Mis.	269–26	Many are *b·* for it,
Hea.	19–20	*b·* man go up higher,

bids

Mis.	335–23	Watcher *b·* them watch,
	348– 8	God *b·* one uncover iniquity,
Un.	4–18	the Father *b·* man have the same Mind
Pul.	3–13	and *b·* tumult cease,
My.	27– 4	Divine Love *b·* me say:
	258– 7	*b·* her bind the tenderest tendril

bier

Ret.	18–13	but laid on the *b·*.
Pul.	1–17	Pass proudly to thy *b·* !
Peo.	14– 3	with flowers laid upon the *b·*,
Po.	26– 6	Pass proudly to thy *b·* !
	27–10	To brighten o'er thy *b·*?
	64– 4	but laid on the *b·*.
	65–21	gathers a wreath for his *b·* ;
My.	326–17	laid on his *b·* the emblems of a

big

Mis.	12–11	the future, *b·* with events.
	216–17	a *b·* protest against injustice ;
	231–16	Why, he made a *b·* hole,
	231–17	with two incisors, in a *b·* pippin,
	241–13	dose of error *b·* enough apparently
	253–14	This period is *b·* with events.
	276– 8	was not *b·* enough to fill the order ;
	400–19	To THE *B·* CHILDREN
Pul.	47–28	* *b·* house, so delightfully remodelled
	49– 1	* *b·*, sunny room which Mrs. Eddy calls
	49–15	"Look at those *b·* elms !
	49–16	almost as *b·* as they are now,
	57–24	* not far from the *b·* Mechanics Building
	63–13	almost as *b·* as they are now,
Po.	69– 7	*To the B· Children*
My.	65–13	* a *b·* church was required,
	75–24	* chapter sub-title
	75–26	* *b·* addition to The Mother Church
	125– 8	*b·* with promise ;

bigger

Mis.	134–15	is *b·* than the shadow,
	191–20	no *b·* than themselves.
Hea.	14– 1	the *b·* lie occupying the field
	14– 2	*b·* animal beats the lesser ;
My.	123–20	outdoor accommodations . . . are *b·* than

biggest

Mis.	123– 9	the serpent's *b·* lie !

bigoted

Un.	11–20	theologian of some *b·* sect,

bigotry

Mis.	365–24	infidelity, *b·*, or sham
Ret.	65– 7	lead to self-righteousness and *b·*,
Pul.	52–21	* wave of materialism and *b·*
My.	93– 4	* have little of the spirit of *b·*.

bilious

My.	335–21	* cause of death as *b·* fever,

bill

Mis.	131–25	itemize a *b·* of this church's gifts
	208– 7	legislative *b·* that governs millions
	289–27	on the basis of a *b·* of rights.
	289–27	Can the *b·* of conjugal rights be
	300–14	spares you the printer's *b·*,
	380–27	a *b·* in equity was filed
Ret.	20–22	compelled to ask for a *b·* of divorce,
Pul.	58–11	* every *b·* being paid.
My.	327–15	* a medical *b·* was proposed

Bill of Rights

Peo.	10–12	our constitutional *B· of R·*.

billow

'02.	20– 2	mounting the *b·* or going down into

billows (see also **billows'**)

Mis.	153– 8	untouched by the *b·*.
	162–10	over their fretted, foaming *b·*.
Po.	10– 2	To the *b·* and the breeze ;
My.	337– 4	To the *b·* and the breeze ;

billows'

Po.	73–10	list the moan Of the *b·* foam,

billowy
Po.	24- 9	From out life's *b·* sea,

bills
Mis.	211–10	Inhuman medical *b·*,
	240- 2	doctor's squills and *b·*
Man.	77- 5	*b·* against the Church,
	77- 9	its endorsement of the *b·*
	78–18	*b·* of immediate necessity
	78–23	for the payment of such *b·*.
Ret.	6–27	Among other important *b·*
My.	27–25	* pay all *b·* in connection with
	30–21	* they were heaped high with *b·*,
	30 23	* Some . . . were one-hundred-dollar *b·*.
	340–17	immediately annulling such *b·*

bind
Mis.	396–20	whose measures *b·* The power of pain,
	398- 5	Thou wilt *b·* the stubborn will,
Ret.	46–11	Thou wilt *b·* the stubborn will,
Un.	12- 5	*b·* it with bands of Soul.
Pul.	17–10	Thou wilt *b·* the stubborn will,
	18- 4	whose measures *b·* The power of pain.
Rud.	4–12	"*b·* the sweet influences of — *Job* 38 : 31.
No.	31–28	"Whatsoever thou shalt *b·* — *Matt.* 16 : 19.
Peo.	11–25	"*b·* heavy burdens," — *Matt.* 23 : 4.
Po.	12- 4	whose measures *b·* The power of pain,
	14- 9	Thou wilt *b·* the stubborn will,
My.	258- 8	*b·* the tenderest tendril of
	350–16	anguish which they blindly *b·*

binder
My.	53- 5	* allow printer and *b·* to send forth

binding
Mis.	296–13	*b·* up the wounds of the
No.	43–14	* *b·* up the broken-hearted,

binds
Mis.	275–15	*b·* up the wounds of bleeding hearts,
	327–32	*b·* up their wounds,
Po.	33- 9	ambition that *b·* us to earth ;
	35- 6	Which *b·* to earth — infirmity of woe!
My.	132–29	It *b·* up the broken hearted ;
	250–17	neither *b·* nor compels the

biographies
Pul.	33–14	* of which Catholic *b·* are full,

birch
Pul.	25–21	* with pews of curly *b·*,
My.	184–15	*b·* bark on which it was written

bird
Mis.	87- 1	as the *b·* in the clear ether of
	124–16	marking the unwinged *b·*,
	267–18	*b·* whose right wing flutters
No.	7–12	"flee as a *b·* — *Psal.* 11 : 1.
Pan.	3–12	lyre of *b·* and brooklet.
Hea.	10 13	Which is first, the egg or the *b·*?
Po. page 34		poem
	34- 1	O for thy wings, sweet *b·*!
	34- 7	*B·* of the airy wing,
	35–13	*B·*, bear me through the sky!
My.	126–27	every unclean . . . *b·*" — *Rev.* 18 : 2.
	129–12	*b·*, brook, blossom, breeze,
	341–11	The *b·* of hope is singing
	347–15	bough, *b·*, and song, to salute me.

birds
Mis.	356–18	and the *b·* of the air,
	387–10	Like brother *b·*, that soar
Po.	6- 4	Like brother *b·*, that soar
My.	182–26	May the *b·* of passage rest

birth
commemorates the
My.	262- 7	commemorates the *b·* of a human,

conception and
Un.	46- 9	human conception and *b·*.

day of the
Pul.	20–23	day of the *b·* and baptism of our

forward the
Un.	57–26	forward the *b·* of immortal being ;

give
My.	133–16	give *b·* to the sowing of Solomon.

give it
Ret.	26–23	Woman must give it *b·*.

given
Mis.	166–20	given *b·* to the corporeal child

giving
'01.	30–13	giving *b·* to nothing and death to

giving it
Mis.	39–12	all her years in giving it *b·*.

his
Mis.	186- 5	embryo-man after his *b·*,
	278–15	cursed the hour of his *b·* ;
No.	36–26	in which he appeared at his *b·*.

human
Mis.	17–22	A material or human *b·* is the

material
Mis.	362- 3	material *b·*, growth, and decay :

birth
new
Mis.	15- 4	chapter sub-title
	15- 5	St. Paul speaks of the new *b·*
	15–13	The new *b·* is not the work of
	15–19	cannot complete, the new *b·* :
	16–25	new *b·* begun in C. S.
	18- 6	spiritual signs of the new *b·*
	386- 8	toiler tireless for Truth's new *b·*
'00.	10- 5	new *b·* of the greatest and best.
Po.	49–13	toiler tireless for Truth's new *b·*
My.	158–13	it points to the new *b·*,

of Christian Science
Pul.	vii- 3	story of the *b·* of C. S.,

of Truth
My.	262–15	*b·* of Truth, the dawn of divine **Love**

second
Mis.	51–26	* as from a second *b·*,

spiritual
Mis.	17–18	spiritual *b·* opens to the enraptured
	17–27	With the spiritual *b·*,

their
Mis.	77–31	miracles of Jesus had their *b·*,

this
Mis.	17–23	This *b·* is more or less prolonged

welcome
Po.	24–10	A wave of welcome *b·*,

without
Chr.	53–39	Life, without *b·* and without end,

wondrous
Po.	31–12	veils the leaflet's wondrous *b·*

Mis.	18- 8	*b·* in the divine order of Science,
	253–25	agonies that gave that child *b·*
	286–21	Human procreation, *b·*, life, and
	321- 3	whose *b·* is less of a miracle than
Chr.	53–25	Yet wherefore signalize the *b·*
Ret.	40–15	at the *b·* of her last babe,
Po.	9- 6	at the *b·* of that beautiful boy.
My.	253–27	by education brightens into *b·*.

birthday
Mis.	225- 4	eighty-second *b·* of his mother
Po.	71–18	freedom's *b·* — blood-bought boon!
My.	148–12	February 22 — Washington's *b·*.

birthdays
Mis.	304–26	* *b·* of the "creators of liberty ;"
My.	235–26	meaningless commemoration of *b·*,

birthmark
'02.	2–23	kind of *b·*, to love the Church ;

birthplace
Pul.	48–14	* point out her own *b·*.
	58- 7	* in Concord, N. H., near her *b·*,
'02.	10–10	* *b·* of civilization is not Athens, but
My.	264–11	* *b·* of Thanksgiving Day,

birthright
Mis.	181 15	When we understand man's true *b·*,
Ret.	9–25	* redeemed her *b·* of the day,
My.	128–11	man's inalienable *b·* — *Liberty*.
	248–10	are they whose new-old *b·*
	283–13	find their *b·* in divine Science.

bishop
'01.	25- 9	the scholasticism of a *b·*,

bishops
Mis.	296- 5	not barmaids, but *b·*

bit
Mis.	159–23	a *b·* of what I said in 1890 :
	231–17	and *b·* the finger

bite
No.	43–27	envy and hatred bark and *b·* at its

bites
'00.	10- 1	Hatred *b·* the heel of love

biteth
Mis.	210–18	as it *b·* at the heel.

bits
My.	70–20	* replete with rare *b·* of art,

bitter
Mis.	27–19	sweet water and *b·*?" — *Jas.* 3 : 11.
	224–25	to neutralize what is *b·* in it,
Pul.	65–22	* one *b·* winter day,
'02.	9–27	Is it cause for *b·* comment
	11–19	gave our glorified Master a *b·* cup
Po.	1–16	Recalling oft the *b·* draft
	34–18	Bearing no *b·* memory at heart ;
My.	97–15	* *Zion's Herald*, a rather *b·* critic
	132–10	waters of Meribah here — *b·* waters ;
	230- 6	nutriment as both sweet and *b·*,
	230- 7	and *b·* in experience
	252- 5	which, if *b·* to sense,
	267–22	*b·* sense of lost opportunities
	350–17	this *b·* searing to the core of love ;

bitterly
My. 218–24 false faith that will end *b*.

bitterness
Mis. 287–26 it will spare you much *b*.
Pul. 84– 4 * wrong be robbed of her *b*
No. 7– 5 any root of *b* to spring up
'00. 14–17 Let no root of *b* spring up

Black, Rev. Hugh
'02. 10–10 Rev. Hugh *B* writes truly :

black
Mis. 210–24 tears the *b* mask from the
333– 8 basis that *b* is not a color
Un. 51– 7 never make one hair white or *b*,
Pul. 83–14 * under the *b* flag of oppression

blacken
My. 130– 8 effort of disloyal students to *b*

blackness
Ret. 69–25 "Above error's awful din, *b*,
Pul. 52–22 * *b* of the Dark Ages,

Blackstone
Mis. 340–14 forsook *B* for gray stone,
Rud. 1–16 *B* applies the word *personal*

blade
Mis. 195–23 He who never unsheathed his *b*
215–31 while the corn is in the *b*,
330–32 to put forth its slender *b*,
Ret. 92– 5 "first the *b*, — Mark 4 : 28.
'01. 35– 6 to bare our bosom to the *b*

Blair's Rhetoric
My. 304– 8 book title

blame
Pul. 80–20 * either to praise or *b*,
No. 43–26 Science often suffers *b* through

blamed
Mis. 111– 9 *b* others more than yourself.
236–27 *b* for all that is not right :

blameless
My. 40–31 * her own *b* and happy life,

blames
Mis. 374–30 he that perceives . . . *b* him not.

blanch
Mis. 395–18 Ere autumn *b* another year,
Po. 58– 3 Ere autumn *b* another year,

blanched
Ret. 31–23 *B* was the cheek of pride.

bland
Mis. 31– 2 is a *b* denial of Truth,

blank
Mis. 325–19 starts up in *b* amazement
Man. 37– 4 *b* has been properly filled out
111– 2 In filling out the application *b*,

blanketed
My. 89–14 * not *b* with debts

blasphemous
No. 18– 1 chapter sub-title
My. 302–20 I regard self-deification as *b*.

blasphemy
No. 18– 2 *B* has never diminished sin
18– 3 *B* rebukes not the godless lie

blast
Mis. 330–31 stoops meekly before the *b* ;

blasts
Mis. 384–11 The cold *b* done,
'00. 15–28 The cold *b* done,
Po. 36–10 The cold *b* done,
46– 4 Nor *b* of winter's angry storm,

blazoned
'02. 14–21 *b* on the forefront of the world
Po. 39–20 *b*, brilliant temperance hall

bleaching
Mis. 393–23 To my heart that would be *b*
Po. 52– 7 To my heart that would be *b*

bled
Ret. 2–16 "Scots wha hae wi' Wallace *b*."
Po. 15–19 pang in the bosom that *b*,

bleeding
Mis. 243–30 *b*, vomiting, death.
266– 1 struggle up, with *b* footprints,
275–15 binds up the wounds of *b* hearts,
Un. 58– 5 Jesus walked with *b* feet
No. 34–23 Love bruised and *b*,
Hea. 18–28 believe he was *b* to death.
19– 8 belief that he was *b* to death,
Po. 27–24 Hearts *b* ere they break
78–10 Tears of the *b* slave
My. 201–14 *b* brow of our blessed Lord,

blemish
Ret. 94–15 and every spot and *b* . . . is removed,
My. 197– 7 without spot or *b*.

blemished
My. 192– 5 make spotless the *b*,

blemishes
My. 121–17 Few *b* can be found in a true

blend
Mis. 387– 9 'Neath which our spirits *b*
No. 26– 3 that good and evil *b* ;
Po. 6– 3 'Neath which our spirits *b*
My. 291–27 Tears *b* with her triumphs.

blended
Mis. 237–18 *b* with the murmuring winds
Rud. 9– 6 more or less *b* with error ;

blending
'01. 25–24 contradictory as the *b* of good and
Hea. 5– 2 and of good and evil *b*.
My. 183–25 *b* with thine my prayer

blends
Chr. 53–37 faith's pale star now *b*
Pul. 76– 6 * *b* harmoniously with the
No. 14–10 *b* with its magic and enchantments.
Po. 3– 1 starlight *b* with morning's hue,

bless
Mis. 16– 3 so comfort, cheer, and *b* one,
32–29 should try to *b* their fellow-mortals.
127–22 inevitable condition . . . is to *b* others :
155– 6 Sacrifice self to *b* one another,
249–26 more tenderly to save and *b*.
273–12 God *b* my enemies, as well as
275–16 and *b* all who mourn.
320–11 *b* man as he reaches forth for
333–26 could heal and *b* ;
348–10 divine Love will *b* this
388–19 To *b* the orphan, feed the poor ;
394– 9 beautify, *b*, and make joyful again.
Ret. 11– 8 And live to *b* mankind.
21–24 but for . . . I *b* God.
Un. 60–13 "*b* we God, — Jas. 3 : 9.
Pul. 87–22 our states of mind, to *b* mankind.
No. 33– 3 lead us to *b* those who curse,
Pan. 9–18 spiritual endeavor to *b* others,
14–15 guide and *b* our chief magistrate,
Hea. 4–12 to *b* what is unfit to be blessed.
Po. 10–12 Returns to *b* a bridal
21– 8 *b* the orphan, feed the poor ;
33– 5 *b* me with Christ's promised rest ;
42–12 beautify, *b*, and make joyful again.
60– 5 And live to *b* mankind.
68– 3 "I'm living to *b* thee ;
My. 23– 7 * *b* us so long as we follow His
132–22 and *b* our enemies.
134–19 *b*, and inspire man's power.
143–23 when these things cease to *b*
158–24 will *b* this dear band of brethren.
185–27 * we *b* Thee, Our God,
194–26 May divine Love abundantly *b* you,
197–28 God will *b* the work of your hearts
202–29 God *b* this vine of His planting.
203–20 God *b* this dear church,
208–24 God *b* the courageous, far-seeing
209– 3 God will abundantly *b* this
220–21 I pray : "God *b* my enemies ;
253–24 in three words : God *b* you.
279–25 pray that God *b* that great nation
280–19 He will *b* all the inhabitants
280–22 Out of His allness He must *b* all
337–13 Returns to *b* a bridal
353–18 but to *b* all mankind.
360–22 God will *b* and prosper you.

Blessed
Mis. 337– 9 immaculate Son of the *B*

blessed
Mis. 8–22 "*B* are ye, when — Matt. 5 : 11.
8–29 "*B* are ye," — Matt. 5 : 11.
15– 7 "*B* are the pure — Matt. 5 : 8.
93– 4 posterity shall call you *b*,
127– 2 He has *b* her.
127–21 condition whereby to become *b*,
155– 7 even as God has *b* you.
185–21 reveals man infinitely *b*,
235–14 is he, whosoever — Matt. 11 : 6.
263– 8 How *b* it is to think of
325– 2 "*B* are the poor in — Matt. 5 : 3.
339–30 wisdom that might have *b* the past
Ret. 42– 2 was a *b* and spiritual union,
82– 7 practitioners of the same *b* faith.
84–22 posterity will call him *b*,
86–24 every man cared for and *b*.
Un. 3– 6 "*B* are the dead — Rev. 14 : 13.
30–16 the Messiah, our *b* Master,

blessed

Pul.	9–21	O glorious hope and b· assurance,
	15– 8	requires the spirit of our b· Master
	44– 9	* era in the b· onward work of C. S.
No.	33–14	The sacrifice of our b· Lord
'01.	3– 4	"B· are ye when — Matt. 5 : 11.
	7–28	b· are they that — John 20 : 29.
'02.	11–22	"B· are ye, when — Matt. 5 : 11.
Hea.	4–13	to bless what is unfit to be b·.
Peo.	12–20	Our b· Master demonstrated this
Po.	34–16	B· compared with me thou art
My.	3– 7	"B· are they that do — Rev. 22 : 14.
	13–31	their loving giving has been b·.
	17–30	He has b· her.
	21–26	* they too will be b·,
	25–21	I shall be with my b· church
	36–17	* with b· accord we are come,
	40–22	* "B· are the peacemakers : — Matt. 5 : 9.
	41– 7	* b· and comforted by divine Love.
	41–12	* "B· are the merciful," — Matt. 5 : 7.
	104–29	"B· are ye, when — Matt. 5 : 11.
	118–16	"B· are they that — John 20 : 29.
	143– 3	are b· in their results.
	158–24	God has b· and will bless this
	191–13	"B· are ye" — Matt. 5 : 11.
	199– 4	B· art thou.
	201–14	bleeding brow of our b· Lord,
	232– 8	mankind b·, and God glorified.
	274–23	I am cheered and b· when
	295– 3	b· assurance that life is not lost ;
	316– 6	"b· are ye, when — Matt. 5 : 11.
	328– 1	* God has dignified, b·, and
	345–16	came like b· relief to me,
	358– 4	you will be b· in your obedience.

blessedness

Mis.	209–26	goodness and b· are one :
	290–27	This individual b· and blessing
My.	40–11	* b· of peacemakers.
	41–13	* allow no one to escape that b·,
	41–24	* his real estate is one of b·.
	162–10	bond of b· such as my beloved
	208–15	in due expectation of just such b·,

blesses

Mis.	8–15	that b· infinitely one and all
	101– 5	that which b· its adoption by
	109–17	seeing the need of . . . b· mortals.
Pul.	21–13	which Christ organizes and b·.
Pan.	9–21	Christianity b· all mankind.
My.	151–14	when it no longer b· this

blessing

Mis.	11–23	and returning b· for cursing.
	18–30	Not to know what is b· you,
	132–22	I retire to seek the divine b·
	134–13	God will pour you out a b·
	139– 5	God will pour you out a b·
	212–12	they received the b·.
	278–16	always a b· to the human race.
	290–27	individual blessedness and b·
	291–19	I would part with a b·
	351– 5	of b· even my enemies.
Un.	60–16	b· and cursing. — Jas. 3 : 10.
Pul.	10–27	breathe Thou Thy b· on
	14–23	Those ready for the b· you impart
	74–18	and the b· it has been to mankind
'00.	8– 9	a b· or a bane upon individuals
'01.	2–19	b· the poor in spirit
	34–20	return b· for cursing ;
'02.	17– 9	is in b· others, and self-immolation
	19– 6	lifting up his hands and b· them,
My.	4–11	b· saint and sinner
	14– 4	b· above the song of angels,
	14– 5	a b· that two millions of
	21–19	* will receive a greater b·
	34– 6	He shall receive the b· — Psal. 24 : 5.
	52– 4	* b· them that curse her,
	66–25	* giving her b· to the structure.
	131–28	pour you out a b·, — Mal. 3 : 10.
	131–30	this great, great b· ;
	132– 5	pour you out a b·," — Mal. 3 : 10.
	154–11	that confers the b·,
	165– 7	I returned b· for cursing.
	165–16	goodness makes life a b·.
	182–15	through God's b· and the faithful
	192–14	May the b· of divine Love
	201– 1	God is b· you, my beloved students
	203–21	if it is ready for the b·.
	209– 6	faith in the b· of fidelity,
	224– 7	the b· which follows obedience
	253–24	you have His rich b· already
	258–26	hallowed by our Lord's b·.
	269–23	pouring out b· for cursing,
	269–28	pour you out a b·, — Mal. 3 : 10.
	297–16	rich b· of disbelief in death,
	323–23	* b· those who would destroy you

blessings

attest the

Mis.	35– 8	attest the b· of this mental system

beautiful as

Mis.	356– 1	radiant sunset, beautiful as b·

brings

Mis.	85– 3	Life eternal brings b·.

filled with

No.	15– 7	filled with b· for the whole human

infinite

Mis.	56–24	and brings b· infinite.
	100–25	crown them with b· infinite.
	238–15	fraught with infinite b·,
Pul.	9–29	and call down b· infinite.
'01.	15–15	infinite b· that divine Love bestows
	31–20	Among the list of b· infinite
My.	281– 8	Faith . . . brings b· infinite,
	354–16	O b· infinite ! O glad New Year !

manifold

My.	262–32	and gives manifold b·.

my

Po.	33– 1	daily remember my b·

of the infinite

My.	118–21	supply the b· of the infinite,

our

My.	256–21	We count our b·

recognition of

My.	352– 1	* chapter sub-title

recognition of the

My.	352– 6	* express our recognition of the b·

rehearsal of

Man.	47–15	More than a mere rehearsal of b·,

rich

Mis.	165–27	to avail himself of the rich b·
My.	132–18	Oh, may these rich b· continue

richest

Mis.	166–28	diffusing richest b·.
My.	149–17	richest b· are obtained by labor.

spreadst

Po.	77– 8	b· spreadst abroad,

temporal

'01.	24–11	* greatest of all temporal b·,

which arose

Ret.	50–28	b· which arose therefrom.

Ret.	78–23	is to conspire against the b·
My.	42–17	* b· which have come into my life
	52– 9	* our indebtedness . . . for these b·,

blest

Mis.	106–13	On to the b· above,
	109–16	Ignorance is only b· by reason of
	205–30	lives on, God-crowned and b·.
	207– 3	heart meets heart reciprocally b·,
	212–12	When they were fit to be b·,
	385– 6	And I am b· !
	386–29	with all the crowned and b·,
Chr.	53– 2	Bright, b·, afar,
	53–49	As in b· Palestina's hour,
Po.	11– 1	Brave Britain, b· America !
	17– 1	B· beings departed !
	29– 1	B· Christmas morn, though murky
	30–15	shadows cast on Thy b· name,
	34– 3	soul of melody by being b·
	37– 6	And I am b· !
	44– 2	Crown the lives thus b·
	50–16	with all the crowned and b·,
My.	31– 5	"B· Christmas morn ;"
	170–28	to kneel with us . . . in b· communion
	202– 1	springs exultant on this b· morn.
	234– 2	Are the holidays b· by
	250–28	make man's being pure and b·.
	257–22	by the branch churches will be b·.
	338– 1	Brave Britain, b· America !

blight

Mis.	88– 1	tends to b· the fruits of
Chr.	53–57	No b·, no broken wing,

blighted

Mis.	360–18	b· flowers of fleeting joys,

blights

Ret.	7–22	* It b· too many hopes ;

blind

Mis.	22–25	and the b·, healed by it,
	66–28	yea, it is "the b· — Matt. 15 : 14.
	66–29	leading the b·." — see Matt. 15 : 14.
	107–24	may become morally b·,
	134–28	but, b· to its own fate,
	168– 4	b·, spiritually and physically,
	170–24	Jesus' proceedings with the b· man
	171– 5	and the b· saw clearly.
	171– 6	anoint the b· man's eyes
	181– 8	requirement of b· obedience
	210–30	Love opens the eyes of the b·,
	211–6, 7	else the b· will lead the b·
	234– 2	remain no longer to b· us

blind

Mis. 241–24   Then, like *b·* Bartimeus,
     242– 9   give sight to one born *b·*.
     244–20   make the *b·* to see,
     258– 7   he restored sight to the *b·*,
     275– 2   "Ye fools and *b·* !" — *Matt.* 23 : 17.
     301–28   harden the heart, *b·* the eyes,
     307–17   opening the eyes of the *b·*
     326– 8   where the *b·* saw them not,
     345–14   Methinks the infidel was *b·*
     362– 8   Scholastic dogma has made men *b·*.
     362– 9   gives sight to these *b·*,
     368– 5   open the eyes of the *b·*,
     370–19   chapter sub-title
     375– 2   *b·* with animality,
Ret.   54–15   *B·* belief cannot say with the
Un.   10–25   He is not the *b·* force of a material
Pul.   55– 1   * "Not in *b·* caprice of will,
No.   8–23   who is too *b·* for instruction,
     20–26   Human reason is a *b·* guide,
'01.   17–15   I healed the deaf, the *b·*,
Hea.   18–24   no *b·* Samson shorn of his locks.
Peo.   11–12   The lame, the *b·*, the sick,
     13–23   The infidel was *b·* who said,
My.   22–11   * let us not be unconsciously *b·*
     105–17   restored sight to the *b·*,
     110–22   solve the *b·* problem of matter.
     140– 2   "And I will bring the *b·* — *Isa.* 42 : 16.
     152–18, 19   the *b·* is leading the *b·*,
     153–22   This trembling and *b·* faith,
     183–20   eyes of the *b·* see out of obscurity.
     224–15   *b·* to his loss of the Golden Rule,
     270–27   opening the eyes of the *b·*
     311– 4   a girl, totally *b·*, knocked
     311– 8   * "If this *b·* girl stays
     311–10   to turn the *b·* girl out,

blinded

Mis. 332–20   *b·* the eyes of reason,

blinding

Rud.   17– 5   *b·* the people to the true character

blindly

Ret.   27–18   * Groping *b·* in the darkness,
My.   350–16   anguish which they *b·* bind

blindness

Ret.   54–14   Belief is virtually *b·*,
Un.   6–19   God's *b·* to error and
My.   80– 5   * they had been cured of *b·*,

Bliss

Mis. 153–29   * Far-off, infinite, *B·* !

bliss

Mis.   19–32   spiritual sense . . . of itself a *b·*,
     83– 2   rhythmic round of unfolding *b·*,
     160– 9   meet and mingle in *b·* supernal.
     263–14   and reflect all *b·*.
     287–12   Soul is the infinite source of *b·* :
     328– 9   which from the summit of *b·*
     330–12   possibilities are infinite, *b·* is eternal,
     344– 7   aught of that which leads to *b·*,
     352– 1   it mocks the *b·* of spiritual being ;
     386–30   to reap, . . . Of *b·* the sum.
Ret.   17– 8   and tremble with accents of *b·*.
     49–16   the *b·* of loving unselfishly,
Un.   57–17   gospel of suffering brought life and *b·*.
Pul. vii–21   the actual *b·* of man's existence
Rud. 14–10   except the *b·* of doing good.
'01.   35–15   And the *b·* of blotted-out sin
Po.   22– 9   *b·* that wipes the tears of time
     31–15   Nor burdened *b·*, but Truth and Love
     50–17   Of *b·* the sum.
     62– 8   tremble with accents of *b·*.
     67– 1   *b·* of life's little day
My.   120–10   *b·* of seeing the risen Christ,
     192– 4   possession of unburdened *b·*.
     267–17   infinite, boundless *b·*.

bloated

Mis. 123–10   pagan priests *b·* with crime ;
Po.   27– 3   *B·* oppression in its awful hour,

block

Peo.   7– 9   * With his marble *b·* before him ;
My.   65–19   * *b·* bounded by Falmouth, Norway, and
     66– 4   * the ownership of the entire *b·*.
     66–10   * the ownership of the entire *b·*.
     66–14   * No *b·* is so well situated for

blood

bayonet and
Peo. 11– 8   not with bayonet and *b·*,
besmeared with
Mis. 274–29   the streets besmeared with *b·*.
brave
Pul. 48–25   * of blue and brave *b·*,
his
Mis. 65–31   shall his *b·* be shed." — *Gen.* 9 : 6.
My. 156–22   "drink of his *b·*'" — see *John* 6 : 53.

blood

human
No. 33–18   human *b·* was inadequate to
     33–20   shedding human *b·* brought to light
     34–20   conception that God requires human *b·*
innocent
Mis. 121–17   the guilt of innocent *b·* — *Deut.* 19 : 13.
man's
Mis. 65–31   "whoso sheddeth man's *b·* — *Gen.* 9 : 6.
of Christ
No. 33–18   to represent the *b·* of Christ,
     34–18   *b·* of Christ speaketh better things
     34–26   significance of the *b·* of Christ.
of Jesus
No. 35– 1   This *b·* of Jesus is everything to
of martyrs
Mis. 121–12   *b·* of martyrs was believed to be
     326–13   licking up the *b·* of martyrs
of the Lamb
Mis. 358–16   in the *b·* of the Lamb ;" — *Rev.* 7 : 14.
Pul. 12– 9   by the *b·* of the Lamb, — *Rev.* 12 : 11.
Peo. 9–10   in the *b·* of the Lamb ;
of the martyrs
My. 125–31   *b·* of the martyrs of Jesus," — *Rev.* 17 : 6.
     177–17   * *b·* of the martyrs is the seed of
of the saints
My. 125–31   with the *b·* of the saints, — *Rev.* 17 : 6.
real
No. 34–22   The real *b·* or Life of Spirit
stained with
'02. 10– 9   footprints . . . are stained with *b·*.
     14– 9   * not like Cæsar, stained with *b·*,
My. 248– 5   * not like Cæsar, stained with *b·*,
young
Pul. 7– 2   * "Had I young *b·* in my veins,

Mis. 180–23   *were born, not of b·*, — *John* 1 : 13.
     182–14   were born, not of *b·*, — *John* 1 : 13.
     246–27   again deluge the earth in *b·* ?
     327–32   wipes away the *b·* stains,
     345–25   baptism not of water but of *b·*,
No. 34–27   *b·*, . . . purchasing the freedom of
Po. 22–21   and *b·* was not its price.

blood-bought

Po. 71–18   freedom's birthday — *b·* boon !

bloodgiving

No. 37–15   as a personal and material *b·*

bloodless

My. 124–12   *b·* sieges and tearless triumphs,

bloodshed

My. 285–10   *B·*, war, and oppression belong to

bloom

Mis.   x– 1   coloring glory of perpetual *b·* ;
     329–17   * "breath all odor and cheek all *b·*."
     389– 1   To form the bud for bursting *b·*,
Chr. 53–31   Sharon's rose must bud and *b·*
Po. 21–15   To form the bud for bursting *b·*,
     46–10   Thus may it ripen into *b·*,

Bloomington, Ill.

Pul. 89–35   * *Leader, B·, I·*.

blossom

Mis. 142– 3   to bud and *b·* as the rose !
     227–18   fresh flowers of feeling *b·*,
Ret. 17–20   Its feathery *b·* and branches
     18– 5   colored softly by *b·* and leaves ;
     95– 2   will *b·* into greater freedom,
Un. 52–24   The most beautiful *b·* is often
Po. 15–16   Here smileth the *b·* and sunshine
     63– 7   Its feathery *b·* and branches
     63–13   colored softly by *b·* and leaves ;
     67–21   flowers of feeling may *b·* above,
My. 129–12   brook, *b·*, breeze, and balm
     201–11   repeat my legacies in *b·*.

blossomed

Pul. 22–21   budded and *b·* as the rose.
My. 141–28   *b·* into spiritual beauty,

blossoming

'02. 1–10   and *b·* as the rose.

blossoms

Mis. 332–15   stately palms, many-hued *b·*,
Pul. 4–19   crown the tree with *b·*.
Peo. 14– 4   amaranth *b·*, evergreen leaves,
Po. 16– 4   hath thy verdure, it *b·* above ;
     32– 5   *b·* whose fragrance and charms
My. 155–29   beautiful *b·* in their Leader's love,
     160–13   with *b·* on its branches
     258–21   *b·* that mock their hope

blot

Mis. 246– 5   to *b·* out all inhuman codes.
Ret. 86–15   should be no *b·* on the escutcheon of
No. 7– 9   and *b·* it out of others.
'01. 5–16   We do not *b·* out the material race

blot
    '01. 20–21 cannot *b·* out its effects on himself
blots
    Mis. 102–20 which *b·* out all our iniquities
blotted
    Pan. 14–25 *b·* out the Spanish squadron.
blotted-out
    '01. 35–15 And the bliss of *b·* sin
blow
    '02. 15– 2 contained threats to *b·* up the hall
    Po. 10–21 His hand averts the *b·*."
    My. 51–11 * would be a serious *b·* to her Cause
    337–22 His hand averts the *b·*."
blowing
    '01. 29–19 adverse winds are *b·*,
blows
    My. 297– 5 knowing that she can bear the *b·*
    297–13 *b·* away the baubles of belief,
blue
    Mis. 87– 1 clear ether of the *b·* temporal sky.
    330–28 violet lifts its *b·* eye to heaven,
    376–25 faint, fairy *b·* and golden flecks
    Pul. 32– 2 * and lighted by luminous *b·* eyes,
    48–25 * of *b·* and brave blood,
    Po. 67–19 like the *b·* hyacinth,
    74– 5 O *b·* eyes and jet,
    My. 110–18 higher in the boundless *b·*.
blue-gray
    My. 342–13 * whether *b·* or grayish brown,
blunder
    Mis. 285– 6 by a *b·* of the gentleman who
    My. 228– 5 Evil minds signally *b·*
blunders
    Ret. 81–17 *b·* which arise from wrong
blush
    Mis. 296–32 *his* shame would not lose its *b·* !
    Ret. 88–22 *b·* to enter unasked
    Pan. 1– 9 roseate *b·* of joyous June
    My. 115– 4 I should *b·* to write of
boa-constrictor
    Mis. 62– 6 holding in thought the form of a *b·*
Board
    Mis. 131–18 *B·* did not act under that By-law ;
    Man. 26–21 a vacancy occurring on that *B·*
    26–25 the discussions of this *B·*,
    27–10 the written consent of said *B·*.
    30–18 *B·* shall attend to the insurance
    51–24 Only the members of this *B·*
    52– 7 shall be laid before this *B·*,
    52–15 shall be deemed sufficient by the *B·*.
    57–15 must have the consent of this *B·*
    69–14 If the author . . . call on this *B·*
    69–15 the *B·* shall immediately appoint
    78– 8 vacancy supplied by the *B·*.
    80–15 such reasons as to the *B·* may
    84–20 Outside of this *B·* each student
    88–14 elected every third year by said *B·*,
    88–19 applying for admission to this *B·*
    90– 4 given certificates by this *B·*
    90– 7 ACTION OF THE *B·*.
    90–16 under the auspices of this *B·*.
    95–13 shall be assigned them by the *B·*.
    95–15 a member of the *B·* may lecture
    100–22 privilege of this *B·* to name the
    100–24 any Committee so named by the *B·*
    101– 4 *B·* shall, . . . appoint an assistant
    Ret. 48–12 *B·* of the Metaphysical College
    My. 62–27 * services rendered to this *B·*
board
    Mis. 231–32 vacant seat at fireside and *b·*.
    Man. 68–12 in addition to rent and *b·*.
    My. 73–22 * concerning rooms and *b·*,
    128– 6 coroner's inquest, a *b·* of health,
    329– 6 * The *b·* only excused them from
    329– 7 * *b·* of medical examiners.
    340–13 a simple *b·* of health,
boarded
    My. 315– 3 * *b·* with me in Littleton,
    323–29 * Mr. Snider and myself *b·* in the
boarding
    '02. 15– 7 rooming and *b·* indigent students
boarding-houses
    My. 82– 9 * Hotels, *b·*, and private houses
Board of Directors
Christian Science
    Mis. 126–17 obedience of the C. S. *B·* of *D·* ;
    130–17 C. S. *B·* of *D·* has borne
    131–13 have the C. S. *B·* of *D·* itemize
    131–29 C. S. *B·* of *D·* to itemize
    Man. 25–18 incorporation of the "C. S. *B·* of *D·*."

Board of Directors
Christian Science
    Man. 26– 9 vote of the C. S. *B·* of *D·*
    26–20 C. S. *B·* of *D·* shall consist of
    27– 3 transacted by its C. S. *B·* of *D·*.
    27–12 duty of the C. S. *B·* of *D·*
    27–19 duty of the C. S. *B·* of *D·*
    28–14 duty of the C. S. *B·* of *D·*
    29– 7 If the C. S. *B·* of *D·* fails
    35–14 signed by the C. S. *B·* of *D·*
    38–12 vote of the C. S. *B·* of *D·*
    39–15 vote of the C. S. *B·* of *D·*.
    51–21 C. S. *B·* of *D·* has power
    56–19 meeting of the C. S. *B·* of *D·*,
    63–22 elected by the C. S. *B·* of *D·*,
    65–22 vote of the C. S. *B·* of *D·*,
    68–20 through the C. S. *B·* of *D·*
    68–24 When the C. S. *B·* of *D·* calls a
    75– 5 C. S. *B·* of *D·*, in behalf of
    75–13 between the C. S. *B·* of *D·*
    75–16 C. S. *B·* of *D·* owns the
    76– 8 duty of the C. S. *B·* of *D·*
    76–19 annually by the C. S. *B·* of *D·*
    77– 1 books of the C. S. *B·* of *D·*
    79– 2 C. S. *B·* of *D·* shall elect
    80– 8 order of the C. S. *B·* of *D·*,
    80–13 C. S. *B·* of *D·* shall have the power
    81– 3 vote of the C. S. *B·* of *D·*,
    81– 7 not accepted by . . . the C. S. *B·* of *D·*
    82–13 vote of the C. S. *B·* of *D·*
    85–22 approval of The C. S. *B·* of *D·*,
    88–12 annually by the C. S. *B·* of *D·*.
    89– 5 meeting of the C. S. *B·* of *D·*
    95– 4 C. S. *B·* of *D·* . . . may call
    97–11 vote of the C. S. *B·* of *D·*
    99–17 elected only by the C. S. *B·* of *D·*.
    99–20 appointed by the C. S. *B·* of *D·*,
    100–13 apparent to the C. S. *B·* of *D·*,
    100–16 The C. S. *B·* of *D·* may notify
    101– 1 any time the C. S. *B·* of *D·* shall
    Pul. 9– 4 Brothers of the C. S. *B·* of *D·*
    59–24 * members of the C. S. *B·* of *D·*
    85–25 * from the C. S. *B·* of *D·*,
    86– 6 * her . . . Students, the C. S. *B·* of *D·*."
    87– 9 * signature
    '02. 13–30 to be known as "The C. S. *B·* of *D·*."
    My. 16–14 * members of the C. S. *B·* of *D·*,
    18–28 members of the C. S. *B·* of *D·*.
    21–32 * signature
    26– 3 * C. S. *B·* of *D·* takes pleasure in
    63– 7 * signature
    142–25 chapter sub-title
    223–24 addressed to the C. S. *B·* of *D·*
    242–20 should be sent to the C. S. *B·* of *D·*
    358–31 and require the C. S. *B·* of *D·* to

    Mis. 131–13 If our *D·* of *D·* is prepared to itemize
    Man. 25– 5 a *B·* of *D·*, a President,
    25–10 elected, . . . by the *B·* of *D·*
    26–14 elected . . . by the *B·* of *D·*,
    27– 8 consulting with the full *B·* of *D·*
    28–19 the *B·* of *D·* shall immediately call
    29– 2 to inform the *B·* of *D·*
    29–16 The salary . . . of the *B·* of *D·*
    30– 8 majority vote of the *B·* of *D·*
    30–16 The *B·* of *D·* shall pay from
    36–22 unanimous vote of the *B·* of *D·*
    50–10 the consent of the *B·* of *D·*.
    50–18 a meeting of the *B·* of *D·*
    53– 3 duty of the *B·* of *D·*
    54– 2 and if, . . . the *B·* of *D·* finds
    55–17 *B·* of *D·* may decide if his loyalty
    56– 2 duty of the *B·* of *D·* to admonish
    56–17 Meetings of *B·* of *D·*.
    57–11 *B·* of *D·* and the Pastor Emeritus
    62– 5 hymn selected by the *B·* of *D·*.
    67–26 *B·* of *D·* shall immediately notify
    77–13 shall be the duty of the *B·* of *D·*
    77–25 shall visit the *B·* of *D·*,
    78–13 sanctioned by the *B·* of *D·*
    78–24 reported, . . . to the *B·* of *D·* and
    104–13 *B·* of *D·*, the Committee on
    Ret. 47–12 *B·* of *D·* of my College,
    Pul. 43–10 * who compose the *B·* of *D·*,
    86–14 * address from the *B·* of *D·*
    My. 26– 8 chapter sub-title
    61–32 * earnest work of our noble *B·* of *D·*.
    76– 6 * became evident to the *B·* of *D·*
    199–10 *B·* of *D·* and Trustees of this church

Board of Education
    Man. 35– 5 by a student of the *B·* of *E·*,
    36– 8 loyal students . . . in the *B·* of *E·*,
    36–10 examination by the *B·* of *E·*,
    38– 6 or a student of the *B·* of *E·*
    65–15 duty . . . of the *B·* of *E·*
    84–10 After 1907, the *B·* of *E·* shall have

Board of Education

Man. 84–26 except it be in the *B· of E·*.
85–16 has taken . . . in the *B· of E·*.
88– 1 heading
88– 4 There shall be a *B· of E·*,
89– 6 vice-president of the *B· of E·*
89–20 may apply to the *B· of E·*
90–10 will open with the *B· of E·*
91– 8 class instruction in the *B· of E·*
91–16 left in the hands of the *B· of E·*
91–23 Normal class in the *B· of E·*
92– 2 Metaphysical College *B· of E·*.
109– 8 students of the *B· of E·*
My. 125–19 The members of the *B· of E·*,
240–29 * certificates from . . . the *B· of E·*,
246– 7 examined . . . by the *B· of E·*,
246–10 chapter sub-title
246–22 *B· of E·* of The Mother Church
251– 9 * class instruction in the *B· of E·*
251–12 after examination in the *B· of E·*,
251–14 taught in the *B· of E·* only.
251–17 mode of instruction in the *B· of E·*.
251–21 examined in the *B· of E·*,
253–19 chapter sub-title
254–17 your article "C. S. *B· of E·*"

Board of Lectureship

Man. 41–15 in the Church or on the *B· of L·*,
73–19 member of the *B· of L·* may lecture
93– 1 heading
93– 5 shall maintain a *B· of L·*,
93–11 It is the duty of the *B· of L·*
93–19 *B· of L·* is not allowed in any wise
95– 6 any member of this *B· of L·*
95–11 to a member of this *B· of L·*
95–18 shall call on the *B· of L·*
96– 2 The *B· of L·* shall not appoint
'02. 4– 5 congratulate our *B· of L·*,
My. 125–12 to the members of our *B· of L·*
248– 1 chapter sub-title
338–15 The members of the *B· of L·*
338–28 *B· of L·* is absolutely inclined to
339– 7 *B· of L·* is specially requested to

Board of Trustees

Man. 79–18 *B· of T·*.
79–18 The *B· of T·*, constituted by
104–14 *B· of T·* shall each keep a copy
My. 135–13 caused me to select a *B· of T·*
136–14 *B· of T·* who own my property :
137–21 influenced me to select a *B· of T·*
360– 8 To the *B· of T·*, First Church of
361–23 * signature
362– 2 Charles A. Dean, Chairman *B· of T·*,

Boards

Man. 27–26 *B·* of Trustees and Syndicates
66–26 either to the *B·* or to the executive

boards

My. 256–24 the festive *b·* are spread,

boast

Pul. 83–22 * It is the proudest *b·* of many
My. 37– 2 * No vainglorious *b·*, . . . has place
161–22 We cannot *b·* ourselves of to-morrow ;
192– 2 *B·* not thyself,

boasted

My. 149–14 a young man vainly *b·*,

boastful

Ret. 86– 2 to offset *b·* emptiness,
Un. 11–13 *b·* sense of physical law
27–13 evil is *egotistic*, — *b·*,

boasting

Mis. 243–17 *B·* is unbecoming
Un. 11–17 cut off this vain *b·*

boasts

Mis. 330–26 mendicant that *b·* and begs,

boat

Mis. 142– 6 chapter sub-title
142– 7 on receipt of a beautiful *b·*
142– 9 The *b·* displays, . . . a number of
142–12 thanks for the beautiful *b·*
142–22 A *b·* song seemed more Olympian
142–26 symbols . . . depicted on the *b·*
143– 5 in beautifying this *b·*

boatbuilder

Un. 14–10 as Burgess, the *b·*, remedies

bodies

Mis. 7– 4 until their *b·* become dry,
60–25 *as many identities as mortal b·?*
61–26 (or *b·*, if you please)
76–12 the *b·* of mortals are mortal,
76–13 hence these *b·* must die
184–10 speaking of presenting our *b·*
240–30 that it takes from their *b·* a
Man. 66–26 the Boards or to the executive *b·*

bodies

Pul. 50–24 * so-called orthodox religious *b·*
Rud. 12–26 subordination to their *b·*,
Peo. 10–23 The emancipation of our *b·*
11–18 the laws that govern their *b·*,
My. 100–13 * organization among religious *b·*,
301–23 on mortal minds and *b·*.

bodily

Mis. 244–12 *b·* penance and torture,
309–23 a *b·* form of existence,
352–16 *b·* belief of the patient
Ret. 57–13 causes all *b·* ailments,
Rud. 1–16 applies . . . to *b· presence*,
3– 3 to heal them of *b·* ills,
My. 110–19 if waking to *b·* sensation
110–19 if *b·* sensation makes us captives

Bodwell, Miss Sarah J.

My. 304– 3 a pupil of Miss Sarah J. *B·*,

body

ablution of the
Peo. 9– 4 not an ablution of the *b·*,
absent from the
Mis. 344–22 absent from the *b·*, — *II Cor.* 5 : 8.
'00. 1– 5 absent from the *b·* and present with
My. 118–14 "absent from the *b·*," — *II Cor.* 5 : 8.
301–29 If mind be absent from the *b·*,
action of the
Peo. 8–18 governs every action of the *b·*
ailments of the
Mis. 6–28 confined to the ailments of the *b·*,
and brain
Po. 47–13 The weary of *b·* and brain
and Mind
Mis. 86–21 the harmony of *b·* and Mind.
and mind
Mis. 163–29 spiritual healing of *b·* and mind.
241– 3 *B·* and mind are correlated
268–19 heals *b·* and mind, head and heart ;
and soul
Mis. 354–19 *b·* and soul in accord with God.
believe that the
Mis. 5–31 believe that the *b·* affects the mind,
247–25 to believe that the *b·* affects mind,
benefit the
Mis. 241– 3 steadfastly in God to benefit the *b·*,
controls the
Mis. 5–24 reality that Mind controls the *b·*.
diseased
My. 218– 1 He restored the diseased *b·* to its
disease in the
Mis. 343– 6 turn from disease in the *b·*
disease on the
Hea. 6–14 mind produces disease on the *b·*,
does not see
Rud. 5–19 The *b·* does not see, hear, smell, or
entire
My. 30–31 * representative of the entire *b·* of
45–11 * only a small part of the entire *b·*
everywhere-present
No. 20–16 notion of an everywhere-present *b·*
finite
No. 20–16 or of . . . starting from a finite *b·*,
function of the
Hea. 19– 5 every function of the *b·*,
get into the
Mis. 240–13 If a cold could get into the *b·*
give to the
Peo. 7–26 give to the *b·* those better
governed
Hea. 14–28 a *b·* governed by this mind.
governs the
Hea. 14–14 to know that mind governs the *b·*
harmonious
Mis. 256– 5 in order to make the *b·* harmonious.
his
Mis. 201– 9 Jesus reproduced his *b·*
355–24 that makes his *b·* sick,
Ret. 57– 7 in order to heal his *b·*.
Hea. 6–19 disease controls his *b·*
6–22 produce a result upon his *b·*.
his own
Ret. 88– 6 He lifted his own *b·* from the
Un. 55– 6 "in his own *b·* — *I Pet.* 2 : 24.
honorable
Mis. 136–23 session of this honorable *b·*
139– 1 I recommend this honorable *b·*
human
My. 218– 7 destruction of the human *b·*,
improve the
Ret. 34–21 renovated to improve the *b·*.
inside of
Mis. 344–17 would place Soul wholly inside of *b·*,
instead of
Mis. 16–25 from Soul instead of *b·*,
237– 4 mortal mind instead of *b·* :

body

in the
  Rud. 13–19 to treat every organ in the *b*.

is an expression
  Mis. 247–26 *b*· is an expression of mind,

is dead
  Chr. 55–16 the *b*· is dead because of— *Rom.* 8: 10.

is governed
  Mis. 34– 6 *b*· is governed by mind ;
  256– 3 *b*· is governed by Mind,

is renewed
  Mis. 34– 7 before the *b*· is renewed

is the servant
  Mis. 47–18 *b*· is the servant of Mind,

its
  Peo. 11– 6 can free its *b*· from disease

its own
  Un. 45–19 telephones over its own *b*·,

limited
  Mis. 102– 7 could originate in a limited *b*·,
  No. 19–12 a limited mind nor a limited *b*·.
  Hea. 4– 2 cannot start from a limited *b*·.

manifest on the
  Mis. 219–26 made manifest on the *b*·,
  Ret. 61– 4 made manifest on the *b*·

man's
  Mis. 198–19 We know that man's *b*·, as matter,

material
  (*see* **material**)

matter, or the
  My. 349– 7 self-evident that matter, or the *b*·,

mind affects the
  Mis. 5–32 the mind affects the *b*.

Mind and
  No. 40–20 obstruct the harmony of Mind and *b*·,

mind and
  (*see* **mind**)

mind or
  Mis. 59–25 away from the human mind or *b*·,
  97–28 a perfect man in mind or *b*·,
  103–22 either as mind or *b*·,
  341– 2 right action of mind or *b*·.

mind over
  Hea. 19– 2 to test the power of mind over *b*· ;

mortal
  Mis. 75–14 not in matter or the mortal *b*·.
  Ret. 34–19 mortal *b*· being but the objective
  Un. 28– 3 Is it a reality within the mortal *b*·?
  Hea. 18– 2 both mortal mind and mortal *b*·

my
  Ret. 10– 2 too large for my *b*·

not in the
  Mis. 75– 7 *and that Soul is not in the b*·

of a female
  Man. 50– 3 the *b*· of a female shall be

of a subject
  Rud. 15–25 *b*· of a subject laid bare for

of believers
  My. 95–11 * prosperous *b*· of believers

of Christ
  My. 126– 1 the *b*· of Christ, Truth ;
  131– 7 For the *b*· of Christ,

of mind or of
  Hea. 9–25 either an error of mind or of *b*·.

of people
  Mis. 312–16 * *b*· of people known as . . . Scientists,
  My. 95–18 * well-dressed *b*· of people.
  99–11 * optimistic *b*· of people,

of Scientists
  My. 30–31 * great *b*· of Scientists joined in

of the church
  My. 38–18 * seats in the *b*· of the church,
  80–30 * in the main *b*· of the church,

of the holy Spirit
  Mis. 70–24 *b*· of the holy Spirit of Jesus was

of the infinite
  Hea. 3–27 the *b*· of the infinite,

one
  My. 316– 2 uniting in one *b*· those who

on the
  Un. 39– 2 is rendered practical on the *b*·.
  Rud. 10–15 thought manifested on the *b*· ;
  Hea. 7– 4 harmonious effect on the *b*·.
  Peo. 7– 3 impress of mind on the *b*·

our own
  Peo. 10–21 We possess our own *b*·,

over the
  Peo. 13–17 triumph of mind over the *b*·,

parts of the
  Rud. 12– 2 nor manipulates the parts of the *b*·

poor
  My. 132–30 heals the poor *b*·,

receptivity of the
  Mis. 229–13 governing the receptivity of the *b*·,

reconstructed the
  Ret. 28–22 Mind reconstructed the *b*·,

body

reconstructed the
  Pul. 35–21 Mind reconstructed the *b*·,

redemption of our
  Mis. 15– 6 redemption of our *b*·."— *Rom.* 8: 23.
  95–23 the redemption of our *b*·,"— *Rom.* 8: 23.
  Peo. 10–26 redemption of our *b*·."— *Rom.* 8: 23.

redemption of the
  Mis. 182–11 the redemption of the *b*·.

reflects God in
  Mis. 184– 7 when man reflects God in *b*·

refresh the
  Peo. 9– 6 The cool bath may refresh the *b*·,

religious
  Ret. 15– 4 My connection with this religious *b*·
  Pul. 50–26 * No one religious *b*· holds the
  My. 49– 5 * The religious *b*· which can direct,

resuscitating the
  My. 293–17 resuscitating the *b*· of the patient.

saviour of the
  My. 108–30 is the saviour of the *b*·."— *Eph.* 5: 23.

scientific
  My. 59–12 * every religious and scientific *b*·

sense of the
  Mis. 47–15 In sleep, a sense of the *b*·

sick
  No. 29–12 * forgiven soul in a sick *b*·

Soul and
  No. 29– 5 false sense of Soul and *b*·.

Soul is not in
  Un. 51–27 whose Soul is not in *b*·,

soulless
  Ret. 74– 5 *corpus sine pectore* (soulless *b*·),

Spirit controls
  Mis. 247–20 understand that Spirit controls *b*·.

spiritual
  My. 218–11 *spiritual b*·, the incorporeal idea,

subjugating the
  '02. 10–13 subjugating the *b*·, subduing matter,

that
  Mis. 312–12 his remarks before that *b*·,
  Ret. 13– 3 having been members of that *b*·

thief's
  Mis. 70–22 The thief's *b*·, as matter,

this
  Mis. 44–20 You call this *b*· matter,

to heal the
  Hea. 7–15 begins in mind to heal the *b*·,

turns to the
  Mis. 101–19 He who turns to the *b*· for

upbuilding of the
  Mis. 169–13 was the upbuilding of the *b*·.

upon the
  Mis. 7–21 depicted in . . . time upon the *b*·,
  70– 6 healing action of Mind upon the *b*·
  Rud. 3 22 manifestation of Truth upon the *b*·
  Hea. 18– 1 destroy their effects upon the *b*·,
  My. 301–30 no curative effect upon the *b*·.

was interred
  My. 333–13 * where the *b*· was interred

whole
  My. 196–13 bridle the whole *b*·."— *Jas.* 3: 2,

your
  Mis. 47–10 when moving your *b*·,
  Man. 47–12 "Glorify God in your *b*·,— *I Cor.* 6: 20.
  My. 139–27 redeem your *b*· from disease ;

  Mis. 3–22 and imparts these states to the *b*· ;
  42–12 not attained by the death of the *b*·,
  76– 9 mortal belief that soul is in *b*·,
  76–21 the so-called soul in the *b*·,
  209–21 without Mind the *b*· is without action ;
  Ret. 61–25 it cannot be found in the *b*·.
  Pul. 82– 1 * make the *b*· not the prison, but the
  Rud. 5–11 who has ever found Soul in the *b*·
  Peo. 4– 6 materialized into a *b*·,
  11–20 while the *b*·, obedient to
  My. 74–21 * intelligent and a happy appearing *b*·,
  91– 1 * immense membership of the *b*· is
  119–31 away from person— from *b*· to Soul,
  217–19 * and not the *b*· itself?"
  269–13 * Whose *b*· nature is, and God the Soul.

Boer
  '02. 3–19 British and *B*· may prosper

Bohemia
  My. 347–22 Special contribution to "*B*·."

boil
  '00. 8–23 will *b*· over the brim of life

boilers
  Pul. 25– 4 * two large *b*· in the basement

bold
  Ret. 17–15 hickory rears his *b*· form,
  Pul. 24–13 inscription carved in *b*· relief :
  Pan. 12–27 *b*· conjecture's sharp point,

bold
  Po. 62–18 hickory rears his *b·* form,
     71– 4 and guilt, grown *b·*,
boldly
  No. 44–10 no hobby, however *b·* ridden
boldness
  Ret. 7–17 * noted for his *b·* and firmness,
Bonaparte
  Mis. 345–16 *B·* declared, "Ever since the
  Peo. 13–24 *B·* said : "Since ever the
bond
  Mis. 77–13 the indissoluble *b·* of union,
     91–11 This *b·* is wholly spiritual
  Ret. 76–19 and *b·* of perfectness.
  Pul. 22– 3 Christian churches have one *b·*
  My. 162–10 *b·* of blessedness such as
     164–22 *unity*, the *b·* of perfectness,
bondage
  Mis. 90–17 Break the yoke of *b·*
     103–16 which must be ever in *b·*,
     241–21 *b·* to sin and sickness.
  Peo. 11–17 children of Israel still in *b·*.
  My. 42–31 * from the *b·* of the Egyptians,
     74–23 * *b·* of the material world,
bonds
  Mis. 135–20 cement the *b·* of Love.
     141–12 *b·* and methods of Truth,
     150– 5 Yours in *b·* of Christ,
     273–13 *b·* of love and perfectness,
     290– 7 break all *b·* that hinder progress.
  Pul. 22–17 *b·* of peace are cemented by
     83–23 * "bound to her by *b·* dearer than
  No. 8– 9 fellowship in the *b·* of Christ.
     26–23 eternal *b·* of Science,
  '02. 19– 3 burst the *b·* of the tomb
  Po. 3–13 Till bursting *b·* our spirits part
  My. 217– 8 invested in safe municipal *b·*
     339– 2 *b·* of Christian brotherhood,
     362–23 * in the *b·* of Christian love
bone
  Mis. 44–17 What you thought was pain in the *b·*
     55–29 and beneath a skull *b·*,
     243–32 "He took a *b·* from— *see* Gen. 2 : 21.
bones
  My. 80– 7 * when having broken *b·* set ;
     105–11 diphtheria and carious *b·*
Bonney, Hon. Charles Carrol
  Mis. 312–11 Hon. Charles Carrol *B·*, President of
Book
  My. 183–20 deaf hear the words of the *B·*,
     295–13 This *B·* of books is also the
book
  above-named
    Mis. 92–23 own a copy of the above-named *b·*
     301– 5 author of the above-named *b·*
  and author
    Man. 32–10 Naming *B·* and Author.
  and the title
    '02. 15–27 both the *b·* and the title.
  clerk's
    My. 311–12 clerk's *b·* shows that I joined the
  covers of the
    My. 178–25 covers of the *b·* were burned up,
  credit of the
    Pul. 80–16 * rather to the credit of the *b·*
  decry the
    My. 114–10 and decry the *b·* which has
  every
    '01. 29–28 every *b·* of mine that they sold.
  first
    Rud. 16–20 the first *b·*, recorded in
  Gerhardt C. Mars'
    My. 351–23 have not read Gerhardt C. Mars' *b·*,
  her
    Mis. 54–14 The reading of her *b·*, "S. and H.
    Pul. 58–25 * with her *b·*, called "S. and H.
     80–12 * her *b·* has many a time
    My. 52–29 * moral rightness of her *b·*."
     53– 6 * send forth her *b·* to the world."
     304–31 the contents of her *b·*,
     336–10 * acknowledgment of this in her *b·*,
  itself
    My. 111–20 and yet the *b·* itself be absurd
  large
    Mis. 276– 1 large *b·* of rare flowers,
  little
    Ret. 6–14 than this little *b·* can afford.
     35– 3 This little *b·* is converted into the
    Rud. v– 1 THIS LITTLE *b·* IS . . . DEDICATED
    My. 323– 7 * I have his little *b·* yet.
  making a
    Po. v– 5 * *not . . . with a view of making a b·*,

book
  Mrs. Eddy's
    Mis. 248–13 mistaken views of Mrs. Eddy's *b·*,
    Pul. 28–17 * the use of Mrs. Eddy's *b·*,
     38– 5 * first edition of Mrs. Eddy's *b·*,
     60–12 * passages . . . from Mrs. Eddy's *b·*.
    My. 334– 5 * Mrs. Eddy's *b·*, "Retrospection and
  my
    Mis. vii– 1 * that tak'st my *b·* in hand,
     274– 4 revise my *b·* "S. and H.
     301–21 It is not right to copy my *b·*
     308–20 scientific notices of my *b·*.
     314–15 shall read from my *b·*, "S. and H.
     383– 7 its pastor is the Bible and my *b·*.
    Ret. 38– 5 to persuade him to finish my *b·*
    Pul. 6–12 thinking she . . . from my *b·*,
     87–17 Through my *b·*, your textbook,
    My. 133–26 my *b·* is not all you know of me.
     228– 2 My *b·* S. and H. names disease,
     266–23 My *b·*, "S. and H. with Key to the
     318– 5 was not my proofreader for my *b·*
     318– 9 critics declared that my *b·* was
     343–17 In 1875 I wrote my *b·*.
  name for the
    '02. 15–21 to suggest a name for the *b·*
  new
    Mis. 375–11 * new *b·* you have given us.
  no other
    My. 114–16 and read no other *b·* but the Bible
  of Revelation
    Pul. 59–15 * read from the *b·* of Revelation
  only
    My. 308–29 Bible was the only *b·* in his
  open
    My. 126– 9 has in his hand a *b·* open
  or an article
    Man. 82– 6 A *b·* or an article of which
  published a
    '01. 23–23 Bishop Berkeley published a *b·*
  read from the
    Mis. 91–27 read from the *b·* as authority for
  sealed
    Pul. 52–24 * The Bible was a sealed *b·*.
  small
    Pul. 69–16 * It would take a small *b·* to explain
  such a
    My. 113– 6 Can such a *b·* be ambiguous,
  Sibyl Wilbur's
    My. 297–30 friends have read Sibyl Wilbur's *b·*,
  that
    Mis. 50– 7 *is contained in that b·*,
     92– 5 inexhaustible topics of that *b·*
    No. 3–14 will put that *b·* in the hands of
    '02. 15–28 God had led me to write that *b·*,
    My. 111– 1 serve to call attention to that *b·*,
  this
    Mis. 50–17 the contents of this *b·*,
     314–24 announcing the full title of this *b·*,
     372–13 Knowing that this *b·* would
    Man. 32–13 commencing to read from this *b·*,
    Ret. 37– 7 "This *b·* is indeed wholly original,
     38–28 learns the letter of this *b·*,
     39– 1 demand for this *b·* increased,
     83– 5 to the teachings of this *b·*,
    Pul. 5–16 and pulpit cannonaded this *b·*,
     5–21 This *b·*, in 1895,
     5–28 This *b·* is the leaven
    My. v–23 * copies of this *b·* have been sold
     43–25 * teachings of this *b·*
     53– 6 * This *b·* has now reached its
     112–16 The earnest student of this *b·*,
     112–25 student of this *b* will tell you
     113– 4 practises the teachings of this *b·*
     114–26 the higher meaning of this *b·*
     114–28 Is it too much to say that this *b·*
     178–26 snatched this *b·* from the flames.
     298– 9 placing this *b·* before the public,
     305–17 the demand for this *b·*
     320–15 * the author of this *b·*
     336–11 * In this *b·* (p. 20) she also states,
  title of the
    Man. 32–14 announce the full title of the *b·*
  unique
    Pul. v– 7 UNIQUE *b·* IS . . . DEDICATED BY
    My. 320–12 * as being a very unique *b·*,
  wonderful
    Mis. 372–11 * pictures in your wonderful *b·*
  write a
    My. 105–27 urged me immediately to write a *b·*
  your
    Mis. 35–19 of what benefit is your *b·*?
     83– 5 *In your b·*, S. and H.,
    Pul. 6–13 * your *b·*, S. and H., was put
    No. 43–10 * "Your *b·* leavens my sermons."
     43–13 * "Your *b·* S. and H. is healing
    My. 238– 3 *Will . . . heal as effectually as your b·*,

book

your

My.	323– 6	* criticism of you and your *b·*
	324– 2	* especially your *b·* S. and H.
	324– 6	* any idea for your *b·*,
	324–17	* the author of your *b·*,
Mis.	x– 8	republish them in *b·* form,
	35–15	*Will the b· S. and H., . . . heal the sick,*
	285–17	*b·* that cast the first stone,
	306– 3	* *b·* which will accompany the bell
	314–22	shall name, . . . the *b·*, chapter, and
Ret.	38–12	finished my copy for the *b·*
	83–24	reading aloud from the *b·* to
Pul.	86–28	* Bible and the *b·* alluded to
Po.	vi– 3	* *in a b· "Gems for You,"*
My.	13– 4	*b·* by Benjamin Wills Newton,
	26–16	too short to be printed in *b·* form,
	112–28	*b·* that through the good it does
	112–32	a *b·* which lies beside the Bible in
	115– 1	written or indicated in the *b·*.
	178–26	not one word in the *b·* was effaced.
	258–31	a child . . . reading a *b·*
	324– 7	* *b·* to have come from any one but

book-borrowing

Ret.	75– 1	*b·* without credit

book-knowledge

Ret.	10– 3	I gained *b·* with far less labor

book-learning

Mis.	366–32	what Jesus had not, namely, mere *b·*,

Book of Life

My.	258– 1	Wherever . . . the *B· of L·* is loved,

books

my

Mis.	32–12	in my *b·*, on this very subject.
	43–14	contemplative reading of my *b·*,
	285– 6	who fills orders for my *b·*
	315– 6	No copies from my *b·* are allowed
	378–20	readers of my *b·* cannot fail to
Ret.	83–11	afforded by the Bible and my *b·*,
Pul.	74–23	"My *b·* and teachings maintain
No.	15– 4	Reading my *b·*, without prejudice,
'00.	1–24	readers of my *b·* and those interested
'01.	25–12	regret their lack in my *b·*,
'02.	13–12	privilege of publishing my *b·*
My.	166–29	for my *b·*, placed in my room
	219– 1	than that which my *b·* afford,
	224–21	My *b·* state C. S. correctly.
	244–22	all loyal students of my *b·*
	296–11	the publisher of my *b·*,
	318– 6	for only two of my *b·*.
Mis.	vii –5	* well made choice of friends and *b·*,
	vii– 7	* making thy friends *b·*, and thy *b·* friends.
	xi– 4	initial "G" on my subsequent *b·*,
	64–14	through no *b·* except the Bible,
	271–12	*b·* which are less than the best.
	348– 5	infringe neither the *b·* nor the business
	381–27	infringing *b·*, to the number of
	382–16	the first *b·* on this subject ;
Man.	27–22	publication and sale of the *b·*
	32– 9	not read from . . . but from the *b·*.
	43–10	*b·* of the Discoverer and Founder of
	44– 8	Obnoxious *B·*.
	44–11	that has for sale obnoxious *b·*.
	59– 8	*b·* or poems of our Pastor Emeritus,
	71–22	shall not write . . . in their church *b·*,
	76– 9	*b·* of the Church Treasurer audited
	76–26	*b·* of the C. S. Board of Directors
	77– 1	*b·* of the Church Treasurer
	77– 3	*b·* are to be audited on May first.
	81– 9	be connected with publishing her *b·*,
	81–25	*B·* to be Published.
	82– 1	publishes the *b·* . . . it sends forth.
	82– 3	disapproves of certain *b·* or
Ret.	2–18	one of my Grandmother Baker's *b·*,
	85– 9	*b·* and teaching are but a ladder
Pul.	45–29	* read from the two *b·* by Readers,
No.	15– 6	enable any one to prove these *b·* to
	43– 9	* the good your *b·* are doing."
'00.	12–22	the magical *b·* in that city were
My.	28– 8	* treasurer's *b·* will show the dollars and
	97–10	* kept no *b·* on the subject,
	224–23	*b·* less correct and therefore less
	238– 6	by reading the above-named *b·*
	295–13	Book of *b·* is also the gift of gifts ;
	354– 4	offering Bibles and other *b·* for sale
	354– 8	*b·* for which my endorsement is

bookstore

Man.	44–10	*b·* that has for sale obnoxious books.

boon

Po.	71–19	freedom's birthday — blood-bought *b·* !

border

Pul.	26–23	* floor of white has a Romanesque *b·*

borders

Mis.	127– 6	and enlarging her *b·*.
	142– 2	how hath He enlarged her *b·* !
	154– 9	enlarge its *b·* with divine Love.
My.	18– 3	and enlarging her *b·*.

bore

Mis.	64– 4	Our Master *b·* the cross
	162–18	Jesus *b·* our infirmities,
	225–11	*b·* testimony to the power of Christ,
	385–13	gales celestial, in sweet music *b·*
Ret.	94–29	Jesus' teachings *b·* much fruit,
Un.	55– 4	In his real self he *b·* no infirmities.
	55– 6	he *b·* not *his* sins, but *ours*,
Po.	25–16	Whose heart *b·* its grief
	48– 6	gales celestial, in sweet music *b·*
My.	326–18	*b·* his remains to their

born

Mis.	72– 2	For the innocent babe to be *b·*
	161– 5	*unto us a child is b·*, — Isa. 9 : 6.
	166–11	unto us a child is *b·*, — Isa. 9 : 6.
	180–22	were *b·*, *not of blood*, — John 1 : 13.
	181–16	"*b·*, not . . . of the will — John 1 : 13.
	181–32	being *b·* not of the human will
	182–14	were *b·*, not of blood, — *John* 1 : 13.
	182–17	*B·* of no doctrine, no human faith,
	183–10	Man is free *b·* :
	184– 8	The child *b·* of a woman has the
	184– 9	man *b·* of Spirit is spiritual,
	184–28	and *is b·* of God !
	205–29	man *b·* of the great Forever,
	242– 9	would give sight to one *b·* blind.
	253–18	devour the child as soon as it was *b·*,
	317– 3	When *b·* of Truth and Love,
	321– 3	"Unto us a child is *b·*," — Isa. 9 : 6.
	370–10	"Unto us a child is *b·*," — Isa. 9 : 6.
Chr.	53–26	the birth Of him ne'er *b·* ?
	55–14	*b·* of a woman — Job 14 : 1.
Ret.	5– 6	In the Baker homestead at Bow I was *b·*,
	19–18	my babe was *b·*.
	26–22	"*b·* of the flesh," — John 3 : 6.
	40–17	her babe was safely *b·*,
Un.	23– 7	divine children are *b·* of law and order,
Pul.	32–18†	* Mary Baker . . . was *b·* in Concord, N. H.,
	48–18	* *b·* and bred in that same
	57–27	* *b·* of an old New Hampshire family,
No.	25–21	That which is *b·* of the flesh
	36–27	a babe *b·* in a manger,
	46–18	that we are *free b·*.
'00.	12–16	night that Alexander the Great was *b·*.
'01.	8–26	was *b·* of a virgin mother,
	27–20	*b·* of the Spirit and not matter.
Hea.	3–16	*b·* in a remote province
	10– 3	as soon as it was *b·*," — Rev. 12 : 4.
Peo.	1– 3	is not *b·* of human wisdom ;
	10–13	"I was free *b·*." — Acts 22 : 28.
Po.	25– 2	Whence the dewdrop is *b·*,
	29– 4	*b·* where storm enshrouds
	70–20	As when this babe was *b·*,
My.	100–20	This church *b·* in my nativity,
	183–12	To-day a nation is *b·*.
	228–13	none greater had been *b·*
	239–25	so-called man *b·* of the flesh,
	261–25	Christ was not *b·* of the flesh,
	261–26	*b·* of God — *b·* of Spirit
	261–27	the Galilean Prophet, was *b·* of
	262– 8	*b·* in a manger amidst the flocks
	262–11	never *b·* and never dying.
	290– 9	*b·* in 1819, married in 1840,
	330–30	my babe was *b·*.
	357– 5	*b·* of God, the offspring of Spirit,

borne

Mis.	130–17	*b·* the burden in the heat of
	147–10	worthy to be *b·* heavenward?
	169–17	*b·* fully to our minds and hearts.
	295–30	and *b·* the English sceptre.
	356–17	has sprung up, *b·* fruit,
	394– 2	*b·* on the zephyr at eventide's hour ;
Pul.	67– 7	* a fact *b·* out by circumstances.
	71– 5	* is not *b·* out by the voluntary
No.	1–11	*b·* on by the current of feeling.
Po.	19– 5	upward and heavenward *b·*.
	27–21	Thou hast *b·* burdens,
	45– 1	*b·* on the zephyr at eventide's hour ;
My.	52– 4	* she has *b·* them bravely,

borrow

Mis.	117–27	*b·* oil of the more provident
	121–30	*b·* their sense of justice from
	342– 7	*b·* the better-tended lamps
My.	130–31	that you *b·* little else from it,

borrowed

Mis.	147–25	He assumes no *b·* appearance.

† *Incorrect newspaper account, quoted as published.*

borrowed

Mis.	371–25	error in *b·* plumes?
Ret.	57–15	Man shines by *b·* light.
Un.	17–12	consolation from *b·* scintillations.
	17–17	despoil error of its *b·* plumes,
Hea.	11– 1	play in *b·* sunbeams,
My.	301– 2	it shines with *b·* rays

borrower

Ret.	30– 5	the dainty *b·* would have fled.
	75–17	the *b·* from it is embraced in the

borrowing

Mis.	276–26	not one of them be found *b·* oil,
Pul.	8–13	no urging, begging, or *b·* ;
My.	130–23	*B·* from my copyrighted works,

borrows

My.	224–17	when he *b·* the thoughts,

bosom

Mis.	125–13	rest on the *b·* of God ;
	145– 8	Does a single *b·* burn for fame
	399– 1	it calls you, — "Come to my *b·*,
Pul.	13–21	has made his *b·* companion,
'01.	35– 5	bare our *b·* to the blade
'02.	9–20	in the *b·* of the Father,
Po.	8– 6	Her *b·* to fill with mortal woes.
	15–18	in the *b·* that bled,
	41– 1	* Come, rest in this *b·*,
	44– 3	With the guerdon of Thy *b·*,
	75– 8	it calls you, — "Come to my *b·*,
My.	203–26	buried . . . in the *b·* of earth
	332– 4	* the feelings of a swelling *b·*.

Boston

Mass.

Mis.	150– 7	*B·*, Mass., 1889.
	161– 2	CHICKERING HALL, *B·*, MASS.
Man.	15– 2	*The First Church* . . . *B·, Mass.*
	19– 1	THE FIRST CHURCH . . . *B·*, MASS.,
	34– 6	The First Church . . . *B·*, Mass.,
	37– 9	The First Church . . . *B·*, Mass.,
	45–16	The First Church . . . *B·*, Mass.,
	58– 8	The First Church . . . *B·*, Mass.,
	65– 5	The First Church . . . *B·*, Mass.,
	72–27	The First Church . . . *B·*, Mass.,
	75– 6	The First Church . . . *B·*, Mass.,
	92–21	The First Church . . . *B·*, Mass.
	102–12	The First Church . . . *B·*, Mass.,
	103– 2	The First Church . . . *B·*, Mass."
	103– 5	The First Church . . . *B·*, Mass.,
	104– 5	The First Church . . . *B·*, Mass.,
Pul. page 1	chapter heading
	23– 8	* *B·*, Mass., December 28.
	77–18	* "The First Church . . . *B·*, Mass.
	78–16	* "The First Church . . . *B·*, Mass.
	88–13	* *Advertiser, B·*, Mass.
	88–19	* *Post, B·*, Mass.
My.	vi–12	*The First Church . . . B·*, Mass.,
	15– 7	The First Church . . *B·*, Mass.,
	23–19	*The First Church . . . B·*, Mass.,
	27–13	*The First Church . . . B·*, Mass.,
	27–19	**B·*, MASS., June 2, 1906.
	44–25	*The First Church . . . B·*, Mass.,
	46–32	**B·*, MASS., June 12, 1906.
	47– 3	*The First Church . . . B·*, Mass.:
	62–16	**B·*, MASS., June 30, 1906.
	63– 9	**B·*, MASS., July 10, 1906.
	135–25	THE FIRST CHURCH . . . *B·*, MASS.
	142– 9	The Mother Church, *B·*, Mass.
	172–10	* The First Church . . . *B·*, Mass.:
	175– 2	my little church in *B·*, Mass.,
	246–24	The Mother Church . . . *B·*, Mass.
	280–13	* *B·*, MASS., June 13, 1905.
	310–16	a large business in *B·*, Mass.
	322– 8	* *B·*, MASS., November 21, 1906.
	352–17	* *B·*, MASS., October 9, 1908.

Massachusetts

Mis.	147– 2	chapter sub-title
	381–30	destroyed, in *B·*, Massachusetts.
My.	244–29	The . . . College of *B·*, Massachusetts,
	289– 9	Mother Church . . . *B·*, Massachusetts,
Mis.	48–13	one of his recent lectures in *B·*
	88–10	a *B·* gentleman whose thought is
	125–22	chapter sub-title
	132–11	*B·*, March 21, 1885.
	133– 3	* prayerless Mrs. Eddy, of *B·*."
	137– 5	a meagre reception in *B·*
	139– 9	chapter sub-title
	139–19	I gave a lot of land — in *B·*,
	141–27	commence building our church in *B·* ;
	141–31	Of our first church in *B·*,
	143–17	"The First Church . . . in *B·*.
	145–31	The Church of Christ, Scientist, in *B·*,
	146– 5	chapter sub-title
	148– 9	Manual of The First Church . . . *B·*,

Boston

Mis.	171–21	chapter sub-title
	193–14	The Church of Christ, Scientist, in *B·*,
	242– 6	the Metaphysical College in *B·*,
	242–26	Also, Mr. C. M. H——, of *B·*,
	249–17	since my residence in *B·* :
	300–23	The Church of Christ, Scientist, in *B·*,
	310–13	gone out of The First Church . . . in *B·*,
	311– 3	unite with The Mother Church in *B·*.
	316– 7	or speak to your church in *B·*
	316– 8	I shall speak to my dear church at *B·*
	320–23	star of Bethlehem is the star of *B·*,
	380–28	the United States Circuit Court in *B·*,
	382–21	edifice of this denomination in *B·* ;
Man.	3– 5	Manual of The First Church . . . *B·*,
	26– 4	general Committee on Publication in *B·*
	30–15	No. 385 Commonwealth Avenue, *B·*,
	97– 6	loyal Christian Scientist who lives in *B·*,
	98–18	in a leading *B·* newspaper
Ret.	6–21	the Hon. Richard Fletcher of *B·*.
	15–13	I was called to preach in *B·*
	16–16	charter for The Mother Church in *B·*
	17– 2	in the beautiful suburbs of *B·*.
	38–16	The afternoon that he left *B·*
	38–16	I started for *B·*
	38–20	he to find me *en route* for *B·*,
	43– 5	Massachusetts Metaphysical College in *B·*,
	45– 1	Church of Christ, Scientist, in *B·*,
	46– 2	Church of Christ, Scientist, in *B·*.
	51– 1	I gave a lot of land in *B·* to
Pul.	v– 6	THE FIRST CHURCH . . . *B·*,
	6–24	the Rev. William R. Alger of *B·*,
	6–26	At a *conversazione* in *B·*,
	7– 4	I love *B·*, and especially the
	7– 8	praised and persecuted in *B·*,
	7–27	The First Church . . . in *B·*.
	8–28	The First Church . . . in *B·*.
	20– 2	The First Church . . . in *B·*.
	23– 3	* THE FIRST CHURCH . . . *B·*
	24– 2	* first C. S. church erected in *B·*
	30– 3	* when a *B·* clergyman remonstrated
	30–10	* is not limited to the *B·* adherents,
	30–25	* church in *B·* was organized by
	31–17	* *B·* atmosphere was largely thrilled and
	36– 2	* the Metaphysical College in *B·*,
	36–23	* most beautiful residences in *B·*.
	37–11	* superintends the church in *B·*,
	40–19	* costly edifice erected in *B·*
	41– 9	* these contributors came to *B·*,
	47–21	* Besides her *B·* home, Mrs. Eddy has
	49–21	* from her busy career in *B·*,
	52–11	* The erection of a massive temple in *B·*
	55–24	* *B·* congregation was organized
	56–11	* the erection of the temple, in *B·*,
	56–25	* C. S. church was dedicated in *B·*
	57–12	* one of the most beautiful buildings in *B·*.
	57–20	* excellent name given to a new *B·* church.
	58– 4	* Coming to *B·* about 1880,
	58– 9	* have joined The Mother Church in *B·*,
	60–15	* had come to *B·* for this
	63– 7	* BUILT IN HER HONOR AT *B·*
	63–23	* was dedicated in *B·*
	64–24	* *B·* has just dedicated the first
	65– 6	* should not overlook the *B·* sect
	65–15	* by the dedication at *B·* of
	65–26	* The *B·* church similarly expresses
	67– 5	* a new faith, go to *B·*,"
	67– 7	* *B·* can fairly claim to be the
	68–19	* The dedication in *B·* last Sunday of
	70–13	* very recently saw completed in *B·*,
	70–26	* She has a palatial home in *B·*
	75–17	* A BEAUTIFUL CHURCH AT *B·*
	75–19	* took part in the ceremonies at *B·*
	76–27	* The First Church . . . *B·*,
	77–11	* erected . . . in the city of *B·*,
	77–22	* "*B·*, January 6th, 1895."
	77–26	* The First Church . . . at *B·*,
	78–10	* erected . . . in the city of *B·*,
	78–20	* "*B·*, January 6, 1895."
	79– 4	* dedication, in *B·*, of a C. S. temple
	80– 8	* *B·* is emphatically the women's
	81– 1	* chimes on the C. S. temple in *B·*
	81– 8	* [*The New Century, B·*, February, 1895]
	84–13	* The First Church . . . in *B·*.
	85–23	* THE FIRST CHURCH . . . IN *B·*
	85–25	* from the C. S. Board of Directors, *B·*,
	86–15	* *B·*, March 20, 1895.
	86–19	* The First Church . . . in *B·*.
	87–13	"The First Church . . . in *B·*
No.	12– 8	Church of Christ, Scientist, in *B·*,
	19– 7	C. S. is no "*B·* craze ;"
	27–19	said, in a lecture in *B·*,
	41–24	a *B·* Baptist clergyman,
	44–25	a Congregational clergyman of *B·*,
	45–13	Let it not be heard in *B·*
'00.	1–19	*B·*, New York, Philadelphia,

Boston

'02. 13–14   The First Church . . . in B·,
13–21   in the B· newspapers,
Po.   vi– 4   * again in B·, in 1856.
vi–12   In 1835 a mob in B·
vi–13   B· has since been the pioneer of
vii– 2   * in the beautiful suburbs of B·
My.   8–26   * annual business meeting in B·,
9–24   enlarge our church edifice in B·.
13–15   The Mother Church . . . in B·.
13–17   pledged to this church in B·
16–12   * The Mother Church in B·
20–25   * annual meeting in B·
20–30   * usual large gathering in B·,
21–11   * forego a visit to B· at this time,
21–28   * the new edifice in B·.
22–31   * The First Church . . . in B·
27– 3   Members of my Church, . . . in B· :
31–18   * by the Scientists in B·
38–29   * The annual meeting . . . in B·,
53–11   * 569 Columbus Avenue, B·.
56–10   * in such suburbs of B· as would
65– 4   * largest . . . meeting ever held in B·
65– 6   * The First Church of Christ, . . . B·,
67–20   * giving B· an edifice that is
72– 5   * chapter sub-title
72– 6   * gates of B· are open wide
72–20   * Scientists who have come to B·
72–29   * church in B· twelve years ago
73–14   * from all over the world to B·
73–28   * due to arrive in B· to-night,
74– 3   * are already in B·.
74–14   * B· is indebted to them for
76–21   * annual church meeting in B·,
76–25   *·will be dedicated in B·
76–29   * was founded in B· by
77– 7   * leading landmark of B·,
77–14   * pilgrims are pouring into B·,
77–26   * believers had gathered in B·.
79–10   * in the heart of the city of B·,
79–15   * this occurred in staid old B·,
80– 1   * close of their visit to B·,
81–17   * audience ever sat in B·.
82– 7   * have been crowding B·
82–21   * indications were that B·
82–27   * came to B· in such numbers
82–29   * to the residents of B·,
83–19   * chapter sub-title
84–12   * B· is the Mecca for
84–17   * B· is near to another great
85–14   * here in B· the zeal and
85–20   * Another glory for B·,
86– 4   * As B· has ever loved its
86–10   * have been pouring into B·
87– 5   * increase of the population of B·
87–17   * B· is to be congratulated
07 21   * in B· during the past few days.
88– 4   * Scientists have assembled at B·
88–10   * The dedication, Sunday, in B·,
88–29   * a great church in B·.
89–23   * The dedication . . . in B·
90–23   * The Mother Church of C. S. at B·,
91–16   * a C. S. temple at B·
91–27   * just been dedicated at B·
92–10   * convention of . . . Scientists in B·
93– 5   * their great church in B·
93–29   * now being held in B·
94–18   * in the recent dedication in B·
95–10   * magnificent C. S. church in B·
95–16   * assembly of . . . Scientists in B·
96– 1   * zeal . . . exhibited at B·,
96–18   * The building they were in B· to
96–28   * Mother Church extension in B·,
97–21   * Mother Church . . . at B·
97–25   * Scientists who descended upon B·
97–28   * B· has not yet recovered from
98–18   * recently dedicated at B·.
98–28   * The erection in B· of the
99–15   * a splendid cathedral in B·,
100– 1   * a C. S. temple in B·
100– 5   * temple recently dedicated at B·
117–28   I left B· in the height of prosperity
134–22   meeting of April 3, 1907, . . . in B·,
135–17   First Reader of my church in B·,
140–15   * The First Church . . . in B·,
141– 9   * members . . . outside of B·
141–15   * The First Church . . . in B·,
141–18   communion season of the B· church
163–17   When I removed from B· in 1889
172–24   * opened the following day in B·
173– 8   members of my church, . . . in B·.
173–17   attend the communion in B·
216–18   The First Church of Christ, . . . B·,
217– 7   The Mother Church . . . in B·,
246–13   closed my College . . . left B·, and
279–23   of The Mother Church . . . in B·,

Boston

My.   292–20   1901, Message to my church in B·,
304–13   Chicago, B·, Portland,
317– 4   * Rev. James Henry Wiggin of B·,
319–21   * entered your Primary class at B·.
322–21   * waiting months in B·
325– 9   * old part of B· in which he lived
338–14   lecture was delivered in B·,

Boston Daily Advertiser
My.   83–20   * [B· D·A·]

Boston Evening Record
My.   84–16   * [B· E·R·]

Boston Evening Transcript (see also **Boston Transcript**)
My.   57–28   * the B· E· T· said :
70– 9   * [B· E· T·]
73–25   * [B· E· T·]
74– 9   * [B· E· T·]
75–23   * [B· E· T·]

Boston Globe (see also **Boston Sunday Globe, Globe**)
My.   65–17   * [B· G·, April, 1903]
69–25   * [B· G·]
71–12   * [B· G·]
72–13   * [B· G·]
73–11   * [B· G·]
75– 5   * [B· G·]
78–25   * [B· G·]
86– 8   * [B· G·]
137– 5   * The B· G·, referring to this
140–10   * [B· G·]
141– 1   * [B· G·]
264– 7   [B· G·, November 29, 1900]
278–15   [B· G·, December, 1904]
281–15   * [B· G·, August, 1905]

Boston Herald
Pul.   40– 7   * [B· H·, January 7, 1895]
Po.   11– 5   B· H·, Sunday, May 15, 1898.
My.   29– 2   * Reprinted from B· H·
79–23   * [B· H·]
82– 4   * [B· H·]
84–11   * [B· H·]
85–19   * [B· H·]
87–19   * [B· H·]
264– 1   [B· H·, May 5, 1900]
268– 1   [B· H·, March 5, 1905]
274–16   * [B· H·, April, 1908]
277– 1   [B· H·, March, 1898]
337– 1   [B· H·, Sunday, May 15, 1898]

Bostonians
Pul.   71– 2   * eight hundred of . . . are B·.

Boston Journal
Pul.   61–19   * [B· J·, January 7, 1895]
My.   65– 1   * [B· J·, June 19, 1902]
71– 6   * [B· J·]
304– 1   [B· J·, June 8, 1903]

Boston Post
My.   66–17   * [B· P·, June 6, 1906]
67– 3   * [B· P·]
70–18   * [B· P·]
72– 4   * [B· P·]
84–25   * [B· P·]
86–21   * [B· P·]
276–15   * [B· P·, November, 1908]

Boston Sunday Globe
Pul.   44–15   * [B· S· G·, January 6, 1895]

Boston Times
My.   99– 1   * B· T·, comments, it is but one of

Boston Transcript
Pul.   50– 9   * [B· T·, December 31, 1894]

Boston Traveler
Mis.   271–24   published in the B· T·
My.   54– 5   * B· T· contained the following

Boswell, Rev. Mr.
'01.   32– 3   Rev. Mr. B·, of Bow, N. H.,

both

Mis.   12–18   interest of b· good and evil
16–18   higher sense of b· God and man.
23–18   b· noumenon and phenomena,
24–23   A knowledge of b· good and evil
35–21   Only because b· are important.
44–15   the mind, or extracting, or b·,
45–20   better b· morally and physically.
51–29   Are b· prayer and drugs necessary to heal?
55–16   Is C. S. based on the facts of b·
60–11   unreality of b· apparent
65–22   C. S. demands b· law and gospel,
65–23   b· in its demonstration, and
65–28   since b· constitute the divine law
68– 3   it requires b· time and eternity.

both

Mis.	72– 7	*b·* good and bad traits
	85–31	way out of *b·* sickness and sin.
	109–22	but, admitting the existence of *b·*,
	118– 2	We cannot obey *b·*
	119– 6	rise and overthrow *b·*.
	121–32	Teacher of *b·* law and gospel
	128–12	have *b·* learned, and received,
	141–15	*b·* the law of God and the
	146–10	*b·* sides of the subject,
	158–11	we *b·* had first to obey,
	161–16	*b·* human and divinely endowed,
	165– 3	*b·* because of the ascension
	167– 8	*B·* son and daughter :
	173–14	says that man is *b·* matter and
	175–29	*b·* animal magnetism and
	180–28	*b·* a material and a spiritual sense.
	187– 1	regeneration of *b·* mind and body,
	187–17	Had *b·* writers and translators
	195– 8	*B·* the spirit and the letter
	197–20	compel us to pattern after *b·* ;
	197–25	that is *b·* good and evil ;
	198–22	knowledge of *b·* good and evil ;
	211– 7	will lead the blind and *b·* shall fall.
	213– 5	Suffering or Science, or *b·*,
	217–21	*b·* cause and effect,
	217–29	to become *b·* finite and infinite ;
	220–22	is patent *b·* to the
	220–23	*B·* should understand
	221–25	against *b·* evil and disease,
	222– 2	gives him a false sense of *b·*
	241– 1	the faith of *b·* youth and adult
	246– 7	*b·* human and divine rights,
	247– 2	*b·* human and divine rights ;
	249–10	*B·* in private and public life,
	267–20	*B·* wings must be plumed
	287–30	preserve affection on *b·* sides.
	292–26	great good, *b·* seen and unseen ;
	295–21	as *b·* untrue and uncivil.
	297–22	mutual consent of *b·* parties,
	314–28	selections from *b·* the Bible and
	333–12	Is it in *b·* evil and good,
	352– 5	*b·* material and spiritual,
	352–26	consciousness of *b·* evil and good,
	367–16	knowledge of *b·* good and evil,
	374–15	hold charge over *b·*,
	381–31	* *b·* founder and discoverer
Man.	37–18	so long as *b·* are loyal
	54–26	member of *b·* The Mother Church and
	74– 3	shall not be a member of *b·*
	87–21	for *b·* teacher and student.''
	92–12	If *b·* husband and wife are
	92–14	either one, not *b·*, should teach
Ret.	1– 1	from *b·* Scotland and England,
	5–11	names of *b·* father and mother
	14– 8	*b·* salvation and condemnation
	38–18	and were *b·* surprised,
	59–16	*b·* in idea and demonstration.
	64– 4	*b·* sinner and sin will be
	67– 6	Sin is *b·* concrete and abstract.
	67– 8	*b·* material and spiritual,
	81– 3	*b·* for the living and the dead.
	84–26	for *b·* teacher and student.
	88–16	*b·* by example and precept.
Un.	7– 7	due *b·* to C. S. and myself
	23–24	knowing *b·* evil and good ;
	24–11	which is *b·* evil and good.
	41–26	appears to *b·* live and die,
	46–19	regarded as *b·* good and evil,
	52– 6	of *b·* God and the universe.
	52–10	consciousness of *b·* good and evil,
	53–19	sums done under *b·* rules
	54–24	*b·* knew and admitted the
	61–23	C. S. is *b·* demonstration and
Pul.	1–10	Time past and time present, *b·*,
	2– 5	*B·* without and within,
	10– 2	healing *b·* mind and body,
	29– 4	* *b·* of whom had formerly been
	46–15	* *b·* in Scotland and England.
	53– 9	* the mind of *b·* healer and patient,
	69– 4	* *B·* were under the instruction of
Rud.	14–26	instructions, *b·* in and out of class.
No.	5–17	*b·* human health and life.
	5–27	in *b·* theory and practice,
	6–20	the evidence in *b·* cases
	10– 2	in *b·* a divine and human sense ;
	12–25	it makes *b·* sense and Soul,
	13– 6	declare *b·* the Principle and idea
	23–15	*b·* a literal and a moral meaning.
	24–10	and denies the actual existence of *b·*
	24–15	claims of evil become *b·* less and more
	31–19	but he treated them *b·*,
	37– 7	to know *b·* evil and good ;
	42–20	declaring itself *b·* true and good.
	45–19	by the noblest of *b·* sexes.
Pan.	5–19	It shows that evil is *b·* liar and lie,

both

'01.	4– 2	for *b·* have the nature of God.
	5–29	explains *b·* His person and nature,
	10–11	*b·* male and female.
	10–13	*b·* the divine and the human,
	10–18	as *b·* Father and Mother.
	28–13	*b·* in Catholic and Protestant
	34– 4	for asserting this, in *b·* cases.
'02.	4–15	*b·* ringing like soft vesper chimes
	8– 4	and *b·* will be fulfilled.
	15–27	*b·* the book and the title.
	17–10	*b·* the old and the new commandment,
Hea.	3– 2	wherewith to heal *b·* mind and body ;
	8– 2	heals *b·* mind and body ;
	8– 8	carrying out this government over *b·*
	10–22	be careful not to talk on *b·* sides,
	11–25	supposed to be *b·* mind and matter.
	13– 1	so weaken *b·* points of action ;
	13– 2	*b·* horns of the dilemma,
	18– 1	*b·* mortal mind and mortal body
My.	vi–29	* *b·* of which, . . . are the property of
	4–18	interests of *b·* medical faculty and
	8–11	* material symbol of *b·* of these,
	12–11	* *b·* as to the amount
	49– 1	* *b·* in public and private.
	62–31	* there was urgent need of *b·*.
	64–16	* *b·* by precept and example
	65–11	* with *b·* unanimity and assurance.
	70–21	* *b·* ancient and modern masters,
	108–19	for *b·* physician and patient.
	137– 9	* in *b·* substance and penmanship :
	147–20	able to heal *b·* sin and disease.
	152–19	and *b·* will stumble into doubt
	179–10	*b·* good and evil, *b·* mind and
	190–10	My experience in *b·* practices
	215–29	to test the effect of *b·* methods
	230– 6	as *b·* sweet and bitter,
	234–18	*b·* sides of the great question
	249–26	If *b·* the First and Second Readers
	251– 8	* *b·* Primary and Normal class
	270–30	control *b·* religion and art
	277– 6	satisfactory to *b·* nations
	292–22	*b·* are equally sincere.
	300– 6	*b·* to will and to do — *Phil.* 2 : 13.
	307–20	which we *b·* desired ;
	309– 9	*B·* entered their pleas,
	324–32	* *B·* Mr. and Mrs. Wiggin frequently
	335– 7	* retained his membership in *b·*
	349– 8	susceptible of *b·* ease and dis-ease,

Botticelli's

Mis.	375–26	* or *B·* 'Madonna' !

bottle

Hea.	18– 7	the *b·* will break and the wine
	18–16	put the new wine into the old *b·*

bottles

Mis.	178– 8	could not be put into old *b·*
No.	43–21	"new wine into old *b·* ;" — *Matt.* 9 : 17.
Hea.	18– 6	put new wine into old *b·* ;
	18–12	put the new wine into old *b·*.

bottom

Mis.	165–12	rends the veil . . . from top to *b·*.
Peo.	5–28	* sunk to the *b·* of the sea,
My.	52–25	* has reached her *b·* dollar,
	301– 8	solid Christianity at the *b·*

bottomless

Mis.	134–29	it will tumble into the *b·*.
No.	42–15	engulfing error in *b·* oblivion,
My.	53– 3	* a *b·* sea of corrections ;
	200–23	*b·* abyss of self-damnation,

bough

My.	347–15	primal presence, *b·*, bird, and song,

boughs

My.	347–10	exquisite design of *b·*
	347–12	* Ah happy, happy *b·*,

bought

Mis.	253– 3	but is *b·* with a price,
Pul.	36–23	* *b·* one of the most beautiful
	49–26	* Once *b·*, the will of the woman
My.	123–13	I had the property *b·* by
	265– 8	and is *b·* at par value ;
	314–10	*b·* a place in North Groton,
	325– 6	* that you had *b·* your house

bound

Mis.	101–18	opening the doors for them that are *b·*.
	143– 7	a closer link hath *b·* us.
	157–13	"as *b·* with you," — see *Heb.* 13 : 3.
	245–18	rights that man is *b·* to respect.
	262–21	to such as are *b·* ;
	275–18	open the prison to them that are *b·*,
	297–20	is held in C. S. as morally *b·*
	345–11	*b·* him to the stake,
Ret.	63–17	Do you not feel *b·* to expose

bound

Un.	7–11	has so *b·* me to Him
Pul.	83–23	* "*b·* to her by bonds dearer than
No.	31–28	shall be *b·* in heaven." — *Matt.* 16 : 19.
	45–15	rights which man is *b·* to respect.
Peo.	13–20	Them they *b·* him to the stake,
Po.	vii– 6	* *b·* volumes of her poems,
My.	48–30	* I am *b·* as an observer
	171–27	* *b·* with burnished brass.

boundaries

Hea.	11– 8	rebels at its own *b·* ;

boundary

Un.	37–11	no *b·* of time can separate

bounded

My.	65–19	* block *b·* by Falmouth,

bounding

Mis.	240– 4	*b·* with sparkling eyes,

boundless

Pul.	3– 4	Can Love be less than *b·* ?
Po.	65–13	from dreams so *b·*
My.	110–18	higher in the *b·* blue.
	267–17	infinite, *b·* bliss.

bounds

Mis.	68–30	* beyond the *b·* of experience,"
My.	138–19	the *b·* of propriety

bounteous

Chr.	53–33	Forever present, *b·*, free,

bounty

Pul.	9–23	a *b·* hidden from the world.
My.	260– 1	*b·* of Life everlasting,

bouquets

Mis.	112–22	* have brought to him *b·*,
	211– 8	supplies criminals with *b·*

Bouton, D. D., Rev. Nathaniel

'01.	32– 2	Rev. Nathaniel *B·*, D. D., of Concord,

Bow

N. H.

'01.	32– 3	Rev. Mr. Boswell, of *B·*, N. H.,
My.	172– 7	* grown on the farm . . . at *B·*, N. H.
	000 7	towns of Loudon and *B·*, N. H.
Ret.	4– 6	towns of Concord and *B·*,
	5– 6	the Baker homestead at *B·*
Pul.	48–16	* on the brow of *B·* hill,
My.	309– 9	and Mark Baker for *B·*.
	309–19	extensive farm situated in *B·*
	309–22	the Baker homestead at *B·* :
	309–28	* at the ancestral home at *B·*.

bow

Mis.	17–13	meekly *b·* before the Christ,
	223 30	arrow shot from another's *b·*
	330–15	let mortals *b·* before the creator,
	388– 6	A *b·* of promise on the cloud.
Pul.	42–28	* fastened with a broad ribbon *b·*.
No.	3– 2	envy will bend its *b·* and shoot
	8–17	*b·* down to the commandments
'02.	20–15	A *b·* of promise on the cloud
Peo.	3–14	the *b·* of omnipotence
Po.	7– 6	A *b·* of promise on the cloud.
	28– 6	Help us to humbly *b·*
	67–11	Should *b·* thee, as winds *b·*
	77–14	to Thee we'll meekly *b·*,
My.	257–20	*b·* and declare Christ's power,
	259– 3	between my *b·* windows,

Bowdoin College

Mis.	178– 3	He is a graduate of *B· C·*

bowed

Mis.	339–22	*b·* the o'erburdened head
	386–18	*B·* to His will.
Hea.	10– 5	the beast *b·* before the Lamb :
Po.	46– 6	leaves have shed or *b·* the stem ;
	50– 2	*B·* to His will.
My.	61–18	* I *b·* my head before the
	258– 9	*b·* in strong . . . anguish,
	309–11	Mr. Pierce *b·* to my father

bowels

Mis.	69–22	even to move his *b·*,

bower

Mis.	354–31	the lark in her emerald *b·*
	394– 6	at the altar or *b·*,
Ret.	11–20	From erudition's *b·*.
Po.	8– 8	naiad from woodland *b·* ;
	18– 9	lark in her emerald *b·* ?
	35– 1	O take me to thy *b·* !
	45– 8	at the altar or *b·*,
	60–18	From erudition's *b·*.

bowers

Ret.	17– 4	In *b·* of beauty,
Po.	25– 9	From your green *b·* free,
	46– 3	Within life's summer *b·* !
	53– 1	Come to thy *b·*, sweet spring,

bowers

Po.	53–18	To empty summer *b·*,
	62– 3	In *b·* of beauty,

Bowring

Pul.	28–23	Robertson, Wesley, *B·*,

Bowring's

Un.	26–20	protest against this stanza of *B·*,

bows

Un.	16– 1	*b·* to the infinite perfection

box

Mis.	148–24	contribution *b·* was presented
Pul.	78–23	* in a white satin-lined *b·*
	86– 3	* contains a solid gold *b·*,
	86–12	* in an elegant plush *b·*.
My.	172–23	* The *b·* containing the gavel
	309–22	* a small, square *b·* building

Boxer's

My.	234–25	more fatal than the *B·* rebellion.

boy

Mis.	ix–20	a Love that is a *b·*,
	162–31	simple as the shepherd *b·*,
Po.	9– 7	the birth of that beautiful *b·*.
My.	60– 8	* "My *b·*, you will be ruined
	313–31	my little *b·* was not welcome in my

boyhood

Mis.	34–20	can return to his *b·*.

bracketed

Pul.	25–25	* On the walls are *b·*

Brahmanism

No.	14–10	from the Oriental philosophy of *B·*,

brain

Mis.	5–25	believe it to be *b·* matter.
	168– 9	"tympanum on the *b·*"
	247–22	believe it to reside in . . . *b·* ;
Ret.	10– 1	taught to believe that my *b·*
Un.	33–14	*B·*, thus assuming to testify,
Pul.	82– 2	* the *b·* for its great white throne.
Pan.	4– 9	located in the *b·* ;
	4–10	conditions of matter, or *b·*,
	4–14	it is patent . . . that *b·* is matter,
'02.	9–19	not the dream of a heated *b·* ;
Hea.	4–10	with softening of the *b·*
	5– 7	the developments of the *b·*
Po.	47–13	The weary of body and *b·* ?
My.	122– 3	from the *b·* of a dreamer.
	301–25	cannot of itself go to the *b·*
	302–11	the specific insanity is that *b·*,

brains

Mis.	210–19	a belief of disordered *b·*,
Un.	22–20	physical senses and material *b·*,
	33–16	that form of matter called *b·*,

branch

Mis.	114– 6	*Quarterly* as an educational *b·*.
	387–11	And on the same *b·* bend.
Man.	54–10	a member of a *b·* of
	54–15	*b·* church's list of membership
	54–26	and a *b·* Church of Christ,
	60–19	and of the *b·* Churches
	73–27	a member of one *b·* Church
	95–10	*b·* Churches of Christ, Scientist,
	95–17	*b·* churches shall call on
Ret.	18–26	from the bent *b·* of a pear tree.
	52–16	*b·* associations in other States,
Pul.	67– 4	* THE MONTREAL *B·*
Rud.	16– 7	in any *b·* of education.
Po.	6 6	And on the same *b·* bend.
	63–24	from the bent *b·* of a pear-tree.
My.	159– 9	rich fruit of this *b·* of his vine,
		(*see also* **church, churches**)

Branch Churches

(*see* **churches**)

branches

Mis.	154– 3	*b·* of The Church of Christ,
	154– 8	prune its encumbering *b·*,
	243– 5	mental *b·* taught in my college ;
	344–11	not studied those *b·*,
	356–19	have lodged in its *b·*.
Man.	45– 6	of The Mother Church and of its *b·*
Ret.	17–20	Its feathery blossom and *b·*
Pul.	46–14	* tracing those *b·* which
	55–27	* all others being *b·*,
Po.	63– 7	Its feathery blossom and *b·*
My.	125– 6	to rejuvenate the *b·*
	160 13	with blossoms on its *b·*,
	192–17	sits smilingly on these *b·*
	257– 1	green *b·* of the Christmas-tree.

Brande

Mis.	68–27	*B·* calls metaphysics "the science

brass

Mis.	316–23	pounding . . . love into sounding *b·* ;
Ret.	2–12	encased in a *b·* scabbard,
Pul.	46–19	* encased in a *b·* scabbard,
	62– 5	* tubes of drawn *b·*

brass

No. 45– 4   "as sounding *b*·,— *I Cor*. 13 : 1.
'01. 26–23   as sounding *b*·,— *I Cor*. 13 : 1.
My. 171–28   bound with burnished *b*·.

brave

Mis. 163–25   After his brief *b*· struggle,
183–29   He is bravely *b*· who dares
240–22   affectionate, and generally *b*·.
376–17   describe the *b*· splendor of a
385–18   *B*· wrestler, lone.
Chr. 53– 4   One lone, *b*· star.
Ret. 17–16   bares a *b*· breast to the lightning
Un. 39–20   be *b*·, and let Science declare
Pul. 48–25   * a tincture of blue and *b*· blood,
Pan. 14–19   remember our *b*· soldiers,
14–23   as at Manila, where *b*· men,
'00. 13– 6   that their words were *b*·
Po. 11– 1   *B*· Britain, blest America !
25–14   Flowers for the *b*·
48–12   *B*· wrestler, lone.
62–20   bares a *b*· breast to the lightning
My. 291–19   was wise, *b*·, unselfed.
338– 1   *B*· Britain, blest America !

bravely

Mis. 137–17   to spread your own so *b*·.
183–28   He is *b*· brave who dares
239–26   so *b*· confessing that she had
239–29   value of saying even more *b*·,
'00. 11–29   His symbolic ethics *b*· rebuke
My. 52– 4   * she has borne them *b*·,

bravery

Ret. 2–15   whose patriotism and *b*·

bravest

Pul. 5–10   *b*· to endure, firmest to suffer,
My. 285–13   best, *b*·, most cultured men and

brawler

My. 106–24   is not a *b*·, an alcohol drinker,

braying

Mis. 370–21   *b*· donkey whose ears stick out

breach

Mis. 283–16   *b*· of good manners and morals ;

breaches

Mis. 316–21   *b*· widened the next hour ;
My. 291– 6   uniting of *b*· soon to widen,

bread

Mis. 127–12   hungry heart petitions . . . for *b*·,
127–15   to feed it with the *b*· of heaven,
170– 7   eating of *b*· and drinking of wine
170–16   "I have *b*· to eat— *see John* 4 : 32.
170–17   The *b*· he ate, which was
175– 7   which says, I am sustained by *b*·,
175–16   unleavened *b*· of— *I Cor*. 5 : 8.
254– 7   *b*· that cometh down from heaven,
399–15   the water, the *b*·, and the wine.
Ret. 91–23   his . . . teaching was the *b*· of Life.
Pul. 30–13   * outward symbols of *b*· and wine,
Pan. 14– 8   *b*· that cometh down from heaven,
Po. 75–22   the water, the *b*·, and the wine.
My. 18– 9   hungry heart petitions . . . for *b*·,
18–11   with the *b*· of heaven, health,
131– 9   *b*· of heaven whereof if a man eat
156–21   *b*· that cometh down from heaven,
196–26   good in being, . . . is your daily *b*·.
196–27   The poor toil for our *b*·,
247–25   cast your *b*· upon the waters
273–12   nor his seed begging *b*·."— *Psal*. 37 : 25.

break

Mis. 19– 3   and will *b*· the rule of C. S.
90–17   *B*· the yoke of bondage
111– 5   and at *b*· of day caught much.
123– 8   That man can *b*· the forever-law
144–31   the universal dawn shall *b*· upon
211–15   Why, then, do you *b*· his peace
283–10   It would be right to *b*· into a burning
283–12   and *b*· through windows
290– 6   must ultimately *b*· all bonds
298–12   my best friend *b*· troth with me?
335–17   to *b*· the Decalogue,
387–14   If thou the bending reed wouldst *b*·
398– 8   *B*· earth's stupid rest.
Man. 54–10   *b*· the rules of its Tenets
67–22   *b*· a rule . . . and are amenable
Ret. 46–14   *B*· earth's stupid rest.
Un. 30–21   to *b*· the cords of matter,
Pul. 9– 6   no Delphian lyre could *b*· the full
13–14   Alas for those who *b*· faith with
17–13   *B*· earth's stupid rest.
Hea. 18– 7   if this be done, the bottle will *b*·
Po. 6– 9   bending reed wouldst *b*·
14–12   *B*· earth's stupid rest.
15– 5   *B*· not on the silence,
27–16   Hearts bleeding ere they *b*·
79–18   The centuries *b*·,

break

My. 117–10   will *b*· one's own dream of
211– 8   *b*· out in devouring flames.
221–17   *b*· the First Commandment of

breaker

My. 282– 2   is its peace maker or *b*·.

breaketh

Ret. 31–18   which *b*· the divine commandments.
Pan. 7– 1   *b*· the First Commandment

breakfast

Mis. 90–28   His spiritually prepared *b*·,

breaking

Mis. 123– 3   *b*· the First Commandment,
311–20   since by *b*· Christ's command,
'02. 20–18   thus *b*· any seeming connection
Po. 41–19   harpstring, just *b*·, reecho again
66–12   'Tis *b*· alone, but a young heart
My. 31– 3   * "The morning light is *b*· ;"
160–20   persist in *b*· the Golden Rule
223–22   *b*· of one of the Church By-laws,
262–16   *b*· upon the gloom of matter

breaks

Mis. 31– 6   *b*· the Golden Rule and
101–17   *b*· their chains,
176– 1   truth that *b*· the dream of sense,
197–27   *b*· the First Commandment of God.
274–19   outrages humanity, *b*· common law,
301–26   *Second* : It *b*· the Golden Rule,
'00. 6–20   and *b*· God's commandments,
'01. 4–30   he *b*· faith with his creed,

breast

Mis. 295–15   lost these sentiments from his own *b*·?
306–24   feathery touch of the *b*· of a dove ;
331–14   calls them to her *b*·,
354–33   than the dream in his *b*·.
389–23   drops down upon the troubled *b*·,
398– 6   Wound the callous *b*·,
Ret. 17–16   And bares a brave *b*· to the
46–12   Wound the callous *b*·,
Pul. 17–11   Wound the callous *b*·,
Po. 5– 3   drops down upon the troubled *b*·,
14–10   Wound the callous *b*·,
18–12   as the dream in his *b*· !
27–23   thy head on time's untired *b*·.
34– 5   dear remembrance in a weary *b*·.
62–20   bares a brave *b*· to the lightning
78–11   Tears . . . poured on her *b*·,
My. 191–24   Immortal courage fills the human *b*·

breast-milk

Rud. 8– 2   or provides *b*· for babes.

breasts

Mis. 240–18   sturdy oak, . . . *b*· the tornado.
Po. 53–16   Their downy little *b*·.

breastworks

My. 62– 1   * stood at the *b*· in the battle,

breath

Mis. 51–22   * from the lips of Truth one mighty *b*·
224–22   so settled that no passing *b*·
233– 7   the *b*· of mental malpractice,
296–30   who utters . . . in the same *b*·?
328–10   with a *b*· of heaven,
329–17   * "*b*· all odor and cheek all bloom."
390– 4   Thy breezes scent the rose's *b*· ;
Ret. 9– 4   I listened with bated *b*·.
19–20   With his parting *b*· he gave
48– 2   drew its *b*· from me,
Un. 60– 5   With the same *b*· he articulates
Pul. 79–24   * as his lungs call for *b*· ;
79–24   * the *b*· of his soul is a belief in God.
No. 14–13   the sweet *b*· of springtide,
Hea. 4– 4   We must give freer *b*· to thought
Po. 16–23   *b*· from the verdant springtime,
25–13   *b*· of the living above.
30–19   and loudest *b*· of praise
55– 5   Thy breezes scent the rose's *b*· ;
My. 195–22   deep-drawn *b*· fresh from God,
256–10   deep-drawn, heartfelt *b*· of thanks
330–32   With his parting *b*· he

breathe

Mis. 7– 2   nor to *b*· the cold air,
152– 8   *b*· a silent benediction over all
Pul. 10–27   *b*· Thou Thy blessing on every
Po. 24– 2   *B*· through the summer air
33–12   *b*· forth a prayer that His love
My. 341– 1   and love to *b*· it to the breeze

breathed

Mis. 189–15   supposition . . . Mind, is *b*· into
396–24   and *b*· in raptured song,
Pul. 18– 8   and *b*· in raptured song,
'02. 5–21   and *b*· in the Sermon on the Mount.
Po. 12– 8   and *b*· in raptured song,

breathes
Mis. 175— 1 *b·* His presence and power,
'00. 11–21 Adelaide A. Proctor *b·* my thought :
Po. 68— 1 she *b·* in my ear,

breathing
Mis. 143–29 *b·* the donor's privileged joy.
293— 2 *b·* new Life and Love
My. 105–22 *b·* at intervals in agony.
188–18 *b·* a benediction for God's largess.
270–18 *b·* love for his enemies,

breathings
Ret. 9–19 * my spirit's *b·* to control,

bred
Pul. 48–18 * was born and *b·* in that same

breeze
Mis. 51–23 * like a whirlwind, scatter in its *b·*
240–17 The sapling bends to the *b·*,
329–16 stirring the soft *b·* ;
329–26 now chirps to the *b·* ;
Po. 10— 2 To the billows and the *b·* ;
53— 4 Bring with thee brush and *b·*.
My. 29–26 * cooling *b·* to temper the heat,
128–10 and whispers to the *b·*
129–12 brook, blossom, *b·*, and balm
208–13 refreshing *b·* of morn,
232— 2 unfurling your banner to the *b·*
337— 4 To the billows and the *b·* ;
341— 2 and love to breathe it to the *b·*

breezes
Mis. 332–16 perfume-laden *b·*, and crystal
390–14 Thy *b·* scent the rose's breath ;
Po. 19— 2 *b·* that waft o'er its sky !
55— 4 Thy *b·* scent the rose's breath ;

brethren
beloved
Mis. 109–28 Beloved *b·*, Christ, Truth,
125–23 *Beloved B·, Children, and*
129— 2 *Beloved B· :* — If a member
148–23 *Beloved B· :* — Until recently,
149–18 *My Beloved B· :* — Lips nor pen
150–10 *Beloved B· :* — Space is no
154— 3 *Beloved B· :* — The spreading
251— 4 My beloved *b·*, who have come
322— 5 *Beloved B· :* — People coming from
Man. 86–10 Those beloved *b·* whose teacher
Pan. 1— 5 Beloved *b·*, since last you
13–10 Beloved *b·*, the love of our loving
'00. 1— 1 My beloved *b·*, methinks even I
11— 3 Beloved *b·*, have no discord over
'01. 1— 1 Beloved *b·*, to-day I extend my
'02. 1— 1 Beloved *b·*, another year of
20–16 Beloved *b·*, are you ready to
My. 3— 4 MY BELOVED *B· :* — The divine might
9–20 thanks to you, my beloved *b·*,
15–12 *My Beloved B· :* — My heart goes out
18–18 "Beloved *b·*, the love of our loving
19–18 *Beloved B· :* — It is conceded that
47— 9 * *Beloved B· of The First Church*
108–26 Finally, beloved *b·* in Christ,
121— 2 MY BELOVED *B· :* — I have suggested
122–16 Beloved *b·*, another Christmas has
124— 6 *My Beloved B· :* — Looking on this
131–18 *My Beloved B· :* — I hope I shall not
133–22 *My Beloved B· :* — I have a secret
139–17 *My Beloved B· :* — When I asked
142–17 My beloved *b·* may some time
144— 4 *My Beloved B· :* — Give yourselves
148–10 *My Beloved B· :* — In the annals of
151–23 *My Beloved B· :* — We learn from
154–15 *My Beloved B· :* — At this, your
155–17 *Beloved B· :* — May this glad Easter
156— 2 *Beloved B· :* — You will accept my
158— 7 *Beloved B· :* — This day
159— 3 *Beloved B· :* — Never more sweet than
164— 8 *My Beloved B· :* — I have yearned to
165–12 *Beloved B· :* — I beg to thank
166–10 *My Beloved B· :* — Your munificent gift
166–27 *Beloved B· :* — I am for the first time
167–23 *Beloved B· :* — Allow me to send
170–12 *Beloved B· :* — Welcome home !
172–11 "*My Beloved B· :* — Permit me to
172–27 "*My Beloved B· :* — You will please
174–17 *Beloved B· :* — I have the pleasure of
176— 5 *My Beloved B· :* — Long ago you
177— 3 BELOVED *B· :* — Most happily would I
183–11 *Beloved B· across the Sea :*
183–18 *Beloved B· :* — I rejoice with you ;
184— 3 *My Beloved B· :* — Have just received
184— 8 *My Beloved B· :* — To-day I am
186–25 *Beloved B· :* — Accept my thanks for
187–22 *My Beloved B· :* — You have met to
189–24 Beloved *b·*, I cannot forget that
191–28 *My Beloved B· :* — Your card of
193–22 *Beloved B· :* — Carlyle writes,

brethren
beloved
My. 195— 3 *Beloved B· :* — You will pardon my
196— 3 *My Beloved B· :* — I congratulate you
196–25 *My Beloved B· :* — The good in being,
197–25 *My Beloved B· :* — At this dedicatory
199–10 *Beloved B· :* — The Board of Directors
200–11 *My Beloved B· :* — The chain of
201–10 *My Beloved B· :* — Your Soul-full words
201–27 *Beloved B· :* — Please accept a line
202–21 *Beloved B· :* — I thank you for
203— 3 *Beloved B· :* — I have nothing new to
204–17 *Beloved B· :* — I congratulate you
205–15 *Beloved B· :* — Love and unity
207— 3 *Beloved B· :* — Your communication
208— 3 *Beloved B· :* — Accept my deep thanks
231–28 *Beloved B· :* — You will accept my
253–11 *Beloved B· :* — I thank you.
253–15 *Beloved B· :* — Accept my love
283— 6 *My Beloved B· :* — Your appointment
341— 9 Beloved *b·* all over our land
360–10 *Beloved B· :* — In consideration of
360–16 My beloved *b·* in First Church
362— 4 *Beloved B· :* — I rejoice with you

Mis. 106–17 *Friends and B· :* — Your Sunday
120–27 *Friends and B· :* — The Biblical
128— 6 "Finally, *b·*, whatsoever — *Phil.* 4 : 8.
152— 3 *Beloved Pastor and B· :*
167–19 they who do the will of . . . are his *b·*.
185–30 with the Corinthian *b·*,
303–11 *b·* in the fullest sense of that word ;
311— 4 welcomed, greeted as *b·*
351–13 to stir up strife between *b·*,
Ret. 22–20 his *b·* are all the children of one parent,
Un. 60–16 My *b·*, these things — *Jas.* 3 : 10.
Pul. 12— 8 accuser of our *b·* — *Rev.* 12 : 10.
87–11 *Beloved Directors and B· :*
Pan. 6— 5 Finally, *b·*, let us continue to
'01. 8— 5 than the belief of our *b·*,
11–26 But, my *b·*, the Scripture saith,
34–20 Finally, *b·*, wait patiently on God ;
'02. 18–15 least of these my *b·*, — *Matt.* 25 : 40.
19–10 *B·*, even as Jesus forgave,
My. 21–22 * their *b·* from far and near,
86–16 * *b·* to give no more money,
125— 4 *B·*, our annual meeting is a
147— 2 *Friends and B· :* — There are
158–24 will bless this dear band of *b·*.
165–12 I beg to thank the dear *b·*
198— 3 *Beloved Students and B· :*
199— 3 BELOVED STUDENTS AND *B· :*
201— 1 beloved students and *b·*.
274–24 unity among *b·*, and love to God
301–10 unite as *b·* in one prayer :
306— 8 * care of her husband's Masonic *b·*,
357–13 When my dear *b·* in New York

brevity
My. 170— 6 The *b·* of my remarks was due to

bribe
Un. 15–25 whom therefore they wish to *b·* with

bric-a-brac
Pul. 76–17 * Pictures and *b·*

brick
My. 66— 2 * a four-story *b·* building

bridal
Mis. 276–16 will always be the *b·* hour,
342— 9 the *b·* of Life and Love,
Ret. 23–14 heart's *b·* to more spiritual
Po. 8— 7 waiting alone for the *b·* hour
10–12 to bless a *b·* Betokened from above.
My. 125–25 beautiful garments — her *b·* robes.
190— 1 falling upon the *b·* wreath,
337–13 to bless a *b·* Betokened from above.

bride
Ret. 19–19 devotion to his young *b·*
My. 125–26 the *b·* (Word) is adorned,
153–27 "the Spirit and the *b·*," — *Rev.* 22 : 17.
(see also **Eddy**)

bridegroom
Mis. 276–21 and the *b·* appears.
342–12 expectancy was to behold the *b·*,
342–17 "The *b·* cometh !" — *Matt.* 25 : 6.
Ret. 23–15 and, lo, the *b·* came !
My. 125–27 and lo, the *b·* cometh !

bridge
Ret. 5— 1 near Concord, just across the *b·*,

Bridgeport, Conn.
Pul. 88–14 * *Farmer, B·, C·.*

Bridgeport (Conn.) Standard
My. 99–26 * [*B· (C·.) S·*]

bridges
No.   1– 9   demolishing *b·* and overwhelming

bridle
My. 196–13   *b·* the whole body." — *Jas.* 3 : 2.

brief
Mis.   96–26   conclusive idea in a *b·* explanation.
      111–22   The Christianity that . . . is *b·*;
      163–25   After his *b·* brave struggle,
      280–23   *b·* address by Mr. D. A. Easton,
      295– 2   deserve and elicit *b·* comment.
      340–12   barrister who never brings out a *b·*.
Ret.   5–17   The following is a *b·* extract from
       19– 7   spared to me for only one *b·* year.
       22– 3   Gospel narratives bear *b·* testimony
Pul.   30–11   * a *b·* "confession of faith,"
       44– 8   * to receive this *b·* message of
       46–11   * touched upon in this *b·* sketch.
No.   22– 5   * once clothed with a "*b·* authority;"
       33–15   the *b·* agony of the cross;
'02.   3–14   in its *b·* occupation of that pearl
Po.   67– 1   *b·* bliss of life's little day
My.   26–17   I thought it better to be *b·*
       65–12   * beyond two *b·* explanations
      113–10   declares . . . in these *b·* sentences:
      312–17   * a *b·* season she taught school."
      333–28   * the *b·* space of six months,
      340–14   clad in a little *b·* authority,

briefly
Mis. 128– 4   to learn or to teach *b·*;
      280–27   allude *b·* to a topic of great import
      285–20   to write *b·* on marriage,
'02.   4–22   *b·* consider these two commandments
My.   72–17   * *B·* that is the notice which
      131–19   I wish to say *b·* that this
      292–15   My answer . . . is *b·* this:
      298– 3   I *b·* declare that nothing has
      305– 8   *b·* express myself unmistakably

Brigham, Mr. Charles
My.   16–18   * Mr. Charles *B·* . . . the architect

bright
Mis. 142–19   with *b·* hues of the spiritual,
      171–30   to keep *b·* their invincible armor;
      354–33   No vision more *b·* than the
      386–20   beckoned me to this *b·* land,
      397– 4   A world more *b·*.
Chr.   53– 2   *B·*, blest, afar,
       55– 4   *b·* and morning star. — *Rev.* 22 : 16.
Ret.   4–19   green pastures *b·* with berries,
       18–11   to the *b·*, laughing day;
Un.   54– 1   The *b·* gold of Truth is
Pul.   18–13   A world more *b·*.
       83–13   * as *b·* as the sun, — see *Song* 6 : 10.
Hea.   10–17   if you will look on the *b·* side;
Po.   2–15   stars, so cold, so glitteringly *b·*,
       12–13   A world more *b·*.
       18–11   What vision so *b·* as the
       27–17   right with *b·* eye wet,
       34–20   in azure *b·* soar far above;
       43–20   Safe in Science, *b·* with glory
       46–15   *B·* as her evening star,
       50– 5   beckoned me to this *b·* land,
       63–22   to the *b·*, laughing day;
       65–14   dreams so boundless and *b·*
       68–21   and *b·* as the star,
       70– 3   A *b·* and golden shower
       73–20   the *b·* truth of the soul.
My.   342–14   * those eyes . . . which are always *b·*.

brighten
Mis. 262– 4   to *b·* so pure a purpose,
Po.   27–10   To *b·* o'er thy bier?
My.   155–22   *b·* their faith with a dawn
      350–25   *B·* the horoscope of crumbling creeds,

brightened
Pan.   10–16   broadened and *b·* before them,

brightening
My.   253– 2   *b·* this lower sphere with the

brightens
My.   253–27   by education *b·* into birth.

brighter
Mis. 321–22   battling for a *b·* crown.
Ret.   6– 4   * to follow her to the *b·* world.
Po.   23–16   In *b·* morn will find

brightest
My.   62–12   * shed its *b·* beams on your pathway,

brightness
Mis.   78– 5   *b·* of His glory encompasseth
      363–20   the *b·* of His coming.
      376–29   the *b·* of His glory.
Un.   18– 4   I can see only the *b·* of

brightness
Pul.   81–16   * who seek the *b·* of truth

brilliant
Mis. 296– 5   profound philosophers, *b·* scholars.
Pul.   6–23   Another *b·* enunciator, seeker,
No.   14–13   *b·* coruscations of the northern sky
Po.   39–20   blazoned, *b·* temperance hall

brilliantly
No.   44–11   boldly ridden or *b·* caparisoned,

brim
'00.   8–23   will boil over the *b·* of life

brimming
Po.   66– 1   nectar our *b·* cup fill,

brimstone
Mis. 237– 2   opinion that hell is fire and *b·*,

bring
Mis.   6– 2   to *b·* man nearer to God,
        7–14   but if you cannot *b·* peace to all,
        8– 3   if we can *b·* to the general thought
       18–32   *b·* to you at His demand
       19–11   and *b·* them out in human lives.
       75–24   does not *b·* out the meaning
       93– 6   *Can fear or sin b· back old beliefs*
       93–22   neither . . . can *b·* on disease
       93–22   or *b·* back disease,
      100–23   *b·* to earth a foretaste of heaven.
      106–20   I can only *b·* crumbs
      139– 4   *b·* your tithes into the storehouse,
      149– 6   Ask them to *b·* what they possess
      149–23   *b·* to your beloved church
      153–18   *b·* forth the fruits of Spirit,
      154–24   *B·* forth fruit
      157–23   shall *b·* it to pass. — *Psal.* 37 : 5.
      157–23   He shall *b·* forth — *Psal.* 37 : 6.
      194–15   *b·* out the entire hues of Deity,
      228–15   This will *b·* us also to look on
      231–23   *b·* the soft little palms patting
      262– 1   designed to *b·* health and happiness
      265–20   can never *b·* forth the real fruits
      269– 1   shall *b·* it to pass." — *Psal.* 37 : 5.
      320–15   sweet immunity these *b·* from sin,
      341– 1   they never *b·* out the right action
      346–25   becomes requisite to *b·* out Truth.
      365– 2   *b·* out the glories of eternity;
      369– 5   *b·* "on earth peace, — *Luke* 2 : 14.
Ret.   30–18   to *b·* him to Christ.
       49–24   *b·* all men to a knowledge of the
       62– 5   *b·* forth better fruits of health,
Un.   13–21   Such a view would *b·* us upon an outworn
       43– 4   cannot *b·* out the infinite reality of
Pul.   14– 2   *b·* the hour when the people will chain,
       51–14   * and with them *b·* different ideas.
Rud.   7–25   * about alteration of species
No.   28–12   is found to *b·* with it health,
       33–25   to *b·* in this glory;
       34–21   propitiate His justice and *b·* His mercy
       39–12   nor *b·* His designs into mortal modes;
'00.   8–14   "*B·* forth things — see *Matt.* 13 : 52.
'01.   12–21   *b·* out the entire hues of God.
       21–22   Christ came not to *b·* death
       35– 2   He shall *b·* forth thy — *Psal.* 37 : 6.
Hea.   5– 1   *b·* out our own erring finite sense
        9–13   to *b·* out in their lives?
Peo.   8– 9   we shall *b·* out these qualities
Po.   39– 5   An offering *b·* to Thee!
       53– 4   *B·* with thee brush and breeze.
My.   14– 6   will *b·* to be discerned in the
       20–12   *B·* all your tithes into
       40–17   * to *b·* health and a cure
       52–15   * *b·* out the perfection of all things,
       74– 5   * night trains of Saturday will *b·*
      131–24   "*B·* ye all the tithes — *Mal.* 3 : 10.
      140– 2   "And I will *b·* the blind — *Isa.* 42 : 16.
      170–24   He shall *b·* it to pass. — *Psal.* 37 : 5.
      170–24   He shall *b·* forth thy — *Psal.* 37 : 6.
      173–12   would *b·* thousands here
      190– 2   *b·* the recompense of human woe,
      193– 3   His presence with you will *b·* to
      213–14   *b·* out glorious results.
      222– 6   *b·* him hither to me." — *Matt.* 17 : 17.
      361– 7   do not *b·* your Leader into a

bringeth
Mis. 235–13   *b·* not forth good fruit;
Ret.   45– 3   "*b·* good tidings, — *Isa.* 52 : 7.
'02.   20– 4   *b·* us into the desired haven,
My.   184–27   *b·* good tidings, — *Isa.* 52 : 7.
      287–22   tree that *b·* not forth good fruit;

bringing
Mis.   41–30   *b·* out the result of the Principle
      139–13   *b· into captivity every* — *II Cor.* 10 : 5.
      201– 5   would oppose *b·* the qualities of
      247–13   those *b·* them do not understand my
      344–30   *b·* Christianity for the first time

bringing

Mis.	392–22	To my busy mem'ry *b·*
Un.	7–25	*b·* out the highest phenomena of
'02.	4– 9	*b·* music to the ear,
Hea.	8– 8	*b·* out the results of this higher
Po.	51– 4	To my busy mem'ry *b·*
My.	14– 3	*Then,* when this *b·* is consummated,
	150–21	*b·* the sinner to repentance,
	202–26	*b·* your sheaves into the storehouse.
	269–20	The vine is *b·* forth its fruit ;

brings

Mis.	9– 3	purification it *b·* to the flesh,
	12– 4	*b·* suffering upon suffering to
	56–24	and *b·* blessings infinite,
	71–16	Law *b·* out Truth, not error ;
	82– 4	*b·* the peace symbolized by a dove ;
	85– 2	Life eternal *b·* blessings.
	96–21	It *b·* to my sense, and to the
	102–22	Human pity often *b·* pain.
	109–11	knowledge . . . that *b·* on repentance
	184–12	*b·* to remembrance the Hebrew strain,
	189–12	*b·* to light the true reflection :
	204–25	*b·* with it wonderful foresight,
	205– 8	*b·* the light which dispels darkness.
	208–20	His soul *b·* to view His love,
	210–13	*b·* the serpent out of its hole,
	282– 3	*b·* to human view an enlarged sense
	292– 2	St. John's Gospel *b·* to view
	292–13	*b·* to human weakness might and
	293–18	*b·* greater torment than ignorance.
	337–16	Science *b·* out harmony ;
	338– 3	*b·* to humanity some great good,
	340–12	barrister who never *b·* out a brief.
	350– 6	*b·* up the question of this society,
	393– 2	Is the moral that it *b·* ;
Chr.	53–45	For C. S. *b·* to view
Ret.	35–14	*b·* out the hues of Deity.
	55– 6	*b·* out the nothingness of evil
	64– 7	*b·* to light, makes apparent,
Un.	7–24	and *b·* us nearer to God,
	38–19	*b·* to light Life and immortality.
	41– 6	*b·* in an unreal sense of suffering
Rud.	4–23	*b·* out the fruits of Spirit
	8– 1	No rock *b·* forth an apple ;
	11– 9	*b·* forward the next proposition
No.	21–23	*b·* in the glories of eternity ;
	24–26	*b·* with it another and more glorious
	26–11	*b·* forth its own sensuous conception.
'01.	19– 5	prayer *b·* the seeker into
Po.	51– 7	Is the moral that it *b·* ;
My.	41 22	* It *b·* into present and hourly
	116–16	*b·* on this contagion.
	132–32	*b·* back the wanderer to
	247 20	loving look which *b·* forth
	253– 4	*b·* to light the perfect original
	278–30	*b·* into human thought
	281– 8	Faith . . . *b·* blessings infinite,

Britain (see also Great Britain)

Po.	11– 1	Brave *B·,* blest America ;
My.	338– 1	Brave *B·,* blest America !

British

Ret.	3– 2	prominent in *B·* politics,
'02.	3–19	*B·* and Boer may prosper in peace,

Britons

Mis.	296–19	Do manly *B·* patronize taprooms

broad

Mis.	99– 2	this *b·* road to destruction.
	81– 1	*b·* and sure foundation
	143– 1	*b·* basis and sure foundation
	154– 5	reaching out their *b·* shelter
	224–24	charity *b·* enough to cover
	253– 8	platform is not *b·* enough for me,
Ret.	4–11	a *b·* picturesque view of the
	4–13	*b·* fields of bending grain
Pul.	42–27	* fastened with a *b·* ribbon bow.
	48– 6	* *b·* piazza on the south side
No.	32–14	cleaves sin with a *b·* battle-axe.
Po.	71– 9	Spans our *b·* heaven of light.
My.	46– 2	* foyer and *b·* stairways,
	68–28	* seven *b·* marble stairways,
	194– 2	Christianity writes in *b·* facts
	245– 6	on a *b·* and liberal basis.
	338–21	unfamiliar with his *b·* views

broadcast

My.	129– 6	Christianity sown *b·*

broaden

Ret.	52– 3	seeking to *b·* its channels

broadened

Ret.	82– 1	lessons are changed, modified, *b·,*
Pan.	10–16	wonderfully *b·* and brightened

broader

Mis.	2–16	deeper and *b·* philosophy

broader

Mis.	136– 6	*b·* and higher views,
	174–13	*b·* than the solar system
	191–32	accept the Scriptures in their *b·,*
Ret.	52–10	the *b·* wants of humanity,

broke

Mis.	111– 6	net has been so full that it *b·* :
Ret.	27–24	Science first *b·* upon my sense,
	45– 2	A new light *b·* in upon it,
Pul.	10–13	*b·* their exalted purpose,
'02.	18–10	who *b·* not the bruised reed
My.	258–10	one word, "Mary," *b·* the gloom

broken

Mis.	111–14	it would not have *b·.*
	224– 7	*b·* the head of his statue
	282–11	would have our houses *b·* open
	285–25	notifies the public of *b·* vows.
	386–19	o'er thy *b·* household band,
Chr.	53–57	no *b·* wing, no moan,
Ret.	60– 4	defines life as a *b·* sphere,
Un.	61–26	the *b·* and contrite heart
Pul.	22–17	doctrinal barriers . . . are *b·,*
	56 21	* We tread upon life's *b·* laws,
	80–14	* fairly *b·* our mental teeth
	83– 9	* a million of *b·* pledges.
Po.	50– 3	o'er thy *b·* household band,
My.	44– 3	* shackles of sin are being *b·,*
	53–30	* must have been very much *b·*
	80– 7	* when having *b·* bones set ;
	232–17	to be *b·* through." — *Luke* 12 : 39.
	257– 2	alas for the *b·* household band !
	318–30	"you have *b·* our agreement.

broken-hearted

Mis.	296–13	binding up the wounds of the *b·,*
No.	43–14	* binding up the *b·,*
My.	132–29	It binds up the *b·* ;

Bronx

My.	363– 8	CHRISTIAN SCIENCE SOCIETY, *B·,*

bronze

Mis.	305–21	* silver, *b·,* copper, and nickel
My.	68–29	* *b·,* marble, and Bedford stone.
	68 31	* *B·* is used in the lighting fixtures,
	69– 2	* the eight *b·* chains,

brood

Mis.	152– 9	*b·* unconsciously o'er the work of
	254– 9	nest of the raven's callow *b·* !
	331–12	dove feeds her callow *b·,*
	356–21	nests of the raven's callow *b·.*
	387– 8	*B·* o'er us with Thy shelt'ring
Po.	6– 1	*B·* o'er us with Thy shelt'ring
	24–17	The barren *b·,* O call

brooded

Mis.	254– 5	love which *b·* tireless
	342–14	darkness profound *b·* over

brooding

Mis.	172–10	charity, *b·* over all,
My.	86– 6	* *b·* elevation, guarding as it were,
	275–27	charity *b·* over all,

brook

'02.	18–19	like the summer *b·,* soon gets dry.
My.	129–12	bird, *b·,* blossom, breeze,

brooklet

Mis.	329–30	*b·* sings melting murmurs
Ret.	27–22	like the *b·* in its meandering
Pan.	3–13	lyre of bird and *b·.*

brooklets

Mis.	395–24	languid *b·* yield their sighs,
Ret.	4–19	*b·,* beautiful wild flowers,
Po.	58– 9	languid *b·* yield their sighs,

BROOKLINE
Mass.

My.	142–23	Box G, *B·,* MASS., June 24, 1908.
	143– 6	*B·,* MASS., June 5, 1909.
	144–10	Box G, *B·,* MASS., June 7, 1909.
	168– 9	Box G, *B·,* MASS., April 12, 1909.
	208– 8	Box G, *B·,* MASS., July 15, 1909.
	208–21	Box G, *B·,* MASS., November 2, 1909.
	237–19	*B·,* MASS., December 24, 1909.
	263–10	Box G, *B·,* MASS., December 25, 1909.
	275– 9	*B·,* MASS., May 1, 1908.
	275–29	Box G, *B·,* MASS., May 15, 1908.
	351–29	Box G, *B·,* MASS., June 24, 1908.
	352–24	Box G, *B·,* MASS., October 12, 1908.
	353– 4	Box G, *B·,* MASS., November 16, 1908.
	354–11	Box G, *B·,* MASS., April 28, 1909.
	358–24	Box G, *B·,* MASS., July 12, 1909.
	359–14	*B·,* MASS., October 12, 1909.
	360– 5	*B·,* MASS., July 23, 1909.
	360–26	*B·,* MASS., November 13, 1909.
	361–13	*B·,* MASS., December 11, 1909.

Brooklyn

N. Y.

My. 183–17 chapter sub-title

My. 363– 5 First Church of Christ, . . . *B·*,
363– 6 Fourth Church of Christ, . . . *B·*,

Brooklyn (N. Y.) Eagle

My. 88–26 *[B· (N. Y.) E·]*

brooks

No. 1– 8 babbling *b·* fill the rivers
Hea. 10–26 hart panteth for the water *b·*,

brother (*see also* **brother's**)

Mis. 50–30 and helping our *b·* man.
129– 4 or to condemn his *b·* without cause,
129– 7 forgive his *b·* and love his enemies.
129–10 tell thy *b·* his fault
151–18 *B·*, sister, beloved in the Lord,
254–11 when *b·* slays *b·*,
353–13 My *b·* was a manufacturer;
353–17 When my *b·* returned and saw it,
387–10 Like *b·* birds, that soar and sing,
Man. 64–21 a tender term such as sister or *b·*.
Chr. 55–24 the same is my *b·*,— *Matt.* 12 : 50.
Ret. 4– 3 and with his *b·*, James Baker,
4– 8 *b·* of the Hon. Henry Moore Baker
6–11 my second *b·*, Albert Baker,
6–15 My *b·* Albert was graduated at
7– 5 wrote of my *b·* as follows :
10– 8 From my *b·* Albert I received
10–10 My *b·* studied Hebrew
19–21 directions to his *b·* masons
Pul. 9– 9 *b·* whose appliances warm this house.
Po. 6– 4 Like *b·* birds, that soar and sing,
10– 1 Hail, *b·* ! fling thy banner
10–14 List, *b·* ! angels whisper
page 23 poem
My. 46–24 * Christly love of God and our *b·*,
296–10 lamented Christian Scientist *b·*
310– 4 My *b·* Albert was a distinguished
310– 9 my youngest *b·*, George . . . Baker,
310–15 My oldest *b·*, Samuel D. Baker,
312–13 * she was met . . . by her *b·* George.
330–32 directions to his *b·* Masons
336– 4 *her *b·*, George S. Baker,
337– 3 Hail, *b·* ! fling thy banner
337–15 List, *b·* ! angels whisper
338–11 last lecture of our dear *b·*,

brotherhood

Mis. 56–20 and the *b·* of man.
318– 3 universal *b·* of man
348– 7 help on the *b·* of men.
Ret. 49–26 uniting them in one common *b·*.
Peo. 13–10 *b·* of man in unity of Mind
My. 85–27 * spirit of faith and *b·*
220–16 I pray . . . for the *b·* of man,
240– 2 one God and the *b·* of man
265–10 *b·* of man should be established,
279–18 will establish the *b·* of man,
280– 9 * universal, loving *b·* on earth
281–10 On this basis the *b·* of all peoples
339– 3 cement the bonds of Christian *b·*,

brotherliness

Man. 40–10 in true *b·*, charitableness, and

brotherly

Mis. 149–22 Christianity, *b·* love, and
Man. 77–19 wisdom, economy, and *b·* love
'00. 14–14 signifies "*b·* love."— *Heb.* 13 : 1.
My. 41–20 * *b·* love which is just and kind
153– 9 the church of *b·* love,
175–26 Let *b·* love continue.
196– 6 "city of *b·* love."
213– 2 *b·* love, spiritual growth and

brother's

Mis. 131– 8 console this *b·* necessity by
My. 329–14 * and of her *b·* letter,

brothers

Mis. 142–28 I longed to say to the masonic *b·* :
167–16 Who are his parents, *b·*, and
Ret. 6–10 my much respected parents, *b·*, and
13– 7 if my *b·* and sisters were to be
14–16 with my *b·* and sisters,
Pul. 9– 4 *B·* of the C. S. Board of Directors,
32–28 * One of her *b·*, Albert Baker,
My. 5– 6 the murderers of their *b·* !
62– 8 * give it to my *b·* and sisters
217– 3 help your parents, *b·*, or sisters.
335– 9 * beloved by his *b·* and companions,

brought

Mis. 3–13 *b·* to the understanding through
56–18 that shall be *b·* to desolation.
75–31 *b·* forth by human thought,
79–27 *persons b· before the courts*
89– 3 *b·* to desolation."— *Matt.* 12 : 25.

brought

Mis. 98–10 *b·* us together to minister and to
112–22 * visitors have *b·* to him bouquets,
112–23 * you have *b·* what will do him good."
136– 8 *b·* to your earnest consideration,
170– 3 resurrection and life immortal are *b·*
201– 6 Sin *b·* death ;
211–18 pitied and *b·* back to life
214–14 The very conflict his Truth *b·*,
217–26 shall be *b·* to desolation.
231–27 *b·* sunshine to every heart.
237–12 *b·* to realize how impossible it is
374–18 To him who *b·* a great light
Man. 66–16 *b·* before a meeting of this Church,
Ret. 2–11 With them they *b·* to New England
20– 2 except what money I had *b·*
72– 9 *b·* into desolation,— *Psal.* 73 : 19.
Un. 57–17 gospel of suffering *b·* life
59–11 the divine idea *b·* to the flesh
Pul. 13–28 *b·* forth the man child.— *Rev.* 12 : 13.
49–16 I had them *b·* here in warm weather,
51–20 * it may, . . . have *b·* a benefit.
56–15 * *b·* hope and comfort to many
63–12 "I had them *b·* here in warm weather,
76–16 * *b·* from the Arctic regions.
80–24 * it has *b·* a hopeful spirit into
83–29 * She *b·* to warring men the
No. 5–22 *b·* to desolation ;"— *Luke* 11 : 17.
33–17 the glory his sacrifice *b·*
Pan. 5–25 *b·* sin, sickness, and death
'01. 1–17 have *b·* you hither.
'02. 6– 7 *b·* death into the world
16– 2 *b·* to me Wyclif's translation of
Hea. 12–18 power of thought *b·* to bear on
My. 14– 2 *b·* their tithes into His storehouse.
28–29 * who has *b·* to the world the
43–12 * *b·* them into the promised land,
43–25 * has *b·* us to this hour.
50–20 * *b·* fresh courage to the
95–10 * has *b·* that cheerful and
100– 1 * *b·* out in connection with the
104–27 What was it that *b·* together this
137–25 before . . . proceedings were *b·*
138– 6 This suit was *b·* without my
149–32 canst be *b·* into no condition,
184–18 *b·* back to me the odor of
187–24 *b·* into the light and liberty of
188– 9 *b·* out of the city of David,
336–13 except what money I had *b·* with me ;
343–18 It *b·* down a shower of abuse
343–29 *b·* all back to union and love
(*see also* **light**)

brow

Mis. 210–25 the shameless *b·* of licentiousness,
225–21 whereon lay the lad with burning *b·*,
325–15 Robust forms, with manly *b·*.
339–20 added one furrow to the *b·* of care?
340– 3 has torn the laurel from many a *b·*
374–26 * "Helen's beauty in a *b·* of Egypt."
386–22 kissed my cold *b·*,
392– 3 Clouds to adorn thy *b·*,
Chr. 53–44 Crowns the pale *b·*.
Pul. 48–15 * on the *b·* of Bow hill,
83–25 * royalty which shines from her *b·*.
'02. 3–22 on the *b·* of good King Edward,
Po. 20– 3 Clouds to adorn thy *b·*,
23– 2 a shadow on thy *b·*
50– 8 kissed my cold *b·*,
My. 201–14 bleeding *b·* of our blessed Lord,

Brown, George T.

Mis. 242–27 George T. *B·*, pharmacist,

brown

My. 342–13 * blue-gray or grayish *b·*, .

Browning

Elizabeth Barrett

Pul. 39– 8 * signature _____

bruise

Mis. 336– 5 handle the serpent and *b·* its head ;
Un. 45– 3 *B·* the head of this serpent,

bruised

Mis. 275– 9 *b·* father bendeth his aching head ;
Un. 55– 7 "He was *b·* for our— *Isa.* 53 : 5.
No. 34–23 Love *b·* and bleeding,
'02. 18–10 who broke not the *b·* reed

brush

Mis. 373– 6 Soul's expression through the *b·*;
377– 2 should move our *b·* or pen
Po. 53– 4 Bring with thee *b·* and breeze.

brushed

My. 92– 7 * Science cannot be *b·* aside by

brutality

'02. 19– 1 treachery, and *b·* that he received.

brute
  Ret. 69– 1   His origin is not, . . . in *b·* instinct,
  Pul. 53–19   * above the level of the *b·*,
brute-force
  Mis. 41– 1   *b·* that only the cruel and evil can
bubbles
  Mis. 328–10   to burst the *b·* of earth
bucket
  Mis. 353–15   to pour a *b·* of water
buckler
  '02. 19–13   his shield and his *b·*.
bud
  Mis. 142– 3   to *b·* and blossom as the rose !
     389– 1   form the *b·* for bursting bloom,
  Chr. 53–31   Sharon's rose must *b·* and bloom
  Po. 21–15   form the *b·* for bursting bloom,
     53– 3   The *b·*, the leaf and wing
budded
  Pul. 22–21   *b·* and blossomed as the rose.
Buddha
  My. 118–25   The doctrine of *B·*,
Buddhism
  '02. 3– 5   *B·* and Shintoism are said to be
  My. 119–11   towards *B·* or any other "ism."
budding
  Mis. 330–18   arranging . . . each *b·* thought.
  Man. 104– 8   adapted to form the *b·* thought
buds
  Ret. 18–10   beauty and perfume from *b·*
  Po. 63–20   beauty and perfume from *b·*
  My. 125– 6   and to vivify the *b·*,
Buffalo
  N. Y.
  Pul. 89– 4   * *News*, *B·*, N. Y.

  Pul. 56– 2   * New York, Chicago, *B·*, Cleveland,
buffetings
  Mis. 228–11   the *b·* of envy or malice
bugle-call
  Rud. 2–24   *b·* to thought and action,
build
  Mis. 5–16   There is nothing to *b·* upon.
     43–24   to *b·* on the downfall of others.
     98–19   *b·* up, through God's right hand,
     133– 4   to *b·* a sentence of so few words
     135–13   though you should *b·* to the heavens,
     135–13   you would *b·* on sand.
     144–19   I will *b·* my church ; — *Matt.* 16 : 18.
     176–18   to *b·* upon the rock of Christ,
     263– 7   I will *b·* my church;" — *Matt.* 16 : 18.
     264– 5   They *b·* for time and eternity.
     298–15   To *b·* on selfishness is to *b·* on sand.
     309– 8   unfitness for fable or fact to *b·* upon.
  Ret. 48– 8   should *b·* on his own foundation,
     52– 4   to *b·* a hedge round about it
  Un. 64– 5   To *b·* the individual spiritual
  Pul. 8–12   helping to *b·* The Mother Church.
     49–22   * *b·* a substantial home that should
  No. 12–16   *b·* on the new-born conception of
     43–19   *b·* a baseless fabric of their own
  '02. 2–14   The wise builders will *b·* on the
     13–13   on which to *b·* The First Church
  Peo. 11– 9   let us *b·* another staging for
  Po. 53–14   And *b·* their cozy nests,
  My. 13 18   with which to *b·* an ample temple
     13–24   to *b·* a temple
     48–21   * will certainly *b·* such truth as
     65– 8   * to *b·* in this city a church
     77–28   * to *b·* the imposing edifice
     98–19   * all of the funds required to *b·* it
     112– 7   and *b·* on its chief corner-stone.
     157– 6   * to *b·* a beautiful church edifice
     162–16   "This man began to *b·*, — *Luke* 14 : 30.
     162–29   may it *b·* upon the rock of ages
     165–30   the means that *b·* to the heavens,
     187–26   *b·* a house unto Him whose name
     192– 1   Ye *b·* not to an unknown God.
     195–25   its united efforts to *b·* an edifice
     195–30   continue to *b·*, rebuild, adorn, and
     357–13   desire to *b·* higher,
     357–18   as they *b·* upon the rock of Christ,
builded
  Mis. 244– 1   *b·* up the woman." — *Gen.* 2 : 21.
  My. 24–10   * *b·* by the prayers and offerings of
builder (God)
  Ret. 48– 9   the one *b·* and maker, God,
builder
  My. 16–20   * the *b·* of the new edifice.
     63– 2   * services of Mr. Whitcomb as *b·*
     162–20   would say to the *b·* of the

builders
  Mis. 5–20   stone that the *b·* have rejected,
     196–24   stone which the *b·* — *Psal.* 118 : 22.
  Man. 18– 1   stone which the *b·* — *Matt.* 21 : 42.
  Pul. 10–19   stone which the *b·* — *Matt.* 21 : 42.
     65–17   * its *b·* call it their "prayer in
  No. 38–13   rock which the *b·* rejected ;
  '00. 5–23   which the *b·* reject for a season ;
  '01. 25– 6   stone which the *b·* reject
  '02. 2–14   The wise *b·* will build on the stone
  Hea. 3– 9   stone which the *b·* rejected
  My. 25–23   *b·* of this church edifice,
     60–12   * stone which the *b·* — *Matt.* 21 : 42.
     71– 3   * discoveries of organ *b·*
     129–20   stone which the *b·* — *Matt.* 21 : 42.
     145– 4   one of Concord's best *b·*
     188– 1   stone which the *b·* rejected
     202–14   on the *b·* of this beautiful temple,
     301– 9   a foundation for the *b·*.
Building
  (*see* **Mother Church**)
building (noun)
  ample
     My. 10– 9   * in a beautiful, ample *b·*,
  beauty of the
     My. 24–23   * The beauty of the *b·*,
  box
     My. 309–23   * a small, square box *b·*
  brick
     My. 66– 2   * a four-story brick *b·* also in the
  burning
     Mis. 283–10   to break into a burning *b·*
     My. 178–22   on a table in a burning *b·*.
  church
     Pul. 30–29   * its own magnificent church *b·*,
     My. 27–15   * the completion of the church *b·*,
     60–26   * dedication of our new church *b·*,
     173–15   beautify our new church *b·*
     174– 1   lawn surrounding their church *b·*,
     175– 7   in repairing your church *b·*.
     208–19   prospect of erecting a church *b·*,
     284–14   service . . . held in my church *b·*,
     284–22   to assemble in my church *b·*,
  College
     Mis. 249–15   to remain in my College *b·*
  cost of the
     My. 76– 8   * the entire cost of the *b·*,
  land and
     Mis. 140– 1   provisions for the land and *b·*
  Mother Church
     My. 357–11   crowned The Mother Church *b·*
  new
     My. 11–24   * the new *b·* will be erected,
     16– 9   * the site of the new *b·*.
     72–25   * subscribed for the new *b·*,
  same
     Man. 27–21   located in the same *b·*,
     My. 123–12   rooms in the same *b·*.
  size of the
     My. 11–26   * The size of the *b·* was decided
  size of this
     My. 69–27   * an idea of the size of this *b·*
  some
     My. 55– 5   * to obtain by purchase some *b·*,
  such a
     My. 22– 8   * adequate to erect such a *b·*
  suitable
     Man. 27–13   suitable *b·* for the publication of
  this
     Mis. 141– 6   This *b·* begun, will go up,
     144– 4   northeast corner of this *b·*,
     My. 28–17   * The significance of this *b·*
     89–13   * remarkable thing in this *b·*
  within the
     My. 69–12   * Everywhere within the *b·*

  ———

  Pul. 57– 2   * The *b·* is fire-proof,
     57– 9   * the significance of the *b·*,
  My. 24– 5   * congratulate you that the *b·* is to
     24–20   * erection of the *b·* is proceeding
     24–29   * *b·* with a seating capacity of
     28– 2   * the completion of the *b·*
     61– 2   * been in the *b·* part of every
     61– 7   * seemed impossible for the *b·* to be
     65–13   * why the *b·* was needed.
     68– 7   * dome surmounting the *b·*
     69–31   * From this point the *b·* and dome
     83–25   * even before the *b·* itself has
     87– 2   * greater than the *b·* could contain.
     89– 5   * The *b·* is of light stone,
     96–18   * The *b·* they were . . . to dedicate
     100– 8   * were present in the *b·*,
     359–21   * then occupied offices in the *b·*

building (adj.)

Man.	75–20	the balance of the b· funds,
	76– 1	b· funds, which can be spared
My.	11–29	date for commencing b· operations.
	14–25	* b· operations have been commenced,
	19–14	* their local church b· funds
	(see also **fund**)	

building (ppr.)

Mis.	141–26	to commence b· our church
	143–24	toward b· The Mother Church.
	144– 3	money for b· "Mother's Room,"
	230–18	in b· air-castles or floating off
	263–10	b· on His foundation,
Ret.	51– 4	b· on the premises
Pul.	44–21	* b· a church by voluntary
	64– 6	* funds for the b· of a new church,
'01.	25– 3	B· on the rock of Christ's
My.	v– 4	* stirring times of church b·,
	21– 6	* b· church homes of their own,
	28–12	* to the b· of this church.
	57–11	* b· a suitable edifice.
	67–18	* for the b· of this addition
	85–16	* the b· of a church structure
	88–29	* the b· of a great church
	98–17	* for the b· of the church
	158– 1	in b· a granite church
	162–13	applied to b·, embellishing,
	192–29	b· for you a house
	321– 1	* b· this church for your followers.

Building Committee

Man.	102– 3	B· C·.
	102– 4	There shall be a B· C·

Building Fund (see also **fund**)

Mis.	140–15	contributions to the B· F·
	143–26	in aid of our Church B· F·,
My.	23–10	* B· F· : Amount on hand
	27–10	* chapter sub-title
	27–18	* Treasurer of the B· F·.

Buildings and buildings

Man.	27–11	Publishing B·.
	75–19	aforesaid premises and b·,
Pul.	45– 7	* get their b· finished on time,
	48– 1	* slopes behind the b·,
	57–12	* one of the most beautiful b·
	62–21	* concert halls, and public b·,
My.	90– 2	* b· should be filled at every
	236– 1	history of our church b·.

builds

Mis.	5–19	b· on the stone that the
	41–19	Mind is the architect that b·
Hea.	1– 9	b· on less than an immortal basis,
Peo.	9– 2	b· on Spirit, not matter ;
My.	164–27	It b upon the rock,
	194–10	b· that which reaches heaven.
	195–27	unselfed love that b· without

built

Mis.	131–11	being b· upon the rock
	140–22	on which our church was to be b·
	140–28	B· on the rock, our church
	149–29	b· the first temple for C. S. worship
	319–22	Our church edifice must be b· in 1894.
	349–23	and b· up the church,
	383–10	and b· upon the rock of Christ.
Man.	19– 2	is designed to be b· on the Rock,
	75–20	After the first church was b·,
	103– 7	the site where it was b·,
Ret.	15– 5	b· on the basis of C. S.,
Un.	9–16	but have b· instead upon the sand
	10– 4	b· on Him as the sole cause.
	28–15	material theories are b· on the
	53–16	not b· on such false foundations,
Pul.	9– 7	May the altar you have b·
	24–22	* church is b· of Concord granite
	40–15	* ROOM WHICH THE CHILDREN B·
	63– 6	* RECENTLY B· IN HER HONOR
	63–26	* b· as "a testimonial to our
	77–13	* b· as a testimonial to Truth,
	78–11	* b· as a testimonial to Truth,
	85– 9	* b· up in human consciousness
No.	38–10	on which he b· his Church
'00.	5–22	On this rock C. S. is b·.
Hea.	1– 9	whoso builds on . . . hath b· on sand.
	2–26	magnifies his name who b·, on Truth,
	11– 9	immortal superstructure is b· on
My.	15– 8	from the site where it was b·,
	17–11	b· up a spiritual house, — I Pet. 2 : 5.
	23–26	* is being b· in our day ;
	66–30	* has such a grand church been b·
	67–28	* it is so proportionately b·
	68– 1	* B· in the Italian Renaissance style,
	68–14	* old church . . . b· twelve years ago,
	71– 9	* b· the C. S. cathedral.
	95– 4	* church which has been b· upon the
	95–12	* They have b· a huge church,

built

My.	97–27	* b· at a cost of two million dollars,
	99–14	* b· a splendid cathedral in Boston,
	157–14	* The church will be b· of the
	172– 3	* It was b· in 1761,
	184–10	having b· First Church of Christ,
	187–30	you have b· this house
	188– 4	house, which thou hast b·, — I Kings 9 : 3.
	302–25	The Mother Church after it was b· and

bullet

My.	277–10	A b· in a man's heart never
	293–11	feared that the b· would

Bulletin

Pul.	88–26	* B·, Auburn, N. Y.
	89–25	* B·, San Francisco, Cal.

bulwark

Mis.	145– 2	b· of civil and religious liberty.

bulwarks

Pul.	9– 2	you are the b· of freedom,

bumper

Mis.	232– 2	in a b· of pudding-sauce

Bunker Hill

Mis.	304–11	* Then it will go to B· H·
My.	45–31	* loftier than the B· H· monument,

buoyancy

Mis.	371–24	with Truth, to give it b·.

buoyant

My.	110–16	b· with liberty and the luxury of

burden

Mis.	130–18	borne the b· in the heat of
	327–18	b· them with their own.
Ret.	86–20	undertakes to carry his b·
Un.	47– 1	Jesus assumed the b· of disproof
Pan.	12–15	lifteth the b· of sharp experience
'00.	9–29	"bear the b· — see Matt. 20 : 12.
My.	120– 9	Bear with me the b· of discovery
	138– 3	relieved of the b· of doing this.
	158–18	b· of proof that C. S. is
	161–29	"My b· is light." — Matt. 11 : 30.

burdened

Mis.	112– 5	ages are b· with material modes.
	251–22	who, b· for an hour,
	328–16	b· by pride, sin, and self,
'02.	19–16	To the b· and weary, Jesus saith :
Po.	31–15	Nor b· bliss, but Truth and Love
My.	162–32	b· with beauty, pointing to the

burdens

Mis.	39–23	bear "one another's b·, — Gal. 6 : 2.
	133–29	Love makes all b· light,
	262–25	yet were our b· heavy but for
	312– 7	speechless and alone, bears all b·,
	320–14	calms man's fears, bears his b·,
	351– 2	to lift the b· imposed by
	374–19	and named his b· light,
	397– 2	sweet mercies show Life's b· light.
Ret.	87–23	They feel their own b· less,
	87–24	bear the weight of others' b·,
Pul.	18–11	sweet mercies show Life's b· light.
Peo.	11–25	"bind heavy b·," — Matt. 23 : 4.
Po.	12–11	sweet mercies show Life's b· light.
	27–21	Thou hast borne b·,
My.	44– 3	* heavy b· are being laid down,
	223–27	b· that time will remove.

burdensome

'02.	10–21	discharges b· baggage,

Burgess

Un.	14–10	as B·, the boatbuilder, remedies

burial

Mis.	201– 9	reproduced his body after its b·,
Man.	50– 3	shall be prepared for b· by
Ret.	2–25	death and b· of George Washington.
	40–13	clothes already prepared for her b· ;
'02.	17– 2	knells tolling the b· of Christ.
My.	312–11	* received a decent b·.

buried

Mis.	78– 1	Life, God, is not b· in matter.
	168– 9	b· in dogmas and physical ailments,
	212–31	and b· it out of their sight.
	393–15	When the b· Master hails us
Ret.	21– 2	that his mother was dead and b·.
	66– 4	no longer b· in materiality,
Un.	62–26	matter, is all that can be b·
	63– 2	The I AM was neither b· nor
No.	37–24	b· in a false sense of being.
'02.	18–25	and it should be b·.
Peo.	5–13	The right ideal is not b·,
Po.	51–20	When the b· Master hails us
My.	110– 4	b· above-ground in material sense.
	159–15	The infinite will not be b· in
	160–11	dead truisms which can be b·
	164–18	b· in the depths of the unseen,

buried
My. 203–25   and *b·* . . . in the bosom of earth
    275–14   is dead, and should be *b·*.

burlesque
My. 278–25   *b·* of uncivil economics.

Burlington, Iowa
Pul. 89–30   * Gazette, B·, I·.

burn
Mis. 145– 8   Does a single bosom *b·* for fame
Hea. 11–13   *b·* upon the altars of to-day ;
My. 160–31   Only the makers of hell *b·* in their fire.
    256–23   the Yule-fires *b·*,

burned
Mis. 214–30   before they can be *b·*,
'00. 12–15   temple was *b·* on the night that
    12–22   books in that city were publicly *b·*.
My. 48–26   * *b·* indelibly upon the mind of
    178–25   covers of the book were *b·* up,
    332–28   * where they were *b·* ;

Burnham, Rev. Abraham
'01. 32– 1   Rev. Abraham *B·* of Pembroke, N. H.,

burning
Mis. 92–11   his own lamp trimmed and *b·*.
    225–21   with *b·* brow, moaning in pain.
    276–25   their lamps trimmed and *b·*
    283–10   right to break into a *b·* building
    335–25   get out of a *b·* house,
Ret. 13–18   as she bathed my *b·* temples,
    84– 8   his own lamp trimmed and *b·*.
Un. 34–16   yet put your finger on a *b·* coal,
Pul. 26–28   * which will be kept always *b·*
    39–15   * The sunset, *b·* low,
    59– 1   * perpetually *b·* in her honor ;
My. 125–28   Are our lamps trimmed and *b·* ?
    160–26   *b·* in torture until the sinner is
    178–22   on a table in a *b·* building.

burnished
My. 171–27   * bound with *b·* brass.

burnishing
Mis. 343–16   *b·* anew the hidden gems of Love,

burns
My. 249–12   heat of hate *b·* the wheat,

burnt
Mis. 51– 3   *B·* offerings and drugs,

burst
Mis. 283–11   but wrong to *b·* open doors
    326– 6   The door is *b·* open,
    328–10   to *b·* the bubbles of earth with
    370–18   *b·* through the lattice
Ret. 18–10   perfume from buds *b·* away,
No. 27– 7   will *b·* upon us in the similitude of
    28– 5   will *b·* the barriers of sense,
'02. 19– 2   as he *b·* the bonds of the tomb
Po. 63–20   perfume from buds *b·* away,
My. 202–18   *b·* upon the spiritual sense of
    318–24   and, addressing me, *b·* out with :

bursting
Mis. 178– 8   into old bottles without *b·* them,
    389– 1   To form the bud for *b·* bloom,
'00. 12– 2   *b·* paraphrases projected from
Po. 3–13   Till *b·* bonds our spirits part
    21–15   To form the bud for *b·* bloom,
My. 81– 7   * *b·* with a desire to testify to
    162–32   *b·* into the rapture of song

bury
Mis. 129–13   dead *b·* their dead," — Matt. 8 : 22.
    169–30   dead *b·* their dead ;— Matt. 8 : 22.
    292–16   It calls loudly on them to *b·* the
    311– 9   so, *b·* the dead past ;
Man. 60–18   dead *b·* their dead," — Matt. 8 : 22.
Ret. 87– 1   dead *b·* their dead." — Matt. 8 : 22.
'01. 16–12   Then let the dead *b·* its dead,
'02. 9– 5   dead *b·* their dead ;" — Matt. 8 : 22.
My. 353–25   dead *b·* their dead," — Matt. 8 : 22.

burying-ground
My. 333–13   * from thence to the Episcopal *b·*,

busier
Mis. 7– 5   mother of one child is often *b·*

busiest
'00. 2–21   are my *b·* workers ;

Business
    (see **Committee on Business**)

business
assigned
Man. 79–10   the *b·* assigned to them
authority for
Man. 66–18   referred to as authority for *b·*,
conduct the
Man. 79–23   and conduct the *b·* of
Father's
Mis. 163–31   forever about the Father's *b·* ;

business
God's
Mis. 140–13   but this was God's *b·*,
her own
My. 276–11   she is minding her own *b·*,
his
Mis. 69–19   he attended to his *b·*.
Man. 46–10   leaflets, which advertise his *b·*
his own
My. 106–23   because he minds his own *b·*
large
Ret. 7–16   * practice of a very large *b·*.
My. 310–15   carried on a large *b·* in Boston,
lucrative
'00. 2–22   will leave a lucrative *b·*
man of
Mis. 147–23   the conscientious man of *b·*,
Master's
'01. 32– 9   busy about their Master's *b·*,
matters of
'02. 12–21   interpolate some matters of *b·*
My. 7– 4   interpolate some matters of *b·*
much
My. 309– 4   called upon to do much *b·*
my
My. 358–22   through whom all my *b·* is
of others
Mis. 348– 5   the books nor the *b·* of others ;
other
Man. 56–20   electing officers and other *b·*,
    57– 2   transaction of such other *b·*
other people's
Mis. 357– 1   trafficking in other people's *b·*,
profits of the
Man. 80– 5   profits of the *b·* shall be paid
regular
My. 8–16   * accommodation for the regular *b·*
such
Man. 79– 6   such *b·* as Mrs. Eddy,
your own
Mis. 283–14   * "Mind your own *b·*,"

Mis. 13– 4   special care to mind my own *b·*.
    141–22   rule this *b·* transaction,
    252–28   encourages and empowers the *b·* man
Man. 27– 1   The *b·* of The Mother Church
    70– 3   nor enter into a *b·* transaction with
Ret. 19– 8   He was in Wilmington, . . . on *b·*,
Pul. 59–22   * *b·* manager of the Publishing Society,
'02. 13– 8   *b·* of The C. S. Publishing Society
My. 8–25   * convened in annual *b·* meeting
    23–19   * in annual *b·* meeting assembled,
    30 12   * *b·* men come from far distant points
    49–15   * first *b·* meeting of the church was
    50–31   * *b·* committee met after the services
    53 25   * annual report of the *b·* committee
    62–27   * by the members of the *b·* committee,
    65– 3   * largest church *b·* meeting
    81–32   * hard-headed shrewd *b·* men.
    96– 6   * in the social and *b·* world,
    106–26   dishonest politician or *b·* man?
    137–28   as to honesty and *b·* capacity,
    312–19   While on a *b·* trip to Wilmington,
    330–18   * who died there while on *b·*

Buskirk's, Hon. Clarence A.
My. 296– 1   chapter sub-title

bustle
Mis. 316–20   my retirement from life's *b·*.
Po. 16–11   *b·* and toil for its pomp and its pride.

busy
Mis. 231– 7   made *b·* many appetites ;
    392–22   To my *b·* mem'ry bringing
Ret. 4–13   But change has been *b·*.
Un. 26–13   * Chance and change are *b·* ever,
Pul. 49–20   * get away from her *b·* career
'01. 32– 9   *b·* about their Master's business,
Po. 51– 4   To my *b·* mem'ry bringing
My. 75– 7   * Yesterday was a *b·* day at
    187– 4   too *b·* to think of doing so
    252– 3   Keep yourselves *b·* with divine Love.
    338–17   owing to my *b·* life,

Busy Bees
Mis. 144– 6   a little band called *B· B·*.
Pul. 8–23   workers were called "*B· B·*."
    42–14   * are known . . . as the "*B· B·*,"
My. 169– 6   *B· B·*, under twelve years of age,
    216–23   drop the insignia of "*B· B·*,"

busybody
Mis. 356–32   Humility is no *b·* :

butcher
Mis. 250– 7   a *b·* fattening the lamb

butchers
Mis. 123– 2   *b·* the helpless Armenians,

buttons
My. 83– 7 * wore tiny white, unmarked *b*·,

buy
Mis. 113– 9 "no man might *b*· — *Rev.* 13 : 17.
140–11 No one could *b*·, sell, or mortgage
149– 2 come ye, *b*·, and eat ; — *Isa.* 55 : 1.
149– 2 *b*· wine and milk — *Isa.* 55 : 1.
269–28 mortals to *b*· error at par value.
269–31 "no man might *b*· — *Rev.* 13 : 17.
342–24 *b*· for yourselves." — *Matt.* 25 : 9.
Man. 43–22 shall neither *b*·, sell, nor circulate
My. 334– 7 * that efforts are being made to *b*·
354– 8 under no obligation to *b*·

buyeth
Mis. 253– 1 all that he hath and *b*· it.
253– 1 *B*· it ! Note the scope

buying
Pul. 50– 5 * one of her motives in *b*·
My. 298– 2 request the privilege of *b*·,

By-Law and By-law
Mis. 131–16 that you waive the church *B*·
131–18 did not act under that *B*· ;
132– 3 had already accepted as a *B*·.
Man. 18–24 *B*· adopted March 17, 1903,
28– 9 hence the necessity of this *B*·
29– 8 to fulfil the requirements of this *B*·,
32–24 This *B*· applies to Readers in
37– 6 A member who violates this *B*·
43–17 This *B*· not only calls
44– 5 the spirit or letter of this *B*·
47–21 This *B*· applies to testimonials
51–18 unless a *B*· governing the case
65–18 Disobedience to this *B*· shall be
68–21 This *B*· takes effect on Dec. 15, 1908.
70– 2 shall not make a church *B*·,
99– 3 For the purposes of this *B*·,
99–15 This *B*· applies to all States except
105– 2 No new Tenet or *B*· shall be
105– 3 nor any Tenet or *B*· amended
My. 15– 2 chapter sub-title
230–11 each Rule and *B*· in this Manual
231–29 interesting report regarding the *B*·,

By-Law and By-law
My. 250– 2 The *B*· of The Mother Church.
250– 8 adopt this *B*· in their churches,
250–12 churches who adopt this *B*·
250–15 The *B*· of The Mother Church
250–18 *B*· applies only to C. S. churches in
250–21 churches adopting this *B*·

By-Laws and by-laws
Mis. 132– 5 to the light of Love — and *B*·.
148– 8 Rules and *B*· in the Manual
382–25 wrote its constitution and *b*·,
382–26 the constitution and *b*· of
Man. 3– 3 Rules and *B*· in the Manual
18–22 Church Tenets, Rules, and *B*·,
18–26 *B*· pertaining to "Executive Members"
28– 6 annulling its Tenets and *B*·.
32–26 Enforcement of *B*·.
33– 4 enforce the discipline and *b*·
36– 3 Article VI, Sect. 2, of these *B*·.
39– 3 according to its *B*·.
50–22 Violation of *B*·.
50–23 found violating any of the *B*·
67–13 case not provided for in its *B*·
71–11 in its *B*· and self-government,
72– 5 A member . . . who obeys its *B*·
78– 2 comply with the *B*· of the Church.
78– 9 debts as are specified in its *B*·.
80–10 *B*· contained in this Manual.
87– 9 authorized by its *B*· to teach
92–24 Article XXVI of these *B*·
100–11 obligations . . . according to these *B*·,
100–15 in accordance with said *B*·.
105– 1 Amendment of *B*·.
My. 15– 4 * Article XLI . . . of the Church *B*·
49–14 * formulate the rules and *b*·,
223–23 breaking of one of the Church *B*·,
254–18 * preamble to our *B*·,
255– 6 publish the foregoing in their *B*·.
343–24 I made a code of *b*·,
358–30 approve the *B*· of The Mother Church,

bypaths
Mis. 169– 4 *b*· of ancient philosophies
No. 20–28 straying into forbidden *b*·

C

cabalistic
No. 9–22 *c*· insignia of philosophy ;

cabinet
My. 166–28 gift to me of a beautiful *c*·,

cable
'02. 11–13 a steam engine, a submarine *c*·,

cabled
My. 259– 6 received the following *c*· message :

Cablegram
My. 295–22 [Copy of *C*·]

cactus
Ret. 18– 4 While *c*· a mellower glory
Po. 63–12 While *c*· a mellower glory

Cæsar (see also Cæsar's)
Mis. 374–24 one renders not unto *C*·
Ret. 71– 5 "Render to *C*· the things — *Mark* 12 : 17.
'02. 14– 9 * not like *C*·, stained with blood,
Hea. 18–23 will cease to assert their *C*· sway
My. 220–10 "Render to *C*· the things — *Mark* 12 : 17.
248– 5 * not like *C*·, stained with blood,
344–25 'Render to *C*· the things — *Mark* 12 : 17.

Cæsar's
Mis. 374–25 things that are *C*· ;" — *Mark* 12 : 17.
376– 9 * taken by Fra Angelico from *C*· Cameo,
Ret. 71– 6 things that are *C*·, — *Mark* 12 : 17.
My. 220–10 things that are *C*·,' — *Mark* 12 : 17.
344–25 things that are *C*·.' — *Mark* 12 : 17.

cage
My. 126–27 *c*· of every unclean . . . bird" — *Rev.* 18 : 2.

Calais, Me.
Pul. 88–12 * *Advertiser, C*·, *M*·.

calamity
Mis. 347– 8 To escape from this *c*·
Ret. 7–23 * It is a public *c*·
71– 2 with the tax it raises on *c*·

calcareous
My. 108– 1 *c*· salts formed by carbonate and

calculated
'02. 1–15 Whatever seems *c*· to displace
My. 97–30 * *c*· to impress the most determined
327–15 * *c*· to limit or stop the

calculating
Hea. 4– 4 before *c*· the results of

calculation
Un. 10–21 attempt the *c*· of His mighty ways,
'01. 21–19 begins his *c*· erroneously ;

calculations
Mis. 376–19 According to terrestrial *c*·,

calculus
Mis. 22–11 infinite *c*· defining the line,
104–10 *c*· of forms and numbers.
'01. 22–20 infinite *c*· of the infinite God.

Calderon
Ret. 32–11 *C*·, the famous Spanish poet,

Caledonia
'02. 13–17 Falmouth and *C*· (now Norway) Streets ;

calendar
Mis. 117–23 According to my *c*·,

calf
Mis. 145–24 *c*· and the young lion and the
307–25 not intended for a golden *c*·,

California and Cal.
Man. 99– 3 State of *C*· shall be considered as
(see also **Los Angeles, Oakland, San Francisco, San Jose**)

call (noun)
accepted the
Man. 18– 6 accepted the *c*·, and was ordained
Ret. 16–19 She accepted the *c*·,
44– 7 I accepted the *c*·,
My. 49–32 * Mrs. Eddy accepted the *c*·.
came
Ret. 9–14 When the *c*· came again
Pul. 33– 9 * The *c*· came, but the little maid
33–11 * if the *c*· came again.
clarion
Mis. 120–16 the clarion *c*· of peace
Ret. 12– 1 nobler far than clarion *c*·
'01. 35– 8 a clarion *c*· to the reign of
Po. 60–21 nobler far than clarion *c*·
cooing
My. 341–12 A lightsome lay, a cooing *c*·,
expert
My. 172–19 your kind, expert *c*· on me."

call (noun)

extended a
- *Man.* 18– 5 extended a *c·* to Mary Baker Eddy
- *Ret.* 16–18 extended a *c·* to Mary B. G. Eddy
- 44– 7 extended a *c·* to me

heart's
- *Po.* 53–17 Come at the sad heart's *c·*,

His
- *Mis.* 151– 2 their ears are attuned to His *c·*.

human
- *Mis.* 81–26 answers the human *c·* for help;
- *Un.* 13– 4 coming at human *c·*;

imperative
- *Mis.* 273–32 the imperative *c·* is for my

imperious
- *Mis.* 177– 1 solemn and imperious *c·*

kind
- *Pul.* 87–12 kind *c·* to the pastorate of

Love's
- *My.* 129–13 They come at Love's *c·*.

mysterious
- *Ret.* 9–16 never again . . . was that mysterious *c·*

quiet
- *Mis.* 143–25 A quiet *c·* from me for this extra

same
- *Ret.* 8–19 the same *c·* was thrice repeated.

spiritual
- *My.* 172–14 material symbol of my spiritual *c·*

that
- *My.* 172–15 and this is that *c·* :

this
- *Mis.* 99–14 Then obey this *c·*.
- *Man.* 68– 7 or who declines to obey this *c·*

to lecture
- *Man.* 96–10 a *c·* to lecture in a place where he

to serve
- *My.* 42–14 * the *c·* to serve you in this

unexplained
- *My.* 243–21 at my unexplained *c·*

- *Man.* 57– 7 upon the *c·* of the Clerk.
- 69–18 in obedience to the *c·*.
- *Ret.* 8–15 the *c·* again came,
- *Pul.* 8– 9 responded to the *c·* for this church
- *My.* 118–12 In a *c·* upon my person,
- 169–18 *c·* of about three thousand

call (verb)

- *Mis.* 9–16 Whom we *c·* friends seem to
- 26–23 this is just what I *c·* matter,
- 44–20 You *c·* this body matter,
- 83–20 *Why did Jesus c· himself*
- 93– 3 posterity shall *c·* you blessed,
- 98–24 and *c·* the world to acknowledge
- 110–28 how fleeting is that which men *c·* great;
- 111–27 Let me specially *c·* the attention of
- 121– 6 cup to which I *c·* your attention,
- 131–28 when you *c·* on the members of the
- 133– 8 I *c·* your attention and
- 181– 1 Jesus said to *c·* no man father;
- 209–12 *c·* in their course to *c·* on me,
- 221–31 or *c·* public attention to that crime!
- 233– 5 *c·* themselves metaphysicians
- 239 1 *C·* at the . . . Metaphysical College,
- 250–16 *c·* for active witnesses to prove it,
- 258–20 and *c·* Mind by the name of matter,
- 282–26 which may *c·* for aid unsought,
- 282–29 The abuse which I *c·* attention to,
- 287– 6 "*C·* no man your father— Matt.* 23 : 9.
- 317– 2 "May I *c·* you mother?"
- 328– 4 will *c·* thee back to the path
- 330– 9 should *c·* his race as gently
- 368–13 who *c·* themselves so.
- 380–11 *c·* for help impelled me to begin
- 387– 3 To *c·* her home,
- *Man.* 28–20 shall immediately *c·* a meeting
- 53– 4 immediately to *c·* a meeting,
- 57–16 before he can *c·* said meeting.
- 69–14 *c·* on this Board for household help
- 76– 4 as the right occasion may *c·* for it.
- 84–20 shall not *c·* their pupils together,
- 95– 5 Mother Church may *c·* on any member
- 95–17 shall *c·* on the Board of Lectureship
- *Ret.* 8– 9 "Mother, who *did c·* me?
- 8–10 I heard somebody *c· Mary,*
- 68–13 "*c·* no man your father— Matt.* 23 : 9.
- 69–11 into what I *c·* matter,
- 84–22 posterity will *c·* him blessed,
- *Un.* 10–28 and *c·* in vain for the mountains of
- 32–16 which I prefer to *c· mortal mind.*
- 32–26 which I *c· mortal mind;*
- 44–15 Human theories *c·*, or miscall,
- 49–24 right to *c·* evil a negation,
- 53– 5 would be truthful to *c·* itself a lie;
- 53–26 "*C·* no man your father— Matt.* 23 : 9.
- 60– 7 We *c·* God omnipotent and
- *Pul.* 9–28 and *c·* down blessings infinite.

call (verb)

- *Pul.* 38–17 * the belief we *c·* spiritualism.
- 52–17 * We *c·* it new.
- 62–13 * and *c·* forth all the purity
- 65–17 * *c·* it their "prayer in stone,"
- 79–24 * as much as his lungs *c·* for breath ;
- 81–12 * dearest ones *c·* her "selfish"
- *Rud.* 9–11 outcome of what I *c· mortal mind,*
- 16–26 *c·* it their first-fruits.
- *Pan.* 8–18 "*C·* no man your father— Matt.* 23 : 9.
- 11–26 are content to *c·* man,
- '00. 3–22 to *c·* the divine name Yahwah,
- 14–14 I *c·* your attention to this
- '01. 7–18 *c·* their God "divine Principle,"
- 10– 5 much more shall they *c· — Matt.* 10 : 25.
- 18–26 Truth, Love— whom men *c·* God
- 25–10 certain individuals *c·* aids to
- '02. 10– 7 *c·* them false or in advance of the
- *Hea.* 16–21 shall we *c·* that reliable evidence
- *Po.* 16–22 And *c·* to my spirit
- 24–17 O *c·* With song of morning lark ;
- 41–17 Was it then thou didst *c·* them
- 50–21 To *c·* her home,
- *My.* 49–30 * to *c·* Mrs. Eddy to the pastorate
- 50–32 * to *c·* a general meeting of the
- 91–17 * serves to *c·* attention to one of
- 104–11 of a man that should *c·* St. Paul a
- 104–13 who shall *c·* a Christian Scientist a
- 110–32 may serve to *c·* attention to
- 150–31 *c·* this "a subtle fraud,"
- 152–23 Principle of good, that we *c·* God,
- 163– 1 *c·* the worshipper to seek the
- 186–21 "Before they *c·*, I will— Isa.* 65 : 24.
- 224– 5 *c·* your attention to this demand,
- 228– 1 I *c·* disease by its name
- 229– 1 I *c·* none but genuine . . . Scientists,
- 240– 7 * *c·* C. S. the higher criticism
- 251–24 *c·* you mine, for all is thine and
- 256–23 Parents *c·* home their loved ones,
- 285–26 way which they *c·* heresy,— Acts* 24 : 14.
- 290–24 where the high and holy *c·* you again
- 319–23 * you suggested that I *c·* on the
- 347–16 *c·* to mind the number of our

called

- *Mis.* 10– 9 Because He has *c·* His own,
- 24–10 I *c·* for my Bible,
- 34–23 All that are *c·* "communications
- 68– 8 * metaphysical healing being *c·* C. S.
- 69–14 once *c·* to visit a sick man
- 84–17 was *c·* the Son of man,
- 89– 4 *If Scientists are c· upon to care for*
- 99–13 *c·* to voice a higher order of
- 112–17 mental state *c·* moral idiocy.
- 131– 3 will be *c·* a moral nuisance,
- 139–21 *c·* The Church of Christ, Scientist.
- 141 6 a little band *c·* Busy Bees,
- 161– 6 *his name shall be c· — Isa.* 9 : 6.
- 162– 2 Jacob was *c·* Israel ;
- 164–17 "His name shall be *c· — Isa.* 9 : 6.
- 173–25 atom or molecule *c·* matter
- 174–21 Shall that be *c·* heresy which
- 176–10 been *c·* for and manifested,
- 180–27 month is *c·* the son of a year.
- 193–23 Christians are properly *c·* Scientists
- 205– 5 *c·* sin, disease, and death.
- 205–28 mortal molecules, *c·* man,
- 234–20 metaphysical healing, *c·* C. S.,
- 248–10 the person they *c·* slanderer,
- 257–20 *c·* it "a murderer"— John* 8 : 44.
- 265–27 constantly *c·* to settle questions
- 272–21 * which may be *c·* a charter,
- 294–12 sometimes *c·* a man,
- 310–22 and upon a meeting being *c·*,
- 312–17 * *c·* to declare the real harmony
- 321– 5 shall be *c·* Wonderful,— Isa.* 9 : 6.
- 337–12 "Jesus *c·* a little child— Matt.* 18 : 2.
- 351– 1 *c·* on students to test their ability
- 380–13 an accident, *c·* fatal to life,
- 380–20 people generally, *c·* for a sign
- *Man.* 17– 3 a church without creeds, to be *c·*
- 50–19 a meeting . . . shall be *c·*,
- 57– 8 *C·* only by the Clerk.
- 64–18 objected to being *c·* thus,
- 65– 5 shall not be *c·* Leader
- 69– 6 has been *c·* to serve our Leader
- 73–19 When *c·* for, a member of the
- 89– 6 shall immediately be *c·*,
- 94– 2 within the city whither he is *c·*
- 95–14 If *c·* for, a member of the Board
- *Ret.* 9–10 when the voice *c·* again,
- 14– 2 John Calvin rightly *c·* his own tenet
- 15–13 I was *c·* to preach in Boston
- 25–11 God I *c· immortal Mind.*
- 25–13 sensuous nature, I *c·* error
- 25–18 Spirit I *c·* the *reality* ;
- 27– 3 my work *c·* S. and H.,

called

Ret. 33– 7 as it has been well c·.
40– 4 c· to speak before the Lyceum
44– 3 to be c· the Church of Christ, Scientist,
47–12 a meeting was c· of the Board
52–20 was c· Journal of C. S.
53– 2 The C. S. Journal, as it was now c·,
54–17 in this mental state c· belief ;
67–16 until the false claim c· sin is
88– 7 c· the physical man from the tomb
91– 3 c· "the pearl of parables,"
91– 5 c· "the diamond sermon."
Un. 15–16 God is commonly c· the sinless,
22–21 c· human intellect and will-power,
33– 5 existence of a substance c· matter.
33–16 that form of matter c· brains,
38–11 transition c· material death,
46– 1 mortal error, c· mind,
54– 3 a false claim, c· sickness,
58–11 through what is humanly c· agony.
Pul. 8–23 youthful workers were c· "Busy Bees."
24– 7 * as it is officially c·,
28–21 * c· the "C. S. Hymnal,"
33– 4 * she heard her name c·
37– 6 * residence, c· Pleasant View.
44–21 * students, as they are c·,
47– 6 * It was c· the Journal of C. S.,
51–18 * c· forth the implements of
55–16 * Her discovery was first c·,
58– 7 * beautiful estate c· Pleasant View ;
58–25 * her book, c· "S. and H.
58–27 * and c· "Mother's Room,"
62–20 * They can be c· into requisition in
65– 3 * what is c· the New England mind
65–14 * progress . . . made by what is c· C. S.
65–20 * c· the Bible of that city.
65–25 * c· the divine spirit of giving,
68–19 * C. S. church, c· The Mother Church,
72– 5 * reporter c· upon a few of the
82–16 * Jews who never c· Abraham "Father,"
Rud. 3–15 c· the Sermon on the Mount,
5–16 either mind which is c· matter,
No. 16–12 c· mortal mind or matter,
31–23 evils c· sin, sickness, and death
41– 4 and contemptuously c· him
'00. 5–29 casting out God's opposites, c· evils,
'01. 3–19 c· in Scripture, Spirit, Love.
7– 7 divine intelligence c· God.
9– 1 Christ Jesus, c· in Scripture the
9–12 crucified Jesus and c· him a
10– 4 "If they have c· the — Matt. 10 : 25.
13– 2 The outcome of evil, c· sin,
24– 4 is generally c· matter
24–20 is c· the Christian era.
'02. 7–27 c· his disciples' special attention to
19– 6 c· one a "fool" — see Luke 24 : 25.
Peo. 4–14 a third person, c· material man,
7–24 objects of sense c· sickness and
Po. v– 7 * c· forth by some experience
My. 13– 4 c· "Thoughts on the Apocalypse,"
21–24 * c· upon to make no less sacrifice
40–22 * c· the children of God." — Matt. 5 : 9.
122–13 It c· forth flattering comment
143–26 c· according to His purpose. — Rom. 8 : 28.
148– 3 c· to do your part wisely
193–27 c· thee by thy name ; — Isa. 43 : 1.
196– 5 c· the "city of brotherly love."
201– 3 whereunto divine Love has c· us
206–25 Him who hath c· you — I Pet. 2 : 9.
228–26 Who shall be c· to Pleasant View?
228–31 such a one was never c· to
229– 9 Scientists, c· to the home of
240– 9 I c· C. S. the higher criticism
244–13 c· of God to contribute my part
244–20 "Many are c·, — Matt. 22 : 14.
245–11 c· out of their hiding-places those
246–22 c· the Board of Education
247–19 c· you to be a fisher of men.
269– 2 image or likeness, c· man,
269– 4 divine Principle, Love, c· God,
291–26 c· to mourn the loss of her
309– 3 c· upon to do much business for
311–32 I was c· by the Rev. R. S. Rust,
317–23 has been c· original.
320–20 * I c· on Mr. Wiggin several times
325– 3 * c· to inquire of his welfare
334–18 * while being c· unreal.
343–14 "I have been c· a pope,
(see also **death**)

calleth

Hea. 11– 4 A dream c· itself a dreamer,

calling

Mis. 4– 6 c· this method "mental science."
245–11 c· forth the vox populi
329–27 c· the feathered tribe back

calling

Mis. 333–18 c· on matter to work out the
348– 2 towards the mark of a high c·.
365–18 that mortal mind is c· for what
Man. 57– 9 Before c· a meeting of the
86–13 who is ready for this high c·,
Ret. 8– 4 c· me distinctly by name,
8–18 "Your mother is c· you !"
8–21 your mother is c· you !"
Un. 53– 6 c· the knowledge of evil good,
Pul. 21–27 spirit of Christ c· us together.
23–15 * and ingenuously c· out a
74–13 c· for an interview
'00. 6– 8 of the high c· of God — Phil. 3 : 14.
'01. 4–28 c· God "divine Principle,"
5–13 c· one the divine Principle
Hea. 6–11 but they take pleasure in c· me a
Po. 15–11 whispering voices are c· away
My. 3–23 Christian Scientist verifies his c·.
147–30 hearts are c· on me for help,
201– 2 Press on towards the high c·
229– 2 unless I mistake their c·.
320– 3 * Upon c· on Mr. Wiggin,

callous

Mis. 398– 6 Wound the c· breast,
Ret. 46–12 Wound the c· breast,
Pul. 17–11 Wound the c· breast,
Po. 14–10 Wound the c· breast,

callow

Mis. 254– 9 nest of the raven's c· brood !
331–12 dove feeds her c· brood,
356–21 nests of the raven's c· brood.

calls

Mis. 27– 2 Science of good c· evil nothing.
68–27 c· metaphysics "the science which
110–29 that which God c· good.
132–20 teaching C. S., receiving c·,
230– 9 making lingering c·,
274– 7 and which God c· me to
283–31 seldom c· on his teacher or
292–16 It c· loudly on them to
325–20 c· out, rubs his eyes,
331–14 c· them to her breast,
370– 1 when their feebleness c· for help,
370–17 and c· forth infinite care from
399– 1 Mourner, it c· you,
399– 6 Sinner, it c· you,
Man. 43–18 c· more serious attention to the
48– 3 whenever God c· a member to
68–18 c· to her home or allows to visit
68–24 C. S. Board of Directors c· a student
95– 2 c· FOR LECTURES.
Ret. 69–26 voice of Truth still c·:
Un. 34–20 could not feel what it c· substance.
59–21 illusion which c· sin real,
59–22 illusion which c· sickness real,
Pul. 49– 1 * room which Mrs. Eddy c· her den
Rud. 8–18 man who c· himself a Christian Scientist,
Hea. 1– 8 c· to higher duties,
15–16 at the same time he c· God almighty
Peo. 11–21 c· its own enactments "laws
Po. 75– 7 Mourner, it c· you,
75–13 Sinner, it c· you,
My. 84– 3 the interest on which c· for
165–23 becomes tired and c· for rest.
180–26 misconstrues . . . and c· them unkind.
228– 7 The evil mind c· it "skulking,"
310– 8 c· my youngest brother,
314– 1 c· Dr. Daniel Patterson,

calm

Mis. 200–25 holy c· of Paul's well-tried hope
227–21 wherein c·, self-respected thoughts
228– 6 is to be c· amid excitement,
229–25 A c·, Christian state of mind
338–17 and c· strength will enrage evil.
Ret. 60–16 and there is a great c·,
'00. 11–25 * With a touch of infinite c·.
'01. 30–25 far-seeing vision, the c· courage,
'02. 19–20 underneath is a deep-settled c·.
Hea. 2– 2 a c· and steadfast communion with
Po. 22–17 life perfected, strong and c·.
My. 127– 8 c· coherence in the ranks of C. S.
139–14 Life, — c·, irresistible, eternal.
150–20 c·, clear, radiant reflection of
204– 5 power which lies concealed in the c·
333–22 * "His end was c· and peaceful,

calmly

Mis. 247– 9 I c· challenge the world,
My. 350– 8 c· and rationally, though faintly,

calms

Mis. 320–13 c· man's fears, bears his burdens,
My. 106–20 divine Mind c· . . . with a word.
166–19 c· of human existence.

calumniator
Mis. 191–27   define him as . . . "c·,"
'01. 16–17   defines *devil* as *accuser*, c·;
      33– 4   "c·" must not be admitted to
My. 305– 3   Failing in . . . the c· has resorted to
     330– 6   * The c· who informed you

calumny
My. 308– 6   It is c· on C. S. to say

Calvary
Mis. 124–24   last act of the tragedy on C·
Ret. 31–26   Bethany, Gethsemane and C·,
Un.   59–15   to suffer before Pilate and on C·,
'02. 10–11   * not Athens, but C·."

Calvin, John
Ret. 14– 1   as John C· rightly called his

Calvinistic
Ret.   2– 3   C· devotion to Protestant liberty

Cambridge
Mass.
My. 53–24   * A. J. Peabody, D.D., of C·, Mass.
     60–22   * C·, Mass., June 12, 1906.

My. 56–13   * C·, Chelsea, and Roxbury.
     69–30   * in Mt. Auburn cemetery in C·,
    318–11   the University Press, C·,

came
Mis. 24– 5   c· to me in an hour of great need ;
      26–13   Whence c· the first seed,
      26–15   Whence c· the infinitesimals,
      82– 8   c· up out of the baptism of
     105– 9   c· from the testimony of the
     143–27   Each donation c· promptly ;
     144– 5   c· from the dear children
     176–22   which c· down from heaven.
     176–23   c· to establish a nation in
     177–26   * c· on the platform.
     178– 8   and he c· to us.
     178–25   * the pastor again c· forward,
     184–29   John c· baptizing with water.
     188–24   c· to her through a spiritual sense
     190–11   *And it c· to pass,— Luke* 11 : 14.
     190–12   that saying c· not from Mind,
     214– 5   c· not to send peace,— *Matt.* 10. 34.
     242– 3   c· not to my notice until January
     261–18   "I c· not to destroy— *see Matt.* 5 : 17.
     281–26   it c· to me more clearly
     327– 3   I c· hither, hoping that I might
     360–28   c· from the Father,"— *see John* 16 : 28.
     372–15   From them c· such replies
     376–25   c· out on a background of
Ret.   2– 7   c· to America seeking
       8–15   the call again c·,
       9–11   The voice c· ; but I was afraid,
       9–14   When the call c· again
      13–21   glow of ineffable joy c· over me.
      14–30   After the meeting was over they c·
      21– 9   and c· to see me in Massachusetts.
      23–16   and, lo, the bridegroom c· !
      24– 6   discovery c· to pass in this way.
      45–14   c· my clue to the uses and
Un.   15– 1   c· "death into the world,
      59– 9   one who c· down from heaven,
      60– 2   Christ Jesus c· to save men,
      62– 4   and c· to save me ;"
Pul.   8–14   and forth c· the money,
       9–11   c· to the rescue as
      29–16   * Then c· his sermon, which dealt
      32–23   * On her father's side Mrs. Eddy c· from
      33– 9   * The call c·, but the little maid
      33–12   * reply if the call c· again.
      33–12   * It c·, and she answered
      33–22   * as to whence the stranger c·
      34– 7   * There c· a Sunday morning when
      34– 8   * her pastor c· to bid her good-by
      35– 1   c· to me with a new meaning,
      35– 6   * Mrs. Eddy c· to perceive that
      36– 7   * To this College c· hundreds
      36–15   * I c· away in a state of exhilaration
      41– 1   * forth from the hands of the
      41– 7   c· to help erect this
      41– 8   * these contributors c· to Boston,
      41–15   * c· parties of forty and fifty.
      43–19   * few minutes of silent prayer c· next,
      46– 3   * c· to hear him preach,
      46–16   * Her family c· to this country
      55– 6   * cyclic changes that c· during the
      57– 4   * contributions for its erection c· from
      64– 8   * Money c· freely from all parts of
      68– 6   * Students c· to it in hundreds
      69– 1   * the pastor, c· to Baltimore
      69– 3   * Miss Cross c· from Syracuse, N. Y.,
      72–22   * other than that which c· from God
      73–11   * c· from her seclusion
No.   42–25   clergyman c· to be healed.

came
'01. 18–19   he c· to do "the will of — *Matt.* 12 : 50.
      21–22   Christ c· not to bring death
      31– 9   "I c· not to send peace— *Matt.* 10 : 34.
'02.   9–22   and knew not whence it c·
      13–16   I c· to the rescue,
      15–22   Its title, S. and H., c· to me
      15–30   voice" that c· to Elijah— *I Kings* 19 : 12.
Hea. 11–22   Mind c· in as the remedy,
      17–27   If sickness . . . c· through mind,
Po.   47– 2   As sweetly they c· of yore,
My.   5–11   Whence, then, c· the creation of
      38–18   * when it c· to the singing,
      42–13   * unexpectedly to me c· the call to
      43–19   * Israel c· over this Jordan
      53– 1   * from every quarter c· important
      61– 9   * Then c· the announcement
      61–16   * conviction . . . c· to me so clearly,
      63–20   * there c· a deeper feeling,
      82–27   * c· to Boston in such numbers
     117–15   and c· unto thee?"— *Matt.* 25 : 39.
     163–18   and c· to Concord, N. H.,
     164– 1   far from my purpose, when I c· here,
     171–23   * carriage c· to a standstill on
     173–15   it c· to me: Why not invite
     184–12   c· when I was so occupied
     217–30   He c· to the world not to
     218–11   c· with the *ascension.*
     247–15   c· out in orderly line to the
     256–22   and see whence they c·
     258–11   Then c· her resurrection and
     275–18   since I c· to Massachusetts.
     310–13   His . . . title of Colonel c· from
     328–16   * how this c· about in Kinston
     343–17   light of the Science c· first to me.
     345–15   c· like blessed relief to me,
     350– 8   c· to the writer's rescue,
     (*see also* **Jesus**)

camels
My. 211– 3   and swallowing c·.
     218–20   and swallowing c·.
     235– 5   one may swallow c·.
     276– 9   strain at gnats or swallow c·

Cameo, Cæsar's
Mis. 076– 0   * the face . . . from Cæsar's C·,

camera
Mis. 264– 8   like c· shadows thrown upon the

camera obscura
My. 164–11   c· o·, a thing focusing light

camomile
Mis. 227–19   like the c·, the more trampled

camp
Pan. 14–20   whether in c· or in battle.

Campbell, Miss Maurine R.
Mis. 144– 7   organized by Miss Maurine R. C·,

Canada and Can.
Man. 94–18   lecture in the United States, in C·,
      97– 8   throughout the United States, C·,
      98–26   United States and in C·
Pul. 44–26   * United States and C·
      67–19   * In C·, also, there is a large
      88– 3   From C· to New Orleans,
My.   77–12   * from C·, from Great Britain,
     136–21   also in C·, Australia, *etc.*
     250–20   in the United States and C·.
     (*see also* **London, Montreal, Toronto**)

Canadian
My. 253–14   chapter sub-title

cancel
Mis. 131–24   opportunity to c· accounts.
No.   7– 9   c· error in our own hearts,

cancelled
Mis. 222–20   c· only through human agony :
     261– 7   c· by repentance or pardon.

cancels
Mis. 338–12   c· not sin until it be destroyed,
'02. 12– 4   c· the disagreement,

cancer
Un.   7–12   a c· which had eaten its way to
Hea.   6–17   whether . . . a flower or a c·,
My.   80– 6   * they had been cured . . . of c· ;
     105–14   I have healed at one visit a c·
     310–18   * "excepting Albert, died of c·,"
     310–21   as caused by c·.
     315–23   declared dying of c·,

cancers
Ret. 15–24   they specified c·.

candidate
Man. 26–22   after the c· is approved by
      65–23   c· shall be subject to the approval
      88–14   c· shall be subject to the approval

candidate
Man.	100– 4	c· for its Committee on Publication,
	100– 5	Readers shall appoint said c·.
Pul.	83– 2	* promise as lover and c·

candidates
Mis.	146– 8	receiving or dismissing c·.
Man.	26–15	names of its c· before they are
	26–17	if she objects, said c· shall not
	56–22	Regular meetings for electing c·
	67– 3	c· for admission to this Church,
	109– 4	are eligible to approve c·
Ret.	14– 3	examination of c· for membership,
My.	57–17	* The number of c· admitted June 5

candle
Pul.	28– 4	* by the light of a single c·,

candle-power
My.	69– 4	* each lamp of thirty-two c·.

candlestick
'00.	12–19	will remove thy c· — Rev. 2 : 5.

candlesticks
'00.	12– 5	seven golden c·'' — Rev. 2 : 1.

candor
Mis.	147–27	full of truth, c·, and humanity.

cane
My.	308–25	saying, "I never use a c·."

canker
'02.	3–23	triumph c· not his coronation,

cannonaded
Pul.	5–16	press and pulpit c· this book,

cannon's
Po.	26–20	Purged by the c· prayer ;

canny
Mis.	xi–15	will find herein a "c·" crumb ;

canon
My.	199–12	receipt of their Christian c·

canonical
'01.	34–11	c· writings of the Fathers,

canonized
My.	104– 4	Mars' Hill orator, the c· saint,
	268–24	Truth, c· by life and love,

cant
Mis.	374– 5	To them it was c· and caricature,

canvas
Mis.	230–27	c· and the touch of an artist
	374–30	thinker and his thought on c·,
Ret.	79– 7	effaced from the c· of mortal mind ;

cap
Mis.	329–22	put the fur c· on pussy-willow,
Pul.	25–24	* The base and c· are of . . . marble.

capabilities
Mis.	43– 1	recognizing the c· of Mind
	193–30	man's c· and spiritual power.
Peo.	2– 1	we learn our c· for good,

capability
Mis.	66–32	to the present c· of the learner,
'00.	3–13	awake the slumbering c· of man.

capable
Mis.	13– 1	of which I feel at present c·,
	273–10	so c· of relieving my tasks
	273–19	good they are c· of accomplishing ;
Pul.	25– 9	* c· of holding fifteen hundred ;
	58–14	* c· of division into seven
Pan.	4–13	will is c· of use and of abuse,
My.	65– 9	* a church edifice c· of seating
	70–24	* or more c· instrument.
	223–16	do not consider myself c· of

capacities
Ret.	82–21	Their liberated c· of mind
'02.	10– 2	Utilizing the c· of the human mind
My.	259–26	in which human c· find the most

capacity
Mis.	49–16	our c· for formulating a dream,
	49–29	c· to err proceeds from
	49–31	never created error, or such a c·,
	76– 2	destitute of . . . derived c· to sin.
	204–18	It develops individual c·,
	228–12	to a c· for a higher life.
	316–14	profited up to their present c·
Un.	26– 2	and the c· to evolve mind.
	36– 3	double c· of creator and creation.
	43–23	divine power to human c·,
Pul.	41–16	* large auditorium, with its c· for
No.	21–12	reflecting God and the divine c·.
My.	8–20	* should have a seating c· of
	24–29	* seating c· of five thousand.
	42–14	* the call to serve you in this c·,
	53–13	* seating c· of which place was
	55–25	* seating c· of six hundred and

capacity
My.	56– 1	* thought the seating c· would be
	57– 5	* would be of great seating c·,
	63– 4	* of Mr. Beman in an advisory c·
	67–10	* Seating c· . . . 5,000
	67–22	* exceeds it in seating c·,
	68–14	* seating c· of twelve hundred,
	69–23	* a cloak-room of the c· of
	77– 4	* seating c· of over five thousand.
	78– 1	* seating c· of the temple is
	137–29	as to honesty and business c·.
	216–21	to your present unfolding c·.
	230–13	invigorate his c· to heal the sick,
	296–29	standing and seating c·,
	325–12	* any c· in which I could serve you,

caparisoned
No.	44–11	boldly ridden or brilliantly c·,

capital
Mis.	48–31	enemy is trying to make c· out of
	304– 9	* coming first to the c·
Pul.	7– 5	whereof this city is the c·.
	47–23	* New Hampshire's quiet c·,
	75–23	* in the great New England c·
'00.	2–20	his dupes are his c· ;
	3– 7	hoards this c· to distribute gain."
	12– 8	the c· of Asia Minor.
My.	157– 7	c· city of your native State.
	199–15	attitude of this church in our c·
	225– 7	A correct use of c· letters
	225–10	where c· letters should be used in
	265– 8	loses c·, and is bought at par
	270– 6	my first religious home in this c·
	289–27	meeting to be held in the c·

capitalization
My.	225– 6	chapter sub-title
	225–14	the c· which distinguishes it from
	318– 1	liberty that I have taken with c·,

capitalized
Man.	112– 5	c· (The), or small (the),

caprice
Pul.	55– 1	* "Not in blind c· of will,

caps
My.	225– 7	c· the climax of the old

capsicum
Mis.	348–19	thea (tea), c· (red pepper) ;

capsize
Pul.	80– 2	* it is ready to c·.

caption
Mis.	242– 2	having the above c·,

captive
Mis.	30–19	opened the door to the c·,
	101–17	and sets the c· free,
	124–16	opening the prison doors to the c·,
	168– 1	he giveth liberty to the c·,
No.	43–15	* preaching deliverance to the c·,
Po.	71–15	Joy for the c· ! Sound it long !
My.	110–26	"led captivity c·," — Psal. 68 : 18.
	133–15	set the c· sense free from self's

captives
Mis.	153–17	as c· are they enchained.
My.	110–20	if bodily sensation makes us c· ?

captivity
Mis.	139–13	bringing into c· every — II Cor. 10 : 5.
'00.	3–21	during the period of c·
My.	110–26	"led c· captive," — Psal. 68 : 18.

captured
Ret.	79–28	its spiritual gates not c·,

car
Mis.	274–28	c· of the modern Inquisition
My.	219–13	to ride to church on an electric c·,

carbonate
My.	108– 1	c· and sulphate of lime ;

Card
Mis.	256– 6	chapter sub-title
	310–10	chapter sub-title
	321–23	chapter sub-title
My.	25–15	chapter sub-title
	136–12	chapter sub-title
	173– 1	chapter sub-title
	316–10	chapter sub-title
	331–17	* heading

card
Mis.	137– 3	my thanks for your c· of invitation,
	157– 9	their c· in The C. S. Journal),
Man.	73– 4	whose c· is published in
	74–16	a c· in The C. S. Journal,
	91–10	c· of free scholarship from the
	91–13	on presentation of the c· to the
My.	184–11	Your kind c·, inviting me to
	186–26	your cordial c· inviting me to

card

My 191–28 Your c· of invitation to this
195– 4 acknowledging your c· of invitation
332–17 * paper containing this c· is

cardinal

Mis. 27–10 the c· point in C. S.,
107–14 Three c· points must be gained
Un. 9–27 What is the c· point of the
No. 25– 3 this c· point of divine Science,
'01. 8– 2 I reiterate this c· point :
My. 339– 4 The c· points of C. S.

cards

Man. 46– 9 on circulars, c·, or leaflets,
49–14 c· of such persons may be
82–10 Removal of C·.
82–10 No c· shall be removed . . . without
My. 223–10 practitioners whose c· are in

care

all
'02. 17–27 will put to flight all c· for
and providence
Pan. 3–29 c· and providence by which he
and responsibility
My. 123–14 c· and responsibility of purchasing it,
and worry
My. 48–25 * the discouragement of c· and worry,
brow of
Mis. 339–20 added one furrow to the brow of c·?
depressing
Mis. 133–26 In the midst of depressing c·
first
Mis. 370–29 His first c· is to separate the
His
Mis. 154– 7 God's love . . . is manifest in His c·.
his
Ret. 91–19 placed themselves under his c·,
infinite
Mis. 370–17 calls forth infinite c· from
of nurse
Ret. 90–17 to the c· of nurse or stranger.
of pupils
Man. 83– 8 C· of Pupils.
of the sick
Man. 49–13 can take proper c· of the sick.
special
Mis. 11–27 I do it with earnest, special c·
13– 4 special c· to mind my own business.
293– 5 special c· of the unerring modes
take
Mis. vii– 1 * take c·, that tak'st my book in hand,
39–13 Can you take c· of yourself?
Man. 69–23 shall not take c· of their churches
My. 138– 2 my property to take c· of
138– 4 to take c· of my property
takes
My. 166– 8 God takes c· of our life.
203–19 for God takes c· of it.
tender
'01. 29– 7 need the watchful and tender c·
under my
Mis. 33–17 place themselves under my c·,
under the
Mis. 304–10 * under the c· of our society.
304–18 * under the c· of the Daughters of the
Ret. 20– 9 under the c· of our family nurse,
87–29 under the c· of a regular physician,
watchful
My. 280– 5 * your watchful c· and guidance

Mis. 89– 4 Scientists are called upon to c· for
139–30 I took c· that the provisions for the
226– 3 * Father of all will c· for him."
238–16 Who should c· for everybody?
238–17 enough, say they, to c· for a few.
370–28 good Shepherd does c· for all,
371– 6 the c· of the great Shepherd,
Ret. 20–28 family to whose c· he was
Pul. 73– 3 * God will c· for us,
79– 7 * no debt had to be taken c· of
Hea. 1– 8 not discharge from c· ;
My. 60–30 * c· to do a little watching
87– 3 * to c· for the multitudes
137–19 carefully taken c· of for
331–24 * extended their c· and sympathy
336– 8 * entrusted herself to the c· of

cared

Ret. 86–24 every man c· for and blessed.

careening

Po. 18– 5 C· in liberty higher and higher

career

Mis. 212– 6 left his glorious c· for our
266–12 An erratic c· is like the comet's
296– 7 work and c· of American women,
Ret. 94–26 affection illustrated in Jesus' c·,

career

Pul. 44–11 * in your eventful c·.
49–20 * her busy c· in Boston,
70– 4 * C· OF REV. MARY BAKER EDDY,
No. 34–17 the endeavor to crush out of a c·
'01. 28–29 After a hard and successful c·

careers

Mis. 356–11 give promise of grand c·.
Un. 4– 1 guides every event of our c·.
'01. 29– 6 in the advancing stages of their c·

careful

Mis. 43–13 c·, . . . reading of my books,
Ret. 45–14 From c· observation and experience
90– 1 student should be most c· not to
Pul. 54–18 * A c· reading of the accounts of
64–20 * After c· study she became convinced
73–20 * made a c· and searching study
'00. 8– 6 hence, be c· of your company.
Hea. 10–22 be c· not to talk on both sides,
My. 237–23 I recommend its c· study to all

carefully

Mis. 306– 3 * entered c· in a book
315–13 thirty-three students, c· selected,
Man. 83– 9 shall c· select for pupils
Ret. 44–17 Examining the situation . . . c·,
Pul. 47–16 * defines c· the difference
62–15 * The tubes are c· tuned,
My. 31–31 * As though trained c· under
38– 8 * c· trained corps of ushers,
137–19 affairs c· taken care of
330–13 * c· investigated the points

careless

Man. 41– 3 C· comparison . . . to Christ Jesus

carelessly

Mis. 339–25 C· or remorselessly thou mayest
My. 12–21 the reliable now is c· lost

cares

Mis. 341–29 neither the c· of this world nor
370–27 good shepherd c· for all
Hea. 4–10 not to forget his daily c·.
My. 52–23 * Little c· she, if only

caressing

Mis. 212– 2 a c· Judas that betrays you,

carfare

My. 65–16 * passing out a nickel for c·.

caricature

Mis. 87– 4 ignorantly to c· God's creation,
374– 5 To them it was cant and c·,

caring

Man. 85– 4 C· for Pupils of Strayed Members.
Rud. 12–20 c· for all the conditions requisite
My. 243–18 c· for their own flocks.

carious

My. 105–11 c· bones that could be dented

Carlyle

'01. 33– 0 C· writes : "Quackery and dupery
My. 154–18 C· wrote : "Wouldst thou plant for
193–22 C· writes, "Give a thing time ;

carnage

Po. 27– 1 "Convulsion, c·, war ;

carnal

Mis. 36–24 "The c· mind . . . is enmity — Rom. 8 : 7.
38–12 reap your c· things?" — I Cor. 9 : 11.
54– 1 The c· mind cannot discern
139–10 not c·, but mighty — II Cor. 10 : 4.
169–26 the reading of the c· mind.
182–16 neither from dust nor c· desire.
214– 3 appeared hate to the c· mind,
Ret. 78– 8 c· and sinister motives, entering
'01. 9–24 disturb the c· and destroy it ;

carnality

'02. 10–27 human error, c·, opposition to
Hea. 2–22 his spirituality rebuked their c·,

carnally

Mis. 24– 3 to be c· minded is death ; — Rom. 8 : 6.
'02. 6–27 to be c· minded is death ; — Rom. 8 : 6.

carnations

Pul. 42–29 * large basket of white c·

carnival

Mis. 274–23 quill-drivers . . . hold high c·.

carobs

Mis. 369–23 c· which he shared with the swine,

Carpenter (see also **Carpenter's**)
Mr.
Mis. 48– 7 Mr. C· deserves praise for his
48–14 Mr. C· made a man drunk on water,

carpenter

Mis. 166–31 a good c·, and a good man,

Carpenter's, Professor
  Mis. 47–27   *Professor C· exhibitions of*

carpenters'
  My. 145–10   One day the *c·* foreman said to me :

carpets
  Mis. 329– 7   between taking up the white *c·* and

carriage
  Mis. 239–12   I observed a *c·* draw up
       239–13   and take from his *c·* the ominous
  Po.   v–16   * *and alighting from her c·*,
  My. 171–23   * Her *c·* came to a standstill
       275–17   I go out in my *c·* daily,
       302–29   went alone in my *c·* to the church,
       346–11   * Mrs. Eddy's *c·* drove into town

carried
  Mis. 113–13   *c·* to the depths of perdition
       191–25   and *c·* the question with Eve.
       226– 5   *c·* the case on the side of God ;
       284–31   those rules must be *c·* out ;
       292–30   and *c·* out my ideal.
       364–28   This error, *c·* to its ultimate,
  Man. 100– 8   *c·* out according to her directions.
  Ret.   6–28   *c·* through the Legislature by
  Pul. 14–10   *c·* away of the flood. — *Rev.* 12 : 15.
       50–21   * thoroughly *c·* away with
  Peo.   8–14   we say that Life is *c·* on through
  My.   8–22   * motion was *c·* unanimously.
       12– 2   * *c·* the implication that work should
       14–26   * will be *c·* on without interruption
       44–18   * motion was *c·* unanimously
       59–16   * my mind was *c·* back to
       68– 2   * *c·* out with the end in view of
       80– 1   * cures that *c·* one back
       138– 7   *c·* on contrary to my wishes.
       145–10   and saw them *c·* out.
       310–15   *c·* on a large business in Boston,
       333–18   * Major Glover's remains were *c·*

carries
  Mis. 346– 2   *c·* this thought even higher,
       353–24   divine Principle *c·* on His harmony.
  Ret.   7–22   * *c·* with it too much of sorrow
       80–22   *c·* his lambs in his arms

carry
  Mis.   7–19   These descriptions *c·* fears
       47– 2   and *c·* about this weight
       117–18   to *c·* out a divine commission
       162–28   To *c·* out his holy purpose,
       356–20   *c·* the fruit of this tree into
  Ret. 44–25   measures were adopted to *c·*
       86–20   undertakes to *c·* his burden
  '01. 16–22   to *c·* a most vital point.
  Hea. 10–22   take the side you wish to *c·*,
  My. 38–25   * *c·* with them the memory of it.
       121–10   the ocean, able to *c·* navies,
       211–19   to *c·* out the designs of
       214–28   with which to *c·* on a Cause
       328–27   * to *c·* them on in this State,

carrying
  Mis. 19– 6   *c·* out what He teaches
  Ret. 16–14   *c·* them on their shoulders.
  Un. 44–19   *c·* out the serpent's assurance :
  Hea.   8– 7   and *c·* out this government

carve
  Peo.   7–20   * *c·* it then on the yielding stone

carved
  Mis. 325– 1   a massive *c·* stone mansion,
  Pul. 24–13   * inscription *c·* in bold relief :
       24–28   * doors of antique oak richly *c·*.
       26– 9   * with richly *c·* seats
       76–12   * in special designs, elaborately *c·*,
  Peo.   7–12   * *c·* the dream on that shapeless stone

carving
  Mis. 231–11   Under the skilful *c·* of the
  Pul. 27– 4   * marble approaches and rich *c·*,

carvings
  My. 69–14   * sculptor added magnificent *c·*
       78–11   * decorative *c·* peculiarly rich

Case, Mr. Henry Lincoln
  Pul. 43– 5   * direction, . . . of Mr. Henry Lincoln *C·*

case
  attorney for the
    Hea. 10–24   You are the attorney for the *c·*,
  carried the
    Mis. 226– 5   carried the *c·* on the side of God ;
  contagious
    My. 220– 7   reporting of a contagious *c·* to the
  difficult
    Rud.   7– 4   as the most difficult *c·* so treated.
  done with the
    Ret. 87–30   until he has done with the *c·*
  either
    Mis. 219–17   remove this feeling in either *c·*,

case
  either
    My. 302– 5   produces the result in either *c·*.
  every
    Mis. 40–19   same results follow not in every *c·*,
       40–20   student does not in every *c·*
       44–10   in every *c·* of disease,
       252– 7   the more the better in every *c·*.
    My. 318– 3   In almost every *c·* where Mr. Wiggin
  following
    Mis. 49– 1   out of the following *c·*.
  given up the
    Ret. 40– 9   The physicians had given up the *c·*
  governing the
    Man. 51–18   By-Law governing the *c·*
  her
    Mis. 378–13   signally failed in healing her *c·*.
    Pul. 34– 6   * her *c·* was pronounced hopeless
  his
    Mis. 69–29   for information about his *c·*.
    Ret. 19–10   which in his *c·* proved fatal.
    Pul. 69– 9   * pronounced his *c·* incurable.
  Mrs. Stebbin's
    Mis. 157–21   relative to Mrs. Stebbin's *c·*.
  my
    Mis. 379– 5   his pennings on my *c·*.
    My. 307–25   At first my *c·* improved
  nature of the
    Mis. 379– 9   and the nature of the *c·* :
    Pul. 80– 6   * inevitable in the nature of the *c·*.
  never loses a
    My. 132–29   Divine Love . . . never loses a *c·*.
  of dropsy
    Hea. 13–18   we cured an inveterate *c·* of dropsy.
  offender's
    Man. 50–20   offender's *c·* shall be tried
  of Jairus' daughter
    Pul. 54–22   * In the *c·* of Jairus' daughter
  of lunacy
    My. 190–15   a severe *c·* of lunacy,
       222– 3   a violent *c·* of lunacy.
  of malignant disease
    My. 227–15   taking a *c·* of malignant disease.
  of necessity
    Man. 100–25   *C·* of Necessity.
  of sprain
    Mis. 243– 7   *c·* of sprain of the wrist-joint,
  one
    Mis. 40– 1   in the one *c·* as in the other.
       63– 2   which is infidel in the one *c·*,
    No.   2–13   by healing one *c·* audibly,
  particulars of the
    Mis. 51–10   We have not the particulars of the *c·*
  rested
    Mis. 140–12   Thus the *c·* rested,
  said
    Man. 67–13   if said *c·* relates to the person
  second
    My. 335–18   * the second *c·* of the dread disease
  seldom the
    Mis. 283–22   but this is seldom the *c·*
  simplest
    Rud.   7– 2   the simplest *c·*, healed in Science,
  single
    Mis. 242–20   if he will heal one single *c·*
  such a
    Mis. 242–25   cured precisely such a *c·* in 1869.
  takes up the
    Mis.   5–19   takes up the *c·* hopefully
  that
    Mis. 52–27   In that *c·* he would be obliged
    My. 222– 8   why they could not heal that *c·*,
  the only
    Mis. 49–10   This is the only *c·* that could be
  this
    Mis. 190–23   In this *c·* it was the evil of
  this being the
    Pan.   4–26   This being the *c·*, what need have we
  your
    Mis. 157–10   questions important for your *c·*,

    Mis. 41–21   There is no other healer in the *c·*.
       195–24   unfit to judge in the *c·* ;
       279–24   in the *c·* of Joshua and his band
       282–26   is a *c·* from accident,
       283– 3   then the *c·* is not exceptional.
    Man. 47– 6   *c·* he cannot fully diagnose,
       67–12   *c·* not provided for in its By-Laws
       77–23   In *c·* of any . . . deviation from
       110–15   as the *c·* may be.
    My. 105– 8   a *c·* which the M.D.'s,
       335–27   * the *c·* was one of yellow fever

cases
  acute
    Mis.   6– 9   the majority of the acute *c·*
       44– 6   Can C. S. cure acute *c·*

cases

both
No.   6–20   evidence in both *c·* to be unreal.
'01. 34– 4   Bible is our authority . . . in both *c·*.

chronic
Man. 46–25   in chronic *c·* of recovery,

desperate
Ret.   41– 4   Many were the desperate *c·*
Pan. 10–20   desperate *c·* of intemperance,

exceptional
Mis. 39–21   There may be exceptional *c·*,
Man. 36–14   Exceptional *C·*.
    96– 9   Exceptional *C·*.

extreme
Mis. 112–15   in extreme *c·*, moral idiocy.

healed
My. 106– 6   The list of *c·* healed by me
   106–13   C. S. has healed *c·* that

his
My. 108– 3   in healing his *c·* without drugs

hopeless
'01. 27–14   has healed hopeless *c·*,

many
Mis. 222– 7   in many *c·* causes the victim

most
Mis. 45–15   more in this than in most *c·* ;
   89–10   advisable in most *c·* that Scientists

notable
Mis. 49–13   notable *c·* of insanity have been

of candidates
Man. 67– 2   *c·* of candidates for admission

of discipline
Man. 67– 2   not . . . on *c·* of discipline,
My. 359– 8   not . . . in *c·* of discipline,

of disease
Mis. 60– 9   healing *c·* of disease and sin

one hundred
My. 127–17   out of one hundred *c·* I healed

some
'01. 17–28   this attenuation in some *c·*

such
Mis.   6–11   such *c·* should certainly prove
  236–20   In such *c·* we have said,
Man 36–12   such *c·* as are provided for
   71–18   except in such *c·* as are specially
  100–21   In such *c·* it shall be the privilege

surgical
My. 345–24   about advice on surgical *c·*."

these
Ret. 15–26   I had not heard of these *c·*

those
Mis.   6–10   those *c·* that are pronounced

Mis. 43– 3   enables one to heal *c·* without even
Man. 46–25   in *c·* where he has not effected a
   52– 1   shall vote on *c·* involving
   67– 4   *c·* of those on trial for dismissal
Ret. 15–24   The *c·* described had been
My. 335–25   * attended *c·* of this terrible disease

cash
Man. 78–21   a petty *c·* fund, to be used by him

casket
Pul.   77– 6   * plush *c·* with white silk linings.
My. 171–27   * a handsome rosewood *c·*
  171–29   * The *c·* contained a gavel

cast
Mis.   7–13   *C·* not your pearls before swine ;
  105 23   the shadow *c·* by this error.
  111–11   *c·* their nets on the right side,
  212–11   *c·* their nets on the right side.
  212–27   *c·* the beam out of his own eye,
  250–18   *c·* aside the word as a sham
  254–20   and *c·* them to the earth.
  280–14   if we *c·* something into the scale
  285–17   the book that *c·* the first stone,
  302– 5   "*c·* lots for his vesture," — see Matt. 27 : 35.
  305–29   * In order that the bell shall be *c·*
  307–21   *C·* not pearls before the unprepared
  326– 4   And *they c· him out.*
  336–15   how to *c·* the mote of evil out of
  355–15   "*C·* the beam out — see Matt. 7 : 5.
  355–22   Learn what . . . and *c·* it out ;
  360– 8   *c·* in the moulds of C. S. :
Un.   29–24   "Why art thou *c·* down, — Psal. 42 : 11.
Pul.   6–17   * I *c·* from me the false remedy
  12– 8   accuser . . . is *c·* down, — Rev. 12 : 10.
  13–28   *c·* unto the earth, — Rev. 12 : 13.
  62– 6   * *c·* bells of old-fashioned chimes.
No.   8–23   no longer *c·* your pearls before this
  22–21   That Jesus *c·* several persons out of
  22–26   indicated his ability to *c·* it out.
  23–11   Jesus *c·* seven devils ;
Pan.   4–21   "Why art thou *c·* down, — Psal. 42 : 11.
  5–27   He . . . *c·* it out of mortal mind,
'01. 26–17   and they *c·* lots for it?

cast
Hea.   7–19   "She hath *c·* in more — see Mark 12 : 43.
Po. 30–15   shadows *c·* on Thy blest name,
My. 190–16   "Why could not we *c·* — Matt. 17 : 19.
  191– 8   and love will *c·* it out.
  206–10   they divide . . . and *c·* lots for it.
  214–27   *c·* my all into the treasury
  227–23   "Neither *c·* ye your pearls — Matt. 7 : 6.
  247–25   *c·* your bread upon the waters

cast out
Mis. 40–21   power to *c·* out the disease.
  70– 4   *c·* out the sick man's illusion,
 131– 5   darkness in one's self must first be *c·* out,
 152–27   no element of earth to *c·* out angels,
 175–30   in thy name *c·* out devils,
 190–21   *c·* out of another person ;
 190–24   *c·* out by the spiritual truth
 191–19   *c·* out of another individual
 326– 1   *c·* out devils, — Matt. 10 : 8.
 336–13   *c·* out your own dislike and hatred
 373–10   serpent *c·* out of his mouth,
Pul.   14– 8   *c·* out of his mouth — Rev. 12 : 15.
  14–12   *c·* out of his mouth. — Rev. 12 : 16.
  29–18   * *c·* out demons." — see Matt. 10 : 8.
  29–23   * *c·* out the demons of evil thought.
  66–13   * *c·* out demons." — see Matt. 10 : 8.
No.   14–19   *c·* out devils" ! — Matt. 10 : 8.
  15–15   *c·* out of another person.
  22–18   *c·* out *devils.*" — Matt. 10 : 8.
  22–23   the *evils* which were *c·* out.
  23–18   in order to *c·* out this devil
  40–23   Truth and Love that *c·* out **fear**
  41–21   *c·* out devils ;" — Matt. 10 : 8.
Pan. 11– 2   *c·* out the unreal or counterfeit.
'01.   9–26   *c·* out evils and heal the sick.
Hea. 1– 2   *shall they c· out devils ; — Mark 16 : 17.*
  6–27   *shall they c· out devils." — Mark 16 : 17.*
Peo.   4–27   cannot heal the sick and *c·* out
My.   47–30   * shall they *c·* out devils ; — Mark 16 : 17.
 192– 5   *c·* out fashionable lunacy.
 288–22   *c·* out devils and healed the sick.
 300– 2   *c·* out the belief in sin
 300–26   *c·* out devils." — Matt. 10 : 8.
  (see also **error, evil, Jesus**)

caste
Mis. 246– 8   interests of wealth, religious *c·*,

casteth
Mis. 184–26   *c·* out all fear, all sin,
 229–21   "*c·* out fear" — I John 4 : 18.
 334–32   Love that *c·* out all fear,
Ret. 61–17   *c·* out fear.' " — I John 4 : 18.
Un. 20–16   "*c·* out fear," — I John 4 : 18.
Peo.   6–10   *c·* out fear ;" — I John 4 : 18.

casting
Mis. 25–18   healing the sick, *c·* out evil,
  77–31   healing the sick, *c·* out evils,
  89–16   *c·* "pearls before swine" — Matt. 7 : 6.
  99–29   *c·* out devils through Beelzebub.
  99–29   *c·* out evils and healing the sick ;
 139–11   *c· down imaginations, — II Cor. 10 : 5.*
 165– 1   *c·* out evils and healing,
 175– 1   *c·* out error and healing
 187– 2   *c· out evils, healing the sick,*
 190–11   *c· out a devil, — Luke 11 : 14.*
 191–13   *c·* out devils — Mark 9 : 38.
 192– 7   in *c·* out error,
 268–13   healing the sick and *c·* out error.
Ret. 65–23   *c·* out evils and healing the sick ;
  66– 2   utilized . . . in *c·* out error,
No. 12–18   *c·* out evil, healing the sick,
'00.   5–28   *c·* out God's opposites,
Peo. 13– 7   *c·* out error and healing the sick.
My. 110– 2   *c·* out evils, healing the sick,
 113–26   men are found *c·* out the evils **of**
 126–13   *c·* out evil and healing the sick.
 153–26   *c·* out evil and healing the sick.

castle
Un. 28– 9   declare some old *c·* to be

Cast out Demons
Pul. 28– 8   * and "*C· out D·.*" — see Matt. 10 : 8.

casts
Mis. 68–17   error which Truth *c·* out.
  73– 3   when Mind *c·* out the suffering.
 191–13   traits, that Christ, Truth, *c·* out.
 193–13   heals the sick, *c·* out error,
 194–25   divine Love that *c·* out all **fear.**
 210–30   rebukes error, and *c·* it out.
 241–26   out sickness as well as sin
Man. 15–12   that *c·* out evil as unreal.
  17–17   *c·* out error, heals the sick,
Ret. 61–20   Love that *c·* out fear.
 81–18   loathes error, and *c·* it aside ;
Hea. 13–23   truth of being that *c·* out error

casts
My. 260–25   c· out evils, heals the sick,
casual
My. 87– 6   * apparent to the most c· observer.
casualties
'01. 24– 8   ills of mortals and the c· of earth.
casualty
Mis. 35– 5   her recovery, . . . from a severe c·
cat
Mis. 216–30   * to conceive a grin without a c·."
218–23   "grin without a c· ;"
218–23   a grin expresses the nature of a c·,
cataracts
Ret. 9–22   * From the far c·
catch
Mis. 229– 6   would c· their state of feeling
Pul. 47–24   * when she wishes to c· a glimpse of
No. 39– 5   ostensibly to c· God's ear,
Hea. 11– 8   would c· the meaning of Spirit.
My. 81–10   * first to c· the Reader's eye.
155– 9   May it c· the early trumpet-call,
227–18   to c· them in their sayings ;
342–13   * shade of which is so hard to c·,
catching
Mis. 228–29   Common consent . . . makes disease c·.
229– 5   If he believed . . . that health is c·
My. 6–28   love c· a glimpse of glory.
344–20   think myself in danger of c· it."
344–28   the fear of c· smallpox is more
catechized
My. 241–19   * c· by a C. S. practitioner
categories
No. 22– 8   circumlocution and cold c· of Kant
category
Mis. 252–12   Continuing this c·, we learn
296–11   same c· with noble women
'02. 7– 6   enter not into the c· of creation
cathedral
Pul. 62–17   * beauties of a great c· chime,
65–18   * story of the c· of Amiens,
My. 67–16   * Corner-stone of c· laid . . . 1904
67–17   * C· to be dedicated . . . 1906
71– 1   * is a set of c· chimes,
71– 9   * that built the C. S. c·.
71–14   * enter this new c· or temple
76–27   * recently built a splendid c·
99–14   * c· erected by the devotees of
182–18   large membership and majestic c·.
188–20   walls of your grand c·
cathedrals
My. 89–10   * finds in the English c·,
Catholic
Mis. 111–25   C· and Protestant sects.
Pul. 33–14   * C· biographies are full,
'01. 28–13   C· and Protestant oratories.
My. 4–15   Scientist loves Protestant and C·,
270–25   promoted by C·, by Protestant,
Catholics
My. 303– 8   Protestants, C·, or any other sect.
catnip
Mis. 52– 5   divided between c· and Christ ;
caught
Mis. 111– 5   at break of day c· much.
228–22   must be c· through mind ;
231–19   Then he was c· walking !
295–12   awake, and c· napping?
326– 7   flames c· in the dwelling
Ret. 16– 2   a soprano, . . . c· my ear.
Un. 15–14   very knowledge c· from God,
Pul. 6–12   mistake of thinking she c·
48–21   * c· her family coat of arms
'01. 9– 6   c· glorious glimpses of the
Peo. 7–15   * c· the angel-vision.
My. 31–21   * sight which the visitors c·
224–15   c· in some author's net,
causation
Mis. 25–13   all other theories of c·,
71–15   c· must interpret omnipotence,
Ret. 24–10   that all c· was Mind,
Pul. 55–19   * that all c· is of Mind,
70–18   certain that "all c· was Mind,
'02. 7– 2   no origin or c· apart from God.
Hea. 19–12   Spirit is c·,
My. 348–22   an actual, unfailing c·,
Cause
great
'01. 17–14   started the great C· that to-day
'02. 14–25   prospered preeminently our great C·,
My. 47–18   * inception of this great C·,
204–21   when starting this great C·,

Cause
of Christian Science
Mis. 153– 2   establishing the C· of C. S.
278–10   connected with the C· of C. S·,
Man. 52–26   advantageous . . . to the C· of C. S.,
'02. 12–30   movements of the C· of C. S.,
My. 10–17   * It is doubtful if the C· of C. S.
37–17   * C· of C. S. has been organized
143–20   The C· of C. S. is prospering
163–20   labor for the C· of C. S.,
199–15   towards the C· of C. S.,
362–17   * C· of C. S. in this community,
our
Mis. x–16   the progress of our C·.
32–27   for the individual, and for our C·.
110–22   unprecedented prosperity of our C·.
148–17   dignity and defense of our C·;
274– 9   might hinder the progress of our C·
351–16   may retard our C·, but they never
Man. 3–14   dignity and defense of our C·;
59–12   for the benefit of our C·.
Ret. 85–25   our C·, is highly prosperous,
'01. 17–23   more difficult stage . . . for our C·.
'02. 13– 3   Christ and our C· my only incentives,
My. 21–13   * our C· throughout the world.
24– 7   * structure is worthy of our C·
45– 3   * for the furtherance of our C·,
224–32   Our C· is growing apace
316–16   a grand defence of our C·
352–15   * testimony of the efficacy of our C·

Mis. 38– 7   to support one's self and a C·
43–22   a vast amount of injury to the C·.
43–30   on the C·, and on the health of
98–16   and the progress of our common C·
263–18   working . . . for our common C·,
Man. 48– 4   and to defend the C· of Christ,
52–20   Working Against the C·
Ret. 85– 7   commend itself as useful to the C·
85–25   The C·, . . . is highly prosperous,
Un. 5–17   neither will it promote the C· of Truth
Pul. 85–27   * in the C· of their common faith.
No. 9– 4   to the hindrance of the C· of Truth.
32–24   a C· which is healing its thousands
'01. 35– 5   sacrifice self for the C· of Christ,
My. v– 6   * growth and prosperity of the C·
v–15   * established the C· on a sound basis
10–25   * importance of . . . to the C·.
10–31   * general welfare of the C·
47–20   * a C· that has rooted itself in so many
50–28   * willing to labor for the C·.
51–11   * would be a serious blow to her C·
51–23   * it was for the interest of the C·,
55–10   * C· itself was spreading over
58– 8   * magnificent growth of this C·,
58–12   * shows the growth of this C·,
157– 9   * prosperity of the C·
214–28   means with which to carry on a C·
214–29   To desert the C· never occurred
cause (noun)
and cure
Hea. 11–23   places all c· and cure as mind ;
11–24   where c· and cure are supposed to
and effect
Mis. 79–18   c· and effect in Science are
93–18   all c· and effect are in God.
155– 2   but one c· and effect.
173–12   Mind is its own . . . c· and effect.
217–22   that matter is both c· and effect,
361–30   are inseparable as c· and effect.
364–15   thought, extension, c· and effect ;
My. 151–26   discovery of all c· and effect.
181– 4   or material c· and effect,
and effects
My. 212– 8   to expose the c· and effects of
and end
Mis. 218–21   Spirit as c· and end,
central
Mis. 295– 9   declares, that the central c· of this
Christ's
Mis. 302–19   working faithfully for Christ's c·
establishment of a
Mis. 238–14   labor for the establishment of a c·
evil
Pul. 56–19   * "And still we love the evil c·,
exciting
Mis. 69–25   the exciting c· of the inflammation
267–26   exciting c· of all defeat and
Ret. 44–18   predisposing and exciting c· of its
final
Mis. 219– 2   science of the final c· of things ;
for bitter comment
'02. 9–27   Is it c· for bitter comment and
for joy
'02. 3– 4   It is c· for joy that among the

cause (noun)

for rejection
 Man. 37–13 to report the c· for rejection.
for rejoicing
 Mis. 72–10 It is c· for rejoicing that this belief
glorious
 Po. 39–15 Work for our glorious c·!
great
 Mis. 79–17 If the great c· is perfect,
 173–12 its own great c· and effect.
greatness of a
 '00. 10– 7 signs . . . of the greatness of a c·
holy
 Mis. 273–17 labor for a good and holy c·.
in effect
 Mis. 219– 3 neither reveals . . . c· in effect,
 My. 149–23 Losing . . . c· in effect, and faith in
 349–32 inductive . . . seeks c· in effect,
insufficient
 Man. 36–17 whose teachers, for insufficient c·,
intelligent
 My. 108– 5 the intelligent c· in pathology?
into effect
 Mis. 362–16 Philosophy . . . puts c· into effect,
its
 Mis. 217–23 antagonistic to its c· ;
judging a
 Pan. 11– 7 judging a c· by its effects?
latent
 Hea. 6–25 latent c· producing the effect
mental
 Ret. 24– 9 physical effects to a mental c· ;
mind is the
 My. 302– 8 mind is the c· of all effect
no
 '01. 28–18 no c· for not following it ;
 My. 339–21 and have no c· to mourn ;
of all disease
 Un. 9– 1 mortal mind is the c· of all disease.
of all sickness
 Ret. 61–13 fear, . . . the c· of all sickness ;
of arbitration
 My. 281–25 * advancement of the c· of arbitration."
of Christ
 My. 165– 6 endured for the c· of Christ,
of Christian Science
 Mis. 288–27 strong impulse from the c· of C. S. :
 Man. 95– 8 as the c· of C. S. demands.
of death
 My. 335–20 * c· of death as bilious fever,
of disease
 Mis. 66–29 Ignorance of the c· of disease
 221–18 If error is the c· of disease,
of human weal
 My. 36–27 * for the c· of human weal,
of its tear
 Po. 65–23 man is the c· of its tear.
of temperance
 Mis. 288–26 c· of temperance receives
of the mischief
 My. 211–27 unless the c· of the mischief is
of the separation
 My. 315– 7 * c· of the separation being wholly
of Truth
 My. 49–28 * labors in the c· of Truth,"
one
 Mis. 25– 3 one c· and one effect,
 155– 2 there is but one c· and effect.
 271– 9 one c· and one effect.
only
 Mis. 23–19 the first and only c·.
 36– 9 only c· is the eternal Mind,
 97–32 The only c· for making this
or effect
 My. 364–12 of any other c· or effect save
other
 Mis. 308– 6 love or hatred or any other c·
 My. 364–12 of any other c· or effect save
present
 My. 152–29 remote, predisposing, and present c·
primal
 Mis. 22–31 primal c·, or Mind-force,
remove that
 Mis. 66–30 can neither remove that c· nor its
removing the
 Mis. 41–23 removing the c· in that so-called
righteous
 Mis. 99–16 ready to suffer for a righteous c·,
sole
 Un. 10– 5 is built on Him as the sole c·.
sufficient
 Man. 65–19 sufficient c· for the removal of the
 111–19 refuse, without sufficient c·, to
supreme
 My. 37–20 * God is the supreme c· of all

cause (noun)

their
 Mis. 288–28 and their c· prospers in proportion
 299– 2 until one is awake to their c·
this
 My. 348– 6 I sought this c·, not within but
true
 Mis. 266– 9 The true leader of a true c·
underlying
 Mis. 169– 8 underlying c· of the long years of
universal
 My. 226– 9 an effect of one universal c·,
 348– 5 the offspring of a universal c·.
which governs
 Mis. 369– 9 c· which governs all effects,
without
 Mis. 129– 4 condemn his brother without c·,
without a
 Mis. 9–11 who have hated thee without a c·
 217– 3 effect without a c· is inconceivable;

 Mis. 33–26 mortal mind is the c· of all "the ills
 46–15 that which is formed is not c·, but
 83– 7 c· of his own sufferings."
 217– 7 whose c· is the self-created Principle,
 255– 6 is not c·, but effect ;
 Man. 49–25 the c· thereof be unknown,
 Ret. 23–22 its substance, c·, and currents
 '01. 24– 7 c· of all the ills of mortals
 Po. 39–13 The c· she elevates.
 My. 295–26 have c· to lament the demise of
 314–15 the c· nevertheless was adultery.

cause (verb)
 Mis. 51–18 c· him to love them,
 66– 3 may c· the innocent to suffer
 67–15 nor c· it to be thought.
 211–16 c· him to suffer in coming to life?
 243–27 c· the coats of the stomach to
 331– 6 c· them to wait patiently
 350–26 c· none to be used in mental practice,
 368– 5 and c· the deaf to hear.
 373–11 c· her to be river-borne."
 Man. 43– 3 c· the name of said member to be
 42– 8 nor c· to be published,
 87–11 or c· or permit others to solicit,
 Ret. 29– 1 can c· a surrender of this effort.
 Pul. 3–10 who or what can c· you to sin
 14–10 c· her to be carried away — Rev. 12 : 15.
 No. 7– 6 nor c· any misapprehension as to
 '01. 17– 4 c· him to return to the Father's
 20–21 sooner or later c· the perpetrator,
 My. 349– 7 matter, . . . cannot c· disease,

caused
 Mis. x–19 c· me, as an author, to
 xi–21 c· me to retain the initial "G"
 24– 9 an injury c· by an accident,
 33– 3 high priests of old c· the crucifixion
 44–15 c· the pain to cease
 89–17 c· our Master to refuse help to
 157– 7 c· my secretary to write,
 212– 9 c· them to remember the
 231–19 c· unconditional surrender.
 267– 8 c· me to exercise most patience.
 374– 2 c· even the publicans to justify
 Ret. 3– 7 c· that prolonged contest
 24–13 an injury c· by an accident,
 40–14 condition was c· by an injury
 47– 3 c· me to dread the . . . popularity of
 Pul. 33–10 * This c· her tears of remorse
 80–21 * c· an army of well-meaning people to
 Pan. 11– 2 it c· St. Paul to write,
 '01. 32–17 c· me to love their doctrines.
 '02. 18–11 who c· not the feeble to fall,
 My. 135–13 c· me to select a Board of Trustees
 307–29 This . . . might have c· my illness.
 310–21 as c· by cancer.

causeless
 Hea. 9–15 * "the curse c· cannot come"

causes
 Mis. 12–20 c· that at former periods in
 18–29 c· much that must be repented of
 41– 6 c· "the wrath of man" — Psal. 76 : 10.
 62–31 its own disease, or that which it c·,
 68–26 * and c· of all things existing,"
 138– 4 if it c· thought to wander
 177– 4 greatest and holiest of all c·.
 222– 5 c· the victim to believe that he is
 222– 7 c· the victim great physical suffering;
 229– 2 certain predisposing or exciting c·.
 289– 1 c· him to degenerate physically
 290–21 cease to judge of c· from a
 292–14 Divine Love eventually c· mortals to
 Man. 53–24 publishes, or c· to be published,
 Ret. 57–13 c· all bodily ailments,

causes
  Un. 8–21 heredity and other physical *c*ˈ.
  Rud. 10–16 *c*ˈ sickness and suffering.
  Pan. 2–20 the deification of natural *c*ˈ,
  8– 2 *c*ˈ a man to be mentally deranged ;
  My. 150–30 if the wisdom you manifest *c*ˈ

causing
  Mis. 2– 8 *c*ˈ great obscuration of Spirit.
  244–19 *c*ˈ him to walk the wave,
  298– 7 *c*ˈ others to go astray,
  328–23 *c*ˈ to stumble, fall, or faint,
  My. 316– 6 *c*ˈ man to love his enemies ;

caution
  Mis. 6–26 *c*ˈ is observed in regard to diet,
  240– 7 by that flippant *c*ˈ,
  Hea. 14– 9 *c*ˈ should be exercised in

cautiously
  Mis. 324–22 Stealing *c*ˈ away from
  Ret. 4–17 the crow caws *c*ˈ,
  My. 245– 5 it should be met . . . . *c*ˈ,

cave
  Mis. 370– 8 and the *c*ˈ of ignorance.

caves
  Mis. 347– 8 people prepare shelter in *c*ˈ

cavil
  Mis. 193– 3 If this be the *c*ˈ, we reply
  223– 9 Science proves, beyond *c*ˈ,
  My. 8– 7 * The necessity . . . is beyond *c*ˈ ;
  91– 1 * established beyond *c*ˈ.
  108– 7 I have proved beyond *c*ˈ that
  181– 2 settle all points beyond *c*ˈ,

caws
  Ret. 4–17 the crow *c*ˈ cautiously,

cease
  Mis. 11– 9 did not *c*ˈ teaching the wayward
  44–16 *caused the pain to c*ˈ
  44–24 You believed . . . the pain would *c*ˈ :
  180– 2 and strive to *c*ˈ my warfare.
  290–21 When will the world *c*ˈ to judge of
  Ret. 60–17 raging of the material elements *c*ˈ?ˈˈ
  60–21 when will my sufferings *c*ˈ?
  Pul. 3–14 and bids tumult *c*ˈ,
  52– 1 * Wonders will never *c*ˈ.
  No. 1–15 stir of contending sentiments *c*ˈ,
  32–20 and shall *c*ˈ to love it.
  35– 7 When human struggles *c*ˈ,
  41– 8 Not that he would *c*ˈ to do the will of
  Hea. 18–23 will *c*ˈ to assert their Cæsar sway
  Po. 35– 8 never dry or *c*ˈ to flow ;
  My. 57–29 * ˈˈWonders will never *c*ˈ.
  110–25 mortals will *c*ˈ to be mortal.
  143–23 when these things *c*ˈ to bless
  143–24 they will *c*ˈ to occur.
  151–13 injustice done by press . . . will *c*ˈ,
  280–16 *c*ˈ special prayer for the peace of
  280–17 and *c*ˈ in full faith that God
  280–28 to *c*ˈ praying for the peace of

ceased
  Mis. 330– 4 Has love *c*ˈ to moan over the
  Ret. 8–16 though I had *c*ˈ to notice it.
  Pul. 33–13 * and after that it *c*ˈ.
  82–30 * *c*ˈ to kiss the iron heel of wrong.
  My. 231–12 *c*ˈ practice herself in order to

ceaseless
  Mis. 224–15 the *c*ˈ action and reaction
  250–24 the silent, *c*ˈ prayer ;
  329–17 rippling all nature in *c*ˈ flow,
  Ret. 30– 5 *C*ˈ toil, self-renunciation, and
  Peo. 1–15 *c*ˈ throbbings and throes of thought

ceases
  Mis. 28– 7 and volition *c*ˈ ;
  34–22 not a moment when he *c*ˈ to exist.
  44–14 *and then the pain c*ˈ,
  44–27 When your belief in pain *c*ˈ,
  324–10 footfalls abate, the laughter *c*ˈ.
  Ret. 67–15 testimony of . . . personal sense *c*ˈ,

ceasing
  Mis. 154–25 Pray without *c*ˈ.
  356–30 ˈˈpray without *c*ˈ,ˈˈ — *I Thess.* 5 : 17.
  No. 40– 1 ˈˈPray without *c*ˈˈˈ — *I Thess.* 5 : 17.
  My. 340– 4 ˈˈPray without *c*ˈ.ˈˈ — *I Thess.* 5 : 17.

ceiling
  Pul. 25–17 * In the *c*ˈ is a sunburst
  25–29 * sunburst in the centre of the *c*ˈ
  58–22 * In the *c*ˈ is a beautiful sunburst
  My. 68– 4 * with its high-domed *c*ˈ,
  69– 5 * *c*ˈ or roof and side walls

ceilings
  My. 68–26 * the great arches and *c*ˈ.

celebrate
  Mis. 91– 1 *c*ˈ in commemoration of the Christ.

celebrate
  Mis. 176–14 The day we *c*ˈ reminds us of
  225– 4 *c*ˈ the eighty-second birthday of
  Chr. 53–18 To *c*ˈ As Truth demands,
  Po. vi–19 *bells are ringing to c*ˈ *the*
  My. 262–12 I *c*ˈ Christmas with my soul,

celebrated
  Mis. 306– 7 * suggestions of events to be *c*ˈ
  Pul. 30–13 * not *c*ˈ by outward symbols of
  31– 1 * on January 6 shall be *c*ˈ.
  75–21 * *c*ˈ the dedication of the church
  My. 50–23 * *c*ˈ her Communion Sabbath as
  304–24 Agassiz, the *c*ˈ naturalist

celebration
  Mis. 304–13 * any great patriotic *c*ˈ

celestial
  Mis. 100–24 unite terrestrial and *c*ˈ joys,
  311– 5 as we journey to the *c*ˈ city.
  323– 3 *c*ˈ city above all clouds,
  376–29 spangled the gloom in *c*ˈ space
  385–13 Soft gales *c*ˈ, in sweet music bore
  Ret. 87–19 to obey the *c*ˈ injunction,
  No. 26–24 Man is a *c*ˈ ;
  Pan. 3–17 * fair wisdom, that *c*ˈ maid.ˈˈ
  3–28 denotes the *c*ˈ harmony of
  3–32 his man-face, the *c*ˈ world.
  Po. 19– 2 *C*ˈ the breezes that waft oˈer its
  ˈ 31– 3 *c*ˈ seed dropped from Loveˈs throne.
  48– 6 Soft gales *c*ˈ, in sweet music bore
  My. 186–11 on to the *c*ˈ hills,

celibacy
  Mis. 288–16 Is marriage nearer right than *c*ˈ?
  341–24 takes the most solemn vow of *c*ˈ

cell
  Mis. 112–16 I visited in his *c*ˈ the assassin
  294–15 hides it in his *c*ˈ of ingratitude.
  Po. 1– 7 sustains thee in thy rock-bound *c*ˈ.

cells
  Ret. 18–11 And ope their closed *c*ˈ to the
  Po. 63–22 And ope their closed *c*ˈ to the

cement
  Mis. 135–20 so *c*ˈ the bonds of Love.
  145– 1 at present is the *c*ˈ of society,
  Pul. 9– 2 *c*ˈ of society, the hope of
  15–20 *c*ˈ of a higher humanity
  My. 189–14 encircle and *c*ˈ the human race.
  339– 2 *c*ˈ the bonds of Christian

cemented
  Pul. 22–17 bonds of peace are *c*ˈ by

cemeteries
  Peo. 14– 4 our *c*ˈ with amaranth blossoms,

cemetery
  Po. vi– 2 * poem
  page 15 poem
  My. 69–30 * Mt. Auburn *c*ˈ in Cambridge,
  312–27 followed the remains . . . to the *c*ˈ.

censor
  Mis. 297–12 surly *c*ˈ ventilating his lofty scorn

censure
  Mis. 278–11 never given occasion for a single *c*ˈ,
  Pul. 51– 8 * though they cannot escape *c*ˈ,
  No. 8– 6 whenever it can substitute *c*ˈ.

census
  Mis. 29–18 The *c*ˈ since 1875
  Pul. 67– 9 * *c*ˈ of the religious faiths

cent
  Mis. 305–25 * asked to contribute one *c*ˈ
  My. 72–26 * every *c*ˈ of it was paid in
  73– 6 * very few of them owe a *c*ˈ.
  86–13 * every *c*ˈ of the estimated cost
  99–17 * not a *c*ˈ of indebtedness left.
  216–11 without a *c*ˈ to sustain it
  216–13 or his truth not worth a *c*ˈ.

Centennial Day
  Ret. 43–22 *C*ˈ *D*ˈ of our nationˈs freedom.

central
  Mis. 162–12 *c*ˈ point of his Messianic mission
  295– 9 *c*ˈ cause of this ˈˈsame original
  357–12 no *c*ˈ emblem, no history.
  Un. 57– 9 The cross is the *c*ˈ emblem of
  Pul. 28– 2 * The *c*ˈ panel represents her
  31–19 * *c*ˈ figure in all this agitation
  42–10 * children in the *c*ˈ pews.
  My. 73–29 * *c*ˈ and western sections of
  236– 6 name for one *c*ˈ Reading Room,

centre
  Mis. 241– 2 should *c*ˈ as steadfastly in God
  308– 1 divine Mind as its sole *c*ˈ
  346– 1 Life, . . . the very *c*ˈ of its faith.
  Ret. 83– 6 than try to *c*ˈ their interest on

centre

Un.	10–19	Alpha and Omega, the c· and
Pul.	25–29	* sunburst in the c· of the ceiling
	26– 3	* the c· being of pure white light,
	37–22	* not to c· too closely around
	42–22	* with a c· of white immortelles,
	56– 5	* and nearly every other c· of
	62–23	* placed on a small c· table.
My.	13–10	* like a sun in the c· of its system,
	75– 4	* holding the c· of the stage
	85–23	* great c· of attraction,
	98– 8	* c· of an enthusiasm and reverence
	236–12	may become equivalent to no c·.

centre-piece

Pul.	8–26	even its c·, — Mother's Room

centres

Mis.	113–28	systematized c· of C. S.
Pul.	8– 8	unemployed in our money c·,
My.	72– 9	* From all the c· of Europe
	236–12	Too many c· may become
	341–21	* interest c· in the personality of

centrifugal

Mis.	19–25	centripetal and c· mental forces

centripetal

Mis.	19–25	c· and centrifugal mental forces

cents

Mis.	305–25	* and twenty-five c· to pay for it.
'01.	29–27	fifty c· on every book
My.	28– 8	* dollars and c· received by him,

centuries

break
Po.	79–18	c· break, the earth-bound wake,

Christian
My.	112– 5	in the early Christian c·

combined
My.	127–22	siege of the combined c·,

coming
'01.	30– 5	bequeathing . . . to the coming c·.

dumb
My.	268–18	as silent as the dumb c·

early
'01.	18–23	followers in the early c·,

eighteen
Mis.	81–12	*Are not the last eighteen c·*
	165– 2	more than eighteen c· ago,
	182–32	more than eighteen c· ago.
	321– 4	less . . . than eighteen c· ago ;

eighteenth
Ret.	2–20	the seventeenth and eighteenth c·,

entire
Mis.	196– 6	through the entire c·,
	312–26	throughout the entire c·,

fifteen
Pul.	52–22	* over the world for fifteen c·,

first
'01.	33–10	what it was in the first c·

forthcoming
Ret.	94–30	and the forthcoming c·,

genius of the
Un.	9–12	talent and genius of the c·

lead on the
My.	347– 3	lead on the c· and reveal my

nineteen
My.	48– 4	* Not until nineteen c· had passed
	220–28	nineteen c· have greatly improved

of spiritual growth
Mis.	380– 8	as if c· of spiritual growth

pass
No.	27–11	Until c· pass, and this vision

passed
No.	13– 9	c· passed after those words were

preceding
Pul.	55– 6	* last quarter of preceding c·.

race of the
My.	126–31	win we the race of the c·.

will intervene
Mis.	92– 4	C· will intervene before the
Ret.	84– 1	C· will intervene before the

Mis.	80–25	in successive generations for c·,
	99–23	winds of time sweep clean the c·,
	203–13	served the imagination for c·.
Ret.	17–19	sturdy horse-chestnut for c· hath
Po.	63– 5	sturdy horse-chestnut for c· hath
My.	117–23	lost to the c· except by
	272– 5	pushes onward the c· ;

century

ago
Ret.	1– 7	English authoress of a c· ago.
My.	147– 4	Over a half c· ago,

closing
Pan.	12–10	This closing c·, and its successors,

century

coming
My.	266– 4	confronting the coming c·

every
Pul.	23–19	* closing years of every c·

first
Mis.	40–12	first c· of the Christian era?''
	189–30	not confined to the first c· ;
Ret.	93– 1	first c· of the Christian era
	94–28	first c· of the Christian era
Pan.	8–15	demonstrated in the first c· by
'01.	28– 8	first c· of the Christian era
My.	107– 1	the Christians in the first c·
	127 11	other religions since the first c·.
	180– 5	practised in the first c· by him
	300–29	from the first c· churches,

half
Mis.	295–29	who for a half c· has
My.	147– 4	a half c· ago, . . . the grand old elm
	229–12	might cost them a half c·.

hence
Pul.	vii– 5	Three quarters of a c· hence,

new
'01.	1– 6	first communion in the new c·
Po.	page 22	poem
My.	290–10	the first month of the new c·.

nineteenth
Mis.	99–12	Men and women of the nineteenth c·,
	382–12	latter half of the nineteenth c·
Pul.	vii– 8	latter half of the nineteenth c·,
	23–18	* last quarter of the nineteenth c·.
	55– 7	* Of our remarkable nineteenth c·
'00.	1–10	last year of the nineteenth c·
My.	127–21	latter days of the nineteenth c·,
	131–23	latter days of the nineteenth c·,
	257–18	the close of the nineteenth c·,
	264–13	* Thanksgiving Day of the nineteenth c·

patient
Po.	22– 1	God-crowned, patient c·,

present
Pul.	23–23	* latter part of the present c·,

quarter
My.	89–28	* marvels of the last quarter c·.

quarter of a
My.	294–27	animated . . . for one quarter of a c·.

quarter of the
Pul.	56–14	* the last quarter of the c·.

third
My.	146– 7	acknowledged since the third c·.

this
Mis.	43–20	great ordeal of this c·.
	166–24	named in this c· C. S.,
'01.	16–24	Shall it be said of this c·
	33–25	proof that a religion in this c· is
My.	192–10	mystery and . . . rule not this c·.
	220– 2	Whatever changes come to this c·
	264–15	last Thanksgiving Day of this c·
	302–19	I stand in relation to this c· as

twentieth
Pul.	vii– 6	elders of the twentieth c·,
	8–30	They belong to the twentieth c·.
	22–10	I predict that in the twentieth c·
'00.	9–20	twentieth c· in the ebb and flow of
'02.	5– 5	spiritual dawn of the twentieth c·
My.	95–20	* miracles . . . in this twentieth c·
	155–16	take step with the twentieth c·,
	199–18	on the verge of the twentieth c·,
	229–23	twentieth c· Church Manual
	248–15	sponsors for the twentieth c·,
	264– 9	* threshold of the twentieth c·,

cerebellum

Un.	45–18	a habitant of the c·,

cerebral

My.	301–25	drug cannot . . . affect c· conditions

ceremonial

Mis.	81–14	c· (or ritualistic) waters
	91– 8	not as a perpetual . . . c· of the
Pul.	30–11	* The c· of uniting is to sign a
No.	34– 4	We shall leave the c· law when we
My.	88–11	* a c· of far more than usual
	170– 2	no formal church c·,

ceremonials

Mis.	91–14	to perpetuate no c· except as

ceremonies

Mis.	17–11	material religion with its . . . c·,
Ret.	89– 8	for sacrificial c·, not for sermons.
Pul.	40–16	* simple c·, four times repeated,
	64–27	* to participate in the c·,
	75–19	* c· at Boston last Sunday
No.	12–10	doctrines, rites, and c·.
My.	29–15	* c· that appealed more to the eye,
	86–12	* take part in the subsequent c·
	86–26	* The attendance at the c·
	333–14	* with the usual c·.

ceremoniously
My. 147–25 never stop *c·* to dedicate halls.
ceremony
Mis. 143–15 with quiet, imposing *c·*,
    282–27 when there is no time for *c·*
Man. 49–19 A Legal *C·*.
    49–20 the *c·* shall be performed by
    60–25 Let the *c·* be devout.
Ret. 19– 3 the *c·* taking place under the
Pul. 38– 3 * *c·* took place in 1881.
My. 19– 6 * The *c·* concluded with
certain
Mis. ix– 1 A *c·* apothegm of a Talmudical
    7– 2 not be allowed to eat *c·* food,
    64–28 as to be *c·* that he *is* in a state of
    71– 8 *c·*, that he healed others who
    71–22 mythical origin and *c·* end.
    80–24 In a *c·* sense, we should
    107–27 in *c·* morbid instances
    159–16 where I deposit a *c·* recollections
    166–22 leaven that a *c·* woman hid
    193–15 *c·* clergyman charitably expressed it,
    220–10 in *c·* directions, and turn them
    229– 1 *c·* predisposing or exciting causes.
    229–11 how much more *c·* would be
    242– 7 if either would reset *c·* dislocations
    272–31 If *c·* natures have not profited
    289–12 agreements to *c·* compacts :
    295– 1 *c·* references to American women
    337– 4 how can you be *c·* of so momentous
    349– 3 a *c·* regular-school physician,
    353–27 *C·* students, being too much
Man. 82– 3 disapproves of *c·* books or
Ret. 1– 8 *c·* manuscripts containing Scriptural
    36– 8 This will account for *c·* published
    37–13 or *c·* German philosophers,
Un. 4– 8 in a *c·* finite human sense,
    7–18 *C·* self-proved propositions
    29– 4 all criminal law, to a *c·* extent.
    45–15 *c·* forms of theology and philosophy,
Pul. 13–13 sweet and *c·* sense that God is Love.
    14– 4 *c·* active yet unseen mental agencies
    29–20 * injunctions could, under *c·* conditions,
    59–10 * *c·* hymns and psalms being omitted.
    69–22 * *c·* Christian and scientific laws,
    70–17 * in 1866 she became *c·* that
    76–10 * in *c·* lights has a shimmer of silver.
Rud. 16–24 originated with *c·* opposing factions,
    17– 1 Like *c·* Jews whom St. Paul
Pan. 3– 8 *C·* moods of mind find an
    4– 1 *c·* forms of pantheism and polytheism.
'00. 8–30 advise students not to do *c·* things
    10–11 *C·* elements in human nature
'01. 25–10 *c·* individuals call aids to
Hea. 5– 4 by *c·* kinds of food.
Peo. 3–25 implanted in our religions *c·*
My. 44– 8 * but one thing is *c·*,
    70– 3 * One thing is *c·* :
    93–27 * *c·* statistics brought to light
    105–32 proved to be more *c·*
    111–27 *c·* class of professionals
    116– 6 *c·* individuals are inclined
    210–19 *C·* individuals entertain the
    221– 4 *c·* purely human views.
    259–23 *C·* occasions, considered
    294– 7 In a *c·* city the Master
    303–13 not wasted in *c·* directions.
    334–12 * *c·* circumstances in 1843,
    342–10 * no mistaking *c·* lines
certainly
Mis. 6–11 should *c·* prove to all minds
    28–22 It *c·* does not signify a
    38– 5 as this teaching *c·* does,
    61–17 * *c·* I saw him, or his effigy,
    87–18 *which is c· a mistake.*
    379–16 He *c·* had advanced views
Un. 4–20 which was *c·* the divine Mind ;
    33–12 it is *c·* not the Mind of Christ,
Pul. 10–23 as progress *c·* demands,
    24– 5 * *c·* the most unique structure in
    31– 2 * *c·* a very remarkable retrospect.
    33–15 * *c·* offer food for meditation.
    33–25 * *c·* true that many and many persons,
No. 6– 2 *c·* would contradict the Science of
    22– 2 has *c·* not touched the hem
Pan. 7–22 *c·* gives to matter and evil
    11–18 as *c·* as the man who
My. 48–21 * will *c·* build such truth
    70– 1 * it *c·* looks imposing
    75– 4 * *c·* holding the centre of the
    79–19 * *c·* must be something more
    87–26 * *c·* imbued with the spirit of
    95–19 * faith of these people is *c·* great.
    244–26 will *c·* not exceed three
    273– 5 * *C·*, Christian Scientists,

certainly
My. 307– 1 *c·* read like words that
    324–19 * He *c·* never gave us the
certainty
Mis. 210– 5 with mathematical *c·*
    220–31 with the *c·* of Science
    279– 3 *c·* of individual punishment
Ret. 24–10 I gained the scientific *c·*
    31– 4 showing this solemn *c·*
Pul. 55–19 * held to be scientific *c·*,
    83–10 * the *c·* of inspiration
'01. 2– 1 *c·* that Christianity is now
    2–13 Absolute *c·* in the practice of
My. 190–19 *c·* of the divine laws of
    295– 5 the *c·* of immortality.
    348–20 *c·* of its value to the race
certificate
Mis. x–25 *c·* of membership made out to
Man. 85–13 unless he has a *c·* to show
    91–21 not having the *c·* of C.S.D.
Ret. 43–13 received a *c·* from Dr. W. W. Keen's
My. 251–22 receive a *c·* of the degree C.S.D.
    329–18 * by the *c·* of a notary public
certificates
Man. 85–11 Teachers must have *C·*.
    90– 3 *C·*.
    90– 4 given *c·* by this Board
    91– 6 shall be on all *c·* issued.
My. 240–28 * who have received *c·* from
    245–23 students . . . have received *c·*,
cerulean
Mis. 376–26 on a background of *c·* hue ;
cessation
Pul. 41– 3 * *c·* of the tide of contributions
chaff
Mis. 79– 6 sift the *c·* from the wheat,
My. 111–11 as *c·* is separated from the wheat.
chagrined
No. 41–22 Church seems almost *c·* that
chain
Mis. 205–23 order of Science is the *c·* of ages,
Pul. 14– 2 hour when the people will *c·*,
Po. 15–15 or die in their *c·*.
    26–19 *c·* and charter I have lived to see
    34–19 Wearing no earthly *c·*,
    72– 1 O not too soon is rent the *c·*
My. 200–11 The *c·* of Christian unity,
    202–18 onward and upward *c·* of being.
    279– 8 *c·* of scientific being
    339– 4 leads upward in the *c·* of being.
chained
Mis. 102– 7 If . . . Mind would be *c·* to finity,
chains
Mis. 101–17 undermines the . . . breaks their *c·*,
    262–20 looseth the *c·* of sickness and sin,
Un. 56–23 be made to fret in their *c·* ;
Peo. 11–14 their *c·* are clasped by the false
My. 69– 2 * the eight bronze *c·*,
chair
Mis. 112–20 he sank back in his *c·*,
Ret. 8–14 I sat in a little *c·* by her side,
Pul. 48– 7 * sit in her swinging *c·*,
Po. 3– 8 I watch thy *c·*, and wish thee here ;
My. 49–20 * with Mrs. Eddy in the *c·*.
Chairman and chairman
My. 173–28 *c·* of the prudential committee
    333– 2 * in the possession of the *c·*
    361–26 * CHARLES DEAN, *C·*,
    362– 2 CHARLES A. DEAN, *C·* BOARD OF TRUSTEES,
chairs
Mis. 325–16 nodding on cushioned *c·*,
Pul. 29–13 * *c·* pressed into service
Chaldee
Mis. 1– 3 The *C·* watched the appearing
    333–30 *C·* hung his destiny out upon
challenge
Mis. 247– 9 I calmly *c·* the world,
'00. 9–21 *c·* the thinkers, speakers,
My. 108– 5 I *c·* matter to act apart from
    163– 3 angelic song chiming chaste *c·*
    248–28 *c·* universal indifference,
challenged
My. 203–27 all chance of being *c·*.
    233– 7 when *c·* by Truth,
challenges
Mis. 131– 1 *c·* the errors of others
challenging
Mis. 329–20 *c·* the sedentary shadows

chamber

Mis.	159–13	Into this upper c·,
	159–15	In this c· is memory's wardrobe,
	202– 5	* c· where the good man meets
	257–29	Even the c· where the good man
	279–23	met together in an upper c· ;
Pul.	54–26	* in the c· with him,

Chamberlin

Hon. Judge

My.	137–10	Hon. Judge C·, Concord, N. H.

Honorable Judge

My.	138–29	* directed to Honorable Judge C·

Judge Robert N.

My.	137– 3	* Judge Robert N. C· of the

chambers

Mis.	292–28	searched the secret c· of sense?
	343–27	haunted c· of memory,
Ret.	8– 2	throng the c· of memory.
Pul.	5– 9	holds in her secret c· those
Po.	26–18	the dim c· of eternity
My.	156–19	the upper c· of thought

chamois

Ret.	11–21	Farther than feet of c· fall,
Po.	60–19	Farther than feet of c· fall,

chance

Mis.	79–30	because they c· to be under arrest
Ret.	14–15	take my c· . . . with my brothers and
Un.	17– 1	A lie has only one c· of
	26–13	* C· and change are busy ever,
	26–18	how can it be also true that c·
	26–23	what place has c· in the divine
Rud.	5–25	football of c· and sinking into
My.	49– 7	* c· of sweeping the world
	120– 7	Accept my gratitude for the c·
	203–26	safe from all c· of being challenged.
	248–28	indifference, c·, and creeds.

chancel

Pul.	26– 8	* corresponding to the c· of
	50–23	* Adjoining the c· is a pastor's

chancery

Mis.	122–24	Neither . . . nor a religious c·

chandeliers

Pul.	25–30	* takes the place of c·.

change (noun)

actual

Mis.	188–27	not . . . an actual c· in the realities

and the grave

Mis.	339–29	C· and the grave may part us ;

another

Mis.	158– 8	another c· in your pulpit

before the

Mis.	42–17	If, before the c· whereby we meet

called death

Mis.	42– 1	*After the c· called death*
No.	27–27	go on after the c· called death,

chance and

Un.	26–13	* Chance and c· are busy ever,
	26–18	can it be . . . that *chance* and c· are

in the actions

Mis.	237– 7	wrought a c· in the actions of men.

in the time

My.	121– 3	suggested a c· in the time for

no present

My.	343– 6	* "No present c· is contemplated

of consciousness

Un.	11–11	c· of consciousness and evidence,

of death

Pul.	38–19	* passed the c· of death

of heart

Mis.	50–18	*Do you believe in c· of heart?*
	50–25	c· of heart would deliver man
	51– 1	c· of heart is essential to
Ret.	14–20	experienced a c· of heart ;

small

My.	78–16	* none proffering small c·.

this

Mis.	50–25	This c· of heart would
	51– 1	This c· of heart is essential
Un.	11–12	effected this c· through the
'02.	20–20	I shall be the loser by this c·,

to health

No.	40–25	comes with the c· to health,

Mis.	50–20	must be a c· from human affections,
	50–22	must be a c· from the belief that
	82–31	not subject to growth, c·, or
Ret.	4–12	But c· has been busy.
Un.	30–22	c· in the mortal sense of things,
	37– 9	a c· in human consciousness,
No.	40–24	If a c· in the religious views of
'01.	23–13	as would a c· of the denominations
My.	60–11	* What a c· in the Christian world !
	341–27	* c· from the misty air outside

change (verb)

Mis.	19–15	can never c· the current of that
	23–31	could not c· its species
	26–31	How, then, can this conclusion c·,
	118–15	nor c· this immutable decree of Love :
	217–28	nature of God must c· in order to
	217–32	and our convictions c· :
	218– 8	mortal mind must c· all its
	219–17	must c· his patient's consciousness
	219–20	must c· the patient's sense of
	219–28	he can c· this evil sense and
	298–30	false consciousness does not c· the
	345–10	* I cannot c· from good to bad."
Un.	35– 2	Let mortal mind c·, and say
	35– 5	C· the mind, and the quality changes.
	56–24	c· from flesh to Spirit,
Rud.	6– 8	when we c· the nature of beauty
No.	39–12	Prayer can neither c· God, nor
	39–13	can and does c· our modes
'02.	17–13	Earth's actors c· earth's scenes ;
Peo.	13–19	* cannot c· at once from
Po.	67–19	c· not with years ;
My.	41– 4	* No one can c· the law of
	321–19	* to c· my opinion one iota

changeableness

Peo.	8– 3	If c· that repenteth itself ;

changed

Mis.	x–17	My signature has been slightly c·
	26–32	or be c·, to mean that good
	50–28	c· from self to benevolence
	50–29	c· to having but *one* God
	52–18	*not dispelled, but only* c·,
	65–17	*Have you c· your instructions*
	68– 5	include also man's c· appearance
	191– 6	c· the meaning of the term,
	220–16	c· his patient's consciousness
	235– 1	man has a c· recognition of
	237– 6	c· belief has wrought a change in
Man.	18–24	c· the title of "First Members"
	64–13	The Title of Mother C·.
Ret.	30– 7	motive of my . . . labors has never c·.
	64–18	God's ways . . . have never c·,
	82– 1	c·, modified, broadened,
Rud.	17–15	ways of Christianity have not c·.
No.	1– 5	only as our natures are c·
Hea.	19– 7	Had they c· the felon's belief
My.	28–31	* c· the whole aspect of medicine
	325–14	* my desire has never c·.
	327–21	* an old law, . . . was c·
	327–24	* was c· to read as follows :

changeful

Pul.	32– 6	* c· expression cannot thus be
Po.	8–16	dreaming alone of its c· sky
	31–14	vassal of the c· hour,
	46– 5	Nor April's c· showers,

changeless

Un.	26–21	If God be c· *goodness,*

changes

Mis.	158– 6	c· about to be made.
	170– 6	which never c· to death.
	175– 9	Science c· this false sense,
	363–13	the c· of matter, or evil.
Un.	7– 4	c· at Andover Seminary
	26–10	the material c·, the *phantasma,*
	35– 6	Change the mind, and the quality c·.
Pul.	55– 5	* cyclic c· that came during
Rud.	7–23	Spirit no more c· its species,
Hea.	5– 5	by c· of temperature,
Peo.	1–16	c· from material to spiritual
My.	66–12	* number of c· will be made
	220– 1	Whatever c· come to this century

changeth

My.	33–24	and c· not.— *Psal.* 15 : 4.

changing

Mis.	268–20	c· the affections,
Un.	11–10	the need of c· this mind
Pan.	6–13	c· the order and harmony of
Hea.	4–27	demonstrate a c· Principle?
My.	215–31	we have no hint of his c·

channel

Mis.	309–15	not the c· through which
	373–18	out of its proper c·,
Ret.	54–19	same c· of ignorant belief.

channels

Mis.	212–20	flow not into one of their c·.
	220–11	turn them into c· of Truth.
	291– 4	forced into personal c·,
	351–29	turns it into the opposite c·.
	359–13	proper c· for development,
Man.	45– 1	supplies within the wide c· of
Ret.	52– 4	seeking to broaden its c·
	79–16	Through the c· of material sense,
No.	44–15	and choke the c· of God.

channels
'01. 19–27 flow through no such *c·*.

chant
Mis. 281– 2 *c·* hymns of victory for triumphs.
Po. 34– 9 Wouldst *c·* thy vespers

chants
Mis. 321– 2 watchful shepherd *c·* his welcome

chaos
Chr. 53– 3 O'er the grim night of *c·*
Ret. 69–25 awful din, blackness, and *c·*,
Un. 13–14 reduce the universe to *c·*.
56– 1 The *c·* of mortal mind
Pul. 14–21 deep waters of *c·* and old night.
Po. 1–10 from *c·* dark set free,

chapel
My. 172– 3 * first *c·* of the college.
184–23 Your rural *c·* is a social success

chapels
Mis. 150–17 *C·* and churches are dotting the

chaplain
My. 309–12 For several years father was *c·* of

chaplet
Mis. 163– 6 its *c·*, a grave

Chapter
115
Mis. 272–12 * Public Statutes, *C·* 115, Section 2,
268
Mis. 272–14 * Statutes of 1883, *C·* 268,
375
Mis. 272– 4 * under Act of 1874, *C·* 375,

My. 335– 9 * officer of the Lodge and *C·*,

Chapter
Mis. 32–13 In Mark, ninth *c·*,
57– 9 in the first *c·* of Genesis.
92–13 in the *c·* on Recapitulation.
92–17 contained in that *c·* of "S· and H·
191– 8 John, sixth *c·* and seventieth verse,
191–12 In Mark, ninth *c·* and
192–25 last *c·* of Mark is emphatic on this
314– 8 *c·* (or portion of the *c·*)
314–22 the book, *c·*, and verses.
332–13 Genesis, third *c·* and ninth verse,
Man. 86–17 teach from the *c·* "Recapitulation"
86–24 said *c·* on "Recapitulation"
Ret. 35– 5 *c·* on Recapitulation in S. and H.
37–22 the *c·* on Animal Magnetism,
38– 2 I had finished . . . as far as that *c·*,
38– 8 in my last *c·* a partial history of
38–21 closing *c·* of my first edition of
83–19 the *c·* for the class-room,
84–10 in the *c·* on Recapitulation.
Un. 43–24 in the third *c·* of Philippians,
Pul. 27–24 * in the Apocalypse, *c·* 12,
Pan. 7–19 the third *c·* of Genesis,
'00. 12– 6 In Revelation, second *c·*,
'02. 7– 5 In the first *c·* of Genesis,
My. 60–17 * the first *c·* of Genesis.
136– 6 as depicted in the *c·*
222– 1 the seventeenth *c·* of the Gospel

chapters
Pul. 38– 9 * It consists of fourteen *c·*,
My. 179– 3 first and second *c·* of Genesis,

character
and divinity
Mis. 197–18 the *c·* and divinity which Jesus
and philanthropy
'00. 14–24 respect the *c·* and philanthropy
and practice
Ret. 28–30 assimilate the *c·* and practice of
and sovereignty
Pan. 7–11 lose the *c·* and sovereignty of
beautiful
Ret. 6–13 To speak of his beautiful *c·*
cause and
Mis. 299– 2 awake to their cause and *c·*.
Christian
My. 332–31 * record and Christian *c·* was found ;
concrete
Mis. 337–25 understood the concrete *c·* of
consecrated
Pul. 32–28 * saintly and consecrated *c·*.
distinguished
Pul. 1– 9 was a distinguished *c·*,
divine
Un. 1–17 nearer to the divine *c·*,
Hea. 4–22 conception of the divine *c·*,
elevated
Ret. 5–25 * She gave an elevated *c·* to
enduring
My. 24–24 * substantial and enduring *c·* of

character
exemplary
Man. 55–17 three years of exemplary *c·*.
give force to
'01. 19–14 That animal natures give force to *c·*
granite
My. 163–26 friendship, and granite *c·*.
health and
Peo. 7–28 health and *c·* of man
her
Ret. 2– 2 had in her *c·* that sturdy
My. 39–30 * strength and beauty of her *c·*.
high-principled
My. 319– 9 for his high-principled *c·*
His
Mis. 102–13 His *c·* admits of no degrees
his
Mis. 148– 3 one part of his *c·* at variance
293–16 if evil dominates his *c·*,
309–11 contemplation of his *c·*.
hue and
Mis. 372–28 with true hue and *c·* of the
human
Mis. 151– 7 purifies the human *c·*,
Un. 29– 2 hypothesis as to its human *c·*.
'00. 8– 9 so the human *c·* comes forth
My. 246–18 revealed through the human *c·*.
identical in
My. 78– 3 * six services, identical in *c·*,
individual
Mis. 81–22 Every individual *c·*,
Ret. 73–14 fail to appreciate individual *c·*.
No. 7–25 distinctions of individual *c·*
Jesus'
Mis. 91–16 real affection for Jesus' *c·*
jewels of
Mis. 201–27 losing those jewels of *c·*,
man's
Hea. 5– 7 saying . . . bias a man's *c·*.
my
My. 306– 2 misrepresents my *c·*,
nature and
Un. 1–12 nature and *c·* of God
3–21 in His own nature and *c·*,
6–18 concerning the divine nature and *c·*
31–18 the nature and *c·* of matter,
of a liar
Mis. 226–21 *c·* of a liar and hypocrite
of Christ
Mis. 367–27 in logic, or in the *c·* of Christ.
of Jesus
Mis. 360–10 and the *c·* of Jesus,
Ret. 22– 8 St. Paul summarized the *c·* of Jesus
of nations
Peo. 2–28 influence upon the *c·* of nations
of the Christ
Ret. 23–16 *c·* of the Christ was illuminated by
of the votaries
Mis. 196–15 the *c·* of the votaries to
of true greatness
My. 150–5 of the *c·* of true greatness :
phases of
Mis. 127–30 Mortal mind presents phases of *c·*
previous
Man. 52–12 and his previous *c·* has been good,
qualities of
Peo. 8– 9 bring out these qualities of *c·*
refines
My. 131– 3 that which refines *c·*
religious
Man. 61–20 of an appropriate religious *c·*
scholarship, and
My. 104–26 talents, scholarship, and *c·*
straightforward
Mis. 233–19 fair-seeming for straightforward *c·*,
subdued
Mis. 354–16 a *c·* subdued, a life consecrated,
true
Rud. 17– 5 true *c·* of C. S.,
My. 121–18 can be found in a true *c·*,
unstable
Mis. 147–18 a loose and unstable *c·*.
whatever
No. 24– 5 He is extension, of whatever *c·*.

Mis. 26–27 in the Greek Testament, *c·*.
67– 9 with his rights of mind and *c·*.
120–28 whose *c·* we to-day commemorate,
224–14 constitution, culture, *c·*,
337–30 again reproduced in the *c·*
Ret. 5–21 * *c·* of Mrs. Abigail Ambrose Baker
My. 4–21 unfolding the true metal in *c·*,
30–11 * the *c·* of the attendance.
85– 1 * remarkable in the *c·* of the
179–22 *c·* of the Nazarene Prophet

characteristic
'02. 2–22 inherent *c·* of my nature,
Hea. 12–15 *c·* peculiarities and
My. 82–20 * *c·* of Christian Scientists,
137– 8 * *c·* in both substance and
184–16 *c·* of our Granite State,

characteristics
Pul. 48–25 * one of her *c·*,
'00. 8– 7 *c·* of tree and flower,
My. 87– 7 * *c·* of this crowd of visitors.

characterize
Mis. 126–21 should *c·* Christian Scientists.
134– 6 *c·* justice and Christianity.
301–12 *c·* the writings of a few professed
Man. 77–19 *c·* all the proceedings of
Pan. 14–13 to *c·* her government,
'01. 1–20 must always *c·* heroic hearts;
My. 4–22 *c·* the seeker and finder of C. S.
245– 7 Law and order *c·* its work

characterized
Mis. 84– 4 This wisdom, which *c·* his sayings,
112–30 is *c·* in this Scripture:
199–31 *c·* and dated the Christian era.
363–31 *c·* by a more spiritual apprehension
Ret. 25–15 God I *c·* as individual entity,
Un. 1– 9 may justly be *c·* as *wonderful.*
Peo. 6–28 Periods and peoples are *c·* by
Po. vii– 2 * *c· by the same lofty trend of*
My. 331–27 * *c·* the people of the South,

characterizes
My. 308–31 whom *McClure's Magazine c·* as

characterizing
Man. 59– 2 or without *c·* their origin

characters
Mis. 191–28 opposite *c·* ascribed to him
357–23 whose Christian *c·* and lives
360– 7 colossal *c·*, Paul and Jesus.
Pul. 5– 9 those *c·* of holiest sort,
Peo. 3– 2 our ideals form our *c·*,
My. 48–22 * into the marrow of their *c·*.
186– 3 writes in living *c·* their lessons
277–14 *c·* and lives of men determine the

charge
Mis. 38– 1 *Why do you c· for teaching C. S.,*
132–19 having *c·* of a church,
155–30 to contemplate the universal *c·*
306–29 give His angels *c· — Psal.* 91: 11.
335–13 others *c·* upon me with
345– 4 against the *c·* of atheism;
374–15 Angels, . . . hold *c·* over both,
Man. 52–11 as to the validity of the *c·*.
63–20 take *c·* of the Reading Rooms
69–11 whatsoever she may *c·*
86–12 who is not in *c·* of an association
Ret. 84–27 A teacher should take *c·* only of
89–28 to take *c·* of their students,
Pul. 87– 1 * take *c·* of any services that may
'00. 14–27 this sin to their *c·.*"— *Acts* 7: 00.
'02. 15– 6 Healing . . . without *c·*,
Po. 33– 1 remember my blessings and *c·*,
My. 12– 6 * those having the work in *c·*
16–15 * who have the work directly in *c·*,
73–20 * It is in *c·* of G. D. Robertson,
135–14 to take the *c·* of my property;
137–21 to take *c·* of my property;
219–18 I would not *c·* Christians with
243–14 who are adequate to take *c·* of
244–27 No *c·* will be made for my services.

chargeable
Mis. 363–16 God is not *c·* with imperfection.

charged
Hea. 7–19 he *c·* home a crime to mind,

charges
Mis. 247–12 The *c·* against my views are false,
311–32 who were reporting false *c·*,
My. 237–15 chapter sub-title
237–17 their *c·* for treatment equal to

charging
My. 204–23 the *c·* of the sick whom you

chariot
My. 115– 2 mighty *c·* of divine Love,

chariot-paths
Pul. 7– 1 from the *c·* of justice,

chariots
Un. 17–10 ties its . . . to the divine *c·*,

chariot-wheels
My. 127– 7 speed of the *c·* of Truth

charitable
Rud. 14– 8 never sought *c·* support,
No. 8– 4 faithful, and *c·* with all.
My. 245–16 let Christian Scientists be *c·*.

charitable
My. 338–29 instructed to be, *c·* towards all,
358–20 to a worthy and *c·* purpose.

charitableness
Man. 40–10 in true brotherliness, *c·*,

charitably
Mis. 78–16 We will *c·* hope, however,
172– 3 Dispensing the Word *c·*,
193–15 clergyman *c·* expressed it,
My. 106– 3 speak *c·* of all mankind

charities
Mis. 245–20 *c·*, and reforms of to-day.
My. 231– 2 endeavors to bestow her *c·*

charity
Mis. ix– 3 * "The noblest *c·* is to
ix– 4 * prevent a man from accepting *c·*;
7– 7 Great *c·* and humility is necessary
13– 2 mercy and *c·* toward every one,
32–23 and *c·* must begin at home.
130– 2 long-suffering, meekness, *c·*,
130–27 he who exercises the largest *c·*,
172–10 white-winged *c·*, brooding over all,
209–30 egotism and false *c·*
210–27 *C·* has the courage of conviction;
210–29 *C·* is Love;
210–31 *C·* never flees before error,
211– 7 sickly *c·* that supplies criminals
224–24 *c·* broad enough to cover the
267– 6 *C·* students, for whom I have
292–23 *C·* thus serves as admonition
311–12 in the full spirit of that *c·*
330–27 boasts and begs, and God denies *c·*.
335–14 having too much *c·*;
338–12 *c·* that suffereth long and is
369–21 white-winged *c·* that heals and
Man. 47–24 *C·* to All.
Ret. 50–15 my list of indigent *c·* scholars
Rud. 14– 1 fed, clothed, and sheltered by *c·*.
14–21 doing *c·* work besides.
No. 45– 3 St. Paul said that without *c·* we
45– 4 "*C·* suffereth long,— *I Cor.* 13: 4.
'00. 14–19 *c·* that seeketh not only her own,
15–24 and *c·*, and service,— *Rev.* 2: 19.
'01. 12–14 yet should not have *c·*,
26–20 a sound faith and *c·*,
26–20 the greatest of which is *c·*
26–23 and have not *c·*,— *I Cor.* 13: 1.
32– 8 Full of *c·* and good works,
34–18 sweet *c·* which seeketh not
My. 19–22 that her *c·*, . . . shall reap richly
149–22 to demonstrate Christian *c·*.
158–15 holiness, patience, *c·*, love.
175–24 fraternity, and Christian *c·*.
187–12 *c·* out of a pure heart,— *I Tim.* 1: 5.
215– 9 without having *c·* scholars,
216–28 that *c·* begins at home,
227– 6 *C·* is quite as rare as wisdom,
227– 7 but when *c·* does appear,
231– 1 chapter sub-title
231–17 "*C·* suffereth long— *I Cor.* 13: 4.
231–18 wisdom must govern *c·*,
262–28 humility, benevolence, *c·*,
275–27 *c·* brooding over all,

charlatan
My. 106–28 * is the Christian Scientist a *c·*?

charlatanism
Mis. 368–14 *C·*, fraud, and malice
'00. 12–23 to purge our cities of *c·*.
Hea. 14–14 ignorance and *c·* are miserable

charlatans
Mis. 80– 7 defense of medical *c·* in general,
243–20 There are *c·* in "mind-cure,"

Charles
Pul. 39–16 * Throws o'er the *C·* its flood of

Charleston
S. C.
Pul. 34– 2 * Colonel Glover, of *C·*, S. C.,
'00. 1–20 cities, such as . . . *C·*, S. C.,
My. 312–19 resided in *C·*, S. C.
330–13 * Christian Scientist of *C·*, S. C.,
330–16 * who she states was of *C·*, S. C.,
335– 3 * resided in *C·*, S. C.,
335–13 * a resident of *C·*, S. C.,

South Carolina
Mis. x–21 Glover of *C·*, South Carolina,
Ret. 19– 2 Glover of *C·*, South Carolina,
'02. 15–17 Glover, of *C·*, South Carolina,

'02. 3– 8 put an end, at *C·*, to any
My. 332–21 * A Christian Scientist in *C·* was
335–22 * to take the remains to *C·*.

Charlestown, Mass.
My. 49–16 * August 16, 1879, in *C·*, *M·*,

charm
Mis. 390– 3   Thou hast a Naiad's *c·* ;
     393– 1   Chief, the *c·* of thy reflecting,
Pul. 81–11   * an added grace— a newer *c·*.
Pan. 3– 7   loneness lacks but one *c·*
Po. 51– 6   Chief, the *c·* of thy reflecting,
     55– 3   Thou hast a naiad's *c·* ;
My. 258–27   A transmitted *c·* rests on them

charms
'00. 13–20   included *c·* and incantations.
Po. 32– 5   blossoms whose fragrance and *c·*

charnel-house
Mis. 293–28   the *c·* of sensuality,
     325–25   Away from this *c·* of the

charred
Peo. 8–25   material systems, already *c·*,
My. 178–24   Instantly the table sank a *c·* mass.

chart
Mis. 356–28   the *c·* of its divine Principle

charter
Mis. 272– 1   * obtained a college *c·*
     272–21   * grant, which may be called a *c·*,
     382–17   obtained the first *c·* for the
     382–21   obtained the first and only *c·* for a
Man. 18– 3   *c·* for the Church was obtained
Ret. 16–16   *c·* for The Mother Church
     43– 5   No *c·* was granted for
     44– 4   *c·* for this church was obtained
     49–19   thank the State for its *c·*,
Pul. 20– 7   and reobtain its *c·*
     38– 1   * *c·* obtained the following June.
     67–28   * and a *c·* was obtained
Po. 26–19   chain and *c·* I have lived to see
     72– 2   *c·*, trampling right in dust !
My. 49– 9   * The *c·* of this little church

chartered
Mis. 271–22   only *c·* College of Metaphysics.
     272–25   * but one legally *c·* college of
Ret. 43– 5   College in Boston, *c·* in 1881,
     48–17   College, *c·* in January, 1881,
'00. 1–11   this first church . . . *c·* in 1879,
My. 244–30   College . . . was *c·* A.D. 1881.

charters
Mis. 272– 8   * no *c·* were granted for
     272–22   * these so-called *c·* bestow no rights to
     272–24   * institutions, under such *c·*,

Chase
Mr.
My. 27–22   * announcement made by Mr. *C·*
Stephen A.
Pul. 43– 9   * On the platform . . . Stephen A. *C·*,
     59–25   * on the platform . . . Stephen A. *C·*,
     86–10   * signatures of . . . and Stephen A. *C·*,
     87– 8   * signature
My. 16– 2   * The report of Mr. Stephen A. *C·*,
     21–30   * signature
     27–17   * signature
     72–17   * the notice which Stephen A. *C·*,

Chase, C.S.D.
Stephen A.
My. 39–16   * Treasurer, Stephen A. *C·*, *C.S.D.* ;

chase
Ret. 17–18   *C·* tulip, magnolia, and fragrant
Po. 63– 3   *C·* tulip, magnolia, and fragrant

chased
Mis. 388– 4   What *c·* the clouds away?
Po. 7– 4   What *c·* the clouds away?

chaste
My. 163– 3   chiming *c·* challenge to praise

chastely
Pul. 77– 3   * one of the most *c·* elegant

chasten
Ret. 21–18   is to *c·* the affections,

chastened
Mis. 209–20   False pleasure will be, is, *c·* ;
     213–15   has *c·* and illumined
     281–10   one will be *c·* for it.
     356–10   cultured intellects, *c·* affections,
Ret. 31–27   spoke to my *c·* sense

chasteneth
Mis. 18– 4   Lord loveth He *c·*,— *Heb.* 12 : 6.
     73– 5   Lord loveth He *c·* ;"— *Heb.* 12 : 6.
     125– 4   Lord loveth He *c·*."— *Heb.* 12 : 6.
     208–20   Lord loveth He *c·*."— *Heb.* 12 : 6.
Ret. 80– 5   Lord loveth He *c·*,— *Heb.* 12 : 6.
Un. 23–12   whom the father *c·* not— *Heb.* 12 : 7.

chastening
Un. 23–10   "If ye endure *c·*,— *Heb.* 12 : 7.

chastens
Mis. 126–14   ordeal refines while it *c·*.

chastens
Mis. 351–28   *c·* its affection, purifies it,
     387–25   *c·* pride and earth-born fear,
Po. 6–20   *c·* pride and earth-born fear,

chastisement
Un. 23–13   if ye be without *c·*,— *Heb.* 12 : 8.

chastisements
Mis. 102–18   His *c·* are the manifestations of
My. 282–10   Through the wholesome *c·* of Love,

Chattanooga, Tenn.
My. 323–15   * *C·*, *T·*, December 4, 1906.

chattel
Pul. 82–13   * they treated woman as a *c·*,

cheating
'00. 2–19   "By *c·*, lying, and crime ;

check
My. 26– 9   *c·* of five thousand dollars,
     159–18   Material theories tend to *c·*
     175– 6   Please accept the enclosed *c·*
     222–30   holding of crime in *c·*,
     289– 4   *c·* for five hundred dollars
     318–20   He held himself well in *c·*

checking
My. 67–11   * *C·* facilities . . . 3,000 garments

checks
Pul. 44–28   * refused to accept any further *c·*

cheek
Mis. 11–29   When smitten on one *c·*,
     329–17   "breath all odor and *c·* all bloom."
Ret. 31–23   Blanched was the *c·* of pride
     45–21   on thy right *c·*,— *Matt.* 5 : 39.
Po. 8–19   parting the ringlets to kiss my *c·*.
My. 227–27   on thy right *c·*,— *Matt.* 5 : 39.

cheeks
Mis. 240– 4   sparkling eyes, and ruby *c·*

cheer
Mis. 16– 3   so comfort, *c·*, and bless one,
     118–24   Be of good *c·* ;
     157–18   I am glad that you are in good *c·*.
     213–27   Christian Scientists, be of good *c·* :
     231–23   look of *c·* and a toy from
     320–11   to *c·*, guide, and bless man
'02. 17–30   *c·* the heart susceptible of light
Po. 10–18   *c·* the hosts of heaven ;
     32–21   *c·* me with hope when 'tis done ;
     66–14   Might *c·* it, perchance,
My. 132– 7   be of good *c·* ;— *John* 16 : 33.
     135–26   *c·* my advancing years.
     175–12   growth and . . . of our city *c·* me.
     202–21   I thank you for the words of *c·*
     261– 3   *c·* the children's Christmas
     337–19   "Wouldst *c·* the hosts of heaven;

cheered
Mis. xii– 5   Supported, *c·*, I take my pen and
My. 11–19   * she will be *c·* and encouraged
     274–23   I am *c·* and blessed when
     302–22   I am less lauded, . . . and *c·*

cheerful
Ret. 5–24   * like the gentle dew and *c·* light,
My. 84–21   * *c·* optimism and energy of its
     87–20   * *c·* looking groups of people
     87–29   * *c·* doing of good.
     91–12   * Its communicants are *c·*
     95–10   * *c·* and prosperous body of

cheerfully
My. 87– 9   * *c·* contented multitude
     118– 2   who *c·* obey God
     222–31   *c·* await the end— justice and
     360–14   *c·* subscribe these words of love :

cheerfulness
My. 31–14   * of light and *c·*,

cheering
Mis. 150–15   The outlook is *c·*.
My. 234–18   regarded on one side only, is *c·*,

cheers
My. 202–23   The taper . . . *c·* the darkness.

Chelsea
My. 56–13   * Cambridge, *C·*, and Roxbury.

chemicalization
Mis. 10–23   This destruction is a moral *c·*,
Pul. 5–30   This spiritual *c·* is the upheaval

chemist
Peo. 6– 9   * *c·*, druggist, or drug

Chemistry and chemistry
Rud. 12–22   with the *c·* of food?
My. 304– 8   *C·*, Blair's Rhetoric,

cherish
Mis. 253–29   *C·* these new-born children

cherish

Mis.	356–30	C· humility, "watch," — *Matt.* 26 : 41.
	370–15	This is the babe we are to c·.
Man.	48– 1	c· no enmity toward those who
Ret.	6–13	his beautiful character as I c· it,
My.	41–21	* unable to c· any enmity.
	251–28	C· steadfastly this fact.
	331–22	* gratitude we owe and c· towards
	362–21	* We revere and c· your friendship,

cherished

Ret.	2–29	for whom she c· a high regard.
My.	40–12	* relinquish their c· resentments,
	195–11	deep love which I c· for you

cherishes

Mis.	131– 1	and c· his own,
	281–10	if one c· ambition unwisely,
'02.	19– 8	Scientist c· no resentment ;

cherries

Ret.	4–15	apples, peaches, pears, and c·

cherubim

My.	188–15	under the wings of the c·,

Cheshire Cat

Mis.	216–19	story of the C· C·,

Chestnut Hill

Mass.

Po.	vii–17	* C· H·, MASS., September 24, 1910.
My.	140– 9	C· H·, MASS.
	140–29	C· H·, MASS., June 21, 1908.
	143–31	C· H·, MASS., June 7, 1909.
	198– 9	C· H·, MASS., June 26, 1909.
	207–26	C· H·, MASS., January 6, 1909.
	255–11	C· H·, MASS., March 6, 1909.
	352– 3	* C· H·, MASS.
	355–16	C· H·, MASS., February 7, 1910.
	356–10	C· H·, MASS., April 20, 1910.
	356–19	C· H·, MASS., July 18, 1910.
	361–18	* MRS. MARY BAKER EDDY, C· H·, MASS.
	362– 7	C· H·, MASS., January 20, 1910.
	362–11	* MRS. MARY BAKER EDDY, C· H·, MASS.

chews

Mis.	240–28	nothing but . . . *naturally* c· tobacco.

Chicago

Ill.

Pul.	89–27	* Elite, C·, Ill.
	90– 9	* Times, C·, Ill.
My.	177– 2	chapter sub-title
	191–27	chapter sub-title
	208–23	chapter sub-title

Mis.	98– 7	at the National Convention in C·,
	98–16	progress of our common Cause in C·,
	134–18	to be in C· on June 13.
	156–14	in the one held at C·
	157–19	Mr. E. A. Kimball, C. S. D., of C·,
	266–19	loyal students in C·, New York,
	275–22	at the grand meeting in C·
	275–26	C· is the wonder of the western
	304– 7	* coming World's Exposition at C·.
	321–24	In reply to all invitations from C·
Pul.	4–29	Parliament of Religions, held in C·,
	23– 1	*Daily Inter-Ocean,* C·,
	28–27	* Judge Hanna, formerly of C·,
	56– 2	* New York, C·, Buffalo, Cleveland,
	79– 1	* [*The Union Signal,* C·]
'00.	1–21	C·, St. Louis, Denver,
My.	36– 4	* Mr. Edward A. Kimball of C·,
	77– 5	* leads the Auditorium of C·.
	146– 1	my dedicatory letter to the C·
	146– 8	in my letter to the church in C·,
	164– 7	heading
	164–15	beginning of C. S. in C·
	177– 6	First Church of Christ, . . . in C·.
	181–23	it is estimated that C· has
	182– 1	Thirty years ago C· had few
	182–12	Scientist Association in C·.
	183– 5	in this great city of C·,
	192–16	hovers around your churches in C·,
	304–13	in New York City, C·, Boston,
	304–21	In a lecture in C·, he said :

Chickering Hall

Mis.	161– 2	IN C· H·, BOSTON, MASS.,
Pul.	28–28	* held its meetings in C· H·;
My.	54–27	* concluded to engage C· H·
	54–31	* Sunday service held in C· H·
	55–10	* attendance . . . in C· H·,
	55–19	* services were held in C· H·.
	55–23	* C· H· was to be remodelled.
	57–15	* in C· H·, October 3, 1893,
	80–15	* Howe and Woolson Halls, C· H·,
	80–24	* Woolson Hall, and C· H·,

chides

Hea.	1–18	* At fifty, c· his infamous delay,

chief

Mis.	163–23	Truth, the c· cornerstone.
	267– 7	whose c· aim is to injure me,
	275– 1	c· actors in scenes like these,
	393– 1	C·, the charm of thy reflecting,
Man.	17–15	the c· corner-stone whereof is,
	111–14	c· points of these instructions
Ret.	15– 6	the c· corner-stone." — *Eph.* 2 : 20.
Pul.	10–18	c· corner-stone in the house of
	43–23	* c· feature of the dedication,
No.	38–15	This is the c· corner-stone,
Pan.	13– 4	C· among the questions herein,
	14–15	guide and bless our c· magistrate,
Po.	51– 6	C·, the charm of thy reflecting,
	78–14	mourners, while yet the c·,
My.	17–15	a c· corner stone, — *I Pet.* 2 : 6.
	112– 8	and build on its c· corner-stone.
	112–30	c· cities and the best families
	158–25	He has laid the c· corner-stone
	166–15	Life's ills are its c· recompense ;
	182– 9	Truth, as the c· corner-stone.
	282– 5	friendship of our c· executive
	290–19	our nation's c· magistrate,
	292–10	comfort the c· mourner

chiefest

Ret.	23–19	"the c·," the only, — *Song* 5 : 10.

chiefly

Mis.	6–27	conversation c· confined to the
	176– 8	c· in the great crises of nations
Hea.	5–12	* the question c· is concerning
My.	159–28	thought c· regards material things,

child (*see also* **child's**)

adopted

Mis.	111–32	or is a spiritually adopted c·,
Man.	46– 3	claims a spiritually adopted c·

another

Ret.	40–17	be delivered of another c·.

appeared as a

Un.	59–14	Jesus appeared as a c·,

complaining

Mis.	236–10	c· complaining of his parents

corporeal

Mis.	166–20	to the corporeal c· Jesus,

give the

Mis.	226– 2	* "Give the c· what he relishes,

God's

Mis.	181–28	preexistence as God's c· ;
Un.	15– 9	Man is God's c· and image.
'02.	8–29	not as . . . but as God's c·.

govern a

Mis.	51–12	*govern a c· metaphysically?*

her

Mis.	253–24	Can a mother tell her c· one tithe

His

No.	30–14	love of a Father for His c·,

his

Un.	48–16	than the . . . enters into his c·.

in sleep

Mis.	215–18	as when a c· in sleep walks

is born

Mis.	161– 5	*unto us a c· is born,* — *Isa.* 9 : 6.
	166–10	unto us a c· is born, — *Isa.* 9 : 6.
	321– 3	"Unto us a c· is born," — *Isa.* 9 : 6.
	370–10	"Unto us a c· is born," — *Isa.* 9 : 6.

little

Mis.	145–25	little c· shall lead them." — *Isa.* 11 : 6.
	337–12	"Jesus called a little c· — *Matt.* 18 : 2.
	337–14	as this little c·, — *Matt.* 18 : 4.
	344–26	as a little c·, — *Luke* 18 : 17.

looks up

My.	257–30	Wherever the c· looks up

man

Pul.	13–29	brought forth the man c·. — *Rev.* 12 : 13.

Mother, and

Mis.	18–19	whereby Father, Mother, and c·

my

Mis.	331–21	Keep Thou my c· on upward wing
	372–12	* book has healed my c·."
	389– 9	Keep Thou my c· on upward wing
Ret.	20–12	night before my c· was taken
	20–25	was to get back my c·,
Po.	4– 7	Keep Thou my c· on upward wing
My.	235– 8	Can I teach my c· the correct

of God

(*see* **God**)

one

Mis.	7– 5	mother of one c· is often

poor

Mis.	239–19	looking up quaintly, the poor c·

spake as a

Mis.	359– 9	I spake as a c·, — *I Cor.* 13 : 11.
My.	135– 3	I spake as a c·, — *I Cor.* 13 : 11.
	261–16	I spake as a c· — *I Cor.* 13 : 11.

child

spiritual
  Mis. 18–15   as God's spiritual c· only,
sweet
  Mis. 239–26   What if that sweet c·,
that
  Mis. 253–24   agonies that gave that c· birth
      253–25   Can that c· conceive of the anguish,
this
  Mis. 166–10   And what of *this* c·?
      166–13   This c·, or spiritual idea,
thought as a
  Mis. 359– 9   I thought as a c· :— *I Cor.* 13 : 11.
  My. 135– 4   I thought as a c· :— *I Cor.* 13 : 11.
tired
  Po. 47–14   Weary of sobbing, like some tired c·
to devour the
  Mis. 253–17   stood ready to devour the c·
  Hea. 10– 3   "to devour the c· — *see Rev.* 12 : 4.
unborn
  Mis. 71–13   *influences on the unborn c·?*
understood as a
  Mis. 359– 9   I understood as a c·, — *I Cor.* 13 : 11.
  My. 135– 3   I understood as a c·, — *I Cor.* 13 : 11.
      261–17   I understood as a c·, — *I Cor.* 13 : 11.
wife and
  Mis. 225– 7   clergyman, his wife and c·.
will demonstrate
  My. 113–21   A c· will demonstrate C. S.
woman, or
  Mis. 336–26   a better man, woman, or c·.
  Rud. 2– 4   * a corporeal man, woman, or c· ;
young
  My. 122–19   to find where the young c· lies,

———

  Mis. 184– 8   The c· born of a woman
      339–19   Art thou a c·,
      359– 8   "When I was a c·, — *I Cor.* 13 : 11.
  No. 18–16   A c·, in his ignorance, may
  '00. 6–12   A c· can measurably understand
      6–15   c· not only accepts C. S.
  My. 135– 3   "When I was a c·, — *I Cor.* 13 : 11.
      258–31   c· with finger on her lip reading a
      261–16   "When I was a c·, — *I Cor.* 13 : 11.
      312–15   * with a c·, but entirely without
      (*see also* **Eddy**)

child-birth
  Ret. 40–19   suffered so little in c·."

childhood (*see also* **childhood's**)
  Mis. 257–24   c·, age, and manhood
      395–15   Written in c·, in a maple grove
  Ret. 1– 8   I remember reading, in my c·,
      2–17   My c· was also gladdened by
      5– 9   During my c· my parents
      8– 2   events connected with my c·
      11– 1   From c· I was a verse-maker.
      31– 9   From my very c· I was
      89–18   which he had frequented in c·.
  My. 184–18   the odor of my c·,
      261–16   inclining thought of c·.

childhood's
  Mis. 238– 4   contrast with that c· wrong
  Ret. 6– 6   My c· home I remember
  '01. 31–19   chapter sub-title
  My. 147– 7   over my c· Sunday noons.

childish
  Mis. 237–30   c· fear clustered round his
      310– 1   c· pleasure of studying Truth
      359–10   put away c· things. — *I Cor.* 13 : 11.
  My. 135– 5   put away c· things." — *I Cor.* 13 : 11.
      261–18   put away c· things." — *I Cor.* 13 : 11.

childlike
  Mis. 15–15   c· trust and joyful adoption
      133–25   with c· confidence that

children (*see also* **children's**)
are destined
  Pul. 8–28   The c· are destined to witness
beloved
  Mis. 110– 4   Beloved c·, the world has need
  My. 216–15   *My Beloved C· :*
big
  Mis. 400–19   To the Big C·
  Po. 69– 7   To the Big C·
Christmas for the
  My. 261– 1   chapter sub-title
created
  Un. 14–16   His created c· proved
dear
  Mis. 144– 5   came from the dear c·
      145–32   and to the dear c·
  My. 217– 8   for my dear c· contributors
      230–24   education of the dear c·,
      258–25   To the dear c· let me say :

children

divine
  Un. 23– 7   divine c· are born of
dusky
  '02. 3–16   her dusky c· are learning
education of
  Mis. 286–11   education of c· will serve
family of
  Mis. 6–29   Take a large family of c·
four thousand
  Mis. 353–26   the Mother's four thousand c·,
gifts from the
  My. 25– 6   * chapter sub-title
God's
  Mis. 170– 9   spiritual refreshment of God's c·
her
  Mis. 152–14   for the welfare of her c·,
      354– 9   "justified of her c·." — *Matt.* 11 : 19.
      374–10   justified of all her c·." — *Luke* 7 : 35.
  Ret. 1–20   thus mingling in her c·.
      6– 1   * to the education of her c·.
      90–16   never willingly neglects her c·
      90–22   and happiness of her c·?
      90–24   till her c· can walk steadfastly
  My. 66–25   * welcoming her c· and
      228–22   justified of her c·." — *Matt.* 11 : 19.
His
  Mis. 373–14   should, does, guide His c·.
  My. 187–25   light and liberty of His c·,
lessons of the
  Man. 62–25   The first lessons of the c·
like
  '01. 29–13   They are like c· that go out
little
  Mis. 189– 3   When, as little c·, we are
      307–23   "Little c·, keep — *I John* 5 : 21.
      400–13   Gift to the Little C·
  Po. 69– 1   Gift to the Little C·
  My. 4–26   become as little c·, — *Matt.* 18 : 3.
      78–28   * little c·, awed by the grandeur
loving
  Mis. 238– 2   Even the loving c· are
My
  Un. 18–12   tears from the eyes of My c·.
new-born
  Mis. 254– 1   Cherish these new-born c·
of darkness
  My. 191–10   you are not c· of darkness.
of God
  Mis. 46–23   we are the c· of God :— *Rom.* 8 : 16.
      199– 9   liberty of the c· of God." — *Rom.* 8 : 21.
      255–15   we are the c· of God :— *Rom.* 8 : 16.
  My. 40–23   * called the c· of God." — *Matt.* 5 : 9.
      242–11   mortals are the c· of God,
      269–10   and are the c· of God." — *Luke* 20 : 36.
of Israel
  Ret. 79–25   c· of Israel were saved by
  Peo. 11–16   c· of Israel still in bondage.
  My. 42–31   * c· of Israel delivered from the
of light
  Mis. 342–29   wiser than the c· of light ;" — *Luke* 16 : 8.
  Ret. 90–29   one of the c· of light.
  My. 191– 9   C· of light, you are
      206–31   walk as c· of light." — *Eph.* 5 : 8.
of men
  Rud. 10–20   c· of men, who are punished
  My. 90–11   * nature endows the c· of men,
      193– 9   to the c· of men." — *Psal.* 107 : 8.
of one parent
  Ret. 22–20   all the c· of one parent,
of our Lord
  Mis. 244–31   especially the c· of our Lord
of this period
  Mis. 253–27   Do the c· of this period dream
of this world
  Mis. 342–28   "The c· of this world — *Luke* 16 : 8.
of to-day
  Pul. vii– 5   c· of to-day are the elders of
precious
  Pul. 8–24   precious c·, your loving hearts
rise up
  Mis. 254–10   whose c· rise up against her ;
Sabbath School
  Man. 62–19   The Sabbath School c· shall
six
  Ret. 5– 7   youngest of my parents' six c·
Sunday School
  Po. page 43   poem
  My. 155–26   May the dear Sunday School c·
      162–12   the dear Sunday School c·,
teaching the
  Man. 62–18   Teaching the C·.
teach the
  Mis. 240–24   Teach the c· early self-government,
their
  Mis. 5– 9   perfect morals in their c·

children
their
Pul. 21– 1   their c· and grandchildren
      82–26   * their husbands, their c·, and
these
Mis.   7– 1   These c· must not be allowed to
Pul. 42–14   * These c· are known in the
thirteen
Ret.   4– 1   grandmother had thirteen c·,
Thy
Mis. 159–25   sense of Thy c· grown to
two
Mis.   6–32   families of one or two c·,
Ret. 21– 7   had a wife and two c·,
understood by the
Mis. 53–26   readily understood by the c· ;
who forget
'01. 29–15   c· who forget their parents'
women and
Pul. 45– 1   * Men, women, and c·
      64– 9   * Men, women, and c· contributed,
your
My. 344–30   let your c· be vaccinated,

Mis. 18–17   as c· of one common Parent,
      46–24   if c·, then heirs ;— Rom. 8: 17.
     110– 5   more as c· than as men
     125–23   Beloved Brethren, C·, and
     240–20   C· not mistaught, naturally love
     255–15   if c·, then heirs ;— Rom. 8: 17.
     315– 1   shall be preached to the c·,
     354–12   the c· are tending the regulator ;
     397–15   where Thine own c· are,
Man. 35– 1   C· when Twelve Years Old.
      35– 2   C· who have arrived at the age
Pul.   v– 3   TWO THOUSAND AND SIX HUNDRED C·
       8–16   Even the c· vied with their
       0– 1   c·, you are the bulwarks of freedom,
      18–24   where Thine own c· are,
      40–14   * ROOM WHICH THE C· BUILT
      42–10   * presence of several hundred c·
      59–26   * c· of believing families
'02.   2–11   making the c· our teachers.
Po.   13– 3   where Thine own c· are,
My.   25– 7   * great interest exhibited by the c·
     133– 5   all earth's c· at last come to
     216–14   chapter sub-title
     258–30   c· who sent me that beautiful
     261– 8   c· should not be taught to believe
     310–28   for her other c· to imitate,
     345– 2   vaccination will do the c· no harm.

children's
Mis. 72–14   c· teeth are set on edge— Ezek. 18: 2.
     240– 7   freshness out of the c· lives by
     252–29   It is the dear c· toy
     315– 4   The c· service shall be
Man. 63– 9   instruction given by the c· teachers
My.   12–29   The dear c· good deeds are
      38–16   * It was "c· day" at noon,
      78–26   * chapter sub-title
     261– 3   How shall we cheer the c· Christmas

child's
Mis. 51–15   a declaration to the c· mind
      51–17   If you make clear to the c· thought
     365– 7   what a c· love of pictures is to art,
No.   18–16   what a c· love of pictures is to art.

chill
Pul. 10–24   rejoice that c· vicissitudes have not
Po.   26– 7   C· was thy midnight day,

chime
Pul. 26–17   * c· of bells includes fifteen,
      62– 8   * a c· of fifteen bells
      62–17   * beauties of a great cathedral c·,
My.   89– 7   * a c· of bells, and

chimed
Pul. 41–28   * were c· until the hour for

chimerical
Ret. 70–11   give c· wings to his imagination,
My. 347–26   that a phenomenon is c·,

chimes
Mis. 126– 5   soft music of our Sabbath c·
     343–26   Among the manifold soft c·
Pul.   8– 4   church c· repeat my thanks
      16– 1   Set to the Church C·
      41–23   * c· in the great stone tower,
      58–13   * In the belfry is a set of . . . c·.
      61–20   * chapter sub-title
      61–22   * listen to the first peal of the c·
      61–27   * The c· were made by
      62– 6   * cast bells of old-fashioned c·.
      62–10   * old-fashioned c· required a strong
      81– 1   * c· on the C. S. temple
'02.   4–15   ringing like soft vesper c·

chimes
My.   30–32   * Before half past seven the c·
      70–10   * chapter sub-title
      70–11   * c· for the new C. S. temple
      70–15   * while the c· were being tested
      71– 1   * a set of cathedral c·,
      77–21   * pealed from the c· a first hymn
     256– 1   chapter sub-title

chiming
My. 163– 3   c· chaste challenge to praise him

China
Pul.   2–16   war between C· and Japan.
       5–25   Greece, Japan, India, and C· ;
       6–20   * missionary to C·, in 1884.
My. 234–15   chapter sub-title
     234–17   C. S. in benighted C·,
     234–25   war on religion in C·

Chinese
Un.   57– 1   More obnoxious than C· stenchpots

chinked
'00.   1– 3   c· within the storied walls of

Chippewa
Ret.   3–12   neighboring battle of C·,

chirps
Mis. 329–26   now c· to the breeze ;

chisel
Peo.   7– 8   * "C· in hand stood a sculptor-boy,
Po.   2– 4   c· of the sculptor's art
My.   69–14   * hammer and c· of the sculptor

chiseled
Po.   76– 8   (Heaven c· squarely good)

chiselled
Mis. 399–24   (Heaven c· squarely good)
Pul. 16– 9   (Heaven c· squarely good)

chiselling
Mis. 360– 4   awaiting the hammering, c·,
Peo.   7– 4   c· to higher excellence,

chivalry
My. 331–13   * Southern c· would have scorned to

choice
Mis. vii– 5   * well made c· of friends and books ;
      19–28   Which, then, shall be our c·,
     227–10   their c· of self-degradation
     269–17   his c· between matter and Mind,
Man. 87– 5   C· of patients is left to
Ret. 71–14   freedom of c· and self-government.
Pul. 66–20   * largely Oriental in its c·.
Pan.   3–15   * C· of the prudent !
Hea. 14– 9   in the c· of physicians.
My.   96–13   * creed of the church of their c·.
      99–29   * no c· but the acceptance of
     283–30   c· of folly never fastens on the

choicest
'01. 28–12   c· memorials of devotion

choir
Ret. 16– 7   not sung before since she left the c·
Pul. 26– 6   * organ and c· gallery is spacious
      37–19   * c· of the new church,
      42–19   * On the wall of the c· gallery
      42–25   * In the c· and the
      43– 2   * the c· of the home church,
      59–11   * There was singing by a c·
Po.   66– 9   To join with the neighboring c· ;

choir organ
(see organ)

choirs
Pul. 43– 1   * Two combined c·

choke
Mis. 343–22   c· the coming clover.
No.   44–15   and c· the channels of God.

choose
Mis. 19–27   c· our course and its results.
     271–13   "C· you this day — Josh. 24: 15.
     289– 9   mortals must first c· between evils,
     289– 9   of two evils c· the less ;
     289–32   whence they can c· only good.
     338–10   cannot c· but to labor and love ;
Un.   60–18   to c· whom they would serve.
'01. 31–12   then I cannot c· but obey.
My.   3–23   C· ye!
       5–27   Continue to c· whom ye will serve.
     165– 3   helping others thus to c·.

choosing
My. 165– 2   namely, of c· the best,

chord
Mis. 187–10   a c· is manifestly the reality of
Ret. 82– 2   law of the c· remains unchanged,
'00.   3– 4   unless he loses the c·.
'01. 34–16   the lost c· of Christ ;

chord

My. 150–11 hallowed by one c· of C. S.,

chords

Mis. 106–29 strains that thrill the c· of feeling
116–16 varied strains of human c·
142–21 c· of feeling too deep for words.
Ret. 17– 7 Wake c· of my lyre,
Pul. 9– 6 break the full c· of such a rest.
'02. 9–13 Loving c· set discords in harmony.
Peo. 8–20 trembling c· of human hope
Po. 62– 7 Wake c· of my lyre,
66– 7 Wake gently the c· of her lyre,

chorus

Mis. 188– 5 grand c· of harmonious being.
My. 59–20 * mighty c· of five thousand voices,

chose

Pul. 49–24 * She c· the stubbly old farm

chosen

Mis. 151–23 Ye are a c· people,
161–14 prophet whose words we have c·
191–10 "Have not I c· you — *John* 6 : 70.
197– 4 Our c· text is one
200–12 that we have c· for a text ;
327– 8 "thou hast c· the good part ;
Man. 26–17 said candidates shall not be c·.
Ret. 42–12 untiring in his c· work.
91–22 students whom he had c·,
Pul. 85–14 * as the one c· of God to this end,
No. 22–25 "Have I not c· you — *John* 6 : 70.
My. 17–10 c· of God, and precious, — *I Pet.* 2 : 4.
70–20 * c· from the works of
125–10 with the sling of Israel's c· one
127–24 garrisoned by God's c· ones,
206–23 "Ye are a c· generation, — *I Pet.* 2 : 9.
244–21 but few are c·." — *Matt.* 22 : 14.

Christ (*see also* Christ's)

according to
Mis. 114–16 enunciation of these according to C·.
Pan. 13– 6 demonstrated according to C·,
'01. 4–10 demonstrate Love according to C·,
adore
Mis. 96–20 I reverence and adore C·
and our Cause
'02. 13– 2 C· and our Cause my only incentives,
appearing of
'00. 7–29 wait for the full appearing of C·
as an example
Pul. 72–26 * we take C· as an example,
ascended
My. 119–17 to the ascended C·, to the Truth
as "the way"
Un. 58–13 C· as "the way." — *John* 14 : 6.
atonement of
Mis. 96–17 Do I believe in the atonement of C·?
261–16 atonement of C· loses no efficacy.
'01. 10–22 atonement of C·, whereby good
at-one-ment with
Mis. 123–21 at-one-ment with C· has appeared
basis that
Hea. 18–21 on the basis that C·, Truth,
behold the
'00. 7–22 behold the C· walking the wave
be in you
Chr. 55–16 If C· be in you, — *Rom.* 8 : 10.
beloved in
My. 150–26 Beloved in C·, what our Master said
blood of
No. 33–19 to represent the blood of C·,
34–18 blood of C· speaketh better things
34–26 significance of the blood of C·.
body of
My. 126– 1 the church, — the body of C·, Truth ;
131– 8 For the body of C·,
bonds of
Mis. 150– 5 Yours in bonds of C·,
No. 8– 9 fellowship in the bonds of C·.
brethren in
My. 108–26 Finally, beloved brethren in C·,
bring him to
Ret. 30–18 schoolmaster, to bring him to C·.
burial of
'02. 17– 2 knells tolling the burial of C·.
came
'01. 21–21 C· came not to bring death but life
cannot leave
Mis. 270–21 we cannot leave C· for
catnip and
Mis. 52– 5 divided between catnip and C· ;
Cause of
Man. 48– 4 to defend the Cause of C·,
'01. 35– 5 sacrifice self for the Cause of C·,
cause of
My. 165– 7 endured for the cause of C·,

Christ

character of
Mis. 367–27 or in the character of C·.
character of the
Ret. 23–16 character of the C· was illuminated
Christianity of
My. 37–12 * rule of the Christianity of C·
179–32 ethics, and Christianity of C·
Church of
(*see* **Church of Christ; Church of Christ, Scientist**)
church of
'00. 13– 3 * Gentiles entered the church of C·'"
closely with
'00. 7–24 would walk more closely with C· ;
comes
Chr. 53–34 C· comes in gloom ;
commandments of
No. 8–18 bow down to the commandments of C·,
command of
Mis. 318–19 so fulfil the command of C·.
Ret. 47–23 so fulfil the command of C·.
Pul. 29–17 * dealt directly with the command of C·
'00. 5–21 to obey . . . the command of C· :
command of the
Ret. 88– 4 Another command of the C·,
conception of the
No. 12–16 new-born conception of the C·,
cross of
Ret. 30–21 and the cross of C·.
cup of
Mis. 144–28 wine poured into the cup of C·
No. 34–11 They drink the cup of C·
days of
Un. 9–26 not . . . since the days of C·.
dear
Po. 29– 7 Dear C·, forever here and near,
debtors to
Mis. 281–22 always as debtors to C·, Truth.
declaration of
'02. 12–14 This declaration of C·, understood,
demands
My. 232–29 watching as C· demands
demonstration of
Man. 47–16 illustrates the demonstration of C·,
direct line in
'01. 2–23 departure from the direct line in C·
disciple of
'00. 6–23 meek and loving disciple of C·,
divine
My. 36–20 * salvation through His divine C·.
doctrines of
Mis. 188– 1 opposed the doctrines of C·
embodied
'00. 8– 2 behold more nearly the embodied C·,
enjoins
Mis. 292–19 C· enjoins it upon man to help
eternal
My. 262–11 my sense of the eternal C·,
even
My. 182– 9 the same, even C·, Truth,
ever-present
Mis. 328– 8 ever-present C·, the spiritual idea
existed
'01. 8–25 C· existed prior to Jesus,
faith in
Rud. 11– 4 leading . . . first to faith in C· ;
feet of
'01. 22–15 I begin at the feet of C·
follow
Ret. 65–13 if they would follow C·,
follower of
Un. 56–13 every follower of C· shares his cup
following
Mis. 170– 2 for by following C· truly,
245–24 thinking that it was following C· ;
No. 34– 5 sense of following C· in spirit,
follows
'01. 34–26 only so far as she follows C·.
'02. 4– 4 only so far as she follows C·.
found
My. 119–32 St. John found C·, Truth,
given by
No. 28–15 way of salvation given by C·,
gospel of
Mis. 18– 7 law and gospel of C·, Truth.
'02. 5–21 reiterated in the gospel of C·,
has said
Mis. 258– 2 C· has said that love is the
has told
Pul. 72–27 * C· has told us to do his work,
healed by
My. 63–30 * had been healed by C·, Truth,
healed the sick
Pul. 66– 2 * as it did when C· healed the sick.
healing
Mis. 154–20 the healing C· will again be

Christic

healing
Pan. 7– 5 demonstration that the healing C·,
'00. 6–12 interprets the healing C·.
'02. 9–19 spirit of the healing C·,
My. 122–17 healing C· that saves from sickness
heart of
Pul. 12–20 nearer to the great heart of C· ;
His
Mis. 177– 7 against the Lord and against His C·,
193–24 commands of our Lord and His C·,
Pul. 12– 7 power of His C·:— Rev. 12 : 10.
My. 260–28 It leaves . . . to God and His C·,
human concept of
Ret. 93– 5 human concept of C· is based on
ideal
Mis. 166– 7 ideal C· — or impersonal infancy,
No. 36–28 while the divine and ideal C· was
ideal, or
Mis. 124–12 rest in the spiritual ideal, or C·.
idea of the
No. 21–26 demonstrably the true idea of the C·,
identify
My. 119–19 could not identify C· spiritually,
I love
'01. 28–19 I love C· more than all the world,
in accord with
Ret. 81– 6 keeping them in accord with C·,
incorporeal
Mis. 164– 7 reveals the incorporeal C· ;
is come
'02. 12– 2 Christian believes that C· is come
is divine
'01. 8– 3 C· is divine — the Holy Ghost, or
is here
My. 44–10 * The C· is here,
is incorporeal
My. 260–30 C· is incorporeal.
is individual
Pul. 74–25 " C· is individual, and one with God,
is meekness
My. 247–11 C· is meekness and Truth enthroned.
is not God
'01. 8–11 C· is not God, but an impartation of
is One
'01. 8– 1 chapter sub-title
is rejected
'01. 9–18 yet C· is rejected of men !
is risen
My. 122–25 Scientist can say his C· is risen
is speaking
My. 257–12 The C· is speaking for himself
is the head
My. 108–29 "C· is the head of the — Eph. 5 : 23.
is the idea
Hea. 3–15 C· is the idea of Truth ;
is the Messiah
'02. 12– 5 on the basis that C· is the Messiah,
is the Truth
My. 261–25 C· is the Truth and Life born of God
is Truth
Mis. 180– 9 "C· is Truth, and Truth is always
joint-heirs with
Mis. 46–25 joint-heirs with C·."— Rom. 8 : 17.
255–16 joint-heirs with C·."— Rom. 8 : 17.
kingdom of
No. 33– 7 by advancing the kingdom of C·
knowledge of
Mis. 360–15 with the true knowledge of C·
360–32 with the true knowledge of C·.
My. 113–15 to aspire to this knowledge of C·
239–14 comes into the knowledge of C·
law of
Mis. 39–24 so fulfil the law of C·."— Gal. 6 : 2.
Ret. 45–23 fulfil the law of C· in
No. 30– 2 law of Life . . . is the law of C·,
leading you to
Rud. 11– 3 schoolmaster, leading you to C· ;
leave all for
Mis. 274–10 therefore I leave all for C·.
My. 138–18 except I leave all for C·.
led to
Mis. 85–30 sick often are thereby led to C·,
Life in
Un. 2–22 to a sense of Life in C·,
life in
Mis. 197–24 does not understand life in, C·.
Life is
My. 185–20 for Life is C·,
life of
No. 10–10 life of C· is the predicate and
41–14 life of C· is the perfect example ;
live in
Mis. 84–25 To lose error thus, is to live in C·,
looks up for
My. 119–15 The Mary of to-day looks up for C·,

Christ

lost chord of
'01. 34–17 again on earth the lost chord of C· ;
love of
Mis. 246–11 when the love of C· would have
Rud. 17– 3 to convert . . . to the love of C·,
loveth
Pul. 21– 3 love wherewith C· loveth us ;
loving
'00. 7–27 tender, loving C· is found near,
lowly in
Mis. 168–11 to the poor — the lowly in C·,
loyal to
Mis. 264– 3 students, who are loyal to C·,
man in
Mis. 15–25 fulness of the stature of man in C·
No. 19–25 fulness of the stature of man in C·.
material
My. 122–26 not the material C· of creeds,
Messiah or
'01. 9– 7 glimpses of the Messiah or C·,
Messiah or the
'02. 12– 1 believes that the Messiah or the C·
metaphysics of
'01. 24–27 metaphysics of C· — healing all
Mind of
Un. 33–12 it is certainly not the Mind of C·,
mind of
My. 142–2 we have the mind of C·.' — I Cor. 2 : 16.
ministries of
Mis. 33– 6 ministers and ministries of C·,
ministry of
My. 327–30 * dignify the ministry of C·
must be spiritual
'01. 10– 9 C· must be spiritual, not material.
name of
Mis. 19–12 has named the name of C·,
223–21 named the name of C·
Pul. 81– 4 * we learn that the name of C·
Hea. 16– 9 named the name of C·
nativity of
My. 262–31 splendor of this nativity of C·
never died
Un. 62–10 In Science, C· never died.
never left
Mis. 180– 9 "C· never left," I replied;
nothing in
Mis. 155– 4 that has nothing in C·.
My. 4–25 that hath nothing in C·.
obedience of
Mis. 139–14 to the obedience of C·.— II Cor. 10 : 5.
obey
My. 241–27 * to obey C· was not to
office of
Mis. 306–28 is the office of C·, Truth,
one
Mis. 22– 1 believe in one God, one C·
Man. 15– 7 We acknowledge His Son, one C· ;
42–11 One C·.
42–17 a belief in more than one C·,
Pul. 75– 1 never can be but one God, one C·,
'00. 7–17 Is there more than one C·,
7–18 There is but one C·.
'01. 8– 3 There is but one C·,
My. 109–20 can be but one God, one C·.
155– 8 have one God, one C·,
191–12 one God and one C·,
303– 2 I believe in one C·, teach one C·,
303– 3 know of but one C·.
303–18 one God, one C , no idolatry,
344– 8 There can be but one C·."
one in
My. 204–11 which makes them one in C·.
oneness of
My. 342–23 the oneness of C· and
organizes
Pul. 21–12 which C· organizes and blesses.
our Lord and
Mis. 276–14 full coming of our Lord and C·.
our Model
Mis. 159–27 our Model, C·, been unveiled to us,
perfect
My. 11– 2 * followers of the perfect C·,
perfectibility through
'00. 7–16 Science of perfectibility through C·,
points the way
Mis. 211– 3 C· points the way of salvation.
power of
(see **power**)
prefers
Ret. 65–19 and prefers C· to creed.
Principle of
My. 149– 6 The Principle of C· is divine Love,
proving the
Ret. 31– 8 paramount . . . in proving the C·.

Christj (left column)

Christ

reach the
  Mis. 309–16 through which we reach the *C·*,
real
  No. 36–12 The real *C·* was unconscious of
reappearing
  No. 46– 7 and the reappearing *C·*,
redemptive
  '01. 11– 8 Through this redemptive *C·*,
reign of the
  My. 64–22 * ideal manhood — the reign of the *C·*
reigns
  My. 183– 7 "When *C·* reigns, and not till then,
rejoiceth
  My. 159– 6 *C·* rejoiceth and comforteth us.
respects the
  My. 259–28 Christmas respects the *C·*
rest in
  '02. 19–18 rest in *C·*, a peace in Love.
return of
  My. 181–29 the year . . . for the return of *C·*
reveals
  My. 119–15 the Principle that reveals *C·*.
risen
  Mis. 159–20 the man of God, the risen *C·*,
      179–31 revealed to me this risen *C·*,
  Un. 63– 2 this appearing as a risen *C·*.
  Peo. 5– 9 spiritual ideal, the risen *C·*,
  Po. 31– 5 Prolong the strain "*C·* risen !"
  My. 120–11 bliss of seeing the risen *C·*,
      155–20 awakened sense of the risen *C·*.
      192– 8 The risen *C·* is thine.
risen with
  Mis. 178–11 be risen with *C·*, — *Col.* 3 : 1.
robe of
  My. 192– 7 ideal robe of *C·* is seamless.
robes of
  My. 247–12 Put on the robes of *C·*,
rock of
    (*see* **rock**)
said
  Mis. 210– 9 *C·* said, "They shall take — *Mark* 16 : 18.
sake of
  No. 42–14 in the name and for the sake of *C·*,
Science of
  My. 103– 9 indeed Science, — the Science of *C·*,
second coming of
  '00. 6–30 the second coming of *C·*.
serving
  Mis. 7–13 if serving *C·*, Truth,
sitteth
  Mis. 178–12 where *C·* sitteth on the — *Col.* 3 : 1.
spirit of
    (*see* **spirit**)
spiritual
  Mis. 84–12 The spiritual *C·* was infallible ;
spiritual sense of
  My. 257–10 to the spiritual sense of *C·*
spoke of the
  Un. 59– 8 spoke of the *C·* as one who
stand for
  My. 344– 4 rays collectively stand for *C·*,
statement of the
  Pul. 74–24 and statement of the *C·*
stature in
  Pan. 11–10 shall his stature in *C·*,
  '01. 11– 1 fulness of his stature in *C·*,
stature of
  Mis. 102– 2 nature and stature of *C·*,
steadfast in
  My. 155– 5 steadfast in *C·*, always abounding
students of the
  My. 190–25 become students of the *C·*,
suffer for
  Mis. 157– 3 worthy to suffer for *C·*, Truth.
  Un. 57–24 worthy to suffer for *C·* ;
summons thee
  Chr. 53–54 *C·* summons thee !
taught
  My. 109–10 *C·* taught his followers to heal
teachings of
  Pul. 38–25 * the literal teachings of *C·*.
the ever
  Po. 31–18 The ever *C·*, and glorified
this
  Mis. 328–13 Hast not thou heard this *C·*
  '00. 7–19 this *C·* is never absent.
  My. 122–28 spiritualized to behold this *C·*,
through
  Mis. 3–14 to the understanding through *C·*,
      41–11 purged through *C·*, Truth,
     114–32 and to be able, through *C·*,
  Man. 16– 1 man is saved through *C·*,
  Un. 51– 9 through *C·* as perfect manhood.
  Rud. 3– 5 to save them from sin through *C·*,
  '01. 15– 8 overcomes them through *C·*,

Christ (right column)

Christ

through
  '02. 6–23 Through *C·*, . . . points the way,
  My. 9–17 * way of salvation through *C·*."
    161–16 is saved through *C·*, Truth.
    349– 5 gained through *C·*, Truth ;
to prove
  My. 119–21 the prints of the nails, to prove *C·*,
truer sense of
  '01. 9– 7 truer sense of *C·* baptized them
trust
  Mis. 369–17 devout enough to trust *C·*
Truth, or
  Pul. 12–23 lay down all for Truth, or *C·*,
  My. 118–27 Truth, or *C·*, finds its paradise
understand
  Ret. 36– 2 understand *C·* as the Truth
  Un. 59–11 By this we understand *C·* to be
understanding of
  Mis. 164–20 grew in the understanding of *C·*,
  My. 344– 2 to my understanding of *C·*
understanding of the
  My. 262–14 human understanding of the *C·*
unlike
  Ret. 49–17 conquering all that is unlike *C·*
veritable
  My. 119–23 the veritable *C·*, Truth,
walketh
  '02. 19–30 *C·* walketh over the wave ;
was not born
  My. 261–25 *C·* was not born of the flesh.
was not crucified
  Chr. 53–29 *C·* was not crucified
was not human
  '01. 10–12 The *C·* was not human.
was "the way"
  Mis. 75– 2 *C·* was "the way ;" — *John* 14 : 6.
what concord hath
  Mis. 333–23 what concord hath *C·* with — *II Cor.* 6 : 15.
white
  Mis. 124–22 adore the white *C·*,
    212–23 Love, the white *C·*, is the
will command
  Pul. 14–24 *C·* will command the wave.
will give
  Pul. 22–13 *C·* will give to Christianity
will rechristen
  Pul. 8–20 *C·* will rechristen them with
words of
  My. 105– 1 even more than the words of *C·*,
works of
  Mis. 196–23 we shall do the works of *C·*,

  Mis. 2–20 *C·*, the spiritual idea of God,
    17–13 meekly bow before the *C·*,
    63–22 If *C· was God, why did Jesus*
    63–26 *C·* as the Son of God was divine.
    76–28 "When *C·*, who is our life, — *Col.* 3 : 4.
    79–24 even so in *C·* — *I Cor.* 15 : 22.
    84–13 Jesus, as material manhood, was not *C·*.
    84–15 *C·*, was the Son of God ;
    84–20 *to live is C·*, — *Phil.* 1 : 21.
    91– 1 in commemoration of the *C·*.
    96–32 It is *C·* come to destroy the
    104– 2 individual being, the *C·*, was at rest
    107– 8 plant the feet steadfastly in *C·*.
    109–28 *C·*, Truth, saith unto you,
    111–31 or is another *C·*,
    151–26 wedded to the spiritual idea, *C·* ;
    151–29 Affectionately yours in *C·*,
    161–11 senses could not cognize the *C·*,
    162–23 The spiritual man, or *C·*, was
    162–27 dethroned his power as the *C·*.
    163–26 *C·* or spiritual idea which leadeth
    166–15 *C·*, the incorporeal idea of God,
    166–29 spiritual idea, or *C·*, entered into
    180– 8 * Has *C·* come again on earth?"
    189–13 *C·* plainly declared, through Jesus,
    191–17 that *C·*, Truth, casts out.
    195– 1 *C·*, the Truth that antidotes all
    234–29 *C·* is clad with a richer illumination
    292–22 leading them, if *possible*, to *C·*,
    310– 5 substituting personality for the *C·*,
    365– 3 which is *C·*, Truth.
    365– 8 whose schoolmaster is not *C·*,
    396–17 poem
    397– 6 I see *C·* walk,
    399–13 Thou the *C·*, and not the creed ;
  Man. 19– 3 to be built on the Rock, *C·* ;
    42–17 even that *C·* whereof the
  Chr. 53–17 Thus *C·*, eternal and divine,
  Ret. 65–17 ruled *C·* out of the synagogues,
    93– 3 *C·*, or the spiritual idea, appeared
  Un. 42–16 With *C·*, Life was not merely a
    59– 5 the *C·* (that is, the divine idea
    60–24 if *C·* be not raised, — *I Cor.* 15 : 17.

Christ

Un.	60–26	*C·* cannot come to mortal and
	62– 3	saith, "*C·* (God) died for me,
Pul.	18– 1	poem
	18–15	I see *C·* walk,
	74–14	'Am I the second *C·*?'
	75– 8	in any manner as a *C·*,
No.	v–11	and if you are babes in *C·*,
	18–19	If the schoolmaster is not *C·*,
	22– 2	not touched the hem of the *C·* garment.
'00.	7–17	hath *C·* a second appearing?
'01.	8–24	*C·* was Jesus' spiritual selfhood ;
	9–17	it is the *C·*, Comforter,
	10– 8	*C·* being the Son of God.
	26– 5	only on *C·*, Truth,
	28–21	*C·*, Truth, is indeed the way
'02.	2–21	wherein *C·* is Alpha and Omega.
	6– 9	*C·*, Truth, demonstrated
	10–24	proof that *C·*, Truth, is the way.
Po.	page 12	poem
	12–15	I see *C·* walk,
	75–20	Thou the *C·*, and not the creed ;
	78–13	Thou who in the *C·* hallowed its
My.	20– 3	Gratefully yours in *C·*,
	104–15	healer of men, the *C·*, the Truth,
	109–12	*C·* is "the same — *Heb.* 13 : 8.
	110–25	*C·* will have "led — *Psal.* 68 : 18.
	129–19	plant thy steps in *C·*, Truth,
	135–20	Lovingly yours in *C·*,
	140–22	*C·*, points the advanced step.
	168– 4	*C·*, the Holy One of Israel,
	174–21	offered me to *C·* in infant baptism.
	185–20	*C·*, as aforetime, heals the sick,
	191–17	*C·*, Truth, has come forth from the
	196–16	"*C·* also suffered for us,— I *Pet.* 2 : 21.
	205– 4	*C·* hath made us free."— *Gal.* 5 : 1.
	219–15	*C·*, Truth, the ever-present
	219–22	*C·*, the great demonstrator of
	238–14	C. S. — the *C·* Science,
	248–23	*C·* mode of understanding Life
	257–13	To-day the *C·* is, more than ever
	260–32	Neither . . . can be or is *C·*.
	339–22	those who have not the *C·*,
	343–13	* heading
	344– 2	been spoken of as a *C·*,
	344– 6	God the Father is greater than *C·*,
	344– 6	*C·* is 'one with the Father,'
	351–18	Lovingly yours in *C·*,
	357– 5	*C·*, born of God,

(see also **Messiah, Model, Saviour, Son, Vine**)

Christ and Christmas

Mis.	32– 5	clergyman's remarks on "*C·* and *C·*"
	33– 8	illustrations in "*C·* and *C·*;"
	307–18	rapid sale . . . of "*C·* and *C·*,"
	308–12	are ready for "*C·* and *C·* ;"
	371–20	chapter sub-title
	372– 7	"*C·* and *C·*" voices C. S.
	372–19	find "*C·* and *C·*" in accord with
	372–22	spirit and mission of "*C·* and *C·*."
	375– 9	illustrations of "*C·* and *C·*" :
Chr.	page 53	poem

Christ-basis

My.	46–16	* heal the sick on the *C·*

Christendom

Mis.	192–27	to all ages and throughout all *C·*.
Pul.	22–14	*C·* will be classified as
'01.	34– 2	prayer, whereby *C·* saves sinners,
My.	4–13	woman has put into *C·* and medicine.
	40–14	* *C·* became divided into
	150–30	wisdom you manifest causes *C·*
	151– 3	attacks of a portion of *C·* :
	339–12	Along the lines of progressive *C·*,

christened

Mis.	121–22	*c·* by John the Baptist,
Un.	17–11	that its vileness may be *c·* purity,
Pul.	8–20	these lambs my prayers had *c·*,

christening

Mis.	320–28	Love, to-day *c·* religion undefiled,

Christ-healing

Mis.	29–10	*C·* was practised even before
Pul.	69–27	* demonstrating the *C·*."
Peo.	3–12	that Christianity and *C·* are
My.	23–26	* with its . . . accompaniment, the *C·*,

Christian (see also **Christian's**)

advancing
'02.	11–21	it is thine, advancing *C·*,

aged
Mis.	226– 4	unbiased youth and the aged *C·*

any
'02.	14–11	only . . . success possible for any *C·*

armor of a
'02.	19–13	Meekness is the armor of a *C·*,

Christian

believes
'02.	12– 2	*C·* believes that Christ is come

best
'02.	11–28	the best *C·* on earth,

consecrated
Mis.	318–22	a devout, consecrated *C·*.
Ret.	47–25	Bible scholar and a consecrated *C·*.

hero, and
Mis.	166– 5	philanthropist, hero, and *C·*.

impels the
My.	9– 8	* impels the *C·* to turn

Jew and
'02.	11–29	while to-day Jew and *C·* can unite

mission of a
Pul.	73–13	* mission of a *C·*, to do good

quickening the
No.	43–16	* and quickening the *C·*."

the word
'01.	12–10	the word *C·* was anciently

true
Mis.	68– 7	* *A true C· would protest*
	281–16	* cost of becoming a true *C·*."
	281–18	* of *not* becoming a true *C·*."
'01.	31– 7	Every true *C·* in the near future
My.	28–14	* qualities which mark the true *C·*,

venerable
Mis.	225–17	he said to this venerable *C·* :

who believes
'02.	12–10	The *C·* who believes in the

Mis.	39–28	A *C·*, or a Christian Scientist,
	86– 4	the *C·* will, must, attain it ;
	108– 2	*C·* asleep, thinks too little of sin.
	234– 9	not lifted ourselves to be, . . . a *C·*.
Ret.	28–29	my endeavor, to be a *C·*,
Un.	62– 3	*C·* saith, "Christ . . . died for me,
Rud.	9– 3	not a *C·*, in the highest sense,
Peo.	2–16	make a *C·* only in theory,
My.	151– 6	I know that no *C·* can or
	160– 1	The *C·*, . . . strives for the spiritual ;
	160–30	the *C·* has no part in it.
	228– 9	how one can be a *C·* and yet

Christian (adj.)

basis
Man.	80– 2	on a strictly *C·* basis,

brotherhood
My.	339– 3	bonds of *C·* brotherhood,

canon
My.	199–12	*C·* canon pertaining to the hour.

centuries
My.	112– 5	Master in the early *C·* centuries

character
My.	332–31	* honorable record and *C·* character

characters
Mis.	357–23	whose *C·* characters and lives

charity
My.	149–22	to demonstrate *C·* charity.
	175–24	fraternity, and *C·* charity.

church
Pul.	22–11	every *C·* church in our land,

churches
Pul.	22– 3	*C·* churches have one bond
Pan.	13–13	Love all *C·* churches
My.	18–21	Love all *C·* churches
	89–18	* all other of the *C·* churches,

clergymen
'01.	31–24	distinguished *C·* clergymen,

compact
Mis.	91–10	The real *C·* compact is love

demonstration
Mis.	156–18	the daily *C·* demonstration

denominations
Mis.	21–13	trend of other *C·* denominations
My.	v– 9	* by other *C·* denominations,

Discoverer
My.	302–19	*C·* Discoverer, Founder, and Leader.

education
My.	230–24	*C·* education of the dear children,

endeavors
Man.	60–19	daily *C·* endeavors for the living

endeavor society
Pul.	21–12	Let this be our *C·* endeavor society,

era
(see **era**)

example
Ret.	26– 4	*C·* example on the cross,
My.	52– 6	* her *C·* example, as well as

faith
Ret.	6– 5	* living illustration of *C·* faith.
Pul.	51– 2	* Neither does the *C·* faith
'02.	6–20	All *C·* faith, hope, and prayer,

fellowship
Man.	51– 7	Violation of *C·* Fellowship.
	51–10	does not live in *C·* fellowship with

Christian (adj.)

fellowship
 Man. 74–20 an attitude of *C·* fellowship.
 Ret. 15–20 we parted in *C·* fellowship,
folk
 Pul. 52– 5 * pity some of our practical *C·* folk
 My. 58– 1 * pity some of our practical *C·* folk
healers
 Mis. 370–26 true fold for *C·* healers,
 '01. 9– 9 made seers of men, and *C·* healers.
healing
  (*see* **healing**)
hero
 Mis. 85– 2 battle-worn and weary *C·* hero,
 '01. 30–26 heart of the unselfed *C·* hero.
 Hea. 2–14 And still another *C·* hero,
history
 Ret. 45– 8 earliest periods in *C·* history.
idea
 '02. 12– 9 Jew unites with the *C·* idea that
lady
 My. 320– 9 * high regard for you as a *C·* lady,
life
 '01. 28– 9 none lived a more devout *C·* life
 My. 200–17 What holds us to the *C·* life is the
lives
 My. 213–11 to live pure and *C·* lives,
love
 My. 362–23 * bonds of *C·* love and fellowship,
manner
 Man. 97–16 to correct in a *C·* manner
metaphysics
 Mis. 205–21 termed in *C·* metaphysics the ideal
  365–26 *C·* metaphysics is hampered by
 No. 11– 8 my system of *C·* metaphysics
 My. 41– 4 * the law of *C·* metaphysics,
motives
 Man. 50–17 shall from *C·* motives make
name
 Mis. x–18 *C·* name, Mary Morse Baker.
 Man. 111– 6 sign her own *C·* name,
names
 Man. 111– 3 one of the *C·* names
people
 Pul. 50–17 * number of *C·* people,
 My. 60–10 * *C·* (?) people at that time.
practice
 Ret. 54–20 whose *C·* practice is far in advance
 '01. 11–19 enough for *C·* practice.
religion
 Pan. 6–22 the *C·* religion has at least
 My. 220–18 establishment of *C·* religion
sacraments
 Mis. 345–26 purpose of *C·* sacraments.
Science
  (*see* **Science**)
Scientist
  (*see* **Scientist**)
Scientist's
  (*see* **Scientist's**)
Scientists
  (*see* **Scientists**)
Scientists'
  (*see* **Scientists'**)
sense
 Pan. 3– 2 the *C·* sense of religion.
sentiments
 My. 316–19 freedom of *C·* sentiments,
service
 My. 36–11 * to a holy *C·* service
spirit
 Man. 77–26 in a *C·* spirit and manner,
standard
 Un. 38–27 the *C·* standard of Life,
standpoint
 No. 12– 2 a purely *C·* standpoint.
state
 Mis. 229–25 calm, *C·* state of mind is a
students
  (*see* **students**)
success
 Mis. 120–14 *C·* success is under arms,
system
 My. 244–31 success of this *C·* system
Theism
 Mis. 13–13 chapter sub-title
tongue
 '01. 28–12 into almost every *C·* tongue,
unity
 My. 200–11 The chain of *C·* unity,
warfare
 Mis. 40–26 In this *C·* warfare the student
  281–19 whatever . . . is hard in the *C·* warfare
 Ret. 44–23 danger to its . . . in *C·* warfare.
woman
 My. 315– 7 * a pure and *C·* woman,

Christian (adj.)

work
 Mis. 5– 7 themselves to this *C·* work.
  242–15 another department of *C·* work,
world
 My. 60–11 * What a change in the *C·* world!
  103 chapter sub-title
worship
 Mis. 345–29 rumor that . . . a part of *C·* worship
 Un. 15–28 Surely this is no *C·* worship!
 My. 47–26 * an era of *C·* worship founded on
zeal
 My. 187– 1 fidelity, faith, and *C·* zeal

 Mis. 22–22 That C. S. is *C·*,
  30–23 * "is neither *C·* nor science!"
  68–11 * *not C·* to believe they are
  269–16 on a *C·*, mental, scientific basis;
  350–13 deliberations were, as usual, *C·*,
 Ret. 25–10 *C·*, because it is compassionate,
 Pul. 69–22 * certain *C·* and scientific laws,
  80–30 * all these ideas are *C·*.
 No. 10– 7 are "*C·*" and "Science."
 Pan. 7–15 Mosaic, the *C·*, and the
 '02. 11–12 neither *C·* nor Science.
 My. 216– 6 *C·*, civil, and educational means,
  245– 5 This *C·* educational system
  257–29 the *C·* traveller's resting-place.

Christianity (*see also* **Christianity's**)

adorns
 My. 285– 9 Whatever adorns *C·* crowns the
advance
 Mis. 50–27 advance *C·* a hundredfold.
age and
 '01. 16–24 to handle with garrulity age and *C·* !
altitude of
 Pan. 12–12 altitude of *C·* openeth, . . . a door
and materialism
 My. 221– 3 distance between *C·* and materialism
and Science
 Pul. 56–16 * Welding *C·* and Science,
 My. 179–25 *C·* and Science, being contingent on
and spiritualism
 Hea. 5–11 * "between *C·* and spiritualism,
antithesis of
 Pul. 6– 3 continue till the antithesis of *C·*,
 Peo. 8–12 not more the antithesis of *C·* than
apostolic
 Mis. 245–26 and rejects apostolic *C·*,
as taught
 Pan. 8–14 *C·*, as taught and demonstrated
 '00. 4–17 *C·* as taught by our great Master ;
authority in
 '01. 25–20 What, . . . is our authority in *C·* for
beginning of
 Pul. 52–19 * At the beginning of *C·* it was taught
bringing
 Mis. 344–30 bringing *C·* for the first time
Christ's
 Mis. 241– 5 Christ's *C·* casts out sickness
 My. 179–21 Christ's *C·* as the perfect ideal.
  220–18 Christian religion — Christ's *C·*.
contemporary of
 Mis. 22– 8 what, but the contemporary of *C·*,
crown of
 Mis. 252–18 C. S. is . . . the crown of *C·*.
crowns
 Mis. 124–27 crowned and still crowns *C·* :
demanded
 Mis. 374– 8 demanded *C·* in life and religion.
demonstrated
 My. 348–25 demonstrated *C·* and proved
demonstration of
 Mis. 149–21 refreshing demonstration of *C·*,
 Pan. 9–21 demonstration of *C·* blesses all
demonstrator of
 '01. 26– 4 demonstrator of *C·* is the Master,
divine Principle of
 Mis. 30– 1 understand the divine Principle of *C·*
elucidates
 '02. 8– 2 elucidates *C·*, illustrates God,
ends of
 No. 12–20 these are the ends of *C·*.
entered
 Mis. 373–21 *C·* entered into synagogues,
equity of
 My. 181–20 universal equity of *C·*.
essential to
 Mis. 51– 1 change of heart is essential to *C·*,
ethics and
 My. 129– 5 spirit of humanity, ethics, and *C·*
Founder of
 Pul. 53– 2 * by the Founder of *C·*
 My. 279– 3 The Founder of *C·* said :
genius of
 Hea. 2– 2 genius of *C·* is works more than

Christianity

genuine
'02. 18–27 ended in the downfall of genuine *C*·,
given to
Pul. vii–16 impetus thereby given to *C*· ;
godliness or
'01. 34–26 Godliness or *C*· is a human necessity :
grandeur of
Pan. 12– 9 chapter sub-title
has withstood
Ret. 45–24 *C*· has withstood less the
healing
My. 180– 7 healing *C*· which applies to all
heart of
Mis. 25– 5 it is the heart of *C*·,
heaven-crowned
Mis. 328– 7 the mountain is heaven-crowned *C*·,
higher
Mis. 162– 5 advent of a higher *C*·.
Hea. 8– 8 results of this higher *C*·,
higher sense of
Mis. 195–30 have given me a higher sense of *C*·.
history of
Peo. 13–25 * "Since ever the history of *C*·
hope of
Mis. 246–31 advancing faith and hope of *C*·,
ideal of
My. 40–25 * has presented . . . the ideal of *C*·,
infant
Mis. 15–29 developed into an infant *C*· ;
is Christlike
Mis. 25–19 *C*· is Christlike only as it
is consistent
'01. 6–19 its consequent *C*· is consistent with
is divine Science
'01. 4–15 and *C*· is divine Science,
is fit only
Mis. 345–14 * "*C*· is fit only for women and
Peo. 13–23 * "*C*· is fit only for women and
is the summons
My. 148–28 *C*· is the summons of divine Love
justice and
Mis. 134– 6 as characterize justice and *C*·.
letter of
My. 246–15 teaching and letter of *C*·
life of
Mis. 199–30 outflowing life of *C*·,
lost
Hea. 3–11 it lost *C*· and the power to heal ;
lower order of
Peo. 13– 4 have a lower order of *C*· than he who
manifestations of
Ret. 65–25 practical manifestations of *C*·
means of
Mis. 260–23 in the proper means of *C*·,
model of
Ret. 22– 9 Jesus as the model of *C*·,
morals and
Mis. 283–20 as well as its morals and *C*·.
nature of
My. 179–19 nature of *C*·, as depicted in
new-old
My. 301– 3 C. S. is the new-old *C*·,
no
'01. 4–16 else there is no Science and no *C*·.
of Christ
My. 37–19 * rule of the *C*· of Christ
179–31 ethics, and *C*· of Christ
one
Pan. 1–19 acknowledge one God and one *C*·.
paragons of
Mis. 316–28 would be on earth paragons of *C*·,
perfect
Mis. 1– 9 ordeal of a perfect *C*·,
pioneers of
My. 104–19 on the pioneers of *C*·
possibilities of
Mis. 30– 7 all the possibilities of *C*·
power of
Mis. 193–26 spirit and power of *C*·.
193–29 power of *C*· to heal ;
No. 44– 7 power of *C*· to heal.
My. 239–10 redemptive power of *C*·
practical
Mis. 232–10 a more perfect and practical *C*·
My. 362–25 * thus demonstrating practical *C*·.
practice of
My. 239– 6 rules, and practice of *C*·
practising
Mis. 5–10 scientific method of practising *C*·.
precedents of
No. 35– 2 how poor the precedents of *C*·!
present
My. 339–21 rejoice in their present *C*·
primitive
Mis. 192–24 as primitive *C*· confirms.

Christianity

primitive
Man. 17–12 should reinstate primitive *C*·
Pul. 69–16 * return to the ideas of primitive *C*·.
Peo. 5–10 ideals of primitive *C*· are nigh,
My. 46–12 should reinstate primitive *C*·
111–16 C. S. maintains primitive *C*·,
245–20 doing the works of primitive *C*·,
Principle of
Mis. 16– 9 The Principle of *C*· is infinite :
144–30 life-giving Principle of *C*·,
privilege of
Hea. 3– 3 The primitive privilege of *C*· was
professed
Mis. 247– 8 I have professed *C*· a half-century ;
progress and
Hea. 7–24 so important to progress and *C*·.
progress of
No. 32– 2 retarded the progress of *C*·
proof of
Hea. 2–23 and gave this proof of *C*·
pure
Mis. 270–16 Gain a pure *C*· ;
Peo. 5–25 a Truth-filled mind makes a pure *C*·
My. 152–12 restoration of pure *C*·
purity of
My. 178– 5 invincible process and purity of *C*·
quintessence of
Mis. 336–23 C. S., . . . the quintessence of *C*·,
realism of
Mis. 374– 2 Immanuel and the realism of *C*·,
reality of
Mis. 251–15 rights and radiant reality of *C*·,
records of
My. 184–21 on the glowing records of *C*·,
reign of
Mis. 345–17 * "Ever since the reign of *C*· began
reinstated
My. 46–17 * requirement of a reinstated *C*·.
requires
Hea. 3– 1 Such *C*· requires neither hygiene nor
reveals God
Ret. 65–30 *C*· reveals God as ever-present Truth
Science and
Peo. 2– 9 unites Science and *C*·,
Science in
My. 127– 2 upward to Science in *C*·,
Science of
(*see* Science)
scientific
Pan. 8–13 chapter sub-title
9–15 attainment of scientific *C*·
'02. 8–21 Scientific *C*· works out the rule of
solid
My. 301– 8 leaving a solid *C*· at the bottom
specific
'01. 6–15 Is this pure, specific *C*· ?
spirit of
My. 246–16 spirit of *C*·, dwelling forever in
spiritual
(*see* spiritual)
standard of
'01. 34–10 look for the standard of *C*·
support the
No. 15–12 to support the *C*· that heals the sick
system of
'01. 34–13 and a new system of *C*·,
Teacher of
My. 338–26 great Teacher of *C*·,
tendency of
Un. 31– 7 tendency of *C*· is to spiritualize
their
My. 107– 1 as a token of their *C*·.
theism in
Pan. 6–21 if . . . what becomes of theism in *C*· ?
this
'00. 4–20 Principle and rules of this *C*·
to elucidate
'02. 16–25 fail to elucidate *C*· :
true
Mis. 113–24 evil can be resisted by true *C*·.
No. 12–14 stimulated true *C*· in all ages,
My. 91–14 * no insignificant element in true *C*·.
turned men
Mis. 345–31 *C*· turned men away from the
unbiased
Mis. 235–24 *C*· unbiased by the superstitions
understanding of
My. 51–15 * to the higher understanding of *C*·,
vital
'01. 30– 4 the object of vital *C*· is
32– 6 lover and student of vital *C*·.
vital spark of
Mis. 132–29 is a vital spark of *C*·.
watchword of
No. 44–27 must be the watchword of *C*·.

Christianity

ways of
Rud. 17–15 ways of C· have not changed.
which heals
My. 300–23 teach the C· which heals,
will give to
Pul. 22–14 Christ will give to C· his
womanhood and
My. 330–11 * whose womanhood and C·
womanhood of
Mis. 16– 7 manhood or womanhood of C·,
work of
My. 30–26 * by evangelists for the work of C·.
would commingle
'00. 4– 6 precedent that would commingle C·,
writes
My. 194– 1 only that which C· writes

Mis. 16–23 C· is a divine Science.
23– 6 C· answers this question.
29–25 will neither flavor C· nor
29–29 they are the signs following C·,
107– 4 C· is not superfluous.
111–21 The C· that is merely of sects,
193–20 supplying the word Science to C·,
242–11 if I should accept his bid on C·,
253– 2 C· is not merely a gift,
307–16 inquiry of mankind as to C·
345–19 * C· must be a divine reality."
357–11 Without . . . C· has no central emblem,
Un. 15–28 In C·, man bows to the infinite
Pul. 6– 8 unites Science to C·.
Pan. 8–17 C· then had one God and one law,
8–21 C·, as he taught and demonstrated
9– 6 in C· they signify
13– 5 C· be demonstrated according to
'01. 2– 1 C· is now what Christ Jesus taught
2–18 C· is ever storming sin
Hea. 11–27 C· of metaphysical healing,
14– 6 What has . . . physics done for C·
Peo. 3–11 C· and Christ-healing are
13–28 * C· must be a divine reality."
My. 4–18 of both medical faculty and C·,
40–16 * C· may more widely reassert its
107– 2 Has C· improved upon its
148–24 C· is not alone a gift, but
214– 8 C· is again demonstrating the Life
219–20 since C· must be predicated of
221–24 All issues of morality, of C·,
239– 4 relegates C· to its primitive proof,
267– 2 C· is fully demonstrated to be
279– 8 C· is the chain of scientific

Christianity's

Mis. 373–19 a sketch of C· state,

Christianization

Mis. 15– 9 C· — of thought and desire,
'02. 6–15 C· of mortals, whereby

Christianized

Mis. 269–20 can only be C· through Mind ;

Christianly

Mis. 259–24 physically, morally, and C·,
Pul. 2–27 do this C· scientific work?
'02. 7–20 proposition can be C· entertained.
My. 105– 4 defined C· and demonstrated

Christian's

Mis. 23–15 matter is not the C· God,
123–16 The C· God is neither,
155–11 valiant in the C· warfare,

Christians

Mis. 29–30 C·, like students in mathematics,
82– 9 Such C· as John cognize the
135– 1 C·, and all *true* Scientists,
193–23 C· are properly called Scientists
200–20 C· to-day should be able to say,
333–31 ancient or modern C·, instructed in
345–23 slanderers affirmed that C· took
345–26 C· met in midnight feasts
383–15 and in the hearts of C·.
Man. 30– 3 exemplary C· and good English
38– 2 known to them to be C·,
Un. 5–22 between C. S. students and C·
14–12 C· are commanded to *grow in grace.*
26–19 Many ordinary C· protest against
43–18 I urge C· to have more faith in
48– 6 I believe more in Him than do most C·,
Pul. 9–23 C· rejoice in secret,
Rud. 2– 5 among Trinitarian C· the word
No. 41– 1 chapter sub-title
42– 1 * C· more and more learn their duty
'01. 7–23 all C· now claim to believe
18–30 C· and clergymen pray for sinners ;
30– 3 since ever the primitive C·,
32– 7 Why I loved C· of the old sort was
32–27 if those venerable C· were here

Christians

'02. 8– 8 are neither C· nor Scientists.
Hea. 7–27 duty and ability of C· to heal
8–25 If we work to become C·
Po. 25–18 Aye, the C· who wind
My. 91– 3 * were already nominal C·,
95–28 * days of the primitive C·,
106–32 the C· in the first century
146– 3 understood by all C·
151–13 this denomination of C·
162–22 in them C· may worship God,
162–23 not that C· may worship church
179–17 C· and Christian Scientists know
190–13 C· who accept our Master
219–18 I would not charge C· with
292–13 "Why did C· of every sect
299–17 Do C·, who believe in sin,

Christian Science

(see **Science**)

Christian Science and Spiritualism

Pul. 38–11 "C· S· and S·,"

Christian Science and the Bible

My. 323– 4 * entitled "C· S· and the B·,"

Christian Science Board of Directors

(see **Board of Directors**)

Christian Science Board of Education

(see **Board of Education**)

Christian Science Board of Lectureship

(see **Board of Lectureship**)

Christian Science Church

(see **Church**)

Christian Science Hall

My. 145– 5 the plan for C· S· H·

Christian Science Hymnal

(see **Hymnal**)

Christian Science Journal, The

(see **Journal**)

Christian Science Monitor, The

(see **Monitor**)

Christian Science Platform

Man. 86–19 and from the C· S· P·,

Christian Science Practice

Pul. 38–14 "C· S· P·,"

Christian Science Publishing Society, The

(see **Publishing Society**)

Christian Science Quarterly

(see **Quarterly**)

Christian Science Quarterly Lessons

Man. 63– 7 may be found in the C· S· Q· L·,

Christian Science Reading Room

My. 236–10 for your name, C· S· R· R·.

Christian Science Sentinel

(see **Sentinel**)

Christian Science Society

Bronx
My. 363– 8 * signature
Flushing, L. I.
My. 363– 9 * signature

Christian Science *versus* Pantheism

p. 13
My. 18–25 (C· S· v· P·, p. 13.)

Christian Scientist

(see **Scientist**)

Christian Scientist Association

Mis. 116– 7 chapter sub-title
271–23 Publishing Committee of the C· S· A·
278–30 membership in the C· S· A·.
382–24 organized the first C· S· A·,
Man. 17– 8 At a meeting of the C· S· A·,
Ret. 43–21 The first C· S· A·
43–24 At a meeting of the C· S· A·
45–17 action of the C· S· A·
52–14 delegations from the C· S· A·
52–19 official organ of the C· S· A·
Pul. 37–26 * The first C· S· A· was organized
67–25 * first C· S· A· was organized by
My. 182–12 formed a C· S· A· in Chicago.
363–19 chapter sub-title
363–21 My address before the C· S· A·
(see *also* **National Christian Scientist Association**)

Christian Scientist's

(see **Scientist's**)

Christian Scientists

(see **Scientists**)

Christian Scientists'

(see **Scientists'**)

Christian Scientists' Association
Mis. 135–26 TO THE MEMBERS OF THE *C· S· A·*

Christ-idea
Mis. 81–11 *C· mingled with the teachings*
   260– 1 intelligent *C·* illustrated by
Chr. 53– 9 The *C·*, God anoints
Pul. 14–19 flood to drown the *C·*?

Christ-image
Mis. 8–18 dethrones the *C·* that you

Christ Jesus (see also Christ Jesus')
Mis. 70–16 *C· J·* lived and reappeared.
   77–21 adopting all this vast idea of *C· J·*,
  188–14 them which are in *C· J·*,— *Rom.* 8 : 1.
  197–21 was also in *C· J·*."— *Phil.* 2 : 5.
  201–18 Spirit of life in *C· J·* — *Rom.* 8 : 2.
  255–11 Mind which was in *C· J·*.
  321–15 Spirit of life in *C· J·* — *Rom.* 8 : 2.
  326– 2 Spirit of life in *C· J·* — *Rom.* 8 : 2.
Man. 15–16 unity with God through *C· J·*
  16–10 which was also in *C· J·* ;
  41– 1 *C· J·* the Ensample.
  41– 4 irreverent reference to *C· J·* is
Ret. 70–10 the Messianic mission of *C· J·* ;
  76–18 was also in *C· J·*,"— *Phil.* 2 : 5.
Un. 2–25 stature of manhood in *C· J·*,
  4–19 was also in *C· J·*,"— *Phil.* 2 : 5.
  43–26 grasped by] *C· J·*,"— *Phil.* 3 : 12.
  60– 2 *C· J·* came to save men,
Pul. 75– 4 that Mind which was in *C· J·*.
Pan. 8–12 infringe the sacredness of one *C· J·*
'00. 4– 7 the righteous Galilean, *C· J·*,
  6– 8 calling of God in *C· J·"* — *Phil.* 3 : 14.
'01. 2– 1 what *C· J·* taught and demonstrated
  9– 1 the spiritual and material *C· J·*,
  9–10 "Spirit of life in *C· J·*," — *Rom.* 8 : 2.
  9–14 *C· J·* possessed it, practised it,
  10–13 but the *C· J·* represented both
  10 20 salvation comes through . . *C· J·*.
  11– 5 the divine nature of *C· J·*
  25–17 *C· J·*, denounced all such
  28–25 *C· J·*, who was not popular
  28–28 is not a student of *C· J·*.
'02. 7–24 *C· J·* saith, "A new — *John* 13 : 34.
  8– 9 The new commandment of *C· J·*
  8–16 life of *C· J·*, his words
  8–26 *C· J·* reckoned man in Science,
  9–12 Spirit of life in *C· J·* — *Rom.* 8 : 2.
Hea. 3–18 *C· J·* was an honorary title ;
My. 24– 2 * truth which *C· J·* revealed
  41–23 "Spirit of life in *C· J·*," — *Rom.* 8 : 2.
  103–13 stature of man in *C· J·*
  113–12 them which are in *C· J·*,— *Rom.* 8 : 1
  113–13 Spirit of life in *C· J·* — *Rom.* 8 : 2.
  129–32 teachings and example of *C· J·*.
  139 6 founded upon the rock, *C· J·*,
  161– 1 *C· J·* paid our debt
  161– 9 Hence these words of *C· J·* :
  205– 2 them which are in *C· J·*,— *Rom.* 8 : 1.
  219–20 what *C· J·* taught and did ;
  221–12 great and good as *C· J·*.
  229–17 according to this saying of *C· J·*
  247– 7 are according to *C· J·* ;
  254–28 are according to *C· J·* ;
  260–17 The basis . . . is the rock, *C· J·* ;
  272– 6 Spirit of life in *C· J·* — *Rom.* 8 : 2.
  293–29 Spirit of life in *C· J·* — *Rom.* 8 : 2.
  318–26 * was such a man as *C· J·* ?"
  339– 6 supreme, infinite, and one *C· J·*.
  347– 1 revealed in a degree through *C· J·*

Christ-Jesus
Mis. 161–13 that made him the *C·*,

Christ Jesus'
Mis. 74–13 *C· J·* sense of matter was
No. 34–27 vital currents of *C· J·* life,
'01. 18–11 of questioning *C· J·* healing,

Christlike
Mis. 16– 8 to become wholly *C·*,
  25–19 Christianity is *C·* only as it
  193–29 this is *C·*, and includes
  373–28 promise that the *C·* shall
Ret. 78–15 wholly *C·* and spiritual.
  95–12 * comforters . . . . Of *C·* touch.
Pul. 21–19 only that which is *C·*,
'01. 27–25 purely spiritual, *C·*,
My. 148–29 summons . . . for man to be *C·*
  149– 7 must be *C·*, or C. S.
  220–26 religion, which . . . cannot be *C·*

Christlikeness
Mis. 162–26 demoralizing his motives and *C·*,
  245–25 in the direction of *C·*,
  313– 8 May the *C·* it reflects
  357– 8 These long for the *C·* that
'02. 9–17 leaves the minor . . . and abides in *C·*.

Christliness
Ret. 86–15 the escutcheon of our *C·*
  92– 7 unloose the latchets of his *C·*,

Christ-love
Mis. 262–25 burdens heavy but for the *C·*

Christly
Mis. 318– 8 who are less lovable or *C·*.
  359– 3 *C·* method of teaching
Ret. 48–28 whose *C·* spirit has led to higher
  93–13 best spiritual type of *C·*
'01. 25–13 No *C·* axioms, practices, or
My. 46–23 * more sincere and *C·* love
  364– 5 treat this mind to be *C·*.

Christ-majesty
Po. 30– 9 With thy still fathomless *C·*.

Christmas
Mis. 159–10 chapter sub-title
  159–18 This is my *C·* storehouse.
  161– 1 chapter sub-title
  161– 3 SUNDAY BEFORE *C·*, 1888.
  309–27 My *C·* poem and its illustrations
  320– 3 chapter sub-title
Man. 67–21 Thanksgiving, *C·*, New Year,
Chr. 53–23 Make merriment on *C·* eves,
Pul. 37–17 * said a gentleman to me on *C·* eve,
Po. page 29 poem
  29– 1 Blest *C·* morn, though murky clouds
My. 31– 5 "Blest *C·* morn ;"
  121–16 gems that adorn the *C·* ring
  122–16 another *C·* has come and gone.
  256– 2 Before the *C·* bells shall ring,
  256– 9 total exemption from *C·* gifts.
  256–16 chapter sub-title
  256–17 Again loved *C·* is here,
  257–23 chapter sub-title
  257–24 your manifold *C·* memorials,
  257–26 my *C·* gift, two words enwrapped,
  258–23 beautiful are the *C·* memories of him
  258–25 Your *C·* gifts are hallowed by
  259– 9 * Loving, grateful *C·* greetings
  259–13 dear churches' *C·* telegrams
  260–14 most pleasing *C·* presents,
  259–22 chapter sub-title
  259–28 *C·* respects the Christ too much to
  260– 3 *C·* would make matter an alien
  260– 9 In C. S., *C·* stands for the real,
  260–17 basis of *C·* is the rock, Christ Jesus ;
  260–22 basis of *C·* is love loving its
  260–24 true spirit of *C·* elevates
  261– 1 chapter sub-title
  261– 3 cheer the children's *C·*
  261–22 chapter sub-title
  261–23 *C·* involves an open secret,
  262– 6 *C·* commemorates the birth of a
  262–12 I celebrate *C·* with my soul,
  262–20 *C·* to me is the reminder of God's
  262–24 ritual of our common *C·*
  262–27 I love to observe *C·* in quietude,
  263 3 chapter sub-title
  263– 6 Mother wishes you all a *happy C·*,

Christmas, 1900
My. 256–16 chapter sub-title

Christmas-tide and Christmastide
Mis. 369– 6 chapter sub-title
My. 257–17 To this auspicious *C·*,

Christmas-tree
My. 257– 1 green branches of the *C·*.

Christ-principle
My. 149– 9 the meekness of the *C·* ;

Christ's
command
  (see **command**)
healing
  (see **healing**)
Sermon
Mis. 21– 4 with *C·* Sermon on the Mount,
  25– 9 *C·* Sermon on the Mount,
  43–30 *C·* Sermon on the Mount,
Rud. 12– 4 practises *C·* Sermon on the Mount.
My. 180– 6 uttered *C·* Sermon on the Mount,
  229–22 ascent of *C·* Sermon on the Mount,
teachings
  (see **teachings**)

———

Mis. 30–30 cleanse our lives in *C·* righteousness ;
  91– 4 to organize materially *C·* church.
  125– 9 Then shall he drink anew *C·* cup,
  199–12 *distresses for C· sake.* — II *Cor.* 12 : 10.
  241– 5 *C·* Christianity casts out sickness
  273–14 one grand family of *C·* followers.
  302–19 working faithfully for *C·* cause
  303–18 and imbibe the spirit of *C·* Beatitudes.
  320– 7 *C·* appearing in a fuller sense

Christ's

Mis.	330–10	to the springtide of C· dear love.
	358–15	C· vestures are put on only when
	362– 8	C· logos gives sight to these blind,
	373–15	clearly delineates C· appearing
Chr.	53–43	C· silent healing, heaven heard,
	53–59	Eternal swells C· music-tone,
Ret.	65–21	tenor of C· teaching and example,
	94– 9	so C· baptism of fire,
	94–27	aid the establishment of C· kingdom
Un.	43–20	I exhort them to accept C· promise,
	52–13	C· immortal sense of Truth,
Pul.	4–14	Each of C· little ones reflects
	13–11	He that touches the hem of C· robe
	14–17	a cup of cold water in C· name,
No.	41–20	have slumbered over C· commands,
	43– 1	and if C· power to heal was not
Pan.	11– 30	And because C· dear demand,
'01.	6–19	is consistent with C· hillside sermon,
	10–22	Love spans the dark passage . . . with C·
	21–23	better way than C· . . . to benefit the race?
	26–12	turns away from C· purely spiritual
	26–14	to preserve C· vesture unrent ;
	28–16	followed exclusively C· teaching,
	34– 7	spiritual obedience to C· mode
'02.	15–16	I became poor for C· sake.
Po.	33– 5	And bless me with C· promised rest ;
My.	147–24	already dedicated to C· service,
	150–20	clear, radiant reflection of C· glory,
	153– 5	if these kind hearts . . . do this in C·
	179–21	C· Christianity as the perfect ideal.
	183– 1	infinite uses of C· creed,
	191–13	C· "Blessed are ye" — Matt. 5: 11.
	220–18	Christian religion — C· Christianity.
	225–17	The coming of C· kingdom on earth
	257–13	C· heavenly origin and aim.
	257–21	should bow and declare C· power,
	258–11	with C· all-conquering love.
	262–26	in commemoration of C· coming.
	269–11	C· plan of salvation from divorce.
	279– 6	C. S. reinforces C· sayings
	300–17	to health in C· name,

Christs
Mis.	175–19	There are false C· that would

Christ Science
(see Science under sub-title Christ)

Christ-spirit
Mis.	40–20	possess sufficiently the C·
Ret.	85–12	bearing on their pinions . . . the C·.
My.	265– 9	the C· will cleanse the earth of

Christ-thought
Mis.	178–31	new, living, impersonal C·

Christus
Chr.	53–21	For heaven's C·, earthly Eves,

Christward
Mis.	85–18	feeble flutterings of mortals C·
My.	148–25	Christianity . . . is a growth C· ;

chronic
Mis.	29–22	c· and acute diseases that had
	41–23	belief of c· or acute disease,
	54–18	was healed of a c· trouble
	204– 6	sometimes c·, but oftener acute.
	355– 7	c· recovery ebbing and flowing,
Man.	46–25	in c· cases of recovery,
Pan.	10–18	c·, and acute diseases that

Chronicle
Pul.	89–26	* C·, San Francisco, Cal.
My.	333–22	* The C· states :
	333–30	* the C·, dated September 25,

chronicles
Mis.	292– 4	he c· this teaching,

chronologically
My.	349– 1	divine Mind was first c·,

Church (see also Church's)
Christian Science
Man.	18–16	reorganized, . . . the C. S. C·
Pul.	28–15	* order of service in the C. S. C·
	30– 6	* C. S. C· did not recruit itself from
	37–13	* recognized head of the C. S. C·.
	56–24	* chapter sub-title
	70–27	* C. S. C· has a membership of
	76–24	* MEMORIALIZED BY A C. S. C·

Clerk of the
Man.	36–26	addressed to the Clerk of the C·.
	37–10	Clerk of the C· shall send
	52– 9	Clerk of the C· shall address a
	52–17	Clerk of the C· shall immediately
	78–17	through the Clerk of the C·,
	98–16	a copy to the Clerk of the C·.
	109–17	to the Clerk of the C·.

this
Man.	18–20	were elected members of this C·,

Church
this
Man.	26– 1	Treasurer of this C·
	27– 7	in the Manual of this C·
	28–16	that the officers of this C·
	28–23	shall be dismissed from this C·,
	28–25	duty of any member of this C·;
	29– 4	or of any other officer in this C·
	29– 9	a member of this C·
	29–14	five suitable members of this C·
	34–18	This C· will receive a member of
	35–20	can unite with this C· only by
	36–19	can apply to the Clerk of this C·,
	38– 6	a Director of this C·,
	38–10	for membership in this C·,
	38–19	been members of this C·,
	38–22	may be received into this C·
	39–19	not again be received into this C·.
	40–11	members of this C· should daily
	41–20	duty of every member of this C·
	42– 5	duty of every member of this C·
	42–15	members of this C· shall neither
	43–14	member of this C· shall not
	43–22	member of this C· shall neither
	44– 9	member of this C· shall not
	44–19	which are the organs of this C· ;
	44–24	Members of this C· shall not unite
	46– 2	be a member of this C·
	46–13	Members of this C· shall hold
	47– 5	If a member of this C· has
	47–25	members of this C· do not
	48– 7	member of this C· shall not
	50– 8	member of this C· shall not debate
	50–14	If a member of this C· shall
	51–12	regular standing with this C·,
	52–21	If a member of this C· shall,
	52–25	advantageous to this C·
	53– 8	If a member of this C·
	53–16	Members of this C· shall not
	53–18	excommunicated from this C·.
	54– 5	from his or her office in this C·
	54–10	member of a branch of this C·
	54–20	If a member of this C·,
	55–22	If a member of this C· is found
	56– 6	dropped from the roll of this C·.
	57– 9	meeting of the members of this C·
	58– 9	continue to preach for this C·
	59– 7	duty of every member of this C·,
	65– 6	by members of this C·,
	65–10	duty of the officers of this C·,
	65–26	If the Clerk of this C· shall
	66– 7	If at a meeting of this C·
	66–17	before a meeting of this C·,
	66–24	Members of this C· shall not
	67– 1	executive bodies of this C·.
	67– 3	for admission to this C·,
	67–11	member of this C· shall not
	67–18	Members of this C· who
	67–22	break a rule of this C·
	68– 2	member of this C· at least three
	69–17	appoint a proper member of this C·
	72– 5	member of this C· who obeys its
	76– 4	used for the benefit of this C·,
	76–17	three members of this C·
	76–23	real estate owned by this C·
	77– 6	Treasurer of this C· shall submit
	78– 9	Donations from this C·
	79–21	Pastor Emeritus of this C·,
	82–16	Members of this C· who practise
	85– 7	of another member of this C·
	85–12	member of this C· shall not
	87– 2	nor a member of this C·
	87–12	No member of this C· shall
	92– 7	that each member of this C·
	92–23	who are members of this C·
	93– 4	This C· shall maintain a
	93–16	mail to the Clerk of this C·
	97–19	Mrs. Eddy or members of this C·
	109– 5	to unite with this C·.
Mis.	121–12	believed to be the seed of the C·.
	144–32	The C·, more than any other institution,
	165– 6	because of the corruption of the C·.
	245–23	I have loved the C· and followed it,
	313–24	chapter sub-title
Man.	18– 3	charter for the C· was obtained
	18– 8	the little C· went steadily on,
	18–19	students and members of her former C·
	19– 6	C· Universal and Triumphant.
	25–12	the annual meeting of the C·.
	33– 8	Rules, and discipline of the C·.
	37–12	neither the Clerk nor the C· shall
	40–16	To be Read in C·
	41–15	disqualifies . . . for office in the C·
	44– 6	involves schisms in our C·
	51–13	withdraw from the C· or be
	52–19	shall dismiss a member from the C·.

Church
Man. 55–14 and forgiven by the C·
56–21 annual meeting of the C·.
61–17 MUSIC IN THE C·.
64–20 this appellative in the C·
66– 3 before presenting it to the C·
66–18 it shall be the duty of the C·
67– 5 on trial for dismissal from the C·.
67– 8 to a member of her C·
75–13 between the . . . Directors and said C·
75–22 belonged to the C·,
76–12 funds which the C· has on hand,
77– 5 paying bills against the C·,
78– 2 comply with the By-Laws of the C·.
78–18 pay from the funds of the C·
87– 5 of the authority of their C·.
102–19 phrase, "Mary Baker Eddy's C·,
110– 8 recorded in the history of the C·
Ret. 13– 2 Congregational (Trinitarian) C·,
Pul. 69–24 * than the C· has had in the past.
No. 12–15 to goodness, in or out of the C·,
38–11 built his C· of the new-born,
41–22 C· seems almost chagrined that
41–26 * as the faith of the C· increases,
44–21 will again unite C· and State,
45–22 anchor the C· in more spiritual
'01. 32– 6 I became early a child of the C·,
'02. 2–23 to love the C· ;
2–24 and the C· once loved me.
2–26 I never left the C·,
2–27 I but began where the C· left off.
My. 8–23 * chapter sub-title
27– 2 To the Beloved Members of my C·,
135–26 My Beloved C· :— Your love
177–18 * is the seed of the C· ;"
183–24 Beloved Students and C· :— Thanks
299– 2 chapter sub-title
(see also Mother Church, The First Church of Christ, Scientist, First Church of Christ, Scientist, Second Church of Christ, Scientist, etc.)

Church (adj.)
Man. 18–14 C· members met and reorganized,
21– 1 heading
25– 1 heading
25– 4 The C· officers shall consist of
28– 3 Duties of C· Officers.
28–24 written on the C· records.
30–17 shall pay from the C· funds
33– 5 C· Reader shall not be a Leader,
44–16 C· Periodicals.
44–23 C· Organizations Ample.
46–18 the offender to C· discipline.
51– 6 from the roll of C· membership.
51–15 No C· discipline shall ensue until
51–20 complaints against C· members ;
52–14 compliance with our C· Rules
53– 6 from the roll of C· membership.
54– 5 suspended . . . from C· membership.
63– 8 read in C· services.
75–18 C· members own the aforesaid
76– 6 proper management of the C· funds :
76–11 to report at the annual C· meeting
77–11 If it be found that the C· funds
79–11 shall be paid from the C· funds.
98–20 letter sent to . . . by the C· members
My. 15– 4 Section 3 . . . of the C· By-laws
223–23 breaking of one of the C· By-laws,

Church, Walter
Mis. 313–17 "The Lamp," by Walter C·,

church (see also **church's**)
action of the
Mis. 310–23 will determine the action of the c·
affairs of the
My. 359– 9 involved in the affairs of the c·
and society
Pul. 20– 2 purchased by the c· and society.
and State
My. 196– 8 to be engrafted in c· and State :
any
Man. 45–17 of any c· whose Readers are not
49– 3 healing work in any c· or locality,
My. 98–25 * record is one of which any c·
any other
Man. 74– 5 or control over any other c·.
My. 71–18 * different from any other c·
around the
Pul. 42– 2 * sidewalks around the c· were all
at Ephesus
'00. 13– 4 commends the c· at Ephesus
at Jerusalem
My. 13– 9 * "The c· at Jerusalem, like a sun
beautiful
Pul. 75–17 * BEAUTIFUL C· AT BOSTON
beloved
Mis. 149–23 bring to your beloved c· a vision of

church
beloved
My. 133–10 My beloved c· will not receive a
169– 2 MY BELOVED C· :— I invite you,
172–14 spiritual call to this my beloved c·
182–30 May this beloved c· adhere to
197– 6 may this beloved c· be glorious,
best
My. 8– 9 * the best c· in the world,
big
My. 65–13 * a big c· was required,
75–24 * chapter sub-title
blessed
My. 25–21 I shall be with my blessed c·
body of the
My. 38–18 * seats in the body of the c·,
80–30 * in the main body of the c·,
Boston
Pul. 57–20 * name given to a new Boston c·.
65–27 * The Boston c· similarly expresses
My. 141–18 * communion season of the Boston c·
branch
Man. 52– 6 belongs to no branch c·
54–17 The Mother Church or a branch c·
71–14 for a branch c· to assume such
72–22 each branch c· shall continue its
72–26 A branch c· of The First Church
74– 3 of both a branch c· and a society ;
74– 6 In C. S. each branch c· shall
100–24 shall be elected by the branch c·.
112– 9 not a member of a branch c·,
My. 142–15 communion of branch c· communicants
building a
Pul. 44–21 * building a c· by voluntary
building of the
My. 98–17 * for the building of the c·
building, or
My. 55– 5 * purchase some building, or c·,
built up the
Mis. 349–24 and built up the c·,
celebrated
My. 50–23 * The c· celebrated her Communion
ceremonial of the
Mis. 91– 8 indispensable ceremonial of the c·.
Chicago
My. 146– 2 dedicatory letter to the Chicago c·
Christian
Pul. 22–11 every Christian c· in our land,
Christian Science
Mis. 382–18 charter for the first C. S. c·,
Pul. 24– 1 * completion of the first C. S. c·
56–25 * A great C. S. c· was dedicated
68–19 * C. S. c·, called The Mother Church,
My. 8–17 * business of the C. S. c·.
30–31 * entire body of the C. S. c·.
58–30 * services at the C. S. c·
65–22 * to the ownership of the C. S. c·,
66– 8 * conveyed by deed to the C. S. c·,
77–20 * temple of the C. S. c·,
78–18 * custom of the C. S. c·,
95–10 * magnificent C. S. c·
99–23 * not a C. S. c· in the land.
329– 2 * healers of the C. S. c·,
Christ's
Mis. 91– 5 organize materially Christ's c·.
Clerk of the
Mis. 310–22 to the Clerk of the c· ;
322– 9 Clerk of the c· can inform
Concord
My. 157– 4 * The members of the Concord c·
171– 9 Concord c· is so nearly completed
conducting the
My. 49–25 * mode of conducting the c·."
connection with the
My. 321–23 * my connection with the c·,
construction of the
My. 63– 3 * the construction of the c·,
cooling of the
Pul. 25– 1 * lighting and cooling of the c·
costly
My. 87–16 * their costly c· fully paid for,
dear
Mis. 125–28 turns to her dear c·,
150– 4 my forever-love to your dear c·.
316– 8 I shall speak to my dear c·
My. 19–20 That this dear c· shall be
155–18 the members of this dear c·
196– 6 May this dear c· militant
203–20 God bless this dear c·,
dedication of the
Pul. 75–22 * celebrated the dedication of the c·
doors of the
My. 31–10 * doors of the c· were thrown open
drag on a
My. 84– 2 * Nothing is more of a drag on a c·
each
Mis. 314– 5 Each c·, or society formed for

church

each
Man. 55– 5 Each c· shall separately and
63–14 Each c· of the C. S. denomination
99–10 Each c· is not necessarily
My. 343–28 I wrote to each c· in tenderness,
enter even the
My. 126– 1 would enter even the c·,
entire
Pul. 27– 9 * the entire c· is a testimonial,
Episcopal
Pul. 26– 8 * chancel of an Episcopal c·
experience of the
Ret. 48– 7 recent experience of the c·
feature of the
Pul. 76– 2 * A striking feature of the c·
filled the
Pul. 41–21 * vast congregations filled the c·
fire-proof
Pul. 70–14 * a handsome fire-proof c·
75–26 * the most nearly fire-proof c·
first
Mis. 141–31 Of our first c· in Boston,
Man. 75–20 After the first c· was built,
Pul. 64–24 * dedicated the first c· of the
'00. 1–10 first c· of our denomination,
My. 47–24 * Mrs. Eddy founded her first c·
67–14 * First c· organized . . . 1879
67–15 * First c· erected . . . 1894
70– 5 * its first c· only twelve years ago,
72–29 * when they erected the first c·
289–10 first c· of C. S. known on earth,
first such
Ret. 44– 4 first such c· ever organized.
form a
Man. 72– 7 to form a c· in conformity with
forming the
My. 49–13 * interested in forming the c·,
founded a
Ret. 15– 5 till I founded a c· of my own,
Frankish
Pul. 65–21 * Frankish c· was reared upon the
grand
My. 66–30 * never before has such a grand c·
great
My. 88–29 * in the building of a great c·
93– 5 * dedication of their great c·
head of the
My. 108–29 the head of the c· : — Eph. 5 : 23.
her
My. vi–23 * all future profits to her c· ;
vi–24 * she presented to her c·
40– 3 * desired for years to have her c·
48–14 * future growth of her c·,
144– 2 * members of her c· in Concord,
172– 9 * to the members of her c·,
His
Mis. 399–25 on this rock . . . Stands His c·,
Pul. 16–10 on this rock . . . Stands His c·,
Po. 76– 9 on this rock . . . Stands His c·,
My. 20–12 what God gives to His c·.
his
My. 300–21 are common to his c·,
history of the
My. 57–19 * largest in the history of the c·
284–16 * first time in the history of the c·
home
Pul. 43– 2 * the choir of the home c·,
huge
My. 95–12 * They have built a huge c·,
in Boston
Mis. 141–31 our first c· in Boston,
316– 7 speak to your c· in Boston?
Pul. 30–25 * c· in Boston was organized by
37–11 * superintends the c· in Boston,
My. 13–17 pledged to this c· in Boston
135–17 First Reader of my c· in Boston,
175– 2 my little c· in Boston, Mass.,
292–20 Message to my c· in Boston,
in Chicago
My. 146– 8 in my letter to the c· in Chicago,
infant
My. 343–28 are dangerous in an infant c·.
in Philadelphia
'00. 13–29 angel of the c· in Philadelphia
14–13 except the c· in Philadelphia
My. 153– 8 c· in Philadelphia," — Rev. 3 : 7.
199– 6 of the c· in Philadelphia :
is the mouthpiece
My. 247– 6 c· is the mouthpiece of C. S.,
254–27 c· is the mouthpiece of C. S.,
Judæo-Christian
'00. 13–28 * of the Judæo-Christian c·."
known in the
Pul. 42–14 * children are known in the c· as

church

land, and the
Mis. 140– 4 The land, and the c· standing on it,
large
'01. 31–13 communicants of my large c·,
My. 132–18 every member of this large c·.
little
Mis. 149–28 little c· that built the first
154– 7 He will dig about this little c·,
My. 47–25 * And this little c·, God's word
49– 9 * The charter of this little c·
50– 1 * first meeting of this little c·
50–26 * little c· in the wilderness,
154–16 congratulate this little c·
155– 4 May this dear little c·,
175– 2 my little c· in Boston,
184–20 God grant that this little c·
185–25 spoke of the little c·
186– 9 tells the tale of your little c·,
local
Man. 55– 4 members of their local c· ;
96–11 local c· is unable to meet the
magnificent
My. 98– 7 * but that magnificent c·,
maintain the
Ret. 44–15 found able to maintain the c·
meeting of the
Man. 100– 2 If prior to the meeting of the c·
My. 49–15 * first business meeting of the c·
50–32 * to call a general meeting of the c·
51–19 * meeting of the c·, December 15, 1880,
57–14 * first annual meeting of the c·
93–28 * meeting of the c· now being held
member of the
Mis. 129– 2 If a member of the c· is inclined
Pul. 73–18 * prominent member of the c·.
My. 98–21 * no member of the c· anywhere,
members of a
Mis. 90–23 members of a c· not organized
members of the
My. 33– 2 * despatch from the members of the c·
55–14 * twelve of the members of the c·
62–29 * services of other members of the c·,
72–22 * members of the c· all over the
141– 8 * Of late years members of the c·
memorial
Pul. 71– 6 * a memorial c· for Mrs. Eddy,
Message to the
My. 57– 7 * Mrs. Eddy's Message to the c·
170– 8 annual Message to the c·
militant
Pul. 3–18 No longer are we of the c· militant,
My. 125–23 grateful that the c· militant
133– 7 c· militant rise to the
154–25 it makes the c· militant,
196– 6 May this dear c· militant
Mind-healing
Ret. 44– 2 Mind-healing c·, without a creed,
misfortune of a
Pul. 37–22 * misfortune of a c· depending on
my
Mis. 126–27 God hath indeed smiled on my c·,
144–19 I will build my c· ; — Matt. 16 : 18.
263– 7 I will build my c· ;" — Matt. 16 : 18.
349–31 accepted no pay from my c·,
Ret. 44–11 my c· increased in members,
45– 5 the prosperity of my c·,
'01. 2–28 my c· of over twenty-one thousand
31–17 every member of my c· would
'02. 13–28 gave to my c· through trustees,
14– 3 is to save it for my c·.
My. 13–29 not only to my c· but to Him who
26–13 ever received from my c·,
118– 2 members of my c· who cheerfully
122–11 my c· tempted me tenderly
135–17 the First Reader of my c·
171– 1 dear members of my c· :
173– 7 to the members of my c·,
215–20 to give my c· The C. S. Journal,
230–21 in the officials of my c·
280–16 that the members of my c· cease
280–28 In no way . . . did I request my c·
281– 3 the daily prayer of my c·,
292–20 Message to my c· in Boston,
my own
Ret. 16–11 occurrence in my own c·
needed a place
My. 55– 3 * c· needed a place of its own,
new
Mis. 149–24 a vision of the new c·,
Pul. 37–19 * for the choir of the new c·,
64– 6 * for the building of a new c·,
79– 3 * chapter sub-title
85–28 * corner-stone of the new c·
My. 30–32 * the chimes of the new c·
70–20 * The new c· is replete with

church

new
My.   72–11   * dedication of the new *c·*
      97–22   * growth of the new *c·*
new-old
My. 182– 8   establishing a new-old *c·*,
Nicolaitan
'00. 12–30   Nicolaitan *c·* presents the
      13–11   denounces the Nicolaitan *c·*.
no other
Man. 71–13   that no other *c·* can fill.
      74– 8   no other *c·* shall interfere
obedient
My. 209– 4   this willing and obedient *c·*
of brotherly love
My. 153– 9   the *c·* of brotherly love,
of Christ
'00. 13– 3   * entered the *c·* of Christ"
of Christian Science
Mis. 383– 6   wherever a *c·* of C. S. is
My. 289–10   first *c·* of C. S. known
of Ephesus
'00. 12– 7   commence with the *c·* of Ephesus.
of Jerusalem
My.   13–13   *c·* of Jerusalem seems to
of our faith
My. 163–29   in this city a *c·* of our faith
of the firstborn
My.   46–30   * *c·* of the firstborn." — Heb. 12: 23.
of their choice
My.   96–13   * of the *c·* of their choice.
old
Mis. 178– 4   He has left his old *c·*,
My.   68–13   * The old *c·* at the corner of
      80–23   * crowded . . . into the old *c·*,
one
Man. 71– 4   where more than one *c·* is
My.   67–21   * But one *c·* in the country
      85– 5   * one *c·* and a mere handful
     243– 5   come together and form one *c·*.
     243– 9   should be more than one *c·* in it.
organize a
Man. 17–10   organize a *c·* designed to
Ret. 44– 1   voted to organize a *c·* to
My.   46–10   organize a *c·* designed to
organized a
Pul. 58– 5   * and organized a *c·*.
or individuals
Pul. 21–21   close the door on *c·* or individuals
or society
Mis. 314– 5   Each *c·*, or society formed for
orthodox
Mis. 111–26   I love the orthodox *c·* ;
our
Mis. 91– 9   If our *c·* is organized,
     126–15   Perhaps our *c·* is not yet
     129–10   the rule of our *c·* is to
     140–14   Our *c·* was prospered by
     140–21   foundation on which our *c·* was
     140–28   our *c·* will stand the storms of ages !
     141–26   to commence building our *c·*
'02.   1– 7   added to our *c·* during the year
      20–19   between the sacrament in our *c·* and
My.   26–24   the true animus of our *c·*
     352–21   for ushering into our *c·* the
     361–19   * We rejoice that our *c·* has
parent
My.   10–26   * a prosperous parent *c·*,
pastorate of the
Pul. 45–24   * from the pastorate of the *c·*,
My.   49–31   * to the pastorate of the *c·*,
pastor of the
Pul. 29– 5   * first pastor of the *c·* here
      43–30   * from a former pastor of the *c·* :
My.   49–19   * to become pastor of the *c·*.
pastorship of the
Pul. 68– 1   * assumed the pastorship of the *c·*
pastor to the
Pul. 28–28   * pastor to the *c·* in this city,
Pergamene
'00. 13–22   The Pergamene *c·* consisted of
prayer in
Man. 42– 1   Prayer in *C·*.
purity of the
'00. 13– 1   unity and the purity of the *c·*.
Reader in
Man. 55–13   a Reader in *c·* or a teacher
Readers in
My. 249–21   chapter sub-title
refers to the
'00. 13–21   refers to the *c·* in this city as
removed
My.   55–24   * the *c·* removed to Copley Hall
reorganized the
My.   55–15   * reorganized the *c·*, and named it

church

reorganize the
Pul. 20– 7   I had to . . . reorganize the *c·*,
rock-ribbed
My. 186– 5   cluster around this rock-ribbed *c·*
ruling
My.   13–12   * a *mother* and a ruling *c·*."
said
My.   51– 6   * now interested in said *c·*,
Science
My.   85–22   * The Science *c·* has become the
seats in the
Man. 59–16   welcomes to her seats in the *c·*,
some
My. 284–19   has been held annually in some *c·*
South Congregational
My. 289–24   in the South Congregational *c·*
students and
My. 358–24   to your dear students and *c·*.
such a
Man. 72–15   the services of such a *c·*
Pul. 57–16   * organization of such a *c·*,
supplied
My. 309–29   * The *c·* supplied the only
that
Mis. 111–26   that *c·* will love C. S.
Man. 100–20   shall be the duty of that *c·*
their
My.   74–17   * paying for their *c·* before
      86–20   * maintain towards their *c·*
      96–18   * generosity . . . towards their *c·*.
     214– 2   on the walls of their *c·*.
their own
My. 359– 4   individuals in their own *c·*
this
Mis. 127– 2   in proportion as this *c·*
     144– 1   granite for this *c·* was taken from
     146–20   cannot be the conscience for this *c·* ;
     153–30   peace be and abide with this *c·*.
     310–18   one's connection with this *c·*,
     382–19   I donated to this *c·* the land
Man. 72–11   This *c·* shall be acknowledged
Ret. 15–15   by the pastor of this *c·*.
      16– 8   When she entered this *c·*
      44– 5   charter for this *c·* was obtained In
      44–20   to defend this *c·* from the envy and
Pul.   7–27   so long as this *c·* is satisfied with
       8–10   responded to the call for this *c·*
      20–13   prosperity of this *c·* is unsurpassed.
      20–21   This *c·* was dedicated on January 6,
      24– 3   * This *c·* is in the fashionable Back Bay,
      28–10   * The cost of this *c·* is
      38– 3   * being ordained in this *c·*,
      57–17   * the adherents of this *c·* have
      66–22   * the dedication of this *c·*,
      86–21   * present this *c·* to you
      86–27   * permanent pastor of this *c·*,
'00. 10– 6   It is written of this *c·*
      13–14   The Revelator writes of this *c·*
      14– 1   approval of this *c·* by our Master
      15–23   write of this *c·*
'02. 12–24   financial transactions of this *c·*,
      13–10   yield this *c·* a liberal income.
My. vii– 5   * its Leader has done for this *c·* ;
       6–27   this *c·* is the one edifice on
       7– 7   financial transactions of this *c·*,
      13–17   pledged to this *c·* in Boston
      17–30   in proportion as this *c·* has
      28–12   * to the building of this *c·*,
      37–23   * that this *c·* owes itself and
      37–27   * your annual Message to this *c·*.
      46– 9   * primary declaration of this *c·*
      47– 6   * steps by which this *c·* has
      55– 9   * rapidly growing in this *c·*
      57–17   * membership of this *c·*
      68– 2   * the interior of this *c·* is
      85–29   * this *c·*, with its noble dome
      89– 1   * This *c·* is one of the largest
     140–29   occasionally attending this *c·*.
     148–11   this *c·* becomes historic,
     155– 8   May this *c·* have one God,
     162–29   This *c·*, born in my nativity,
     163–10   come to the dedication of this *c·*,
     165–13   thank the dear brethren of this *c·*
     165–18   may each member of this *c·*
     165–29   God grant that this *c·*
     177–20   nurtured and nourished this *c·*
     182– 7   my early love for this *c·*
     186–19   May our God make this *c·*
     195–24   praiseworthy success of this *c·*,
     199–11   Trustees of this *c·* will please
     199–14   attitude of this *c·* in our
     230– 9   This *c·* is impartial.
     259–12   To this *c·* across the sea
     321– 1   * building this *c·* for your

church

to examine the
  My. 38–15   * tarry to examine the *c*·.
to leave the
  My. 56–27   * obliged to leave the *c*·
to ride to
  My. 219–12   To say that it is sin to ride to *c*·
triumphant
  Pul. 3–19   but of the *c*· triumphant ;
  My. 133– 7   rise to the *c*· triumphant,
  154–26   foreshadowing of the *c*· triumphant.
  174–30   rejoice in the *c*· triumphant ?
two-million-dollar
  My. 86–12   * new two-million-dollar *c*·,
  98–28   * two-million-dollar *c*· of the
unique
  Pul. 61–16   * every part of this unique *c*·,
Unitarian
  My. 171–22   * the lawn of the Unitarian *c*·
  173–29   committee of the Unitarian *c*·,
unite with the
  Ret. 14–13   could I unite with the *c*·,
vestibule of the
  My. 320–31   * in the vestibule of the *c*·
voted
  My. 53–15   * the *c*· voted to wait upon
  57– 9   * *c*· voted to raise any part of
was filled
  My. 30–27   * Though the *c*· was filled
  38–11   * The *c*· was filled for each service
was founded
  Pul. 37–28   * 1879, the *c*· was founded
  67–27   * The *c*· was founded in April,
went into the
  Ret. 16–13   pale cripples went into the *c*·
will be built
  My. 157–14   * The *c*· will be built of the
without creeds
  Man. 17– 3   forming a *c*· without creeds,
work of the
  My. 51–26   * this very early work of the *c*·,
yields to the
  Pul. 6– 5   yields to the *c*· established by
your
  Mis. 155– 9   win the . . . stranger to your *c*·,
  159– 5   read this letter to your *c*·,
  316– 7   or speak to your *c*· in Boston ?
  My. 23–18   * The members of your *c*·,
  36– 9   * The members of your *c*·
  62–20   * We, the Directors of your *c*·,
  191–29   the dedication of your *c*·
  192–21   at the dedication of your *c*·.
  194–18   fair escutcheon of your *c*·.
  194–27   guide and guard you and your *c*·
  195– 5   dedicatory services of your *c*·.
  352– 5   * we, the ushers of your *c*·,
  360–19   unite with those in your *c*·

  Mis. 35–20   and then go to *c*· to hear it
  129–12   drop this member's name from the *c*·,
  131– 8   kneels on a stool in *c*·,
  132–19   having charge of a *c*·,
  349–25   When the *c*· had sufficient
  Man. 29– 1   the First Reader of a *c*·,
  33– 4   the *c*· in which he is Reader.
  33– 9   shall not be a President of a *c*·.
  96– 8   paid by the *c*· that employs him.
  99–27   Readers of the *c*· employing said
  100– 3   send to the First Reader of the *c*·
  Ret. 44–24   recommended that the *c*· be dissolved.
  Un. 26–12   the hymn-verse so often sung in *c*· :
  Pul. 20– 5   gave back the land to the *c*·.
  20–10   regive the land to the *c*·.
  24–22   * *c*· is built of Concord granite
  30– 8   * *c*· numbers now four thousand
  44–22   * *c*· which will be dedicated to-day
  52– 1   * Here is a *c*· whose treasurer
  63– 6   * C· COSTING $250,000
  77– 1   * which the *c*· has just erected.
  Pan. 14–10   chapter sub-title
  Peo. 14–12   thou of the *c*· of the new-born ;
  My. 8–19   * *c*· of twenty-four thousand members
  14–27   * until the *c*· is finished.
  29–28   * began to congregate about the *c*·
  30– 8   * drawn to the *c*· from curiosity,
  36– 3   * telegram from the *c*· to Mrs. Eddy
  49–20   * August 27 the *c*· held a meeting,
  50– 3   * her Communion Sabbath as a *c*·,
  50–25   * members were added to the *c*·."
  50–31   * her farewell sermon to the *c*·.
  53– 9   * voted that the *c*· hold its
  53–19   * establishing itself as a *c*·
  53–26   * business committee of the *c*·,
  55–22   * *c*· was obliged to seek other
  57–29   * *c*· whose Treasurer has

church

  My. 61– 1   * watching at the *c*·.
  66–13   * will enable the *c*· to expand,
  69– 1   * *c*· is unusually well lighted,
  75–27   * No *c*· has ever yet been
  91–24   * the *c*· has continued to grow.
  94– 4   * figures given out by the *c*·
  94–26   * "crowning ultimate" of the *c*·
  95– 4   * *c*· which has been built upon the
  123–22   less sufficient to receive a *c*· of
  171–25   * greeted in behalf of the *c*· by
  171–26   * as a love-token for the *c*·
  172–21   * in behalf of the *c*·,
  173–30   and to the *c*· itself,
  174–22   until I had a *c*· of my own,
  187– 3   *c*· in Salt Lake City hath not
  259–10   * members London, England, *c*·.
  299– 7   * by the *c*· or the Bible,
  302–29   went alone . . . to the *c*·,
  308–23   as they were about to start for *c*·.
  328–22   * a prominent healer of the *c*·,

church (adj.)

  Mis. 131–16   that you waive the *c*· By-law
  141– 8   and against this *c*· temple
  177–23   hour for the *c*· service
  284–30   rules of *c*· government,
  310–19   comply with the *c*· rules.
  Man. 70– 2   shall not make a *c*·By-Law,
  71–22   in their *c*· books,
  72– 9   *c*· services conducted by
  72–18   under one *c*· government.
  75– 1   heading
  75–23   balance of the *c*· building funds,
  Ret. 89– 6   There was no *c*· preaching,
  Pul. 8– 4   *c*· chimes repeat my thanks
  9–17   *c*· services were maintained by
  16– 1   Set to the C· Chimes
  20–11   ministry and *c*· government.
  29–26   * heading
  39–21   * on the gray *c*· tower,
  44–19   * chapter sub-title
  66– 4   * first *c*· organization of this faith
  75–26   * most nearly fire-proof *c*· structure
  77– 7   * golden key of the *c*· structure.
  78–22   * gold key to the *c*· door.
  '02. 1– 4   our *c*· communicants constantly
  My. v– 4   * stirring times of *c*· building,
  vi–12   * devised its *c*· government,
  19–14   * their local *c*· building funds
  19–29   * towards its *c*· building fund.
  21– 6   * building *c*· homes of their own,
  29–13   * more gorgeous *c*· pageantries
  29–15   * have been *c*· ceremonies that
  49–14   * tenets and *c*· covenant.
  50– 4   * left their former *c*· homes,
  65– 3   * largest *c*· business meeting
  66–15   * so well situated for *c*· purposes
  71–19   * all the traditions of *c*· interior
  72– 3   * interior *c*· architecture.
  74– 6   * numbers of belated *c*· members
  76–11   * by the thousands of *c*· members
  76–17   * support of their *c*· work,
  76–20   * in their annual *c*· meeting
  83–31   * necessary expense of *c*· work,
  84– 5   * how a "*c*· debt" cramps and
  85–16   * in the building of a *c*· structure
  121– 4   our semi-annual *c*· meetings,
  170– 2   no formal *c*· ceremonial,
  170– 4   request of my *c*· members that
  171–11   invite all my *c*· communicants
  186–26   on the day of your *c*· dedication.
  203– 7   C· laws which are obeyed without
  223– 5   which pertain to *c*· difficulties
  236– 1   history of our *c*· buildings.
  250– 3   three years' term for *c*· Readers,
  250–10   acceptable service as *c*· Readers,
  311–16   my first *c*· membership,
  352– 7   * enjoy in this *c*· work.
  360–13   settle this *c*· difficulty amicably
  (*see also* **building, edifice, edifices, home**)

Church-building
  Man. 102– 1   heading

Church Building Fund
  Mis. 143–26   in aid of our C· B· F·,

Church Business
  Man. 27– 1   C· B·.

Church Directors
  (*see* **Directors**)

Churches and churches (*see also* **churches'**)

action of the
  Man. 70–20   unity and action of the *c*·
all
  Pul. 69–25   * All *c*· have prayed for the cure of

Churches and **churches**

all the
Mis. 383– 2   pastor, on this planet, of all the c.
Pul. 56– 7   * members of all the c·
'00. 14–12   inspired rebuke to all the c·
'01. 11–14   the pastor for all the c·
My. 301– 9   I would that all the c· on earth
342–21   It will embrace all the c·,

and associations
Mis. 358–22   organizing c· and associations.

and societies
Man. 74–17   c· and societies are required to
74–18   other C. S. c· and societies
My. 207– 7   * representatives of c· and societies
362–23   * will unite the c· and societies

are united
Pan. 13–14   c· are united in purpose.
My. 18–22   c· are united in purpose.

branch
Man. 31– 3   AND OF ITS BRANCH C·.
31– 6   Readers . . . of all its branch c·
32–17   Readers in Branch C·.
32–25   Readers in all the branch c·.
40–18   the branch c· by the First Reader
45–21   branch c· of this denomination
48–19   nor that of the branch c·.
54–25   Members of Branch C·.
61–11   Communion of Branch C·.
61–13   be observed in the branch c· on
70– 8   heading
71– 1   Branch c· of The Mother Church
71– 7   before titles of branch c·,
71–17   no Church . . . that has branch c·
71–21   Branch c· shall not write the
72– 1   Branch c· shall not adopt,
72–16   branch c· shall be individual,
72–26   Organizing Branch C·.
73–23   branch c· shall not confine their
74–13   or rooms in the branch c·,
93–18   No Disruption of Branch C·.
94– 1   organization of branch c·.
95– 9   From Branch C·.
95–10   branch C· of Christ, Scientist,
95–17   branch c· shall call on
98–24   In Branch C·.
98–25   three largest branch c· in each
99– 8   its three largest branch c·,
112– 1   When branch c· are designated by
112– 6   before titles of branch c·.
120– 2   heading
125– 2   heading
127– 3   heading
'02. 1– 9   our branch c· are multiplying
My. 10–27   * prosperity of the branch c· ;
19–13   * branch c· which contributed
21– 4   * made by many of the branch c·
21– 9   * erection of many branch c·.
40– 6   * we are sure that now the branch c·
56–10   * necessary to organize branch c·
56–12   * three branch c· were organized,
56 18   * organization of branch c·
56–22   * more branch c· were established
57–22   * total number of branch c·
141–26   "The branch c· continue their
243– 7   of the rules for branch c·
250–18   nor compels the branch c· to
250–23   the branch c· can wait for the
250–28   is done . . . by the branch c·.
359– 5   with the members of branch c·.

chapels and
Mis. 150–17   Chapels and c· are dotting the

Christian
Pul. 22– 3   Christian c· have one bond
Pan. 13–13   Love all Christian c·
My. 18–21   Love all Christian c·
89–18   * almost all other of the Christian c·,

Christian Science
Man. 32– 2   First Readers in the C. S. c·
42– 2   prayers in C. S. c· shall be
64– 5   Reading Rooms of a C. S. C·
71–10   its relation to other C. S. c·,
74–18   all other C. S. c· and societies
My. 250–19   applies only to C. S. c· in
255– 5   C. S. c· have my consent to
362–13   * Readers of all the C. S. c·
363–15   C. S. c· in Greater New York

conference of
Man. 70–16   No conference of c· shall be held,

Congregational
My. 182– 2   Chicago had few Congregational c·.

dear
My. 164–16   Now [1904] six dear c· are there,
175–13   Its dear c·, reliable editors,

dedicate
Mis. 91– 6   ordain pastors and to dedicate c· ;

dozens of
My. 73– 4   * They have erected dozens of c·

Churches and **churches**

each other's
Man. 85– 2   Pupils may visit each other's c·,

Eastern
Pul. 65– 4   * Eastern c· and the Anglican fold

erect
Pul. 45– 6   * effect cures . . . and erect c·,

evangelical
Mis. 249–13   devout members of evangelical c·
Man. 17– 5   were members of evangelical c·,
Ret. 64–30   If evangelical c· refuse
My. 182– 6   recommendation to evangelical c·

first century
My. 300–30   from the first century c·,

five
My. 343–26   they had five c· under discipline.

form
Mis. 137–30   My students can now . . . form c·,

from halls to
Mis. 125–30   the rapid transit from halls to c·,

halls and
Ret. 40–23   a hearing in their halls and c·.

have risen
My. 85– 8   * its c· have risen by hundreds,

messages to the
'00. 12– 7   his messages to the c·

more
Man. 63–16   two or more c· may unite in
My. 243–15   to take charge of three or more c·.

new
My. 8–30   * one hundred and five new c·

old
Mis. 179– 1   The old c· are saying,

or associations
No. 41–13   perfection in c· or associations.

organize
Ret. 50–24   continue to organize c·, schools,

organizing
Mis. 358–22   organizing c· and associations.
Man. 72– 4   Organizing C·.

other
Man. 70–12   no . . . official control of other c·,
Ret. 44–21   molestation of other c·,
Pul. 30– 7   * not recruit itself from other c·,
66–10   * conversions from other c·,
My. 13–10   * other c·, like so many planets,
284–23   only as other c· had done.

our
Mis. 91– 3   observed at present in our c·.
113–29   Our c·, The C. S. Journal, and
158–29   as our c· ordain ministers.
Man. 70–17   our c·, located in the same
My. 189– 9   The silent prayers of our c·,
214– 2   Otherwise, as our c· multiply,
249–29   What our c· need is

pastors of
Mis. 143–20   editors, and pastors of c·,

seven
'00. 14– 6   He goes on to portray seven c·,

several
My. 240 4   the several c· in New York City

shall decide
Man. 94– 5   the c· shall decide their action.

small
Man. 72–18   not more than two small c· shall

some
Pul. 56– 7   * In some c· a majority of

some of the
My. 10–12   * and some of the c·

strong
Pul. 67–20   * Toronto and . . . have strong c·,

such
Man. 71– 8   nor written . . . in naming such c·.
My. 99–24   * hundreds of such c·.

their
Man. 69–23   take care of their c· or attend to
94– 4   for their c· a less lecture fee ;
My. 76–18   * dedicate their c· free of debt
250– 8   adopt this By-law in their c·,

these
My. 182– 3   said to have a majority of these c·

Unitarian
Pul. 28–26   * hymn-books of the Unitarian c·.

unity with
Pul. 21–26   Our unity with c· of other

unto the
'00. 11–27   saith unto the c·." — Rev. 2 : 7.
14–10   what the Spirit saith unto the c· ;
14–20   angel that spake unto the c·

within the city
Man. 94– 2   can invite c· within the city

your
My. 192–16   My heart hovers around your c·
214– 4   on the walls of your c·.

Mis. 158–26   directions sent out to the c·.

Churches and churches
Mis. 257–26 c·, schools, and mortals.
Man. 41–11 misrepresented by the c· or
Ret. 85– 5 continue the organization of c·,
Pul. 22–16 doctrinal barriers between the c·
      30– 5 * unite with c· already established
'00. 2– 2 C· of this denomination are
'02. 2–28 When the c· and I round the
My. 56–20 * three foregoing named c·
      164– 7 heading
      199–21 c· of our denomination
      243– 1 chapter sub-title
      250–12 c· who adopt this By-law
      250–20 c· adopting this By-law will
      259–17 c· will remember me only thus.
      300–31 Are the c· opening fire on their own
      340–11 as witness her schools, her c·,
churches'
My. 259–13 our dear c· Christmas telegrams
Churches and Societies of C. S. in Missouri
My. 207–16 * signature
Churches of Christ, Scientist
Man. 58–13 of the branch C· of C·, S·,
      95–10 The branch C· of C·, S·, may apply
My. 213–30 to the dear C· of C·, S·.
church-fund
Mis. 349–32 I have put into the c·
churchman
Ret. 15–28 c· agreeably informed the
Church Manual (*see also* **Manual**)
Article I.
Man. 25– 3 NAMES, ELECTION, AND DUTIES.
      78–15 (See A· I, Sect. 6.)
Article II.
Man. 29–19 READERS OF THE MOTHER CHURCH.
Article III.
Man. 31– 2 DUTIES OF READERS OF THE MOTHER CHURCH
            AND OF ITS BRANCH CHURCHES.
Article IV.
Man. 34– 3 QUALIFICATIONS FOR MEMBERSHIP.
Article V.
Man. 35– 9 APPLICATIONS FOR MEMBERSHIP.
      37–20 provided for in A· V, Sect. 4.
      109–13 as required by A· V, Sect. 6,
      111–20 (see A· V, Sect. 4),
Article VI.
Man. 36– 2 as provided in A· VI, Sect. 2,
      37–15 RECOMMENDATION AND ELECTION.
Article VII.
Man. 38–16 PROBATIONARY MEMBERSHIP.
Article VIII.
Man. 40– 3 GUIDANCE OF MEMBERS.
Article IX.
Man. 49–18 MARRIAGE AND DECEASE.
Article X.
Man. 50– 6 DEBATING IN PUBLIC.
Article XI.
Man. 50–12 COMPLAINTS.
      56– 3 according to A· XI, Sect. 4.
Article XII.
Man. 55– 9 TEACHERS.
      85– 9 the provisions of A· XII, Sect. 1,
Article XIII.
Man. 56– 9 REGULAR AND SPECIAL MEETINGS.
Article XIV.
Man. 58– 3 THE C. S. PASTOR.
Article XV.
Man. 58–19 READING IN PUBLIC.
Article XVI.
Man. 59–14 WELCOMING STRANGERS.
Article XVII.
Man. 60– 2 SERVICES UNINTERRUPTED.
Article XVIII.
Man. 61– 7 COMMUNION.
Article XIX.
Man. 61–17 MUSIC IN THE CHURCH.
My. 230–19 amendments to A· XIX.,
Article XX.
Man. 62– 7 SUNDAY SCHOOL.
My. 230–30 A· XX., Sections 2 and 3
      231–30 A· XX., Section 3
Article XXI.
Man. 63–12 READING ROOMS
Article XXII.
Man. 64–10 RELATION AND DUTIES OF MEMBERS TO PASTOR
            EMERITUS
      68–25 in accordance with A· XXII, Sect. 11,
      69– 7 in accordance with A· XXII, Sect. 11,
My. 353–20 chapter sub-title
Article XXIII.
Man. 70– 7 THE MOTHER CHURCH AND BRANCH CHURCHES.
      112– 6 See A· XXIII, Sect. 2.
Article XXIV.
Man. 75– 1 GUARDIANSHIP OF CHURCH FUNDS.

Church Manual
Article XXV.
Man. 64–25 See also A· XXV, Sect. 7.
      79–15 THE C. S. PUBLISHING SOCIETY.
Article XXVI.
Man. 83– 3 TEACHERS.
      92–24 named in Sect. 9 of A· XXVI
Article XXVII.
Man. 86– 2 PUPILS.
Article XXVIII.
Man. 88– 3 ORGANIZATION.
Article XXIX.
Man. 89–10 APPLICANTS AND GRADUATES.
Article XXX.
Man. 90– 7 ACTION OF THE BOARD.
Article XXXI.
Man. 93– 3 ORGANIZATION AND DUTIES.
Article XXXII.
Man. 95– 2 CALLS FOR LECTURES.
Article XXXIII.
Man. 97– 1 COMMITTEE ON PUBLICATION.
Article XXXIV.
Man. 102– 1 CHURCH-BUILDING.
My. 15– 3 * Section 3 . . . XXXIV in revised edition
Article XXXV.
Man. 72– 3 See Article XXXV, Sect. 1.
      104– 1 C· M·.
Article XLI.
My. 15– 3 * Section 3 of Article XLI
p. 17
My. 46–13 (C· M·, p. 17.)
                    ⸻
Man. 68–26 in accordance with . . . our C· M·
      69– 4 time specified in the C· M·.
      69– 8 Article XXII, Sect. II of the C· M·.
      104– 1 heading
      104– 4 C· M· of The First Church
      104–16 subsequent editions of the C· M·;
'02. 14– 1 is published in our C· M·.
My. vi–14 * wrote its C· M· and Tenets,
      46–26 * admonitions of our C· M·
      229–24 the twentieth century C· M·
      230– 2 eternity awaits our C· M·,
      230–20 amendments . . . in our C· M·.
      231–30 Article XX., Section 3 of C· M·
      237–21 The article on the C· M· by
      243– 8 as published in our C· M·.
      359– 2 contrary to the rules of the C· M·,
church-member
Man. 34–19 not a c· from a different
Pan. 11–14 best c· or moralist on earth,
church-members
Ret. 14–29 even the oldest c· wept.
'02. 20–22 the faces of my dear c· ;
Church Membership
Man. 34– 1 heading
      87– 1 C· M·.
      109– 2 *Regarding Applications for* C· M·
churchmen
'01. 32–21 Such c· and the Bible,
Church of Christ
Mis. 140–25 for upbuilding the C· of C·
      145– 3 religious element, or C· of C·,
My. 49–24 * their duties in the C· of C·,
      50–19 * outlook of the C· of C·.''
      51– 5 * members of the C· of C·,
      345–28 light the way to the C· of C·.
Church of Christ, Scientist
Mis. 90–21 *pastor of the* C· of C·, S·.
Man. 17– 4 to be called the "C· of C·, S·.''
      33– 2 First Reader in a C· of C·, S·,
      34–19 member of another C· of C·, S·,
      38–20 members of the C· of C·, S·,
      55– 1 and a branch C· of C·, S·,
      60–24 Corner Stone of a C· of C·, S·.
      61– 3 A C· of C·, S·, shall not hold
      62–10 classes of any C· of C·, S·,
      62–12 from another C· of C·, S·,
      62–14 Sunday School of any C· of C·, S·,
      70–14 Each C· of C·, S· shall have
      71–15 no C· of C·, S·, shall be
      72–12 publicly as a C· of C·, S·,
      74– 1 member of one branch C· of C·, S·,
      99–14 with another C· of C·, S·,
      100–17 may notify any C· of C·, S·,
Ret. 44– 3 to be called the "C· of C·, S·,
      45– 1 C· of C·, S·, in Boston,
      46– 1 pastor of the C· of C·, S·, in Boston.
      65– 1 fellowship with the C· of C·, S·,
No. 12– 7 College and C· of C·, S·,
My. 186–28 erected a C· of C·, S·,
      (*see also* **The Church of Christ, Scientist; The First Church of Christ, Scientist**)

Church of England
'01.   21– 9   * Berkeley of the C· of E·
Church Officers
Man.   21– 1   names of
     25– 1   heading
     28– 3   Duties of C· O·.
Church of Rome
My.   294–26   animated the C· of R·
Church Purposes
Man.   136– 2   heading
Church Rule
Man.   40–17   C· R· shall be read in
Church's
Man.   75– 8   this C· love and gratitude,
church's
Mis.   131–26   bill of this c· gifts to Mother ;
Man.   54–15   branch c· list of membership
Ret.   44–18   noting the c· need, and the
Pul.   45–13   * declared that the c· completion
     87–24   our c· tall tower detains the sun,
My.   123– 1   this c· gifts to me are
Church Services
Man.   58– 1   heading
Church Tenets
Man.   18–22   The C· T·, Rules, and
     40–20   the C· T· are to be read.
Church Treasurer
Man.   44–15   forwarded each year to the C· T·.
     76– 9   the books of the C· T·
     77– 1   books of the C· T· audited annually
     (see also **Treasurer**)
Church Universal and Triumphant
Man.   19– 6   reflect . . . the C· U· and T·.
church-yards
Peo.   14– 6   dismal gray stones of c·
cigarette
Mis.   240–26   If they see their father with a c·
Cincinnati
Pul.   56– 2   * Buffalo, Cleveland, C·,
cipher
My.   235– 9   and never name a c·?
circle
Ret.   19– 5   parting with the dear home c·
     19–14   lamented by a large c· of friends
Un.   12– 5   sickle of Mind's eternal c·,
Pul.   47– 4   * her c· of pupils and admirers
'02.   2–28   in the c· of love, we shall meet
My.   330–26   lamented by a large c· of friends
circles
Ret.   5–26   * in the c· in which she moved,
Pul.   51–17   * a sensation in religious c·,
     57–21   * few people outside its own c·
circling
Chr.   53– 1   Fast o· on, from zone to zone,
'02.   1–21   C. S., ... is c· the globe,
My.   115– 2   is c· the whole world.
Circuit Lecturer
Man.   94–14   C· L·.
     94–16   Mother Church shall appoint a C· L·.
circuitous
Mis.   139 23   transferred in a c·, novel way,
circular
Mis.   305–11   * this c· is sent to every member
     305–31   * every one receiving this c·
Pul.   24–10   * Romanesque tower with a c· front
circulars
Man.   46– 9   on c·, cards, or leaflets,
circulate
Man.   43–22   shall neither buy, sell, nor c·
     98–14   c· in large quantities the papers
My.   298–11   to publish and c· this work.
circulated
Mis.   285– 4   and not one of them c·,
Man.   97–20   or c· literature of any sort.
My.   305–10   "vulgar" defamers have c·,
circulates
Mis.   126–23   yet nothing c· so rapidly :
circulating
My.   136–20   c· in the five grand divisions of
     297–29   said to be c· regarding my history,
     298– 2   buying, c·, and recommending it
circulation
Mis.   382– 6   manuscripts of mine were in c·.
Pul.   47– 7   * c· with the members of this
My.   76– 4   * notices . . . had been in c·,
     175–27   counterfeit letters in c·,
     333–32   * reports of . . . are in c·.''

circumference
Un.   10–20   God is . . . the centre and c·.
circumlocution
No.   22– 8   The c· and cold categories
circumscribed
Un.   21–11   said, . . . your intellect will be c·
circumstance
Mis.   91–13   at all times and under every c·,
     117–32   hasten to follow under every c·.
     118– 7   Honesty . . . under every c·,
     119–12   more stubborn than the c·,
     155– 3   pride of c· or power
     160– 6   through time and c·,
Ret.   40–24   This c· is cited simply to show
Pul.   55– 8   * not the least eventful c·
My.   248–18   No fatal c· of idolatry can
     330–22   * Mrs. Eddy says of this c· :
circumstances
Mis.   17–25   the timely or untimely c·,
     90–12   under c· exceptional,
     146–10   would need to know the c·
     178–28   but will yield to c·.
     200–26   met no obstacle or c· paramount
     229– 4   c· which he believes produce it.
     276– 7   c· demanded my attention
     288–14   nearest right under the c·,
     298–10   Under the same c·,
     326–16   under every hue of c·,
Man.   46–20   shall not, under pardonable c·,
Ret.   8– 1   Many peculiar c· and events
     13– 4   some c· are noteworthy.
     38– 1   will be seen in the following c·.
     38–25   motives and c· unknown to me.
     53– 4   prosperous under difficult c·,
Pul.   15–16   At all times and under all c·,
     67– 7   * fact borne out by c·.
'01.   30–27   under all c· to obey
'02.   11– 4   to and fro by adverse c·,
My.   37– 3   * no pride of c· has place
     52–31   * peculiar knowledge of the c·.
     118–14   such c· embarrass the
     195– 5   Adverse c·, loss of help,
     204–20   recommend it under the c·.
     321–17   * nothing in the c· which have
     334–12   * this critic places certain c·
citadel
Pul.   2–20   strengthen your c· by every means
My.   213–22   strengthen your own c·
citadels
Mis.   211–27   Jesus stormed sin in its c·
'01.   2–19   ever storming sin in its c·,
citations
My.   34–14   * c· from the Bible and "S. and **H.**
cite
Mis.   300–25   I gave permission to c·,
My.   107– 7   I will c· a modern phase of
cited
Mis.   296– 9   unknown author c· by Mr Wakeman
Man.   104–18   shall be c· as authority.
Ret.   40–24   circumstance is c· simply to show
     76– 7   it is c·, and quoted deferentially.
My.   281– 6   I c·, as our present need, faith
cites
'00.   6–29   c· 1875 as the year of the
     14–20   angel that spake . . . c· Jesus as
cities
Mis.   81–17   c· and towns of Judea,
     257–26   Earthquakes engulf c·, churches,
Ret.   82–14   locate in large c·, in order to
     82–16   population of our principal c·
     89– 9   scattered about in c· and villages,
Pul.   5–23   public libraries of the principal c·,
     79–13   * or village — to say nothing of c·
No.   1– 9   demolishing bridges and . . . c·.
'00.   1–19   in most of the principal c·,
     2– 3   springing up in the above-named c·,
     12–23   to purge our c· of charlatanism.
My.   112–31   into the chief c·
citing
Ret.   75– 8   c· from the works of other authors
citizen
Mis.   147–24   the public-spirited c·.
My.   277–22   every c· would be a soldier
citizens
'01.   33–29   Christian Scientists are harmless c·
My.   173– 6   to thank the c· of Concord for
     227–10   c· are arrested for manslaughter
     331– 5   * of Wilmington's best c·,
     333– 5   * found by one of your own c·,

citizenship
 Pul. 50– 8 * better home life and *c*.
city
 above the
  My 67– 1 * raises its dome above the *c·*
 American
  My. 85–31 * sky-lines in an American *c·*,
 another
  My. 14–12 * from a friend in another *c·*,
 any
  Pul. 23– 5 * Most Unique Structure in Any *C·*
  24– 6 * most unique structure in any *c·*.
 beleaguered
  Mis. 326–18 wanderers in a beleaguered *c·*,
 best
  My. 8–12 * and in the best *c·* in the world.
 capital
  My. 157– 8 * capital *c·* of your native State.
 celestial
  Mis. 311– 5 as we journey to the celestial *c·*.
  323– 3 celestial *c·* above all clouds,
 certain
  My. 294– 7 In a certain *c·* the Master
 convention
  My. 83– 4 * residing in the convention *c·*.
 entire
  '00. 12–26 The entire *c·* is now in ruins.
  My. 69–29 * seems to dominate the entire *c·*,
 great
  My. 183– 5 in this great *c·* of Chicago,
 guests of the
  My. 74–26 * are as the guests of the *c·*,
 heavenly
  Pul. 27–13 * one representing the heavenly *c·*
 historic
  My. 85–25 * this historic *c·* is the Mecca
 home
  My. 157– 9 * the Cause in your home *c·*,
  174–11 editors in my home *c·*
 illustrious
  '00. 12– 8 Ephesus as an illustrious *c·*,
 intellectual
  Pul. 80– 7 * in the most intellectual *c·*
 light of the
  No. 27–10 Spirit will be the light of the *c·*,
 other
  My. 74–15 * in this or any other *c·*,
  182– 3 any other *c·* in the United States.
 our
  My. 154–17 this little church in our *c·*,
  175–12 growth and prosperity of our *c·*
 picturesque
  My. 175–17 Our picturesque *c·*, however,
 pleasant
  My. 163–24 people of this pleasant *c·*
 renowned
  My. 177–16 In your renowned *c·*,
 streets of a
  Mis. 324– 3 streets of a *c·* made with hands.
 that
  Ret. 19– 8 when the yellow-fever raged in that *c·*,
  Pul. 65–20 * called the Bible of that *c·*.
  '00. 12–22 the magical books in that *c·*
  12–24 During St. Paul's stay in that *c·*
  13– 3 church of Christ" in that *c·*.
  My. 89–24 * not . . . to that *c·* alone,
  92–11 * than it has evoked in that *c·*,
  335–19 * the dread disease in that *c·*,
 this
  Mis. 251–10 voicing the friendship of this *c·*
  Pul. 7– 5 whereof this *c·* is the capital.
  28–28 * pastor to the church in this *c·*,
  50–12 * house of worship in this *c·*,
  68–16 * was organized in this *c·*
  71–13 * Christian Scientists in this *c·*,
  72– 4 * feeling of Scientists in this *c·*
  78– 1 * Mary Baker Eddy of this *c·*,
  '00. 12–11 items concerning this *c·*.
  13–21 refers to the church in this *c·* as
  13–25 * "In this *c·* the amalgamation of
  My. 65– 9 * to build in this *c·* a church edifice
  67–27 * surpass any church . . . in this *c·*.
  74– 7 * who will arrive in this *c·*
  77–10 * rapidly gathering in this *c·*
  83–21 * Christian Scientists in this *c·*
  141– 5 * held annually . . . in this *c·*,
  148– 1 your pioneer work in this *c·*,
  158– 3 church edifice for . . . in this *c·*.
  163–29 in this *c·* a church of our faith
  164– 4 give to many in this *c·* a church
  328–19 * C. S. healers in this *c·*.
 town and
  My. 92– 1 * in every important town and *c·*
 within the
  Man. 94– 2 can invite churches within the *c·*

city
 your
  My. 177–10 able to take the trip to your *c·*,
  187– 1 Church of Christ, . . . in your *c·*.
  187– 4 at some near future visit your *c·*,
  330–10 * Christian Scientist of your *c·*,
  331– 9 * irreproachable standing in your *c·*

  Mis. 323– 2 "a *c·* set upon a hill," — *see Matt.* 5 : 14.
  Ret. 20–23 in the *c·* of Salem, Massachusetts.
  Pul. 77–11 * in the *c·* of Boston,
  78–10 * in the *c·* of Boston,
  '00. 13–12 founded the *c·* of Smyrna,
  13–17 *c·* of Pergamos was devoted to a
  13–24 deity in the *c·* of Thyatira was Apollo.
  '01. 28–17 persecuted from *c·* to *c·*.
  My. 3–10 gates into the *c·*." — *Rev.* 22 : 14.
  46–28 * *c·* of the living God, — *Heb.* 12 : 22.
  66–16 * in a fine part of the *c·*.
  70– 1 * in their relation to the *c·* itself,
  71–11 * great adornment to the *c·*.
  72– 7 * Never before has the *c·* been more
  75– 9 * into the *c·* from every direction
  78– 8 * from every quarter of the *c·*,
  79–10 * in the heart of the *c·* of Boston,
  82–26 * trains pulled out of the *c·*
  122–15 in our good *c·* of Concord.
  123–11 finest localities in the *c·*,
  188–10 brought out of the *c·* of David,
  196– 5 "*c·* of brotherly love."
  196–12 that taketh a *c·*." — *Prov.* 16 : 32.
  206–20 "The *c·* had no need of — *Rev.* 21 : 23.
  270– 7 this capital *c·* of Concord, N. H.,
  271–13 * in the *c·* of Concord,
  285–23 nor in the *c·* : — *Acts* 24 : 12.

city (adj.)
  Po. vi–17 that the *c·* authorities could
  My. 174– 8 the efficient *c·* marshal and his
  175–19 favor of our *c·* government ;

City of Mexico, Mex.
  My. 95– 8 * [*Mexican Herald, C· of M·, M·*.]

civic
  '00. 10–12 *c·*, social, and religious rights
  My. 285– 8 industrial, *c·*, and national peace.

Civic League of San Francisco
  My. 285– 3 on behalf of the *C· L· of S· F·*,

civil
  Mis. 145– 2 *c·* and religious liberty.
  206– 2 natural, *c·*, or religious,
  246– 5 *c·* and religious reform.
  246– 9 *c·* and political power.
  251–12 *c·* and religious freedom,
  Ret. 70–28 *c·*, moral, and religious reform.
  Pul. 20–17 *c·* and religious reform
  No. 15–10 *c·* and religious arms
  44–22 the *c·* arm of government,
  My. 216– 6 *c·*, and educational means,
  268–13 the justice of *c·* codes,

civilization
  Pul. 66–27 * with which our *c·* has developed.
  '02. 10–10 * "The birthplace of *c·* is not
  My. 29–14 * and in an older *c·*,
  265–10 that *c·*, peace between nations,
  278–20 elevating power of *c·*
  278–24 have no right to engraft into *c·*

civilized
  Pul. 79–11 * in every part of the *c·* world,
  My. 59–12 * scientific body in the *c·* world.
  77–13 * practically every *c·* country,
  90–25 * from all over the *c·* world,
  273– 9 * covers practically the *c·* world.

Civil War
  My. 332–27 * during the *C· W·* many Masonic

clad
  Mis. 104–16 *c·* in a false mentality,
  162–14 *C·* with divine might,
  171–29 all *c·* in the shining mail
  234–29 *c·* with a richer illumination
  262– 7 *c·* in Truth-healing's new
  373–16 as *c·* not in soft raiment
  374– 3 *c·* in panoply of power,
  Ret. 28–16 we must be *c·* with divine power.
  Pul. 1– 5 promise *c·* in white raiment,
  15–18 *C·* in the panoply of Love,
  35–20 we must be *c·* with divine power.
  No. 29–22 though *c·* in soft raiment,
  My. 189– 1 *C·* in invincible armor,
  191–18 *c·* in immortality.
  210– 8 *c·* therewith you are completely
  340–13 *c·* in a little brief authority,

claim (noun)

any
Un. 54–12 To admit that sin has any c·
No. 30–12 to rebuke any c· of another law.
being worthless
No. 27– 3 and the c·, being worthless,
claimant or a
Mis. 259– 8 that evil is a claimant or a c·.
cope with the
My. 227–17 their ability to cope with the c·,
diviner
Mis. 140–25 The diviner c· and means for
evil
Mis. 284–22 neither an evil c· nor an
false
Mis. 53– 1 out of this dream or false c·
53– 3 before this false c· can be
108–11 Not to know that a false c· is false,
258– 5 unrelenting false c· of matter
Ret. 64–23 and error being a false c·,
67– 1 Sin existed as a false c·
67–16 until the false c· called sin is
Un. 32– 2 and that evil is a false c·,
32–15 misnamed mind is a false c·,
32–26 but the false c· to personality,
47– 5 false c· to existence or consciousness.
54– 3 To say there is a false c·, called
54– 4 it is nothing but a false c·.
54– 5 one must lose sight of a false c·.
54– 8 regard sickness as a false c·,
No. 16– 7 If God knows evil even as a false c·,
17–24 If God could know a false c·,
27– 3 It issues a false c· ;
'01. 14– 8 evil, as a false c·, false entity,
'02. 6–14 is seen to obtain in a false c·,
falsity of the
Un. 32–28 demonstrate the falsity of the c·.
fraudulent
Mis. 272–25 * is a fraudulent c·.
great
Pul. 31–27 * with great c· to personal beauty.
his
Mis. 261–29 one will either abandon his c·
381–12 evidence to support his c·
idolatrous
Un. 31–11 first idolatrous c· of sin is,
illusive
Pan. 6– 6 illusive c· that God is not supreme,
its
Mis. 31–11 Its c· to power is in proportion to
108–13 reducing its c· to its proper
Ret. 35–20 its c· is substantiated,
mortal
Mis. 198–10 the mortal c· to life, substance, or
no
No. 27– 4 in reality no c· whatever.
'00. 15–14 thence to see that sin has no c·,
My. 279– 0 no c· that man is equal to God,
no other
Mis. 193–10 established on no other c·
of error
Mis. 100–10 c· of error for Truth to deny
293–23 creator of the c· of error.
Un. 8–20 nothingness of every c· of error,
54–10 insensible to every c· of error.
'01. 15– 5 We must condemn the c· of error
of evil
Mis. 55– 0 is the universal c· of evil
115–18 delivered from every c· of evil,
Ret. 64–11 as the opposite c· of evil is one.
of insanity
Mis. 49–11 distorted into the c· of insanity
of matter
Mis. 258– 5 unrelenting false c· of matter
Un. 32– 3 Hence the c· of matter usurps the
of sin
Un. 31–11 c· of sin is, that matter exists ;
'00. 15–14 awakened to see . . . the c· of sin,
'01. 13–28 first detect the c· of sin ;
pushed that
Un. 54–27 serpent, who pushed that c·
sin, as a
Ret. 63–19 Sin, as a c·, is more dangerous
sin's
Un. 54–14 for if sin's c· be allowed
their
No. 38– 5 by knowing their c·.
My. 134–14 will never lose their c· on us.
this
Mis. 39–10 risen up in a day to make this c· ;
109– 9 how much of this c· you admit
to error
No. 30–20 forbids . . . even a c· to error.
valid
Mis. 261–30 or else make the c· valid.

claim (noun)
Mis. 63– 4 the c· that one erring mind cures
Ret. 35–21 a c· too immanent to fall to the
Un. 32–26 a c· which C. S. uncovers.
54– 6 If the c· be present to the thought,
54– 9 the so-called fact of the c·
claim (verb)
Mis. 3– 3 shall c· no especial gift from our
43– 6 Do all who at present c· to be
196– 3 c· no mind apart from God.
199– 4 erring mind can c· to do thus,
255–20 I c· for healing by C. S.
303–16 privileges that we c· for ourselves.
349–17 I c· no jurisdiction over any
367–14 to c· that He is ignorant of anything ;
Man. 92–11 Science to be all that we c· for it.
Ret. 34–10 I c· for healing scientifically the
Pul. 66–11 * c· to have been rescued from death
67– 8 * Boston can fairly c· to be the hub
74–16 I c· nothing more than what I am,
No. 27– 4 Matter is not Mind, to c· aught ;
'01. 7–24 God whom all Christians now c·
Hea. 15–15 why should man . . . c· another mind
My. 26–21 or that I c· their homage.
245–24 all who c· to teach C. S.
299– 8 * c· the allegiance of mankind.''
299–18 those who c· to pardon sin,
305–21 I c· no special merit of any kind.
320–16 * c· to be a Christian Scientist,
354– 4 which they c· have been endorsed by
claimant
Mis. 259– 8 supposition that evil is a c·
Un. 54–17 even as a false c·,
54–18 then acquaintance with that c·
No. 24–22 evil has no . . . and was never a c· ;
claimants
Mis. 263–27 especially by unprincipled c·,
No. 42–21 C. S. is beset with false c·,
claimed
Mis. 60–26 Evil in the beginning c· the power,
349–15 which he c· to be practising ;
352–16 what has c· to produce it,
Ret. 25 17 The real I c· as eternal ;
68– 2 as a serpent it c· to originate
68– 4 it c· to beget the offspring of evil,
Un. 46–19 as is still c· by the worldly-wise.
Pul. 72–21 * had never c·, nor did she believe
82–12 * In olden times the Jews c· to be
Hea. 17–18 had c· audience with a serpent.
18–19 or c· to reach that woe :
Po. v– 7 * experience that c· her attention.
My. 14–13 * c· to have good authority for
73– 6 * it is c· that very few of them
303– 5 and I have never c· to be.
330–18 * as c· in your issue
333–16 * It has never been c· by Mrs. Eddy
354– 9 for which my endorsement is c·.
claiming
Mis. 39–29 c· to work with God
108– 5 c·, as they do, that good is
174– 3 it is a lie, c· to talk
184– 1 by c· that God is Spirit,
223 16 c· full faith in the divine
255–10 not c· equality with,
Un. 25–12 c· to be something beside God,
claims (noun)
accepted the
Mis. 297–19 accepted the c· of the marriage
all
Mis. 185– 7 it strips matter of all c·,
all the
Mis. 293– 3 all the c· and modes of evil ;
297–21 morally bound to fulfil all the c·
298–19 all the c· of sensuality.
divine
Mis. 19–13 accepted the divine c· of Truth
diviner
Peo. 11–10 another staging for diviner c·,
erroneous
My. 161–18 to destroy its erroneous c·,
false
Mis. 24–32 effect arising from false c·
109–26 to escape from the false c· of sin.
higher
Mis. 67– 3 higher c· of the law and gospel
Peo. 11– 4 struck the keynote of higher c·,
his
No. 2–18 student . . . is modest in his c·
infinite
Mis. 16–11 Principle hath infinite c· on man,
its
Mis. 284–26 aggressive, and enlarges its c· ;
lawful
Pul. 82–18 * women had few lawful c·

claims (noun)
Mrs. Eddy's
  My. 332–24 * corroborate Mrs. Eddy's *c·*.
no
  Ret. 64–23 they are no *c·* at all.
  No. 24–21 evil has no *c·*
of envy
  My. 167–28 illegitimate *c·* of envy, jealousy,
of error
  Mis. 293–13 against the opposite *c·* of error.
  Ret. 64–22 supposititious *c·* of error ;
of evil
  Mis. 114–23 deliverance from the *c·* of evil.
  No. 23–20 we need to discern the *c·* of evil,
       24–15 *c·* of evil become both less and more
of matter
  Un. 31– 9 annulled the *c·* of matter,
      36–18 rejection of the *c·* of matter
of physique
  Mis. 28–29 annulled the *c·* of physique
of politics
  My. 266– 5 *c·* of politics and of human power,
of sense
  Mis. 172– 8 defeat the *c·* of sense and sin,
of Spirit
  Mis. 140–10 superiority of the *c·* of Spirit
of the corporeal senses
  Ret. 54– 6 the *c·* of the corporeal senses
of the law
  Mis. 67– 3 higher *c·* of the law and gospel
       348– 3 *c·* of the law and the gospel.
of the senses
  My. 222–14 from admitting the *c·* of the senses
of these senses
  Mis. 198–15 if we deny the *c·* of these senses
other
  Mis. 286–28 shut out all sense of other *c·*.
Scientist
  My. 81–24 * demonstration of the Scientist *c·*,
sensible
  No. 38– 4 that . . . and death are sensible *c·*,
statements and
  Mis. 78–19 false statements and *c·*.
strong
  Pan. 12–11 will make strong *c·* on religion,
such
  Mis. 297–22 unless such *c·* are relinquished by
their
  Mis. 172– 1 their *c·* and lives steadfast in
these
  Mis. 16–11 these *c·* are divine, not human ;
  Ret. 54– 9 deny these *c·* and learn the divine
  No. 23–21 fight these *c·*, . . . as illusions ;

  Mis. 181–10 *c·* of the divine Principle.

claims (verb)
  Mis. 27–22 matter *c·* something besides God,
       62–15 *mind-cure c· to heal without it?*
      109– 9 how much, sin *c·* of you ;
      138–12 divine Principle which he *c·*
      183–25 for it *c·* another father.
      243–14 *c·* more than it practises.
      363– 4 "ego" that *c·* selfhood in error,
  Man. 46– 2 who *c·* a spiritually adopted child
  Ret. 56–21 Whatever else *c·* to be mind,
       70– 5 and *c·* God as their author ;
  Un. 39–15 *c·* another father, and denies
  Pul. 47–15 * She *c·* that no human reason has
       72–12 * *c·* to have been healed
  No. 3– 3 which *c·* only its inheritance,
  My. 300–20 If, as this kind priest *c·*,
       314–13 as *McClure's Magazine c·*,

clairvoyant
  My. 313–23 * never was "an amateur *c·*,"

clambering
  Mis. 341– 8 after much slipping and *c·*,

clamor
  No. 45–25 The people *c·* to leave cradle
  '02. 2– 4 without *c·* for distinction or

clamorous
  My. 203– 7 not *c·* for worldly distinction.

clanging
  My. 31– 7 * "Oh, the *c·* bells of time ;"

clans
  Mis. 172– 9 regardless of the bans or *c·*
       274–21 inordinate, unprincipled *c·*.

clap
  Mis. 168–20 pure in heart *c·* their hands.
       330– 1 the leaves *c·* their hands,

Clarendon Street
  My. 55–24 * Copley Hall on *C· S·*,

clarion
  Mis. 120–16 the *c·* call of peace
  Ret. 12– 1 nobler far than *c·* call
  '01. 35– 8 It is a *c·* call to the reign of
  Po. 60–21 nobler far than *c·* call

clasp
  Mis. 143– 8 I reach out my hand to *c·* yours,
       152– 4 in love continents *c·* hands,
       392– 3 skies *c·* thy hand,
  Pul. 84– 5 * revenge shall *c·* hands with pity,
  Po. 20– 4 skies *c·* thy hand,

clasped
  Peo. 11–14 their chains are *c·* by the false

claspeth
  Po. 65–17 love *c·* earth's raptures not long,

clasping
  Mis. 306–27 it is not the *c·* of hands,

Class
    (*see* **Primary Class**)

class (noun)
another
  No. 9– 6 or established among another *c·*
any
  Man. 92–17 instructions in C. S. in any *c·*
  My. 93– 8 * to attract any *c·* save the
       223– 7 any *c·* of individual discords.
better
  '00. 14–25 the better *c·* of M.D.'s
certain
  My. 111–27 may irritate a certain *c·* of
College
  Mis. 49– 1 A young lady entered the College *c·*
  Man. 90–13 members of the College *c·*
each
  Mis. 315–12 Each *c·* shall consist of
enter a
  Rud. 15–13 diseased people not to enter a *c·*.
       15–20 can advantageously enter a *c·*,
first
  My. 59– 3 * member of your *first c·* in Lynn,
healed in a
  Rud. 15– 3 student, if healed in a *c·*,
healed in the
  Rud. 14–28 and were healed in the *c·* ;
her
  Mis. 49–14 have been cured in her *c·*.
higher
  '01. 30–17 higher *c·* of critics in theology
his
  Mis. 92–13 textbook of C. S. into his *c·*,
       92–21 When closing his *c·*, the teacher
in Christian Science
  Mis. 239– 6 commence a large *c·* in C. S.
       316– 6 When will you take a *c·* in C. S.
       316–10 The date of a *c·* in C. S.
  My. 182–11 In 1884, I taught a *c·* in C. S.
juvenile
  Man. 63– 6 are adapted to a juvenile *c·*,
larger
  My. 244– 5 if a larger *c·* were advantageous
my
  My. 104–24 in my *c·* on C. S. were many
my last
  My. 125–22 The students in my last *c·*
no favored
  No. v– 2 to benefit no favored *c·*,
Normal
  Mis. 143–19 Normal *c·* graduates of my College,
       264–13 enter the Normal *c·* of my College
  Man. 84–11 Normal *c·* not exceeding thirty
       86–17 teachers of the Normal *c·* shall
       90– 1 eligible to enter the Normal *c·*.
       90–19 be given to each Normal *c·*
       91–22 may enter the Normal *c·* in
  Ret. 47–18 Normal *c·* student who partakes
  My. 251– 8 * Primary and Normal *c·* instruction
       251–13 eligible to enter the Normal *c·*,
       323–31 * Normal *c·* in the fall of 1887?
Obstetric
  Ret. 43–17 taught the . . . Obstetric *c·*
of aspirants
  Rud. 16–25 fusing with a *c·* of aspirants
of people
  Mis. 80–15 with a wrong *c·* of people.
of students
  Mis. 32–16 the above-named *c·* of students
one
  Man. 84– 8 shall teach but one *c·* yearly,
       84–11 shall have one *c·* triennially,
       92–14 should teach yearly one *c·*.
  Ret. 50–16 as many as seventeen in one *c·*.
  No. 9– 5 errors of one *c·* of thinkers
  My. 215–10 a dozen or upward in one *c·*.

class (noun)

or creed
My. 157–10 * without regard to *c·* or creed,

Primary
Mis. 273–24 applications . . . for the Primary *c·*
273–29 if I should teach that Primary *c·*,
280–18 students of this Primary *c·*,
318–15 instructions in a Primary *c·*
Man. 86–23 teachers of the Primary *c·*
89–12 taught in a Primary *c·* by Mrs. Eddy
Ret. 43–18 taught one Primary *c·*, in 1889,
47–16 A Primary *c·* student,
47–19 instructions in a Primary *c·*
Rud. 14–13 never taught a Primary *c·* without
My. 245–32 given to students of the Primary *c·* ;
319–21 * I entered your Primary *c·*
320–21 * while I was in your Primary *c·*
322–19 * to enter the next Primary *c·*

privileged
Mis. 244–27 not for a privileged *c·* or

read to the
Man. 90–22 shall be read to the *c·*,

same
My. 111– 7 same *c·* of minds to deal with

second
My. 323–31 * studying in the second *c·*

this
Man. 90– 1 All members of this *c·* must
My. 104–27 that brought together this *c·*
254–14 faithful teacher of this *c·*

your
My. 321–22 * and entered your *c·*,
324–27 * to sit through your *c·*.

Mis. 49–12 in a *c·* of Mrs. Eddy's ;
92–19 point out the lesson to the *c·*,
242–29 before leaving the *c·* he took
273–26 *c·* which contains that number.
280–26 met the *c·* to answer some questions
316– 5 chapter sub-title
317–13 to be taught in a *c·*,
Man. 84– 9 *c·* shall consist of not more than
90–21 One student in the *c·* shall
Ret. 84–11 When closing the *c·*,
Rud. 14–26 both in and out of *c·*.
Pan. 10–13 best students in the *c·* averred·
My. 93– 1 * Christian Scientists, as a *c·*,
100–15 * of a *c·* who are reputable,
243–19 chapter sub-title
254– 4 chapter sub-title
254– 9 chapter sub-title
319– 6 nothing further from him in the *c·*,
320–28 * several times after the *c·* closed,

class (adj.)

Mis. 11–10 at close of the *c·* term,
211–10 medical bills, *c·* legislation,
256–17 intervals between my *c·* terms,
273–28 waiting for the same *c·* instruction ;
274–24 shout for *c·* legislation,
315–17 not only through *c·* term, but
Man. 83–16 not only during the *c·* term but
87–13 against *c·* instruction.
91– 8 Tuition of *c·* instruction
Pul. 36– 9 * I was present at the *c·* lectures
Rud. 16– 7 to thorough *c·* instruction
My. 128– 6 or *c·* legislation is less than the
340–12 and her frown on *c·* legislation,
(see also **teaching**)

classed

'01. 28–12 *c·* with the choicest memorials of
My. 340– 4 He *c·* the usage of special days

classes

Mis. 41–18 *Can all c· of disease be healed*
256–13 that this must prevent my *c·*
273–29 the other three *c·*
296–15 This writer *c·* C. S. with
315–11 can teach annually three *c·* only.
Man. 62– 9 received in the Sunday School *c·*
87–12 shall not solicit, . . . for their *c·*.
90–15 no Primary *c·* shall be taught under
91–14 President gives free admission to *c·*.
Rud. 14–11 The only pay . . . was from *c·*,
14–19 No discount . . . made on higher *c·*,
14–19 their first *c·* furnished students with
14–24 unprepared to enter higher *c·*,
'02. 3– 5 among the educated *c·*
My. 88– 7 * among *c·* above the average in
181–18 *c·* and masses of mankind,
251–10 * become teachers of Primary *c·* ?"
265–30 reaching out to all *c·* and peoples.
318–16 to visit one of my *c·*

classic

Ret. 86– 8 as said the *c·* Grecian motto.
Hea. 1–15 A *c·* writes, — "At thirty, man
My. 224–30 let us adopt the *c·* saying,

classical

Ret. 17–17 palm, bay, and laurel, in *c·* glee,
Po. 63– 1 palm, bay, and laurel, in *c·* glee,

classification

My. 107–25 entitled to a *c·* as truth or
109– 7 When this scientific *c·* is
224–18 borrows the thoughts, words, and *c·*

classifications

Mis. 86–13 scientific *c·* of the unreal

classified

Mis. 112–13 strictly *c·* in metaphysics as
Pul. 22–15 Christendom will be *c·* as
Pan. 4– 8 reason and will are properly *c·* as

classifies

Mis. 252– 8 C. S. *c·* thought thus :

classify

Mis. 36– 3 *c·* evil and error as mortal mind,
Ret. 64–21 *c·* sin, sickness, and death as

class-room

Mis. 91–25 textbook with him into the *c·*,
279–27 We, to-day, in this *c·*,
Ret. 83–19 the chapter for the *c·*,
91–26 The grove became his *c·*,

class-rooms

Pul. 27– 7 * opening from it are three large *c·*
58–15 * division into seven excellent *c·*,

claws

Mis. 294–21 their stings, and jaws, and *c·* ;

clay

Mis. 326–17 driven out of their houses of *c·*
Pan. 11–12 allow mortals to turn from *c·* to
Po. 2– 3 to sport at mortal *c·*
67– 4 cold in this spot as the spiritless *c·*,
My. 344–10 inhabiting *c·* and then withdrawn

clean

Mis. 79– 4 swept *c·* by the winds of history.
99–23 The winds of time sweep *c·*
398–20 Shepherd, wash them *c·*.
Ret. 46–26 Shepherd, wash them *c·*.
Pul. 17–25 Shepherd, wash them *c·*.
Po. 14–24 Shepherd, wash them *c·*.
My. 34– 3 He that hath *c·* hands, *Psal.* 24 : 4.
228–20 washing it *c·* from the taints of

cleanliness

Mis. 184–30 a type of physical *c·*

cleanse

Mis. 30–30 *c·* our lives in Christ's
271–13 *C·* your mind of the cobwebs
399– 7 *C·* the foul senses within ;
Ret. 86–11 *C·* every stain from this
Pul. 90–18 * *c·* the lepers, — *Matt.* 10 : 8.
29–22 * to *c·* the leprosy of sin,
66–12 * *c·* the lepers, — *Matt.* 10 : 8.
Po. 39–12 will watch to *c·* from dross
75–14 *C·* the foul senses within ;
My. 265– 9 *c·* the earth of human gore;
300–26 *c·* the lepers, — *Matt.* 10 : 8.

cleansed

Mis. 153–14 Israel, . . . *c·* of the flesh,
153–21 *c·* my heart in vain." — *Psal.* 73 : 13.
168– 7 moral lepers are *c·* ;
Pul. 53–11 * When the ten lepers were *c·*
No. 1–20 healed the sick and *c·* the sinful.
My. 265–25 *c·* of self and permeated with

cleanseth

Mis. 322–21 healeth the sick and *c·* the sinner.

Cleanse the Lepers

Pul. 28– 8 * "*C·* the *L·*," — *Matt.* 10 : 8.

cleansing

Mis. 124–17 healing the sick, *c·* the leper,
185–12 *c·* mortals of all uncleanness,
204–13 spirit of Truth *c·* from all sin ;

clear

Mis. 51–16 If you make *c·* to the child's thought
79– 6 until it is *c·* to human comprehension
87– 1 as the bird in the *c·* ether of the
140–27 * "read our title *c·*"
181–31 *c·* discernment of divine Science :
211– 6 Our own vision must be *c·*
215–14 and be *c·* that it is Love,
347–15 Where my vision begins and is *c·*,
357–22 it has been *c·* to my thought
Man. 66– 4 and obtain a *c·* understanding of
Ret. 16– 1 a soprano, *c·*, strong, sympathetic,
34– 7 Neither ancient nor . . . could *c·* the clouds
93–20 It is quite *c·* that as yet this
Pul. 21–24 a *c·* expression of God's likeness,
59–19 * in a *c·* emphatic style.
60– 7 * *c·*, manly, and intelligent tones,
Rud. 9–25 imbued with a *c·* conviction of

clear
No.	13–14	c· and profound deduction from
'00.	9–16	till the mental atmosphere is c·.
'01.	25– 2	becomes c· to the godly.
	30–25	like the c·, far-seeing vision,
	31– 1	by a c· elucidation of truth,
My.	113–22	have a c· perception of it.
	137– 7	* c·, plain-speaking English."
	149–19	c· perception of divine justice,
	150–20	calm, c·, radiant reflection of
	155–19	a c· vision of heaven here,
	234– 5	they only cloud the c· sky,
	297–18	c·, correct teaching of C. S.
	342–20	* she said, in her c· voice,

cleared
Ret.	30– 6	have c· its pathway.

clearer
Mis.	13–23	and reveals in c· divinity the
	13–27	c· discernment of good.
	78–23	will some time appear all the c· for
	84–30	a c· and nearer sense of Life
	277– 4	Truth is speaking louder, c·,
	324–17	c· pane of his own heart
Ret.	23– 6	As these pungent lessons became c·,
	82–29	makes the subject-matter c·
Un.	25– 4	nothing can be c· than the
	49–24	gives me a c· right to call evil a
Pul.	12–19	rises c· and nearer to the
No.	9– 7	c· and more conscientious
My.	207–11	* for the c· understanding and
	265–27	in c· skies, less thunderbolts,
	324–11	* c· nomenclature for S. and H.

clear-headed
Mis.	266–13	c· and honest Christian Scientist

clearing
Mis.	174– 6	a c· up of abstractions.
	343–13	c· the gardens of thought
My.	57–11	* The labor of c· the land

clearly
Mis.	37– 8	recognized this relation so c·
	42–10	S. and H. c· states that
	92–1C	He who sees most c·
	95–19	but I c· understand that no
	107– 9	we behold more c· that
	113–21	Already I c· recognize that
	156–10	will see c· the signs of Truth
	164– 8	continue to be seen more c·
	171– 5	and the blind saw c·.
	186–18	let us not lose this . . . but gain it c· ;
	261–28	apprehending the moral law so c·
	281–26	came to me more c· this morning
	336–15	that hinders your seeing c·
	373–15	One great master c· delineates
Ret.	50–23	I see c· that students in C. S.
	84– 7	He who sees c· and enlightens
Un.	7– 9	When I have most c· seen
Pul.	12–24	This rule c· interprets God as
No.	1–17	read more c· the tablets of Truth.
	39–22	It shows us more c· than we
'01.	9– 4	C. S. shows us that God is
	27– 7	* who will interpret . . . more c·,
My.	45–22	* As c· as in retrospect we see the
	61–16	* conviction . . . came to me so c·,
	225–27	In their textbook it is c· stated
	317–14	enable me to explain more c·
	322–26	* which were so c· stated that I

clearness
Mis.	220–23	understand with equal c·,

clears
Mis.	75–20	*sense* for *soul* c· the meaning,
	355–17	To strike . . . never c· the vision ;

cleave
Mis.	2– 7	determination of mankind to c· to

cleaves
No.	32–13	c· sin with a broad battle-axe.

cleaving
No.	42–21	c· to their own vices.

clemency
Mis.	274–19	it discounts c·, mocks morality,
	295–29	dignity, virtue, c·, and

clergy
Mis.	225– 1	chapter sub-title
Ret.	6– 7	to the c· were accorded
	40–22	so stirred the doctors and c·

clergyman (see also clergyman's)
Mis.	193–15	c· charitably expressed it,
	225– 6	c·, his wife and child.
Man.	49–21	a c· who is legally authorized.
Pul.	30– 3	* when a Boston c· remonstrated
No.	41–24	a Boston Baptist c·,
	42–25	distinguished c· came to be healed.

clergyman
No.	44–24	Congregational c· of Boston,
'01.	21–12	This c· gives it as his opinion
My.	84– 4	* Many a c· can testify
	118– 8	chapter sub-title
	331– 6	* Rev. Mr. Reperton, a Baptist c·,

clergyman's
Mis.	32– 4	what about that c· remarks on
	32–31	c· comments on my illustrated poem,
	225–13	c· son was taken violently ill.
	225–14	Then was the c· opportunity to
	226– 6	c· son returned home — *well.*
	229–12	c· conversion of sinners.
	300–13	gives you the c· salary
Ret.	15– 2	the good c· heart also melted,

clergymen
Mis.	33– 7	All c· may not understand the
Ret.	42–10	c· of other denominations
Pul.	5– 1	one of the very c· who had
	29– 4	* formerly been Congregational c·.
	47– 1	* c· of other denominations
'01.	18–30	Christians and c· pray for sinners ;
	31–25	distinguished Christian c·,
Hea.	5–11	One of our leading c·
My.	53–22	* by c· of different denominations,
	95–21	* c· of other denominations

clerical
Mis.	246– 1	pulpit and press, c· robes and

Clerk (see also Clerk's)
Mis.	310–21	send in their petitions . . . to the C·
	322– 9	the C· of the church can inform
Man.	25– 6	a President, a C·, a Treasurer,
	25–15	C· and Treasurer.
	25–16	The term of office for the C·
	29–10	shall complain thereof to the C·
	36–19	can apply to the C· of this Church,
	36–24	Addressed to C·.
	36–26	addressed to the C· cf the Church.
	37–10	C· of the Church shall send to the
	37–11	neither the C· nor the Church shall
	52– 8	C· of the Church shall address a
	52–16	C· of the Church shall immediately
	56–15	reports of Treasurer, C·, and
	57– 7	upon the call of the C·.
	57– 8	Called only by the C·.
	57–11	shall be the duty of the C·
	57–14	C· must have the consent of
	65–26	If the C· of this Church shall
	66–11	duty of the C· to report to her
	78–17	through the C· of the Church,
	78–21	sum of $500 with the C·,
	93–16	mail to the C· of this Church
	98–16	sending a copy to the C·
	109–17	before sending them to the C·
	111–21	on application to the C·.
Ret.	49–31	C. A. FRYE, C·.
My.	38– 7	* WILLIAM B. JOHNSON, C·.
	39–14	* list of officers . . . was read by the C·
	39–16	* C·, William B. Johnson, C.S.D.
	46–31	* WILLIAM B. JOHNSON, C·.
	47– 1	* heading
	49–17	* August 22 the C·, by instructions
	49–30	* voted to instruct the C· to call
	51–16	* It was moved to instruct the C· to
	242–23	leave these duties to the C· of The
	280–12	* WILLIAM B. JOHNSON, C·.
	283– 5	MR. JOHN D. HIGGINS, C·.
	289– 7	MR. WILLIAM B. JOHNSON, C.S.B., C·.
	361–27	* ARTHUR O. PROBST, C·.

clerk (see also clerk's)
My.	314–21	instructed the c· to record the

Clerk of the Court
My.	137– 4	* in the office of the C· *of the* C·,

Clerk's
My.	22– 2	* *Extract from the* C· *Report*

clerk's
My.	311–12	c· book shows that I joined the

clerks
Man.	95–11	may apply through their c·

Cleveland
Ohio
Ret.	52–23	its meeting in C·, Ohio,
Pul.	89–36	* *Leader,* C·, Ohio.
My.	195– 2	chapter sub-title

Pul.	56– 2	New York, Chicago, Buffalo, C·.

clew
Pul.	64–18	* without finding a c· ;

Cliff
Mis.	393–12	Crowns life's C· for such as we.
	393–24	To thy whiteness, C· of Wight.
Po.	51–17	Crowns life's C· for such as we.
	52– 8	To thy whiteness, C· of Wight.

cliffs
　Mis. 323–19　climbing its rough *c*·,
climax
　No. 17–13　Man is the *c*· of creation ;
　My. 225– 8　caps the *c*· of the old
climb
　Mis. 215–10　not seek to *c*· up some other way,
　　　327– 5　"Wilt thou *c*· the mountain,
　Un. 64–15　Mortals may *c*· the smooth glaciers,
　No. 44– 9　To *c*· up by some other way
　My. 152–15　or do I *c*· up some other way?
climbed
　Pul. 9–13　a woman *c*· with feet and hands
climbing
　Mis. 323–19　*c*· its rough cliffs,
　My. 61–14　* I was *c*· over stones and
clime
　No. 44–26　In every age and *c*·,
climes
　My. 127–32　all times, *c*·, and races.
cling
　Mis. 310– 8　rather than *c*· to personality
　Pul. 40– 2　* thoughts of you forever *c*· to me :
　My. 116– 7　inclined to *c* to the personality
clinging
　Mis. 275– 4　*c*· faith in divine power
clings
　Mis. 308– 6　*c*· to my material personality,
　Ret. 73–19　He who *c*· to personality,
　'01. 14– 3　that *c*· fast to iniquity.
　My. 334–21　that *c*· fast to iniquity.
clip
　Ret. 88–28　not be allowed to *c*· the wings of
cloak
　'01. 30–24　* man "clouting his own *c*·"
cloak-room
　My. 69–23　* in the basement is a *c*·
clod
　Mis. 187–25　Did the substance . . . become a *c*·,
　　　395– 7　His home the *c*· !
　Po. 57–14　His home the *c*· !
clog
　Mis. 234– 2　and *c*· the wheels of progress.
clogging
　Rud. 17– 4　*c*· the wheels of progress by
　My. 215–22　*c*· the wheels of C. S.
clogs
　Mis. 156–20　*c*· the progress of students.
close
　Mis. 11–10　at *c*· of the class term,
　　　49– 3　to withdraw before its *c*·,
　　　127–31　need *c*· attention and examination.
　　　128– 5　Therefore I *c*· here, with the
　　　133– 2　at the *c*· of your article,
　　　136 23　*c*· your meetings for the summer ;
　　　137– 6　at the *c*· of the first convention
　　　185–21　so-called material senses would *c*·,
　　　271–18　chapter sub-title
　　　273– 5　I *c*· my College in order to work in
　　　274–13　I *c*· my College.
　　　277–23　No evidence . . . can *c*· my eyes to
　　　280–19　at *c*· of the lecture on the fourth
　　　304– 7　* After the *c*· of the Exhibition
　　　355–30　at the *c*· of a balmy autumnal day,
　Man. 73–22　No *C*· Communion.
　Ret. 3–12　towards the *c*· of the War of 1812.
　　　6–17　talented, *c*·, and thorough
　　　15–19　At the *c*· of my engagement
　　　43–19　judged it best to *c*· the institution.
　　　48–10　to *c*· my flourishing school,
　Un. 55–10　must keep *c*· to his path,
　Pul. 12– 4　stillness . . . indicated *c*· attention.
　　　21–21　and *c*· the door on church or
　　　31–15　* *c*· contact with public feeling
　　　34–10　* that she would be alive at its *c*·.
　　　45–12　* one month before the *c*· of the year
　　　84–13　* *c*· of the year, Anno Domini 1894,
　No. 45–27　material history is drawing to a *c*·.
　Pan. 7–18　*c*· study of the . . . Testaments
　　　13–15　*c*· the war between flesh and
　'00. 2– 8　*c*· observer reports three types
　　　11–23　* Like the *c*· of an angel's psalm,
　'02. 3–18　*c*· of the conflict in South Africa ;
　　　3–20　wiser at the *c*· than the beginning
　Hea. 20– 1　following hymn was sung at the *c*· :
　My. 15–16　I *c*· with Kate Hankey's . . . hymn,
　　　18–23　*c*· the war between flesh and
　　　29–31　* until the *c*· of the evening service,
　　　78–17　* At the *c*· of the Lesson-Sermon,
　　　80– 1　* *c*· of their visit to Boston :

close
　My. 81–25　* a fitting *c*· to a memorable week.
　　　108–28　and will *c*· with his own words :
　　　256–12　*c*· the door of mind
　　　257–17　*c*· of the nineteenth century,
closed
　Mis. 214–12　*c* — to the senses — that wondrous
　　　244– 1　*c*· up the wound — see *Gen.* 2 : 21.
　　　317–11　when my College *c*·,
　　　328–14　and *c*· it against Truth,
　　　332– 6　doors that *c*· on C. S.
　　　358–26　Metaphysical College, . . . is *c*·.
　Man. 69–27　shall hereafter be *c*· to visitors.
　Ret. 18–11　ope their *c*· cells to the bright,
　Pul. 36– 4　* *c*· (in 1889) in the very zenith of
　　　42– 1　* had *c*· the large vestry room
　　　68– 8　* The college was *c*· in 1889,
　'02. 9–24　opened my *c*· eyes.
　Hea. 2– 5　synagogues as of old *c*· upon it,
　Po. 63–22　ope their *c*· cells to the bright,
　My. 79– 3　* in absolute stillness, their eyes *c*·
　　　246–12　*c*· my College in the midst of
　　　320–28　* several times after the class *c*·,
　　　333–15　* which was *c*· in due form."
　　　353–23　shall hereafter be *c*· to visitors.
closely
　Mis. 114–22　or bar their doors too *c*·,
　　　376– 5　* very *c*· resemble in detail
　Pul. 37–23　* not to centre too *c*· around
　'00. 7–24　would walk more *c*· with Christ ;
　My. 10–30　* is *c*· interwoven with the
closer
　Mis. 143– 7　a *c*· link hath bound us.
　Un. 1–18　*c*· to the true understanding of God
　Pul. 23–15　* calling out a *c*· inquiry into
　'01. 19– 6　*c*· proximity with divine Love,
closes
　Mis. 88–18　*c*· the task of talking to deaf ears
　　　276–30　it *c*· the door on itself.
　　　304–16　* until that Exhibition *c*·.
　　　319– 5　*c*· the argument of aught besides
　　　324– 2　His converse . . . in the valley *c*·,
closest
　Pul. 54–24　* with his *c*· friends and followers,
closet
　Mis. 133–14　enter into thy *c*·, — *Matt.* 6 : 6.
closing
　Mis. 92–21　When *c*· his class,
　　　244– 7　*c*· the incisions of the flesh.
　Ret. 38–21　*c*· chapter of my first edition of
　　　84–11　When *c*· the class, each member
　Pul. 23–19　* *c*· years of every century
　Pan. 3–12　evening's *c*· vespers,
　　　12–10　This *c*· century, and its successors,
　My. 29– 7　* Such was the *c*· incident
　　　185–26　*c*· my remarks with the words of
cloth
　Mis. 203–14　new *c*· of metaphysics ;
　'01. 2– 8　new-old *c*· of Christian healing.
clothe
　No. 26–26　*c*· the grass of the field, — *Matt.* 6 : 30.
　　　26–27　much more *c*· you, — *Matt.* 6 : 30.
　Peo. 14– 2　we *c*· our thoughts of death with
　My. 154–18　to *c*· the human race.
clothed
　Mis. 6–30　keeping them *c*· and fed,
　　　104–14　*C*·, and in its right Mind,
　　　185–16　and man be *c*· with might,
　　　251–21　*c*· more lightly,
　Pul. 83–27　* a woman *c*· with the sun, — *Rev.* 12 : 1.
　Rud. 13–27　to be fed, *c*·, and sheltered
　No. 22– 5　*c*· with a "brief authority ;"
　'00. 6–23　*c*· and in his right mind,
　'01. 29– 1　housed, fed, *c*·, or visited
　My. 117–14　or naked, and *c*· thee? — *Matt.* 25 : 38.
　　　349–14　at the feet of Jesus *c*· in truth,
clothes
　Ret. 40–12　*c*· already prepared for her burial ;
clothing
　Mis. 294–18　from wolves in sheep's *c*·
　　　323–19　wolves in sheep's *c*· are ready to
　　　325– 6　Christian Scientists in sheep's *c*· ;
　　　370–21　a wolf in sheep's *c*·
　Hea. 4– 7　*C*· Deity with personality,
　My. 215–21　wolves in sheep's *c*·," — see *Matt.* 7 : 15.
cloud
　Mis. ix–16　darkness of storm and *c*·
　　　149–28　Guided by the pillar and the *c*·,
　　　204– 2　a dark, impenetrable *c*· of error ;
　　　257–23　Electricity, . . . sparkles on the *c*·,
　　　277–30　the *c*· of the intoxicated senses.

cloud
Mis. 347– 6   A conical c·, hanging like a
    360–16   When C. S. has melted away the c· of
    386–28   farewells c· not o'er our ransomed rest
    388– 6   A bow of promise on the c·.
Ret.   23– 7   c· of mortal mind seemed to
No.   21–28   like a c· without rain,
'02.   20–15   A bow of promise on the c·.
Peo.   3–17   like a promise upon the c·,
Po.   7– 6   A bow of promise on the c·.
    50–14   farewells c· not o'er our ransomed rest
My.   45–20   * by day in a pillar of c·
    45–25   * pillar of c· by day, — see Exod. 13 : 22.
    178– 3   c· not the spiritual meaning
    234– 5   they only c· the clear sky,

cloud-crowned
Po.   1–13   Proud from yon c· height

cloudless
Mis. 395–26   sunny days and c· skies,
Po.   58–11   sunny days and c· skies,

clouds
Mis. 277–25   Though c· are round about Him,
    323– 3   celestial city above all c·,
    355–26   Let no c· of sin gather
    377– 5   in c· and darkness !
    388– 4   What chased the c· away?
    392– 3   C· to adorn thy brow,
Ret.   9–26   * And won, through c·, to Him,
    18–24   But c· are a presage,
    34– 7   Neither . . . could clear the c·,
Pul.   9–12   as sunshine from the c· ;
'02.   20–13   That swept the c· away ;
Po.   7– 4   What chased the c· away?
    20– 3   C· to adorn thy brow,
    29– 2   though murky c· Pursue thy way,
    30–18   Piercing the c· with its triumphal
    54– 3   O come to c· and tears
    64–20   But c· are a presage,
    70– 1   Beyond the c·, away
My. 149–27   C· parsimonious of rain,
    252–14   work midst c· of wrong,

clouting
'01.   30–23   * "c· his own cloak"

clover
Mis. 343–22   to choke the coming c·.

club-house
My. 174– 7   opening their spacious c·

clubs
Mis. 336– 6   resort to stones and c·,
My. 224–14   Avoid . . . public debating c·.

clue
Ret. 45–14   my c· to the uses and abuses of

cluster
My. 186– 5   c· around this rock-ribbed church

clustered
Mis. 237–30   fear c· round his coming.

coal
Un. 34–16   put your finger on a burning c·,

coast
Pul.   41– 9   * from the far-off Pacific c·
My.   30–17   * from Hawaii, from the c· States.

coat
Pul. 48–21   * her family c· of arms

coated
Pul. 25–14   * are of iron, c· with plaster ;

coat-of-arms
My. 311–18   facts regarding the McNeil c·
    311–21   presented me my c·,
    311–23   with her own family c·.
    311–24   I have another c·, which is

coats
Mis. 243–27   the c· of the stomach to thicken

coax
Mis. 119– 6   If a criminal c· the unwary

coaxed
Mis. 203–12   you have c· in their course
My. 152–32   florist has c into loveliness

cobelievers
Pul. 71–22   * By her followers and c· she is

cobwebs
Mis. 271–14   Cleanse your mind of the c·

cocaine
Mis. 244–30   discoverers of quinine, c·, etc.,

code
Mis. 257–15   It is a c· whose modes
My. 343–23   I made a c· of by-laws,

codes
Mis. 246– 5   to blot out all inhuman c·.
Peo.   5–12   barbarisms of spiritless c·.
    11–19   as men . . . enact penal c· ;
My. 266–17   all c·, modes, hypotheses,
    268–13   the justice of civil c·, and the

coelbow
Mis. 138–10   but sometimes to c· !

coequal
Mis. 319– 4   can neither be coeval nor c ,

coercive
Mis.   80–16   unjust c· legislation
    297– 6   by legally c· measures,

coeternal
Mis.   79–23   coexistent and c· with God.
    360–30   coexistent and c· with God,
Ret.   59–23   as coexistent and c· with God,
No.   25–18   coexistent and c· with Him.

coeval
Mis.   93–15   its c·, is without divine authority.
    319– 4   can neither be c· nor coequal,

coexist
Un.   64– 4   than the sun can c· with darkness.
'00.   4–26   Man and the universe c· with God
'02.   8–24   Love, purity, meekness, c· in
My. 349–22   and c· with the God of nature

coexistence
Mis. 47–24   spiritual c· with his Maker.

coexistent
Mis.   57–26   if he was c· with God?
    79–23   c· and coeternal with God.
    190– 8   man is c· with Mind,
    360–29   c· and coeternal with God,
Ret.   59–23   c· and coeternal with God,
Un.   49– 4   man is c· with God,
No.   25–17   c· and coeternal with Him.
'01.   5–25   are c· and eternal,
'02.   7–18   man and the universe c· with God.
My.   5– 9   His idea, c· with Him

coexists
My. 239– 2   The Science of . . . c· with God ;

coffea
Mis. 348–19   not even c· (coffee),

coffee
Mis. 348–19   not even coffea (c·),
No.   42–27   * and drink strong c· to support

coffers
My. 52–26   * has always filled her c· anew.

cognate
My. 106–11   the folly of the c· declaration

cognizance
Mis.   28– 8   Matter takes no c· of matter.
    218–13   can take no c· of Spirit
    228–21   in any way takes c· of,
Ret.   60–26   no c· of the spiritual facts
Un.   28–18   five senses take no c· of Soul,
    28–19   so they take no c· of God.
    38– 1   no c· of spiritual individuality,
No.   6– 8   take c· of their own phenomena,
    19–22   A sinner can take no c· of

cognizant
Mis. 208– 6   He is c· only of good.
Un.   8– 4   of which the physical senses are c·?
    15– 6   declare Him absolutely c· of sin?

cognize
Mis.   72–29   it cannot c· aught material,
    74–12   how did Jesus, . . . c· it?
    82– 9   c· the symbols of God,
    97–26   more than personal sense can c·,
    161–11   could not c· the Christ,
Un.   23–25   has no sense whereby to c·
    28– 7   The five physical senses do not c· it.
    34–22   could not c· its own so-called
No.   25– 9   c· through the material senses.

cognized
Mis. 22–29   simple fact c· by the senses,

cognizes
Rud. 5–19   consciousness which c· being.

cognomen
Mis. 108–26   This c· makes it less dangerous ;
    336–22   c· of all true religion,

coherence
My. 127– 8   calm c· in the ranks of C. S.

coherent
'01. 5– 6   and become less c· than the

cohesion
Mis. 173–29   Have attraction and c· formed it?
Ret.   45– 8   this material form of c·

coin
My. 170–16   It is His c·, His currency ;

coincide
Mis. 223– 8   logic, and revelation c·.
'02.   8–25   Lust, hatred, revenge, c· in
My. 278– 1   To c· with God's government

coincidence
Mis. 100–21   c· of the divine with the human,
Un.   52– 9   in the c· of God and man,
Pul.   55–12   * regard it as a mere c·
'02.   8–12   The c· between the law and
My. 114–17   a strange c· or relationship
181–31   It is a marked c· that those dates
265–22   c· of the human and divine,
327– 3   Is it not a memorable c·

coincident
My.   28– 1   * c· with the completion of the
326– 8   * this recognition should be c·

coincides
'00.   5– 3   c· with the First Commandment

colaborers
My. 173–30   his c· on said committee

cold
Mis.   7– 2   nor to breathe the c· air,
239–10   * chapter sub-title
239–20   * "I've got c·, doctor."
240– 1   "I have not got c·."
240– 3   through the c· air the little one
240– 8   flippant caution, "You will get c·."
240–13   If a c· could get into the body
339–16   with finger grim and c· it points
343–15   picking away the c·, hard pebbles
384–11   The c· blasts done,
386–22   kissed my c· brow,
398–13   So, when day grows dark and c·,
Ret.   46–19   So, when day grows dark and c·,
Un.   34–19   is hot or c·?
Pul.   14–17   Give them a cup of c· water
16–18   C·, silent, stately stone,
17–18   So, when day grows dark and c·,
21–20   To perpetuate a c· distance
82– 3   * the c· haunts of sin and sorrow,
No.   20– 9   it may seem distant or c·,
22– 8   c· categories of Kant
'00.   15–28   The c· blasts done,
Hea.   5– 8   if a man has taken c· by doing good
5– 9   will punish him now for the c·,
Peo.   5– 7   into the c· materialisms of dogma
10– 5   as we struggle through the c· night of
Po.   2–15   so c·, so glitteringly bright,
14–17   So, when day grows dark and c·,
26–14   phantom finger, grim and c·,
36–10   The c· blasts done,
50– 7   kissed my c· brow,
67– 3   Grow c· in this spot as the
My. 113–22   Then, is C. S. a c·, dull
252–31   by the c· impulse of a lesser gain !
265–28   extremes of heat and c· ;

Cole
Mrs.
Pul.   73–20   Mrs. C· has made a careful
Mrs. Henrietta N.
Pul.   73–17   * Mrs. Henrietta N. C· is also a very

Coligny, Admiral
Mis. 281–12   Admiral C·, in the time of the

collapse
Un.   10–15   they cannot c·, or lapse into
No.   26–14   man can no more relapse or c·
My. 106–15   Without . . . the universe would c· ;

collect
Mis.   x– 5   to c· my miscellaneous writings
148–25   c· no moneyed contributions from
305–26   * to c· two dollars from others,

collected
Pul.   59–27   * c· the money for the Mother's Room,
My.   21– 5   * money which had been c· for
185–23   an attentive audience c· in

collection
Man.   62– 3   time required to take the c·.
Po.   vi–23   * are included in this c·,
My.   32–23   * C·.

collections
Mis. 159–17   and rare grand c·
My.   30–19   * The six c· were large,
30–25   * record c· secured by evangelists

collective
Ret.   67–21   c· as well as individual.

collectively
Mis. 164–28   reveal man c·, as individually,
Man.   42– 3   offered for the congregations c·

collectively
My. 134– 9   keep the faith individually and c·,
259–23   considered either c· or
344– 4   then all his rays c· stand for

College and college
Mis.   4–14   come to the C· and to the
5– 5   Our C· should be crowded with
35–23   and then study it at c·?
38–13   How happened you to establish a c·
49– 1   A young lady entered the C· class
49– 4   before entering the C·,
64– 9   prospective students of the C·
135–23   chapter sub-title
143–19   Normal class graduates of my C·,
243– 6   mental branches taught in my c· ;
249–15   None are permitted . . . in my C·
249–22   students, expelled from my C·
264–13   enter the Normal class of my C·
272– 1   * obtained a c· charter in January, 1881,
272– 6   * Mrs. Eddy's grant for a c·,
272–25   * but one legally chartered c· of
273– 5   I close my C· in order to work in
274– 4   when I opened my C·.
274– 8   outside of C· work,
274–13   I close my C·.
317–11   was shut when my C· closed.
349– 1   to take lessons outside of my C·,
349–10   mode of obstetrics taught in my C·.
358–24   only C· for teaching C· S·
382–22   for a metaphysical medical c·,
Man.   35–10   Students of the C·.
73–10   students in any university or c·,
73–12   at such university or c·,
73–15   graduates of said university or c·,
73–18   the rules of the university or c·
73–20   said university or c· organization.
80– 1   Presidency of C·.
90–13   teacher and members of the C· class
91– 5   and of the President of the C·
Ret.   10–11   studied Hebrew during his c· vacations.
43– 7   It is the only C·, hitherto, for
43–10   taught two terms in my C·.
43–20   the only assistant teachers in the C·.
44–13   accumulating work in the C·,
45–18   connected with my C·
47– 4   unprecedented popularity of my C·.
47– 7   persons desiring to enter the C·,
47–13   Board of Directors of my C·,
49–20   only one ever granted to a legal c·
50– 6   one course of lessons at my C·,
Pul.   36– 7   * To this C· came hundreds
68– 8   * The c· was closed in 1889,
No.   43–22   Such students come to my C· to
'01.   29–30   * our tuition for the c· course."
My. 172– 3   * the first chapel of the C·
246–12   closed my C· in the midst of
246–22   the result is an auxiliary to the C·

College Association
Mis. 135–23   chapter sub-title

College of Metaphysics
Mis. 271–22   the only chartered C· of M·,

colleges
Mis.   38–21   metaphysics at other c· means,
272– 8   * no . . . granted for similar c·,
272–19   * "All the mind-healing c·
272–24   * Hence to name these . . . c·,
Pul.   5–23   c·, and universities of America ;

collisions
Mis. 339–13   In the mental c· of mortals
Un.   6–12   forcible c· of thought
Peo.   1–12   intellectual wrestling and c·

colloquialism
Pul.   31– 7   * At the risk of c·,

colloquy
Mis. 168–15   Here ends the c· ;
Un.   27– 2   word employed in the foregoing c·.
Pan.   6–20   c· between good and evil,

Colonel
Mis.   x–20   my first marriage, to C· Glover
Ret.   19– 1   C· George Washington Glover
19–19   C· Glover's tender devotion
Pul.   34– 1   was married to C· Glover,
'02.   15–16   My husband, C· Glover,
My. 310–13   His military title of C· came from
330–30   C· Glover's tender devotion

Colonial
Pul.   48–27   * C· and Revolutionary days,

colony
My. 309–20   paid the largest tax in the c·.

color
Mis.   86–19   sensations . . . of form and c·,
87–10   substance of form, light, and c·,
147–18   give the c· of virtue to

color

Mis.	333– 8	basis that black is not a *c·*
Un.	52–22	elaborate in beauty, *c·*, and form,
Rud.	6–14	* He says that "*c·* is in *us*,"
My.	36–26	* all the beauty of *c·* and design,
	68–18	* *c·* scheme for all the auditorium

Colorado and Col.

Pul. 60– 6 * who was a *C·* lawyer
(*see also* **Colorado Springs, Denver**)

Colorado Springs, Col.

My. 19–17 FIRST CHURCH OF . . . *C· S·, C·.*

colored

Mis.	246–13	The cry of the *c·* slave
Ret.	18– 5	light *c·* softly by blossom and
Pul.	58–21	* windows are of *c·* glass,
Peo.	11– 3	rights of the *c·* man
Po.	63–13	light *c·* softly by blossom and

coloring

Mis.	ix–22	*c·* glory of perpetual bloom ;
Pul.	32–21	* *c·* and the elastic bearing of
	48–10	* gorgeous October *c·* of the

colors

Rud. 6– 4 *assuming manifold forms and c·,*

colossal

Mis. 360– 7 unpretentious yet *c·* characters,

Columbia

My. 332–28 * records were transferred to *C·,*

Columbian Liberty Bell

Mis. 304– 4 * to create a *C· L· B·,*

Columbian Liberty Bell Committee

Mis. 304– 1 * *C· L· B· C·,* . . . WASHINGTON, D. C.

Columbus (Avenue)

Pul. 36–20 * from *C·* to Commonwealth Avenue,

Columbus Avenue

569
My. 53–11 * 569 *C· A·,* Boston.
571
Mis. 132–10 571 *C· A·,* BOSTON,
279–11 METAPHYSICAL COLLEGE, 571 *C· A·,*

Pul. 31–24 * at a spacious house on *C· A·.*

Columbus, Ohio

Pul. 89–33 * *Journal, C·, O·.*
My. 204–13 chapter sub-title

columns

My.	vi–19	* principal contributor to its *c·* ;
	331–18	* Through the *c·* of your paper,
	346–19	* in the *c·* of the *New York Herald*,

combat

Mis.	216– 2	your own state of *c·* with error.
	241–15	by constant *c·* and direful struggles,
Pul.	2–19	single-handed to *c·* the foe
Po.	71–12	Injustice to the *c·* sprang ;

combated

My. 94– 6 * concrete and cannot be *c·.*

combating

Mis. 285– 1 *c·* evil only, rather than person.

combination

'02.	16– 6	Wyclif's use of that *c·* of words,
My.	70–25	* it is a *c·* of six organs,

combination pedals

(*see* **organ**)

combinations

Un. 9–15 its *c·*, phenomena, and outcome,

combine

My. 225–29 Mind, Soul, which *c·* as *one*.

combined

Mis.	245– 8	*c·* efforts of the materialistic
	249–21	from the *c·* efforts of
Pul.	43– 1	* Two *c·* choirs — that of
Pan.	2–17	* *c·* forces and laws which
'02.	1–11	*c·* in formidable conspiracy,
My.	127–22	siege of the *c·* centuries,
	308– 2	all the powers of earth *c·*

combines

Mis.	97–16	*c·* faith with understanding,
	217– 1	*c·* in logical sequence,
'01.	26– 9	that *c·* matter with Spirit.

combustible

Pul. 75–26 * the only *c·* material used

come

Mis.	4–14	*c·* to the College and to the
	16– 4	heaven to *c·* down to earth.
	18– 1	baptismals that *c·* from Spirit,
	20– 4	"*C·* unto me, — *Matt.* 11 : 28.
	22–14	they *c·* from God and return to
	26–10	believes that his crops *c·* from the
	34–18	can no more *c·* to those they have

come

Mis.	42–14	shall have *c·* upon the same plane
	55– 6	will *c·* when the student possesses
	59–19	"*C·* now, and let us reason — *Isa.* 1 : 18.
	63–11	*why did Jesus c· to save sinners?*
	70–12	rest from physical agony would *c·*
	70–15	paradise of Spirit would *c·* to Jesus,
	80–30	*c·* to understand the medical system
	83–24	the hour is *c· ; — John* 17 : 1.
	83–26	The hour had *c·* for the avowal of
	96–32	It is Christ *c·* to destroy the
	98–17	*c·* to strengthen and perpetuate our
	99–28	and *c·* up hither."
	107– 6	these *c·* to the rescue of mortals,
	112– 3	not knowing whence they *c·*,
	116–15	tones whence *c·* glad echoes
	120–17	and *c·* more sweetly to our ear
	122– 4	needs be that offenses *c· ; — Matt.* 18 : 7.
	122–18	that good may *c· ! — Rom.* 3 : 8.
	135– 2	*c·* into the ranks !
	136–15	"Wherefore *c·* out — *II Cor.* 6 : 17.
	143– 9	May the kingdom of heaven *c·*
	146–22	that desired to *c·*, into its fold,
	149– 1	*c·* ye to the waters, — *Isa.* 55 : 1.
	149– 1	*c·* ye, buy, and eat ; — *Isa.* 55 : 1.
	149– 2	*c·*, buy wine and milk — *Isa.* 55 : 1.
	163–28	must needs *c·* in C. S.
	166–28	*c·* to be seen as diffusing
	168–16	seems to say, "*C·* and see." — *Rev.* 6 : 1.
	169–11	had *c·* physical rejuvenation.
	174– 7	Let us *c·* into the presence of Him
	174–25	"Thy kingdom *c· ;" — Matt.* 6 : 10.
	176– 2	*c·* in with healing, and peace,
	177– 4	The hour is *c·*.
	179–21	*c·* into the spiritual resurrection
	180– 8	* Has Christ *c·* again on earth?"
	195–11	Son of man is *c· — Matt.* 18 : 11.
	199– 8	*c·* into their rightful heritage,
	208–11	*c·* into sympathy with it,
	211–31	"Thy kingdom *c·." — Matt.* 6 : 10.
	214– 5	"Think not that I am *c·* to — *Matt.* 10 : 34
	214– 6	For I am *c·* to — *Matt.* 10 : 35.
	223– 3	"*C·* not thou into — *Gen.* 49 : 6.
	229–19	*c·* nigh thy dwelling." — *Psal.* 91 : 10.
	251– 4	who have *c·* all the way from
	253–19	*c·*, let us kill him, — *Luke* 20 : 14.
	254–14	*c·*, let us kill him, — *Luke* 20 : 14.
	254–26	will *c·* and destroy — *Mark* 12 : 9
	279– 1	"Offenses will *c· : — Luke* 17 : 1.
	279– 2	through whom they *c·." — Luke* 17 : 1.
	280– 9	You have *c·* to be weighed ;
	281–15	to *c·* out and confess his faith,
	281–28	But, whatever may *c·* to you,
	293– 7	punishing of sin must, will *c·*,
	298– 5	that good may *c· ? — Rom.* 3 : 8.
	299–10	that this query has finally *c·*
	311– 2	*c·* and unite with The Mother Church
	312–14	* has *c·* in recent years,
	332– 8	seedtime has *c·* to enrich earth
	335– 7	shall *c·* in a day — *Matt.* 24 : 50.
	335–29	that good may *c·*,
	339–30	may *c·* too late.
	345–10	* "Let them *c·* ; I cannot change
	350–18	If harm could *c·* from the
	356–13	the harvest hour has *c·* ;
	362–22	revelation must *c·* tc the rescue
	365–30	impostors that *c·* in its name.
	384– 1	poem
	384– 2	*C·*, in the minstrel's lay ;
	384– 6	*C·* Thou ! and now, anew,
	384–18	* "The seasons *c·* and go :
	386– 4	Where mortal yearnings *c·* not,
	386–27	Thy child, shall *c·*
	387–24	*C·* from that Love, divinely near,
	397– 7	And *c·* to me, and tenderly,
	399– 1	"*C·* to my bosom,
	399– 6	"*C·* to this fountain,
Man.	41–21	"Thy kingdom *c· ;" — Matt.* 6 : 10.
	46–16	*c·* to them by reason of their relation
	57– 2	as may properly *c·* before these
	59–18	*c·* to listen to the Sunday sermon
	59–23	*c·* to attend the morning services.
	66–21	authority supposed to *c·* from her
	69– 1	said student shall *c·* under a
Chr.	55–27	I will *c·* in to him, — *Rev.* 3 : 20.
Ret.	22–16	but this triumph will *c· !*
	38–19	and had *c·* to tell me
	38–24	He had *c·* to a standstill
	44–19	I saw that the crisis had *c·*
	49– 8	the hour has *c·* wherein the
	79–19	*c·* short of the wisdom requisite
Un.	1–18	*c·* closer to the true understanding
	9– 7	That time has partially *c·*,
	19–10	how could it have *c·* into the world?
	22–17	Whatever exists must *c·* from God,
	26– 4	From Him *c·* my forms,

come

Un.	41–12	must *c·* to all sooner or later ;
	45–10	egotist must *c·* down and learn,
	58– 7	*c·* down from the cross." — *Mark* 15 : 30.
	59– 1	why did the Messiah *c·*
	59–17	never saw the Saviour *c·* and go,
	60–26	Christ cannot *c·* to mortal and
Pul.	5–17	* "I have *c·* to comfort you."
	9– 1	into the building fund have *c·*
	12– 6	Now is *c·* salvation, — *Rev.* 12 : 10.
	12–13	the devil is *c·* down — *Rev.* 12 : 12.
	18–16	And *c·* to me, and tenderly,
	21–28	It cannot *c·* from any other source.
	22– 7	"Thy kingdom *c·*. — *Matt.* 6 : 10.
	35–28	* a physician who had *c·* into
	40– 3	* wonder how the seasons *c·* and go
	41–29	* hour for the dedication service had *c·*.
	49–11	* has *c·* forth all this beauty !"
	53–18	* salvation in the world to *c·*.
	60–14	* thousands of adherents who had *c·*
Rud.	9–19	and similar effects *c·* from pride,
No.	v–10	"*C·* and drink ;"
	11–13	those who *c·* falsely in its name.
	18–10	physical and . . . *c·* with Science,
	31–25	"*C·* out of him, — *Mark* 9 : 25.
	34–15	pangs which *c·* to one upon whom
	41–18	will never admit such as *c·* to steal
	43– 4	"*C·* unto me, — *Matt.* 11 : 28.
	43–22	Such students *c·* to my College to
	46–10	he that should *c* ?" — *Matt.* 11 : 3.
Pan.	1– 6	winter winds have *c·* and gone ;
'00.	2–23	doom of such workers will *c·*,
	9–11	art thou *c·* hither — *Matt.* 8 : 29.
	15– 2	you have *c* to a sumptuous feast,
	15–18	To-day you have *c·* to Love's feast,
'01.	9–21	art thou *c·* to destroy us? — *Mark* 1 : 24.
	28–30	Has the thought *c·* to Christian Scientists,
'02.	5–23	"Think not that I am *c·* — *Matt.* 5 : 17.
	5–24	am not *c·* to destroy, — *Matt.* 5 : 17.
	10– 6	"Art thou *c·* hither to — *Matt.* 8 : 29.
	12– 1	believes . . . Christ has not yet *c·* ;
	12– 2	believes that Christ is *c·*
	12– 9	the Christian idea that God is *c·*,
	19–16	"*C·* unto me." — *Matt.* 11 : 28.
Hea.	2–17	"*C·* unto me, — *Matt.* 11 : 28.
	6– 3	and so *c·* back to the world?
	9–16	* "the curse causeless cannot *c·*"?
	10–16	when sorrow seems to *c·*,
	16–13	*c·* nearer your hearts
Peo.	13–19	* "Let them *c·* ; I cannot change
Po.	6–19	*C·* from that Love, divinely near,
	12–16	And *c·* to me, and tenderly,
	16– 7	Ambition, *c·* hither !
	10–20	They *c·* with a breath
	22– 2	Thine hour hath *c·* !
	23– 6	*C·* ever o'er thy heart?
	24– 1	*C·* to me, joys of heaven !
	24– 8	*C·* to me, peace on earth !
	24–15	*C·* when the shadows fall,
	page 36	poem
	36– 1	*C·*, in the minstrel's lay ;
	36– 5	*C·* Thou ! and now, anew,
	36–17	* "The seasons *c·* and go :
	41– 1	* *C·*, rest in this bosom,
	49– 6	Where mortal yearnings *c·* not,
	50–13	Thy child, shall *c·*
	53– 1	*C·* to thy bowers, sweet spring,
	53–13	Bid faithful swallows *c·*
	53–17	*C·* at the sad heart's call,
	54– 3	O *c·* to clouds and tears
	73– 2	I *c·* to thee O'er the moonlit sea,
	75– 7	"*C·* to my bosom,
	75–13	"*C·* to this fountain.
My.	3–21	good which has *c·* into his life,
	22–23	* In years to *c·* the moral and
	30–12	* *c·* from far distant points
	34–11	King of glory shall *c·* — *Psal.* 24 : 9.
	36–18	* we are *c·*, in humility, to
	42–17	* blessings which have *c·* into my life
	44–10	* *c·* to individual consciousness ;
	49– 2	* '*C·*' thou with us, and we will
	56– 2	* adequate for years to *c·*.
	62– 6	* Whence did it *c·*?
	63–23	* has *c·* to the present age.
	63–27	* of the thousands who had *c·*,
	66–23	* will *c·* from her beautiful home,
	69– 5	* roof and side walls *c·* together
	72–11	* who *c·* to attend the dedication
	72–20	* Scientists who have *c·* to Boston to
	73–15	* for several days to *c·*,
	93–24	* part it has *c·* to play in the
	93–29	* *c·* in the nature of a revelation.
	116–23	has *c·* from injustice and
	118–24	should *c·* from conscience.
	122–16	another Christmas has *c·* and gone.
	125– 8	You *c·* from feeding your flocks,

come

My.	125– 9	you *c·* with the sling of Israel's
	125–26	hour is *c·* ; the bride (Word) is
	126–14	"*C·* out of her, my people" — *Rev.* 18 : 4.
	126–20	plagues *c·* in one day, — *Rev.* 18 : 8.
	129–13	They *c·* at Love's call.
	132–13	may there *c·* this benediction :
	133– 5	at last *c·* to acknowledge God,
	142– 5	* communicants who *c·* long distances
	153– 7	have *c·* to fulfil the whole law.
	153–29	*C·*, and I will give thee rest,
	155–24	heaven's symphonies that *c·* to
	156–19	may these communicants *c·* with
	163–10	so kindly *c·* to the dedication
	166–14	of shade and shine may *c·* and go,
	170–27	*c·* long distances to kneel with us
	171– 4	*c·* to Zion with songs — *Isa.* 35 : 10.
	171–12	to *c·* to Concord,
	173–13	gifts had *c·* from Christian Scientists
	183–19	day has *c·* when the forest
	183–27	for thy light is *c·*, — *Isa.* 60 : 1.
	191–18	*c·* forth from the tomb of the past,
	219–24	"Think not that I am *c·* to — *Matt.* 5 : 17.
	219–25	I am not *c·* to destroy, — *Matt.* 5 : 17.
	220– 2	Whatever changes *c·* to this century
	221–25	must *c·* through a correct or
	225– 2	*c·* to the surface to pass off,
	229– 3	No mesmerist . . . is fit to *c·* hither.
	229–18	and *c·* after me, — *Luke* 14 : 27.
	232–15	the thief would *c·*, — *Luke* 12 : 39.
	243– 4	*c·* together and form one church.
	244–23	teachers have *c·* so to regard them.
	247–24	Do you *c·* to your little flock
	273–26	lapse and relapse, *c·* and go,
	277–12	that the answer . . . shall *c·* from God
	281– 4	"Thy kingdom *c·*, — *Matt.* 6 : 10.
	288–26	lest a worse thing *c·* — *John* 5 : 14.
	319–17	* not *c·* under the observation of
	324– 7	* *c·* from any one but yourself.
	336– 5	* *c·* to her after her husband's death,
	352– 6	* blessings that have *c·* to us

comeliness

Mis.	302– 8	the form without the *c·*,
My.	42– 2	* depicted its form and *c·*.
	257– 9	*c·* of the divine ideal,

comers

My.	223– 2	no *c·* are received . . . without

comes

Mis.	1–12	new idea that *c·* welling up from
	5–18	Then metaphysics *c·* in, armed with
	9– 2	*c·* through affliction rightly understood,
	10–27	Heaven *c·* down to earth,
	26–29	From this premise *c·* the
	69–30	Now *c·* the question :
	73–29	the spiritualization that *c·* from
	140– 7	good *c·* to Christian Scientists,
	158–10	*c·* the interpretation thereof.
	171–10	When one *c·* to the age with
	178– 1	I have met one who *c·* from
	199– 5	thence *c·* man's ability to annul
	215– 8	*c·* into the intermediate space,
	218–17	Truth *c·* to the rescue of reason
	227– 8	crime *c·* within its jurisdiction.
	231–31	through which the loved one *c·* not,
	246–14	there *c·* another sharp cry of
	276–19	Out of the gloom *c·* the glory
	276–21	the true sense *c·* out,
	287–31	mischief *c·* from attempts to
	290–27	blessedness and blessing *c·*
	335–24	when the hour of trial *c·*
	339– 7	out of defeat *c·* the secret of
	340–28	*c·* out in the darkness to shine
	341–13	*c·* of honesty and humility.
	346–10	whence *c·* the evil?
	394– 8	It *c·* through our tears,
Chr.	53–34	Christ *c·* in gloom ;
Ret.	2–15	*c·* that heart-stirring air,
	81–16	there *c·* an overwhelming sense
Un.	4– 9	that God *c·* to us and pities us ;
	15–13	his destruction *c·* through the
	20– 6	Through . . . evil *c·* into authority :
	27– 1	From various friends *c·* inquiry
	34–10	Here *c·* in the summary of the
	40–22	*c·* through our ignorance of Life,
	56– 5	all suffering *c·* from mind,
	62– 5	that neither *c·* nor goes,
Pul.	13–21	*c·* back to him at last
	26–12	* The great organ *c·* from Detroit.
	48–24	* lawful pride that *c·* with
	69–10	* believing that disease *c·* from
	71– 7	* money *c·* from C. S. believers
	73–23	* but that all *c·* from God.
	82– 3	* she *c·* like the south wind
No.	1– 4	which *c·* to our recognition
	40–25	*c·* with the change to health.

comes

Pan.	12– 3	*c·* from the rejection of evil
'00.	8– 9	so the human character *c·* forth
'01.	1–19	Truth *c·* from a deep sincerity
	10–19	man's salvation *c·* through
Hea.	6–28	The word *devil c·* from
Po.	2– 5	* but *c·* not to the heart.''
	45–10	It *c·* through our tears,
My.	5– 8	C. S. *c·* to reveal man as God's
	12–22	it *c·* not back again.
	54– 3	* inconvenience that *c·* from crowding,
	66– 3	* now *c·* the purchase of the last
	118–17	saving faith *c·* not of a person,
	134–18	Love *c·* to our tears like a
	147– 3	past *c·* forth like a pageant
	196–29	The beauty of holiness *c·*
	208–13	*c·* your dear letter to my waiting
	239–13	*c· into the knowledge of Christ*
	252–28	the impetus *c·* from above
	292– 4	*c·* from God and human faith in

comest

Mis.	326–31	"Wherefore *c·* thou hither?''

cometh

Mis.	37–19	whence *c·* all evil.
	101–11	Now *c·* a third struggle ;
	109–31	and thus, *c·* repentance,
	118–32	*c·* out of the mouth, — *Matt.* 15 : 11.
	122– 5	the offense *c·* !'' — *Matt.* 18 : 7.
	145– 3	But the time *c·* when the
	149–24	that *c·* down from heaven,
	251–16	kingdom of God *c·* — *Luke* 17 : 20.
	254– 7	that *c·* down from heaven,
	286–19	The time *c·*, and now is,
	321–13	"The hour *c·*, — *John* 4 : 23.
	340– 9	that which *c·* from God,
	342–17	"The bridegroom *c·* !'' — *Matt.* 25 : 6.
Ret.	79– 4	nor *c·* this apprehension from
	79–17	Through . . . pride, *c·* no success in
Un.	11–28	then *c·* the harvest,
	22–19	*c·* not from the eternal Spirit,
Pul.	4–25	with it *c·* the full power of being.
	27–13	* "*c·* down from God — *see Rev.* 3 : 12.
No.	34– 9	"The hour *c·*, — *John* 4 : 23.
Pan.	14– 8	bread that *c·* down from heaven,
'00.	15–11	after this Passover *c·* victory,
'01.	12–11	"When the Son of man *c·*, — *Luke* 18 : 8.
'02.	18– 3	wilt know when the thief *c·*.
Hea.	10–18	and joy *c·* with the light.
	16–28	man *c·* unto the Father,
My.	38– 2	* every perfect gift *c·* from above,
	125–27	and lo, the bridegroom *c·* !
	156–21	bread that *c·* down from heaven,
	257–15	*c·* into the world,'' — *John* 1 : 9.
	364–12	save that which *c·* from God.

comet's

Mis.	266–12	is like the *c·* course,

comfort (*see also* comfort's)

Mis.	16– 3	so *c·*, cheer, and bless one,
	118–20	His rod and His staff *c·* you.
	232– 1	God *c·* them all !
	275–15	*c·*, encourage, and bless all
Pul.	5–18	* "I have come to *c·* you.''
	56–15	* brought hope and *c·* to many
	87–16	If it will *c·* you in the least,
'00.	3– 6	no heart his *c·*.
Po.	24–14	Is all I need to *c·* mine.
	32–20	*c·* my soul all the wearisome day,
	78–15	Give to the pleading hearts *c·*
My.	38– 3	* in God is all consolation and *c·*,
	92–29	* for some such *c·* as it promises.
	174– 2	open their doors for the *c·* and
	206–18	words of the Scriptures *c·* you:
	230–13	to *c·* such as mourn,
	292– 9	His rod and His staff *c·* the living
	292–10	may His love shield, . . . and *c·*

comfortable

Mis.	ix– 8	their *c·* fortunes are acquired by
Pul.	58–17	* in its exceedingly *c·* pews.
	58–20	* rather dark, . . . for *c·* reading,
My.	87–15	* these *c·* acquaintances

comfortably

My.	71–23	* and seat them *c·*.
	80–31	* the auditorium was *c·* filled.

comforted

Pul.	50–19	* *c·* and strengthened by them.
My.	41– 7	* blessed and *c·* by divine Love.

Comforter

Mis.	174–31	Divine Science ; the *C·* ;
	189– 6	*C·* that leadeth into all truth.
	195–32	by divine Science, the *C·* ;
Man.	15– 8	Holy Ghost or divine *C·* ;
'01.	9–17	it is the Christ, *C·*,

comforter

Un.	18–15	our *c·* always from outside and above

comforters

Ret.	95–11	* And *c·* are needed much

comforteth

My.	159– 7	Christ rejoiceth and *c·* us.

comforting

Mis.	124–15	*c·* such as mourn,
My.	154–10	*c·* to the dear sick,

comfortless

Mis.	249–24	will never leave me *c·*,

comfort's

Ret.	95– 5	* give thee skill In *c·* art :

comforts

My.	132–31	*c·* such as mourn,
	295– 2	knowing our dear God *c·* such

comical

Mis.	239–22	Her apparent pride . . . was *c·*.

coming

Mis.	81–13	*c· up straightway out of the*
	136–26	members *c·* from a distance
	211–16	cause him to suffer in *c·* to life?
	213–26	when he seeth the wolf *c·*.
	237–30	fear clustered round his *c·*.
	249–25	*c·* nearer in my need,
	276–14	*c·* of our Lord and Christ.
	304– 6	* in the *c·* World's Exposition
	304– 9	* *c·* first to the capital
	322– 5	People *c·* from a distance
	323– 9	working and watching for his *c·*.
	335– 4	delayeth his *c·* ; — *Matt.* 24 : 48.
	343–22	to choke the *c·* clover.
	363–21	brightness of His *c·*.
Man.	36– 5	*c·* from pupils of loyal students
Chr.	55– 6	The hour is *c·*, — *John* 5 : 25.
Un.	13– 3	*c·* at human call ;
	28–12	going in or *c·* out.
	58– 8	*c·* down from the cross,
	61– 2	*C·* and going belong to
Pul.	44–27	* and it kept *c·* until the custodian
	58– 3	* *C·* to Boston about 1880,
	60– 6	* before *c·* into this work,
	82– 9	* could stop the *c·* of spring.
'00.	6–29	the second *c·* of Christ.
	7–23	we believe in the second *c·*,
'01.	19–10	because of your often *c·*
	30– 5	bequeathing . . . to the *c·* centuries.
Po.	47– 1	Are the dear days ever *c·* again,
My.	17– 9	"To whom *c·*, as unto — *I Pet.* 2 : 4.
	20– 8	The holidays are *c·*,
	25– 3	* special effort during the *c·* week
	30– 2	* either *c·* from a service or
	42– 6	* President for the *c·* year,
	73–26	* chapter sub-title
	87– 4	* multitudes going and *c·*.
	99–18	* *c·* from all parts of the world,
	100– 8	* *c·* from all, or nearly all, parts
	223–20	All inquiries, *c·* directly or
	225–17	The *c·* of Christ's kingdom on earth
	241–25	* after *c·* to the light of Truth,
	262–26	in commemoration of Christ's *c·*.
	266– 4	dangers confronting the *c·* century
	307–19	referred to the *c·* anew of Truth,

command

another

Ret.	88– 4	Another *c·* of the Christ,

Christ's

Mis.	194– 9	permanence of Christ's *c·*
	311–21	since by breaking Christ's *c·*,
Ret.	71–17	transgressing Christ's *c·*.
'01.	12–15	Christ's *c·* to heal in all ages,
My.	227–26	side by side with Christ's *c·*,
	300–24	according to Christ's *c·*,

divine

Mis.	10–14	If they mistake the divine *c·*,
Ret.	71– 5	obedient to the divine *c·*,
My.	224– 6	the human need, the divine *c·*,
	351–11	is indeed a divine *c·*,

first

Mis.	347– 1	this first *c·* of Solomon,

full

Mis.	193–25	no one is following his full *c·*

God's

Mis.	223– 5	according to God's *c·*.
	298–17	he did not say that it was God's *c·* ;
Peo.	7–18	* Waiting the hour when at God's *c·*

His

Mis.	153– 9	At His *c·*, the rock became

his

Mis.	282–15	metaphysical tone of his *c·*,

Jesus'

Ret.	35–24	perpetuity of Jesus' *c·*,
	45–20	following Jesus' *c·*,

command

Lord's
Ret. 88–25   The Lord's *c·* means this,
Master's
My. 233– 2   spirit of our Master's *c·*?
obedience to the
My. 43–15   * In obedience to the *c·*
of Christ
Mis. 318–18   and so fulfil the *c·* of Christ.
Ret. 47–22   and so fulfil the *c·* of Christ.
Pul. 29–17   * dealt directly with the *c·* of Christ
'00.   5–21   to obey . . . the *c·* of Christ :
of the Master
My. 128–20   following the *c·* of the Master,
prime
Ret. 88– 5   his prime *c·*, was that his
proper
Mis. 138–26   God will give . . . the proper *c·*,
remains
Mis. 23–12   and the *c·* remains,
sacred
'02.   5–29   sacred *c·*, "Thou shalt have — *Exod.* 20 : 3.
second
Mis. 158–15   second *c·*, to drop the use of notes,
this
Ret. 88–10   significance of this *c·*,
My. 156–18   In obedience to this *c·*
transverse
Mis. 348–14   Solomon's transverse *c·* :

Mis. xii– 3   *c·* and countermand ;
56–25   *Why did God c·*,
214–13   the *c·*, "Put up thy sword." — *John* 18 : 11.
227–32   *c·* of almighty wisdom ;
Pul. 14–24   Christ will *c·* the wave.
My. 122–13   such as to *c·* respect everywhere.
325–14   * *C·* me at any time, in any way,

commanded

Ret. 4–10   *c·* a broad picturesque view of
87–16   as the Master *c·*.
Un. 11– 6   he *c·* the winds,
14–12   are *c·* to *grow in grace.*
'01.   19–17   *c·* even the winds and waves,
'02.   9– 5   Jesus *c·*, "Follow me ; — *Matt.* 8 : 22.
My. 106–31   *c·* his followers to do likewise.

commanding

'00.   11–15   tones intricate, profound, *c·*.

Commandment

Mis. 292– 1   chapter sub-title
'02.   page 1 heading
(*see also* **First Commandment**)

commandment

Mis. 28–24   Then the *c·* means,
73–13   and a *c·* to the wise.
292– 4   "A new *c·* I give — *John* 13 : 34.
292– 7   Love had a new *c·* even for him.
Man. 43–18   more serious attention to the *c·*
Ret. 69–30   and keeping His *c·*?' "
'02.   4–14   new *c·* in the gospel of peace,
5–12   subordinated to this *c·*,
7–25   "A new *c·* I give — *John* 13 : 34.
7–27   special attention to his *new c·*.
8– 9   *c·* of Christ Jesus shows what
8–14   between the old and the new *c·*,
17–10   obey both the old and the new *c·*,
My. 64–17   * how to obey this *c·* and rule,
109– 8   *c·*, "Love thy neighbor — *Lev.* 19 : 18.
153–16   the great and first *c·*,
187–12   end of the *c·* is charity — *I Tim.* 1 : 5.
187–27   would glorify in a new *c·*
364– 7   includes and inculcates the *c·*,

Commandments

(*see* **Ten Commandments**)

commandments

Mis. 67–15   Obedience to these *c·* is
118–16   "Keep My *c·*." — *John* 15 : 10.
123–25   love God, and keep His *c·*,
268– 8   hearkened to My *c·* ! — *Isa.* 48 : 18.
311– 1   love God and keep His *c·*,
318–11   love God and keep His *c·*.
Ret. 31–18   which breaketh the divine *c·*.
No. 8–17   it will bow down to the *c·*
'00.   6–20   licentious, and breaks God's *c·*,
'01.   32–20   love God and keep His *c·*
'02.   4–22   briefly consider these two *c·*
17– 3   keep my *c·*." — *John* 14 : 15.
My. 3– 8   they that do His *c·*, — *Rev.* 22 : 14.
130–26   to him who keeps the *c·*.
160–21   or in disobeying the *c·*
268–14   Two *c·* of the Hebrew Decalogue,

commands

Mis. 18–11   These *c·* of infinite wisdom,
193–24   who follow the *c·* of our Lord
301–30   the *c·* of our hillside Priest,

commands

Mis. 358–29   awaiting, with staff in hand, God's *c·*.
Un. 3–10   those who have obeyed God's *c·*,
38–21   no divine fiat *c·* us to believe
49–26   *c·* mortals to shun or relinquish,
No. 14–21   are obeying these *c·* ;
41–20   have slumbered over Christ's *c·*,
Pan. 12–12   inspired Scriptural *c·* be fulfilled.
'01.   17–14   *c·* the respect of our best thinkers.
'02.   8– 3   *c·* man to love as Jesus loved.
My. 23– 8   * so long as we follow His *c·*.
47–27   * founded on the *c·* of Jesus :
52–17   * to establish these our Master's *c·*
118–13   spiritual sense demands and *c·* us ;
131– 4   humbles, exalts, and *c·* a man,
226–12   *c·* the waves and the winds,

commemorate

Mis. 120–28   whose character we to-day *c·*,
159–18   *c·*, . . . the man of God,
251–12   To-day we *c·* not only
Man. 17–10   *c·* the word and works of our Master,
Ret. 44– 1   *c·* the words and works of our Master,
'01.   1–10   *c·* in unity the life of our Lord,
My. 46 10   *c·* the word and works of our Master,
131– 8   life that we *c·* and would emulate,
158–26   temple which to-day you *c·*,
262–13   and so *c·* the entrance into

commemorated

Mis. 306– 8   * names to be *c·*.
My. 235–29   in deed or in word

commemorates

Mis. 166– 3   *c·* the earthly life of a martyr ;
My. 262– 6   *c·* the birth of a human, . . . babe

commemorating

No. 34– 8   *c·* his death with a material rite.

commemoration

Mis. 91– 1   in *c·* of the Christ.
Pul. 64–25   * in *c·* of the Founder of that sect,
My. 188– 8   Your feast days will not be in *c·*,
235–26   meaningless *c·* of birthdays,
262–25   in *c·* of Christ's coming.

commence

Mis. 15–10   Time may *c·*, but it cannot complete,
51–25   * reign of Mind *c·* on earth,
141–26   Delay not longer to *c·* building
198– 5   one must *c·* by turning away from
239– 5   about to *c·* a large class in C. S.
314–24   *c·* by announcing the full title of
'00.   12– 7   *c·* with the church of Ephesus.
'01.   16–27   Shall the hope for our race *c·* with

commenced

Mis. 380–15   and *c·* teaching.
Ret. 15–16   accepted the invitation and *c·* work.
My. 12– 2   * work should be *c·* as soon as
14–26   * building operations have been *c·*,
54– 8   * one hour before the service *c·*,

commences

Mis. 327–15   The journey *c·*.

commencing

Mis. 32–13   *c·* at the thirty-third verse,
Man. 32–12   before *c·* to read from this book,
Un. 10–23   It is like *c·* with the minus sign,
My. 11–28   * date for *c·* building operations,
12–12   * the date of *c·* building work,

commend

Mis. 97–22   I *c·* the Icelandic translation :
Ret. 83– 4   *c·* students and patients to
85– 7   *c·* itself as useful to the Cause

commendable

Mis. 297–10   Smart journalism . . . is *c·* ;

commendation

Mis. 313– 1   chapter sub-title

commending

My. 124– 3   *c·* ourselves to every — *II Cor.* 4 : 2.

commends

'00.   13– 3   *c·* the church at Ephesus

commensurate

Mis. 261– 2   suffering is *c·* with evil,
My. 288–22   suffering is *c·* with sin ;

comment

Mis. 295– 2   which deserve and elicit brief *c·*.
No. 44– 2   incapacitates him for correct *c·*.
'01.   11–18   read each Sunday without *c·*
'02.   9–27   Is it cause for bitter *c·*
My. v– 7   * wonderment and frequent *c·*,
122–14   It called forth flattering *c·*
209– 1   chapter sub-title
232–10   *C·* ON AN EDITORIAL WHICH APPEARED

commentaries

No. 15– 8   *c·* are employed to explain

commentators

My. 95–11 * the press gallery of c·.

comments

Mis. 32–31 in regard to some clergyman's c·
Ret. 27– 1 I wrote . . . c· on the Scriptures,
27– 5 If these notes and c·,
27–10 These early c· are valuable
My. 99– 1 * contemporary, the *Boston Times*, c·,

commerce

'02. 4– 1 Competition in c·, deceit in councils,
My. 265–28 agriculture, manufacture, c·,

Commercial

Pul. 89–17 * C·, Louisville, Ky.

commercial

My. 91– 6 * in this so-called c· age.

commingle

Mis. 333– 3 The supposition is, that . . . c·,
'00. 4– 5 This precedent that would c·

commingled

Mis. ix–13 sigh, and smile c·,
379–16 they c· error with truth,

commingling

My. 189–13 c· in one righteous prayer,

commiserate

Mis. 80–24 c· the lot of regular doctors,

commission

Mis. 87–19 I never c· any one to
117–18 to carry out a divine c·

commissioned

Pul. 81–24 * c· to complete all that the

commissions

Mis. 18–32 or that those whom He c·

commit

Mis. 19–19 most fearful sin that mortals can c·.
52–19 if . . . why not c· suicide?
61–13 image of God, does not c· sin.'
67– 5 shalt not c· adultery ;" — *Exod.* 20 : 14.
119– 7 unwary man to c· a crime,
130– 7 to be wronged, than to c· wrong?
130–25 greatest sin that one can c·
157–22 "C· thy way unto — *Psal.* 37 : 5.
261–10 suffer from the wrong they c·,
268–32 "C· thy way unto — *Psal.* 37 : 5.
335–17 to murder, steal, c· adultery,
Man. 79– 8 such business as . . . shall c· to it.
'01. 14– 2 To assume . . . and yet c· sin,
'02. 19–11 c· an offense against me that I
My. 170–23 C· thy way unto — *Psal.* 37 : 5.
252– 9 the wrong you may c· must,
268–15 shalt not c· adultery" — *Exod.* 20 : 14.
334–20 "To assume . . . and yet c· sin,

commits

Mis. 61–14 * *What c· theft? Or who does murder?*
113–16 c· his way to God,
212– 3 betrays you, and c· suicide.
269– 4 c· his moral sense to a dungeon.
'01. 16–11 outdoes itself and c· suicide.

committal

My. 211–16 c· of acts foreign to the

committed

Mis. 163–15 c· to the providence of God.
222–22 The crimes c· under this
Man. 54– 3 finds that the offense has been c·,
Ret. 20–28 family to whose care he was c·
Pul. 7–18 c· in the name of religion.
20–12 c· to the providence of God,
'01. 20–23 crimes c· under this new-old
My. 136–24 c· the hard earnings of my pen,
156– 9 have c· unto Him — *II Tim.* 1 : 12.
196–19 c· himself to Him that — *I Pet.* 2 : 23.
228–29 have c· unto him — *II Tim.* 1 : 12.
231–16 They are c· to the waste-basket
248–25 I have largely c· to you,
301–20 c· to insane asylums

Committee and committee

Mis. 114– 2 C· on Sunday School Lessons
271–23 the Publishing C· of
305– 1 * c· of women representing
Man. 17–14 Mrs. Eddy was appointed on the c·
27– 6 action to be taken by said C·
77– 7 submit them all to said c·
77– 7 This c· shall decide thereupon
79– 9 While the members of this C· are
98– 5 which has been forwarded to this C·
98– 9 C· shall immediately apply for aid
99–12 in selecting this C·,
99–18 C· for the counties in which London,
100– 1 church employing said C·.
100–19 another C· to fill the vacancy ;
100–22 name the C· if it so desires,
100–23 any C· so named by the Board

Committee and committee

Man. 102– 5 this c· shall not be dissolved until
102– 7 This c· shall elect, dismiss, or
My. 49–13 * Mrs. Eddy was appointed on the c·
50–31 * business c· met after the services
53–25 * annual report of the business c·
62–28 * by the members of the business c·,
83– 6 * members of the local arrangement c·
141–14 * Alfred Farlow of the publication c·
173–29 chairman of the prudential c·
173–30 to his colaborers on said c·
242–18 publication c· work, reading-room work,
282–19 International Conciliation C·,
333– 3 * the C. S. publication c·.
363–10 * By the C·.
(see also **Building Committee, Publication Committee, State Committee**)

Committee on Bible Lessons

Man. 104–13 the C· on B· L·, and the Board

Committee on Business

Man. 79– 1 C· on B·.
79– 3 elect annually a C· on B·,
98–10 apply for aid to the C· on B·.

Committee on Finance

Man. 76–16 There shall be a C· cn F·,
77–25 C· on F· shall visit the
78–25 Board of Directors and the C· on F·,

Committee on Publication

Man. 26– 3 manager of the general C· on P·
27– 4 manager of the general C· on P·
29– 2 the failure of the C· on P·
78–12 the manager of the C· on P·
79– 7 C· on P· shall commit to it
97– 1 heading
97– 4 C· on P·, which shall consist of
97–16 duty of the C· on P· to correct
98– 1 C· on P· shall be responsible for
98– 6 the correction by the C· on P·
98–11 the C· on P· shall read
98–17 duty of the C· on P· to have published
98–22 under the direction of this C· on P·.
99– 1 appoint a C· on P· to serve
99– 9 appoint a C· on P·
99–13 can appoint a C· on P·
99–16 C· on P· is elected only by the
100– 4 candidate for its C· on P·,
100– 7 special request to any C· on P·,
100– 9 If the C· on P· neglects to
100–18 to remove its C· on P·
100–26 not obtainable for C· on P·,
101– 3 manager of the general C· on P·

Committees and committees

Man. 56–16 reports of Treasure, Clerk, and C·,
My. 208–23 chapter sub-title
208–24 The C· :
208–25 God bless the courageous, . . . c·

Committees on Publication

Man. 65–13 members of the C· on P·,
82– 4 The C· on P· are in no manner
97– 7 manager of the C· on P·
98–21 The State C· on P·
99–22 District Manager of the C· on P·
99–24 C· on P· shall consist of men

committing

Mis. 53– 3 C· suicide to dodge the question
115– 1 is c· an offense against God
221–31 a crime that he himself is c·,
331– 3 c· their way unto Him who
Rud. 16–13 some impostors are c· this error.
My. 130– 5 This hidden method of c· crime

commodious

My. 46– 1 * in c· foyer and broad stairways,
157–11 * c· and beautiful church home

common

Mis. 11–16 in accordance with c· law,
18–18 children of one c· Parent,
26–26 in the c· version of Hebrews
40–27 those elements of evil too c·
49–21 the c· belief in the opposite of
78–21 this abuse, has become too c· :
98–15 the progress of our c· Cause
125–24 Apart from the c· walks of mankind,
138–11 the guidance of our c· Father
145–19 may melt into one, and c· dust,
155–26 to Him as our c· Parent,
201–22 beyond the c· apprehension of
202– 6 * beyond the walks of c· life,
219–14 In c· parlance, one person feels
228–28 C· consent is contagious,
247–24 seems, to the c· estimate, solid
263–18 working assiduously for our c· Cause,
274–20 outrages humanity, breaks c· law,
285–27, 28 c· law, c· sense, and c· honesty,
300– 7 in c· parlance, it is an *ignorant*

common

Mis.	348–22	*Natrum muriaticum* (*c·* salt).
	357–10	beyond the walks of *c·* life,
	365–17	form the *c·* want,
	365–28	is held back by the *c·* ignorance
	371– 9	guidance of our *c·* Father,
Ret.	49–25	uniting them in one *c·* brotherhood.
	75–25	no warrant in *c·* law and
Un.	28–13	The *c·* hypotheses about souls
Pul.	23–13	* each having the *c·* identity of
	39– 1	* all meet on *c·* ground in the
	85–27	* in the Cause of their *c·* faith.
No.	1– 1	*c·* sentiment of regard for the
	3–25	so *c·* it is becoming odious
	11–12	*c·* ignorance of what it is
	18–22	health and . . . are the *c·* wants ;
	20–20	*c·* idolatry of man-worship.
'02.	14–16	so counter to the *c·* convictions of
My.	165–24	a relapse into the *c·* hope.
	168– 4	with the demand of our *c·* Christ,
	189– 6	in the *c·* walks of life,
	220– 3	safely submit . . . to *c·* justice,
	226– 1	not be written or used as a *c·* noun
	226– 6	termed in *c·* speech the principle of
	247– 4	by the *c·* consent of the governed,
	254–25	by the *c·* consent of the governed,
	262–24	ritual of our *c·* Christmas
	300–21	are *c·* to his church,
	316–17	in behalf of *c·* justice and truth
	(*see also* sense)	

commonly

Mis.	75–29	*c·* accepted view is that *soul*
	81–10	*c· accepted teachings of the day*,
	280–13	As we *c·* think,
Ret.	91– 7	*c·* known as the Sermon on the Mount,
Un.	15–16	God is *c·* called the *sinless*,
	32– 7	By matter is *c·* meant mind,

commonplace

Mis.	142–24	send my answer in a *c·* letter.
	379– 7	The composition was *c·*,

Commonwealth and Huntington Avenues

Pul.	24– 4	* between *C·* and *H· A·*.

Commonwealth Avenue

No. 385

Man.	30–15	No. 385 *C· A·*, Boston.

Pul.	36–21	* removed from Columbus to *C· A·*,
My.	325– 7	* your house on *C· A·*,

commotion

Ret.	79–19	quicksands of worldly *c·*,
My.	121– 5	*c·* of the season's holidays.

commune

Pan.	14– 5	*c·* at the table of our Lord
My.	36– 9	* assembled at this sacred time to *c·*

communicants

'00.	1–12	sixteen thousand *c·* in unity,
'01.	2–29	over twenty-one thousand . . . *c·*
	31–13	*c·* of my large church,
'02.	1– 4	our church *c·* constantly increase
	12–23	a privilege to acquaint *c·* with
My.	7– 6	a privilege to acquaint *c·* with
	90–24	* tremendous outpouring of eager *c·*
	91–12	* Its *c·* are cheerful
	141–25	forty-eight thousand *c·*,
	142– 5	* *c·* who come long distances
	142–15	communion of branch church *c·*
	148–17	membership of seventy-four *c·*,
	156–18	In obedience to . . . may these *c·*
	171–11	invite all my church *c·*
	175– 3	thirty-six thousand *c·*,

communicate

Mis.	34–15	If the departed were to *c·* with us,
	42–16	then we shall be able to *c·* with
	60–20	or for one who sleeps to *c·* with
My.	203– 3	I have nothing new to *c·* ;

communicates

Ret.	83–15	*c·*, . . . his misconception of Truth,

communicating

Mis.	60–18	reveals the impossibility of . . . *c·*,
'02.	10–28	like sentencing a man for *c·* with

communication

Mis.	132–12	In your *c·* to *Zion's Herald*,
Man.	65–26	*c·* from the Pastor Emeritus
	67– 7	*c·* from the Pastor Emeritus
Pul.	38–21	* no possibility of *c·*.
My.	207– 3	Your *c·* is gratefully received.
	272–24	* will be interested in this *c·*
	329–25	* give your readers the following *c·*.

communications

Mis.	34–23	called "*c·* from spirits,"
Man.	46–14	all private *c·* made to them
	65–25	Understanding *C·*.

communications

Man.	66– 6	Interpreting *C·*.
	66– 9	*c·* of the Pastor Emeritus
	67– 6	Private *C·*.
Hea.	5–13	* trustworthiness of the *c·*,

communing

Mis.	171–14	This does not mean *c·* with spirits
My.	154–27	*C·* heart with heart,
	154–30	Such *c·* uplifts man's being ;

Communion and communion (noun)

1898

Pan.	1– 3	heading

January 2, 1898

My.	121– 1	chapter sub-title

June 4, 1899

My.	124– 5	chapter sub-title

1904

My.	15–11	chapter sub-title

Mis.	60–13	*deny the possibility of c· with*
	90–22	*administer the c·*,
	90–24	*shall . . . receive the c·?*
	90–30	*c·* which . . . Scientists celebrate
	149–25	whose *c·* is fellowship with saints
	282–18	person with whom you hold *c·*
	333–22	"What *c·* hath light with— *II Cor.* 6 : 14.
	344– 1	chapter sub-title
Man.	61– 7	*C·*.
	61– 8	No more *C·*.
	61–11	*C·* of Branch Churches.
	61–12	*C·* shall be observed in the
	73–22	No Close *C·*.
Ret.	15– 3	he received me into their *c·*,
	18–21	sacred *c·* with home's magic spell !
Pul.	30–12	* *c·*, which is not celebrated by
'01.	1– 6	Our first *c·* in the new century
	1–16	human in *c·* with the Divine,
Hea.	2– 3	calm and steadfast *c·* with God ;
Po.	64–14	sacred *c·* with home's magic spell !
My.	19–10	*c·* of the Holy Ghost,— *II Cor.* 13 : 14.
	20–24	* at the *c·* and annual meeting
	25–19	at our annual *c·*
	26– 5	* on the date of the annual *c·*,
	26 17	This *c·* and dedication include
	29– 4	* kneeling in silent *c·* ;
	32– 3	* after five minutes of silent *c·*
	32–29	* After the reading . . . silent *c·*,
	38–24	* than the silent *c·*.
	54–13	* *c·* was held at Odd Fellows Hall,
	61– 8	* *c·* would likely be postponed
	63–11	* Our annual *c·* and the dedication
	78–19	* congregation knelt in silent *c·*,
	79– 2	* kneeling for silent *c·*
	139–25	material to the spiritual *c·* ;
	140–11	* chapter sub-title
	140–20	Relinquishing a material form of *c·*
	140–25	Dropping the *c·* of The Mother Church
	141–29	*c·* universal and divine.
	149 15	*c·* of branch church communicants
	154–26	embodied in a visible *c·*,
	170–28	to kneel with us . . . in blest *c·*
	171–12	communicants who attend this *c·*,
	173–16	invite those who attend the *c·*

Communion and communion (adj.)

Mis.	120–26	chapter sub-title
	314–28	observed at the *C·* service ;
	398–21	poem
Man.	40–20	On *C·* day the Church Tenets
	61–10	shall observe no more *C·* seasons,
'02.	4– 8	pray at this *C·* season for
Po.	page 75	poem
My.	5–24	memorable dedication and *c·* season,
	27– 6	our annual meeting and *c·* service,
	29– 3	* chapter sub-title
	56–32	* Our *c·* services and annual meetings
	140–13	* dropping the annual *c·* service
	141– 2	* chapter sub-title
	141– 3	* general *c·* service of the
	141–10	* not . . . to attend the *c·* seasons
	141–16	* to abolish its famous *c·* seasons.
	141–17	* *c·* season of the Boston church
	141–26	branch churches continue their *c·*
	141–27	no more *c·* season in The
	142–11	abolishing the *c·* season of The
	142–14	The Mother Church *c·* season

Communion Day

Mis.	315– 5	on the Sunday following *C· D·*.

Communion Doxology

My.	33– 1	* Singing the *C· D·*.

Communion Hymn

My.	31– 1	* first the "*C· H·*,"
	32–24	* Solo, "*C· H·*,"
	(*see also* Appendix A)	

communions
  My.   91– 4   * did not find in other *c·*.
Communion Sabbath
  My.   50– 1   * *C· S·* was held at the home of
       50–14   * for deliberation before *C· S·*
       50–23   * church celebrated her *C· S·*
Communion Services
  in Branch Churches
  Man. 125– 1   heading
Communion Sunday
  Mis. 314–32   first Sunday of . . . except *C· S·*,
  02.   12–27   their presence on *C· S·*.
  My.   7–11   their presence on *C· S·*.
       50–19   * *C. S.*, . . . brought fresh courage
communities
  My.   95– 7   * intelligence of many *c·*
community
  Mis.   43–31   the health of the *c·*.
       115–11   ignorance of the *c·* on this subject
       271–26   * "To benefit the *c·*,
  No.   3–21   to be safe members of the *c·*.
  '01.   31–16   individual and the *c·*.
  My.   94–10   * growth of the sect in every *c·*
       362–17   * Cause of C. S. in this *c·*,
compact
  Mis.   91–10   The real Christian *c·* is love for
       290– 1   *c·* of two hearts.
  Ret.   47– 3   wars with Love's spiritual *c·*,
compacts
  Mis. 289–13   agreements to certain *c·* :
companion
  Pul.   13–21   has made his bosom *c·*,
  My. 124–24   time-table, log, traveller's *c·*,
       130–28   used as a *c·* to the Bible
companionless
  Po.   35–13   in the cringing crowd *C· !*
companions
  My. 335–10   * beloved by his brothers and *c·*,
company
  Mis. 153–12   great was the *c·* of — *Psal.* 68 : 11.
       272–21   * such as any stock *c·* may obtain
       324–21   he seeks to leave the odious *c·*
       378– 9   in *c·* with several other patients,
  Pul.   66–26   * to supplant those in *c·* with
  '00.   8– 7   be careful of your *c·*.
  '01.   12– 9   only . . . would be seen in such *c·*."
  My.   46–29   * innumerable *c·* of angels, — *Heb.* 12 : 22.
comparative
  Rud.   3– 2   Hence their *c·* acquiescence
  '01.   17–21   *c·* ease of healing
comparatively
  Pul.   67–21   * have strong churches, *c·*,
  '00.   9– 9   but few, *c·*, see it ;
  My.   29–22   * A *c·* new religion
       85– 5   * it was *c·* unknown ;
       271– 8   of *c·* little importance
compare
  Man. 109–14   *c·* them with the forms here given,
  No.   41–14   to *c·* mortal lives with this model
  '01.   21–18   or to *c·* its literature.
  My. 107– 3   *C·* the lives of its professors with
       164–14   *c·* the beginning of C. S.
compared
  Mis.   67– 9   *c·* with his rights of mind and
       239–22   her dividend, when *c·* with
       317–15   *c·* with the whole of the Scriptures
  No.   22–11   *C·* with the inspired wisdom
  Po.   34–16   Blessed *c·* with me thou art
  My.   96– 8   * in no sense, save one, be *c·* with
comparing
  Mis. 382– 8   *c·* those with the joy of
  My. 127–11   *C·* our scientific system of
       197–15   *C·* such students with those
comparison
  Mis. 102–14   admits of no degrees of *c·*.
       294–24   chapter sub-title
  Man.   41– 3   Careless *c·* or irreverent reference
  My.   92–19   * give a feeble impression in *c·* with
       96–15   * *c·* with other creeds.
       123– 2   gifts to me are beyond *c·*
       127– 9   On *c·*, it will be found that C. S.
       238– 5   *c·* between the effects produced by
comparisons
  Mis. 267–15   * *C· are odorous.* — SHAKESPEARE.
  My. 338–22   his *c·* and ready humor.
compass
  Ret.   70–15   No person can *c·* or fulfil the
  Un.   58–16   test the full *c·* of human woe,
  Pul.   26–13   * It is of vast *c·*,
       60–22   * It is of three-manual *c·*,

compass
  Pul.   60–23   * pedal *c·*, C. C. C. to F. 30.
  Hea.   4– 6   the *c·* of infinite Life,
  Po.   18–10   higher he soareth to *c·* his rest,
       (*see also* **organ**)
compassed
  '02.   14–15   *c·* on any other foundation,
compassion
  My.   39–26   * Our hearts were thrilled by her *c·*,
compassionate
  Ret.   25–10   *c·*, helpful, and spiritual.
  Pan.   15– 3   as she has been *c·* in peace.
  '02.   18–13   Jesus was *c·*, true,
  My.   37– 5   * incense of gratitude and *c·* love
compatible
  Mis. 289–18   *c·* with home and heaven.
compel
  Mis. 197–20   *c·* us to pattern after both ;
compelled
  Ret.   20–22   *c·* to ask for a bill of divorce,
  Un.   50–13   though we are *c·* to use the phrase
  Pul.   64–11   * *c·* to refuse further contributions,
  No.   42– 6   mortals are not *c·* to have other gods
  My. 160–16   until *c·* to glance at it.
compelling
  Ret.   80–24   under his *c·* rod.
compels
  Mis.   85–27   pain *c·* human consciousness to
       200–23   *c·* me to seek the remedy for it,
       209–15   *c·* mortals to learn that
       265–32   until suffering *c·* the downfall of
  My.   3–21   *c·* him to think genuine,
       250–17   nor *c·* the branch churches to
       308–13   *c·* me . . . to speak.
compensate
  Mis.   65–27   is inadequate to *c·* for the
       111–12   *c·* loss, and gain a higher sense
       322–25   to *c·* your zealous affection for
  Ret.   58– 4   trying to *c·* for the absence of
  My. 212–26   tries to *c·* himself for his own loss
compensated
  '00.   11–12   answered and *c·* by divine love.
compensates
  My.   21–15   * divine Love more than *c·* for
compensateth
  Mis. 363– 8   *c·* vanity with nothingness.
compensation
  Mis.   38–10   should expect no *c·*.
compete
  Ret.   31– 3   Nothing can *c·* with C. S.,
       82–25   *c·* with ecclesiastical fellowship
competent
  Man.   77– 2   by an honest, *c·* accountant.
competition
  '02.   4– 1   *C·* in commerce, deceit in councils,
  My. 266– 7   insufficient freedom of honest *c·* ;
competitor
  Mis.   22–19   It hath no peer, no *c·*,
compilation
  Mis. 300– 6   reading it publicly as your own *c·*,
  Pul.   28–20   * *c·* called the "C. S. Hymnal,"
compilations
  No.   3–26   such *c·*, instead of possessing
compilers
  Ret.   91– 8   *c·* and translators of the Bible,
compiling
  Mis. xi–27   In *c·* this work, I have tried
       300– 3   *c·* them in connection with
       301– 1   *c·* and delivering that sermon
complacently
  Mis. 222–13   listen *c·* to audible falsehoods
  '01.   20–13   People may listen *c·* to the
complain
  Man.   29–10   shall *c·* thereof to the Clerk
  Pul.   56–20   * And of the just effect *c·* ;
complainant
  Mis. 381–18   ordered that the *c·* (Mrs. Eddy)
  Man.   29– 6   the name of the *c·*.
complained
  Man.   52–10   to the member *c·* of
  '01.   9–11   the mysticism *c·* of
complaining
  Mis. 236–10   the child *c·* of his parents
complains
  '01.   11–28   St. Paul *c·* of him whose god is

complaint
Man. 29–10 and the c· be found valid,
52– 4 A c· against a member of
52– 6 and if this c· is not for
53–1, 2 upon her c· or the c· of a member
53–10 upon her c· that member should
53–18 No member shall enter a c· of
54– 1 upon c· by another member,
54–12 on c· of Mrs. Eddy
54–13 this c· being found valid,
68– 8 upon Mrs. Eddy's c· thereof
'02. 19–19 The thought of it stills c· ;

complaints
Mis. 6– 4 but little time free from c·
Man. 50–12 C·.
51–25 c· against Church members ;
82–15 for the examination of c·.
No. 9–14 repeated c· and murmurings
My. 223– 4 that I neither listen to c·,
354– 2 In view of c· from the field,

complete
Mis. 15–18 it cannot c·, the new birth :
35–11 most concise, yet c·, summary
50–10 a c· textbook of C. S. ;
75–17 used and make c· sense.
137– 4 all of which are c·.
393–16 From the shores afar, c·.
Ret. 37– 2 the c· statement of C. S.,
60– 3 Science reveals Life as a c· sphere,
78– 6 is c· in S. and H. ;
Un. 43– 9 c· triumph over death,
Pul. 73–27 * c· and yet concise idea
81–25 * commissioned to c· all that the
No. 37– 3 nature and manhood were forever c·,
'00. 14– 7 signifies a c· time or number
Po. 51–21 From the shores afar, c·.
My. 14–14 * entire amount required to c·
14–24 * the building fund is not c·,
22–12 * in order to c· this great work,
23–14 * Amount necessary to c· the sum
29–17 * c· unanimity of thought
58– 5 * no more funds are needed to c·
66–21 * spacious and elegant edifice c·
81– 5 * so c· this self-abnegation,
113– 9 truth of the c· system of C. S.
158–26 to-morrow c·, and thereafter dedicate
194–11 a c· subordination of self.
212–13 to c· the sum total of sin.
221–13 a more c·, natural, and divine

completed
Man. 102– 7 new church edifice is c·.
Pul. 45–15 * that it could not be c· before
70–10 * very recently saw c· in Boston,
84–24 * and that our temple is c·
86– 1 * the new church . . . just c·,
My. 20 28 * should he c· as early as possible,
40– 1 * this c· extension of
61– 7 * for the building to be c·
72–27 * work was actually c·
76–31 * structure, which is now c·,
83–26 * building itself has been c·.
86–14 * before the actual work was c·,
148–11 having c· its organization
171–10 church is so nearly c·
311–30 * c· her education when she

completely
Pul. 71–20 * Mrs. Eddy has resigned herself c· to
My. v–17 * reforming the sinner . . . c·,
59–31 * or so c· vindicated.
127–13 divine metaphysics c· overshadows
210– 8 c· shielded from the attacks of

completeness
No. 10– 5 of the c· of Science.

completing
My. 24–31 * appropriate time for c· the
197–11 c· and dedicating your church

completion
Mis. 158–25 you will find the forthcoming c·
Pul. 23– 3 * C· of The First Church of Christ,
24– 1 * c· of the first C. S. church
45–13 * c· within the year 1894
84–14 * 1894, witnessed the c· of
84–23 * all obstacles to its c·
86–18 * the c· of The First Church of Christ,
My. 21–- 8 * c· of The Mother Church,
21–27 * c· of the new edifice
27–14 * c· of the church building,
28– 2 * coincident with the c· of
43–30 * c· and dedication of our
62–11 * which crowns the c· of this
62–21 * c· of the magnificent extension

complex
My. 239–20 compound, c· idea or likeness of

complexion
Mis. 379– 8 general appearance, height, and c·
Pul. 32– 5 * her beautiful c· and

compliance
Mis. 244– 9 without c· to ordained conditions.
Man. 52–14 his c· with our Church Rules
Peo. 9– 6 as c· with a religious rite may
My. 180–23 drop c· with their desires,
204–15 in C· with the State Laws
231– 3 Giving merely in c· with

complied
Man. 110– 6 conditions be exactly c· with,
My. 217–15 provided he has c· with my request

compliment
Ret. 89–14 hortatory c· to a stranger,

compliments
My. 184–17 I treasure it next to your c·.

comply
Mis. x– 5 c· with an oft-repeated request ;
109–10 claim you admit . . . or c· with.
194–30 we must c· with the first condition
286– 8 ability to c· with absolute Science,
310–19 one must c· with the church rules.
Man. 65–15 c· with any written order,
78– 1 c· with the By-Laws of the Church.
100–20 duty of that church to c· with
'00. 9– 1 they c· with my counsel ;
My. 177– 3 Most happily would I c· with your

compose
Ret. 76– 6 he cannot dishonestly c· C. S.
Pul. 43– 9 * who c· the Board of Directors,

composed
Mis. 106–17 Sunday Lesson, c· of Scripture and
381– 3 manuscripts originally c· by
Pul. 27–30 * c· of three separate panels,
29–28 * entire congregation was c· of
76–15 * rug c· entirely of skins of
My. 276–10 try to be c· and resigned

composite
Pul. 81–14 * represents the c· beauty,
My. 359–19 * quotations from a c· letter,

composition
Mis. 379– 6 The c· was commonplace,
'00. 11– 15 his c· is the triumph of art,
My. 225– 7 correct use of capital letters in c·

compound
Mis. 167– 8 c· idea of all that resembles God.
Pul. 74–26 Love and its c· divine ideal.
'01. 22– 8 I do not believe in such a c·,
22– 9 Truth and Truth is not a c· ;
My. 239–20 c·, complex idea or likeness of
269– 2 c· idea, image of likeness,
292–16 a c· of prayers in which
292 20 mind is a c· of faith and doubt,
293– 6 this c· of mind and matter

compounded
Mis. 248–12 falsehoods uttered about me were c·,
271– 7 notion that c· metaphysics
Rud. 1–14 Latin verb personare is c· of

compounds
Mis. 270–27 chapter sub-title
271– 1 exclusion of c from its pharmacy,
271–14 which spurious " c·" engender.
'01. 22–10 Spirit and matter, are c·
23 18 all error, amalgamation, and c·.

comprehend
Mis. 23–24 who c· what C. S. means by
82–21 see and c· only as abstract glory.
197–12 to c· the meaning of the text,
255–12 He should c·, in divine Science,
Ret. 90–18 c· the needs of her babe
My. 39–29 * enables us to c· better the
41–32 * c· the " beauty of—' Psal. 29 : 2.
42–25 * begin to c·, even in small degree,
225– 9 reader who does not c· where

comprehended
Mis. 164– 9 Saviour, which is Truth, be c·.
187–17 fully c· the later teachings
Ret. 75–16 If one's spiritual ideal is c·
No. 20–13 As the divine Principle is c·,
My. 110– 9 darkness c· it not."— John 1 : 5.

comprehendeth
Mis. 368– 4 the darkness c· it not,
Un. 63–11 the darkness c it not.

comprehending
Mis. 46–20 but c· at every point,
My. 117– 9 the c· of the divine order

comprehends
Mis. 362– 6   c' and reflects all real mode,
Pul. 44–12   * c' its full significance.
No. 9–25   More . . . than this period c'.

comprehension
Mis. 79– 7   until it is clear to human c'
200–15   remote from the general c' of
Pul. 84–22   * unfold it to the c' of mankind.
No. 15– 5   The c' of my teachings would
28–22   neither the c' of its Principle nor

comprehensive
My. 45– 2   * c' means by you provided
149–22   Losing the c' in the technical,

comprise
Mis. 101–32   c' the elements of all forms
No. 4– 7   c' the whole of mortal existence,

comprised
My. 107–26   c' in a knowledge or understanding
306–24   these c' the manuscripts which

compromise
Mis. 53–15   by any c' with matter ;
101–15   enters into no c' with
My. 41–16   * makes no c' with evil,

compromises
Pul. 51–22   * c' have been welcomed.

compulsory
My. 344–30   Where vaccination is c',

compute
My. 23– 3   * c' by the total membership of

comrades
Mis. 324–23   Stealing cautiously away from his c',

Comstock's Natural Philosophy
My. 304– 7   book title

con
Pul. vii–16   to c' the facts surrounding the

Conant
Mrs.
My. 32– 8   * Mrs. C' could be heard perfectly
34–17   * read by Mr. McCrackan and Mrs. C' :
Mrs. Laura Carey
My. 31–24   * Second Reader, Mrs. Laura Carey C',

conceal
My. 335–27   * could not c' the fact that the case

concealed
Mis. 22–32   c' in the treasure-troves of
209–25   false basis that evil should be c'
My. 160–32   C' crimes, the wrongs done
166–18   virtues that lie c' in the
204– 5   the power which lies c'
241-- 8   * cunningly c' to prevent

concede
No. 23–14   c' that the Scriptures have
My. 347–24   Most thinkers c' that Science is

conceded
Mis. 13–25   only needs to be c'.
218–12   when it is c' that the five
My. 19–18   It is c' that our shadows

concedes
'02. 7– 2   c' no origin or causation apart from

conceit
Mis. 234–13   his vain c', the Phariseeism of
267–18   c', cowardice, or dishonesty.
348–16   wise in his own c'." — Prov. 26 : 5.
No. 2–24   C' cannot avert the effects of

conceivable
Pul. 25– 7   * as literally fire-proof as is c'.
36–17   * walked any c' distance.
'01. 6–27   lose all c' idea of Him as
7– 1   consistently c' as the
My. 212–27   hindering in every way c'
259– 2   sweetest sculptured face and form c',

conceive
Mis. 96–11   worship that of which I can c',
216–27   * to c' the universe as a
216–29   * to c' a grin without a cat."
217– 4   all should c' and understand
253–25   Can that child c' of the anguish,
259–11   too evil to c' of good
Un. 23–23   c' of God only as like itself,
Pul. 66–14   * what they c' to be the literal
Rud. 2–12   We do not c' rightly of God, if we
No. 18–18   Thus falsely may the human c' of
20– 1   so far as he can c' of personality.
23– 2   To c' of God as resembling
'01. 4–24   c' of God as One
6–11   Who can c' either of three
14–19   to c' of error as either right or
15–17   I can c' of little short of

conceive
'02. 5–26   why should mortals c' of a law,
My. 248–22   to c' God aright you must

conceived
Mis. 71–21   Whatever is humanly c'
108–14   c' of only as a delusion.
108–21   that which is truly c' of,
No. 13–20   No greater opposites can be c' of,
Pan. 2–16   * the universe, c' of as
2–20   c' as one personified nature,
'01. 7–24   cannot be c' of on that basis ;
My. 262–14   c' of Spirit, of God

conceives
Un. 40–28   It c' and beholds nothing but

concentrated
Mis. 242–22   in its most c' form,
Ret. 93–12   c' and immovably fixed
Hea. 12–17   the c' power of thought

concentric
Mis. 107–12   A pure affection, c',

concept
human
   (see **human**)
___
Mis. 89–25   Mortal man is a false c'
353– 7   If one asks me, Is my c' of you
Ret. 67– 2   hence one's c' of error is
67– 5   human or physical c'.
68– 1   material c' was never a creator,
68–10   human material c' is unreal,
68–10   divine c' or idea is spiritually
Un. 32– 7   universe, is His spiritual c'.
41– 2   has but a feeble c' of immortality.
No. 23– 1   incorrect c' of the nature of evil
36–25   from human sense to a higher c'
36–27   Mankind's c' of Jesus was
'01. 24– 2   * impossible and unreal c'."
'02. 6–16   mortal c' and all it includes
My. 224–11   its right or its wrong c',

conception
above
My. 59– 7   * It was above c'
convey a
My. 81–29   * impossible to convey a c' of
divine
Mis. 287– 1   the most exalted divine c'.
false
Rud. 6–10   beauty is marred, through a false c',
frail
Mis. 87–11   Matter is a frail c' of mortal mind ;
heathen
No. 34–20   infinitely beyond the heathen c'
'00. 3–26   In the heathen c' Yahwah,
higher
Pul. 85–10   * a better and higher c' of God
holier
Mis. 17–19   much higher and holier c' of
human
   (see **human**)
humanized
Ret. 54– 8   a humanized c' of His power,
infantile
Mis. 215–17   not according to the infantile c'
maturing
My. 181– 8   Progress is the maturing c' of
my
Mis. 354– 2   It exceeds my c' of human nature.
My. 262–29   express my c' of Truth's appearing.
no possible
'01. 5– 1   has no possible c' of ours,
of God
Ret. 25–20   I knew the human c' of God to be
Pul. 85–10   * better and higher c' of God
of man
Mis. 186–10   even separates its c' of man from
of sin
'01. 13–18   destroy the c' of sin as something,
of Spirit
My. 152–10   c' of Spirit and its all-power.
of the Christ
No. 12–16   new-born c' of the Christ,
of Truth
Ret. 83–13   may mistake in his c' of Truth,
original
Mis. 263–29   or a single original c',
proper
Ret. 25–26   inadequate to form any proper c' of
Hea. 4–21   can we ever arrive at a proper c'
sensual
Mis. 361– 4   When the belief in . . . sensual c',
sensuous
No. 26–11   brings forth its own sensuous c'.
spiritual
Mis. 286–11   more spiritual c' and education

conception

true
Mis. 108–15 This true *c·* would remove
My. 267–25 to darken the true *c·* of
your own
Mis. 8–12 the object of your own *c·*?

Mis. 108–22 *c·* of it at all as something

conceptions

Mis. 6–19 *c·* of Life, Truth, and Love
68–22 * science of the *c·* and relations
170–14 wrong and foolish, *c·* of God
218– 9 mortal mind must change all its *c·*
325– 7 small *c·* of spiritual riches,
375– 2 material *c·* and personality
Rud. 7– 5 infinite and subtler *c·*
No. 15–16 These *c·* of Deity and devil
Peo. 2– 6 material *c·* of spiritual being,
2–14 It is the false *c·* of Spirit,
8– 8 our *c·* of Deity,
8–13 finite and material *c·* of Deity.
12–17 advance to truer *c·*,

concepts

Mis. 71–28 even human *c·*, mortal shadows
294– 3 the *c·* of his own creating,
351–19 chapter sub-title
353– 3 Human *c·* run in extremes ;
361–10 spiritual *c·* testifying to
375– 3 are not my *c·* of angels.
My. 293– 2 but differing human *c·*

concern

Rud. 12–22 *c·* themselves with the chemistry of
'02. 9– 7 pride, and ease *c·* you less,
My. 104–17 of the utmost *c·* to the world
143– 9 *To Whom It May C·* :
276– 2 chapter sub-title
354– 1 chapter sub-title

concerned

Mis. 141–17 actuating all the parties *c·*
My. 99–13 * whenever their . . . religion is *c·*.
342–16 * all now *c·* in its government
351–26 Scientists are not *c·* with

concerning

Mis. 65– 9 *c·* the greater subject of human weal
72–13 proverb *c·* the land of — *Ezek.* 18 : 2.
78–23 of the public thought *c·* it.
79–13 error *c·* himself and his origin :
197–14 an opinion entertained *c·* Jesus
236–16 to give, . . . advice *c·* difficulties
287–23 important questions *c·* their
311–31 when rehearsing facts *c·* others
335–28 remember the Scripture *c·* those
372–22 declaration *c·* the spirit and
Un. 6–17 *c·* the divine nature and character
33–16 when they testify *c·* Spirit,
33– 7 from their own evidence, and *c·*
44– 1 misrepresentations are made *c·* my
Pul. 47–10 * knowledge *c·* the physical side
57–15 * *c·* the organization of
No. 24–26 great fact *c·* all error
Pan. 2–25 belief *c·* Deity in theology.
'00. 12–11 St. Paul's life furnished items *c·*
'01. 18– 4 woeful warnings *c·* C. S. healing
Hea. 5–12 * the question chiefly is *c·*
Peo. 8–15 speculate *c·* material forces.
My. 73–22 * information *c·* rooms and board,
220– 9 *c·* obedience to human law,
329–27 * facts *c·* Mrs. Mary Baker Eddy,
330–13 * *c·* Major Glover's history

concerns

Mis. 63–18 the great reality that *c·* man,
65–12 your query *c·* a negative
321–30 wisdom . . . that *c·* me, and you,
Ret. 88–11 The spiritual . . . most *c·* mankind.
88–18 a part which *c·* us intimately,

concert

Mis. 314– 9 repeat in *c·* with the congregation
Pul. 62–21 * *c·* halls, and public buildings,

concession

Mis. 91– 7 let it be in *c·* to the period,

conciliate

My. 284–26 efficacy of divine Love to *c·*

Conciliation

My. 282–19 International *C·* Committee,

concise

Mis. 35–11 most *c·*, yet complete, summary
Pul. 73–27 * *c·* idea of her belief

conclave

Mis. 148–10 originated not in solemn *c·*
Man. 3– 5 originated not in solemn *c·*

conclude

Mis. 47–27 What should one *c·* as to
56–13 to *c·* that Spirit constitutes
161–22 it is natural to *c·* that
165–31 before man can truthfully *c·*
327–19 they *c·* to stop and
'01. 4–30 we naturally *c·* that he breaks faith

concluded

Mis. 169–19 divines of the world have *c·* ;
Pul. 70–21 * *c·* that the way of salvation
My. 19– 6 * ceremony *c·* with the
32–30 * *c·* with the audible repetition of
54–27 * *c·* to engage Chickering Hall
307–18 afterwards I *c·* that he only

concluding

My. 135– 6 *c·* declaration may be applied to

conclusion

any
Mis. 288–12 any *c·* drawn therefrom is not
correct
Mis. 344–19 would seek a correct *c·*.
final
Ret. 33– 2 my final *c·* that mortal belief,
follows
Mis. 269–22 *c·* follows that the correct
his
My. 111–24 proving that his *c·* was logical
illogical
My. 225–24 and by no illogical *c·*,
inevitable
Un. 38–25 Hence the inevitable *c·* that
latter
Rud. 5–28 latter *c·* is the simple solution
logical
Mis. 26– 6 The only logical *c·* is that
26–30 logical *c·* that God is
93–11 logical *c·* drawn from the
'02. 7–19 No other logical *c·* can be
must be met
Ret. 94– 4 the *c·* must be met that
of the sermon
Mis. 178–25 * At the *c·* of the sermon,
one
Pul. 74–23 teachings maintain but one *c·*
opposite
Mis. 367–25 opposite *c·*, that darkness dwelleth
premise and
Mis. 101–28 On this proof rest premise and *c·*
195–21 one correct premise and *c·*,
200– 9 an error of premise and *c·*,
My. 112–14 with its logical premise and *c·*,
premise and in
My. 111–17 logical in premise and in *c·*.
rash
Mis. 288– 9 A rash *c·* that regards only
such a
Mis. 195–15 the authority for such a *c·*,
this
Mis. 9–10 Wherein is this *c·* relative to
95–11 Christ's Sermon . . . confirms this *c·*.
26–31 How, then, can this *c·* change,
119–17 This *c·* is not an argument
My. 340– 1 The fact that . . . confirms this *c·*.

Mis. 216–16 justifies one in the *c·* that he
245–17 The *c·* cannot now be pushed,
'01. 3–23 is not lost by the *c·*,
3–27 the *c·* is not properly drawn.

conclusions

Mis. 27– 6 *c·* that destroy their premise
46–13 premises or *c·* of C. S.,
101–19 bases his *c·* on mortality,
228–26 reliability of its *c·*,
291–32 over his emotions and *c·*.
309– 5 must result in erroneous *c·*.
312–23 *c·* which . . . cannot fasten upon.
366–23 mortal *c·* start from this false
Ret. 21–28 if spiritual *c·* are separated from
21–30 argument, with its rightful *c·*,
Un. 5–16 No stubborn purpose to force *c·*
9–14 their arguments and *c·* as to the
My. 175–29 to *c·* the very opposite of
224– 8 Hurried *c·* as to the public thought
350– 1 draws its *c·* of Deity and man,

conclusive

Mis. 96–25 any *c·* idea in a brief explanation.
192–28 Nothing can be more *c·* than this :
My. 85–13 * This is *c·* ;
321–25 * *c·* to me in every detail,

conclusively

Un. 9– 1 it proves my view *c·*,
My. 103– 8 show *c·* that C. S. is indeed
348– 4 proved *c·* that all effect must be

concomitants
  Mis. 14–16   facts of existence and its *c·* :
  Un. 46–21   sickness, and death were evil's *c·*.
  My. 129– 6   all *c·* of C. S.

Concord (*see also* **Concord's**)
New Hampshire
  Mis. 203– 3   Pleasant View, in *C·*, New Hampshire,
  Pul. 43–11   * a native of *C·*, New Hampshire.
N. H.
  Mis. xii–10   *C·*, N. H. January, 1897
  116– 5   PLEASANT VIEW, *C·*, N. H.,
  138–32   *C·*, N. H., May 23, 1890.
  251– 2   chapter sub-title
  294–25   Since my residence in *C·*, N. H.,
  Pul. 32–18 † * and was born in *C·*, N. H.,
  37– 5   * in her removal to *C·*, N. H.,
  43–25   * remained at her home in *C·*, N. H.,
  58– 6   * she has lived in *C·*, N. H.,
  63–12   * country home in *C·*, N. H.
  70–27   * a country-seat in *C·*, N. H.
  74– 4   * *C·*, N. H., February 4, 1895.
  76–21   * *C·*, N. H., February 27, 1895
  77–23   * *People and Patriot*, *C·*, N. H.,
  '01. 32– 2   Nathaniel Bouton, D. D., of *C·*, N. H.,
  Po. 22–22   *C·*, N. H., *January*, 1901.
  24–22   Pleasant View, *C·*, N. H., 1899.
  25–20   *C·*, N. H., *May* 21, 1904.
  31–23   *C·*, N. H., *April* 18, 1900.
  44– 5   *C·*, N. H., *April* 3, 1899.
  79–22   *C·*, N. H., *January*, 1900.
  My. 9–29   *C·*, N. H., July 21, 1902.
  20– 5   *C·*, N. H., September 1, 1904.
  20–20   *C·*, N. H., October 31, 1904.
  25–29   *C·*, N. H., April 8, 1906.
  26–27   *C·*, N. H., April 23, 1906.
  44–22   * Pleasant View, *C·*, N. H.
  58–27   * Pleasant View, *C·*, N. H.
  60–24   * Pleasant View, *C·*, N. H.
  62–18   * Pleasant View, *C·*, N. H.
  66–24   * Pleasant View, in *C·*, N. H.,
  91–21   * Mary Baker Eddy of *C·*, N. H.
  123–10   To-day in *C·*, N. H., we have a
  133–19   *C·*, N. H., May 11, 1903.
  135–22   *C·*, N. H., March 22, 1907.
  136–10   *C·*, N. H., April 2, 1907.
  136–23   National State Capital Bank, *C·*, N. H.
  136–30   *C·*, N. H., April 3, 1907.
  137–10   HON. JUDGE CHAMBERLIN, *C·*, N. H.
  138–23   *C·*, N. H., May 16, 1907.
  144– 2   * her church in *C·*, N. H. :
  144– 3   FIRST CHURCH . . . *C·*, N. H.
  145– 5   C. S. Hall in *C·*, N. H.
  162–15   our church edifice in *C·*, N. H.
  163–18   and came to *C·*, N. H.,
  165–14   First Church . . . in *C·*, N. H.
  166–12   First Church . . . *C·*, N. H.,
  166–30   First Church . . . *C·*, N. H.,
  169– 3   *C·*, N. H., on July 5,
  169–11   *C·*, N. H., June 30, 1897.
  169–17   I was happy to receive at *C·*, N. H.,
  171–17   *C·*, N. H., June 11, 1904.
  173– 2   * in the *C·* (N. H.) newspapers
  174–15   Congregational Church, *C·*, N. H.,
  174–20   Congregational Church in *C·*, N. H.,
  175– 8   *C·*, N. H., November 14, 1905.
  187–18   *C·*, N. H., November 16, 1898.
  193–11   *C·*, N. H., November 20, 1902.
  197–29   *C·*, N. H., July 27, 1907.
  230–28   *C·*, N. H., November 14, 1904.
  236–21   *C·*, N. H., July 8, 1907.
  259– 8   * PLEASANT VIEW, *C·*, N. H.
  261–19   *C·*, N. H., December 28, 1905.
  270– 7   in this capital city of *C·*, N. H.,
  271–14   * in the city of *C·*, N. H.,
  272–17   PLEASANT VIEW, *C·*, N. H.
  279–29   *C·*, N. H., June 13, 1905.
  280– 2   * Pleasant View, *C·*, N. H.
  280–24   *C·*, N. H., June 27, 1905.
  282–29   *C·*, N. H., April 3, 1907.
  284– 8   *C·*, N. H., April 22, 1907.
  284–20   in some church in *C·*, N. H.
  284–29   *C·*, N. H., May 28, 1907.
  285–31   PLEASANT VIEW, *C·*, N. H.
  289–21   *C·*, N. H., January 27, 1901.
  290–30   *C·*, N. H., September 14, 1901.
  295–30   *C·*, N. H., August 31, 1907.
  296– 7   *C·*, N. H., October 14, 1907.
  296–22   *C·*, N. H., December 10, 1907.
  297– 9   *C·*, N. H., January 10, 1908.
  299– 5   First Church . . . *C·*, N. H.,
  301–12   *C·*, N. H., March 22, 1899.
  309–19   situated in Bow and *C·*, N. H.
  327– 8   *C·*, N. H., October 16, 1903.
  335– 2   * formerly of *C·*, N. H.

† *Incorrect newspaper account, quoted as published.*

Concord
N. H.
  My. 346–16   * *C·*, N. H., Tuesday, April 30, 1901.
  351–20   *C·*, N. H., February 9, 1906.

  Mis. 251– 9   welcomed you to *C·* most graciously,
  Ret. 4– 5   adjoining towns of *C·* and Bow,
  5– 1   near *C·*, just across the bridge,
  5–10   eighteen miles from *C·*,
  7– 5   Hon. Isaac Hill, of *C·*,
  Pul. 24–22   * church is built of *C·* granite
  47–26   * so picturesque all about *C·*
  49–23   * do honor to that precinct of *C·*.
  49–24   * old farm on the road from *C·*,
  '02. 20–20   a pilgrimage to *C·*?
  My. 122–15   in our good city of *C·*.
  145–15   Mr. George H. Moore of *C·*,
  148– 6   May the good folk of *C·*
  153– 2   Christian Scientists in *C·*
  153– 7   gospel ministry of my students in *C·*
  157– 4   * members of the *C·* church
  157–14   * of the same beautiful *C·* granite
  158– 6   chapter sub-title
  162–21   Scientists' church edifice in *C·* :
  164–10   gift to First Church . . . in *C·*,
  169– 1   chapter sub-title
  169–14   chapter sub-title
  170–10   minds of all present here in *C·*.
  171– 8   chapter sub-title
  171– 9   *C·* church is so nearly completed
  171–12   invite all . . . to come to *C·*,
  171–19   * heading
  173– 6   thank the citizens of *C·*
  173–15   our new church building in *C·*,
  175–11   say to the good folk of *C·*
  243–21   Your prompt presence in *C·*
  284–18   Since my residence in *C·*,
  346–10   * Soon after I reached *C·*

concord
  Mis. 116–18   gain of its sweet *c·*,
  333–23   what *c·* hath Christ with — *II Cor.* **6: 15.**

Concord Church
  My. 148– 9   chapter sub-title
  157– 2   * chapter sub-title

Concord Evening Monitor
  Pul. 85–20   * [*C· E· M·*, March 23, 1895]

Concord Monitor
  My. 157–18   * first announced in the *C· M·*

Concord* (N. H.) *Daily Patriot
  My. 284–10   [*C·* (*N.H.*) *D· P·*]

Concord* (N. H.) *Monitor
  My. 88– 9   * [*C·* (*N.H.*) *M·*]
  157– 1   * [*C·* (*N.H.*) *M·*]
  266–10   [*C·* (*N.H.*) *M·*, July, 1902]

Concord (N. H.) Street Fund
  My. 176– 4   TOWARDS THE *C·* (*N.H.*) *S· F·*

Concord Publishing Company
  My. 298– 8   Miss Wilbur and the *C· P· C·*

Concord's
  My. 145– 4   one of *C·* best builders
  163–20   opportunity in *C·* quiet

Concord School of Philosophy
  Pul. 5–11   founder of the *C· S· of P·*

concourse
  Mis. 225– 3   *c·* of friends had gathered

concrete
  Mis. 82–20   Infinite progression is *c·* being,
  337–25   understood the *c·* character of
  Ret. 67– 6   Sin is both *c·* and abstract.
  My. 92–20   * so huge and *c·* a demonstration
  94– 5   * evidence appears in the *c·*

concur
  '02. 8– 4   The law and the gospel *c·*,

concurrence
  My. 148–16   and the father of our nation in *c·*.
  246–20   light and might of the divine *c·*

condemn
  Mis. 22–26   is incompetent to *c·* it;
  55– 1   and then, . . . *c·* the pupil
  126–22   Most people *c·* evil-doing,
  129– 3   or to *c·* his brother without cause,
  171–12   right action is not to *c·*
  '01. 15– 5   must *c·* the claim of error
  My. 249– 1   You may *c·* evil in the abstract
  249– 2   *c·* persons seldom, if ever.

condemnation
  Mis. 188–13   now no *c·* to them — *Rom.* 8: 1.
  285– 5   because I had been personal in *c·*.
  300–14   does it spare you our Master's *c·*?
  Ret. 14– 9   salvation and *c·* depended,
  Pan. 13–11   stern *c·* of all error,

condemnation

My. 18–19 stern c· of all error,
113–11 now no c· to them — Rom. 8 : 1.
205– 2 now no c· to them — Rom. 8 : 1.

condemned

Mis. 48– 5 should be conscientiously c·.
Man. 42–10 and justified or c·.
Un. 29– 3 Jewish law c· the sinner to death,
54–25 c· the knowledge of sin
No. 23– 3 personality that Jesus c· as
Hea. 2– 7 c· at every advancing footstep,
My. 196–14 shalt be c·." — Matt. 12 : 37.

condemneth

Ret. 94–18 he that c· not himself — Rom. 14 : 22.

condemning

Mis. 95– 6 * public letter c· her doctrines ;
Man. 40–13 prophesying, judging, c·,
93–13 reply to public topics c· C. S.,

condition

diseased
Ret. 40–14 said the diseased c· was caused by
every
Mis. 118– 6 Honesty in every c·,
'02. 9–14 Every c· implied by the
first
Mis. 109–18 Ignorance was the first c· of sin
194–30 first c· set forth in the text,
form the
Un. 52–26 The senses, . . . form the c· of
higher
Rud. 8–15 higher c· of thought and action.
inevitable
Mis. 127–21 inevitable c· whereby to become
its
Ret. 44–19 exciting cause of its c·,
mental
(see mental)
no
My. 149–32 canst be brought into no c·,
normal
Ret. 13–23 in a normal c· of health.
of mortality
Mis. 64–25 put into this c· of mortality?
of salvation
Mis. 192–26 making healing a c· of salvation,
of sin
Mis. 109–18 Ignorance was the first c· of sin
overcrowded
My. 56–11 * relieve the overcrowded c· of
56–25 * the overcrowded c· of
perplexed
Pul. 8– 6 Notwithstanding the perplexed c· of
present
Mis. 98– 3 whereby to improve his present c· ;
real
No. 5–23 normal and real c· of man,
spiritual
Un. 7–13 In the same spiritual c· I have
their
Mis. 371–13 he who deprecates their c·
this
Mis. 64–25 into this c· of mortality?
Pul. 79–28 * this c· can never long continue.
wretched
Mis. 52–15 wretched c· of human existence.

Mis. 193–31 The c· insisted upon is,
Pul. 53– 7 * c· which Jesus of Nazareth,
My. 318–18 on c· that I should not ask

conditional

My. 260–12 Nothing c· or material belongs to

conditioned

Mis. 64–28 wherefore man is thus c·,

conditions

aforesaid
My. 144– 7 either of the aforesaid c·
all
My. 260–26 appeals to all c·,
all the
Rud. 12–20 as caring for all the c·
My. 294–14 to control all the c·
certain
Pul. 29–21 * could, under certain c·, be
cerebral
My. 301–26 or affect cerebral c· in any manner
ethical
Mis. 297– 8 bases its work on ethical c·
fulfils the
Mis. 73–16 Belief fulfils the c· of a
fulfil the
Mis. 212– 1 to fulfil the c· of our
intermediate
No. 28– 7 intermediate c· — the purifying

conditions

its own
Rud. 11– 1 or . . . frame its own c·,
material
(see material)
mental
Mis. 91–15 types of these mental c·,
Un. 56–27 Such mental c· as ingratitude,
mortal
Un. 59–17 this conformity to mortal c· ;
of environment
Pul. 54–20 * c· of environment and harmonious
of matter
Pan. 4–10 depend on c· of matter,
of mortals
No. 22– 9 fail to improve the c· of mortals,
of salvation
Mis. 244–11 are the c· of salvation mental,
ordained
Mis. 244– 9 compliance to ordained c·.
other
My. 212–21 impossible under other c·,
requisite
Pul. 54–10 * c· requisite in psychic healing
Rud. 12–20 c· requisite for the well-being of man.
strict
Man. 110– 5 these seemingly strict c·
their
My. 250–22 its adaptability to their c·.
these
Mis. 73–17 these c· destroy the belief.
those
Mis. 244–10 those c· named in Genesis

My. 69–12 * where c· permitted it

condolence

My. 289–25 send a few words of c·,

conduct

Mis. 297–25 consequences of his own c· ;
301–27 a divine rule for human c·.
Man. 31–16 duty of the First Readers to c· the
53– 7 No Unchristian C·.
54–11 unjust and unmerciful c·
73–11 form and c· a C. S. organization
79–23 and c· the business of
81–20 Rule of C·.
86–14 c· the meetings of their association.
88–19 nor on their course or c·.
'00. 1–15 fast forming themselves into c·.
'02. 18–25 ignoble c· of his disciples
My. 71–26 * two Readers who c· the services
161–25 because one's thought and c·
223– 1 chapter sub-title

conducted

Mis. 44–10 c· by one who understands
314– 4 c· by Readers in lieu of pastors.
Man. 72– 9 church services c· by reading the
81–17 copyrighted and c· according to
My. 10–21 * c· by the First Reader,

conducting

My. 49–25 * mode of c· the church."

confer

Mis. 262– 3 c· increased power to be good
272–23 * bestow no rights to c· degrees.
272–26 * with powers to c· diplomas
Man. 47– 9 to c· with an M.D. on Ontology,
70–18 c· on a statute of said State,
70–18 c· harmoniously on individual unity
88–20 students can c· with their teachers
My. 362–15 * to c· harmoniously and unitedly

conference

Man. 70–15 No c· of churches shall be held,
My. 207– 9 * in annual c· assembled,
208–23 chapter sub-title
208–25 God bless the . . . committees in c·

conferred

Mis. 90–27 this prerogative being c· by
272–16 * or authorizes to be c·,
Man. 67–15 personally c· with her
Ret. 78–23 the blessings otherwise c·,
My. 42–15 * the honor c· upon me.
245–30 c· by the President

conferring

My. 244– 8 prior to c· on any or all

confers

Mis. 272–15 * c·, or authorizes to be conferred,
Ret. 70– 1 c· animal names and natures
Un. 7–21 c· a power nothing else can.
'02. 17–24 what God gives, . . . c· happiness :
My. 154–11 not he . . . that c· the blessing,

confess
Mis. 281–15 come out and c· his faith,
My. 88–27 * stoutest enemies of C. S. will c·
285–25 this I c· unto thee, — Acts 24 ; 14.
confessed
Mis. 299–30 c· that they are the property of
confessedly
Un. 23–17 c· incompetent to speak.
confessing
Mis. 239–26 c· that she had something that she
344–10 On Justin's c· that he had not
confession
Man. 52–13 his c· of his error and
Pul. 30–11 * a brief "c· of faith,"
30–15 * The " c· of faith" includes
My. 42– 8 * "witnessed a good c·" — I Tim. 6 : 13.
confessions
Peo. 13–15 forcing . . . shameful c·,
confidence
Mis. 33–18 Patients naturally gain c· in
133–25 c· that He will reward
137–28 teach with increased c·.
229–20 The c· of mankind in
256– 7 acknowledging the public c·
257–17 suspicion where c· is due,
323–15 meets . . . attacks with serene c·.
Man. 46–13 shall hold in sacred c· all
Ret. 15– 7 In c· of faith, I could say
27–25 before gathering experience and c·
Pul. 3–11 Our surety is in our c·
21–25 abide in c· and hope.
Peo. 9–19 full c· in their efficacy,
My. 44–29 * unshaken c· in the unerring
137–27 because I had implicit c· in
208–25 their c· in His ways
332–23 * we had full c· that it would
340–25 tend to enhance their c·
confident
My. 21–25 * we are c· that they too
37–26 * c· and favorable expectation.
44–30 * and their c· assurance
confidently
My. 318–12 c· awaited the years to declare the
confine
Mis. 95–12 c· myself to questions and answers.
339– 2 If people would c· their talk to
Man. 73–24 shall not c· their membership to the
confined
Mis. 6–27 conversation chiefly c· to the
42–30 Mind is not c· to limits ;
60–21 c· and conformed to the Science of
150–25 God is universal ; c· to no spot,
189–29 not c· to the first century ;
Man. 99–11 church is not necessarily c· to
Pul. 65– 1 * not c· to its original apostles
No. 14–22 not c· to Jesus' students
confines
My. 37– 4 * sacred c· of this sanctuary.
confining
Un. 62–25 Mortal sense, c· itself to matter,
confirm
Mis. 13–20 what the shifting mortal senses c·
153– 3 God will c· His inheritance.
'02. 7–24 serves to c· C. S.
My. 319–13 * c· her statement regarding the
confirmation
Un. 57–20 Suffering was the c· of Paul's
confirms
Mis. 25–10 c· this conclusion.
192–24 as primitive Christianity c·.
Un. 36– 6 it unwittingly c· Truth,
'02. 8–14 c· the fact that God and Love are
My. 339–30 c· this conclusion.
conflict
Mis. xii– 7 above the smoke of c·
16–31 c· between the flesh and Spirit.
45–19 in a single instance decides the c·,
73– 7 materially, these passages c· ;
102–27 c· between sense and Soul.
105–12 Science would have no c· with Life
184– 4 Science and sense c·,
195–24 unequal to the c·,
214–14 The very c· his Truth brought,
246–20 c· more terrible than the battle of
Ret. 30– 2 I stood alone in this c·,
Un. 39–28 Science and material sense c·
'00. 10– 5 C· and persecution are the truest
10– 8 Such c· never ends till
'02. 3–19 close of the c· in South Africa ;
Po. 77–12 joy and tears, c· and rest,

conflict
My. 306– 3 into a c· for fame.
358– 8 whereby the c· against Truth
361– 8 into a personal c·.
conflicting
No. 2–27 c· theories and practice.
My. 134– 9 c· elements must be mastered.
293–13 c· states of the human mind,
conflicts
Mis. 260– 2 By c·, defeats, and triumphs,
'01. 27–28 * people say it c· with the Bible.
'02. 12–14 c· not at all with another
My. 103– 3 severest c· of the ages
304–26 * people say it c· with the Bible.
conform
Mis. 114–10 Teachers must c· strictly to the
Un. 59–20 to which he seemed to c· :
conformed
Mis. 21–23 c· to the text of the
60–21 c· to the Science of being.
127–15 it will be c· to a fitness
My. 18–12 c· to a fitness to receive
221–21 Our Master c· to this law,
conforming
Mis. 138– 6 detail of c· to society,
Man. 62– 2 the offertory c· to the time
conformity
Mis. 315–28 educate their students in c· to
Man. 72– 7 to form a church in c· with
83–19 in c· with the unerring laws of God,
Un. 59–16 this c· to mortal conditions ;
confounded
Mis. 4–21 in many minds it is c· with
No. 27–18 the two should not be c·.
My. 17–16 shall not be c·." — I Pet. 2 : 6.
245–16 Babel of confusion worse c·,
confounding
Rud. 7–27 thus confusing and c· the
confront
Pul. 2–25 The enemy we c· would
My. 229–24 Heaps upon heaps of praise c· me,
confronted
My. 214–21 I was c· with the fact that I
confronting
My. 266– 3 imminent dangers c· the
confronts
Mis. 346– 7 c· each generation anew.
346– 8 It c· C. S.
Confucius
No. 21– 6 C· and Plato but dimly discerned,
confuse
My. 211–25 into his mind, fret and c· it,
218–18 tends to c· the mind of
confused
My. 170– 8 should not be c· with other
confusing
Rud. 7–27 thus c· and confounding the
confusion
Man. 110– 4 c· that might result therefrom.
My. 38– 9 * was no c· in finding seats,
245–15 Babel of c· worse confounded,
confutes
Mis. 363–26 c· the astronomer, exposes the
congenial
My. 87– 8 * pleasant, c·, quietly happy,
congratulate
'02. 4– 5 I cordially c· our Board
My. 24– 4 * We c· you that the building
87–15 * c· these comfortable acquaintances
154–16 permit me to c· this little church
184– 9 to c· the Christian Scientists
196– 3 I c· you upon erecting
204–17 I c· you tenderly on the
208–18 I c· you on the prospect of
270– 9 the leading editors . . . c· me ;
congratulated
My. 87–17 * Boston is to be c· upon the
309–11 bowed to my father and c· him.
congratulation
Pul. 44– 8 * receive this brief message of c·.
congratulations
Pul. 44– 6 * I send my hearty c·.
My. 62–20 * send you loving greetings and c·
63–18 * even the greetings and c· of
197–27 I send loving c·,
234– 3 writing or reading c·?
281–20 * expression of c· and views
285– 5 and accept my hearty c·.

congratulatory
Man. 67–20 sending gifts, *c·* despatches

congregate
My. 29–27 * thousands who began to *c·*
289–11 should upon this solemn occasion *c·* ;

congregation
Mis. 150–13 dwelleth in the *c·* of the faithful,
314–10 repeat in concert with the *c·*
314–17 alternately in response to the *c·*,
322– 9 present to address this *c·*,
Ret. 15–17 The *c·* so increased in number
15–28 agreeably informed the *c·*
Pul. 29–10 * a *c·* whose remarkable earnestness
20–27 * I was told that almost the entire *c·*
30– 4 * enticing a separate *c·*
41–30 * At 9 a. m. the first *c·* gathered,
43–16 * hymn, . . . was sung by the *c·*.
45–30 * elected each year by the *c·*.
55–24 * Boston *c·* was organized
59–11 * singing by a choir and *c·*.
59–13 * *c·* repeating one sentence
68–15 * C. S. *c·* was organized
68–24 * The Baltimore *c·* was organized
74– 7 * pastor of the C. S. *c·*
My. 29– 6 * rising in unison from the vast *c·*,
31–27 * *c·* had taken their seats,
32– 4 * *c·* began to repeat the
35–28 * read to the *c·* the . . . Message
54–26 * large *c·* was present.
55–28 * *c·* worshipped in Copley Hall
78–19 * *c·* knelt in silent communion,
78–21 * *c·* singing in perfect unison.
81– 3 * prosperity of the great *c·*.
97 18 * evidently wealthy *c·*
188–12 your tabernacle of the *c·*
249–30 thought which spiritualizes the *c·*.

Congregational
Ret. 13– 1 admitted to the *C·* . . . Church,
Pul. 29– 4 * formerly been *C·* clergymen.
No. 44–24 Rev. S. E. Herrick, a *C·* clergyman
My. 182– 1 Chicago had few *C·* churches.

Congregational Church
Mis. 178– 2 the *C· C·*.
Ret. 5– 4 first *C· C·* in Pembroke.
'01. 31–21 my early culture in the *C· C·* ;
My. 174–23 I was a member of the *C· C·*
182– 4 I received from the *C· C·*
311–13 I joined the Tilton *C· C·*

Congregationalist
'01. 32– 4 Rev. Corban Curtis, *C·* ;

Congregationalists
'01. 32– 2 of Concord, N. H., *C·* ;

congregations
Man. 42– 3 offered for the *c·* collectively
Pul. 40–17 * presence of four different *c·*,
41–21 * four vast *c·* filled the church
55–29 * members of different *c·*
My. 8–30 * one hundred and five new . . . *c·*
30–12 * In those huge *c·* were
30–21 * having been through the *c·*,
85– 8 * its *c·* meet in Europe and in
91–31 * *c·* in every important town

Congress and **congress**
Ret. 7– 1 nomination to *C·* on a majority vote
Pan. 14–16 give to our *c·* wisdom,
Po. vi–20 *resolution in C· prohibiting*
My. 278–13 President and *C·* of our favored land
310– 7 was nominated for *C·*,

congressman
Mis. 253– 9 the speakers . . . one a *c·*

conical
Mis. 347– 6 A *c·* cloud, hanging like a

conjectural
Mis. 290–22 *c·* and misapprehensive !

conjecture's
Pan. 12–27 unpierced by bold *c·* sharp point,

conjectures
Un. 28–14 than ordinary material *c·*,
My. 346–22 * Various *c·* having arisen

conjoined
'01. 23–29 * *c·* by the operations of the

conjugal
Mis. 289–26 Science touches the *c·* question
289–27 Can the bill of *c·* rights be fairly

conjugality
Mis. 285–23 may conjure up a new-style *c·*,
285–29 the *rôle* of a superfine *c·* ;

conjure
Mis. 285–22 may *c·* up a new-style conjugality,
Un. 60– 8 and then *c·* up, from the dark

Conn. (State)
(see **Bridgeport, Hartford, New Haven, New London**)

connected
Mis. 278– 9 in my history as *c·* with the
309–20 and whatever is *c·* therewith,
Man. 27–24 and of other literature *c·* therewith.
74–14 nor in rooms *c·* therewith.
81– 8 shall in no manner be *c·* with
82– 5 are in no manner *c·* with these
Ret. 3– 4 *c·* with Capt. John Lovewell
6–17 ever *c·* with that institution.
8– 1 events *c·* with my childhood
24– 4 in no wise *c·* with this event,
45–18 Association *c·* with my College
Un. 47– 3 Nowhere in Scripture is evil *c·* with
Pul. 59–25 * gentlemen officially *c·* with the
'01. 23–28 * phenomena *c·* by association
My. 125–12 Board of Lectureship *c·* with The
175– 4 organizations *c·* therewith,
321– 3 * in a way *c·* with your work,

connecting
Mis. 393– 3 Nature, with the mind *c·*,
Po. 51– 8 Nature, with the mind *c·*,

connection
Mis. x–27 in *c·* with my published works.
60–23 *what is the c· between*
127– 3 Throughout my entire *c·* with
300– 4 compiling them in *c·* with
310–18 one's *c·* with this church,
Man. 65– 7 used in *c·* with C. S.
Ret. 13– 3 In *c·* with this event,
15– 3 My *c·* with this religious body
Un. 7–19 in *c·* with these experiences ;
Pul. 86–27 * in *c·* with the Bible
Pan. 7–18 in *c·* with the original text
'02. 15–12 *c·* between justice and being
20–19 breaking any seeming *c·* between
Hea. 18– 8 no *c·* between Spirit and matter.
My. 17–31 Throughout my entire *c·* with
27–25 * in *c·* with the extension of
100– 1 * brought out in *c·* with the
112–26 S. and H. in *c·* with the Bible.
200–28 *c·* with its divine Principle,
311–22 in *c·* with her own family
315– 2 is of interest in this *c·* :
321–22 * my *c·* with the church,

connects
My. 205–19 This idealism *c·* itself with

conquer
Mis. 6–20 we *c·* sickness, sin, and death.
40–30 requires more . . . to *c·* this sin
163– 1 to *c·* the three-in-one of error :
235– 4 to *c·* sin, sickness, and death ;
Un. 18–24 and thus I *c·* death ;
'00. 9–18 before he can *c·* others.
My. 125– 2 Have you learned to *c·* sin,

conquered
Mis. 74–28 He met and *c·* the resistance of
Pul. 83–16 * Amazons who *c·* the invincibles,
No. 35–10 *c·* also the drear subtlety of death.
36–23 nor could he have *c·* the malice
'00. 9–17 and he must have *c·* himself
My. 43– 3 * that wilderness must be *c·*.

conquering
Ret. 49–16 *c·* all that is unlike Christ

conqueror
'02. 10 15 happier than the *c·* of a world.

conquerors
Mis. 176–17 not as the flying nor as *c·*,

conquers
Mis. 126–13 sustains us, and finally *c·*
135–10 *c·* all opposition, surmounts all
'01. 13–20 fear, unconquered, *c·* him.

conquest
Pul. 12–18 mighty *c·* over all sin?
My. 127–28 it is not . . . surrendered in *c·*,
192–11 *c·* over sin and mortality,

conscience (see also **conscience'**)
Mis. 43–23 at the expense of his *c·*,
146–20 I cannot be the *c·* for this church ;
147–16 Truth and the voice of his *c·*
176–24 true freedom, in the rights of *c·*.
228–16 just person, faithful to *c·*
236–12 but you have the rights of *c·*,
237–11 such a cup of gall that *c·* strikes
237–16 is not essentially one of *c·* :
246–17 to shackle *c·*, stop free speech,
299–30 but does this silence your *c·*?
339–27 surge dolefully at the door of *c·*,
Un. 5–19 Let us respect the rights of *c·*
25– 3 stultify my intellect, insult my *c·*,

conscience

Pul.	10– 3	that raised the deadened *c*·,
	10–12	they planted . . . the rights of *c*·,
No.	44–15	and so abrogate the rights of *c*·
'01.	33–15	allowed the rights of *c*·
'02.	18– 1	at the temple gate of *c*·,
Peo.	13–14	putting man to the rack for his *c*·,
My.	118–24	should come from *c*·.
	124– 4	to every man's *c*·." — *II Cor.* 4: 2.
	128–16	dictates of his own rational *c*·
	160–25	even the fire of a guilty *c*·,
	168– 3	the dictates of enlightened *c*·,
	187–13	and of a good *c*·, — *I Tim.* 1: 5.
	197– 3	which is least distinct to *c*·.
	220–31	should share alike liberty of *c*·,
	222–27	liberty of *c*· held sacred.

conscience'

Mis.	261–28	for *c*· sake, one will either

consciences

Mis.	274–22	those quill-drivers whose *c*·

conscientious

Mis.	80–12	cultured and *c*· medical men,
	147–23	the *c*· man of business,
	220–22	to the *c*· Christian Scientist
	340–20	The *c*· are successful.
	375–18	* *c*· application to detail,
Ret.	48– 5	*c*· scruples about diplomas,
Un.	25–21	Evil is not conscious or *c*· Mind ;
	31–16	Hence my *c*· position,
Pul.	51– 5	* a number of *c*· followers
No.	v– 7	hearts of all *c*· laborers
	2–18	is modest . . . *c*· in duty,
	9– 7	more *c*· in their convictions ;
Peo.	6– 6	* "I declare my *c*· belief,
My.	112–26	result of his *c*· study
	213–10	*c*· in their desire to do right

conscientiously

Mis.	48– 5	should be *c*· condemned.
	146– 6	I cannot *c*· lend my
	262–14	who are at work *c*·
	365–31	it must be *c*· understood
Ret.	55– 2	enter . . . and work *c*·.
Rud.	14– 5	and then *c*· *earn their wages,*
No.	11–14	understood and *c*· introduced.

conscious

Mis.	42– 7	still in a *c*· state of existence ;
	42–12	but by a *c*· union with God.
	42–15	same plane of *c*· existence
	73– 1	or that God is *c*· of it.
	103–15	true substance, because eternally *c*·.
	219–29	a good sense, or *c*· goodness,
	283–18	*c*· trespass on the rights of mortals.
	283–25	*c*·, meanwhile, that God worketh
	363– 1	the more *c*· it becomes of
Ret.	61– 8	actually *c*· of the truth of C. S.,
	64–24	scientific to abide in *c*· harmony,
Un.	4–17	if God be *c*· of it?
	13–13	If God could be *c*· of sin,
	18–24	to be ever *c*· of Life
	18–25	is to be never *c*· of death.
	24–24	becomes *c*·, and is able to see,
	25–16	honors *c*· human individuality
	25–21	Evil is not *c*· or conscientious
	36–23	to say that the divine Mind is *c*· of
	36–23	yet is not *c*· of matter,
	44–22	[you shall be *c*· matter],
	45–13	teaching that matter can be *c*· ;
	45–14	*c*· matter implies pantheism.
	45–28	Matter is not truly *c*· ;
	48–13	as infinite and *c*· Life,
	48–19	I believe that of which I am *c*·
	50–24	Matter and evil cannot be *c*·,
	56–19	Their *c*· being was not fully exempt
	57–28	The only *c*· existence in the flesh
	64– 5	*c*· of only health, holiness, and
	64– 7	which is *c*· of sickness, sin, and
Pul.	13– 8	*c*· of the supremacy of Truth,
No.	17–10	*c*· of aught but good.
	19–14	gratefully and lovingly *c*· of
	36– 9	Jesus' true and *c*· being
	36–13	was *c*· only of God,
	36–17	*c*· reality and royalty of his
	36–21	Had he been as *c*· of those
'01.	23–30	* nothing more than *c*· experience.
	24– 1	* Matter apart from *c*· mind
'02.	8–30	*c*· that God is his Father,
	17–24	*c*· worth satisfies the hungry heart,
My.	221–26	since matter is not *c*·,
	294–18	*c*· understanding of omnipotence,
	349–15	*c*· of the allness of God

consciously

Mis.	212–24	If, *c*· or unconsciously, one is
Ret.	81–19	is *c*· untrue to the light,
'00.	8– 5	exhales *c*· and unconsciously his

consciousness

accompanying

Mis.	189–23	accompanying *c*· of spiritual power

affectional

Ret.	81–12	spiritual sense, affectional *c*·,

all

Ret.	56–18	All *c*· is Mind,
Un.	4–16	we lose all *c*· of error,
	24– 3	proceedeth all Mind, all *c*·,
	24–12	All *c*· is Mind ;
No.	10–18	all *c*· is Mind and eternal,

and life

Un.	36– 1	evidence of *c*· and life
My.	203– 6	distinct in our *c*· and life,

any other

Mis.	179– 9	any other *c*· than that of good?

awakened

Mis.	16–24	awakened *c*· is wholly spiritual ;
No.	40– 9	pure pearls of awakened *c*·,
'00.	15–18	feast for this awakened *c*·,
My.	257– 7	To the awakened *c*·, the Bethlehem

being, or

Un.	3–21	and is perfect being, or *c*·.

change of

Un.	11–11	demanded a change of *c*·

disk of

Ret.	94–15	blemish on the disk of *c*·

divine

(*see* **divine**)

diviner

Mis.	96–13	ascends the scale . . . to diviner *c*·,

evil in

Un.	49–14	So long as I hold evil in *c*·,

existence or

Un.	47– 5	false claim to existence or *c*·.

false

Mis.	222– 6	This state of false *c*·
	298–30	false *c*· does not change the fact,
Un.	52–10	false *c*· of both good and

falsity of

Un.	35–27	outlined falsity of *c*·,

finite

Un.	24–10	*Evil.* I am a finite *c*·,
	24–13	and not a finite *c*·.
	24–16	There is . . . no finite *c*·.

force the

Mis.	288–18	to force the *c*· of scientific

glorified

Un.	49–12	a glorified *c*· of the only

His

No.	17–25	would be a part of His *c*·.

his

Mis.	352–24	his *c*· is the reflection of the divine,

His own

No.	16–21	no . . . inference but His own *c*·,

his own

Mis.	302– 6	preserves in his own *c*·
My.	161–15	within his own *c*·,
	364–10	excludes from his own *c*·,

human

(*see* **human**)

idea in

My.	263– 1	spiritual idea in *c*·,

identity or

Mis.	205–17	man's identity or *c*· reflects only

individual

Un.	8–12	individual *c*· is permanent.
	21–13	individual *c*· and existence.
	21–17	Individual *c*· in man is
	24–14	reflected in individual *c*·,
'01.	1–12	rise . . . higher in the individual *c*·
My.	42–24	* unfolds in each individual *c*·
	44–10	* has come to individual *c*· ;

individual in

My.	119– 9	individual in *c*· — in Mind,

infinite

Mis.	258–24	infinite *c*·, ever-presence,
No.	37– 6	eternal God and infinite *c*·

in Science

My.	117– 9	divine order and *c*· in Science,

interchange of

No.	14– 6	can be no interchange of *c*·,

is Mind

Ret.	56–18	All *c*· is Mind,
Un.	24–12	All *c*· is Mind ;
No.	10–18	all *c*· is Mind and eternal,

left to

'02.	7–14	nothing is left to *c*· but Love,

material

Mis.	179–28	We must lay aside material *c*·,
Un.	42– 6	results of material *c*· ;
	42– 6	material *c*· can have no real

mental

Ret.	94–13	no matter, to the mental *c*·.

misguide

'01.	20–16	bewilder, darken, or misguide *c*·,

consciousness

misled
Mis. 222–12 In this state of misled *c*,
mode of
Un. 8– 6 What you see, . . . is a mode of *c*,
modes and
Mis. 268– 1 materializes human modes and *c*,
mortal
Un. 61– 3 belong to mortal *c*.
Po. 35– 5 mortal *c* Which binds to earth
my
Mis. 222–31 Truth had flowed into my *c*
My. 270–11 nearer my *c* than before,
no
Mis. 259– 9 no *c* or knowledge of evil ;
Un. 3–24 no *c* of anything unlike Himself ;
21–15 With Him is no *c* of evil,
No. 36–22 no *c* of human error,
of corporeality
Mis. 309–19 The *c* of corporeality,
of disease
Mis. 308–26 holding in mind the *c* of disease
of ease
Mis. 219–18 *c* of ease and loss of suffering ;
of error
Un. 4–14 lose our own *c* of error.
4–16 we lose all *c* of error,
of evil
Un. 21–15 With Him is no *c* of evil,
50–19 The less *c* of evil . . . mortals have,
of God
Mis. 352–11 quickens the true *c* of God,
'02. 8–30 *c* of God as Love gives man power
of good
Mis. 9– 1 *c* of good, grace, and peace,
259– 9 *c* of good has no . . . knowledge of
of harmony
Rud. 11–15 absolute *c* of harmony
of health
Mis. 311–17 to gain the abiding *c* of health,
My. 349– 4 health is a *c* of health,
of heaven
My. 118–28 *c* of heaven within us
of Life
Un. 41– 3 true knowledge and *c* of Life,
of light
No. 30–22 *c* of light is like the
of Mind
My. 131–31 I say with the *c* of Mind
of sickness
Mis. 179–16 Have we left the *c* of sickness
of the unreality
Rud. 11–13 *c* of the unreality of pain
of Truth
My. 63–13 * our expanding *c* of Truth,
old
Mis. 179–12 This is the old *c*.
179–22 old *c* of Soul in sense.
one
No. 38–20 Having one God, one Mind, one *c*,
our
Mis. 179– 8 Is our *c* in matter or in God?
179–11 We are wrong if our *c* is in sin,
290–24 it should not, to our *c*,
My. 203– 6 distinct in our *c* and life,
patient's
Mis. 219–18 change his patient's *c* of dis-ease
220–17 changed his patient's *c* from
perfect
No. 31–18 until a perfect *c* is attained.
plane of
Pul. 38–19 * entirely different a plane of *c*
pure
Un. 57–14 His pure *c* was discriminating,
real
Rud. 5–18 Soul is the only real *c*
realm and
No. 21–17 mingle in the same realm and *c*.
rise in
My. 116– 3 endeavor to rise in *c*
roused
Ret. 31–15 acting . . . on my roused *c*,
same
Mis. 364–27 it has the same *c*,
sensation and
Mis. 228–23 perception, sensation, and *c*
360–23 spiritual sensation and *c*.
sense and
Mis. 219–28 change this evil sense and *c*
sense or
Mis. 93–29 a sinning sense or *c*
Un. 7–24 the sense or *c* of sin,
sensual
Un. 9– 5 Material and sensual *c* are
silences
Mis. 198– 9 *c* silences the mortal claim

consciousness

spiritual
Un. 23–25 good and spiritual *c*
35–24 Spirit is *spiritual c* alone.
35–25 spiritual *c* can form nothing unlike
spiritualize
No. 11–27 spiritualize *c* with the dictum and
stages of
Un. 50–16 states or stages of *c*,
state of
Mis. 219–25 state of *c* made manifest
367–22 evil is a different state of *c*.
'02. 9–16 urging a state of *c* that
supercilious
'00. 15–12 supercilious *c* that saith
supreme in
My. 205–20 makes God more supreme in *c*,
temporary
Un. 4– 7 To gain a temporary *c* of
their
Mis. 267– 3 steadfast in their *c* of the
the only
Un. 21–20 and this is the only *c*
this
Mis. 180– 4 through this *c*, I was delivered
278– 8 There is great joy in this *c*,
Un. 24–13 This *c* is reflected in
My. 258–27 this *c* of God's dear love
true
Mis. 298–25 true *c* is the true health.
352–11 quickens the true *c* of God,
Un. 4–13 God is all true *c* ;
untrue
'02. 6–14 a false claim, an untrue *c*,
without
Mis. 47–11 without *c* of its weight
your own
'01. 1–23 define God to your own *c*

Mis. 205–20 individual Spirit-substance and *c*
330–12 *c* thereof is here and now
352–32 the *c* be allowed to rejoice
Ret. 56–21 claims to be mind, or *c*,
69–26 *C*, where art thou?
Un. 50–22 a *c* which is without Mind
50–24 *c* should not be evil.
'01. 30– 8 *c* which is most imbued
'02. 7– 6 category of creation or *c*.
My. 349– 4 a *c* gained through Christ,

consecrate
Mis. 5– 6 willing to *c* themselves to this
109–27 *c* one's life anew.
Hea. 5–26 elevate, and *c* man;
My. 36–10 *c* all that we are or hope to be
187–22 to *c* your beautiful temple

consecrated
Mis. x– 2 *c* life wherein dwelleth peace,
177–15 become real and *c* warriors
318–22 a devout, *c* Christian.
350–30 My life, *c* to humanity
354–17 character subdued, a life *c*,
Man. 55–20 consistent, *c* Christian Scientist
Ret. 47–25 good Bible scholar and a *c* Christian,
95– 6 * That thou may'st *c* be
Pul. 32–27 * a saintly and *c* character.
My. 28–19 * *c* leadership of Mrs. Eddy,

consecrates
Mis. 8–19 sanctifies, and *c* human life,
252–26 *c* and inspires the teacher

consecrating
Mis. 291–26 refreshing, and *c* mankind.

consecration
Mis. 177– 3 an absolute *c* to the greatest
Pul. 30–30 * its *c* service on January 6
59– 5 * sentence or prayer of *c*,
85– 2 * devotion and *c* to God
My. 41–28 * through long years of *c*
46–23 * pledge ourselves to a deeper *c*,

consecutive
Man. 68–14 remain with her three *c* years,
91–25 diplomas are for three *c* years
Ret. 6–27 faithfully for two *c* years.

consecutively
Man. 68– 5 to remain . . . three years *c*.

consent
Mis. 77– 7 and *c* to that infinite demand
83–13 with the *c* of his own belief.
113–14 depths of perdition by his own *c*.
119–27 Would you *c* that others should tear
228–28 Common *c* is contagious,
282– 8 without their knowledge or *c*?
283– 6 without his knowledge or *c*,
289–22 except by mutual *c*.

consent

Mis. 289–25	by mutual *c*·, . . . she may win
297–22	by mutual *c*· of both parties,
300–17	When I *c*· to this act,
301– 3	without the author's *c*·,
301–22	and read it publicly *without my c*·.
349– 1	received my *c*· and even the offer of
Man. 26–10	the *c*· of the Pastor Emeritus
27–10	the written *c*· of said Board.
30– 9	the *c*· of the Pastor Emeritus,
43– 1	without her or their *c*·
50–10	the *c*· of the Board of Directors.
53–13	unnecessarily and without her *c*·,
57–15	the *c*· of this Board and the
67– 9	without her written *c*·.
68– 7	without the Directors' *c*·
76–20	the *c*· of the Pastor Emeritus.
78–10	written *c*· of the Pastor Emeritus.
81– 3	the *c*· of the Pastor Emeritus
82– 9	without her knowledge or written *c*·.
87– 4	*c*· of the authority of their Church.
97–11	the *c*· of the Pastor Emeritus
103– 7	written *c*· of the Pastor Emeritus,
104–11	written *c*· of its author.
105– 4	written *c*· of Mary Baker Eddy,
Ret. 71–10	without the *c*· or knowledge of
71–16	if he would *c*· to this ;
88–24	without the *c*· of the stated occupant
Pan. 8– 1	or by the *c*· of Mind !
My. 15– 9	written *c*· of the Pastor Emeritus,
61–24	* the human mind was giving its *c*·.
247– 4	the common *c*· of the governed,
254–25	the common *c*· of the governed,
255– 5	churches have my *c*· to publish
302–16	But without my *c*·, the use of
356–16	nor *c*· to have my picture issued,

consented

Man. 64–19	afterward *c*· on the ground that
My. 164– 3	demand increased, and I *c*·,
284–22	I *c*· thereto only as other
318–17	he *c*· on condition that I
320– 4	* he readily *c*· to assist me,

consents

'00. 4– 4	unwittingly *c*· to many minds

consequence

Pan. 8–28	and dying in *c*· of it.
My. 56– 4	* in *c*· two services were held,

consequences

Mis. 108–16	mortals' ignorance and its *c*·,
109–21	knowledge of sin and its *c*·,
297–24	count the *c*· of his own conduct ;
Pul. 14–17	and never fear the *c*·.
No. 17– 3	He must produce its *c*·.
'02. 6–13	God made neither evil nor its *c*·.

consequent

Mis. 26–24	God's *c*· is the spiritual cosmos.
337–10	*c*· disaffection for all evil,
No. 6–11	the *c*· cure of the sick,
16–28	Death is the *c*· of an
'01. 6–18	its *c*· Christianity is consistent
My. 266–13	*c*· vacancies occurring in the

consequently

Mis. 31–12	*c*· to the lack of faith in good.
Ret. 6–22	He was *c*· admitted to the bar
59– 3	*c*· a mortal mind and soul
68–23	*c*· no transference of mortal thought
Un. 34–12	*c*· there is no matter.
Pul. 46– 4	* *C*· the new rules were formulated.
No. 17– 7	*c*· it is impossible for the true man
My. 14–16	* *c*· further payments or

conservation

My. 226– 7	*c*· of number in geometry,

conservative

Mis. 226–30	*c*· swindler, who sells himself
My. 345–24	*c*· about advice on surgical cases.''

conservators

Pul. 82–12	* *c*· of the world's morals

consider

Mis. 31– 1	*c*· to be mental malpractice?
65–14	not *c*· the false side of existence
131–19	just to *c*· the great struggles with
297–25	will *c*· the effects, on himself
Chr. 55–13	neither *c*· the operation — *Isa.* 5 : 12.
Ret. 22– 9	'' *C*· him that endured — *Heb.* 12 : 3.
50–12	if they *c*· three hundred dollars
83–28	when we *c*· the necessity of
Pul. 39– 9	poem that I *c*· superbly sweet
49– 3	* *c*· her their spiritual Leader
No. 28–15	The proof . . . I *c*· well established.
'02. 4–22	*c*· these two commandments
My. 138– 4	I *c*· this agreement a great benefit
196–20	'' *C*· him that endured — *Heb.* 12 : 3.

consider

My. 223–15	do not *c*· myself capable of
227–16	*c*· well their ability to cope with
236–27	I *c*· the information there given
237– 6	I do not *c*· a precedent for

considerable

Pul. 64– 5	* There is usually *c*· difficulty in
My. 66– 5	* *c*· activity has been going on
74– 5	* will bring *c*· numbers of

consideration

Mis. 13–10	urge upon the solemn *c*·
133– 9	*c*· to the following Scripture,
134–17	Let no *c*· bend or outweigh
136– 9	brought to your earnest *c*·,
247– 4	*proofs* . . . be allowed due *c*·,
350– 8	subject given out for *c*·
350–19	the *c*· of these two topics,
Ret. 88–17	leads inevitably to a *c*· of
'01. 33– 1	piety was the all-important *c*·
My. 54–28	* *c*· of places for meeting
85–29	* Aside from every other *c*·,
297– 4	in *c*· of all that Miss Barton
360–10	In *c*· of the present momentous

considerations

Mis. 317–19	These *c*· prompt my answers
Ret. 48– 9	all these *c*· moved me to
No. 7– 4	No personal *c*· should allow
'01. 30–20	destroying all lower *c*·.

considered

Mis. 289–15	This fact should be duly *c*·
378– 3	A patient *c*· incurable left that
Man. 44– 1	spirit . . . shall be definitely *c*·.
53–14	it shall be *c*· an offense.
53–22	shall be *c*· a sufficient evidence
71–16	no Church . . . shall be *c*· loyal that
99– 4	*c*· as though it were two States,
Un. 8– 1	Let another query now be *c*·,
57– 3	Anatomically *c*·, the design of
Rud. 5–10	*c*· apart from Mind.
'02. 5–13	God must be intelligently *c*·
15–17	My husband, . . . was *c*· wealthy,
My. 54–17	* different places were *c*·,
55– 6	* Several places were *c*·,
259–23	occasions, *c*· either collectively
314– 9	*c*· a rarely skilful dentist.
319–27	* I *c*· the time an important

considering

Mis. 92– 1	*c*· the necessity for
271–15	*c*· a subject that is unworthy
My. 319–18	* *c*· the questions which have

consign

Mis. 350–27	which *c*· people to suffering.

consigned

My. 273–27	at length they are *c*· to dust.

consigning

Ret. 90–17	*c*· them to the care of nurse

consigns

Mis. 293–28	*c*· sensibility to the charnel-house

consist

Mis. 315–13	class shall *c*· of not over
Man. 25– 5	The Church officers shall *c*· of
26–20	Board of Directors shall *c*· of
63– 5	The next lessons *c*· of
64– 5	literature sold . . . shall *c*· only of
76–16	shall *c*· of three members of
79– 4	shall *c*· of not less than three
84– 9	class shall *c*· of not more than
97– 5	*c*· of one loyal Christian Scientist
99–25	Committees on . . . shall *c*· of men
Pul. 45–28	* sermons hereafter will *c*· of

consisted

'00. 13–22	The Pergamene church *c*· of
My. 34–14	* The Lesson-Sermon *c*· of

consistencies

Rud. 7– 5	conceptions and *c*· of C. S.

consistency

'01. 26– 1	unity and *c*· of Jesus' theory
My. 214–16	letters questioning the *c*· of

consistent

Mis. 191–21	destroys all *c*· supposition of
223–15	disbelieves in . . . and is *c*·.
312– 4	Love is *c*·, uniform,
Man. 55–20	*c*·, consecrated Christian Scientist,
'01. 6–19	*c*· with Christ's hillside sermon,
Hea. 4–28	*c*· with our inconsistent statement
My. vii–11	* *c*· and constant right thinking
94–10	* steady, *c*· growth of the sect
291–17	uniform, *c*·, sympathetic,

consistently

Mis. 105–13	if this sense were *c*· sensible.
'01. 4–24	Scientists *c*· conceive of God as One

consistently
'01.	7– 1	c· conceivable as the personality of
	7–14	c· say, "Our Father-Mother God"
My.	313–20	I have always c· declared

consisting
Mis.	132–16	c· in part of dictating answers
Man.	88– 7	c· of three members,
	102– 4	c· of not less than three members,
My.	80–17	* services were identical, c· of

consists
Un.	4–23	"life eternal" c· in — *John* 17 : 3.
	22– 3	this likeness c· in a sense of
Pul.	38– 8	* It c· of fourteen chapters,
'02.	17–22	Happiness c· in being . . . good ;
Peo.	6–12	* "The art of medicine c· in
My.	108–11	c· in this forcible fact :

consolation
Un.	17–12	c· from borrowed scintillations.
My.	38– 3	* in God is all c· and comfort,
	283–27	C· and peace are based on
	290–13	for your support, c·, and victory.

console
Mis.	131– 8	let the leaner sort c· this brother's
	275–18	c· the innocent, and throw wide the
Un.	18–13	in order to c· it.
	18–14	you oftenest c· others in
'02.	19– 3	hastened to c· his unfaithful

consolidate
Man.	72–18	shall c· under one church

consolidating
My.	200– 3	c· the genius of C. S.

consoling
Mis.	327–24	c· their afflictions, and helping

consonance
Mis.	364– 1	c· with the textbook of C. S.
Man.	51– 2	in c· with the Scriptural demand
	72–23	in c· with The Mother Church Manual.
Ret.	93– 7	in c· with their Principle.

consonant
My.	277–16	Killing men is not c· with

conspicuous
Mis.	83–21	meekness was as c· as
My.	272–26	* and leads with such c· success

conspicuously
My.	85–13	* it is c· manifest.
	356– 3	where God dwells most c·

conspiracy
Mis.	177– 6	leagued together in secret c·
Ret.	63–16	nothing but a c· against man's
	63–18	feel bound to expose this c·,
'02.	1–11	combined in formidable c·,

conspirator
My.	128–25	as effectually as does a subtle c· ;

conspire
Ret.	78–22	to c· against the blessings

conspires
Peo.	11–27	Scientific guessing c· unwittingly

constancy
Po.	page 3	poem
My.	37–14	* c· of your obedience during

constant
Mis.	115–16	c· watchfulness and prayer
	147–14	one who makes it his c· rule
	236–15	yielding to c· solicitations
	241–15	c· combat and direful struggles,
	263–18	their c· petitions for the same,
Ret.	32–17	* Whose most c· substance seems
	38– 7	I yielded to a c· conviction
Pul.	9–25	c· prayers, prophecies, and
No.	46– 9	must answer the c· inquiry:
'01.	23–28	* "only the c· relation between
'02.	18– 4	c· spectacle of sin thrust upon
Po.	15–20	c· as love that outliveth the
	16– 2	c· and hopeful though winter
My.	vii–11	* consistent and c· right thinking
	48–18	* c· daily reading of the Bible
	86– 3	* will be c· and sincere.
	89–19	* almost as c· as petitions
	134– 1	c· battle against the world,
	160– 6	in c· relation with the divine,
	175– 4	requires my c· attention and time,
	192–24	c· recurring demands upon my time
	294–19	in spite of the c· stress of

Constantine
Mis.	224– 7	courtier told C· that a mob

constantly
Mis.	62– 4	opposite image . . . kept c· in mind,
	133–27	I turn c· to divine Love
	160–11	gaining c· in the knowledge
	177–29	I am c· homesick for heaven.

constantly
Mis.	206–19	Scientist is c· accentuating harmony
	238–28	falsehoods kept c· before the public.
	265–27	c· called to settle questions
	353–30	they c· go to her for help,
Ret.	73–21	C· to scrutinize physical
	82– 2	yet their core is c· renewed ;
Un.	30– 3	c· uses the word *soul*
Rud.	9– 4	c· sowing the seeds of discord
Pan.	8–28	They c· reiterate the belief of
	12– 6	how can Spirit be c· passing
'02.	1– 5	church communicants c· increase
Hea.	5–19	grand truth which is c· covered,
	9– 5	We are c· thinking and talking
Peo.	2–26	held c· before the people's
My.	11– 5	* has been c· at her post
	22– 5	* the c· increasing attendance
	76– 5	* new contributions were c· being
	95– 5	* c· strengthened by members
	211–24	lies, poured c· into his mind,
	231–19	Mrs. Eddy is c· receiving
	305–17	demand for this book c· increases.
	308–27	household law, c· enforced,

constellation
Mis.	340–27	Every luminary in the c· of

constituency
No.	4–22	true c· of being.

constituent
No.	4– 7	human error, a c· part of

constituents
Mis.	296– 4	among its c· and managers
My.	340–23	has suggested to his c·

constitute
Mis.	v– 6	c· THE SUCCESS OF A STUDENT
	65–28	c· the divine law of healing
	234–25	c· physical and mental perfection,
Ret.	65–25	c· the only evangelism.
	67– 4	human thought does not c· sin,
	68–29	good, and pure c· his ancestry.
	76–20	c· the Mind-healer a wonder-worker,
Un.	24–20	God and the universe — c· all
	56–27	c· the miasma of earth.
No.	10–27	c· the phenomena of being,
	11– 6	c· his individuality in the
	38–21	and loving . . . c· C. S.,
Pan.	10–30	c· no part of man, but obscure man.
'01.	1–14	c· mental and physical perfection.
	5– 4	he believes three persons c· the
My.	5–16	c· a Christian Scientist,
	88–17	* externals c· the smallest feature of
	136–13	c· the Board of Trustees
	259–19	c· man, and nothing less is man

constituted
Mis.	56–14	c· laws to that effect,
	217–15	nature is c· of and by Spirit.
Man.	79–19	c· by a Deed of Trust
Ret.	65–16	If the religion of to-day is c· of
My.	80– 8	* c· a severe tax upon
	107–26	the c· religious rights in
	318– 2	c· a new style of language.

constitutes
Mis.	9–30	false sense of what c· happiness
	56–13	to conclude that Spirit c·
	86–27	c· our mortal environment.
	86–29	c· their present earth and heaven :
	185– 8	c· a so-called material man,
	206–16	nor lack of what c· true manhood,
	233–26	rule of C. S. is what c· its utility :
	375–14	* idea of what c· true art.
Man.	28– 4	Law c· government,
Ret.	28–20	increases, diminishes, c·, and
	67– 4	c· the human or physical concept.
Un.	53– 7	it c· the lie an evil.
Pul.	53–21	* c· the power of the human soul.
'01.	2–14	Absolute certainty . . . c· its utility
	7– 5	c· the individuality of the infinite
My.	64–18	* c· the high standing of C. S.

constituting
Mis.	56–11	Every indication of matter's c· life
	364–15	c· and governing all identity,
Rud.	2– 6	subjects, or agents, c· the

Constitution
My.	128– 7	C· of the United States,
	200– 2	individual rights under the C·
	222–22	C· of the United States
	282– 3	in our C·, and in the laws of God.

constitution
Mis.	224–14	different history, c·, culture,
	382–25	wrote its c· and by-laws,
	382–26	also the c· and by-laws of
Pul.	79–22	* something in the c· of man

constitutional
'01. 33–16 c· laws of their land ;
Peo. 10–12 our c· Bill of Rights.
My. 227–22 justice, c· individual rights,
340–18 through c· interpretations.

constrained
My. 360–12 I am c· to say, if I can settle this

construct
Mis. 330–32 c· the stalk, instruct the ear,
My. 71–28 * c· an auditorium that would

constructed
Pul. 75–22 * the church c· in the great
My. 157–16 * Building in Washington is c·.

constructing
Mis. 244– 5 Mind alone c· the human system,

construction
Pul. 65–19 * whose architectural c·
76– 1 * material used in its c·
My. 24–24 * enduring character of its c·,
63– 3 * the c· of the church,
71–15 * been in process of c·,
75–29 * any part of the expense of its c·
83–24 * the c· of the new temple
318–12 to defend my grammatical c·,
338–21 may have overlooked the c· that

construed
Mis. 121–32 c· the substitution of a good man
291–11 is often c· as direct orders,
No. 9–26 humanly c·, and according to Webster,
My. 329– 1 * This was c· to include

construes
Mis. 301– 9 what the law c· as crime.

consult
Man. 47– 7 may c· with an M. D. on the anatomy
'02. 17–25 C· thy every-day life ;
My. 338–16 not allowed to c· me relative to

consultation
Mis. 378– 8 After much c· among ourselves,

consulted
Mis. 146–13 have hitherto declined to be c·
289–30 Mutual interests . . . should be c·,
348–32 student who c· me on this
349–12 he c· me on the feasibility of
Man. 67– 2 is not to be c· on cases of
70– 1 Pastor Emeritus to be C·.
87– 7 is not to be c· on this subject.
88–16 President not to be C·.
88–17 President is not to be c·
My. 114–15 I c· no other authors and
137–26 c· Lawyer Streeter about the method.

consulting
Man. 27– 8 without c· with the full Board
70– 5 without first c· her on said subject

consume
Mis. 51–31 that ye may c· it — Jas. 4: 3.
366– 3 attention that human hypotheses c·.
No. 40– 2 c· it on your lusts."— see Jas. 4: 3.
My. 124–31 that they c· in their own fires
160–23 will eventually c· this planet.

consumed
Mis. 82–26 is c· as a moth,
230– 4 great amount of time is c· in
326–12 they c· the next dwelling ;
Ret. 72–10 c· with terrors."— Psal. 73 : 19.
My. 25–18 the time c· in travel,
105–10 the lungs were mostly c·.
160–26 until the sinner is c·,

consumes
Mis. 117–21 each step be taken, c· time,
Ret. 94–10 c· whatsoever is of sin.

consuming
Mis. 151– 6 God is a c· fire.
326–15 "God is a c· fire."— Heb. 12 : 29.
Ret. 79– 6 In this c· heat false images
'02. 18–12 nor spared . . . the c· tares.

consummate
Mis. 194–29 c· naturalness of the Life
200– 1 c· naturalness of Truth
213– 7 c· the joys of acquiescence
355–10 To c· this desideratum,
Ret. 82–22 to c· much good or else evil ;
My. 23– 6 * to c· the erection of the
274– 7 so c· man's being with the

consummated
Ret. 20–27 A plot was c· for
My. 14– 3 when this bringing is c·,
292– 7 and the joy of acquiescence c·.

consummates
'02. 6–18 and c· the First Commandment,

consummation
Mis. 98–22 * "c· devoutly to be wished."
322–22 For this c· He hath given you
Un. 17–19 * c· devoutly to be wished."
Pul. 8–19 earn a few pence toward this c·.
45–11 * features of this glorious c·
My. 60–28 * to perform in this wonderful c·.
181–16 * c· devoutly to be wished"
283–11 prayed and labored for the c· of

consumption
Mis. 58– 1 If one has died of c·,
58– 7 learns that c· did not kill him.
Ret. 16– 8 since she . . . was in c· !
Pul. 54–30 of incipient pulmonary c·.
'01. 17–16 the last stages of c·, pneumonia,
My. 80– 5 * cured of blindness, of c·
105– 7 I healed c· in its last stages,

contact
Mis. 110– 9 lose them not through c· with the
229– 5 catching when exposed to c· with
236– 7 from c· with family difficulties,
Pul. 31–15 * close c· with public feeling
36– 6 * to retire from active c· with
68–10 * to retire from active c· with

contagion
Mis. 228–20 chapter sub-title
229–26 a better preventive of c·
My. 116– 1 chapter sub-title
116– 5 fact . . . realized will stop a c·.
116– 8 it is a c· — a mental malady,
116–15 danger and darkness of personal c·.
116–16 Forgetting . . . brings on this c·.
116–23 from injustice and personal c·.
118– 4 the disobedient spread personal c·,

contagious
Mis. 228–28 Common consent is c·,
228–30 infectious and c· diseases,
229–10 good is more c· than evil,
229–20 confidence of mankind in c· disease
My. 116– 2 At a time of c· disease,
116–20 not a symptom of this c· malady,
190– 9 of c· and organic diseases?
219–28 infectious and c· diseases
220– 7 reporting of a c· case to
226–30 infectious or c· diseases."
344–23 infectious and c· diseases.

contain
Mis. 16–20 more than a person, . . . can c· ;
76–12 but they c· immortal souls !
309–30 which c· all and much more
311–23 The works . . . c· absolute Truth,
366– 6 they c· and offer Science,
Hea. 4– 1 finite cannot c· the infinite,
12– 1 c· no medicinal properties,
My. 50–21 * records c· these simple . . . words,
87– 2 * greater than the building could c·.
179–13 Testaments c· self-evident truths
334–10 * still c· the original account of

contained
Mis. 50– 7 c· in that book,
92–16 c· in that chapter of "S. and H.
199–27 so-called miracles c· in Holy Writ
302–29 divine teachings c· in "S. and H.
Man. 34– 9 teaching c· in the C. S. textbook,
43– 9 is c· in the books of the
63–10 C. S. c· in their textbook.
80–10 By-Laws c· in this Manual.
Ret. 2–24 c· a full account of the
91– 6 c· in what is commonly known as
Pul. 53–10 * c· in the one word — faith.
55–22 * c· in the volume entitled "S. and H.
'00. 3–24 c· this divine appellative
'02. 15– 1 letters mailed to me c· threats
My. 17–14 c· in the scripture, — I Pet. 2 : 6.
18–28 It c· the following articles :
54– 5 * Boston Traveler c· the following
138–28 * statements c· in the annexed letter
171–29 * The casket c· a gavel
199–13 joint resolutions c· therein

containing
Mis. 217–18 presuppose . . . person c· infinite
280–21 c· beautiful hand-painted flowers
Man. 98–15 papers c· such an article,
Ret. 1– 9 manuscripts c· Scriptural sonnets,
37– 2 c· the complete statement of C. S.,
Pul. 28– 5 * c· the C. S. seal,
60–20 * c· pneumatic wind-chests
My. 172–23 * box c· the gavel was opened
223–13 c· questions about secular affairs,
332–17 * paper c· this card is now in

contains
Mis. 273–26 class which c· that number.
Un. 2–18 c· neither discord nor disease.

contains
Un. 14– 1 platform, which c· such planks as
Pul. vii– 1 c· scintillations from press and
86– 2 * c· a solid gold box,
'01. 6–14 We hear . . . this Person c· three
Hea. 7–28 it c· no argument for a creed
My. 53–26 * c· some very interesting
68– 6 * c· about one mile and a half of pews.
69–16 * auditorium c· seven galleries,
98–14 * c· a . . . remarkable announcement
112–18 c· a Science which is demonstrable
146–13 C. S. c· infinitely more than
180–12 C. S. c· no element whatever of
299–11 c· the entire truth of

contaminating
Ret. 52– 5 c· influences of those who

contemned
My. 33–22 vile person is c· ; — Psal. 15 : 4.

contemplate
Mis. 16–28 earnestly to c· this new-born
155–29 were they to c· the universal
321–29 wisdom and Love to c·,
'01. 15–14 to c· the infinite blessings

contemplated
My. 137–24 I had c· doing this
237– 1 c· reference in S. and H.
343– 6 * "No present change is c·

contemplating
Mis. 64–12 Persons c· a course at the
308–25 c· personality impedes spiritual
380– 7 When c· the majesty and
Man. 94–10 should go away c· truth ;
Po. v–10 * c· this lofty New Hampshire crag,
My. 216–30 C· these important wants,
290– 2 c· this sudden international

contemplation
Mis. 98– 3 that his c· regarding himself
136–11 turning aside for one hour from c·
309–10 true c· of his character.
322– 2 earnestly invite you to its c·

contemplative
Mis. 43–13 c· reading of my books,

contemporary
Mis. 22– 7 what, but the c· of Christianity,
My. 98–30 * our c·, the Boston Times,

contempt
Mis. 170–27 expressing the utmost c·.
170–28 recorded as having expressed c·
My. 324– 4 * thought of c· for the unlearned,

contemptible
Mis. 226–21 liar and hypocrite is so c·,
230– 8 one of which is c·,

contemptuously
No. 41– 4 Pharisees . . . c· called him

contending
No. 1–15 noise and stir of c· sentiments
Hea. 9–13 C· for the reality of
My. 148–27 to gain power over c· sects

content
Pan. 11–20 Mortals, c· with something less
11–26 lost image that mortals are c· to
My. 151–26 They were c· to look no higher

contented
My. 80– 2 * prosperous, c· men and women,
87– 9 * and cheerfully c· multitude
95–17 * c· and well-dressed body of people.

contentiously
Mis. 156–25 listening . . . amicably, or c·,

contents
Mis. 9–21 the c· of this cup of selfish
50–16 understanding of the c· of this book,
My. 178–27 c· of "S. and H. with Key to the
304–30 she has stolen the c· of
338–11 The c· of the last lecture

contest
Mis. 101–10 they began and ended in a c· for
188–11 a c· between Truth and error ;
Ret. 3– 7 caused that prolonged c·
56–13 this c· must go on until

contests
Peo. 2–19 demoniacal c· over religion.

context
Mis. 194–19 The c· of the foregoing
Hea. 8– 9 perceive the meaning of the c·,

contexts
My. 110–32 torn from their necessary c·,

continent
Ret. 47– 5 Students from all over our c·,
Pul. 75–26 * most nearly fire-proof . . . on the c·,

continent
Peo. 10–28 slavery was abolished on this c·,
My. 85–10 * Atlantic to the Pacific on this c·.
88– 5 * C. S., as now before this c·,

continents
Mis. 152– 4 in love c· clasp hands,
My. 124–12 heart meeting heart across c·
194– 2 in broad facts over great c·

contingent
Ret. 67–22 in no way c· on Adam's thought,
No. 43– 3 Truth is not c· on matter.
My. 179–26 being c· on nothing written
293–23 c· on the power of God,

continual
Mis. 316–20 c· recapitulation of tired aphorisms
Un. 41–17 c· presence and power of good,
No. 37–17 demands His c· presence,

continually
Mis. 92– 7 needs c· to study this textbook.
130–10 looking c· for a fault in
151–25 c· be full of oil,
362–20 c·, until self-extinguished by
Man. 48–13 c· stroll by her house,
Un. 9–24 Healing has gone on c· ;
No. 20–28 c· straying into forbidden by-paths
My. 9–11 * c· move us to utter our gratitude
130–14 to be c· pursuing a lie
346– 1 * her views, . . . were c· surprising.

continuance
Peo. 2– 2 which insures man's c·
My. 198– 7 God grant not only the c· of

continue
Mis. xii– 3 With armor on, I c· the march,
42– 2 does life c· in thought only
86– 6 must c· to strive with sickness,
92–23 to c· the study of this textbook.
154–23 C· in His love.
164– 7 this will c· to be seen
164–22 Thus it will c·, . . . until man
256–18 c· to send to each applicant
273–19 c·, as at present, to send
286– 7 will c· unprohibited in C. S.
004 16 * will c· until that Exhibition closes.
310–18 To c· one's connection with this
312–25 Truth that will c· to reverberate
359– 5 you c· the mental argument
Man. 58– 9 will c· to preach for this Church
61–23 should c· about eight or nine minutes
72–22 c· its present form of government
90–12 will c· not over one week.
Ret. 22–15 c· till its involved errors are
50–24 c· to organize churches,
65–18 it will c· to avoid whatever
81– 7 and our friendship will surely c·.
84– 4 should c· to study this textbook,
84–12 c· to study and assimilate this
85– 4 to c· the organization of churches,
Pul. 6– 8 It will c· till the antithesis of
79–28 this condition can never long c·.
83– 1 * c· to demand woman's love
No. 7– 7 and c· to do so unto the end.
46–22 I shall c· to labor and wait.
Pan. 6– 5 let us c· to denounce evil
6– 6 c· to fight it until it disappears,
14–12 c· to characterize her government,
'01. 19– 9 c· to ask, and because of your
My. 5–27 C· to choose whom ye will serve.
10–33 c· to "prosper — Isa. 55 : 11.
37–10 * all that you have done and c· to do
122– 9 plant will c· to grow.
123– 4 I must c· to prize love even more
123– 8 c· to urge the perfect model
132–18 Oh, may these rich blessings c·
141–26 branch churches c· their communion
166– 3 will c· with divine approbation.
175–26 Let brotherly love c·.
191– 8 C· steadfast in love
195–29 c· to build, rebuild, adorn, and
200–29 For this I shall c· to pray.
246– 2 c· for three years as practitioners
261– 7 Let it c· thus with one exception :
267– 4 Nothing can . . . c· forever which is

continued
Mis. 110–21 thanksgiving for the c· progress
192–16 name shall be c· — Psal. 72 : 17.
Man. 60– 3 C· Throughout the Year.
60– 5 c· twelve months each year,
Ret. 8–10 c· until I grew discouraged,
45– 9 c· organization retards spiritual
Pul. 37–21 * "Mother feels very strongly," he c·,
41– 4 * contributions which c· to flow in
49–15 * she c· : "Look at those big elms !
64–12 * to stop the c· inflow of money

continued
No. 20–26 c· series of mortal hypotheses,
Po. v–22 * c· to reach the author
My. 44–28 * desire to express their c· loyalty
55–20 * c· there until March, 1894,
56–31 * c· growth, this c· overcrowding,
91–24 * the church has c· to grow.
222–10 c· : "If ye have faith — Matt. 17 : 20.
318–27 would have c· with a long argument,

continues
Mis. 188–22 c· the explanation of the power
365–21 but it c·, and increases,
No. 19– 4 That it c· to rise,
'00. 9–14 reformer c· his lightning,
'02. 6–10 c· to demonstrate this grand
My. 5–21 c· to love more and to serve
94– 1 * growth c· in like proportion
236– 7 this name c· to be multiplied,

continuing
Mis. 252–12 C· this category, we learn

continuity
Pan. 4– 3 owes its origin and c· to
My. 53–29 * even though the c· of thought
342–19 c· of The Church of Christ,

continuous
Pul. 59– 6 * c· services were held from nine to

continuously
Man. 85–18 members who have not been c·

contract
Mis. 243–28 and the organ to c· ;
289–16 when by the marriage c·
290– 5 animus of the c is preserved
297–21 claims growing out of this c·,
297–23 or this c· is legally dissolved.

contractors
Mis. 289–22 must not be retaken by the c·,

contracts
My. 12– 4 * justified the letting of c·.

contradict
Mis. 190–17 will c· the interpretations that
382– 2 my experience would c· it
Rud. 7–14 Science and spiritual sense c· this,
No. 6– 2 would c· the Science of Mind-healing

contradicted
Mis. 295–21 not only be queried, but flatly c·,
My. 334– 7 * allegation . . . she has c· herself,

contradicting
Pan. 4–28 By admitting . . . and then c· them,
6–12 talking serpent, c· the word of God
My. 294–10 unrighteous c· minds of mortals,
330– 8 * thus c· his own statement,

contradiction
Mis. 83–11 *please explain this seeming c·?*
361–14 c· of human hypotheses ;
Ret. 22–10 endured such c· of sinners — Heb. 12 : 3.
Un. 38– 4 Death is a c· of Life,
My. 196–20 endured such c· of sinners — Heb. 12 : 3.

contradictions
Un. 16– 3 unheard-of c·, — absurdities ;
Pan. 7–21 or a vague apology for c·.
Hea. 4–23 with such self-evident c·?

contradictory
Mis. 190–15 too limited and c·.
372– 2 incorrect, c·, unscientific,
Ret. 34– 6 the reply was dark and c·.
59– 4 have no c· significations.
No. 5–26 Any c· fusion of Truth with error,
'01. 25–23 as c· as the blending of good and

contradicts
Mis. 14– 3 material view which c· the
96–31 Science c· this evidence ;
195–17 divine logic, ... c· this inference,
221–24 Such denial also c· the doctrine
Ret. 60–25 Material sense c· Science,
94– 5 and yet c· divine Science

contradistinction
Mis. 36– 4 in c· to good and Truth,
73–30 in c· to the testimony of
Un. 52– 1 in c· to the supposition that
52– 9 c· to the false consciousness of
'01. 24–24 In c· to his views I
'02. 2– 8 in c· to all error,

contrary
Mis. 29–28 on the c·, they fulfil His laws ;
350–12 On the c·, our deliberations were,
350–28 On the c·, I cannot serve two
Man. 55–23 c· to the statement thereof
86–22 shall teach nothing c· thereto.
Ret. 38–10 I set to work, c· to my inclination,
72– 4 is c· to the law of God ;

contrary
Un. 4–18 on the c·, the Father bids man
14–28 but the c·, that by this knowledge,
19– 5 are c· to His creative will,
19–15 On the c·, evil is only a delusive
Pul. 45–18 * repeatedly asseverated to the c·.
54–13 * On the c·, the whole transaction
84–16 * to the c· notwithstanding.
Rud. 11– 1 c· to the law of Spirit.
No. 21– 1 c· to the life and teachings
'00. 9– 3 c· to their inclination.
My. 106–12 On the c·, C. S. has healed cases
138– 7 carried on c· to my wishes.
215–25 on the c·, he bade them take script.
308–30 On the c·, my father was
351–25 any assertions to the c· are false.
359– 2 These Directors do not act c· to

contrast
Mis. 238– 4 to c· with that childhood's wrong

contrasted
Ret. 30–14 as c· with the foibles
41– 2 as c· with its present welcome

contribute
Mis. 156– 1 they would c· oftener to the pages
240–12 All education should c· to
305–24 * asked to c· one cent
My. 7–19 * we agree to c· any portion of
9– 5 * agree to c· any portion of
9–22 to c· any part of two millions
10–20 * not expected to c· money against
20–30 * to ask the members to c· to
21–12 * in order to c· more liberally
96–20 * invited to c· what they could
98–22 * no member . . . was asked to c·
216–24 and no longer c· to The
244–14 to c· my part towards this result.

contributed
Mis. 203– 2 pretty pond c· to Pleasant View,
Pul. 64– 9 * Men, women, and children c·,
My. 19–13 * of the many branch churches which c·
22– 9 * Christian Scientists have c· already
28– 6 * experience of many who have c·
31–12 * c· from over the entire world.
58–13 * c· to the erection of these mighty
86–14 * c· before the actual work was

contributes
My. 68–23 * c· not a little to the imposing

contributing
My. 78–16 * high with bank-notes, everybody c·,

contribution
Mis. 143–25 call from me for this extra c·,
148–24 I was not aware that the c· box
Pul. 71– 5 * c· of a quarter of a million dollars
My. 12–14 * promptness of his own c·.
99–19 * c· baskets when passed around
347–22 Special c· to "Bohemia."

contributions
Mis. 140–15 c· to the Building Fund
143–21 c· of one thousand dollars each,
148–26 c· from the people present
156– 8 send in your c· as usual
303–26 will respond to this letter by c·.
305–16 * small c· from many persons
305–17 * rather than large c· from a few.
306–12 * C· should be sent to the
349–29 the c·, when I preached,
350– 1 two thousand dollars of my own c·.
Man. 96–13 and trust to c· for his fee.
Pul. v– 4 c· OF $4,460 WERE DEVOTED
41– 3 * a cessation of the tide of c·
44–21 * building a church by voluntary c·,
57– 4 * c· for its erection came from
63–24 * by the voluntary c· of
64–12 * compelled to refuse further c·,
'01. 27– 3 * "The best c· that have been made
My. 14–29 * c· to the building fund
23– 1 * to delay our c·
25– 9 * their c· to the building fund.
30–22 * Some of these c· were
76– 5 * c· were constantly being received ;
76– 9 * no more c· to the building fund
76–21 * all c· have been voluntary.
98–23 * C· were entirely voluntary.

contributor
Mis. 305–28 * name of each c·.
My. 217–11 in equal shares to each c·.
217–13 each c· will receive his dividend
(*see also* **Eddy**)

contributors
Mis. 141–29 to the several c·,
313–12 c· to *The C. S. Journal*
Pul. 41– 8 * four thousand of these c·

contributors
Pul. 42–11   * little c· to the building fund,
     86–20   * all c· wherever they may be,
My. 27–10   * chapter sub-title
     27–11   * The c· to the building fund
     42–10   * helpful c· to our periodicals,
     216–14   chapter sub-title
     217– 9   bonds for my dear children c·
     217–12   c· shall have arrived at legal age,

contrite
Un. 61–27   c· heart soonest discerns this truth,

contrition
Mis. 134– 3   as you have expressed c·

control
Mis. 37–11   under the c· of God,
     45– 4   enables you to c· pain.
     69–32   want of c· over "the fish — Gen. 1 : 26.
     97–13   All human c· is animal magnetism,
     137–24   c· appetite, passion, pride,
     140– 1   such as error could not c·.
     199–20   manifest in the c· it gave him
     220–13   harmonious thought has the full c·
Man. 70–12   no . . . c· of other churches,
     74– 5   or c· over any other church.
     83–12   shall not assume personal c· of,
Ret. 9–19   * my spirit's breathings to c·,
Pul. 32– 8   * to dominate, to lead, to c·,
Rud. 16– 1   If publicity and material c· are
No. 40–21   c· aright the thought
'01. 14–24   c· it in the first instance,
     14–25   or it will c· you in the second.
Po. 23–10   Above the world's c·
My. 49– 5   * c·, in no arbitrary sense,
     159–26   could not c· human will,
     270–30   c· both religion and art in unity
     293–25   law of Spirit to c· matter,
     294–14   c· all the conditions of man
     318–23   could c· himself no longer

controlled
Mis. 66–18   material sense must be c· by
     354–24   all is c·, . . . by wisdom, Truth, and
Man. 70–13   shall be c· by none other.
Ret. 82– 6   not . . . be c· by other students,
My. 275– 7   until they are c· by divine Love ;

controller
Rud. 10– 2   throne of the c· of all mankind.

controllers
No. 11– 2   not the creators, c·, nor

controls
Mis. 5–24   reality that Mind c· the body.
     175–23   supposition . . . that one mind c·
     247–20   understand that Spirit c· body.
Man. 87–18   "The less the teacher personally c·
Ret. 84–24   The less the teacher personally c·
Rud. 12–18   c· the health or existence of
'01. 17–27   must be mind that c· the effect ;
Hea. 6–19   Man thinks . . . disease c· his body
Peo. 8–10   c· the muscles of the arm,

controversies
Mis. 125–26   the c· which baffle it,

controversy
Mis. 89–22   for information, not for c·,
Un. 5–21   Let no enmity, no untempered c·,
No. 8–19   hold no c· or enmity over
'00. 12–30   presents the phase of a great c·,
     13– 2   * "a c· was inevitable when
My. 129–32   Refrain from public c· ;
     306– 8   newspaper c· over a question

controvert
Mis. 109– 6   try to reverse, . . . or c·, Truth ;

controverted
My. 322– 4   * facts which cannot be c·

contusions
Mis. 243– 7   students treat sprains, c·, etc.,

convene
Mis. 315–23   c· as often as once in three months.
Man. 57–14   for which the members are to c·.
     70–17   c· to confer on a statute
     84–17   pupils of loyal teachers shall c·
My. 289–12   c· for the sacred purpose of

convened
Mis. 147– 4   another annual meeting has c·,
     350–14   second P. M. c· in about one week
My. 8–25   * c· in annual business meeting
     251–26   You have c· only to convince
     333– 7   * was c· for the purpose of

convenience
Pul. 27– 2   * French mirrors and every c·.
My. 174– 3   c· of the Christian Scientists

conveniences
Pul. 58–28   * furnished with all c· for living,

convenient
Mis. 52–12   That it is often c·,
     150–17   C· houses and halls can now
'00. 2–27   working when it is c·."
     9–10   and wait for a more c· season ;
My. 119– 1   It is c· for history to record
     211– 2   sticklers for a false, c· peace,

conveniently
Man. 27–20   provide suitable rooms, c· and

convening
Mis. 136–24   c· once in four months ;

convention
Mis. 137– 6   close of the first c· of the
     138– 4   to prepare for this national c·
     276–12   the third c· of our National
     370–25   gather . . . into a "national c·"
Ret. 52–17   general c· at New York City,
My. 83– 3   * the holding of a great c·
     83– 4   * residing in the c· city.
     92– 9   * prodigious c· of Christian Scientists

converge
Un. 10–13   Spiritual phenomena never c· toward

convergence
Pul. 22– 4   one nucleus or point of c·,

conversant
My. 319–16   * I am c· with some facts

conversation
Mis. 6–27   c· chiefly confined to the
     225– 8   c· drifted to . . . C. S. ;
     225–13   Soon after this c·,
Man. 91–26   under Mrs. Eddy's daily c·
Ret. 5–26   * elevated character to the tone of c·
Pul. 5–19   c· with a beauty all its own
My. 48–32   * manifest in their faces, their c·,
     315– 5   * c· with him about his wife,
     319–22   * in c· with you about the
     319–29   * recall very plainly the c·
     320–29   * last c· I had with him
     322–13   * reminds me of a c· I had with

conversations
Pul. 72– 6   * number of very interesting c·
My. 306–30   holding long c· with him
     307– 3   In his c· with me
     320–24   * c· were at times somewhat long
     321–24   * my many c· with you,
     321–30   * c· with people who knew you

conversazione
Pul. 6–26   At a c· in Boston, he said,

converse
Mis. 148–28   Let the invitation to this sweet c·
     324– 1   His c· with the watchers
Pul. 72–10   * agreeable lady, ready to c·,
My. 320– 6   * to c· about you and your work,

conversed
My. 149–15   * c· with many wise men,"

conversion
Mis. 229–12   clergyman's c· of sinners,
My. 82– 2   * same stories of their c·,

conversions
Pul. 66– 9   * than from c· from other churches,

convert
Mis. 279–27   enough to c· the world if we are
Rud. 17– 2   Jews whom St. Paul had hoped to c·

converted
Mis. 261–13   was c· to Protestantism through
Ret. 14– 5   c· and rescued from perdition,
     35– 3   c· into the chapter on Recapitulation
Pul. 69– 6   * c· to C. S. by being cured
My. 92– 6   * large numbers . . . c· to it

convertible
'01. 4– 3   major premise must be c· to the

converting
Mis. 39–30   than in c· the sinner.

converts
Pul. 70–13   * over one hundred thousand c·,
My. 94–12   * adherence of its c· to the faith,
     343–19   it won c· from the first.

convey
My. 44–26   * c· to you their sincere greetings
     78–27   * No mere words can c· the
     81–29   * impossible to c· a conception of
     188–27   c· all impressions to man,
     226– 5   and c· its meaning in C. S.

conveyed
Mis. 140– 4   must be c· through a type
     140–12   my gift as I had it c·.
Man. 79–23   manage the property therein c·,

conveyed
Ret.	51– 5	on the premises thereby *c·*,
'02.	13–27	land legally *c·* to me,
My.	66– 7	* estates having been *c·* by deed
	¶7–26	* Word was *c·* to them that
	157–23	which *c·* to them the sum of
	324–24	* Everything he said *c·* this

conveying
Mis.	133– 5	*c·* ideas more opposite to the fact.
Man.	136– 1	heading

conveys
Mis.	378–17	"Because it *c· electricity*
No.	20–12	fully *c·* the ideas of God,

convict
My.	110–28	Robert Ingersoll's attempt to *c·*

convicting
No.	43–15	* *c·* the infidel, alarming the

conviction
Mis.	210–27	Charity has the courage of *c·* ;
	222– 8	*c·* of his wrong state of
	222– 9	failing of *c·* and reform,
	299–11	with the courage of *c·*
Ret.	30–13	Why was this *c·* necessary to
	38– 7	I yielded to a constant *c·*
	48– 7	growing *c·* that every one should
Un.	7–20	and here is one such *c·* :
	55–21	as expressed in his *c·*,
Pul.	34–18	* From that hour dated her *c·* of
Rud.	9–25	clear *c·* of the omnipotence
No.	40–12	thoughts are our honest *c·*.
'00.	15–15	it yields to sharp *c·*
My.	24–26	* have gone away with the *c·* that
	61–15	* and the *c·* that the work
	79–27	* *c·* that they would be believed,
	121– 8	a true, tried mental *c·*

convictions
Mis.	31–19	against his own *c·* of good
	99– 9	courage of his *c·* fell
	116–19	the courage of honest *c·*,
	217–32	and our *c·* change ;
	238– 6	honest to their *c·*,
	247– 3	his honest *c·* and *proofs*
	288– 2	sincere and courageous *c·*
Ret.	71–22	they proceed from false *c·*
Un.	5–12	following upward individual *c·*,
No.	9– 7	conscientious in their *c·* ;
'00.	1–14	right *c·* fast forming
'01.	32–13	courage of their *c·* was seen.
	32–15	Their *c·* were honest,
'02.	14–17	counter to the common *c·* of mankind

convince
No.	15– 4	*c·* all that their purpose is right.
My.	94–14	* much to *c·* the skeptic.
	251–27	*c·* yourselves of this grand verity :

convinced
Mis.	6–23	once *c·* of the uselessness of
	358–31	leaving the material
Pul.	35–23	* Mrs. Eddy became *c·* of the
	64–20	* *c·* that the curative Principle was
'01.	24–11	* *c·* that under Providence I
My.	146–18	I am *c·* of the absolute truth of

convinces
Un.	4–13	*c·* us that, as we get still nearer

convincing
Ret.	93–24	give to the world *c·* proof of

convulsion
Po.	27– 1	"*C·*, carnage, war ;

convulsions
My.	201–17	scan the *c·* of mortal mind,

cooing
My.	341–12	A lightsome lay, a *c·* call,

Cooke, Mr.
My.	332– 9	* Many thanks are due Mr. *C·*,

Cook's, Mr.
Mis.	95– 5	* was presented to Mr. *C·* audience,

cool
Mis.	225–26	a *c·* perspiration spread over it,
	227–27	bathes it in the *c·* waters of peace
	323–30	rest in its *c·* grottos,
	332–14	walking in the *c·* of the day
Ret.	18– 3	*C·* waters at play with the
Peo.	9– 6	The *c·* bath may refresh the body,
	14– 5	*c·* grottos, smiling fountains,
Po.	63–10	*C·* waters at play with the

cooling
Pul.	25– 1	* lighting and *c·* of the church
	25– 2	* for *c·* is a recognized feature
My.	29–26	* *c·* breeze to temper the heat,

coolly
Mis.	285–25	*c·* notifies the public of

cooperate
Mis.	138– 9	is not always to *c·*,
	152– 8	*c·* with the divine power,
	364–23	must either *c·* or quarrel

cooperates
Peo.	11–11	wherein man *c·* with and

cooperation
Mis.	40– 2	healing demands such *c·* ;
	305–12	* asking for her personal *c·*
My.	162– 9	Unity is spiritual *c·*,

copartnership
Mis.	59–21	Any *c·* with that Mind

cope
Mis.	183– 9	there is no matter to *c·* with.
My.	227–16	their ability to *c·* with the claim,

Copeland
Mrs.
Pul.	72– 9	* Mrs. *C·* is a very pleasant and
	72–12	* Mrs. *C·* claims to have been healed
	72–16	* past eleven years," said Mrs. *C·*,
	72–19	* In regard to Mrs. Eddy, Mrs. *C·* said
	73–19	* of the same theory as Mrs. *C·*.

Mrs. D. W.
Pul.	72– 8	* Mrs. D. W. *C·* of University Avenue

Copernicus
No.	6–23	*C·* has shown that what appears

copied
Mis.	381– 2	but had been *c·* by her,
Pul.	88– 8	To those which are *c·*
My.	317–11	Mr. Calvin A. Frye *c·* my writings,
	328– 7	* following article, *c·* from the
	331–10	* *c·* from the *Wilmington Chronicle*

copies
Mis.	300–12	from *c·* of my publications
	301–13	have read *c·* of my works
	302–21	destroyed the *c·* at once
	315– 6	No *c·* from my books
	376–12	* *c·* of an engraving cut in a stone.
Man.	32– 8	shall not read from *c·*
	93–16	*c·* of his lectures
Ret.	37– 9	edition numbered one thousand *c·*.
Pul.	5–22	edition of one thousand *c·*.
My.	v–22	* over four hundred thousand *c·*
	53– 8	* each of one thousand *c·*.
	329–13	* photographed *c·* of the notice
	334– 5	* allegation that *c·* of Mrs. Eddy's

Copley Hall
Pul.	29– 1	* held its meetings . . . later in *C· H·*,
	29– 9	* service held in *C· H·*.
My.	55–24	* the church removed to *C· H·*
	55–29	* congregation worshipped in *C· H·*

Copley Square
Pul.	29– 2	* Studio Building on *C· S·*.

copper
Mis.	305–21	* gold, silver, bronze, *c·*, and

copy
Mis.	92–22	to own a *c·* of the above-named book
	144– 8	laid away a *c·* of this address,
	153–23	to whom I presented a *c·* of
	281–13	through a stray *c·* of the Scriptures
	299–13	* "Is it right to *c·* your works
	300– 4	taking this *c·* into the pulpit
	300– 9	If you should print and publish your *c·*
	300–19	Your manuscript *c·* is liable.
	301–20	"Is it right to *c·* your works
	301–21	It is not right to *c·* my book
	302–26	derived from making his *c·*,
	372–26	Not by aid of . . . could I *c·* art,
	379– 6	I read the *c·* in his presence,
Man.	91– 2	shall not allow it or a *c·* of it
	98–14	published according to *c·* ;
	98–16	sending a *c·* to the Clerk of the
	104–15	a *c·* of the Seventy-third Edition
Ret.	38–11	finished my *c·* for the book.
	38–14	finished printing the *c·* he had
	38–17	with my finished *c·*.
	38–19	printed all the *c·* on hand,
	84–11	should own a *c·* of S. and H.,
'02.	13–30	A *c·* of this deed is published in our
	16– 2	happy possessor of a *c·* of Wyclif,
Po.	v–21	* *each* requested a *c·*,
My.	189–28	from which I *c·* this verse:
	295– 9	GIFT OF A *C·* OF MARTIN LUTHER'S
	295–22	[*C·* of Cablegram]
	307– 3	which I, ... added to his *c·*
	333–30	* we *c·* the following :

copying
Mis.	300– 3	*C·* my published works
	302–20	*c·* and reading my works
	302–23	desist from further *c·* of my

copyright

Mis.	300–10	arrest for infringement of *c·*,
	302– 5	encourages infringement of my *c·*,
Ret.	36– 5	after taking out my first *c·*,
	39– 2	the *c·* was infringed.
	39– 3	entered a suit at law, and my *c·* was
	76– 3	nor would protection by *c·* be
My.	116–25	*C·*, 1909, by Mary Baker Eddy.
	159–29	*C·*, 1904, by Mary Baker G. Eddy.
	210–22	*C·*, 1909, by Mary Baker G. Eddy.
	273–32	*C·*, 1907, by Mary Baker G. Eddy.

copyrighted

Mis.	xi– 2	*c·* at the date of its issue, 1875,
	381– 1	*c·* works of Mrs. Eddy
Man.	43–16	from Mary Baker Eddy's *c·* works
	71–20	Tenets *C·*.
	71–25	*c·* in S. AND H. WITH KEY TO THE
	81–16	*c·* and conducted according to
	104– 6	written by Mary Baker Eddy and *c·*,
Ret.	35– 1	I *c·* the first publication on
	76– 2	C. S. is not *c·* ;
My.	130–23	Borrowing from my *c·* works,

cord

My.	105–16	so that it stood out like a *c·*.

cordial

My.	177– 4	comply with your *c·* invitation
	184–14	and to return my *c·* thanks
	186–25	Accept my thanks for your *c·* card

cordiality

Mis.	276– 4	purely Western in its *c·*

cordially

Mis.	149 4	Invite all *c·* and freely to this
	306– 9	* Very *c·* yours,
	310–27	would *c·* invite all persons who
Pul.	87– 1	* most *c·* invite you to be present
'02.	4– 5	I *c·* congratulate our Board

cords

Un.	30–22	to break the *c·* of matter,
'02.	3– 3	loosening *c·* of non-Christian

core

Mis.	251–10	loyal to the heart's *c·* to religion,
Ret.	82– 1	yet their *c·* is constantly renewed ;
My.	350–17	bitter searing to the *c·* of love ;

Corinthian

Mis.	185–29	reasoning . . . with the *C·* brethren.

Corinthians

first epistle to (xv. 45)

Un.	30–13	In his first epistle to the *C·* (xv. 45)

II. (13 : 14)

My.	19– 8	* benediction, 2 *C·* 13 : 14 :

corn

Mis.	215–21	while the *c·* is in the blade,
	330–31	patient *c·* waits on the elements
	331– 1	crown the full *c·* in the ear,
Ret.	92– 6	full *c·* in the ear." — *Mark* 4 : 28.

corner

Mis.	144– 4	tower on the northeast *c·*
	196–24	head stone of the *c·*," — *Psal.* 118. 22.
	306–13	* *c·* Liberty and West Streets,
Man.	18– 2	the head of the *c·*." — *Matt.* 21 : 42
Ret.	7–12	* explored their every nook and *c·*,
Pul.	10–20	the head of the *c·*." — *Matt.* 21 : 42.
	61–23	* *c·* of Falmouth and Norway Streets,
No.	38–14	the head of the *c·*." — *Matt.* 21 : 42.
'00.	5–25	will become the head of the *c·*,
'01.	25– 7	the crown and head of the *c·*,
'02.	2–15	on the stone at the head of the *c·* ;
	13–17	*c·* of Falmouth and Caledonia
Hea.	3–10	become the head of the *c·*.
My.	16–26	a precious *c·* stone, — *Isa.* 28 : 16.
	17–15	a chief *c·* stone, — *I Pet.* 2 : 6.
	29– 9	* *c·* of Falmouth and Norway Streets,
	48– 7	* "the head of the *c·*" — *Matt.* 21 : 42.
	67– 1	* *c·* of Falmouth and Norway Streets.
	68–13	* *c·* of Falmouth and Norway Streets,
	70–16	* on every *c·* in the neighborhood.
	73–19	* *c·* of Huntington and Massachusetts
	188– 2	have made the head of the *c·*.

corners

Mis.	133–13	*c·* of the streets, — *Matt.* 6 : 5.
Pul.	24–12	* stone porticos and turreted *c·*.

Corner Stone and corner-stone

Mis.	143–13	chapter sub-title
	143–15	*c·* of "The First Church of Christ,
	145–10	in this *c·* of our temple :
	163–23	eternal as Truth, the chief *C·*.
	399–17	*c·* of The Mother Church
Man.	17–16	the chief *c·* whereof is,
	60–22	Laying a *C· S·*.
	60–24	when laying the *C· S·* of a Church
Ret.	15– 6	being the chief *c·*." — *Eph.* 2 : 20.

Corner Stone and corner-stone

Un.	14–20	but the *c·* of living rock,
Pul.	10–18	*c·* in the house of our God.
	16– 2	poem
	43–15	* for the *c·* laying last spring,
	85–28	* It was a facsimile of the *c·*
No.	38–15	This is the chief *c·*,
Po.	76– 1	the *c·* of The Mother Church.
My.	16–10	* chapter sub-title
	16–11	* *c·* of the new auditorium
	18–27	* The *c·* was then laid by the
	55–32	* the *c·* of The Mother Church
	57–12	* the *c·* was laid July 16, 1904.
	60–13	* *c·* of this wonderful temple
	67–16	* *C·* of cathedral . . . 1904.
	112– 8	and build on its chief *c·*.
	158– 6	chapter sub-title
	158–25	He has laid the chief *c·* of the
	182–10	Christ, Truth, as the chief *c·*.
	203–24	You have laid the *c·* of

coronals

My.	258–20	*c·* of meekness, diadems of love.

coronation

'02.	3–23	triumph canker not his *c·*,

coroner's

My.	128– 6	*c·* inquest, a board of health,

corporation

Mis.	272–15	* agent, or servant of any *c·*
Ret.	49–28	all debts of the *c·* have been
	49–29	deemed best to dissolve this *c·*,

corporeal

Mis.	51–21	to resort to *c·* punishment.
	97–30	*c·* man is this lost image ;
	102– 3	A *c·* God, as often defined
	152–11	I, as a *c·* person, am not in
	161– 4	*C·* and Incorporeal Saviour.
	162–18	*c·* Jesus bore our infirmities,
	163–26	crucifixion of the *c·* man,
	164– 2	incorporeal and *c·* are distinguished
	166–20	given birth to the *c·* child Jesus,
	205–15	the last scene in *c·* sense.
	205–27	*c·* or mortal man disappears
	308–29	invisible to *c·* sense.
	309–20	*C·* falsities include all obstacles
Ret.	45–11	even as the *c·* organization
	54– 7	the claims of the *c·* senses
	73– 2	material, *c·*, and temporal.
	76–24	never abuses the *c·* personality,
	89–29	*C·* and selfish influence is human,
	91–21	His power . . . was spiritual, not *c·*.
Rud.	2– 3	* a *c·* man, woman, or child ;
'01.	4–18	is not *c·* nor anthropomorphic.
	6–23	the *c·* or anthropomorphic sense.
	12–26	embodies itself in the so-called *c·*,
My.	100–15	whose person is not *c·*,
	257–10	has passed from a *c·* to the
	260–19	tradition, usage, or *c·* pleasures,
		(*see also* **personality**)

corporeality

Mis.	162–24	without *c·* or finite mind.
	165– 9	fetters of the flesh, or *c·*.
	165–14	The material *c·* disappears ;
	309– 2	their own or others' *c·*,
	309–19	The consciousness of *c·*,
Ret.	25–16	but His *c·* I denied.
	73–12	personal *c·* became less to me
	73–21	sure victim of his own *c·*.
	74– 1	increases one's sense of *c·*,
	74– 6	the false sense of *c·*,
No.	22–17	greater than the *c·* we behold.

corporeally

Mis.	60–19	even if touching each other *c* ;
	123–32	as attends eating and drinking *c·*.

corps

My.	38– 8	* carefully trained *c·* of ushers,

corpse

My.	302– 7	Neither . . . can be produced on a *c·*,

corpuscle

No.	26–21	never originated in molecule, *c·*,

corpus sine pectore

Ret.	74– 4	defines it by his own *c· s· p·*

correct

Mis.	14–13	we begin with the *c·* statement,
	65– 6	If man's *ipse dixit* . . . is *c·*,
	81–19	*if all this be a fair or c· view*
	86– 9	*Is it c· to say of material objects,*
	86–11	words which need *c·* definition.
	195–20	but one *c·* premise and conclusion,
	202– 3	are found to *c·* the discords of
	264–21	whether those be *c·* or incorrect.
	266–24	If I *c·* mistakes which may be made
	269–23	*c·* Mind-healing is the proper means
	344–19	would seek a *c·* conclusion.

correct
Man. 43–24   C. S. literature which is not $c\cdot$
    97–16   to $c\cdot$ in a Christian manner
    109–17   If not $c\cdot$, the applicant will be
Un. 7–17   views here promulgated . . . are $c\cdot$.
    25– 1   thus affirms is mainly $c\cdot$.
Rud. 5– 3   Which testimony is $c\cdot$?
No. v– 4 $c\cdot$ involuntary as well as voluntary
    44– 2   incapacitates him for $c\cdot$ comment.
'01. 3–22   The first proposition is $c\cdot$,
    27–10   nothing . . . that is $c\cdot$ on this subject
'02. 4– 6 $c\cdot$ analysis of C. S.
    10–19   his predicate tending thereto is $c\cdot$,
Hea. 7–16   begins in motive to $c\cdot$ the act,
    9–21   only $c\cdot$ answer to the question,
    16–27   gain our . . . from the $c\cdot$ source.
Peo. 4–17   mysterious ideas . . . are far from $c\cdot$.
My. 107– 5   and you have the $c\cdot$ answer.
    130– 1 $c\cdot$ the false with the true
    221–25 $c\cdot$ or incorrect state of thought,
    224–20   more fashionable but less $c\cdot$.
    224–23   books less $c\cdot$ and therefore less
    225– 7   A $c\cdot$ use of capital letters in
    235– 8 $c\cdot$ numeration of numbers
    237–11   my teachings that I know to be $c\cdot$
    241–15   * absolute and $c\cdot$ teaching.
    242– 2   scientifically $c\cdot$ in your statement
    249– 3 $c\cdot$ sin through your own perfectness.
    249–24   The report . . . I desire to $c\cdot$.
    267– 3   Nothing can be $c\cdot$ . . . which
    284–17   next issue please $c\cdot$ this mistake.
    297–18   clear, $c\cdot$ teaching of C. S.
    301–23   supposition that we can $c\cdot$ insanity by
    317–10   to $c\cdot$ my diction.
    349–27   is $c\cdot$ only as it is spiritual,
    356–28   only possible $c\cdot$ version of C. S.

corrected
Mis. 109–13   must be seen . . . in order to be $c\cdot$;
    141–18   it can easily be $c\cdot$
    198–25   is $c\cdot$ alone by Science,
    256– 4   mortal mind must be $c\cdot$ in order to
    285– 7   mistaken for the $c\cdot$ edition,
    356– 3   a life $c\cdot$ illumine its own
Man. 98– 2 $c\cdot$ a false newspaper article
Ret. 81– 9 $c\cdot$ by a diviner sense of liberty
    83–14   is sure to be $c\cdot$.
'01. 27–20   and appetites of mankind $c\cdot$,
My. 304– 2   chapter sub-title
    307– 3   his copy when I $c\cdot$ it.

correcting
Man. 98– 2   shall be responsible for $c\cdot$
Ret. 57– 7   would be like $c\cdot$ the principle of
No. 1–21 $c\cdot$ the individual thought,
Hea. 7– 3 $c\cdot$ error in thought,
    7–12   and there $c\cdot$ the motive,
My. 322–10   * your statement $c\cdot$ mistakes

correction
Mis. 137–24   self-examination and $c\cdot$;
Man. 98– 6   If the $c\cdot$ by the Committee
    98– 8   desirable that this $c\cdot$ shall appear,
My. 217–16   chapter sub-title
    284–11   chapter sub-title

corrections
Mis. 133– 1   you will not delay $c\cdot$ of the
My. 53– 3   * a bottomless sea of $c\cdot$;
    272–22   * with the $c\cdot$ on the manuscript

correctly
Mis. 43– 7   Do all . . . teach it $c\cdot$?
    58–11   read and studied $c\cdot$,
Man. 38–11   whose applications are $c\cdot$ prepared,
    110– 2   that are not $c\cdot$ made out.
Rud. 16–18   Whatever is said and written $c\cdot$
'01. 22–29   is not taught $c\cdot$ by those who
My. 224– 9   are not apt to be $c\cdot$ drawn.
    224–21   My books state C. S. $c\cdot$.
    242–13   you must state its Principle $c\cdot$,
    298– 4   experience which, if $c\cdot$ narrated
    313– 2 $C\cdot$ quoted, it is as follows,

correctness
Mis. 13–26   opportunity for proof of its $c\cdot$
    56–23   proves the $c\cdot$ of my statements,

corrects
Mis. 37–19   Mind, which $c\cdot$ mortal thought,
    287–11   Science $c\cdot$ this error with the
    363–25   This Word $c\cdot$ the philosopher,
'01. 12– 3   and it $c\cdot$ the material sense
Hea. 7–12   it $c\cdot$ the act that results from

correlated
Mis. 241– 4   Body and mind are $c\cdot$

correlative
Mis. 106–18   its $c\cdot$ in "S. and H.
Man. 32– 3 $c\cdot$ texts in S. AND H.
Man. 58–15 $c\cdot$ Biblical texts in the

correlative
My. 33– 5   * $c\cdot$ Scripture, 1 John 3 : 1–3.

correlatives
My. 218–16   introduction of . . . without their $c\cdot$,

correspond
Mis. 32–18   If I had the time to . . . $c\cdot$ with
    217– 8 $c\cdot$ in quality and quantity.

correspondence
Mis. 74– 1   divine $c\cdot$ of noumenon and
    155–17   all of her interesting $c\cdot$,
    205–23   maintain their obvious $c\cdot$,
Pul. 23– 8   * December 28. — Special Correspondence.
    37–10   * attends to a vast $c\cdot$;
My. 279– 9   its obvious $c\cdot$ with the Scriptures

correspondent
Mis. 295–14   has our American $c\cdot$ lost
My. 341–25   * received the Herald $c\cdot$.

correspondents
Mis. 155–15   chapter sub-title
    322–10   Clerk of the church can inform $c\cdot$.
My. 25–16   Will one and all of my dear $c\cdot$

corresponding
Mis. 279–18 $c\cdot$ to the seven days of creation :
Pul. 26– 7   * $c\cdot$ to the chancel of
'00. 12–11 $C\cdot$ to its roads, its gates,

correspondingly
Ret. 22– 1   becomes $c\cdot$ obscure.

corresponds
Mis. 158–28 $c\cdot$ to the example of our Master.
Chr. 55– 2   whereto their number $c\cdot$.

corridors
Mis. xi–25   through the dim $c\cdot$ of years,
'02. 4–16   adown the $c\cdot$ of time,
My. 189–10   through the dim $c\cdot$ of time,

corroborate
Ret. 83–24   to $c\cdot$ what they teach.
My. 332–23   * $c\cdot$ Mrs. Eddy's claims.
    338– 9   * will fully $c\cdot$ this statement.

corroborating
'00. 5– 6   words of our Master $c\cdot$ this

corroborative
My. 317–20   quoting $c\cdot$ texts of Scripture.

corrupt
Mis. 223– 7   impure streams flow from $c\cdot$ sources.

corruption (see also corruption's)
Mis. 165– 5   because of the $c\cdot$ of the Church.
    228– 8   and pure amid $c\cdot$.
No. 14– 8   Theosophy is a $c\cdot$ of Judaism.
    14– 8   This $c\cdot$ had a renewal in the
'00. 12– 1   His types of purity pierce $c\cdot$

corruption's
Po. 71– 6 $C\cdot$ band Is driven back ;

Corser, Rev. Enoch
'01. 32– 4   Rev. Enoch $C\cdot$, . . . Congregationalists ;

coruscations
No. 14–13   brilliant $c\cdot$ of the northern sky

Cosmopolitan
My. 272–18   * [$C\cdot$, November, 1907]
    272–20   * The $C\cdot$ presents this month
    272–32   * $C\cdot$ gives no editorial indorsement

cosmopolitan
My. 81–16   * No more $c\cdot$ audience ever

cosmos
Mis. 26–25   God's consequent is the spiritual $c\cdot$.
    362–25   spiritual $c\cdot$ and Science of Soul.
Un. 56– 2   to the $c\cdot$ of immortal Mind.
My. 180–32   the whence and why of the $c\cdot$
    226–19   immortality of man and the $c\cdot$
    350–10   the $c\cdot$ and Science of man.

cost
Mis. 84– 8   This $c\cdot$ them their lives,
    99– 7   It $c\cdot$ Galileo, what?
    165–24   This $c\cdot$, none but the sinner can pay ;
    199–15 $c\cdot$ him the hatred of the rabbis.
    211–22   protects himself at his neighbor's $c\cdot$,
    212–15   One step away . . . $c\cdot$ them — what?
    222–29   I shall not forget the $c\cdot$ of
    236–29   doing our duty, . . . at whatever $c\cdot$.
    273– 4   although it will $c\cdot$ him much,
    281–16   * to count the $c\cdot$ of becoming a true
    281–17   * to count the $c\cdot$ of not becoming a
    288–21   To reckon the universal $c\cdot$ and gain,
    300– 1   and so avoiding the $c\cdot$ of hiring
    342–25   It should $c\cdot$ you something :
    381–19   recover of the defendant her $c\cdot$ of
    382– 7 $c\cdot$ more than thirty years of
Man. 96– 7   the $c\cdot$ of hall shall be paid by
Pul. 26–14   * $c\cdot$ eleven thousand dollars.
    28–10   * The $c\cdot$ of this church is
    50–13   * $c\cdot$ two hundred thousand dollars,

cost

Pul. 52–12 * c· of over two hundred thousand
  57– 3 * c· over two hundred thousand
  58–10 * c· of over two hundred thousand
  60–17 * at a c· of eleven thousand dollars,
  62– 7 * economy of space, as well as of c·,
  63–22 * c· of two hundred and fifty thousand
  68–20 * c· over two hundred thousand
  70–15 * c· two hundred and fifty thousand
'00. 11– 1 c· me a tear !
Hea. 11– 2 Did we survey the c· of sublunary
My. 31–11 * the c· of which approximates
  67– 6 * C· . . . $2,000,000
  76– 8 * entire c· of the building,
  76–19 * estimated c· of the extension
  86–13 * every cent of the estimated c·
  89–14 * although it c· two million dollars,
  90–23 * paid-up c· of two million dollars
  91–27 * The temple . . . c· two million dollars,
  95–13 * c· them about two million dollars,
  96–19 * c· approximately two million dollars.
  97–27 * at a c· of two million dollars,
  98–18 * c· about two million dollars,
  99–15 * at a c· of two million dollars,
  100– 5 * c· about two million dollars
  123–16 original c· of the estate was
  127–26 not costly as men count c·,
  167– 2 self-sacrifice it may have c·
  229–12 might c· them a half century.

costing

Mis. 280–20 album c· fifty dollars,
Pul. 30–29 * c· over two hundred thousand
  63– 6 * Сниксн C· $250,000
  79– 5 * c· over two hundred thousand
My. 166–28 c· one hundred and seventy-five

costly

Mis. 110– 1 The c· balm of Araby,
  117–22 experiments ofttimes are c·.
  262– 8 new and c· spring dress.
  281–24 most beautiful and the most c·,
  356–11 chastened affections, and c· hopes,
Ret. 30– 4 bequests of C. S. are c·,
Pul. 10 18 * c· edifice erected in Boston
  87–11 your c· offering, and kind call
My. 87–16 * their c· church fully paid for,
  127–25 not c· as men count cost,

costs

Mis. 108–23 conception of it . . . c· much.
  138– 6 c· you what it would
'01. 2–23 c· a return under difficulties ;

cot

My. 287–12 Love lived in a court or c·

cottage

My. 113– 2 sinners in court and in c·,

couch

Mis. 388–32 And hover o'er the c· of woe ;
Po. 21–12 And hover o'er the c· of woo ;
My. 313–13 with a c· or cradle

cough

Mis. 239–18 suffused eyes, c·, and tired look,

councils

'01. 10– 4 deliver you up to the c·'' — Matt. 10 : 17.
'02. 4– 1 deceit in c·, dishonor in nations,

counsel

Mis. 138–20 My c· is applicable to the state of
  146– 7 I cannot conscientiously lend my c·
  146–22 and c· and help him to
  230– 8 weary with study to c· wisely
  236–20 "Take no c· of a mortal,
  243–24 Did he refer to that questionable c·,
  263–16 The need of their teacher's c·,
  301–18 my private c· they disregard.
  347–18 I follow his c·, take a few steps,
  349–19 My c· to all of them was
  359–28 Men give c· ; but they give not
  370– 5 they went away and took c·
  381– 6 present personally and by c·.
  381– 8 gave notice through his c·
  381–11 to inquire of defendant's c·
  381–13 her c· asked the defendant's c·
  381–17 drawn up and signed by c·.
Man. 83–19 and patiently c· his pupils
Ret. 81–23 puts this pious c· into a father's
Un. 1–13 I c· my students to defer this
Pul. 33–20 * high c· and serious thought.
No. 8–11 c· each other to work out his
  8–28 This c· is not new,
Pan. 13–12 I c· thee, rebuke and exhort
'00. 9– 2 and they comply with my c· ;
'01. 30–27 I c· Christian Scientists under all
'02. 13–19 paying for it . . . through my legal c·.
  13–21 were instituted by my c·
  13–27 conveyed to me, by my c·.

counsel

My. 18–20 I c· thee, rebuke and exhort
  37–29 * its wise c· and admonition.
  44– 9 * c· of our ever faithful Leader.
  49– 6 * but through sane c·,
  55–15 * upon Mrs. Eddy's c·, reorganized
  62–23 * appreciation of your wise c·,
  129–29 Accept my c· and teachings only as
  196– 7 accept my tender c· in these words
  309– 5 even acting as c· in a lawsuit
  309– 8 was the c· for Loudon

counseling

Man. 40–14 condemning, c·, influencing

counselling

My. 362–20 * we rejoice . . . in your wise c·.

Counsellor

Mis. 161– 7 C·, The mighty God, — Isa. 9 : 6.
  164–18 C·, The mighty God, — Isa. 9 : 6.
  321– 5 C·, The mighty God, — Isa. 9 : 6.
  (see also **Eddy**)

counsellor

Mis. 288– 5 sure of being a fit c·.
  (see also **Eddy**)

count

Mis. 8–17 c· your enemy to be that which
  149–11 c· the baskets full of accessions
  281–16 * "It is wise to c· the cost of
  281–17 * wiser to c· the cost of not
  281–19 we must c· as nothing,
  281–21 c· ourselves always as debtors to
  297–24 he will c· the consequences of his
  391– 8 Will c· their mercies o'er,
'00. 6– 4 "I c· not myself to have   Phil. 3 : 13.
'01. 31–20 blessings infinite I c· these dear :
Po. 38– 7 Will c· their mercies o'er,
My. 127–26 not costly as men c· cost,
  256–21 We c· our blessings and see

counted

Mis. 176–15 c· not their own lives dear
Man. 55–16 shall not be c· loyal till after

countenance

Mis. 148 1 never shows us a smiling c·
Ret. 42–14 smile . . . resting on his serene c·.
Un. 29–26 health of my c·, — Psal. 42 : 11.
Pan. 4–24 health of my c·, — Psal. 42 : 11.
My. 249–17 c· such evil tendencies.

counter

Mis. 301–30 c· to the commands of our
'02. 14–16 so c· to the common convictions of

counteract

Mis. 7–21 A periodical of our own will c·
  291–30 c· the influence of envious minds
My. 129– 9 c· the trend of mad ambition.
  249– 7 c· its most gigantic falsities.

counteracting

Mis. 223–22 no c· influence can hinder
My. 294– 9 because of the mental c· elements,

counteracts

'02. 9–29 c· ignorance and superstition

counterfeit

Mis. 60–28 has its c· in some matter belief.
  61– 5 against the material . . . c· sciences.
  71–27 is the c· of the divine,
  173–26 the c· of man's creator
  250–19 cast aside the word as a . . . c·,
  375– 4 c· of the spiritual
No. 25–25 sinful mortal is but the c· of
Pan. 11– 2 to cast out the unreal or c·.
My. 175–27 am sure that the c· letters

counterfeits

Mis. 351–20 Evil c· good :
Rud. 4– 5 of which . . . are the c·.

countermand

Mis. xii– 4 command and c· ;
  10–15 c· their order, retrace their
  119–29 reverse your rules, c· your orders,
  124– 3 would tend to . . . c· the Scripture
  346–26 c· this first command of Solomon,

counterpart

Mis. 173–26 not the c· but the counterfeit

counterpoised

My. 129–16 c· his origin from dust,

countersign

Man. 37– 3 c· an application for membership
  109– 6 No persons are eligible to c·

countersigned

Man. 35– 4 c· by one of Mrs. Eddy's loyal
  38– 8 application must be c· by

countersigners
Man. 110–11 applicants, approvers, or c,

Countess of Dunmore and Family
My. 295–23 C of D and F , 55 Lancaster Gate

counties
Man. 99–18 Committee for the c in which

counting
My. 178–12 * "c the legs of insects"?

countless
My. vi– 1 * to well-nigh c numbers
42–17 * gratitude for the c blessings

countries
Pul. 53– 3 * though practised in other c
My. 73– 5 * in other c since that time,
94–23 * foreign c were in attendance.
315–30 in our own and in other c,

country (see also **country's**)
Mis. 251–11 religion, home, friends, and c.
303–24 profitable to the heart of our c.
Ret. 7–15 * distinguished men in the c.
48–22 and sent to all parts of our c,
Pul. 23–11 * has swept over the c,
30–10 * includes those all over the c.
36– 8 * from Europe as well as this c.
46–16 * Her family came to this c
47–22 * Mrs. Eddy has a delightful c home
47–26 * driving rather into the c,
58– 8 * believers throughout this c
60–16 * from all parts of the c.
62– 2 * a novelty in this c,
63–12 * her delightful c home in Concord,
63–25 * Christian Scientists all over the c,
66– 8 * societies in every part of the c.
66–19 * uncommon development in this c
68–11 * c residence in her native State.
70–16 * Christian Scientists all over the c.
71–14 * and in fact all over the c,
78– 3 * ever wrought in this c.
80– 7 * the freest c in the world
Pan. 3–27 patron of c life,
14–10 chapter sub-title
14–11 Pray for the prosperity of our c,
14–20 Oh, may their love of c,
'00. 10–29 serving his c in that torrid zone
'02. 11– 3 mortals who seek for a better c
15– 5 protection of the laws of my c.
My. 29–14 * pageantries have been seen in this c
67–22 * But one church in the c exceeds
71–17 * church edifices in the c
73– 5 * churches all over this c
74– 1 * western sections of this c.
77–13 * practically every civilized c,
79–19 * intelligence and wisdom of the c
85–18 * architectural beauties of the c.
91–18 * this c or any other c
92–18 * every other sect in the c
97–21 * has opened the eyes of the c
98– 4 * C. S. army in this c
98–22 * in this c or elsewhere,
100– 9 * nearly all, parts of the c,
104–27 in this or any other c.
129– 8 throughout our beloved c
167–30 In our c the day of heathenism,
234–24 teaching C. S. in her c.
278–19 him who dies in defence of his c,
284–16 * history of the church in this c
291–30 work for their own c,
311– 3 his c home in North Groton, N. H.,
313–23 * nor did "the superstitious" c folk
329–22 * when the whole c is recognizing

country's
Po. 10– 8 Didst rock the c cradle
My. 337– 9 Didst rock the c cradle

Country-Seat and **country-seat**
Ret. page 17 poem
Pul. 70–26 * c in Concord, N. H.
Po. vi–29 * poem
page 62 poem

county
Man. 99– 6 Each c of Great Britain

couple
My. 59–18 * scarce fill a c of pews
118–30 which would . . . c evil with good.
314–26 the means of reconciling the c.

coupled
'02. 17– 1 c with selfishness, worldliness,

couplers
(see **organ**)

couples
'00. 4– 1 misnomer c love and hate,
My. 108–13 c faith with spiritual understanding

couplet
Un. 44– 7 if the . . . c may be so paraphrased
My. 347–11 illustrated by Keats' touching c,

courage
Mis. 30–26 Take c, dear reader,
99– 9 c of his convictions fell
116–18 the c of honest convictions,
210–27 Charity has the c of conviction ;
257–18 fear where c is requisite,
294–22 but thank God and take c,
299–11 come with the c of conviction
Pul. 83– 6 * moral strength and c
'01. 30–25 far-seeing vision, the calm c,
32–13 c of their convictions was seen.
My. 50–20 * brought fresh c to the
131– 5 gives him c, devotion, and
140–18 *Christian Scientists :* — Take c.
191–24 Immortal c fills the human breast
209– 7 fidelity, c, patience, and grace.
211–22 fear where c should be

courageous
Mis. 288– 2 and c convictions regarding
My. 208–24 God bless the c, far-seeing

course
above-named
Mis. 349–11 had taken the above-named c
college
'01. 29–30 * our tuition for the college c."
comet's
Mis. 266–12 career is like the comet's c,
erroneous
Mis. 352– 8 error of its present erroneous c,
free
Man. 91–12 a free c in this department
No. 45–24 Let the Word have free c
native
Pul. 6–30 the native c of whose mind
of lessons
Ret. 50– 5 one c of lessons at my College,
Primary
Mis. 264–14 not fitted for it by the Primary c.
regular
Rud. 14–27 regular c of instruction from me,
right
Mis. 212–19 rush in against the right c ;
straight to the
Mis. 268–14 Scientist keeps straight to the c.
such a
Mis. 349– 7 Such a c with such a teacher
their
Mis. 41–13 keep the faith and finish their c.
203–12 you have coaxed in their c
280–29 the rocks and sirens in their c,
Man. 88–19 nor on their c or conduct.
Ret. 11–14 That widen in their c.
Po. 60–11 That widen in their c.
this
Mis. 220–12 He persists in this c until the
My. 200–25 gap between this c and C. S.
unswerving
Mis. 291–22 true and unswerving c of a
─────
Mis. ix–15 To preserve a long c of years
19–27 choose our c and its results.
39– 2 c of instruction in C. S.
64–12 Persons contemplating a c at the
79–26 What c should Christian Scientists
225– 8 In the c of the evening,
Man. 68–13 members whom she teaches the c
Ret. 14– 4 I was of c present.
Pul. 32– 9 * Of c such a personality,
82– 9 * no more turn her from her c than
No. 45– 9 is of c out of the question.
Po. 19– 1 My c, like the eagle's,
68–22 Be its c through our heavens,
My. 12– 1 * of c carried the implication
21– 7 * c suggested will not only
92– 1 * Of c the new idea will never
232– 1 you are recognizing the proper c,
304– 5 finished my c of studies under
343–21 but of c the term pope is

courses
Un. 17– 6 the stars in their c — Judg. 5 : 20.

Court
Mis. 380–29 by decree and order of the C,
381–22 under the seal of the said C,
My. 137– 7 * office of the Clerk of the C,
327– 3 in the C of New Hampshire,
(see also **Superior Court**)

court
Rud. 1–17 appearance (in c, for example)
Pan. 3–17 * We c fair wisdom,

court
My. 113– 2 in c· and in cottage,
188–23 C. S. has a place in its c·,
287–12 Love lived in a c· or cot is
294–30 c· of the Vatican mourns him ;
314–13 the c· record may state
314–17 who were present in c·
314–20 the c· instructed the clerk to
courtesy
Ret. 88– 1 The same c· should be observed
Pul. 36–15 * by her hospitable c·,
36–27 * to whose c· I am much indebted
My. 123–13 by the c· of another person
174– 6 c· extended to my friends
174– 8 c· of the efficient city marshal
271–21 * requesting the c· of a reply :
271–28 To your c· and to your question
341– 2 breathe it to the breeze as God's c·.
court-house
My. 346–12 * made several turns about the c·
courtier
Mis. 224– 7 c· told Constantine that a mob
court-room
My. 185–12 in the pulpit, in the c·,
courts
Mis. 79–27 *persons brought before the c·*
373–18 as living feebly, in kings' c·.
Man. 48–10 impertinent towards . . . the c·,
My. 326– 3 * legislatures and c· are thus
340–17 c· immediately annulling such
cousin
Ret. 3– 9 A c· of my grandmother
8–13 One day, when my c·, Mehitable
8–17 surprised, my c· turned to me
8–24 my c· had heard the voice,
9– 2 led my c· into an adjoining
9– 6 My c· answered quickly,
Pul. 48–17 * her c·, was born and bred in that
covenant
Mis. 285–24 severs the marriage c·,
297–19 claims of the marriage c·,
My. 49–15 * also the tenets and church c·.
131–13 seals the c· of everlasting love.
177–24 everlasting c· with them.'' — *Isa.* 61 : 8.
188– 9 your ark of the c· will not be
cover
Mis. 19–18 wherewith to c· iniquity,
147–26 He seeks no mask to c· him,
172–10 shall c· with her feathers
209 31 to c· iniquity and punish it not,
210–29 foolhardiness to c· iniquity.
224–24 to c· the whole world's evil,
263– 8 ''He shall c· thee — *Psal.* 91 : 4,
Pul. 86– 3 * upon the c· of which
86– 8 * On the under side of the c·
My. 127–31 a c· and a defence adapted to
212–31 he says this to c· his crime of
covered
Mis. 263 11 and c· from the devourer
352–31 while sickness must be c· with the
Ret. 4–21 herds, c· areas of rich acres,
'01. 10– 7 there is nothing c·,— *Matt.* 10 : 20.
Hea. 5–19 grand truth which is constantly c·,
covereth
Mis. 153–16 wherein violence c· men
213– 9 ''He that c· his sins — *Prov.* 28 : 13.
covering
Mis. 335–21 notion that one is c· iniquity
Pul. 26– 1 * c· one hundred and forty-four
52–22 * c· it with the blackness of the
My. 328–23 * act of the Legislature c· it
coverings
Mis. 7– 4 loaded down with c·
covers
Mis. 208– 4 it c· all sin and its effects.
246– 2 that cradles and c· the sins of
Ret. 63–19 Whosoever c· iniquity becomes
My. 178–25 c· of the book were burned up,
273– 9 * c· practically the civilized world.
covert
Mis. 144–16 c· from the tempest ;— *Isa.* 32 : 2.
My. 182–29 and a c· from the tempest.
coveted
My. 163–23 retirement I so much c·,
covetousness
Mis. 19– 2 c·, lust, hatred, malice,
118–21 c·, envy, revenge, are foes to
123– 6 idolatry, envy, jealousy, c·,
coward
My. 225– 1 in which the c· and the hypocrite

cowardice
Mis. 210–28 neither the c· nor the foolhardiness
211–21 C · is selfishness.
267–18 from individual conceit, c·, or
'02. 18– 8 c· and self-seeking of his disciples
cowardly
Mis. 211– 4 His mode is not c·, uncharitable,
My. 211– 4 too c·, too ignorant, or too wicked
coworker
Pan. 6–18 creator or c· with God?
coworkers
'01. 29–15 grand c· for mankind,
cozy
Po. 53–14 And build their c· nests,
Crabtre
No. 23–12 According to C ·, these devils were
cradle
Mis. 321– 2 over the c· of a great truth,
329–20 rocking the oriole's c· ;
331–15 remember *their* c· hymns,
Ret. 11–18 The c· of her power,
Pul. vii–17. c· of this grand verity
No. 45–25 to leave c· and swaddling-clothes.
'01. 31–23 my c· hymn and the Lord's Prayer,
Po. 10– 8 Didst rock the country's c·
29– 8 No c· song, No natal hour
60–15 The c· of her power,
My. 257– 5 the new c· of an old truth.
257– 6 from c· to crown.
313–13 with a couch or c·
315–28 from the c· and the grave,
337– 9 Didst rock the country's c·
cradled
My. 122–21 not . . . finitized, cribbed, or c·,
cradles
Mis. 246– 2 c· and covers the sins of the world,
craft
'01. 30–15 they have no c· that is in danger.
craftily
My. 241– 7 * beware the net that is c· laid
craftiness
Mis. 191– 1 ''dishonesty, c·,— *see II Cor.* 4 : 2.
'01. 16–15 world's god as dishonesty, c·,
My. 124– 1 not walking in c·,— *II Cor.* 4 : 2.
craftsmen
My. 66–20 * c· are hurrying on with their
crag
Po. v–11 * *this lofty New Hampshire c·*,
cramps
My. 84– 6 * a ''church debt'' c· and retards
crannies
My. 186– 6 in the c· of the rocks,
crass
Pul. 79–18 * from the c· materialism of
crave
Mis. 369–28 c· the privilege of saying to
craving
Mis. 227–26 the mind c· a higher good,
No. 46– 6 c· health and holiness,
cravings
Mis. 16– 2 the c· for immortality,
287–13 can satisfy immortal c·.
325– 8 few c· for the immortal,
My. 189–20 satisfies the immortal c·
craze
No. 19– 8 C. S. is no ''Boston c· ;''
My. 302–10 c· is that matter masters mind ;
create
Mis. 25–28 if He could c· them otherwise,
26–18 to evolve or c· itself :
174– 1 to evolve or to c· matter
187–25 c· a sick, sinning, dying man?
304– 4 * c· a Columbian Liberty Bell,
306–25 love they c· in our hearts.
362–17 and out of nothing would c·
Un. 23–21 can He c· anything so wholly unlike
Pan. 5– 6 What, then, can matter c·,
5– 8 Did God c· evil?
My. 122– 2 this would c· for one's self
149–11 tides of truth . . . c· and govern it ;
created
Mis. 25–27 If God c· drugs good,
25–29 and if He c· drugs for healing
49–31 Truth never c· error,
56–30 first spiritually c· the universe,
56–30 implies that Spirit, . . . c· man over
57–23 universe with man c· spiritually.
57–24 and the universe c· materially.
61–12 was c· in the image of God,

created

Mis.	97–23	"He *c·* man in the image and
	97–24	likeness of Mind *c·* He him."
	182–16	*c·* neither from dust nor
	186– 2	*c·* man in His own image
	247–29	Everything that God *c·*,
	346– 9	If God *c·* only the good,
Ret.	22–18	nor is he ever *c·* through the flesh ;
	60– 9	sense adds that the divine Spirit *c·*
	67–18	The sinner *c·* neither himself nor
	67–19	sin *c·* the sinner ;
	69–22	God *c·* all through Mind,
Un.	14–16	*c·* children proved sinful ;
	15– 8	God *c·* all things,
	20– 7	*First:* The Lord *c·* it.
	23–20	unless God has *c·* them?
	64– 1	All that *is*, God *c·*.
Pul.	82–14	* because she was *c·* after man,
	82–15	* was *c·* solely for man.
No.	17– 9	*c·* in the eternal Science of being
Pan.	7– 9	*c·* all things spiritually,
	11– 6	Him that *c·* him." — *Col.* 3 : 10.
'01.	5–12	the creator and the *c·*,
	18–17	If God *c·* drugs for medical use,
Hea.	16–24	shall we say that God hath *c·*
	17– 7	personal senses were *c·* by God?
My.	87–12	* The impression *c·* is that of
	122–14	*c·* surprise in our good city of
	182–22	that *c·* and governs the universe
	232–25	man *c·* by and of Spirit,
	239–26	spiritual man, *c·* by God,

creates

Mis.	27– 4	That God, good, *c·* evil,
	27– 5	or that Spirit *c·* its opposite,
Un.	48–14	Father and Mother of all He *c·* ;
My.	189–16	love it *c·* in the heart of man ;
	225–19	the names of that which He *c·*.
	262– 1	God *c·* man perfect and eternal

creating

Mis.	37– 2	*c·* or governing man or the universe.
	294– 4	the concepts of his own *c·*,
	305–13	* In *c·* the bell it is particularly

Creation

Pul.	38–10	"*C·*," "Science of Being,"

creation (*see also* creation's)

bases
Ret.	68–21	it bases *c·* on materiality"

category of
'02.	7– 6	not into the category of *c·*

climax of
No.	17–13	Man is the climax of *c·* ;

creator and
Un.	36– 3	double capacity of creator and *c·*.
My.	103–10	of the creator and *c·*.

error of
Mis.	57–23	The false sense and error of *c·*

every
Mis.	60–27	every *c·* or idea of Spirit

Genesis of
Mis.	258–12	In the spiritual Genesis of *c·*,

God's
Mis.	87– 5	to caricature God's *c·*,
	286–13	in the dawn of God's *c·*,
Pan.	6–14	order and harmony of God's *c·*.

His
Mis.	22–18	untruths belong not to His *c·*,
	362–14	part and parcel of His *c·*?
Un.	30–17	interpretation of God and His *c·*
	48–15	no more enters into His *c·* than
	48–16	His *c·* is not the Ego,
Pan.	3–20	reveals Himself . . . to His *c·*,
	9– 3	means one God and His *c·*,
'02.	7– 8	understanding . . . of God and His *c·*,

His own
Mis.	354–21	to govern His own *c·*,

impossible
'02.	6–15	human woe . . . an impossible *c·*,

its own
Un.	45–20	imaginary sphere of its own *c·*

law of
Mis.	258–15	This is the law of *c·* :
	259–14	Lawgiver was the only law of *c·*,

material
Pan.	7– 9	belief, . . . a material *c·* took place,

named in the
'00.	14– 7	number of days named in the *c·*,

no other
My.	235–22	no other creator and no other *c·*.

of Adam
Mis.	186– 3	In the *c·* of Adam from dust,

of the schools
'01.	34–14	but a *c·* of the schools

other
Mis.	57– 5	what evidence . . . of any other *c·*?

creation

Principle of
Mis.	361–27	God, . . . divine Principle of *c·*,

reckons
My.	349–31	reckons *c·* as its own creator,

reflection is
Mis.	23–23	God, whose reflection is *c·*,

regards
Mis.	362–15	regards *c·* as its own creator,

Science of
Mis.	57–22	Science of *c·* is the universe with
	57–27	Science of *c·* is stated in

seven days of
Mis.	279–18	to the seven days of *c·* :

spiritual
My.	179– 5	account of the spiritual *c·*,

support of
No.	38–15	the basis and support of *c·*,

true
Mis.	57– 8	the true *c·* was finished,

understood
Mis.	286–32	*c·* understood as the most exalted

vast
Po.	1– 8	when first *c·* vast began,

work of
'00.	3–28	improved on his work of *c·*,

Mis.	8–10	thing outside thine own *c·*?
	23–11	Was it Mind or . . . that spake in *c·*,
	27–23	*C ·*, evolution, or manifestation,
	57–25	a *c·* of the sixth and last day,
	185–31	namely, that *c·* is material :
	188– 4	*c·* joined in the grand chorus
My.	5–11	Whence, then, came the *c·* of matter,

creation's

Mis.	388– 2	Which swelled *c·* lay :
'02.	20–11	Which swelled *c·* lay,
Po.	7– 2	Which swelled *c·* lay :
	70–19	To hail *c·* glorious morn

creations

Ret.	69–18	believing that . . . are *c·* of God,

creative

Mis.	57– 5	The *c·* "Us" made all,
	361–27	is by no means a *c·* partner
Un.	19– 5	contrary to His *c·* will,

creator

and creation
Un.	36– 3	double capacity of *c·* and creation.
My.	103–10	Science . . . of the *c·* and creation.

and preserver
Pan.	4– 5	*c·* and preserver of man.

and the created
'01.	5–12	God and man, the *c·* and the created,

before the
Mis.	330–16	let mortals bow before the *c·*,

evil is not a
Un.	25–20	Evil is not a *c·*.

his
Mis.	46–19	in the scale *with* his *c·* ;
	294–11	and honors his *c·*.
Un.	14–26	which is everlasting in his *c·*
	15–15	for his likeness to his *c·*.
My.	247– 5	whereby man governed by his *c·* is
	254– 1	one *with* his *c·*,
	254–26	whereby man governed by his *c·* is

intelligent
Pan.	6–18	intelligent *c·* or coworker with God?

its own
Mis.	362–16	regards creation as its own *c·*,
My.	349–32	reckons creation as its own *c·*,

man's
Mis.	173–26	counterfeit of man's *c·*

Mind was the
Mis.	57– 6	and Mind was the *c·*.

no other
My.	235–22	no other *c·* and no other creation.

of man
Pan.	4–16	He is the *c·* of man,

of the claim
Mis.	293–23	*c·* of the claim of error.

one
Mis.	361–11	testifying to one *c·*,

the only
Mis.	56– 9	Life is God, the only *c·*,
	286–17	Spirit, God, is the only *c·* :
Un.	25–21	God, good, is the only *c·*.
	32– 6	Spirit is the only *c·*,
	35–26	Spirit is the only *c·*,
No.	6– 6	God is the only *c·*,

underived from its
Mis.	46–16	no power underived from its *c·*.

was never a
Ret.	68– 1	material concept was never a *c·*,

creator

Mis.	26–32	or the *c·* of evil?
	72– 4	Science sets aside man as a *c·*,
Un.	25–18	*Evil.* I am a *c·*,
	32– 4	saying, "I am a *c·*.
Pan.	4–16	but that man also is a *c·*,
My.	32– 6	* in a heartfelt appeal to the *c·*.
	235–20	Is mortal man a *c·*,

creators

Mis.	57–19	ye shall be as gods," *c·*. — *Gen.* 3 : 5.
	304–26	* birthdays of the "*c·* of liberty ;"
No.	11– 2	desire, and fear, are not the *c·*,
Pan.	4–17	making two *c·* ;

creature

Mis.	8–10	Is it a *c·* or a thing
	8–14	or any other *c·* separate you
	175– 4	showeth them unto the *c·*,
Ret.	25– 1	and show them to the *c·*,
Un.	15–14	and the *c·* is punished for
'01.	9–23	showeth them unto the *c·* ;
My.	47–29	* gospel to every *c·*. — *Mark* 16 : 15.
	253–28	Let the *c·* become one with
	300–25	gospel to every *c·*," — *Mark* 16 : 15.

credentials

Man.	89–15	such *c·* as are required to
My.	245–24	these *c·* are still required

credible

My.	85 26	* Last Sunday it was entirely *c·*

credibly

Mis.	49– 3	We are *c·* informed that,

credit

Mis.	238–29	I accord these evil-mongers due *c·*
	263–28	without *c·*, appreciation, or a
	264– 1	and give them *c·* for every
Ret.	75– 1	book-borrowing without *c·*
	75– 8	give *c·* when citing from the works
Pul.	73–28	* She placed no *c·* whatever in the
	80–16	* rather to the *c·* of the book
My.	vi–10	* *c·* for this extraordinary work.
	70– 6	* fine church edifices to its *c·*
	130–24	without *c·*, is inadmissible
	224–19	at the same time giving full *c·*

credited

Mis.	220–19	* "Not to be *c·* when he
My.	118–22	*c·* only by human belief,

credulity

My.	80– 9	* severe tax upon frail human *c·*,

creed

Mis.	176–21	frozen ritual and *c·* should forever
	195–28	but deed, not *c·*, and
	331–23	frozen crust of *c·* and dogma,
	338–31	* A great and noble *c·*."
	399–13	Thou the Christ, and not the *c·* ;
Ret.	44 3	Mind-healing church, without a *c·*,
	65–19	and prefers Christ to *c·*.
	69–20	and they need no *c·*.
Pul.	65– 1	* belief in that curious *c·*
'01.	5– 1	he breaks faith with his *c·*,
	5–28	necessitates a *c·* to explain both
	33–14	platform, a *c·*, or a diploma
Hea.	7–28	contains no argument for a *c·*
Po.	29–19	Or cruel *c·*, or earth-born taint :
	75–20	Thou the Christ, and not the *c·* ;
My.	47–26	* in the wilderness of dogma and *c·*,
	50–12	* against the currents of dogma, *c·*,
	85–15	* followers of this *c·*
	87–28	* whatever one's special *c·* may be,
	96–12	* attesting their faith in the *c·*
	148–25	it is not a *c·* or dogma,
	157–10	* without regard to class or *c·*,
	183– 1	infinite uses of Christ's *c·*.
	205–24	human hypotheses, matter, *c·* and
	266– 7	ritual, *c·*, and trusts in place of
	288–15	*c·*, dogma, or *materia medica*.
	301– 7	dogma and *c·* will pass off in scum,

creedal

Ret.	14–18	even if my *c·* doubts left me outside

creeds

Man.	17– 3	forming a church without *c·*,
Pul.	67–12	* enumeration of John Bull's *c·*.
No.	15– 9	explain and prop old *c·*,
	15–13	notions . . . to be found in *c·*
	24–16	human philosophies or *c·* :
'00.	7– 5	*c·* and dogmas have been sifted,
My.	96–15	* comparison with other *c·*.
	122–26	not the material Christ of *c·*,
	248–28	indifference, chance, and *c·*.
	299–13	portions of truth may be found in *c·*.
	299–16	and lacking in the *c·*.
	307–27	*materia medica*, dogma, and *c·*,
	350–25	horoscope of crumbling *c·*,

creeping

Mis.	111– 6	human pride, *c·* into its meshes,

crept

Mis.	326–13	*c·* unseen into the synagogue,

crescendo

Mis.	116–15	As *c·* and *diminuendo* accent music,

crescent

Mis.	276– 2	and the *c·* with a star.

crest

Un.	45– 5	rears its *c·* proudly,
Po.	1– 2	unfallen still thy *c·* !

crib

Chr.	53–24	O'er babe and *c·*.

cribbed

My.	122–21	finitized, *c·*, or cradled.

cricket's

Mis.	396– 5	*c·* sharp, discordant scream
Po.	58–17	*c·* sharp, discordant scream

cried

Pul.	44–27	* custodian of funds *c·* "enough"
My.	81–16	* "Dresden !" "Peoria !" they *c·*.
	211–10	unclean spirits *c·* out,
	290–16	have I *c·* unto Thee." — *Psal.* 130 : 1.

cries

Mis.	204– 4	humble before God, he *c·*,
Ret.	4–17	now the lone night-bird *c·*,

crieth

'01.	9–20	*c·* out, "Let us alone ; — *Mark* 1 : 24.

crime

Mis.	61–15	* is held responsible for the *c·* ;
	112–12	The mental stages of *c·*,
	112–18	He had no sense of his *c·* ;
	119– 7	coax the unwary man to commit a *c·*,
	122– 1	to suffer for evil-doers — a *c·*
	122–22	lessens not . . . the criminal's *c·* ;
	123–10	pagan priests bloated with *c·* ;
	221–30	Who would tell another of a *c·* that
	221–31	or call public attention to that *c·* ?
	227– 3	no fraternity where its *c·* may stand
	227– 8	*c·* comes within its jurisdiction.
	240– 9	all unmitigated systems of *c·* ;
	301– 9	for what the law construes as *c·*.
	362–30	And pleasure is no *c·* except when
Pul.	7–17	power to wash away, . . . every *c·*,
No.	32– 6	can neither extinguish a *c·* nor
'00.	2–19	"By cheating, lying, and *c·* ;
Hea.	7–20	he charged home a *c·* to mind,
	7–22	knew that adultery is a *c·*,
Po.	71– 2	When earth, inebriate with *c·*,
My.	130– 5	hidden method of committing *c·*
	212–31	he says this to cover his *c·*
	222–29	holding of *c·* in check,

crimes

Mis.	222–22	*c·* committed under this new
'01.	20 33	*c·* committed under this new-old
	20–29	darkest and deepest of human *c·*.
My.	160–32	Concealed *c·*, the wrongs done

criminal (*see also* criminal's)

Mis.	70–13	rest . . . would come to the *c·*, if
	119– 6	If a *c·* coax the unwary man to
	211–17	Then, if a *c·* is at peace,
Un.	15–26	*c·* appeases, with a money-bag,
	29– 4	as does all *c·* law,
No.	30–10	*c·* who is punished by the law
	92– 4	pardon may encourage a *c·*
Hea.	7–22	and *mind* is the *c·*.
My.	276– 3	watched, as one watches a *c·*

criminal's

Mis.	122–21	hater's hatred nor the *c·* crime ;

criminals

Mis.	211– 8	supplies *c·* with bouquets

crimson

Mis.	376–27	gold, orange, pink, *c·*, violet ;
Ret.	17– 9	peers out, from her *c·* repose,
'00.	11–22	* It flooded the *c·* twilight
Po.	16–12	flitting through far *c·* glow,
	62– 9	peers out, from her *c·* repose,

cringing

Po.	35–12	And in the *c·* crowd

cripples

Ret.	16–12	Many pale *c·* went into the church
Peo.	3– 5	helpless invalids and *c·*.

crises

Mis.	176– 8	in the great *c·* of nations

crisis

Ret.	44–19	I saw that the *c·* had come

crisp

My.	137– 7	* *c·*, clear, plain-speaking English."

critic

Mis. 88–14   c· who knows whereof he speaks.
'01.   21–14   I am sorry for my c·,
     21–23   Does this c· know of a better
     27– 3   My c· also writes :
My. 97–15   * a rather bitter c· of Mrs. Eddy
     330–15   * are questioned by this c·,
     334–12   * since this c· places certain

critical

Mis. 245–12   directing more c· observation to

critically

Rud. 15–25   may be dissected more c·

criticise

Mis. 353–31   c· and disobey her ;
'01.   21–18   manifest unfitness to c· it

criticism

Mis. 88–16   glows in the shadow of darkling c·
     216–16   conclusion that he is a power in c·,
     224– 2   makes another's c· rankle,
Pan.   6–15   But the higher c· is not satisfied
'00.   11–27   His allegories are the highest c·
My.   3–19   higher c·, the higher hope ;
     40– 8   * subsidence of c· among workers.
     118–15   embarrass the higher c·.
     136–28   spiritual thought and the higher c·.
     237– 2   reference . . . to the "higher c·"
     240– 5   chapter sub-title
     240– 8   * call C. S. the higher c·
     240– 9   I called C. S. the higher c·
     240–16   higher c· because it criticizes evil,
     323– 6   * unfair c· of you and your book
     329–29   * c· of this good woman

criticisms

'01.   18– 4   weak c· and woeful warnings
'02.   14–28   forever silence all private c·,
My. 317–12   so as to avail myself of his c·
     317–13   which c· would enable me to

criticized

My. 142–13   important events are c·.
     146– 9   has been quoted and c· :
     179–15   the Scriptures are c·.
     276– 5   therefore to be c· or judged

criticizes

My. 240–16   higher criticism because it c· evil,

critics

Mis. 66–22   Cynical c· misjudge my meaning
     193–19   when c· attacked me for
     372– 1   c· declared that it was incorrect,
     372–14   I sought the judgment of sound c·
Ret. 37– 6   the c· took pleasure in saying,
'01.   30–17   higher class of c· in theology
My. 95–23   * higher c· and the men of science
     98–10   * c· who seek the light
     318– 8   c· declared that my book was

critique

Mis. 88– 7   *author of that genuine c· in*

crook

Pan.   3–29   his shepherd's c·,

crooked

My. 140– 5   c· things straight.— Isa. 42 : 16.

crops

Mis. 26–10   believes that his c· come from the

Cross, Miss

Pul. 69– 2   * Miss C· came from Syracuse,

cross

agony of the
No. 33–15   the brief agony of the c· ;
and the crown
Mis. 135–15   take this c·, and the crown
Pul. 28– 9   * The c· and the crown and the star
bearing the
Hea. 19–23   bearing the c· meekly along the
bear the
Mis. 211–32   refuses to bear the c· and to
'02.   20–23   but in this, . . . I can bear the c·,
bore the
Mis. 64– 4   Our Master bore the c·
down from the
Un. 58– 7   come down from the c·."— Mark 15 : 30.
     58– 9   coming down from the c·,
endured the
Ret. 22–12   endured the c·,— Heb. 12 : 2.
My. 258–15   endured the c·,— Heb. 12 : 2.
example on the
Ret. 26– 5   Christian example on the c·,
glorifies the
'02.   19–28   divine Science glorifies the c·
his
Ret. 86–18   taking up his c· and following
My.   4– 8   taketh not his c·,— Matt. 10 : 38.
     229–17   doth not bear his c·,— Luke 14 : 27.

cross

his
My. 233–24   taketh not his c·,— Matt. 10 : 38.
is the central emblem
Un. 57– 9   c· is the central emblem of
kiss the
Mis. 397– 3   I kiss the c·, and wake to know
Pul. 18–12   I kiss the c·, and wake to know
Po. 12–12   I kiss the c·, and wake to know
last at the
Mis. 100– 5   woman, "last at the c·,"
     388–20   Last at the c· to mourn her Lord,
No. 45–14   woman, "last at the c·
Po. 21– 9   Last at the c· to mourn her Lord,
     39–10   And she— last at the c·,
no
Hea.   1–13   "Then there were no c· to take up,
of Christ
Ret. 30–21   and the c· of Christ.
soldiers of the
Mis. 138–26   to all His soldiers of the c·
Un. 39–20   As soldiers of the c· we must
take up the
Mis. 115–13   take up the c· as I have done,
Ret. 65–12   Mortals must take up the c·
No.   2–11   deny self, sense, and take up the c·.
this
Mis. 135–15   Then take this c·,
     158–18   obedience in bearing this c·.
thy
Mis. 328–31   bear thy c· up to the throne
to crown
My. 163– 5   from c· to crown, from sense to Soul,
wait at the
My. 305–22   I still wait at the c· to learn
without the
Mis. 357–11   Without the c· and healing,

Mis. 135–14   Is it a c· to give one week's time
     138–16   love made perfect through the c·.
     162–11   c· became the emblem of Jesus'
     212–30   friends took down from the c·
'01.   25– 6   the c·, which they reject
My.   6–19   modest edifice . . . began with the c· ;
     155–30   in the flowers and the c· from
     180–27   But this is the c·.

cross-bearing

Mis. 213– 4   through c·, self-forgetfulness,
Ret. 54– 5   It demands less c·,

crossed

Mis. 285–15   first c· swords with free-love,
Ret.   2– 9   c· the Atlantic more than a
     2–23   nor had they c· the ocean ;

crossing

Mis. 10–17   c· swords with temptation,
My. 43–12   * The c· of the Jordan

Croton oil

Mis. 69–15   given three doses of C· o·,
My. 292–23   c· o· is not mixed with morphine

crouching

Mis. 246–21   awaits the c· wrong that refused

croup

Mis. 44– 7   *acute cases . . . as in membranous c·?*

crow

Ret.   4–17   the c· caws cautiously,
Pul. 48–15   * Straight as the c· flies,

crowd

Mis. 339–12   The elbowing of the c·
Ret. 16– 4   pushing their way through the c·.
Po. 35–12   in the cringing c· Companionless
My. 30–29   * the largest c· of the day
     87– 7   * the characteristics of this c·

crowded

Mis.   5– 6   c· with students who are
Pul. 60– 1   * vestibule and street . . . were c·
     60–13   * The place was again c·,
My. 54– 8   * c· one hour before the service
     55– 1   * at this service . . . the hall was c·.
     55–21   * was c· to overflowing.
     75–19   * C· as the hall was yesterday,
     80–21   * c· into the auditorium
     304–12   lectured in large and c· halls

crowding

My. 54– 4   * inconvenience that comes from c·,
     82– 7   * c· Boston the last week
     323–20   * c· thoughts of gratitude

crowds

My. 30– 1   * held large c· of people,
     54–24   * c· had besieged the doors
     73–29   * c· of Christian Scientists
     82–17   * edifice was emptied of its c·

crown
Mis. 100–25 c· them with blessings infinite.
135–15 take this cross, and the c· with it.
155–12 and peace will c· your joy.
231– 2 formed a c· of glory ;
252–18 the c· of Christianity.
295–30 worn the English c·
321–22 And battling for a brighter c·.
330–29 and c· imperial unveils its regal
331– 1 c· the full corn in the ear,
340– 9 win and wear the c· of the faithful.
388–16 Her dazzling c·, her sceptred throne,
389– 2 The hoary head with joy to c· ;
392– 9 her noonday glories c·?
Ret. 85–26 will c· the effort of to-day
86– 2 to c· patient toil, and rejoice in
Pul. 4–19 c· the tree with blossoms.
4–22 his diadem a c· of crowns.
28– 9 * The cross and the c· and the star
83–29 * a c· of twelve stars."— Rev. 12 : 1.
'00. 13–15 give thee a c· of life."— Rev. 2 : 10.
14– 5 that no man take thy c·."— Rev. 3 : 11.
'01. 25– 7 whereby is won the c·
'02. 18– 9 helped c· with thorns the life of
Hea. 2–15 passed from his execution to a c·,
Po. 20–13 her noonday glories c·
21– 4 Her dazzling c·, her sceptred
21–16 The hoary head with joy to c· ;
44– 2 C· the lives thus blest
My. 6–19 its excelsior extension is the c·.
84–14 * Its stately cupola is a fitting c·
125–22 stars in my c· of rejoicing.
128–13 No c· nor sceptre nor rulers
150– 9 joy and c· of such a pilgrimage
163– 5 from cross to c·, from sense to
180–27 Take it up,— it wins the c· ;
201–13 Even the c· of thorns,
253– 9 * manhood's glorious c· to gain."
257– 6 from cradle to c·.
274–25 this is my c· of rejoicing,
347–16 beautiful pearls that c· this cup

crowned
Mis. 124–26 c· and still crowns Christianity :
320– 4 c· with the history of Truth's idea,
360–14 When shall earth be c· with
376–21 c· with an acre of eldritch ebony.
386–29 with all the c· and blest,
Pul. 1–15 path behind thee is with glory c· ;
'00. 1–11 c· with unprecedented prosperity ;
Po. 26– 3 track behind thee is with glory c· ;
50–16 with all the c· and blest,
My. 256–18 c· with the dearest memories
350–26 Truth delightful, c· with endless
357–11 c· The Mother Church building

crowneth
My. 13–21 who c· thee with— Psal. 103 . 4.

crowning
My. 6–22 Its c· ultimate rises to
94–26 "c· ultimate" of the church
192–28 c· your endeavors, and
208–15 c· the hope and hour of
323–22 * Your c· triumph over error

crowns
Mis. 118–27 obedience c· persistent effort
124–27 crowned and still c· Christianity :
267–29 and c· them with success ;
393–12 C· life's Cliff for such as we.
Chr. 53–44 C· the pale brow.
Ret. 71– 4 not the forager . . . that God thus c·,
Pul. 4–22 his diadem a crown of c·.
'02. 19–28 c· the association with our Saviour
Po. 51–17 C· life's Cliff for such as we.
My. 62–11 * glory which c· the completion of
250– 6 and c· honest endeavors,
285– 9 c· the great purposes of life

crucial
My. 225– 1 This is a c· hour,

crucible
Mis. 79– 2 dissolved in the c· of Truth,

crucified
Mis. 187–32 such as c· our Master,
345–28 and talked of the c· Saviour ;
Chr. 53–29 Christ was not c·
Un. 56– 7 "c· the Lord of glory,"— I Cor. 2 : 8.
'01. 9–12 rabbis, who c· Jesus
14– 5 self-righteousness c· Jesus.
My. 119–16 away from the supposedly c·
333–20 * on the merits of a c· Redeemer.
334–23 self-righteousness c· Jesus."

crucifixion
Mis. 33– 4 c· of even the great Master ;
63–28 through the c· of the human,

crucifixion
Mis. 121–21 arrest, trial, and c· of
122– 2 foretelling his own c·,
163–25 c· of the corporeal man,
Man. 16– 5 We acknowledge that the c· of
Ret. 26– 7 to allay the tortures of c·.

crucifixions
Mis. 107– 6 self-denials, and c· of the flesh.

crucify
Mis. 270–22 schools which c· him,

crude
Mis. 360– 3 encumbered with c·, rude fragments,
Un. 4–28 at the present c· hour,
Pul. 32– 8 * not by any c· self-assertion,
My. 111– 5 false psychics, c· theories or modes

cruder
Pul. 79–19 * materialism of the c· science

crudest
Peo. 3– 3 c· ideals of speculative theology

cruel
Mis. 19– 1 is unjust,— is wrong and c·.
41– 1 brute-force that only the c· and evil
257–13 is c· and merciless.
324–21 odious company and the c· walls,
Un. 23– 1 c· treatment received by old Gloster
Po. 29–19 c· creed, or earth-born taint :

cruelly
Man. 53– 9 disrespectfully and c·,
My. 138–13 c·, unjustly, and wrongfully accused.

crumb
Mis. xi–15 will find herein a "canny" c· ;
369–19 c· that falleth from his table.

crumble
Mis. 140–30 though . . . should c· into dust,
Pul. 7–22 tabernacles c· with dry rot.

crumbled
Peo. 14 7 churchyards have c· into decay,

crumbling
Peo. 1– 5 c· away of material elements
My. 200–21 on c· thrones of justice
350–25 horoscope of c· creeds,

crumbs
Mis. 106–20 c· fallen from this table of Truth,
My. 133–12 These c· and monads will feed the

crush
No. 34–16 the endeavor to c· out of a career its

crushed
Ret. 32– 8 is c· as the moth.
My. 128– 9 Truth c· to earth springs . . . upward,

crushing
My. 350–18 This c· out of health and peace,

crust
Mis. 331–23 frozen c· of creed and dogma,

crutches
Mis. 168– 6 or hobbling on c·,
Ret. 16–13 went into the church leaning on c·

cry
Mis. 63–22 why did Jesus c· out,
64– 2 human c· which voiced that struggle ;
81–23 c· in the desert of earthly joy ;
209 6 and c·, "Peace, peace ;— Jer. 6 : 14.
246–13 The c· of the colored slave
246–15 another sharp c· of oppression.
342–19 Hear that human c· :
369– 6 chapter sub-title
Pul. 82–28 * remain deaf to their c·?
'00. 7–26 fails, and we c·, "Save,— Matt. 8 : 25.
9–11 or as of old c· out :
'02. 10– 5 and mortals c· out,
Po. 71–22 "C· aloud !"— Isa. 58 : 1.
73–13 The sea-mew's lone c·,

crying
Mis. 99–26 voice of one c· in the wilderness,
231–22 instead of a real set-to at c·,
246–23 was heard c· in the wilderness,

crystal
Mis. 332–16 c· streams of the Orient,
Pul. 7–15 Those c· globes made morals for

crystallized
No. 2– 2 that c· expression, C. S.
My. 13–31 c· into a foundation for our

C. S.
Man. 46– 7 Use of Initials "C. S."
46– 9 the initials "C. S." after his name

C. S. B.
Man.   92–19   nor receive the degree of *C. S. B.*
My.   245–32   The first degree (*C. S. B.*) is given

C. S. D.
Man.   89–17   to receive the degree of *C. S. D.*
     91–22   not having the certificate of *C. S. D.*
     92–19   the degree of C. S. B. or *C. S. D.*,
My.   244– 9   the degree of *C. S. D.*,
     246– 1   second degree (*C. S. D.*) is given to
     251–22   certificate of the degree *C. S. D.*

Cuba
Pan.   14–29   for the liberty of *C*·.
'02.   3–12   inauguration of home rule in *C*·,
My.   81–15   * "Des Moines !" "Glasgow !" "*C*· !"

Cubans
My.   278– 4   so that the *C*· may learn to

cuckoo
Mis.   329–26   *c*· sounds her invisible lute,

Cullis, Dr.
Mis.   132–15   * "like to hear from Dr. *C*· ;
     132–28   * misrepresented either Dr. *C*· or

culminate
Mis.   366–25   *c*· in sickness, sin, disease, and
My.   311–15   seemed to *c*· at twelve years

culminates
Mis.   21– 5   *c*· in the Revelation of
     85–13   it *c*· in the fulfilment of

culminating
My.   127–22   *c*· in fierce attack,

culpable
Mis.   115– 5   *c*· ignorance of the workings of
     234– 7   nor gained by a *c*· attempt
     283–17   mistaken kindness, a *c*· ignorance,

culprit
Mis.   61–23   A *c*·, a sinner, — anything but a

cult
My.   77– 2   * the *c*· which it represents.
     77–11   * feature in the life of their *c*·.
     85– 4   * growth of this *c*· is the marvel of
     88–28   * debt to that great and growing *c*·,
     94–18   * magnificent new temple of the *c*·.
     96–26   * evident that the *c*· will soon
     97–16   * critic of Mrs. Eddy and her *c*·,
     99– 7   * a *c*· able to promote its faith
     100–10   * number of the followers of the *c*·.
     341–22   * the Founder of the *c*·.

cultivated
Ret.   4– 7   are still *c*· and owned by
My.   309– 3   *c*· in mind and manners.

cultivation
No.   1–13   silent *c*· of the true idea

cults
My.   95– 1   * included among the *c*·

culture
Mis.   v– 5   INDISPENSABLE TO THE *C*· AND
     88–12   intellectual *c*·, reading, writing,
     224–14   constitution, *c*·, character,
     265–26   is not in the *c*· but the soil.
     317–26   *c*·, and singleness of purpose
'01.   31–21   my early *c*· in the Congregational
My.   211–31   admits of no intellectual *c*·
     304–23   * sound education and liberal *c*·."

cultured
Mis.   80–12   better to be friendly with *c*·
     356–10   My students, with *c*· intellects,
My.   285–14   most *c*· men and women

cumbereth
Mis.   151–12   why *c*· it the ground?" — *Luke* 13 : 7.

cunning
Pul.   55– 2   * Not in *c*· sleight of skill,

cunningly
My.   241– 7   * craftily laid and *c*· concealed

cup
bitter
'02.   11–19   gave our glorified Master a bitter *c*·
Christ's
Mis.   125– 9   Then shall he drink anew Christ's *c*·,
drain the
Ret.   30–21   No one else can drain the *c*·
drop in the
'02.   19–30   no redundant drop in the *c*·
his
Mis.   212–32   had not yet drunk of his *c*·,
Un.   56–14   shares his *c*· of sorrows.
Jesus'
Ret.   54– 9   drinking Jesus' *c*·,
life's
Mis.   9–16   friends seem to sweeten life's *c*·

cup
Master's
Mis.   125– 1   indeed drink of our Master's *c*·,
My.   258–21   they who drink their Master's *c*·
my
Mis.   211–26   drink indeed of my *c*·." — *Matt.* 20 : 23.
My.   161–20   drink indeed of my *c*·, — *Matt.* 20 : 23.
of Christ
Mis.   144–28   wine poured into the *c*· of Christ.
No.   34–11   They drink the *c*· of Christ
of cold water
Pul.   14–16   Give them a *c*· of cold water
of gall
Mis.   237–11   earth gives them such a *c*· of gall
of martyrdom
Mis.   121– 7   even the *c*· of martyrdom :
of salvation
Pan.   14– 9   drink of the *c*· of salvation,
of their Lord
My.   161–17   *c*· of their Lord and Master
take the
Mis.   311–28   ought not that one to take the *c*·,
this
Mis.   9–17   We lift this *c*· to our lips ;
     9–22   this *c*· of selfish human enjoyment
     211–28   He drank this *c*· giving thanks,
Ret.   30–24   without tasting this *c*·.
My.   347–11   design . . . encircling this *c*·,
     347–16   pearls that crown this *c*·

Mis.   121– 6   is not the *c*· to which I call your
Po.   66– 1   pure nectar our brimming *c*· fill,
My.   126–18   *c*· which she hath filled — *Rev.* 18 : 6.
     131–10   *c*· red with loving restitution,

cupola
My.   84–14   * Its stately *c*· is a fitting crown

curative
Ret.   25– 1   reveal the great *c*· Principle,
     33–21   Mind, the *c*· Principle, remains,
     34– 1   utility of using a material *c*·.
Pul.   64–16   * search for the great *c*· Principle.
     64–20   * the *c*· Principle was the Deity.
     70–20   * to find the great *c*· Principle
Hea.   13–20   Mind as the only *c*· Principle.
My.   105–28   my *c*· system of metaphysics.
     106– 1   proved to be more certain and *c*·
     301–30   drugs can produce no *c*· effect

cure (noun)
all
Mis.   3–19   The Principle of all *c*· is God,
cause and
Hea.   11–23   places all cause and *c*· as mind ;
     11–25   where cause and *c*· are supposed
effected the
Mis.   243–11   effected the *c*· in less than one week.
instantaneous
Mis.   355– 8   not guesswork, . . . but instantaneous *c*·.
inventor of this
Pul.   71– 7   * Mrs. Eddy, the inventor of this *c*·.
its
Mis.   343– 6   to find disease . . . and its *c*·,
not effected a
Man.   46–26   where he has not effected a *c*·.
of disease
Pul.   69–25   * prayed for the *c*· of disease,
Rud.   3– 1   harder than the *c*· of disease ;
     3–18   He wrought the *c*· of disease
of the sick
No.   6–11   the consequent *c*· of the sick,
     30–26   *c*· of the sick demonstrates
Principle of
Mis.   209–12   demonstrates this Principle of *c*·
Principle of his
Mis.   260–11   Principle of his *c*· was God,
producing a
Mis.   53–12   *to assist in producing a c*·,
Truth being the
Mis.   221–19   Truth being the *c*·,
work a
Pul.   69–13   * if they . . . they can work a *c*·.
     69–22   * to work a *c*· the practitioner must

Pul.   69–10   * but rely on Mind for *c*·,
My.   40–18   * power to bring health and a *c*· to
     82– 2   * through a *c*· to themselves or
     268– 2   chapter sub-title

cure (verb)
Mis.   37–16   *Can your Science c*· *intemperance?*
     38–28   to *c*· his present disease,
     44– 6   *Can C. S. c*· *acute cases*
     48–26   Mind-healing would *c*· the insane.
     62–31   can *c*· its own disease,
     242–24   to *c*· that habit in three days,

cure (verb)

Mis.	359– 6	until you can *c·* without it
	399– 9	That exalts thee, and will *c·*
Ret.	33–17	would *c·* patients not affected by
Pul.	53–11	* Can drugs suddenly *c·* leprosy?
Rud.	8–24	whom he is supposed to *c·*,
	12– 7	strengthen . . . instead of *c·* it ;
Hea.	12– 9	when matter cannot *c·* it,
	13–27	while it is supposed to *c·* another,
Po.	75–16	That exalts thee, and will *c·*
My.	106–14	impossible for the surgeon . . . to *c·*.
	190–14	Jesus' students, failing to *c·* a
	222– 3	once failed mentally to *c·*

cured

Mis.	45–12	*profane man be c· by metaphysics,*
	49–14	have been *c·* in her class.
	242–25	I *c·* precisely such a case in 1869.
	243– 2	*c·* her perfectly of this habit,
	256– 2	*c·* of their belief in disease,
Ret.	15–24	Among other diseases *c·*
Pul.	69– 7	* being *c·* by Mrs. Eddy of a
	73– 6	* *c·* herself of a deathly disease
Hea.	13–14	*c·* the incipient stage of fever.
	13–17	*c·* an inveterate case of dropsy.
My.	80– 5	* *c·* of blindness, of consumption
	81–19	* gratitude for ills *c·*,
	90– 9	* it has *c·* them of diseases many
	228– 1	and have *c·* it thus ;

cures

Mis.	40–11	perform as instantaneous *c·* as
	63– 4	claim that one erring mind *c·*
	255–25	and *c·* where they fail,
Ret.	34–15	*c·* when they fail, or only relieve ;
	54– 2	some of the *c·* wrought through
Un.	7–16	bear witness to these *c·*.
Pul.	45– 6	* can effect *c·* of disease
Hea.	12– 9	*c·* it thus when matter cannot
Peo.	6–12	* while nature *c·* the disease."
My.	79–28	* told of *c·* from diseases,
	80– 1	* *c·* that carried one back
	81–27	* account of the marvellous *c·*
	227–31	Statistics show that C. S. *c·*

curing

Mis.	33–30	*c·* where these fail,
	54–15	*c·* hundreds at this very time ;
	268–21	*c·* alike the sin and the

curiosity

Mis.	348–24	I wanted to satisfy my *c·*
	379– 2	I had a *c·* to know
My.	30– 9	* from *c·*, and from sympathy, too.

curious

Pul.	23–19	* History shows the *c·* fact that
	65– 1	* belief in that *c·* creed

curly

Pul.	25–21	* with pews of *c·* birch,

currency

My.	14– 5	two millions of love *c·*
	170–16	It is His coin, His *c·* ;
	216– 9	regulated by a government *c·*,

current

Mis.	19–16	can never change the *c·* of that life
	126–24	even gold is less *c·*.
	228–25	Floating with the popular *c·*
	234–22	even the entire *c·* of mortality,
Ret.	2–19	with the phraseology *c·* in the
No.	1–12	borne on by the *c·* of feeling.
My.	19– 2	*c·* numbers of *The Christian Science Journal,*
	214–25	to meet my own *c·* expenses.

currents

Mis.	135–16	Sending forth *c·* of Truth,
	157–28	the eternal *c·* of Truth.
	212–18	*c·* of human nature rush in
Ret.	23–22	its substance, cause, and *c·*
Un.	11– 3	*c·* of matter, or mortal mind.
No.	34–27	the vital *c·* of Christ Jesus' life,
'01.	19–26	*c·* of God flow through no such
My.	50–11	* against the *c·* of dogma,

curse

Mis.	17–17	from under the *c·* of materialism,
	278–15	a *c·* on sin is always a blessing
	292–21	and therefore *c·* him ;
Un.	60–14	therewith *c·* we men, — *Jas.* 3 : 9.
No.	33– 4	lead us to bless those who *c·*,
'02.	6– 4	*c·* . . . . was pronounced upon a lie,
Hea.	9–15	* "the *c·* causeless cannot come"
My.	52– 4	* blessing them that *c·* her,

cursed

Mis.	278–14	he *c·* the hour of his birth ;
	295– 5	* "*c·* barmaid system" in England
Hea.	9–17	God never *c·* man,
My.	213– 8	Because this age is *c·* with

cursing

Mis.	11–23	returning blessing for *c·*.
Un.	60–16	blessing and *c·*. — *Jas.* 3 : 10.
'01.	34–21	return blessing for *c·* ;
My.	165– 7	I returned blessing for *c·*.
	269–23	pouring out blessing for *c·*,

curtail

Mis.	302–25	injunction did not *c·* the benefit

curtailed

My.	127–27	it is not *c·* in peace,

curtain

Mis.	205–16	drops the *c·* on material man
	346–26	lift the *c·*, let in the light,
	395–11	The *c·* drops on June ;
'02.	17–14	the *c·* of human life should be
Po.	57–18	The *c·* drops on June ;
My.	268–25	lifts the *c·* on the Science of being,
	305–31	to lift the *c·* on wrong,

curtains

My.	296–27	lifting the *c·* of mortal mind,

Curtice, Rev. Corban

'01.	32– 4	Rev. Corban *C·*, Congregationalist ;

curve

Pul.	26–10	* following the sweep of its *c·*,

curved

My.	69– 7	* gently *c·* and panelled surface,

curving

Un.	12– 4	*c·* sickle of Mind's eternal circle,

cushioned

Mis.	325–15	nodding on *c·* chairs,

custodian

Pul.	44–27	* kept coming until the *c·* of funds
	64–11	* the *c·* of the funds was

custodians

Man.	77–17	of which they are the *c·*.

custom

Ret.	89–13	It was the *c·* to pay this
Pul.	43–27	* her *c·* to discourage among her
My.	75–25	* *c·* of the Christian Scientists,
	78–18	* *c·* of the C. S. church,
	83– 2	* *c·* Christian Scientists have
	96–25	* It is the *c·* to sneer at C. S.,
	202– 9	*c·* to whom *c·* ; — *Rom.* 13 : 7.
	201– 6	according to the *c·* of the age

cut

Mis.	151–11	"*C·* it down ; — *Luke* 13 : 7.
	233–16	into a more fashionable *c·*
	235–13	to *c·* down all that bringeth not
	335–10	shall *c·* him asunder, *Matt.* 24 : 51.
	335–24	would *c·* off somebody's ears.
	370–12	* an engraving *c·* in a stone.
Un.	11–17	*c·* off this vain boasting
	28– 6	nor *c·* with the dissecting-knife.
Pul.	25–30	* There is a disc of *c·* glass in
	78– 6	* inscription, *c·* in script letters ;
My.	122– 7	To *c·* off the top of a plant

cuts

My.	160–14	trenchant truth that *c·* its way

cycle

Pul.	23–22	* assert that the end of a *c·*,
My.	270– 3	*c·* of good obliterates the

cycles

Un.	11–24	Jesus required neither *c·* of time
My.	13–26	all *c·* of systems and spheres.
	160–28	This may take millions of *c·*,

cyclic

Pul.	55– 5	* *c·* changes that came during

cyclone

Mis.	347– 7	foreshadows a *c·*.

cyclones

Mis.	257–27	*C·* kill and destroy,

cymbal

No.	45– 4	or a tinkling *c·* ;" — *I Cor.* 13 : 1.
'01.	26–24	or a tinkling *c·*." — *I Cor.* 13 : 1.

cynical

Mis.	66–22	*C·* critics misjudge my meaning

cynically

Mis.	255– 2	It is sometimes said, *c·*,
My.	93–10	* It has been said *c·*

cynosure

My.	77– 1	* been the *c·* of all eyes

cypress

Po.	16– 1	gentle *c·*, in evergreen tears,
	67–17	The *c·* may mourn with

D

dabbled
My. 313–22 * never "*d·* in mesmerism,"

Daily
Pul. 88–27 * *D·*, York, Pa.

daily
Mis. 7–10 has *d·* to be exemplified ;
19–14 is *d·* departing from evil ;
29–20 *D·* letters inform me that a perusal
47–3 *and carry about this weight d·*
102–30 proves *d·* that "one on God's side
127–9 pray *d·* for themselves ;
156–18 *d·* Christian demonstration thereof.
256–8 confidence manifested in *d·* letters
294–26 I have read the *d·* paper,
307–2 they give you *d·* supplies.
311–15 My deepest desires and *d·* labors
366–30 and this is being done *d·*.
373–31 *d·* demonstration of Truth and Love.
397–17 My prayer, some *d·* good to do
Man. 40–12 should *d·* watch and pray
41–19 *D·* Prayer.
42–6 to defend himself *d·* against
60–19 appeal to *d·* Christian endeavors
91–26 under Mrs. Eddy's *d·* conversation
97–19 by the *d·* press, by periodicals or
Ret. 83–20 to God's *d·* interpretation.
Pul. 4–11 and *d·* demonstrate this.
19–1 My prayer, some *d·* good to do
31–16 * editorial work in *d·* journalism
37–2 * "for it is the great *d·* that is
37–9 * she takes a *d·* walk and
79–13 * a *d·* paper in town or village
No. 43–2 *d·* meat and drink.
43–13 specimen of those received *d·* :
Pan. 14–6 if *d·* adoring, imploring, and
'01. 31–22 *d·* Bible reading and family prayer ;
Hea. 4–10 not to forget his *d·* cares.
Po. 13–5 My prayer, some *d·* good to do
28–16 Give us this day our *d·* food
33–1 To *d·* remember my blessings
My. 15–13 *d·* desire that the Giver of all good
18–6 pray *d·* for themselves ;
36–23 * devotion to the *d·* life and purpose
42–29 * performance of her *d·* tasks.
43–6 * order aright the affairs of *d·* life.
48–19 * constant *d·* reading of the Bible
77–13 * *d·* trainloads of pilgrims are
128–30 Watch, and pray *d·* that evil
134–7 inasmuch as our *d·* lives serve to
143–11 am seen *d·* by the members of my
175–5 with the exception of a *d·* drive.
177–6 *d·* duties require attention
196–26 The good . . . is your *d·* bread.
233–4 in yourself, in your *d·* life,
237–14 give *d·* attention thereto.
244–12 need of which I *d·* discern.
275–17 I go out in my carriage *d·*,
275–20 that prevents my *d·* drive.
276–6 *d·* drive or a dignified stay at home,
281–3 *d·* prayer of my church,
286–3 I have prayed *d·* that there be
352–14 * that our *d·* living may be
353–2 and read our *d·* newspaper.

Daily Inter-Ocean (*see also Inter-Ocean*)
Pul. 23–1 *D· I·*, Chicago, December 31, 1894

dainty
Mis. 329–22 Her *d·* fingers put the fur cap on
Ret. 30–5 the *d·* borrower would have fled.
Po. 47–3 the olden and *d·* refrain,

daisies
Mis. 329–19 turning up the *d·*,

dale
Po. 32–7 scattered o'er hillside and *d·* ;

Dallas, Tex.
Pul. 89–22 * *Times-Herald, D·, T·*.

damaging
Mis. 43–29 *d·* effects these leave

damnation
Mis. 122–18 whose *d·* is just." — *Rom.* 3 : 8.
298–6 whose *d·* is just." — *Rom.* 3 : 8.
335–29 "whose *d·* is just ;" — *Rom.* 3 : 8.
No. 14–26 the doctrine of eternal *d·*,
My. 6–9 smile and deceit of *d·*.

damned
Mis. 368–26 the destinies of the *d·*.

damning
My. 211–1 error that is *d·* men.

damp
My. 341–26 * raining all day and was *d·*

damsel
Peo. 8–22 "*D·*, I say unto thee, — *Mark* 5 : 41.

dancing-halls
Mis. 324–7 *d·*, and banquet-rooms.

danger
Mis. 7–3 because there is *d·* in it ;
9–29 great and only *d·* in the path
12–19 *d·* of yielding to temptation
67–20 if you see the *d·* menacing
108–11 is to be in *d·* of believing it ;
126–1 from *d·* to escape,
240–9 Predicting *d·* does not dignify life,
257–20 where there is most *d·*.
284–11 in no *d·* of mistaking their way.
318–26 Two points of *d·* beset mankind ;
319–7 mortals are in *d·* of not
347–4 To avoid *d·* from this source
Ret. 13–14 in the *d·* of endless punishment,
44–22 from the *d·* to its members
54–16 There is *d·* in this mental state
Pul. 15–14 stewards who have seen the *d·*
37–21 * feels very strongly," . . . "the *d·*
Un. 57–4 warn mortals of the approach of *d·*
No. 23–4 is fraught with spiritual *d·*.
'01. 18–11 *d·* of questioning Christ Jesus'
30–15 they have no craft that is in *d·*.
'02. 19–23 A *d·* besets thy path?
My. 116–14 Hence the sin, the *d·* and
129–3 I reluctantly foresee great *d·*
211–24 where there is most *d·* ;
234–23 there would be no *d·* in
234–30 is fraught with *d·*.
344–20 I should think myself in *d·* of

dangerous
Mis. 7–18 reflects that it is *d·* to live,
108–27 This cognomen makes it less *d·* ;
209–14 that destroy its more *d·* pleasures.
252–6 its largest dose is never *d·*,
385–11 thy bark is past The *d·* sea,
Ret. 63–20 is more *d·* than sickness,
71–22 selfish motives . . . are *d·* incentives ;
Un. 8–9 *d·* to rest upon the evidence of
54–12 is to admit a *d·* fact.
Po. 48–3 thy bark is past The *d·* sea,
My. 179–15 Some *d·* skepticism exists as to
224–10 is helpful or *d·* only in
283–29 Lured by fame, . . . success is *d·*,
343–27 Dissensions are *d·*
344–29 more *d·* than any material infection,
364–1 is more or less *d·*.

dangers
Ret. 47–9 Example had shown the *d·*
My. 266–3 To my sense, the most imminent *d·*

dangle
Mis. 61–22 or *d·* at the end of a rope?

dangling
Mis. 61–17 * *d·* at the end of a rope.

Daniel's
My. 181–28 one expositor of *D·* dates

Dante
No. 18–17 may imagine the face of *D·* to be

dare
Mis. 22–5 Who *d·* say that matter or mortals
238–5 for all who *d·* to be true,
Peo. 9–18 to invoke the divine aid of Spirit
Po. 27–4 I, dying, *d·* abhor !"
My. 253–27 *D·* to be faithful to God

dared
Mis. 110–26 *d·* the perilous defense of Truth,

dares
Mis. 183–29 *d·* at this date refute the evidence
Un. 28–8 Who, then, *d·* define Soul as

daring
Ret. 2–4 poetic *d·* and pious picturesqueness

dark
Mis. 51–24 * *d·* pile of human mockeries ;
53–30 but to . . . the ungodly, it is *d*
117–25 he works somewhat in the *d·* ;
180–5 the *d·* shadow and portal of death,
204–2 a *d·*, impenetrable cloud of error ;
228–2 a deception *d·* as it is base
250–28 lighting the *d·* places of earth.
265–5 He grows *d·*, and cannot regain,
276–31 In the *d·* hours, . . . stand firmer

dark

Mis.	330– 2	make melody through *d·* pine groves.
	360–28	to sensitive ears and *d·* disciples.
	385–21	The *d·* unknown.
	398–13	So, when day grows *d·* and cold,
Ret.	4–18	low requiems through *d·* pine groves.
	18– 8	*D·* sentinel hedgerow is guarding
	20–13	knelt by his side throughout the *d·* hours,
	23–10	The world was *d·.*
	34– 6	the reply was *d·* and contradictory.
	46–19	So, when day grows *d·* and cold,
Un.	40– 4	*d·* shadow of material sense,
	60– 8	the *d·* abyss of nothingness,
	64–15	leap the *d·* fissures,
Pul.	17–18	So, when day grows *d·* and cold,
	32– 1	* her face, framed in *d·* hair
	58–19	* It is rather *d·*, often too much so
'01.	10–21	Divine Love spans the *d·* passage of sin,
Po.	1–10	from chaos *d·* set free,
	14–17	So, when day grows *d·* and cold,
	22–18	The *d·* domain of pain
	24–16	And night grows deeply *d·* ;
	26–15	*d·* record of our guilt unrolled,
	30–15	And stern, *d·* shadows cast
	34– 8	In what *d·* leafy grove
	42– 3	sunshine without a *d·* spot ;
	48–15	The *d·* unknown.
	63–17	*D·* sentinel hedgerow is guarding
	67–15	o'er the *d·* wavy grass.
My.	61–26	* *d·* stillness of the night,
	222–15	in those *d·* days Jesus was not
	256–24	the gifts glow in the *d·* green
	297–13	*d·* hour that precedes the dawn.
	340–27	*d·* days of our forefathers
	350–12	did'st not Thou the *d·* wave treading

Dark Ages

Pul.	52–23	* the blackness of the *D· A·,*

darken

Ret.	18–24	they *d·* my lay :
Pul.	21–29	aught that can *d·* in any degree
'01.	20–15	could not bewilder, *d·*, or
Po.	64–20	they *d·* my lay :
Mis.	206– 9	*d·* the discernment of Science ;
	267–25	*d·* the true conception of man's

darkened

Mis.	169– 5	insight had been *d·* thereby,
Ret.	35–15	*d·* the glow and grandeur
My.	350–20	mortal sense is *d·* unto death

darkens

Mis.	291– 6	*d·* the understanding that

darker

My.	285–11	war, and . . . belong to the *d·* ages,

darkest

'01.	20–28	*d·* and deepest of human crimes.

darkling

Mis.	88–16	the shadow of *d·* criticism
Po.	79–10	*d·* sense, arise, go hence !

darkly

Mis.	359–11	see through a glass, *d·* ; — *1 Cor.* 13 : 12.

darkness

and death
Po.	65–18	*d·* and death like mist melt away,

and doubt
Ret.	68–20	*D·* and doubt encompass thought,

and gloom
Mis.	320–20	wading through *d·* and gloom,

cannot see
Mis.	367–24	sees light, and cannot see *d·.*

cheers the
My.	202–23	taper unseen in . . . cheers the *d·.*

children of
My.	191–10	you are not children of *d·.*

clouds and
Mis.	377– 5	radiant relief in clouds and *d·* !

coexist with
Un.	64– 4	than the sun can coexist with *d·.*

danger and
My.	116–14	danger and *d·* of personal contagion.

deeper
Ret.	81–20	so sinks into deeper *d·.*

discern
Mis.	131– 6	in order rightly to discern *d·*

dispels
Mis.	205– 9	light which dispels *d·.*

doubt and
Mis.	342– 4	thus they were in doubt and *d·.*
'00.	7–20	In doubt and *d·* we say as did Mary
My.	152–20	stumble into doubt and *d·*,

flies in
Mis.	145–15	hooded hawk which flies in *d·.*

for light
Mis.	174–27	We do not look into *d·* for light.

darkness

illumine the
Mis.	276–18	light will illumine the *d·.*

in one's self
Mis.	131– 4	*d·* in one's self must first be

its
Un.	17–11	and its *d·* get consolation from

light and
Mis.	34–27	as direct opposites as light and *d·.*

light with
Mis.	333–22	hath light with *d·?* — *II Cor.* 6 : 14.

melt into
Mis.	264– 9	they melt into *d·.*

mental
Mis.	355–18	Mental *d·* is senseless error,

no
Mis.	113– 3	spiritual light, wherein is no *d·.*
No.	16–17	because it has no *d·* to emit.
	30–21	light wherein there is no *d·*,
'02.	16–20	in whom there is no *d·*,

of belief
Pul.	13–16	in the deep *d·* of belief.

or doubt
My.	187– 8	exclude all *d·* or doubt,

our
My.	232–13	as living lights in our *d·* :

out of
Mis.	130–31	out of *d·* into light.
My.	206–25	called you out of *d·* — *I Pet.* 2 : 9.

pierce the
Mis.	320–25	pierce the *d·* and melt into dawn.

place of
My.	199– 4	In place of *d·*, light hath

power of
My.	206 20	from the power of *d·*, — *Col.* 1 : 13.

powers of
'02.	14– 8	against the powers of *d·*,

profound
Mis.	342–14	*d·* profound brooded over

shineth in
Mis.	368– 3	let the light that shineth in *d·*,
Un.	63–10	that light which shineth in *d·*,
My.	110– 8	"shineth in *d·* ; — *John* 1 : 5.

sometimes
My.	206–30	" Ye were sometimes *d·*, — *Eph.* 5 : 8.

that
Ret.	27–19	* Touch God's right hand in that *d·*,
	81–22	how great is that *d·* !" — *Matt.* 6 : 23.
Un.	19–13	how great is that *d·* !" — *Matt.* 6 : 23.

to daylight
Mis.	126– 3	yea, from *d·* to daylight,

walked in
Chr.	55– 8	that walked in *d·* — *Isa.* 9 : 2.

within
No.	30–21	holding *d·* within itself.

works of
Rud.	4–24	extinguishes forever the works of *d·*

Mis.	ix–16	*d·* of storm and cloud and tempest,
	165–14	neither *d·*, doubt, disease, nor
	212–16	reign of difficulties, *d·*, and
	319– 1	in the *d·* of all the ages,
	340–29	comes out in the *d·* to shine
	367–25	conclusion, that *d·* dwelleth in light,
	368– 4	the *d·* comprehendeth it not,
Ret.	27–18	* Groping blindly in the *d·*,
	61–15	you are *d·*, nothingness.
	81–21	light that is in thee be *d·*, — *Matt.* 6 : 23.
Un.	19–14	light that is in thee be *d·*, — *Matt.* 6 : 23.
	63–11	the *d·* comprehendeth it not.
'00.	6–24	is not *d·* but light.
'01.	2–23	*d·*, doubt, and unrequited toil
My.	110– 8	*d·* comprehended it not." — *John* 1 : 5.
	140– 4	I will make *d·* light — *Isa.* 42 : 16.

Dartmouth

Pul.	32–29	* Albert Baker, graduated at *D·*

Dartmouth College

Ret.	6–15	graduated at *D· C·* in 1834,

darts

Mis.	387–13	*D·* not from those who watch
Po.	6– 8	*D·* not from those who watch

Darwin

Mis.	361–15	Berkeley, Tyndall, *D·*,
'01.	24–18	Leibnitz, Berkeley, *D·*,

dashing

Mis.	206– 5	*d·* against the receding shore,
	266–12	comet's course, *d·* through space,

dastardly

My.	340–20	paltering, timid, or *d·* policy,

data

Mis.	x–13	To some articles are affixed *d·*,
Pul.	36–28	* some of the *d·* of this paper.

date

Mis.	xi– 2	the *d·* of its issue, 1875,
	xii– 2	and to retain at this *d·* the
	4–12	At this *d·*, 1883,
	29–16	Since that *d·* I have known of
	29–18	the *d·* of the first publication
	39– 8	abroad at this early *d·*
	81–23	at some *d·* must cry in the
	139– 2	to three years from this *d·* ;
	183–29	who dares at this *d·* refute the
	271–20	Much is said at this *d·*, 1889,
	293– 7	will come, at some *d·*,
	314– 3	From this *d·* the Sunday services
	316–10	The *d·* of a class in C. S. should
	316–16	the word spoken at this *d·*.
	366–16	At this *d·*, poor jaded humanity
	372– 9	*d·* of its publication in December,
Ret.	26–19	gave the world a new *d·* in the
Pul.	53– 4	* in other countries at an earlier *d·*.
	67–23	* *d·* of the Declaration of Independence,
	82–28	* The *d·* is no longer B. C.
	86–11	* with the *d·*, "1895."
'00.	15– 2	a new one that is up to *d·*.
Po.	vi– 9	* *under the d· of February* 3, 1865.
My.	10–15	* as to amount and *d·* of payment.
	11–28	* *d·* for commencing building
	12–12	* and the *d·* of commencing work,
	16– 6	* $226,285.73 on hand on that *d·*,
	26– 5	* on the *d·* of the annual communion,
	26–22	should *d·* some special reform,
	55– 1	* This *d·* is memorable as the one
	56– 6	* The *d·* of the inauguration of
	57–16	* membership at that *d·* was 1,545.
	148–13	Memorable *d·*, all unthought of
	169– 7	requested to visit me at a later *d·*,
	184–14	my cordial thanks at an earlier *d·*.
	216–22	I request that from this *d·*
	217–14	dividend with interest thereon up to *d·*,
	266–26	points . . . at that *d·* undisturbed,
	307–16	At that *d·* I was a staunch orthodox,
	309–25	style of architecture at that *d·*.
	311–16	*d·* of my first church membership.
	318– 8	because at that *d·* some critics
	334– 3	* newspaper reports of that *d·*
	351– 3	* publish her letter of recent *d·*,

dated

Mis.	163– 8	He who *d·* time, the Christian era,
	199–31	*d·* the Christian era.
Man.	41– 2	He who *d·* the Christian era
Pul.	34–18	* From that hour *d·* her conviction of
My.	138–29	* and *d·* May 16, 1907,
	180– 8	by him . . . who *d·* time.
	333–30	* *Chronicle, d·* September 25, 1844,
	359–19	* composite letter, *d·* July 19,

dates

145 (A. D.)		
My.	178–31	written in A.D. 145,
325		
'02.	18–28	about the year 325,
1620		
My.	183– 6	what John Robinson wrote in 1620
1710		
'01.	23–23	published a book in 1710
1722–1725		
Ret.	3– 7	Indian troubles of 1722–1725,
1733		
My.	295–11	PRINTED IN NUREMBERG IN 1733
1761		
My.	172 –4	* It was built in 1761,
1812		
Mis.	304–12	* battle-field of New Orleans (1812),
Ret.	3–12	towards the close of the War of 1812.
1814		
Ret.	3–11	and won distinction in 1814
1819		
My.	290– 9	this noble woman, born in 1819,
1820–'30		
Pul.	32–19	* in the early decade of 1820–'30.
1834		
Ret.	6–16	at Dartmouth College in 1834,
1835		
Po.	vi–12	*In* 1835 *a mob in Boston*
1837		
Ret.	6–23	In 1837 he succeeded to the
1840		
My.	290–10	married in 1840,
1841		
Ret.	6–30	In 1841 he received further
1843		
Ret.	19– 1	In 1843 I was united to my first husband,
My.	330– 3	* in Wilmington in 1843,
	330–18	* in 1844, not in 1843, as claimed
	334–13	* certain circumstances in 1843,
1844		
Pul.	34– 3	* to her father's home — in 1844

dates

1844		
'02.	15–19	sell them at his decease in 1844,
My.	189–28	a poem written in 1844,
	330–18	* in 1844, not in 1843, as claimed
	332–30	* George Washington Glover in 1844
	334–13	* records show really existed in 1844,
1844, June		
My.	312– 7	* in *J·*, 1844, . . . he died
	333– 6	* twenty-eighth day of *J·*, 1844,
	335–16	* Wilmington, N. C., in *J·*, 1844,
1844, July 3		
My.	333–19	* *Wilmington Chronicle* of *J·* 3, 1844,
1844, August 21		
My.	329–17	* issues of July 3 and *A·* 21, 1844,
	331–11	* *Wilmington Chronicle* of *A·* 21, 1844,
1844, September 25		
My.	333–30	* *Chronicle,* dated *S·* 25, 1844,
1845		
My.	334–27	* obituary which appeared in 1845
1850		
Po.	vi– 4	* *in Manchester, N. H., in* 1850,
1853		
Peo.	10– 8	succored a fugitive slave in 1853,
My.	13– 6	in London, England, in 1853,
1856		
Po.	vi– 4	* *and again in Boston, in* 1856.
1862		
Mis.	378– 1	About the year 1862, while the author
My.	306–22	In 1862, when I first visited
1865		
Po.	page 26	poem
1866		
Mis.	179–31	In 1866, when God revealed to me
	246–23	the spiritual famine of 1866,
	379–28	I discovered, in 1866, the momentous
Ret.	24– 9	and in the latter part of 1866
Pul.	vii– 3	birth of C. S., in 1866,
	5– 1	my form of prayer since 1866 ;
	34– 4	* until 1866 no special record is
	34– 5	* In 1866, while living in Lynn,
	64–15	* she discovered C. S. in 1866.
	70–17	* Mrs. Eddy asserts that in 1866
Po.	vi– 6	* *in Lynn, Mass., in* 1866,
My.	v–15	* discovered C. S. in 1866,
	22–15	* Since 1866, almost forty years ago,
	67–13	* C. S. discovered . . . 1866
	181–21	(1866) C. S. was discovered
	181–28	fixed the year 1866 or 1867
	343–16	It was in 1866 that the light of
1866–'69		
Pul.	34–24	* From 1866–'69 Mrs. Eddy withdrew
1866, January		
My.	306–26	*J·*, 1866, Dr. Quimby had
1866, February		
Ret.	24– 1	in *F·*, 1866, and after the death
1867		
Mis.	29–15	In 1867, I taught the first
Ret.	43– 1	In 1867 I introduced the first
My.	181–28	fixed the year 1866 or 1867
1868		
Pul.	54–28	About 1868, the author of S. and H.
Po.	page 28	poem
1869		
Mis.	242–25	cured precisely such a case in 1869.
My.	105–19	About the year 1869, I was wired
1870		
Ret.	35– 1	In 1870 I copyrighted the first
1874		
Mis.	272– 4	* Act of 1874, Chapter 375, Section 4.
My.	315– 3	* About the year 1874, Dr. Patterson
1875		
Mis.	xi– 2	at the date of its issue, 1875,
	29–18	The census since 1875
	285–14	about the year 1875 that S. and H.
Ret.	27– 4	S. and H., published in 1875.
	37– 5	was published in 1875.
Pul.	38– 6	* S. and H., was issued in 1875.
	55–14	* have been published in 1875.
Rud.	16–20	which I published in 1875.
'00.	6–29	cites 1875 as the year of
My.	v–19	in 1875, after nine years of
	266–24	"S. and H. . . . published in 1875.
	343–17	In 1875 I wrote my book.
1876		
Ret.	43–22	and six of my students in 1876,
1876, July 4		
Pul.	37–27	* was organized on *J·* 4, 1876,
	67–24	* when on *J·* 4, 1876, the first
1877		
Ret.	42– 4	last marriage . . . in the year 1877.
Pul.	35–27	* In 1877 Mrs. Glover married
	46–27	* marriage was in the spring of 1877,
My.	266–22	Since 1877, these special "signs

dates

1878
Ret. 15–13 In the year 1878 I was called
No. 3– 9 in 1878, some irresponsible people
1879
Man. 17– 1 In the spring of 1879, a little band
38–20 organized in 1879 by Mary Baker Eddy,
'00. 1–11 first church . . . chartered in 1879,
My. 67–14 * First church organized . . . 1879
1879, April
Pul. 37–28 * A·, 1879, the church was founded
67–27 * church was founded in A·, 1879,
1879, April 12
Man. 17– 9 A· 12, 1879, on motion of
Ret. 43–24 A· 12, 1879, it was voted
Pul. 30–26 * meeting held on A· 12, 1879.
55–25 * was organized A· 12, 1879,
1879, June
Man. 18– 4 was obtained J·, 1879,
Ret. 16–17 was obtained J·, 1879,
44– 5 was obtained in J·, 1879,
1879, August 16
My. 49–16 * was held A· 16, 1879,
1879, August 23
My. 49–10 * was obtained A· 23, 1879,
1879, October 19
My. 49–26 * meeting held O· 19, 1879,
1880
Pul. 58– 4 * Coming to Boston about 1880,
Peo. 10–10 practice of medicine in 1880.
'80's
Pul. 31–14 * some year in the early '80's
1880, January 2
My. 50– 3 * Communion . . . J· 2, 1880.
1880, January 4
My. 50–22 * "Sunday, J· 4, 1880.
1880, May 23
My. 50–29 * record of M· 23, 1880,
1880, December 15
My. 51–19 * meeting . . . D· 15, 1880,
1881
Man. 18– 7 was ordained A.D. 1881.
Ret. 16–20 was ordained A. D. 1881.
43– 5 chartered in 1881.
44– 8 was ordained in 1881,
Pul. 38– 4 * ceremony took place in 1881.
68– 2 * and in 1881 was ordained,
68– 5 * by Mrs. Eddy in 1881,
My. 244–30 was chartered A.D. 1881.
1881, January
Mis. 272– 2 * charter in J·, 1881,
272– 9 * from J·, 1881, till
Ret. 48–17 chartered in J·, 1881,
1881, July 20
My. 51–27 * record . . . of J· 20, 1881,
1882
Ret. 42–13 In 1882 he passed away,
Pul. 36– 1 * Dr. Eddy died in 1882,
47– 3 * He died in 1882.
1882, January
Mis. 272–10 * said Act in J·, 1882.
1882, January 31
Mis. 272– 6 * from and after J· 31, 1882.
1882, September 8
My. 53– 9 * S· 8, 1882, it was voted
1883
Mis. 4–12 At this date, 1883,
35– 7 In 1883, a million of people
272–14 * In accordance with Statutes of 1883,
Ret. 43– 6 No charter was . . . after 1883.
My. vi–12 * founded The C. S. Journal in 1883,
304–16 1883, I started The C. S. Journal,
1883, April
Mis. x– 7 published . . . since A·, 1883,
139–15 A·, 1883, I started the Journal
380–27 A·, 1883, a bill in equity was
Ret. 52–21 I started it, A·, 1883,
1883, October 22
My. 53–15 * At a meeting O· 22, 1883,
1883, November
My. 53–12 * until N·, 1883,
1884
Pul. 6–20 * a missionary to China, in 1884.
My. 182–11 In 1884, I taught a class in
1884, December
Mis. 242–28 he was my student in D·, 1884 ;
1885
Mis. 39– 5 In 1885, this knowledge
245– 9 the pulpit and press in 1885,
1885, February 8
My. 54–13 * F· 8, 1885, communion was held
1885, March 16
Mis. 95– 3 * on Monday, M· 16, 1885,
1885, October 18
My. 54–26 * On O· 18, 1885, the rooms

dates

1885, October 25
My. 54–32 * first Sunday service . . . O· 25, 1885.
1885, December 7
My. 53–26 * year ending D· 7, 1885,
1886
Ret. 52–12 to my students, in 1886,
1886, February 11
Ret. 52–18 at New York City, F· 11, 1886.
1887
My. 306–24 manuscripts which in 1887
323–31 * Normal class in the fall of 1887
1887, January
My. 319–21 * J·, 1887, I entered your
1887, Jan. 10
My. 322–19 * Primary class (J· 10, 1887).
1888
Mis. 134–11 and meet en masse, in 1888,
161– 3 SUNDAY BEFORE CHRISTMAS, 1888.
274–22 At this period, 1888, those quill-drivers
275–23 Scientist Association in 1888.
My. 185–22 In 1888 I visited these
1888, June 13
Mis. 98– 8 Convention in Chicago, J· 13, 1888.
1889
Mis. 239– 2 Metaphysical College, in 1889,
271–20 Much is said at this date, 1889,
Ret. 43–18 taught one Primary class, in 1889,
Pul. 36– 4 * and it was closed (in 1889)
68– 8 * The college was closed in 1889,
My. 163–17 I removed from Boston in 1889
246–11 In the year 1889, to gain a
284–18 my residence in Concord, 1889,
1889, Feb. 25
Mis. 279–12 THAT ASSEMBLED F· 25, 1889,
1889, June
Ret. 52–23 in Cleveland, Ohio, J·, 1889,
1889, Oct. 29
Ret. 48–13 College Corporation, O· 29, 1889,
1889, December
Ret. 51– 1 In D·, 1889, I gave a lot of
1889, December 10
Mis. 139–18 D· 10, 1889, I gave
1890
Mis. 159–23 a bit of what I said in 1890 :
309–32 See the revised edition of 1890,
379–32 revised edition of 1890,
Ret. 82–28 my last revision, in 1890,
My. 92–15 * since 1890 its following had
93–29 * In 1890 the faith had but
1891, April 15
My. 178–21 A· 15, 1891, the C. S. textbook
1891, June 3
Mis. 135–25 Association, J· 3, 1891.
1891, September
Ret. 37–10 S·, 1891, it had reached
1892
Ret. 51– 3 valued in 1892 at about
Pul. 20– 6 In 1892 I had to recover the land
1892, September
Man. 18–12 twenty-third day of S·, 1892,
My. 55–13 * twenty-third day of S·, 1892,
1892, September 1
My. 55–11 * S· 1, 1892, Mrs. Eddy gave
1893
Pul. 1– 8 1893 was a distinguished character,
4–26 In 1893 the World's Parliament of
My. 172– 4 * razed in 1893 to make room for
304–18 In 1893, Judge S. J. Hanna became
1893, October 3
My. 57–15 * Chickering Hall, O· 3, 1893,
1893, December
Mis. 372– 9 its publication in D·, 1893,
1894
Mis. x–24 In 1894, I received from the
131–21 encountered in Anno Domini 1894,
310–26 year of religious jubilee, 1894,
319–22 edifice must be built in 1894.
382–20 1894 was erected the first church
Man. 103– 4 The edifice erected in 1894 for
Pul. 1–12 garner the memory of 1894 ;
6–13 wrote to me in 1894,
24–15 * erected Anno Domini 1894.
42–24 * "Love-Children's Offering — 1894."
45–13 * completion within the year 1894
78– 8 * During the year 1894 a church
84–14 * year, Anno Domini 1894,
My. 15– 6 * edifice erected in 1894 for The
23– 6 * of the present edifice in 1894.
67–15 * First church erected . . . 1894
eighteen hundred and ninety-four
Pul. 77– 9 * year e· h· and n·

dates

1894, February 27
  Pul. 68–26 * meeting . . . on *F·* 27, 1894.
1894, March
  My. 55–20 * continued there until *M·*, 1894,
1894, 21st day of May, A. D.
  Mis. 143–15 On the 21st *d· of M·*, A. D. 1894,
1894, December 30
  My. 55–28 * for occupancy, *D·* 30, 1894.
1895
  Mis. 382–32 In 1895 I ordained that the Bible,
  Pul. 5–21 book, in 1895, is in its ninety-first
    20–10 In 1895 I reconstructed my
    45–16 * before April or May of 1895.
    86–11 * with the date, "1895."
  '00. 7– 6 In 1895 it was estimated that
  My. 57–28 * before the dedication . . . in 1895,
    76–14 * time of the dedication . . . in 1895,
    320–31 * time of the dedication . . . in 1895.
1895, February
  Pul. 78–15 * *F·*, 1895, at high noon.
eighteen hundred and ninety-five
  Man. 64–14 year *e· h· and n·*,
eighteen hundred and ninety-five, February
  Pul. 77–16 * *F·, e· h· and n·*,
eighteen hundred and ninety-five, March
  Pul. 87– 4 * *M·, e· h· and n·*,
1895, March 20
  Man. 75– 4 Whereas, on *M·* 20, 1895,
1896
  Mis. 383– 8 In 1896 it goes without saying,
1896, April 26
  My. 56– 7 * The date of . . . was *A·* 26, 1896.
1897
  My. 121–17 by my students in 1897.
1897, October
  My. 145– 3 in *O·*, 1897, I proposed to
1897, October 29
  My. 145– 7 From that time, *O·* 29, 1897,
1898
  Mis. 347–31 *The C. S. Journal* . . . up to 1898.
  My. vi–20 * Publishing Society, which in 1898,
    125–22 students in my last class in 1898
1898, January twenty-fifth
  Man. 79–22 on *J· t·*, 1898,
1898, January 31
  My. 157–22 On *J·* 31, 1898, I gave a
1898, March 19
  My. 157–19 * *Concord Monitor* of *M·* 19, 1898.
1898, November 21
  My. 104–24 On *N·* 21, 1898, in my class
1899, Oct. 12
  My. 217–17 the last *Sentinel* [*O·* 12, 1899]
1900
  Mis. 304–14 * until 1900, when it will be sent to
  My. 8–29 * "Since the last report, in 1900,
    256–16 chapter sub-title
1901
  My. 334–19 * Message to The Mother Church [1901] :
1901, May 16
  My. 346–26 * Associated Press, *M·* 16, 1901 :
1901, June
  My. 292–19 In the *J·*, 1901, Message
1901, August
  My. 330– 2 * in your paper in *A·*, 1901.
1902
  Man. 86–21 revised editions since 1902,
  '02. 20–17 in 1902 to begin omitting our *annual*
  My. 22– 3 * In the year 1902 our Leader
    23–15 * pledged at the annual meeting, 1902,
    57– 7 * Message to the church in 1902
    76–21 * church meeting in Boston, in 1902,
    259–17 I hope that in 1902 the churches
1902, June
  '02. 1– 8 during the year ending *J·*, 1902,
  My. 22– 7 * annual meeting in *J·*, 1902,
1902, June 19
  My. 23–12 * total receipts *J·* 19, 1902
1903
  My. 13– 6 was presented to me in 1903
    305–18 in the *National Magazine* (1903)
    327– 5 in 1903, made it legal to
nineteen hundred and three
  Man. 64–22 year *n· h· and t·*
1903, March
  Man. 102–15 deeds given by . . . in *M·*, 1903 ;
1903, March 1
  My. 25–12 * *M·* 1, 1903 to February 29, 1904,
1903, March 17
  Man. 18–24 By-Law adopted *M·* 17, 1903,
1903, June
  My. 57–21 * 2,194 more than . . . of *J·*, 1903.
1903, July 16
  My. 347–10 presented *J·* 16, 1903.
1903, October
  My. 57–12 * was begun in *O·*, 1903,

dates

1903, October 24
  My. 329–12 * appeared . . . *O·* 24, 1903.
1904
  My. 67–16 * Corner-stone . . . 1904
    159–29 Copyright, 1904, by
    164–16 Now [1904] six dear churches are
    173– 4 * visit of . . . Scientists in 1904 :
    254–20 * in the June *Journal* of 1904,
1904, February 29
  My. 25–12 * March 1, 1903 to *F·* 29, 1904,
1904, March 1
  My. 25–13 * *M·* 1, 1904 to February 28, 1905,
1904, May 31
  My. 16– 5 * up to and including *M·* 31, 1904,
1904, June 1
  My. 23–11 * expenditures *J·* 1, 1904
1904, June 13
  My. 171–14 Monday, *J·* 13, 1904.
1904, July 16
  My. 16–12 * Saturday, *J·* 16, 1904,
    57–13 * corner-stone . . . laid *J·* 16, 1904.
1905
  My. 56–24 * In the spring of 1905
    270– 5 In 1905, the First Congregational
1905, February 28
  My. 25–13 * March 1, 1904 to *F·* 28, 1905,
1905, March 1
  My. 25–13 * *M·* 1, 1905 to February 28, 1906,
1905, May 31
  My. 23–11 * June 1, 1904 to *M·* 31, 1905,
1905, June 1
  My. 23–10 * Amount on hand *J·* 1, 1905,
    23–13 * June 19, 1902 to *J·* 1, 1905,
1905, September 23
  My. 232–11 SENTINEL, *S·* 23, 1905
1905, October 1
  My. 56–28 * beginning *O·* 1, 1905,
1906
  My. 67–17 * Cathedral to be dedicated . . . 1906
1906, February 28
  My. 25–14 * March 1, 1905 to *F·* 28, 1906,
1906, April 23
  My. 26–10 generous check . . . *A·* 23, 1906,
1906, June 10
  My. 26– 6 * annual communion, . . . *J·* 10, 1906.
    240–11 Message . . . *J·* 10, 1906,
1906, December 1
  My. 317– 2 * *Sentinel* of *D·* 1, 1906,
1907
  Man. 84–10 After 1907, the Board of Education
    88–12 Beginning with 1907, the teacher
    91–24 beginning A.D. 1907 ;
  My. 273–32 Copyright, 1907, by
1907, January
  My. 308–13 *McClure's Magazine, J·*, 1907,
1907, April 3
  My. 134–21 * meeting of *A·* 3, 1907,
1907, May
  My. 138–26 * sixteenth day of *M·*, 1907,
1907, May 16
  My. 138–29 * and dated *M·* 16, 1907,
1908
  Mis. 21–24 1908 edition of S. and H.
1908, January 6
  My. 296–25 *New York American, J·* 6, 1908,
1908, February 29
  My. 236–27 will be issued *F·* 29 [1908].
1908, July 8
  Man. 18–26 On *J·* 8, 1908, the By-Laws
1908, Dec. 15
  Man. 68–22 takes effect on *D·* 15, 1908.
1909
  Mis. 318–28 See edition of 1909.
  My. 116–25 Copyright, 1909, by
    210–22 Copyright, 1909, by
1909, June 7
  My. 142–28 annual meeting . . . *J·* 7, 1909.
1909, July 31
  My. 359–17 * In the *Sentinel* of *J·* 31, 1909,
1909, August 30
  My. 361–10 not written to her since *A·* 30, 1909.
1910, May
  Po. vii– 5 * *In M·*, 1910, *Mrs. Eddy requested*
1910, September 10
  My. 237–22 in the *Sentinel* of *S·* 10 [1910]
1913
  My. 34–30 * according to the 1913 edition.

  Mis. 148–14 were written at different *d·*,
  Man. 3–10 were written at different *d·*,
  Pul. 20–22 one of the many *d·* selected
  '01. 24–18 It *d·* beyond Socrates,
  My. 67–12 * *Notable D· in C. S.*
    181–28 one expositor of Daniel's *d·*
    181–31 those *d·* were the first two years of

dates
  My. 319–26   * These *d·* are very well fixed in
      (*see also* **months**)

dates — addresses
  1888, June 13
    Mis. 98– 8
  1895, June 3
    Mis. 116– 6

dates — affidavits
  1902, Jan'y
    My. 315–16 *
  1907, May 16
    My. 138–24

dates — chapter sub-titles
  1885, January 18
    Mis. 171–22
  1893
    Mis. 116– 9
  1895
    Mis. 110–14
  1895, May 26
    Mis. 106–16
  1896
    Mis. 125–22
  1896, January
    Mis. 120–26
  1897
    Mis. 251– 3
  1897, July 4
    My. 169– 1
  1897, December 12
    My. 147– 1
  1898
    My. 243–19
  1898, January 2
    My. 121– 1
  1898, December
    My. 256– 1
  1899
    My. 339–11
  1899, February
    My. 148– 9
  1899, April 19
    My. 151–21
  1899, June 4
    My. 124– 5
  1899, June 6
    My. 131–17
  1900
    My. 256–16
  1900, January 11
    My. 154–14
  1901
    My. 109–11
  1902
    My. 155–16
  1902, June 15
    My.   7– 2
  1903
    My. 251–23
         252–18
  1903, June
    My. 133–21
         170–11
  1903, July 20
    My. 294–22
  1904
    My. 15–11
         167–14
         171– 8
         253–10
         253–14
  1904, July 17
    My. 159– 2
  1904, December
    My. 253–20
  1905
    My. 254– 4
         254– 9
  1905, January 6
    My. 156– 1
  1906, June 10
    My.   3– 3

dates — headings
  1895, January 6
    Pul. page 1
  1898
    Pan.   1– 3
  1902, June 18
    My.   7–13
  1904, June 14
    My. 16– 1 *
  1905, May
    My. 20–22 *

dates — headings
  1905, June 13
    My. 22– 1 *
  1906, June 12
    My. 38–27 *

dates — interview
  1901, April 30
    My. 346–17 *

dates — letters from Mrs. Eddy
  1885, March 21
    Mis. 132–11
  1889
    Mis. 150– 7
  1890, May 23
    Mis. 138–32
  1895, Feb. 12
    Mis. 146–28
  1895, March 25
    Pul. 87–28
  1895, Sept. 30
    Mis. 148– 6
  1897, June 30
    My. 169–12
  1898, November 16
    My. 187–19
  1899, March 22
    My. 301–13
  1902, July 21
    My.   9–30
  1902, November 20
    My. 193–12
  1903, May 11
    My. 133–20
  1903, October 16
    My. 327– 9
  1904, June 11
    My. 171–18
  1904, September 1
    My. 20– 6
  1904, October 31
    My. 20–21
  1904, November 14
    My. 230–29
  1905, June 10
    My. 279–30
  1905, June 27
    My. 280–25
  1905, November 14
    My. 175– 9
  1905, December 28
    My. 261–20
  1906, February 9
    My. 351–21
  1906, April 8
    My. 25–30
  1906, April 23
    My. 26–28
  1907, March 22
    My. 135–23
  1907, April 2
    My. 136–11
  1907, April 3
    My. 136–31
         282–30
  1907, April 22
    My. 284– 9
  1907, May 28
    My. 284–30
  1907, July 8
    My. 236–22
  1907, July 27
    My. 197–30
  1908, June 21
    My. 140–30
  1908, June 24
    My. 142–24
  1908, October 12
    My. 352–25
  1908, November 16
    My. 353– 5
  1909, March 6
    My. 255–12
  1909, April 12
    My. 168–10
  1909, June 5
    My. 143– 7
  1909, June 7
    My. 144–11
  1909, June 26
    My. 198–10
  1909, July 12
    My. 358–28
  1909, July 15
    My. 208– 9

dates — letters from Mrs. Eddy
1909, July 23
 My. 360— 6
1909, November 2
 My. 208—22
1909, December 11
 My. 361—14
1909, December 25
 My. 263—11
1910, January 20
 My. 362— 8
1910, February 7
 My. 355—17
1910, April 20
 My. 356—11 *

dates — letters to a newspaper
1844, August 12
 My. 332—16 *

dates — letters to Mrs. Eddy
1895, January 6
 Pul. 77—22 *
   78—20 *
1895, March 20
 Pul. 86—15 *
1903, October 11
 My. 328— 6 *
1905, June 13
 My. 280—13 *
1906, June 12
 My. 60—22 *
1906, June 30
 My. 62—16 *
1906, July 10
 My. 63— 9 *
1906, November 21
 My. 322— 8 *
1906, December 4
 My. 323—16 *
1906, December 7
 My. 325—20 *
1908, October 9
 My. 352—17 *
1910, January 19
 My. 361—29 *
1910, February 5
 My. 363—12 *

dates — newspaper articles
1894, December 31
 Pul. 23— 1 *
   50— 9 *
1895, January
 Pul. 84— 9 *
1895, January 6
 Pul. 44—15 *
1895, January 7
 Pul. 40— 7 *
   61—19 *
1895, January 9
 Pul. 71— 3 *
1895, January 10
 Pul. 65—10 *
1895, January 12
 Pul. 75—13 *
1895, January 14
 Pul. 68—12 *
1895, January 18
 Pul. 70— 1 *
1895, January 19
 Pul. 56—23 *
1895, January 20
 Pul. 52— 8 *
1895, January 26
 Pul. 57—18 *
1895, February
 Pul. 81— 8 *
1895, February 1
 Pul. 71— 9 *
1895, February 2
 Pul. 63— 1 *
   67— 1 *
1895, February 6
 Pul. 74— 1 *
1895, February 7
 Pul. 64—22 *
1895, February 27
 Pul. 76—21 *
   77—23 *
1895, March 23
 Pul. 85—20 *
1895, July
 My. 363—17
1898, March
 My. 277— 1
1900, May 5
 My. 264— 1

dates — newspaper articles
1900, November 29
 My. 264— 7
1900, December
 My. 266— 1
1901, May 1
 My. 341—17 *
1902, June 19
 My. 65— 1 *
1902, July
 My. 266—10
1903, April
 My. 65—17 *
1903, May 16
 My. 10— 1 *
   11—22 *
1903, May 30
 My. 12—15 *
1903, June 8
 My. 304— 1
1904, January 2
 My. 14—10 *
1904, March 5
 My. 15— 1 *
1904, December
 My. 278—15
1905, February
 My. 267—13
1905, March 5
 My. 268— 1
1905, June 17
 My. 279—20
1905, July 1
 My. 280—14
1905, July 22
 My. 280—26
1905, August
 My. 281—15 *
1905, November 25
 My. 24—16 *
1906, March 17
 My. 25— 5 *
1906, April 14
 My. 26— 1
1906, April 28
 My. vii—15 *
   26— 7 *
1906, June 6
 My. 66—17 *
1906, June 9
 My. 27—20 *
1906, June 16
 My. 29— 1 *
1906, June 23
 My. 63—10 *
1906, November
 My. 269—15
1907, January 19
 My. 316— 9
1907, August
 My. 271—11 *
1907, November
 My. 272—18 *
1908, April
 My. 274—16 *
1908, May
 My. 286— 1
1908, May 1
 My. 275—10
1908, May 15
 My. 275—30
1908, May 16
 My. 276— 1
1908, November
 My. 276—15 *
1908, November 25
 My. 353— 7
1909, November 13
 My. 360—27
   363—18
1910, July 18
 My. 356—20

dates — notices
1906, June 2
 My. 27—19 *
1908, June 24
 My. 351—30
1909, April 28
 My. 354—12
1909, June 7
 My. 143—32
1909, October 12
 My. 359—15
1909, December 24
 My. 237—19
1910, September 28
 My. 242—26

dates—poem by Lilian Whiting
 1888, April 15
  Pul. 40– 6 *

dates—poems by Mrs. Eddy
 1865, February 3
  Po. vi–10
   72– 5
 1865, August 24
  Po. 68–24
 1865, December 7
  Po. 78–17
 1866, January 1
  Po. 27–25
 1866, August 4
  Po. 40– 5
 1866, August 25
  Po. 66–15
 1866, September 3
  Po. 9–12
 1866, November 8
  Po. 23–23
 1866, December 8
  Po. 46–18
 1867, March 3
  Po. 74– 7
 1868, January 1
  Po. 28–18
 1868, February 19
  Po. 42– 8
 1871, April
  Po. 70–26
 1871, September 3
  Po. 47–23
 1876, May 6
  Po. 21–19
 1898, May 15
  Po. 11– 5
  My. 337– 1
 1898, December
  Po. 29–23
 1899
  Po. 24–22
 1899, April 3
  Po. 44– 5
 1900, January
  Po. 79–22
 1900, April 18
  Po. 31–23
 1901, January
  Po. 22–22
 1904, May 21
  Po. 25–20
 1910, January 1
  My. 354–14

dates—prefaces
 1895, February
  Pul. vii–24
 1897, January
  Mis. xii–11
 1910, September 24
  Po. vii–17 *

dates—telegrams, cablegrams
 1895, February 4
  Pul. 74– 4 *
 1901, December 24
  My. 259–11 *
 1906, June 12
  My. 46–32 *
 1909, January 5
  My. 207–19 *
 1909, January 6
  My. 207–27

dates—tributes
 1901, January 27
  My. 289–22
 1901, September 14
  My. 290–31
 1907, August 31
  My. 295–31
 1907, October 14
  My. 296– 8
 1907, December 10
  My. 296–23
 1908, January 10
  My. 297–10

dating
 Mis. xi–12 d· the unseen, and enabling
 Man. 26– 4 d· from the time of election
   80–25 d· from the time of election
 Po. v– 3 * d· from her early girlhood

daughter
 Mis. 126–28 my church,— this d· of Zion:
   167– 7 Is the babe a son, or d·?
   167– 8 Both son and d·:

daughter
 Mis. 214– 7 d· against her mother,— *Matt.* 10 : 35.
 Ret. 1–15 Marion Moor McNeil had a d·,
   4–24 d· of Deacon Nathaniel Ambrose
   16– 6 " Did you hear my d· sing?
 Pul. 27–16 * the raising of the d· of Jairus.
   32–17 * Mary Baker was the d· of
   54–22 * In the case of Jairus' d·
   54–27 * he raised the d· to life.
 My. 233–17 the d· of my people— *Jer.* 6 : 14.
   282–24 importance to every son and d·

daughter-in-law
 Mis. 214– 8 the d· against her — *Matt.* 10 : 35.

Daughter of the Revolution
 (*see* **Eddy**)

daughters
 Mis. 182–26 the Elohim, His sons and d·.
   295–16 the dignity of her d·
 Pul. 83–17 * we must look now to their d·
 Po. 40– 2 Good " Sons," and d·, too,
 My. 185–29 d· of the Granite State
   310– 1 All my father's d· were

Daughters and Sons of the American Revolution
 Mis. 305– 4 * D· and S· of the A· R·,

Daughters of the American Revolution
 Mis. x–24 from the D· of the A· R· :
   304– 3 * To THE D· of the A· R· :
   304–18 * care of the D· of the A· R·.
   304–30 * of the D· of the A· R·.
   305–10 * of the D· of the A· R·

Daughters of the Revolution
 Pul. 48–22 * Society of the D· of the R·.

dauntless
 Pan. 14–23 led by the d· Dewey,
 My. 50–10 * d· Leader and teacher,

David (*see also* **David's**)
 Mis. 151–15 D· sang, " Whom have I — *Psal.* 73 : 25.
   162–30 Of the lineage of D·,
   196–23 and, in the words of D·,
   200–21 D· said, " Before I was — *Psal.* 119 : 67.
   229–16 would teach man as D· taught :
 Chr. 55– 4 the offspring of D·,— *Rev.* 22 : 16.
 Un. 30–12 restoreth my soul," says D·.— *Psal.* 23 : 3.
 Pul. 83–19 * D· sang— " God shall help — *Psal.* 46 : 5.
 '00. 14–21 hath the key of D· ;— *Rev.* 3 : 7.
 My. 188–10 out of the city of D·,
   244–15 place," whereof D· sang,— *Psal.* 91 : 1.
   273–10 King D·, the Hebrew bard, sang,

David's
 Ret. 15– 7 I could say in D· words,

Davis
 Dr.
 My. 105–20 Dr. D· of Manchester, N. H.
 Mr.
 My. 282–21 *Dear Mr. D· :—* Deeply do I thank you
 Mr. Hayne
 My. 282–18 MR. HAYNE D·, American Secretary,

dawn
 Mis. 78– 2 the spiritual d· of the Messiah,
   144–31 the universal d· shall break
   174–28 Death can never usher in the d·
   286–13 the d· of God's creation,
   313–10 d·, kindling its glories in the east,
   320–26 pierce the darkness and melt into d·.
   390– 6 lark's shrill song doth wake the d· :
 Un. 61–10 twilight and d· of earthly vision,
 No. 20–15 omnipresence will d· on mortals,
   22–14 as Stygian night to the kindling d·.
 '01. 35–14 Doth it d· on you and me?
 '02. 5– 1 As silent night foretells the d·
   5– 4 d· of the twentieth century
   20– 5 hues of heaven, tipping the d·
 Po. 17– 1 Ye echoes at d· !
   27– 8 d· with wisdom's light
   29– 6 Nor d· nor day !
   55– 7 lark's shrill song doth wake the d· :
 My. 110– 9 But the day will d·
   155–22 d· that knows no twilight
   254– 6 am glad you enjoy the d· of C. S. ;
   262–16 d· of divine Love breaking upon
   282–10 no uncertain ray of d·.
   290–21 Through a . . . mist he beheld the d·.
   297–13 dark hour that precedes the d·.
   350–26 D· Truth delightful, crowned with

dawned
 Mis. 1– 4 d· on the dome of being
   24– 6 daystar that d· on the night of
   24–12 healing Truth d· upon my sense ;
   169– 9 Truth d· upon her understanding.

dawned

Ret. 14–24 the new light *d·* within me.
No. 46–20 has *d·* on the sick-bound and
My. 265–14 Science of Christianity has *d·*
307–31 had already *d·* on me.

dawning

Mis. 320–13 *d·* upon human imperfection,
385–27 radiant glory sped The *d·* day.
Po. 28– 5 Of truth, this *d·* year !
49– 2 radiant glory sped The *d·* day.

dawns

Mis. 17–28 *d·* on human thought,
84–11 which *d·* by degrees on mortals.
213–28 night is far spent, the day *d·* ;
222–32 as easily as *d·* the morning light
'00. 6–10 *d·* the spiritual meaning thereof ;
7–30 morning *d·* on eternal day.
My. 185– 3 day *d·* and the harvest bells are

Day

My. 252–25 in England on New Year's *D·*,

day. (see also day's)

after day
My. 52–32 * "*D·* after day flew by,
all
My. 341–26 * It had been raining all *d·*
ancient
Po. 10– 7 Thy palm, in ancient *d·*,
My. 337– 8 Thy palm, in ancient *d·*,
and night
Mis. 177– 9 are engaged *d·* and night in
341–26 replenished with oil *d·* and night,
Pul. 12– 9 *d·* and night. — *Rev.* 12 : 10.
26–28 * kept always burning *d·* and night.
autumnal
Mis. 355–30 close of a balmy autumnal *d·*,
before
My. 322–17 * I had seen you the *d·* before
before the
My. 96–21 * before the *d·* set for the
break of
Mis. 111– 5 and at break of *d·* caught much.
busy
My. 75– 7 * Yesterday was a busy *d·* at the
by day
My. 31– 6 * "*D·* by day the manna fell ;"
207–10 * strive more earnestly, *d·* by day,
children's
My. 38–16 * It was "children's *d·*" at noon,
Communion
Man. 40–20 On Communion *d·* the Church Tenets
cool of the
Mis. 332–14 walking in the cool of the *d·*
dawning
Mis. 385–27 radiant glory sped The dawning *d·*.
Po. 49– 2 radiant glory sped The dawning *d·*.
dawns
Mis. 213–28 night is far spent, the *d·* dawns ;
My. 185– 3 *d·* dawns and the harvest bells
dedication
Pul. 79– 7 * taken care of on dedication *d·*
My. 77–17 * chapter sub-title
77–22 * It was dedication *d·*,
distant
My. 59– 6 * might be true in some far distant *d·*
147– 8 And now, at this distant *d·*,
during the
Pul. 43–25 * in Concord, N. H., during the *d·*,
My. 29–11 * repeated six times during the *d·*.
174– 4 Christian Scientists during the *d·*.
each
Mis. 142–12 Each *d·* since they arrived
Man. 41–21 duty of . . . to pray each *d·* :
60–16 should abide in every heart each *d·*
My. 161–23 sufficient unto each *d·* is the
174–27 Each *d·* I know Him nearer,
220–14 Each *d·* I pray for the
220–21 Each *d·* I pray : " God bless my
279–24 pray each *d·* for the . . . settlement of
endless
Mis. 399– 5 glories of one endless *d·*."
Po. 75–12 glories of one endless *d·*."
eternal
'00. 7–30 morning dawns on eternal *d·*.
Po. 22–11 And bask in one eternal *d·*.
everlasting
Mis. vii–18 sprung from Spirit, In everlasting *d·* ;
'02. 20– 6 tipping the dawn of everlasting *d·*,
every
Mis. 33–14 that is being asked every *d·*.
99–18 and be in the battle every *d·*
348–20 every *d·*, and especially at dinner,
My. 48–11 * make, every *d·*, a prayerful study
48–27 * every *d·* through its reading.
145– 8 I inspected the work every *d·*,

day

every
My. 167–21 this and every *d·*.
340– 3 every *d·* and every hour.
eye of
Po. 8–10 Ravished with beauty the eye of *d·*.
facts of
My. 110–21 unfold in part the facts of *d·*,
following
'02. 15–25 The following *d·* I showed it to my
My. 172–24 * was opened the following *d·*
glad
My. 158– 8 it is a glad *d·*, in attune with
173–21 It was a glad *d·* for me
grayest
My. 87–23 * make sunshine on the grayest *d·*.
grows dark
Mis. 398–13 So, when *d·* grows dark and cold,
Ret. 46–19 So, when *d·* grows dark and cold,
Pul. 17–18 So, when *d·* grows dark and cold,
Po. 14–17 So, when *d·* grows dark and cold,
has come
My. 183–18 *d·* has come when the forest becomes
heat of the
Mis. 130–18 the burden in the heat of the *d·*,
'00. 9–30 heat of the *d·*." — *Matt.* 20 : 12.
hours of the
My. 94–21 * at different hours of the *d·*,
in Concord
My. 171–19 * heading
interesting
Mis. 320– 4 This interesting *d·*, crowned with
is at hand
My. 202– 7 and the *d·* is at hand.
is not distant
Pan. 1–17 *d·* is not distant in the horizon
last
Mis. 57–26 *the sixth and last d·*,
laughing
Ret. 18–11 to the bright, laughing *d·* ;
Po. 63–23 to the bright, laughing *d·* ;
little
Po. 67– 2 brief bliss of life's little *d·*
memorable
Mis. 144– 8 On this memorable *d·* there are
midnight
Po. 26– 7 Chill was thy midnight *d·*,
next
Mis. 69–18 next *d·* he attended to his
night and
My. 66–19 * artists are working night and *d·*
no
My. 129–10 there is no *d·* but in His smile.
no distant
Mis. 6–14 At no distant *d·*, Christian healing
of dedication
Pul. 57– 7 * services on the *d·* of dedication.
of heathenism
My. 167–30 In our country the *d·* of heathenism,
of rest
Mis. 279–20 the seventh is the *d·* of rest,
of the birth
Pul. 20–23 *d·* of the birth and baptism of our
one
Mis. 339– 8 and is one *d·* beyond it,
353–13 one *d·* a workman in his mills,
Ret. 8–13 One *d·*, when my cousin,
Un. 14– 2 the belief that God must one *d·*
Pul. 33–17 * at work in a field one *d·*
My. 126–21 plagues come in one *d·*, — *Rev.* 18 : 8.
145–10 One *d·* the carpenters' foreman
307– 5 till one *d·* I declared to him
one especial
My. 325– 2 * spoke of one especial *d·* when
oppressive
My. 29–30 * inconveniences of an oppressive *d·*.
or night
Pul. 58–29 * make it a home by *d·* or night.
or two
Pul. 75–20 * and for the *d·* or two following,
other
My. 70–15 * were being tested the other *d·*.
96–28 * The dedication of . . . the other *d·*,
our
My. 23–27 * is being built in our *d·* ;
pillar by
My. 164–21 pillar by *d·*, kindling, guiding,
same
Mis. 243–10 removed these appliances the same *d·*
seventh
My. 336– 2 * would have died on the seventh *d·*.
sixteenth
My. 138–26 * On the sixteenth *d·* of May, 1907,
teachings of the
Mis. 81–11 *accepted teachings of the d·*,
tenth
My. 319–20 * On the tenth *d·* of January, 1887,

day

that
Mis. 70–25   That *d·* the thief would be with
    304–30   * organization on that *d·* of the
Pul. 60– 9   * happened that *d·* to be on Jesus'
Po. vi–26   * *various publications of that d·.*
My. 156–10   against that *d·.*" — *II Tim.* 1 : 12.
    228–30   against that *d·.*" — *II Tim.* 1 : 12.

that thou eatest
Mis. 367–17   "In the *d·* that thou eatest — *Gen.* 2 : 17.

the other
Hea. 6– 4   When I was told the other *d·,*

third
Mis. 24–10   On the third *d·* thereafter,
My. 335–23   * third *d·* of her husband's illness,

this
Mis. 271–13   "Choose you this *d·* — *Josh.* 24 : 15.
Po. 28–16   Give us this *d·* our daily food
My. 158– 7   This *d·* drops down upon the
    158–10   This *d·* is the natal hour of my

three times a
Mis. 133–22   Three times a *d·,* I retire to seek

throughout the
My. 31– 2   * following hymns throughout the *d·* :

20th
Pul. 78–14   * on the 20th *d·* of February, 1895,

twentieth
Pul. 77–16   * on the twentieth *d·* of February,

twenty-eighth
My. 333– 6   twenty-eighth *d·* of June, 1844,

twenty-fourth
Pul. 87– 3   * on the twenty-fourth *d·* of March,

twenty-third
Man. 18–12   On the twenty-third *d·* of September,
My. 55–13   * On the twenty-third *d·* of September,

wearisome
Po. 32–20   all the wearisome *d·,*

we celebrate
Mis. 176–14   The *d·* we celebrate reminds us

when all people
Pan. 1–18   even the *d·* when all people

will dawn
My. 110– 9   *d·* will dawn and the daystar

winter
Pul. 65–22   * bitter winter *d·,* a Roman soldier

Mis. 7–17   the newspapers of the *d·,*
    39–10   risen up in a *d·* to make this claim ;
    57–16   "In the *d·* that thou eatest — *Gen.* 2 : 17.
    226–16   * must follow, as the night the *d·,*
    335– 7   *d·* when he looketh not — *Matt.* 24 : 50.
Ret. 9–25   * redeemed her birthright of the *d·,*
    81–25   * must follow, as the night the *d·,*
Un. 5–13   every Life-problem in a *d·.*
    17–22   in the *d·* when they should partake of
    44–20   "In the *d·* ye eat thereof — *Gen.* 3 : 5.
Po. vi–27   * poem
    29– 6   Nor dawn nor *d·* !
    page 32   poem
My. 30–29   * by far the largest crowd of the *d·*
    45–19   * by *d·* in a pillar of cloud
    45–25   * pillar of cloud by *d·,* — see *Exod.* 13 : 22.
    75–20   * and warm as the *d·* was,
    148–13   unthought of till the *d·* had passed !
    153–12   healed from the *d·* my flowers
    173–17   on the *d·* when there are no formal
    186–26   on the *d·* of your church dedication.
    187–24   Since the *d·* in which you were
    327–29   * and look forward to the *d·,*

daybreak
Un. 27–14   fleeing like a shadow at *d·* ;
My. 77–19   * began to gather at *d·*

day-dream
Mis. 47–13   tend to elucidate your *d·,*

day-dreams
Ret. 12– 5   echoes still my *d·* thrill,
Po. 61– 3   echoes still my *d·* thrill,
My. 109– 3   Matter has no . . . in our *d·*

day-god
Po. 16–14   when the *d·* is low ;

daylight
Mis. 126– 3   yea, from darkness to *d·,*

day's
My. 92–12   * hardly more than a *d·* wonder.

days (see also days')
apostolic
Ret. 43– 2   since the apostolic *d·.*
beginning of
Chr. 55–20   neither beginning of *d·,* — *Heb.* 7 : 3.
dark
My. 222–15   Even in those dark *d·* Jesus was not
    340–27   The dark *d·* of our forefathers
dear
Po. 47– 1   Are the dear *d·* ever coming again,

days

early
Mis. 345–27   midnight feasts in the early *d·,*
My. 63– 3   * early *d·* of the construction of

eight
My. 323–32   * eight *d·* in Mr. and Mrs. Wiggin's

endless
My. 350–26   crowned with endless *d·,*

end of
Un. 13–18   or end of *d·.*" — see *Heb.* 7 : 3.
My. 119–25   without beginning or end of *d·.*

feast
My. 188– 7   Your feast *d·* will not be in

few
Mis. 80–17   must be "of few *d·,* — *Job* 14 : 1.
    373– 7   A few *d·* afterward, the following
Chr. 55–14   is of few *d·,* — *Job.* 14 : 1.
My. 14–11   * A few *d·* ago we received a
    86–10   * into Boston in the past few *d·*
    87–22   * in Boston during the past few *d·.*
    145–12   * "I want to be let off for a few *d·.*
    247–26   after many or a few *d·*
    319–22   * A few *d·* later, in conversation

for prayer
My. 340– 3   St. Paul's *d·* for prayer were

full number of
'00. 14– 7   full number of *d·* named in the

later
My. 63– 4   * advisory capacity in the later *d·* ;
    319–22   * A few *d·* later, in conversation

latter
Mis. 112–13   seem to belong to the latter *d·,*
My. 127–21   latter *d·* of the nineteenth century.
    131–22   in this hour of the latter *d·*

length of
Mis. 29–26   nor advance health and length of *d·.*
    67–17   happiness, and length of *d·.*

many
My. 13–30   returns it unto them after many *d·,*

may be few
Po. 33–17   I ponder the *d·* may be few

nine
My. 312–21   and died in about nine *d·.*
    335–17   * and at the end of nine *d·*
    335–29   * In these nine *d·* and nights

of Christ
Un. 9–25   since the *d·* of Christ.

of Eden
Un. 44–10   In the *d·* of Eden, humanity was

of shade
My. 166–13   *D·* of shade and shine may come

pioneer
Mis. x–10   in the early pioneer *d·,*

Revolutionary
Pul. 48–28   * in Colonial and Revolutionary *d·,*

seven
Mis. 279–18   corresponding to the seven *d·* of

several
My. 73–15   * as they have been for several *d·*
    73–15   * will be for several *d·* to come,

six
Mis. 279–18   the six *d·* are to find out the

special
My. 340– 5   usage of special *d·* and seasons

sunny
Mis. 395–26   Of sunny *d·* and cloudless skies,
Po. 58–11   Of sunny *d·* and cloudless skies,

ten
Man. 52– 8   within ten *d·* thereafter,
    68– 3   to go in ten *d·* to her,
My. 76– 3   * Up to within ten *d·*

these
Pul. 51– 4   * a great privilege in these *d·.*

those
Ret. 89– 5   In those *d·* preaching and
    93– 2   The evangelists of those *d·*
Pul. 82–18   * In those *d·* women had few lawful

three
Mis. 242–24   cure that habit in three *d·,*
Pul. 3– 5   in three *d·* I will — *John* 2 : 19.

thy
My. 252–16   "As thy *d·,* so shall thy — *Deut.* 33 : 25.
    270–17   "as thy *d·,* so shall thy — *Deut.* 33 : 25.

Mis. 167–13   Of his *d·* there is no beginning
    304–24   * anniversaries of the *d·* on which
Pul. 34–20   * *d·* when Jesus of Nazareth
'02. 15–12   *d·* wherein the connection between
My. 95–28   * since the *d·* of the primitive

days'
Mis. 239– 5   had but four *d·* vacation
My. 74– 4   * within two or three *d·* ride,
    214–11   Jesus' three *d·* work in the sepulchre
    322–22   * few *d·* instruction by Mrs. Eddy

dayspring
Pul. 10–25   descended like d· from on high.
Po. 30– 7   O gladsome d· ! 'reft of mortal sigh

daystar
Mis. 24– 6   d· that dawned on the night of
165–10   d· of this appearing is the light of
'02. 2– 2   sees through the mist . . . this d·,
My. 110–10   d· will appear, lighting the gloom,

dazzling
Mis. 162– 6   From this d·, God-crowned summit,
376–22   over a deeply d· sunlight,
388–16   Her d· crown, her sceptred throne,
'02. 3–21   The d· diadem of royalty
Po. 21– 4   Her d· crown, her sceptered throne,
My. 193– 7   d· glory in the Occident,

D. C. (District of Columbia)
(see **Washington**)

D. D.
My. 4–15   Protestant and Catholic, D.D. and

D. D. S.
My. 314– 9   He had the degree D.D.S.,

deacon
My. 60– 7   * my uncle, the good old d· of

Deacons
My. 174–16   Ballard, . . . Morrison, D·.

dead
Mis. 25–19   and raising the spiritually d·.
28–28   healed the sick and raised the d·.
60–13   d· only in belief?
74–19   he raised the d·, and
95–16   the so-called d· and living.
124–18   raising the d·, saving sinners.
129–13   d· bury their d·,'' — Matt. 8 : 22.
168– 9   the d·, those buried in dogmas
169–30   d· bury their d· ; — Matt. 8 : 22.
170– 4   to us there can be no d·.
187– 2   healing the sick, and raising the d·.
237–27   in honor of the d· hero
238–27   allegement that I . . . am d·,
244–21   and the d· to be raised
248–19   not more true than that I am d·,
249–20   The report that I was d· arose
292–17   bury the d· out of sight ;
311– 9   so, bury the d· past ;
326– 1   raise the d· ; — Matt. 10 : 8.
385–20   Man is not mortal, never of the d·:
Man. 60–18   d· bury their d·,'' — Matt. 8 : 22.
Chr. 53– 7   rouse the living, wake the d·,
55– 6   d· shall hear the voice — John 5 : 25.
55–16   body is d· because of — Rom. 8 : 10.
Ret. 20–19   life is d·, bereft of all, with thee,
21– 2   was d· and buried.
66– 2   in casting out error, in raising the d·.
81– 3   both for the living and the d·.
87–1, 2   d· bury their d·.'' — Matt. 8 : 22.
88– 5   "raise the d·.'' — Matt. 10 : 8.
88– 8   so-called d· forthwith emerged into a
88–11   "Raise the d·,'' — Matt. 10 : 8.
Un. 3– 7   "Blessed are the d· — Rev. 14 : 13.
41–11   Resurrection from the d·
61– 8   neither d· nor risen.
62–24   the living among the d· ? — Luke 24 : 5.
Pul. 9–29   without works is d·.'' — James 2 : 26.
29–18   * raise the d·, — Matt. 10 : 8.
66–13   * raise the d·, — Matt. 10 : 8.
No. 25– 5   that being d· wherein — Rom. 7 : 6.
37–23   saved the sinner and raised the d·,
'01. 16–12   Then let the dead bury its d·,
19–17   healed the sick, raised the d·,
'02. 9–5, 6   d· bury their d· ;'' — Matt. 8 : 22.
Hea. 2–24   not in the power of . . . a d· rite
6–12   the so-called d· and the living.
Peo. 12–21   healing the sick and raising the d·
Po. 15–17   blossom and sunshine not d·
25–12   Fragrance fresh round the d·,
48–14   Man is not mortal, never of the d· :
53–19   and d· are all The vernal songs
67–10   memory of dear ones deemed d·
78– 1   our honored d· fought on
My. 110– 3   healing the sick, and raising the d·
128– 4   repentance from d· works.'' — Heb. 6 : 1.
133–14   "d· in trespasses — Eph. 2 : 1.
139– 3   She is neither d· nor
150–22   d· in trespasses and sins
158–20   letter without the spirit is d· :
160–11   willingly accept d· truisms
185–18   "was d·, and is alive — Luke 15 : 32.
189–31   D· is he who loved me dearly :
191–19   The sepulchres give up their d·.
192– 5   raise the living d·,
206– 1   would unite d· matter with
218–10   The power . . . to raise the d·
219–16   spiritual idea, who raises the d·,

dead
My. 269– 7   resurrection from the d·, — Luke 20 : 35.
270–15   Mary Baker Eddy is not d·,
275–14   is d·, and should be buried.
296–12   Joseph Armstrong, C.S.D., is not d·,
300–26   raise the d·, — Matt. 10 : 8.
306– 4   to tread on the ashes of the d·
353–25   d· bury their d·,'' — Luke 9 : 60.

deadened
Pul. 10– 3   raised the d· conscience,
My. 91–11   * no person's . . . were ever d·

deadly
Mis. 28–32   drink any d· thing, — Mark 16 : 18.
177–10   Their feeling and purpose are d·,
249– 6   drink any d· thing, — Mark 16 : 18.
368–16   more d· than the upas-tree
Un. 54–16   its most potent and d· enemy.
'01. 32–15   they armed quickly, aimed d·,
Hea. 1– 3   drink any d· thing, — Mark 16 : 18.
7–26   drink any d· thing, — Mark 16 : 18.
15–11   drink any d· thing, — Mark 16 : 18.
Peo. 12– 4   drink any d· thing, — Mark 16 : 18.
My. 48– 1   * drink any d· thing, — Mark 16 : 18.
146– 4   drink any d· thing, — Mark 16 : 18.

deaf
Mis. 22–24   with the sick, the lame, the d·,
88–18   task of talking to d· ears
168– 7   the d· — those who, having ears,
244–21   the d· to hear, the lame to walk,
362– 9   ears to these d·, feet to these lame,
368– 6   and cause the d· to hear.
Pul. 82–28   * remain d· to their cry?
'00. 11–13   The d· Beethoven besieges you with
'01. 17–15   It was that I healed the d·,
My. 105–17   sight to the blind, hearing to the d·,
183–19   the d· hear the words of the Book,

deal
Mis. 4–25   must require a great d· of faith
64–19   are those which d· with facts
Peo. 12–10   D·, then, with this fabulous law
My. 98–12   * would d· with the phenomenon
111– 7   same class of minds to d· with

dealeth
Un. 23–11   d· with you as with sons ; — Heb. 12 : 7.

dealing
Ret. 71–19   is not d· justly and loving
82– 3   d· with a simple Latour exercise
My. 121–14   Peace, like plain d·,
121–15   plain d· is a jewel as beautiful as
181– 4   d· with human hypotheses,

dealt
Mis. 12–23   d· with by divine justice.
211– 8   d· with summarily by
284–16   so d· with at the outset.
284–20   sin must now be d· with as evil,
Pul. 29–17   * d· directly with the command of

Dean,
Charles
My. 361–26   * signature
Charles A.
My. 362– 2   Charles A. D·, Chairman

dear
Mis. 16–27   d· reader, pause for a moment
30–26   Take courage, d· reader,
42–17   we meet the d· departed,
61–11   * "D· Mrs. Eddy :— In the October
81– 5   by right of God's d· love,
132–12   D· Sir :— In your communication
134– 3   d· sir, as you have expressed
137–17   d· ones, if you take my advice
142–17   your d· hearts expressed in their
145–18   friendship, delicate as d·,
176–15   counted not their own lives d·
180– 7   A d· old lady asked me,
239– 1   let me say to you, d· reader :
252–29   It is the d· children's toy
262– 1   D· readers, our Journal is designed to
266–22   They are essentially d· to me,
313– 8   rest on the d· readers,
317– 9   The d· ones whom I would have
319–18   Will all the d· Christian Scientists
320– 6   d· to the heart of Christian Scientists ;
328– 6   D· reader, dost thou suspect that
330–10   the springtide of Christ's d· love.
Ret. 19– 5   parting with the d· home circle
21–13   It is well to know, d· reader,
Un. 20–15   Try this process, d· inquirer,
Pul. v– 2   To THE D· . . . CHILDREN
7–10   were our d· Master in our
44– 2   * "D· Teacher, Leader, Guide :
77– 9   * "D· Mother :— During the year
78– 8   * "D· Mother :— During the year 1894
82–11   * many things d· to the soul

dear

Pan.	11–30	because Christ's d· demand,
'01.	31–20	of blessings infinite I count these d· :
'02.	20–21	faces of my d· church-members ;
Po.	24–20	D· heart of Love,
	29– 7	D· Christ, forever here and near,
	34– 5	d· remembrance in a weary breast.
	47– 1	Are the d· days ever coming again,
	67– 9	memory of d· ones deemed dead
	77–17	some d· lost guest
My.	12–29	d· children's good deeds are gems
	25–16	all of my d· correspondents
	58 28	* My D· Teacher : — Of the many
	60–25	* D· Leader and Guide :
	82– 3	* one near and d· to them.
	90–12	* for self or d· ones.
	118–19	My D· Sir : — I beg to thank you
	122–12	deportment of its d· members
	145– 2	D· Editors : — You are by this time
	148–21	of this d· little flock,
	154–10	comforting to the d· sick,
	155– 4	May this d· little church,
	155 26	d· Sunday School children
	156– 3	my gratitude for your d· letter,
	158–24	will bless this d· band of brethren.
	162–11	d· Sunday School children,
	163–17	D· Editor : — When I removed from
	164–16	Now . . . six d· churches are there,
	165–12	I beg to thank the d· brethren
	166–22	d· ones, let us together sing
	167– 2	may have cost the d· donors.
	167–19	Give to all the d· ones my love,
	168– 6	people of my d· old New Hampshire.
	171– 1	d· members of my church :
	173– 5	D· Mr. Editor : — Allow me
	175–12	Its d· churches, reliable editors,
	175–23	d· as the friendship of
	175–29	minds of this d· people
	176– 5	Long ago you of the d· South
	189– 4	So d·, so due, to God is obedience,
	197– 5	be upon this d· people,
	199–16	C. S., so d· to our hearts
	202–25	From the d· tone of your letter,
	206–30	kingdom of His d· Son '' — Col, 1 : 13.
	208–14	your d· letter to my waiting heart,
	213–30	d· Churches of Christ, Scientist.
	254–14	this class and its d· members.
	254–17	* D· Leader : — May we have permission
	257– 3	His d· love that heals the
	258–28	consciousness of God's d· love for you
	259–13	d· churches' Christmas telegrams
	270–18	words of our d·, departing Saviour,
	274–10	D· reader, right thinking,
	274–20	Will the d· Christian Scientists
	275–21	my d· friends' and my d· enemies'
	276–12	all her d· friends and enemies.
	283–21	D· Mr. Davis : — Deeply do I thank
	284–12	D· Editor : — In the issue of
	290–12	D· Mrs. Mckinley : — My soul reaches
	302–27	d· members wanted to greet me
	319–16	* D· Teacher : — I am conversant
	326–12	D· Editor : — I send for publication
	327–22	* representative men of our d· State
327–31 *,	328– 1	* as lived by our d·, d· Leader,
	338–11	lecture of our d· brother,
	357–13	When my d· brethren in New York

(see also children, church, God, student, students)

dearer

Pul.	83–23	* by bonds d· than freedom,''

dearest

Ret.	6–12	the very d· of my kindred.
Pul.	81–12	* Some of her d· ones
My.	129–22	and be thy d· allies.
	256–18	d· memories in human history
	271–22	* ''What is nearest and d·
	271–30	what is ''nearest and d·''

dearly

Chr.	53–15	understanding, d· sought,
My.	189–31	Dead is he who loved me d· :
	279–22	D· Beloved : — I request that
	313–27	My oldest sister d· loved me,

dearth

Po.	33– 7	selfishness, sinfulness, d·,

death (see also death's)

after

Mis.	2–21	Man's probation after d·
	2–24	If man should not progress after d·,
	28–18	shown by his ascension after d·,
	34–17	after d·, they can no more come
	222–19	suffer its full penalty after d·.

agony and

'01.	20–20	Even the agony and d· that it

alone

My.	273–30	d· alone does not awaken man
	274– 5	D· alone does not absolve man

death

and burial

Ret.	2–25	d· and burial of George Washington.

and humanity

My.	258–24	love, grief, d·, and humanity.

and the grave

Un.	30–19	victorious over d· and the grave.
Peo.	5–14	overcome d· and the grave,
My.	218–15	absolved from d· and the grave.

before

Mis.	34–16	see them as they were before d·,
My.	344–14	better than he was before d·.

belief in

Un.	40–10	subordinates the belief in d·,
	41–12	(that is, from the belief in d·)

belief of

Mis.	170– 1	salvation from the belief of d·,

believes in

My.	300–14	Does he who believes in d·

believing in

Un.	40–14	by believing in d·,

bleeding to

Hea.	18–28	believe he was bleeding to d·.
	19– 8	belief that he was bleeding to d·,

brought

'02.	6– 7	brought d· into the world

called

Mis.	42– 1	After the change called d·
	42– 5	through the belief called d·.
	42–13	passed the ordeal called d·,
Un.	2–28	this transition, called d·,
	40– 4	shadow of material sense, called d·,
No.	14– 5	the transition called d·,
	27▪27	after the change called d·,
	28– 3	after the transition called d·,
My.	206–14	through the shadow called d·,

came

Un.	15– 2	came ''d· into the world,

can be nowhere

Un.	42– 1	must follow that d· can be nowhere ;

can never

Mis.	174–27	D· can never usher in the dawn of
Un.	40–20	D· can never alarm or

cause of

My.	335–21	* cause of d· as bilious fever,

changed, by

Mis.	52–19	but only changed, by d·,

change of

Pul.	38–19	* passed the change of d·

conquer

Un.	18–24	saith, . . . thus I conquer d· ;

darkness and

Po.	65–18	darkness and d· like mist melt away,

demonstration over

Un.	43– 4	strong demonstration over d·,

deprives

Un.	48–10	deprives d· of its sting,

destroy

Mis.	193–10	C. S., . . . will destroy d·.

destroys

Mis.	235– 5	reflect Him who destroys d·
	336–24	heals disease . . . and destroys d·!

disbelief in

My.	297–17	blessing of disbelief in d·,

disease and

(see disease)

disease, nor

Mis.	165–14	darkness, doubt, disease, nor d·.

disease, sin, and

Un.	10– 1	unreality of disease, sin, and d·,
My.	106–20	expressed in disease, sin, and d·,

dissolving

Po.	24– 4	Dissolving d·, despair !

does not destroy

Mis.	28–14	d· does not destroy the beliefs of

door named

Mis.	84–30	through the door named d·,

dream of

Mis.	58– 6	Waking from the dream of d·,
My.	273–28	''Man awakes from the dream of d·

early

My.	335–10	* who mourn his early d·.

ends in

Mis.	361– 6	its miscalled life ends in d·,
Ret.	69–15	false sense . . . which ends in d·''

error and

Hea.	8– 5	that destroy error and d·.

fear of

'02.	3–22	the muffled fear of d·

has lost

My.	191–23	D· has lost its sting,

has no

Un.	38–20	D· has no quality of Life ;
	41–14	second d· has no power.

death

her husband's
My. 329–14 * notice of her husband's *d·*
336– 5 * come to her after her husband's *d·*,
his
Mis. 71– 4 John B. Gough . . . until his *d·* ;
84– 5 did not prophesy his *d·*,
Ret. 7–18 * His *d·* will be deplored,
No. 34– 8 by commemorating his *d·* with a
My. 331–31 * extended to her after his *d·*,
335–15 * for many years after his *d·*.
illness and
My. 335–12 * regarding . . . his illness and *d·*,
illusion that
Un. 59–23 illusion that *d·* is as real as
into Life
Un. 41–18 portal from *d·* into Life ;
is a contradiction
Un. 38– 4 *D·* is a contradiction of Life,
is at war
Mis. 217–23 *d·* is at war with Life,
is not the goal
Un. 45–22 *d·* is not the goal which Truth seeks.
issues of
Mis. 222– 1 holds the issues of *d·* to the
is the consequent
No. 16–28 *D·* is the consequent of an
itself
Mis. 361– 6 *d·* itself is swallowed up in
jaws of
Pan. 14–25 victoriously through the jaws of *d·*
know
Un. 41– 8 to know *d·*, or to believe in it,
last enemy
My. 185–21 destroys the last enemy, *d·*.
law of
My. 154– 6 transcending the law of *d·*.
leadership and
Ret. 3– 6 whose gallant leadership and *d·*,
lead to
Mis. 61– 7 vain strivings . . . that lead to *d·*,
life and
(*see* **life**)
life from
My. 139–29 redeem . . . your life from *d·*.
life nor
My. 302– 6 Neither life nor *d·*, health nor
Life, not
Un. 39–24 and embodies Life, not *d·*.
My. 239– 1 it demonstrates Life, not *d·* ;
life, not
Mis. 346– 1 Life, not *d·*, was and is the
Life, not of
Un. 3–19 of Life, not of *d·*.
Life over
Mis. 61–10 and of Life over *d·*.
321–12 of Life over *d·*,
material
Un. 38–12 transition called *material d·*,
Mr. Quimby's
Mis. 379–27 It was after Mr. Quimby's *d·*
must know
Un. 18–22 Error says God must know *d·*
never changes to
Mis. 170– 7 which never changes to *d·*.
never conscious of
Un. 18–25 is to be never conscious of *d·*.
never see
Mis. 76– 5 shall never see *d·*." — *John* 8 : 51.
No. 31–27 shall never see *d·*;" — *John* 8 : 51.
My. 300–19 shall never see *d·*." — *John* 8 : 51.
no
Mis. 179–32 this Life that knows no *d·*,
183– 3 Love, and . . . that know no *d·*.
194–27 sense of Life that knows no *d·*,
Un. 37–14 to believe there is no *d·* ?
39– 8 that Life which knows no *d·*.
43– 5 namely, that there is no *d·*,
43–27 Life which knows no *d·*,
55– 3 namely, that there is no *d·*.
No. 13–13 in Life that knows no *d·*,
My. 297–11 chapter sub-title
297–15 no evil, no disease, no *d·* ;
300–14 aver that there is no *d·*,
no spiritual
Un. 29– 8 there can be, no spiritual *d·*.
not through
Un. 41–20 not through *d·*, but through Life ;
My. 181–11 not through *d·*, but through the
not to bring
'01. 21–22 came not to bring *d·* but life
of an individual
'01. 21–15 *d·* of an individual who loves God
of a sparrow
Mis. 184– 4 from . . . to the *d·* of a sparrow.

death

of her husband
My. 329– 9 * reference to the *d·* of her husband,
of Pope Leo XIII
My. 294–22 chapter sub-title
of sinners
Un. 50–27 maturity, and *d·* of sinners,
or the grave
Mis. 104– 5 not subject . . . to *d·*, or the grave.
pain or
My. 90–12 * pain or *d·* for self or dear ones.
pangs of
Peo. 1–17 Even the pangs of *d·* disappear,
physical
Mis. 37–21 leads to moral or physical *d·*.
portal of
Mis. 180– 5 dark shadow and portal of *d·*,
power over
Mis. 64– 4 to show his power over *d·* ;
No. 33–22 Love and its power over *d·*.
putting him to
Mis. 182– 3 impossibility of putting him to *d·*,
put to
No. 29– 2 put to *d·* for his own sin,
'02. 11–27 put to *d·* the Galilean Prophet,
recording the
My. 332–29 * papers recording the *d·* of
rescued from
Pul. 66–11 * claim to have been rescued from *d·*
second
Mis. 2–26 second *d·* hath no power" — *Rev.* 20 : 6.
Un. 3– 8 the second *d·*, of which we read
41–14 the second *d·* has no power.
sense of
Un. 2–22 awake from a sense of *d·*
40–19 A sense of *d·* is not requisite
shadow of
Chr. 55– 9 land of the shadow of *d·*, — *Isa.* 9 : 2.
My. 294–29 passed through the shadow of *d·*
sickness and
(*see* **sickness**)
sickness, disease, or
Mis. 65– 4 sin, sickness, disease, or *d·*,
sickness or
Peo. 12– 6 The only law of sickness or *d·*
sickness, sin, and
(*see* **sickness**)
sin and
(*see* **sin**)
sin brought
Mis. 201– 7 Sin brought *d·* ; and death is an
sin, disease, and
(*see* **sin**)
sin, disease, or
My. 146–27 the side of sin, disease, or *d·*.
sin, or
Mis. 30–11 they were without pain, sin, or *d·*.
Un. 62–16 sin, or *d·* is a false sense of
sin, sickness, and
(*see* **sin**)
sin, sickness, or
Mis. 17– 6 law of sin, sickness, or *d·*.
Un. 4– 3 finite sense of sin, sickness, or *d·*,
Hea. 9– 7 less . . . of sin, sickness, or *d·*,
16–18 evidence . . . of sin, sickness, or *d·*
sin unto
Mis. 120– 9 whether of sin unto *d·*, or — *Rom.* 6 : 16.
source of
Ret. 59– 7 *Life* never means . . . source of *d·*,
sting of
Po. 31–21 wipes away the sting of *d·*
stung to
Pul. 13–24 The dragon is at last stung to *d·*
subjection to
Mis. 67–28 without his subjection to *d·*,
subtlety of
No. 35–10 also the drear subtlety of *d·*.
suffering and
Un. 41– 6 unreal sense of suffering and *d·*.
My. 161–32 triumph over . . . suffering, and *d·*.
surrenders to
Mis. 257–30 where the good man surrenders to *d·*
their
Mis. 304–28 * anniversaries of their *d·*.
thoughts of
Peo. 14– 3 clothe our thoughts of *d·* with
to all
'01. 30–13 birth to nothing and *d·* to all,
tragic
My. 312– 4 the tragic *d·* of my husband,
triumph over
Un. 43–10 complete triumph over *d·*,
twin sister of
Po. 65–11 Ah, sleep, twin sister of *d·*
ultimate
Mis. 257–16 lead to immediate or ultimate *d·*.

death

until
Mis. 286– 4 * "until *d·* do us part ;"
unto
Mis. 351–25 life that leads unto *d·*,
'00. 13–15 faithful unto *d·*, — Rev. 2 : 10.
My. 80– 8 * that when wasted unto *d·*
350–20 sense is darkened unto *d·*
unto the
Pul. 12–11 their lives unto the *d·*. — Rev. 12 : 11.
violent
'02. 18–28 violent *d·* of all his disciples
what is termed
Hea. 18–26 You must admit that what is termed *d·*
word
My. 235– 3 without using the word *d·*,

Mis. 17– 3 the material law of *d·* ;
23– 9 disease, *d·*, winds, and waves,
24– 3 carnally minded is *d·* ; — Rom. 8 : 6.
27–12 inharmony, sin, disease, *d·*
30–11 *D·* was not the door to
42–11 not attained by the *d·* of the body,
76–14 theory that *d·* must occur,
76–27 wages of sin is *d·*." — Rom. 6 : 23.
76–32 overcame the last enemy, *d·*.
96– 3 robbed . . . *d·* of its sting.
105–16 its opposites — *d·*, disease, and
105–28 the thought of sin, sickness, *d·*,
123–27 not through the *d·* of a man,
170– 5 may still believe in *d·* and
174–26 did not teach us to pray for *d·*
180–17 of Life, and not of *d·*,
196–27 not through *d·*, but Life,
201– 7 *d·* is an element of matter,
211–11 wish to save him from *d·*.
243–30 bleeding, vomiting, *d·*.
259– 6 law of Life, not of *d·* ;
332–24 third, suffering ; fourth, *d·*.
Ret. 24– 2 after the *d·* of the
Un. 29– 4 condemned the sinner to *d·*,
37– 7 *d·* is not the real stepping-stone
38– 6 *D·*, then, is error, opposed to
58– 1 sin, pain, *d·*, — a false sense of
No. 13– 7 *d·* must be swallowed up in Life,
17–27 Then . . . *d·* as real as Life ;
Pan. 12– 7 passing out of mankind by *d·*
'01. 21–20 *D·* is neither the predicate nor
'02. 6–27 carnally minded is *d·* ; — Rom. 8 : 6.
My. 126–21 *d·*, and mourning, and — Rev. 18 : 8.
180–17 C. S. meets . . . *d·* with Life,
192–12 living way to Life, not to *d·*.
248–24 and their penalty, *d·*
288–21 Jesus cast out evil, disease, *d·*,
310–19 there was never a *d·* in my

death-bed
Mis. 24– 6 give it to you as *d·* testimony

death-blow
Mis. 299– 4 The error . . . has received its *d·* ;

death-couch
Mis. 385–25 faith triumphant round thy *d·*
Po. 48–21 faith triumphant round thy *d·*

death-dealing
Mis. 257–25 go down in the *d·* wave.

deathless
Mis. 75–30 accepted view is that *soul* is *d·*.
104–15 individuality is sinless, *d·*,
184– 3 that Deity is *d·*,
187–29 dying, before *d·*,
Ret. 64–25 *d·* Truth and Love.
Un. 39–26 that Deity is *d·*,
40– 7 in order to prove man *d·*.
41–23 Life, therefore, is *d·*,
42– 3 Soul, Spirit, is *d·*.
42–10 dying before he can be *d·*,
Pul. 4–22 His existence is *d·*,
5– 8 the glow of some *d·* reality.
No. 29– 4 and a *d·* sense of being.
Peo. 5– 6 they have resurrected a *d·* life
Po. 28– 3 Help us to write a *d·* page
29–16 living Love, And *d·* Life !
My. 195–24 lives, moves, and has *d·* being.
214–12 He proved Life to be *d·*

deathly
Pul. 73– 7 * cured herself of a *d·* disease

death-penalty
Un. 40–22 *d·* comes through our ignorance of

death-rate
'00. 7– 3 statistics show the annual *d·*
My. 181–26 the *d·* was at its maximum.

death's
Mis. 386–13 "When, severed by *d·* dream,
Po. 49–19 "When, severed by *d·* dream,

deaths
Mis. 29–16 but fourteen *d·* in the ranks of
48–21 tragic events and sudden *d·*

death's-head
Mis. 233– 8 *d·* at the feast of Truth ;
'01. 2–18 *d·* at the feast of Love,

debar
My. 140–15 * need not *d·* distant members from

debased
My. 91–11 * or his moral standards *d·*

debate
Man. 50– 8 shall not *d·* on C. S. in public

debaters
Mis. 88–19 deaf ears and dull *d·*.

debating
Man. 50– 6 *d·* IN PUBLIC.
50– 7 No Unauthorized *D·*.
50– 9 in public *d·* assemblies,
My. 224–14 Avoid . . . public *d·* clubs.

débris
Mis. 393– 5 Soul, sublime 'mid human *d·*,
Po. 51–10 Soul, sublime 'mid human *d·*,

debt
Mis. xi– 8 one's *d·* of gratitude to God,
261–12 pays his full *d·* to divine law,
Man. 78– 6 *D·* and Duty.
Ret. 6–29 abolition of imprisonment for *d·*.
Pul. 44–24 * dedicated to-day . . . and free of *d·*.
79– 6 * no *d·* had to be taken care of
My. 75–27 * dedicated to-morrow free from *d·*.
76–18 * free of *d·* without exception.
77–27 * open its doors absolutely free of *d·*,
84– 3 * heavy *d·*, the interest on which
84– 5 * "church *d·*" cramps and retards
84– 9 * until it be wholly free from *d·*.
88–28 * æsthetic *d·* to that great and
91–30 * Church is absolutely free from *d·*.
94–20 * the structure was free from *d·*,
98– 8 * dedicated free from *d·*,
98–21 * dedicated absolutely free of *d·*,
98–30 * and its dedication free from *d·*
161– 2 paid our *d·* and set us free
352– 8 * acknowledge our *d·* of gratitude

debtor
Mis. 382–11 comparing those . . . I am the *d·*.

debtors
Mis. 281–22 always as *d·* to Christ, Truth.
My. 161– 3 for which we are still his *d·*,

debts
Man. 76– 2 after the *d·* are paid,
78– 7 not . . . responsible for the *d·* of
78– 8 except such *d·* as are specified
Ret. 49–28 all *d·* of the corporation
My. 81–18 * *d·* of gratitude for ills cured,
89–14 * not blanketed with *d·*
232– 7 whereby all our *d·* are paid,

decade
Pul. 23–10 * paralleled during the last *d·* by
32–19 * in the early *d·* of 1820–'30.
66–20 * during the last *d·*,
67 16 * practically unknown a *d·* since,
'02. 2–12 Within the last *d·* religion
My. 94– 2 * through another *d·*

Decalogue
Mis. 254– 2 to which the *D·* points
335–17 to break the *D·*, — to murder,
Man. 43 10 commandment of the *D·*,
Ret. 65–12 in the gospel or the *D·*.
Pan. 7– 2 First Commandment in the *D·*.
'00. 5– 4 First Commandment of the *D·*,
5–19 First Commandment of the *D·*:
'01. 32–22 First Commandment of the *D·*,
My. 221–18 First Commandment of the *D·*,
264–18 First Commandment of the *D·*

decapitated
Mis. 274–24 *d·* reputations, headless trunks,

decay
Mis. 362– 3 material birth, growth, and *d·* :
395–20 Touched by the finger of *d·*
Ret. 81–12 and falsity must thus *d·*,
Peo. 14– 7 churchyards have crumbled into *d·*,
Po. 58– 5 Touched by the finger of *d·*
My. 189–20 that which defies *d·*

decaying
Mis. 100– 3 articulated in a *d·* language,
121– 1 written in a *d·* language,
'01. 33– 8 * *d·* stages of religion,

decays
Un. 26–14 * Man *d·* and ages move ;
26–19 that *man d·* ?

decease
Man.	49–18	MARRIAGE AND *d·*.
	49–23	Sudden *D·*.
	49–24	If a member . . . shall *d·* suddenly,
Ret.	20– 4	until after my mother's *d·*.
'02.	15–19	I declined to sell them at his *d·*
My.	294–23	*d·* of Pope Leo XIII,
	306–26	Before his *d·*, in January, 1866,
	312–23	At his *d·* I was surrounded by
	331–25	* bereaved widow after his *d·*.
	335– 7	* membership in both till his *d·*.
	336–15	after my mother's *d·*.''

deceased
Man.	36–15	*d·*, absent, or disloyal,
	111–17	*d·*, absent, or disloyal,
My.	290–10	*d·* the first month of the new
	331–23	* towards those friends of the *d·*
	331–30	* the *d·* during his late illness,
	333–12	* the residence of the *d·*,

deceit
No.	2–25	cannot avert the effects of *d·*.
'02.	4– 1	*d·* in councils, dishonor in nations,
	18–17	no emulation, *d·* enters into
My.	5–32	Indulging *d·* is like the defendant
	6– 9	smile and *d·* of damnation.
	261–10	*d·* or falsehood is never wise.

deceitfully
Mis.	78–15	word of God *d·*.'' — *II Cor.* 4 : 2.
'01.	16–15	handling the word of God *d·*.
My.	34– 5	nor sworn *d·*. — *Psal.* 24 : 4.
	124– 2	word of God *d·* ; — *II Cor.* 4 : 2.

deceive
Mis.	78–15	which would *d·*, if possible,
	175–20	"*d·*, if it were — *see Matt.* 24 : 24.
	341–14	Do human hopes *d·*?
My.	258–19	hopes that cannot *d·*,

deceived
My.	212–22	are being *d·* and misled.

deceiver
'01.	9–12	called him a "*d·*." — *Matt.* 27 : 63.

deceives
Mis.	334– 7	the belief that it has, *d·* itself.

deceiveth
Pan.	10– 4	he *d·* himself.'' — *Gal.* 6 : 3.

December
(*see* months)

decent
My.	312–11	* and thus received a *d·* burial.

decently
Mis.	310–16	*d·* and in order.'' — *I Cor.* 14 : 40.

deception
Mis.	14–18	This awful *d·* is evil's umpire
	228– 2	a *d·* dark as it is base
	338–16	will subject one to *d·* ;
Un.	17– 1	one chance of successful *d·*,
	19–16	evil is only a delusive *d·*,

decide
Mis.	65–11	Science must and will *d·*.
	81– 8	patiently wait on God to *d·*,
Man.	55–18	may *d·* if his loyalty has been
	77– 8	This committee shall *d·*
	94– 5	the churches shall *d·* their action.

decided
Mis.	2–32	While we entertain *d·* views
	243– 3	with *d·* improvement in health.
	306– 5	* motto has not yet been *d·* upon,
Man.	55–11	it may be *d·* that a teacher has
My.	11–26	* The size of the building was *d·*
	20–29	* *d·* to omit this year the
	54–29	* *d·* that this hall was too large,
	237– 3	I have since *d·* not to publish.
	309–10	After it was *d·*, Mr. Pierce bowed to
	324– 9	* so original and so very *d·*

decides
Mis.	45–19	when Science in a single instance *d·*

decision
Mis.	65–11	Left to the *d·* of Science,
Ret.	50–11	the wisdom of this *d·* ;
My.	6– 1	*d·* which the defendant knows will
	11–27	* there still remained for definite *d·*
	12– 9	* *d·* of these remaining problems.
	76–13	* A similar *d·* was reached
	190–21	divine *d·* in behalf of Mind.
	204–18	*d·* you have made as to the
	314–17	the *d·* was given by the judge

declaims
'01.	26–10	In one sentence he *d·* against

declaration
Mis.	28–30	his *d·*, "These signs — *Mark* 16 : 17.
	46–22	apostle meant by the *d·*,

declaration
Mis.	48–17	*d·* as to the animus of
	51–14	virtually a *d·* to the child's mind
	76–16	rendered void by Jesus' divine *d·*,
	172–30	*d·* in Scripture that God is good ;
	187–30	is but the *d·* of the material senses
	192–30	*d·* of our Master settles the
	193–28	unmistakable *d·* of the right
	201– 3	*d·* resolves the element misnamed
	278–13	*d·* that Job sinned not
	372–21	gives no uncertain *d·* concerning
	373–26	is followed by Jesus' *d·*,
	381–32	*d·* were either a truism or a rule,
Ret.	35–19	the authenticity of this *d·*,
Un.	30–24	understood the meaning of the *d·*
	32–20	To this *d·* C. S. responds,
Pul.	4–16	therefore is the seer's *d·* true,
	30–15	* "confession of faith" includes the *d·*
No.	13–13	the *d·* is nevertheless true,
Pan.	2– 2	a *d·* from the pulpit that
'01.	15– 1	*d·* that evil is unreal,
'02.	8– 1	*d·*, "God is Love," — *I John* 4 : 8.
	12–14	This *d·* of Christ, understood,
My.	46– 9	* primary *d·* of this church
	106–11	folly of the cognate *d·* that
	135– 6	*d·* may be applied to old age,
	190–17	This *d·* of our Master,
	326– 8	* the *d·* of this recognition

Declaration of Independence
Pul.	67–24	* from the date of the *D· of I·*,

declarations
Un.	6–24	our *d·* about sin and Deity
Pul.	45–20	* oft-repeated *d·* of our textbooks,

declare
Mis.	23–18	Reason and revelation *d·* that
	46– 2	Scriptures *d·*, "To whom — *Rom.* 6 : 16.
	55–26	Spirit, as the Scriptures *d·*,
	63–21	as the Scriptures *d·*.
	93– 8	Scriptures plainly *d·* the allness
	141–28	you yourselves *d·* you have had no
	166–17	how to *d·* its spiritual origin,
	172– 4	*d·* the positive and the negative
	174–20	first to *d·* against this kingdom
	183–32	Scriptures *d·* reflects his Maker,
	189–20	Scriptures *d·* Life to be the
	243–19	works alone should *d·* them,
	258–23	did *d·* a mighty individuality,
	312–17	* to *d·* the real harmony between
	346–17	and the Scriptures *d·* that
	362–12	Scriptures *d·* that all that He made
	363–17	His modes *d·* the beauty of
Man.	80–14	to *d·* vacancies in said trusteeship,
Ret.	37–12	*d·* Bishop Berkeley, David Hume,
Un.	2– 1	*d·* that God is too pure to
	2– 2	they also *d·* that God pitieth
	15– 6	may *d·* Him absolutely cognizant of
	25–13	this lie I *d·* an illusion.
	28– 9	As well might you *d·* some old castle
	39–21	*d·* the immortal status of man,
	56– 3	suffered, as the Scriptures *d·*,
Pul.	13–23	Scriptures *d·* that evil is temporal,
	74–16	to *d·* in His infinite mercy.
	75– 7	they can justly *d·* it.
No.	5– 8	to *d·* error real would be to
	13– 5	*d·* both the Principle and idea
Pan.	5– 4	The Scriptures plainly *d·*,
	11–10	shall his stature . . . *d·* him?
'01.	7–11	as the Scriptures *d·* ;
	7–17	as the Scriptures *d·* He will
	15– 1	*d·* that he must awake from his
Hea.	3–24	The Scriptures *d·* that
Peo.	5–17	to *d·* His omnipotence.''
	6– 6	* "I *d·* my conscientious belief,
	9– 7	religious rite may *d·* one's belief ;
My.	9–12	* *d·* the depth of our affection
	37– 9	* *d·* again our high appreciation
	127–16	I deliberately *d·* that when I
	155– 9	Saviour whom the Scriptures *d·*.
	242– 4	*d·* yourself to be immortal
	257–21	bow and *d·* Christ's power,
	271– 1	If, as the Scriptures *d·*,
	298– 3	*d·* that nothing has occurred in my
	300– 8	*d·* that there is no sickness or
	305– 5	defamer will *d·* as honestly (?),
	318–13	*d·* the moral and spiritual effect
	359– 8	I hereby publicly *d·*

declared
Mis.	24–29	*d·* that his followers should handle
	30–12	gates thereof he *d·* were inlaid
	57–18	*d·*, "God doth know — *Gen.* 3 : 5.
	83–22	he *d·* his sonship with God ;
	96–14	as to the apostle who *d·* it,
	121–16	prophet *d·*, "Thou shalt — *Deut.* 19 : 13.
	172–26	*d·* on the side of immutable right,

declared

Mis.	189–13	Christ plainly *d·*, through Jesus,
	201–17	*d·* that "the law of the — *Rom.* 8: 2.
	225–16	what the Christian Scientist had *d·*;
	345–16	Bonaparte *d·*, "Ever since the
	372– 1	critics *d·* that it was incorrect,
Ret.	8–23	earnestly *d·* my cousin had heard the
	15–11	hitherto have I *d·* — *Psal.* 71 : 17.
	30–17	St. Paul *d·* that the law was
	56–14	until peace be *d·* by
Un.	1– 5	such as the apostle Peter *d·*
	37– 1	Jesus not only *d·* himself
Pul.	45–12	* *d·* that the church's completion
	45–17	* hopeful, trustful ones, who *d·*
	53– 9	* *d·* to be essential,
Pan.	7–10	*d·* that man should die,
'01.	23–27	In later publications he *d·*
'02.	12–13	is not God, as he himself *d·*,
Hea.	8–20	what the Scriptures have *d·*,
My.	45–17	* *d·* you to be *in extremis.*
	94–26	* greetings in which she *d·*
	98– .2	* but these, it is *d·*, are but
	105– 9	*d·* incurable because the lungs
	105–23	*d·* that she could not live.
	152– 6	and our Master *d·*,
	228–14	Referring to . . . our Master *d·* :
	307– 5	till one day I *d·* to him
	313–20	I have always consistently *a·*
	315–23	*d·* dying of cancer,
	318– 9	some critics *d·* that my book
		(*see also* **Jesus**)

declares

Mis.	26–11	even while the Scripture *d·*
	30–20	law of Life, which St. Paul *d·*
	71–23	St. Paul *d·* astutely,
	122–17	denounces him that *d·*,
	123–29	Holy Writ *d·* that God is Love,
	176– 2	harmony of Science that *d· Him,*
	192–24	as the above Scripture plainly *d·*,
	217–13	Nature *d·*, throughout the mineral,
	218– 5	visible universe *d·* the invisible
	218– 6	by reversion, as error *d·* Truth.
	259–19	*d·* that God knows iniquity !
	295– 9	anonymous talker further *d·*,
	309– 7	this *d·* its unfitness for fable
	351–26	*d·* itself the antipode of Love ;
Ret.	60–12	*d·* that evil is the absence of
	60–28	*d·* that there is but one Truth,
	61– 3	*d·* that sickness is a belief,
Un.	4– 5	*d·* that Truth is All,
	4–23	John's Gospel *d·* (xvii. 3) that
	17–21	*d·* God told our first parents
	29–10	Science *d·* God to be the Soul
	30–20	*d·* can never be seen or measured
	31– 2	"God is Spirit"), *d·* the Scripture
	32–17	*d·* itself material, in sin, sickness,
	33–26	*d·* that matter sees through the
	34– 2	*d·* that matter is the master
	40–12	*d·* that they who believe
Pul.	63–26	* *d·* that it was built as
	64–16	* she *d·*, in a search for the
Pan.	5–25	as the Scripture *d·*,
'02.	1 –12	The Scripture *d·*,
My.	107–24	Scripture *d·*, God made all
	113– 9	Paul *d·* the truth of the
	178–12	The Scripture *d·* that God is All.
	224–25	since the Scripture *d·*,
	308–29	*McClure's Magazine* also *d·*
	334–19	* She *d·* in her Message

declaring

Mis.	108–30	while *d·* that they have no
	109– 1	*d·* the unity of Truth,
	334– 9	does this as a lie *d·* itself,
	354– 1	*d·* they "never disobey Mother" !
Ret.	14–12	*d·* that never could I unite with
Un.	38–15	by *d·* that not He alone
No.	42–19	by *d·* itself both true and good.
My.	116–18	*D·* the truth regarding an
	326– 3	* courts are thus *d·* the liberties of
	346– 7	* *d·* Mrs. Eddy non-existent

decline

Mis.	342– 6	hence the steady *d·* of
Pul.	87–14	permit me, respectfully, to *d·*
My.	138–15	*d·* to receive solely because I
	194–24	but I must *d·* to receive
	226–29	*d·* to doctor infectious or

declined

Mis.	146–12	hence I have hitherto *d·* to
Man.	75–10	*d·* to receive this munificent gift,
Pul.	71– 4	* The idea that C. S. has *d·*
'02.	15–18	I *d·* to sell them at his decease
My.	302–28	but I *d·* and went alone
	308–24	*d·* to accept the stick,
	336– 7	* she *d·* on this ground,

declines

Man.	68– 7	or who *d·* to obey this call

declineth

Ret.	21–17	shadow when it *d·*." — *see Psal.* 102 : 11.

declining

Mis.	163–14	language of a *d·* race,
'02.	15–15	*d·* dictation as to what I should

decoction

No.	21– 4	an unsafe *d·* for the race.

decomposition

My.	107–31	stops *d·*, removes enteritis,

decorated

Pul.	26–24	* *d·* with sprays of fig leaves
	28– 6	* *d·* with emblematic designs,

decoration

Pul.	76– 7	* pale green and gold *d·*
	76–14	* Mexican onyx with gold *d·*

decorations

Mis.	142– 9	among other beautiful *d·*,

decorative

Pul.	26– 1	* disc of cut glass in *d·* designs,
	28–10	* in appropriate *d·* effect.
My.	78–11	* in soft gray with *d·* carvings

decrease

My.	266–12	article on the *d·* of students in

decreased

My.	181–27	Since that time it has steadily *d·*.

decree

Mis.	66–10	always according to divine *d·*.
	118–15	this immutable *d·* of Love :
	121–14	a divine *d·*, a law of Love !
	122–11	predestined to fulfil a divine *d·*,
	341–20	implicit treason to divine *d·*.
	380–28	by *d·* and order of the Court,
	381–16	a *d·* in favor of Mrs. Eddy
Ret.	14– 1	"horrible *d·*" of predestination

decry

My.	114– 9	*d·* the book which has moulded their

dedicate

Mis.	v 1	*d·* THESE PRACTICAL TEACHINGS
	91– 6	to ordain pastors and to *d·* churches ;
Po.	39–21	temperance hall To Thee we *d·*.
	40– 3	We *d·* this temperance hall
My.	13–19	an ample temple *d·* to God,
	76–17	* enables them to *d·* their churches
	96–18	* building they were in Boston to *d·*
	97–26	* to *d·* the new temple,
	147–25	never stop ceremoniously to *d·*
	158–27	*d·* to Truth and Love.
	182–19	*d·* this beautiful house of worship
	193– 1	*d·* your temple in faith unfeigned,

dedicated

Pul.	v– 7	THIS UNIQUE BOOK IS TENDERLY *d·* BY
	11– 5	*d·* to the ever-present God
	20–21	church *d·* on January 6,
	40–22	* *d·* to the worship of God.
	44–23	* church which will be *d·* to-day
	50–13	* which will be *d·* to-morrow,
	56–25	* church was *d·* in Boston
	59– 3	* *d·* on New Year's Sunday
	61–24	* Church . . . *d·* yesterday.
	63–23	* Church . . . was *d·* in Boston.
	64–24	* has just *d·* the first church of
Rud.	v– 3	TENDERLY AND RESPECTFULLY *d·*
My.	26– 5	* will be *d·* on the date of the
	36–21	* *d·* to the only true God,
	67–17	* Cathedral to be *d·* . . . 1906
	75–26	* *d·* to-morrow free from debt.
	75–28	* *d·* by this denomination
	76–25	* *d·* in Boston to-morrow
	84– 8	* may not be formally *d·* until
	91– 9	* paid for before they are *d·*.
	91–27	* which has just been *d·* at Boston
	98– 7	* church, . . . *d·* free from debt,
	98–17	* was recently *d·* at Boston.
	98–20	* *d·* absolutely free of debt,
	99–16	* when it was *d·* there was not
	100– 4	* temple recently *d·* at Boston
	147–24	already *d·* to Christ's service,
	193–25	*d·* to God and humanity,
	302–26	after it was built and *d·*

dedicating

My.	74–17	* paying for their church before *d·* it.
	193–17	You are *d·* yours to Him.
	197–12	completing and *d·* your church

dedication (noun)

at Boston

Pul.	65–14	* by the *d·* at Boston of

attend the

My.	72–11	* attend the *d·* of the new church

dedication (noun)

church
My. 186–27 on the day of your church d·.

communion and
My. 26–18 communion and d· include enough

completion and
My. 43–30 * completion and d· of our

day of
Pul. 57– 7 * four services on the day of d·.

historical
My. 26–22 This historical d· should date

in Boston
Pul. 68–18 * The d· in Boston last Sunday
79– 4 * d·, in Boston, of a C. S. temple
My. 94–17 * in the recent d· in Boston

in June
My. 25–19 the d· in June next of

its
My. 88–15 * its d· abounds in remarkable
184–12 to be present at its d·,

of the church
Pul. 75–21 * celebrated the d· of the church

of the edifice
My. 86–22 * The d· of the edifice of the

of the extension
My. 3– 2 chapter sub-title
29–25 * the d· of the extension of
63–11 * the d· of the extension of
96– 3 * the d· of the extension of

of The Mother Church
Pul. 40– 9 * chapter sub-title
88– 6 the d· of The Mother Church.
My. 57–27 * the d· of The Mother Church
76–14 * the d· of The Mother Church
90–22 * The d· of The Mother Church

of this church
Pul. 66–22 * marked by the d· of this church,
My. 163–10 come to the d· of this church,

of your church
My. 191–29 the d· of your church
192–21 present at the d· of your church,

recent
My. 99–30 * recent d· of a C. S. temple

your
My. 183–25 Thanks for invitation to your d·.

———

Pul. 43–24 * chief feature of the d·,
56–12 * d· taking place on the 6th of
75–16 * D· TO THE FOUNDER OF THE ORDER
81– 3 * morning of the d·.
Po. vi– 5 * poem
page 39 poem
My. 26– 2 * chapter sub-title
29– 3 * chapter sub-title
38–23 * impressive feature of the d·
45–10 * physically present at the d·
60–26 * d· of our new church building,
73–16 * d· of the new temple.
77–15 * will participate in the d·.
78– 2 * all might participate in the d·,
79– 9 * to read the account of the d·
84–26 * d· of the beautiful structure on
86–11 * to be present at the d·
88–10 * The d·, Sunday, in Boston,
89–22 * d· of the new Mother Church
91–16 * d· of a C. S. temple
92–20 * the d· of this vast temple.
93– 5 * d· of their great church in Boston
95– 9 * d· of the magnificent C. S. church
96–22 * before the day set for the d·
96–27 * The d· of what is known as
98–29 * its d· free from debt
100– 7 * On the Sunday of the d·,
159– 1 chapter sub-title
177– 5 d· of First Church of Christ,
198– 4 d· of your magnificent church
320–30 * d· of the first Mother Church

dedication (adj.)

Pul. 41–29 * hour for the d· service
79– 7 * no debt . . . on d· day,
My. 5–24 d· and communion season,
72–21 * to attend the d· exercises,
77–17 * chapter sub-title
77–22 It was d· day,

Dedication of a Temperance Hall

Po. vi– 5 * poem
(see also **Appendix A**)

dedicatory

Pul. 59–28 * at the second d· service.
Po. vi– 8 * sung . . . as a d· hymn.
My. 29– 7 * closing incident of the d· services
31–29 * opening of the d· service.
36– 1 * d· Message from their teacher
58–29 * attended the d· services
64–11 * d· Message to The Mother Church,

dedicatory

My. 82–14 * d· services of The Mother Church
94–20 * d· services were being held
99–18 * attended the d· exercises,
146– 1 In explanation of my d· letter
195– 4 d· services of your church.
197–25 d· season of your church edifice
240–10 d· Message to The Mother Church,

deduced

My. 349–28 induced by love and d· from God,

deduction

No. 13– 5 scientific d· from the Principle of
13–14 profound d· from C. S.
My. 273–13 I for one accept his wise d·,

deductive

My. 349–27 d· reasoning is correct only as it

deed

Mis. 195–28 d·, not creed, and practice more than
198–24 belief, fear, theory, or bad d·,
206–20 harmony in word and d·,
224– 3 that makes another's d· offensive,
250–23 unselfish d· done in secret ;
384– 7 To thought and d· Give sober speed,
399–14 Thou the Truth in thought and d· ;
Ret. 79–22 temperate in thought, word, and d·.
'02. 13–30 A copy of this d· is published in
Hea. 5–10 reward of his good d· hereafter.
Po. 36– 6 To thought and d· Give sober speed,
75–21 Thou the Truth in thought and d· ;
79– 8 in thought and d·
My. 9– 9 * glory in every good d· and thought
65–22 * d· being taken by Ira O. Knapp
66– 7 * conveyed by d· to the C. S. church,
157–18 * in her original d· of trust,
157–22 I gave a d· of trust to three individuals
205–18 * "As the thought is, so is the d· ;
235–29 commemorated in d· or in word
260–29 the Way, in word and in d·,
338–25 he stands alone in word and d·,

Deed Conveying Land

for Church Purposes
Man. 136– 1 heading

deeded

My. 217– 6 I have d· in trust to

Deed of Trust

Man. 25–17 See under "D· of T·" for
79–19 constituted by a D· of T·
81–18 the provisions in the D· of T·
128– 1 heading

deeds

Mis. 210–14 Good d· are harmless.
257–14 and repays our best d· with
292–23 by loving words and d·.
341– 7 then put . . . words into d· ;
370– 4 saw Jesus do such d· of mercy,
Man. 102–10 Designation of D·.
102–14 All d· of further purchases of
102–14 in the d· given by Albert Metcalf
102–18 shall be incorporated in all such d·
No. 27–21 old man and his d·," — see Col. 3 : 9.
Pan. 11– 4 old man with his d· ; — Col. 3 : 9.
'00. 13– 5 d· of the Nicolaitanes, — Rev. 2 : 6.
13– 7 words were brave and their d· evil.
'01. 2–11 substitute good words for good d·,
26– 6 supported it by his words and d·.
'02. 8–17 his d·, demonstrate Love.
Hea. 19–26 rays in the sunlight of our d· ;
My. vii–10 * D·, not words, are the sound test
12–29 dear children's good d· are gems
218– 3 and in explanation of his d· he said,
277–20 immortal words and d· of men
283–14 Right thoughts and d· are the
309– 4 making out d·, settling quarrels,
350–27 in prayer, in word, and d·.

deem

Mis. 80–27 of what they d· pathology,
112– 4 may d· these delusions verities,
Po. 47–18 reaping the harvest we d·,
My. 289– 8 Beloved Student : — I d· it proper that
306– 7 I d· it unwise to enter into a

deemed

Mis. 193– 5 or d· it safe to say at that time.
228– 3 by those d· at least indebted friends
349–17 he should do as he d· best,
386–14 She d· I died, and could not know
Man. 52–15 d· sufficient by the Board
85– 8 so strayed as justly to be d·,
92–25 d· loyal teachers of C. S.
Ret. 7–18 * advocacy of the side he d· right.
45–11 d· requisite in the first stages of
49–29 d· best to dissolve this corporation,
Peo. 6–23 should no longer be d· treason to

deemed
 Po. 49–21 She *d·* I died, and could not know
   67–10 memory of dear ones *d·* dead
 My. 89– 4 * are *d·* by its professors not to exist
deems
 Po. 31–19 which *d·* no suffering vain
deep
 Mis. ix–17 *d·* draughts from the fount of
   3–31 *d·* demand for the Science of
   107–26 and of *repentance* therefor, *d·*,
   133– 9 *d·* consideration to the following
   142–21 chords of feeling too *d·* for words.
   225–26 The *d·* flush faded from the face.
   285–18 *d·* down in human consciousness,
   387– 2 joy divinely fair, the high and *d·*,
   388–18 The right to worship *d·* and pure,
 Ret. 17– 5 while I worship in *d·* sylvan spot,
   42–11 listened to him with *d·* interest.
   69– 6 the Adam-dream, the *d·* sleep,
 Un. 29–22 *d·* meaning of the Scriptures
 Pul. 13–16 in the *d·* darkness of belief.
   73–10 * *d·* into the Biblical passages,
   76–10 * hangings of *d·* green plush,
 Rud. 15–10 and *d·* systematic thinking
 No. 34–25 this is the *d·* significance of the
   35– 5 through *d·* humility and adoration
 '01. 1–19 Truth comes from a *d·* sincerity that
 '02. 20– 2 or going down into the *d·*,
 Hea. 17–16 "*d·* sleep" — *Gen. 2: 21.*
 Po. 2–19 thy *d·* silence is unbroken still.
   21– 7 The right to worship *d·* and pure,
   23–12 With utterance *d·* and strong,
   31– 8 *D·* loneliness, tear-filled tones of
   50–20 divinely fair, the high and *d·*,
   53– 6 On vale and woodland *d·* ;
   62– 5 while I worship in *d·* sylvan spot,
   68–11 Enchant *d·* the senses,
 My. 42–22 * *d·* significance of this momentous
   44–26 * greetings and their *d·* love.
   113–31 the *d·* thinkers, the truly great
   154–19 * *d·* infinite faculties of man."
   157– 5 * *d·* gratitude that your generous
   167– 1 Accept my *d·* thanks therefor,
   195–11 *d·* love which I cherished for you
   195–18 best way to silence a *d·* discontent
   197–11 express my *d·* appreciation
   203–18 A *d·* sincerity is sure of success,
   208– 3 Accept my *d·* thanks for your
   248–10 reaching *d·* down into the universal
   271–23 * read with *d·* interest by all
   289–13 expressing our *d·* sympathy with
   348– 4 induced a *d·* research,
   (*see also* **waters**)
deep-drawn
 My. 195–22 *d·* breath fresh from God,
   256–10 *d·*, heartfelt breath of thanks
deeper
 Mis. 2–10 a *d·* and broader philosophy
 Ret. 81–20 so sinks into *d·* darkness.
 Pul. 2– 9 a thought higher and *d·*
   36– 5 * *d·* foundation of her religious work
 '00. 11–17 measures himself against *d·* grief.
 Po. 34–12 thy love-lorn note— In *d·* solitude,
 My. 46–22 * to a *d·* consecration,
   63–21 * there came a *d·* feeling,
deepest
 Mis. 311–15 My *d·* desires and daily labors
 '01. 20–28 darkest and *d·* of human crimes.
deeply
 Mis. 176– 6 *d·* and solemnly expounded
   256–10 I feel, *d·*, that of necessity this
   274–11 *D·* regretting the disappointment
   317–24 My sympathies are *d·* enlisted
   376–22 over a *d·* dazzling sunlight
   392–16 *d·* rooted in a soil of love ;
 Pul. 1–13 and records *d·* engraven,
 Po. v– 6 * *outpouring of a d· poetic nature*
   20–20 *d·* rooted in a soil of love ;
   24–16 And night grows *d·* dark ;
 My. 6–16 *d·* do I thank you for this proof
   28– 2 * will be *d·* significant.
   37–28 * We are *d·* touched by its
   58–30 * one so *d·* impressed
   125–23 *d·* grateful that the church militant
   149–20 too *d·* read in scholastic theology
   175– 1 *d·* interesting anniversary,
   194–22 I *d·* appreciate it,
   245– 2 became *d·* interested in it.
   282–21 *D·* do I thank you
   326–13 *d·* interesting letter from
   326–19 *D·* grateful, I recognize the divine
   338–23 Christian Scientists *d·* recognize

deep-settled
 '02. 19–20 underneath is a *d·* calm.
deep-toned
 Mis. 204–16 freedom, *d·* faith in God ;
deer
 Po. 41– 1 * my own stricken *d·*.
defaces
 Mis. 8–18 defiles, *d·*, and dethrones the
defacing
 Mis. 337–23 possessing these *d·* deformities.
defame
 '01. 32–10 to *d·* their fellow-men.
defamer
 My. 305– 5 Lastly, the *d·* will declare
defamers
 '01. 16–12 surviving *d·* share our pity.
 My. 305–10 "vulgar" *d·* have circulated,
defeat
 Mis. 172– 7 *d·* the claims of sense and sin,
   204– 8 hope, sorrow, joy, *d·*, and triumph.
   267–26 cause of all *d·* and victory
   339– 7 out of *d·* comes the secret of
 '00. 10– 1 Success in sin is downright *d·*.
 My. 134–10 *D·* need not follow victory.
   278–26 Victory in error is *d·* in Truth.
defeats
 Mis. 126–26 honesty always *d·* dishonesty.
   260– 3 By conflicts, *d·*, and triumphs,
   268– 2 divine Principle . . . *d·* them.
   268– 7 victories of rivalry . . . are *d·*.
 My. 43– 9 * in the wilderness they suffered *d·*
defence (*see also* **defense**)
 My. 127–31 a *d·* adapted to all men,
   161–26 a sufficient *d·* against it.
   264– 2 chapter sub-title
   278–19 dies in *d·* of his country,
   316–15 grand *d·* of our Cause
defend
 Mis. 112– 9 can neither *d·* the innocent nor
   115–22 relying on God to *d·* us
   295–16 *d·* the dignity of her daughters
   315–32 how to *d·* themselves against
   371–20 has no truth to *d·*.
 Man. 42– 5 *d·* himself daily against aggressive
   48– 4 to *d·* the Cause of Christ,
   84– 2 how to *d·* themselves against
 Ret. 44–20 to *d·* this church from the envy
 Pul. 2–26 behooves us to *d·* our heritage.
 My. 318–12 to *d·* my grammatical construction,
   364–13 to *d·* themselves from all evil,
defendant (*see also* **defendant's**)
 Mis. 380–32 Answer was filed by the *d·*,
   001– 6 *d·* being present personally
   381– 7 testimony on the part of the *d·*
   381–10 recover of the *d·* her cost of suit,
   381–22 restraining the *d·* from directly or
 My. 5–32 like the *d·* arguing for
   6– 2 decision which the *d·* knows will be
defendant's
 Mis. 381–10 inquire of *d·* counsel why he
   381–13 asked the *d·* counsel this question,
defenders
 Peo. 11– 2 *d·* of the rights of the
defending
 Mis. 345– 3 *d·* himself against the charge of
 My. 207–23 mastering evil and *d·* good,
defends
 My. 316–18 It *d·* human rights
defense (*see also* **defence**)
 Mis. 80– 7 *d·* of medical charlatans in general,
   110–26 dared the perilous *d·* of Truth,
   115–16 protection and *d·* from sin
   148–17 dignity and *d·* of our Cause ;
   229–28 Love" . . . is a sure *d·*.— *I John 4 : 18.*
   238– 7 no time to give in *d·* of his own
   258–16 "My *d·* is of God,— *Psal. 7 : 10.*
   338–18 move majestically to your *d·*
 Man. 3–14 dignity and *d·* of our Cause ;
   84– 1 *D·* against Malpractice.
 Ret. 91– 1 God is their sure *d·* and refuge.
 Pul. 2–21 remain within the walls for its *d·*
 No. 15–10 religious arms in their *d·* ;
defenses
 Mis. 10–10 furnished them *d·* impregnable.
defer
 Un. 1–14 to *d·* this infinite inquiry,
deference
 Mis. 60– 6 To regard . . . death with less *d·*,
 My. 225–14 giving unto His holy name due *d·*,

deferentially
   Ret. 76– 8 cited, and quoted *d·*.

deferred
   Mis. 17–29 travail of mortal mind, hope *d·*,
       262–19 heart grown faint with hope *d·*.
       389–15 For hope *d·*, ingratitude, disdain !
   Po. 4–14 For hope *d·*, ingratitude, disdain !

defiance
   Pul. 54– 7 * not in *d·*, suppression, or

defiant
   Mis. 190– 4 Life, *d·* of error or matter.
   Un. 42–24 Truth, *d·* of error or matter,
   No. 2–23 the most *d·* forms of disease.

deficiency
   Mis. 115– 6 even the teacher's own *d·*

defied
   Mis. 29–22 diseases that had *d·* medical skill.
       199–17 denied and *d·* their superstition.
       223– 2 mystery of error . . . at first *d·* me.

defies
   Mis. 86–23 is something that *d·* a sneer.
   Un. 31–19 all that denies and *d·* Spirit,
   My. 189–20 that which *d·* decay

defiled
   Un. 50– 2 how can infinite Mind be *d·*?

defilement
   Mis. 109– 7 a sure pretext of moral *d·*.
   Un. 50– 2 implies the possibility of its *d·* ;

defiles
   Mis. 8–17 *d·*, defaces, and dethrones

defileth
   Mis. 118–32 *d·* a man ;— *Matt.* 15 : 11.
       119– 1 this *d·* a man." — *Matt.* 15 : 11.

define
   Mis. 13–29 then *d·* good as God,
       191–26 the original texts *d·* him as
       269–10 a man who can better *d·* ethics,
   Ret. 59–20 five material senses *d·* Mind and
   Un. 28– 8 Who, then, dares *d·* Soul as
       29–16 that which the senses cannot *d·*
   Rud. 1– 1 How would you *d·* C. S.?
   '01. 1–22 As Christian Scientists you seek to *d·*
       3–16 to *d·* Love in divine Science
   '02. 7–13 Use these words to *d·* God,
   Po. 42– 6 Without heart to *d·* them,
   My. 235– 4 to *d·* truth and not name its

defined
   Mis. 68–21 metaphysics is *d·* thus :
       102– 3 A corporeal God, as often *d·*
       150–25 God is . . . *d·* by no dogma,
       180–27 word "son" is *d·* variously ;
       193–12 as *d·* and practised by Jesus,
   Ret. 32–11 is graphically *d·* by Calderon,
       58–12 Life, as *d·* by Jesus,
   Un. 42–21 As *d·* by Jesus, Life had no
   No. 9–25 Divinely *d·*, Science is the
       22–24 Jesus *d·* devil as a mortal who
   '01. 5– 2 *d·* strictly by the word Person,
       ¶–15 their personality is *d·* spiritually,
       6– 1 human person, as *d·* by C. S.,
       6– 6 Person is *d·* differently by
   My. 105– 4 Æsculapius, *d·* Christianly and

defines
   Mis. 68–24 Worcester *d·* it as "the philosophy
       102–32 Science *d· omnipresence* as
       190–31 and then *d·* this god as
       191– 4 then *d·* this serpent as
       192– 5 *d·* devil as a "liar." — *John* 8 : 44.
       300–11 law *d·* and punishes as theft.
   Ret. 59–23 Science *d·* man as immortal,
       60– 1 *d·* life as something apart from
       60– 4 sense *d·* life as a broken sphere,
       74– 4 *d·* it by his own *corpus sine pectore*
   Un. 29–17 C. S. *d·* as material sense ;
   Pul. 47–16 * *d·* carefully the difference
   Rud. 2–18 Science *d·* the individuality of
   '01. 16–14 St. Paul *d·* this world's god as
       16–16 original text *d· devil* as *accuser*,
   My. 180–32 *d·* noumenon and . . . spiritually,

defining
   Mis. 22–11 infinite calculus *d·* the line,
   Rud. 2– 9 in *d· person* as especially a
   My. 248– 8 grasping and *d·* the demonstrable,
       317– 2 * *d·* her relations with the

definite
   Un. 49– 3 man is as *d·* and eternal as God,
   Pul. 24– 2 * keynote of *d·* attention.
   Rud. 6–25 *d·* and absolute form of healing,
   No. 23–26 He is *d·* and individual,
   Peo. 8–11 *d·* form of a national religion,
   My. 11–27 * remained for *d·* decision

definite
   My. 43– 5 * *d·* rule of action whereby to
       51–22 * "she gave no *d·* answer,
       343–11 * Here, then, was the *d·* statement
       358– 1 C. S. abides by the *d·* rules

definitely
   Man. 44– 1 spirit . . . shall be *d·* considered.
       57–13 state *d·* the purpose for which
   Rud. 2– 7 God is *d·* individual,
   My. 235–12 should *d·* name the error,
       305–23 to learn *d·* more from my

definition
   Mis. 68–31 is a further *d·*.
       86–12 which need correct *d·*.
       108– 6 in his *d·* of Satan
       108–26 Jesus' *d·* of sin as a *lie.*
       190–14 Its *d·* as an individual is
       216–13 might add to the above *d·*
       258–29 the divine *d·* of Deity
       371–23 in a *d·* of purpose,
   Rud. 1–12 misapprehension, as well as *d·*.
   No. 22–26 His *d·* of evil indicated
       23–10 not a *devil*, after the accepted *d·*.
       27–28 learn the *d·* of immortal being ;
   Pan. 5– 7 chapter sub-title
       5–18 Jesus' *d·* of devil (evil) explains
   '01. 3–11 adopt Webster's *d·* of God,
       3–12 Standard dictionary's *d·* of God,
       3–14 higher *d·* derived from the Bible,
   '02. 5–19 This absolute *d·* of Deity
   My. 221–10 establish the *d·* of omnipotence,

definitions
   Mis. 52–14 Marriage is susceptible of many *d·*.
   Pul. 47–20 * *d·* of these two healing arts.
   Rud. 2– 1 Other *d·* of *person*,
       2–21 introduces us to higher *d·*.
   No. 25–14 Man outlives finite mortal *d·* of

deformed
   Mis. 107–26 lack of seeing one's *d·* mentality,
       167– 5 Is he *d·*?

deformities
   Mis. 337–23 possessing these defacing *d·*.

deformity
   Mis. 203–22 rends the veil that hides mental *d·*.
       332–20 masked with *d·* the glories of
   My. 121–21 No *d·* exists in honesty.

defrauds
   Rud. 15– 1 has shown that this *d·* the scholar,

deft
   Pul. 8–25 loving hearts and *d·* fingers

degenerate
   Mis. 289– 1 causes him to *d·* physically

degrade
   Pan. 10–28 does not *d·* man's personality.

degree
any
   Mis. 371–22 To sympathize in any *d·* with error,
   Un. 54–14 if sin's claim be allowed in any *d·*,
   Pul. 21–29 aught that can darken in any *d·* our
C.S.D.
   My. 251–26 a certificate of the *d·* C.S.D.
diploma or
   Mis. 272–16 * who confers, . . . any diploma or *d·*,
final
   Mis. 86– 3 final *d·* of regeneration is saving,
first
   My. 245–31 first *d·* (C.S.B.) is given to
       246– 2 after receiving the first *d·*,
great
   Pul. 37– 8 * retains in a great *d·* her energy
greater
   Pul. 75– 6 a greater *d·* of this spirit than in
highest
   Mis. 334–20 of the highest *d·* of nothingness :
   Un. 50–12 of which evil is the highest *d·* ;
holds a
   Man. 38– 7 student . . . who holds a *d·*.
large
   My. 74– 2 * to a large *d·* are already in Boston.
last
   Mis. 85–16 The last *d·* of regeneration rises
of comparison
   My. 238– 5 exact *d·* of comparison between
of C.S.B.
   Man. 92–18 nor receive the *d·* of C.S.B.
of C.S.D.
   Man. 89–16 to receive the *d·* of C.S.D.
   My. 244– 9 conferring . . . the *d·* of C.S.D.,
of M. D.
   Mis. 349– 6 students with the *d·* of M. D.,
receive the
   Man. 68–15 receive the *d·* of the . . . College.
       89–16 to receive the *d·* of C.S.D.

degree

remarkable
Ret. 83– 3   purpose to a remarkable *d*·.
My. 287– 6   used in a remarkable *d*·

second
My. 246– 1   the second *d*· (C.S.D.)

small
Rud. 7– 3   as . . . scientific, in a small *d*·,
No. 38– 3   to-day proving in a small *d*·,
'00. 7–15   lived, and learned, in a small *d*·,
My. 42–25   * comprehend, even in small *d*·,

smallest
Rud. 13– 7   even in the smallest *d*·.

some
Mis. 195–10   every one can prove, in some *d*·,
Man. 19– 6   thus to reflect in some *d*· the
Un. 39–17   must reflect, in some *d*·, the power
Pul. 31–10   * some *d*· of familiarity with the
'01. 6–20   which is set aside to some *d*·,
My. 63–19   * in some *d*· sharing in our joy.
112–17   demonstrates in some *d*· the truth

Man. 109– 9   who have been given a *d*·,
Pul. 85–12   * in the *d*· in which she has
'00. 6–26   in the *d*· that you accept it,
'02. 6–25   In the *d*· that man becomes
My. 314– 9   He had the *d*· D.D.S.,
335– 5   * *d*· of a Royal Arch Mason
347– 1   been revealed in a *d*· through

degrees
Mis. 84–12   dawns by *d*· on mortals.
86 7   strive . . . though in lessening *d*·
102–13   admits of no *d*· of comparison.
165– 3   spiritual idea . . . disappeared by *d*· ;
272– 3   * *(including the right to grant d·)*
272–23   * bestow no rights to *confer d*·)
272–26   * to confer diplomas and *d*·,
359–25   Science is demonstrated by *d*·,
'01. 18– 2   attenuated one thousand *d*· less
My. 245–27   *d*· that follow the names of
245–29   indicate, . . . *d*· of Bachelor and

de Hirsch

Baron and Baroness
My. 287– 2   chapter sub-title
287– 4   the late Baron and Baroness *de H*·

My. 289– 5   *De H*· monument fund.

deific
Mis. 45–16   *d*· law that supply invariably meets
Ret. 70– 6   usurps the *d*· prerogatives
Un. 17– 5   Be allied to the *d*· power,
Pul. 4–13   thus demonstrating *d*· Principle.
Rud. 1– 9   these are the *d*· Principle.
My. 262–19   *d*· presence or power.

deification
Mis. 307–11   chapter sub-title
307–20   the *d*· of finite personality.
Pul. 72– 4   * the reported *d*· of Mrs. Eddy,
74–24   statement of the Christ and the *d*· of
Rud. 17– 9   pride, rivalry, or the *d*· of self.
Pan. 2–20   the *d*· of natural causes,

deified
Mis. 308–11   revelators . . . will not be *d*·.
Pul. 6– 9   not the *d*· drug, but the goodness of
71–10   * chapter sub-title
73–25   * accredited as having been *d*·,

deify
My. 359–29   allowing your students to *d*·

deities
Mis. 255– 3   on pedestals, as so many petty *d*· ;
No. 36– 2   did not teach that there are two *d*·,
Peo. 4–23   as material as the heathen *d*·
4–25   inquired of these heathen *d*·

Deity

and man
My. 350– 1   draws its conclusions of *D*· and man,
applied to
'00. 5–10   Applied to *D*·, Father and Mother are
belief concerning
Pan. 2–25   belief concerning *D*· in theology.
conceptions of
No. 15–16   These conceptions of *D*· and devil
Peo. 8– 9   if . . . are our conceptions of *D*·,
8–14   material conceptions of *D*·.
definition of
Mis. 258–29   divine definition of *D*·
'02. 5–19   This absolute definition of *D*·
dethrone
Mis. 260–22   seeking to dethrone *D*·.
dethroning
Mis. 3–28   denying . . . and dethroning *D*·.

Deity

drugs to
My. 139–25   advanced . . . from drugs to *D*· ;
entertained of
Hea. 8–17   mistaken views entertained of *D*·
essence of
Mis. 121–19   nature and essence of *D*·,
fact of
'00. 4–30   this fundamental fact of *D*· as the
foreknows
Un. 19– 3   What *D*· *foreknows*, Deity must
good
Un. 15–23   who worship not the good *D*·,
hues of
Mis. 194–15   bring out the entire hues of *D*·,
Ret. 35–14   brings out the hues of *D*·.
ideal of
Peo. 6–18   spiritual and true ideal of *D*·
ideas of
Ret. 56– 1   The following ideas of *D*·,
Peo. 12–17   As our ideas of *D*· advance
14– 1   As our ideas of *D*· become more
infinite
Un. 10–14   toward aught but infinite *D*·.
is deathless
Mis. 184– 3   claiming . . . *D*· is deathless, but
Un. 39–26   presuppose . . . *D*· is deathless, but
its
Peo. 2–17   and form its *D*· out of the worst
knoweth
Un. 64–18   can never turn back what *D*· knoweth,
misconception of
Mis. 124–11   Moslem's misconception of *D*·,
monument of
Pv. 1–12   Ye rose, a monument of *D*·,
must foreordain
Un. 19– 3   *foreknows*, *D*· must *foreordain;*
name of
Mis. 75–24   name of *D*· used in that place
nature of
Mis. 79– 1   antagonistic to . . . the nature of *D*·,
192– 9   terms and nature of *D*· and devil
not absorbed in
No. 25–19   Man is not absorbed in *D*· ;
personal
No. 19–10   chapter sub-title
possible in
Un. 15–17   if . . . could be possible in *D*·,
recognition of
Mis. 1–16   to a higher recognition of *D*·.
relation to
Mis. 181–21   his spiritual relation to *D*· :
scoff at
Mis. 69– 3   sneer at metaphysics is a scoff at *D*· ;
sense of
      (see sense)
signify
No. 20– 8   Principle is used to signify *D*·
sin and
Un. 6–24   our declarations about sin and *D*·
statement of
Hea. 5– 1   our inconsistent statement of *D*·,
term for
Mis. 75–15   Soul is a term for *D*·,
192– 3   Hebrew term for *D*· was "good,"
their
Peo. 2–22   has their *D*· become good ;
to indicate
Ret. 59–13   *Life* is a term used to indicate *D*· ;
truth of
Peo. 9–27   This truth of *D*·, understood,
understanding of
Un. 13–13   gain the true understanding of *D*·.
was forever
Mis. 218– 3   fact that *D*· was forever Mind,
wholeness of
Un. 5– 4   of the wholeness of *D*·,
would fashion
No. 20– 6   Error would fashion *D*· in a manlike

Mis. 217–18   and that *D*· is a finite person
218–15   they make *D*· unreal and
Ret. 25– 2   great curative Principle,— *D*·.
Un. 15–18   would *D*· then be sinless
19–13   if . . . there would be sin in *D*·,
Pul. 64–21   * curative Principle was the *D*·.
70–20   * great curative Principle— the *D*·
No. 23–22   *D*· can have no such warfare
Hea. 4– 7   Clothing *D*· with personality,
15–22   as if drugs were superior to *D*·.
Peo. 12–25   As if *D*· would not if He could,

deity
Mis. 123–16   Jehovah, was the Jewish tribal *d*·.
Un. 15–24   the bad *d*·, who seeks to do
Pan. 2–24   mythological *d*· of that name ;

deity
Pan.   3– 1   mythical d· may please the fancy,
    3– 3   Pan, as a d·, is supposed to
'00.   13–24   principal d· in the city of
Peo.   13– 2   have a more material d·,
My.   189– 8   You worship no distant d·,

delay
Mis.   133– 1   you will not d· corrections
    141–26   D· not longer to commence building
    151–20   d· not to make Him thy
    341–22   the evil of inaction and d·.
Hea.   1–18   * chides his infamous d·,
My.   23– 1   * not necessary for us to d· our
    195– 3   You will pardon my d·

delayed
Mis.   237–24   Honor to faithful merit is d·,
    273–30   classes . . . would be d·.
Pul.   83– 8   * sunlight cannot long be d·.

delayeth
Mis.   335– 4   d· his coming ; — Matt. 24 : 48.

delegates
Mis.   276–10   My students, our d·,

delegations
Ret.   52–14   d· from the . . . Association

deleterious
Un.   8–15   arises from their d· effects,

deliberately
My.   127–16   I d· declare that when I was

deliberation
Ret.   49–27   due d· and earnest discussion
    85–18   without due d· and light,
My.   50– 1   * meeting of this little church for d·
    50–14   * "The tone of this meeting for d·

deliberations
Mis.   350–12   On the contrary, our d·
Man.   17– 2   went into d· over forming

delicacy
Mis.   133–20   I should feel a d· in making

delicate
Mis.   145–18   friendship, d· as dear,

delicious
Mis.   9–26   d· forms of friendship,
    231–14   d· pie, pudding, and fruit

delight
Mis.   375–21   * to my amazement and d·
Ret.   50–17   Loyal students speak with d· of
Pul.   46–12   * Mrs. Eddy takes d· in
    61–26   * people, who listened with d·.
My.   170–21   D· thyself also in — Psal. 37 : 4.

delighted
Mis.   372–18   d· to find "Christ and Christmas"

delightful
Pul.   47–21   * a d· country home one mile from
    63–11   * d· country home in Concord,
My.   350–26   Truth d·, crowned with endless days,

delightfully
Pul.   47–28   * big house, so d· remodelled

delighting
Pul.   46–24   * d· in philosophy, logic, and

delights
Mis.   131–23   sense of gratitude which d· in

delineate
Mis.   375– 7   it demands more . . . to d· this art.

delineated
Mis.   309–10   been so unnaturally d·
Ret.   82–13   orderly methods herein d·.

delineates
Mis.   373–15   d· Christ's appearing in the flesh,

delineations
Mis.   372–18   * d· from the old masters."
Peo.   7–26   give to the body those better d·.

delirious
Pul.   34–13   * believing her d·.

delirium
Mis.   243– 1   without it . . . she would have d·

deliver
Mis.   50–26   would d· man from heart-disease,
    81–28   d· mortals out of the depths of
    114–28   He will d· us from temptation
    298–18   Trials purify mortals and d· them
    301– 2   you d· without the author's consent,
Ret.   91–13   Where did Jesus d· this great lesson
'01.   10– 3   d· you up to the councils" — Matt. 10 : 17.
My.   150– 4   to save, to heal, and to d·,
    233– 6   "D· us from evil" — Matt. 6 : 13.
    233–12   better adapted to d· mortals from

deliverance
Mis.   114–23   d· from the claims of evil.
No.   43–15   * preaching d· to the captive,
Po.   33– 6   To hourly seek for d· strong
My.   43– 1   * but this d· did not put them in

delivered
Mis.   115–18   d· from every claim of evil,
    161– 2   D· IN CHICKERING HALL,
    171–21   chapter sub-title
    178–10   * d· an interesting discourse
    180– 4   I was d· from the dark shadow
    211–13   I d· thee." — Psal. 81 : 7.
    281–31   righteous shall be d·." — Prov. 11 : 21.
Man.   40–12   pray to be d· from all evil,
Ret.   40–16   d· of another child.
Pul.   1 —   chapter heading
No.   25– 5   we are d· from the law, — Rom. 7 : 6.
'01.   14–20   d· from believing in what is unreal,
Hea.   19– 1   felon was d· to them for experiment
My.   36–13   * d· from beds of sickness
    36–22   * we who have been d· from the
    42–31   * children of Israel d· from the
    206–28   d· us from the power of — Col. 1 : 13.
    338–13   after the lecture was d·

deliverer
Mis.   399–11   Strongest d·, friend of the
Po.   75–18   Strongest d·, friend of the
My.   132–15   this benediction : . . . I am thy d·.
    252–15   wait on God, the strong d·,

delivering
Mis.   235–10   d· mankind from all error
    301– 1   compiling and d· that sermon
Man.   93–17   his lectures before d· them.

delivers
Mis.   298–21   then Truth d· you from the

dell
Mis.   390–13   Through woodland, grove, and d· ;
Po.   55–14   Through woodland, grove, and d· ;

Delphian
Pul.   9– 5   no D· lyre could break the

Delsarte
Pul.   31–28   * flexible . . . as that of a D· disciple ;

delude
Ret.   18–14   Earth's beauty and glory d·
Po.   64– 5   Earth's beauty and glory d·

deluded
Mis.   107–21   d· sense must first be shown its
    254–24   filling with hate its d· victims,
'01.   15–19   waken such a one from his d· sense ;
    15–19   for all sin is a d· sense,

deluding
Mis.   3–27   d· reason, denying revelation,
    260–20   d· reason and denying revelation,

deluge
Mis.   246–27   again d· the earth in blood?
    355–25   like the dove from the d·.
Pan.   2– 8   higher than Mt. Ararat above the d·.

delusion
Mis.   11– 1   wake from his d· to suffer
    15– 3   endure the effects of his d·
    108–15   conceived of only as a d·.
    109–32   your superiority to a d· is won.
Ret.   32–15   * Fleeting pleasure, fond d·,
    69– 6   in which originated the d·
Un.   30– 4   under the d· that the senses
    33–16   only through error and d·
    53–14   which will die of its own d· ;
    56–21   Until he awakes from his d·,
Pul.   14–28   the great d· of mortal mind,
No.   4– 8   material sensation and mental d·.
    34– 1   d· of all human error,
Pan.   5–19   liar and lie, a d· and illusion.
Hea.   17–26   did not mind originate the d· ?
My.   5– 8   this illusion and d· of sense,

delusions
Mis.   112– 4   may deem these d· verities,

delusive
Mis.   65– 1   d· evidence, Science has dethroned
Un.   19–16   evil is only a d· deception,

delved
Pul.   73– 9   * d· deep into the Biblical passages,

delving
Mis.   340–14   dug into soils instead of d· into

demand
accommodate the
My.   82–13   * enough to accommodate the d·.
and example
No.   14–24   The d· and example of Jesus
and supply
My.   216– 8   subsist on d· and supply,

demand

dear
Pan. 11–30 because Christ's dear *d·*,
deep
Mis. 3–31 Hence the deep *d·* for the Science of
every
My. 41–29 * has obeyed its every *d·*,
feasibility of the
Hea. 19–21 or doubts the feasibility of the *d·*.
for this book
Ret. 39– 1 *d·* for this book increased,
My. 305–17 *d·* for this book . . . increases.
great
Mis. 132–16 great *d·* upon my time,
His
Mis. 18–32 bring to you at His *d·* that which
his
My. 339–27 not sufficient to meet his *d·*.
immediate
Mis. 148–16 immediate *d·* for them as a help
Man. 3–12 immediate *d·* for them as a help
imperative
My. 134–13 some imperative *d·* not yet met.
increased
My. 164– 3 But the *d·* increased, and I
infinite
Mis. 77– 7 infinite *d·* made upon the eunuch
its
Mis. 8–27 its *d·* and sentence,
Master's
Mis. 287– 5 and the Master's *d·*,
meets
Mis. 45–16 law that supply invariably meets *d·*,
meet the
Mis. 91– 9 it is to meet the *d·*
Ret. 48–23 to meet the *d·* of the age
Pul. 8–17 vied with . . . to meet the *d·*.
No. 39–28 silent prayer can meet the *d·*,
met the
Mis. 276– 9 my heart's desire met the *d·*.
of mortal thought
Mis. 44–24 *d·* of mortal thought once met,
of the times
Mis. 232–21 healing, . . . is a *d·* of the times.
of this age
My. 40–15 * *d·* of this age is for peacemaking,
of this hour
My. 132– 1 Love . . . is the *d·* of this hour
present
My. 237–11 adapted to the present *d·*.
Scriptural
Man. 51– 2 consonance with the Scriptural *d·*
special
My. 132– 2 fulfilment of . . . the special *d·*.
spiritual
Pul. 23–14 * common identity of spiritual *d·*.
Hea. 19–20 makes a more spiritual *d·*,
that
My. 224 3 understand the importance of that *d·*
this
No. 18–25 This *d·* militates against the
My. 46–18 * pledge ourselves anew to this *d·*,
224– 5 call your attention to this *d·*,
wide
My. 245– 3 wide *d·* for this universal benefice
would diminish
Mis. 365–21 If . . . the *d·* would diminish ;

Mis. 136– 4 as society and our societies *d·*,
225–15 opportunity to *d·* a proof of
232–23 would desire and *d·* it,
247– 1 *d·* for man his God-given heritage,
Man. 78– 1 *d·* that each member thereof
Ret. 61–26 Posterity will have the right to *d·*
Pul. 83– 1 * *d·* woman's love and woman's help
No. 19– 4 and the *d·* to increase,
Pan. 12–11 and *d·* that the inspired Scriptural
'01. 10–28 This is what the Scriptures *d·*
My. 168– 4 with the *d·* of our common Christ,
219–30 I recommend, if the law *d·*,

demanded

Mis. 19– 5 obedience *d·* of His servants
158– 8 change in your pulpit would be *d·*.
276– 7 circumstances *d·* my attention
283–12 if no emergency *d·* this.
298–18 implied that the period *d·* it.
374– 8 *d·* Christianity in life and
Un. 11–11 *d·* a change of consciousness
'01. 25–25 which Satan *d·* in the beginning,
My. 103– 5 The faith and works *d·* of man
348–18 since Science *d·* a rational proof

demanding

Mis. 23– 2 Science, *d·* more, pushes the
Ret. 26– 1 *d·* neither obedience to

demanding

Pul. 82–24 * They are *d·* the right to help
My. 231–15 letters from invalids *d·* her help

demands (noun)

dictatorial
Mis. 148–11 not . . . opinions nor dictatorial *d·*,
Man. 3– 7 not . . . opinions nor dictatorial *d·*,
eternal
My. 159–22 only legitimate and eternal *d·*
Father's
Peo. 3–27 obedience to our Father's *d·*,
great
Mis. 204–20 great *d·* of spiritual sense are
My. 222–17 his great *d·* on the faith of
highest
No. 45–26 urging its highest *d·* on mortals,
holy
My. 291– 2 Imperative, accumulative, holy *d·*
immortal
Mis. 201– 2 meets the immortal *d·* of Truth.
important
My. 231–20 important *d·* on her time
increasing
Pul. 37– 4 * increasing *d·* of the public
My. 135–11 increasing *d·* upon my time
137–17 increasing *d·* upon my time,
indispensable
Mis. 318–23 These are the indispensable *d·*
manifold
Mis. x– 9 manifold *d·* on my time
of Love
Peo. 9– 8 or meet the *d·* of Love.
of matter
No. 18–26 so-called *d·* of matter,
Peo. 12–16 lifts man above the *d·* of matter.
of the hour
Mis. 70–18 not equal to the *d·* of the hour ;
of the law
My. 43– 7 * Obedience to the *d·* of the law
recurring
My. 192–24 recurring *d·* upon my time and
sacred
My. 163–14 sacred *d·* on my time and
strong
Mis. 250–16 I make strong *d·* on love,
sweet
Mis. 316–19 sweet *d·* rest on my retirement

My. 46–14 * *d·* of this early pronouncement
118–20 furnishing the *d·* upon the finite
275–19 *d·* upon my time at home,

demands (verb)

Mis. 2–13 the outlook *d·* labor,
3– 2 shall express these views as duty *d·*,
16–29 this statement *d·* demonstration.
37–29 least difficult of the labor that C. S. *d·*.
40– 2 healing *d·* such cooperation ;
45–14 moral status of the man *d·* the
65–21 C. S. *d·* both law and gospel,
65–30 The Jewish religion *d·* that
67–19 mercy *d·* that if you see the danger
112–11 this knowledge *d·* our time and attention
119–25 *d·* of all trespassers upon the
123–11 a religion that *d·* human victims
215–12 C. S. *d·* order and truth.
244–15 * *d·* the employment of visible
264–12 *d·* oneness of thought and action.
299– 7 which *d·* our present attention.
317– 8 demonstrate, as this period *d·*,
318– 4 and *d·* to be demonstrated.
375– 6 it *d·* more than a Raphael
Man. 95– 8 as the cause of C. S. *d·*.
Chr. 53–19 To celebrate As Truth *d·*,
Ret. 54– 5 It *d·* less cross-bearing,
57– 1 *d·* mighty wrestlings with mortal
87–12 *d·* implicit adherence to fixed rules,
Pul. 10–23 as progress certainly *d·*,
No. 37–16 *d·* His continual presence,
Pan. 11–26 *d·* man's unfallen spiritual
My. 3– 5 *d·* well-doing in order to
118–13 spiritual sense *d·* and commands
152–25 God *d·* all our faith and love ;
232–22 Can watching as Christ *d·*
316–18 truth *d·* public attention.
355– 9 However, if the occasion *d·* it,

dematerialized

Peo. 2–21 has been *d·* and unfinited
8– 1 Religion and medicine must be *d·*

dematerializing

No. 10–24 *d·* and spiritualizing mortals

demean

Mis. 32– 3 *How shall we d· ourselves towards*

dementia

Mis. 113–22 insanity, *d·*, or moral idiocy.

demerit

Mis. 80–14 on its own merit or *d·*,
My. 306–17 Human merit or *d·* will find its

demise

Mis. 248–21 alleged to have reported my *d·*,
My. 295–26 lament the *d·* of Lord Dunmore ;
334–10 * account of her husband's *d·*

democratic

Man. 74– 7 distinctly *d·* in its government,
My. 247– 3 Essentially *d·*, its government is
254–24 Essentially *d·*, its government is
361–21 * *d·* and liberal government.

demolish

My. 127–23 cannot *d·* our strongholds.

demolished

Man. 103– 6 *d·*, nor removed from the site
Pul. 3– 2 *d·*, or even disturbed?
My. 15– 7 *d·* nor removed from the site

demolishing

No. 1– 8 *d·* bridges and overwhelming cities.

demon

'01. 16– 8 whereby the *d·* of this world,

demoniacal

Peo. 2–19 *d·* contests over religion.

demons

Mis. 19–15 endeavors of suppositional *d·*
Un. 28–10 peopled with *d·* or angels,
Pul. 29–19 * cast out *d·*." — see *Matt.* 10 : 8.
29–23 * cast out the *d·* of evil thought.
66–13 * cast out *d·*." — see *Matt.* 10 : 8.

demonstrable

Mis. 26– 3 truth, as *d·* as mathematics.
150–27 God *d·* as divine Life, Truth, and
193– 7 self-evident *d·* truth.
Man. 49–10 *d·* knowledge of C. S. practice,
Ret. 56– 3 *d·* rules in C. S.,
Un. 49– 5 This is *d·* by the simple appeal to
Pan. 2– 6 neither hypothetical nor . . . but *d·*,
'00. 4–20 being *d·*, they are undeniable ;
'01. 2–15 divine and *d·* Principle and rule
21– 5 students of a *d·* Science
My. 58–20 * revealed a *d·* way of salvation.
112–19 it contains a Science which is *d·*
143–21 an eternal and *d·* Science,
179–32 as make even God *d·*,
248– 8 grasping and defining the *d·*,
260–20 fundamental and *d·* truth,
299–14 presents the *d·* divine Principle
348–26 a *d·* Principle and given rule.

demonstrably

Mis. 12–27 aught else . . . *d·* is not Love.
80–32 C. S. Mind-healing rests *d·* on
Rud. 7– 3 as *d·* scientific, in a small degree,
No. 10– 3 C. S. is *d·* as true,
21–25 Divine philosophy is *d·* the true
28–20 What is *d·* true cannot be gainsaid ;
Pan. 12–23 is *d·* the self-existent Life,
My. 4–31 divinely natural and *d·* true,

demonstrate

Mis. v– 7 AND *d·* THE ETHICS OF C. S.
3– 7 *d·* in our lives the power of
22–27 a willing sinner, cannot *d·* it.
30– 7 *d·* all the possibilities of
30–19 enabled man to *d·* the law of
44–11 to *d·* its highest possibilities.
52–23 failing to *d·* one rule
55– 5 ability to *d·* to the extent
59– 3 can neither understand nor *d·* its
65–22 in order to *d·* healing,
75–10 or it is impossible to *d·* the
111– 2 to *d·* what you have adopted
115–19 till you intelligently know and *d·*,
138–12 Principle which he claims to *d·*,
148–19 requisite to *d·* genuine C. S.,
181– 5 power to *d·* his divine Principle,
185– 3 to discern fully and *d·* fairly
195– 6 is unable to *d·* this Science ;
201–30 you can *d·* the triumph of good
220– 1 *d·* this rule, which obtains in
243–16 can *d·* only in proportion as he
247–16 *d·* this Science by healing the sick ;
258–21 could neither name nor *d·* Spirit.
264–11 and to *d·* the divine One,
282– 1 going out to *d·* a living faith,
283–27 genius of C. S. to *d·* good,
317– 6 to *d·* self-knowledge and
317– 8 and to *d·*, as this period demands,
322–13 the Love they *d·*,
334–32 *d·* the might of perfect Love
344–20 *d·* the Science of Life,
366– 5 *d·* what they teach
380– 9 to *d·* what I had discovered :

demonstrate

Man. 3–15 so requisite to *d·* genuine C. S.,
92– 8 *d·* by his or her practice,
Chr. 53–20 this living Vine Ye *d·*.
Ret. 28– 6 to *d·*, even in part,
38–29 in order to *d·* C. S.
78–19 an attempt to *d·* the facts
88–15 its power to *d·* immortality.
Un. 8–21 You *d·* the process of Science
10– 1 you *d·* the allness of God.
32–27 to *d·* the falsity of the claim.
48–20 faintly able to *d·* Truth and Love.
55–10 *d·* "the way" — *John* 14 : 6.
Pul. 4–11 and daily *d·* this.
Rud. 8– 7 *How should I undertake to d· C. S.*
No. 11–19 and *d·* what these works teach,
11–24 are inadequate . . . to *d·* it.
12– 6 to understand and to *d·* God.
26– 9 to *d·* my metaphysics.
33– 9 and *d·* what these volumes teach,
38–22 must *d·* the nothingness of
Pan. 11–14 will *d·* man to be superior
'00. 4–23 Does it *d·* its doctrines?
6– 2 Principle and rules which *d·* it.
'01. 4– 9 destroys the ability to *d·* Love
15– 3 to understand and *d·* its unreality.
23–14 cannot *d·* C. S. except
24–26 to *d·* the divine Science of
'02. 6–10 to *d·* this grand verity,
8–17 his deeds, *d·* Love.
Hea. 3–23 or we cannot *d·* it in part.
4–27 how can we *d·* a changing Principle?
Peo. 13– 6 can *d·* in part this great
My. 3– 5 in order to *d·* truth,
5–29 they cannot *d·* the omnipotence
111–16 shows how to *d·* it,
113–21 A child will *d·* C. S.
119– 3 or on such a basis to *d·* the
149–21 or to *d·* Christian charity.
187–10 to *d·* the perfect man
203– 4 Pray aright and *d·* your prayer ;
233–13 can you *d·* over the effects of
234–27 to teach and to *d·* C. S.
242– 3 You can never *d·* spirituality until
242– 9 you have no Principle to *d·*
242–14 or you forfeit your ability to *d·* it.
254– 7 Watch, pray, *d·*.
279–18 *d·* "on earth peace, — *Luke* 2 : 14.
303–17 to *d·* Science and its pure
357–14 *d·* C. S. to a higher
358– 1 which *d·* the true following of
(see also **Principle**)

demonstrated

Mis. 22–23 *d·* it, according to the rules
23– 7 *d·* a divine intelligence
25– 6 that Jesus taught and *d·*.
28–16 he *d·* that divine Science alone can
40–15 and *d·* on, the same Principle
41–28 if *d·*, is sufficient for all
52–26 first rule was not easily *d·* ?
54– 5 discovered, *d·*, and teaches C. S. ?
57–13 after the truth of man had been *d·*,
70– 3 I *d·* its truth when I
74–26 *d·* the lifelessness of matter,
76– 6 is true, and remains to be *d·*,
92– 6 sufficiently . . . to be absolutely *d·*.
101– 3 divine Mind is understood and *d·*
104–26 divine Principle and idea are *d·*,
107–15 is regenerated and C. S. is *d·* :
172–21 understood, and *d·* in our lives.
183– 5 must be acknowledged and *d·*.
188– 2 that *d·* the opposite, Truth.
251–27 will fall before Truth *d·*,
258– 9 he *d·* the healing power and
270– 9 He who *d·* his power over sin,
286–29 *d·* in the offspring of divine Mind,
318– 4 is stated and demands to be *d·*
334–26 By the substitution of Truth *d·*,
342– 2 the joy of divine Science *d·*.
359–25 Science is *d·* by degrees,
367–12 goodness and harmony — is *d·*.
Man. 16– 2 Love as *d·* by the Galilean Prophet
17–17 taught and *d·* by our Master,
Ret. 26– 9 *d·* for all time and peoples
35–19 was and is *d·* as practical,
61–27 stated and *d·* in its godliness
71–26 wheat can be garnered and C. S. *d·*.
84– 3 sufficiently understood to be fully *d·*.
93–21 has not been fully *d·*,
Un. 1–13 little apprehended and *d·* by mortals,
53– 9 they are here to be seen and *d·* ;
55– 2 rule of Life can be *d·*,
Pul. 21– 8 live, to see this love *d·*.
63–19 * *d·* in a very tangible and
70–22 * way of salvation *d·* by Jesus

demonstrated

Pul. 85– 9 * unfolded and *d·* divine Love,
    85–13 * she has *d·* the system of healing
No. 13–12 before that saying is *d·* in Life
    14– 2 nor misconceived, when properly *d·*.
    21–10 Science *d·* the Principle of all
    28–18 Truth, as *d·* by Jesus,
    36– 1 *d·* the infinite as one,
Pan. 8–14 Christianity, as taught and *d·* in
    8–21 Christianity, as he taught and *d·* it,
    9– 8 that hath *d·* one God
    11–29 grand realism . . . is *d·* by C. S.
    13– 5 When shall Christianity be *d·*
'01. 2– 2 what Christ Jesus taught and *d·*
    4–14 and *d·* as divine Love ;
    23–20 he *d·* his power over matter, sin,
    23–22 as no other person has ever *d·* it.
    25–21 He *d·* what he taught.
'02. 6– 9 Christ, Truth, *d·* and continues to
Peo. 12–20 Our blessed Master *d·* this great
My. 37–15 * you have *d·* this Science
    103–20 I have *d·* through Mind
    105– 4 defined Christianly and *d·*
    105– 5 rules *d·* prove one's faith
    112–20 is fully understood when *d·*.
    113–24 is *d·* on a fixed Principle
    146–13 infinitely more than has been *d·*,
    146–21 has not been *d·* in this age.
    152–28 understood and *d·*, is found to be
    162–12 have *d·* in gifts to me
    181–14 which, *d·* on the Golden Rule,
    205–27 it is *d·* by perfect rules ;
    238– 9 discerned, understood, and *d·*.
    267– 3 fully *d·* to be divine Science?
    275–27 spiritually understood and *d·*,
    300–12 Principle of C. S., *d·*, heals
    348–24 *d·* Christianity and proved
    357–25 upon which this Science can be *d·*.
    (*see also* **Jesus**)

demonstrates

Mis. 67–18 gospel of healing *d·* the law of Love.
    85– 7 and *d·* what he understands.
    98–20 *d·* God and the perfectibility of man.
    101–22 omnipotence *d·* but one power,
    116–26 Obeying the divine . . . *d·* Truth.
    166– 1 which alone *d·* the divine Principle
    189–31 *d·* Life without beginning or end.
    190– 5 *d·* Mind as dispelling a false sense
    209– 9 rule of this Principle *d·* Love,
    209–11 Metaphysics also *d·* this Principle
    252–22 *d·* the divine Principle, rules and
    259–24 Truth *d·* good, and is natural ;
    261– 8 *d·* this verity of being ;
    265–13 *d·* its Principle according to rule,
    291– 6 *d·* above personal motives,
    300–29 C. S. *d·* that the patient
    338–14 only rule . . . which *d·* C. S.
Man. 92– 4 *d·* what we affirm of
Ret. 65–21 it *d·* the power of Christ
    88–28 Mind *d·* omnipresence and
Un. 40–10 *d·* Life as imperative in the
No. 4–14 Science *d·* the reality of Truth
    6–28 and C. S. *d·* this.
    30–26 cure of the sick *d·* this grand
Pan. 9–16 Whoever *d·* the highest humanity,
'01. 15–11 *d·* the Science of Christianity.
    22– 2 whosoever *d·* the truth of these
'02. 6–24 points the way, *d·* heaven here,
My. 5–10 understanding which *d·* C. S.,
    112–17 *d·* in some degree the truth of
    181– 9 it *d·* the scientific, sinless
    238–19 Science is reached that *d·* God.
    238–23 is Science, for it *d·* Life,
    274– 1 *d·* the Principle of life eternal ;
    274–14 *d·* health, holiness, and
    274–25 for it *d·* C. S.
    275– 5 it lives love, it *d·* love.
    279– 7 Principle of C. S. *d·* peace.
    285– 9 and *d·* the Science of being.
    288– 9 *d·* Truth and reflects divine Love.

demonstrating

Mis. 42–31 false admissions prevent us from *d·*
    54–11 she is *d·* the power of C. S.
    64– 5 *d·* the nothingness of sickness,
    116–22 doing, the Word — *d·* Truth
    147– 7 *d·* the divine Principle of C. S.
    163–28 *d·* the spiritual healing of body
    185–13 *d·* the true image and likeness.
    270–12 used in *d·* Life scientifically,
    380– 3 human modus for it *d·*
    380–24 *d·* the Science of metaphysical
Man. 45–12 *d·* the rules of divine Love.
Ret. 37–17 *d·* the spiritual Principle of
    79–20 *d·* the victory over self and sin.
Pul. 4–13 thus *d·* deific Principle.

demonstrating

Pul. 69–27 * *d·* the Christ-healing.''
Rud. 1– 3 *d·* the divine Principle
No. 4– 3 *d·* it understandingly
Hea. 9– 4 employed our thoughts more in *d·* it.
    16– 6 How much are you *d·* of this
    16–11 unless you do this you are not *d·* the
My. 214– 8 *d·* the Life that is Truth,
    297–23 *d·* the fundamental truth of C. S.
    362–24 * thus *d·* practical Christianity.

demonstration

absolute
  Mis. 136–18 absolute *d·* of C. S.
    355– 9 absolute *d·* of Science must be
and fruition
  Un. 61–23 C. S. is both *d·* and fruition,
Christian
  Mis. 156–19 daily Christian *d·* thereof.
daily
  Mis. 373–32 daily *d·* of Truth and Love.
demands
  Mis. 16–29 this statement demands *d·*.
dethrones
  Mis. 221–22 Such denial dethrones *d·*,
feeble
  Mis. 30– 2 in at least some feeble *d·* thereof,
gospel, or
  Mis. 367– 1 letter without law, gospel, or *d·*,
grand
  My. 321– 1 * grand *d·* in building this church
great
  My. 84–17 * near to another great *d·* of
higher
  Mis. 355–16 gives scope to higher *d·*.
  No. 44– 5 higher *d·* of medicine and religion.
his
  Mis. 3–11 his *d·* hath taught us
    74–20 His *d·* of Spirit
    192– 7 his *d·* of Truth in casting out
    215–29 used at the *end* of his *d·*.
  '01. 11– 3 his *d·* over sin, disease, and death,
idea and
  Ret. 59–17 both in idea and *d·*.
inquiry and
  Mis. 268–15 His whole inquiry and *d·*
its
  Mis. 19– 4 and prevent its *d·* ;
    56–22 its *d·* proves the correctness
    65–23 I have taught them both in its *d·*,
    214–13 summed up its *d·* in the command,
    357–32 Divine Love . . . the basis of its *d·*,
  Ret. 31– 3 C. S., and its *d·*
    94– 3 a struggle for its *d·*.
  Un. 25–13 Truth and its *d·* in C. S.,
  My. 113–14 knowledge of Christ and its *d·*,
    242–10 and no rule for its *d·*.
    361–20 * has promptly made its *d·*
manifestation, and
  My. 357– 8 manifestation, and *d·*.
marvellous
  No. 37–14 this most marvellous *d·*,
of being
  Ret. 26–29 *d·* of being, in Science,
of Christ
  Man. 47–16 illustrates the *d·* of Christ,
of Christianity
  Mis. 149–21 refreshing *d·* of Christianity,
  Pan. 9–20 *d·* of Christianity blesses all
of Christian Science
  Mis. 136–18 absolute *d·* of C. S.
    338– 6 but by *d·* of C, S.,
  Man. 43–25 rules and the *d·* of C. S.
  Ret. 78–10 will prevent the *d·* of C. S.
  '01. 23–12 Principle, rule, or *d·* of C. S.,
    28–20 my *d·* of C. S. in healing
  My. 136– 3 At this period my *d·* of C. S.
of divine Life
  No. 18–14 *d·* of divine Life and Love ;
of divine power
  Mis. 268–10 the *d·* of divine power,
of God
    (*see* **God**)
of healing
  '01. 18–21 is above a *d·* of healing,
of infinity
  Ret. 59–12 in *d·* of infinity.
of Jesus
  Mis. 244–26 teachings and *d·* of Jesus
of Love
  Mis. 214– 2 was full of Love, and a *d·* of Love,
of the Science
  Rud. 11–18 *d·* of the Science of Mind-healing
of the science
  Ret. 59–10 *d·* of the science of numbers ;

demonstration

of the truth
Mis. 87–27 indispensable to the *d·* of the truth
of the unreality
Ret. 62– 7 A *d·* of the *unreality* of evil
of Truth
Mis. 192– 7 and to his *d·* of Truth
373–32 *d·* of Truth and Love.
Ret. 75–11 writings on ethics, and *d·* of Truth,
No. 11–28 dictum and the *d·* of Truth
origin and
Mis. 58–23 not human, in origin and *d·*.
our
Mis. 359–25 our *d·* rises only as we rise
Un. 61–24 our *d·* and realization of this
perfection and
Ret. 57–30 perfection and *d·* of metaphysical,
practical
Un. 36–26 interfere with its practical *d·*.
Rud. 6–23 best understood in practical *d·*.
My. 81–24 * It was a practical *d·* of the
prevents the
Pan. 7– 5 and thus prevents the *d·*
Principle and
Mis. 69– 7 Science rests on Principle and *d·*.
progress is
Mis. 235– 8 progress is *d·*, not doctrine.
rule and
Mis. 336–12 insist on the rule and *d·* of
Ret. 94–24 in Principle, rule, and *d·*.
rule, and the
My. 272–14 rule, and the *d·* of this idealism.
rules for
Mis. 307–28 Principle and rules for *d·*.
scientific
Mis. 288–20 would prevent scientific *d·*.
Ret. 40–21 This scientific *d·* so stirred the
Pul. 45–19 * indeed, then, a scientific *d·*.
strong
Un. 43– 3 for any strong *d·* over death,
supreme in
Ret. 28–15 For Spirit to be supreme in *d·*,
Pul. 35–19 For Spirit to be supreme in *d·*,
teaching and
Ret. 25– 7 Jesus' teaching and *d·*,
that
My. 79–22 * higher pedestal by that *d·*
their
Mis. 215–23 at the beginning of their *d·*;
thereof
Mis. 30– 2 some feeble *d·* thereof,
55– 4 understanding and *d·* thereof
156–19 daily Christian *d·* thereof.
Ret. 87–13 in the orderly *d·* thereof.
Peo. 5–20 *d·* thereof in healing the sick.
My. 348–20 the *d·* thereof was made,
this
Mis. 105– 7 this *d·* is the foundation of C. S.
Man. 92– 6 nothing can substitute this *d·*.
Rud. 11–19 This *d·* is based on a true
understanding and
Mis. 55– 4 least understanding and *d·* thereof
Man. 19– 3 understanding and *d·* of divine Truth,
wonderful
My. 95–29 * wonderful *d·* of religious faith

Mis. 252–15 My proof of these . . . is *d·*,
346– 3 *d·* of moral and spiritual healing
365–12 for it rests alone on *d·*.
Un. 36–16 is the *d·*, according to C. S.,
No. 13– 4 *d·* of moral and physical growth,
18– 8 *d·* of God's supremacy
'01. 25–14 *d·* of matter minus, and God all,
Hea. 3– 6 a *d·*, more than a doctrine.
My. 25– 4 * of this feature of the *d·*.
47–22 * *d·* of the knowledge of God,
92–20 * so huge and concrete a *d·*
221– 9 the *d·* which was to destroy sin,

demonstrations

Mis. 4–26 faith to make your *d·*."
48– 1 I measure its *d·* as a false belief,
70–28 wonderful *d·* of divine power,
105– 5 Master's individual *d·* over sin,
172– 1 to keep their *d·* modest,
187–18 the later teachings and *d·* of
263–25 Science is hampered by immature *d·*,
Un. 31– 8 *d·* of Jesus annulled the
Pul. 51–29 * other great *d·* of religious belief
'01. 17–11 my first *d·* of C. S.
My. 103–24 *d·* of our great Master
111–31 attest with their individual *d·*.

demonstratively

Mis. 288– 3 must be *d·* right yourself,

demonstrator

'00. 6– 3 Only the *d·* can mistake or
'01. 26– 3 great teacher, preacher, and *d·*
My. 219–23 great *d·* of C. S., said,
338–25 visible discoverer, founder, *d·*,
348–27 The human *d·* of this Science

demoralize

Ret. 81– 9 tends to *d·* mortals,

demoralized

My. 122–20 our sense of Truth is not *d·*,

demoralizes

Ret. 71–28 *d·* the person who does this,

demoralizing

Mis. 162–26 *d·* his motives and Christlikeness,

Demosthenes

Mis. 345– 4 place where *D·* had pleaded

demurrer

My. 307–17 I entered a *d·* which rebuked him.

den

Pul. 49– 1 * which Mrs. Eddy calls her *d·*

denial

Mis. 31– 2 malpractice is a bland *d·* of Truth,
183–24 is a *d·* of man's spiritual sonship ;
194–10 this *d·* would dishonor that office
221–19 *d·* of this fact in one instance
221–21 Such *d·* dethrones demonstration,
221–23 Such *d·* also contradicts the doctrine
247–32 must be met, . . . with a *d·* by Truth.
Un. 25–14 This *d·* enlarges the human intellect
31–16 in the *d·* of matter,
45–12 These falsities need a *d·*.
No. 29–16 a *d·* of God's power?
42–22 *D·* of the authorship of "S. and H.
My. 275–12 chapter sub-title

denials

Pul. 83– 9 * not be disheartened by a thousand *d·*

denied

Mis. 7–26 Oftentimes we are *d·* the
184–20 he has *d·* the power of Truth,
199–17 *d·* and defined their superstition.
348–31 afterwards *d·* this and objected to
Ret. 25–16 His corporeality I *d·*.
35–24 and *d·* the perpetuity of Jesus'
Un. 21–12 your personal senses be *d·*.
50– 5 something to be *d·* and destroyed
54–13 Hence the fact must be *d·* ;
Pul. 46– 5 * at C. S. headquarters this is *d·* ;
Pan. 5–27 He *d·* it, cast it out of mortal mind,
'00. 14– 2 hast not *d·* my name.— *Rev.* 3 : 8.
My. 195–13 We must resign . . . what we are *d·*,

denies

Mis. 31–14 *d·* the grand verity of this Science,
102–23 supports harmony, *d·* suffering,
211–32 when the heart *d·* it,
221–14 if he *d·* it, the good effect is lost.
330–27 boasts and begs, and God *d·*
Un. 31–19 all that *d·* and defies Spirit,
39–16 and *d·* spiritual sonship ;
Rud. 12–12 *d·* the Principle of Mind-healing.
No. 18– 4 lie that *d·* Him as All-in-all,
24– 9 *d·* . . . both matter and evil.
'01. 24– 2 He *d·* the existence of matter,
Hea. 15–17 admits in . . . what he *d·* in proof?

denominated

Mis. 112–15 *d·*, in extreme cases, moral idiocy.
190–28 "devil" is *d·* Abaddon ;— *Luke* 11 : 14.
Ret. 25–14 Soul I *d·* substance,

denomination (*see also* denomination's)

Mis. 168–26 * would speak before the Scientist *d·*
314– 3 Sunday services of our *d·*
334–21 reduce this falsity to its proper *d·*,
382–20 first church edifice of this *d·*
383– 3 all the churches of the C. S. *d·*.
Man. 34–20 members from a different *d·*
45–21 read in branch churches of this *d·*
48–23 The periodicals of our *d·*
63–15 Each church of the C. S. *d·*
Ret. 28–18 to their own mental *d·*,
Un. 35–10 Reduced to its proper *d·*,
Pul. 21–20 between our *d·* and other sects,
24–20 * and the first pastor of this *d·*."
31– 3 * the Founder of this *d·*
40–14 * MARY BAKER EDDY, FOUNDER OF THE *D·*
41–13 * members of the *d·* gathered ;
45– 9 * a publication of the new *d·* :
64– 4 * the first pastor of this *d·*."
70–10 * first pastor of the C. S. *d·*,
'00. 1–10 this first church of our *d·*,
2– 3 Churches of this *d·* are
'01. 11–15 churches of the C. S. *d·*,
84–24 Bible and the textbook of our *d·* ;

denomination
My. 8– 4 * "Our d· is palpably outgrowing
8–28 * Leader of our religious d·
26–24 animus of our church and d·.
65– 6 * Mother Church of the d·,
70– 7 * any other d· in the world,
75–28 * been dedicated by this d·
90–27 * the Founder of a great d·
96– 4 * The Mother Church of that d·.
99–24 * d· has grown with a rapidity
141– 4 * communion service of the C. S. d·,
148–10 In the annals of our d·
151–13 injustice done . . . to this d·
151–14 when it no longer blesses this d·.
189–25 first church edifice of our d·
194–17 attested by the Founder of your d·
196– 4 the first edifice of our d·
199–21 between the churches of our d·

denominational
Mis. 32–25 d· and social organizations
155–28 reading-matter for our d· organ.
382–28 our d· form of Sunday services,
My. 139–21 the d· to the doctrinal,
173–18 exercises at the d· headquarters

denomination's
My. 90–30 * d· peculiar department of healing,

denominations
Mis. 21–13 trend of other Christian d·
Man. 34–17 Free from Other D·.
59–17 persons of all sects and d·
Ret. 42–10 clergymen of other d· listened
Pul. 21–15 in all d· of·religion,
21–26 unity with churches of other d·
47– 1 * many clergymen of other d·
'01. 23–13 change of the d· of mathematics ;
30– 2 as all other religious d· have
My. v– 9 * extended . . . by other Christian d·,
53–23 * by clergymen of different d·,
74–16 * other d· might profit by
84– 7 * It is a rule in some d·
91– 7 * a good example to other d·
95–21 * clergymen of other d· are avowing
112– 8 Our religious d· interpret the

denominator
Mis. 108–13 reducing its claim to its proper d·,

denotes
Pan. 3–28 d· the celestial harmony of
My. 220–14 Injustice d· the absence of law.

denounce
Pan. 6– 5 let us continue to d· evil
My. 210–21 and only d· error in general,

denounced
Mis. 57–15 is seen when Truth, God, d· it,
Ret. 65–10 hence Jesus d· it.
'01. 25–17 d· all such gilded sepulchres
My. 218–19 ultimates in what Jesus d·.

denounces
Mis. 122–17 Holy Writ d· him that declares,
'00. 13–11 he d· the Nicolaitan church.

dens
Un. 11– 5 beard the lions in their d·.

densely
Mis. 108–28 * Hawthorne Hall was d· packed,

dented
My. 105–12 could be d· by the finger,

dentist
My. 314– 2 * second husband, "an itinerant d·."
314–10 considered a rarely skilful d·.
315– 3 * Dr. Patterson, a d·, boarded with

dentistry
Mis. 45–11 in the practice of d·.

denunciation
Ret. 63–12 this d· must precede its
'01. 32–15 aimed deadly, and spared no d·.
My. 104–22 what can atone for the vulgar d·

denunciations
My. 112– 2 always been first met with d·.

Denver
Mis. 152– 2 chapter sub-title
'00. 1–21 St. Louis, D·, Salt Lake City,

Denver (Col.) News
My. 89–21 *[D· (C·) N·]

Denver (Col.) Republican
My. 99–10 *[D· (C·) R·]

deny
Mis. 58–11 d· the evidences of the senses
60–12 to d· the possibility of communion
100–11 for Truth to d· or to destroy.
171–13 not to condemn and d·, but to

deny
Mis. 193– 7 Doctrines that d· the substance
194– 8 yet should d· the validity or
198–15 if we d· the claims of these senses
199– 2 d· the supposed power of matter to
335–18 Those who d· my wisdom or right
374–23 doggedly d· or frantically affirm
Ret. 54– 8 d· these claims and learn the
63–11 When we d· the authority of sin,
Un. 10– 3 these so-called existences I d·,
25– 1 If you, O good, d· this,
25– 1 then I d· your truthfulness.
36–21 To d· the existence or reality of
38–22 or to d· that He is Life eternal.
39–21 d· the evidence of the material senses,
46– 7 I do not d·, I maintain, the
Rud. 3–17 they will . . . prescribe drugs, or d· God.
5– 2 but d· the testimony of the
No. 2–11 d· self, sense, and take up the cross.
Pan. 5–22 d· it and prove its falsity.
8– 9 d· the self-existence of God?
'01. 12–15 d· the validity and permanence of
23–25 to d·, on received principles of
Hea. 15–14 why should man d· all might to
Po. 32–16 reason with appetite, pleasures d·,
My. 74–24 * to d· them the satisfaction
217–18 * why do we d· the existence of
217–21 We d· first the existence of disease,
224–25 We would not d· their authors a

denying
Mis. 3–28 deluding reason, d· revelation,
198– 5 d· material so-called laws and
260–21 deluding reason and d· revelation,
333–13 d· that God, good, is supreme,
Un. 25–12 d· Truth and its demonstration
No. 6–14 healed by d· its validity;
My. 143–14 d· or asserting the personality
211– 5 by d· that this evil exists.

Deo volente
Mis. 67–21 you shall, D· v·, inform them
My. 123–19 I will see you in this hall, D· v·;

depart
Mis. 21–13 to d· from the trend of
215– 7 let us d· from the material sense
270– 6 Shall we d· from the example of
270–20 We cannot d· from his holy example,
316–13 and d· farther from the primitives
398–19 White as wool, ere they d·,
399–21 Lifted higher, we d·,
Man. 50–14 If a member of this Church shall d·
94–12 opportunity to d· in quiet thought
Ret. 46–25 White as wool, ere they d·,
00–12 and d· on their united pilgrimages.
Un. 24– 5 to d· from the supreme sense of
Pul. 16– 6 Joyous, risen, we d·
17–24 White as wool, ere they d·
'01. 4– 6 To d· from the rule of mathematics
Po. 14–23 White as wool, ere they d·,
24– 7 A sign that never can d·.
31– 9 D· ! Glad Easter glows with gratitude
76– 5 Lifted higher, we d·,
My. 161– 9 "D· from me,— Luke 13 : 27.
228– 9 yet d· from Christ's teachings.

departed
Mis. 34–15 If the d· were to communicate with
34–19 than we, . . . can go to the d·
42–17 change whereby we meet the dear d·,
00–13 d· friends — dead only in belief
171–15 supposed to have d· from the earth,
385– 9 poem
No. 12–22 in nothing else has she d· from the
'01. 17– 7 prodigal — d· from his better self
22–29 those who have d· from its
Hea. 5–14, 15 think the d· are not d·,
Po. 17– 1 Blest beings d· ! Ye echoes at dawn !
34–22 O'er joys d·, unforgotten love.
page 48 poem
My. 97–28 * have mostly d·, but Boston
267–17 the d· enter heaven in proportion to
290– 5 The d· Queen's royal and imperial
302– 7 a corpse, whence mind has d·.
308–10 my duty to be just to the d·

departeth
Mis. 335–30 whoso d· from divine Science,

departing
Mis. 19–14 is daily d· from evil ;
101– 4 d· from the thraldom of the senses
Ret. 58– 2 then d· from this statement
Pul. 83–30 * and he, d·, left his scepter
My. 82–28 * d· with such remarkable expedition,
270–18 words of our dear, d· Saviour,
292– 9 comfort the living as it did the d·.

department

Mis. 115– 7 deficiency in this *d·*.
242–15 At present, I am in another *d·*
Man. 91–12 a free course in this *d·*
Rud. 15–15 to fill . . . the *d·* of healing.
My. 90–30 * denomination's peculiar *d·* of

departments

Rud. 15–16 should have separate *d·*,

departs

Mis. 268–11 who *d·* from Mind to matter,
324–23 Stealing cautiously away . . . he *d·* ;
325–28 As he *d·*, he sees robbers
'00. 6– 9 Any mystery in C. S. *d·* when
My. 220–25 which *d·* from the instructions
254– 1 mysticism *d·*, heaven opens,

departure

Mis. 71–21 is a *d·* from divine law ;
136– 2 it was a *d·*, socially, publicly,
234–28 In this new *d·* of metaphysics,
247–10 to furnish a single instance of *d·*
Man. 41–13 A *d·* from this rule
44– 4 A *d·* from the spirit or letter of this
50–13 *D·* from Tenets.
Ret. 78–21 *d·* from the Science of Mind-healing.
Pul. 31– 9 * and take, as the point of *d·*,
66–21 * *d·* from long respected views
Rud. 16–16 *d·* from Science is an irreparable
'01. 2–22 a *d·* from the direct line in Christ
4– 7 a *d·* from the Principle and rule
6– 5 Here is the *d·*.
6–25 Our *d·* from theological personality
14–10 Our only *d·* from ecclesiasticism
19–15 flat *d·* from Jesus' practice
23–11 This *d·*, however, from the
'02. 8–28 a *d·* from God, or His lost likeness,
My. 151–27 This *d·* from Spirit, . . . was
181–10 *d·* from matter to Spirit,
197– 1 comes with the *d·* of sin.
289–14 in the sudden *d·* of the late
300–29 C. S. is not a *d·* from
331– 8 * to the train on her *d·*,
348–11 *d·* from divine Science sprang from
348–14 writer's *d·* from such a religion
364– 6 *d·* from this golden rule is

departures

Mis. 265–29 growing out of the *d·* from Science
278–32 and led to some startling *d·*
Ret. 57–24 Human systems . . . are *d·* from C. S.

depend

Mis. 77– 1 *Did the salvation of the eunuch d·*
316–10 *d·* on the fitness of things,
Pul. 13–26 must *d·* upon sin's obduracy.
Pan. 4–10 *d·* on conditions of matter,
My. 226–20 *d·* on Him for your existence.
244–25 This, however, must *d·* on results.
342–11 * *d·* upon the osseous structure ;

depended

Ret. 14– 9 salvation and condemnation *d·*,

dependence

Ret. 28–14 and *d·* on spiritual things.
Pul. 35–18 and *d·* on spiritual things.
Peo. 3–26 such as *d·* on personal pardon

dependent

Mis. 28– 5 *d·* on the beliefs that
Ret. 59–21 mutually *d·*, each on the other,
No. 3–12 People *d·* on the rules of this
5–14 *d·* on material conditions.
'02. 15– 9 while *d·* on the income from the

depending

Pul. 37–22 * *d·* on any one personality.

depends

Mis. 47–29 *d·* upon what one accepts as
88–28 *d·* upon what kind of a doctor it is.
230– 2 Success in life *d·* upon persistent
Man. 31– 9 prosperity of C. S. largely *d·*
Pul. 82–26 * *d·* the welfare of their husbands,
My. 108– 4 allopath who *d·* upon drugs.

depict

Ret. 76–26 sees each mortal in an impersonal *d·*.
Pul. 26– 7 * beyond the power of words to *d·*.

depicted

Mis. 7–20 *d·* in some future time upon the
142–26 symbols of freemasonry *d·* on the
My. 42– 1 * *d·* its form and comeliness,
136– 6 as *d·* in the chapter Atonement
179–19 as *d·* in the life of our Lord,
296–28 she *d·* its rooms, guests,

depictive

Po. 43– 1 *picture d· of Isaiah xi.*

depicts

Rud. 11–27 never *d·* the muscular, vascular,

deplorable

Mis. 107–24 this *d·* mental state is moral idiocy.
'01. 15–14 *d·* sight is to contemplate the

deplorably

Mis. 25–25 sick are more *d·* situated than

deplored

Ret. 7–19 * His death will be *d·*,

deportment

My. 122–12 The *d·* of its dear members

deposit

Mis. 159–16 where I *d·* certain recollections
159–20 Here I *d·* the gifts that
Man. 76– 2 should remain on safe *d·*,
78–20 keep on *d·* the sum of $500

deposits

My. 135–10 investments, *d·*, expenditures,
137–13 investments, *d·*, expenditures,

depot

Ret. 38–17 We met at the Eastern *d·* in **Lynn,**

depraved

Mis. 354–10 When *d·* reason is preferred to
Rud. 7–13 material, fallen, sick, *d·*,

depravity

Mis. 2–10 admit the total *d·* of mortals,
112–32 exemplification of total *d·*,

deprecate

Mis. 97–12 Such suppositional healing I *d·*.
284–29 I *d·* personal animosities

deprecates

Mis. 371–13 he who *d·* their condition

depressing

Mis. 133–23 In the midst of *d·* care and labor

depression

Mis. 51– 6 *accompanied by great mental d·*,

deprivation

My. 21–16 * every seeming trial and *d·*

deprive

Mis. 281– 8 could neither *d·* me of something **nor**
291–20 could not *d·* them of it.
My. vii– 6 * not unwittingly made to *d·*

deprives

Mis. 14–29 *d·* evil of all power,
41– 7 It *d·* those who practise it
Un. 48–10 *d·* death of its sting,

depth

Mis. 8–14 Can height, or *d·*, or any other
122–13 in the *d·* of the sea'' — *Matt.* 18 : 6.
My. 9–12 * declare the *d·* of our affection
81–21 * the *d·* of sincerity.
128– 2 *d·* of desire can find no other

depths

Mis. 81–28 out of the *d·* of ignorance
111–11 like Peter, they launch into the *d·*,
113–14 *d·* of perdition by his own consent.
211–13 "Out of the *d·* — *Psal.* 130 : 1.
Ret. 73– 9 great fact leads into profound *d·*.
My. 36–22 * have been delivered from the *d·*
37– 8 * *d·* of tenderest gratitude,
164–19 buried in the *d·* of the unseen,
194–28 guard you . . . through the *d·* ;
200–27 spare this plunge, lessen its *d·*,
258–24 all *d·* of love, grief, death, and
290–16 "Out of the *d·* — *Psal.* 130 : 1.

deputy

Rud. 1–18 (in court, for example) by *d·*

deranged

Pan. 8– 3 causes a man to be mentally *d·* ;

Derby's, J. C.

Pul. 78–26 * window of J. C. *D·* jewelry store.

deride

Mis. 126–28 to *d·* her is to incur the penalty
Man. 94–10 who goes to hear and *d·* truth,

derided

No. 41– 7 work most *d·* and envied

derision

Mis. 126–32 shall have them in *d·*.'' — *Psal.* 2 : 4.

derisively

My. 162–17 This was spoken *d·*.

derivation

Pan. 2–12 Webster's *d·* of the English word

derivative

Mis. 14–25 cannot be, the *d·* of good.
14–26 neither a primitive nor a *d·*,

derive

Mis. 33–20 recognize the help they *d·*

derived
Mis. 76– 2 self-created or d· capacity
103–21 Any inference of the divine d· from
162–15 his power, d· from Spirit,
244–17 d· from the life and teachings of
302–26 d· from making his copy,
316–26 could have d· most benefit from
Un. 6– 7 higher selfhood, d· from God,
No. 10– 1 * and from which it is d·."
Pan. 2–10 d· from two Greek words
'01. 3–14 definition d· from the Bible,
Hea. 3–15 was d· from the word good.

derives
My. 189–15 government of divine Love d· its

dernier ressort
Mis. 357– 5 the schoolroom is the d· r·.

descant
Un. 60–11 yet we d· upon sickness, sin,
No. 46–12 Theologians d· pleasantly upon

descanting
'01. 24– 9 d· on the virtues of tar-water,

Descartes
No. 22– 4 Leibnitz, D·, Fichte,

descend
Ret. 85–11 angelic thoughts ascend and d·,

descendants
No. 46–16 As dutiful d· of Puritans,

descended
Pul. 10–25 which d· like day-spring
My. 97–25 * Christian Scientists who d· upon

descending
My. 342– 3 * lady slowly d· the stairs.

descent
Mis. 323–10 d· and ascent are beset with
Chr. 55–20 without mother, without d·,— Heb. 7 : 3.

describe
Mis. 376–17 d· the brave splendor of a
My. 313–25 I never went into a trance to d·

described
Ret. 15–24 cases d· had been treated
25–18 the temporal, I d· as unreal.
Un. 28– 5 has not descried nor d· Soul.
Pul. 60–20 * and is d· as containing
62–22 * from those d· down to little sets
76– 6 * d· as "particularly beautiful,
My. 95–16 * were d· in the newspapers
315–24 dummy heretofore d·?

describes
Mis. 259–20 rhythm that the Scripture d·,
My. 271–12 * chapter sub-title

describing
Mis. 24–28 or rather the allegory d· it.
My. 105–25 a work d· my system of healing.
300–21 d· the Baker homestead

descried
Un. 28– 4 has not d· nor described Soul.

description
Mis. 306– 2 * send fullest historical d·.
376– 9 * from a d·, in The Galaxy,
Man. 47–18 shall not include a d· of
Un. 21– 1 we read the apostle's d· of
Pul. 23– 4 * D· OF THE MOST UNIQUE
57–11 * From the d· we judge that
My. v–24 * record for a work of this d· ;
13–13 According to his d·, the church
67– 4 * chapter sub-title
150– 5 Pliny gives the following d·
297– 6 said d· of her soul-visit,

descriptions
Mis. 7–19 These d· carry fears to many
Man. 48–23 d· of our church edifices,
My. 306–23 his scribblings were d· of

descriptive
Mis. 379– 7 d· of the general appearance,

desert
Mis. 81–23 in the d· of earthly joy ;
150–22 and the d· a resting-place
154–26 never d· the post of spiritual
246–22 to yield its prey the peace of a d·,
325–24 grieve Him in the d·."— Psal. 78 : 40.
Pul. 14–15 weary wanderers, athirst in the d·
'00. 15–16 it waits in the d·
My. 214–29 To d· the Cause never
332–10 * but did not d· her

desertion
My. 314–15 granted on the ground of d·,

deserts
'01. 3–25 d· its premise, and expresses
My. 167–10 Love . . . which never d· us.
361– 2 and though it be through d·

deserve
Mis. 295– 2 which d· and elicit brief comment.
My. 160–10 than that we d· it.

deserved
My. 83–22 * takes on a tone of d· satisfaction,
258– 4 lifts a system . . . to d· fame?
284– 4 accorded me more than is d·,

deserves
Mis. 48– 7 Mr. Carpenter d· praise for his
Pul. 50– 4 * he d· to have a home and
51–27 * get the share of attention it d·,
Hea. 4–12 d· to be punished,
Peo. 9–15 sin that d· to be punished
My. 130– 7 and punished as it d·.
150– 6 * "Doing what d· to be written,
150– 7 * writing what d· to be read ;

deserving
My. 46–20 * obedient, d· disciples.

Desha
Mary
Mis. 306–10 * signature
Miss Mary
Mis. 306–15 * notification . . . to Miss Mary D·,

desideratum
Mis. 355–10 To consummate this d·,

design
Mis. 205–24 all periods in the divine d·.
249–23 of their mental d· to do this
Un. 57– 3 the d· of the material senses
Pul. 24–10 * the d· a Romanesque tower
25–26 * silver lamps of Roman d·,
Rud. 3–18 in its nature, method, and d·.
My. 10– 9 * embodying the best of d·,
36–26 * all the beauty of color and d·,
68– 3 * the beauty and strength of the d·.
85–28 * symmetrical and appropriate d·.
190– 3 merciful d· of divine Love,
279–10 all periods in the d· of God.
347–10 exquisite d· of boughs

designate
Ret. 14–21 could not d· any precise time.
Pul. 15–13 d· those as unfaithful stewards

designated
Man. 112– 1 branch churches are d· by number,
My. 108–23 our Master d· as his best work,
137–20 I have d· by my last will,

designation
Man. 102–10 D· of Deeds.
My. 268–30 the d· man meaning woman as well,

designed
Mis. 84–24 discipline of the flesh is d· to
262– 1 is d· to bring health and happiness
351–13 falsehood d· to stir up strife
Man. 17–10 church d· to commemorate the word
19– 2 d· to be built on the Rock, Christ ;
Ret. 53– 5 d· to bear aloft the standard of
Pul. 25–10 * d· for the exclusive use of
28– 1 * d· to be wholly typical of the
My. 46–10 church d· to commemorate the word
244–11 This opportunity is d· to impart
353–11 d· to put on record the

designs
Pul. 26– 1 * cut glass in decorative d ,
28– 6 * decorated with emblematic d·,
76– 8 * floor is of mosaic in elegant d·,
76–12 * white mahogany in special d·,
No. 39–12 nor bring His d· into mortal modes ;
My. 211–19 tools to carry out the d· of
212–32 in furtherance of unscrupulous d·.

desirable
Mis. 4– 3 potent and d· remedial agent
97–10 by no means a d· . . . healer.
109–20 Their mental state is not d·,
139–23 I had this d· site transferred
Man. 98– 8 periodical in which it is d· that
Un. 54–21 Satan held it up . . . as something d·
My. 14–29 * it is d· that the contributions
121–15 peace is d·, and plain dealing is a

desire (noun)
and fear
No. 11– 2 human will, intellect, d·, and fear,
and motives
No. 12–13 The same affection, d·, and motives
and thought
Pul. 55–20 * has its origin in d· and thought.
awakened
No. 39–20 an awakened d· to be and do good.

desire (noun)

carnal
Mis. 182–16 neither from dust nor carnal *d·*.
daily
My. 15–13 daily *d·* that the Giver of all
depth of
My. 128– 2 depth of *d·* can find no other
devout
'02. 6–21 all devout *d·*, virtually petition,
due to a
My. 170– 6 was due to a *d·* on my part
for notoriety
Mis. 296–26 from a *d·* for notoriety and a
for services
My. 54–21 * *d·* for services was so great
for something
Ret. 31–10 *d·* for something higher
heart's
Mis. 276– 9 my heart's *d·* met the demand.
hope and
My. 9–16 * modestly renew the hope and *d·*
human
Mis. 317–20 Human *d·* is inadequate to adjust
360– 1 Meekness, moderating human *d·*,
My. 3– 7 not alone in accord with human *d·*
292–21 the effect of one human *d·*
humble
'01. 14– 4 Publican's wail won his humble *d·*,
My. 334–22 Publican's wail won his humble *d·*,
its
Mis. 127–16 to receive the answer to its *d·* ;
My. 18–13 to receive the answer to its *d·* ;
kindling
No. 38–26 kindling *d·* loses a part of its
may belie
No. 40–10 Words may belie *d·*,
my
Mis. 133–19 my *d·* to set you right on this
291–17 and is far from my *d·* ;
310–14 my *d·* is that all shall be
My. 128– 1 cannot quench my *d·* to say this ;
159– 8 every pulse of my *d·* for the
325–13 * my *d·* has never changed.
352–29 My *d·* is that every
no
Mis. 198– 2 will have no *d·* to sin.
321–27 no *d·* to see or to hear what
no time or
'01. 32–10 no time or *d·* to defame their
prayer is a
Peo. 9–22 Silent prayer is a *d·*, fervent,
quenchless
Po. 18– 6 unfolding a quenchless *d·*.
retain a
'00. 8–28 retain a *d·* to follow your own
rightful
Mis. 179– 4 rightful *d·* in the hour of loss,
stronger
Mis. 235–17 and a stronger *d·* for it.
tender
My. 292–17 one earnest, tender *d·* works
their
Mis. 239– 1 due credit for their *d·*,
My. 213–11 in their *d·* to do right
284–21 the Veterans indicated their *d·*
thought and
Mis. 15–10 Christianization— of thought and *d·*,
to be just
Mis. 132–29 Even the *d·* to be just is a
to testify
My. 81– 7 * bursting with a *d·* to testify
untamed
Ret. 31–18 untamed *d·* which breaketh the
worldly
Mis. 354–29 inflated with worldly *d·*.
your
My. 361–21 * in accordance with your *d·* for

No. 38–25 All prayer that is *d·* is
My. 23– 5 * divine Love that prompted the *d·*,
92–28 * nothing save the *d·* in the human heart
275–14 (and I trust the *d·* thereof)

desire (verb)
Mis. 90–15 Do you *d·* to be freed from sin?
148–25 I specially *d·* that you collect no
151–17 *d·* beside thee."— *Psal.* 73 : 25.
232–23 would *d·* and demand it,
274– 4 I *d·* to revise my book
282–21 If the friends of a patient *d·* you to
291–12 I *d·* the equal growth and prosperity
294–22 *d·* to help even such as these.
310–20 All who *d·* its fellowship,
363–15 a perfect man would not *d·* to
Man. 89–19 pupils who so *d·* may apply to
Ret. 74– 9 for I *d·* never to think of it,

desire (verb)
Pul. 85–16 * *d·* a better and grander humanity,
87– 3 * We especially *d·* you to be present
87–20 more of earth now, than I *d·*,
'00. 9– 4 "You may do it if you *d·*."
'02. 13–12 no personal benefit . . . and *d·* none
My. 12–30 The good they *d·* to do,
17– 6 *d·* the sincere milk — *I Pet.* 2 : 2.
42–14 * *d·* to improve this opportunity
44–28 * *d·* to express their continued
138–15 persons whom I *d·* to see
204– 1 not accomplished all you *d·*,
249–24 The report . . . I *d·* to correct.
293–31 "What things soever ye *d·*,— *Mark* 11 : 24.
352– 5 * *d·* to express our recognition
357–13 brethren in New York *d·* to
358–13 however much I *d·* to read all

desired
Mis. 86–16 beauty . . . is something to be *d·*.
127– 7 One thing I have greatly *d·*,
146–21 every reformed mortal that *d·*
276– 6 all with whom I *d·* to,
305–14 * *d·* that the largest number of
Un. 53– 6 and greatly to be *d·*,
'00. 9–26 I have *d·* to step aside
'02. 20– 4 bringeth us into the *d·* haven,
My. 14–17 * further payments . . . were not *d·*.
18– 4 "One thing I have greatly *d·*,
40– 3 * She has *d·* for years to
164– 3 retirement I so much *d·*.
292–19 would prevent the result *d·*.
307–20 Truth, which we both *d·* ;
336– 6 * he *d·* to go to her assistance,

desires
Mis. 32– 1 if indeed he *d·* success in this
37– 5 manifest in all thoughts and *d·*
50–20 human affections, *d·*, and aims,
71–12 *law of transmission, prenatal d·*,
155–18 (however much she *d·* thus to do),
235–11 It gives to the race loftier *d·*
266–26 in accordance with my students' *d·*,
282–18 should know that the person . . . *d·* it.
311–15 My deepest *d·* and daily labors
356–18 uplifted *d·* of the human heart,
371–19 Whoever *d·* to say, "good right,
Man. 69– 3 remain with Mrs. Eddy if she so *d·*,
100–23 name the Committee if it so *d·*,
Ret. 79–12 purification of the affections and *d·*.
Pul. 3–23 when all human *d·* are quenched,
'00. 9–13 Strong *d·* bias human judgment
My. 12–11 * that his individual *d·*,
170–22 *d·* of thine heart.— *Psal.* 37 : 4.
180–23 drop compliance with their *d·*,
287–20 wakens lofty *d·*, new possibilities,
359–12 individual who *d·* to inform himself

desiring
Ret. 47– 7 persons *d·* to enter the College,
86–17 *d·* growth in the knowledge of Truth,

desirous
My. 170– 1 *d·* that it should be understood

desist
Mis. 302–23 *d·* from further copying of my
358–22 or to *d·* from organizing churches

desk
Mis. 273–24 applications lying on the *d·*
283– 7 to enter a house, unlock the *d·*,
379– 2 and write at his *d·*.
Pul. 42–26 * *d·* was wreathed with ferns

Des Moines
My. 81–15 * "*D· M·*!" "Glasgow!" "Cuba!"

desolate
Mis. 231–30 But, alas ! for the *d·* home ;
326–28 left unto you *d·*."— *Matt.* 23 : 38.
Po. 34–14 Divinely *d·* the shrine to paint?
My. 292–11 mourner at the *d·* home !

desolating
Mis. 257–27 *d·* the green earth.

desolation
Mis. 56–18 that shall be brought to *d·*.
81–25 *d·* of human understanding,
89– 3 is brought to *d·*."— *Matt.* 12 : 25.
217–27 shall be brought to *d·*.
Ret. 72– 9 brought into *d·*,— *Psal.* 73 : 19.
No. 5–22 brought to *d·* ;"— *Luke* 11 : 17.

despair
Mis. 30– 5 *d·* of ultimately reaching them,
275–11 looks in dull *d·* at the vacant
Un. 64–13 the hope . . . must yield to *d·*,
Po. 24– 4 Dissolving death, *d·* !
My. 150– 2 Therefore *d·* not nor murmur,
350–13 Lift from *d·* the struggler

despairing
Mis. 327–18 D· of gaining the summit,

despatch
Pul. 74–13 d· is given me, calling for
My. 33– 2 * d· from the members of the church
44–16 * read the following d·,
44–20 * The d· was as follows :
65–15 * pledged with the readiness and d·
184– 3 Have just received your d·.

despatches
Man. 67–20 congratulatory d· or letters
My. 79–17 * According to the d·,
223–11 Letters and d· from individuals

desperate
Mis. 177– 8 Large numbers, in d· malice,
Ret. 41– 4 Many were the d· cases
Pan. 10–20 d· cases of intemperance,

despicable
Mis. 97–13 more. d· than all other

despise
Mis. 269– 8 and d· the other. — *Matt.* 6 : 24.
My. 356–23 and d· the other. — *Matt.* 6 : 24.

despising
Ret. 22–12 d· the shame, — *Heb.* 12 : 2.
My. 258–15 d· the shame, — *Heb.* 12 : 2.

despite
Ret. 45– 5 D· the prosperity of my church,
Un. 11–13 d· the boastful sense of
Pul. 59–30 * (d· the snowstorm)
Pan. 8– 1 d· of Mind, or by the consent of
Peo. 9–20 d· the authority of Jesus
My. 91–23 * d· the obstacles put in the way
153– 1 d· our winter snows.

despitefully
Mis. 11–22 persecute and d· use one,
147 –12 hate you and d· use you
Man. 41–10 However d· used and misrepresented
Ret. 29– 4 "d· use you — *Matt.* 5 : 44.
My. 6–11 men may revile us and d· use us,
52– 5 * loving them that d· use her,

despoil
Un. 17–17 d· error of its borrowed plumes,

despot
Ret. 11–10 No d· bears misrule,
Po. 60– 7 No d· bears misrule,

despotic
Mis. 48– 7 its so-called power is d·,

despotism
My. 260– 5 The d· of material sense

destined
Mis. 148–20 doctrines d· for future generations
Man. 3–17 doctrines d· for future generations
Pul. 8–28 The children are d· to witness
Pul. 33–26 * whose life has been d· to more than
'02. 11– 2 Our heavenly Father never d·
My. 266–29 C. S. is d· to become the one and

destines
Mis. 147–20 d· him to do nothing but what is

destinies
Mis. 368–25 working out the d· of the damned.
My. 291– 4 Presiding over the d· of a nation

destiny
Mis. 1– 4 to him, no higher d· dawned
119–17 in the scale against man's high d·.
232–12 standard . . . that regulates human d·.
333–30 Chaldee hung his d· out upon
Ret. 48–21 fulfilled its high and noble d·,
No. 34–17 endeavor to crush . . . its divine d·.
45–23 and so fulfil her d·.
46–19 Man has a noble d· ;
46–20 full-orbed significance of this d·
Po. 78– 9 star whose d· none may outrun ;
My. 122– 3 d· more grand than can issue from
229–30 Truth is strong with d· ;

destitute
Mis. 76– 2 d· of . . . derived capacity to sin.
Un. 49–22 Being d· of Principle,
50–18 Like evil, it is d· of Mind,
No. 16–13 d· of time and space ;

destroy
Mis. 4–30 but to d· sin in mortal thought.
24–31 thus d· any supposed effect
27– 6 conclusions that d· their premise
28– 6 D· the belief that you can walk,
28–14 death does not d· the beliefs
31–19 so d· his power to be or to do good,
37–20 God can and does d· the
40–17 power of Truth to d· error,
45– 8 d· the necessity for ether
46– 7 to d· the appearance of evil

destroy
Mis. 47–22 Truth does not d· but substantiates
56– 5 disorganization would d· Spirit
60– 8 is the only way to d· them ;
73–17 these conditions d· the belief.
85–29 tends to d· error :
97– 1 to d· the power of the flesh ;
97– 4 and d· mortal discord with
100–11 for Truth to deny or to d·.
105– 3 disdain the fears and d· the discords
105–28 D· the thought of sin, sickness,
105–29 and you d· their existence.
116– 1 d· your own sensitiveness to the
157–27 Error has no power but to d· itself.
193–13 casts out error, and will d· death.
201–11 its powerlessness to d· good,
209–13 that d· its more dangerous pleasures.
209–19 d· the peace of a false sense.
254–26 will come and d· — *Mark.* 12 : 9.
257–27 Cyclones kill and d·,
261–19 to d· the law," — *Matt.* 5 : 17.
334–25 Can belief d· belief?
352–20 enable one to d· it and its effects.
365–11 If C. S. lacked . . . it would d· itself ;
366–27 To d· sin and its sequence,
Man. 91– 3 but shall d· this paper.
Ret. 55– 4 sufficient knowledge of error to d· it
63– 9 to d· this belief and save him
Un. 9– 2 D· the mental sense of the disease,
9– 3 D· the sense of sin,
18– 8 and d· everything that is unlike
18–20 eventually d·, every supposition of
20–17 then see if this Love does not d·
25–19 *Evil.* . . . I give life, and I can d· life.
35– 6 D· the belief, and the
49–27 relinquish, lest it d· them.
54– 8 does not d· the so-called fact of the
62–15 D· this sense of sin,
62–16 D· this trinity of error,
Pul. 3– 5 "D· this temple, — *John* 2 : 19.
Rud. 5–21 d· this belief of seeing with the
5–26 D· the five senses as
10–25 an error which Truth will d·.
No. 5–17 material conditions can and do d·
6 3 attempt to d· the realities of
30–16 could not d· our woes totally if
31–15 d· the works of — *I John* 3 : 8.
'00. 3–19 would d· this man's goodness.
13– 1 ready to d· the unity and
'01. 9–21 art thou come to d· us? — *Mark* 1 : 24.
9–25 they disturb the carnal and d· it ;
13–10 take possession of us and d· us,
13–18 d· the conception of sin as
13–19 and you d· the fear
'02. 5–23 to d· the law, — *Matt.* 5 : 17.
5–24 not come to d·, — *Matt.* 5 : 17.
6– 8 Love and Truth d· this
16–26 they never d· one iota of hypocrisy,
Hea. 8–5 that d· error and death.
18– 1 d· their effects upon the body,
My. 132–24 will also rebuke and d· disease,
132 95 d· the belief of life in matter.
161– 5 would d· himself eternally,
161–18 to d· its erroneous claims,
217–31 not to d· the law of being,
218– 9 to d· all disease and
219–24 to d· the law, — *Matt.* 5 : 17.
219–25 not come to d·, — *Matt.* 5 : 17.
221– 9 demonstration which was to d· sin,
260–25 not d· the fruits of — *Mal.* 3 : 11.
296–14 to harm, to hinder, or to d·
301–28 Drugs cannot . . . . d· disease
323–24 * blessing those who would d· you

destroyed
Mis. 37–22 sin of every sort, is d· by Truth.
42–13 or d· this last enemy,
58– 9 When the belief . . . is d·,
67–23 discerned, disarmed, and d·.
118–19 until all error is d·
194– 4 sickness, disease, and death are d· ;
210– 6 when found out, is two-thirds d·,
213–13 evil which, if seen, can be d·.
302–21 each and all d· the copies
338–13 but cancels not sin until it be d·,
343–20 not always d· by the first uprooting ;
352–30 *uncovered* before it can be d·,
355–14 Error found out is two-thirds d·.
356– 7 that they be d· through suffering ;
381–29 and their unlawful existence d·,
Ret. 64– 5 d· by the supremacy of good.
64–28 illusion, error, may be d· ;
Un. 11–18 and d· human pride by
15–12 If man must be d· by the
50– 5 something to be denied and d·
Pul. 81–17 * not as the moth to be d·
No. 29–21 sin, disease, and death are d·.

destroyed

No.	30– 5	will not let sin go until it is *d·*,
'01.	13–24	never punishes it only as it is *d·*,
	16– 6	till the sin is *d·*.
Peo.	9–15	can be *d·* only through suffering.
My.	108–22	if they did . . . they would be *d·*.
	111– 5	cannot be *d·* by false psychics,
	130–18	lie left to itself is not so soon *d·*
	160–27	sinner is consumed,— his sins *d·*.
	207–13	* by which sin and sickness are *d·*
	211–28	cause . . . is found out and *d·*.

destroyer

Mis.	210–26	save him from his *d·*.
My.	161– 5	The intentional *d·* of others
	161–28	avenging itself on its *d·*,

destroyers

No.	11– 3	nor *d·* of life or its harmonies.

destroying

Mis.	40– 7	Truth is as effectual in *d·* sickness
	70–18	sin was *d·* itself,
	185–13	*d·* all suffering,
	214–28	prevent the possibility of *d·* the
	261–21	by Truth's *d·* error.
	352–18	in *d·* this belief.
Ret.	57– 8	for the purpose of *d·* discord.
	71–30	will end in *d·* health and morals.
	94–12	divine mercy, *d·* all error,
Un.	47– 1	*d·* sin, sickness, and death,
No.	30– 2	*d·* all sense of sin and death.
Pan.	15– 2	*d·* millions of her money,
'01.	30–19	*d·* all lower considerations.
Peo.	6–22	*d·* sin, sickness, and death ;
My.	126– 3	purpose of the *d·* angel,
	194– 9	healing sickness and *d·* sin,
	265–18	mitigating and *d·* sin, disease, and

destroys

Mis.	3–23	*d·* these material elements
	14–20	that good, . . . forcibly *d·*.
	14–30	*d·* all error, sin, sickness,
	41– 8	*d·* their own possibility of
	78– 4	*d·* all sense of sin, sickness, and
	101–24	This virtually *d·* matter and evil,
	102–23	denies suffering, and *d·* it
	105–15	*d·* the too common sense of
	107–30	so severe that it *d·* them,
	184–22	*d·* his self-deceived sense
	189–11	antidotes and *d·* the errors of
	189–25	*d·* sin, disease, and death.
	191–21	*d·* all consistent supposition of
	194–26	in the Truth that *d·* all error,
	235– 5	to reflect Him who *d·* death
	260–17	*d·* any suppositional or
	283–29	mandate of Truth which *d·* all error.
	297– 8	*d·* the appetite for alcoholic drinks.
	336–23	heals disease and sin and *d·* death !
Ret.	62– 8	A demonstration of . . . *d·* evil.
	67–14	reforms the sinner and *d·* sin.
Un.	4– 7	Truth *d·* every phase of error.
	4–11	*d·* our sense of imperfection,
	32–12	*d·* all sense of matter as substance,
	48–10	heals all my ills, *d·* my iniquities,
	54–14	if . . . then sin *d·* the *at-one-ment*,
	56–12	C. S. first eliminates and then *d·*.
Rud.	3–20	*d·* the mental error made manifest
No.	2–24	Dishonesty *d·* one's ability to heal
	4–12	*d·* the feasibility of disease ;
	13– 2	*d·* sin quickly and utterly.
	30– 8	God's law reaches and *d·* evil
	30– 9	He need not know the evil He *d·*,
	32–22	domination of good *d·* the
Pan.	11–24	good supreme *d·* all sense of evil,
'00.	6–21	which *d·* his false appetites
'01.	4– 7	To depart from . . . *d·* the proof of
	4– 9	*d·* the ability to demonstrate
	10–23	whereby good *d·* evil,
	13–12	such a sense of its nullity as *d·* it.
	13–16	*d·* it on the very basis of
	18–27	if God *d·* the popular triad
Peo.	9–27	*d·* discord with the higher and
My.	119–12	C. S. *d·* such tendency.
	119–23	*d·* the false sense with the
	185–21	*d·* the last enemy, death.
	212–25	*d·* the true sense of Science,
	233–22	*d·* his peace in error,
	278–20	civilization *d·* such illusions
	288–27	through love that *d·* sin.
		(*see also* **error, Truth**)

destructibility

Un.	50– 1	notion of the *d·* of Mind

destruction

Mis.	10–23	This *d·* is a moral chemicalization,
	32– 2	in this broad road to *d·*.
	40– 7	as in the *d·* of sin.

destruction

Mis.	55–22	in the final *d·* of all that
	56–18	final *d·* of this false belief
	82–13	*after the d· of mortal mind*
	215– 1	and the final *d·* of error
	237–22	can only work out its own *d·* ;
Man.	15–11	forgiveness of sin in the *d·* of sin
Ret.	63–13	denunciation must precede its *d·*.
Un.	1– 7	unto their own *d·*."— II *Pet.* 3 : 16
	15–13	then his *d·* comes through the
Rud.	6–18	*d·* of the evidence of the
No.	6–10	indispensable to the *d·* of false
	23– 1	hinders the *d·* of evil.
	24–20	exposure is nine points of *d·*.
	31–12	which is the sure *d·* of sin ;
	31–13	I insist on the *d·* of sin
	42–10	God's pardon is the *d·* of
'01.	15–24	* swallowed up in everlasting *d·*.
My.	13–21	thy life from *d·* ;— *Psal.* 103 : 4.
	218– 6	the *d·* of the human body,
	219–14	the *d·* of disease germs.
	249–11	let loose for one's own *d·*.
	360– 1	It will be your *d·* if you

destructive

Mis.	103– 7	materiality, and *d·* forces,

detail

Mis.	35–26	who explains it in *d·*.
	138– 5	The *d·* of conforming to society,
	148–18	simple, scientific basis, and *d·*
	375–18	* conscientious application to *d·*,
	376– 5	* very closely resemble in *d·*
Man.	3–15	simple, scientific basis, and *d·*
Un.	31–22	It can be shown, in *d·*,
Pul.	46–10	* much is told of herself in *d·*
My.	320–25	* *d·* regarding your work,
	321–26	* conclusive to me in every *d·*,

detailed

Mis.	299– 8	I have no time for *d·* report

details

My.	145– 9	suggested the *d·* outside and inside
	173–26	for arranging the *d·* and

detains

Pul.	87–24	church's tall tower *d·* the sun,
'01.	34– 5	interval that *d·* the patient from

detect

Mis.	112– 9	neither defend the innocent nor *d·*
'01.	13–27	first *d·* the claim of sin ;

detected

Un.	57–16	for it was *d·* and dismissed.

deter

Mis.	236–28	must not *d·* us from doing our duty,

deteriorates

Ret.	72– 5	*d·* one's ability to do good,

determination

Mis.	2– 7	*d·* of mankind to cleave to
My.	273– 8	* remarkable skill, *d·*, and energy

determine

Mis.	310–23	will *d·* the action of the church
Man.	101– 2	C. S. Board of Directors shall *d·*
Ret.	65–27	As well expect to *d·*, without a
No.	42–17	with power to *d·* the fact
My.	277–14	characters and lives of men *d·* the
	306–12	Time and goodness *d·* greatness.

determined

Mis.	224–25	*d·* not to be offended when no
	304– 4	* It has been *d·* to create a
	327–21	*d·* not to part with their baggage.
My.	11–26	* The location is, therefore, *d·*.
	92– 2	* *d·* its real position in the
	98– 1	* impress the most *d·* skeptic.
	238– 7	can only be *d·* by personal proof.

determines

Pul.	80–29	* *d·* where we shall be hereafter
No.	6–19	Science *d·* the evidence in both
My.	117– 4	*d·* the right or the wrong of
	270–24	What we love *d·* what we are.

deterrent

My.	129– 1	a *d·* of Truth and Love,

dethrone

Mis.	260–21	and seeking to *d·* Deity.
No.	21–13	philosophy would *d·* perfection,
	30–24	would *d·* God as Truth,
My.	116–10	would *d·* the First Commandment,

dethroned

Mis.	65– 2	delusive evidence, Science has *d·*
	162–27	would have *d·* his power
Un.	20–10	evil must be *d·* :

dethrones

Mis. 8–18 defiles, defaces, and *d·* the
221–22 Such denial *d·* demonstration,
My. 193–16 Nothing *d·* His house.

dethroning

Mis. 3–28 denying revelation, and *d·* Deity.

detonation

Mis. 356– 6 need no terrible *d·* to free them.

detonations

Mis. 17– 1 before the awful *d·* of Sinai.

detract

Mis. 302–26 nor *d·* from the good that
349– 9 nor *d·* from the metaphysical mode

detraction

'02. 1–18 met with opposition and *d·* ;

Detroit

Mich.
Pul. 89–29 * *Free Press, D·*, Mich.
My. 183–23 chapter sub-title

Pul. 26–13 * great organ comes from *D·*.
56– 3 * Philadelphia, *D·*, Toledo,
60–17 * Farrand & Votey in *D·*,

Deuteronomy

26: 1, 2, 5–10 (first sentence)
My. 32–15 * *D·* 26 : 1, 2, 5–10 (first sentence).

Rud. 13–14 In *D·* (iv. 35) we read :

devastating

Mis. 343–21 they reappear, like *d·* witch-grass,

develop

Mis. 14–10 through which to *d·* good.
18– 2 *d·*, step by step, the original
Un. 42–26 mortal does not *d·* the immortal,
No. 37– 2 offspring had to grow, *d·* ;
Hea. 14–19 educate and *d·* the spiritual sense
My. 100– 16 they *d·* hidden strength.
342–28 Its government will *d·* as

developed

Mis. 15–28 *d·* into an infant Christianity ;
201–23 they tested and *d·* latent power.
247–18 healing force *d·* by C. S.
278–31 This has *d·* higher energies
Ret. 27– 9 Science *d·* itself to me until
Pul. 66–27 * which our civilization has *d·*.
69–20 * power fully *d·* to heal the sick.
No. 24– 6 *d·* through the lower orders of
My. 355– 9 conflict , . . is engendered and *d·*.

developing

'00. 10– 3 asserting and *d·* good.
'01. 1–21 man's nature *d·* itself.

development

Mis. 75– 5 man's possible earthly *d·*.
264–27 aid the mental *d·* of the student ;
356–22 second stage of mental *d·* is
Mis. 359–13 proper channels for *d·*,
Pul. 31–10 * *d·* of some degree of familiarity
53– 1 * fresh *d·* of a Principle that
66–19 * has shown an uncommon *d·*
79–17 * reasons for this remarkable *d·*,
My. 48–20 * a means of spiritual *d·*
84–24 * Its hold and *d·* are most notable.
88– 6 * is the *d·* of a short lifetime.
88–20 * material *d·* in evidence of

developments

Hea. 5– 6 Phrenology will be saying the *d·* of

develops

Mis. 204–18 It *d·* individual capacity,
Pan. 11–21 may believe that evil *d·* good,

deviate

Man. 63– 9 children's teachers must not *d·* from
Rud. 3–14 will no more *d·* morally from

deviating

Mis. 92– 3 present liability of *d·* from C. S.
Ret. 83–29 liability of *d·* from absolute C. S.

deviation

Man. 77–24 In case of any . . . *d·* from duty,
Ret. 85–15 any *d·* from the order prescribed by
My. 363–28 Any *d·* from this direct rule

device

Mis. 372–25 Not by aid of foreign *d·*

devices

Mis. 119– 4 instead of aiding other people's *d·*
159–28 rich *d·* in embroidery, silver,
Pan. 4–18 chapter sub-title

devil

Mis. 68–15 Jesus cast out a *d·*,
97– 8 "He is a *d·*," — *see John* 6 : 70.
163– 2 the world, the flesh, and the *d·*.
190–11 *casting out a d·*, — *Luke* 11 : 14.
190–12 *d· was gone out*, — *Luke* 11 : 14.
190–13 meaning of the term "*d·*" — *Luke* 11 : 14.
190–21 the *d·* herein referred to was
190–28 In the Hebrew, "*d·*" — *Luke* 11 : 14.
191– 2 the term "*d·*" — *Luke* 11 : 14.
191– 9 refers to a wicked man as the *d·* :
191–10 one of you is a *d·* ?" — *John* 6 : 70.
191–11 if *d·* is an individuality,
191–12 if . . . there is more than one *d·*.
191–15 indicating . . . more than one *d·* ;
191–22 existence of one personal *d·*.
191–23 our text refers to the *d·* as dumb ;
191–24 the original *d·* was a great talker.
192– 4 we mean not that he is a personal *d·*,
192– 5 defines *d·* as a "liar." — *John* 8 : 44.
192– 9 nature of Deity and *d·* be understood.
248–11 word synonymous with *d·*.
Ret. 63–22 * "The *d·* is but the ape of God."
67–24 the "*d·*" (*alias* evil), — *John* 8 : 44.
Un. 17–14 the *d·*, was the would-be murderer
52–11 good and evil, God and *d·*,
52–18 world, the flesh, and the *d·*.
Pul. 12–13 *d·* is come down — *Rev.* 12 : 12.
13–12 the *d·* knoweth his time is short.
No. 15–17 conceptions of Deity and *d·*
22–15 chapter sub-title
22–19 shows that the term *d·* is generic,
22–20 that there is more than one *d·*.
22–24 *d·* as a mortal who is full of evil.
22–25 one of you is a *d·* ?" — *John* 6 : 70.
23– 9 and therefore was not a *d·*,
23–17 moral sense of the word *d·*,
23–18 in order to cast out this *d·* ?
24–22 for behold evil (or *d·*) is,
31–15 the works of the *d·*" — *I John* 3 : 8.
32–16 the *d·* was "a liar, — *John* 8 : 44.
42–18 said that the *d·* is the ape of God.
Pan. 5–12 your father, the *d·*, — *John* 8 : 44.
5–18 Jesus' definition of *d·* (evil)
'00. 5– 8 opposite of God . . . named *d·*
'01. 13–14 evil, *alias d·*, sin, is a lie
16–13 In the Greek *d·* is named *serpent*
16–16 defines *d·* as accuser,
Hea. 6–27 word *d·* comes from the Greek
Peo. 3–13 mysterious God and a natural *d·*.
4–13 personal God and a personal *d·*
7– 1 by their God and their *d·*.
My. 14–20 * If the *d·* were really an entity,
60– 9 * it is the work of the *d·*."
252– 3 and you will have no *d·*.
269–22 "the world, the flesh and the *d·*,"

devilish

No. 23– 4 that Jesus condemned as *d·*,
My. 278–26 War is . . . barbarous, *d·*.

devils

Mis. 97– 9 casting out *d·* through Beelzebub.
175–30 in thy name cast out *d·*.
191–14 casting out *d·* — *Mark* 9 : 38.
326– 1 cast out *d·*, — *Matt.* 10 : 8.
No. 14–19 cast out *d·*" ! — *Matt.* 10 : 8.
22–18 cast out *d·*." — *Matt.* 10 : 8.
23–11 Jesus cast seven *d·* ;
22–12 these *d·* were the diseases
41–21 cast out *d·* ," — *Matt.* 10 : 8.
Hea. 1– 2 *shall they cast out d·* ; — *Mark* 16 : 17.
6–27 shall they cast out *d·*." — *Mark* 16 : 17.
Peo. 4–28 and cast out *d·*, error.
My. 47–30 * shall they cast out *d·* ; — *Mark* 16 : 17.
126–26 the habitation of *d·*, — *Rev.* 18 : 2.
288–23 cast out *d·* and healed the sick.
300–27 cast out *d·*." — *Matt.* 10 : 8.

devious

My. 260–14 philosophy may pursue paths *d·*,

deviously

Mis. 111–29 inclining mortal mind more *d·* :

devise

My. 51– 1 * to *d·* means to pay our pastor,

devised

My. vi–12 * *d·* its church government,

devoid

Un. 49–23 it is *d·* of Science.

devote

Mis. 5– 2 *d·* our best energies to the work.
Man. 31– 6 *d·* a suitable portion of their time
82–20 *d·* ample time for faithful practice
My. 358–19 I shall *d·* it to a worthy

devoted

Mis.	4–16	has been d· to their answer.
	4–17	periodical d· to this work
	37–26	Her time is wholly d· to instruction,
	48–19	purpose to which it can be d·,
	318– 7	love some of those d· students
Pul.	v– 4	WERE d· TO THE MOTHERS'S ROOM
	8–17	never before d· to menial
	42–12	* was d· to the "Mother's Room,"
	58– 2	* d· herself to imparting this
	58–27	* a room d· to her,
	63–17	* among her d· followers,
	71–22	* thousands . . . are now so entirely d·.
'00.	13–17	d· to a sensual worship.
My.	30–14	* professional men, d· women
	49–28	* d· labors in the cause of Truth,"
	88–24	* by a noble and d· woman,
	272–23	* Mrs. Eddy's own d· followers,
	321– 7	* your d· and faithful friends,
	328– 3	* With d· love,

devotedly

My.	335– 7	* He was d· attached to Masonry,

devotees

Un.	15–22	There are, or have been, d· who
Pul.	79– 8	* never have been, d· of
My.	76–27	* erected by the d· of a religion

devotes

Pul.	44–18	* chapter sub-title

devoting

Mis.	375–15	* d· every moment to the study of

devotion

Mis.	176– 9	supreme d· to Principle
	177– 2	fervent d· and an absolute
	342– 1	keep aglow the flame of d·
Ret.	2– 3	that sturdy Calvinistic d· to
	19–19	tender d· to his young bride
Pul.	85– 2	* d· and consecration to God
'01.	28–13	choicest memorials of d·
My.	30–10	* d· of the members to their
	36–23	* the measure of our d· to
	41–31	* supports such selfless d·,
	86–19	* the generosity of the d·
	131– 5	courage, d·, and attainment.
	330–30	Colonel Glover's tender d· to his

devotional

Pul.	28–22	* those d· hymns from Herbert,
	28–24	* other recognized d· poets,

devour

Mis.	82–28	the errors which d· it.
	253–17	stood ready to d· the child
	323–13	wolves . . . are ready to d· ;
Hea.	10– 3	d· the child as soon— see Rev. 12 : 4.
	10– 4	ready to d· the idea of Truth.

devourer

Mis.	263–11	covered from the d· by
'00.	12–29	Balaam as the d· of the people.
My.	269–24	"I will rebuke the d· — Mal. 3 : 11.

devouring

My.	211– 8	break out in d· flames.
	245–12	poisonous reptiles and d· beasts,

devout

Mis.	249–12	The most d· members of
	318–22	a d·, consecrated Christian.
	337–24	Only the d· Marys, and such as
	369–17	d· enough to trust Christ
Man.	60–25	Let the ceremony be d·.
	64– 1	and a d· Christian Scientist.
Ret.	54–20	The faith-cure has d· followers,
Pul.	10–22	if you are as d· as they,
	80–24	* women more thoughtful and d· ;
'00.	3–30	not the incentive of the d· Jew
	14–26	as the d· St. Stephen said :
'01.	28– 9	none lived a more d· Christian life
	31–21	D· orthodox parents ;
'02.	6–21	hope, and prayer, all d· desire,
My.	5–19	enables the d· Scientist to
	38–24	* D· Scientists said after the service
	90– 3	* d· worshippers, wooed by no
	249–29	d·, unselfed quality of thought

devoutly

Mis.	98–23	* "consummation d· to be wished."
Un.	17–19	* consummation d· to be wished."
Peo.	5– 2	d· recommends the more spiritual
My.	181–16	* consummation d· to be wished"

dew

Mis.	291–23	The d· of heaven will fall gently
	394– 3	It falls on the heart like the d·
Ret.	5–24	* like the gentle d· and cheerful light,
Po.	3– 3	I miss thee as the flower the d· !
	45– 3	It falls on the heart like the d·

dewdrop

Ret.	17–11	d· is shed On the heart of the pink
Pul.	4–14	A d· reflects the sun.
Po.	25– 2	Whence the d· is born,
	62–13	d· is shed On the heart of the pink

Dewey

Pan.	14–24	led by the dauntless D·,

dews

Mis.	154– 8	water it with the d· of heaven,
	343–11	watered by the heavenly d· of Love,
	360–17	d· of divine grace, falling upon
Ret.	95– 1	watered by d· of divine Science,
No.	14–26	d· of divine Truth,
My.	208–12	Like the gentle d· of heaven

dewy

Po.	73–12	Night's d· eye,

dexterous

Mis.	231–13	d· use of knife and fork,

dexterously

My.	6–13	d· and wisely provided for

diabolical

Mis.	41– 2	is given vent in the d· practice of
Un.	54–27	audacity of d· and sinuous logic

diabolism

Mis.	334–18	d· of suppositional evil
'01.	20–24	new-old régime of necromancy or d·

diabolos

Hea.	6–28	word devil comes from the Greek d· ;

diadem

Ret.	85–27	with a d· of gems from the
Pul.	4–21	his d· a crown of crowns.
'02.	3–21	The dazzling d· of royalty
Po.	46– 8	A gem in beauty's d·,
My.	201–15	with a d· of duties done.

diadems

My.	258–20	coronals of meekness, d· of love.

diagnose

Man.	47– 6	case he cannot fully d·,

diagnosed

My.	310–25	these "fits" were d· by Dr. Ladd

diagnoses

Hea.	12– 8	he d· disease as mind,

diagnosis

Mis.	69–25	According to their d·,

dial

Mis.	71–29	flitting across the d· of time.
Ret.	23–11	were indicated by no floral d·.

diameter

My.	68– 8	* having a d· of eighty-two feet

diametrical

Mis.	220–18	d· opposite of what it was

diametrically

Pul.	38–22	* They are d· opposed

diamond

Mis.	376–27	d·, topaz, opal, garnet,
Ret.	91– 5	be called "the d· sermon."
No.	13–25	and sparkle like a d·,
My.	121–18	a d· of the first water ;

diamonds

Pul.	8–14	forth came the money, or d·,
My.	175–23	richer than the d· of Golconda,

Diana

'00.	12–14	D·, the tutelary divinity

diapason

Mis.	206–21	repeating this d· of heaven :
My.	189–11	a d· of heart-beats,
		(see also organ)

Dickey

Adam H.

Po.	vii–16	* signature

Mr. Adam

My.	240–24	* through her student, Mr. Adam D·,
	358–21	Mr. Adam D· is my secretary,

dictate

My.	223– 5	nor d· replies to letters which
	276–19	* no one should seek to d· the

dictated

My.	114–24	which d· "S. and H. with Key to

dictates

My.	128–16	d· of his own rational conscience
	168– 2	d· of enlightened conscience,

dictating

Mis.	132–17	d· answers through my secretary,

dictation

'02.	15–15	declining d· as to what I should write.

dictator
Mis. 152–12 as a *d·*, arbiter, or ruler,

dictatorial
Mis. 148–11 arbitrary opinions nor *d·* demands,
Man. 3– 7 arbitrary opinions nor *d·* demands,

diction
Mis. 341–28 and the *d·* purely Oriental.
Ret. 27–15 express in feeble *d·* Truth's ultimate.
My. 317–10 to correct my *d·*.
317–17 left my *d·* quite out of the
317–22 My *d·*, as used in explaining C. S.,

dictionary (*see also* **dictionary's**)
Mis. 252–30 the wise man's spiritual *d·* ;
363–29 the ignorant man's *d·*,

dictionary's
'01. 3–12 Standard *d·* definition of God,

dictum
Mis. 133–18 following the *d·* of Jesus
No. 11–28 *d·* and the demonstration of Truth

did
Mis. 40–12 as *d·* those in the first century of
47–10 *d·* this without consciousness of
54–26 as Jesus and his disciples *d·*,
55– 6 to the extent that Jesus *d·*,
77– 3 It *d·* ; but this believing was more
165–19 rich legacy of what he said and *d·*,
178– 4 left his old church, as I *d·*,
182–31 will yield to it, even as they *d·*
237–27 dead hero who *d·* the hard work,
244–22 he *d·* this for man's example ;
253– 4 knoweth as *d·* our Master
373–6 the person who *d·* it.
293–23 *d·* this even as a surgeon
Man. 28–12 neither *d·* according to — Luke 12 : 47.
Ret. 9–10 bade me, . . . to reply as he *d·*,
89–11 he *d·* so informally, and because
90–13 This he *d·*, even though one of the
Un. 32–21 even as *d·* our Master ;
50– 9 We should subjugate it as Jesus *d·*,
62–20 Jesus seemed to die, though he *d·* not.
Pul. 33– 8 * bade her,			reply as he *d·* :
34–13 * and reluctantly they *d·* so,
51– 2 * If it *d·*, it would be a prodigy.
66– 2 * exists as much to-day as it *d·* when
74–11 * which she *d·* in this letter,
No. 31– 7 in subtler forms than they *d·*
46–11 rejoicing, as Paul *d·*,
'00. 7–12 as they *d·* after reading
7– 20 we say as *d·* Mary of old :
'02. 11–28 for the truths he said and *d·* :
18–21 how much of what he *d·*
Hea. 8–15 Plato *d·* better ; he said,
18–18 never *d·* anything for sickness
My. 3–22 to think genuine, whoever *d·* it.
59–25 * "Some say she *d·* not."
59–27 * "Send those who say she *d·* not
112– 5 *d·* just what he enjoined
190–28 would remain, even as it *d·*,
212–18 If they *d·*, there would be unity
215– 5 bade me do what I *d·*,
219–21 what Christ Jesus taught and *d·* :
220–32 seems more divine to-day than it *d·*
235–16 Did God make all . . . He *d·*.
292– 9 as it *d·* the departing.
294 7 "*d·* not many mighty — Matt. 13 : 58.
307–21 better than some others *d·*
313–14 *d·* everything they could think of
319–14 * work which the Rev. Mr Wiggin *d·*
319–25 * which I *d·* about the twentieth of
320– 5 * consented to assist me, which he *d·*.
321–31 * knew you years before I *d·*,

die
Mis. 57–17 thou shalt surely *d·*." — Gen. 2 : 17.
58– 7 and that he did not *d·* ;
69–16 and then had left him to *d·*.
70–17 He was too good to *d·* ;
70–19 and had already begun to *d·*,
75–28 it shall *d·*," — Ezek. 18 : 4.
75–29 mortal man . . . that sinneth, shall *d·* ;
76–13 hence these bodies must *d·*
76–23 sense, which sinneth and shall *d·* ;
76–26 Now if Soul sinned, it would *d·* :
79–24 "As in Adam all *d·*, — I Cor. 15 : 22.
84–20 and to *d·* is gain." — Phil. 1 : 21.
208– 3 "Thou shalt surely *d·*." — Gen. 2 : 17.
209–22 Evil passions *d·* in their own flames,
235– 3 to sin, be sick, and *d·*
258– 1 lawless law which dooms man to *d·*
367–17 thou shalt surely *d·*." — Gen. 2 : 17.
Chr. 55–28 shall never *d·*." — John 11 : 26.
Un. 2–21 if they *d·* in the Lord
3– 7 which *d·* in the Lord." — Rev. 14 : 13.

die
Un. 17–23 declares . . . they must surely *d·*.
22– 7 ye shall not touch it, lest ye *d·*.
28– 2 it shall *d·*." — Ezek. 18 : 4.
37– 4 Must man *d·*, then, in order to
38–18 all that dies, or appears to *d·*.
40–13 who believe his sayings will never *d·* ;
40–26 mortals *d·*, in belief,
41–26 matter appears to both live and *d·*,
53–14 will *d·* of its own delusion ;
62–19 The fleshly Jesus seemed to *d·*,
Pul. 3– 3 Can Life *d·* ?
No. 1–16 flames *d·* away on the mount of
13– 9 shall never *d·*." — John 11 : 26.
28–26 it shall *d·*." — Ezek. 18 : 20.
Pan. 7–11 declared that man should *d·*,
9–13 shall never *d·*." — John 11 : 26.
'01. 33–12 * that they were about to *d·*."
Po. 15–14 or *d·* in their chain.
My. 128–15 to live or to *d·* according to
164–30 man must live, he cannot *d·* ;
195–22 mortals expect to live and *d·*.
269– 9 neither can they *d·* — Luke 20 : 36.
333–24 * assurance of his willingness to *d·*,

died
Mis. 17– 7 before the flames have *d·*
58– 1 If one has *d·* of consumption,
58– 6 proves to him who thought he *d·*
238–26 or that I *d·* of palsy,
248–21 said that I *d·* of poison,
386–14 She deemed I *d·*,
Un. 62– 3 saith, "Christ (God) *d·* for me,
62–18 In Science, Christ never *d·*.
62–19 In material sense Jesus *d·*,
Pul. 34–15 "and they thought I had *d·*,
36– 1 * Dr. Eddy *d·* in 1882,
47– 3 * He *d·* in 1882.
49–17 big elms ! . . . and not one *d·*."
63–14 and not one *d·*."
'01. 11– 3 never suffered and never *d·*.
Po. 49–21 She deemed I *d·*,
My. 97– 8 * a larger proportion have *d·*
189–26 There my husband *d·*,
241–24 * lived or *d·* according to the
297–23 and realize that he never *d·* ;
310– 9 * but *d·* before the election.
310–18 * "excepting Albert, *d·* of cancer."
312– 8 * he *d·* of yellow fever.
312–21 *d·* in about nine days.
330–17 * *d·* there while on business
333– 9 * *d·* on the night of the
333–21 * *d·* on Thursday night,
335– 1 * *D·* at Wilmington, N. C., on the
336– 1 * would have *d·* on the seventh day.

dies
Mis. 2–22 for good *d·* not
184– 3 by claiming that . . . man *d·*.
209–10 and *d·* of its own physics.
208–30 error *d·* of its own elements.
277– 7 its voice *d·* out in the distance.
Ret. 25–12 That which sins, suffers, and *d·*,
Un. 38–18 false sense of life is all that *d·*,
39–22 which testify that man *d·*,
39–26 presuppose . . . that man *d·*,
40– 2 It is mortality only that *d·*.
40– 5 but man in Science never *d·*.
41–25 hence matter neither lives nor *d·*.
43–14 that man *d·* not,
45–21 until it finally *d·* in order to
45 22 But Truth never *d·*,
62– 4 God *d·* not, and is the ever-presence
No. 20– 3 mortal sense, sins and *d·*.
My. 194– 5 The letter of your work *d·*,
227–12 *d·* while the others recover,
278–18 *d·* in defence of his country,
297–16 Scientist who believes that he *d·*,
344–13 absurd to say that when a man *d·*,

diet
Mis. 6–27 observed in regard to *d·*,

differ
Mis. 117–23 God's time and mortals' *d·*.
252– 4 allopathy and homœopathy *d·*.
288–30 People will *d·* in their opinions
Un. 5–23 wholly or partially *d·* from them
Pul. 28–16 * does not *d·* widely from that of
38–27 * may *d·* among themselves,

difference
Mis. x–15 *d·* between then and now,
42–21 The *d·* between a belief of
111–23 no greater *d·* existed between
271–27 * *d·* between true and false teachers
352–28 *d·* between the healing of sin and
Ret. 68– 8 *d·* between these opposites
Un. 9–27 the cardinal point of the *d·* in

difference

Un.	10– 2	This d· wholly separates my
	27– 4	really have a shade of d·
Pul.	47–17	* defines carefully the d·
	57–14	* whatever d· of opinion there may be
Rud.	16–23	shades of d· in Mind-healing
Hea.	1–20	The d· between religions is,
My.	75–16	* it would not make much d·,
	108–10	* d· between metaphysics in
	319– 2	would make no d· to me.

different

Mis.	60–18	sleepers, in d· phases of thought,
	100–30	d· stages of man's recovery
	148–13	were written at d· dates,
	191–29	d· phases of sin or disease
	224–12	thousand million d· human wills,
	224–13	each person has a d· history,
	224–16	action . . . of these d· atoms.
	237–13	All the d· phases of error
	325– 5	These are believers of d· sects,
	367–21	evil is a d· state of consciousness.
	370–12	In d· ages the divine idea assumes d·
Man.	3–10	were written at d· dates,
	34–20	church member from a d· denomination
Ret.	33– 7	I sought knowledge from the d· schools,
	61– 4	d· forms of fear or disease.
	80– 7	As the poets in d· languages have
	87–30	and d· aid is sought.
Un.	9–23	So they have, but in a far d· form.
Pul.	23–12	* under several d· aspects
	38–19	* entirely d· a plane of consciousness
	40–17	* four d· congregations,
	47–11	* d· schools of allopathy,
	51–13	* others who have d· methods,
	51–14	* with them bring d· ideas.
	55–29	* members of d· congregations
'00.	13–25	* amalgamation of d· pagan religions
'01.	7–13	thoughts that express the d· mentalities
	22–22	and the d· religious sects
Po.	v– 2	* were written at d· periods
My.	24–22	* fifteen d· trades represented.
	29–23	* d· status before the world !
	47–22	* many of d· races and tongues
	53–22	* clergymen of d· denominations,
	53–31	* d· ones address them on the
	54–17	* d· places were considered,
	71–18	* d· from any other church
	89–17	* d· from almost all other
	94–21	* held at d· hours of the day,
	95– 7	* in d· parts of the world.
	179–24	d· renderings or translations of
	293– 4	act as the d· properties of drugs
	315– 5	* During his stay, at d· times,
	328–26	* enumerating the d· professions

differently

'01.	6– 6	defined d· by theology,

differing

Mis.	380–17	practised in slightly d· forms.
'01.	7–16	d· needs of the individual mind
	22–23	and the d· schools of medicine
Hea.	11–24	d· in this from homœopathy,
My.	293– 2	d· human concepts as to the
	321–15	* said anything . . . d· from what he

differs

Mis.	258–29	d· essentially from the human.

difficult

Mis.	37–28	is in reality the least d· of
	52– 3	It is d· to say how much
	52– 5	but not so d· to know that
	52–25	a rule farther on and more d·
	53–12	when it is d· to start the
	53–24	d· to make the rulers understand,
	53–28	abstract or d· to perceive.
	54– 1	to . . . the ungodly, it is dark and d·.
	117–18	It is d· for me to carry out a
	133– 4	d· to build a sentence of
	242–14	I performed more d· tasks
	245–20	It is d· to say which may be
Ret.	53– 4	prosperous under d· circumstances,
	63–20	more subtle, more d· to heal.
	83–17	find it more d· to rekindle
Un.	10– 5	It would be d· to name any
Pul.	37–23	* d· not to centre too closely
Rud.	7– 4	as the most d· case so treated.
'01.	17–20	overcome a d· stage of the work,
	17–22	more d· stage of action
Po.	27–13	let today grow d· and vast

difficulties

Mis.	53–16	acknowledging that under d·
	131–20	perplexities and d· which
	212–16	return under the reign of d·,
	236– 7	shrunk from contact with family d·,
	236–16	advice concerning d· and the
'01.	2–23	costs a return under d· ;

difficulties

'01.	29–27	a tithe of my own d·,
My.	220–15	pacification of all national d·,
	223– 5	which pertain to church d·
	277– 3	d· between the United States and
	277– 7	d· between individuals and
	291–18	fathomed the abyss of d·
	359– 3	trouble me with their d·

difficulty

Mis.	379–30	there remained the d· of
Pul.	64– 5	* considerable d· in securing
My.	134– 1	D·, abnegation, constant battle
	360–13	settle this church d· amicably

diffusing

Mis.	166–28	d· richest blessings.

dig

Mis.	154– 7	d· about this little church,

digest

Mis.	313– 5	It is a d· of good manners,
Rud.	3–15	that divine d· of Science

digested

My.	230– 8	d· only when Soul silences the

digestion

My.	229–19	chapter sub-title
	230– 5	d· of spiritual nutriment

dignified

Mis.	226–26	d· natures cannot stoop to
Man.	61–22	d· and suitable manner.
My.	276– 6	daily drive or a d· stay at home,
	309– 2	The man . . . was uniformly d·
	316–16	a d·, eloquent appeal to the press
	327–27	* this d· legal protection
	328– 1	* d·, blessed, and prospered it.

dignify

Mis.	111– 3	work, well done, would d· angels.
	199– 4	and d· the result with the name of
	240– 9	Predicting danger does not d· life,
My.	327–30	* will d· the ministry of Christ

dignitaries

Pul.	71–17	* various d· of the faith.

dignity

Mis.	126–12	lift us to that d· of Soul
	148–17	d· and defense of our Cause
	295–16	defend the d· of her daughters
	295–29	such d·, clemency, and virtue
Man.	3–13	d· and defense of our Cause ;
Un.	54–24	admitted the d· of evil.
My.	39–24	* her graciousness and d·.
	58–11	* d· of this church edifice

dilates

Mis.	356– 2	d· and kindles into rest.

dilemma

Mis.	134– 5	you are placed in this d· :
Hea.	13– 2	both horns of the d·,
My.	350– 7	It was in this d· that

diligence

My.	340–31	which man's d· has utilized.

diligently

Mis.	154–26	Watch d· ; never desert the
	206–26	all who d· seek God.
Ret.	23–18	He whom my affections had d·
	31–12	seek d· for the knowledge of God
My.	122–18	Are we still searching d·

dim

Mis.	xi–25	the d· corridors of years,
	368– 8	* behind the d· unknown,
	383–13	go down the d· posterns of time
Chr.	53–58	Truth's fane can d· ;
Ret.	9–20	* His presence in the vast and d·
	33– 5	d· mazes of materia medica,
Po.	18– 7	Would a tear d· his eye,
	26–18	the d· chambers of eternity
	70– 2	In the d· distance, lay
My.	189–10	the d· corridors of time,

dimension

Mis.	22–12	fourth d· of Spirit.
Pul.	86– 2	* about six inches in each d·,

dimensions

My.	77– 8	* its d· are only half as great.

diminish

Mis.	365–21	the demand would d· ;
Un.	5– 8	their . . . will proportionately d·.

diminished

No.	18– 2	never d· sin and sickness,
'00.	7– 4	death-rate to have gradually d·.

diminishes

Ret.	28–19	d·, constitutes, and sustains,
	67–16	sin d·, until the false claim

diminishing
Mis. 8- 2 abating suffering and d· sin,
No. 32-25 d· the percentage of sin.
My. 107-17 d· of the drug does not disprove

diminuendo
Mis. 116-15 *crescendo* and d· accent music,

diminution
Mis. 82-31 not subject to growth, change, or d·,

dimly
Mis. 87-10 what I now through you discern d· ;
Pul. 39-17 * D·, as in a dream, I watch the flow
39-23 * D·, as in a dream, I see the
No. 21- 6 Plato but d· discerned,

dimmed
Mis. 92-28 have d· the power and glory of
324-16 have so d· their sight
Un. 54- 1 bright gold of Truth is d· by

dims
Mis. 1-19 removing the dust that d· them.
291- 5 it d· the true sense of God's
354-30 No tear d· his eye

din
Mis. 120-17 heard above the d· of battle,
Ret. 69-25 "Above error's awful d·,
'02. 5- 1 foretells the dawn and d· of morn ;
My. 245-18 dire d· of mortal nothingness,

dine
My. 322-16 * to d· with the Wiggin family.

dinner
Mis. 230-26 chapter sub-title
348-21 every day, and especially at d·,

dinner-table
Mis. 231- 6 Four generations sat at that d·.

dip
My. 125-11 d· my pen in my heart to say,

diphtheria
My. 105-11 I healed malignant d·
107-32 pneumonia, d·, and ossification

diploma
Mis. 272-16 * any d· or degree,
Pul. 40 22 * d· given her by the Society of
'01. 33-14 platform, a creed, or a d·

diplomacy
My. 277- 5 by statesmanship and d·,

diplomas
Mis. 272-26 * with powers to confer d·
Man. 91-25 provided their d· are for three
Ret. 48- 6 conscientious scruples about d·,

dipped
My. 296-26 Clara Barton d· her pen in my heart,

dire
My. 245-17 the d· din of mortal nothingness,

direct
Mis. 25-10 d· application to human needs,
34-26 as d· opposites as light and darkness.
44- 9 and its application d·,
55-20 d· antipodes of the so-called facts
56-12 d· opposite of immortal Life,
146- 7 to d· your action on receiving or
147-29 the fair, open, and d· one,
157- 6 He that marketh . . . will d· thy way.
212-14 One step away from the d· line
282- 9 d· rule for practice of C. S.
291-11 is often construed as d· orders,
319-26 Christian Scientists can d· attention,
Ret. 37-16 Scriptures gave no d· interpretation
Un. 11- 7 in d· opposition to human philosophy
Pul. 50-22 * simple and d· as they are,
Rud. 9-22 without a d· effort,
'01. 2-23 departure from the d· line in Christ
35- 1 He shall d· thy paths ;" — Prov. 3 : 6
My. 49- 5 * The religious body which can d·,
129-29 Trust God to d· your steps.
161-27 "He shall d· thy paths." — Prov. 3: 6.
177-23 "I will d· their work — Isa. 61: 8.
361- 3 He will d· you into the paths of
363-28 Any deviation from this d· rule

directed
Mis. 264-19 As mortal mind is d·,
313-25 as I believe, divinely d·,
345-32 d· them to spiritual attainments.
Ret. 5-26 * d· attention to themes
Pul. 65-13 * Attention is d· to the progress
Pan. 2-22 the religious sentiment is d·.
Hea. 15- 8 spiritual power divinely d·.
My. 73-23 * to which all mail may be d·,
138-28 * d· to Honorable Judge Chamberlin
156-11 Jesus d· his disciples to
342-29 * d· by a single earthly ruler?"

directing
Mis. 245-12 d· more critical observation to

direction
Mis. 78-10 than can science in any other d·.
80- 9 aid individual rights in a wrong d·
115-32 Using mental power in the right d·
127-23 know yourself, under God's d·,
156-28 growth and understanding in this d·.
172-17 nor of human d·.
212-25 If, . . . one is at work in a wrong d·,
229-13 encourage faith in God in this d·,
245-25 to go no further in the d· of
246-14 from another d· there comes
297- 5 In the d· of temperance it has
304-31 * and the d· of its use,
347-16 Take the opposite d· !
381- 2 copied by her, or by her d·,
Man. 98-22 under the d· of this Committee
Ret. 84-29 place themselves under his d· ;
Pul. 43- 4 * led the singing, under the d·,
No. 39-15 in the d· that is unerring.
'01. 13-21 conquers him, in whatever d·.
Hea. 14- 8 encourage faith in an opposite d·?
My. 10-13 * have taken steps in this d·,
75- 9 * into the city from every d·
117- 7 helping a leader in God's d·,
117-27 only in the right d· !
146-25 in the right or in the wrong d·.
213-18 to drift in the wrong d·
215-31 no hint of his changing this d· ;
241- 9 advancement in this d·.
250-27 whatever is done in this d·
266-15 flux and flow in one d·,

directions
Mis. 33-18 and follow the d· given.
66-11 precept is verified in all d·
89- 8 *to follow the doctor's d·?*
158-26 divine d· sent out to the churches.
220-10 words, and actions, in certain d·,
273- 5 in order to work in other d·,
Man. 100- 8 carried out according to her d·.
Ret. 19-21 pathetic d· to his brother masons
My. 231- 5 working in wrong d·.
303-13 wit was not wasted in certain d·.
330-32 pathetic d· to his brother Masons
361- 1 Follow the d· of God

directly
Mis. 37-23 yields to Science as d· and
44-29 applying this . . . d· to your belief,
381-22 d· or indirectly printing,
Pul. 29-17 * dealt d· with the command of
Hea. 8-25 as d· upon a divine Principle,
8-27 as d· as we do to the rule of
12-13 God, d· or indirectly, through His
19- 5 is governed d· and entirely by
Peo. 8-19 as d· as it moves a planet
11-18 as d· as men pass legislative acts
My. 16-15 * have the work d· in charge,
82-30 * leading d· to Horticultural Hall.
223-20 All inquiries, coming d· or

Director
Man. 29- 5 D· shall not make known the
35- 5 by a D·, or by a student of
38- 6 a D· of this Church, or a student of
78- 2 If any D· fails to heed this

Directors (*see also* **Board of Directors, Directors'**)
Mis. 131-21 difficulties which the D· encountered
322- 8 notify the D· when I shall be present
Man. 26-17 The D· shall fix the salaries of
26-19 D·
29-11 the D· shall resign their office or
30- 1 D· shall select intelligible Readers
44-20 the duty of the D· to see that these
75-22 remained in the hands of the D·,
75-23 not solely to the D·.
76- 7 Report of D·.
79- 7 such business as Mrs. Eddy, the D·, or
95- 3 From the D·.
100-14 it shall be the duty of the D·
109- 8 D·, and students of the Board of
Pul. 20-10 and through D· regive the land
86- 9 * facsimile signatures of the D·,
87-11 *Beloved D· and Brethren:*
My. 20-22 * chapter sub-title
60-30 * was asked by one of the D·
62-19 * We, the D· of your church,
82-16 * pride of the Church D· that the
359- 1 D· do not act contrary to the
360-18 support the D· of The Mother Church,
360-20 supporting The Mother Church D·.

Directors'
Man. 68- 6 without the D· consent

directors'
Pul. 25–11 * "d· room," and the vestry.
      25–20 * "Mother's Room," and the d· room.
      27– 3 * d· room is very beautiful

directory
Mis. 363–29 the wise man's d·.

directs
Mis. 117–31 Be sure that God d· your way;
My. 143– 2 Watch and pray that God d· your
      231–14 as God, not man, d·.

direful
Mis. 241–16 by constant combat and d· struggles,
Pul.   2–15 d· scenes of the war

dirge
Mis. 400– 7 D· and song and shoutings low
Pul. 16–19 D· and song and shoutings low,
Po.   76–18 D· and song and shoutings low
My. 189–27 the song and the d·,
      326–18 in long procession with tender d·

dirty
Mis. 329– 9 various apartments are dismally d·.

disabilities
Mis. 185– 7 abilities or d·, pains or pleasures.

disable
My.   4– 5 dishonesty, sin, d· the student;

disadvantage
Mis. 156–15 I saw no advantage, but great d·,

disaffection
Mis. 337–18 consequent d· for all evil,

disaffections
Mis. 265–27 questions and d· toward C. S.

disagree
Mis. 81– 7 agree to d·, and then patiently
      243–25 Even doctors d· on that
      327–16 encumbered travellers halt and d·.
      345–16 even infidels may d·.
No.   45–22 we should agree to d·;
'02.   2–25 at least agree to d·, in love,
Peo. 13–24 infidels d·; for Bonaparte said:

disagreement
Man. 66– 7 a doubt or d· shall arise
Un.   41–28 implies perpetual d· with Spirit.
'02. 12– 4 cancels the d·, and settles the

disagreements
My. 286– 8 National d· can be, and

disallowed
My.   17– 9 d· indeed of men, — I Pet. 2: 4.

disappear
Mis. 28– 1 and the stone itself would d·,
       41–24 the effect or disease will d·
       72–19 do they d· only to the natural sense?
      165–16 eternal, appears — never to d·.
      166–26 and all materialism d·.
      198–17 the temptation will d·.
      217–30 matter must d·, for Spirit to appear.
      290–10 whatever is false should d·.
      361– 9 When every form and mode of evil d·
      367– 9 will d· in the proportion that
      395–16 Quickly earth's jewels d·;
Un.   60–23 Without Him, the universe would d·,
No.   16–23 sin, sickness, and death — d·
       17–23 would d·, and the eternal, infinite
       20–17 and the notion . . . will d·.
Pan.   6– 3 will never d· in any other way.
Hea.   9–14 Contending for . . . what should d·
       18– 5 mortality shall d· and immortality be
Peo.   1–17 Even the pangs of death d·,
Po.   58– 1 Quickly earth's jewels d·;
My. 197–18 else C. S. will d· from
      260– 8 the inaccuracy of . . . would d·.

disappearance
Mis. 68– 4 means more than mere d·
      271– 3 the point of its d· as matter

disappeared
Mis. 165– 3 spiritual idea . . . . d· by degrees;
Un.   63– 6 never d· to spiritual sense,

disappearing
Mis. 338– 2 involves the d· of evil.
Un.   63– 8 appearing, d·, and reappearing
My. 266–27 agitated, modified, and d·,

disappears
Mis. 165–15 The material corporeality d·;
      205–27 mortal man d· forever.
Ret. 33–18 d· in the higher attenuations of
       73– 7 as the fleshly nature d·
Un.   9– 3 and the disease itself d·.
        9– 4 and sin itself d·.

disappears
Un.   35– 7 Destroy the belief, and the quality d·.
       50–27 as the history of man, d·,
       57– 5 as this sense d· it foresees the
       62–15 Destroy this sense of sin, and sin d·.
No.   38–19 and material incumbrance d·.
Pan.   6– 7 continue to fight it until it d·,
'01. 13–20 destroy the fear . . . and sin d·.
      13–29 sin d·, and its unreality is proven.
Hea. 12–24 drug d· by your process
My.   25–26 all vanity of victory d·
      232–24 material error finally d·,

disappointed
Mis. 316–21 aphorisms and d· ethics;
      322– 7 People . . . are frequently d·.
'02. 11– 3 d· travellers, tossed to and fro
My. 229–28 my d· hope and grateful joy.

disappointment
Mis. ix–12 joy, sorrow, hope, d·,
      274–11 Deeply regretting the d·
My. 142– 4 * has only abolished the d·

disappointments
My.   43–10 * suffered defeats and met with d·,

disapprove
Mis. 109– 4 as authority for what I d·,

disapproves
Man. 82– 2 d· of certain books
My. 240–18 approves or d· according to

disarm
Mis. 134–27 can neither silence nor d· God's
      162–31 to d· the Goliath.
'02. 19– 4 and to d· their fears.

disarmed
Mis. 67–23 discerned, d·, and destroyed.
My. 364– 9 are d· by the practitioner who

disarrangement
Pan.   8– 2 it follows that the d· of matter

disastrous
Mis.   9–31 more d· to human progress
Man. 71–14 such position would be d· to C. S.

disastrously
Mis. 31– 4 a manner that can d· affect

disband
My. 216–22 that from this date you d·

disbelief
My.   95–22 * their d· in the miraculous.
      297–16 blessing of d· in death,

disbelieves
Mis. 223–14 individual d· in Mind-healing,

disbursal
My. 217–11 This d· will take place when the

disbursed
My. 217–10 on interest till it is d·

disbursements
My.   14–30 * keep pace with the d·.

disc
Pul. 25–30 * There is a d· of cut glass in

discern
Mis.   1– 7 d· the face of the — Matt. 16: 3.
        1– 8 d· the signs of — Matt. 16: 3.
        2– 1 d· the power of Truth and Love
       49–20 to d· between the real and the
       54– 1 carnal mind cannot d· spiritual
       57– 4 that which you admit cannot d·
       66–17 to d· God's perfect ways
       73– 8 once d· their spiritual meaning,
       77– 7 d· and consent to that infinite
       87–10 what I now through you d·
      103–25 so far as material sense could d·
      109–26 must d· the nothingness of evil,
      117– 5 d· between the thought, motive, and
      131– 5 in order rightly to d· darkness
      185– 3 shall be able to d· fully
      188–28 that we can d· more of them.
      223–12 sufficiently strong to d· what
      287–16 until progress lifts mortals to d·
      347– 9 d· the face of the skies
      347–10 cannot always d· the mental signs
      352– 6 able for the first time to d·
      355–23 then thou wilt d· the error
Un.   62–27 Mary had risen to d· faintly
No.   23–20 need to d· the claims of evil,
       34–12 who d· his true merit,
'00.   9– 2 I d· that this obedience is
My.   45–23 * we now d· the fulfilment of
      114– 1 d· the signs of — Matt. 16: 3.
      244–12 need of which I daily d·.

di

DISCUSSIONS

d· for you divine Science,

d·,
...Science :
My. 51–21 ...must be used
and his own spiritual *d·*,
My. 22–21 * spiritual *d·* of the needs of
206– 9 they darken the *d·* of Science ;

discerns
Un. 61–27 contrite heart earnest *d·* this

discharge
Hea. 1– 8 not *d·* from care ;

discharged
No. 8–11 Having *d·* this duty,
My. 119–21 *d·* evidence of material sense

discharges
'02. 10–21 *d·* burdensome baggage,

disciple
Mis. 28–15 proved to his doubting *d·*,
151– 2 In the words of the loving *d·*,
Pul. 32– 1 * as that of a Delsarte *d·*;
'00. 6–23 meek and loving *d·* of Christ,
'01. 28–24 enough for the *d·* — *Matt.* 10 : 25.
My. 44–11 * faithful *d·* rejoices in prophecy
113– 8 not an immediate *d·* of our Lord,
113–17 not a *d·* of the personal Jesus
119–18 doubting *d·* could not identify
229–18 cannot be my *d·*.'' — *Luke* 14 : 27.
244–21 In the highest sense of a *d·*,

disciples (*see also* disciples')
and prophets
Mis. 84– 7 *d·* and prophets thrust disputed
dark
Mis. 360–28 to sensitive ears and dark *d·*,
deserving
My. 46–20 * faithful, obedient, deserving *d·*.
dull
Mis. 100– 2 artless listeners and dull *d·*.
163–11 to arrant hypocrite and to dull *d·*
337–27 to itching ears and to dull *d·*
first
My. 347–17 our great Master's first *d·*,
her
My. 48–20 * has given to her *d·* a means of
his
Mis. 54–26 *healing as Jesus and his d· did,*
90–25 administered to his *d·* the Passover,
90–29 after his *d·* had left their nets
212–31 His *d·*, who had not yet drunk
274– 1 history of Jesus and of his *d·*,
344– 4 the wish to become one of his *d·*.
Ret. 90– 7 towns whither he sent his *d·* ;
Pul. 52–20 * practised by Jesus and his *d·*.
'00. 10–16 of Jesus and his *d·*.
'01. 18–12 and taught his *d·* none other.
18–18 Jesus and his *d·* would have
23–19 and taught his *d·* and followers
'02. 18– 9 self-seeking of his *d·*
18–25 ignoble conduct of his *d·*
18–28 all his *d·* save one.
My. 150–27 our Master said unto his *d·*,
156–11 directed his *d·* to prepare
180– 7 taught his *d·* the healing
190–22 Jesus gave his *d·* (students)
222– 7 When his *d·* asked him
339–24 Jesus said to his *d·*,

disciples
immediate
Mis. 29– 5 only to his immediate *d·*,
Ret. 91–16 primarily to his immediate *d·*.
Jesus'
'01. 2–21 Jesus' *d·* of old experienced,
met together
Mis. 279–22 picture is of the *d·* met together
Mrs. Eddy's
Pul. 68–14 * chapter sub-title
my
My. 156–16 passover with my *d·* ? — *Luke* 22 : **11.**
339–20 My *d·* rejoice in their
of Christian Science
Pul. 41– 6 * love-offerings of the *d·* of C. S.
of Jesus
My. 222– 2 even the *d·* of Jesus once failed
of Mary Baker Eddy
Pul. 52–13 * of the *d·* of Mary Baker Eddy,
of old
'01. 2–21 Jesus' *d·* of old experienced,
My. 212–19 Being like the *d·* of old,
of St. John
My. 339–17 *d·* of St. John the Baptist said
thy
My. 339–19 thy *d·* fast not?'' — *Matt.* 9 : 14.
true
Mis. 171–18 By these signs are the true *d·*

Mis. 279–26 the *d·*, too, were of one mind.
Ret. 76–21 the *d·* were of one accord.

disciples'
'02. 7–27 called his *d·* special attention

discipleship
My. 188–30 be God-endowed for *d·*.

discipline
Mis. 6– 2 *d·* to bring man nearer to God,
84–23 *d·* of the flesh is designed to
Man. 33– 3 to enforce the *d·* and by-laws of
33– 7 Rules, and *d·* of the Church.
40– 1 heading
41–16 renders this member liable to *d·*
46–18 subject the offender to Church *d·*.
46–22 on penalty of *d·*
51–15 No Church *d·* shall ensue until
51–21 Board of Directors has power to *d·*,
52– 2 involving The Mother Church *d·*,
55– 6 and independently *d·* its own
67– 2 not to be consulted on cases of *d·*,
Ret. 77– 1 for laxity in *d·* and
80–15 receptive of the heavenly *d·*.
'00. 8–13 till God's *d·* takes it off
My. 343–27 had five churches under *d·*.
359– 8 not to interfere in cases of *d·*,

disciplined
Man. 37– 6 member who . . . shall be *d·*.
43– 1 A member . . . shall be *d·*,
54–22 shall immediately be *d·*,

disclaim
Mis. 174– 3 claiming to talk and *d·* against

disclaimer
My. 150–30 or the *d·* against God

disclaims
Ret. 56–15 Divine Science *d·* sin,

disclose
My. 224–13 the future must *d·* and dispel.

discomfited
Pul. 71–14 * startled and greatly *d·*

discomfort
Mis. 219–21 a sense of *d·* in sin
My. 233–11 Is not *d·* from sin

discomforted
Mis. 241–30 sick who are dis-eased, *d·*,

discomforts
My. 75–22 * *d·* they might have endured

disconnected
Ret. 93–11 is not fragmentary, *d·*,

disconsolate
Mis. 262–17 and hope to the *d·* ;

discontent
Mis. 332– 7 * long winter of our *d·*.''
My. 195–19 deep *d·* with our shortcomings.

discontinue
Hea. 9–12 subjects they would gladly *d·* to

discontinued
Ret. 47–15 voted that the school be *d·*.
My. 51–12 * to have the public services *d·*
141–22 * these gatherings will be *d·* :

discord
Mis.	40–17	*d·* of whatever sort.
	65– 3	no more proof of human *d·*,
	97– 4	destroy mortal *d·* with immortal
	187– 8	*d·*, as seen in disease and death,
	187–11	and *d·* the unreality.
	187–27	extinguished in a night of *d·*.
	236–24	the remedy for all human *d·*.
	247–27	and reflects harmony or *d·*
	265–18	whose minds . . . disturbed by this *d·*,
	283–28	good, not evil, — harmony, not *d·* ;
	287– 8	To an ill-attuned ear, *d·* is harmony ;
Ret.	57– 8	for the purpose of destroying *d·*.
	69– 5	parent of all human *d·*
Un.	2–19	contains neither *d·* nor disease.
	13– 8	principle . . . knows nothing of *d·*.
	18–21	every supposition of *d·*.
Rud.	9– 5	the seeds of *d·* and disease.
	13–20	and *d·* is the unreal,
No.	16– 4	and *d·* must be eternal.
'00.	11– 3	have no *d·* over music.
Peo.	9–27	destroys *d·* with the higher and
Po.	70–16	*d·* ne'er in harmony began !
My.	90–15	* that *d·* is poisonous,

discordant
Mis.	396– 5	cricket's sharp, *d·* scream
Peo.	10–22	harmonious or *d·* according to
Po.	58–17	cricket's sharp, *d·* scream

discords
Mis.	105– 3	*d·* of this material personality.
	202– 3	correct the *d·* of sense,
No.	10–22	earth's *d·* have not the reality
'02.	9–13	Loving chords set *d·* in harmony.
My.	223– 7	any class of individual *d·*.

discount
Rud.	14–18	No *d·* on tuition was made

discountenanced
'00.	13–26	* *d·* by the authorities of

discounts
Mis.	274–18	it *d·* clemency, mocks morality,

discourage
Pul.	43–27	* *d·* . . . that sort of personal worship

discouraged
Ret.	8–11	continued until I grew *d·*,

discouragement
My.	48–24	* with the *d·* of care and worry,

discouraging
My.	50–18	* apparently *d·* outlook of the

discourse
Mis.	149– 9	has opened his lips to *d·*
	178–10	* delivered an interesting *d·*
Pul.	29–19	* In his admirable *d·* Judge Hanna
	29–24	* *d·* was able, and helpful
My.	155–23	May those who *d·* music to-day,
	296– 2	able *d·* of our "learned judge,"

discourses
Mis.	126– 2	from fragmentary *d·* to one

discoursing
My.	339– 8	wise in *d·* on the great subject

discourteous
My.	327–22	* did not wish to be "*d·*

discover
Mis.	380–14	had driven me to *d·* the Science of
Un.	50–26	you will *d·* the material origin,

discovered
Mis.	34–30	*d·* the Science of healing
	54– 5	Who is it that *d·*, demonstrated,
	75–26	she *d·* the spiritual origin of man.
	165–29	secret stores of wisdom must be *d·*,
	188–21	found it, when she *d·* C. S.
	337– 1	Have I *d·* and founded at this period
	370–23	What manner of man . . . has *d·* an
	379–27	I *d·*, in 1866, the momentous facts
	380–10	to demonstrate what I had *d·* :
	382–12	I *d·* the Science of Christianity
Ret.	24– 4	I *d·* the Science of divine
Un.	30–21	When I *d·* the power of Spirit
Pul.	64–14	* she *d·* C. S. in 1866.
	70– 3	* chapter sub-title
Pan.	5– 3	Can . . . be *d·* in matter?
'01.	27–29	* say it has been *d·* before.
Hea.	12–10	*d·* that all physical effects
My.	v–14	* Mary Baker Eddy *d·* C. S.
	41–27	* not only *d·* C. S., but
	61–29	* As I *d·* the many intricate
	67–13	* C. S. *d·* . . . 1866
	103–19	just as I have *d·* them.
	133–29	even as your heart has *d·* it.
	181–21	C. S. was *d·* in America.
	304–27	* say it has been *d·* before.

dis-covered
Mis.	334–28	an

Discoverer
(see **Eddy***)*

discoverer
Mis.	381–32	both foun
My.	143–18	the *d·* of a
	338–25	visible *d·*, f

(see also **Eddy***)*

discoverers
Mis.	244–30	Are the *d·* of qu

discoveries
Mis.	244–32	because of their m
No.	39–21	new and scientific
	41–22	by new *d·* of Truth
My.	71– 2	* intricate *d·* of organ
	237– 9	in his earliest studies

discovering
Pul.	35–24	* *d·* that the more atten

discovers
Mis.	352– 9	when it *d·* the truth,

discovery
Mis.	22– 9	the *d·* of even a portion of
	121–10	up to a point of *d·* ;
	188–29	At the moment of her
	263–25	by the infancy of its *d·*, and *d·*,
	263–28	to appropriate my ide C. S.,
	297– 2	elapsed since the *d·* by the *d·* of C. S.
	310– 6	amplified in this C. S.,
	379–29	and named m of this Science.
	382– 4	prior to my ounding of C. S.
	382– 6	The *d·* a d of C. S.
Ret.	10–11	After came to pass in this way.
	24– 6	Th uring twenty years prior to my *d·*
	24– 8	the *d·* how to be well myself,
	24–1	*d·* of the Science of being
	26–2	divine Science must be a *d·*.
	26–23	*d·* of the absolute Science o
	27– 7	I had not fully voiced my *d·*.
	27–13	
Pul.	55–16	* Her *d·* was first called,
'01.	27– 1	experience, and final *d·*,
'02.	9–25	Morse's *d·* of telegraphy?
Peo.	7–27	Scientific *d·* and the inspiration of
My.	66–28	* Since the *d·* by Mrs. Eddy,
	91–20	* a *d·* of Mary Baker Eddy
	105– 7	After my *d·* of C. S.,
	120–10	Bear with me the burden of *d·*
	151–26	thus missing the *d·* of all cause
	181–32	first two years of my *d·* of C. S.
	214–19	Four years after my *d·* of C. S.
	238–13	*d·*, and presentation of C. S.
	296–29	gave her *d·* to the press.
	348– 1	My *d·* that mankind is absolutely
	348–15	was based upon her *d·* that

discredit
Mis.	223–13	and to say, if it must, "I *d·*
'02.	1–15	calculated to displace or *d·*

discrepancy
Man.	104–17	if a *d·* appears in any
Un.	29–18	herein lies the *d·* between

discretion
Mis.	287–32	venturing on valor without *d·*,
Man.	96– 5	left to the *d·* of the lecturer.

discriminate
Mis.	302–11	*d·* between error and Truth,
My.	250–21	*d·* as regards its adaptability

discriminates
Mis.	119–23	*d·* between the real and the unreal
'01.	5–11	*d·* between God and man,

discriminating
Un.	57–14	His pure consciousness was *d·*,

discriminations
No.	7–26	*d·* and guidance thereof

discussed
Man.	90–23	thoroughly *d·*, and understood ;
My.	271–15	* most *d·* woman in all the world.

discussing
'01.	22–23	schools of medicine are *d·* them

discussion
Ret.	49–27	deliberation and earnest *d·*
Un.	6–23	provoked *d·* and horror,
My.	107– 7	general subject under *d·*,

discussions
Man.	26–25	shall neither report the *d·* of
Un.	1–14	in their *d·* of C. S.

disdain

Mis. 105– 3   *d·* the fears and destroy the discords
    389–15   hope deferred, ingratitude, *d·* !
Po.   4–14   hope deferred, ingratitude, *d·* !

disdainfully

My. 129–18   O ye who leap *d·* from this rock

disease

acute
Mis.   41–23   belief of chronic or acute *d·*,
all
Un.   9– 1   mortal mind is the cause of all *d·*.
No.   4–26   All *d·* must be . . . healed on this
My. 204–30   its therapeutics, . . . heals all *d·*.
    218–10   to destroy all *d·* and to raise the
all classes of
Mis.   41–18   *Can all classes of d· be healed*
all manner of
Ret.   60–18   saith to all manner of *d·*,
My. 239–10   by healing all manner of *d·*,
    245– 1   system of healing all manner of *d·*,
and death
Mis.   14–31   sin, sickness, *d·*, and death.
    36–21   includes all evil, *d·*, and death ;
    187– 3   sin, sickness, *d·*, and death.
    187– 8   discord, as seen in *d·* and death,
    194– 4   *d·*, and death are destroyed ;
No.   6– 9   sickness, *d·*, and death.
Pan. 10–27   no necessity for *d·* and death.
My. 172–24   cast out evil, *d·*, and death ;
    180–16   sin, sickness, *d·*, and death.
    240–17   it criticizes evil, *d·*, and death
and sin
Mis.   60– 9   healing cases of *d·* and sin
    105–16   opposites — death, *d·*, and sin.
    336–23   heals *d·* and sin and destroys death !
No.   31– 6   *D·* and sin appear to-day in subtler
    31– 8   *d·* and sin are unreal,
any
Mis.   54–23   not to be subject again to any *d·*
    229– 3   prepares one to have any *d·*
arises
No.   5– 9   *D·* arises from a false and material
becomes
Un.   54– 6   then *d·* becomes as tangible as
No.   5–20   *D·* becomes indeed a stubborn
belief in
Mis. 256– 2   not only cured of their belief in *d·*,
belief of
Mis. 198–20   belief of *d·* is as much the product of
beliefs of
Mis.   93– 6   *beliefs of d· that have been healed*
bring back
Mis.   93–22   neither . . . can . . . bring back *d·*,
bring on
Mis.   93–22   neither fear nor sin can bring on *d·*
cannot cause
My. 349– 7   the body, cannot cause *d·*,
cast out
Mis.   6– 4   Jesus cast out *d·* as evil.
cast out the
Mis.   40–21   power to cast out the *d·*.
cause of
Mis.   66–29   Ignorance of the cause of *d·*
    221–18   If error is the cause of *d·*,
consciousness of
Mis. 308–26   holding . . . the consciousness of *d·*
contagious
Mis. 229–20   confidence . . . in contagious *d·*
My. 116– 2   At a time of contagious *d·*,
controls
Hea.   6–19   when he is sick, *d·* controls
cure of
Pul. 69–26   * prayed for the cure of *d·*,
Rud.   3– 1   harder than the cure of *d·* ;
    3–19   He wrought the cure of *d·* through
cures of
Pul.   45– 6   * they can effect cures of *d·*
cures the
Peo.   6–13   * says : . . . nature cures the *d·*.''
deathly
Pul. 73– 7   * cured herself of a deathly *d·*
destroy
My. 132–24   will also rebuke and destroy *d·*,
    301–28   or destroy *d·* without the aid of
diagnoses
Hea. 12– 8   he diagnoses *d·* as mind,
discord and
Rud.   9– 5   seeds of discord and *d·*.
discord nor
Un.   2–19   contains neither discord nor *d·*.
dread
My. 335–19   * the second case of the dread *d·*
effect or
Mis.   41–24   the effect or *d·* will disappear

disease

eradicate
No.   31– 1   you cannot eradicate *d·* if you
every case of
Mis.   44–10   heal in every case of *d·*,
evidence for
No.   6–19   as . . . real as the evidence for *d·* ;
evidence of
No.   6–13   error indicates, the evidence of *d·*
evil and
Mis. 221–25   struggle against both evil and *d·*,
Un.   37–16   Evil and *d·* do not testify of
Pan.   6– 1   His treatment of evil and *d·*,
    6– 3   because evil and *d·* will never
fear or
Ret. 61– 5   different forms of fear or *d·*.
feasibility of
No.   4–13   destroys the feasibility of *d·* ;
feel
Mis. 234– 1   feel *d·* only by reason of our belief
forms of
No.   2–23   the most defiant forms of *d·*.
heal
My. 117–11   heal *d·*, and make one a
    180–18   overcome evil and heal *d·*.
    300– 9   Does he . . . thus heal *d·* ?
    300–11   heal *d·*, for the reason that
healed
No.   31–19   He healed *d·* as he healed sin ;
healed of
My. 113– 5   and thereby is healed of *d·*.
healed of the
Mis.   34– 5   not only healed of the *d·*,
healing
Mis.   33–22   *ordinary methods of healing d·?*
    51– 3   effect physically . . . healing *d·*.
My. 190–20   divine laws . . . in healing *d·*,
    302– 1   all modes of healing *d·*
healing of
Mis.   63–14   to the healing of *d·*,
health nor
My. 302– 6   life nor death, health nor *d·*,
health, not
My. 239– 1   Life, not death ; health, not *d·* ;
heart
My.   80– 6   * been cured . . . of heart *d·*,
his
Ret. 34–18   not only healed of his *d·*, but
idea about a
My. 344–19   harbored that idea about a *d·*,
in error
Mis.   85–29   *D·* in error, more than ease
insidious
Ret. 19– 9   attacked by this insidious *d·*,
My. 334– 3   * some insidious *d·* was raging
in the body
Mis. 343– 5   turn from *d·* in the body
in the mortal mind
Mis. 343– 6   to find *d·* in the mortal mind,
intruding
My. 221–29   open to the intruding *d·*,
is more
No.   4– 6   *D·* is more than *imagination* ;
is treated
Hea. 14– 4   until *d·* is treated mentally
is unreal
Rud. 12–28   in Science, *d·* is unreal ;
No.   4–16   proposition, . . . that *d·* is unreal ;
itself
Mis.   40–31   nullify either the *d·* itself or
Un.   9– 2   the *d·* itself disappears.
its own
Mis.   62–31   notion that . . . can cure its own *d·*.
loaded with
Mis.   7–18   so loaded with *d·* seems the
malignant
My. 227–15   taking a case of malignant *d·*.
material
Rud. 10–12   of material *d·* and mortality.
medium of
Hea.   6–19   thinks he is a medium of *d·* ;
mental
Mis. 112–24   This mental *d·* at first shows
more
No.   2–15   I have healed more *d·* by the
named
No.   4–10   error of belief, named *d·*,
name of the
Man. 47–20   the generic name of the *d·*
names
My. 228– 3   S. and H. names *d·*,
no
Mis.   93–23   since there is in reality no *d·*.
    334–14   since there is no *d·* ?

disease

no
Un. 7–10 the infinite recognizes no *d·*,
My. 297–15 in reality no evil, no *d·*,
nor death
Mis. 165–14 darkness, doubt, *d·*, nor death.
one
Hea. 13–26 Mesmerism makes one *d·* while it
on the body
Hea. 6–13 mind produces *d·* on the body,
origin of
Hea. 19–11 The illusive origin of *d·*
pain and
Mis. 68–10 * maintained that pain and d· are not
68–15 is the very pain and *d·*.
Rud. 11–14 the unreality of pain and *d·* ;
pain or
Rud. 10–14 see, or report pain or *d·*.
power of
Mis. 58– 9 belief in the power of *d·*
present
Mis. 38–28 in order to cure his present *d·*,
producing
My. 302– 2 vehicle . . . of producing *d·*.
propagation of
My. 344–17 * theory of the propagation of *d·?"*
regarding
Mis. 130–13 acting thus regarding *d·*
return of the
Mis. 54–21 return of the *d·* that you were
said to
No. 31–25 but Jesus said to *d·* :
same
My. 227–11 patients, having the same *d·*
seizure of
My. 336–16 * seizure of *d·* was so sudden
sense of
Ret. 61–24 If you rule out every sense of *d·*
Rud. 12– 7 strengthen the sense of *d·*, instead of
sense of the
Un. 9– 2 Destroy the mental sense of the *d·*,
sickness and
Pul. 73– 2 * worry . . . about sickness and *d·?*
Peo. 7–24 To remove . . . sickness and *d·*,
My. 364–16 heals all manner of sickness and *d·*,
sickness or
My. 300– 9 there is no sickness or *d·*,
sickness, . . . or death
Mis. 65– 4 sin, sickness, *d·*, or death,
sin and
Mis. 101–25 evil, including sin and *d·*.
No. 4–19 Sin and *d·* are not scientific,
My. 147–21 able to heal both sin and *d·*
221–20 with which to heal sin and *d·*.
sin, and death
Un. 10– 1 unreality of *d·*, sin, and death,
My. 106–19 expressed in *d·*, sin, and death,
sin, . . . and death
(see sin)
sin or
Mis. 191–30 phases of sin or *d·* made manifest.
sin, . . . or death
My. 146–27 the side of sin, *d·*, or death.
sin, sickness, and
Mis. 251–29 Sin, sickness, and *d·* flee before
smites with
Mis. 257–28 pitiless power smites with *d·*
so-called
My. 228– 4 so-called *d·* is a sensation of mind,
348– 2 absolutely healed of so-called *d·*
spread
My. 336– 3 * The *d·* spread so rapidly
storms of
'01. 24–13 when the storms of *d·* beat against
subject to
Mis. 39– 4 To avoid being subject to *d·*,
terrible
My. 335–25 * attended cases of this terrible *d·*
that
Mis. 58– 2 and he has no remembrance of that *d·*
58– 2 does that *d·* have any more power
their
Ret. 25–30 as to their *d·* or its symptoms,
'01. 33–11 * was not the health . . . but their *d·*,
to rob
No. 2– 9 scientific to rob *d·* of all reality ;
treat
Mis. 334–13 Why do Christian Scientists treat *d·*
treating
Mis. 35– 9 mental system of treating *d·*.
65–18 the right way of treating *d·?*
97–14 all other methods of treating *d·*.
368–18 Science of treating *d·* through Mind.
Hea. 14– 4 at the science of treating *d·*

disease

treatment of
Hea. 14–21 the metaphysical treatment of *d·* ;
My. 103–19 application to the treatment of *d·*
treatment of a
My. 204–23 The too long treatment of a *d·*,
unreal
No. 4– 5 chapter sub-title
13– 3 makes *d·* unreal, and this heals it.
worse than the
My. 118– 7 remedy is worse than the *d·*.

———

Mis. 23– 9 *d·*, death, winds, and waves,
27–12 inharmony, sin, *d·*, death
58– 9 belief . . . destroyed, *d·* cannot return.
66–23 *D·* that is superinduced by sin
181–26 *d·*, sickness, sin, and death
198–18 *d·* also is treated and healed.
228–28 and it makes *d·* catching.
334–13 Why . . . treat disease as *d·*,
Pul. 69–10 * believing that *d·* comes from evil
Rud. 10–15 *D·* is a thing of thought
11–11 What seem to be *d·*, vice, and
No. 2– 6 To aver that *d·* is normal,
2–12 healers who admit that *d·* is real
5– 5 and *d·* is one of the severe
5–18 If *d·* is as real as health,
6– 1 If *d·* is real it is not illusive,
6–14 If, . . . then *d·* cannot be healed by
Peo. 11– 6 can free its body from *d·*
My. v–25 * has healed multitudes of *d·*
139–27 redeem your body from *d·* ;
217–19 * deny the existence of *d·*
217–21 deny first the existence of *d·*,
219–14 the destruction of *d·* germs.
228– 1 I call *d·* by its name and have
288–21 cast out evil, *d·*, death,
300–11 do not believe in the reality of *d·*,
349– 5 while *d·* is a mental state
349– 8 *d·* is in a sense susceptible of

dis-ease

Mis. 219–18 his patient's consciousness of *d·*
'01. 15–20 *d·* in sin is better than ease.
My. 233–11 should we prefer, ease or *d·* in sin?
349– 9 susceptible of both ease and *d·*,

diseased

Ret. 40–14 *d·* condition was caused by
78– 1 acts like a *d·* physique,
Rud. 13–21 according to their own belief is *d·*,
15–12 advising *d·* people not to enter a
My. 106–18 overcomes the evidence of *d·*
218– 1 He restored the *d·* body to its

dis-eased

Mis. 241–30 the sick who are *d·*,
Un. 58– 3 must become *d·*, disquieted,

diseases

acute
Mis. 29–22 chronic and acute *d·* that had defied
Pan. 10–19 acute *d·* that M.D.'s have failed to
all manner of
'01. 2– 5 Science of healing all manner of *d·*.
24–27 healing all manner of *d·*.
34– 3 in the healing of all manner of *d·*.
'02. 15– 6 Healing all manner of *d·* without
My. 190–23 power over all manner of *d·* ;
214–21 and for healing all manner of *d·*,
219–18 healing, . . . all manner of *d·*.
contagious
Mis. 228–30 in infectious and contagious *d·*,
My. 219–28 so-called infectious and contagious *d·*
226–30 to doctor infectious or contagious *d·*."
344–23 of infectious and contagious *d·*.
cures from
My. 79–28 * Scientists told of cures from *d·*,
healeth all our
Mis. 174– 8 and healeth all our *d·*.
imaginary
My. 106–12 limited to imaginary *d·* !
infectious
My. 344–21 * heading
inflammatory
My. 107–30 organic and inflammatory *d·*,
inveterate
Rud. 9–23 oftentimes healed inveterate *d·*.
My. 300–13 heals the most inveterate *d·*.
malignant
My. 227–32 a larger per cent of malignant *d·*
many
My. 90– 9 * has cured them of *d·* many
mysterious
Mis. 221–17 practitioners and mysterious *d·*.
of mortal mind
Rud. 10–13 *d·* of mortal mind, and not of

diseases

organic
My. 106– 1 in functional and organic d·
106– 7 organic d· of almost every kind.
190– 9 of contagious and organic d·?

other
Ret. 15–24 Among other d· cured

our
Mis. 102–21 and heals all our d·.
320–19 all our d· ;" — see Psal. 103 : 3.
My. 37– 1 * natural healer of all our d·

their
My. 28–27 * and healed them of their d·

thy
Mis. 184–13 healeth all thy d·." — Psal. 103 : 3.
Man. 47–17 healeth all thy d·." — Psal. 103 : 3.
Pul. 10– 7 healeth all thy d·." — Psal. 103 : 3.
Pan. 4–25 healeth all thy d·." — Psal. 103 : 3.
Peo. 12–14 healeth all thy d·." — Psal. 103 : 3.
My. 13–20 healeth all thy d· ;— Psal. 103 : 3.
119–17 "healeth all thy d·" — Psal. 103 : 3.

venereal
Mis. 210–24 belief in venereal d· tears the

No. 23–12 these devils were the d·

disembodied
Mis. 205–19 d· individual Spirit-substance
Pul. 38–20 * between the embodied and d·

disengage
Mis. 344– 8 d· the soul from objects of sense,

disgorging
My. 82–10 * d· trunks and smaller articles

disgrace
Mis. 41– 5 malpractice would d· Mind-healing,
No. 43–23 which they go away to d·.

disgraces
Mis. 226–27 d· human nature more than

disguise
Pan. 11–22 whatever strips off evil's d·
'00. 15–13 awakened to see through sin's d·
My. 121–20 to d· internal vulgarity and

disguised
My. 180–24 the d· or the self-satisfied mind,

disguises
Mis. 210– 2 strips off its d·,

disgusted
Ret. 38–23 had grown d· with my printer,

disgusting
Mis. 233– 5 feverish, d· pride of those who

disheartened
Mis. 264– 4 will not be d· in the midst
325–13 Somewhat d·, he patiently
Pul. 83– 8 * will not be d· by a thousand

dishonest
Mis. 288–23 the shift of a d· mind,
Hea. 12–28 it would be d· and divide one's
My. 106–26 d· politician or business man?

dishonestly
Ret. 76– 6 he cannot d· compose C. S.

dishonesty
Mis. 190–26 honesty always defeats d·.
191– 1 "d·, craftiness, — see II Cor. 4 : 2.
267–18 conceit, cowardice, or d·.
366–27 d·, self-will, envy, and lust.
Ret. 75–20 d· retards spiritual growth
79–13 D·, envy, and mad ambition
No. 2–24 D· destroys one's ability to heal
3–19 D· necessarily stultifies
39– 8 no d· or vanity influences the
'01. 16–15 defines this world's god as d·,
'02. 4– 2 dishonor . . . d· in trusts,
My. 4– 5 d·, sin, disable the student ;
124– 1 hidden things of d·, — II Cor. 4 : 2.
203–16 D· is a mental malady
233–20 d·, sin, follow in its train.

dishonor
Mis. 194–10 denial would d· that office
236–10 restore harmony and prevent d·.
'01. 12–16 he would d· that office
'02. 4– 1 d· in nations, dishonesty

dishonored
Mis. 163– 6 a grave to mortal sense d·
Pul. 83– 4 * better self is shamed and d·,
No. 43–17 C. S. Mind-healing is d· by

dishonors
Mis. 367–14 it d· God to claim that He

disinterested
Ret. 50–11 I beg d· people to ask my

disk
Ret. 94–15 on the d· of consciousness

dislike
Mis. 336–13 d· and hatred of God's idea,

dislocated
Un. 7–14 able to replace d· joints

dislocations
Mis. 242– 7 reset certain d· without the

disloyal
Mis. 32– 4 the students of d· students?
Man. 36–16 are deceased, absent, or d·,
111–18 are deceased, absent, or d·,
'01. 20–11 he is d· to God and man ;
'02. 3– 2 ten thousand loyal . . . to one d·,
My. 130– 4 d· to the teachings of C. S.
130– 8 The effort of d· students
229– 3 nor d· Christian Scientist

dismal
Peo. 14– 6 d· gray stones of church-yards

dismally
Mis. 329– 9 various apartments are d· dirty.

dismayed
Mis. 278– 3 but I am not d·,
My. 294–16 faithful M.D. is not d· by a

dismiss
Man. 26–24 shall d· a member.
52–18 shall d· a member from the Church.
102– 8 This committee shall elect, d·, or

dismissal
Mis. 101– 6 and the d· of sorrow.
280–27 some questions before their d·,
Man. 28–23 his d· shall be written on the
41–17 d· from The Mother Church.
67– 4 on trial for d· from the Church.
My. 182– 5 letter of d· and recommendation

dismissed
Mis. 280–18 d· the fifth of March,
344–11 he was d· by the professor.
Man. 28–23 shall be d· from this Church,
39– 7 Members once D·.
78– 3 he may be d· from office
Un. 57–16 for it was detected and d·.

dismissing
Mis. 140– 7 on receiving or d· candidates.

disobedience
Mis. 267–29 d· to this divine Principle
Man. 28– 4 d· to the laws of The Mother Church
65–18 D· to this By-Law shall be
Un. 15– 1 by man's first d·, came
Rud. 10–21 d· to His spiritual law.
My. 224– 8 enforcing obedience and punishing d·.
224– 8 and the bane which follows d·.

disobedient
Mis. 117–29 The d· make their moves before
My. 118– 4 d· spread personal contagion,

disobey
Mis. 73–13 The foolish d· moral law,
208–16 and so d· the divine order.
353–31 criticise and d· her ;
354– 1 declaring they "never d· Mother" !

disobeying
My. 160–20 d· the commandments of God.

disordered
Mis. 210–19 begets a belief of d· brains,
375– 1 Pictures which present d· phases
My. 301–27 cannot . . . restore d· functions,

disorderly
My. 131–19 I hope I shall not be found d·,

disorganization
Mis. 50– 5 if . . . d· would destroy Spirit

disorganize
Mis. 137–19 D· the National . . . Association !
139– 2 adjourn, if it does not d·,
139– 3 if it does d·, to meet again
Un. 34– 1 D· the so-called material structure,

disowned
Un. 54–26 and d· its acquaintance,

disparagement
No. 29–15 Is not this a d· of the person

dispassionately
My. 249– 6 Meet d· the raging element of

dispel
Mis. 368– 4 d· this illusion of the senses,
My. 224–13 future must disclose and d·.

dispelled
Mis. 52–18 If this life is a dream not d·,
53– 3 false claim can be wholly d·.

dispelling
Mis. 190– 5 as d· a false sense
Un. 42–24 Science, d· a false sense

dispels
Mis. 205– 9 the light which d· darkness.
Un. 7–23 realization of this fact d· even

dispensation
Ret. 87–22 In this orderly, scientific d·
My. 110– 2 belongs not to a d· now ended,
221– 7 foresaw the new d· of Truth

dispense
Mis. ix– 5 * enable a man to d· with alms.''
My. 139–17 When I asked you to d· with

dispensing
Mis. 172– 3 D· the Word charitably,

dispersed
Po. vi–14 In 1835 a mob . . . d· a meeting

displace
Mis. 283– 7 unlock the desk, d· the furniture,
'02. 1–15 Whatever seems calculated to d·

displacing
Mis. 294– 5 and d· his fellows.

display
Man. 60–23 No large gathering of people nor d·

displayed
Mis. 66– 5 the genius whereof is d· in
Ret. 88–30 and its power is d·

displays
Mis. 142– 9 boat d·, among other beautiful

displeasure
Pul. 15– 9 and so risk human d·

disporting
Mis. 112– 1 d· itself with the subtleties of

disposal
Man. 80– 4 D· of Funds.
My. 167–24 noble d· of the legislative question
281– 6 faith in God's d· of events.

dispose
My. 25– 3 * d· fully and finally of this feature

disposed
Mis. 4–14 questions important to be d· of
My. 93–19 * too often d· to touch upon it

disposer
Un. 26– 5 author, authority, governor, d·.

disposing
Mis. 381–24 d· of, the enjoined pamphlet,

disposition
Man. 80– 9 is authorized to order its d·
My. 211–26 spoiling that individual's d·,
310–27 often presented my d· as
311– 2 as illustrative of my d· :

dispositions
Un. 57– 1 d· which offend the spiritual sense.

dispossess
Pul. 3– 8 nothing can d· you of this
No. 42–12 to d· the divine Mind of

dispraise
Mis. 245–22 the praise or the d· of men.

disproof
Un. 47– 1 Jesus assumed the burden of d·

disprove
Mis. 101–29 d· the evidence of the senses.
My. 107–18 does not d· the efficiency of

disproved
My. 303–16 If . . . C. S. would be d· ;

dispute
Un. 25– 3 and d· self-evident facts ;
'02. 10– 7 and mortals . . . d· the facts,

disputed
Mis. 84– 7 prophets thrust d· points
Peo. 12– 9 d· and trampled under the feet
My. 111– 8 d· his teachings on practically

disputing
My. 285–21 in the temple d· with — Acts 24 : 12.

disqualifies
Man. 41–14 d· a member for office

disquieted
Un. 58– 3 must become dis-eased, d·,
Pan. 4–22 why art thou d· within — Psal. 42 : 11.

disregard
Mis. 301–18 my private counsel they d·.
Ret. 72– 3 To d· the welfare of others
My. 41–25 * d· his lawful inheritance,

disrespectfully
Man. 53– 9 to treat the author of our textbook d·

disrupt
Man. 93–20 to meddle with nor to d· the

disruption
Man. 93–18 No D· of Branch Churches.

dissected
Rud. 15–24 mind of the pupil may be d·

dissecting-knife
Un. 28– 6 nor cut with the d·.

dissension
My. 212–15 Why is there so much d·

dissensions
My. 343–27 D· are dangerous in an infant church.

dissent
Mis. 109– 3 assent where they should d· ;
Pul. 51– 4 * Freedom to believe or to d·
My. 94–12 * absence of d· among them
291– 6 a quiet assent or d·.

dissented
My. 317–19 d· from what I had written,

dissenting
Ret. 44–26 passing without a d· voice.

dissever
My. 306– 5 to d· any unity that may exist

dissimulation
Un. 56–26 Love which is without d·

dissolve
Mis. 70–23 d· into its native nothingness ;
291–23 will at length d· into thin air.
358–21 to d· their organizations,
Ret. 49–29 deemed best to d· this corporation,
87–26 such efficacy as to d· error.
Un. 60–28 must yield . . . and so d·.

dissolved
Mis. 53– 6 d· only as we master error
79– 2 beliefs will be purged and d·
297–23 or this contract is legally d·.
350–17 I d· the society,
364–25 impossible partnership is d·.
Man. 34–21 until that membership is d·.
102– 6 shall not be d· until the
Ret. 44–24 recommended that the church be d·.
49–30 and the same is hereby d·.

dissolves
Mis. 205–26 d· all supposed material life
361– 4 d· through self-imposed suffering,

dissolving
Mis. 1–17 from the ashes of d· self,
290– 9 Mistaken views ought to be d· views,
Ret. 45–18 when d· that organization,
Po. 24– 4 D· death, despair !

distance
Mis. x–15 as mile-stones measuring the d·,
79–14 he cannot get out of the focal d· of
120–21 members reside a long d· from
136–26 members coming from a d·
263–17 especially by those at a d·,
277– 7 its voice dies out in the d·.
322– 5 People coming from a d·
Ret. 65–28 magnitude and d· of the stars,
Un. 20–22 outside of His own focal d·.
Pul. 21–20 To perpetuate a cold d· between
36–17 * could have walked any conceivable d·.
47–23 * an easy driving d· for her
'02. 10–21 shortens the d·,
Po. 70– 2 In the dim d·, lay
My. 221– 2 moral d· between Christianity and
332– 1 * restore her to her friends at a d·

distanced
Mis. 297– 3 has d· all other religious

distances
My. 142– 5 * communicants who come long d·
170–27 some of you have come long d·

distant
Mis. 6–14 At no d· day, Christian healing
347– 3 d· rumbling and quivering of the
Pul. 41–15 * and even from the d· States
No. 20– 9 it may seem d· or cold,
Pan. 1–17 day is not d· in the horizon of
Po. 31– 8 tear-filled tones of d· joy,
My. 30–12 * come from far d· points
47–21 * rooted itself in so many d· lands,
59– 6 * true in some far d· day
140–15 * need not debar d· members from
140–26 does not prevent its d· members
147– 8 And now, at this d· day,
189– 8 You worship no d· deity,
290– 4 the near seems afar, the d· nigh,
327–29 * not far d·, when the laws

distilled
Mis.	278– 2	are the d· spirits of evil,
Pul.	8–25	d· the nectar and painted the
My.	178– 9	d· in the laboratory of

distinct
Mis.	32–25	D· denominational and social
Ret.	34– 8	or give me one d· statement
	59–21	define Mind and matter as d·,
Un.	54–22	d· addition to human wisdom,
Pul.	47–14	* gave her any d· statement of
	64–19	* gave her no d· statement of
My.	179– 3	were in two d· manuscripts.
	197– 3	is least d· to conscience.
	203– 6	should be d· in our consciousness

distinction
Mis.	36–19	What is the d· between
	203– 3	I make no d· between my
	227–10	is the nice d· by which
	257– 6	d· between that which
Ret.	3–11	won d· in 1814 at the
Rud.	1–17	in d· from one's appearance
'02.	2– 4	without clamor for d· or
My.	87–11	* visitors of title and d·,
	203– 7	not clamorous for worldly d·.
	343–15	I have sought no such d·.

distinctions
Un.	27–12	Applying these d· to evil and
No.	7–25	d· of individual character

distinctive
'00.	13–10	d· feature the apostle justly regards
My.	100–12	* as a d· organization

distinctly
Man.	32–13	d· announce the full title
	74– 7	d· democratic in its government,
Ret.	8– 4	calling me d· by name,
	14–14	D· do I recall what followed.
Un.	17–13	Jesus d· taught the arrogant
Pul.	33– 5	* heard her name called d·,
My.	39–27	* even more d· may we realize

distinguish
Ret.	74– 5	fails to d· the individual,
Un.	14–28	learning to d· evil from good,

distinguished
Mis.	68–25	* d· from that of matter,
	68–29	* d· from its phenomenal modifications."
	164– 3	incorporeal and . . . are d· thus :
	168–29	* The d· speaker began by saying :
	372–30	the ancient and most d· artists.
Ret.	5–21	* d· for numerous excellences.
	7–14	* made himself one of the most d· men
Pul.	1– 8	1893 was a d· character,
	43–11	* Mrs. Henrietta Clark Bemis, a d·
	48–19	* Hon. Hoke Smith, another d· relative,
No.	42–25	A d· clergyman came to be healed.
	43–10	A d· Doctor of Divinity said :
'00.	7– 9	d· members of the bar and bench,
	14–29	being told they are d· individuals,
	15– 4	d· above human title
'01.	31–24	with d· Christian clergymen,
My.	105–20	the patient of a d· M.D.,
	174–10	d· editors in my home city
	298– 7	has d· all my working years.
	305–13	best and most d· men
	310– 4	Albert was a d· lawyer.
	335–24	* sent for the d· physician

distinguishes
Pul.	69–13	* He d· C. S. from the
My.	225–14	capitalization which d· it

distinguishing
Man.	59– 3	d· them from the writings of
Ret.	94–25	the modesty and d· affection
My.	82–19	* is a d· characteristic of

distorted
Mis.	49–11	d· into the claim of insanity
	250–11	is d· into human qualities,

distorting
Mis.	345–25	thus d· or misapprehending the

distress
'02.	5– 6	C. S. stills all d·

distresses
Mis.	199–12	in d· for Christ's sake. — II Cor. 12 : 10.

distribute
Mis.	149– 9	d· what God has given him
'00.	3– 8	hoards this capital to d· gain."

distributed
Pul.	25– 4	* d· by the four systems

distributing
Mis.	381–24	selling, giving away, d·, or
Ret.	36– 7	and d· them unsparingly.
My.	252– 4	like the bee, always d· sweet

distribution
Man.	77–16	proper d· of the funds ·
Po.	vii– 7	* her poems, for private d·.

district
My.	77–29	* edifice in the Back Bay d·
	309–30	* the d· school practically all the

District Manager
Man.	99–22	act as D· M· of the Committees

distrust
My.	202– 3	from human ambition, fear, or d·
	211–21	suspicious d· where honor is due,

disturb
Mis.	124– 2	would tend to d· the divine order,
'01.	9–24	they d· the carnal and destroy it ;

disturbance
Mis.	224–23	no passing breath nor accidental d·

disturbed
Mis.	265–18	must be, d· by this discord,
Pul.	3– 2	be demolished, or even d· ?
My.	126– 4	the d· human mind

ditch
Mis.	230–20	drop human life into the d·

diverged
Mis.	322–17	must not be diverted or d·,

divergence
Mis.	265– 5	if he . . . this d· widens.
Rud.	17– 1	slight d· is fatal in Science.

diverges
Mis.	265– 2	if he d· from Science
Ret.	56– 5	d· from the one divine Mind,

diverse
Mis.	265– 8	D· opinions in Science are
My.	90–10	* of diseases many and d·.

diversions
My.	309–30	* supplied the only social d·,

diversities
Mis.	347–13	d· of operation by the same spirit.

diverted
Mis.	322–16	must not be d· or diverged,

divest
Mis.	14– 2	D· your thought, then, of the mortal

divests
Mis.	92–32	d· himself of pride and self,
Ret.	84–19	d· himself most of pride and self,

divide
Mis.	194–14	to d· the rays of Truth,
Ret.	60–30	Any attempt to d· these
	85–23	to d· the ranks of C. S.
'01.	12–20	to d· the rays of Truth,
Hea.	12–28	dishonest and d· one's faith
My.	206–10	they d· Truth's garment

divided
Mis.	52– 4	d· between catnip and Christ;
	56–17	a kingdom d· against itself,
	89– 2	d· against itself — Matt. 12 : 25.
	197–26	that is d· against itself,
	217–26	a kingdom d· against itself,
	237–30	a period of . . . d· interests,
Un.	33–23	find them d· in evidence,
	00– 4	a kingdom d· against itself.
No.	5–21	d· against itself — Luke 11 : 17.
'01.	25–29	a kingdom d· against itself,
My.	40–15	* d· into warring sects ;

dividend
Mis.	239–22	her d·, when compared with
My.	217–13	will receive his d· with interest

divides
Ret.	28–19	d·, subdivides, increases,
	35–13	d· its rays and brings out the
	56– 6	Whatever . . . d· Mind into minds,
Rud.	10– 7	d· His power with nothing evil
My.	316– 3	d· between sect and Science

dividing
Man.	99– 5	d· line being the 36th parallel
Peo.	9–12	d· our homage and obedience

Divina
My.	268–19	centuries without a living D·.

Divine
Un.	50– 6	and is unknown to the D·.
Rud.	4– 6	or only of D· or C. S.?
No.	18–19	the human conceive of the D·.
'01.	1–17	human in communion with the D·,
'02.	10–13	above itself towards the D·,

divine

adventure
My.	158– 9	an age of Love's d· adventure

afflatus
Mis.	166– 7	moves in our midst a d· afflatus.

divine

aid
  Peo. 9–18 invoke the *d·* aid of Spirit
  My. 166–20 When we . . . . *d·* aid is near.
All
  Un. 31– 6 the *d·* All must be Spirit.
antidote
  Mis. 255–26 because it is this *d·* antidote,
appellative
  '00. 3–24 contained this *d·* appellative
approbation
  My. 166– 3 will continue with *d·* approbation.
Arbiter
  Un. 30–27 reflect the Life of the *d·* Arbiter.
art
  Pul. 66– 1 * what they term the *d·* art of healing,
authority
  Mis. 93–16 fear, . . . is without *d·* authority.
  Un. 33– 7 yet we have it on *d·* authority :
  '01. 14–27 wrong has no *d·* authority ;
beauty
  Mis. 86–24 It is next to *d·* beauty
Being
  Pan. 4– 4 a self-existent *d·* Being,
  '01. 3–19 intelligent, *d·* Being,
benedictions
  Mis. 320– 8 with *d·* benedictions for mankind.
  My. 256–17 full of *d·* benedictions
blessing
  Mis. 133–22 to seek the *d·* blessing
capacity
  No. 21–12 reflecting God and the *d·* capacity.
character
  Un. 1–16 draw nearer to the *d·* character,
  Hea. 4–22 conception of the *d·* character,
chariots
  Un. 17–10 evil ties its . . . to the *d·* chariots,
children
  Un. 23– 7 *d·* children are born of law and
Christ
  My. 36–20 * salvation through His *d·* Christ.
claims
  Mis. 19–13 accepted the *d·* claims of Truth
Comforter
  Man. 15– 8 Holy Ghost or *d·* Comforter ;
command
  Mis. 10–14 If they mistake the *d·* command,
  Ret. 71– 5 obedient to the *d·* command,
  My. 224– 6 the human need, the *d·* command,
  351–11 is indeed a *d·* command,
commandments
  Ret. 31–18 breaketh the *d·* commandments.
commission
  Mis. 117–18 to carry out a *d·* commission
concept
  Ret. 68–10 *d·* concept . . . is spiritually real.
conception
  Mis. 287– 1 most exalted *d·* conception.
concurrence
  My. 246–20 *d·* concurrence of the spirit and
consciousness
  Mis. 366–14 or can be *d·* consciousness.
  Un. 51–20 The Ego is *d·* consciousness,
  No. 4–22 do not arise from the *d·* consciousness
  16– 1 found in the *d·* consciousness.
  17–16 *d·* consciousness and God's verity.
correspondence
  Mis. 74– 1 *d·* correspondence of noumenon and
decision
  My. 190–21 *d·* decision in behalf of Mind.
declaration
  Mis. 76–16 void by Jesus' *d·* declaration,
decree
  Mis. 66–10 always according to *d·* decree.
  121–14 even a *d·* decree, a law of Love !
  122–10 predestined to fulfil a *d·* decree,
  341–20 implicit treason to *d·* decree.
definition
  Mis. 258–28 *d·* definition of Deity
design
  Mis. 205–24 unites all periods in the *d·* design.
destiny
  No. 34–17 to crush out . . . its *d·* destiny.
digest
  Rud. 3–15 that *d·* digest of Science
directions
  Mis. 158–26 *d·* directions sent out to the
economy
  Un. 26–23 *chance* in the *d·* economy?
efficacy
  Rud. 17– 6 its *d·* efficacy to heal.
effulgence
  My. 262–19 *d·* effulgence, deific presence
element
  Mis. 337–21 they obscure its *d·* element,

divine

emanation
  '01. 10– 8 a spiritual, *d·* emanation,
energies
  Mis. 176–12 more of the *d·* energies of good,
  352–23 Through the *d·* energies alone
  360–22 fill earth with the *d·* energies,
  Ret. 88–13 its practicality, its *d·* energies,
  '02. 10– 4 spiritual forces, the *d·* energies,
energy
  Mis. 166–27 This action of the *d·* energy,
  176–28 up to the acme of *d·* energy
  208– 3 This law is a *d·* energy.
  292–13 partly illustrate the *d·* energy
  343– 8 for the *d·* energy to move it
  My. 355–13 in our ranks of *d·* energy,
Esse
  My. 202–25 the underived glory, the *d·* *Esse*.
essence
  Mis. 163–30 This idea or *d·* essence was,
  Un. 39– 6 quenched in the *d·* essence,
ever-presence
  My. 192–28 *d·* ever-presence, answering your
Father
  Mis. 33–11 our *d·* Father and Mother.
Father-Mother
  Mis. 102–15 loving, *d·* Father-Mother God.
  127–11 petitions the *d·* Father-Mother God
  My. 18– 8 petitions the *d·* Father-Mother God
fiat
  Un. 38–21 no *d·* fiat commands us to
food
  My. 247–24 so filled with *d·* food
God is
  Pan. 4–12 reason and will are human ; God is *d·*.
good
  Mis. 164– 4 idea that represents *d·* good,
  Ret. 56–17 omnipresence of God, or *d·* good.
  80– 2 this is the pledge of *d·* good
  Un. 24– 4 My Mind is *d·* good,
government
  Mis. 56–15 opposed to the *d·* government.
grace
  Mis. 360–17 and the dews of *d·* grace,
hand
  Ret. 27–29 *d·* hand led me into a new world
  My. 326–20 I recognize the *d·* hand in
healing
  Mis. 2–17 a more rational and *d·* healing
  Ret. 28– 7 the perfect Mind and *d·* healing.
  Pul. 34–17 * heading
  34–19 * the Principle of *d·* healing,
  67–13 * the Principle of *d·* healing,
  My. 308– 3 the advent of *d·* healing
help
  Mis. 39–30 *D·* help is as necessary in the one
  158–17 a lack of faith in *d·* help,
  380–15 I again, in faith, turned to *d·* help,
history
  Ret. 10–15 *d·* history, voicing the idea of
honors
  Mis. 358– 5 will graduate under *d·* honors,
idea
  Mis. 18–20 divine Principle and *d·* idea,
  186–16 the *d·* idea named man ;
  370–12 *d·* idea assumes different forms,
  Un. 49– 4 as being the eternally *d·* idea.
  59– 5 *d·* idea of the divine Principle
  59–11 *d·* idea brought to the flesh
  59–18 the *d·* idea is always present.
  No. 26– 8 than . . . belief resembles the *d·* idea.
  My. 350– 9 spiritually discerned the *d·* idea
  357– 4 even the *d·* idea of C. S.,
ideal
  Mis. 103–26 exchanges this . . . for the *d·* ideal,
  Un. 51–26 *d·* ideal, whose Soul is not in body,
  Pul. 74–26 Love and its compound *d·* ideal.
  My. 257– 9 form and comeliness of the *d·* ideal,
  272–11 and ever shall be the *d·* ideal,
illumination
  Pul. 34–11 * became aware of a *d·* illumination
impetus
  My. 248–21 fall for lack of the *d·* impetus.
import
  '00. 14–11 seek thou the *d·* import of the
infinitude
  Un. 20–20 as you realize the *d·* infinitude
influence
  No. 40–27 are made better only by *d·* influence.
influx
  My. 206– 4 hinder the *d·* influx and lose
intelligence
  Mis. 23– 8 demonstrated a *d·* intelligence
  82–31 *d·* intelligence, or Principle, of all
  336–27 the fiat of *d·* intelligence,
  '01. 7– 6 infinite Person or *d·* intelligence

divine

interpretation
My. 114–21 the influx of *d·* interpretation

justice
Mis. 12–24 dealt with by *d·* justice.
277–25 *d·* justice and judgment are
289–19 Neither *d·* justice nor human
My. 149–20 clear perception of *d·* justice,
227–13 turn to *d·* justice for support

knowledge
Un. 4–22 no part of the *d·* knowledge.

largess
My. 349–12 a *d·* largess, a gift of God

law
Mis. 65–28 constitute the *d·* law of healing.
71–22 is a departure from *d·* law ;
73–28 It is the appearing of *d·* law
104–23 *d·* law and order of being.
107–23 oft-repeated violations of *d·* law,
119–25 prominent statute in the *d·* law,
261– 6 According to *d·* law, sin and
261–12 pays his full debt to *d·* law,
Ret. 24–21 perfect scientific accord with *d·* law.
26–16 the operation of the *d·* law.
Un. 13– 6 in obedience to *d·* law,
13–17 I show My pity through *d·* law,
56–16 but the *d·* law is supreme,
Pul. 34–24 scientific accord with the *d·* law."
35– 7 * natural fulfilment of *d·* law
No. 26–23 immutable harmony of *d·* law.
My. 106– 4 for love fulfils *d·* law
129–22 *d·* law gives to man health
131–23 much of the *d·* law and the gospel.
131–24 The *d·* law has said to us :
153–23 unmindful of the *d·* law of Love,
154– 8 to infringe the *d·* law of Love
190–26 with power (knowledge of *d·* law)

laws
My. 100 19 certainty of the *d·* laws of Mind

liberty
Mis. 163–20 and are the basis of *d·* liberty,

Life
Mis. 2–17 The time approaches when *d·* Life,
123–27 but through a *d·* Life,
150 27 God demonstrable as *d·* Life,
167–17 His Father and Mother are *d·* Life,
331–19 O Life *d·*, that owns each waiting
389– 7 O Life *d·*, that owns each waiting
Un. 61–12 nightless radiance of *d·* Life.
Pul. 30–22 * the possibilities of the *d·* Life.
No. 15–24 estranges mortals from *d·* Life
18–14 demonstration of *d·* Life and Love ;
33–21 efficacy of *d·* Life and Love
Pan. 14– 7 living the *d·* Life, Truth, Love,
'01. 18–26 The *d·* Life, Truth, Love
Peo. 2–23 but the *d·* Life, Truth, and Love,
14–17 power of *d·* Life and Love
Po. 4– 3 O Life *d·*, that owns each waiting
22– 8 New themes seraphic, Life *d·*,
My. 109–21 reflex images of this *d·* Life,
150–14 to reflect the *d·* Life, Truth, and
153–32 up to the one source, *d·* Life
257–22 the reign of Truth and Life *d·*
348–20 *D·* Life, Truth, Love is the basic

life
Po. 70 0 Making this life *d·*,

light
Mis. 113– 7 and *d·* light to be obscured,
223– 8 *d·* light, logic, and revelation
Un. 6–11 presented to the people in *d·* light,
My. 187– 6 May the *d·* light of C. S.
194–14 human self lost in *d·* light,
258– 7 seems illuminated . . . with *d·* light.

likeness
Ret. 60– 2 as very far from the *d·* likeness.
Un. 39–27 losing the *d·* likeness.
No. 36– 5 when we awake in the *d·* likeness.
My. 121–23 and reflects the *d·* likeness.

logic
Mis. 195–17 Master's *d·* logic, as seen in
My. 350– 5 minus *d·* logic and plus human

Love
Mis. ix–18 draughts from the fount of *d·* Love.
20– 2 with the radiance of *d·* Love ;
28–27 together with his *d·* Love,
81–26 *d·* Love hears and answers the human
111– 8 losing hold of *d·* Love, you lost
113–24 *D·* Love is our hope, strength, and
121–28 greater than human pity, is *d·* Love,
122–20 Love *d·* spurned, lessens not the
122–27 *D·* Love knows no hate ;
123–20 majestic atonement of *d·* Love.
125–13 rest; in the understanding of *d·* Love
127–14 faithfully asks *d·* Love to feed it
127–17 the tributary of *d·* Love,
133–27 I turn constantly to *d·* Love

divine

Love
Mis. 144–29 To-day I pray that *d·* Love,
154–10 and enlarge its borders with *d·* Love.
154–16 the purpose of *d·* Love to resurrect
155–30 wherewith *d·* Love has entrusted us,
158–10 has obeyed the message of *d·* Love,
160–11 knowledge of Truth and *d·* Love.
165–26 this account is settled with *d·* Love,
186–15 that God is *d·* Love :
186–15 *d·* Love is the divine Principle
194–25 *d·* Love that casts out all fear.
208–13 motion of the law of *d·* Love
209–32 *D·* Love, . . . pursues the evil
213– 8 acquiescence in the methods of *d·* Love.
223–20 *d·* Love so permeate the affections
236–23 seek in *d·* Love the remedy
261–21 No greater type of *d·* Love can be
262–19 *d·* Love which looseth the chains of
276–20 *d·* Love is found in affliction.
292–14 *D·* Love eventually causes mortals to
303– 7 be governed by *d·* Love alone
307– 3 *d·* Love is an ever-present help ;
317–28 *d·* Love will open the way
328–25 Whatever . . . *d·* Love will remove ;
335–15 path made luminous by *d·* Love.
348– 9 *d·* Love will bless this
351–27 Love *d·* punishes the joys of
357–31 *D·* Love is the substance of C. S.,
384–15 Light, Love *d·* Is here,
386– 3 infinite appear Life, Love *d·*,
Man. 40– 7 *d·* Love alone governs man ;
45–12 demonstrating the rules of *d·* Love.
104– 9 hedge it about with *d·* Love.
Un. 55–22 here shall I behold God, *d·* Love.
Pul. 3–15 *d·* Love gives us the true sense of
3–21 is a tributary of *d·* Love,
74 26 with God, in the sense of *d·* Love
77–14 * as revealed by *d·* Love through you
78–12 * as revealed by *d·* Love through you
85– 9 * unfolded and demonstrated *d·* Love,
Rud. 12–19 induces rest in God, *d·* Love,
No. 19–18 feel no sensation of *d·* Love,
35– 8 to the purpose of *d·* Love,
Pan. 14–22 May the *d·* Love succor and
'00. 4–28 *d·* Love includes and reflects all
5–17 divine Science of *d·* Love,
5–28 utilize the power of *d·* Love in
15– 6 partake of what *d·* Love hath
15–17 all this time *d·* Love has
'01. 1–24 practical possibilities of *d·* Love;
4–14 demonstrated as *d·* Love;
4–28 Principle," meaning *d·* Love,
7–23 may attend their petitions to *d·* Love.
9–14 the spirit of *d·* Love,
10–20 *D·* Love spans the dark passage of sin,
15–15 blessings that *d·* Love bestows
17– 5 quickly to return to *d·* Love,
19– 6 closer proximity with *d·* Love,
21–27 or felt the incipient touch of *d·* Love
35–11 Love *d·* that plucks us From the human
'02. 2– 5 to wait on *d·* Love ;
5–10 almost unconceived light of *d·* Love,
6–22 image and likeness of *d·* Love.
7– 9 the true idea of God— *d·* Love
11– 6 *D·* Love waits and pleads to save
19–22 It is *d·* Love that doeth it,
20– 9 with the fulness of *d·* Love."
Po. 3–14 Love *d·* doth fill my heart.
24–12 O Love *d·*, This heart of Thine
36–14 Love *d·* Is here, and thine ;
49– 5 infinite appear Life, Love *d·*,
My. 4–12 with the leaven of *d·* Love
12–26 Faith in *d·* Love supplies the
18–11 faithfully asks *d·* Love to
18–14 the tributary of *d·* Love,
21–15 * *d·* Love more than compensates for
23– 4 * The *d·* Love that prompted the desire,
27– 3 *D·* Love bids me say :
28– 4 "*D·* Love always has met
41– 7 * blessed and comforted by *d·* Love.
61–19 * the might of *d·* Love,
63–15 * to work out the purposes of *d·* Love.
73– 9 "*D·* Love always has met
113–19 in the arms of *d·* Love,
115– 2 mighty chariot of *d·* Love,
123– 5 great guerdon of *d·* Love,
132– 1 fulfilment of *d·* Love in our lives
132–16 *D·* Love has strengthened the hand
132–19 *D·* Love hath opened the gate
132–24 *D·* Love will also rebuke and
132–28 *D·* Love is our only physician,
135–30 understand that God is *d·* Love,
138–11 test my trust in *d·* Love
139–27 so doth the *d·* Love redeem your body
148–29 Christianity is the summons of *d·* Love
149– 6 Principle of Christ is *d·* Love,

divine

Love

My. 153–18 spiritual help of *d·* Love.
161– 7 balancing his account with *d·* Love,
162–28 their understanding of *d·* Love.
179–32 the *d·* Love practical,
181– 9 maturing conception of *d·* Love ;
182–20 *d·* Love that reigns above the
184–25 precious in the sight of *d·* Love,
188–11 When *d·* Love gains admittance to
189–15 government of *d·* Love derives its
190– 3 merciful design of *d·* Love,
192– 3 thou ransomed of *d·* Love,
192–15 May the blessing of *d·* Love
194–25 May *d·* Love abundantly bless
197–20 I thank *d·* Love for the hope
200–14 the glorious beatitudes of *d·* Love.
201– 3 whereunto *d·* Love has called us
204–10 in one Principle, of *d·* Love,
214– 5 *D·* Love always has met
223–28 Just now *d·* Love and wisdom saith,
240– 1 all men shall know Him (*d·* Love)
252– 3 Keep yourselves busy with *d·* Love.
262– 4 inherent unity with *d·* Love,
262–16 dawn of *d·* Love breaking upon
265–20 *d·* Love, impartial and universal,
265–26 and permeated with *d·* Love,
270–10 *D·* Love, nearer my consciousness
275– 4 As the sequence of *d·* Love
275– 7 they are controlled by *d·* Love ;
278– 7 government of *d·* Love is supreme.
284–25 in the full efficacy of *d·* Love
287– 6 as instruments of *d·* Love.
287– 7 *D·* Love reforms, regenerates,
287– 9 *D·* Love is the noumenon
288– 9 and reflects *d·* Love.
288–20 the functions of Spirit, *d·* Love.
290–17 *D·* Love is never so near as when
292– 5 Through *d·* Love the right government
293–24 power of *d·* Love to overrule the
295– 4 *d·* Love holds its substance safe
295–25 *D·* Love is your ever-present help.
301– 4 and is the revelation of *d·* Love.
308– 1 *d·* Love will accomplish what
350–24 Love *d·*, whose kindling mighty rays

love

Mis. 388– 9 Fed by Thy love *d·* we live,
'00. 11–12 and compensated by *d·* love.
Po. 7– 9 Fed by Thy love *d·* we live,

Master

Mis. 187–19 our human and *d·* Master,

means

No. 21–14 for *d·* means and ends.

mercy

Mis. 11–14 Love metes . . . but *d·* mercy.
Ret. 94–11 this purgation of *d·* mercy,
My. 89–20 * constant as petitions for *d·* mercy.

metaphysics

Mis. 38–20 makes *d·* metaphysics needful,
68–19 know the meaning of *d·* metaphysics,
69– 1 *D·* metaphysics is that which
70– 7 only explanation in *d·* metaphysics.
252– 3 mental medicine of *d·* metaphysics
293– 8 teacher of *d·* metaphysics should impart
Ret. 30–19 the mazes of *d·* metaphysics
'01. 2–13 in the practice of *d·* metaphysics
5–11 *d·* metaphysics discriminates between
8–21 logic of *d·* metaphysics makes
10–14 Science of *d·* metaphysics removes the
24–15 from *d·* metaphysics to tar-water !
25–11 call aids to *d·* metaphysics,
'02. 5–16 *D·* metaphysics and St. John
6–23 *d·* metaphysics points the way,
7– 1 *D·* metaphysics concedes no
7–17 authority for *d·* metaphysics
My. 109–23 *D·* metaphysics is not to be scoffed
115– 7 harmonies of heaven in *d·* metaphysics,
127–13 *d·* metaphysics completely overshadows
206– 5 lose the Principle of *d·* metaphysics
228– 5 signally blunder in *d·* metaphysics ;
279–17 understood in its *d·* metaphysics,
287–10 practice of *d·* metaphysics.
294– 3 on the subject of *d·* metaphysics ;
301–16 Is faith in *d·* metaphysics insanity?
349–11 *d·* metaphysics or its therapeutics.

method

My. 103–15 Alluding to this *d·* method,

might

Mis. 138–19 unity is *d·* might,
162–14 Clad with *d·* might,
My. 3– 4 *d·* might of Truth demands well-doing

Mind

Mis. 33–29 mortal mind's opposite, — the *d·* Mind.
39–18 for this medicine is *d·* Mind ;
56– 8 substance of Spirit is *d·* Mind.
59–28 *d·* Mind, who is the only physician ;
59–28 *d·* Mind is the scientific healer.

divine

Mind

Mis. 62–29 the action of the *d·* Mind,
75–30 Soul is the *d·* Mind,
95–20 *d·* Mind reveals itself to humanity
101– 2 how the *d·* Mind is understood
103–14 which dwell forever in the *d·* Mind,
113–15 influenced by any but the *d·* Mind,
199–19 the qualities of the *d·* Mind
205– 3 practical C. S. is the *d·* Mind,
255–24 may be found in God, the *d·* Mind.
257–10 force of immortal and *d·* Mind.
260– 9 The *d·* Mind was his only
264–29 must take its hue from the *d·* Mind.
269–18 *d·* Mind to be the only physician.
269–22 Science is a law of *d·* Mind.
286–30 demonstrated in the offspring of *d·* Mind,
308– 1 *d·* Mind as its sole centre and
363– 3 *d·* Mind and true happiness.
364–19 it is good, reflects the *d·* Mind,
Ret. 28– 1 *d·* Mind alone must answer,
56– 5 diverges from the one *d·* Mind,
Un. 4–20 which was certainly the *d·* Mind ;
36–23 to say that the *d·* Mind is
Pul. 3–24 pleasing to the *d·* Mind.
15– 2 good resident in *d·* Mind,
58– 2 * healed by the power of *d·* Mind,
Rud. 3–19 cure of disease through the *d·* Mind,
11–11 no . . . death in the *d·* Mind.
12–26 *d·* Mind, not material law,
No. 24– 1 immeasurable idea of *d·* Mind.
25–16 immortal mode of the *d·* Mind.
27–16 *d·* Mind and that Mind's idea.
37–16 is known to the *d·* Mind,
42–12 to dispossess the *d·* Mind of
Pan. 3–24 * proceeding from the *d·* Mind
'01. 7–12 our heavenly Parent — the *d·* Mind
20– 6 guided by . . . Truth, the *d·* Mind.
Hea. 15–14 why . . . deny all might to the *d·* Mind,
Peo. 4– 5 an infinite and *d·* Mind ;
My. 3–15 This Science is a law of *d·* Mind,
5–30 *d·* Mind that heals the sick
61– 5 * of the power of *d·* Mind
106–20 *d·* Mind calms . . . with a word.
108– 7 action of the *d·* Mind is salutary
108–14 based on the law of *d·* Mind.
108–16 *d·* Mind is the sovereign appeal,
108–18 nothing in the *d·* Mind to attenuate.
153–25 as the *d·* Mind, not as matter,
221–28 shall we have no faith . . . in the *d·* Mind,
221–29 forgetting that the *d·* Mind,
240–11 "This Science is a law of *d·* Mind,
241–21 * immortal idea of the one *d·* Mind.
246–17 dwelling forever in the *d·* Mind
279–13 God is the *d·* Mind.
288–15 *d·* Mind was his only instrumentality
292–27 *d·* Mind is the same yesterday,
348–18 proof that the *d·* Mind heals
349– 1 *d·* Mind was first chronologically,
349–23 The laws of God, or *d·* Mind,

Mind-force

Mis. 331–23 *d·* Mind-force, filling all space

ministry

My. 24– 4 * all who accept its *d·* ministry.

mission

Pul. 71–23 * having a *d·* mission to fulfil,

modes

Mis. 361–32 *d·* modes and manifestations
My. 267–30 all the *d·* modes, means, forms,
349–20 *D·* modes or manifestations

music is

'00. 11–18 Music is *d·*.

mystery

No. 38– 9 This *d·* mystery of godliness

name

'00. 3–22 to call the *d·* name Yahwah,

nature

Mis. 104–22 In obedience to the *d·* nature,
392– 4 Nature *d·*, in harmony profound,
Un. 6–18 verity concerning the *d·* nature
No. 37– 2 his *d·* nature and manhood
'01. 11– 4 the *d·* nature of Christ Jesus
'02. 19– 5 Again : True to his *d·* nature,
Hea. 17– 4 get nearer his *d·* nature
Po. 20– 5 Nature *d·*, in harmony profound,
My. 110– 1 it is the *d·* nature of God,
119– 8 is not absorbed in the *d·* nature,

noumenon

My. 350– 4 To begin with the *d·* noumenon,

One

Mis. 264–11 to demonstrate the *d·* One,

oneness

Mis. 131–12 upon the rock of *d·* oneness,
No. 1–19 *d·* oneness of the trinity,

order

Mis. 18– 8 in the *d·* order of Science,
79– 1 views antagonistic to the *d·* order

divine

order
Mis. 122–14   d· order is the acme of mercy :
    124– 2   tend to disturb the d· order,
    136–14   its fulfilment of d· order.
    208–16   and so disobey the d· order.
Ret. 87–17   they must follow the d· order
    91–19   always leading them into the d· order,
Un. 40–10   imperative in the d· order of being.
    56–13   In the d· order of Science
My. 117– 9   comprehending of the d· order
    238–15   became requisite in the d· order.

origin
Mis. 3– 3   no especial gift from our d· origin,
    232–13   next to appear as its d· origin.
Ret. 56–10   is of human instead of d· origin.
Pul. 39– 3   * the d· origin of humanity
'02. 9–23   was the proof of its d· origin,

overtures
My. 13–25   reach the stars with d· overtures,

pardon
No. 31–11   d· pardon is that divine presence

Parent
Un. 48–14   d· Parent no more enters into His

peace
Peo. 11– 8   not by . . . warfare, but in d· peace.

perfection
Mis. 320–12   infant idea of d· perfection

Person
My. 117–29   and to seek the one d· Person,

persons
'01. 6– 2   theology's three d· persons,

philosophy
Mis. 364–12   It is the soul of d· philosophy,
    364–32   reproduces the d· philosophy of Jesus
No. 21–25   D· philosophy is demonstrably the

potency
Ret. 80– 2   d· potency of this spiritual mode

power
Mis. 17–21   man reflects the d· power to heal
    59– 7   d· power understood, as in C. S. ;
    63– 6   and to hide his d· power.
    69– 9   man shall utilize the d· power.
    70–29   wonderful demonstrations of d· power,
    97–12   in no way allied to d· power.
    152– 9   cooperate with the d· power,
    171– 9   for the d· power to filter from
    175–29   both animal magnetism and d· power,
    183–23   equips man with d· power
    194–16   lens of Science magnifies the d· power
    201–32   illustrates through the flesh the d· power
    225–24   through the d· power, she healed him.
    244– 5   was performed by d· power,
    268–10   the demonstration of d· power,
    275– 4   clinging faith in d· power?
    360– 2   and procures d· power.
Ret. 26– 3   the d· power which heals.
    28–16   we must be clad with d· power.
    50– 4   knowledge of that d· power
Un. 43–22   This will interpret the d· power
Pul. 35 20   we must be clad with d· power.
    73– 5   * His unlimited and d· power.
Rud. 12–31   As power d· is the healer,
No. 12–27   It removes all limits from d· power.
    29–19   shocking reflection on the d· power,
'01. 2–10   into harmony with d· power,
    12–22   magnifies the d· power to human
    19– 3   They believe that d· power, besought,
    24– 5   impression produced by d· power
    33–22   might and majesty of d· power
'02. 18– 7   d· power manifested through man ;
Hea. 15–25   to pray for a proof of d· power,
My. 114–23   d· power of Truth and Love,
    131– 3   endues with d· power ;
    293– 3   d· power and purpose of
    293–19   The d· power and poor human sense
    315–27   of the d· power of C. S.,

precept
Mis. 235–27   tried to follow the d· precept,
    289–16   according to the d· precept,

presence
Mis. 71–19   not the factors of d· presence
    110–17   when encompassed by d· presence,
Pul. 10–27   D· presence, breathe Thou Thy
No. 31–12   divine pardon is that d· presence
Pan. 14–14   Pray that the d· presence may still
'02. 16–14   is to recognize the d· presence

presumption
My. 228–27   has the d· presumption to say :

Principle
Mis. 17–16   d· Principle that redeems man
    18–19   d· Principle and divine idea,
    19– 9   d· Principle and rules of C. S.
    22– 5   law of God, its d· Principle.
    22–23   the rules of its d· Principle,
    30– 1   the d· Principle of Christianity

divine

Principle
Mis. 32– 9   rules and d· Principle of C. S.
    34–13   C. S. is based on d· Principle ;
    41–27   d· Principle which governs the universe,
    46–25   represents his d· Principle.
    46–29   the Father, his d· Principle, is perfect.
    62–24   attempts to solve its d· Principle
    71–16   Law . . . unfolds d· Principle,
    77–12   d· Principle and spiritual idea ;
    79–22   immortal man's d· Principle.
    85– 8   the d· Principle of his being,
    87–22   d· Principle and rules of
    89–29   saved on this d· Principle,
    96–14   d· Principle, — which I worship ;
    98–25   acknowledge its d· Principle.
    104–26   d· Principle and idea are demonstrated,
    116–25   Obeying the d· Principle which
    118–26   d· Principle worketh with you,
    120– 5   d· Principle of life's long problem,
    121–30   justice from the d· Principle,
    138–12   d· Principle which he claims to
    140–32   a perpetual type of the d· Principle
    147– 8   demonstrating the d· Principle of
    164– 1   Its d· Principle interprets the
    165–10   as eternal as its d· Principle.
    166– 1   d· Principle and spiritual idea of
    181– 6   power to demonstrate his d· Principle,
    181–11   the claims of the d· Principle.
    182– 6   in and of his d· Principle,
    185– 3   demonstrate fairly the d· Principle
    186–16   d· Principle of the divine idea
    188–10   d· Principle and idea of being,
    189– 4   d· Principle and rule of being,
    195– 3   d· Principle of metaphysical healing.
    198–26   d· Principle, and its spiritual laws.
    100–24   d· Principle is discerned in C. S.,
    200–28   involved in its d· Principle, God :
    204–28   God, the d· Principle of C. S.,
    221– 6   learns more of its d· Principle.
    223–16   full faith in the d· Principle,
    252–22   demonstrates the d· Principle,
    268– 1   while disobedience to this d· Principle
    290–11   d· Principle, which is Love,
    290–13   misapprehension of the d· Principle
    307–28   adhere to the d· Principle
    308–15   healing the sick on its d· Principle.
    308–28   is taught through its d· Principle,
    309–16   true idea of man's d· Principle.
    335– 1   you turn away from this d· Principle
    353–23   d· Principle carries on His harmony.
    354–13   the knowledge of the d· Principle
    356–28   its d· Principle and rule of practice.
    361–26   the only substance and d· Principle
    364–11   a postulate of the d· Principle,
    379–15   the d· Principle of all healing.
    380– 2   if a d· Principle alone heals,
    380– 4   d· Principle heals the sick,
Man. 43–24   its statement of the d· Principle
    62–22   simpler meanings of the d· Principle
    67 18   from the d· Principle of being
    83–15   the understanding of d· Principle,
Ret. 55– 7   vindicates the d· Principle,
    56– 8   unerring d· Principle of Science,
    57–25   Mistaking d· Principle for
    58– 1   Stating the d· Principle,
    82–10   rest on d· Principle for guidance,
    93– 6   incorporeal d· Principle of man,
Un. 10–10   for God is their d· Principle.
    46– 8   but I do so on a d· Principle,
    51–27   God, — the d· Principle of man.
    59– 6   d· Principle which made heaven
    61–14   but the d· Principle and Spirit
Pul. 4– 9   protected by his d· Principle, God
    13– 1   interprets God as d· Principle,
    85–11   * the d· Principle of all things
Rud. 1– 3   demonstrating d· Principle
    3–26   d· Principle of all being,
    9–14   the d· Principle of man's being ;
No. 4–20   embody not the idea of d· Principle,
    11– 4   d· Principle, and an eternal being.
    20– 8   term d· Principle is used to signify
    20–13   As the d· Principle is comprehended,
    25–14   the eternal idea of his d· Principle,
    26–15   his d· Principle, or Father,
Pan. 11–10   Governed by the d· Principle of his
'00. 4–20   The d· Principle and rules of this
'01. 3–17   phrase for God — d· Principle.
    3–28   Love is d· Principle ;
    4– 1   d· Principle or Person stands for God
    4–28   calling God "d· Principle,"
    5–13   the d· Principle of all.
    7–18   call their God "d· Principle,"
    8– 4   spiritual idea of the d· Principle,
    22–21   its d· Principle and rules,
    23–12   d· Principle, rule, or demonstration
Hea. 3–13   d· Principle that begets the quality,

divine

Principle
Hea. 3–22 understand in part this *d·* Principle,
8–26 as directly upon a *d·* Principle,
14– 7 the *d·* Principle of healing
Peo. 2–11 *d·* Principle, — Life, Truth, Love ;
4–19 three terms for one *d·* Principle
6–20 *d·* Principle, understood in part,
My. 40–27 * She has obeyed the *d·* Principle,
45–16 * fidelity to the *d·* Principle
105– 5 the *d·* Principle whose rules
109–14 the ever-operative *d·* Principle
116–13 God is *d·* Principle, Love.
116–16 Forgetting *d·* Principle brings on
117–24 sinking its *d·* Principle in
119– 4 demonstrate the *d·* Principle
125–13 Loyal to the *d·* Principle
149– 2 know somewhat of the *d·* Principle
152–16 *d·* Principle of all that really is,
152–22 Then the *d·* Principle of good,
152–27 the *d·* Principle of nature
179–27 based on the *d·* Principle of being,
180–14 *d·* Principle, or Life, Truth, and
200–29 with its *d·* Principle, Love.
204–29 based . . . on this *d·* Principle,
205–26 full idea of its *d·* Principle,
218–13 demonstrated the *d·* Principle
218–17 leaves the *d·* Principle of C. S.
225–21 C. S. names God as *d·* Principle,
225–27 God is *d·* Principle
225–29 *d·* Principle includes them all.
226–15 Withdraw God, *d·* Principle, from
226–20 intelligent *d·* Principle, Love.
239– 5 reason, revelation, the *d·* Principle,
248–29 found nearest the *d·* Principle
267–26 man's *d·* Principle, Love,
269– 3 infinite *d·* Principle,
270–29 The *d·* Principle of C. S. will
272–13 C. S. reveals the *d·* Principle,
299–14 the demonstrable *d·* Principle
299–22 the *d·* Principle of C. S.,
300–11 the *d·* Principle of C. S..
303– 9 following the *d·* Principle
348–12 rather than his *d·* Principle,
348–23 enshrined in the *d·* Principle

process
Un. 11–23 neither . . . hindered the *d·* process.
protection
Mis. 263–11 by *d·* protection and affection.
Providence
Mis. 312–14 * interposition of *d·* Providence
320– 1 seize them, trust the *d·* Providence
purpose
Ret. 37–23 *d·* purpose that this should be done,
83– 3 accomplishing the *d·* purpose
realism
Mis. 87– 6 unjust . . . to the *d·* realism.
reality
Mis. 345–20 * Christianity must be a *d·* reality."
Peo. 13–28 * Christianity must be a *d·* reality."
rebuke
Ret. 80–12 *d·* rebuke is effectual to the
reflection
'00. 1– 8 in the glow of *d·* reflection.
My. 129–13 richly fraught with *d·* reflection.
repentance
Un. 14– 1 such planks as the *d·* repentance,
requirements
Mis. 261–19 *d·* requirements typified in
346–21 grasped in all its *d·* requirements.
retreat
Pan. 3–14 * "O sacred solitude ! *d·* retreat !
rights
Mis. 246– 7 both human and *d·* rights,
247– 2 both human and *d·* rights ;
My. 303–14 eschews *d·* rights in human beings.
royalty
Mis. 121–24 shameless insult to *d·* royalty,
rule
Mis. 85–13 this *d·* rule in Science :
209– 8 the *d·* rule of this Principle
301–26 a *d·* rule for human conduct.
ruling
Mis. 204–30 *d·* ruling gives prudence and energy;
scale
My. 146–31 in the *d·* scale of being
Science
(see **Science**)
Science is
Mis. 58–22 All Science is *d·*,
172–16 Science is *d·* :
219– 3 (and all Science is *d·*)
261–31 All Science is *d·*.
My. 260–11 Science is *d·* ;
Scientist
Ret. 26–17 a natural and *d·* Scientist.

divine

sense
Un. 21–21 true individuality, or a *d·* sense of being.
'02. 6–17 lets in the *d·* sense of being,
significance
Mis. 250–10 The *d·* significance of Love
sin
Un. 16– 2 such terms as *d· sin* and
source
Mis. 19–17 flowing on to God, its *d·* source.
22– 7 if not from the *d·* source,
333–18 the *d·* source of being,
Pul. 4–11 sense of unity with your *d·* source,
Spirit
Mis. 40–16 action of the *d·* Spirit,
49–23 opposes the leadings of the *d·* Spirit
55– 7 as much of the *d·* Spirit as
Ret. 24–19 *d·* Spirit had wrought the miracle
60– 9 adds that the *d·* Spirit created
Pul. 20–16 whose substance is the *d·* Spirit,
34–21 *d·* Spirit had wrought a miracle,"
No. 42– 7 *d·* Spirit supplies all human needs.
My. 225–20 gives to the *d·* Spirit the name God.
294–14 ever-present power of *d·* Spirit
spirit
Pul. 65–25 * the *d·* spirit of giving,
standard
Mis. 50–21 change from . . . to the *d·* standard,
statute
'02. 4–20 a *d·* statute for yesterday, and
statutes
Peo. 12– 2 these *d·* statutes of God :
strength
Mis. 170–17 was refreshment of *d·* strength,
358–15 humility, and love are *d·* strength.
Un. 39–12 removes human weakness by *d·* strength,
substance
Mis. 68– 1 *d·* substance, intelligence, Life,
Talitha cumi
Peo. 8–21 swept by the *d· Talitha cumi,*
teachings
Mis. 302–29 *d·* teachings contained in "S. and **H.**
theology
My. 180–30 between *d·* theology and C. S.,
things
Ret. 31–10 hunger and thirst after *d·* things,
thought
Un. 5– 6 toward the perfect thought *d·*.
tone
'00. 11–19 if the *d·* tone be lacking,
trinity
Mis. 63– 8 this *d·* trinity is one infinite remedy
Truth
Mis. 241–28 When *d·* Truth and Love heal,
284–18 vindicated *d·* Truth and Love
Man. 19– 4 demonstration of *d·* Truth,
41–22 reign of *d·* Truth, Life, and Love
87–20 trusts them to the *d·* Truth and **Love,**
Ret. 50–21 strict adherence to *d·* Truth
84–25 trusts them to the *d·* Truth and **Love,**
93–14 and imparting *d·* Truth,
No. 15– 1 dews of *d·* Truth,
understanding
Mis. 40–29 it requires more *d·* understanding to
Un. 30–10 till *d·* understanding takes away
Us
Mis. 18–20 *d·* "Us"— one in good, and good in One.
verities
Mis. 81–27 utters the *d·* verities of being
visions
Ret. 18–15 of real joy and of visions *d·* ;
Po. 64– 6 of real joy and of visions *d·* ;
way
Ret. 54– 9 and learn the *d·* way,
No. 12–20 *d·* way impels a spiritualization
Whole
Mis. 16–16 God is a *d· Whole,* and *All,*
will
Mis. 141–21 but let the *d·* will . . . rule
wisdom
Mis. 209– 4 prerogative of *d·* wisdom,
293– 6 unerring modes of *d·* wisdom.
My. 5–31 may . . . mislead man ; *d·* wisdom, never.
215–32 his *d·* wisdom should temper
Word
Mis. 192–19 practicability of the *d·* Word,
Pul. 73– 9 * meditated over His *d·* Word.
No. 29–17 Better . . . than to the *d·* Word.

Mis. 16–11 and these claims are *d·*,
16–22 Love, a *d·*, infinite Principle ;
63– 8 the Son of God was *d·*.
69– 8 The Principle of C. S. is *d·*.
71–28 is the counterfeit of the *d·*,
99–20 seemed Jesus of Nazareth more *d·*
100–21 coincidence of the *d·* with the human,

divine

Mis.	103–21	Any inference of the *d·*
	121– 9	the human struggles against the *d·*,
	121–19	whatever belittles, . . . is not *d·*.
	125–20	All that is real is *d·*
	163–16	less human and more *d·*
	172–12	*D·* and unerring Mind measures man,
	184–32	submerged in the humane and *d·*,
	199–23	Principle of these marvellous works is *d·* ;
	208–18	*d·* Truth's negativing error
	212–22	human will is lost in the *d·* ;
	234–12	things most essential and *d·*.
	309–24	human concept antagonizes the *d·*.
	337– 6	its effect on yourself to be— *d·*.
	338– 7	that its Principle is *d·*.
	352–25	consciousness is the reflection of the *d·*,
	353– 9	relinquish your human . . . and find the *d·*,
	394–11	rainbow of rapture, o'erarching, *d·* ;
	399–12	Life of all being *d·* :
Man.	15–15	evidence of *d·*, efficacious Love,
Chr.	53–17	Thus Christ, eternal and *d·*,
Ret.	24– 5	Science of *d·* metaphysical healing
	28–26	Its Principle is *d·*, not human,
	37– 4	*d·*, or spiritual, Science of
	50–20	subordination of the human to the *d·*,
	89–30	but incorporeal impulsion is *d·*,
Un.	10–15	Their gradations are spiritual and *d·* ;
	15–20	become only an echo of the *d·* ?
	42– 8	a *d·* and intelligent — reality.
	52– 8	consciousness should become *d·*,
Pul.	70–24	* the *d·* or spiritual Science of
Rud.	13– 9	the *d·* and spiritual image of God.
No.	10– 2	in both a *d·* and human sense ;
	13– 6	both the Principle and idea to be *d·*.
	21–17	modes, wherein the human and *d·*
	30–18	His sympathy is *d·*, not human.
	36–18	mortal as unreal, and the *d·* as real.
	36–28	while the *d·* and ideal Christ was
Pan.	3– 7	but one charm to make it half *d·*
	7– 6	the omnipotence of one *d·*, infinite
	8– 7	one the *d·*, infinite Person,
	12–22	this *d·* infinite Principle,
'00.	15–10	of all human experience is the most *d·* ;
'01.	2–14	it has a *d·* and demonstrable Principle
	4–13	The Science of God must be, is, *d·*,
	5– 7	one *d·* infinite triune Principle,
	8– 1	chapter sub-title
	8– 3	one Christ, and Christ is *d·*
	10–13	both the *d·* and the human,
	31– 7	neither personal nor human, but *d·*.
'02.	8–20	The energy that saves . . . is *d·* :
Hea.	20– 7	* In notes almost *d·*."
Peo.	10–16	*d·* as well as human.
Po.	39– 1	of all *d·* Gifts, lofty, pure,
	45–14	rainbow of rapture, o'erarching, *d·*;
	75–19	Life of all being *d·* :
My.	27– 6	the *d·* and not the human
	111–25	conclusion was logical and *d·*
	132–21	one Mind and that *d·* ;
	139–22	from the human to the *d·*.
	141–29	communion universal and *d·*.
	160– 6	constant relation with the *d·*,
	178–10	Science is naturally *d·*,
	186– 2	prophetic of the finger *d·*
	220–30	That the innocent . . . seems less *d·*.
	220 01	seems more *d·* to-day than
	221–17	other than the spiritual and *d·*,
	220–10	the one *d·* intelligent Principle
	244–19	put off the human for the *d·*.
	252–29	it is moral, spiritual, *d·*.
	265–22	coincidence of the human and *d·*,
	283–26	only as it patterns the *d·*.

Divine Being

Peo.	13– 5	*D· B·* is more than a person,

divinely

Mis.	26–30	naturally and *d·* infinite good.
	81–24	be heard *d·* and humanly.
	121–11	good, as *d·* attested.
	161–16	both human and *d·* endowed,
	163– 4	preparing to heal and teach *d·* ;
	192–13	words of him who spake *d·*,
	209–22	To suffer for . . . is *d·* wise.
	246–11	would have washed it *d·* away
	313–25	and, as I believe, *d·* directed,
	360– 6	good, because fashioned *d·*,
	387– 2	With joy *d·* fair,
	387–24	Come from that Love, *d·* near,
	397– 8	and tenderly, *D·* talk.
Ret.	26–13	*d·* natural and apprehensible ;
	32– 1	*d·* appointed human mission,
Pul.	18–17	and tenderly, *D·* talk.
No.	9–25	*D·* defined, Science is the
Pan.	12–28	It is *d·* true, and every hour
'01.	19– 1	*d·* appointed means of grace
Hea.	15– 7	spiritual power *d·* directed.

divinely

Po.	6–19	that Love, *d·* near,
	12–17	and tenderly, *D·* talk.
	34–14	*D·* desolate the shrine to paint?
	50–20	With joy *d·* fair,
	77–10	Love, and Truth, — *d·* God !
My.	4–31	Whatever is not *d·* natural
	28–28	* labors of one *d·* guided woman,
	258–22	*D·* beautiful are the Christmas
	267– 4	which is not *d·* scientific,
	288–10	Good is *d·* natural.
	349–13	*d·* natural to him who sits
	351–13	hem of his garment who spake *d·*.

diviner

Mis.	68– 5	changed appearance and *d·* form
	96–13	ascends . . . to *d·* consciousness,
	140–25	The *d·* claim and means for
	330–22	purer peace and *d·* energy,
	385–17	To Soul's *d·* sense,
Ret.	81–10	*d·* sense of liberty and light.
Un.	4–12	a *d·* sense that God is all
No.	3–11	but I obeyed a *d·* rule.
Peo.	5–19	*d·* sense of Life and Love,
	11–10	another staging for *d·* claims,
Po.	48–11	To Soul's *d·* sense,

diviners

Mis.	363–27	and drives *d·* mad.

divines

Mis.	169–19	most eminent *d·* of the world
No.	23–14	eminent *d·*, in Europe
'01.	31–28	taught by some grand old *d·*,
My.	149–20	and *d·* be too deeply read

Divine Science

Mis.	174–31	The leaven . . . is *D· S·* ;
	336–20	chapter sub-title
Rud.	14– 6	strictly practising *D· S·*,

divine Science

(*see* **Science**)

Divinity (*see also* **Doctor of Divinity**)

Man.	68–13	teaches the course in *D·*,

divinity

Mis.	13–23	reveals in clearer *d·* the
	63–27	This *d·* was reaching humanity
	96– 1	reveals the infinitude of *d·*
	102–21	destroys it with the *d·* of Truth.
	197–18	character and *d·* which Jesus
	292– 2	*d·* of St. John's Gospel
	372–30	shades to the shadows of *d·*,
Ret.	57–29	status and rule of *d·*
	91–14	lessons — on humanity and *d·*
Pul.	15–21	unite all interests in the one *d·*.
No.	v–10	life-giving waters of a true *d·*,
	7– 2	The rule of *d·* is golden ;
Pan.	11– 1	required the *d·* of our Master
'00.	6– 4	proving its power and *d·*
	12– 2	projected from *d·* upon humanity,
	12–14	tutelary *d·* of Ephesus.
Hea.	4–13	to drop *d·* long enough to
Peo.	14–11	our ideas of *d·* form our
My.	25–26	and the glory of *d·* appears
	63–23	* revelation of *d·* which has come
	107–20	nothing beyond illimitable *d·*.
	118–26	represents not the *d·* of
	179–23	Principle and practice of a true *d·*
	291–16	weighed in the scales of *d·*,
	306–18	*D·* alone solves the problem
	307–30	want of *d·* in scholastic theology,

division

Pul.	58–14	* *d·* into seven excellent class-rooms,
My.	311–31	* reached long *d·* in arithmetic,"

divisions

'00.	1–17	five grand *d·* of the globe ;
My.	136–20	five grand *d·* of our globe ;

divorce

Ret.	20–22	to ask for a bill of *d·*,
My.	268– 2	chapter sub-title
	268– 5	frequency of *d·* shows that
	268–11	*D·* and war should be exterminated
	268–17	will eliminate *d·* and war.
	269–11	Christ's plan of salvation from *d·*.
	314–14	my *d·* from Dr. Patterson
	314–21	to record the *d·* in my favor.
	314–30	up to the time of the *d·*.

divorced

Mis.	289–19	nor human equity has *d·*
Pul.	56–17	* Christianity and Science, hitherto *d·*
My.	349–26	human will *d·* from Science.

divorces

Mis.	221–23	and *d·* his work from Science.

divulged

Ret.	15–27	persons who *d·* their secret joy

do

Mis.	4– 9 its power to *d·* good, not evil.
	5– 2 It cannot fail to *d·* this if we
	5–15 says, "I can *d·* no more.
	6– 7 C. S. practitioners have plenty to *d·*,
	10– 6 whatever these try to *d·*, shall
	11–20 *d·* them good whenever opportunity
	11–26 I can *d·* much general good to such
	11–27 I *d·* it with earnest, special care
	21– 9 that I *d·* shall ye *d·* — see *John* 14 : 12.
	29– 3 I *d·*, and that his promise is
	31–20 power to be or to *d·* good,
	32–19 gladly *d·* my best towards helping those
	37–23 as directly and surely as *d·*
	38– 2 *all the good we can d·*
	41– 3 power of liberated thought to *d·* good,
	45– 6 *d·* more than to heal a toothache.
	52– 4 how much one can *d·* for himself,
	52– 6 he could *d·* vastly more.
	57–11 *d·* quickly." — *John* 13 : 27.
	67–27 If your question refers to . . . I *d·*.
	71– 9 unquestionably right to *d·* right ;
	71–10 is a very right thing to *d·*.
	89–15 to *d·* him all the good you can ;
	90–14 should *d·* to you, — *Matt.* 7 : 12.
	90–14 *d·* ye even so — *Matt.* 7 : 12.
	91–30 sufficiently to *d·* this,
	93–18 Sin can *d·* nothing :
	96–18 I *d·* ; and this atonement becomes
	108– 5 Scientists, claiming, as they *d·*,
	112–23 * have brought what will *d·* him good."
	116– 1 as you would have them *d·* to you,
	119–32 should *d·* to you, — *Matt.* 7 : 12.
	119–32 *d·* ye even so — *Matt.* 7 : 12.
	122–18 "Let us *d·* evil, — *Rom.* 3 : 8.
	127–20 one must *d·* good to others.
	127–23 *d·* His will even though
	128–13 and seen in me, *d·* : — *Phil.* 4 : 9.
	130–22 Where the motive to *d·* right exists,
	131–15 prepared to itemize . . . let it *d·* so ;
	135–10 as ye would have they should *d·* unto you,
	137–18 you will *d·* — what?
	146– 8 To *d·* this, I should need to be
	146–19 should *d·* unto you, — see *Matt.* 7 : 12.
	146–19 *d·* ye even so — *Matt.* 7 : 12.
	147–20 *d·* nothing but what is honorable,
	148–20 which will *d·* for the race what
	155–19 she desires thus to *d·*
	158–11 to *d·* this through faith,
	158–23 and God will *d·* the rest.
	167–18 they who *d·* the will of his Father
	175–25 nothing to *d·* with the Science of
	177–13 What will you *d·* about it?
	180–18 Let us *d·* our work ;
	192–10 *that I d· shall he d·* — *John* 14 : 12.
	192–11 *than these shall he d·* ; — *John* 14 : 12.
	193–27 that I *d·* shall he *d·*," — *John* 14 : 12.
	195–19 that I *d·* shall he *d·* — *John* 14 : 12.
	196–22 we shall *d·* the works of Christ,
	199– 3 supposed power of matter to *d·* it,
	199– 4 erring mind can claim to *d·* this,
	208–14 But who is willing to *d·* His will
	211–19 Or, are you afraid to *d·* this
	214–22 need to *d·* this even to understand
	215– 5 I *d·* it all in love ;
	215–11 as we shall *d·* if we take
	218–28 "How *d·* you *d·*?"
	221–11 The evil-doer can *d·* little at
	226–28 more than *d·* most vices.
	228– 5 is to *d·* good to thyself ;
	228–26 we *d·* what others *d·*,
	230– 6 as to what one should *d·*.
	232–10 never *d·* to be behind the times
	235–28 should *d·* unto you, — see *Matt.* 7 : 12.
	235–29 *d·* ye even so — *Matt.* 7 : 12.
	238–18 the love that foresees more to *d·*,
	241–12 and try to make others *d·* likewise,
	248–25 could *d·* no more for me.
	249–23 of their mental design to *d·* this
	251–16 that I *d·* shall he *d·*" ; — *John* 14 : 12.
	251–23 good they would *d·*, that they *d·*,
	251–24 and the evil they would not *d·*,
	251–24 that they *d·* not.
	254–26 Lord of the vineyard *d·* ? — *Mark* 12 : 9.
	262– 4 to be good and to *d·* good.
	265–24 Those who abide by them *d·* well.
	265–25 If others, . . . *d·* ill,
	266–12 that nobody else can or will *d·*.
	273– 7 where none other can *d·* the work.
	273–25 I cannot *d·* my best work for a
	274– 5 in order to *d·* this I must
	282–10 should *d·* to you, — *Luke* 6 : 31.
	282–23 it is sometimes wise to *d·* so,
	284– 1 for each one to *d·* his own work well,
	287–27 pleasanter to *d·* right than wrong ;
	298– 5 Let us *d·* evil, — *Rom.* 3 : 8.

do

Mis.	299–25 permission to *d·* this,
	299–27 What right have I to *d·* this?
	301– 6 would have others *d·* unto you?
	315–25 nor allow their students to *d·* thus,
	317– 5 to *d·* their own work ;
	317–22 "What I *d·* — *John* 13 : 7.
	323–18 "What *d·* ye here?
	334–26 understanding is required to *d·* this.
	335–29 who *d·* evil that good may come,
	338– 7 All must go and *d·* likewise,
	349–16 he should *d·* as he deemed best,
	358–27 *d·* their present work,
	359–16 as he was able to *d·* this ;
	370– 4 saw Jesus *d·* such deeds of mercy,
	384– 9 Thy will to know, and *d·*.
	397–17 My prayer, some daily good to *d·*
Man.	3–16 will *d·* for the race what
	16–11 to *d·* unto others
	16–11 as we would have them *d·* unto us ;
	28–22 then failing to *d·* either,
	29–13 Failing to *d·* thus,
	41– 8 *d·* it, but without hard words.
	41–12 *d·* good unto your enemies
	42–23 should *d·* to you, — *Matt.* 7 : 12.
	42–24 *d·* even so — *Matt.* 7 : 12.
	46–17 failure to *d·* this shall subject the
	48– 5 he shall *d·* it with love
Chr.	55–23 For whosoever shall *d·* — *Matt.* 12 : 50.
Ret.	5–16 the pen can never *d·* justice.
	9–13 resolving to *d·*, next time,
	13–20 as I was wont to *d·*,
	64–25 To *d·* this, mortals must first
	68–25 In C. S., man can *d·* no harm,
	72– 5 deteriorates one's ability to *d·* good,
	75–14 which shall *d·* a miracle — *Mark* 9 : 39.
	78– 3 to *d·* either too much or too little.
	82–15 in order to *d·* the greatest good
	86– 5 and that is to *d·* it !
	86–20 carry his burden and *d·* his work,
	87–20 should *d·* to you, — *Matt.* 7 : 12.
	87–21 *d·* ye even so — *Matt.* 7 : 12.
	90–27 * " I believe the proper thing for us to *d·*
Un.	14– 2 must one day *d·* His work over again,
	15–24 who seeks to *d·* them mischief,
	17–10 or seeks so to *d·*,
	21–11 If you *d·* not, your intellect will be
	44– 4 know not what they *d·*." — *Luke* 23 : 34.
	46– 8 I *d·* so on a divine Principle,
	48– 6 I believe more in Him than *d·* most
Pul.	2–21 Likewise should we *d·* as
	2–27 How can we *d·* this Christianly
	19– 1 My prayer, some daily good to *d·*
	21– 6 This we all must *d·*
	32– 4 * No photographs can *d·* the least
	49–22 * *d·* honor to that precinct of Concord.
	50– 6 * *d·* something for the toilers,
	72–28 * Christ has told us to *d·* his work,
	73–13 * to *d·* good and heal the sick,
Rud.	14– 4 To *d·* this, they must at present
	14–12 in order to *d·* gratuitous work.
	14–16 must of necessity *d·* better
No.	7– 8 and continue to *d·* so
	39–20 desire to be and *d·* good.
	41– 8 to *d·* the will of his Father
Pan.	5–13 ye will *d·*. — *John* 8 : 44.
	9–14 wise enough to *d·* himself no harm,
	13–20 we *d·* "live, and move, — *Acts* 17 : 28.
'00.	6– 5 this one thing I *d·*, — *Phil.* 3 : 13.
	8–30 not to *d·* certain things
	9– 1 know it were best not to *d·*,
	9– 4 "You may *d·* it if you desire."
	9– 6 not because it is the best thing to *d·*,
	9–21 workers to *d·* their best.
	14–17 should *d·* to you, *d·* ye." — *Luke* 6 : 31.
'01.	5–15 They *d·*, but their personality is
	9–15 taught his followers to *d·* likewise.
	9–20 what have we to *d·* with — *Mark* 1 : 24.
	11–23 forgets what Christian Scientists *d·* not,
	18–19 he came to *d·* "the will of — *Matt.* 12 : 50.
	23–20 and followers to *d·* likewise ;
	27–23 than others *d·* in proportion,
'02.	18–20 what more could he *d·* ?
	18–22 that I *d·* shall he *d·*." — *John* 14 : 12.
Hea.	5–23 to *d·* our work for us,
	8–27 as directly as we *d·* to the rule of
	8–28 *d·* more than we are now doing,
	12– 6 it can *d·* nothing,
	16–11 unless you *d·* this you are
Po.	13– 5 some daily good to *d·*
	36– 8 Thy will to know, and *d·*.
My.	vii– 4 * can never *d·* for its Leader what
	3– 8 *d·* His commandments, — *Rev.* 22 : 14.
	9–25 but I *d·* now,
	13– 1 The good they desire to *d·*,
	15–25 * As nothing else can *d·*.

do

My. 37–10   * you have done and continue to *d·*
   49– 3   * and we will *d·* thee good,'
   60– 5   * she would doubtless *d·* so.
   60–30   * care to *d·* a little watching
   61–27   * "What cannot God *d·*?"
   66–14   * to *d·* so it was necessary to have
   72– 2   * To *d·* this it was necessary to
   73– 7   * If you ask . . . how they *d·* it,
  106–31   his followers to *d·* likewise.
  114– 5   *D·* unto others as ye
  114– 6   would have others *d·* to you.
  129–21   *d·* thy errands, and
  140– 6   These things will I *d·* — *Isa.* 42 : 16.
  147–26   I have a work to *d·*
  148– 1   to *d·* your pioneer work in
  148– 3   called to *d·* your part wisely
  149– 3   "Go, and *d·* thou likewise." — *Luke* 10 : 37.
  153– 4   *d·* this in Christ's name,
  156– 5   "able to *d·* exceeding — *Eph.* 3 : 20.
  163–15   which I think *d·* them more good.
  170–20   in the Lord, and *d·* good ; — *Psal.* 37 : 3.
  180–29   know not what they *d·*." — *Luke* 23 : 34.
  191– 2   "No man can *d·* these — *John* 3 : 2.
  194– 5   as *d·* all things material,
  195–14   for we cannot *d·* more than we
  195–15   To *d·* good to all
  200–14   Striving to be good, to *d·* good,
  203–10   All that is worth . . . is what we *d·*,
  211–11   what have we to *d·* with — *Mark* 1 : 24.
  212– 2   victim is led to believe and *d·*
  212– 3   never, otherwise, think or *d·*
  212–11   matter, wherewith to *d·* evil ;
  213–11   in their desire to *d·* right
  213–12   be more zealous to *d·* good,
  214–24   which I yearned to *d·*,
  215– 5   bade me *d·* what I did,
  216–10   What, then, can a man *d·*
  216–20   by which you can *d·* much good
  221–21   that I *d·* shall he *d·* — *John* 14 : 12.
  229– 5   all that *d·* these things — *Deut.* 18 : 12.
  235–10   cannot *d·* this in mathematics,
  235–25   Do you adopt as truth . . . I *d·*.
  246–25   "What I *d·* thou knowest not — *John* 13 : 7.
  251– 2   "What I *d·* thou knowest not — *John* 13 : 7.
  252– 8   good you *d·* unto others you *d·* to
  258–12   to know and to *d·* God's will,
  261– 9   aught to *d·* with this pastime.
  264– 4   may *d·* so honestly and not
  266– 9   should *d·* to you, — *Matt.* 7 : 12.
  266– 9   *d·* ye even so — *Matt.* 7 : 12.
  270–20   know not what they *d·*." — *Luke* 23 : 34.
  274– 6   holiness, and love *d·* this,
  275–24   as we would that they *d·* by us,
  276–18   * entitled to vote should *d·* so,
  281–21   * Will you *d·* us the kindness
  283–23   "To *d·* justly, — *Mic.* 6 : 8.
  288– 6   The good done and the good to *d·*
  289– 2   what we *d·*, not what we say.
  300– 6   both to will and to *d·* — *Phil.* 2 : 13.
  303–29   proved by the good I *d·*.
  305–25   simply how to *d·* his works.
  307– 8   nothing to *d·* with matter,
  309– 4   called upon to *d·* much business
  310–31   * "Read it, for it will *d·* you good.
  314–23   imploring him not to *d·* it.
  319–28   * and *d·* so still.
  320–13   * having had something to *d·*
  324–29   * if he found you could *d·* so,
  345– 2   will *d·* the children no harm.
  345– 4   I *d·* not suppose their
  358–14   I have not the time to *d·* so.
  360– 1   if you do not *d·* this.

dock root
My. 122– 7   Sin is like a *d· r·*.

Doctor
Man. 45–25   titles of Reverend and *D·*,
My. 245–29   degrees of Bachelor and *D·*

doctor (*see also* doctor's)
Mis. 88–27   to treat with a *d·*?
   88–28   depends upon what kind of a *d·*
  239–20   * "I've got cold, *d·*."
  243– 8   regular *d·* had put on splints
  252–27   equips the *d·* with safe and
  378–11   the aforesaid *d·* in Portland.
Ret. 13–11   family *d·* was summoned,
   24– 2   magnetic *d·*, Mr. P. P. Quimby,
No. 29– 9   and then they *d·* this soul
'01. 18–20   *d·* who teaches that a human
My. 226–30   decline to *d·* infectious or
  314– 5   * The *d·* practised in several towns,

doctored
Ret. 57– 6   which must be *d·* in order to

Doctor of Divinity
No. 43–10   A distinguished *D· of D·* said :

doctor's
Mis. 89– 7   to follow the *d·* directions?
  229–11   more certain would be the *d·* success,
  240– 2   *d·* squills and bills would have

doctors
Mis. 80–25   regular *d·*, who, in successive
   88–30   drop one of these *d·* when you
  240– 6   Parents and *d·* must not take the
  243–25   Even *d·* disagree on that
  365–23   Even *d·* agree that infidelity,
Ret. 40–21   demonstration so stirred the *d·*
Pul. 69– 8   * *d·* had pronounced his case incurable.
No. 10– 5   Even *d·* will agree that infidelity,
My. 111–10   now assumed by many *d·* and
  345–14   *d·* said I would live if the

doctrinal
Pul. 22–16   *d·* barriers between the churches
'01. 33–14   not to be judged on a *d·* platform,
'02. 12– 3   explains these *d·* points,
My. 139–21   the denominational to the *d·*,

doctrine
Mis. 46– 8   *d·* previously entertained.
   76–10   That *d·* is not theism,
  121–13   would make this fatal *d·* just
  182–17   Born of no *d·*,
  189–16   a pantheistic *d·* that presents
  189–27   astonished at his *d·* : — *Matt.* 7 : 28.
  221–24   contradicts the *d·* that we must
  235– 9   demonstration, not *d·*.
  366– 5   to learn the *d·* of theology,
  382– 5   my first work on this *d·*,
Ret. 13– 5   the *d·* of unconditional election,
   13–10   aroused by this erroneous *d·*,
   14–13   if assent to this *d·* was essential
   15–20   if not in full unity of *d·*.
   58–10   astonished at his *d·* :   *Matt.* 7 : 28.
Un. 1– 1   no *d·* of C. S. rouses so much
   8–20   even the *d·* of heredity
  42–18   astonished at his *d·* ; — *Matt.* 7 : 28.
  54– 1   *d·* of mind in matter.
Pul. 52–26   * No new *d·* is proclaimed,
No. 12–21   method, beyond *d·* and ritual ;
  14–25   the *d·* of eternal damnation,
  22– 1   wind of *d·*." — *Eph.* 4 : 14.
Pan. 2–15   * "The *d·* that the universe,
   2–20   pantheism is the *d·* of the
   4– 2   the *d·* that the universe
   8–10   *d·* that Mohammed is the only **prophet**
'00. 13– 8   system supported by their *d·*
'01. 19– 5   I love this *d·*, for I know
  24–29   to prove the *d·* of Jesus,
'02. 2–20   either in heart or in *d·* ;
   5–26   formulate a *d·*, or speculate
  11–29   Jew and Christian can unite in *d·*
Hea. 3– 6   a demonstration, more than a *d·*.
   7–28   no argument for a creed or *d·*,
  18–18   The *d·* of atonement never
Peo. 5– 7   cold materialisms of dogma and *d·*
   5–18   points away from matter and *d·*,
My. 87–29   * this *d·* of health, happiness,
  93–17   * who do not accept the *d·* of
  112– 9   interpret the Scriptures to fit a *d·*,
  118–25   The *d·* of Buddha,
  148– 5   judge our *d·* by its fruits.
  221– 4   precludes Jesus' *d·*, now as then,
  282– 3   believe strictly in the Monroe *d·*,
  300–22   make known his *d·* to the world,

doctrines
absolute
  Mis. 148–20   absolute *d·* destined for future
  Man. 3–17   absolute *d·* destined for future
and hypotheses
  Ret. 56– 2   theories, *d·*, and hypotheses,
and traditions
  No. 8–20   enmity over *d·* and traditions,
beliefs and
  Pul. 73–22   * versed in all their beliefs and *d·*.
effete
  Ret. 79–11   ridding the thought of effete *d·*,
erroneous
  Mis. 366–26   Erroneous *d·* never have abated
goodness, not
  Pul. 9–27   goodness, not *d·*,
her
  Mis. 95– 7   * public letter condemning her *d·* ;
his
  Mis. 111–24   his *d·* and those of Jesus,
human
  '00. 4–18   beaten path of human *d·*
  My. 262–18   Human *d·* or hypotheses
its
  '00. 4–23   Does it demonstrate its *d·*?

doctrines

my
Un. 44– 2 made concerning my *d·*,
Pul. 75–11 more of heathenism than of my *d·*.

new-old
'00. 10–16 new-old *d·* of the prophets

of Christ
Mis. 188– 1 teachings opposed the *d·* of Christ

of Christian Science
Man. 34– 8 believer in the *d·* of C. S.,

of men
Mis. 366–19 "beware of . . . *d·* of men, — *Matt.* 16 : 6.

of theosophy
Man. 47–25 not believe in the *d·* of theosophy,

of the world
My. 92– 3 * real position in the *d·* of the world

opinions and
Mis. 17– 9 human opinions and *d·*,

personal
Mis. 232–15 theories, personal *d·* and

Presbyterian
Ret. 14– 6 of the strictest Presbyterian *d·*.

such
Man. 48– 2 those who do believe in such *d·*,
No. 29–17 Better far that we impute such *d·* to

taught
My. 112– 9 *d·* taught by divine Science

that deny
Mis. 193– 7 *D·* that deny the substance and

their
'01. 32–17 caused me to love their *d·*.

——

No. 12–10 *d·*, rites, and ceremonies,
Pan. 8–24 *d·* that embrace pantheism,
11– 8 *d·*, and dogmas of men
My. 85–11 * the *d·* of Mrs. Eddy

document
My. 137– 6 *Boston Globe*, referring to this *d·*,
179– 7 In this allegorical *d·* the power

dodge
Mis. 53– 4 to *d·* the question is not

doer
My. 210–15 the proud talker and *d·*.

doers
My. 125– 3 not only sayers but *d·* of the law?
197–21 in the Word and in the *d·* thereof,
352–22 the hearers and the *d·* of God's Word.

does
Mis. 6–13 surely *d·*, to many thinkers,
15–19 eternity *d·* this ;
33–25 *d·* away with all material medicines,
37–26 She now *d·* not.
38– 5 as this teaching certainly *d·*,
43–22 *d·* a vast amount of injury to
61–23 If not, what *d·* ?
87–20 he *d·* best in the investigation of
92–31 That teacher *d·* most for his students
145– 8 *D·* a single bosom burn for fame
179–24 God *d·* all this through His
190– 7 nor *d·* the material ultimate in
229– 7 and with better effect than he *d·*
240–10 forecasting liberty and joy *d·*;
255–22 It *d·* away with material medicine,
266– 7 Whoever *d·* this may represent
280–11 Because God *d·* all,
334– 8 *d·* this as a lie declaring itself,
365–29 what it is and of what it *d·*,
369–18 to trust Christ more than it *d·* drugs.
Ret. 34–11 It *d·* away with all material medicines,
71–28 demoralizes the person who *d·* this,
74– 3 He who *d·* this is ignorant of the
75– 5 *d·* violence to the ethics of C. S.
84–19 That teacher *d·* most for his students who
86–19 If he *d·* this not, and another one
Un. 13– 2 on the same principle that it *d·*
29– 4 as *d·* all criminal law,
30– 4 This it *d·* under the delusion
46–27 as it *d·* of the present.
Rud. 5–20 Human belief says that it *d·* ;
No. 11–12 what it is and what it *d·*,
18– 6 C. S. *d·* this.
30– 3 It *d·* more than forgive the
'00. 3– 4 thinker and worker *d·* his best,
3– 5 *d·* the thinking for the ages.
'01. 18–29 *d·* it and so proves their nullity.
22– 7 since Science *d·* not
29–24 *d·* most, and sacrifices most
Peo. 2– 7 what God is, and what God *d·*.
Po. 43– 2 Jesus loves you ! so *d·* mother :
My. 106–23 more than *d·* the average man,
108– 3 as *d·* the allopath who depends upon
112–28 through the good it *d·*
122– 8 To cut off the top . . . *d·* no good ;

does
My. 128–18 Men cannot punish . . . God *d·* that.
128–25 as *d·* a subtle conspirator ;
227–32 than *d· materia medica.*
232–26 Does the textbook . . . It *d·*.
232–29 does that watch accord . . . It *d·* not.
240–26 * She most assuredly *d·*,
271– 9 the good that a man *d·*
273–29 "Man awakes . . . . *d·* he not?"

doest
Mis. 57–11 "That thou *d·*, — *John* 13 : 27.
334– 3 What *d·* Thou?" — *Dan.* 4 : 35.
347–28 None can say unto Him, What *d·* Thou?
Po. 77–16 learned of Truth what Thou *d·* now
My. 191– 3 miracles that thou *d·*, — *John* 3 : 2.
200– 8 "What *d·* thou?" — *Dan.* 4 : 35.
280–21 nor say unto Him, What *d·* Thou?

doeth
Mis. 334– 1 "He *d·* according to His — *Dan.* 4 : 35.
'02. 19–22 It is divine Love that *d·* it,
My. 33–19 nor *d·* evil to his — *Psal.* 15 : 3.
33–26 He that *d·* these things — *Psal.* 15 : 5.
99– 5 * merry heart that *d·* good

doff
Mis. 177–14 *d·* your lavender-kid zeal,

doggedly
Mis. 374–23 *d·* deny or frantically affirm
My. 308–16 * tramping *d·* along the highway,

dogma
Mis. 150–26 defined by no *d·*, appropriated by no
331–23 frozen crust of creed and *d·*,
362– 8 Scholastic *d·* has made men blind.
Ret. 31– 7 paramount to rubric and *d·*
65– 6 Ritualism and *d·* lead to
Pul. 56–17 * *d·* and truth could not unite,
No. 24–17 evil that is hidden by *d·* and
42–12 vain power of *d·* and philosophy
Peo. 5– 7 cold materialisms of *d·* and
5–19 from matter and doctrine, or *d·*,
My. 47–26 * in the wilderness of *d·* and creed,
50–11 * against the currents of *d·*,
148–26 it is not a creed or *d·*,
205–24 wholly apart from . . . creed and *d·*,
288–15 creed, *d·*, or *materia medica.*
301– 7 *d·* and creed will pass off in scum,
307–27 *materia medica*, *d·*, and creeds,

dogmas
Mis. 168– 9 buried in *d·* and physical ailments,
232–15 personal doctrines and *d·*,
Ret. 14– 7 unbelievers in these *d·* lost,
No. 14–25 frozen *d·*, persistent persecution,
Pan. 11– 8 doctrines, and *d·* of men
'00. 7– 5 creeds and *d·* have been sifted,

dogmatical
Pan. 2– 6 neither hypothetical nor *d·*,

dogmatism
'02. 2–20 *d·*, relegated to the past,

doing
Mis. 9–13 they are *d·* thee good
67–12 but shalt know that by *d·* thus
114–24 Thus *d·*, Scientists will silence
115–32 *d·* to others as you would have
116–22 not merely saying, but *d·*,
131– 9 console . . . by *d·* likewise.
135– 9 *d·* unto others as ye would they
153– 4 not weary in well *d·*." — *see Gal.* 6 : 9.
199– 8 so *d·*, male and female come into
215–22 and what he was *d·*.
223–17 while *d·* unto others what
230– 5 in talking nothing, *d·* nothing,
230–22 * "Let us, then, be up and *d·*,
236–28 not deter us from *d·* our duty,
262–15 for the good you are *d·* .
263– 1 much pleasure in thus *d·*,
266– 7 may represent me as *d·* it ;
266–11 *d·* the work that nobody else can
284– 2 hinder others from *d·* theirs
290–19 this person was *d·* well,
292–20 who know not what he is *d·*
301– 4 *d·* to the author of the
317– 3 *Yes*, if you are *d·* God's work.
Ret. 84–22 Thus *d·*, posterity will call him
85– 2 for *d·* their own work well.
87–17 In so *d·* they must follow the
Un. 13– 5 *d·* their own work in obedience
45– 4 as Truth and . . . are *d·* in C. S.,
58– 8 This was the very thing he *was d·*,
Pul. 4–13 in being and *d·* right,
15–10 for the sake of *d·* right
Rud. 14–21 *d·* charity work besides.
No. 41–26 * and it is *d·* it to-day ;
43– 9 * the good your books are *d·*."

doing

'00. 3-15 not far from saying and d·.
8-18 d· rightly by yourself and others.
8-19 d· the work that belongs to another.
'02. 18-21 how much of what he did are we d·?
Hea. 9- 1 more than we are now d·,
12- 5 to learn what matter is doing
My. v-17 * d· this work "without money — Isa. 55 : 1.
12-24 God prepares the way for d· ;
13- 1 they insist upon d· now.
14-20 * was entirely right in d· so.
28-20 * d· the works which Jesus
64-18 * her success in so d·
87-29 * the cheerful d· of good.
99- 3 * good things that this sect is d·.
137-24 I had contemplated d· this
138- 3 relieved of the burden of d· this.
142-12 sought God's guidance in d· it,
149- 3 by d· as he bade :
150- 6 *"D· what deserves to be written,
165- 4 But in d· this the Master
185- 4 * Let us, then, be up and d·,
187- 5 too busy to think of d· so
203-28 d· so much to benefit mankind
204- 1 nor will you be long in d· more.
245-20 d· the works of primitive
252-12 to make one enjoy d· right,
275-24 D· unto others as we would
358- 3 d· as you say you are,
363-25 sure that one is not d· this,
(see also **good**)

doinge
Mis. 253-12 * chapter sub-title

doings
My. 279- 6 Christ's sayings and d·.

doleful
Ret. 14-11 ready for his d· questions,

dolefully
Mis. 339-27 surge d· at the door of

dollar
Man. 44-14 tax of not less than one d·
Mis. 141-27 or else return every d·
My. 52-25 * reached her bottom d·,
98-23 * asked to contribute a d·.
(see also **values**)

dollars
My. 28- 8 * will show the d· and cents
53- 3 * hundreds of d· were sunk
(see also **values**)

domain
Mis. 320-24 the zenith of Truth's d·,
Po. 22-18 d· of pain and sin
My. 278-27 War is not in the d· of good ;

dome
Mis. 1- 4 dawned on the d· of being
Pul. 2- 8 soft shimmer of its starlit d·.
Po. 30- 6 A temple, whose high d·
My. 29-20 * the d· of the great edifice
36-25 * by this sheltering d· ;
46- 3 * towering, overshadowing d·,
61-26 * stood under the great d·,
67- 1 * raises its d· above the city
68- 7 * d· surmounting the building
68- 8 * twice the size of the d· on
68-10 * d· is two hundred and twenty-four feet
69- 7 * presenting an oval and d· appearance
69-28 * in which the d· seems to dominate
69-31 * building and d· can be seen
70-12 * are worthy of the d·.
77- 6 * d· of the Massachusetts State House,
78- 6 * massive d· rising to a height of
81-23 * rose tingling to the great d·,
85-30 * noble d· of pure gray tint,
86- 5 * loved its golden State House d·,
89- 6 * d· over two hundred and twenty feet
95-13 * d· which rivals that of the
186- 8 Though neither d· nor turret

domestic
Pul. 49-19 * something of her d· arrangements,

dominance
Pul. 31-18 * in the d· of mind over matter,
No. 33- 3 gives the d· to God,

dominant
Mis. 293-14 If spiritual sense is not d· in
297-24 If the man is d· over the animal,
Ret. 20-24 My d· thought in marrying again
31- 2 sunders the d· ties of earth
Un. 50- 9 by a d· understanding of Spirit.

dominate
Man. 83-13 or attempt to d· his pupils.
Pul. 32- 7 * to d·, to lead, to control,
My. 69-28 * seems to d· the entire city,

dominates
Mis. 293-15 if evil d· his character,
Pul. 2- 6 spirit of beauty d· The
My. 96- 9 * where fanaticism d· everything
193-15 The spiritual d· the temporal.

dominating
Pul. 32-13 * d· her followers like any abbess
Pan. 7-27 lapses into evil d· good,
My. 309- 1 * d·, passionate, fearless."

domination
No. 32-22 d· of good destroys the sense of evil.

dominion
Mis. 16-14 reflect the full d· of Spirit
69-12 let them have d· Gen. 1 : 26.
69-30 Had that sick man d· over the fish
125- 8 d· over his own sinful sense
145-12 to whom God gave "d· — Gen. 1 : 26.
167-22 He has d· over the whole earth ;
183-28 in proof of man's "d· — Gen. 1 : 26.
331- 7 rich heritage, — "d· over — Gen. 1 : 26.
373-24 God gave man d· over all things ;
Un. 39-18 giveth man d· over all the earth.
Pul. 53-19 * d· over the physical world.
Peo. 12- 3 Let them have "d· Gen. 1 : 26.
My. 93-13 * or attaining d· over others,
119-18 gives d· over all the earth.

donated
Mis. 140-20 The lot of land which I d·
143-23 d· the munificent sum of
382-19 I d· to this church the land

donating
Pul. 64-10 * others d· large sums.

donation
Mis. 143-27 Each d· came promptly ;
My. 10-14 * d· to be specifically subscribed

donations
Man. 78- 9 D· from this Church
My. 12- 5 * spontaneous and liberal d·

done
Mis. 5- 1 This work well d· will elevate
5-16 I have d· all that can be d·.
7-25 great work already has been d·,
7-26 work yet remains to be d·.
8- 7 we shall have d· more.
11-13 I had d· my whole duty to students.
23-11 "and it was d·" — Psal. 33 : 9.
38- 2 must be d· freely?
41-17 struggle with sin is forever d·.
42-18 proves to have been well d·,
45- 2 This is not d· by will-power,
57- 8 This work had been d· ;
91- 6 but if this be d·, let it be in
96-24 How is the healing d· in C. S.?
96-27 some means by which it is not d·.
111- 3 work, well d·, would dignify angels.
115-13 take up the cross as I have d·,
122-25 or the "Well d·, — Matt. 25 : 23.
129- 6 having d· this, one will naturally,
141-19 Let this be speedily d·.
141-30 what might be d· with their money.
147- 5 and has another duty been d·
175-31 and d· many wonderful works?
198- 8 must be d· with the understanding
208- 1 chapter sub-title — Matt. 6 : 10.
208-12 and to let His will be d·.
208-15 to do His will or to let it be d·
212-21 but Thine, be d·," — Luke 22 : 42.
213-30 be d· on earth as in heaven.
216- 4 must first have d· our work,
223-18 we would resist to the hilt if d·
236-17 d· this to the best of our ability,
238-18 the good d·, and the love that
250-23 unselfish deed d· in secret ;
274- 7 The work that needs to be d·,
283-22 d· without incriminating the
292-30 as to just how this should be d·,
308- 2 Until this be d·, man will
308-21 messenger has d· its work,
310-16 be d· decently — I Cor. 14: 40.
334-15 This is d· only as one gives
334-21 and you have d· with it.
335-31 has d· himself harm.
355- 7 "well d· ;" — Matt. 25 : 21.
359- 3 when it has d· its work,
366-30 and this is being d· daily.
380-22 that something was being d·
384-11 The cold blasts d·,
391-11 That when a wrong is d· us,
391-19 Then if we've d· to others
399-18 Laus Deo, it is d· !
Man. 97-18 injustices d· Mrs. Eddy or members of
Ret. 28-23 How it was d·,

done

Ret.	33–13	the better the work is d· ;
	37–23	divine purpose that this should be d·,
	50–18	what it has d· for them,
	52–14	This was immediately d·,
	62– 7	than *a belief . . . has ever d·.*
	64–28	if this is not d·, mortals will
	87–30	until he has d· with the case
	91–28	teacher, d· for the human race?
	91–29	Ask, rather, what has he *not d·.*
	92–10	it shall be d· unto you." — *John* 15 : 7.
Un.	14– 3	was not at first d· aright.
	53–19	sums d· under both rules would
	58–11	d· through what is humanly called
Pul.	9– 5	your tireless tasks are d· — well d·
	16– 3	*Laus Deo,* it is d· !
	21–22	however much this is d· to us
	22– 7	Thy will be d· — *Matt.* 6 : 10.
	25– 3	* are d· by electricity,
	43–14	* "*Laus Deo,* it is d· !"
	44– 2	* '*Laus Deo,* it is d· !'
	51–19	* While it has d· this,
	51–29	* which have d· something good
	53– 5	* that which is d· — *Eccl.* 1 : 9.
	53– 6	* that which shall be d· : — *Eccl.* 1 : 9.
	69–26	* have not d· so in an intelligent
No.	1– 3	but this must be d· gradually,
	9– 8	but this one thing can be d·,
	37–26	but he could not have d· this if
	38– 1	so far as this could be d·
	40–26	our Father has d· this.
Pan.	13–17	and d· on earth as in heaven.
'00.	3–15	worker has said and d·,
	15–28	The cold blasts d·,
'01.	27–20	why was it not d· ?
'02.	17–15	duty d· and life perfected,
	18–14	ye have d· it unto — *Matt.* 25 : 40.
	18–15	d· it unto me." — *Matt.* 25 : 40.
Hea.	7–21	would not have d· to-day.
	14– 6	What has physiology, . . . d·
	18– 7	if this be d·, the bottle will break
	18–13	If that could be d·,
Peo.	11– 3	scarcely d· with their battles
Po.	26–16	And smiling, say'st, " 'Tis d· !
	27–20	Thy work is d·, and well :
	32–21	with hope when 'tis d· ;
	36–10	The cold blasts d·,
	38–10	That when a wrong is d· us,
	38–18	Then if we've d· to others
	76– 2	LAUS DEO, it is d· !
My.	vii– 4	* what its Leader has d· for
	6– 7	is to be d· forever with the sins
	8–15	* something d·, and d· immediately,
	12–23	Whatever needs to be d·
	12–23	which cannot be d· now,
	12–25	that which can be d· now,
	18–25	and d· on earth as in heaven."
	20– 1	this also that she hath d· — *Mark* 14 : 9.
	24–28	* as well as this can be d· by a
	37–10	* of all that you have d·
	38– 6	* all that you have d· for us.
	53– 5	* that her duty was wholly d·,
	58–23	* as she has d·, verifying
	61–23	* to admit that the work could be d·,
	62– 2	* "Well d·, — *Matt.* 25 : 23.
	64– 7	* gratitude and love for all that she has d·.
	78–10	* an interior d· in soft gray
	84– 7	* that would otherwise be d·.
	98–11	* must have d· with scoffs and jeers
	122– 9	Now I am d· with homilies
	124–13	"well d·." — *Matt.* 25 : 23.
	134–11	and work well d· should not
	136–27	and I have so d· that I may have
	142–19	as they so often have d·,
	150–25	it shall be d· unto you." — *John* 15 : 7.
	151–12	injustice d· by press and pulpit
	152–30	of all that is rightly d·.
	160–32	the wrongs d· to others,
	162–21	"Well d·, — *Matt.* 25 : 23.
	201–15	crowned with a diadem of duties d·.
	202–13	"Well d·, — *Matt.* 25 : 23.
	207–21	"Well d·, — *Matt.* 25 : 21.
	225– 4	"Well d·, — *Matt.* 25 : 23.
	229–16	as she has d·,
	235–11	it cannot be d· in metaphysics,
	235–28	Had I known what was being d·
	240–27	* when the teaching is d· by those who
	247–29	has all been d· through love,
	250–27	whatever is d· in this direction
	261–11	Too much cannot be d· towards
	281– 4	Thy will be d· — *Matt.* 6 : 10.
	284–23	only as other churches had d·.
	288– 6	The good d· and the good to do
	315– 8	* if he had d· as he ought,
	319–30	* told me that he had d· some literary
	320– 7	* statement of what he had d· for you

done

My.	324–31	* no man could have d· so any better.
	327–14	* This is the result of the work d· at
	345–21	"The work d· by the surgeon

donkey

Mis.	370–21	braying d· whose ears stick out

donor (*see also* **donor's**)

Pul.	26–16	* healing of the wife of the d·.

donor's

Mis.	143–29	breathing the d· privileged joy.

donors

Mis.	142– 6	chapter sub-title
	142–13	Let me write to the d·,
Pul.	8–11	d· all touchingly told their
My.	167– 2	it may have cost the dear d·.

doom

Mis.	354– 5	lead the innocent to d· ?
Chr.	53–29	that d· Was Jesus' part ;
Un.	57– 6	it foresees the impending d·
Pul.	7–21	stumble onward to their d· ;
'00.	2–23	d· of such workers will come,
Po.	34–15	Yet wherefore ask thy d· ?
My.	125–29	The d· of the Babylonish woman,
	211–27	and sealing his d·,
	350–19	Thou infinite — dost d· above.

doomed

Mis.	261– 1	evil, as *mind,* is d·,
	362–19	an evil mind already d·,
	385–23	flesh was weak, and d· To pass away.
Ret.	13– 8	among those who were d· to
Po.	48–19	flesh was weak, and d· To pass away.

dooms

Mis.	258– 1	this lawless law which d· man to

door

Mis.	30–12	Death was not the d· to this
	30–18	opened the d· to the captive,
	74–19	rolled away the stone from the d·
	83–14	error which knocks at the d·
	84–30	through the d· named death,
	106–12	Out through the d· of Love,
	133–15	when thou hast shut thy d·, — *Matt.* 6 : 6.
	155– 8	woo the weary wanderer to your d·,
	180–14	I found the open d· from this
	201–28	is awakened to bar his d·
	250–26	out of a side d· ;
	250–27	the d· that turns toward want
	275– 5	from the d· of this sepulchre
	276–29	quickly learned when the d· is shut.
	276–30	and it closes the d· on itself.
	303–14	knock instead of push at the d·
	317–10	d· to my teaching was shut when
	324– 5	The d· is shut.
	324–12	him who waiteth at the d·.
	326– 6	The d· is burst open,
	328–13	heard this Christ knock at the d· of
	339–27	at the d· of conscience,
	342–22	The d· is shut.
	391–18	Find items at our d·.
	398–11	We would enter by the d·,
Chr.	55–26	I stand at the d·, — *Rev.* 3 : 20.
	55–27	and open the d·, — *Rev.* 3 : 20.
Ret.	9– 3	The d· was ajar,
	23–14	When the d· opened,
	46–17	We would enter by the d·,
	80–24	sees the d· and turns away from it,
Pul.	17–16	We would enter by the d·,
	21–21	and close the d· on church or
	26–21	over the d·, . . . is the word "Love."
	35–30	* on the sign at his d·.
	78–22	* gold key to the church d·.
Pan.	12–13	a d· that no man can shut ;
'01.	14–23	even as one guards his d· against
Peo.	5–11	are nigh, even at our d·.
Po.	14–15	We would enter by the d·,
	38–17	Find items at our d·.
My.	54–11	* was turned from the d·
	90–13	* the d· to this gospel for many,
	152–14	Do I enter by the d·
	210– 5	no d· through which evil can enter,
	221–28	thus throwing the d· wide open to
	256–12	close the d· of mind on this subject,
	311– 5	knocked at the d· and was admitted.

doors

Mis.	101–18	opening the d· for them that
	114–22	or bar their d· too closely,
	124–16	opening the prison d· to the
	262–21	opening the prison d· to such as
	280–30	d· of animal magnetism open wide
	281– 3	d· that this animal element
	283–12	wrong to burst open d·
	325–30	without watchers and the d· unbarred !
	332– 6	d· that closed on C. S.
Ret.	14–18	even if . . . left me outside the d·.

doors

Pul.	24–27	* with *d·* of antique oak
	59–30	* auditors left by the rear *d·*,
	76– 2	* that used in the *d·* and pews.
No.	41–17	trying to force the *d·* of Science
My.	29–29	* for the opening of the *d·*
	31– 9	* *d·* of the church were thrown open
	34–11	ye everlasting *d·* ; — *Psal.* 24 : 9.
	54–24	* crowds had besieged the *d·*
	77–27	* open its *d·* absolutely free of
	94–19	* *d·* were opened to the public,
	110–22	open the prison *d·*
	174– 2	throwing open their *d·* for the
	276– 8	preference to remain within *d·*

dormant

Pul.	72–24	* power of Christ has been *d·* in
My.	211–29	Other minds are made *d·* by it,
	260–25	raises the *d·* faculties.

dose

Mis.	241–10	give to the immoralist a mental *d·*
	241–13	so taking a *d·* of error
	252– 6	its largest *d·* is never dangerous,
Ret.	33–18	not affected by a larger *d·*.
'01.	18– 3	that was my favorite *d·*.
Hea.	12–19	made the infinitesimal *d·* effectual.
	13–17	with this original *d·* we cured an

dosed

My.	345–13	I was *d·* with drugs until

doses

Mis.	69–15	given three *d·* of Croton oil,
	249– 2	some large *d·* of morphine,
	348–21	*d·* of *Natrum muriaticum*
	348–26	Hence I tried several *d·* of
'01.	17–28	where the allopathic *d·* would not.

dotted

Pul.	48– 3	* *d·* with beds of flowering shrubs,

dotting

Mis.	150–17	churches are *d·* the entire land.

dottings

My.	252–19	Your letter and *d·* are an

double

Un.	36– 3	endows with the *d·* capacity of
My.	82–26	* trains pulled out . . . in *d·* sections.
	126–17	*d·* unto her *d·* — *Rev.* 18 : 6.
	126–19	fill to her *d·* — *Rev.* 18 : 6.
	315–24	or is it her alleged *d·* or

doubled

Mis.	349–30	contributions, . . . *d·* that amount.

doubleminded

Mis.	198–23	the "*d·*" senses, — *Jas.* 4 : 8.

doubly

My.	85–31	* this church, . . . is *d·* welcomed.

doubt

and darkness

Mis.	342– 4	they were in *d·* and darkness.
'00.	7–19	In *d·* and darkness we say as did
My.	152–19	will stumble into *d·* and darkness,

any

My.	61–20	* never more did I have any *d·*.

beyond a

Ret.	89– 4	is proven beyond a *d·*
'01.	28–21	has proven to me beyond a *d·*
My.	180– 4	knows beyond a *d·* that its

darkness and

Ret.	68–20	Darkness and *d·* encompass thought,

darkness or

My.	187– 8	exclude all darkness or *d·*,

every

Mis.	120–29	puts to flight every *d·* as to the

excludes

My.	293– 2	The knowledge that . . . excludes *d·*,

faith and

My.	292–29	is a compound of faith and *d·*,

fear or

No.	8–13	his own salvation, without fear or *d·*,

natural

Un.	1– 2	rouses so much natural *d·*

no

Mis.	6–19	we exist in God, . . . there is no *d·*,
	49– 6	no *d·* she could have been
	52– 8	has no *d·* of God's power,
	249–20	no *d·* from the combined efforts of
	319–28	No *d·* must intervene
My.	19–27	no *d·* fill the memory
	42– 9	* no *d·* already acquainted with him
	74– 5	* no *d·* the night trains

of their reality

Hea.	5–14	* not the *d·* of their reality."

or disagreement

Man.	66– 7	If . . . a *d·* or disagreement shall

doubt

period of

Mis.	237–19	This is a period of *d·*, inquiry,

prayer of

Mis.	59–16	prayer of *d·* and mortal belief

single

My.	294–13	would mightily rebuke a single *d·*

without

Pul.	70–10	* is without *d·* one of the

Mis.	30– 5	and *d·* its higher rules,
	165–14	darkness, *d·*, disease, nor death.
	204– 7	attended throughout with *d·*,
	226– 2	* *d·* not that the Father of all
	250– 6	and *d·* what it is.
	341–20	To *d·* this is implicit treason
Pul.	54– 8	* That Jesus . . . we cannot *d·*.
'01.	2–24	*d·*, and unrequited toil will beset
	22– 2	Science is Science, who can *d·* ;

doubted

My.	311–23	I never *d·* the veracity of

doubtful

Un.	23–15	*d·* or spurious evidence of
'02.	2·13	Protestantism to *d·* liberalism.
	5– 6	*d·* interpretations of the Bible ;
My.	10–17	* It is *d·* if the Cause of C. S.
	58–30	* it is *d·* if there was one so
	95–28	* It is *d·* if, since the days of
	260–15	*d·* sense that falls short of

doubting

Mis.	28–15	our Master proved to his *d·* disciple,
	241–24	*d·* heart looks up through faith,
	307– 4	if you wait, never *d·*,
My.	119–18	The *d·* disciple could not identify
	219–18	not charge Christians with *d·*

doubtingly

Mis.	241–14	else he will *d·* await the result ;

doubtless

Mis.	137–11	Since then you have *d·* realized
	239–24	*d·* their familiarity with
Ret.	49– 6	will *d·* follow the example of
Pul.	50–18	* and *d·* have been comforted
	51–23	* erection of this temple will *d·* help
My.	60– 5	* she would *d·* do so.
	83–14	* policemen, who will *d·* have fewer
	215–29	*D·* to test the effect of both
	250–20	*D·* the churches adopting this

doubts

Ret.	14–18	even if my creedal *d·*
	33–24	insufficient to satisfy my *d·*
Un.	27– 9	which *d·* all existence except
Hea.	19–21	*d·* the feasibility of the demand.

Douma

My.	282– 9	The *D·* recently adopted in

dove (*see also* dove's)

Mis.	81–21	*hear this voice, or see the d·*,
	82– 5	*peace symbolized by a d·* ;
	306–24	touch of the breast of a *d·* ;
	330– 6	no arrow wounds the *d·* ?
	331–12	*d·* feeds her callow brood,
	355–25	like the *d·* from the deluge.
	387·12	arrow that doth wound the *d·*
Po.	6– 7	arrow that doth wound the *d·*
	10–11	Our eagle, like the *d·*,
	24–21	Send us thy white-winged *d·*.
	43– 7	Gentle as the *d·*,
My.	192–16	the *d·* of peace sits smilingly
	337–12	Our eagle, like the *d·*,

dove-like

Mis.	ix–14	now hope sits *d·*.

dove's

Po.	28–13	The *d·* to soar to Thee !

doves

Mis.	210–11	harmless as *d·*." — *Matt.* 10 : 16.
	270– 3	them that sold *d·*," — *Matt.* 21 : 12.
My.	150–29	harmless as *d·*." — *Matt.* 10 : 16.
	205– 6	harmless as *d·*." — *Matt.* 10 : 16.

Dowager Empress

My.	234–22	If the *D· E·* could hold her nation

down

Mis.	5–28	weighed *d·* as is mortal thought
	7– 4	loaded *d·* with coverings
	10–27	Heaven comes *d·* to earth.
	16– 4	heaven to come *d·* to earth.
	24–30	put *d·* all subtle falsities
	36–12	lion that lieth *d·* with the lamb.
	120–15	with armor on, not laid *d·*.
	125–11	shall sit *d·* at the Father's right hand :
	125–12	*sit d·*; not stand waiting
	139–11	*pulling d· of strong holds*; — *II Cor.* 10 : 4.

down

Mis.	139–11	casting *d·* imaginations,— *II Cor.* 10 : 5.
	145–23	lie *d·* with the kid ;— *Isa.* 11 : 6.
	151–11	"Cut it *d·* ; — *Luke* 13 : 7.
	212–10	friends took *d·* from the cross
	225–20	sat *d·* beside the sofa whereon
	235–13	cut *d·* all that bringeth not forth
	250–15	taken *d·* on rare occasions
	257–23	and strikes *d·* the hoary saint.
	257–25	*d·* in the death-dealing wave.
	261–14	pressed *d·*, and running over.
	285–18	deep *d·* in human consciousness,
	320– 9	The star that looked lovingly *d·*
	320–24	looketh *d·* on the long night of
	321–21	Still treading each temptation *d·*,
	327–20	lay *d·* a few of the heavy weights,
	329– 8	putting *d·* the green ones,
	356–25	gone *d·* in his own esteem.
	373–28	sit *d·* at the right hand of the Father.
	376–10	* handed *d·* from the *living reality.*
	383–13	*d·* the dim posterns of time
	389–23	No night drops *d·* upon
	392– 8	pouring *d·* Thy sheltering shade,
Ret.	22–12	set *d·* at the right hand of — *Heb.* 12 : 2.
	35– 5	basis it laid *d·* for physical and
	40–23	notices for a second lecture pulled *d·*,
	80–13	pulling *d·* of sin's strongholds,
	85–10	a ladder let *d·* from the heaven of
Un.	1– 4	this may be set *d·* as
	12– 1	I say, Look up, not *d·*,
	29–24	"Why art thou cast *d·*,— *Psal.* 42 : 11.
	45–10	The egotist must come *d·* and learn,
	58– 7	come *d·* from the cross."— *Mark* 15 : 30.
	58– 8	coming *d·* from the cross,
Pul.	9–28	and call *d·* blessings infinite.
	12– 8	accuser of . . . is cast *d·*,— *Rev.* 12 : 10.
	12–13	for the devil is come *d·* — *Rev.* 12 : 12.
	12–22	Self-abnegation, by which we lay *d·* all
	27–13	* "cometh *d·* from God— see *Rev.* 3 : 12.
	28– 4	* star of Bethlehem shines *d·* from above.
	45–24	* gladly laid *d·* his responsibilities
	49– 8	* Looking *d·* from the windows
	50–28	* live *d·* any attempted repression.
	60–11	* as set *d·* for him,
	62–22	* from those described *d·* to
Rud.	16–19	practice laid *d·* in S. and H.,
No.	8–17	bow *d·* to the commandments of
	19– 3	the premium would go *d·*.
Pan.	4–21	"Why art thou cast *d·*,— *Psal.* 42 : 11.
'01.	16– 1	* at this moment drop *d·* into
'02.	18–19	Jesus laid *d·* his life for mankind ;
	20– 2	or going *d·* into the deep,
Po.	2–13	The moon looks *d·* upon
	5– 2	No night drops *d·* upon the
	20–11	from thy lofty summit, pouring *d·*
	41– 6	earth-stricken lay *d·* their woes,
My.	21–19	* "good measure, pressed *d·*,— *Luke* 6 : 38
	44– 4	* heavy burdens are being laid *d·*,
	110– 5	looks *d·* upon the long night of
	119–13	she *stooped d·* and looked into the
	127–28	nor laid *d·* at the feet of progress
	155–11	lay *d·* the low laurels of vain glory,
	158– 7	This day drops *d·* upon
	200–22	by pulling *d·* its benefactors,
	212– 9	put *d·* the evil effects of alcohol.
	248–15	reaching deep *d·* into the universal
	258–16	set *d·* at the right hand of— *Heb.* 12 : 2.
	343–18	It brought *d·* a shower of abuse
		(*see also* **heaven**)

downfall

Mis.	43–24	or to build on the *d·* of others,
	265–32	compels the *d·* of his self-conceit.
'02.	18–27	*d·* of genuine Christianity,

downright

'00.	10– 1	Success in sin is *d·* defeat.

downtrodden

Mis.	127–24	even though your pearls be *d·*.
	331– 4	When *d·* like the grass,

downward

Mis.	267–20	while the left beats its way *d·*,
	323– 7	Stranger wending his way *d·*,
	362–24	millstone that is dragging them *d·*,

downy

Po.	53–16	Their *d·* little breasts.

Doxology

My.	31– 8	* following hymns . . . *D·*.

dozen

My.	81–13	* up leaped half a *d·* Scientists.
	107–15	administers half a *d·* or less
	215–10	sometimes a *d·* or upward in one
	243–12	duties of half a *d·* or more

dozens

My.	73– 4	* have erected *d·* of churches

Dr.——

Mis.	218–30	*D·* says : "The recognition of

Dr.——'s

Mis.	218–27	illustrate *D·* views

draft

Man.	17–15	committee to *d·* the Tenets of
Po.	1–16	Recalling oft the bitter *d·*

drag

My.	84– 2	* Nothing is more of a *d·* on a

dragged

Mis.	237–26	through which Garrison was *d·*

dragging

Mis.	362–23	millstone that is *d·* them downward,

dragon

Mis.	253 -17	*d·* that stood ready to devour
	254–18	great red *d·* of this hour,
Pul.	13–24	*d·* is at last stung to death
	13–27	when the *d·* saw that— *Rev.* 12 : 13.
	14–12	flood which the *d·* — *Rev.* 12 : 16.
	14–18	What if the old *d·* should
Hea.	10– 2	The *d·* that was wroth

drain

Ret.	30–21	No one else can *d·* the cup

drama

My.	281– 1	foresight of the nations' *d·*

drank

Mis.	121– 5	*d·* from their festal wine-cup.
	211–28	*d·* this cup giving thanks,
	232– 3	*d·* to peace, and plenty,
'02.	11–19	which he *d·*, giving thanks,

draped

Mis.	237–26	*d·* in honor of the dead hero

drapery

Mis.	376– 5	* face, figure, and *d·* of Jesus,
	376– 6	* face, figure, and *d·* of that

drap'ry

Po.	65–12	My thoughts 'neath thy *d·*

draughts

Mis.	ix–17	deep *d·* from the fount

draw

Mis.	37– 5	*d·* mankind toward purity,
	239–12	I observed a carriage *d·* up
Ret.	88–27	as will *d·* men unto us.
	93– 9	will *d·* all men unto— *John* 12 : 32.
Un.	1–16	until they *d·* nearer to the
No.	7–21	*d·* no lines whatever between
My.	9–25	*d·* on God for the amount
	202– 6	may his salvation *d·* near,
	247–13	will *d·* all men unto you.

drawing

Pul.	64–26	* *d·* together six thousand people
No.	45–27	material history is *d·* to a close.

drawing-room

Pul.	37–17	* sat in the beautiful *d·*,

drawings

My.	335–14	* *d·* and specifications of which

drawn

Mis.	93–11	conclusion *d·* from the Scriptures,
	214–17	the sword must have been *d·*
	288–12	conclusion *d·* therefrom is not
	341–22	parable is *d·* from the sad history of
	381–17	decree in favor of Mrs. Eddy was *d·*
Pul.	46– 7	* no such inference is to be *d·*
	62– 5	* substitution of tubes of *d·* brass
'01.	3–27	conclusion is not properly *d·*,
	26–27	I was not *d·* to them by a
'02.	7–19	No other logical conclusion can be *d·*
My.	30– 8	* other faiths, *d·* to the church
	49– 4	* one is wholly *d·* over,
	185– 9	sword of the Spirit is *d·* ;
	189–23	we are *d·* towards God.
	224– 9	are not apt to be correctly *d·*.

draws

Peo.	1– 4	it *d·* not its life from human
Po.	22– 3	Eternity *D·* nigh
My.	350– 1	*d·* its conclusions of Deity and

dread

Mis.	396– 6	Fills mortal sense with *d·* ;
Ret.	47– 3	to *d·* the unprecedented popularity
Un.	64–12	hope of ever eluding their *d·* presence
Po.	58–18	Fills mortal sense with *d·* ;
My.	335–18	* second case of the *d·* disease

dreaded

Ret.	13–16	to win me from *d·* heresy.

dream

angel
Peo.   7–11   * angel d· passed o'er him.

apart from the
Hea.   11– 5   wholly apart from the d·.

asleep in a
Mis.   44–21   or when asleep in a d·.

calleth itself
Hea.   11– 4   d· calleth itself a dreamer,

carved the
Peo.   7–12   * He carved the d· on that

death's
Mis.   386–13   "When, severed by death's d·,
Po.   49–19   "When, severed by death's d·,

disease or
Mis.   58– 2   no remembrance of that disease or d·,

formulating a
Mis.   49–16   capacity for formulating a d·,

has no place
Ret.   21–15   d· has no place in the Science

has passed
Hea.   11– 4   but when the d· has passed,

life
Peo.   7–19   * Our life d· passes o'er us.

life is a
Mis.   28–11   so-called life is a d· soon told.
    52–18   If this life is a d·

like a
Ret.   10–13   vanished like a d·.

material
Mis.   28–12   this mortal and material d·,

memory's
Po.   66– 5   songs float in memory's d·.

mortal
Mis.   393– 8   Lighting up this mortal d·.
Po.   51–13   Lighting up this mortal d·.
My.   5– 7   apart from this mortal d·,
    296–16   mortal d· of life, substance, or

nothingness of the
Mis.   49–24   the nothingness of the d·,

of avarice
Pul.   10–12   No d· of avarice or ambition

of death
Mis.   58– 5   Waking from the d· of death,
My.   273–28   "Man awakes from the d· of death

of dying
Mis.   70–13   if the d· of dying should

of life
Mis.   16–16   the d· of life in matter,
Hea.   9–27   the d· of life in matter,
Peo.   14–16   this d· of life in matter,
My.   267–20   his d· of life in matter
    296–16   mortal d· of life, substance, or

of material sensation
Mis.   331–29   their d· of material sensation,

of other dreams
Ret.   32–18   * But the d· of other dreams.

of sense
Mis.   176– 1   that breaks the d· of sense,

of sickness
Rud.   11–17   awake from the d· of sickness;

of Spirit
Mis.   180– 1   the d· of Spirit in the flesh

of suffering
Mis.   70–14   from the d· of suffering.

one's own
My.   117–10   one's own d· of personal sense,

or error
Mis.   49–15   is a d· or error,

passing
My.   46– 7   * it were but a passing d·.

this
Mis.   53– 1   out of this d· or false claim
Hea.   9–26   sickness, and death are this d·.
    17–15   explains this d· of material life,
Peo.   14–16   this d· of life in matter,

troubled
Un.   50–22   awake from the troubled d·,

vanish as a
Mis.   205–29   molecules, . . . vanish as a d· ;

waking from a
Mis.   58– 4   Waking from a d·, one learns

waking from the
Mis.   58– 5   Waking from the d· of

Mis.   23– 5   * or d· in the animal,
    42– 3   only as in a d·?
    42–22   is a d· and unreal,
    44–23   is but a d· at all times.
    58– 7   proves to him . . . that it was a d·,
    253–27   Do the children of this period d· of
    354–33   more bright than the d· in his breast.
Pul.   39–17   * Dimly, as in a d·, I watch the flow
    39–23   * Dimly, as in a d·,
'02.   9–18   man is not the d· of a heated brain ;

dream

Hea.   9–25   Life in matter is a d· :
    10–19   Then will your sorrow be a d·,
    17–11   sickness, and death, are but a d·,
    17–15   d· of the "deep sleep" — Gen. 2: 21.
Po.   3–10   To d· of thee, to d· of thee !
    18–11   as the d· in his breast !
    47–21   and the gladness a d·,
My.   109– 5   d· which is mortal and God-condemned
    132–28   satisfied to sleep and d·.

dreamed

Mis.   78–11   never d· that either of these
    91–24   never d·, until informed thereof,
Pul.   33– 2   * saw visions and d· dreams.

dreamer

Hea.   11– 4   dream calleth itself a d·,
My.   122– 4   from the brain of a d·.
    132–26   It will waken the d·

dreaming

Mis.   325–17   d· away the hours.
Po.   8–16   I'm d· alone of its changeful sky
My.   132–26   sinner, d· of pleasure in sin ;
    132–27   the sick, d· of suffering matter ;

dreams

Mis.   28– 8   In d·, things are only what
    28–10   phenomena of mortal life are as d· ;
    36–28   as in the d· of sleep.
    209–16   neither oblivion nor d· can
    252–10   possessing the nature of d·.
    257– 4   d· in the animal,
Ret.   21–14   history is but the record of d·,
    32–18   * But the dream of other d·.
Un.   26–25   a product of human d·.
Pul.   8–29   which will eclipse Oriental d·.
    33– 2   * saw visions and dreamed d·.
Pan.   9– 2   * d· in the animal,
Hea.   10–28   Earth's fading d· are empty streams,
Po.   65– 5   meeting with loved ones in d·
    65–13   d· so boundless and bright
My.   110–16   my early d· of flying
    236– 2   Let us have no more of echoing d·.

dreamt

Pul.   6–28   * more than is d· of

dreamy

Mis.   9–21   d· objects of self-satisfaction ;
    206–14   manifests . . . no d· absentness,

drear

No.   35–10   also the d· subtlety of death.
Po.   2–12   still art thou d· and lone !

dreary

Po.   65– 9   enchained to life's d· night,
    65–15   We waken to life's d· sigh.

dregs

Ret.   30–22   cup which I have drunk to the d·

Dresden

My.   81–16   * "D· !" "Peoria !" they cried.

dress

Mis.   262– 8   new and costly spring d·.
Pul.   54– 2   * The healing of his seamless d·

dressed

Mis.   24–13   I rose, d· myself, and
Ret.   13–22   I rose and d· myself,
    40–11   rose from her bed, d· herself,

drew

Mis.   121–24   d· from the great Master this answer
    168–27   * d· a large audience.
    340–15   d· up logs instead of leases.
Ret.   48– 1   * its breath from me,
My.   145– 5   He d· the plan,

drift

Mis.   81– 5   d·, by right of God's dear love,
Un.   24– 5   and cannot d· into evil.
Peo.   1–13   d· into more spiritual latitudes.
My.   166–15   will live on and never d· apart.
    213–18   to d· in the wrong direction

drifted

Mis.   225– 8   conversation d· to . . . C. S. ;

drifting

No.   45–21   D· into intellectual wrestlings,
My.   307–27   and d· whither I knew not.

driftwood

No.   29–23   d· on the ocean of thought ;

drilled

Un.   6–26   not yet thoroughly d· in the

drills

Peo.   12–23   Having faith in drugs and hygienic d·,

drink

Mis.   28–32   d· any deadly thing, — Mark 16: 18.
    71– 4   an appetite for alcoholic d·

drink
Mis. 125– 1 he will indeed *d·* of our Master's cup,
125– 9 Then shall he *d·* anew Christ's cup,
207– 3 *d·* with me the living waters of the
211–26 "Ye shall *d·* indeed — *Matt.* 20 : 23.
211–29 "*D·* ye all of it," — *Matt.* 26 : 27.
211–29, 30 *d·* it all, and let all *d·* of it.
245– 4 What shall we *d·*?" — *Matt.* 6 : 31.
249– 6 *d·* any deadly thing, — *Mark* 16 : 18.
289– 2 Strong *d·* is unquestionably an evil,
311–28 to take the cup, *d·* all of it,
323–21 and *d·* from its living fountains?
328–14 *d·* with the drunken" — *Matt.* 24 : 49.
335– 6 *d·* with the drunken ; — *Matt.* 24 : 49.
Ret. 26– 5 on the cross, when he refused to *d·*
Pul. 1– 2 *d· of the river of* — *Psal.* 36 : 8.
3–17 *d·* of the river of — *Psal.* 36 : 8.
3–23 We *d·* of this river when all
7–30 *d·* of the river of — *Psal.* 36 : 8.
9–20 "*d·* from the river — *see Psal.* 36 : 8.
14–16 watching for rest and *d·*.
No. v–10 it saith tenderly, "Come and *d·* ; "
34–11 They *d·* the cup of Christ
42–27 * eat beefsteak and *d·* strong coffee
43– 2 to the power of daily meat and *d·*.
Pan. 14– 9 *d·* of the cup of salvation,
'02. 11–20 gave it to his followers to *d·*.
Hea. 1– 3 *d· any deadly thing*, — *Mark* 16 : 18.
7–25 *d·* any deadly thing, — *Mark* 16 : 18.
15–11 *d·* any deadly thing, — *Mark* 16 : 18.
Peo. 12– 3 *d·* any deadly thing, — *Mark* 16 : 18.
Po. 32– 1 and *d·* in the view
My. 48– 1 * *d·* any deadly thing, — *Mark* 16 : 18.
126– 6 such as *d·* of the living water.
146– 4 *·d·* any deadly thing, — *Mark* 16 : 18.
156–22 "*d·* of his blood" — *see John* 6 : 53.
161–17 *d·* sufficiently of the cup
161–19 "Ye shall *d·* indeed — *Matt.* 20 : 23.
258–21 who *d·* their Master's cup

drinker
My. 106–24 a brawler, an alcohol *d·*,

drinking
Mis. 90– 9 *for d· and smoking?*
123–32 eating and *d·* corporeally.
170– 7 eating of bread and *d·* of wine
Ret. 54– 9 *d·* Jesus' cup, being baptized
No. 19–19 *d·* in the nature and essence of
'01. 12– 5 came neither eating nor *d·*,
My. 78–30 * *d·* in every word of the

drinks
Mis. 15–30 it *d·* in the sweet revealings
243–27 will tell you that alcoholic *d·*
297– 9 appetite for alcoholic *d·*.
'01. 12– 2 spiritual sense *d·* it in,

drive
Man. 48–13 shall not haunt Mrs. Eddy's *d·*
My. 171–20 * While on her regular afternoon *d·*
175– 5 with the exception of a daily *d·*.
229– 7 doth *d·* them out from — *Deut.* 18 : 12.
275–18 have omitted my *d·* but twice
275–20 is all that prevents my daily *d·*.
276– 6 judged by either a daily *d·* or
276– 9 because . . . she omits her *d·*,

driven
Mis. 326–17 *d·* out of their houses of clay
328–15 Hast thou been *d·* by suffering
380–14 had *d·* me to discover the
No. 22– 1 "*d·* about by every wind — *see Eph.* 4 : 14.
Po. 71– 7 Corruption's band Is *d·* back ;

drives
Mis. 263–27 mad ambition *d·* them to
363–27 and *d·* diviners mad.
Pul. 37– 9 * and *d·* in the afternoon.

driving
Pul. 47–23 * an easy *d·* distance for her
47–25 * *d·* rather into the country,
My. 313–12 *d·* into Franklin, N. H.,

drooped
Mis. 385–23 Thy pinions *d·* ; the flesh was weak,
Po. 48–18 Thy pinions *d·* ; the flesh was weak,

drooping
Mis. 376–22 *d·* over a deeply dazzling sunlight,
Pul. 1– 6 Can ne'er refresh a *d·* earth,
Po. 3– 9 Till sleep sets *d·* fancy free

droops
Mis. 329–18 Whatever else *d·*, spring is gay :

drop
Mis. 42–26 *d·* our false sense of Life in sin
88–30 *d·* one of these doctors when you
129–12 *d·* this member's name from the church,
158–16 command, to *d·* the use of notes,
230–20 *d·* human life into the ditch of

drop
Man. 45–24 *d·* the titles of Reverend and Doctor,
53– 4 *d·* forever the name of the member
65– 1 *d·* the word *mother*
Ret. 33–14 One *d·* of the thirtieth attenuation
Pul. 4– 4 'So small a *d·* as I
4–18 *d·* of water may help to hide the stars,
5–15 bedew my hope with a *d·* of humanity.
'01. 16– 1 * at this moment *d·* down into hell,
'02. 12–16 *d·* of water is one with the ocean,
15–26 advised me to *d·* both the book and
19–30 no redundant *d·* in the cup
Hea. 4–13 to *d·* divinity long enough to
13–12 *d·* of this harmless solution,
My. 180–22 *d·* compliance with their desires,
202–24 a *d·* from His ocean of love,
216–23 *d·* the insignia of "Busy Bees,"

dropped
Mis. x–21 I *d·* the name of Morse
288– 6 *d·* into the balances of God
Man. 43– 3 name of said member to be *d·*
51– 6 his name shall be *d·* from the roll
56– 5 his or her name shall be *d·*
Hea. 7–18 *d·* her mite into the treasury,
13–11 *d·* into a tumblerful of water
Po. 31– 3 celestial seed *d·* from

dropping
My. 140–13 * *d·* the annual communion
140–25 *D·* the communion of

drops
Mis. 1–17 mounting sense . . . *d·* the world.
205–15 *d·* the curtain on material man
389–23 No night *d·* down upon the
395–11 The curtain *d·* on June ;
Pul. 7–13 sacred *d·* were but enshrined
Po. 5– 2 No night *d·* down upon the
57–18 The curtain *d·* on June ;
66– 1 But *d·* of pure nectar
My. 158– 7 This day *d·* down upon the

dropsy
Hea. 13–18 an inveterate case of *d·*.

dross
Mis. 151– 6 separates the *d·* from the gold,
205– 8 separates the *d·* from the gold,
Ret. 94– 9 As *d·* is separated from gold,
Po. 39–12 will watch to cleanse from *d·*

drove
My. 346–11 * Mrs. Eddy's carriage *d·* into town

drown
Pul. 14–19 flood to *d·* the Christ-idea?
14–19 can neither *d·* your voice
My. 126– 4 to *d·* the strong swimmer

drowned
Mis. 122–12 and that he were *d·* — *Matt.* 18 : 6.
My. 48–28 * *d·* in frivolity, or paralyzed by
91– 6 * has been *d·* out in this so-called

drowning
Mis. 211–14 *d·* man just rescued from
Pul. 13–18 their heads above the *d·* wave.

drowsy
Po. 30– 5 murmurs from the *d·* rills

drug
any
Mis. 48–16 effect of alcohol, or of any *d·*,
attenuated the
Pul. 35–25 * the more attenuated the *d·*,
attenuation of a
Mis. 271– 2 attenuation of a *d·* up to
diminishing of the
My. 107–18 diminishing of the *d·* does not
disappears
Ret. 33–18 The *d·* disappears in the higher
Hea. 12–24 for when the *d·* disappears
gives the
My. 154– 4 not the person who gives the *d·*
had no effect
Mis. 249– 4 "The *d·* had no effect upon me
instead of the
Ret. 33–14 mortal belief, instead of the *d·*,
killed by a
My. 302– 4 can he be . . . killed by a *d·* ;
knife or the
My. 294–17 use of the knife or the *d·*,
power of a
Mis. 194– 2 power of a *d·* to heal the sick !
so-called
Hea. 13–10 then the so-called *d·* loses its power

Mis. 45–10 follow the use of that *d·*
229–26 is a better preventive . . . than a *d·*,
249–17 neither purchased nor ordered a *d·*
Pul. 6– 9 not the deified *d·*, but

drug
'01.   17–26   the *d·* is utterly expelled,
     18– 1   one grain of the *d·* was
Hea.   12–21   cannot shake the poor *d·* without
     13–16   leave the *d·* out of the question
Peo.   6– 9   * chemist, druggist, or *d·*
My.   107–12   have not an iota of the *d·* left
     154– 4   nor the *d·* itself that heals,
     301–25   *d·* cannot of itself go to the brain

drugged
My.   48–28   * are not *d·* by scandal,

drugging
Mis.   233–13   to put into the old garment of *d·*
Ret.   48–24   higher than physic or *d·* ;

drugging-doctor
Mis.   19–20   more faith in an honest *d·*,

druggist
Peo.   6– 9   * chemist, *d·*, or drug

drugs
administer
Peo.   9–19   and then administer *d·* with
and prayers
Mis.   40– 5   hygienic rules, *d·*, and prayers
depends upon
My.   108– 4   allopath who depends upon *d·*.
dosed with
My.   345–13   I was dosed with *d·* until
effect of
Mis.   348–25   curiosity as to the effect of *d·* on
faith in
Mis.   6–22   overcome the patient's faith in *d·*
Peo.   12–23   faith in *d·* and hygienic drills,
healing by
My.   345–12   false science — healing by *d·*.
healing with
Mis.   88–29   Mind-healing, and healing with *d·*,
hygiene and
Peo.   4– 3   more faith in hygiene and *d·* than
hygiene nor
Hea.   3– 1   requires neither hygiene nor *d·*
hygiene or
Hea.   15– 6   no faith in hygiene or *d·* ;
if God created
Mis.   25–27   If God created *d·* good,
'01.   18–17   If God created *d·* for medical use,
inanimate
'01.   19–22   the use of inanimate *d·* to
medicine or
Pul.   72–17   * medicine or *d·* of any kind,
more effectual than
Mis.   33–30   It is more effectual than *d·* ;
     255–25   It is more effectual than *d·*,
Ret.   34–15   It is more effectual than *d·*,
never recommended
'01.   25–19   He never recommended *d·*,
no
Mis.   348–19   I use no *d·* whatever,
no remedies in
Mis.   96– 6   no remedies in *d·*,
partook not of
Mis.   260– 8   His faith partook not of *d·*,
poisonous
'01.   33–19   not kill people with poisonous *d·*,
prayer and
Mis.   51–29   *Are both prayer and d· necessary*
prescribe
Rud.   3–17   manipulate invalids, prescribe *d·*,
prescribing
Ret.   26– 2   nor prescribing *d·* to support
properties of
My.   293– 5   different properties of *d·*
those
My.   292–24   those *d·* are supposed to
to Deity
My.   139–25   advanced . . . from *d·* to Deity ;
use of
Mis.   108–30   believed in the use of *d·*,
My.   301–24   use of *d·* is in itself a species
without
My.   106–29   because he heals the sick without *d·*?
     108– 3   healing his cases without *d·*

Mis.   3–16   *D·*, inert matter, never are needed
     8– 4   *d·* do not, cannot, produce health
     25–29   if He created *d·* for healing
     51– 3   and *d·*, God does not require.
     52– 2   to such as . . . take *d·* to
     245– 2   or recommended others to use, *d·* ;
     248–28   since which time I have not taken *d·*,
     348–27   *d·* have no beneficial effect
     366–22   *d·*, electricity, and animal magnetism
     369–18   trust Christ more than it does *d·*.
Pul.   53–10   * Can *d·* suddenly cure leprosy?
Pan.   4–26   what need have we of *d·*,

drugs
Hea.   15–21   as if *d·* were superior to Deity.
Peo.   4–25   inquired . . . what *d·* to prescribe.
My.   301–26   *D·* cannot remove inflammation,
     301–29   *d·* can produce no curative effect
     345–14   if the *d·* could be made to act on me.
     345–19   How could I believe in . . . *d·*?"
     348– 2   *d·*, surgery, hygiene, electricity,

drunk
Mis.   48–14   made a man *d·* on water,
     212–32   had not yet *d·* of his cup,
     225–10   who had *d·* at its fount,
Ret.   30–22   which I have *d·* to the dregs
Pul.   83– 5   * from Philip *d·* to Philip sober,
My.   125–32   "*d·* with the wine of — *Rev.* 17 : 2.

drunkard
Mis.   71– 5   yet he saved many a *d·*

drunkards
'02.   20– 6   "No *d·* within, no sorrow, no pain ;

drunken
Mis.   325– 7   "*d·* without wine." — *see Isa.* 29 : 9.
     328–15   drink with the *d·*" — *Matt.* 24 : 49.
     335– 6   drink with the *d·* ; — *Matt.* 24 : 49.
My.   125–30   "*d·* with the blood of — *Rev.* 17 : 6.
     212– 5   which makes mankind *d·*.

drunkenness
Mis.   277–31   *d·* produced by animality.
     289– 4   *D·* is sensuality let loose,
     324–14   *d·*, witchcraft, variance, envy,

Dr. Vail's Hydropathic Institute
Mis.   378– 2   *D· V· H· I·* in New Hampshire,

dry
Mis.   7– 5   until their bodies become *d·*,
     38–15   *such a d· and abstract subject*
     88–17   far from *d·* and abstract.
     251–28   as *d·* leaves fall to enrich the soil
Pul.   7–22   tabernacles crumble with *d·* rot.
'02.   18–19   like the summer brook, soon gets *d·*.
Po.   35– 8   streams will never *d·* or cease to
My.   43–20   * over this Jordan on *d·* ground.

dual
Mis.   161–15   the appearing of this *d·* nature,
     169–18   *d·* meaning to every Biblical passage,
     322–10   Your *d·* and impersonal pastor,
'01.   8–28   as to his *d·* personality,

Dublin
'00.   1–22   Edinburgh, *D·*, Paris,

duck
Pul.   76–16   * skins of the eider-down *d·*,

due
Mis.   x–11   without *d·* preparation.
     199–23   for the suffering *d·* to sin.
     209– 1   attaches to sin *d·* penalties
     238–29   I accord these evil-mongers *d·* credit
     242–10   thanks *d·* to his generosity ;
     247– 4   be allowed *d·* consideration,
     257–17   suspicion where confidence is *d·*,
     308–23   only to reappear in *d·* season.
     373–21   in *d·* time Christianity entered into
     374–20   homage is indeed *d·*,
Man.   30–11   gives *d·* evidence of having
Ret.   1–17   in *d·* time was married to an
     49–22   everlasting gratitude is *d·* to
     49–27   After *d·* deliberation and earnest
     85–18   *d·* deliberation and light,
Un.   7– 7   *d·* both to C. S. and myself
Pul.   1–11   For *d·* refreshment garner the
     21–14   While we entertain *d·* respect
     32–22   * *d·* to the principles of C. S.
'00.   8–19   We lose a percentage *d·* to
'02.   13–20   note therewith became *d·*,
     13–24   amount *d·* on the mortgage.
Peo.   2– 4   *d·* to the people's improved views of
My.   20–16   rich portion in *d·* season.
     73–27   * trains are *d·* to arrive
     83– 1   * This fact will be *d·* to the
     92–27   * *d·* apparently to nothing save
     116–19   praise to whom praise is *d·*,
     170– 6   *d·* to a desire on my part
     173–25   Special thanks are *d·*
     189– 5   so *d·*, to God is *obedience*,
     202– 9   to whom tribute is *d·* ; — *Rom.* 13 : 7.
     208–14   waiting in *d·* expectation of just
     211–21   distrust where honor is *d·*,
     225–14   unto His holy name *d·* deference,
     332– 9   * Many thanks are *d·* Mr. Cooke,
     333–15   * which was closed in *d·* form."
     354– 5   it is *d·* the field to state that

dues
My.   202– 8   to all their *d·* : — *Rom.* 13 : 7.

dug
Mis. 340–14   *d·* into soils instead of

dull
Mis. 88–19   deaf ears and *d·* debaters.
100– 1   artless listeners and *d·* disciples.
100– 5   was to awaken the *d·* senses,
163–11   arrant hypocrite and to *d·* disciples
275–11   looks in *d·* despair at the vacant
320–21   addressing to *d·* ears and
324– 9   the music is *d·*, the wine is unsipped,
337–27   to itching ears and to *d·* disciples
No. 40– 8   to hide from *d·* and base ears
My. 113–23   is C. S. a cold, *d·* abstraction,

dullards
My. 162– 8   better than a wilderness of *d·*

dulness
'02. 5– 2   *d·* of to-day prophesies renewed

Duluth, Minn.
Pul. 90– 1   * *News-Tribune, D·, M·.*
My. 186–17   chapter sub-title
186–18   *First Church of Christ, ... D·, M·:*

duly
Mis. 176–26   Are we *d·* aware of our own great
289–15   This fact should be *d·* considered
Man. 86– 4   *d·* authorized to be a teacher of
91–20   Students of C. S., *d·* instructed
92–12   *d·* qualified to teach C. S.,
Ret. 27–23   can *d·* express it to the ear,
No. 9–27   * "knowledge, *d·* arranged and
'00. 3– 9   worker's servitude is *d·* valued,
My. 26–10   generous check . . . is *d·* received.
191–29   invitation . . . was *d·* received.
192–21   Your kind letter, . . . *d·* received.
240–27   * by those who are *d·* qualified,
351– 8   letter was handed to me *d·*.
358–12   have been *d·* informed by me

dumb
Mis. 68–15   cast out a devil, and the *d·* spake ;
190–11   *a devil, and it was d·.— Luke* 11 : 14.
190–12   *the d· spake.— Luke* 11 : 14.
191–23   refers to the devil as *d·* ;
'01. 16–20   refer to an evil spirit as *d·*,
17–16   the blind, the lame,
Po. 71–10   Righteousness ne'er— awestruck or *d·*
My. 105–17   hearing to the deaf, speech to the *d·*,
149–28   with *d·* thunderbolts,
268–18   as silent as the *d·* centuries

dumbness
Mis. 190–23   it was the evil of *d·*,

dummy
My. 315–24   * her alleged double or *d·*

Duncan, Mrs. Elizabeth Patterson
Ret. 20– 6   to Mrs. Elizabeth Patterson *D·*,

dungeon
Mis. 99–14   Go, if you must, to the *d·* or
269– 5   commits his moral sense to a *d·*.
No. 44–14   sentence men to the *d·* or stake

Dunmore
Countess of
My. 295–23   Countess of *D·* and Family,
Lord
My. 295–26   lament the demise of Lord *D·* ;

Dunstable
Ret. 3– 5   Capt. John Lovewell of *D·*,

duodecillions
Pul. 4–12   as important a factor as *d·*

dupe
Mis. 119– 7   our laws punish the *d·* as

dupery
'01. 33– 7   * "Quackery and *d·* do abound

dupes
'00. 2–20   his *d·* are his capital ;

duplicate
Mis. 306–14   * a *d·* letter written,
My. 303–27   her *d·*, antecedent, or

duplicated
Man. 110– 3   to prevent applications being *d·*

Dura lex, sed lex
My. 40–30   * hence the proverb : *D· l·, s· l·*

during
Mis. 42–29   *without being present d· treatment?*
241–11   *d·* which interim, by constant combat
321–25   *d·* the great wonder of the world,
Man. 30–13   *d·* his term of Readership,
32–16   made but once *d·* the lesson.
60– 6   *d·* the months of July and August
69– 3   *d·* the time specified in the
69–11   *d·* the time of such service.
83–16   not only *d·* the class term but after

during
Man. 95–21   *d·* his term of Readership.
Ret. 5– 9   *D·* my childhood my parents removed
10–10   *d·* his college vacations.
24– 7   *D·* twenty years prior to my discovery
44– 5   *d·* the same month the members,
50–13   *d·* twelve half-days,
Pul. vii– 4   *d·* the ensuing thirty years.
23–10   * paralleled *d·* the last decade by
31–14   * *d·* some year in the early '80's
34–10   * *D·* this time she suddenly
34–26   *"D·* this time," she said,
38– 6   * *D·* these succeeding twenty years it
43–25   * in Concord, N. H., *d·* the day,
53– 8   * *d·* the three years of his ministry
55– 6   * cyclic changes that came *d·* the
66–19   * *d·* the last decade,
68– 1   * of the church *d·* its early years,
77– 9   * *D·* the year eighteen hundred and
78– 8   * *D·* the year 1894
81– 5   * than it was *d·* those services,
85– 3   * *d·* the intervening years
'00. 3–21   *d·* the period of captivity
7– 7   *d·* the past three years
12–24   *D·* St. Paul's stay in that city
'02. 1– 7   *d·* the year ending June, 1902,
13– 5   *D·* the last seven years
Po. vi–24   * *d· the years she resided in Lynn,*
My. 11– 5   * *d·* all the storms that have
11– 8   * *d·* these years she has not
25– 3   * special effort *d·* the coming week
29–11   * six times *d·* the day.
35–27   * *D·* the progress of each service,
37–14   * obedience *d·* forty years
43– 8   * *D·* their sojourn in the
52– 1   * *d·* the past year.
54–16   * *D·* the summer vacation,
55–21   * *d·* the last year the hall was
55–28   * *D·* the months that the
57–21   * admitted *d·* the last year
66– 5   * *D·* the past two weeks
78– 3   * *d·* the morning, afternoon, and
87–21   * *d·* the past few days.
90– 1   * *d·* her lifetime ;
91–22   * *d·* the first years of her
95–15   * *D·* the great assembly of
97–30   * incidents witnessed *d·* the week
174– 3   convenience of . . . *d·* the day.
230– 7   *d·* the senses' assimilation
312– 2   *d·* her temporary absence.
314– 4   * *D·* the following nine years
315– 4   * *D·* his stay,
321–22   * *D·* that time, from my
321–28   * *d·* the past twenty years.
322–19   * *D·* the evening my friend spoke of
323–30   * *d·* the time of our studying in
331–23   * *d·* his last sickness,
331–30   * *d·* his late illness,
332–26   * *d·* the Civil War
333–23   * attended him *d·* his illness

dusky
'02. 3–16   her *d·* children are learning

dust
Mis. vii–10   And mankind from the *d·* ;
1–19   removing the *d·* that dims them.
23–21   it is not organized *d·*.
57– 7   Man originated not from *d·*,
140–30   though the . . . should crumble into *d·*,
145–19   melt into one, and common *d·*,
145–21   to quicken even *d·* into
170–25   he is said to have spat upon the *d·*.
182–16   created neither from *d·* nor
186– 4   In the creation of Adam from *d·*,
325–26   wipes off the *d·* from his feet
363– 9   compensateth . . . *d·* with *d·* !
Ret. 22–18   The real man is not of the *d·*,
71– 1   monuments which weigh *d·*,
86–12   wipe the *d·* from his feet
Pul. 10– 9   pomp and power lie low in *d·*.
No. 26–28   *d·* returning to *d·*,
Po. 31–13   rare footprints on the *d·* of earth.
72– 2   trampling right in *d·* !
My. 5– 3   man is supposed to start from *d·*
129–16   counterpoised his origin from *d·*,
162– 7   not in atom or in *d·*.
179– 7   allegory, of . . . and man made of *d·*.
179– 9   enters non-intelligent *d·*
273–27   they are consigned to *d·*.
350– 1   from atom and *d·* draws its

duties
Man. 25– 3   Names, election, and *d·*.
28– 3   *D·* of Church Officers.
29– 4   to perform his official *d·*.
31– 2   *d·* of readers of the
31–15   First Readers' *D·*.

duties

Man. 64–10 heading
93– 3 ORGANIZATION AND *d·*.
95–22 *d·* alone of a Reader are ample.
97–15 *D·*.
99–22 in addition to his other *d·*,
Hea. 1– 8 they are calls to higher *d·*,
My. 49–24 * *d·* in the Church of Christ,
177– 6 daily *d·* require attention
201–15 crowned with a diadem of *d·* done.
242–23 leave these *d·* to the Clerk of The
243–12 the *d·* of half a dozen or more
250–29 *d·* and attainments beckoning them.
325– 2 * when amidst all your *d·*
358–16 It is part of their *d·* to relieve

dutiful

Mis. 255– 7 it is possible, and *d·*,
Man. 45– 2 *d·* and sufficient occupation
No. 46–16 As *d·* descendants of Puritans,
My. 308–13 compels me as a *d·* child

duty

Mis. 3– 2 shall express these views as *d·* demands,
11–13 I had done my whole *d·* to students.
46–17 man's *d·*, so to throw the weight of
147– 5 and has another *d·* been done
147–15 rule to follow the road of *d·*,
236–28 must not deter us from doing our *d·*,
293–22 includes the whole *d·* of man :
Man. 27–12 *d·* of the C. S. Board of Directors
27–18 *d·* of the C. S. Board of Directors
28–14 *d·* of the C. S. Board of Directors
28–25 *d·* of any member of this Church,
31 16 *d·* of the First Readers to conduct the
33– 1 *d·* of every member of The
41–19 *d·* of every member of this Church
42– 4 Alertness to *D·*.
42– 5 *d·* of every member of this Church
42– 8 nor to neglect his *d·* to God,
44–17 privilege and *d·* of every member,
44–20 shall be the *d·* of the Directors
45– 5 *d·* of the members of The
47– 4 *D·* to Patients.
53– 3 *d·* of the Board of Directors
56– 2 *d·* of the Board of Directors
57–11 *d·* of the Clerk to inform the
59– 6 *d·* of every member of this Church,
59–21 *d·* and privilege of the local members
64–24 *d·* of Christian Scientists to drop the
65–10 *d·* of the officers of this Church,
66–11 *d·* of the Clerk to report to her
66–18 *d·* of the Church to inquire
67–17 *D·* to God.
68– 3 *d·* of the member thus notified
68– 8 or who declines to obey this call to *d·*,
70 8 *d·* of the C. S. Board of Directors
77–12 *d·* of the Board of Directors
77 24 possible future deviation from *d·*,
78– 6 Debt and *D·*.
93–10 *D·* of Lecturers.
93–10 *d·* of the Board of Lecturership
97–15 *d·* of the Committee on Publication
98–17 *d·* of the Committee on Publication
100–13 *d·* of the Directors immediately to act
100–20 *d·* of that church to comply with this
Ret. 70–29 post of *d·*, unpierced by vanity,
86–20 the *d·* will *not be accomplished.*
88–20 *d·* should not be so warped
89–13 *d·* at that particular moment.
Pul. 73–13 * this *d·* she faithfully performed.
81–16 * love and her handmaiden *d·*
No. 2–18 conscientious in *d·*, waiting and
8–11 Having discharged this *d·*,
12–11 sacred *d·* for her to impart to others
42– 1 * Christians more and more learn their *d·*
'00. 2–26 says : "It is my *d·* to take some time
'01. 32–21 the whole *d·* of man.
'02. 17–15 *d·* done and life perfected,
Hea. 7–27 *d·* and ability of Christians to heal
9–15 Is it a *d·* for any one to believe that
9–16 Then it is a higher *d·* to know that
My. 22–27 * Is it not therefore the *d·* of
39–22 * it was my pleasant *d·* to preside at
51– 7 * Mrs. Eddy, feels it her *d·* to
51–23 * her *d·*, to go into new fields
53– 4 * satisfied that her *d·* was
85–25 * Mecca of their love and *d·*.
161–23 each day is the *d·* thereof.
248–27 labor, *d·*, liberty, and love,
308–10 *d·* to be just to the departed

dwarf

Mis. 278–26 and so *d·* their experience.
My. 118–30 would *d·* individuality in personality

dwell

Mis. 103–14 *d·* forever in the divine Mind
145–23 *d·* with the lamb,— *Isa.* 11: 6.

dwell

Mis. 152–16 mercy, and love *d·* forever in the
184– 6 and *d·* among mortals, only when
290–24 it should not, . . . *d·* elsewhere,
309– 1 not to *d·* in thought upon their own
400– 9 *D·* serene,— and sorrow? No,
Chr. 55– 8 they that *d·* in the land — *Isa.* 9: 2.
Ret. 18–20 the spot where affection may *d·*
Un. 22– 4 in which no evil can possibly *d·*.
41–22 never *d·* in its antagonist, matter.
Pul. 12–12 ye that *d·* in them. — *Rev.* 12: 12.
16–21 *D·* serene, — and sorrow? No,
84– 5 * love shall *d·* in the tents of hate ;
Po. 16–22 my spirit with seraphs to *d·* ;
32– 3 home where I *d·* in the vale,
64–13 the spot where affection may *d·*
76–20 *D·* serene, — and sorrow? No,
My. 33–16 *d·* in thy holy hill? — *Psal.* 15: 1.
33–29 they that *d·* therein. — *Psal.* 24: 1.
170–20 *d·* in the land, — *Psal.* 37: 3.
228–23 *d·* in Thy holy hill? — *Psal.* 15: 1.

dweller

Mis. 189–21 not a *d·* in matter.
Po. 1– 3 Primeval *d·* where the wild
My. 3–13 C. S. is not a *d·* apart

dwellers

Mis. 325– 2 saith unto the *d·* therein,
Ret. 18–12 *d·* in Eden, earth yields
Pul. 3–12 indeed *d·* in Truth and Love,
13–16 *d·* still in the deep darkness of
Po. 64– 1 *d·* in Eden, earth yields

dwelleth

Mis. x– 2 consecrated life wherein *d·* peace,
22 20 for it *d·* in Him
93–10 in Him *d·* no evil
134–14 He who *d·* in eternal light
150–12 God *d·* in the congregation of
367–23 He *d·* in light ;
367–25 conclusion, that darkness *d·* in
Un. 64–19 *d·* in the eternal Mind
My. 186–14 in whom *d·* all life, health,

dwelling

Mis. 227–22 *d·* upon a holy hill,
229–19 come nigh thy *d·*." — *Psal.* 91: 10.
324– 4 at the threshold of a palatial *d·*,
324–10 from the window of this *d·*
324–17 he alone who looks from that *d·*,
325–14 he patiently seeks another *d·*,
325–29 finding ready ingress to that *d·*
326– 8 flames caught in the *d·* of luxury,
326–12 they consumed the next *d·* ;
326–30 groped his way from the *d·* of
Ret. 69–27 Art thou *d·* in the belief that
82–24 found *d·* together in harmony,
Un. 18– 4 *D·* in light, I can see only the
Pul. 47–18 * *d·* particularly upon the terms
'00. 13–21 church in this city as *d·*
My. 246–10 *d·* forever in the divine Mind

dwelling-house

My. 335–13 * where he erected a fine *d·*,

dwelling-place

Mis. 206–30 the *d·* of our God,
326– 5 Once more he seeks the *d·*

dwellings

Mis. 201–25 We protect our *d·* more securely

dwells

Mis. 290–23 When thought *d·* in God,
Po. 23– 1 *D·* there a shadow on thy brow
My. 356– 3 where God *d·* most conspicuously

dwelt

No. 37– 3 *d·* forever in the Father.
'02. 9–19 *d·* forever in the bosom of the Father,
Hea. 18–10 good and evil never *d·* together.

dye

Ret. 17–14 flowers with exquisite *d·*.
Po. 62–17 flowers with exquisite *d·*.

dyed

My. 150–16 willowy banks *d·* with emerald.

dying

Mis. 36– 1 erring, sinful, sick, and *d·*,
42– 6 belief of *d·* passes from mortal mind,
70–10 *when he said to the d· thief,*
70–13 if the dream of *d·* should startle
70–20 The *d·* malefactor and our Lord
79–19 A mortal who is sinning, sick, and *d·*,
187–25 a sick, sinning, *d·* man?
187–28 *d·*, before deathless ;
Ret. 9–21 * where *d·* thunders roll
40– 6 her next-door neighbor was *d·*.
Un. 2–21 the *d·* — if they die in the Lord

dying

Un. 7–14 raise the *d·* to instantaneous health.
42–10 *d·* before he can be deathless,
43–19 more faith in living than in *d·*.
Pan. 8–28 and *d·* in consequence of it.
Peo. 4–21 sinning, sick, and *d·* mortals.
Po. 27– 4 I, *d·*, dare abhor !''
My. 58–10 * statements . . . that ''C. S. is *d·* out.''
105–21 The patient was pronounced *d·*
262–12 Truth, never born and never *d·*.
267–17 The *d·* or the departed
300–16 and raise the *d·* to health?

dying

My. 300–16 Scientists raise the *d·* to health
315–23 declared *d·* of cancer,

dynamics

Mis. 258–31 eternal *d·* of being,
'01. 17–24 *d·* of medicine is Mind.

dysentery

My. 292–24 not mixed with . . . to remedy *d·*,

dyspepsia

My. 230– 8 silences the *d·* of sense.

E

each

Mis. xi–14 At *e·* recurring holiday
26– 4 *E·* successive period of progress
38–27 not necessary to make *e·* patient a
81– 6 let *e·* society of practitioners,
117–21 then watch that *e·* step be taken,
119– 8 *E·* individual is responsible for
120– 4 *e·* and every injunction of the
137–20 and *e·* one return to his place
137–25 *e·* one of the innumerable errors
138–10 *E·* student should seek alone
143– 9 May the kingdom of heaven come in *e·*
143–21 contributions of one thousand dollars *e·*,
143–27 *E·* donation came promptly ;
144–21 be this hope in *e·* of our hearts,
224–13 *e·* person has a different history,
256–18 continue to send to *e·* applicant
280–21 hand-painted flowers on *e·* page,
283–24 *E·* student should, must, work out his
284– 1 *e·* one to do his own work well,
289–13 *e·* party voluntarily surrenders
290–26 and *e·* share the benefit of
291–14 *e·* and every one has equal
294–14 with sting ready for *e·* kind touch,
302–21 *provided*, they *e·* and all
303–14 and allow to *e·* and every one
305– 1 * women representing *e·* State and
305– 2 * representative from *e·* Republic
305–28 * the name of *e·* contributor.
308–19 I thank you, *e·* and all,
314– 5 *E·* church, or society formed for
314–21 shall name, at *e·* reading,
314–32 On the first Sunday of *e·* month,
315–12 *E·* class shall consist of not over
321– 7 *e·* receding year sees the steady
321– 9 *e·* recurring year witnesses the
321–21 Still treading *e·* temptation down,
330–18 arranging . . . *e·* budding thought.
330–21 With *e·* returning year,
331–19 that owns *e·* waiting hour ;
338–28 * Speak truly, and *e·* word of thine
342–11 *E·* moment's fair expectancy
346– 8 It confronts *e·* generation anew.
349–28 fifteen dollars *e·* Sunday
375–20 * I went on to study *e·* illustration
389– 7 that owns *e·* waiting hour,
Man. 26– 4 one year *e·*, dating from the
29–17 two thousand five hundred dollars *e·*
40–19 on the first Sunday of *e·* month.
55– 5 *E·* church shall separately and
63–14 *E·* church of the C. S. denomination
70–14 *E·* Church of Christ, Scientist,
72–21 *e·* branch church shall continue its
74– 6 In C. S. *e·* branch church
80–25 one year *e·*, dating from the
84–26 *e·* student occupies only his own
85– 2 Pupils may visit *e·* other's churches,
85– 3 attend *e·* other's associations.
90–19 shall be given to *e·* Normal class
93–11 include in *e·* lecture a true and
98–25 largest branch churches in *e·* State
99– 6 *E·* county of Great Britain and Ireland,
99–10 *E·* church is not necessarily
99–25 *E·* State Committee shall be appointed
104–14 shall *e·* keep a copy of the
110–13 given names of *e·*, written in full.
Ret. 50– 5 price for *e·* pupil in one course
59–22 dependent, *e·* on the other,
70–18 *E·* individual must fill his own niche
76–26 sees *e·* mortal in an impersonal depict.
82–19 the prosperity of *e·* worker ;
83–26 study *e·* lesson before the recitation.
86–22 God will help *e·* man who
Un. 21– 5 *e·* mortal is not two personalities,
Pul. 4–14 *E·* of Christ's little ones
23–13 * *e·* having the common identity
26– 4 * *e·* ray under prisms which reflect
38–26 * Yet *e·* and all these movements,

each

Pul. 38–29 * good that *e·* and all shall prosper,
41–21 * *e·* of the four vast congregations
42–15 * *e·* of them wore a white satin badge
55–27 * *e·* is entirely independent in the
60–10 * *E·* paragraph he supplemented
60–26 * 61 pipes *e·*.
60–30 * 61 pipes *e·*.
61– 3 * 61 pipes *e·*.
61– 5 * 30 pipes *e·*.
86– 2 * about six inches in *e·* dimension,
87–18 I already speak to you *e·* Sunday.
Rud. 5–22 with *e·* of the physical senses.
No. v– 1 *e·* edition of this pamphlet
7–20 performance of *e·* one of them.
22–16 *E·* is greater than the corporeality
Pan. 7–15 Does not *e·* of these religions
'01. 5– 8 *e·* of these possesses the nature of
11–17 read *e·* Sunday without comment
'02. 11–14 *e·* in turn has helped mankind,
13– 3 *e·* success incurred a sharper fire
17–19 square accounts with *e·* passing hour.
Po. v– 5 * *e·* poem being the spontaneous
v–21 * *e·* requested a copy,
4– 3 that owns *e·* waiting hour,
46–17 While beauty fills *e·* bar.
My. 11–11 * to grow into readiness for *e·* step,
12–10 * *E·* person interested must remember,
23– 4 * what amount *e·* shall send
35–27 * During the progress of *e·* service,
38–12 * church was filled for *e·* service
42–24 * in *e·* individual consciousness
45–26 * *e·* advancing step has logically
47–16 * are precious *e·* and all.
47–18 * by *e·* landmark of progress
52– 9 * *e·* and all, will make greater efforts
53– 7 * *e·* of one thousand copies.
56–12 * *e·* of the following named places :
56–29 * three services were held *e·* Sunday,
69– 2 * *e·* suspending seventy-two lamps,
69– 3 * *e·* lamp of thirty-two candle-power.
71–30 * *e·* of whom could see the Readers,
72– 1 * *e·* person could hear what was said.
74–30 * and *e·* is interesting,
80–16 * At *e·* of the meetings the
81–30 * *e·* tells his or her experience.
83–31 * bear *e·* his or her share
86–29 * At *e·* of the identical services,
114–30 trace its teachings in *e·* step
137–28 implicit confidence in *e·* one
148–21 and what is *e·* heart in this
173–21 my heart welcomed *e·* and all.
215– 8 tuition of three hundred dollars *e·*,
216– 9 by which *e·* is provided for
217–11 in equal shares to *e·* contributor.
217–13 and *e·* contributor will receive his
230–11 *e·* Rule and By-law in this Manual
330–19 * by Masonic records in *e·* place
343–24 *e·* one was the fruit of experience
343–28 I wrote to *e·* church in tenderness,
344– 4 *e·* separate ray for men and women.
(*see also* **day, member, year**)

each other

Mis. 4– 8 and their relation to *e·* other.
60–19 even if touching *e·* other corporeally ;
156–25 listening to *e·* other amicably,
224–16 action and reaction upon *e·* other
236–22 Be not estranged from *e·* other
266–26 thus we mutually aid *e·* other,
327–29 grumbling, and fighting *e·* other,
No. 8–10 Advise students to rebuke *e·* other
8–12 counsel *e·* other to work out
My. 120– 5 and know *e·* other there,
173–22 fellow-citizens vied with *e·* other

eager

Mis. 98–14 to watch with *e·* joy the
Ret. 14– 6 He was apparently as *e·* to have

eager

'01. 32– 6 an *e·* lover and student of
My. 90–24 * outpouring of *e·* communicants

eagle (see also eagle's)

Mis. 354–26 Go gaze on the *e·*,
Po. 10–11 Our *e·*, like the dove,
My. 290–22 where no arrow wounds the *e·*
337–12 Our *e·*, like the dove,

eagle-plumed

Mis. 385–22 hope soared high, and joy was *e·*,
Po. 48–16 hope soared high, and joy was *e·*,

eagle's

Po. 18– 1 in the azure the *e·* proud wing,
19– 1 My course, like the *e·*,
28–12 Give us the *e·* fearless wing,
My. 13–24 renewed like the *e·*,"— *Psal.* 103 : 5.

eaglet

Ret. 18–16 as the *e·* that spurneth the sod,
Po. 64– 7 as the *e·* that spurneth the sod,

ear

Mis. 120–18 come more sweetly to our *e·*
126– 6 Sabbath chimes saluting the *e·*
127–28 on the *e·* or heart of the hearer ;
166–14 has evolved a more ready *e·*
215–32 nor yet when it is in the *e·* ;
287– 8 To an ill-attuned *e·*, discord is
331– 1 construct the stalk, instruct the *e·*,
331– 2 crown the full corn in the *e·*.
Ret. 16– 3 a soprano, . . . caught my *e·*.
27–23 can duly express it to the *e·*,
79– 3 Not by the hearing of the *e·*
92– 6 "first the blade, then the *e·*,— *Mark* 4 : 28.
92– 6 the full corn in the *e·*."— *Mark* 4 : 28.
Un. 28–22 nor *e·* heard."— *I Cor.* 2 : 9.
Pul. 9–28 gain the *e·* and right hand of
Rud. 5 14 in the material *e·*,
No. 39– 6 ostensibly to catch God's *e·*,
'00. 14– 9 Beloved, let him that hath an *e·*
'02. 4– 9 bringing music to the *e·*,
Peo. 13–12 On the startled *e·* of humanity
Po. 68– 2 she breathes in my *e·*,
My. 109–16 by the hearing of the *e·*,
184– 5 have not heard with the *e·*,

earlier

Pul. 53– 4 * in other countries at an *e·* date.
'00. 12–15 The *e·* temple was burned
My. 45–23 * in retrospect we see the *e·* leading,
107– 2 improved upon its *e·* records,
184–14 cordial thanks at an *e·* date.

earliest

Ret. 30– 7 motive of my *e·* labors
45– 7 *e·* periods in Christian history.
Hea. 6– 7 From my *e·* investigations
Po. vi–26 * *Among her e· poems*
16–25 waken my joy, as in *e·* prime.
My. 237– 9 in his *e·* studies or discoveries.
051 8 my *e·* moment in which to .

early

Mis. ix– 6 In the *e·* history of C. S.,
x–10 my time in the *e·* pioneer days,
x–18 Timidity in *e·* years caused me,
39– 8 There are abroad at this *e·* date
43–17 The sad fact at this *e·* writing is,
141–20 Do not, . . . stain the *e·* history of
169– 6 E· training, through the
240–19 incline the *e·* thought rightly,
240–24 Teach the children *e·*
345–27 midnight feasts in the *e·* days,
373–20 *e·* part of the Christian era,
Ret. 22– 7 history of the *e·* life of Jesus.
27–10 These *e·* comments are valuable to me
32– 5 E· had I learned that whatever
90–17 in their *e·* and sacred hours,
Pul. vii–14 on the *e·* footsteps of C. S.
31–14 * during some year in the *e·* '80's
32–19 * in the *e·* decade of 1820–'30.
33–28 * voices or visions in their *e·* youth.
34– 1 * At an *e·* age Miss Baker was married
51–15 * It is too *e·* to predict where this
68– 2 * the church during its *e·* years,
83–20 * and that right *e·*."— *Psal.* 46 : 5.
Pan. 3–12 the gentle murmur of *e·* morn,
'01. 18–23 his followers in the *e·* centuries,
31–21 my *e·* culture in the Congregational
31–24 my *e·* association with distinguished
32– 5 I became *e·* a child of the Church,
34– 1 *e·* employment of an M.D.
'02. 12–29 institutions and *e·* movements of
Po. v– 3 * *dating from her e· girlhood*
19– 6 Written in *e·* years.
My. 20–28 * completed as *e·* as possible,
29–28 * as *e·* as half past five in the
46–14 * this *e·* pronouncement

early

My. 51–25 * *e·* work of the church,
60– 1 * knew of your *e·* struggles.
60– 2 * *e·* history of C. S.
63– 3 * *e·* days of the construction of
80–29 * as *e·* as three o'clock
82–25 * to the utmost from *e·* morning,
86–30 * at intervals from *e·* morning
110–16 *e·* dreams of flying in airy space,
112– 5 in the *e·* Christian centuries
155–10 catch the *e·* trumpet-call,
182– 7 my *e·* love for this church
217– 4 *e·*, generous incentive for action,
256– 1 chapter sub-title
273–16 should be *e·* presented to youth
304– 3 I was *e·* a pupil of
304– 7 Among my *e·* studies were
321–26 * I was among your *e·* students
335–10 * who mourn his *e·* death.
350–22 old foundations of an *e·* faith

earn

Pul. 8–18 to *e·* a few pence toward
Rud. 14– 6 *conscientiously e· their wages,*
My. 125–14 they *e·* their laurels.
216– 4 must *e·* it in order to help
216–31 you should begin now to *e·*

earned

Pul. 53–24 * *e·* the title of Saviour
Hea. 8–23 receive only what we have *e·*.
My. 215–16 I *e·* the means with which

earnest

Mis. 11–27 I do it with *e·*, special care
87 26 to be honest, *e·*, loving, and
106–22 long been a question of *e·* import,
136– 9 brought to your *e·* consideration,
156– 3 a vast number of *e·* readers,
177–14 equally in *e·* for the truth?
246–32 *e·* seeking after practical truth
276–11 Scientists, active, *e·*, and loyal,
317–21 subjects of such *e·* import.
Man. 17– 1 band of *e·* seekers after Truth
Ret. 49–27 due deliberation and *e·* discussion
Un. 8– 2 much trouble to many *e·* thinkers
Pul. 32– 4 * she was magnetic, *e·*, impassioned.
37–14 * It is her most *e·* aim to
'02. 2– 1 *e·*, honest investigator sees
Po. 23– 7 Or give those *e·* eyes
My. v–11 * *e·* and loyal Christian Scientists
50–21 * fresh courage to the *e·* band,
51–31 * appreciation of her *e·* endeavors,
61–31 * *e·* work of our noble Board
96–11 * Scientists are thoroughly in *e·*
112–16 The *e·* student of this book,
150–13 be honest and in *e·*
240– 6 An *e·* student writes to me :
202–17 one *e·*, tender desire works
352 19 * It is our *e·* prayer that

earnestly

Mis. 16–27 *e·* to contemplate this
127– 7 and again *e·* request,
306 30 *e·* advise all Christian Scientists
322– 2 *e·* invite you to its contemplation
Ret. 8–23 Then I *e·* declared
14–29 This was so *e·* said,
Pul. 49–18 * talked *e·* of her friendships.
'00. 9–28 I strove *e·* to fit others
Hea. 19–22 let us work more *e·*
My. vi– 3 * those who are *e·* seeking Truth ;
18– 4 and again *e·* request,
80– 4 * *e·* assure thousands of auditors
105–26 he asked *e·* if I had a work
207–10 * strive more *e·*, day by day,
221–31 *e·* ask : Shall we not believe
264– 5 honestly and not too *e·*,
322–29 * spoke *e·* and beautifully of you

earnestness

Pul. 29–10 * *e·* impressed the observer.
36–10 * such *e·* of attention
My. 52–24 * More than once, in her *e·*,
76–15 * show the *e·* and loyalty

earnings

'02. 13– 1 my own private *e·*
My. 136–25 hard *e·* of my pen,

earns

'00. 2–14 *e·* his money and gives it wisely
2–16 idler *e·* little and is stingy ;

ears

Mis. 88–18 deaf *e·* and dull debaters.
99– 4 and *e·* ye hear not ;— *see Mark* 8 : 18.
151– 1 their *e·* are attuned to His call.
168– 8 those who, having *e·*, hear not,
170–29 and *e·*, ye hear not,
301–29 the *e·* of understanding,

ars

Mis.	320–21	dull *e·* and undisciplined beliefs
	335–24	would cut off somebody's *e·*.
	337–27	to itching *e·* and to dull disciples
	360–28	saying to sensitive *e·*
	362– 9	*e·* to these deaf, feet to these lame,
	370–21	braying donkey whose *e·* stick out
Man.	58–21	To pour into the *e·* of listeners
Ret.	91– 6	ever fell upon human *e·*
No.	40– 8	to hide from dull and base *e·*
Hea.	16– 3	having *e·*, hear and understand.
My.	188– 6	mine *e·* attent unto the— *II Chron.* 7 : 15.

earshot
My.	70–12	* The effect on all within *e·* is

earth (*see also* earth's)
above the
Mis.	158– 4	than the heavens above the *e·*
Pul.	41–24	* which rises . . . above the *e·*,

again on
Mis.	180– 8	* Has Christ come again on *e·* ?"
'01.	34–16	Give us, dear God, again on *e·*

all the
Mis.	145–13	over all the *e·*," — *Gen.* 1 : 26.
	152– 8	silent benediction over all the *e·*,
	183–28	over all the *e·*." — *Gen.* 1 : 26.
	331– 8	over all the *e·*" — *Gen.* 1 : 26.
Un.	39–19	dominion over all the *e·*.
Peo.	12– 3	over all the *e·*." — *Gen.* 1 : 26.
My.	119–18	gives dominion over all the *e·*.
	185–10	reign triumphant over all the *e·*.
	208– 7	its heavenly rays over all the *e·*.

and heaven
Mis.	30– 9	He saw the real *e·* and heaven.
	86–29	their present *e·* and heaven :
	228–18	existence fit for *e·* and heaven.
Un.	59– 7	never absent from the *e·* and heaven ;

and in heaven
Mis.	113–26	to enjoy on *e·* and in heaven.
	151–15	on *e·* and in heaven.
'00.	2– 6	best people on *e·* and in heaven.

and mortals
Un.	52–22	Why are *e·* and mortals so

and sky
Rud.	6– 3	*sounds and glories of e· and sky,*

armies of
Mis.	338–19	armies of *e·* press hard upon you.

best Christian on
'02.	11–28	the best Christian on *e·*,

best queen on
Mis.	295–28	unquestionably the best queen on *e·* ;

bind on
No.	31–28	thou shalt bind on *e·* — *Matt.* 16 : 19.
My.	350–17	which they blindly bind On *e·*,

binds to
Po.	35– 6	consciousness Which binds to *e·*

binds us to
Po.	33– 9	ambition that binds us to *e·* ;

bosom of
My.	203–26	in the bosom of *e·* safe from

bring to
Mis.	100–23	bring to *e·* a foretaste of heaven.

brotherhood on
My.	280–10	* loving brotherhood on *e·*

bubbles of
Mis.	328–10	to burst the bubbles of *e·*

came to
Un.	59– 5	Jesus came to *e·* ;

cast unto the
Pul.	13–28	cast unto the *e·*, — *Rev.* 12 : 13.

casualties of
'01.	24– 8	and the casualties of *e·*.

caves of the
Mis.	347– 8	shelter in caves of the *e·*.

Christian Scientist on
'01.	27–17	without a Christian Scientist on *e·*,

cleanse the
My.	265– 9	will cleanse the *e·* of human gore ;

comes down to
Mis.	10–27	Heaven comes down to *e·*,

come to
My.	155–25	heaven's symphonies that come to *e·*.

commence on
Mis.	51–25	* reign of Mind commence on *e·*,

crushed to
My.	128– 9	Truth crushed to *e·* springs

dark places of
Mis.	250–29	lighting the dark places of *e·*.

deluge the
Mis.	246–27	again deluge the *e·* in blood?

down to
Mis.	16– 5	enough of heaven to come down to *e·*.

drooping
Pul.	4– 5	Can ne'er refresh a drooping *e·*,

dust of
Po.	31–13	footprints on the dust of *e·*.

earth
elements of
Mis.	9– 8	from the elements of *e·*.
	383–11	elements of *e·* beat in vain

ends of the
My.	282– 8	all the ends of the *e·*." — *Isa.* 45 : 22.

enrich
Mis.	332– 8	seedtime has come to enrich *e·*

face of the
Peo.	6–10	* or drug on the face of the *e·*,

fair
Mis.	329–29	fair *e·* and sunny skies.

falls to the
Mis.	267–20	The bird . . . falls to the *e·*.

fall to the
My.	166– 5	fail . . . and fall to the *e·*.

fill
Mis.	360–22	fill *e·* with the divine energies,

from the
Mis.	30–28	a mist from the *e·* — *Gen.* 2 : 6.
	171–15	to have departed from the *e·*,
	179–26	before it sprang from the *e·* :
	378–23	than the . . . is from the *e·*.
Ret.	93– 9	lifted up from the *e·*, — *John* 12 : 32.

gives
Mis.	237–10	*e·* gives them such a cup of gall

green
Mis.	257–27	desolating the green *e·*.

has not known
My.	221–11	*E·* has not known another

heaven and
　　(*see* **heaven**)

held
Po.	68– 7	*E·* held but this joy,

helped the woman
Pul.	14–10	*e·* helped the woman, — *Rev.* 12 : 16.

holds the
Rud.	4–11	holds the *e·* in its orbit.
My.	226–11	holds the *e·* in its orbit

inhabitants of the
Mis.	334– 2	inhabitants of the *e·* ; — *Dan.* 4 : 35.
My.	280–20	all the inhabitants of the *e·*,

inhabiters of the
Pul.	12–13	inhabiters of the *e·* — *Rev.* 12 : 12.

inherit the
Mis.	145–14	"inherit the *e·*." — *Psal.* 37 : 11.
'01.	26–19	the meek that inherit the *e·* ;
My.	228–18	Who shall inherit the *e·*?
	228–22	they shall inherit the *e·*,

in the
Mis.	26–12	before it was in the *e·*." — *Gen.* 2 : 5.
	266–29	running to and fro in the *e·*,
	277– 6	walking to and fro in the *e·*,
Hea.	19–15	before it was in the *e·*." — *Gen.* 2 : 5.

is full
Mis.	361–11	*e·* is full of His glory,

is the Lord's
My.	33–28	The *e·* is the Lord's, — *Psal.* 24 : 1.

kingdom on
My.	225–17	coming of Christ's kingdom on *e·*

known on
Pul.	20–18	greatest . . . reform ever known on *e·*.
My.	289–10	first church of C. S. known on *e·*,

known to
Ret.	80–26	no greater miracles known to *e·*

launched the
My.	182–22	launched the *e·* in its orbit,

mantled the
Ret.	31–26	humility, . . . mantled the *e·*.

material
My.	181–30	material *e·* or antipode of heaven.

matter and the
Mis.	179–27	yet we look into matter and the *e·*

meekest man on
Mis.	163– 9	was the meekest man on *e·*.

miasma of
Un.	56–28	constitute the miasma of *e·*.

ministry on
Pul.	53– 8	* three years of his ministry on *e·*,

more of
Pul.	87–20	more of *e·* now, than I desire,

new
Mis.	21– 7	new heaven and a new *e·*," — *Rev.* 21 : 1.

no element of
Mis.	152–27	there enters no element of *e·*

old
Po.	22– 6	Again shall bid old *e·* good-by

omnipotent on
'01.	25– 4	omnipotent on *e·*, encompassing time

on the
Ret.	94–28	Christ's kingdom on the *e·*.
'01.	12–12	find faith on the *e·* ?" — *Luke* 18 : 8.
My.	126– 8	his left foot on the *e·*," — *Rev.* 10 : 2.

opened her mouth
Pul.	14–11	the *e·* opened her mouth, — *Rev.* 12 : 16.

earth
  our
    My. 160–22   internal fires of our *e·*
  parts of the
    My. 147–28   to the utmost parts of the *e·*,
  passes from
    Pul.   5– 7   passes from *e·* to heaven,
  peace on
    (*see* peace)
  peoples
    Po.   1–15   insignificance that peoples *e·*,
  powers of
    Mis. 134–20   the powers of *e·* and hell
    My. 308– 2   powers of *e·* . . . can never prevent
  quivering of the
    Mis. 347– 3   rumbling and quivering of the *e·*
  reach
    Mis. 275–18   Thy light and Thy love reach *e·*,
  rejoice
    Mis. 277–22   let the *e·* rejoice." — *Psal.* 97 : 1.
  replenish the
    Mis. 56–26   *and replenish the e·,"* — *Gen.* 1 : 28.
  revolution of the
    Un. 40– 1   from the revolution of the *e·*
  solidity of the
    Pan.   3–31   goat's feet, the solidity of the *e·* ;
  things of
    Mis. 390–24   like things of *e·*,
    Po. 56– 3   like things of *e·*,
  this
    Mis. 368–28   this *e·* shall some time rejoice
    Po.   9–10   wishing this *e·* more gifts from
  throughout the
    My. 185– 1   acceptance throughout the *e·*,
    240– 4   and acknowledged throughout the *e·*.
  ties of
    Ret. 31– 2   sunders the dominant ties of *e·*
  to heaven
    Pul.   5– 7   passes from *e·* to heaven,
    '00. 11– 9   away from *e·* to heaven ;
    '02. 10–16   and rise . . . from *e·* to heaven.
    19– 7   he rose from *e·* to heaven,
    My. 202– 3   the path from *e·* to heaven
  tumult on
    Hea.   2– 3   tumult on *e·*, — religious factions
  upheaves the
    Mis. 331–24   having all power, upheaves the *e·*.
  upon
    Mis. 151–16   there is none upon *e·* — *Psal.* 73 : 25.
    Pul. 85–18   * kingdom of heaven upon *e·*
    '01. 28– 5   heaven within us and upon *e·*,
    My. 200– 7   ruleth in heaven and upon *e·*,
    274–28   may be known upon *e·*, — *Psal.* 67 : 2.
  upon the
    Mis. 287– 6   father upon the *e·* : — *Matt.* 23 : 9.
    Ret. 68–14   father upon the *e·* — *Matt.* 23 : 9.
    Un. 53–27   father upon the *e·* — *Matt* 23 : 9.
    Pan.   8–19   father upon the *e·*, — *Matt.* 23 : 9.
  verdant
    My. 129–11   The oracular skies, the verdant *e·*
  walked the
    Pul. 34–20   * Jesus of Nazareth walked the *e·*.
  was without form
    Mis. 280– 1   when the *e·* was without form,
  whole
    Mis. 167–22   has dominion over the whole *e·* ;
    330–30   grass, inhabiting the whole *e·*,
    Pul. 84– 3   * shall subdue the whole *e·*
  will help the woman
    Pul. 14–21   the *e·* will help the woman ;
  writ on
    Po. 22–12   'Tis writ on *e·*, on leaf and flower :
  yields
    Ret. 18–12   *e·* yields you her tear,
    Po. 64– 1   *e·* yields you her tear,

    Mis.   4– 3   desirable remedial agent on the *e·*.
    21– 6   while on *e·* and in the flesh,
    86–16   *E·* is more spiritually beautiful
    104– 1   while his personality was on *e·*
    145–27   *e·* will float majestically
    145–29   on *e·* peace, — *Luke* 2 : 14.
    213–30   and *His* will be done on *e·* as in heaven.
    254–20   and cast them to the *e·*,
    302–19   for Christ's cause on *e·*,
    316–27   there would be on *e·* paragons of
    329– 6   sets the *e·* in order ;
    337– 8   Wonder in heaven and on *e·*,
    339– 4   would happen very frequently on *e·*,
    360–14   When shall *e·* be crowned with the
    360–31   then will the *e·* be filled with
    369– 5   "on *e·* peace, — *Luke* 2 : 14.
    373–27   in heaven and in *e·*," — *Matt.* 28 : 18.
    386– 7   tidings from our loved on *e·*,
    392– 7   Guard'st thou the *e·*,
    Ret. 87–12   most systematic . . . people on *e·*,

earth
  Un. 14– 6   *e·*, man, animals, plants,
  Pul. 22– 7   every praying assembly on *e·*,
    22– 8   Thy will be done in *e·*, — *Matt.* 6 : 10.
    41–25   * "On *e·* peace, — *Luke* 2 : 14.
  No.   6–17   evidence that the *e·* is motionless
    6–22   revolution of the sun around the *e·*
    36– 7   never left heaven for *e·*.
    44–26   "On *e·* peace, — *Luke* 2 : 14.
  Pan.   3–25   * heaven, *e·*, sea, the eternal fire,
    11–15   to the best church member . . . on *e·*,
    13–17   and done on *e·* as in heaven
  '01. 11– 3   because of Jesus' great work on *e·*,
    35– 9   to the kingdom of heaven . . . on *e·*,
  Po. 20– 9   Guard'st thou the *e·*,
    49–12   tidings from our loved on *e·*,
    67–22   yield *e·* the fragrance of goodness
    71– 2   When *e·*, inebriate with crime,
  My. vi– 6   * That no one on *e·* to-day,
    6–27   the one edifice on *e·* which most
    18–25   and done on *e·* as in heaven."
    90–19   * "on *e·* peace, — *Luke* 2 : 14.
    127–30   "on *e·* peace, — *Luke* 2 : 14.
    158–11   natal hour of my lone *e·* life ;
    159–12   greatest man or woman on *e·*
    167–11   "on *e·* peace, — *Luke* 2 : 14.
    279–19   "on *e·* peace, — *Luke* 2 : 14.
    281– 4   Thy will be done in *e·*, — *Matt.* 6 : 10.
    281– 9   "on *e·* peace, — *Luke* 2 : 14.
    283–11   "on *e·* peace, — *Luke* 2 : 14.
    286– 5   prayed that all the peoples on *e·*
    301– 9   I would that all the churches on *e·*
    346–28   I did not mean any man to-day on *e·*.
    355–22   are the happiest group on *e·*.

earth-born
  Mis. 387–25   chastens pride and *e·* fear,
  Po.   6–20   chastens pride and *e·* fear,
    29–19   cruel creed, or *e·* taint :
earth-bound
  Mis. 328–16   *e·*, burdened by pride,
  Po. 79–18   centuries break, the *e·* wake,
earth-life
  Mis. 86–25   It lives with our *e·*,
earthliness
  Ret. 32– 8   hope, if tinged with *e·*,
earthly
  Mis. 74–15   His *e·* mission was to
    75– 5   man's possible *e·* development.
    81–24   must cry in the desert of *e·* joy ;
    86–17   more *e·* to the eyes of Eve.
    144–26   may our *e·* sowing bear fruit
    166– 4   the *e·* life of a martyr ;
    268– 4   *E·* glory is vain ;
    320– 5   its *e·* advent and nativity,
    321–30   infinitely beyond all *e·* expositions
    395–21   Is every *e·* love ;
  Chr. 53–21   For heaven's *Christus*, *e·* Evos,
  Ret. 10–17   and no *e·* or inglorious theme.
    20–20   Star of my *e·* hope,
    23– 3   things *e·* must ultimately yield
    47– 9   placed on *e·* pinnacles,
  Un. 61–11   twilight and dawn of *e·* vision,
    61–19   *e·* acme of human sense.
  '01. 24–19   its *e·* advent is called
    90–10   all the best of his *e·* years.
  Po. 34–19   Wearing no *e·* chain,'
    58– 6   Is every *e·* love ;
  My. 221– 1   *e·* price of spirituality
    241–28   * the beliefs of an *e·* mortal.
    256–19   *e·* advent and nativity of
    290–17   when all *e·* joys seem most afar,
    342–30   * directed by a single *e·* ruler?"
    358–11   Leader and best *e·* friend.
    361– 1   above . . . any *e·* friend.
earthquake
  Un. 46–24   This ego was in the *e·*,
  '02. 16– 1   after the *e·* and the fire.
earthquakes
  Mis. 257–25   *E·* engulf cities,
  Un. 52–20   lightnings, *e·*, poisons,
  Po. 18–17   and *e·* may shock,
earth-road
  Un. 58– 5   Jesus walked . . . the thorny *e·*,
earth's
  Mis. 65– 5   that the *e·* surface is flat,
    87– 3   To take all *e·* beauty into
    107– 2   sweetness and beauty . . . are *e·* accents,
    144–25   from *e·* pillows of stone,
    313–10   the east, lightens *e·* landscape.
    331– 3   tosses *e·* mass of wonders into
    331–30   *e·* hieroglyphics of Love,
    342–15   over *e·* lazy sleepers.
    342–20   *e·* fables flee, and heaven is

earth's

Mis. 374–13 envy, and hatred— e· harmless thunder
389–24 e· tear-drops gain,
394–13 No place for e· idols,
395–16 Quickly e· jewels disappear ;
397– 5 And o'er e· troubled, angry sea
398– 8 Break e· stupid rest.
Ret. 18–14 E· beauty and glory delude
21–17 heavenly intent of e· shadows
46–14 Break e· stupid rest.
Un. 57–18 This is e· Bethel in stone,
Pul. 17–13 Break e· stupid rest.
18–14 And o'er e· troubled, angry sea
No. 10–22 e· discords have not the reality of
'00. 7–22 walking the wave of e· troubled sea,
'02. 17–13 E· actors change e· scenes ;
19–21 e· pleasures, its ties and
20– 7 the glory of e· woes is risen
Hea. 10–28 E· fading dreams are empty streams,
Po. 5– 4 e· tear-drops gain,
12–14 o'er e· troubled, angry sea
14–12 Break e· stupid rest.
30–17 a patient love above e· ire,
45–17 No place for e· idols,
58– 1 e· jewels disappear ;
64– 5 E· beauty and glory delude
65–17 love claspeth e· raptures not long,
My. 133– 5 So shall all e· children
189–19 how soon e· fables flee
283–15 sovereign remedies for all e· woe.
290–20 has passed e· shadow

earth-stricken

Po. 41– 5 Where the weary and e·

earth-task

Mis. 64– 5 relinquished his e· of teaching

earthward

My. 154–29 not looking nor gravitating e·,

earth-weary

'02. 11– 8 the e· and heavy-laden

earth-weights

Mis. 328–27 give up thy e· ;

ease

Mis. 85–29 Disease in error, more than e·
219–19 to a consciousness of e·
219–20 patient's sense of sinning at e·
241–29 the sinner who is at e· in sin,
293–29 e·, self-love, self-justification,
343– 2 the temptation of e· in sin ;
Ret. 82–20 the e· and welfare of the workers.
Un. 58– 2 if at e· in so-called existence,
'00. 2–13 takes no time for amusement, e·,
'01. 15–13 A sinner ought not to be at e·,
15–20 dis-ease in sin is better than e·.
17–22 the comparative e· of healing
30–21 by the hope of e·, pleasure, or
'02. 9– 7 pride, and e· concern you less,
My. 233–11 should we prefer, e· or dis-ease in
233–13 better adapted . . . than e· in sin?
253– 8 * "Thou art not here for e· or pain,
308– 7 only by e·, pleasure, or recompense.
349– 8 susceptible of both e· and dis-ease,

easel

Mis. ix–10 e· of time presents pictures
373– 5 My artist at the e·

easier

Mis. 5–30 e· for people to believe that
240–19 e· to incline the early thought
241–27 e· to heal the physical than
247–25 e· for people to believe that
Ret. 54– 4 it is e· to believe that
Un. 50–20 the e· it is for them to evade
'02. 3–21 diadem of royalty will sit e· on the

easily

Mis. 5–27 is something not e· accepted,
52–26 first rule was not e· demonstrated?
141–18 it can e· be corrected
222–32 as e· as dawns the morning light
247–23 is not so e· accepted.
361–18 which doth so e· beset us,— Heb. 12 : 1.
'01. 20–24 are not e· reckoned.

easily-besetting

Mis. 307–22 Idolatry is an e· sin

East

Ret. 80–22 The kindly shepherd of the E·
Pul. 20–22 dates selected and observed in the E·
My. 193– 6 from E· to West,

east

Mis. 313–10 kindling its glories in the e·,
376–20 above the horizon, in the e·,
Pul. 83– 7 * But the e· is rosy,
My. 63–28 * "from the e·, and from— Psal. 107 : 3.

East Boston

Mis. 243–12 107 Eutaw Street, E· B·.

Easter

Mis. 177–21 chapter sub-title
180–16 I love the E· service :
Man. 60–12 E· Observances.
60–14 nor gifts at the E· season
67–22 Christmas, New Year, or E·,
Pul. 42–26 * palms and ferns and E· lilies.
Po. page 30 poem
31– 9 Glad E· glows with gratitude
My. 155–16 chapter sub-title
155–17 May this glad E· morn
155–27 gathering E· lilies of love
191–15 This glad E· morning witnesseth
202– 5 him who hallowed this E· morn.

Eastern

Ret. 38–17 We met at the E· depot in Lynn,
Pul. 65– 4 * In inviting the E· churches and

eastern

Mis. 368–16 in the e· archipelago.

Eastern States

Pul. 88–11 * heading

Easter Sunday

My. 54– 7 * had their meeting E· S·

Eastertide

Po. 43– 3 Glad thy E· :

Easton

Mr.
Mis. 177–27 * introduced Mr. E· as follows :
178–10 * Mr E· then delivered an
Mr. D. A.
Mis. 280–23 brief address by Mr. D. A. E·,
Rev. D. A.
Mis. 177–25 * accompanied by Rev. D. A. E·,
Pul. 9–17 lamented pastor, Rev. D. A. E·,
29– 3 * Rev. D. A. E· and

Eastport, Me.

Pul. 88–22 * Sentinel, E·, M·.

eastward

Pul. 48–13 * truant river, as it wanders e·.

easy

Mis. 200– 2 that made his healing e· and
262–26 and renders the yoke e·.
347–23 ascent is e· and the summit can be
Pul. 47–23 * an e· driving distance for her
No. 15–14 It is no e· matter to believe
Hea. 2–11 * the parting will be e·."

eat

Mis. 7– 2 not be allowed to e· certain food,
149– 2 come ye, buy, and e· ; — Isa. 55 : 1.
170–16 " I have bread to e·— see John 4 : 32.
245– 4 What shall we e·?— Matt. 6 : 31.
328–14 "e· and drink with the— Matt. 24 : 49.
335– 6 e· and drink with the— Matt. 24 : 49.
345–29 to kill and e· a human being.
Un. 21–10 "Ye shall e· of every tree— see Gen. 3 : 1.
22– 5 e· of the fruit of Godlikeness,
22–10 to e· or be eaten, to eat or be seen,
44–20 "In the day ye e· thereof— Gen. 3 : 5.
Rud. 12–23 what ye shall e·."— Matt. 6 : 25.
No. 42–26 * and have to e· beefsteak
My. 131– 9 whereof if a man e·
156–15 where I shall e· the passover — Luke 22 : 11.
186–20 those that plant the vineyard e·

eaten

Mis. 72–14 have e· sour grapes,— Ezek. 18 : 2.
Un. 7–12 e· its way to the jugular vein.
22–10 to eat or be e·, to eat or be seen,
My. 105–15 e· the flesh of the neck

eatest

Mis. 57–16 day that thou e· thereof— Gen. 2 : 17.
367–17 day that thou e· thereof,— Gen. 2 : 17.

eating

Mis. 69–26 e· smoked herring.
123–32 e· and drinking corporeally.
170– 7 e· of bread and drinking of wine
226– 5 after e· several ice-creams,
'01. 12– 5 came neither e· nor drinking,
My. 216– 3 live without e·, and obtain their
339–26 Merely to abstain from e· was not

ebb

Mis. 384–21 * But knows no e· and flow.
'00. 9–20 the e· and flow of thought
Po. 36–20 * But knows no e· and flow.

ebbing

Mis. 355– 8 chronic recovery e· and flowing,
My. 183–13 no e· faith, no night.

ebony

Mis. 376–21 with an acre of eldritch e·.

Eddy

Rev. Mary Baker
Man. 79–20   given by Rev. Mary Baker *E·*,
    91–11   the President, Rev. Mary Baker *E·*,
Pul. page 1   heading
    page 16   heading
    page 20   heading
    24–16   * beloved teacher, the Rev. Mary Baker *E·*,
    31– 3   * Rev. Mary Baker *E·*, the Founder
    40–13   * SERMON BY REV. MARY BAKER *E·*,
    40–22   * Founder of C. S., Rev. Mary Baker *E·*,
    44– 1   * "To Rev. Mary Baker *E·*.
    57– 2   * Founder of C. S., the Rev. Mary Baker *E·*.
    63– 9   * Rev. Mary Baker *E·*, the "Mother" of C. S.,
    63–27   * beloved teacher, Rev. Mary Baker *E·*,
    64– 7   * experience of Rev. Mary Baker *E·*.
    64–26   * Founder . . . the Rev. Mary Baker *E·*,
    68– 3   * known as the Rev. Mary Baker *E·*.
    70– 4   * CAREER OF REV. MARY BAKER *E·*,
    70– 6   * Rev. Mary Baker *E·*, Discoverer and
    75–24   * Founder of C. S., Rev. Mary Baker *E·*,
    76–23   * REV. MARY BAKER *E·* MEMORIALIZED BY
    76–25   * Rev. Mary Baker *E·*, Discoverer of C. S.,
    78–19   * "To the Rev. Mary Baker *E·*,
    85–22   * To REV. MARY BAKER *E·*, FROM THE
    85–24   * Rev. Mary Baker *E·* received
My. 18–31   * writings of the Rev. Mary Baker *E·*,
    32–14   * Words by the Rev. Mary Baker *E·*.
    32–25   * words by the Rev. Mary Baker *E·*,
    32–27   * Message from . . . Rev. Mary Baker *E·*.
    34–16   * by the Rev. Mary Baker *E·*,
    36– 7   * REV. MARY BAKER *E·*, Pastor Emeritus.
    43–23   * Leader, the Rev. Mary Baker *E·*.
    44–21   * To THE REV. MARY BAKER *E·*,
    54–10   * pastor, the Rev. Mary Baker *E·*,
    62–17   * REV. MARY BAKER *E·*, Pleasant View,
    140–13   * Rev. Mary Baker *E·* explains
    172– 6   * father of the Rev. Mary Baker *E·*,
    280– 1   * REV. MARY BAKER *E·*, Pleasant View,
    338– 6   * views of the Rev. Mary Baker *E·*
    346–20   * Rev. Mary Baker *E·*, Discoverer and

Rev. Mary Baker G.
Mis. 177–24   * pastor, Rev. Mary Baker G. *E·*,
    272– 1   * "Rev. Mary Baker G. *D·* obtained a

Rev. Mary Baker Glover
Pul. 57–26   * of Rev. Mary Baker Glover *E·*,

Rev. Mary B. G.
Mis. 168–25   * Rev. Mary B. G. *E·* would speak
Ret. 48–30   President, the Rev. Mary B. G. *E·*,

Rev. Mrs.
Mis. 272–28   * of which Rev. Mrs. *E·* is founder
My. 259– 7   * REV. MRS. *E·*, PLEASANT VIEW,

author
Mis. x–19   caused me, as an *a·*, to assume
    34 20   *a·* of "S. and H. with Key to the
    35–26   taught its Science by the *a·*
    144–12   other works written by the same *a·*,
    301– 5   the *a·* of the above-named book
    314–25   with the name of its *a·*,
    315– 8   except by their *a·*,
    378– 1   the *a·* of this work was at Dr. Vail's
    378– 9   *a·*, in company with several other
    378–15   never occurred to the *a·* to learn his
    382–16   *a·* and publisher of the first books
Man. 27–23   is, or may be, the *a·*,
    32–10   Naming Book and *A·*.
    53– 8   the *a·* of our textbook
    53–20   *a·* of S. AND H. shall bear witness
    59–10   announce the name of the *a·*.
    64– 8   and other writings by this *a·* ;
    64–15   given to the *a·* of their textbook,
    69–13   If the *a·* of the C. S. textbook call on
    71–23   they give the name of their *a·*
    82– 7   of which Mrs. Eddy is the *a·*
    104–11   the written consent of its *a·*,
    105– 5   the *a·* of our textbook, S. AND H.
Ret. 70–17   No person can take the place of the *a·*
    75–13   misrepresent or misrepresent the *a·*.
Pul. 5–17   introduced himself to its *a·*
    24–17   * *a·* of "S. and H. with Key to the
    52–14   * *a·* of the textbook from which,
    54–28   About 1868, the *a·* of S. and H.
    64– 1   * *a·* of its textbook, 'S. and H.
    70– 7   * *a·* of its textbook, "S. and H.
    86–24   * *a·* of its textbook, "S. and H.
    88– 4   From Canada to . . . the *a·* has
Rud. 14– 8   *a·* never sought charitable support,
Po. v– 5   * in the life of the *a·*,
    v–10   * written while the *a·* was
    v–23   * requests continued to reach the *a·*
    vi–10   * A note from the *a·*,
    vii–13   * from this spiritually-minded *a·*
My. 23–22   * Founder of C. S. and *a·* of its
    115– 6   were I, apart from God, its *a·*.
    224–18   borrows . . . of one *a·* without
    305–15   I am the *a·* of the C. S. textbook,

Eddy

author
My. 310–32   * it so resembles the *a·*."
    320–10   * *a·*, and as a student of ability.
    320–14   * always spoke of you as the *a·*
    320–15   * *a·* of all your works.
    320–23   * referred to you as the *a·* of
    324–17   * that you were the *a·* of

authoress
My. 53– 4   * yet not until the *a·* was satisfied

author's
Mis. 300– 5   announcing the *a·* name,
    300–28   a special privilege, and the *a·* gift.
    301– 3   without the *a·* consent,
Man. 32–14   and give the *a·* name.
    58–20   Announcing *A·* Name.
No. 12– 9   of the *a·* religious experience.
    46–14   The *a·* ancestors were
Po. vi–22   * All of the *a·* best-known hymns
My. 130–22   must have the *a·* name added

bride
Po. 8–20   thinking alone of a fair young *b·*,
My. 312– 6   * took his *b·* to Wilmington,
    330–31   devotion to his young *b·*

child
Mis. 386–12   What of my *c·*?"
    386–27   Thy *c·*, shall come
Ret. 2–28   listening, when a *c·*, to grandmother's
    8– 8   "Nothing, *c·*! What do you mean?"
Pul. 33– 1   * heading
    33– 2   * As a *c·* Mary Baker saw visions
'01. 32– 5   I became early a *c·* of the Church,
Po. 49–18   What of my *c·*?"
    50–13   Thy *c·*, shall come
My. 308–13   compels me as a dutiful *c·*
    310–23   * Mary, a *c·* ten years old,
    341– 3   a *c·* of the Republic,
    345–13   I was a sickly *c·*.

contributor
My. vi–19   * principal *c·* to its columns ;

Counsellor
My. 362–12   * Revered Leader, *C·*, and Friend:

counsellor
My. vi–16   * wise and unerring *c·*.

Daughter of the Revolution
My. 341– 3   a *D·* of the *R·*,

Discoverer
Mis. 144–13   *D·* and Founder of C. S. ;
Man. 43–10   *D·* and Founder of C. S.
Ret. 30–22   *D·* and teacher of C. S. ;
    70–17   *D·* and Founder of C. S.
Pul. 24–16   * *D·* and Founder of C. S. ;
    31– 4   * *D·* of C. S., as they term her
    40–21   * *D·* and Founder of C. S.,
    57– 1   * *D·* and Founder of C. S.,
    64– 1   * *D·* and Founder of C. S.,
    70– 6   * *D·* and Founder of C. S.,
    74– 9   * the C. S. "*D·*," to-day.
    74–17   *D·* and Founder of C. S.
    75–23   * *D·* and Founder of C. S.,
    76–25   * *D·* of C. S., has received from the
    84–20   * *D·* and Founder of C. S.,
    86– 5   * *D·* and Founder of C. S.,
    86–23   * *D·* and Founder of C. S.,
Rud. 17–10   *D·* of this Science could tell you
My. 18–31   * *D·* and Founder of C. S. ;
    23–21   * *D·* and Founder of C. S.
    143–17   history of its *D·* and Founder.
    229–10   *D·* and Founder of C. S.
    302–10   *D·*, Founder, and Leader.
    315–12   * *D·* and Founder of C. S.,
    346–21   * *D·* and Founder of C. S.,
    359– 6   *D·* and Founder of C. S.

discoverer
Mis. 383–10   is founded by its *d·*,
'01. 16–25   its greatest *d·* is a woman

editor
Mis. 382–23   *e·* and proprietor of the first
Ret. 52–21   as *e·* and publisher.
Pul. 47– 5   * *e·* and publisher of the first official
My. vi–18   * was its first *e·* and for years
    304–17   sole *e·* of that periodical.
    304–20   he knew my ability as an *e·*.

Founder
Mis. 34–28   Who is the *F·* of mental healing?
    39–11   the *F·* of genuine C. S. has been
    40–21   The *F·* of C. S. teaches her
    144–13   Discoverer and *F·* of C. S. ;
    295–32   *F·* of this system of religion,
Man. 43–10   Discoverer and *F·* of C. S.
    64–16   author of their textbook, the *F·* of C. S.,
Ret. 70–18   Discoverer and *F·* of C. S.
Pul. 24– 7   * termed by its *F·*, "Our prayer
    24–16   * Discoverer and *F·* of C. S. ;
    31– 3   * the *F·* of this denomination
    40–13   * *F·* OF THE DENOMINATION

Eddy

Founder

Pul. 40–21   * Discoverer and *F·* of C. S.,
     57– 1   * Discoverer and *F·* of C. S.,
     64– 1   * Discoverer and *F·* of C. S.,
     64–25   * in commemoration of the *F·* of that
     69– 5   * the *F·* of the movement.
     70– 6   * Discoverer and *F·* of C. S.,
     71–12   * MARY BAKER EDDY, F· OF THE FAITH
     72–20   * was the *F·* of the faith,
     74–17   Discoverer and *F·* of C. S.,
     75–16   * DEDICATION TO THE *F·* OF THE
     75–23   * Discoverer and *F·* of C. S.,
     78– 1   * the *F·* of C. S.,
     84–29   * Discoverer and *F·* of C. S.,
     86– 5   * Discoverer and *F·* of C. S.,
     86–23   * Discoverer and *F·* of C. S.,
My. 19– 1   * Discoverer and *F·* of C. S. ;
     22–16   * Mrs. Eddy, the *F·* of C. S.,
     23–21   * Discoverer and *F·* of C. S.,
     90–27   * *F·* of a great denomination
     94–24   * Mrs. Eddy, the *F·* of C. S.,
     143–17   history of its Discoverer and *F·*.
     194–16   *F·* of your denomination
     229–10   Discoverer and *F·* of C. S.,
     249–19   I am the *F·* of C. S.
     271–16   * *F·* and Leader of C. S.,
     302–19   Discoverer, *F·*, and Leader.
     315–13   * Discoverer and *F·* of C. S.,
     316–13   Attacks on C. S. and its *F·*,
     341–22   * the *F·* of the cult.
     346–21   * Discoverer and *F·* of C. S.,
     359– 7   Discoverer and *F·* of C. S.

founder

Mis. 272–28   * of which Rev. Mrs. Eddy is *f·*
My. 305–30   the *f·* of C. S.

Friend

My. 362–12   * *Leader, Counsellor, and F· :*

guardian

My. vi–15   * its guide, *g·*, Leader, and

Guide

Pul. 44– 2   * *"Dear teacher, Leader, G· :*
My. 60–25   * *Dear Leader and G· :*

guide

My. vi–15   * its *g·*, guardian, Leader, and

head

Man. 72–20   her place as the *h·* or Leader of
Pul. 37–13   * *h·* of the C. S. Church.

helper

My. 229–14   go to help their *h·*, and thus

her

Mis. 35– 1   healing embodied in *h·* works.
     35– 2   revealed to *h·* the fact that Mind,
     35– 4   and subsequently *h·* recovery,
     35–10   the following words of *h·* husband,
     35–13   * are the outgrowths of *h·* life.
     37–26   *H·* time is wholly devoted to instruction,
     37–27   leaving to *h·* students the work of
     39–12   been all *h·* years in giving it birth.
     40–22   teaches *h·* students that they must
     48–30   solely to injure *h·* or *h·* school.
     49–14   have been cured in *h·* class.
     54– 3   *Has Mrs. Eddy lost h· power to heal?*
     54– 9   are *h·* students, and they bear witness
     54–11   Instead of losing *h·* power to heal,
     54–13   malice would fling in *h·* path.
     54–13   reading of *h·* book, "S. and H.
     58–12   *She had to use h· eyes to read.*
     95– 7   * public letter condemning *h·* doctrines ;
     125–28   turns to *h·* dear church,
     130– 2   Has *h·* life exemplified long-suffering,
     130– 5   to those who know *h·*.
     131–26   let *h·* state the value thereof,
     141– 4   and of your hearts' offering to *h·*
     155–17   all of *h·* interesting correspondence,
     155–19   you, *h·* students' students,
     155–21   write such excellent letters to *h·*,
     169– 2   the way of *h·* researches therein,
     169– 3   whenever *h·* thoughts had wandered
     169– 5   *h·* spiritual insight had been
     169– 9   dawned upon *h·* understanding,
     188–24   this power came to *h·* through
     188–29   At the moment of *h·* discovery,
     188–31   This knowledge did become to *h·*
     254–11   whose children rise up against *h·*;
     353–30   they constantly go to *h·* for help,
     353–31   criticise and disobey *h·* ;
     378–12   seemed at first to relieve *h·*,
     378–13   failed in healing *h·* case.
     378–18   the sum of what he taught *h·*
     381– 2   were not original with *h·*,
     381– 2   copied by *h·*, or by *h·* direction,
     381–10   Mrs. Eddy requested *h·* lawyer to inquire
     381–12   was the author of *h·* writings !
     381–13   *h·* counsel asked the defendant's
     381–19   *h·* cost of suit, taxed at

Eddy

her

Mis. 386–11   This hour looks on *h·* heart
     386–25   the remembrance of *h·* loyal life,
     387– 3   To call *h·* home,
     389–25   And mother finds *h·* home
Man. 18–14   twelve of *h·* students
     18–15   reorganized, under *h·* jurisdiction,
     18–19   and members of *h·* former Church
     26–11   given in *h·* own handwriting.
     30–23   are satisfactory to *h·*.
     43– 1   treats our Leader or *h·* staff
     43– 1   without *h·* or their consent
     43–16   without *h·* permission,
     43–17   shall not plagiarize *h·* writings.
     48–14   continually stroll by *h·* house,
     48–14   or make a summer resort near *h·*
     53– 1   upon *h·* complaint or the
     53– 2   complaint of a member for *h·*
     53–10   upon *h·* complaint that member should
     53–11   without *h·* having requested
     53–12   shall trouble *h·* on subjects
     53–13   and without *h·* consent,
     59–16   to *h·* seats in the church,
     66– 2   he shall inform *h·* of this fact
     66–11   report to *h·* the vexed question
     66–12   await *h·* explanation thereof.
     66–21   authority supposed to come from *h·*
     67– 8   to a member of *h·* Church
     67– 9   without *h·* written consent.
     67–16   personally conferred with *h·*
     68– 3   to go in ten days to *h·*,
     68– 6   leaves *h·* in less time without
     68–14   remain with *h·* three consecutive
     68–18   calls to *h·* home or allows to visit
     69– 8   leaves *h·* before the expiration
     69–22   employed by Mrs. Eddy at *h·* home
     69–24   affairs outside of *h·* house.
     70– 5   without first consulting *h·*
     70– 6   adhering strictly to *h·* advice
     71–23   *h·* permission to publish them
     72–20   *h·* place as the head or Leader
     79–14   for *h·* written approval.
     80–21   subject to *h·* approval.
     81– 4   given in *h·* own handwriting.
     81– 9   connected with publishing *h·* books,
     82– 8   without *h·* knowledge or written
     89– 2   resign over *h·* own signature
     89– 3   or vacate *h·* office of President
     89– 7   on receiving *h·* approval
     97–12   given in *h·* own handwriting,
     100– 8   according to *h·* directions.
Ret. 19–22   accompanying *h·* on *h·* sad journey
     49–23   for *h·* great and noble work,
     90–23   Mother in Israel give all *h·* hours
     90–24   till *h·* children can walk steadfastly
Pul. 23– 6   * MRS. EDDY'S WORK and *H·* INFLUENCE
     28– 2   * The central panel represents *h·*
     31– 4   * as they term *h·* work in affirming
     31– 9   * my first meeting with *h·*
     31–11   * familiarity with the work of *h·* life
     31–20   * To a note which I wrote *h·*,
     31–27   * *H·* figure was tall,
     32– 1   * *h·* face, framed in dark hair
     32– 5   * *h·* beautiful complexion and
     32–10   * *h·* large and enthusiastic following
     32–13   * was dominating *h·* followers
     32–14   * She told me the story of *h·* life,
     32–20   * At the time I met *h·*
     32–23   * On *h·* father's side
     32–25   * was a relative of *h·* grandmother.
     32–25   * Deacon Ambrose, *h·* . . . grandfather,
     32–26   * *h·* mother was a religious enthusiast,
     32–28   * One of *h·* brothers,
     33– 4   * for a year she heard *h·* name
     33– 5   * would often run to *h·* mother
     33– 6   * the mother related to *h·* the story of
     33– 7   * bade *h·*, if she heard the voice
     33–10   * caused *h·* tears of remorse
     33–13   * as *h·* mother had bidden *h·*,
     34– 3   * returned to *h·* father's home
     34– 6   * *h·* case was pronounced hopeless
     34– 8   * *h·* pastor came to bid *h·* good-by
     34–12   * She requested those with *h·* to
     34–13   * they did so, believing *h·* delirious.
     34–18   * From that hour dated *h·* conviction
     35–29   * sympathy with *h·* own views,
     36– 1   * a year after *h·* founding of the
     36– 6   * foundation of *h·* religious work
     36–11   * given to *h·* morning talks by
     36–14   * by *h·* hospitable courtesy,
     36–15   * I went to *h·* peculiarly fatigued.
     37– 5   * in *h·* removal to Concord,
     37– 7   * *H·* health is excellent,
     37– 7   * although *h·* hair is
     37– 8   * *h·* energy and power ;

Eddy
her

Pul. 37–14 * it is h· most earnest aim to
43–25 * remained at h· home in Concord,
43–26 * it is h· custom
43–27 * to discourage among h· followers
44–18 * chapter sub-title
46–16 * H· family came to this country
46–18 * belonging to h· grandparents
46–23 * applied herself, . . . to h· studies,
46–27 * H· last marriage was in the
47–4 * Mrs. Eddy is known to h· circle of
47–9 * In recounting h· experiences
47–14 * No ancient . . . philosophy gave h· any
47–21 * Besides h· Boston home,
47–24 * easy driving distance for h·
48–5 * straight to h· beloved "lookout"
48–7 * can sit in h· swinging chair,
48–14 * pleased h· to point out h· own
48–15 * Straight as the crow flies, from h· piazza,
48–17 * Congressman Baker . . . h· cousin,
48–21 * h· family coat of arms
48–22 * diploma given h· by the
48–25 * one of h· characteristics,
48–29 * figure largely in h· genealogy,
49–1 * which Mrs. Eddy calls h· den
49–2 * speaking of h· many followers
49–3 * consider h· their spiritual Leader
49–7 * gifts of h· loving pupils.
49–18 * talked earnestly of h· friendships.
49–10 * h· domestic arrangements,
49–20 * h· busy career in Boston,
49–21 * return to h· native granite hills.
50–1 * using h· money to promote
50–5 * one of h· motives in buying
50–7 * thus add h· influence toward
55–16 * H· discovery was first called,
58–3 * imparting this faith to h·
58–7 * near h· birthplace,
58–25 * the Bible, with h· book,
58–27 * a room devoted to h·,
58–30 * portrait of h· in stained glass ;
59–1 * burning in h· honor ,
59–2 * has not yet visited h· temple,
59–16 * book of Revelation and h· work
63–6 * RECENTLY BUILT IN H· HONOR
63–11 * shade h· delightful country home
63–17 * among h· devoted followers
64–18 * modern philosophy gave h· no
68–9 * interests of h· religious work
68–11 * country residence in h· native State.
70–14 * a testimonial to h· labors,
70–10 * Taking h· text from the Bible,
71–22 * h· followers and cobelievers
72–1 * inspired in h· great task
73–7 * through the mediation of h· God.
73–11 * came from h· seclusion
73–12 * H· mission was then the mission of
73–15 * fulfilled His promises to h·
73–28 * concise idea of h· belief
80–12 * h· book has many a time been sent
85–5 * in part, understand h· mission,
85–6 * gratitude to h· for h· great work,
85–26 * the appreciation of h· labors
86–6 * from h· affectionate Students,
Rud. 14–9 fully seven-eighths of h· time
14–10 The only pay taken for h· labors
17–13 miraculous vision to sustain h·,
No. 12–11 sacred duty for h· to impart to
12–15 nerved h· purpose to
Po. v–3 * dating from h· early girlhood
v–7 * that claimed h· attention.
v–15 * take form in h· thought,
v–16 * alighting from h· carriage,
v–18 * who made h· acquaintance,
v–19 * asked h· what she was writing,
vi–26 * Among h· earliest poems
vii–4 * in h· later productions.
vii–5 * requested h· publisher to prepare
vii–6 * a few bound volumes of h· poems,
vii–8 * this became known to h· friends,
vii–8 * they urged h· to allow a popular
5–6 mother finds h· home and
9–1 glance of h· husband's watchful eye
49–15 gathered from h· parting sigh :
49–16 looks on h· heart with pitying eye,
50–11 remembrance of h· loyal life,
50–21 To call h· home,
My. vi–8 * from h· and from h· writings,
vi–9 * only as they give h· full credit
vi–23 * all future profits to h· church ;
vi–24 * she presented to h· church
vi–27 * for the publishing of h· works ;
11–5 * has been constantly at h· post
11–6 * storms that have surged against h·
20–11 and name your gifts to h·.

Eddy
her

My. 20–12 Send h· only what God gives
20–14 would expend for presents to h·,
20–16 let this suffice for h· rich portion
20–17 Send no gifts to h·
22–19 * justification of h· labors is the fruit.
28–20 * and following h· example,
39–24 * h· graciousness and dignity.
39–25 * harmonious tones of h· gentle voice.
39–25 * were thrilled by h· compassion,
39–27 * realize h· presence with us to-day.
39–29 * beauty of h· character.
40–2 * evidence to us of h· hospitable love.
40–3 * desired for years to have h· church
40–31 * h· own blameless and happy life,
40–32 * as well as by h· teachings,
41–30 * as well as for h· own ;
42–1 * to be truly grateful to h·
42–27 * faithful is h· allegiance to God,
42–28 * how untiring are h· efforts,
42–29 * performance of h· daily tasks.
47–24 * Mrs. Eddy founded h· first church
48–9 * h· textbook, "S. and H.
48–11 * insisted that h· students
48–14 * future growth of h· church,
48–15 * appreciation of h· efforts
48–18 * in h· insistence upon the constant
48–19 * and h· own writings,
48–20 * has given to h· disciples a means of
50–23 * celebrated h· Communion Sabbath
51–1 * so as to keep h· with us,
51–2 * who could take h· place
51–7 * feels it h· duty to tender h·
51–11 * serious blow to h· Cause
51–23 * h· duty, to go into new fields
51–31 * h· earnest endeavors, h· arduous labors,
52–4 * blessing them that curse h·,
52–5 * them that despitefully use h·,
52–6 * giving in h· Christian example,
52–6 * as well as h· instructions,
52–8 * acknowledge our indebtedness to h·,
52–10 * to sustain h· in h· work.
52–23 * if only through h· work
52–24 * More than once, in h· earnestness,
52–25 * reached h· bottom dollar,
52–26 * to hear h· word
52–26 * has always filled h· coffers anew.
52–29 * the moral rightness of h· book."
53–4 * satisfied that h· duty was
53–6 * send forth h· book to the world."
53–22 * by h· students and by clergymen
58–21 * May h· example inspire us
58–21 * to follow h· in preaching,
59–27 * I heard h· talk it before
64–2 * h· relation to the experiences
61–5 * through h· spiritual attainments
64–5 * and h· years of toil,
64–11 * in h· dedicatory Message
64–15 * in all h· writings,
64–15 * all the years of h· leadership,
64–16 * has been teaching h· followers
64–18 * h· success in so doing
64–20 * warn all h· followers against
66–24 * h· beautiful home, Pleasant View,
66–25 * welcoming h· children and giving h·
90–1 * thousands during h· lifetime ;
90–28 * and the sources of h· power
91–22 * the first years of h· preaching
97–16 * Mrs. Eddy and h· cult,
97–19 * their teacher and h· utterances."
104–28 to learn of h· who, thirty years ago,
134–27 * a letter from h· to me.
134–29 * it shows h· usual mental
144–2 * to the members of h· church
157–17 * in h· original deed of trust,
171–20 * h· regular afternoon drive
171–23 * H· carriage came to a standstill
172–9 * to the members of h· church,
231–2 endeavors to bestow h· charities
231–15 invalids demanding h· help
231–15 letters from . . . do not reach h·.
231–16 committed to the waste-basket by h·
231–20 important demands on h· time
231–22 unwise for h· to undertake
240–23 * replies, through h· student,
270–16 H· life is proven under trial,
271–12 * chapter sub-title
271–19 * has made h· famous.
272–22 * reproduced in h· own handwriting.
272–26 * h· very great following.
273–4 * vindicate in h· own person
273–4 * the value of h· teachings.
273–7 * from all attacks upon h·.
276–4 begs to say, in h· own behalf,
276–8 or because . . . she omits h· drive,

Eddy

her

My.	276–11	she is minding *h·* own business,
	276–12	all *h·* dear friends and enemies.
	276–22	* expression of *h·* political views,
	304–30	the contents of *h·* book,
	309–28	* passed *h·* first fifteen years at
	310–23	*h·* father, a gray-haired man
	311–30	* completed *h·* education when
	312–13	*h·* father's home by *h·* brother
	312–14	* *H·* position was an embarrassing one.
	315– 6	* He spoke of *h·* being a pure and
	315–24	or is it *h·* alleged double
	317– 3	* defining *h·* relations with the
	319–13	* confirm *h·* statement regarding
	319–14	* which the Rev. Mr. Wiggin did for *h·*,
	326–10	* which Mrs. Eddy has made *h·* home.
	328– 2	* blessed, and prospered it, and *h·*.
	329– 9	* the death of *h·* husband,
	329–13	* has in *h·* possession
	329–14	* notice of *h·* husband's death
	329–14	* and of *h·* brother's letter,
	329–28	* some incidents of *h·* life
	330–16	* relating to *h·* husband
	331– 1	accompanying *h·* on *h·* sad journey
	331– 7	* accompanied *h·* to the train
	331– 8	* on *h·* departure,
	331– 8	* *h·* irreproachable standing
	331–31	* sympathy extended to *h·*
	332– 1	* to restore *h·* to *h·* friends
	332–10	* who engaged to accompany *h·*
	332–11	* but did not desert *h·*
	332–11	* until he saw *h·* in the
	332–12	* in the fond embrace of *h·* friends.
	334–10	* account of *h·* husband's demise
	334–16	* to quote *h·* own words.
	334–17	* Nothing could be further from *h·*
	334–19	* She declares in *h·* Message
	335–23	* third day of *h·* husband's illness,
	335–29	* save the life of *h·* husband.
	335–30	* for *h·* husband's recovery,
	336– 1	* but for *h·* prayers
	336– 4	* *h·* brother, George S. Baker.
	336– 5	* come to *h·* after *h·* husband's
	336– 5	* to take *h·* back to the North.
	336– 6	* he desired to go to *h·* assistance,
	336– 8	* *h·* husband's Masonic brethren,
	336– 9	* performed their obligation to *h·*.
	336–10	* acknowledgment of this in *h·* book,
	338– 8	* held and expressed by *h·*.
	338– 9	* reference to *h·* writings will
	342–20	* she said, in *h·* clear voice,
	343– 4	* a question in *h·* own way,
	345–32	* *h·* views, strictly and always
	346– 2	* has lived with *h·* subject
	346– 5	* another view of *h·* religion.
	346–15	* expression of . . . was on *h·* face.
	346–22	* *h·* successor would be a man.
	348–15	was based upon *h·* discovery
	351– 3	* publish *h·* letter of recent date,
	354–27	* The members of *h·* household
	355– 1	* were with *h·* at the time,
	355– 2	* in *h·* spiritualized thought

hers

Mis.	272– 8	* similar colleges, except *h·*,

herself

Man.	30–22	does not occupy the house *h·*
Pul.	29– 6	* Mrs. Eddy *h·*, of whose work I
	46–10	* much is told of *h·* in detail
	46–23	* applied *h·*, like other girls,
	49– 4	* that marks its hostess *h·*.
	58– 1	* found *h·* . . . healed by the power of
	58– 2	* devoted *h·* to imparting this
	71–19	* resigned *h·* completely to the study
	73– 6	* cured *h·* of a deathly disease
	73– 8	* secluded *h·* from the world
	73–14	* She of *h·* had no power.
	73–26	* Mrs. Eddy had *h·* written,
Po.	v–16	* seated *h·* by the roadside
My.	vi–27	* reserving for *h·* only a
	231–12	has ceased practice *h·*
	334– 8	* allegation . . . has contradicted *h·*,
	336– 7	* entrusted *h·* to the care of
	342– 8	* but Mrs. Eddy *h·*.
	343–12	* like *h·*, be the ruler.

hostess

Pul.	49– 4	* that marks its hostess herself.

I

Mis.	11–28	with tears have *I* striven for it.
	238–26	or that *I* died of palsy,
	239–15	"Ah!" thought *I*, "somebody has to
	248–21	have said that *I* died of poison,
	277–29	*I* thunder His law to the sinner,
	299–27	What right have *I* to do this?
	303–16	If ever *I* wear out from serving
	350–17	*I* dissolved the society,

Eddy

I

Mis.	371–12	*I* as their teacher can say,
	372–26	Not by aid of . . . could *I* copy art,
	376–30	Then thought *I*, What are we,
Man.	58– 4	*I*, Mary Baker Eddy, ordain
Ret.	13– 9	So perturbed was *I* by the
	24– 5	which *I* afterwards named C. S.
	28–28	Am *I* a believer in spiritualism?
	38–18	*I* to learn that he had printed
	73–10	as *I* floated into more spiritual
Un.	9–21	it is said, . . . that *I* monopolize;
	40– 3	To say that you and *I*, as mortals
Pul.	1–19	Were *I* present, methinks
	74–14	'Am *I* the second Christ?'
Pan.	13–25	Have *I* wearied you with the
'02.	2–27	*I* but began where the Church
	2–28	When the churches and *I*
Hea.	14–18	most arduous task *I* ever performed.
My.	20–10	May *I* relieve you of selecting.
	62– 8	* may *I* not take this precious truth
	115– 6	were *I*, apart from God, its author.
	127–16	*I* deliberately declare that when
	129– 3	*I* reluctantly foresee great danger
	148–18	*I*, as usual at home and alone,
	163–23	retirement *I* so much coveted,
	164– 2	retirement *I* so much desired.
	166–16	Had *I* never suffered for
	173–11	*I* scarcely supposed that a note,
	174– 5	*I* greatly appreciate the courtesy
	189–32	Am *I* not alone in soul?
	194–22	*I* deeply appreciate it,
	201–19	Rich hope have *I* in him
	214–25	*I* therefore halted from necessity.
	219– 7	*I* by no means would pluck their plumes.
	220–18	*I* also have faith that
	223– 4	*I* neither listen to complaints, . . . nor
	228– 8	*I* fail to know how one can
	233– 9	*I* surely should.
	235–28	Had *I* known what was being done
	249–20	*I* alone know what that means.
	256– 8	that *I* be permitted total exemption
	260–31	Neither the you nor the *I* in the
	264– 3	*I* even hope that those who are
	271– 5	*I* little understood all that *I*
	295–25	You, *I*, and mankind have cause
	302–14	*I* begged the students who first
	306–22	when *I* first visited Dr. Quimby
	307– 2	and which *I*, at his request,
	313–13	*I* only know that my father and
	313–27	but *I* wounded her pride
	315–25	If indeed it be *I*, allow me to
	318– 7	*I* especially employed him on
	344–18	If *I* harbored that idea
	351–15	May you and *I* and all mankind

I abide

My.	227–28	*I* abide by this rule

I accepted

Mis.	349–27	*I* accepted, for a time,
Ret.	15–15	*I* accepted the invitation
	44– 7	*I* accepted the call,
My.	145– 6	showed it to me, and *I* accepted it.

I accord

Mis.	238–29	*I* accord these evil-mongers

I add

Pul.	39– 9	*I* add on the following page

I adhere

'01.	22–19	*I* adhere to my text,

I admire

My.	282– 4	While *I* admire the faith and

I admonish

Mis.	141–25	*I* admonish you :
My.	106– 2	*I* admonish Christian Scientists

I adopted

My.	313–28	when *I* adopted C. S.,

I advertised

My.	306–24	*I* advertised that I would pay

I advise

My.	360–17	*I* advise you with all my soul

I afterwards

'02.	13–28	*I* afterwards gave to my church

I again

Mis.	380–15	*I* again, in faith, turned to
'02.	4– 3	*I* again repeat, Follow your

I agree

Mis.	117–10	*I* agree with Rev. Dr. Talmage,
	243–13	*I* agree with the Professor
My.	154–22	*I* agree with him :

I agreed

My.	318–19	*I* agreed not to question him

I aimed

Mis.	372–24	*I* aimed to reproduce, . . . the modest

I allowed

Mis.	302–18	*I* allowed, . . . the privilege of
'01.	29–27	*I* allowed them for several years

Eddy

I already
Pul. 87–18 I already speak to you each Sunday.
I also saw
Ret. 45–23 I also saw that Christianity has
I always try
My. 163–12 I always try to be just,
I am
Mis. 22– 1 I am strictly a theist
48– 8 I am opposed to it,
88– 9 I am pleased to inform this inquirer,
115– 3 I am astounded at the apathy of
133– 6 your statement that I am a pantheist,
136– 5 I am still with you on the field
150–11 I am with all who are with Truth,
157–18 I am glad that you are in good cheer.
177–29 I am constantly homesick for heaven.
193–15 of which I am pastor,
193–17 I am thankful even for his allusion
238–25 allegement that I am "sick,
242–15 I am in another department
248–16 that I am an infidel,
248–19 not more true than that I am dead,
249–28 I am in awe before it.
262–15 I am grateful to you for giving to
265–27 I am constantly called to
273– 2 I am thankful that the neophyte
284–32 I am opposed to all personal
295–32 I am a Christian Scientist,
372–18 I am delighted to find
382–11 I am the debtor.
385– 6 And I am blest!
Ret. 94–25 I am persuaded that only by
Un. 48–19 that of which I am conscious
Pul. 21– 8 I am seeking and praying for it
74–15 What I am is for God to declare
74–17 claim nothing more than what I am,
No. 28– 8 Of his intermediate . . . I am ignorant.
'00. 1– 1 I am touched with the tone of your
1– 6 I am with thee, heart answering to
1– 9 I am grateful to say that in the
'01. 21–14 I am sorry for my critic,
22– 7 I am a spiritual homœopathist
'02. 16– 7 To-day I am the happy possessor of
Po. 37– 6 And I am blest!
73– 8 I am with thee in spirit
My. 5–24 I am with you "in spirit — John 4 : 23.
9–19 I am bankrupt in thanks
9–26 till I am satisfied with
122– 9 Now I am done with homilies
136–13 I am pleased to say that the
144– 5 lies afloat that I am sick,
144– 6 public report that I am in
146–18 I am convinced of the absolute
146–20 I am equally sure that
147–30 and I am helping them.
151– 1 I am patient with the newspaper
160–19 I am asked, "Is there a hell?"
166–27 I am for the first time informed of
170– 1 I am especially desirous that
175–27 I am sure that the counterfeit
177– 7 and I am glad to say
177– 9 I am quite able to take the trip
183–25 I am blending with thine my prayer
184– 8 To-day I am privileged to
203–20 and I am sure that He will
219– 1 unless I am personally present,
228– 6 hence I am always saying
230–11 I am sure, that each Rule
233–10 made better by watching? I am.
235–24 Are you a Christian Scientist? I am.
248– 2 I am more than satisfied
249–19 I am the Founder of C. S.
254– 5 I am glad you enjoy the dawn of
268–18 I am as silent as the
274–22 I am cheered and blessed
275–13 the report that I am sick
275–15 I am well and keenly alive
276–23 I am asked, "What are your politics?"
284–23 But here let me say that I am
289–27 I am interested in a meeting
295–12 I am in grateful receipt of your
302–21 I am less lauded, pampered,
303–28 What I am remains to be proved
305–15 I am the author of the
305–17 I am rated in the
305–21 All that I am in reality,
313–11 stories . . . I am ignorant of.
316–21 I am pleased to find this
345–23 At present I am conservative
360–12 I am constrained to say,
I am not
Mis. 95–15 I am not, and never was.
133–18 I hope I am not wrong
249–11 I am not a spiritualist,
253– 6 I am not enough the new woman

Eddy

I am not
Mis. 265–22 I am not morally responsible for
278– 3 but I am not dismayed,
310–15 I am not unmindful that
Po. 19– 3 I am not alone
My. 5–23 Beloved, I am not with you
119–28 for I am not there.
274–21 I am not fond of an abundance of
303– 4 I know that I am not that one,
359– 8 I am not personally involved
I answer
Mis. 301–21 I answer : It is not right
I answered
Ret. 14–11 I answered without a tremor,
I answered not
Ret. 8–18 I answered not, till again
I anticipated
My. 163–25 more than I anticipated.
I apprehended
Ret. 25– 6 I apprehended for the first time,
Pul. 35– 1 I apprehended the spiritual meaning
I approve
My. 358–30 I approve the By-laws
I, as a
Mis. 152–11 I, as a corporeal person,
152–11 I, as a dictator, arbiter, or
152–12 but I, as a mother
I as an individual
Mis. 310–26 I as an individual would
I ask
Un. 34–18 I ask : What evidence does
35– 1 I ask, Which was first, matter or
'02. 14–24 I ask : What has shielded and
My. 19–19 I ask for more, even this :
117–31 is all that I ask of mankind.
130–15 Therefore I ask the help of others
130–18 I ask that according to
175–18 May I ask in behalf of the public
I asked
Ret. 40– 7 I asked permission to see her.
My. 139–17 When I asked you to dispense with
I a spiritualist?
Mis. 95–14 Am I a spiritualist?
I assert
My. 106–13 I assert it would have been
I availed
My. 318–10 I availed myself of the name of
I aver
My. 193–23 Here I aver that you have
I awoke
Mis. 180– 1 I awoke from the dream of Spirit
I became
'01. 32– 5 I became early a child of the
'02. 15–15 I became poor for Christ's sake.
I become
Ret. 76–29 I become responsible, as a teacher,
I beg
Ret. 50–11 I beg disinterested people to
My. 118– 9 I beg to thank you for your
165–12 I beg to thank the dear brethren
256– 9 I beg to send to you all a
I began
Ret. 43– 2 I began by teaching one
My. 304–10 I began writing for the leading
318–21 I began my attack on agnosticism.
I begin
'01. 22–15 I begin at the feet of Christ
I beheld
Ret. 25–29 I beheld with ineffable awe
I behold
Mis. 389–11 Can I behold the snare, the pit,
Po. 4–10 Can I behold the snare, the pit,
I believe
Mis. 67–29 I believe in this removal being
70– 2 That the Bible is true I believe,
96– 7 Do I believe in a personal God?
96– 8 I believe in God as the Supreme
96–17 Do I believe in the atonement of
132–23 what I believe and teach,
141–16 I understand, — yea, I understand,
313–25 as I believe, divinely directed,
Ret. 28–28 I believe in no ism.
Un. 48– 6 I believe more in Him than
48–19 I believe that of which I am
49– 2 I believe in the individual man,
49– 7 I believe less in the sinner,
50– 4 I believe in matter only as
50– 4 only as I believe in evil,
'01. 32–26 I believe, if those venerable
My. 146– 5 I believe this saying
220–12 I believe in obeying the laws
234–20 I believe that all our great
282– 3 I believe strictly in the Monroe
303– 2 I believe in one Christ,

Eddy

I believe
   My. 303– 3   I believe in but one incarnation,
       345–18   could *I* believe in a science of

I bend
   Ret. 17– 4   I bend to thy lay,
   Po. 62– 3   I bend to thy lay,

I be present
   Mis. 322–19   though *I* be present or absent,

I bless God
   Ret. 21–24   for those lucid . . . I bless God.

I briefly
   My. 298– 3   I briefly declare that nothing has
      305– 7   I briefly express myself

I by firing first
   Mis. 11– 6   and *I* by firing first could kill him

I call
   Mis. 26–23   I call matter, *nothing.*
      121– 6   to which *I* call your attention,
      133– 8   I call your attention and
      282–29   abuse which *I* call attention to,
   Un. 32–26   which *I* call *mortal mind;*
   Rud. 9–11   of what *I* call *mortal mind,*
   '00. 14–14   I call your attention to this
   My. 228– 1   I call disease by its name
      229– 1   I call none but genuine Christian
      251–24   I call you mine, for all is

I called
   Mis. 24–10   I called for my Bible,
   Ret. 25–11   God *I* called *immortal Mind.*
      25–13   sensuous nature, *I* called *error*
      25–18   Spirit *I* called the *reality;*
   My. 240– 9   I called C. S. the higher criticism

I calmly
   Mis. 247– 9   I calmly challenge the world,

I came
   '02. 13–15   I came to the rescue,
   My. 164– 1   far from my purpose, when *I* came
      275–18   since *I* came to Massachusetts.

I can
   Mis. 11–26   I can do much general good
      62– 2   I can improve my own,
      96–11   that of which *I* can conceive,
      96–26   I can name some means by which
      106–20   I can only bring crumbs fallen from
      115– 7   I can account for this state of mind
      239– 3   I can talk — and laugh too !
   Un. 44– 3   I can only repeat the Master's
   Rud. 8–10   I can give you here nothing but
   '01. 15–17   I can conceive of little short of
      31–14   I can use the power that God gives
   '02. 14– 4   I can neither rent, mortgage, nor
      20–22   I can bear the cross,
   My. 145–22   I can serve equally my friends and
      192–26   Of this, however, *I* can sing :
      268–21   I can only solace the sore ills of
      270–22   I can appeal to Him as my witness
      277– 6   I can see no other way of
      343– 8   I can answer that.
      360–12   if *I* can settle this
      360–14   as many students think *I* can,

I cannot
   Mis. 136– 9   I cannot feel justified in turning
      146– 6   I cannot conscientiously lend my
      146– 9   I cannot accept hearsay,
      146–20   I cannot be the conscience for this
      266–21   I cannot find it in my heart not to
      273–25   I cannot do my best work for
      277–30   I cannot help loathing the
      318– 6   I cannot but love some of those
      350–28   I cannot serve two masters ;
   Ret. 5–15   I cannot speak as I would,
   Un. 43–12   I *cannot* speak of myself as
      49–14   So long as . . . *I* cannot be wholly good.
   '01. 31–12   then *I* cannot choose but obey.
   '02. 19–12   no person . . . that *I* cannot forgive.
   My. 25–18   I cannot be present *in*
      115– 8   I cannot be super-modest in
      127–32   I cannot quench my desire to say
      138–16   I cannot "serve two — *Matt.* 6 : 24.
      138–17   I cannot be a . . . Scientist except
      145–18   but *I* cannot go upon the
      163–12   and *I* cannot show
      189–24   I cannot forget that yours is the first
      233–15   by indifference thereto? *I* cannot.
      234– 4   I cannot watch and pray while
      251– 1   What these are *I* cannot yet say.
      285– 6   I cannot spare the time requisite to
      307–13   saying what *I* cannot forget
      343–10   "*I* cannot answer that now."

I cast
   Mis. 250–18   I cast aside the word as a sham

I celebrate
   My. 262–12   I celebrate Christmas with my soul,

I challenge
   My. 108– 5   I challenge matter to act

Eddy

I characterized
   Ret. 25–15   God *I* characterized as

I cherish
   Ret. 6–13   beautiful character as *I* cherish it,

I cherished
   My. 195–11   deep love which *I* cherished

I cited
   My. 281– 6   I cited, as our present need,

I claim
   Mis. 255–20   I claim for healing by C. S.
      349–17   I claim no jurisdiction over any
   Ret. 34–10   I claim for healing scientifically
   Pul. 74–16   I claim nothing more than
   My. 26–21   or that *I* claim their homage.
      305–21   I claim no special merit

I claimed
   Ret. 25–16   The real *I* claimed as eternal ;

I clearly
   Mis. 95–19   I clearly understand that no
      113–21   I clearly recognize that

I close
   Mis. 128– 5   Therefore *I* close here,
      273– 5   I close my College in order to
      274–13   I close my College.
   My. 15–16   I close with Kate Hankey's
      256–12   Thus may *I* close the door

I closed
   My. 246–11   I closed my College

I come
   Po. 73– 2   I come to thee

I commend
   Mis. 97–22   I commend the Icelandic

I comply
   My. 177– 3   Most happily would *I* comply

I concluded
   My. 307–18   But afterwards *I* concluded that

I congratulate
   My. 196– 3   I congratulate you upon erecting
      204–17   I congratulate you tenderly
      208–18   I congratulate you on the

I consent
   Mis. 300–17   When *I* consent to this act,

I consented
   My. 164– 3   demand increased, and *I* consented,
      284–22   I consented thereto only as other

I consider
   Pul. 39– 9   that *I* consider superbly sweet
   No. 28–15   I consider well established.
   My. 138– 4   I consider this agreement
      236–27   I consider the information there

I consulted
   My. 114–15   I consulted no other authors

I continue
   Mis. xii– 3   I continue the march,

I copy
   My. 189–28   from which *I* copy this verse :

I copyrighted
   Ret. 35– 1   I copyrighted the first publication

I cordially
   '02. 4– 5   I cordially congratulate our Board

I correct
   Mis. 266–24   If *I* correct mistakes which may be

I corrected
   My. 307– 3   his copy when *I* corrected it.

I could
   Mis. 19–22   than *I* could or would have
      106– 4   if *I* could write the history in
      351– 9   would not if *I* could,
      379– 4   asked if *I* could see his pennings
      380–18   Although *I* could heal mentally,
   Ret. 14–24   I could only answer him in the
      15– 7   I could say in David's words,
      24–19   I could only assure him that
      50– 2   I could think of no financial
   '02. 15–19   I could never believe that a

I could not
   Mis. 351– 8   I could not if I would,
   Ret. 14–21   I could not designate any precise
      24–18   I could not then explain the *modus*
   Pul. 34–22   "How, *I* could not tell,
   '01. 32– 7   I could not help loving them.
   My. 114–18   I could not write these notes after
      311– 7   I could not refuse her.

I counsel
   Un. 1–13   I counsel my students to defer
   Pan. 13–12   I counsel thee, rebuke and
   '01. 30–27   I counsel Christian Scientists
   My. 18–20   I counsel thee, rebuke and

I count
   '01. 31–20   I count these dear :

I cured
   Mis. 242–24   I cured precisely such a case

I daily
   My. 244–12   need of which *I* daily discern.

Eddy

I declare
'01. 15– 1   I declare that he must awake

I declared
My. 307– 5   one day I declared to him

I declined
'02. 15–18   I declined to sell them
My. 302–28   I declined and went alone in my

I dedicate
My. 182–19   I dedicate this beautiful house

I deem
My. 289– 8   I deem it proper that The
306– 7   I deem it unwise to enter into

I demonstrated
Mis. 70– 3   I *demonstrated* its truth when I

I denied
Ret. 25–16   His corporeality I denied.

I denominated
Ret. 25–14   Soul I denominated *substance*,

I deny
Un. 10– 3   reality of these . . . I deny,

I deposit
Mis. 159–16   I deposit certain recollections
159–20   Here I deposit the gifts that my

I deprecate
Mis. 97–12   Such . . . healing I deprecate.
284–29   I deprecate personal animosities

I described
Ret. 25–18   temporal, I described as unreal.

I desire
Mis. 274– 4   I desire to revise my book
291–12   I desire the equal growth and
Ret. 74– 9   I desire never to think of it,
Pul. 87–20   more of earth now, than I desire,
My. 138–15   persons whom I desire to see
249–24   The report . . . I desire to correct.
358–13   however much I desire to read all

I desired
Mis. 276– 6   all with whom I desired to,

I did
Mis. 178– 4   left his old church, as I did,
311–25   I did this even as a surgeon
Ret. 9–15   I did answer, in the words of
My. 215– 5   bade me do what I did,
312–30   I did open an infant school,
346–27   "I did say that a man would be

I did not
Mis. 276– 5   I did not hold interviews with all
Ret. 35– 7   I did not venture . . . until later,
My. 340–28   I did not mean any man

I disapprove
Mis. 100– 4   authority for what I disapprove,

I discern
'00. 9– 2   I discern that this obedience

I discerned
Ret. 26– 3   Adoringly I discerned the Principle
Un. 30–23   I discerned the last Adam as a

I discovered
Mis. 337– 1   Have I discovered and founded
379–27   I discovered, . . . the momentous facts
382–12   I discovered the Science of
Ret. 24– 4   I discovered the Science of
Un. 30–21   When I discovered the power of Spirit

I do
Mis. 11–27   I do it with earnest, special care
29– 3   Do you believe his words? I do,
67–27   If your question refers to . . . I do.
96–18   Do I believe in the . . . I do ;
Un. 46– 8   I do so on a divine Principle,
My. 9–25   but I do now,
219–21   I do say that C. S. cannot annul
235–25   Do you adopt as truth . . . I do.
284–24   I do believe implicitly in the
303–29   to be proved by the good I do.

I donated
Mis. 140–20   The lot of land which I donated
382–19   I donated to this church the land

I do not
Mis. 267– 9   * those whom I do not love,"
358–20   Be it understood that I do not
Ret. 76–28   but if I do not insist upon
Un. 46– 7   I do not deny, . . . the individuality
'01. 22– 6   I do not try to mix matter and
22– 8   I do not believe in such a compound.
22–16   I do not say that one added to one
My. 143–22   I do not regard this . . . as a trial,
223–13   secular affairs, I do not answer.
223–15   I do not consider myself capable of
223–19   either of which I do not entertain.
237– 6   I do not consider a precedent for
242–10   I do not mean that mortals are
255– 7   I do not mean that minor officers
318–31   I do not find my authority for
345– 3   I do not suppose their
361– 4   I do not presume to give you

Eddy

I dropped
Mis. x–21   I dropped the name of Morse

I dwell
Po. 32– 3   home where I dwell in the vale,

I earned
My. 215–16   I earned the means with which to

I earnestly
Mis. 308–32   I earnestly advise . . . Scientists
322– 2   I earnestly invite you to its
Ret. 8–23   Then I earnestly declared

I employ
No. 10– 1   I employ this awe-filled word

I employed
My. 307–11   terms which I employed
317– 9   mistake to say that I employed

I enclose
Mis. 157–18   I enclose you the name of
My. 289– 4   I enclose a check for

I endeavor
Mis. 66–31   I endeavor to accommodate my

I endeavored
Ret. 73–14   I endeavored to lift thought above

I engaged
My. 317–11   I engaged Mr. Wiggin so as to

I enjoin
No. 8–19   I enjoin it upon my students to

I enter
Mis. 299–18   If I enter Mr. Smith's store
347–20   I enter the path.
My. 188–17   In spirit I enter your inner

I entered
Ret. 39– 3   I entered a suit at law,
My. 307–17   I entered a demurrer which

I entertain
Mis. 292–12   higher sense I entertain of Love,

I entitled
My. 353–12   the second I entitled *Sentinel*,

I esteem
Ret. 29– 2   I esteem all honest people,

I exercised
Mis. 70– 3   when I exercised my power

I exhort
Un. 43–19   I exhort them to accept Christ's

I exist
My. 143–11   I exist in the flesh,

I experimented
Mis. 249– 2   I experimented by taking

I extend
'01. 1– 1   to-day I extend my

I fain
Mis. 394–19   * I fain would keep the gates ajar,
Po. 57– 5   * I fain would keep the gates ajar,

I fed
My. 247–16   I fed these sweet little thoughts

I feel
Mis. 13– 1   only justice of which I feel
146–23   I feel sure that as Christian Scientists
256–10   I feel, . . . this imposes on me the
266–20   I speak of them as I feel,
303–24   I feel assured that many
My. 138– 7   I feel that it is not for my benefit

I felt
Mis. 281–25   I felt the weight of this yesterday,
Ret. 14–23   asked me to say how I felt
Pul. 34–20   "I felt that the divine Spirit

I find
Mis. 132–20   I find it inconvenient to
281– 6   I find also another mental
My. 137–30   I find myself able to select
138–16   solely because I find that I

I first proved
Mis. 338– 5   I first proved to myself,

I follow
Mis. 347–18   I follow his counsel,

I followed
My. 343–19   I followed it up, teaching

I foresaw
My. 185–24   Then and there I foresaw this hour,

I foresee
Mis. 363–30   I foresee and foresay that
My. 26–20   as I foresee, the need of it.

I for one
Mis. 131–24   I, for one, would be pleased
My. 273–13   I for one accept his wise

I found
Mis. 69–16   I found him barely alive,
180–14   I found the open door from this
247– 7   I found health in just
348–23   When I found myself under this
Ret. 24–21   I found to be in perfect scientific
33–10   I found, in the two hundred and
56– 2   I found to be demonstrable
Pul. 34–23   I found it to be in perfect scientific
'01. 24–24   I found it necessary to follow
My. 343–26   I found at one time that they had

Eddy

I found
My. 345–16 but I found that when I
348– 6 I found it was God made manifest

I founded
Ret. 15– 4 till I founded a church of my own,

I fully
Pul. 87–15 I fully appreciate your kind

I furnished
'02. 12–30 I furnished the money

I gained
Ret. 10– 3 I gained book-knowledge
24– 9 I gained the scientific certainty

I gave
Mis. 137– 5 I gave you a meagre reception
139–18 I gave a lot of land
300–25 I gave permission to cite,
Ret. 43–10 After I gave up teaching,
51– 1 I gave a lot of land in Boston
'02. 15–27 To this, . . . I gave no heed,
My. 138– 1 I gave them my property to
157–22 I gave a deed of trust

I gazed
Ret. 31–22 I gazed, and stood abashed.

I give
Mis. 24– 5 I give it to you as
My. 119–26 Should I give myself the pleasant

I go
My. 275–17 I go out in my carriage daily,

I greatly rejoice
Mis. 137–14 I greatly rejoice over the growth of

I greet
Mis. 251– 6 beloved brethren, . . . I greet you ;

I grew discouraged
Ret. 8–10 until I grew discouraged,

I group
My. 257–25 I group you in one benison

I had
Mis. 11–13 I had done my whole duty
24–14 better health than I had before
32–17 If I had the time to talk with all
139–23 I had this desirable site transferred
140–11 as I had it conveyed.
237–30 I had heard the awful story
285– 4 because I had been personal
300–23 which I had organized
300–24 I had for many years been pastor,
373– 9 I had never before seen it :
379– 2 I had a curiosity to know if he
379–20 I had already experimented
380–10 demonstrate what I had discovered :
Ret. 8–16 though I had ceased to notice it.
10– 6 latter I had to repeat every Sunday.
10–12 knowledge I had gleaned from
14–19 when I had experienced a change
14–20 tearfully I had to respond
14–22 I had been truly regenerated,
20– 2 except what money I had brought
20–10 I had no training for self-support,
23–23 I had touched the hem of C. S.
24– 8 I had been trying to trace
28– 9 I had learned that thought must
28–22 I had learned that Mind reconstructed
38– 1 I had finished that edition as far as
38– 3 I had already paid him
38– 9 I had already observed
38–23 I had grown disgusted with
40– 9 I had stood by her side
44– 8 though I had preached five years
Pul. 20– 6 In 1892 I had to recover the land
34–15 they thought I had died,
35–13 "I had learned that thought must
35–21 I had learned that Mind reconstructed
49–15 I had them brought here
63–12 "I had them brought here
'01. 17–19 I had overcome a difficult stage
17–24 I had learned that the dynamics
'02. 13–25 price I had paid for it,
15–22 book I had been writing.
My. 13– 7 first that I had even heard of it.
105–25 he asked earnestly if I had a
123–13 I had the property bought
137–23 I had contemplated doing this
137–25 I had consulted Lawyer Streeter
137–27 I had implicit confidence in each one
174–22 until I had a church of my own,
214–21 I had no monetary means
214–27 I had cast my all into the treasury of
271– 7 truth of what I had written.
317–19 dissented from what I had written,
336–13 except what money I had brought
348–21 I had found unmistakably an

I had not
Mis. 290–18 I had not thought of the writer
Ret. 15–26 I had not heard of these cases
27–13 I had not fully voiced my

Eddy

I had not
Ret. 38–12 although I had not thought of
'01. 24–21 I had not read one line of Berkeley's

I half wish
Mis. 126– 4 I half wish for society again ;

I hate no one
Mis. 311–18 I hate no one ;

I have
Mis. xi–27 In compiling this work, I have
11–29 When smitten on one cheek, I have
11–30 I have but two to present.
13– 7 I have long endured at the hands of
24–16 I have since tried to make plain to
29–16 I have known of but fourteen
39–14 I have faith in His promise,
47–30 I have no knowledge of mesmerism,
65–23 I have taught them both in its
115–13 take up the cross as I have done,
127– 1 I have observed that in proportion as
127– 4 I have seen, that in the ratio of
127– 7 One thing I have greatly desired,
142–13 since they arrived I have said,
146–12 I have hitherto declined to be
157– 7 I have written, or caused my
177–30 I have met one who
213– 3 All that I have written,
231– 9 would I have had the table
239– 4 I have had but four days' vacation
245–23 I have loved the Church
247– 8 I have professed Christianity
249– 8 false report that I have appropriated
249–16 I have neither purchased nor
249–23 I have proof, but no fear.
266–18 assertion that I have said
267– 6 for whom I have sacrificed the most
272–29 I have endeavored to act toward all
278–10 can be proven that I have never
278–15 I have learned that a curse on sin
278–24 I have felt for some time that
278–29 I have been gradually withdrawing
281– 9 I have now one ambition
294–25 I have read the daily paper,
299– 8 I have no time for detailed report
307–13 I have thought best to stop its
308–24 The knowledge that I have gleaned
311–23 works I have written on C. S.
311–32 I have been sorry that I spoke
318– 4 I have a large affection,
321–27 I have no desire to see or to hear what
321–29 I have a world of . . . to contemplate,
334–28 Because I have uncovered evil,
338–13 only rule I have found which
348–18 I have to repeat this,
348–29 I have by no means encouraged
349– 5 I have students with the degree of
349–30 I have accepted no pay from my
349–31 I have put into the church-fund
351– 1 I have sometimes called on
351– 7 I have no skill in occultism ;
Ret. 28–25 I have since understood it.
30–21 the cup which I have drunk
50–16 I have had as many as seventeen in
52– 1 I have endeavored to find new ways
52– 7 I have worked to provide a home for
76–27 I have long remained silent
83– 7 Students whom I have taught
Un. 7– 8 When I have most clearly seen
7–13 I have been able to replace
43–12 I have by no means spoken of myself,
48– 6 I have no faith in any other thing
Pul. 7–24 I have ordained the Bible and
74–22 not what I have taught her,
74–22 not at all as I have heard her talk.
87–19 I have more of earth now, than
Rud. 8– 9 I have given you only an epitome of
No. 2–15 I have healed more disease by
8–11 in love, as I have rebuked them.
9–16 I have opposed occasionally
40–12 I have no objection to audible prayer
Pan. 13–26 I have only traversed my subject that
'00. 9–25 I have desired to step aside
10–25 I have learned it was a private
'01. 11–13 True, I have made the
26–14 I have passed through deep waters
26–26 I have read little of their writings.
26–28 What I have given to the world
27–14 I have in one to three interviews
27–22 I have put less of my own
27–23 I have taken out of its
'02. 2–29 I have always taught the student to
13– 5 I have transferred to The Mother Church,
14–12 only success I have ever achieved
Po. 65– 5 in dreams I have had,
My. 15–14 Already I have said to you
17–29 "Hitherto, I have observed that in

Eddy

I have

My.
18– 1 *I* have seen, that in the ratio of
18– 4 "One thing *I* have greatly desired,
25–23 *I* have faith in the givers
26–13 that *I* have ever received
103–18 *I* have set forth C. S.
103–19 just as *I* have discovered them.
103–20 *I* have demonstrated through Mind
103–22 *I* have found nothing in ancient or
104 1 *I* have had no other guide
105–14 *I* have healed at one visit a cancer
105–16 *I* have physically restored sight
105–32 *I* have proved to be more certain
108– 6 *I* have proved beyond cavil
114–25 *I* have been learning the higher
115– 5 blush to write of . . . as *I* have, were it
119–28 *I* have risen to look and wait
121– 2 *I* have suggested a change
125–11 *I* have only to dip my pen in my
125 16 *I* have felt the touch of the
130–10 whom *I* have assisted pecuniarily
130–13 *I* have neither the time nor the
133–22 *I* have a secret to tell you
135– 8 *I* have heretofore personally
136–24 To my . . . Trustees *I* have committed
136–27 *I* have so done that I may have
137–11 *I* have attended personally to my
137–14 *I* have personally selected all my
137–20 *I* have designated by my last will,
143– 0 *I* have the pleasure to report
145–17 *I* have worked even harder
147– 8 *I* have provided for you a
147–22 *I* have purchased a pleasant place
147–26 *I* have a work to do
152–31 *I* have the sweet satisfaction of
163–23 *I* have also received from
164– 8 *I* have yearned to express my
174–17 *I* have the pleasure of thanking you
203– 3 *I* have nothing new to communicate ;
217– 5 *I* have deeded in trust to The
219–26 *I* have expressed my opinion
223–11 with whom *I* have no acquaintance
223–12 of whom *I* have no knowledge,
229– 3 *I* have no use for such,
236–13 *I* have the joy of knowing that
237– 3 *I* have since decided not to publish.
242–21 *I* have requested my secretary not to
244– 1 *I* have awaited your arrival
244–13 *I* have awaited the right hour,
244–24 What *I* have to say may not require
247–28 The little that *I* have accomplished
248–24 *I* have largely committed to you,
250–20 *I* have faith that whatever is done
259– 4 *I* have named it my *white student.*
270 21 *I* have returned good for evil,
276–23 *I* have none, in reality,
296– 3 *I* have prayed daily that there be no
303– 4 and *I* have never claimed to be.
303–12 of which *I* have seen only extracts,
304–12 *I* have lectured in large and crowded
306–10 *I* have quite another purpose
311–24 *I* have another coat-of-arms,
313– 3 so *I* have been told :
313–19 *I* have always consistently declared
314–28 just as *I* have stated them.
316– 1 the truth *I* have promulgated
317–23 liberty that *I* have taken with
318– 3 *I* have erased them in my revisions.
341– 1 *I* have one innate joy,
343–14 "*I* have been called a pope,
343–14 *I* have sought no such distinction.
343–15 *I* have simply taught as I learned
344– 1 *I* have even been spoken of as a
353– 9 *I* have given the name to all the
356–15 *I* have given no assurance,
357–11 *I* have crowned The Mother Church
357–28 *I* have just finished reading your

I have not

Mis.
32–21 But *I* have not moments enough
65–19 *I* have not ; and this important fact
97–27 *I* have not seen a perfect man
243– 5 *I* have not yet made surgery one of
248–28 *I* have not taken drugs,
264–14 whom *I* have not fitted for it
317– 1 students whom *I* have not seen
My.
138–19 Trusting that *I* have not exceeded
165– 6 which *I* have not endured for the
195– 9 privileges *I* have not had time to
223–14 *I* have not sufficient time to waste
243–13 *I* have not yet had the privilege of
297–27 *I* have not had sufficient interest in the
303–26 *I* have not the inspiration nor the
351–23 *I* have not read Gerhardt C. Mars' book,
351–24 therefore *I* have not endorsed it,
355– 8 *I* have not infrequently hinted at

Eddy

I have not

My.
358–13 *I* have not the time to do so.
361– 9 *I* have not seen Mrs. Stetson for

I healed

Ret. 40– 1 four successive years *I* healed,
'01. 17–15 It was that *I* healed the deaf,
My. 105– 7 *I* healed consumption in its last stages,
105–10 *I* healed malignant diphtheria
127–17 *I* healed ninety-nine to the ten of
145–13 *I* healed him on the spot.

I hear

Mis. 106–25 methinks *I* hear the soft, sweet
Po. 16–20 'Mid graves do *I* hear the glad
My. 153– 1 *I* hear that the loving hearts

I heard

Ret. 8– 9 *I* heard somebody call *Mary,*
'02. 9–21 When first *I* heard the life-giving sound
My. 319– 5 *I* heard nothing further from him

I hereby

Mis. 297–16 *I* hereby state, in unmistakable
313–25 *I* hereby ordain the Bible, and
My. 171–11 *I* hereby invite all my church
223– 2 *I* hereby notify the public that
242–16 *I* hereby announce to the C. S. field
359– 8 and *I* hereby publicly declare that

I herewith

My. 289–25 *I* herewith send a few words of
360–14 *I* herewith cheerfully subscribe these

I hold

Mis. 350– 1 *I* hold receipts for $1,489.50
Un. 49–13 So long as *I* hold evil in
My. 319– 8 *I* hold the late Mr. Wiggin in
344–12 *I* hold it absurd to say that when

I hope

Mis. 133–18 *I* hope I am not wrong in
391– 3 *I* hope the heart that's hungry
396–14 *I* hope it's better made,
Po. 38– 2 *I* hope the heart that's hungry
59– 6 *I* hope it's better made,
My. 120– 4 *I* hope and trust that you and I
131–18 *I* hope I shall not be found disorderly,
169– 7 date, which *I* hope soon to name
259–16 *I* hope that in 1902 the churches

I impart

Mis. 292–11 Could *I* impart to the student

I implore

Mis. 141–19 Do not, *I* implore you,

I indited

My. 271– 5 little understood all that *I* indited ;

I indulge

Mis. 348–21 *I* indulge in homoeopathic doses of

I infer

Mis. 32– 6 *I* infer that some of my students

I inferred

Mis. 379–10 from his remarks *I* inferred that

I inform

My. 135–18 *I* inform you of this,

I insist

Mis. 283–19 *I* insist on the etiquette of C. S.,
Un. 43–13 *I* insist only upon the fact,
No. 10– 3 *I* insist that C. S. is
31–13 *I* insist on the destruction of sin

I insisted

Mis. 158– 6 When *I* insisted on your speaking
373– 3 *I* insisted upon placing the serpent

I inspected

My. 145– 8 *I* inspected the work every day,

I instantly

Ret. 41– 4 desperate cases *I* instantly healed,

I instruct

No. 40–14 *I* instruct my students to pursue

I intervened

My. 343–27 *I* intervened.

I introduce

Mis. 247–14 of the Science *I* introduce,

I introduced

Ret. 43– 1 In 1867 *I* introduced the first

I invite

My. 169– 2 *I* invite you, one and all,

I invited

My. 318–16 *I* invited Mr. Wiggin

I issue

Mis. 350–26 *I* issue no arguments,

I joined

My. 311–13 *I* joined the Tilton Congregational

I judged

Ret. 43–18 *I* judged it best to close the

I just

Mis. 262–13 *I* just want to say, I thank you,

I kiss

Mis. 397– 3 *I* kiss the cross, and wake to know
Pul. 18–12 *I* kiss the cross, and wake to know
Po. 12–12 *I* kiss the cross, and wake to know

I knelt

Ret. 20–13 *I* knelt by his side throughout

Eddy

I knew
Mis. 140– 1   I knew that to God's gift,
  267–12   when I knew they were secretly
  290–19   I knew that this person was
Ret. 25–20   I knew the human conception of
Hea.   6– 8   I knew it was misinterpreted,
My. 137–25   or I knew aught about them,

I knew not
My. 307–28   drifting whither I knew not.

I know
Mis. 78–10   I know not how to teach either
 157–25   This I know, for God is for us.
'00.   8–30   I know it were best not to do,
'01. 19– 5   I know that prayer brings the
'02. 12–24   so far as I know them,
My.   7– 7   so far as I know them,
 138– 9   I know it was not needed
 151– 6   I know that no Christian can
 174–27   Each day I know Him nearer,
 223–17   that of which I know nothing.
 237–10   that I know to be correct
 271–29   insomuch as I know myself,
 303– 4   I know that I am not that one,
 357–30   I know that every true follower
 360–22   This I know, for He has proved it

I know not
Mis. 96– 8   I know not what the person of

I lay
Mis. 335–16   I lay bare the ability, in belief,

I leaned
'02. 15– 5   I leaned on God, and was safe.

I learned
Mis. 24–18   I learned that mortal thought
 281– 7   I learned long ago that the world
Ret. 25–24   I learned that these material senses
 32– 5   Early had I learned that
Hea.   6–13   I learned how mind produces
  6–14   I learned how it produces the
My. 271– 7   then I learned the truth
 343–15   I have simply taught as I learned

I leave all
Mis. 274–10   therefore I leave all for Christ.
My. 138–17   except I leave all for Christ.

I led
Ret. 30–19   Even so was I led into the

I left
My. 117–28   I left Boston in the height of

I listened
Ret.   9– 3   I listened with bated breath.

I little knew
Mis. 158– 7   I little knew that so soon another

I little thought
Mis. 158– 5   I little thought of the changes

I live
Un. 48– 9   Because He lives, I live.

I lived
My. 314–28   I lived with Dr. Patterson

I'll think
Po. 17– 3   I'll think of its glory, and rest

I long
Pul. 21– 7   I long, and live, to see

I longed
Mis. 142–28   I longed to say to the masonic

I look
Mis. 159–28   I look at the rich devices in
 203– 6   as I look on this smile of C. S.,

I lost
Ret. 20– 1   I lost all my husband's property,
My. 311–11   so I lost my housekeeper.
 336–12   I lost all my husband's property,

I love
Mis. 33– 5   I love all ministers and
 111–25   I love the orthodox church ;
 180–16   I love the Easter service :
 311–16   I love my enemies
 397–16   I love to be.
Pul.   7– 4   I love Boston, and especially the
 18–25   I love to be.
'01. 19– 5   I love this doctrine,
 28–19   I love Christ more than all
Po. 13– 4   I love to be.
 35– 4   as I love life less !
My. 105–30   and I love them ;
 133–23   Do you know how much I love
 163–25   I love its people
 234– 7   know how much I love them,
 262–27   I love to observe Christmas
 270–24   I love the prosperity of Zion,

I loved
'01. 32– 7   I loved Christians of the old sort

I love you
Mis. 11–32   "I love you, and would

I lovingly
Mis. v– 4   I LOVINGLY DEDICATE THESE

Eddy

I'm
Po. page 8   poem
  8– 1   I'm sitting alone where the shadows
  8– 7   I'm waiting alone for the bridal
  8–11   I'm watching alone o'er the starlit
  8–16   I'm dreaming alone of its changeful
  8–20   I'm thinking alone of a fair young
  9– 3   I'm picturing alone a glad young
  9– 8   I'm weeping alone that the vision is

I made
My. 343–23   I made a code of by-laws,

I maintain
Un. 46– 7   I do not deny, I maintain,

I make
Mis. 203– 3   I make no distinction between
 250–16   I make strong demands on love,
 299–20   can I make this right by saying,

I may
Mis. 58–16   I may read the Scriptures through a
 142–29   If as a woman I may not unite with
 143– 6   I may hope that a closer link
 322– 7   I may hereafter notify the Directors
Po. 33–12   that His love I may know,
My. 120– 4   that you and I may meet in truth
 136–27   that I may have more peace,
 146–10   I may then be even younger
 187– 3   I may at some near future
 302–20   I may be more loved,

I mean
Mis. 261–24   by mankind I mean mortals,
Ret. 50–19   By loyalty in students I mean this,
Rud.   3–26   I mean the infinite and divine
  8–25   By this I mean that mortal mind

I measure
Mis. 48– 1   as I measure its demonstrations

I met
Mis. 280–26   I met the class to answer some

I might
My. 163–18   that I might find retirement

I miss
Po.   3– 3   I miss thee as the flower

I mistake
My. 229– 2   unless I mistake their calling.

I modify
Mis. 67–29   I modify my affirmative answer.

I must
Mis. 58–17   I must spiritually understand them
 105–18   I must ever follow this line
 274– 6   I must stop teaching at present.
 307–20   I must stand on this absolute
Ret. 34– 1   I must know more of the
 38– 8   I must insert in my last chapter
My. 123– 4   I must continue to prize love
 194–24   I must decline to receive that

I must not
Mis. 301–16   I must not leave persistent
My. 163–10   I must not allow myself the

I name
My. 106– 7   I name those mentioned above

I named
Ret. 25–10   I named it Christian, because
 25–12   I named mortal mind.
My. 353–15   the next I named Monitor,

individual
Mis. 266–11   this i· is doing the work that
'01. 21–15   an i· who loves God and man ;
My. 116–18   the truth regarding an i·

I need
Po. 24–14   Is all I need to comfort mine.
My. 137–30   to select the Trustees I need
 234– 8   I need every hour wherein to

I need not
My. 130–24   But I need not say this
 200–19   I need not say this to you,

I neglect
Mis. 351– 5   The fact is, . . . I neglect myself.

I never
Mis. 87–19   I never commission any one to
 91–24   I never dreamed, until informed
 94– 3   I never knew a person who
 239– 3   I never was in better health.
 292–28   I never knew a student who
 349–28   I never received more than
 351– 5   I never have practised by
 374–20   I never looked on my ideal of
 379–13   I never heard him say that
'00. 10–24   from a person I never saw.
'02.   2–26   I never left the Church,
 15– 2   yet I never lost my faith
My.   9–24   I never before felt poor in
 311–23   I never doubted the veracity
 313–21   I never was especially interested,
 313–24   I never went into a trance

I noticed
My. 307–10   I noticed he used that word,

Eddy

I now
Mis.	13– 9	This law *I* now urge upon the
	158–25	completion (as *I* now think)
	273– 6	*I* now seem to be most needed,
	311–19	As *I* now understand C. S.,
No.	9–19	*I* now point steadfastly to the
My.	240–15	*I* now repeat another proof,
	280–16	*I* now request that the members

instructor
Pul. 58–24   * their prime *i·* has ordained

I obeyed
No. 3–11   *I* obeyed a diviner rule.

I objected
Mis. 349–13   *I* objected on the ground that

I observed
Mis. 239–11   *I* observed a carriage

I offer
Mis. 242–19   *I* offer him three thousand dollars

I often
Mis. 159–14   *I* often retreat, sit silently,

I omitted
My. 184–13   so occupied that *I* omitted

I once
Mis.	138–17	*I* once thought that in unity
	195–25	*I* once believed that
	278–13	*I* once wondered at the Scriptural

I opened
Mis. 274– 3   when *I* opened my College.

I ordained
Mis. 382–32   *I* ordained that the Bible,

I ordered
Mis. 285– 3   pamphlets *I* ordered to be laid away

I ought
My. 224– 6   knowing a little, as *I* ought,

I owe
My. 9–26   for the amount *I* owe you,

I paid
Pul. 20– 4   therefore *I* paid it,

I performed
Mis. 242–14   *I* performed more difficult tasks

I ponder
Po. 33–17   'Twill be sweet when *I* ponder

I practise
My. 220–12   *I* practise and teach this

I practised
My.	204–20	*I* practised gratuitously
	271– 6	*I* practised its precepts,

I pray
Mis.	144–29	*I* pray that divine Love,
	151–19	*I* pray thee as a Christian Scientist,
	276–24	*I* pray that all my students
My.	167–11	*I* pray that heaven's messages of
	220–15	*I* pray for the pacification of
	220–21	Each day *I* pray : "God bless my

I prayed
Ret.	13–21	*I* prayed ; and a soft glow of
My.	283–10	Many years have *I* prayed and labored

I preached
Mis.	349–23	*I* preached four years,
	349–28	each Sunday when *I* preached,
	349–29	contributions, when *I* preached,
'02.	15– 2	the hall where *I* preached ;

I predict
Pul. 22–10   *I* predict that in the twentieth century

I prefer
Un.	32–16	which *I* prefer to call *mortal mind.*
Rud.	2–14	*I* prefer to retain the proper sense of
My.	249–22	The report that *I* prefer to have a

I prescribed
My. 345–16   *I* prescribed pellets without any

I present
My. 216–19   which *I* present to your thought,

I presented
Mis. 153–23   to whom *I* presented a copy of

I proceeded
My. 318–21   As *I* proceeded, Mr. Wiggin

I proposed
Mis.	156–13	*I* proposed to merge the
My.	145– 4	*I* proposed to one of

I published
Rud.	16–20	a work which *I* published in 1875.
'01.	24–21	when *I* published my work S. and H.,

I query
My. 299–17   *I* query : Do Christians, who believe

I quickly saw
Mis. 49– 2   *I* quickly saw, had a tendency to

I quieted
My. 317–20   *I* quieted him by quoting

I reach
Mis.	143– 8	*I* reach out my hand to clasp yours,
Un.	49–11	*I* reach, in thought,

I read
Mis.	24–11	As *I* read, the healing Truth
	58–13	*I* read the inspired page
	132–26	*I* read in your article these words:

Eddy

I read
Mis.	379– 5	*I* read the copy in his presence,
My.	230–18	*I* read with pleasure your approval

I realized
Mis. 281–27   *I* realized what a responsibility

I rebuke
Mis. 277–32   *I* rebuke it wherever I see it.

I recall
Ret.	14–14	*I* recall what followed.
Pul.	7– 7	Yet when *I* recall the past,

I receive
'02. 13–10   *I* receive no personal benefit

I received
Mis.	x–24	*I* received from the Daughters of
	137–10	*I* received no reply.
Ret.	10– 9	*I* received lessons in the ancient
'00.	10–23	*I* received a touching token
My.	182– 4	*I* received from the Congregational Church
	259– 6	*I* received the following cabled

I recognize
Mis.	102–15	*I* recognize the loving, divine
My.	326–19	*I* recognize the divine hand

I recollect
My. 309–13   as *I* recollect it, he was justice of

I recommend
Mis.	120–20	*I* recommend that this Association
	131–16	*I* recommend that you waive the
	136–22	*I* recommend that the June session
	139– 1	*I* recommend this honorable body
	302–32	*I* recommend that students stay
Man.	92– 7	*I* recommend that each member
Ret.	78–11	*I* recommend students not to
No.	7–21	*I* recommend that Scientists draw no
My.	219–29	*I* recommend, if the law demand,
	237–23	*I* recommend its careful study to all
	354– 5	*I* recommend nothing but what is

I recommended
Ret. 44–23   *I* recommended that the church

I reconstructed
Pul. 20–10   In 1895 *I* reconstructed my

I redeemed
Mis.	140–20	*I* redeemed from under mortgage.
'02.	14– 2	the land when *I* redeemed it.

I refer
My. 292–20   *I* refer to the effect of one

I refuse
My. 302–24   and *I* refuse adulation.

I regard
My. 302–20   *I* regard self-deification as

I regarded
Ret. 20–11   my home *I* regarded as very

I regret
My. 245–11   *I* regret to say,

I reiterate
'01. 8– 9   *I* reiterate this cardinal point :

I rejoice
Mis.	270– 6	*I* rejoice with those who rejoice,
'01.	14–28	*I* rejoice in the scientific
'02.	3– 7	*I* rejoice that the President
My.	183–18	Brethren :— *I* rejoice with you ;
	190– 3	BRETHREN :— *I* rejoice with thee.
	285– 7	*I* rejoice with you in all your wise
	362– 4	*I* rejoice with you in the victory of

I relinquished
'01. 24–29   *I* relinquished the form to attain

I remain
My.	108–28	*I* remain steadfast in St. Paul's faith.
	138–21	*I* remain most respectfully yours,
	175–25	must remain so long as *I* remain.

I remember
Mis.	137– 9	*I* remember my regret,
	237–28	*I* remember, when a girl,
Ret.	1– 8	*I* remember reading, in my childhood,
	6– 6	My childhood's home *I* remember as
My.	313–11	Nor do *I* remember any such stuff

I removed
Mis.	69–19	*I* removed the stoppage,
My.	163–17	*I* removed from Boston in 1889

I repeat
Mis.	135– 2	*I* repeat, person is not in the
My.	170–30	*I* repeat to these dear members
	285–20	In the words of St. Paul, *I* repeat :

I repeatedly
Ret. 8– 4   *I* repeatedly heard a voice,

I replied
Mis.	180– 9	"Christ never left," *I* replied ;
Ret.	14–24	*I* replied that I could only answer

I reply
Mis.	353– 7	*I* reply, The human concept is
My.	251– 5	*I* reply to the following question

I request
Mis.	133– 7	*I* request you to read my sermons
My.	216–21	*I* request that from this date
	236–24	*I* request the Christian Scientists

Eddy

I request
My. 279–22   I request that every member of The
    280–28   In no way nor manner did *I* request
I requested
Mis. 158– 5   When *I* requested you to be
I respect
Mis. 223–11   I respect that moral sense which
My. 163–27   I respect their religious beliefs,
I respectfully
My. 224– 5   I respectfully call your attention to
I rest
My. 250–25   I rest peacefully in knowing that
I retain
'02. 14– 3   only interest I retain in this property
I retire
Mis. 133–22   I retire to seek the divine blessing
I retired
Mis. 136– 1   I retired from the field of labor,
I return
My. 259–12   I return my heart's wireless love.
I returned
Ret. 19–16   A month later *I* returned
My. 165– 7   I returned blessing for cursing.
    215–12   I returned this money
    330–28   I returned to New Hampshire,
I reverence
Mis. 96–20   I reverence and adore Christ
I revised
No. 3– 8   When *I* revised "S. and H.
I rose
Mis. 24–13   I rose, dressed myself,
Ret. 13–22   I rose and dressed myself.
'02. 15–24   I rose and recorded the
I said
Mis. 159–23   what *I* said in 1890 :
    180–11   I said, in the words of
    380–22   I said, "Suffer it to be so— *Matt.* 3 : 15.
Hea. 6– 9   misinterpreted, and *I* said it.
My. 229–25   That which *I* said in my heart
    240–11   June 10, 1906, when *I* said,
    307– 1   words that *I* said to him,
    307–21   and understood what *I* said
    318–30   "Now, Mr. Wiggin," *I* said,
I sat
Ret. 8–14   I sat in a little chair by her
I saw
Mis. 156–14   because *I* saw no advantage,
    267–10   when *I* saw an opportunity
Ret. 44–19   I saw that the crisis had come
    45–21   I saw these fruits of Spirit,
Hea. 6–11   I saw the impossibility,
    6–15   I saw how the mind's ideals
I say
Mis. 12– 1   *Because* I thus feel, I say
    249– 4   I say with tearful thanks,
    282–15   I say, When you enter
    298–26   I say, You mistake ;
    321–26   I say, Do not expect me.
Un. 11–28   I say, Look up,
    17– 4   I say, Be allied to the
'01. 29–11   I say this not because reformers
'02. 19–11   I say it with joy,
My. 131–11   I say with the consciousness of
    216–18   I say : The purpose of God
    344–25   "I say, 'Render to Caesar— *Mark* 12 : 17.
    344–29   I say : Where vaccination is
    361– 5   All *I* say is stated in C. S.
I see
Mis. 277–32   I rebuke it wherever *I* see it.
    347–19   I see the way now.
    397– 6   I see Christ walk,
Ret. 50–23   I see clearly that students
Un. 49– 8   the more *I* see it to be sinless,
Pul. 18–15   I see Christ walk,
Rud. 16–11   but *I* see that some novices,
'00. 5–14   I see no other way
Po. 12–15   I see Christ walk,
    17– 3   and rest till *I* see
My. 216–30   I see that you should begin now
I seek
My. 118–13   hence *I* seek to be
I seldom
My. 215– 8   I seldom taught without having
    313–19   but *I* seldom took one.
I selected
My. 137–27   I selected said Trustees because
I send
Mis. 142–23   So *I* send my answer in a
My. 159– 7   Sitting at his feet, *I* send
    197–26   I send loving congratulations,
    253–21   I send with this a store of wisdom
    326–12   I send for publication in our
I sent
Ret. 52–23   June, 1889, *I* sent a letter,

Eddy

I set to work
Ret. 38–10   I set to work, contrary to my
I shall
Mis. 95–12   I shall confine myself to questions
    132– 3   I shall take this as a favorable
    155–25   I shall be apt to forward their
    256–18   I shall continue to send to each
    263– 2   I shall have the unselfish joy
    278– 6   I shall fulfil my mission,
    316– 8   I shall speak . . . very seldom.
    322– 8   when *I* shall be present
No. 46–22   I shall continue to labor and wait.
'01. 27–15   I shall rejoice in being informed
'02. 4–21   I shall briefly consider these two
    20–20   I shall be the loser by this change,
My. 25–21   I shall be with my blessed church
    147–25   I shall be with you personally
    154– 7   I shall scarcely venture to send
    177–11   I shall then be even younger
    200–29   For this *I* shall continue to pray.
    240–20   I shall refer to this.
    347–20   I shall treasure my loving-cup
    358–19   I shall devote it to a worthy
I shall not
Mis. 222–29   I shall not forget the cost of
My. 131–18   I hope I shall not be found disorderly
I should
Mis. 19–20   I should have more faith in an
    133–20   I should feel a delicacy in
    146– 8   I should need to be with you.
    242–11   if *I* should accept his bid on
    273–28   if *I* should teach my Primary class,
    302–22   When *I* should so elect
    311–22   I should lose my hope of heaven.
Pul. 1–18   what need that *I* should be present
    2– 1   I should be much like the Queen of
'02. 15–15   as to what *I* should write,
My. 115– 4   I should blush to write of
    249–27   I should prefer that student who is
    297– 3   I should shrink from such salient
    307–23   I should still think that it was
    319– 2   I should still know that
    344–19   I should think myself in danger of
    344–27   I should tremble for mankind ;
I should not
'01. 21–26   I should not have known
My. 318–18   on condition that *I* should not ask
I showed
'02. 15–26   I showed it to my literary friends,
I shrank
Ret. 50– 8   I shrank from asking it,
I shuddered
Mis. 180–12   I shuddered at her material
I smiled
Hea. 6– 4   pardon me if *I* smiled.
I sometimes
'00. 8–29   I sometimes advise students not to
    9– 3   I sometimes withdraw that advice
I sought
Mis. 372–13   I sought the judgment of
Ret. 33– 7   I sought knowledge from the
    34– 5   If *I* sought an answer from the
My. 142–12   I sought God's guidance
    348– 5   I sought this cause, not within but
I speak
Mis. 266–20   I speak of them as I feel,
My. 107– 9   Here *I* speak from experience.
I specially desire
Mis. 148–25   I specially desire that you
I spoke
Mis. 312– 1   sorry that *I* spoke at all,
I stand
Mis. 158–20   I stand with sandals on and staff
    347–16   Between the two *I* stand still;
    392– 2   at whose feet *I* stand,
Po. 20– 2   at whose feet *I* stand,
My. 302–18   I stand in relation to this century
I started
Mis. 139–15   April, 1883, *I* started the *Journal*
Ret. 38–16   I started for Boston
    52–20   I started it, April, 1883,
My. 304–16   I started The C. S. *Journal*,
I still
My. 302–17   I still must think the name is not
    305–22   I still wait at the cross
    316– 4   I still hear the harvest song
I stood
Ret. 30– 1   I stood alone in this conflict,
My. 247–14   when *I* stood silently beside it,
    247–16   to the rim where *I* stood.
I stopped him
My. 318–29   but *I* stopped him.
I stoutly
Ret. 14–14   I stoutly maintained that

Eddy

I strove
'00. 9–27 *I* strove earnestly to fit others
I struggled
'02. 15– 8 *I* struggled on through many
I submit
My. 26–19 enclosed notice *I* submit to you,
299–10 *I* submit that C. S. has
I suggest
'02. 14– 6 *I* suggest as a motto for every
My. 236–14 the one which *I* suggest,
I suggested
Ret. 52–11 *I* suggested to my students,
My. 236– 5 *I* suggested the name
I supposed
Mis. 91–28 *I* supposed that students had
140–12 *I* supposed the trustee-deed
I sympathize
My. 151– 4 Because *I* sympathize with
295– 1 *I* sympathize with those who
I take
Mis. xii– 5 *I* take my pen and
231– 8 *I* take no stock in spirit-rappings
248–16 That *I* take opium ; . . . is not
262–29 *I* take so much pleasure in
I talk
Mis. 159–22 Here *I* talk once a year,
I taught
Mis. 11– 8 if *I* taught indigent students
29–15 *I* taught the first student
382–11 *I* taught the first student
Ret. 36– 5 *I* taught the Science of
'02. 15– 8 indigent students that *I* taught
My. 182–11 In 1884, *I* taught a class
I teach
Mis. 247– 7 in just what *I* teach.
350–28 *I* teach the use of such
Un. 9–25 healing, as *I* teach it,
No. 10–11 postulate of all that *I* teach,
I temporarily
Mis. 350– 3 *I* temporarily organized a
I thank
Mis. 262–13 *I* thank you, my dear students,
308–18 *I* thank you, each and all,
313–12 *I* thank the contributors to *The*
My. 6–16 *I* thank you for this proof of your
142–26 *I* thank you for your kind
159–10 *I* thank God who hath sent forth His
174–10 *I* thank the distinguished editors
197–20 *I* thank divine Love for the hope
201–12 *I* thank you out of a full heart.
202–21 *I* thank you for the words of cheer
253–11 *Brethren:* — *I* thank you.
254–19 *I* thank the faithful teacher
270–31 *I* thank God that for the
282–21 Deeply do *I* thank you for the
295–16 *I* thank you for it.
298– 8 *I* thank Miss Wilbur and the Concord
341– 3 *I* thank God that He has
352–29 *I* thank you not only for your
357–29 *I* thank you for acknowledging me as
358–18 *I* thank you for the money
I then left
Ret. 8–21 *I* then left the room,
I then withdrew
Ret. 24–22 *I* then withdrew from society
I think
Pul. 74–20 "*I* think Mrs. Lathrop was not
Po. 3– 6 *I* think of thee, *I* think of thee!
My. 133– 3 *I* think of this in the great light of
163–15 which *I* think do them more good.
171–10 *I* think you would enjoy seeing it.
I thought
Mis. 11– 7 *I* thought, also, that if *I*
Ret. 8– 5 *I* thought this was my mother's
My. 26–16 *I* thought it better to be brief
I thus feel
Mis. 12– 1 *Because I* thus feel, I say to
I thus speak
Un. 7– 6 though *I* thus speak, and from my
I took
Mis. 139–30 *I* took care that the provisions for
248–24 prescribed morphine, which *I* took,
My. 313–19 when *I* took an evening walk,
I touch
No. 32–11 when *I* touch this subject
I tread
Mis. 395–17 The turf, whereon *I* tread,
Po. 58– 2 The turf, whereon *I* tread,
I treasure
My. 184–16 *I* treasure it next to your
I tried
Mis. 348–26 *I* tried several doses of medicine,
I trow
Mis. 395– 8 And yet *I* trow,
Po. 57–15 And yet *I* trow,

Eddy

I trow
My. 20– 8 *I* trow you are awaiting
I trust
My. 167–27 will, *I* trust, never be marred
275–13 (and *I* trust the desire thereof)
I try
Un. 45–15 *I* try to show its all-pervading
I turn
Mis. 133–27 *I* turn constantly to divine Love
I understand
Mis. 34–14 so far as *I* understand it,
95–15 *I* understand the impossibility of
06– 3 *I* understand that God is an
141–16 *I* believe, — yea, *I* understand,
Ret. 29– 1 As *I* understand it, spiritualism is the
Un. 49– 2 *I* understand that man is as
49– 8 *I* understand true humanhood,
My. 13–16 *I* understand that the members
146– 6 because *I* understand it,
313– 1 is, *I* understand, a paraphrase
I unite
Ret. 14–12 never could *I* unite with the
I unveil
Un. 45–14 This pantheism *I* unveil.
I urge
Mis. 75– 8 *I* urge this fundamental fact
Un. 43–18 *I* urge Christians to have more faith
I use
Mis. 348–18 *I* use no drugs whatever,
Pul. 5– 3 adoration in the words *I* use,
I used to think
Mis. 11– 4 *I* used to think it sufficiently just
I've
Mis. vii–19 Whereof, I've more to glory,
Po. 18– 1 I've watched in the azure
I vindicate
Mis. 141–15 *I* vindicate both the law of God
No. 2– 1 only Mind-healing *I* vindicate ;
I visited
Mis. 112–15 *I* visited in his cell the
My. 185–22 *I* visited these mountains
I waited
'02. 15–21 Six weeks *I* waited on God
Hea. 14–22 *I* waited many years for a
I wandered
Ret. 33– 5 *I* wandered through the dim mazes
I want
'00. 11–17 *I* want not only quality,
I wanted
Mis. 348–24 *I* wanted to satisfy my curiosity
My. 138–2 *I* wanted it protected
I warn
Mis. 309–18 *I* warn students against
I was
Mis. 60 14 *I* was once called to visit a
180– 4 *I* was delivered from the dark shadow
223– 2 *I* was saying all the time,
249–20 The report that *I* was dead
311–26 *I* was a scribe under orders ;
313–14 *I* was impressed by the articles
349–15 *I* was willing, and said so,
Ret. 2–27 *I* was fond of listening,
5– 6 at Bow *I* was born,
8– 3 when *I* was about eight years old,
9–12 *I* was afraid, and did not answer.
10– 4 *I* was as familiar with
11– 1 *I* was a verse-maker.
13– 1 *I* was admitted to the Congregational
13– 6 *I* was unwilling to be saved, if
13–20 as *I* was wont to do,
14– 4 *I* was of course present.
14–10 *I* was ready for his doleful questions,
14–15 *I* was willing to trust God,
15–13 *I* was called to preach in Boston
19– 1 *I* was united to my first husband,
20–22 *I* was compelled to ask for a bill of
21– 4 *I* was then informed that my son
23–15 *I* was waiting and watching ;
25– 4 questions as to how *I* was healed ;
31– 9 *I* was impelled, by a hunger
33– 6 *I* was weary of "scientific
40– 4 *I* was called to speak before the
44–10 When *I* was its pastor,
46– 1 Lines penned when *I* was pastor of
48– 2 *I* was yearning for retirement.
50– 4 *I* was led to name three hundred
Pul. 34–28 by which *I* was restored to health ;
'00. 11– 5 Once *I* was passionately fond of
'01. 26–26 *I* was not drawn to them by
Hea. 6– 3 *I* was told the other day,
My. 105–19 *I* was wired to attend the patient of
115– 6 *I* was only a scribe echoing the
127–16 when *I* was in practice,
169–17 *I* was happy to receive at Concord,
169–19 *I* was rejoiced at the appropriate

Eddy

I was

My.	174–23	*I* was a member of the Congregational
	184–12	came when *I* was so occupied that
	214–21	*I* was confronted with the fact that
	215– 2	*I* was above begging
	304– 3	*I* was early a pupil of
	306–29	while *I* was his patient in Portland
	307–16	*I* was a staunch orthodox,
	307–26	*I* was gradually emerging from
	310– 5	*I* was privately tutored by him.
	311– 3	*I* was living with Dr. Patterson
	311–25	When *I* was last in Washington,
	311–31	*I* was called by the
	312–21	*I* was with him on this trip.
	312–23	*I* was surrounded by friends,
	313–15	to help me when *I* was ill.
	313–16	*I* was never "given to long and
	313–17	*I* was always accompanied by
	313–29	*I* was obliged to be parted from
	314– 7	When *I* was married to him,
	314–25	*I* was also the means of
	343–20	*I* was the mother,
	345–12	*I* was a sickly child.
	345–13	*I* was dosed with drugs until
	348– 8	Then *I* was healed,

I was not

Mis.	148–23	*I* was not aware that the
My.	313–20	*I* was not a medium for spirits.

I watch

Po.	3– 8	*I* watch thy chair, and wish

I ween

Mis.	393– 6	Paints the limner's work, *I* ween,
Po.	51–11	Paints the limner's work, *I* ween,

I welcome

My.	154–23	*I* welcome the means and methods,

I went

Ret.	13–19	if *I* went to Him in prayer,
	19– 5	*I* went with him to the South ;
	40– 8	*I* went to the invalid's house.

I wept

Ret.	9–12	*I* wept, and prayed that God would

I were

Mis.	146–20	if *I* were, I would gather every
	312– 1	wished *I* were wise enough to

I will

Mis.	33– 1	*I* will say : It is the righteous
	69–27	*I* will send his address to any one
	104–29	*I* will love, if another hates.
	104–30	*I* will gain a balance on the side of
	158– 2	In reply to your letter *I* will say :
	349–22	*I* will state that I preached
	398– 1	*I* will listen for Thy voice,
	398– 3	*I* will follow and rejoice
Ret.	46– 7	*I* will listen for Thy voice,
	46– 9	*I* will follow and rejoice
Un.	48– 3	yet ask, and *I* will answer.
Pul.	17– 6	*I* will listen for Thy voice,
	17– 8	*I* will follow and rejoice
Po.	14– 5	*I* will listen for Thy voice,
	14– 7	*I* will follow and rejoice
My.	107– 7	*I* will cite a modern phase of
	123–19	Ere long *I* will see you in this hall,
	142–28	*I* will attend the meeting,
	146– 2	*I* will say : It is understood by all
	214–18	In reply . . . *I* will say :
	277– 6	*I* will say I can see no other way
	297– 6	*I* will say, Amen, so be it.
	310–18	*I* will say that there was never a
	311– 1	*I* will relate the following incident,
	355– 9	*I* will repeat that men are very

I wish

Hea.	7–23	*I* wish the age was up to his
My.	131–19	*I* wish to say briefly that this meeting

I wished

Mis.	178–27	*I* wished to be excused from

I withdraw

Mis.	273– 7	*I* withdraw from an overwhelming

I wonder

Pul.	7– 9	*I* wonder whether, were our dear

I worship

Mis.	96–10	*I* worship that of which
	96–15	divine Principle, — which *I* worship ;
Ret.	17– 5	while *I* worship in deep sylvan spot,
Po.	62– 5	while *I* worship in deep sylvan spot,

I would

Mis.	11–31	*I* would enjoy taking by the hand
	32–19	*I* would gladly do my best towards
	146–21	*I* would gather every reformed mortal
	291–19	*I* would part with a blessing
	311– 6	*I* would extend a tender invitation
	311–19	*I* would as soon harm myself as
	317– 9	dear ones whom *I* would have
	335–27	*I* would have you already out,
	349–24	before *I* would accept the slightest
	350–11	which *I* would hesitate to

Eddy

I would

Mis.	351– 8	and I could not if *I* would,
	392–23	Scenes that *I* would see again.
Ret.	5–15	I cannot speak as *I* would,
	8– 9	Then *I* would say,
Pan.	9–19	*I* would kiss the feet of such a
'01.	17–20	*I* would put patients into the
Po.	15–14	*I* would live in their empire,
	51– 5	Scenes that *I* would see again.
My.	166–17	she nor *I* would be practising
	170–14	*I* would present a gift
	175– 1	*I* would love to be with you
	244– 4	to whom *I* would gladly give it
	270–28	*I* would no more quarrel with
	270–29	than *I* would because of his art.
	301– 9	*I* would that all the churches
	306–25	I advertised that *I* would pay
	345–14	doctors said *I* would live if

I would not

Mis.	280– 9	*I* would not weigh you,
Ret.	27–11	which *I* would not have effaced.
My.	219–18	*I* would not charge Christians

I write

Pan.	14– 4	Once more *I* write,
Po.	32–12	inspires my pen as *I* write ;
My.	258–32	To the children . . . *I* write :

I wrote

Ret.	27– 1	*I* wrote also, at this period,
My.	114–17	What *I* wrote had a strange
	146–21	what *I* wrote is true,
	215– 6	*I* wrote "S. and H. with Key to
	237– 5	What *I* wrote on C. S.
	271– 4	When *I* wrote "S. and H.
	304–11	for many years *I* wrote
	343– 7	In 1875 *I* wrote my book.
	343–28	*I* wrote to each church

I yearned

My.	214–24	which *I* yearned to do,

I yielded

Ret.	38– 7	*I* yielded to a constant conviction

lady

My.	271–15	* This *l·* with sweet smile and
	320– 9	* regard for you as a Christian *l·*,
	331–21	* and his bereaved *l·*,
	342– 3	* *l·* slowly descending the stairs.

Leader

Mis.	159–22	and to their lone *L·*.
Man.	37–19	loyal to their *L·* and to the
	42– 8	his duty to God, to his *L·*, and
	42–26	malpractises upon or treats our *L·*
	54– 1	injurious, to C. S. or to its *L·*,
	54–21	to or of the *L·* and Pastor Emeritus,
	65– 1	and to substitute *L·*,
	67–24	Opportunity for Serving the *L·*.
	68–10	Members thus serving the *L·*
	69– 1	to the home of their *L·*,
	69– 6	has been called to serve our *L·*
	72–20	her place as the head or *L·*
Pul.	44– 2	* "*Dear Teacher, L·, Guide:* — 'Laus Deo,
	49– 3	* consider her their spiritual *L·*
	71–17	* the acknowledged C. S. *L·*,
	84–28	* our beloved teacher and *L·*,
	86–17	* *our Beloved Teacher and L·:*
'01.	34–25	follow your *L·* only so far as she
'02.	4– 3	Follow your *L·*, only so far as she
My.	vi–15	* its guide, guardian, *L·*,
	vii– 4	* can never do for its *L·*
	vii– 4	* what its *L·* has done for
	vii– 7	* not . . . to deprive their *L·* of
	vii–14	* service which . . . can render their *L·*.
	6–20	The room of your *L·* remains
	8–27	* *L·* of our religious denomination
	11– 4	* *L·* of this movement,
	20– 9	awaiting on behalf of your *L·*
	22– 3	* our *L·* saw the need of a larger
	22–15	* our beloved *L·* and teacher,
	22–25	* our Pastor Emeritus and *L·*,
	23–17	* *Beloved Teacher and L·* :
	28– 3	* Our *L·* has said in S. and H.
	36– 1	* Message from their teacher and *L·*,
	36– 8	* *Beloved Teacher and L·* :
	40–24	* Our *L·*, Mrs. Eddy, has presented
	40–32	* our *L·* has induced a multitude
	41–27	* Our *L·* and teacher not only
	42– 6	* faithful follower of this *L·*
	42–27	* inaugurated by our beloved *L·*,
	43–22	* revealed to our beloved *L·*,
	44– 9	* counsel of our ever faithful *L·*.
	44–17	* forwarded at once to our *L·*,
	44–23	* *Beloved Teacher and L·* :
	50–10	* guided by their dauntless *L·*
	58–19	* our revered *L·* and teacher,
	60–25	* *Dear L· and Guide:*
	62–19	* *Beloved L· and Teacher:*
	64– 2	* achievements of our beloved *L·*

Eddy

Leader

My.	64– 9	* it is because our *L·* has made the
	129–28	Lean not too much on your *L·*.
	134–26	* been secured from our beloved *L·*
	139– 2	Rest assured that your *L·*
	143– 3	your *L·* will then be sure
	157– 3	* "BELOVED TEACHER AND *L·* :
	170– 4	might see the *L·* of C. S.
	207– 7	* *Beloved L· :* — The representatives
	210– 1	chapter sub-title
	241–17	* instruction from their *L·*
	244– 1	unity with your *L·*.
	254–17	* *Dear L· :* — May we have permission
	256–12	to send to your *L·*.
	271–17	* Founder and *L·* of C. S.,
	273– 6	* being able to point to a *L·*
	280– 3	* *Beloved L· :* — We acknowledge
	302–20	Discoverer, Founder, and *L·*.
	308–14	and the *L·* of C. S.
	315–29	beloved *L·* of millions of
	316–12	defence of our Cause and its *L·*.
	323–21	* giving this age such a *L·*
	325–15	* Command me . . . beloved *L·*.
	326– 2	* enclosures received from our *L·*.
	327–11	* *Beloved L· :* — I know the enclosed
	328– 1	* as lived by our dear, dear *L·*,
	351– 1	* chapter sub-title
	352– 4	* *Beloved L· :* — Informally assembled,
	357–30	acknowledging me as your *L·*,
	358– 2	true following of their *L·* ;
	358–11	cannot separate you from your *L·*
	358–25	Lovingly your teacher and *L·*,
	359– 6	My province as a *L·*
	361– 7	do not bring your *L·* into
	361–19	* *Beloved L· :* — We rejoice that
	362–12	* *L·, Counsellor, and Friend:*

leader

Mis.	266– 9	true *l·* of a true cause
My.	116– 8	personality of its *l·*.
	116–18	regarding an individual or *l·*,
	117– 7	whereas helping a *l·*
	117– 8	and giving this *l·* time

Leader's

Mis.	129–22	*L·* precepts and example !
Man.	59–15	The *L·* Welcome.
My.	9–18	chapter sub-title
	155–29	blossoms in their *L·* love,
	341–10	your *L·* Spring greeting,
	351– 2	* With our *L·* kind permission,

Mary

My.	119–15	*M·* of to-day looks up for Christ,

me

Mis.	x– 4	for *m·* to comply with an
	x–19	caused *m·*, as an author,
	xi– 3	caused *m·* to retain the initial "G"
	11–27	general good to such as hate *m·*,
	11 29	since they permit *m·* no other way,
	11–31	all who love *m·* not,
	13– 3	so far as one and all permit *m·* to
	13– 8	wrought out for *m·* the law of
	16–27	pause for a moment with *m·*,
	19–22	more faith in an honest . . . healing *m·*,
	24– 5	came to *m·* in an hour of great need ;
	29–21	Daily letters inform *m·* that a
	38–16	Metaphysics, as taught by *m·* at the
	48–11	enough for *m·* to know that
	74–30	If you will admit, with *m·*,
	94– 4	to understand *m·*, or himself.
	95–11	the time so kindly allotted *m·*
	96–13	God becomes to *m·*,
	96–18	this atonement becomes more to *m·*
	102– 5	a theory to *m·* inconceivable.
	104–31	gives *m·* the forces of God
	109– 4	who take *m·* as authority for
	111–27	Let *m·* specially call the attention
	112–21	The jailer thanked *m·*, and said,
	117–18	difficult for *m·* to carry out a
	132–30	inspire *m·* with the hope
	133 3	when referring to *m·*,
	133–28	It affords *m·* great joy to be able to
	135– 8	not one . . . can be separated from *m·* ;
	135–28	You may be looking to see *m·*
	136–12	seem to you as to *m·*,
	136–19	can well afford to give *m·* up,
	142–13	Let *m·* write to the donors,
	142–30	nor you with *m·* in C. S.,
	143–18	It gives *m·* great pleasure to say
	143–25	A quiet call from *m·* for this
	145–32	let *m·* say, 'T is sweet to
	149–19	the joy you give *m·*
	149–21	to send him to aid *m·*.
	155–25	when they address *m·* I shall be apt
	157–26	Write *m·* when you need *m·*.
	180– 6	beholding *m·* restored to health.
	180– 7	A dear old lady asked *m·*,

Eddy

me

Mis.	180–11	person, more material, met *m·*,
	180–16	it speaks to *m·* of Life,
	193–19	when critics attacked *m·*
	195–29	given *m·* a higher sense
	203–12	in their course to call on *m·*,
	207– 3	drink with *m·* the living waters
	223– 2	mystery of error . . . at first defied *m·*.
	239– 1	let *m·* say to you, dear reader :
	242– 5	offered *m·*, as President of
	247– 7	those who know *m·*, know that
	248–11	falsehoods uttered about *m·*
	248 -25	he could do no more for *m·*.
	248–26	revelations of C. S. saved *m·*
	248–27	and made *m·* well,
	249– 5	drug had no effect upon *m·*
	249–22	combined efforts . . . to kill *m·* :
	249–24	will never leave *m·* comfortless,
	253– 8	platform is not broad enough for *m·*,
	256–11	imposes on *m·* the severe task of
	262–28	little need of . . . encouragement from *m·*,
	262–28	Perhaps it is even selfish in *m·*
	265– 1	and gives *m·* as authority for it ;
	266– 7	may represent *m·* as doing it ;
	266– 8	but he mistakes *m·*,
	266–22	They are essentially dear to *m·*,
	267– 7	whose chief aim is to injure *m·*,
	267– 8	caused *m·* to exercise most patience.
	267– 9	When they report *m·* as
	267–13	secretly striving to injure *m·*.
	273–24	lying on the desk before *m·*,
	274– 3	This point, . . . had not impressed *m·*
	274– 7	which God calls *m·* to
	275–22	satisfaction that you afforded *m·*.
	275–25	moved *m·* to speechless thanks.
	278– 1	vision of the . . . is before *m·*.
	278– 4	my peace returns unto *m·*.
	278–19	who are absent from *m·*,
	281– 7	fills *m·* with joy.
	281– 8	neither deprive *m·* of something
	281– 8	nor give *m·* anything,
	281–26	but it came to *m·* more clearly
	290–15	A person wrote to *m·*,
	291– 9	is attached to *m·* as authority
	299–10	the following question sent to *m·* ;
	299–22	but you must pay *m·*,
	303–22	oblige *m·* by giving place in your *Journal*
	308– 4	Whosoever looks to *m·* personally
	308–22	mayhap taught *m·* more than
	309– 6	All will agree with *m·* that
	311–19	more than they can love *m·*.
	313– 2	Permit *m·* to say that your editorial
	318–15	from *m·*, or from a loyal student
	319–19	grant *m·* this request,
	319 -21	without one gift to *m·*.
	321–27	Do not expect *m·*,
	321–30	that concerns *m·*, and you,
	322– 2	its contemplation with *m·*,
	322– 6	expecting to hear *m·* speak
	335–12	One mercilessly assails *m·*
	335–13	others charge upon *m·*
	335–15	neither moves *m·* from
	347–15	Two individuals, . . . advise *m·*.
	347–20	The guardians . . . go before *m·*.
	348–32	A student who consulted *m·*
	349–12	consulted *m·* on the feasibility
	349–26	and refused to give *m·* up
	353– 7	If one asks *m·*, Is my concept of
	353– 9	your human concept of *m·*,
	353–11	People give *m·* too much attention
	373– 9	New Testament was handed to *m·*,
	376–18	burst through the lattice for *m·*,
	380– 9	to enable *m·* to elucidate
	380–11	call for help impelled *m·* to
	380–14	driven *m·* to discover the Science
	380–24	taught *m·* the impossibility of
	389–13	His arm encircles *m·*,
	389–14	O make *m·* glad for every
	392–12	of life, that teacheth *m·*
	397– 7	And come to *m·*, and tenderly,
	397– 9	Thus Truth engrounds *m·*
	397–20	God leadeth *m·*.
	397–22	Shepherd, show *m·* how to go
	398–25	And was found by you and *m·*
Chr.	53–35	grace towards you and *m·*,
Ret.	8– 4	a voice, calling *m·* distinctly
	8– 7	to tell *m·* what she wanted.
	8– 9	"Mother, who *did* call *m·*?
	8–17	my cousin turned to *m·*
	8–22	asked her if she had summoned *m·* ?
	9– 1	said that mother wanted *m·*.
	9– 1	she returned with *m·* to
	9– 8	my mother read to *m·*
	9– 9	bade *m·*, when the voice called **again,**
	9–13	prayed that God would forgive *m·*,

Eddy

me

Ret.	9–14	as my mother had bidden *m*.
	10– 2	kept *m*. much out of school,
	13– 6	predestination, greatly troubled *m*. ;
	13–11	pronounced *m*. stricken with fever.
	13–16	to win *m*. from dreaded heresy.
	13–19	bade *m*. lean on God's love,
	13–19	which would give *m*. rest,
	13–22	ineffable joy came over *m*.
	14– 2	forever lost its power over *m*.
	14–18	doubts left *m*. outside the doors.
	14–19	wished *m*. to tell him
	14–23	asked *m*. to say how I felt
	14–24	when the new light dawned within *m*.
	15– 1	they came and kissed *m*.
	15– 2	received *m*. into their communion,
	15– 3	and my protest along with *m*.
	18–20	Oh, give *m*. the spot where
	19– 6	he was spared to *m*. for only
	19–16	helped to support *m*. in this
	20– 3	money I had brought with *m*. ;
	20– 8	was sent away from *m*.,
	20–13	before my child was taken from *m*.,
	20–23	granted *m*. in the city of Salem,
	20–26	he should have a home with *m*.
	21– 9	came to see *m*. in Massachusetts.
	23– 1	too eventful to leave *m*. undisturbed
	24–14	the falling apple that led *m*. to
	24–17	physician who attended *m*.,
	25– 4	had to *m*. a new meaning,
	26–13	had before seemed to *m*. supernatural,
	27– 9	Science developed itself to *m*.
	27–11	valuable to *m*. as waymarks
	27–29	divine hand led *m*. into a new world
	28–24	It was a mystery to *m*. then,
	30–11	why C. S. was revealed to *m*.
	34– 8	give *m*. one distinct statement of
	36–10	did not originate with *m*.
	37– 3	the term employed by *m*. to
	38– 2	the printer informed *m*.
	38–15	started for Lynn to see *m*.
	38–19	come to tell *m*. he wanted more,
	38–20	to find *m*. *en route* for Boston,
	38–26	circumstances unknown to *m*.
	40– 6	my hostess told *m*. that
	40–12	they showed *m*. the clothes
	40–13	told *m*. that her physicians
	40–19	The mother afterwards wrote to *m*.,
	40–23	refused *m*. a hearing in their halls
	44– 7	call to *m*. to become their pastor.
	46– 3	Shepherd, show *m*. how to go
	47– 3	caused *m*. to dread the
	47–19	instructions in a Primary class from *m*.,
	48– 2	drew its breath from *m*.,
	48–10	moved *m*. to close my flourishing
	50– 1	impelled *m*. to set a price on
	50– 8	This amount greatly troubled *m*.
	50–10	God has since shown *m*.,
	73–13	corporeality became less to *m*.
	74– 8	afflicteth *m*. not wittingly :
	74–10	and it cannot think of *m*.
	81– 5	Nothing . . . can separate them from *m*.
	81–29	led *m*. to the feet of C. S.,
	87– 7	Experience has taught *m*. that
	90–26	One of my students wrote to *m*.
Un.	7–10	has not separated *m*. from God,
	7–11	has so bound *m*. to Him as to
	7–11	enable *m*. instantaneously to heal
	9–21	by those who fail to understand *m*.,
	48–12	To *m*. God is All.
	49–10	To *m*. the reality and substance of
	49–24	gives *m*. a clearer right to call evil a
Pul.	2–12	think for a moment with *m*. of
	5– 2	who had publicly proclaimed *m*.
	5–20	his conversation . . . reassured *m*.
	6–13	wrote to *m*. in 1894,
	6–25	signalled *m*. kindly as my lone bark rose
	17– 2	Shepherd, show *m*. how to go
	18–16	And come to *m*., and tenderly,
	18–18	Truth engrounds *m*. on the rock,
	19– 4	God leadeth *m*.
	21–10	Who will unite with *m*. in
	35– 1	it came to *m*. with a new meaning,
	74–13	"A despatch is given *m*.,
	74–15	"Even the question shocks *m*.
	75– 7	But to think or speak of *m*.
	87–14	But permit *m*., respectfully,
	87–16	make *m*. your *Pastor Emeritus*,
	87–19	when asking *m*. to accept your
Rud.	14–27	course of instruction from *m*.,
No.	31–11	To *m*. *divine pardon* is
'00.	10–26	soldier who sent to *m*.,
	10–30	send *m*. some of his hard-earned
	11– 1	cost *m*. a tear !
	11– 1	it gave *m*. more pleasure than

Eddy

me

'00.	11– 7	weaned *m*. from this love
	11– 8	wedded *m*. to spiritual music,
	11–15	To *m*. his composition is the triumph
	11–20	human tone has no melody for *m*.
'01.	21–24	My faith assures *m*. that God
	26–26	allow *m*. to add I have read little of
	28–21	proven to *m*. beyond a doubt
	29–29	students wrote *m*.,
	31–11	Has God entrusted *m*. with a
	31–14	they regard *m*. with no vague,
	31–15	the power that God gives *m*.
	32–17	caused *m*. to love their doctrines.
	35–14	Doth it dawn on you and *m*.?
'02.	2–24	and the Church once loved *m*.
	12–21	allow *m*. to interpolate some matters
	13–27	land legally conveyed to *m*.,
	14–23	afforded *m*. neither favor nor
	15– 1	anonymous letters mailed to *m*.
	15–11	paid *m*. not one dollar of royalty
	15–23	came to *m*. in the silence of night,
	15–26	advised *m*. to drop both
	15–28	God had led *m*. to write that book,
	15–30	It was to *m*. the "still, — *I Kings* 19 : 12.
	16– 2	brought to *m*. Wyclif's translation
	19–12	no . . . offense against *m*. that I
	20–16	are you ready to join *m*.
	20–21	for it gives *m*. great joy
Hea.	6– 4	pardon *m*. if I smiled.
	6– 9	spiritualists abused *m*. for it then,
	6–11	calling *m*. a medium.
Peo.	7–28	have taught *m*. that the health
Po.	4–12	His arm encircles *m*.,
	4–13	O make *m*. glad for every
	12–16	And come to *m*., and tenderly,
	12–18	Thus Truth engrounds *m*.
	13– 8	God leadeth *m*.
	14– 1	Shepherd, show *m*. how to go
	17– 4	in glory still waiting for *m*.
	19– 3	God's eye is upon *m*.
	20–16	of life, that teacheth *m*.
	24– 1	Come to *m*., joys of heaven !
	24– 6	To *m*. thou art
	24– 8	Come to *m*., peace on earth !
	32–21	And cheer *m*. with hope
	33– 5	And bless *m*. with Christ's
	33–19	That waft *m*. away to my **God.**
	34–16	Blessed compared with *m*.
	35– 1	O take *m*. to thy bower !
	35– 4	To make *m*. love thee
	35–13	bear *m*. through the sky !
	43– 1	*sent m*. *the picture depictive of*
	64–12	Oh, give *m*. the spot where
page 65		poem
	65– 1	O sing *m*. that song !
	65–10	sing *m*. "Sweet hour of
	68– 1	So one heart is left *m*.
	74– 2	Think kindly of *m*.,
	74– 4	Smile on *m*. yet,
	75– 5	was found by you and *m*.
	79–14	Love looseth thee, and lifteth *m*.,
My.	7– 4	allow *m*. to interpolate some matters
	13– 6	was presented to *m*. in 1903
	26–21	*the lie* that students worship *m*.
	27– 4	Divine Love bids *m*. say :
	31– 3	"Shepherd, show *m*. how to go ;"
	105–24	restored by *m*. without material aid,
	105–27	urged *m*. immediately to write a book
	106– 6	The list of cases healed by *m*.
	110–15	remind *m*. of my early dreams of
	114–20	leave *m*. until the rising of the sun.
	114–24	divine power . . . infinitely above *m*.,
	117–31	To give *m*. this opportunity
	118–11	with which you honor *m*.
	118–12	you would not see *m*., for
	119–28	you would not see *m*. thus,
	120– 2	Those who look for *m*. in person,
	120– 3, 4	lose *m*. instead of find *m*.
	120– 7	gratitude for the chance you give *m*.
	120– 9	Bear with *m*. the burden of discovery
	120–10	share with *m*. the bliss of seeing the
	121–17	Christmas ring presented to *m*.
	122–11	tempted *m*. tenderly to be proud !
	123– 2	this church's gifts to *m*. are
	123– 3	To *m*., however, love is the greater
	123– 8	this encourages *m*. to continue
	130– 8	effort of . . . to blacken *m*. and
	130–12	failed too often for *m*. to fear it.
	131–12	given to *m*. in a little symbol,
	131–20	this meeting is very joyous to *m*.
	131–22	something suggestive to *m*.
	133–11	will not receive a Message from *m*.
	133–27	my book is not all you know of *m*.
	134–15	And here let *m*. add :
	135–13	caused *m*. to select a Board of Trustees

Eddy
me

My.	136– 1	enough for you and *m·* to know
	137–21	influenced *m·* to select a Board of Trustees
	137–29	No person influenced *m·* to make
	138– 4	agreed with *m·* to take care of my
	138– 5	a great benefit to *m·* already.
	138–14	ask *m·* to receive persons whom I
	138–20	statements herein made by *m·*,
	142–18	learn this and rejoice with *m·*,
	143–23	do not regard this attack upon *m·* as a
	145– 6	He drew the plan, showed it to *m·*,
	145–11	carpenters' foreman said to *m·* :
	145–21	makes *m·* the servant of the race
	147–30	calling on *m·* for help,
	147–31	You have less need of *m·* than
	148– 1	must not expect *m·* further to do
	154–16	permit *m·* to congratulate this little
	156– 3	allow *m·* to reply in words of
	159– 4	seem to *m·*, and must seem to thee,
	162–12	have demonstrated in gifts to *m·*
	163–22	Here let *m·* add that,
	165–14	presented to *m·* for First Church of
	166–28	gift to *m·* of a beautiful cabinet,
	167–23	Allow *m·* to send forth a pæan
	169– 7	to visit *m·* at a later date,
	172–11	Permit *m·* to present to you
	172–19	your kind, expert call on *m·*."
	172–28	accept from *m·* the accompanying gift
	173– 5	Allow *m·* through your paper to
	173–16	it came to *m·* : Why not invite
	173–21	It was a glad day for *m·*
	174– 9	extended to *m·* throughout.
	174–21	my parents first offered *m·* to Christ
	174–27	and omnipotence enfolds *m·*.
	175–11	Allow *m·* to say to the good folk of
	175–12	and prosperity of our city cheer *m·*.
	177–11	fourscore (already imputed to *m·*),
	184–11	inviting *m·* to be present
	184–14	beautiful birch bark . . . pleased *m·* ;
	184–18	brought back to *m·* the odor of
	186–26	inviting *m·* to be with you
	186–27	It gives *m·* great pleasure to know
	188–19	He surely will not shut *m·* out
	188–21	cannot prevent *m·* from entering
	188–22	heart of a Southron has welcomed *m·*.
	189– 6	affords even *m·* a perquisite of joy.
	189–29	why throng in pity round *m·* ?
	189–31	Dead is he who loved *m·* dearly :
	192–20	inviting *m·* to be present
	192–22	It would indeed give *m·* pleasure
	192–25	demands upon . . . pin *m·* to my post.
	194–20	you present to *m·* the princely gift
	198– 4	informing *m·* of the dedication of
	199–15	towards *m·* and towards the Cause
	201–27	Please accept a line from *m·* in lieu of
	214–29	To desert . . . never occurred to *m·*,
	215– 5	bade *m·* do what I did,
	215–11	sent *m·* the full tuition money.
	215–13	it was again mailed to *m·*
	215–14	in letters begging *m·* to accept it,
	218–30	receiving instruction from *m·*;
	219– 2	anticipate being helped by *m·*
	223– 8	not read by *m·* or by my
	228– 7	when to *m·* it is wisdom to
	229–25	heaps of praise confront *m·*,
	232– 1	It rejoices *m·* that you are
	234– 9	give *m·* the holidays for this work
	236– 7	you will permit *m·* to make
	240– 6	An earnest student writes to *m·* :
	244– 7	invited hither to receive from *m*
	247–14	must have felt *m·* when I . . . silently
	247–17	thoughts that, not fearing *m·*,
	247–18	sought their food of *m·*.
	248– 3	its grandeur almost surprises *m·*.
	253– 1	It rejoices *m·* to know that you
	254–11	to your kind letter, let *m·* say :
	256– 2	allow *m·* to improvise some new
	256– 8	you must grant *m·* my request
	258–25	To the dear children let *m·* say :
	258–30	children who sent *m·* that beautiful
	258–32	Fancy yourselves with *m·* ;
	259–14	Christmas telegrams to *m·* are
	259–15	and give *m·* more time to think and work
	259–17	churches will remember *m·* only thus.
	261–22	chapter sub-title
	261–23	To *m·* Christmas involves an open
	262–20	Christmas to *m·* is the reminder of
	264– 4	kind enough to speak well of *m·*
	270– 7	kindly invited *m·* to its
	270– 9	leading editors . . . congratulate *m·* ;
	271–29	to your question permit *m·* to say
	273–24	You will agree with *m·* that the
	274–21	allow *m·* to say that I am not fond of
	275–13	Permit *m·* to say, the report that I
	283– 6	Your appointment of *m·* as *Fondateur*

Eddy
me

My.	284– 4	you may have accorded *m·* more
	284–23	But here let *m·* say that I
	289–23	inconvenient for *m·* to attend the
	295–15	kind of you to give it to *m·*.
	297–21	he visited *m·* a year ago.
	298– 5	nothing . . . could injure *m·* ;
	302–15	gave *m·* the endearing appellative
	302–16	not to name *m·* thus.
	302–18	name is not applicable to *m·*.
	302–22	than others before *m·*
	302–26	My first visit to . . . pleased *m·*,
	302–27	wanted to greet *m·* with escort
	303– 5	It suffices *m·* to learn the Science of
	304–29	The first attack upon *m·* was :
	305–22	All that I am . . . God has made *m·*.
	306– 4	Far be it from *m·* to tread on
	307– 4	In his conversations with *m·*
	307–12	startled *m·* by saying
	307–31	had already dawned on *m·*.
	308–11	attack on *m·* and my late father
	308–13	compels *m·* as a dutiful child
	311– 6	to be allowed to remain with *m·*,
	311– 8	my good housekeeper said to *m·* :
	311–21	presented *m·* my coat-of-arms,
	312–28	took *m·* to my father's home
	312–29	My salary . . . gave *m·* ample support.
	312–32	rhyme attributed to *m·* by
	313–11	being hired to rock *m·*,
	313–13	cradle for *m·* in his wagon.
	313–15	to help *m·* when I was ill.
	313–27	My oldest sister dearly loved *m·*,
	314–23	was a letter from *m·* to
	314–26	A Christian Scientist has told *m·*
	314–29	he was kind to *m·* up to the time of
	315–25	allow *m·* to thank the enterprising
	315–28	snatched *m·* from the *cradle* and the
	315–29	made *m·* the beloved Leader of
	317–13	enable *m·* to explain more clearly
	318–20	refrained from questioning *m·*.
	318–24	addressing *m·*, burst out with:
	319– 2	would make no difference to *m·*.
	330–27	helped to support *m·* in this
	336–14	money I had brought with *m·* ;
	338–13	unknown to *m·* till after the
	338–16	not allowed to consult *m·*
	343–17	light of . . . came first to *m·*.
	343–20	and trust in *m·* grew.
	345–14	until they had no effect on *m·*.
	345–15	if . . . could be made to act on *m·*.
	345–16	came like blessed relief to *m·*,
	347– 9	their beautiful gift to *m·*,
	347–15	bird, and song, to salute *m·*.
	348–10	the hope that was within *m·*.
	351– 8	letter was handed to *m·* duly.
	351–15	to remember *m·* as the widow of a
	352–21	your tender letter to *m·*,
	354– 5	claim have been endorsed by *m·*,
	357–29	acknowledging *m·* as your Leader,
	358–12	have been duly informed by *m·*
	358–13	to read all that you send to *m·*,
	358–17	to relieve *m·* of so much labor.
	358–18	for the money you send *m·*
	359– 3	neither do they trouble *m·* with
	359–29	temptation . . . to deify you and *m·*.
	360–23	for He has proved it to *m·*

messenger
| *Mis.* | 158– 9 | now, after His *m·* has obeyed |

mine
Mis.	13– 9	the law of loving *m·* enemies.
	87–19	to teach students of *m·*.
	140–14	God's business, not *m·*.
	203– 5	*m·* through gratitude and affection.
	225– 5	a friend of *m·*,
	243– 9	a student of *m·* removed these
	264– 2	random thought in line with *m·*.
	266– 8	state of his own mind for *m·*.
	283–15	For a student of *m·* to
	318– 2	*M·* and thine are obsolete terms
	318– 8	some of *m·* who are less lovable
	322–16	personal presence, or word of *m·*,
	329– 2	*M·* is an obstinate *penchant* for
	382– 6	a few manuscripts of *m·*
	389–10	Love is our refuge ; only with *m·* eye
	389–13	encircles me, and *m·*, and all.
Ret.	43–19	These students of *m·* were the only
Un.	9–22	ideas akin to *m·* have been held
No.	26–11	*M·* is the spiritual idea which
'00.	1– 7	and *m·* to thine in the glow of
'01.	29–28	every book of *m·* that they sold.
Po.	4– 9	Love is our refuge ; only with *m·* eye
	4–12	encircles me, and *m·*, and all.
	24–14	Is all I need to comfort *m·*.
My.	119–27	the opportunity of seeing *m·*,
	163–28	for helping to form *m·*.

Eddy

mine

My.	193– 5	privilege remains *m·* to watch
	251–18	A Primary student of *m·*
	251–24	I call you *m·*,
	251–25	for all is thine and *m·*.
	313– 1	The rhyme . . . is not *m·*,

Mother

Mis.	125–27	*M·*, thought-tired, turns to-day to
	128–14	With love, *M·*,
	131–26	a bill of this church's gifts to *M·* ;
	141– 4	It will speak to you of the *M·*,
	155–16	Because *M·* has not the time
	353–29	They do not love *M·*,
	354– 2	declaring they "never disobey *M·*" !
Man.	64–13	The Title of *M·* Changed.
	64–17	endearing term of *M·*.
Pul.	37–21	* "*M·* feels very strongly,"
	63– 4	* THE "*M·*" OF THE IDEA
	63–10	* the "*M·*" of C. S.,
	77– 9	* *Dear M· :* — During the year
	78– 8	* "*Dear M· :* — During the year
My.	169– 5	as simply seeing *M·*.
	169– 9	With love, *M·*,
	263– 5	*M·* wishes you all a *happy*
	302–15	endearing appellative "*M·*,"

mother

Mis.	389–25	And *m·* finds her home
Man.	65– 1	to drop the word *m·*
Chr.	53–48	gleaming through Mind, *m·*, man.
Ret.	21– 2	informing him that his *m·*
	21– 8	learned that his *m·* still lived,
Po.	5– 6	And *m·* finds her home
	43– 2	Jesus loves you ! so does *m·* :
My.	343–20	I was the *m·*, but of course

Mother in Israel

Ret.	90–23	Thus must the *M· in I·*

mother in Israel

Pul.	44–11	* yet the *m· in I·*, alone

Mother's

Mis.	253–28	the spiritual *M·* sore travail,
	353–25	*M·* four thousand children,
	354– 8	When the *M·* love can no longer
	389– 5	poem
	400–13	*M·* NEW YEAR GIFT TO THE
Po.	page 4	poem
	69– 1	*M· New Year Gift to the*
		(*see also* **Mother's Room** and **room**)

mother's

Po.	9– 4	young face, Upturned to his *m·*

my

Mis.	vii–17	*M·* world has sprung from Spirit,
	ix– 2	suits *m·* sense of doing good.
	ix– 6	among *m·* thousands of students
	x– 6	to collect *m·* miscellaneous
	x– 9	manifold demands on *m·* time
	x–17	*M·* signature has been
	x–17	changed from *m·* Christian name,
	x–20	After *m·* first marriage, to
	x–22	to retain *m·* maiden name,
	x–27	connection with *m·* published works.
	xi– 2	in *m·* name of Glover,
	xi– 3	initial "G" on *m·* subsequent books.
	xii– 5	I take *m·* pen and pruning-hook,
	xii– 7	lift *m·* readers above the smoke of
	11– 6	aim a ball at *m·* heart,
	11– 7	and save *m·* own life,
	11–11	if *m·* instructions had healed them
	11–13	I had done *m·* whole duty
	13– 4	special care to mind *m·* own business.
	21–15	*M·* first plank in the platform of
	24– 8	wrought *m·* immediate recovery
	24–11	I called for *m·* Bible,
	24–12	Truth dawned upon *m·* sense ;
	25– 5	to *m·* understanding it is the heart of
	29–17	in the ranks of *m·*
	29–19	first publication of *m·* work,
	29–21	perusal of *m·* volume is healing the
	32– 6	I infer that some of *m·* students
	32–12	*m·* books, on this very subject.
	32–14	you will find *m·* views
	32–15	*M·* sympathies extend
	32–19	I would gladly do *m·* best towards
	32–22	in which to give to *m·* own flock
	33– 1	comments on *m·* illustrated poem,
	33–17	to place themselves under *m·* care,
	43–14	contemplative reading of *m·* books,
	46–11	A reader of *m·* writings would not
	56–23	the correctness of *m·* statements,
	62– 1	*right* idea of man in *m·* mind,
	62– 2	I can improve *m·* own,
	65–20	*m·* instructions on this question.
	66–22	critics misjudge *m·* meaning
	66–31	to accommodate *m·* instructions
	67–29	I modify *m·* affirmative answer.
	68–13	*M·* proof of this is,

Eddy

my

Mis.	69–16	Upon *m·* arrival I found him
	70– 4	exercised *m·* power over the fish,
	86–14	*M·* sense of the beauty of
	86–17	spiritually beautiful to *m·* gaze
	87–22	*M·* students are taught the
	88– 1	to blight the fruits of *m·* students.
	89–24	in *m·* published works.
	91–29	had followed *m·* example,
	95–17	always attended *m·* life phenomena
	96–21	to *m·* sense, and to the sense of all
	97–25	To *m·* sense, we have not seen all of
	98– 7	*m·* Address at the National Convention
	104–31	on the side of good, *m·* true being.
	105–20	C. S. is *m·* only ideal ;
	106–15	chapter sub-title
	110–15	*M· Beloved Students:* — Weeks have
	112–19	*M·* few words touched him ;
	115–13	May God enable *m·* students to
	116–11	*M· Beloved Students:* — This question,
	116–12	ever nearest to *m·* heart,
	117–22	According to *m·* calendar,
	126–27	hath indeed smiled on *m·* church,
	127– 3	*m·* entire connection with The
	129– 2	*M· Beloved Brethren:*
	132–16	the great demand upon *m·* time,
	132–17	answers through *m·* secretary,
	132–24	to *m·* various publications,
	132–24	and to *m·* Christian students.
	133– 7	read *m·* sermons and publications.
	133–10	voices *m·* impressions of prayer :
	133–19	were it not because of *m·* desire
	133–23	with *m·* face toward the Jerusalem
	135–28	*M· Beloved Students:* — You may be
	135–29	to see me in *m·* accustomed place
	136– 9	so grow upon *m·* vision that I
	136–14	necessity for *m·* seclusion,
	136–19	*m·* last revised edition of S. and H.
	137– 2	*M· Dear Students and Friends:*
	137– 2	Accept *m·* thanks
	137– 9	I remember *m·* regret,
	137–14	rejoice over the growth of *m·* students
	137–17	dear ones, if you take *m·* advice
	137–28	*M·* students can *now* organize
	138–20	*M·* counsel is applicable to the
	139–25	to *m·* spiritual perception,
	140–11	No one could . . . mortgage *m·* gift
	142–11	Accept *m·* thanks for the
	142–15	*M·* first impression was to indite
	142–15	*m·* second, a psalm ;
	142–16	*m·* third, a letter.
	142–19	*m·* Muse lost her lightsome lyre,
	142–23	So I send *m·* answer
	143– 4	*M·* dear students may have explained
	143– 8	I reach out *m·* hand to clasp yours,
	143–19	class graduates of *m·* College,
	144– 2	New Hampshire, *m·* native State.
	145–32	children that *m·* heart folds within it,
	146– 6	*M· Beloved Students:* — I cannot
	146– 7	conscientiously lend *m·* counsel
	146–11	not *m·* present province ;
	147– 3	*M· Beloved Students:* — Another year
	149–18	*M· Beloved Brethren:* — Lips nor
	150– 4	*m·* forever-love to your dear church.
	153–24	*m·* first edition of "S. and H.
	155–24	If *m·* own students cannot spare time
	156–18	through the study of *m·* works
	157– 2	*M· Dear Student:* — It is a great
	157– 7	or caused *m·* secretary to write,
	157–15	Yes, *m·* student, *m·* Father is your
	158– 2	*M· Beloved Student:* — In reply to
	159–11	*M·* heart has many rooms :
	159–12	sacred to the memory of *m·* students.
	159–21	the gifts that *m·* heart hope
	160–13	It satisfies *m·* present hope.
	177–30	In *m·* long journeyings I have met
	178– 1	the place of *m·* own sojourning
	178–27	*M·* friends, I wished to be excused
	180– 3	and strive to cease *m·* warfare.
	180– 5	*m·* friends were frightened
	180–12	in the words of *m·* Master,
	180–13	then *m·* heart went out to God,
	203– 4	*m·* students and your students ;
	203– 6	From *m·* tower window,
	203– 7	this gift from *m·* students
	207– 4	the spirit of *m·* life-purpose,
	213– 4	*m·* faith in the right.
	213–14	May *m·* friends and *m·* enemies
	214–19	*M·* students need to search the
	214–22	even to understand *m·* works,
	215–23	*M·* students are at the beginning of
	222–31	flowed into *m·* consciousness
	224–31	a question in *m·* mind,
	227–15	Would that *m·* pen or pity
	237–29	he visited *m·* father,

Eddy
my

Mis. 238– 5 reverence of *m·* riper years
239– 8 *m·* shadow is not growing less ;
242– 4 came not to *m·* notice until January
242– 6 one of *m·* students,
242–10 Will the gentleman accept *m·* thanks
242–28 he was *m·* student in December,
243– 6 mental branches taught in *m·* college ;
243–18 *M·* Christian students are proverbially
243–19 *m·* system of medicine
244–17 Will he accept *m·* reply
247– 6 Those familiar with *m·* history
247–10 in one of *m·* works
247–12 charges against *m·* views are false,
247–13 do not understand *m·* statement
248–17 or that *m·* hourly life is prayerless,
248–20 to have reported *m·* demise,
248–22 and bequeathed *m·* property to
248–24 *m·* regular physician prescribed
249– 9 that I have . . . in *m·* works,
249–11 especially through *m·* teachings,
249–14 *m·* intimate acquaintances.
249–15 remain in *m·* College building
249–17 since *m·* residence in Boston ;
249–17 and to *m·* knowledge,
249–18 not one has been sent to *m·* house,
249–22 expelled from *m·* College
249–23 *M·* heavenly Father will
249–25 coming nearer in *m·* need,
251– 4 *M·* beloved brethren, who have come
251– 6 *m·* land may not touch yours to-day
251– 7 *m·* heart will with tenderness
251–10 and of *m·* native State
252–14 *M·* proof of these novel propositions
256–13 prevent *m·* classes from forming
256–17 intervals between *m·* class terms,
262–13 I thank you, *m·* dear students,
262–29 to relieve *m·* heart of its secrets,
263– 1 but if *m·* motives are sinister,
263–28 *m·* ideas and discovery,
264– 3 *M·* noble students, who are loyal to
264–13 Normal class of *m·* College
264–15 taught their first lessons by *m·* students ;
264–20 Some students leave *m·* instructions
265–23 *M·* teachings are uniform.
266–18 about *m·* loyal students
266–21 I cannot find it in *m·* heart
266–23 *m·* own endeavors and prayers.
266–26 accordance with *m·* students' desires,
272–31 not profited by *m·* rebukes,
273– 5 I close *m·* College in order to
273– 8 *M·* students have never expressed so
273– 9 grateful a sense of *m·* labors
273–10 capable of relieving *m·* tasks
273–12 God bless *m·* enemies,
273 13 and gather all *m·* students,
273–25 cannot do *m·* best work for
273–32 call is for *m·* exclusive teaching.
274– 4 when I opened *m·* College
274– 4 I desire to revise *m·* book
274– 9 more than *m·* teaching would
274–13 I close *m·* College.
275–29 floral offerings sent to *m·* apartments
276– 7 circumstances demanded *m·* attention
276– 7 *m·* personality was not big enough
276– 9 *m·* heart's desire met the demand.
276–10 *M·* students, our delegates,
276–24 I pray that all *m·* students
277–23 No evidence . . . can close *m·* eyes
278– 4 *m·* peace returns unto me.
278– 6 I shall fulfil *m·* mission,
278– 9 throughout *m·* labors,
278– 9 in *m·* history as connected with
278–11 when *m·* motives and acts are
278–12 seen as *m·* Father seeth them.
278–18 *m·* beloved students, who are absent
278–19 shared less of *m·* labors
278–25 perpetual instruction of *m·* students
278–25 might substitute *m·* own for
279–13 *M·* students, three picture-stories
279–14 present themselves to *m·* thought ;
281–23 Among the gifts of *m·* students,
285– 6 who fills orders for *m·* books,
287–23 the substance of *m·* reply is :
290–20 *m·* affections involuntarily flow out
291–15 to be benefited by *m·* thoughts
291–17 this is not *m·* fault,
291–17 and is far from *m·* desire ;
292–29 who fully understood *m·* instructions
293– 1 and carried out *m·* ideal.
294–25 Since *m·* residence in Concord,
300– 3 Copying *m·* published works
300– 9 your copy of *m·* works,
300–12 from copies of *m·* publications
300–15 You literally publish *m·* works

Eddy
my

Mis. 300–26 from *m·* work S. and H.,
301– 8 made up of *m·* publications,
301–13 *M·* Christian students who have read
301–14 copies of *m·* works
301–18 *m·* private counsel they disregard.
301–19 question of *m·* true-hearted students,
301–21 It is not right to copy *m·* book
301–22 publicly *without m· consent.*
301–22 *M·* reasons are as follows :
302– 4 infringement of *m·* copyright,
302– 9 *M·* students are expected
302–20 copying and reading *m·* works
302–24 from further copying of *m·* writings
308– 6 clings to *m·* material personality,
308–20 scientific notices of *m·* book.
309–27 *M·* Christmas poem and its
310– 2 neither the intent of *m·* works
310–11 *M·* answer to manifold letters
310–13 *m·* affections plead for all
310–14 *m·* desire is that all shall be
311–15 *M·* deepest desires and daily labors
311–16 I love *m·* enemies and would help all
311–22 I should lose *m·* hope of heaven.
311–24 *m·* necessity was to tell it ;
311–31 never escaped from *m·* lips,
314–15 First Reader shall read from *m·* book,
315– 6 No copies from *m·* books are allowed
316– 8 I shall speak to *m·* dear church
316–17 *M·* juniors can tell others
316–19 rest on *m·* retirement
316–25 had *m·* students achieved the point
317– 2 *m·* heart replies, *Yes,* if you
317–10 the door to *m·* teaching was shut
317–11 when *m·* College closed.
317–19 *m·* answers to the above questions.
317–24 *M·* sympathies are deeply enlisted
317–29 *M·* soul abhors injustice,
318– 1 chapter sub-title
318– 5 not alone for *m·* students,
318–21 latest editions of *m·* works,
319–18 accept *m·* tender greetings
321– 7 *M·* heart is filled with joy,
322–11 Shepherd that feedeth *m·* flock,
322–18 *m·* often-coming is unnecessary ;
322–23 *m·* past poor labors and love.
329–10 Spring is *m·* sweetheart,
331–21 Keep Thou *m·* child on upward wing
335–16 In *m·* public works I
335–18 Those who deny *m·* wisdom
347–11 Where *m·* vision begins and is clear,
348–24 I wanted to satisfy *m·* curiosity
349– 1 received *m·* consent and even
349– 2 take lessons outside of *m·* College,
349–10 obstetrics taught in *m·* College.
349–16 notwithstanding *m·* objection,
349–19 *M·* counsel to all of them was
349–26 or to receive *m·* gratuitous services,
349–30 accepted no pay from *m·* church
350– 1 two thousand dollars of *m·* own
350–13 and like *m·* public instruction.
350–30 *M·* life, consecrated to humanity
350–32 its own proof of *m·* practice.
351– 5 blessing even *m·* enemies,
353–13 *M·* brother was a manufacturer ;
353–16 When *m·* brother returned
354– 2 It exceeds *m·* conception of
355–29 rainbow seen from *m·* window
356–10 *M·* students, with cultured
356–19 Now let *m·* faithful students
357–22 it has been clear to *m·* thought
371–14 *m·* heart pleads for them
373– 4 *M·* artist at the easel objected,
373– 5 *m·* sense of Soul's expression
374–20 never looked on *m·* ideal of the
374–22 the one illustrating *m·* poem
374–31 *m·* ideal of an angel is
375– 3 not *m·* concepts of angels.
376–19 for me, on *m·* bed?
378–20 The readers of *m·* books cannot
379– 5 see his pennings on *m·* case.
379–29 named *m·* discovery C. S.
380–17 *M·* students at first practised
380–19 *m·* students' patients, and people
382– 1 *m·* experience would contradict it
382– 4 *m·* discovery of this Science.
382– 5 *m·* first work on this doctrine,
383– 7 pastor is the Bible and *m·* book.
385– 5 Oh, Thou hast heard *m·* prayer ;
385– 9 poem
389– 9 Keep Thou *m·* child on upward
392–11 To *m·* lone heart thou art a
392–14 and patient be *m·* life as thine ;
392–21 To *m·* sense a sweet refrain ;
392–22 To *m·* busy mem'ry bringing

Eddy
my

Mis. 393–23 To *m·* heart that would be bleaching
395–19 May rest above *m·* head.
395–22 For joy, to shun *m·* weary way,
396– 2 To scare *m·* woodland walk,
396–13 *M·* heart unbidden joins rehearse ;
396–17 poem
397–17 *M·* prayer, some daily good to do
398– 2 Lest *m·* footsteps stray ;
398–22 Saw ye *m·* Saviour?

Ret. 1– 1 *M·* ancestors, according to the flesh,
1–2, 3 *m·* great-grandfather, on *m·* father's
1– 4 His wife, *m·* great-grandmother,
1– 8 remember reading, in *m·* childhood,
1–10 which *m·* grandmother said
1–11 written by *m·* great-grandmother.
1–11 But because *m·* great-grandmother
1–18 became *m·* paternal grandmother,
2–17 *M·* childhood was also gladdened
2–17 one of *m·* Grandmother Baker's books,
2–26 relative of *m·* Grandfather Baker was
2–30 *m·* Grandmother Baker's family
3– 4 *M·* grandparents were likewise
3– 9 A cousin of *m·* grandmother
4– 2 youngest of whom was *m·* father,
4– 4 inherited *m·* grandfather's farm
5– 7 youngest of *m·* parents' six children
5– 9 During *m·* childhood *m·* parents
5–14 *M·* father possessed a strong
5–15 Of *m·* mother I cannot speak
5–19 and knew *m·* sainted mother
6– 6 *M·* childhood's home I remember
6– 9 *m·* much respected parents,
6–11 *m·* second brother, Albert Baker,
6–11 who was, next to *m·* mother,
6–12 the very dearest of *m·* kindred.
6–15 *M·* brother Albert was graduated at
7– 5 wrote of *m·* brother as follows :
8– 2 connected with *m·* childhood
8– 6 I thought this was *m·* mother's voice,
8–11 and *m·* mother was perplexed
8–13 One day, when *m·* cousin,
8–17 *m·* cousin turned to me
8–21 went to *m·* mother,
8–24 *m·* cousin had heard the voice,
9– 2 and led *m·* cousin into an adjoining
9– 6 *M·* cousin answered quickly,
9– 8 *m·* mother read to me
9–14 as *m·* mother had bidden me.
10– 1 *M·* father was taught to believe
10–1, 2 that *m·* brain was too large for *m·* body
10– 7 *M·* favorite studies were
10– 8 From *m·* brother Albert I received
10–10 *M·* brother studied Hebrew
10–11 After *m·* discovery of C. S.,
11– 2 Poetry suited *m·* emotions
11– 3 one of *m·* girlhood productions.
12– 5 echoes still *m·* day-dreams thrill,
13– 2 *m·* parents having been members
13– 7 if *m·* brothers and sisters were to
13–13 *M·* father's relentless theology
13–18 *M·* mother, as she bathed *m·*
14–15 and take *m·* chance of
14–16 with *m·* brothers and sisters,
14–18 if *m·* creedal doubts left me
15– 3 and *m·* protest along with me.
15– 3 *M·* connection with this
15– 5 founded a church of *m·* own,
15–19 At the close of *m·* engagement
15–23 healed through *m·* preaching.
15–30 healed under *m·* preaching,
16– 3 a soprano, . . . caught *m·* ear.
16–11 occurrence in *m·* own church
16–12 for the sick to be healed by *m·*
17– 7 Wake chords of *m·* lyre,
18–24 they darken *m·* lay:
19– 1 I was united to *m·* first husband,
19–11 *M·* husband was a freemason,
19–18 *m·* babe was born.
20– 1 I lost all *m·* husband's property,
20– 3 and remained with *m·* parents
20– 3 until after *m·* mother's decease.
20– 5 before *m·* father's second marriage,
20– 7 *m·* little son, about four years of age,
20–11 *m·* home I regarded as very precious.
20–12 night before *m·* child was taken
20–15 *m·* poem, "Mother's Darling,"
20–20 Star of *m·* earthly hope,
20–20 babe of *m·* soul.
20–21 *M·* second marriage was very
20–24 *M·* dominant thought in marrying again
20–25 was to get back *m·* child,
21– 1 a letter was read to *m·* little son,
21– 3 Without *m·* knowledge a guardian was
21– 4 informed that *m·* son was lost.

Eddy
my

Ret. 21– 5 Every means within *m·* power
23–17 *M·* heart knew its Redeemer.
23–18 *m·* affections had diligently sought
24– 7 years prior to *m·* discovery
24–12 *M·* immediate recovery from
24–18 rejoiced in *m·* recovery,
24–19 the *modus* of *m·* relief.
24–23 to ponder *m·* mission,
25– 3 The Bible was *m·* textbook.
25– 3 It answered *m·* questions
27– 3 so laid the foundation of *m·* work
27– 7 after *m·* discovery of the absolute
27–13 had not fully voiced *m·* discovery.
27–14 *m·* first jottings were but efforts to
27–24 first broke upon *m·* sense,
28–29 *m·* endeavor, to be a Christian,
30– 7 The motive of *m·* earliest labors
31– 9 From *m·* very childhood I was
31–15 acting . . . on *m·* roused consciousness,
31–23 *M·* heart bent low before the
31–27 spoke to *m·* chastened sense
32– 2 bearing . . . to *m·* apprehension,
33– 2 sustaining *m·* final conclusion
33–24 insufficient to satisfy *m·* doubts
36– 5 after taking out *m·* first copyright,
36– 7 writing out *m·* manuscripts for
37– 1 first edition of *m·* most important work,
37–21 *M·* reluctance to give the public,
37–21 in *m·* first edition of S. and H.,
38– 3 could not go on with *m·* work.
38– 4 and yet he stopped *m·* work.
38– 5 to persuade him to finish *m·* book
38– 8 I must insert in *m·* last chapter
38–10 contrary to *m·* inclination,
38–11 and finished *m·* copy for the book.
38–13 *m·* printer resumed his work
38–17 started for Boston with *m·* finished copy.
38–21 *m·* first edition of S. and H.
38–24 had grown disgusted with *m·* printer,
39– 3 and *m·* copyright was protected.
40– 3 refusing to take any pay for *m·* services
40– 5 On *m·* arrival *m·* hostess told me
40– 8 and with *m·* hostess I went to the
40–22 *m·* notices for a second lecture
42– 1 *M·* last marriage was with
43– 9 *M·* husband, Asa G. Eddy,
43– 9 taught two terms in *m·* College.
43–10 *m·* adopted son, Ebenezer J. Foster-Eddy,
43–22 myself and six of *m·* students in 1876,
44–11 *m·* church increased in members,
44–24 No sooner were *m·* views made
45– 5 the prosperity of *m·* church,
45–14 *m·* clue to the uses and abuses
45–16 in accord with *m·* special request,
45–18 connected with *m·* College
46– 8 Lest *m·* footsteps stray ;
47– 4 popularity of *m·* College.
47–13 Directors of *m·* College,
47–14 being informed of *m·* intentions,
47–24 latest editions of *m·* works,
48– 5 *M·* conscientious scruples
48– 7 fresh in *m·* thoughts,
48–10 close *m·* flourishing school,
50– 1 set a price on *m·* instruction
50– 6 course of lessons at *m·* College,
50–12 ask *m·* loyal students if they
50–13 equivalent for *m·* instruction
50–15 *m·* list of indigent charity scholars
50–26 *m·* necessity is not necessarily theirs ;
51– 1 *m·* student, Mr. Ira O. Knapp
52–12 I suggested to *m·* students,
54–23 *M·* Christian students,
74– 8 *M·* own corporeal personality
75– 7 Why withhold *m·* name,
75– 7 while appropriating *m·* language
82– 5 *m·* students should not allow
82–14 *m·* students should locate in large cities,
82–28 arrangement of *m·* last revision,
83–11 the Bible and *m·* books,
90–26 One of *m·* students wrote to me :
93–19 identical with *m·* own :

Un. 1–13 I counsel *m·* students to defer this
7– 6 from *m·* heart of hearts,
7–16 Herein is *m·* evidence, from on high,
7–18 pour into *m·* waiting thought
8–13 *M·* insistence upon a proper
8–22 and it proves *m·* view
9– 7 or *m·* words would not have been spoken.
9–27 difference in *m·* metaphysical system
10– 2 separates *m·* system from all others.
10– 8 If there be any *monopoly* in *m·*
31–16 Hence *m·* conscientious position,
44– 1 concerning *m·* doctrines,
48– 2 repeat *m·* twice-told tale,

Eddy

my

Eddy
my

My.
26–11 imagine *m·* gratitude and emotion
26–13 ever received from *m·* church,
26–15 *M·* Message for June 10 is ready
27– 2 *To the Beloved Members of m· Church,*
62– 8 * and give it to *m·* brothers
103–23 on which to found *m·* own,
103–25 Bible has been *m·* only authority.
104–24 in *m·* class on C. S.
105– 7 After *m·* discovery of C. S.,
105–26 work describing *m·* system
105–28 *m·* curative system of metaphysics.
110–16 remind me of *m·* early dreams
114–14 *M·* first writings on C. S. began
114–22 pour in upon *m·* spiritual sense
115– 8 *m·* estimate of the C. S. textbook.
118– 1 *M·* soul thanks the loyal,
118– 2 beloved members of *m·* church
118– 9 *M· Dear Sir:—* I beg to thank you
118–12 In a call upon *m·* person,
120– 3 or elsewhere than in *m·* writings,
120– 7 Accept *m·* gratitude for the chance
120– 9 *m·* honest position.
121– 2 *M·* Beloved Brethren:— I have
121–17 presented to me by *m·* students
122–11 *m·* church tempted me tenderly
123–19 *m·* outdoor accommodations at
123–21 *M·* little hall, which holds
124– 6 *M· Beloved Brethren:—* Looking on
125–11 dip *m·* pen in *m·* heart to say,
125–21 students in *m·* last class in 1898
125–22 stars in *m·* crown of rejoicing.
127–32 I cannot quench *m·* desire to say
129–29 Accept *m·* counsel and teachings
130– 8 effort . . . to keep *m·* works from
130–17 *m·* students reprove, rebuke, and
130–21 published quotations from *m·* works
130–23 Borrowing from *m·* copyrighted works,
130–31 hence *m·* request, that you
131–18 *M· Beloved Brethren:—* I hope
133–10 *M·* beloved church will not receive
133–11 for *m·* annual Message is
133–22 *M· Beloved Brethren:—* I have a secret
133–24 *m·* sacred secret is incommunicable,
133–26 *m·* book is not all you know of me.
133–28 uncovers *m·* life,
134– 2 tell *m·* long-kept secret
135– 9 to *m·* secular affairs,— to *m·* income,
135–10 to *m·* employees.
135–11 increasing demands upon *m·* time
135–12 *m·* yearning for more peace
135–12 in *m·* advancing years,
135–14 take the charge of *m·* property;
135–17 First Reader of *m·* church
135–26 *M· Beloved Church:—* Your love
135–26 cheer *m·* advancing years.
136– 3 *m·* demonstration of C. S.
136–14 Trustees who own *m·* property :
136–24 To *m·* aforesaid Trustees I have
136–25 hard earnings of *m·* pen,
137–12 *m·* secular affairs, to *m·* income,
137–13 to *m·* employees.
137–14 selected all *m·* investments
137–17 increasing demands upon *m·* time,
137–18 *m·* property and affairs
137–20 designated by *m·* last will,
137–22 take charge of *m·* property ;
138– 1 I gave them *m·* property to
138– 4 to take care of *m·* property
138– 6 suit was brought without *m·*
138– 7 carried on contrary to *m·* wishes.
138– 8 not for *m·* benefit in any way,
138– 8 but for *m·* injury,
138– 9 not needed to protect *m·* person or
138–10 test *m·* trust in divine Love.
138–11 *M·* personal reputation is assailed
138–12 some of *m·* students and trusted
139–17 *M· Beloved Brethren:—* When I asked
139–18 purpose of *m·* request was sacred.
142–10 Accept *m·* thanks for your approval
142–17 *M·* beloved brethren may some time
143–10 one and all of *m·* beloved friends
143–12 by the members of *m·* household
144– 4 *M· Beloved Brethren:—* Give yourselves
145– 2 *M·* Dear Editors:— You are
145–22, 23 *m·* friends and *m·* enemies.
146– 1 *m·* dedicatory letter to the Chicago
146– 8 statement in *m·* letter to the church
146–10 "If wisdom lengthens *m·* sum of years
146–17 and *m·* poor prophecy,
147– 9 *m·* childhood's Sunday noons.
148–10 *M· Beloved Brethren:—* In the annals of
148–20 and *m·* heart is asking:
151–23 *M· Beloved Brethren:—* We learn
152–32 flowers that *m·* skilful florist has

Eddy
my

My
153– 3 floral offerings in *m·* name to
153– 7 gospel ministry of *m·* students
153–12 healed from the day *m·* flowers
153–14 from *m·* poor personality.
154–15 *M· Beloved Brethren:—* At this, **your**
155– 4 nestled so near *m·* heart
156– 2 *m·* gratitude for your dear letter,
158–10 natal hour of *m·* lone earth life ;
159– 8 every pulse of *m·* desire for
162–10 such as *m·* beloved Christian Scientists
162–29 This church, born in *m·* nativity,
163–13 cannot show *m·* love for them in
163–14 sacred demands on *m·* time
164– 1 was far from *m·* purpose,
164– 8 *M· Beloved Brethren:—* I have yearned
164– 8 yearned to express *m·* thanks
166–10 *M· Beloved Brethren:—* Your munificent
166–22 *m·* dear ones, let us together sing
166–29 for *m·* books, placed in *m·* room
167– 1 Accept *m·* deep thanks therefor,
167–19 *m·* love, and *m·* prayer
167–26 by the laws of *m·* native State.
168– 5 of *m·* dear old New Hampshire.
169– 2 *M· Beloved Church:—* I invite **you,**
169– 6 *M·* precious Busy Bees,
169–18 believers of *m·* faith,
170– 3 simply *m·* acquiescence in
170– 3 request of *m·* church members
170– 6 brevity of *m·* remarks was due **to**
170– 6 desire on *m·* part that the
170– 7 in *m·* annual Message to **the church**
170–13 your home in *m·* heart !
170–18 it is *m·* sacred motto,
171– 1 dear members of *m·* church:
171–11 invite all *m·* church communicants
172–11 "*M· Beloved Brethren:—* Permit me
172–13 symbol of *m·* spiritual call
172–14 to this *m·* beloved church
172–18 please accept *m·* thanks for your
172–27 "*M· Beloved Brethren:—* You will **please**
173– 7 to the members of *m·* church,
173–20 exceeded *m·* expectation,
173–20 *m·* heart welcomed each and all.
173–22 *m·* fellow-citizens vied with
174– 6 courtesy extended to *m·* friends **by**
174–10 editors in *m·* home city
174–21 where *m·* parents first offered
174–22 until I had a church of *m·* own,
174–25 *m·* soul can only sing and soar.
175– 2 *m·* little church in Boston, Mass.,
175– 4 requires *m·* constant attention
175–25 song of *m·* soul must remain
175–28 purporting to have *m·* signature,
175–30 opposite of *m·* real sentiments.
176– 5 *M· Beloved Brethren:—* Long **ago**
176– 6 way to *m·* forever gratitude,
177– 8 of *m·* personal presence at your
177–10 lengthens *m·* sum of years to
181–32 of *m·* discovery of C. S.
182– 4 Thirty years ago at *m·* request
182– 6 *m·* early love for this church
183–26 blending with thine *m·* prayer
184– 3 *M· Beloved Brethren:—* Have just
184– 8 *M· Beloved Brethren:—* To-day I am
184– 9 Christian Scientists of *m·* native State
184–14 to return *m·* cordial thanks
184–18 brought back to me the odor of *m·*
185–26 closing *m·* remarks with the words **of**
186–25 Accept *m·* thanks for your cordial
187–22 *M· Beloved Brethren:—* You have
189–26 sunny South — once *m·* home.
189–26 There *m·* husband died,
189–27 and the dirge, surging *m·* being,
190– 9 *M·* experience in both practices
191–28 *M· Beloved Brethren:—* Your card
191–30 Accept *m·* thanks.
192–15 *M·* heart hovers around your
192–25 demands upon *m·* time
192–25 demands upon . . . pin me to *m·* post
192–26 *M·* love can fly on wings of joy
193– 4 that you will not feel *m·* absence.
195– 3 You will pardon *m·* delay in
195– 7 hitherto prevented *m·* reply.
196– 3 *M· Beloved Brethren:—* I congratulate
196– 7 accept *m·* tender counsel
196–25 *M· Beloved Brethren:—* The good in
197–11 *m·* deep appreciation of your labor
197–25 *M· Beloved Brethren:—* At this
197–26 in the home of *m·* heart,
199– 3 *M·* Beloved Students and Brethren :
199–11 accept *m·* grateful acknowledgment
200–11 *M· Beloved Brethren:—* The chain of
201– 1 God is blessing you, *m·* beloved
201–10 *M· Beloved Brethren:—* Your Soul-full

Eddy
my

My. 201–11 repeat *m·* legacies in blossom.
201–22 Lest *m·* footsteps stray ;
201–28 in lieu of *m·* presence
202–23 *M·* work is reflected light,
204– 1 *M·* faith in God
208– 3 Accept *m·* deep thanks for your
208–14 dear letter to *m·* waiting heart,
214–19 after *m·* discovery of C. S.,
214–20 taking no remuneration for *m·* labors,
214–25 to meet *m·* own current expenses.
214–27 cast *m·* all into the treasury of
215–19 give *m·* church *The C. S. Journal,*
215–21 preying upon *m·* pearls,
216–15 *M· Beloved Children :* — Tenderly
217– 8 municipal bonds for *m·* dear children
217–15 complied with *m·* request as above
218–24 *M·* published works are teachers
218–25 *M·* private life is given to
219– 1 other than that which *m·* books
219– 6 *M·* good students have all the
219–26 have expressed *m·* opinion publicly
220–19 faith that *m·* prayer availeth,
220–21 I pray : "God bless *m·* enemies ;
223– 8 by me or by *m·* secretaries.
224–21 *M·* books state C. S. correctly.
228– 2 *M·* book S. and H.
229–25 which I said in *m·* heart would never
229–28 hence *m·* disappointed hope
230–21 in the officials of *m·* church
230–22 give *m·* solitude sweet surcease.
231–28 accept *m·* thanks for your
236– 2 accept *m·* full heart's love for them
236– 5 *M· Beloved Christian Scientists :*
237–10 wise to accept only *m·* teachings
240– 9 in *m·* dedicatory Message
242–21 I have requested *m·* secretary not to
243– 2 *M· BELOVED STUDENTS :* — According to
243 21 at *m·* unexplained call
244– 2 before informing you of *m·* purpose
244–14 called of God to contribute *m·* part
244–22 students of *m·* books are indeed *m·*
244–27 No charge will be made for *m·*
246–12 I closed *m·* College in the midst of
247–14 The little fishes in *m·* fountain
248–25 to you, *m·* faithful witnesses.
249–24 *M·* preference lies with
249–26 If both . . . Readers are *m·* students,
251–16 misapprehension of *m·* meaning
251–20 *m·* Primary student can himself be
251–24 *M· Beloved Students :* — I call you
252–20 an oasis in *m·* wilderness.
253– 0 *M·* heart and hope are with you
253–15 Accept *m·* love and these words of
253–21 accept *m·* profound thanks for
253 25 His rich blessing already and *m·* joy
255– 5 C. S. churches have *m·* consent to
256– 4 adapted to the key of *m·* feeling
256– 7 *m·* beloved Christian Scientists,
256– 8 you must grant me *m·* request
257–26 send you *m·* Christmas gift,
259– 1 take a peep into *m·* studio ;
259– 3 pedestal between *m·* bow windows,
259– 4 I have named it *m· white student.*
259–12 I return *m·* heart's wireless love.
262 11 *m·* sense of the eternal Christ,
262–12 with *m·* soul, *m·* spiritual sense,
262–29 express *m·* conception of Truth's
263– 4 *M·* HOUSEHOLD.
264– 6 learn more of *m·* meaning
264– 6 can speak justly of *m·* living.
266– 3 To *m·* sense, the most imminent
266–23 *M·* book, "S. and H.
268–20 time-world flutters in *m·* thought
270– 6 *m·* first religious home
270– 9 newspapers of *m·* native State
270–10 records of *m·* ancestry attest
270–11 nearer *m·* consciousness than before,
270–19 Those words . . . fill *m·* heart :
270–20 *M·* writings heal the sick,
270–23 as *m·* witness to the truth of
271–30 "nearest and dearest" to *m·* heart
274–21 *m·* thanks for their magnificent
274–25 this is *m·* crown of rejoicing,
275–17 I go out in *m·* carriage daily,
275–18 omitted *m·* drive but twice
275–19 Either *m·* work,
275–19 demands upon *m·* time at home,
275–20 is all that prevents *m·* daily drive.
275–21 *m·* dear friends' and *m·* dear enemies'
276–25 *m·* neighbor as myself.
280–16 request that the members of *m·* church
280–28 In no way . . . did I request *m·* church to
281– 3 daily prayer of *m·* church,
282– 6 *m·* hope must still rest in God,
283– 6 *M· Beloved Brethren :* — Your

Eddy
my

My. 283–10 leading impetus of *m·* life.
284– 1 Because of *m·* rediscovery of C. S.,
284–14 held in *m·* church building,
284–18 Since *m·* residence in Concord,
284–22 to assemble in *m·* church building,
285– 2 Please accept *m·* thanks for
285– 5 accept *m·* hearty congratulations.
287– 4 enlists *m·* hearty sympathy.
289–28 capital of *m·* native State
290–12 *M· Dear Mrs. McKinley :* — *M·* soul reaches
292–13 *M·* answer to the inquiry,
292–20 Message to *m·* church in Boston,
296–11 the publisher of *m·* books,
296–26 dipped her pen in *m·* heart,
297–18 *M·* beloved Edward A. Kimball,
297–29 regarding *m·* history,
297–30 *m·* friends have read Sibyl Wilbur's
298– 3 in *m·* life's experience
298– 7 distinguished all *m·* working years.
298–10 they have *m·* permission
299– 4 kindly referring to *m·* address
302–16 But without *m·* consent,
302–25 *M·* first visit to The Mother Church
302–29 went alone in *m·* carriage
303– 1 fell mysteriously upon *m·* spirit.
303–15 *m·* statement of C. S.
304– 5 finished *m·* course of studies
304– 7 Among *m·* early studies were
304 20 knew *m·* ability as an editor.
305–10 letters in *m·* possession,
305–23 from *m·* great Master,
305–27 *M·* recent reply to the reprint
305–31 *m·* purpose was to lift the
306– 2 misrepresents *m·* character,
306– 3 attempts to narrow *m·* life
306–31 *m·* views of mental therapeutics.
307–16 *m·* theological belief was offended
307–23 related to *m·* personality,
307–25 At first *m·* case improved
307–29 might have caused *m·* illness.
307–31 *M·* idealism, however, limped,
308–10 *m·* duty to be just to the departed
308–12 *m·* late father and his family
308–15 refers to *m·* father's "tall, gaunt
308–18 *M·* father's person was erect and
308–20 One time when *m·* father
308–23 *M·* father thanked the Governor,
308–26 attributes to *m·* father
308–30 *m·* father was a great reader.
309–10 *m·* father won the suit.
309–11 Mr. Pierce bowed to *m·* father and
309–14 *M·* father was a strong believer in
309–23 *M·* father's house had a sloping
310– 1 All *m·* father's daughters were
310– 4 *M·* brother Albert was
310– 5 In addition to *m·* academic training,
310– 8 calls *m·* youngest brother,
310–14 *M·* oldest brother, Samuel D. Baker,
310–19 death in *m·* father's family
310–26 *M·* mother often
310–27 often presented *m·* disposition as
311– 2 illustrative of *m·* disposition :
311– 6 *m·* tenderness and sympathy
311– 8 *m·* good housekeeper said to me :
311–10 It was not in *m·* heart to
311–11 so I lost *m·* housekeeper.
311–12 *M·* reply to the statement
311–14 *m·* religious experience seemed to
311–16 *m·* first church membership.
311–21 presented me *m·* coat-of-arms,
311–24 which is of *m·* mother's ancestry.
312– 4 Regarding *m·* first marriage
312– 4 tragic death of *m·* husband,
312–18 *M·* first husband,
312–24 their provisions in *m·* behalf
312–26 the remains of *m·* beloved one
312–28 Free Masons selected *m·* escort,
312–28 took me to *m·* father's home
312–29 *M·* salary for writing gave me
313– 9 stories told . . . about *m·* father
313–14 only know that *m·* father and mother
313–24 frequently" seek *m·* advice.
313–27 *M·* oldest sister dearly loved me,
313–30 parted from *m·* son,
313–30 after *m·* father's second marriage
313–31 *m·* little boy was not welcome
313–31 not welcome in *m·* father's house.
314– 1 calls . . . *m·* second husband,
314– 3 says that after *m·* marriage we
314–14 *m·* divorce from Dr. Patterson was
314–21 record the divorce in *m·* favor.
315– 1 which is in *m·* possession,
317–10 to correct *m·* diction.
317–12 *m·* statement of C. S.,

Eddy

my
My. 317–16 Calvin A. Frye copied *m·* writings,
317–17 left *m·* diction quite out of the
317–22 *M·* diction, as used in explaining
318– 4 I have erased them in *m·* revisions.
318– 5 not *m·* proofreader for *m·* book
318– 6 for only two of *m·* books.
318– 9 critics declared that *m·* book was
318–12 defend *m·* grammatical construction,
318–16 to visit one of *m·* classes
318–21 began *m·* attack on agnosticism.
318–31 find *m·* authority for C. S.
319– 5 *M·* saying touched him,
326–14 the State where *m·* husband,
327– 4 *m·* native State,
330–23 "*M·* husband was a Free Mason,
330–29 where, . . . *m·* babe was born.
336–12 I lost all *m·* husband's property,
336–14 remained with *m·* parents until
336–15 after *m·* mother's decease."
338–17 owing to *m·* busy life,
343– 7 whether *m·* successor will be
343–17 In 1875 I wrote *m·* book.
343–18 shower of abuse upon *m·* head,
344– 2 to *m·* understanding of Christ
346–27 would be *m·* future successor.
347– 3 and reveal *m·* successor,
347– 8 accept *m·* heartfelt acknowledgment
347–20 I shall treasure *m·* loving-cup
348– 1 *M·* discovery that mankind is
351– 8 *m·* earliest moment in which to
352–27 *m·* thanks for your successful plans
352–29 *M·* desire is that every
354– 8 books for which *m·* endorsement is
356–16 nor consent to have *m·* picture
357–13 When *m·* dear brethren in New York
358–21 Mr. Adam Dickey is *m·* secretary,
358–22 through whom all *m·* business is
358–23 Give *m·* best wishes and love to
359– 6 *M·* province as a Leader
359–10 *m·* written and published rules,
359–27 *M· Dear Student:* — Awake and
360–16 *M·* beloved brethren in First Church
360–17 I advise you with all *m·* soul
360–29 *M· Dear Student:* — Your favor
363–21 *M·* address . . . has been misrepresented

myself
Mis. 24–13 I rose, dressed *m·*,
95–12 shall confine *m·* to questions
263– 2 they will harm *m·* only,
291–20 would part with a blessing *m·*
296– 2 have allowed *m·* to be elected
299–19 array *m·* in them,
299–20 put *m·* and them on exhibition,
311–20 as soon harm *m·* as another;
338– 5 I first proved to *m·*,
348–23 found *m·* under this new *régime*
348–27 so proved to *m·* that drugs
351– 5 for want of time, . . . I neglect *m·*.
Ret. 13–23 I rose and dressed *m·*,
24–15 how to be well *m·*,
27– 6 never been read by any one but *m·*,
43–22 organized by *m·* and six of my
Un. 7– 7 both to C. S. and *m·*
43–12 by no means spoken of *m·*,
43–13 I *cannot* speak of *m·* as
Pul. 74–14 an interview to answer for *m·*,
'02. 3– 1 used no other means *m·*;
My. 114–23 not *m·*, but the divine power
119–26 give *m·* the pleasant pastime of
137–30 I find *m·* able to select the
138– 2 and *m·* relieved of the burden of
163–11 must not allow *m·* the pleasure of
223–15 I do not consider *m·* capable of
271–30 as I know *m·*, what is "nearest and
276–25 and my neighbor as *m·*.
305– 8 I briefly express *m·*
311–26 Mrs. Judge Potter and *m·* knelt
315–22 Is it *m·*, the veritable Mrs. Eddy,
317–12 to avail *m·* of his criticisms
318–10 I availed *m·* of the name of
344–19 I should think *m·* in danger of

one
Mis. 54– 6 That *o·*, whoever it be,
234–18 That *o·* should have ventured
My. 48– 4 * *o·* ready to receive the inspiration,
58–19 * the *o·* through whom God has revealed
62–10 * thank God enough for such an *o·*,
321– 4 * referred to you as the *o·* who had
346– 2 * as *o·* who has lived with her subject

organizer
Pul. 29– 5 * The *o·* and first pastor of
our
Mis. 3– 3 shall claim no especial gift from *o·*
195–17 divine logic, as seen in *o·* text,

Eddy

our
Mis. 197– 4 *O·* chosen text is one
236– 3 Throughout *o·* experience
236–18 to the best of *o·* ability,
Pastor
Pul. 1— chapter heading
pastor
Mis. 177–24 * the *p·*, Rev. Mary Baker G. Eddy,
177–26 * The *p·* introduced Mr. Easton
178–25 * the *p·* again came forward,
193–15 of which I am *p·*,
300–25 had for many years been *p·*,
382–19 and was its first *p·*.
Man. 18– 6 to become their *p·*.
Ret. 16–19 to become their *p·*.
44– 7 to become their *p·*.
44–10 When I was its *p·*,
46– 1 Lines penned when I was *p·*
Pul. 24–19 * first *p·* of this denomination."
29– 5 * and first *p·* of the church
64– 4 * first *p·* of this denomination."
70– 9 * *p·* of the C. S. denomination,
86–27 * the permanent *p·* of this church,
My. 49–11 * Mrs. Eddy to become its *p·*.
49–19 * to become *p·* of the church.
50– 2 * held at the home of the *p·*,
50–30 * "Our *p·*, Mrs. Eddy, preached her
51– 1 * devise means to pay our *p·*,
51– 7 * sincerely regret that our *p·*,
51–17 * have our *p·* remain with us
51–29 * tender to our beloved *p·*,
52–14 * taught and expressed by our *p·*,
53–32 * When our *p·* preached for us
54– 9 * before the arrival of the *p·*,
Pastor Emeritus
Man. 25– 5 *P· E·*, a Board of Directors,
25– 9 approval of the *P· E·*,
26–10 consent of the *P· E·*
26–15 shall inform the *P· E·*
26–22 approved by the *P· E·*.
28– 2 approval of the *P· E·*
29– 9 If . . . the *P· E·* shall complain
29–13 the *P· E·* shall appoint five
30– 9 the consent of the *P· E·*,
30–14 the house of the *P· E·*.
51– 9 aggrieve or vilify the *P· E·*
52–23 or the interests of our *P· E·*
54–12 on complaint of Mrs. Eddy our *P· E·*
54–21 represents falsely to . . . *P· E·*
55– 3 to The Mother Church, or to the *P· E·*,
57–12 Board of Directors and the *P· E·*
57–15 consent of this Board and the *P· E·*,
59– 8 books or poems of our *P· E·*,
64–11 heading
66– 1 communication from the *P· E·*
66–10 communications of the *P· E·*
66–15 or a message from the *P· E·*
67– 1 *P· E·* is not to be consulted
67– 7 communication from the *P· E·*
67–20 or letters to the *P· E·*
67–25 written request of the *P· E·*,
70– 1 *P· E·* to be Consulted.
72–19 If the *P· E·*, . . . should relinquish
76–20 with the consent of the *P· E·*.
78–11 written consent of the *P· E·*.
79–20 the *P· E·* of this Church,
80–17 *P· E·* reserves the right to fill the
81– 3 and the consent of the *P· E·*
81– 6 who is not accepted by the *P· E·*
87– 2 Neither the *P· E·* nor a member
88–15 to the approval of the *P· E·*.
93– 8 to the approval of the *P· E·*.
93–15 pertaining to the life of the *P· E·*.
97–12 and the consent of the *P· E·*
98–19 letter sent to the *P· E·*
101– 5 with the approval of the *P· E·*,
103– 8 written consent of the *P· E·*,
Pul. 87–16 make me your *P· E·*, nominally.
My. 15– 9 writable consent of the *P· E·*,
22–25 * position taken by our *P· E·*
27– 5 residence of your *P· E·*
32–26 * Message from the *P· E·*,
36– 7 * REV. MARY BAKER EDDY, *P· E·*.
39–23 * *P· E·*, Mrs. Eddy, was present.
133–21 chapter sub-title
216–17 the room of the *P· E·*
217– 9 the room of the *P· E·*.
223–25 and not to the *P· E·*.
pastor's
Pan. 1– 1 heading
My. 52–17 * and our *p·* teachings,
President
Mis. 242– 5 *P·* of the Metaphysical College
Man. 88– 6 *P·* of the . . . Metaphysical College
88–16 *P·* not to be Consulted.

Eddy

President

Man.	88–17	P· is not to be consulted
	89– 2	Should the P· resign
	89– 3	or vacate her office of P·
	91– 5	of the P· of the College
	91–10	free scholarship from the P·,
	91–14	Only the P· gives free
Ret.	48–30	P·, the Rev. Mary B. G. Eddy,
	49–23	gratitude is due to the P·,
My.	245–30	conferred by the P· or

president

Mis.	272–28	* Rev. Mrs. Eddy is founder and p·."
	382–23	its first and only p· ;
Man.	88– 7	a p·, vice-president, and teacher
Pul.	24–18	* p· of the . . . Metaphysical College,
	64– 3	* p· of the . . . Metaphysical College,
	70– 8	* p· of the . . . Metaphysical College,

proprietor

| Mis. | 382–23 | p· of the first C. S. periodical ; |
| My. | 304–17 | p· and sole editor of |

publisher

Mis.	382–16	author and p· of the first
Ret.	52–21	I started it, . . . as editor and p·.
Pul.	47– 5	* editor and p· of the first official

pupil

| My. | 304– 3 | p· of Miss Sarah J. Bodwell, |

revelator

| My. | vii– 7 | * her rightful place as the r· |

scribe

| Mis. | 311–26 | I was a s· under orders ; |
| My. | 115– 7 | I was only a s· echoing the |

she

Mis.	37–26	S· now does not.
	54–11	s· is demonstrating the power of
	58–10	*How does Mrs. Eddy know that s·*
	58–12	S· had to use her eyes to read.
	130– 4	S· readily leaves the answer to
	155–18	however much s· desires thus to do
	155–19	s· hereby requests : First,
	169– 1	Within Bible pages s· had found
	169– 2	all the divine Science s· preaches ;
	169– 6	till s· was God-driven back
	169– 9	years of invalidism s· endured
	160–14	S· affirmed that the Scriptures
	170–12	So, also, s· spoke of the hades,
	170–19	material record of the Bible, s· said,
	170–31	s· explained as the putting forth
	188–21	when s· discovered C. S.
	188–22	And s· has *not* left it,
	188–29	s· knew that the last Adam,
	188–32	s· beheld the meaning of
	210–17	s· puts her foot on the head of
	234–23	s· has made some progress,
	378–15	s· did ask him how manipulation
	386–14	S· deemed I died,
	386–22	S· that has wept o'er thee.
	387– 4	S· shall mount upward unto
Man.	18– 6	S· accepted the call,
	26–16	and if s· objects,
	43–11	Sometimes s· may strengthen the faith
	48–13	not haunt Mrs. Eddy's drive when s·
	52–24	what s· understands is advantageous
	66–17	or s· is referred to as authority
	66–25	an order . . . that s· has not sent,
	68–13	members whom s· teaches the course
	68–19	those individuals whom s· engages
	69– 9	remain with Mrs. Eddy if s· so desires,
	69–10	whatsoever s· may charge
	69–11	what s· has taught him or her
	75– 9	s·, with grateful acknowledgments
	75–11	s· now understands the financial
	80–19	but if s· does not elect to
	100– 6	if s· shall send a special request
Ret.	16–19	S· accepted the call,
Pul.	31–21	* s· most kindly replied,
	31–22	* s· would receive me.
	31–25	* S· impressed me as . . . graceful
	32– 3	* s· was magnetic, earnest,
	32– 7	* s· had the temperament to dominate.
	32–12	* What had s· originated?
	32–14	* S· told me the story of her life,
	32–20	* s· must have been some sixty years
	32–20	* yet s· had the coloring and the
	32–22	* this, s· told me, was due to
	33– 3	* s· began, like Jeanne d'Arc,
	33– 4	* s· heard her name called
	33– 6	* questioning if s· were wanted.
	33– 7	* if s· heard the voice again
	33–11	* s· prayed for forgiveness,
	33–12	* It came, and s· answered as
	34– 2	* S· returned to her father's home
	34–10	* no probability that s· would be alive
	34–11	* s· suddenly became aware of a
	34–12	* S· requested those with her to
	34–14	* s· walked into the adjoining room,

Eddy

she

Pul.	34–16	* they thought I had died, . . . s· said.
	34–21	* s· said, in reference to this
	34–26	* s· said, in reply to my questions,
	35–10	* begotten of spirituality," s· says,
	36–23	* s· bought one of the most beautiful
	37– 6	* where s· has a beautiful residence,
	37– 8	* s· retains in a great degree her
	37– 9	* s· takes a daily walk
	37– 9	* S· personally attends to a vast
	37–12	* s· is the recognized head of the
	46–28	* s· became the wife of
	47–10	* s· states that s· sought knowledge
	47 15	* S· claims that no human reason has
	47–16	* s· also defines carefully
	47–24	* when s· wishes to catch a glimpse of
	47–25	* s· lives very much retired,
	48– 7	* s· can sit in her swinging chair,
	48–16	* s· paused and reminded the reporter
	48–26	* S· had a long list of worthy
	49–13	* "Four years !" s· ejaculated ;
	49–15	* s· continued : "Look at those
	49–19	* S· told something of her domestic
	49–20	* s· had long wished to get away
	49–24	* S· chose the stubbly old farm
	49–29	* S· employs a number of men
	50– 2	* in whom s· takes a vital interest.
	50– 6	* that s· might do something for
	55–14	* Since then s· has revised it
	55–17	* Afterward s· selected the name
	58– 4	* about 1880, s· began teaching,
	58– 6	* s· has lived in Concord, N. H.,
	58–29	* should s· wish to make it a home
	59– 2	* s· has not yet visited her temple,
	63– 4	* S· HAS AN IMMENSE FOLLOWING
	63–10	* s· pointed to a number of large elms
	63–19	* hold s· has upon this army
	64–14	* Mrs. Eddy says s· discovered C. S.
	64–15	* S· studied the . . . s· declares,
	64–16	* S· investigated allopathy,
	64–20	* s· became convinced that
	68– 5	* s· taught the principles of the
	68–10	* S· now lives in a beautiful
	70–11	* S· has within a few years
	70–17	* in 1866 s· became certain that
	70–19	* s· endeavored in vain to find
	70–21	* s· concluded that the way of
	70–25	* Mind-healing, which s· termed C. S.
	70–25	* S· has a palatial home in Boston
	71–10	* chapter sub-title
	71–22	* s· is unquestionably looked upon as
	72–19	* s· was the Founder of the faith,
	73– 6	* S· had faith in Him,
	73– 6	* s· cured herself of a deathly disease
	73– 8	* s· secluded herself from the world
	73 9	* S· delved deep into the
	73–13	* this duty s· faithfully performed.
	74–11	* which s· did in this letter,
	85– 8	* s· has unfolded and demonstrated
	85–13	* s· has demonstrated the system
	85–14	* surely s·, as the one chosen of God
	88– 8	s· can append only a few of
Rud.	14–12	S· has never taught . . . without
	17–12	s· needed miraculous vision to
No.	12–22	in nothing else has s· departed from
'01.	34–25	only so far as s· follows Christ.
'02.	4– 4	only so far as s· follows Christ.
Po.	v–16	* s· seated herself by the roadside
	v–19	*asked her what s· was writing,*
	v–19	*s· replied by reading the poem*
	vi–24	*years s· resided in Lynn,*
	vii– 9	*to which s· assented.*
	49–21	S· deemed I died,
	50– 7	S· that has wept o'er thee,
	50–22	S· shall mount upward unto
My.	v–20	* s· wrote and published the
	vi–19	* s· organized The C. S. Publishing
	vi–22	* s· made over to trustees
	vi–23	* s· presented to her church
	vi–28	* s· established the *C. S. Sentinel*
	11– 7	* S· has been the one of all the world
	11– 9	* s· has not tried to guide us by
	11–11	* In all this time s· has never
	11–14	* s· quietly alluded to the need of
	11–15	* S· knew that we were ready ;
	11–16	* s· expressed much gratification
	11–18	* s· will be cheered and encouraged
	22–18	* purpose s· has set in motion,
	22–20	* s· has shown wisdom, faith, and
	40– 2	* S· has desired for years to
	40–25	* s· is an exact metaphysician.
	40–26	* S· has illustrated what the poet
	40–27	* S· has obeyed the divine Principle,
	42–28	* and how successful s· is in the

Eddy

she

My. 43–23 * s· gave us our textbook,
48–13 * s· founded the future growth of
51– 8 * s· has not met with the support
51– 9 * s· should have reason to expect,
51–10 * hope s· will remain with us.
51–14 * who is so able as s· to lead us
52– 2 * s· had many obstacles to
52– 4 * s· has borne them bravely,
52–23 * Little cares s·, if only
52–24 * s· has reached her bottom dollar,
52–27 * s· has made sacrifices
53– 5 * would s· allow printer and binder
53–16 * ascertain if s· would preach for
53–18 * which invitation s· accepted.
53–21 * when s· could give the time to
54– 4 * eternal truth s· taught them."
57– 7 * s· suggested the need of a larger
58–23 * as s· has done, verifying Jesus'
59–25 * Some say s· did not."
59–27 * "Send those who say s· did not to me.
60– 4 * s· would doubtless do so.
64– 7 * for all that s· has done.
64–16 * s· has been teaching her followers
64–20 * Fearlessly does s· warn all her
94–25 * s· sent greetings in which s·
139– 3 S· is neither dead nor
139– 4 s· is keenly alive to the reality of
155–29 their Leader's love, which s· sends
171–24 * s· was greeted in behalf of
171–26 * s· presented as a love-token for
229–15 lose all selfishness, as s· has
229–16 as s· has done, according to
231– 6 s· has suffered most from those
231– 6 whom s· has labored much to
231– 8 to whom s· has given large sums
231– 9 S· has, therefore, finally resolved
231–11 S· has qualified students for
240–26 * S· most assuredly does,
270–15 of those who say that s· is
275–12 chapter sub-title
276– 4 s· begs to say, in her own behalf,
276– 5 that s· is neither ;
276– 8 When . . . s· omits her drive,
276–11 s· is minding her own business,
276–18 * s· has also believed that in such
276–22 * s· has given out this statement :
304–30 second, s· has stolen the contents
311–30 * when s· finished Smith's grammar
312– 9 * S· was far from home
312–12 * s· was met and taken to her father's
312–14 * S· was a grown woman,
312–17 * a brief season s· taught school."
330–16 * who s· states was of Charleston,
331– 5 * among whom s· remembers
334– 7 * because s· has contradicted
334–18 * S· declares in her Message
336– 7 * s· declined on this ground,
336– 9 * S· makes grateful acknowledgment
336–11 * In this book . . . s· also states,
342– 4 * S· entered with a gracious smile,
342–15 * for weak s· was not.
242–20 * s· said, in her clear voice,
343– 2 * S· has a rapt way of talking,
343– 5 * S· explained : "No present change
343–22 * position of authority," s· went on,
346– 2 * S· talks as one who has
346– 9 * s· is in the flesh and in health.
346–13 * S· was inside, and as s· passed
346–23 * as to whether s· had in mind any
350– 9 s· spiritually discerned the divine

sister

My. 331–29 * to Mrs. Glover (my s·)

St. Catherine

Pul. 32–12 * this modern St. C·,

student

My. 320–10 * as a s· of ability.

Teacher

Pul. 44– 2 * "Dear T·, Leader, Guide :
86– 4 * "To our Beloved T·,
86–17 * Beloved T· and Leader :
My. 23–17 * Beloved T· and Leader :
36– 8 * Beloved T· and Leader :
44–23 * Beloved T· and Leader :
58–28 * Dear T· :— Of the many thousands
62–19 * Beloved Leader and T· :
157– 3 * "BELOVED T· AND LEADER :
319–16 * Dear T· :— I am conversant
322– 9 * Beloved T· :— I have just
323–17 * Beloved T· :— My heart has

teacher

Mis. 137– 9 a few words aside to your t·.
138–30 Your loving t·,
144–12 the same author, your t·,
280–20 presented their t· with an

Eddy

teacher

Mis. 280–25 thanks to their t·.
302–12 sparing their t· a task
371–12 I as their t· can say,
Ret. 77– 1 I become responsible, as a t·,
Pul. 24–15 * testimonial to our beloved t·,
41–12 * sent them by the t·
63–27 * testimonial to our beloved t·,
84–28 * our beloved t· and Leader,
My. 22–15 * our beloved Leader and t·,
36– 1 * from their t· and Leader,
41–27 * Our Leader and t· not only
50–10 * dauntless Leader and t·,
58–19 * revered Leader and t·,
97–19 * their t· and her utterances."
323–21 * such a Leader and t·
358–25 Lovingly your t· and Leader,
360– 3 As ever, lovingly your t·,

thee

Po. 68– 3 "I'm living to bless t· ;

toiler

Mis. 386– 8 t· tireless for Truth's new birth
Po. 49–13 t· tireless for Truth's new birth

we

Mis. 2–32 w· entertain decided views
3– 2 w· shall claim no especial gift
35–28 w· refer you to "S. and H.
36– 3 w· shall classify evil and error
41–19 W· answer, Yes.
48–19 has, w· trust, been made in season
49– 3 W· are credibly informed that,
161–14 whose words w· have chosen
193– 3 w· reply in the affirmative
195–15 W· ask what is the authority
197– 6 w· fear . . . this text is not yet recognized.
200–12 that w· have chosen for a text ;
236– 4 w· have been made the repository
236–10 w· have said, "Love and honor thy
236–17 w· have done this to the best of our
236–20 In such cases w· have said,
244– 9 But, w· ask, have those conditions
285–20 W· have taken the precaution to write
286– 7 W· look to future generations for
300– 7 W· answer, It is a mistake ;
368–12 W· regret to be obliged to say that
Pan. 7–14 W· know of but three theistic
10–21 which, w· regret to say,
'00. 2–22 Here w· add : The doom of such
Hea. 12–10 w· discovered that all physical effects
12–12 w· learned from the Scripture
12–17 w· saw at once the concentrated
13–10 W· have attenuated a grain of
13–15 highest attenuation w· ever
13–17 w· cured an inveterate case of
13–19 w· resigned the imaginary medicine
My. 212–15 W· answer, Because they do not
300–21 w· propose that he make known his

who

Mis. 35–26 author of that work, w· explains it
My. 272–25 w·, nearly eighty-seven years of

widow

My. 331–25 * lone, feeble, and bereaved w·
335–15 * were kept by his w·
351–15 as the w· of a Mason.

wife

Mis. 386–26 my w·, Thy child, shall come
Pul. 46–28 * became the w· of Asa Gilbert Eddy.
Po. 50–12 my w·, Thy child, shall come
My. 312– 8 He left his young w· in
315– 6 * conversation with him about his w·,
315–11 * no knowledge of who his w· was.
333–27 * He has left an amiable w·,
335–30 * young w· prayed incessantly for

woman

Pul. 7– 3 * I would help that w·."
44–18 * chapter sub-title
49–26 * the will of the w· set at work,
'01. 16–25 its greatest discoverer is a w·
My. 4–12 w· has put into Christendom
28–29 * one divinely guided w·,
85–12 * this wonderful w· is a world power.
88–24 * a noble and devoted w·,
89–30 * That a w· should found a
231–21 one w· is sufficient to
271–15 * most discussed w· in all the
271–19 * aged w· of world-wide renown
271–26 * personality of this remarkable w·.
272–25 * w· who, nearly eighty-seven years
304–22 * a w· of sound education and
305–12 * w· in New Hampshire."
312–15 * She was a grown w·,
315– 7 * a pure and Christian w·,
315–14 * the above-mentioned w·.
330– 1 * criticism of this good w·

Eddy

writer

Mis. 188–21 where the present *w·* found it,

writer's

My. 348–14 *w·* departure from such a religion
350– 8 came to the *w·* rescue,

you

Mis. 4–24 is often said, "Y· must have
31– 1 *What do y· consider to be mental*
35–15 *S. and H. that y· offer for sale*
35–18 *if one is obliged to study under y·,*
38– 1 *Why do y· charge for teaching C. S.,*
38–13 *How happened y· to establish a*
39–13 *Can y· take care of yourself?*
46–10 *Do y· teach that y· are equal with*
50–18 *Do y· believe in change of heart?*
52–11 *What do y· think of marriage?*
53–11 *Do y· sometimes find it advisable*
60– 1 *How can y· believe there is no sin,*
60– 3 *How can y· believe there is no*
64–10 *Do y· regard the study of*
65–17 *Have y· changed your instructions*
67–24 *Do y· believe in translation?*
75– 6 *Why do y· insist that there is but*
83– 5 *y· say : "Every sin is the*
83– 8 *y· say: "Sickness is a*
83–10 *Will y· please explain this*
87–15 *if y· sent Mrs. —— to —— .*
87–16 *She said that y· sent her there*
112–22 * y· have brought what will do him good."
180– 7 * "How is it that y· are restored
299–24 Did he give y· permission
299–25 or loan them to y·?
299–26 have y· asked yourself this question
299–30 because y· have confessed that
299–32 and y· wished to handle them,
299–32 does it justify y· in appropriating
317– 2 "May I call y· mother?"
353– 7 Is my concept of y· right?
375–11 * new book y· have given us.
375–32 * "All that I can say to y·,
376–14 * Y· have given us back our Jesus,

Ret. 8– 8 "Nothing, child ! What do y· mean?"
8–18 "Your mother is calling y· !"
8–20 "Why don't y· go?
8–21 your mother is calling y· !"
90–28 * in the path y· have pursued !"

Un. 48– 5 *Do y· believe in God?*
49– 1 *Do y· believe in man?*
50– 3 *Do y· believe in matter?*
51–13 *What say y· of woman?*
52–15 *What say y· of evil?*

Pul. 5–18 * "I have come to comfort y·."
44– 3 * y· begin to see the fruition of that y·
44– 6 * Y· are fully occupied, but
44– 7 * I thought y· would willingly pause
77–14 * revealed by divine Love through y·
77–14 * Y· are hereby most lovingly invited
78–12 * revealed by divine Love through y·
78–13 * Y· are hereby most lovingly invited
86–17 * We are happy to announce to y·
86–22 * we hereby present this church to y·
86–26 * extend to y· the invitation
86–29 * which y· have already ordained as
87– 1 * invite y· to be present

Rud. 1– 1 *How would y· define C. S.?*
1–10 *Do y· mean by this that God*
3–24 *do y· mean that God has*

Hea. 6– 4 * "People say y· are a medium,"

My. 8–26 * send our greeting to y·,
23–20 * loving greetings to y·,
24– 5 * We congratulate y·
24– 8 * which inspires y· to welcome all
24–12 * Through y· has been revealed
37–11 * y· have demonstrated this Science
37–14 * and bestow upon y· the balm of
38– 1 * story of our love for y·
38– 5 * and for all that y· are
38– 6 * and all that y· have done for us.
44–26 * convey to y· their sincere
45–16 * divine Principle revealed to y·
45–17 * mortal sense declared y· to be
45–18 * Y· followed unswervingly
45–19 * of Him who went before y·
59– 2 * whom y· will recall as a member
59– 4 * y· told us that the truth y·
59–14 * which has been reared by y·,
60– 6 * Possibly y· may remember the
60– 8 * told that I had studied with y·.
60–15 * little Bible which y· gave me
60–27 * to tell y· of the interesting
62–10 * ever thank y· enough for your
62–20 * send y· loving greetings and
63– 1 * through y· we were enabled to
117–16 But when may we see y·,

Eddy

you

My. 157–10 * y· are so highly esteemed,
157–12 * y· have so freely bestowed.
157–12 * We thank y· for this
207– 9 * unite in loving greetings to y·,
207–12 * truth which y· have unfolded
240– 7 * "Would it be asking too much of y·
240– 7 * explain more fully why y· call
280– 8 * in this new reminder from y·
307–14 * "I see now what y· mean,
307–14 * I see that I am John, and that y·
311– 9 * "If this blind girl stays with y·,
319–19 * may interest y· to be advised that
310–22 * later, in conversation with y·
319–23 * y· suggested that I call on
319–29 * conversation with y· in general
319–30 * Y· told me that he had done some
320– 1 * literary work for y·
320– 6 * pleased to converse about y·
320– 7 * of what he had done for y·
320– 8 * agreed with what y· had told me.
320– 9 * as to his high regard for y·
320–14 * spoke of y· as the author of
320–22 * he always referred to y· as
320–27 * proud of his acquaintance with y·.
321– 4 * referred to y· as the one who
321– 8 * one who knew who and what y· are,
321– 9 * he always gave y· that position
321–14 * of y· and your relations to your
321–21 * twenty years since I first saw y·
321–24 * many conversations with y·,
321–31 * who knew y· years before I did,
322– 2 * told me she knew y· when y· were
322–12 * attitude towards y· ;
322–12 * Edward P. Bates' letter to y·
322–17 I had seen y· the day before
322–30 * of y· and your work.
323– 6 * criticism of y· and your book
323– 8 * y· have so identified yourself with
323– 9 * y· are not going to lie
323–18 * to tell y· in words all that your
323–24 * blessing those who would destroy y·
323–24 * if God did not hold y· up
323–28 * I wonder if y· will remember
323–31 * in the second class with y·
324– 2 * about y· and your work,
324– 5 * had given y· any idea for
324– 6 * he said y· and your ideas were
324– 8 * said y· were so original and so
324–10 * of much service to y·,
324–12 * telling y· of this, and y· explained
324–13 * y· had waited on the Lord
324–14 * those very terms revealed to y·.
324–16 * that y· were the author of
324–19 * had helped y· write it.
324–22 * Mr. Wiggin regarded y· as quite
324–23 * pleased in numbering y· among his
324–25 * regarded y· as entirely unique
324–29 * we asked him if he found y· could
325– 1 * kindnesses y· had shown them,
325– 2 * y· personally called to inquire
325– 5 * that I think will amuse y· :
325– 6 * troubled that y· had bought
325– 8 * never be worth what y· then paid
325–12 * I offered my services to y·
325–13 * in which I could serve y·,
343– 9 * "Can y· name the man?"
344–16 * "Do y· reject utterly the
345– 7 * Do y· oppose it?"
352– 8 * our debt of gratitude to y·
362–18 * send y· their loving greetings.
362–21 * assure y· that it is our intention

your

Mis. 4–26 to make y· demonstrations."
33–21 *advantages of y· system of healing,*
35–17 *under y· personal instruction*
35–19 *of what benefit is y· book?*
37–16 *Can y· Science cure intemperance?*
38–25 *Is it necessary to study y· Science*
41–18 *healed by y· method*
54–17 *Must I study y· Science in order to*
54–19 *treatment by one of y· students.*
54–25 *Because none of y· students have*
65–17 *Have you changed y· instructions*
83– 5 *In y· book, S. and H.,*
87–15 *inform us, through y· Journal,*
88– 6 *give us, through y· Journal,*
255–18 *of y· system of healing?*
290–16 * "I felt the influence of y· thought
299–13 * "Is it right to copy y· works
299–28 it saves y· purchasing these
299–30 does this silence y· conscience?
301–20 "Is it right to copy y· works
316– 7 speak to y· church in Boston?
372–11 * pictures in y· wonderful book

Eddy's

Mrs.
My. 355–21 Christian Scientists at Mrs. *E·*
    361–15 chapter sub-title
    362– 1 heading
    362– 9 * chapter sub-title
    363–13 heading

Rev. Mrs.
Mis. 272–20 * (except Rev. Mrs. *E·*)
Pul. 87–10 * heading

Eddy-signatures

Letters to branch churches
Mis. 151–30 Mary Baker Eddy.
    153–32 " " "
    155–14 " " "
My. 20– 4 " " "
    144– 9 " " "
    158–30 " " "
    168– 8 " " "
    169–10 " " "
    284– 7 " " "
    360–25 " " "

Mis. 150– 6 Mary Baker G. Eddy.

Letters to students
Mis. 159– 9 Mary Baker Eddy.
My. 20–19 " " "
    135–21 " " "
    142–22 " " "
    171–16 " " "
    263– 9 " " "
    285–30 " " "
    351–19 " " "
    358–26 " " "
    360– 4 " " "
    361–12 " " "
    362– 6 " " "
    363–16 " " "

Mis. 160–17 Mary Baker G. Eddy.

Mis. 156–30 Mary B. G. Eddy.
    157–30 " " "

Letters to the . . . Christian Scientist Association
Mis. 135–22 Mary Baker Eddy.
My. 364–18 " " "

Mis. 138–31 Mary Baker G. Eddy.

Mis. 139– 7 M. B. G. E.

Letters to the Directors
Pul. 87–27 Mary Baker Eddy.
My. 26–26 " " "
    143– 6 " " "

Letters to The Mother Church
Mis. 132– 7 Mary Baker Eddy.
    142– 5 " " "
    146–27 " " "
    149–15 " " "
Pan. 15–11 " " "
My. 9–28 " " "
    27– 9 " " "
    133–18 " " "
    136– 9 " " "
    140–28 " " "
    279–28 " " "
    280–23 " " "

Mis. 128–15 Mary Baker G. Eddy.

Letters to the Press
Pul. 75–12 Mary Baker Eddy.
My. 158– 5 " " "
    272–16 " " "
    276–14 " " "
    282–16 " " "
    284–28 " " "
    316–26 " " "
    327– 7 " " "
    339–10 " " "
    353–19 " " "
    356–18 " " "

Mis. 274–14 Mary Baker G. Eddy.

Letter to the College Association
Mis. 136–29 Mary B. G. Eddy.

to an Affidavit
My. 138–22 Mary Baker Eddy.

to a Notice
Mis. 303–27 Mary Baker Eddy.

to Dedications
Mis. v– 9 Mary Baker Eddy.
Pul. v– 8 " " "
Rud. v– 8 " " "

to Inscriptions
My. 214– 7 Mary Baker Eddy.
    214–10 " " "
    214–14 " " "

Eddy-signatures

to Poems
Mis. vii–21 Mary Baker Eddy.
My. 354–25 " " "

to Prefaces
Mis. xii– 9 Mary Baker Eddy.
Pul. vii–23 " " "
No. v–14 " " "

to Tenets
Man. 16–13 Mary Baker Eddy.

to the First (or Executive) Members
Mis. 148– 5 Mary Baker Eddy.
My. 140– 8 " " "

to Tributes
My. 289–20 Mary Baker Eddy.
    290–29 " " "
    295–29 " " "
    296– 6 " " "
    296–21 " " "
    297– 8 " " "
    297–25 " " "
    298–12 " " "

Miscellaneous signatures
Mis. 143–12 Mary Baker Eddy.
    156– 5 " " "
My. 25–28 " " "
    136–29 " " "
    143–30 " " "
    240–21 " " "
    242–25 " " "
    282–28 " " "
    351–28 " " "
    352–23 " " "
    353– 3 " " "
    353–27 " " "
    354–10 " " "
    355–15 " " "
    356– 9 " " "
    359–13 " " "

Mis. 134– 8 Mary Baker G. Eddy.
    256–20 " " "

Pul. 39–12 M. B. Eddy.
    54–30 " " "

Eden
Mis. 109–19 Adam and Eve in the garden of *E·*.
    287–12 and restores lost *E·*.
Ret. 18–12 dwellers in *E·*, earth yields you
Un. 44–10 In the days of *E·*, humanity was
Po. 64– 1 dwellers in *E·*, earth yields you

Edgar
Un. 23– 5 His lawful son, *E·*,

edge
Mis. 72–15 teeth are set on *e·*? — *Ezek.* 18 : 2.
    195–23 to try the *e·* of truth in C. S.,
    381–28 put under the *e·* of the knife,

edict
My. 278– 8 and its *e·* hath gone forth:

edifice

church
Mis. 139–21 erected thereon a church *e·*
    319–22 church *e·* must be built in 1894.
    382–20 church *e·* of this denomination
Man. 75– 3 Church *E·* a Testimonial.
    75– 8 church *e·* as a Testimonial
    102– 7 new church *e·* is completed.
    102–17 erection of a church *e·*.
Ret. 51– 5 church *e·* to be used as a
Pul. 24–21 * heading
    77–10 * a church *e·* was erected at
    78– 8 * a church *e·* was erected at
    87–19 to accept your grand church *e·*.
'02. 12–26 and enlarge our church *e·*
    14– 4 nor sell this church *e·*
My. 7– 9 and enlarge our church *e·*
    9–24 to enlarge our church *e·*
    25–24 builders of this church *e·*,
    55– 7 * thought of obtaining a church *e·*,
    57– 8 * need of a larger church *e·*,
    58–11 * the dignity of this church *e·*
    65– 9 * to build in this city a church *e·*
    67–26 * any church *e·* erected in this city.
    84– 8 * church *e·* may not be formally
    157– 7 * to build a beautiful church *e·*
    158– 2 in building a granite church *e·*
    162–14 furnishing our church *e·* in Concord,
    162–20 church *e·* in Concord :
    167–17 in our new church *e·*,
    173–17 to take a peep at this church *e·*
    189–25 first church *e·* of our denomination

editorial

My. 63-10 * E· in C. S. Sentinel,
88- 1 * chapter sub-title
232-10 COMMENT ON AN E· WHICH APPEARED
272-32 * gives no e· indorsement to
334-27 * extract from an e· obituary
353- 6 Extract from the leading E·

editor-in-chief

My. 136-19 e· of the C. S. periodicals,
226-26 e· of the C. S. Sentinel,
227-21 above quotation by the e·

editor's

Mis. 168-21 chapter sub-title
My. 272-20 * E· NOTE.— The Cosmopolitan presents

editors

Mis. 126-18 able e· of The C. S. Journal,
143-20 teachers, e·, and pastors
155-22 e· of The C. S. Journal
301- 7 authors and e· of pamphlets
Man. 26- 1 also for the e· and the manager
65-11 e· of the C. S. Journal,
80-22 E· and Manager.
80-23 term of office for the e·
Pul. 36-26 * e· of The C. S. Journal,
My. 83-19 * chapter sub-title
145- 2 MY DEAR E· :— You are by this time
174-10 I thank the distinguished e·
175-13 Its dear churches, reliable e·,
270- 8 leading e· and newspapers of

Edmund

Un. 23- 2 his bastard son E·

educate

Mis. 51-19 e· him to love God, good,
235-23 e· the affections to higher
315-27 strive to e· their students
Hea. 14-19 e· and develop the spiritual sense

educated

Mis. 9-27 wherewith mortals become e· to
53-27 only the thought e· away from it
178-30 in which we have been e·,
Man. 32-20 read understandingly and be well e·.
64- 1 shall be well e·, and a devout
'01. 32-24 e· my thought many years,
'02. 3- 5 among the e· classes
My. 246- 7 Students . . . must be well e·

Education

(see Board of Education)

education

Mis. 38- 8 our whole system of e·,
61- 4 e· of the future will be
240-11 All e· should contribute to
273-21 from these sources of e·,
286-11 more spiritual . . . e· of children
Ret. 5-00 * to the e· of her children.
Rud. 16- 7 in any branch of e·.
My. 217- 2 for your own school e·.
230-24 Christian e· of the dear children,
252-11 entire purpose of true e·
253-27 by e· brightens into birth.
289- 1 All e· is work,
304-22 * a woman of sound e·
306- 2 my character, e·, and authorship,
309-27 * received a liberal e·.
310- 2 were given an academic e·
311-30 * completed her e· when she

educational

Mis. 114- 5 Quarterly as an e· branch.
203-23 e· system of C. S.
My. 216- 6 Christian, civil, and e· means,
245- 6 This Christian e· system
312-31 starting that e· system

educed

Mis. 122-20 Good is not e· from its opposite :
Pan. 12- 2 good is not e· from evil,

Edward, King

'02. 3-22 on the brow of good King E·,

Edwards, Jonathan

Pul. 23-10 * of the time of Jonathan E·
'01. 15-22 thunderbolt of Jonathan E· :

e'en

Po. 30-10 E· as Thou gildest gladdened joy,
43- 8 Fondling e· the lion furious,

e'er

Po. 1- 5 Beyond the ken of mortal e· to tell
73-20 E· to mock the bright truth

E. E. Sturtevant Post

My. 284-14 Memorial service of the E· E· S· P·

efface

Mis. 18- 3 e· the mark of the beast.
Ret. 64- 6 to e· sin, alias the sinner,

effaced

Ret. 6- 3 * impressions . . . can never be e·,
27-12 I would not have e·.
79- 7 false images are e·.
My. 178-26 not one word in the book was e·.

effect

all

My. 302- 9 mind is the cause of all e·
348- 4 all e· must be the offspring of

any

My. 98-12 * if they would deal . . . with any e·.

appreciable

My. 107-14 and without appreciable e·.

artistic

My. 67-24 * never was a more artistic e·

better

Mis. 229- 7 and with better e· than he

cause and

(see cause)

cause in

Mis. 219- 4 neither reveals . . . cause in e·,
My. 149-23 cause in e·, and faith in sight,
349-32 seeks cause in e·,

cause into

Mis. 362-16 puts cause into e·,

cause or

My. 364-12 of any other cause or e·

controls the

'01. 17-27 mind that controls the e· ;

curative

My. 301-30 no curative e· upon the body.

decorative

Pul. 28-10 * in appropriate decorative e·.

every

Mis. 261-11 every e· and amplification of wrong
Ret. 24-11 every e· a mental phenomenon.
Pul. 55-20 * every e· has its origin in desire
70-18 every e· a mental phenomenon.''
My. 288-24 every e· or amplification of wrong

fails in

Mis. 129-11 If this rule fails in e·,

good

Mis. 221-14 if he denies it, the good e· is lost.

harmonious

Hea. 7- 4 harmonious e· on the body.

imposing

My. 68-21 * imposing e· of the interior.

is antagonistic

Mis. 217-22 the e· is antagonistic to its cause ;

its

Mis. 51- 2 will have its e· physically
66-30 that cause nor its e·.
79-17 its e· is perfect also ;
218-22 and end, with matter as its e·,
249- 4 see if . . . could not obviate its e· ;
337- 5 By proving its e· on yourself
Ret. 62- 3 Test C. S. by its e· on society,
My. 3-20 its e· on man is mainly this

just

Pul. 56-20 * And of the just e· complain ;

laws to that

Mis. 50-14 constituted laws to that e·,

manifestation in

Mis. 271- 4 its manifestation in e· as a thought,

no

Mis. 249- 5 drug had no e· upon me
My. 345-14 until they had no e· on me.

no beneficial

Mis. 348-28 drugs have no beneficial e·

of a fear

Ret. 61- 7 experiencing the e· of a fear

of alcohol

Mis. 48-16 could produce the e· of alcohol,

of both methods

My. 215-29 to test the e· of both methods

of drugs

Mis. 348-25 as to the e· of drugs on one who

of mesmerism

Mis. 59- 5 produces the e· of mesmerism.

of power

Mis. 334-10 may have the e· of power ;

of prayer

'01. 34- 1 e· of prayer, . . . as salutary in the

of self-mesmerism

My. 118- 5 is the e· of self-mesmerism,

of sin

Mis. 221-11 removing the e· of sin on himself,

one

Mis. 25- 4 one cause and one e·,
271- 9 one cause and one e·.

on society

Ret. 62- 3 Test C. S. by its e· on society.

opposite

My. 348-24 never producing an opposite e·,

effect

or disease
Mis. 41–24 the *e·* or disease will disappear
pictorial
Pul. 25– 1 * are very rich in pictorial *e·*.
produced the
Mis. 221–13 sin has produced the *e·*
producing the
Hea. 6–25 cause producing the *e·* we see.
slightest
Mis. 221– 1 does not, produce the slightest *e·*,
spiritual
My. 318–14 the moral and spiritual *e·* upon the
supposed
Mis. 24–31 thus destroy any supposed *e·*
takes
Man. 68–22 By-Law takes *e·* on Dec. 15, 1908.
this
Mis. 310–21 send in their petitions to this *e·*
Un. 38–26 the popular views to this *e·*
took
Mis. 383– 4 ordinance took *e·* the same year,

Mis. 46–15 is not cause, but *e·*,
217– 3 *e·* without a cause is inconceivable ;
255– 6 is not cause, but *e·* ;
277–16 through which to *e·* the purposes of
Pul. 45– 5 * can *e·* cures of disease
No. 28– 8 necessary to *e·* this end
Pan. 10–22 other . . . teachers are unable to *e·*.
10–23 the *e·* of God *understood.*
My. 70–12 * The *e·* on all within earshot is
98–15 * announcement to the *e·* that
226– 9 an *e·* of one universal cause,
281–23 * *e·* on the two parties
292–20 *e·* of one human desire or belief
317– 5 * to the *e·* that Mr. Wiggin

effected

Mis. 243–10 *e·* the cure in less than one week.
Man. 46–26 where he has not *e·* a cure.
Un. 11–12 *e·* this change through the
No. 13–22 S. and H. has *e·* a revolution

effecting

Mis. 261–22 *e·* so glorious a purpose.

effective

'02. 18–23 we shall have more *e·* healers
My. 28–25 * it is as *e·* to-day as it was
155– 2 which is *e·* here and now.
233– 5 which prevents an *e·* watch?

effects

action and
Mis. 12–22 The action and *e·* of this
after
Mis. 34– 1 none of the harmful "after *e·*"
all
Mis. 369– 9 cause which governs all *e·*,
architectural
My. 86– 2 * to fine architectural *e·*,
bad
Mis. 69–20 neutralized the bad *e·*
baneful
Mis. 115–28 baneful *e·* of sin
My. 301–22 baneful *e·* of illusion
beautiful
My. 71– 4 * produce the most beautiful *e·*
cause and
My. 212– 8 expose the cause and *e·* of
consider the
Mis. 297–25 consider the *e·*, on himself
damaging
Mis. 43–29 damaging *e·* these leave
deleterious
Un. 8–15 from their deleterious *e·*,
demonstrate over the
My. 233–14 can you demonstrate over the *e·*
harmonious
'02. 8–10 its harmonious *e·* on the sick
its
Mis. 12–27 in its *e·* upon mankind,
208– 5 covers all sin and its *e·*.
352–21 to destroy it and its *e·*.
Pul. 35–26 * the more potent was its *e·*.
Pan. 11– 8 judging a cause by its *e·* ?
'01. 20–21 cannot blot out its *e·* on himself
My. 41– 6 * nor in any wise alter its *e·*
350– 6 human hypothesis, with its *e·*,
natural
My. 205–29 Hence . . . are its natural *e·*.
occasions
Mis. 350–22 occasions *e·* on patients which
of alcohol
My. 212–10 the evil *e·* of alcohol.
of an injury
Ret. 24–12 the *e·* of an injury caused by

effects

of belief
My. 233–12 the *e·* of belief in sin
of Christian Science
Pan. 10– 6 *e·* of C. S. on the lives
of deceit
No. 2–25 cannot avert the *e·* of deceit.
of his delusion
Mis. 15– 3 endure the *e·* of his delusion
of infinite Love
Hea. 4– 5 the *e·* of infinite Love,
of Truth
Mis. 188–17 *e·* of Truth on the material senses ;
My. 103–20 *e·* of Truth on the health,
opposite
Ret. 57–27 such opposite *e·* as good and evil,
My. 292–26 and so to produce opposite *e·*.
physical
(*see* **physical**)
produced
My. 97–29 * *e·* produced by that stupendous
238– 5 *e·* produced by reading the
similar
Rud. 9–19 similar *e·* come from pride,
their
Hea. 18– 1 to destroy their *e·* upon the body,
witness the
Mis. 241–11 and witness the *e·*.

Mis. 222–17 From the *e·* of mental malpractice
My. 107–32 *e·* of calcareous salts

effectual

Mis. 33–30 It is more *e·* than drugs ;
40– 7 as *e·* in destroying sickness
45–17 *e·* in treating moral ailments.
255–25 It is more *e·* than drugs,
263–19 should be met in the most *e·* way.
Ret. 34–14 It is more *e·* than drugs,
80–12 Though the divine rebuke is *e·*
Pul. 87–22 More *e·* than the forum
No. 40–13 but the inaudible is more *e·*.
Pan. 6– 2 more *e·* than all other means ;
Hea. 12–19 made the infinitesimal dose *e·*.

effectually

My. 128–24 as *e·* as does a subtle
238– 2 *Will the Bible, . . . heal as e·*

effervescing

Hea. 18–16 if it could prevent its *e·*

effete

Ret. 12– 4 Are loosed, and not *e·* ;
79–11 ridding the thought of *e·* doctrines,
Po. 61– 2 Are loosed, and not *e·* ;

efficacious

Mis. 97–11 by no means a desirable or *e·* healer.
Man. 15–15 evidence of divine, *e·* Love,

efficacy

Mis. 3–27 their only supposed *e·* is in
89–30 avail himself of the *e·* of Truth,
261–17 atonement of Christ loses no *e·*.
282–22 they believe in the *e·* of
Ret. 83– 5 and the healing *e·* thereof,
87–26 Truth beams with such *e·* as to
Rud. 17– 6 and its divine *e·* to heal.
No. 4–17 and the *e·* of my system,
33–21 the *e·* of divine Life and Love
34– 7 meaning and *e·* of Truth and Love,
37–20 work of Jesus would lose its *e·*
43– 1 if the atonement had lost its *e·*
Peo. 9–19 with full confidence in their *e·*,
My. 90–31 * the *e·* of which to some extent is
284–25 full *e·* of divine Love
352–14 * testimony of the *e·* of our Cause

efficiency

My. 107–18 does not disprove the *e·* of the
107–19 It enhances its *e·*,

efficient

Mis. 126–19 to our *e·* Publishing Society.
'01. 19–13 notion that . . . is wise or *e·*,
My. 4– 6 practice or *e·* teaching of C. S.,
174– 8 courtesy of the *e·* city marshal

efficiently

Man. 79– 6 transact . . . *e·* such business as

effigy

Mis. 61–17 * certainly I saw him, or his *e·*,

effort

Mis. 11–25 general *e·* to benefit the race.
69–23 their *e·* to accomplish this result,
115–25 every *e·* to hurt one will only help
118–27 obedience crowns persistent *e·* with
171– 3 Jesus' first *e·* to realize Truth
230– 2 depends upon persistent *e·*,
234–14 his *e·* to steal from others

effort

Mis.	303–17	e· to help them to obey
Ret.	29– 1	cause a surrender of this e·.
	85–27	crown the e· of to-day
Un.	46–28	The fight was an e· to
Pul.	84–27	* zealous e· on the part of our
Rud.	9–22	without a direct e·,
No.	8– 4	To this small e· let us add
	9–13	whereas you may err in e·,
'02.	1– 4	With no special e· to achieve this
	12–25	united e· to purchase more land
My.	7– 8	united e· to purchase more land
	9–14	* the e· for righteous reform,
	25– 3	* making a special e·
	47–19	* showed a forward e· into the
	55–16	* This e· of Mrs. Eddy was
	130– 7	e· of disloyal students to
	164– 2	knowing that such an e· would
	312–16	* one e· at self-support.
	332– 6	* for so noble an e· in behalf of

efforts

Mis.	139–29	e· in the interest of C. S.,
	236–26	in one's e· to help another,
	245– 8	The combined e· of the
	249–21	e· of some malignant students,
Ret.	5–28	* untiring in her e· to
	27–14	* to express in feeble diction
	38– 5	e· to persuade him to finish
	71–27	Secret mental e· to obtain help
	87–10	unsettled and spasmodic e·.
Rud.	3– 4	obstinate resistance to all e·
No.	45–11	such e· arise from a spiritual lack,
Hea.	14–13	and his e· are salutary ;
Po.	32–17	health may my e· repay ;
My.	28–10	* a hint of the unselfish e·,
	42–28	* how untiring are her e·,
	48–15	* appreciation of her e·
	52–10	* will make greater e·
	55– 4	* e· were made to obtain
	62–30	* freely of their time and e·
	84–15	* for the other architectural e·
	93– 3	* without e· at proselytizing ;
	166– 2	e· to be great will never
	195–25	e· to build an edifice
	224–27	speak in loving terms of their e·,
	284– 2	honest e· (however meagre)
	304– 6	* e· are being made to buy

effulgence

Mis.	336–25	wherever one ray of its e·
My.	262–19	afford little divine e·,

egg

Hea.	19–13	Which is first, the e· or the bird?

Ego

Un.	48–16	His creation is not the E·,
	48–17	but the reflection of the E·.
	48–17	The E· is God Himself,
	51–20	The E· is divine consciousness,
	51–22	The E· is revealed as Father,

ego

Mis.	196– 1	e· is found not in matter
	196–25	the e· does arise to
	363– 4	"e·" that claims selfhood in error,
	363– 5	is no e·, but is simply
	375– 3	What is the material e·,
Un.	44–13	This abortive e·, this fable of
	45–11	evil e·, and his assumed power,
	45–24	evil e· has but the visionary
	46–20	evil was even more the e· than
	46–22	evil e· they believed must extend
	46–24	This e· was in the earthquake,
	52–16	God is not the so-called e· of evil ;
No.	26–17	Man's real e·, or selfhood, is
'02.	8–23	the e·, or I, goes to the Father,
Peo.	5–23	The e· is not self-existent

egoism

Un.	27– 8	E· is a more philosophical word,

egoist

Un.	27–10	An e·, therefore, is one

egoistic

Un.	26– 1	Evil. . . . and matter is e·,
	27–14	while God is e·, knowing only His

egotism

Mis.	209–29	e· and false charity say,
	224– 3	our e· that feels hurt by
	319–10	are beset with e· and hypocrisy.
Un.	27– 6	E· implies vanity and self-conceit.
'00.	8–17	is always e· and animality.

egotist

Un.	27– 6	e· is one who talks much of himself.
	45–10	e· must come down and learn,

egotistic

Ret.	74– 6	sense of corporeality, or e· self.
Un.	27–13	we shall find that evil is e·,

egotistical

Mis.	265–14	e· theorist or shallow moralist
Ret.	73–24	violent and e· personality,
	74– 2	a perpetually e· sensibility.

egregious

'01.	19–15	e· nonsense — a flat departure

Egypt

Mis.	374–26	* "Helen's beauty in a brow of E·."
Hea.	11–12	like the great pyramid of E·,
My.	127–16	rods of the magicians of E·.

Egyptians

My.	43– 1	* from the bondage of the E·,

eider-down

Pul.	76–16	* entirely of skins of the e· duck,

eight

Mis.	7– 6	busier than the mother of e·.
	341–23	a little girl of e· years,
Man.	61–24	about e· or nine minutes
Ret.	8– 3	when I was about e· years old,
Pul.	26–12	* silver lamps, e· feet in height.
	33– 3	* When e· years of age she began,
	62– 9	* not more than five by e· feet.
My.	16–13	* at e· o'clock in the forenoon.
	69– 2	* the e· bronze chains,
	323–32	* We were at that time some e· days
		(see also **numbers**)

eighteen

Mis.	81–12	Are not the last e· centuries
	165– 2	more than e· centuries ago,
	182–32	more than e· centuries ago.
	321– 4	than e· centuries ago ;
Ret.	5–10	e· miles from Concord,
Pul.	69– 3	* about e· months ago.
My.	52–20	* E· years ago, the Rev. . . . Wiggin,
		(see also **dates**)

eighteenth

Ret.	2–19	seventeenth and e· centuries.

eighth

Pul.	78– 5	* an e· of an inch thick.
My.	305–19	* e· in a list of twenty-two

eighties

'02.	15– 1	In the e·, anonymous letters

eighty

(see **values**)

eighty-four

(see **numbers**)

eighty-second

Mis.	225– 4	e· birthday of his mother

eighty-seven

My.	272–25	* nearly e· years of age,

eighty-six

My.	271–14	* at e· years of age

eighty-two

My.	68– 9	* a diameter of e· feet

either

Mis.	14– 6	e· to the origin or ultimate
	40–30	nullify e· the disease itself or
	47–29	what one accepts as e· useful or
	55–30	e· a godless and material Mind, or
	67–14	shalt not utter a lie, e· mentally or
	78–11	e· Euclid or the Science of Mind
	78–12	never dreamed that e· of these
	83– 9	e· your own thought or another's."
	86–12	They e· mean formations of
	93–28	cannot go unpunished e· here or
	103–22	the human, e· as mind or body,
	105–21	If e· is misunderstood or maligned,
	105–27	has no right e· to be pitied or to
	107–32	e· too much or too little of sin.
	119–18	not an argument e· for pessimism or
	123– 5	it is e· idolizing something
	132–28	e· Dr. Cullis or Mrs. Eddy,
	214–27	e· in the recognition or
	218–16	e· as mind or matter ;
	219–17	remove this feeling in e· case,
	221–14	E· of these states of mind
	241–12	E· he will hate you,
	242– 7	one thousand dollars if e·
	242– 9	two thousand dollars if e·
	250– 4	e· as a quality or as an entity?
	257– 1	e· excludes God from the universe, or
	257– 8	e· a moral or an immoral force.
	261–29	one will e· abandon his claim
	268–29	e· vacillating good or
	269– 7	e· he will hate the one, — Matt. 6 : 24.
	293–25	makes mortals e· saints or sinners.
	309– 2	e· as good or evil.

either

Mis.	315– 7	*e·* in private or in public assemblies,
	318–27	seem *e·* too large or too little :
	319–13	*e·* be overcoming sin in themselves,
	335–19	*e·* willing participants in wrong,
	352–23	*e·* get out of himself and into God
	353– 4	*e·* an excess of action or
	364–23	*e·* cooperate or quarrel
	364–29	This error, . . . would *e·* extinguish God
	374–23	*e·* doggedly deny or
	382– 1	*e·* a truism or a rule,
Man.	28–20	*e·* to resign his place or
	28–22	failing to do *e·*, said officer shall
	43– 9	Whatever is requisite for *e·* is
	51–12	*e·* withdraw from the Church or
	54–20	*e·* by word or work,
	66–26	*e·* to the Boards or to the
	92–13	*e·* one, not both, should teach
	112– 4	*e·* capitalized (The), or small
Ret.	64–18	*e·* in Principle or practice.
	78– 3	*e·* too much or too little.
	82–23	their examples *e·* excel or fall short
Pul.	26–11	* with a lamp stand . . . on *e·* end,
	29–28	* persons who had *e·* been
	80–20	* *e·* to praise or blame,
Rud.	5–15	*e·* mind which is called matter, or
	5–27	*e·* become non-existent, or
No.	3– 5	error murders *e·* friend or foe
	23–26	through the person of *e·*.
'01.	4– 1	Love as *e·* divine Principle or
	6–11	*e·* of three persons as one
	6–29	That God is *e·* inconceivable, or
	13–17	*e·* because he fears it or loves it.
	14–19	To conceive of error as *e·* right or
	19–13	*e·* in medicine or in religion,
	20– 7	to harm *e·* man or beast.
	23– 8	evil must *e·* exist in good, or
	33–30	*e·* by their practice or by
'02.	2–26	*e* in heart or in doctrine ;
Hea.	9–10	has not saved them from *e·*,
	9–24	*e·* an error of mind or of body.
	13– 3	accomplish less on *e·* side.
My.	30– 2	* *e·* coming from a service or
	69–16	* two on *e·* side
	71–25	* *e·* on floor or galleries,
	82– 2	* *e·* through a cure to themselves or
	106– 2	I admonish . . . Scientists *e·* to
	114–32	these progressive steps *e·* written or
	143–14	fustian of *e·* denying or asserting
	144– 7	*e·* of the aforesaid conditions
	146–25	*e·* in the right or in the wrong
	216–11	*E·* his life must be a miracle
	218–23	belief that an individual can *e·*
	223–18	*e·* of which I do not entertain.
	225–24	*e·* in speaking or in writing,
	259– 3	on *e·* side lace and flowers.
	259–23	considered *e·* collectively or
	275–19	*E·* my work, . . . or the weather,
	276– 6	judged by *e·* a daily drive or
	302– 5	produces the result in *e·* case.
	356–22	*e·* he will hate the one, — *Matt.* 6: 24.

ejaculated

Pul.	49–13	* "Four years !" she *e·* ;

ejection

My.	222–30	will aid the *e·* of error,

elaborate

Un.	52–22	*e·* in beauty, color, and form,
Pul.	56–10	* Space does not admit of an *e·*
My.	66–21	* *e·* observances of Sunday,
	68–26	* with *e·* plaster work

elaborately

Pul.	76–12	* special designs, *e·* carved,

elaborates

Mis.	13–14	theology *e·* the proposition

elaborating

Mis.	38–22	*e·* a man-made theory,

elapsed

Mis.	297– 1	short time that has *e·* since
Man.	39–10	when sufficient time has *e·*

elastic

Pul.	32–21	* *e·* bearing of a woman of thirty,

elate

Po.	39–16	be your waiting hearts *e·*,

elbow

Mis.	32–28	should never envy, *e·*, slander,

elbowed

Mis.	80–28	*e·* by a new school of practitioners,

elbowing

Mis.	294– 3	*e·* the concepts of his own creating,
	339–12	The *e* of the crowd

elders

Pul.	vii– 5	*e·* of the twentieth century,
'00.	12–12	the Ephesian *e·* travelled to
My.	38–20	* not a whit behind their *e* ,
	261– 4	The wisdom of their *e·*,
	340–19	Not the tradition of the *e·*,

eldritch

Mis.	376–21	with an acre of *e·* ebony.

elect

Mis.	78–16	if possible, the very *e·*.
	175–20	the very *e·*," — *Matt.* 24: 24.
	302–22	When I should so *e·*
	314– 6	shall *e·* two Readers :
Man.	79– 2	Directors shall *e·* annually
	80–19	but if she does not *e·* to
	86–11	can *e·* an experienced
	102– 7	This committee shall *e·*,
Ret.	14– 7	to have *e·* believers converted
	90–10	"the *e·* lady" — *II John* 1 : 1.
My.	17–15	corner stone, — *I Pet.* 2: 6.
	229–30	should be happier than the *e·*.

elected

Mis.	296– 2	have allowed myself to be *e·*
Man.	18–20	were *e·* members of this Church,
	18–21	others that have since been *e·*
	25– 9	The President shall be *e·*,
	26– 7	or new officers *e·*,
	26–13	Readers shall be *e·*
	26–16	its candidates before they are *e·* ;
	38–11	*e·* by majority vote
	63–21	*e·* by the C. S. Board of Directors,
	81– 1	or new officers *e·*,
	88–11	vice-president shall be *e·* annually
	88–13	teacher shall be *e·* every third year
	89– 8	*e·* to fill the vacancy.
	93– 6	members of which shall be *e·* annually
	97– 9	He shall be *e·* annually
	99–17	Committee . . . is *e·* only by
	100–24	*e·* by the branch church.
	100–27	suitable woman shall be *e·*.
Ret.	6–25	soon *e·* to the Legislature
Pul.	45–30	* *e·* each year by the congregation.

electing

Man.	56–19	*e·* officers and other business,
	56–22	meetings for *e·* candidates
My.	49–17	* for the purpose of *e·* officers.

election

Man.	25– 3	NAMES, *e·*, AND DUTIES.
	25–13	eligible for *e·* but once in
	26– 5	dating from the time of *e·*
	29–20	*E·*
	37–15	RECOMMENDATION AND *e·*.
	38– 9	*E·*.
	80–25	dating from the time of *e·*
	88–10	*E·*.
	93– 4	*E·*.
	100– 2	for the *e·* of officers,
Ret.	7– 4	before his *e·*.
	13– 6	doctrine of unconditional *e·*,
Peo.	3– 6	the *e·* of the minority to be saved
My.	310– 8	died before the *e·*.

electric

Pul.	25– 5	* systems with motor *e·* power.
	26– 2	* *e·* lights in the form of a star,
	58–30	* *e·* light, behind an antique
	62–11	* rung from an *e·* keyboard,
My.	219–12	to ride to church on an *e·* car,

electrical

My.	110–13	*e·* forces annihilating time and

electricity

Mis.	257–22	*E·*, governed by this so-called law,
	366–22	drugs, *e·*, and animal magnetism
	378–17	"Because it conveys *e·* to them."
	379–14	*e·* was not as potential or
Ret.	33– 8	homœopathy, hydropathy, *e·*, and
Pul.	25– 3	* are done by *e·*,
	64–17	* allopathy, homœopathy, and *e·*,
My.	307– 8	nothing to do with matter, *e·*, or
	345–10	* *e·*, engineering, *che* telephone,
	348– 3	*e·*, magnetism, or will-power,

elects

Peo.	8– 4	*e·* some to be saved and others to be

elegant

Mis.	280–20	*e·* album costing fifty dollars,
Pul.	76– 8	* floor is of mosaic in *e·* designs,
	76–22	chapter sub-title
	77– 3	* one of the most chastely *e·*
	86–12	* encased in an *e·* plush box.
My.	66–21	* spacious and *e·* edifice

element

animal

Mis.	281– 3	doors that this animal *e·* flings open

element
divine
Mis. 337–21 they obscure its divine *e*·,
essential
Pul. 53–20 * the essential *e*· of success
great
Peo. 1– 3 The great *e*· of reform
lost
Mis. 252–25 restores its lost *e*·,
Man. 17–13 its lost *e*· of healing.
My. 46–12 its lost *e*· of healing."
magnetic
'01. 2– 9 the fatal magnetic *e*·
male
My. 355–11 The male *e*· is a strong
material
Hea. 3–10 the personal and material *e*·
misnamed matter
Mis. 201– 4 resolves the *e*· misnamed matter
mortal
Mis. 2–28 out of evil, their mortal *e*·,
no
Mis. 152–27 there enters no *e*· of earth
My. 180–12 no *e*· whatever of hypnotism
no insignificant
My. 91–13 * no insignificant *e*· in true
of action
Peo. 10– 2 the stronger *e*· of action ;
of brute-force
Mis. 40–32 An *e*· of brute-force that
of error
Un. 58– 3 their native *e*· of error,
of matter
Mis. 201– 7 death is an *e*· of matter,
of personality
Pul. 37–14 * eliminate the *e*· of personality
opposing
'01. 31 - 3 The only opposing *e*· that
My. 293–22 possessed no opposing *e*·,
raging
My. 249– 6 raging *e*· of individual hate
religious
Mis. 145– 3 when the religious *e*·,
spiritual
Ret. 65– 7 which freeze out the spiritual *e*·.

My. 278–30 an *e*· opposed to Love,
elementary
Mis. 260–18 *e*· opposite to Him who
My. 181– 5 are aided . . . with *e*· truths,
elements
animal
My. 245–14 Towards the animal *e*·
angry
Mis. 162– 9 stem these rising angry *e*·,
certain
'00. 10–11 Certain *e*· in human nature
conflicting
My. 134– 9 conflicting *e*· must be mastered.
counteracting
My. 294– 9 mental counteracting *e*·,
English
Ret. 1–19 Scotch and English *e*·
grosser
Peo. 2– 7 yields its grosser *e*·,
its own
Mis. 268–30 error dies of its own *e*·.
jarring
'00. 11– 6 jarring *e*· among musicians
material
Mis. 3–24 material *e*· of sin and death.
Ret. 60–17 raging of the material *e*·
Peo. 1– 5 crumbling away of material *e*·
of all forms
Mis. 101–32 comprise the *e*· of all forms
of earth
Mis. 9– 8 refuge at last from the *e*· of earth.
383–10 *e*· of earth beat in vain against
of evil
Mis. 40–27 has to master those *e*· of evil
pent-up
Mis. 356– 5 pent-up *e*· of mortal mind
self-destroying
Un. 52–19 self-destroying *e*· of this world,
spiritual
Mis. 2–30 putting on the spiritual *e*·
such
Ret. 65–17 constituted of such *e*· as
My. 201–11 Such *e*· of friendship, faith, and
these
'00. 10–15 These *e*· assail even the new-old
waits on the
Mis. 330–32 patient corn waits on the *e*·

Un. 25–24 *e*· which belong to the eternal All,

elevate
Mis. 5– 1 will *e*· and purify the race.
38– 4 *e*· man in every line of life,
Hea. 5–26 purify, *e*·, and consecrate man ;
elevated
Ret. 5–25 * She gave an *e*· character to
93– 6 Science has *e*· this idea
My. 255– 9 *e*· to offices for which they are not
elevates
Pul. 53–18 * attribute of mind which *e*· man
Po. 39–13 The cause she *e*·.
My. 130–13 the lever which *e*· mankind.
260–24 *e*· medicine to Mind ;
elevating
Mis. 3– 1 *e*· the race physically, morally,
Pan. 6–26 It is plain that *e*· evil to the
Peo. 2–27 a benign and *e*· influence
My. 278–19 *e*· power of civilization
elevation
Ret. 88–11 an *e*· of the understanding
My. 86– 6 brooding *e*·, guarding as it were,
elevator
Mis. 259–23 spiritual *e*· of the human race,
My. 288– 8 *e*· of the human race ;
eleven
Pul. 72–16 * "And for the past *e*· years,"
(*see also* **numbers, values**)
elicit
Mis. 295– 2 deserve and *e*· brief comment.
eligibility
Man. 30– 1 E·.
89–23 furnish evidence of their *e*·
eligible
Man. 25–13 *e*· for election but once in
39–13 *e*· to probationary membership
72– 7 is *e*· to form a church
74–15 In order to be *e*· to a card in *The*
79–12 Before being *e*· for office
89–16 *e*· to receive the degree of C.S.D.
89–23 *e*· to enter the Normal class.
109– 4 *e*· to approve candidates
109– 6 No persons are *e*· to countersign
My. 251–13 *e*· to enter the Normal class,
251–21 if found *e*·, receive a certificate
Elijah
'02. 16– 1 came to E· after the earthquake
eliminate
Pul. 37–14 * to *e*· the element of personality
My. 208–16 will *e*· divorce and war.
eliminated
Mis. 218–26 neither *e*· nor retained by Spirit.
259–11 not a quality to be known or *e*· by
My. 268–30 sex or gender *e*· ;
eliminates
Un. 56–12 first *e*· and then destroys.
Elisha
Mis. 134–23 Like E·, look up, and behold :
Elite
Pul. 89–27 * E·, Chicago, Ill.
Elizabeth's, Queen
No. 44–13 In Queen E· time Protestantism could
Ellen
Po. page 65 poem
elm
My. 147– 6 old *e*· on North State Street
elms
Pul. 49–15 "Look at those big *e*· !
63–11 * pointed to a number of large *e*·
My. 174– 4 The wide-spreading *e*·
elocutionist
Pul. 43–11 * Mrs. . . . Bemis, a distinguished *e*·,
59–18 * read by a professional *e*·,
Elohim
Mis. 182–25 eternal heritage of the E·,
eloping
My. 314–20 for *e*· with his wife,
eloquence
Mis. 345– 6 immortal strains of *e*·.
Hea. 2–24 it was not in the power of *e*·
My. 90– 4 * wooed by no *e*· of orator
247–21 not so much *e*· as
eloquent
Mis. 101– 1 feeble lips are made *e*·,
Ret. 15–21 memorable by *e*· addresses
Pul. 1–10 time *improved* is *e*· in God's
46– 1 * that Judge Hanna was so *e*·
My. 262–28 *e*· silence, prayer, and praise
316–16 *e*· appeal to the press

eloquently
Pul. 5–18 Then *e·* paraphrasing it,
My. 46– 4 * *e·* beckoning us on

else
Mis. 9–21 *e·*, the contents of this cup of
12–27 Whatever manifests aught *e·*
63–20 none *e·* beside Him,"— *Deut.* 4: 35.
64–16 are narrow, *e·* extravagant,
70– 1 *e·* the Scriptures misstate man's power.
97–19 and there is none *e·*,— *Isa.* 45: 5.
128– 1 *e·* it grows hard and
130–10 for a fault in somebody *e·*,
141–27 or *e·* return every dollar that
178–20 * 'Much learning' — or something *e·*
192–31 *e·* we are entertaining the startling
211– 6 *e·* the blind will lead the blind
236– 5 little *e·* than the troubles,
236–29 doing our duty, whatever *e·* may
241–14 *e·* he will doubtingly await the result ;
260–20 Then, whatever *e·* seemeth to be
261–30 or *e·* make the claim valid.
265– 4 or wiser than somebody *e·*,
266–11 work that nobody *e·* can or will do.
269– 7 *e·* he will hold to— *Matt.* 6: 24.
276– 4 like all *e·*, was purely Western
319– 6 aught *e·* than good.
319–15 *e·* they are self-deceived sinners
329–18 Whatever *e·* droops, spring is gay :
365–30 more than all *e·*,
367–19 if He did know aught *e·*,
Man. 43–12 as no one *e·* can.
Ret. 23– 4 or *e·* be merged into the
28– 5 *e·* we cannot understand the
30–21 No one *e·* can drain the cup
48– 3 Who *e·* could sustain this institute,
56–21 Whatever *e·* claims to be mind,
81–18 or *e·* that heart is consciously untrue
82–23 consummate much good or *e·* evil ;
Un. 19– 4 *e·* He is not omnipotent,
19–10 *e·* how could it have come
21– 3 *e·* excusing one another."— *Rom.* 2: 15.
38–16 but that something *e·* also is
53–22 or *e·* he has lost his true
53–24 *e·* the immortal and unerring
Pul. 33–22 * no one *e·* had seen him,
Rud. 12– 7 *e·* quiet the fear of the sick
13–15 none *e·* beside Him."— *Deut.* 4: 35.
16–27 or *e· post mortem* evidence.
No. 27–28 *e·* their present mistakes would
Pan. 9– 4 no reality in aught *e·*.
'00. 9–14 misguide action, *e·* they uplift
9–29 no one *e·* has seemed equal to
'01. 4–15 *divine,* . . . *e·* there is no Science
'02. 7–16 than which there is naught *e·*.
20–22 but in this, as all *e·*,
Hea. 15–19 everything *e·* besides God,
19– 5 *e·* those functions could not
Peo. 2–17 *e·* of wood or stone.
6–27 for which we are to leave all *e·*.
My. 10–22 * on the part of some one *e·*.
37– 4 * Naught *e·* than the grandeur
90– 7 * Whatever *e·* it is, this faith
96–10 * dominates everything *e·*.
130–31 that you borrow little *e·*
152–18 than which there is none *e·*
153–19 Faith in aught *e·* misguides
178–31 all *e·* reported as his sayings
197–18 * C. S. will disappear
231–18 *e·* love's labor is lost
340–26 example in this, as in all *e·*,
347–19 in exchange for all *e·*.
356–23 *e·* he will hold to the one,— *Matt.* 6 : 24.
(see also **nothing**)

elsewhere
Mis. 127– 9 Scientists, here and *e·*,
178–24 * *to* preach, here or *e·*.''
290–24 and it should not, . . . dwell *e·*,
My. 18– 5 Scientists, here and *e·*,
74– 7 * from New York and *e·*
98–22 * in this country or *e·*,
120– 3 or *e·* than in my writings,
177– 7 daily duties require attention *e·*,
243–16 students in New York and *e·*

elucidate
Mis. 47–13 tend to *e·* your day-dream,
159– 3 to *e·* His Word.
269–11 *e·* the Principle of being,
380– 9 to enable me to *e·* or
Man. 87–16 *e·* the Principle and rule of C. S.,
Ret. 83– 1 *e·* scientific healing and teaching.
Un. 29–22 Often we can *e·* the
Rud. 13–17 *e·* my meaning.
'02. 16–25 fail to *e·* Christianity :

elucidates
Mis. 261– 8 C. S. not only *e·* but
309–26 ''S. and H. . . . *e·* this topic.
361–28 He *e·* His own idea,
Rud. 16–21 *e·* a pathological Science
'02. 8– 1 *e·* Christianity, illustrates God,
My. 251–25 What God gives, *e·*, armors, and

elucidation
'01. 31– 1 by a clear *e·* of truth,
My. 241– 4 * *e·* of the Principle and rule of

eluding
Un. 64–12 *e·* their dread presence

emanate
Rud. 11–24 whence *e·* health, harmony, and

emanates
Mis. 16–24 *e·* from Soul instead of body,

emanating
Rud. 6– 7 beauty and goodness . . . *e·* from God ;
No. 1– 2 spiritual idea *e·* from the infinite,
My. 29–19 * *e·* from the thousands who
154–24 *e·* from the pulpit and press.

emanation
'01. 10– 8 a spiritual, divine *e·*,
My. 226–10 an *e·* of the one . . . Principle

emancipate
Mis. 385–14 Spirit *e·* for this far shore
Po. 48– 7 Spirit *e·* for this far shore
My. 267–27 whereby soul is *e·*

emancipating
My. 190– 4 *e·* it with the morning beams

emancipation
Pul. 55–10 * *e·* from many of the thraldoms,
Peo. 10–23 *e·* of our bodies from sickness
My. 74–25 * springs from a belief in such *e·*.
248–13 adequate for the *e·* of the race.

emasculation
Mis. 206–14 no *e·*, no illusive vision,

embark
My. 132–10 knows they *e·* for infinity

embarrass
My. 118–15 *e·* the higher criticism.

embarrassing
My. 312–14 * position was an *e·* one.

embellishing
My. 162–14 building, *e·*, and furnishing

emblazoned
No. 2– 1 on its standard have *e·*
My. 194–17 *e·* on the fair escutcheon
341– 4 *e·* on the escutcheon

emblem
Mis. 162–11 the cross became the *e·*
357–12 no central *e·*, no history.
Un. 57– 9 The cross is the central *e·*
'00. 13–19 the *e·* of Æsculapius.

emblematic
Pul. 27–14 * *e·* of the six water-pots
28– 6 * decorated with *e·* designs,

emblems
My. 326–17 the *e·* of a master Mason,

embodied
Mis. 34–30 Science of healing *e·* in her works.
Pul. 38–20 * between the *e·* and disembodied
'00. 8– 2 behold more nearly the *e·* Christ,
My. 154–25 *e·* in a visible communion,
285–15 *e·* in the Association for

embodies
Mis. 191– 2 The Hebrew *e·* the term
Un. 39–24 and *e·* Life, not death.
'01. 12–26 Incorporeal evil *e·* itself

embodiment
Mis. 61–28 Naming these His *e·*,
Un. 3–23 every *e·* of Life and Mind.
Pan. 5–21 nor believe that it hath *e·*
'00. 7–24 so far from the *e·* of Truth
'01. 13– 4 annihilates its own *e·* :
Peo. 5– 4 the *e·* of a living faith;
My. 130–29 *e·* and substance of the truth

embodiments
Mis. 61–26 mortals are the *e·* . . . of error,

embody
No. 4–19 because they *e·* not the idea

embodying
My. 10– 9 * *e·* the best of design,

embound
Po. 29–13 Beloved, replete, by flesh *e·*

embrace

Mis.	392– 7	earth, asleep in night's *e*·,
	400– 2	Slumbers not in God's *e*· ;
Pul.	16–14	Slumbers not in God's *e*· ;
	66–10	* most of those who *e*· the faith
Pan.	8–24	doctrines that *e*· pantheism,
Po.	20–10	earth, asleep in night's *e*·,
	76–13	Slumbers not in God's *e*· ;
My.	332–12	* fond *e*· of her friends.
	342–21	It will *e*· all the churches,

embraced

Mis.	103–30	individuality is *e*· in Mind,
Ret.	43–15	*e*· the teachings of C. S.,
	75–17	*e*· in the author's own mental mood,
Un.	6–18	as is *e*· in the theory of

embraces

Mis.	2–15	*e*· a deeper and broader philosophy
'02.	4–13	My subject to-day *e*· the

embracing

My.	86– 6	* *e*· as it may be, the hosts of

embroidery

Mis.	159–28	rich devices in *e*·, silver, gold,

embryo

Mis.	15–26	In mortal . . . goodness seems in *e*·.

embryo-man

Mis.	186– 5	Soul is supposed to enter the *e*·

emerald

Mis.	354 31	To gaze on the lark in her *e*· bower
Po.	18– 9	To gaze on the lark in her *e*· bower
	30– 3	new-born beauty in the *e*· sky,
My.	150–16	willowy banks dyed with *e*·.

emerge

'01.	10–27	we *e*· gently into Life everlasting.

emerged

Ret.	88– 8	*e*· into a higher manifestation of
No.	20–24	*e*· from the ark,

emergencies

Mis.	5–14	do not fail in the greatest *e*·.
	41–28	is sufficient for all *e*·.
Man.	78–16	E·.

emergency

Mis.	283–12	if no *e*· demanded this.

emerges

My.	200–16	man *e*· from mortality

emerging

My.	273– 7	* *e*· triumphantly from all attacks
	307–26	*e*· from *materia medica*,

Emeritus

(see **Eddy, Pastor Emeritus**)

Emerson (see also **Emerson's**)

Ralph Waldo

Ret.	37–13	David Hume, Ralph Waldo *E*·,
My.	306– 7	for such was Ralph Waldo *E*· ;

Un.	17– 4	*E*· says, "Hitch your wagon to a

Emerson's

Ralph Waldo

My.	305– 4	Ralph Waldo *E*· philosophy

eminence

Pul.	32–20	* achieved *e*· as a lawyer.

eminent

Mis.	169–18	most *e*· divines of the world
	346– 4	spiritual healing as *e*· proof
No.	23–14	The most *e*· divines, in Europe

eminently

My.	97–17	* good-looking, *e*· respectable,

emissaries

My.	213– 7	by no means a right of . . . its *e*·.

emit

No.	16–17	because it has no darkness to *e*·.
'00.	8– 7	odors *e*· characteristics of

emits

Mis.	290–29	it *e*· light because it reflects ;

emitting

Chr.	53–40	Life, . . . *E*· light !
My.	282–15	to all mankind a light *e*· light.
	301– 2	from Light *e*· light.

emoluments

Mis.	44– 3	are not working for *e*·,

emotion

My.	26–12	imagine my gratitude and *e*·

emotionalism

My.	vii–12	* untainted by the *e*· which

emotions

Mis.	291–31	his *e*· and conclusions.
Ret.	11– 2	Poetry suited my *e*· better
	79–18	If beset with misguided *e*·,

emotions

My.	296–27	its *e*·, motives, and object.
	332– 5	* *e*· of the thankful heart,

emperor

Mis.	224– 8	The *e*· lifted his hands to his head,
'01.	30–23	no *e*· is obeyed like the

Emperor Augustus

'00.	12–10	in the time of the Roman *E*· *A*·.

emperors

My.	112–29	palaces of *e*· and kings,

emphasis

Mis.	312–26	reverberate and renew its *e*·
Pul.	57–10	* truths which will find *e*·

emphasize

My.	113–29	*e*· the answer to this
	291–20	*e*· humane power, and

emphasized

Ret.	9–7	and *e*· her affirmation.
	13–13	theology *e*· belief in a
Pul.	73–18	* When seen yesterday she *e*·
My.	170– 9	*e*· in the minds of all present

emphasizes

Pul.	33–15	* which history not infrequently *e*·,
'02.	7–28	*e*· the apostle's declaration,

emphasizing

Mis.	116–13	*e*· its grand strains,

emphatic

Mis.	192–25	last chapter of Mark is *e*· on this
Pul.	59–19	* in a clear *e*· style.
Rud.	2–26	*e*· purpose of C. S. is the
	3–10	His history is *e*· in our hearts,
My.	12–17	This was an *e*· rule of St. Paul :

emphatically

Un.	31– 9	as *e*· as they annihilated sin.
Pul.	80– 8	* Boston is *e*· the women's paradise.
'01.	3 13	Also, we accept God, *e*·, in the
My.	14–18	* *e*· pronounced the story a
	256– 5	*e*· phrasing strict observance

empire

Mis.	14–19	evil's umpire and *e*·,
Po.	15–14	I would live in their *e*·,

Empire City

My.	243– 8	The *E*· *C*· is large,

(see also **New York**)

empires

Mis.	268–27	From lack of moral strength *e*· fall.
Peo.	2–19	Such a theory has overturned *e*·
My.	162– 9	stronger than the might of *e*·.

empirical

Mis.	234–15	*E*· knowledge is worse than useless :

employ

Mis.	25–30	why did not Jesus *e*· them
	78–17	that some people *e*· the
	89– 1	when you *e*· the other.
	270–11	To seek or *e*· other means
Man.	41–11	*e*· no violent invective,
	67–11	shall not *e*· an attorney,
	70– 4	a Christian Scientist in the *e*· of
Ret.	85– 6	at present they can *e*·
No.	10– 1	I *e*· this awe-filled word
	42– 6	and *e*· material forms to
Hea.	14–10	If you *e*· a medical practitioner,
My.	128–15	man's right . . . to *e*· a physician,

employed

Mis.	49– 7	friends *e*· a homœopathist,
	75–16	this term should seldom be *e*·
	91–17	*e*· in the service of C. S.
	95–20	no human agencies were *e*·,
	184–29	He *e*· a type of physical
	191–20	The term, being here *e*· in its
Man.	69–22	Students *e*· by Mrs. Eddy
Ret.	21– 5	Every means . . . was *e*· to find him,
	37– 3	term *e*· by me to express
	59–14	name . . . if properly *e*·,
Un.	27– 2	*e*· in the foregoing colloquy.
No.	15– 9	commentaries are *e*·
Hea.	9– 4	and *e*· our thoughts more in
	13–20	*e*· Mind as the only curative
My.	307–11	other terms which I *e*·
	317– 9	great mistake to say that I *e*·
	318– 7	I especially *e*· him on

employees

Man.	81– 5	Suitable *E*·.
My.	135–10	personally attended . . . to my *e*·.
	137–14	attended personally . . . to my *e*·.

employing

Mis.	89– 5	*who is e· a regular physician*,
Man.	99–27	church *e*· said Committee.
Ret.	89–23	for *e*· another student to take
Hea.	15– 4	*e*· no other remedy than Truth,

employment
Mis. 118–26 it gives one plenty of e·,
244–16 * the e· of visible agencies
'01. 34– 1 or by preventing the early e· of

employs
Man. 96– 8 paid by the church that e· him.
Pul. 49–29 * She e· a number of men

emporium
'00. 12– 9 especially flourished as an e

empowered
Mis. 235– 3 e· to conquer sin, sickness,

empowers
Mis. 252–28 and e· the business man

Empress of India
My. 289–16 Queen of Great Britain and E· of I·,
289–29 Queen of Great Britain and E· of I·.

emptied
Mis. 168–13 e· of vainglory and vain knowledge,
My. 38–13 * and was e· in twelve,
82–17 * edifice was e· of its crowds
82–22 * would be e· of its twenty thousand
149–18 must be e· before it can be refilled.

emptiness
Ret. 86– 2 to offset boastful e·,

empty
Mis. 93– 1 to e· his students' minds,
Ret. 84–21 to e· his students' minds of error,
Rud. 15–27 as are required to e· and to
Hea. 10–28 Earth's fading dreams are e· streams,
Po. 53–18 To e· summer bowers,
My. 231–23 has not an e· apartment in his

emulate
Mis. 7– 9 we must strive to e·.
My. 131– 9 that we commemorate and would e·,
148–30 to e· the words and the works of

emulation
Mis. 324–14 envy, e·, hatred, wrath,
'02. 18–17 no e·, no deceit, enters into

enable
Mis. ix– 4 * e· a man to dispense with alms."
115–12 May God e· my students
352–20 in order to e· one to destroy it
380– 9 requisite to e· me to elucidate
Ret. 82–22 e· Christian Scientists to
88–12 will e· thought to apprehend
Un. 7–11 to e· me instantaneously to
18–19 which alone e· Me to rebuke,
43–23 e· us to apprehend, or lay hold
No. 15– 6 would e· any one to prove
'00. 5–18 it would e· man to escape
My. 63–14 * e· us better to work out the
66–13 * will e· the church to expand,
71– 3 * e· the organist to produce
150–18 ask God to e· you to reflect God,
317–13 e· me to explain more clearly

enabled
Mis. 30–10 e· man to demonstrate the law of
201–17 e· him to triumph over them,
'01. 29–15 e· them to be grand coworkers
My. 12– 5 * liberal donations which e·
63– 1 * e· to secure the services of
122–17 Has it e· us to know more of the

enables
Mis. 43– 3 e· one to heal cases without
45– 4 e· you to control pain.
49–19 e· man to discern between
125– 7 This knowledge e· him to
352–17 e· the practitioner to act
369– 7 e· us to stand erect
Pan. 11–23 God e· us to know that
'00. 5–27 e· one to utilize the power of
Hea. 15– 9 it e· mind to govern matter,
My. 5–19 e· the devout Scientist to worship,
39–28 * e· us to comprehend their churches
76–17 * e· them to dedicate their churches
274–13 To begin rightly e· one to end rightly,

enabling
Mis. xi–12 e· him to walk the untrodden
Pul. 40–11 * E· Six Thousand Believers to Attend
My. 161– 2 and set us free by e· us to pay it ;
300– 3 e· the sinner to overcome sin

enact
Peo. 11–19 pass legislative acts and e· penal

enacted
No. 30–11 is punished by the law e·.

enactments
Peo. 11–21 calls its own e· "laws of

encased
Ret. 2–12 sword, e· in a brass scabbard,
Pul. 46–19 * sword, e· in a brass scabbard,

encased
Pul. 77– 5 * e· in a handsome plush casket
78–23 * e· in a white satin-lined box
86–11 * is e· in an elegant plush box.

enchained
Mis. 153–17 and as captives are they e·.
Po. 65– 9 is e· to life's dreary night,

enchant
Po. 68–11 E· deep the senses,

enchanting
Pul. 2–12 sublunary views, however e·,

enchantment
Mis. 394–20 * So full of sweet e· are
Po. 15– 9 Here gloom hath e·
41–21 a strain of e· that flowed
57– 6 * So full of sweet e· are

enchantments
No. 14–11 blends with its magic and e·.

encircle
My. 189–14 e· and cement the human race.

encircles
Mis. 389–13 His arm e· me, and mine,
Po. 4–12 His arm e· me, and mine,

encircling
My. 347–11 design of boughs e· this cup,

enclose
Mis. 157–18 I e· you the name of
My. 289– 4 I e· a check for five hundred

enclosed
Pul. 60–30 * e· in separate swell-box,
My. 26–19 The e· notice I submit to you,
172–25 e· note from Mrs. Eddy was read :
175– 6 Please accept the e· check
327–11 * I know the e· article will

enclosures
My. 326– 2 * e· received from our Leader.

encompass
Ret. 68–20 Darkness and doubt e· thought,

encompassed
Mis. 110–17 when e· by divine presence,
153–15 e· not with pride, hatred,
My. 64– 6 * The glories of . . . e· us,

encompasseth
Mis. 78– 5 brightness of His glory e·

encompassing
'01. 25– 5 e· time and eternity.

encounter
Mis. 210–32 lest it should suffer from an e·.
237–14 must e· and help to eradicate.
'01. 31– 4 opposing element that . . . can e·

encountered
Mis. 131–21 e· in Anno Domini 1894,
Ret. 41– 1 which C. S. e· a quarter-century
50–30 e· in the beginning of pioneer work.
My. 11– 7 * e· the full force of antagonism.

encourage
Mis. 229–13 e· faith in God in this direction,
275–16 e·, and bless all who mourn.
No. 32– 4 pardon may e· a criminal to
Hea. 14– 7 and e· faith in an opposite
My. 217– 4 Further to e· your early,

encouraged
Mis. 348–29 I have by no means e·
Un. 5– 9 Every one should be e· not to
My. 6–16 Greatly impressed and e· thereby,
11–19 * cheered and e· to know that,
132–17 e· the heart of every member
141– 9 * have not been e· to attend the
213– 7 ought not to be e· in it.

encouragement
Mis. 262–27 words of approval and e·
'01. 14–30 evil-doer receives no e· from
My. 62–24 * words of e· when they were so
356–15 I have given no assurance, no e·

encourages
Mis. 252–27 it e· and empowers the business man
302– 4 e· infringement of my copyright,
Ret. 63–24 recollect that it e· sin to say,
My. 123– 7 this e· me to continue to

encouraging
Mis. 262–18 e· the heart grown faint
Rud. 12– 8 e· them in the belief of error

encroachment
Pul. 66–24 * this e· upon prevailing faiths,

encumbered
Mis. 327–15 e· travellers halt and disagree.
360– 3 e· with crude, rude fragments,
Pul. 1– 6 e· with greetings

encumbering
  Mis. 154– 8 prune its *e*· branches,
      205–28 *e*· mortal molecules,

end (noun)
  accomplished its
    Ret. 45– 9 has accomplished its *e*·,
  await the
    My. 222–31 will cheerfully await the *e*·
  beginning or
    Mis. 189–32 Life without beginning or *e*·.
    No. 37–10 He cannot know beginning or *e*·.
    My. 119–25 without beginning or *e*· of days.
  cause and
    Mis. 218–21 notion of Spirit as cause and *e*·,
  certain
    Mis. 71–22 mythical origin and certain *e*·.
  either
    Pul. 26–11 * a lamp stand . . . on either *e*·,
  for the beginning
    Mis. 215–11 if we take the *e*· for the beginning
  gaining the
    Ret. 54–10 gaining the *e*· through persecution
  great
    Mis. 361–17 To this great *e*·, Paul admonished,
  have an
    Hea. 4–18 to become finite, and have an *e*· ;
  his
    My. 333–22 * "His *e*· was calm and peaceful,
  institutional
    My. 8– 5 * outgrowing the institutional *e*·
  in view
    My. 68– 2 * with the *e*· in view of
  is attained
    Mis. 220–14 *e*· is attained, and the patient says
  knows the
    Mis. 208–23 knows the *e*· from the beginning,
  means and
    My. 278– 5 this means and *e*· will be
  no
    My. 267–12 hath no beginning and no *e*·,
  of a cycle
    Pul. 23–22 * assert that the *e*· of a cycle,
  of a rope
    Mis. 61–18 * dangling at the *e*· of a rope.
      61–23 or dangle at the *e*· of a rope?
  of days
    Un. 13–17 or *e*· of days." — *see Heb.* 7 : 3.
    My. 119–25 Life without beginning or *e*· of days.
  of four months
    Ret. 19–17 at the *e*· of four months, my babe
    My. 330–29 at the *e*· of four months, my babe
  of his demonstration
    Mis. 215–28 at the *e*· of his demonstration.
  of idolatry
    My. 220–16 *e*· of idolatry and infidelity,
  of life
    Chr. 55–21 nor *e*· of life ; — *Heb.* 7 : 3.
  of nine days
    My. 335–17 * at the *e*· of nine days he passed away.
  of summer
    My. 61– 8 * completed before the *e*· of summer,
  of that man
    Ret. 42–15 the *e*· of *that* man is — *Psal.* 37 : 37.
  of the period
    Pul. 73–10 * and at the *e*· of the period
  of the service
    My. 32– 3 * communion at the *e*· of the service,
  of the world
    My. 44–12 * unto the *e*· of the world." — *Matt.* 28 : 20.
  pulpit
    Pul. 42–19 * The pulpit *e*· of the auditorium
  put an
    '02. 3– 8 has put an *e*·, at Charleston, to any
    My. 248–10 is to put an *e*· to falsities
  steadfast to the
    Ret. 26– 8 Way-shower, steadfast to the *e*·
  successful
    '02. 14–15 successful *e*· could never have been
  this
    Ret. 21–27 To this *e*·, but only to this *e*·,
      88–15 This *e*· Jesus achieved,
    Pul. 85–15 * chosen of God to this *e*·,
    No. 28– 8 revolutions necessary to effect this *e*·
    My. 10–23 * the money necessary to this *e*·,
      178– 8 it hastens hourly to this *e*·.
  unto the
    Chr. 57– 2 my works unto the *e*·, — *Rev.* 2 : 26.
    Ret. 89–20 and guarded them unto the *e*·,
    No. 7– 8 and continue to do so unto the *e*·.
    My. 44–12 * even unto the *e*· — *Matt.* 28 : 20.
      159– 6 even unto the *e*·." — *Matt.* 28 : 20.
      285–18 my works unto the *e*·, — *Rev.* 2 : 26.
  without
    Chr. 53–39 without birth and without *e*·,
    Un. 40–23 without beginning and without *e*·,

end (noun)
  without
    '02. 7–15 without beginning and without *e*·,
    Hea. 4–20 without beginning and without *e*·.
    Mis. 140– 8 to the *e*· of taxing their faith
      216–20 * beginning with the *e*· of the tail,
      282–23 sometimes . . . *e*· justifies the means ;
    Un. 19–13 this would be the *e*· of infinite
    Pul. 13–19 What must the *e*· be?
    My. 99–25 * and the *e*· is not yet.
      187–11 *e*· of the commandment is — *I Tim.* 1 : 5.
      344–12 preserving individuality . . . to the *e*·.
      345– 6 will overthrow false . . . in the *e*·."

end (verb)
  Mis. vii–11 Till time shall *e*· more timely,
    106–25 praise that shall never *e*·
    113–22 will *e*· in insanity, dementia, or
  Ret. 71–29 will *e*· in destroying health and
  Pul. 3– 3 Can eternity *e*·?
  No. 37– 7 to begin and *e*·,
  My. 166– 2 will never *e*· in anarchy
    204– 8 can begin and never *e*·.
    218–24 false faith that will *e*· bitterly.
    274–13 enables one to *e*· rightly,
    279–18 *e*· wars, and demonstrate
    281–28 War will *e*· when nations are
    296–19 evil will *e*· in harmony,
    350– 4 to *e*· with the phenomenon, matter,

endearing
  Man. 64–17 individual, *e*· term of Mother.
  My. 302–15 *e*· appellative "Mother,"

endeavor
  Mis. 41–15 scales the mountain of human *e*·,
    66–31 I *e*· to accommodate my
    204–27 gives . . . success to *e*·.
    227–11 *e*· to get their weighty stuff
    348–10 divine Love will bless this *e*·
  Man. 49– 2 shall not *e*· to monopolize the
  Ret. 28–29 my *e*·, to be a Christian,
  Un. 10–27 would *e*· to hide from His presence
    50–14 the *e*· to express the underlying
  Pul. 21–12 our Christian *e*· society,
    53–21 * in every field of human *e*·.
  Rud. 12–24 practitioner should also *e*· to
  No. 8– 3 should *e*· to be long-suffering,
    34–16 in the *e*· to crush out
  Pan. 9–17 spiritual *e*· to bless others,
  '02. 13– 1 In this *e*· self was forgotten,
  Hea. 19–17 spiritualize thought, motive, and *e*·.
  My. 42–18 * I shall *e*· to perform this service
    116– 2 *e*· to rise in consciousness
    253– 6 can nerve your *e*·
    282–26 May God guide . . . this good *e*·.
    300– 2 On this basis they *e*· to cast out

endeavored
  Mis. 272–29 I have *e*· to act toward all
  Ret. 52– 1 I have *e*· to find new ways
    73–14 I *e*· to lift thought above
  Pul. 70–10 * who *e*· in vain to find
  Rud. 11–14 has *e*· to take the full price of

endeavoring
  Mis. 311– 4 *e*· to walk with us hand in hand,
  Ret. 30– 2 *e*· to smite error with the
    80–27 by *e*· to influence other minds

endeavors
  Mis. 19–15 wicked *e*· of suppositional demons
    227–14 responsible for kind(?) *e*·.
    266–20 in unison with my own *e*·
    351–18 nor benefit mankind by such *e*·.
    365– 6 their highest *e*· are to Science
  Man. 60–20 Christian *e*· for the living
  Rud. 3– 3 in your *e*· to heal them of
  No. 18–15 highest *e*· are, to divine Science,
  My. 51–31 * appreciation of her earnest *e*·,
    192–29 crowning your *e*·, and
    231– 2 *e*· to bestow her charities
    250– 6 and crowns honest *e*·.
    285– 7 wise *e*· for industrial, civic,

ended
  Mis. 85–25 the warfare is not *e*·
    101–10 *e*· in a contest for the true idea,
    285–17 warfare of sensuality was not then *e*·
  No. 22– 6 Berkeley *e*· his metaphysical theory
  '02. 18–27 *e*· in the downfall of genuine
  My. 30–10 * my modest task will be *e*·.
    110– 2 not to a dispensation now *e*·,
    291–12 and it *e*· with a universal good

ending
  Mis. 47–25 That . . . must have an *e*·.
    167–13 there is no beginning and no *e*·.
    216–21 * and *e*· with the grin,
  Ret. 59– 6 without beginning or *e*·.

ending
Ret. 60– 2 apart from God, beginning and e·,
'02. 1– 7 during the year e· June, 1902,
Peo. 2–24 Life without beginning or e·,
My. 53–26 * the year e· December 7, 1885,
281–22 * on the e· of the war,

endings
My. 123–26 small beginnings have large e·.

endless
Mis. 77–16 it holds man in e· Life
82–17 the e· beatitudes of Being ;
104–10 for individuality is e· in the
399– 5 Midst the glories of one e· day."
Ret. 13–14 in the danger of e· punishment,
Po. 75–12 Midst the glories of one e· day."
My. 202–17 e· hopes, and glad victories
340– 7 fables, and e· genealogies.
350–26 crowned with e· days,

endorse
Man. 36–17 refuse to e· their applications
37– 2 shall not e· nor countersign an
My. 320–18 * did not e· all the statements

endorsed
My. 59–31 * so thoroughly e· or so
351–24 therefore I have not e· it,
354– 4 they claim have been e· by me,

endorsement
Man. 77– 9 and its e· of the bills shall
My. 354– 8 books for which my e· is claimed.

endorsing
Man. 37– 1 E· Applications.

endowed
Mis. 161–16 both human and divinely e·,
161–23 specially e· with the Holy Spirit ;
Un. 31–14 matter, being so e·,
My. 14–21 * e· with genius and inspiration,

endows
Un. 36– 2 e· with the double capacity of
'01. 26–10 in the next he e· it with·
My. 90–11 * nature e· the children of men,

ends
Mis. vii– 6 * I love thee, and behold thy e·
62–25 fails, and e· in a parody
102–30 outmasters it, and e· the warfare.
112–28 it e· in a total loss of
118–29 e· in the fiery punishment of the
122–30 and he e· — with suicide.
137–22 the sublime e· of human life.
168–15 Here e· the colloquy ;
244–16 * visible agencies for specific e·?"
288–31 to promote the e· of temperance ;
347–12 grows indistinct and e·.
358–30 fulfilled all the good e· of
361– 6 miscalled life e· in death,
Ret. 32–16 * Short-lived joy, that e· in sadness,
47–11 promotion of spiritual e·.
69–15 false sense . . . which e· in death"
Pul. 3–13 assurance e· all warfare,
No. 12–20 these are the e· of Christianity.
21–14 for divine means and e·.
'00. 10– 9 Such conflict never e· till
'01. 25–15 e· in some specious folly.
My. 259–29 temporary means and e·.
260–12 with human means and e·,
282– 8 all the e· of the earth." — Isa. 45: 22.

endues
My. 131– 2 and e· with divine power ;

endurance
Mis. 238– 9 silent e· of his love.
My. 227– 8 known by its patience and e·.

endure
Mis. 15– 2 e· the effects of his delusion
192–15 "His name shall e· — Psal. 72: 17.
Un. 23–10 "If ye e· chastening, — Heb. 12: 7.
Pul. 5–10 bravest to e·, firmest to suffer,
My. 52– 3 * many mental hardships to e·,

endured
Mis. 13– 7 e· at the hands of others
169– 9 long years of invalidism she e·
Ret. 22–10 "Consider him that e· — Heb. 12: 3.
22–11 e· the cross, — Heb. 12: 2.
My. 75–22 * discomforts they might have e·
165– 6 e· for the cause of Christ, Truth,
196–20 "Consider him that e· — Heb. 12: 3.
258–15 e· the cross, — Heb. 12: 2.

endures
Mis. 312– 7 e· all piercing for the sake of
Ret. 90–20 e· with her patience,

endureth
Un. 24–17 Spirit is all that e·,
56–26 and e· all things.

endureth
Pul. 7–23 word of the Lord e· — I Pet. 1: 25.
Hea. 10–17 sorrow e· but for the night,
Po. 16– 6 it e· and liveth in love.
My. 158–12 it e· all things ;

enduring
Mis. 117–12 * wit, humor, and e· vivacity
Ret. 21–23 lucid and e· lessons of Love
My. 24–23 * e· character of its construction,
36–29 * stand as an e· monument,
54– 3 * e· the inconvenience
268– 9 affections are e· and achieving.

enemies (see also enemies')
forgiving
Ret. 45–19 forgiving e·, returning good for
friends and
My. 276–13 all her dear friends and e·.
harmless
My. 205–21 and e· harmless.
hates
My. 41–20 * admires friends and hates e·,
his
Mis. 129– 8 forgive his brother and love his e·.
'00. 3–28 revenged himself upon his e·.
My. 4–16 and he loves his e·
270–19 breathing love for his e·,
316– 6 causing man to love his e· ;
its
Mis. 124–26 Love forgiving its e·.
Pan. 9–22 it loves its e·
9–23 and this love benefits its e·
My. 260–22 love loving its e·,
love your
Mis. 8– 8 chapter sub-title
210–32 Love your e·, or you will
mine
Mis. 13– 9 the law of loving mine e·.
my
Mis. 213–14 May my friends and my e·
273–12 God bless my e·,
311–16 go to prove that I love my e·
351– 5 purpose of blessing even my e·,
My. 145–23 my friends and my e·.
220–21 "God bless my e· ;
no
Mis. 9–10 "Thou hast no e·."
10– 4 We have no e·.
10–28 "I have no e·."
of Christian Science
My. 88–27 * stoutest e· of C. S. will confess
297–28 the e· of C. S. are said to be
one's
Mis. 11–24 doing good to one's e·
227–31 one's self upon one's e·,
'02. 17–19 to hate no man, to love one's e·,
My. 204–27 loving one's e·, and overcoming
249– 9 hating even one's e· excludes
our
Mis. 11–18 We must love our e·
Ret. 29– 4 and hold to loving our e·
No. 7– 7 We must love our e·,
Pan. 15– 7 midst of our e·," — see Psal. 23: 5.
My. 132–23 and bless our e·.
their
Mis. 371–21 * "men are known by their e·."
Pul. 21– 5 Moreover, they love their e·,
thine
Mis. 9– 9 "Love thine e·" — see Matt. 5: 44.
worst
Mis. 267– 5 Our worst e· are the best friends
My. 211–19 the designs of their worst e·,
your
Man. 41–13 do good unto your e·
My. 128–29 God will reward your e· according to
191– 5 Your e· will advertise for you.

Mis. 10–31 erroneous belief that you have e· ;

enemies'
My. 275–22 my dear e· health, happiness, and

enemy (see also enemy's)
Mis. 8– 9 Who is thine e·
8–11 Can you see an e·,
8–12 except you first formulate this e·
8–17 count your e· to be that which
8–20 Whatever purifies, . . . is not an e·,
9–32 all that an e· or enmity can
10–30 and this one e· is yourself
10–32 Soon or late, your e· will wake
42–14 or destroyed this last e·,
48–31 The e· is trying to make capital
76–32 overcame the last e·, death.
170– 1 the last e· to be overthrown ;
223–27 * "If I wished to punish my e·,
Un. 54–16 its most potent and deadly e·.

enemy

Pul.	2–18	fiercely besieged by the e·.
	2–25	e· we confront would overthrow
No.	7–13	away from the e· of sinning sense,
My.	185–21	destroys the last e·, death.
	213–19	Be ever on guard against this e·.
	283–15	Sin is its own e·.
	300–15	overcome "the last e·" — *I Cor.* 15 : 26.
	358–10	pray that the e· of good cannot

enemy's

Mis.	xi–27	sadly to survey . . . the e· losses.

energies

Mis.	5– 3	devote our best e· to the work.
	97– 3	eternal e· of Truth,
	176–12	of the divine e· of good,
	278–31	This has developed higher e·
	352–23	Through the divine e· alone
	360–22	fill earth with the divine e·,
Ret.	30–14	infinite e· of Truth and Love,
	88–14	its practicality, its divine e·,
Pul.	11– 7	means, e·, and prayers helped
'02.	10– 4	divine e·, and their power over
My.	287–21	new possibilities, . . . and e· ;

energize

Ret.	86– 1	To e· wholesome spiritual warfare,

energizing

Mis.	291–26	truth which is e·, refreshing, and

energy

divine

    (*see* **divine**)

Mis.	23–21	material force or e· ;
	190– 2	It is neither the e· of matter,
	204–31	gives prudence and e· ;
	245–11	giving it new impetus and e· ;
	330 22	a purer peace and diviner e·,
Ret.	6–28	carried . . . by his persistent e·
Pul.	36–16	* state of exhilaration and e·
	37– 8	* retains in a great degree her e·
'00.	10–10	gained fresh e· and final victory.
'02.	5– 2	prophesies renewed e· for to-morrow,
	8–19	The e· that saves sinners and heals
My.	24–21	* being pushed with the utmost e·,
	52–16	* more e· and unselfish labor
	75– 3	* its enthusiasm, its e·, and
	84–21	* optimism and e· of its followers
	273– 8	* skill, determination, and e·
	204–25	moral, and religious e·

enfolded

My.	291–14	e· a wealth of affection,

enfolds

Pul.	74–19	which eternity e·.
My.	174–27	and omnipotence e· me.
	290–14	Him whose love e· thee.

enforce

Man.	33– 3	to e· the discipline and by-laws
Pul.	82–25	* at least to help e· the laws
Peo.	11–15	that e· new forms of oppression

enforced

Mis.	6–26	laws of health are strictly e·,
My.	308–27	his household law, constantly e·,

enforcement

Man.	32–26	E· of By-Laws.
My.	343–25	Entrusting their e· to others,

enforcing

My.	159–23	spiritual laws e· obedience

engage

My.	27– 7	should e· our attention at this
	54–27	* concluded to e· Chickering Hall

engaged

Mis.	177– 9	e· day and night in organizing
Man.	79– 9	are e· in the transaction of the
	82–19	e· in the work of C. S.,
Pul.	37–11	* e· on further writings on C. S.
My.	317–11	I e· Mr. Wiggin so as to
	332– 9	* Mr. Cooke, who e· to accompany her

engagement

Ret.	15–19	At the close of my e·

engages

Man.	68–19	only those individuals whom she e·
My.	295–19	It e· the attention and

engaging

'02.	1–21	e· the attention of philosopher

engender

Mis.	271–15	which spurious "compounds" e·.

engendered

Mis.	105– 1	faith e· by C. S.,
	291–21	False views, however e·,
My.	191– 8	e· by their fear,
	358– 9	conflict against Truth is e·

engendering

Pul.	6– 3	e· the limited forms of a

engenders

My.	213– 5	starts factions and e· envy

engine

'02.	9–27	inventor of a steam e·
	11–13	a steam e·, a submarine cable,
My.	345–11	* the telephone, the steam e·

engineering

My.	345–10	* electricity, e·, the telephone,

engirdle

My.	164–24	bond . . . that will e· the world,

England

Mis.	295– 5	"cursed barmaid system" in E·
Ret.	1– 2	from both Scotland and E·,
Pul.	5–26	Victoria Institute, E· ;
	46–15	* both in Scotland and E·.
	62– 4	* especially in E·.
My.	30–15	* from India, from E·, from Germany
	252–24	instituted in E· on New Year's
	289–17	is heard no more in E·,
		(*see also* **London**)

English

Mis.	294–24	chapter sub-title
	295– 3	noted E· leader, whom he quotes
	295–21	E· sentiment is not wholly
	295–30	worn the E· crown
	295–30	and borne the E· sceptre.
	296–10	barmaids of E· alehouses
Man.	30– 3	Christians and good E· scholars.
	90– 2	must be thorough E· scholars.
Ret.	1– 6	pious and popular E· authoress
	1–19	Scotch and E· elements
Un.	27– 3	two E· words, often used as if they
Pul.	32–24	* Scotch and E· ancestry,
Pan.	2–12	derivation of the E· word "pantheism"
'02.	7–11	*omni*, . . . used as an E· prefix
My.	89–10	* finds in the E· cathedrals,
	137– 7	* crisp, clear, plain-speaking E·."

English Barmaids

Mis.	294–24	chapter sub-title

Englishman

Ret.	1–17	was married to an E·,

engraft

Mis.	10– 1	or e· upon its purposes and
No.	43–21	can never e· Truth into error.
My.	278–24	no right to e· into civilization

engrafted

My.	196– 8	e· in church and State:
	268– 7	some fundamental error is e·

engraved

Mis.	121– 3	e· upon eternity's tablets.
Pul.	77– 5	* scroll of solid gold, suitably e·,

engraven

Mis.	376–13	* living Saviour e· on the heart.
Pul.	1–13	and records deeply e·,
My.	194–13	The tender memorial e· on
	341– 5	e· on his granite rocks,

engraving

Mis.	376–12	* an e· cut in a stone.

engrossed

Hea.	3–13	e· the attention of the ages.

engrounds

Mis.	397– 9	Truth e· me on the rock,
Pul.	18–18	Truth e· me on the rock,
Po.	12–18	Truth e· me on the rock,

engulf

Mis.	257–26	Earthquakes e· cities,

engulfing

No.	42–15	While Science is e· error

enhance

Mis.	10– 2	wherewith to . . . e· its sorrows.
	154–11	to e· the means and measure
My.	134– 7	our daily lives serve to e·
	340–24	tend to e· their confidence

enhances

My.	107–19	It e· its efficiency,

enhancing

Mis.	395–27	E· autumn's gloom.
Po.	58–12	E· autumn's gloom.

enigmas

Ret.	1–10	other verses and e·

enigmatical

02.	16–18	e· seals of the angel,

enjoin

Mis.	24– 1	e· the First Commandment ;
	310–16	that the Scriptures e·,
	315–29	shall e· upon them habitually

enjoin
Man. 83–21 e· them habitually to study
No. 8–19 I e· it upon my students
Peo. 6–24 the Scriptures e· us to

enjoined
Mis. 381–25 disposing of, the e· pamphlet,
Ret. 76–16 e· upon the Galatians.
'01. 33–23 e· his students to teach
My. 112– 6 did just what he e·

enjoining
Peo. 8–11 Judaism, e· the limited and

enjoins
Mis. 292–19 Christ e· it upon man to help
292–21 e· taking them by the hand

enjoy
Mis. 11–31 I would e· taking by the hand
113–26 but everything to e· on earth
200–22 e· the touch of weakness,
My. 169– 4 if you would e· so long a trip
171–10 I think you would e· seeing it.
252–12 to make one e· doing right,
254– 5 glad you e· the dawn of
352– 7 * the peculiar privileges we e·

enjoyed
Mis. 24–14 than I had before e·.

enjoying
Pul. 51– 6 * they are e· that liberty
My. 139– 3 living, loving, acting, e·.
197– 1 E· good things is not evil,

enjoyment
Mis. 9–22 this cup of selfish human e·
209–18 loss of gustatory e·
210–23 pretense of . . . innocent e·,
'02. 3–13 the e· of self-government

enjoys
'01. 14– 9 something that e·, suffers,

enkindling
Po. 32– 8 sunbeams e· the sky

enlarge
Mis. 154– 9 and e· its borders with
Ret. 89–25 to e· their sphere of action.
'02. 12–26 and e· our church edifice
Po. 33– 4 my faith and my vision e·,
My. 7– 9 and e· our church edifice
9–23 to e· our church edifice
10– 3 * e· the favorable expectation,
40– 6 * also e· their hospitality,
357–14 to e· their phylacteries

enlarged
Mis. 142– 1 how hath He e· her borders!
193–26 this e· sense of the spirit
282– 3 an e· sense of Deity.
Un. 31–21 This subject can be e·.
Pul. 38– 7 * greatly revised and e·,
My. 129–16 And how is man, . . . e·,

enlarges
Mis. 284–26 aggressive, and e· its claims ;
Un. 25–14 e· the human intellect
Rud. 2–19 e· our sense of Deity,
No. 12–24 so e· our sense of God
'02. 9–30 Whatever e· man's facilities

enlarging
Mis. 127– 6 and e· her borders.
My. 18– 3 and e· her borders.
362–16 * e· the activities of the Cause

enlighten
Mis. 38–19 e· and reform the sinner,
82– 8 to e· and redeem mortals.
Ret. 83–18 to rekindle his own light or to e·
Un. 5–18 or e· the individual thought.
No. 3–16 students, whom it would e·.

enlightened
Mis. 7–32 not . . . e· on this great subject.
173– 3 most e· sense herein sees
340–31 have not sufficiently e· mankind.
343–19 freshness and sunshine of e· faith
Ret. 81–17 The e· heart loathes error,
Pul. 9–30 foundation of e· faith is
No. 45–16 measure of e· understanding
Hea. 14–12 as a physician is e· and liberal
Peo. 11– 5 mind, e· and spiritualized,
My. 95–30 * religious faith and e· zeal
128–16 conscience and e· understanding.
168– 2 dictates of e· conscience,
187– 7 lighteth every e· thought
249–16 marvel is, that at this e· period
283–27 e· sense of God's government.

enlightening
Mis. 268–20 e· the misguided senses,
'02. 2–17 e· the world with the
My. 245–20 and e· the world.

enlightenment
Mis. 4–16 Further e· is necessary
162– 1 even as, at times of special e·,
246– 4 requires the e· of these worthies,
Pan. 2– 2 At this period of e·,
My. 340– 9 The e·, the erudition,

enlightens
Mis. 92–10 e· other minds most readily,
Ret. 84– 7 sees clearly and e· other minds
My. 147–16 e· the people's sense of C. S.

enlisted
Mis. 317–24 My sympathies are deeply e·
'01. 15– 7 Scientist has e· to lessen sin,

enlists
My. 108–12 e· faith in the pharmacy of
287– 4 e· my hearty sympathy.

en masse
Mis. 134–10 Meet together and meet e· m·,

enmity
Mis. 9–32 all that an enemy or e· can
36–25 is e· against God ; — Rom. 8 : 7.
74– 5 e· of mortal man toward God.
169–26 carnal mind, which is e· toward God
177–11 sworn e· against the lives of our
Man. 48– 1 cherish no e· toward those who
Ret. 61– 1 e· to God and divine Science.
81– 1 envy, ingratitude, and e·,
Un. 5–21 no e·, no untempered controversy,
No. 8–20 e· over doctrines and traditions,
'02. 13– 4 incurred a sharper fire from e·.
My. 41–21 * unable to cherish any e·.
164–28 rock, against which envy, e·, or

ennobling
Mis. 41–12 ready for victory in the e· strife.

enormous
My. 67–27 * Notwithstanding its e· size,
130–27 has an e· strain put upon it,

enormously
My. 90–18 * The world is e· richer for this

enough
Mis. 16– 4 this is e· of heaven
32–22 But I have not moments e·
39–20 e· of the leaven of Truth to
48–11 e· for me to know that
224–24 charity broad e· to cover the
224–25 sweet e· to neutralize what is bitter
224–31 e· of a flatterer, a fool, or
233–25 unwilling to work hard e·
238–17 It is e·, say they,
241–13 e· apparently to neutralize
253– 6 I am not e· the new woman
253– 8 platform is not broad e· for me,
268– 5 not vain e· to attempt
271– 6 understand e· of this to keep out
276– 8 not big e· to fill the order ;
279–27 e· to convert the world
294–19 just e· to reform and transform them,
307– 3 it is e· that divine Love is an
312– 1 and wished I were wise e· to
353– 5 excess of action or not action e· ;
369–17 This method is devout e· to
Un. 6–11 is radical e· to promote as
Pul. 44–27 * the custodian of funds cried "e·"
61–22 * fortunate e· to listen to the
84–22 * It is e· for us now to know that
Rud. 15–14 until there were e· practitioners
No. 16–25 It is not e· to say that matter
25–11 uttering this great thought is not e· !
27– 6 When we get near e· to God
39– 7 speaking loud e· to be heard ;
Pan. 9–14 What mortal to-day is wise e·
'00. 2–30 but I work hard e· to be so."
10–28 Surely it is e· for a soldier
'01. 11–19 would be e· for Christian practice.
28–23 e· for the disciple — Matt. 10 : 25.
Hea. 4–14 to drop divinity long e· to hate.
6–18 if . . . is strong e· to manifest it.
My. 26–18 include e· of their own.
62– 9 * How can we ever thank God e·
62–10 * ever thank you e· for your
72–16 * do not send . . . money — we have e· !"
76– 7 * e· money was on hand to provide for
82–12 * e· to accommodate the demand.
86–17 * no more money, since he had e·.
86–18 * which indicates plainly e· the
124–15 e· to make this hour glad.
131–28 room e· to receive it." — Mal. 3 : 10.
136– 1 e· for you and me to know
221–23 This is e·.
264– 3 kind e· to speak well of me
268–28 Look high e·, and you see the
268–29 Look long e·, and you see
269–28 room e· to receive it." — Mal. 3 : 10.

Enquirer
  Pul. 89–28   * E·, Oakland, Cal.

enrage
  Mis. 338–17   calm strength will e· evil.

enraptured
  Mis. 17–18   opens to the e· understanding
      390–11   E· by thy spell,
  Po. 55–12   E· by thy spell,

enrich
  Mis. 154– 9   e· its roots, and enlarge its
      251–28   to e· the soil for fruitage.
      332– 8   seedtime has come to e· earth
  Man. 41–24   e· the affections of all mankind,

enriched
  Ret. 84–23   tired tongue of history be e·.

enriches
  My. 295–19   e· the being of all men.

enrobe
  Mis. 332– 8   e· man in righteousness;

en route
  Mis. 378–10   left the water-cure, e· r· for
  Ret. 38–20   to find me e· r· for Boston,
  My. 124–27   and the number e· r·.

Ensample
  Mis. 258– 4   Our great E·, Jesus of Nazareth,
  Man. 41– 1   Christ Jesus the E·.
      41– 2   is the E· in C. S.

enshrined
  Pul. 7–13   but e· for future use,
  My. 348–22   e· in the divine Principle

enshrouds
  Po. 29– 5   born where storm e·

ensign
  Mis. 135– 2   marching under whatsoever e·,
      313–19   The field waves its white e·,
  My. 291–23   our nation's e· of peace
      341– 6   the e· of religious liberty

ensigns
  Mis. xii– 1   signs and e· of war,

enslave
  Peo. 10–14   injustice and error e· him.

ensnare
  My. 14–22   * lie with which to e·
      252– 7   which weaves webs that e·.

ensue
  Man. 51–15   No Church discipline shall e· until
  My. 127–20   e· a purer Protestantism

ensuing
  Pul. vii– 4   during the e· thirty years.
  My. 20–17   no gifts to her the e· season,
      30–13   * officers for the e· year
      51–21   * pastorate for the e· year;

ensure
  Pul. 15– 6   to e· the avoidance of the evil?

entails
  My. 20–25   * e· the expenditure of a

enter
  Mis. 3–15   e· this line of thought or action.
      77–22   e· the spiritual sanctuary
      77–29   e· unshod the Holy of Holies,
      88–23   * who do not e· into its sublimity
      115–17   that you e· not into temptation
      122–26   e· thou into the joy — *Matt.* 25 : 23.
      133–14   e· into thy closet, — *Matt.* 6 : 6.
      186– 4   Soul is supposed to e· the
      241– 5   man will no more e· heaven sick than
      262– 3   wherein it is permitted to e·,
      264–13   e· the Normal class of my College
      274–16   *and equity cannot e·.* — *Isa.* 59 : 14.
      280–32   when you are ready to e·
      282–14   "When ye e· a house, — *see Matt.* 10 : 12.
      282–16   When you e· mentally the personal
      283– 4   no more right to e· the mind of a
      283– 6   than one has to e· a house,
      296–25   Do they e· this line of
      299–18   If I e· Mr. Smith's store
      318–17   can e· upon the gospel work of
      328–25   are striving to e· the path,
      342– 1   to e· into the joy of divine Science
      343– 2   that we e· not into the temptation
      344–26   shall in no wise e·— *Luke* 18 : 17.
      347–21   I e· the path.
      348–30   to e· medical schools,
      398–11   We would e· by the door,
  Man. 49– 5   to e· into this holy work,
      53–18   No member shall e· a complaint
      70– 3   nor e· into a business transaction
      89–23   eligible to e· the Normal class.

enter
  Man. 91–22   may e· the Normal class
  Ret. 46–17   We would e· by the door,
      47– 7   persons desiring to e· the College,
      47–21   can e· upon the gospel work of
      54–18   error may e· through this same channel
      55– 1   e· this strait and narrow path,
      88–23   blush to e· unasked another's
  Un. 37– 4   to inherit eternal life and e· heaven
      40– 3   will not e· this dark shadow
      50– 7   pray that we e· not into the
  Pul. 17–16   We would e· by the door,
  Rud. 14–24   unprepared to e· higher classes.
      15– 5   to immediately e· upon its
      15–13   diseased people not to e· a class.
      15–20   can advantageously e· a class,
  No. 31–26   e· no more into him." — *Mark* 9 : 25.
      41–17   trying to force the doors . . . and e· in ;
  Pan. 6–19   e· into the Scriptural allegory,
  '01. 14–22   that he e· not into temptation
      28– 6   e· the strait and narrow way,
  '02. 7– 6   e· not into the category
  Peo. 4– 9   could e· finite man through his
  Po. 14–15   We would e· by the door,
      22–10   will e·, when they may,
      22–19   Love doth e· in,
  My. 3– 9   e· in through the gates — *Rev.* 22 : 14.
      4–27   ye shall not e· into — *Matt.* 18 : 3.
      6–15   wherein to e· and pray.
      40–10   * shall willingly e· into the
      62– 3   * e· thou into the joy — *Matt.* 25 : 23.
      71–14   * When these people e· this
      126– 1   would e· even the church,
      152–14   Ask thyself, Do I e· by the door
      159–14   struggling to e· into the
      188–17   In spirit I e· your
      207–21   e· thou into the joy — *Matt.* 25 : 21.
      210– 4   death cannot e· them.
      210– 6   no door through which evil can e·,
      218–28   an individual should not e·
      244–18   mortals do not e· without a
      246– 5   Students who e· the . . . College,
      251–13   eligible to e· the Normal class,
      267–17   e· heaven in proportion to
      306– 8   I deem it unwise to e· into
      322–18   * received your permission to e·
      348–31   nothing that worketh ill can e·
      358– 5   e· not into temptation." — *Matt.* 26 : 41.

entered
  Mis. 49– 1   A young lady e· the College class
      166–29   e· into the minutiæ of
      206–24   you have e· the path.
      216– 5   e· into our rest,
      260– 7   never e· into the line of
      297–18   voluntarily e· into wedlock,
      306– 2   * e· carefully in a book
      327–10   Many there were who had e· the
      349–18   He e· the medical school,
      373–22   in due time Christianity e· into
  Ret. 16– 8   e· this church one hour ago
      39– 3   I e· a suit at law,
      89–17   once again e· the synagogue which
      90– 7   ever e· the towns whither he sent
  Pul. 31–25   * Mrs. Eddy e· the room.
  '00. 13– 2   * Gentiles e· the church of Christ"
  Heu. 13– 9   Spirit never e· and it never
  Peo. 4– 7   belief . . . eternal e· the temporal.
      4–13   error that . . . personal devil e·
  My. 92–24   * worshippers who e· its portals
      94– 8   * worshippers who e· its portals
      178–23   e· the house through a window
      235–30   would never have e· into the history
      302–29   e· it, and knelt in thanks
      307–17   and I e· a demurrer
      309– 9   Both e· their pleas,
      319–21   * I e· your Primary class
      321–22   * I first saw you and e· your class.
      342– 4   * She e· with a gracious smile,
      355– 4   * on which we have just e·.

entereth
  Pan. 12–17   that he who e· it may run

entering
  Mis. 18–25   e· into a state of evil
      49– 4   before e· the College,
      262– 6   e· upon its fifth volume,
      316–24   Before e· the Massachusetts
      318–19   Before e· this sacred field
      342– 8   e· the guest-chamber of Truth,
      348–31   and objected to their e·
      349–12   feasibility of e· a medical school ;
  Ret. 47–23   before e· this field of labor
      71–21   selfish motives e· into mental
      78– 9   sinister motives, e· into
  No. 28–13   to-day is none too soon for e·
  '02. 15–13   Before e· upon my great life-work,

entering
My.	81– 1	* Upon *e·* The Mother Church
	188–21	cannot prevent me from *e·*

enteritis
Mis.	69–19	healed him of *e·*,
My.	107–31	removes *e·*, gastritis,

enterprising
My.	315–25	to thank the *e·* historians

enters
Mis.	101–15	*e·* into no compromise with
	152–27	there *e·* no element of earth
	208– 9	*e·* unconsciously the human heart
	325– 1	*e·* a massive carved stone mansion.
	325–31	Next he *e·* a place of worship,
Un.	48–15	no more *e·* into His creation
	48–16	than the human father *e·* into
'02.	18–17	no deceit, *e·* into the heart that
My.	68–19	* *e·* so largely into the
	179– 9	*e·* non-intelligent dust

entertain
Mis.	2–32	While we *e·* decided views as to
	9–14	present sense which thou canst *e·* of
	16–18	we must *e·* a higher sense of
	18–23	necessarily *e·* habitual love for
	28– 6	beliefs that mortals *e·*.
	47– 5	*e·* an adipose belief of yourself as
	74–14	opposite of that which mortals *e·* :
	96–21	all who *e·* this understanding
	292–12	higher sense I *e·* of Love,
Man.	42–16	shall neither *e·* a belief nor
Un.	8– 7	than the sense you *e·* of it.
Pul.	21–14	*e·* due respect and fellowship for
Peo.	5–22	and not *e·* the angel unawares.
My.	74–31	* Whatever opinions we many *e·*
	210–19	Certain individuals *e·* the notion
	223–19	either of which I do not *e·*.

entertained
Mis.	46– 9	any doctrine previously *e·*.
	197–14	It means more than an opinion *e·*
Ret.	5–29	* She ever *e·* a lively sense of
'02.	7–21	no other . . . can be Christianly *e·*.
Hea.	8–17	mistaken views *e·* of Deity
My.	241–24	* according to the beliefs I *e·*
	331–12	* love and respect *e·* for Mrs. Eddy

entertaining
Mis.	49–20	*E·* the common belief in
	192–31	else we are *e·* the startling

entertainment
My.	82–19	* when the *e·* is over

entertains
'00.	6–19	sense which the adult *e·* of it.
'02.	19–13	He *e·* angels who

enthrall
'01.	10–15	used to *e·* my sense of the Godhead,
My.	4– 4	world's *nolens volens* cannot *e·* it.

enthrone
Mis.	74– 7	affections which *e·* the Son of man
Un.	38–13	such misbelief must *e·* another
	46–28	The fight was an effort to *e·* evil.
No.	42–16	material senses would *e·* error as

enthroned
Mis.	66–19	and Truth be *e·*,
	277–26	justice and judgment are *e·*.
My.	201– 7	are *e·* now and forever.
	247–12	meekness and Truth *e·*.

enthrones
Un.	32–13	*e·* God in the eternal qualities of

enthusiasm
My.	75– 2	* respectful acknowledgment of its *e·*,
	79–13	* shows an *e·* for C. S.
	85–15	* zeal and *e·* of the followers
	98– 8	* centre of an *e·* and reverence
	322–24	* to banter me on such *e·*,

enthusiast
Pul.	32–27	* her mother was a religious *e·*,

enthusiastic
Pul.	32–10	* her large and *e·* following
	64–13	* money from *e·* Christian Scientists.
My.	273– 5	* Scientists, *e·* in their belief,

enthusiasts
My.	99–13	* *e·* whenever their form of religion

entices
My.	211–13	*e·* its victim by unseen, silent

enticing
Pul.	30– 4	* *e·* a separate congregation

entire
Mis.	50– 6	*e· method of metaphysical healing,*
	92–15	Throughout his *e·* explanations,
	118–10	to make incorrect your *e·* problem,

entire
Mis.	127– 3	Throughout my *e·* connection with
	150–17	churches are dotting the *e·* land.
	154– 5	broad shelter to the *e·* world.
	194–15	bring out the *e·* hues of Deity,
	196– 6	subtleties through the *e·* centuries,
	201– 1	supports the *e·* wisdom of the text ;
	234–21	the *e·* current of mortality,
	260–23	Mind as absolute and *e·*,
	312–26	throughout the *e·* centuries,
	382–30	*e·* system of teaching and
Ret.	78– 4	*e·* wisdom of Mind-practice.
	84– 9	Throughout his *e·* explanations
Pul.	27– 9	* the *e·* church is a testimonial,
	29–27	* almost the *e·* congregation was
	30–23	* *e·* membership of Christian Scientists
'00.	12–26	The *e·* city is now in ruins.
'01.	12–21	bring out the *e·* hues of God.
My.	10–14	* for this *e·* donation to be
	14–14	* *e·* amount required to complete
	17–31	Throughout my *e·* connection with
	30–30	* representative of the *e·* body of the
	31–13	* from over the *e·* world.
	45–11	* small part of the *e·* body
	66– 4	* ownership of the *e·* block.
	66–10	* ownership of the *e·* block.
	69–29	* dominate the *e·* city,
	76– 8	* the *e·* cost of the building,
	78–19	* the *e·* congregation knelt
	137– 7	* *e·* letter is in Mrs. Eddy's own
	232–22	*e·* mortal, material error
	252–10	*e·* purpose of true education
	299–11	contains the *e·* truth of the
	301–19	*e·* testimony of the material

entirely
Mis.	71– 1	*when I am not e· well myself?*
Pul.	30–30	* and *e·* paid for when its
	38–19	* in so *e·* different a plane
	55–27	* though each is *e·* independent
	57– 3	* It is *e·* paid for,
	71–22	* are now so *e·* devoted.
	76–15	* rug composed *e·* of skins
Hea.	19– 5	governed directly and *e·* by mind,
My.	14–20	* was *e·* right in doing so.
	83–12	* men go *e·* unadorned.
	85–26	* it was *e·* credible that the
	93–24	* many of us have missed *e·*
	98–23	* Contributions were *e·* voluntary.
	118–29	*e·* apart from limitations,
	312– 9	* and *e·* without money
	312–15	* but *e·* without means
	323– 1	* *e·* in accordance with what
	324–25	* *e·* unique and original.
	344–18	"Oh," . . . "*e·*.

entitled
Mis.	62–22	her work *e·* "Mind-cure on a
	313–15	*e·* "The New Pastor," by
Man.	45–20	is not *e·* to hold office
	91–11	shall be *e·* to a free course
Ret.	35– 2	*e·* "The Science of Man."
	75–23	is he *e·*, when he leaves the
Pul.	28–17	* Mrs. Eddy's book, *e·* "S. and H.
	54– 1	* in a poem *e·* "The Master,"
	55–22	* volume *e·* "S. and H.
	85–15	* *e·* to the gratitude and love of all
'01.	23–23	book . . . *e·* "Treatise Concerning the
My.	107–25	*e·* to a classification as truth
	250– 4	was *e·* to and has received
	276–18	* those who are *e·* to vote
	316–12	*e·* "The Recent Reckless and
	323– 3	* pamphlet *e·* C. S. and the Bible,"
	353–12	the second I *e· Sentinel,*

entity
Mis.	45–23	It never . . . existed as an *e·*.
	250– 4	either as a quality or as an *e·*.
	346–12	Evil never did exist as an *e·*.
Ret.	25–16	God I characterized as individual *e·*,
'01.	13–12	Sin can have neither *e·*, verity, nor
	14– 8	evil, as a false claim, false *e·*, and
My.	14–21	If the devil were really an *e·*,

entrance
Mis.	100–31	and his *e·* into Science
	170–10	*e·* into their understanding is
	280–31	open wide for the *e·* of error.
Pul.	25–16	* *e·* to this magnificent temple.
	26–20	* an *e·* of Italian marble,
	36–22	* at the *e·* to the Back Bay Park,
My.	54– 2	* could not obtain *e·* ;
	221–30	Truth and Life, can guard the *e·*
	262–13	*e·* into human understanding of the

entrances
Pul.	24–26	* The *e·* are of marble,
	25–18	* *e·* leading to the auditorium,
My.	78– 9	* *e·* beneath a series of arches

entreaty
Mis. 254– 3   gentle *e·*, the stern rebuke
My. 10–22   * *e·* on the part of some one else.
    37–28   * deeply touched by its sweet *e·*,

entrusted
Mis. 155–30   wherewith divine Love has *e·* us,
Ret. 6– 2   * especially *e·* to her watch-care,
'01. 31–11   *e·* me with a message to mankind
My. 336– 7   * *e·* herself to the care of

entrusting
My. 343–25   *E·* their enforcement to others,

enumerated
Ret. 33–11   remedies *e·* by Jahr,

enumerating
My. 328–26   * *e·* the different professions

enumeration
Pul. 67–11   * Max O'Rell's famous *e·* of

enunciated
Pul. 54– 9   * Jesus *e·* and exemplified the

enunciates
'00. 4–30   St. Paul beautifully *e·* this

enunciating
My. 188–15   *e·*, "God is Love." — *I John* 4 : 8.

enunciation
Mis. 114–15   *e·* of these according to Christ.

enunciator
Pul. 6–23   Another brilliant *e·*, seeker, and

envied
No. 41– 7   work most derided and *e·*

envies
My. 17– 5   hypocrisies, and *e·*, and — *I Pet.* 2 : 1.

envious
Mis. 129–15   If a man is jealous, *e·*, or
    291–30   counteract the influence of *e·* minds

environed
Ret. 50–29   Students are not *e·* with such
My. 267–27   *e·* with everlasting Life.

environment
Mis. 85–22   *e·* of mortals, suggests
    86–27   constitutes our mortal *e·*.
    372–26   Not by aid of foreign device or *e·*
Un. 56– 9   quickened sense of false *e·*,
Pul. 54–20   * the conditions of *e·* and
    54–27   * most perfect obtainable *e·*,

environments
Mis. 76–15   set a human soul free from its *e·*,
    263–22   without a full knowledge of the *e·*.
My. 257– 8   swaddling-clothes (material *e·*)

envy
Mis. 10– 4   Whatever *e·*, hatred, revenge
    19– 1   *E·*, evil thinking, evil speaking,
    32–28   they should never *e·*, elbow,
    54–12   over all obstacles that *e·* and malice
    118–22   *e·*, revenge, are foes to grace,
    123– 6   spirit of idolatry, *e·*,
    137–25   passion, pride, *e·*, evil-speaking,
    201–31   banishes forever all *e·*, rivalry,
    222– 3   It inflames *e·*, passion,
    228–11   the buffetings of *e·* or malice
    254–18   *E·*, the great red dragon of
    274–20   gives impulse to violence, *e·*,
    277–17   the purposes of *e·* and malice
    278– 2   The wines of fornication, *e·*, and
    281– 4   rivalry, jealousy, *e·*, revenge.
    324–14   witchcraft, variance, *e·*,
    337–19   evil-speaking, lust, *e·*, hate.
    343–14   weeds of passion, malice, *e·*,
    347–31   Loyal Scientists are targets for *e·*,
    356– 6   *E·*, rivalry, hate need no
    357– 1   no place for *e·*,
    366–27   self-will, *e·*, and lust.
    368–25   Others, from malice and *e·*,
    374–13   ignorance, *e·*, and hatred
    383– 9   preeminent over ignorance or *e·*,
Ret. 44–21   *e·* and molestation of other
    79–13   *e·*, and mad ambition are
    81– 1   *e·*, ingratitude, and enmity,
Rud. 9–20   *e·*, lust, and all fleshly vices.
No. 3– 2   How sad it is that *e·* will bend its
    43–27   while *e·* and hatred bark and bite
Pan. 3–15   * *e·* of the great !
'01. 16– 9   lusts, falsities, *e·*, and hate,
'02. 3–28   *E·* is the atmosphere of hell.
    11–10   *E·* or abuse of him who,
    14–20   with mockery, *e·*, rivalry, and falsehood
    16–27   pride, self-will, *e·*, or hate.
Hea. 10– 4   the vision of *e·*, sensuality, and
    17– 2   the pride of life, *e·*, hypocrisy,
    18–22   Pride, appetites, passions, *e·*,
My. 164–28   rock, against which *e·*, enmity, or

envy
My. 167–28   the illegitimate claims of *e·*,
    213– 5   starts factions and engenders *e·*
    228–21   self-righteousness, hypocrisy, *e·*,
    252–14   wrong, injustice, *e·*, hate ;
    316–20   foaming torrents of ignorance, *e·*,

enwrapped
My. 257–26   Christmas gift, two words *e·*,

Ephesian
'00. 12–12   whence the *E·* elders travelled

Ephesus
'00. 12– 7   commence with the church of *E·*.
    12– 8   records *E·* as an illustrious city,
    12–15   the tutelary divinity of *E·*.
    12–17   Magical arts prevailed at *E·* ;
    13– 4   commends the church at *E·*

Epictetus
My. 149–15   *E·* made answer, "And I with many
    159–25   *E·*, a heathen philosopher

Epicurean
Mis. 162– 8   Gnostic, *E·*, and Stoic.

epicycle
My. 270– 3   obliterates the *e·* of evil.

Epigram
Mis. vii– 3   * BEN JONSON : *E· I.*
    vii– 8   * BEN JONSON : *E· 86.*

Episcopal
Pul. 26– 8   * chancel of an *E·* church
My. 333–12   * thence to the *E·* burying-ground,

epistle
Un. 30–13   his first *e·* to the Corinthians

epistles
Ret. 90–11   addressed one of his *e·*

epithet
'01. 4–29   If . . . we merit the *e·* "godless,"
Hea. 3–19   which *e·* the great goodness and
My. 104– 6   That *e·* points a moral.

epithets
My. 151– 2   present schoolboy *e·* and attacks

epitome
Rud. 8– 9   only an *e·* of the Principle,

epitomize
Pul. vii– 2   *e·* the story of the birth of

epitomizes
My. 364–16   *e·* what heals all manner of

epoch
Mis. 363–30   every advancing *e·* of Truth
Man. 18– 9   at every *e·* saying,
Ret. 93– 4   At the present *e·* the human concept
My. 66–27   * an *e·* in the history of C. S.
    220– 2   to this century or to any *e·*,

epoch-making
My. 30–19   * in gratitude for the *e·* event.

epoch-marking
My. 47–14   * *e·* stages of its growth,

equal
Mis. 40–14   *e·* the ancient prophets as healers.
    41–20   may not always prove *e·* to
    46–10   *Do you teach that you are e· with*
    46–14   Man is not *e·* with his Maker ;
    53–10   former is not *e·* to the latter.
    62–11   offsets an *e·* positive quantity,
    70–18   thief was not *e·* to the demands
    70–29   none could *e·* his glory.
    90–19   are *e·* to your motives ;
    138–25   *e·* to the march triumphant,
    220–23   understand with *e·* clearness,
    255– 5   Man is not *e·* to his Maker.
    291–13   *e·* growth and prosperity of all
    291–15   *e·* opportunity to be benefited
Ret. 34– 9   Human reason was not *e·* to it.
Un. 38–27   or *e·* to the reality of being,
Pul. 28–19   * *e·* measure to its use of the Bible.
    47–16   * no human reason has been *e·* to
    84– 6   * side by side, *e·* partners in
Rud. 6– 2   *e·* inference that there is no matter.
No. 43– 2   *e·* to the power of daily meat and
'00. 9–29   But no one else has seemed *e·* to
'01. 16– 7   scarcely *e·* the modern nondescripts,
    27–18   an *e·* number of sick healed,
My. 190– 8   Does C. S. *e· materia medica* in
    217–11   *e·* shares to each contributor.
    219–14   to believe that . . . is not *e·* to
    219–16   is *e·* to the giving of life and health
    237–17   charges for treatment *e·* to those of
    247– 8   *e·* rights and privileges,
    255– 1   *e·* rights and privileges,
    269– 9   *e·* unto the angels ; — *Luke* 20 : 36.
    272– 9   no claim that man is *e·* to God,

equal
My. 323–19   * Neither do I now feel at all e· to
324–22   * as quite his literary e·,
equality
Mis. 255–10   not claiming e· with,
294–29   true ideas of humanity and e·.
My. 247– 9   e· of the sexes, rotation in office.
255– 2   e· of the sexes, rotation in office.''
equalled
Pul. 36–12   * I never saw e·.
equalling
My. 190–12   not only e· but vastly excelling
equally
Mis. 46–20   not weighing e· with Him,
177–13   Will you be e· in earnest for the
290–30   all who are receptive share this e·.
Ret. 64–10   good is e· one and all,
Un. 46–23   being e· identical and
No. 15–11   should not these be e· extended to
My. 145–22   I can serve e· my friends and
146–20   e· sure that what I wrote is true,
230–10   but to one and all e·.
292–22   though both are e· sincere.
equals
Mis. 194– 1   believe that the power of God e·
equanimity
Mis. 224–22   with an e· so settled that
No. 8–26   while you walk on in e·,
equations
Mis. 54–29   not ask the pupil in simple e· to
equatorial
Mis. 88–25   * miraculous to the e· African,
equipoise
Mis. 65–25   restoring the e· of mind and body,
equipped
Mis. 10– 9   armed them, e· them, and
88–13   have e· him as a critic
Hea. 14–13   In proportion . . . is he e· with Truth,
equips
Mis. 183–23   e· man with divine power
252–27   e· the doctor with safe and sure
equitable
My. 277– 9   wholesome tribunals, e· laws,
equity
Mis. 274–16   and e· cannot enter.— Isa. 59 : 14.
289–19   Neither divine justice nor human e·
380–27   April, 1883, a bill in e· was filed
My. 181–20   universal e· of Christianity.
277–18   eternal scale of e· and mercy,
equivalent
Mis. 67–26   by e· words in another,
300–31   withholds a slight e· for health.
Ret. 50– 3   I could think of no financial e·
50–13   e· for my instruction
Rud. 1–12   In French the e· word is personne.
My. 236–12   may become e· to no centre.
era
Christian
Mis. 29–11   even before the Christian e· ;
40–12   first century of the Christian e· ?''
163– 8   dated time, the Christian e·,
199–31   and dated the Christian e·.
373–20   early part of the Christian e·,
Man. 41– 2   He who dated the Christian e·
Ret. 26–20   a new date in the Christian e·,
93– 1   In the first century of the Christian e·
94–28   In the first century of the Christian e·
'01. 24–20   advent is called the Christian e·.
28– 9   first century of the Christian e·
My. 107– 5   at the beginning of the Christian e·,
340– 7   belonging not to the Christian e·,
340–27   suffices for the Christian e·.

Pul. 44– 9   * an e· in the blessed onward work
My. 29–23   * launching upon a new e·,
47–26   * an e· of Christian worship
154–23   in our e· of the world
212– 6   In this e· it is taking the place of
eradicate
Mis. 237–15   encounter and help to e·.
No. 31– 1   cannot e· disease if you admit
eradicated
My. 122– 8   the roots must be e· or the
erased
Man. 54–14   her name shall be e· from The
My. 318– 3   I have e· them in my revisions.
erases
Rud. 12–16   C. S. e· from the minds of invalids

ere
Mis. 227–13   e· that one himself become aware,
395–18   E· autumn blanch another year,
398–19   White as wool, e· they depart,
Ret. 46–25   White as wool, e· they depart,
81–12   falsity must thus decay, e· spiritual
Un. 56–24   e· he can change from flesh to
Pul. 17–24   White as wool, e· they depart
51–20   * E· this many a new project
Hea. 2–14   e· he passed from his execution to a
Peo. 8–26   will e· long stop trusting where
Po. 14–23   White as wool, e· they depart,
27– 6   E· thou grow tremulous with
27–16   Hearts bleeding e· they break
58– 3   E· autumn blanch another year,
My. 123–18   E· long I will see you
130– 6   will e· long be unearthed
181–15   would have solved e· this
erect
Mis. 79–16   is e· in goodness and perpetual in
369– 7   enables us to stand e·
383–12   E· and eternal, it will go on
Pul. 8–15   to e· this "miracle in stone."
11– 7   helped e· The Mother Church,
41– 7   * to help e· this beautiful
45– 6   * can effect cures . . . and e· churches,
My. 22– 8   * to e· such a building
287– 3   movement to e· a monument to
308–18   My father's person was e·
erected
Mis. 139–21   having e· thereon a church edifice
382–20   was e· the first church edifice
Man. 103– 4   The edifice e· in 1894
Pul. 2– 2   house Solomon had e·.
24– 2   * first C. S. church e· in Boston
24–14   * e· Anno Domini 1894.
40–19   * costly edifice e· in Boston
58–10   * e· this edifice at a cost of
63–21   * e· at a cost of
77– 2   * which the church has just e·.
77–10   * a church edifice was e· at the
78– 9   * 1894 a church edifice was e·
84–13   * The First Church . . . is e·.
My. 11–24   * the new building will be e·,
15– 6   edifice e· in 1894 for The
66–29   * houses of worship have been e·,
67–15   * First church e· . . . 1894
67–26   * surpass any church edifice e· in
70– 4   * e· its first church only
72–29   * when they e· the first church
73– 4   * have e· dozens of churches
76–27   * cathedral e· by the devotees of
186–28   * a Church of Christ, Scientist,
189–25   e· in the sunny South
195–26   temples e· first in the hearts of
335–13   * where he e· a fine dwelling-house.
erecting
Ret. 5– 4   gave the money for e· the
My. 196– 3   I congratulate you upon e· the
208–18   e· a church building,
erection
Mis. 131–14   since the e· of the edifice of
Man. 102–17   e· of a church edifice.
Ret. 51– 4   to be appropriated for the e·,
Pul. 50–12   * e· of a visible house of worship
51–23   * The e· of this temple will
52–11   * e· of a massive temple in
56–11   * e· of the temple, in Boston,
57– 4   * contributions for its e· came from
85– 4   * have made its e· possible.
My. 21– 9   * e· of many branch churches.
22–29   * e· of the new edifice of The
23– 6   * e· of the present edifice in 1894,
23–28   * in the work of its e·.
24–19   * e· of the building is proceeding
58–14   * e· of these mighty walls.
98–28   * The e· in Boston of the
err
Mis. 49–29   that the capacity to e· proceeds from
168–22   Ye do e·, not knowing the— Matt. 22 : 29.
219– 6   "Ye do e·, not knowing the— Matt. 22 : 29.
No. 9–13   whereas you may e· in effort,
37– 4   "Ye do e·, not knowing the— Matt. 22 : 29.
'01. 30– 4   We e· in thinking the object of
errancy
Ret. 73–24   Such e· betrays a violent and
errand
Mis. 250–25   on an e· of mercy,
errands
My. 129–21   do thy e·, and be thy dearest
erratic
Mis. 266–12   An e· career is like the

erring

Mis.
3–20 the e˙ or mortal thought holds in itself
5–25 an e˙ or mortal mind,
13–22 testimony of the five e˙ senses,
27–28 To e˙ material sense, No !
36– 1 e˙, sinful, sick, and dying,
63– 4 claim that one e˙ mind cures
97–10 E˙ human mind is by no means a
139–28 the e˙ mind's apprehension.
186– 9 this e˙ belief even separates its
199– 4 only mortal, e˙ mind can claim
199– 6 annul his own e˙ mental law,
257–11 immoral force of e˙ mortal mind,
260–14 Jesus knew that e˙ mortal thought
286–22 states of the human e˙ mind ;
362–24 refute e˙ reason with the spiritual
362–32 an e˙ so-called mind

Ret.
59– 2 a finite and e˙ mind,

Rud.
9–10 in e˙ human will,

No.
4– 9 an e˙ sense of existence,
5– 4 In e˙ mortal thought

Hea.
5– 1 our own e˙ finite sense of God,

erroneous

Mis.
10–30 e˙ belief that you have enemies ;
73– 3 this supposition is proven e˙
218–11 It is e˙ to accept the evidence of
309– 5 must result in e˙ conclusions.
352– 8 error of its present e˙ course,
360–26 E˙ doctrines never have

Ret.
13–10 aroused by this e˙ doctrine,

Un.
36–14 matter is e˙, transitory, unreal.
36–24 or to say that . . . is e˙.

Rud.
10–23 e˙ physical and mental state,

No.
10–20 former position, . . . is proven e˙.

My.
161–18 to destroy its e˙ claims.
219– 3 Such practice would be e˙,

erroneously

Mis.
276–27 or at work e˙,

Man.
40–15 influencing or being influenced e˙.

'01.
21–19 begins his calculation e˙ ;

error (see also error's)

above
Mis.
234– 4 we attempt to mount above e˙ by
absorbed in
Mis.
333– 6 could be absorbed in e˙ !
against
My.
193–18 Protesting against e˙, you unite with
all
Mis.
14–30 and thereby destroys all e˙,
104–32 wherewith to overcome all e˙.
118–19 until all e˙ is destroyed
194–26 the Truth that destroys all e˙,
195– 2 the Truth that antidotes all e˙,
235–10 delivering mankind from all e˙
251–26 all e˙, physical, moral, or
283–29 Truth which destroys all e˙.
301–28 All e˙ tends to harden the heart,
Ret.
94–12 divine mercy, destroying all e˙,
Un.
17– 2 Evil seeks to fasten all e˙ upon
Pul.
70–23 * power of Truth over all e˙,
No.
9–23 it excludes all e˙ and
24–26 This great fact concerning all e˙
Pan.
13–11 stern condemnation of all e˙,
'01.
23–17 laid the axe at the root of all e˙,
31– 5 Truth opposed to all e˙,
'02.
2– 8 in contradistinction to all e˙,
My.
18–20 stern condemnation of all e˙,
all forms of
Un.
8–17 All forms of e˙ are uprooted
always strives
Mis.
371–22 e˙ always strives to unite,
and death
Hea.
8– 5 that destroy e˙ and death.
and delusion
Un.
33–15 only through e˙ and delusion.
and nothingness
Mis.
201–12 e˙ and nothingness of supposed life
and shadow
Ret.
25–13 senses, . . . I called e˙ and shadow.
and sickness
Mis.
221– 9 e˙ and sickness are one,
and sin
No.
37–26 if e˙ and sin existed in the
My.
323–22 * triumph over e˙ and sin,
and Truth
Mis.
302–11 discriminate between e˙ and Truth,
annihilates
Mis.
14–29 Science of Truth annihilates e˙,
antagonism of
Mis.
320–21 doth meet the antagonism of e˙ ;
asks
My.
211– 9 All that e˙ asks is to be let alone ;
atone for
Mis.
118–14 sympathy can neither atone for e˙,

error

attacks of
My.
210– 9 shielded from the attacks of e˙
before
Mis.
210–31 Charity never flees before e˙,
belief of
Rud.
12– 9 encouraging them in the belief of e˙
belief or
Mis.
79–13 cannot lapse into a . . . belief or e˙
bid
Po.
23–22 Bid e˙ melt away !
blended with
Rud.
9– 6 more or less blended with e˙ ;
blindness to
Un.
6–19 theory of God's blindness to e˙
cancel
No.
7– 9 we can cancel e˙ in our own hearts,
cannot antidote
Mis.
334–24 Then it cannot antidote e˙.
casting out
Mis.
175– 2 casting out e˙ and healing the sick.
192– 7 casting out e˙, — sickness, sin,
268–13 healing the sick and casting out e˙.
Ret.
66– 2 healing the sick, in casting out e˙,
Peo.
13– 7 casting out e˙ and healing the sick.
cast out
Mis.
247– 1 truth that shall cast out e˙
No.
42–13 or to cast out e˙ with error,
Hea.
2–25 cast out e˙ and heal the sick.
3– 4 to make men better, to cast out e˙,
7– 3 power of Truth to cast out e˙ ;
Peo.
8– 2 cast out e˙ and heal the sick.
casts out
Mis.
193–13 heals the sick, casts out e˙,
Man.
17–18 casts out e˙, heals the sick,
Hea.
13–24 casts out e˙ and thus heals
claim of
(see claim)
claims of
Mis.
293–13 opposite claims of e˙.
Ret.
64–23 supposititious claims of e˙ ;
claim to
No.
30–20 existence of even a claim to e˙.
cloud of
Mis.
204– 2 impenetrable cloud of e˙ ;
combat with
Mis.
216– 3 your own state of combat with e˙.
commingled
Mis.
379–17 they commingled e˙ with truth,
conceive of
'01.
14–19 to conceive of e˙ as either right or
concept of
Ret.
67– 2 hence one's concept of e˙ is
consciousness of
Un.
4–15 lose our own consciousness of e˙.
4–16 we lose all consciousness of e˙,
could not control
Mis.
140– 1 such as e˙ could not control.
declares
Mis.
218– 6 as e˙ declares Truth.
denounce
My.
210–21 only denounce e˙ in general,
despoil
Un.
17–17 despoil e˙ of its borrowed plumes,
destroy
Mis.
40–17 power of Truth to destroy e˙,
85–30 tends to destroy e˙ ;
Hea.
8– 5 that destroy e˙ and death.
destroying
Mis.
261–21 by Truth's destroying e˙.
destroys
Mis.
105–24 Truth destroys e˙.
204– 5 neutralizes and destroys e˙.
299– 3 To know the . . . destroys e˙.
370–24 by which e˙ destroys e˙,
Ret.
61–20 Truth that destroys e˙
My.
232–23 Truth which destroys e˙,
destroys the
Mis.
241–21 Truth destroys the e˙ that insists on
destruction of
Mis.
215– 1 final destruction of e˙ through this
discern the
Mis.
355–23 then thou wilt discern the e˙
disease in
Mis.
85–29 Disease in e˙, more than ease
dissolve
Ret.
87–27 such efficacy as to dissolve e˙.
dose of
Mis.
241–13 taking a dose of e˙ big enough
dream or
Mis.
49–15 all that is mortal is a dream or e˙,
ejection of
My.
222–30 will aid the ejection of e˙,
element of
Un.
58– 3 in their native element of e˙,

error

engulfing
No. 42–15 engulfing *e·* in bottomless oblivion,

entrance of
Mis. 280–31 open wide for the entrance of *e·*,

every
No. 7–11 to see every *e·* they possess,

every phase of
Un. 4– 7 destroys every phase of *e·.*

evil and
Mis. 36– 3 classify evil and *e·* as mortal mind,

evil, or
Ret. 57–19 Evil, or *e·*, is not Mind ;

existence of
Un. 22–11 To admit the existence of *e·*

expose
Mis. 335–19 right to expose *e·*,

fable of
Un. 44–13 This abortive ego, this fable of *e·*,

fails
Mis. 6–17 ultimately succeed where *e·* fails.

faith in
My. 292–30 faith in truth and faith in *e·.*

fall into
No. 9–16 students who fall into *e·*,

find
Mis. 334–17 You must find *e·* to be *nothing:*

firm of
Mis. 361–28 by no means . . . in the firm of *e·*,

form of
Mis. 48– 9 as to every form of *e·*,

found out
Mis. 355–13 *E·* found out is two-thirds destroyed,

froth of
Mis. 78–21 we will hope it is the froth of *e·*

fundamental
Ret. 31–16 fundamental *e·* of faith in things
My. 268– 7 fundamental *e·* is engrafted on it.

giveth no light
Mis. 276–29 *E·* giveth no light,

handle the
Mis. 221– 4 opportunity to handle the *e·*,

has no hobby
No. 44–10 *E·* has no hobby, however boldly

has no life
Un. 38– 8 *E·* has no life, and is virtually

has no power
Mis. 157–26 *E·* has no power but to destroy

her
Un. 57–15 he neither held her *e·* by affinity nor

his
Man. 52–13 his confession of his *e·*

human
(*see* **human**)

illusion and
Mis. 68–17 illusion and *e·* which Truth casts out.

in borrowed plumes
Mis. 371–24 *e·* in borrowed plumes

incapable of
Mis. 210– 1 as unconscious as incapable of *e·*,

indicates
No. 6–13 If, as the *e·* indicates,

injustice and
Peo. 10–14 injustice and *e·* enslave him.

in practice
Mis. 66–28 is met with *e·* in practice ;

in premise
Mis. 66–27 *E·* in premise is met with
265–19 An *e·* in premise can never
309– 5 personality is an *e·* in premise,

in thought
Hea. 7– 3 correcting *e·* in thought,

is annihilated
Un. 58– 4 before *e·* is annihilated.

is not Mind
Mis. 367– 8 showing that *e·* is not Mind,
Ret. 57–19 Evil, or *e·*, is not Mind ;

is not Truth
'01. 14–17 self-evident that *e·* is not Truth ;

is the unreal
Hea. 10–15 Truth is the real ; *e·* is the unreal.

is walking
Mis. 277– 5 *E·* is walking to and fro

its own
Mis. 145–16 wounded sense of its own *e·*,

Jesus said of
Mis. 57–11 Jesus said of *e·*,

knowledge of
Ret. 55– 4 sufficient knowledge of *e·* to
My. 232–21 "A knowledge of *e·* and of its

lapse or
Peo. 2–25 Truth without a lapse or *e·*,

last
Mis. 293–17 last *e·* will be worse than the first

likeness of
Rud. 13–11 but the likeness of *e·*

error

loathes
Ret. 81–18 The enlightened heart loathes *e·*,

material
My. 232–24 material *e·* finally disappears,

may enter
Ret. 54–18 *e·* may enter through this same

may say
Un. 18– 6 *E·* may say that God can never

meets
My. 180–16 C. S. meets *e·* with Truth,

mental
Rud. 3–21 mental *e·* made manifest physically,

mists of
No. 28– 4 mists of *e·*, . . . will melt

mortal
Mis. 21–19 matter is mortal *e·.*
56–15 to conclude that . . . is a mortal *e·*,
77–28 could fall into mortal *e·* ;
Un. 46– 1 mortal *e·*, called *mind*, is not

mystery of
Mis. 223– 1 the metaphysical mystery of *e·*

name the
My. 235–12 definitely name the *e·*, uncover it,

negation, or
Mis. 334–22 How shall we treat a negation, or *e·*

negativing
Mis. 208–18 by divine Truth's negativing *e·*

neutralizing
Pul. 6– 2 when Truth is neutralizing *e·*

never created
Mis. 49–31 that Truth never created *e·*,

never to repeat
Mis. 346–25 rule in C. S. never to repeat *e·*

ninety-nine parts of
No. 21– 3 philosophy has ninety-nine parts of *e·*

no
Mis. 77–18 Truth that knows no *e·*,
Un. 4– 6 Truth is All, and there is no *e·.*
No. 5– 7 To Truth there is no *e·.*

no sympathy for
No. 30–25 Truth has no sympathy for *e·.*

nothingness of
Pul. 13– 9 nothingness of *e·* is seen ;
13–10 nothingness of *e·* is in proportion to

not through
Un. 41–21 not through *e·*, but through Truth.

of anti-Christ
Mis. 309–18 falling into the *e·* of anti-Christ.

of belief
Mis. 45–27 This *e·* of belief is idolatry.
220–31 he knows that an *e·* of belief
No. 4– 9 *e·* of belief, named disease,

of believing
Ret. 69–17 *e·* of believing that there is life in

of creation
Mis. 57–23 The false sense and *e·* of creation

of material sense
Mis. 190–23 dumbness, an *e·* of material sense,

of mind
Hea. 9–24 an *e·* of mind or of body.

of premise
Mis. 200– 8 an *e·* of premise and conclusion,
344–18 from *e·* of premise would seek a

of sickness
Mis. 62–18 *e·* of sickness, sin, and death,

of statement
Mis. 56–21 Organic life is an *e·* of statement

of supposed life
Mis. 53– 5 *e·* of supposed life . . . in matter,

of the revolution
No. 6–21 *e·* of the revolution of the sun

of the senses
Un. 42–11 is an *e·* of the senses ;

of thought
No. 4–13 hence *e·* of thought becomes fable
My. 211–15 mortal mind into *e·* of thought,

opaque
Mis. 347–11 peer through the opaque *e·.*

opposite
Mis. 57–17 The opposite *e·* said, "I am true,"

or Adam
Mis. 258–19 *E·*, or Adam, might give names to

or evil
Mis. 259–25 *e·*, or evil, is really non-existent,

or false sense
Mis. 76–24 it is an *e·* or false sense of

or matter
Mis. 190– 4 Life, defiant of *e·* or matter.
Un. 42–24 Truth, defiant of *e·* or matter,

outside of the
Mis. 352– 9 facts of Truth outside of the *e·* ;

overcome
Mis. 89–27 saved from error, or *e·* overcome.

pantheistic
Ret. 69– 8 pantheistic *e·*, or so-called

error

peace in
  My. 233–23   destroys his peace in *e*,
penalty of
  Un. 11– 2   from the penalty of *e*.
phase of
  Mis. 25– 8   matter is a phase of *e*,
phases of
  Mis. 237–13   All the different phases of *e*
postulate of
  Mis. 57–13   postulate of *e* must appear.
qualities of
  Mis. 332–28   but are qualities of *e*.
rage
  My. 270–14   Let *e* rage and imagine a vain
rebukes
  Mis. 210–30   rebukes *e*, and casts it out.
  No. 43– 6   Truth rebukes *e* ;
remain in
  Mis. 2–25   If man . . . should remain in *e*,
renders
  Mis. 333– 6   this renders *e* a palpable falsity,
repeats itself
  '00. 10–17   History shows that *e* repeats itself
results of
  Mis. 288–11   works out the results of *e*.
root of
  Mis. 285–19   laying the axe at the root of *e*.
rule of
  No. 44–21   no Reign of Terror or rule of *e*
saved from
  Mis. 89–27   saved from *e*, or error overcome.
says
  Mis. 367–13   *E*· says that knowing all things
  Un. 17–20   *E*· says God must know evil
       18–13   *E*· says you must know grief
       18–22   *E*· says God must know death
seen aright as
  Mis. 299– 4   error that is seen aright as *e*,
see the
  Mis. 352– 7   must first see the *e* of its
self-assertive
  Mis. 268–30   self-assertive *e* dies of its own
self-destroying
  No. 10–16   matter, . . . is a self-destroying *e*.
selfhood in
  Mis. 363– 4   "ego" that claims selfhood in *e*,
senseless
  Mis. 355–19   Mental darkness is senseless *e*,
sense of
  Mis. 352–31   aroused to reject the sense of *e* ;
  Un. 1–19   they lose all sense of *e*.
side of
  My. 146–28   Others who take the side of *e*
smite
  Ret. 30– 2   endeavoring to smite *e* with
statements of
  Un. 20– 4   We undo the statements of *e* by
states of
  Mis. 007– 5   states of *e* or mortal mind.
strives
  My. 310– 4   When *e* strives to be heard
subtlety of
  Ret. 64–27   forms, methods, and subtlety of *e*,
such an
  Mis. 276–28   Such an *e* and loss will be
suggestion of
  My. 243– 5   This is a suggestion of *e*,
supersedes
  Un. 40– 8   As Truth supersedes *e*,
surging sea of
  Pul. 13–17   They are in the surging sea of *e*,
take
  Mis. 214–26   cannot . . . take *e* along with Truth,
tempest of
  Hea. 2– 7   and stills the tempest of *e* ;
that
  My. 197– 2   That *e* is most forcible which
that is seen
  Mis. 299– 3   *e* that is seen aright as error,
their
  Mis. 212– 9   had suffered, and seen their *e*.
the unreal
  Hea. 18–11   Truth is the real ; *e*, the unreal.
this
  Mis. 45–27   This *e* of belief is idolatry,
       83–16   to reject or to accept this *e* ;
     105–23   shadow cast by this *e*.
     184–21   suffer for this *e* until he learns
     212–26   and open his eyes to see this *e* ?
     265– 6   This *e* in the teacher
     287–11   Science corrects this *e*
     288–10   this *e* works out the results of
     364–28   This *e*, carried to its ultimate,
  Ret. 69–13   This *e* has proved itself to be

error

this
  Ret. 75– 3   This *e* violates the law
      83–14   this *e* . . . is sure to be corrected.
  Un. 36–24   This *e* stultifies the logic of
     42–12   very opposite of this *e* is the
  Rud. 9– 6   this *e* will spring up in the
     16–13   impostors are committing this *e*.
  No. 5– 6   severe realities of this *e*.
  Pan. 7–24   the logical sequence of this *e*
  My. 268– 7   What is this *e* ?
thrall of
  No. 11–26   rescue reason from the thrall of *e*.
three-in-one of
  Mis. 163– 1   to conquer the three-in-one of *e* :
throe of
  Mis. 285–22   some extra throe of *e* may
to buy
  Mis. 269–28   mortals to buy *e* at par value.
to declare
  No. 5– 8   it follows that to declare *e* real
to lose
  Mis. 84–25   To lose *e* thus, is to live in Christ,
to mix with
  Hea. 4–15   expect infinite Truth to mix with *e*,
to pay for
  Mis. 342–25   to pay for *e* and receive nothing
trespassing
  No. 3– 5   while the trespassing *e* murders
trinity of
  Un. 62–17   Destroy this trinity of *e*,
Truth and
  Mis. 65–10   question between Truth and *e*,
     188–12   contest between Truth and *e* ;
  '01. 22–10   Truth and *e*, Spirit and matter,
truth and
  Un. 60– 5   he articulates truth and *e*.
  Pan. 8–26   matter and Spirit, truth and *e*,
Truth, not
  Mis. 71–16   Law brings out Truth, not *e* ;
     297–28   Trust Truth, not *e* ;
  My. 239– 1   Truth, not *e* ; Love, not hate.
Truth over
  (*see* **Truth**)
Truth to
  Mis. 208– 2   the law of Truth to *e*,
     268–12   from Truth to *e*, in pursuit of
Truth versus
  Mis. 346–22   chapter sub-title
uncondemned
  '01. 15– 4   *E*· uncondemned is not nullified.
uncovers the
  Mis. 352–10   uncovers the *e* and quickens the
unfolding of
  Mis. 293– 4   the righteous unfolding of *e*
unreality of
  No. 17–19   Hence the unreality of *e*,
unreality of the
  No. 4–15   the unreality of the *e*.
versus
  Mis. 332–22   *E*· versus Truth :
victory in
  My. 278–26   Victory in *e* is defeat in Truth.
voicing
  No. 8– 6   Avoid voicing *e* ;
voluntary
  No. v– 5   involuntary as well as voluntary *e*.
warfare against
  Pul. 12–23   in our warfare against *e*,
warfare with
  Mis. 215–24   they have a long warfare with *e*
ways of
  Un. 55–16   self-destroying ways of *e*
we master
  Mis. 53– 5   only as we master *e* with Truth.
when found out
  Mis. 210– 5   certainty that *e*, when found out,
whole of
  Ret. 67– 3   is not the whole of *e*.
will hate
  Mis. 278– 5   *E*· will hate more as it realizes
witnesses for
  Un. 33–21   Examine these witnesses for *e*,
workings of
  Mis. 51– 9   malicious workings of *e*
would enthrone
  No. 42–16   material senses would enthrone *e*
would fashion
  No. 20–5   *E*· would fashion Deity in a manlike
wrestle with
  Mis. 336– 4   your province to wrestle with *e*,
yielding
  Mis. 107–20   pass through . . . before yielding *e*.
yields
  Mis. 204– 9   *e* yields up its weapons

error

Mis.	24–22	e·, the opposite of Truth ;
	36–30	The belief that . . . . is an e· ;
	49–18	wrong, sinful, or an e·?
	50– 2	e· is an illusion of mortals ;
	61–27	of e·, not of Truth ;
	80– 2	By rendering e· such a service,
	83–13	e· which knocks at the door of
	105–26	senses join issue with e·,
	112– 8	e·, given new opportunities,
	118–19	willing to suffer patiently for e·
	134–25	E· is only fermenting,
	141–12	e·, which hates the bonds
	177–19	salvation of the world from e·,
	221– 6	E· produces physical sufferings,
	221–18	If e· is the cause of disease,
	222–24	E· is more abstract than Truth.
	222–30	methods and power of e·.
	258–20	e· could neither name nor
	266– 6	to abridge a . . . privilege is an e·.
	266–29	e·, running to and fro
	269–27	E· is vending itself on trust,
	298–22	the seeming power of e·,
	299– 3	the what, when, and how of e·,
	348–13	E·, left to itself, accumulates.
	352– 4	to behold aright the e·,
	352– 4	the e· of regarding Life,
	354–10	e· to Truth, and evil to good,
	371–22	To sympathize in any degree with e·,
Ret.	57–17	Matter is substance in e·,
	59– 3	mortal mind . . . is e·.
	64–23	e· being a false claim,
	64–28	e·, may be destroyed ;
	64–29	will become the victims of e·.
	67–19	e· made its man mortal,
	69–10	saying, . . . I will make e· as real
	69–14	proved itself to be e·.
	71–11	an e· of much magnitude.
	84–21	empty his students' minds of e·,
Un.	22– 8	would taste and know e· for
	22– 9	not admit that e· is something
	22–18	Evil. . . . E·, even, is His offspring.
	38– 6	Death, then, is e·,
	57–28	existence in the flesh is e·
Rud.	8–17	e· has the majority.
	10– 3	if you have power in e·,
	10–25	e· which Truth will destroy.
No.	5– 5	an antipode,— the reality of e· ;
	5–26	contradictory fusion of Truth with e·,
	42–13	or to cast out error with e·,
	43–21	can never engraft Truth into e·.
'01.	22–12	Truth is true, . . . e·, is not ;
Hea.	17–20	Sin, sickness, and death are e· ;
Peo.	4–13	the e· that a personal God
	4–28	and cast out devils, e·.
Po.	70–15	Then, e·, get thee hence,
My.	211– 1	of e· that is damning men.
	217–25	improved belief is one step out of e·,
	235– 4	not name its opposite, e·.
	349 –6	e· that Truth destroys.

error's

Mis.	277– 8	becomes the mark for e· shafts.
Ret.	69–25	"Above e· awful din,
	81–16	overwhelming sense of e· vacuity,
Un.	45–16	it becomes e· affirmative

errors

are based
Mis.	71–18	E· are based on a mortal or

barefaced
Mis.	43–29	barefaced e· that are taught

his
Mis.	212–28	tries to show his e· to him
My.	233–22	to know what his e· are ;

history of the
Mis.	277–21	* history of the e· of the human mind."

innumerable
Mis.	137–26	each one of the innumerable e·

involved
Ret.	22–15	till its involved e· are vanquished

of flesh
Mis.	189–11	destroys the e· of flesh,

of others
Mis.	131– 1	challenges the e· of others
	236– 6	indiscretions, and e· of others ;

of the members
Man.	55– 3	e· of the members of their

of thought
Rud.	10–12	Mortal ills are but e· of thought,

old
'01.	21– 4	or new editions of old e· ;

our own
Mis.	224–28	Nothing short of our own e· should

prejudices, and
No.	9– 5	prejudices, and e· of one class of

these
Man.	55– 5	strive to overcome these e·.

errors

which devour
Mis.	82–28	the e· which devour it.

Mis.	234–15	e· which can never find a place in

errs

Mis.	308– 7	greatly e·, stops his own progress,
Ret.	59–15	Whatever e· is mortal,
	94– 7	seems to be good, and yet e·,

erudite

Ret.	31–28	E· systems of philosophy and

erudition (see also erudition's)

No.	2–21	beacon-lights along the shores of e· ;
My.	340– 9	The enlightenment, the e·,

erudition's

Ret.	11–20	From e· bower.
Po.	60–18	From e· bower.

escape

Mis.	53– 8	e· the weariness and wickedness of
	64– 3	way he made for mortals' e·.
	76–14	to e· and be immortal.
	85–27	to e· from sense into the
	105–11	to e· from the material body.
	109–25	to e· from the false claims of sin.
	113–18	of e· from the latter-day ultimatum
	119–30	and e· the penalty therefor?
	126– 1	from danger to e·,
	162–20	to e· from the sins of the flesh.
	261– 3	evil finds no e· from itself ;
	269– 4	He cannot e· from barriers
	347– 5	e· from their houses to the open
	347– 7	To e· from this calamity
Un.	14–24	How then could man e·,
	14–25	or hope to e·,
	64–18	nor e· from identification with
Pul.	15–13	E· from evil, and designate those
	51– 8	* though they cannot e· censure,
No.	17– 4	From this logic there is no e·.
	17–18	no e· from the focal radiation of
Pan.	12–14	way of e· from sin, disease, and
'00.	5–18	enable man to e· from idolatry
My.	41–13	* no one to e· that blessedness,

escaped

Mis.	311–30	never e· from my lips,
Hea.	18– 9	never e· from matter ;
My.	74–22	* e· from the bondage of the

escapes

My.	159–15	the true thought e· from

eschew

Mis.	271–11	e· all magazines and books which

eschewed

My.	288–17	so-called laws of matter he e· ;

eschewing

Peo.	4–28	E· a materialistic and idolatrous

eschews

Mis.	80– 9	A league . . . which C. S. e·
My.	303–14	e· divine rights in human beings.

escort

My.	302–27	wanted to greet me with e·
	312–28	The Free Masons selected my e·,

Esculapius (see also Æsculapius)

Peo.	4–24	Apollo and E· the gods of medicine,

escutcheon

Ret.	86–15	no blot on the e· of our Christliness
My.	194–17	fair e· of your church.
	341– 4	on the e· of this State,

esoteric

Mis.	29–24	e· magic and Oriental barbarisms

especial

Mis.	3– 3	shall claim no e· gift from
My.	325– 2	* and spoke of one e· day
	329–10	* gives e· interest to the

especially

Mis.	62–26	e· when she tells them that she
	128– 4	e· within the limits of a letter.
	138–13	e· should he prove his faith
	176– 9	devotion to Principle has e·
	244–30	e· the children of our Lord
	249–10	and e· through my teachings,
	263–17	e· by those at a distance,
	263–26	e· by unprincipled claimants,
	276– 1	e· the large book of rare flowers,
	277–26	Love is e· near in times of hate,
	315– 2	e· adapted to the occasion,
	320– 6	e· dear to the heart of
	348–20	every day, and e· at dinner,
Man.	28–26	e· of one who has been or
Ret.	5–30	* e· in regard to the education of
	6– 2	* e· entrusted to her watch-care,
Un.	23–16	e· when they testify concerning

especially

Pul. 7– 4 and e· the laws of the State
59–28 * seats were e· set apart for them
62– 3 * in the Old Country, e· in England.
87– 2 * We e· desire you to be present
Rud. 2– 3 * e·, a living human being,
2–10 as e· a finite *human being;*
No. 9–17 e· in the first edition
'00. 12– 9 It e· flourished as an emporium
'01. 32–22 e· the First Commandment of the
'02. 12–24 e· before making another united
My. 7– 8 e· before making another united
167– 1 e· for the self-sacrifice
170– 1 I am e· desirous that it should
299–18 e· those who claim to pardon sin,
313–17 * e· at night," as stated by
313–21 I never was e· interested in
318– 7 I e· employed him on "S. and H.
324– 2 * e· your book S. and H.
326– 7 * It is e· gratifying to them
351– 5 * This letter is e· interesting

essayed

Ret. 22– 6 e· in the Apocryphal New Testament

Esse

My. 202–25 underived glory, the divine *E·.*

essence

Mis. 69– 2 His e·, relations, and attributes.
121–18 belies the nature and e· of Deity,
163–30 This idea or divine e· was, and is,
394– 4 infinite e· from tropic to pole,
Ret. 33–20 rarefied to its fatal e·,
Un. 39– 6 quenched in the divine e·,
No. 12– 3 e· of this Science is right thinking
19–19 e· of the individual infinite.
'00. 5–13 the e· and source of the
'01. 4–26 and these three are one in e·
Peo. 10– 1 Thought is the e· of an act,
Po. 45– 5 infinite e· from tropic to pole,
My. 159–27 * "What is the e· of God?
178– 8 This Science is the e· of religion,
204–10 that sacred *ave* and e· of Soul
212– 5 the e·, or spirit, of evil,
342–27 Its e· is evangelical.

essences

Peo. 10 1 E· are refinements that lose
My. 345–28 They seek the finer e·.

essential

Mis. 13–16 e· to a rounded sense of the
50–15 it is e· that the student
51– 1 This change of heart is e·
61–22 Does God's e· likeness sin,
62–15 *hold that their theology is e· to*
76–30 e· to the fulfilment of this
232–11 behind the times in things most e·,
234–12 to things most e· and divine.
264–10 Unity is the e· nature of C. S.
349– 8 not necessitate e· materialization
Man. 88–21 subjects e· to their progress.
Ret. 14–13 if assent to this doctrine was e·
83–27 That these e· points are
Un. 22–14 e· to happiness and life.
Pul. 80– 5 * as Mrs. Eddy felt it e· to
53– 9 * which Jesus . . . declared to be e·,
53–20 * the e· element of success
54–21 * that are e· to success.
72–28 * naming as one great e·
'01. 1–12 most e· to your growth
30– 6 are e· to its propagation.
My. 46–17 * e· requirement of a reinstated
99– 6 * a pleasure and an e· ;
303–19 it is e· to understand the spiritual

essentially

Mis. 237–16 This period is not e· one of
258–29 differs e· from the human.
266–22 They are e· dear to me,
Ret. 94–17 preaching, and practice be e· one.
My. 247– 2 E· democratic, its government
254–24 E· democratic, its government

essentials

Pul. 39– 2 * great e· of love to God
No. 3–27 possessing the e· of C. S.,
My. 93–26 * have overlooked these e· of

establish

Mis. 38–13 *How happened you to e· a college*
176–23 The Pilgrims came to e· a nation
234–19 to e· this mighty system of
Pul. 85–17 * believe it to be possible to e·
Pan. 6– 1 Science will restore and e·,
15– 7 e· us in the most holy faith,
My. 52–17 * to e· these our Master's commands
111–18 e· their practice of healing
214–23 or to e· a C. S. home
215–18 to e· a Metaphysical College,

establish

My. 221–10 e· the definition of omnipotence,
279–17 e· the brotherhood of man,

established

Mis. 187– 6 He e· health and harmony,
193–10 can be e· on no other claim
383– 6 wherever a church of C. S. is e·,
Man. 41–22 e· in me, and rule out of me all sin ;
49–15 under rules e· by the publishers.
71– 4 more than one church is e· in the
Ret. 93– 7 e· its rules in consonance with
Un. 6– 8 e· on everlasting foundations.
33–25 every word may be e·." — *Matt.* 18 : 16.
Pul. 6– 5 church e· by the Nazarene Prophet
30– 5 * unite with churches already e·
No. 9– 6 must not be introduced or e· among
28–15 The proof . . . I consider well e·.
38– 6 He e· the only true idealism
Hea. 11–18 it has e· this axiom,
15– 3 e· upon this Principle,
18–20 he e· his Messiahship on the basis
My. v–15 * e· the Cause on a sound basis
vi–28 * she e· the C. S. *Sentinel*
9– 1 * those previously e· have had
33–30 * it upon the floods. — *Psal.* 24 : 2.
47–10 * After a work has been e·,
56–20 * foregoing named churches were e·,
56–22 * more branch churches were e·
90–31 * e· beyond cavil.
241– 4 * that for which it was e· ;
245– 6 e· on a broad and liberal basis.
265–11 brotherhood of man should be e·,
281–11 brotherhood of all peoples is e· ;
348–21 its value to the race firmly e·.

establishes

Mis. 73–10 e· the reality of what is spiritual,
101–14 scientific sense of being which e·
Rud. 3–21 e· the opposite manifestation

establishing

Mis. 153– 2 e· the Cause of C. S.
177–17 work of e· the truth,
Ret. 63– 4 e· the recognition that God *is* All,
My. 53–18 * After e· itself as a church
163–29 e· in this city a church
182– 8 by e· a new-old church,

establishment

Mis. 238–14 labor for the e· of a cause
Man. 63–14 E·.
Ret. 48– 4 e· of *genuine* C. S. healing
94–27 the e· of Christ's kingdom
Un. 8–18 by the e·, through reason,
Rud. v– 6 e· OF THE SCIENCE OF MIND-HEALING
'01. 30–20 the e· of a new-old religion
My. 220–17 e· of Christian religion
280– 9 * things which make for the e· of
310–12 manufacturing e· in Tilton,

estate

Mis. 64– 7 and rose to his native e·,
77–26 fallen away from his first e· ;
167–20 Is he heir to an e· ?
182–13 his perfect and eternal e·.
Pul. 49–27 * a strikingly well-kept e·
50– 6 * in buying so large an e·
58– 7 * e· called Pleasant View ;
My. 41–24 * his real e· is one of blessedness.
123–16 The original cost of the e·
(*see also* **real estate**)

estates

My. 66– 7 * ten e· having been conveyed

esteem

Mis. 84– 9 the world's temporary e· ;
356–25 gone down in his own e·.
Ret. 29– 2 I e· all honest people,
'01. 24–10 * "I e· my having taken this
My. 9–13 * depth of our affection and e·.

esteemed

Ret. 19–13 highly e· and sincerely lamented
My. 157–10 * where, . . . you are so highly e·,
330–25 highly e· and sincerely lamented

esteems

Mis. 289–24 if the wife e· not this privilege,

Esther

Pul. 82–20 * there were Miriam and *E·,*

Esthers

Pul. 82–22 * there are ten thousand *E·,*

estimable

My. 324–15 * neither Mr. Wiggin nor his e· wife

estimate

Mis. 247–24 seems, to the common e·,
248– 9 Greeks showed a just e· of
Ret. 21–20 to spiritual joy and true e· of being.

estimate

Ret.	49–14	must learn to lose their e· of
Pul.	30– 9	* but this e·, as I understand,
No.	43– 8	* He who knows all things can e·
Hea.	7–11	where Jesus formed his e· ;
My.	115– 8	my e· of the C. S. textbook.
	357–17	proportionably e· their success

estimated

Mis.	131–27	if, indeed, it could be e·.
'00.	7– 7	e· that during the past three years
My.	76–18	* e· cost of the extension
	77–14	* it is e· that not less than
	77–25	* e· that nearly forty thousand
	86–13	* every cent of the e· cost
	181–22	e· that Chicago has gained from

estimation

Mis.	383–14	in the e· of thinkers

estranged

Mis.	236–22	Be not e· from each other

estrangement

'02.	18–16	No e·, no emulation,

estranges

No.	15–24	e· mortals from divine Life

et cetera

Mis.	78–17	some people employ the e· c· of
	114–20	and all the e· c· of evil.
	357– 2	all the e· c· of the ways and means
My.	25–18	consumed in travel, e· c·,
	110–15	all the e· c· of mortal mind
	124–24	log, traveller's companion, e· c·,

et ceteras

'01.	21– 3	They are not the addenda, the e· c·,

eternal

absolute and

'00.	4–22	found final, absolute, and e·.
My.	260–10	the real, the absolute and e·,

All

Un.	25–24	elements which belong to the e· All,

and divine

Chr.	53–17	Thus Christ, e· and divine,

as God

Un.	49– 3	as definite and e· as God,
	59–13	Salvation is as e· as God.
No.	17–28	would be as e· as God.

as Truth

Mis.	163–23	are as e· as Truth,

attribute

Mis.	2–12	the e· attribute of Truth,

being

Un.	43– 1	e· being and its perfections,
No.	11– 4	divine Principle, and an e· being.

bliss is

Mis.	330–12	why not, since . . . bliss is e·,

bonds

No.	26–22	God holds man in the e· bonds of

Christ

My.	262–11	my sense of the e· Christ, Truth,

Christian Science

My.	357–21	to salvation and e· C. S.

Christmas

My.	260– 3	An e· Christmas would make matter an

circle

Un.	12– 5	curving sickle of Mind's e· circle,

coexistent and

'01.	5–26	are coexistent and e·,

currents

Mis.	157–28	cannot stop the e· currents of Truth.

damnation

No.	14–26	doctrine of e· damnation,

day

'00.	7–30	morning dawns on e· day.
Po.	22–11	And bask in one e· day.

definite and

Un.	49– 3	man is as definite and e· as God,

demands

My.	159–22	legitimate and e· demands upon man ;

dynamics

Mis.	258–31	explains the e· dynamics of being,

energies

Mis.	97– 3	e· energies of Truth,

erect and

Mis.	383–12	Erect and e·, it will go on

existence

Mis.	206– 9	interpret man's e· existence,
	286–19	spiritual and e· existence

fact

My.	143–16	the e· fact of C. S.

fire

Pan.	3–25	* heaven, earth, sea, the e· fire,

God

No.	37– 6	e· God and infinite consciousness

God is

No.	37– 8	evil is temporal and God is e·,

eternal

good

(see good)

harmonies

Mis.	72– 5	unfolds the e· harmonies of the

harmonious and

Mis.	5– 4	spiritual, harmonious, and e·.
	235–21	the real man, harmonious and e·.
Rud.	4– 4	perfect beings, harmonious and e·,
No.	6– 6	spiritual, harmonious, and e·,
My.	119– 5	is real, harmonious, and e·
	146–29	voices the harmonious and e·,

harmony

(see harmony)

haven

Ret.	57– 2	as we sail into the e· haven

heritage

Mis.	182–25	e· heritage of the Elohim,

idea

Mis.	79–12	the e· idea of Truth,
Un.	61– 7	even the e· idea of God,
No.	25–14	Man is the e· idea of

identity

No.	25–22	flesh is not man's e· identity.

image

'01.	5–27	His e· image and likeness.

immutable and

Un.	29–13	absolutely immutable and e·,
No.	11– 1	immutable and e· laws of God ;

individuality

Mis.	361–25	and all e· individuality.

infinite and

Peo.	4– 9	Life, which is infinite and e·,
My.	159–20	towards God, the infinite and e·

inseparable and

Mis.	182–28	man and . . . are inseparable and e·.

intact and

'02.	7– 1	nature of Love intact and e·.

joys

Mis.	xi–16	become footsteps to joys e·.

justice

Ret.	80– 3	though e· justice be graciously

law

Mis.	123–23	through the e· law of justice ;
No.	30–22	like the e· law of God,

laws

No.	11– 1	immutable and e· laws of God ;

Life

(see Life)

life

(see life)

Life is

Un.	37–13	God is Life, all Life is e·.

light

Mis.	134–14	He who dwelleth in e· light
Po.	70–10	Truth is e· light,

likeness

Un.	22– 2	made after God's e· likeness,

lore

Mis.	125–17	the e· lore of Love ;

Love

Mis.	206–31	baptismal font of e· Love.
	286–10	the unity of e· Love.

man is

Mis.	287– 3	forever fact that man is e·

mansion

Pul.	3–12	Truth and Love, man's e· mansion.

meridian

My.	177–12	and nearer the e· meridian

Mind

(see Mind)

noon

Mis.	385– 4	* And one e· noon."
Po.	37– 4	And one e· noon."

perfect and

Mis.	165–16	perfect and e·, appears
	182–13	recognize his perfect and e· estate.
	187–23	self-existent, perfect, and e·
	369–26	perfect and e· Principle of man.
Ret.	69–23	made all perfect and e·.
No.	28– 6	man be found perfect and e·.
My.	262– 1	God creates man perfect and e·

presence

Un.	60–28	must yield to His e· presence,

Principle

Mis.	369–26	e· Principle of man.
Pul.	4–23	unfolding its e· Principle.

punishment

'01.	16– 4	a future and e· punishment

qualities

Un.	32–14	the e· qualities of His being.

real and

(see real)

reality

Un.	36–12	Spirit is Truth and e· reality ;
	49–11	Through the e· reality of existence

eternal

real nor
Mis. 286–25   and neither real nor *e*.
right and
Mis. 71–30   Whatever is real is right and *e*;
341– 5   that is real, right, and *e*
roasting
Peo. 3– 6   *e* roasting amidst noxious vapors;
round
Mis. 77–17   *e* round of harmonious being.
scale
My. 277–18   weighs in the *e* scale of equity
Science
No. 17– 9   in the *e* Science of being
self-existent and
'01. 3–13   * Being, self-existent and *e*."
self-sustaining and
My. 275–26   is self-sustaining and *e*.
sense
Mis. 67–11   not strike at the *e* sense of Life
sermon
Mis. 126– 2   from . . . to one *e* sermon ;
somethingness
Ret. 55– 7   brings out . . . the *e* somethingness,
Son of God
'01. 11– 2   *c* Son of God, that never suffered
Spirit
Un. 22–19   cometh not from the *e* Spirit,
spiritual and
Mis. 188– 8   is primal, spiritual, and *e*.
286–19   for spiritual and *e* existence
Rud. 5– 7   man is spiritual and *e*,
No. 25–16   for he is spiritual and *e*,
37– 1   Son of God, spiritual and *e*.
stillness
Ret. 89– 1   *e* stillness and immovable Love.
sunshine
Mis. 279– 7   *e* sunshine and joy unspeakable.
My. 252–21   the *e* sunshine of Love,
supersensible
Un. 10–11   Spirit, the supersensible *e*.
Truth
Mis. 182–30   *e* Truth will be understood ;
Un. 17– 3   make the lie seem part of *e* Truth.
61– 2   takes hold of *e* Truth.
No. 10–14   rests on Mind, the *e* Truth.
truth
My. 54– 4   * for the sake of the *e* truth
143 18   discoverer of an *e* truth
unity
Mis. 77–11   *e* unity of man and God,
upright and
Mis. 79–15   God is upright and *e*,
verities
Mis. 55–21   the *e* verities of Spirit assert
363–19   in glimpses of the *e* verities.
No. 27–15   *e* verities of God and man
verity
My. 232–24   *e* verity, man created by

Mis. 19–30   spiritual, joy-giving, and *e*
61– 3   priceless, *e*, and just at hand.
70–24   holy Spirit of Jesus was *e*.
93–12   is in reality none besides the *e*,
100–18   and teach the *e*.
103– 5   while the other is *e*,
103–19   Neither does the temporal know the *e*.
104–15   sinless, deathless, harmonious, *e*.
136– 8   The *e* and the infinite, already
165–10   *e* as its divine Principle.
187–26   primal facts of being are *e*,
217–11   that matter and Spirit are one and *e* ;
268–28   is irresistible, permanent, *e*.
Chr. 53–59   E* swells Christ's music-tone,
Ret. 25–17   The real I claimed as *e* ;
59– 5   Life is not temporal, but *e*,
60– 3   as *e*, self-existent Mind ;
68–12   One is temporal, but the other is *e*.
73– 2   spiritual, individual, and *e*,
90– 1   divine, infallible, and *e*.
Un. 13–16   they must be *e* ;
24–21   must be spiritual, perfect, *e*.
51– 4   and hence that sin is *e*,
62– 7   which are not seen are *e*."— *II Cor.* 4: 18.
Pul. 2–11   are temporal, not *e*.
2–14   *e* in the heavens."— *II Cor.* 5: 1.
13–24   evil is temporal, not *e*.
No. 4–25   being, to be *e*, must be harmonious.
10–18   all consciousness is Mind and *e*,
16– 4   then . . . discord must be *e*.
17–23   the *e*, infinite harmony
'00. 5–14   *e*, infinite individuality.
'01. 9– 3   his *e* spiritual selfhood
25– 4   superstructure *e* in the heavens,
Peo. 2–25   Love universal, infinite, *e*.

eternal

Peo. 4– 7   and the *e* entered the
My. 44– 5   * promised land of *e*, harmonious
139–15   Life, — calm, irresistible, *e*.
143–21   an *e* and demonstrable Science,
160– 7   the spiritual, and the *e*,
179–28   are, irrefutable and *e*.
188–14   *e* in the heavens ;"— *II Cor.* 5: 1.
192–29   "*e* in the heavens."— *II Cor.* 5: 1.
194– 8   *e* in the heavens,"— *II Cor.* 5: 1.
195–28   *e* in the heaven of Spirit.
248– 9   defining the demonstrable, the *e*.
259–30   It represents the *e* informing Soul
348–29   the law of God — infallible, *e*.

eternally

Mis. 103–15   because *e* conscious.
Ret. 87– 3   poet's line, . . . is so *e* true,
94–23   since Science is *e* one,
Un. 10–17   and they are *e* perfect,
49– 4   being the *e* divine idea.
51–20   *e* radiating throughout all space
No. 16– 2   must truly and *e* exist.
Peo. 3– 7   majority to be *e* punished ;
8– 8   punishes man *e*,
My. 126–28   One thing is *e* here ;
161– 6   would destroy himself *e*,

eternity (*see also* eternity's)

all
Un. 17– 9   predestined from all *e* ;
awaits
My. 230– 2   *e* awaits our Church Manual,
chambers of
Po. 26–18   To the dim chambers of *e*
enfolds
Pul. 74–19   mankind which *e* enfolds.
glories of
Mis. 365– 2   bring out the glories of *e* ;
No. 21–23   brings in the glories of *e* ;
hoary with
Mis. 336–28   hoary with *e*, touches time only to
inhabits
Mis. 189–31   extends to all time, inhabits *e*,
keep pace with
Mis. 107–19   it cannot keep pace with *e*.
of joy
Mis. 135–18   is in itself an *e* of joy
plant for
'01. 33– 4   To plant for *e*,
My. 154–19   * "Wouldst thou plant for *e*,
rounds of
'02. 4–17   the measureless rounds of *e*.
seal of
My. 214–12   set the seal of *e* on time.
shoreless
Mis. 82– 6   as a river into a shoreless *e*.
shore of
Mis. 82–11   stand upon the shore of *e*,
spanned
Mis. 163– 9   He who . . . spanned *e*,
takes hold of
No. 13–18   It takes hold of *e*,
time and
   (*see* time)
time and for
'02. 5–10   the theme for time and for *e* ;

Mis. 15–19   *e* does this ; for progress is the law
292–10   such as *e* is ever sounding.
Pul. 3– 2   Can *e* end?   Can Life die?
Pan. 13– 1   in time and in *e* will witness more
Po. 22– 2   E* Draws nigh
30– 8   To glorify all time — *e*

eternity's

Mis. 121– 3   engraved upon *e* tablets.
Hea. 2–26   on Truth, *e* foundation stone.

ether

Mis. 26– 7   worlds, in the most subtle *e*,
45– 8   and destroy the necessity for *e*
87– 1   as the bird in the clear *e*

ethereal

'02. 5– 9   It is this *e* flame,
Peo. 10– 4   simply because it is more *e*.

etherialized

My. 345–27   more *e* ways of living.

ethical

Mis. 295–23   high and pure *e* tones
297– 8   bases its work on *e* conditions
My. 178– 1   *e* tenets, do not mislead

ethically

Mis. 138–13   *e*, physically, and spiritually.

ethics

Mis. v– 7   AND DEMONSTRATE THE *e* OF C. S.
64–17   *e* which guide thought spiritually

ethics
Mis. 247–11	from the highest possible *e·*.
264–30	mistake . . . in *e·*, is more fatal than
265–21	explaining spiritual Truth and its *e·*
269–10	who can better define *e·*,
316–21	tired aphorisms and disappointed *e·* ;
340–30	Material philosophy, human *e·*,
344– 3	Pythagorean professor of *e·*,
Ret. 21–26	illustrate the *e·* of Truth.
75– 5	does violence to the *e·* of C. S.
75–11	and one's writings on *e·*,
Un. 13–10	not infringed in *e·* any more than in
No. 44– 8	swerves not from the highest *e·*
'00. 11–29	His symbolic *e·* bravely rebuke
'02. 2–10	religions, *e·*, and learning,
2–16	*e·*, medicine, and religion,
My. 4–32	in *e·*, philosophy, or religion,
114–31	each step . . . in religion and *e·*,
129– 5	humanity, *e·*, and Christianity
179–31	therapeutics, *e·*, and Christianity
260–27	hygiene, medicine, *e·*,
351–12	*morale* of Free Masonry is above *e·*

etiology
Mis. 74–10	systems of *e·* and teleology.

etiquette
Mis. 283–19	I insist on the *e·* of C. S.,
342–30	the *e·* of the exchange,

Eton of America
Pul. 49–25	* "*E·* of *A·*," St. Paul's School.

Etta
Po. page 46	poem

etymology
Ret. 10–15	*E·* was divine history,

Eucharist
Pul. 38–13	"Atonement and *E·*,"
My. 136– 7	chapter Atonement and *E·*,

Euclid
Mis. 78–11	either *E·* or the Science of Mind
Un. 6–21	about the problems of *E·*.

eulogy
Ret. 5–17	*e·* of the Rev. Richard S. Rust,

eunuch
Mis. 77– 1	*Did the salvation of the e·*
77– 8	demand made upon the *e·*
77–21	the *e·* was to *know* in whom

euphonious
Ret. 27–26	manifestation is beautiful and *e·*,

euphony
My. 291–20	renew *e·*, emphasize humane power,

Europe (see also Europe's)
Mis. 170–20	history of *E·* and America ;
345– 1	bringing Christianity . . . into *E·*.
Ret. 47– 5	all over our continent, and from *E·*,
Pul. 36– 8	* students, from *E·* as well as this
No. 23–14	eminent divines, in *E·* and America,
My. 72– 9	* From all the centres of *E·*
85– 9	* meet in *E·* and in the antipodes,

Europe's
Pul. 49– 6	* some of *E·* masterpieces,

Eutaw Street
Mis. 243–12	107 *E· S·*, East Boston.

evade
Mis. 226–25	manages to *e·* the law,
227– 8	Thus, to *e·* the penalty of law,
300–16	and thus *e·* the law,
Un. 50–20	*e·* sin, sickness, and death,

evangel
Mis. 251–29	flee before the *e·* of Truth
My. 113– 3	not less the *e·* of C. S.
188–15	your oracle, . . . is Truth's *e·*,

evangelic
Ret. 65–20	C. S. is the pure *e·* truth.

evangelical
Mis. 193– 9	Doctrines that deny . . . cannot be *e·* ;
193– 9	*e·* religion can be established
194–11	and misinterpret *e·* religion.
249–13	devout members of *e·* churches
Man. 17– 5	They were members of *e·* churches,
Ret. 35–15	glow and grandeur of *e·* religion.
64–30	If *e·* churches refuse fellowship
'01. 12–17	and misinterpret *e·* religion.
34–11	Have we misread the *e·* precepts
My. 182– 6	recommendation to *e·* churches
342–27	Its essence is *e·*.

evangelism
Ret. 65–26	constitute the only *e·*,

evangelistic
Ret. 88–20	*e·* duty should not be so warped

evangelists
Ret. 93– 2	*e·* of those days wandered about.
My. 30–25	* record collections secured by *e·*

Eve
Mis. 86–18	more earthly to the eyes of *E·*.
109–18	allegory of Adam and *E·*
191–25	carried the question with *E·*.
Un. 51–17	not one . . . is an *E·* or an Adam.

eve
Pul. 37–17	* Christmas *e·*, as I sat in the
'02. 19– 5	he rebuked them on the *e·* of
Po. 53–11	Till heard at silvery *e·*

eve-bird's
Mis. 390– 7	The *e·* forest flute
Po. 55– 8	The *e·* forest flute

even (see also e'en)
Mis. 4–21	with isms, and *e·* infidelity,
6– 2	*e·* though sickness often leaves
10–29	*E·* in belief you have but one
11–19	must *e·* try not to expose their
16–14	*e·* its supremacy over sin,
18–14	*e·* in substance ;
18–20	*e·* the divine "Us"
22– 9	discovery of *e·* a portion of it?
23–16	Matter cannot *e·* talk ;
23–27	*e·* as the human likeness
26–11	*e·* while the Scripture declares
29–10	*e·* before the Christian era ;
30– 6	*e·* though failing at first to
33– 4	crucifixion of *e·* the great Master ;
43– 3	heal cases without *e·* having seen the
45–24	*e·* the belief that God is not
46–26	*e·* as the idea of sound,
46–29	man is perfect *e·* as the Father,
52– 8	*e·* the might of Truth,
58–28	*e·* one human mind governing another,
60–18	*e·* if touching each other
61– 7	*e·* when aping the wisdom
62– 9	*e·* as in mathematics.
63–24	*E·* as the struggling heart,
69–21	His physicians had failed *e·*
70–28	*e·* in the silent tomb,
71–28	*e·* human concepts,
77–11	*e·* the eternal unity of man and God,
79–24	*e·* so in Christ shall — *I Cor.* 15 : 22.
84–29	*e·* though it be through the
85–14	*e·* as your Father — *Matt.* 5 : 48.
86–22	*E·* the human conception of beauty,
86–30	*e·* this pleasing thraldom,
88– 2	*e·* sometimes feel the need of
90–14	do ye *e·* so to them." — *Matt.* 7 : 12.
93–29	to indulge . . . *e·* one moment.
93–31	*e·* if you suffer for it
95–12	*e·* a synopsis of C. S.,
103–32	*E·* while his personality was
107– 1	*e·* the sweetness and beauty in
109–12	*e·* a mild mistake must be seen
109–25	*e·* the power to escape from the
112– 3	*E·* honest thinkers, not knowing
114–29	*e·* its utter nothingness
115– 6	*e·* the teacher's own deficiency
116–22	*e·* as the fruits of watchfulness,
119–22	*e·* in the least,
119–32	do ye *e·* so to them." — *Matt.* 7 : 12.
121– 7	*e·* the cup of martyrdom:
121–14	*e·* a divine decree, a law of Love !
126–23	*e·* gold is less current.
127–19	*e·* that joy which finds one's
127–23	*e·* though your pearls be downtrodden.
132– 5	*e·* wider than before,
132– 8	*E·* the desire to be just
137–19	*E·* this : Disorganize the
138–11	*e·* the divine Principle which
139– 5	as you *e·* yet have not received.
140– 7	*e·* after the manner that all
141–14	*e·* the annihilating law of Love.
145–14	*E·* vanity forbids man to be vain ;
145–21	remains, to quicken *e·* dust
146–19	do ye *e·* so to them." — *Matt.* 7 : 12.
151–23	God is — what? *E·* All.
154–14	*e·* that vine whereof our Father is
155– 6	*e·* as God has blessed you.
155–17	Mother has not the time *e·* to
162– 1	*e·* as, at times of special
166–18	Judæan religion *e·* required the
166–27	*e·* if not acknowledged,
167– 8	*e·* the compound idea of
175–13	*e·* as the leaven expands the loaf.
180–22	*e· to them that believe* — *John* 1 : 12.
181– 2	your Father," *e·* God. — *Matt.* 23 : 9.
182–18	*e·* the understanding that
182–31	*e·* as they did . . . centuries ago.
184–17	*e·* as when saying,
184–31	*e·* mortal mind purged of the

even

Mis. 186– 9 e· separates its conception of man
186–31 e· the sense of the real man
187– 9 e· as in Science a chord is
191–25 supposed to have out-talked e· Truth,
193– 4 Jesus did mean all, and e· more
193–17 thankful e· for his allusion to truth ;
194– 2 e· the power of a drug to heal
214–22 e· to understand my works,
217– 6 e· the ideal world
222–25 E· the healing Principle,
224–27 when no wrong is meant, nor e· when
226–22 e· of those who have lost their honor
228–11 e· while seeking to raise those
229–17 e· the most High — Psal. 91 : 9.
234–21 e· the entire current of mortality,
235–29 do ye e· so to them," — Matt. 7 : 12.
236–20 e· though it be your best friend ;
238– 2 E· the loving children are
239–29 value of saying e· more bravely,
243–25 E· doctors disagree on that
244– 4 e· a "surgical operation"
247–15 to be taught it, e· gratuitously.
251–13 e·, the liberty of the sons of God,
251–27 e· as dry leaves fall to enrich the
253– 2 e· that Christianity is not merely
254– 7 e· the bread that cometh down
257–29 E· the chamber where the good man
258–24 e· the everlasting Father,
261–29 e· a knowledge of this Science,
262– 2 e· through this white-winged messenger,
262–28 Perhaps it is e· selfish in me
275– 3 e· woman's trembling, clinging faith
278–14 e· when he cursed the hour of his birth ;
284– 6 E· the humanitarian at work
286–30 e· as the Father is perfect,
288– 1 E· your sincere . . . convictions
292– 8 a new commandment e· for him.
294–23 desire to help e· such as these.
296–17 by no means identical — nor e· similar.
308–14 e·   they know its practicality only
308–25 e· as holding in mind the
309– 7 often fails to express e· mortal man,
310– 4 E· the teachings of Jesus
311–25 I did this e· as a surgeon
312– 5 e· that which lays all upon the
313– 9 e· as the dawn,
319– 3 e· as God is good,
329–11 e· as the heart may be ;
330–24 and e· pride should sanction
333– 4 e· that every ray of Truth,
336–13 e· that you first cast out your
337–22 E· the life of Jesus was belittled
345–15 but e· infidels may disagree.
346– 2 C. S. carries this thought e· higher,
348–19 not e· coffea (coffee), thea (tea),
349– 1 e· the offer of pecuniary assistance
351– 5 blessing o· my enemies,
363–19 E· through the mists of mortality
365–23 E· doctors agree that infidelity,
366–19 e· as Jesus admonished.
368– 3 E· so, Father, let the light
369–19 e· a crumb that falleth from
374– 2 caused e· the publicans to justify
380–13 E· as when an accident,

Man. 16– 7 e· the allness of Soul, Spirit,
19– 3 e· the understanding and
31–13 e· that spiritual animus
42–17 one Christ, e· that Christ whereof
42–24 do ye e· so to them." — Matt. 7 : 12.

Ret. 14–18 e· if my creedal doubts
14–29 e· the oldest church-members wept.
15– 9 e· of Thine only. — Psal. 71 : 16.
22– 3 bear brief testimony e· to the
23– 8 not e· fringed with light.
24–17 E· to the homœopathic physician
28– 7 demonstrate, e· in part,
30–18 E· so was I led into the mazes of
32– 3 e· the possibilities of spiritual
33–21 is found to be e· more active.
37–16 E· the Scriptures gave no direct
41– 6 without e· an acknowledgment of the
45–11 e· as the corporeal organization
50–14 or e· in half as many lessons.
59–11 e· as mortals apply finite terms to
64– 8 e· God's "image and — see Gen. 1 : 26.
64–10 e· the opposite claim of evil is one.
68– 7 E· the spiritual idea, or ideal man,
70–24 e· the reflection,
82– 6 e· if they are teachers and
82–25 if e· they compete with
83–16 communicates, e· unintentionally,
84–16 e· the power and glory of the
87–21 do ye e· so to them." — Matt. 7 : 12.
89–20 e· according to his promise,
90–13 e· though one of the twelve

even

Un. 6–14 e· the thinkers are not
7–23 dispels e· the sense or
8–20 e· the doctrine of heredity
22–18 Evil. . . . Error, e·, is His offspring.
28–13 are e· more vague than
32–20 responds, e· as did our Master :
38– 6 e· the unreality of mortal mind,
40–21 can never alarm or e· appear
46–20 To them evil was e· more the ego
54–17 e· as a false claimant,
58–12 E· the ice-bound hypocrite
60–13 e· the Father ; — Jas. 3 : 9.
61– 7 e· the eternal idea of God,
61–27 e· as the helpless sick are
64–10 e· if it were (or could be) God,

Pul. 2–14 e· the "house not — II Cor. 5 : 1.
3– 2 demolished, or e· disturbed?
7–17 e· when mistakenly committed in
8–16 E· the children vied with their
8–26 e· its centre-piece, — Mother's Room
20–15 e· that shadow whose substance
21– 5 e· those that hate them.
41–14 * and e· from the distant States
42– 7 * scarcely e· a minor variation
45– 7 * e· when the feat seems impossible
50–27 * show e· some one side of it
62–12 * e· when rung by hand
67–11 * e· Max O'Rell's famous enumeration
74–15 "E· the question shocks me.

Rud. 9– 5 E· the truth he speaks is
9–22 or e· a mental argument,
13– 6 e· in the smallest degree.

No. 16– 7 If God knows evil e· as a
19– 5 E· doctors will agree that
24– 1 e· the immeasurable idea of
25–11 e· as the infinite idea of Truth is
29–10 as if it were not e· a material sense.
30–19 of e· a claim to error.
33– 1 e· the wrath of man shall praise Him.
36– 7 e· while mortals believed it was here.
36–28 e· while the divine and ideal Christ
39–26 as photography grasps the solar
42–14 e· in the name and for the sake of

Pan. 1–18 e· the day when all people
9–11 e· as your Father — Matt. 5 : 48.
10– 2 what saith the apostle? e· this :

'00. 1– 1 methinks e· I am touched with the
10–15 assail e· the new-old doctrines

'01. 6–21 its theory e· seldom named.
7–17 e· as the Scriptures declare He will
8–15 e· as your Father — Matt. 5 : 48.
12– 9 e· the word Christian was anciently
14–22 e· as one guards his door
15–21 may e· need to hear the following
17– 6 loves e· the repentant prodigal
19–18 commanded e· the winds and waves,
20–20 E· the agony and death that
22–28 E· the numeration table of C. S.
28–25 well to know that e· Christ Jesus,
29– 3 or e· known of his sore necessities?
29– 9 e· as he has sacrificed for others
30– 1 persecuted e· as all other
30–16 E· religion and therapeutics

'02. 7–15 e· the forever I AM,
11–16 e· the knowledge of salvation
12–18 e· so God and man,
19–10 Brethren, e· as Jesus forgave,

Hea. 4– 9 e· as we ask a person with
10–19 e· the triumph of Soul over sense.
17–15 dream of material life, e· the dream

Peo. 1–16 E· the pangs of death disappear,
3–21 e· the quality or the quantity of
5–10 are nigh, e· at our door.
9–17 e· dare to invoke the divine aid
10– 2 e· as steam is more powerful than
11–10 e· the supremacy of Soul

Po. vii– 2 * yet, e· these are characterized by

My. 5–21 understanding e· in part,
6–24 e· the outcome of their hearts,
13– 7 first that I had e· heard of it.
18–15 e· that joy which finds one's
19–20 but I ask for more, e· this :
29–25 * E· the sun smiled kindly upon the
34–10 e· lift them up, — Psal. 24 : 9.
39–26 * But e· more distinctly may we
40– 9 * It may e· imply that some who
42–25 * comprehend, e· in small degree,
44–12 * e· unto the end — Matt. 28 : 20.
53–29 * e· though the continuity of thought
56– 8 * e· this provision was inadequate
56–27 * there was not e· standing-room.
63–17 * e· the greetings and congratulations
63–26 * e· more impressive than this
65–12 * It was not e· talked over,
73– 2 * e· to return more than

even

My.
74–12   * e· to those who are unable to
74–21   * e· if those outside are unable
83–25   * e· before the building itself has
84–2   * impress e· the man who
86–28   * Not e· the great size of the
89–15   * e· to the flagstones in front
91–25   * but e· stranger is its increase
92–10   * worthy of perhaps e· more interest
94–28   e· the outcome of their hearts,
105– 1   e· more than the words of Christ,
110–23   e· mortals can mount higher
119–31   e· to the true image
122–26   Truth, e· as Jesus declared ;
123– 4   prize love e· more than the gifts
126– 1   would enter e· the church,
127–14   e· as Aaron's rod swallowed up the
133–28   e· as your heart has discovered it.
139– 6   e· the spiritual idea of Life,
145–18   worked e· harder than usual,
146–11   be e· younger than now.
150–20   e· the calm, clear, radiant reflection
152–20   e· as the ages have shown.
154– 9   to infringe . . . e· in thought.
159– 5   e· unto the end." — Matt. 28 : 20.
159–25   E· Epictetus, a heathen philosopher
160–12   e· though it be a sapling
160–25   e· the fire of a guilty conscience,
177–12   I shall then be e· younger
179–32   make e· God demonstrable,
182– 9   e· Christ, Truth, as the chief
185–18   e· that which "was dead, — Luke 15 : 32.
188–11   e· the omniscience of
189– 6   affords e· me a perquisite of joy.
190–28   would remain, e· as it did,
196–25   e· the spiritually indispensable,
200–13   e· to the glorious beatitudes
201–13   E· the crown of thorns,
211– 9   e· as in Jesus' time
211–19   their worst enemies, e· those who
214–24   e· to meet my own current expenses.
216–31   to earn for a purpose e· higher,
218–10   e· the self-same Lazarus.
220–10   e· while you render
222– 2   e· the disciples of Jesus
222–15   E· in those dark days
226–22   e· as you value His all-power,
232– 6   e· the way of Truth and Love
233– 1   e· the spirit of our Master's
244–17   e· the inner sanctuary
249– 9   hating e· one's enemies excludes
264– 3   I e· hope that those who are
266– 9   do ye e· so to them." — Matt. 7 : 12.
269–22   rays of reality — e· C. S.,
274– 2   e· the Life that is Soul
274– 9   e· its all-power, all-presence,
281– 2   e· to know how to pray
283–16   e· though it be betrayed.
293–11   E· the physicians may have feared this.
307–12   He e· acknowledged this himself,
309– 5   e· acting as counsel in a lawsuit
328– 1   * e· as God has dignified, blessed,
340–29   e· the full beneficence of the laws
344– 1   I have e· been spoken of as a
357– 4   e· the divine idea of C. S.,

evening (see also evening's)

Mis.
148–25   presented at your Friday e· meetings.
225–8   In the course of the e·,
389– 5   poem
Man.
31–18   and the Wednesday e· meetings.
31–21   part of the Wednesday e· services,
47–23   at the Wednesday e· meeting.
96– 1   No Wednesday E· Lectures.
96– 3   not appoint a lecture for Wednesday e·.
Un.
61– 9   e· and the morning of human thought.
Pul.
31–22   * e· on which she would receive me.
36–14   * the e· that I first met Mrs. Eddy
Pan.
3–16   * or in thy e· shade,
Po.
3– 7   With e·, memories reappear
page 4   poem
46–15   Bright as her e· star,
My.
29–31   * until the close of the e· service,
78– 4   * morning, afternoon, and e·.
79–24   * chapter sub-title
87– 1   * from early morning until the e·,
134–21   * At the Wednesday e· meeting
241–19   * "Last e· I was catechized by a
289–25   on Sunday e·, February 3,
313–19   when I took an e· walk,
322–19   * During the e· my friend spoke of
323– 3   * Before we left that e·,

Evening Monitor
Pul.
76–21   * [E· M·, Concord, N. H.,

Evening Reporter
Pul.
88–29   * E· R·, Lebanon, Pa.

evening's
Pan.
3–12   the e· closing vespers,

event
Mis.
162– 3   third e· of this eventful period,
197–17   belief in any historical e·
319–29   between the promise and e· ;
Ret.
7–21   * This sad e· will not be soon forgotten.
13– 4   In connection with this e·,
24– 4   in no wise connected with this e·,
Un.
3–28   and guides every e· of our
Pul.
79– 7   * The dedication, . . . is a notable e·.
No.
37–13   full-orbed glory of that e· ;
My.
21– 2   * expended in such an e·.
30–19   * gratitude for the epoch-making e·.
60–25   * the great e·, the dedication
90–25   * is an e· of impressiveness
100– 2   * in connection with the e·
284–16   * first time . . . that such an e·

eventful
Mis.
162– 3   third event of this e· period,
Ret.
23– 1   too e· to leave me undisturbed
Pul.
44–11   * auspicious hour in your e· career.
55– 7   * not the least e· circumstance

eventide (see also eventide's)
Po.
66– 6   Sweet spirit of love, at soft e·

eventide's
Mis. 394– 2   borne on the zephyr at e· hour ;
Po. 45– 1   borne on the zephyr at e· hour ;

events
Mis.
12–11   the future, big with e·.
48–21   hidden nature of some tragic e·
148–15   the logic of e·,
209–29   scientific logic and the logic of e·,
253–14   This period is big with e·.
269–13   in relation to human e·?
304–24   * days on which great e· have
306– 7   * welcome suggestions of e· to be
339–26   mayest have sent along the ocean of e·
Man.
3–12   the logic of e·,
Ret.
8– 1   e· connected with my childhood
21–25   personal e· are frivolous
70–13   recurrence of such e·.
Un.
19– 5   e· which are contrary to His
Pul.
32–15   * so far as outward e· may
'02.
20– 1   on the ocean of e·,
My.
31–22   * one of the e· of their lives.
45– 7   * e· associated with this,
142–13   most important e· are criticized
224– 4   should wait on the logic of e·
272– 4   logic of e· pushes onward the
281– 7   faith in God's disposal of e·.

eventually
Mis.
292–14   Divine Love e· causes mortals to
323–16   Stranger e· stands in the valley
Ret.
32– 6   corporeal personality, is e· lost.
Un.
18–20   e· destroy, every supposition of
Pul.
13–19   must e· expiate their sin
66–26   * e· to supplant those in
My.
160–23   will e· consume this planet.

ever (see also e'er)
Mis.
ix–21   a Psyche who is e· a girl.
24–13   e· after was in better health than
27–13   no species e· produces its opposite.
27–22   though God is e· present ;
46–18   be e· found in the scale with
48–23   Was e· a person made insane by
49–11   e· having occurred in a class
56–14   or e· has constituted laws to that
85– 4   Is a Christian Scientist e· sick,
103–16   must be e· in bondage,
105–18   I must e· follow this line of light
116–11   question, e· nearest to my heart,
147–22   we find him e· the same,
149–18   Lips nor pen can e· express
157–29   E· with love,
172– 7   a higher sense than e· before,
173– 5   Who has e· learned of the schools that
173– 8   Who has e· learned from the schools,
182–20   since he is and e· was the image and
185–24   how much of a man he e· has been:
238–10   All that e· was accomplished,
245– 1   no record showing that our Master e·
276–32   stand firmer than e· in their
277– 5   more imperatively than e·.
292–10   such as eternity is e· sounding.
303–16   If e· I wear out from serving students,
327–21   more than e· determined
345–16   * "E· since the reign of Christianity
370–14   more intelligently than e· before,
386– 6   Thine, e· thine.
386–17   a hope that e· upward yearns,
Ret.
5–29   * She e· entertained a lively sense
6– 7   The needy were e· welcome,

ever

Ret.
6–17 e· connected with that institution.
22–18 nor is he e· created through the
44– 4 first such church e· organized.
49–20 only one e· granted to a *legal college*
62– 7 than *a belief in their reality has* e· done.
83–27 That these essential points are e·
90– 7 to show that Jesus e· entered
91– 6 e· fell upon human ears

Un.
18–24 to be e· conscious of Life
23– 5 Edgar, was to his father e· loyal.
26–13 * Chance and change are busy e·,
28–11 not a spectre had e· been seen
37–11 Because God is e· present,
60–21 God is e· present,
64–12 e· eluding their dread presence

Pul.
12–19 than has e· before reached high heaven,
20–18 greatest . . . religious reform e· known
72–30 * e· hear of Jesus' taking medicine
77– 4 * elegant memorials e· prepared,
78– 3 * of the goldsmith's art e· wrought in

Rud.
5–11 who has e· found Soul in the body
5–12 who has e· seen spiritual substance

No.
20–18 Ever-present Love must seem e· absent to
20–23 Satan's reasoning, e· since the
30–12 this perfect law is e· present to

Pan.
8–22 must e· rest on the basis of the
12– 5 * Spirit, is e· in universal nature."

'01.
1– 8 better appreciated, than e· before,
2–19 e· storming sin in its citadels,
23–22 as no other person has e· demonstrated
27– 9 the first e· published on C. S.,
30– 2 since e· the primitive Christians,

'02.
12–10 that God is come, and is e· present.
14–12 the only success I have e· achieved
17–17 Who of the world's lovers e· found

Hea.
4–21 e· arrive at a proper conception of
6–10 abused me for it then, and have e· since;
13–15 highest attenuation we e· attained
14–18 most arduous task I e· performed.

Peo.
13–25 * "Since e· the history of Christianity

Po.
23– 6 Come e· o'er thy heart?
23–11 So may their gaze be e· fraught
31–18 The e· Christ, and glorified
02 6 fragrance and charms e· new
43–11 E· thus as Thine !
47– 1 Are the dear days e· coming again,
47– 5 Oh, e· and nevermore?
47– 6 E· to gladness and never to tears,
47– 7 E· the gross world above ;
47– 9 E· to Truth and to Love?
47–11 Outside this e· of pain?
49–10 Thine, e· thine.
50– 1 hope that e· upward yearns,

My.
vii– 3 * Strive it e· so hard,
10–15 * No appeal has e· been made in this
10–17 * none will be made or e· be needed.
15–13 goes out to you as e·
26–13 that I have e· received
29–19 * will e· be able to forget.
37–13 * which has e· healed the sick.
38–25 * they would e· carry with them
44– 9 * of our e· faithful Leader.
56–19 * increased faster than e·.
59–28 * before it was e· written.
60–28 * before it was e· printed."
62– 9 * How can we e· thank God enough
62–10 * e· thank you enough for your
62–28 * who were e· ready to assist us
65– 3 * e· held in Boston
65– 4 * e· held in the United States
75–27 * e· yet been dedicated by
79–22 * than it e· occupied before.
81–17 * No more cosmopolitan audience e·
86– 4 * As Boston has e· loved its
87–20 * I do not think I have e· seen
91–11 * spiritual aspirations were e·
91–19 * country has e· known.
110– 2 e· present, casting out evils,
136–17 highest fee e· received by
144– 8 With love, e· yours,
145–16 * "I am as well as I e· was."
148– 2 and more than e· persistently,
149–32 no condition, be it e· so severe,
159– 6 Thus may it e· be that Christ
213–19 Be e· on guard against this enemy.
239–29 going on since e· time was.
249– 3 condemn persons seldom, if e·.
257–14 Christ is, more than e· before,
265– 4 knocks more loudly than e· before
272–11 * e· shall be the greatest
282–26 prosper e· this good endeavor.
292– 3 All good that e· was written,
310–28 * "When do you e· see Mary angry?"
318–25 * "How do you know that there e·
321–13 * cannot believe that he has e· said
325–16 * e· faithfully your student,

ever

My.
347–13 * nor e· bid the Spring adieu !
360– 3 As e·, lovingly your teacher,

ever-conscious

Un.
18–23 God saith, I am e· Life,

ever-flowing

Mis.
360–23 e· tides of spiritual sensation

My.
149–10 its might is the e· tides of truth

evergreen

Mis.
ix–22 is not the e· of Soul ;

Peo.
14– 4 amaranth blossoms, e· leaves,

Po.
16– 1 gentle cypress, in e· tears,
67–17 cypress may mourn with her e· tears,

My.
139– 9 verdure and e· that flourish when

everlasting

Mis.
vii–18 sprung from Spirit, In e· day ;
74–26 was an e· victory for Life ;
105–17 C. S. is an e· victor,
118–28 persistent effort with e· victory.
161– 7 The e· Father, — Isa. 9 : 6.
163– 7 a sublime and e· victory !
164–18 The e· Father, — Isa. 9 : 6.
258–24 even the e· Father,
261–26 already saved with an e· salvation.
277–11 right wins the e· victory.
321– 6 The e· Father, — Isa. 9 : 6.
328–31 up to the throne of e· glory.
336–29 That it rests on e· foundations,

Ret.
14–28 lead me in the way e·."–Psal. 139 : 24.
49–22 And e· gratitude is due to the

Un.
6– 9 established on e· foundations.
14–20 firmer than e· hills.
14–25 a knowledge which is e·
40–13 can no more receive e· life by
51– 1 and the e· facts of being appear,

Pul.
12–21 her primal and e· strain.

No.
25–20 but what this e· individuality is,
34–26 Nameless woe, e· victories,

'00.
7–18, 19 from e· to e· this Christ is never

'01.
15–24 * swallowed up in e· destruction.

'02.
20– 6 tipping the dawn of e· day,

My.
33–12 lead me in the way e·." — Psal. 139 : 24.
34–11 ye e· doors :— Psal. 24 : 9.
37–10 * e· advantage of this race.
129–23 gives to man health and life e·
131–13 seals the covenant of e· love.
171– 9 songs and e· joy — Isa. 35 : 10.
177–24 e· covenant with them." — Isa. 61 : 8.
193– 3 whom to know aright is life e·.
206–19 unto thee an e· light, — Isa. 60 : 19.
253– 3 higher and e· harmony,
(see also **Life**)

ever-living

Mis.
124–14 the ever-loving, e· Life,

ever-loving

Mis.
124–14 the e·, ever-living Life,

evermore

Mis.
100–20 the e· of Truth is triumphant.
384–13 And Love, the e·.

Pul.
53–30 * Is e· the same.

'00.
15–30 And love, the e·.

Po.
36–12 And Love, the e·.
47–19 E· gathering in woe

ever-operative

My.
109–13 the e· divine Principle

ever-presence

Mis.
14– 3 the e· and all-power of good;
196–19 e· and power of God,
258–25 as infinite consciousness, e·,

Un.
62– 4 e· that neither comes nor goes,
62–27 to discern faintly God's e·,
63– 8 so-called . . . reappearing of e·,

Rud.
11–23 all-power and e· of good,

Peo.
13–10 His all-power and e·,

My.
192–28 whisper to you of the divine e·.

ever-present

Mis.
174–19 No : it is e· here.
183– 2 e· good, omnipotent Love,
238–19 and are an e· reward.
268–18 the omnipotent and e· good.
307– 3 divine Love is an e· help ;
328– 8 the Stranger the e· Christ.

Ret.
31–13 e· relief from human woe.
60–13 good is God e·,
65–30 reveals God as e· Truth and Love,

Un.
43–26 e· Life which knows no death,
52– 7 the e· reign of harmony,
60– 2 through e· and eternal good.
62–10 omnipotent and e· good

Pul.
11– 5 dedicated to the e· God

Rud.
3–27 e· I AM, filling all space,

No.
17– 6 God is good, e· and All.

ever-present

No. 17–14   God is not without an *e·* witness,
20–18   *E·* Love must seem
20–18   ever absent to *e·* selfishness
'00.   1– 5   *e·* Love filling all space, time,
'02.   16–19   spiritual idea of the *e·* God
My. 219–15   Truth, the *e·* spiritual idea,
254–13   will find the *e·* God
273–23   *e·* good, and therefore life eternal.
288– 6   good done and . . . are his *e·* reward.
294–14   *e·* power of divine Spirit
     (*see also* **help**)

ever-recurring

'02.   5–14   *e·* human question and wonder,

ever-self

Mis. 385–19   Now see thy *e·* ; Life never fled ;
Po.   48–13   Now see thy *e·* ; Life never fled ;

every

Mis.   v– 3   SCIENTISTS IN THIS AND *e·* LAND
13– 2   mercy and charity toward *e·* one,
18– 4   scourgeth *e·* son whom — *Heb.* 12 : 6.
18–13   its opposite, in *e·* God-quality,
26–11   "*e·* plant of the field — *Gen.* 2 : 5.
37–21   sin of *e·* sort, is destroyed by
38– 4   elevate man in *e·* line of life,
39–14   God giveth to *e·* one this *puissance;*
46–20   comprehending at *e·* point,
48– 9   opposed to it, as to *e·* form of error,
56–11   *E·* indication of matter's constituting
60–27   *e·* creation or idea of Spirit
60–28   *E·* material Mind hints the existence of
64–18   must benefit *e·* one ;
65–10   *E·* question between Truth and error,
67–19   Justice uncovers sin of *e·* sort ;
81–22   *E·* individual character, like the
83– 6   "*E·* sin is the author of itself,
83– 6   and *e· invalid the cause of his own*
85– 9   *e·* thought and act leading to good.
86– 8   manifest growth at *e·* experience.
89– 2   "*E·* kingdom divided — *Matt.* 12 : 25.
90–17   Break the yoke of bondage in *e·* wise
91–13   and under *e·* circumstance,
115–18   delivered from *e·* claim of evil,
115–25   *e·* effort to hurt one will only help
117–32   follow under *e·* circumstance.
118– 6   Honesty in *e·* condition,
118– 7   under *e·* circumstance,
118–28   *E·* attempt of evil to harm good
120– 5   obey implicitly each and *e·* injunction
120–29   puts to flight *e·* doubt
139–12   *e·* high thing that — *II Cor.* 10 : 5.
139–13   *into captivity e· thought* — *II Cor.* 10 : 5.
141–27   or else return *e·* dollar that you
146–21   *e·* reformed mortal that desired to come,
148–29   "Ho, *e·* one that thirsteth, — *Isa.* 55 : 1.
152–13   pulsates with *e·* throb of theirs
157–12   *E·* true Christian Scientist will feel
160–13   *e·* trial of our faith in God
169–18   dual meaning to *e·* Biblical passage,
175–10   increase by *e·* spiritual touch,
179–25   and He made *e·* flower
183–16   can fulfil the Scriptures in *e·* instance ;
185–12   flows into *e·* avenue of being,
187– 5   over and above *e·* sense of matter,
192–23   belongs to *e·* period ;
195–10   *e·* one can prove, in some degree,
197– 3   the motive-power of *e·* act.
200–13   applicable to *e·* stage and state
200–19   *e·* supposed material law.
220– 1   in *e·* line of mental healing,
232–22   *e·* woman would desire and demand it,
241– 6   as well as sin of *e·* sort.
243–13   *e·* system of medicine claims
247–31   must be met, in *e·* instance,
256–23   while *e·* quality of matter
257– 2   in *e·* mode and form of evil.
264– 1   *e·* random thought in line with mine.
288–22   in *e·* state and stage of being.
291–14   each and *e·* one has equal opportunity
303–15   *e·* one the same rights and
305–31   * *e·* one receiving this circular
307– 5   will have all you need *e·* moment.
307– 9   to suffering of *e·* sort.
307–30   *E·* human thought must turn
310–14   plead for all and *e·* one,
317–18   progress of *e·* Christian Scientist.
326–16   under *e·* hue of circumstances,
333– 4   even that *e·* ray of Truth,
339–16   it points to *e·* mortal mistake ;
340–27   *E·* luminary in the constellation
353–16   *e·* ten minutes on the regulator.
360–19   lift *e·* thought-leaflet
361– 9   *e·* form and mode of evil
361–18   lay aside *e·* weight, — *Heb.* 12 : 1.
363–30   *e·* advancing epoch of Truth

every

Mis. 375–15   * *e·* moment to the study of music
383–14   and on *e·* battle-field rise higher
389–14   glad for *e·* scalding tear,
389–16   Wait, and love more for *e·* hate,
391–15   That *e·* ragged urchin,
395–21   Is *e·* earthly love ;
Man. 18– 9   and at *e·* epoch saying,
26–12   *E·* third year Readers shall be
88–13   shall be elected *e·* third year
Ret.   7–12   * explored their *e·* nook and corner,
10– 7   the latter I had to repeat *e·* Sunday.
21– 4   *E·* means within my power was
28– 5   guiding our *e·* thought and action ;
35–16   true followers in *e·* period,
44–10   and in the pulpit *e·* Sunday,
48– 8   *e·* one should build on his own
52– 8   *e·* true seeker and honest worker
59–13   *e·* other name for the Supreme
61–24   If you rule out *e·* sense of
76–25   thinks of *e·* one in his real quality,
80– 6   scourgeth *e·* son whom — *Heb.* 12 : 6.
81–30   at *e·* stage of advancement.
86–11   Cleanse *e·* stain from this wanderer's
94–14   *e·* spot and blemish on the disk of
Un.   3–23   *e·* embodiment of Life and Mind.
3–28   guides *e·* event of our careers.
4– 7   Truth destroys *e·* phase of error.
5– 9   *E·* one should be encouraged
5–13   *e·* Life-problem in a day.
8–20   nothingness of *e·* claim of error,
18–20   *e·* supposition of discord.
21–10   *e·* tree of the garden." — *Gen.* 3 : 1.
29– 1   in this relation to *e·* hypothesis
33–25   *e·* word may be — *Matt.* 18 : 16.
35– 3   If *e·* mortal mind believed
47– 4   with *e·* passing hour it is
48– 1   fair to ask of *e·* one a reason for
54–10   insensible to *e·* claim of error.
56–13   *e·* follower of Christ shares his cup
Pul.   2–20   by *e·* means in your power,
7–17   power to wash away, . . . *e·* crime,
13– 3   *E·* mortal at some period,
22– 6   *e·* praying assembly on earth,
22–10   *e·* Christian church in our land,
23–19   * the closing years of *e·* century
27– 2   * French mirrors and *e·* convenience.
29–12   * *e·* seat in the hall was filled
37–12   * In *e·* sense she is the recognized
41– 2   * with *e·* stone paid for
41– 5   * From *e·* State in the Union,
45–12   * *e·* evidence of material sense
51–11   * *E·* truth is more or less in a
53–21   * *e·* field of human endeavor.
56– 4   * nearly *e·* other centre of population,
57– 4   * from *e·* State in the Union,
58–11   * *e·* bill being paid.
74– 7   * meets *e·* Sunday in Hodgson Hall,
80–10   * socially, indeed *e·* way.
Rud. 10–23   removes *e·* erroneous physical and
11–21   takes away *e·* human belief,
13–18   to treat *e·* organ in the body.
No.   3–16   *E·* teacher must pore over it in secret,
7–11   to see *e·* error they possess,
7–13   stubborn will, and *e·* imperfection
7–16   *E·* loving sacrifice for the good of
8–15   *e·* germ of goodness will at last
8–16   *e·* sin will so punish itself
20–24   specimens of *e·* kind emerged
22– 1   *e·* wind of doctrine." — *Eph.* 4 : 14.
44–20   pours the healing . . . into *e·* wound.
'00.   5–19   escape from idolatry of *e·* kind,
5–30   attend *e·* footstep of C. S.
'01.   15– 5   the claim of error in *e·* phase
20–11   he has *e·* opportunity to
27–27   * "*E·* great scientific truth
28–12   into almost *e·* Christian tongue,
29–28   *e·* book of mine that they sold.
31– 7   *E·* true Christian in the
32–30   governing impulse of *e·* action ;
'02.   9–14   *E·* condition implied by the
9–15   *e·* promise fulfilled, was loving and
14– 6   motto for *e·* Christian Scientist,
14–18   *e·* forward step has been met
Hea.   2– 7   condemned at *e·* advancing footstep,
5– 4   limiting His power at *e·* point,
13– 6   thirty times at *e·* attenuation.
19– 4   *e·* organ of the system, *e·* function of
19–14   "*e·* plant of the field — *Gen.* 2 : 5.
Peo.   8–18   governs *e·* action of the body
Po.   4–13   glad for *e·* scalding tear,
4–15   Wait, and love more for *e·* hate,
28– 2   Of *e·* rolling sphere,
38–14   That *e·* ragged urchin,
43–18   Temper *e·* trembling footfall,
58– 6   Is *e·* earthly love ;
71–14   Joy is in *e·* belfry bell

every

My.	9– 9	* glory in e˙ good deed
	21–15	* compensates for e˙ seeming trial
	22–18	* e˙ purpose she has set in motion,
	28– 5	will meet e˙ human need,''
	30– 3	* precisely the same in e˙ respect,
	31–16	* were heard on e˙ hand
	38– 2	* e˙ perfect gift cometh from above,
	38–21	* In e˙ respect their service was
	41–29	* has obeyed its e˙ demand,
	47–28	* to e˙ creature. — Mark 16: 15.
	53– 1	* from e˙ quarter came important
	56– 3	* until e˙ seat was filled
	59–11	* e˙ religious and scientific body
	61– 2	* in the building part of e˙ night
	62–28	* to assist us in e˙ way possible ;
	63–17	* as friend met friend at e˙ turn
	70–16	* living reproductions on e˙ corner
	71–24	* e˙ person seated in the auditorium,
	72–25	* e˙ cent of it was paid
	73–10	will meet e˙ human need.''
	75– 9	* poured into the city from e˙
	77–12	* practically e˙ civilized country,
	77–28	* e˙ penny of the two million
	78– 7	* from e˙ quarter of the city.
	78–15	* e˙ basket piled high with
	78–30	* e˙ word of the exercises
	83– 4	* patent to e˙ one residing in
	85–29	* Aside from e˙ other consideration,
	86–13	* e˙ cent of the estimated cost
	90– 2	* should be filled at e˙ meeting
	91–31	* in e˙ important town and city
	92–17	* e˙ other sect in the country
	94– 2	* e˙ other sect will be left behind
	94–10	* in e˙ community in which
	94–22	* from e˙ State in the Union
	97– 1	* almost e˙ one is inclined to
	103–11	and at its e˙ appearing.
	106– 7	diseases of almost e˙ kind.
	106 –10	matter in e˙ mode and form,
	112–14	ninety-nine out of e˙ hundred
	116–22	E˙ loss in grace and growth
	124– 3	to e˙ man's conscience.'' — II Cor. 4: 2.
	126–26	e˙ foul spirit, — Rev. 18: 2.
	126–27	a cage of e˙ unclean — Rev. 18: 2.
	149–30	solicit e˙ root and e˙ leaf
	156– 8	to e˙ good work,'' — II Cor. 9: 8.
	159– 8	the throbbing of e˙ pulse
	187– 7	lighteth e˙ enlightened thought
	210– 9	attacks of error of e˙ sort.
	212–27	hindering in e˙ way conceivable
	213–23	through e˙ attack of your foe,
	214– 5	will meet e˙ human need.
	238–22	applicable to e˙ human need.
	249– 3	Improve e˙ opportunity
	255– 8	removed e˙ three years.
	260–26	supplies e˙ need of man.
	277–22	e˙ citizen would be a soldier
	282–24	to e˙ son and daughter
	292–13	''Why did Christians of e˙ sect
	300–25	to e˙ creature,'' — Mark 16: 15.
	304–22	* from e˙ point of view a woman of
	304–25	* ''E˙ great scientific truth
	321–12	* told the same story to e˙ one
	321–25	* is conclusive to me in e˙ detail,
	327–29	* when the laws of e˙ State will
	334– 9	* advertised in e˙ weekly issue of
	339– 3	whose e˙ link leads upward
	340–32	light their fires in e˙ home.
	341– 9	all over our land and in e˙ land,
	345– 5	But e˙ thought tells,
	352–29	My desire is that e˙ . . . Scientist,
	357–30	I know that e˙ true follower

(see also **age, case, day, effect, heart, hour, man, member, part, step**)

everybody

Mis.	80–10	Anybody and e˙, who will
	238–16	Who should care for e˙?
	313– 7	pinnacle, that e˙ needs.
My.	78–15	* e˙ contributing,

every-day

'02.	17–25	Consult thy e˙ life ;

everything

Mis.	113–26	e˙ to enjoy on earth and in heaven.
	217–31	To the material sense, e˙ is matter ;
	224–19	appreciation of e˙ beautiful,
	247–29	E˙ that God created,
	364–10	C. S. refutes e˙ that is not
Un.	8– 5	E˙ is as real as you make it,
	18– 8	e˙ that is unlike Myself.
	27–10	uncertain of e˙ except his own
	44–10	into e˙ that exists,
No.	35– 1	is e˙ to human hope and faith.
Hea.	15–19	trying e˙ else besides God,
My.	61–23	* e˙ seemed to move as by magic ;

everything

My.	89–15	* E˙, even to the flagstones
	96–10	* where fanaticism dominates e˙
	203–11	best of e˙ is not too good,
	313–14	did e˙ they could think of
	324–24	* E˙ he said conveyed this impression

everywhere

Mis.	173–20	If God . . . is e˙, matter is nowhere
	385– 8	Thou, here and e˙.
Ret.	61–18	God is e˙.
Un.	42– 1	Life, God, being e˙, it must follow
Pul.	51–24	* Pilgrims from e˙ will go
	76–17	* Pictures and bric-a-brac e˙
No.	35–27	God's kingdom is e˙ and supreme,
'02.	1–10	branch churches are multiplying e˙
	12– 7	now and forever, here and e˙.
Po.	37– 8	Thou, here and e˙.
My.	40– 7	* seekers e˙ may be satisfied.
	69–12	* E˙ within the building
	122–13	such as to command respect e˙.
	128–12	God is e˙.
	173–14	from Christian Scientists e˙
	329–24	* fair attitude of the press e˙,

everywhere-present

No.	20–15	notion of an e˙ body

Eves

Chr.	53–21	For heaven's Christus, earthly E˙,

eves

Chr.	53–23	Make merriment on Christmas e˙,

evidence

accept the
Mis.	218–11	It is erroneous to accept the e˙ of

according to the
Rud.	7–12	According to the e˙ of the so-called

all
Peo.	9–24	remove all e˙ of any other power

another
Mis.	238–27	another e˙ of the falsehoods

appears
My.	94– 5	* e˙ appears in the concrete

built on the
Un.	28–15	built on the e˙ of the material

consciousness and
Un.	11–11	change of consciousness and e˙

contradicts this
Mis.	96–31	Science contradicts this e˙ ;

delusive
Mis.	65– 1	delusive e˙, Science has dethroned

deny the
Un.	39–21	deny the e˙ of the material senses,

destruction of the
Rud.	6–18	destruction of the e˙ of the material

discharged
My.	119–21	discharged e˙ of material sense

divided in
Un.	33–23	find them divided in e˙,

due
Man.	39–11	due e˙ of having genuinely repented

false
Mis.	99– 3	It annuls false e˙,
No.	6–10	destruction of false e˙,

falsity of the
No.	38– 3	falsity of the e˙ of the . . . senses

for disease
No.	6–19	as the e˙ for disease ;

furnish
Man.	89–22	furnish e˙ of their eligibility

in both cases
No.	6–19	e˙ in both cases to be unreal.

its
Un.	25–15	by removing its e˙

material
Mis.	380–21	material e˙ wherewith to
Un.	11–19	taking away the material e˙.
Rud.	7–16	material e˙ being wholly false.
My.	93– 6	* material e˙ of their prosperity ;

mistaken
Mis.	66– 3	false testimony or mistaken e˙

mortal
Mis.	13–19	basis of material and mortal e˙

my
Un.	7–16	Herein is my e˙,

no
Mis.	72–31	passage quoted affords no e˙ of
	277–23	No e˙ before the material senses
	381–15	''There is no e˙ to present.''
Ret.	90– 6	There is no e˙ to show
	90– 8	no e˙ that he there taught
'02.	8–17	We have no e˙ . . . except
Hea.	5–16	we have no e˙ of the fact
	16–20	the senses afford no e˙ of

no such
Rud.	5– 1	spiritual senses afford no such e˙

evidence
  of consciousness
    Un. 36– 1 additional e· of consciousness
  of disease
    No. 6–13 If, . . . e· of disease is not false,
  of his compliance
    Man. 52–14 e· of his compliance with
  of His presence
    '01. 7–26 gain any e· of His presence
  of Life
    Un. 61– 1 to the true e· of Life,
  of material sense
    Mis. 47–19 reverses the e· of material sense
        183–29 refute the e· of material sense
    Pul. 45–12 * every e· of material sense
    My. 119–21 e· of material sense gave the
  of mortal sense
    My. 61–12 * with the e· of mortal sense
  of Soul
    My. 119–24 e· of Soul, immortality,
  of spiritual verity
    Pul. 3–26 e· of spiritual verity in me
  of that beauty
    My. 88–20 * e· of that beauty and serenity
  of the loyalty
    Man. 35–15 e· of the loyalty of the applicants.
  of the senses
    Mis. 65– 7 e· of the senses is false.
        97– 2 rise above the e· of the senses,
      101–29 disprove the e· of the senses.
    Un. 8– 9 to rest upon the e· of the senses,
      11–15 nor to the e· of the senses.
      13– 1 Science reverses the e· of the senses
      23–15 spurious e· of the senses
  only
    Mis. 64–29 only e· of the existence of a
    Hea. 16–17 only e· we have of sin,
  overcomes the
    My. 106–18 overcomes the e· of diseased
  post mortem
    Rud. 16–27 or else *post mortem e·*.
  present
    Mis. 381–11 why he did not present e· to
  rebuke the
    Ret. 26–22 in order to rebuke the e·.
  reliable
    Hea. 16–22 shall we call that reliable e·
  renewed
    My. 157–13 * renewed e· of your unselfish love."
  Science affords the
    Mis. 164–31 Science affords the e· that God is
  slightest
    My. 75–20 * not the slightest e· of temper,
  stand in
    My. 305–11 and the manuscripts . . . stand in e·.
  sufficient
    Man. 53–22 considered a sufficient e· thereof.
  their
    No. 38– 5 God substantiates their e·
  their own
    Un. 33– 6 can only testify from their own e·,
  this
    Un. 8–10 this e· is not absolute,
  transcending the
    Un. 29– 9 Transcending the e· of the
  transcends the
    '01. 18–14 transcends the e· of the
  true
    Un. 61– 1 the true e· of Life,
    Rud. 6–20 *true e· of spiritual sense*
      7–15 afford the only true e· of
  unseen
    My. 260–16 things hoped for and the e· unseen.
  what
    Un. 34–18 What e· does mortal mind afford

    Mis. 57– 3 what e· have you — apart from the e· of
      96–30 the e· before the personal senses,
     101–19 He who turns to the body for e·,
     131–11 e· of its being built upon the rock
    Man. 15–14 e· of divine, efficacious Love,
    Un. 10–22 e· before the material senses,
     21–12 e· of your personal senses
    Pul. 45–21 * e· of the mortal senses is
     52–16 * e· of the rapid growth of the new
    No. 6–17 The e· that the earth is
    My. 40– 2 * e· to us of her hospitable love.
     134– 3 e· a heart wholly in protest
     226–19 e· of the immortality of man
     314–18 After the e· had been submitted

evidenced
    My. 12–13 * e· by the liberality

evidences
  based on the
    Peo. 2–15 based on the e· gained from the

evidences
  in Christian Science
    Peo. 9–28 more potent e· in C. S. of
  of Life
    Hea. 16–26 gain our e· of Life from
  of sin
    Hea. 17–10 with all their e· of sin,
  of Spirit
    Ret. 56–12 waged between the e· of Spirit and
  of the senses
    Mis. 58–11 *deny the e· of the senses?*
    Hea. 15– 1 repudiates the e· of the senses
  other
    My. 83–27 * other e· of the strength and
  trial, and
    My. 270–17 proven under trial, and e·

    Mis. 14–15 from e· before him he is
     172–18 e· whereof are taken in by
    Ret. 56–13 e· of the five physical senses ;
     65– 3 e· of the physical senses,
    My. 20–17 e· of glorious growth in C. S.
     58– 7 * e· of the magnificent growth of

evidencing
    My. 6–21 e· the praise of babes

evident
    Man. 50–18 from Christian motives make this e·,
    Ret. 28– 1 It became e· that the divine Mind
    My. 56– 8 * It was soon e· that even this
     74–19 * not only e· from their addresses
     76– 6 * e· to the Board of Directors
     96–26 * e· that the cult will soon be
     215–31 That he preferred the latter is e·,

evidently
    Mis. 75–25 It was e· an illuminated sense
     216–11 Phare Pleigh e· means more than
    Pul. 72–10 * e· very much absorbed in the work
    My. 97–18 * e· wealthy congregation
     251–16 e· some misapprehension
     363–22 e· misunderstood by some students.

evil (*see also* **evil's**)
  absolute
    Mis. 299–17 is the only absolute e·.
  abuses from
    Mis. 338–16 uses of good, to abuses from e· ;
  accompanying
    Un. 37–18 e· accompanying physical personality
  acquaintance with
    Un. 4–21 man's acquaintance with e·.
  activity of
    Mis. 339–11 the supposed activity of e·.
  Adam-dream of
    My. 296–19 waking out of his Adam-dream of e·
  admitting
    Mis. 18–25 Only by admitting e· as a reality,
  against
    Mis. 367–22 It was not against e·, but against
  alias
    Ret. 67–24 the "devil" (*alias e·*), — *John* 8 : 44.
  all
    Mis. 36–21 Mortal mind includes all e·,
     37–19 whence cometh all e·.
     97– 7 that holds within itself all e·.
     125– 8 the world, the flesh, and all e·,
     337–19 disaffection for all e·,
    Man. 40–13 to be delivered from all e·,
    My. 37– 2 * salvation of all men from all e·.
     268–25 axe at the root of all e·,
     357–19 magnetism, — the name of all e·,
     364–14 defend themselves from all e·,
  all manner of
    Mis. 8–24 all manner of e· — *Matt.* 5 : 11.
    '01. 3– 5 all manner of e· — *Matt.* 5 : 11.
    '02. 11–23 all manner of e· — *Matt.* 5 : 11.
    My. 104–31 all manner of e· — *Matt.* 5 : 11.
     316– 8 all manner of e· — *Matt.* 5 : 11.
  and disease
    Mis. 221–25 against both e· and disease,
    Un. 37–16 E· and disease do not testify of
    Pan. 5–28 His treatment of e· and disease,
     6– 3 because e· and disease will never
  and error
    Mis. 36– 3 we shall classify e· and error
  and God
    Un. 27–12 these distinctions to e· and God,
  and good
    Mis. 222– 2 false sense of both e· and good.
     333–12 Is it in both e· and good,
     352–26 consciousness of both e· and good,
    Un. 23–24 knowing both e· and good ;
     24–11 consciousness, . . . both e· and good.
    No. 37– 8 to know both e· and good ;

evil

and matter
  Mis. 27–20   *e·* and matter are negation :
  '01. 25–28   excludes *e·* and matter.
appearance of
  Mis. 46– 7   destroy the appearance of *e·*
armies of
  Pul. 83–18   * our own allied armies of *e·*
as a false claim
  '01. 14– 8   *e·*, as a false claim, false entity, and
as a lie
  '01. 14–14   We regard *e·* as a lie,
as a supposition
  Un. 52–16   *e·*, as a supposition, is the father of
as mind
  Mis. 261– 1   *e·*, as *mind*, is doomed,
as personified
  Pan. 6–10   chapter sub-title
attempt of
  Mis. 118–28   Every attempt of *e·* to harm good
attenuation of
  Mis. 260–32   is the highest attenuation of *e·*.
author of
  Hea. 9–22   "Who is the author of *e·*?"
avoidance of the
  Pul. 15– 6   ensure the avoidance of the *e·*
beautiful
  Un. 52–27   form the condition of beautiful *e·*,
belief in
  Mis. 221–32   belief in *e·* and in the process of
belief . . . that
  Ret. 69–28   the belief . . . that *e·* is mind,
believe that
  Pan. 11–21   believe that *e·* develops good,
  '01. 14– 6   Do . . . Scientists believe that *e·*
besetments of
  Mis. 10–19   with fear and the besetments of *e·* ;
call
  Un. 49–24   clearer right to call *e·* a negation,
calls
  Mis. 27– 2   Science of good calls *e·* *nothing*.
can neither
  No. 23– 4   *E·* can neither grasp
can never
  Un. 25–25   *e·* can never take away.
casting out
  Mis. 25–18   healing the sick, casting out *e·*,
  No. 12–18   Living a true life, casting out *e·*,
  My. 126–13   casting out *e·* and healing the sick.
  153–26   casting out *e·* and healing the sick.
cast out
  Mis. 211– 5   to handle serpents and cast out *e·*.
  Pan. 5–24   our Master cast out *e·*,
  My. 114– 5   cast out *e·* and heal the sick ;
  172–17   cast out *e·*, disease, and death ;
  288–21   Jesus cast out *e·*, disease, death,
casts out
  Man. 15–19   understanding that casts out *e·* as
claim of
  Mis. 55– 9   is the universal claim of *e·*
  115–18   delivered from every claim of *e·*.
  Ret. 64–11   as the opposite claim of *e·*
claims of
  Mis. 114–23   deliverance from the claims of *e·*.
  No. 23–20   we need to discern the claims of *e·*,
  24–15   claims of *e·* become both less and
combating
  Mis. 285– 1   combating *e·* only, rather than
comes
  Un. 20– 5   *e·* comes into authority :
commensurate with
  Mis. 261– 2   suffering is commensurate with *e·*,
condemn
  My. 249– 1   You may condemn *e·* in the abstract
consciousness of
  Un. 50–19   The less consciousness of *e·*
conscious of
  Un. 36–23   to say that . . . is conscious of *e·*,
counterfeits good
  Mis. 351–20   *E·* counterfeits good : it says,
criticizes
  My. 240–16   because it criticizes *e·*, disease,
cruel and
  Mis. 41– 1   only the cruel and *e·* can
dealt with as
  Mis. 284–20   must now be dealt with as *e·*,
definition of
  No. 22–26   His definition of *e·* indicated
  Pan. 5– 7   chapter sub-title
deliver us from
  My. 233– 6   "Deliver us from *e·*"— *Matt.* 6: 13.
denounce
  Pan. 6– 5   let us continue to denounce *e·*
departing from
  Mis. 19–14   is daily departing from *e·* ;

evil

deprives
  Mis. 14–29   deprives *e·* of all power,
destroys
  Ret. 62– 8   demonstration of . . . destroys *e·*.
  No. 30– 8   reaches and destroys *e·* by
  '01. 10–23   whereby good destroys *e·*,
destruction of
  No. 23– 2   hinders the destruction of *e·*.
dignity of
  Un. 54–24   and admitted the dignity of *e·*.
disappearing of
  Mis. 338– 2   involves the disappearing of *e·*.
does not obtain
  Un. 31–22   *e·* does not obtain in Spirit,
doeth
  My. 33–20   nor doeth *e·* to his— *Psal.* 15: 3.
dominates
  Mis. 293–15   if *e·* dominates his character,
drift into
  Un. 24– 5   and cannot drift into *e·*.
ego of
  Un. 52–16   not the so-called ego of *e·* ;
elements of
  Mis. 40–27   has to master those elements of *e·*
elevating
  Pan. 6–26   It is plain that elevating *e·*
enrage
  Mis. 338–17   calm strength will enrage *e·*.
enthrone
  Un. 46–28   an effort to enthrone *e·*.
epicycle of
  My. 270– 3   obliterates the epicycle of *e·*.
error, or
  Mis. 259–25   error, or *e·*, is really non-existent,
escape from
  Pul. 15–13   Escape from *e·*, and designate
et cetera of
  Mis. 114–21   and all the *et cetera* of *e·*.
explains
  Pan. 5–18   Jesus' definition . . . explains *e·*.
fact that
  '01. 14–12   takes hold of the fact that *e·*
faith in
  Mis. 31–11   is in proportion to the faith in *e·*,
  31–18   to relinquish his faith in *e·*
  31–22   in order to retain his faith in *e·*
  46– 2   perpetuates the belief or faith in *e·*.
  346–17   perpetuates faith in *e·* ;
falsity of
  Mis. 201–10   myth or material falsity of *e·* ;
familiar with
  Un. 14–21   if this Mind is familiar with *e·*,
fear of
  Mis. 279– 5   and not the fear of *e·*,
finds
  Mis. 261– 3   *e·* finds no escape from itself;
  No. 27– 5   *e·* finds no place in good.
flesh, and
  Mis. 2– 8   the world, the flesh, and *e·*,
  My. 134– 2   the world, the flesh, and *e·*,
foreknow
  Un. 19–12   predestine or foreknow *e·*,
for evil
  Mis. 19– 8   Never return *e·* for evil ;
  316– 2   never to return *e·* for evil,
  Man. 84– 4   never to return *e·* for evil,
  My. 128–26   Return not *e·* for evil,
form of
  Mis. 257– 3   every mode and form of *e·*.
forms of
  Mis. 115–23   against the subtler forms of *e·*,
from good
  Un. 14–28   to distinguish *e·* from good,
fruit of
  Un. 17–23   partake of the fruit of *e·*,
full of
  No. 22–24   a mortal who is full of *e·*.
gives
  '00. 5– 5   It gives *e·* no origin,
good and
  (see **good**)
good for
  (see **good**)
good, not
  Mis. 4–10   its power to do good, not *e·*.
  42–24   learn that good, not *e·*, lives
  101–23   this power is good, not *e·* ;
  283–27   to demonstrate good, not *e·*,
good or
  Mis. 309– 3   corporeality, either as good or *e·*.
  No. 23–24   amount of good or *e·* he possesses.
good or of
  No. 22–16   the person of good or of *e·*.
good over
  Ret. 26–10   supremacy of good over *e·*,

evil

great
No. 32–23 It seems a great e· to belie
growing
Ret. 76–27 a growing e· in plagiarism ;
guard against
Mis. 114–31 guard against e· and its silent modes,
gust of
My. 297–12 A suppositional gust of e·
handling
Mis. 292–30 on this point of handling e·,
hands of
My. 128–24 betrays Truth into the hands of e·
has no claims
No. 24–21 namely, that e· has no claims
has no power
My. 296–13 E· has no power to harm,
He destroys
No. 30– 9 He need not know the e· He destroys,
hidden
My. 288– 3 and uncovers hidden e·.
immunity from
Mis. 298–28 than immunity from e·.
impersonal
Mis. 190–22 referred to was an impersonal e·,
impotence of
Mis. 121–10 namely, the impotence of e·,
incapable of
Pan. 4–14 while God is incapable of e· ;
in consciousness
Un. 49–13 So long as I hold e· in consciousness,
incorporeal
'01. 12–26 Incorporeal e· embodies itself in
indulged
Mis. 94– 3 a person who knowingly indulged e·,
infirmity of
Mis. 294– 2 last infirmity of e· is so-called
'02. 10–26 is the infirmity of e·,
in human nature
'01. 9–19 The e· in human nature foams
insists
Mis. 366–20 e· insists on the unity of good and
introduces
Pan. 6–11 Mosaic theism introduces e·,
is a false claim
Un. 32– 1 and that e· is a false claim,
is a lie
Pan. 5–25 Knowing that e· is a lie,
is a negation
Mis. 107–17 E· is a negation :
is a quality
No. 23–18 E· is a quality, not an individual.
is egotistic
Un. 27–13 we shall find that e· is *egotistic*,
is illusion
'00. 10– 4 E· is illusion, that after a fight
is impotent
Mis. 119–10 E· is impotent to turn the righteous
Hea. 10– 9 therefore e· is impotent.
is naught
Mis. 260–24 e· is naught, although it seems to
279–20 e· is naught and good is all.
Un. 21– 8 e· is naught, and good only is
is never present
Mis. 367–21 To good, e· is never present;
is no part
Un. 4–21 e· is no part of the divine
is not a creator
Un. 25–20 E· is not a creator.
is not a quality
Mis. 259–10 e· is not a quality to be known
is not Mind
Rud. 4–16 Good is Mind, but e· is not Mind.
is not self-made
Pan. 5– 9 Since e· is not self-made,
is not something
Mis. 284–24 E· is not something to fear
is not spiritual
Un. 25–22 E· is not spiritual, and therefore
is not the medium
Pan. 11–24 e· is not the medium of good,
is powerless
Mis. 336– 3 this lesson . . . e· is powerless,
is self-destroying
No. 26–18 for e· is self-destroying.
is self-destructive
Mis. 2–22 and e· is self-destructive,
is temporal
Mis. 93–13 E· is temporal : it is the illusion
Pul. 13–23 e· is temporal, not eternal.
No. 37– 8 e· is temporal and God is eternal,
is the absence
Ret. 60–12 e· is the absence of good ;
No. 17– 4 e·, is the absence of Spirit
is unnatural
My. 288–10 E· is unnatural ; it has no origin

evil

is unreal
Ret. 60–13 e· is unreal and good is all
'01. 15– 1 declaration that e· is unreal,
Hea. 9–23 statement that e· is unreal ;
My. 178–19 revelation . . . that e· is unreal ;
knowing
Mis. 108–12 utility of knowing e· aright,
367–14 implies the necessity of knowing e·,
367–23 but against *knowing e·*,
knowledge of
(see **knowledge**)
know not
Un. 18– 3 therefore I know not e·.
knows
Un. 15–10 If God knows e·, so must man,
18– 1 God must perish, if He knows e·
19– 7 If God knows e· at all,
No. 16– 7 If God knows e· even as a false
lapses into
Pan. 7–27 lapses into e· dominating
league with
My. 200–25 to relinquish its league with e·.
let alone
Mis. 284–25 E· let alone grows more real,
licensed
My. 211– 7 mistaken way, . . . has licensed e·,
lie of
No. 42–19 lie of e· holds its own by declaring
like
Un. 50–18 Like e·, it is destitute of Mind,
likeness of
Ret. 67–20 the image and likeness of e·,
loses all place
No. 24– 2 e· loses all place, person, and
loss of faith in
Mis. 204–17 marked loss of faith in e·,
lurks an
Mis. 302– 1 Behind the scenes lurks an e·
made
Mis. 362–12 believing that God, . . . made e· ;
Pan. 5–10 who or what hath made e·?
made neither
'02. 6–12 God made neither e· nor its
make
No. 23– 5 nor make e· omnipotent and
manifest
No. 16– 8 this knowledge would manifest e·
manifestations of
Mis. 362–20 material manifestations of e·,
mastering
My. 207–23 mastering e· and defending good,
master of
Mis. 209–28 good is the master of e·.
material world and
Rud. 3– 7 the material world and e·.
matter and
(see **matter**)
matter, or
Mis. 363–13 changes of matter, or e·.
No. 17– 4 Matter, or e·, is the absence of
meditates
Mis. 148– 2 while he meditates e· against us
mental
My. 212–13 highest form of mental e·,
mode of
Mis. 361– 9 every form and mode of e·
modes as
Mis. 364–27 same power or modes as e·,
modes of
Mis. 293– 3 all the claims and modes of e· ;
moral
Un. 36–22 and yet admit . . . moral e·, sin, or
more contagious than
Mis. 229–10 good is more contagious than e·,
more natural than
Mis. 199–29 goodness is more natural than e·.
222–28 should seem more natural than e·.
mote of
Mis. 336–15 mote of e· out of other eyes.
must be dethroned
Un. 20–10 e· must be dethroned :
mysterious
Mis. 237–21 marvellous good, and mysterious e·.
mythology of
Mis. 363–10 mythology of e· and mortality
named
Mis. 196– 9 separate mind . . . named e· ;
Ret. 63–16 Its opposite, nothing, named e·,
Un. 60– 9 presence named e·.
No. 32–18 its opposite, named e·, must
nature of
No. 23– 1 incorrect concept of the nature of e·
never did exist
Mis. 346–11 E· never did exist as an entity.

evil

never made
Un. 20–12   *First:* God never made e·.
45–11   God never made e·.

no
Mis. 93–10   in Him dwelleth no e·.
229–18   shall no e· befall thee, — *Psal.* 91 : 10.
311–13   charity which thinketh no e· ;
Ret. 63– 6   there is in reality no e·,
Un. 22– 4   in which no e· can possibly dwell.
46–15   In his identity there is no e·.
62–14   there is no e·.
No. 24–28   there can be no e·.
45– 6   thinketh no e·, — *I Cor.* 13 : 5.
'01. 34–19   yea, which *knoweth* no e·.
My. 297–14   for there is in reality no e·,

no compromise with
My. 41–17   * C. S. makes no compromise with e·,

no consciousness of
Un. 21–16   With Him is no consciousness of e·,

no faith in
Mis. 118– 4   We shall have no faith in e·

no intelligent
Mis. 36–30   for there is no intelligent e·,

no Life in
Un. 62–11   learn that there is no Life in e·.

non-intelligent
Mis. 267–25   *matter,* or *non-intelligent e·,*

no reality in
Un. 59– 1   there is no reality in e·,

not educed from
Pan. 12– 2   good is not educed from e·,

nothingness of
Mis. 108– 8   attested the . . . nothingness — of e· :
109–27   must discern the nothingness of e·,
176–11   learn . . . the nothingness of e·,
Ret. 55– 7   brings out the nothingness of e·

not overcome of
Mis. 334–30   "Be not overcome of e·, — *Rom.* 12 : 21.
'01. 34–21   be not overcome of e·,

of dumbness
Mis. 190–23   it was the e· of dumbness,

offspring of
Ret. 68– 4   claimed to beget the offspring of e·,

of inaction
Mis. 341–22   e· of inaction and delay.

one
Mis. 112– 1   in other words, the one e·
My. 130–15   the one e· or the evil one.

opposes
Mis. 119–16   whatever or whoever opposes e·,

or error
Ret. 57–19   E·, or error, is not Mind ;

original
Mis. 295–10   * cause of this "same original e·"
Ret. 68– 3   claimed to originate . . . original e· ;

origin of
Mis. 24–25   Speaking of the origin of e·,
346– 6   chapter sub-title
346– 7   origin of e· is the problem of ages.

or sin
'01. 12–25   chapter sub-title

outcome of
'01. 13– 2   The outcome of e·, called sin,

out of
Mis. 2–27   those who progress . . . out of e·,

overcome
Mis. 66–21   "overcome e· with good." — *Rom.* 12 : 21.
116– 1   will overcome e· with good,
334–30   overcome e· with good," — *Rom.* 12 : 21.
352–27   through argument . . . overcome e·.
Man. 47– 2   seeks to overcome e· with good.
Pul. 15–16   overcome e· with good.
No. 9–20   overcome e· with good.
33– 4   thus we may overcome e· with good.
'01. 34–22   overcome e· with good ;
'02. 2–30   overcome e· with good,
My. 128–27   "overcome e· with good." — *Rom.* 12 : 21.
180–18   overcome e· and heal disease.
228– 8   "overcome e· with good." — *Rom.* 12 : 21.
278–21   overcome e· with good.

overcoming
My. 204–28   overcoming e· with good,
291–13   universal good overcoming e·.

persists in
Mis. 184–20   If he . . . persists in e·,

personal
Rud. 7–17   Jesus said of personal e·,

personality of
Mis. 190–30   Paul refers to this personality of e·

phenomenal
My. 349–25   phenomenal e·, which is lawless and

point out the
Pul. 15– 3   point out the e· in human thought,

possible
Mis. 302–28   intended to forestall the possible e·

evil

powerless
My. 296–19   e· powerless, and God, . . . omnipotent

powerlessness of
Mis. 114–29   show us the powerlessness of e·,

powers of
Mis. 177– 5   powers of e· are leagued together

presence of
Mis. 103– 1   precludes the presence of e·.

proceedeth not
Mis. 198–13   e· proceedeth not from God,

process of
Mis. 221–32   belief . . . in the process of e·,

punishment of
My. 296–18   and punishment of e·

pursues the
Mis. 210– 1   pursues the e· that hideth

really
Ret. 94– 8   and yet errs, . . . is really e·.

reduction of
No. 33– 2   The reduction of e·, in Science,

regard
My. 119– 2   to regard e· as real,

rejection of
Pan. 12– 3   comes from the rejection of e·

resists
My. 210–14   Goodness involuntarily resists e·.

result in
Mis. 27– 5   or aught that can result in e·,

return of
Mis. 13– 6   sharp return of e· for good

reward of
Mis. 340– 4   Good is never the reward of e·,

said of
Pan. 5–12   He said of e· : "Ye are of — *John* 8 : 44.

seeks
Un. 17– 2   *E·* seeks to fasten all error upon

seems as real
Mis. 108–19   wherein e· seems as real as good,

seems to predominate
Mis. 113– 6   when e· seems to predominate

seething
Mis. 338–11   in the midst of seething e· ;

self-existent
Mis. 198–28   a belief in self-existent e·,
Pan. 5– 8   or is e· self-existent,

sense of
(*see* sense)

sensible
Ret. 73–17   where sensible e· is lost

should not be
Un. 50–25   consciousness should not be e·.

signifies
Mis. 27–21   e· signifies the absence of good,

spirit of
Mis. 370– 6   spirit of e· is still abroad ;
My. 212– 5   the essence, or spirit, of e·,

spirits of
Mis. 278– 2   the distilled spirits of e·,

states of
No. 16–12   The subjective states of e·,

subordinates good
No. 24–13   e· subordinates good in personality.

substratum of
No. 16–26   matter is the substratum of e·,

suppositional
Mis. 334–19   diabolism of suppositional e·
367– 8   the lie of suppositional e·,

supposition of
Mis. 260–15   holds . . . the supposition of e·,

supposition that
Mis. 259– 8   silences the supposition that e·

that is hidden
No. 24–17   e· that is hidden by dogma

this
Mis. 113–23   this e· can be resisted
254–16   kill this e· in "self"
284–15   The hour has passed for this e· to
368–17   This e· obtains in the present
Un. 44–15   miscall, this e· a child of God.
No. 32–26   reduce this e· to its lowest terms,
My. 211– 6   denying that this e· exists.

to attack
Mis. 90–13   inexpedient to attack e·.

to behold
My. 300– 1   than to behold e·." — *Hab.* 1 : 13.

to cognize
Un. 24– 1   whereby to cognize e·.

to know
Un. 54–20   God forbade man to know e·

to produce
Mis. 174– 2   than has good to produce e·.

treatment of
Pan. 5–28   His treatment of e· and disease,

ultimating in
Mis. 122–16   nor good ultimating in e·.

evil

ultimatum of
Mis. 113–19   latter-day ultimatum of *e*˙,
uncontaminated with
Man. 31–11   uncontaminated with *e*˙,
uncovered
Mis. 210– 2   *e*˙, uncovered, is self-destroyed.
    334–28   Because I have uncovered *e*˙,
unreality of
Mis. 319– 2   the unreality of *e*˙ is lost.
 Ret. 62– 7   demonstration of the *unreality* of *e*˙
 My. 334–16   * teaching on the unreality of *e*˙
unseen
 '01. 20–19   This unseen *e*˙ is the sin of sins ;
victory over
 Pul. 15–18   occasion for a victory over *e*˙.
wail of
Mis. 267– 2   wail of *e*˙ never harms Scientists,
was avenging
 My. 161–27   When *e*˙ was avenging itself on its
was even more
 Un. 46–20   To them *e*˙ was even more the ego
was loquacious
 '01. 16–20   in its origin *e*˙ was loquacious,
where is
 Pan. 6–16   what and where is *e*˙ ?
whisper
Mis. 119– 2   If malicious suggestions whisper *e*˙
wholly
 No. 23– 9   could not have been wholly *e*˙,
with good
Mis. 217–23   at war with Life, *e*˙ with good,
 My. 118–30   and couple *e*˙ with good.
    204–28   overcoming *e*˙ with good,
    (*see also sub-title* **overcome**)
world's
Mis. 224–24   to cover the whole world's *e*˙,

Mis.   2–23   therefore *e*˙ must be mortal
   3– 5   good as more natural than *e*˙,
   6– 5   Jesus cast out disease as *e*˙.
  10–31   erroneous belief . . . that *e*˙ is real ;
  13–15   proposition that *e*˙ is a factor of
  13–16   to believe in the reality of *e*˙
  14– 2   neither place nor power left for *e*˙.
  14– 6   where will you see or feel *e*˙,
  14–10   that requires *e*˙ through which to
  14–17   to him *e*˙ is as real and eternal as
  14–22   to be the necessity for *e*˙,
  14–24   *e*˙, good's opposite, has no Principle,
  14–26   *e*˙ is neither a primitive nor a
  14–32   he makes a great reality of *e*˙,
  22–15   transmitting human ills, or *e*˙,
  26–32   to mean that good is *e*˙,
  27– 1   or the creator of *e*˙ ?
  27– 4   That God, good, creates *e*˙,
  45–22   *where did e*˙ *originate?*
  45–26   opposite intelligence . . . termed *e*˙.
  46– 1   admission of the reality of *e*˙
  46– 5   *e*˙, good's opposite, is unreal.
  49–22   that *e*˙ is as real as good,
  60–26   *E*˙ in the beginning claimed the
  107–22   knowledge of evil as *e*˙, so-called.
  108–22   of what we need to know of *e*˙,
  115–19   *e*˙ has neither prestige, power, nor
  116– 2   sensitiveness to the power of *e*˙.
  122–15   it is not *e*˙ producing good,
  122–18   "Let us do *e*˙,— *Rom.* 3 : 8.
  123– 3   *E*˙ was, and is, the illusion of
  174– 4   Matter is . . . *e*˙, having presence
  181–29   not of God's opposite,— *e*˙,
  184– 3   by claiming that . . . man is *e*˙ ;
  184–23   self-deceived sense of power in *e*˙.
  196–10   and make you know *e*˙,
  196–11   thus become material, sensual, *e*˙.
  200– 4   and *e*˙ as the abnormal ;
  209–24   false basis that *e*˙ should be concealed
  213–12   against the *e*˙ which, if seen,
  251–23   and the *e*˙ they would not do,
  259– 7   of good, not of *e*˙.
  259–16   moral power of good, not of *e*˙ :
  261– 3   and lasts as long as the *e*˙.
  287–14   should preponderate over the *e*˙,
  289– 2   Strong drink is unquestionably an *e*˙,
  289– 2   and *e*˙ cannot be used temperately :
  289– 7   What is *e*˙ ?   It is suppositional
  298– 5   Let us do *e*˙,— *Rom.* 3 : 8.
  299–16   the *e*˙ which these senses see not
  335–17   ability, in belief, of *e*˙ to break the
  335–29   concerning those who do *e*˙
  346–10   whence comes the *e*˙ ?
  346–16   mortal admission of the reality of *e*˙
  354–11   error to Truth, and *e*˙ to good,
  362–13   Then, was *e*˙ part and parcel of
  364–23   matter of Spirit and *e*˙ of good ;
  364–30   or give reality and power to *e*˙

evil

Mis. 367–21   *e*˙ is a different state of consciousness.
 Ret. 55– 5   *E*˙ is not mastered by *e*˙ ;
   57–10   it is the flesh that is *e*˙.
   64– 4   such is the unity of *e*˙ ;
   82–23   consummate much good or else *e*˙ ;
 Un.   3–18   likeness of good, not of *e*˙ ;
   15– 9   Was *e*˙ among these good things?
   17– 9   *e*˙ ties its wagon-load of offal
   17–20   Error says God must know *e*˙
   18– 1   *e*˙ necessarily leads to extinction
   19–15   *e*˙ is only a delusive deception,
   21–10   *E*˙.   God hath said,
   22– 1   *E*˙.   Why is this so?
   22– 8   *E*˙.   But I would taste and know
   22–13   *E*˙.   But there is something besides
   23–19   *E*˙.   But mortal mind and sin really
   24–10   *E*˙.   I am a finite consciousness,
   24–22   *E*˙.   I am something separate from
   25–18   *E*˙.   I am a creator,
   25–21   *E*˙ is not conscious or conscientious
   26– 1   *E*˙.   I am intelligent matter ;
   26– 7   shirk all responsibility . . . as *e*˙,
   26– 9   *Good.*   You mistake, O *e*˙ !
   31–23   *e*˙ *does*, according to belief,
   39–26   They presuppose that . . . man is *e*˙,
   41– 4   Of *e*˙ we can never learn it,
   44–18   Human wisdom says of *e*˙,
   47– 3   Nowhere . . . is *e*˙ connected with **good,**
   49–22   *E*˙ is without Principle.
   50– 4   only as I believe in *e*˙,
   50–12   mortal mind, of which *e*˙ is the
   51–22   and not of His opposite, *e*˙.
   52–15   *What say you of e*˙ *?*
   53– 2   So *e*˙ and all its forms are
   53– 4   or it would not be *e*˙.
   53– 7   constitutes the lie an *e*˙.
   53–12   that *e*˙ is Mind, is a
 Rud.   4–17   Good is not in *e*˙, but in God only.
   6–10   to the material senses, *e*˙ takes the place
 No. 16– 9   matter, *e*˙, sin, sickness, and death
   17–26   Then *e*˙ would be as real as good,
   21–19   supposed power and reality of *e*˙
   24– 4   *e*˙ in human thought.
   24–12   By the same token, *e*˙ is not only
   24–18   *e*˙, being thus uncovered, is
   24–22   for behold *e*˙ (or devil) is,
   24–25   never a moment in which *e*˙ was **real.**
   26–18   If man's individuality were *e*˙,
 Pan.   5– 8   Did God create *e*˙ ?
   5–15   no truth [reality] in him [*e*˙].
   5–18   Jesus' definition of devil (*e*˙)
   5–19   shows that *e*˙ is both liar and lie,
   6–22   For if . . . *e*˙ also is mind,
   6–25   what power hath *e*˙ ?
 '00.   5– 8   *e*˙ — "is a liar,— *John* 8 : 44.
 '01. 12–27   *E*˙ is neither quality nor quantity :
   13–13   *e*˙, *alias* devil, sin, is a lie
   23– 7   yet that *e*˙ exists and is real,
   23– 8   thence it would follow that *e*˙
 '02.   1–10   *E*˙, though combined in
 Peo.   4–12   was named a person, and *e*˙ another
 My. 178–16   therefore if *e*˙ exists,
   197– 2   Enjoying good things is not *e*˙,
   210– 6   no door through which *e*˙ can enter,
   210– 6   no space for *e*˙ to fill
   211–12   in its ascending steps of *e*˙,
   212–11   wherewith to do *e*˙ ;
   213– 5   and give activity to *e*˙.
   213– 7   is by no means a right of *e*˙
   265– 7   *e*˙ flourishes less, invests less
   278–25   War is in itself an *e*˙,
   288–31   *e*˙ is not a fatherly grace.
   334–17   * than that *e*˙ could be indulged

evil (adj., adv.)

Mis. 11– 1   to suffer for his *e*˙ intent ;
  18–25   entering into a state of *e*˙ thoughts,
  19–1, 2   *e*˙ thinking, *e*˙ speaking,
  41– 4   to accomplish an *e*˙ purpose.
  72– 1   nothing *e*˙, or unlike Himself.
  89–16   "be *e*˙ spoken of."— *Rom.* 14 : 16.
  103– 2   which say that sin is an *e*˙ power,
  113–17   suggestions from an *e*˙ source.
  114–24   Scientists will silence *e*˙ suggestions,
  187–28   That man must be *e*˙ before he
  191–29   could only be possible as *e*˙ beliefs,
  204–32   *e*˙ thinking, *e*˙ speaking
  209–22   *E*˙ passions die in their own **flames,**
  219–28   if he can change this *e*˙ sense
  227–10   to extend their *e*˙ intent,
  247–30   Hence *that* is only an *e*˙ belief
  252–11   *e*˙ thoughts are impotent,
  259–11   iniquity, too *e*˙ to conceive of good
  284–21, 22   neither an *e*˙ claim nor an *e*˙ **person**
  332–19   to have formed an *e*˙ sense

evil (adj., adv.)

Mis.	335– 3	"But and if that *e·* servant — *Matt.* 24 : 48.
	340– 1	relinquishment of right in an *e·* hour,
	340–21	through *e·* or through good report,
Man.	81–24	no *e·* speaking shall be allowed.
Ret.	68– 5	*alias* an *e·* offspring.
	75–15	lightly speak *e·* of me." — *Mark* 9 : 39.
Un.	23–22	An *e·* material mind, so-called,
	43– 8	the possibility that Life can be *e·*.
	45–11	*e·* ego, and his assumed power,
	45–24	*e·* ego has but the visionary
	46–16	only as . . . not as material or *e·*.
	46–22	This *e·* ego they believed must
	53–10	*e·* belief that renders them obscure.
Pul.	29–23	* cast out the demons of *e·* thought.
	56–19	* "And still we love the *e·* cause,
	69–11	* *e·* and sick-producing thoughts,
Rud.	10– 8	with nothing *e·* or material ;
No.	7– 3	*e·* influences waver the scales
Pan.	9– 7	a good Spirit and an *e·* spirit.
'00.	8– 5	but the *e·* man also
	8– 6	exhales . . . his *e·* nature
	13– 7	words were brave and their deeds *e·*.
'01.	16–20	once refer to an *e·* spirit as *dumb*,
Hea.	10–11	it has no *e·* side ;
My.	17– 5	all *e·* speakings, — *I Pet.* 2 : 1.
	128–30	*e·* suggestions, in whatever guise,
	130– 3	guard . . . against *e·* suggestions
	210–12	self-seeking pride of the *e·* thinker
	210–14	The *e·* thinker is the proud talker
	211–32	induced by this secret *e·* influence
	212– 9	effects of this *e·* influence,
	212–10	the *e·* effects of alcohol.
	223–18	or by "*e·* suggestions,"
	228– 5	*E·* minds signally blunder
	249–17	countenance such *e·* tendencies.
	297–12	gust of evil in this *e·* world
		(*see also* **mind**)

evil-doer

Mis.	118–30	punishment of the *e·*.
	221–11	*e·* can do little at removing
	222– 1	issues of death to the *e·*.
	284–20	not as an *e·* or personality.
'01.	14–30	*e·* receives no encouragement from

evil-doers

Mis.	122– 1	good man to suffer for *e·*
My.	135–28	because of *e·* ;" — *Psal.* 37 : 1.

evil-doing

Mis.	126–22	condemn *e·*, evil-speaking ;

evilly

Mis.	119– 3	no apology for acting *e·*.
'00.	2–17	means, but he uses them *e·*.

evil-minded

Ret.	36–10	the *e·* would insinuate

evil-mongers

Mis.	238–29	I accord these *e·* due credit

evil one

Mis.	111–32	The belief in . . . is the *e· o·*
My.	14–19	* a fabrication of the *e· o·*,
	130–15	the one evil or the *e· o·*.

evil's

Mis.	14–18	*e·* umpire and empire,
Un.	46–21	Sin, sickness, and death were *e·*
Pul.	15– 3	*e·* hidden mental ways
Pan.	11–22	whatever strips off *e·* disguise

evils

called

'00.	5–29	God's opposites, called *e·*,

called sin

No.	31–23	If the *e·* called sin, sickness,

casting out

Mis.	77–32	healing the sick, casting out *e·*,
	99–30	casting out *e·* and healing the sick ;
	165– 2	casting out *e·* and healing,
	187– 2	casting out *e·*, *healing the sick*,
Ret.	65–23	casting out *e·* and healing the sick ;
My.	110– 3	casting out *e·*, healing the sick,

cast out

No.	31–17	Jesus cast out *e·*,
'01.	9–26	cast out *e·* and heal the sick.

casts out

My.	260–25	casts out *e·*, heals the sick,

choose between

Mis.	289– 9	must first choose between *e·*,

of mortal thought

My.	113–27	casting out the *e·* of mortal thought,

refer to the

No.	22–23	passage must refer to the *e·*

these

No.	36–21	Had he been as conscious of these *e·*

two

Mis.	289– 9	of two *e·* choose the less ;
	302–16	of two *e·* the less would be

evils

what

Un.	59– 2	from what *e·* was it his purpose to
Mis.	191–17	*e·*, apparent wrong traits,
Un.	59– 4	*e·* from which he saves

evil-speaking

Mis.	126–23	Most people condemn evil-doing, *e·* ;
	137–25	envy, *e·*, resentment, and
	222– 3	inflames envy, passion, *e·*, and
	337–19	*e·*, lust, envy, hate.

evinced

My.	293–14	*e·* a lack of . . . understanding

evoked

My.	92–11	* more interest than it has *e·* in

evokes

Mis.	364– 4	naturally *e·* new paraphrase

evolution (*see also* **evolution's**)

Mis.	27–24	Creation, *e·*, or manifestation,
Pul.	23–17	* potent factors in the social *e·*

evolution's

Mis.	vii–13	Thenceforth to *e·* Geology,

evolutions

Mis.	1–21	by the *e·* of advancing thought,

evolve

Mis.	22– 6	say that . . . mortals can *e·* Science?
	23–32	Spirit, could not . . . *e·* matter.
	26–18	not . . . able to *e·* or create itself :
	174– 1	no more power to *e·* or to create
Un.	26– 2	the capacity to *e·* mind.
My.	190– 3	so help to *e·* that larger sympathy
	342–27	"It will *e·* scientifically.

evolved

Mis.	166–13	has *e·* a more ready ear
	295– 5	is *e·* by the same power
	331–25	divine Science *e·* nature as thought,
Hea.	6–16	were *e·* and made tangible ;
My.	226–11	by *e·* spiritual power,

evolves

Mis.	24–18	*e·* a subjective state
	190– 7	mortal *e·* not the immortal,
	364–20	or *e·* the universe.

evolving

Rud.	7–24	by *e·* matter from Spirit,

Ewing, Judge William G.

My.	8– 8	* Judge William G. *E·*, in seconding the

exact

Mis.	78–27	the *e·* nature of its Principle,
My.	40–25	* she is an *e·* metaphysician.
	238– 5	*e·* degree of comparison between
	311–16	as to the *e·* date of my first
	322–30	* The *e·* words I do not recall,

exactly

Man.	110– 6	conditions be *e·* complied with,
Pul.	07–23	* It was *e·* one hundred years
My.	71–22	* *e·* five thousand and twelve people
	317– 2	* *e·* defining her relations with the
	320– 7	* *e·* agreed with what you had told me.

exactness

Mis.	233–24	with the *e·* of the rule
Ret.	80–11	* With *e·* grinds He all.

exaggerating

Mis.	112–27	an *e·* sense of other people's.

exalt

Peo.	7– 7	to beautify and *e·* our lives.

exalted

Mis.	130–28	renews his strength, and is *e·*
	162–32	in the strength of an *e·* hope,
	196–26	is *e·*, — not through death,
	287– 1	as the most *e·* divine conception.
	289–25	*e·* and increased affections,
	341–10	and its strength in *e·* purpose.
Ret.	91– 6	No purer and more *e·* teachings
	92– 2	nor was his power so *e·*
Pul.	10–13	No dream . . . broke their *e·* purpose,
	71–17	*e·* by various dignitaries
My.	335– 5	* soon *e·* to the degree of

exalteth

Mis.	139–12	*high thing that e· itself* — *II Cor.* 10 : 5.
	167–29	he *e·* the lowly ;

exalts

Mis.	399– 9	That *e·* thee, and will cure
Ret.	70–29	*e·* a mortal beyond human praise,
No.	12– 3	heals the sick and *e·* the race.
Po.	75–16	That *e·* thee, and will cure
My.	131– 4	*e·*, and commands a man,

examination

Mis.	127–31	need close attention and *e·*.
Man.	36–10	*e·* by the Board of Education,

examination

Man. 51–25 meetings for the e· of complaints
77– 7 shall submit them . . . for e·.
82–14 or for the e· of complaints.
Ret. 14– 3 e· of candidates for membership,
Un. 35– 8 senses are found, upon e·, to be
Rud. 15–26 laid bare for anatomical e·.
My. 3–21 e· compels him to think genuine,
251–12 after e· in the Board of Education,
310–20 by physician or post-mortem e·
329– 7 * excused them from a medical e·

examine

Mis. 109– 8 E· yourselves, and see what,
Un. 33–16 E· that form of matter called *brains*,
33–21 E· these witnesses for error,
Pul. 50–18 * tempted to e· its principles,
'01. 3– 9 Let us e· this.
My. 38–14 * to e· the church.
128–32 Ofttimes e· yourselves, and see if
233–30 Let us e· it for ourselves.

examined

Man. 90– 3 Students are e· . . . by this Board
My. 246– 6 are e· under its auspices
251–20 e· in the Board of Education,

examiners

My. 329– 8 * before a board of medical e·.

examines

Hea. 12– 4 feels the pulse, e· the tongue, etc.,

examining

Ret. 44–17 E· the situation prayerfully

example

and precept
Ret. 88–16 both by e· and precept.
and suffering
Mis. 165–27 e·, and suffering of our Master.
better
My. 215–26 Can we find a better e·
character and
Mis. 91–16 Jesus' character and e·.
Christ as an
Pul. 72–26 * we take Christ as an e·,
Christian
Ret. 26– 5 his holy heroism and Christian e·
My. 52– 6 * in her Christian e·, as well as
demand and
No. 14–24 The demand and e· of Jesus were
follows the
Ret. 65–18 follows the e· of our Lord
follow the
Mis. 359– 1 follow the e· of the *Alma Mater*.
Ret. 49– 6 follow the e· of the *Alma Mater*
55– 3 Let us follow the e· of Jesus,
give
Mis. 216– 6 as the Scriptures give e·.
good
Mis. 126–21 silent lesson of a good e·.
My. 91– 7 * Christian Scientists set a good e·
had shown
Ret. 47– 8 E· had shown the dangers
her
Peo. 10–11 States had followed her e·
My. 28–20 * and following her e·,
58–21 * May her e· inspire us to follow
his
Mis. 165–19 the heirs to his e· ;
359–22 but his e· was right,
Rud. 3–12 His e· is, to Christian Scientists,
'00. 2–12 benefits society by his e·
holy
Mis. 270–21 cannot depart from his holy e·,
instructions and
My. 220–25 the instructions and e· of the
Jesus'
Mis. 30– 3 according to Jesus' e·
My. 340–26 Jesus' e· in this, as in all else,
man's
Mis. 244–23 he did this for man's e· ;
my
Mis. 91–29 had followed my e·,
of our Master
Mis. 158–28 corresponds to the e· of our Master.
of the Master
Mis. 270– 7 e· of the Master in C. S.,
our
Mis. 212– 7 glorious career for our e·.
particular
My. 83–30 * But of this particular e·
perfect
No. 41–14 life of Christ is the perfect e· ;
precept and
'01. 18–22 Metaphysician's precept and e·,
My. 64–17 * by precept and e· how to obey

example

precepts and
Mis. 129–22 your Leader's precepts and e· !
269–12 whose precepts and e· have
previous
Mis. 52–28 and work out the previous e·,
teaching and
Ret. 65–21 Christ's teaching and e·,
teachings, and
Pul. 75– 6 my writings, teachings, and e·
My. 127–10 Christ's teachings and e·
129–32 teachings and e· of Christ Jesus.
their
My. 74–16 * might profit by their e· of
this
Mis. 149–26 This e· of yours is a light
your
Mis. 110–11 to know that your e·,

Ret. 49–17 Christ and the e· he gave ;
Rud. 1–18 (in court, for e·)
My. 137– 6 * an e· of crisp, clear,
196–16 leaving us an e·, — *I Pet.* 2 : 21.
272–13 reveals . . . the e·, the rule,

examples

Mis. 223–23 or taint their e·.
Ret. 82–23 their e· either excel or
Pul. 78– 2 * one of the most magnificent e·
My. 218– 6 Neither . . . furnishes reasons or e·

exceed

Mis. 111–18 Jesus' faith . . . must not e· that of
Man. 84–14 shall not e· $100.00 per pupil.
My. 208–16 nothing can e· its ministrations of
244–26 certainly not e· three in number.

exceeded

'01. 17–12 e· that of other methods,
My. 138–19 Trusting that I have not e· the
173–20 e· my expectation,

exceedeth

Pul. 2– 5 e· the fame which— *I Kings* 10 : 7.

exceeding

Man. 78–19 not e· $200 for any one transaction,
84–12 Normal class not e· thirty
Ret. 80– 9 * Yet they grind e· small ;
'02. 11–24 be e· glad :— *Matt.* 5 : 12.
My. 156– 5 to do e· abundantly — *Eph.* 3 : 20.
270– 1 and be e· glad :— *Matt.* 5 : 12.

exceedingly

Pul. 58–17 * in its e· comfortable pews.
Pan. 13–14 e· glad that the churches
My. 18–22 e· glad that the churches
139–26 Rejoice and be e· glad,

exceeds

Mis. 354– 2 It e· my conception of
Pul. 30–24 * e· two hundred thousand people.
My. 67–22 * But one church in the country e·

excel

Ret. 82–23 examples either e· or fall short

excellence

Mis. 340– 5 There is no e· without labor ;
Man. 61–21 standard of musical e· ;
Hea. 11–28 this e· above other systems.
Peo. 7– 4 chiselling to higher e·,

excellences

Ret. 5–22 * distinguished for numerous e·.

excellent

Mis. 155–20 who write such e· letters
313–22 more laborers of the e· sort,
Pul. 9–17 e· sermons from the editor
37– 7 * Her health is e·,
57–20 * Such is the e· name
58–14 * into seven e· class-rooms,
My. 15–17 Kate Hankey's e· hymn,
118–10 for your most e· letter.
120– 8 to answer your e· letter.

excelling

My. 190–12 vastly e· the former.

excelsior

My. 6–19 its e· extension is the crown.

except

Mis. x–27 e· in connection with my
8–11 e· you first formulate this enemy
21–14 e· by increase of spirituality.
64–14 e· the Bible, and "S. and H.
75–16 e· where the word *God* can be
83–12 e· it be with the consent of
91–14 e· as types of these mental
226–27 cannot stoop to notice, e· legally,
272– 8 * no charters were granted . . . e· hers,
272–19 * colleges (e· Rev. Mrs. Eddy's)
289–22 e· by mutual consent.

EXCEPT   321   EXECUTIVE

except
Mis. 314–32　e· Communion Sunday,
315– 8　e· by their author.
315–25　e· the individual needing it
362–29　e· when it is necessary to
362–30　pleasure is no crime e· when
Man. 36–12　e· in such cases as are
37–20　e· as provided for in Article V,
45– 9　e· those specified in the
45–22　e· by invitation.
45–25　e· those who have received
46–11　e· as a C. S. practitioner.
62–15　None e· the officers, teachers, and
71–18　e· in such cases as are specially
71–22　e· they give the name
78– 8　e· such debts as are specified
82–12　e· by a majority vote of the
84–25　e· it be in the Board of Education.
87– 4　e· it be with the written consent of
99– 6　e· as hereinafter specified,
99–15　all States e· Massachusetts,
109– 7　e· loyal students of Mrs. Eddy,
Ret. 20– 2　e· what money I had brought
81– 4　Nothing e· sin, in the students
Un. 2– 6　no refuge from sin, e· in God,
27– 9　doubts all existence e· its own.
27–11　everything e· his own existence.
42– 5　nothing e· the results of material
51– 7　hair white or black, e· in belief ;
Pul. 52– 2　* no sums e· those already subscribed
Rud. 14– 9　e· the bliss of doing good.
'00. 12–20　e· thou repent."— Rev. 2 : 5.
14　13　o· the church in Philadelphia
'01. 6–13　e· He be a Person,
20– 4　e· it be to serve God
23–15　e· on its fixed Principle
27– 2　all other authors e· the Bible.
31–15　in no way e· in the interest of
'02. 8–18　e· we possess this inspiration,
13–11　e· the privilege of publishing
Hea. 5–16　no evidence of the fact e·
My. vi– 7　* e· as he has learned it
4–26　"E· ye . . . become as — Matt. 18 : 3.
57–30　* e· those already subscribed
82–30　* e· perhaps those living in the
103–23　e· the teachings and demonstrations
117–24　lost to the centuries e· by
137–15　e· in one or two instances,
138–17　e· I leave all for Christ.
141–10　* e· on the triennial gatherings,
191– 3　e· God be with him."— John 3 : 2.
261–24　unutterable e· in C. S.
336–13　e· what money I had brought

excepting
Man. 57–10　(e· its regular sessions)
82–18　e· those members who
Pul. 47–22　* nothing is left e· the angles
My. 310–18　* that all the family, "e· Albert,

exception
Mis. 7 1　sickness is by no means the e·.
248–28　with the following e· :
282–19　the following is an e·
283–13　e· to the old wholesome rule,
382– 2　contradict it and prove an e·.
Ret. 82– 8　e· to this rule should be very rare.
Hea. 19–11　is not an e· to the origin
My. 76–18　* free of debt without e·.
83–13　* Therefore, with the e· of the
175– 5　with the e· of a daily drive.
261– 8　continue thus with one e· :

exceptional
Mis. 39–21　There may be e· cases,
90–12　under circumstances e·,
283– 4　then the case is not e·.
Man. 36–14　E· Cases.
96– 9　E· Cases.

exceptions
Mis. 282–18　There are solitary e· to most
Man. 94– 8　there may occur e·.

excess
Mis. 353– 4　either an e· of action or
My. 340–10　in e· of other States,

exchange
Mis. 76–20　e· the term soul for sense
78–20　taking its money in e· for this
274–26　in e· for money, place, and
342–30　with the etiquette of the e·,
My. 236–14　will e· the present name for
347–19　in e· for all else.

exchanged
My. 36–15　* e· the tears of sorrow for
339–14　Massachusetts has e· Fast Day,

exchanges
Mis. 103–26　e· this human concept of Jesus

excite
Pul. 66–23　* may reasonably e· wonder

excited
Pul. 32–11　* that her . . . following e·,
My. 75–18　* They do not get e· over trifles.

excitement
Mis. 228– 7　is to be calm amid e·,
My. 121– 5　e· and commotion of the season's
335–19　* in the hope of allaying the e·

exciting
Mis. 69–25　e· cause of the inflammation
229– 2　predisposing or e· causes.
267–26　predisposing and e· cause of all
Ret. 44–18　predisposing and e· cause of its

exclaim
Mis. 326–25　Well might this heavenly messenger e·,
Pul. 3–19　with Job of old we e·,

exclaimed
Un. 30– 1　e·, "My soul...doth magnify — Luke 1 : 46.
Pul. 49– 9　* e· : "You have lived here only four

exclaims
Mis. 167–23　e·, "I thank Thee, O Father,— Luke 10 : 21.

exclamation
Mis. 75–21　e·, "My soul doth magnify — Luke 1 : 46.

exclude
Mis. 194–32　e· all faith in any other remedy
My. 187– 8　e· all darkness or doubt,

excluded
Un. 4–27　the vision of sin is wholly e·.

excludes
Mis. 257– 2　either e· God from the universe, or
Ret. 75–18　Science of Mind e· opposites,
No. 9–23　e· all error and includes all Truth.
'01. 25–28　e· evil and matter.
My. 249– 9　hating even one's enemies e· goodness.
293– 1　The knowledge that . . . e· doubt,
364–10　e· from his own consciousness,

exclusion
Mis. 271– 1　e· of compounds from its pharmacy,
Man. 49– 3　not . . . to the e· of others,

exclusive
Mis. 273–32　call is for my e· teaching.
Pul. 25–10　* designed for the e· use of
28–11　* e· of the land
No. 4–25　rests on the e· truth that being,

exclusively
Mis. 375–30　* as belonging to them e·,
Man. 42– 3　collectively and e·.
Pul. 71– 8　* from C. S. believers e·.
'01. 28–15　those who have followed e·

ex-common sense
Mis. 112– 7　microbes, X-rays, and e· s·,

excommunicate
Man. 51–23　e· members of The Mother Church.

excommunicated
Man. 39– 9　who has been e· once,
50–21　put on probation, or e·.
51–13　withdraw from the Church or be e·.
53–10　that member should be e·.
53–17　on penalty of being e· from
68– 9　e· from The Mother Church.

excommunication
Man. 99–17　twice notified of his e·,

excursion
My. 312–23　would need on such an e·.

excuse
Mis. 113–20　so that all are without e·.
Un. 9– 9　so plain that all are without e·
'01. 29–20　this is no e· for waiting
My. 211– 5　and e· themselves by denying

excused
Mis. 178–27　I wished to be e· from speaking
My. 329– 6　* The board only e· them from

excusing
Un. 21– 3　or else e· one another."— Rom. 2 : 15.

executed
My. 222–16　was not arrested and e·

execution
Hea. 2–15　passed from his e· to a crown.

executive
Man. 66–26　to the Boards or to the e· bodies
Pan. 14–15　associated with his e· trust,
My. 281–29　is not an e· power,
282– 5　friendship of our chief e·

Executive Members (*see also* **Executive Members'**)
Man. 18–25 "First Members" to "*E· M·*."
    18–26 pertaining to "*E· M·*"
My. 347– 7 *E· M·* of The Mother Church

Executive Members'
My. 139–18 the *E· M·* meeting,

exegesis
'*00* 6–28 *e·* on the prophetic Scriptures.

Exemplar
My. 106–30 Our great *E·*, the Nazarene Prophet,
    180–28 in the spirit of our great *E·* pray:
    217–28 Thus it is that our great *E·*,

exemplar
Pul. 65–26 * unbelieving *e·* afterward became

exemplary
Man. 30– 2 Readers who are *e·* Christians
    55–17 after three years of *e·* character.
    72– 6 loyal *e·* Christian Scientist
My. 19–26 with acknowledgment of *e·* giving,
    310–27 presented my disposition as *e·*

exemplification
Mis. 112–32 *e·* of total depravity,
Ret. 86– chapter sub-title

exemplified
Mis. 7–10 has daily to be *e·*;
    130– 2 Has her life *e·* long-suffering,
    176– 7 has been *e·* in all ages,
    293–21 sum total of Love reflected is *e·*,
Pul. 54– 9 * enunciated and *e·* the Principle;
My. 287–13 Love lived . . . is God *e·*,

exemplify
Mis. 333–29 *e·* the power of Truth and Love.
Man. 60–20 whereby is *e·* our risen Lord.
My. 181–19 *e·* in all things the universal equity
    182– 6 *e·* my early love for this church

exemplifying
Mis. 311–10 *e·* what we profess.

exempt
Mis. 257–30 is not *e·* from this law.
Un. 56–19 not fully *e·* from physicality

exemption
Mis. 119–19 full *e·* from all necessity to
My. 256– 8 total *e·* from Christmas gifts.

exercise
Mis. 13– 3 permit me to *e·* these sentiments
    137– 3 badge, and order of *e·*,
    152–30 *E·* more faith in God
    267– 8 caused me to *e·* most patience.
Man. 74– 4 neither shall he *e·* supervision
    80–19 not elect to *e·* this right,
Ret. 82– 4 dealing with a simple Latour *e·* or
Pan. 4–11 depend on . . . for their proper *e·*.
My. 259–27 appropriate and proper *e·*.

exercised
Mis. 70– 3 *e·* my power over the fish,
Hea. 14– 9 caution should be *e·* in the choice of

exercises
Mis. 130–27 he who *e·* the largest charity,
Man. 62–17 attend the Sunday School *e·*.
Pul. 40–12 * TO ATTEND THE *E·*
    42– 7 * variation in the *e·*
    43– 7 * presided over the *e·*.
    43–13 * simplicity marked the *e·*.
    59– 8 * *e·* four times repeated.
My. 72–21 * to attend the dedication *e·*,
    78–30 * every word of the *e·*
    86–13 * ceremonies and *e·*.
    99–19 * attended the dedicatory *e·*,
    173–18 when there are no formal *e·*

exercising
Mis. 24–32 *e·* their supposed power

exerted
My. 281–24 * which President Roosevelt has *e·*

exhale
Man. 31–12 the mental atmosphere they *e·*

exhales
'*00.* 8– 5 *e·* consciously and unconsciously

exhaling
Mis. 20– 3 *e·* the aroma of Jesus' own

exhaustion
My. 165–26 and never stop from *e·*.
    232–27 produces fear or *e·*

exhaustless
Mis. 39–18 this saving, *e·* source
My. 149–12 mysteries of *e·* being.

exhibit
Mis. 299–23 pay me, not him, for this *e·*?

exhibited
Man. 64– 4 *e·* in the Reading Rooms
    81–21 *e·* in the rooms where
My. 25– 7 * great interest *e·* by the
    95–30 * as that *e·* at Boston,

Exhibition
Mis. 304– 7 * After the close of the *E·*
    304–16 * until that *E·* closes.

exhibition
Mis. 299–20 and put myself and them on *e·*,
Pul. 78–25 * The scroll is on *e·*

exhibitions
Mis. 47–28 *Professor Carpenter's e·*
    322– 1 earthly expositions or *e·*.

exhibits
'*01.* 21–17 *e·* a startling ignorance of

exhilaration
Pul. 36–16 * a state of *e·* and energy

exhort
Mis. 197– 5 *e·* people to turn from sin
Ret. 89–16 as Jesus was once asked to *e·*,
Un. 43–19 I *e·* them to accept Christ's promise,
No. v– 3 "reprove, rebuke, *e·*," — *II Tim.* 4 : 2.
Pan. 13–12 rebuke and *e·* one another.
My. 18–20 rebuke and *e·* one another.
    130–17 my students reprove, rebuke, and *e·*.

exhortation
Pan. 13– 9 chapter sub-title
My. 343–29 in tenderness, in *e·*, and in rebuke,

exigencies
My. 224– 3 to meet the *e·* of the hour

exigency
Pul. 9–13 quibbled over an architectural *e·*,

exiled
Po. 2–13 upon thine *e·* height ;

exist
Mis. 6–18 we *e·* in God, perfect,
    34–23 not a moment when he ceases to *e·*.
    50–24 we *e·* in Mind, live thereby,
    86–10 *e·* only in imagination ?
    101–28 no other . . . intelligence can *e·*.
    105–27 no right either to be pitied or to *e·*,
    105–27 and what does not *e·* in Science.
    145– 4 shall *e·* alone in the affections,
    173–17 Does an evil mind *e·*
    183– 4 the verities of being *e·*,
    190–27 and *e·* in Mind.
    337–20 Where these *e·*, C. S. has no sure
    346–12 Evil never did *e·* as an entity.
Ret. 61–16 saith to fear, . . . You do not *e·*,
    61–17 and have no right to *e·*,
Un. 23–19 *Evil.* But mortal mind and sin . . . *e·* !
    23–20 *Good.* How can they *e·*,
    47– 6 All that can *e·* is God and His idea.
Pul. 85–12 * all things which really *e·*,
Rud. 5–28 *e·* in Mind only ;
No. 16– 3 must truly and eternally *e·*.
    16– 3 If . . . matter can *e·* in Mind,
Pan. 5– 6 how can it *e·*?
'*01.* 14– 9 evil, as a false claim, . . . does *e·*
    23– 8 either *e·* in good, or *e·* outside of
My. 89– 5 * deemed by its professors not to *e·*
    143–11 I *e·* in the flesh, and am seen daily
    226–16 and the universe would no longer *e·*.
    246–15 scientific unity which must *e·*
    306– 5 any unity that may *e·* between

existed
Mis. 5–29 That which never *e·*,
    45–23 never originated or *e·*
    56–26 *e·* from the beginning,
    57–30 *e·* in and of the Mind that
    111–23 no greater difference *e·*
    382– 3 No works on the subject of C. S. *e·*,
Ret. 67– 1 Sin *e·* as a false claim
No. 37–27 if error and sin *e·* in
'*01.* 8–25 Christ *e·* prior to Jesus,
My. 319– 1 If there had never *e·* such a
    334–13 * which records show really *e·*

existence

acknowledge the
Mis. 247–20 They acknowledge the *e·* of
actual
Mis. 182– 6 perceive man's actual *e·*
No. 24–10 denies the actual *e·* of both
admitting the
Mis. 109–22 but, admitting the *e·* of both,
all
Un. 27– 9 doubts all *e·* except its own.
and rulership
Un. 38–16 affirming the *e·* and rulership

existence

conscious
Mis. 42–15 same plane of conscious e·
Un. 57–28 The only conscious e· in the flesh
consciousness and
Un. 21–14 individual consciousness and e·.
denies the
'01. 24– 2 He denies the e· of matter,
eternal
Mis. 206– 9 interpret man's eternal e·,
286–20 spiritual and eternal e·
evidence of the
Mis. 64–29 The only evidence of the e· of
facts of
Mis. 14–16 facts of e· and its concomitants :
false side of
Mis. 65–14 not consider the false side of e·
form of
Mis. 309–23 above a bodily form of e·,
genuine
No. 30–19 forbids the genuine e· of
goal of
Mis. 85–11 Perfection, the goal of e·,
harmonious
My. 44– 6 * eternal, harmonious e·.
health or
Rud. 12–19 health or e· of mankind,
hints the
Mis. 60–29 hints the e· of spiritual reality ;
his
Mis. 122–30 his e· is a parody,
Pul. 4–22 His e· is deathless,
his own
Mis. 182– 1 antedated his own e·,
Un. 27–11 everything except his own e·.
human
(*see* **human**)
indicating the
Mis. 191–15 assertion indicating the e· of
individual
Mis. 85–17 spiritual, individual e·.
in relation to
Mis. 218– 7 testimony of . . . in relation to e·
intelligence and
Ret. 59–22 for intelligence and e·.
its
Mis. 14– 6 or find its e· necessary
legitimate
My. 37–21 * activities of legitimate e·,
life or
Mis. 105–14 Man's real life or e·
man's
Mis. 52–21 Man's e· is a problem to be
Pul. vii–21 bliss of man's e· in Science.
material
Mis. 42–21 a belief of material e·
Ret. 30–16 finite mind and material e .
32–10 termed mortal and material e·
mortal
(*see* **mortal**)
no longer in
My. 332–26 * lodge was no longer in e·,
no other
Un. 36– 0 beside which there is no other e·.
of anything
'02. 5–27 or speculate on the e· of anything
of a substance
Un. 33– 5 as to the e· of a substance called
of error
Un. 22–11 To admit the e· of error
of God
Mis. 69– 1 treats of the e· of God,
of good
Mis. 13–16 rounded sense of the e· of good.
13–23 e· of good only ;
or consciousness
Un. 47– 5 false claim to e· or consciousness.
origin and
Mis. 79–10 Man's origin and e· being in Him,
origin nor
No. 15–22 have neither origin nor e·
origin or
Un. 45–27 It has no origin or e· in Spirit,
or reality
Un. 36–21 deny the e· or reality of matter,
other
No. 16–18 inference of some other e·
plane of
Mis. 34–25 on this present plane of e·,
power, nor
Mis. 115–20 neither prestige, power, nor e·,
present
Mis. 196–19 illumines our present e·
pretence of
Un. 64– 2 If sin has any pretense of e·,

existence

real
Mis. 30–14 understanding of man's real e·,
Ret. 21–14 not of man's real e·,
25–23 witnesses to . . . the real e· of
Un. 42– 7 can have no real e·,
realities of
Mis. 53– 2 spiritual realities of e·,
reality of
Mis. 24–18 the sole reality of e·.
Un. 49–11 eternal reality of e·
roving
My. 314– 5 * led a roving e·.
sense of
(*see* **sense**)
sensual side of
Peo. 1– 9 pass from the sensual side of e· to
so-called
Un. 58– 2 Mortals, if at ease in so-called e·,
spiritual
Mis. 17–28 primitive, sinless, spiritual e·
182–16 man's primal, spiritual e·,
Ret. 23–14 heart's bridal to more spiritual e·.
stages of
Mis. 56–28 *successive stages of e·*
statement of
Mis. 182–26 metaphysical statement of e·
state of
Mis. 34–19 in our present state of e·,
34–21 We may pass on to their state of e·,
42– 7 in a conscious state of e· ;
42–28 and recognize a better state of e·.
states of
Un. 49–17 two opposite states of e·.
supposed
No. 35–16 supposed e· apart from God.
supposition of the
Mis. 191–22 supposition of the e· of
196– 4 supposition of the e· of many minds
their
Mis. 105–29 and you destroy their e·.
My. 99–28 * their e· points out their meaning
Truth of
Mis. 182– 7 receive the Truth of e· ;
unlawful
Mis. 381–20 their unlawful e· destroyed,
unstimulating
My. 309–29 * a lonely and unstimulating e·.
310– 1 * "lonely and unstimulating e·."
weave an
Mis. 228–18 weave an e· fit for earth and
without
Un. 38– 9 is virtually without e·.
your
My. 226–23 depend on Him for your e·.

Mis. 131–18 it was not in e· all of the year.
Ret. 61– 7 a fear whose e· you do not realize ;
60–15 false sense of an e· which ends in
Rud. 4–26 testify to the e· of matter.
10–28 to believe in the e· of matter,
Hea. 10–14 of a good and a bad side to e·.
My. 217–19 * deny the e· of disease
217–21 We deny *first* the e· of disease,

existences
Un. 10– 3 these so-called e· I deny,

existent
Mis. 12–21 at former periods . . . were not e·.
Un. 46–14 taught no selfhood as e· in matter.

existing
Mis. 09–27 * causes of all things e·,"
Un. 37–20 E· here and now,
No. 9–18 e· wrongs of the nature referred to.
Pan. 2–18 * manifested in the e· universe."
My. 165–22 and my reason for e·.

exists
Mis. 10–32 that aught but good e· in Science.
25– 8 neither one really e·,
42–25 e· only in spiritual perfection,
72–26 it e· only to material sense.
93–20 and e· only as fable.
111–24 e· between the Catholic and Protestant
130–22 Where the motive to do right e·,
354–21 Principle of all that really e·,
Ret. 61–21 reveals the fact that, if suffering e·,
Un. 22–16 Whatever e· must come from God,
24–20 constitute all that e·.
31–12 claim of sin is, that matter e· ;
43–14 fact, as it e· in divine Science,
44–17 into everything that e·,
62–14 Sin e· only as a sense,
Pul. 66– 2 * e· as much to-day as it did when
No. 29– 6 believes that . . . Soul, e· in matter.
'01. 14– 6 Do . . . Scientists believe that evil e·?

exists

'01.	23– 7	yet that evil e· and is
My.	95–25	* no religion . . . e· without faith
	121–21	No deformity e· in honesty,
	178–16	if evil e·, it e· without God.
	179–15	Some dangerous skepticism e·
	180–30	No warfare e· between divine
	211– 6	by denying that this evil e·.

exits

My.	68–28	* There are twelve e·

exodus

My.	82– 5	* chapter sub-title

Exodus 20: 3—17

Man.	63– 1	Ten Commandments (E· 20 : 3–17),

ex officio

My. 250– 9		their Readers will retire e· o·,

exonerated

Man.	50–20	said member e·, put on probation, or

exordium

My.	343– 5	* after a prolonged e·.

expand

My.	66–13	* will enable the church to e·,

expanding

My.	63–13	* our e· consciousness of Truth,

expands

Mis.	175–13	as the leaven e· the loaf.
My.	202–28	but it e· as we walk in it.

expansion

Mis.	111– 7	extended it beyond safe e· ;
Ret.	52– 2	e· of scientific Mind-healing,
My.	164–23	e· that will engirdle the world,

expansive

My.	46– 2	* exquisite and e· auditorium,

expatiates

My.	129–27	e·, strengthens, and exults.

expect

Mis.	7–12	where one would least e· it,
	38– 6	is it unreasonable to e·
	38– 9	should e· no compensation.
	136– 1	this you must no longer e·.
	195–14	does not authorize us to e· the
	321–27	Do not e· me.
Ret.	65–27	As well e· to determine, without
	65–28	e· to obtain health, harmony,
Rud.	14–17	yet will e· and require others to
No.	40– 4	mortals seek, and e· to receive,
	40– 5	they e· also what is impossible,
Hea.	4–13	We e· infinite Love to
	4–14	We e· infinite Truth to
	4–17	We e· infinite Life to
	15–18	but should you e· this when you
My.	21–17	* it is but right to e· that
	51– 9	* should have reason to e·,
	147–31	must not e· me further to do
	195–21	by which we poor mortals e·

expectancy

Mis.	342–11	Each moment's fair e· was
My.	230– 6	sweet in e· and bitter in experience

expectation

My.	10– 4	* enlarge the favorable e·,
	37–26	* confident and favorable e·.
	54–20	* e· that some place would
	173–20	number . . . exceeded my e·,
	208–14	waiting in due e· of
	218–29	e· of receiving instruction

expectations

Mis.	224–18	with the smallest e·,

expected

Mis.	130–19	it ought not to be e·
	226–23	e· that from the violation of
	302–10	e· to know the teaching of C. S.
Ret.	7–20	* e· no more than they realized
Rud.	13–25	not be e·, more than others,
My.	10–20	* not e· to contribute money
	216–27	it is to be e· you will feel more
	225–23	e· to stick to their text,

expecting

Mis.	322– 6	e· to hear me speak

expedient

Man.	80–15	to the Board may seem e·.

expedition

My.	82–28	* with such remarkable e·,

expelled

Mis.	249–21	e· from my College
'01.	17–26	the drug is utterly e·,

expend

My.	20–14	what you would e· for presents
	217– 1	money that you e· for flowers.

expended

Pul.	44–23	* quarter of a million dollars e·
My.	11–28	* the amount to be e·
	12–12	* the amount to be e·
	21– 2	* which they would have e·

expending

Ret.	84–30	e· his labor where there are other

expenditure

My.	20–25	* e· of a large amount of money,

expenditures

Man.	76–13	of its e· for the last year.
My.	23–11	* e· June 1, 1904 to May 31, 1905,
	135–10	investments, deposits, e·,
	137–13	investments, deposits, e·,

expense

Mis.	43–23	at the e· of his conscience,
	135–14	to give one week's time and e·
Man.	96–12	unable to meet the e·,
Pul.	62–18	* with infinitely less e·.
My.	75–29	* e· of its construction
	83–31	* his or her share of the necessary e·

expenses

Man.	96– 6	E·.
	96– 7	The lecturer's traveling e·
'02.	13– 1	to meet the e· involved.
My.	123–17	repairs and other necessary e·
	214–25	to meet my own current e·.
	215–29	with, provision for their e·

experience

and wisdom

My.	273–15	acquired by e· and wisdom,

another sphere of

Un.	3– 5	awake only to another sphere of e·,

benefited by

Mis.	273– 3	neophyte will be benefited by e·,

bitter in

My.	230– 7	sweet in expectancy and bitter in e·

bounds of

Mis.	68–31	* soars beyond the bounds of e·,"

conscious

'01.	24– 1	* nothing more than conscious e·.

dwarf their

Mis.	278–26	and so dwarf their e·.

every

Mis.	86– 8	manifest growth at every e·.

fruit of

My.	343–24	each one was the fruit of e·

gathering

Ret.	27–25	gathering e· and confidence

has shown

Rud.	14–28	e· has shown that this defrauds

has taught

Ret.	87– 7	E· has taught me that the rules of

her

My.	81–30	* tells his or her e·.

his own

My.	84– 5	* can testify from his own e·

holy

My.	63–13	* this happy and holy e·

human

'00.	15–10	of all human e· is the most divine ;

is victor

Mis.	339– 6	E· is victor, never the vanquished ;

learned from

My.	21–14	* Scientists have learned from e·
	43–10	* but they learned from e·
	43–26	* We have learned from e·,

learn from

Mis.	359–20	He had to learn from e· ;

mortal

Mis.	205– 7	In mortal e·, the fire of

my

Mis.	382– 1	my e· would contradict it
My.	190– 9	My e· in both practices
	319–28	* important one in my e·,

my life's

My.	298– 4	occurred in my life's e·

need of

Mis.	73–16	we have need of e·.

observation and

Ret.	45–14	careful observation and e·

of many

My.	28– 6	* true in the e· of many
	84– 9	* e· of many generations

our

Mis.	236– 3	Throughout our e·

past

Un.	14– 8	gain wisdom and power from past e·

personal

My.	105–32	from personal e· I have proved

proves

Mis.	309–13	E· proves this true.

recent

Ret.	48– 6	recent e· of the church

experience

religious
No. 12– 9 of the author's religious e'.
My. 311–14 my religious e' seemed to
rich in
Mis. 231– 4 grandmother, rich in e',
sharp
Pan. 12–16 it lifteth the burden of sharp e'
My. 244–18 without a struggle or sharp e',
short
Mis. 24–15 That short e' included a glimpse of
shows
Mis. 354–22 E' shows that humility is the first
some
Po. v– 7 * called forth by some e'
standpoint of
No. 9–10 from their own standpoint of e',
this
Mis. 212– 9 This e' caused them to remember
Pul. 34–22 * in reference to this e'.
35–12 * In writing of this e', Mrs. Eddy
36–19 * always with this e' repeated.
My. 43–13 * this e' was almost as marvellous
321–27 * have had this e'
verdict of
Mis. 73–18 Hence the verdict of e' :
wisdom or
Mis. 2– 4 have the least wisdom or e' ;

Mis. 124–29 to patience, e' ;
124–29 to e', hope ;
149–10 what God has given him of e',
156–26 E' and, above all, obedience,
293–12 E' weighs in the scales of God
380–23 E', however, taught me
Man. 63–24 shall have had e' in the Field,
Pul. 64– 7 * not the e' of Rev. Mary Baker Eddy.
'01. 27– 1 e', and final discovery,
My. 107– 9 Here I speak from e'.
205– 7 won through faith, prayer, e' ;

experience-acquired
My. 306–16 Age, with e' patience

experienced
Man. 86–11 can elect an e' Christian Scientist,
Ret. 14–19 e' a change of heart ;
'01. 2–21 What Jesus' disciples of old e',
My. 21–21 * always e' much pleasure in

experiences
Mis. 165–22 by their own growth and e'.
Ret. 79– 4 from the e' of others.
Un. 7–19 in connection with these e' ;
Pul. 32–15 * translate those inner e'
33–14 * e', of which Catholic biographies
33–27 * have had e' of voices or visions
47– 9 * her e' as the pioneer of C. S.,
My. 64– 3 * her relation to the e' of the hour
236–30 in their individual e'.

experiencing
Ret. 61– 7 e' the effect of a fear
My. 100– 4 mortals are e' the Adam-dream

experiment
Hea. 19– 1 felon was delivered to them for e'

experimental
Ret. 80–11 golden scholarship of e' tuition.

experimented
Mis. 249– 2 e' by taking some large doses of
379–20 I had already e' in medicine

experiments
Mis. 117–22 and e' ofttimes are costly.
Hea. 13–18 After these e' you cannot

expert
My. 172–19 your kind, e' call on me."
335–25 * an e' (Dr. McRee we think it was),
335–31 * was told by the e' physician

experts
Man. 50– 2 shall be made by qualified e'.

expiate
Pul. 13–19 e' their sin through suffering.

expiration
Man. 39– 3 at the e' of said one year,
69– 8 before the e' of the time
Ret. 21–11 and at its e' was appointed

expired
Mis. 381– 8 The time . . . having nearly e',
'02. 13–19 After the mortgage had e'

expires
Mis. 341–27 so that the flame never e'.
Man. 30–19 attend to the insurance before it e',

expiring
Po. 27–19 Thou fast e' year,

explain
Mis. 50– 6 Does "S. and H. . . . . e' the entire
68–26 * object is to e' the principles
83–10 Will you please e' this seeming
84–19 Please e' Paul's meaning in the
317–22 words of our Master e' this hour :
Ret. 24–18 I could not then e' the modus
83–19 should e' only Recapitulation,
Pul. 69–16 * would take a small book to e' fully
No. 15– 9 to e' and prop old creeds,
'01. 4–23 should be able to e' God's
5–29 to e' both His person and nature,
32–18 e' in a few words a good man.
My. 105–28 e' to the world my curative system
240– 7 * to e' more fully why you call
317–13 would enable me to e' more clearly

explained
Mis. 30–27 is e' in the Scripture,
143– 4 e' to the kind participants
163–11 he e' the Word of God,
169–31 passages e' metaphysically.
170–31 e' as the putting forth of power,
My. 136– 5 it is best e' by its fruits.
324–12 * you e' how long you had waited
343– 5 * She e' : "No present change is
344– 7 mystery is scientifically e'.

explaining
Mis. 265–21 thoroughly e' spiritual Truth
My. 59–15 * your words e' the Scriptures,
151– 8 opportunity for e' C. S. :
317–22 diction, as used in e' C. S.,

explains
Mis. 25–14 e' the teachings . . . of our Lord.
35–26 author of that work, who e' it in detail.
194–19 Scriptural text e' Jesus' words,
258–30 e' the eternal dynamics of being,
Pan. 5–18 Jesus' definition . . . e' evil.
'01. 2–27 e' its rapid growth.
5–29 God e' Himself in C. S.
8–27 e' that mystic saying of the Master
9– 2 e' it as referring to his eternal
10–17 C. S. e' the nature of God
'02. 12– 3 e' these doctrinal points,
Hea. 15–12 e' to any one's perfect satisfaction
17–15 e' this dream of material life,
My. 140–13 * Rev. Mary Baker Eddy e'
275– 4 it e' love, it lives love,

explanation
Mis. 70– 6 its only e' in divine metaphysics.
96–26 any conclusive idea in a brief e'.
188–22 continues the e' of the power of Spirit
220– 8 by audible e', attestation, and
Man. 66–12 to await her e' thereof.
Ret. 78– 5 The textual e' of this practice
Pul. 60– 5 * e' of Bible or their textbook.
My. 146– 1 In e' of my dedicatory letter
218– 2 in e' of his deeds he said,
280–27 chapter sub-title

explanations
Mis. 92–15 Throughout his entire e',
Ret. 84– 9 Throughout his entire e' he
My. 65–12 * beyond two brief e'

explanatory
Man. 32–21 no remarks e' of the Lesson-Sermon

explicitly
My. 199–14 show e' the attitude of this church

explored
Ret. 7–12 * e' their every nook and corner,

expose
Mis. 11–10 even try not to e' their faults,
335–19 my wisdom or right to e' error,
Ret. 63–17 feel bound to e' this conspiracy,
Pul. 15– 3 e' evil's hidden mental ways
My. 212– 8 e' the cause and effects of this evil

exposed
Mis. 229– 5 e' to contact with healthy people,
My. 105–15 and e' the jugular vein

exposes
Mis. 363–26 e' the subtle sophist,
367– 5 e' the lie of suppositional evil,

expositions
Mis. 322– 1 infinitely beyond all earthly e'
My. 179–30 e' of the therapeutics, ethics, and

expositor
Pan. 12– 4 scholarly e' of the Scriptures,
My. 181–28 one e' of Daniel's dates

exposure
Mis. 48– 8 praise for his public e' of it.
129–23 spare his e' so long as a hope
Pul. 15– 5 since e' is necessary to ensure
No. 24–19 e' is nine points of destruction.

expound
Ret. 36– 3   *e·* the gospel according to Jesus.
expounded
Mis. 35–21   go to church to hear it *e·*
     176– 6   so deeply and solemnly *e·*
My. 59– 4   * the truth you *e·*
expounder
Ret. 14– 5   pastor was an old-school *e·* of
expounding
Mis. 159– 2   reading the Scriptures and *e·* them ;
ex-President
Mis. 306–20   * Mrs. Harrison, wife of the *e·*,
express
Mis. 3– 2   *e·* these views as duty demands,
     26–25   phrase, "*e·* image," — *Heb.* 1 : 3.
     36– 7   Beasts, as well as men, *e·* Mind
     36–15   *e·* the lower qualities of the
     50–12   necessity to *e·* the metaphysical in
     74–25   recognize or *e·* pain and pleasure.
     78–27   *e·* the exact nature of its Principle,
     116–16   *e·* life's loss or gain,
     145– 5   need no organization to *e·* it.
     145– 7   to *e·* Soul and substance.
     149–18   *e·* the joy you give me
     181–10   *e·* the claims of the divine Principle.
     218–25   matter does not *e·* the nature of
     250– 8   What the lower propensities *e·*,
     262–20   more grateful than words can *e·*,
     309– 7   often fails to *e·* even mortal man,
     365–27   terms in which to *e·* what it means.
     375–27   * joy as no words can *e·*,
Ret. 27–15   *e·* in feeble diction Truth's ultimate.
     27–23   can duly *e·* it to the ear,
     37– 3   to *e·* the divine, or spiritual,
Un. 50–14   to *e·* the underlying thought.
Pul. 81– 7   * *e·* image of God for love.
No. 39– 1   if the lips try to *e·* it.
'01. 7–13   *e·* the different mentalities of man
'02. 16–23   *e·* the life of Godlikeness.
Peo. 14– 1   *e·* them by objects more beautiful.
My. 24– 5   * to *e·* in its ample auditorium
     42–15   * *e·* my thanks for the honor
     44–28   * *e·* their continued loyalty
     62–22   * *e·* our thankful appreciation
     82–12   * secured *e·* wagons enough
     123– 5   gifts which would *e·* it.
     164– 8   to *e·* my thanks for your
     195–10   I have not had time to *e·*,
     197–10   *e·* my deep appreciation
     234– 8   wherein to *e·* this love
     262–29   *e·* my conception of Truth's
     305– 8   *e·* myself unmistakably
     317–18   * wouldn't *e·* it that way."
     318– 1   capitalization, in order to *e·*
     331–21   * *e·* the feeling of gratitude
     352– 5   * desire to *e·* our recognition of
expressed
Mis. 4–19   interest is awakened and *e·*
     102–17   His pity is *e·* in modes above the
     102–20   fully *e·* in divine Science,
     134– 3   as you have *e·* contrition
     142–17   Because your dear hearts *e·*
     170–27   *e·* contempt for the belief of
     171–11   *e·* in literal or physical terms,
     177– 7   *e·* and operative in C. S.
     193–16   clergyman charitably *e·* it,
     273– 8   *e·* so grateful a sense of my
     280–24   * his fellow-students' thanks
     344– 3   *e·* the wish to become one of
Ret. 80– 7   different languages have *e·* it :
Un. 55–20   as *e·* in his conviction,
Pul. vii–20   *e·* in the absolute power of Truth
     61–21   * Much admiration was *e·*
     66–15   * Bible as *e·* in its poetical
     84–19   * It can be better felt than *e·*.
My. 8–13   * *e·* the universal voice of
     11–16   * she *e·* much gratification
     24–13   * purpose which is thus *e·*,
     52–14   * taught and *e·* by our pastor,
     60–10   * *e·* the thought of all the
     106–19   *e·* in disease, sin, and death,
     157–16   * wish of Mrs. Eddy,
     219–26   *e·* my opinion publicly
     252–25   It *e·* your thanks,
     320– 8   * He also *e·* himself freely
     338– 8   * uniformly held and *e·* by her.
expresses
Mis. 67–25   *e·* the sense of words
     218–23   a grin *e·* the nature of a cat,
Pul. 53–16   * *e·* the whole law of
     65–27   * *e·* the faith of those who
     75– 1   Whoever in any age *e·* most
No. 10– 9   unfolds, and *e·* the ALL-God.
'01. 3–23   Love *e·* the nature of God ;

expresses
'01. 3–26   *e·* God only in metaphor,
My. 76–12   * feebly *e·* the gratification.
expressing
Mis. 170–26   method of *e·* the utmost contempt.
My. 289–13   *e·* our deep sympathy with the
     323–19   * *e·* the crowding thoughts of
     332– 3   * *e·* the feelings of a swelling bosom.
expression
Mis. 4–28   we meet with an *e·* of incredulity.
     247–26   body is an *e·* of mind,
     373– 6   my sense of Soul's *e·*
Ret. 27–27   written *e·* increases in power
Pul. 21–24   a clear *e·* of God's likeness,
     32– 6   * beautiful complexion and changeful *e·*
     38–28   * higher spirituality seeking *e·*.
     67–14   * to give *e·* to a higher spirituality.
No. 2– 2   that crystallized *e·*, C. S.
     11– 8   In its literary *e·*, my system
Pan. 8– 4   find *e·* in sun worship, lunacy,
Peo. 4–15   the error . . . obtained *e·*.
My. 8–10   * the best *e·* of the religion of
     90– 6   * in the history of religious *e·*.
     189–27   gave *e·* to a poem written in 1844,
     248–30   nearest the scientific *e·* of Truth.
     267–30   divine modes, means, forms, *e·*,
     276–21   * an *e·* of her political views,
     281–19   * for the *e·* of congratulations
     346–13   * same *e·* of looking forward,
expressionless
Mis. 376–11   * *e·* copies of an engraving
expressions
Mis. 275–24   *e·* of love and loyalty
My. 31–15   * *e·* of surprise and of admiration
     87–24   * gives such serene, beautiful *e·*,
expressive
Mis. 124–21   *e·* silence wherein to muse His
Un. 44–17   whether *e·* or not *e·* of the Mind
Pul. 2– 2   In the *e·* language of Holy Writ,
My. 124–22   *E·* silence, or with finger pointing
expunged
Ret. 22– 2   and the material record *e·*.
exquisite
Ret. 17–14   To sprinkle the flowers with *e·* dye.
Po. 62–17   To sprinkle the flowers with *e·* dye.
My. 46– 2   * in *e·* and expansive auditorium,
     347–10   The *e·* design of boughs
extant
Ret. 36– 9   unpublished manuscripts *e·*,
extemporaneously
My. 354–26   * above lines were written *e·*
Extempore
Mis. 176– 5   *E·* REMARKS
My. 354–13   poem
extend
Mis. 32–16   My sympathies *e·* to the
     98–13   to quicken and *e·* the interest
     227–10   to *e·* their evil intent,
     311– 6   I would *e·* a tender invitation to
Man. 58–16   shall *e·* from Genesis to Revelation.
Un. 46–22   must *e·* throughout the universe,
Pul. 86–26   * *e·* to you the invitation
No. 14–22   but they *e·* to this age,
'01. 1– 1   I *e·* my heart-and-hand-fellowship to
Peo. 8–10   *e·* their influence to others.
My. 331–14   * *e·* such unrestrained hospitality
extended
Mis. 111– 7   *e·* it beyond safe expansion ;
Man. 18– 5   *e·* a call to Mary Baker Eddy
Ret. 16–18   *e·* a call to Mary B. G. Eddy
     44– 6   *e·* a call to me
No. 15–11   should not these be equally *e·* to
'01. 1– 7   new century finds C. S. more *e·*,
Hea. 18–20   Jesus' mission *e·* to the sick
My. v– 8   * *e·* to this people by other Christian
     49–10   * members *e·* a unanimous invitation to
     51–20   * an invitation was *e·* to Mrs. Eddy
     173– 7   generous hospitality *e·*
     174– 6   courtesy *e·* to my friends
     174– 9   courtesy . . . *e·* to me throughout.
     326– 5   * not because a favor has been *e·*,
     331–24   * *e·* their care and sympathy
     331–30   * sympathy *e·* to her after his death,
extends
Mis. 189–30   it *e·* to all time,
     192–26   salvation, that *e·* to all ages
     265–18   which *e·* along the whole line of
extension
Mis. 364–15   thought, *e·*, cause, and effect ;
Un. 7– 3   glorified in the wide *e·* of belief
No. 21– 9   space, immortality, thought, *e·*.

extension

No.	24– 5	He is *e·*, of whatever character.
My.	3– 2	chapter sub-title
	6–19	its excelsior *e·* is the crown.
	24–19	* progress of the work on the *e·*
	26– 4	* *e·* of The Mother Church
	27–11	* fund for the *e·* of The
	27–25	* all bills in connection with the *e·*
	29– 8	* dedicatory services of the *e·*
	29–26	* dedication of the *e·* of The
	38–29	* in the *e·* of The Mother Church,
	40– 1	* completed *e·* of The Mother Church
	42–21	* in the *e·* of The Mother Church.
	58– 5	* *e·* of The Mother Church,
	61–10	* held in the new *e·* on June 10.
	62–21	* completion of the magnificent *e·*
	63–11	* dedication of the *c·*
	67– 4	* chapter sub-title
	67– 5	* *E· of The Mother Church*
	76–19	* estimated cost of the *e·*
	80–10	* Meetings were held in the *e·*
	80–11	* in the *e·* vestry,
	80–22	* the *e·* of The Mother Church,
	82–15	* services of The Mother Church *e·*
	96– 3	* dedication of the *e·* of The
	96–28	* known as The Mother Church *e·*

extensive

Mis.	88–12	reading, writing, *e·* travel,
Pul.	57–21	* Few people . . . realize how *e·* is
My.	309–18	an *e·* farm situated in Bow

extent

Mis.	7–22	will counteract to some *e·* this
	40– 8	to an *e·* beyond the power of
	55– 5	to the *e·* that Jesus did,
	64–23	and languages, to a limited *e·*,
	366–23	To a greater or less *e·*,
Un.	29– 5	all criminal law, to a certain *e·*.
Pul.	65– 4	* penetrated . . . to an unlooked-for *e·*.
No.	9– 3	would have prevented, to a great *e·*,
'01.	5–23	to the *e·* of extinguishing
	22– 3	to some *e·* a Christian Scientist.
My.	90–31	* the efficacy of which to some *e·* is
	357–15	demonstrate C. S. to a higher *e·*,

exterminate

Mis.	348– 9	uncover iniquity, in order to *e·* it,
'00.	8–21	We must *e·* self

exterminated

No.	31–21	as mortal beliefs to be *e·*.
'00.	10–17	error repeats itself until it is *e·*.
My.	268–11	Divorce and war should be *e·*
	277–17	wrong and injustice are . . . *e·*.

exterminating

My.	248–23	*e·* sin and suffering

external

'01.	23–26	of an *e·* material world.
My.	88–16	* remarkable *e·* manifestations
	121–19	*e·* gentility and good humor

externalized

My.	10– 6	* impulse for good . . . *e·* itself,

externals

My.	88–17	* *e·* constitute the smallest feature

extinction

Un.	18– 2	and evil necessarily leads to *e·*
'01.	20–22	till he suffers up to its *e·*

extinguish

Mis.	199–17	*e·* whatever denied and defied
	337–22	and thus seem to *e·* it.
	364–29	would either *e·* God and
No.	28– 1	would *e·* human existence.
	32– 6	can neither *e·* a crime nor the

extinguished

Mis.	84–22	so far *e·* the latter as
	187–26	never *e·* in a night of discord.
	209–23	but are punished before *e·*.
'00.	8–24	and the fire . . . will be *e·*.

extinguishes

Ret.	81–10	*e·* false thinking,
Rud.	4–23	*e·* forever the works of darkness

extinguishing

'01.	5–23	to the extent of *e·* anything that

extolling

Mis.	372– 9	letters *e·* it were pouring in

extra

Mis.	143–25	for this *e·* contribution,
	285–22	some *e·* throe of error may
My.	73–27	* *e·* sections of trains are due

extract

Mis.	106–15	chapter sub-title
	148– 7	chapter sub-title
	159–10	chapter sub-title
	171–21	chapter sub-title

extract

Mis.	375– 8	*e·* from a letter reverting to
Man.	3– 1	heading
Ret.	5–17	following is a brief *e·* from
Pul.	40– 8	* from *Boston Herald*
	44–16	* from *Boston Sunday Globe*
	50–10	* from *Boston Transcript*
	52– 9	* from *Jackson Patriot*
	63– 2	* from *The Republic*
	64–23	* from *New York Tribune*
	65–11	* from *Journal*, Kansas City, Mo.
	67– 2	* from *Montreal Daily Herald*
	68–13	* from *The American*, Baltimore, Md.
	70– 2	* from *The Reporter*, Lebanon, Ind.
	75–14	* from *The Globe*, Toronto, Canada
	79– 2	* from *The Union Signal*, Chicago
	84–10	* from *Christian Science Journal*
No.	43–12	following *e·* from a letter
My.	7– 3	from Mrs. Eddy's Message, June 1902.
	16– 1	* chapter sub-title
	22– 2	* *E·* from the Clerk's Report
	23– 9	* *E·* from the Treasurer's Report
	241–11	* *e·* from a letter to Mrs. Eddy,
	254–19	* following *e·* from your article
	334–26	* *e·* from an editorial
	341–18	* from *New York Herald*
	353– 6	*E·* from the leading Editorial

extracted

Mis.	44–14	*until I have the tooth e·*,
	44–24	if the tooth were *e·*,

extracting

Mis.	44–15	*has the mind, or e·, or both,*

extracts

Mis.	168–21	chapter sub-title
	216– 9	some *e·* from, "Scientific Theism,"
	216–19	One of these *e·* is the story of
My.	17–27	* *e·* from Mrs. Eddy's writings
	303–12	of which I have seen only *e·*,
	336–19	* These letters and *e·* are of

extra-natural

Mis.	88–23	* supernatural, or *e·*,

extraordinary

My.	vi–10	* full credit for this *e·* work.
	69– 2	* one of the *e·* features is
	86–17	* regarded as an *e·* achievement,
	272–24	* communication from the *e·* woman

extravagant

Mis.	64–16	theories are narrow, else *e·*,

extreme

Mis.	42– 8	a moment of *e·* mortal fear,
	112–15	in *e·* cases, moral idiocy.
	112–24	shows itself in *e·* sensitiveness ;
	215– 3	go from one *e·* to another :
Pul.	14– 6	another *e·* mortal mood,
	14– 7	one *e·* follows another.
	80– 3	* pendulum that has swung to one *e·*
My.	89–11	* to achieve its *e·* of beauty.

extremes

Mis.	206– 4	from *e·* to intermediate.
	353– 3	Human concepts run in *e·* ;
My.	265–27	*e·* of heat and cold ;

extremists

Mis.	374–23	*E·* . . . either doggedly deny or

exuberant

Mis.	231– 3	infancy, *e·* with joy,
Rud.	15– 8	satisfies the thought with *e·* joy.

exudes

Mis.	144–27	*e·* the inspiration of the wine

exultant

Ret.	32– 8	*E·* hope, if tinged with earthliness
My.	201–29	Hope springs *e·* on this blest morn.

exultation

My.	63–16	* to repress a feeling of *e·*

exults

My.	129–27	expatiates, strengthens, and *e·*.

ex-Vice-President General, D. A. R.

Mis.	306–11	* MARY DESHA, *e· G·*, D. A. R.

eye (*see also* **eye's**)

blue

Mis.	330–28	violet lifts its blue *e·* to heaven,

bright

Po.	27–17	and right with bright *e·* wet,

dewy

Po.	73–12	Night's dewy *e·*,

God's

Po.	18–13	God's *e·* is upon him.
	19– 3	God's *e·* is upon me

hath not seen

Mis.	82–12	what *e·* hath not seen.
	205–18	*e·* hath not seen it,
Un.	28–22	"*e·* hath not seen, — *I Cor.* 2 : 9.

eye

his
Mis. 354–26 the eagle, his *e·* on the sun,
354–30 No tear dims his *e·*,
Po. 18– 7 Would a tear dim his *e·*,
his own
Mis. 212–27 cast the beam out of his own *e·*,
mind's
Pul. 2–15 With the mind's *e·* glance at the
mine
Mis. 389–10 only with mine *e·* Can I behold
Po. 4– 9 only with mine *e·* Can I behold
My. 109–17 "But now mine *e·* — *Job* 42 : 5.
my
Pul. 48–21 * my *e·* caught her family coat of arms
of day
Po. 8–10 Ravished with beauty the *e·* of day.
pitying
Mis. 228–13 We should look with pitying *e·* on
386–11 looks on her heart with pitying *e·*,
Po. 49–17 looks on her heart with pitying *e·*,
Reader's
My. 81–10 * first to catch the Reader's *e·*.
seeing with the
Rud. 5–21 this belief of seeing with the *e·*,
spiritual
Po. 32–11 illumines my spiritual *e·*,
thine own
Mis. 355–21 out of thine own *e·*." — *Matt.* 7 : 5.
to eye
Mis. 117–15 We see *e·* to eye and know as we
watchful
Po. 9– 1 her husband's watchful *e·*
your own
Mis. 336–14 the beam in your own *e·*

———

Mis. 58–15 As matter, the *e·* cannot see ;
Rud. 5–13 who has ever seen . . . with the *e·*,
Po. 70– 8 glory that *e·* cannot see.
My. 29–16 * appealed more to the *e·*,
184– 5 neither hath the *e·* seen, what God

eye's
Un. 34– 5 pictured on the *e·* retina.

eyes

admiring
My. 86– 1 * greeting of admiring *e·*,
all
My. 77– 1 * the cynosure of all *e·*
blind man's
Mis. 171– 6 anoint the blind man's *e·* with
blind the
Mis. 301–29 blind the *e·*, stop the ears
blue
Pul. 32– 2 * lighted by luminous blue *e·*,
Po. 74– 5 O blue *e·* and jet,
closed
'02. 9–24 opened my closed *e·*.
earnest
Po. 23– 7 give those earnest *e·* yet back
face and
Mis. 285–27 in the face and *e·* of common law,
green
Mis. 129–18 for other green *e·* to gaze on :
half open
Mis. 325–18 with *e·* half open, the porter
having
Mis. 58–13 "Having *e·*, see ye not?" — *Mark* 8 : 18.
99– 4 "Having *e·* ye see not, — see *Mark* 8 : 18.
170–29 Having *e·*, ye see not ;
her
Mis. 58–12 *She had to use her e· to read.*
366–17 needs to get her *e·* open
Ret. 16– 5 tears of joy flooding her *e·*
his
Mis. 83–24 lifted up his *e·* to heaven,
212–26 open his *e·* to see this error
325–20 calls out, rubs his *e·*,
371– 5 opened his *e·* to see the need of

eyes

his
Ret. 86–13 and the tears from his *e·*,
Hea. 19– 9 removed the bandage from his *e·*,
material
Mis. 170–28 belief of material *e·* as having any
mine
My. 188– 4 mine *e·* and mine heart — *I Kings* 9 : 3.
188– 6 mine *e·* shall be open, — *II Chron.* 7 : 15.
my
Mis. 277–24 No evidence . . . can close my *e·* to
My. 61–15 * I raised my *e·*,
of Eve
Mis. 86–18 more earthly to the *e·* of Eve.
of My children
Un. 18–12 tears from the *e·* of My children.
of reason
Mis. 332–20 blinded the *e·* of reason,
of sinful mortals
No. 7–10 *e·* of sinful mortals must be opened
of the blind
Mis. 307–17 God's love opening the *e·* of the blind
368– 5 open the *e·* of the blind,
My. 183–20 *e·* of the blind see out of obscurity.
270–27 opening the *e·* of the blind
of Truth
Mis. 233–17 worse in the *e·* of Truth
one's
My. 213–15 Unless one's *e·* are opened to the
opened the
My. 97–21 * has opened the *e·* of the country
opens the
Mis. 210–30 Love opens the *e·* of the blind,
open the
Mis. 48–20 to open the *e·* of the people
211– 6 to open the *e·* of others,
277–18 open the *e·* to the truth of
368– 5 open the *e·* of the blind,
Pul. 15– 1 to open the *e·* of the people
other
Mis. 336–16 mote of evil out of other *e·*.
our
Mis. 9–19 to fall in fragments before our *e·*.
pure
'01. 15–28 * provoking His pure *e·* by
purer
'01. 15–25 * He is of purer *e·* than to bear to
My. 300– 1 "of purer *e·* than to — *Hab.* 1 : 13.
sore
Mis. 71– 8 that he had sore *e·* ;
sparkling
Mis. 240– 4 bounding with sparkling *e·*,
suffused
Mis. 239–18 red nose, suffused *e·*, cough,
tear-filled
Mis. 231–30 tear-filled *e·* looking longingly
tears flood the
Mis. 203–22 Tears flood the *e·*, agony struggles,
their
Mis. 253–29 opened their *e·* to the light
Ret. 64–26 must first open their *e·*
'00. 9–10 shut their *e·* and wait for a
My. 79– 3 * kneeling . . . their *e·* closed
those
My. 342–12 * those *e·* the shade of which
wet
My. 326–16 with wet *e·* the Free Masons
your
Mis. 57–18 your *e·* shall be opened, — *Gen.* 3 : 5.
196–10 shall open your *e·*
Un. 44–21 your *e·* shall be opened — *Gen.* 3 : 5.

My. 33–22 In whose *e·* a vile person — *Psal.* 15 : 4.
342–12 * there is no mistaking the *e·*

eyesight
Mis. 58–17 through a belief of *e·* ;

Ezekiel
Mis. 72–12 saith, through the prophet *E·*,

F

F——, Mrs. M. A.
Mis. 243–11 Reference, Mrs. M. A. *F·*,

Faber
Pul. 28–23 * *F·*, Robertson, Wesley, Bowring,

fable
Mis. 93–21 and exists only as *f·*.
309– 8 its unfitness for *f·* or fact
Un. 44–13 This abortive ego, this *f·* of error,
No. 4–13 error of thought becomes *f·*.
My. 301–18 insanity which mistakes *f·* for fact

fables
Mis. 64–20 resist speculative opinions and *f·*.
191–31 St. Paul's injunction to reject *f·*,
342–20 no light ! earth's *f·* flee,
Ret. 30–15 the foibles and *f·* of finite mind
My. 189–19 to see how soon earth's *f·* flee
340– 7 to traditions, old-wives' *f·*,

fabric
Mis. 228–17 as the only suitable *f·*
Pul. 8–26 in the *f·* of this history,
No. 43–19 or think to build a baseless *f·*

fabrication
- *Mis.* 48–30 baseless *f·* offered solely to injure
- 334–10 whole *f·* is found to be a lie,
- *Pul.* 2–29 true temple is no human *f·*,
- *My.* 14–19 * pronounced the story a *f·*

fabulous
- *Peo.* 12–11 Deal, then, with this *f·* law

Fabyan House
- *My.* 185–23 in the hall at the *F· H·*.

Fabyans, N. H.
- *My.* 314–32 White Mountain House, *F·*, *N. H.*,

facades
- *My.* 78–10 * arches in the several *f·*.

face
  and eyes
  - *Mis.* 285–27 in the *f·* and eyes of common law,
  and form
  - *My.* 259– 2 sweetest sculptured *f·* and form
  answereth to
  - *Mis.* 152– 3 *f·* answereth to *f·*,"— *Prov.* 27 : 19.
  - 203– 9 *f·* answereth to *f·*,— *Prov.* 27 : 19.
  familiar
  - *Mis.* 177–29 greets with joy a familiar *f·*.
  her
  - *Pul.* 32– 1 * her *f·*, framed in dark hair
  - *My.* 346–15 * expression of . . . was on her *f·*.
  human
  - *Po.* v–12 * *resemble the profile of a human f·.*
  its
  - *Pul.* 78– 6 * bears upon its *f·* the following
  lit up
  - *Peo.* 7–10 * his *f·* lit up with a smile of joy
  looks out
  - *Mis.* 321–11 from the window . . . a *f·* looks out,
  my
  - *Mis.* 133–23 my *f·* toward the Jerusalem of Love
  of Dante
  - *No.* 18–17 may imagine the *f·* of Dante to be
  of Jesus
  - *Mis.* 309– 9 The *f·* of Jesus has uniformly
  - *No.* 18–18 the rapt *f·* of Jesus.
  of mortals
  - *Mis.* 332–21 shamed the *f·* of mortals.
  of the earth
  - *Peo.* 6– 9 * on the *f·* of the earth,
  of the Nazarite
  - *Mis.* 374–21 the *f·* of the Nazarite Prophet ;
  of the skies
  - *Mis.* 347– 9 They who discern the *f·* of the skies
  of the sky
  - *Mis.* 1– 7 discern the *f·* of the sky ;— *Matt.* 16 : 3.
  one
  - *Pul.* 39–25 * 'mid them all I only see *one f·*,
  portray the
  - *No.* 39–27 portray the *f·* of pleasant thought.
  shining
  - *My.* 355–20 * He hides a shining *f·* ."
  sweet
  - *Mis.* 289–17 Just then a tiny, sweet *f·* appeared
  thy
  - *My.* 34– 9 seek thy *f·*, O Jacob.— *Psal.* 24 : 6.
  to face
  - *Mis.* 16–30 you stand *f·* to face with the laws of
  - 359–11 but then *f·* to face."— *I Cor.* 13 : 12.
  young
  - *Po.* 9– 3 I'm picturing alone a glad young *f·*,

  - *Mis.* 99–17 take the front rank, *f·* the foe,
  - 112– 5 look the illusions in the *f·*,
  - 225–26 The deep flush faded from the *f·*,
  - 376– 4 * *f·*, figure, and drapery of Jesus,
  - 376– 6 * *f·*, figure, and drapery of that
  - 376– 8 * the *f·* having been taken by
  - *My.* 99–30 * at their *f·* value.
  - 248–26 *f·* the foe with loving look

faces
- *'00.* 1– 3 and can see your glad *f·*,
- *'02.* 20–21 to look into the *f·* of my
- *My.* 48–32 * already manifest in their *f·*,
- 74–20 * but reflected in their *f·*,
- 79– 4 * little *f·* turned upward.
- 81– 5 * No pessimistic *f·* there !
- 87–22 * Their happy *f·* would make
- 124– 8 garlanded with glad *f·*,
- 355–22 *f·* shine with the reflection of

facetiousness
- *My.* 93–20 * with the tongue of *f·*.

facilities
- *'02.* 10– 1 *f·* for knowing and doing good,
- *My.* 67–11 * Checking *f·* . . . 3,000 garments
- 82–24 * Transportation *f·* at the two
- 87– 2 * transportation *f·* of the town

facing
- *'01.* 29–22 won for them by *f·* the winds.

facsimile
- *Pul.* 85–28 * *f·* of the corner-stone of
- 86– 8 * *f·* signatures of the Directors,
- *My.* 272–21 * *f·* of an article sent to us

fact
  accessory to the
  - *Mis.* 119– 8 punish . . . as accessory to the *f·*.
  against the
  - *Un.* 36– 5 false witness against the *f·*
  change the
  - *Mis.* 298–30 false . . . does not change the *f·*,
  confirms the
  - *'02.* 8–14 confirms the *f·* that God and Love
  curious
  - *Pul.* 23–19 * History shows the curious *f·*
  dangerous
  - *Un.* 54–13 is to admit a dangerous *f·*.
  determine the
  - *No.* 42–18 power to determine the *f·*
  eternal
  - *My.* 143–16 stands the eternal *f·* of C. S.
  fable for
  - *My.* 301–19 which mistakes fable for *f·*
  fable or
  - *Mis.* 309– 8 for fable or *f·* to build upon.
  faith in the
  - *Mis.* 77– 4 faith in the *f·* that Jesus was the
  far from the
  - *My.* 206–16 far from the *f·* that portrays Life,
  final
  - *Mis.* 63–18 and understand the final *f·*,
  forcible
  - *My.* 108–12 consists in this forcible *f·* :
  forever
  - *Mis.* 287– 3 forever *f·* that man is eternal
  - *My.* 41– 6 * forever *f·* that the meek and lowly
  - 226–17 would remain the forever *f·*,
  foundation in
  - *Mis.* 108– 9 being without foundation in *f·*,
  fundamental
  - *Mis.* 75– 8 I urge this fundamental *f·*
  - *'00.* 4–30 enunciates this fundamental *f·*
  further
  - *My.* 20–20 * further *f·* that it is important
  great
  - *Mis.* 8– 4 to the general thought this great *f·*
  - 16–17 great *f·* that *God is the only Life;*
  - 24–15 included a glimpse of the great *f·*
  - 43– 1 demonstrating this great *f·*,
  - 181–23 The apostle urges . . . this great *f·* :
  - *Ret.* 73– 9 great *f·* leads into profound depths.
  - *No.* 24–26 great *f·* concerning all error
  - *Peo.* 9–25 whereby we learn the great *f·*
  - 12– 8 When this great *f·* is understood,
  - *My.* 116– 5 this great *f·* in C. S. realized
  - 266–20 since this great *f·* is to be verified
  ignorant of the
  - *Mis.* 295–23 Nor is the world ignorant of the *f·*
  important
  - *Mis.* 65–19 and this important *f·* must be,
  instead of
  - *No.* 4–14 becomes fable instead of *f·*.
  is found out
  - *Hea.* 13– 8 until the *f·* is found out
  is made obvious
  - *Ret.* 64–12 In C. S. the *f·* is made obvious
  matter of
  - *My.* 14–24 * As a matter of *f·*, the building fund
  - 310–10 As a matter of *f·*, he was
  metaphysical
  - *Mis.* 237– 3 yielded . . . to the metaphysical *f·*
  must be denied
  - *Un.* 54–13 Hence the *f·* must be denied ;
  no evidence of the
  - *Hea.* 5–16 we have no evidence of the *f·*
  notable
  - *'00.* 6–17 This notable *f·* proves that the
  noticeable
  - *Mis.* 6–25 It is a noticeable *f·*,
  notwithstanding the
  - *My.* 11– 1 * Notwithstanding the *f·* that as
  of being
  - *Mis.* 186–25 is not the scientific *f·* of being ;
  - *My.* 109– 6 not the spiritual *f·* of being.
  of divine substance
  - *Mis.* 68– 1 up to the . . . *f·* of divine substance,
  of its nothingness
  - *Mis.* 93–25 sin and the *f·* of its nothingness,
  one
  - *Un.* 55– 1 accepted the one *f·* whereby
  one more
  - *Mis.* 277–20 * one more *f·* to be recorded

fact

opposite to the
Mis. 133– 5 ideas more opposite to the *f*.
overlook the
My. 227–17 should not overlook the *f*. that
prove the
Mis. 45– 1 prove the *f*. that Mind is supreme.
really remains
Un. 62– 1 when the *f*. really remains,
recognizes the
Mis. 33–26 recognizes the *f*. that, as mortal
 255–23 recognizes the *f*. that the antidote
recognize the
My. 85–12 * to recognize the *f*. that
remains
Mis. 372– 4 *f*. remains, that the textbook
Hea. 6–20 the *f*. remains, in metaphysics,
rests in the
My. 204– 2 rests in the *f*. that He is infinite
rests on the
Un. 31–17 rests on the *f*. that matter usurps
reveals the
Ret. 61–21 C. S. reveals the *f*. that,
No. 28–16 reveals the *f*. that Truth is
sad
Mis. 43–17 sad *f*. at this early writing is,
scientific
Mis. 186–25 not the scientific *f*. of being ;
Ret. 94– 2 perceived, . . . this scientific *f*.,
self-evident
My. 302– 8 self-evident *f*. is proof that
shocking
My. 276–11 resigned to the shocking *f*.
significant
Pul. 79–12 * significant *f*. that one cannot
simple
Mis. 22–29 simple *f*. cognized by the senses,
so-called
Un. 54– 9 does not destroy the so-called *f*.
spiritual
Mis. 42–22 and the spiritual *f*. of Life is,
My. 109– 6 not the spiritual *f*. of being.
state the
Pul. 80–18 * but simply state the *f*.
that evil
'01. 14–12 takes hold of the *f*. that evil
that Mind
Mis. 35– 2 *f*. that Mind, instead of matter,
this
Mis. 27–16 Scriptures maintain this *f*.
 54–10 they bear witness to this *f*.
 62–21 acknowledges this *f*. in her work
 82– 4 Understanding this *f*. in C. S.,
 221–19 denial of this *f*. in one instance
 289–15 This *f*. should be duly considered
Man. 66– 3 shall inform her of this *f*.
 89–16 as are required to verify this *f*.,
Ret. 82–18 This *f*. interferes in no way with
Un. 7–23 realization of this *f*. dispels now
No. 6–27 This *f*. intimates that the laws of
'02. 3– 2 bear testimony to this *f*.
My. 83– 1 * This *f*. will be due to
 117–25 Christian Scientists ponder this *f*.,
 251–29 Cherish steadfastly this *f*.,
 275– 6 senses do not perceive this *f*. until
unfolds the
Mis. 218– 2 Science unfolds the *f*. that Deity
was heralded
My. 79–15 * *f*. was heralded in flaming
welcome the
My. 52–12 * welcome the *f*. of the spreading
well-known
My. 145–21 This well-known *f*. makes me
witnesses of the
Mis. 150–23 with living witnesses of the *f*.

Mis. 334– 6 in *f*., no intelligence ;
 351– 4 *f*. is, that for want of time,
 367– 6 *f*. of there being no mortal mind,
Ret. 33–13 a *f*. which seems to prove
Un. 1–15 In *f*., they had better leave the
 43–14 I insist only upon the *f*.,
Pul. 67– 7 * *f*. borne out by circumstances.
 71–13 in *f*. all over the country,
Rud. 6–16 *f*. "almost universally accepted,
My. 20–23 * In view of the *f*. that a general
 24–20 in *f*., it is being pushed
 27–26 * *f*. that he has been able to
 38–13 in spite of the *f*. that many
 58– 3 * The *f*. that a notice was published
 71–19 * In *f*., nearly all the traditions of
 87–16 * the *f*. that they have their costly
 96–31 * The *f*. is that C. S. just
 110–14 in *f*., all the *et cetera* of mortal
 214–21 I was confronted with the *f*. that I
 275–15 *f*. that I am well and keenly alive

fact

My. 302–14 It is a *f*. well understood that I
 328–12 * *f*. that the law recognizes them
 335–27 * he could not conceal the *f*. that
 339–29 *f*. that he healed the sick man

factions

Rud. 16–24 opposing *f*., springing up
No. 9– 3 the *f*. which have sprung up
Hea. 2– 4 religious *f*. and prejudices
My. 213– 5 starts *f*. and engenders envy

factor

Mis. 13–15 proposition that evil is a *f*.
Pul. 4–12 is as important a *f*. as
 37– 5 * *f*. in her removal to Concord,

factors

Mis. 71–19 not the *f*. of divine presence
Un. 26–19 can it be . . . are universal *f*.,
Pul. 23–17 * one of the most potent *f*.
My. 355–10 important *f*. in our field of labor

facts

additional
My. 335–11 * Additional *f*. regarding Major Glover,
all
My. 89– 4 * all *f*. inhospitable to it
and figures
My. 99–27 * *F*. and figures are stubborn things,
 100– 2 * some of the *f*. and figures belonging
based on the
Mis. 55–16 Is C. S. based on the *f*. of both
 55–18 C. S. is based on the *f*. of Spirit
broad
My. 194– 2 which Christianity writes in broad *f*.
circumstances and
Mis. 146–10 circumstances and *f*. regarding both
con the
Pul. vii–17 to con the *f*. surrounding the
deal with
Mis. 64–19 are those which deal with *f*.
demonstrate the
Ret. 78–19 an attempt to demonstrate the *f*.
dispute the
'02. 10– 7 dispute the *f*., call them false
following
My. 314–18 and who know the following *f* :
foundational
Mis. 200–18 foundational *f*. of C. S.
given
My. 336–20 * the *f*. given by Mrs. Eddy
historical
My. v–13 * recalling the following historical *f* :
immortal
Mis. 14– 5 take in only the immortal *f*.
interesting
My. 329–27 * put before them some interesting *f*.
misrepresent
Mis. 109– 3 Beware of those who misrepresent *f* ;
momentous
Mis. 379–28 momentous *f*. relating to Mind
No. 28– 9 these momentous *f*. in the Science
nor supported by
Mis. 93–20 nor supported by *f*.,
of being
Mis. 37– 7 spiritual *f*. of being.
 187–26 primal *f*. of being are eternal ;
 234–24 into the spiritual *f*. of being
Un. 51– 1 everlasting *f*. of being appear,
of day
My. 110–21 unfold in part the *f*. of day,
of existence
Mis. 14–16 knowing the *f*. of existence
of Science
Mis. 183–30 with the *f*. of Science,
Un. 30– 5 spiritual *f*. of Science,
of Spirit
Mis. 55–18 C. S. is based on the *f*. of Spirit
of Truth
Mis. 352– 8 able to behold the *f*. of Truth
opposite
Un. 36– 9 opposite *f*., or phenomena.
real
No. 31–10 never actual persons or real *f*.
rehearsing
Mis. 311–31 rehearsing *f*. concerning others
self-evident
Un. 25– 4 and dispute self-evident *f* ;
so-called
Mis. 55–20 so-called *f*. of matter ;
some
My. 319–16 * I am conversant with some *f*.
speak
My. 84– 1 * *f*. speak more plainly than
spiritual
  (*see* **spiritual**)

facts

testimony to the
Man. 93–14 to bear testimony to the *f·*

these
Mis. 24– 1 These *f·* enjoin the
55–20 these *f·* are the direct antipodes of
My. 314–28 related these *f·* to her

two
Hea. 7–24 two *f·*, so important to progress

Mis. 101–29 *f·* that disprove the evidence of
105– 2 *f·* of man's spirituality,
My. vi– 1 *f·* which prove, (1) that S. and H.
124–25 *f·* relating to the thitherward,
311–18 *f·* regarding the McNeil coat-of-arms
322– 4 *f·* which cannot be controverted
332–19 *f·* regarding Major Glover's
359–12 desires to inform himself of the *f·*.

faculties

Mis. 332–27 not *f·* of Mind,
Pan. 4–10 functions of these *f·* depend on
'01. 23– 3 little left that the sects and *f·*
My. 154–20 *infinite *f·* of man."
260–25 raises the dormant *f·*,

faculty

Mis. 80–11 who will fight the medical *f·*,
243–26 some of the medical *f·* will tell you
Man. 73– 9 members of the *f·*, instructors, or
No. 2– 4 ostracized by the medical *f·*,
Hea. 9–19 not a *f·* or power underived from
14–20 spiritual sense or perceptive *f·*
My. 4–18 both medical *f·* and Christianity,
175–13 intelligent medical *f·*,

fad

My. 79–20 * more than a *f·* in C. S.,
218–22 *f·* of belief is the fool of mesmerism.

fade

Ret. 18–19 radiance and glory ne'er *f·*.
79– 8 material pigment beneath *f·* into
Po. 64–11 radiance and glory ne'er *f·*.

faded

Mis. 225–26 flush *f·* from the face,
396– 9 Yet here, upon this *f·* sod,
Po. 9– 9 leaves all *f·*, the fruitage shed,
59– 1 Yet here, upon this *f·* sod,

fadeless

'02. 17–16 wherein joy is real and *f·*.

fading

Mis. 15–27 gradual *f·* out of the mortal
342– 5 their *f·* warmth of action ;
Un. 8–13 is illusive and *f·*.
'01. 33– 3 seems to be *f·* so sensibly
Hea. 10–28 Earth's *f·* dreams are empty streams,
Peo. 8–26 fast *f·* into ashes ;

fagots

Mis. 345–11 set fire to the *f·*,
Peo. 13–21 set fire to the *f·*,

fail

Mis. 5– 2 It cannot *f·* to do this if we
5–13 Truth and Love, and these do not *f·*
34– 1 curing where these *f·*,
44– 9 It cannot *f·* to heal in every case
78–27 cannot *f·* to express the exact nature of
135–12 or *f·* to fulfil this Golden Rule,
147–30 rather *f·* of success than attain it by
255–26 and cures where they *f·*,
378–20 readers of my books cannot *f·* to
Ret. 6– 3 * can hardly *f·* to induce them to follow
31–15 and cures when they *f·*,
73–13 who *f·* to appreciate individual
Un. 9–20 by those who *f·* to understand me,
Pul. 13–15 and *f·* to strangle the serpent of sin
No. 22– 9 cold categories of Kant *f·*
'00. 6– 3 demonstrator can mistake or *f·*
9–23 Whosoever attempts . . . will signally *f·* ;
'02. 16–24 *f·* to elucidate Christianity :
Hea. 6– 2 should this rule *f·* hereafter,
My. 111–28 professionals who *f·* to understand it,
166– 4 *f·* to succeed and fall to the earth.
175–28 must *f·* to influence the minds
205–29 The practitioner may *f·*,
271–25 * cannot *f·* to be impressed by the
292–14 *f·* in their prayers to save

failed

Mis. 55– 1 *f·* to get the right answer,
60–10 after all other means have *f·*.
69–21 His physicians have *f·*
267–11 never was a time when I . . . *f·* to
282–25 when other means have *f·*.
378–13 signally *f·* in healing her case.
Pan. 10–19 that M.D.'s have *f·* to heal ;
My. 130–12 has *f·* too often for me to fear it.

failed

My. 151–24 Baalites or sun-worshippers *f·* to
222– 2 even the disciples of Jesus once *f·*.
306–27 to get them published and had *f·*.

failest

Mis. 63–25 Why *f·* thou me?

failing

Mis. 30– 6 even though *f·* at first
52–23 *f·* to demonstrate one rule
220–28 publish . . . that he is *f·*,
222– 9 *f·* of conviction and reform,
Man. 28–22 *f·* to do either, said officer
29–13 F· to do thus, the Pastor
My. 190–14 Jesus' students, *f·* to cure a
305– 2 F· in these attempts,

fails

Mis. 6–17 ultimately succeed where error *f·*.
62–25 *f·*, and ends in a parody on
129–11 If this rule *f·* in effect,
309– 7 often *f·* to express even mortal man,
Man. 28–18 If an officer *f·* to fulfil
29– 7 If the C. S. Board of Directors *f·*
78– 3 If any Director *f·* to heed
Ret. 74– 5 *f·* to distinguish the individual,
Pul. 4– 1 is naught and my faith *f·*."
'00. 7–26 this attempt measurably *f·*,
My. 130–19 Truth never falters nor *f·* ;
130–20 it is our faith that *f·*.
165–15 Goodness never *f·* to receive its

failure

Mis. 9–25 And wherefore our *f·*
Man. 29– 2 *f·* of the Committee on Publication
46–17 A *f·* to do this shall subject the
No. 44– 3 This *f·* should make him modest.
My. 110–29 made his life an abject *f·*.

failures

Mis. 285–10 too short for foibles or *f·*.

fain

Mis. 394–19 I *f·* would keep the gates ajar,
Po. 57– 5 *I *f·* would keep the gates ajar,

faint

Mis. ix–11 once fragmentary and *f·*
2–15 first *f·* view of a more spiritual
262–18 heart grown *f·* with hope deferred.
328–24 causing to stumble, fall, or *f·*,
376–24 Fleecy, *f·*, fairy blue and golden
My. 8–17 * with my *f·* knowledge of
123–32 "We *f·* not ;— II Cor. 4 : 1.
132–31 whose whole heart is *f·* :
196–21 lest ye be wearied and *f·* — Heb. 12 : 3.
254– 8 not be weary, walk and not *f·*.

fainting

Mis. 212–30 the *f·* form of Jesus,

faintly

Un. 48–20 *f·* able to demonstrate Truth
62–27 discern *f·* God's ever presence.
My. 350– 9 calmly and rationally, though *f·*,

fair

Mis. 81–19 if all this be a *f·* or correct view
132– 4 a *f·* token that heavy lids
147–29 no path but the *f·*, open, and direct one,
239– 7 *f·* proof that my shadow is not
247– 9 the world, upon *f·* investigation,
329–29 prophesies of *f·* earth and sunny skies.
342–11 Each moment's *f·* expectancy
387– 2 With joy divinely *f·*,
Ret. 18–22 are fragrant and *f·*,
Un. 48– 1 It is *f·* to ask of every one a reason
Pul. 37– 2 * it is the great daily that is so *f·*
82–29 * and in this *f·* land at least
83–12 * "as *f·* as the morn, — see Song 6 : 10.
Pan. 3–17 *f·* wisdom, that celestial maid."
'01. 2–11 a *f·* opening for right being,
31–27 my *f·* fortune to be often taught by
'02. 2–25 remain friends, or . . . part *f·* foes.
14–29 an open field and *f·* play.
Po. 8–20 thinking alone of a *f·* young bride,
25–10 F· floral apostles of love,
46– 1 F· girl, thy rosebud heart
50–20 With joy divinely *f·*,
64–17 are fragrant and *f·*,
My. 154– 1 Send flowers and all things *f·*
182–27 amid the *f·* foliage of this vine
194–17 *f·* escutcheon of your church.
329–24 *f·* attitude of the press

fairly

Mis. 185– 3 demonstrate *f·* the divine Principle
269–16 has *f·* proven his knowledge
289–28 *f·* stated by a magistrate,
Pul. 67– 8 * Boston can *f·* claim to be
80–14 *f·* broken our mental teeth
My. 81– 3 * Scientists *f·* radiate good nature

fairly

My. 124–25 prove *f·* the facts relating to
187– 2 faith, and Christian zeal *f·* indicate
286– 9 arbitrated wisely, *f·* ;

fairness

Mis. 255– 4 no *f·* or propriety in the aspersion.
377– 2 brush or pen to paint frail *f·*
My. 48–31 * to say, in all *f·*,

fair-seeming

Mis. 233–19 *f·* for straightforward character,

fairy

Mis. 376–24 *f·* blue and golden flecks

fairy-land

Mis. 216–25 * "When philosophy becomes *f·*,

fairy-peopled

Mis. 390–10 The *f·* world of flowers,
Po. 55–11 The *f·* world of flowers,

faith (*see also* faith's)

abiding
Mis. 100–29 abiding *f·*, and affection,
abound in
'01. 34–22 abound in *f·*, understanding, and
all
Mis. 194–32 exclude all *f·* in any other remedy
348–26 one who had lost all *f·* in them.
Hea. 15– 7 reposes all *f·* in mind,
Peo. 9–23 rest all *f·* in Spirit,
My. 158–16 Having all *f·* in C. S.,
ancient
Pul. 52–14 * reviver of the ancient *f·*
and doubt
My. 292–29 is a compound of *f·* and doubt,
and friendship
My. 282– 5 *f·* and friendship of our chief
and good works
'00. 15–11 victory, *f·*, and good works.
'02. 20– 9 thy unfaltering *f·* and good works
and hope
Mis. 246–31 *f·* and hope of Christianity,
Un. 55–17 Job's *f·* and hope gained him
My. 201–12 friendship, *f·*, and hope
and Love
Mis. 152–24 strong tower of hope, *f·*, and Love,
and love
Mis. 176–17 steadfast in *f·* and love,
My. 64–23 * with renewed *f·* and love
152–25 God demands all our *f·* and love ;
156–20 with hope, *f·*, and love ready
and purity
'00. 6–13 through his simple *f·* and purity,
and resolve
Mis. 319–29 *f·* and resolve are friends to Truth ;
and understanding
Mis. 149–10 hope, *f·*, and understanding,
162–32 hope, *f·*, and understanding,
Ret. 28–17 *f·*, and understanding must
My. 132– 8 spiritual *f·* and understanding
187– 7 illumine your *f·* and understanding,
222– 3 cure by their *f·* and understanding
and works
My. 103– 5 The *f·* and works demanded of man
armed
My. 278–11 *f·* armed with the understanding
aspiration and
My. 88–14 * symbolisms of aspiration and *f·*,
assurance of
Pul. 83–10 * With the assurance of *f·* she prays,
banish
My. 95–24 * may think they can banish *f·*
blessed
Ret. 82– 7 practitioners of the same blessed *f·*.
blind
My. 153–22 This trembling and blind *f·*,
break
Pul. 13–14 Alas for those who break *f·* with
breaks
'01. 4–30 conclude that he breaks *f·* with
Christian
Ret. 6– 5 * living illustration of Christian *f·*.
Pul. 51– 3 * Neither does the Christian *f·* produce
'02. 6–20 Christian *f·*, hope, and prayer,
Christian Science
My. 88–11 * Mother Church of the C. S. *f·*
88–18 * smallest feature of the C. S. *f·*,
97–20 * Mother Church of the C. S. *f·*
clinging
Mis. 275– 4 woman's trembling, clinging *f·*
common
Pul. 85–27 * in the Cause of their common *f·*.
confession of
Pul. 30–12 * sign a brief "confession of *f·*,"
30–15 * The "confession of *f·*" includes the
confidence of
Ret. 15– 7 In confidence of *f·*, I could say

faith

converts to the
My. 94–12 * adherence of its converts to the *f·*,
couples
My. 108–13 couples *f·* with spiritual understanding
dignitaries of the
Pul. 71–18 * various dignitaries of the *f·*.
early
My. 350–22 old foundations of an early *f·*
ebbing
My. 183–13 no more sea, no ebbing *f·*, no night.
embrace the
Pul. 66–10 * most of those who embrace the *f·*
encourage
Hea. 14– 8 and encourage *f·* in an opposite
enlightened
Mis. 343–19 sunshine of enlightened *f·*?
Pul. 9–30 enlightened *f·* is Christ's teachings
expresses the
Pul. 65–27 * expresses the *f·* of those who believe
false
Mis. 31–13 false *f·* finds no place in,
My. 218–24 false *f·* that will end bitterly.
fast-increasing
Pul. 47– 8 * members of this fast-increasing *f·*.
firm
My. 97– 3 * They believe that firm *f·*
foundation of the
Pul. 71–20 * foundation of the *f·* to which
Founder of the
Pul. 71–12 * FOUNDER OF THE *F·*
72–20 * she was the Founder of the *f·*,
full
Mis. 223–16 full *f·* in the divine Principle,
270–18 full *f·* in his prophecy,
My. 280–18 in full *f·* that God does not
294–12 accords not with a full *f·*
full-fledged
My. 281– 7 *F·* full-fledged, soaring to the
great deal of
Mis. 4–25 must require a great deal of *f·*
growth of a
Pul. 65–12 * chapter sub-title
half-persuaded
My. 166– 4 It is insincerity and a half-persuaded *f·*
have
Mis. 33–12 *Must I have f· in C. S.*
39–15 I have *f·* in His promise,
Pul. 72–29 * we have *f·* in him.
73– 4 * send to us those who have *f·*,
73–16 * If you have *f·*, you can
'01. 21– 1 they have *f·*, but they have Science,
My. 25–23 I have *f·* in the givers
158–17 we must have *f·* in whatever
220–19 I also have *f·* that my prayer
222–10 "If ye have *f·* as a — *Matt.* 17 : 20.
250–27 So I have *f·* that whatever
having
Hea. 4–26 having *f·* in it, how can we
Peo. 12–23 Having *f·* in drugs and hygienic
healing
My. 153–15 healing *f·* is a saving faith ;
Hebrew
Un. 14–15 Jehovah of limited Hebrew *f·*
his
Mis. 31–18 to relinquish his *f·* in evil,
31–22 in order to retain his *f·* in evil
99–20 his *f·* in the immortality of
138–13 prove his *f·* by works,
260– 8 His *f·* partook not of drugs,
281–15 come out and confess his *f·*,
Peo. 8–27 gorging his *f·* with skill
My. 4– 1 by losing his *f·* in matter
222–16 because of his *f·* and his great
294–20 reason for his *f·* in what
holy
Pan. 15– 7 establish us in the most holy *f·*,
hope and
(*see* hope)
human
Mis. 182–18 Born of . . . no human *f·*,
My. 292–18 human *f·* in the right.
illumed by
Mis. 396–24 thoughts, illumed By *f·*,
Pul. 18– 8 thoughts, illumed By *f·*,
Po. 12– 8 thoughts, illumed By *f·*,
illumined
Mis. 338– 9 *F·* illumined by works ;
implicit
Mis. 105– 1 implicit *f·* engendered by C. S.,
inactive
Pul. 10– 3 paralyzed by inactive *f·*,
in Christ
Rud. 11– 4 first to *f·* in Christ ;

faith

in Christian Science
Mis. 33–12   *Must I have f· in C. S.*
My. 158–16   Having all f· in C. S.,
in divine Love
My. 12–26   F· in divine Love supplies the
in drugs
Mis. 6–22   overcome the patient's f· in drugs
Peo. 12–23   f· in drugs and hygienic drills,
in error
My. 292–30   faith in truth and f· in error.
in evil
(*see* evil)
inexplicable
My. 97–17   * stupendous, inexplicable f·
in God
(*see* God)
in Him
Pul. 72–23   * f· in Him and His teachings.
73– 6   * She had f· in Him,
in him
Pul. 72–29   * we have f· in him.
in His promise
Mis. 39–15   I have f· in His promise,
in humanity
Mis. 338–15   a pure f· in humanity
in hygiene
Hea. 15– 6   It places no f· in hygiene
Peo. 4– 3   more f· in hygiene and drugs
in man
My. 152– 9   By reposing f· in man
in matter
Mis. 334– 9   mortals' f· in matter may
Peo. 9–20   showing our greater f· in matter,
My. 4– 1   losing his f· in matter and sin,
in metaphysics
My. 301–15   chapter sub-title
in Mind
Mis. 229–14   f· in Mind over all other influences
in omnipotence
Peo. 12–24   we lose f· in omnipotence,
in sight
My. 149–24   Losing . . . f· in sight, we lose the
insufficient
My. 292–16   Insufficient f· or spiritual
interesting
Pul. 65– 8   * undoubtedly an interesting f·
in the blessing
My. 209– 6   f· in the blessing of fidelity,
in the givers
My. 25–23   I have f· in the givers
in the pharmacy
My. 108–12   enlists f· in the pharmacy of
in things material
Ret. 31–16   error of f· in things material ;
in truth
My. 292–30   f· in truth and faith in error.
iris of
Mis. 355–29   iris of f·, more beautiful than
is belief
Ret. 54– 3   Because f· is belief,
is divided
Mis. 59– 4   whose f· is divided between
is fruition
My. 253–24   If f· is fruition, you have
its
Mis. 346– 2   the very centre of its f·.
My. 75– 3   * its f· in its fundamentals.
99– 7   * a cult able to promote its f·
152– 3   anchored its f· in troubled waters.
155–15   finds the full fruition of its f·,
Jesus'
Mis. 111–18   Jesus' f· in Truth
keep the
Mis. 41–13   keep the f· and finish their course.
278– 7   and keep the f·.
My. 134– 8   To triumph in truth, to keep the f·
kept the
Hea. 2–16   I have kept the f·."— II Tim. 4 : 7.
lack of
Mis. 31–12   lack of f· in good.
158–16   rebuke a lack of f· in divine help,
My. 222– 9   unbelief" (lack of f·) ;— Matt. 17 : 20.
little
No. 26–27   O ye of little f·?"— Matt. 6 : 30.
live by the
Un. 61–21   I live by the f· of— Gal. 2 : 20.
living
Mis. 197– 1   they require a living f·,
282– 1   to demonstrate a living f·,
Ret. 69–29   art thou in the living f·
Pul. 30–21   * and the need of living f·
Peo. 5– 4   embodiment of a living f·,
lofty
Peo. 13–16   But the lofty f· of the

faith

loss of
Mis. 204–16   marked loss of f· in evil,
members of that
Pul. 75–21   * by which the members of that f·
members of the
Pul. 72– 6   * leading members of the f·
meritorious
Mis. 118–17   guerdon of meritorious f·
molecule of
My. 278–10   Let us have the molecule of f·
more
Mis. 19–20   I should have more f· in an
152–30   Exercise more f· in God
Un. 43–19   more f· in living than in dying.
Peo. 4– 3   more f· in hygiene and drugs
My. 162– 2   our want of more f· in His
more than
Mis. 4–28   more than f· is necessary,
77– 3   more than f· in the fact
mounts upward
My. 129–26   where f· mounts upward,
my
Mis. 213– 5   and my f· in the right.
Pul. 4– 1   you may say, . . . my f· fails."
63– 8   "My f· has the strength to
'01. 21–24   My f· assures me that God
'02. 15– 3   never lost my f· in God,
Hea. 5–24   my f· by my works."— Jas. 2 : 18.
Po. 33– 3   Increase Thou my f·
My. 169–18   three thousand believers of my f·,
204– 1   My f· in God and in His
new
Pul. 67– 5   * found a new f·, go to Boston,"
My. 92–13   * swift growth of the new f·
no
Mis. 31–20   because he has no f· in the
33–16   had no f· whatever in the Science,
89–14   have no f· in your method,
118– 4   We shall have no f· in evil
Un. 48– 7   have no f· in any other thing
Hea. 15– 6   no f· in hygiene or drugs ;
15–25   that you have little or no f·
My. 221–27   shall we have no f· in God,
not of
Ret. 94–19   whatsoever is not of f·— Rom. 14 : 23.
not sufficient
Mis. 5–12   but have not sufficient f·
of ages
Ret. 33–17   mixed with the f· of ages,
of Christian Science
My. 69– 9   * illustrative of the f· of C. S.
of his followers
My. 222–17   demands on the f· of his followers,
of the Church
No. 41–26   * as the f· of the Church increases,
of these people
My. 95–19   * The f· of those people is
one
Mis. 131–12   one f·, one God, one baptism.
Peo. 1– 1   one f·, one baptism.— Eph. 4 : 5.
5– 3   one f·, one baptism."— Eph. 4 : 5.
9– 1   C. S. has one f·, one Lord,
14–19   one f·, one baptism."— Eph. 4 : 5.
one's
Hea. 12–28   divide one's f· apparently between
My. 105– 6   prove one's f· by his works.
only
Un. 61–19   Only f· and a feeble understanding
on the earth
'01. 12–12   find f· on the earth?"— Luke 18 : 8.
our
Mis. 100–14   every trial of our f· in God
361–21   finisher of our f·."— Heb. 12 : 2.
'01. 14–11   our f· takes hold of the fact that
17– 6   author and finisher of our f·,
My. 63–18   * of those not of our f·
130–20   it is our f· that fails.
152–25   God demands all our f· and love ;
163–29   a church of our f·
258–14   finisher of our f· ;— Heb. 12 : 2.
349–16   finisher of our f·."— Heb. 12 : 2.
patient
'01. 35–18   do we walk in Patient f·
Paul's
Un. 57–20   confirmation of Paul's f·.
power of
Pul. 80–22   * in God and the power of f·,
power of the
My. 81– 8   * healing power of the f·,
prayer of
No. 41–25   * prayer of f· shall save— Jas. 5 : 15.
My. 221–32   prayer of f· shall save— Jas. 5 : 15.
primeval
My. 139– 8   primeval f·, hope, love.

faith

principles of the
Pul. 68– 6 * taught the principles of the f·
pure
Mis. 338–15 a pure f· in humanity
Peo. 13–21 and his pure f· went up
reasonable
Mis. 200–27 triumph of a reasonable f·
reason for the
Un. 48– 1 a reason for the f· within.
receivers of the
Pul. 56– 6 * receivers of the f· among the
religious
My. 89–27 * this form of religious f·
95–30 * demonstration of religious f·
301– 5 present flux in religious f·
saving
My. 118–17 saving f· comes not of
153–16 healing faith is a saving f· ;
serenity of
My. 88–21 * beauty and serenity of f·,
service, and
'00. 15–24 service, and f·,— Rev. 2 : 19.
sound
'01. 26–20 sound f· and charity,
My. 164–17 not only possess a sound f·,
spirit of
My. 85–26 * spirit of f· and brotherhood
spreads
Po. 33–16 f· spreads her pinions abroad,
St. Paul's
My. 108–28 remain steadfast in St. Paul's f·,
strengthen the
Man. 43–12 she may strengthen the f· by
strong
Mis. 345–12 his pure and strong f· rose
sublime
Mis. 131–11 substance of our sublime f·,
system of
My. 59– 8 * new system of f· and worship,
that
My. 89– 3 * held to symbolize that f· which
164–17 that f· also possesses them.
their
Mis. 140– 8 taxing their f· in God,
Pul. 57–17 * proved their f· by their works.
My. 30–11 * the devotion . . . to their f·,
74–18 * to the sincerity of their f· ;
79– 8 * stagger their f· not a little
90–12 * grips hold of their f·
96–12 * take joy in attesting their f·
155–22 brighten their f· with a dawn
162–27 may their f· never falter
162–28 their f· in and their understanding
222– 3 by their f· and understanding
this
Pul. 58– 3 * imparting this f· to her
66– 4 * church organization of this f·
Peo. 9– 2 this f· builds on Spirit,
My. 90– 8 * this f· is real and is given
103– 7 the practicality of this f·
through
Mis. 158–11 do this through f·, not sight.
241–25 doubting heart looks up through f·,
Pul. 72–23 * through f· in Him and His teachings.
My. 205– 7 Wisdom is won through f·,
thy
Pul. 53–13 * thy f· hath made— Luke 17 : 19.
My. 3–12 "Show me thy f·— Jas. 2 : 18.
152– 6 "Thy f· hath made— Matt. 9 : 22.
153–13 Thy f· hath healed thee.
trembling
My. 293–14 trembling f·, hope, and of fear,
triumphant
Mis. 385–25 f· triumphant round thy
Po. 48–21 f· triumphant round thy
unfaltering
Mis. 163–17 in his unfaltering f· in the
'02. 20– 9 glorifying thy unfaltering f·
My. 155– 6 unfaltering f· in the prophecies,
unfeigned
Mis. 136–11 and of the f· unfeigned.
My. 187–13 and of f· unfeigned ;"— I Tim. 1 : 5.
193– 1 your temple in f· unfeigned,
unflinching
My. 62– 1 * unflinching f· and unfailing
unity of
My. 170–29 unity of f·, understanding,
uplift
Man. 16– 6 served to uplift f·
vested in
Mis. 298–22 f· vested in righteousness
waning
Mis. 312–18 * restore the waning f· of many
without
My. 95–25 * without f· in the things unseen.

faith

without proof
'02. 18–24 f· without proof loses its life,
without works
Pul. 9–29 "F· without works is dead."— Jas. 2 : 26.
My. 3–10 sear leaves of f· without works,
with understanding
Mis. .97–16 combines f· with understanding,
your
Mis. 154– 5 Your f· has not been without works,
Un. 60–25 your f· is vain ;— I Cor. 15 : 17.
My. 148– 4 let your f· be known by your works.
187– 7 illumine your f· and understanding,

Mis. 97–15 C. S. is not a remedy of f· alone,
118– 5 when f· finds a resting-place
124–29 to experience, hope ; to hope, f· ;
124–30 to f·, understanding ;
149–30 shall abide steadfastly in the f·
210–15 He who has f· in woman's special
229–22 f· in the power of God to heal
241– 1 the f· of both youth and adult
380–15 in f·, turned to divine help,
385– 1 * "F·, hope, and tears, triune,
387–21 For f· to kiss, and know ;
Pul. 37–15 * to eliminate . . . from the f·.
52– 4 * f· of the mustard-seed variety.
52– 6 * have not a f· approximate to the
53–10 contained in the one word— f·.
'01. 10–28 f· according to works.
Po. 6–16 For f· to kiss, and know ;
37– 1 * "F·, hope, and tears, triune,
My. 3–18 hope, f·, understanding.
6–28 self-abnegation, hope, f· ;
22–20 * she has shown wisdom, f·, and
23–24 * not only to f· but also to sight ;
25–24 f· in the grandeur and sublimity of
57–31 * f· of the mustard-seed variety.
58– 1 * a f· approximate to that of
89– 3 * that faith which is so much a f·
90–14 * A f· which teaches that hate is
93–30 * In 1890 the f· had but
96–13 * It is a f· based upon reason,
99– 3 * "A f· which is able to raise
99–17 * Thirty thousand of the f·,
153–18 F· in aught else misguides the
187– 1 fidelity, f·, and Christian zeal
189–19 and f· grows wearisome,
202– 4 f·, meekness, and might of him who
203– 5 sing in f·.
234–13 from f· to achievement,
240–14 hope, f·, understanding."
281– 6 f· in God's disposal of events.
301–16 f· in divine metaphysics

faith-cure

Ret. 54–19 The f· has devout followers,
Pul. 47–17 * between f· and C. S.,
69–14 * distinguishes C. S. from the f·,
69–21 * It is not f·, but it is an

faith-cures

Ret. 54– 1 Why are f· sometimes more speedy

faith-curists

'01. 21– 1 mind-curists, nor f· ;

faithful

Mis. 7–15 if f· laborers in His vineyard.
88– 1 A f· student may even
110– 6 unselfishness, f· affection,
114–28 if found f·, He will deliver us
116–28 "f· over a few things."— Matt. 25 : 23.
122–25 good and f· servant,— Matt. 25 : 23.
150–13 in the congregation of the f·,
155–11 pressing meekly on, be f·,
158–15 in reward for your f· service,
158–22 Let us be f· and obedient,
213–18 But the f· adherents of Truth
228–16 just person, f· to conscience
237–24 Honor to f· merit is delayed,
238–22 Are you f· ?   Do you love?
275– 8 the f·, stricken mother,
287–24 Be f· over home relations ;
317–17 by the most f· seekers ;
339–17 f· over a few things."— Matt. 25 : 23.
340–10 wear the crown of the f·.
340–16 He has not been f· over a few things.
340–24 hast been f· over a few things.
342– 8 better-tended lamps of the f·.
342–32 f· over the few things of Spirit,
343–28 "Thou hast been f· !"— Matt. 25 : 23.
354– 6 f· Christian Scientists
356–19 Now let my f· students
392–14 F· and patient be my life as thine ;
Man. 38– 2 f·, loyal students of the textbook,
82–21 devote ample time for f· practice.
Ret. 90– 4 Does the f· shepherd forsake
Pul. 5– 8 Memory, f· to goodness,

faithful

Pul.	13– 6	*f·* over a few things, — *Matt.* 25 : 23.
No.	8– 3	*f·*, and charitable with all.
Pan.	14–21	and their *f·* service thereof,
'00.	13–14	"Be thou *f·* unto death, — *Rev.* 2 : 10.
'01.	1– 2	heart-and-hand-fellowship to the *f·*,
'02.	18– 1	*f·* at the temple gate of conscience,
	18–13	*f·* to rebuke, ready to forgive.
Po.	20–18	*F·* and patient be my life
	53–13	Bid *f·* swallows come
	79– 9	in thought and deed — To *f·* His.
My.	6– 4	Are we honest, just, *f·*?
	42– 5	* a *f·* follower of this Leader
	42–27	* how *f·* is her allegiance to God,
	44– 9	* counsel of our ever *f·* Leader.
	44–11	* *f·* disciple rejoices in prophecy
	46–19	* are we *f·*, obedient, deserving
	61–31	* the *f·*, earnest work of our noble
	62– 3	* good and *f·* servant ; — *Matt.* 25 : 23.
	84–19	* wealth, vigor, and *f·* adherence.
	158–21	makes the heart tender, *f·*, true.
	162–21	"Well done, good and *f·*." — *Matt.* 25 : 23.
	167– 9	in that Love which is *f·*,
	182–15	*f·* labor of loyal students,
	202–13	"Well done, good and *f·*," — *Matt.* 25 · 23.
	205–21	friends more *f·*,
	207–21	"Well done, thou good and *f·* — *Matt.* 25 : 21.
	225– 5	"Well done, good and *f·*," — *Matt.* 25 : 23.
	226–25	Our *f·* laborers in the field
	230–23	*f·* over foundational trusts,
	235– 6	guided by love, *f·* to her instincts,
	244–23	your wise, *f·* teachers
	248–25	committed to you, my *f·* witnesses.
	253–28	Dare to be *f·* to God and man.
	254–14	thank the *f·* teacher of this class
	294–16	skilful surgeon or the *f·* M.D.
	321– 7	* your devoted and *f·* friends,
	335– 8	* *f·* as a member and officer
	355–13	the strong, the *f·*, the untiring

faithfully

Mis.	111– 4	*F·*, as meekly, you have toiled
	127–14	*f·* asks divine Love to feed it
	302–19	working *f·* for Christ's cause
	318–20	student must have studied *f·*
	340–20	They follow *f·* ;
Man.	28–21	to perform his office *f·* ;
	29–12	or perform their functions *f·*.
Ret.	6–26	he served the public interests *f·*
	19–24	performed their obligations most *f·*.
Pul.	21–11	*f·* struggle till it be accomplished
	73–14	* and this duty she *f·* performed.
'01.	31–26	used *f·* God's Word,
My.	18–11	*f·* asks divine Love to feed it
	50– 5	* had labored *f·* and ardently,
	52–10	* more *f·* to sustain her
	60–20	* Respectfully and *f·* yours,
	148– 1	*F·* and more than ever persistently,
	328–16	* over *f·* your student,
	331– 3	performed their obligations most *f·*."
	336– 8	* *f·* performed their obligation to her.

faithless

Mis.	340– 2	*f·* tarrying, has torn the laurel
Ret.	81–19	*f·* to itself and to others,
My.	222– 5	"O *f·* and perverse — *Matt.* 17 : 17.

faith-lighted

Mis.	15–22	What a *f·* thought is this !

faith's

Chr.	53–37	*f·* pale star now blends
My.	158– 8	in attune with *f·* fond trust.

faiths

Mis.	251–25	falling leaves of old-time *f·*
	331–22	falling leaves of old-time *f·*,
Pul.	66–25	* encroachment upon prevailing *f·*,
	67– 9	* census of the religious *f·*
Peo.	1–13	collisions with old-time *f·*,
My.	30– 8	* but many hundreds of other *f·*,

falchion

Ret.	30– 3	smite error with the *f·* of Truth.

falcon

Po.	2– 8	trained *f·* in the Gallic van,

fall

Mis.	xi–19	intolerance will *f·* to the ground,
	9–18	to *f·* in fragments before our eyes.
	10–11	if they *f·* they shall rise again,
	22–30	to which it seemed to *f·*
	77–28	could *f·* into mortal error ;
	80–13	who leave C. S. to rise or *f·*
	115–30	you will *f·* the victim of your own
	127–27	garrulous talk may *f·* to the ground,
	157– 5	He that marketh the sparrow's *f·*
	195–21	and it cannot *f·* to the ground
	211– 7	will lead the blind and both shall *f·*.
	215–21	would *f·* immediately if he knew

fall

Mis.	231– 5	had seen sunshine and shadow *f·* upon
	233–27	if some *f·* short, others will approach
	251–27	will *f·* before Truth demonstrated,
	251–28	as dry leaves *f·* to enrich the soil
	268–27	From lack of moral strength empires *f·*.
	279–25	in order that the walls might *f·* ;
	291–24	dew of heaven will *f·* gently on the
	296–23	Why *f·* into such patronage,
	325–10	*f·* upon the Stranger,
	327–28	they *f·* behind and lose sight of
	328–24	causing to stumble, *f·*, or faint,
	355–27	Let no clouds of sin gather and *f·*
	357–13	seeds of Truth *f·* by the wayside,
	357–14	*f·* on stony ground and shallow soil.
	389–11	behold the snare, the pit, the *f·* :
Ret.	11–21	Farther than feet of chamois *f·*,
	35–21	too immanent to *f·* to the ground
	61– 8	but if you *f·* asleep,
	82–23	their examples either excel or *f·* short
Un.	40– 1	to the *f·* of a sparrow.
No.	3– 6	better to *f·* into the hands of God,
	9–16	students who *f·* into error,
	26–16	than his divine Principle, . . . can *f·*
	44–10	To climb up by . . . is to *f·*.
'01.	2–15	if some *f·* short of Truth,
	24–15	and great was the *f·*
'02.	18–11	who caused not the feeble to *f·*,
Po.	4–10	the snare, the pit, the *f·* :
	8– 2	alone where the shadows *f·*
	24–15	Come when the shadows *f·*,
	60–19	Farther than feet of chamois *f·*,
My.	128–29	it will *f·* powerless,
	166– 4	and *f·* to the earth.
	194–30	* Ne'er in a sunny hour *f·* off."
	226–13	that marks the sparrow's *f·*,
	248–21	*f·* for lack of the divine impetus.
	262– 3	an ideal which cannot *f·*
	278–28	*f·*, pierced by its own sword.
	323–31	* Normal class in the *f·* of 1887

fallacy

Mis.	74–22	he proved the *f·* of the theory
	217–10	*f·* of an unscientific statement
My.	307–29	*f·* of *materia medica*,

fallen

Mis.	14– 9	has *f·* into the imperfection
	77–26	has *f·* away from his first estate ;
	78–25	*Has man f· from a state of*
	106–20	crumbs from this table of Truth,
	181–29	God's opposite, — evil, or a *f·* man.
	186– 7	material belief has *f·* far below
	259–19	man is not *f·* : he is governed in
	262–17	lifting the *f·* and strengthening the
	274–16	*Truth is f· in the street,* — *Isa.* 59 : 14.
	328–26	uplift the *f·* and strengthen the
	357–17	*f·* into the good and honest hearts
Pul.	10– 8	Rome's *f·* fanes and silent
Rud.	7–13	material, *f·*, sick, depraved,
No.	17–17	In Science there is no *f·* state
Pan.	11–16	If man is spiritually *f·*,
	11–29	image of God, not *f·* or inverted
My.	126–24	The Babylonish woman is *f·*,

falleth

Mis.	369–20	crumb that *f·* from his table.

fallibility

Mis.	351–19	chapter sub-title
Ret.	60–30	arises from the *f·* of sense,

fallible

Mis.	332– 5	Mind is Love, — but not *f·* love.
	353– 5	Human concepts . . . are *f·* ;
	353–11	of the misguided, *f·* sort,
Ret.	89–29	and selfish influence is human, *f·*,

falling

Mis.	22–28	A *f·* apple suggested to Newton
	174–11	from the *f·* of a sparrow
	204– 2	*f·* on the bended knee of prayer,
	251–25	*f·* leaves of old-time faiths
	309–18	*f·* into the error of anti-Christ.
	331–22	*f·* leaves of old-time faiths,
	360–17	*f·* upon the blighted flowers of
Ret.	24–14	the *f·* apple that led me to
No.	15– 1	*f·* on the sick and sinner,
My.	190– 1	*f·* upon the bridal wreath,

falls

Mis.	267–20	*f·* to the earth.
	390–14	soft thy footstep *f·* upon
	394– 3	*f·* on the heart like the dew
No.	34–16	*f·* with its leaden weight
Pan.	11–19	the man who *f·* physically
Po.	45– 3	*f·* on the heart like the dew
	55–15	soft thy footstep *f·* upon
My.	260–15	sense that *f·* short of substance,
	262–10	*f·* far short of my sense of the

Falmouth

'02. 13–17 corner of *F·* and Caledonia

Falmouth and Norway Streets

Pul. 61–23 * corner of *F·* and *N· S·*,
77–11 * intersection of *F·* and *N· S·*,
78– 9 * intersection of *F·* and *N· S·*,
My. 29– 9 * corner of *F·* and *N· S·*,
30– 1 * *F·* and *N· S·* held large crowds
67– 2 * corner of *F·* and *N· S·*,
68–13 * corner of *F·* and *N· S·*,

Falmouth, Norway, and St. Paul Streets

My. 65–19 * bounded by *F·*, *N·*, and St. *P· S·*,

Falmouth Street

95 and 97
My. vi–25 * property at 95 and 97 *F· S·*,

My. 84–27 * beautiful structure on *F· S·*,

_____

false

Mis. 24–32 effect arising from *f·* claims
31–12 *f·* faith finds no place in,
32– 8 the students of *f·* teachers,
39– 8 incorrect and *f·* teachers
42–31 *f·* admissions prevent us from
57–19 This was *f·* ; and the Lord God never
65– 8 evidence of the senses is *f·*.
65–14 We must not consider the *f·* side of
66– 2 *f·* testimony or mistaken evidence
67–13 not bear *f·* witness ;" — *Exod.* 20 : 16.
72–11 as *f·* as it is remorseless.
73–20 subjective states of *f·* sensation
76– 8 or proven true upon a *f·* premise,
78–18 *f·* statements and claims.
89–25 Mortal man is a *f·* concept
89–26 saved from . . . whatever is *f·*.
99– 3 It annuls *f·* evidence,
104–16 clad in a *f·* mentality,
104–20 stand the friction of *f·* selfhood
107–19 *f·* senses pass through three
108–11 Not to know that a false claim is *f·*,
109–26 to escape from the *f·* claims of sin.
111–28 *f·* beliefs inclining mortal mind
118– 3 *f·* suggestions, self-will,
171–28 ignorance or *f·* knowledge
175–19 There are *f·* Christs that would
209–20 *F·* pleasure will be, is, chastened ;
209–24 has no foothold on the *f·* basis
209–30 egotism and *f·* charity say,
210–22 under the *f·* pretense of human need,
218– 7 in relation to existence is *f·* ;
218–14 *f·* realistic views sap the Science
220– 3 and a *f·* rule the opposite way.
221– 3 to harm by a *f·* mental argument ;
222– 6 This state of *f·* consciousness
222–15 because the *f·* seems true.
226–12 *f·* to themselves as to others?
226–17 * canst not then be *f·* to any man.
247–12 charges against my views are *f·*,
249– 8 *f·* report that I have appropriated
260–20 whatever else seemeth to be . . . is *f·*,
266–20 is utterly *f·* and groundless.
271–27 * *f·* teachers of mental healing,
287–10 may place love on a *f·* basis
290–10 whatever is *f·* should disappear.
291–21 *F·* views, however engendered,
298–30 *f·* consciousness does not change the
311–32 others who were reporting *f·* charges,
332–25 Is man the supposer, *f·* believer,
332–27 Supposing, *f·* believing, suffering
351–24 pleasure that is *f·*,
358– 9 hounded footsteps, *f·* laurels.
360–17 the cloud of *f·* witnesses ;
366–24 start from this *f·* premise,
366–31 *f·* theories whose names are legion,
368–17, 18 present *f·* teaching and *f·* practice
Man. 53–25 an article that is *f·* or unjust,
98– 2 corrected a *f·* newspaper article
Ret. 30–12 *f·* testimony of the physical senses.
58– 5 physical, *f·*, and finite substitute.
68–11 One is *f·*, while the other is true.
71–22 they proceed from *f·* convictions
73–18 whereby the *f·* personality is laid off.
79– 6 In this consuming heat *f·* images
81–11 Truth extinguishes *f·* thinking,
81–26 * canst not then be *f·* to any man.
94– 6 seems true, and yet . . . is *f·* ;
Un. 32– 2 *f·* to God, *f·* to Truth and Life.
32– 8 but a *f·* form of mind.
33–20 self-testimony of . . . senses is *f·*.
36– 4 this lie was the *f·* witness
36– 8 C. S., which reverses *f·* testimony
39–14 That selfhood is *f·* which opposes
44–10 misled by a *f·* personality,
46– 2 These are the shadowy and *f·*,
51– 3 Reasoning from *f·* premises,

false

Un. 52–10 *f·* consciousness of both good and
53–16 not built on such *f·* foundations,
54–17 even as a *f·* claimant,
55–19 how *f·* are the pleasures and pains
56– 9 a quickened sense of *f·* environment,
61– 1 Rising above the *f·*, to the true
63– 9 *f·* human sense of that light
Pul. 6–18 * I cast from me the *f·* remedy
7–20 *f·* prophets in the present
75– 9 statement would not only be *f·*,
Rud. 6–10 marred, through a *f·* conception,
7–16 material evidence being wholly *f·*.
8–19 yet is *f·* to God and man,
9–12 *f·* and temporal sense of Truth,
12– 8 else quiet the fear . . . on *f·* grounds,
No. 5– 9 a *f·* and material sense,
6–10 destruction of *f·* evidence,
6–13 If, . . . evidence of disease is not *f·*,
17– 1 *f·* assumption of the realness of
17–25 *f·* knowledge would be a part of
24–11 *f·* philosophy and scholastic theology,
42–21 C. S. is beset with *f·* claimants,
'00. 6–21 which destroys his *f·* appetites
'01. 14– 8 *f·* entity, and utter falsity,
15– 6 to prove it *f·*, therefore unreal.
19–14 The notion . . . is proven *f·*.
22–11 if one is true, the other is *f·*.
26– 2 my tired sense of *f·* philosophy
'02. 6– 5 *f·* knowledge, the fruits of the flesh
10– 7 dispute the facts, call them *f·*
16–22 self-defense against *f·* witnesses,
18–12 nor spared through *f·* pity
Hea. 17–23 appeared through the *f·* supposition
Peo. 2–14 *f·* conceptions of Spirit,
3– 9 *f·* beliefs that have produced sin,
4–26 *f·* ideals of the Supreme Being
11–14 are clasped by the *f·* teachings,
11–15 *f·* theories, *f·* fears,
Po. 79–12 *F·* fears are foes
My. 111– 5 cannot be destroyed by *f·* psychics,
112– 3 A fiction or a *f·* philosophy
125– 2 *f·* affections, motives, and aims,
130– 1 correct the *f·* with the true
144– 7 The public report . . . is utterly *f·*.
211– 2 a *f·*, convenient peace,
218–24 *f·* faith that will end bitterly.
274– 5 a *f·* material sense of life,
306– 9 The *f·* should be antagonized
323–11 * leave any *f·* impression.
345– 6 C. S. will overthrow *f·* knowledge
345–12 *f·* science — healing by drugs.
351–25 assertions to the contrary are *f·*.
    (*see also* **belief, claim, sense**)

falsehood

Mis. 13– 5 *f·*, ingratitude, misjudgment,
226–19 by uttering a *f·*,
248– 8 chapter sub-title
248–23 The opium *f·* has only this to it :
269– 3 By using *f·* to regain his liberty,
277– 3 *F·* is on the wings of the winds,
348–17 To quench the growing flames of *f·*,
351–12 *f·* designed to stir up strife
Un. 52–18 From this *f·* arise the
Rud. 8–20 uttering *f·* about good.
'01. 20–14 suggestion of the inaudible *f·*,
'02. 14–20 mockery, envy, rivalry, and *f·*
My. 261–10 deceit or *f·* is never wise.
306– 1 *f·* which persistently misrepresents

falsehoods

Mis. 222–13 *f·* that once he would have resisted
238–27 another evidence of the *f·*
248–11 *f·* uttered about me
277–15 by slanderous *f·*, and
'01. 16–27 one hundred *f·* told about it

falsely

Mis. 8–24 against you *f·*, — *Matt.* 5 : 11.
Man. 54–21 represents *f·* to or of the Leader
Ret. 25–24 material senses testify *f·*,
Un. 39–25 material senses testify *f·*,
Rud. 8–25 mortal mind should not be *f·*
No. 11–13 those who come *f·* in its name.
18–18 Thus *f·* may the human conceive of
'01. 3– 6 against you *f·*, — *Matt.* 5 : 11.
'02. 11–24 against you *f·*, — *Matt.* 5 : 11.
My. 104–31 against you *f·*, — *Matt.* 5 : 11.
316– 8 against you *f·*, — *Matt.* 5 : 11.

falsities

Mis. 24–30 put down all subtle *f·*
309–21 Corporeal *f·* include all obstacles to
Un. 10–28 under their own *f·*,
45–12 An evil ego, and . . . are *f·*.
45–12 These *f·* need a denial.
'01. 16– 8 its lusts, *f·*, envy, and hate,

falsities
My. 248–10   put an end to *f·* in a wise way
249– 8   counteract its most gigantic *f·*.

falsity
Mis. 57–20   history of a *f·* must be told
65– 2   by repeated proofs of its *f·*.
84–26   A true sense of the *f·* of material
107–21   must first be shown its *f·*
108– 9   since a lie, . . . is merely a *f·* ;
201– 8   element of matter, or material *f·*,
201–10   myth or material *f·* of evil ;
333– 7   renders error a palpable *f·*,
334–20   reduce this *f·* to its proper
Ret. 61–14   you are a self-constituted *f·*,
81–11   and *f·* must thus decay,
86– 9   Note well the *f·* of this mortal self !
Un. 32–28   to demonstrate the *f·* of the claim.
33–21   witnesses for error, or *f·*,
35–27   an outlined *f·* of consciousness,
45–13   The *f·* is the teaching that
Rud.   8–20   *f·* shuts against him the Truth
No. 38– 3   *f·* of the evidence of the material
Pan.   5–23   deny it and prove its *f·*.
'01. 14– 8   false entity, and utter *f·*,
My. 161–30   *f·* of supposititious life

falter
Mis. 135–12   If you *f·*, or fail to fulfil this
My. 11– 3   * although we may *f·* or stumble
162–28   may their faith never *f·*
248–19   No . . . can fold or *f·* your wings.

faltering
Mis. 331–20   guards the nestling's *f·* flight !
389– 8   guards the nestling's *f·* flight !
Po.   4– 5   guards the nestling's *f·* flight !

falters
My. 130–19   Truth never *f·* nor fails ;

fame
Mis. 145– 8   Does a single bosom burn for *f·*
270– 4   such as barter . . . for money and *f·*.
327–12   and to search for wealth and *f·*.
Ret.   2–27   Henry Knox of Revolutionary *f·*.
Pul.   2– 5   the *f·* which I heard." — *1 Kings* 10 ; 7.
46–22   * Wallace of mighty Scottish *f·*.
No. 43–19   motives, for wealth and *f·*,
'00. 13–18   the god of medicine, acquired *f·* ;
Hea. 16– 7   wealth and *f·*, or Truth and Love?
Po. 42– 5   for glory and *f·*, Without heart
My. 258– 4   lifts a system . . . to deserved *f·*
283–29   Lured by *f·*, pride, or gold,
306– 3   into a conflict for *f·*.

fame-honored
Ret. 17–15   *f·* hickory rears his bold form,
Po. 62–18   *f·* hickory rears his bold form,

familiar
Mis. 177–29   greets with joy a *f·* face.
247– 6   Those *f·* with my history
364– 9   and posterity your *f·* !
372–14   critics *f·* with the works of masters
372–17   * seems quite *f·* with delineations
Ret. 10– 5   *f·* with Lindley Murray's Grammar
Un. 14–21   if this Mind is *f·* with evil,
Pul. 41–27   * Old *f·* hymns — "All hail
My. 92–14   * has in general way been *f·* ;
134–29   * with which I have been *f·* for several

familiarity
Mis. 239–24   their *f·* with what the stock paid,
Pul. 31–10   * *f·* with the work of her life

families
Mis.   6–25   *f·* where laws of health are strictly
6–32   small *f·* of one or two children,
Pul. 30– 1   * members of their own *f·*,
59–26   * children of believing *f·*
My. 112–31   chief cities and the best *f·*

family
all the
My. 310–18   all the *f·*, "excepting Albert,
grand
Mis. 273–14   one grand *f·* of Christ's followers.
her
Ret.   1– 5   her *f·* is said to have been
5–29   * to secure the happiness of her *f·*.
Pul. 46–16   * Her *f·* came to this country
his
My. 308–12   my late father and his *f·*
his father's
My. 309–17   the youngest of his father's *f·*,
home and
Pul. 50– 5   * a home and *f·* of his own.
human
Mis. 18–21   of the whole human *f·*,
98–12   helping the whole human *f·* ;
No. 15– 7   blessings for the whole human *f·*.
My. 208–20   prayer for the whole human *f·*.

family
large
Mis.   6–29   large *f·* of children where the
member of the
Mis. 89– 5   *to care for a member of the f·*,
my father's
My. 310–19   a death in my father's *f·*
New Hampshire
Pul. 57–27   * born of an old New Hampshire *f·*,
peace in the
Mis. 354– 9   promote peace in the *f·*,
remained
Ret.   5–10   and there the *f·* remained
same
My. 227–12   same disease and in the same *f·*,
Wiggin
My. 322–16   * to dine with the Wiggin *f·*.

Mis. 236– 7   shrunk from . . . *f·* difficulties,
Ret.   2–30   my Grandmother Baker's *f·*
13–11   the *f·* doctor was summoned,
17– 1   while visiting a *f·* friend
20– 9   under the care of our *f·* nurse,
20–27   *f·* to whose care he was
Pul. 48–21   * her *f·* coat of arms
'01. 31–22   daily Bible reading and *f·* prayer ;
'02.   3–10   reinstating the old national *f·* pride
Po. vii– 1   * *while visiting a f· friend*
My. 295–23   Countess of Dunmore and F·,
311–22   her own *f·* coat-of-arms.

famine
Mis. 246–23   the spiritual *f·* of 1866,
338–27   * Shall the world's *f·* feed ;
Ret. 23 20   Soulless *f·* had fled.
My. 126–21   and mourning, and *f·* ; — *Rev.* 18 : 8.
263– 7   feast of Soul and a *f·* of sense,

famishing
No. 43– 6   whether stall-fed or *f·*,

famous
Ret. 32–11   Calderon, the *f·* Spanish poet,
Pul. 67–11   * Max O'Rell's *f·* enumeration of
'01. 21– 8   * "To the *f·* Bishop Berkeley
My. 68–16   * Mrs. Eddy's *f·* room will be
95–14   * *f·* old Massachusetts State House.
141–16   * its *f·* communion seasons.
271–19   * thought that has made her *f·*.

fan
Po. 30–12   *f·* Thou the flame Of right

fanatic
Po. 71– 8   Rescued by the "*f·*" hand,

fanaticism
Mis. 48–10   whether of ignorance or *f·*,
My. 79–25   * without a trace of *f·*,
90 7   * slightest trace of *f·*.
96– 9   * where *f·* dominates everything else.

fancied
Ret. 12– 6   Woke by her *f·* feet.
Po. 61– 4   Woke by her *f·* feet.
My. 314–11   which he *f·*, for a summer home.

fancies
Mis. 15– 1   *f·* he finds pleasure in it,

fancy
Mis. 12– 9   do not *f·* that you have been wronged
393– 4   Gives the artist's *f·* wings.
396– 3   And frightened *f·* flees,
Ret. 11– 5   If *f·* plumes aerial flight,
Un. 18–10   Many *f·* that our heavenly Father
Pan.   3– 1   mythical deity may please the *f·*,
Po.   3– 9   Till sleep sets drooping *f·* free
51– 9   Gives the artist's *f·* wings
58–15   And frightened *f·* flees,
60– 1   If *f·* plumes aerial flight,
My. 258–32   F· yourselves with me ;

fane
Chr. 53–58   Truth's *f·* can dim ;
My. 151–17   * "Pass ye proud *f·* by,

fanes
Pul. 10– 8   Rome's fallen *f·* and silent

fanned
Mis. 233– 7   *f·* by the breath of mental

Fantasie in E minor, Merkel
My. 32–11   * organ voluntary — F· *in E m·*, M·

fantastic
Un. 26–24   there is in God naught *f·*.

far
Mis.   6–15   will rank *f·* in advance of allopathy
9–14   good *f·* beyond the present sense
12–32   imparting, so *f·* as we reflect them,
13– 2   just so *f·* as one and all permit me

far

Mis.	19– 8	task of healing the sick is *f·* lighter
	22– 8	*f·* in advance of human knowledge
	34–13	so *f·* as I understand it,
	38–17	*f·* from dry and abstract.
	43–14	*f·* more advantageous to the sick
	84–22	so *f·* extinguished the latter as
	103– 4	*f·* more impregnable and solid than
	103–24	so *f·* as material sense could
	123–31	*f·* apart from physical sensation
	158– 3	not as our ways ; but higher *f·*
	180– 2	so *f·* as to take the side of Spirit,
	186– 7	material belief has fallen *f·* below
	213–28	the night is *f·* spent,
	234–24	has seen *f·* into the spiritual facts of
	291–17	and is *f·* from my desire ;
	297– 5	has achieved *f·* more than
	344–23	Such philosophy is *f·* from
	352–24	out of himself and into God so *f·* that
	371–12	They know *f·* more of C. S. than
	385–14	emancipate for this *f·* shore
	385–16	and *f·* from mortal joys,
Ret.	9–22	* From the *f·* cataracts?
	10– 3	with *f·* less labor than is usually
	12– 1	nobler *f·* than clarion call
	38– 1	I had finished that edition as *f·*
	54–20	*f·* in advance of their theory.
	60– 2	very *f·* from the divine likeness.
	76–15	This affection, so *f·* from being
	87– 8	can be *f·* more thoroughly and
Un.	2–24	their lives have grown so *f·* toward the
	6–16	and the world is *f·* from ready to
	9–23	but in a *f·* different form.
	45– 9	very *f·* from God's likeness.''
Pul.	3–28	so *f·* from victory over the death
	32–14	* so *f·* as outward events may translate
	57–24	* not *f·* from the big Mechanics Building
	82–11	* *f·* better than her teachers.
Rud.	6–21	so *f·* as you perceive and understand
No.	15–13	are *f·* more mystic than
	20– 1	so *f·* as he can conceive of
	29–16	Better *f·* that we impute such
	38– 1	so *f·* as this could be done
Pan.	1–17	The night is *f·* spent,
'00.	3–15	not *f·* from saying and doing.
	7–24	find ourselves so *f·* from the
'01.	34–25	only so *f·* as she follows Christ.
'02.	4– 4	only so *f·* as she follows Christ.
	12–24	so *f·* as I know them,
Peo.	4–16	are *f·* from correct.
Po.	1– 9	And *f·* the universal fiat ran,
	16–12	through *f·* crimson glow,
	22– 7	*f·* heaven is nigh !
	25– 8	*F·* do ye flee,
	29–17	so *f·* above All mortal strife,
	34–20	in azure bright soar *f·* above ;
	48– 7	emancipate for this *f·* shore
	48– 9	and *f·* from mortal joys,
	60–21	Strains nobler *f·* than clarion call
My.	7– 7	so *f·* as I know them,
	21–22	* their brethren from *f·* and near,
	30–12	* business men come from *f·* distant
	30–28	* by *f·* the largest crowd of the day
	41–13	* howsoever *f·* he may stray,
	59– 6	* might be true in some *f·* distant day
	74– 2	* from abroad and from the *f·* West
	75–21	* no matter how *f·* they had travelled
	79– 6	* chapter sub-title
	79–21	* placed upon a *f·* higher pedestal
	88–12	* of *f·* more than usual ecclesiastic
	93– 1	* so *f·* as the writer knows them,
	97– 4	* *f·* towards making the patient well.
	97–13	* the advantage so *f·* as this goes.
	152– 7	*f·* lower in the scale of thought,
	163–29	was *f·* from my purpose, when I came
	197–13	ready hands of our *f·* Western
	202– 6	for the night is *f·* spent
	206–16	belief, which is *f·* from the fact
	229–13	Better *f·* that Christian Scientists
	242–12	I do not mean that . . . *f·* from it.
	262–10	*f·* short of my sense of the
	273– 6	* a Leader *f·* beyond the allotted years of
	291–18	and so *f·* as it fathomed
	306– 4	*F·* be it from me to tread on the
	312– 9	* She was *f·* from home
	313–25	to describe scenes *f·* away,
	322–20	* journeying from the *f·* South,
	323– 7	* some minister in the *f·* West
	327–29	* to the day, not *f·* distant,
	346– 4	* and so *f·* from being puzzled

farce

Mis.	288–25	real suffering would stop the *f·*.

fare

Mis.	275–28	and the *f·* is appetizing.
My.	312–12	* Masons also paid Mrs. Glover's *f·*

farewell

Po.	27–24	Illustrious year, *f·* !
My.	50–30	* her *f·* sermon to the church.

farewells

Mis.	386–28	Where *f·* cloud not o'er
Po.	50–14	Where *f·* cloud not o'er

Farlow

Alfred

My.	141–13	* Alfred *F·* of the publication committee

Mr. Alfred

My.	16–16	* Mr. Alfred *F·*, President of The

farm

Ret.	4– 4	inherited my grandfather's *f·*
	4– 7	One hundred acres of the old *f·*
Pul.	33–18	* on his father's *f·* at Lexington,
	48–11	* that lies below, across the *f·*,
	49–24	* She chose the stubbly old *f·*
	49–30	* to keep the grounds and *f·*
My.	172– 5	* grown on the *f·* of Mark Baker,
	309–18	an extensive *f·* situated in Bow

Farmer

Pul.	88–14	* *F·*, Bridgeport, Conn.
	88–30	* *F·*, Bridgeport, N. Y.

farm-house

Ret.	4–10	*f·*, situated on the summit of

far-off

Mis.	153–29	* music of this *F·*, infinite, Bliss !
Pul.	22–11	and a few in *f·* lands,
	41– 9	* from the *f·* Pacific coast

Farrand & Votey

Pul.	60–16	* organ, made by *F·* & *V·*

far-reaching

My.	236–18	a *f·* motive and success,

far-seeing

Mis.	254– 3	loving warning, the *f·* wisdom,
'01.	30–25	clear, *f·* vision, the calm courage,
My.	208–24	courageous, *f·* committees

farther

Mis.	52–25	a rule *f·* on and more difficult
	73–15	can get no *f·* than to say,
	316–13	depart *f·* from the primitives of
	378–21	*f·* removed from such thoughts
Ret.	11–21	*F·* than feet of chamois fall,
Po.	60–19	*F·* than feet of chamois fall,

Far West

Ret.	20–29	then regarded as the *F· W·*.

fascinated

Pul.	32–11	* *f·* the imagination.

fashion

Mis.	219–14	think also after a sickly *f·*.
	354–32	Whenever he soareth to *f·* his nest,
Rud.	12–13	aided in this mistaken *f·*,
No.	20– 5	Error would *f·* Deity in a manlike
	39– 6	after the *f·* of Baal's prophets,
My.	121–14	is somewhat out of *f·*.

fashionable

Mis.	111–22	sects, the pulpit, and *f·* society,
	233–16	into a more *f·* cut
Pul.	24– 3	* church is in the *f·* Back Bay,
My.	192– 6	cast out *f·* lunacy.
	224–20	more *f·* but less correct.

fashioned

Mis.	360– 6	good, because *f·* divinely,

fashions

Mis.	376–30	He who *f·* forever such forms

fast

Mis.	117–24	inclined to be too *f·* or too slow :
	154– 4	*f·* reaching out their broad shelter
	307–18	*f·* fitting all minds for the
	354–27	*F·* gathering strength for a flight
	363–24	hold *f·* to the Principle of C. S.
	400–24	Be it slow or *f·*,
Chr.	53– 1	*F·* circling on, from zone to zone,
Ret.	78– 2	being too *f·* or too slow.
'00.	1–14	right convictions *f·* forming
	14– 5	Hold that *f·* which thou — *Rev. 3 : 11.*
'01.	14– 3	sin itself, that clings *f·* to
	31–25	held *f·* to whatever is good,
Peo.	8–26	*f·* fading into ashes ;
Po.	27–19	Thou *f·* expiring year,
	69–12	Be it slow or *f·*,
My.	44– 7	* our progress may be *f·* or
	82–11	* disgorging trunks . . . so *f·* that
	129– 2	"hold *f·* that which — *I Thess. 5 : 21.*
	190– 7	*f·* answering this question :
	201– 3	*f·* fulfilling the promises.
	205– 3	"Stand *f·* therefore — *Gal. 5 : 1.*
	334–21	that clings *f·* to iniquity.
	335–20	* excitement which was *f·* arising,
	339–19	Pharisees *f·* oft, — *Matt. 9 : 14.*

fast

My. 339–19 thy disciples *f·* not?" — *Matt.* 9 : 14.
339–25 but he did not appoint a *f·.*
339–30 observance of a material *f·*

Fast Day

in New Hampshire, 1899
My. 339–11 chapter sub-title

My. 339–14 has exchanged *F· D·,*

fasten

Mis. 312–24 which reason . . . cannot *f·* upon.
Ret. 18–17 soar above matter, to *f·* on God,
Un. 17– 2 seeks to *f·* all error upon God,
Po. 64– 8 soar above matter, to *f·* on God,

fastened

Pul. 42–27 * pure white roses *f·* with

fastens

My. 283–30 never *f·* on the good

faster

Mis. 327–17 ascend *f·* than themselves,
Hea. 9– 1 and progress *f·* than we are
My. 56–19 * increased *f·* than ever.

fast-increasing

Pul. 47– 7 * members of this *f·* faith.

fasting

Mis. 156–21 by prayer and *f·.*" — *Matt.* 17 : 21.
'02. 16–23 *f·,* feasting, or penance.
My. 190–17 by prayer and *f·.*" — *Matt.* 17 : 21.
222–13 by prayer and *f·.*" — *Matt.* 17 : 21.
339–25 by prayer and *f·,*" — *Matt.* 17 : 21.

fasts

'00. 15–16 and *f·* in the wilderness.
My. 340– 2 of his observing appointed *f·.*

fat

Mis. 326–11 fed by the *f·* of hypocrisy

fatal

Mis. 24– 9 pronounced *f·* by the physicians.
45– 9 *f·* results that frequently follow
71– 5 from this *f·* appetite.
72–10 to impart to man this *f·* power.
93–28 Nothing is more *f·* than to
121–13 would make this *f·* doctrine just
222–16 malicious mental argument . . . is *f·,*
233–14 *f·* magnetic force of mortal mind,
264–30 more *f·* than a mistake in physics.
380–14 an accident, called *f·* to life,
Ret. 19–10 which in his case proved *f·.*
33–20 its *f·* essence, mortal mind ;
71–23 false convictions and a *f·* ignorance.
Un. 52–21 rabid beasts, *f·* reptiles, and mortals
Rud. 17– 1 A slight divergence is *f·* in Science.
'01. 2– 9 *f·* magnetic element of human will
34– 7 cannot be *f·* to the patient.
My. 234–25 more *f·* than the Boxers' rebellion.
248–18 No *f·* circumstance of idolatry
249–13 mental miasma *f·* to health,
293–11 that the bullet would prove *f·.*

fate

Mis. 83–17 arbiter of your own *f·,*
134–28 blind to its own *f·,* it will
200 5 * where the good man meets his *f·*
230–23 * With a heart for any *f·* ;
291–18 is the irony of *f·,*
Ret. 23– 4 yield to the irony of *f·,*
No. 42–18 fact and *f·* to being.
My. 165– 2 Of two things *f·* cannot rob us;
185– 5 * With a heart for any *f·* ;

Father (see also Father's)

adoption with the
Mis. 182–10 their adoption with the *F·* ;
and Mother
Mis. 33–11 God, our divine *F·* and Mother.
96–11 as a loving *F·* and Mother ;
113– 5 Spirit is our *F·* and Mother,
154–23 thy *F·* and Mother, God.
167–17 *F·* and Mother are divine Life,
186–14 the universal *F·* and Mother of man ;
Un. 48–14 *F·* and Mother of all He creates ;
'00. 5–10 *F·* and Mother are synonymous
'01. 10–18 God as both *F·* and Mother.
and son
'02. 12–18 *F·* and son, are one in being.
begotten of the
Mis. 164–26 the only begotten of the *F·,*
bids man
Un. 4–18 *F·* bids man have the same Mind
bosom of the
'02. 9–20 forever in the bosom of the *F·,*
came from the
Mis. 360–29 "I came from the *F·,*" — see *John* 16 : 28.
even the
Un. 60–13 "bless we God, even the *F·* ; — *Jas.* 3 : 9.

Father

everlasting
Mis. 161– 7 *The everlasting F·,* — *Isa.* 9 : 6.
164–19 *The everlasting F·,* — *Isa.* 9 : 6.
258–24 even the everlasting *F·,*
321– 6 *The everlasting F·,* — *Isa.* 9 : 6.
God is
My. 279–16 God is *F·,* infinite, and
God the
My. 344– 5 God the *F·* is greater than Christ,
goes to the
'02. 8–23 the ego, or I, goes to the *F·,*
go to the
Mis. 195–31 The "I" will go to the *F·* — *John* 14 : 12.
Un. 41–20 and we shall go to the *F·,*
great
My. 50–18 * feeling of trust in the great *F·,*
heavenly
Mis. 72–20 *heavenly F· knoweth* — *Matt.* 6 : 32.
249–24 My heavenly *F·* will never leave me
Ret. 37–18 until our heavenly *F·* saw fit,
Un. 18–10 Many fancy that our heavenly *F·*
'02. 11– 2 Our heavenly *F·* never destined
My. 9– 9 * thankfulness to his heavenly *F·*
36–10 * with our infinite heavenly *F·*
327–27 * We thank our heavenly *F·*
his
Mis. 74– 8 Son of man in the glory of his *F·* ;
167–17 His *F·* and Mother are divine Life,
167–18 they who do the will of his *F·*
Ret. 69– 4 God is his *F·,*
Un. 53–25 or else . . . God, is not his *F·* ;
No. 41– 8 to do the will of his *F·*
41–11 and the glory of his *F·.*
'01. 9–29 the spirit of his *F·* speaketh
'02. 8–30 conscious that God is his *F·,*
honored
Mis. 81–15 *benediction of an honored F·,*
is perfect
Mis. 286–31 even as the *F·* is perfect,
live in the
'01. 6– 2 live in the *F·* and have no
loved of the
Hea. 2–21 Jesus, the loved of the *F·,*
love of a
No. 30–14 love of a *F·* for His child,
loving
Mis. 96–11 as a loving *F·* and Mother ;
Un. 53–25 man's origin and loving *F·,*
man's
Un. 53–23 Man's *F·* is not a mortal mind
my
Mis. 37– 9 "I and my *F·* are one." — *John* 10 : 30.
157–15 my *F·* is your Father ;
192–11 *I go unto my F·* — *John* 14 : 12.
194–20 I go unto my *F·.*" — *John* 14 : 12.
278–12 as my *F·* seeth them.
Chr. 55–93 the will of my *F·* — *Matt* 12 : 50.
Un. 46–13 "I and my *F·* are one." — *John* 10 : 30.
Pan. 8–20 "My *F·* is greater than I." — *John* 14 : 28.
'01. 8– 8 "I and my *F·* are one," — *John* 10 : 30.
8– 8 "my *F·* is greater than I," — *John* 14 : 28.
'02. 12–15 "I and my *F·* are one," — *John* 10 : 30.
My. 202–28 "Herein is my *F·* — *John* 15 : 8.
of all
Mis. 226– 3 * *F·* of all will care for him."
Pan. 13–23 *F·* of all, who is above — *Eph.* 4 : 6.
'00. 4–30 "*F·* of all, who is above — *Eph.* 4 : 6
My. 288–11 and He is the *F·* of all.
of lights
Un. 14–17 "the *F·* of lights, — *Jas.* 1 : 17.
of man
Mis. 164–32 God is the *F·* of man,
of the universe
My. 148–15 the *F·* of the universe
one
My. 198– 6 gratitude to our one *F·.*
one with the
Un. 61– 7 he was one with the *F·,*
My. 344– 6 Christ is 'one with the *F·,*'
our
Mis. 100–30 symptoms by which our *F·*
113– 5 Spirit is our *F·* and Mother,
151–13 God is our *F·* and our Mother,
154–14 our *F·* is husbandman.
369–27 the vine which our *F·* tends.
Rud. 1– 7 our *F·* which is in heaven.
No. 40–26 our *F·* has done this ;
'02. 19–30 cup that our *F·* permits us.
Peo. 8–24 We thank our *F·* that to-day
9–14 after the model of our *F·,*
12–27 our *F·* bestows heaven
our common
Mis. 138–11 guidance of our common *F·*
371– 9 guidance of our common *F·,*

Father

prayer to the
Mis. 133–24   in silent prayer to the F·

Principle, or
No. 25–14   his divine Principle, or F·.
26–15   his divine Principle, or F·,

relation to the
No. 36–16   higher self and relation to the F·,

represented by the
Pul. 13– 1   Life, represented by the F· ;

similitude of the
Mis. 162–24   after the similitude of the F·,

their
Mis. 278–18   reflect the image of their F·.

thy
Mis. 133–15   pray to thy F· — *Matt.* 6: 6.
133–16   thy F· which seeth in — *Matt.* 6: 6.
154–23   thy F· and Mother, God.

unto the
My. 206–26   "Giving thanks unto the F·, — *Col.* 1: 12.

was glorified
Ret. 94–29   the F· was glorified therein.

will of the
'01. 18–19   "the will of the F·." — *see Matt.* 12: 50.

worship the
Mis. 124– 4   those who worship the F·
150–19   worship the F· "in spirit — *John* 4: 23.
321–14   worship the F· in spirit — *John* 4: 23.
Ret. 65–13   worship the F· "in spirit — *John* 4: 23.
No. 34–10   worship the F· in spirit — *John* 4: 23.

your
Mis. 85–14   your F· which is in heaven — *Matt.* 5: 48.
157–15   my Father is your F· ;
181– 1   "for one is your F·," — *Matt.* 23: 9.
287– 7   for one is your F·, — *Matt.* 23: 9.
Ret. 68–14   for one is your F·, — *Matt.* 23: 9.
Un. 53–27   for one is your F·, — *Matt.* 23: 9.
Pan. 8–19   for one is your F·, — *Matt.* 23: 9.
9–12   your F· which is in heaven — *Matt.* 5: 48.
'01. 8–16   your F· which is in heaven — *Matt.* 5: 48.

Mis. 18–19   F·, Mother, and child are the
46–29   man is perfect even as the F·,
83–24   F·, the hour is come ; — *John* 17: 1.
103–31   therefore is forever with the F·.
167–23   "I thank Thee, O F·, — *Luke* 10: 21.
182–22   than he hath seen the F·.
184–28   that saith Abba, F·,
196–16   the "I" does go unto the F·, — *John* 14: 12.
206– 6   the F· and Mother's welcome,
275–17   F·, we thank Thee that
368– 3   Even so, F·, let the light
373–29   at the right hand of the F·.
397–15   F·, where Thine own children are,
Un. 51–22   The Ego is revealed as F·, Son, and
Pul. 18–24   F·, where Thine own children are,
82–16   * who never called Abraham "F·,"
No. 8– 1   F·, whose wisdom is unerring
37– 4   and dwelt forever in the F·.
44–28   "I thank Thee, O F·, — *Luke* 10: 21.
'00. 5–11   F·, Son, and Holy Ghost
Hea. 16–28   cometh unto the F·, — *John* 14: 6.
Po. 13– 3   F·, where Thine own children are,
43–10   F·, in Thy great heart hold them
My. 180–28   "F·, forgive them ; — *Luke* 23: 34.
270–19   "F·, forgive them ; — *Luke* 23: 34.
301–10   F·, teach us the life of Love.
350–12   F·, did'st not Thou the dark wave

father (see also father's)

and mother
Ret. 5–11   names of both f· and mother
22–19   his f· and mother are the one Spirit,
Pul. 54–24   * permitting only the f· and mother,
'01. 29–23   who honor their f· and mother.
My. 313–14   I only know that my f· and mother

another
Mis. 183–25   for it claims another f·.
Un. 39–15   claims another f·,

bruised
Mis. 275– 9   bruised f· bendeth his aching

chasteneth not
Un. 23–12   the f· chasteneth not? — *Heb.* 12: 7.

Franklin Pierce's
My. 308–21   President Franklin Pierce's f·,

her
My. 310–23   * her f·, a gray-haired man of fifty,

her late
My. 311–27   on the mound of her late f·,

his
Mis. 214– 7   variance against his f·, — *Matt.* 10: 35.
Ret. 22–19   his f· and mother are the one Spirit,
Un. 23– 5   was to his f· ever loyal.

human
Un. 48–16   than the human f· enters into his

father

Mark Baker's
My. 309–20   Mark Baker's f· paid the largest tax

my
Mis. 237–29   and he visited my f·,
Ret. 4– 2   youngest of whom was my f·,
5–14   My f· possessed a strong intellect
10– 1   My f· was taught to believe
My. 308–20   my f· was visiting Governor Pierce,
308–23   My f· thanked the Governor,
308–26   attributes to my f· language
308–30   my f· was a great reader.
309–10   and my f· won the suit.
309–11   Mr. Pierce bowed to my f·
309–14   My f· was a strong believer in
313– 9   stories . . . about my f·
313–14   know that my f· and mother

my late
My. 308–12   my late f· and his family

of every age
Po. 28– 1   F· of every age,

of itself
Un. 52–17   evil, . . . is the f· of itself,

of lies
Rud. 7–21   "the f· of lies ;" — *see John* 8: 44.

of man
Mis. 77–28   or, that man is the f· of man.
Ret. 68– 6   neither indeed can be, the f· of man.

of nothingness
'01. 13–14   and the f· of nothingness.

of our nation
My. 148–15   and the f· of our nation

or mother
Man. 69–19   loveth f· or mother more — *Matt.* 10: 37.

their
Mis. 240–25   see their f· with a cigarette
Un. 17–14   their f·, the devil,
'01. 29–23   honor their f· and mother.

was chaplain
My. 309–12   several years f· was chaplain

without
Chr. 55–20   Without f·, without mother, — *Heb.* 7: 3.

your
Mis. 287– 6   "Call no man your f· — *Matt.* 23: 9.
Ret. 68–14   "call no man your f· — *Matt.* 23: 9.
Un. 53–26   "Call no man your f· — *Matt.* 23: 9.
Pan. 5–12   "Ye are of your f·, — *John* 8: 44.
5–13   lusts of your f· ye will — *John* 8: 44.
8–18   "Call no man your f· — *Matt.* 23: 9.

Mis. 24–27   and the f· of it." — *John* 8: 44.
83–18   and the f· of it — *John* 8: 44.
121–19   Who, then, shall f· or favor
181– 1   Jesus said to call no man f· ;
196–14   and the f· of it ;" — *John* 8: 44.
259– 5   and the f· of it." — *John* 8: 44.
Ret. 67–25   and the f· of it. — *John* 8: 44.
Un. 32–23   and the f· of it." — *John* 8: 44.
No. 32–16   and the f· of it. — *John* 8: 44.
Pan. 5–16   and the f· of it — *John* 8: 44.
'00. 5– 8   and the f· of it" — *John* 8: 44.
My. 172– 6   * f· of the Rev. Mary Baker Eddy,
270–16   are the f· of their wish.

fatherliness

Mis. 234–31   God's f· as Life, Truth, and Love,
No. 19–14   f· of this Supreme Being.

fatherly

My. 288–32   evil is not a f· grace.

Father-Mother

Mis. 102–15   loving, divine F· God
127–11   petitions the divine F· God
400–14   F· God, Loving me,
400–20   F· good, lovingly Thee I seek,
Rud. 4– 1   Mind, the one F· God.
Pan. 15– 5   May our F· God, who in times past
'01. 3– 3   benediction of our F· God
7– 9   all-knowing, all-loving F·,
7–15   consistently say, "Our F· God"
Po. 69– 2   F· God, Loving me,
69– 8   F· good, lovingly Thee I seek,
My. 18– 8   petitions the divine F· God
186–12   anthem of one F· God,
265–31   we thank our F· God.
281–13   God, good, the F· Love,
347– 4   likeness of the F· God,

Father's

Mis. 77–15   This is the F· great Love
81–29   This *is* the F· benediction.
125–11   sit down at the F· right hand :
150– 1   your F· good pleasure — *Luke* 12: 32.
163–31   forever about the F· business ;
321–17   your F· good pleasure — *Luke* 12: 32.
326–18   forced to seek the F· house,
369–25   we would find our F· house

Father's
Ret. 50–27 it was the F· opportunity
Pul. 9–22 your F· good pleasure — Luke 12 : 32.
'01. 17– 4 to return to the F· house
Peo. 3–27 obedience to our F· demands,
My. 133– 1 F· house in which are many

father's
Mis. 124–17 with more than a f· pity ;
Ret. 1– 3 great-grandfather, on my f· side,
13–13 My f· relentless theology
20– 5 my f· second marriage,
81–23 puts this pious counsel into a f·
Pul. 32–23 * On her f· side Mrs. Eddy came
33–18 * one day on his f· farm
34– 3 * returned to her f· home
My. 308–15 my f· "tall, gaunt frame"
308–18 My f· person was erect
309–17 youngest of his f· family,
309–18 inherited his f· real estate,
309–23 f· house had a sloping roof,
310– 1 All my f· daughters were
310–19 death in my f· family
312–13 * taken to her f· home by her
312–28 took me to my f· home
313–30 after my f· second marriage
313–31 not welcome in my f· house.

Fathers
'01. 34–12 canonical writings of the F·,
(see also **Pilgrim Fathers**)

fathers (see also **fathers'**)
Mis. 72–14 f· have eaten sour grapes, — Ezek. 18 : 2.
96–16 manner of my f·, — see Acts 24 : 14.
245– 6 slept with his f·." — II Chron. 16 : 13.
Ret. 64–15 generation of his f· ; — Psal. 49 : 19.
'02. 6–11 Jesus said a lie f· itself,
My. 43– 8 * revealed the God of their f·,
192–13 God of our f·, the infinite Person
285–26 God of my f·, — Acts 24 : 14.

fathers'
My. 185–28 Our God, our f· God !

fathom
Po. 2– 7 Ah, who can f· thee !

fathomed
No. 17–24 infinite harmony would be f·.
My. 291–18 so far as it f· the abyss of

fathomless
'02. 4–10 f· peace between Soul and sense
Po. 30– 9 With thy still f· Christ-majesty.

fatigued
Man. 60– 8 Scientist is not f· by prayer,
Pul. 36–15 * I went to her peculiarly f·.

fatiguing
No. 15– 7 F· Bible translations

fatling
Mis. 145–24 young lion and the f· — Isa. 11 : 6.
My. 177–20 as a f· of the flock.

fatness
Pul. 1– 1 with the f· of Thy house; — Psal. 36 : 8.
3–16 with the f· of Thy house ; — Psal. 30 : 8.
4–26 with the f· of Thy house." — Psal. 36 : 8.
7–29 with the f· of Thy house ; — Psal. 36 : 8.

fattened
Mis. 240– 5 f· by metaphysical hygiene.

fattening
Mis. 250– 7 f· the lamb to slay it.

fatuous
Un. 10–22 To attempt the calculation . . . is f·.

fault
Mis. 38– 8 whole system . . . is at f·,
129–10 to tell thy brother his f·
130–10 for a f· in somebody else,
233–24 finds f· with the exactness of
265–25 the f· is not in the culture
284–18 and told him his f·,
291–17 this is not my f·,
335–22 is a f· of zealots,
340–11 law-school is not at f· which
Rud. 14–23 it is their own f·,
My. 104– 9 they could find no f· in him,

faultless
'01. 6–18 logic of divine Science being f·,

faults
Mis. 11–20 try not to expose their f·,
112–27 inability to see one's own f·,
129–20 will see somebody's f· to magnify
223–29 To punish ourselves for others' f·,
224– 5 wounded by our own f·,
224– 6 to be miserable for the f· of others.
317–28 penalty for other people's f· ;

faults
Ret. 72– 7 portrays the result of secret f·,
Pul. 15– 9 to tell a man his f·,

faulty
Mis. 66– 2 obedience thereto may be found f·,

favor
Mis. 121–19 father or f· this sentence
164–21 it grew in f· with them.
285– 1 in f· of combating evil only,
381–16 a decree in f· of Mrs. Eddy
Pul. 31–21 * begging the f· of an interview
'02. 12–27 annually f· us with their presence
14–23 neither f· nor protection
My. 6– 1 in f· of a decision which the
7–10 annually f· us with their presence
92–26 * things to be said in f· of C. S.
175–19 this f· of our city government ;
221– 4 now as then, from finding f· with
314–21 to record the divorce in my f·.
326– 5 * a f· has been extended,
341–24 * a special f· that Mrs. Eddy
360–29 Your f· of the 10th instant

favorable
Mis. 132– 4 I shall take this as a f· omen,
370–20 What figure is less f· than
My. 10– 4 * enlarge the f· expectation,
37–26 * confident and f· expectation.

favorably
Pul. 62– 3 * f· known in the Old Country,

favored
Pul. 10–10 Our land, more f·,
No. v– 2 benefit no f· class,
My. 219– 3 through some f· student.
250–23 wait for the f· moment to act
278–13 Congress of our f· land

favorite
Ret. 10– 7 My f· studies were
'01. 18– 3 that was my f· dose.
Peo. 3– 9 torture of His f· Son,

favors
Hea. 1– 7 Heaven's f· are formidable :
My. 198– 7 the continuance of His f·,

fear (noun)
abate the
Un. 54– 8 is to abate the f· of it ;
action of
Mis. 41–22 through the action of f·,
all
Mis. 184–26 which casteth out all f·,
194–25 Love that casts out all f·.
335– 1 Love that casteth out all f·,
allay
Mis. 45– 7 although its power to allay f·,
and hope
My. 102–30 compound of . . . f· and hope,
and trembling
My. 300– 5 with f· and trembling. — Phil 2 ; 12.
and weakness
Mis. 245–15 indicate f· and weakness,
casteth out
Mis. 229–28 "casteth out f·." — I John 4 : 18.
Ret. 61–17 casteth out f·.'" — I John 4 : 18.
Un. 20–16 "casteth out f·." — I John 4 : 18.
Peo. 6–16 casteth out f· ;" — I John 4 : 18.
cast out
No. 40–23 cast out f· and heal the sick,
casts out
Ret. 61–20 Love that casts out f·.
childish
Mis. 237–30 childish f· clustered round his
desire, and
No. 11– 2 intellect, desire, and f·,
destroy the
'01. 13–19 you destroy the f· and the
earth-born
Mis. 387–25 chastens pride and earth-born f·,
Po. 6–20 chastens pride and earth-born f·,
effect of a
Ret. 61– 7 experiencing the effect of a f·
has ceased
Pul. 82–30 * f· has ceased to kiss the iron heel
is a belief
Mis. 93–18 F· is a belief of sensation in
is the procurator
Rud. 10–16 f· is the procurator of the
is the weapon
Mis. 99–10 F· is the weapon in the
latent
Ret. 61– 4 a latent f·, made manifest
man's
'01. 13–20 A man's f·, unconquered,
mortal
Mis. 42– 9 moment of extreme mortal f·,

fear

no
Mis. 249–23 I have proof, but no *f·*.
My. 61–17 * said aloud, "Why, there is no *f·* ;
144– 4 Give yourselves no *f·*
nor sin
Mis. 93–21 neither *f·* nor sin can bring on
of death
'02. 3–22 the muffled *f·* of death
of evil
Mis. 279– 5 love of God, and not the *f·* of evil,
of the senses
Ret. 74– 1 begets a *f·* of the senses
of the sick
Rud. 12– 7 quiet the *f·* of the sick
or disease
Ret. 61– 5 different forms of *f·* or disease.
or distrust
My. 202– 3 human ambition, *f·*, or distrust
or doubt
No. 8–12 without *f·* or doubt,
or exhaustion
My. 232–27 produces *f·* or exhaustion
or malice
No. 45–10 weakness, *f·*, or malice ;
or sin
Mis. 93– 6 *Can f· or sin bring back old beliefs*
or suffering
Ret. 61–11 cannot awake in *f·* or suffering
My. 267–22 relief from *f·* or suffering,
removes
My. 131– 2 removes *f·*, subdues sin,
sin and
No. 40–20 Only when sickness, sin, and *f·*
that
Mis. 237– 9 but remove that *f·*, and the
their
Mis. 10–21 their *f·* is self-immolated.
My. 191– 8 engendered by their *f·*,
247–22 *persuasion that takes away their f·*,
this
Ret. 61– 5 This *f·* is formed unconsciously
Rud. 10–17 Remove this *f·* by the true
without
Man. 48– 5 do it with love and without *f·*.
No. 8–12 without *f·* or doubt,

Mis. 10–18 with *f·* and the besetments of evil ;
93–15 *f·*, its coeval, is without divine
99– 9 His *f·* overcame his loyalty ;
115– 9 and *f·* of being found out.
198–24 to some belief, *f·*, theory, or
237– 8 serve God (or try to) from *f·* ;
257–17 *f·* where courage is requisite,
Ret. 61–13 saith to *f·*, "You are the cause of
My. 211–21 *f·* where courage should be
293–14 trembling faith, hope, and of *f·*,
344–28 *f·* of catching smallpox is more

fear (verb)

Mis. 109–29 *f·* not sin, lest thereby it
109–30 only *f· to sin.*
113–25 We have nothing to *f·* when Love is
149–30 "*F·* not, little flock ;— *Luke* 12 : 32.
197– 6 we *f·* the full import of this
284–24 Evil is not something to *f·*
321–16 "*F·* not, little flock ;— *Luke* 12 : 32.
325–10 *f·* not to fall upon the Stranger,
389–16 *f·* No ill,— since God is good,
Un. 2– 3 God pitieth them who *f·* Him ;
20–14 *Third :* We therefore need not *f·* it.
Pul. 14–17 never *f·* the consequences.
'01. 10– 6 *F·* them not therefore :— *Matt.* 10 : 26.
Peo. 6–15 Believing that . . . we naturally *f·*
Po. 4–15 *f·* No ill,— since God is good,
My. 33–23 them that *f·* the Lord.— *Psal.* 15 : 4.
130–12 failed too often for me to *f·* it.
193–27 "*F·* not :— *Isa.* 43 : 1.

feared

Mis. 284–23 is neither to be *f·* nor
Po. 71–11 *F·* for an hour the tyrant's heel !
My. 293–10 *f·* that the bullet would
293–12 physicians may have *f·* this.

fearful

Mis. 19–19 most *f·* sin that mortals can
368–24 and at a *f·* stake.

fearfully

'01. 33– 9 * they have *f·* abounded ;

fearing

'01. 14–20 delivered . . . from *f·* it,
My. 247–17 not *f·* me, sought their food of me

fearless

Mis. 213–20 *f·* wing and firm foundation.
'01. 2–26 *f·* wing and a sure reward.

fearless

Po. 28–12 Give us the eagle's *f·* wing,
My. 309– 1 * dominating, passionate, *f·*,"

fearlessly

No. 5– 2 Scientists are vindicating, *f·* and
My. 64–19 * *F·* does she warn all her followers
160– 4 and follows Truth *f·*.

fears

Mis. 7–19 descriptions carry *f·* to many minds,
105– 3 disdain the *f·* and destroy the
307– 9 to all human *f·*, to suffering
320–14 calms man's *f·*, bears his burdens,
Un. 10–27 pursued by their *f·*,
'00. 7–28 and we are saved from our *f·*.
'01. 13–17 because he *f·* it or loves it.
'02. 19– 4 to disarm their *f·*.
Peo. 11–15 false theories, false *f·*,
Po. 47– 8 Never to toiling and never to *f·*,
79–12 False *f·* are foes
My. 182–26 *f·* turn hither with satisfied hope.

feasibility

Mis. 349–12 *f·* of entering a medical school ;
No. 2–13 test the *f·* of what they say
4–12 destroys the *f·* of disease ;
10–21 *f·* and immobility of C. S.
Hea. 19–21 doubts the *f·* of the demand.

feast

Mis. 121– 4 partook of the Jews' *f·*
149– 5 this *f·* and flow of Soul.
175–14 keep the *f·* of Life,
233– 8 the death's-head at the *f·*
Pan. 1– 6 at the *f·* of our Passover,
'00. 14–28 When invited to a *f·*
15– 3 come to a sumptuous *f·*,
15– 5 and this *f·* is a Passover.
15–17 Love has been preparing a *f·*
15–19 you have come to Love's *f·*,
'01. 2–18 the death's-head at the *f·*
My. 188– 7 Your *f·* days will not be in
191–29 invitation to this *f·* of soul
263– 6 a *f·* of Soul and a famine of sense.

feasting

Ret. 65–10 *F·* the senses, gratification of
'02. 16–23 Fasting, *f·*, or penance,

feasts

Mis. 345–27 Christians met in midnight *f·*
Chr. 55–12 are in their *f·* :— *Isa.* 5 : 12.
'00. 13– 7 orgies of their idolatrous *f·*
My. 340– 1 Jesus attended *f·*,

feat

Pul. 45– 7 * even when the *f·* seems impossible

feather (*see also* **feather's**)

Mis. 127–32 human heart, like a *f·* bed,

feathered

Mis. 329–27 calling the *f·* tribe back

feather's

Mis. 372– 3 had not one *f·* weight

feathers

Mis. 152–26 He will hide you in His *f·*
172–10 shall cover with her *f·*
263– 6 two words . . . *rock* and *f·* :
263– 8 cover thee with His *f·*."— *Psal.* 91 : 4.
374–32 without *f·* on her wings,

feather-some

Po. 18– 3 majestic, and *f·* fling

feathery

Mis. 306–24 nor feel the *f·* touch
Ret. 17–20 *f·* blossom and branches
Po. 63– 7 *f·* blossom and branches

feature

Pul. 25– 2 * cooling is a recognized *f·*
27– 8 * remarkable *f·* of this temple.
43–23 * chief *f·* of the dedication,
76– 2 * striking *f·* of the church
'00. 13–10 *f·* the apostle justly regards as
My. 25– 4 * this *f·* of the demonstration.
38–23 * no more impressive *f·* of the
61–21 * One *f·* about the work
69–20 * Another unusual *f·* is the foyer,
77–11 * notable *f·* in the life of their cult.
88–18 * smallest *f·* of the C. S. faith,
96–16 * A remarkable *f·*,

features

Mis. 112–14 many *f·* and forms of
Pul. vii–19 *f·* of the vast problem of
25– 8 * The principal *f·* are
45–10 * grandest and most helpful *f·*
'01. 20– 2 yielding to its aggressive *f·*.
My. 32– 2 * striking *f·* of the services.
69– 2 * one of the extraordinary *f·*
78–21 * remarkable *f·* of the services

February
(*see* **months**)

fed
Mis.	6–31	keeping them clothed and *f·*,
	106–19	Your Sunday Lesson, . . . has *f·* you.
	153– 7	they were *f·* with manna :
	254– 6	love that hath *f·* them with Truth,
	326–11	*f·* by the fat of hypocrisy
	369–24	whom he *f·* that wholesome . . . food.
	388– 9	F· by Thy love divine we live,
Rud.	13–27	to be *f·*, clothed, and sheltered
Pan.	15– 1	*f·* her starving foe,
'01.	29– 1	Have we housed, *f·*, clothed, or
Po.	7– 9	F· by Thy love divine we live,
My.	170–21	verily thou shalt be *f·*.— *Psal.* 37 : 3.
	247–16	*f·* these sweet little thoughts

fee
Man.	94– 4	a less lecture *f·* ;
	96– 4	Lecture F·.
	96– 4	lecture *f·* shall be left to the
	96–13	trust to contributions for his *f·*.
Ret.	50– 9	finally led, . . . to accept this *f·*.
My.	136–17	highest *f·* ever received by
	204–24	a full *f·* for treatment,
	328–29	* shall pay a license *f·*
	329– 6	* from paying this *f·*,

feeble
Mis.	30– 2	in at least some *f·* demonstration
	85–18	*f·* flutterings of mortals Christward
	100–32	*f·* lips are made eloquent,
	104–16	wages *f·* fight with his
	172–10	*f·* sense of the infinite law
	196–31	*f·* acceptance of the truths
Ret.	27–15	to express in *f·* diction
	27–17	* But the *f·* hands and helpless,
Un.	41– 1	*f·* concept of immortality.
	61–19	faith and a *f·* understanding
'02.	18–11	caused not the *f·* to fall,
My.	59–22	* *f·* attempts to lead the singing.
	92–19	* statistics give a *f·* impression
	162–25	Shepherd of this *f·* flock
	331–25	* lone, *f·*, and bereaved widow

feebleness
Mis.	101–16	with finiteness and *f·*.
	370– 1	their *f·* calls for help,

feeblest
Peo.	11– 5	it was found that the *f·* mind,

feebly
Mis.	80–21	Tyranny can thrive but *f·* under
	373–18	living *f·*, in kings' courts.
My.	76–11	* *f·* expresses the gratification.
	174–29	seeking and finding (though *f·*),

feed
Mis.	127–14	faithfully asks divine Love to *f·* it
	338–27	* Shall the world's famine *f·* ;
	388–19	To bless the orphan, *f·* the poor ;
	397–21	poem — *John* 21 . 10.
	397–25	How to *f·* Thy sheep ;
	398–17	F· the hungry, heal the heart,
Ret. page 46	poem — *John* 21 : 16.
	46– 6	How to *f·* Thy sheep ;
	46–23	F· the hungry, heal the heart,
Pul.	17– 1	poem — *John* 21 : 16.
	17– 5	How to *f·* Thy sheep ;
	17–22	F· the hungry, heal the heart,
Po. page 14	poem — *John* 21 : 16.
	14– 4	How to *f·* Thy sheep ;
	14–21	F· the hungry, heal the heart,
	21– 8	bless the orphan, *f·* the poor ;
My.	18–11	asks divine Love to *f·* it
	48–30	* They *f·* the higher nature
	123–24	to *f·* the multitude ;
	133–13	monads will *f·* the hungry,

feedeth
Mis.	322–14	Shepherd that *f·* my flock,
	322–19	God that *f·* the hungry heart,

feeding
Mis.	15–29	*f·* at first on the milk of
My.	125– 8	You come from *f·* your flocks,

Feed My Sheep
(*see* **Appendix A**)

feeds
Mis.	150–31	He guards, guides, *f·*,
	331–12	dove *f·* her callow brood,
Pul.	21–30	*f·* and fills the sentiment
My.	247–23	Love alone that *f·* them.
	303–20	what *f·* a few *f·* all.

feel
Mis.	12– 1	*Because* I thus *f·*, I say to others :
	13– 1	The only justice of which I *f·*
	14– 6	where will you see or *f·* evil,
	28– 3	neither see, hear, *f·*, taste, nor

feel
Mis.	86–28	What mortals hear, see, *f·*,
	88– 2	*f·* the need of physical help,
	133–20	*f·* a delicacy in making the following
	136–10	I cannot *f·* justified in
	142–30	yet as friends we can *f·* the
	146–23	I *f·* sure that as Christian Scientists
	157–13	true Christian Scientist will *f·*
	218– 8	can neither see, hear, nor *f·*,
	224– 5	Well may we *f·* wounded by
	224–10	* I don't *f·* hurt in the least."
	234– 1	that we see and *f·* disease only by
	237–17	few *f·* and live now as when
	256–10	I *f·*, deeply, . . . the severe task
	266–20	I speak of them as I *f·*,
	279–29	will *f·* the influence of this Mind ;
	303–24	I *f·* assured that many
	306–24	nor *f·* the feathery touch of the
	306–26	Oh, may you *f·* *this* touch,
	319–26	and *f·* themselves alone among
	326– 9	but the flesh at length did *f·* them ;
Ret.	9–20	* And *f·* His presence in the vast
	61– 7	awaken from sleep and *f·* ill,
	63–17	Do you not *f·* bound to expose this
	85–16	*f·* that God ordains you.
	87–23	They *f·* their own burdens less,
	90–18	Who can *f·* and comprehend the
Un.	4– 8	to *f·*, in a certain finite human
	8– 6	What you see, hear, *f·*, is a
	22–11	to see or be seen, to *f·* or be felt.
	24–25	taste, hear, *f·*, smell.
	34–15	says that matter cannot *f·* matter ;
	34–17	material nerves, *do f·* matter.
	34–20	matter could not *f·* what it calls
	57– 5	the pain they *f·* and occasion ;
Pul.	3–27	I *f·* so far from victory over the
	6–21	* I *f·* the truth is leading us to
	36–17	* made me *f·* I could have
Rud.	10– 5	must *f·* and know that
	10–14	cannot *f·*, see, or report pain
No.	19–17	*f·* no sensation of divine Love,
Hea.	16–21	They can neither see, hear, *f·*,
My.	21–10	* We therefore *f·* sure that all
	21–24	* will *f·* that they have been called
	51– 8	* while we *f·* that she has not
	64– 8	* we *f·* a pardonable pride
	87–17	* we *f·* that Boston is to be
	133– 7	I *f·* that it is not for my benefit
	145–12	* I do not *f·* able to keep about.
	193– 4	you will not *f·* my absence.
	216–28	you will *f·* more than at present
	323–19	* Neither do I now *f·* at all equal

feeling
Mis.	106–29	that thrill the chords of *f·*
	142–21	chords of *f·* too deep for words.
	177–10	Their *f·* and purpose are deadly,
	219–16	if he would remove this *f·*
	222– 8	conviction of his wrong state of *f·*
	227–18	flowers of *f·* blossom,
	229– 7	would catch their state of *f·*
	343–18	Are we *f·* the vernal freshness
Ret.	18–22	flowers of *f·* are fragrant
	81–11	false thinking, *f·*, and acting ;
Pul.	31–15	* close contact with public *f·*
	51–21	* religious belief has stirred up *f·*,
	72– 3	* learning the *f·* of Scientists
No.	1–12	borne on by the current of *f·*,
	6–24	to material sense and *f·*,
'01.	1–23	by *f·* and applying the nature
'02.	15–28	*f·* sure that God had led me
Po.	64–16	flowers of *f·* are fragrant
	67–21	flowers of *f·* may blossom
My.	50–17	* there was a *f·* of trust
	63–16	* to repress a *f·* of exultation
	63–21	* there came a deeper *f·*,
	63–21	* a *f·* of awe and of reverence
	145–13	* I am *f·* an old ailment
	256– 5	adapted to the key of my *f·*
	273–14	spiritual sense of thinking, *f·*,
	274–10	right thinking, right *f·*,
	331–21	* express the *f·* of gratitude
	331–26	* the high *f·* of honor

feelingly
Ret.	15–22	from persons who *f·* testified

feelings
My.	332– 3	* attempt at expressing the *f·*

feels
Mis.	219–15	one person *f·* sick,
	219–15	another *f·* wicked.
	219–27	*f·* wickedly and acts wickedly,
	220–15	patient says and *f·*, "I am well,
	224– 4	our egotism that *f·* hurt by
	228–21	Whatever man sees, *f·*, or
Ret.	25–25	neither sees, hears, nor *f·* Spirit,

feels

Un.	11–17	looks very real and *f·* very real ;"
	25– 9	It sees, hears, *f·*, tastes, smells
Pul.	37–16	* Mrs. Eddy *f·* very strongly,"
	37–21	* "Mother *f·* very strongly,"
'00.	3– 6	No hand that *f·* not his help,
Hea.	12– 4	matter-physician *f·* the pulse,
My.	51– 7	* Mrs. Eddy, *f·* it her duty to

fees

My.	204–15	TO PRACTISE WITHOUT *F·*

feet

and hands
Pul.	9–14	climbed with *f·* and hands

another's
My.	188–24	lies at another's *f·*.

bare
Mis.	391–16	With bare *f·* soiled or sore,
Po.	38–15	With bare *f·* soiled or sore,

bleeding
Un.	58– 5	Jesus walked with bleeding *f·*

eight
Pul.	26–12	* eight *f·* in height.
	62– 9	* not more than five by eight *f·*.

eighty-two
My.	68– 9	* a diameter of eighty-two *f·*

fancied
Ret.	12– 6	Woke by her fancied *f·*.
Po.	61– 4	Woke by her fancied *f·*.

fifty-one
My.	68– 9	* and a height of fifty-one *f·*.

goat's
Pan.	3–31	goat's *f·*, the solidity of the earth ;

hands and
Mis.	375–24	* hands and *f·* of the figures
	375–25	* hands and *f·* in Angelico's 'Jesus,'

her
Mis.	142– 1	how beautiful are her *f·* !
Pul.	83–28	* the moon under her *f·*, — *Rev.* 12 : 1.

his
Mis.	325–26	wipes off the dust from his *f·*
Ret.	86–13	wipe the dust from his *f·*
My.	159– 7	Sitting at his *f·*,

hundred and twenty-six
Pul.	41–24	* rises one hundred and twenty-six *f·*

Jesus'
Mis.	388–25	The right to sit at Jesus' *f·* ;
Po.	21–14	The right to sit at Jesus' *f·* ;

kiss the
Mis.	124–22	to kiss the *f·* of Jesus,
Pan.	9–19	kiss the *f·* of such a messenger,

kneeling at the
Peo.	13–15	Galileo kneeling at the *f·* of

little
Mis.	250–26	little *f·* tripping along the sidewalk ;
	329–18	her little *f·* trip lightly on,
	400–17	Guide my little *f·*
Po.	69– 5	Guide my little *f·*

Master's
Mis.	110– 2	poured on our Master's *f·*,
	369–19	we kneel at our Master's *f·*,
My.	222–21	the sandals of thy Master's *f·*.

of Christ
'01.	22–15	I begin at the *f·* of Christ

of Christian Science
Ret.	81–29	led me to the *f·* of C. S.,

of Jesus
Mis.	17–12	to sit at the *f·* of Jesus.
	124–22	to kiss the *f·* of Jesus,
	361–16	sit at the *f·* of Jesus.
Pul.	27–22	*Mary washing the *f·* of Jesus,
My.	349–13	to him who sits at the *f·* of Jesus

of Love
Mis.	204– 9	and kisses the *f·* of Love,

of progress
My.	127–28	nor laid down at the *f·* of progress

of Truth
Peo.	12–10	trampled under the *f·* of Truth.
My.	228–19	meek, who sit at the *f·* of Truth,

one hundred and twenty
Pul.	24–25	* tower is one hundred and twenty *f·* in

our
Mis.	339–12	plants our *f·* more firmly.
Pan.	15– 8	plant our *f·* firmly on Truth,

their
Mis.	176–20	planted their *f·* on Plymouth Rock,
	325–16	their *f·* resting on footstools,
	326–24	to wash their *f·*,
My.	227–25	under their *f·*, — *Matt.* 7 : 6.

thirty-two
My.	70–30	* which is thirty-two *f·* long.

to these lame
Mis.	362– 9	ears to these deaf, *f·* to these lame,

twenty-nine
My.	68–11	* altitude twenty-nine *f·* higher

feet

twenty-one and one half
Pul.	24–26	* twenty-one and one half *f·* square.

two hundred and twenty
My.	89– 6	* over two hundred and twenty *f·* high,

two hundred and twenty-four
My.	45–30	* two hundred and twenty-four *f·*,
	68–10	* two hundred and twenty-four *f·*
	78– 7	* two hundred and twenty-four *f·*

Way-shower's
My.	161– 4	washing the Way-shower's *f·*

Mis.	107– 8	plant the *f·* steadfastly in Christ.
	392– 2	at whose *f·* I stand,
Ret.	11–21	Farther than *f·* of chamois fall,
Po.	20– 2	at whose *f·* I stand,
	60–19	Farther than *f·* of chamois fall,
My.	129–25	whose *f·* can never be moved.
	184–27	*f·* of him that bringeth — *Isa.* 52 : 7.

felicity

Pul.	53–16	* expresses the whole law of human *f·*

fell

Mis.	99–10	courage of his convictions *f·*
	281–14	copy of . . . that *f·* into his hands.
	285–15	and the latter *f·* *hors de combat;*
Ret.	91– 6	ever *f·* upon human ears
Pul.	6–25	as my lone bark rose and *f·*
'01.	24–15	he *f·*, and great was the fall
Hea.	10– 7	*f·* before the womanhood of God,
	17–16	sleep" that *f·* upon Adam — *Gen.* 2 : 21.
My.	31– 6	* "Day by day the manna *f·* ;"
	194– 3	*f·* forests and remove mountains,
	220–27	*f·* a victim to those laws.
	303– 1	*f·* mysteriously upon my spirit.

fellow

No.	41– 5	called him "this *f·*." — *Luke* 23 : 2.
My.	104– 5	a "pestilent *f·*," — *Acts* 24 : 5.
	104– 6	of this "pestilent *f·*." — *Acts* 24 : 5.

fellow-apostle

Un.	1– 5	taught by his *f·* Paul,

fellow-being

Mis.	31– 5	affect the happiness of a *f·*

fellow-beings

Pul.	58– 3	* imparting this faith to her *f·*.
My.	286– 5	no more . . . slaughtering of our *f·* ;

fellow-citizens

My.	173–22	my *f·* vied with each other to

fellow-man

Mis.	18–24	habitual love for his *f·*.

fellow-men

Mis.	170–15	conceptions of God and our *f·*.
'01.	32–10	or desire to defame their *f·*.

fellow-mortals

Mis.	32–30	should try to bless their *f·*.
	213–12	forewarn and forearm our *f·*
'02.	11–12	hastens to help on his *f·*,

Fellow of the Royal College of Physicians

Peo.	6– 3	Dr. Abercrombie, *F· of the R· C· of P·*

fellows

Mis.	294– 5	and displacing his *f·*.

fellow-saint

Ret.	86–14	*f·* of a holy household.

fellow-servants

Mis.	335– 5	begin to smite his *f·*, — *Matt.* 24 : 49.

fellowship

Mis.	149–25	*f·* with saints and angels.
	310–20	All who desire its *f·*,
	357–24	should receive full *f·* from us,
Man.	51– 7	Violation of Christian *F·*.
	51–10	does not live in Christian *f·*
	74–21	attitude of Christian *f·*.
	99–13	who is in good *f·* with another
Ret.	15–20	we parted in Christian *f·*,
	45– 9	material form of cohesion and *f·*
	64–30	refuse *f·* with the Church
	82–26	with ecclesiastical *f·*
Pul.	21–14	entertain due respect and *f·*
No.	8– 9	*f·* in the bonds of Christ.
My.	v– 8	* hand of *f·* is being extended
	275– 2	chapter sub-title
	275– 4	does produce universal *f·*.
	360–20	Abide in *f·* with and
	362–24	* Christian love and *f·*,

fellow-students

Mis.	280–24	expressed his *f·* thanks

felon (*see also* felon's)

Hea.	19– 1	A *f·* was delivered to them

felon's

Hea.	19– 8	*f·* belief that he was bleeding

felt
Mis. 98-13 already f· in a higher mode of
113-32 animus is f· throughout the land.
127-29 but a tender sentiment f·,
183- 7 seen and f· in health, happiness, and
263-16 f· by students, especially by those
278-24 I have f· for some time that
281-25 I f· the weight of this yesterday,
290-16 * "I f· the influence of your thought
312- 3 may the love that is talked, be f· !
375-10 * I did not utter all I f·
398-23 F· ye the power of the Word?
Ret. 5-24 * was f· by all around her.
14-23 and asked me to say how I f·
89- 1 its presence f· in eternal stillness
Un. 7- 9 most sensibly f· that the infinite
22-11 to see or be seen, to feel or be f·.
34-24 Nothing would remain to be seen or f·.
51- 5 is neither seen, f·, heard, nor
57-12 must have f· the influence
57-13 for it is written that he f· that
Pul. 34-20 "I f· that the divine Spirit
36- 5 * as Mrs. Eddy f· it essential to the
68- 9 * as Mrs. Eddy f· it necessary
84-18 * can be better f· than expressed.
No. 45-11 f·, though unacknowledged.
'01. 12- 2 it is not f· with the fingers ;
13- 5 it ought not to be seen, f·, or
21-27 or f· the incipient touch of
Po. 75- 3 F· ye the power of the Word?
My. 3-17 Its presence is f·,
9-24 never before f· poor in thanks,
50- 7 * Pilgrims f· the strangeness of
50-12 * f· a peculiar sense of isolation,
55- 3 * it was f· that the church needed a
57- 4 * need was f· of an auditorium
80- 6 * that they had f· no pain
125-16 f· the touch of the spirit of
165-31 f· the infinite source where is all,
185-11 thought, f·, spoken, or written,
240-12 Its presence is f·,
247-14 must have f· me when
290- 1 a love and a loss f· by
291-15 not talked but f· and lived.

female
Mis. 18-16 all-harmonious "male and f·,"— Gen. 1 : 27.
199- 8 male and f· come into their rightful
295- 7 * from f· suffrage, past a score of
295-10 * "a f· passion for some manner of
296-27 a wish to promote f· suffrage
314- 6 two Readers : a male, and a f·.
Man. 50- 3 body of a f· shall be
'01. 7-11 made them male and f·
10-12 generic term for both male and f·.
My. 268-30 and you see male and f· one

Female Anti-Slavery Society
Po. vi-14 *a meeting of the F· A· S·.*

feminine
Mis. 296-20 note or foster a f· ambition
Un. 32-24 neither masculine nor f·.

fermentation
My. 301- 6 found to be a healthy f·,

fermenting
Mis. 134-25 Error is only f·,
Pul. 5-28 is the leaven f· religion ;
'02. 2-17 rapidly f·, and enlightening the world

fern
Ret. 4-22 scrub-oak, poplar, and f· flourish.

Fernald, Mr. Josiah E.
My. 135-16 namely, . . . Mr. Josiah E. F·.
136-22 Josiah E. F·, justice of the peace
137-23 namely, . . . Mr. Josiah E. F·.

ferns
Pul. 42-26 * palms and f· and Easter lilies.
42-27 * with f· and pure white roses

ferocious
Mis. 36-10 f· mind seen in the beast

fervent
Mis. xi- 9 the f· heart and willing hand
177- 2 f· devotion and an absolute
Un. 58-12 hypocrite melts in f· heat,
No. 28- 4 in the f· heat of suffering,
Peo. 9-22 a desire, f·, importunate :

fervently
Mis. 114-22 cannot . . . pray to God too f·,
'00. 14-18 hold in your full hearts f·
My. 293-21 Had prayer so f· offered

fervid
My. 25-17 my answer to their f· question :
248-12 f· affection for the race

fervor
'01. 3- 2 virtue, f·, and fidelity.
My. 81- 6 * that at the very height of f·,
81-30 * conception of the f· of belief

festal
Mis. 121- 5 drank from their f· wine-cup.
My. 170- 2 this was no f· occasion.

festive
Po. 77-17 Why from this f· hour
My. 256-24 the f· boards are spread,

festivities
Man. 60-14 no special observances, f·, nor gifts
94- 7 no receptions nor f· after

festivity
Mis. 324- 6 sounds of f· and mirth ;
'00. 14-30 prepare accordingly for the f·.

fetishism
My. 248-19 No f· with a symbol can fetter

fetter
My. 248-20 No fetishism . . . can f· your flight.

fettered
Peo. 10-19 they alone have f· free limbs,

fetters
Mis. 165- 8 without the f· of the flesh,
173-24 pains, f·, and befools him.
237-28 loosing the f· of one form of
246-16 to forge anew the old f· ;
359-14 or by holding it in f·.
394- 7 And loosens the f· of pride
Pul. 14- 2 will chain, with f· of some sort,
Peo. 3-24 and assigns them mortal f·
11-13 their f· are gnawing away life
Po. 45- 9 loosens the f· of pride

fever
Ret. 13-12 pronounced me stricken with f·.
13-22 The f· was gone, and I rose
Hea. 13-15 cured the incipient stage of f·.
My. 312- 8 * he died of yellow f·.
312-20 was suddenly seized with yellow f·
335-17 * was attacked with yellow f·
335-21 * cause of death as bilious f·,
335-27 * case was one of yellow f·

fevered
'00. 11-24 * And it lay on my f· spirit

feverish
Mis. 233- 5 f·, disgusting pride of those
'01. 2-17 f· pride of sects and systems

few
Mis. ix- 7 among my thousands of students f·
x-12 a f· articles are herein
2-14 the laborers seem f·.
23-24 F· there are who comprehend what
139-24 a f· persons have since scrupled ;
171-26 F· people at present know
237- 7 Not a f· individuals serve God
237-16 f· feel and live now as when
238-17 It is enough, say they, to care for a f·.
301-12 a f· professed Christian Scientists.
305-17 * large contributions from a f·.
323- 8 a f· laborers in a valley
323-23 and f· there be that find it."
325- 8 f· cravings for the immortal,
327-20 lay down a f· of the heavy weights,
347-18 take a f· steps,
354-16 a f· truths tenderly told,
378- 4 in a f· weeks returned
382- 5 a f· manuscripts of mine
Ret. 20- 5 f· months before my father's
90- 8 taught a f· hungry ones,
Un. 9-22 a f· spiritual thinkers
12- 3 laborers are f· in this vineyard of
Pul. 8-19 to earn a f· pence toward this
22-11 and a f· in far-off lands,
43-19 * A f· minutes of silent prayer
49- 6 * a f· of which had been the gifts
57-21 * f· people outside its own circles
72- 5 * a f· of the leading members
82-18 * women had f· lawful claims
88- 8 can append only a f· of the names
Rud. 15-13 F· were taken besides invalids for
'00. 9- 9 but f·, comparatively, see it ;
'01. 28- 7 f· there be that find it." — Matt. 7 : 14.
'02. 4-22 a f· of their infinite meanings,
Peo. 8- 7 the sins of a f· tired years
12-14 F· there be who know what a power
Po. vii- 6 * to prepare a f· bound volumes
33-18 I ponder the days may be f·
My. 17-24 * f· moments of silent prayer
47- 7 * a f· of the stages of its progress,
50-26 * and f· knew of its teachings,
50-27 * those f· saw the grandeur
51-17 * remain with us for a f· Sundays

few

My.	52–27	* Within a *f·* months she has made
	73– 6	* very *f·* of them owe a cent.
	80–28	* A *f·* were upon the scene
	85–31	* one of the *f·* perfect sky-lines
	91–21	* The *f·* thousand persons who followed
	121–17	*F·* blemishes can be found in a
	146–12	*F·* believe this saying.
	146–12	*F·* believe that C. S. contains
	182– 1	Chicago had *f·* Congregational
	237– 2	in the *Sentinel* a *f·* weeks ago,
	244–20	but *f·* are chosen." — *Matt.* 22 : 14.
	261–24	an open secret, understood by *f·*
	290– 5	and the tried and true seem *f·*.
	290– 8	*F·* sovereigns have been as venerable,
	303–20	what feeds a *f·* feeds all.
	322–21	* a *f·* days' instruction by Mrs. Eddy
	327–18	* a *f·* other Scientists who stayed
	334– 6	* allegation that copies . . . are *f·*,

(*see also* **days, things, words, years**)

fewer

My.	83–14	* will doubtless have *f·* questions

fiat

Mis.	336–27	Science is the *f·* of divine
Un.	38–21	no divine *f·* commands us to
'01.	5–18	leave all sin to God's *f·*
Po.	1– 9	far the universal *f·* ran,

fibre

Un.	13–17	in the very *f·* of His being,

fibres

Mis.	142–27	touched tender *f·* of thought,

Fichte

No.	22– 4	Leibnitz, Descartes, *F·*,

fiction

My.	48–29	* or paralyzed by sentimental *f·*.
	112– 3	A *f·* or a false philosophy

fidelity

Mis.	270–23	*F·* to his precepts and practice
	286– 4	the solemn vow of *f·*,
	339– 1	chapter sub-title
	341– 9	*F·* finds its reward
Ret.	91–17	and with such *f·*,
Pul.	22– 9	attest their *f·* to Truth,
	38–24	* They hold with strict *f·* to
	66–13	* They hold with strict *f·* to
'01.	3– 2	virtue, fervor, and *f·*.
My.	5–26	your generosity and *f·*,
	37–13	* By your *f·* and the constancy of
	45–16	* *f·* to the divine Principle
	62– 1	* unflinching faith and unfailing *f·*
	90–12	* insures *f·* in pain or death
	135–26	Your love and *f·* cheer my
	187– 1	your *f·*, faith, and Christian zeal
	209– 6	*f·*, courage, patience, and grace.
	230–21	fitness and *f·* such as thine
	243–21	witnesses your *f·* to C. S.

Field

Man.	56–16	general reports from the *F·*.
	64– 1	experience in the *F·*,
	72– 7	Scientist working in the *F·*,

field

at work in a

Pul.	33–17	* at work in a *f·* one day

beasts of the

Mis.	191– 5	beasts of the *f·*." — see *Gen.* 3 : 1.

complaints from the

My.	354– 2	In view of complaints from the *f·*,

every

Pul.	53–21	* every *f·* of human endeavor.

fruitful

My.	183–19	forest becomes a fruitful *f·*,

grass of the

No.	26–26	clothe the grass of the *f·*, — *Matt.* 6 : 30.

occupying the

Hea.	14– 1	occupying the *f·* for a period ;

of battle

Mis.	136– 5	with you on the *f·* of battle,

of labor

Mis.	136– 1	I retired from the *f·* of labor,
	318–19	entering this sacred *f·* of labor,
Man.	84–23	A Single *F·* of Labor.
	85– 1	occupies only his own *f·* of labor.
Ret.	47–23	before entering this *f·* of labor
No.	7–25	in this *f·* of labor.
My.	347–19	purchases our *f·* of labor
	355–10	factors in our *f·* of labor

of medicine

Mis.	366–10	imposition in the *f·* of medicine

of Mind-healing

Rud.	8–17	in the *f·* of Mind-healing.

of Science

My.	226–25	laborers in the *f·* of Science

of work

My.	216–19	indicates another *f·* of work

field

open

'02.	14–29	an open *f·* and fair play.

plant of the

Mis.	26–12	"every plant of the *f·* — *Gen.* 2 : 5.
Hea.	19–14	"every plant of the *f·* — *Gen.* 2 : 5.

student in the

My.	355– 6	letter from a student in the *f·*

this

Mis.	284– 7	in this *f·* of limitless power
Ret.	47–23	before entering this *f·* of labor
No.	7–25	in this *f·* of labor.
My.	362–23	* churches and societies in this *f·*

whole

My.	297–20	inspiration to the whole *f·*,

Mis.	54– 8	*f·* of metaphysical healing,
	313–19	The *f·* waves its white ensign,
My.	162–11	Scientists all over the *f·*,
	195– 6	problems to be worked out for the *f·*,
	242–16	I hereby announce to the C. S. *f·*
	327–18	* Scientists who stayed on the *f·*
	354– 5	it is due the *f·* to state that I
	355– 2	as it will be to the *f·*,

fields

Mis.	xi–14	unexplored *f·* of Science.
	xi–26	to survey the *f·* of the slain
	80–26	sown and reaped in the *f·*
	120–25	from their own *f·* of labor.
	302–32	stay within their own *f·*
Ret.	4–13	Where once stretched broad *f·*
	30– 4	have won *f·* of battle
Un.	12– 1	your *f·* are already white
My.	51–23	* her duty, to go into new *f·*
	243–17	remain in their own *f·* of labor

fierce

Chr.	53–16	With *f·* heart-beats ;
My.	127–22	culminating in *f·* attack,

fiercely

Pul.	2–17	*f·* besieged by the enemy.

fiery

Mis.	118–29	*f·* punishment of the evil-doer.

fifteen

Mis.	242–14	more difficult tasks *f·* years ago.
Ret.	40–10	stood by her side about *f·* minutes
Pul.	26–17	* chime of bells includes *f·*,
	30–27	* and within *f·* years it has grown
	52–22	* over the world for *f·* centuries,
	62– 8	* a chime of *f·* bells
	66– 5	* was founded *f·* years ago
	79–10	* starting *f·* years ago,
My.	24–22	* *f·* different trades represented.
	309–28	* passed her first *f·* years at

(*see also* **numbers, values**)

fifth

Mis.	262– 7	entering upon its *f·* volume,
	280–18	dismissed the *f·* of March,
	280–26	On the morning of the *f·*,
My.	122–11	On the *f·* of July last,

Fifth Avenue

542

My.	282–20	542 *F· A·*, New York City.

Fifth Church of Christ, Scientist

My.	363– 3	* signature

fifty

Mis.	221–26	that five times ten are *f·*
	221–27	saying . . . ten times five are not *f·* ;
Un.	6–28	in less than another *f·* years
Pul.	41–15	* parties of forty and *f·*.
Hea.	1–18	* At *f·*, chides his infamous delay,
My.	234– 1	*f·* telegrams per holiday
	310–24	* a gray-haired man of *f·*

(*see also* **numbers, values**)

fifty-one

My.	68– 9	* a height of *f·* feet.

fig

Pul.	26–24	* with sprays of *f·* leaves

fight

Mis.	41–12	The good *f·* must be fought
	80–11	will *f·* the medical faculty,
	104–17	wages feeble *f·* with his
	204– 8	When the good *f·* is fought,
	278–6, 7	*f·* the good *f·*,
	321–30	Untiring in your holy *f·*,
Un.	46–28	The *f·* was an effort to enthrone evil.
Pul.	3–14	good *f·* we have waged is over,
No.	7–20	must now *f·* their own battles.
	23–21	*f·* these claims, not as realities,
Pan.	6– 7	continue to *f·* it until it disappears,
	13–16	*f·* the good *f·*
'00.	9–23	no one can *f·* against God,
	10– 4	illusion, that after a *f·* vanisheth

fight

'02.	10– 2	has a *f·* with the flesh.
Hea.	2–16	"I have fought a good *f·*, — II Tim. 4: 7.
	14– 2	it is the *f·* of beasts,
Po.	10–10	The hoar *f·* is forgotten ;
My.	18–24	to *f·* the good *f·* till God's will
	212– 7	A harder *f·* will be necessary
	337–11	The hoar *f·* is forgotten ;

fighting

Mis.	140–24	not be found *f·* against God.
	327–29	grumbling, and *f·* each other,
My.	278–22	Nothing is gained by *f·*,

figs

Mis.	27–17	or *f·* of thistles?" — Matt. 7 : 16.
	336–18	nor *f·* of thistles.

fig-tree

Mis.	151–11	He saith of the barren *f·*,
	154–13	beneath your own vine and *f·*

figurative

Pul.	66–15	* highly *f·* language.

figuratively

Mis.	258– 7	*f·* and literally spat upon matter ;
My.	343–21	the term pope is used *f·*.

figure

Mis.	370–20	What *f·* is less favorable than
	376– 4	* face, *f·*, and drapery of Jesus,
	376– 6	* the face, *f·*, and drapery of
	376– 9	* the *f·* and garments from a
	392–13	love the Hebrew *f·* of a tree.
Pul.	31–19	* central *f·* in all this agitation
	31–27	* Her *f·* was tall, slender, and
	48–28	* *f·* largely in her genealogy,
Po.	20–17	love the Hebrew *f·* of a tree.

figures

Mis.	375–24	* "The hands and feet of the *f·*
My.	8–18	* and the relationship of *f·*,
	25–10	* *f·* are taken from the report
	94– 3	* *f·* given out by the church
	96– 5	* many of them prominent *f·* in
	97–11	* if the *f·* could be given
	99–27	* Facts and *f·* are stubborn things,
	100– 2	* some of the facts and *f·*
	345–29	make them our *f·* of speech.

filed

Mis.	380–27	a bill in equity was *f·*
	380–32	Answer was *f·* by the defendant,
My.	137– 4	following affidavit, . . . was *f·*

filial

Mis.	254– 1	*f·* obedience to which the Decalogue

fill

Mis.	9–17	*f·* it with the nectar of the gods.
	39–19	they intend to *f·* the human mind
	43–23	*f·* one's pocket at the expense of
	276– 8	not big enough to *f·* the order ;
	343–26	*f·* the haunted chambers of memory,
	360–22	*f·* earth with the divine energies,
	386–15	to *f·* That waking with a love
Man.	26–21	They shall *f·* a vacancy occurring
	29–14	five suitable members . . . to *f·*
	71–13	position that no other church can *f·*.
	80–18	reserves the right to *f·* the same
	80–20	trustees shall *f·* the vacancy,
	89– 8	shall be elected to *f·* the vacancy.
	100–19	Committee to *f·* the vacancy ;
	112– 9	*f·* out his application
Ret.	70–19	*f·* his own niche in time and eternity.
Pul.	60–19	* to *f·* the recess behind the
	69–12	* *f·* the mind with good thoughts
Rud.	15–15	to *f·* in the best possible manner
	15–28	to *f·* anew the individual mind.
No.	1– 8	*f·* the rivers till they rise in floods,
	45–16	right of woman to *f·* the highest
Pan.	15– 9	and *f·* us with the life and
'01.	32–19	They *f·* the ecclesiastic measure,
Po.	3–14	Love divine doth *f·* my heart.
	8– 6	Her bosom to *f·* with mortal woes.
	29–20	*F·* us today With all thou art
	49–23	to *f·* That waking with a love
	66– 2	our brimming cup *f·*,
My.	19–27	no doubt *f·* the memory
	59–18	* would scarce *f·* a couple of pews
	62–13	* *f·* your heart with the joy of Love's
	126–18	*f·* to her double — Rev. 18: 6.
	167–12	may *f·* your hearts
	195–30	*f·* these spiritual temples with grace,
	210– 6	and no space for evil to *f·*
	270–19	Those words . . . *f·* my heart :

filled

Mis.	93– 2	that they may be *f·* with Truth.
	111–14	had He *f·* the net,
	124–19	man's true sense is *f·* with peace,
	183–17	if he open his mouth it shall be *f·*

filled

Mis.	321– 7	My heart is *f·* with joy,
	360–31	*f·* with the true knowledge of
	386– 5	and hearts are found and *f·*,
Man.	37– 4	after the blank has been properly *f·*
	109–12	*f·* out by the applicants,
Ret.	84–21	that they may be *f·* with Truth.
Pul.	28–27	* has *f·* the office of pastor
	29–13	* the hall was *f·*
	41–21	* vast congregations *f·* the church
	42– 3	* *f·* with a waiting multitude.
	42–30	* *f·* with beautiful pink roses.
	53–29	* power that *f·* his garment's hem
No.	15– 7	*f·* with blessings for the whole
Po.	49– 9	hearts are found and *f·*,
My.	30–27	* church was *f·* for the service
	38–10	* seating space had been *f·*
	38–12	* church was *f·* for each service
	38–17	* They *f·* all the seats
	42–16	* a heart *f·* with gratitude
	52–26	* always *f·* her coffers anew.
	56– 3	* until every seat was *f·*
	77–19	* *f·* the streets leading to the
	80–27	* these places had all been *f·*,
	80–32	* auditorium was comfortably *f·*.
	90– 2	* great buildings should be *f·*
	126–18	cup which she hath *f·* — Rev. 18: 6.
	157– 4	* are *f·* with profound joy
	210– 3	*f·* with Truth and Love,
	210– 7	in a mind *f·* with goodness.
	247–24	so *f·* with divine food
	250–28	have *f·* this sacred office
	291–25	sheaves garnered, her treasury *f·*,
	362–19	* *f·* with gratitude to God,

filling

Mis.	116–12	*f·* the measures of life's music
	254–23	*f·* with hate its deluded victims,
	331–24	*f·* all space and having all power,
Man.	111– 2	*f·* out the application blank,
Rud.	3–27	ever-present I AM, *f·* all space,
'00	1– 6	ever-present Love *f·* all space,
'01.	15–16	*f·* up the measure of wickedness
My.	255– 7	*f·* their positions satisfactorily

fills

Mis.	13–30	it *f·* all space, being omnipresent ;
	173–20	God is Mind and *f·* all space,
	228–10	*f·* the world with its fragrance,
	281– 7	*f·* me with joy.
	285– 6	*f·* orders for my books,
	396– 6	*F·* mortal sense with dread ;
Pul.	21–30	*f·* the sentiment with unworldliness,
Po.	46–17	While beauty *f·* each bar.
	58–18	*F·* mortal sense with dread ;
My.	191–24	Immortal courage *f·* the human breast

filter

Mis.	171– 9	*f·* from vertebræ to vertebræ.

final

Mis.	55–22	the *f·* destruction of all that
	56–18	*f·* destruction of this false belief
	63–18	and understand the *f·* fact,
	86– 3	This *f·* degree of regeneration
	99– 1	Science is absolute and *f·*.
	116–19	*f·* obedience to spiritual law.
	205–13	*f·* immersion of human consciousness
	215– 1	the *f·* destruction of error
	219– 2	science of the *f·* cause of things ;
	318–10	third and fourth and *f·* generation
	361–21	So shall mortals soar to *f·* freedom,
Ret.	13–14	belief in a *f·* judgment-day,
	33– 2	my *f·* conclusion that mortal belief,
	47– 2	*f·* outcome of material organization,
	56–14	by the *f·* triumph of Spirit
	78–24	your own success and *f·* happiness,
'00.	4–22	*f·*, absolute, and eternal.
	10–10	gained fresh energy and *f·* victory.
'01.	5–18	*f·* manifestation of the real
	27– 1	experience, and *f·* discovery,
Peo.	1– 7	*f·* unity between man and God.
My.	266–17	*f·* spiritualization of all things,

finale

Un.	2–11	as the *f·* in Science :
My.	303–24	rather is it the pith and *f·* of

finally

Mis.	100–15	*f·* show the fruits of Love.
	126–12	and *f·* conquers them ;
	128– 6	"F·", brethren, — Phil. 4: 8.
	136– 2	socially, publicly, and *f·*
	205–26	abandonment of sin *f·* dissolves all
	299–10	that this query has *f·* come
	369– 4	God's law, . . . shall be *f·* understood;
	373– 6	but, as usual, he *f·* yielded.
	373–28	*f·* sit down at the right hand
Ret.	45–12	mortal existence is *f·* laid off,

finally

Ret.	50– 8	was *f·* led, . . to accept this fee.
	67–16	*f·* lost for lack of witness.
Un.	45–21	until it *f·* dies in order to
Pul.	14– 5	*f·* be shocked into another
	50–25	* skirmishing, *f·* subsides.
Rud.	11– 5	*f·* to the *understanding* of God
No.	9–12	separate wisely and *f·* ;
Pan.	6– 5	*F·*, brethren, . . . denounce evil
'01.	20–26	flagrance will *f·* be known,
	34–20	*F·*, brethren, wait patiently
'02.	10–15	will *f·* gain the scope of
	10–17	becomes *f·* spiritual.
Po.	vi– 1	* *f· found its way into print,*
My.	25– 4	* to dispose fully and *f·*
	43–11	* *f·* became willingly obedient
	108–26	*F·*, beloved brethren
	174–29	*f·* may we not together
	231– 9	*f·* resolved to spend no
	232–24	material error *f·* disappears,
	278–28	*f·* fall, pierced by its own

Finance

(*see* **Committee on Finance**)

finance

Mis.	327–11	policy, religion, politics, *f·*,

Finance Committee

Man.	76–15	*F· C·*.

finances

Mis.	131–17	By-law relating to *f·*
Pul.	8– 7	condition of our nation's *f·*,

financial

Mis.	131–14	a report of the first *f·* year
	131–28	After this *f·* year, when you
Man.	75–11	understands the *f·* situation
	75–15	*F·* Situation.
Ret.	50– 3	no *f·* equivalent for
'02.	12–23	*f·* transactions of this church,
My.	7– 7	*f·* transactions of this church,

find

Mis.	xi–15	will *f·* herein a "canny" crumb ;
	11– 2	to *f·* that, though thwarted,
	13–29	you will *f·* it to be good ;
	13–30	will *f·* that good is omnipotence,
	14– 6	or *f·* its existence necessary
	28–25	*f·* neither pleasure nor pain therein.
	32–14	will *f·* my views on this subject ;
	38–14	*other institutions f· little interest in*
	53–11	*Do you sometimes f· it advisable*
	76–22	will *f·* the right meaning indicated.
	86–30	and *f·* wings to reach the glory of
	89–23	will *f·* the proper answer to this
	98–18	and to *f·* strength in union,
	117–10	and always *f·* him there.
	124– 5	cannot *f·* God in matter,
	124–11	*f·* rest in the spiritual ideal,
	129–19	*f·* somebody in his way,
	130– 7	What do we *f·* in the Bible,
	132–21	I *f·* it inconvenient to accept
	133–28	I turn constantly to . . . and *f·* rest.
	147–21	we *f·* him ever the same,
	148– 2	We shall never *f·* one part of
	155– 9	*f·* access to the heart of humanity.
	157– 8	*f·* their card in *The C. S. Journal*
	158–25	*f·* the forthcoming completion
	176– 1	*f·* the truth that breaks the dream
	182– 9	*f·* their adoption with the Father ;
	200–24	to seek . . . and to *f·* happiness,
	211–24	*f·* the Life that cannot be lost.
	217– 4	nor reason attempts to *f·* one ;
	220– 2	*f·* that a good rule works one way,
	227–13	*f·* himself responsible for kind(?)
	234–15	which can never *f·* a place in Science.
	266–21	cannot *f·* it in my heart not to love
	279–19	*f·* out the nothingness of matter ;
	281– 6	But I *f·* also another mental condition
	287–17	*f·* the highway of holiness.
	298–26	One says, "I *f·* relief from pain in
	323–24	and few there be that *f·* it."
	324–22	and to *f·* the Stranger.
	324–25	only to *f·* the lights all wasted
	325–14	only to *f·* its inmates asleep
	327–26	for my sake, shall *f·* it." — *Matt.* 10 : 39.
	334–17	You must *f·* error to be *nothing:*
	341–19	and you *f·* Life eternal :
	343– 6	to *f·* disease in the mortal mind,
	353– 9	and *f·* the divine,
	357– 7	and yearn to *f·* living pastures
	362–25	We all must *f·* shelter from the
	369–25	would *f·* our Father's house again
	372–19	to *f·* "Christ and Christmas"
	375–21	* *f·* an almost identical resemblance,
	385– 3	* *F·* peace in God,
	390–22	And thou wilt *f·* that harmonies,
	391– 5	Will *f·* within its portals

find

Mis.	391–18	*F·* items at our door.
Man.	111–14	Applicants will *f·* the chief points
Ret.	2– 5	*f·* so graphically set forth in the
	18–23	*f·* a happiness rare ;
	21– 5	employed to *f·* him,
	24–23	*f·* the Science of Mind
	38–20	to *f·* me *en route* for Boston,
	52– 1	endeavored to *f* new ways and means
	62– 4	*f·* that the views here set forth
	83–17	he will *f·* it more difficult to
	85– 3	Teachers of C. S. will *f·* it advisable
	89–22	*f·* any precedent for employing
	90–28	It is gladdening to *f·*, in such a student,
Un.	20–19	*f·* yourself losing the knowledge
	21– 4	we shall *f·* that we are perpetually
	26–12	as we *f·* in the hymn-verse
	33–17	and you *f·* no mind therein.
	33–23	*f·* them divided in evidence,
	62–17	and you *f·* Truth.
Pul.	4–12	will *f·* that one is as important a
	6–27	* *f·* in Mrs. Eddy's metaphysical
	11– 8	*f·* within it home, and *heaven.*
	38–30	* *f·* in one form of belief or another
	57–10	* truths which will *f·* emphasis
	69–19	* We *f·* in this view of the Bible
	70–20	* to *f·* the great curative Principle
	75– 5	"If Christian Scientists *f·* in my
	80– 3	* will surely *f·* the other.
No.	7–14	*f·* rescue and refuge in Truth
	36–16	*f·* rest from unreal trials in
Pan.	3– 9	*f·* an indefinable pleasure in
	8– 4	*f·* expression in sun worship,
	13–19	*f·* life in Him in whom we
'00.	7–24	*f·* ourselves so far from the
'01.	2–12	*f·* the standard of Christ's healing
	12–12	*f·* faith on the earth?" — *Luke* 18 : 8.
	28– 7	few there be that *f·* it." — *Matt.* 7 : 14.
'02.	11– 8	*f·* and point the path
	12–22	*f·* no place in my Message.
	19–27	*f·* divine Science glorifies the
Peo.	4–20	*f·* no reflection in
Po.	23–16	In brighter morn will *f·*
	37– 3	* *F·* peace in God,
	38– 4	Will *f·* within its portals
	38–17	*F·* items at our door.
	56– 1	thou wilt *f·* that harmonies,
	64–18	*f·* a happiness rare ;
My.	7– 5	that ordinarily *f·* no place in
	23– 2	* in order to *f·* out how much our
	71–15	* they will *f·* themselves in one of
	86– 5	* *f·* pleasure in this new symbol,
	91– 4	* something they did not *f·* in other
	104– 9	they could *f·* no fault in him,
	105– 3	*f·* in them man's only medicine
	114–31	and *f·* these progressive steps
	120– 2	and there we *f·* him.
	120– 4	lose me instead of *f·* me.
	122–19	to *f·* where the young child lies,
	127–13	we *f·* that divine metaphysics
	128– 2	*f·* no other outlet to liberty.
	137–30	I *f·* myself able to select the
	138–16	I *f·* that I cannot
	142– 5	* and then *f·* no seats in The
	155–17	May this glad Easter morn *f·*
	155–28	To-day may they *f·* some sweet
	163–18	that I might *f·* retirement from
	182–28	*f·* shelter from the storm
	184–29	*f·* utterance and acceptance
	212–28	will *f·* this practitioner saying
	215–26	Can we *f·* a better example
	221–13	can we *f·* a better moral philosophy,
	233–27	for my sake shall *f·* it." — *Matt.* 10 : 39.
	254–13	*f·* the ever-present God
	259–27	in which human capacities *f·* the
	283–13	*f·* their birthright in divine Science.
	306–17	Human merit or demerit will *f·*
	316–21	I am pleased to *f·* this
	318–31	I do not *f·* my authority for
	323– 8	* before the people *f·* out that
	361– 6	Please *f·* it there, and do not

finder

My.	4–22	seeker and *f·* of C. S.

findeth

Mis.	252–32	if a man *f·*, he goeth and selleth

finding

Mis.	98–11	*f·* ways and means for helping
	182–24	*f·* their place in God's great love,
	324–26	*F·* no happiness within,
	324–27	seeking peace but *f·* none.
	325–28	sees robbers *f·* ready ingress to
	389–20	Seeking and *f·*, with the angels sing :
Pul.	64–18	* without *f·* a clew ;
'02.	4–28	and past *f·* out.
Po.	4–19	Seeking and *f·*, with the angels sing :

finding
My. 38— 9 * no confusion in *f·* seats,
174—29 seeking and *f·* (though feebly),
188—29 and *f·* it, be God-endowed
221— 4 precludes . . . from *f·* favor with

finds
Mis. 15— 1 fancies he *f·* pleasure in it,
16— 7 one *f·* so much lacking,
31—13 false faith *f·* no place in,
53—27 *f·* it abstract or difficult to
118— 5 when faith *f·* a resting-place
127—19 *f·* one's own in another's good.
233—23 *f·* fault with the exactness of
261— 3 evil *f·* no escape from itself ;
341—10 Fidelity *f·* its reward
389—25 And mother *f·* her home
Man. 54— 2 *f·* that the offense has been committed,
Pul. 39—3, 4 * *f·* no rest until it *f·* the peace of
No. 15—20 *f·* Spirit neither in matter nor
27— 5 evil *f·* no place in good.
Pan. 10—25 individual who *f·* the highest joy,
'01. 1— 7 *f·* C. S. more extended,
19— 7 thus he *f·* what he seeks,
'02. 10—20 reformer who *f·* the more spiritual
Po. 5— 6 And mother *f·* her home
My. 4— 1 *f·* the spirit of Truth,
18—16 *f·* one's own in another's good."
88—21 * *f·* its temple in the heart of
89—10 * *f·* in the English cathedrals,
118—27 *f·* its paradise in Spirit,
155—14 *f·* the full fruition of its faith,
265— 4 and that it *f·* admittance ;

fine
Mis. 272—17 * shall be punished by a *f·*
Pul. 26—17 * of *f·* range and perfect tone.
Hea. 14— 3 in *f·*, much ado about nothing.
My. 66—16 * in a *f·* part of the city.
70— 6 * C. S. has more *f·* church edifices
86— 2 * *f·* architectural effects,
220— 1 * he was a *f·* literary student
335—13 * erected a *f·* dwelling-house,

finely
Pul. 29—16 * were *f·* read by Judge Hanna.

finer
My. 345—27 *f·*, more etherealized ways of
345—27 They seek the *f·* essences.

finesse
Mis. 373—12 Neither material *f·*, standpoint, nor

finest
Pul. 8—25 painted the *f·* flowers in the
My. 74—15 * *f·* architectural achievements
91—28 * one of the *f·* places of worship
123—11 in one of the *f·* localities

finger
Mis. 129— 4 let him put his *f·* to his lips,
166— 3 monument whose *f·* points upward,
231—17 and bit the *f·*
330—16 with *f·* grim and cold it points
388— 5 'T was Love whose *f·* traced aloud
395—20 Touched by the *f·* of decay
Ret. 85—18 wait for God's *f·* to point the way.
Un. 34—15 yet put your *f·* on a burning coal,
'02. 20—14 'T was Love whose *f·* traced aloud
Po. 7— 5 'Twas Love whose *f·* traced aloud
26—13 Thou point'st thy phantom *f·*,
58— 5 Touched by the *f·* of decay
My. 105—12 could be dented by the *f·*,
121—11 yielding to the touch of a *f·*.
124—23 with *f·* pointing upward,
186— 3 prophetic of the *f·* divine
258—31 a child with *f·* on her lip

fingers
Mis. 329—22 Her dainty *f·* put the fur cap on
Pul. 8—25 your loving hearts and deft *f·*
'01. 12— 2 is not felt with the *f·* ;
Peo. 11—27 "with one of their *f·*." — Matt. 23 : 4.
14—10 * white *f·* pointing upward."

finish
Mis. 41—13 keep the faith and *f·* their course.
215—25 long warfare with error . . . to *f·*,
Ret. 38— 5 to persuade him to *f·*
My. 68—20 * largely into the interior *f·*.
68—25 * form the interior *f·*,
162—17 was not able to *f·*." — Luke 14 : 30.

finished
Mis. 57— 8 the true creation was *f·*,
Ret. 38— 1 I had *f·* that edition
38—11 *f·* my copy for the book.
38—14 *f·* printing the copy
38—17 started for Boston with my *f·* copy.
Pul. 45— 7 * get their buildings *f·* on time,
My. 14—27 * until the church is *f·*.

finished
My. 45—13 * The great temple is *f·* !
45—28 * The great temple is *f·* !
68—29 * and *f·* with bronze,
126—11 how the first is *f·*
145— 8 remodelling of the house was *f·*,
304— 5 *f·* my course of studies
311—30 * when she *f·* Smith's grammar
357—28 I have just *f·* reading your

finisher
Mis. 361—20 *f·* of our faith." — Heb. 12 : 2.
'01. 17— 6 the author and *f·* of our faith,
My. 258—14 *f·* of our faith ;— Heb. 12 : 2.
349—16 *f·* of our faith." — Heb. 12 : 2.

finishes
Hea. 10—13 that *f·* the question

finishing
My. 66—18 * chapter sub-title

finite (noun)
Mis. 75—13 infinite is not within the *f·* ;
173—16 Can the infinite be within the *f·* ?
Ret. 67—10 *f·* was self-arrayed against the
Hea. 3—28 the *f·* cannot contain the infinite,
My. 118—21 the demands upon the *f·*
230— 1 measures the infinite against the *f·*.
272— 9 the *f·* is not the altitude of the infinite.

finite (adj.)
Mis. 16—20 more than a person, or *f·* form,
70—25 *f·* and material sense of relief ;
82—20 which *f·* mortals see and comprehend
102— 4 is only an infinite *f·* being,
102— 8 and the infinite forever *f·*.
162—24 without corporeality or *f·* mind.
172—19 presents but a *f·*, feeble sense of
182—23 no personal plan . . . partial and *f·* ;
217—18 and that Deity is a *f·* person
217—29 or to become both *f·* and infinite ;
219— 6 or that the personality of . . . is *f·*
307—20 deification of *f·* personality.
308—31 a *f·* person is not the model
309—14 Pondering on the *f·* personality of
Ret. 30—15 foibles and fables of *f·* mind
56— 1 antagonized by *f·* theories,
58— 3 taking the rule of *f·* matter,
58— 6 physical, false, and *f·* substitute.
59— 2 to believe man has a *f·* and
59—11 even as mortals apply *f·* terms
73— 3 Physical personality is *f·* ;
Un. 4— 8 in a certain *f·* human sense,
24—10 *Evil.* I am a *f·* consciousness,
24—13 infinite, and not a *f·* consciousness.
24—15 There is no really *f·* mind,
24—16 no *f·* consciousness.
43— 7 too *f·* for anchorage in infinite
Rud. 2—10 especially a *f·* human being;
2—13 The human person is *f·* ;
2—21 assigned to God by *f·* thought,
3—25 do you mean that God has a *f·* form?
No. 24—16 starting from a *f·* body,
25—11 is beyond a *f·* belief.
25—12 Man outlives *f·* mortal definitions
36— 3 one infinite and the other *f·* ;
Pan. 8— 8 a human *f·* personality?
'01. 4—19 God is not *f·* ;
6— 7 reckons . . . the Infinite in a *f·* form,
6— 9 infinite Mind inhabit a *f·* form?
6—10 a *f·* or an infinite Person?
6—28 idea of Him as a *f·* Person
Hea. 4— 8 we limit . . . to the *f·* senses.
4—15 and become *f·* for a season ;
4—18 expect infinite Life to become *f·*,
Peo. 3—20 is based on *f·* premises,
4— 9 said that . . . could enter *f·* man
8—13 our *f·* and material conceptions of Deity.
My. 109—15 is not corporeal, not *f·*.
159—15 will not be buried in the *f·* ;
159—21 the temporary and *f·*.
(see also **sense**)

finiteness
Mis. 101—15 no compromise with *f·*
Ret. 73— 4 without *f·* of form or Mind.
Un. 25—15 from *f·* into infinity.

finitized
My. 122—21 *f·*, cribbed, or cradled,

finity
Mis. 102— 7 Mind would be chained to *f·*,
Ret. 67—10 manifestation of sin was a *f·*.
Peo. 4— 7 belief that . . . infinity became *f·*,

fire
Mis. 1—17 *f·* from the ashes of dissolving self,
125— 2 be purified as by *f·*,
151— 6 God is a consuming *f·*.

fire

Mis. 172– 9 clans pouring in their f· upon us ;
    176–22 melted away in the f· of love
    205– 7 the f· of repentance first
    213–18 pass through a baptism of f·.
    215– 2 the sifting and the f·.
    237– 2 that hell is f· and brimstone,
    326– 7 that house is on f· !
    326–15 "God is a consuming f·." — Heb. 12 : 29.
    328–20 wakened through the baptism of f· ?
    345–11 set f· to the fagots,
Ret. 94–10 * so Christ's baptism of f·,
Pan. 3–25 * heaven, earth, sea, the eternal f·,
'00. 8–23 f· that purifies sense with Soul
'01. 12– 6 with the Holy Ghost and with f·,
'02. 13– 4 a sharper f· from enmity.
    16– 1 after the earthquake and the f·.
Peo. 13–21 set f· to the fagots,
    13–22 through the baptism of f·
My. 45–21 * by night in a pillar of f·
    45–25 * pillar of f· by night," — Exod. 13 : 22.
    160–24 unpunished sin is this internal f·,
    160–25 even the f· of a guilty conscience,
    160–31 makers of hell burn in their f·.
    164–21 What is this . . . phœnix f·,
    300–31 Are the churches opening f· on

fired

My. 29–22 * f· the imagination.

fire-proof

Pul. 25– 7 * as literally f· as is conceivable.
    57– 2 * The building is f·,
    70–14 * a handsome f· church
    75–25 * believed to be the most nearly f·

fires

Mis. 125– 2 the f· of suffering ;
    237–10 belch forth their latent f·.
Pul. 9– 8 kindle perpetually its f·.
'02. 5– 7 lights the f· of the Holy Ghost,
    19–26 Master triumphed in furnace f·.
Hea. 11–13 f· of ancient proscription
My. 124–31 they consume in their own f·
    160–22 internal f· of our earth
    340–32 light their f· in every home.

fireside

Mis. 231–32 vacant seat at f· and board

firesides

My. 126–29 need it in our homes, at our f·,

firing

Mis. 11– 6 by f· first could kill him

firm

Mis. 77– 5 to be f·, — yea, to understand
    77–20 To believe is to be f·.
    134–13 F· in your allegiance to
    213–20 fearless wing and f· foundation.
    232–24 its infinite value and f· basis.
    299–31 property of a noted f·,
    361–27 partner in the f· of error,
'01. 2–25 Only a f· foundation in Truth can
My. 97– 3 * f· faith on the part of a

firmer

Mis. 160–14 f· in understanding and obedience.
    276–32 f· than ever in their allegiance to
Un. 14–20 f· than everlasting hills.

firmest

Pul. 5–10 bravest to endure, f· to suffer,

firmly

Mis. 225–11 f· bore testimony to the power
    339–12 plants our feet more f·.
Un. 6–14 Until . . . is f· grounded,
Pan. 15– 8 plant our feet f· on Truth,
Peo. 5–27 * "I f· believe that if the whole
My. 299–20 f· subscribe to this statement ;
    348–21 value to the race f· established.

firmness

Ret. 7–17 * noted for his boldness and f·,

First

Man. 99–26 by the F· and Second Readers
    112– 3 must be written F·, Second,
Pul. 37–25 * heading
My. 249–26 the F· and Second Readers

first

Mis. x–20 After my f· marriage, to
    xi– 1 f· edition of S. and H. having been
    2–11 Adam legacy may be seen,
    2–14 but the f· faint view of a
    8–11 except you f· formulate this enemy
    11– 6 by firing f· could kill him
    15–29 feeding at f· on the milk of the
    21– 5 My f· plank in the platform of C. S.
    23–17 Satan, the f· talker in its behalf,
    23–19 the f· and only cause.

first

Mis. 26–13 Whence came the f· seed,
    27–31 f· admitting that it is substantial.
    29–15 In 1867, I taught the f· student
    29–18 the f· publication of my work,
    30– 6 even though failing at f· to
    33–25 F· : It does away with all material
    36– 8 The f· and only cause is
    52–26 because the f· rule was not easily
    56–29 f· spiritually created the universe,
    57– 2 If the f· record is true,
    57– 9 in the f· chapter of Genesis.
    59–10 is worse than the f·.
    63– 5 was at f· gotten up to hinder his
    67– 4 F· is the law, which saith :
    75– 8 F· : I urge this fundamental fact
    77–26 has fallen away from his f· estate ;
    85–17 f· feeble flutterings of mortals
    90–18 F·, be sure that your means for
    93–31 suffer for it in the f· instance,
    94– 5 He must f· see himself and the
    96–11 f·, as a loving Father and Mother ;
    106–15 chapter sub-title
    107–21 must f· be shown its falsity
    108–17 f· state, . . . knowledge of one's self,
    109–18 Ignorance was the f· condition
    112–24 This mental disease at f·
    117– 4 f· separate the tares from the wheat ;
    129– 5 One's f· lesson is to
    131– 5 darkness in one's self must f· be
    131–14 f· financial year since the erection
    137– 6 close of the f· convention of the
    138–15 f· and last lesson of C. S. is love,
    138–24 growth of these at f· is more gradual ;
    142–15 My f· impression was to indite a poem ;
    149–29 f· temple for C. S. worship
    151–21 make Him thy f· acquaintance.
    153–24 my f· edition of "S. and H.
    153–28 * Hear the f· music of this
    155–19 she hereby requests : F·, that you,
    158–11 we both had f· to obey,
    164–13 At f·, the babe Jesus seemed small
    171– 3 Jesus' f· effort to realize Truth
    172–28 f· and fundamental rule of Science
    174–20 f· to declare against this kingdom
    176–20 When f· the Pilgrims
    179– 4 The f· rightful desire
    185–27 The f· man Adam — I Cor. 15 : 45.
    185–30 f· spake from their standpoint of
    187–14 presuppose a material man to be the f·
    188– 4 when the stars f· sang together,
    188– 6 presents as being f· that which
    188–16 St. Paul f· reasons upon the basis
    188–30 was the f·, the only man.
    189– 1 "The last shall be f·, — Matt. 20 : 16.
    189– 1 and the f· last." — Matt. 20–16.
    189–13 "the f· man," — I Cor. 15 : 45.
    191–16 and by omitting the f· letter,
    193–31 condition insisted upon is, f·,
    194–30 must comply with the f· condition
    203–19 F· : The baptism of repentance
    205– 7 repentance f· separates the dross
    215–13 must f· understand the Principle
    216– 4 must f· have done our work,
    223– 2 mystery of error . . . at f· defied me.
    231–26 his f· sitting-at-table on Thanksgiving
    249– 1 f· undertaken by a mesmerist,
    255–22 F· : It does away with material
    264–15 are taught their f· lessons by my
    264–21 the bias of their f· impressions,
    270–14 "Seek ye f· the kingdom — Matt. 6 : 33.
    272– 7 * the f· on record in history,
    279–15 The f· is that of Joshua
    285–15 f· crossed swords with free-love,
    285–18 book that cast the f· stone,
    289– 8 mortals must f· choose between
    293–17 last error will be worse than the f·
    301–24 F· : This method is an unseen
    304– 9 * coming f· to the capital
    305–19 * F· : Material that can be made a
    305–30 * the f· President of the United States,
    314–31 On the f· Sunday of each month,
    315–23 f· few years, convene as often as
    326–23 f·, to meet with joy his own,
    330–23 Nature's f· and last lessons
    332–22 f·, a supposition ;
    336–13 even that you f· cast out your
    338– 2 f· brings to humanity some great
    338– 5 I f· proved to myself,
    341– 6 F· purify thought,
    343–21 not . . . by the f· uprooting ;
    347– 1 f· command of Solomon,
    350– 8 The f· subject given out for
    350–15 in about one week from the f·
    352– 7 But it must f· see the error of its
    354–23 humility is the f· step in C. S.,

first.

	⌐5–12　F·, self-knowledge.
	358–23　the f· and only College for
	360–13　stars of the f· magnitude
	366–20　From f· to last, evil insists on
	370–29　f· care is to separate the sheep
	371– 1　among the f· lessons on healing
	372– 1　When the latter was f· issued,
	375–17　* "The f· thing that impressed me
	378–12　treatment seemed at f· to relieve her,
	380–12　teach the f· student in C. S.
	380–17　My students at f· practised in
	382– 5　my f· work on this doctrine.
	382–13　f· patient healed in this age by
	382–15　I taught the f· student in C. S.
	382–16　the f· books on this subject ;
	382–17　obtained the f· charter for
	382–17　the f· C. S. church,
	382–19　and was its f· pastor.
	382–20　erected the f· church edifice
	382–21　obtained the f· and only charter
	382–22　its f· and only president ;
	382–23　the f· C. S. periodical,
	382–24　f· Christian Scientist Association,
	386–15　At f· to fill That waking with
	388–21　F· at the tomb to hear his word :
Man.	40–19　f· Sunday of each month.
	56–12　following the f· Sunday in June.
	57– 4　preceding the f· Sunday in June,
	57– 5　f· Friday in November of each year.
	59– 9　f· to announce the name of the
	62–24　The f· lessons of the children
	64–18　At f· Mrs. Eddy objected to being
	70– 5　without f· consulting her on said
	77– 4　books are to be audited on May f·.
	78–24　on the f· of the following month,
	90–10　on the f· Wednesday of December.
	110–13　Initials only of f· names will not
Chr.	55–10　seek ye f· the kingdom — Matt. 6 : 33.
Ret.	5– 4　f· Congregational Church in Pembroke.
	19– 1　I was united to my f· husband,
	26–26　could f· state this Principle,
	27–14　f· jottings were but efforts to
	27–21　ripples in one's f· thoughts of it
	27–24　Science f· broke upon my sense,
	28–12　The f· must become last.
	31–13　f· spontaneous motion of Truth
	34–11　F· : It does away with all material
	35– 1　copyrighted the f· publication on
	36– 5　after taking out my f· copyright,
	37– 1　f· edition of my most important work,
	37– 6　When it was f· printed,
	37– 9　f· edition numbered one thousand copies.
	37–21　in my f· edition of S. and H.,
	38–21　closing chapter of my f· edition
	42– 4　Dr. Eddy was the f· student publicly
	42– 7　He was the f· organizer of
	43– 1　f· purely metaphysical system
	43–21　The f· Christian Scientist Association
	44– 4　The f· such church ever organized.
	45–12　deemed requisite in the f· stages of
	49–12　spiritual formation f·, last, and
	49–13　in human growth material . . . is f· ;
	52–19　The f· official organ of the
	64–26　mortals must f· open their eyes to
	67– 9　f· . . . manifestation of sin was
	81–28　f· led me to the feet of C. S.,
	81–30　Though our f· lessons are changed,
	87– 3　* "Order is heaven's f· law,"
	87–15　F· : Christian Scientists are to
	89–28　action not f· made known to them
	90–23　to those f· sacred tasks,
	92– 5　"f· the blade, then the ear, — Mark 4 : 28.
Un.	14– 3　because it was not at f· done
	15– 1　man's f· disobedience,
	17–21　God told our f· parents that
	20– 7　F· : The Lord created it.
	20–12　F· : God never made evil.
	30–13　f· epistle to the Corinthians
	30–14　"The f· man Adam — I Cor. 15 : 45.
	30–25　f· shall be last," — Matt. 19 : 30.
	31–11　f· idolatrous claim of sin is,
	35–15　Which was f·, matter or power?
	35–15　That which was f· was God,
	56–12　f· eliminates and then destroys.
	56–23　f· be made to fret in their chains ;
	61– 5　Jesus f· appeared as a helpless
Pul.	1——　chapter heading
	5–15　the f· to bedew my hope with a
	7–28　This is my f· ordination.
	20– 2　was f· purchased by the church
	20–14　From f· to last The Mother Church
	24– 1　* completion of the f· C. S. church
	24–19　* the f· pastor of this denomination."
	29– 5　* f· pastor of the church here
	30–26　* f· meeting held on April 12, 1879.

Pul.	31– 9　* my f· meeting with her
	35–16　The f· must become last.
	35–29　* the f· to place "Christian Scientist" on
	36–14　* evening that I f· met Mrs. Eddy
	37–26　* f· Christian Scientist Association
	38– 5　* f· edition of Mrs. Eddy's book,
	41–30　* At 9 a. m. the f· congregation
	44–22　* the f· of its kind ;
	46–29　* He was the f· organizer of a
	47– 5　* publisher of the f· official organ
	49–27　* f· impression given to the visitor
	55–13　* the f· edition of Mrs. Eddy's
	55–16　* Her discovery was f· called,
	60–10　* Each paragraph he supplemented f·
	61–22　* f· peal of the chimes in the tower
	64– 4　* the f· pastor of this denomination."
	67–25　* f· Christian Scientist Association
	70– 9　* f· pastor of the C. S. denomination,
	72– 9　* one of the f· to be seen.
	79–18　* The f· is that a revolt was inevitable
Rud.	9– 2　worse than the f·." — Matt. 12 : 45.
	11– 4　f· to faith in Christ ;
	12–10　belief that they are f· made sick
	14–19　f· classes furnished students with
	16–20　This was the f· book,
	17–13　when taking the f· footsteps
No.	6– 1　last state . . . worse than the f·.
	9–17　the f· edition of this little work
	45–14　and f· at the sepulchre,"
	46–14　the f· settlers of New Hampshire.
Pan.	6– 1　f·, because it was more effectual
	6–11　f·, in the form of a talking serpent,
	9– 9　four f· rules pertaining thereto,
'00.	7– 2　"S. and H. . . . was f· published.
	8–26　learn f· what obedience is.
	10–26　in the name of a f· lieutenant of the
	12–19　hast left thy f· love— Rev. 2 : 4.
	15–23　not left thy f· love, — see Rev. 2 : 4.
	15–26　more than the f·." — Rev. 2 : 19.
'01.	1– 6　f· communion in the new century
	3–22　The f· proposition is correct,
	3–24　last . . . does not illustrate the f·,
	13–27　f· detect the claim of sin ;
	14–24　control it in the f· instance, or
	17–11　my f· demonstrations of C. S.
	27– 9　the f· ever published on C. S.,
	27–28　* F·, people say it conflicts with
	28– 1　Having passed through the f· two stages,
	33–13　Christian Scientists f· and last
	33–26　just what it was in the f· centuries
'02.	2– 5　to write truth f· on the
	3–30　the f· lie and leap into perdition
	7– 5　In the f· chapter of Genesis,
	9–21　When f· I heard the life-giving sound
	15–11　not one dollar of royalty on its f·
	16– 6　This was my f· inkling of Wyclif's
Hea.	11–14　the f· to be intolerant.
	13–28　that one is worse than the f· ;
	14–19　You must f· mentally educate and
	17 01　sin was f· in the allegory,
	19–13　Which is f·, the egg or the bird?
Peo.	4–11　When f· good, God, was named a
Po.	1– 8　when f· creation vast began,
	3–11　Since f· we met, in weal or woe
	21–10　F· at the tomb to hear his word :
	39–11　F· at the tomb, who waits
	49–23　At f· to fill That waking with a
My.	vi–18　* was its f· editor and
	13– 7　the f· that I had even heard of it.
	31– 1　* f· the "Communion Hymn,"
	31–10　* public had its f· glimpse of the
	31–13　* f· impression was of vastness,
	31–20　* f· sight which the visitors caught
	40–19　* f· pure, then peaceable, — Jas. 3 : 17.
	42–20　* welcome you to our f· annual meeting
	49–15　* f· business meeting of the church
	49–32　* f· meeting of this little church
	54–23　* stated that from the f· of September
	54–31　* f· Sunday service held in Chickering
	56–30　* being repetitions of the f· service.
	57–14　* The f· annual meeting of the church
	59– 3　* your f· class in Lynn, Mass.,
	59–16　* back to that f· public meeting
	60–17　* of the f· chapter of Genesis.
	61– 6　* At f· I thought that,
	68–27　* floors of the f· story are of marble.
	73–28　* the f· instalments of the crowds
	74– 8　* in time for the f· Sunday service.
	76–26　* f· great monument to C. S.,
	77–21　* f· hymn of thanksgiving at six o'clock
	81–10　* f· to catch the Reader's eye.
	91–22　* the f· years of her preaching
	95– 4　* tenets f· presented by Mrs. Eddy
	112– 2　Science has always been f· met with
	114–14　My f· writings on C. S. began

first

firstborn

First Cause

First Church

First Church of Christ, Scientist

First Church of Christ, Scientist

First Commandment

First Commandment
My.   64–12   F· C· of the Hebrew Decalogue,
    116–10   would dethrone the F· C·,
    221–17   F· C· of the Decalogue,
    264–17   F· C· of the Decalogue
    279–11   F· C· in the Hebrew Decalogue

First Congregational Church
My.   60– 7   * deacon of the F· C· C·
    147– 5   afternoon services of the F· C· C·,
    174–12   chapter sub-title
    174–14   Pastor of the F· C· C·,
    174–20   our time-honored F· C· C·
    270– 5   In 1905, the F· C· C·,

firstfruits
Mis.   131–17   this year of your f·.
Rud.   16–26   call it their f·, or else

First Members
Mis.   147– 1   chapter sub-title
    310–23   F· M· will determine the action
Man.   18–21   were known as "F· M·."
    18–25   changed the title of "F· M·"
My.   289–12   special meeting of its F· M·

First Reader (see also First Reader's)
Mis.   314–10   F· R· shall give out any notices
    314–15   F ·R· shall read from my book,
Man.   29– 1   the F· R· of a church,
    30–12   F· R· of The Mother Church shall
    33– 2   F· R· in a Church of Christ,
    40–18   by the F· R· on the first Sunday
    100– 3   send to the F. R· of the church
My.   16–17   * Prof. Hermann S. Hering, F· R· ;
    16–22   * conducted by the F· R·,
    31–23   *F· R· William D. McCrackan,
    31–27   * the F· R· announced simply
    35–27   * F· R· William D. McCrackan read
    134–23   * F· R·, Mr. William D. McCrackan,
    135–17   F· R· of my church in Boston,
    142– 9   F· R·, The Mother Church,
    217–10   chapter sub-title
    249–23   for F· R· in The Church of Christ,

First Reader's
Man.   30–11   F· R· Residence.

First Readers (see also First Readers')
Man.   31–16   shall be the duty of the F· R·
    31–19   The F· R· shall read, as a part of
    32– 1   F· R. in the C. S. churches shall

First Readers'
Man.   31–15   F· R· Duties.

fish (see also fish's)
Mis.   69–12   over the f· of the sea, — Gen. 1 : 26.
    69–31   dominion over the f·
    69–32   "the f· of the sea" — Gen. 1 : 26.
    70– 4   exercised my power over the f·,
    393–14   Those who f· in waters deep,
Ret.   18– 3   at play with the gold-gleaming f· ;
Po.   51–10   Those who f· in waters deep,
    63–11   at play with the gold-gleaming f· ;

fisher
My.   247–19   God has called you to be a f· of men.

fishermen
My.   295–18   It guides the f·.

fishers
Mis.   111–10   "f· of men" — Mark 1 : 17.
My.   295–17   Christian Scientists are f· of men.

fishes
Mis.   111– 8   you lost your f·,
Pul.   60– 9   * Jesus' miracle of loaves and f·.
Peo.   6– 1   * and all the worse for the f·,"
My.   123–24   "five loaves and two f·" — Matt. 14 : 17.
    247–14   The little f· in my fountain

fishing-boat
Ret.   91–23   a f· became a sanctuary,

fish's
My.   216– 3   obtain their money from a f· mouth,

fissures
Un.   64–16   leap the dark f·,

fit
Mis.   212–12   When they were f· to be blest,
    228–18   an existence f· for earth and heaven.
    288– 5   sure of being a f· counsellor.
    315–10   who are letterly f·
    344– 9   f· habitation for the intelligences
    345–15   * f· only for women and weak men" ;
Man.   55–12   so strayed as not to be f· for the
Ret.   37–18   until our heavenly Father saw f·,
Rud.   16– 5   to f· students for practice
'00.   9–28   strove earnestly to f· others for
Peo.   13–23   * f· only for women and weak-minded
My.   112– 9   the Scriptures to f· a doctrine,
    200–28   and f· their being to recover its
    229– 3   No mesmerist . . . is f· to come hither.

fitful
Po.   65– 3   Life's pulses move f· and slow ;

fitly
Mis.   346–23   "A word f· spoken — Prov. 25 : 11.
My.   24–14   * "f· framed together — Eph. 2 : 21.

fitness
Mis.   127–16   f· to receive the answer to its
    316–11   should depend on the f· of things,
Un.   11–25   to mature f· for perfection
My.   18–12   f· to receive the answer to its
    230–20   Be assured that f· and fidelity
    267–18   in proportion to their f·

fits
My.   310–25   * these "f·" were diagnosed by

fitted
Mis.   197– 9   no man can be wholly f· for
    264–14   whom I have not f· for it
    315–10   spiritually f· for teachers,
My.   249–25   individual best f· to perform this

fittest
Mis.   140–30   the f· would survive,
No.   25–13   * "the survival of the f·."
My.   166– 6   but the f· survives ;

fitting
Mis.   307–18   is fast f· all minds for the
    374–17   most f· that Christian Scientists
Pul.   25–16   * vestibule is a f· entrance
My.   45–15   * edifice stands a f· monument of
    58–15   * f· testimonial in stone,
    81–25   * a f· close to a memorable week.
    84–14   * stately cupola is a f· crown
    352–14   * f· testimony of the efficacy of

five
Mis.   13–22   testimony of the f· erring senses,
    28– 4   Perception by the f· personal senses
    65– 1   gathered from the f· personal senses.
    99– 3   saith to the f· material senses,
    100–12   f· personal senses, that grasp neither
    172–18   taken in by the f· personal senses,
    172–25   Science, and the f· personal senses,
    218–13   f· personal senses can take no
    221–26   f· times ten are fifty
    221–26   while ten times f· are not
    351–23   f· senses give to mortals pain,
Man.   26–20   Board of Directors shall consist of f·
    29–14   f· suitable members of this Church
Ret.   25–22   f· physical senses are so many
    36– 5   F· years after taking out my
    44– 8   though I had preached f· years
    56–13   evidences of the f· physical senses ;
    59–20   the f· material senses define
Un.   25– 5   testimony of the f· senses.
    28– 6   f· physical senses do not cognize it.
    28–18   f· senses take no cognizance of Soul,
Pul.   38– 2   * in other parishes for f· years
    62– 9   * not more than f· by eight feet,
Rud.   4–26   f· material senses testify to the
    5–26   Destroy the f· senses as
'00.   1–17   f· grand divisions of the globe ;
'01.   18–15   of the f· personal senses,
    26– 7   f· personal senses can have
Hea.   16–16   about the f· personal senses,
My.   29–28   * half past f· in the morning
    32– 3   * f· minutes of silent communion
    123–23   the "f· loaves — Matt. 14 : 17.
    136–20   in the f· grand divisions
    273–25   the f· personal senses are
    273–29   of the f· personal senses,
    343–26   f· churches under discipline.
    356–14   within the last f· years
    (see also numbers, values)

five-dollar
'00.   10–27   ten f· gold pieces

fix
Man.   26–18   f· the salaries of the Readers.
Ret.   11– 6   Go f· thy restless mind
Po.   60– 2   Go f· thy restless mind

fixed
Mis.   147–19   is guided by a f· Principle,
    232–24   f· Principle of all healing is God ;
    240–18   with form and inclination f·,
    320–17   f· in the heavens of divine Science,
    360–13   f· stars in the heavens of Soul.
    366– 7   with f· Principle, given rule, and
Ret.   87–13   implicit adherence to f· rules,
    93–12   immovably f· in Principle.
No.   11–21   with f· Principle, given rule, and
    33–10   divine Science, with f· Principle,
'01.   23–15   its f· Principle and given rule,
My.   v– 5   * attention . . . is f· on C. S.,
    106–18   rests on the basis of f· Principle,
    113–24   demonstrated on a f· Principle

fixed
My. 122– 5 *f·* in one's own moral make-up.
181–28 *f·* the year 1866 or 1867 for the
319–26 * well *f·* in my memory,
347–27 manifestation of a *f·* Principle

fixtures
My. 68–31 * Bronze is used in the lighting *f·*,

flag
Pul. 83–14 * black *f·* of oppression
Po. 71–20 O war-rent *f·* ! O soldier-shroud !

flagrance
'01. 20–26 its hidden modus and *f·*

flagstones
My. 89–15 * even to the *f·* in front

flame
Mis. 82–27 treacherous glare of its own *f·*
341–27 so that the *f·* never expires.
341–32 to keep aglow the *f·* of devotion
345–13 though the baptism of *f·*.
'02. 5– 9 It is this ethereal *f·*,
Po. 30–13 fan Thou the *f·* Of right with might ;

flames
Mis. 17– 7 before the *f·* have died away
209–23 Evil passions die in their own *f·*,
237– 5 in place of material *f·* and odor,
326– 7 *f·* caught in the dwelling
348–17 quench the growing *f·* of falsehood,
No. 1–16 *f·* die away on the mount of
Hea. 9–14 furnishing fuel for the *f·*.
My. 178–24 snatched this book from the *f·*.
211– 9 break out in devouring *f·*.

flaming
My. 79–16 * fact was heralded in *f·* headlines

flash
My. 296– 2 his *f·* of flight and insight,

flat
Mis. 65– 5 that the earth's surface is *f·*,
325–16 or, *f·* on their backs,
'01. 19–15 a *f·* departure from Jesus' practice

flatly
Mis. 295–20 *f·* contradicted, as both untrue and

flatterer
Mis. 224–31 a *f·*, a fool, or a liar,
363– 7 greatest *f·*, identification,

flattering
My. 122–14 called forth *f·* comment

flattery
'02. 17–28 world's soft *f·* or its frown.

flaunting
Mis. 295–18 *f·* and floundering statements
My. 83– 8 * has been no *f·* of badges
151–18 * aisles by *f·* folly trod,

flavor
Mis. 9–23 enjoyment having lost its *f·*,
29–25 neither *f·* Christianity nor

flavored
Mis. 294–28 *f·* with the true ideas

flax
'02. 18–11 quenched not the smoking *f·*,

flecked
Ret. 4–20 and *f·* with large flocks

flecks
Mis. 376–25 golden *f·* came out on a

fled
Mis. 112–21 his flippancy had *f·*.
324–26 all wasted and the music *f·*.
385–19 see thy ever-self ; Life never *f·* ;
396– 8 It voices beauty *f·*.
Ret. 23–21 Soulless famine had *f·*.
30– 5 borrower would have *f·*.
Pan. 1– 9 frown and smile . . . have *f·* ;
'02. 15–24 when slumber had *f·*,
Po. 9– 8 weeping alone that the vision is *f·*,
41–15 waters had *f·* to the sea,
47–17 Watching the husbandman *f·* ;
48–13 see thy ever-self ; Life never *f·* ;
58–20 It voices beauty *f·*.
65– 7 it *f·* with the light,

fledgling
Po. 18–15 notice the frail *f·* hath.

flee
Mis. 222–32 light and shadows *f·*,
251–29 Sin, sickness, and disease *f·*
284–24 to fear and *f·* before,
342–20 earth's fables *f·*,
No. 7–12 "*f·* as a bird to your — *Psal.* 11 : 1.
Po. 3– 5 length'ning shadows *f·*,
25– 8 Far do ye *f·*,

flee
My. 171– 7 shall *f·* away." — *Isa.* 35 : 10.
189–19 how soon earth's fables *f·*
260– 6 would *f·* before such reality,
350–23 whither shall he *f·* ?

fleecy
Mis. 376–24 *F·*, faint, fairy blue

fleeing
Un. 27–13 *f·* like a shadow at daybreak ;

flees
Mis. 210–31 Charity never *f·* before error,
396– 3 And frightened fancy *f·*,
Po. 58–15 And frightened fancy *f·*,

fleet
Mis. 396–10 O happy hours and *f·*,
Po. 59– 2 O happy hours and *f·*,

fleetest
Po. 65–16 moments most sweet are *f·*

fleeth
Mis. 213–25 *f·* when he seeth the wolf

fleeting
Mis. ix–21 The *f·* freshness of youth,
9–25 to relish this *f·* sense,
110–28 You have learned how *f·* is that which
360–18 blighted flowers of *f·* joys,
Ret. 32–15 * *F·* pleasure, fond delusion,

flesh
according to the
Ret. 1– 1 My ancestors, according to the *f·*,
after the
Mis. 188–14 walk not after the *f·*, — *Rom.* 8 : 1.
360–20 "Israel after the *f·*," — *I Cor.* 10 : 18.
My. 113–12 walk not after the *f·*, — *Rom.* 8 : 1.
205– 3 walk not after the *f·*, — *Rom.* 8 : 1.
and evil
Mis. 2– 8 the world, the *f·*, and evil,
My. 134– 2 the world, the *f·*, and evil,
and Spirit
Mis. 16–32 conflict between the *f·* and Spirit.
188–11 a war between the *f·* and Spirit,
Pul. 20–15 warfare between the *f·* and Spirit,
Pan. 13–16 war between *f·* and Spirit,
My. 18–24 war between *f·* and Spirit,
and the devil
Mis. 163– 2 the world, the *f·*, and the devil.
Un. 52–18 world, the *f·*, and the devil.
My. 268–22 "the world, the *f·* and the devil,"
beliefs of the
Mis. 28–14 not destroy the beliefs of the *f·*,
72– 7 According to the beliefs of the *f·*,
born of the
Ret. 26–22 to one "born of the *f·*," — *John* 3 : 6.
No. 25–22 That which is born of the *f·*
My. 239–26 so-called man born of the *f·*,
261–25 Christ was not born of the *f·*.
brings to the
Mis. 9– 3 purification it brings to the *f·*,
brought to the
Un. 59–11 divine idea brought to the *f·*
cleansed of the
Mis. 153–14 cleansed of the *f·*,
crucifixions of the
Mis. 107– 6 self-denials, and crucifixions of the *f·*.
discipline of the
Mis. 84–23 discipline of the *f·* is designed to
errors of
Mis. 189–11 destroys the errors of *f·*,
fetters of the
Mis. 165– 8 man, without the fetters of the *f·*,
fight with the
'02. 10– 2 has a fight with the *f·*.
fruits of the
'02. 6– 6 fruits of the *f·* not Spirit.
human will or
Mis. 181–32 born not of the human will or *f·*,
incisions of the
Mis. 244– 7 closing the incisions of the *f·*.
in the
Mis. 21– 6 while on earth and in the *f·*,
103–24 Jesus' personality in the *f·*,
162–20 and suffered in the *f·*,
167– 3 manner of a mother in the *f·*,
178–28 In the *f·*, we are as a partition
180– 2 the dream of Spirit in the *f·*
214–21 personal Jesus' labor in the *f·*
292– 7 he gave his life (in the *f·*)
373–16 Christ's appearing in the *f·*,
Un. 55–12 "The way," in the *f·*, — *John* 14 : 6.
56–14 He also suffereth in the *f·*,
57–28 conscious existence in the *f·*
61–21 now live in the *f·* — *Gal.* 2 : 20.
'01. 10–30 fulfilled his mission in the *f·*
My. 143–11 I exist in the *f·*, and am seen daily

flesh

in the
My. 260–31 Neither the you nor the I in the *f·*
346– 9 * she is in the *f·* and in health.
(see also sub-title **manifest in the)**

is heir
Mis. 33–27 * "the ills that *f·* is heir to,"
No. 42–10 * ills that *f·* is heir to."
Hea. 15– 6 all ills that *f·* is heir to.

leaves no
Ret. 94–12 destroying all error, leaves no *f·*,

lust of the
Un. 39– 5 lust of the *f·* and the pride of
My. 205–25 lust of the *f·* and the pride of

lusts of the
Mis. 182–32 lusts of the *f·* and the pride of
Ret. 79–14 "lusts of the *f·*," — *see I John* 2 : 16.
Hea. 17– 2 lusts of the *f·*, the pride of life,

made
Mis. 182–29 When the Word is made *f·*,
184– 6 The Word will be made *f·*
Un. 39– 1 "the Word" is "made *f·*." — *John* 1 : 14.

manifest in the
Mis. 44–20 thought made manifest in the *f·*
78– 4 God is made manifest in the *f·*,
154–21 be made manifest in the *f·*
Chr. 53–61 manifest in the *f·*." — *I Tim.* 3 : 16.
'01. 9–16 God is made manifest in the *f·*,
12–27 and thus is manifest in the *f·*.
My. 109–25 "manifest in the *f·*," — *I Tim.* 3 : 16.
124–28 "manifest in the *f·*," — *I Tim.* 3 : 16.
348– 7 God made manifest in the *f·*,

matter, or the
Mis. 124– 7 by means of matter, or the *f·*,

my
Un. 55–21 in my *f·* shall I see God ;" — *Job.* 19 : 26.
Pul. 3–20 in my *f·* shall I see God." — *Job.* 19 : 26.
My. 218– 5 "In my *f·* shall I see God." — *Job.* 19 : 26.
241–23 * I still lived in my *f·*.
241–23 * I did not live in my *f·*,
241–24 * my *f·* lived or died according to

not of the
Mis. 181–18 of Spirit, and not of the *f·* ;

of the neck
My. 105–15 that had eaten the *f·* of the neck

one
Mis. 94– 7 the twain that are one *f·*,
289–17 twain shall be one *f·*." — *Matt.* 19 : 5.

out of the
Un. 55–12 suffering which leads out of the *f·*.
No. 33–26 show them that the way out of the *f·*,

over the
Mis. 30–18 superiority of Mind over the *f·*,
356–23 This virtue triumphs over the *f·* ;
Pul. 3–28 so far from victory over the *f·*

prevailed
My. 293–20 to mortal sense the *f·* prevailed.

sense of the
Un. 55–14 from the false sense of the *f·*

sin and
00. 8– 1 if sin and *f·* are put off,

sins of the
Mis. 162–21 to escape from the sins of the *f·*.
My. 6– 8 with the sins of the *f·*,

somebody in the
Mis. 111–30 belief . . . that somebody in the *f·*

Spirit and
Mis. 85–21 Spirit and *f·* antagonize.

spirit and the
My. 293–20 the spirit and the *f·* — struggled,

strives
Mis. 119–15 for the *f·* strives against Spirit,

suffering of the
Mis. 200–23 pain, and all suffering of the *f·*,

sufferings of the
Un. 3–12 through the sufferings of the *f·*
55–18 sufferings of the *f·* are unreal.
'01. 11–10 the sins and sufferings of the *f·*,

temptations of the
Mis. 104– 4 to the temptations of the *f·*,

thorn in the
Mis. 71– 6 Paul had a thorn in the *f·* :
Un. 57–21 "a thorn in the *f·*" — *II Cor.* 12 : 7.

through the
Mis. 201–32 it illustrates through the *f·*
Ret. 22–19 nor is he ever created through the *f·* ;
Rud. 3– 7 through the *f·*, from the flesh,

to Spirit
Un. 56–24 change from *f·* to Spirit,

unknown to the
My. 167– 3 is unknown to the *f·*,

vale of the
Mis. 328–10 surveys the vale of the *f·*,

veil of the
Mis. 165–12 rends the veil of the *f·*

flesh

was weak
Mis. 385–23 the *f·* was weak, and doomed
Po. 48–18 the *f·* was weak, and doomed

weakness of
Mis. 64– 1 Jesus assumed . . . weakness of *f·*,

will of the
Mis. 180–23 *nor of the will of the f·,* — *John* 1 : 13.
181–16 of the will of the *f·,* — *John* 1 : 13.
182–15 nor of the will of the *f·.*" — *John* 1 : 13.

Mis. 96–32 not of the *f·*, but of the Spirit.
97– 1 to destroy the power of the *f·* ;
125– 8 overcome the world, the *f·*, and
153–19 the fruits of Spirit, not *f·* ;
326– 9 but the *f·* at length did feel them ;
Ret. 57–10 it is the *f·* that is evil.
Un. 36–13 the *f·* at war with Spirit ;
46– 4 from Spirit, not from *f·*.
Rud. 3– 7 the *f·*, — the material world and evil.
Po. 29–13 Beloved, replete, by *f·* embound
My. 108– 9 *f·* profiteth nothing." — *John* 6 : 63.
119– 9 Man is free from the *f·*
260– 6 the *f·* would flee before such

fleshly
Mis. 86– 2 these have no *f·* nature.
345–32 from the thought of *f·* sacrifice,
Ret. 73– 6 as the *f·* nature disappears
94–14 When all *f·* belief is annihilated,
Un. 46–11 subordinate the *f·* perceptions
62–19 The *f·* Jesus seemed to die,
Rud. 9–20 envy, lust, and all *f·* vices.

Fletcher, Hon. Richard
Ret. 6–21 Hon. Richard *F·* of Boston.

flew
My. 52–32 * "Day after day *f·* by,

flexible
Pul. 31–28 * tall, slender, and as *f·* in movement

flies
Mis. 145–15 hawk which *f·* in darkness.
Pul. 48–15 * Straight as the crow *f·*,

flight
Mis. 120–29 puts to *f·* every doubt as to the
267–21 rarefied atmospheres and upward *f·*.
331–20 guards the nestling's faltering *f·* !
354–27 strength for a *f·* well begun,
356– 2 blessings when they take their *f·*,
389– 8 guards the nestling's faltering *f·* !
Ret. 11– 5 If fancy plumes aerial *f·*,
'02. 17–27 will put to *f·* all care for the
Po. 4– 6 guards the nestling's faltering *f·* !
60– 1 If fancy plumes aerial *f·*,
My. 186– 7 preen their thoughts for upward *f·*.
248–20 No fetishism . . . can fetter your *f·*.
206– 3 his flash of *f·* and insight,

fling
Mis. xi–20 no battledores to *f·* it back and forth.
54–13 malice would *f·* in her path.
I'o. 10 1 *f·* thy banner To the billows and
18– 4 majestic, and feathersome *f·*
My. 337– 3 *f·* thy banner To the billows

flings
Mis. 281– 3 this animal element *f·* open

flippancy
Mis. 112–20 his *f·* had fled.

flippant
Mis. 240– 7 by that *f·* caution,

flit
Po. 2–16 On wings of morning gladly *f·*

flitting
Mis. 71–29 *f·* across the dial of time.
Po. 16–12 The tired wings *f·* through

float
Mis. 145–28 earth will *f·* majestically
Po. 66– 5 *f·* in memory's dream.

floated
Ret. 73–10 *f·* into more spiritual latitudes
Po. 8–17 rainbows of rapture *f·* by !

floating
Mis. 228–24 *F·* with the popular current
230–19 *f·* off on the wings of sense :
Ret. 16– 2 *f·* up from the pews,

flock
Mis. 9– 6 passes all His *f·* under His rod
32–22 in which to give to my own *f·*
146–23 to walk in the footsteps of His *f·*.
150– 1 "Fear not, little *f·* ; — *Luke* 12 : 32.
154– 6 God's love for His *f·* is manifest
303– 6 and tends his own *f·*.
321–17 "Fear not, little *f·* ; — *Luke* 12 : 32.

flock

Mis. 322–14 Shepherd that feedeth my *f·*,
     399–27 and understood By His *f·*.
Ret. 90– 5 salary for tending the home *f·*
Pul.   9–20 giving this *f·* "drink — *Psal.* 36 : 8.
      16–12 and understood By His *f·*.
Rud. 17–17 and the footsteps of His *f·*.
Po.   76–11 and understood By His *f·*.
My. 148–21 of this dear little *f·*,
     162–25 loving Shepherd of this feeble *f·*
     167–18 good will for yourselves, your *f·*,
     177–20 this church as a fatling of the *f·*.
     247–24 Do you come to your little *f·*

flocking

My.   73–13 * *f·* from all over the world

flocks

Mis. 371– 3 large *f·* of metaphysicians are
Ret.   4–20 flecked with large *f·* and herds,
Pan.   3–28 guardian of *f·* and herds.
My. 125– 8 You come from feeding your *f·*,
     186–19 make this church the fold of *f·*,
     243–18 caring for their own *f·*.
     262– 8 *f·* and herds of a Jewish village.

flood

Mis. 203–22 Tears *f·* the eyes,
     339–27 will some time *f·* thy memory,
Pul. 14– 9 water as a *f·*, — *Rev.* 12 : 15.
      14–12 carried away of the *f·*. — *Rev.* 12 : 15.
      14–12 swallowed up the *f·* — *Rev.* 12 : 16.
      14–19 a new *f·* to drown the Christ-idea?
      39–16 * its *f·* of golden light.
No.   20–24 ever since the *f·*,
My. 106–20 in tempest and in *f·*,

flooded

'00. 11–22 * It *f·* the crimson twilight

flood-gates

Mis. 185–11 opens the very *f·* of heaven ;
'01. 32–29 through the *f·* of Love ;

flooding

Ret. 16– 5 tears of joy *f·* her eyes
      47– 5 Students . . . were *f·* the school.
No.   2–27 *f·* our land with conflicting theories

floods

Mis. 257–23 *F·* swallow up homes and
Pul.   7–17 in *f·* of forgiveness,
No.   1– 8 fill the rivers till they rise in *f·*,
'02.   5– 8 *f·* the world with the baptism of
My.   33–31 established it upon the *f·*. — *Psal.* 24 : 2.

floor

Mis. 231–22 soft as thistle-down, on the *f·* ;
     325–17 lie stretched on the *f·*,
     391– 4 For things above the *f·*,
Un.   44–21 [when you, lie, get the *f·*],
Pul. 25–22 * *f·* is in white Italian mosaic,
      26–23 * mosaic marble *f·* of white has a
      76– 8 * The *f·* is of mosaic
Po.   38– 3 For things above the *f·*,
My.   71–23 * people on *f·* and galleries,
      71–25 * either on *f·* or galleries,

flooring

Pul.   2– 7 from its mosaic *f·* to the

floors

Pul. 25– 6 * *f·* of marble in mosaic
      58–18 * The *f·* are all mosaic,
My.   68–27 * The *f·* of the first story

Flora

Ret. 17–13 *F·* has stolen the rainbow
Po.   62–16 *F·* has stolen the rainbow

floral

Mis. 179–24 These flowers are *f·* apostles.
     275–29 The *f·* offerings sent to my
Ret. 23–11 indicated by no *f·* dial.
'00.   8– 7 in the *f·* kingdom odors emit
Po.   25–10 Fair *f·* apostles of love,
My. 153– 3 send these *f·* offerings in my name

florist

My. 152–32 flowers that my skilful *f·*

floundering

Mis. 295–18 flaunting and *f·* statements

flourish

Ret.   4–22 scrub-oak, poplar, and fern *f·*.
My.   95– 2 * cults which *f·* for a time
     104– 5 institutions *f·* under the name of
     139– 9 that *f·* when trampled upon.

flourished

'00. 12– 9 *f·* as an emporium

flourishes

My. 112– 3 false philosophy *f·* for a time
     265– 7 signifies . . . that evil *f·* less,

flourishing

Ret. 48–10 moved me to close my *f·* school,

flow

Mis. 127–16 then will *f·* into it the
     149– 5 this feast and *f·* of Soul.
     160– 8 Thus may our lives *f·* on
     212–19 happiness, and life *f·* not into
     223– 7 impure streams *f·* from corrupt
     290–20 my affections involuntarily *f·* out
     329–17 rippling all nature in ceaseless *f·*,
     384–21 * But knows no ebb and *f·*.
     387–23 Whence joys supernal *f·*,
Ret. 11–13 from this fount the streamlets *f·*,
      18– 7 lap of the pear-tree, with musical *f·*.
Pul.   3–22 and *f·* into everlasting Life.
       7–12 O ye tears ! Not in vain did ye *f·*.
      39–17 * as in a dream, I watch the *f·*
      39–20 * Repeats its glory in the river's *f·* ;
      41– 4 * which continued to *f·* in
'00.   9–20 in the ebb and *f·* of thought
'01. 19–26 *f·* through no such channels.
Po.   6–18 Whence joys supernal *f·*,
       8–12 O'er the silv'ry moon and ocean *f·* ;
      35– 9 will never dry or cease to *f·* ;
      36–20 * But knows no ebb and *f·*.
      60–10 from this fount the streamlets *f·*,
      63–16 with musical *f·*.
My.   18–13 then will *f·* into it the
     266–15 This flux and *f·* in one direction,

flowed

Mis. 213– 4 *f·* through cross-bearing,
     222–31 Truth had *f·* into my consciousness
Pul. 44–25 * money has *f·* in from all parts
Po.   41–21 strain of enchantment that *f·*

Flower (see also Flower's)

Mr. B. O.

My. 316–15 scholarly editor, Mr. B. O. *F·*,

flower

Mis. 179–25 He made every *f·* in Mind
     394– 3 like the dew on the *f·*,
'00.   8– 8 characteristics of tree and *f·*,
Hea.   6–17 whether that ideal is a *f·* or a
Po.   3– 3 I miss thee as the *f·* the dew !
      22–12 'Tis writ on earth, on leaf and *f·* :
      45– 4 like the dew on the *f·*,
My. 216–25 The Mother Church *f·* fund.

flowering

Pul. 48– 3 * dotted with beds of *f·* shrubs,

Flower's, Mr.

My. 316–22 under Mr. *F·* able guardianship

flowers

Mis. 179–24 These *f·* are floral apostles.
     227–18 fresh *f·* of feeling blossom,
     276– 1 large book of rare *f·*,
     280–21 hand-painted *f·* on each page,
     294–15 the *f·* of human hearts
     360–18 blighted *f·* of fleeting joys,
     390–10 The fairy-peopled world of *f·*,
     394–15 * "The *f·* of June
     394–17 * The *f·* of June
     394–21 * The *f·* of June."
Ret.   4–20 beautiful wild *f·*,
      17–14 sprinkle the *f·* with exquisite dye.
      18–22 *f·* of feeling are fragrant
Pul.   8–26 and painted the finest *f·*
      42–19 * rich with the adornment of *f·*.
Peo. 14– 3 with *f·* laid upon the bier,
Po.   15–18 *F·* fresh as the pang in the bosom
     page 25 poem
      25–14 *F·* for the brave
      25–17 *F·* for the kind
      53–20 The vernal songs and *f·*.
      55–11 fairy-peopled world of *f·*,
      57– 1 * The *f·* of June
      57– 3 * The *f·* of June
      57– 7 * The *f·* of June.
      62–17 sprinkle the *f·* with exquisite dye.
      64–16 *f·* of feeling are fragrant
      67– 8 bedewing these fresh-smiling *f·* !
      67–21 *f·* of feeling may blossom above,
My. 152–32 *f·* that my skilful florist has
     153–12 my *f·* visited his bedside :
     153–13 *f·* were imbued and associated with
     153–30 *f·* should be to us His apostles,
     154– 7 I shall scarcely venture to send *f·*
     154– 9 Send *f·* and all things fair
     154–11 it is not he who gives the *f·*
     155–30 which she sends . . . in the *f·*
     217– 1 money that you expend for *f·*.
     259– 4 and on either side lace and *f·*.

floweth

Mis. 82– 5 this peace *f·* as a river

flowing

Mis. 19–16 steadfastly *f·* on to God,
165–27 blessings *f·* from the teaching,
355– 8 chronic recovery ebbing and *f·*,

flows

Mis. 185–12 *f·* into every avenue of being,
316–11 tide which *f·* heavenward,
Ret. 18– 9 songlet and streamlet that *f·*
Pul. 39– 6 * God's greatness *f* around our
Po. 63–19 songlet and streamlet that *f·*

flung

Mis. 332– 8 doors that closed . . . are open *f·*.
My. 147– 7 *f·* its foliage in kindly shelter

flush

Mis. 225–26 deep *f·* faded from the face,

Flushing, L. I.

My. 363– 9 C. S. SOCIETY, F·, L. I.,

flute

Mis. 390– 7 The eve-bird's forest *f·*
Po. 55– 8 The eve-bird's forest *f·*

flutterings

Mis. 85–18 *f·* of mortals Christward

flutters

Mis. 267–19 right wing *f·* to soar,
My. 268–20 This time-world *f·* in my thought

flux

Mis. 206– 3 from *f·* to permanence,
My. 266–15 *f·* and flow in one direction,
301– 5 present *f·* in religious faith

fly

Hea. 6– 6 *f·* too high or too low.
My. 192–26 My love can *f·* on wings of joy

flying

Mis. 176–17 not as the *f·* nor as
My. 110–16 dreams of *f·* in airy space,

fly-leaf

My. 60–18 * this inscription on the *f·*

foam

Mis. 385–12 moored at last Beyond rough *f·*.
Po. 48– 5 moored at last Beyond rough *f·*.
73–10 list the moan Of the billows' *f·*,

foaming

Mis. 162–10 over their fretted, *f·* billows.
My. 316–20 *f·* torrents of ignorance, envy, and

foams

'01. 9–19 *f·* at the touch of good ;
'02. 19–19 life's troubled sea *f·* itself away,

focal

Mis. 79–14 *f·* distance of infinity.
Un. 20–22 outside of His own *f·* distance.
No. 17–18 *f·* radiation of the infinite.

focusing

My. 164–11 a thing *f·* light

foe

Mis. 32–15 towards friend and *f·*.
99–17 take the front rank, face the *f·*,
114–17 resist the *f·* within and without.
206–12 idleness is the *f·* of progress.
290–26 whether it be friend or *f·*,
Ret. 31–17 unseen sin, the unknown *f·*,
Pul. 2–19 single-handed to combat the *f·* ?
15–11 telling mankind of the *f·* in ambush
15–12 informer one who sees the *f·* ?
No. 3– 5 error murders either friend or *f·*
Pan. 15– 1 which fed her starving *f·*,
Po. 33–10 kindly pass over a wound, or a *f·*
My. 213– 9 lurking *f·* to human weal,
213–24 through every attack of your *f·*,
248–26 face the *f·* with loving look

foes

Mis. 118–22 envy, revenge, are *f·* to grace,
126–25 race to run, and *f·* in ambush ;
214– 9 a man's *f·* shall be— *Matt.* 10 : 36.
No. 36–24 conquered the malice of his *f·*,
'02. 2–26 why not . . . part fair *f·*.
19–10 the malice of his *f·*.
Po. 79–12 False fears are *f·*
My. 98– 6 * anything that its *f·* try to prove

fog

'00. 6–17 proves that the so-called *f·*

fogs

Mis. 374–11 Above the *f·* of sense

foibles

Mis. 285–10 too short for *f·* or failures.
Ret. 30–15 *f·* and fables of finite mind

fold

Mis. 9– 7 under His rod into His *f·* ;
146–22 that desired to come, into its *f·*

fold

Mis. 244–25 which are not of this *f·*."— *John* 10 : 16.
270–19 one *f·*, and one shepherd ;"— *John* 10 : 16.
303– 5 kindly shepherd has his own *f·*
310–28 all persons who have left our *f·*,
357– 6 having strayed from the true *f·*,
357–28 that have sought the true *f·*
370–26 the true *f·* for Christian healers,
388–22 To *f·* an angel's wings below ;
398–15 Lead Thy lambkins to the *f·*
Chr. 55–25 one *f·*, and one shepherd.— *John* 10 : 16.
Ret. 46–21 Lead Thy lambkins to the *f·*,
80–23 older sheep pass into the *f·*
90– 6 while he is serving another *f·* ?
Pul. 17–20 Lead Thy lambkins to the *f·*,
65– 5 * Anglican *f·* to unity with Rome,
Po. 14–19 Lead Thy lambkins to the *f·*,
21–11 *f·* an angel's wings below ;
34– 7 and *f·* thy plumes?
41– 3 Was that *f·* for the lambkin
My. 186–19 God make this church the *f·*
248–18 can *f·* or falter your wings.

folds

Mis. 145–32 that my heart *f·* within it,
151– 1 *f·* the sheep of His pasture ;
Ret. 52–11 provide *f·* for the sheep
Un. 7– 5 of other religious *f·*

foliage

Po. 15– 1 zephyrs through *f·* and vine !
My. 147– 7 flung its *f·* in kindly shelter
182–27 amid the fair *f·* of this vine

folk

Pul. 52– 5 * our practical Christian *f·*
My. 58– 1 * our practical Christian *f·*
148– 6 May the good *f·* of Concord
175–11 say to the good *f·* of Concord
313–24 * "the superstitious country *f·*

folks

Mis. 117–20 *modus operandi*, of other *f·*,
238– 2 * 'niggers' kill the white *f·* !"
353–18 Some people try to tend *f·*,

follow

Mis. 28–31 "These signs shall *f·* — *Mark* 16 : 17.
33–18 *f·* the directions given.
40–18 reason that the same results *f·* not
45– 9 fatal results that frequently *f·* the
89– 7 *f· the doctor's directions?*
90–30 left their nets to *f·* him,
105–19 I must ever *f·* this line
117–30 or make them too late to *f·* Him.
117–31 *f·* under every circumstance.
127–18 great growth in C. S. will *f·*,
136– 7 with the hope that you will *f·*.
147–15 to *f·* the road of duty,
151– 3 and they *f·* me ;— *John* 10 : 27.
169–30 *f·* thou me,"— see *Matt.* 8 : 22.
170– 3 If we *f·* him, to us there can be no
192–29 these signs shall *f·* — *Mark* 16 : 17.
103–24 *f·* the commands of our Lord
195– 2 Thence will *f·* the absorption
213–22 and they *f·* me :— *John* 10 : 27.
215–30 If you would *f·* in his footsteps,
219–30 the fruits of goodness will *f·*,
226–16 * And it must *f·*, as the night the day,
235–27 tried to *f·* the divine precept,
236–13 must *f·* God in all your ways."
237–25 but it is sure to *f·*."
265–10 all *who f· the Principle and rule*
270–22 and yet *f·* him in healing.
311– 8 so, should we *f·* Christ's teachings ;
321– 1 The wise men *f·* this guiding star ;
327– 3 hoping that I might *f·* thee
327– 9 hast chosen the good part ; *f·* me."
332–10 autumn *f·* with hues of heaven,
340–29 They *f·* faithfully ;
347–18 I *f·* his counsel,
359– 1 *f·* the example of the *Alma Mater.*
398– 3 I will *f·* and rejoice
Man. 60–19 "*F·* thou me," — *John* 21 : 22.
Ret. 6– 4 * can hardly fail to induce them to *f·*
16–15 *f·* them that believe."— *Mark* 16 : 17.
42– 6 He forsook all to *f·* in this line
46– 9 I will *f·* and rejoice
49– 6 *f·* the example of the *Alma Mater*
55– 3 Let us *f·* the example of Jesus,
65–13 if they would *f·* Christ,
81–25 * And it must *f·*, as the night the day,
87– 1 Master said, "*F·* me ;— *Matt.* 8 : 22.
87–17 they must *f·* the divine order
90–27 * to *f·*, as nearly as we can,
Un. 17–23 Would it not absurdly *f·* that
42– 1 must *f·* that death can be nowhere ;
Pul. 17– 8 I will *f·* and rejoice
'00. 8–28 a desire to *f·* your own

follow

'01.	8–22	if we *f·* the teachings of the
	23– 8	thence it would *f·* that evil
	24–25	necessary to *f·* Jesus' teachings,
	28–19	only apology for trying to *f·* it is
	34–25	*f·* your Leader only so far as she
'02.	3–26	It does not *f·* that power must
	4– 3	*F·* your Leader, only so far as she
	9– 5	Jesus commanded, "*F·* me ; — *Matt.* 8 : 22.
	16–12	"*F·* peace with all men, — *Heb.* 12 : 14.
	18–26	showing their unfitness to *f·* him,
Hea.	1– 1	*And these signs shall f·* — *Mark* 16 : 17.
	6–26	"And these signs shall *f·* — *Mark* 16 : 17.
	19–26	and "these signs shall *f·* — *Mark* 16 : 17.
Peo.	10–24	*f·* the mind's freedom from sin ;
Po.	14– 7	I will *f·* and rejoice
My.	4–10	We *f·* Truth only as we
	4–10	*f·* truly, meekly, patiently,
	9–16	* that we may worthily *f·* with you
	18–15	great growth in C. S. will *f·*,
	19–19	our shadows *f·* us in the sunlight
	23– 7	* so long as we *f·* His commands.
	47–29	* And these signs shall *f·* — *Mark* 16 : 17.
	58–21	* inspire us to *f·* her in preaching,
	122– 1	If one would *f·* the advice
	125–15	their works will *f·* them.
	134–10	Defeat need not *f·* victory.
	196–17	should *f·* his steps :— *I Pet.* 2: 21.
	201–23	I will *f·* and rejoice
	233–21	dishonesty, sin, *f·* in its train.
	241–18	* question and Mrs. Eddy's reply *f·*.
	245–27	degrees that *f·* the names of
	250–18	nor compels the branch churches to *f·*
	278–17	*F·* that which is good.
	296–13	and his works do *f·* him.
	297– 6	which may *f·* said description
	361– 1	*F·* the directions of God

followed

Mis.	11–11	*f·* them with precept upon precept ;
	73–23	*ye which have f· me,* — *Matt.* 19 : 28.
	91–29	supposed that students had *f·* my
	245–23	loved the Church and *f·* it,
	340–13	*f·* agriculture instead of
	373–25	is *f·* by Jesus' declaration,
Ret.	14–14	Distinctly do I recall what *f·*.
	44–27	This measure was immediately *f·* by
	45–16	*f·* that noble, unprecedented action
Pul.	43–19	* *f·* by the recitation of the
	59– 9	* program was for some reason not *f·*,
'01.	28–15	*f·* exclusively Christ's teaching,
Peo.	10–11	if the sister States had *f·*
My.	17–24	* *f·* by a few moments of
	32–17	* Silent prayer, *f·* by the
	39–11	* Then *f·* a short silent prayer
	45–18	* *f·* unswervingly the guidance
	45–26	* logically *f·* the preceding one.
	76– 2	* would be *f·* with this new
	78–19	* *f·* by the audible repetition
	91–22	* few thousand persons who *f·*
	312–26	*f·* the remains of my beloved one
	343–19	I *f·* it up, teaching and

follower

Mis.	152–20	worshipper in truth, the *f·* of
Un.	56–13	every *f·* of Christ shares
Pul.	73– 5	* ardent *f·* after God.
My.	42– 5	* a faithful *f·* of this Leader
	62–14	* Your sincere *f·*,
	113– 8	St. Paul was a *f·* but not
	330– 4	* noteworthy *f·* of our Lord
	357–30	I know that every true *f·*

followers

Christ's
Mis.	273–15	grand family of Christ's *f·*.

conscientious
Pul.	51– 5	* a number of conscientious *f·*

devoted
Pul.	63–18	* among her devoted *f·*.
My.	272–23	* Mrs. Eddy's own devoted *f·*,

devout
Ret.	54–20	The faith-cure has devout *f·*,

friends and
Pul.	54–25	* closest friends and *f·*,
My.	143–10	my beloved friends and *f·*

her
Pul.	32–13	* was dominating her *f·*
	43–27	* discourage among her *f·*
	71–22	* her *f·* and cobelievers
My.	64–16	* has been teaching her *f·*
	64–20	* Fearlessly does she warn all her *f·*

His
Mis.	179–25	God does all this through His *f·* ;
My.	204– 2	My faith in God and in His *f·*
	204– 3	He gives His *f·* opportunity to

followers

his
Mis.	24–29	declared that his *f·* should
	165–19	makes his *f·* the heirs to his example ;
	197–10	way which Jesus . . . bade his *f·*
	211–29	and he said to his *f·*,
Ret.	88– 5	command, was that his *f·* should
'00.	8–14	Our Master saith to his *f·* :
'01.	2–21	his *f·* of to-day will prove,
	9–15	taught his *f·* to do likewise.
	18–23	his *f·* in the early centuries,
'02.	11–20	then gave it to his *f·* to drink.
My.	28–21	* mark the lives of his *f·*.
	106–31	commanded his *f·* to do likewise.
	109–10	Christ taught his *f·* to heal
	111–22	unwittingly misguide his *f·*?
	221–21	and instructed his *f·*, saying,
	222–17	demands on the faith of his *f·*,
	330– 6	* he prophesied that his *f·* would be

hundred thousand
Pul.	70– 5	* OVER ONE HUNDRED THOUSAND *F·*

its
My.	10– 5	* achievements of its *f·*.
	37–18	* its *f·* have been prospered,
	84–21	* optimism and energy of its *f·*
	89–31	* that its *f·* should number
	107– 4	its *f·* at the beginning of

many
Pul.	49– 3	* speaking of her many *f·*

Mrs. Eddy's
'01.	27– 5	* have been by Mrs. Eddy's *f·*.

of the Master
My.	112– 4	*f·* of the Master in the early

of this creed
My.	85–15	* enthusiasm of the *f·* of this creed

true
Mis.	278–32	on the part of true *f·*,
Ret.	35–16	his true *f·* in every period,
My.	204– 9	unites its true *f·* in one Principle,
	213–21	into harmony with His true *f·*.

unfaithful
'02.	19– 4	to console his unfaithful *f·*

will gain
Pul.	50–27	* will gain *f·* and live down any

your
My.	60– 2	* solicited by many of your *f·*
	157– 7	* church edifice for your *f·*
	321– 2	* building this church for your *f·*.

Pul.	57–26	* *f·* of Rev. Mary Baker Glover Eddy,
'01.	23–20	taught his disciples and *f·*
My.	11– 2	* as yet but imperfect *f·* of the
	100–10	* of the *f·* of the cult.
	271–18	* *f·* of the thought that has

followeth

My.	4– 8	*f·* after me, — *Matt.* 10 : 38.
	233–24	*f·* after me, — *Matt.* 10 : 38.

following (noun)

Mis.	357–21	irrespective of self, rank, or *f·*.
Pul.	32–11	* her large and enthusiastic *f·*
	63– 5	* SHE HAS AN IMMENSE *F·*
Pan.	6–13	obtaining . . . a large *f·*,
'00.	1–16	C. S. already has a hearing and *f·* in
My.	90–29	* sources of her power and *f·*
	92–16	* since 1890 its *f·* had increased
	93–30	* had but an insignificant *f·*.
	117– 5	right or the wrong of this *f·*.
	272–27	* her very great *f·*.
	358– 2	true *f·* of their Leader ;

following (adj.)

Mis.	33–23	Healing by C. S. has the *f·* advantages:
	35– 9	*f·* words of her husband,
	48–31	to make capital out of the *f·*
	61–12	* In the . . . *Journal* I read the *f·* :
	88–15	His allusion to C. S. in the *f·*
	111–28	to the *f·* false beliefs
	133– 9	consideration to the *f·* Scripture,
	178–26	* came forward, and added the *f·* :
	216–23	illustrate the author's *f·* point?
	248–28	with the *f·* exception :
	255–20	I claim for . . . C. S. the *f·*
	271–25	in the *Boston Traveler* the *f·* :
	271–28	* the *f·* history and statistics
	272–12	* with the *f·* important restrictions :
	282–19	the *f·* is an exception to
	297–16	the *f·* statute in the *morale* of
	299– 7	*f·* mistake, which demands
	299– 9	simply answer the *f·* question
	303–22	giving place . . . to the *f·* notice.
	304–22	* The *f·* is the proposed use of
	318–12	*f·* is an amendment of the
	349–22	to a question on the *f·* subject,
	372–16	came such replies as the *f·* :
	373– 7	*f·* from Rotherham's translation

following (adj.)
Mis. 375– 8   The f· is an extract from a letter
    376– 4   * most authentic in the f· sense :
Man. 76– 5   The f· indicates the proper management
    78–24   reported, on the first of the f· month,
Ret. 5–17   The f· is a brief extract from
    11– 2   f· is one of my girlhood
    20–14   The f· lines are taken from
    34–10   I claim for . . . the f· advantages :
    37–24   seen in the f· circumstances.
    48–11   the f· resolutions were passed :
    48–13   the f· are some of the resolutions
    56– 1   The f· ideas of Deity,
Pul. 12– 1   f· selections from "S. and H.
    24–12   * the f· inscription carved in
    38– 1   * charter obtained the f· June.
    39– 9   on the f· page a little poem
    45– 8   * Read the f·, from a
    75–20   * and for the day or two f·,
    78– 6   * upon its face the f· inscription,
    86–13   * f· address from the Board of Directors :
No. 43–12   The f· extract from a letter
'01. 15–21   to hear the f· thunderbolt of
'02. 15–25   The f· day I showed it to my
Hea. 20– 1   f· hymn was sung at the close :
My. v–13   * the f· historical facts :
    7–14   * offered the f· motion :
    13– 9   attention was arrested by the f· :
    17–27   * f· extracts from Mrs. Eddy's
    18–29   It contained the f· articles :
    25– 9   * The f· figures are taken from
    31– 2   * succeeded by the f· hymns
    34–14   * f· citations from the Bible
    39–13   * f· list of officers for
    44–16   * read the f· despatch,
    48–14   * f· splendid appreciation of her
    51– 4   * f· resolutions were passed :
    54– 5   * Boston Traveler contained the f·
    56–13   * in each of the f· named places :
    136–13   f· members constitute the Board
    137– 2   * f· affidavit, in the form of
    140–16   * The f· is Mrs. Eddy's letter :
    141–25   hence the f· :
    150– 5   Pliny gives the f· description of
    172–23   * opened the f· day in Boston
    213–28   The f· three quotations from
    217–18   was the f· question :
    219–28   my opinion . . . in the f· words :
    232–12   Master left to us the f· sayings
    251– 5   I reply to the f· question from
    254–18   * f· extract from your article
    259– 6   received the f· cabled message :
    274–18   * has sent the f· to the Herald :
    311– 1   I will relate the f· incident,
    314– 4   * During the f· nine years
    314–18   who know the f· facts :
    314–31   f· affidavit by R. D. Rounsevel
    319–12   * f· letters from students
    320– 1   * publish the f· interesting letter
    326–13   f· deeply interesting letter from
    328– 7   * The f· article, copied from
    329–25   * to give your readers the f·
    333–31   * we copy the f· :
    334–26   * f· extract from an editorial
    338– 6   * f· views of the Rev. Mary Baker Eddy
    346–25   * the f· to the Associated Press,
    (see also letter, signs, statement)

following (ppr.)
Mis. 133–18   f· the dictum of Jesus ;
    170– 2   for by f· Christ truly,
    193–25   is f· his full command
    194–21   in f· him, you understand God
    245–24   thinking that it was f· Christ ;
    315– 5   on the Sunday f· Communion Day.
Man. 56–12   Monday f· the first Sunday in June.
Ret. 45–20   in f· Jesus' command,
    86–18   taking up his cross and f· Truth.
Un. 5–11   by f· upward individual convictions,
Pul. 26– 9   * seats f· the sweep of its curve,
No. 34– 5   truer sense of f· Christ in spirit,
'00. 14–15   f· the more perfect way,
'01. 14–21   from fearing it, f· it, or
    28–18   no cause for not f· it ;
My. 4– 9   how many are f· the Way-shower?
    28–19   * and f· her example,
    32–11   * F· the organ voluntary
    45–21   * results of such f· have been
    128–20   f· the command of the Master,
    303– 9   f· the divine Principle

follows
Mis. 21–16   My first plank . . . is as f· :
    88–17   f· like a benediction
    95– 4   * as will be seen by what f·,
    101–26   it f· that all must be good ;
    123–30   it f· that those who worship Him,

follows
Mis. 168–24   * The C. S. Journal reported as f· :
    177–27   * introduced Mr. Easton as f· :
    220–29   it f· that he will believe that he
    245– 3   his words, and the prophet's, as f· :
    269–22   The conclusion f· that the
    301–23   My reasons are as f· :
    328–22   who f· the Way-shower,
Man. 75–14   said Church to be as f· :
Ret. 7– 6   wrote of my brother as f· :
    65–18   f· the example of our Lord
    68–18   transference of thought, as f· :
Un. 2–11   Then f· this, as the finale in
    13–19   f· that He knows something which
Pul. 14– 7   for one extreme f· another.
    38– 9   * chapters, whose titles are as f· :
Rud. 8–12   it f· thou wilt be strong in God,
No. 5– 8   f· that to declare error real would
    22–20   it f· that there is more than one
    35–27   it f· that the human kingdom is
Pan. 8– 2   f· that the disarrangement of matter
'01. 14–17   then it f· that it is untrue :
    34–25   only so far as she f· Christ.
'02. 4– 4   only so far as she f· Christ.
Po. vi–11   * A note from the author, . . . read as f· :
My. 15– 4   * been amended to read as f· :
    16–22   * order of the services, . . . was as f· :
    19–15   * Mrs. Eddy wrote as f· :
    32–12   * order of service was as f· :
    39– 5   * Bible and S. and H. as f· :
    44–20   * The despatch was as f· :
    52–21   * wrote as f· : "Whatever is to be
    141–14   * The announcement . . . as f· :
    146– 9   statement in my letter . . . as f·,
    160– 3   and f· Truth fearlessly.
    172– 9   * Mrs. Eddy spoke as f·
    224– 7   blessing which f· obedience
    224– 8   bane which f· disobedience.
    311–19   The facts are as . . . f· :
    313– 2   Correctly quoted, it is as f·,
    327–21   * was changed as f·,
    327–25   * was changed to read as f· :
    328–17   * in the Kinston Free Press as f· :
    359–26   * wrote to Mrs. Stetson as f· :

folly
Mis. 223–30   is superlative f·.
    327–24   showing them their f·,
    347– 2   according to his f·, — Prov. 26 : 4.
    348–15   according to his f·, — Prov. 26 : 5.
    353–23   f· of tending it is no mere jest.
'01. 11–27   according to his f·, — Prov. 26 : 4.
    25–16   ends in some specious f·.
Po. 33– 8   vanity, f·, and all that is wrong
My. 106– 8   simply to show the f· of
    106–11   f· of the cognate declaration that
    151–18   * aisles by flaunting f· trod,
    283–30   choice of f· never fastens on

fond
Ret. 2–27   I was f· of listening,
    7–10   * He was f· of investigating
    32–15   * Fleeting pleasure, f· delusion,
'00. 11– 6   f· of material music,
My. 124–10   "What a f· fool is hope"?
    158– 9   in attune with faith's f· trust.
    274–22   I am not f· of an abundance of
    332–12   * in the f· embrace of her friends.

Fondateur
My. 283– 2   chapter sub-title
    283– 7   Your appointment of me as F·

fondest
'02. 17–26   thy aims, motives, f· purposes,

fondling
Po. 43– 8   F· e'en the lion furious,

fondness
Un. 2– 9   takes away man's f· for sin

font
Mis. 206–31   baptismal f· of eternal Love.

food
Mis. 7– 2   not be allowed to eat certain f·,
    369–24   wholesome but unattractive f·.
Pul. 33–16   * offer f· for meditation.
Rud. 12–22   with the chemistry of f·?
Hea. 5– 5   certain kinds of f·
Po. 28–16   Give us this day our daily f·
My. 154–20   * "If the poor . . . toil that we have f·,
    247–18   sought their f· of me.
    247–25   so filled with divine f·

fool
Mis. 30–24   f· hath said in his heart, — Psal. 14 : 1.
    112–30   f· hath said in his heart, — Psal. 14 : 1.
    212– 2   is a f· that saith in his heart,
    224–31   a flatterer, a f·, or a liar,
    347– 1   "Answer not a f· — Prov. 26 : 4.

fool
　Mis. 348–15　"Answer a f·— Prov. 26 : 5.
　'01. 11–27　"Answer not a f·— Prov. 26 : 4.
　　18–24　f· hath said in his heart,— Psal. 14 : 1.
　'02. 19– 6　called one a "f·"— see Luke 24 : 25.
　Hea. 1–16　man suspects himself a f· ;
　My. 124–10　"What a fond f· is hope"?
　　218–22　fad of belief is the f· of mesmerism.
　　227–29　f· hath said in his heart,— Psal. 14 : 1.

foolhardiness
　Mis. 210–28　neither the cowardice nor the f·

fooling
　Mis. 271–17　* "Trust her not, she's f· thee ;"

foolish
　Mis. 73–13　The f· disobey moral law,
　　170–14　wrong and f·, conceptions of God
　　342– 3　The f· virgins had no oil
　　342–23　and they said to the f·,
　Ret. 37–11　formerly sneered at it, as f·

fools
　Mis. 226–11　he loses the homage of f·,
　　275– 2　"Ye f· and blind !"— Matt. 23 : 17.

foot
　Mis. 210–17　her f· on the head of the serpent,
　　265–31　stop at the f· of the grand ascent,
　　274–28　rights are trodden under f·,
　　323– 8　valley at the f· of the mountain
　　323–17　valley at the f· of the mountain.
　　324–30　valley at the f· of the mountain,
　　325–18　Balancing on one f·,
　　328–16　to the f· of the mount,
　　369– 1　f· of the mount of revelation,
　Ret. 11–11　knowledge plants the f· of power
　Pan. 6– 8　putteth his f· upon a lie.
　Hea. 11–16　lifting its f· against its neighbor,
　Peo. 10– 9　put her humane f· on a
　Po. 60– 8　knowledge plants the f· of power
　My. 45–30　* one f· loftier than
　　126– 8　"right f· upon the sea,— Rev. 10 : 2.
　　126– 8　his left f· on the earth,"— Rev. 10 : 2.

football
　Rud. 5–25　believe . . . to be the f· of chance

footfall
　Po. 43–18　Temper every trembling f·,

footfalls
　Mis. 324– 9　wine is unsipped, the f· abate,

foothold
　Mis. 209–24　no f· on the false basis that
　　337–20　has no sure f· :
　My. 94–11　* in which it has found a f·.

footprints
　Mis. 266– 2　struggle up, with bleeding f·,
　'02. 10– 8　Hence the f· of a reformer are
　Po. 31–13　rare f· on the dust of earth.

footstep
　Mis. 390–14　And soft thy f· falls upon
　'00. 5–30　might and majesty attend every f·
　Hea. 2– 7　condemned at every advancing f·,
　Po. 55–15　And soft thy f· falls upon

footsteps
　Mis. xi–16　become f· to joys eternal.
　　67–30　f· requisite have been taken
　　81–13　f· of Truth being baptized of John,
　　146–23　to walk in the f· of His flock.
　　215–30　If you would follow in his f·,
　　358– 9　hounded f·, false laurels.
　　398– 2　Lest my f· stray ;
　Ret. 46– 8　Lest my f· stray ;
　Pul. vii–14　on the early f· of C. S.
　　17– 7　Lest my f· stray ;
　Rud. 17–13　the first f· in this Science.
　　17–17　and the f· of His flock.
　'01. 2–25　beset all their returning f·.
　　29–25　who soonest will walk in his f·.
　Hea. 17– 1　through the f· of Truth.
　Peo. 1– 8　f· of thought, as they pass from
　Po. 14– 6　Lest my f· stray ;
　　15– 3　echoing moans from the f· of time !
　My. 117–30　f· from sense to Soul.
　　139– 7　advancing f· of progress,
　　201–22　Lest my f· stray ;
　　205–11　* He plants His f· in the sea
　　224–11　and the forward f· it impels
　　355–23　their f· are not weary ;
　　356– 7　* "He plants His f· in the sea

Footsteps of Truth
　Pul. 38–10　"F· of T·," "Creation,"

footstools
　Mis. 325–16　their feet resting on f·,

forager
　Ret. 71– 3　f· on others' wisdom

forbade
　Un. 54–20　God f· man to know evil

forbearance
　No. 8–28　gained from your f·.

forbearing
　Mis. 84– 1　was shown by his f· to speak,

forbid
　Un. 4–20　f· man's acquaintance with evil.
　'01. 26–17　cast lots for it? God f· !

forbidden
　Man. 43– 5　Formulas F·.
　　45–14　F· Membership.
　Un. 3–14　This knowledge is not the f· fruit
　　4–17　God has not f· man to know Him ;
　　54–19　this knowledge would not be f· ;
　No. 20–28　straying into f· by-paths
　'02. 6– 4　The knowledge of . . . is f·.

forbids
　Mis. 145–14　Even vanity f· man to be vain ;
　No. 30–19　f· the genuine existence of even
　'01. 30– 7　The magnitude of its meaning f·
　'02. 6– 1　f· the thought of any other reality,

force
　Mis. 23–21　atomic action, material f· or
　　220– 7　he supports this silent mental f·
　　233–15　magnetic f· of mortal mind,
　　247–18　healing f· developed by C. S.
　　257– 8　a moral or an immoral f·.
　　257– 9　a moral and spiritual f·.
　　257–11　f· of erring mortal mind,
　　257–12　This so-called f·, or law,
　　288–18　But to f· the consciousness
　Ret. 79–27　violent take it by f· !"— Matt. 11 : 12.
　Un. 5–16　to f· conclusions on this subject
　　10–26　He is not the blind f· of a
　　35–13　F·. What is gravitation?
　　35–14　a material power, or f·.
　Pul. 13–22　at last with accelerated f·,
　Rud. 4–10　a moral and spiritual f·,
　　4–11　This f· is Spirit,
　No. 41–17　trying to f· the doors of
　Pan. 6–24　how can matter be f·
　'01. 19–14　That animal natures give f· to
　My. 11– 8　* the full f· of antagonism.
　　74–11　* Scientists are here in f·,
　　344–26　cannot f· perfection on the

forced
　Mis. 291– 3　f· into personal channels,
　　326–18　f· to seek the Father's house,
　　373–17　f· out of its proper channel,
　Hea. 4–16　f· in and out of matter
　My. 11–10　* by means of f· marches,

forces
　Mis. 19–25　mental f· of material and spiritual
　　100–15　leads on irresistible f·,
　　103– 7　destructive f·, such as sin,
　　104–31　gives me the f· of God
　　173–30　are these f· laws of matter,
　Un. 35–17　f· of Truth are moral and
　　35–18　not the merciless f· of matter.
　　35–19　the so-called f· of matter?
　　52–19　its unkind f·, its tempests,
　Pan. 2–17　* combined f· and laws which are
　'02. 3–12　our military f· withdrawing,
　　10– 4　unfolds spiritual f·,
　Peo. 8–16　speculate concerning material f·.
　My. 48–25　* f· that make for righteousness.
　　110–13　electrical f· annihilating time and

forcible
　Un. 6–12　as f· collisions of thought
　My. 108–11　consists in this f· fact :
　　197– 3　That error is most f· which

forcibly
　Mis. 14–19　that good, . . . f· destroys.

forcing
　Mis. 359–12　Growth is restricted by f· humanity
　Peo. 13–14　f· from the lips of manhood

fore
　My. 341–20　* C. S. has been so much to the f·

forearm
　Mis. 213–11　forewarn and f· our fellow-mortals
　My. 273–17　forewarn and f· humanity.

forecasting
　Mis. 240– 9　f· liberty and joy

foreclosed
　'02. 13–26　the mortgage was f·,

forefathers (see also forefathers')
　Pul. 10–21　less appreciated . . . than your f·,
　'00. 10–18　wisdom of our f· is not added
　My. 340–27　dark days of our f·

forefathers'
Mis. 237–18 our f· prayers blended with the
forefelt
Mis.   1– 8 for he f· and foresaw the ordeal
forefront
'02. 14–21 blazoned on the f· of the world
My.   9–14 * you, who are standing in the f· of
forego
My. 21–11 *f· a visit to Boston at this time,
21–17 * to f· their anticipated visit
foregoing
Mis. 194–19 context of the f· Scriptural text
349–20 in substance the same as the f·,
Un. 27– 2 word employed in the f· colloquy.
My. 56–19 * three f· named churches
255– 6 publish the f· in their By-laws.
foreign
Mis. 177–28 homesick traveller in f· lands
372–25 f· device or environment
Ret. 48–22 our country, and into f· lands,
Un. 23–22 unlike Himself and f· to
26–21 its sentiment is f· to C. S.
'02. 10–29 communicating with f· nations
11– 1 to leave on a f· shore.
My. 68–17 * a beautiful f· marble,
94–23 * and from many f· countries
112–31 in our own and in f· lands,
129– 8 country and in f· lands,
211–16 committal of acts f· to
foreknew
Un. 19– 8 if He f· it, He must virtually
foreknow
Un. 19–12 could predestine or f· evil,
foreknowing
'01. 21–16 such foreseeing is not f·,
foreknowledge
Un. 19– 1 With God, knowledge is necessarily f·;
19– 2 f· and foreordination must
19– 7 have had f· thereof ;
foreknows
Un. 19– 3 What Deity f·, Deity must
forelock
My. 193–24 taking the first by the f·
foreman
My. 145–11 carpenters' f· said to me :
foremost
Mis. 57–31 wherein man is f·.
270–29 Among the f· virtues of
Pul. 67–26 * of whom the f· was Mrs. Eddy.
My. 305–19 * the f· living authors.''
forenoon
My. 16–13 * eight o'clock in the f·.
39– 1 * at ten o'clock in the f·,
73–19 * open to visitors this f·
foreordain
Un. 19– 3 What . . . Deity must f· ;
foreordained
Mis. 122–10 God f· and predestined
Un. 19– 9 ordered it aforetime, — f· it ;
foreordination
Un. 19– 2 foreknowledge and f· must
foresaw
Mis.   1– 9 he forefelt and f· the
My. 185–24 Then and there I f· this hour,
201– 6 as the Revelator f·,
221– 7 f· the new dispensation
foresay
Mis. 363–30 I foresee and f· that every
foresee
Mis. 363–30 I f· and foresay that every
My. 26–20 trust that you will see, as I f·,
129– 3 I reluctantly f· great danger
foreseeing
'01. 21–16 such f· is not foreknowing,
foresees
Mis. 238–18 love that f· more to do,
Un. 19– 5 f· events which are contrary to
57– 6 it f· the impending doom
foreshadow
Mis. 184–30 to f· metaphysical purity,
foreshadowed
Mis.   1– 5 f· by signs in the heavens.
278–23 since necessities and . . . are f·.
'02.   5– 4 but f· the spiritual dawn
foreshadowing
My. 154–26 the f· of the church triumphant.
303–30 f· and foretasting heaven

foreshadows
Mis. 232–13 f· what is next to appear
347– 7 A conical cloud, . . . f· a cyclone.
My. 194– 7 f· the idea of God,
foresight
Mis. 204–25 It brings with it wonderful f·,
My. 173–31 kindly f· in granting permission,
281– 1 f· of the nations' drama
foresplendor
My. 302–30 f· of the beginnings of truth
forest
Mis. 237–19 murmuring winds of their f· home.
390– 7 The eve-bird's f· flute
Po. 55– 8 The eve-bird's f· flute
My. 183–19 f· becomes a fruitful field,
forestall
Mis. 302–28 to f· the possible evil of
forestalling
Mis. 107–13 forgiving wrongs and f· them,
forests
Pan.   3– 5 poetical phase of the genii of f·.
My. 50– 8 * vast gloom of the mysterious f·,
186– 2 f· of our native State
194– 3 fell f· and remove mountains,
foretaste
Mis. 100–24 bring to earth a f· of heaven.
foretasting
My. 303–31 foreshadowing and f· heaven
foretell
Mis. 347– 3 f· the internal action of
foretelling
Mis. 82– 7 He who knew the f· Truth,
122– 2 f· his own crucifixion,
foretells
Un. 57– 6 and f· the pain.
'02.   5– 1 silent night f· the dawn
foretold
Mis. 164–17 In our text Isaiah f·,
214–30 Jesus f· the harvest hour
Po. 71– 1 the hour they then f·
Forever
Mis. 205–29 man born of the great F·,
forever
  abide
'02.   9–20 should abide f· in man.
  abode
No. 36– 7 It abode f· above,
  accompany
Un. 64–14 f· accompany our being.
  at once and
Ret. 31–16 banished at once and f·
  at strife
Mis. 333– 3 commingle, and are f· at strife ;
  banishes
Mis. 204–31 it banishes f· all envy,
  based
My. 205–27 it is f· based on Love,
  cling
Pul. 40– 2 * thoughts of you f· cling to me :
  complete
No. 37– 3 were f· complete,
  continue
My. 267– 4 Nothing can . . . continue f· which is
  disappears
Mis. 205–28 mortal man disappears f·.
  done
Mis. 41–17 struggle with sin is f· done.
My.   6– 7 done f· with the sins of the flesh,
  drop
Man. 53– 4 drop f· the name of the member
  dropped
Man. 43– 4 dropped f· from The Mother Church.
  dwell
Mis. 103–14 dwell f· in the divine Mind
152–16 mercy, and love dwell f·
  dwelling
My. 246–16 dwelling f· in the divine Mind
  dwelt
No. 37– 4 dwelt f· in the Father.
'02.   9–19 dwelt f· in the bosom of the Father,
  endureth
Pul.   7–23 endureth f·.''—I Pet. 1 : 25.
  extinguishes
Rud.   4–24 extinguishes f· the works of
  fact
Mis. 287– 3 f· fact that man is eternal
My. 41– 6 * a f· fact that the meek
226–17 would remain the f· fact,
  fashions
Mis. 376–30 fashions f· such forms

forever
finite
Mis. 102– 8 and the infinite f· finite.
forbids
'02. 5–30 and f· forbids the thought of
good
Mis. 104–12 and good is f· good.
great
Mis. 183– 4 In the great f·, the verities
My. 267–10 supreme, infinite, the great f·,
294–29 passed . . . into the great f·.
harmonious
No. 26–25 individual and f· harmonious.
here
Po. 29– 7 f· here and near,
higher
My. 110–18 higher and f· higher
I AM
'02. 7–15 without end, even the f· I AM,
individual
Ret. 70–24 f· individual, incorporeal
No. 25–19 he is f· individual ;
26–25 he is f· individual
learn
Mis. 125–18 learn f· the infinite meanings
live
My. 131–10 shall live f·,"— John 6 : 51.
lose
Un. 4–14 f· lose our own consciousness of
lost
Ret. 14– 2 f· lost its power over me.
Mind
Mis. 218– 3 Deity was f· Mind, Spirit ;
near
Po. 70–11 A help f· near ;
now and
No. 35–23 one with Him now and f·.
'02. 12– 6 this ideal of God is now and f·, here
My. 201– 7 enthroned now and f·.
of happiness
Po. 47–10 Can the f· of happiness be
permeated
Mis. 205–21 f· permeated with eternal life,
present
Chr. 53–33 F· present, bounteous, free,
reflection
Rud. 11– 7 the f· reflection of goodness.
reflects
Un. 39–23 man f· reflects and embodies Life,
reigns
Un. 63– 5 lives and reigns f·.
remained
Un. 63– 7 remained f· in the Science of being.
saith
Un. 62–21 saith f·, "I am the living God,
silence
'02. 14–27 f· silence all private criticisms,
stands
My. 143–21 stands f· as an eternal and
to-day and
Ret. 94–23 to-day, and f·,"— Heb. 13 : 8.
Un. 61– 4 to-day, and f·."— Heb. 13 : 8.
'02. 4–21 yesterday, and to-day, and f·.
My. 109–13 to-day, and f·."— Heb. 13 : 8.
292–28 yesterday, to-day, and f· ;
unfoldeth
No. 45–28 it unfoldeth f·.
unfolding
Mis. 82–17 man is f· unfolding
Pul. 4–22 f· unfolding its eternal Principle.
vast
Mis. 312–27 into the vast f·.
My. 291–22 bear its banner into the vast f·.
yesterday and
My. 246–29 to-day as yesterday and f·.

Mis. 57–30 always was and f· is ;
79– 4 will know them no more f·,
83– 2 holding man f· in the rhythmic
84–22 f· to quench his love for it.
90–13 This rule is f· golden :
103–31 is f· with the Father.
156–12 harmony be supreme and f· yours.
163–30 f· about the Father's business ;
176–21 should f· have melted away in the
188– 3 perfect now, and henceforth, and f·,
192–15 name shall endure f· : — Psal. 72 : 17.
197–32 neither be sick nor f· a sinner.
206– 7 saying f· to the baptized of
368– 7 * "Truth f· on the scaffold,
368– 7 * Wrong f· on the throne.
Un. 62– 5 man is f· His image and likeness.
No. 16–16 f· giving forth more light,
'00. 10–22 habitation of His throne f·.
'02. 5–18 answered this great question f·
My. 126–29 supreme to-day, to-morrow, f·.

forever
My. 168– 5 f· the privileges of the people
176– 6 paved the way to my f· gratitude,
188– 4 put my name there f· ; — I Kings 9 : 3.
193– 8 and to thank God f·
forever-existing
Mis. 362– 3 f· realities of divine Science ;
forever-law
Mis. 123– 8 the f· of infinite Love,
forever-love
Mis. 150– 4 Give my f· to your dear church.
forewarn
Mis. 213–11 f· and forearm our fellow-mortals
My. 273–17 f· and forearm humanity.
forewarned
Mis. 367–23 against knowing evil, that God f·.
forfeit
Rud. 10– 3 f· the power that Truth bestows,
No. 40–18 f· their ability to heal in Science.
My. 242–13 f· your ability to demonstrate it.
forfeited
Mis. 67–13 by doing thus . . . shall be f·.
forfeits
Mis. 268–29 human pride f· spiritual power,
forgave
'02. 19–10 as Jesus f·, forgive thou.
forge
Mis. 246–16 to f· anew the old fetters ;
forget
Mis. 12– 6 If . . . wronged, forgive and f· :
154–30 F· not for a moment, that
155– 7 F· self in laboring for mankind ;
222–29 I shall not f· the cost of
292–17 to forgive and f· whatever is
343– 3 not f· that others before us have
353– 2 but something to f·.
368–27 let us not f· that the Lord reigns,
Man. 42– 7 not be made to f· nor to neglect
'01. 29–16 f· their parents' increasing years
Hea. 4–10 not to f· his daily cares.
Po. 27–11 Or we the past f·,
My. v– 2 * Lest we f·— lest we f· !
29–13 * will ever be able to f·.
63– 1 * not f· that it was through you
189–24 I cannot f· that yours is the first
225–25 to f· their prayer,
227–19 neither should they f· that
259–18 Do not f· that an honest, wise zeal,
307–13 by saying what I cannot f·
forgets
'01. 11–23 f· what Christian Scientists do not,
forgettest
Mis. 339–23 and f· to be grateful?
forgetting
Mis. 107–12 f· self, forgiving wrongs and
328–28 "F· those things which— Phil. 3 : 13.
'00. 6– 5 f· those things which— Phil. 3 : 13.
My. 5–28 F· the Golden Rule and indulging sin,
116–16 F· divine Principle brings on
221–29 f· that the divine Mind,
forgive
Mis. 12– 6 If . . . f· and forget :
118–12 human affections yearn to f·
129– 5 f· others as he would be
129– 7 f· his brother and love his enemies.
292–17 to f· and forget whatever is
Ret. 9–13 prayed that God would f· me,
No. 30– 3 It does more than f·
'02. 18–13 faithful to rebuke, ready to f·.
19–10 even as Jesus forgave, f· thou.
19–12 no person . . . that I cannot f·.
Hea. 4–11 We ask infinite wisdom to . . . f·
My. 120– 8 f·, if it needs forgiveness,
180–28 "Father, f· them ; — Luke 23 : 34.
201–16 mercifully f·, wisely ponder,
270–19 "Father, f· them ; — Luke 23 : 34.
forgiven
Mis. 129– 5 forgive others as he would be f·.
Man. 55–14 repentant and f· by the Church
No. 29–12 * "The f· soul in a sick body
30– 1 chapter sub-title
30– 6 until nothing is left to be f·,
30– 6 F· thus, sickness and sin
31–23 f· in the generally accepted sense,
31–25 returned, to be again f· ;
42– 9 "Thy sins are f· thee ; — see Luke 5 : 23.
'01. 20–19 sin of sins ; it is never f·.
forgiveness
Mis. 100–29 patience, f·, abiding faith,
227– 2 can retire for f· to no fraternity

forgiveness
  Man. 15–10 We acknowledge God's *f·* of sin
       40–11 charitableness, and *f·*.
       52–16 deemed sufficient by the Board for *f·*
  Pul. 7–17 wash away, in floods of *f·*,
       30–20 * the *f·* of sin by God,
       33–11 * she prayed for *f·*,
  No. 32– 5 *f·*, in the popular sense of the word,
  My. 120– 8 Forgive, if it needs *f·*,

forgiveth
  Pul. 10– 6 *f·* all thine iniquities ; — *Psal.* 103 : 3.
  Pan. 4–24 *f·* all thine iniquities ; — *Psal.* 103 : 3.
  Peo. 12–13 *f·* all thine iniquities ; — *Psal.* 103 : 3.
  My. 13–19 *f·* all thine iniquities ; — *Psal.* 103 : 3.

forgiving
  Mis. 107–12 forgetting self, *f·* wrongs
     124–26 *Love f· its enemies.*
  Man. 47– 1 he is benevolent, *f·*,
  Ret. 45–19 *f·* enemies, returning good for

forgotten
  Mis. 54– 4 Has the sun *f·* to shine,
      92–26 It must not be *f·* that
    283–21 may momentarily be *f·* ;
    295–15 Has he *f·* how to honor
  Ret. 7–22 * sad event will not be soon *f·*.
  '02. 13– 2 In this endeavor self was *f·*,
  Po. 10–10 The hoar fight is *f·* ;
  My. 55– 8 * given up for a time, was not *f·*.
      95– 3 * and are then *f·*.
    149–28 seen and *f·* in the same hour ;
    337–11 The hoar fight is *f·* ;

fork
  Mis. 231–14 dexterous use of knife and *f·*.

form (noun)
  according to the
  Man. 112–10 according to the *f·* on page 114.
  and color
  Mis. 86 10 sensations . . . of *f·* and color,
  and comeliness
  My. 42– 1 * depicted its *f·* and comeliness.
    257– 9 *f·* and comeliness of the divine ideal,
  and inclination
  Mis. 240–18 with *f·* and inclination fixed,
  and individuality
  Mis. 103–12 *f·* and individuality are never lost,
  and tangibility
  Mis. 56– 7 substance, *f·*, and tangibility,
  angel
  Peo. 5 16 beside the sepulchre in angel *f·*,
  another
  Mis. 246–15 Another *f·* of inhumanity
  My. 152– 1 turned to another *f·* of idolatry,
  appeared
  Mis. 280– 1 Mind spake and *f·* appeared,
  better
  Mis. 376–15 * and in a much better *f·*."
  bodily
  Mis. 309–23 above a bodily *f·* of existence,
  bold
  Ret. 17–15 hickory rears his bold *f·*,
  Po. 62–19 hickory rears his bold *f·*,
  book
  Mis. x– 8 republish them in book *f·*,
  My. 26–16 too short to be printed in book *f·*,
  color, and
  Un. 52–23 elaborate in beauty, color, and *f·*,
  concentrated
  Mis. 242–22 in its most concentrated *f·*,
  definite
  Peo. 8–11 definite *f·* of a national religion,
  denominational
  Mis. 382–29 our denominational *f·* of
  different
  Un. 9–24 but in a far different *f·*.
  diviner
  Mis. 68– 5 changed appearance and diviner *f·*
  due
  My. 333–15 * which was closed in due *f·*."
  every
  Mis. 48– 9 as to every *f·* of error,
    361– 9 every *f·* and mode of evil
  face and
  My. 259– 2 sweetest sculptured face and *f·*
  fainting
  Mis. 212–31 the fainting *f·* of Jesus,
  finite
  Mis. 16–20 more than a person, or finite *f·*,
  Rud. 3–25 *that God has a finite f·?*
  '01. 6– 7 reckons . . . the infinite in a finite *f·*,
    6– 9 infinite Mind inhabit a finite *f·*?
  finiteness of
  Ret. 73– 5 without finiteness of *f·* or
  hero
  Po. 78– 6 Till molds the hero *f·*?

form (noun)
  highest
  My. 212–12 highest *f·* of mental evil,
  its
  Mis. 382–18 originated its *f·* of government,
  My. vi–13 * originated its *f·* of public worship,
    42– 1 * depicted its *f·* and comeliness.
  lowest
  Mis. 57–28 beginning with the lowest *f·*
  material
  Ret. 45– 8 this material *f·* of cohesion
  My. 140–20 a material *f·* of communion
    140–21 The material *f·* is a
  mode and
  Mis. 257– 3 every mode and *f·* of evil.
  My. 106–10 above matter in every mode and *f·*,
  new
  Mis. 44–26 your belief assumed a new *f·*,
  octagonal
  Pul. 24–11 * circular front and an octagonal *f·*,
  of a boa-constrictor
  Mis. 62– 6 the *f·* of a boa-constrictor
  of action
  Man. 28– 7 Without a proper . . . *f·* of action,
  of a gold scroll
  Pul. 78– 4 * in the *f·* of a gold scroll,
  of a letter
  My. 137– 2 * affidavit, in the *f·* of a letter
  of a quotation
  My. 73– 8 * in the *f·* of a quotation from
  of a star
  Pul. 26– 2 * electric lights in the *f·* of a star,
  of a talking serpent
  Pan. 6–11 first, in the *f·* of a talking serpent,
  of Christian healing
  Mis. 370–14 the *f·* of Christian healing.
  of error
  Mis. 48– 9 as to every *f·* of error,
  of evil
  Mis. 257 3 every mode and *f·* of evil.
  of Godlikeness
  Mis. 213– 2 in the *f·* of Godlikeness.
  of godliness
  Mis. 145– 5 this *f·* of godliness seems as
  '02. 16–27 The mere *f·* of godliness,
  of government
  Mis. 382–18 originated its *f·* of government,
  Man. 70–15 its own *f·* of government.
    71–18 The Mother Church's *f·* of government
    72–23 its present *f·* of government
  of healing
  Rud. 6–25 definite and absolute *f·* of healing,
  of matter
  Un. 33–16 that *f·* of matter called *brains,*
  of mind
  Un. 32 8 a false *f·* of mind.
  of practice
  Mis. 380–25 any outward *f·* of practice.
  of prayer
  Pul. 4–29 my *f·* of prayer since 1866 ;
  of religion
  Mis. 345–22 an advanced *f·* of religion,
  My. 99–13 * whenever their *f·* of religion is
  of Truth
  Mis. 310– 6 impersonal *f·* of Truth,
  one
  Mis. 237–28 one *f·* of human slavery.
  Pul. 38–30 * in one *f·* of belief or another
  personality, or
  No. 23– 3 in personality, or *f·*
  pleasing
  My. vi– 5 * simpler or more pleasing *f·*.
  relinquished the
  '01. 24–30 I relinquished the *f·* to attain
  spiritual
  Pul. 33–24 * that his visitor was a spiritual *f·*
  substance of
  Mis. 87– 9 spiritual reality and substance of *f·*,
  take
  Po. v–15 * began to take *f·* in her thought,
  that
  Mis. x–26 adopted that *f·* of signature,
  Un. 33–16 that *f·* of matter called *brains,*
  this
  Mis. 145– 5 this *f·* of godliness seems as
    314–27 This *f·* shall also be observed
  My. 89–27 * this *f·* of religious faith
  unseen
  Mis. 301–24 an unseen *f·* of injustice
  veiled
  Mis. 250–25 veiled *f·* stealing on an errand of
  whatever
  Mis. 289– 5 in whatever *f·* it is made manifest.
  without
  Mis. 280– 1 earth was without *f·*,

form (noun)
  without the comeliness
    Mis. 302– 8   the *f·* without the comeliness,
  worst
    Mis. 233– 4   in the worst *f·* of medicine,
    My. 335–28   * yellow fever in its worst *f·*,

    Mis. 181–14   who can tell what is the *f·* of
          362– 6   reflects all real mode, *f·*,
    Un.   28–10   never a light or *f·* was discerned
    Peo.   4– 4   the belief that God is a *f·*,
form (verb)
    Mis. 137–30   My students can *now* . . . *f·* churches,
        146–11   to *f·* a proper judgment.
        193– 6   *f·* propositions of self-evident
        315–22   Teachers shall *f·* associations
        365–16   *f·* the common want,
        389– 1   To *f·* the bud for bursting bloom,
    Man.   72– 7   is eligible to *f·* a church
        73–10   *f·* and conduct a C. S. organization
        104– 8   to *f·* the budding thought
    Ret.   25–26   to *f·* any proper conception of
    Un.   35–25   can *f·* nothing unlike itself, Spirit,
        52–26   *f·* the condition of beautiful
    Peo.   2–17   and *f·* its Deity out of the worst
        3– 2   our ideals *f·* our characters,
        4–14   would *f·* a third person,
       14–11   *f·* our models of humanity.
    Po.   21–15   *f·* the bud for bursting bloom,
        32–13   *f·* resolutions, with strength from
    My.   68–25   * stone and marble *f·* the interior
       163–28   for helping to *f·* mine.
       243– 5   and *f·* one church.
Form 1
    Man. 111–15   instructions illustrated in *F·* 1
Form 2
    Man. 111–15   illustrated in Form 1 and *F·* 2,
formal
    My.   29–20   * edifice whose *f·* opening
        76– 8   *f·* announcement was made that
       170– 2   no *f·* church ceremonial,
       173–18   there are no *f·* exercises
formally
    Pul.   76–27   * an invitation *f·* to accept
        77–15   *f·* accept this testimonial
        78–14   *f·* accept this testimonial
    My.   84– 8   * may not be *f·* dedicated
formation
    Mis.   71–18   based on a mortal or material *f·* ;
       184– 8   has the *f·* of his parents ;
      287–16   discern the Science of mental *f·*
    Ret.   49–12   spiritual *f·* first, last, and always,
formations
    Mis.   86–12   *f·* of . . . vague human opinions,
    No.   6– 5   God's *f·* are spiritual,
formed
    Mis. vii– 9   If worlds were *f·* by matter,
       46–15   that which is *f·* is not cause,
       71–26   nothing can be *f·* apart from
       75–31   Soul cannot be *f·* or
      104– 5   *F·* and governed by God,
     173–29   Have attraction and cohesion *f·* it?
     231– 1   almond-blossom *f·* a crown of glory ;
     255– 5   That which is *f·* is not cause,
     276–11   *f·* a goodly assemblage
     289–12   partnerships are *f·* on agreements
     314– 5   society *f·* for Sunday worship,
     332–19   afterwards to have *f·* an evil sense
     350– 7   with advice of . . . it was *f·*.
    Man.   28– 1   *f·* by The Mother Church,
    Ret.   61– 5   This fear is *f·* unconsciously
       67– 2   a false claim before . . . sin was *f·* ;
    Un.   35–23   matter, is not *f·* by Spirit ;
    No.   19–26   Person is *f·* after the manner of
    Hea.   7–11   where Jesus *f·* his estimate ;
    My.   55– 2   * Sunday School was *f·*.
      108– 1   calcareous salts *f·* by
     182–12   *f·* a Christian Scientist Association
     185–15   Love *f·* this trinity,
     333–11   * "A procession was *f·*,
former
    Mis.   12–20   at *f·* periods in human history
       42–22   the *f·* is a dream and unreal,
       53–16   the *f·* is not equal to the latter.
     104–19   the *f·* revolve in their own orbits,
     117– 8   arrest the *f·*, and obey the latter.
     139–29   all *f·* efforts in the interest of
     164– 3   the *f·* is the spiritual idea
     206– 2   the *f·* being servant to the latter,
     264–23   influence of their *f·* teacher.
    Man.   18–19   members of her *f·* Church
       86– 7   jurisdiction of his *f·* teacher.
    Pul.   43–30   * from a *f·* pastor of the church :

former
    Rud.   16– 3   the *f·* can never give a thorough
    No.   10– 7   The *f·* is the highest style of man ;
      10–18   *f·* position, that sense is organic
    Hea.   3– 8   reestablished on its *f·* basis.
    My.   39–21   * thoughts revert to a *f·* occasion,
       50– 4   * left their *f·* church homes,
     108–12   *f·* enlists faith in the pharmacy of
     128–23   without the *f·* the latter were
     141–17   * In *f·* years, the annual communion
     190–12   vastly excelling the *f·*.
     197–17   translucent atmosphere of the *f·*
     318–10   name of the *f·* proofreader for
formerly
    Mis. 242–26   *f·* partner of George T. Brown,
    Man.   69–26   *f·* known as "Mother's Room"
    Ret.   37–11   Those who *f·* sneered at it,
    Pul.   28–26   * Judge Hanna, *f·* of Chicago,
       29– 4   *f·* been Congregational clergymen.
       59–22   * Joseph Armstrong, *f·* of Kansas,
    My.   56–23   * *f·* been attendants at The
      327–23   * *f·* read, "pretended healers,"
     335– 2   * *f·* of Concord, N. H.
     339–14   and all that it *f·* signified,
     353–22   *f·* known as "Mother's Room"
formidable
    Pan.   15– 3   will be as *f·* in war as
    '02.   1–11   combined in *f·* conspiracy,
    Hea.   1– 7   But Heaven's favors are *f·* :
    My. 185–11   Truth, Life, and Love are *f·*,
forming
    Mis. 256–13   from *f·* as frequently as
    Man.   17– 3   *f·* a church without creeds,
    Ret.   52–12   *f·* a National . . . Association.
    '00.   1–14   right convictions fast *f·*
    My.   49–12   * interested in *f·* the church,
       69– 7   * and *f·* a gently curved
       85–30   * *f·* one of the few perfect sky-lines
     256–11   *f·* themselves in your thoughts
forms (noun)
  all
    Mis. 101–32   the elements of all *f·*
    Un.   8–17   All *f·* of error are uprooted in
  all its
    Un.   53– 3   evil and all its *f·* are
    My.   6–10   overcome sin in all its *f·*,
  and colors
    Rud.   6– 4   *assuming manifold f· and colors,*
  and hues
    Mis. 377– 1   such *f·* and hues of heaven,
  and numbers
    Mis. 104–10   calculus of *f·* and numbers.
  and representations
    Mis.   55–19   its *f·* and representations,
  application
    Man. 113– 1   heading
  certain
    Un.   45–16   in certain *f·* of theology
    Pan.   4– 1   certain *f·* of pantheism
  delicious
    Mis.   9–26   delicious *f·* of friendship,
  different
    Mis. 370–13   assumes different *f·*,
    Ret.   61– 4   in different *f·* of fear
  differing
    Mis. 380–18   in slightly differing *f·*.
  features and
    Mis. 112–14   some of the many features and *f·*
  fresh
    Mis.   1–16   mounting sense gathers fresh *f·*
  here given
    Man. 109–15   compare them with the *f·* here given,
  illusive
    Ret.   64–26   all the illusive *f·*, methods, and
  limited
    Pul.   6– 4   the limited *f·* of a national
  majestic
    Mis. 385–26   But faith . . . shed Majestic *f·* ;
    Po.   49– 1   But faith . . . shed Majestic *f·* ;
  material
    Mis. 358–32   by leaving the material *f·*
    No.   42– 7   material *f·* to meet a mental want.
  milder
    '01.   19–28   the milder *f·* of animal magnetism
  moods and
    Mis. 329– 3   nature in all her moods and *f·*,
  my
    Un.   26– 4   my *f·*, near or remote.
  myriad
    Mis. 114–19   appearing in its myriad *f·* :
      325–27   sensualism in its myriad *f·*.
     361– 7   whose myriad *f·* are neither
  new
    Peo.   11–15   that enforce new *f·* of oppression,

forms (noun)
of disease
  No. 2–23 the most defiant *f·* of disease.
of matter
  My. 212–11 use of higher *f·* of matter,
of religion
  '02. 16–24 merely outside *f·* of religion,
of sin
  No. 41–16 subtlest *f·* of sin are trying
other
  Ret. 71–29 the same as other *f·* of stealing,
  My. 212– 7 and other *f·* of intoxication.
regular
  Man. 111– 9 regular *f·* of application.
robust
  Mis. 325–15 Robust *f·*, with manly brow
special
  Man. 111–20 will be furnished special *f·*
spiritual
  Mis. 91–19 the most spiritual *f·* of thought
subtler
  Mis. 115–23 against the subtler *f·* of evil,
  No. 31– 6 appear to-day in subtler *f·*
their
  Mis. 192– 8 disease, and death, in all their *f·*,
varied
  Mis. 198– 7 its varied *f·* of pleasure and pain.
various
  Ret. 75– 1 various *f·* of book-borrowing
worse
  No. 31– 8 will multiply into worse *f·*,
worst
  Mis. 296–24 the worst *f·* of vice
  My. 190– 8 in healing the worst *f·* of

  My. 267–30 of all the divine modes, means, *f·*,
forms (verb)
  My. 265–22 *f·* the coincidence of the human and

formulas
  Man. 43– 5 F· Forbidden.
        43– 6 No member shall use written *f·*,
formulate
  Mis. 8–11 except you first *f·* this enemy
  '02. 5–26 *f·* a doctrine, or speculate on
  My. 49–14 * *f·* the rules and by-laws,
formulated
  Mis. 78–30 *f·* views antagonistic to
  Pul. 46– 4 * the new rules were *f·*.
formulating
  Mis. 49–16 *our capacity for f· a dream,*
fornication
  Mis. 278– 1 wines of *f·*, envy, and
  My. 125–32 with the wine of her *f·*," — *Rev.* 17 : 2.
fornicator
  My. 106–25 swearer, an adulterer, a *f·*,
fornicators
  Mis. 324–13 adulterers, *f·*, idolaters ;
forsake
  Mis. 123–24 repent, *f·* sin, love God,
  Ret. 85–17 Never *f·* your post without due
       90– 4 Does the faithful shepherd *f·* the
  '01. 15– 3 repent and *f·* it, in order to
  My. 40–13 * *f·* animosity, and abandon their
     140– 6 and not *f·* them." — *Isa.* 42 : 16.
     258–22 and friends that *f·*.
forsaken
  Mis. 63–23 *why hast Thou f· me?"* — *Mark* 15 : 34.
  Po. 41–11 When the herd had *f·*,
  My. 273–12 not seen the righteous *f·*, — *Psal.* 37 : 25.
forsaking
  My. 221–27 like a watchman *f·* his post,
forsook
  Mis. 340–13 *f·* Blackstone for gray stone,
  Ret. 7–11 * he never *f·* them until he
      42– 6 He *f·* all to follow in this line
      90–15 and others *f·* him.
fort
  Pul. 2–17 in a poorly barricaded *f·*,
forth
  Mis. xi–20 to fling it back and *f·*.
     27–18 "Doth a fountain send *f·* — *Jas.* 3 : 11.
     41– 1 only the cruel and evil can send *f·*,
     75–31 Soul cannot be formed or brought *f·*
     81–17 *before it shall go f·*
   131–10 so shadow *f·* the substance of
   135–16 Sending *f·* currents of Truth,
   153– 6 When God went *f·* before His people,
   153–18 Christian Scientists bring *f·* the
   154–24 Bring *f·* fruit

forth
  Mis. 156–21 "this kind goeth not *f·* — *see Matt.* 17 : 21.
   157–23 And He shall bring *f·* — *Psal.* 37 : 6.
   162–30 like him he went *f·*,
   170–31 explained as the putting *f·* of power.
   187–16 as set *f·* in original Holy Writ.
   194–31 first condition set *f·* in the text,
   201–12 he also showed *f·* the error
   224–17 Then, we should go *f·* into life
   227–20 the sweeter the odor they send *f·*
   235–13 that bringeth not *f·* good fruit ;
   237– 9 belch *f·* their latent fires.
   245–11 calling *f·* the *vox populi*
   265–20 can never bring *f·* the real fruits of
   311– 9 go *f·* to the full vintage-time,
   313–21 to send *f·* more laborers
   320–12 reaches *f·* for the infant idea
   328–29 reaching *f·* unto those — *Phil.* 3 : 13.
   330–32 to put *f·* its slender blade,
   339–28 and pour *f·* the unavailing tear.
   340–11 sends *f·* a barrister who never
   368–15 sending *f·* a poison more deadly
   370– 2 "Stretch *f·* thy hand, — *Matt.* 12 : 13.
   370–17 calls *f·* infinite care from
  Man. 51– 1 Rules herein set *f·*,
     82– 2 literature it sends *f·*.
  Ret. 2– 5 find so graphically set *f·* in the
   11–13 F· from this fount the streamlets
   27– 2 setting *f·* their spiritual
   56–22 The sun sends *f·* light,
   62– 4 find that the views here set *f·*
   62– 5 bring *f·* better fruits of health,
   70– 4 puts *f·* its own qualities,
  Un. 5–25 shadowed *f·* in scientific thought.
   42–28 *f·* in the radiance of eternal being
   45–20 goes *f·* into an imaginary sphere
  Pul. 2–18 Would you rush *f·* single-handed to
   8–14 and *f·* came the money,
   12–21 Love sends *f·* her primal and
   13–29 brought *f·* the man child. — *Rev.* 12 : 13.
   14–18 send *f·* a new flood to drown the
   41– 1 * *f·* from the hands of the artisans
   47–12 * homœopathy, and so *f·*,
   49–11 * has come *f·* all this beauty !"
   51–18 * called *f·* the implements of
   54–22 * they are fully set *f·*.
   62–13 and call *f·* all the purity
   80–19 * speak of the system it sets *f·*,
   81– 6 * set *f·* as the power of God
  Rud. 7– 6 set *f·* in my work S. and H.
   8– 1 No rock brings *f·* an apple ;
   8– 5 in Science, Spirit sends *f·* its own
  No. 10–16 forever giving *f·* more light,
   26–11 brings *f·* its own sensuous conception.
   40–11 and pour *f·* a hypocrite's prayer ;
  '00. 6– 6 reaching *f·* to those — *see Phil.* 3 : 13.
   8– 9 comes *f·* a blessing or a bane
   8–14 "Bring *f·* things — *see Matt.* 13 : 52.
  '01. 35– 2 He shall bring *f·* thy — *Psal.* 37 : 6.
  Hea 4– 2 infinite can neither go *f·* from,
   20– 3 " could we sound the glories *f·*,
  Po. v– 7 * called *f·* by some experience
   33–12 To breathe *f·* a prayer that
   60–10 F· from this fount the streamlets
  My. 53– 6 * send *f·* her book to the world."
   72–19 * sent *f·* to the thirty thousand
   103–18 I have set *f·* C. S.
   122–14 called *f·* flattering comment
   147– 3 past comes *f·* like a pageant
   150–27 he sent them *f·* to heal
   151–20 * Go *f·*, and worship God."
   159–10 sent *f·* His word to heal
   167–23 send *f·* a pæan of praise
   170–25 He shall bring *f·* thy — *Psal.* 37 : 6.
   179– 2 Scriptures, as set *f·* in the
   189–10 go *f·* in waves of sound,
   191–18 come *f·* from the tomb of the past,
   206–24 show *f·* the praises — *I Pet.* 2 : 9.
   208– 5 mirrored *f·* by your loving hearts,
   215– 4 God stretched *f·* His hand.
   215–23 first sent *f·* his students,
   215–28 Why did he send *f·* his students
   216– 1 set *f·* in the Scriptures,
   247–20 a loving look which brings *f·*
   248–26 You go *f·* to face the foe
   249–12 sends *f·* a mental miasma
   269– 3 showing *f·* the infinite
   269–20 vine is bringing *f·* its fruit ;
   269–22 sending *f·* their rays of reality
   278– 8 its edict hath gone *f·* :
   287–22 bringeth not *f·* good fruit ;
forthcoming
  Mis. 82– 7 beheld the *f·* Truth,
   158–25 will find the *f·* completion
   319–19 greetings for the *f·* holidays,
  Ret. 94–30 this period and the *f·* centuries,

forthwith
Ret. 88– 8 so-called dead f· emerged into
My. 334– 1 * f· strives to give the impression
fortified
Rud. 15–17 should be f· on all sides
fortify
My. v–11 * f· themselves against the mesmerism
fortress
Pul. 2–25 would overthrow this sublime f·,
forts
My. 127–23 f· of C. S., garrisoned by God's
fortunate
Pul. 61–21 * those f· enough to listen to the
My. 241–16 * Christian Scientists are f·
273– 6 * f· in being able to point to a
fortune
'01. 31–27 my fair f· to be often taught by
fortunes
Mis. ix– 8 their comfortable f· are acquired by
forty
Pul. 41–15 * parties of f· and fifty.
'01. 18– 6 the sneers f· years ago
Hea. 1–17 * Knows it at f·, and reforms his
My. 22–14 * 1866, almost f· years ago,
22–14 * almost f· years in the wilderness,
37–14 * your obedience during f· years
43–15 * f· years before.
43–21 * F· years ago the Science of
59– 3 * nearly f· years ago.
59– 8 * in less than f· years
137–11 It is over f· years that I have
174–22 For nearly f· years
270–21 f· years I have returned good for
360–23 for f· years in succession.
(see also **values**)
forty-eight
Mis. 243– 2 in f· hours cured her perfectly
(see also **numbers**)
forty-five
(see **numbers, values**)
forty-four
(see **numbers**)
Forty-second Psalm
Un. 29–23 soul, as in the F· P· :
forty-two
(see **values**)
forum
Pul. 87–22 More effectual than the f·
forward
Mis. 18– 8 prominent laws which f· birth
136– 5 taking f· marches, broader and
155–25 I shall be apt to f· their letters
178–26 * pastor again came f·, and added the
212–25 who will step f· and open his
227–12 one may give it a f· move,
348– 1 They press f· towards the mark
Un. 57–26 f· the birth of immortal being ;
61–14 retreats, and again goes f· ;
Pul. 43–23 * which was looked f· to as
Rud. 11– 9 brings f· the next proposition
'00. 4–11 the new and f· steps in religion,
15– 7 Christian Scientists start f· with
'02. 3–11 Our nation's f· step was the
14–18 every f· step has been met
My. 14–28 * work will be pushed f·
47–19 * that showed a f· effort
155–12 f· in the onward march of Truth,
224–11 the f· footsteps it impels
327–28 * look f· to the day,
346–14 * expression of looking f·,
forwarded
Man. 44–15 which shall be f· each year
98– 4 f· to this Committee
Pul. 77–26 f· to Mrs. Mary Baker Eddy
My. 44–17 * f· at once to our Leader,
359–23 * This letter was f· to Mrs. Eddy
forwarding
Mis. 306– 1 * In f· material to be melted
fossil
Mis. 30–23 the f· of wisdomless wit,
fossils
Peo. 8–25 f· of material systems,
Foster, Bishop
No. 27–18 Bishop F· said, in a lecture
foster
Mis. 296–20 f· a feminine ambition
Foster-Eddy, Ebenezer J.
Ret. 43–11 adopted son, Ebenezer J. F·,

fosters
Mis. 257–17 f· suspicion where confidence is due,
Rud. 12–11 This f· infidelity,
My. 211–21 f· suspicious distrust
fought
Mis. 41–12 The good fight must be f·
204– 8 When the good fight is f·,
Ret. 3–10 general who f· at Lundy's Lane,
Un. 17– 6 f· against Sisera. — Judg. 5 : 20.
46–26 Pharisees f· Jesus on this issue.
Hea. 2–16 "I have f· a good fight, — II Tim. 4 : 7.
10– 6 it was supposed to have f· the
Po. 78– 1 our honored dead f· on in gloom !
My. 61–12 * I f· hard with the evidence of
foul
Mis. 206– 3 from f· to pure, from torpid to
354– 7 to overbalance this f· stuff.
399– 7 Cleanse the f· senses within ;
Po. 75–14 Cleanse the f· senses within ;
My. 126–26 hold of every f· spirit, — Rev. 18 : 2.
found
Mis. xi–17 be f· to surpass imagination,
2–18 will be f· alone the remedy for sin,
10–20 f· their strength made perfect in
15–23 until man is f· to be the image of
25– 7 it is f· that matter is a phase of
27– 9 Here also is f· the pith of
28–13 will be f· to be the only Life.
32–11 are to be f· in the Scriptures,
33–28 f· in mortal mind's opposite,
46– 6 f· true, and adapted to destroy the
46–19 f· in the scale with his creator ;
53–23 f· it difficult to make the rulers
61– 2 f· the type and representative of
64– 1 Spirit might be f· "All-in-all."
66– 2 obedience thereto may be f· faulty,
69–17 I f· him barely alive,
80–23 until right is f· supreme.
96– 5 have f· Him so ;
112–16 f· him in the mental state called
114–27 then, if f· faithful,
115– 9 and fear of being f· out.
119–12 always be f· arguing for itself,
119–21 is f· powerless in C. S.
131–30 these will be f· already itemized,
139–27 it will be f· that this act was
140–24 we would not be f· fighting against
143–26 f· you all "with one accord — Acts 2 : 1.
157– 2 to be f· worthy to suffer for
164–23 f· in the actual likeness of
165–31 f· in the order, mode, and
169– 1 she had f· all the divine Science
178– 7 He f· that the new wine
178–21 * If I had not f· C. S. a new gospel,
178–23 * if I had not f· it truth,
180–14 f· the open door from this sepulchre
183– 8 will be f· that Mind is All-in-all,
188–21 where the present writer f· it,
189– 6 will be f· to be the Comforter
190–18 these terms will be f· to include the
191–16 name of his satanic majesty is f·
195–16 not to be f· in the Scriptures.
196– 1 ego is f· not in matter
202– 3 are f· to correct the discords of
210– 5 error, when f· out, is two-thirds
227– 6 Law has f· it necessary to offer to
236– 1 has not f· that human passions
247– 7 know that I f· health in just what I
248– 5 f· in the "new tongue," — see Mark 16 : 17.
255–10 Man should be f· not claiming
255–24 f· in God, the divine Mind.
260– 4 and f· able to heal them.
263– 6 the sweetest similes to be f·
276–13 an assemblage f· waiting and
276–20 divine Love is f· in affliction.
276–26 not one of them be f· borrowing oil,
279–20 when it is f· that evil is naught
286– 9 f· to be man's oneness with God,
288– 8 and not be f· wanting.
290– 3 f· within their precincts.
291–24 who are f· worthy to suffer for
303– 3 sought and f· as healers
308– 2 f· harmonious and immortal.
312– 4 we be not f· wanting.
334–11 fabrication is f· to be a lie,
338–14 afford the only rule I have f·
348–23 f· myself under this new régime
355–14 Error f· out is two-thirds destroyed,
361– 5 its substances are f· substanceless,
365– 6 Human theories . . . are f· wanting ;
386– 5 and hearts are f· and filled,
398–25 And was f· by you and me
Man. 29–11 and the complaint be f· valid,
30– 6 be f· at any time inadequate
39– 4 If, . . . they are f· worthy,

found

Man. 39– 5   but if not *f·* worthy
50–15   be *f·* having the name without
50–23   *f·* violating any of the By-Laws
52–11   If a member is *f·* guilty of
54–13   and this complaint being *f·* valid,
55–22   is *f·* trying to practise or to
63– 7   *f·* in the C. S. Quarterly Lessons,
77–11   If it be *f·* that the Church funds
89– 7   vice-president of . . . being *f·* worthy,
90– 4   if *f·* qualified to receive them.
92–12   *f·* duly qualified to teach C. S.,

Ret. 24–21   *f·* to be in perfect scientific accord
28– 2   *f·* as the Life, or Principle,
33–10   I *f·*, in the . . . remedies
33–21   is *f·* to be even more active.
44–14   *f·* able to maintain the church
56– 2   *f·* to be demonstrable rules in C. S.,
61–25   it cannot be *f·* in the body.
69–14   Its life is *f·* to be not Life,
73– 7   man is *f·* in the reflection of
82–24   *f·* dwelling together in harmony,
94–16   immortal Truth be *f·* true,

Un. 3–17   man is *f·* in the image and
10– 4   they are not to be *f·* in God,
15–21   *f·* in heathen religious history.
30–26   shall be *f·* a quickening Spirit ;
35– 8   so-called material senses are *f·*,
51–23   Truth is *f·* only in divine Science,
57–23   rejoiced that he was *f·* worthy

Pul. 6–15   * realized I had *f·* that for which
28–25   * are *f·* in the hymn-books of the
34–23   *f·* it to be in perfect scientific accord
58– 1   * *f·* herself in Lynn, Mass.,
58–18   * Scarcely any woodwork is to be *f·*.
67– 5   * "If you would *f·* a new faith,
67–10   * faiths which are to be *f·* there
67–22   * little knots of them are to be *f·*.

Rud. 5–11   who has ever *f·* Soul in the body
5–13   who has *f·* sight in matter,

No. 8–23   If one be *f·* who is too blind for
12–27   be *f·* all instead of a part of being,
15–13   notions of personality to be *f·* in
16– 1   *f·* in the divine consciousness.
18–14   Human theories, . . . are *f·* unequal to
20–11   Principle is *f·* to be the only
24–19   being thus uncovered, is *f·* out,
28– 6   man be *f·* perfect and eternal.
28–12   is *f·* to bring with it health,

Pan. 5– 1   is *f·* in scholastic theology.
12– 1   it will be *f·* possible to fulfill it.
13–12   condemnation of all error, wherever *f·*.

'00. 1–11   is *f·* crowned with unprecedented
4–21   and they must be *f·* final, absolute,
7–27   loving Christ is *f·* near,

'01. 24–24   I *f·* it necessary to follow Jesus'
26–11   quality not to be *f·* in God !

'02. 17–17   Who . . . ever *f·* her true?

Hea. 12– 2   *f·* out that Mind instead of
13– 9   *f·* out they have taken no medicine,

Peo. 6–22   are *f·* destroying sin, sickness, and
11– 1   liberty of the sons of God as *f·* in C. S.
11– 5   was *f·* that the feeblest mind,

Po. vi– 1   * *finally f· its* way into print,
49– 8   and hearts are *f·* and filled,
75– 5   was *f·* by you and me

My. 4–16   *f·* that, instead of opposing,
18–20   all error, wherever *f·*.
28–17   * not to be *f·* in the material
42– 2   * We have *f·* it true that
43–27   * *f·* in C. S. that which heals
53–32   * it was *f·* that the Hawthorne Rooms
54–18   * no place suitable could be *f·*
56– 9   * *f·* necessary to organize
63–30   * *f·* the kingdom of God.
73– 1   * *f·* necessary to issue a
78–15   * *f·* every basket piled high
78–23   * were *f·* to be perfect.
88–22   * *f·* the truths of C. S. to be
89–30   * *f·* a religious movement
94–11   * in which it has *f·* a foothold.
103–22   I have *f·* nothing in ancient or
103–23   on which to *f·* my own,
111–12   will tell you that he has *f·*
113–26   men are *f·* casting out the evils
119–32   St. John *f·* Christ, Truth,
121–18   Few blemishes can be *f·*
127– 9   it will be *f·* that C. S.
129– 1   see if there be *f·* anywhere a
131–18   I hope I shall not be *f·* disorderly,
147–20   *f·* able to heal both sin and
152–23   *f·* an ever-present help
152–28   is *f·* to be the remote,
165–31   *f·* and felt the infinite
185–19   lost, and is *f·* ;" — *Luke* 15 : 32.

found

My. 189–21   is sought and *f·*.
211–27   is *f·* out and destroyed.
229– 4   cannot be *f·* at Pleasant View
241–26   * I had *f·* that I lived and moved
248–12   *f·* adequate for the emancipation
248–29   *f·* nearest the divine Principle
251–13   your pupils are *f·* eligible to
251–21   if *f·* eligible, receive a
285–21   they neither *f·* me in — *Acts* 24 : 12.
291–16   His humanity, . . . was not *f·* wanting.
299–13   may be *f·* in creeds.
301– 5   *f·* to be a healthy fermentation,
320– 6   * I *f·* that his statement
324–29   * if he *f·* you could do so,
330–15   * *f·* Mrs. Eddy's statements,
332–31   * a roll of papers . . . was *f·* ;
333– 5   * *f·* by one of your own citizens,
343–26   I *f·* at one time that they had
345–16   I *f·* that when I prescribed
348– 6   I *f·* it was God made manifest
348–21   I had *f·* unmistakably

foundation

and superstructure
Mis. 140– 2   *f·* and superstructure,
357–32   yea, its *f·* and superstructure.

another's
No. 43–20   on another's *f·*.

deeper
Pul. 36– 5   * deeper *f·* of her religious work

firm
Mis. 213–20   fearless wing and firm *f·*.
'01. 2–25   Only a firm *f·* in Truth can give

for our temple
My. 13–31   a *f·* for our temple,

for the builders
My. 301– 8   a *f·* for the builders.

His
Mis. 263–11   building on His *f·*,

his own
Ret. 48– 8   build on his own *f·*,

in nature
Mis. 367–26   neither precedent nor *f·* in nature,

laid the
Ret. 27– 3   so laid the *f·* of my work
Hea. 11–17   homœopathy has laid the *f·* stone of

no
Mis. 334– 6   Necromancy has no *f·*,

of all systems
'00. 5–25   the *f·* of all systems of religion.

of Christian Science
Mis. 105– 7   demonstration is the *f·* of C. S.
My. 117–22   is the *f·* of C. S.

of Love
Pul. 2–30   reared on the *f·* of Love,

of repentance
My. 128– 4   *f·* of repentance from — *Heb.* 6 : 1.

of right thinking
Hea. 3– 6   It was the *f·* of right thinking

of Science
Mis. 81– 1   broad and sure *f·* of Science ;

of the world
My. 185–17   from the *f·* of the world," — *Rev.* 13 : 8.

of this temple
Pul. 85– 1   * to lay the *f·* of this temple,

of true art
Mis. 375–19   * the *f·* of true art.

of unbelief
Mis. 109–23   often is the *f·* of unbelief

other
Mis. 365– 2   "other *f·* can no man — *I Cor.* 3 : 11.
Un. 64– 8   "other *f·* can no man — *I Cor.* 3 : 11.
No. 21–23   other *f·* can no man — *I Cor.* 3 : 11.
'02. 14–16   on any other *f·*,

solid
My. 45–32   * In solid *f·* in symmetrical

spiritual
   (*see* **spiritual**)

study and
Pul. 71–20   * study and *f·* of the faith

sure
Mis. 81– 1   broad and sure *f·* of Science ;
143– 2   broad basis and sure *f·*
152–23   beat against this sure *f·*,
My. 16–26   corner stone, a sure *f·* : — *Isa.* 28 : 16.

without
Mis. 108– 1   being without *f·* in fact,
My. 334– 8   * allegation . . . is without *f·*.

———

Mis. 140–21   The *f·* on which our church
Pul. 9–30   *f·* of enlightened faith is
52–15   * with the New Testament at the *f·*,
Hea. 2–27   Truth, eternity's *f·* stone,
My. 16–25   for a *f·* stone, — *Isa.* 28 : 16.

foundational
Mis. 200–17 The f· facts of C. S.
My. 230–23 faithful over f· trusts,

foundations
everlasting
Mis. 336–29 it rests on everlasting f·,
Un. 6– 9 established on everlasting f·.
false
Un. 53–16 not built on such false f·,
its
My. 187–30 laid its f· on the rock
of Christian Science
My. 191–11 f· of C. S. — one God and one Christ.
of human affection
Mis. 287–19 lays the f· of human affection
of mortality
Mis. 101–16 undermines the f· of mortality,
of their testimony
Un. 33–22 observe the f· of their testimony,
of these assertions
Un. 44– 5 The f· of these assertions,
old
My. 350–22 old f· of an early faith
scientific
Ret. 83– 8 scientific f· are already laid
sure
Mis. 82–10 reach the sure f· of time,

Mis. 163–22 yet the f· he laid are
Un. 64– 6 on the f· of an eternal Mind
Hea. 13–22 the f· of metaphysical healing
My. 145– 9 from the f· to the tower,
182– 8 the f· of which are the same,

founded
Mis. 13–18 f· upon the basis of material and
152–22 f· upon the rock of Christ,
337– 1 f· at this period C. S.,
383– 9 C. S. is f· by its discoverer,
Ret. 15– 4 till I f· a church of my own,
Pul. 37–28 * f· with twenty-six members,
66– 4 * was f· fifteen years ago
67–15 * F· twenty-five years ago,
67–27 * The church was f· in April, 1879,
68– 4 * College was f· by Mrs. Eddy
68–24 * C. S. was f· by Mrs. Mary Baker Eddy
70–12 * has within a few years f· a sect that
No. 10– 1 * principles on which it is f·,
'00. 13–12 f· the city of Smyrna,
'01. 26– 4 f· his system of metaphysics
Peo. 3–19 religion f· upon C. S.
6– 7 * f· on long observation
My. vi–17 * f· The C. S. Journal in 1883,
33–30 hath f· it upon the seas, — Psal. 24 : 2.
47–24 * Mrs. Eddy f· her first church
47–27 * f· on the commands of Jesus :
48–13 * f· the future growth of her church,
76–28 * f· . . . by Mrs. Mary Baker Eddy
112–10 f· squarely . . . on the Scriptures.
139– 5 f· upon the rock, Christ Jesus,

Founder
Pul. 53– 2 * by the F· of Christianity
My. 279– 3 The F· of Christianity said :
(see also **Eddy**)

founder
Mis. 381–31 * both f· and discoverer
Pul. 5–11 f· of the Concord School of
My. 305– 2 and that he is the f· of
338–25 discoverer, f·, demonstrator,
(see also **Eddy**)

founding
Mis. 382– 7 discovery and f· of C. S.
Pul. 36– 1 * a year after her f· of the
'02. 12–29 f· the institutions and early

fount
Mis. ix–18 from the f· of divine Love.
92– 9 open f· of Truth and Love.
225–11 had drunk at its f·,
Ret. 11–13 from this f· the streamlets flow,
18–15 shrine Or f· of real joy
84– 6 this open f· of Truth and Love.
Hea. 10–27 for the true f· and Soul's baptism.
12– 7 metaphysician goes to the f·
Po. 60–10 from this f· the streamlets flow,
64– 6 shrine Or f· of real joy

fountain
Mis. 27–18 "Doth a f· send forth — Jas. 3 : 11.
117–28 God is the f· of light,
153– 9 the rock became a f· ;
399– 6 it calls you, — "Come to this f·,
Pul. 48– 4 * with here and there a f· or
Hea. 7–14 makes pure the f·,
Po. 41– 7 f· and leaflet are frozen

fountain
Po. 75–13 it calls you, — "Come to this f·,
My. 79–10 * supposed f· of knowledge
247–14 little fishes in my f·

fountains
Mis. 113–29 life-giving f· of truth.
223– 6 necessarily have pure f· ;
323–22 drink from its living f· ?
Ret. 31–28 Frozen f· were unsealed.
Hea. 10–28 f· play in borrowed sunbeams,
Peo. 14– 5 cool grottos, smiling f·,
Po. 9– 5 unsealed f· of grief and joy
My. 186– 2 meadows, f·, and forests

four
Mis. 136–25 convening once in f· months ;
231– 6 F· generations sat at that
239– 4 but f· days' vacation for the past year,
304–27 * at f· o'clock it will toll on the
349–23 will state that I preached f· years,
Man. 73– 2 f· of whom are members of The
Ret. 19–17 at the end of f· months,
20– 8 my little son, about f· years of age,
40– 1 f· successive years I healed,
65–22 as taught in the f· Gospels.
89–22 Nowhere in the f· Gospels
Un. 11–27 ye say, There are yet f· months,
Pul. 25– 4 * distributed by the f· systems
27–20 * pictorial story of the f· Marys
40–12 * THE SERVICE REPEATED F· TIMES
40–16 * simple ceremonies, f· times repeated,
40–17 * presence of f· different congregations,
41–21 * f· vast congregations filled the
49–10 * "You have lived here only f· years,
49–13 "F· years !" she ejaculated ;
57– 7 * was thronged at the f· services
59– 6 * were held from nine to f· o'clock,
59– 8 * exercises f· times repeated.
Pan. 9– 9 f· first rules pertaining thereto,
'01. 4– 5 f· times three is twelve,
4– 6 three times f· is twelve.
My. 68– 5 * f· arches springing from the
69–30 * some f· miles away.
70–25 * six organs, with f· manuals,
214–19 F· years after my discovery
330–29 where, at the end of f· months,
(see also **numbers, values**)

fourfold
My. 199–20 f· unity between the churches

fourscore
Po. 71–16 Ye who have wept f·
My. 146–10 sum of years to f·,
177–11 sum of years to f·

four-story
My. 66– 2 * f· brick building also

fourteen
Mis. 29–16 but f· deaths in the ranks
Pul. 8– 9 within f· months, responded
38– 8 * consists of f· chapters,
(see also **numbers, values**)

fourth
Mis. 22–12 f· dimension of Spirit.
176– 4 chapter sub-title
280–19 close of the lecture on the f·
309–25 third and f· paragraphs,
318–10 f· and final generation
332–24 third, suffering ; f·, death.
Un. 31–14 f·, that matter, being so endowed,

Fourth Church of Christ, Scientist
Brooklyn
My. 363– 6 * signature

My. 363– 2 * signature
Fourth of July
Mis. 251– 1 chapter sub-title

fowl
Mis. 69–12 over the f· of the air." — Gen. 1 : 26.

fowler
Mis. 389–22 no f·, pestilence or pain ;
Po. 5– 1 no f·, pestilence or pain ;

fowls
Mis. 357–15 f· of the air pick them up.

foxes
My. 123–30 "the little f· — Song 2 : 15.

foyer
My. 46– 1 * f· and broad stairways,
69–20 * unusual feature is the f·,
69–21 * Adjoining this f· are

Fra Angelico
Mis. 376– 8 * having been taken by F· A·

fraction
Mis. 269–14　*f·* of the actual Science
No. 29–21　more than a *f·* of himself.

fragmentary
Mis. ix–11　pictures — once *f·* and faint
126– 2　from *f·* discourses
Ret. 93–11　Truth is not *f·*,

fragments
Mis. 9–18　fall in *f·* before our eyes.
106–21　and gather up the *f·*.
149–11　gather up the *f·*, and count
360– 4　with crude, rude *f·*,
My. 133–13　*f·* gathered therefrom

fragrance
Mis. 228–10　fills the world with its *f·*,
330–23　freshen the *f·* of being.
Po. 25–12　F· fresh round the dead,
32– 5　blossoms whose *f·* and charms
67–22　*f·* of goodness and love ;

fragrant
Ret. 17–18　magnolia, and *f·* fringe-tree ;
18–22　flowers of feeling are *f·* and fair,
Peo. 14– 5　*f·* recesses, cool grottos,
Po. 46–11　Fresh as the *f·* sod,
63– 3　magnolia, and *f·* fringe-tree ;
64–16　flowers of feeling are *f·* and fair,

frail
Mis. 13–18　This *f·* hypothesis is founded upon
13–20　*f·* human reason accepts.
87–11　*f·* conception of mortal mind ;
377– 2　brush or pen to paint *f·* fairness
Po. 18–15　notice the *f·* fledgling hath.
My. 80– 9　* tax upon *f·* human credulity,
342–14　* when I say *f·*, let it not

frailer
My. 342– 7　*f·*, but Mrs. Eddy herself.

frailty
Mis. 336–28　only to take away its *f·*.
Ret. 81–28　*f·* of mortal anticipations,

frame
Rud. 11– 1　*f·* its own conditions,
11–28　nervous operations of the human *f·*.
My. 308–16　* "tall, gaunt *f·*"

framed
Pul. 32– 1　* her face, *f·* in dark hair
My. 24–14　* "fitly *f·* together — *Eph.* 2 : 21.
68–29　* *f·* of iron and finished with
318–28　long argument, *f·* from his

frames
Pul. 25–13　* window *f·* are of iron,
76–11　* furniture *f·* are of white

France
Mis. 304–15　* takes place at Paris, F·.
372–15　masters in F· and Italy.
Pul. 5–24　F·, Germany, Russia,

Frankish
Pul. 65–21　* F· church was reared upon the spot

Franklin
N. H.
My. 313–12　driving into F·, N. H.,
314– 8　was located in F·, N. H.
314–12　owned a house in F·, N. H.

My. 314– 4　* then moved to F·.

Franklin's, Benjamin
Mis. 277–18　truth of Benjamin F· report

frankly
'02. 14–27　answered *f·* and honestly,

frantically
Mis. 374–23　*f·* affirm what is what :

fraternity
Mis. 227– 2　no *f·* where its crime may
My. 175–24　*f·*, and Christian charity.

fraud
Mis. 368–14　Charlatanism, *f·*, and malice
My. 143–19　cannot be a temporal *f·*.
150–31　to call this "a subtle *f·*,"

fraudulent
Mis. 51– 8　the ignorant, the *f·*,
272–24　* Hence . . . is a *f·* claim.

fraught
Mis. 238–14　*f·* with infinite blessings,
253–14　F· with history, it repeats the
320– 8　*f·* with divine benedictions.
No. 23– 4　*f·* with spiritual danger.
Po. 23–11　may their gaze be ever *f·*
My. 129–13　*f·* with divine reflection.
234–29　is *f·* with danger.
258– 6　so *f·* with opposites,

free
Mis. 6– 3　leaves mortals but little time *f·*
30–20　"hath made me *f·* from — *Rom.* 8 : 2.
76–15　to set a human soul *f·* from its
83–15　you are a *f·* moral agent
90–15　Then help others to be *f·* ;
101–18　and sets the captive *f·*,
103–17　eternal Mind is *f·*, unlimited,
113– 7　*f·* moral agency is lost ;
119–19　a plea for *f·* moral agency,
154–19　Through the word . . . are you made *f·*.
157–13　*f·* in Truth and Love,
183–10　Man is *f·* born :
185–22　upright, pure, and *f·* ;
201–19　hath made me *f·* from — *Rom.* 8 : 2.
241–23　truth shall make you *f·*." — *John* 8 : 32.
246– 2　and the prohibiting of *f·* speech,
246–17　stop *f·* speech, slander, vilify ;
264–20　before they are quite *f·* from
316– 3　to know the truth that makes *f·*,
321–16　hath made me *f·* from — *Rom.* 8 : 2.
326– 3　hath made you *f·* from — see *Rom.* 8 : 2.
356– 6　need no terrible detonation to *f·* them.
388– 8　F· us from human strife.
398–24　'T was the Truth that made us *f·*,
Man. 34–17　F· from Other Denominations.
84– 5　to know the truth that makes *f·*,
91– 7　Remuneration and F· Scholarship.
91–10　card of *f·* scholarship from
91–12　a *f·* course in this department
91–14　gives *f·* admission to classes.
Chr. 53–33　Forever present, bounteous, *f·*,
Ret. 11–12　In our God-blessed *f·* school.
11–22　F· as the generous air,
Un. 60–18　Mortals are *f·* moral agents,
Pul. 44–24　* a church . . . *f·* of debt.
Rud. 12–24　*f·* the minds of the healthy
13–22　it will *f·* his patient.
14–14　sometimes seventeen, *f·* students in it ;
No. 45–24　Let the Word have *f·* course
46–12　upon *f·* moral agency ;
46–18　rejoicing, . . . that we are *f·* born.
'01. 10– 2　truth shall make you *f·*." — *John* 8 : 32.
'02. 9–12　hath made me *f·* from — *Rom.* 8 : 2.
15– 7　keeping a *f·* institute,
Peo. 10–13　Paul said, "I was *f·* born." — *Acts* 22 : 28.
10–14　Justice and truth make man *f·*,
10–19　they alone have fettered *f·* limbs,
11– 6　can *f·* its body from disease
Po. 1–11　from chaos dark set *f·*,
3– 9　sleep sets drooping fancy *f·*
7– 8　F· us from human strife.
25– 9　From your green bowers *f·*,
39– 2　Gifts, lofty, pure, and *f·*,
47–12　Will the hereafter from suffering *f·*
00– 9　In our God-blessed *f·* school.
00–20　F· as the generous air,
75– 4　'Twas the Truth that made us *f·*,
My. 24– 3　* the truth which makes *f·*
75–27　* dedicated to-morrow *f·* from debt.
76–18　* dedicate their churches *f·* of debt
77–27　* absolutely *f·* of debt,
84– 9　* until it be wholly *f·* from debt.
91–30　* is absolutely *f·* from debt.
94–19　* structure was *f·* from debt.
98– 8　* dedicated *f·* from debt,
98–21　* absolutely *f·* of debt,
98–29　* its dedication *f·* from debt
113–14　hath made me *f·* from — *Rom.* 8 : 2.
117–26　give their talents . . . *f·* scope
119– 8　Man is *f·* from the flesh
133–15　set the captive sense *f·*
161– 2　set *f·* by enabling us to
205– 5　Christ hath made us *f·*." — *Gal.* 5 : 1.
272– 6　hath made me . . . *f·* from — *Rom.* 8 : 2.
293–29　hath made me *f·* from — *Rom.* 8 : 2
350–15　the pathway glad and *f·*

freed
Mis. 90–15　Do you desire to be *f·* from sin?

freedom (see also freedom's)
air and
Mis. 356– 9　stifled from lack of air and *f·*.
and greatness
Mis. 331–11　its springtide of *f·* and greatness.
No. 8–16　struggle into *f·* and greatness,
and supremacy
Ret. 45–13　gain spiritual *f·* and supremacy.
bulwarks of
Pul. 9– 2　you are the bulwarks of *f·*,
dearer than
Pul. 83–23　* by bonds dearer than *f·*,"
final
Mis. 361–21　So shall mortals soar to final *f·*,
from pain
Mis. 298–28　gains *f·* from pain

freedom

from sin
Peo. 10–24 mind's *f·* from sin ;
great
Mis. 120–14 great *f·* for the race ;
greater
Ret. 95– 2 blossom into greater *f·*,
growing
Ret. 31– 4 solemn certainty in growing *f·*
heritage of
My. 128–14 vital heritage of *f·*
insufficient
My. 266– 2 chapter sub-title
266– 7 and insufficient *f·* of honest
missionary of
Mis. 304– 9 * as a missionary of *f·*,
nation's
Ret. 43–23 Centennial Day of our nation's *f·*.
native
My. 120–12 gives to soul its native *f·*.
of choice
Ret. 71–14 *f·* of choice and self-government.
of health
Mis. 101–12 for the *f·* of health, holiness, and
of mortals
No. 34–28 *f·* of mortals from sin and death.
pleaded for
Mis. 345– 5 pleaded for *f·* in immortal strains
Principle of
Mis. 258–18 this infinite Principle of *f·*,
reigned
Mis. 259–14 *f·* reigned, and was the heritage of
religious
Mis. 251–13 civil and religious *f·*,
My. 167–22 chapter sub-title
rights of
Mis. 297–29 belongs to the rights of *f·*.
strength and
Mis. 240–12 physical strength and *f·*.
struggling for
No. 40–22 the thought struggling for *f·*.
this
Mis. 259–16 this *f·* was the moral power of
to believe
Pul. 51– 3 * *F·* to believe or to dissent
to worship
Ret. 2– 8 seeking "*f·* to worship God ;"
My. 168– 1 *F·* to worship God according to
341– 6 * "*F·* to worship God."
true
Mis. 176–23 to establish a nation in true *f·*,

Mis. 141–13 *f·*, might, and majesty of Spirit,
204–15 *f·*, deep-toned faith in God ;
My. 154–22 * he have light, . . . *f·*, immortality ?"
316–19 the *f·* of Christian sentiments,

freedom's

Ret. 11– 9 sword is sheathed, 't is *f·* hour,
12– 2 Wake *f·* welcome,
Po. 60– 6 sword is sheathed, 'tis *f·* hour,
60–22 Wake *f·* welcome,
71–18 *f·* birthday — blood-bought boon !

free-love

Mis. 285–15 first crossed swords with *f·*,
285–26 up from the ashes of *f·*,

freely

Mis. 38– 2 *good we can do must be done f·*
149– 4 Invite all cordially and *f·*
Ret. 18–18 *f·* adore all His spirit hath made,
Pul. 64– 5 * Money came *f·* from all parts
Po. 64– 9 *f·* adore all His spirit hath made,
My. 62–30 * gave *f·* of their time and efforts
69–21 * where five thousand people can *f·*
157–12 * church home you have so *f·* bestowed.
172–17 '*F·* ye have received,— *Matt.* 10 : 8.
172–18 *f·* give.'— *Matt.* 10 : 8.
320– 9 * He also expressed himself *f·*
321–15 * talked so *f·* in my presence.
324– 1 * He often spoke his thoughts *f·*

Free Mason

My. 312–10 Glover, however, was a *F· M·*,
330–23 "My husband was a *F· M·*,

freemason

Ret. 19–11 My husband was a *f·*,

Free Masonry

My. 351– 6 * its beautiful tribute to *F· M·*.
351–11 *morale* of *F· M·* is above ethics

freemasonry

Mis. 142–26 symbols of *f·* depicted on
142–29 I may not unite with you in *f·*,

Free Masons

My. 312–27 *F· M·* selected my escort,
326–17 *F· M·* laid on his bier the emblems

Freemason's Monthly Magazine

My. 334–28 * appeared in 1845 in the *F· M· M·*,

Free Press

Pul. 89–29 * *F· P·*, Detroit, Mich.
90–13 * *F· P·*, London, Can.

freer

Hea. 4– 4 must give *f·* breath to thought

freest

Pul. 80– 7 * *f·* country in the world

freeth

Un. 56–16 *f·* him from the law of sin

freeze

Mis. 88–26 * had never seen water *f·*."
Ret. 65– 7 *f·* out the spiritual element.

French

Pul. 27– 2 * *F·* mirrors and every convenience.
Rud. 1–12 In *F·* the equivalent word is

French Commisioners

Mis. 277–19 report before the *F· C·*

French Huguenots

Mis. 281–12 in the time of the *F· H·*,

frequency

My. 268– 4 The *f·* of divorce shows

frequent

Mis. 238–25 The *f·* public allegement that I am
Man. 84–22 for more *f·* meetings.
Pul. 25–26 * *f·* illuminated texts from the
My. v– 7 * wonderment and *f·* comment,
332–24 * After *f·* searchings and much

frequented

Ret. 89–18 he had *f·* in childhood.
My. 72– 7 * *f·* by members of the

frequently

Mis. 6–21 *F·* it requires time to
45– 9 fatal results that *f·* follow
197– 4 text is one more *f·* used
256–13 classes from forming as *f·* as
322– 7 are *f·* disappointed.
339– 4 would happen very *f·* on earth,
No. 32–11 *F·* when I touch this subject
'01. 4–29 meaning divine Love, more *f·* than
My. 83– 9 * Scientists *f·* wear a small pin,
310–24 * *f·* set the house in an uproar,"
313–24 * *f·*" seek my advice.
324–32 * Mr. and Mrs. Wiggin *f·* mentioned

fresh

Mis. 1–16 mounting sense gathers *f·* forms
51–26 * *f·*, as from a second birth,
144–24 *f·* as a summer morn,
227–18 *f·* flowers of feeling blossom,
240–23 over the *f·*, unbiased thought.
Ret. 27–30 a *f·* universe — old to God,
48– 7 experience . . . *f·* in my thoughts,
Pul. 53– 1 * *f·* development of a Principle
'00. 10–10 *f·* energy and final victory.
Hea. 19–19 *f·* opportunities every hour ;
Po. 15–18 Flowers *f·* as the pang in the bosom
25–12 Fragrance *f·* round the dead,
46–11 *F·* as the fragrant sod,
My. 50–20 * brought *f·* courage to the
155–19 a pure peace, a *f·* joy,
195–22 breath *f·* from God,
244–11 designed to impart a *f·* impulse

freshen

Mis. 330–23 *f·* the fragrance of being.

freshness

Mis. ix–21 fleeting *f·* of youth,
240– 6 must not take the sweet *f·* out
269–13 perpetual *f·* in relation to
343–18 vernal *f·* and sunshine

fresh-smiling

Po. 67– 7 bedewing these *f·* flowers !

fret

Un. 56–23 made to *f·* in their chains;
My. 135–28 "*F·* not thyself — *Psal.* 37 : 1.
211–25 *f·* and confuse it, spoiling that

fretful

My. 10–19 * *f·* or reluctant sacrifice

fretfulness

Mis. 6– 4 free from complaints and *f·*,

fretted

Mis. 162–10 over their *f·*, foaming billows.

friction

Mis. 104–20 the *f·* of false selfhood
224–20 the *f·* of the world

Friday

Mis. 148–24 at your *F·* evening meetings.
Man. 57– 3 held on the *F·* preceding

Friday
  Man. 57– 5 the first *F·* in November
  Pul. 85–24 * received *F·*, from the C. S. Board
Friend
  (*see* **Eddy**)
friend
 and foe
  Mis. 32–15 admissible towards *f·* and foe.
 best
  Mis. 236–21 though it be your best *f·* ;
       298–12 best *f·* break troth with me?
 earthly
  My. 358–11 your Leader and best earthly *f·*.
       361– 1 your healer, or any earthly *f·*.
 family
  Ret. 17– 1 while visiting a family *f·*
  Po. vii– 1 * *while visiting a family f·*
 happy
  Mis. 385–10 "Joy for thee, happy *f·* !
  Po. 48– 1 Joy for thee, happy *f·* !
 met friend
  My. 63–16 * as *f·* met friend at every turn
 my
  Pul. 39–10 from my *f·*, Miss Whiting,
  My. 322–20 * During the evening my *f·* spoke of
 of mine
  Mis. 225– 5 his mother— a *f·* of mine,
 or foe
  Mis. 290–26 whether it be *f·* or foe,
  No. 3– 5 error murders either *f·* or foe
 our
  My. 14–18 * Our *f·* very promptly and
 trusty
  Mis. 147–22 at all times the trusty *f·*,
 without
  Mis. 227– 5 without *f·* and without apologist.
 your
  Mis. 364– 8 made the public your *f·*,
  My. 332–13 * Your *f·* and obedient servant,

  Mis. 89– 5 or a *f·* in sickness, who is
      118–13 and pass a *f·* over it smoothly,
      339–23 Hast thou a *f·*, and forgettest to be
      399–11 Strongest deliverer, *f·* of the
  Pul. 33–23 * so a *f·* has told me,
  Pan. 3– 7 a *f·*, with whom to whisper,
  Po. 75–18 Strongest deliverer, *f·* of the
  My. 14–11 * we received a letter from a *f·*
      322–15 * a *f·* and I were the guests
friendless
  Mis. 399–11 friend of the *f·*,
  Po. 41– 9 And the mountains more *f·*,
     75–18 friend of the *f·*,
friendlessness
  Rud. 17–11 *f·*, toil, agonies, and
friendly
  Mis. 80–12 It is better to be *f·*
     294–17 O *f·* hand ! keep back thy
     330– 9 man, more *f·*, should call his
  My. 320–19 * but his tendency was *f·*.
friends (*see also* **friends'**)
 admires
  My. 41–20 * admires *f·* and hates enemies,
 and books
  Mis. vii– 5 * well made choice of *f·* and books ;
 and brethren
  Mis. 106–17 *F·* and Brethren :— Your Sunday Lesson,
     120–27 *F·* and Brethren :— The Biblical record
  My. 147– 2 *F·* and Brethren :— There are
 and country
  Mis. 251–11 religion, home, *f·*, and country.
 and enemies
  My. 276–12 all her dear *f·* and enemies.
 and followers
  Pul. 54–25 * with his closest *f·* and followers,
  My. 143–10 my beloved *f·* and followers
 beloved
  My. 42–13 * *Beloved F·* :— Most unexpectedly
     143–10 my beloved *f·* and followers
 best
  Mis. 9–13 are virtually thy best *f·*.
     267– 5 are the best *f·* to our growth.
 circle of
  Ret. 19–14 lamented by a large circle of *f·*
  My. 330–26 lamented by a large circle of *f·*
 concourse of
  Mis. 225– 3 happy concourse of *f·* had gathered
 departed
  Mis. 60–13 *departed f· — dead only in belief*
 faithful
  My. 321– 7 * your devoted and faithful *f·*,
 her
  Mis. 49– 7 Her *f·* employed a homœopathist,
     49– 9 opinion given to her *f·*,

friends
 her
  Po. vii– 8 * *When this became known to her f·*,
  My. 332– 1 * to restore her to her *f·*
     332–12 * in the fond embrace of her *f·*.
 indebted
  Mis. 228– 4 deemed at least indebted *f·*
 interested
  Pul. 80–13 * sent us by interested *f·*,
 literary
  '02. 15–26 I showed it to my literary *f·*,
  My. 324–23 * among his literary *f·*.
 loving
  Pul. 76–18 * the tribute of loving *f·*.
 my
  Mis. 178–27 My *f·*, I wished to be excused from
     180– 5 my *f·* were frightened
     213–14 May my *f·* and my enemies
  Po. 73– 1 inscribed to my *f·* in Lynn.
  My. 145–22 serve equally my *f·* and my enemies.
     174– 6 courtesy extended to my *f·*
     297–30 my *f·* have read Sibyl Wilbur's book,
 number of
  Ret. 7–20 * by a large number of *f·*,
 of a patient
  Mis. 282–21 If the *f·* of a patient desire
 other
  Pul. 37–20 * one or two other *f·* were gathered.
 our
  Mis. 11–19 whereby we love our *f·* ;
  Ret. 80–27 We love our *f·*, but ofttimes we
  My. 332– 8 * will our *f·* at Wilmington
 personal
  My. 138–12 students and trusted personal *f·*
 pitying
  Mis. 212–30 Pitying *f·* took down from the
 relatives and
  My. 331–19 * relatives and *f·* of the late
 remain
  '02. 2–25 Then why not remain *f·*,
 students and
  Mis. 137– 2 *My Dear Students and F·* :
     142–11 *Beloved Students and F·* :
 surrounded by
  My. 312–24 I was surrounded by *f·*,
 that forsake
  My. 258–22 and *f·* that forsake.
 their
  My. 76–11 * church members and their *f·*
 those
  My. 331–22 * those *f·* of the deceased
     333–23 * those *f·* who attended him during
 Thy
  My. 220–22 make them Thy *f·* ;
 thy
  Mis. vii– 7 * In making thy *f·* books,
 to Truth
  Mis. 319–29 faith and resolve are *f·* to Truth ;
 truest
  My. 213–10 are the truest *f·* of mankind,
 various
  Un. 27– 1 From various *f·* comes inquiry
 were requested
  My. 98–16 * *f·* were requested to send no
 without money or
  My. 312–10 * and entirely without money or *f·*.

  Mis. vii– 7 * and thy books *f·*.
     9–16 *f·* seem to sweeten life's cup
     89–13 *f·* have no faith in your method,
     142–30 as *f·* we can feel the touch of heart
     177–28 *F·* :— The homesick traveller in
     253– 6 *F·*, I am not enough the new woman
     308–18 *F·*, strangers, and
  Hea. 4–21 *F·*, can we ever arrive at a
     16–25 *F·*, it is of the utmost importance
  Po. 74– 1 *F·*, will not ye Think kindly of me,
  My. 27–15 * *f·* are requested to send no more
     44– 7 * *F·*, our progress may be fast or
     189–29 *f·*, why throng in pity round me?
     205–21 *f·* more faithful, and
friends'
  My. 275–21 praying for my dear *f·*
friendship (*see also* **friendship's**)
  Mis. 9–26 delicious forms of *f·*,
     100–23 Pure humanity, *f·*, home,
     145–18 In our rock-bound *f·*,
     251– 9 voicing the *f·* of this city
  Ret. 80–27 perfection and an unbroken *f·*.
     81– 7 our *f·* will surely continue.
     82–26 ecclesiastical fellowship and *f·*.
  Pul. 5– 6 light of one *f·* after another
  Po. 68–19 star of our *f·* arose
  My. 124–10 The fruition of *f·*,
     163–26 *f·*, and granite character.

friendship
 My. 175–23 the *f·* of those we love,
 201–11 Such elements of *f·*, faith,
 282– 5 *f·* of our chief executive
 362–21 * revere and cherish your *f·*,
friendship's
 Mis. 143– 2 *f·* "level" and the "square"
friendships
 Pul. 49–18 * talked earnestly of her *f·*.
 My. 204– 7 mutual *f·* such as ours
frieze
 Pul. 25–23 * with *f·* of the old rose,
fright
 Pul. 34–14 * to their bewilderment and *f·*,
frighten
 '01. 14–12 cannot be made so real as to *f·*
frightened
 Mis. 180– 6 *f·* at beholding me restored
 396– 3 And *f·* fancy flees,
 Un. 5–12 undisturbed by the *f·* sense
 Po. 58–15 And *f·* fancy flees,
 My. 123–25 is not *f·* at miracles,
frightens
 My. 160–14 a live truth, . . . *f·* people.
 216–12 a miracle that *f·* people,
 233– 7 challenged by Truth, *f·* you,
fringed
 Ret. 23– 8 was not even *f·* with light.
fringe-tree
 Ret. 17–18 magnolia, and fragrant *f·* ;
 Po. 63– 3 magnolia, and fragrant *f·* ;
frivolity
 '00. 2–14 no time for amusement, ease, *f·* ;
 My. 48–29 * drugged by scandal, drowned in *f·*,
 260– 7 shadow of *f·* and the
frivolous
 Ret. 21–25 personal events are *f·*
frocks
 My. 83–11 * laces of the women's *f·*,
front
 Mis. 23–29 actions of the object in *f·* of it.
 99–17 take the *f·* rank, face the foe,
 106– 9 Priestcraft in *f·* of them,
 Un. 6–25 if hastily pushed to the *f·*
 Pul. 24–10 * tower with a circular *f·*
 24–12 * On the *f·* is a marble tablet,
 59–30 * the *f·* vestibule and street
 My. 31–19 * a place in the *f·* rank of the
 31–26 * Stepping to the *f·* of the platform,
 44–16 * advanced to the *f·* of the platform,
 71–27 * in *f·* of the great organ.
 89–16 * even to the flagstones in *f·*
 110–15 mortal mind pressing to the *f·*,
 313– 9 road in *f·* of his house
frost
 Mis. 240–15 takes the *f·* out of the ground
froth
 Mis. 78–21 *f·* of error passing off ;
frown
 Pan. 1– 8 *f·* and smile of April,
 '02. 17–28 world's soft flattery or its *f·*.
 My. 129–10 no night but in God's *f·* ;
 134–17 pride— its pomp and its *f·*
 340–12 her *f·* on class legislation.
frowning
 My. 355–19 * "Behind a *f·* providence
frozen
 Mis. 176–21 *f·* ritual and creed should forever
 331–23 *f·* crust of creed and dogma,
 Ret. 31–28 F· fountains were unsealed.
 No. 14–25 *f·* dogmas, persistent persecution,
 Po. 41– 7 fountain and leaflet are *f·* and
fruit
 bear
 Mis. 144–27 may our earthly sowing bear *f·*
 151– 8 Those who bear *f·* He purgeth,
 My. 128–32 in your thought nor bear *f·*.
 bearing
 Mis. 357–18 and is bearing *f·*.
 Un. 6– 3 "bearing *f·* after its kind."— *see Gen.* 1 : 11.
 Pul. 26–24 * sprays of fig leaves bearing *f·*.
 bears
 Mis. 220–21 has power and bears *f·*,
 borne
 Mis. 356–17 has sprung up, borne *f·*,
 bring forth
 Mis. 154–24 Bring forth *f·*
 eat the
 My. 186–20 plant the vineyard eat the *f·*

fruit
 forbidden
 Un. 3–14 knowledge is not the forbidden *f·*
 good
 Mis. 235–14 bringeth not forth good *f·* ;
 My. 287–22 bringeth not forth good *f·* ;
 hothouse
 My. 325– 4 * and to leave luscious hothouse *f·*.
 its
 Mis. 223–10 tree is known by its *f·* ;
 My. 111–21 Is not the tree known by its *f·* ?
 112–24 The tree is known by its *f·*.
 269–20 vine is bringing forth its *f·* ;
 300–28 The tree is known by its *f·*.
 legitimate
 '02. 14–14 growth and . . . are its legitimate *f·*
 more
 Mis. 151– 9 that they may bear more *f·*.
 much
 Ret. 94–29 Jesus' teachings bore much *f·*,
 My. 202–29 that ye bear much *f·*."— *John* 15 : 8.
 of evil
 Un. 17–22 partake of the *f·* of evil,
 of experience
 My. 343–24 each one was the *f·* of experience
 of Godlikeness
 Un. 22– 5 may eat of the *f·* of Godlikeness,
 of righteousness
 My. 40–20 * the *f·* of righteousness— *Jas.* 3 : 18.
 of rightness
 My. 281– 9 is the *f·* of rightness,
 of the Spirit
 My. 167– 4 "the *f·* of the Spirit."— *Gal.* 5 : 22.
 of the tree
 Mis. 198–21 *f·* of the tree of the knowledge
 367–15 this *f·* of the tree of knowledge
 of this tree
 Mis. 356–20 carry the *f·* of this tree into the
 of ungodliness
 Un. 22– 5 but as to the *f·* of ungodliness,
 pudding, and
 Mis. 231–14 delicious pie, pudding, and *f·*
 rich
 My. 159– 9 rich *f·* of this branch of his vine,
 ripened
 My. 198– 8 their abundant and ripened *f·*.

 —

 Un. 3–15 it is the *f·* which grows on the
 My. 22–19 * justification . . . is the *f·*.
 218–26 *f·* of which all mankind may share.
fruitage
 Mis. 251–28 to enrich the soil for *f·*.
 308–24 I have gleaned from its *f·*
 Po. 9– 9 leaves all faded, the *f·* shed,
fruite
 Mis. 253–12 * chapter sub-title
fruitful
 Mis. 56–25 *f·, and multiply,*— *Gen.* 1 : 28.
 338–29 * Shall be a *f·* seed ;
 343– 8 human life more *f·*,
 '00. 3– 2 right, active, and they are *f·* ;
 My. 183–19 the forest becomes a *f·* field,
fruition
 Mis. 231– 2 the full *f·* of happiness ;
 281– 1 the *f·* of your labors,
 Ret. 92– 8 reach the *f·* of his promise :
 Un. 61–23 both demonstration and *f·*,
 Pul. 44– 3 * At last you begin to see the *f·*
 No. 9–13 may err . . . and lose your *f·*.
 My. 19–21 *f·* of her unselfed love,
 124–10 The *f·* of friendship,
 155–11 the full *f·* of its faith,
 253–24 If faith is *f·*, you have His
fruitless
 Pul. 33–22 * All inquiry . . . was *f·* ;
 '01. 31–14 no vague, *f·*, inquiring wonder.
 My. 294–17 by a *f·* use of the knife
fruits
 blight the
 Mis. 88– 1 to blight the *f·* of my students.
 immortal
 My. 182–15 sprang immortal *f·* through
 its
 My. 136– 5 is best explained by its *f·*,
 136–26 labor that is known by its *f·*,
 148– 5 judge our doctrine by its *f·*.
 204–28 these are its *f·* ;
 260–18 its *f·* are inspiration and
 of Christian Science
 Mis. 343–11 *f·* of C. S. spring upward,
 My. 204–26 are not the *f·* of C. S.,
 213– 1 *f·* of C. S. Mind-healing

fruits

of goodness
Mis. 219–29 f· of goodness will follow,
Ret. 54–13 without bearing the f· of goodness,
of health
Ret. 62– 5 bring forth better f· of health,
of Love
Mis. 100–15 finally show the f· of Love.
Un. 40– 8 and bears the f· of Love,
of Spirit
Mis. 153–18 bring forth the f· of Spirit,
303–10 peace and joy, the f· of Spirit,
331–10 will ripen the f· of Spirit,
Ret. 45–22 I saw these f· of Spirit,
Rud. 4–23 brings out the f· of Spirit
of the flesh
'02. 6– 6 f· of the flesh not Spirit.
of Truth
Mis. 265–20 bring forth the real f· of Truth.
of watchfulness
Mis. 116–23 f· of watchfulness, prayer,
of your ground
My. 269–25 f· of your ground.'' — Mal. 3 : 11.
of your labors
'00. 2–28 what of the f· of your labors?
prove
Mis. 354–14 whose f· prove the nature of their
purpose, and
Mis. 223– 2 its hidden paths, purpose, and f·
their
Mis. 90–20 then judge them by their f·.
Man. 49– 6 ''by their f· ye shall — Matt. 7 : 20.
No. 15– 2 ''By their f· ye shall — Matt. 7 : 20.
Pan. 10– 5 ''By their f· ye shall — Matt. 7 : 20.
My. 233– 4 ''by their f· ye shall — Matt. 7 : 20.
306–19 ''By their f· ye shall — Matt. 7 : 20.

My. 136–25 the f· of honest toil,
283–12 f· of said grand Association,
309–32 what were the f· of this

Frye

C. A.
Ret. 49–31 signature
Mr. Calvin A.
My. 138–14 Mr. Calvin A. F· and other students
317–16 Mr. Calvin A. F· copied my writings,

fuel

Hea. 9–14 furnishing f· for the flames.

fugitive

Peo. 10– 8 succored a f· slave in 1853,

fulfil

Mis. 29–28 on the contrary, they f· His laws ;
30–24 f· the law of Christ.'' — Gal. 6 : 2.
122–10 to f· a divine decree,
135–12 If you falter, or fail to f· this
193–15 man can f· the Scriptures
212– 1 f· the conditions of our petition
261–20 ''but to f·'' — Matt. 5 : 17.
278– 6 I shall f· my mission,
284–31 to f· that trust those rules must be
297–21 f· all the claims growing out of this
318–18 so f· the command of Christ.
Man. 28–18 If an officer fails to f· all the
29– 8 f· the requirements of this By-Law,
100–10 f· the obligations of his office
Ret. 38–11 to f· this painful task,
45–22 f· the law of Christ
47–22 so f· the command of Christ.
70–15 No person can compass or f·
90–12 until they were able to f· his
Un. 13– 6 f· the intended harmony of being.
Pul. 72– 1 * having a divine mission to f·,
83– 3 * what we never f· as husband and
No. 45–23 and so f· her destiny.
Pan. 12– 1 it will be found possible to f· it.
'02. 5–24 but to f·. — Matt. 5 : 17.
7–10 to f· the First Commandment.
My. 46–19 * f· the pledge in righteous living,
153– 5 will f· the law in righteousness.
153– 7 have come to f· the whole law.
162– 4 f· all righteousness.'' — Matt. 3 : 15.
217–31 but to f· it in righteousness.
218– 4 f· all righteousness.'' — Matt. 3 : 15.
219–25 but to f·.'' — Matt. 5 : 17.

fulfilled

Mis. 8–28 can only be f· through the
84–10 but the prophecies were f·,
141– 2 will be the prophecy f·,
286– 2 has already been f·.
308–21 f· its mission, retired with honor
358–30 When students have f· all the
Ret. 48–21 f· its high and noble destiny,
Un. 43–17 till all be f·.'' — Matt. 5 : 18.
Pul. 5–20 That prophecy is f·.

fulfilled

Pul. 13– 7 f·, when we are conscious of
29–21 * interpreted and f· literally,
73–15 * God has f· His promises to her
No. 13– 8 and the prophecy of Jesus f·,
37–28 and it must be f·.
Pan. 12–12 Scriptural commands be f·.
'00. 12–20 This prophecy has been f·.
'01. 10–30 After Jesus had f· his mission
'02. 4– 8 a more f· life and spiritual
8– 4 and both will be f·.
9–15 every promise f·, was loving and
18–23 prophecy of the great Teacher is f·
My. 36–28 * have f· a high resolve
44–11 * rejoices in prophecy f·,
125–30 The doom . . . is being f·.
171– 3 To-day is f· the prophecy of Isaiah :
177–23 this prophecy of Isaiah is f·
193–27 may the prophecy of Isaiah be f·:
202–11 hath f· the law.'' — Rom. 13 : 8.

fulfilling

Mis. 11– 3 Love is the f· of the law :
12–30 f· the law of Love,
155–27 thus f· their moral obligation to
258– 2 love is the f· of the law.
262– 5 aid our prospect of f· it by
285– 9 Love is the f· of the law.
304–20 * f· its mission throughout the
Ret. 65–23 Love, f· the law
'02. 9–11 f· the apostle's saying :
My. 131–23 f· much of the divine law
190–31 who are f· Jesus' prophecy
201– 3 and is fast f· the promises.

fulfilment

Mis. 76–30 the f· of this glorious prophecy
85–13 in the f· of this divine rule
136–14 and its f· of divine order.
192–33 The f· of the grand verities of
208– 4 Mortals cannot prevent the f· of
Pul. 9–11 and nerved its grand f·.
35– 7 * natural f· of divine law
My. 45–24 * the f· of the later prophecy,
132– 1 f· of divine Love in our lives
133– 4 might and light of the present f·.

fulfils

Mis. 66– 4 f· the law in righteousness,
73–16 Belief f· the conditions of a belief,
117–15 it f· the law.
209–10 belief f· the law of belief,
Ret. 76–16 f· the law of Love which Paul
'02. 6–18 f· the law in righteousness,
6–20 f· the law and the gospel,
My. 106– 4 love f· divine law
265–23 f· the saying of our great Master,
275–25 self-oblivious love f· the law

full

Mis. 16–13 reflect the f· dominion of Spirit
45– 3 The f· understanding that God is
46–21 f· significance of what the apostle
56–19 the f· revelation of Spirit,
80–18 and f· of trouble.'' — Job 14 : 1.
95– 7 * which reply was taken in f·
111– 6 net has been so f· that it broke :
119–19 f· exemption from all necessity to
147–27 f· of truth, candor, and
149–12 f· of accessions to your love,
151–25 lamp of our light continually be f·
164–26 f· of grace and Truth,
192–18 Principle of a f· salvation.
193–25 following his f· command
197– 6 the f· import of this text is not yet
197– 7 It means a f· salvation,
214– 2 While Jesus' life was f· of Love,
220–13 Thought has the f· control
222–19 suffer its f· penalty after death.
223–10 f· faith in the divine Principle,
227–28 grows into the f· stature of wisdom,
231– 2 f· fruition of happiness ;
261–12 pays his f· debt to divine law,
261–13 f·, pressed down, and
263–22 without a f· knowledge of the
270–18 have f· faith in his prophecy,
276–14 the f· coming of our Lord and Christ.
292–25 C. S., f· of grace and truth,
311–10 go forth to the f· vintage-time,
311–12 in the f· spirit of that charity
314–24 announcing the f· title of this book,
331– 1 crown the f· corn in the ear,
331– 6 f· of good odor.
338–25 * To give the lips f· speech.
357–24 should receive f· fellowship from us,
361–11 earth is f· of His glory,
377– 4 yet so near and f· of radiant relief
394–20 * So f· of sweet enchantment

full

Man.	27– 8	without consulting with the f· Board
	32–13	announce the f· title of the book
	39– 5	received into f· membership,
	39– 7	A f· member or a probationary member,
	110–13	given names of each, written in f·.
	111– 3	names must be written in f·.
Chr.	55–14	few days, and f· of trouble. — Job 14 : 1.
Ret.	2–24	contained a f· account of the
	15–20	if not in f· unity of doctrine.
	92– 6	the f· corn in the ear." — Mark 4 : 28.
Un.	51–23	the f· Truth is found only in
	58–16	f· compass of human woe,
Pul.	4–25	with it cometh the f· power of being.
	9– 6	the f· chords of such a rest.
	33–15	* Catholic biographies are f·,
	41– 4	* after the f· amount needed was
	44–12	* comprehends its f· significance.
	81–20	* she is as f· of beautiful possibilities
Rud.	14–15	to take the f· price of tuition
No.	22–24	as a mortal who is f· of evil.
	31–13	the only f· proof of its pardon.
'00.	7–29	wait for the f· appearing
	14– 6	f· numbers of days named
	14–18	hold in your f· hearts fervently
'01.	32– 8	F· of charity and good works,
'02.	9– 8	f· significance of this saying
Peo.	9–19	f· confidence in their efficacy,
	11– 1	f· liberty of the sons of God
Po.	57– 6	* So f· of sweet enchantment
My.	vi– 9	* only as they give her f· credit
	11– 8	* the f· force of antagonism.
	96–22	*fund was f· to overflowing
	107–13	a vial f· of the pellets
	149–18	vessel f· must be emptied
	150–12	can accomplish the f· scale ;
	155–14	finds the f· fruition of its faith,
	167–17	f· of love, peace, and good will
	201–13	I thank you out of a f· heart.
	204–24	charging . . . a f· fee for treatment,
	205–26	f· idea of its divine Principle,
	210– 5	added to the mind already f·.
	215–11	sent me the f· tuition money.
	224–19	giving f· credit to another
	236– 3	accept my f· heart's favor
	237– 8	not attained the f· understanding
	256–17	f· of divine benedictions and
	261– 6	f· supply of juvenile joy.
	280–17	and cease in f· faith that God
	284–25	f· efficacy of divine Love to
	294–12	f· faith and spiritual knowledge
	323–17	* My heart has been too f· to
	332–23	* as we had f· confidence that it
	333–25	*f· reliance for salvation on the
	338–19	a heart f· of love towards God
	340–30	f· beneficence of the laws of the

fuller

Mis.	320– 7	Christ's appearing in a f· sense

fullest

Mis.	169–32	In their f· meaning,
	223–21	name of Christ in its f· sense,
	303–11	brethren in the f· sense
	306– 2	*f· historical description.

full-fledged

Mis.	335–13	charge upon me with f· invective
My.	281– 7	Faith f·, soaring to the

full-length

Pul.	27– 2	* with f· French mirrors

full-orbed

Mis.	355– 3	f· promise, and a gaunt want.
No.	37–12	unfolds the f· glory of that event;
	46–19	f· significance of this destiny
'01.	8–10	but it is not the f· sun.
My.	265–15	to appear f· in millennial glory ;

fully

Mis.	102–20	f· expressed in divine Science,
	169–17	borne f· to our minds and hearts.
	185– 3	discern f· and demonstrate fairly
	187–17	f· comprehended the later teachings
	292–28	who f· understood my instructions
Man.	47– 6	case he cannot f· diagnose,
	66– 2	which he does not f· understand,
Ret.	27–13	had not f· voiced my discovery.
	84– 3	sufficiently . . . to be f· demonstrated.
	93–21	has not been f· demonstrated,
Un.	40–21	to him who f· understands Life.
	56–19	not f· exempt from physicaiity
Pul.	44– 6	* You are f· occupied,
	54–22	* they are f· set forth.
	69–16	* take a small book to explain f·
	69–20	* power f· developed to heal
	87–15	f· appreciate your kind intentions.
Rud.	14– 9	f· seven-eighths of her time

fully

No.	20–12	f· conveys the ideas of God,
	27–12	f· interpreted by divine Science,
My.	25– 3	* to dispose f· and finally of
	87–16	* their costly church f· paid for,
	91– 8	* church edifices to be f· paid for
	112–19	f· understood when demonstrated.
	136– 4	cannot be f· understood,
	146–16	are not f· scaled.
	240– 7	* to explain more f· why you
	242– 8	Unless you f· perceive that
My.	267– 2	since Christianity is f· demonstrated
	286– 9	wisely, fairly ; and f· settled.
	338– 9	* her writings will f· corroborate

fulness

Mis.	15–25	f· of the stature of man
	172–14	arrives at f· of stature ;
Pul.	85– 7	* will, in the f· of time, see
No.	19–24	f· of the stature of man
'01.	11– 1	f· of his stature in Christ,
'02.	20– 9	with the f· of divine Love."
Po.	vii– 4	*f· in her later productions.
My.	33–28	and the f· thereof ; — Psal. 24 : 1.
	357– 3	the spiritual f· of God,

function

Un.	34– 8	whole f· of material sight
Hea.	19– 4	every f· of the body,
My.	249–26	perform this important f·.

functional

Rud.	13– 2	hence Life is not f·,
Pan.	10–18	heal f·, organic, chronic,
My.	106– 1	in f· and organic diseases

functions

Mis.	260–27	performs the vital f·
Man.	28–16	f· of their several offices
	29–12	perform their f· faithfully.
	65–17	applies to their official f·.
	82– 6	connected with these f·.
Pan.	4– 9	the f· of these faculties
Hea.	19– 6	else those f· could not
My.	218– 2	its normal action, f·, and
	288–19	to perform the f· of Spirit,
	301–27	restore disordered f·,
	303–30	love to perform the f· of

fund (see also Building Fund)

building

Pul.	9– 1	into the building f· have come
	42–12	* contributors to the building f·,
My.	14–15	* building f· had been paid in ;
	14–24	* the building f· is not complete,
	14–30	* contributions to the building f·
	16– 3	* treasurer of the building f·
	19–15	* The Mother Church building f·,
	19–30	towards its church building f·.
	20–15	The Mother Church building f·,
	20–27	* building f· of The Mother Church
	21– 1	* contribute to the building f·
	21–12	* contribute . . . to the building f·
	22–11	* further needs of the building f·,
	24–31	* completing the building f·
	25– 9	* contributions to the building f·.
	27–11	* contributors to the building f·
	27–24	* treasurer of the building f·,
	28– 7	* contributed to the building f·.
	72–18	* treasurer of the building f·
	76– 9	* contributions to the building f·
	86–15	* building f· of the great temple

Man.	78–22	as a petty cash f·,
My.	10–11	* paid in towards the f·,
	21– 5	* transferring to this f· the money
	27–16	* no more money to this f·.
	28–13	* the giving to this f· has
	96–22	*f· was full to overflowing
	176– 4	Concord (N. H.) Street F·
	216–25	The Mother Church flower f·.
	289– 5	De Hirsch monument f·.
	318–28	f· of historical knowledge,

fundamental

Mis.	75– 8	I urge this f· fact
	172–28	first and f· rule of Science
	186–21	torn apart from its f· basis.
	221– 8	f· Principle of C. S. ;
	233– 1	without knowing its f· Principle.
Ret.	31–16	f· error of faith in things material
	49–11	f· principle for growth in C. S.
Pul.	69–17	*f· idea is that God is Mind,
'00.	4–30	enunciates this f· fact
'01.	3–18	f·, intelligent, divine Being,
My.	260–20	f· and demonstrable truth,
	268– 6	some f· error is engrafted
	297–23	f· truth of C. S.
	347–23	chapter sub-title

fundamentals
   My. 75– 3   * its faith in its *f·*.
funds
   Man. 30–17   shall pay from the Church *f·*
        75– 1   heading
        75–21   the balance of the building *f·*,
        76– 1   balance of the church building *f·*,
        76– 6   management of the Church *f·* :
        76–11   *f·* which the Church has on hand,
        76–23   and the amount of *f·* received
        76–25   individually responsible for said *f·*.
        77–11   If it be found that the Church *f·*
        77–16   proper distribution of the *f·*
        78–18   pay from the *f·* of the Church
        79–11   shall be paid from the Church *f·*.
        80– 4   Disposal of *F·*.
        91–15   Surplus *F·*.
        91–15   Any surplus *f·* left in the
   Ret. 53– 2   and the *f·* belonging thereto.
   Pul. 44–27   * until the custodian of *f·*
        64– 6   * securing sufficient *f·* for
        64–11   * the custodian of the *f·* was
   '02. 13– 6   my personal property and *f·*,
        13–15   when a loss of *f·* occurred,
   My. 19–14   * their local church building *f·*
        27–14   * sufficient *f·* have been received
        27–23   * sufficient *f·* have been received
        58– 4   * no more *f·* are needed
        98–19   * the *f·* required to build it
fungus
   Mis. 131– 3   a *f·*, a microbe, a mouse
fur
   Mis. 329–22   the *f·* cap on pussy-willow,
furious
   Po. 43– 8   Fondling e'en the lion *f·*,
furnace
   Mis. 151– 8   through the *f·* of affliction.
        278–17   are tried in the *f·*
   '02. 19–26   triumphed in *f·* fires.
   My. 269-18   molten in the *f·* of Soul.
        303–32   molten in the *f·* of affliction.
furnish
   Mis. 155–28   to *f·* some reading-matter
        157–11   *f·* all information possible.
        247–10   to *f·* a single instance of
   Man. 30–19   suitably *f·* the house,
        89–22   *f·* evidence of their eligibility
   No. 9–20   "*f·* a table in — *Psal.* 78 : 19.
   My. 166–11   with which to *f·* First Church
        173–14   to help *f·* and beautify our
        180   1   *f·* rules whereby man can
furnished
   Mis. 10–10   *f·* them defenses impregnable.
   Man. 111–20   will be *f·* special forms
   Un. 46–26   *f·* the battle-ground of
   Pul. 58–28   * *f·* with all conveniences
   Rud. 14–19   *f·* students with the means
   No. 2–19   Institutes *f·* with such teachers
   '00. 12–11   *f·* items concerning this city.
   '02. 12–30   I *f·* the money from my own
   Hea. 16–18   is *f·* by these senses ;
   My. 123–15   *f·* him the money to pay for it.
        156–17   upper room *f·* : — *Luke* 22 : 12.
        342– 1   * the ample, richly *f·* house
furnishes
   Mis. 242–18   C. S. that *f·* its own proof.
        258–27   *f·* man with the only suitable
        350–31   *f·* its own proof of my practice.
   Ret. 57– 4   *f·* a scientific basis for the
   My. 218– 6   *f·* reasons or examples for the
furnishing
   Ret. 50–27   *f·* a new rule of order
   Pul. 76– 5   * The *f·* of the "Mother's Room"
   Hea. 9–14   like *f·* fuel for the flames.
   My. 118–20   *f·* the demands upon the finite
        162–14   embellishing, and *f·* our church
furnishings
   Pul. 23– 6   * Beautiful Temple and Its *F·*
furniture
   Mis. 283– 7   unlock the desk, displace the *f·*,
   Pul. 76–11   * *f·* frames are of white mahogany
furrow
   Mis. 339–19   added one *f·* to the brow of care?
further
   Mis. 4–16   *F·* enlightenment is necessary
        68–31   is a *f·* definition.
        201–28   bar his door against *f·* robberies.
        244– 8   He *f·* states that God cannot

further
   Mis. 245–25   to go no *f·* in the direction of
        295– 9   anonymous talker *f·* declares,
        302–23   desist from *f·* copying of my
   Man. 102–11   *f·* purchases of land
   Ret. 6–30   *f·* political preferment,
   Un. 36–16   A *f·* proof of this is the
   Pul. vii–19   scan *f·* the features of the
        30– 2   * I was *f·* told that once
        37–11   * *f·* writings on C. S.
        44–28   * refused to accept any *f·* checks
        64–12   * refuse *f·* contributions,
   My. 14–16   * *f·* payments or subscriptions
        20–26   * *f·* fact that it is important
        22–11   * *f·* needs of the building fund,
        42–11   * *f·* words of mine are unnecessary.
        50–17   * as the records *f·* relate,
        56–26   * still *f·* provision must be made,
        148– 1   must not expect me *f·* to
        217– 4   *F·* to encourage your
        319– 5   heard nothing *f·* from him
        328–28   * The section, . . . *f·* says,
        333–10   * record this *f·* proceeding :
        334–17   * Nothing could be *f·* from
        334–26   * Of *f·* interest in this matter
furtherance
   Ret. 50–25   *f·* and unfolding of Truth,
   '02. 9– 2   gives man power with untold *f·*.
   My. 45– 2   * for the *f·* of our Cause,
        212–32   in *f·* of unscrupulous designs.
furthermore
   Man. 98–11   *F·*, the Committee on Publication
fury
   Po. vi–16   *such f· that the city authorities*
fused
   Mis. 305–22   * copper, and nickel can be *f·*.
        305–25   * to be *f·* into the bell,
fusing
   Rud. 16–25   *f·* with a class of aspirants
fusion
   No. 5–26   Any contradictory *f·* of
fussing
   My. 71– 8   * no need of *f·* about the
fustian
   My. 143–14   Above all this *f·* of either
futile
   Mis. 118–29   attempt of evil to harm good is *f·*,
future
   Mis. 7–20   to be depicted in some *f·* time
        12–11   the *f·*, big with events.
        61– 4   The education of the *f·* will be
        100– 8   Past, present, *f·*, will show the
        139–26   transaction will in *f·* be regarded
        148–20   destined for *f·* generations
        230– 6   If one would be successful in the *f·*,
        253–15   and portends much for the *f·*.
        264–23   the *f·* mental influence of their
        281–32   You will need, in *f·*, *practice*
        285–22   In the present or *f·*,
        285–30   will have no past, present, or *f·*.
        286– 8   We look to *f·* generations for
        339– 9   robes the *f·* with hope's rainbow
        368– 8   * Yet that scaffold sways the *f·*,
   Man. 3–18   destined for *f·* generations
        77–23   Provision for the *f·*.
        77–24   any possible *f·* deviation
   Pul. 7–13   were but enshrined for *f·* use,
        65– 8   * may have a *f·* before it,
        84–21   * the *f·* will tell the story
   No. 28–16   The present, as well as the *f·*,
   Pan. 10–15   present and *f·* of those students
   '01. 16– 3   chapter sub-title
        16– 4   a *f·* and eternal punishment
        31– 8   in the near *f·* will learn
   '02. 4–24   past, present, and *f·*.
   Hea. 2–26   Past, present, *f·* magnifies his
   My. vi–23   * *f·* profits to her church ;
        12–20   We own no past, no *f·*,
        13– 2   on the past, present, nor *f·*,
        14– 6   to be discerned in the near *f·*
        22–22   * needs of the present and of the *f·*
        43–17   * In *f·* generations when it was asked,
        48–13   * the *f·* growth of her church,
        52–22   * to be Mrs. Eddy's *f·* reputation
        85–21   * for *f·* generations to reverence
        187– 4   at some near *f·* visit your city,
        220–24   Past, present, or *f·* philosophy
        224–13   *f·* must disclose and dispel.
        325–10   * as having a greater *f·*
        346–27   would be my *f·* successor.

G

Gabriel
Hea. 20– 6 * vie with *G·*, while he sings,
gagged
Mis. 274–17 When the press is *g·*,
gain (noun)
Mis. 6–24 once convinced . . . the *g·* is rapid.
  84–20 *and to die is g·.*" — *Phil.* 1 : 21
  116–17 express life's loss or *g·*,
  288–21 reckon the universal cost and *g·*,
  321– 8 *g·* of Truth's idea in C. S. ;
  358– 7 their *g·* is loss to the . . . Scientist.
  389–17 since God is good, and loss is *g·*.
Pul. vii–13 *g·* of intellectual momentum,
'00. 3– 8 to distribute *g·*."
'02. 17–20 Then thy *g·* outlives the sun,
Po. 4–16 since God is good, and loss is *g·*.
My. 252–31 cold impulse of a lesser *g·* !
gain (verb)
Mis. 33–18 Patients naturally *g·* confidence in C. S.
  38– 3 ability to *g·* and maintain health,
  40–23 must *g·* the power over sin
  50–16 *g·* the spiritual understanding of
  53– 9 *g·* heaven, the harmony of being.
  65–15 to *g·* the true solution of Life
  86–19 until we *g·* the glorified sense of
  104–28 or would not *g·* the true ideal of Life
  104–30 I will *g·* a balance on the side of
  111–12 *g·* a higher sense of the true idea.
  116–18 *g·* of its sweet concord,
  172–28 To *g·* this scientific result,
  174–26 whereby to *g·* heaven.
  181–27 in the proportion that they *g·* the
  186–18 but *g·* it clearly ;
  203–20 *g·* severe views of themselves ;
  215– 8 *g·* a spiritual understanding
  226–18 asked what a person could *g·* by
  227– 1 traffic by which he can *g·* nothing.
  234– 9 we *g·* a true sense of Love as God ;
  254–16 *g·* the kingdom of God.
  270–16 *G·* a pure Christianity ;
  311–16 *g·* the abiding consciousness of
  341–19 and you find Life eternal : you *g·* all.
  389–24 aftersmile earth's tear-drops *g·*,
Ret. 34– 3 to *g·* the Science of Mind,
  38–28 must also *g·* its spiritual significance,
  45–13 *g·* spiritual freedom and supremacy.
  55– 4 *g·* sufficient knowledge of error
Un. 2–18 *g·* that spiritual sense of harmony
  4– 7 To *g·* a temporary consciousness of
  13–12 as we *g·* the true understanding
  14– 8 *g·* wisdom and power from past
Pul. 9–28 *g·* the ear and right hand of
  50–27 * will *g·* followers and live down any
  69–24 * may *g·* a better understanding than
No. 23–16 Which . . . is the more important to *g·*,
  34– 4 when we *g·* the truer sense
'01. 1–24 to *g·* the absolute and supreme
  7–26 nor can they *g·* any evidence of
'02. 10–15 *g·* the scope of Jacob's vision,
Hea. 4–22 *g·* a right idea of the Principle
  16–22 evidence through which we can *g·* no
  16–26 *g·* our evidences of Life from
Po. 5– 5 aftersmile earth's tear-drops *g·*,
  43–19 Till they *g·* at last
My. 39– 2 * *g·* admittance at that hour
  48–21 * build such truth as they do *g·*
  79–12 * to *g·* admission to the temple
  148–27 struggling to *g·* power over
  194–11 *g·* greatness who *g·* themselves
  246–11 to *g·* a higher hope for the race,
  253– 9 manhood's glorious crown to *g·*."
  287–15 In love for man we *g·* the only
gained
Mis. vii–15 Nothing have we *g·* therefrom,
  10–17 *g·* by crossing swords with
  24–21 knowledge *g·* from mortal sense
  43–17 letter is *g·* sooner than the spirit
  80– 3 you lose much more than can be *g·*
  107–14 Three cardinal points must be *g·*
  126–11 We also have *g·* higher heights ;
  206–11 are *g·* through growth, not
  226– 9 What has an individual *g·* by
  234– 7 nor *g·* by a culpable attempt to
  278–27 the sooner this lesson is *g·*
  293–10 *g·* from instruction, observation,
  298– 2 Nothing is *g·* by wrong-doing.
  338– 3 must have *g·* its height beforehand,
  347–24 and the summit can be *g·*.
  353–10 you have *g·* the right one
Ret. 10– 3 *g·* book-knowledge with far less
  24– 9 I *g·* the scientific certainty

gained
Ret. 30–23 neither can . . . be *g·* without
Un. 5– 4 understanding they have already *g·*
  51– 9 *g·* through Christ as perfect
  55–17 *g·* him the assurance that
Pul. 79–11 * *g·* to itself adherents
No. 8–28 *g·* from your forbearance.
  12– 1 C. S. Mind-healing can only be *g·* by
'00. 10–10 *g·* fresh energy and final victory.
Peo. 2–15 evidences *g·* from the material
  13– 8 understanding is *g·* in C. S.,
My. 181–23 *g·* from a population of 238,000 to
  278–22 Nothing is *g·* by fighting,
  349– 5 consciousness *g·* through Christ,
gaining
Mis. 113–12 not *g·* a higher sense of Truth
  160–10 knowing that one is *g·* constantly
  327–19 Despairing of *g·* the summit,
Ret. 54–10 *g·* the end through persecution and
My. 233– 1 *g·* the spirit of true watching,
gains
Mis. 17–31 *g·* a truer sense of Spirit
  41–15 *g·* the summit in Science
  43–12 sense one *g·* of this Science
  182–11 man *g·* the power to become the
  221– 5 *g·* in the rules of metaphysics,
  252– 5 *g·* no potency by attenuation,
  298–28 *g·* freedom from pain
Ret. 76–23 *g·* the God-crowned summit of C. S.
Un. 2–12 *g·* a higher sense of God,
  36– 8 and *g·* a knowledge of God
Pan. 12–20 *g·* and points the path.
My. 83–29 * made steady *g·* in recent years.
  112– 4 where Science *g·* no hearing.
  161–14 He who *g·* self-knowledge,
  188–31 When divine Love *g·* admittance to
  297–16 *g·* a rich blessing of disbelief in
gainsaid
No. 16–11 positives that cannot be *g·*.
  28–21 What is . . . true cannot be *g·* ;
gainsay
Mis. 265–14 Nobody can *g·* this.
'gainst
Mis. 397–11 '*G·* which the winds and waves
Pul. 18–20 '*G·* which the winds and waves
Po. 12–20 '*G·* which the winds and waves
Galatians
Ret. 76–17 Paul enjoined upon the *G·*.
gales
Mis. 385–13 *g·* celestial, in sweet music bore
Po. 48– 6 *g·* celestial, in sweet music bore
Galilean
'00. 4– 7 teaching of the righteous *G·*,
Galilean Prophet
Man. 16– 3 as demonstrated by the *G· P·*
'02. 11–27 Jews put to death the *G· P·*,
My. 111– 6 master Metaphysician, the *G· P·*,
  220–26 example of the great *G· P·*,
  261–27 Jesus, the *G· P·*, was born of
  288–12 The great *G· P·* was,
  319– 1 such a person as the *G· P·*,
Galilee
Pan. 8– 6 Jesus, the man of *G·*,
Galileo
Mis. 99– 7 It cost *G·*, what?
  269– 3 *G·* virtually lost it.
Peo. 13–15 *G·* kneeling at the feet of
gall
Mis. 237–11 earth gives them such a cup of *g·*
Ret. 26– 6 "vinegar and *g·*," — *see Matt.* 27 : 34.
gallant
Ret. 3– 6 *g·* leadership and death,
galleries
Pul. 25–13 * *g·* are in plaster relief,
  26– 5 * *g·* are richly panelled
  58–16 * auditorium has wide *g·*,
My. 69–16 * auditorium contains seven *g·*,
  71–23 * five thousand . . . on floor and *g·*,
  71–25 * either on floor or *g·*,
  78–13 * mahogany pews and in triple *g·*.
gallery
Pul. 26– 6 * organ and choir *g·* is spacious
  27–27 * In the *g·* are windows
  42–19 * On the wall of the choir *g·*
My. 59–13 * *g·* of that magnificent temple,
  95–11 * the press *g·* of commentators.

Gallic
Po. 2– 8 falcon in the *G·* van,
gamesters
My. 203–14 hero is a mark for *g·*,
gamut
Mis. 295– 7 * a *g·* of isms and ists,
gap
My. 200–25 Wide yawns the *g·* between
garbling
No. 43–23 Stealing or *g·* my statements
garden
Mis. 109–19 Adam and Eve in the *g·* of Eden.
Un. 21–11 every tree of the *g·*.'' — *Gen.* 3 : 1.
gardener
Mis. 343–22 O stupid *g·* ! watch their
gardens
Mis. 343–13 clearing the *g·* of thought
Garfield, President
Mis. 112–16 assassin of President *G·*,
garlanded
My. 124– 8 *g·* with glad faces,
garment (*see also* **garment's**)
Mis. 75– 2 touched the hem of the *g·*
97–17 touch the hem of His *g·* ;
153–16 covereth men as a *g·*,
233–13 put into the old *g·* of drugging
Pul. 65–23 * gave half of the *g·* to a
No. 22– 3 touched the hem of the Christ *g·*.
'00. 8–12 and wear the purloined *g·*
15– 1 Putting aside the old *g·*,
15–20 a wedding *g·* new and old,
15–21 touch of the hem of this *g·*
'01. 2– 7 trying to put into the *old g·*
Hea. 16–15 touch but the hem of Truth's *g·*.
My. 108–21 the *g·* of Christian Scientists,
206–10 they divide Truth's *g·*
351–12 touches the hem of his *g·*
garment's
Pul. 53–29 * power that filled his *g·* hem
garments
Mis. 142– 1 how beautiful are her *g·* !
299–18 *g·* that are on sale,
299–21 These *g·* are Mr. Smith's ;
299–28 saves your purchasing these *g·*,
376– 9 * the figure and *g·* from a
Ret. 45 3 more beautiful became the *g·*
86–12 wanderer's soiled *g·*,
Pul. 22–20 put on her most beautiful *g·*,
Pan. 1–12 outgrown, wornout, or soiled *g·*
My. 67–11 * Checking facilities . . . 3,000 *g·*
125–25 put on her beautiful *g·*
garner
Mis. 313–22 *g·* the supplies for a world,
Pul. 1–11 *g·* the memory of 1894 ;
garnered
Ret. 71–25 before the wheat can be *g·*
Po. v– 1 * *g·* up in *this little volume*
My. 291–25 sheaves *g·*, her treasury filled,
garnet
Mis. 376–28 opal, *g·*, turquoise, and sapphire
Garrison
William Lloyd
Po. vi–16 *the person of William Lloyd G·*

Mis. 237–26 streets through which *G·* was dragged
garrisoned
My. 127–24 *g·* by God's chosen ones,
garrisons
Mis. 303– 9 *g·* these strongholds of C. S.,
garrulity
'01. 16–23 to handle with *g·* age and
garrulous
Mis. 127–27 Wise sayings and *g·* talk
gas
Mis. 347– 4 action of pent-up *g.*
gastric
Mis. 243–29 secretions of the *g·* juice,
gastritis
My. 107–31 removes enteritis, *g·*, hyperæmia,
gate
'02. 18– 1 at the temple *g·* of conscience,
My. 132–19 Divine Love hath opened the *g·*
gates
Mis. 30–12 *g·* thereof he declared were inlaid
141– 8 ''the *g·* of hell'' — *Matt.* 16 : 18.
144–20 the *g·* of hell — *Matt.* 16 : 18.
146– 3 and her *g·* with praise !

gates
Mis. 150–13 and loveth the *g·* of Zion.
185–20 opens the *g·* of paradise
275–19 throw wide the *g·* of heaven.
394–16 * The *g·* of memory unbar :
394–19 * I fain would keep the *g·* ajar,
Ret. 71– 3 to open the *g·* of heaven.
79–28 its spiritual *g·* not captured,
86–11 within thy *g·*.'' — *Exod.* 20 : 10.
No. 38–11 against which the *g·* of hell
'00. 12–12 its *g·*, whence the Ephesian elders
Po. 57– 2 * The *g·* of memory unbar :
57– 5 * I fain would keep the *g·* ajar,
My. 3– 9 enter in through the *g·* — *Rev.* 22 : 14.
34–10 your heads, O ye *g·* ; — *Psal.* 24 : 9.
72– 5 * chapter sub-title
72– 6 * The *g·* of Boston are open wide
Gath
My. 123–13 ''Tell it not in *G·*'' ! — *II Sam.* 1 : 20.
gather
Mis. 27–17 ''Do men *g·* grapes of — *Matt.* 7 : 16.
82–11 grasp and *g·* — in all glory
106–21 and *g·* up the fragments.
146–21 I would *g·* every reformed mortal
149–11 *g·* up the fragments,
215–31 must not try to *g·* the harvest while
273–13 and *g·* all my students, in the
336–17 we *g·* not grapes of thorns,
355–26 Let no clouds of sin *g·*
370–25 would *g·* all sorts into a
397–24 How to *g·*, how to sow,
Ret. 46– 5 How to *g·*, how to sow,
Un. 12– 2 and *g·* the harvest by mental,
35–27 which can *g·* additional evidence
Pul. 17– 4 How to *g·*, how to sow,
Hea. 10–15 *g·* the importance of this saying,
Po. 14– 3 How to *g·*, how to sow,
My. 77–18 * multitude which began to *g·*
208–19 to *g·* in praise and prayer
gathered
Mis. 64–30 *g·* from the five personal senses.
200–18 are *g·* from the supremacy of
225– 3 concourse of friends had *g·*
386–10 *g·* from her parting sigh :
Pul. 37–20 * one or two other friends were *g·*.
41–14 * members of the denomination *g·* ;
41–30 * At 9 a. m. the first congregation *g·*.
58– 4 * *g·* an association of students,
Pan. 1– 5 since last you *g·* at the feast
Po. 49–15 *g·* from her parting sigh :
My. 29–21 * they had *g·* to observe,
47– 4 * *g·* here from all parts
77–26 * believers had *g·* in Boston,
133–13 the fragments *g·* therefrom
362–14 * *g·* in one place with one accord,
gathering
Mis. 354–27 *g·* strength for a flight
Man. 60–23 No large *g·* of people nor display
Ret. 27–25 *g·* experience and confidence
'02. 20–18 *annual g·* at Pleasant View,
Po. 47–19 Evermore *g·* in woe
My. 20–29 usual large *g·* in Boston,
73–12 * chapter sub-title
77–10 * rapidly *g·* in this city
79–18 * that assembly was not a *g·* of
84–20 * story which the *g·* here tells.
84–26 * The *g·* of Christian Scientists
87–13 * a great *g·* of people
96– 7 * The *g·* can in no sense,
96–17 * the most remarkable, of the *g·*
97–29 * produced by that stupendous *g·*.
141–18 * *g·* of vast multitudes
155–26 *g·* Easter lilies of love
173–10 *g·* at this annual meeting
gatherings
My. 22– 6 * *g·* at the annual meeting ;
45– 8 * *g·* of Christian Scientists
141–10 * except on the triennial *g·*,
141–21 * these *g·* will be discontinued :
gathers
Mis. 1–16 mounting sense *g·* fresh forms
Po. 65–21 *g·* a wreath for his bier ;
gauge
Pan. 11– 9 *g·* the animus of man?
gaunt
Mis. 355– 4 full-orbed promise, and a *g·* want.
My. 308–15 * my father's ''tall, *g·* frame''
gave
Mis. 17–14 *g·* of the power of God to heal
75– 3 *g·* us, through a human person,
137– 5 *g·* you a meagre reception in Boston
139–18 I *g·* a lot of land
142–20 *g·* place to chords of feeling

gave

Mis. 145–12 to whom God g· "dominion— Gen. 1 : 26.
153–11 "the Lord g· the word :— Psal. 68 : 11.
180–21 g· he power to become— John 1 : 12.
181–24 g· he power to become— John 1 : 12.
185–18 g· he power to become— John 1 : 12.
185–25 g· he power to become— John 1 : 12.
199–21 is manifest in the control it g· him
253–24 agonies that g· that child birth?
292– 6 who so loved the world that he g·
300–25 I g· permission to cite,
373–24 God g· man dominion over all things ;
375–27 * "It g· me such a thrill of joy
381– 8 g· notice through his counsel
382–27 and g· it The C. S. Journal ;
388– 1 who g· that word of might
Ret. 2– 3 g· those religionists the
5– 4 g· the money for erecting the
5–25 * She g· an elevated character to the
19–21 he g· pathetic directions to
26–19 g· the world a new date in the
37–16 Even the Scriptures g· no direct
43–10 After I g· up teaching,
49–17 Christ and the example he g· ;
51– 1 I g· a lot of land in Boston to
90–11 he g· personal instruction,
90–11 and g· in plain words,
Un. 39–18 who g· and giveth man dominion
Pul. 8–18 and babes g· kisses to
20– 5 g· back the land to the church.
29– 8 * Last Sunday g· myself the pleasure of
47–14 * g· her any distinct statement of
53–23 * g· to mankind the key to health
64–18 * modern philosophy g· her no
65–23 * g· half of the garment to
Rud. 14– 8 g· fully seven-eighths of her time
No. 23– 8 he to whom our Lord g· the keys of the
Pan. 5–11 g· the proper answer for all time
7– 5 demonstration that . . . Truth, g·
'00. 11– 1 it g· me more pleasure than
'02. 11–18 g· our glorified Master a bitter cup
11–19 g· it to his followers to drink.
13–28 I afterwards g· to my church
15–27 To this, however, I g· no heed,
20–10 'T was God who g· that word
Hea. 2–22 g· this proof of Christianity
Po. 7– 1 Through God, who g· that word
41–24 to welcome the murmur it g·
43– 6 through Him who g· you to us,
My. 30–18 * They g· generously of their means
30–24 * g· a sum surpassing some of
43–23 * she g· us our textbook,
51–21 * "she g· no definite answer,
55–11 * Mrs. Eddy g· the plot of ground
60–15 * little Bible which you g· me
62–30 * g· freely of their time and efforts
119–22 g· the real proof of his Saviour,
138– 1 I g· them my property to
157–22 I g· a deed of trust to
179– 4 The first g· an account of
189–27 g· expression to a poem
190–22 Jesus g· his disciples (students)
215– 1 or g· it a halfpenny.
252–26 and g· to the "happy New Year"
296–29 g· her discovery to the press.
302–15 g· me the endearing appellative
312–29 salary for writing g· me ample
321– 9 * he always g· you that position
323– 3 * Mr. Wiggin g· me a pamphlet
324–20 * never g· us the impression that
330–32 he g· pathetic directions to his
333–23 * he g· the repeated assurance of his
335–20 * authorities g· the cause of death as
346–25 * Mrs. Eddy g· the following to

gavel

My. 171–29 * The casket contained a g·
172– 2 * wood of the head of the g·
172– 8 * presenting this g· to President Bates,
172–23 * The box containing the g·

gay

Mis. 329–18 Whatever else droops, spring is g· :
376–23 softened, grew gray, then g·,

gayly

Mis. 324– 7 manhood, and age g· tread the

gaze

Mis. 86–17 spiritually beautiful to my g·
129–18 for other green eyes to g· on :
354–26 Go g· on the eagle,
354–31 To g· on the lark in her
355–28 Hold thy g· to the light,
Pul. 39–22 * G· on the world below.
Po. 18– 9 To g· on the lark in her
23 -11 So may their g· be ever
32– 8 To g· on the sunbeams

gaze

My. 37–15 * the g· of universal humanity.
114–12 to the g· of many men,

gazed

Ret. 31–22 I g·, and stood abashed.

Gazette

Pul. 89–30 * G·, Burlington, Iowa.

gazing

Mis. 231–32 g· silently on the vacant seat
My. 59–14 * g· across that sea of heads,

gem

Po. 46– 8 A g· in beauty's diadem,
My. 184–20 church shall prove a historic g·
351–10 the title of your g· quoted,

gems

Mis. 343–17 the hidden g· of Love,
Ret. 85–27 with a diadem of g· from the
Po. vi– 3 * book "G· for You,"
vii–12 * these g· of purest thought
My. 12–29 children's good deeds are g·
121–16 g· that adorn the Christmas ring

Gems for You

Po. vi– 3 * in a book "G· for Y·,"

gender

Un. 32–24 liar was in the neuter g·,
My. 239–23 G· means a kind.
268–30 sex or g· eliminated ;

genealogies

My. 340– 8 old-wives' fables, and endless g·.

genealogy

Pul. 48–29 * figure largely in her g·,

General

Ret. 2–26 G· Henry Knox of Revolutionary fame.
2–28 stories about G· Knox,
Pul. 48–28 the McNeils and G· Knox
My. 311–27 G· John McNeil, the hero of

general

Mis. 8– 4 if we can bring to the g· thought
11–25 g· effort to benefit the race.
11–26 Because I can do much g· good to
80– 8 medical charlatans in g·,
137–10 having asked in g· assembly if you
138–20 applicable to the state of g· growth
155–21 as a g· rule, send them to
200–15 g· comprehension of mankind
236–27 as a g· rule, one will be blamed
291–14 and the world in g· ;
293– 5 (as a g· rule)
293– 9 g· knowledge that he has gained from
379– 7 descriptive of the g· appearance,
Man. 26– 3 g· Committee on Publication
27– 4 g· Committee on Publication
56–16 g· reports from the Field.
70–12 shall assume no g· official control
101– 3 g· Committee on Publication
Ret. 3–10 John Macneil, the New Hampshire g·
40– 2 and taught in a g· way,
52–17 g· convention at New York City,
82– 5 A g· rule is, that my students
No. 9–28 * referred to g· truths
'02. 10–17 Religions in g· admit that
Hea. 12–16 g· and moral symptoms
My. v– 7 * matters of g· wonderment
10–31 * g· welfare of the Cause.
20–23 * g· attendance of the members
46–29 * to the g· assembly— Heb. 12 : 23.
50–32 * a g· meeting of the church
88– 1 * chapter sub-title
92–14 * the public has in a g· way
107– 6 g· subject under discussion,
141– 3 * g· communion service of the
159–28 The g· thought chiefly regards
210–21 denounce error in g·,
302–10 g· craze is that matter masters
319–29 * conversation with you in g·
345– 7 * your attitude to science in g·?

General Assembly

My. 329– 4 * last G· A· of North Carolina

General Association

My. 251–23 chapter sub-title
253–10 chapter sub-title

General Committee

Mis. 305–11 * representing . . . upon the G· C·,

generally

Mis. 6–31 and health is g· the rule ;
89–15 but your good will g·
237– 5 g· accepted as the penalty
240–21 affectionate, and g· brave.
243–20 my system . . . is not g· understood.
380–20 people g·, called for a sign
Man. 99–25 shall consist of men g·.

generally

Pul.	68–15	* It is not *g·* known that a
No.	31–24	in the *g·* accepted sense,
Pan.	10–12	The students . . . *g·*, were the average
'01.	24– 4	that which is *g·* called matter
My.	100–15	* of a class who are reputable,
	178– 7	is not *g·* understood,
	236– 9	please adopt *g·* for your name,
	266–16	so *g·* apparent,
	272–23	* public *g·*, will be interested

generate

My.	194– 1	song and sermon *g·* only that

generated

Pul.	25– 3	* *g·* by two large boilers

generating

'01.	9– 5	*g·* or regenerating power.

generation

Mis.	74– 4	false sense of *g·*,
	286–16	maintain morality and *g·*,
	287– 2	offspring of an improved *g·*,
	318– 6	students of the second *g·*.
	318–10	final *g·* of those who
	342–28	in their *g·* wiser— *Luke* 16 : 8.
	346– 8	confronts each *g·* anew.
Ret.	64–15	*g·* of his fathers ;— *Psal.* 49 : 19.
Un.	43– 3	This *g·* seems too material
Pul.	vii–15	the pathway of this *g·* ;
My.	11– 6	* surged against her for a *g·*.
	34– 8	*g·* of them that seek— *Psal.* 24 : 6
	49– 8	* sweeping the world within a *g·*."
	59–30	* No human being in this *g·*
	88–24	* revelation given to this *g·*
	99–22	* Less than a *g·* ago
	206–23	a chosen *g·*,— *I Pet.* 2 : 9.
	222 5	perverse *g·*,— *Matt.* 17 : 17.
	272–31	* so much influence on this *g·*.

generations

Mis.	80–25	in successive *g·* for centuries,
	148–21	doctrines destined for future *g·*
	231– 6	Four *g·* sat at that dinner-table.
	286– 8	We look to future *g·* for
Man.	3–18	doctrines destined for future *g·*
Pul.	21– 2	grandchildren to the latest *g·*,
My.	43–18	* In future *g·* when it was asked,
	84–10	* And the experience of many *g·*
	85–21	* in the illustrious list for future *g·*
	177–22	the joy of many *g·* awaits it,

generic

Man.	47–20	*g·* name of the disease
Un.	51–14	the *g·* term for all humanity.
	51–15	the *g·* term for all women ;
No.	22–19	the term devil is *g·*,
'01.	10–11	*g·* term for both male and female.
My.	185–14	Love is the *g·* term for God.
	230–19	*g·* term for men and women.
	247 5	man the *g·* term for mankind."

generosity

Mis.	242–10	my thanks due to his *g·* ;
Pul.	85–27	* her labors and loving *g·*
My.	5–26	thanking your *g·* and fidelity,
	86–19	* *g·* of the devotion that the
	96–17	* *g·* of its adherents towards
	331–27	* the noble *g·* of heart which

generous

Mis.	231–11	skilful carving of the *g·* host,
	347–14	all the goodness of *g·* natures,
Ret.	11–22	Free as the *g·* air,
No.	3– 4	modest, *g·*, and sincere !
Po.	60–20	Free as the *g·* air,
My.	14–23	* to ensnare a *g·* and loyal people.
	26– 9	*g·* check of five thousand dollars,
	46– 1	* in *g·* hallways, in commodious foyer
	121–12	*g·*, reliable, helpful,
	157– 5	* *g·* gift of one hundred thousand
	163–12	I always try to be just, if not *g·* ;
	165–27	He who is afraid of being too *g·*
	173– 6	*g·* hospitality extended yesterday
	217– 4	your early, *g·* incentive

generously

Mis.	140–16	*g·* poured into the treasury.
My.	28–11	* those who have given so *g·*
	30–18	* They gave *g·* of their means

Genesis

Mis.	57–10	in the first chapter of *G·*.
	69–10	In *G·* i. 26, we read :
	244–10	those conditions named in *G·*
	258–12	In the spiritual *G·* of creation,
	332–13	In the allegory of *G·*,
	366–10	from *G·* to Revelation.
	373–24	In *G·* we read that God
Man.	58–17	shall extend from *G·* to Revelation.

Genesis

Pul.	38–16	*G·*, Apocalypse, and Glossary.
No.	37–21	From *G·* to Revelation the Scriptures
Pan.	7–20	in the third chapter of *G·*,
'02.	7– 5	In the first chapter of *G·*,
My.	60–17	* of the first chapter of *G·*.
	179– 3	first and second chapters of *G·*,

genesis

Mis.	57–27	In its *g·*, the Science of creation
My.	177–16	*g·* of C. S. was allied to

genial

Mis.	224–20	with a temper so *g·* that
'01.	30–19	kindles the inner *g·* life of a man,
Po.	2–17	sun's more *g·*, mighty ray ;

genii

Pan.	3– 5	poetical phase of the *g·* of forests.

genius

Mis.	66– 5	*g·* whereof is displayed in the
	283–26	It is the *g·* of C. S.
	354–29	*g·* inflated with worldly desire.
	356–23	it is the *g·* of C. S.
	365–12	Its *g·* is right thinking
Un.	9–12	talent and *g·* of the centuries
Pul.	83–11	* with the patience of *g·* she waits.
'00.	9–18	Sincerity is more successful than *g·*
Hea.	2– 1	*g·* of Christianity is works
Po.	18– 6	*g·* unfolding a quenchless desire.
My.	14–21	* endowed with *g·* and inspiration,
	200– 3	consolidating the *g·* of C. S.

Gennesaret

Mis.	212– 7	On the shore of *G·*

Gentiles

'00.	13– 2	* *G·* entered the church of Christ"

gentility

My.	121–19	external *g·* and good humor

gentle

Mis.	153–27	* Souls that are *g·* and still
	213–16	by *g·* benedictions.
	250–27	the *g·* hand opening the door
	254– 3	the *g·* entreaty, the stern rebuke
	330–28	When *g·* violet lifts its blue eye
	331–18	O *g·* presence, peace and joy
	389– 6	O *g·* presence, peace and joy
	390– 2	Whence are thy wooings, *g·* June?
Ret.	5–24	* *g·* dew and cheerful light,
	80– 4	though . . . justice be graciously *g·*,
Pul.	82– 8	* she is soft and *g·*,
Pan.	3–11	the *g·* murmur of early morn,
Hea.	2–12	Said the more *g·* Melanchthon :
Po.	4– 1	O *g·* presence, peace and joy
	16– 1	*g·* cypress, in evergreen tears,
	29–15	Thou *g·* beam of living Love,
	43– 7	*G·* as the dove,
	55 1	thy wooings, *g·* June
My.	28–13	* *g·* qualities which mark the true
	39–25	* harmonious tones of her *g·* voice.
	93 2	* happy, *g·*, and virtuous.
	208–12	Like the *g·* dews of heaven

gentleman (*see also* gentleman's)

Mis.	48– 3	by the *g·* referred to,
	68–18	Does the *g·* above mentioned
	88–10	Boston *g·* whose thought is
	239–13	a portly *g·* alight, and take
	242–10	Will the *g·* accept my thanks
	285– 6	*g·* who fills orders for my books,
	371– 3	the *g·* aforesaid states,
Pul.	37–16	* said a *g·* to me on Christmas eve,
	60–18	* a wealthy Universalist *g·*,
My.	153–11	would say to the aged *g·*

gentleman's

Mis.	296–21	in this unknown *g·* language,

gentlemen

Pul.	59–25	* *g·* officially connected with the

gentleness

Ret.	80–16	mingled sternness and *g·*

gently

Mis.	137–15	kind of you to part so *g·* with the
	240–14	nature would take it out as *g·*,
	291–24	will fall *g·* on the hearts
	330– 9	should call his race as *g·*
	387– 1	the heart-strings *g·* sweep,
Un.	5– 5	work gradually and *g·* up
Pan.	12–18	pass *g·* on without man
'01.	10–27	emerge *g·* into Life everlasting.
Po.	30– 1	*G·* thou beckonest from the
	50–19	the heartstrings *g·* sweep
	66– 7	Wake *g·* the chords of her lyre,
My.	69– 7	*g·* curved and panelled surface,
	162–26	*g·* into "green pastures— *Psal.* 23 : 2.

genuine

Mis.	39–11	the Founder of *g·* C. S. has
	88– 7	*author of that g· critique in the*
	148–19	requisite to demonstrate *g·* C. S.,
	207– 5	the *g·* recognition of practical,
Man.	3–16	requisite to demonstrate *g·* C. S.,
Ret.	48– 5	establishment of *g·* C. S. healing
	53– 5	bear aloft the standard of *g·* C. S.
	81–13	*g·* goodness become so apparent
	87–10	*G·* Christian Scientists are,
Un.	22–15	*g·* as Truth, though not so legitimate
	42–12	is the *g·* Science of being.
	49–13	only living God and the *g·* man.
Rud.	3–14	*G·* Christian Scientists will no more
No.	3–14	which sustains the *g·* practice,
	30–19	forbids the *g·* existence of even
'02.	14–11	only *g·* success possible for
	18–27	downfall of *g·* Christianity,
My.	3–22	compels him to think *g·*,
	4–14	A *g·* Christian Scientist loves
	111–12	*g·* Christian Scientist will tell you
	224–29	which is not absolutely *g·*.
	229– 1	I call none but *g·* Christian Scientists,

genuinely

Man.	39–12	evidence of having *g·* repented

genuineness

Mis.	39– 6	can be obtained in its *g·*

genus

Mis.	26–21	neither a *g·* nor a species

geology

Mis.	vii–14	to evolution's *G·*, we say,

geometry

Mis.	344– 6	music, astronomy, and *g·*,
	344–14	Of what avail would *g·* be
My.	226– 8	conservation of number in *g·*,

George

(see **Baker**)

Georgia and Ga.

(see **Atlanta**)

germ

No.	8–15	rejoice that every *g·* of goodness

German

Ret.	37–13	or certain *G·* philosophers,
My.	295–10	TRANSLATION INTO *G·* OF THE
	295–13	time-worn Bible in *G·*.

Germany

Pul.	5–24	France, *G·*, Russia,
My.	30–15	* from England, from *G·*,

germinating

My.	261–11	guarding and guiding well the *g·*

germs

Ret.	79–14	which uproot the *g·* of growth
My.	219–15	destruction of disease *g·*.

get

Mis.	55– 1	he failed to *g·* the right answer,
	73–15	can *g·* no farther than to say,
	79–14	cannot *g·* out of the focal distance of
	169–19	to *g·* at the highest, or
	225–30	* "Wait until we *g·* home,
	227–11	to *g·* their weighty stuff into the
	240– 8	flippant caution, "You will *g·* cold."
	240–13	If a cold could *g·* into the body
	241–16	you *g·* the victory and Truth heals
	280–13	We must *g·* rid of that notion.
	335–25	*g·* out of a burning house,
	352–23	one must either *g·* out of himself
	366–16	humanity needs to *g·* her eyes open
Ret.	20–24	was to *g·* back my child,
Un.	4–14	as we *g·* still nearer Him,
	17–12	its darkness *g·* consolation from
	44–20	[when you, lie, *g·* the floor],
Pul.	45– 7	* *g·* their buildings finished
	49–20	* long wished to *g·* away from
	51–27	* *g·* the share of attention it deserves,
No.	23– 7	"*G·* thee behind me, Satan ;" — *Matt.* 16 : 23.
	27– 6	*g·* near enough to God to see this,
'01.	13–29	and then we *g·* the victory,
Hea.	17– 4	*g·* nearer his divine nature
Po.	70–15	Then, error, *g·* thee hence,
My.	8–21	* if they are all to *g·* in."
	22–28	* to *g·* immediately into the
	60–19	* *g·* understanding." — *Prov.* 4 : 7.
	69–27	* If one would *g·* an idea of the size
	75–18	* They do not *g·* excited over trifles.
	82– 8	* were trying to *g·* away at the
	82–19	* this ability to *g·* away
	117–16	to *g·* some good out of
	306–26	tried to *g·* them published
	359–30	*g·* your students to help you

Gethsemane

Ret.	31–26	Bethany, *G·* and Calvary,

gets

Mis.	52–19	*if one g· tired of it,*
	365– 8	*g·* things wrong,
No.	18–20	If . . . the school *g·* things wrong,
'00.	2–18	Ask how he *g·* his money,
'02.	18–19	the summer brook, soon *g·* dry.

getting

Mis.	368–14	*g·* into the ranks of the good
No.	28–21	*g·* the letter and omitting the spirit
Hea.	13–28	one lie *g·* the better of another,
My.	60–19	* "With all thy *g·* — *Prov.* 4 : 7.
	97– 6	* *g·* well without the use of medicine.

Gettysburg

Mis.	246–20	more terrible than the battle of *G·*

ghosts

Mis.	396– 4	Where *g·* and goblins stalk.
Po.	58–16	Where *g·* and goblins stalk.

giant

Mis.	55–13	This *g·* sin is the sin against the
Po.	30– 2	thou beckonest from the *g·* hills
My.	76–24	* chapter sub-title
	341– 6	lifted to her *g·* hills the ensign

gift

accompanying

My.	172–28	accept from me the accompanying *g·*

author's

Mis.	300–28	privilege, and the author's *g·*.

beautiful

My.	347– 9	their beautiful *g·* to me,

beneficent

My.	26–12	Your beneficent *g·* is the largest

Christmas

My.	257–26	and send you my Christmas *g·*,

from Mrs. Eddy

Pul.	28–12	* a *g·* from Mrs. Eddy

generous

My.	157– 5	* gratitude that your generous *g·*

God's

Mis.	140– 2	I knew that to God's *g·*,

great

My.	262–21	reminder of God's great *g·*,

healing

Pul.	53–27	* That healing *g·* he lends to them

her

My.	311–23	never doubted the veracity of her *g·*.

invaluable

'02.	16– 8	Wyclif, the invaluable *g·* of

little

My.	172–12	present to you a little *g·*

lovely

Mis.	142–17	expressed in their lovely *g·*

Mrs. Eddy's

My.	157– 2	* chapter sub-title
	159– 2	chapter sub-title

munificent

Man.	75–11	to receive this munificent *g·*,
My.	164– 9	thanks for your munificent *g·*
	166–10	munificent *g·* of ten thousand

my

Mis.	140–11	my *g·* as I had it conveyed.

New Year

Mis.	400–13	MOTHER'S NEW YEAR *G·* TO THE
Po.	69– 1	*Mother's New Year G· to the*

no especial

Mis.	3– 3	we shall claim no especial *g·*

of gifts

My.	295–14	This Book . . . the *g·* of gifts ;

of God

Mis.	382–11	this *g·* of God to the race,
'01.	11– 9	it is the *g·* of God ;
My.	349–12	a divine largess, a *g·* of God

of joy

Po.	28– 8	Whate'er the *g·* of joy or woe,

one

Mis.	319–21	pass without one *g·* to me.

our

Ret.	86–16	we offer our *g·* upon the altar.

perfect

My.	38– 2	* every perfect *g·* cometh from

personal

Mis.	181– 3	sonship a personal *g·* to man,
	181–22	it is not, then, a personal *g·*,

princely

My.	194–20	princely *g·* of your magnificent

that

My.	19–28	because of that *g·* which you

this

Mis.	203– 7	this *g·* from my students
	382–11	this *g·* of God to the race,
My.	170–15	this *g·* is already yours.

gift

this
My.	170–17	This *g·* is a passage of
	172–21	* "I accept this *g·* in behalf of

your
Mis.	203– 2	your *g·* of the pretty pond
My.	166–28	your *g·* to me of a beautiful
	259– 1	look again at your *g·*,

Mis.	140– 5	the true nature of the *g·* ;
	253– 3	Christianity is not merely a *g·*,
Pul.	26–14	* *g·* of a single individual
	60–17	* *g·* of a wealthy Universalist
	85–21	* chapter sub-title
My.	148–25	Christianity is not alone a *g·*,
	170–14	I would present a *g·* to you
	176– 3	A *G·* OF FIFTY DOLLARS IN GOLD
	262–22	a *g·* which so transcends mortal,
	295– 9	*G·* OF A COPY OF MARTIN LUTHER'S
	347– 6	chapter sub-title

gifted
Ret.	7– 8	*G·* with the highest order of
Pul.	37–24	* a highly *g·* personality."

gift-giving
My.	259–26	mere merry-making or needless *g·*

gifts
Mis.	131–26	this church's *g·* to Mother;
	159–21	*g·* that my dear students offer
	159–29	*g·* of Christian Scientists
	281–23	Among the *g·* of my students,
	345– 1	Spirit bestows spiritual *g·*,
Man.	60–14	nor *g·* at the Easter season
	67–19	*g·*, congratulatory despatches or
Pul.	49– 7	* *g·* of her loving pupils.
'01.	29– 3	*G·* he needs not.
Po.	9–10	more *g·* from above,
	39– 2	*G·*, lofty, pure, and free,
My.	20– 7	chapter sub-title
	20–11	name your *g·* to her,
	20–16	Send no *g·* to her
	25– 6	* chapter sub-title
	123– 2	this church's *g·* to me
	123– 4	even more than the *g·*
	162–12	have demonstrated in *g·* to me
	164– 6	chapter sub-title
	173–13	as many *g·* had come from
	256– 9	exemption from Christmas *g·*.
	256–24	*g·* glow in the dark green branches
	257–23	chapter sub-title
	258–18	*g·* greater than those of
	258–25	Your Christmas *g·* are hallowed by
	262–32	Material *g·* and pastimes tend to
	274–21	my thanks for their magnificent *g·*,
	295–14	is also the gift of *g·* ;

gigantic
Po.	1– 1	*G·* sire, unfallen still thy crest !
My.	249– 7	counteract its most *g·* falsities.

gilded
Mis.	366–31	*g·* with sophistry and what
'01.	25–18	denounced all such *g·* sepulchres

gildest
Po.	30–10	as Thou *g·* gladdened joy,

Gilead
My.	175–22	Sweeter than the balm of *G·*,

gilt
Pul.	42–17	* "Mother's Room," in *g·* letters.

girders
Pul.	25–12	* The *g·* are all of iron,

girl
Mis.	ix–21	Psyche who is ever a *g·*.
	237–29	I remember, when a *g·*,
	341–23	a little *g·* of eight years,
Po.	46– 1	Fair *g·*, thy rosebud heart
My.	311– 4	a *g·*, totally blind,
	311– 8	* "If this blind *g·* stays with you,
	311–10	to turn the blind *g·* out,

girlhood
Ret.	11– 3	one of my *g·* productions.
Pul.	6–16	* for which I had hungered since *g·*,
Pan.	3–23	(one of my *g·* studies),
Po.	v– 3	* dating from her early *g·*
	vi–24	* many poems written in *g·*
	33–20	Written in *g·*.
	59– 9	Written in *g·*, in a maple grove.

girls
Pul.	46–23	* applied herself, like other *g·*,

girt
Ret.	35–23	Though a man were *g·* with the
Peo.	14–16	*g·* with a higher sense of
My.	277–23	armed with power *g·* for the hour.

gist
My.	363–23	*g·* of the whole subject

give
Mis.	11–17	would one sooner *g·* up his own?
	15–10	can *g·* the true perception of God
	17–10	*g·* up your more material religion
	20– 5	and I will *g·* you rest." — *Matt.* 11 : 28.
	24– 5	*g·* it to you as death-bed testimony
	32–22	to *g·* to my own flock all the
	80– 6	obligates its members to *g·* money
	88– 6	*Please g· us, through your Journal,*
	96–25	to *g·* you any conclusive idea
	114– 3	cannot *g·* too much time and
	115–26	for God will *g·* the ability to
	131–22	May God *g·* unto us all that loving
	135–14	Is it a cross to *g·* one week's time
	136–19	You can well afford to *g·* me up,
	137– 7	simply to *g·* you the privilege,
	137–23	*g·* much time to self-examination
	137–27	*g·* to the world the benefit of
	138– 7	to *g·* time and attention to hygiene
	138–25	God will *g·* to all His soldiers
	146–16	but will *g·* them immediate attention,
	147–17	may some time *g·* the color of virtue to
	149–19	the joy you *g·* me in parting . . . with
	150– 2	*g·* you the kingdom." — *Luke* 12 : 32.
	150– 2	May He soon *g·* you a pastor ;
	150– 4	*G·* my forever-love to your dear
	155–23	*g·* to us all the pleasure of
	159– 7	God of all grace *g·* you peace.
	160– 5	it may *g·* no material token,
	177–16	*g·* yourselves wholly and irrevocably
	179–27	to *g·* us these smiles of God !
	183–19	to *g·* utterance to Truth.
	190–18	interpretations that the senses *g·*
	196– 8	will *g·* you a separate mind from
	213–23	*g·* unto them eternal life ; — *John* 10 : 28.
	215– 6	*g·* I unto thee. — see *John* 14 : 27.
	216– 5	as the Scriptures *g·* example.
	226– 2	* "*G·* the child what he relishes,
	227–12	may *g·* it a forward move,
	231– 9	*g·* a spiritual groan for the
	236–16	to *g·*, to one or the other, advice
	238– 7	no time to *g·* in defense of his own
	239– 7	*g·* fair proof that my shadow is not
	241–10	*g·* to the immoralist a mental dose
	242– 9	would *g·* sight to one born blind.
	254–27	will *g·* the vineyard unto — *Mark* 12 : 9.
	258–19	might *g·* names to itself,
	264– 1	and *g·* them credit for every
	268– 3	*g·* point to human action :
	281– 8	nor *g·* me anything,
	292– 5	I *g·* unto you, — *John* 13 : 34.
	296–12	*g·* their time and strength to
	297–28	and Truth will *g·* you all that
	299–24	Did he *g·* you permission to do this,
	302–23	so elect and *g·* suitable notice,
	306–29	"He shall *g·* His angels — *Psal.* 91 : 11.
	307– 2	and in turn, they *g·* you daily supplies.
	314–11	*g·* out any notices from the pulpit,
	320– 2	God will *g·* the benediction.
	321–17	to *g·* you the kingdom." — *Luke* 12 : 32.
	322–12	and the Life these *g·*,
	328–26	Therefore, *g·* up thy earth-weights ;
	338–25	* To *g·* the lips full speech.
	349–26	refused to *g·* me up or to
	351–23	the five senses *g·* to mortals pain,
	353–11	People *g·* me too much attention
	356–11	*g·* promise of grand careers.
	359–28	Men *g·* counsel ;
	359–28	they *g·* not the wisdom to
	364–29	or *g·* reality and power to evil
	366– 9	Scriptures *g·* the keynote of C. S.
	371–24	with Truth, to *g·* it buoyancy.
	384– 8	*G·* sober speed,
	388– 7	to whose power our hope we *g·*,
Man.	32–14	and *g·* the author's name.
	48–25	or *g·* incidental narratives.
	59–22	*g·* their seats, if necessary,
	71–23	*g·* the name of their author
Chr.	55–18	such as I have *g·* I — *Acts* 3 : 6.
	57– 2	*g·* power over the — *Rev.* 2 : 26
	57– 4	*g·* him the MORNING STAR. — *Rev.* 2 : 28.
Ret.	13–19	which would *g·* me rest,
	18–20	*g·* me the spot where affection
	26–23	Woman must *g·* it birth.
	34– 8	or *g·* me one distinct statement
	37–21	My reluctance to *g·* the public,
	38–20	to *g·* him the closing chapter of
	48–17	*g·* instruction in scientific methods
	70–11	*g·* chimerical wings to his
	75– 8	*g·* credit when citing from the
	90–25	Mother in Israel *g·* all her hours to
	93–24	*g·* to the world convincing proof of
	95– 4	* Ask God to *g·* thee skill

give

Un.	25–19	*Evil.* . . . I *g·* life,
	33– 4	*g·* the only pretended testimony
Pul.	9–22	to *g·* you the kingdom." — *Luke* 12 : 32.
	14–16	G· them a cup of cold water
	22– 1	can *g·* peace and good will towards
	22–13	Christ will *g·* to Christianity
	37– 1	* pleasure to *g·* any information
	67–14	* *g·* expression to a higher spirituality.
	81–19	* those who have so much to *g·*
	87–23	God *g·* you grace.
Rud.	8–10	*g·* you here nothing but an outline
	13–20	and then *g·* special attention to
	13–26	to *g·* all their time to C. S.
	14– 3	They must *g·* Him all their services,
	16– 3	can never *g·* a thorough knowledge of
No.	20– 5	imagination, and revelation *g·* us no
	43– 5	and I will *g·* you rest." — *Matt.* 11 : 28.
Pan.	14–16	*g·* to our congress wisdom,
'00.	13–15	*g·* thee a crown of life." — *Rev.* 2 : 10.
'01.	2–25	Truth can *g·* a fearless wing
	13–28	hold it invalid, *g·* it the lie,
	19–14	That animal natures *g·* force to
	26– 2	*g·* my tired sense of false philosophy
	34–16	G· us, dear God, again on earth
'02.	7– 9	can *g·* man the true idea of God
	7–25	I *g·* unto you, — *John* 13 : 34.
	17–23	what we *g·* ourselves and others
Hea.	2–19	and I will *g·* you rest." — *Matt.* 11 : 28.
	4– 4	must *g·* freer breath to thought
Peo.	7–26	and *g·* to the body those better
	12–24	and *g·* the healing power to
	12–26	*g·* health to man ;
Po.	7– 7	to whose power our hope we *g·*,
	23– 7	*g·* those earnest eyes yet back
	23–21	G· peaceful triumph to the truth,
	28–12	G· us the eagle's fearless wing,
	28–16	G· us this day our daily food
	30–12	G· risen power to prayer ;
	36– 7	To thought and deed G· sober speed,
	64–12	*g·* me the spot where affection may
	70–23	G· God's idea sway,
	78–15	G· to the pleading hearts comfort
My.	vi– 9	* only as they *g·* her full credit
	26–23	*g·* the true animus of our church
	28– 9	* they can *g·* no more than a hint of
	37–30	* *g·* heed and ponder and obey.
	40– 3	* *g·* more adequate reception to
	45–21	* pillar of fire to *g·* you light,
	53–21	* *g·* the time to preach,
	62– 8	* *g·* it to my brothers and sisters?"
	80–26	* wanted to *g·* testimony
	81– 9	* *g·* precedence to another
	81–26	* to *g·* any account of the
	86–16	* to *g·* no more money,
	92–19	* *g·* a feeble impression
	117–25	and *g·* their talents
	117–31	To *g·* me this opportunity
	119–26	*g·* myself the pleasant pastime
	119–27	or *g·* you the opportunity of
	120– 7	chance you *g·* me to
	133–16	*g·* birth to the sowing of
	144– 4	G· yourselves no fear
	153–29	Come, and I will *g·* thee rest,
	164– 4	to *g·* to many in this city
	167–19	G· to all the dear ones
	170–22	and He shall *g·* thee— *Psal.* 37 : 4.
	172–18	freely *g·*.' — *Matt.* 10 : 8.
	191–19	sepulchres *g·* up their dead.
	192–22	*g·* me pleasure to visit you,
	193–22	* Carlyle writes, "G· a thing time ;
	213– 4	*g·* activity to evil.
	215–19	to *g·* my church *The C. S. Journal,*
	216– 2	Till Christian Scientists *g·* all
	220–22	*g·* them to know the joy and
	230–21	*g·* my solitude sweet surcease.
	234– 5	and they *g·* the appearance of
	234– 9	would gladly *g·* me the holidays
	237–14	and *g·* daily attention thereto.
	241–28	* Please *g·* the truth in the *Sentinel,*
	243–17	*g·* all possible time and attention
	244– 5	to whom I would gladly *g·* it
	257– 2	God *g·* to them more of His dear love
	258–20	*g·* you the might of love,
	259–15	*g·* me more time to think
	259–24	*g·* the activity of man infinite
	279– 4	peace I *g·* unto you :— *John* 14 : 27.
	279– 4	*g·* I unto you." — *John* 14 : 27.
	285–19	to him will I *g·* power— *Rev.* 2 : 26.
	295–15	kind of you to *g·* it to me.
	324–10	* thought he could *g·* a clearer
	329–25	* we ask you to *g·* your readers
	334– 1	* strives to *g·* the impression that
	348– 9	to *g·* a reason for the hope
	354–21	G· us not only angels' songs,
	358–23	G· my best wishes and love

give

My.	361– 4	I do not presume to *g·* you personal
		(*see also* **thanks**)

given

Mis.	6– 9	acute cases are *g·* to the M. D.'s,
	8– 1	thought is *g·* to material illusions
	33–18	and follow the directions *g·*.
	41– 2	*g·* vent in the diabolical practice of
	49– 9	his opinion *g·* to her friends,
	59–13	God *has g·* all things to
	69–15	had *g·* three doses of Croton oil,
	112– 8	error, *g·* new opportunities, will
	120–29	what is *g·*, puts to flight every
	127–12	it is not *g·* a stone,
	128– 1	and *g·* a variety of *turns,*
	136–17	All our thoughts should be *g·* to
	147– 5	another space of time has been *g·*
	149–10	what God has *g·* him of experience,
	158–27	order therein *g·* corresponds to
	159– 2	God has *g·* to this age "S. and H.
	161– 5	*unto us a son is g·* :— *Isa.* 9 : 6.
	161–23	he was *g·* the new name,
	165–30	reproduced and *g·* to the world,
	166–11	unto us a son *is g·* :— *Isa.* 9 : 6.
	166–20	*g·* birth to the corporeal child
	168–18	"Unto us a son is *g·*." — *Isa.* 9 : 6.
	178–32	has been *g·* to the world to-day.
	195–29	have *g·* me a higher sense of
	216–12	*g·* to the Anglo-Saxon tongue,
	227– 4	*g·* up to the hisses of the multitude,
	242–16	no signs be *g·* them," — *see Matt.* 12 : 39.
	278–11	never *g·* occasion for a single censure,
	282–19	exceptions to most *g·* rules :
	286–14	nor are *g·* in marriage,
	307– 6	*g·* to us through the understanding
	322–22	He hath *g·* you C. S.,
	350– 8	The first subject *g·* out for
	350–10	There was no advice *g·*,
	350–15	subject *g·* out at that meeting
	370–11	unto us a son is *g·*." — *Isa.* 9 : 6.
	373–26	power is *g·* unto me— *Matt.* 28 : 18.
	375–11	* new book you have *g·* us.
	376–14	* You have *g·* us back our Jesus,
	387–20	that wisdom's rod is *g·*
Man.	26–11	*g·* in her own handwriting.
	47–22	*g·* at the Wednesday evening meeting.
	63– 8	instruction *g·* by the children's
	64–15	Christian Scientists had *g·* to the author
	79–20	a Deed of Trust *g·* by Rev. . . . Eddy,
	81– 4	*g·* in her own handwriting.
	90– 4	*g·* certificates by this Board
	90–19	*g·* to each Normal class
	91– 1	this paper shall be *g·* to the teacher,
	95–21	No lecture shall be *g·* by a Reader
	97–12	*g·* in her own handwriting,
	102–14	deeds *g·* by Albert Metcalf and
	109– 9	who have been *g·* a degree,
	109–15	compare them with the forms here *g·*,
	110–12	one, at least, of the *g·* names
Ret.	15–25	treated and *g·* over by physicians
	17–19	*g·* Its feathery blossom
	40– 9	physicians had *g·* up the case
	44–20	time and attention must be *g·*
	75– 4	violates the law *g·* by Moses,
	78–18	or any name *g·* to it other than C. S.,
	91– 8	this name has been *g·* it by
Pul.	vii– 7	inclination *g·* their own thoughts
	vii–16	impetus thereby *g·* to Christianity ;
	8–10	Not a mortgage was *g·*
	15–14	yet have *g·* no warning.
	36–11	* *g·* to her morning talks by the
	40– 9	* chapter sub-title
	43–21	* as *g·* in the C. S. textbook.
	48–22	* diploma *g·* her by the Society of
	49–28	* first impression *g·* to the visitor
	57–20	* name *g·* to a new Boston church.
	61–17	* the name *g·* by Mrs. Eddy.
	72–11	* work to which she has *g·* so much
	72–14	* *g·* up by a number of well-known
	74–13	"A despatch is *g·* me,
Rud.	2– 1	definitions of *person,* as *g·* by
	8– 9	I have *g·* you only an epitome
No.	10– 5	as any proof that can be *g·*
	12–14	and *g·* impulse to goodness,
	13–23	and *g·* impulse to reason
	28–15	way of salvation *g·* by Christ,
'00.	10– 6	are the truest signs that can be *g·* of
	11– 2	than millions of money could have *g·*.
'01.	15–26	* There is no other reason to be *g·*
	15–30	* nothing else . . . *g·* as a reason
	19– 3	*g·* to them in times of trouble,
	19–10	it shall be *g·* unto you,"
	26–29	What I have *g·* to the world
Hea.	2–23	that religions had not *g·*.
	16– 1	and *g·* its spiritual version,

given

Peo.	4– 1	It has g· to all systems of
Po.	6–15	wisdom's rod is g·
	41–16	but one g· to suffer and be?
	46–16	Be all thy life in music g·,
	63– 6	for centuries hath g·
	68– 6	to my lone heart was g·,
My.	17–26	* as g· in the C. S. textbook,
	18– 9	it is not g· a stone,
	23– 2	* how much our neighbor has g·,
	28–11	* those who have g· so generously
	32–18	* as g· in the C. S. textbook.
	43– 4	* The law was g· that they might
	48–20	* has g· to her disciples a means of
	55– 7	* although g· up for a time,
	56–18	* branch churches had g·,
	88–24	* revelation g· to this generation
	90– 8	* and is g· very real tests.
	94– 3	* figures g· out by the church
	97–11	* if the figures could be g·
	131–12	g· to me in a little symbol,
	133–12	in sundries already g· out.
	141–21	* just g· out to the press,
	170–16	God hath g· it to all mankind.
	173– 9	C. S. periodicals had g· notice
	199– 6	reward of thy hands is g· thee
	218–25	My private life is g· to a
	231– 8	g· large sums of money,
	236–27	information there g· to
	245–32	g· to students of the Primary class ;
	246– 1	second degree (C.S.D.) is g· to
	253–17	whom Thou hast g· me, — John 17: 11.
	269– 8	nor are g· in marriage :— Luke 20: 35.
	276–22	* she has g· out this statement :
	310– 2	g· an academic education,
	313–16	* I was never "g· to
	314–17	decision was g· by the judge
	315–26	testimony they have thereby g·
	324– 5	* Mr. Quimby had g· you
	336–20	* amplification of the facts g· by
	353– 9	I have g· the name to
	356–15	I have g· no assurance,
	358–19	g· you by your students.
	(see also **rule**)	

Giver

| My. | 15–13 | desire that the G· of all good |
| | 127– 6 | We thank the G· of all good |

giver

| Pul. | 4–24 | the lord and g· of Life. |
| My. | 205– 8 | and God is the g·. |

givers

| My. | 25–23 | I have faith in the g· |
| | 123– 7 | will reward these g·, |

gives

Mis.	25–17	It g· God's infinite meaning to
	50–14	that g· one the power to heal ;
	81–29	It g· lessons to human life,
	97– 2	g· man ability to rise above the
	104 31	This alone g· me the forces of God
	113– 2	God's presence g· spiritual light,
	118–25	g· one plenty of employment,
	124–28	it g· to suffering, inspiration ;
	143–18	It g· me great pleasure to say that
	181– 5	g· him power to demonstrate
	184–23	g· back the lost likeness and
	189–22	g· him not merely a sense of
	204–26	g· steadiness to resolve,
	204–30	divine ruling g· prudence
	208–13	the law of divine Love g·,
	213–20	C. S. g· a fearless wing
	221– 4	it g· one opportunity to
	222– 2	g· him a false sense of both
	235–11	It g· to the race loftier desires
	235–16	g· a keener sense of Truth
	237–11	g· them such a cup of gall that
	260–25	g· out an atmosphere that heals
	265– 1	and g· me as authority for it ;
	274–20	g· impulse to violence, envy,
	299–28	g· to the public new patterns
	300–12	g· you the clergyman's salary
	307– 1	God g· you His spiritual ideas,
	334–15	only as one g· the lie to a lie ;
	355–15	g· scope to higher demonstration.
	362– 9	g· sight to these blind,
	372–21	C. S. Journal g· no uncertain
	372–29	S. and H. g· scopes and shades to
	375–32	* one who g· no mean attention to
	390– 5	Old Time g· thee her palm.
	390– 8	G· back some maiden melody,
	393– 4	G· the artist's fancy wings.
Man.	39–11	g· due evidence of having
	91–14	Only the President g· free admission
Ret.	66– 3	C. S. g· vitality to religion,
Un.	8– 1	g· much trouble to many
	49–24	This g· me a clearer right to call evil a

gives

Pul.	3–15	divine Love g· us the true sense
	53–19	* g· dominion over the physical
Rud.	3–19	which g· all true volition,
No.	32–14	It g· the lie to sin,
	33– 2	g· the dominance to God,
	37– 6	Mortal thought g· the
Pan.	2–13	g· the meaning of pantheism
	6–26	altitude of mind g· it power,
	7– 6	gave and g· in proof of
	7–22	It certainly g· to matter and evil
'00.	2–11	he g· little time to society
	2–14	earns his money and g· it wisely
	5– 5	g· evil no origin, no reality.
'01.	20– 7	g· neither moral right nor might to
	21–12	clergyman g· it as his opinion
'02.	2–20	g· place to a more spiritual
	9– 1	g· man power with untold
	17– 5	when obedience g· him happiness.
	20–21	for it g· me great joy to
Hea.	7– 9	g· the spiritual instead of the
Peo.	2– 8	g· another letter to the word God
Po.	51– 9	G· the artist's fancy wings.
	55– 6	Old Time g· thee her palm.
	55– 9	G· back some maiden melody,
My.	9–27	with what my heart g·
	12– 7	* g· promise of the speedy
	12–27	g· the power to "act in the
	66– 3	* g· to the above society the
	66–10	* g· them the ownership of the
	87–23	* If C. S. g· such serene,
	118–19	Soul, not sense, receives and g· it.
	119–18	g· dominion over all the earth.
	120–12	g· to soul its native freedom.
	129–22	divine law g· to man health
	129–23	g· a soul to Soul,
	131– 5	g· him courage, devotion, and
	150– 5	Pliny g· the following description
	154– 3	not the person who g· the drug
	154–11	not he who g· the flowers
	186–27	It g· me great pleasure to
	193–16	Love g· nothing to take away.
	204– 3	He g· His followers opportunity
	225–20	g· to the divine Spirit the name God.
	234–20	g· the subject quite another aspect.
	262–32	and g· manifold blessings.
	268–23	g· man the victory over himself.
	272–32	* g· no editorial indorsement to the
	273–31	g· the true sense of life
	280– 4	* g· assurance of your watchful care
	288– 4	g· little thought to self-defence ;
	328–13	* it g· them a license to heal.
	329–10	* g· especial interest to the
	(see also **God**)	

giveth

Mis.	39–14	g· to every one this *puissance* ;
	133 30	it g· a peace that passeth
	158–19	g· this 'new name' — Rev. 3: 12.
	167–28	He g· power, peace, and holiness ;
	167–29	he g· liberty to the captive,
	213–11	opportunities which God g·,
	215– 6	not as the world g·, — John 14: 27.
	276–29	Error g· no light, and it closes the
	317–31	g· not the Spirit by — John 3: 34.
	322–20	that g· grace for grace,
Ret.	65– 8	Spirit g· Life.
Un.	39–18	gave and g· man dominion
'01.	9–30	the spirit g· him liberty :
Po.	77–12	g· joy and tears, conflict and rest,
My.	156–23	which g· victory over sin,
	279– 4	not as the world g·, — John 14: 27.

giving

Mis.	9– 7	g· them refuge at last from the
	39–12	all her years in g· it birth.
	121–20	g· the signet of God to the
	138–19	g· to human power, peace.
	175– 9	g· better views of Life.
	184–32	g· back the lost sense of man in
	186– 1	not at this point g· the history of
	190– 5	g· the true sense of itself, God,
	204–13	g· mortals new motives,
	211–28	He drank this cup g· thanks,
	236– 8	g· advice on personal topics.
	245–10	g· it new impetus and energy ;
	262–15	g· to the sick relief from pain ;
	262–16	for g· joy to the suffering
	287–20	g· them strength and permanence.
	300–27	passages g· the spiritual meaning
	303–22	by g· place in your *Journal* to
	320–29	g· to it a new name,
	381–23	publishing, selling, g· away,
Pul.	9–20	with the Sunday School g· this
	33–20	* g· him high counsel and serious
	45– 2	* some g· a mite and some
	64– 9	* some g· a pittance,

giving

Pul.	65–25	* called the divine spirit of g·,
	73– 1	* or g· it to others?''
Rud.	14– 1	g· only a portion of their time to
No.	16–16	yet forever g· forth more light,
'01.	30–13	g· birth to nothing and death to
'02.	9– 3	g· life, health, holiness ;
	11–19	which he drank, g· thanks,
	13–22	g· opportunity for those who
Hea.	12–27	g· the unmedicated sugar
Peo.	13–16	and g· the lie to science.
Po.	70– 8	G· the glory that eye cannot see.
My.	5–10	God g· all and man having all
	6–25	g· to the material a spiritual
	13–30	their loving g· has been blessed.
	19–27	acknowledgment of exemplary g·,
	22–13	* the absolute necessity of g·.
	28–13	* that the g· to this fund
	49–24	* g· some useful hints as to
	52– 5	* g· in her Christian example,
	61–24	* human mind was g· its consent.
	66–25	* and g· her blessing to the
	67–20	* in g· Boston an edifice
	94–29	g· to the material a spiritual
	96–23	* members were asked to quit g·.
	117– 7	g· this leader time and retirement
	131– 7	we unite in g· thanks.
	182–23	guarding, guiding, g· grace,
	206–26	"G· thanks unto the— Col. 1 : 12.
	219–16	g· of life and health to man
	224–19	g· full credit to another
	225–13	g· unto His holy name
	231– 3	G· merely in compliance with
	231–18	else love's labor is lost and g· is
	262–22	mortal, material, sensual g·
	287– 7	g· to human weakness strength,
	323–21	* g· this age such a Leader
	332–30	* g· best praises to his

givings

My.	20–14	please add to your g·

glaciers

Un.	64–15	may climb the smooth g·,
My.	196–28	Over the g· of winter

glad

Mis.	93– 5	heart of history shall be made g· !
	116–15	tones whence come g· echoes
	157–12	They will be g· to help you.
	157–18	I am g· that you are in good cheer.
	262–19	We are made g· by the
	299–10	g·, indeed, that this query has
	329–10	whose voices are sad or g·,
	357–29	ready and g· to help them
	369– 4	and the gospel of g· tidings
	387– 5	waiting, in what g· surprise,
	389–14	g· for every scalding tear,
	398–22	Heard ye the g· sound?
Ret.	13–24	Mother saw this, and was g·.
Pul.	51–12	* are g· to welcome others
Rud.	15– 6	g· surprise of suddenly regained
Pan.	13–14	g· that the churches are united
'00.	1– 3	g· faces, aglow with gratitude
	13–15	A g· promise to such as wait
'01.	29– 9	who are not g· to sacrifice for him
'02.	11–24	and be exceeding g· :— Matt. 5 : 12.
Po.	4–13	g· for every scalding tear,
	9– 3	picturing alone a g· young face,
	16–20	hear the g· voices that swell,
	31– 9	G· Easter glows with gratitude
	43– 3	G· thy Eastertide!
	50–23	waiting, in what g· surprise,
	66–13	but a young heart and g·
	70– 5	the soul's g· immortality,
	70–18	while the g· stars sang
	75– 2	Heard ye the g· sound?
My.	18–22	g· that the churches are united
	21–27	* rejoice in the g· reunion
	37–31	* We would be g· if our prayers,
	124– 8	garlanded with g· faces,
	124–15	enough to make this hour g·.
	139–26	Rejoice and be exceedingly g·,
	155–17	May this g· Easter morn
	155–30	which she sends to them this g· morn
	158– 8	it is a g· day, in attune with
	173–21	It was a g· day for me
	177– 7	and I am g· to say
	191–15	This g· Easter morning
	202–17	endless hopes, and g· victories
	241–11	* We are g· to have the privilege of
	254– 5	g· you enjoy the dawn of C. S. ;
	270– 1	and be exceeding g· :— Matt. 5 : 12.
	321–26	* g· that I was among your early
	326– 1	* g· to publish the following
	327–12	* will make your heart g·,
	327–12	* as it has made g· the hearts of

glad

My.	350–15	pathway g· and free
	354–17	O g· New Year !
	355– 3	* a symbol of the g· New Year

gladdened

Ret.	2–17	My childhood was also g· by
Po.	30–10	E'en as Thou gildest g· joy,

gladdening

Mis.	377– 3	glow with g· gleams of God,
Ret.	90–28	g· to find, in such a student,

gladly

Mis.	32–19	I would g· do my best towards
Ret.	21–19	turn it g· from a material, false
Pul.	45–24	* g· laid down his responsibilities
'02.	17– 4	g· obeys when obedience gives him
Hea.	9–12	subjects they would g· discontinue
	11– 3	g· waken to see it was unreal.
Po.	2–16	On wings of morning g· flit away,
My.	21–11	* g· forego a visit to Boston
	41– 2	* become g· obedient to law,
	61– 1	* I g· answered in the affirmative,
	145–21	g· thus, if in this way
	234– 9	g· give me the holidays
	244– 4	to whom I would g· give it

gladness

Po.	47– 6	Ever to g· and never to tears,
	47–20	are the sheaves and the g·
My.	171– 6	obtain joy and g·,— Isa. 35 : 10.
	194– 4	songs of joy and g·

gladsome

Po.	30– 7	O g· dayspring !

glance

Pul.	2–15	With the mind's eye g· at the
Po.	9– 1	g· of her husband's watchful eye
My.	160–16	until compelled to g· at it.

glare

Mis.	82–27	treacherous g· of its own flame

glared

No.	2– 4	naturally g· at by the pulpit,

Glasgow

My.	81–15	* "Des Moines !" "G· !" "Cuba !"

glass

Mis.	359–11	through a g·, darkly ;— I Cor. 13 : 12.
Pul.	vii– 9	rise of the mercury in the g·
	24–28	* The windows of stained g·
	25–30	* There is a disc of cut g· in
	58–21	* windows are of colored g·,
	58–30	* portrait of her in stained g· ;

gleam

Mis.	1–11	kindle all minds with a g· of
My.	14– 6	as a g· of reality ;
	163– 6	from g· to glory, from matter to

gleaming

Chr.	53–47	g· through Mind, mother, man.

gleams

Mis.	377– 3	with gladdening g· of God,
My.	258–19	g· of glory, coronals of meekness,

glean

Ret.	79– 5	We g· spiritual harvests

gleaned

Mis.	308–24	have g· from its fruitage
Ret.	10–12	g· from schoolbooks
My.	47– 8	* as g· from the pages of its history.

glee

Ret.	17–17	bay, and laurel, in classical g·,
Po.	28–11	Above the tempest's g· ;
	63– 2	bay, and laurel, in classical g·,
My.	350–21	shadow of a world of g·) ;

glide

Mis.	110–25	increase rapidly as years g· on.

glided

Mis.	376–23	g· into a glory of

glimpse

Mis.	24–15	a g· of the great fact
Pul.	47–24	* to catch a g· of the world.
My.	6–29	love catching a g· of glory.
	31–11	* g· of the great structure,

glimpses

Mis.	363–19	in g· of the eternal verities.
'01.	9– 6	glorious g· of the Messiah

glittering

Un.	54–27	g· audacity of diabolical . . . logic

glitteringly

Po.	2–15	stars, so cold, so g· bright,

Globe (*see also Boston Globe*)
The
Pul. 75–13   * *The G·*, Toronto, Canada,

My. 264–10   * send through the *G·* to the people
    281–27   To the Editor of the *G·* :

globe
Ret. 85–26   rapidly spreading over the *g·* ;
'00.   1–17   five grand divisions of the *g·* ;
'02.   2– 1   is circling the *g·*,
My. 77–23   * from all quarters of the *g·*
    136–21   five grand divisions of our *g·* ;

globes
Pul. 7–15   Those crystal *g·* made morals for

globules
My. 107–16   dozen or less of these same *g·*,

gloom
Mis. 276–19   Out of the *g·* comes the glory of
    320–20   through darkness and *g·*,
    342– 7   the midnight *g·* upon them,
    376–28   spangled the *g·* in celestial space
    395–27   Enhancing autumn's *g·*.
    399– 3   will lift the shade of *g·*,
Chr. 53–34   Christ comes in *g·* ;
Peo. 1–11   guardians of the *g·* are the
Po. 15– 9   Here *g·* hath enchantment in
  58–12   Enhancing autumn's *g·*.
  75–10   will lift the shade of *g·*,
  78– 2   fought on in *g·* !
My. 50– 8   * *g·* of the mysterious forests,
  90–16   * teaches . . . that *g·* is sin,
  110–10   will appear, lighting the *g·* ,
  158–11   to-day hath its *g·* and glory :
  191–22   Mortality's thick *g·* is pierced.
  192– 9   mystery and *g·* of his glory
  257– 6   has traversed night, through *g·*
  258–10   one word, "Mary," broke the *g·*
  262–16   breaking upon the *g·* of matter

glooms
Pan. 3– 6   My sense of nature's rich *g·*
Po. 34–10   chant thy vespers 'mid rich *g·* ?

glories
Mis. 313–10   kindling its *g·* in the east,
    332–21   the *g·* of revelation,
    365– 2   bring out the *g·* of eternity ;
    392– 9   shade, her noonday *g·* crown?
    399– 5   the *g·* of one endless day."
Rud. 6– 3   *g·* of earth and sky,
No. 21–23   brings in the *g·* of eternity ;
Hea. 20– 3   * could we sound the *g·* forth,
Po. 20–12   shade, her noonday *g·* crown?
  75–12   the *g·* of one endless day."
My. 64– 4   * The *g·* of the realm of
  158– 8   upon the *g·* of summer ;

glorieth
Mis. 270–26   "He that *g·*,— *I Cor.* 1 : 31.

glorified
Mis. 86–20   gain the *g·* sense of substance
    154–22   Christ will again be . . . *g·*.
    166–32   before it could make him the *g·*.
Ret. 85–14   the Son of man will be *g·*,
  94–29   the Father was *g·* therein.
Un. 7– 2   as already He is *g·* in the
  49–12   a *g·* consciousness of the only
Pul. 82– 7   * one whom her love had *g·*
No. 39–10   Prophet and apostle have *g·* God
  45–24   have free course and be *g·*.
'00. 12– 5   the radiance of *g·* Being.
'02. 11–18   gave our *g·* Master a bitter cup
  16–18   a *g·* spiritual idea of the
  79–19   God's glorified ! Who doth His will
Po. 31–18   The ever Christ, and *g·* behest,
My. 52–24   * through her work Truth may be glorified.
  133– 8   church triumphant, and Zion be glorified.
  202–28   "Herein is my Father glorified, — *John* 15 : 8.
  232– 8   mankind blessed, and God glorified.
  355–27   glorified in His reflection

glorifies
'02. 19–28   *g·* the cross and crowns

glorify
Mis. 83–25   *g·* Thy Son, — *John* 17 : 1.
    83–25   Son also may *g·* Thee." — *John* 17 : 1.
Man. 47–11   "*G·* God in your body, — *I Cor.* 6 : 20.
'02. 1–12   Evil, . . . is made to *g·* God.
Po. 30– 8   To *g·* all time — eternity
My. 187–27   *g·* in a new commandment

glorifying
'02. 20– 8   *g·* thy unfaltering faith

glorious
Mis. 76–31   fulfilment of this *g·* prophecy
    105–14   Life and its *g·* phenomena.
    151–22   *G·* things are spoken of you

glorious
Mis. 159–24   "O *g·* Truth ! O Mother Love !
    199– 9   "into the *g·* liberty — *Rom.* 8 : 21.
    212– 6   left his *g·* career for our example.
    234–32   makes His sovereignty *g·*.
    245–17   remove with *g·* results.
    248–26   the *g·* revelations of C. S.
    250–22   *g·* significance of affection
    261–22   effecting so *g·* a purpose.
    307– 5   a *g·* inheritance is given to us
    386– 1   "Intensely grand and *g·*
    387–22   greetings *g·* from high heaven,
Chr. 53–27   rehearse the *g·* worth
Pul. 9–21   O *g·* hope and blessed assurance,
  45–11   * features of this *g·* consummation
No. 24–27   another and more *g·* truth,
  35–20   The *g·* truth of being
'01. 9– 6   *g·* glimpses of the Messiah
'02. 10–17   O *g·* hope ! there remaineth a rest
Peo. 4–18   *g·* Godhead is Life, Truth, and Love,
Po. 6–17   greetings *g·* from high heaven,
  39–15   Work for our *g·* cause !
  49– 3   grand and *g·* life's sphere,
  70–19   To hail creation's *g·* morn
My. 20–17   *g·* growth in C. S.
  154–21   * high and *g·* toil for him
  197– 6   may this beloved church be *g·*,
  200–13   *g·* beatitudes of divine Love.
  213–14   bring out *g·* results.
  253– 9   * manhood's *g·* crown to gain."

gloriously
My. 114–22   as *g·* as the sunlight on the

glory (*see also* **glory's**)
abstract
Mis. 82–21   only as abstract *g·*.
all
Mis. 82–12   and gather — in all *g·*
and fame
Po. 42– 4   will be victor, for *g·* and fame,
and permanence
Mis. 47– 7   *g·* and permanence of Spirit :
another
My. 85–20   * Another *g·* for Boston,
beauty and
Ret. 18–14   Earth's beauty and *g·* delude
Po. 64– 5   Earth's beauty and *g·* delude
bright with
Po. 43–20   Safe in Science, bright with *g·*
Christ's
My. 150–20   radiant reflection of Christ's *g·*,
coloring
Mis. ix 22   coloring *g·* of perpetual bloom ;
crowned
Pul. 1–15   path behind thee is with *g·* crowned ;
Po. 26– 3   track behind thee is with *g·* crowned ;
crown of
Mis. 231– 2   formed a crown of *g·* ;
dazzling
My. 193– 7   dazzling *g·* in the Occident,
earthly
Mis. 268– 5   Earthly *g·* is vain ;
everlasting
Mis. 328–32   the throne of everlasting *g·*.
full-orbed
No. 37–12   full-orbed *g·* of that event ;
giving the
Po. 70– 8   Giving the *g·* that eye cannot see.
gleams of
My. 258–19   gleams of *g·*, coronals of meekness,
gleam to
My. 163– 6   gleam to *g·*, from matter to Spirit.
glimpse of
My. 6–29   love catching a glimpse of *g·*.
gloom and
My. 158–12   to-day hath its gloom and *g·* :
gloom to
My. 257– 6   through gloom to *g·*,
God's
My. 117– 1   let them alone in, God's *g·*,
gone
My. 189–22   last-drawn sigh of a *g·* gone,
grace and
'02. 11– 7   warrant and welcome, grace and *g·*,
My. 339–16   joy, grace, and *g·* of liberty.
grandeur, and
Mis. 87–13   grandeur, and *g·* of the immortal
greater
My. 253– 5   what greater *g·* can nerve your
His
Mis. 78– 5   His *g·* encompasseth all being.
    361–12   earth is full of His *g·*,
    376–29   with the brightness of His *g·*.
My. 263– 2   leaving one alone and without His *g·*.

glory

his
Mis. 70–30 in which none could equal his *g*.
73–24 *in the throne of his g*,— *Matt.* 19 : 28.
My. 15–20 * Of Jesus and his *g*,
192– 9 mystery and gloom of his *g*
His riches in
My. 186–15 according to His riches in *g*.
imperishable
Pul. 10–12 rights of conscience, imperishable *g*.
insure the
No. 33–16 insufficient to insure the *g*
invested with
My. 349–17 great Way-shower, invested with *g*,
its
Po. 17– 3 Then I'll think of its *g*,
My. 134– 8 to enhance or to stay its *g*.
King of
My. 34–11 King of *g* shall come in.— *Psal.* 24 : 9.
34–12 Who is this King of *g* ?— *Psal.* 24 : 10.
34–13 he is the King of *g*.— *Psal.* 24 : 10.
lean
My. 245–15 persecution, and lean *g*,
Lord of
Un. 56– 8 "crucified the Lord of *g*,"— *I Cor.* 2 : 8.
loved ones in
Po. 17– 4 My loved ones in *g*
marvel of
Mis. 163– 5 mission was a marvel of *g* :
Master's
'01. 35–13 O the Master's *g* won thus,
mellower
Ret. 18– 4 While cactus a mellower *g* receives
Po. 63–12 While cactus a mellower *g* receives
mild
My. 150–17 moon ablaze with her mild *g*.
millennial
My. 265–16 appear full-orbed in millennial *g* ;
modest
Mis. 372–25 the modest *g* of divine Science.
My own
Un. 18– 5 brightness of My own *g*.
noonday
My. 190– 5 noonday *g* of C. S.
of achievement
My. 357–18 success and *g* of achievement
of divinity
My. 25–26 *g* of divinity appears in all its
of earth's woes
'02. 20– 7 *g* of earth's woes is risen
of God
My. 206–21 *g* of God did lighten it,— *Rev.* 21 : 23.
of good
My. 4–28 *g* of good, healing the sick
of his Father
Mis. 74– 8 in the *g* of his Father ;
No. 41–10 and the *g* of his Father.
of His presence
My. 177–21 *g* of His presence rests upon it,
356– 5 liberty and *g* of His presence,
of human life
No. 33–23 The *g* of human life is in
of immortality
Peo. 2– 2 is the true *g* of immortality.
of infinite
My. 262–17 with the *g* of infinite being.
of mottled marvels
Mis. 376–24 glided into a *g* of mottled marvels.
of our Lord
Mis. 276–19 comes the *g* of our Lord,
of the Lord
My. 183–27 *g* of the Lord is risen— *Isa.* 60 : 1.
of the resurrection
My. 202–15 *g* of the resurrection morn
of the strife
Mis. 341–12 *g* of the strife comes of honesty
power and
Mis. 92–28 power and *g* of the Scriptures,
Ret. 84–17 power and *g* of the Scriptures,
No. 18– 5 all presence, power, and *g*.
presence and
No. 20–22 only power, presence, and *g*.
radiance and
Ret. 18–19 radiance and *g* ne'er fade.
Po. 64–10 radiance and *g* ne'er fade.
radiant
Mis. 385–26 radiant *g* sped The dawning day.
Po. 49– 1 radiant *g* sped The dawning day.
reflected
My. 301– 1 C. S. is a reflected *g* ;
reflection and
Mis. 187–24 man is their reflection and *g*.
repeats its
Pul. 39–20 * Repeats its *g* in the river's flow ;
scenes of
My. 15–30 * And when, in scenes of *g*,

glory

songs of
My. 176–10 palms of victory and songs of *g*.
task of
My. 258–12 resurrection and task of *g*,
temptation nor
Un. 57–10 neither temptation nor *g*.
that
My. 122– 5 That *g* only is imperishable which
this
No. 33–25 all mortals to bring in this *g* ;
My. 303–31 This *g* is molten in the furnace
throne of
No. 34–24 yet mounting to the throne of *g*
thy
My. 206–20 thy God thy *g*."— *Isa.* 60 : 19.
to God
Mis. 145–29 "*G* to God in the— *Luke* 2 : 14.
underived
My. 202–24 underived *g*, the divine *Esse*.
unfathomable
Mis. 323– 4 serene azure and unfathomable *g* :
unseen
No. 34–13 unseen *g* of suffering for others.
wonder of
No. 37–13 to regard this wonder of *g*,

Mis. vii–19 Whereof, I've more to *g*,
76–29 appear with him in *g*."— *Col.* 3 : 4.
86–31 the *g* of supersensible Life ;
231–13 His was the *g* to vie with guests in
270–26 let him *g* in the Lord."— *I Cor.* 1 : 31.
320–20 through . . . gloom, on to *g*.
'02. 2–18 *g* of untrammelled truth.
Po. 16– 9 The sequel of power, of *g*,
71–21 Thine be the *g*
My. 4–29 *G* be to Thee, Thou God most high
9– 9 * *g* in every good deed and thought
62–11 * *g* which crowns the completion of

glory's

Pul. 10– 8 silent Aventine is *g* tomb ;

Glossary

Chr. page 55 heading
Pul. 38–16 Apocalypse, and *G*.

Gloster

Un. 23– 1 treatment received by old *G*

Glover (*see also* Glover's)

Brother
My. 335– 3 * Brother *G* resided in Charleston,
Brother George W.
My. 333– 8 * respect to Brother George W. *G*,
Colonel
Mis. x–20 my first marriage, to Colonel *G*
Pul. 34– 2 * was married to Colonel *G*,
'02. 15–16 My husband, Colonel *G*,
Colonel George Washington
Ret. 19– 2 husband, Colonel George Washington *G*
George Washington
My. 312– 5 * "He [George Washington *G*] took his
332–30 * death of George Washington *G*
Jane
My. 313– 4 * Go to Jane *G*, Tell her I love her ;
Major
My. 335–11 * facts regarding Major *G*,
Major George W.
My. 312–18 Major George W. *G*, resided in
326–15 Major George W. *G*, passed on
329–10 * her husband, Major George W. *G*,
331–10 * the late Major George W. *G*
333–20 * Major George W. *G*, died
335– 2 * Major George W. *G*, formerly
Mr.
My. 335–16 * Mr. *G* was attacked with yellow fever
336–15 * Mr. *G* had made no will
Mrs. (*see also* Eddy)
Pul. 35–27 * Mrs. *G* married Dr. Asa Gilbert Eddy,
My. 312–16 * Mrs. *G* made only one effort at
331–28 * yet when we listen to Mrs. *G*
335–23 * Mrs. *G* (now Mrs. Eddy)
336– 3 * disease spread so rapidly that Mrs. *G*

Mis. xi– 3 in my name of *G*,
My. 312–10 * *G*, however, was a Free Mason,

Glover's

Colonel
Ret. 19–19 Colonel *G* tender devotion to
My. 330–30 Colonel *G* tender devotion to
Major
My. 330–14 * concerning Major *G* history
332–19 * facts regarding Major *G*
333–17 * never been claimed . . . that Major *G*
334–25 * heading

Glover's

Mrs. (*see also* **Baker, Eddy**)
  My. 312–12 * Mrs. G· fare to New York City,

glow

Mis. x– 1 spiritual g· and grandeur of
  356– 4 spiritual g· and understanding.
  377– 3 words that g· with gladdening
Ret. 13–21 a soft g· of ineffable joy
  35–15 g· and grandeur of evangelical
Pul. 5– 7 g· of some deathless reality.
'00. 1– 8 in the g· of divine reflection.
Po. 8–11 watching alone o'er the starlit g·,
  16–13 flitting through far crimson g·,
  77–19 Bears hence its sunlit g·
My. 256–24 gifts g· in the dark green branches

glowed

Po. 74– 6 when parting thy sympathy g· !

glowing

My. 184–20 g· records of Christianity,

glows

Mis. 88–16 g· in the shadow of darkling
Po. 31– 9 Glad Easter g· with gratitude
My. 196–29 Over the glaciers . . . the summer g·.

gnashing

My. 161–11 weeping and g· of teeth, — *Luke* 13 : 28.

gnats

My. 211– 2 straining at g· and swallowing
  218–20 straining at g· and swallowing
  235– 5 Straining at g·, one may
  276– 9 do not strain at g· or

gnawing

Mis. 131– 4 g· at the vitals of humanity.
Peo. 11–13 their fetters are g· away life

Gnostic

Mis. 162– 8 G·, Epicurean, and Stoic.

go

Mis. 19–26, 27 we g· into or we g· out of materialism
  34–19 than we, . . . can g· to the departed
  35–20 g· to church to hear it expounded
  37–12 we g· on to leave the animal for the
  37–14 "G· ye into all the world — *Mark* 16 : 15.
  41–14 Mental purgation must g· on :
  63–13 g· to the bedside and address
  81–16 to g· up into the wilderness,
  81–17 g· forth into all the cities
  93–27 because it cannot g· unpunished
  99–14 G·, if you must, to the dungeon
  121–27 nor let me g·." — *Luke* 22 : 68.
  134–19 g· to its rescue.
  141– 6 This building begun, will g· up,
  151–24 May mercy and truth g· before you :
  166–19 Virgin-mother to g· to the temple
  168– 3 G·, and tell what things ye shall see
  168–28 * g· away unable to obtain seats.
  192–11 I g· unto my Father. — *John* 14 : 12.
  194–20 I g· unto my Father." — *John* 14 : 12.
  195–31 The "I" will g· to the — *John* 14 : 12.
  196–25 the "I" does g· unto — *John* 14 : 12.
  201–30 G· to the bedside of pain,
  215– 3 g· from one extreme to another :
  215– 7 Arise, let us g· hence ; — *John* 14 : 31.
  224–17 we should g· forth into life with
  245–25 allows the people to g· no further
  257–25 g· down in the death-dealing wave.
  273–16 g· on in their present line of labor
  281–30 shall not g· unpunished : — *see Prov.* 11 : 21.
  286–31 human speculation will g· on,
  287– 2 will g· out before the forever fact
  298– 7 causing others to g· astray,
  304–11 * Then it will g· to Bunker Hill
  311– 9 g· forth to the full vintage-time,
  311–15 g· to prove that I love my
  318– 9 goodness must g· on *ad libitum*
  324–24 he is afraid to g· on
  325–32 "G· ye into all the world ; — *Mark* 16 : 15.
  338– 7 All must g· and do likewise.
  341– 8 you will g· up the scale of Science
  342–23 "G· to them that sell, — *see Matt.* 25 : 9.
  347–15 One says, G· this way ;
  347–20 The guardians of . . . g· before me.
  353–29 interested in themselves . . . g· their way.
  353–30 they constantly g· to her for help,
  354–26 G· gaze on the eagle,
  356–24 One can never g· up, until
  383–12 Erect and eternal, it will g· on
  383–13 g· down the dim posterns of time
  384–18 * "The seasons come and g· :
  397–22 Shepherd, show me how to g·
Man. 68– 3 to g· in ten days to her,
  69–17 shall g· immediately in obedience to
  94–10 should g· away contemplating truth ;
Ret. 8–20 said sharply, "Why don't you g· ?
  11– 6 G· fix thy restless mind

go

Ret. 15– 8 g· in the strength — *Psal.* 71 : 16.
  38– 3 could not g· on with my work.
  46– 3 Shepherd, show me how to g·
  56–14 must g· on until peace be declared
  64–15 "He shall g· to the — *Psal.* 49 : 19.
  88–21 signify that we must or may g·,
Un. 41–19 and we shall g· to the Father,
  41–27 appear to g· on *ad infinitum* ;
  42–28 g· forth in the radiance of
  59–17 never saw the Saviour come and g·,
Pul. 17– 2 Shepherd, show me how to g·
  21–23 G· not into the way of the
  40– 3 * I wonder how the seasons come and g·
  51–15 * predict where this movement will g·,
  51–24 * will g· there in search of truth,
  53–13 * "Arise, g· thy way : — *Luke* 17 : 19.
  67– 5 * found a new faith, g· to Boston,"
No. 14–18 "G· ye into all the world" — *Mark* 16 : 15.
  19– 3 the premium would g· down.
  27–27 probation of mortals must g· on
  30– 5 will not let sin g· until it is
  41–20 "G· ye into all the world, — *Mark* 16 : 15.
  43–23 a system which they g· away to disgrace.
'00. 8– 3 g· on till we awake in his likeness.
'01. 16–26 g· to mock, and g· away to pray
  19–22 to g· from the use of inanimate
  29–13 g· out from the parents
  29–17 g· not to help mother but to
Hea. 4– 2 can neither g· forth from,
  9–11 why do they g· on thus,
  17–28 so must they g· ;
  19–20 bidding man g· up higher,
Peo. 14–15 g· to the bed of anguish,
Po. 14– 1 Shepherd, show me how to g·
  36–17 * "The seasons come and g· :
  60– 2 G· fix thy restless mind
  79–10 darkling sense, arise, g· hence !
My. 19–19 sunlight wherever we g· ;
  31– 4 "Shepherd, show me how to g· ;"
  47–27 * "G· ye into all the world, — *Mark* 16 : 15.
  51–23 * to g· into new fields to teach
  83–11 * g· entirely unadorned.
  95–19 * They g· about telling of
  97– 4 * will g· far towards making the
  118– 3 g· on promoting the true Principle
  128– 3 g· on unto perfection ; — *Heb.* 6 : 1.
  128–21 they g· into all the world,
  132– 5 and we g· to the Gospels,
  145–18 cannot g· upon the platform
  149– 3 "G·, and do thou — *Luke* 10 : 37.
  151–20 * G· forth, and worship God."
  166–14 shade and shine may come and g·,
  172–10 'G· into all the world,' — *Mark* 16 : 15.
  229–14 g· to help their helper,
  245–19 g· on *ad infinitum*,
  248–26 g· forth to face the foe with
  273–26 lapse and relapse, come and g·,
  275–17 I g· out in my carriage daily,
  300–24 "G· ye into all the world, — *Mark* 16 : 15.
  301–25 cannot of itself g· to the brain
  313– 4 * G· to Jane Glover.
  313– 7 * I will g· to her.
  324–18 * to allow the thought to g· out
  336– 6 * to g· to her assistance,

goal

Mis. 63–25 reaching toward a higher g·,
  85–11 Perfection, the g· of existence,
Un. 3–13 reached the g· in divine Science,
  45–22 death is not the g· which Truth
  58–15 was immortality's g·.
No. 44– 9 swerves not . . . from the spiritual g·.
Hea. 11–21 When you have reached this high g·
Po. 73–17 afar from life's turmoil its g·.

goat (*see also* goat's)

Pan. 3– 4 half g· and half man,

goat's

Pan. 3–31 g· feet, the solidity of the

goats

Mis. 370–29 separate the sheep from the g· ;

goblins

Mis. 396– 4 Where ghosts and g· stalk.
Po. 58–16 Where ghosts and g· stalk.

God (*see also* God's)

accept
'01. 3–13 we accept G·, emphatically,
acceptable to
No. 41– 8 most acceptable to G· ?
My. 17–13 acceptable to G· by — *I Pet.* 2 : 5.
acceptable unto
My. 36–12 * shall be acceptable unto G·.
accords all to
'02. 7– 3 It accords all to G·, Spirit,

God

acknowledge
Rud. 10–26 learn to acknowledge G·
My. 133– 5 come to acknowledge G·,
acquainted with
Mis. 151–19 art thou acquainted with G·?
acquaints us with
Mis. 175–26 which acquaints us with G·
action of
Hea. 4– 8 we limit the action of G·
against
Mis. 115– 2 offense against G· and humanity.
140–24 not be found fighting against G·.
224–27 unless the offense be against G·.
'00. 9–23 no one can fight against G·,
My. 150–31 or the disclaimer against G·
all
My. 132–21 G· all, one, — one Mind
allegiance to
Mis. 276–32 in their allegiance to G·.
Ret. 50–20 allegiance to G·, subordination
My. 42–27 * faithful is her allegiance to G·,
all-inclusive
Mis. 331–30 adorable, all-inclusive G·,
all is
Rud. 4–21 all is G·, and there is naught beside
allness of
Un. 10– 1 demonstrate the allness of G·.
Rud. 10–27 understanding of the allness of G·,
No. 30– 8 by virtue of the allness of G·.
My. 349–15 conscious of the allness of G·
All of
Mis. 174–22 the All of G·, and His omnipresence?
allude to
Mis. 379–15 allude to G· as·the divine
alone
Mis. 236–21 be guided by G· alone ;"
250– 2 the *alone* G·, is Love.
358– 9 G· alone is his help,
Un. 38– 3 To G· alone belong the indisputable
Rud. 10– 5 G· alone governs man ;
alone to
My. 180–13 It appeals alone to G·,
alone with
Mis. 118–18 willing to work alone with G·
'01. 30–24 working alone with G·,
and a serpent
Pan. 6–20 between . . . G· and a serpent?
and devil
Un. 52–10 good and evil, G· and devil,
and good
Mis. 27– 3 terms G· and good, as Spirit,
and heaven
Un. 37– 7 G· and heaven, or Life, are present,
and His creation
Un. 30–17 interpretation of G· and His creation
Pan. 9– 3 one G· and His creation,
'02. 7– 8 of G· and His creation,
and His idea
Mis. 13–24 that is, of G· and His idea.
332–29 supposition is, that G· and His idea
Ret. 23–23 were G· and His idea.
60–11 C. S. reveals G· and His idea as
63– 1 G· and His idea are the only realities,
Un. 47– 6 All . . . is G· and His idea.
and His ideas
Un. 24–19 G· and His ideas
and His universe
Mis. 186–26 sense of G· and His universe
and humanity
Mis. 115– 2 offense against G· and humanity.
Pul. 85– 2 * consecration to G· and humanity
'01. 1– 4 for G· and humanity ;
My. 158–29 stand . . . for G· and humanity !
193–26 dedicated to G· and humanity,
and Love
'02. 8–14 G· and Love are one.
and man
Mis. 16–19 higher sense of both G· and man.
50–29 and love for G· and man ;
77–25 to understand G· and man :
82– 2 G· and man as the Principle and idea
124– 1 intervening between G· and man,
126– 6 with love for G· and man.
188– 9 misconception of G· and man,
189– 9 inseparability of G· and man,
361–29 Principle and idea, G· and man,
362– 4 wherein G· and man are perfect,
369–10 strong in the unity of G· and man.
Un. 52– 4 Science of G· and man is the
52– 9 in the coincidence of G· and man
Rud. 7–15 evidence of the being of G· and man,
8–19 yet is false to G· and man,
11– 5 *understanding* of G· and man
No. 10– 8 reveals and interprets G· and man ;
27–15 eternal verities of G· and man

God

and man
'01. 5–12 discriminates between G· and man,
5–24 G· and man in divine Science,
10–14 divine and the human, G· and man.
20–11 he is disloyal to G· and man ;
21–16 individual who loves G· and man ;
'02. 8– 2 "G· and man as His likeness,
9–18 The unity of G· and man is
12–18 even so G· and man, Father and son,
Peo. 4–16 mysterious ideas of G· and man
14–13 holier love for G· and man ;
Po. 11– 4 The love for G· and man.
My. 103–10 the Science of G· and man,
119– 6 one infinite G·, and man,
158–17 manifests love for G· and man.
159–14 perfect love of G· and man.
199–17 loyal lovers of G· and man.
200–17 the love of G· and man.
253–28 be faithful to G· and man.
274–24 and love to G· and man ;
295–27 the servant of G· and man,
338– 4 The love for G· and man.
338–20 love towards G· and man.
and Saviour
My. 155– 8 that one the G· and Saviour
and sin
Un. 6–16 leading questions about G· and sin,
and the universe
Mis. 190– 6 G·, and the universe ;
218–18 real nature of G· and the universe
Un. 24–19 G· and the universe — constitute all
34–25 reality of G· and the universe
52– 6 harmony of both G· and the universe.
anoints
Mis. 130–29 meek and loving, G· anoints
Chr. 53– 9 The Christ-idea, G· anoints
answers
'01. 19– 1 G· answers their prayers,
antipode of
Ret. 67–12 a sinner was the antipode of G·.
No. 35–19 which is the antipode of G·,
apart from
Mis. 71–26 nothing can be formed apart from G·,
183–24 Asserting a selfhood apart from G·,
196– 3 claim no mind apart from G·.
333– 2 sin — yea, selfhood — is apart from G·,
Ret. 60– 1 as something apart from G·,
No. 35–16 supposed existence apart from G·.
'02. 7– 3 no . . . causation apart from G·.
My. 115– 6 were I, apart from G·, its author.
ape of
Ret. 63–23 * "The devil is but the ape of G·."
No. 42–19 the devil is the ape of G·.
appeal to
Ret. 54– 7 and appeal to G· for relief
apprehension of
Un. 5– 7 increase their apprehension of G·,
approach
Un. 13– 5 Men must approach G· reverently,
as a person
No. 20– 4 and of G· as a person,
Hea. 3–12 and the qualities of G· as a person,
aside from
Mis. 335–31 seeking power or good aside from G·,
as infinite
No. 36– 4 He knew G· as infinite,
as its source
Un. 25–17 by showing G· as its source.
ask
Ret. 95– 4 * Ask G· to give thee skill
My. 150–18 ask G· to enable you to
as Love
'02. 4–18 chapter sub-title
9– 1 consciousness of G· as Love
My. 152–16 Do I understand G· as Love,
as old as
'01. 24–19 It is as old as G·,
as omnipotent
Mis. 197–30 recognize G· as omnipotent,
assigned to
Rud. 2–20 assigned to G· by finite thought,
assured that
Mis. 114–26 Rest assured that G· in His wisdom
as Truth
No. 30–25 sickness would dethrone G· as Truth,
atmosphere of
No. 9–26 Science is the atmosphere of G· ;
at-one-ment with
No. 33–20 man's at-one-ment with G· ;
aught besides
Mis. 358–11 He that seeketh aught besides G·,
'00. 5– 5 idolatry or aught besides G·,
authority of
Un. 31–17 matter usurps the authority of G·,

God

avails with
Mis. 33– 2 prayer that avails with G·.
balances of
Mis. 288– 7 dropped into the balances of G·
365– 5 weighed in the balances of G·
banishment from
Ret. 13– 9 perpetual banishment from G·.
becomes
Mis. 96–13 G· becomes to me,
No. 25– 2 G· becomes the All and Only of our
'02. 9– 2 G· becomes to him the All-presence
before
Mis. 117–30 their moves before G· makes His,
204– 3 humble before G·, he cries,
behold
Un. 55–22 Now and here shall I behold G·,
being infinite
My. 356–28 G· being infinite, He is the only basis of
being is
Mis. 72–28 Being is G·, infinite Spirit ;
being of
Un. 47– 4 good, the being of G·,
Rud. 7–15 of the being of G· and man,
belief in
Pul. 79–25 * breath of his soul is a belief in G·.
Rud. 11– 4 belief in G· as omnipotent ;
belief of
Peo. 2–21 belief of G·, in every age,
belief that
Mis. 45–24 even the belief that G· is not
Un. 14– 2 the belief that G· must one day
Peo. 4– 4 the belief that G· is a form,
believe in
Un. 48– 5 Do you believe in G·?
Pul. 80–22 * believe in G· and the power of
'01. 6–27 We believe in G· as the infinite
believe that
Peo. 13– 3 those who believe that G· is a
belongs to
Mis. 107–10 the heart's homage belongs to G·.
No. 42–11 All power belongs to G· ;
My. 225–12 all belongs to G·, for God is All ;
bereft of its
Un. 51–10 bereft of its G·, whose place is
beside
Ret. 60– 7 there is nothing beside G· ;
Un. 25–12 claiming to be something beside G·,
No. 16–13 there is none beside G·
16–19 beside G· and His true likeness,
besides
Mis. 27–23 claims something besides G·,
37– 1 no power besides G·, good.
333–25 believed that something besides G·
Ret. 60– 8 says . . . is something besides G·.
'02. 6– 7 of something besides G·, good,
Hea. 15–20 trying everything else besides G·,
My. 300– 3 or in aught besides G·,
bids one
Mis. 345– 5 When G· bids one uncover iniquity,
bless
Mis. 273–12 G· bless my enemies,
Ret. 21–24 but for those . . . I bless G·.
My. 202–29 G· bless this vine of His planting.
203–19 G· bless this dear church,
208–24 G· bless the courageous,
220–21 "G· bless my enemies ;
353 23 three words : G· bless you.
279–25 G· bless that great nation
bless we
Un. 60–13 "bless we G·,— Jas. 3 : 9.
born of
Mis. 184–28 and is born of G· !
My. 261–26 Truth and Life born of G·
357– 5 born of G·, the offspring of Spirit,
bosom of
Mis. 125–13 but rest on the bosom of G· ;
breeze of
My. 232– 2 banner to the breeze of G·,
called
'01. 7– 7 divine intelligence called G·.
My. 269– 4 Principle, Love, called G·,
called of
My. 244–13 called of G· to contribute
calling
'01. 4–28 calling G· "divine Principle,"
calls
Mis. 274– 7 work . . . which G· calls me to
Man. 48– 3 whenever G· calls a member to
Hea. 15–16 calls G· almighty and admits
calls good
Mis. 110–29 that which G· calls good.
came from
Pul. 72–23 * that which came from G·
cannot believe of
Un. 19–11 But this we cannot believe of G· ;

God

cannot be obscured
Mis. 333– 6 G· cannot be obscured,
caught from
Un. 15–14 knowledge caught from G·,
channels of
No. 44–16 choke the channels of G·.
character of
Un. 1–12 nature and character of G·
child of
Mis. 185–10 identity as the child of G·,
Un. 22–16 not so legitimate a child of G·.
44–15 miscall, this evil a child of G·.
53–23 as a perfect child of G·.
My. 242– 9 the child of G·, hence perfect,
children of
(see **children**)
chosen of
Pul. 85–14 * chosen of G· to this end,
My. 17–10 but chosen of G·,— I Pet. 2 : 4.
Christian's
Mis. 23–16 matter is not the Christian's G·,
123–16 The Christian's G· is neither,
Christ is not
'01. 8–12 Christ is not G·, but an impartation
claims
Ret. 70– 5 claims G· as their author ;
coeternal with
Mis. 79–24 coexistent and coeternal with G·.
360–30 coexistent and coeternal with G·,
Ret. 59–24 coexistent and coeternal with G·,
coexistent with
Mis. 57–26 he was coexistent with G·
Un. 49– 4 man is coexistent with G·,
'02. 7–18 universe coexistent with G·.
coexists with
My. 239– 2 Science of the . . . coexists with G· ;
coexist with
'00. 4–26 Man and the universe coexist with G·
come from
Mis. 22–17 come from G· and return to Him,
Un. 22–17 Whatever exists must come from G·,
My. 277–13 shall come from G·
comes from
Pul. 73–23 * that all comes from G·.
My. 292– 4 All good . . . comes from G·
comes to us
Un. 4– 9 that G· comes to us and pities us ;
cometh down from
Pul. 27–13 * "cometh down from G·— see Rev. 3 : 12.
cometh from
Mis. 340– 9 than that which cometh from G·,
My. 364–13 save that which cometh from G·.
comfort them
Mis. 232– 1 G· comfort them all !
commandments of
My. 160–21 disobeying the commandments of G·.
communion with
Hea. 9– 9 steadfast communion with G· ;
conceive of
Un. 23–23 can conceive of G· only as
No. 23– 2 To conceive of G· as resembling
'01. 4–24 consistently conceive of G· as One
conception of
Ret. 25–20 the human conception of G·
Pul. 85–11 * conception of G· as Life,
conceptions of
Mis. 170–15 conceptions of G· and our
consciousness of
Mis. 352–11 the true consciousness of G·,
'02. 9– 1 consciousness of G· as Love
conscious only of
No. 36–13 and was conscious only of G·,
control of
Mis. 37–11 ourselves under the control of G·,
corporeal
Mis. 102– 3 corporeal G·, as often defined
coworker with
Pan. 6–18 creator or coworker with G·?
created
Mis. 25–27 If G· created drugs good,
247–29 Everything that G· created,
346– 9 If G· created only the good,
Ret. 69–22 G· created all through Mind,
Un. 15– 8 G· created all things,
64– 1 All that is, G· created.
'01. 18–17 If G· created drugs for
created by
Hea. 17– 7 personal senses were created by G·?
My. 239–26 spiritual man, created by G·,
creates
My. 262– 1 G· creates man perfect and eternal
currents of
'01. 19–26 currents of G· flow through no such
dealeth
Un. 23–11 G· dealeth with you as— Heb. 12 : 7.

God

dear
'01. 34–16 Give us, dear *G·*, again on earth
Po. 22–14 Dear *G·* ! how great, how good
30–11 Thou gildest gladdened joy, dear *G·*,
My. 62– 7 * "Dear *G·*, may I not
295– 2 knowing our dear *G·* comforts such

declares
Un. 17–21 declares *G·* told our first parents
29–10 declares *G·* to be the Soul of all being,

declare that
Un. 2– 1 declare that *G·* is too pure to

dedicated to
My. 193–26 lofty temple, dedicated to *G·*

dedicate to
My. 13–19 an ample temple dedicate to *G·*,

deduced from
My. 349–28 deduced from *G·*, Spirit ;

defense is of
Mis. 258–16 "My defense is of *G·*, — *Psal.* 7 : 10.

definition of
'01. 3–11 Webster's definition of *G·*,
3–12 dictionary's definition of *G·*,

demands
My. 152–25 *G·* demands all our faith and love ;

demonstrable
Mis. 150–27 *G·* demonstrable as divine Life,
My. 179–32 make even *G·* demonstrable,

demonstrate
No. 12– 6 to understand and to demonstrate *G·*.

demonstrates
Mis. 98–20 Science demonstrates *G·*
My. 238–19 Science . . . that demonstrates *G·*.

demonstration of
Mis. 63–29 momentous demonstration of *G·*,
186–30 Messias whose demonstration of *G·*
Ret. 66– 6 scientific demonstration of *G·*.
Un. 51– 8 demonstration of *G·*, as in C. S.,
My. 221– 8 demonstration of *G·* in His

denies
Mis. 330–26 A mere mendicant that . . . *G·* denies

denounced it
Mis. 57–14 *G·*, denounced it, and said :

deny
Rud. 3–17 prescribe drugs, or deny *G·*.

departure from
'02. 8–28 Adam, a departure from *G·*,

derived from
Un. 6– 7 higher selfhood, derived from *G·*,

design of
My. 279–10 all periods in the design of *G·*.

destroys
'01. 18–27 if *G·* destroys the popular triad

dies not
Un. 62– 4 yet *G·* dies not,

directions of
My. 361– 1 Follow the directions of *G·*

directs
Mis. 117–31 Be sure that *G· directs* your way ;
My. 143– 2 pray that *G·* directs your meetings

discoveries of
No. 39–21 new and scientific discoveries of *G·*,

dishonors
Mis. 367–14 says . . . that it dishonors *G·* to

divinely
Po. 77–11 Love, and Truth, — divinely *G·* !

does
Peo. 2– 7 what God is, and what *G·* does.
My. 128–18 Men cannot punish . . . *G·* does that.

does all
Mis. 280–11 Because *G·* does all,

does all this
Mis. 179–24 *G·* does all this through His

does forbid
Un. 4–20 but *G·* does forbid man's

does not limit
Mis. 282– 2 a sense that does not limit *G·*,

does not recognize
Mis. 60– 1 *G· does not recognize any*,
74–11 If *G· does not recognize matter*,

dominance to
No. 33– 3 gives the dominance to *G·*,

doth lighten it
Mis. 323– 6 for *G·* doth lighten it.

due, to
My. 189– 5 so due, to *G·* is *obedience*,

duty to
Man. 42– 8 nor to neglect his duty to *G·*,
67–17 Duty to *G·*.

dwelleth in
Mis. 150–12 *G·* dwelleth in the congregation of

dwells
My. 356– 2 where *G·* dwells most conspicuously

dwells in
Mis. 290–23 When thought dwells in *G·*,

God

emanating from
Rud. 6– 7 in and of Mind, emanating from *G·* ;

enables us
Pan. 11–23 *G·* enables us to know that

enmity against
Mis. 36–25 is enmity against *G·* ; — *Rom.* 8 : 7.

enmity to
Ret. 61– 1 enmity to *G·* and divine Science.

enmity toward
Mis. 169–27 mind, which is enmity toward *G·*,

enthrones
Un. 32–13 enthrones *G·* in the eternal

entrusted
'01. 31–11 Has *G·* entrusted me with a message

essence of
My. 159–27 * "What is the essence of *G·* ? Mind."

eternal
No. 37– 6 eternal *G·* and infinite consciousness

eternal as
Un. 49– 3 as definite and eternal as *G·*,
59–13 Salvation is as eternal as *G·*.
No. 17–28 would be as eternal as *G·*.

even
Mis. 181– 2 is your Father," even *G·*. — *Matt.* 23 : 9.
My. 179–32 make even *G·* demonstrable,

ever-present
Ret. 60–13 good is *G·* ever-present,
Pul. 11– 5 dedicated to the ever-present *G·*
'02. 16–19 spiritual idea of the ever-present *G·*
My. 254–13 find the ever-present *G·*

evil and
Un. 27–12 these distinctions to evil and *G·*,

excludes
Mis. 257– 2 excludes *G·* from the universe, or

exemplified
My. 287–13 Love lived . . . is *G·* exemplified,

existence of
Mis. 69– 2 treats of the existence of *G·*,

exist in
Mis. 6–18 we exist in *G·*, perfect,

explains
'01. 5–29 *G·* explains Himself in C. S.

extinguish
Mis. 364–29 would either extinguish *G·* and His

faith in
Mis. 140– 9 taxing their faith in *G·*,
152–30 Exercise more faith in *G·*
160–14 every trial of our faith in *G·*
204–16 deep-toned faith in *G·* ;
229–13 would encourage faith in *G·*
345–18 * a practical faith in *G·*
'02. 15– 3 never lost my faith in *G·*,
Peo. 13–26 * had a practical faith in *G·* ;"
My. 204– 2 My faith in *G·* and in His
221–28 shall we have no faith in *G·*,

false to
Un. 32– 2 false to *G·*, false to Truth
Rud. 8–19 yet is false to *G·* and man,

fasten on
Ret. 18–17 soar above matter, to fasten on *G·*,
Po. 64– 8 soar above matter, to fasten on *G·*,

Father-Mother
Mis. 102–16 divine Father-Mother *G·*.
127–12 petitions the divine Father-Mother *G·*
400–14 Father-Mother *G·*, Loving me,
Rud. 4– 1 Mind, the one Father-Mother *G·*.
Pan. 15– 5 May our Father-Mother *G·*,
'01. 3– 3 benediction of our Father-Mother *G·*
7–15 "Our Father-Mother *G·*"
Po. 69– 2 Father-Mother *G·*, Loving me,
My. 18– 9 petitions the divine Father-Mother *G·*
186–13 anthem of one Father-Mother *G·*,
265–32 we thank our Father-Mother *G·*,
347– 5 likeness of the Father-Mother *G·*,

fathers'
My. 185–28 * Our God, our fathers' *G·* !

fear
Peo. 6–15 Believing . . . we naturally fear *G·*

find
Mis. 124– 5 cannot find *G·* in matter,

First Commandment of
Mis. 197–28 breaks the First Commandment of *G·*.

follow
Mis. 236–13 must follow *G·* in all your ways."

follower after
Pul. 73– 6 * an ardent follower after *G·*.

forbade
Un. 54–20 *G·* forbade man to know evil

forbid
'01. 26–17 cast lots for it? *G·* forbid !

forces of
Mis. 104–32 gives me the forces of *G·*

foreordained
Mis. 122–10 of him whom *G·* foreordained

God

forewarned
Mis. 367–23 It was . . . that G· forewarned.
found in
Mis. 255–24 may be found in G·, the divine Mind.
Un. 10– 4 they are not to be found in G·,
'01. 26–11 quality not to be found in G· !
fresh from
My. 195–23 deep-drawn breath fresh from G·,
fulness of
My. 357– 3 at the spiritual fulness of G·,
gave
Mis. 145–12 less than man to whom G· gave
373–24 G· gave man dominion over all
gift of
Mis. 382–11 this gift of G· to the race,
'01. 11– 9 it is the gift of G· ;
My. 349–12 a divine largess, a gift of G·
give
Mis. 131–22 May G· give unto us all that loving
Pul. 87–23 G· give you grace.
My. 257– 2 G· give to them more of
given to
Pul. 40– 9 * chapter sub-title
gives
Mis. 111–13 Nothing is lost that G· gives :
307– 1 G· gives you His spiritual ideas,
'01. 31–15 the power that G· gives me
'02. 17–23 what G· gives, . . . confers happiness :
My. 5–10 man having all that G· gives.
20–12 Send her only what G· gives
251–25 What G· gives, elucidates, armors,
giveth
Mis. 39–14 G· giveth to every one this
153–19 G· giveth this "new name"— Rev. 3 : 12.
213–11 opportunities which G· giveth,
317–31 for G· giveth not the— John 3 : 34.
giving all
My. 5– 0 G· giving all and man having all
gleams of
Mis. 377– 3 with gladdening gleams of G·,
glorified
No. 39–10 glorified G· in secret prayer,
My. 232– 8 mankind blessed, and G· glorified.
glorify
Man. 47–11 "Glorify G· in your— I Cor. 6 : 20.
'02. 1–12 Evil, . . . is made to glorify G·.
glory of
My. 206–21 for the glory of G·— Rev. 21 : 23.
glory to
Mis. 145–29 "Glory to G· in the Luke 2 : 14.
good as
Mis. 13–29 then define good as G·,
good is
Mis. 24–24 (when good is G·, and God is All)
319– 3 good is G·, even as God is good,
Ret. 60–13 good is G· ever-present,
goodness of
Pul. 0– 9 goodness of G·— healing
good or
Un. 2–16 the Mind which is good, or G·,
24–22 separate from good or G·.
governed by
Mis. 104– 6 Formed and governed by G·,
198–16 man as governed by G·,
government and
Mis. 59– 1 one government and G·.
government of
Hea. 18– 3 yield to the government of G·,
Peo. 12– 7 just government of G·.
governs
My. 165–10 and by it G· governs.
grace from
Mis. 129– 7 through grace from G·, forgive
grace of
Un. 7– 3 the impartial grace of G·,
Pan. 10–23 accomplished by the grace of G·,
grant
Peo. 8–20 G· grant that the trembling
My. 165–29 G· grant that this church is
176– 7 G· grant that such great goodness,
184–19 G· grant that this little church
195–28 G· grant that this unity remain,
198– 7 May G· grant not only the
gratitude to
Mis. xi– 9 one's debt of gratitude to G·,
My. 36–19 * pour out our gratitude to G·
362–19 * filled with gratitude to G·,
guide
My. 282–26 May G· guide and prosper
guided by
Mis. 236–21 be guided by G· alone ;"
had led me
'02. 15–28 feeling sure that G· had led me

God

hand of
Mis. 319–24 in the outstretched hand of G·.
hands of
No. 3– 6 better to fall into the hands of G·,
harmony with
Hea. 14–27 a mind in harmony with G·,
has all power
My. 294– 4 on the basis that G· has all power,
has appointed
No. 7–18 G· has appointed . . . high tasks,
has blessed
Mis. 155– 6 even as G· has blessed you.
My. 158–24 G· has blessed and will bless
has called
My. 247–19 G· has called you to be a fisher of
has created
Un. 23–20 unless G· has created them
has dignified
My. 328– 1 * G· has dignified, blessed, and
has fulfilled
Pul. 73–15 * G· has fulfilled His promises
has given
Mis. 59–13 G· has given all things to
149– 9 what G· has given him of experience,
159– 2 G· has given to this age "S. and H.
has made
My. 288–30 the best of what G· has made.
305–22 All that I am . . . G· has made me.
has no bastards
Un. 23– 6 G· has no bastards to turn again
has no opposite
No. 5– 6 G· has no opposite in Science.
has not forbidden
Un. 4–17 G· has not forbidden man to know Him ;
has prepared
Mis. 152–18 heritage that G· has prepared for
has provided
'01. 29– 4 G· has provided the means for him
has revealed
My. 58–20 * one through whom G· has revealed
hath all-power
Mis. 101–21 saith to man, "G· hath all-power."
hath created
Hea. 16–23 shall we say that G· hath created
hath given
My. 170–15 G· hath given it to all mankind.
hath joined
My. 268– 9 What G· hath joined together,
hath not joined
Mis. 94– 8 but which G· hath not joined together.
hath prepared
My. 184– 5 what G· hath prepared for them
hath remembered
My. 126–16 and G· hath remembered— Rev. 18 : 5.
hath said
Un. 21–10 Evil, G· hath said,
hath seen
No. 27–24 Who living hath seen G·
heals
Pul. 14–26 When G· heals the sick or the
My. 348–16 G·, heals and saves mankind.
heart of
Mis. 253–22 love touches the heart of G·,
heirs of
Mis. 46–24 heirs of G·, and joint-heirs— Rom. 8 : 17.
255–16 heirs of G·, and joint-heirs— Rom. 8 : 17.
He is
Mis. 63–20 "that the Lord He is G· ;— Deut. 4 : 35.
366–11 the Lord He is G·,— Deut. 4 : 35.
Rud. 13–15 "The Lord, He is G· ;— Deut. 4 : 35.
her
Pul. 73– 7 * through the mediation of her G·.
high calling of
'00. 6– 8 of the high calling of G·— Phil. 3 : 14.
holds man
No. 26–22 G· holds man in the eternal
honoring
My. 225–18 by honoring G· and sacredly holding
honors
'02. 1–19 a system that honors G·
hope anchors in
'00. 10–21 our hope anchors in G· who reigns,
hope thou in
Un. 29–25 Hope thou in G·— Psal. 42 : 11.
Pan. 4–23 hope thou in G· :— Psal. 42 : 11.
house of
'01. 15–28 * sat here in the house of G·,
My. 37– 7 * heavenward from this house of G·.
hues of
'01. 12–21 bring out the entire hues of G·.
[human concept] of
Un. 60–15 [human concept] of G·.— Jas. 3 : 9.
I believe in
Mis. 96– 8 I believe in G· as the Supreme

God

ideal of
Ret. 93–10   ideal of *G·* is no longer impersonated
'02.   12– 6   this ideal of *G·* is *now* and *forever,*
Peo.   5–16   our ideal of *G·* has risen

idea of
Mis.   2–20   Christ, the spiritual idea of *G·,*
  78–27   man is the idea of *G· ;*
  165– 8   wholly spiritual idea of *G·*
  166–16   Christ, the incorporeal idea of *G·,*
  176–18   Christ, the true idea of *G·*
  328–23   presence and idea of *G·.*
Ret. 10–15   voicing the idea of *G·* in man's
  70–21   the advancing idea of *G·,*
Un. 51–21   in the idea of *G·,* good,
  61– 7   even the eternal idea of *G·,*
'00.   6– 9   in the true idea of *G·.*
'02.   7– 9   can give man the true idea of *G·*
My. 194– 7   foreshadows the idea of *G·,*
  206–15   not seeing the spiritual idea of *G· ;*

ideas of
No. 20–12   fully conveys the ideas of *G·,*
Peo.   4–16   mysterious ideas of *G·* and man

illustrates
'02.   8– 2   illustrates *G·,* and man as His

image of
Mis. 61–13   created in the image of *G·,*
Un. 32–25   not man (the image of *G·*) who lied,
  39–23   As the image of *G·,* or Life,
Pul. 81– 7   * express image of *G·* for love.
Rud. 13– 9   spiritual image of *G·.*
No. 17–18   therein is no inverted image of *G·,*
Pan.   9–26   chapter sub-title
  11–28   man is the true image of *G·,*

impelled me
Ret. 50– 1   When *G·* impelled me to set a price

in accord with
Mis. 354–19   body and soul in accord with G.

in Christian Science
'01.   6–16   is *G·* in C. S. no God

indebtedness to
My. 12–26   increases our indebtedness to *G·.*

indicates
My. 231– 3   purposes only as *G·* indicates.

indites
Mis. 311–27   transcribing what *G·* indites,

individual
Rud.   2–15   the phrase an individual *G·,*

individuality of
Mis. 103–23   presence, and individuality of *G·*
Rud.   2–18   defines the individuality of *G·*
  3–24   *By the individuality of G·, do you*

infinite
Mis. 93–13   the eternal, infinite *G·,* good.
Man. 15– 7   one supreme and infinite *G·.*
Ret. 70–25   reflection, . . . of the infinite *G·.*
No. 37–22   Scriptures teach an infinite *G·,*
'01. 22–20   calculus of the infinite *G·.*
  25–27   as the infinite *G·,* — good,
My. 119– 6   based on one infinite *G·,*
  235–15   Is *G·* infinite? Yes.
  239–20   and likeness of the infinite *G·,*
  281–13   by which the infinite *G·* good,

infinity of
Pan.   7–16   oneness and infinity of *G·,*

in place of
Mis. 175–21   and its methods in place of *G·,*

intended
Pul. 84–25   * as *G·* intended it should be.

interpretation of
Un. 30–17   interpretation of *G·* and His

interprets
Pul. 12–24   interprets *G·* as divine Principle,
No. 10– 8   reveals and interprets *G·* and man ;

is above
My. 360–30   *G·* is above your teacher,

is a consuming fire
Mis. 151– 6   *G·* is a consuming fire.
  326–14   "*G·* is a consuming fire." — *Heb.* 12 : 29.

is All
Mis. 24–24   (when good is God, and *G·* is All)
  26–22   *G·* is All, in all.
  101–26   If *G·* is All, and God is good,
  208– 5   *G·* is All, and by virtue of this
  258– 9   the great truth that *G·* is All,
  293–24   *G·* is All and there is no sickness
  350–16   "*G·* is All ; there is none — see *Deut.* 4 : 35.
Ret. 63– 5   the recognition that *G· is All,*
Un.   7–23   because *G·* is All,
  31– 5   If God is Spirit, and *G·* is All,
  34–11   *G·* is All, and God is Spirit ;
  48–12   To me *G·* is All.
  60– 6   *G·* is All, and there is none beside
No. 38– 6   on the basis that *G·* is All,
Hea. 10–13   *G·* is All, and in all :
Po. 79–17   Life is light, . . . And *G·* is All.

God

is All
My. 109–19   God is one because *G·* is All.
  178–13   Scripture declares that *G·* is All.
  225–12   belongs to God, for *G·* is All ;
  299–19   and that *G·* is *All*

is All-in-all
Mis. 21–18   for *G·* is All-in-all.
  125–20   for *G·* is All-in-all.
  155– 1   Forget not . . . that *G·* is All-in-all
  319– 4   for *G·* is All-in-all.
Un.   3–20   *G·* is All-in-all.
  24– 8   I say unto you, *G·* is All-in-all ;
Rud. 5– 5   Scriptures imply, *G·* is All-in-all,
No. 15–24   *G·* is All-in-all.
  23–26   *G·* is All-in-all ;
My. 123–31   people whose *G·* is All-in-all,
  127– 4   people whose *G·* is All-in-all,
  181– 3   basis that *G·* is All-in-all ;

is all-power
Mis. 173–21   *G·,* is all-power and all-presence,
Ret. 60–18   *G·* is all-power and all-presence,

is a Person
'01.   11–24   namely, that *G·* is a Person,

is a Spirit
Mis. 219– 8   "*G·* is a Spirit :— *John* 4 : 24.
Un. 31– 1   "*G·* is a Spirit" — *John* 4 : 24.

is blessing
My. 201– 1   *G·* is blessing you, my beloved

is come
'02.   12– 9   Christian idea that *G·* is come,

is commonly called
Un. 15–16   *G·* is commonly called the *sinless,*

is divine
Pan.   4–12   *G·* is divine.

is divine Love
Mis. 186–15   that *G·* is divine Love :
My. 135–30   understand that *G·* is divine Love,

is divine Principle
My. 116–13   for *G·* is divine Principle, Love.
  225–27   stated that *G·* is divine Principle

is egoistic
Un. 27–14   *G·* is *egoistic,* knowing only His own

is eternal
No. 37– 8   evil is temporal and *G·* is eternal,

is ever present
Mis. 27–22   though *G·* is ever present ;
Un. 37–11   Because *G·* is ever present,
  60–21   If *G·* is ever present, He is

is everywhere
Ret. 61–18   *G·* is everywhere.
My. 128–12   *G·* is everywhere.

is Father
My. 279–16   *G·* is Father, infinite, and

is for us
Mis. 157–25   This I know, for *G·* is for us.

is glorified
My. 355–27   *G·* is glorified in His reflection

is God
Po. 72– 3   Till *G·* is God no longer

is good
Mis. 71–31   law of Science, that *G·* is good only,
  93– 9   *G·* is good : in Him dwelleth no evil.
  101–26   If God is All, and *G·* is good,
  153–13   *G·* is good to Israel,
  172–31   *G·* is good ; hence, good is
  184– 2   that *G·* is good, but man is
  199–28   *G·* is good, and goodness is
  206–22   "Good is my God, and my *G·* is good.
  206–25   *G·* is good, and good is the reward
  218– 2   Spirit is God, and *G·* is good.
  319– 3   If good is God, even as *G·* is good.
  389–17   since *G·* is good, and loss is gain.
Ret. 63–14   *G·* is good, hence goodness is
Un. 25– 7   Spirit is God, and *G·* is good ;
  39–25   presuppose that *G·* is good
  40–16   Life is God, and *G·* is good.
Rud. 9–27   *G·* is good, and the producer only of
  11– 6   whereby you learn that *G·* is good.
No. 17– 5   *G·* is good, ever-present, and All.
'01.   22– 7   That *G·* is good, that Truth is true,
  23– 6   that *G·* is good and infinite,
Po.   4–16   since *G·* is good, and loss is gain.
  79–11   Our *G·* is good.
My. 299–19   believe that *G·* is good,

is his Father
Ret. 69– 3   *G·* is his Father, and Life is the law
'02.   8–30   conscious that *G·* is his Father,

is individual
Mis. 101–31   *G·* is individual Mind.
No. 19–15   *G·* is individual, and man is His

is infinite
Ret. 73– 4   but *G·* is infinite.
No. 19–11   *G·* is infinite.
Pan.   7– 1   Spirit, *G·,* is infinite,
'01.   5–20   *G·* is infinite Spirit or Person,
My. 239–18   *G·* is *infinite* and so includes *all*

God

is infinite good
Mis. 367–18   *G·* is infinite good,
Pan.   6–15   If *G·* is *infinite* good,
My. 356–26   and this *G·* is infinite good.

is infinite Love
'02.   6–29   wherein *G·* is infinite Love,

is infinite Mind
Rud.   4–15   *G·* is infinite Mind,

is just
Mis.   2– 9   remember that *G·* is just,
Pul.   7– 9   remember also that *G·* is just,

is leading
My. 140–18   *G·* is leading you onward

is Life
Un.   37– 2   *G·* is Life ;
     37–13   because *G·* is Life,
     37–15   *G·* is Life and All-in-all.

is light
'01.   3–21   * *G·* is light, but light is not God."

is Love
Mis.   96–14   "*G·* is Love," — *I John* 4 : 8.
     123–29   Holy Writ declares that *G·* is Love,
     125–19   "*G·* is Love ;" — *I John* 4 : 8.
     150–24   "*G·* is Love." — *I John* 4 : 8.
     206–23   Love is my God, and my *G·* is Love."
     250– 2   the *alone G·*, is Love.
     399–26   *G·* is Love, and understood
Pul.   13–13   certain sense that *G·* is Love.
     16–11   *G·* is Love, and understood
Rud.   10–18   true sense that *G·* is Love,
No.   19–12   *G·* is Love ; and Love is Principle,
'01.   3–16   "*G·* is Love." — *I John* 4 : 8.
     3–20   * It is sometimes said : "*G·* is Love,
     3–28   logical that because *G·* is Love,
'02.   5–18   "*G·* is Love." — *I John* 4 : 8.
     5–25   Since *G·* is Love, and infinite,
     8– 1   "*G·* is Love," — *I John* 4 : 8.
     8 7   "*G·* is Love ;" — *I John* 4 : 8.
Hea.   3–24   "*G·* is Love, Truth, and Life,"
Po.   70–10   *G·* is Love, and understood
My. 109–13   "*G·* is Love." — *I John* 4 : 8.
     180–21   in mercy, *G·* is Love.
     188–15   "*G·* is Love." — *I John* 4 : 8.
     278–29   power is God, and *G·* is Love.

is love
Un.   26–16   * God is wisdom, *G·* is love.

is made manifest
Mis.   78– 3   when *G·* is made manifest
'01.   9–16   *G·* is made manifest in the flesh,

is man's origin
Un.   53–25   *G· is* man's origin and loving

is Mind
Mis.   45– 3   understanding that *G·* is Mind,
     58–29   if you agree that *G·* is Mind,
     105–31   Because *G·* is Mind, and this
     173–20   *G·* is Mind and fills all space,
Un.   14–21   As *G·* is Mind, if this Mind is
Pul.   60–10   * idea is that *G·* is Mind,
Rud.   5– 6   since *G·* is Mind.
Pan.   4–17   but *G·* is Mind and one.
My. 349– 1   *G·* is Mind, and divine Mind

is no respecter
'01.   27–20   *G·* is no respecter of persons.

is not finite
'01.   4–19   understand that *G·* is not finite ;

is not in matter
Mis.   75–13   *G·* is not in matter or the

is not mocked
Pul.   7–22   "*G·* is not mocked," — *Gal.* 6 : 7.
My.   6– 5   "*G·* is not mocked :— *Gal.* 6 : 7.

is not part
Mis. 102–14   *G·* is not part, but the whole.

is not personal
Mis. 102– 9   lower sense *G·* is not personal.

is not unable
No.   42– 5   *G·* is not unable or unwilling

is omnipotent
Mis.   63–19   *G·* is omnipotent and omnipresent ;
     90– 1   know that *G·* is omnipotent ;
Hea.   5– 3   admitting that *G·* is omnipotent,

is omnipresence
Mis. 229–10   since *G·* is omnipresence,

is One
Mis. 258–14   In divine Science, *G·* is One
'00.   4–24   believe that *G·* is *One* and *All?*

is one
My. 109–19   *G·* is one because God is All.
     116–12   If *G·* is one and God is Person,
     239–17   *G·* is one, and His idea,

is our Father
Mis. 151–13   *G·* is our Father and our Mother,

is our Life
Mis.   50–24   understanding that *G·* is our Life,

God

is our Shepherd
Mis. 150–31   hence *G·* is our Shepherd.

is over all
Ret.   22–17   *G·* is over all.

is Person
'01.   6–22   *G·* is Person in the infinite
My. 116–12   If God is one and *G·* is Person,

is personal
Rud.   2–10   but *G·* is personal, if by person
'01.   4–17   *G·* is personal in a scientific

is really All
Mis.   27–23   when *G·* is really *All.*

is recognized
Mis.   85– 8   *G·* is recognized as the divine
No.   20–21   *G·* is recognized as the only power,

is regarded
Mis. 234–28   *G·* is regarded more as absolute,

is responsible
Mis. 347–25   *G·* is responsible for the mission of
Un.   64– 2   If . . . *G·* is responsible therefor ;

is seen
Mis.   23–25   *G·* is seen only in that which

is self-existent
'00.   5–12   *G·* is self-existent, the essence

is Spirit
Mis.   55–26   If *G·* is Spirit, as the Scriptures
     75–11   synonym of Spirit, and *G·* is Spirit.
     113– 4   "*G·* is Spirit," — *see John* 4 : 24.
     184– 1   by claiming that *G·* is Spirit,
Un.   31– 2   accurately translated, "*G·* is Spirit"
     31– 5   If *G·* is Spirit, and God is All,
     34–11   that God is All, and *G·* is Spirit ;
Rud.   4–21   "*G·* is Spirit ;" — *see John* 4 : 24.
     13–16   "*G·* is Spirit." — *see John* 4 : 24.
'01.   3–15   "*G·* is Spirit," — *see John* 4 : 24.
     22– 5   Mind of God — and *G·* is Spirit.
     23– 5   would admit that *G·* is Spirit
Peo.   7–30   Because *G·* is Spirit, our thoughts must
My. 221–16   *G·* is Spirit. Then modes of healing,
     266–19   *G·* is Spirit and the origin of all
     270–31   *G·* is Spirit,

is supposed
Mis.   72– 9   *G·* is supposed to impart to man

is supreme
Mis.   3–25   *G·* is supreme and omnipotent,
     259–17   Science, in which *G·* is supreme,

is the Alpha
Un.   10–19   *G·* is the Alpha and Omega,

is the author
'01.   4–12   *G·* is the author of Science

is the Father
Mis. 164–31   *G·* is the Father of man,

is the fountain
Mis. 117–27   *G·* is the fountain of light,

is the giver
My. 205– 8   and *G·* is the giver.

is the law
Mis. 259– 5   *G·* is the law of Life,

is the only creator
Mis. 280–26   Spirit, *G·*, is the only creator :
No.   6– 6   *G·* is the only creator,

is the only Life
Mis.   16–17   great fact that *G· is the only Life;*
     194–28   *know* that *G·* is the only Life.

is the only Mind
Mis. 361–24   *G·* is the only Mind,
No.   35–21   *G·* is the only Mind, Life,

is the Principle
Mis.   78–26   If *G·* is the Principle of man
Hea.   3–21   *G·* is the Principle of Christian healing,

is "the same
Un.   61– 3   *G·* is "the same yesterday, — *Heb.* 13 : 8.

is the temple
Mis. 323– 4   for *G·* is the temple thereof ;

is this Principle
Mis. 194– 4   and *G·* is this Principle.

is Truth
Mis.   25– 8   since *G·* is Truth, and All-in-all.
     49–30   *G·* is Truth, the Scriptures aver ;
Un.   35–16   But *G·* is Truth,

is understandable
My. 238–21   *G·* is understandable, knowable,

is understood
Mis. 346– 4   proof that *G·* is understood
Un.   6– 5   selfhood of *G·* is understood,

is universal
Mis. 150–25   *G·* is universal ; confined to no spot,

is upright
Mis.   79–15   *G·* is upright and eternal,

is wisdom
Un.   26–16   * *G·* is wisdom, God is love.

justify
Mis. 374– 3   even the publicans to justify *G·*.

God

kingdom of
   (*see* **kingdom**)
knowing
  My. 356– 5 privilege of knowing *G·*,
knowledge of
   (*see* **knowledge**)
known of
  My. 120– 6 know as we are known of *G·*.
known to
  No. 7–17 loving sacrifice . . . is known to *G·*,
knows
  Mis. 259–12 declares that *G·* knows iniquity !
  Un. 1– 3 *G·* knows no such thing as sin.
   13–18 If *G·* knows that which is not
   15–10 If *G·* knows evil, so must man,
   19– 7 If *G·* knows evil at all, He must
   22–13 *G·* knows that a knowledge of
   54–17 If *G·* knows sin, even as a
  No. 16– 7 If *G·* knows evil even as a
   17– 2 If *G·* knows the antecedent,
   37–27 What *G·* knows, He also predestinates ;
  '01. 21–24 faith assures me that *G·* knows
Lamb of
  Mis. 121–23 "the Lamb of *G·*." — *John* 1 : 29.
law of
   (*see* **law**)
laws of
   (*see* **laws**)
leadeth me
  Mis. 397–20 whereto *G·* leadeth me.
  Pul. 19– 4 whereto *G·* leadeth me.
  Po. 13– 8 whereto *G·* leadeth me.
lead you to
  My. 213–21 whether they lead you to *G·*
leaned on
  '02. 15– 5 I leaned on *G·*, and was safe.
learn
  Mis. 235–19 learn *G·* aright, and know
  Peo. 6–16 but when we learn *G·* aright,
learn that
  Peo. 2–10 learn that *G·*, good, is universal,
leave with
  Ret. 90–30 leave with *G·* the government
leaving self for
  Peo. 9– 6 it is love leaving self for *G·*.
Life and
  Un. 37–16 do not testify of Life and *G·*.
Life as
  Mis. 189–20 Life in God and Life *as G·*.
  Un. 38–23 Life as *G·*, moral and spiritual
  My. 273–22 understanding of Life as *G·*,
Life in
  Mis. 189–19 Life in *G·* and Life *as* God.
life in
  Mis. 64– 8 indestructible eternal life in *G·*.
  My. 150–23 raising . . . to life in *G·*.
Life is
   (*see* **Life**)
Life, or
  Ret. 59–16 antipodes of Life, or *G·*,
  Un. 38– 4 a contradiction of Life, or *G·* ;
Life that is
  Mis. 194–30 naturalness of the Life that is *G·*,
   196–21 When the Life that is *G·*, good,
light is not
  '01. 3–22 * God is light, but light is not *G·*."
light of
  Mis. 340–29 shine with the reflected light of *G·*.
likeness of
  Mis. 61–22 image and likeness of *G·*.
   97–22 image and likeness of *G·*.
   182–20 image and likeness of *G·*,
   186– 9 in the image and likeness of *G·* ;
   188–30 the true likeness of *G·*,
   308–31 man in the image and likeness of *G·*.
  Rud. 7–10 He is the likeness of *G·* ;
  No. 25–17 Man is the image and likeness of *G·*,
  '02. 8– 5 likeness of *G·*, Spirit, is spiritual,
  Hea. 17– 5 present the image and likeness of *G·*.
  My. 36–24 * in the image and likeness of *G·*.
   119–32 true image and likeness of *G·*.
lives also in
  Pul. 4–20 Who lives in good, lives also in *G·*,
lives in
  Un. 40–17 abides in good, if he lives in *G·*,
living
  Mis. 372–28 character of the living *G·*,
  Un. 49–13 consciousness of the only living *G·*
   62–22 "I am the living *G·*, and man is My
  My. 46–28 * city of the living *G·*, — *Heb.* 12 : 22.
Lord is
  Un. 21–15 The Lord is *G·*.
lose with
  Mis. 341–19 O learn to lose with *G·* !

God

love
  Mis. 10– 7 to them that love *G·*." — *Rom.* 8 : 28.
   51–19 educate him to love *G·*, good,
   123–25 love *G·*, and keep His commandments,
   240–21 Children . . . naturally love *G·* ;
   311– 1 love *G·* and keep His commandments,
   318–11 love *G·* and keep His commandments.
   367– 4 and to love *G·* supremely.
  '00. 11–11 to them that love *G·*," — *Rom.* 8 : 28.
  '01. 32–20 love *G·* and keep His commandments
  My. 4–15 loves all who love *G·*,
   6– 3 Do we love *G·* supremely?
   143–26 to them that love *G·*, — *Rom.* 8 : 28.
   233–29 Do Christian Scientists love *G·* as
   276–25 to love *G·* supremely,
   286– 7 love *G·* supremely,
love and
  Mis. 395– 4 Is out of tune With love and *G·* ;
  Po. 57–11 Is out of tune With love and *G·* ;
Love as
  Mis. 234–10 true sense of Love as *G·* ;
love for
   (*see* **love**)
Love is
  '01. 3–21 * this is no argument that Love is *G·* ;
love of
  Mis. 279– 4 It is the love of *G·*, and not the
  No. 7– 8 By the love of *G·* we can cancel
  My. 19–10 and the love of *G·*, — *II Cor.* 13 : 14.
   46–23 * love of *G·* and our brother,
   159–14 perfect love of *G·* and man.
   187–16 the grace and love of *G·*
   200–17 the love of *G·* and man.
loves
  Mis. 100–27 because he loves *G·* most.
  '01. 21–16 individual who loves *G·* and man ;
love to
  Pul. 39– 2 * love to *G·* and love to man
  My. 274–24 and love to *G·* and man ;
loving
  Mis. 328–30 Then, loving *G·* supremely
  Rud. 10–20 look up to the loving *G·*,
  Po. 43– 4 Loving *G·* and one another,
loyal to
  Mis. 277–10 a heart loyal to *G·* is patient
made
  Mis. 45–21 *If G· made all that was made,*
   50– 1 *G·* made all that was made.
   186–14 We learn . . . that *G·* made all ;
  Un. 14– 6 after *G·* made the universe,
   32– 4 saying, . . . *G·* made me, and I make man
  '01. 7– 9 *G·* made man in His own image
   8–14 more transcendental than *G·* made him?
   8–19 As *G·* made man, is he not wholly
  '02. 6–12 *G·* made neither evil nor its
  Hea. 9–23 *G·* made all that was made,
   17– 8 *G·* made all that was made ;
  My. 107–24 *G·* made all that was made,
   124–28 *G·* made "manifest — *I Tim.* 3 : 16.
   178–15 all that *G·* made "good ;" — *Gen.* 1 : 31.
   288–31 all is good because *G·* made all,
made by
  Hea. 9–18 man made by *G·* had
made manifest
  Mis. 77–10 *G·* made manifest through man,
  My. 348– 6 *G·* made manifest in the flesh,
makes
  Mis. 111–10 *G·* makes "fishers of men" — *Mark* 1 : 17.
   117–30 make their moves before *G·* makes His,
   177– 2 *G·* makes to us all, right here,
   353–19 *G·* makes *us* pay for tending the
  Un. 13– 3 theology makes *G·* tributary to man,
  '01. 7– 3 theology makes *G·* manlike ;
   24– 7 Here he makes *G·* the cause of
  My. 205–20 so makes *G·* more supreme
man and
  Mis. 77–11 eternal unity of man and *G·*,
   332–17 pondered the things of man and *G·*.
  Ret. 60–27 or of the real man and *G·*.
  Peo. 1– 7 final unity between man and *G·*.
manhood of
  Mis. 33–11 as well as in the manhood of *G·*,
  Hea. 10– 6 fought the manhood of *G·*,
manifest
  My. 109–24 *G·* "manifest in the flesh," — *I Tim.* 3 : 16.
manifestation of
  '00. 10– 3 is some manifestation of *G·*
manlike
  Mis. 178– 6 not satisfied with a manlike *G·*,
  '01. 7– 3 theology makes *G·* manlike ;
man of
  Mis. 159–19 as the man of *G·*, the risen Christ,
man or
  Ret. 71–19 without the permission of man or *G·*,

God

man to
    Un. 51–25 scientific relation of man to *G·*,
man with
    Un. 5–24 marvellous unity of man with *G·*
men call
    '01. 18–26 Truth, Love— whom men call *G·*
message from
    '02. 11–16 new-old message from *G·*,
methods of
    Mis. 270–25 modes and methods of *G·.*
mighty
    Mis. 161– 7 *The mighty G·,— Isa. 9 : 6.*
    164–18 The mighty *G·,— Isa. 9 : 6.*
    321– 6 The mighty *G·,— Isa. 9 : 6.*
mills of
    Ret. 80– 8 * mills of *G·* grind slowly,
Mind is
    (see **Mind**)
Mind of
    No. 37–27 existed in the Mind of *G·.*
    '01. 22– 5 It is the Mind of *G·*
    27–25 the Mind of *G·* and not of man
Mind, or
    Mis. 69– 6 Mind, or *G·,* and His attributes.
    Ret. 56– 5 the one divine Mind, or *G·,*
    No. 5–20 then Mind, or *G·,* does not
Mind that is
    Mis. 4– 7 Science of the Mind that is *G·,*
    57–18 existed in and of the Mind that is *G·,*
    113– 1 Mind that is *G·* is not in matter ;
    My. 267– 8 law of the Mind that is *G·,*
Mind which is
    Mis. 36– 9 eternal Mind, which is *G·,*
    Un. 44–18 expressive of the Mind which is *G·.*
    56– 6 in the Mind which is *G·.*
must be One
    '01. 6–14 *G·* must be One although He is three.
must know
    Un. 17–20 Error says *G·* must know evil
    18–22 Error says *G·* must know death
my
    Mis. 63–22 "*My G·, why hast Thou — Mark* 15 : 34.
    206–22 "Good is my *G·,*
    206–22 my *G·* is good.
    206–22 Love is my *G·,*
    206–23 my *G·* is Love."
    Un. 29–27 my *G·* [my Soul, — *Psal.* 42 : 11.
    Pan. 4–24 and my *G·.— Psal.* 42 : 11.
    Po. 33–19 waft me away to my *G·.*
mysterious
    Peo. 3–13 make a mysterious *G·* and a
name
    Mis. 15–24 infinite good that we name *G·,*
    26–28 Scriptures name *G·* as good,
    My. 225–21 to the divine Spirit the name *G·.*
named
    Rud. 2–17 whom mortals have named *G·.*
named Himself
    Mis. 258–18 *G·* named Himself, I AM
namely
    Mis. 189–22 namely *G·,* the eternal good,
    My. 226–14 the infinite, — namely, *G·.*
name of
    '00. 10–14 and this, too, in the name of *G·,*
    My. 190–30 Then, in the name of *G·,*
    233–19 taking the name of *G·* in vain.
names
    My. 225–21 C. S. names *G·* as divine Principle,
nature of
    Mis. 104–12 not in the nature of *G·,*
    217–28 nature of *G·* must change in order to
    218–18 unfolds the real nature of *G·*
    259– 4 partakes not of the nature of *G·,*
    Pan. 5– 9 possessed of the nature of *G·

;*
    '01. 3–23 Love expresses the nature of *G·* ;
    3–25 loses the nature of *G·,* Spirit,
    4– 2 both have the nature of *G·.*
    5–26 nature of *G·* must be seen in man,
    10–17 C. S. explains the nature of *G·*
    My. 110– 1 it is the nature of *G·,*
    288–11 has no origin in the nature of *G·,*
nature's
    Po. v–15 * *through nature, unto nature's G·,"*
    My. 151–25 "through nature up to nature's *G·,"*
near enough to
    No. 27– 6 get near enough to *G·* to see this,
nearer to
    Mis. 6– 2 to bring man nearer to *G·,*
    Un. 7–25 and brings us nearer to *G·,*
neither slumbers
    Mis. 209–17 *G·* neither slumbers nor sleeps.
never made
    Mis. 122–28 *G·* never made it,
    241–19 "*G·* never made you sick :
    Un. 20–12 *First: G·* never made evil.

God

never made
    Un. 45–11 that *G·* never made evil.
    53– 3 *G·* never made them ;
    '01. 13– 1 and *G·* never made it.
    Hea. 9–17 *G·* never made a wicked man ;
never said
    Un. 14–27 *G·* never said that man would
noblest work of
    Mis. 294– 1 noblest work of *G·* is man
no cognizance of
    Un. 28–19 they take no cognizance of *G·.*
no other
    Mis. 182– 8 no other *G·,* no other Mind,
nor acknowledged
    No. 18– 3 nor acknowledged *G·* in all His ways.
not asking
    No. 39–17 True prayer is not asking *G·* for
not of
    Un. 11– 9 laws of mortal mind, not of *G·.*
    '02. 6–15 something that is not of *G·.*
    My. 4–32 not of *G·* but originates in the
not ordained of
    Ret. 49–15 powers that are not ordained of *G·,*
noumenon is
    My. 347–28 Principle whose noumenon is *G·*
obedience to
    Mis. 12–30 measured by our obedience to *G·,*
    267–28 that action, in obedience to *G·,*
obey
    My. 118– 2 obey *G·* and steadily go on
of all grace
    Mis. 116– 3 The *G·* of all grace be with you,
    159– 7 *G·* of all grace give you peace.
    My. 148– 7 and may the *G·* of all grace,
of Christian Science
    '01. 6– 4 the *G·* of C. S. is not a person,
of harvest
    Mis. 313 21 *G·* of harvest to send forth more
of harvests
    My. 291–28 to pray, that the *G·* of harvests
of Israel
    My. 182–20 the *G·* of Israel, the divine Love
of my fathers
    My. 285–26 *G·* of my fathers, — *Acts* 24 : 14.
of nature
    My. 349–22 coexist with the *G·* of nature
of our fathers
    My. 192–13 May the *G·* of our fathers,
of peace
    Mis. 128–13 *G·* of peace shall be — *Phil.* 4 : 9.
    153–30 *G·* of peace be and abide with this
of spirituality
    Un. 49–16 and the *G·* of spirituality.
of their fathers
    My. 43– 7 * revealed the *G·* of their fathers,
of theology
    '01. 6– 3 says the *G·* of theology is a Person.
    6–9 Is the *G·* of theology a finite or an
omnipotence of
    Mis. 31–21 faith in the *omnipotence* of *G·,*
omnipotent
    '01. 5– 9 *G·* omnipotent, omnipresent,
omnipresence of
    Ret. 56–17 omnipotence and omnipresence of *G·,*
    Rud. 9–26 omnipotence and omnipresence of *G·* ;
omnipresent
    '02. 12– 8 he has one omnipresent *G·* :
    Po. 23–19 Supreme and omnipresent *G·,*
One
    Pan. 12–22 strictly monotheism, — it has ONE *G·.*
one
    Mis. 22– 1 a theist — believe in one *G·,*
    23–23 synonymous for the one *G·,*
    25– 3 That there is but one *G·*
    36–10 and there is but one *G·.*
    50–29 changed to having but *one G·*
    55–24 knows that he can have one *G·* only,
    56–20 one *G·,* and the brotherhood of man.
    75–12 There is but one *G·,*
    131–12 one faith, one *G·,* one baptism.
    196– 1 lead to the one *G·* :
    196– 2 for there is but one *G·,*
    196– 5 supposition . . . more than one *G·,*
    252–22 It has one *G·.*
    341– 8 whole human race have one *G·,*
    364–20 nothing apart from this Mind, one *G·,*
    Ret. 69–30 there is and can be but one *G·,*
    Un. 10– 9 utter reliance upon the one *G·,*
    24– 8 assumptions . . . more than the one *G·* ;
    29–12 There is but one *G·,* one Soul,
    37– 3 as there is but one *G·,*
    Pul. 74–27 never can be but one *G·,*
    Rud. 13–12 saith there is more than one *G·,*
    No. 38–16 the interpreter of one *G·,*
    38–19 Having one *G·,* one Mind,

God

one

Pan. 1–19   know and acknowledge one *G·*
    3–22   In religion, it is a belief in one *G·*, or in
    7– 4   signifies more than one *G·*,
    8–13   chapter sub-title
    8–17   Christianity then had one *G·*
    9– 3   one *G·* and His creation,
    9– 9   one *G·* and the four first rules
    13–22   "one *G·* and Father— *Eph.* 4 : 6.
'00. 4– 4   real and normal as the one *G·*,
    4–10   the perfect worship of one *G·*.
    5–11   they signify one *G·*.
    5–16   whereby to have one *G·*,
'01. 5– 5   lose the nature of one *G·*,
'02. 12–12   the Jew's belief in one *G·*,
Peo. 13– 9   revealing the one *G·* and His
My. 109– 8   we shall have one Mind, one *G·*,
    109–20   there can be but one *G·*,
    116–11   Thou shalt have one *G·*.
    155– 8   May this church have one *G·*,
    191–12   one *G·* and one Christ.
    240– 2   one *G·* and the brotherhood of man
    252– 2   Have one *G·* and you will have no
    281–11   namely, one *G·*, one Mind,
    286– 6   have one *G·*, one Mind ;
    303–18   its pure monotheism— one *G·*,
    339– 6   one *G·*, supreme, infinite,

oneness of

Mis. 93– 9   the allness and oneness of *G·*
    152– 5   the oneness of *G·* includes
My. 342–23   simplicity of the oneness of *G·* ;

oneness with

Mis. 286–10   found to be man's oneness with *G·*,
Un. 54–15   *at-one-ment,* or oneness with *G·*,

one with

Mis. 245–29   * "one with *G·* is a majority."
Pul. 74–25   one with *G·*, in the sense of

only

Mis. 55–24   he can have one *G·* only,
Rud. 4–17   Good is not in evil, but in *G·* only.
'01. 3–26   expresses *G·* only in metaphor,
Peo. 12–12   acknowledge only *G·* in all thy ways,

only waits

Mis. 154–10   *G·* only waits for man's worthiness

opposed to

Mis. 49–27   not only a power opposed to *G·*,
Pul. 13– 5   belief in a power opposed to *G·*.

opposition to

Mis. 197–29   theory that is in opposition to *G·*,
'02. 10–27   opposition to *G·* and His power

oracles of

Mis. 107– 3   mistaken for the oracles of *G·*.

ordains

Ret. 85–17   you do not feel that *G·* ordains you.

or good

Ret. 54–12   believing in *G·*, or good,
Un. 31–23   *G·*, or good, is Spirit alone ;

originates in

Mis. 186– 2   man who originates in *G·*,

origin in

No. 18– 7   proof of its origin in *G·*,

or Life

Mis. 25– 3   there is but one *G·* or Life,
Un. 39–23   As the image of *G·*, or Life,

or man

No. 23–25   cannot understand *G·* or man,
    27–23   personality of *G·* or man is

or Spirit

Un. 10–11   Life is *G·*, or Spirit,
No. 16–13   none beside *G·* or Spirit

other than

'02. 6– 4   apart or other than *G·* — good

our

Mis. 124–13   so great a God as our *G·* !"— *Psal.* 77 : 13.
    129– 9   The law of our *G·*
    206–30   the dwelling-place of our *G·*,
    308–16   Lord our *G·* is one Lord."— *Deut.* 6 : 4.
Pul. 10–18   corner-stone in the house of our *G·*,
    12– 7   kingdom of our *G·*,— *Rev.* 12 : 10.
    12– 9   accused them before our *G·* — *Rev.* 12 : 10.
Po. 79–11   Our *G·* is good.
My. 185–28   * Our *G·*, our fathers' God !
    186–19   May our *G·* make this church
    280–15   chapter sub-title— *Deut.* 6 : 4.

outstretched to

No. 44–18   weak hand outstretched to *G·*.

overrules it

Mis. 41– 6   were it not that *G·* overrules it,

pardoned by

No. 29–19   A mortal pardoned by *G·* is

peace in

Mis. 385– 3   * Above the sod Find peace in *G·*,
Po. 37– 3   * Above the sod Find peace in *G·*,

peace of

No. 8– 8   "the peace of *G·*,— *Phil.* 4 : 7.

God

peace with

Mis. 211–28   and kept peace with *G·*.
'01. 2–20   keeping peace with *G·*.

people of

Mis. 216– 4   Sabbath rest for the people of *G·* ;

perception of

Un. 20–18   perception of *G·* as All-in-all.

perfect in

Mis. 5–27   perfect in *G·*, in Truth, Life, and

personal

Mis. 96– 7   Do I believe in a personal *G·* ?
Rud. 2–16   rather than *a personal G·* ;
'01. 11–25   a sermon from his personal *G·* !
Peo. 3–20   A personal *G·* is based on
    4–13   the error that a personal *G·*

pities

No. 30–13   *G·* pities our woes with the love of a

pitieth

Un. 2– 3   *G·* pitieth them who fear Him ;

possible to

Mis. 183–13   possible to *G·*, is possible to man
Un. 18–27   If such . . . were possible to *G·*,
My. 293– 1   all things are possible to *G·*

power of

(*see* **power**)

praise

My. 148–18   you have met to praise *G·*.
    207– 4   wrath of men shall praise *G·*,

praise to

My. 323–21   * gratitude and praise to *G·*

praising

My. 245–19   go on *ad infinitum*, praising *G·*,

pray to

Mis. 114–22   cannot . . . pray to *G·* too fervently,

prepares

My. 12–24   *G·* prepares the way for

prerogative of

Un. 32– 3   usurps the prerogative of *G·*,
No. 23– 5   neither grasp the prerogative of *G·*

preserving

My. 344–11   *G·* preserving individuality and

Principle is

Un. 38– 2   immortality, whose Principle is *G·*.
    38–28   being, whose Principle is *G·*.

Principle that is

Peo. 5–20   yea, to the Principle that is *G·*,

proceedeth not from

Mis. 198–14   evil proceedeth not from *G·*,

proceed from

Mis. 76– 1   must proceed from *G·* ;
'00. 4–25   must proceed from *G·*, from Mind,

proceeds from

Mis. 49–29   belief . . . to err proceeds from *G·*.
    58–22   order that proceeds from *G·*.

proceeds not from

Mis. 36–12   harmful and proceeds not from *G·* ;

prophet of

Pan. 8–11   the only prophet of *G·*

providence of

Mis. 80–19   through the providence of *G·*,
    100– 4   left to the providence of *G·*.
    163–15   committed to the providence of *G·*.
Ret. 30–20   providence of *G·*, and the cross of
Pul. 20–12   committed to the providence of *G·*,
My. 148– 3   through the providence of *G·*,
    220– 3   submit to the providence of *G·*,

purpose of

Mis. 366–21   as the purpose of *G·* ;
My. 216–18   purpose of *G·* to youward

quality of

Pan. 5– 2   Can a single quality of *G·*,

reaches others

Mis. 39–26   *by which G· reaches others*

reaches out to

My. 290–12   My soul reaches out to *G·* for your

realities of

No. 5–24   the realities of *G·* and His laws.

reality of

Un. 34–25   What is the reality of *G·*
My. 248–17   reality of *G·*, man, nature,

reconciliation with

No. 35–22   needs no reconciliation with *G·*,

referring to

My. 225–31   Principle, when referring to *G·*,

refer to

Mis. 59–19   Scriptures refer to *G·* as saying,

reflect

'00. 4–27   they reflect *G·* and nothing else.
My. 150–19   enable you to reflect *G·*,

reflecting

No. 21–12   showed man as reflecting *G·*

reflection of

Rud. 7– 9   the manifest reflection of *G·*,

reflects

Mis. 184– 7   only when man reflects *G·*

God

reflects
  Ret. 56–23   *G·* reflects Himself, or Mind,
        57–15   He reflects *G·* as his Mind,

regards
  Mis. 55–25   regards *G·* as the only Mind,

reigns
  Mis. 80–22   *G·* reigns, and will . . . until

relation to
  Mis. 235– 2   recognition of his relation to *G·*.

relying on
  Mis. 115–22   necessity for relying on *G·*

remember
  Mis. 175–32   remember *G·* in all thy ways,

removes
  '01. 13–22   *G·* removes the punishment for sin

render to
  My. 220–11   render 'to *G·* the things— *Mark* 12 : 17.

representatives of
  Mis. 200– 5   better representatives of *G·*

represents
  Mis. 336– 8   that which represents *G·* most,
  Ret. 63–15   represents *G·*, the Life of man.
  No. 26–13   All real being represents *G·*,

requires
  Man. 44–26   *G·* requires our whole heart,
        77–18   *G·* requires wisdom, economy,
  No. 34–20   heathen conception that *G·* requires

resembles
  Mis. 167–9   idea of all that resembles *G·*.

rest in
  Rud. 12–19   and induces rest in *G·*,
  My. 282– 6   my hope must still rest in *G·*,

rests on
  No. 24– 9   which rests on *G·* as One and All,

revealed
  Mis. 179–31   when *G·* revealed to me this risen
  My. v–25   * revealed *G·* to well-nigh countless

reveals
  Mis. 82– 2   and reveals *G·* and man as
       210– 9   neither reveals *G·* in matter,
  Ret. 60–11   C. S. reveals *G·* and
       65–30   reveals *G·* as ever-present Truth and

right hand of
  Mis. 178–13   on the right hand of *G·"*— *Col.* 3 : 1.

rising to
  Mis. 144–26   our visible lives are rising to *G·*.

robs
  Un. 38–15   material sense of life robs *G·*,

rod of
  Mis. 19– 5   but the rod of *G·*,

saith
  Un. 18–23   *G·* saith, I am ever-conscious Life,

save
  My. 289–17   "*G·* save the Queen"

says
  Mis. 367–15   but *G·* says of this fruit of the tree
  Un. 18– 7   *G·* says, I am too pure to behold
       18–14   *G·* says you oftenest console others
       18–17   *G·* says, I show My pity

scale of
  Mis. 312– 4   when weighed in the scale of *G·*

scales of
  Mis. 293–12   weighs in the scales of *G·*
      372– 4   weight in the scales of *G·*.

Science of
  (*see* **Science**)

see
  Mis. 15– 8   they shall see *G·".*— *Matt.* 5 : 8.
      185– 2   pure in heart shall see *G·*,
  Ret. 26–25   none but the pure in heart can see *G·*,
  Un. 51–24   where we see *G·* as Life,
      55–21   in my flesh shall I see *G· ;"*— *Job* 19 : 26.
  Pul. 3–20   in my flesh shall I see *G·".*— *Job* 19 : 26.
      35–11   'pure in heart' can see *G·".*— *Matt.* 5 : 8.
  '01. 26–18   left to such as see *G·*
  My. 132–20   where we may see *G·* and live,
      218– 5   "In my flesh shall I see *G·".*— *Job* 19 : 26.

seek
  Mis. 206–26   all who diligently seek *G·*.

seemed
  '01. 32–10   *G·* seemed to shield the whole

sees
  Mis. 361– 2   pure heart that sees *G·*.
  Un. 49–25   something which *G·* sees and knows,

self-existence of
  Pan. 8–10   deny the self-existence of *G·*?

self-existent
  Pan. 3–19   supreme, holy, self-existent *G·*,

self-same
  Un. 3–27   this self-same *G·* is our helper.

self-sustained by
  Mis. 316– 9   must be self-sustained by *G·*.

sense of
  (*see* **sense**)

God

separate from
  Mis. 36–29   in matter and separate from *G·*,
  Ret. 60– 6   as something separate from *G·*.
      67– 9   yet are separate from *G·*.

serve
  Mis. 237– 8   serve *G·* (or try to) from fear ;
      269– 9   cannot serve *G·* and— *Matt.* 6 : 24.
  01. 20– 4   serve *G·* and benefit mankind.
  '02. 3–28   true ambition is to serve *G·*
  My. 5–29   indulging sin, men cannot serve *G·* ;
      356–24   cannot serve *G·* and— *Matt.* 6 : 24.

shall help her
  Pul. 83–20   * "*G·* shall help her, — *Psal.* 46 : 5.

shall reveal
  Mis. 348–12   *G·* shall reveal His rod,

signet of
  Mis. 121–21   thereby giving the signet of *G·*

smiles of
  Mis. 179–27   to give us these smiles of *G·* !

so clothe
  No. 26–26   "If God so clothe— *Matt.* 6 : 30.

Son of
  (*see* **Son**)

son of
  (*see* **son**)

sonship with
  Mis. 83–23   declared his sonship with *G·* :
      360–11   scientific sonship with *G·*.

sons of
  Mis. 176–13   the liberty of the sons of *G·*.
      180–22   *become the sons of G·,* — *John* 1 : 12.
      181–25   *become the sons of G·."* — *John* 1 : 12.
      185–19   *become the sons of G·."* — *John* 1 : 12.
      185–26   *become the sons of G·."* — *John* 1 : 12.
      251–14   the liberty of the sons of *G·*,
      259–21   sons of *G·* shouted — *Job* 38 : 7.
  Un. 5–20   the liberty of the sons of *G·*,
      42–15   sons of *G·* shouted — *Job* 38 : 7.
  Peo. 11– 1   full liberty of the sons of *G·*

Soul must be
  Un. 28–17   Soul must be *G·* ;

source in
  Pul. 3–22   living waters have their source in *G·*,

speaks
  '00. 8–27   When *G·* speaks to you through

Spirit is
  (*see* **Spirit**)

spirit of
  My. 344–10   "It is not the spirit of *G·*,

Spirit, or
  Rud. 5– 8   made in the image of Spirit, or *G·*.

standeth
  Mis. 368– 9   * Standeth *G·* within the shadow,

stands for
  '01. 4– 2   Principle or Person stands for *G·*
  My. 344– 3   If we say that the sun stands for *G·*,

statutes of
  Peo. 12– 2   these divine statutes of *G·* :

steadfastly in
  Mis. 241– 2   should centre as steadfastly in *G·*

strong in
  Rud. 8–12   thou wilt be strong in *G·*,

substance of
  Mis. 104– 8   yea, the substance of *G·*,
      187–24   Did the substance of *G·*, Spirit,

substantiates
  No. 38– 5   and that *G·* substantiates their

supremacy of
  Hea. 15– 2   rests upon the supremacy of *G·*.

Supreme
  My. 36–31   * proof that our Supreme *G·*,

surrender to
  Mis. 15–15   moments of surrender to *G·*,

symbols of
  Mis. 82–10   cognize the symbols of *G·*,

takes care
  My. 166– 8   *G·* takes care of our life.
      203–19   for *G·* takes care of it.

taught of
  My. 230–27   all taught of *G·".*— *John* 6 : 45.
      239–14   *and all are taught of G·*

temporary loss of
  Un. 41– 9   involves a temporary loss of *G·*,

term for
  Mis. 13–28   Seek the Anglo-Saxon term for *G·*,
      26–29   Saxon term for *G·* is also good.
  Pul. 6– 7   Good, the Anglo-Saxon term for *G·*,
  My. 185–14   Love is the generic term for *G·*.

testify of
  Un. 2–14   is ready to testify of *G·*

thank
  Mis. 113–23   Thank *G·* ! this evil can be resisted
      294–12   thank *G·* and take courage,
      331–15   thank *G·* for those redemptive words
  Ret. 16–10   thank *G·*, she is healed !"

God

thank
My. 62– 9   * How can we ever thank *G·* enough
127–19   thank *G·* for persecution
159–10   I thank *G·* who hath sent forth
193– 8   and to thank *G·* forever
270–21   I thank *G·* that for the past
341– 4   thank *G·* that He has emblazoned

thanks to
'00. 2– 4   thanks to *G·*, the people most

that feedeth
Mis. 322–19   *G·* that feedeth the hungry heart,

the Father
My. 344– 5   *G·* the Father is greater than

their
Mis. 10–11   Their *G·* will not let them be lost ;
10–13   The good cannot lose their *G·*,
'01. 3– 9   because their *G·* is not a person.
7–18   call their *G·* "divine Principle,"
Peo. 7– 1   by their *G·* and their devil.

theological
'01. 5–28   The theological *G·* as a Person

the perfect Mind
Mis. 37–18   antidote . . . is *G·*, the perfect Mind,

the preserver
Pan. 7–10   *G·*, the preserver of man, declared

the term
Hea. 3–14   the term *G·* was derived from

the word
Mis. 75–17   where the word *G·* can be used
Peo. 2– 9   another letter to the word *G·*
My. 226– 3   substitute the word *G·*

things of
Mis. 175– 3   takes of the things of *G·* and
Ret. 24–24   should take the things of *G·*
'01. 9–23   takes of the things of *G·*

think of
Un. 18– 2   Rather let us think of *G·* as

this is
Mis. 173– 6   one Mind, and that this is *G·*,

this phrase for
'01. 3–17   we use this phrase for *G·*

this spirit is of
My. 292–27   but this spirit is of *G·*,

throne of
Ret. 22–13   the throne of *G·*."— *Heb.* 12 : 2.
My. 258–16   the throne of *G·*."— *Heb.* 12 : 2.

thus crowns
Ret. 71– 4   wisdom that *G·* thus crowns,

thy
My. 183– 2   love the Lord thy *G·* — *Luke* 10 : 27.
184–28   Thy *G·* reigneth !"— *Isa.* 52 : 7.
206–19   thy *G·* thy glory."— *Isa.* 60 : 19.
229– 7   thy *G·* doth drive them out — *Deut.* 18 : 12.

to define
'01. 1–22   As . . . Scientists you seek to define *G·*
'02. 7–14   Use these words to define *G·*,

to hide from
Ret. 78–22   or for yourself to hide from *G·*,

told
Un. 17–21   *G·* told our first parents

to man
Ret. 31– 5   "the ways of *G·*" to man — *Job* 40 : 19.
68–27   passing from *G·* to man"
My. 208–17   ministrations of *G·* to man.

to the rescue
Po. 71–13   *G·* to the rescue — Liberty, peal!

towards
My. 159–19   the tendency towards *G·*,
189–23   we are drawn towards *G·*.
338–20   heart full of love towards *G·*

to work for
Mis. 116–28   never unready to work for *G·*,

true
Mis. 333–15   from the only living and true *G·*,
Ret. 49–25   knowledge of the true *G·*,
59–19   the only living and true *G·*,
Un. 4–24   knowledge of the only true *G·*,
38–14   the living and true *G·*.
My. 36–21   * dedicated to the only true *G·*,
187–24   worship of the only true *G·*.

true perception of
Mis. 15–10   can give the true perception of *G·*

trust
Mis. 25–26   if the sick cannot trust *G·* for help
Ret. 14–15   I was willing to trust *G·*,
My. 129–28   Trust *G·* to direct your steps.

trust in
My. 161–26   Trust in *G·*, and "He shall — *Prov.* 3 : 6.

Truth is
Un. 4– 5   Truth is *G·*, and in God's law.

truth of
No. 8– 7   utter the truth of *G·*
'00. 4–19   truth of *G·*, and of man

God

turns to
Mis. 386–17   a love that steady turns To *G·* ;
Po. 50– 1   a love that steady turns To *G·* ;

understand
Mis. 42–24   Only as we understand *G·*,
77–25   It was to understand *G·* and man :
94– 6   love good in order to understand *G·*.
194–21   in following him, you understand *G·*
194–32   understand *G·* sufficiently to
No. 23–25   cannot understand *G·* or man,
Hea. 15–26   because you do not understand *G·*,
15–28   as we understand *G·* better.
Peo. 6–23   deemed treason to understand *G·*,
My. 152–16   Do I understand *G·* as Love,

understanding of
Mis. 342–11   higher understanding of *G·*.
Ret. 28–12   understanding of *G·* in divine Science.
Un. 1–18   closer to the true understanding of *G·*
3–16   This is the understanding of *G·*,
38–19   opposite understanding of *G·*
61–26   the understanding of *G·* ;
Pul. 35–16   understanding of *G·* in divine Science.
Rud. 11– 5   *understanding* of *G·* and man
11–20   based on a true understanding of *G·*
Pan. 15–10   life and understanding of *G·*,
'02. 11–11   spiritual understanding of *G·*,
Hea. 8– 2   beyond the understanding of *G·*,
My. 44– 2   * Through the understanding of *G·*
107–27   knowledge or understanding of *G·*,
152–10   reached the understanding of *G·*,

understand that
Mis. 96– 4   I understand that *G·* is an
Hea. 8–19   When we understand that *G·* is

understood
Mis. 14–19   that good, *G·*, understood,
196–27   but Life, *G·* understood.
Pan. 10–23   the effect of *G· understood.*

unfolded
My. 348–19   *G·* unfolded the way,

union with
Mis. 42–12   but by a conscious union with *G·*.

unity of
Mis. 266–16   inseparable from the unity of *G·*.
369–10   strong in the unity of *G·* and man.
'02. 9–18   The unity of *G·* and man

unity with
Mis. 181– 7   his sonship, or unity with *G·*,
Man. 15–16   unfolding man's unity with *G·*

universe of
Mis. 217– 6   the universe of *G·* is spiritual,

unknown
My. 5–20   worship, not an unknown *G·*, but
192– 2   Ye build not to an unknown *G·*.
193– 2   not to the unknown *G·*,
338–12   "The Unknown *G·* Made Known,"

unlike
Mis. 217–21   a third quality unlike *G·*.
Un. 38–22   in aught which is unlike *G·*,
No. 37–16   that what is unlike *G·*
37–26   whatever is unlike *G·* ;
My. 64–24   * overcoming all that is unlike *G·*,
240–17   all that is unlike *G·*, good

waited on
'02. 15–21   I waited on *G·* to suggest a name for

waiting on
Mis. 331– 2   mortals looking up, waiting on *G·*,

wait on
Mis. 81– 8   patiently wait on *G·* to decide,
'02. 17–17   to be willing to wait on *G·*,
My. 227–14   turn to . . . and wait on *G·*.
252–15   wait on *G·*, the strong deliverer,

wait patiently on
'01. 34–20   brethren, wait patiently on *G·* ;

waits on
Mis. 130–28   waits on *G·*, renews his strength,
My. 103– 4   summons the . . . and waits on *G·*.
306–17   Age, . . . waits on *G·*.

warned man
Mis. 24–27   *G·* warned man not to believe the

was manifest
Chr. 53–61   "*G·* was manifest — *I Tim.* 3 : 16.

was not outlined
Mis. 103–28   This *G·* was not outlined.

ways of
Ret. 31– 5   vindicating "the ways of *G·*" — *Job* 40 : 19.

we call
Un. 60– 7   We call *G·* omnipotent
My. 152–23   good, that we call *G·*,

we can know
Mis. 79– 8   whereby we can know *G·*.

weds himself with
Un. 17– 8   man thus weds himself with *G·*,

we learn
Un. 28–18   only as we learn *G·*,

God

went forth
Mis. 153– 6   *G·* went forth before His people,
went out to
Mis. 180–14   my heart went out to *G·,*
what is
'02.   5–15   question and wonder, What is *G·?*
where is
Ret. 60–21   Material sense saith, . . . Where is *G·?*
which worketh
My. 300– 5   it is *G·* which worketh— *Phil.* 2 : 13.
who gave
Mis. 388– 1   *G·,* who gave that word of might
'02. 20–10   *G·* who gave that word of might
Po.   7– 1   *G·,* who gave that word of might
who is Love
Mis. 337–11   its Principle, *G·* who is Love.
will bless
My. 197–28   *G·* will bless the work of your
360–21   *G·* will bless and prosper you.
will care for
Pul. 73– 3   * *G·* will care for us, and will send
will confirm
Mis. 153– 3   *G·* will confirm His inheritance.
will give
Mis. 115–26   for *G·* will give the ability to
138–25   *G·* will give to all His soldiers
320– 2   *G·* will give the benediction.
will guide you
Mis. 287–24   *G·* will guide you.
will help
Ret. 86–22   *G·* will help each man who
will make
No.   8–13   knowing that *G·* will make the
will of
Mis. 185– 4   The will of *G·,* or power of Spirit,
will recompense
Mis. 12– 6   *G·* will recompense this wrong,
will reward
My. 128–20   *G·* will reward your enemies
234–11   *G·* will reward their kind motives,
will supply
Pul. 15–17   *G·* will supply the wisdom
wisdom of
Mis. 210–12   wisdom of *G·,* as revealed in C. S.,
359–29   To ask wisdom of *G·,*
My. 261– 5   their elders, who seek wisdom of *G·,*
without
Ret. 61–16   without *G·* in the world.'— *Eph.* 2 : 12.
My. 178–17   if . . . it exists without *G·.*
with us
Mis. 103–28   Immanuel, or "*G·* with us."— *Matt.* 1 : 23.
331–27   "*G·* with us," the I AM.— *Matt.* 1 : 23.
My. 218– 8   proof of "*G·* with us."— *Matt.* 1 : 23.
womanhood of
Hea. 10– 7   fell before the womanhood of *G·,*
My. 346–30   manhood and womanhood of *G·*
Word of
     (*see* **Word**)
word of
     (*see* **word**)
words of
Mis. 317–31   speaketh the words of *G·* : — *John* 3 : 34.
Word that is
Mis. 363–25   Word that *is G·,* Spirit, and
My. 184–29   Word that is *G·* must at some time
Word was
Mis. 29–12   the Word was *G·.*"— *John* 1 : 1.
Pan.   5– 4   "The Word was *G·* ;"— *John* 1 : 1.
My. 117–19   the Word was *G·*"— *John* 1 : 1.
Word was with
Mis. 29–11   "the Word was with *G·,* — *John* 1 : 1.
My. 117–19   the Word was with *G·,* — *John* 1 : 1.
worketh
Mis. 283–25   *G·* worketh with him,
'01. 10–25   for *G·* worketh with us,
working for
Mis. 343– 7   in working for *G·.*
work of
Ret. 77– 3   * the noblest work of *G·* ;"
work with
Mis. 39–29   work with *G·* in healing the sick,
worship
Ret.   2– 8   seeking "freedom to worship *G·* ;"
My. 151–20   * Go forth, and worship *G·.*"
162–23   that in them Christians may worship *G·,*
168– 2   Freedom to worship *G·*
341– 7   * "Freedom to worship *G·.*"
worship of
Pul. 40–23   * dedicated to the worship of *G·.*
would forgive
Ret.   9–13   prayed that *G·* would forgive me,
wouldst teach
Mis. 209– 4   and wouldst teach *G·* not to

God

wrath of
No. 35–11   not to appease the wrath of *G·,*
Peo.   3– 8   the wrath of *G·,*
wrought
Mis. 333–26   They believed . . . that *G·* wrought

Mis.   2–19   when *G·,* man's saving Principle,
3–19   The Principle of all cure is *G·,*
11–23   leaving all retribution to *G·*
14–18   as real and eternal as good, *G·* !
16–10   it is indeed *G·* ;
16–12   ability to meet them is from *G·* ;
16–19   *G·* is infinitely more than a person,
16–21   *G·* is a divine *Whole,*
18–23   never separate himself from good, *G·* ;
18–28   to separate Life from *G·.*
18–31   to believe that aught that *G·* sends
19–16   steadfastly flowing on to *G·,*
22–10   C. S. translates Mind, *G·,*
23–18   *G·* is both noumenon and phenomena,
23–22   *G·,* Spirit, . . . are terms synonymous
23–31   *G·,* Spirit, could not change its
26– 2   whatever is of *G·,* hath life
26–24   *G·,* has no antecedent ;
26–30   *G·* is naturally and divinely
27– 4   That *G·,* good, creates evil, or
27–21   evil signifies the absence of good, *G·,*
30–25   There is no *G·.*"   *Psal.* 14 : 1.
31–15   *G·,* good, has *all* power.
37– 1   *G·* would not be omnipotent if
37–19   *G·* can and does destroy the
46–10   *Do you teach that you are equal with G·?*
46–26   the Life and Love that are *G·,*
47–20   *G·,* Spirit, is the only substance ;
48–12   animal magnetism is neither of *G·* nor
49–27   presupposes . . . that *G·* is not All-in-all,
50– 3   that *G·* is not its author,
51– 3   and drugs, *G·* does not require.
55–31   *G·* in matter,— which are theories
56– 7   If . . . *G·* is substanceless ;
56–25   *Why did G· command,*
57–18   "*G·* doth know— *Gen.* 3 : 5.
58–23   If *G·* does not govern the action of
63–22   *If Christ was G·, why did Jesus*
72– 6   only living and true origin, *G·.*
73– 1   or that *G·* is conscious of it.
74– 5   enmity of mortal man toward *G·.*
75–13   Soul is one, and is *G·* ;
77–24   the All-Father-Mother *G·,*
78– 1   Life, *G·,* is not buried in matter.
87–22   most reliant on himself and *G·.*
93–18   all cause and effect are in *G·.*
96–16   so worship I *G·.*"— *see Acts* 24 : 14.
97–19   there is no *G·* beside me."— *Isa.* 45 : 5.
102–12   *G·* is like Himself
103–32   a *G·* at hand,— *Jer.* 23 : 23.
104–27   *G·* and the real man.
105–32   *G·* is the sum total of the universe.
112–31   There is no *G·.*"— *Psal.* 14 : 1.
113–16   commits his way to *G·,*
115–12   May *G·* enable my students to
115–20   since *G·,* good, is All-in-all.
118– 2   cannot obey both *G·,* good, and evil,
124–13   "who is so great a *G·* — *Psal.* 77 : 13.
124–23   stretch out our arms to *G·.*
126–27   *G·* hath indeed smiled on my church
134–13   *G·* will pour you out a blessing
139– 4   *G·* will pour you out a blessing
139–11   *but mighty through G·* — *II Cor.* 10 : 4.
141–32   *G·* is in the midst of her :
150–21   "If *G·* be for us, — *Rom.* 8 : 31.
151–23   chosen person, whose *G·* is— what?
154–23   Honor thy Father and Mother, *G·.*
155–24   cannot spare time to write to *G·,*
158–22   and *G·* will do the rest.
173–27   Surely not from *G·,*
179– 8   consciousness in matter or in *G·?*
180–24   *but of G·.— John* 1 : 13.
181–17   but of *G·,*"— *John* 1 : 13.
184–19   If he says, "I am of *G·,*
184–22   good because it is of *G·,*
186–10   its conception of man from *G·,*
186–20   his perfect Principle, *G·,*
187–22   *G·,* — Life, Truth, Love.
187–23   perfect, and eternal are *G·* ;
192– 2   we do not mean that man is *G·*
196– 8   a separate mind from *G·*
196–13   *G·* was not the author of it ;
197–15   as the Son of God, or as *G·* ;
198– 4   this point of unity of Spirit, *G·,*
198–28   supposition of another . . . than *G·* ;
199– 1   *G·* does not reward . . . with penalties ;
199–27   Life, and intelligence are *G·.*
200– 9   *G·* was the only substance,
200–28   involved in its divine Principle, *G·* :

God.

Mis.
204–28   *G·*, the divine Principle of C. S.,
206–19   law-abiding Principle, *G·*,
212– 2   saith in his heart, "No *G·*"— *Psal.* 53 : 1.
218–12   whence to reason out *G·*,
218–32   * purely spiritual personality in *G·*."
226– 5   carried the case on the side of *G·* ;
232–25   Principle of all healing is *G·* ;
232–28   understood to be of *G·*,
244– 8   He further states that *G·* cannot save
257– 4   presupposes that *G·* sleeps in the
259–27   belongs not to nature nor to *G·*.
260–11   Principle of his cure was *G·*,
277–24   proof that *G·*, good, is supreme.
282– 5   sense of personality in *G·* or in man,
317–30   "Whom *G·* hath sent— *John* 3 : 34.
321–10   balance . . . more on the side of *G·*,
331– 7   cause them to wait patiently on *G·*
333–13   denying that *G·*, good, is supreme,
346–13   belief . . . opposite intelligence to *G·*.
346–15   belief . . . wood or stone is *G·*.
352–24   out of himself and into *G·* so far that
361–26   *G·*, the only substance and
362–11   believing that *G·*, having made *all*,
363–16   *G·* is not chargeable with
364–11   of the divine Principle, *G·*.
367–29   *G·* is too pure to behold iniquity ;
396–11   songsters' matin hymns to *G·*

Ret.
14–25   "Search me, O *G·*,— *Psal.* 139 : 23.
15–10   *G·*, Thou hast taught me— *Psal.* 71 : 17.
25–11   *G·* I called *immortal Mind.*
25–15   *G·* I characterized as individual
27–30   old to *G·*, but new to His
28– 3   one must acquaint himself with *G·*,
48– 9   the one builder and maker, *G·*,
50–10   *G·* has since shown me,
56–21   not the subdivision, of *G·*.
57–11   Soul is the synonym of Spirit, *G·* ;
57–22   All must be of *G·*,
59–12   mortals apply finite terms to *G·*,
68–25   Life and being are of *G·*.
69–12   seem to have life as much as *G·*,
69–19   that . . . are creations of *G·*,
71– 6   and to *G·* the things— *Mark* 12 : 17.
73–16   spiritual individuality in *G·*,
85–24   "if *G·* be for us,— *Rom.* 8 : 31.
91– 1   *G·* is their sure defense and refuge.

Un.
1–11   *Does G· know or behold sin,*
2– 6   no refuge from sin, except in *G·*,
4–12   *G·* is all true consciousness ;
4–16   if *G·* be conscious of it?
7–10   has not separated me from *G·*,
10–16   *G·* is their divine Principle.
10–25   *G·* was not in the whirlwind.
13– 8   *G·* is harmony's selfhood.
13–13   If *G·* could be conscious of sin,
13–15   If *G·* has any real knowledge of sin,
14–13   Was it necessary for *G·* to grow
14–19   *G·* is not the shifting vane
15– 3   more just than *G·*?"— *Job.* 4 : 17.
15– 5   incubus which *G·* never can throw off?
15– 6   Do mortals know more than *G·*,
15–18   Would *G·* not of necessity take
16– 4   sheer nonsense, if *G·* has, or can
17– 3   seeks to fasten all error upon *G·*,
18– 1   absurdly follow that *G·* must perish,
18– 6   Error may say that *G·* can never
19– 1   With *G·*, *knowledge* is necessarily
25–20   *G·*, good, is the only creator.
26– 3   *Evil. . . . G·* is in matter,
26– 3   *Evil. . . .* matter reproduces *G·*.
26– 5   *G·* is my author,
26– 9   O evil ! *G·* is not your authority
26–21   If *G·* be *changeless goodness*,
26–23   there is in *G·* naught fantastic.
29– 7   Soul is sinless, and is *G·*.
31–22   evil does not obtain in Spirit, *G·* ;
35–15   That which was first was *G·*,
35–22   is a misstatement of Mind, *G·*.
39– 5   sin, and death yield . . . to *G·*.
39–15   which opposes itself to *G·*,
41– 8   loss of the true sense of good, *G·* ;
41–23   *G·* cannot be the opposite of
42– 1   Life, *G·*, being everywhere,
43– 7   anchorage in infinite good, *G·*,
46–24   identical and self-conscious with *G·*.
48–17   The Ego is *G·* Himself,
51–27   Soul is not in body, but is *G·*,
52–16   *G·* is not the so-called ego of evil ;
52–23   if *G·* has no part in them?
52–26   The senses, not *G·*, Soul, form the
53–24   immortal and unerring Mind, *G·*,
54–24   representation that *G·* both knew and
54–25   *G·*, who condemned the knowledge
60–19   If *G·*, then let them serve Him,
60–27   material sense, which sees not *G·*.

God

Un.
62– 3   saith, "Christ (*G·*) died for me,
62– 9   *G·*, good, is never absent,
64– 3   *G·* can no more behold it,
64–11   even if it were (or could be) *G·*,

Pul.
2–24   *G·*, the eternal harmony of
4– 9   protected by his divine Principle, *G·*?
7–13   *G·* has now unsealed their
30–20   * forgiveness of sin by *G·*,
74–15   What I am is for *G·* to declare
79–21   * "If there were no *G·*, we should

Rud.
1– 6   It is *G·*, the Supreme Being,
1–10   *Do you mean by this that G· is a*
2– 7   In C. S. we learn that *G·* is
2–12   We do not conceive rightly of *G·*,
3–24   *do you mean that G· has a finite*
4– 6   *Is G· the Principle of all science,*
5– 3   "Let *G·* be true,— *Rom.* 3 : 4.
14– 2   a portion of their time to *G·*,

No.
5–14   independent of *G·*, and dependent on
9–11   *G·* will well regenerate
9–20   *G·* will "furnish a table— *Psal.* 78 : 19.
10–25   turns . . . all hope and faith to *G·*,
12–27   *G·* must be found all
15–17   presuppose an impotent *G·*
16– 1   For *G·* to know, is to be ;
17–13   *G·* is not without an ever-present
17–22   *G·* who has no knowledge of sin
17–24   If *G·* could know a false claim,
21–15   philosophy has an undeveloped *G·*,
24– 3   to Spinoza's philosophy *G·* is
24–11   According to . . . *G·* is three persons
31– 2   if you admit that *G·* sends it
36–21   *G·*, wherein there is no
39–12   Prayer can neither change *G·* nor
39–24   most of all, it shows us what *G·* is.

Pan.
2–16   * conceived of as a whole, is *G·* ;
2–17   * no *G·* but the combined forces
4–14   *G·* is incapable of evil ;
4–20   *G·*, Spirit, is indeed the preserver
5– 8   Did *G·* create evil?
5–14   not in the truth [*G·*],
6– 6   claim that *G·* is not supreme,
6–22   For if *G·*, good, is Mind,
6–24   if *G·*, good, is omnipotent,
7– 8   belief, that after *G·*, Spirit, had
7–24   which implies Mind, Spirit, *G·* ;
8– 7   belief that Jesus, . . . is *G·*,
8– 9   belief that Mary was the mother of *G·*
12– 5   * "*G·*, Spirit, is ever in universal

'00.
5– 7   Jesus said the opposite of *G·*
5–12   *G·*, man, and divine Science.

'01.
3– 7   chapter sub-title
3– 8   We hear it said the . . . have no *G·*
4–22   *G·* is the infinite One instead of
5– 3   for if Person is *G·*,
6– 5   not a person, hence *G·* ?
6–13   We hear that *G·* is not *G·* except
6–16   is God in C. S. no *G·* because
6–29   that *G·* is either inconceivable, or
7– 8   *G·* being infinite Mind, He is the
7–23   The *G·* whom all Christians now claim
8– 6   who regard Jesus as *G·*
8–16   Is *G·* Spirit? He is.
9– 4   C. S. shows clearly that *G·* is the
9–22   the Holy One of *G·*."— *Mark* 1 : 24.
18–25   There is no *G·*."— *Psal.* 53 : 1.
23– 5   yet that *G·* has an opposite
25–15   matter minus, and *G·* all,
34–13   originating not in *G·*,

'02.
2–14   *G·* speed the right !
5–13   *G·* must be intelligently considered
12– 2   that Christ is come and is *G·*.
12–13   Jesus Christ is not *G·*,

Hea.
4– 8   We pray for *G·* to remember us,
4–24   *G·* must be our model,
5– 9   saying, . . . *G·* will punish him now
5–23   relying not on the person of *G·*
8– 3   *G·*,— not a person to whom we should
9– 3   what is not the person of *G·*,
9–17   know that *G·* never cursed man,
10– 9   remember that *G·* — good— is omnipotent ;
12–13   *G·*, . . . never made a man sick.
15–18   You pray for *G·* to heal you,
16– 5   no other Life, substance, and . . . but *G·*.
16–21   neither see, hear, . . . nor smell *G·* ;

Peo.
2– 7   we shall learn what *G·* is,
4– 3   in hygiene and drugs than in *G·*.
4–12   When first good, *G·*, was named a
6–19   *G·* is no longer a mystery
6–25   thyself with Him [*G·*],— *Job.* 22 : 21

Po.
40– 4   To *G·*, to Truth, and you !
46–13   An offering pure to *G·*.
59– 3   songsters' matin hymns to *G·*
70– 9   In *G·* there is no night,

God

Po.	77– 1	G· of the rolling year !
	79– 7	G· able is To raise up seed
My.	4–30	Thou G· most high and nigh.
	6–22	proceedeth out of the mouth of G·.
	9–25	will draw on G· for the amount
	14– 1	[G·, Spirit] sent it." — Isa. 55 : 11.
	14– 3	G· will pour them out a blessing
	33–10	"Search me, O G·, — Psal. 139 : 23.
	34– 7	G· of his salvation. — Psal. 24 : 5.
	37–20	* G· is the supreme cause of all
	38– 3	* G· is all consolation and comfort,
	52– 9	* to G·, for these blessings,
	61–25	* I should be willing to let G· work.
	61–27	* "What cannot G· do?"
	120– 1	in the Word which is G·.
	131–20	Where G· is we can meet,
	131–21	where G· is we can never part.
	143–28	If G· be for us, — Rom. 8 : 31.
	151–14	for G· is for me" — Psal. 56 : 9.
	151–16	"If G· be for us, — Rom. 8 : 31.
	152–27	G·, the divine Principle of nature
	164–29	Man . . . has his being in G·, Love.
	183–14	G· will multiply thee.
	183–26	G· is with thee.
	191– 3	except G· be with him." — John 3 : 2.
	193–19	G· guard and guide you.
	199– 6	May G· say this of the church
	200–27	G· spare this plunge,
	205– 9	* "G· moves in a mysterious way
	205–26	of its divine Principle, G· ;
	209– 3	G· will abundantly bless
	215– 4	G· stretched forth His hand.
	223–29	know that I am G·." — Psal. 46 : 10.
	226–14	Withdraw G·, divine Principle, from
	227–30	fool hath said . . . no G·." — Psal. 14 : 1.
	231–14	as G·, not man, directs.
	235–15	Did G· make man?
	235–16	Did G· make all that was made?
	235–16	Is G· Spirit?
	238– 9	G· being Spirit, His language and
	239– 6	acquaint the student with G·.
	239–15	for G· to be represented by
	241–27	* and had my being in G·,
	248–20	to conceive G· aright you must be
	260–28	leaves hygiene, medicine, . . . to G·
	262–15	Christ conceived of Spirit, of G·
	267– 9	remember that G· is not the,
	269–13	* and G· the Soul.
	269–17	G· hath thrust in the sickle,
	271– 1	G·, Spirit, is infinite,
	272– 9	no claim that man is equal to G·,
	275– 8	know that I am G·." — Psal. 46 : 10.
	278–29	The Principle of all power is G·,
	279–13	G· in the divine Mind.
	280–18	in full faith that G· does not
	292– 7	May G· sanctify our nation's sorrow
	296–20	G·, good, omnipotent and infinite.
	299–22	G·, the divine Principle of C. S.,
	303– 9	following the divine Principle — G·,
	323–24	* if G· did not hold you up
	348–13	his divine Principle, G·,

(see also **All, All-in-all, All-power, Almighty, Almighty God, Arbiter, Being, Blessed, builder, Cause, Comforter, creator, Deity, Ego, Elohim, Esse, Father, Father-Mother, Forever, Giver, Godhead, He, Herself, Him, Himself, His, Holy Father, Holy Ghost, Holy One, Holy Spirit, I, I AM, Immanuel, King, Life, Light, Lord, Lord of Hosts, Love, Maker, Me, Mind, Minister, Most High, Mother, My, One, Only, Parent, Person, Physician, Principle, Providence, Ruler Supreme, Soul, Spirit, Supreme Being, Supreme God, Thee, Thou, Thy, Truth, Unseen, Us, Wonderful**)

god

Mis.	123–13	appease the anger of a so-called g·
	123–14	Merodach, or the g· of sin,
	123–15	was the "lucky g· ;"
	190–29	serpent, liar, the g· of this world,
	190–31	"the g· of this world ;" — II Cor. 4 : 4.
	190–31	and then defines this g·
Un.	54–23	would make man a g·,
Pan.	2–11	words meaning "all" and "g·."
	2–13	His uncapitalized word "g·"
	3–26	Pan was the g· of shepherds
	8– 3	and the Babylonian sun g·,
	8– 4	moon g·, and sin g·
'00.	3–26	Jehovah, was a g· of hate and of
	13–18	Æsculapius, the g· of medicine,
'01.	11–28	him whose g· is his belly :
	16–14	the g· of this world;
	16–14	St. Paul defines this world's g·

God-anointed

Mis.	161–24	Jesus Christ, — the G· ;

God-bestowed

No.	2– 6	aver that disease is normal, a G·
My.	22–22	* nothing less than G·

God-blessed

Ret.	11–12	In our G· free school.
Po.	60– 9	In our G· free school.

God-condemned

My.	109– 5	dream which is mortal and G·

God-crowned

Mis.	162– 6	From this dazzling, G· summit,
	205–30	lives on, G· and blest.
	266– 2	to the G· summit of
Ret.	76–23	the G· summit of C. S.
Pul.	27–24	* and the woman . . . G·.
Po.	22– 1	G·, patient century,
My.	133– 6	G· summit of divine Science ;

God-driven

Mis.	169– 6	till she was G· back to the

God-endowed

My.	188–29	be G· for discipleship.

God-endued

My.	190–26	become G· with power

God-given

Mis.	117– 7	G· intent and volition
	247– 1	demand for man his G· heritage,
	394–12	G· mandate that speaks from
Peo.	10–12	Discerning the G· rights of man,
Po.	45–15	G· mandate that speaks from

God-governed

My.	222–25	Mankind will be G·

Godhead

Rud.	2– 6	agents, constituting the G·.
'01.	5– 4	constitute the G·,
	7– 4	trinity of the G· in C. S.
	8– 7	third person in the G·
	10–16	enthrall my sense of the G·,
Peo.	4–18	G· is Life, Truth, and Love,

Godhood

Un.	42–26	true sense of selfhood and G· ;

God-idea

Ret.	70–23	scientific ultimate of this G·
Po.	29–11	Thou G·, Life-crowned,

godless

Mis.	55–30	either a g· and material
	212– 3	This g· policy never knows
No.	18– 4	g· lie that denies Him as All-in-all,
'01.	4–30	merit the epithet "g·,"

Godlike

Mis.	122–23	the suffering of the G· for
	161–13	Christ-Jesus, the G·,
	178– 6	wanted to become a G· man.
Un.	46– 1	mortal error, called mind, is not G·.
No.	20– 7	Truth is moulding a G· man.
'01.	7– 4	C. S. makes man G·.
'02.	6–26	degree that . . . he becomes G·.
	8–24	whereby man is G·.
My.	14– 8	G· agency of man.
	161–28	the G· man said,

Godlikeness

Mis.	213– 2	in the form of G·.
Chr.	55–16	Spirit [G·] is life — Rom. 8 : 10.
Un.	22– 5	eat of the fruit of G·,
'02.	16–11	chapter sub-title
	16–23	express the life of G·.

godliness

Mis.	53–29	is the mystery of g· ;
	53–29	g· is simple to the godly ;
	145– 5	Till then, this form of g· seems
	328–12	with the mystery of g·,
Ret.	37–20	"mystery of g·." — I Tim. 3 : 16.
	61–27	stated and demonstrated in its g·
Un.	5–14	mystery of g·," — I Tim. 3 : 16.
	62– 8	This is the mystery of g·
No.	38–10	This divine mystery of g·
'01.	25– 1	spirit or mystery of g·.
	34–26	G· or Christianity is a
	34–28	nor happiness without g·.
'02.	16–27	The mere form of g·,
My.	124–28	The mystery of g·,
	126–11	the mystery of g·,

godly

Mis.	53–30	godliness is simple to the g· ;
Pul.	3– 1	how can our g· temple possibly be
	32–26	* was known as a "g· man,"
'01.	25– 2	becomes clear to the g·.

God-made

Mis.	49–17	is it not G·;
	49–17	if G·, can it be wrong,
Un.	53– 8	reality and . . . of man are good and G·

God-quality
Mis. 18–13 in every *G·*, even in substance ;

God's
acres
Mis. 140–26 Our title to *G·* acres will be safe
action
Mis. 354–22 pride would regulate *G·* action.
allness
Mis. 206– 9 can interpret . . . *G·* allness,
all-power
Mis. 141– 5 *G·* all-power, all-presence,
altar
Mis. 87–31 help anybody and steady *G·* altar
appointing
Mis. 208–19 in the way of *G·* appointing.
avenging angel
Mis. 275– 5 Who— but *G·* avenging angel !
best witnesses
'02. 10–25 martyrdom of *G·* best witnesses
blessing
My. 182–15 through *G·* blessing and the
blindness to error
Un. 6–19 the theory of *G·* blindness to error
business
Mis. 140–13 but this was *G·* business,
child
Mis. 181–28 preexistence as *G·* child ;
Un. 15– 9 Man is *G·* child and image.
'02. 8–29 He spake of man . . . as *G·* child.
children
Mis. 170– 9 refreshment of *G·* children
chosen ones
My. 127–24 garrisoned by *G·* chosen ones,
command
Mis. 223– 4 according to *G·* command.
298–17 did not say that it was *G·* command ;
Peo. 7–18 * Waiting the hour when at *G·* command
commandments
'00. 6–20 breaks *G·* commandments,
commands
Mis. 358–28 awaiting, . . . *G·* commands.
Un. 3–10 have obeyed *G·* commands,
consequent
Mis. 26–24 *G·* consequent is the spiritual cosmos.
courtesy
My. 341– 2 breathe it to . . . as *G·* courtesy.
creation
Mis. 87– 5 to caricature *G·* creation,
286–13 usher in the dawn of *G·* creation,
Pan. 6–14 order and harmony of *G·* creation.
dear love
Mis. 81– 5 by right of *G·* dear love,
My. 258–27 consciousness of *G·* dear love
direction
Mis. 127–23 know yourself, under *G·* direction,
My. 117– 7 helping a leader in *G·* direction,
discipline
'00. 8–12 till *G·* discipline takes it off
disposal
My. 281– 6 faith in *G·* disposal of events.
ear
No. 39– 6 ostensibly to catch *G·* ear,
embrace
Mis. 400– 2 Slumbers not in *G·* embrace ;
Pul. 16–14 Slumbers not in *G·* embrace ;
Po. 76–13 Slumbers not in *G·* embrace ;
essential likeness
Mis. 61–22 Does *G·* essential likeness sin,
eternal likeness
Un. 22– 2 made after *G·* eternal likeness,
ever-presence
Un. 62–27 discern faintly *G·* ever-presence,
eye
Po. 18–13 *G·* eye is upon him.
19– 3 *G·* eye is upon me
fatherliness
Mis. 234–31 *G·* fatherliness as Life, Truth, and
fiat
'01. 5–17 leave all sin to *G·* fiat
finger
Ret. 85–18 wait for *G·* finger to point the way.
forgiveness
Man. 15–10 acknowledge *G·* forgiveness of sin
formations
No. 6– 5 *G·* formations are spiritual,
frown
My. 129–10 no night but in *G·* frown ;
gift
Mis. 140– 2 I knew that to *G·* gift,
glorified
Po. 79–19 *G·* glorified !
glory
My. 117– 1 let them alone in, *G·* glory,

God's
government
Mis. 199– 7 spiritual law,— *G·* government.
My. 222–26 as *G·* government becomes apparent,
278– 1 coincide with *G·* government
283–28 enlightened sense of *G·* government.
great gift
My. 262–20 reminder of *G·* great gift,
great love
Mis. 182–24 their place in *G·* great love,
greatness
Pul. 39– 6 * *G·* greatness flows around our
grooves
Mis. 104–18 The latter move in *G·* grooves
guidance
My. 142–12 sought *G·* guidance in doing it,
hand
'01. 16– 1 * *G·* hand has held you up."
hands
My. 278–14 President and . . . are in *G·* hands.
help
Ret. 86–21 No one . . . without *G·* help,
My. 197– 4 Attempt nothing without *G·* help.
hour
Mis. 134–19 In *G·* hour, the powers of
household
'01. 9–27 He of *G·* household who loveth
idea
Mis. 261–25 Man as *G·* idea is already saved
336–14 dislike and hatred of *G·* idea,
Pul. 75– 3 the Principle of *G·* idea,
Po. 70–23 Give *G·* idea sway,
ideas
Mis. 164–30 The limited view of *G·* ideas
image
(*see* **image**)
impersonality
My. 117–20 great truth of *G·* impersonality
infinite meaning
Mis. 25–17 It gives *G·* infinite meaning
interpretation
Mis. 258–27 *G·* interpretation of Himself
kingdom
No. 35–26 *G·* kingdom is everywhere
largess
My. 188–18 a benediction for *G·* largess.
law
(*see* **law**)
laws
Mis. 29–27 no infraction of *G·* laws ;
Ret. 26– 9 in his obedience to *G·* laws,
No. 11– 5 *G·* laws, and their intelligent and
My. 203– 8 without mutiny are *G·* laws.
likeness
(*see* **likeness**)
little ones
Mis. 130–25 one of *G·* "little ones."— *Matt.* 18 : 6.
My. 186– 4 May *G·* little ones cluster around this
love
(*see* **love**)
man
Mis. 36– 2 is neither *G·* man nor Mind ;
167– 2 infantile thought of *G·* man,
Un. 46– 6 for he is *G·* man ;
mercy
My. 162– 1 *G·* mercy for mortal ignorance
mere pleasure
'01. 15–23 * *G·* mere pleasure that keeps you
messages
Mis. 171–11 spiritual translations of *G·* messages,
methods
Mis. 135–16 *G·* methods and means of healing,
miracles
My. 107–22 wouldst thou mock *G·* miracles
most tender mercies
Mis. 391–17 Share *G·* most tender mercies,
Po. 38–16 Share *G·* most tender mercies,
nestlings
Mis. 152–25 you, . . . are *G·* nestlings ;
offspring
Un. 24–20 Man, as *G·* offspring, must
No. 37– 1 In human conception *G·* offspring
omnipotence
No. 20–14 *G·* omnipotence and omnipresence
My. 293–15 understanding of *G·* omnipotence,
open secret
My. 289– 2 *G·* open secret is seen through grace,
opposite
Mis. 181–29 and not of *G·* opposite,— evil,
opposites
'00. 5–28 in casting out *G·* opposites,
orbits
Mis. 22–17 true thoughts revolve in *G·* orbits :

God's

own image
Mis. 330–17 man in G· own image and likeness,
No. 23–28 is G· own image and likeness,
Peo. 14–18 reinstate man in G· own image
My. 244–16 man's spiritual state in G· own image
own likeness
Mis. 77–27 man, made in G· own likeness,
own plan
My. 283–23 G· own plan of salvation.
own time
My. 306–19 and that in G· own time.
pardon
No. 42– 9 G· pardon is the destruction of
paths
Mis. 99–27 "Make straight G· paths ;
people
Mis. 117–12 * enduring vivacity among G· people."
perfect likeness
Mis. 79– 7 was, and is, G· perfect likeness,
perfect ways
Mis. 66–17 G· perfect ways and means,
personality
'01. 4–23 able to explain G· personality
6–25 G· personality must be as infinite
phenomena
My. 249– 6 produce G· phenomena.
plan
Peo. 12–18 G· plan of redemption,
power
(see **power**)
praise
Pul. 1–11 eloquent in G· praise.
No. 44–17 the mouth lisping G· praise;
preparations
Mis. 208–22 G· preparations for the sick
presence
Mis. 113– 2 G· presence gives spiritual light,
345– 1 G· presence and providence.
Un. 2– 7 G· presence, power, and love,
My. 354–19 Of G· presence here.
problems
My. 348–32 the solution of G· problems.
providence
Mis. 278–23 necessities and G· providence
reflection
Mis. 18–17 spiritual origin, G· reflection,
183–13 possible to man as G· reflection.
291– 5 true sense of G· reflection,
representative
My. 227– 3 spake as G· representative
requirement
Man. 77–18 G· Requirement.
revelation
Mis. 92–25 substituted for G· revelation.
Ret. 84–14 substituted for G· revelation.
right hand
Mis. ix–12 the touch of G· right hand.
08–19 build up, through G· right hand,
364–13 G· right hand grasping the
Ret. 27–19 * Touch G· right hand in that
servants
Mis. 158–19 All G· servants are minute men
service
My. 195–16 use in G· service the one talent
side
Mis. 102–31 "one on G· side is a majority."
Pul. 4–16 "one on G· side is a majority."
No. 45–28 "One on G· side is a majority ;"
sight
Mis. 144–22 precious in G· sight
My. 184–22 service acceptable in G· sight.
spiritual child
Mis. 18–15 as G· spiritual child only,
spiritual idea
My. 120–11 G· spiritual idea that takes away all sin,
spiritual ideal
My. 319– 3 G· spiritual ideal is the only
supremacy
No. 18– 8 demonstration of G· supremacy
Hea. 7– 5 those who understand G· supremacy,
temple
Mis. 140–17 to know who owned G· temple,
time
Mis. 117–23 G· time and mortals' differ.
My. 13– 3 act in G· time.
universal kingdom
Mis. 213–28 G· universal kingdom will appear,
universe
Mis. 65–13 G· universe and man are immortal.
verity
No. 17–16 divine consciousness and G· verity.
voice
Mis. 134–27 neither silence nor disarm G· voice.
way
My. 293– 8 believed . . . martyrdom was G· way.

God's

ways
(see **ways**)
Way-shower
My. 140–22 so soon as G· Way-shower, Christ,
whole plan
Peo. 12–21 as G· whole plan,
will
Pan. 13–16 till G· will be witnessed
My. 18–24 till G· will be witnessed
258–12 to know and to do G· will,
window
Ret. 90– 2 G· window which lets in light,
wisdom
Mis. 362– 5 at rest in G· wisdom,
Un. 51–18 in the economy of G· wisdom
Word
'01. 31–26 used faithfully G· Word,
My. 352–22 hearers and the doers of G· Word.
word
My. 47–25 * G· word in the wilderness
work
Mis. 317– 3 Yes, if you are doing G· work.
My. 231–13 in order to help G· work
works
My. 294–21 shown him by G· works?
Zion
Mis. 146– 1 remember thee, and G· Zion,

Man. 47–12 which are G·." — I Cor. 6 : 20.
Ret. 71– 6 the things that are G·." — Mark 12 : 17.
77– 4 * "An honest G· the noblest
83–20 to G· daily interpretation.
90– 3 or seek to stand in G· stead.
'01. 1– 5 can never lack G· outstretched arm
'02. 1– 1 G· loving providence for His people
My. 128– 8 less than G· benign government,
220–11 the things that are G·.'" — Mark 12 : 17.

Gods

Pan. 6–23 religion has at least two G·.
8– 7 imply two G·, one the divine,

gods

alias
No. 26– 5 spirits, or souls, — alias g·.
are just
Un. 23– 3 * The g· are just, and of our
human
Mis. 123–12 human passions and human g·,
many
Mis. 333–16 and g· many." — see I Cor. 8 : 5.
No. 21–21 in the pantheon of many g·,
Pan. 2–14 " g· many," — I Cor. 8 : 5.
3–22 belief in one God, or in many g·.
'00. 4– 5 many minds and many g·.
master of the
My. 160–26 Zeus, the master of the g·,
material
Mis. 198– 5 turning away from material g· ;
more
Un. 38–17 rulership of more g· than one.
nectar of the
Mis. 9–17 with the nectar of the g·,
no other
Mis. 18–10 no other g· before me ;" — Exod. 20 : 3.
21– 3 no other g· before me." — Exod. 20 : 3.
23–13 no other g· before me." — Exod. 20 : 3.
28–21 no other g· before me." — Exod. 20 : 3.
96– 5 and would have no other g·,
123– 4 no other g· before me :" — Exod. 20 : 3.
Pan. 9–10 no other g· before me :" — Exod. 20 : 3.
'00. 5–20 no other g· before me :" — Exod. 20 : 3.
'02. 4–20 no other g· before me," — Exod. 20 : 3.
5–29 no other g· before me," — Exod. 20 : 3.
6–19 no other g· before me," — Exod. 20 : 3.
My. 5–14 no other g· before me," — Exod. 20 : 3.
64–13 no other g· before me,' — Exod. 20 : 3.
152–22 and serve no other g·,
153–17 no other g· before me" — Exod. 20 : 3.
221–18 no other g· before me." — Exod. 20 : 3.
278– 9 no other g· before me," — Exod. 20 : 3.
279–12 no other g· before me." — Exod. 20 : 3.
364– 8 no other g· before me." — Exod. 20 : 3.
of medicine
Peo. 4–24 the g· of medicine,
of paganism
Pan. 7–12 and hint the g· of paganism
other
Mis. 40– 6 thus serve "other g·." — Exod. 20 : 3.
45–27 "other g· before me." — Exod. 20 : 3.
174– 4 idolatry, having other g· ;
196–15 votaries to "other g·" — Exod. 20 : 3.
209–21 "other g· before me," — Exod. 20 : 3.
No. 42– 6 not compelled to have other g·
Pan. 7–25 this error is idolatry — other g·.
'00. 3–25 idolatry, — other g·.

gods

shall be as
Mis.	57–19	ye shall be as *g·*," — *Gen.* 3 : 5.
Ret.	69–10	'Ye shall be as *g·* ;' — *Gen.* 3 : 5.
Un.	44–22	ye shall be as *g·*, — *Gen.* 3 : 5.

Mis.	196– 8	will make you as *g·* ;" — *see Gen.* 3 : 5.
	255– 1	chapter sub-title
	364–31	this veil of the temple of *g·*,
Pan.	9– 5	in paganism they stand for *g·* ;

Godspeed
My.	99– 9	* and bidden *G·*."

Godward
Mis.	49–23	that are helping man *G·* :

goes
Mis.	15–14	and *g·* on with years ;
	21– 3	It *g·* on in perfect unity
	254–15	*g·* on to learn that he must
	306– 4	* accompany the bell wherever it *g·*.
	327–31	*g·* back and kindly binds up their
	334–11	away *g·* all its supposed power
	383– 8	it *g·* without saying,
Man.	48–13	Mrs. Eddy's drive when she *g·* out,
	94– 9	*g·* to hear and deride truth,
	94–11	and he who *g·* to seek truth
Ret.	45– 1	spiritually organized Church . . . *g·* on.
Un.	45– 5	and *g·* on saying, "Am I not myself?
	45–19	*g·* forth into an imaginary sphere
	61–14	retreats, and again *g·* forward ;
	62– 5	that neither comes nor *g·*,
'00.	14– 6	He *g·* on to portray seven churches,
'01.	27–27	* *g·* through three stages.
'02.	8–23	the ego, or I, *g·* to the Father,
Hea.	12– 7	metaphysician *g·* to the fount to
My.	15–12	My heart *g·* out to you
	76–15	* all of which *g·* to show
	96–31	* C. S. just *g·* a little beyond
	97–13	* advantage so far as this *g·*.
	228–30	It *g·* without saying that such
	275–23	the true sense of being *g·* on.
	277–11	The mental animus *g·* on,
	304–25	* *g·* through three stages.

goest
Mis.	327– 4	withersoever thou *g·*."

goeth
Mis.	118–31	which *g·* into the mouth — *Matt.* 15 : 11.
	156–20	"this kind *g·* not — *Matt.* 17 : 21.
	252–32	*g·* and selleth all that he hath
	328– 5	path that *g·* upward."
My.	190–17	"This kind *g·* not — *Matt.* 17 : 21.
	222–13	"This kind *g·* not — *Matt.* 17 : 21.
	339–24	"This kind *g·* not — *Matt.* 17 : 21.

going
Mis.	206–28	Way-shower, who, *g·* before you,
	282– 1	You are *g·* out to demonstrate a
Ret.	9– 8	That night, before *g·* to rest,
Un.	28–12	*g·* in or coming out.
	61– 3	Coming and *g·* belong to mortal
Pul.	46–13	* *g·* back to the ancestral tree
	72–27	* *g·* about doing good and healing the
'02.	20– 2	or *g·* down into the deep,
My.	44– 5	* *g·* up to possess the promised land
	54– 2	* hundreds *g·* away who could not
	66– 6	* activity has been *g·* on
	82–29	* their *g·* will not be noticeable
	83– 2	* never *g·* about labelled
	87– 4	* multitudes *g·* and coming.
	229–13	incentive for *g·* thither.
	239–28	*g·* on since ever time was.
	323–10	* not *g·* to lie about anything

goings
Mis.	245–10	the stately *g·* of C. S.,
Un.	5–26	stately *g·* of this wonderful part

Golconda
My.	175–23	richer than the diamonds of *G·*,

gold
Mis.	126–23	even *g·* is less current.
	151– 7	He separates the dross from the *g·*,
	159–28	devices in embroidery, silver, *g·*,
	205– 8	separates the dross from the *g·*,
	305–21	*g·*, silver, bronze, copper, and
	346–23	apples of *g·* in pictures of — *Prov.* 25 : 11.
	376–27	*g·*, orange, pink, crimson, violet ;
Ret.	94– 9	As dross is separated from *g·*,
Un.	54– 1	The bright *g·* of Truth
Pul.	26–26	* The mantel is of onyx and *g·*.
	76– 7	* the pale green and *g·* decoration
	76–13	* in white and *g·* tapestry.
	76–14	* Mexican onyx with *g·* decoration
	76–20	* heavily plated with *g·*."
	77– 4	* a scroll of solid *g·*,
	78– 4	* in the form of a *g·* scroll,

gold
Pul.	78–21	* *g·* key to the church door.
	86– 3	* contains a solid *g·* box,
'00.	10–27	ten five-dollar *g·* pieces
Po.	16– 9	of power, cf glory, or *g·* ;
My.	30–22	* with silver, and with *g·*.
	176– 3	FIFTY DOLLARS IN *G·*
	260–15	may pursue . . . the lure of *g·*,
	283–29	Lured by fame, pride, or *g·*,

golden
Mis.	90–13	This rule is forever *g·* :
	307–25	not intended for a *g·* calf,
	376–25	fairy blue and *g·* flecks
Ret.	79–28	nor its *g·* streets invaded.
	80–20	win the *g·* scholarship
Pul.	26–21	* *g·* letters on a marble tablet,
	39–16	* its flood of *g·* light.
	42–16	* *g·* beehive stamped upon it,
	77– 7	* *g·* key of the church structure.
No.	7– 2	The rule of divinity is *g·* ;
'00.	12– 5	*g·* candlesticks" — *Rev.* 2 : 1.
Hea.	19–25	*g·* rays in the sunlight
Po.	70– 3	A bright and *g·* shower
My.	86– 4	* *g·* State House dome,
	364– 6	departure from this *g·* rule

Golden Rule
Mis.	31– 6	breaks the *G· R·* and subverts the
	51–19	love God, good, and obey the *G· R·*,
	135–12	or fail to fulfil this *G· R·*,
	266–27	aid each other, and obey the *G· R·*.
	282– 9	practice of C. S. is the *G· R·*,
	287–25	obey the *G· R·* for human life,
	301–26	*Second :* It breaks the *G· R·*,
	334–31	to understand this *G· R·*
	337–10	the *G· R·* and its Principle,
Man.	42–22	practised according to the *G· R·* :
	44– 3	strict adherence to the *G· R·*,
	48–11	The *G· R·*.
'00.	14–16	the more perfect way, or *G· R·* :
'01.	30–11	observing the *G· R·*,
	30–28	to obey the *G· R·*,
My.	4– 2	then he practises the *G· R·*
	5–14	Hebrew Decalogue, . . . and the *G· R·*
	5–28	Forgetting the *G· R·* and
	64–14	Hebrew Decalogue, . . . and the *G· R·*
	160–20	who persist in breaking the *G· R·*
	181–14	demonstrated on the *G· R·*,
	213–24	and the *G· R·* will not fail
	222–26	*G· R·* utilized, and the rights of
	224–16	blind to his loss of the *G· R·*,
	266– 8	trusts in place of the *G· R·*,
	281–16	* chapter sub-title
	282–14	what we already know of the *G· R·*,

Golden Text
My.	33– 9	* *G· T·* : "Search me, — *Psal.* 139 : 23.

gold-gleaming
Ret.	18– 3	at play with the *g·* fish ;
Po.	63–10	at play with the *g·* fish ;

gold-headed
My.	308–22	handed him a *g·* walking-stick

goldsmith's
Pul.	78– 3	* examples of the *g·* art

Goliath
Mis.	162–31	shepherd boy, to disarm the *G·*.
	195–25	shepherd's sling would slay this *G·*.

Goliaths
My.	125–10	chosen one to meet the *G·*.

gone
Mis.	42– 2	*do we meet those g· before?*
	42–15	existence with those *g·* before,
	48–27	That persons have *g·* away from
	190–12	*when the devil was g· out,* — *Luke* 11 : 14.
	213–19	adherents of Truth have *g·* on
	216–22	* some time after the rest of it had *g·*."
	234–19	should have *g·* on to establish this
	284–17	*g·* personally to the malpractitioner
	310–12	return of members that have *g·* out
	342–19	our lamps have *g·* out, — *see Matt.* 25 : 8.
	356–25	*g·* down in his own esteem.
Ret.	13–22	The fever was *g·*, and I rose
Un.	9–24	Healing has *g·* on continually ;
	57–13	"virtue had *g·* out of him." — *Mark* 5 : 30.
Pul.	51–22	* but as time has *g·* on,
Pan.	1– 7	winter winds have come and *g·*
'01.	15–27	* why you have not *g·* to hell
	16–10	hatred *g·* mad becomes imbecile
	21–14	after Mrs. Eddy has *g·*.
My.	24–26	* have *g·* away with the conviction
	59–24	* In years *g·* by I have been asked,
	83–18	* realize that the Scientists have *g·*.
	122–16	another Christmas has come and *g·*.
	189–22	last-drawn sigh of a glory *g·*,
	278– 8	and its edict hath *g·* forth :

good (*see also* **good's**)

abides in
Un. 40–17 abides in man, if man abides in *g*·,
absence of
Mis. 27–21 evil signifies the absence of *g*·,
289– 7 It is suppositional absence of *g*·.
363– 6 supposition that the absence of *g*· is
Ret. 60–12 evil is the absence of *g*· ;
absolute
Mis. 299–16 is the only absolute *g*· ;
364–28 If . . . there is no absolute *g*·.
accomplished
My. 298– 6 of the *g*· accomplished therein,
achievement of
Mis. 340–22 work on to the achievement of *g*· ;
adoption of
Mis. 15–16 childlike trust and joyful adoption of *g*· ;
aggregation of
My. 99– 8 * aggregation of *g*· and beneficial
all
Mis. 82– 3 Principle and idea of all *g*·.
337–18 growing affection for all *g*·,
No. 24–28 none beside Him, and He is all *g*·,
My. 15–13 desire that the Giver of all *g*·
127– 6 We thank the Giver of all *g*·
292– 3 All *g*· that ever was written,
356– 2 their present ownership of all *g*·,
all is
Mis. 105–32 all is *g*· and all is Mind.
Ret. 63– 6 all is *g*·, and there is . . . no evil,
My. 288–31 all is *g*· because God made all,
allness of
My. 364–15 supremacy and allness of *g*·.
All of
Mis. 250– 1 the infinite All of *g*·,
all power of
Mis. 14– 4 ever-presence and all-power of *g*· ;
all that is
Un. 17– 5 all that is *g*· will aid your journey,
all the
Mis. 38– 2 *all the g· we can do*
89–15 do him all the *g*· you can ;
273–18 all the *g*· they are capable of
and evil
Mis. 12–18 in the interest of both *g*· and evil
24–23 A knowledge of both *g*· and evil
118– 2 cannot obey both God, *g*·, and evil,
121– 8 *g*· and evil, seem to grapple,
197–26 that is both *g*· and evil ;
198–22 the knowledge of *both g*· and evil ;
319– 3 *g*· and evil can neither be coeval
333– 3 *g*· and evil, life and death,
366–21 insists on the unity of *g*· and evil
367–16 knowledge of *both g*· and evil,
Ret. 56–24 into minds, *g*· and evil.
57–27 such opposite effects as *g*· and evil,
59– 7 source of death, and of *g*· and evil.
Un. 21– 7 In like manner *g*· and evil talk
44–22 knowing *g*· and evil— *Gen.* 3 : 5.
46–19 regarded as both *g*· and evil,
52–10 consciousness of both *g*· and evil,
Pul. 1– 9 notable for *g*· and evil.
No. 26– 3 believe . . . that *g*· and evil blend ;
Pan. 6–20 colloquy between *g*· and evil,
'*00.* 4– 2 couples love and hate, *g*· and evil,
'*01.* 25–24 as the blending of *g*· and evil,
Hea. 5– 2 finite sense . . . of *g*· and evil
18–10 *g*· and evil never dwelt together.
Peo. 4–11 said . . . of *g*· and evil,
My. 179–10 both *g*· and evil, both mind and
and pure
Mis. 368–15 ranks of the *g*· and pure,
Ret. 68–28 The beautiful, *g*·, and pure
and Truth
Mis. 36– 4 in contradistinction to *g*· and Truth,
Peo. 3–16 spiritual idea of *g*· and Truth
another's
Mis. 127–19 finds one's own in another's *g*·.
184–27 not her own, but another's *g*· ;
No. 3–23 not so much thine own as another's *g*·,
'*00.* 14–20 not only her own, but another's *g*·.
'*01.* 34–19 not her own but another's *g*·,
My. 18–16 finds one's own in another's *g*·.''
19–23 "seeketh . . . another's *g*·,— *I Cor.* 13 : 5.
appearing of
Mis. 338– 1 appearing of *g*· in an individual
attendant
Un. 37–19 *g*· attendant upon spiritual
aught but
Mis. 10–32 belief . . . that aught but *g*· exists
No. 17–10 to be conscious of aught but *g*·.
being
Ret. 86– 6 but one way of *being g*·,
being real
Mis. 46– 5 *g*· being real, evil, . . . is unreal.
346–20 *g*· being real, its opposite is . . . unreal,

good

cannot lose
Mis. 10–12 The *g*· cannot lose their God,
capabilities for
Peo. 2– 1 learn our capabilities for *g*·,
choose only
Mis. 289–32 whence they can choose only *g*·.
consciousness of
Mis. 9– 1 consciousness of *g*·, grace, and peace,
259– 9 The consciousness of *g*· has no
convictions of
Mis. 31–19 against his own convictions of *g*·
cycle of
My. 270– 3 cycle of *g*· obliterates the
daily
Mis. 397–17 My prayer, some daily *g*· to do
Pul. 19– 1 My prayer, some daily *g*· to do
Po. 13– 5 My prayer, some daily *g*· to do
defending
My. 207–23 mastering evil and defending *g*·,
define
Mis. 13–29 then define *g*· as God,
demonstrates
Mis. 259–25 Truth demonstrates *g*·,
derivative of
Mis. 14–25 cannot be, the derivative of *g*·.
destroys evil
'*01.* 10–23 whereby *g*· destroys evil,
detract from the
Mis. 302–27 nor detract from the *g*·
developing
'*00.* 10– 4 asserting and developing *g*·.
dies not
Mis. 2–22 for *g*· dies not
discernment of
Mis. 13–27 clearer discernment of *g*·.
divine
Mis. 164– 4 idea that represents divine *g*·,
Ret. 56–17 omnipresence of God, or divine *g*·.
80– 2 this is the pledge of divine *g*·
Un. 24– 4 My Mind is divine *g*·,
does no
My. 122– 8 To cut off the top . . . does no *g*· ;
doeth
My. 99– 5 * merry heart that doeth *g*·
doing
Mis. ix– 2 suits my sense of doing *g*·.
11–24 doing *g*· to one's enemies
12–30 law of Love, doing *g*· to all ;
90–18 be sure that your means for doing *g*·
163– 3 Three years he went about doing *g*·.
198–29 seems to punish man for doing *g*·,
198–31 in doing *g*·, therefore he must
Ret. 29– 4 loving our enemies and doing *g*· to
80– 5 but one way of *doing g*·,
93– 2 Jesus went about doing *g*·.
Pul. 21–15 doing *g*· in all denominations
72–27 * doing *g*· and healing the sick.
Rud. 14–10 except the bliss of doing *g*·.
'*01.* 30–11 too occupied with doing *g*·,
'*02.* 10– 1 knowing and doing *g*·,
17–22 in being and in doing *g*· ;
Hea. 5– 8 doing *g*· to his neighbor,
doing of
My. 87–30 * in the cheerful doing of *g*·.
domain of
My. 278–27 War is not in the domain of *g*· ;
dominating
Pan. 7–27 hypothesis of . . . evil dominating *g*·,
domination of
No. 32–22 The domination of *g*· destroys the
eliminated by
Mis. 259–11 to be known or eliminated by *g*· :
enemy of
My. 358–10 pray that the enemy of *g*· cannot
energies of
Mis. 176–12 more of the divine energies of *g*·,
estimate the
No. 43– 9 * can estimate the *g*· your books are
eternal
Mis. 189–22 namely God, the eternal *g*·,
Ret. 22–21 of one parent, the eternal *g*·.
Un. 60– 3 through ever-present and eternal *g*·.
Rud. 8–13 strong in God, the eternal *g*·.
Peo. 3–22 or the quantity of eternal *g*·.
eternal as
Mis. 14–18 real and eternal as *g*·, God !
ever-presence of
Rud. 11–23 all-power and ever-presence of *g*·,
ever-present
Mis. 183– 2 in the ever-present *g*·,
268–18 omnipotent and ever-present *g*·,
Un. 62–13 omnipotent and ever-present *g*·
My. 273–23 Life as God, good, ever-present *g*·,
evil and
(*see* **evil**)

good

evil counterfeits
Mis. 351–20 Evil counterfeits *g·* :
evil from
Un. 14–28 learning to distinguish evil from *g·*,
evil subordinates
No. 24–14 evil subordinates *g·* in personality.
evil with
(*see* evil)
existence of
Mis. 13–17 sense of the existence of *g·*.
13–23 the existence of *g·* only ;
factor of
Mis. 13–15 is a factor of *g·*,
faith in
Mis. 31–12 the lack of faith in *g·*.
falsehood about
Rud. 8–20 uttering falsehocd about *g·*.
flows
Mis. 185–11 *g·* flows into every avenue of being,
follower of
Mis. 152–21 the follower of *g·*.
for evil
Mis. 277–28 and render *g·* for evil.
Ret. 45–19 returning *g·* for evil,
My. 204–27 while returning *g·* for evil,
260–23 returning *g·* for evil,
270–22 I have returned *g·* for evil,
general
Mis. 11–26 can do much general *g·*
glory of
My. 4–28 the glory of *g·*,
God and
Mis. 27– 3 terms God and *g·*, as Spirit,
God as
Mis. 26–28 Scriptures name God as *g·*,
Peo. 3–23 sense of God as *g·*
God calls
Mis. 110–29 that which God calls *g·*.
God is
(*see* God)
God, or
Ret. 54–12 Millions are believing in God, or *g·*,
Un. 31–23 God, or *g·*, is Spirit alone ;
great
Mis. 292–26 is accomplishing great *g·*,
338– 3 brings to humanity some great *g·*,
Peo. 6–26 great *g·* for which we are to leave all
greatest
Mis. 288– 4 work out the greatest *g·* to the
Ret. 82–15 greatest *g·* to the greatest number,
Pul. 54–17 * where the greatest *g·* could be
harmony and
Mis. 17– 5 law of omnipotent harmony and *g·*,
has all power
Mis. 31–15 that God, *g·*, has *all* power.
He is
No. 38– 7 He is *g·*, and good is Spirit ;
higher
Mis. 227–26 satisfies the mind craving a higher *g·*,
if we regard
Mis. 3– 4 If we regard *g·* as more natural
immortal
Mis. 82–29 Mind is God, immortal *g·* ;
immutable
Un. 51– 2 reflection of immutable *g·*.
impulse for
My. 10– 6 * this mighty impulse for *g·*
in being
My. 196–25 The *g·* in being,
inclusive
Mis. 104– 8 the one inclusive *g·*.
inexhaustible
Mis. 83– 4 perpetual idea of inexhaustible *g·*.
infinite
Mis. 15–24 infinite *g·* that we name God,
26–31 naturally and divinely infinite *g·*.
100–14 Science . . . unfolds infinite *g·*,
282– 2 a true sense of the infinite *g·*,
367–18 If God is infinite *g·*,
Ret. 56–19 and that one is the infinite *g·*,
Un. 18– 3 saying, I am infinite *g·* ;
43– 7 anchorage in infinite *g·*, God,
61–17 Our highest sense of infinite *g·*
Pan. 6–16 God is *infinite g·*,
My. 42–24 * only as infinite *g·* unfolds
152–17 infinite *g·*, than which there is none else
204– 3 fact that He is infinite *g·*,
356–26 and this God is infinite *g·*.
infinity of
Ret. 68– 8 he reflects the infinity of *g·*.
influence for
My. 47–12 * touched by its influence for *g·*,
in good
My. 132–20 see God and live, see *g·* in good,

good

in One
Mis. 18–21 one in good, and *g·* in One.
inseparable from
Un. 21–18 is inseparable from *g·*.
intelligent
Mis. 267–23 governed by Spirit, intelligent *g·*.
in the name of
Mis. 334–19 evil at work in the name of *g·*,
inverted
Un. 53– 3 all its forms are inverted *g·*.
is all
Mis. 279–21 evil is naught and *g·* is all.
Ret. 60–14 evil is unreal and *g·* is all
is equally one
Ret. 64–10 teaches that *g·* is equally *one* and *all*,
is forever good
Mis. 104–12 and *g·* is forever good.
is God
Mis. 24–24 *g·* is God, and God is All
319– 3 *g·* is God, even as God is good,
Ret. 60–13 *g·* is God ever-present,
is great
No. 32–18 *G·* is great and real.
is infinite
Mis. 108– 5 *g·* is infinite, All.
is made
Mis. 339–10 *g·* is made more industrious
is Mind
Rud. 4–16 *G·* is Mind, but evil is not Mind.
Pan. 6–22 For if God, *g·*, is Mind,
is more contagious
Mis. 229– 9 *g·* is more contagious than evil,
is my God
Mis. 206–22 "*G·* is my God, and my God is good.
is never
Mis. 340– 3 *G·* is never the reward of evil,
Un. 62– 9 God, *g·*, is never absent,
is not educed
Mis. 122–20 *G·* is not educed from its opposite :
Pan. 12– 2 *g·* is not educed from evil,
is omnipotence
Mis. 13–30 will find that *g·* is omnipotence,
is omnipotent
Mis. 172–31 hence, *g·* is omnipotent
Pan. 6–24 if God, *g·*, is omnipotent,
Hea. 10– 9 God — *g·* — is omnipotent ;
is one
Rud. 11– 8 Therefore *g·* is one and All.
is Spirit
No. 38– 7 He is good, and *g·* is Spirit ;
is supreme
No. 24–27 truth, that *g·* is supreme.
is the master
Mis. 209–27 *g·* is the master of evil.
is the only creator
Un. 25–20 God, *g·*, is the only creator.
is the only substance
Un. 25– 7 *g·* is the only substance,
is the reward
Mis. 206–25 *g·* is the reward of all who
it wrought
No. 33–17 and the *g·* it wrought.
knowledge of
Mis. 109–23 third stage, — the knowledge of *g·* ;
law of
Rud. 1– 2 the law of God, the law of *g·*,
leading to
Mis. 85– 9 thought and act leading to *g·*.
learn it of
Un. 41– 4 we must learn it of *g·*.
Life and
Un. 62–16 false sense of Life and *g·*.
Life of
Un. 62–11 as they reach the Life of *g·*,
likeness of
Un. 3–18 the image and likeness of *g·*,
lives in
Pul. 4–20 Who lives in *g·*, lives also in God,
love
Mis. 94– 6 he must repent, and love *g·*
206–27 if you love *g·* supremely,
'00. 11–11 love God," — love *g·*. — *Rom.* 8 : 28.
love of
Mis. 232–26 sought from the love of *g·*,
marvellous
Mis. 237–21 marvellous *g·*, and mysterious evil.
My. 288– 3 Love unfolds marvellous *g·*
may come
Mis. 122–18 that *g·* may come ! — *Rom.* 3 : 8.
298– 5 that *g·* may come? — *Rom.* 3 : 8.
335–29 those who do evil that *g·* may come,
medium of
Pan. 11–24 evil is not the medium of *g·*,

good

Mind is
Mis. 105–31 and this Mind is *g·*,
Mind, or
Ret. 56–24 does not subdivide Mind, or *g·*,
Un. 45–28 in Spirit, immortal Mind, or *g·*.
modes of
My. 211–14 Reversing the modes of *g·*,
more
My. 163–15 which I think do them more *g·*.
much
Mis. 302–14 Much *g·* has been accomplished
Ret. 82–22 to consummate much *g·* or else
My. 216–20 by which you can do much *g·*
mysticism of
My. 167– 3 mysticism of *g·* is unknown to
none beside
Un. 62–10 and there is none beside *g·*.
no place in
No. 27– 5 evil finds no place in *g·*.
not evil
Mis. 4– 9 its power to do *g·*, not evil.
42–24 learn that *g·*, not evil, lives
101–23 this power is *g·*, not evil ;
283–27 to demonstrate *g·*, not evil,
nothing but
Mis. 367–18 He knows nothing but *g·* ;
offspring of
Mis. 181–29 offspring of *g·*, and not of
of others
No. 7–16 sacrifice for the *g·* of others
omnipotence of
Mis. 121–11 and the omnipotence of *g·*,
200–27 faith in the omnipotence of *g·*,
omnipresence of
Ret. 28– 6 understand the omnipresence of *g·*
omnipresent
Mis. 8–15 Love that is omnipresent *g·*,
one in
Mis. 18–20 one in *g·*, and good in One.
oneness of
Mis. 259– 7 infinitude and oneness of *g·*
one side to
Hea. 10–10 There is but one side to *g·*,
only
Un. 21– 8 and *g·* only is reality.
on the side of
Mis. 104–31 gain a balance on the side of *g·*,
opposed to
Mis. 198–25 law, so-called as opposed to *g·*,
198–28 belief in . . . evil, opposed to *g·* ;
opposite to
Mis. 55– 9 Opposite to *g·*, is the
or evil
Mis. 309– 2 either as *g·* or evil.
No. 23–24 amount of *g·* or evil he possesses.
or God
Un. 2–16 Mind which is *g·*, or God,
24–22 separate from *g·* or God.
or of evil
No. 22–16 person of *g·* or of evil.
or Truth
Mis. 196–13 came not from Mind, *g·*, or Truth.
overcome evil with
(*see* **evil**, *sub-title* **overcome**)
overcome with
Ret. 55– 6 it can only be overcome with *g·*.
over evil
Ret. 26–10 supremacy of *g·* over evil,
paralyze
My. 213– 4 aim of . . . is to paralyze *g·*
place of
Rud. 6–11 takes the place of *g·*.
power and
Mis. 284– 7 this field of limitless power and *g·*
power is
Mis. 101–23 this power is *g·*, not evil ;
184–22 learns that all power is *g·*
power of
Mis. 259–16 moral power of *g·*, not of evil :
Un. 41–17 presence and power of *g·*,
Pul. 15– 1 power of *g·* resident in
power or
Mis. 335–31 seeking power or *g·* aside from
practical
My. 287–16 love for God, practical *g·*,
Principle of
My. 152–22 Principle of *g·*, that we call God,
producing
Mis. 122–15 it is not evil producing *g·*,
proportions of
Mis. 55–10 seeks the proportions of *g·*.
quality of
Mis. 78–29 to present the quality of *g·*.

good

real as
Mis. 49–22 belief . . . that evil is as real as *g·*,
108–20 wherein evil seems as real as *g·*,
No. 17–26 If . . . evil would be as real as *g·*,
24–13 not only as real as *g·*, but
reality and
My. 164–26 the sum of all reality and *g·*.
reflects
Mis. 23–26 reflects *g·*, Life, Truth, Love
reward of
My. 296–17 reward of *g·* and punishment of evil
Science of
Mis. 27– 2 Science of *g·* calls evil *nothing*.
352– 7 discern the Science of *g·*.
No. 24– 2 In the Science of *g·*,
sense of
Mis. 222– 2 man's proper sense of *g·*,
341–18 to win the spiritual sense of *g·*.
Un. 41– 8 loss of the true sense of *g·*,
some
Mis. 391–20 Some *g·* ne'er told before,
Po. 38–19 Some *g·* ne'er told before,
My. 117–16 some *g·* out of your personality
Spirit and
Ret. 60–10 as real as Spirit and *g·*.
Spirit or
No. 17– 5 absence of Spirit or *g·*.
spiritual
Mis. 140– 7 all spiritual *g·* comes to
Un. 38–23 moral and spiritual *g·*,
standpoint of
Mis. 289– 8 From a human standpoint of *g·*,
substance of
Mis. 103–12 for who knoweth the substance of *g·*?"
Ret. 57–17 the substance of *g·*.
Un. 61–18 symbol, not the substance of *g·*.
supersensible
Ret. 73–17 evil is lost in supersensible *g·*.
supremacy of
Ret. 26–10 supremacy of *g·* over evil,
64– 5 destroyed by the supremacy of *g·*.
supreme
Un. 19–12 for if the supreme *g·* could
Rud. 2–19 supreme *g·*, Life, Truth, Love.
Pan. 11–24 *g·* supreme destroys all sense of
the word
Hea. 3–15 derived from the word *g·*.
to bad
Mts. 345–10 * cannot change from *g·* to bad."
to conceive of
Mis. 259–12 too evil to conceive of *g·*
to develop
Mis. 14–10 through which to develop *g·*.
to harm
Mis. 118–28 Every attempt of evil to harm *g·*
touch of
'01. 9–19 foams at the touch of *g·* ;
to understand
Mis. 109–26 To understand *g·*, one must discern
trinity of
Rud. 3– 8 this trinity of *g·*
triumph of
Mis. 201–31 demonstrate the triumph of *g·*
ultimate of
Mis. 14– 7 origin or ultimate of *g·*
understanding of
Mis. 31–21 with his understanding of *g·*,
107–17 the understanding of *g·*.
unity of
(*see* **unity**)
universal
My. 165–18 identifies man with universal *g·*.
186– 1 and *g·* universal.
291–12 universal *g·* overcoming evil.
unlike
Pan. 14– 1 nature of whatever is unlike *g·*,
uses of
Mis. 338–16 uses of *g·*, to abuses from evil ;
utility of
Mis. 60–27 power, wisdom, and utility of *g·* ;
vacillating
Mis. 268–30 vacillating *g·* or self-assertive error
wholly
Un. 49–14 cannot be wholly *g·*.
worketh
'00. 10– 3 All that worketh *g·* is
work together for
'00. 11–10 work together for *g·* — *Rom.* 8 : 28.
My. 143–25 work together for *g·* — *Rom.* 8 : 28.
your
Mis. 89–15 your *g·* will generally

Mis. 2–28 and into *g·* that is immortal ;
9–14 doing thee *g·* far beyond the present sense

good

Mis.
9–15 which thou canst entertain of *g*·
10– 6 "work together for *g*· — *Rom.* 8 : 28.
11–20 to do them *g*· whenever
13– 6 sharp return of evil for *g*·
14–19 that *g*·, God, understood,
14–23 G· is the primitive Principle of
18–23 could never separate himself from *g*·,
26–29 Saxon term for God is also *g*·.
26–32 changed, to mean that *g*· is evil,
27– 4 That God, *g*·, creates evil, or
31–20 power to be or to do *g*·,
31–21 the *omnipotence* of God, *g*·.
37– 1 no power besides God, *g*·.
41– 3 liberated thought to do *g*·,
51–19 educate him to love God, *g*·,
71–26 God, *g*·, the all-knowing Mind.
93–13 the eternal, infinite God, *g*·.
101–27 it follows that all must be *g*·
112–23 * you have brought what will do him *g*·."
115–20 since God, *g*·, is All-in-all.
122–16 nor *g*· ultimating in evil.
127–20 one must do *g*· to others.
174– 2 than has *g*· to produce evil.
179– 9 other consciousness than that of *g*·?
181– 8 unity with God, *g*·.
182–21 image and likeness of God, *g*·.
184–19 says, "I am of God, therefore *g*·,"
192– 3 Hebrew term for Deity was "*g*·,"
194–30 the Life that is God, *g*·,
196– 9 a separate mind from God (*g*·),
196–19 ever-presence and power of God, *g*·.
196–21 When the Life that is God, *g*·,
198–14 evil proceedeth not from God, *g*·,
200– 3 Jesus regarded *g*· as the normal state
201–11 its powerlessness to destroy *g*·,
201–14 somethingness of the *g*· we possess,
205–17 *g*·, whose visible being is
208– 6 He is cognizant only of *g*·.
213– 3 taught, or lived, that is *g*·,
222–27 *g*· should seem more natural than
228– 5 is to do *g*· to thyself;
238–17 Yet the *g*· done,
251–23 the *g*· they would do, that they do,
259– 6 law . . . of *g*·, not of evil.
262– 4 power to be good and to do *g*·.
262–14 for the *g*· you are doing.
277–24 proof that God, *g*·, is supreme.
287–10 The *g*· in human affections
299–15 *g*· which the material senses see not
319– 6 aught else than *g*·.
322–26 zealous affection for seeking *g*·,
333–14 God, *g*·, is supreme, *all* power and
338–11 hope holding steadfastly to *g*·
346–10 God created only the *g*·,
352–11 true consciousness of God, *g*·.
354–11 error to Truth, and evil to *g*·,
360– 6 *g*·, because fashioned divinely,
364–18 it is *g*·, reflects the divine Mind,
364–23 matter of Spirit and evil of *g*· ;
364–26 *g*· has the same power or modes
367–21 To *g*·, evil is never present ;
400–20 Father-Mother *g*·.
Man. 41–12 do *g*· unto your enemies
Ret. 67–21 likeness of evil, not of *g*·.
68– 3 in the name of "the Lord," or *g*·,
72– 5 one's ability to do *g*·,
Un. 14–22 all cannot be *g*· therein.
21–15 G·. The Lord is God.
22– 2 G·. Because man is made after
22– 9 G·. Thou shalt not admit
22–13 *Evil.* . . . something besides *g*·.
22–19 G·. Whatever cometh not from
23–20 G·. How can they exist, unless
24–12 G·. All consciousness is Mind ;
25– 1 If you, O *g*·, deny this,
25– 6 G·. Spirit is the only substance.
25–20 G·. Evil is not a creator.
26– 9 G·. You mistake, O evil !
46–20 even more the ego than was the *g*·.
47– 3 Nowhere . . . is evil connected with *g*·,
49–10 reality and substance of being are *g*·,
51–21 in the idea of God, *g*·,
53– 6 calling the knowledge of evil *g*·,
Pul. 6– 7 G·, the Anglo-Saxon term for God,
73–13 * to do *g*· and heal the sick,
81–24 * the true, the beautiful, the *g*·,
Rud. 4–17 G· is not in evil, but in God only.
9–27 and the producer only of *g*· ;
13– 2 that Life is God, *g*· ;
No. 36–14 conscious only of God, of *g*·.
39–20 awakened desire to be and do *g*·.
Pan. 5– 9 possessed of the nature of God, *g*·
11–22 may believe that evil develops *g*·,
'00. 5– 5 or aught besides God, *g*·.
5– 8 opposite of God — *g*· — named devil

good

'00. 8–25 not Science for . . . the *g*· to weep.
'01. 23– 8 must either exist in *g*·, or
25–27 as the infinite God, — *g*·,
31–25 who held fast to whatever is *g*·,
'02. 6– 4 law, apart or other than God — *g*·
6– 7 of something besides God, *g*·,
Hea. 18–11 There is in reality but the *g*· :
Peo. 2– 9 and makes it *g*·,
2–10 learn that God, *g*·, is universal,
4–11 When first *g*·, God, was named a
Po. 28–14 All-merciful and *g*·,
69– 8 Father-Mother *g*·,
My. 3–20 *g*· which has come into his life,
4–16 loves all who love God, *g*· ;
12–30 The *g*· they desire to do,
49– 3 * and we will do thee *g*·,'
79– 7 * who seem to see no *g*· in C. S.,
112–28 book that through the *g*· it does
129– 2 that which is *g*·." — *I Thess.* 5 : 21.
170–20 "Trust . . . and do *g*· ; — *Psal.* 37 : 3.
195–16 To do *g*· to all because we love all,
200–14 Striving to be good, to do *g*·,
213–12 should be more zealous to do *g*·,
240–17 all that is unlike God, *g*·
252– 8 the *g*· you do unto others
271– 9 the *g*· that a man does
273–23 understanding of Life as God, *g*·,
281–13 God, *g*·, the Father-Mother Love,
283–30 never fastens on the *g*· or the great.
288– 6 The *g*· done and the *g*· to do
288– 9 G· is divinely natural.
296–20 God, *g*·, omnipotent and infinite.
303–29 remains to be proved by the *g*· I do.
310–31 * "Read it, for it will do you *g*·.

good (adj.)

Mis. 13–29 you will find it to be *g*· ;
25–27 If God created drugs *g*·,
41–12 The *g*· fight must be fought by
45–21 *all that was made, and it was g*·,
70–17 He was too *g*· to die ;
71–12 *g*· or bad influences on the unborn
72– 7 both *g*· and bad traits of the
118–24 Be of *g*· cheer ;
122–25 *g*· and faithful servant, — *Matt.* 25 : 23.
126–20 the silent lesson of a *g*· example.
128–10 are of *g*· report ; — *Phil.* 4 : 8.
153–14 *g*· to His Israel
157–18 I am glad that you are in *g*· cheer.
159–14 are pure and of *g*· report.
166–31 an honest man, a *g*· carpenter,
187–28 evil before he can be *g*· ;
204– 8 When the *g*· fight is fought,
210–14 G· deeds are harmless.
211– 9 by the *g*· judgment of people
213–27 Christian Scientists, be of *g*· cheer :
216–26 * nor the laws of reason hold *g*·,
219–28 a *g*· sense, or conscious goodness,
220– 2 a *g*· rule works one way,
221–14 if he denies it, the *g*· effect is lost.
224–20 beautiful, great, and *g*·,
233–18 Substituting *g*· words for a *g*· life,
235–13 that bringeth not forth *g*· fruit ;
236–25 notwithstanding one's *g*· intentions,
245–19 in all the *g*· tendencies, charities,
247–29 that God created, He pronounced *g*·.
252–10 G· thoughts are potent ;
257–28 *g*· Samaritan ministering to
262– 3 confer increased power to be *g*·
273–17 labor for a *g*· and holy cause.
278– 6 fight the *g*· fight, and keep the
283–16 breach of *g*· manners and morals ;
298–14 "It is not *g*· to marry." — *Matt.* 19 : 10.
313– 5 It is a digest of *g*· manners,
318–21 be a *g*· Bible scholar
327– 9 "thou hast chosen the *g*· part ;
330–18 It is *g*· to talk with our past hours,
331– 6 obedient, full of *g*· odor,
340–21 through evil or through *g*· report,
355– 6 Less teaching and *g*· healing
357–17 fallen into the *g*· and honest hearts
358–30 all the *g*· ends of organization,
362–13 all that He made was *g*·.
365–16 G· health and a more spiritual
370–27 the *g*· shepherd cares for all
370–28 *g*· Shepherd does care for all,
371–19 * "*g*· right, and *g*· wrong,"
379–23 with phenomenally *g*· results ;
399–24 (Heaven chiselled squarely *g*·)
Man. 30– 3 and *g*· English scholars.
30–20 keep the property in *g*· repair,
36–21 members thereof in *g*· standing,
50–17 another member in *g*· standing
51–11 *g*· and regular standing with
52–13 previous character has been *g*·.

good (adj.)

Man. 73– 8   *g·* standing with The Mother Church,
  73–13   Also members in *g·* standing with
  76–17   members of this Church in *g·* standing.
  83–10   such only as have *g·* past records
  91–21   and with *g·* moral records,
  99–13   who is in *g·* fellowship with
Ret. 15– 1   the *g·* clergyman's heart also
  45– 3   "bringeth *g·* tidings, — *Isa.* 52 : 7.
  47–24   be a *g·* Bible scholar
  86– 6   and that is to *be g·* !
  94– 7   whatsoever seems to be *g·*,
Un. 8–11   All that is beautiful and *g·*
  15– 8   and pronounced them *g·*.
  15– 9   Was evil among these *g·* things?
  15–23   who worship not the *g·* Deity,
  23–24   a purely *g·* and spiritual consciousness
  46–16   only as spiritual and *g·*,
  53– 8   are *g·* and God-made,
Pul. 3–14   *g·* fight we have waged is over,
  16– 9   (Heaven chiselled squarely *g·*)
  21–15   and fellowship for what is *g·*
  38–29   * *g·* that each and all shall prosper,
  46–14   * identified with *g·* and great names
  51–30   * which have done something *g·*
  69–12   * so fill the mind with *g·* thoughts
No. 3–22   How *g·* and pleasant a thing it is
  18–22   *G·* health and a more spiritual
  42–20   declaring itself both true and *g·*.
  43– 7   stimulate and sustain a *g·* sermon.
Pan. 9– 7   a *g·* Spirit and an evil spirit.
  13–16   to fight the *g·* fight
'00. 2–28   Well, all that is *g·*.
  3–11, 12   a *g·* work or *g·* workers
  8–11   may steal other people's *g·* thoughts,
'01. 2–10   to substitute *g·* words for *g·* deeds,
  5–24   anything that is real, *g·*, or true ;
  14–27   it is *g·* to know that wrong has no
'02. 3–22   on the brow of *g·* King Edward,
  14–10   * But only great as I am *g·*."
  20–25   *g·* people welcome Christian Scientists.
Hea. 1–14   less need of publishing the *g·* news."
  2–16   "I have fought a *g·* fight, — *II Tim.* 4 : 7.
  5–10   reward of his *g·* deed
  7– 1   "that which is *g·* for nothing,
  10–12   and that is the *g·* side.
  10–14   question of a *g·* and a bad side
Peo. 2–22   has their Deity become *g·* ;
  13–20   * cannot change . . . from *g·* to bad."
Po. 22–14   how great, how *g·* Thou art
  40– 2   *G·* "Sons," and daughters,
  76– 8   (Heaven chiseled squarely *g·*)
My. 9– 9   * glory in every *g·* deed and thought
  11–20   * made *g·* the pledge.
  12–29   The dear children's *g·* deeds
  13–23   with *g·* things ;— *Psal.* 103: 5.
  14–13   * *g·* authority for the statement
  18–24   to fight the *g·* fight
  21–19   * "*g·* measure, pressed down, — *Luke* 6 : 38.
  32– 7   * So *g·* are the acoustic properties
  42– 8   * a *g·* confession" — *I Tim.* 6 : 13.
  60– 7   * my uncle, the *g·* old deacon
  62– 3   * *g·* and faithful servant ;— *Matt.* 25 : 23.
  81– 3   * Scientists fairly radiate *g·* nature
  81– 5   * So ingrained is this *g·* nature,
  91– 7   * Scientists set a *g·* example
  99– 2   * *g·* things that this sect is doing.
  111–19   models of *g·* morals,
  121–19   external gentility and *g·* humor
  122–14   in our *g·* city of Concord.
  129–24   wherein the *g·* man's heart
  132– 6   be of *g·* cheer ;— *John* 16 : 33.
  134–11   Joy over *g·* achievements
  148– 6   May the *g·* folk of Concord
  156– 9   abound to every *g·* work," — *II Cor.* 9 : 8.
  162–21   *g·* and faithful." — *Matt.* 25 : 23.
  175–11   to the *g·* folk of Concord
  178–16   all that God made "*g·*;"— *Gen.* 1 : 31.
  184–27   bringeth *g·* tidings, — *Isa.* 52 : 7.
  187–13   and of a *g·* conscience, — *I Tim.* 1 : 5.
  195–13   We must resign with *g·* grace
  197– 1   Enjoying *g·* things is not evil,
  200–14   Striving to be *g·*, to do good,
  202–13   *g·* and faithful," — *Matt.* 25 : 23.
  203–11   best of everything is not too *g·*,
  203–13   to be great, — only as *g·*.
  205–18   * as the thing made is *g·* or bad,
  207–21   *g·* and faithful — *Matt.* 25 : 21.
  210– 7   *G·* thoughts are an impervious
  219– 6   My *g·* students have all the
  221–12   so great and *g·* as Christ Jesus.
  225– 4   *g·* and faithful," — *Matt.* 25 : 23.
  227–10   *g·* citizens are arrested for
  232–28   exhaustion and no *g·* results,
  246– 3   in *g·* and regular standing.
  246– 8   three years with *g·* success.

good (adj.)

My. 248– 6   * But only great as I am *g·*."
  248–22   to conceive God aright you must be *g·*.
  251–19   after three years of *g·* practice,
  278–17   Follow that which is *g·*.
  282–26   prosper ever this *g·* endeavor.
  284–12   issue of your *g·* paper,
  287–22   bringeth not forth *g·* fruit ;
  311– 8   my *g·* housekeeper said to me :
  315–29   *g·* men and women in our own
  320– 2   * and a *g·* proofreader.
  322–25   * *g·* points in the Science,
  330– 1   * criticism of this *g·* woman
  330–12   * by a Mason of *g·* standing
  331–16   * the assailant of a *g·* woman :
    (*see also* **man, pleasure, will, works**)

good-by

Pul. 34– 8   * came to bid her *g·*
Po. 22– 6   shall bid old earth *g·*

good-looking

My. 97–17   * *g·*, eminently respectable,

goodly

Mis. 276–11   formed a *g·* assemblage
My. 162–31   towering top of its *g·* temple

goodman

My. 156–13   say to the *g·* of the house :
  232–14   *g·* of the house— *Luke* 12 : 39.

good-natured

My. 75–19   * They are very patient and *g·*.

good-naturedly

My. 75–17   * would take it all very *g·*.

goodness

achievements of
  My. 0–20   beauty, and achievements of *g·*.
  94–30   beauty, and achievements of *g·*."
affection for
  Mis. 318– 9   natural affection for *g·*
all the
  Mis. 347–14   all the *g·* of generous natures,
and benevolence
  My. 165–24   *G·* and benevolence never tire.
and blessedness
  Mis. 209–26   *g·* and blessedness are one :
and greatness
  Mis. 270–24   pathway of *g·* and greatness
  My. 123– 6   hearts of men to *g·* and greatness,
and happiness
  My. 267–31   manifestation of *g·* and happiness.
and harmony
  Mis. 367–11   reality of being — *g·* and harmony
and love
  Po. 67–22   fragrance of *g·* and love ;
and philanthropy
  My. 203– 8   *G·* and philanthropy begin with work
and power
  No. 39–21   of God, of His *g·* and power.
  Pan. 4– 5   possesses all wisdom, *g·*, and power,
and utility
  Mis. 365–10   proof of its *g·* and utility,
and virtue
  No. 13–24   reason and revelation, *g·* and virtue.
beauty and
  Rud. 6– 7   All beauty and *g·* are in and of
  6– 8   the nature of beauty and *g·*
changeless
  Un. 26–21   If God be *changeless g·*,
conscious
  Mis. 219–29   good sense, or conscious *g·*,
erect in
  Mis. 79–16   man as His likeness is erect in *g·*
excludes
  My. 249–10   abandon of hating . . . excludes *g·*.
faithful to
  Pul. 5– 8   Memory, faithful to *g·*,
filled with
  My. 210– 7   in a mind filled with *g·*.
fruits of
  Mis. 219–29   the fruits of *g·* will follow,
  Ret. 54–13   without bearing the fruits of *g·*,
genuine
  Ret. 81–13   genuine *g·* become so apparent
germ of
  No. 8–15   rejoice that every germ of *g·*
given impulse to
  No. 12–15   and given impulse to *g·*,
grasp of
  My. 283–17   until his grasp of *g·* grows
great
  Hea. 3–20   great and wonderful works
  My. 176– 8   God grant that such great *g·*,
greatness and
  No. 46–22   health, greatness, and *g·*,

goodness

healing-power of
Mis. 199–30   marvellous healing-power of *g·*
hieroglyphs of
My. 205–16   Love and unity are hieroglyphs of *g·*,
His
Mis. 69– 3   at His *g·*, mercy, and might.
No. 39–21   of God, of His *g·* and power.
My. 193– 9   "for His *g·*, — *Psal.* 107 : 8.
his
Mis. 165–22   His *g·* and grace purchased
his own
My. 227– 6   the minifying of his own *g·*
infinite
Rud. 2–25   higher range of infinite *g·*.
in man
Mis. 164– 5   human presentation of *g·* in man.
in others
Pul. 21–17   true sense of *g·* in others,
is greatness
My. 272– 4   *G·* is greatness, and the logic of
is immortal
Mis. 70–17   for *g·* is immortal.
is something
Ret. 63–14   hence *g·* is something,
learned through
Peo. 2–12   is learned through *g·*,
Life and
Ret. 63–17   against man's Life and *g·*.
man's
'00. 3–20   would destroy this man's *g·*.
never fails
My. 165–15   *G·* never fails to receive
not doctrines
Pul. 9–26   *g·*, not doctrines, . . . gain the ear
of God
Pul. 6– 9   *g·* of God — healing and
opposite of
Mis. 49–21   belief in the opposite of *g·*,
Un. 24– 2   sin the opposite of *g·*.
outpouring of
My. 118–10   It is an outpouring of *g·*
peace in
Mis. 219–21   discomfort in sin and peace in *g·*.
perpetual
'02. 8–23   it prompts perpetual *g·*,
power and
No. 13– 1   reflection of His power and *g·*.
preeminent
My. 161–28   his preeminent *g·*,
proceed from
Mis. 155– 5   and proceed from *g·*.
purposes of
Mis. 152– 6   unite in the purposes of *g·*.
reflection of
Rud. 11– 8   the forever reflection of *g·*.
reveals
Mis. 1–19   *G·* reveals another scene
reward of
My. 19–24   reap richly the reward of *g·*.
ripening
My. 155–28   happy hearts and ripening *g·*.
their
Peo. 3–23   thought and action in their *g·*,
time and
My. 306–12   Time and *g·* determine greatness.
to grandeur
My. 163– 5   meekness to might, *g·* to grandeur,
transcendent
Mis. 199–20   his transcendent *g·* is manifest

Mis. 15–26   In mortal and material man, *g·* seems
78–28   any more than *g·*, to present
199–29   *g·* is more natural than evil.
250–21   *g·* without activity and power.
294–10   the might and majesty ! — of *g·*.
331–10   *g·* will have its springtide of
333– 5   omnipotence, omnipresence, *g·*,
No. 26–17   Man's real ego, or selfhood, is *g·*.
'00. 8– 5   The good man imparts . . . *g·* ;
My. 123–29   not overlook small things in *g·*
165–16   *g·* makes life a blessing.
165–17   *g·* identifies man with
167– 4   *g·* is "the fruit of the — *Gal.* 5 : 22.
210–13   *G·* involuntarily resists evil.
274– 6   but *g·*, holiness, and love do this,
295–15   and kindness . . . is *g·*.

good's
Mis. 14–24   evil, *g·* opposite, has no Principle,
46– 5   evil, *g·* opposite, is unreal.

goods
Mis. 159–18   Its *g·* commemorate,

Good Templars
Po. 40– 1   "*G· T·*" one and all,

Good-will
Mis. 153–26   * Peace on earth and *G·* !

Gordon, Rev. Dr. A. J.
No. 41–24   Rev. Dr. A. J. *G·*, a Boston Baptist

Gordon's, Dr.
No. 29–11   Dr. *G·* sermon on The Ministry of

gore
Mis. 246–10   purged of that sin by human *g·*,
My. 265– 9   cleanse the earth of human *g·* ;

gorgeous
Mis. 230–28   render it pathetic, tender, *g·*.
373–17   not in soft raiment or *g·* apparel ;
Pul. 48– 9   * in the *g·* October coloring
My. 29–13   * more *g·* church pageantries
193– 7   *g·* skies of the Orient

gorgeously
Mis. 324– 7   *g·* tapestried parlors,

gorging
Peo. 8–27   *g·* his faith with skill

Gospel
Mis. 292– 2   The divinity of St. John's *G·*
Ret. 22– 3   *G·* narratives bear brief testimony
Un. 4–23   John's *G·* declares (xvii. 3) that
My. 222– 1   *G·* according to St. Matthew.

gospel (*see also* gospel's)

appeal to the
My. 219–31   and then appeal to the *g·*
expound the
Ret. 36– 3   not expound the *g·* according to
is preached
Mis. 168–12   to the poor . . . the *g·* is preached.
171–20   to the poor the *g·* is preached.
Jesus'
My. 28–24   * Jesus' *g·* was for all time
law and
    (*see* law)
law and the
    (*see* law)
new
Mis. 178–22   * found C. S. a new *g·*,
of Christ
Mis. 18– 7   under the law and *g·* of Christ,
'02. 5–20   reiterated in the *g·* of Christ,
of glad tidings
Mis. 369– 4   the *g·* of glad tidings bring
of grace
'02. 2–28   round the *g·* of grace,
of healing
Mis. 67– 3   law and *g·* of healing.
67–18   *g·* of healing demonstrates the
208–21   interprets . . . the *g·* of healing.
Ret. 32– 1   It was the *g·* of healing,
Pul. 7– 7   how the *g·* of healing was
of health
Mis. 241–25   rejoices in the *g·* of health.
of Love
Mis. 135–17   so spreading the *g·* of Love,
of marriage
Mis. 286– 3   *g·* of marriage is not without
of peace
'02. 4–15   new commandment in the *g·* of peace,
of suffering
Ret. 30–20   through the *g·* of suffering,
Un. 57–17   This *g·* of suffering brought life
old
My. 90–19   * reincarnation of the old, old *g·*
or demonstration
Mis. 367– 1   without law, *g·*, or demonstration,
preaching the
Ret. 88–19   C. S. work, . . . preaching the *g·*.
No. 12–19   preaching the *g·* of Truth,
My. 128–21   preaching the *g·* and healing the sick.
preach the
Mis. 325–32   preach the *g·*, — *Mark* 16 : 15.
No. 41–21   preach the *g·* ;" — *Mark* 16 : 15.
My. 46–16   * preach the *g·* and heal the sick
47–28   * preach the *g·* — *Mark* 16 : 15.
52–18   * heal the sick, and preach the *g·*,
147–16   preach the *g·* which heals
150–28   heal the sick and preach the *g·*,
300–25   preach the *g·* — *Mark* 16 : 15.
saving
My. 24– 9   * this healing and saving *g·*.
this
Un. 57–17   This *g·* of suffering brought life
My. 90–13   * door to this *g·* for many,

Mis. 66– 4   *g·* that fulfils the law in
151–11   in the *g·*, He saith of
177–17   establishing the truth, the *g·*,
300–16   thus evade the law, *but not the g·*.
318–17   *g·* work of teaching C. S.,

gospel

Ret.	47–21	student can enter upon the *g·* work of
	65–11	have no warrant in the *g·* or
	75–25	no permission in the *g·* for
Pul.	44–17	* chapter sub-title
'00.	4– 6	the *g·* of the New Testament
My.	19–31	Wheresoever this *g·* shall be
	147–11	*g·* with "signs following,"— *Mark* 16: 20.
	153– 6	*g·* ministry of my students
	179– 1	beginning of the *g·* writings.
	179–18	Old Testament and *g·* narratives
	227–23	and the *g·* injunction,

gospel-opposing
Mis.	301–11	law-breaking and *g·*

gospel's
Mis.	8–29	through the *g·* benediction.
Pan.	13–13	Love all . . . for the *g·* sake ;
My.	18–21	Love all . . . for the *g·* sake ;

Gospels
Mis.	193–11	the authenticity of the *G·*,
Ret.	65–22	as taught in the four *G·*.
	89–22	Nowhere in the four *G·* will
My.	132– 5	go to the *G·*, and there we hear :

gossip
Mis.	227–12	stuff into the hands of *g·* !
Man.	81–23	No idle *g·*, no slander,
'01.	16– 9	supply sacrilegious *g·* with the

gossiping
Mis.	230– 9	*g·* mischief, making lingering calls,

got
Mis.	239–10	* chapter sub-title
	239–20	* "I've *g·* cold, doctor."
	240– 1	"I have *not g·* cold."
	375–13	* *g·* quite an idea of what constitutes

gotten
Mis.	63– 5	at first *g·* up to hinder his
	239–28	must be *g·* rid of,

Gough, John B.
Mis.	71– 3	John B. *G·* is said to have

govern
Mis.	10– 5	motives that *g·* mortal mind
	51–12	*g·* a child metaphysically?
	51–16	Motives *g·* acts,
	58–24	If God does not *g·*
	58–25	if He does *g·* it,
	59–21	should and does *g·* man.
	108–20	has no power to *g·* itself ;
	354–21	to *g·* His own creation,
Man.	41–25	all mankind, and *g·* them !
Rud.	10– 9	which *g·* mortals wrongfully.
Hea.	12– 7	goes to the fount to *g·*
	15– 9	it enables mind to *g·* matter,
Peo.	11–18	the laws that *g·* their bodies,
My.	149–11	that . . . create and *g·* it ;
	231–18	wisdom must *g·* charity,
	363–14	that sanity and Science *g·*

governed
Mis.	34– 6	The body is *g·* by mind ;
	40–15	All true healing is *g·* by,
	104– 5	Formed and *g·* by God,
	146–17	be *g·* therein by the spirit
	198– 1	wholly *g·* by the one perfect Mind,
	198–16	recognize man as *g·* by God,
	206–17	Growth is *g·* by intelligence ;
	256– 4	The body is *g·* by Mind,
	257–22	Electricity, *g·* by this so-called
	259–19	he is *g·* in the same rhythm
	267–23	*g·* by Spirit, intelligent good.
	291– 2	they are not *g·* by the Principle
	291– 3	a mind *g·* by Principle
	303– 7	*unmolested,* be *g·* by divine Love
	353–21	regulator is *g·* by the principle that
	353–22	and because it *is* thus *g·*,
	364–19	is good, . . . is *g·* by it ;
Ret.	33– 3	*g·* the action of material medicine.
	78– 7	for it is *g·* by its Principle,
Pul.	4– 8	*g·* and protected by his divine
No.	10–28	*G·* by the immutable and
Pan.	11–10	*G·* by the divine Principle
Hea.	14–28	a body *g·* by this mind.
	19– 5	is *g·* directly and entirely by mind,
My.	247– 4	by the common consent of the *g·*,
	247– 5	man *g·* by his creator
	254–25	by the common consent of the *g·*,
	254–26	man *g·* by his creator
	265–29	wealth should be *g·* by honesty,
	303–15	If the individual *g·* human
	342–25	* "How will it be *g·*

governing
Mis.	37– 2	*g·* man or the universe.
	58–28	one human mind *g·* another ;
	229–14	*g·* the receptivity of the body,

governing
Mis.	258–14	*g·* Himself, He governs the universe.
	332– 3	Wisely *g·*, informing the universe,
	364–16	constituting and *g·* all identity,
Man.	51–18	By-Law *g·* the case
Pan.	7–27	hypothesis of . . . matter *g·* Mind,
'01.	32–30	Love was the *g·* impulse
My.	287– 9	*g·* all that really is.
	287–13	*g·* governments, industries,
	299–21	understand it and the law *g·* it,

Government
Mis.	80–21	can thrive but feebly under our *G·*.

government

benign
My.	128– 8	less than God's benign *g·*,

church
Mis.	284–30	intrusted with the rules of church *g·*,
Man.	72–18	consolidate under one church *g·*.
Pul.	20–11	system of ministry and church *g·*.
My.	vi–13	* devised its church *g·*,

city
My.	175–19	this favor of our city *g·* ;

civil arm of
No.	44–22	through the civil arm of *g·*,

constitutes
Man.	28– 4	Law constitutes *g·*,

divine
Mis.	56–16	opposed to the divine *g·*.

form of
Mis.	382–18	originated its form of *g·*,
Man.	70–15	its own form of *g·*.
	71–18	the Mother Church's form of *g·*,
	72–22	shall continue its present form of *g·*

God's
Mis.	199– 7	spiritual law,— God's *g·*.
My.	222–26	as God's *g·* becomes apparent,
	278– 1	To coincide with God's *g·*
	283–28	enlightened sense of God's *g·*.

her
Pan.	14–13	continue to characterize her *g·*,

highest places in
No.	45–17	and the highest places in *g·*,

His
Mis.	59–16	under His *g·*,
Rud.	10– 6	His *g·* is harmonious ;
Hea.	8– 2	and obedience to His *g·*,

its
Man.	74– 7	democratic in its *g·*,
My.	247– 3	its *g·* is administered by
	254–24	its *g·* is administered by
	342–26	* all now concerned in its *g·*
	342–28	Its *g·* will develop as it progresses."

liberal
My.	361–22	* truly democratic and liberal *g·*.

nature and
'00.	5– 2	nature, and *g·* of all things

of a nation
My.	282– 1	*g·* of a nation is its peace maker or

of divine Love
My.	189–15	The *g·* of divine Love derives its
	278– 7	*g·* of divine Love is supreme.

of God
Hea.	18– 2	shall yield to the *g·* of God,
Peo.	12– 7	merciful and just *g·* of God.

of man
Ret.	90–30	leave with God the *g·* of man.

one
Mis.	59– 1	one *g·* and God.

our
'02.	3–14	It is well that our *g·*,

right
My.	292– 5	Through divine Love the right *g·* is

righteous
My.	276–24	help support a righteous *g·* ;

system of
Man.	28– 7	system of *g·* and form of

this
Hea.	8– 7	and carrying out this *g·*

wisdom and
Un.	51–19	of God's wisdom and *g·*.

Mis.	161– 6	*g·* shall be upon his — *Isa.* 9: 6.
	166–11	*g·* shall be upon his — *Isa.* 9: 6.
	167–21	*g·* shall be upon his — *Isa.* 9: 6.
My.	216– 9	regulated by a *g·* currency,

governmental
My.	220– 4	submit . . . to *g·* usages.

governments
My.	278–23	*G·* have no right to
	287–13	governing *g·*, industries,
	293–32	Human *g·* maintain the right

Governor
Po.	vi–18	*To-day, by order of G· Andrew,*
My.	308–20	father was visiting *G·* Pierce,

Governor
My. 308–21 Franklin Pierce's father, the *G·*
308–23 My father thanked the *G·*,
310–14 the *G·* of New Hampshire.
312–25 The *G·* of the State and his
331– 7 * and the *G·* of the State,
340–22 the *G·* of New Hampshire

governor
Un. 26– 5 my author, authority, *g·*,

governs
Mis. 6–18 Mind *g·* all.
41–27 Principle which *g·* the universe,
51–16 and Mind *g·* man.
204–29 *g·* the aims, ambition, and acts
208– 7 *g·* millions of mortals
208–10 enters . . . the human heart and *g·* it.
258–15 He *g·* the universe.
258–17 infinite Mind *g·* all things.
287–19 higher nature of man *g·* the lower.
369– 9 peering into the cause which *g·* all
380– 5 *g·* the universe, time, space,
Man. 40– 8 divine Love alone *g·* man ;
Un. 10–18 because He is perfect, and *g·* them
34– 4 declares . . . that non-intelligence *g·*.
Rud. 10– 5 know that God alone *g·*
No. 13–19 voices the infinite, and *g·* the
35–19 and yet *g·* mankind.
Pan. 3–30 he *g·* the universe ;
Hea. 14–16 to know that mind *g·* the body
Peo. 8–18 Mind, that *g·* the universe,
8–18 *g·* every action of the body
My. 165–10 and by it God *g·*.
182–22 created and *g·* the universe
226–13 *g·* all from the infinitesimal to

gown
'01. 16–23 under sanction of the *g·*,

grace
added
Pul. 81–11 * an added *g·* —a newer charm.
administer
My. 129–21 Then will angels administer *g·*,
all
Mis. 116– 3 God of all *g·* be with you,
159– 7 God of all *g·* give you peace.
My. 148– 7 God of all *g·*, truth, and love
156– 7 all *g·* abound toward you ;— II Cor. 9: 8.
and glory
'02. 11– 7 warrant and welcome, *g·* and glory,
My. 339–16 *g·*, and glory of liberty.
and growth
My. 116–22 Every loss in *g·* and growth
and love
My. 187–16 May the *g·* and love of God
and peace
Mis. 9– 1 consciousness of good, *g·*, and peace,
and Truth
Mis. 164–26 full of *g·* and Truth,
and truth
Mis. 292–25 C. S., full of *g·* and truth,
beauty and the
My. 31–17 * for the beauty and the *g·* of
divine
Mis. 360–17 dews of divine *g·*,
fatherly
My. 288–32 evil is not a fatherly *g·*.
foes to
Mis. 118–22 envy, revenge, are foes to *g·*,
from God
Mis. 129– 7 through *g·* from God,
giving
My. 182–23 giving *g·*, health, and immortality
good
My. 195–13 must resign with good *g·* what we
goodness and
Mis. 165–22 His goodness and *g·* purchased
gospel of
'02. 2–28 round the gospel of *g·*,
grace for
Mis. 322–20 that giveth grace for *g·*,
grow in
Un. 14–12 commanded to *grow in g·*.
14–13 necessary . . . to grow in *g·*,
His
Mis. 154–11 means and measure of His *g·*.
'01. 10–20 "the riches of His *g·*" — Eph. 1: 7.
his
My. 257–19 We own his *g·*,
lightness and
My. 89– 8 * joined lightness and *g·* to
means of
Mis. 115–25 becomes a means of *g·*.
127–25 Ofttimes the rod is His means of *g·* ;
'01. 19– 2 divinely appointed means of *g·*

grace
miracle of
Mis. 77–30 where the miracle of *g·* appears,
Peo. 4–21 No miracle of *g·* can make
more
Mis. 127–13 more *g·*, obedience, and love.
354–15 more *g·*, a motive made pure,
'02. 4– 8 Let us all pray . . . for more *g·*,
My. 18– 9 more *g·*, obedience, and love.
nations'
Po. 10–17 Allied by nations' *g·*,
My. 337–18 Allied by nations' *g·*,
of God
Un. 7– 3 impartial *g·* of God,
Pan. 10–23 accomplished by the *g·* of God,
of the Lord
My. 19– 9 "The *g·* of the Lord — II Cor. 13: 14.
pardon and
Po. 32–19 pardon and *g·*, through His Son,
patience, and
My. 209– 7 fidelity, courage, patience, and *g·*.
playful
Po. 9– 4 to his mother's in playful *g·* ;
power of
No. 9–19 point steadfastly to the power of *g·*
spiritual
Un. 57–21 spiritual *g·* was sufficient for him.
startling
My. 9–21 pledged yourselves with startling *g·*
supernal
Ret. 85–16 order prescribed by supernal *g·*.
tender
My. 206– 5 tender *g·* of spiritual understanding,

Mis. 11– 3 it is *g·*, mercy, and justice.
Chr. 53–35 with *g·* towards you and me,
Pul. 87–24 God give you *g·*.
Rud. 15–18 thorough guardianship and *g·*.
'02. 7– 9 neither philosophy, nature, nor *g·*
My. 195–31 fill these spiritual temples with *g·*,
289– 3 God's open secret is seen through *g·*,

graceful
Pul. 31–26 * singularly *g·* and winning
My. 67–29 * in the *g·* outlines.

gracefully
Ret. 4–14 waving *g·* in the sunlight,
Po. 46– 7 But *g·* it stands

graces
Mis. 149–22 all the rich *g·* of the Spirit.
My. 121–22 adds to these *g·*, and reflects the

gracious
My. 15–16 your *g·* reception of it
17– 8 the Lord is *g·*.— I Pet. 2: 3.
283– 8 Your appointment . . . is most *g·*.
342– 4 * entered with a *g·* smile,

graciously
Mis. 251– 9 welcomed you to Concord most *g·*,
Ret. 80– 3 eternal justice be *g·* gentle,
'01. 31–26 yielded up *g·* what He
My. 171–21 * Mrs. Eddy responded *g·*

graciousness
My. 39–24 * We remember her *g·* and dignity.

gradations
Un. 10–14 Their *g·* are spiritual

grades
Mis. 371–15 but mixing all *g·* of persons

gradual
Mis. 15–27 the *g·* fading out of the
85–12 regeneration leading thereto is *g·*,
138–24 at first is more *g·* ;
My. 344–15 must make *g·* approaches to

gradually
Mis. 278–29 I have been *g·* withdrawing
Un. 5– 5 work *g·* and gently up
No. 1– 3 this must be done *g·*,
'00. 7– 3 death-rate to have *g·* diminished.
My. 56– 3 * Attendance . . . *g·* increased,
307–26 *g·* emerging from *materia medica*,

graduate
Mis. 178– 3 a *g·* of Bowdoin College
358– 5 *g·* under divine honors,
Ret. 43–11 Ebenezer J. Foster-Eddy, a *g·* of
Un. 6–20 a *g·* of Wellesley College,

graduated
Ret. 6–15 My brother Albert was *g·*
Pul. 32–28 * Albert Baker, *g·* at Dartmouth

graduates
Mis. 143–19 the Normal class *g·*
Man. 73–14 *g·* of said university
89–10 APPLICANTS AND *g·*.

graduation
Pan. 10–13 after *g*·, the best students

Grafton S. S.
My. 315–16 * *G· S. S.* Jan'y, 1902.

grain
Ret. 4–14 broad fields of bending *g*·
Un. 12– 4 to the waiting *g*· the curving sickle
'01. 18– 1 "mother tincture" of one *g*·
Hea. 13– 5 hundredth part of a *g*· of medicine
.13–10 We have attenuated a *g*· of aconite
My. 222–10 faith as a *g*· of mustard — *Matt.* 17 : 20.

grammar
Ret. 10–14 Learning was so illumined, that *g*·
My. 311–31 * when she finished Smith's *g*·

grammatical
My. 318–12 defend my *g*· construction,

grand
Mis. 5–23 do not understand the *g*· reality
19–31 sense of Life and its *g*· pursuits
28–27 practical knowledge of this *g*· verity,
31–15 it denies the *g*· verity of this Science,
75– 8 fundamental fact and *g*· verity
79– 5 *g*· verities of Science will sift the
97– 5 the *g*· verities of being.
106– 5 parody on Tennyson's *g*· verse,
116–13 emphasizing its *g*· strains,
118–25 warfare with one's self is *g*· ;
124–26 *g*· act crowned and still crowns
159–17 recollections and rare *g*· collections
181– 5 Man's knowledge of this *g*· verity
188– 5 *g*· chorus of harmonious being.
192–22 *g*· verities of Christian healing
197–31 placing his trust in this *g*· Truth,
250–17 *g*· achievements as its results.
264–27 teacher's mind must be pure, *g*·, true,
265–31 must stop at the foot of the *g*· ascent,
273–14 one *g*· family of Christ's followers.
275–22 at the *g*· meeting in Chicago
330– 7 join in nature's *g*· harmony,
333–28 the *g*· realities of Mind,
337–32 this *g*· verity in Science,
356–11 give promise of *g*· careers.
386– 1 "Intensely *g*· and glorious
393–22 Lessons long and *g*·,
Ret. 59– 1 C. S. reveals the *g*· verity,
Un. 6–17 such a *g*· and all-absorbing verity
Pul. vii–17 cradle of this *g*· verity
9–11 nerved its *g*· fulfilment.
87–19 to accept your *g*· church edifice.
No. 5– 2 *g*· verity of Mind-healing.
24–20 the *g*· verity of C. S. :
27–15 *g*· and eternal verities of God and
30–26 demonstrates this *g*· verity
Pan. 11–28 *g*· realism that man is the true
'00. 1–17 five *g*· divisions of the globe ;
01. 14–29 apprehension of this *g*· verity.
29–15 *g*· coworkers for mankind,
31–28 taught by some *g*· old divines,
'02. 6–10 demonstrate this *g*· verity,
Hea. 5–19 obscure the one *g*· truth
9–28 this *g*· truth of being.
Peo. 6–21 *g*· realities of Life and Truth
Po. 39–19 "Social," or *g*·, or great,
49– 3 *g*· and glorious life's sphere,
52– 6 Lessons long and *g*·,
My. 22–10 * this *g*· and noble purpose,
37–19 * Recognizing the *g*· truth
43–29 * this *g*· achievement,
59–19 * in this *g*· amphitheatre ;
66–30 * never before has such a *g*· church
122– 3 for the world a destiny more *g*·
136–20 five *g*· divisions of our globe ;
147– 6 *g*· old elm on North State Street
165– 5 The *g*· must stoop to the menial.
180–19 refuses to see this *g*· verity
188–20 walls of your *g*· cathedral
194– 8 *g*· man or woman,
194–13 engraven on your *g*· edifice
203–12 Be great not as a *g*· obelisk,
251–27 convince yourselves of this *g*· verity :
283–12 fruits of said *g*· Association,
285–15 *g*· object embodied in the
316–15 *g*· defence of our Cause
321– 1 * your *g*· demonstration in
351–14 truly Masonic, tender, *g*· in you

grandchildren
Mis. 125–23 *Beloved Brethren, Children, and G*· :
Pul. 21– 1 Scientists, their children and *g*·

grander
Mis. 110– 9 What *g*· ambition is there
Pul. 85–16 * a better and *g*· humanity,

grandest
Mis. 319–25 opportunity for the *g*· achievement
Ret. 93–21 this *g*· verity has not been
Pul. 45–10 * *g*· and most helpful features
45–25 * succeeded by the *g*· of ministers
53–25 * Whittier, *g*· of mystic poets,

grandeur
Mis. x– 1 spiritual glow and *g*· of
86–22 human conception of beauty, *g*·, and
86–24 divine beauty and the *g*· of Spirit.
87–13 *g*·, and glory of the immortal Mind."
99–28 *g*· of the word, the power of Truth,
354– 6 *g*· of the loyal, self-forgetful,
Ret. 35–15 glow and *g*· of evangelical religion.
61–28 demonstrated in its godliness and *g*·,
Pan. 12– 9 chapter sub-title
'01. 18–21 the *g*· of our great master
Peo. 1–12 impart *g*· to the intellectual
Po. v–13 *Inspired by the g· of this*
My. 25–24 faith in the *g*· and sublimity of
29–17 * its *g*· sprang from the
37– 4 * *g*· of humility and the incense of
50–27 * those few saw the *g*· of its work
59– 1 * *g*· and magnitude of your work
67–26 * will in its simple *g*· surpass any
78–29 * awed by the *g*· of the great room
124– 8 health, harmony, growth, *g*·,
163– 5 meekness to might, goodness to *g*·,
248– 3 its *g*· almost surprises me.

Grandfather
Ret. 2–26 A relative of my *G*· Baker
5– 3 *G*· Ambrose was a very

grandfather (*see also* **grandfather's**)
Pul. 32–26 * Deacon Ambrose, her maternal *g*·

grandfather's
Ret. 4– 4 he inherited my *g*· farm

Grand Lodge of Massachusetts
My. 334–29 * Secretary of the *G· L· of M*· :

grandly
Mis. 392–17 *g*· rising to the heavens above.
Po. 20–21 *g*· rising to the heavens above.
My. 63–24 * *G*· does our temple symbolize

Grandmother
Ret. 2–17 one of my *G*· Baker's books,
2–30 the line of my *G*· Baker's family

grandmother (*see also* **grandmother's**)
Mis. 231– 4 The sober-suited *g*·,
Ret. 1–10 which my *g*· said were written
1–18 so became my paternal *g*·,
3– 9 A cousin of my *g*· was
4– 1 *g*· had thirteen children,
8–15 same room with *g*·,
Pul. 32–25 * a relative of her *g*·.

grandmother's
Ret. 2–21 Among *g*· treasures were
2–28 *g*· stories about General Knox,
9– 1 returned with me to *g*· room,

grandpa
Mis. 231–20 *g*· was taken napping.

grandparents
Ret. 3– 4 *g*· were likewise connected with
Pul. 46–18 * as belonging to her *g*·

Grand Rapids, Mich.
Pul. 89–31 * *Herald, G· R·, M·*.
My. 271–11 * *The Evening Press, G· R·, M·*,

Grand Secretary
My. 333– 1 with the seal of the *G· S·*,
334–29 * Charles W. Moore, *G· S·* of the

grandson
Ret. 4– 8 owned by Uncle James Baker's *g*·,

granite
Mis. 144– 1 *g*· for this church was taken from
Pul. 24–22 * church is built of Concord *g*·
24–23 * pink *g*· of New Hampshire,
49–21 * return to her native *g*· hills,
65–16 * beautiful structure of gray *g*·,
86– 1 * corner-stone . . . being of *g*·,
My. 45–29 * massive pile of New Hampshire *g*·
157–15 * of the same beautiful Concord *g*·
158– 2 building a *g*· church edifice
163–26 friendship, and *g*· character.
341– 5 engraven on her *g*· rocks,

Granite State (*see also* **New Hampshire**)
My. 184–16 characteristic of our *G· S·*,
185–29 sons and daughters of the *G· S·*
305–14 natives of the *G· S·*.

granitic
Pul. 80–14 * over its *g*· pebbles.

grant
Mis. xi–21 *vox populi* is inclined to g· us peace,
272– 3 * *the right to g· degrees*
272– 6 * Mrs. Eddy's g· for a college,
272–20 * simply an incorporated g·,
319–19 and g· me this request,
Pul. 20– 9 refused to g· it,
Peo. 8–20 God g· that the trembling chords of
My. 165–29 God g· that this church is rapidly
176– 7 God g· that such great goodness,
184–19 God g· that this little church
195–29 God g· that this unity remain,
198– 7 May God g· not only the
256– 8 you must g· me my request

granted
Mis. 272– 8 * no charters were g· for similar
Ret. 20–23 g· me in the city of Salem,
40– 7 It was g·,
43– 6 No charter was g· for similar
49–20 only one ever g· to a *legal college*
My. 314–15 g· on the ground of desertion,

granting
My. 173–31 foresight in g· permission,
341–23 * g· of interviews is not usual,

grapes
Mis. 27–17 "Do men gather g· of — *Matt.* 7 : 16.
72–14 have eaten sour g·, — *Ezek.* 18 : 2.
336–18 we gather not g· of thorns,

graphic
Mis. xi–11 g· guide-book, pointing the path,
294–27 terse, g·, and poetic style

graphically
Ret. 2– 5 so g· set forth in the pages of
32–10 g· defined by Calderon,

grapple
Mis. 121– 8 good and evil, seem to g·,
Pul. 13– 4 must g· with and overcome the
Rud. 15–20 g· with this subject,
'01. 23– 4 sects and faculties can g·.

grappled
Mis. 284–25 not . . . more real when it is g· with.

grapples
Mis. 62–23 the author g· with C. S.,

grasp
Mis. 9–18 but it slips from our g·,
82–11 g· and gather — in all glory
100–12 that g· neither the meaning nor
100–17 inadequate to g· the word of Truth,
140–22 rescued from the g· of legal power,
Man. 62–21 to g· the simpler meanings of
No. 11–24 to g· the Principle of C. S.,
17–21 If mortals could g· these two words
23– 5 Evil can neither g· the
My. 122–21 risen to g· the spiritual idea
283–17 his g· of goodness grows stronger.

grasped
Mis. 346–21 g· in all its divine requirements.
Un. 43–25 "apprehended of [or g· — *Phil.* 3 : 12.
No. 21– 8 g· in spiritual law the universe,
Po. 26– 8 While Justice g· the sword
My. 90–17 * can be readily g· by sick or well.
193–24 have g· time and labor,

grasping
Mis. 364–14 right hand g· the universe,
My. 189– 2 g· the sword of Spirit,
248– 8 g· and defining the demonstrable,

grasps
No. 39–26 photography g· the solar light
Peo. 10–15 g· the standard of liberty,

grass
Mis. 329–15 weaving the wavy g·,
330–30 g·, inhabiting the whole earth,
331– 5 When downtrodden like the g·,
390–15 The verdant g· it weaves ;
Pul. 39–26 * Under the meadow g·.
No. 26–26 so clothe the g· — *Matt.* 6 : 30.
Po. 53–10 The patient, timid g·,
55–16 The verdant g· it weaves ;
67–16 o'er the dark wavy g·.

grateful
Mis. 94– 4 never knew a person who . . . to be g· ;
262–15 I am g· to you for
262–22 more g· than words can express,
273– 9 so g· a sense of my labors
274–12 g· acknowledgments to the public
339–24 and forgettest to be g· ?
Man. 75– 9 and she, with g· acknowledgments
'00. 1– 9 I am g· to say that in the last year
Po. vii–10 * *With g· acknowledgment,*
77– 3 holiest hymn in g· praise !
My. 42– 1 * truly g· to her who has

grateful
My. 63– 5 * we are g·.
125–23 deeply g· that the church
134– 6 we cannot be too g· nor too
199–11 accept my g· acknowledgment
229–29 hence my . . . g· joy.
259– 9 * Loving, g· Christmas greetings
295–12 I am in g· receipt of your
319– 8 in loving, g· memory
326–19 Deeply g·, I recognize the
332– 4 * silent gush of g· tears
332– 8 * tribute of g· hearts
336– 9 * She makes g· acknowledgment

gratefully
Mis. 256– 7 While g· acknowledging the
306– 6 * will be g· received ;
No. 19–14 g· and lovingly conscious of the
'02. 20–23 g· appreciating the privilege of
My. 20– 3 G· yours in Christ,
63– 6 * Lovingly and g· yours, students,
81–19 * spoke simply and g·,
182–19 Humbly, g·, trustingly,
194–23 g· accept the spirit of it ;
207– 3 Your communication is g· received.
362–26 * G· yours,

gratification
Mis. 9–27 educated to g· in personal
Ret. 65–10 g· of appetite and passion,
My. 11–17 * she expressed much g·
76–12 * only feebly expresses the g·.

gratified
My. 117– 5 A personal motive g· by
324–22 * was g· and pleased in

gratifying
My. 25–11 * and are most g· :
93–12 * g· the passions or
326– 4 * is most g· to our people ;
326– 7 * It is especially g· to them
355– 1 * it was g· to them,

gratitude
aglow with
'00. 1– 3 glad faces, aglow with g·,
and affection
Mis. 203– 5 mine through g· and affection.
and love
(*see* love)
and praise
My. 323–20 * thoughts of g· and praise
debt of
Mis. xi– 9 debt of g· to God,
My. 352– 8 * our debt of g· to you
debts of
My. 81–18 * debts of g· for ills cured,
deep
My. 157– 5 * deep g· that your generous gift
everlasting
Ret. 49–22 * everlasting g· is due to the
feeling of
My. 331–22 * express the feeling of g·
filled with
My. 42–16 * With a heart filled with g·
362–19 * hearts filled with g· to God,
forever
My. 176– 6 paved the way to my forever g·,
gleam of
Mis. 1–11 kindle all minds with a gleam of g·,
glows with
Po. 31– 9 Glad Easter glows with g·
great
My. 198– 6 great g· to our one Father.
grief and
Pul. 1– 7 redolent with grief and g·.
incense of
My. 37– 5 * incense of g· and compassionate love
instinctive
My. 9– 7 * instinctive g· which not only
joy and
My. 45– 6 * witnessing with joy and g·
justice and
Mis. 291–28 station justice and g· as sentinels
love and
Man. 75– 9 this Church's love and g·,
Pul. 86–22 * testimonial of love and g·
My. 58–17 * love and g· of a great multitude
325–16 * With increasing love and g·,
loving
My. 323–12 * In loving g· for your
my
My. 26–11 You can imagine my g·
120– 7 Accept my g· for the chance
156– 2 You will accept my g· for
offering of
Pul. 26–15 * a votive offering of g·

atitude

our

My. 9–11 * to utter our *g·* to you
36–18 * pour out our *g·* to God

real

My. 352–10 * we know that the real *g·* is

sense of

Mis. 131–23 that loving sense of *g·*

tears of

My. 314–27 with tears of *g·*

tenderest

My. 37– 8 * from the depths of tenderest *g·*,

thanks and

My. 51–30 * heartfelt thanks and *g·*

to God

Mis. xi– 9 one's debt of *g·* to God,
My. 36–18 * pour out our *g·* to God
362–19 * hearts filled with *g·* to God,

Pul. 85– 6 * *g·* to her for her great work,
My. 30–18 * in *g·* for the epoch-making event.
164–11 What is *g·* but a powerful

gratuitous

Mis. 349–27 or to receive my *g·* services,
Rud. 14–12 in order to do *g·* work.

gratuitously

Mis. 11– 8 taught indigent students *g·*,
247–15 unwilling to be taught it, even *g·*.
My. 122– 1 advice that one *g·* bestows
204–20 I practised *g·* when starting

grave

Mis. 12– 5 throughout time and beyond the *g·*.
74–25 His triumph over the *g·*
96– 3 robbed the *g·* of victory
104– 5 to death, or the *g·*.
146–15 These are matters of *g·* import ;
163– 6 a *g·* to mortal sense dishonored
234–22 is matter of *g·* wonderment
291– 5 but the notion . . . is a *g·* mistake ;
330– 4 to moan over the new-made *g·*,
339–29 Change and the *g·* may part us ;
388–14 *G·* on her monumental pile :
392–12 A lesson *g·*, of life,
400– 6 *G·*, silent, steadfast stone,
Un. 30–20 victorious over death and the *g·*.
48–11 robs the *g·* of its victory.
Peo. 5–14 overcome death and the *g·*,
Po. 15–21 love that outliveth the *g·*,
20–16 A lesson *g·*, of life,
21– 1 *G·* on her monumental pile :
73–15 Pleasant a *g·* By the "Rock"
76–17 *G·*, silent, steadfast stone,
My. 5–18 rob the *g·* of its victory.
125– 4 annual meeting is a *g·* guardian.
191–23 and the *g·* its victory.
218–15 absolved from death and the *g·*.
315–28 from the *cradle* and the *g·*,
355– 6 *g·* need for more men in C. S.

grave-clothes

Mis. 370– 8 risen from the *g·* of tradition
My. 191–17 With *g·* laid aside,

graven

Mis. 28–23 does not signify a *g·* idol,
218–25 and matter's *g·* grins
335– 2 shall you turn . . . to *g·* images?
346–15 an image *g·* on wood or stone

graves

Mis. 170– 5 weep over the *g·* of their beloved ;
Po. 16–20 'Mid *g·* do I hear the glad voices
My. 36–14 * or withheld from open *g·*

graveyards

Pul. 30– 7 * but from the *g·* !
66– 9 * proceeds more from the *g·*

gravitate

Mis. 267–22 must *g·* from sense to Soul,
Ret. 76–10 *g·* naturally toward Truth.

gravitating

My. 154–29 not looking nor *g·* earthward,

gravitation

Mis. 23– 1 Newton named it *g·*,
23– 3 what is the power back of *g·*,
256–22 to speak of *g·* as a law of matter ;
Un. 35–13 *Force.* What is *g·*?
35–13 Mortal mind says *g·* is a

gravitations

Mis. 19–26 of material and spiritual *g·*,

gray

Mis. 340–14 forsook Blackstone for *g·* stone,
376–23 softened, grew *g·*, then gay,
Pul. 24–22 * Concord granite in light *g·*,
39–21 * angels, on the *g·* church tower,
65–16 * beautiful structure of *g·* granite,

gray

Peo. 14– 6 *g·* stones of church-yards
Po. 53– 2 paint the *g·*, stark trees,
My. 68–19 * auditorium is of a warm *g·*,
78– 5 * imposing structure of *g·* stone
78–11 * an interior done in soft *g·*
85–30 * its noble dome of pure *g·* tint,

grayest

My. 87–23 * sunshine on the *g·* day.

gray-haired

My. 310–23 * her father, a *g·* man of fifty,

grayish

My. 342–13 * whether blue-gray or *g·* brown,

great

Mis. 2– 8 causing *g·* obscuration of Spirit.
4–25 "It must require a *g·* deal of faith
6–26 *g·* caution is observed in regard to
7– 7 *G·* charity and humility is necessary
7–32 enlightened on this *g·* subject.
9–29 *g·* and only danger
14–32 he makes a *g·* reality of evil,
15– 7 *g·* Nazarene Prophet said,
24– 5 came to me in an hour of *g·* need ;
30–16 *g·* Way-shower illustrated Life
38–11 is it a *g·* thing if we — *I Cor. 9 : 11.*
43–19 qualify students for the *g·* ordeal
47–22 This *g·* Truth does not destroy
51– 5 *accompanied by g· mental depression,*
53–25 their *g·* lack of spirituality.
54–26 *as g· miracles in healing as Jesus*
63–17 the *g·* reality that concerns man,
65–16 Life and its *g·* realities.
77– 6 *g·* truths asserted of the Messiah :
77–15 This is the Father's *g·* love
79–17 If the *g·* cause is perfect,
107–11 More love is the *g·* need of
110–28 fleeting is that which men call *g·* ;
120–12 achieved *g·* guerdons in the
120–14 a *g·* freedom for the race :
120–28 Biblical record of the *g·* Nazarene,
124–13 "who is so *g·* a God — *Psal. 77 : 13.*
124–25 Love's *g·* legacy to mortals :
127–18 *g·* growth in C. S. will follow,
131– 9 *g·* struggles with perplexities
132–16 the *g·* demand upon my time,
133–28 affords *g·* joy to be able to
143–18 It gives me *g·* pleasure to say
144–17 shadow of a *g·* rock — *Isa. 32 : 2.*
150– 3 already you have the *g·* Shepherd
151–14 our Minister and the *g·* Physician :
153–12 *g·* was the company of — *Psal. 68 : 11.*
156–14 no advantage, but *g·* disadvantage,
157– 2 *g·* thing to be found worthy to
173–12 Mind is its own *g·* cause and effect.
176– 6 *g·* theme so deeply and solemnly
176– 8 chiefly in the *g·* crises of nations
176–26 *g·* opportunities and responsibilities
177– 4 *g·* battle of Armageddon is upon us.
182–24 their place in God's *g·* love,
183– 3 In the *g·* forever,
187– 4 The *g·* Metaphysician wrought,
191–24 original devil was a *g·* talker,
192–17 his words reveal the *g·* Principle
201–13 *g·* somethingness of the good
204–20 *g·* demands of spiritual sense
205–29 man born of the *g·* Forever,
222– 7 causes the victim *g·* physical
224–19 everything beautiful, *g·*, and good,
228– 9 To be a *g·* man or woman,
230– 4 A *g·* amount of time is consumed
238– 8 no sacrifice is too *g·* for the
241– 9 the *g·* alterative, Truth :
252–23 rules and practice of the *g·* healer
253– 3 bought with a price, a *g·* price ;
253–17 *g·* red dragon that stood ready to
254–18 Envy, the *g·* red dragon of this hour,
258– 4 Our *g·* Ensample, Jesus of Nazareth,
263– 0 shadow of a *g·* rock — *Isa. 32 : 2.*
269–30 heard the *g·* Red Dragon *whispering*
275–13 May the *g·* Shepherd that
278– 8 *g·* joy in this consciousness,
280–28 *g·* import to the student of C. S.,
287–31 *G·* mischief comes from attempts **to**
292–26 *g·* good, both seen and unseen ;
295–18 statements of the *g·* unknown
304–13 * any *g·* patriotic celebration
304–24 * days on which *g·* events have
312–10 chapter sub-title
317– 9 *g·* pleasure in instructing,
321–26 the *g·* wonder of the world,
322–14 *g·* Shepherd that feedeth my flock,
338– 3 brings to humanity some *g·* good,
338–31 * A *g·* and noble creed.''
340–26 lives of *g·* men and women

great

Mis.	357– 7	have lost their *g·* Shepherd
	357–28	true fold and the *g·* Shepherd,
	358–10	his shield and *g·* reward.
	360– 6	*G·* only as good,
	361–17	To this *g·* end, Paul admonished,
	363– 2	*g·* reality of divine Mind and
	371– 6	care of the *g·* Shepherd,
	373–15	One *g·* master clearly delineates
	374– 1	so *g·* a proof of Immanuel
	374–18	To him who brought a *g·* light
	375–12	* old masters and their *g·* works
	379–24	solution of this *g·* question :
Man.	41– 6	*g·* gulf between C. S. and theosophy,
Chr.	53–46	The *g·* I Am,
	55– 8	have seen a *g·* light :— *Isa.* 9 : 2.
Ret.	25– 1	the *g·* curative Principle,— Deity.
	25–29	our *g·* Master's purpose in not
	26– 8	*g·* Way-shower, steadfast to the end
	27– 8	Mind-healing, like all *g·* truths,
	31–12	the one *g·* and ever-present relief
	44–27	a *g·* revival of mutual love,
	49– 8	*g·* need is for more of the spirit
	49–23	for her *g·* and noble work,
	60–15	and there is a *g·* calm.
	68– 8	The *g·* difference between these
	71– 7	*G·* temptations beset an ignorant
	81–22	how *g·* is that darkness !"— *Matt.* 6 : 23.
	91–13	Where did Jesus deliver this *g·* lesson
	91–14	this series of *g·* lessons
Un.	5–10	personal opinion on so *g·* a matter,
	5–14	"*G·* is the mystery of — *I Tim.* 3 : 16.
	19–15	how *g·* is that darkness !"— *Matt.* 6 : 23.
Pul.	1–13	*g·* is the value thereof.
	6–18	* turned to the '*g·* Physician.'
	12–14	having *g·* wrath,— *Rev.* 12 : 12.
	12–20	nearer to the *g·* heart of Christ ;
	14–27	*g·* benefit which Mind has wrought.
	14–28	the *g·* delusion of mortal mind,
	20–19	shadow of a *g·* rock — *Isa.* 32 : 2.
	23– 9	* The "*g·* awakening" of the time
	26–12	* The *g·* organ comes from Detroit.
	26–26	* Before the *g·* bay window
	27–20	* Another *g·* window tells its
	31–27	* with *g·* claim to personal beauty.
	37– 2	* the *g·* daily that is so fair
	37– 8	* retains in a *g·* degree her energy
	39– 2	* *g·* essentials of love to God and
	41–23	* the chimes in the *g·* stone tower,
	46–14	* identified with good and *g·* names
	47– 7	* *g·* circulation with the members of
	51– 4	* a *g·* privilege in these days.
	51–28	* alongside other *g·* demonstrations
	52–20	* The Master was the *g·* healer.
	56–25	* A *g·* C. S. church was dedicated
	62– 7	* *g·* economy of space,
	62–17	* beauties of a *g·* cathedral chime,
	63–19	* *g·* hold she has upon this army
	64–16	* search for the *g·* curative Principle.
	67– 6	* said by a *g·* American writer.
	70–20	* to find the *g·* curative Principle
	72– 1	* inspired in her *g·* task
	72–28	* one *g·* essential that we have faith
	75–22	* in the *g·* New England capital
	81–18	* soars and sings to the *g·* sun.
	82– 2	* brain for its *g·* white throne.
	83–27	* a *g·* wonder in heaven, — *Rev.* 12 : 1.
Rud.	8– 1	confounding the three *g·* kingdoms.
No.	9– 2	have prevented, to a *g·* extent,
	9–15	too *g·* leniency, on my part.
	25– 1	uttering this *g·* thought is not enough !
	25– 3	won through *g·* tribulation
	32–18	Good is *g·* and real.
	32–23	*g·* evil to belie and belittle C. S.,
Pan.	3–15	* envy of the *g·* !
	10– 4	*g·* Nazarene Prophet said,
	14–27	*G·* occasion have we to rejoice
'00.	7–14	This is my *g·* reward for
	9–28	fit others for this *g·* responsibility.
	12–30	phase of a *g·* controversy,
'01.	1–13	*g·* realities of being,
	17–14	and started the *g·* Cause
	18–22	*g·* master Metaphysician's precept
	19–16	*g·* Metaphysician healed the sick,
	24–15	and *g·* was the fall
	25–17	*g·* Metaphysician, Christ Jesus,
	26– 3	the *g·* teacher, preacher, and
	27–27	* "Every *g·* scientific truth goes
	28– 2	the *g·* naturalist's prophecy.
	30–25	*g·* heart of the unselfed Christian
'02.	5–17	have answered this *g·* question
	11–25	for *g·* is your reward — *Matt.* 5 : 12
	14– 9	* "*G·* not like Cæsar, stained
	14–10	* But only *g·* as I am good."
	14–18	beginning of the *g·* battle
	14–24	nor protection in the *g·* struggle.

great

'02.	14–25	prospered preeminently our *g·* Cause,
	15–14	entering upon my *g·* life-work,
	18–22	prophecy of the *g·* Teacher
	20–21	*g·* joy to look into the faces of
Hea.	1–12	the *g·* subject of Christian healing ;
	3–20	*g·* goodness and wonderful works
	11–12	the *g·* pyramid of Egypt,
	14– 9	*G·* caution should be exercised
Peo.	1– 3	*g·* element of reform is not
	6–26	something of that *g·* good
	13– 6	this *g·* impersonal Life, Truth, and
Po.	2–11	*G·* as thou art,
	22–14	how *g·*, how good Thou art
	26–11	Lincoln's own *G·* willing heart
	39–19	"Social," or grand, or *g·*,
	43–10	Father, in Thy *g·* heart hold them
My.	6–11	"for *g·* is [our] reward — *see Matt.* 5 : 12.
	18–15	*g·* growth in C. S. will follow,
	25– 2	* there would be *g·* propriety in
	25– 7	* *g·* interest exhibited by the children
	29–20	* dome of the *g·* edifice
	31–11	* first glimpse of the *g·* structure,
	31–31	* the *g·* body of Scientists
	41– 1	* how *g·* no man can number
	42–20	* It affords me *g·* pleasure to
	42–25	* how *g·* is the work that has
	45–13	* The *g·* temple is finished !
	45–28	* The *g·* temple is finished !
	46– 3	* the *g·* structure stands,
	47–10	* has grown to *g·* magnitude,
	47–17	* inception of this *g·* Cause,
	49– 7	* *g·* chance of sweeping the world
	50–18	* trust in the *g·* Father,
	54–21	* desire for services was so *g·*
	57– 5	* of *g·* seating capacity,
	58–17	* gratitude of a *g·* multitude
	60–25	* Now that the *g·* event,
	61–26	* stood under the *g·* dome,
	68– 4	* The *g·* auditorium, with its
	68– 5	* tops of *g·* stone piers,
	68–21	* *g·* organ is placed back of the
	68–26	* plaster work for the *g·* arches
	71–11	* *g·* adornment to the city.
	71–27	* in front of the *g·* organ.
	73–12	* chapter sub-title
	75–13	* of a *g·* number of visitors
	76–26	* first *g·* monument to C. S.,
	77– 1	* because of its *g·* size,
	77– 8	* its dimensions are only half as *g·*.
	78–29	* awed by the grandeur of the *g·* room
	80–25	* to accommodate the *g·* throngs
	81– 3	* prosperity of the *g·* congregation.
	81–23	* song rose tingling to the *g·* dome,
	83– 3	* the holding of a *g·* convention
	84–17	* near to another *g·* demonstration
	85–22	* the *g·* centre of attraction,
	86–15	* building fund of the *g·* temple
	86–28	* *g·* size of the auditorium
	87–13	* a *g·* gathering of people
	88– 4	* opening of their *g·* new temple.
	88–28	* debt to that *g·* and growing cult,
	88–29	* in the building of a *g·* church
	90– 2	* hundreds of *g·* buildings
	90–27	* Founder of a *g·* denomination
	93– 5	* dedication of their *g·* church
	93–28	* by the *g·* meeting of the church
	95–15	* During the *g·* assembly of
	95–19	* faith of these people is certainly *g·*.
	99– 2	* *g·*, and really good things
	99– 7	* with so *g·* an aggregation of
	104– 7	*g·* master of metaphysics,
	106–30	Our *g·* Exemplar, the Nazarene
	113–32	truly *g·* men and women
	123– 5	The *g·* guerdon of divine Love,
	129– 3	I reluctantly foresee *g·* danger
	131–12	signet of the *g·* heart,
	131–30	this *g·*, *g·* blessing ;
	133– 3	in the *g·* light of the present,
	138– 5	a *g·* benefit to me already.
	146–15	heights of the *g·* Nazarene's sayings
	153–16	*g·* and first commandment,
	164–18	A *g·* sanity, a mighty something
	166– 2	efforts to be *g·* will never end in
	176– 8	God grant that such *g·* goodness,
	177–19	the *g·* Shepherd has nurtured
	180–28	in the spirit of our *g·* Exemplar
	183– 5	in this *g·* city of Chicago,
	186–27	gives me *g·* pleasure to know
	190–15	asked their *g·* Teacher,
	194– 2	broad facts over *g·* continents
	197–13	*g·* hearts and ready hands of our
	198– 6	*g·* gratitude to our one Father.
	203–12	Be *g·* not as a grand obelisk,
	203–13	nor by setting up to be *g·*,
	204–21	when starting this *g·* Cause,

great

My.	217–28	Thus it is that our *g·* Exemplar,
	219–19	Bible record of our *g·* Master's life
	219–23	the *g·* demonstrator of C. S.,
	220–25	example of the *g·* Galilean Prophet,
	221–12	so *g·* and good as Christ Jesus.
	222–17	his *g·* demands on the faith of
	234–18	both sides of the *g·* question
	234–21	all our *g·* Master's sayings
	236–28	*g·* importance at this stage
	244–12	the *g·* need of which I daily discern.
	248– 5	* "*G·*, not like Caesar, stained
	248– 6	* But only *g·* as I am good."
	248– 7	You are not setting up to be *g·* ;
	262–20	the reminder of God's *g·* gift,
	267–10	infinite, the *g·* for ever,
	267–28	Our *g·* Teacher hath said :
	272–25	* plays so *g·* a part in the world
	272–27	* and leads . . . her very *g·* following.
	273– 9	* a very *g·* organization
	279–25	God bless that *g·* nation
	284– 1	never fastens on the good or the *g·*.
	285– 9	crowns the *g·* purposes of life
	288–12	The *g·* Galilean Prophet was,
	294–29	passed . . . into the *g·* forever.
	304–25	* "Every *g·* scientific truth
	306– 6	philosophy of a *g·* and good man,
	306–11	than to be thought *g·*.
	308–30	my father was a *g·* reader.
	309–16	slavery he regarded as a *g·* sin.
	317– 9	It is a *g·* mistake to say that I
	322–28	* my *g·* interest in the subject,
	338–20	*g·* Teacher of Christianity,
	339– 8	discoursing on the *g·* subject
	347–17	our *g·* Master's first disciples,
	349–17	*g·* Way-shower, invested with glory,
		(*see also* **fact, Master, truth, work**)

Great Britain (*see also* **Britain**)

Mis.	295–27	Philosophical Society of *G· B·*,
Man.	94–19	in Canada, in *G· B·* and Ireland.
	97– 0	Canada, *G· B·* and Ireland.
	00– 6	Each county of *G· B·* and Ireland,
	99–23	Committees on Publication for *G· B·*
Pul.	5–24	same in *G· B·*, France, Germany,
Po.	page 10	poem
My.	77–12	* from Canada, from *G· B·*,
	259– 6	From . . . in London, *G· B·*,
	289–15	Victoria, Queen of *G· B·*
	289–29	Victoria, Queen of *G· B·*
	337– 2	poem

greater

Mis.	7–25	*g·* work yet remains to be done.
	65– 9	concerning the *g·* subject of
	111–23	but no *g·* difference existed
	121–28	*g·* than human pity, is divine Love.
	145–11	Am I *g·* for them?
	192–11	*g· works than these — John* 14 : 12.
	251–13	but a *g·* even, the liberty of
	261–21	No *g·* type of divine Love can be
	293–18	brings *g·* torment than ignorance.
	000–23	To a *g·* or less extent, all mortal
	370– 7	*g·* spirit of Christ is also abroad,
Ret.	80–26	no *g·* miracles known to earth
	95– 2	blossom into *g·* freedom,
Un.	6– 1	and the whole is *g·* than its parts.
Pul.	67–10	* show a *g·* number of them
	75– 6	a *g·* degree of this spirit
No.	13–19	No *g·* opposites can be conceived of,
	22–17	*g·* than the corporeality we behold.
	33–15	the brief agony of the cross ;
Pan.	8–20	"My Father is *g·* than I." — *John* 14 : 28.
'00.	4–12	indicate a renaissance *g·* than
	7– 6	*g·* love of the Scriptures
'01.	2– 4	*g·* power in the perfected Science
	8– 8	"my Father is *g·* than I," — *John* 14 : 28.
Peo.	9–20	showing our *g·* faith in matter,
My.	21–18	* will receive a *g·* blessing
	52–10	* each and all, will make *g·* efforts
	87– 1	* the attendance was *g·* than
	123– 3	love is the *g·* marvel,
	164–25	into the *g·* and better,
	209– 5	No *g·* hope have we than
	228–13	none *g·* had been born of women
	228–15	is *g·* than he." — *Matt.* 11 : 11.
	253– 5	what *g·* glory can nerve your
	258–18	gifts *g·* than those of Magian kings,
	325–10	* as having a *g·* future
	344– 5	God the Father is *g·* than Christ,

Greater New York (*see also* **New York**)

My.	362–14	* C. S. churches . . . of *G· N· Y·*,
	363–15	C. S. churches in *G· N· Y·*

greatest

Mis.	5–14	not fail in the *g·* emergencies.
	111– 1	proven that the *g·* piety

greatest

Mis.	130–24	*g·* sin that one can commit
	177– 3	*g·* and holiest of all causes.
	268– 4	Who shall be *g·*?
	288–4, 5	the *g·* good to the *g·* number,
	303–12	"who shall be *g·*." — *see Mark* 9 : 34.
	337–14	*g·* in the kingdom of — *Matt.* 18 : 4.
	357–20	*g·* of all stages and states of
	358–25	the *g·* work of the ages,
	363– 7	its *g·* flatterer, identification,
Ret.	75– 3	Who shall be *g·*?
	82–15	the *g·* good to the *g·* number,
	91– 4	and our Master's *g·* utterance
Pul.	20–17	the *g·* moral, physical, civil,
	54–17	* *g·* good could be accomplished."
	73–11	* one of the *g·* Biblical scholars
'00.	10– 5	new birth of the *g·* and best.
'01.	16–25	its *g·* discoverer is a woman
	24–11	* *g·* of all temporal blessings,
	26–20	the *g·* of which is charity
'02.	4– 3	"Who shall be *g·*?" — *see Mark* 9 : 34.
Hea.	9– 8	The *g·* sinner and the most
My.	12–18	lost opportunity is the *g·* of losses.
	45– 7	* *g·* and most important
	89–29	* *g·* religious phenomenon
	159–12	*g·* man or woman on earth
	228–12	Who shall be *g·*?
	228–17	he that hath . . . shall be *g·*.
	240– 2	from the least to the *g·*,
	305–29	"Who shall be *g·*?" — *see Mark* 9 : 34.
	306–12	The *g·* reform, . . . must wait to
	348– 8	*g·* of all questions was solved

great-grandfather

Ret.	1– 2	my *g·*, on my father's side,

great-grandmother

Ret.	1– 4	my *g·*, was Marion Moor,
	1–11	were written by my *g·*.
	1–11	because my *g·* wrote a

greatly

Mis.	35–25	it is *g·* to your advantage
	57–15	*g·* multiply thy sorrow." — *Gen.* 3 : 16.
	127– 7	One thing I have *g·* desired,
	137–14	I *g·* rejoice over the growth of
	139–27	in future be regarded as *g·* wise,
	308– 7	*g·* errs, stops his own progress, and
	327–14	which must *g·* hinder their ascent.
	358– 1	Love is *g·* needed, and must be had
Ret.	8–17	*G·* surprised, my cousin turned
	13– 6	predestination, *g·* troubled me ;
	50– 7	This amount *g·* troubled me.
Un.	53– 6	and *g·* to be desired,
Pul.	38– 7	* *g·* revised and enlarged,
	51–16	* and how *g·* it will affect the
	71–14	* startled and *g·* discomfited
Peo.	11–22	*g·* responsible for all the woes
My.	6–15	*G·* impressed and encouraged
	18– 4	"One thing I have *g·* desired,
	23–23	* We rejoice *g·* that the walls
	130–20	you have been *g·* recompensed.
	174– 5	I *g·* appreciate the courtesy
	175–17	*g·* needs improved streets.
	220–28	*g·* improved human nature
	236–29	it will *g·* aid the students
	328–10	* *g·* pleased at the law

greatness

Mis.	270–25	pathway of goodness and *g·*
	331–11	its springtide of freedom and *g·*.
	340–28	in the constellation of human *g·*,
Pul.	39– 6	* God's *g·* flows around our
No.	8–16	struggle into freedom and *g·*,
	46–22	health, *g·*, and goodness,
'00.	10– 6	*g·* of a cause or of an individual,
My.	118–11	outpouring of goodness and *g·*
	123– 7	hearts of men to goodness and *g·*,
	150– 6	character of true *g·*:
	194–11	Only those men and women gain *g·*
	272– 4	Goodness is *g·*,
	306–12	Time and goodness determine *g·*.

great organ

(*see* **organ**)

Grecian

Mis.	260– 6	Pagan mysticism, *G·* philosophy,
Ret.	86– 9	as said the classic *G·* motto.

Greece

Pul.	5–25	*G·*, Japan, India, and China ;
	5–27	in the Academy of *G·*,

greed

My.	257–20	all human hate, pride, *g·*, lust

Greek

Mis.	1– 2	ancient *G·* looked longingly for
	190–29	in the *G·*, Apollyon, serpent, liar,
Ret.	10–10	Hebrew, *G·*, and Latin.
Pul.	46–26	* Hebrew, *G·*, and Latin.

Greek

Pan.	2–11	derived from two G· words
	2–23	*Pan* is a G· prefix,
'01.	16–13	In the G· *devil* is named *serpent*
Hea.	6–28	*devil* comes from the G· *diabolos;*
My.	288–14	G· philosophy, creed, dogma, or
	305–24	not of the G· nor of the Roman

Greeks

Mis.	248– 9	G· showed a just estimate of

Greek Testament

Mis.	26–26	is, in the G· T·, *character.*

green

Mis.	129–18	for other g· eyes to gaze on :
	153–10	g· isles of refreshment,
	227–24	mind can rest in g· pastures,
	257–27	desolating the g· earth.
	329– 8	putting down the g· ones,
Ret.	4–19	g· pastures bright with berries,
Pul.	26–25	* The room is toned in pale g·
	48– 2	* g· stretches of lawns,
	76– 7	* pale g· and gold decoration
	76–10	* rich hangings of deep g· plush,
	78–24	* satin-lined box of rich g· velvet.
Po.	25– 9	From your g· bowers free,
	41–13	From the g· sunny slopes of the
My.	95– 2	* like a g· bay-tree,
	129–26	g· pastures beside still waters,
	162–26	into "g· pastures — *Psal.* 23 : 2.
	173–27	visitors to assemble on the g·
	257– 1	g· branches of the Christmas-tree.

greenness

Pul.	48– 9	* spring and summer g·.

greensward

My.	174– 4	soft g· proved an ideal
	193– 6	the g· and gorgeous skies

greenwood

Po.	34–17	Unto thy g· home

greet

Mis.	251– 6	beloved brethren, . . . I g· you ;
	384– 4	And true hearts g·,
Pul.	61–15	* Beautiful suggestions g· you
Po.	36– 3	And true hearts g·,
My.	302–27	members wanted to g· me

greeted

Mis.	311– 4	g· as brethren endeavoring to
My.	169–20	time and place which g· them.
	171–24	* g· in behalf of the church

greeting

My.	8–23	* chapter sub-title
	8–26	* send our g· to you,
	23–16	* G· to *Mrs. Eddy from the*
	86– 1	* the g· of admiring eyes,
	163–16	chapter sub-title
	341– 8	chapter sub-title
	341–10	your Leader's Spring g·,
	342– 5	* after a kindly g· took a seat

greetings

Mis.	319–19	accept my tender g·
	387–22	g· glorious from high heaven,
Pul.	1– 6	and encumbered with g·
Po.	6–17	g· glorious from high heaven,
My.	23–20	* their loyal and loving g·
	44–26	* convey to you their sincere g·
	62–20	* send you loving g·
	63–18	* even the g· and congratulations
	94–25	* she sent g· in which she
	142–17	and merge into a meeting for g·.
	171–21	* the silent g· of the people
	175–10	chapter sub-title
	207– 9	* unite in loving g· to you,
	259– 9	* Christmas g· from members
	362–18	* send you their loving g·.

greets

Mis.	177–29	g· with joy a familiar face.

grew

Mis.	164–20	g· in the understanding of Christ,
	164–21	it g· in favor with them.
	231–12	turkey g· beautifully less.
	376–23	softened, g· gray, then gay,
Ret.	8–11	until I g· discouraged,
	23– 6	pungent lessons . . . g· sterner.
	26–13	g· divinely natural and
	43– 4	From this seed g· the
	73–10	human concept g· beautifully less
Un.	59–14	and g· to manhood,
My.	56–22	* The Mother Church steadily g·,
	343–20	and trust in me g·.

grief

Mis.	397–13	From tired joy and g· afar,
Ret.	7–19	* with the most poignant g·,
Un.	18–13	Error says you must know g·

grief

Un.	55– 5	and acquainted with g·," — *Isa.* 53 : 3.
Pul.	1– 6	redolent with g· and gratitude.
	18–22	From tired joy and g· afar,
'00.	11–17	measures himself against deeper g·.
Po.	9– 5	unsealed fountains of g· and joy
	13– 1	From tired joy and g· afar,
	25–16	Whose heart bore its g·
	78–13	in the Christ hallowed its g·,
My.	258–24	all depths of love, g·, death,

grieve

Mis.	325–24	g· Him in the desert." — *Psal.* 78 : 40

grim

Mis.	339–16	with finger g· and cold it points
Chr.	53– 3	O'er the g· night of chaos
Po.	26–13	phantom finger, g· and cold,

grin

Mis.	216–21	* and ending with the g·,
	216–29	* a g· without a cat."
	218–22	"g· without a cat ;"
	218–23	a g· expresses the nature of a cat,

grind

Ret.	80– 8	* mills of God g· slowly,
	80– 9	* Yet they g· exceeding small ;

grinds

Ret.	80–11	* With exactness g· He all.

grins

Mis.	218–26	matter's graven g· are neither

grips

My.	90–11	* g· hold of their faith

groan

Mis.	231–10	spiritual g· for the unfeasted ones.

grooves

Mis.	104–18	The latter move in God's g·
	322–27	laboring in its widening g·
My.	107–21	nearer the g· of omnipotence.

groped

Mis.	326–29	one who had g· his way

groping

Ret.	27–18	* G· blindly in the darkness,

Gross, Mr.

My.	42–12	* Mr. G·, on assuming office, said :

gross

Po.	47– 7	Ever the g· world above ;
My.	48–23	* The scorn of the g· and sensual,

Gross, C.S.B.

Willis F.

My.	39–15	* President, Willis F. G·, C.S.B. ;
	42– 7	* Willis F. G·, C.S.B.,

grosser

Peo.	2– 6	yields its g· elements,

grossly

Mis.	39– 8	g· incorrect and false teachers

grot

Ret.	17– 6	soft echoes to kindle the g·.
Po.	62– 6	soft echoes to kindle the g·.

grotto

Ret.	18– 9	Midst g· and songlet
Po.	63–18	Midst g· and songlet

grottos

Mis.	323–21	rest in its cool g·,
Peo.	14– 5	cool g·, smiling fountains,

ground

Mis.	xi–19	intolerance will fall to the g·,
	27–15	accept divine Science on this g·?
	127–27	garrulous talk may fall to the g·,
	151–12	cumbereth it the g·?" — *Luke* 13 : 7.
	195–21	it cannot fall to the g·
	234–19	ventured on such unfamiliar g·,
	240–15	as it takes the frost out of the g·
	349–13	on the g· that it was inconsistent
	357–14	They fall on stony g·
Man.	64–19	consented on the g· that this
Ret.	35–21	too immanent to fall to the g·
Pul.	1–16	whereon thou troddest was holy g· ;
	24– 9	* on a triangular plot of g·,
	39– 1	* that all meet on common g·
	49–11	* of most unpromising g·
No.	4–11	On the g· that harmony is the truth
	27–26	tread lightly, for this is holy g·.
Pan.	10– 1	on the g· that it takes away
Po.	26– 5	where thou hast trod is holy g·.
My.	43–20	* came over this Jordan on dry g·.
	55–12	* Mrs. Eddy gave the plot of g·
	268– 6	marriage relation is losing g·,
	269–25	fruits of your g·." — *Mal.* 3 : 11.
	308–17	* regularly beating the g· with a
	314–15	on the g· of desertion,
	336– 7	* she declined on this g·,

grounded
Un. 6–14 Until . . . is firmly g·,
groundless
Mis. 266–20 is utterly false and g·.
grounds
Mis. 68–28 * regards the ultimate g· of being,
Pul. 49–29 * a number of men to keep the g·
Rud. 12– 8 on false g·,
My. 111– 9 on practically the same g·
groundwork
Mis. 264– 7 without the g· of right,
Un. 25–23 therefore has no g· in Life,
group
Mis 230–27 It was a beautiful g· !
My. 162– 7 A small g· of wise thinkers
257–25 I g· you in one benison
355–22 the happiest g· on earth.
355–26 happy g· of Christian Scientists ;
groups
Po. 8– 3 In somber g· at the vesper-call,
My. 87–21 * cheerful looking g· of people
grove
Mis. 390–13 Through woodland, g·, and dell ;
395–15 Written in childhood, in a maple g·
Ret. 91–25 The g· became his class-room,
Po. vi–28 * (written in a maple g·),
34– 8 In what dark leafy g·
55–14 Through woodland, g·, and dell ;
59– 9 Written in girlhood, in a maple g·.
groves
Mis. 330– 2 make melody through dark pine g·.
Ret. 4–18 requiems through dark pine g·.
grow
Mis. 86–30 we must g· out of even this
136– 9 so g· upon my vision that I
Un. 14–12 commanded to g· in grace.
14–13 Was it necessary for God to g·
No. v–12 until you g· to apprehend the
37– 2 had to g·, develop ;
Hea. 6– 2 and we g· more material,
Peo. 3–27 whereby we g· out of sin
7–31 our methods g· more spiritual
Po. 27– 6 Ere thou g· tremulous
27–13 let today g· difficult and vast
67– 3 G· cold in this spot as the
My. 11–10 * g· into readiness for each step,
17– 7 ye may g· thereby :— I Pet. 2 : 2.
91–25 * church has continued to g·.
122– 9 the plant will continue to g·.
213–23 you will g· wiser and better
216–20 As you g· older, advance in the
groweth
My. 24–14 * g· unto an holy temple— Eph. 2 : 21.
growing
Mis. 239– 8 my shadow is not g· less ;
255–11 g· into, that altitude of Mind
265–28 g· out of the departures from
273–21 g· interest in C. S. Mind-healing.
284–19 This g· sin must now be dealt with
297–21 g· out of this contract,
324–20 g· more and more troubled,
337–18 a g· affection for all good,
348–17 the g· flames of falsehood,
365–24 the g· wants of humanity.
Ret. 18–26 alder g· from the bent branch
31– 4 solemn certainty in g· freedom
48– 7 and the g· conviction
71–23 tares g· side by side with the
76–27 a g· evil in plagiarism ;
Pul. 14– 3 g· occultism of this period.
56– 5 * a large and g· number
67–19 * and is rapidly g·.
No. 19– 6 the g· wants of humanity.
Po. 63–24 g· from the bent branch
My. 55– 9 * the attendance rapidly g·
88–28 * that great and g· cult,
224–32 Our Cause is g· apace
342–20 It is g· wonderfully.
grown
Mis. 138–18 g· to know that human strength
159–25 g· to behold Thee !
165– 4 he had g· beyond the
262–18 encouraging the heart g· faint
358–27 who have g· to self-sacrifice
Ret. 38–23 g· disgusted with my printer,
Un. 2–24 their lives have g· so far toward
Pul. 30–27 * within fifteen years it has g·
66– 6 * number of believers has g·
Peo. 4–26 g· out of such false ideals
14– 8 have g· more spiritual ;
Po. 71– 4 and guilt, g· bold,
My. 47–10 * has g· to great magnitude,

grown
My. 99–24 * The denomination has g·
172– 5 * g· on the farm of Mark Baker,
312–15 * She was a g· woman,
grows
Mis. ix–20 youth that never g· old ;
16– 6 g· into the manhood or womanhood
128– 2 variety of turns, else it g· hard
227–28 g· into the full stature of wisdom,
254–12 g· weak with wickedness
265– 5 He g· dark, and cannot regain,
284–26 Evil let alone g· more real,
339–15 if it yields not, g· stronger.
347–12 theirs g· indistinct and ends.
398–13 So, when day g· dark and cold,
Ret. 46–19 So, when day g· dark and cold,
Un. 3–15 fruit which g· on the
Pul. 17–18 So, when day g· dark and cold,
Hea. 1– 6 to-morrow g· out of to-day.
Po. 14–17 when day g· dark and cold,
24–16 night g· deeply dark ;
My. 23–29 * the stately structure g·,
189–19 and faith g· wearisome,
283–18 grasp of goodness g· stronger.
growth
and decay
Mis. 362– 3 material birth, g·, and decay :
and establishment
My. 220–17 g· and establishment of
and experiences
Mis. 165–22 their own g· and experiences.
and progress
My. 8– 6 * our own g· and progress.
and prosperity
Mis. 291–13 equal g· and prosperity of all
'02. 14–13 g· and prosperity of C. S.
My. v– 6 * g· and prosperity of the Cause
175–12 g· and prosperity of our city
and understanding
Mis. 156–28 tests of g· and understanding
and vitality
My. 95–25 * religion of g· and vitality
consistent
My. 94–10 * consistent g· of the sect
continued
My. 56–31 * This continued g·, . . . proved
continues
My. 94– 1 * if the g· continues
desiring
Ret. 86–17 A student desiring g· in the
future
My. 48–13 * future g· of her church,
gained through
Mis. 206–12 gained through g·, not accretion ;
general
Mis. 138–20 general g· in the members
glorious
My. 20–18 glorious g· in C. S.
great
Mis. 127–18 great g· in C. S. will follow,
My. 18–15 great g· in C. S. will follow,
human
Mis. 286– 6 Until time matures human g·,
Ret. 49–13 in human g· material organization
in Christian Science
Mis. 127–18 great g· in C. S. will follow,
Ret. 49–11 principle for g· in C. S.
My. 18–15 great g· in C. S. will follow,
20–18 glorious g· in C. S.
individual
Mis. 98–14 individual g· of Christian Scientists,
98–18 it must begin with individual g·,
118–15 advance individual g·, nor
in love
My. 39–28 * our own g· in love and unity
in Science
Ret. 79–14 uproot the germs of g· in Science
is governed
Mis. 206–17 G· is governed by intelligence ;
is restricted
Mis. 359–12 G· is restricted by forcing humanity
its
My. 47–14 * epoch-marking stages of its g·,
91–25 * Its g· in numbers is remarkable,
92–27 * Its g· has been wonderfully rapid,
manifest
Mis. 86– 7 manifest g· at every experience.
mental
Mis. 357–19 third stage of mental g· is
of a faith
Pul. 65–12 * chapter sub-title
of attendance
My. 56–16 * room for g· of attendance
of Christian Science
Pul. 50–11 * The g· of C. S. is properly

growth
of Christian Scientists
   Mis. 98–14 individual *g·* of Christian Scientists,
   107–28 the *g·* of Christian Scientists.
of illusion
   Mis. 83– 8 *"Sickness is a g· of illusion,*
of its principles
   Pul. 51–24 * help on the *g·* of its principles.
of mankind
   Mis. 237–23 push on the *g·* of mankind.
of my students
   Mis. 137–14 rejoice over the *g·* of my students
of spirituality
   Mis. 154–13 as the *g·* of spirituality
of this Cause
   My. 58– 8 * magnificent *g·* of this Cause,
   58–12 * shows the *g·* of this Cause,
of this cult
   My. 85– 4 * *g·* of this cult is the marvel of
origin and
   Pul. 67– 4 * SKETCH OF ITS ORIGIN AND *G·*
our
   Mis. 267– 5 the best friends to our *g·.*
personal
   Mis. 356–28 indispensable to personal *g·,*
physical
   No. 13– 4 moral and physical *g·,*
present
   My. 47– 7 * church has reached its present *g·,*
prosperous
   My. 10–28 * prosperous *g·* of this movement
rapid
   Mis. 6–14 as the rapid *g·* of the work shows.
   Pul. 52–17 * rapid *g·* of the new movement.
   '01. 2–28 explains its rapid *g·.*
   My. 52–11 * while we realize the rapid *g·,*
remarkable
   My. 94–16 * remarkable *g·* and the apparent
rewarded by
   Mis. 84–11 motives were rewarded by *g·*
scientific
   Mis. 206–13 scientific *g·* manifests no weakness,
spiritual
   (*see* **spiritual**)
stages of
   Mis. 355–11 pass through three stages of *g·.*
strength and
   My. 83–28 * strength and *g·* of their organization,
strongest
   Ret. 82– 9 widest power and strongest *g·*
subject to
   Mis. 82–31 Mind, then, is not subject to *g·,*
swift
   My. 92–13 * swift *g·* of the new faith
their
   Mis. 223–22 no . . . influence can hinder their *g·*
   278–25 substitute my own for their *g·,*
this
   Pul. 66– 8 * This *g·,* it is said, proceeds
tremendous
   My. 93–24 * missed entirely its tremendous *g·*
wonderful
   My. 98– 4 * and this is the wonderful *g·*
your
   Mis. 206–26 Your *g·* will be rapid, if you
   '01. 1–12 most essential to your *g·*

   Mis. 138–24 *g·* of these at first is more gradual ;
   Un. 50–26 material origin, *g·,* maturity, and
   My. 84–18 * *g·* of the C. S. idea
   89–27 * The *g·* of this form of religious faith
   97–22 * *g·* of the new church
   124– 7 health, harmony, *g·,* grandeur, and
   148–25 it is a *g·* Christward ;
   229–20 beloved students, whose *g·* is
   245–10 The *g·* of human inquiry
gruel
   Mis. 225–31 * you shall have some *g·."*
grumbling
   Mis. 327–29 stumbling and *g·,* and fighting]
Grundmann Studio Building
   Pul. 29– 1 * in the new *G· S· B·*
guaranteed
   My. 167–25 rights and privileges *g·* to you
guard
   Mis. 114–31 how to *g·* against evil
   116–27 never off *g·,* never ill-humored,
   126– 9 has his own thoughts to *g·,*
   134–15 *g·* and guide His own.
   281– 5 will-power that you must *g·* against.
   307–29 must *g·* against the deification of
   312– 1 to *g·* against that temptation.
   400–16 *G·* me when I sleep ;
   Ret. 81– 5 we should *g·* thought and action,

guard
   Ret. 85–13 *G·* yourselves against the
   '02. 18– 2 gate of conscience, wakefully *g·* it ;
   Po. 43–12 Shield and guide and *g·* them ;
   69– 4 *G·* me when I sleep ;
   My. 130– 2 Watch and *g·* your own thoughts
   193–19 God *g·* and guide you.
   194–27 guide and *g·* you and your church
   213–19 Be ever on *g·* against this enemy.
   213–22 *G·* and strengthen your own citadel
   221–30 Truth and Life, can *g·* the entrance
   353–13 intended to hold *g·* over Truth,
guarded
   Ret. 89–20 *g·* them unto the end,
guardian
   Ret. 21– 3 a *g·* was appointed him,
   Pan. 3–27 *g·* of flocks and herds.
   My. 125– 4 our annual meeting is a grave *g·.*
   (*see also* **Eddy**)
guardians
   Mis. 347–20 *g·* of His presence go before me.
   Peo. 1–11 *g·* of the gloom are the angels of
   My. 261– 2 loving parents and *g·* of youth
guardianship
   Man. 75– 1 heading
   Rud. 15–18 with suitable and thorough *g·*
   My. 316–22 under Mr. Flower's able *g·*
guarding
   Ret. 18– 8 sentinel hedgerow is *g·* repose,
   Po. 63–17 sentinel hedgerow is *g·* repose,
   My. 86– 6 * brooding elevation, *g·* as it were,
   164–22 guiding, and *g·* your way
   182–23 *g·,* guiding, giving grace,
   261–11 *g·* and guiding well the
guards
   Mis. 150–31 He *g·,* guides, feeds,
   331–20 Love that *g·* the nestling's
   389– 8 Love that *g·* the nestling's
   '01. 14–22 even as one *g·* his door
   Po. 4– 5 Love that *g·* the nestling's
guard'st
   Mis. 392– 7 *G·* thou the earth,
   Po. 20– 9 *G·* thou the earth,
guerdon
   Mis. 118–16 *g·* of meritorious faith
   Po. 44– 3 With the *g·* of Thy bosom,
   My. 123– 5 The great *g·* of divine Love,
guerdons
   Mis. 120–12 and achieved great *g·*
guessing
   Ret. 33– 6 till I was weary of "scientific *g·,"*
   '01. 33–15 or a diploma for scientific *g·.*
   Peo. 6– 5 * "Medicine is the science of *g·."*
   11–27 Scientific *g·* conspires unwittingly
guesswork
   Mis. 355– 7 a healing that is not *g·,*
   My. 92–22 * ridiculed by the hostile as mere *g·,*
   94– 5 * ridiculed by the hostile as mere *g·,*
guest
   Po. 77–18 some dear lost *g·* Bears hence its
guestchamber and **guest-chamber**
   Mis. 342– 9 By entering the *g·* of Truth,
   My. 156–15 Where is the *g·,* — *Luke* 22 : 11.
guests
   Mis. 225– 6 Among the *g·,* were an orthodox
   231–13 to vie with *g·* in the dexterous use of
   '00. 14–29 ask who are to be the *g·.*
   15– 4 The *g·* are distinguished above human
   My. 74–26 * as the *g·* of the city,
   296–28 she depicted its rooms, *g·,*
   322–15 * when a friend and I were the *g·*
guidance
   Mis. 133–27 constantly to divine Love for *g·,*
   138–11 *g·* of our common Father
   194–24 accept God's power and *g·,*
   324–32 receive his heavenly *g·.*
   371– 9 *g·* of our common Father,
   Man. 40– 3 *g·* OF MEMBERS.
   Ret. 13–21 seeking His *g·*
   27–28 under the *g·* of the great Master.
   82–11 rest on divine Principle for *g·,*
   Un. 5–27 left to the supernal *g·.*
   Pul. 39– 1 * their best aid and *g·,*
   No. 7–26 discriminations and *g·* thereof
   My. 45–18 * *g·* of Him who went before
   142–12 I sought God's *g·* in doing it,
   150– 4 if thou seekest this *g·.*
   280– 5 * your watchful care and *g·*
   338–18 higher source for wisdom and *g·.*

Guide
(see **Eddy**)

guide
Mis.	64–17	ethics which *g·* thought spiritually
	134–15	guard and *g·* His own.
	136–21	S. and H. your teacher and *g·*.
	216– 2	to *g·* your own state of combat
	228– 1	safer *g·* than the promptings of
	287–24	God will *g·* you.
	320–11	to cheer, *g·*, and bless man
	327–28	and lose sight of their *g·* ;
	371– 8	Is it that he can *g·* . . . better than
	371– 9	they, . . . can *g·* themselves?
	373–13	should, does, *g·* His children.
	400–17	G· my little feet
Man.	15– 4	sufficient *g·* to eternal Life.
Pul.	30–16	* are the *g·* to eternal Life ;
	30–19	* as the teacher and *g·* to salvation ;
No.	20–26	Human reason is a blind *g·*,
Pan.	14–14	*g·* and bless our chief magistrate,
Po.	23–20	G· him in wisdom's way !
	43–12	Shield and *g·* and guard them ;
	69– 5	G· my little feet
	79– 2	So Love doth *g·* ;
My.	11– 9	* not tried to *g·* us by means of
	104– 1	I have had no other *g·*
	150– 4	will *g·* thee, if thou seekest this
	193–19	God guard and *g·* you.
	194–27	*g·* and guard you and your church
	234–11	*g·* them every step of the way
	282–26	May God *g·* and prosper

(see also **Eddy**)

guide-book
Mis.	xi–11	a graphic *g·*, pointing the path,

guided
Mis.	147–17	not *g·* merely by affections
	147–19	The upright man is *g·* by
	149–28	G· by the pillar and the cloud,
	236–21	be *g·* by God alone ;''
	290–11	*g·* by the divine Principle,
Man.	84–18	pupils shall be *g·* by the BIBLE,
'01.	20– 5	*g·* by no other mind than Truth,
Po.	2– 9	G· and led, can never reach to
My.	28–23	* labors of one divinely *g·* woman,
	50–10	* *g·* by their dauntless Leader
	235– 6	tender mother, *g·* by love,

guides
Mis.	77–18	*g·* him by Truth that knows no error,
	81–30	*g·* the understanding,
	118– 6	scientific understanding *g·* man.
	150–31	He guards, *g·*, feeds,
	152–28	which *g·* you safely home.
	373–12	Neither . . . *g·* the infinite Mind
Ret.	83–12	and are their best *g·*.

guides
Un.	3–28	*g·* every event of our careers.
'02.	2– 3	this daystar, and whither it *g·*.
My.	295–18	It *g·* the fisherman.

guiding
Mis.	59–25	*g·* them with Truth.
	303– 8	teaching and *g·* their students.
	321– 1	The wise men follow this *g·* star ;
Ret.	28– 4	*g·* our every thought and action ;
My.	110–10	*g·* the steps of progress
	164–22	*g·*, and guarding your way
	182–23	guarding, *g·*, giving grace, health,
	261–11	guarding and *g·* well the
	273– 8	* *g·* with remarkable skill,

guile
My.	17– 4	all malice, and all *g·*, — I Pet. 2 : 1.

guilt
Mis.	115– 9	*g·* as a mental malpractitioner,
	121–10	the *g·* of innocent blood — Deut. 19 : 13.
Po.	26–15	dark record of our *g·* unrolled,
	71– 3	and *g·*, grown bold,

guilty
Mis.	66– 3	innocent to suffer for the *g·*.
	112–10	nor detect the *g·*, unless he
	121–15	suffer for the *g·*, is inhuman.
	121–31	punishes the *g·*, not the innocent.
Man.	52–11	If a member is found *g·* of
	53– 5	member *g·* of this offense
Ret.	31–20	he is *g·* of all.'' — Jas. 2 : 10.
	80–25	and turns away from it, is *g·*,
My.	160–25	even the fire of a *g·* conscience,
	220–30	suffer for the *g·*,

guise
Pul.	23–14	* under the *g·* of C. S.,
My.	128–31	evil suggestions, in whatever *g·*,

gulf
Man.	41– 6	*g·* between C. S. and theosophy,

Gulf States
Pul.	41– 9	* far-off Pacific coast and the G· S·

gulp
Mis.	87– 3	into one *g·* of vacuity

gush
My.	332– 4	* The silent *g·* of grateful tears alone

gushed
Po.	9– 6	fountains of grief and joy That *g·*

gust
My.	207–12	A suppositional *g·* of evil
	297–13	This *g·* blows away the baubles

gustatory
Mis.	200–18	The loss of *g·* enjoyment

H

H——, Mr. C. M.
Mis.	242–26	Also, Mr. C. M. H·, of Boston,

habit
Mis.	240–26	the *h·* of smoking is not nice,
	242–24	he is to cure that *h·* in three days,
	243– 2	cured her perfectly of this *h·*,
	319–11	*h·* of mental and audible protest
My.	212–10	alcoholic *h·* is the use of

habitant
Un.	45–18	make mind-matter a *h·* of the

habitation
Mis.	229–17	most High thy *h·* ; — Psal. 91 : 9.
	328–18	tarried in the *h·* of the senses,
	344– 9	fit *h·* for the intelligences?''
	389–12	His *h·* high is here,
'00.	10–22	*h·* of His throne forever.
Po.	4–11	His *h·* high is here,
My.	120–26	become the *h·* of devils, — Rev. 18 : 2.

habits
Mis.	119–13	its *h·*, tastes, and indulgences.
Man.	63–24	He or she shall have no bad *h·*,
Pan.	10–26	no pleasure in loathsome *h·*
'01.	27–19	*h·* and appetites of mankind corrected,

habitual
Mis.	18–24	*h·* love for his fellow-man.

habitually
Mis.	315–29	*h·* to study His revealed Word,
Man.	83–21	*h·* to study the Scriptures

hades
Mis.	170–12	*h·*, or hell of Scripture,
'01.	16–10	with the verbiage of *h·*.

Hahnemann Medical College
Ret.	43–11	the H· M· C· of Philadelphia,

hail
Mis.	141–10	*h·* with joy this proposed type
Pul.	41–27	* ''All *h·* the power of Jesus' name,''
	81– 2	* ''All *h·* the power of Jesus' name,''
Po.	10– 1	H·, brother ! fling thy banner
	70–19	*h·* creation's glorious morn
My.	16–29	*h·* shall sweep away — Isa. 28 : 17.
	252–29	All *h·* to this higher hope
	337– 3	H·, brother ! fling thy banner

hails
Mis.	393–15	When the buried Master *h·* us
Po.	51–20	When the buried Master *h·* us

hair
Un.	51– 7	never make one *h·* white or black,
Pul.	32– 1	* her face, framed in dark *h·*
	37– 7	* although her *h·* is white,
My.	271–16	* sweet smile and snowy *h·*

half
Mis.	126– 4	I *h·* wish for society again ;
	295–29	for a *h·* century has with such dignity,
	325–18	with eyes *h·* open, the porter starts up
	339– 5	silence for the space of *h·* an hour.
	382–12	latter *h·* of the nineteenth century
Ret.	50–14	or even in *h·* as many lessons.
Pul.	vii– 8	latter *h·* of the nineteenth century,
	2– 4	the *h·* was not told me : — I Kings 10 : 7.
	9–19	who, with his better *h·*, is a
	59– 7	* every hour and a *h·*,
	65–23	* gave *h·* of the garment to
No.	29–12	* is not *h·* a man.
Pan.	3– 4	*h·* goat and *h·* man,

G
H

half
  Pan.   3– 7   one charm to make it *h·* divine
  '01.   22–17   three, or one and a *h·*,
  '02.   13–15   about one *h·* the price paid,
  Hea.   13–14   at intervals of *h·* an hour
  My.   29–28   * *h·* past five in the morning
      30–27   * the service at *h·* past seven,
      30–32   * Before *h·* past seven the chimes
      31– 9   * Promptly at *h·* past six
      38–16   * service at *h·* past twelve
      54– 9   * *h·* an hour before the arrival
      68– 6   * one mile and a *h·* of pews.
      77– 8   * its dimensions are only *h·* as great.
      78–28   * of the *h·* past twelve service ;
      81–13   * up leaped *h·* a dozen Scientists.
      107–15   administers *h·* a dozen or less
      147– 4   Over a *h·* century ago,
      229–12   might cost them a *h·* century.
      243–12   duties of *h·* a dozen or more
      (*see also* **numbers**)

half-century and **half century**
  Mis.   247– 8   professed Christianity a *h·* ;
      295–29   for a *h· c·* has with such dignity
  Ret.   13– 3   members of that body for a *h·*.
  Un.   6–22   a *h·* ago the assertion
  My.   147– 4   Over a *h· c·* ago,
      229–12   might cost them a *h· c·*.

half-days
  Ret.   50–14   during twelve *h·*,

half-hostility
  '02.   3– 9   the North's *h·* to the South,

halfpenny
  My.   215– 1   but nobody . . . gave it a *h·*.

half-persuaded
  My.   49– 3   * the hitherto *h·* one
      166– 4   insincerity and a *h·* faith

half-way
  My.   260–12   it hath . . . no *h·* stations.

hall
  Mis.   178–16   * I strayed into this *h·*,
  Man.   96– 7   cost of *h·* shall be paid by
  Pul.   29–13   * every seat in the *h·* was filled
  '02.   15– 2   contained threats to blow up the *h·*
  Po.   vi– 6   * poem
    page 39   poem
      39–20   brilliant temperance *h·*
      40– 3   We dedicate this temperance *h·*
  My.   54–29   * decided that this *h·* was too large,
      55– 1   * the *h·* was crowded.
      55–21   * *h·* was crowded to overflowing.
      59–17   * little *h·* on Market Street, Lynn,
      75–19   * Crowded as the *h·* was yesterday,
      123–10   we have a modest *h·* in one of
      123–19   I will see you in this *h·*,
      123–21   My little *h·*, which holds
      147– 9   provided for you a modest *h·*,
      147–23   work-rooms and a little *h·*,
      154– 7   to send flowers to this little *h·*
      185–16   audience collected in the *h·*
      214–22   to hire a *h·* in which to speak,
      342–17   * smaller parlor across the *h·*,

hallow
  '02.   3–25   *h·* the ring of state.
  My.   176– 9   *h·* your Palmetto home with
      226–21   in this you learn to *h·* His name,

hallowed
  '02.   15–25   recorded the *h·* suggestion.
  Po.   78–13   in the Christ *h·* its grief,
  My.   150–11   *h·* by one chord of C. S.
      188– 2   This house is *h·* by His promise :
      188– 3   "I have *h·* this house, — *I Kings* 9 : 3.
      202– 4   him who *h·* this Easter morn.
      225–25   "*H·* be Thy name." — *Matt.* 6 : 9.
      258–26   *h·* by our Lord's blessing.

hallows
  Mis.   287–28   *h·* home, — which is woman's world.
  My.   257–17   *h·* the close of the nineteenth

halls
  Mis.   125–30   rapid transit from *h·* to churches,
      150–18   Convenient houses and *h·*
  Ret.   40–23   refused me a hearing in their *h·*
  Pul.   62–21   * concert *h·*, and public buildings,
  My.   147–25   never stop . . . to dedicate *h·*.
      304–13   lectured in large and crowded *h·*

hallucination
  Mis.   3–32   thus to annihilate *h·*.
      94– 5   see himself and the *h·* of sin ;
  Hea.   5–16   sleight-of-hand and *h·*

hallways
  My.   46– 1   * in generous *h·*, in commodious

halt
  Mis.   327–16   travellers *h·* and disagree.
      347–18   take a few steps, then *h·*.

halted
  My.   214–25   I therefore *h·* from necessity.

halting
  Mis.   168– 5   *h·* between two opinions
  Un.   61–16   neither . . . retreating, nor *h·*.

halts
  Un.   61–13   *h·*, retreats, and again goes
  No.   46– 7   advancing hope . . . *h·* for a reply ;

Hamilton, A. E.
  Ret.   95–13   signature

hamlet
  My.   134–16   Truth happifies life in the *h·* or
      257–29   the Alpine *h·*,

hammer
  My.   69–13   * *h·* and chisel of the sculptor

hammering
  Mis.   360– 4   awaiting the *h·*, chiselling, and

Hammond, Dr.
  Pul.   69– 1   * Dr. *H·*, the pastor,
      69– 6   * Dr. *H·* says he was converted to

hampered
  Mis.   263–24   *h·* by immature demonstrations,
      365–26   Christian metaphysics is *h·* by
  No.   11– 9   Christian metaphysics is *h·* by

hand
  at
  Mis.   61– 3   priceless, eternal, and just at *h·*.
      103–32   "I am a God at *h·*, — *see Jer.* 23 : 23.
  Un.   37– 6   heaven is at *h·*." — *Matt.* 10 : 7.
  No.   35–25   kingdom of God is at *h·*," — *Mark* 1 : 15.
  My.   10–13   * but the time is at *h·*,
      58–22   * heaven is at *h·*," — *Matt.* 3 : 2.
      121–13   helpful, and always at *h·*.
      202– 7   and the day is at *h·*.
      360–30   Your favor . . . is at *h·*.
  chisel in
  Peo.   7– 8   * "Chisel in *h·* stood a sculptor-boy,
  divine
  Ret.   27–29   divine *h·* led me into a new world
  My.   326–20   I recognize the divine *h·*
  every
  My.   31–16   * were heard on every *h·*
  fanatic
  Po.   71– 8   Rescued by the "fanatic" *h·*,
  friendly
  Mis.   294–17   O friendly *h·* !
  gentle
  Mis.   250–27   gentle *h·* opening the door
  God's
  '01.   16– 2   * God's *h·* has held you up."
  helping
  Pul.   45– 1   * children lent a helping *h·*,
  My.   259–19   a true heart, and a helping *h·*
  her
  Pul.   82– 5   * Her *h·* is tender
      84– 1   * not in her *h·*, but in her soul.
  His
  Mis.   152–10   o'er the work of His *h·*.
      171– 1   "His *h·* is not shortened — *see Isa.* 59 : 1.
      334– 3   none can stay His *h·*, — *Dan.* 4 : 35.
      347–27   Those who . . . take His *h·*,
      360– 5   transfiguration from His *h·*.
  Po.   10–21   His *h·* averts the blow."
  My.   200– 7   none can stay His *h·*
      215– 5   God stretched forth His *h·*.
      280–20   none can stay His *h·*
      337–22   His *h·* averts the blow."
  his
  '02.   11– 1   with a letter in his *h·*
  My.   126– 9   has in his *h·* a book open
  in hand
  Mis.   311– 4   walk with us *h·* in hand,
  join in hand
  Mis.   281–29   "Though *h·* join in hand, — *Prov.* 11 : 21.
  mighty
  My.   42–30   * "With a mighty *h·*, —*Deut.* 26 : 8.
  my
  Mis.   143– 8   I reach out my *h·* to clasp yours,
      151– 5   out of my *h·*." — *John* 10 : 28.
      213–25   out of my *h·*." — *John* 10 : 28.
      251– 6   my *h·* may not touch yours
  no
  '00.   3– 5   No *h·* that feels not his help,
  of God
  Mis.   178–13   right *h·* of God" — *Col.* 3 : 1.
      319–24   the outstretched *h·* of God.
  of love
  '01.   33– 6   *h·* of love must sow the seed.

hand

open
Ret. 6– 7 as one with the open h·.
other
Mis. 241–18 On the other h·, . . . administer this
279– 1 departures on the other h·.
Pul. 51–20 * it may, on the other h·,
our
Po. 10– 4 With our h·, though not our knees.
My. 337– 6 With our h·, though not our knees.
palsied
Un. 11–13 The palsied h· moved,
right
Mis. ix–12 by the touch of God's right h·.
98–19 through God's right h·,
125–11 sit down at the Father's right h· :
140–14 right h· of His righteousness,
178–13 right h· of God"— Col. 3 : 1.
364–14 God's right h· grasping the
373–28 right h· of the Father.
Ret. 22–13 right h· of the throne— Heb. 12 : 2
27–19 * Touch God's right h· in that
Pul. 9–28 and right h· of omnipotence,
'00. 12– 4 stars in His right h·— Rev. 2 : 1
My. v– 8 * right h· of fellowship is being
258–16 right h· of the throne— Heb. 12 : 2.
323–25 * right h· of His righteousness,
rung by
Pul. 62–12 * even when rung by h·
same
Chr. 53–51 same h· unfolds His power,
senseless
Un. 11–22 for restoring his senseless h· ;
staff in
Mis. 158–20 with sandals on and staff in h·,
358–28 awaiting, with staff in h·,
strengthened the
My. 132–17 Divine Love has strengthened the h·
taking by the
Mis. 11–31 taking by the h· all who love me not,
thy
Mis. 370– 3 "Stretch forth thy h·,— Matt. 12 : 13.
392– 3 skies clasp thy h·,
Po. 20– 4 skies clasp thy h·,
to hand
Mis. 143– 1 heart to heart and h· to hand,
weak
No. 44–18 weak h· outstretched to God.
willing
Mis. xi–9 fervent heart and willing h·
withered
Un. 11–16 "That withered h· looks very real

Mis. vii– 1 * that tak'st my book in h·,
170–32 "H·," in Bible usage,— Isa. 59 : 1.
292–21 enjoins taking them by the h· and
307–13 and many orders on h·,
Man. 76–12 funds which the Church has on h·,
Ret. 38–15 printing the copy he had on h·,
38 19 printed all the copy on h·,
My. 12– 3 * as soon as the money in h·
16– 6 * $226,285.73 on h· on that date,
23–10 * Amount on h· June 1, 1905,
76– 7 * enough money was on h·

handed

Mis. 373– 8 the following . . . was h· to me,
376 10 * a small sketch h· down
My. 308–21 h· him a gold-headed walking-stick
351– 7 letter was h· to me duly.

handful

My. 59–18 * preached to a h· of people
85– 6 * a mere h· of members

handiwork

Po. v–13 * masterpiece of nature's h·,

handkerchief

My. 152– 4 the h· of St. Paul

handle

Mis. 24–30 followers should h· serpents ;
108–21 that which . . . we can h· ;
211– 5 teaches mortals to h· serpents
221– 4 opportunity to h· the error,
299–32 you wished to h· them,
315–25 shall not silently . . . h· it,
334–18 then, and only then, do you h· it
336– 4 h· the serpent and bruise its head ;
'01. 16–23 to h· with garrulity age and
20–21 laws of our land will h· its thefts,
My. 172– 5 * wood in the h· was grown on the farm
364– 4 to h· no other mentality

handled

Mis. 350–21 in the mind that h· them.
Un. 36– 7 confirms Truth, when h· by C. S.,

handles

Mis. 203–15 h· it with so-called science,
210–14 h· it, and takes away its sting.
My. 107–29 homœopathist h· in his practice

handling

Mis. 191– 1 h· the word of God— II Cor. 4 : 2.
292–29 on this point of h· evil,
'01. 16–15 h· the word of God deceitfully.
My. 75–13 * h· of a great number
124– 2 h· the word of God— II Cor. 4 : 2.
338–17 their subjects or the h· thereof,

handmaid

Mis. 261–17 Justice is the h· of mercy,
Man. 69–15 household help or a h·,

handmaiden

Pul. 81–16 * love and her h· duty

hand-painted

Mis. 280–21 containing beautiful h· flowers

hands

and feet
Mis. 375–24 * "The h· and feet of the figures
375–25 * h· and feet in Angelico's 'Jesus,'
clap their
Mis. 168–20 pure in heart clap their h·.
clasp
Mis. 152– 4 in love continents clasp h·,
Pul. 84– 5 * shall clasp h· with pity,
clasping of
Mis. 306–27 it is not the clasping of h·,
clean
My. 34– 3 He that hath clean h·,— Psal. 24 : 4.
feeble
Ret. 27–17 * But the feeble h· and helpless,
feet and
Pul. 9–14 climbed with feet and h·
God's
My. 278–14 are in God's h·.
hearts and
My. 153– 2 loving hearts and h· of the
197–28 work of your hearts and h·.
His
Chr. 55–13 operation of His h·.— Isa. 5 : 12.
My. 232– 3 with the helm in His h·.
his
Mis. 224– 9 emperor lifted his h· to his head,
281–14 that fell into his h·.
Rud. 12– 1 never lays his h· on the patient,
'02. 19– 6 lifting up his h· and blessing them,
human
Mis. 171– 3 to signify human h·.
302–30 putting . . . into human h·,
little
Pul. 8–17 Little h·, never before devoted to
loving
Pul. 77–12 * loving h· of four thousand members,
78–10 * loving h· of four thousand members.
made with
Mis. 324– 3 city made with h·.
men's
My. 6–24 above the work of men's h·,
94–28 above the work of men's h·,
my
Pul. 6–14 * S. and H., was put into my h·.
'02. 13–26 to take the property off my h·,
not made with
Pul. 2–14 "house not made with h·,— II Cor. 5 : 1.
My. 188–13 "house not made with h·,— II Cor. 5 : 1.
194– 8 "house not made with h·,— II Cor. 5 : 1.
of aspirants
Mis. 351–14 in the h· of aspirants for place
of evil
My. 128–24 betrays Truth into the h· of evil
of God
No. 3– 6 better to fall into the h· of God,
of gossip
Mis. 227–11 weighty stuff into the h· of gossip !
of my students
'01. 17–21 into the h· of my students
of omnipotence
My. 127–29 through the h· of omnipotence.
of others
Mis. 13– 7 endured at the h· of others
of the artisans
Pul. 41– 1 * from the h· of the artisans
of their patients
No. 3–14 in the h· of their patients,
of tyrants
Mis. 99–10 weapon in the h· of tyrants.
on the sick
(see sick)
our
Mis. 110–19 our h· have wrought steadfastly
outstretched
Un. 26– 6 to be in His outstretched h·,

hands

ready
  My. 197–13   the great hearts and ready *h·*
ruthless
  Po. 46– 9   Unplucked by ruthless *h·*.
strengthened
  My. 199–20   of strengthened *h·*, of unveiled hearts,
swift
  My. 124–14   waiting only your swift *h·*,
their
  Mis. 330– 1   the leaves clap their *h·*,
        331– 4   wonders into their *h·*?
Thy
  Mis. 248– 7   works of Thy *h·*." — *Psal.* 92 : 4.
thy
  My. 199– 5   reward of thy *h·* is given
use of
  Mis. 242– 8   without the use of *h·*,
willing
  My. 124– 9   with glad faces, willing *h·*,
without
  My. 195–28   love that builds without *h·*,
wrong
  Mis. 351–17   never can place it in the wrong *h·*

  Mis. 170–30   putting on of *h·* . . . she explained as
        216–11   means more than "*h·* off."
        216–14   "laying on of *h·*," — *Heb.* 6 : 2.
        304–32   * have been placed in the *h·* of
  Man. 75–21   remained in the *h·* of the Directors,
        91–16   surplus funds left in the *h·* of
  Hea. 14–12   in the *h·* of a quack.
  My. 331– 5   Mrs. Eddy received at the *h·* of

handsome

  Pul. 63–23   * This *h·* edifice was paid for
        70–14   * a *h·* fire-proof church
        77– 5   * encased in a *h·* plush casket
  My. 87–18   * an edifice so *h·* architecturally.
       171–27   * *h·* rosewood casket

handsomely

  '01. 28–30   usually are *h·* provided for.

hand-trunk

  Mis. 239–14   the ominous *h·*.

handwriting

  Mis. 144–10   names in your own *h·*,
  Man. 26–11   given in her own *h·*.
        81– 4   given in her own *h·*.
        97–12   given in her own *h·*,
  My. 60–18   * on the fly-leaf in your *h·*,
       134–28   * letter is in Mrs. Eddy's own *h·*,
       137– 8   * letter is in Mrs. Eddy's own *h·*
       272–22   * reproduced in her own *h·*.

hanged

  Mis. 61–16   * where a man was said to be '*h·*
       122–12   were *h·* about his neck, — *Matt.* 18 : 6.

hanging

  Mis. 347–6   *h·* like a horoscope in the air,

hangings

  Pul. 76– 9   * *h·* of deep green plush,

hangs

  Pul. 26–27   * *h·* an Athenian lamp

Hankey's, Kate

  My. 15–17   Kate *H·* excellent hymn,

Hanna

Judge
  Pul. 28–26   * Judge *H·*, formerly of Chicago,
       29– 3   * Preceding Judge *H·* were
       29–16   * were finely read by Judge *H·*.
       29–19   * In his admirable discourse Judge *H·* said
       30– 3   * remonstrated with Judge *H·*
       43–18   * were read by Judge *H·* and Dr. Eddy,
       45–23   * Judge *H·* withdrew from the pastorate
       46– 1   * Judge *H·* was so eloquent
       60– 6   * Judge *H·*, who was a Colorado lawyer
Judge and Mrs.
  Pul. 36–25   * now occupied by Judge and Mrs. *H·*,
       37–18   * Judge and Mrs. *H·*, Miss Elsie Lincoln,
Judge Septimus J.
  My. 44–15   * Judge Septimus J. *H·* then advanced
Judge S. J.
  Pul. 5– 5   read by Judge S. J. *H·*,
       43– 6   * Judge S. J. *H·*, editor of
  My. 304–18   Judge S. J. *H·* became editor of
Mrs.
  Pul. 37– 2   * remarked Mrs. *H·*,

haply

  Mis. 84– 2   *H·* he waited for a preparation

happen

  Mis. 339– 4   *h·* very frequently on earth,

happened

  Mis. 38–13   *How h· you to establish a*
  Pul. 60– 8   * which *h·* that day to be

happier

  Mis. 229–24   holier, *h·*, and longer lived.
  Pul. 56–16   * makes people better and *h·*.
  '02. 19–15   *h·* than the conqueror of a world.
  My. 150– 8   * rendering the world *h·*
       229–30   The redeemed should be *h·* than
       296–15   healthier and *h·*, than yesterday.
       355–26   Mrs. Eddy is *h·* because of them ;

happiest

  My. 355–22   the *h·* group on earth.

happifies

  Mis. 394– 6   Hope *h·* life, at the altar
  Po. 45– 8   Hope *h·* life, at the altar
  My. 134–16   Truth *h·* life in the hamlet

happily

  Mis. 13– 8   *h·* wrought out for me
  My. 110–29   *H·*, the misquoting of "S. and **H.**
       177– 3   Most *h·* would I comply with **your**

happiness

all
  Mis. 118–24   they will uproot all *h·*.
and heaven
  Mis. 308– 8   health, *h·*, and heaven.
       311–17   health, *h·*, and heaven.
and holiness
  Mis. 15–11   health, *h·*, and holiness.
       183– 7   in health, *h·*, and holiness :
  My. 167–20   their health, *h·*, and holiness
       275–22   health, *h·*, and holiness,
and life
  Mis. 212–19   *h·*, and life flow not into
  Un. 22–15   essential to *h·* and life.
another's
  Ret. 72– 2   that hazards another's *h·*,
confers
  '02. 17–24   only what God gives, . . . confers *h·* :
consists
  '02. 17–22   *H·* consists in being and in doing
constitutes
  Mis. 9–31   false sense of what constitutes *h·*
final
  Ret. 78–24   your own success and final *h·*,
find
  Mis. 200–24   find *h·*, apart from the
forever of
  Po. 47–10   Can the forever of *h·* be
fruition of
  Mis. 231– 3   the full fruition of *h·* ;
gives him
  '02. 17– 5   obedience gives him *h·*.
goodness and
  My. 267–31   manifestation of goodness and *h·*.
health and
  Mis. 240–11   promoters of health and *h·*.
       262– 2   bring health and *h·* to all
  My. 165–21   impart truth, health, and *h·*,
highest
  '02. 17– 8   learn that man's highest *h·*,
hope, nor
  '01. 34–28   no intelligence, health, hope, nor *h·*
human
  Ret. 81–27   shifting scenes of human *h·*
in manhood
  My. 274–12   intellectuality, and *h·* in manhood.
Life and
  Un. 37– 8   stepping-stone to Life and *h·*.
life and
  Mis. 209–25   life and *h·* should still attend it.
       341–18   a material sense of life and *h·*
  Ret. 21–19   false sense of life and *h·*,
  Un. 58– 1   a false sense of life and *h·*.
no
  Mis. 324–26   Finding no *h·* within,
of a fellow-being
  Mis. 31– 5   affect the *h·* of a fellow-being
of her family
  Ret. 5–29   * secure the *h·* of her family.
power and
  Mis. 155– 5   All power and *h·* are spiritual,
procurator of
  Mis. 351–26   not the procurator of *h·*,
rare
  Ret. 18–23   those we most love find a *h·* rare ;
  Po. 64–18   those we most love find a *h·* rare ;
their
  Mis. 287–23   questions concerning their *h·*,
the side of
  Hea. 10–21   argue with yourself on the side of *h·* ;
this
  Po. 68– 7   Earth held but this joy, or this *h·*

happiness

true
Mis. 363– 3 reality of divine Mind and true *h·*.
welfare and
Ret. 90–22 welfare and *h·* of her children

Mis. 67–16 indispensable to health, *h·*, and
212– 4 never knows what *h·* is,
227–29 by the amount of *h·* it has
339–21 its all of *h·* to thy keeping
My. 87–29 * in this doctrine of health, *h·*,
249–13 mental miasma fatal to health, *h·*,

happy

Mis. 216–23 a *h·* hit at idealism,
225– 3 a *h·* concourse of friends
232– 4 peace, and plenty, and *h·* households.
385–10 "Joy for thee, *h·* friend !
388–17 Affection's wreath, a *h·* home ;
396–10 O *h·* hours and fleet,
Ret. 94–18 " *H·* is he that — *Rom.* 14 : 22.
Pul. 56–18 * Welding . . . was a *h·* inspiration.
86–17 * We are *h·* to announce to you
'00. 1– 2 with the tone of your *h·* hearts,
'02. 16– 7 I am the *h·* possessor of a copy
Hea. 10–20 If you wish to be *h·*,
Po. 21– 6 Affection's wreath, a *h·* home ;
48– 1 Joy for thee, *h·* friend !
59– 2 O *h·* hours and fleet,
My. 40–31 * her own blameless and *h·* life,
63–12 * this *h·* and holy experience
74–21 * a *h·* appearing body,
87– 8 * congenial, quietly *h·*, well-to-do,
87–22 * Their *h·* faces would make sunshine
93– 1 * *h·*, gentle, and virtuous.
127– 4 *H·* are the people whose God is
155–27 *h·* hearts and ripening goodness.
169–17 I was *h·* to receive at Concord,
174–11 their reports of the *h·* occasion.
252–26 gave to the "*h·* New Year"
256–20 At this *h·* season
263 6 wishes you all a *h·* Christmas,
315– 9 * *h·* home as one could wish for.
347–12 * Ah *h·*, *h·* boughs, that cannot
355–26 *h·* group of Christian Scientists ;

harbinger

Un. 57–25 Sorrow is the *h·* of joy.

harbor

'00. 12–14 At the head of the *h·* was the temple of

harbored

My. 344–19 If I *h·* that idea

hard

Mis. 128– 2 else it grows *h·* and uncomfortable
230–14 have become such by *h·* work ;
233–25 to work *h·* enough to practise it
234–14 and avoid *h·* work ;
237–27 dead hero who did the *h·* work,
261–15 "the way of *·* is *h·*." *Prov.* 13 . 15.
266 18 assertion that I have said *h·* things
281–19 So, whatever we meet that is *h·*
338–19 armies of earth press *h·* upon you.
343–15 cold, *h·* pebbles of selfishness,
Man. 41– 8 but without *h·* words.
Un. 1– 4 *h·* to be understood," — *II Pet.* 3 : 16.
'00. 2–30 I work *h·* enough to be so."
'01. 28–29 After a *h·* and successful career
My. vii– 3 * Strive it ever so *h·*,
40–30 * *H·* is the law, nevertheless it is
61–12 * I fought *h·* with the evidence of
136–24 *h·* earnings of my pen,
342–12 * shade of which is so *h·* to catch,

hard-earned

'00. 10–30 send me some of his *h·* money

harden

Mis. 301–28 All error tends to *h·* the heart,

hardened

Un. 56–22 suffers least . . . who is a *h·* sinner.

harder

Rud. 2–27 task, sometimes, may be *h·* than
My. 145–18 worked even *h·* than usual,
212– 7 A *h·* fight will be necessary

hard-headed

My. 81–32 * *h·* shrewd business men.

hardly

Mis. 224– 5 we can *h·* afford to be miserable
Ret. 2– 9 *h·* have crossed the Atlantic
6– 3 * can *h·* fail to induce them to
Pul. 31–24 * I was *h·* more than seated
My. 90– 7 * Unaccountable? *H·* so.
92–12 * *h·* more than a day's wonder.
98– 9 * as religious annals *h·* parallel

hardships

My. 52– 3 * many mental *h·* to endure,

harlequin

Mis. 233– 9 monkey in *h·* jacket

harlot

My. 126– 2 retaining the heart of the *h·*

harm

Mis. 12– 1 would not knowingly *h·* you."
31– 5 *h·* him morally, physically, or
55–12 to *h·* rather than to heal,
118–28 Every attempt of evil to *h·* good
157–27 It *cannot h· you ;*
221– 3 to *h·* by a false mental argument ;
263– 2 they will *h·* myself only,
311–20 as soon *h·* myself as another ;
335–32 has done himself *h·*.
350–18 If *h·* could come from the
351– 9 would not if I could, *h·* any one
Man. 48– 2 and will not *h·* them.
Ret. 68–26 In C. S., man can do no *h·*,
Un. 15–23 who will not *h·* them,
No. 33– 1 slander loses its power to *h·* ;
Pan. 9–15 wise enough to do himself no *h·*,
'01. 20– 7 neither moral right nor might to *h·*
'02. 19– 9 that would *h·* him more than
My. 107–14 can be swallowed without *h·*
210–13 when he would *h·* others.
232–29 Can watching as Christ demands *h·*
296–14 Evil has no power to *h·*,
345– 3 will do the children no *h·*.

harmful

Mis. 25–28 they cannot be *h·* ;
34– 1 none of the *h·* "after effects"
36–11 mortal mind, which is *h·*

harming

My. 249– 1 without *h·* any one

harmless

Mis. 210–11 *h·* as doves." — *Matt.* 10 : 16.
210–15 Good deeds are *h·*.
224– 1 mental arrow . . . is practically *h·*,
374–13 envy, and hatred — earth's *h·* thunder
Rud. 8– 5 sends forth its own *h·* likeness.
'01. 33–29 Christian Scientists are *h·* citizens
Hea. 13–12 single drop of this *h·* solution,
My. 128–22 Therefore be wise and *h·*,
150–29 *h·* as doves." — *Matt.* 10 : 16.
205– 5 *h·* as doves." — *Matt.* 10 : 16.
205–23 friends more faithful, and enemies *h·*.

harmlessly

Mis. 240–15 or let it remain as *h·*,

harmonies

Mis. 72– 5 unfolds the eternal *h·* of
202– 2 whereby the sweet *h·* of C. S.
329–12 sweet rhythm of unforgotten *h·*,
333–20 securing the sweet *h·* of Spirit
390–22 And thou wilt find that *h·*,
394–18 * Such old-time *h·* retune,
Pul. 81–21 * all the *h·* of the universe
No. 11– 3 of life or its *h·*.
Po. 56– 1 thou wilt find that *h·*,
57– 4 * Such old-time *h·* retune,
My. 115– 7 scribe echoing the *h·* of heaven

harmonious

Mis. 5– 4 reveals man as spiritual, *h·*, and
34– 8 before the body is renewed and *h·*,
72–18 Are . . . things real when they are *h·*,
77–17 one eternal round of *h·* being.
104–15 sinless, deathless, *h·*, eternal.
188– 5 grand chorus of *h·* being.
220–12 *h·* thought has the full control
235–21 the real man, *h·* and eternal.
256– 5 in order to make the body *h·*.
258–32 nature and man are as *h·* to-day as
308– 2 be found *h·* and immortal.
Ret. 59–19 Mind, as *h·*, immortal, and
Un. 51–18 have none of them lost their *h·* state
Pul. 54–21 * environment and *h·* influence that
Rud. 4– 3 perfect beings, *h·* and eternal,
10– 6 His government is *h·* ;
No. 4–25 to be eternal, must be *h·*.
6– 5 God's formations are spiritual, *h·*,
11– 6 their intelligent and *h·* action,
26–25 forever individual and forever *h·*.
'02. 8–10 its *h·* effects on the sick
Hea. 7– 4 produces the *h·* effect on the body.
Peo. 10–21 and make it *h·* or discordant
My. 39–24 * *h·* tones of her gentle voice.
44– 6 * land of eternal, *h·* existence.
119– 4 that which is real, *h·*, and eternal
146–29 voices the *h·* and eternal,
226– 6 principle of *h·* vibration,

harmoniously

Man.	70–19	confer h· on individual unity
Pul.	76– 7	* blends h· with the pale green
My.	268–27	h· ascends the scale of life.
	283–21	unite h· on the basis of justice,
	362–15	* to confer h· and unitedly

harmonize

'00.	11– 5	h·, unify, and unself you.
My.	68–19	* to h· with the Bedford stone

harmony (see also **harmony's**)

accentuating
Mis. 206–20 accentuating h· in word and deed,
all
Mis. 41–20 produces all h· that appears.
No. 13– 5 from the Principle of all h·,
and health
Rud. 3–22 upon the body in h· and health.
and heaven
No. 34– 2 up to health, h·, and heaven.
and holiness
Ret. 65–29 to obtain health, h·, and holiness
and immortality
Un. 22– 3 sense of h· and immortality,
Peo. 10– 1 of man's h· and immortality.
and its Principle
Mis. 14–13 with h· and its Principle ;
and Life
Un. 32–19 of holiness, h·, and Life."
Rud. 11–24 health, h·, and Life eternal.
and prosperity
Ret. 44–15 in its previous h· and prosperity.
basis of
Ret. 60–24 C. S. is the only sure basis of h·.
brings out
Mis. 337–16 Science brings out h· ;
celestial
Pan. 3–29 denotes the celestial h· of
conscious
Ret. 64–24 scientific to abide in conscious h·,
consciousness of
Rud. 11–15 the absolute consciousness of h·
establishes
Mis. 101–14 being which establishes h·,
eternal
Mis. 104– 2 at rest in the eternal h·.
259–18 In this eternal h· of Science,
Un. 52– 5 unbroken and eternal h·
Pul. 2–24 eternal h· of infinite Soul.
No. 10–27 Eternal h·, perpetuity, and
everlasting
My. 253– 4 higher and everlasting h·,
goodness and
Mis. 367–11 reality of being — goodness and h·
grand
Mis. 330– 7 join in nature's grand h·,
health, alias
Mis. 41–25 health, alias h·, is the normal
health and
Mis. 8– 5 cannot, produce health and h·,
59–15 to restore health and h·,
187– 6 He established health and h·,
heaven is
My. 267–16 Heaven is h·, — infinite,
His
Mis. 353–24 Principle carries on His h·.
holy
My. 13–26 divine overtures, holy h·,
hope, and
Ret. 48–20 restore health, hope, and h·
hum of
Pan. 3–11 is voiced with a hum of h·,
immortal
Mis. 97– 4 destroy . . . discord with immortal h·,
immutable
Ret. 56–15 triumph of Spirit in immutable h·.
No. 26–23 immutable h· of divine law.
increased
Mis. 204–24 permeates with increased h·
infinite
No. 17–23 infinite h· would be fathomed.
is heaven
Mis. 337–16 H· is heaven.
is perfect
Pul. 62–16 * so that the h· is perfect.
is real
Un. 60–10 We say that h· is real,
is the real
Rud. 13–19 To aver that h· is the real
is the truth
No. 4–11 On the ground that h· is the truth of
knowledge of
Un. 18–19 My knowledge of h· (not inharmony)

harmony

Life, and
No. 36–14 of good, of eternal Life, and h·.
maintain
My. 211– 7 in order to maintain h·,
man's
Ret. 61–10 man's h· is no more to be invaded
Peo. 10– 1 man's h· and immortality.
moral
Mis. 261–32 produce physical and moral h·.
365–13 right acting, physical and moral h· ;
No. 18–10 right acting, physical and moral h·,
moves all in
Mis. 174–11 Principle that moves all in h·,
not discord
Mis. 283–28 good, not evil, — h·, not discord ;
not in
Mis. 350–22 not in h· with Science
obstruct the
No. 40–20 obstruct the h· of Mind and body,
of being
Mis. 53– 9 gain heaven, the h· of being.
106–28 Music is the h· of being ;
116–14 swelling the h· of being with
268– 6 way to heaven, the h· of being.
Un. 13– 7 fulfil the intended h· of being.
of body
Mis. 86–21 h· of body and Mind.
of divine Science
Ret. 27–24 so the h· of divine Science first
of heaven
My. 274– 7 with the h· of heaven ;
of man's being
Un. 53–15 h· of man's being is not built on
of Science
Mis. 176– 2 h· of Science that declares Him,
259–18 In this eternal h· of Science,
of Soul
Mis. 85–28 immortality and h· of Soul.
omnipotent
Mis. 17– 5 law of omnipotent h· and good,
only in
My. 259–30 Soul recognized only in h·,
order and
Pan. 6–14 order and h· of God's creation.
or discord
Mis. 247–27 reflects h· or discord according to
or holiness
Rud. 9–28 health, h·, or holiness,
peace and
Mis. 156–11 Let the reign of peace and h·
perfect
Pul. 54– 6 * Jesus operated in perfect h· with
perpetual
Mis. 72–25 nothing which . . . is in perpetual h·.
physical
Un. 6–10 The Science of physical h·,
present
My. 129–24 a present h· wherein the
Principle and its
Mis. 14–15 lost his Principle and its h·,
profound
Mis. 392– 4 Nature divine, in h· profound,
Po. 20– 5 Nature divine, in h· profound,
real
Mis. 312–17 * the real h· between religion and
reign of
Mis. 154–17 reign of h· already within us.
344–28 way to heaven and the reign of h·.
Ret. 79–30 the reign of h· within us,
Un. 52– 7 reign of h·, already with us.
represents
Mis. 46–27 sound, in tones, represents h· ;
restore
Mis. 236–19 to restore h· and prevent dishonor.
rule of
Mis. 187–11 This rule of h· must be accepted
scale of
Mis. 290– 6 higher in the scale of h·,
Science supports
Mis. 102–23 Science supports h·, denies suffering,
sense of
Un. 2–18 gain that spiritual sense of h·
22– 3 consists in a sense of h·
24– 6 from the supreme sense of h·.
'00. 11– 4 Hold . . . the true sense of h·,
take hold of
No. 38–18 they take hold of h·,
this
Mis. 337–17 this h· is not understood unless
No. 45–22 this h· would anchor the Church
together in
Ret. 82–25 dwelling together in h·,
unity and
My. 270–31 religion and art in unity and h·.

harmony
universal
    Mis. 99–28 health, holiness, universal *h·*,
         134–19 the reign of universal *h·*,
    Rud.   1– 4 Principle and rule of universal *h·*.
veil of
    Mis. 352–32 must be covered with the veil of *h·*,
will end in
    My. 296–19 the waking . . . will end in *h·*,
with divine power
    '01.   2– 9 into *h·* with divine power,
with God
    Hea. 14–26 to attain a mind in *h·* with God,
with Life
    Mis. 105–14 in *h·* with Life and its glorious
with the laws
    Pul. 80–28 * into *h·* with the laws of God,

    Mis. 287– 8 To an ill-attuned ear, discord is *h·* ;
    '02.   9–13 Loving chords set discords in *h·*.
    Po. 70–16 Thy discord ne'er in *h·* began !
    My. 118–29 health, *h·*, holiness,
         124– 7 health, *h·*, growth, grandeur, and
         213– 2 *h·*, brotherly love, spiritual growth
         213–21 into *h·* with His true followers.

harmony's
    Un. 13– 9 God is *h·* selfhood.

harms
    Mis. 7–12 although skepticism . . . it *h·* not ;
          8–13 What is it that *h·* you?
        40–32 *h·* himself or another.
       267– 2 wail of evil never *h·* Scientists,
       398–14 Tear or triumph *h·*,
    Ret. 46–20 Tear or triumph *h·*,
    Pul. 17–19 Tear or triumph *h·*,
    Po. 14–18 Tear or triumph *h·*,

harp
    Mis. 394–10 The *h·* of the minstrel,
    Pul. 81–21 * as a perfect *h·*,
    Po. 45–13 The *h·* of the minstrel,

harpstring
    Po. 41–19 *h·*, just breaking, reecho again

harpstrings
    Mis. 106–30 awaken the heart's *h·*.
       396–18 O'er waiting *h·* of the mind
    Pul. 18– 2 O'er waiting *h·* of the mind
    Po. 12– 1 O'er waiting *h·* of the mind
    My. 31– 8 * "O'er waiting *h·* of the mind ;"

Harrisburg, Pa.
    Pul. 88–32 * *Independent, H·, P·.*

Harrison
  Mary Hatch
    My. 334–24 * signature
  Miss
    My. 329–10 * presented to Mrs. Eddy by Miss *H·*.
  Miss Mary Hatch
    My. 327–17 * obtained by Miss Mary Hatch *H·*
  Mrs.
    Mis. 306–19 * request of the late Mrs. *H·*,

Harrison's
  Miss Mary Hatch
    My. 329–20 * heading

hart
    Hea. 10–26 *h·* panteth for the water brooks,

Hartford, Conn.
    Pul. 88–20 * *Post, H·, C·.*

Harvard College
    Ret. 75–21 If a student at *H· C·*

Harvard Medical School
    Peo. 5–26 in a lecture before the *H· M· S·* :

harvest
    Mis. 214–30 Jesus foretold the *h·* hour
       215–31 not try to gather the *h·* while the
       313–21 pray ye therefore the God of *h·*
       332–10 ripened sheaves, and *h·* songs.
       356–13 the *h·* hour has come ;
    Un. 11–28 and *then* cometh the *h·*,
        12– 1 fields are already white for the *h·* ;
        12– 2 gather the *h·* by mental,
    Po. 47–18 Nevermore reaping the *h·* we deem,
    My. 269– 3 the *h·* bells are ringing.
       269–16 chapter sub-title
       269–19 Its *h·* song is world-wide,
       316– 5 *h·* song of the Redeemer

harvest-home
    Mis. 85– 1 are ripe for the *h·*.

harvests
    Ret. 79– 5 We glean spiritual *h·* from our
    My. 291–28 to pray, that the God of *h·*

---

hast
    Mis. 9– 9 "Thou *h·* no enemies."

haste
    Mis. x–11 originally written in *h·*,
    '01. 30– 8 forbids headlong *h·*,
    '02. 2– 9 Truth makes *h·* to meet and to
    My. 16–27 shall not make *h·*.— *Isa.* 28 : 16.

hasten
    Mis. 84– 6 and thereby *h·* or permit it.
       109–22 *h·* through the second to the third
       117–31 then, *h·* to follow
    My. 21– 8 * *h·* the completion of The

hastened
    '02. 19– 3 he *h·* to console his unfaithful

hastens
    Ret. 18–25 This life is a shadow, and *h·* away.
    '02. 11–11 *h·* to help on his fellow-mortals,
    Po. 04–22 This life is a shadow, and *h·* away.
    My. 178– 7 it *h·* hourly to this end.

hastily
    Un. 6–25 if *h·* pushed to the front

hate (*see also* **hate's**)
all
    Un. 20–17 all *h·* and the sense of evil.
animality, and
    Pul. 13–12 mortal beliefs, animality, and *h·*,
annihilates
    Un. 39– 7 Love which annihilates *h·*,
appeared
    Mis. 214– 3 it appeared *h·* to the carnal mind,
envy, and
    Mis. 274–20 impulse to violence, envy, and *h·*,
    '01. 16– 9 its lusts, falsities, envy, and *h·*,
envy, or
    '02. 16–27 pride, self-will, envy, or *h·*.
error and
    Mis. 284–19 against human error and *h·*.
every
    Mis. 389–16 love more for every *h·*,
    Po. 4–15 love more for every *h·*,
filling with
    Mis. 254–23 filling with *h·* its deluded
god of
    '00. 3–27 a god of *h·* and of love,
heat of
    My. 249–12 the heat of *h·* burns the wheat,
human
    My. 257–20 all human *h·*, pride, greed,
individual
    My. 249– 7 raging element of individual *h·*
ingratitude and
    '01. 15–10 their ingratitude and *h·*,
is atheism
    My. 90–15 * teaches that *h·* is atheism,
jaws of
    Mis. 106–11 Into the jaws of *h·*,
jealousy and
    Mis. 250–13 become jealousy and *h·*.
love and
    '00. 4– 2 love and *h·*, good and evil,
Love, not
    My. 239– 2 Truth, not error ; Love, not *h·*.
master of
    Mis. 336– 1 Love is the master of *h·* ;
    My. 214–13 Love to be the master of *h·*.
no
    Mis. 122–27 Divine Love knows no *h·* ;
nothingness of
    No. 35–12 nothingness of *h·*, sin, and death,
or the hater
    Mis. 122–27 for *h·*, or the hater, is nothing :
purposes of
    My. 293–25 overrule the purposes of *h·*
tents of
    Pul. 84– 6 * dwell in the tents of *h·* ;
times of
    Mis. 277–27 Love is . . . near in times of *h·*,

    Mis. 40–28 *h·* that is holding the purpose to
       337–19 evil-speaking, lust, envy, *h·*.
       351–22 it is *h·* instead of Love ;
       356– 6 Envy, rivalry, *h·* need no
    Un. 56–27 ingratitude, lust, malice, *h·*,
    My. 180–17 C. S. meets . . . *h·* with Love,
       249–10 *H·* is a moral idiocy let loose
       252–14 wrong, injustice, envy, *h·* ;

hate (verb)
    Mis. 11–27 good to such as *h·* me,
        12– 2 *H·* no one ; for hatred is a
       32–29 slander, *h·*, or try to injure,
      147–12 manifest love for those that *h·* you
      223–28 * I should make him *h·* somebody."
      238– 3 to believe a lie, and to *h·* reformers.

hate (verb)
Mis. 241–12 Either he will *h·* you, and
269– 7 either he will *h·* the one, — *Matt.* 6 : 24.
278– 5 Error will *h·* more as it
311–18 I *h·* no one ; and love others
336–10 Then you would *h·* Jesus if you saw
Pul. 21– 6 even those that *h·* them.
'00. 13– 5 which I also *h·*.'' — *Rev.* 2 : 6.
'02. 17–18 to *h·* no man, to love one's enemies,
Hea. 2–20 why should the world *h·* Jesus,
4–14 to drop divinity long enough to *h·*.
My. 356–22 either he will *h·* the one, — *Matt.* 6 : 24.

hated
Mis. 1– 9 perfect Christianity, *h·* by sinners.
9–11 *h·* thee without a cause

hater (see also **hater's**)
Mis. 122–27 hate, or the *h·*, is nothing :

hater's
Mis. 122–21 lessens not the *h·* hatred
122–29 The *h·* pleasures are unreal ;

hate's
Po. 79–15 lifteth me, Ayont *h·* thrall :

hates
Mis. 104–30 I will love, if another *h·*.
141–12 *h·* the bonds and methods of Truth,
My. 41–20 * admires friends and *h·* enemies,

hatest
'00. 13– 4 "Thou *h·* the deeds of the — *Rev.* 2 : 6.

hating
Mis. 123– 5 either idolizing . . . or *h·* them :
267– 9 * When they report me as "*h·*
'02. 8– 7 mortals *h·*, or unloving,
My. 249– 9 *h·* even one's enemies
339– 1 charitable towards all, and *h·* none.

hatred
Mis. 10– 4 Whatever envy, *h·*, revenge
12– 2 *h·* is a plague-spot
19– 2 covetousness, lust, *h·*, malice,
114–20 passion, appetites, *h·*,
122–21 lessens not the hater's *h·*
153–15 encompassed not with pride, *h·*,
199–16 cost him the *h·* of the rabbis.
278– 2 fornication, envy, and *h·*
308– 6 by reason of human love or *h·*
324–15 emulation, *h·*, wrath,
336–13 *h·* of God's idea,
374–13 ignorance, envy, and *h·*
Pul. 15–19 human *h·* cannot reach you.
No. 43–27 while envy and *h·* bark and bite
'00. 10– 1 *H·* bites the heel of love
'01. 16–10 *h·* gone mad becomes imbecile
'02. 8–25 Lust, *h·*, revenge, coincide in
17– 1 worldliness, *h·*, and lust,
My. 41–14 * lawlessness of *h·* he may practise
104– 9 they vented their *h·* of Jesus
213– 6 engenders envy and *h·*,

haunt
Man. 48–12 shall not *h·* Mrs. Eddy's drive

haunted
Mis. 87–29 *h·* by obsequious helpers,
343–26 fill the *h·* chambers of memory,

haunting
Un. 64–13 and the *h·* sense of evil
My. 192– 9 *h·* mystery and gloom

haunts
Ret. 91–26 and nature's *h·* were the
Pul. 82– 3 * into the cold *h·* of sin

have
Mis. vii–16 And nothing *h·* to pray :
vii–20 Wherefor, *h·* much to pay.
2– 3 who *h·* the least wisdom or
2– 5 they *h·* so little of their own.
4–24 is often said, "You must *h·*
5–11 but *h·* not sufficient faith
5–12 that I *h·* the power to heal.''
6– 6 C. S. practitioners *h·* plenty to do,
8– 6 and *h·* our being,'' — *Acts* 17 : 28.
10– 4 We *h·* no enemies.
10–28 the lesson, "I *h·* no enemies.''
10–29 Even in belief you *h·* but one
10–31 belief that you *h·* enemies ;
11–30 I *h·* but two to present.
13–11 what thank *h·* ye? — *Luke* 6 : 32.
18– 9 *h·* no other gods — *Exod.* 20 : 3.
19–20 I should *h·* more faith in an
19–23 or would *h·* in a smooth-tongued
21– 3 *h·* no other gods — *Exod.* 20 : 3.
23–12 *h·* no other gods — *Exod.* 20 : 3.
28–20 *h·* no other gods — *Exod.* 20 : 3.
32–21 But I *h·* not moments enough
34–17 and *h·* them with us ;

have
Mis. 36– 6 *Do animals and beasts h· a mind?*
36–15 beasts that *h·* these propensities
42–19 we shall not *h·* to repeat it ;
44–13 *If I h· the toothache,*
47–26 must *h·* an ending.
47–30 I *h·* no knowledge of mesmerism,
49– 6 *h·* no doubt she could have been
50–25 live thereby, and *h·* being.
51– 2 will *h·* its effect physically as well
51– 9 We *h·* not the particulars of
52–29 Mortals *h·* the sum of being to
55–24 knows that he can *h·* one God only,
57– 3 what evidence *h·* you
57–21 or it would *h·* no seeming.
58– 2 *h· any more power over him?*
65– 3 We *h·* no more proof of
65– 4 than we *h·* that the earth's
65–19 I *h·* not ; and this important
69–11 let them *h·* dominion — *Gen.* 1 : 26.
72–16 shall not *h·* occasion — *Ezek.* 18 : 3.
72–20 *knoweth that ye h· need* — *Matt.* 6 : 32.
73–15 He knoweth that we *h·* need
73–18 We *h·* need of *these* things ;
73–19 *h·* need to know that the so-called
74–31 you may *h·* all that is left of it ;
79– 9 we live, move, and *h·* being.
82–30 and *h·* our being.'' — *Acts* 17 : 28.
86– 2 these *h·* no fleshly nature.
89–13 attendant and friends *h·* no faith
91–21 *Should not the teacher of C. S. h·*
96– 5 *h·* found Him so ; and would *h·* no other
99–22 and they *h·* not.
105–12 would *h·* no conflict with Life
106– 4 Scientists will, *must*, *h·* a history ;
108–30 they *h·* no intrinsic quality
113–25 We *h·* nothing to fear when Love
114–17 They must always *h·* on armor,
115–32 as you would *h·* them do to you,
118– 4 We shall *h·* no faith in evil
123– 4 *h·* no other gods — *Exod.* 20 : 3.
125– 8 *h·* dominion over his own sinful sense
126–24 Scientists *h·* a strong race to run,
126–31 *h·* them in derision.'' — *Psal.* 2 : 4.
131–24 I, for one, would be pleased to *h·*
131–26 to *h·* them let her state the value
136–19 you *h·* in my last revised edition
150– 3 you *h·* the great Shepherd
151–15 "Whom *h·* I in heaven — *Psal.* 73 : 25.
154–12 You *h·* already proof of the
154–29 *H·* no ambition, affection, nor
158–30 *h·* no record that he used notes
163–20 they *h·* not : they still live ;
170–16 "I *h·* bread to eat — *see John* 4 : 32.
174– 6 Let us *h·* a clearing up of
179– 8 *h·* we any other consciousness
179– 9 If we *h·*, He is saying to us
180–18 *h·* part in his resurrection.
182– 7 and these *h·* no other God,
183–27 will *h·* power to reflect His
184–17 saying, "I *h·* the power to sin
198– 2 will *h·* no desire to sin.
199– 2 we *h·* the right to deny the
208–11 Mortals *h·* only to submit to the
209–31 then shall mortals *h·* peace.''
210– 9 reptiles because they *h·* stings?
215–24 they *h·* a long warfare with error
223– 6 necessarily *h·* pure fountains ;
225–30 * and you shall *h·* some gruel.''
228– 9 to *h·* a name whose odor fills the
229– 1 that any one is liable to *h·* them
229– 3 prepares one to *h·* any disease
230–18 when they *h·* nothing to say,
235–19 we shall *h·* it,
236–12 you *h·* the rights of conscience,
236–13 as we all *h·*,
239–27 something that she ought not to *h·*,
240–22 *h·* slight sway over the fresh,
241–11 says, "You *h·* no pleasure in sin,''
243– 1 she would *h·* delirium
244– 3 we *h·* the Professor on the
244–24 "And other sheep I *h·*, — *John* 10 : 16.
245– 1 We *h·* no record showing that
245– 2 but we *h·* his words,
245–18 that women *h·* no rights
246–28 we *h·* a spiritual Christianity
249–23 I *h·* proof, but no fear.
262–11 to those who *h·* hearts.
262–27 you *h·* little need of words of
263– 2 I shall *h·* the unselfish joy of
265– 9 All must *h·* one Principle
265–10 *h·* but one opinion of it.
269–12 *h·* a perpetual freshness
270–18 *h·* full faith in his prophecy,
272–20 *h·* simply an incorporated grant,
274– 2 *h·* no Biblical authority for

have

Mis.	276–17	The wise will *h·* their lamps
	276–24	*h·* their lamps trimmed
	285–29	will *h·* no past, present, or
	298–13	*h·* special application to
	299–27	What right *h·* I to do this?
	301– 6	would *h·* others do unto you
	303– 6	should *h·* their own institutes
	305–15	* shall *h·* a part in it.
	307– 4	will *h·* all you need
	307– 8	more we cannot *h·*.
	315–14	*h·* promising proclivities toward
	317– 9	would *h·* great pleasure in
	321–27	I *h·* no desire to see or to
	321–29	I *h·* a world of wisdom and Love
	325– 7	They *h·* small conceptions
	325–10	they *h·* plenty of pelf,
	331–10	goodness will *h·* its springtide of
	334–10	may *h·* the effect of power ;
	335–25	*h·* me get out of a burning
	335–27	I would *h·* you already out,
	341– 2	human race *h·* one God,
	343– 4	all that we *h·* to sacrifice,
	347– 5	*h·* to escape from their houses
	348–18	I *h·* to repeat this,
	348–27	drugs *h·* no beneficial effect
	349– 6	I *h·* students with the degree of
	359–20	from experience ; so *h·* we.
	367– 2	*h·* no place in C. S.
	391–10	*H·* many items more ;
Man.	16–11	as we would *h·* them do
	57–14	must *h·* the consent of this Board
	63–15	shall *h·* a Reading Room,
	63–24	shall *h·* no bad habits,
	70–14	shall *h·* its own form of
	74–12	shall not *h·* their offices or rooms in
	76– 9	to *h·* the books of the Church
	76–26	*h·* the books of the C. S.
	80–13	*h·* the power to declare vacancies
	83–10	such only as *h·* good past records
	84–11	shall *h·* one class triennially,
	85–11	Teachers may *h·* Certificates.
	87–14	must *h·* the necessary moral and
	94–12	should *h·* the opportunity to
Chr.	55–18	such as I *h·* give I thee :— *Acts 3 : 6.*
Ret.	20–26	he should *h·* a home with me.
	23– 8	seemed to *h·* a silver lining ;
	28–11	in order to *h·* the least
	33–12	the less material medicine we *h·*,
	37–24	may *h·* an interest for the reader,
	52– 6	*h·* a small portion of its letter
	59– 4	*h·* no contradictory significations.
	61–16	and *h·* no right to exist,
	61–26	Posterity will *h·* the right to
	65–11	*h·* no warrant in the gospel or
	69–12	shall seem to *h·* life as much as
	93–18	and *h·* our being."— *Acts 17 : 28.*
Un.	3–24	He can *h·* no consciousness of
	4–18	bids man *h·* the same Mind
	8– 7	can *h·* no other reality than
	9–23	So they *h·*, but in a far different
	16– 4	if God has, or can *h·*,
	18–15	troubles that you *h·* not.
	28–14	hypotheses . . . *h·* less basis ;
	33– 7	we *h·* it on divine authority :
	34–23	so-called mind would *h·* no identity.
	41–13	*h·* part in this resurrection
	42– 7	can *h·* no real existence,
	43–19	*h·* more faith in living than in
	48– 7	I *h·* no faith in any other
	50–19	less consciousness of . . . mortals *h·*,
	53–19	would *h·* one quotient.
Pul.	vii– 6	*h·* not only a record of
	2–23	and *h·* our being"— *Acts 17 : 28.*
	3–22	*h·* their source in God,
	4– 9	*h·* simply to preserve a scientific,
	9–23	*h·* a bounty hidden from the world.
	22– 3	*h·* one bond of unity,
	35–15	in order to *h·* the least
	50– 4	* he deserves to *h·* a home
	51–13	* others who *h·* different methods,
	52– 4	* Christian Scientists *h·* a faith of
	52– 5	* *h·* not a faith approximate to that
	62– 6	* They *h·* the advantage of
	62–16	* They *h·* all the beauties of a
	65– 8	* and may *h·* a future before it.
	67–20	* *h·* strong churches,
	80–10	* *h·* the largest individuality,
	80–17	* we *h·* no opinion to pronounce,
	81–19	* of those who *h·* so much to give
	81–29	* *h·* some measure of understanding
	87–20	*h·* more of earth now, than I desire
Rud.	10– 1	Note this, that if you *h·* power in
	15–16	should *h·* separate departments,
No.	2–21	*h·* large practices and some
	10–22	earth's discords *h·* not the reality of

have

No.	13–26	parts of it *h·* no lustre.
	15–10	*h·* the civil and religious arms
	15–22	matter and mortal mind *h·* neither
	16–20	can *h·* no knowledge or inference but
	17– 7	and *h·* our being ;"— *Acts 17 : 28.*
	23–15	Scriptures *h·* both a literal and a
	23–22	Deity can *h·* no such warfare
	29– 7	mind-quacks *h·* so slight a
	30– 7	sickness and sin *h·* no relapse.
	35– 5	what hope *h·* mortals but
	39–23	what we already *h·* and are ;
	42– 6	not compelled to *h·* other gods
	42–26	* and *h·* to eat beefsteak
	45–24	Let the Word *h·* free course
	46– 3	Shall we *h·* a practical,
	46– 5	or shall we *h·* material medicine
Pan.	4–26	what need *h·* we of drugs,
	9–10	*h·* no other gods — *Exod. 20 : 3.*
	9–25	what reward *h·* ye?" — *Matt. 5 : 46.*
	13–20	and *h·* our being" — *Acts 17 : 28.*
	13–22	*h·* "one God and — *Eph. 4 : 6.*
	14–27	Great occasion *h·* we to rejoice
'00.	5–15	whereby to *h·* one God,
	5–20	*h·* no other gods — *Exod. 20 : 3.*
	9–26	to *h·* some one take my place
	11– 3	*h·* no discord over music.
	11–10	we *h·* the promise that
	12–18	*h·* somewhat against thee, — *Rev. 2 : 4.*
	15–19	May you *h·* on a wedding garment
'01.	3– 8	said the Christian Scientists *h·* no
	4– 2	both *h·* the nature of God.
	6– 3	*h·* no separate identity
	8–11	we *h·* the authority of Jesus for
	9–20	what *h·* we to do— *Mark 1 : 24.*
	12–14	yet should not *h·* charity, or
	13–12	Sin can *h·* neither entity, verity,
	15–25	* to *h·* you in His sight.
	20– 3	*h·* no moral right and no
	21– 2	they *h·* Science, understanding, and
	25– 3	we *h·* a superstructure eternal in
	26– 7	personal senses can *h·* only a
	26–22	and *h·* not charity, — *I Cor. 13 : 1.*
	30–15	*h·* no craft that is in danger.
	34–12	or must we *h·* a new Bible
'02.	4–19	*h·* no other gods — *Exod. 20 : 3.*
	5–29	*h·* no other gods — *Exod. 20 : 3.*
	6– 2	to *h·* aught unlike the infinite.
	6–19	*h·* no other gods — *Exod. 20 : 3.*
	7–16	we *h·* Scriptural authority for
	8–17	We *h·* no evidence of
	9– 9	we shall *h·* better practitioners,
	12–20	and *h·* our being." — *Acts 17 : 28.*
	18–23	we shall *h·* more effective healers
	19–23	"Ye *h·* need of — *Matt. 6 : 32.*
Hea.	4–18	become finite, and *h·* an end ;
	4–24	God must be our model, or we *h·* none ;
	5–15	although we *h·* no evidence of
	6–10	abused me . . . and *h·* ever since ;
	9– 2	We should *h·* no anxiety about
	15–25	that you *h·* little or no faith
	16–18	only evidence we *h·* of sin,
Peo.	2–27	*h·* a benign and elevating influence
	12– 2	Let them *h·* "dominion— *Gen. 1 : 26.*
	13– 1	*h·* a more material deity,
	13– 4	*h·* a lower order of Christianity
Po.	38– 9	*H·* many items more ;
My.	3– 8	*h·* right to the tree of — *Rev. 22 : 14.*
	5–13	*h·* no other gods — *Exod. 20 : 3.*
	8– 9	* "As we *h·* the best church
	8–10	* *h·* the best expression of the
	8–11	* let us *h·* the best material symbol
	8–20	* should *h·* a seating capacity of
	14–13	* claimed to *h·* good authority for
	16–14	* *h·* the work directly in charge,
	23–27	* we *h·* the privilege of
	32– 9	* did not *h·* to lift their voices
	40– 3	* to *h·* her church able to give
	41– 9	* because they *h·* thoughts adverse to
	43– 5	* that they might *h·* a definite rule
	51–17	* to *h·* our pastor remain
	57– 5	* *h·* the sacred atmosphere of a
	57–31	* Christian Scientists *h·* a faith
	58– 1	* *h·* not a faith approximate to
	60–15	* I *h·* yet the little Bible
	61–19	* never more did I *h·* any doubt.
	64–13	*h·* no other gods — *Exod. 20 : 3.*
	66–14	* necessary to *h·* this property.
	72–14	* chapter sub-title
	72–15	* do not send . . . money — we *h·* enough !"
	82– 1	* they all *h·* the same stories
	83– 2	* the custom Christian Scientists *h·*
	83–14	* will doubtless *h·* fewer questions
	83–16	* *h·* time to rest and sleep,
	87–14	* people we . . . like to *h·* here.
	87–16	* they *h·* their costly church

have

My. 93– 4   * h· little of the spirit of bigotry.
97–12   * h· a little the advantage
106– 9   h· not power over and above
107– 5   you h· the correct answer.
107–11   h· not an iota of the drug
107–12   lower attenuations h· so little
109– 7   we shall h· one Mind,
109–23   and h· our being." — Acts 17 : 28.
111– 8   as we h· in our time.
113–21   h· a clear perception of it.
114– 6   as ye would h· others do to you.
115– 5   blush to write . . . as I h·, were it
116–11   Thou shalt h· one God.
123–10   we h· a modest hall
123–27   Seeing that we h· to attain to
126–31   We h· it only as we live it.
130–13   I h· neither the time nor the
130–21   must h· the author's name added
132– 6   ye shall h· tribulation ; — John 16 : 33.
133–22   I h· a secret to tell you
136–27   that I may h· more peace,
137–18   to h· my property and affairs
142– 2   we h· the mind of Christ.' — I Cor. 2 : 16.
143–12   those with whom I h· appointments.
147–30   You h· less need of me
147–31   less need of me than h· they,
148– 6   May the good folk of Concord h·
149–19   to h· a clear perception of divine justice,
153–17   h· no other gods — Exod. 20 : 3.
154–20   * If the poor toil that we h· food,
154–22   * that we h· light, freedom,
155– 8   May this church h· one God,
166– 7   so long as we h· the right ideal,
171– 2   and h· no other trusts.
174–17   I h· the pleasure of thanking
175–28   purporting to h· my signature,
182– 2   it is said to h· a majority
183– 8   * will the world h· rest."
190–24   should h· the same opportunity
195–17   the one talent that we all h·,
203– 3   I h· nothing new to communicate ;
211–11   what h· we to do with — Mark 1 : 24.
215–31   we h· no hint of his changing
219– 6   h· all the honor of their success
221–18   h· no other gods — Exod. 20 : 3.
221–27   shall we h· no faith in God,
223–12   with whom I h· no acquaintance
223–12   of whom I h· no knowledge,
223–14   because I h· not sufficient time
229– 4   I h· no use for such,
236– 1   h· no more of echoing dreams.
240–29   * h· the necessary moral and spiritual
241–11   * We are glad to h· the privilege of
242– 9   h· no Principle to demonstrate
244–24   What I h· to say may not require
249–22   The report that I prefer to h· a
250–29   h· beyond it duties and
252–2, 3   H· one God and you will h· no devil.
253–24   you h· His rich blessing already
254–17   May we h· permission to print,
255– 5   C. S. churches h· my consent to
257–28   Scientists h· their record in the
269–21   beams of right h· healing in the
276–23   politics?"   I h· none, in reality,
278– 9   h· no other gods — Exod. 20 : 3.
278–10   Let us h· the molecule of faith
278–24   Governments h· no right to
279–12   h· no other gods — Exod. 20 : 3.
286– 6   h· one God, one Mind ;
293–32   and ye shall h· them." — Mark 11 : 24.
295–26   h· cause to lament the demise of
298–10   h· my permission to publish
299– 6   * h· any truth to reveal
303– 7   Scientists h· no quarrel with
303–26   I h· not the inspiration nor
311– 9   * I shall h· to leave ;
311–24   I h· another coat-of-arms,
319–20   * I h· this information.
323– 7   * I h· his little book yet.
324–13   * to h· those very terms
336– 4   * was afraid to h· her brother,
339–21   h· no cause to mourn ;
339–22   only those who h· not the Christ,
340– 1   h· no record of his observing
341– 1   I h· one innate joy,
351–27   Science is all they need, or can h·
353–26   spiritual h· all place and power.
358–13   I h· not the time to do so.
364– 8   h· no other gods — Exod. 20 : 3.
(see also **faith**)

haven

Mis. 152–26   Into His h· of Soul
316–18   turn them slowly toward the h·.
Ret. 57 –2   we sail into the eternal h·

haven

'02. 20– 4   bringeth us into the desired h·,
My. 163– 2   to seek the h· of hope,

having

Mis. 28– 3   h· no sensation of its own.
45–27   h· "other gods before me." — Exod. 20 : 3.
50–29   changed to h· but one God
51–20   without your h· to resort to
58–13   "H· eyes, see ye not?" — Mark 8 : 18.
59– 1   H· no true sense of the
99– 4   " H· eyes ye see not, — see Mark 8 : 18.
125–15   whom, not h· seen, we love.
132–19   h· charge of a church,
168– 7   those who, h· ears, hear not,
170–28   as h· any power to see.
170–29   H· eyes, ye see not ;
174– 4   idolatry, h· other gods ;
174– 4   evil, h· presence and power over
185–22   h· no need of statistics
189–28   as one h· authority, — Matt. 7 : 29.
195– 9   h· these, every one can prove,
197–30   omnipotent, h· all-power ;
209–21   for h· "other gods — Exod. 20 : 3.
223–13   h· the power to heal.'
232–19   will be one h· more power,
232–19   h· perfected in Science
233–27   h· a true standard,
241– 8   one h· morals to be healed,
241– 8   the other h· a physical ailment.
242– 2   h· the above caption,
250–19   h· no ring of the true metal.
262–26   H· his word, you have
285–29   but, h· no Truth, it will
298–11   by h· my best friend break troth
323– 4   h· no temple therein,
327–16   h· less baggage, ascend faster
331–24   filling all space and h· all power,
335–14   as they say, h· too much charity ;
399–22   we depart, H· one.
Man. 50–15   be found h· the name without
63–17   may unite in h· Reading Rooms,
91–21   not h· the certificate of C.S.D.
98– 5   for the purpose of h· him reply to it.
Chr. 55–20   h· neither beginning of— Heb. 7 : 3.
Ret. 58–11   as one h· authority, — Matt. 7 : 29.
Un. 26– 2   h· its own innate selfhood
33– 3   (matter really h· no sense)
42–19   as one h· authority, — Matt. 7 : 29.
Pul. 12–14   h· great wrath, — Rev. 12 : 12.
16– 7   we depart H· one.
23–13   * each h· the common identity of
54–26   * and h· thus the most perfect
60–21   * h· an Æolian attachment.
71–23   * h· a divine mission to fulfil,
No. 38–19   H· one God, one Mind,
44– 6   h· its best interpretation in
'02. 8–27   h· the kingdom of heaven within
11–10   abuse of him who, h· a new idea
Hea. 4–26   Or, h· faith in it,
16– 3   h· ears, hear and understand.
Peo. 9–11   H· one Lord, we shall not
12–23   H· faith in drugs and hygienic
14–19   h· "one Lord, one faith, — Eph. 4 : 5.
Po. 76– 6   we depart, H· one.
My. 5–10   man h· all that God gives.
12– 6   * those h· the work in charge
53–30   * by h· so many different ones
68– 8   * h· a diameter of eighty-two feet
155– 6   h· unfaltering faith in the
155–18   h· a pure peace, a fresh joy,
156– 7   h· all sufficiency — II Cor. 9 : 8.
158–16   H· all faith in C. S.,
163– 9   Not h· the time to receive all
179–29   We are indeed privileged in h· the
215– 9   h· charity scholars,
227–11   h· the same disease
325–10   * as h· a greater future

Hawaii

My. 30–16   * from South Africa, from H·,

Hawaiian Islands

'00.   1–18   Philippine Islands, H· I· ;

hawk

Mis. 145–15   pride is a hooded h·

Hawthorne Hall

Mis. 168–27   * H· H· was densely packed,

Hawthorne Rooms

My. 53–12   * H· R·, at No. 3 Park Street,
53–19   * as a church in the H· R·,
54– 1   * H· R· were inadequate
54– 7   * H· R·, which were crowded
54–15   * At this time the H· R·,
54–21   * H· R· were again secured.
54–24   * besieged the doors at the H· R·,

He

'01. 7– 8   *H·* is the all-wise, all-knowing,
      7–17   as the Scriptures declare *H·* will
      7–25   *H·* cannot be apprehended through the
      8–17   Is God Spirit?   *H·* is.
    15–25   * *H·* is of purer eyes than to
    18–29   remember it is *H·* who does it
    19– 4   and that *H·* worketh with them
    21–25   for did *H·* not know all things
    31–27   and yielded up graciously what *H·*
    35– 1   *H·* shall direct thy paths ;" — *Prov.* 3 : 6.
    35– 2   *H·* shall bring forth thy — *Psal.* 37 : 6.
'02. 17– 4   *H·* knew that obedience is the test
Hea. 4–11   *H·* knows deserves to be punished,
     5– 4   saying *H·* is beaten by certain kinds of
     9–24   *H·* never made sin or sickness,
   15–20   something *H·* cannot reach,
   19–14   *H·* made "every plant — *Gen.* 2 : 5.
Peo. 6–17   *H·* is found altogether lovely.
   12–25   As if Deity would not if *H·* could,
   12–26   or could not if *H·* would,
Po. 18–13   *H·* penciled his path
My. 17–30   *H·* has blessed her.
   34–12   *h·* is the King of glory. — *Psal.* 24 : 10.
   37–21   * recognize that *H·* has made known
   45–24   * "*H·* took not away the — *Exod.* 13 : 22.
  132–15   begat *H·* us with the — *Jas.* 1 : 18.
  153– 9   *H·* that is holy." — *Rev.* 3 : 7.
  156– 5   that *H·* is able" — *II Tim.* 1 : 12.
  158–25   *H·* has laid the chief corner-stone
  161–26   "*H·* shall direct thy paths." — *Prov.* 3 : 6.
  162–27   May *H·* increase its members,
  170–22   *H·* shall give thee — *Psal.* 37 : 4.
  170–24   *H·* shall bring it to pass. — *Psal.* 37 : 5.
  170–24   *H·* shall bring forth — *Psal.* 37 : 6.
  178–17   impossible . . . for *H·* made all
  186–13   Rest assured that *H·* in whom
  188–18   *H·* surely will not shut me out
  203–20   *H·* will if it is ready
  204– 2   the fact that *H·* is infinite
  204– 3   *H·* gives His followers opportunity
  205–11   * *H·* plants His footsteps in the sea
  207– 5   remainder thereof *H·* will restrain.
  215– 5   *H·* it was that bade me
  220–19   *H·* who is overturning will overturn
  220–20   *H·* whose right it is shall reign.
  225–19   names of that which *H·* creates.
  235–16   Did God make all . . . *H·* did.
  235–17   Is God Spirit? *H·* is.
  267–10   *H·* is supreme, infinite,
  269–17   *H·* is separating the tares from
  280–19   *H·* will bless all the inhabitants
  280–21   *H·* must bless all with His
  288–11   *H·* is the Father of all.
  341– 4   thank God that *H·* has emblazoned
  355–20   * *H·* hides a shining face."
  356– 7   * "*H·* plants His footsteps in the sea
  357– 1   *H·* is the only basis of Science ;
  360–22   *H·* has proved it to me
  361– 3   *H·* will direct you into the paths of

head

aching
  Mis. 275– 9   bendeth his aching *h·* ;
and heart
  Mis. 160– 9   sweet rhythm of *h·* and heart,
      268–19   heals body and mind, *h·* and heart ;
at the
  Ret. 70–28   virtually stands at the *h·* of all
  '00. 12–13   At the *h·* of the harbor
her
  Pul. 83–29   * upon her *h·* a crown — *Rev.* 12 : 1.
his
  Mis. 224– 9   lifted his hands to his *h·*, saying :
  Pan. 6– 8   but lifteth his *h·* above it
hoary
  Mis. 231– 1   Age, on whose hoary *h·*
      389– 2   The hoary *h·* with joy to crown ;
  Po. 21–16   The hoary *h·* with joy to crown ;
hydra
  Mis. 246–16   inhumanity lifts its hydra *h·*
its.
  Mis. 336– 5   handle the serpent and bruise its *h·* ;
  '00. 10– 2   that is treading on its *h·*
man's
  My. 188–24   one man's *h·* lies at another's feet.
my
  Mis. 395–19   May rest above my *h·*.
  Po. 58– 4   May rest above my *h·*.
  My. 61–18   * I bowed my *h·* before the might of
      343–18   a shower of abuse upon my *h·*,
o'erburdened
  Mis. 339–22   hast bowed the o'erburdened *h·*
of his statue
  Mis. 224– 8   broken the *h·* of his statue
of Jesus
  Pul. 27–21   * Mary anointing the *h·* of Jesus,

head

of the church
  My. 108–29   the *h·* of the church : — *Eph.* 5 : 23.
of the corner
  Man. 18– 2   *h·* of the corner." — *Matt.* 21 : 42.
  Pul. 10–20   *h·* of the corner." — *Matt.* 21 : 42.
  No. 38–14   *h·* of the corner." — *Matt.* 21 : 42.
  '00. 5–25   it will become the *h·* of the corner.
  '01. 25– 7   the crown and the *h·* of the corner.
  '02. 2–15   stone at the *h·* of the corner ;
  Hea. 3– 9   again become the *h·* of the corner.
  My. 48– 7   * *h·* of the corner" — *Matt.* 21 : 42.
      188– 2   made the *h·* of the corner.
of the gavel
  My. 172– 1   * wood of the *h·* of the gavel
of the serpent
  Mis. 210–17   her foot on the *h·* of the serpent,
of this serpent
  Un. 45– 3   Bruise the *h·* of this serpent,
of this sketch
  Pul. 61–13   * stands at the *h·* of this sketch.
pillow thy
  Po. 27–23   Pillow thy *h·* on time's
plays round the
  Po. 2– 5   * "Plays round the *h·*, but comes not
whole
  My. 132–30   body, whose whole *h·* is sick
willow's
  Po. 67–12   winds bow the tall willow's *h·* !
your
  Mis. 355–18   to lift your *h·* above it,

  Mis. 196–24   *h·* stone of the corner," — *Psal.* 118 : 22.
        (see also **Eddy**)

headed

  Pul. 80– 5   * the revolt was *h·* by them ;
  My. 75–10   * most of them *h·* straight for

heading

  Mis. 132–13   March 18, under the *h·*,
  My. 359–18   appeared under the *h·*

headless

  Mis. 274–25   *h·* trunks, and quivering hearts

headlines

  My. 79–16   * heralded in flaming *h·*

headlong

  Mis. 254–25   laurels of *h·* human will.
      266–13   dashing through space, *h·* and alone.
      327–30   plunge *h·* over the jagged rocks.
  '01. 30– 7   The magnitude . . . forbids *h·* haste,

headquarters

  Mis. 156– 8   All is well at *h·*,
  Pul. 46– 5   at C. S. *h·* this is denied ;
      79–15   * they are held at "*h·*."
  My. 73–18   * The *h·* was thrown open
      75– 7   * a busy day at the *h·*
    173–19   at the denominational *h·*?

heads

  Mis. 240–29   "Battle-Axe Plug" takes off men's *h·* ;
      271– 7   keep out of their *h·* the notion
  Pul. 13–18   not struggling to lift their *h·*
  My. 34–10   Lift up your *h·*, — *Psal.* 24 : 9.
      59–14   * across that sea of *h·*,
      77–18   * Over the *h·* of a multitude which
    171– 5   joy upon their *h·* : — *Isa.* 35 : 10.

heal

  Mis. 4–25   said, . . . strong will-power to *h·*,"
     17–14   the power of God to *h·*
     33–15   not proved impossible to *h·*
     38– 4   to *h·* and elevate man
     38–19   *h·* the sick,
     39–26   *by which God reaches others to h·*
     43– 3   enables one to *h·* cases
     44– 9   It cannot fail to *h·*
     45– 6   is able to do more than to *h·* a
     50–17   in order to *h·*.
     51–29   *prayer and drugs necessary to h·?*
     52– 9   to *h·*, through divine Science,
     54–27   *they do not h· on the same basis*
     55–12   to harm rather than to *h·*,
     62–15   *mind-cure claims to h· without it?*
    137–28   *h·* and teach with increased
    151–26   then will you *h·*, and teach,
    163– 4   preparing to *h·* and teach
    193–29   power of Christianity to *h·*;
    194– 9   Christ's command to *h·* in all ages,
    215– 4   saying, "I wound to *h·*,"
    220– 5   another would *h·* mentally.
    225–18   * "If you *h·* my son,
    229–22   faith in the power of God to *h·*
    241–27   easier to *h·* the physical than the
    241–28   When divine Truth and Love *h·*,
    241–30   how much more should these *h·*,
    242–20   if he will *h·* one single case of
    260– 5   and found able to *h·* them.

heal

Mis.	311–26	even as a surgeon who wounds to h·.
	333–26	could h· and bless ;
	355–26	"Physician, h· thyself."— *Luke* 4 : 23.
	380–18	Although *I* could h· mentally,
	398–17	Feed the hungry, h· the heart,
Man.	47– 5	a patient whom he does not h·,
Ret.	46–23	Feed the hungry, h· the heart,
	57– 7	in order to h· his body.
	60–23	cannot, or does not, h·."
	63–11	in order to h· them.
	63–21	more difficult to h·.
Un.	7–12	h· a cancer which had eaten its way
Pul.	17–22	Feed the hungry, h· the heart,
Rud.	3– 3	endeavors to h· them of bodily ills,
	8–13	*H·* through Truth and Love ;
	8–23	may say the unchristian . . . can h· ;
	9–13	To h·, in C. S., is to
	17– 7	and its divine efficacy to h·.
No.	2– 7	but that you can h· it,
	2–24	destroys one's ability to h·
	3–15	their patients, whom it will h·,
	6–15	trying to h· on a material basis.
	15– 1	the sick and sinner, to h· them,
	39– 4	potent prayer to h· and save.
	40–19	forfeit their ability to h· in Science.
	42– 5	not unable or unwilling to h·,
	43–28	A man's inability to h·.
	44– 7	power of Christianity to h·.
Pan.	10–18	Scientists h· functional, organic,
	10–19	that M.D.'s have failed to h· ;
'01.	12–16	Christ's command to h· in all ages,
	19– 7	power of God to h· and to save.
	33–20	in order to h· them.
'02.	8–11	No person can h· . . . unless
Hea.	3– 2	wherewith to h· both mind and body ;
	7–15	It begins in mind to h· the body,
	15– 5	to h· all ills that flesh is heir to.
	15–18	You pray for God to h· you,
Peo.	12–15	what a power mind is to h·
	14–18	power of divine Life and Love to h·
Po.	14–21	Feed the hungry, h· the heart,
	22–15	To h· humanity's sore heart ;
	27–12	h· her wounds too tenderly
My.	24– 4	* is ready to h· all who accept its
	117–11	h· disease, and make one a
	147–20	able to h· both sin and disease.
	150– 3	seeketh to save, to h·, and
	152–26	matter, man, or woman can never h·
	159–10	sent forth His word to h·
	180–18	overcome evil and h· disease.
	218–23	teach or h· by proxy is a false faith
	221–20	with which to h· sin and disease.
	222– 8	why they could not h· that case,
	238– 2	*Will the Bible,* . . . *h· as effectually*
	300– 9	and thus h· disease
	300–11	h· disease, for the reason that the
	308–11	* it gives them a license to h·.
	363–27	and practise only to h·.
		(*see also* **power, sick**)

healed

Mis.	3–14	is man h· and saved.
	11–12	if my instructions had h· them
	22–25	the deaf, and the blind, h· by it,
	33–13	*in order to be h· by it.*
	34– 4	One who has been h· by C. S.
	34– 5	is not only h· of the disease,
	38–25	*in order to be h· by it*
	39– 5	the understanding of how you are h·.
	41–18	*Can all classes of disease be h·*
	54–18	*I was h· of a chronic trouble*
	54–20	When once you are h· by Science,
	54–22	disease that you were h· of.
	54–24	Science by which you were h·.
	63– 3	said of old . . . that Jesus h· through
	66–24	not h· like the more physical
	69–19	h· him of enteritis,
	70– 5	sick man's illusion, and h· him.
	71– 8	he h· others who were sick.
	93– 7	have been h· by C. S.
	133–32	behold the sick who are h·,
	162–19	through his stripes we are h·.
	163– 9	He h· and taught by the
	171–19	the sick are h· ;
	187–30	in order to be h· and saved,
	198–18	disease also is treated and h·.
	210– 4	C. S. never h· a patient without
	214–24	mortal mind in being h· morally,
	225–25	through the divine power, she h· him.
	241– 8	one having morals to be h·,
	256– 1	Persons who have been h· by C. S.
	260– 2	"stripes we are h·."— *Isa.* 53 : 5.
	300–30	patient who pays . . . for being h·,
	307–26	look and be h·.
	352–14	sickness is h· upon the same
	352–15	by the same rule that sin is h·.

healed

Mis.	364– 4	whereby the sick are h·,
	364– 7	to have h·, through Truth,
	372–12	* wonderful book has h· my child."
	378– 5	having been h·, as he informed the
	382–14	patient h· in this age by C. S.
	387–17	Who loved and h· mankind :
Ret.	15–23	having been h· through my preaching.
	15–27	till the persons . . . were h·.
	15–29	others present had been h·
	16–10	thank God, she is h· !"
	16–12	sick to be h· by my sermon.
	25– 4	as to how I was h· ;
	25–30	not questioning those he h·
	34–17	A person h· by C. S.
	34–18	is not only h· of his disease,
	39– 2	were h· simply by reading it,
	40– 1	four successive years I h·, preached,
	41– 4	desperate cases I instantly h·,
	60–20	and the sick are h·.
	92– 4	he h· by Truth and Love.
Un.	8–18	basis whereby sickness is h·,
	54– 5	To be h·, one must lose sight of a
	55– 8	stripes we are h·."— *Isa.* 53 : 5.
	61–28	helpless sick are soonest h·
Pul.	vii–18	the sick are h· and sinners saved,
	6–16	* was h· instantaneously
	30– 1	* h· by C. S. treatment ;
	54–28	h· Mr. Whittier with one visit,
	58– 1	* h· by the power of divine Mind,
	72–12	* h· a number of years ago
Rud.	7– 2	but that the simplest case, h· in Science,
	9–23	oftentimes h· inveterate diseases.
	14–25	h· by means of my instructions,
	14–28	and were h· in the class ;
	15– 3	a student, if h· in a class,
No.	2–15	I have h· more disease by the
	4–26	can only be — h· on this basis.
	6–14	then disease cannot be h· by
	31– 4	but has not h· mortals ;
	31–18, 19	He h· disease as he h· sin ;
	42–25	clergyman came to be h·.
Pan.	5–28	and thus h· sickness and sin.
'01.	11– 8	we are h· and saved,
	17–15	It was that I h· the deaf, the blind,
	17–28	attenuation in some cases h·
	27–14	If any one as yet has h· hopeless
	27–19	an equal number of sick h·,
Hea.	14– 5	man is h· morally and physically.
Po.	6–12	loved and h· mankind :
My.	v–24	* h· multitudes of disease
	24–11	* have been h· through C. S.,
	28–23	* our Master h· and reformed them.
	38–27	* h· them of their diseases
	44– 3	* the sick are being h·,
	58–17	* great multitude that has been h·
	63–30	* had been h· by Christ, Truth,
	105– 7	I h· consumption in its last stages,
	105–11	I h· malignant diphtheria
	105–14	I have h· at one visit a cancer
	106– 6	The list of cases h· by me
	106–13	C. S. has h· cases that I assert
	106–30	Nazarene Prophet, h· through Mind,
	111–32	They have themselves been h·
	112– 1	h· others by means of the Principle
	113– 5	and thereby is h· of disease.
	127–17	I h· ninety-nine to the ten of
	145–13	I h· him on the spot.
	153–12	h· from the day my flowers
	153–13	Thy faith hath h· thee.
	178– 6	sick are h· and sinners saved.
	192– 8	thou art being h·.
	204–24	sick whom you have not h·
	228– 3	thousands are h· by learning that
	233–16	"They have h· also the hurt — *Jer.* 6 : 14.
	258– 2	and the sick are h·.
	339–29	The fact that he h· the sick man
	348– 1	h· of so-called disease
	348– 8	Then I was h·,
		(*see also* **sick**)

healer

Mis.	41–21	no other h· in the case.
	59–26	That individual is the best h· who
	59–29	Mind is the scientific h·.
	97–11	by no means a desirable . . . h·.
	220– 5	h· begins by mental argument.
	252–23	rules and practice of the great h·
Ret.	47–17	a better h· and teacher
Pul.	52–20	* The Master was the great h·.
	53– 9	* the mind of both h· and patient,
Rud.	8–14	there is no other h·.
	11–25	The lecturer, teacher, or h·
	12–21	As power divine is the h·,
	13–22	if the h· *realizes* the truth,
No.	6–15	mistaken h· is not successful,
'01.	18–27	the Christian Scientists' h· ;

healer

My.	36–31	* *h·* of all our diseases
	104–15	the *h·* of men, the Christ,
	328–22	* a prominent *h·* of the church,
	349– 2	*h·* to whom all things are possible.
	360–30	your *h·*, or any earthly friend.

healers

Mis.	40–14	ancient prophets as *h·*.
	40–25	or they cannot be instantaneous *h·*.
	303– 3	as *h·* physical and moral.
	370–26	true fold for Christian *h·*,
Man.	82–18	shall not advertise as *h·*,
Ret.	87–22	*h·* become a law unto themselves.
	88– 2	professional intercourse of C. S. *h·*
Pul.	57–23	* several sects of mental *h·*,
No.	2–12	*h·* who admit that disease is real
'01.	9– 9	seers of men, and Christian *h·*.
'02.	18–23	we shall have more effective *h·*
My.	111–19	become successful *h·* and
	218–25	My published works are teachers and *h·*.
	327–24	* formerly read, "pretended *h·*,"
	328–13	* the law recognizes them as *h·*,
	328–19	* two C. S. *h·* in this city.
	328–20	* first to be issued to the *h·*
	329– 1	* construed to include the *h·*
	329– 5	* relieved the *h·* of this sect

healest

Mis.	209– 7	*h·* the wounds of my people

healeth

Mis.	173– 6	*h·* all our sickness and sins?
	174– 8	and *h·* all our diseases.
	184–13	*h·* all thy diseases." — *Psal.* 103 : 3.
	320–18	"*h·* all our diseases ;" — see *Psal.* 103 : 3.
	322–21	*h·* the sick and cleanseth
Man.	47–17	*h·* all thy diseases" — *Psal.* 103 : 3.
Pul.	10– 7	*h·* all thy diseases." — *Psal.* 103 : 3.
Pan.	4–25	*h·* all thy diseases." — *Psal.* 103 : 3.
'01.	9–30	worketh well and *h·* quickly,
Peo.	12–13	*h·* all thy diseases." — *Psal.* 103 : 3.
My.	13–20	*h· all thy diseases;* — *Psal.* 103 : 3.
	119–17	"*h·* all thy diseases" — *Psal.* 103 : 3.

healing (noun)

aid its

Mis.	58–19	*Does the theology of C. S. aid its h·?*

all

Mis.	232–25	Principle of all *h·* is God ;
	379–15	divine Principle of all *h·*.
Rud.	7– 1	Not that all *h·* is Science,
My.	154– 2	Science of all *h·* is based on Mind

and peace

Mis.	176– 3	*h·*, and peace, and perfect love.

and salvation

Mis.	244–24	way of *h·* and salvation.

and teaching

Ret.	78– 3	In *h·* and teaching the student has not
	83– 1	scientific *h·* and teaching.

art of

My.	327–26	* practise the art of *h·*,"
	328–29	* practise the art of *h·* for pay,

Christian

Mis.	6–15	Christian *h·* will rank far in advance
	88–22	* that Christian *h·* is
	192–22	grand verities of Christian *h·*
	359– 6	in the practice of Christian *h·*
	370–15	the form of Christian *h·*.
Ret.	62– 1	Science of Christian *h·* will again be
'01.	2– 8	new-old cloth of Christian *h·*.
Hea.	1–12	great subject of Christian *h·* ;
	3–22	God is the Principle of Christian *h·*,
	15– 2	Christian *h·*, established upon this
My.	43–21	* Science of Christian *h·* was revealed
	274–23	when beholding Christian *h·*,

Christian Science

Mis.	307–19	proper reception of C. S. *h·*.
Man.	89–14	practised C. S. *h·* acceptably
	89–21	practised C. S. *h·* successfully
Ret.	48– 5	establishment of *genuine* C. S. *h·*
'01.	18– 5	woeful warnings concerning C. S. *h·*
My.	153–27	C. S. *h·* is "the Spirit and — *Rev.* 22 : 17.
	219–11	chapter sub-title

Christ Jesus'

'01.	18–11	of questioning Christ Jesus' *h·*,

Christ's

Mis.	302– 9	without the Science, of Christ's *h·*.
Ret.	26–15	ignorantly pronounce Christ's *h·*,
Pul.	6– 6	spiritual foundation of Christ's *h·*.
	35– 6	* Christ's *h·* was not miraculous,
'01.	2–12	find the standard of Christ's *h·*
Hea.	12–12	from the Scripture and Christ's *h·*

cross and

Mis.	357–11	Without the cross and *h·*,

demonstrate

Mis.	65–22	in order to demonstrate *h·*,

healing

demonstration of

'01.	18–21	is above a demonstration of *h·*,

department of

Rud.	15–15	the department of *h·*.
My.	90–31	* peculiar department of *h·*,

divine

(see **divine**)

divine art of

Pul.	66– 1	* what they term the divine art of *h·*,

form of

Rud.	6–25	definite and absolute form of *h·*,

good

Mis.	355– 6	Less teaching and good *h·*

gospel

Pul.	44–17	* chapter sub-title

gospel of

(see **gospel**)

has gone on

Un.	9–24	*H·* has gone on continually ;

his

Mis.	200– 2	that made his *h·* easy

in its wings

'02.	9–10	with *h·* in its wings,

Jesus'

Rud.	3–17	Jesus' *h·* was spiritual

last

My.	345–21	* last *h·* that will be vouchsafed

law of

Mis.	65–29	constitute the divine law of *h·*.

lessons on

Mis.	371– 1	among the first lessons on *h·*

lost element of

Man.	17–13	and its lost element of *h·*.
My.	46–13	and its lost element of *h·*."

means of

Mis.	135–17	God's methods and means of *h·*,
'01.	34– 7	Christ's mode and means of *h·*,

mental

(see **mental**)

metaphysical

Mis.	4– 2	Science of metaphysical *h·*,
	4–20	on the subject of metaphysical *h·*,
	45– 6	Principle of metaphysical *h·*,
	50– 6	*entire method of metaphysical h·*,
	54– 9	in the field of metaphysical *h·*,
	68– 8	* *protest against metaphysical h·*
	195– 4	divine Principle of metaphysical *h·*.
	232–21	Metaphysical *h·*, or C. S.,
	233–12	standard of metaphysical *h·*
	234–20	mighty system of metaphysical *h·*,
	241– 7	Test, if you will, metaphysical *h·* on
	369–15	Metaphysical *h·* seeks a wisdom that
	370–24	C. S., a "metaphysical *h·*"
	380–25	the Science of metaphysical *h·*
Man.	34–16	and practising metaphysical *h·*.
Ret.	24– 5	Science of divine metaphysical *h·*
	25– 9	spiritual Science and metaphysical *h·*,
Pul.	35– 4	spiritual Science and metaphysical *h·*
No.	5–25	Metaphysical *h·* is a lost jewel
'01.	17–12	C. S. or metaphysical *h·*
	26–30	subject of metaphysical *h·* or C. S.
Hea.	11–27	Christianity of metaphysical *h·*,
	13–22	foundations of metaphysical *h·*?
	14–15	Metaphysical *h·* includes
	16–12	Science of metaphysical *h·*.

method of

Mis.	40–10	the same method of *h·*
	50–11	metaphysical method of *h·*

ministry and

Mis.	138– 8	in your ministry and *h·*.

ministry of

Mis.	195–14	ministry of *h·* at this period.

miracles in

Mis.	54–26	as great miracles in *h·*

modes of

My.	221–16	Then modes of *h·*, other than

of disease

Mis.	63–14	address himself to the *h·* of disease,

of sickness

Mis.	352–29	and the *h·* of sickness is,

of sin

Mis.	352–28	difference between the *h·* of sin and
Rud.	2–26	purpose of C. S. is the *h·* of sin ;

of the sick

Man.	47–13	in regard to the *h·* of the sick
My.	104–32	It was the *h·* of the sick,
	182–16	the *h·* of the sick,

of the wife

Pul.	26–16	* *h·* of the wife of the donor.

on her wings

Mis.	146–2	with *h·* on her wings.

physical

Rud.	3–11	his spiritual than his physical *h·*.

practice of

My.	111–18	establish their practice of *h·*

healing

Principle of
- *Mis.* 40– 2 scientific Principle of *h·* demands
- *Ret.* 37–18 the spiritual Principle of *h·*,
- *Hea.* 14– 7 obscure the divine Principle of *h·*

proof of
- *Pul.* 13–13 rejoices in the proof of *h·*,

psychic
- *Pul.* 54–10 * conditions requisite in psychic *h·*

Science of
- (*see* **Science**)

scientific
- *Ret.* 83– 1 elucidate scientific *h·* and teaching.
- *Rud.* 16–14 *school of scientific h·?*

silent
- *Chr.* 53–43 Christ's silent *h·*, heaven heard,

so-called
- *Mis.* 254–23 hurling its so-called *h·* at random,

spiritual
- *Mis.* 163–29 demonstrating the spiritual *h·* of
- 246–26 Christianity and a spiritual *h·*,
- 346– 4 spiritual *h·* as eminent proof that

suppositional
- *Mis.* 97–11 Such suppositional *h·* I deprecate.

system of
- (*see* **system**)

teaching and
- *Mis.* 162–13 good will, love, teaching, and *h·*.
- *Rud.* 15–16 Teaching and *h·* should have

their
- *No.* 3–13 rules of this practice for their *h·*,

true
- *Mis.* 40–14 All true *h·* is governed by,

Truth of
- *Rud.* 9–17 is the Truth of *h·*.

two poles of
- *My.* 74–29 * of the two poles of *h·*,

work of
- *Mis.* 7– 8 necessary in this work of *h·*.
- 37–27 to her students the work of *h·* ;
- *Ret.* 54–22 work of *h·*, in the Science of Mind,

- *Mis.* 6–11 The *h·* of such cases
- 80–29 outdoing the *h·* of the old.
- 96–24 How is the *h·* done in C. S.?
- 104–27 are demonstrated, in *h·*,
- 192–26 making *h·* a condition of salvation,
- 194–22 turn from matter to Spirit for *h·* ;
- 232–20 most important of all arts, — *h·*.
- 242– 1 chapter sub-title.
- 255–20 I claim for *h·* by C. S.
- 270–22 yet follow him in *h·*,
- 355– 7 a *h·* that is not guesswork,
- *Man.* 92– 3 *H·* Better than Teaching.
- *Ret.* 49–24 will prove a *h·* for the nations,
- *Un.* 0 24 yet *h·*, as I teach it,
- *Pul.* 54– 2 * The *h·* of his seamless dress
- *My.* 59– 9 * as well as of *h·*,
- 122–32 see the power of Truth in *h·*.
- 153– 6 The *h·* and the gospel ministry
- 219– 7 success in teaching or in *h·*.
- 219–19 our great Master's life of *h·*,
- 269–21 have *h·* in their light.

healing (adj.)
- *Mis.* 7–24 with *h·*, purifying thought.
- 24–12 *h·* Truth dawned upon my sense ;
- 59– 2 the *h·* theology of Mind,
- 70– 6 *h·* action of Mind upon the body
- 222–25 Even the *h·* Principle, whose power
- 247–18 *h·* force developed by C. S.
- 373–32 Its *h·* and saving power was
- *Man.* 49– 2 to monopolize the *h·* work
- *Ret.* 31–30 Love unveiled the *h·* promise
- 83– 5 and the *h·* efficacy thereof.
- *Pul.* 47–20 * definitions of these two *h·* arts.
- 53–27 * That *h·* gift he lends to them
- *No.* 22– 7 on the *h·* properties of tar-water,
- 44–19 *h·* balm of Truth and Love
- *'01.* 2– 6 the *h·* standard of C. S.
- *My.* 22–27 * touched the *h·* hem of C. S.,
- 24– 9 * this *h·* and saving gospel.
- 153–14 no intrinsic *h·* qualities from my
- 153–15 scientific, *h·* faith is a saving
- 180– 7 *h·* Christianity which applies to all
- (*see also* **Christ, power**)

healing (ppr.)
- *Mis.* ix– 9 *h·* mankind morally, physically,
- 19–22 more faith in an honest . . . *h·* me,
- 29–21 *h·* the writers of chronic and acute
- 33–22 *ordinary methods of h· disease*
- 33–23 *H·* by C. S. has the following
- 51– 3 spiritually, *h·* disease.
- 60– 9 *h·* cases of disease and sin
- 74–23 *h·* through Mind, he removed any

healing (ppr.)
- *Mis.* 88–29 Mind-healing, and *h·* with drugs,
- 101– 1 *h·* becomes spontaneous,
- 165– 2 casting out evils and *h·*,
- 189–29 spiritual power, *h·* sin and sickness,
- 300–32 *H·* morally and physically are one.
- 352–18 Thus it is in *h·* the moral sickness;
- 358– 5 and teaches by *h·*,
- 378–13 signally failed in *h·* her case.
- *Man.* 19– 4 *h·* and saving the world
- 83– 6 *h·* and uplifting the race.
- *Ret.* 34–10 I claim for *h·* scientifically
- 63– 3 insist on the need of *h·* sickness
- 85–20 or of *h·* on a material basis.
- 95– 3 the *h·* of the nations." — *Rev.* 22 : 2.
- *Pul.* 6–10 *h·* and saving mankind.
- 10– 2 *h·* both mind and body,
- *Rud.* 2–23 *H·* physical sickness is the smallest
- *No.* 2–13 by *h·* one case audibly,
- 2–22 marked success in *h·*
- 5–27 prevents one from *h·* scientifically,
- 32–24 a Cause which is *h·* its thousands
- 44–17 instead of *h·*, it palsied
- *'01.* 9–16 *h·* and saving men,
- 17–22 the comparative ease of *h·*
- 24–27 *h·* all manner of diseases.
- 27–13 C. S. is *h·* and reforming mankind.
- 28–21 my demonstration of C. S. in *h·*
- 33–21 *h·* them through the might and
- 34– 3 *h·* of all manner of diseases.
- *'02.* 15– 6 *H·* all manner of diseases
- *My.* 108– 3 *h·* his cases without drugs
- 113–16 *h·* sin and sickness,
- 190– 8 *h·* the worst forms of contagious
- 190–20 and *above matter* in *h·* disease,
- 194– 9 *h·* sickness and destroying sin,
- 214–20 *h·* all manner of diseases,
- 219–17 *h·*, . . . of all manner of diseases.
- 239–10 by *h·* all manner of disease,
- 257–16 *h·* all sorrow, sickness, and sin.
- 257–19 his grace, reviving and *h·*.
- 302– 1 all modes of *h·* disease
- 345–12 false science — *h·* by drugs.
- (*see also* **sick**)

healing-power
- *Mis.* 199–30 marvellous *h·* of goodness

healings
- *Pul.* 54–18 * the accounts of his *h·*,

heals
- *Mis.* 20– 2 *h·* man spontaneously,
- 102–21 and *h·* all our diseases.
- 222– 9 reforms him, and so *h·* him :
- 241–16 *h·* him of the moral malady.
- 260–25 gives out an atmosphere that *h·*
- 268–19 *h·* body and mind, head and heart ;
- 336–23 Christianity, that *h·* disease and sin
- 358– 4 student who *h·* by teaching
- 369–21 charity that *h·* and saves ;
- 380– 2 if a divine Principle alone *h·*,
- *Ret.* 26– 3 the divine power which *h·*.
- 50– 4 that divine power which *h·* ;
- 63– 4 *h·* sin as it *h·* sickness,
- *Un.* 48– 9 He *h·* all my ills,
- *Pul.* 82– 5 * which *h·* the stricken soul.
- *No.* 13– 3 makes disease unreal, and this *h·* it.
- 21–26 wherein Principle *h·* and saves.
- *'01.* 12– 3 *h·* the sinning and the sick.
- *Hea.* 8– 2 *h·* both mind and body
- *My.* 3–15 not a law . . . that *h·* only the sick.
- 43–28 * that which *h·* and saves.
- 52– 7 * giving . . . the love that *h·*.
- 107–29 *h·* the most violent stages of
- 132–30 *h·* the poor body,
- 154– 4 nor the drug itself that *h·*,
- 180–15 *h·* sin, sickness, disease,
- 183 12 unfolds, transfigures, *h·*.
- 204–30 divine Principle, *h·* all disease.
- 206– 6 holiness which *h·* and saves.
- 257– 3 that *h·* the wounded heart.
- 260– 2 that *h·* and saves mankind.
- 300–12 *h·* the most inveterate diseases.
- 300–23 the Christianity which *h·*,
- 348–13 and that *materia medica h·*
- 348–16 but God, *h·* and saves mankind.
- 364–16 *h·* all manner of sickness
- (*see also* **sick**)

health

advance
- *Mis.* 29–26 nor advance *h·* and length of days.

alias harmony
- *Mis.* 41–25 *h·*, *alias* harmony, is the normal

and character
- *Peo.* 7–28 the *h·* and character of

health

and happiness
Mis. 240–11   promoters of h· and happiness.
262– 1   designed to bring h· and happiness
My. 165–20   impart truth, h·, and happiness,
and harmony
Mis. 8– 5   produce h· and harmony,
59–15   or to restore h· and harmony,
187– 6   He established h· and harmony,
and heaven
Pul. 53–24   * the key to h· and heaven,
and holiness
Mis. 179–17   for that of h· and holiness?
194–12   redolent with love, h·, and holiness,
Man. 31–12   shall promote h· and holiness,
Ret. 59–16   the antipodes . . . of h· and holiness,
No. 46– 6   craving h· and holiness,
Pan. 10–28   statuesque being, h·, and holiness
My. 146–32   scale of being — for h· and holiness,
186–14   dwelleth all life, h·, and holiness,
196–28   work for their h· and holiness.
210–17   can only reflect . . . h·, and holiness.
211–15   allurements to h· and holiness,
and immortality
My. 182–23   giving grace, h·, and immortality
and Life
Un. 39– 4   yield to holiness, h·, and Life,
and life
Rud. 12–27   maintains human h· and life.
No. 5–17   destroy both human h· and life.
'01. 33–10   * it was not the h· and life of religion,
Peo. 8–17   and lean upon it for h· and life.
My. 129–22   gives to man h· and life
and morals
Mis. 62– 3   individuality, h·, and morals ;
Ret. 71–30   end in destroying h· and morals.
No. 18–11   need of better h· and morals.
and peace
Mis. 169–24   h· and peace and hope for all.
My. 350–18   crushing out of h· and peace,
and sickness
Ret. 57–27   good and evil, h· and sickness,
'00. 4– 2   good and evil h· and sickness,
and strength
Mis. 7–29   they think that h· and strength
Pul. 52–16   * receive light, h·, and strength,
as real as
No. 5–18   If disease is as real as h·,
better
Mis. 24–14   and ever after was in better h·
239– 4   I never was in better h·.
365–15   universal need of better h·
No. 18–11   universal need of better h·
board of
My. 128– 6   A coroner's inquest, a board of h·,
340–13   a simple board of h·,
bring
My. 40–18   * its pristine power to bring h·
change to
No. 40–26   comes with the change to h·,
consciousness of
Mis. 311–17   abiding consciousness of h·,
My. 349– 4   consciousness of h·, holiness,
demonstrates
My. 274–14   demonstrates h·, holiness, and
doctrine of
My. 87–29   * this doctrine of h·, happiness,
equivalent for
Mis. 300–32   withholds a slight equivalent for h·.
fatal to
My. 249–13   mental miasma fatal to h·,
felt in
Mis. 183– 7   felt in h·, happiness, and holiness :
found
Mis. 247– 7   I found h· in just what I teach.
freedom of
Mis. 101–12   freedom of h·, holiness, and
fruits of
Ret. 62– 6   bring forth better fruits of h·,
good
Mis. 365–16   Good h· and a more spiritual
No. 18–22   Good h· and a more spiritual
gospel of
Mis. 241–26   rejoices in the gospel of h·.
harmony and
Rud. 3–23   upon the body in harmony and h·.
her
Pul. 37– 7   * Her h· is excellent,
his
Mis. 308– 4   for his h· or holiness,
My. 211–26   undermining his h·,
holiness and
Mis. 25– 2   against his holiness and h·.
human
Rud. 12–27   maintains human h· and life.
No. 5–17   both human h· and life.

health

improvement in
Mis. 243– 4   decided improvement in h·.
indispensable to
Mis. 67–16   indispensable to h·, happiness,
instantaneous
Un. 7–15   raise the dying to instantaneous h·.
is catching
Mis. 229– 5   If he believed . . . h· is catching
law of
Un. 6–13   Until the heavenly law of h·,
laws of
Mis. 6–26   where laws of h· are strictly enforced,
life and
(see life)
maintain
Mis. 38– 4   ability to gain and maintain h·,
moral
Ret. 35– 5   for physical and moral h·
nor disease
My. 302– 6   life nor death, h· nor disease,
normal condition of
Ret. 13–23   in a normal condition of h·.
not disease
My. 239– 1   h·, not disease ; Truth, not error ;
not of sickness
Un. 3–18   of h·, not of sickness ;
obstacles to
Mis. 309–21   include all obstacles to h·,
of my countenance
Un. 29–26   h· of my countenance, — Psal. 42 : 11.
Pan. 4–23   h· of my countenance, — Psal. 42 : 11.
of the community
Mis. 43–31   the h· of the community.
or existence
Rud. 12–18   h· or existence of mankind,
or holiness
Mis. 308– 4   for his h· or holiness,
or morals
Mis. 62– 5   improve h· or morals,
over sickness
Mis. 321–11   triumphs . . . of h· over sickness,
path to
Mis. 308– 8   and loses the path to h·,
perfect
Mis. 5– 8   perfect h· and perfect morals
physical
My. 93–14   * physical h· and spiritual peace.
Principle of
Mis. 163–31   heralding the Principle of h·,
promote
Mis. 350–29   promote h· and spiritual growth.
Man. 31–12   promote h· and holiness,
real as
No. 17–27   would be . . . as real as h·,
redolent with
'01. 12–18   redolent with h·, holiness, and
regained
Rud. 15– 6   surprise of suddenly regained h·
restore
Ret. 48–20   to restore h·, hope, and harmony
No. 5–16   restore h· and perpetuate life,
restored to
Mis. 180– 6   beholding me restored to h·.
Pul. 34–28   by which I was restored to h· ;
results in
Mis. 15–11   results in h·, happiness, and
saving
My. 274–28   thy saving h· among all — Psal. 67 : 2.
sickness to
Mis. 220–17   from sickness to h·.
state of
Mis. 219–25   a state of h· is but a state of
My. 349– 3   A scientific state of h· is
tendency to
No. 46–22   this upward tendency to h·,
their
My. 167–20   my prayer for their h·,
to man
Peo. 12–26   He would, give h· to man ;
My. 219–16   giving of life and h· to man
to obtain
Ret. 65–29   expect to obtain h·, harmony,
to the sick
Mis. 168– 1   h· to the sick, salvation from
true
Mis. 298–25   true consciousness is the true h·.
undertaken in
No. 4– 4   had better be undertaken in h·
will be restored
Mis. 41–25   and h· will be restored ;
without
Peo. 12–28   without h· there could be no heaven.

Mis. 6–31   h· is generally the rule ;
37– 6   toward purity, h·, holiness, and

health

Mis.	99–27	make way for *h·*, holiness,
	127–15	bread of heaven, *h·*, holiness,
	172–27	*h·*, holiness, and immortality
	212–19	*h·*, happiness, and life
	238–15	*h·*, virtue, and heaven ;
	245–13	its uplifting influence upon the *h·*,
	259– 6	of *h·*, not of sickness ;
	315–18	prove sound in sentiment, *h·*, and
Chr.	53–36	For *h·* makes room.
Ret.	88– 7	from the tomb to *h·*,
Un.	64– 6	conscious of only *h·*, holiness, and
Rud.	8–26	If by such lower means the *h·* is
	9–28	whatever militates against *h·*,
	11–13	*H·* is the consciousness of
	11–24	*h·*, harmony, and Life eternal.
No.	4– 2	has restored the sick to *h·* ;
	28–12	is found to bring with it *h·*,
	34– 2	leading up to *h·*, harmony, and
'01.	2– 2	demonstrated — *h·*, holiness,
	34–27	no intelligence, *h·*, hope, nor
'02.	9– 3	All-power — giving life, *h·*, holiness ;
Peo.	12–27	heaven more willingly than *h·* ;
Po.	32–17	That *h·* may my efforts repay ;
My.	18–12	bread of heaven, *h·*, holiness,
	103–21	*h·*, longevity, and morals of men;
	118–28	*h·*, harmony, holiness,
	124– 7	*h·*, harmony, growth, grandeur, and
	153–30	will give thee rest, peace, *h·*,
	155–13	run in joy, *h·*, holiness,
	160–17	for actual being, *h·*, holiness,
	205–28	Hence *h·*, holiness, immortality,
	247– 8	its rules are *h·*, holiness, and
	255– 1	*h·*, holiness, and immortality,
	275–22	and my dear enemies' *h·*,
	300–16	and raise the dying to *h·*?
	300–17	raise the dying to *h·* in Christ's
	344–22	* the *h·* laws of the States
	346– 9	* she is in the flesh and in *h·*.

Heal the Sick

Pul.	28– 7	* " *H·ʼ the Sʼ*," — *Matt.* 10 : 8.

healthful

Mis.	170–10	understanding is *h·* life.

health-giving

Mis.	19–32	*h·* and joy-inspiring.
Ret.	64–25	in *h·*, deathless Truth and Love.
	88–14	*h·* and life-bestowing qualities,

healthier

Mis.	229–24	become *h·*, holier, happier, and
My.	296–15	He is wiser to-day, *h·* and happier,

health-seeking

My.	90–13	* while *h·* is the door . . . for many,

healthy

Mis.	229– 6	exposed to contact with *h·* people,
	252–13	*h·* thoughts are reality
Rud.	12–25	free the minds of the *h·* from any
Peo.	5–25	a *h·* mind and body.
My.	14–25	* it is in such a *h·* state that
	81– 4	* *h·* satisfaction with life.
	301– 6	found to be a *h·* fermentation,

heaped

Pul.	45–17	* Much was the ridicule *h·* upon
My.	30–21	* they were *h·* high with bills,

heaps

My.	229–24	*H·* upon *h·* of praise

hear

Mis.	6– 1	We *h·* from the pulpits that
	17– 1	*h·* and record the thunderings
	28– 3	neither see, *h·*, feel, taste,
	35–21	go to church to *h·* it expounded
	81–20	*why does not John h· this voice,*
	86–28	What mortals *h·*, see, feel,
	99– 4	and ears ye *h·* not ; — *see Mark* 8 : 18
	106–25	methinks I *h·* the soft, sweet sigh
	126– 5	to *h·* the soft music of our Sabbath
	132–14	* "like to *h·* from Dr. Cullis"
	151– 3	"My sheep *h·* my voice, — *John* 10 : 27.
	153–28	* *H·* the first music of this
	168– 3	what things ye shall see and *h·* :
	168– 8	those who, having ears, *h·* not,
	168– 9	how the deaf . . . *h·* ;
	170–29	and ears, ye *h·* not,
	213–22	"My sheep *h·* my voice, — *John* 10 : 27.
	218– 8	matter can neither see, *h·*, nor feel,
	244–21	the blind to see, the deaf to *h·*,
	248– 3	interpretation they refuse to *h·*
	269– 5	*H·* the Master on this subject :
	306–23	When angels visit us, we do not *h·* the
	308–16	" *H·*, O Israel : — *Deut.* 6 : 4.
	321–27	no desire to see or to *h·* what
	322– 6	expecting to *h·* me speak
	342–18	*H·* that human cry :
	368– 6	and cause the deaf to *h·*.

hear

Mis.	388–21	First at the tomb to *h·* his word :
Man.	94– 9	goes to *h·* and deride truth,
Chr.	55– 7	*h·* the voice of the — *John* 5 : 25.
	55– 7	they that *h·* shall live. — *John* 5 : 25.
	55–26	if any man *h·* my voice, — *Rev.* 3 : 20.
Ret.	9– 5	if she really did *h·* Mary's name
	16– 6	"Did you *h·* my daughter sing?
	93– 8	*H·* this saying of our Master,
Un.	8– 6	What you see, *h·*, feel, is a
	24–25	see, taste, *h·*, feel, smell.
Pul.	33– 4	* like Jeanne d'Arc, to *h·* "voices,"
	46– 3	* came to *h·* him preach,
	72–30	* "Did you ever *h·* of Jesus' taking
Rud.	5–19	body does not see, *h·*, smell, or taste.
No.	14–18	*H·* the words of our Master :
'00.	3– 3	cannot *h·* himself, unless he
	14–10	*h·* what the Spirit saith unto
'01.	3– 8	We *h·* it said the . . . have no God
	6–13	We *h·* that God is not God
	11–24	willing to *h·* a sermon
	15–21	*h·* the following thunderbolt
Hea.	16– 3	having ears, *h·* and understand.
	16–20	They can neither see, *h·*, feel, taste,
Po.	16–20	'Mid graves do I *h·* the glad voices
	21–10	at the tomb to *h·* his word :
My.	15–29	* To *h·* it like the rest.
	52–26	* interest of the world to *h·* her
	71–25	* can see and *h·* the two Readers
	72– 1	* could *h·* what was said.
	80– 2	* To *h·* prosperous, contented men
	80–26	* or who wanted to *h·* it.
	132– 5	go to the Gospels, and there we *h·* :
	152–21	if ye would *h·* His voice,
	153– 1	I *h·* that the loving hearts
	182–20	the deaf *h·* the words of the Book,
	186–22	yet speaking, I will *h·*." — *Isa.* 65 : 24.
	196– 9	every man be swift to *h·*, — *Jas.* 1 : 19.
	280–15	chapter sub-title — *Deut.* 6 : 4.
	280–18	does not *h·* our prayers only because
	296– 9	chapter sub-title — *Deut.* 6 : 4.
	316– 4	I still *h·* the harvest song

heard

Mis.	81–24	be *h·* divinely and humanly.
	120–17	call of peace will at length be *h·*
	128–12	and *h·*, and seen — *Phil.* 4 : 9.
	171–18	would prove his right to be *h·*
	206– 6	is *h·* the Father and Mother's welcome,
	237–30	had *h·* the awful story
	246–13	scarcely been *h·* and hushed, when
	246–22	was *h·* crying in the wilderness,
	267– 1	screaming, to make itself *h·* above
	269–30	*h·* the great Red Dragon *whispering*
	277– 5	trying to be *h·* above Truth,
	328–13	Hast not thou *h·* this Christ knock
	329–25	voice of the turtle is *h·* — *Song* 2 : 12.
	342–17	they *h·* the shout,
	360–27	is *h·* as of you saying
	379–13	I never *h·* him say that
	385– 5	Thou hast *h·* my prayer ;
	398–22	*H·* ye the glad sound?
Chr.	53–43	silent healing, heaven *h·*,
Ret.	8– 4	I repeatedly *h·* a voice,
	8– 9	I *h·* somebody call *Mary*,
	8–16	so loud that Mehitable *h·* it,
	8–24	my cousin had *h·* the voice,
	15–26	I had not *h·* of these cases
	61–19	voice is not *h·* ;" — *Psal.* 19 : 3.
Un.	2– 4	no place where His voice is not *h·*;
	28–22	nor ear *h·*." — *I Cor.* 2 : 9.
	51– 5	is neither seen, felt, *h·*, nor
Pul.	2– 5	the fame which I *h·*." — *I Kings* 10 : 7.
	12– 5	I *h·* a loud voice — *Rev.* 12 : 10.
	33– 4	* she *h·* her name called
	33– 7	* if she *h·* the voice again
	41–20	* until all who wished had *h·* and
	59– 8	* *h·* these exercises four times
	74–22	not at all as I have *h·* her talk.
No.	39– 6	offered to be *h·* of men,
	39– 7	speaking loud enough to be *h·* ;
	45–13	Let it not be *h·* in Boston
'01.	11–21	nor too transcendental to be *h·*
'02.	9–21	When first I *h·* the life-giving sound
Peo.	1–14	beatings of our heart can be *h·* ;
Po.	37– 5	Oh, Thou hast *h·* my prayer ;
	53–11	Till *h·* at silvery eve
	71–22	Is *h·* your "Cry aloud !" — *Isa.* 58 : 1.
	75– 1	*H·* ye the glad sound?
My.	13– 7	first that I had even *h·* of it.
	31–16	* expressions of surprise . . . were *h·*
	32– 8	* Mrs. Conant could be *h·* perfectly
	59–19	* as I *h·* the sonorous tones of the
	59–27	* I *h·* her talk it before it was
	78–31	* understanding all they *h·*,
	126–14	And a voice was *h·*, saying,
	184– 4	men have not *h·* . . . what God hath

heard
My. 187–14 message that ye *h·* — *I John* 3 : 11.
    245–17 voice of Truth and Love be *h·*
    249– 5 error strives to be *h·* above Truth,
    289–17 is *h·* no more in England,
    319– 5 I *h·* nothing further from him

hearer
Mis. 127–28 on the ear or heart of the *h·* ;

hearers
Mis. 302–27 the good that his *h·* received
My. 124–16 hearts of these *h·* and speakers,
    352–21 the *h·* and the doers of God's Word.

hearest
My. 290–25 Thou *h·* me always,'' — *John* 11 : 42.

heareth
Ret. 9–11 for Thy servant *h·*.'' — *I Sam.* 3 : 9.
Pul. 33– 9 * for Thy servant *h·*.'' — *I Sam.* 3 : 9.

hearing
Mis. 155–23 the pleasure of *h·* from you.
    344– 2 *h·* of a Pythagorean professor
Ret. 40–23 refused me a *h·* in their halls
    79– 3 Not by the *h·* of the ear
Rud. 5–13 *h·* in the material ear,
'00. 1–16 C. S. already has a *h·*
My. 105–17 sight to the blind, *h·* to the deaf,
    109–16 by the *h·* of the ear,
    112– 4 where Science gains no *h·*.
    224–25 would not deny their authors a *h·*,

hearken
Peo. 12– 1 *h·* to the higher law of God,
My. 126–14 (*h·* not to her lies),

hearkened
Mis. 268– 8 *h·* to My commandments ! — *Isa.* 48 : 18.

hears
Mis. 81–26 divine Love *h·* and answers
    324– 5 He *h·* the sounds of festivity
Ret. 25–25 matter neither sees, *h·*, nor feels
Un. 25– 8 *h·*, feels, tastes, smells as Mind,

hearsay
Mis. 146– 9 I cannot accept *h·*,

heart (*see also* **heart's**)
another's
Mis. 98–28 * another's *h·* would'st reach.''
answering to
'00. 1– 7 *h·* answering to *h·*,
bore its grief
Po. 25–16 *h·* bore its grief and is still !
change of
Mis. 50–18 *Do you believe in change of h·?*
    50–26 This change of *h·* would deliver man
    51– 1 This change of *h·* is essential to
Ret. 14–20 experienced a change of *h·* ;
cheer the
'02. 17–30 cheer the *h·* susceptible of light
clergyman's
Ret. 15– 2 the good clergyman's *h·* also
contrite
Un. 61–27 contrite *h·* soonest discerns this
dear
Po. 24–20 Dear *h·* of Love,
denies it
Mis. 211–32 when the *h·* denies it,
doubting
Mis. 241–24 doubting *h·* looks up through faith,
each
My. 148–22 what is each *h·* in this house
encouraged the
My. 132–17 encouraged the *h·* of every member
engraven on the
Mis. 376–13 * living Saviour engraven on the *h·*.
enlightened
Ret. 81–18 The enlightened *h·* loathes error,
every
Mis. 213–29 Love will reign in every *h·*,
    231–28 brought sunshine to every *h·*.
Man. 60–16 love should abide in every *h·*
Ret. 95–10 * weight of ill In every *h·* ;
Pul. 10–28 Thy blessing on every *h·*
No. 7– 3 to be . . . true rejoices every *h·*.
My. 132–13 at this time and in every *h·*
falls on the
Mis. 394– 3 falls on the *h·* like the dew
Po. 45– 3 falls on the *h·* like the dew
fervent
Mis. xi– 9 fervent *h·* and willing hand
for any fate
My. 185– 5 * With a *h·* for any fate ;
full
My. 201–13 I thank you out of a full *h·*.
    338–19 *h·* full of love towards God

heart
generosity of
My. 331–27 * the noble generosity of *h·*
good man's
My. 129–24 good man's *h·* takes hold on heaven,
great
Pul. 12–20 nearer to the great *h·* of Christ ;
'01. 30–26 great *h·* of the unselfed Christian
Po. 43–10 Father, in Thy great *h·* hold them
My. 131–12 signet of the great *h·*,
grown faint
Mis. 262–18 *h·* grown faint with hope deferred.
harden the
Mis. 301–28 error tends to harden the *h·*,
head and
Mis. 160– 9 sweet rhythm of head and *h·*,
    268–20 body and mind, head and *h·* ;
heal the
Mis. 398–17 Feed the hungry, heal the *h·*,
Ret. 46–23 Feed the hungry, heal the *h·*,
Pul. 17–22 Feed the hungry, heal the *h·*,
Po. 14–21 Feed the hungry, heal the *h·*,
her
Mis. 386–11 This hour looks on her *h·*
Po. 49–16 This hour looks on her *h·*
My. 126–19 she saith in her *h·*, — *Rev.* 18 : 7.
    341–13 And in her *h·* is beating
his
Mis. 30–25 fool hath said in his *h·*, — *Psal.* 14 : 1.
    70– 8 ''thinketh in his *h·*, — *Prov.* 23 : 7.
    112–31 fool hath said in his *h·*, — *Psal.* 14 : 1.
    148– 2 meditates evil against us in his *h·*.
    212– 2 a fool that saith in his *h·*,
    335– 3 shall say in his *h·*, — *Matt.* 24 : 48.
'01. 18–24 fool hath said in his *h·*, — *Psal.* 14 : 1.
Peo. 3– 2 ''thinketh in his *h·*, — *Prov.* 23 : 7.
My. 33–18 the truth in his *h·*. — *Psal.* 15 : 2.
    201–20 in him who says in his *h·* :
    227–30 fool hath said in his *h·*, — *Psal.* 14 : 1.
    228–17 in the least in his *h·*, — *Matt.* 11 : 11.
    228–25 the truth in his *h·*.'' — *Psal.* 15 : 2.
his own
Mis. 324–17 the clearer pane of his own *h·*
homeless
Po. 28–15 Hover the homeless *h·* !
honest
Ret. 83–14 this error, in an honest *h·*,
human
    (*see* **human**)
humble
My. 188–31 admittance to a humble *h·*,
hungry
Mis. 127–11 When a hungry *h·* petitions
    322–20 God that feedeth the hungry *h·*,
'02. 17–25 worth satisfies the hungry *h·*,
My. 18– 8 When a hungry *h·* petitions
hushed in the
Po. 35–11 Hushed in the *h·* whereunto
hushed is the
Mis. 395–13 Hushed is the *h·*.
Po. 57–20 Hushed is the *h·*.
little
Po. 24– 5 O little *h·*, To me thou art
lone
Mis. 392–11 To my lone *h·* thou art a power
Po. 20–15 To my lone *h·* thou art a power
    68– 5 sweet pledge to my lone *h·*
long-hushed
Mis. 390–20 Ask of its June, the long-hushed *h·*,
Po. 55–21 Ask of its June, the long-hushed *h·*,
loving
Mis. 149–25 whose altar is a loving *h·*,
    370–18 infinite care from His loving *h·*.
    399–19 Rolled away from loving *h·*
Pul. 16– 4 Rolled away from loving *h·*
Po. 76– 3 Rolled away from loving *h·*
lowly in
My. 41– 7 * meek and lowly in *h·* are blessed
loyal
Mis. 277– 9 a *h·* loyal to God is patient and
loyal at
My. 225– 3 while the loyal at *h·*
man's
My. 277–10 A bullet in a man's *h·*
many a
Mis. 340– 3 and repose from many a *h·*.
meeting heart
My. 124–11 *h·* meeting heart across continents
meets heart
Mis. 207– 2 *h·* meets heart reciprocally blest,
merry
My. 99– 5 * merry *h·* that doeth good
mine
My. 188– 5 mine eyes and mine *h·* — *I Kings* 9 : 3.
music in the
Mis. 330– 8 make music in the *h·*.

heart

my
Mis.	11– 6	should aim a ball at my *h·*,
	116–12	question, ever nearest to my *h·*,
	145–32	children that my *h·* folds within it,
	153–21	cleansed my *h·* in vain." — *Psal.* 73 : 13.
	159–11	My *h·* has many rooms :
	180–13	then my *h·* went out to God,
	251– 7	but my *h·* will with tenderness
	262–29	to relieve my *h·* of its secrets,
	266–21	I cannot find it in my *h·* not to
	317– 2	my *h·* replies, *Yes,* if you are doing
	321– 7	My *h·* is filled with joy,
	345–19	* "My *h·* has always assured and
	371–14	and my *h·* pleads for them
	393–23	To my *h·* that would be bleaching
	396–13	My *h·* unbidden joins rehearse ;
Ret.	14–26	and know my *h·* : — *Psal.* 139 : 23.
	23–17	My *h·* knew its Redeemer.
	31–23	My *h·* bent low before the
Un.	7– 6	from my *h·* of hearts,
Pan.	13– 5	and nearest my *h·*,
Hea.	10–27	so panteth my *h·* for the true fount
Peo.	13–27	* "My *h·* has assured and reassured me
Po.	3–14	Love divine doth fill my *h·*.
	16– 4	My *h·* hath thy verdure.
	52– 7	To my *h·* that would be bleaching
	59– 5	My *h·* unbidden joins rehearse,
My.	9–27	satisfied with what my *h·* gives
	15–12	My *h·* goes out to you
	33–10	and know my *h·* : — *Psal.* 139 : 23.
	125–11	to dip my pen in my *h·*
	148–20	and my *h·* is asking :
	155– 4	church, nestled so near my *h·*
	170–13	To your home in my *h·* !
	173–20	my *h·* welcomed each and all.
	192–15	My *h·* hovers around your churches
	197–26	in the home of my *h·*,
	229–25	That which I said in my *h·*
	253– 6	My *h·* and hope are with you.
	270–19	Those words . . . fill my *h·* :
	271–30	"nearest and dearest" to my *h·*
	296–26	Clara Barton dipped her pen in my *h·*,
	311–10	It was not in my *h·* to turn the
	323–17	* My *h·* has been too full

my own
Pul.	21– 9	praying for it to inhabit my own *h·*

nation's
Pul.	10–11	they planted a nation's *h·*,

no
'00.	3– 6	no *h·* his comfort.

of a moonbeam
Ret.	31–25	soft as the *h·* of a moonbeam,

of a rock
Mis.	144–15	secret in the *h·* of a rock,

of Christianity
Mis.	25– 5	it is the *h·* of Christianity,

of God
Mis.	253–22	mother's love touches the *h·* of God,

of history
Mis.	93– 4	*h·* of history shall be made glad !

of humanity
Mis.	155–10	find access to the *h·* of humanity.
	294– 8	he inscribes on the *h·* of humanity
Pan.	12–16	from off the *h·* of humanity,
My.	257–11	is winning the *h·* of humanity
	265– 4	at the *h·* of humanity
	268–28	and you see the *h·* of humanity

of man
Mis.	203–10	so the *h·* of man to man." — *Prov.* 27 : 19.
My.	189–16	love it creates in the *h·* of man ;

of millions
My.	289–18	lives on in the *h·* of millions.

of our country
Mis.	303–24	profitable to the *h·* of our country.

of the city
My.	79– 9	* in the *h·* of the city of Boston,

of the harlot
My.	126– 2	retaining the *h·* of the harlot

of the hearer
Mis.	127–28	on the ear or *h·* of the hearer ;

of the leaves
Po.	16–18	To the *h·* of the leaves

of the pink
Ret.	17–12	On the *h·* of the pink
Po.	62–15	On the *h·* of the pink

of Truth
Ret.	75–21	strikes at the *h·* of Truth.

one
Po.	68– 1	So one *h·* is left me
My.	189–12	from one *h·* to another,

one in
Mis.	135– 7	and we shall be one in *h·*,

one's own
'02.	2– 6	on the tablet of one's own *h·*,

heart

or in doctrine
'02.	2–26	either in *h·* or in doctrine ;

our
Peo.	1–14	beatings of our *h·* can be heard ;

overflow of
Mis.	338–24	* It needs the overflow of *h·*,

pierced the
Mis.	339–21	and hast pierced the *h·*

prays
No.	39– 7	when the *h·* prays, and not the lips,

preparation of
Mis.	115–14	need of a proper preparation of *h·*

preparation of the
Rud.	9–15	requires a preparation of the *h·*

pulsates
Mis.	152–13	as a mother whose *h·* pulsates with

pure
Mis.	361– 2	pure *h·* that sees God.
My.	34– 3	and a pure *h·* ; — *Psal.* 24 : 4.
	187–12	charity out of a pure *h·*, — *I Tim.* 1 : 5.

pure in
Mis.	15– 8	pure in *h·* : — *Matt.* 5 : 8.
	168–20	pure in *h·* clap their hands.
	185– 2	None but the pure in *h·* shall see
Ret.	26–25	none but the pure in *h·* can see
Pul.	35–10	'pure in *h·*' — *Matt.* 5 : 8.

rapture to the
'02.	4–10	music to the ear, rapture to the *h·*

reach not the
'02.	16–25	reach not the *h·* nor renovate it ;

records of the
Mis.	390–25	In records of the *h·*.
Po.	56– 4	In records of the *h·*.

rejoices the
Mis.	12–25	law of Love rejoices the *h·* ;

rosebud
Po.	46– 1	Fair girl, thy rosebud *h·* rests warm

searching the
Mis.	204– 5	Truth, searching the *h·*,

secret
Pul.	83– 4	* In our secret *h·* our better self is

self-forgetful
Mis.	250–24	self-forgetful *h·* that overflows ;

signs of the
Po. page 24		poem

sings to the
Mis.	204–10	sings to the *h·* a song of angels.

smite the
Ret.	81– 1	smite the *h·* and threaten

softened
Mis.	354–16	a *h·* softened, a character subdued,

sore
Po.	22–15	To heal humanity's sore *h·* ;

speaks
Mis.	262–10	When the *h·* speaks,

stricken to the
Mis.	329–28	stricken to the *h·* with winter's snow,

struggling
Mis.	63–24	Even as the struggling *h·*,

sympathizing
Ret.	5–23	* sympathizing *h·*, and a placid spirit.

tender
My.	158–21	makes the *h·* tender, faithful,

tendril of the
My.	258– 8	bind the tenderest tendril of the *h·*

thankful
My.	332– 5	* emotions of the thankful *h·*,

that
Ret.	81–19	else that *h·* is consciously untrue
Po.	66–10	tell how that *h·* is silent and sad,

that loves
'02.	18–17	*h·* that loves as Jesus loved.

that's hungry
Mis.	391– 3	I hope the *h·* that's hungry
Po.	38– 2	I hope the *h·* that's hungry

thine
Mis.	298– 1	with all thine *h·* ; — *Prov.* 3 : 5.
'01.	34–30	with all thine *h·* ; — *Prov.* 3 : 5.
My.	170–23	desires of thine *h·*. — *Psal.* 37 : 4.

thine own
Mis.	328–14	at the door of thine own *h·*,

this
Mis.	127–13	If this *h·*, humble and trustful,
Ret.	80–14	this *h·* becomes obediently
Po.	24–13	O Love divine, This *h·* of Thine
My.	18–10	If this *h·*, humble and trustful,
	150–12	this *h·* must be honest

thy
Mis.	98–28	* Thy *h·* must overflow,
	400– 8	In thy *h·* Dwell serene,
Pul.	16–20	In thy *h·* Dwell serene,
Po.	23– 6	Come ever o'er thy *h·* ?
	76–19	In thy *h·* Dwell serene,
My.	161–24	say not in thy *h·* : Sickness is possible
	183– 2	with all thy *h·*, — *Luke* 10 : 27.

heart
to heart
Mis. 143– 1 can feel the touch of h· to heart
262– 9 chapter sub-title
388–11 life most sweet, as h· to heart
Po. 7–11 life most sweet, as h· to heart
My. 162–10 spiritual cooperation, h· to heart,
touched
My. 150–11 A h· touched and hallowed by
touches the
My. 294–24 touches the h· and will move the
touch the
My. 186– 9 song and sermon will touch the h·,
true
My. 259–19 a true h·, and a helping hand
upright in
Mis. 258–17 saveth the upright in h·.'' — Psal. 7 : 10.
waiting
Mis. 384–14 Be patient, waiting h· :
Po. 36–13 Be patient, waiting h· :
My. 208–14 dear letter to my waiting h·,
weary
Po. vii–15 * a balm to the weary h·.
what other
Ret. 90–20 What other h· yearns with her
whole
Man. 44–26 God requires our whole h·,
My. 132–31 and whose whole h· is faint ;
willing
Po. 26–11 Lincoln's own Great willing h·
with heart
My. 154–27 Communing h· with heart,
without
Po. 42– 6 Without h· to define them,
without the
Mis. 302– 8 the skeleton without the h·,
wounded
My. 257– 3 love that heals the wounded h·.
written on the
Mis. 172–20 which law is written on the h·,
yearning of the
Mis. 178– 5 from a yearning of the h· ;
young
Po. 66–12 but a young h· and glad
your
'00. 14–26 say in your h· as the devout
My. 62–13 * fill your h· with the joy of
133–29 your h· has discovered it.
150–18 This will stir your h·.
271–22 * nearest and dearest to your h·
327–12 * article will make your h· glad,
your heart's
My. 188–18 inner sanctuary, your heart's h·,

Mis. ix–19 There is an old age of the h·,
50–23 the belief that the h· is matter
227–23 speaking the truth in the h· ;
230–23 * With a h· for any fate ;
320– 6 dear to the h· of Christian Scientists;
329–11 even as the h· may be ;
336–25 looks in upon the h·,
Ret. 81–15 supreme advent of Truth in the h·,
Po. 2– 6 * but comes not to the h·.''
34–18 Bearing no bitter memory at h·;
My. 42–16 * With a h· filled with gratitude
88–22 * in the h· of all that increasing host
134– 3 a h· wholly in protest
160– 4 The h· that beats mostly for self is
188–21 where the h· of a Southron has
heart-and-hand-fellowship
'01. 1– 1 I extend my h·
heart-beats
Chr. 53–16 With fierce h· ;
My. 189–11 a diapason of h·,
heart-disease and **heart disease**
Mis. 50–26 would deliver man from h·,
My. 80– 6 * of h· d·, of cancer ;
heartfelt
Mis. 231–29 echo such tones of h· joy
My. 32– 6 * h· appeal to the creator.
51–29 * h· thanks and gratitude
256–10 deep-drawn, h· breath of thanks
347– 8 accept my h· acknowledgment of
hearth
Pul. 76–15 * before the h· is a large rug
heart's
Mis. 106–30 awaken the h· harpstrings.
107–10 all the h· homage belongs to God.
251–10 loyal to the h· core to religion,
276– 9 my h· desire met the demand.
Ret. 23–13 h· bridal to more spiritual
31–18 h· untamed desire which breaketh
Po. 53–17 Come at the sad h· call,

heart's
My. 188–17 your inner sanctuary, your h· heart,
236– 3 my full h· love for them
259–12 I return my h· wireless love.
hearts (see also **hearts'**)
abides in the
My. 124–16 abides in the h· of these hearers
all love
Po. 9–11 reason made right and h· all love.
and hands
My. 153– 2 loving h· and hands of the
197–28 work of your h· and hands.
and lives
Mis. 291–24 fall gently on the h· and lives of
are found
Mis. 386– 5 home and peace and h· are found
Po. 49– 8 home and peace and h· are found
are inspired
Mis. 101– 1 how h· are inspired,
bleeding
Mis. 275–15 the wounds of bleeding h·,
Po. 27–16 H· bleeding ere they break
dear
Mis. 142–17 Because your dear h· expressed
filled
My. 362–19 * h· filled with gratitude to God,
full
'00. 14–18 hold in your full h· fervently
grateful
My. 332– 9 * a tribute of grateful h·?
great
My. 197–13 great h· and ready hands of our
happy
'00. 1– 2 the tone of your happy h·,
My. 155–27 happy h· and ripening goodness.
heart of
Un. 7– 7 and from my heart of h·,
heroic
'01. 1–20 characterize heroic h· ;
honest
Mis. 357–17 the good and honest h·
human
Mis. 294–15 the flowers of human h·
303–14 at the door of human h·,
hungry
My. 147–29 heavenly homesick or hungry h·
kind
My. 153– 4 if these kind h· will only
lifted up
My. 81–19 * h· lifted up, spoke simply
loving
Pul. 8–24 loving h· and deft fingers
My. 13–17 loving h·, pledged to this
117–26 their talents and loving h·
153– 2 loving h· and hands of the
208– 9 mirrored forth by your loving h·,
minds and
Mis. 169–17 borne fully to our minds and h·.
no separator of
Mis. 150–10 Space is no separator of h·.
of all
No. v– 7 transparent to the h· of all
My. 327–12 * made glad the h· of all
of Christians
Mis. 383–15 and in the h· of Christians.
of Christian Scientists
Mis. 145–26 When the h· of Christian Scientists
of men
Mis. 121– 2 inscribed upon the h· of men :
My. 123– 6 which moves the h· of men
of this people
My. 187–26 has been in the h· of this people
our
Mis. 110–18 Our h· have kept time together,
135– 4 Principle, . . . is next to our h·,
144–21 be this hope in each of our h·,
306–26 love they create in our h·.
344–24 His words, living in our h·,
Pul. 9– 7 never be shattered in our h·,
Rud. 3–10 His history is emphatic in our h·,
My. 39–25 * Our h· were thrilled by her
199–16 C. S., so dear to our h·
257–18 our h· are kneeling humbly.
our own
No. 7– 9 cancel error in our own h·,
overflowing
Mis. 348– 6 with h· overflowing with love
pleading
Po. 78–15 Give to the pleading h· comfort
quivering
Mis. 274–25 headless trunks, and quivering h·
stout
Mis. 222–23 will make stout h· quail.
strong
My. 290– 1 the strong h· of New England

hearts

swell the
My. 19–27 swell the h· of the members

their
Mis. 277– 1 their h· are not troubled.
Pul. 85– 6 * turn their h· in gratitude
'01. 32–11 shield the whole world in their h·,
My. 6–25 even the outcome of their h·,
94–29 even the outcome of their h·,
160–17 Then they open their h· to it

the very
My. 122–31 the very h· that rejected it

true
Mis. 384– 4 And true h· greet,
Po. 36– 3 And true h· greet,

two
Mis. 290– 2 to the compact of two h·.
384– 3 When two h· meet,
Po. 36– 2 When two h· meet,

unveiled
My. 199–20 of strengthened hands, of unveiled h·,

waiting
Po. 39–16 And be your waiting h· elate,

warm
My. 124– 9 willing hands, and warm h·,

weary
My. 93–14 * it has rare lures for weary h·,

were thrilled
My. 64– 6 * h· were thrilled with tender

your
Mis. 143–10 in each of your h· !
156–11 heaven of Love within your h·.
Hea. 16–14 come nearer your h·
My. 167–12 may fill your h·
193– 4 bring to your h· so much of heaven
197–28 work of your h· and hands.

Mis. 150–12 h· to-day are repeating their joy
152– 6 whose h· unite in the purposes of
152–17 h· of those who worship in this
262–12 acceptable to those who have h·.
Ret. 6– 2 * h· of those especially entrusted to
'01. 1– 2 to those whose h· have been
My. 195–27 in the h· of its members
326–20 turning the h· of the noble Southrons

hearts'

Mis. 141– 4 of your h· offering to her
Pul. 11– 6 rehearse your h· holy intents.
Po. 43–14 their pure h· off'ring,

heart-stirring

Ret. 2–15 h· air, "Scots wha hae wi' Wallace

heart-strings

Mis. 387– 1 the h· gently sweep,
Po. 50–18 the h· gently sweep
68–15 To sweep o'er the h·

hearty

Pul. 44– 6 * I send my h· congratulations.
My. 285– 5 accept my h· congratulations.
287– 4 enlists my h· sympathy.

heat

Mis. 130–18 burden in the h· of the day,
134–25 fermenting, and its h· hissing at
Ret. 79– 6 In this consuming h· false images
Un. 58–12 hypocrite melts in fervent h·.
Pul. 25– 3 * h· generated by two large boilers
No. 14–14 solar h· and light.
28– 4 melt in the fervent h· of suffering,
'00. 9–30 h· of the day." — Matt. 20 : 12.
My. 29–27 * breeze to temper the h·,
249–11 Unless withstood, the h· of hate
265–28 extremes of h· and cold ;

heated

'02. 9–18 is not the dream of a h· brain ;

heathen

Un. 15–21 found in h· religious history.
No. 34–20 infinitely beyond the h· conception
'00. 3–25 In the h· conception Yahwah,
3–29 the animus of h· religion
13–10 the apostle justly regards as h·,
Peo. 4–23 as material as the h· deities.
4–25 they inquired of these h· deities
My. 103–16 "Why do the h· rage, — Psal. 2 : 1.
118–29 which rests on a h· basis
159–25 Epictetus, a h· philosopher
200– 5 Let "the h· rage, — Psal. 2 : 1.
234–19 introducing C. S. into a h· nation,
234–26 prayer in and for a h· nation

heathenism

Pul. 75–10 would savor more of h· than of
My. 167–30 In our country the day of h·.

heating

Pul. 25– 2 * cooling . . . as well as h·

heaven (see also heaven's)

and earth
Mis. 86–20 as in the new h· and earth,
99–21 " H· and earth shall pass — Matt. 24 : 35.
111–17 " H· and earth shall pass — Matt. 24 : 35.
163–18 " H· and earth shall pass — Matt. 24 : 35.
167–24 Lord of h· and earth, — Luke 10 : 21.
Un. 59– 6 Principle which made h· and earth
No. 44–28 Lord of h· and earth, — Luke 10 : 21

antipode of
My. 181–30 material earth or antipode of h·.

army of
Mis. 334– 2 in the army of h·, — Dan. 4 : 35.

attainment of
Mis. 101–13 holiness, and the attainment of h·.

be praised
My. 200– 4 H· be praised for the signs of

bestows
Peo. 12–27 when our Father bestows h·

bound in
No. 32– 1 shall be bound in h·." — Matt. 16 : 19.

bread of
Mis. 127–15 to feed it with the bread of h·,
My. 18–12 to feed it with the bread of h·,
131– 9 bread of h· whereof if a man eat

breath of
Mis. 328–11 with a breath of h·,

comes down
Mis. 10–27 H· comes down to earth,

consciousness of
My. 118–28 the consciousness of h· within

demonstrates
'02. 6–24 points the way, demonstrates h·

dew of
Mis. 291–23 The dew of h· will fall

dews of
Mis. 154– 9 water it with the dews of h·,
My. 208–13 Like the gentle dews of h·

diapason of
Mis. 206–21 repeating this diapason of h· :

down from
Mis. 149–24 that cometh down from h·,
176–22 which came down from h·.
254– 7 that cometh down from h·
Un. 59– 9 one who came down from h·,
Pan. 14– 8 that cometh down from h·,
My. 156–21 that cometh down from h·,

earth and
Mis. 30–10 He saw the real earth and h·.
86–29 their present earth and h· :
228–19 fit for earth and h·.
Un. 50– 7 never absent from the earth and h· ;

earth and in
Mis. 113–27 to enjoy on earth and in h·,
151–15 real relative on earth and in h·.
'00. 2– 6 best people on earth and in h·.

earth to
(see earth)

enough of
Mis. 16– 4 enough of h· to come down to

enter
Mis. 241– 5 man will no more enter h· sick
Un. 37– 5 inherit eternal life and enter h· ?
My. 267 17 enter h· in proportion to their

far
Po. 22– 7 lo, the light ! far h· is nigh !

fitted for
Mis. 197– 9 fitted for h· in the way which

flood-gates of
Mis. 185–11 opens the very flood-gates of h· ;

foretaste of
Mis. 100–24 bring to earth a foretaste of h·.

gain
Mis. 53– 9 gain h·, the harmony of being.
174–26 whereby to gain h·.

gates of
Mis. 275–19 throw wide the gates of h·.
Ret. 71– 3 to open the gates of h·.

God and
Un. 37– 7 God and h·, or Life, are present,

happiness, and
Mis. 308– 8 path to health, happiness, and h·.
311–17 health, happiness, and h·.

harmonies of
My. 115– 7 echoing the harmonies of h·

harmony, and
No. 34– 3 up to health, harmony, and h·.

harmony is
Mis. 337–16 Harmony is h·.

harmony of
My. 274– 7 with the harmony of h· ;

health and
Pul. 53–24 * key to health and h·,

heaven

high
Mis. 122–25 Neither . . . can win high *h*·,
387–22 greetings glorious from high *h*·,
Pul. 12–19 reached high *h*·,
Po. 6–17 greetings glorious from high *h*·,
My. 189–5 that it reaches high *h*·

highway to
No. 33–13 Self-sacrifice is the highway to *h*·.

holiness and
Mis. 309–22 health, holiness, and *h*·.
Un. 64–6 health, holiness, and *h*·,

home and
Mis. 289–18 compatible with home and *h*·.
Pul. 11–8 find within it home, and *h*·.

homesick for
Mis. 177–30 I am constantly homesick for *h*·.

hope of
Mis. 311–22 lose my hope of *h*·.

hosts of
Po. 10–18 cheer the hosts of *h*· ;
My. 337–19 cheer the hosts of *h*· ;

hues of
Mis. 332–10 follow with hues of *h*·,
377–1 such forms and hues of *h*·,
'02. 20–5 hues of *h*·, tipping the dawn

husbands
'02. 5–10 *divine Love*, that *h*· husbands

insignia of
Ret. 80–2 and the insignia of *h*·.

is afar off
Mis. 342–20 and *h*· is afar off.''

is harmony
My. 267–16 *H*· is harmony,

is spiritual
My. 267–16 *H*· is spiritual.

joys of
Po. 24–1 Come to me, joys of *h*· !

kingdom of
(see **kingdom**)

less of
Pul. 87–20 more of earth . . . and less of *h*· ;

livery of
Mis. 19–18 But, taking the livery of *h*·

Lord of
Mis. 167–24 Lord of *h*· and earth, — Luke 10 : 21.
No. 44–28 Lord of *h*· and earth, — Luke 10 : 21.

message from
Po. 15–7 canst bear A message from *h*·

most of
'02. 17–8 that which has most of *h*·

never left
No. 36–7 conscious being never left *h*·

new
Mis. 21–7 beheld "a new *h*· — Rev. 21 : 1.
86–20 as in the new *h*· and earth,

of His presence
Un. 37–12 and the *h*· of His presence ;

of light
Po. 71–9 Spans our broad *h*· of light.

of Love
Mis. 156–10 *h*· of Love within your hearts.

of my youth
Po. 8–13 sketching in light the *h*· of my youth

of Soul
Mis. 394–5 the home, and the *h*· of Soul.
Po. 45–6 the home, and the *h*· of Soul.
My. 163–2 haven of hope, the *h*· of Soul,

of Spirit
My. 195–28 eternal in the *h*· of Spirit.

of Truth
Ret. 85–10 down from the *h*· of Truth and Love,

path to
'02. 11–9 and point the path to *h*·.
My. 176–8 pointing the path to *h*·

plan of
Mis. 296–14 and live on the plan of *h*· ?

poetry of
Po. 46–14 Sweet as the poetry of *h*·,

points to
Ret. 31–2 loss of . . . points to *h*·.

point to
Mis. 389–4 * "To point to *h*· and lead the way."
Po. 21–18 * "To point to *h*· and lead the way."

rang
Po. 70–17 Immortal Truth, — since *h*· rang,

rapid transit to
Mis. 206–1 take rapid transit to *h*·,

reaches
Un. 57–19 ladder which reaches *h*·.
My. 194–10 builds that which reaches *h*·.

realization of
My. 297–17 and a higher realization of *h*·.

recorded in
'02. 14–22 achievement . . . recorded in *h*·.

heaven

reign of
Mis. 384–12 The reign of *h*· begun,
'00. 15–29 The reign of *h*· begun,
Po. 36–11 The reign of *h*· begun,

reward in
'02. 11–25 reward in *h*· : — Matt. 5 : 12.
My. 6–12 reward in *h*·.'' — Matt. 5 : 12.

ruleth in
My. 200–6 ruleth in *h*· and upon earth,

so much of
My. 193–4 bring to your hearts so much of *h*·

stars of
Ret. 28–27 higher than the stars of *h*·.

takes hold on
My. 129–25 man's heart takes hold on *h*·,

this
Mis. 30–12 was not the door to this *h*·.

to reach
Mis. 235–3 no longer . . . die to reach *h*·,
Hea. 8–21 to reach *h*· through Principle

under
Mis. 185–15 There is no other way under *h*·
'00. 5–15 no other way under *h*·

unto
My. 126–16 reached unto *h*·, — Rev. 18 : 5.

verge of
Mis. 202–7 * Quite on the verge of *h*·.''
357–11 quite on the verge of *h*·.

virtue, and
Mis. 238–15 health, virtue, and *h*· ;

vision of
My. 155–19 a clear vision of *h*· here,

voice from
Mis. 168–15 voice from *h*· seems to say,

way to
Mis. 268–6 pointing the way to *h*·,
344–27 point out the way to *h*·

which is in
Mis. 85–15 Father which is in *h*· — Matt. 5 : 48.
287–7 Father, which is in *h*·.'' — Matt. 23 : 9.
Chr. 55–23 Father which is in *h*·, — Matt. 12 : 50.
Ret. 68–15 Father, which is in *h*·.'' — Matt 23 : 9.
Un. 53–28 Father, which is in *h*·.'' — Matt. 23 : 9.
59–10 *which is in h*·.'' — John 3 : 13.
Rud. 1–8 It is our Father which is in *h*·.
No. 36–9 which is in *h*·,'' — John 3 : 13.
Pan. 8–19 Father, which is in *h*· — Matt. 23 : 9.
9–12 Father which is in *h*· — Matt. 5 : 48.
'01. 8–16 Father which is in *h*· — Matt. 5 : 48.

windows of
My. 131–27 windows of *h*·, — Mal. 3 : 10.
132–4 windows of *h*·, — Mal. 3 : 10.
269–22 windows of *h*· are sending forth
269–27 windows of *h*·, — Mal. 3 : 10.

within us
My. 155–19 *h*· within us,
260–21 because of the *h*· within us.
303–31 foretasting *h*· within us.

wonder in
Mis. 337–8 Wonder in *h*· and on earth,
Pul. 83–27 * a great wonder in *h*·, — Rev. 12 : 1.

Mis. 33–5 they lost, and he won, *h*·.
67–28 removal of a person to *h*·,
83–24 lifted up his eyes to *h*·, — John 17 : 1.
151–16 "Whom have I in *h*· — Psal. 73 : 25.
205–22 with eternal life, holiness, *h*·.
213–30 *His* will be done on earth as in *h*·.
251–20 *H*· right here,
330–28 violet lifts its blue eye to *h*·,
339–4 took place once in *h*·,
373–27 in *h*· and in earth,'' — Matt. 28 : 18.
399–24 (*H*· chiselled squarely good)
Chr. 53–43 silent healing, *h*· heard,
Ret. 17–20 blossom and branches to *h*·.
Pul. 12–6 voice saying in *h*·, — Rev. 12 : 10.
16–9 (*H*· chiselled squarely good)
22–8 in earth, as it is in *h*·,'' — Matt. 6 : 10.
27–14 * from God out of *h*·,'' — see Rev. 3 : 12.
Pan. 3–25 * *h*·, earth, sea, the eternal fire,
13–17 and done on earth as in *h*·.
Hea. 19–25 up the steep ascent, on to *h*·,
Peo. 12–28 without health there could be no *h*·.
Po. 63–7 feathery blossom and branches to *h*·.
68–8 or this happiness *h*· !
76–8 (*H*· chiseled squarely good)
My. 18–25 and done on earth as in *h*·.''
139–11 life-lease of hope, home, *h*· ;
158–13 *h*· here, the struggle over ;
201–12 hope repossess us of *h*·.
203–15 suffering here and of *h*· hereafter.
254–1 *h*· opens, right reigns,
267–14 chapter sub-title
267–15 Is *h*· spiritual?

heaven
My. 267–19 quality and the quantity of *h*.
267–23 *H* is the reign of divine Science.
278–18 Japanese may believe in a *h* for
281– 5 in earth, as it is in *h*." — *Matt.* 6 : 10.
heaven-appointed
My. 221–19 no other *h* means than
heaven-born
Mis. 15–17 *h* hope, and spiritual love.
374–14 pluck not their *h* wings.
heaven-crowned
Mis. 328– 7 mountain is *h* Christianity,
358–18 *h* summit of C. S.
heavenly
Mis. 140–28 our title clear" to *h* mansions.
324–31 receive his *h* guidance.
326–25 Well might this *h* messenger exclaim,
343–11 watered by the *h* dews of Love,
387–18 Seek holy thoughts and *h* strain,
389–25 finds her home and *h* rest.
Ret. 21–17 *h* intent of earth's shadows
80–15 receptive of the *h* discipline.
Un. 6–13 Until the *h* law of health,
51–12 of the *h* sovereignty.
Pul. 3–13 *h* assurance ends all warfare,
27–13 * one representing the *h* city
'01. 7–12 our *h* Parent — the divine Mind
7–15 does not this *h* Parent know
Hea. 20– 5 * We'd soar and touch the *h* strings,
Peo. 5–21 Let us then heed this *h* visitant,
7–22 * Its *h* beauty shall be our own,
Po. 5– 6 finds her home and *h* rest.
6–13 Seek holy thoughts and *h* strain,
My. 38 1 * balm of *h* joy,
40–28 the *h* Jerusalem, — *Heb.* 12 : 22.
109–12 teaching them the same *h* lesson.
147–29 *h* homesick or hungry hearts
208– 6 to reflect its *h* rays over all
257–13 Christ's *h* origin and aim.
(*see also* **Father**)
Heaven's
Hea. 1– 7 *H* favors are formidable :
19–16 *H* signet is Love.
heaven's
Mis. 145–28 float majestically *h* heraldry,
312– 9 for the kingdom of *h* sake.
380–24 When *h* aftersmile
Chr. 53–21 For *h* *Christus*, earthly Eves,
53–60 In *h* hymn.
Ret. 87– 3 * "Order is *h* first law,"
Peo. 7–14 * With *h* own light the sculptor
Po. 5– 4 When *h* aftersmile
30–22 *h* lyres and angels' loving lays,
My. 155–24 sing as the angels *h* symphonies
167–11 I pray that *h* messages
heavens
above
Mis. 158– 4 higher far than the *h* above
392–17 grandly rising to the *h* above.
Po. 20–21 grandly rising to the *h* above.
build to the
Mis. 135–13 though you should build to the *h*,
My. 165–30 means that build to the *h*,
eternal in the
Pul. 2–15 eternal in the *h*." — *II Cor.* 5 : 1.
'01. 25– 4 superstructure eternal in the *h*,
My. 188–14 eternal in the *h*;" — *II Cor.* 5 : 1.
192–30 "eternal in the *h*." — *II Cor.* 5 : 1.
194– 8 eternal in the *h*," — *II Cor.* 5 : 1.
moral
Peo. 3–15 spans the moral *h* with light,
of divine Science
Mis. 320–17 fixed in the *h* of divine Science,
of Soul
Mis. 360–13 fixed stars in the *h* of Soul.
of thought
Mis. 355–31 will span thy *h* of thought.
our
Po. 68–22 Be its course through our *h*,
our own
Mis. 170–13 we make our own *h*
pointing to the
My. 162–32 temple . . . pointing to the *h*,
signs in the
Mis. 1– 5 foreshadowed by signs in the *h*.
sitteth in the
Mis. 126–31 "He that sitteth in the *h* — *Psal.* 2 : 4.
spiritual
Mis. 254–20 stars from the spiritual *h*,
the very
Mis. 338–17 But the very *h* shall laugh
upon the
Mis. 333–31 hung his destiny out upon the *h* ;
Pul. 12–12 Therefore rejoice, ye *h*, — *Rev.* 12 : 12.

heavenward
Mis. 147–10 worthy to be borne *h* ?
316–11 the tide which flows *h*,
Pul. 11– 1 bear you outward, upward, *h*.
Po. 19– 4 onward and upward and *h*
My. 37– 6 * can acceptably ascend *h*
154–29 whereby we are looking *h*,
204– 7 It is only by looking *h*
316– 4 and renews the *h* impulse ;
heavily
Pul. 76–20 * is all *h* plated with gold."
heaving
'02. 19–19 *h* surf of life's troubled sea
heavy
Mis. 20– 4 labor and are *h* laden, — *Matt.* 11 : 28.
132– 4 token that *h* lids are opening,
262–25 yet were our burdens *h*
327–12 had *h* baggage of their own,
327–20 lay down a few of the *h* weights,
Man. 60–11 rest the weary and *h* laden.
Ret. 2–11 brought to New England a *h* sword,
95– 9 * For *h* is the weight of ill
Pul. 20– 3 Owing to a *h* loss,
46–18 * a *h* sword, encased in a
62– 6 * *h* cast bells of old-fashioned
No. 43– 5 labor and are *h* laden, — *Matt.* 11 : 28.
Hea. 2–18 labor and are *h* laden, — *Matt.* 11 : 28.
Peo. 11–25 "bind *h* burdens," — *Matt.* 23 : 4.
Po. vii–14 * a joy to the *h* laden
My. 44– 3 * *h* burdens are being laid down,
84– 3 * *h* debt, the interest on which
291– 7 began with *h* strokes,
heavy-laden
Mis. 208–14 to the weary and *h*,
'02. 11– 8 earth-weary and *h* who find
Hebrew
Mis. 8–27 The *H* law with its
126–29 penalty of which the *H* bard spake
142–23 spiritual strains of the *H* bard.
170–26 Spitting was the *H* method of
180–26 In the *H* text, the word "son"
184–12 brings to remembrance the *H* strain,
190–28 In the *H*, "devil" is — *Luke* 11 : 14.
191– 2 The *H* embodies the term
192– 2 *H* term for Deity was "good,"
192–14 The *H* bard saith,
193–32 "belief;" the *H* of which implies
297–29 The *H* bard wrote,
392–13 To love the *H* figure of a tree.
Ret. 10– 9 ancient tongues, *H*, Greek, and
10–10 My brother studied *H*
Un. 14–15 limited *H* faith might need
28– 1 We read in the *H* Scriptures,
Pul. 46–26 * ancient languages, *H*, Greek,
Pan. 4–21 words of the *H* singer,
'00. 12–29 It refers to the *H* Balaam
'01. 34–29 words of the *H* writers :
Hea. 6–28 in *H* it is *belial*,
Peo. 2– 8 The *H* term that gives
Po. 20–17 love the *H* figure of a tree.
My. 273–10 King David, the *H* bard,
Hebrew Decalogue
Mis. 21– 2 First Commandment of the *H* *D*,
114–14 teach others to practise, the *H* *D*,
'02. 4–14 First Commandment in the *H* *D*,
My. 5–13 First Commandment of the *H* *D*,
64–12 First Commandment of the *H* *D*,
268–15 Two commandments of the *H* *D*,
279–11 First Commandment in the *H* *D*
Hebrews
Mis. 26–26 common version of *H* i. 3,
Un. 23–10 Scripture, in *H* xii. 7, 8 :
hedge
Man. 104– 9 *h* it about with divine Love.
Ret. 52– 4 build a *h* round about it
hedgerow
Ret. 18– 8 sentinel *h* is guarding repose,
Po. 63–17 sentinel *h* is guarding repose,
heed
Mis. 368–11 chapter sub-title
Man. 78– 3 fails to *h* this admonition,
'02. 15–28 To this, however, I gave no *h*,
Peo. 5–21 Let us then *h* this heavenly visitant,
My. 37–31 * pray that we may give *h*
heeded
Mis. 254– 4 the stern rebuke have been *h*,
326–10 slumberers who *h* them not,
342– 5 They *h* not their sloth,
Un. 11–16 He *h* not the taunt,
No. 9– 2 if it had been *h* in times past
heed'st
My. 350–14 *h* Thou not the scalding

heel
Mis.	210–18	as it biteth at the *h·*.
Un.	45– 5	and it stings your *h·*,
Pul.	82–30	* ceased to kiss the iron *h·* of wrong.
'00.	10– 2	Hatred bites the *h·* of love
Hea.	11–15	may not recover from the *h·* of allopathy
Po.	71–11	Feared for an hour the tyrant's *h·* !

heels
No.	43–27	bark and bite at its *h·*.

Hegel
No.	22– 4	Leibnitz, Descartes, Fichte, *H·*,
	22– 7	*H·* was an inveterate snuff-taker.

height
Mis.	8–13	Can *h·*, or depth, or any other
	338– 4	gained its *h·* beforehand,
	379– 8	appearance, *h·*, and complexion
Ret.	48–30	*h·* of prosperity in the institution,
Pul.	24–26	* twenty feet in *h·*
	26–12	* lamps, eight feet in *h·*.
Po.	1–13	from yon cloud-crowned *h·*
	2–14	upon thine exiled *h·* ;
My.	4–29	*h·* of my hope must remain.
	45–29	* Bedford stone, rising to a *h·* of
	67– 8	* *H· . . . .* 224 ft.
	68– 9	* a *h·* of fifty-one feet.
	78– 6	* massive dome rising to a *h·* of
	81– 6	* at the very *h·* of fervor,
	117–28	I left Boston in the *h·* of
	281– 7	soaring to the Horeb *h·*,

heightens
Mis.	1–18	*h·* immortal attributes

heights
Mis.	126–11	have gained higher *h·* ;
	369– 8	stand erect on sublime *h·*,
My.	146–15	*h·* of the great Nazarene's sayings

heir
Mis.	33–27	* "the ills that flesh is *h·* to,"
	167–20	Is he *h·* to an estate?
	253–19	"This is the *h·* : — *Luke* 20 : 14.
	254–14	"This is the *h·* : — *Luke* 20 : 14.
No.	42–10	* "the ills that flesh is *h·* to."
Hea.	15– 6	to heal all ills that flesh is *h·* to.

heirs
Mis.	46–24	if children, then *h·* ; — *Rom.* 8 : 17.
	46–24	*h·* of God, — *Rom.* 8 : 17.
	165–19	makes his followers the *h·* to
	255–15	if children, then *h·* ; — *Rom.* 8 : 17.
	255–16	*h·* of God, — *Rom.* 8 : 17.

held
Mis.	61–15	* the man is *h·* responsible for the crime ;
	61–18	* This 'man' was *h·* responsible
	98– 2	perfect model should be *h·* in mind,
	156–14	the one *h·* at Chicago,
	195– 8	*h·* back by reason of the lack of
	274–25	and quivering hearts are *h·* up
	297–20	is *h·* in·C. S. as morally bound
	304– 4	* great patriotic celebration is being *h·*,
	315– 5	*h·* on the Sunday following
	365–28	*h·* back by the common ignorance
Man.	26– 8	annual meeting *h·* for this purpose,
	38–13	meetings *h·* for this purpose.
	56–11	*h·* annually, on Monday following
	56–20	*h·* on Monday preceding the
	57– 3	shall be *h·* on the Friday preceding
	57– 6	Special meetings may be *h·*
	70–16	No conference . . . shall be *h·*,
	82–14	meeting *h·* for this purpose
	91–23	which will be *h·* once in three years
Ret.	3– 2	*h·* the position of ambassador to
	14– 3	meeting was *h·* for the examination
Un.	9–22	*h·* by a few spiritual thinkers in
	14– 5	Can it be seriously *h·*, by any
	54–21	Satan *h·* it up before man as
	57–15	he neither *h·* her error by affinity
Pul.	4–28	Parliament of Religions, *h·* in
	28–28	* *h·* its meetings in Chickering Hall,
	29– 9	* service *h·* in Copley Hall.
	30–26	* first meeting *h·* on April 12,
	55–18	* *h·* to be scientific certainty,
	59– 6	* continuous services were *h·*
	68–25	* meeting *h·* at the present location
	79–15	* in most instances they are *h·* at
	87– 2	* services that may be *h·* therein.
No.	11–11	this system is *h·* back by the
	13–17	not . . . *h·* as a mere theory.
	25– 6	wherein we were *h·* ; — *Rom.* 7 : 6.
'01.	16– 2	* God's hand has *h·* you up."
	31–25	*h·* fast to whatever is good,
Peo.	2–26	*h·* constantly before the people's
Po.	68– 7	Earth *h·* but this joy,
My.	30– 1	* *h·* large crowds of people,
	38–29	* was *h·* in the extension of The
	39– 2	* second session was *h·* at two

held
My.	42–21	* first annual meeting *h·* in the
	49–16	* meeting of the church was *h·*
	49–20	* August 27 the church *h·* a meeting,
	49–26	* meeting *h·* October 19, 1879,
	50– 2	* *h·* at the home of the pastor,
	53–12	* services were *h·* there until
	54–13	* *h·* at Odd Fellows Hall,
	54–31	* *h·* in Chickering Hall
	55–19	* were *h·* in Chickering Hall,
	55–26	* Sunday services were *h·*
	56– 5	* two services were *h·*,
	56–29	* three services were *h·* each Sunday,
	57–14	* was *h·* in Chickering Hall,
	61–10	* *h·* in the new extension
	65– 4	* largest . . . ever *h·* in Boston
	65– 4	* largest ever *h·* in the
	66–22	* six services will be *h·*,
	78– 3	* were *h·* during the morning,
	80–10	* Meetings were *h·* in the extension
	80–31	* where the largest meeting was *h·*,
	89– 3	* may be *h·* to symbolize that faith
	93–28	* now being *h·* in Boston
	94–21	* *h·* at different hours of the day,
	141– 4	* *h·* annually in The First Church
	141– 8	* the last to be *h·*.
	141–11	* would have been *h·* next year.
	159–25	heathen philosopher who *h·* that
	222–28	liberty of conscience *h·* sacred.
	284–14	*h·* in my church building,
	284–19	been *h·* annually in some church
	289–27	meeting to be *h·* in the capital
	318–20	He *h·* himself well in check
	338– 8	* *h·* and expressed by her.

Helen's
Mis.	374–25	* "*H·* beauty in a brow of Egypt."

hell
Mis.	134–20	earth and *h·* are proven powerless.
	141– 9	"the gates of *h·*" — *Matt.* 16 : 18.
	144–20	the gates of *h·* — *Matt.* 16 : 18.
	170–12	hades, or *h·* of Scripture,
	235– 6	Him who destroys death and *h·*.
	237– 2	olden opinion that *h·* is fire and
Un.	56–24	pangs of *h·* must lay hold of him
No.	38–11	against which the gates of *h·*
'01.	15–18	the old orthodox *h·*
	15–27	* why you have not gone to *h·*
	16– 1	* drop down into *h·*,
'02.	3–29	Envy is the atmosphere of *h·*.
My.	160–19	I am asked, "Is there a *h·*?"
	160–19	Yes, there is a *h·* for all who
	160–29	this *h·* is mental, not material,
	160–31	makers of *h·* burn in their fire.

hells
Mis.	170–13	our own heavens and our own *h·*,

helm
Mis.	113–26	at the *h·* of thought,
My.	232– 3	with the *h·* in His hands.

help (noun)
affords
'00.	7–27	Christ is found near, affords *h·*,

apply for
Mis.	39– 1	Many who apply for *h·*

call for
Mis.	81–26	answers the human call for *h·* ;
	380–11	imperative call for *h·*

calls for
Mis.	370– 1	feebleness calls for *h·*,

divine
Mis.	39–30	Divine *h·* is as necessary in the
	158–17	a lack of faith in divine *h·*,
	380–15	in faith, turned to divine *h·*.

ever-present
Mis.	96– 4	God is an ever-present *h·*
	157–17	He is the ever-present *h·*
	225–24	spiritual source and ever-present *h·*,
	307– 4	divine Love is an ever-present *h·* ;
My.	3–17	unerring impetus, an ever-present *h·*.
	12–27	supplies the ever-present *h·*
	44– 2	* God as an ever-present *h·*,
	152–23	ever-present *h·* in all things,
	167– 9	ever-present *h·* in trouble,
	240–12	Science . . . an ever-present *h·*.
	254–13	God an ever-present *h·*.
	295–25	Divine Love is your ever-present *h·*.

God's
Ret.	86–22	save himself without God's *h·*,
My.	197– 4	Attempt nothing without God's *h·*.

her
My.	231–15	invalids demanding her *h·*

his
Mis.	268–18	His "*h·* is from — *see Psal.* 121 : 2.
	358–10	God alone is his *h·*,
'00.	3– 6	No hand that feels not his *h·*,

help

household
Man. 69–15 household *h·* or a handmaid,

loss of
My. 195– 6 Adverse circumstances, loss of *h·*,

needed
My. 324–21 * he thought you needed *h·*,

no more
Mis. 197–16 would be of no more *h·*

of others
My. 130–15 I ask the *h·* of others
138– 1 without the *h·* of others.

of truth-telling
My. 130–19 with the *h·* of truth-telling.

personal
Mis. 283–32 The only personal *h·* required

physical
Mis. 88– 3 feel the need of physical *h·*,

prayer for
Mis. 70–20 poor thief's prayer for *h·*

present
Un. 2– 5 very present *h·* — Psal. 46 : 1.
My. 162– 3 "very present *h·* — Psal. 46 : 1.

rather than
My. 219– 5 hindrance rather than *h·*.

recognize the
Mis. 33–19 recognize the *h·* they derive

refuse
Mis. 89–17 caused our Master to refuse *h·* to

shriek for
Mis. 326– 7 sufferers shriek for *h·* :

special
Mis. 357–27 and need special *h·*.

spiritual
My. 153–18 spiritual *h·* of divine Love.

their
Mis. 10–13 their *h·* in times of trouble.

to obtain
Ret. 71–27 Secret mental efforts to obtain *h·*

woman's
Pul. 83– 2 * woman's love and woman's *h·*

Mis. 25–26 if the sick cannot trust God for *h·*
115–24 more unreservedly to Him for *h·*,
148–16 immediate demand for them as a *h·*
157–16 when *h·* is most needed,
353–30 they constantly go to her for *h·*,
Man. 3–12 immediate demand for them as a *h·*
69–13 *H·*.
83–23 and S. AND H. . . . as a *h·* thereto.
'01. 26–13 for *h·* in times of need.
Po. 70–11 A *h·* forever near ;
My. 147–30 hearts are calling on me for *h·*,

help (verb)
Mis. 87–30 imagine they can *h·* anybody
90–18 Then *h·* others to be free ;
115–26 every effort to hurt one will only *h·*
129–10 and thereby *h·* him.
131– 2 can neither *h·* himself nor others ;
146–22 *h·* him to walk in the footsteps of
149– 6 to *h·* leaven your loaf
157–12 They will be glad to *h·* you.
211– 1 you will *h·* to reform them.
236–26 in one's efforts to *h·* another,
237–14 must encounter and *h·* to eradicate.
267–11 I saw an opportunity really to *h·*
277–30 I cannot *h·* loathing the
292–19 enjoins it upon man to *h·* those
294–23 that you desire to *h·* even such as
303–17 effort to *h·* them to obey
311–16 I love my enemies and would *h·* all
328– 1 and would *h·* them on ;
348– 6 *h·* on the brotherhood of men.
357–29 ready and glad to *h·* them
371– 7 to *h·* them by his own leadership
Ret. 80–22 and God will *h·* each man who
Pul. 4–18 drop of water may *h·* to hide
7– 2 * I would *h·* that woman."
14–22 the earth will *h·* the woman ;
41– 7 * to *h·* erect this beautiful structure,
51–23 * *h·* on the growth of its principles.
82–24 * the right to *h·* make the laws,
82–25 * at least to *h·* enforce the laws
83–20 * "God shall *h·* her, — Psal. 46 : 5.
No. 43–25 reconstruct . . . and *h·* humanity.
Pan. 9–20 to *h·* such a one is to *h·* one's self.
'01. 29– 7 those who want to *h·* them.
29–17 not to *h·* mother but to recruit
29–19 attempt to *h·* their parents,
32– 8 I could not *h·* loving them.
'02. 3–28 to serve God and to *h·* the race.
11–11 hastens to *h·* on his fellow-mortals,
Po. 28–3 *H·* us to weave a deathless page
28– 6 *H·* us to humbly bow
My. 47–18 * we cannot *h·* being touched by

help (verb)
My. 165– 8 The best *h·* the worst ;
166– 1 it can *h·* its neighbor.
166–19 willing to *h·* and to be helped,
173–14 to *h·* furnish and beautify your
190– 3 *h·* to evolve that larger sympathy
201–18 may *h·* us, not to a start, but to
216– 4 in order to *h·* mankind with it.
217– 3 to *h·* your parents,
229–14 go to *h·* their helper,
229–15 and thereby *h·* themselves
231–13 in order to *h·* God's work
276–24 *h·* support a righteous government ;
284– 3 to *h·* human purpose and peoples,
313–15 to *h·* me when I was ill.
359–30 to *h·* you rise out of it.

helped
Mis. 238– 1 * story that "he *h·* 'niggers'
382–10 the sick are *h·* thereby,
Man. 18–11 hath the Lord *h·* us." — I Sam. 7 : 12.
Ret. 19–15 sympathy *h·* to support me
Pul. 9–14 and *h·* settle the subject.
11– 7 *h·* erect The Mother Church,
14–11 *h·* the woman, — Rev. 12 : 16.
'02. 11–14 each in turn has *h·* mankind,
11–15 when the race is *h·* onward
18– 9 disciples *h·* crown with thorns
My. 116–24 Had the ages *h·* their leaders
166–20 to help and to be *h·*,
219– 2 anticipate being *h·* by me
282–11 nations are *h·* onward
302– 3 can he be *h·* or be killed
322–24 * Mr. Wiggin kindly *h·* me
324–19 * that he had *h·* you
330–27 sympathy *h·* to support me

helper
Ret. 86–24 To the unwise *h·* our Master
Un. 3–27 this self-same God is our *h·*.
(see also **Eddy**)

helpers
Mis. 87–29 haunted by obsequious *h·*,

helpful
Ret. 25–11 compassionate, *h·*, and spiritual.
Pul. 29–24 * discourse was able, and *h·*
45–10 * grandest and most *h·* features
56–13 * *h·*, and powerful movements
My. 42–10 * one of the *h·* contributors
121–13 generous, reliable, *h·*,
224–10 public sentiment is *h·* or

helpfulness
My. vii–11 * *h·* of consistent and constant
87–27 * spirit of unselfishness and *h·*,

helping
Mis. 32–19 *h·* those unfortunate seekers
49–23 are *h·* man Godward :
50–30 *h·* our brother man.
98–12 ways and means for *h·*
327–25 *h·* them on, saying,
353–29 to think of *h·* others,
371–10 incapable of *h·* themselves
Pul. 8–12 privileged joy at *h·* to build
45– 1 * children lent a *h·* hand,
81–13 * her whole time *h·* others.
My. 117– 7 whereas *h·* a leader
147–30 calling on me for help, and I am *h·*
163–28 thank their ancestors for *h·*
165– 3 *h·* others thus to choose.
259–19 true heart, and a *h·* hand

helpless
Mis. 72– 8 to their *h·* offspring,
115–11 *h·* ignorance of the community
123– 2 butchers his *h·* Armenians,
221–16 This accounts for many *h·* mental
Ret. 27–17 * But the feeble hands and *h·*,
Un. 61– 5 appeared as a *h·* human babe ;
61–27 *h·* sick are soonest healed by it.
Peo. 3– 5 *h·* invalids and cripples.
My. 144– 6 lies afloat that I am sick, *h·*, or

helplessness
Mis. 281–20 *h·* without this understanding,
Hea. 3– 3 or, lacking these, to show its *h·*.

helpmeet
Pul. 82–18 * woman as man's proper *h·*.

helps
Mis. 157–16 *h·* us most when help is most needed,

hem
Mis. 75– 1 touched the *h·* of the garment
97–17 touch the *h·* of His garment ;
Ret. 23–23 I had touched the *h·* of C. S.
Pul. 13–11 touches the *h·* of Christ's robe
53–29 * power that filled his garment's *h·*
No. 22– 2 has certainly not touched the *h·*

hem

'00. 15–20 the touch of the *h·* of this garment
Hea. 16–15 *h·* of Truth's garment.
My. 22–27 * touched the healing *h·* of C. S.,
108–20 slang, and malice touch not the *h·* of
192– 8 Thou hast touched its *h·*,
205–23 touches but the *h·* of C. S.,
351–12 touches the *h·* of his garment

Hemans, Mrs.

Ret. 9–27 signature
My. 185–26 words of Mrs. *H·* :

hemisphere

Mis. 275–26 wonder of the western *h·*.

hence

Mis. 3–30 *H·* the deep demand for the Science
12–19 *h·* the need of watching,
14– 1 *h·*, there is neither place nor power
15– 2 *h·* the sinner must endure the
28–30 *h·* his declaration,
55–30 *h·* it is either a godless and
64– 2 *H·*, the human cry which voiced
66– 4 *H·* the gospel that fulfils the law
68–16 *h·* it is right to know that the works of
71–22 *h·* its mythical origin and
71–30 *h·* the immutable and just law
73–17 *H·* the verdict of experience :
75–13 *h·* Soul is one, and is God ;
76– 1 *h·* it must be sinless, and destitute of
76–13 *h·* these bodies must die
83–16 *h·*, you are the arbiter of your
90– 2 *h·*, that sin is impotent.
97–31 *h·*, it doth not appear
103–31 *H·* the Scripture,
108–12 *h·* the utility of knowing
123–29 *h·* it follows that those who
146–12 *h·* I have hitherto declined
147–21 *h·* we find him ever the same,
148–17 *h·* their simple, scientific basis,
150–31 *h·* God is our Shepherd.
164– 2 *h·* the incorporeal and
172–31 *h·*, good is omnipotent
182– 2 *h·* the impossibility of
187– 9 opposite of man, *h·* the unreality ;
196–13 *h·* the words of our Master :
215– 7 Arise, let us go *h·* ; — *John* 14 : 31.
217– 6 *h·* that the universe of God is
232–18 *h·* a more spiritual Christianity
247–16 *h·* the injustice of their interpretations.
247–30 *H·* *that* is only an evil belief
264–15 *h·* the aptness to assimilate pure and
268–16 *h·* he suffers no shipwreck in a
272–23 * *H·* to name these institutions,
284–22 *h·* is neither to be *feared* nor
287– 4 *H·* the Scripture : "It is He— *Psal.* 100 : 3.
289– 3 *h·* the only temperance is total
308–31 *H·*, a finite person is not the model
318–11 *H·* the following is
342– 6 *h·* the steady decline of
348–14 *H·*, Solomon's transverse command :
348–26 *H·* I tried several doses of
350–24 *H·* it prevents the normal action,
357–29 *h·* we should be ready and glad to
364–23 *h·* these opposites must
Man. 3–14 *h·* their simple, scientific basis,
28– 9 *h·* the necessity of this By-Law
53–26 *h·* injurious, to C. S.
Ret. 56–18 *H·* there is but one Mind ;
57–11 *h·* there is but one Soul,
63–14 God is good, *h·* goodness is
65–15 *h·* Jesus denounced it.
67– 2 *h·* one's concept of error is
83–18 *H·*, as a rule, the student should
Un. 3– 4 *H·* they awake only to another
3–20 *H·* He is in Himself only,
9– 5 *H·* they must, some time
24–17 and *h·* is the only substance.
25– 7 *h·* good is the only substance,
25–10 *h·*, whatever it appears to say
29– 6 *H·*, as Spirit, Soul is sinless,
30– 8 *H·* this lower sense sins
31–16 *H·* my conscientious position,
32– 2 *H·* the claim of matter usurps
32–24 *H·* it was not man
33–17 *H·* the logical sequence,
35–24 *H·* this spiritual consciousness
36–14 *h·*, that matter is erroneous,
38–24 *H·* the inevitable conclusion
40–16 *H·* Life abides in man,
41–25 *h·* matter neither lives nor dies.
43– 4 *h·* cannot bring out the
49–23 *H·* it is undemonstrable,
51– 4 and *h·* that sin is eternal,
52– 1 *H·* Soul is sinless and immortal,
52– 7 *H·* the need that human
53–26 *h·* that saying of Jesus,

hence

Un. 54–13 *H·* the fact must be denied ;
59– 7 *h·* the phraseology of Jesus,
Pul. vii– 5 Three quarters of a century *h·*,
41–19 * *H·* the service was repeated
Rud. 3– 2 *H·* their comparative acquiescence in
4–15 *h·* there is no other Mind.
9–28 *h·*, that whatever militates against
13– 2 *h·* Life is not functional,
13–10 *h·* it is not the truth of being,
No. 4–13 *h·* error of thought becomes fable
16–18 *h·* their inference of some other
17–19 *H·* the unreality of error,
20–19 *H·* this asking amiss
22–22 *H·* the passage must refer to
23–25 *H·* we cannot understand
26– 8 *H·* it is impossible for those
32–18 *H·* its opposite, named *evil*, must
35–26 *H·* there is no sin,
36–14 *H·* the human Jesus had
38– 7 *h·* there is no intelligent sin,
'00. 8– 6 *h·*, be careful of your company.
12–17 *h·* the Revelator's saying :
'01. 6– 5 says . . . not a person, *h·* no God?
12–11 *h·* the Scripture,
13–25 *h·* the hope of universal salvation.
17–26 *h·* it must be mind that
25– 1 *H·* the mysticism, so called,
28–27 *h·* the inference that he who
'02. 5–22 *H·* our Master's saying,
10– 8 *H·* the footprints of a reformer are
Hea. 11–27 *h·* the Christianity of . . . healing,
Peo. 13– 2 *h·* a lower order of humanity,
Po. 70–15 error, get thee *h·*,
70–25 sin, and death are banished *h·*.
77–19 Bears *h·* its sunlit glow
79–10 darkling sense, arise, go *h·* !
My. 40–29 * rebels against law, *h·* the proverb :
108– 9 *H·* our Master's saying,
108–16 *H·* the divine Mind is the
116–14 *H·* the sin, the danger and
118–13 *h·* I seek to be
130–30 *h·* my request, that you
136– 1 *h·* it is enough for you and me
141–25 *h·* the following :
161– 9 *H·* these words of Christ Jesus :
178–18 *H·* the inevitable revelation
205–28 *H·* health, holiness, immortality,
222–11 Remove *h·* to yonder place ; — *Matt.* 17 : 20.
225–13 *h·* the propriety of giving unto
228– 6 *h·* I am always saying the
229–28 *h·* my disappointed hope
231–14 *H·*, letters from invalids
235–21 *h·* there can be no other creator
237– 9 *H·*, it were wise to accept
238–12 *H·* the revelation, discovery, and
239–23 *H·* mankind . . . a kind of man
242– 9 the child of God, *h·* perfect,
262– 2 *H·* man is the image, idea, or
268– 6 *h·* that some fundamental error
272– 5 *h·* the Scripture, "The law of— *Rom.* 8 : 2.
275– 7 *h·* the Scripture, "Be still,— *Psal.* 46 : 10.
279–14 *H·* the sequence?
288–25 *h·* his saying, "Sin no more,— *John* 5 : 14.
311–15 *H·* a mistake may have occurred
341–23 * *h·* it was a special favor
357– 1 *h·* materiality is wholly apart from
364– 1 *h·* the Scripture, "Judge no— *John* 8 : 15.

henceforth

Mis. 144–18 *h·* to whisper our Master's promise,
188– 3 Man is as perfect now, and *h·*,
Po. 1–14 to look *h·* On insignificance
My. 86– 1 * *H·* the greeting of admiring eyes,
148– 8 be and abide with you *h·*.

Herald

The

Pul. 43–26 * as heretofore stated in *The H·*,

Pul. 74– 3 * [By Telegraph to the *H·*]
74– 5 * article published in the *H·*
74–12 * addressed to the editor of the *H·* :
88–31 * *H·*, Rochester, N. Y.
89–31 * *H·*, Grand Rapids, Mich.
89–32 * *H·*, St. Joseph, Mo.
My. 274–19 * sent the following to the *H·* :
341–24 * received the *H·* correspondent.
346– 9 * learn authoritatively from the *H·*

heralded

My. 79–15 * *h·* in flaming headlines

heralding

Mis. 163–31 *h·* the Principle of health,

heraldry

Mis. 145–28 will float majestically heaven's *h·*,
Po. 70–21 A painless *h·* of Soul, not sense,

Herbert

Pul. 28–22   * devotional hymns from *H·*, Faber,

Herculean

Mis. 130–20   such *H·* tasks as they have

herd

Po. 41–11   When the *h·* had forsaken,

herds

Ret. 4–21   with large flocks and *h·*,
Pan. 3–28   guardian of flocks and *h·*.
My. 262– 8   *h·* of a Jewish village.

here

Mis. vii–12   There's nothing *h·* to trust.
2–27   progress *h·* and hereafter out of
16–16   *H·*, then, is the awakening from
16–30   *H·* you stand face to face with
27– 7   *H·* is where C. S. sticks to its
27– 9   *H·* also is found the pith of the
30–14   to be recognized *h·* and now.
68– 6   visible to those beholding him *h·*.
74– 2   are *h·* signified.
77– 4   *H·* the verb *believe* took its
93–28   cannot go unpunished either *h·* or
127– 8   Christian Scientists, *h·* and
127–22   but *h·*, you must so know yourself,
128– 5   Therefore I close *h·*
150–20   *H·* I deposit the gifts that my
159–22   *H·* I talk once a year,
162–11   *H·* the cross became the emblem
168–15   *H·* ends the colloquy ;
174–19   No : it is ever-present *h·*.
174–29   spiritual facts of man's Life *h·*
177– 2   God makes to us all, right *h·*,
178–24   * to preach, *h·* or elsewhere.''
179– 1   ''He is not *h·* ;'' — *Luke* 24 : 6.
179–13   ''He is not *h·* ; — *Luke* 24 : 6.
180–10   Truth is always *h·*,
180–25   *H·*, the apostle assures us that
191–14   *H·* is an assertion indicating
191–20   The term, being *h·* employed in
203– 4   for *h·*, thine becomes mine through
223– 7   *H·*, divine light, logic, and
244– 3   *H·* we have the Professor on the
251–20   Heaven right *h·*, where
319–10   *H·* Christian Scientists must be most
323–18   ''What do ye *h·*?
330–13   consciousness thereof is *h·* and now
332– 6   Spring is *h·* ! and doors that
362–22   *H·* revelation must come to the
373–23   it has rich possession *h·*,
384–16   Love divine Is *h·*, and thine ;
385– 8   Thou, *h·* and *everywhere*.
389–12   His habitation high is *h·*,
396– 9   Yet *h·*, upon this faded sod,
Man. 100 15   compare them with the forms *h·* given,
Chr. 53–42   Are *h·*, and now
Ret. 17– 9   *H·* morning peers out,
17–15   *H·* fame-honored hickory rears his
18– 1   *H·* is life !   *H·* is youth !
18– 1   *H·* the poet's world-wish,
19–22   *H·* it is but justice to record,
62– 4   find that the views *h·* set forth
87–14   Let some of these rules be *h·* stated.
94–21   ''lo *h·* ! or lo there !'' — *Luke* 17 : 21.
Un. 7–17   views *h·* promulgated on this subject
7–19   and *h·* is one such conviction :
11–26   kingdom of heaven is *h·*,
32–23   *H·* it appears that a *liar* was
34–10   *H·* comes in the summary of the
37– 9   They are now and *h·* ;
37–20   Existing *h·* and now,
46– 5   not see much of the real man *h·*,
46–10   scientific man and his Maker are *h·* ;
53– 9   *h·* to be seen and demonstrated,
55–22   Now and *h·* shall I behold God,
62–24   He is not *h·*, but is risen.'' — *Luke* 24 : 6.
Pul. 13– 3   at some period, *h·* or hereafter,
13–23   *H·* the Scriptures declare that evil
29– 5   * first pastor of the church *h·*
48– 4   * with *h·* and there a fountain
49–10   * ''You have lived *h·* only four years,
49–16   brought *h·* in warm weather,
52– 1   * *H·* is a church whose treasurer has
63–13   brought *h·* in warm weather,
68– 5   * *h·* she taught the principles of
80–10   * *H·* they have the largest individuality,
80–27   * *h·* to be trained into harmony with
80–28   * what we are *h·* determines where
Rud. 8–10   give you *h·* nothing but an outline
No. 28–26   *H·* soul means sense and organic life ;
36– 8   even while mortals believed it was *h·*.
42–28   *H·* a skeptic might well ask
Pan. 1–10   roseate blush of joyous June is *h·*
13– 7   Lo, *h·* ! or, lo there ! — *Luke* 17 : 21.
'00. 2–22   *H·* we add : The doom of such

here

'00. 5– 6   *H·* note the words of our Master
7–28   Thus it is we walk *h·* below,
10–20   *H·* our hope anchors in God
'01. 5– 5   does not Person *h·* lose the nature of
6– 5   *H·* is the departure.
15–27   * since you have sat *h·* in the house
16– 6   punishing itself *h·* and hereafter
24– 7   *H·* he makes God the cause of
32–27   if those venerable Christians were *h·*
'02. 6–13   *H·* all human woe is seen to
6–24   demonstrates heaven *h·*,
7–23   *H·* we proceed to another
12– 3   *H·* C. S. intervenes,
12– 6   *now* and *forever*, *h·* and *everywhere*.
12–21   *H·* allow me to interpolate some
Hea. 6– 1   The more spiritual we become *h·*,
Peo. 1–18   that we are spiritual beings *h·*
9–22   *h·* metaphysics is seen to rise above
Po. 3– 8   watch thy chair, and wish thee *h·* ;
4–11   His habitation high is *h·*, and nigh,
15– 9   *H·* gloom hath enchantment in
15–16   *H·* smileth the blossom and sunshine
16–16   The voice of the night-bird must *h·*
29– 7   Dear Christ, forever *h·* and near,
36–15   Love divine Is *h·*, and thine ;
37– 8   Thou, *h·* and *everywhere*.
41–10   their home is not *h·*
59– 1   Yet *h·*, upon this faded sod,
62– 9   *H·* morning peers out,
62–18   *H·* fame-honored hickory rears his
63– 8   *H·* is life!   *H·* is youth!
63– 8   *H·* the poet's world-wish,
68– 4   for this are we *h·*.''
68– 9   *H·* the rock and the sea and the
70–12   For sinless sense is *h·*
My. 7– 4   *H·* allow me to interpolate
8– 6   * The necessity *h·* indicated
18– 5   that Christian Scientists, *h·* and
36–13   * Most of us are *h·* because
44–10   * Christ is *h·*, has come to
47– 4   * gathered *h·* from all parts of
54–23   * should be *h·* stated that
57–29   * is a church whose Treasurer
71–20   * *h·* are neither nave, aisles,
73–21   * *h·* the visitors will receive
73–23   * There is *h·* also a post-office
74–11   * Christian Scientists are *h·* in force,
74–28   * we have had *h·* the representatives
84–20   * story which the gathering *h·* tells.
85–14   * And *h·* In Boston the zeal
87–14   * people we . . . like to have *h·*.
89–17   * is an occasion for joy
107– 9   *H·* I speak from experience.
122–23   he is not *h·* : — *Mark* 16 : 6.
126–28   One thing is eternally *h·*,
132– 9   pass through the waters of Meribah *h·*
134–15   And *h·* let me add :
155– 2   which is effective *h·* and now.
155–19   a clear vision of heaven *h·*,
158–13   heaven *h·*, the struggle over ;
163–22   *H·* let me add that,
164– 1   far from my purpose, when I came *h·*,
170–10   of all present *h·* in Concord.
173–13   would bring thousands *h·* yesterday ;
186–20   *H·* let His promise be verified :
193–23   *H·* I aver that you have grasped
203–15   the summary of suffering *h·*
232–18   *H·* we ask : Are Christ's teachings
236–13   *H·* I have the joy of knowing
248– 7   you are *h·* for the purpose of
253– 8   * ''Thou art not *h·* for ease or pain,
256–17   Again loved Christmas is *h·*,
267– 8   *H·* let us remember that God is
273–18   The ultimatum of life *h·* and
284–23   But *h·* let me say that I
297–20   is *h·* now as veritably as when
297–22   If . . . we should see him *h·*
314–16   Individuals are *h·* to-day
324–17   * and were he *h·* to-day
331– 2   *H·* it is but justice to record,
343–11   * *H·*, then, was the definite statement
345–32   * are *h·* touched upon,
348–17   *H·*, however, has no stopping-place,
354–19   Of God's presence *h·*.

hereafter

Mis. 2–27   progress here and *h·* out of evil,
93–28   either here or *h·*.
120–20   this Association *h·* meet triennially :
136–24   that *h·* you hold three sessions
155–21   will *h·*, as a general rule,
313–27   to be *h·* the only pastor of
317–23   thou shalt know *h·*.'' — *John* 13 : 7.
322– 7   I may *h·* notify the Directors
Man. 45– 8   shall not *h·* become members of
69–27   shall *h·* be closed to visitors.

hereafter
- *Man.* 76– 3 *h·* used for the benefit of
- *Pul.* 13– 3 here or *h·*, must grapple with
- 42–20 * where the organ is to be *h·* placed,
- 45–28 * The sermons *h·* will consist of
- 80–29 * determines where we shall be *h·*
- *'01.* 16– 6 punishing itself here and *h·*
- *Hea.* 5–10 reward of his good deed *h·*.
- 6– 2 should this rule fail *h·*,
- *Po.* 47–12 Will the *h·* from suffering free
- *My.* 203–15 and of heaven *h·*.
- 246–26 thou shalt know *h·* ;"— *John* 13 : 7.
- 251– 3 thou shalt know *h·*." — *John* 13 : 7.
- 273–18 of life here and *h·*
- 353–23 shall *h·* be closed to visitors.

hereby
- *Mis.* 155–19 she *h·* requests : First, that you,
- 297–16 I *h·* state, in unmistakable
- 313–25 I *h·* ordain the Bible, and "S. and H.
- *Ret.* 49–30 the same is *h·* dissolved.
- *Pul.* 77–14 * *h·* most lovingly invited
- 78–13 * You are *h·* most lovingly invited
- 86–21 * we *h·* present this church to you
- *My.* 27–13 * *h·* notified that sufficient funds
- 44–25 * *h·* convey to you their sincere
- 46–22 * we do *h·* pledge ourselves
- 171–11 I *h·* invite all my church
- 173–25 due and are *h·* tendered to
- 223– 2 I *h·* notify the public that no
- 242–16 I *h·* announce to the C. S. field
- 298–10 and *h·* say that they have my
- 359– 8 I *h·* publicly declare that I

heredity
- *Un.* 8–21 even the doctrine of *h·*

herein
- *Mis.* x–12 a few articles are *h·* appended.
- xi–15 find *h·* a "canny" crumb ;
- 104–10 *H·* sin is miraculous
- 173– 3 most enlightened sense *h·*
- 190–21 the devil *h·* referred to
- 252– 2 *H·* the mental medicine of
- *Man.* 51– 1 Rules *h·* set forth
- *Ret.* 82–13 orderly methods *h·* delineated.
- *Un.* 7–16 *H·* is my evidence,
- 29–18 *h·* lies the discrepancy
- *Pan.* 13– 4 among the questions *h·*,
- *My.* 138–20 statements *h·* made by me,
- 202–28 " *H·* is my Father — *John* 15 : 8.

hereinafter
- *Man.* 99– 7 except as *h·* specified,

heresy
- *Mis.* 174–21 Shall that be called *h·*.
- *Ret.* 13–17 to win me from dreaded *h·*.
- *My.* 285–26 which they call *h·*, — *Acts* 24 : 14.

heretics
- *No.* 44–25 * " *H·* of yesterday are martyrs

heretofore
- *Mis.* x–12 To those *h·* in print,
- 314–30 from the *Quarterly*, as *h·*,
- 337–31 sensualism, as *h·*, would hide
- *Man.* 38–18 who have *h·* been members
- *Pul.* 43–26 * *h·* stated in *The Herald*,
- *My.* 135– 8 *h·* personally attended to
- 245– 4 it should be met as *h·*,
- 315–24 dummy *h·* described?
- 356–17 *h·* presented in S. and H.

herewith
- *My.* 131–26 prove me now *h·*, — *Mal.* 3 : 10.
- 132– 3 "Prove me now *h·*, — *Mal.* 3 : 10.
- 269–26 "Prove me now *h·*, — *Mal.* 3 : 10.
- 289–25 I *h·* send a few words of
- 360–14 I *h·* cheerfully subscribe

Hering, Prof. Hermann S.
- *My.* 16–17 * Prof. Hermann S. *H·*, First Reader ;

heritage
- *Mis.* 152–18 *h·* that God has prepared
- 182–25 *h·* of the Elohim,
- 199– 9 into their rightful *h·*,
- 247– 2 demand for man his God-given *h·*,
- 259–15 was the *h·* of man ;
- 331– 7 for man's rich *h·*,
- *Pul.* 2–26 behooves us to defend our *h·*.
- 3– 9 dispossess you of this *h·*
- *My.* 128–14 the vital *h·* of freedom

hero
- *Mis.* 85– 2 battle-worn and weary Christian *h·*,
- 166– 5 philanthropist, *h·* and Christian.
- 237–27 draped in honor of the dead *h·*
- *Ret.* 11–15 *H·* and sage arise to show
- *Pul.* 48–29 * as well as the *h·* who killed the
- *'00.* 9–16 reformer must be a *h·* at all points,
- *'01.* 30–26 heart of the unselfed Christian *h·*.
- *Hea.* 2–14 And still another Christian *h·*

hero
- *Po.* 60–12 *H·* and sage arise to show
- 78– 6 Till molds the *h·* form?
- *My.* 203–13 A spiritual *h·* is a mark for
- 311–28 John McNeil, the *h·* of Lundy Lane.

heroes
- *Mis.* 176–14 *h·* and heroines who counted not
- *'01.* 32–14 They were *h·* in the strife ;
- *Po.* 78– 8 Shades of our *h·* !
- *My.* 248– 9 Spiritual *h·* and prophets

heroic
- *'01.* 1–20 always characterize *h·* hearts ;

heroines
- *Mis.* 176–15 heroes and *h·* who counted not

heroism
- *Ret.* 26– 4 Principle of his holy *h·*

Herold, Der
der Christian Science
- *Man.* 27–15 *C. S. Sentinel, Der H· der C. S.*,
- 81–11 *C. S. Sentinel, Der H· der C. S.*,
- *My.* vi–29 * and authorized *Der H· der C. S.*,
- 19– 4 * *C. S. Sentinel, Der H· der C. S.*,
- 353–13 the third, *Der H· der C. S.*,

- *Man.* 65–12 *C. S. Journal, Sentinel*, and *Der H·*,

Herrick
Rev. S. E.
- *No.* 44–24 Rev. S. E. *H·*, a Congregational

- *Mis.* 253–13 signature

herring
- *Mis.* 69–26 eating smoked *h·*.

Herself
- *Mis.* 367–20 nothing beyond Himself or *H·*

hesitate
- *Mis.* 350–11 no transactions . . . which I would *h·*

hesitated
- *'00.* 3–22 Israelites in Babylon *h·* not to

hesitation
- *My.* 320–24 * without any *h·* or restriction.

heterodox
- *Ret.* 64– 9 opposite theory is *h·*

hiatus
- *No.* 13–11 though the *h·* be longer still

hickory
- *Ret.* 17–15 *h·* rears his bold form,
- *Po.* 62–18 *h·* rears his bold form,

hid
- *Mis.* 149–27 a light that cannot be *h·*.
- 166–22 *h·* in three measures of meal,
- 167–24 *h·* these things from — *Luke* 10 : 21.
- 171–24 *h·* in three measures — *Matt.* 13 : 33.
- 174–30 *h·* in three measures of meal,
- 303– 2 lights that cannot be *h·*,
- 348–11 "Nothing is *h·* — see *Matt.* 10 : 26.
- *No.* 45– 1 *h·* these things from — *Luke* 10 : 21.
- *'02.* 2–16 leaven *h·* in three measures of meal,

hidden
- *Mis.* 48–21 *h·* nature of some tragic events
- 114–25 and stop their *h·* influence upon the
- 194–16 which scholastic theology has *h·*.
- 223– 1 its *h·* paths, purpose, and fruits
- 343–17 the *h·* gems of Love,
- *Ret.* 7–13 * however *h·* and remote.
- 85–13 against the subtly *h·* suggestion
- *Pul.* 9–24 bounty *h·* from the world.
- 15– 3 expose evil's *h·* mental ways
- *No.* 24–17 the evil that is *h·* by dogma
- *'01.* 20–25 its *h·* modus and flagrance
- *My.* 83–10 * *h·* away in the laces of
- 110–13 *H·* electrical forces annihilating
- 124– 1 *h·* things of dishonesty, — *II Cor.* 4 : 2.
- 130– 5 *h·* method of committing crime
- 160–24 shows that *h·* unpunished sin
- 166–16 they develop *h·* strength.
- 195–11 under an appearance of
- 204– 4 opportunity to use their *h·* virtues,
- 288– 3 Love . . . uncovers *h·* evil.

hide
- *Mis.* 63– 5 and to *h·* his divine power.
- 152–25 He will *h·* you in His feathers
- 210–12 wisdom of a serpent is to *h·*
- 323–11 serpents *h·* among the rocks,
- 337–31 sensualism, as heretofore, would *h·*
- 337–32 Sin of any sort tends to *h·*
- *Ret.* 78–22 or for yourself to *h·* from God,
- *Un.* 10–28 would endeavor to *h·* from His presence
- *Pul.* 4–18 may help to *h·* the stars,
- *No.* 7–17 wrath of man cannot *h·* it
- 40– 8 wise to *h·* from dull and base ears

hides
Mis. 103–22 h· the actual power, presence,
    203–22 veil that h· mental deformity.
    210–22 h· itself under the false pretense
    294–15 h· it in his cell of ingratitude.
My. 355–20 * He h· a shining face."

hideth
Mis. 210– 1 pursues the evil that h· itself,

hiding
Mis. 144–16 h· place from the wind,— Isa. 32 : 2.
My. 17– 1 overflow the h· place."— Isa. 28 : 17.
    211– 6 This mistaken way, of h· sin

hiding-places
My. 245–12 have called out of their h·

hierarchy
My. 342–29 * "Will there be a h·,

hieroglyphics
Mis. 331–31 all earth's h· of Love,

hieroglyphs
My. 205–15 Love and unity are h· of goodness,

Higdon, Mr. John C.
My. 351– 4 * addressed to Mr. John C. H·

Higgins, Mr. John D.
My. 283– 5 Mr. John D. H·, Clerk.

higgles
Mis. 296–22 * "poises and poses, h· and

High
(see **Most High**)

high
Mis. 19–22 as h· a basis as he understands,
    33– 3 The h· priests of old caused
    80–26 subjective state of h· thoughts.
   116– 4 wickedness in h· places." Eph. 6 : 12.
   119–17 scale against man's h· destiny.
   126–28 she sitteth in h· places ;
   134–28 wickedness is standing in h· places ;
   139–12 and every h· thing that— II Cor. 10 : 5.
   233–22 who think the standard of C. S. too h·
   274–23 whose consciences . . . hold h· carnival.
   285–11 hold h· the banner of Truth and
   287–12 only h· and holy joy can satisfy
   295–23 that h· and pure ethical tones do
   320–23 h· in the zenith of Truth's
   348– 2 towards the mark of a h· calling.
   385– 7 This is Thy h· behest :
   385–22 "When hope soared h·,
   387– 2 divinely fair, the h· and deep,
   389–12 His habitation h· is here,
   302– 0 majestic oak, from yon h· place
Man. 86 13 ready for this h· calling,
Chr. 53–28 Of his h· morn?
Ret. 2–29 for whom she cherished a h· regard.
    48 21 fulfilled its h· and noble destiny,
Un. 7–16 Herein is my evidence, from on h·,
Pul. 10–26 like day-spring from on h·.
    33–20 * giving him h· counsel and serious
    77–17 * twentieth day of . . . at h· noon.
    78–15 * 20th day of February, . . . at h· noon.
No. 7–18 God has appointed . . . h· tasks,
   19– 1 regulates the present h· premium
Pan. 12–13 h· above the so-called laws of matter,
'00. 6– 8 the h· calling of God in— Phil. 3 : 14.
'01. 2–13 Christ's healing too h· for them.
Hea. 6– 7 opinions of people fly too h· or
   11–21 When you have reached this h· goal
Po. 4–11 His habitation h· is here,
  19– 1 like the eagle's, oh, still be it h·,
  20– 8 majestic oak, from yon h· place
  32–14 with strength from on h·,
  37– 7 This is Thy h· behest :
  39– 6 A temple, whose h· dome
  48–16 "When hope soared h·,
  50–20 the h· and deep,
My. 4–30 Thou God most h· and nigh.
  6–23 h· above the work of men's hands,
  30–21 * they were heaped h· with bills,
  36–28 * have fulfilled a h· resolve
  37– 9 * declare again our h· appreciation
  64–18 * constitutes the h· standing of C. S.
  64–23 * h· and holy task of overcoming
  78–15 * piled h· with bank-notes,
  89– 6 * two hundred and twenty feet h·,
  94–27 * h· above the work of men's hands,
  154–21 * must not the h· and glorious
  171–23 * and of the h· school.
  173–27 green surrounding the h· school ;
  201– 2 Press on towards the h· calling
  268–28 Look h· enough, and you see
  290–23 h· and holy call you again to
  320– 9 * h· regard for you as a Christian
  331–26 * of the h· feeling of honor
(see also **heaven**)

high-domed
My. 68– 4 * auditorium, with its h· ceiling

higher
Mis. 1– 4 to him, no h· destiny dawned
   1–15 stepping-stone to a h· recognition
  17–19 a much h· and holier conception of
  28–30 by the superiority of the h· law ;
  29–31 h· rules of Life which Jesus taught
  30– 5 and doubt its h· rules,
  52–17 that tends to lift mortals h·.
  58–14 through a h· than mortal sense.
  63–24 reaching toward a h· goal,
  66–19 the h· spiritual sense,
  67– 3 h· claims of the law and gospel
  98–13 in a h· mode of medicine ;
  99–13 called to voice a h· order of Science
  126–11 We also have gained h· heights ;
  136– 6 broader and h· views,
  158– 3 h· far than the heavens above
  162– 5 advent of a h· Christianity.
  174–13 h· than the atmosphere of our planet,
  227–26 satisfies the mind craving a h· good,
  228–13 to a capacity for a h· life.
  235–23 educate the affections to h·
  244–19 by the h· law of Spirit,
  270– 8 mankind hath no h· ideal
  276–22 a purer, h· affection and ideal.
  278–31 This has developed h· energies
  287–18 the h· nature of man governs
  287–25 they lead to h· joys :
  289–26 she may win a h·.
  290– 6 h· in the scale of harmony,
  330–21 h· joys, holier aims,
  342–10 a h· understanding of God.
  345–12 pure and strong faith rose h·
  346– 3 carries this thought even h·,
  354 28 he rests in a liberty h·
  355–16 gives scope to h· demonstration.
  358–32 a h· spiritual unity is won,
  369–16 h· than a rhubarb tincture
  383–14 rise h· in the estimation of
  399–21 Lifted h·, we depart,
Man. 87–17 h· meaning of the Scriptures.
Ret. 28–27 h· than the stars of heaven.
  31–11 a desire for something h·
  33–18 disappears in the h· attenuations
  48–24 h· than physic or drugging ;
  48–29 has led to h· ways, means, and
  88– 8 h· manifestation of Life.
Un. 6– 7 h· selfhood, derived from God,
  11–12 through the h· laws of God.
Pul. 2– 9 a thought h· and deeper than
  15–20 cement of a h· humanity will unite
  38–28 * manifestations of a h· spirituality
  67–15 * give expression to a h· spirituality.
  85–10 * better and h· conception of God
Rud. 2–21 introduces us to h· definitions.
  2–25 h· range of infinite goodness.
  8–15 from a lower to a h· condition
  14–19 No discount . . . made on h· classes,
  14–20 their tuition in the h· instruction,
  14–24 unprepared to enter h· classes.
No. 36–15 Jesus had a resort to his h· self
  36–25 risen from human sense to a h·
  44– 4 h· demonstration of medicine
  46–17 let us lift their standard h·,
Pan. 2– 7 h· than Mt. Ararat above the deluge.
  6–14 h· criticism is not satisfied
  10–24 A h· manhood is manifest,
'01. 1–11 to rise h· and still h·
  3–14 h· definition derived from the
  30–17 and the h· class of critics
Hea. 1– 8 they are calls to h· duties,
  5–26 lead our lives to h· issues ;
  8– 8 results of this h· Christianity,
  9–16 Then it is a h· duty to know that
  11–28 h· attenuations of homœopathy
  12–23 h· attenuations prove that
  12–26 admit the h· attenuations are
  13– 7 h· natures are reached
  13– 8 soonest by the h· attenuations,
  16– 9 Christ with a h· meaning,
  19–20 bidding man go up h·,
Peo. 5–13 risen h· to our mortal sense,
  7– 4 chiseling to h· excellence,
  9–27 destroys discord with the h· and
  11– 4 struck the keynote of h· claims,
  12– 1 hearken to the h· law of God,
  14–13 awake to a h· and holier love
Po. 18– 5 Careening in liberty h· and h·
  18–10 When h· he soareth to compass his
  23–17 Life hath a h· recompense
  76– 5 Lifted h·, we depart, Having one.
My. 3–19 It is the h· criticism,
  46– 5 * h· and more spiritual plane of
  48–30 * feed the h· nature through the mind,

higher

My.	51–14	* *h·* understanding of Christianity,
	68–12	* *h·* than that of the State House.
	79– 6	* chapter sub-title
	79–21	* upon a far *h·* pedestal
	95–23	* *h·* critics and the men of science
	110–17, 18	rising *h·* and forever *h·*
	110–24	*h·* in the altitude of being.
	110–25	Mounting *h·*, mortals will cease to
	112–25	his *h·* life is the result of
	114–26	*h·* meaning of this book
	118–15	embarrass the *h·* criticism.
	136–28	and the *h·* criticism.
	142–19	step *h·* in their passage from sense
	151–27	They were content to look no *h·*
	152– 1	it took a step *h·* ;
	159–17	whereby we reach our *h·* nature.
	191–16	*h·* human sense of Life and
	212–11	*h·* forms of matter,
	216–31	to earn for a purpose even *h·*,
	221– 6	something *h·* than the systems
	237– 2	"*h·* criticism" announced in the
	240– 5	chapter sub-title
	240– 8	* why you call C. S. the *h·* criticism?"
	240– 9	I called C. S. the *h·* criticism
	240–16	C. S. is the *h·* criticism because
	241– 5	* *h·* meaning of the Scriptures.
	246–14	*h·* understanding of the absolute
	250–10	*h·* usefulness in this vast vineyard
	252–26	gave to . . . a *h·* hint.
	253– 3	the *h·* and everlasting harmony,
	277–16	not consonant with the *h·* law
	297–17	a *h·* realization of heaven.
	308– 8	*h·*, nobler, more imperative
	338–18	and they seek a *h·* source
	357–14	desire to build *h·*,
	357–15	demonstrate C. S. to a *h·* extent,
	(*see also* **hope, sense**)	

highest

Mis.	15– 9	yea, the *h·* Christianization
	44–12	to demonstrate its *h·* possibilities.
	88–21	* Jesus was the *h·* type of
	145–29	"Glory to God in the *h·*, — *Luke* 2 : 14.
	146–25	*h·* understanding of justice and mercy.
	164–24	*h·* human concept of the man Jesus,
	169–20	to get at the *h·*, or metaphysical,
	247–11	from the *h·* possible ethics
	260–32	the *h·* attenuation of evil.
	334–19	the *h·* degree of nothingness :
	336– 8	His *h·* idea as seen to-day
	348– 1	But the Scientists aim *h·*.
	365– 6	their *h·* endeavors are to Science
	379–21	*h·* attenuation in homœopathy,
Ret.	7– 8	* *h·* order of intellectual powers,
Un.	7–25	*h·* phenomena of the All-Mind.
	32– 8	not the *h·* Mind,
	50–12	of which evil is the *h·* degree ;
	51–15	Woman is the *h·* species of man,
	61–17	Our *h·* sense of infinite good
Pul.	81–26	* of missions— the *h·* of all
Rud.	9– 4	not a Christian, in the *h·* sense,
No.	10– 7	former is the *h·* style of man ;
	16–26	its *h·* attenuation is mortal mind ;
	18–15	and their *h·* endeavors are,
	44– 8	swerves not from the *h·* ethics
	45–16	fill the *h·* measure of enlightened
	45–17	the *h·* places in government,
	45–26	urging its *h·* demands on mortals,
Pan.	9–16	demonstrates the *h·* humanity,
	10–25	individual who finds the *h·* joy,
'00.	11–27	*h·* criticism on all human action,
'01.	2– 3	The *h·* spiritual Christianity
	17–25	*h·* attenuations of homœopathy
	28–10	up to his *h·* understanding
'02.	17– 8	learn that man's *h·* happiness,
Hea.	10– 8	presented the *h·* ideal of Love.
	13–15	*h·* attenuation we ever attained
Peo.	6–28	by their *h·* or their lowest ideals,
My.	52– 7	* *h·* type of womanhood,
	96– 4	* *h·* order of intelligence,
	104–25	men and women of the *h·* talents,
	136–17	*h·* fee ever received by
	146–14	altitude of its *h·* propositions
	212–12	*h·* form of mental evil,
	231–13	its *h·* and infinite meanings,
	244–21	In the *h·* sense of a disciple,
	248–29	*h·* inspiration is found nearest the
	283–17	a man's *h·* idea of right

highly

Man.	47–14	Testimony . . . is *h·* important.
Ret.	19–13	He was *h·* esteemed
	83–25	It is also *h·* important
	85–25	our Cause, is *h·* prosperous,
Pul.	37–24	* a *h·* gifted personality."
	66–15	* *h·* figurative language.

highly

My.	157–10	* you are so *h·* esteemed,
	208– 4	your *h·* interesting letter.
	330–25	He was *h·* esteemed

high-principled

My.	319– 9	his *h·* character and

highway

Mis.	287–17	find the *h·* of holiness.
No.	33–13	Self-sacrifice is the *h·* to heaven.
My.	3–18	*h·* of hope, faith, understanding.
	240–13	*h·* of hope, faith, understanding."
	308–17	* tramping doggedly along the *h·*,

Hill, Hon. Isaac

Ret.	7– 5	Hon. Isaac *H·*, of Concord,

hill

Mis.	227–22	dwelling upon a holy *h·*,
	232–16	ascend the *h·* of Science,
	323– 2	city set upon a *h·*," — *see Matt.* 5 : 14.
	323–23	up the *h·* it is straight and narrow,
	328–21	ascends the *h·* of C. S.
	344–30	stood on Mars' *h·* at Athens,
Ret.	4–10	situated on the summit of a *h·*,
Pul.	48–16	* on the brow of Bow *h·*,
My.	33–16	dwell in thy holy *h·* — *Psal.* 15 : 1.
	34– 1	into the *h·* of the Lord — *Psal.* 24 : 3.
	133– 6	inhabit His holy *h·*,
	228–23	dwell in Thy holy *h·* — *Psal.* 15 : 1.

hills

Un.	14–20	rock, firmer than everlasting *h·*.
Pul.	49–21	* return to her native granite *h·*,
Po.	30– 2	beckonest from the giant *h·*
My.	155– 5	near my heart and native *h·*,
	185–27	* For the strength of the *h·*,
	186–11	and on to the celestial *h·*,
	341– 6	and lifted to her giant *h·*

Hillsborough

Ret.	6–18	he read law at *H·*,

hillside

Mis.	301–30	the commands of our *h·* Priest,
	397–23	O'er the *h·* steep,
Ret.	46– 4	O'er the *h·* steep,
	91–15	On a *h·*, near the sloping shores
	91–28	What has this *h·* priest,
Pul.	17– 3	O'er the *h·* steep,
'01.	6–19	consistent with Christ's *h·* sermon,
Po.	14– 2	O'er the *h·* steep,
	32– 7	scattered o'er *h·* and dale ;

hilltops and hill-tops

Pul.	53–23	* from the *h·* of Palestine,
'01.	35– 7	asleep upon the *h·* of Zion.

hilt

Mis.	223–18	what we would resist to the *h·*

Him

Mis.	xi–10	nor unrewarded by *H·*.
	8– 5	"in *H·* [Mind] we live, — *Acts* 17 : 28.
	22–18	come from God and return to *H·*,
	22–20	for it dwelleth in *H·*
	41– 7	wrath of man" to praise *H·*. — *Psal.* 76 : 10.
	45–25	Scriptures imply *H·* to be,
	45–28	were made by *H·* ; — *John* 1 : 3.
	45–29	without *H·* was not — *John* 1 : 3.
	46–20	not weighing equally with *H·*,
	49–28	as the Scriptures imply *H·* to be,
	50–30	and loving *H·* supremely,
	55–30	it is in something unlike *H·* ;
	59–13	all things to those who love *H·* ;
	63–20	none else beside *H·*," — *Deut.* 4 : 35.
	71–24	"For of *H·*, — *Rom.* 11 : 36.
	71–24	and through *H·*, — *Rom.* 11 : 36.
	71–24	and to *H·*, — *Rom.* 11 : 36.
	79– 9	In *H·* we live, move, and
	79–10	origin and existence being in *H·*,
	93–10	in *H·* dwelleth no evil.
	96– 5	have found *H·* so ;
	107– 1	your many-throated organ, . . . praises *H·*;
	107– 2	in and of this temple that praise *H·*,
	115–24	turns us more unreservedly to *H·*
	117–30	or make them too late to follow *H·*.
	118–15	to work alone with God and for *H·*,
	123–30	it follows that those who worship *H·*,
	123–31	must worship *H·* spiritually,
	124– 4	must worship *H·* in spirit.
	124– 7	neither do we love and obey *H·* by
	127–26	cannot avoid . . . if we reflect *H·*.
	150–28	His people are they that reflect *H·*
	151–20	make *H·* thy first acquaintance.
	153–20	who honors *H·* not by positive proof
	155–26	forward their letters to *H·*
	157–22	trust also in *H·* ; — *Psal.* 37 : 5.
	173–25	whence, then, is something besides *H·*
	174– 7	come into the presence of *H·*

Him

Mis. 176– 2   harmony of Science that declares H,
194– 6   know H better, and love H more.
196–22   "we shall be like H ; " — I John 3 : 2.
219– 9   they that worship H — John 4 : 24.
219– 9   must worship H in spirit — John 4 : 24.
235– 5   to reflect H who destroys death
257– 2   or includes H in every mode and
258–28   only suitable or true idea of H ;
259– 1   were made by H ; — John 1 : 3.
259– 1   without H was not — John 1 : 3.
260–18   opposite to H who is All.
269– 1   trust also in H ; — Psal. 37 : 5.
277–25   Though clouds are round about H,
319– 5   the argument of aught besides H,
325–23   "provoke H in the — Psal. 78 : 40.
325–24   grieve H in the desert." — Psal. 78 : 40.
331– 3   committing their way unto H
332–30   that there is something besides H ;
333–27   that which does not reflect H
334– 1   the prophet better understood H
334– 3   or say unto H, — Dan. 4 : 35.
347–28   None can say unto H,
350–16   none beside H." — see Deut. 4 : 35.
360–27   Jesus, as the true idea of H,
363– 8 H who compensateth vanity
366–12   none beside H." — see Deut. 4 : 35.
366–14   nothing that . . . maketh a lie is in H,
Ret. 9–18   * that I may worship H,
9–26   * won, through clouds, to H,
13–20   if I went to H in prayer,
57–23   not our own, separated from H.
59–19   and all that is made by H,
60–20   there is nothing beside H ;"
60–22   saith, . . . is something besides H,
63– 5   and there is none beside H,
93–17   in H we live, — Acts 17 : 28.
Un. 2– 3   God pitieth them who fear H ;
3–13   by knowing H in whom they have
4– 1   He is near to them who adore H.
4– 2   To understand H, without a single taint
4–3, 4   approach H and become like H.
4–14   as we get still nearer H,
4–18   has not forbidden man to know H ;
7–11   has so bound me to H as to enable me
10– 5   this system is built on H
13–11   To H there is no moral inharmony ;
15– 6   that they may declare H absolutely
21–15   With H is no consciousness of evil,
21–16   because there is nothing beside H
21–17   or outside of H.
26– 4   From H come my forms,
29–26   I shall yet praise H, — Psal. 42 : 11.
31– 3   they that worship H — John 4 : 24.
31– 3   must worship H in spirit — John 4 : 24.
37–12   no . . . can separate us from H
39–18   power of H who gave and giveth
41–19   "we shall be like H," — I John 3 : 2.
48– 6   I believe more in H than do most
60– 6   and there is none beside H,
60–19   then let them serve H,
60–22   Without H, the universe would
Pul. 72–23   * faith in H and His teachings.
73– 6   * She had faith in H,
Rud. 2–12   if we think of H as less than
4–21   and there is naught beside H.
4–22   we can only learn and love H
9–27   there can be none beside H ;
13–15   none else beside H." — Deut. 4 : 35.
14– 3   give H all their services,
No. 7–17   cannot hide it from H.
8–14   the wrath of man to praise H,
16– 8   would manifest evil in H
16– 8   and proceeding from H.
16–19   of something unlike H.
17– 7   "In H we live, — Acts 17 : 28.
17–21   "none beside H." — see Deut. 4 : 35.
18– 4   lie that denies H as All-in-all,
18– 5   nor does it ascribe to H all presence,
24–28   As there is none beside H,
25–18   coexistent and coeternal with H.
26–13   represents God, and is in H.
30–23   revealing H and nothing else.
33– 2   the wrath of man shall praise H.
35–22   one with H now and forever.
37–22   infinite God, and none beside H ;
39–14   uplifting us to H.
42– 6   to have other gods before H,
Pan. 4–23   for I shall yet praise H, — Psal. 42 : 11.
5– 5   were made by H," — John 1 : 3.
11– 6   after the image of H — Col. 3 : 10.
13–18   Sooner or later all shall know H,
13–19   and find life in H in whom
'01. 6–22   infinite scientific sense of H,
6–28   idea of H as a finite Person
6–30   is not my sense of H.

Him

'01. 7–20   know not where they have laid H.
8–12   but an impartation of H.
32–12   willing to renounce all for H.
35– 1   acknowledge H, and He — Prov. 3 : 6.
'02. 12–19   in H we live, — Acts 17 : 28.
Hea. 16–25   impossible to approach H?
Peo. 6–15   more than we love H ;
6–17   we love H, because
6–25   "acquaint now thyself with H — Job 22 : 21.
7–31   must spiritualize to approach H,
Po. 43– 5   You in H abide.
43– 6   Ours through H who gave
My. 5– 9   His idea, coexistent with H
5–20   not an unknown God, but H whom,
13–19   to H "who forgiveth — Psal. 103 : 3.
13–29   to H who returns it unto them
43– 8   * and they learned to know H.
45–19   * guidance of H who went before
154–12   "in H was life," — John 1 : 4.
156–10   have committed unto H — II Tim. 1 : 12,
170–24   trust also in H ; — Psal. 37 : 5.
174–27   I know H nearer, love H more,
174–28   humbly pray to serve H
184– 6   for them that wait upon H
187–26   to build a house unto H
192– 2   Ye worship H whom ye serve.
193– 2   unto H whom to know aright
193–17   You are dedicating yours to H.
196–19   committed himself to H — I Pet. 2 : 23.
206–25 H who hath called you — I Pet. 2 : 9.
209– 5   those that seek and serve H.
226–23   depend on H for your existence.
240– 1   till all men shall know H
267– 7   were made by H ; — John 1 : 3.
267– 7   without H was not — John 1 : 3.
270–23   and that I can appeal to H
270–32   "they that worship H — John 4 : 24.
270–32   must worship H in spirit — John 4 : 24.
280–21   nor say unto H, What doest Thou?
290–13   Trust in H whose love enfolds thee.
295– 6   "In H was life ; — John 1 : 4.

Himself

Mis. 72– 2   nothing evil, or unlike H.
102–12   God is like H and like nothing else.
258–13   who was a law to H.
258–14   governing H, He governs the universe.
258–18   God named H, I AM.
258–27   God's interpretation of H furnishes
366–13   He is in nothing unlike H ;
367–20   Mind knows nothing beyond H
367–32   abideth in H, the only Life,
Ret. 56–29   God reflects H, or Mind,
Un. 3–20   Hence He is in H only,
3–23   Within H is every embodiment of
3–25   no consciousness of anything unlike H ;
3–26   there can be nothing outside of H.
23–22   anything so wholly unlike H
41–24   God cannot be the opposite of H.
48–17   The Ego is God H,
60–21   neither absent from H nor from the
No. 15–25   in nothing is He unlike H.
17–14   witness, testifying of H.
21–16   who unfolds H through
23–22   no such warfare against H.
26–16   out of H into something below
Pan. 9–19   God, who reveals H
'01. 5–30   God explains H in C. S.
'02. 7– 1   producing nothing unlike H,

hinder

Mis. 63– 5   to h his benign influence
111–16   the tares cannot h it.
223–22   no counteracting influence can h
274– 8   might h the progress of our Cause
284– 2   and never try to h others
290– 7   break all bonds that h progress.
327–14   greatly h their ascent.
No. 45– 8   To h the unfolding truth,
Pan. 9–15   to h not the attainment of
'01. 14–13   so h our way to holiness.
My. 189– 4   who shall h you?
206– 3 h the divine influx and lose
296–14   Evil has no power to harm, to h,

hindered

Mis. 154–25   that your prayers be not h.
Un. 11–23   neither . . . h the divine process.
Pan. 9–18   ought to be aided, not h,

hindering

My. 212–27 h in every way conceivable

hinders

Mis. 234–12   What h man's progress is his
336–14   beam in your own eye that h
No. 23– 1 h the destruction of evil.
My. 296– 4   whatever h the Science of being.

hindrance

Ret.	89– 2	*h·* opposed to it by material motion,
No.	9– 4	*h·* of the Cause of Truth.
My.	219– 5	a *h·* rather than help.

hindrances

My.	294–20	*h·* previously mentioned,

Hindu

My.	96– 9	* Mecca and the *H·* shrines,

Hinds, Father

'01.	32– 5	Father *H·*, Methodist Elder.

hinge

Mis.	206– 1	*h·* on which have turned all

hint

Mis.	278–22	This may be a serviceable *h·*,
Pan.	7–12	and *h·* the gods of paganism
My.	28– 9	* a *h·* of the unselfish efforts,
	215–31	we have no *h·* of his changing
	252–27	gave to . . . a higher *h·*.

hinted

My.	324–10	* *h·* that he thought he could give
	355– 8	I have not infrequently *h·* at this.

hints

Mis.	60–29	*h·* the existence of spiritual
	225– 1	chapter sub-title
Ret.	33– 1	aided by *h·* from homœopathy,
My.	49–24	* useful *h·* as to the mode of

hire

Pul.	50– 4	* worthy of his *h·*," — *Luke* 10 : 7.
My.	214–15	chapter sub-title
	214–22	*h·* a hall in which to speak,
	215–25	worthy of his *h·*." — *Luke* 10 : 7.

hired

My.	313–10	being *h·* to rock me,

hireling

Mis.	213–25	"an *h·*'" — *John* 10 : 13.

hiring

Mis.	300– 1	avoiding the cost of *h·*

His

Mis.	7–15	laborers in *H·* vineyard.
	9– 5	are these uses of *H·* rod !
	9– 6	passes all *H·* flock under *H·* rod
	9– 7	passes all . . . into *H·* fold ;
	10– 9	He has called *H·* own,
	10–16	and reinstate *H·* orders,
	18–32	bring to you at *H·* demand
	19– 5	demanded of *H·* servants
	23–27	manifests all *H·* attributes
	36–12	*H·* beast is the lion that
	39–15	I have faith in *H·* promise,
	59–16	lost under *H·* government.
	60– 2	He sent *H·* Son to save from sin,
	61–28	Naming these *H·* embodiment,
	69– 2	*H·* essence, relations, and attributes.
	69– 3	at *H·* goodness, mercy, and might.
	69– 6	of Mind, or God, and *H·* attributes.
	78– 5	*H·* glory encompasseth all being.
	97–17	may touch the hem of *H·* garment ;
	101–31	This one Mind and *H·* individuality
	102–10	*H·* infinity precludes the possibility
	102–11	*H·* being is individual, but not
	102–13	*H·* character admits of no degrees
	102–14	In *H·* individuality I recognize
	102–17	*H·* pity is expressed in modes
	102–18	*H·* chastisements are the manifestations
	102–19	sympathy of *H·* eternal Mind
	106–27	and resound *H·* praise."
	114–26	Rest assured that God in *H·* wisdom
	117–30	their moves before God makes *H·*,
	118–19	*H·* rod and *H·* staff comfort you.
	121–21	crucifixion of *H·* beloved Son,
	123–25	and keep *H·* commandments,
	124–21	silence wherein to muse *H·* praise,
	127– 2	smiled on *H·* "little ones," — *Matt.* 18 : 6.
	127–17	"river of *H·* pleasure," — *see Psal.* 36 : 8.
	127–24	the rod is *H·* means of grace ;
	134–15	will guard and guide *H·* own.
	138–26	God will give to all *H·* soldiers
	146–23	to walk in the footsteps of *H·* flock.
	151– 1	folds the sheep of *H·* pasture ;
	151– 2	ears are attuned to *H·* call.
	151–22	spoken of you in *H·* Word.
	152–25	He will hide you in *H·* feathers
	152–26	Into *H·* haven of Soul
	152–30	faith in God and *H·* spiritual means
	153– 3	God will confirm *H·* inheritance.
	153– 9	At *H·* command, the rock became a
	153–14	good to *H·* Israel
	154– 6	God's love for *H·* flock
	154– 7	is manifest in *H·* care.
	154–11	means and measure of *H·* grace.
	154–12	proof of the prosperity of *H·* Zion.
	154–19	Abide in *H·* word.
	157–14	safe under the shadow of *H·* wing.

His

Mis.	158– 4	is *H·* wisdom above ours.
	158– 9	after *H·* messenger has obeyed
	159– 4	to elucidate *H·* Word.
	170– 9	having rightly read *H·* Word,
	173–27	man in *H·* own likeness.
	174–22	God, and *H·* omnipresence?
	175–22	there are other minds than *H·* ;
	177– 7	the Lord and against *H·* Christ,
	179–25	God does all this through *H·*
	182–25	*H·* sons and daughters.
	186– 3	in *H·* own image and likeness.
	186–26	sense of God and *H·* universe
	193–24	our Lord and *H·* Christ, Truth ;
	208–20	*H·* rod brings to view
	209– 5	shut the mouth of *H·* prophets,
	215–16	in the way of *H·* appointment,
	234–32	makes *H·* sovereignty glorious.
	246–24	make *H·* paths straight." — *Matt.* 3 : 3.
	263– 8	with *H·* feathers." — *Psal.* 91 : 4.
	263–10	safe in *H·* strength,
	263–10	building on *H·* foundation,
	268–23	potions of *H·* own qualities.
	268–25	*H·* preparations for the sick
	276–20	*H·* divine Love is found in affliction.
	277–29	I thunder *H·* law to the sinner,
	306–29	give *H·* angels charge — *Psal.* 91 : 11.
	307– 1	God gives you *H·* spiritual ideas,
	311– 1	and keep *H·* commandments,
	315–30	to study *H·* revealed Word,
	318–11	and keep *H·* commandments.
	322–24	the amplitude of *H·* mercy,
	322–24	the justice of *H·* judgment,
	336– 8	*H·* highest idea as seen to-day
	347–26	Those who know no will but *H·*
	348–12	when God shall reveal *H·* rod,
	353–24	divine Principle carries on *H·* harmony.
	354–21	to govern *H·* own creation,
	361–12	earth is full of *H·* glory,
	361–24	*H·* manifestation is the spiritual
	361–29	He elucidates *H·* own idea,
	361–32	*H·* ways are not as our way.
	363–17	*H·* modes declare the beauty of
	363–18	*H·* manifold wisdom shines through
	363–20	the brightness of *H·* coming.
	364–29	God and *H·* modes,
	366–29	according to *H·* mode of C. S. ;
	367–30	*H·* ignorance of that which is not,
	368– 1	*H·* own image and likeness.
	368– 9	* keeping watch above *H·* own."
	368–29	rejoice in *H·* supreme rule,
	370–18	care from *H·* loving heart.
	370–28	*H·* first care is to separate the
	373–14	does, guide *H·* children.
	376–29	the brightness of *H·* glory.
	389–12	*H·* habitation high is here,
	389–13	*H·* arm encircles me,
	389–18	the shadow of *H·* mighty wing ;
	397– 1	Then *H·* unveiled, sweet mercies
	399–25	Stands *H·* church,
	399–27	and understood By *H·* flock.
Man.	15– 7	We acknowledge *H·* Son,
Chr.	53–41	Truth, the Life — *H·* word
	55–13	operation of *H·* hands. — *Isa.* 5 : 12.
Ret.	9–23	* learned at last to know *H·* voice
	13–20	seeking *H·* guidance.
	18–18	all *H·* spirit hath made,
	25–16	but *H·* corporeality I denied.
	27–30	new to *H·* "little one." — *see Matt.* 10 : 42.
	59–24	in *H·* own image and likeness
	60– 8	sense says that matter, *H·* antipode,
	69–30	keeping *H·* commandment?' "
	91– 1	and He anoints *H·* Truth-bearers,
Un.	2– 4	no place where *H·* voice is not heard ;
	3–20	in *H·* own nature and character,
	4–12	our sense . . . of *H·* absence,
	7– 1	*H·* name will be magnified
	10–21	the calculation of *H·* mighty ways,
	13– 9	*H·* universal laws, *H·* unchangeableness,
	13–13	*H·* infinite power would
	13–17	in the very fibre of *H·* being,
	14– 2	do *H·* work over again,
	14– 9	upon *H·* own previous work,
	14–14	rectify *H·* spiritual universe?
	14–16	because *H·* created children proved
	18–28	it would lower *H·* rank.
	19– 5	contrary to *H·* creative will,
	20–22	outside of *H·* own focal distance.
	22–18	*Evil.* . . . Error, even, is *H·* offspring.
	23–22	unlike Himself and foreign to *H·* nature?
	24– 9	can never be outside of *H·* oneness.
	24–19	God and *H·* ideas
	26– 6	I am proud to be in *H·* outstretched
	26–15	* But *H·* mercy waneth never,
	27–15	knowing only *H·* own all-presence,
	32– 7	universe, is *H·* spiritual concept.

His

Un.	32–14	the eternal qualities of *H·* being.
	38– 5	not in accordance with *H·* law,
	51–22	and not of *H·* opposite, evil.
	60–28	yield to *H·* eternal presence,
Pul.	3–21	river of *H·* pleasures is a
	7–14	with *H·* outstretched arm.
	9–21	river of *H·* pleasures." — *see Psal.* 36: 8.
	10–29	this is *H·* redeemed ; this, *H·* beloved.
	12– 7	the power of *H·* Christ : — *Rev.* 12: 10.
	16–10	Stands *H·* church,
	16–12	and understood By *H·* flock.
	18–10	Then *H·* unveiled, sweet mercies
	30–17	* Supreme Being, and *H·* Son,
	39– 7	* Round our restlessness, *H·* rest.
	72–23	* faith in Him and *H·* teachings.
	73– 4	* *H·* unlimited and divine power.
	73– 9	* meditated over *H·* divine Word.
	73–15	* God has fulfilled *H·* promises to her
	74–16	to declare in *H·* infinite mercy.
Rud.	4–23	love Him through *H·* spirit,
	4–24	by *H·* marvellous light.
	10– 6	*H·* government is harmonious ;
	10–21	disobedience to *H·* spiritual law.
	10–22	*H·* law of Truth, when obeyed,
	10–26	acknowledge God in all *H·* ways.
	17–16	are the paths of *H·* testimony
	17–17	and the footsteps of *H·* flock.
No.	10–26	*H·* omnipotence and omnipresence.
	16–19	God and *H·* true likeness,
	16–21	but *H·* own consciousness,
	17–25	a part of *H·* consciousness.
	18– 3	acknowledged God in all *H·* ways.
	19–16	man is *H·* individualized idea.
	20– 2	*H·* person and perfection are
	30–14	the love of a Father for *H·* child,
	30–17	*H·* sympathy is divine, not human.
	34–21	propitiate *H·* justice and bring *H·* mercy
	37–16	demands *H·* continual presence,
	38–20	which includes only *H·* own nature,
	39–12	nor bring *H·* designs into mortal modes ;
	39–21	discoveries of God, of *H·* goodness
'00.	4– 3	makes *H·* opposites as real and
	4–25	and is *H·* reflection and Science.
	5–24	Science of God and *H·* universe,
	8 27	through one of *H·* little ones,
	10–22	habitation of *H·* throne forever.
	12– 4	seven stars in *H·* right hand — *Rev.* 2: 1.
'01.	1– 6	so long as you are in *H·* service.
	5–27	*H·* eternal image and likeness,
	5–29	explain both *H·* person and nature,
	7 10	man in *H·* own image and likeness,
	10–20	"the riches of *H·* grace" — *Eph.* 1: 7.
	15–26	* to bear to have you in *H·* sight.
	15–28	* provoking *H·* pure eyes by your sinful,
	16 00	* attending *H·* solemn worship.
	32–20	love God and keep *H·* commandments
'02.	7– 3	*H·* infinite manifestations of love
	8–29	departure from God, or *H·* lost likeness,
	17–24	ourselves and others through *H·* tenure,
Hea.	8– 2	and obedience to *H·* government.
	9–17	man, *H·* own image and likeness.
	12–13	directly or indirectly, through *H·* providence
	19–22	work more earnestly in *H·* vineyard,
Peo.	3– 9	torture of *H·* favorite Son,
	5–17	to declare *H·* omnipotence."
	13– 9	one God and *H·* all-power
Po.	4–17	shadow of *H·* mighty wing ;
	12–10	*H·* unveiled, sweet mercies show
	32–19	pardon and grace, through *H·* Son,
	64– 9	adore all *H·* spirit hath made,
	76– 9	on this rock . . . Stands *H·* church,
	76–11	understood By *H·* flock.
	79– 9	in thought and deed — To faithful *H·*.
My.	3– 8	that do *H·* commandments, — *Rev.* 22: 14.
	14– 2	their tithes into *H·* storehouse,
	15–14	*H·* own image and likeness.
	17–30	on *H·* 'little ones,' — *Matt.* 18: 6.
	18–14	'river of *H·* pleasure,' — *see Psal.* 36: 8.
	20–12	what God gives to *H·* church.
	20–13	your tithes into *H·* storehouse,
	23– 7	* so long as we follow *H·* commands.
	36–20	* salvation through *H·* divine Christ.
	109–21	but specks in *H·* universe,
	113–20	to perfect *H·* praise.
	129–11	no day but in *H·* smile.
	129–26	These are *H·* green pastures
	132–15	"Of *H·* own will — *Jas.* 1: 18.
	133– 6	inhabit *H·* holy hill,
	143–27	according to *H·* purpose. — *Rom.* 8: 31.
	150–19	*H·* own image and likeness,
	152–21	hear *H·* voice, listen to *H·* Word
	153–31	should be to us *H·* apostles,
	159–10	sent forth *H·* word to heal
	162– 2	*H·* "very present help — *Psal.* 46: 1.
	167–17	one acceptable in *H·* sight,

His

My.	170–16	It is *H·* coin, *H·* currency ;
	182–28	this vine of *H·* husbanding,
	186–15	according to *H·* riches in glory.
	186–21	Here let *H·* promise be verified :
	187–25	light and liberty of *H·* children,
	187–29	majesty of *H·* might
	188– 3	This house is hallowed by *H·* promise :
	190–30	wherefore vilify *H·* prophets
	193– 8	"for *H·* goodness, — *Psal.* 107: 8.
	193– 9	*H·* wonderful works — *Psal.* 107: 8.
	193–16	Nothing dethrones *H·* house.
	198– 7	continuance of *H·* favors,
	202–24	a drop from *H·* ocean of love,
	202–30	God bless this vine of *H·* planting.
	204– 2	faith in God and in *H·* followers
	204– 3	gives *H·* followers opportunity
	205–10	* *H·* wonders to perform ;
	205–11	* plants *H·* footsteps in the sea
	206–26	*H·* marvellous light." — *I Pet.* 2: 9.
	206–30	kingdom of *H·* dear Son." — *Col.* 1: 13.
	208–25	their confidence in *H·* ways
	213–21	harmony with *H·* true followers.
	221– 8	God in *H·* more infinite meanings,
	225–13	giving unto *H·* holy name
	225–18	sacredly holding *H·* name apart
	225–28	*H·* synonyms are Love, Truth, Life,
	226–21	you learn to hallow *H·* name,
	226–22	*H·* all-power, all-presence,
	232– 3	with the helm in *H·* hands.
	238–10	*H·* language and meaning are
	251–26	armors, and tests in *H·* service,
	251–26	and we are *H·*.
	253–24	you have *H·* rich blessing
	257– 3	*H·* dear love that heals
	260–28	religion to God and *H·* Christ,
	262– 1	eternal in *H·* own image.
	262–21	*H·* spiritual idea, man
	263– 2	alone and without *H·* glory.
	278– 2	If *H·* purpose for peace is to be
	280–21	Out of *H·* allness He must
	280–22	with *H·* own truth and love.
	281 14	we are *H·* in divine Science.
	288–27	*H·* rod is love.
	292–8, 9	*H·* rod and *H·* staff comfort
	300– 6	*H·* good pleasure." — *Phil.* 2: 13.
	323–22	* to reveal to us *H·* way.
	347– 2	through . . . *H·* two witnesses.
	355–27	God is glorified in *H·* reflection
	356– 3	in *H·* reflection of love and
	356– 7	* plants *H·* footsteps in the sea

(see also **creation, hand, idea, image, laws, likeness, love, people, power, presence, righteousness, will**)

hisses

Mis.	227– 4	to the *h·* of the multitude,

hissing

Mis.	134–25	fermenting, and its heat *h·*
	323–19	hushing the *h·* serpents,

historians

My.	315–26	thank the enterprising *h·*

historic

Mis.	305–20	* articles of *h·* interest will be
Ret.	21–25	*h·* incidents and personal events
My.	85–25	* this *h·* city is the Mecca of
	90–20	* *h·* place of Mrs. Eddy as the
	148–11	this church becomes *h·*,
	184–20	*h·* gem on the glowing records of

historical

Mis.	197–16	belief in any *h·* event or person.
	306– 2	* send fullest *h·* description.
'00.	12–28	rather than personal or *h·*.
My.	v–13	* recalling the following *h·* facts:
	26–22	This *h·* dedication should
	318–28	ample fund of *h·* knowledge,

historically

Ret.	3– 8	known *h·* as Lovewell's War.
Pul.	8– 2	press has spoken out *h·*,

history
all

My.	89–29	* religious phenomenon of all *h·*.

Biblical

Un.	44–12	according to Biblical *h·*.

Christian

Ret.	45– 8	earliest periods in Christian *h·*.

different

Mis.	224–14	each person has a different *h·*,

divine

Ret.	10–15	Etymology was divine *h·*,

early

Mis.	ix– 6	In the early *h·* of C. S.,
	141–20	stain the early *h·* of C. S.
My.	60– 2	* about the early *h·* of C. S.

history
  following
    Mis. 271–28   * following *h·* and statistics
  fraught with
    Mis. 253–14   Fraught with *h·*, it repeats the past
  heart of
    Mis. 93– 4   heart of *h·* shall be made glad !
  his
    Rud. 3–10   His *h·* is emphatic in our hearts,
    My. 291–19   May his *h·* waken a tone of truth
  human
    (*see* **human**)
  its
    My. 47– 9   * from the pages of its *h·*.
  Jesus'
    Mis. 162–11   became the emblem of Jesus' *h·* ;
  Major Glover's
    My. 330–14   * concerning Major Glover's *h·*
  material
    No. 45–27   material *h·* is drawing to a close.
  McClure
    My. 315–21   * the *McClure* "*h·*," so called,
  mortal
    Ret. 21–14   mortal *h·* is but the record of
  Mrs. Eddy's
    My. 297–26   chapter sub-title
  my
    Mis. 247– 6   Those familiar with my *h·*
         278– 9   my *h·* as connected with the Cause
    My. 297–30   circulating regarding my *h·*,
  natural
    Mis. 26–20   Natural *h·* shows that neither a
  needs
    Mis. 354– 5   *H·* needs it,
  no
    Mis. 357–12   no central emblem, no *h·*.
  of a seed
    Mis. 26– 9   ponders the *h·* of a seed,
        144–26   As in the *h·* of a seed,
  of Christianity
    Peo. 13–25   * "Since ever the *h·* of Christianity
  of Christian Science
    Mis. ix– 6   In the early *h·* of C. S.,
        141–20   stain the early *h·* of C. S.
    '01. 2–27   *h·* of C. S. explains its
    '02. 1– 3   marked the *h·* of C. S.
    My. 60– 2   * about the early *h·* of C. S.
        66–27   * an epoch in the *h·* of C. S.
  of Europe
    Mis. 170–20   *h·* of Europe and America ;
  of its Discoverer
    My. 143–16   the honest *h·* of its Discoverer
  of man
    Un. 50–27   as the *h·* of man, disappears,
  of Mind-healing
    No. 3–18   *h·* of Mind-healing notes this hour.
  of the Church
    Man. 110– 8   recorded in the *h·* of the Church
  of the church
    My. 57–18   * largest in the *h·* of the church
        284–15   * first time in the *h·* of the church
  of the errors
    Mis. 277–20   * *h·* of the errors of the human mind."
  of the spiritual man
    Mis. 186– 1   giving the *h·* of the spiritual man
  our
    My. 45– 9   * in the annals of our *h·*.
  partial
    Ret. 38– 9   partial *h·* of what I had already
  place in
    Mis. 308–10   their proper place in *h·*,
  recorded in
    Rud. 16–21   first book, recorded in *h·*, which
  records
    '00. 12– 7   *H·* records Ephesus as an
  religious
    Un. 15–21   found in heathen religious *h·*.
  repeats itself
    No. 41– 3   *H·* repeats itself.
    Hea. 1– 6   *H·* repeats itself ;
    My. 58– 6   * "*H·* repeats itself."
  sad
    Mis. 341–23   the sad *h·* of Vesta,
  scant
    Mis. 274– 1   From the scant *h·* of Jesus
  shows
    Pul. 23–18   * *H·* shows the curious fact that
    '00. 10–17   *H·* shows that error repeats itself
    '01. 28–15   Sacred *h·* shows that those who
  society and
    Mis. 296– 6   American society and *h·*,
  temporal
    My. 134– 1   spiritual bespeaks our temporal *h·*.
  this
    Mis. 57–20   This *h·* of a falsity
    Pul. 8–26   in the fabric of this *h·*,

history
  tired tongue of
    Ret. 84–23   tired tongue of *h·* be enriched.
  traditional
    Ret. 22– 7   traditional *h·* of the early life of
  veritable
    Mis. 312–20   honest utterance of veritable *h·*,
  web of
    Mis. 145–27   their names in the web of *h·*,
  winds of
    Mis. 79– 5   swept clean by the winds of *h·*.
  write the
    Mis. 106– 4   write the *h·* in poor parody on

    Mis. 106– 4   Scientists will, *must*, have a *h·* ;
        238–11   more than *h·* has yet recorded.
        272– 7   * is the first on record in *h·*,
        320– 4   the *h·* of Truth's idea,
    Ret. 44–29   The *h·* of that hour holds this true
    Pul. 33–15   * *h·* not infrequently emphasizes,
    Peo. 7– 3   on the body as well as on *h·*
    My. 89–26   * not to this time alone, but to *h·*.
        90– 5   * in the *h·* of religious expression.
       119– 1   It is convenient for *h·* to record
       125–14   *H·* will record their words,
       236– 1   *h·* of our church buildings.
       292– 2   more than *h·* has yet recorded.
       318–32   I do not find my authority . . . in *h·*,

hit
    Mis. 216–23   a happy *h·* at idealism,
    Hea. 6– 6   The pioneer . . . is never *h·* :
hitch
    Un. 17– 4   * "*H·* your wagon to a star."
    My. 75–15   * not been the slightest *h·*
hither
    Mis. 99–28   come up *h·*."
       326–31   "Wherefore comest thou *h·*?"
       327– 3   I came *h·*, hoping that I
       386–29   *H·* to reap, with all the crowned
    '00. 9–11   art thou come *h·* to — *Matt.* 8 : 29.
    '01. 1–17   have brought you *h·*.
    '02. 10– 6   "Art thou come *h·* to — *Matt.* 8 : 29.
    Po. 16– 7   Ambition, come *h·* !
       50–16   *H·* to reap, with all the crowned
    My. 182–26   turn *h·* with satisfied hope.
       222– 6   bring him *h·* — *Matt.* 17 : 17.
       229– 3   No mesmerist . . . is fit to come *h·*.
       244– 7   You have been invited *h·*
hitherto
    Mis. xi– 7   what they have *h·* achieved
       xi–13   in the *h·* unexplored fields
       125–25   the *h·* untouched problems
       127– 1   *H·*, I have observed that
       146–12   I have *h·* declined to be
    Man. 18–11   "*H·* hath the Lord — *I Sam.* 7 : 12.
    Ret. 15–10   *h·* have I declared — *Psal.* 71 : 17.
       43– 7   the only College, *h·*,
    Pul. 56–17   * Christianity and Science, *h·* divorced
    '01. 35–16   And the working *h·*
    My. 17–29   "*H·*, I have observed that
       49– 3   * the *h·* half-persuaded
       57–20   * the *h·* largest admission,
       195– 7   have *h·* prevented my reply.
       217– 5   your *h·* unselfish toil,
       299–15   *h·* undiscovered in the translations
hits
    Mis. 347–32   whoever *h·* this mark is well paid
hived
    Mis. 294–13   a *h·* bee, with sting ready
hoar
    Po. 10–10   The *h·* fight is forgotten ;
    My. 337–11   The *h·* fight is forgotten ;
hoards
    '00. 3– 7   he *h·* this capital to distribute
hoarse
    Po. 73– 4   *h·* wave revisits thy shore !
hoary
    Mis. 231– 1   on whose *h·* head the almond-blossom
       257–23   and strikes down the *h·* saint.
       336–27   *h·* with eternity, touches time
       389– 2   The *h·* head with joy to crown ;
    No. 13–18   It is *h·* with time.
    Pan. 5–11   answer for all time to this *h·* query.
    Po. 21–16   The *h·* head with joy to crown ;
hobbling
    Mis. 168– 5   or *h·* on crutches,
hobby
    No. 44–10   Error has no *h·*,
Hodgson Hall
    Pul. 74– 7   * meets every Sunday in *H· H·*,

Hogue, Blanche Hersey
    My. 237–22 The article . . . by Blanche Hersey *H·*,

hold
  Mis. 62–14 *Why do Christian Scientists h·*
        63–17 might lay *h·* of eternal Life,
        97– 3 take *h·* of the eternal energies
      111– 8 losing *h·* of divine Love,
     136–24 *h·* three sessions annually,
     137–30 *h·* these organizations of their own,
     140– 3 could *h·* a wholly material title.
     199– 6 *h·* himself amenable only to
     216–26 * nor the laws of reason *h·* good,
     266–15 *h·* justice and mercy as inseparable
     269– 8 will *h·* to the one, — *Matt.* 6 : 24.
     274–23 those quill-drivers . . . *h·* high carnival.
     276– 5 I did not *h·* interviews with all
     282–18 person with whom you *h·* communion
     285–11 *h·* high the banner of Truth
     290–25 *h·* a place in one's memory,
     315–15 *h·* himself morally obligated to
     333–11 Where do we *h·* intelligence to be?
     350– 1 I *h·* receipts for $1,489.50 paid in,
     351–17 they never can . . . *h·* it there,
     355–28 *H·* thy gaze to the light,
     363–24 *h·* fast to the Principle of C. S.
     374–15 Angels, . . . *h·* charge over both,
  Man. 25–12 President shall *h·* office for one year,
      45–20 is not entitled to *h·* office
      46–13 shall *h·* in sacred confidence
      61– 4 shall not *h·* two or more
      76–21 They shall *h·* quarterly meetings
      79–22 *h·* and manage the property
      80– 7 shall *h·* this money subject to
      83–13 *h·* himself morally obligated
  Ret. 29– 3 and *h·* to loving our enemies
  Un. 43–23 to *apprehend,* or lay *h·* upon,
     49–13 So long as I *h·* evil in consciousness,
     56–24 lay *h·* of him ere he can change
     61– 2 that takes *h·* of eternal Truth.
  Pul. 38–24 * They *h·* with strict fidelity to
     63–19 * The great *h·* she has upon this army
     66–13 * They *h·* with strict fidelity to
  Rud. 12– 9 until they *h·* stronger than before
  No. 8–19 students to *h·* no controversy or
     13–18 It takes *h·* of eternity,
     38–18 they take *h·* of harmony,
  '00. 11– 3 *H·* in yourselves the true sense of
     14– 4 *H·* that fast which thou— *Rev.* 3 : 11.
     14–18 *h·* in your full hearts fervently
  '01. 13–28 *h·* it invalid, give it the lie,
     14–11 our faith takes *h·* of the fact that
  Hea. 13– 2 *h·* of both horns of the dilemma,
  Peo. 11–16 *h·* the children of Israel still in
  Po. 20– 8 grasped the sword to *h·* her throne,
     43–10 in Thy great heart *h·* them
  My. 53–10 * *h·* its meetings of worship in the
     84–23 * Its *h·* and development are
     85–17 * *h·* place among the architectural
     90–11 * grips *h·* of their faith
     93–27 * its *h·* upon the public,
    126–26 *h·* of every foul spirit, — *Rev.* 18 : 2
    129– 2 "*h·* fast that which is— *I Thess.* 5 : 21.
    129– 7 taking strong *h·* of the public
    129–24 takes *h·* on heaven,
    146–23 Scientists *h·* as a vital point
    234–22 If the Dowager Empress could *h·*
    243–10 *h·* important, responsible offices,
    290–26 *H·* this attitude of mind,
    319– 8 *h·* the late Mr. Wiggin in . . . memory
    323–24 * if God did not *h·* you up
    344–12 I *h·* it absurd to say
    353–12 intended to *h·* guard over Truth,
    356–23 else he will *h·* to the one, — *Matt.* 6 : 24.

holdeth
  '00. 12– 3 "*h·* the seven stars — *Rev.* 2 : 1.

holding
  Mis. 40–28 If it is hate that is *h·* the purpose
      62– 1 *H·* the *right* idea of man in
      62– 5 *h·* in thought the form of a
      83– 1 *h·* man forever in the
    204–21 *h·* sway over human consciousness.
    308–26 even as *h·* in mind the
    327–27 Obstinately *h·* themselves back,
    338–10 hope *h·* steadfastly to good
    359–13 or by *h·* it in fetters.
  Man. 74– 2 C. S. society *h·* public services,
  Un. 40–25 *H·* a material sense of Life,
     56– 9 *H·* a quickened sense of
  Pul. 25– 9 * capable of *h·* fifteen hundred ;
     41–16 * capacity for *h·* from fourteen hundred
  No. 26– 9 *h·* such material and mortal
     30–21 not light *h·* darkness within itself.
     36–17 *h·* the mortal as unreal,
  My. 75– 4 * *h·* the centre of the stage
     83– 3 * the *h·* of a great convention

holding
  My. 98– 7 * church, *h·* five thousand people,
    121– 3 time for *h·* our semi-annual
    184–25 *h·* unwearied watch over a world.
    222–29 in the *h·* of crime in check,
    225–18 sacredly *h·* His name apart
    306–30 *h·* long conversations with him

holds
  Mis. 3–20 mortal thought *h·* in itself all sin,
      77–16 it *h·* man in endless Life
      97– 7 human mind that *h·* within itself
    139–11 *pulling down of strong h·;— II Cor.* 10 : 4.
    221–32 *h·* the issues of death to
    260–14 mortal thought *h·* only in itself the
  Man. 38– 7 student of . . . who *h·* a degree,
  Ret. 44–29 that hour *h·* this true record.
  Un. 40–17 who *h·* Life by a spiritual and not by
  Pul. 5– 9 Memory, *h·* in her secret chambers
     50–26 * No one . . . *h·* the whole of truth,
     68–17 * now *h·* regular services in the
  Rud. 4–11 which *h·* the earth in its orbit.
     15– 7 this *h·* and satisfies the thought
  No. 26–22 God *h·* man in the eternal
     42–19 The lie of evil *h·* its own by
  My. 84– 6 * *h·* back work that would otherwise
     93–11 * which it *h·* out to its votaries ;
    123–21 My little hall, which *h·* a trifle over
    200–17 What *h·* us to the Christian life
    226–11 *h·* the earth in its orbit
    205– 4 Love *h·* its substance safe

hole
  Mis. 210–14 brings the serpent out of its *h·*,
    231–16 made a big *h·*, with two incisors,

holiday
  Mis. xi–14 At each recurring *h·*
  My. 20– 7 chapter sub-title
    234– 1 and fifty telegrams per *h·*
    309–16 and the observance of the *h·*

holidays
  Mis. 319–19 greetings for the forthcoming *h·*,
  My. 20– 8 The *h·* are coming,
    121– 6 commotion of the season's *h·*.
    166–21 If all our years were *h·*,
    234– 2 Are the *h·* blest by absorbing
    234– 9 give me the *h·* for this work

holier
  Mis. 17–19 much higher and *h·* conception
    220–24 become healthier, *h·*, happier,
    330–22 higher joys, *h·* aims,
  Peo. 14–13 higher and *h·* love for God

holiest
  Mis. 177– 4 greatest and *h·* of all causes.
  Pul. 5– 9 characters of *h·* sort,
  Po. 77– 3 A nation's *h·* hymn
  My. 258– 8 to all of *h·* worth.

holiness
  and health
    Mis. 25– 1 against his *h·* and health.
  and heaven
    Mis. 309–20 health, *h·*, and heaven.
    Un. 64– 6 only health, *h·*, and heaven,
  and immortality
    Mis. 163–32 health, *h·*, and immortality.
      172–27 health, *h·*, and immortality of man.
    No. 28–12 health, *h·*, and immortality,
    My. 160–17 health, *h·*, and immortality.
      247– 8 health, *h·*, and immortality,
      255– 1 health, *h·*, and immortality,
     274–15 health, *h·*, and immortality.
  and Life
    Un. 42– 4 outcome of Spirit, *h·*, and Life.
  and love
    '01. 12–19 redolent with health, *h·*, and love.
    My. 274– 2 goodness, *h·*, and love do this,
  apart from
    Mis. 154–30 nor aim apart from *h·*.
  beauty of
    (see **beauty**)
  happiness, and
    Mis. 15–12 health, happiness, and *h·*.
      183– 7 health, happiness, and *h·* :
    My. 167–20 their health, happiness, and *h·*
      275–22 health, happiness, and *h·*,
  harmony, and
    Ret. 65–29 obtain health, harmony, and *h·*
  harmony, or
    Rud. 10– 1 against health, harmony, or *h·*,
  health and
    (see **health**)
  health or
    Mis. 308– 4 for his health or *h·*,
  highway of
    Mis. 287–17 find the highway of *h·*.

holiness
love-linked
  My. 206– 6 love-linked *h·* which heals
mount of
  Mis. 206–30 stands upon the mount of *h·*,
peace, and
  Mis. 167–29 He giveth power, peace, and *h·* ;
  '02. 16–14 To attain peace and *h·*
  My. 252–23 into paths of peace and *h·*.
reign of
  My. 228–16 kingdom of heaven, the reign of *h·*,
sin to
  Un. 37–10 from sin to *h·*,
  '02. 10–23 yea, from sin to *h·*
strive after
  Mis. 197– 6 to strive after *h·* ;
typifies
  Mis. 86–15 that beauty typifies *h·*,
way to
  '01. 14–14 so hinder our way to *h·*.
yield to
  Un. 39– 4 yield to *h·*, health, and Life,

———

  Mis. 37– 6 toward purity, health, *h·*, and
  99–27 health, *h·*, universal harmony,
  101–12 for the freedom of health, *h·*, and
  127–15 bread of heaven, health, *h·*,
  200– 4 *h·*, life, and health as the better
  205–22 with eternal life, *h·*, heaven.
  Un. 32–19 the opposite of Spirit, of *h·*,
  '01. 2– 2 demonstrated — health, *h·*,
  '02. 9– 4 All-power — giving life, health, *h·* ;
  16–12 *h·*, without which no man — *Heb.* 12 : 14.
  My. 18–12 bread of heaven, health, *h·*,
  118–29 harmony, *h·*, entirely apart from
  153–30 give thee rest, peace, health, *h·*.
  155–13 run in joy, health, *h·*,
  158–15 lends a new-born beauty to *h·*,
  205–28 Hence health, *h·*, immortality,
  349– 4 consciousness of health, *h·*,

Hollis, Allen
  My. 138–30 * signature
Holmes
Mr. Marcus
  My. 13– 7 presented . . . by Mr. Marcus *H·*.
Oliver Wendell
  Peo. 5–26 Oliver Wendell *H·* said, in a lecture
holy
  Mis. 51–28 * transparent like some *h·* thing.''
  70–24 body of the *h·* Spirit of Jesus
  122– 8 instrument in this *h·* (?) alliance
  162–28 To carry out his *h·* purpose,
  184–11 presenting our bodies *h·* and acceptable,
  200–25 *h·* calm of Paul's well-tried hope
  227–22 dwelling upon a *h·* hill,
  270–21 cannot depart from his *h·* example,
  273–17 labor for a good and *h·* cause.
  280– 7 messengers of pure and *h·* thoughts
  280– 7 hurt not the *h·* things of Truth.
  287–13 only high and *h·* joy can satisfy
  301–25 injustice standing in a *h·* place.
  321–20 Untiring in your *h·* fight,
  387–18 *h·* thoughts and heavenly strain,
  Man. 4– 5 to enter into this *h·* work,
  Ret. 26– 4 Principle of his *h·* heroism
  86–14 the fellow-saint of a *h·* household.
  91–25 *h·* messages from the All-Father.
  91–30 His *h·* humility, unworldliness,
  Pul. 1–16 spot whereon thou troddest was *h·*
  11– 6 rehearse your hearts' *h·* intents.
  82– 6 * steel tempered with *h·* resolve,
  No. 27–26 tread lightly, for this is *h·* ground.
  Pan. 3–19 one supreme, *h·*, self-existent God,
  9–19 not hindered, in his *h·* mission.
  15– 7 establish us in the most *h·* faith,
  Po. 6–13 *h·* thoughts and heavenly strain,
  23–13 Yielding a *h·* strength to right,
  26– 5 where thou hast trod is *h·* ground.
  71–17 *h·* meaning of their song.
  My. 13–25 *h·* harmony, reverberating
  17–12 an *h·* priesthood, — *I Pet.* 2 : 5.
  19–25 words of our *h·* Way-shower,
  24–14 * unto an *h·* temple — *Eph.* 2 : 21.
  33–16 dwell in thy *h·* hill? — *Psal.* 15 : 1.
  34– 2 stand in his *h·* place? — *Psal.* 24 : 3.
  36–11 * to a *h·* Christian service
  63–13 * this happy and *h·* experience
  64–23 * to the high and *h·* task of
  81–22 * *h·* song rose tingling to the
  133– 6 inhabit His *h·* hill,
  153–10 He that is *h·*.'' — *Rev.* 3 : 7.
  206–23 an *h·* nation, — *I Pet.* 2 : 9.
  225–13 giving unto His *h·* name
  228–23 dwell in Thy *h·* hill? — *Psal.* 15 : 1.

holy
  My. 283– 9 To aid in this *h·* purpose
  290–23 the high and *h·* call you again
  291– 2 *h·* demands rested on the
Holy Bible (*see also* **Bible**)
  My. 18–29 * The *H· B·* ; ''S. and H.
Holy Father
  Pul. 65– 5 * the *H· F·* should not overlook
  My. 253–16 ''*H· F·*, keep through — *John* 17 : 11.
Holy Ghost
  Mis. 55–14 sin against the *H· G·*
  174–32 the *H· G·* that leadeth into
  204–12 The baptism of the *H· G·*
  Man. 15– 8 the *H· G·* or divine Comforter ;
  Un. 51–23 as Father, Son, and *H· G·*;
  52– 4 This Science . . . is the *H· G·*,
  Pul. 30–17 * and His Son, and the *H· G·*,
  '00. 5–11 Father, Son, and *H· G·*
  '01. 8– 3 the *H· G·*, or spiritual idea
  8– 6 who regard . . . the *H· G·* as
  12– 6 he baptized with the *H· G·*
  '02. 5– 7 it lights the fires of the *H· G·*,
  My. 19–10 communion of the *H· G·*, — *II Cor.* 13 : 14.
Holy of Holies
  Mis. 77–29 It was to enter unshod the *H· of H·*,
Holy One
  Mis. 268– 7 The *H· O·* saith,
  '01. 9–22 the *H· O·* of God.'' — *Mark* 1 : 24.
  My. 168– 4 the *H· O·* of Israel,
Holy Scriptures
  Mis. 132–24 refer you to the *H· S·*,
Holy Spirit
  Mis. 161–23 specially endowed with the *H· S·* ;
  '01. 9–22 The *H· S·* takes of the things of God
Holy Writ
  Mis. 122–17 *H· W·* denounces him that declares,
  123–29 *H· W·* declares that God is Love,
  187–16 set forth in original *H· W·*.
  199–27 so-called miracles contained in *H· W·*
  217–25 According to *H· W·*, it is a
  Man. 28–10 the warning of *H· W·* :
  Un. 17–21 *H· W·* declares God told our
  30–25 meaning of the declaration of *H· W·*,
  Pul. 2– 3 expressive language of *H· W·*,
  '01. 8–18 according to *H· W·*
  16–17 according to *H· W·* these qualities
  '02. 3–29 According to *H· W·*, the first lie
  My. 155– 7 promises, and proofs of *H· W·*.
  162–16 We read in *H· W·* :
  178– 4 spiritual meaning of *H· W·*
  339–17 We read in *H· W·* that the disciples

homage
  Mis. 107–10 heart's *h·* belongs to God.
  226–11 he loses the *h·* of fools,
  262–24 With all the *h·* beneath the skies,
  374–19 *h·* is indeed due,
  Peo. 9–12 dividing our *h·* and obedience
  My. 26–22 *the lie . . . that I claim their h·*.
home (*see also* **home's**)
ancestral
  My. 309–28 * the ancestral *h·* at Bow.
and family
  Pul. 50– 4 * deserves to have a *h·* and family
and heaven
  Mis. 289–18 compatible with *h·* and heaven.
  Pul. 11– 8 find within it *h·*, and *heaven.*
and peace
  Mis. 386– 5 *h·* and peace and hearts are found
  Po. 49– 8 *h·* and peace and hearts are found
at last
  My. 155–14 *h·* at last, it finds the full
beautiful
  My. 66–24 * her beautiful *h·*, Pleasant View,
begin at
  Mis. 32–24 charity must begin at *h·*.
Boston
  Pul. 47–21 * Besides her Boston *h·*, Mrs. Eddy has
call her
  Mis. 387– 3 To call her *h·*,
  Po. 50–21 To call her *h·*,
childhood's
  Ret. 6– 6 My childhood's *h·* I remember as
Christian Science
  My. 214–23 C. S. *h·* for indigent students,
  215–17 C. S. *h·* for the poor worthy student,
church
  '01. 31–19 chapter sub-title
  My. 54–16 * been regarded as the church *h·*,
  55–18 * plans were made for a church *h·*.
  57– 6 * sacred atmosphere of a church *h·*,
  157–11 * commodious and beautiful church *h·*
  164– 5 to many in this city a church *h·*.

home

country
Pul. 47–22   * has a delightful country h·
    63–12   * her delightful country h· in Concord,
My. 311– 4   at his country h· in North Groton,

desolate
Mis. 231–30   alas ! for the desolate h· ;
My. 292–11   mourner at the desolate h· !

every
My. 340–32   light their fires in every h·.

far from
My. 312– 9   * She was far from h·

father's
Pul. 34– 3   * She returned to her father's h·
My. 312–13   * met and taken to her father's h·
    312–28   took me to my father's h· in Tilton,

forest
Mis. 237–19   murmuring winds of their forest h·.

get
Mis. 225–30   * "Wait until we get h·,

greenwood
Po. 34–17   Unto thy greenwood h·

hallows
Mis. 287–28   ruler over one's self and hallows h·,

happy
Mis. 388–17   Affection's wreath, a happy h· ;
Po. 21– 6   Affection's wreath, a happy h· ;
My. 315– 9   * happy h· as one could wish for.

her
Mis. 389–25   And mother finds her h·
Man. 68–18   calls to her h· . . . only those
    69–22   employed by Mrs. Eddy at her h·
Pul. 43–25   * Mrs. Eddy remained at her h·
Po. 5– 6   And mother finds her h·
My. 314–25   kept her a prisoner in her h·,
    326–10   * which Mrs. Eddy has made her h·.

his
Mis. 305– 7   His h· the clod !
Pul. 54–29   at his h· in Amesbury,
Po. 57–14   His h· the clod !

Mrs. Eddy's
My. 53–11   * in the parlors of Mrs. Eddy's h·,
    355–21   Scientists at Mrs. Eddy's h·

my
Ret. 20–11   my h· I regarded as very precious.
My. 189–26   the sunny South —once my h·.

new
My. 31–17   * The new h· for worship
    50– 8   * strangeness of their new h·,

of Love
Mis. 84–24   turn one, . . . to the h· of Love.

of love
Po. 8–21   light of a h· of love and pride ;

of their Leader
Man. 68–26   to the h· of their Leader,

of the pastor
My. 50– 2   * was held at the h· of the pastor,

of the President
My. 112–30   h· of the President of the United

of vice
Un. 52–25   sometimes the h· of vice.

old
'01. 29–17   whenever they return to the old h·

palatial
Pul. 70–26   * She has a palatial h· in Boston

Palmetto
My. 176– 9   hallow your Palmetto h· with palms

provide a
Ret. 52– 8   provide a h· for every true seeker

radiant
Po. 17– 2   O tell of their radiant h·

religious
My. 270– 6   my first religious h·

returned
Mis. 226– 6   clergyman's son returned h· — well.

sackcloth of
Mis. 275– 8   lift the veil on the sackcloth of h·,

stately
Pul. 44–17   * chapter sub-title

substantial
Pul. 49–22   * there to build a substantial h·

summer
My. 314–11   which he fancied, for a summer h·.

their
Po. 41–10   their h· is not here?

thy
Mis. 385–15   Thee to thy h·.
Po. 48– 8   Thee to thy h·.
My. 290–27   remove the sackcloth from thy h·.

your
My. 170–12   To your h· in my heart !

Mis. 100–23   Pure humanity, friendship, h·,
    152–29   which guides you safely h·.
    237–11   cup of gall that conscience strikes h· ;
    251–11   religion, h·, friends, and country.

home

Mis. 304–19   * Washington will be its h·,
    394– 5   the h·, and the heaven of Soul.
Ret. 20–26   he should have a h· with me.
Un. 17–18   into a h· of marvellous light,
Pul. 40–20   * h· for The First Church of Christ,
    58–29   * to make it a h· by day or night.
'01. 14–16   traveller on his way h·.
    17– 9   and to welcome him h·.
Hea. 7–20   he charged h· a crime to mind,
Po. 32– 3   h· where I dwell in the vale,
    45– 6   the h·, and the heaven of Soul.
My. 22– 4   * for the h· of The Mother Church,
    139–11   his is a life-lease of hope, h·,
    145–19   at h· attending to the machinery
    148–19   I, as usual at h· and alone,
    170–12   Beloved Brethren: — Welcome h· !
    197–26   in the h· of my heart,
    216–29   charity begins at h·,
    229–10   Scientists, called to the h· of
    256–23   Parents call h· their loved ones,
    271–13   * modest, pleasantly situated h·
    275–19   demands upon my time at h·,
    276– 6   or a dignified stay at h·,
    323–29   * h· of the late Rev. J. Henry Wiggin
    324– 1   * in Mr. and Mrs. Wiggin's h·.

home (adj.)

Mis. 287–24   Be faithful over h· relations ;
    303– 2   shine from their h· summits
Ret. 19– 5   parting with the dear h· circle
    90– 5   salary for tending the h· flock
Pul. 43– 2   * the choir of the h· church,
    50– 8   * better h· life and citizenship.
'02. 3–12   inauguration of h· rule in Cuba,
My. 157– 9   * the Cause in your h· city,
    174–11   distinguished editors in my h· city
    291–14   His h· relations enfolded a wealth of

home-harmony
Mis. 353–31   interrupt the h·, criticise and

homeless
Mis. 326–17   h· wanderers in a beleaguered city,
Po. 28–15   Hover the h· heart !

homelessness
Mis. 373–21   as h· in a wilderness.

homely
My. 262–10   This h· origin of the babe Jesus

home's
Ret. 18–21   communion with h· magic spell !
Po. 64–14   communion with h· magic spell !

homes
Mis. 7–24   able to reach many h·
    99–32   by the wayside, in humble h·.
    163–10   by the wayside, in humble h· :
    231–28   How many h· echo such tones
    257–24   Floods swallow up h·
    321–25   hospitality of their beautiful h·
    329–28   back to their summer h·.
    337–27   by the wayside, in humble h·,
Pul. 80–25   * the h· of unnumbered invalids.
Pan. 14–19   In your peaceful h· remember
Hea. 16–14   nearer your hearts and into your h·
My. 21– 6   * church h· of their own,
    50– 5   * left their former church h·,
    113– 1   in thousands of h·,
    126–29   We need it in our h·,
    185–13   by the wayside, or in our h·.

homesick
Mis. 177–28   h· traveller in foreign lands
    177–29   I am constantly h· for heaven.
My. 147–29   heavenly h· or hungry hearts

homestead
Ret. 4– 3   who inherited the h·,
    5– 6   In the Baker h· at Bow
Pul. 47–29   * modernized from a primitive h·
My. 309–21   describing the Baker h· at Bow:

homilies
My. 122– 9   Now I am done with h·

homœopathic
Mis. 348–21   h· doses of Natrum muriaticum
Ret. 24–17   Even to the h· physician who
My. 107– 8   namely, the h· system, to which
    107–18   efficiency of the h· system.
    108– 2   the h· physician succeeds as well in

homœopathist
Mis. 49– 8   Her friends employed a h·,
'01. 22– 8   I am a spiritual h· in that
My. 107–14   Yet the h· administers
    107–29   The h· handles in his practice

homœopathists
Hea. 12–25   h· admit the higher attenuations

homœopathy

Mis.	6–16	in advance of allopathy and h;
	35– 2	practical proof, through h,
	252– 4	allopathy and h differ.
	270–28	H is the last link in
	271– 1	Among the foremost virtues of h
	378–14	Having practised h,
	379–22	the highest attenuation in h,
Ret.	33– 2	aided by hints from h,
	33– 8	allopathy, h, hydropathy,
	33–19	the higher attenuations of h,
Pul.	35–23	* Through h, too, Mrs. Eddy
	47–12	* schools of allopathy, h,
	64–17	* allopathy, h, and electricity,
'01.	17–26	highest attenuations of h
	18– 6	at the medicine of h;
Hea.	11–15	H may not recover from the
	11–17	h has laid the foundation stone of
	11–24	differing in this from h,
	12– 1	higher attenuations of h
	12–19	on the pharmacy of h,
	13– 4	The pharmacy of h is
My.	107–10	In h, the one thousandth
	108–10	between metaphysics in h and
	345–15	h came like blessed relief

honest

Mis.	19–20	faith in an h drugging-doctor,
	41–10	h student of C. S.
	44– 1	H students speak the truth
	48–17	h declaration as to the animus of
	87–26	to be h, earnest, loving, and
	112– 3	Even h thinkers, not knowing
	116–19	the courage of h convictions,
	128– 7	whatsoever things are h, — Phil. 4: 8.
	166–30	It made him an h man,
	227–18	wider aims of a life made h :
	227–26	sublime summary of an h life
	228–17	and h beyond reproach,
	238– 5	all who dare to be true, h
	247– 3	his h convictions and proofs of
	266–14	and h Christian Scientist will
	312–20	h utterance of veritable history,
	357–17	fallen into the good and h hearts
	367– 3	This Science requires man to be h,
Man.	77– 2	by an h, competent accountant.
Ret.	28–10	It must become h,
	29– 3	I esteem all h people,
	52– 8	every true seeker and h worker in
	75–18	and is therefore h.
	77– 3	* h man's the noblest work of God ;"
	77– 4	* h God's the noblest work of man."
	79– 1	h metaphysical theory and
	83–14	error, in an h heart,
Pul.	14– 1	h investigation will bring the hour
	35–14	become h, unselfish, and pure,
Rud.	8–11	Be h, be true to thyself,
No.	2–17	The h student of C. S.
	3–26	becoming odious to h people ;
	39– 3	an h and potent prayer to heal
	40–11	thoughts are our h conviction.
Pan.	10– 7	h verdict of humanity
'00.	10– 8	provided this warfare is h
'01.	30–29	* h, sensible, and well-bred man
	32–16	Their convictions were h,
'02.	2– 1	earnest, h investigator
Hea.	8–22	this will make us h and laborious,
My.	vi– 9	* Scientists are h only as they
	6– 4	Are we h, just, faithful?
	112–15	h, intelligent, and scholarly
	114– 4	be h, just, and pure ;
	120– 9	Forgive, . . . my h position.
	136–25	the fruits of h toil,
	143–16	h history of its Discoverer
	150–13	this heart must be h
	248–11	h, fervid affection for the race
	250– 6	and crowns h endeavors.
	259–18	Do not forget that an h, wise zeal,
	266– 7	insufficient freedom of h
	272– 1	an h man or woman
	284– 2	h efforts . . . to help human purpose
	321–11	* Mr. Wiggin was an h man

honestly

Mis.	62–21	h acknowledges this fact in
	160– 3	unite more h in uttering the word
	283–30	h laboring to learn the principle
Ret.	76– 6	if he writes h,
No.	5– 2	vindicating, fearlessly and h,
'02.	14–27	answered frankly and h,
Hea.	8–25	work to become Christians as h
	13–20	h employed Mind as the only
My.	264– 4	h and not too earnestly,
	305– 5	the defamer will declare as h (?),

honesty

Mis.	88–17	Its manly h follows like a
	118– 6	H in every condition,

honesty

Mis.	126–16	meekness, h, and obedience
	126–26	h always defeats dishonesty.
	252–29	secures the success of h.
	285–28	common sense, and common h,
	341–13	glory of the strife comes of h
Ret.	34– 1	as to the h or utility of using a
My.	4–21	h and justice characterize the
	121–21	No deformity exists in h,
	137–28	as to h and business capacity.
	139–13	Justice, h, cannot be abjured ;
	200–18	seven-fold shield of h,
	265–29	should be governed by h,
	270–10	attest h and valor.
	274–11	h, purity, unselfishness

honey

Mis.	294–14	makes h out of the flowers

Honor

his

Mis.	251– 8	His H, Mayor Woodworth,
My.	173–26	to his H, the Mayor,

honor

Mis.	49– 8	had the skill and h to state,
	154–23	H thy Father and Mother, God.
	158–15	faithful service, thus to h it.
	226–22	even of those who have lost their h
	236–11	"Love and h thy parents,
	237–24	H to faithful merit is delayed,
	237–26	draped in h of the dead hero
	295–15	Has he forgotten how to h his
	308–22	fulfilled its mission, retired with h
Ret.	64–16	Man that is in h, — Psal. 49 : 20.
Un.	26– 5	This is my h,
Pul.	49–22	* home that should do h to
	59– 2	* perpetually burning in her h ;
	63– 7	* WAS RECENTLY BUILT IN HER H
'01.	29–22	All h and success to those who
	29–23	h their father and mother.
My.	42–15	* for the h conferred upon me.
	118–11	greatness with which you h me.
	125–11	All h to the members of our
	182–31	h the name of C. S.,
	202– 9, 10	h to whom h. — Rom. 13 : 7.
	211–21	distrust where h is due,
	219– 6	have all the h of their success
	277–22	if our nation's rights or h
	331–26	* high feeling of h and the noble

honorable

Mis.	136–26	June session of this h body
	139– 1	recommend this h body to adjourn,
	147–20	do nothing but what is h,
My.	277– 5	h and satisfactory to both
	324–18	* he would be too h to
	332–31	* his h record and Christian

honorary

Hea.	3–19	Christ Jesus was an h title ;

honored

Mis.	81–15	benediction of an h Father,
	284–23	neither to be feared nor h.
'01.	18– 7	more h and respected to-day
Po.	78– 1	our h dead fought on in gloom !
My.	64–10	* made the name an h one
	289–16	long h, revered, beloved.
	326–16	so signally h his memory,

honoreth

My.	33–23	h them that fear the — Psal. 15 : 4.

honoring

My.	225–18	begins in the minds of men by h God

honors

Mis.	153–20	no man who h Him not
	294–11	and h his creator.
	358– 5	will graduate under divine h,
	358– 7	State h perish.
Un.	25–16	h conscious human individuality
'02.	1–19	a system that h God
My.	290– 5	Queen's royal and imperial h
	333–26	* were interred with Masonic h.

hooded

Mis.	145–15	h hawk which flies in darkness.

hoofed

Pan.	3– 4	horned and h animal,

hope (see also hope's)

and comfort

Pul.	56–15	* brought h and comfort to many

and desire

My.	9–15	* modestly renew the h and desire

and faith

Mis.	63–25	appeals to its h and faith,
	207– 2	in h and faith, where heart meets
No.	330– 7	Human h and faith should join
	10–25	turns . . . all h and faith to God,
	35– 1	everything to human h and faith.

hope

and harmony
Ret. 48–20 health, *h·*, and harmony to man,
and hour
My. 208–15 crowning the *h·* and hour
and prayer
'*02.* 6–20 All Christian faith, *h·*, and prayer,
15–29 to my waiting *h·* and prayer.
My. 155–15 fruition of its faith, *h·*, and prayer.
and tears
Mis. 385– 1 * "Faith, *h·*, and tears, triune,
Po. 37– 1 * "Faith, *h·*, and tears, triune,
bare
My. 322–21 * bare *h·* of a few days' instruction
benediction and
No. 8–25 quietly, with benediction and *h·*,
bird of
My. 341–11 The bird of *h·* is singing
cheer me with
Po. 32–21 cheer me with *h·* when 'tis done ;
common
My. 165–24 a relapse into the common *h·*.
confidence and
Pul. 21–25 there abide in confidence and *h·*.
deferred
Mis. 17–29 travail of mortal mind, *h·* deferred,
262–19 heart grown faint with *h·* deferred.
389–15 *h·* deferred, ingratitude, disdain !
Po. 4–14 *h·* deferred, ingratitude, disdain !
disappointed
My. 229–29 hence my disappointed *h·*
earthly
Ret. 20–20 Star of my earthly *h·*,
exalted
Mis. 162–32 in the strength of an exalted *h·*,
exultant
Ret. 32– 8 Exultant *h·*, if tinged with
faith and
Mis. 240–31 faith and *h·* of Christianity,
Un. 55–17 Job's faith and *h·* gained him
My. 201–12 friendship, faith, and *h·*
fear and
My. 292–30 compound . . . of fear and *h·*,
for our race
'*01.* 16–26 Shall the *h·* for our race
glorious
Pul. 9–21 O glorious *h·* and blessed
'*02.* 19–17 O glorious *h·* !
happifies life
Mis. 394– 6 *H·* happifies life,
Po. 45– 8 *H·* happifies life,
haven of
My. 163– 2 seek the haven of *h·*,
heart and
My. 253– 6 My heart and *h·* are with you.
heaven-born
Mis. 15–17 heaven-born *h·*, and spiritual love.
her
Ret. 90–21 waits with her *h·*, and labors with
higher
'*01.* 3– 1 higher *h·*, and increasing virtue,
My. 3–19 higher criticism, the higher *h·* ;
199–19 sounded the tocsin of a higher *h·*,
246–11 to gain a higher *h·* for the race,
252–30 All hail to this higher *h·*
highway of
My. 3–18 unfolding the highway of *h·*,
240–14 unfolding the highway of *h·*,
human
Mis. 330– 7 Human *h·* and faith should join in
No. 35– 1 everything to human *h·* and faith.
Peo. 8–21 trembling chords of human *h·*
hungry
Mis. 16– 2 These nourish the hungry *h·*,
life and
Peo. 11–14 gnawing away life and *h·* ;
life-lease of
My. 139–11 life-lease of *h·*, home, heaven ;
my
Mis. 311–22 I should lose my *h·* of heaven.
Pul. 3–29 present realization of my *h·*
5–15 was the first to bedew my *h·*
My. 4–29 The height of my *h·* must remain.
282– 6 my *h·* must still rest in God,
no greater
My. 209–19 No greater *h·* have we than in
nor happiness
'*01.* 34–28 health, *h·*, nor happiness
of ease
'*01.* 30–21 by the *h·* of ease, pleasure,
of ever eluding
Un. 64–12 until the *h·* of ever eluding their
of our race
Pul. 9– 2 children, . . . the *h·* of our race !
of relieving
My. 214–18 the *h·* of relieving the questioners'

hope

of that parent
Mis. 254–10 what of the *h·* of that parent
of the race
Mis. 163–21 medium of Mind, the *h·* of the race.
No. 46– 6 The advancing *h·* of the race,
of universal salvation
'*01.* 13–25 hence the *h·* of universal salvation.
our
Mis. 113–24 Divine Love is our *h·*,
388– 7 Thou to whose power our *h·* we give,
'*00.* 10–21 Here our *h·* anchors in God
Po. 7– 7 Thou to whose power our *h·* we give,
peace and
Mis. 169–25 health and peace and *h·* for all.
perishless
Pul. 9–10 warmed also our perishless *h·*,
present
Mis. 160–13 It satisfies my present *h·*.
reason for
Mis. 5–17 no longer any reason for *h·*."
reason for the
My. 348– 9 to give a reason for the *h·*
rejoice in
Peo. 14–14 rejoice in *h·* ;
remained
Mis. 130– 1 so long as a *h·* remained
rich
My. 201–19 Rich *h·* have I in him who
satisfied
My. 182–26 turn hither with satisfied *h·*.
soared high
Mis. 385–22 "When *h·* soared high,
Po. 48–16 "When *h·* soared high,
springs
My. 201–29 *H·* springs exultant on this blest
their
My. 155–21 span the horizon of their *h·*
258–22 blossoms that mock their *h·*
this
Mis. 144–21 be this *h·* in each of our hearts,
to the disconsolate
Mis. 262–17 giving . . . *h·* to the disconsolate ;
tower of
Mis. 152–24 sheltered in the strong tower of *h·*,
upspringing
My. 192–10 Thine is the upspringing *h·*,
well-tried
Mis. 200–25 holy calm of Paul's well-tried *h·*
without
Ret. 61–15 without '*h·*, and without God — *Eph.* 2 : 12.
woman's
My. 258– 7 seems illuminated for woman's *h·*

Mis. ix–12 joy, sorrow, *h·*, disappointment,
ix–13 now *h·* sits dove-like.
124–29 to experience, *h·* ; to *h·*, faith ;
132–30 those words inspire me with the *h·*
136– 6 with the *h·* that you will follow.
149–10 *h·*, faith, and understanding,
204– 7 doubt, *h·*, sorrow, joy, defeat, and
338–10 *h·* holding steadfastly to good
386–17 a *h·* that ever upward yearns,
394– 1 poem
Ret. 18–16 But *h·*, as the eaglet
No. 35– 5 and what *h·* have mortals but
Po. vii–12 * in the *h·* that these gems
page 45 poem
50– 1 *h·* that ever upward yearns,
64– 7 *h·*, as the eaglet that spurneth the
My. 6–28 self-abnegation, *h·*, faith ;
124–10 "What a fond fool is *h·*"
139– 2 progress, primeval faith, *h·*, love.
156–20 with *h·*, faith, and love ready
197–20 *h·* set before us in the Word
293–14 of trembling faith, *h·*, and of fear,
335–19 * *h·* of allaying the excitement

hope (verb)

Mis. 78–16 We will charitably *h·*, however,
78–21 we will *h·* it is the froth of error
133–18 I *h·* I am not wrong in
143– 6 *h·* that a closer link hath bound us.
391– 3 I *h·* the heart that's hungry
394–13 but *h·* thou, and love.
396–14 I *h·* it's better made,
Un. 14–25 How then . . . *h·* to escape,
29–25 *H·* thou in God [Soul] : — *Psal.* 42 : 11.
Pan. 4–22 *h·* thou in God : — *Psal.* 42 : 11.
'*00.* 2–24 than the adversary can *h·*.
Po. 38– 2 I *h·* the heart that's hungry
45–17 but *h·* thou, and love.
59– 6 I *h·* it's better made,
My. 36–11 * all that we are or *h·* to be
51–10 * *h·* she will remain with us.
120– 4 I *h·* and trust that you and I may

hope (verb)
My. 131–18 I *h·* I shall not be found disorderly,
169– 7 date, which I *h·* soon to name
259–16 I *h·* that in 1902 the churches
264– 3 *h·* that those who are kind enough

hoped
Mis. 27–30 of things *h·* for.'' — *Heb.* 11 : 1.
47– 8 that which is *h·* for but unseen,
103– 9 substance of things *not h·* for.
175–11 of things *h·* for.'' — *Heb.* 11 : 1.
Rud. 17– 2 Jews whom St. Paul had *h·* to convert
Pan. 15– 9 of things *h·* for'' — *Heb.* 11 : 1.
My. 226–18 of things *h·* for ;'' — *Heb.* 11 : 1.
260–16 substance, the things *h·* for

hopeful
Mis. 109–11 most *h·* stage of mortal mentality.
134– 1 sorrowful who are made *h·*,
Pul. 45–17 * the *h·*, trustful ones,
80–25 * brought a *h·* spirit into the
Po. 16– 2 and *h·* though winter appears.

hopefully
Mis. 5–19 takes up the case *h·*
324–30 whence he may *h·* look for
'01. 21–15 my critic, who reckons *h·* on the

hopefulness
My. 74–30 * one for its *h·* and the other for

hopeless
Pul. 34– 7 * her case was pronounced *h·*
'01. 27–14 healed *h·* cases, such as I have
Hea. 9– 8 sinner and the most *h·* invalid
My. 106– 7 *h·* organic diseases of almost every

hopelessly
Mis. 371–28 as *h·* original as is ''S. and H.
Ret. 35– 6 basis . . . was so *h·* original,
Pul. 41–17 * was *h·* incapable of receiving

hopelessness
Mis. 169–24 foundation of unbelief and *h·*.

hope's
Mis. 339– 9 with *h·* rainbow hues.
Pul. 10–14 the wish to reign in *h·* reality

hopes
Mis. 341–14 Do human *h·* deceive?
356–11 chastened affections, and costly *h·*,
Ret. 7–22 * It blights too many *h·* ;
Po. 8–15 Its starry *h·* and its waves of truth.
My. 202–17 endless *h·*, and glad victories
258–18 *h·* that cannot deceive,

hopeth
Pan. 1–15 what a man seeth he *h·* not for,
1–15 *h·* for what he hath not seen,

hoping
Mis. 327– 3 *h·* that I might follow thee
Ret. 13–16 *h·* to win me from dreaded heresy.
20–14 *h·* for a vision of relief
No. 9–14 *H·* to pacify repeated complaints
Pan. 1–11 mortals are *h·* and working,
My. 164– 4 *h·* thereby to give to many

hordes
Mis. 325–29 in the midst of murderous *h·*,

Horeb
My. 281– 7 soaring to the *H·* height,

horizon
Mis. 376–20 above the *h·*, in the east,
Pan. 1–18 in the *h·* of Truth
'02. 17–30 like the sun beneath the *h·*,
My. 155–21 span the *h·* of their hope

horned
Pan. 3– 4 a *h·* and hoofed animal,

horns
Hea. 13– 2 both *h·* of the dilemma,

horoscope
Mis. 347– 6 hanging like a *h·* in the air,
My. 350–25 the *h·* of crumbling creeds,

horrible
Ret. 13–24 ''*h·* decree'' of predestination

horror
Un. 6–23 provoked discussion and *h·*,

horrors
No. 44–22 the *h·* of religious persecution.

hors de combat
Mis. 285–15 the latter fell *h· de c·* ;

horse-chestnut
Ret. 17–19 sturdy *h·* for centuries hath given
Po. 63– 5 sturdy *h·* for centuries hath given

hortatory
Ret. 89–14 pay this *h·* compliment

Horticultural Hall
Exhibition Hall
My. 80–13 * *H· H·* (Exhibition Hall),
Lecture Hall
My. 80–13 * *H· H·* (Lecture Hall),

My. 73–19 * this forenoon in *H· H·*,
75– 8 * Christian Scientists in *H· H·*.
75–10 * headed straight for *H· H·*.
80–23 * *H· H·*, Jordan Hall, Potter Hall,
83– 1 * leading directly to *H· H·*.
83– 5 * Up at *H· H·* the one hundred

hospitable
Pul. 36–14 * met Mrs. Eddy by her *h·* courtesy,
My. 40– 2 * evidence to us of her *h·* love.

hospitality
Mis. 321–25 *h·* of their beautiful homes
Pul. 49– 4 * the air of *h·* that marks its
My. 40– 7 * will also enlarge their *h·*,
173– 6 for the generous *h·* extended
331–14 * such unrestrained *h·*

hospitals
My. 188–24 in which, like beds in *h·*,

host
Mis. 231–11 carving of the generous *h·*,
My. 46–22 * in the presence of this assembled *h·*,
88–22 * all that increasing *h·* who have
98– 2 * truly make up a mighty *h·*,

hostess
Ret. 40– 6 On my arrival my *h·* told me
40– 8 with my *h·* I went to the invalid's
(see also **Eddy**)

hostile
My. 92–21 * have been ridiculed by the *h·*
94– 4 * been ridiculed by the *h·*

Hosts
My. v– 1 * Lord God of *H·*, be with us yet ;

hosts
Po. 10–18 cheer the *h·* of heaven ;
My. 34–12 The Lord of *h·*, — *Psal.* 24 : 10.
86– 7 * the *h·* of a new religion.
131–26 saith the Lord of *h·*, — *Mal.* 3 : 10.
269–26 saith the Lord of *h·*, — *Mal.* 3 : 10.
337–19 cheer the *h·* of heaven ;

hot
Un. 34–19 is substantial, is *h·* or cold?

hotel
My. 83–15 * the *h·* and restaurant keepers,

Hotel Brookline
My. 66– 2 * which is known as the *H· B·*,

hotels
My. 73–22 * rooms and board, *h·*, railroads, *etc.*
75–11 * rooms in *h·* or lodging-houses,
82– 9 * *H·*, boarding-houses, and private

hothouse
My. 325– 4 * to leave luscious *h·* fruit.

hounded
Mis. 358– 9 *h·* footsteps, ralse laurels.

hour
adapted to the
Mis. 313–14 thought, so adapted to the *h·*,
appointed
Pul. 29–12 * Before the appointed *h·*
auspicious
Pul. 44–10 * It is a most auspicious *h·*
awful
Po. 27– 3 oppression in its awful *h·*,
bridal
Mis. 276–16 will always be the bridal *h·*,
Po. 8– 7 waiting alone for the bridal *h·*
bring the
Pul. 14– 2 investigation will bring the *h·*
burdened for an
Mis. 251–22 burdened for an *h·*, spring into
changeful
Po. 31–14 the vassal of the changeful *h·*,
cometh
Mis. 321–13 *h·* cometh, and now is, — *John* 4 : 23.
No. 34– 9 *h·* cometh, and now is, — *John* 4 : 23.
crucial
My. 225– 1 This is a crucial *h·*, in which the
crude
Un. 4–28 Nevertheless, at the present crude *h·*,
dark
My. 297–13 dark *h·* that precedes the dawn.
demands of the
Mis. 70–18 not equal to the demands of the *h·* ;
eventide's
Mis. 394– 2 on the zephyr at eventide's *h·* ;
Po. 45– 2 on the zephyr at eventide's *h·* ;

hour

every
Pul. 59– 7   * every *h·* and a half, so long as
Pan. 12–28   every *h·* in time and in eternity
Hea. 19–19   fresh opportunities every *h·* ;
My. 31– 5   * "I need Thee every *h·* ;"
      234– 8   and how I need every *h·*
      340– 4   every day and every *h·*.

evil
Mis. 340– 2   relinquishment of right in an evil *h·*,

exigencies of the
My. 224– 3   to meet the exigencies of the *h·*

feared for an
Po. 71–11   Feared for an *h·* the tyrant's

festive
Po. 77–17   Why from this festive *h·* some

freedom's
Ret. 11– 9   't is freedom's *h·*,
Po. 60– 6   'tis freedom's *h·*,

girt for the
My. 277–23   armed with power girt for the *h·*.

God's
Mis. 134–20   In God's *h·*, the powers of earth

had come
Mis. 83–26   *h·* had come for the avowal of

half an
Mis. 339– 5   silence for the space of half an *h·*.
Hea. 13–14   at intervals of half an *h·*
My. 54– 9   * half an *h·* before the arrival of

harvest
Mis. 214–30   Jesus foretold the harvest *h·*
     356–13   the harvest *h·* has come ;

has passed
Mis. 284–14   *h·* has passed for this evil to

has struck
Mis. 249– 5   The *h·* has struck,
     317– 5   The *h·* has struck for

hope and
My. 208–16   crowning the hope and *h·* of

immortal
My. 257–20   At this immortal *h·*,

is come
Mis. 83–24   Father, the *h·* is come ; — *John* 17 : 1.
     177– 4   The *h·* is come.
My. 125–26   The *h·* is come ;

is coming
Chr. 55– 6   The *h·* is coming, — *John* 5 : 25.

is imminent
My. 223–27   The *h·* is imminent.

memory's
Po. 68–16   o'er the heartstrings in memory's *h·*.

midnight
Mis. 117–26   his lamp at the midnight *h·*
     276–15   In C. S. the midnight *h·* will

miracle of the
Hea. 11–11   it stands and is the miracle of the *h·*,

momentous
My. 45–17   * revealed to you in that momentous *h·*

named
Pul. 31–23   * At the *h·* named I rang the bell

natal
Po. 29– 9   No natal *h·* and mother's tear,
My. 158–10   natal *h·* of my lone earth life ;

next
Mis. 316–22   breaches widened the next *h·* ;

of great need
Mis. 24– 5   came to me in an *h·* of great need ;

of his birth
Mis. 278–15   he cursed the *h·* of his birth ;

of loss
Mis. 179– 4   rightful desire in the *h·* of loss,

of prayer
Po. 65–10   "Sweet *h·* of prayer" !

of trial
Mis. 335–24   and when the *h·* of trial comes

one
Mis. 69–18   In one *h·* he was well,
     136–10   in turning aside for one *h·*
     225–28   In about one *h·* he awoke,
Ret. 16– 8   entered this church one *h·* ago
My. 54– 8   * crowded one *h·* before the service

outweighs an
Mis. 135–19   joy that outweighs an *h·*.

Palestina's
Chr. 53–49   As in blest Palestina's *h·*,

passing
Un. 47– 4   and with every passing *h·*
'02. 17–19   square accounts with each passing *h·*.

pertaining to the
My. 199–13   Christian canon pertaining to the *h·*.

puppets of the
Mis. 368–23   Some of the mere puppets of the *h·*

radiant
Po. 70– 4   At sunset's radiant *h·*,

right
My. 244–13   I have awaited the right *h·*,

hour

same
Man. 61– 5   Sunday services at the same *h·*.
My. 149–29   and forgotten in the same *h·* ;

sunny
My. 194–30   * Ne'er in a sunny *h·* fall off."

that
Ret. 44–29   that *h·* holds this true record.
     73–12   From that *h·* personal corporeality
Pul. 34–18   * From that *h·* dated her conviction
Peo. 10–28   yet that *h·* was a prophecy of
My. 39– 2   * could not gain admittance at that *h·*
     351–16   meet in that *h·* of Soul

thine
Po. 22– 2   Thine *h·* hath come !

this
Mis. 37–28   work of healing ; which, at this *h·*,
     253–21   are type and shadow of this *h·*.
     254–18   the great red dragon of this *h·*,
     317–22   words of our Master explain this *h·* :
     320–10   lends its . . . light to this *h·* :
     386–11   This *h·* looks on her heart
Pul. 7–11   New England metropolis at this *h·*,
No. 3–18   history of Mind-healing notes this *h·*.
'01. 3– 4   benediction . . . rests upon this *h·* :
Po. 49–16   This *h·* looks on her heart
My. 43–26   * has brought us to this *h·*.
     124–15   enough to make this *h·* glad.
     131– 6   For this *h·*, for this period,
     131–22   in this *h·* of the latter days
     131–30   There is with us at this *h·*
     132– 2   is the demand of this *h·*
     132–12   Oh, may this *h·* be prolific,
     185–24   Then and there I foresaw this *h·*,
     269–18   This *h·* is molten in the furnace
     286–10   however, that at this *h·*

until the
Pul. 41–28   * until the *h·* for the dedication

waiting
Mis. 331–19   that owns each waiting *h·* ;
     389– 7   that owns each waiting *h·*,
Po. 4– 4   that owns each waiting *h·*,

waiting the
Peo. 7–18   * Waiting the *h·* when

woman's
Mis. 245–19   This is woman's *h·*,
No. 45–19   This is woman's *h·*,

Mis. 177–23   * the *h·* for the church service
     316–12   the *h·* best for the student.
     335– 8   in an *h·* that he is not   *Matt.* 24 : 50.
Ret. 49– 8   *h·* has come wherein the great need
Po. 71– 1   the *h·* they then foretold
     71– 6   This is the *h·* !
My. 64– 3   * the experiences of the *h·*
     232–15   *h·* the thief would come, — *Luke* 12 : 39.

hourly
Mis. 248–17   or that my *h·* life is prayerless,
Un. 17– 7   *H·*, in C. S., man thus
Po. 33– 6   *h·* seek for deliverance strong
My. 41–22   * into present and *h·* application
     178– 8   it hastens *h·* to this end.

hours

dark
Mis. 276–31   In the dark *h·*, . . . stand firmer
Ret. 20–13   throughout the dark *h·*,

different
My. 94–21   * at different *h·* of the day,

forty-eight
Mis. 243– 2   in forty-eight *h·* cured her

happy
Mis. 396–10   O happy *h·* and fleet,
Po. 59– 2   O happy *h·* and fleet,

her
Ret. 90–23   Mother in Israel give all her *h·*

lagging
Po. 35– 2   the lagging *h·* of weariness

laughing
Mis. 390–12   Looks love unto the laughing *h·*,
Po. 55–13   Looks love unto the laughing *h·*,

long-buried
Po. 67– 6   at work with the long-buried *h·*,

oncoming
Ret. 23–10   The oncoming *h·* were indicated by no

pass into
Mis. 230–15   moments before they pass into *h·*,

past
Mis. 147– 9   Have you improved past *h·*,
     330–19   It is good to talk with our past *h·*,

sacred
Ret. 90–17   in their early and sacred *h·*,

twenty-four
Mis. 243– 1   if . . . without it twenty-four *h·*

vanished
Po. 23– 5   a thought of vanished *h·*

hours

waking
Mis. 47–12 If never in your waking *h*·,

Mis. 230–16 *h*· that other people may occupy in
325–18 dreaming away the *h*·.

house

big
Pul. 47–28 * big *h*·, so delightfully remodelled
build a
My. 187–26 build a *h*· unto Him whose name
burning
Mis. 335–26 have me get out of a burning *h*·,
enter a
Mis. 282–14 "When ye enter a *h*·, — *see Matt.* 10 : 12.
283– 7 than one has to enter a *h*·,
entered the
My. 178–23 Christian Scientist entered the *h*·
Father's
Mis. 326–19 forced to seek the Father's *h*·,
369–25 would find our Father's *h*· again
'01. 17– 4 cause him to return to the Father's *h*·
My. 133– 1 Father's *h*· in which are many
father's
My. 309–24 My father's *h*· had a sloping roof,
313–31 not welcome in my father's *h*·.
furnished
My. 342– 1 * ample, richly furnished *h*·
furnish the
Man. 30–20 suitably furnish the *h*·,
her
Man. 48–14 continually stroll by her *h*·,
69–24 affairs outside of her *h*·.
His
My. 193–17 Nothing dethrones His *h*·.
his
My. 231–23 not an empty apartment in his *h*·,
232–16 not have suffered his *h*· — *Luke* 12 : 39.
308–30 only book in his *h*·.
313– 9 road in front of his *h*·
invalid's
Ret. 40– 8 I went to the invalid's *h*·.
is on fire
Mis. 326– 7 that *h*· is on fire !
master of the
'01. 10– 5 master of the *h*· — *Matt.* 10 : 25.
mine
My. 131–25 meat in mine *h*·, — *Mal.* 3 : 10.
my
Mis. 249–18 not one has been sent to my *h*·,
of God
'01. 15–27 * sat here in the *h*· of God,
My. 37– 7 * heavenward from this *h*· of God.
of our God
Pul. 10–18 corner-stone in the *h*· of our God.
of slumberers
Mis. 326–10 spread to the *h*· of slumberers
of the Pastor
Man. 30–14 the *h*· of the Pastor Emeritus,
of worship
Pul. 50–12 * visible *h*· of worship in this city,
My. 182–20 beautiful *h*· of worship
owned a
My. 314–12 he owned a *h*· in Franklin, N. H.
publishing
Man. 44–10 publishing *h*· or bookstore
'02. 13–12 in their publishing *h*·,
real
Pul. 2–23 The real *h*· in which
returns to the
Mis. 324–25 So he returns to the *h*·,
roof of the
Mis. 215–19 summit of the roof of the *h*·
saw the
Pul. 2– 2 saw the *h*· Solomon had erected.
spacious
Pul. 31–23 * spacious *h*· on Columbus Avenue,
spiritual
My. 17–11 built up a spiritual *h*·, — *I Pet.* 2 : 5.
this
Mis. 325–23 They in this *h*· are those that
Pul. 9–10 whose appliances warm this *h*·,
10–25 timely shelter of this *h*·,
10–28 blessing on every heart in this *h*·.
My. 37– 7 heavenward from this *h*· of God.
61–17 * this *h*· will be ready for
148–22 what is each heart in this *h*·
187–30 you have built this *h*·
188– 2 This *h*· is hallowed by His
188– 3 hallowed this *h*·, — *I Kings* 9 : 3.
Thy
Pul. 1– 2 *fatness of Thy h*·; — *Psal.* 36 : 8.
3–16 *fatness of Thy h*·; — *Psal.* 36 : 8.
4–27 *fatness of Thy h*·." — *Psal.* 36 : 8.
7–29 *fatness of Thy h*·; — *Psal.* 36 : 8.

house

your
Mis. 326–27 Behold, your *h*· — *Matt.* 23 : 38.
My. 325– 6 * that you had bought your *h*·

Mis. 327– 2 When I went back into the *h*·
Man. 30–21 Mrs. Eddy does not occupy the *h*·
Pul. 2–13 think . . . of the *h*· wherewith
2–14 "*h*· not made with hands, — *II Cor.* 5 : 1.
36–25 * *h*· is now occupied by
48– 7 * second story of the *h*·,
My. 141–23 *h*· of The Mother Church seats
145– 7 remodelling of the *h*·
156–14 say to the goodman of the *h*· :
188–13 "*h*· not made with hands, — *II Cor.* 5 : 1.
192–29 building for you a *h*·
194– 7 "*h*· not made with hands, — *II Cor.* 5 : 1.
232–15 goodman of the *h*· — *Luke* 12 : 39.
309–22 * *h*· itself was a small, square
310 24 * set the *h*· in an uproar,"

housed
'01. 29– 1 Have we *h*·, fed, clothed,

household
Mis. 214– 9 of his own *h*·." — *Matt.* 10 : 36.
239–23 with that of the *h*· stockholders,
386–19 o'er thy broken *h*· band,
Man. 69–15 for *h*· help or a handmaid,
Ret. 6– 8 accorded special *h*· privileges.
86–14 fellow-saint of a holy *h*·.
'01. 9–27 He of God's *h*· who loveth
10– 6 call them of his *h*· — *Matt.* 10 : 25.
Po. 50– 3 o'er thy broken *h*· band,
My. 143–12 by the members of my *h*·
257– 2 alas for the broken *h*· band !
263– 4 My *H*·.
308–27 his *h*· law, constantly enforced,
355– 1 * members of her *h*· were with her

households
Mis. 232– 4 peace, and plenty, and happy *h*·.
257–24 Floods swallow up homes and *h*· ;
262– 2 health and happiness to all *h*·

housekeeper
My. 311– 8 my good *h*· said to me :
311–11 so I lost my *h*·.

housekeeping
Mis. 353–27 set up *h*· alone.

houses
Mis. 150–18 Convenient *h*· and halls
282–11 Who of us would have our *h*· broken
326–17 driven out of their *h*· of clay
347– 5 people have to escape from their *h*·
373–23 rich possession here, with *h*· and
'00. 12–26 he labored . . . also in private *h*·.
My. 31–19 * front rank of the world's *h*·
66–29 * many beautiful *h*· of worship
82– 9 * boarding-houses, and private *h*·
149–26 could not see London for its *h*·.

housewife
Mis. 329– 6 nature like a thrifty *h*·

hover
Mis. 388–23 *h*· o'er the couch of woe ;
Po. 21–12 *h*· o'er the couch of woe ;
28–15 *H*· the homeless heart !

hovers
My. 192–15 My heart *h*· around your churches

Howe and Woolson Halls
My. 80–14 * *H*· and W· *H*·, Chickering Hall.

however
Mis. ix–21 freshness of youth, *h*·,
8–20 *h*· much we suffer in the process.
29–12 There is, *h*·, no analogy between
78–16 We will charitably hope, *h*·,
93–24 Bear in mind, *h*·, that human
118–12 *H*· keenly the human affections
120–16 rejoice, *h*·, that the clarion call
121– 6 This, *h*·, is not the cup to which
141–11 not so, *h*·, with error,
155–18 (*h*· much she desires thus to do),
158–27 It is satisfactory to note, *h*·,
239–22 *H*·, her dividend, when compared
262–10 *h*· simple the words,
274– 3 This point, *h*·, had not impressed me
287– 2 improved generation, *h*·,
291–21 False views, *h*· engendered,
294–29 In an issue of January 17, *h*·,
340–23 *h*· slow, thy success is sure :
355– 4 need, *h*·, is not of the letter, but
380–24 Experience, *h*·, taught me
Man. 41–10 *H*· despitefully used and
47–18 testimony, *h*·, shall not include
Ret. 2–22 Some of these, *h*·, were not very
7–13 * *h*· hidden and remote.

however

Ret.	14–10	H·, I was ready for his doleful
	26–22	h·, divine Science must be
	61–28	that h· little be taught or learned,
	64– 5	This, h·, does not annihilate
	68– 5	H·, the human concept never was,
Un.	2– 7	must, h·, realize God's presence,
	48–20	h· faintly able to demonstrate
Pul.	2–12	sublunary views, h· enchanting,
	20– 7	not, h·, through the State
	21–22	h· much this is done to us
	38–26	* h· they may differ among
	42– 8	* At 10:30 a. m., h·, the scene was
	59–20	* solo singer, h·, was a Scientist,
	88– 6	They were, h·, too voluminous
No.	44–10	Error has no hobby, h· boldly
Pan.	2–25	H·, Pan in imagery is preferable to
'00.	2–26	h·, I believe in working
	3–29	H·, the animus of heathen religion
	6–19	H·, to a man who uses tobacco,
'01.	23–11	This departure, h·, from the
	32–13	When infidels assailed them, h·,
'02.	15–27	To this, h·, I gave no heed,
My.	12–10	* must remember, h·, that
	28–12	* Suffice it to say, h·, that
	39–19	* allow me, h·, the privilege
	40–11	* Nothing will be lost, h·,
	50–20	* Communion Sunday, h·, brought
	55–22	* In March, h·, the church was
	97– 5	* physicians, h·, ridicule the idea
	121–22	C. S., h·, adds
	123– 3	To me, h·, love is the greater
	160– 1	The Christian, h·, strives for
	175–17	Our picturesque city, h·,
	180–10	The obstinate sinner, h·, refuses
	192–26	Of this, h·, I can sing:
	195– 7	H·, it is never too late to
	215–12	H·, I returned this money
	244–25	This, h·, must depend on results.
	272– 9	presents, h·, no claim that man
	284– 2	honest efforts (h· meagre)
	286–10	It is unquestionable, h·,
	307–32	My idealism, h·, limped,
	311– 7	Shortly after, h·, my good housekeeper
	312–10	* Glover, h·, was a Free Mason,
	340–26	H·, Jesus' example in this,
	348–17	Here, h·, was no stopping-place,
	355– 8	H·, if the occasion demands
	358–12	h· much I desire to read all

howl

Mis.	390– 1	winds mutter, h·, and moan,
Po.	58–13	winds mutter, h·, and moan,

howsoever

My.	41–13	* h· far he may stray,

Hub and hub

Pul.	67– 8	* h· of the logical universe,
My.	95–17	* described in the newspapers of the H·

huddle

Mis.	275–12	little ones, wondering, h· together,

Hudson

Pul.	53–15	* H· says: "That word, more than
	54–12	* We accept the statement of H· :

hue

Mis.	264–29	take its h· from the divine Mind.
	326–16	under every h· of circumstances,
	372–28	true h· and character of the living
	376–26	on a background of cerulean h· ;
Po.	3– 2	starlight blends with morning's h·,

hues

Mis.	142–19	with bright h· of the spiritual,
	194–15	bring out the entire h· of Deity,
	332–10	autumn follow with h· of heaven,
	339– 9	with hope's rainbow h·.
	376–21	one rod of rainbow h·,
	377– 1	such forms and h· of heaven,
Ret.	4–16	in the mellow h· of autumn,
	35–14	brings out the h· of Deity.
'01.	12–21	bring out the entire h· of God.
'02.	20– 5	h· of heaven, tipping the dawn

huge

Pul.	42–21	* a h· seven-pointed star was hung
My.	30–11	* In those h· congregations
	92–19	* so h· and concrete a demonstration
	95–12	* They have built a h· church,
	308–18	* with a h· walking-stick."

hum

Pan.	3–11	voiced with a h· of harmony,

human

abandon

Mis.	250–12	which in their h· abandon

human

action

Mis.	268– 3	queries give point to h· action :
	288–13	Wisdom in h· action begins with
Ret.	93–16	becomes the model for h· action.
'00.	11–28	highest criticism on all h· action,

affairs

Mis.	204–24	all the minutiæ of h· affairs.
	267–22	h· affairs should be governed by
	312–14	* divine Providence in h· affairs
My.	215–32	wisdom should temper h· affairs,

affection

Mis.	287–19	lays the foundations of h· affection
My.	234–12	from h· affection to spiritual
	268– 8	If the motives of h· affection are

affections

Mis.	10–25	tendencies of h· affections
	50–20	a change from h· affections,
	50–27	h· affections need to be changed
	118–12	the h· affections yearn to
	287–14	The good in h· affections

agencies

Mis.	95–20	understand that no h· agencies

agony

Mis.	222–20	cancelled only through h· agony :
'01.	35–12	From the h· agony !

aims

Mis.	9–24	tasteless and unworthy of h· aims.

ambition

My.	202– 3	h· ambition, fear, or distrust

anatomy

Rud.	11–26	the subject of h· anatomy ;

apprehension

'01.	11– 5	has risen to h· apprehension,

babe

Un.	61– 6	appeared as a helpless h· babe ;

being

Mis.	345–29	to kill and eat a h· being.
Rud.	2– 3	* h· being, a corporeal man,
	2–10	especially a finite h· being;
'02.	15–20	never believe that a h· being
My.	59–29	* No h· being in this generation
	303–11	worshippers of a h· being.

beings

Un.	37–17	H· beings are physically mortal,
Pul.	51– 7	* inherent right as h· beings,
My.	294–28	two hundred and fifty million h· beings
	303–14	eschews divine rights in h· beings.

belief

Mis.	34–15	speculative opinion and h· belief.
	76–11	According to h· belief the bodies of
	86–18	pleasant sensations of h· belief,
	209–10	h· belief fulfils the law of belief,
Rud.	5–20	H· belief says that it does ;
	11–19	rests on the strength of h· belief.
	11–21	takes away every h· belief,
	13– 4	Whatever saps, with h· belief,
	13–12	h· belief which saith there is
No.	26– 7	or the h· belief resembles the
My.	118–23	credited only by h· belief,
	206–16	but it is seeing a h· belief,

beliefs

Mis.	320–25	on the long night of h· beliefs,
Rud.	10– 8	material laws are only h· beliefs,
My.	44– 1	* out of the wilderness of h· beliefs
	206– 8	Schisms, imagination, and h· beliefs

birth

Mis.	17–22	h· birth is the appearing of a

blood

No.	33–18	h· blood was inadequate
	33–20	shedding h· blood brought to light
	34–20	conception that God requires h· blood

body

My.	218– 7	destruction of the h· body,

breast

My.	191–24	Immortal courage fills the h· breast

call

Mis.	81–26	answers the h· call for help ;
Un.	13– 4	coming at h· call ;

capacities

My.	259–26	not that in which h· capacities

capacity

Un.	43–23	will interpret . . . to h· capacity,

character

Mis.	151– 7	purifies the h· character,
Un.	29– 1	hypothesis as to its h· character.
'00.	8– 8	so the h· character comes forth a
My.	246–18	revealed through the h· character.

chords

Mis.	116–16	varied strains of h· chords

comprehension

Mis.	79– 6	until it is clear to h· comprehension

concept

Mis.	103–26	this h· concept of Jesus
	164–24	highest h· concept of the man Jesus,

human

concept
Mis. 309–23 h· concept antagonizes the divine.
353– 8 h· concept is always imperfect ;
353– 8 relinquish your h· concept of me,
Ret. 67– 1 before the h· concept of sin
68– 4 in the name of h· concept,
68– 5 However, the h· concept never
68–17 treats of the h· concept,
73–10 h· concept grew beautifully less
93– 5 h· concept of Christ is based on
Un. 60–15 [h· concept] of God. — Jas. 3 : 9.

conception
Mis. 56–15 a h· conception opposed to
86–22 Even the h· conception of beauty,
Ret. 25–20 h· conception of God
Un. 46– 9 not based on a h· conception
No. 37– 1 In h· conception God's offspring

concepts
Mis. 71–28 h· concepts, mortal shadows
351–19 chapter sub-title
353– 3 H· concepts run in extremes ;
My. 293– 2 differing h· concepts as to the

conduct
Mis. 301–27 a divine rule for h· conduct.

consciousness
Mis. 85–27 pain compels h· consciousness to
93–24 h· consciousness does not test sin
107–20 states and stages of h· consciousness
108–17 second stage of h· consciousness,
203–20 stricken state of h· consciousness,
204–21 holding sway over h· consciousness.
205–14 immersion of h· consciousness in
285–18 deep down in h· consciousness,
352–26 argument and the h· consciousness
Ret. 21–18 to rebuke h· consciousness
93– 3 appeared to h· consciousness
Un. 11–14 Jesus stooped not to h· consciousness,
37– 9 a change in h· consciousness,
49– 5 simple appeal to h· consciousness.
50– 5 destroyed to h· consciousness,
52– 8 h· consciousness should become
Pul. 85–10 * built up in h· consciousness
My. 48– 5 * to restore to h· consciousness
113–28 uplifting h· consciousness to
124– 7 assemblage of h· consciousness,
160– 5 keep h· consciousness in constant
303–15 governed h· consciousness,

control
Mis. 97–13 h· control is animal magnetism,

credulity
My. 80– 9 * tax upon frail h· credulity,

crimes
'01. 20–28 darkest and deepest of h· crimes.

cry
Mis. 64– 2 h· cry which voiced that struggle ;
342–18 Hear that h· cry :

débris
Mis. 393– 5 Soul, sublime 'mid h· débris,
Po. 51–10 Soul, sublime 'mid h· débris,

demonstrator
My. 348–27 h· demonstrator of this Science

desire
Mis. 317–20 H· desire is inadequate to
360– 1 Meekness, moderating h· desire,
My. 3– 6 not alone in accord with h· desire
292–21 effect of one h· desire or belief

desires
Pul. 3–23 when all h· desires are quenched,

destiny
Mis. 232–12 right that regulates h· destiny.

devices
Pan. 4–18 chapter sub-title

direction
Mis. 172–17 nor of h· direction.

discord
Mis. 65– 3 no more proof of h· discord,
236–24 remedy for all h· discord.
Ret. 69– 5 parent of all h· discord

displeasure
Pul. 15– 9 risk h· displeasure for the sake of

doctrines
'00. 4–18 beaten path of h· doctrines
My. 262–18 H· doctrines or hypotheses

dreams
Un. 26–25 is a product of h· dreams.

ears
Ret. 91– 6 ever fell upon h· ears

economy
Mis. 286– 5 this verity in h· economy

endeavor
Mis. 41–15 scales the mountain of h· endeavor,
Pul. 53–21 * in every field of h· endeavor.

enjoyment
Mis. 9–22 this cup of selfish h· enjoyment

human

equity
Mis. 289–19 Neither divine justice nor h· equity

error
Mis. 208–17 All states and stages of h· error
284–19 against h· error and hate.
Un. 62–21 undisturbed by h· error,
No. 4– 6 Disease . . . is a h· error,
34– 1 delusion of all h· error,
36–22 no consciousness of h· error,
'02. 10–26 modus operandi of h· error,

ethics
Mis. 340–30 Material philosophy, h· ethics,

events
Mis. 269–13 in relation to h· events

existence
Mis. 52–15 wretched condition of h· existence.
200–14 stage and state of h· existence.
Un. 9–19 perplexing problem of h· existence.
No. 28– 1 would extinguish h· existence.
My. 166–19 seasons and calms of h· existence.

experience
'00. 15–10 of all h· experience is the most

fabrication
Pul. 2–29 true temple is no h· fabrication,

face
Po. v–12 * resemble the profile of a h· face.

faith
Mis. 182–18 Born of no doctrine, no h· faith,
My. 292– 4 and h· faith in the right.

family
Mis. 18–27 those of the whole h· family,
98–12 helping the whole h· family ;
No. 15– 7 blessings for the whole h· family.
My. 208–20 for the whole h· family.

father
Un. 48–15 than the h· father enters into

fears
Mis. 307– 9 to all h· fears, to suffering

felicity
Pul. 53–16 * law of h· felicity and power

frame
Rud. 11–28 nervous operations of the h· frame.

gods
Mis. 123–12 human passions and h· gods,

gore
Mis. 246–10 purged of that sin by h· gore,
My. 265– 9 cleanse the earth of h· gore ;

governments
My. 293–32 H· governments maintain the

greatness
Mis. 340–28 in the constellation of h· greatness,

growth
Mis. 286– 6 Until time matures h· growth,
Ret. 49–13 in h· growth material organization

hands
Mis. 171– 2 can never . . . signify h· hands.
302–30 evil of putting . . . into h· hands,

happiness
Ret. 81–27 shifting scenes of h· happiness,

hate
My. 257–20 h· hate, pride, greed, lust

hatred
Pul. 15–19 h· hatred cannot reach you.

health
Rud. 12–27 maintains h· health and life.
No. 5–17 destroy both h· health and life.

heart
Mis. 84– 3 a preparation of the h· heart
127–32 h· heart, like a feather bed, needs
208– 9 enters unconsciously the h· heart
245–21 most mischievous to the h· heart,
290–13 its workings in the h· heart.
293–27 rolls on the h· heart a stone ;
356–18 uplifted desires of the h· heart,
Chr. 53–32 bud and bloom In h· heart.
Ret. 80–13 it may stir the h· heart to
My. 62– 7 * love that trembled in one h· heart
92–28 * desire in the h· heart for some such
164–12 and all within the h· heart

hearts
Mis. 294–15 out of the flowers of h· hearts
303–14 at the door of h· hearts,

history
Mis. 12–21 former periods in h· history
267–16 Through all h· history, the vital
Ret. 22– 1 h· history needs to be revised,
Un. 57– 9 central emblem of h· history.
My. 256–18 dearest memories in h· history

hope
Mis. 330– 7 H· hope and faith should join
No. 35– 1 everything to h· hope and faith.
Peo. 8–20 trembling chords of h· hope

hopes
Mis. 341–14 Do h· hopes deceive?

human

hypotheses
Mis.	3–15	No . . . *h·* hypotheses enter this
	25–32	No *h·* hypotheses, whether in
	78–29	*H·* hypotheses are always
	361–14	contradiction of *h·* hypotheses ;
	364–22	*H·* hypotheses predicate·matter of
	366– 3	attention that *h·* hypotheses consume,
Ret.	35–14	*H·* hypotheses have darkened the
'02.	5–16	by *h·* hypotheses or philosophy.
My.	181– 4	dealing with *h·* hypotheses,
	205–24	apart from *h·* hypotheses,

hypothesis
Mis.	71–17	neither *h·* hypothesis nor matter.
'01.	18–20	teaches that a *h·* hypothesis is
My.	350– 5	minus . . . and plus *h·* hypothesis,

ideal
'02.	2– 7	and my *h·* ideal.
My.	271–12	* chapter sub-title

idolatry
No.	35–17	the shocking *h·* idolatry

ills
Mis.	22–15	impossibility of transmitting *h·* ills,

images
Mis.	96–29	*h·* images of thought

imperfection
Mis.	320–13	dawning upon *h·* imperfection,

indignation
Pul.	14– 6	into *h·* indignation ;

individuality
Un.	25–16	honors conscious *h·* individuality

inquiry
My.	245–10	growth of *h·* inquiry

intellect
Un.	22–21	*h· intellect* and *will-power*,
	25–14	This denial enlarges the *h·* intellect

Jesus
Mis.	199–19	through the *h·* Jesus.
No.	36–14	*h·* Jesus had a resort to his higher

judgment
'00.	9–13	Strong desires bias *h·* judgment

justice
Mis.	11–14	Love metes not out *h·* justice,
	11–21	To mete out *h·* justice
	275– 2	Oh, tardy *h·* justice !

ken
My.	45–22	* marvellous beyond *h·* ken.

kingdom
No.	35 27	*h·* kingdom is nowhere,

knowledge
Mis.	22– 8	far in advance of *h·* knowledge
	288–17	*H·* knowledge inculcates that it is,

language
Un.	30– 3	*H·* language constantly uses the

law
My.	149–19	may know too much of *h·* law
	220– 9	concerning obedience to *h·* law,
	283–26	*H·* law is right only as it

laws
My.	220–27	Jesus obeyed *h·* laws

liberty
Mis.	101–11	for *h·* liberty and rights.

life
Mis.	8–20	sanctifies, and consecrates *h·* life,
	81–30	It gives lessons to *h·* life,
	92– 8	and to spiritualize *h·* life,
	137–22	the sublime ends of *h·* life.
	224–15	*h·* life is the work, the play,
	230–20	all of which drop *h·* life into the
	285– 9	*H·* life is too short for foibles
	287–26	obey the Golden Rule for *h·* life,
	289–10	scientific rules to *h·* life
	330– 3	What is the anthem of *h·* life?
	343– 8	and *h·* life more fruitful,
Ret.	23– 1	The trend of *h·* life was
	84– 5	his own thoughts and *h·* life
No.	33–23	glory of *h·* life is in overcoming
'02.	17–14	curtain of *h·* life should be lifted
My.	6– 8	the wrongs of *h·* life,

likeness
Mis.	23–28	*h·* likeness thrown upon the mirror
	308–30	*h·* likeness is the antipode of man

lives
Mis.	19–11	bring them out in *h·* lives.
	360– 2	*H·* lives are yet uncarved,

love
Mis.	107–13	should swell the lyre of *h·* love.
	290–10	To suppose that *h·* love,
	308– 5	He that by reason of *h·* love

manifestation
Mis.	84–16	*h·* manifestation of the Son of God

means
Mis.	52– 9	beyond all *h·* means and methods.
My.	260–11	no partnership with *h·* means

meekness
Mis.	141–22	nobility of *h·* meekness

human

mentality
My.	106–19	*H·* mentality, expressed in disease,

merit
My.	306–17	*H·* merit or demerit will find its

mind
Mis.	12–22	effects of this so-called *h·* mind
	39–19	to fill the *h·* mind with
	58–28	even one *h·* mind governing another ;
	59–25	away from the *h·* mind or body,
	62–24	rule of *h·* mind, fails, and ends in
	62–29	divine Mind over the *h·* mind
	62–30	notion that the *h·* mind can cure
	97– 6	*h·* mind that holds within itself
	97–10	Erring *h·* mind is by no means
	113–11	mentally manipulating *h·* mind,
	277–21	* history of the errors of the *h·* mind."
	360–32	No advancing modes of *h·* mind
No.	40–26	*h·* mind and body are made better only
'01.	19–23	misuse of the *h·* mind,
	20–12	to mislead the *h·* mind,
'02.	10– 3	capacities of the *h·* mind
	10–12	When the *h·* mind is advancing
My.	61–24	* *h·* mind was giving its consent.
	108–13	pharmacy of the *h·* mind,
	126– 4	the disturbed *h·* mind
	190–19	over the *h·* mind and *above matter*
	265–25	atmosphere of the *h·* mind,
	292–29	the *h·* mind is a compound of
	293–13	conflicting states of the *h·* mind,

mind-cure
Mis.	58–27	leaving it a *h·* "mind-cure,"

misjudgment
Mis.	66– 8	no *h·* misjudgment can pervert it ;

mission
Ret.	32– 2	divinely appointed *h·* mission,

misstatement
Mis.	188– 9	Because of *h·* misstatement

mockeries
Mis.	51–24	* dark pile of *h·* mockeries ;

mockery
My.	262 24	a *h·* mockery in mimicry

modes
Mis.	268– 1	*h·* modes and consciousness,

modus
Mis.	380– 3	what is the *h·* modus for

nature
Mis.	212–18	The currents of *h·* nature
	226–27	disgraces *h·* nature more than
	228– 1	the promptings of *h·* nature.
	237–14	phases of error in *h·* nature
	289 33	*H·* nature has bestowed on a wife
	354– 2	exceeds my conception of *h·* nature.
Un.	6– 6	*h·* nature will be renovated,
'00.	2 9	three types of *h·* nature
	10–11	Certain elements in *h·* nature
'01.	9–19	The evil in *h·* nature foams
My.	4–21	iron in *h·* nature rusts away ;
	220–28	have greatly improved *h·* nature

necessity
'01.	34–26	Christianity is a *h·* necessity :

need
Mis.	210–22	false pretense of *h·* need,
My.	28– 5	will meet every *h·* need,"
	73–10	will meet every *h·* need."
	214– 0	will meet every *h·* need.
	224– 6	the *h·* need, the divine command,
	238–22	applicable to every *h·* need.

needs
Mis.	25–10	direct application to *h·* needs,
	192–20	its adaptability to *h·* needs,
	263–13	meet all *h·* needs and reflect
No.	42– 8	Spirit supplies all *h·* needs.
'01.	27– 8	* more rationally to *h·* needs."

obligations
Mis.	204 4	are loyal to . . . *h·* obligations.

obstructions
My.	61– 5	* to remove *h·* obstructions

opinion
Pan.	2–14	of pantheism as a *h·* opinion

opinions
Mis.	17– 9	*h·* opinions and doctrines,
	86–13	indefinite and vague *h·* opinions,
	372– 3	those *h·* opinions had not
Ret.	78– 8	not by *h·* opinions ;
My.	288–13	travesties of *h·* opinions,

organizations
Peo.	1– 4	not . . . from *h·* organizations ;

origin
Mis.	71–27	seems to be of *h·* origin
	172–16	it is neither of *h·* origin nor of
	287– 4	and has no *h·* origin.
Rud.	4– 9	neither is it of *h·* origin.
My.	115– 5	were it of *h·* origin,

human

passions
  Mis. 123-12 h· passions and human gods,
       236- 1 h· passions in their reaction
       237- 9 and the worst of h· passions
       294- 3 maëlstrom of h· passions,
perception
  Un. 61-12 H· perception, advancing toward
person
  Mis. 75- 4 through a h· person,
  Rud.   2-13 The h· person is finite ;
  '01.   5-30 h· person, as defined by C. S.,
philosophies
  No. 24-16 in h· philosophies or creeds :
philosophy
  Mis. 361-13 overshadowed all h· philosophy,
  Un.   9-10 h· philosophy, or mystic psychology.
        11- 7 direct opposition to h· philosophy
        51- 6 H· philosophy and human reason
  No. 11-23 Ancient and modern h· philosophy
        20-25 veins of all h· philosophy.
        21- 2 H· philosophy has ninety-nine parts of
        21-12 H· philosophy would dethrone
        21-15 H· philosophy has an undeveloped God,
  My. 262-18 or vague h· philosophy
       349-21 natural sciences and h· philosophy,
pity
  Mis. 102-21 H· pity often brings pain.
       121-28 Infinitely greater than h· pity,
policy
  Mis. 118- 4 selfish motives, and h· policy.
       204-17 h· policy, ways, and means.
       212- 1 H· policy is a fool that saith
possibility
  Pul. 45-14 * transcended h· possibility.
power
  Mis. 138-19 giving to h· power, peace.
  My. 219- 8 H· power is most properly used in
       266- 6 claims of politics and of h· power,
praise
  Ret. 71- 1 exalts a mortal beyond h· praise,
presentation
  Mis. 164- 4 h· presentation of goodness
pride
  Mis. 111- 6 h· pride, creeping into its meshes,
       162-25 worldliness, h· pride, or self-will,
       183-23 while it shames h· pride.
       268-28 h· pride forfeits spiritual
       358-13 H· pride is human weakness.
  Un. 11-18 destroyed h· pride by taking away
procreation
  Mis. 286-21 H· procreation, birth, life,
progress
  Mis.   9-31 more disastrous to h· progress
propaganda
  My. 303-18 no idolatry, no h· propaganda
purpose
  My. 284- 3 to help h· purpose and peoples,
qualities
  Mis. 250-11 Love is distorted into h· qualities,
  Peo.   2-17 out of the worst h· qualities,
quality
  Mis. 75-19 warped to signify h· quality,
       250-21 As a h· quality, the glorious
question
  '02.   5-14 ever-recurring h· question
race
  Mis. 176- 8 crises of nations or of the h· race.
       194-13 for the whole h· race.
       229-23 h· race would become healthier,
       259-23 spiritual elevator of the h· race,
       278-16 is always a blessing to the h· race.
       341- 2 When will the whole h· race have
  Ret. 79- 1 against the progress of the h· race
        91-29 done for the h· race?
  Un.   6- 4 the whole h· race will learn that,
  Rud.   2- 4 * an individual of the h· race.''
  No. 44-19 legitimate to the h· race,
  My. 136-26 its fruits,— benefiting the h· race ;
       152- 9 h· race has not yet reached
       154-18 and to clothe the h· race.
       189-14 encircle and cement the h· race.
       288- 8 is the elevator of the h· race ;
reason
  Mis. 13-20 and frail h· reason accepts.
       100-16 H· reason is inaccurate ;
       173- 1 h· reason, or man's theorems,
  Ret. 34- 9 H· reason was not equal to it.
  Un.   9-16 upon the sand of h· reason.
        51- 6 Human philosophy and h· reason
  Pul. 47-15 * no h· reason has been equal to
  No. 20- 4 h· reason, imagination, and
        20-26 H· reason is a blind guide,
        24-17 hidden by dogma and h· reason
  My. 161-23 Lest h· reason becloud

human

reason
  My. 165-23 H· reason becomes tired
       260-13 H· reason and philosophy may
       283-19 When pride, self, and h· reason
       350- 7 revelation, uplifting h· reason,
reflection
  Un. 28-20 h· reflection, reason, or belief
right
  Mis. 266- 6 to abridge a single h· right
rights
  '00. 10-13 h· rights, and self-government
  Peo. 11- 9 Above the platform of h· rights
  My. 181-15 religious liberty and h· rights.
       287- 4 industries, h· rights, liberty,
       316-18 It defends h· rights and the
sacrifice
  My. 125- 1 altars for h· sacrifice.
self
  Mis. 162-29 he must be oblivious of h· self.
  My. 194-14 h· self lost in divine light,
sense
  Mis. 68- 4 disappearance to the h· sense ;
        77-32 and resurrecting the h· sense
        87- 5 which is unjust to h· sense
       164-27 become so magnified to h· sense,
       165- 5 had grown beyond the h· sense
       212-13 h· sense of ways and means
       352- 3 When h· sense is quickened
  Un.   4- 8 in a certain finite h· sense,
        61-20 the earthly acme of h· sense.
        63- 9 false h· sense of that light
  No. 10- 2 in both a divine and h· sense ;
        36-25 risen from h· sense to a higher
  My. 40-29 * H· sense often rebels against law,
       191-16 h· sense of Life and Love,
       293-19 divine power and poor h· sense
senses
  My. 189-18 When the h· senses wake from
shadows
  Mis. 352-11 May the h· shadows of thought
sigh
  '00. 11-11 The h· sigh for peace and love
sight
  Mis. 194-17 magnifies the divine power to h· sight ;
  '01. 12-22 magnifies the divine power to h· sight ;
sin
  Un. 15-19 and h· sin become only an echo of
skill
  Mis. 232-12 H· skill but foreshadows what is
slavery
  Mis. 237-28 fetters of one form of h· slavery.
soul
  Mis. 76-15 to set a h· soul free from its
        76-22 misnamed h· soul is material sense,
  Un. 51-26 man is reflected not as h· soul,
  Pul. 53-22 * power of the h· soul.
speculation
  Mis. 286-31 h· speculation will go on,
standpoint
  Mis. 289- 8 From a h· standpoint of good,
statutes
  My. 220-29 human nature and h· statutes.
strength
  Mis. 138-17 that in unity was h· strength ;
       138-18 h· strength is weakness,
  My. 132-14 no longer to appeal to h· strength,
strife
  Mis. 388- 8 Free us from h· strife.
  Po.   7- 8 Free us from h· strife.
struggles
  No. 35- 7 When h· struggles cease,
suffering
  Mis. 179- 3 rolled away by h· suffering.
  Ret. 62- 2 and h· suffering will increase.
sympathy
  Mis. 253-23 should it not appeal to h· sympathy?
system
  Mis. 48-16 of any drug, on the h· system,
       244- 6 constructing the h· system,
systems
  Mis. 74- 9 all h· systems of etiology and
  Ret. 57-24 H· systems of philosophy and
theorems
  Mis. 312-22 h· theorems or hypotheses,
theories
  Mis. 365- 5 H· theories weighed in the balances
  Un. 44-15 H· theories call, or miscall,
  No. 18-13 H· theories, when weighed in the
thought
  Mis. 17-28 existence dawns on h· thought,
        75-31 or brought forth by h· thought,
       166-25 leavening the lump of h· thought,
       204-23 By purifying h· thought,
       205-10 Truth and Love on the h· thought,

human
thought
Mis. 217–31   but spiritualize *h·* thought,
     282–16   personal precincts of *h·* thought,
     307–30   *h·* thought must arise instinctively
     352–22   not sufficient . . . in the *h·* thought
     361– 9   disappear to *h·* thought,
Ret. 67– 3   *h·* thought does not constitute sin,
     93–14   method for uplifting *h·* thought
Un. 61–10   the morning of *h·* thought,
Pul. 15– 3   point out the evil in *h·* thought,
No. 24– 4   in evil in *h·* thought.
     40–15   never to touch the *h·* thought
'02.   9– 9   Truth will arise in *h·* thought
Peo.   3–23   limits *h·* thought and action
My. 114–29   the whole lump of *h·* thought?
     151–29   *h·* thought discerned its idolatrous
     153–28   to all *h·* thought and action,
     191–21   but *h·* thought has risen !
     265–15   has dawned upon *h·* thought
     278–30   Whatever brings into *h·* thought
thoughts
Mis. 393–10   the misty Mine of *h·* thoughts,
Un. 21– 2   processes wherein *h·* thoughts
Po. 51–15   the misty Mine of *h·* thoughts,
title
'00. 15– 4   are distinguished above *h·* title
tone
'00. 11–20   *h·* tone has no melody for me.
tribunals
Mis. 121–29   *H·* tribunals, if just, borrow their
understanding
Mis. 73–28   divine law to *h·* understanding ;
     81–25   desolation of *h·* understanding,
No. 37–24   uplifting the *h·* understanding,
My. 228–19   bathing the *h·* understanding with
     262–14   entrance into *h·* understanding
use
'01. 6–21   impracticable for *h·* use,
vagaries
Mis. 78–30   hypotheses are always *h·* vagaries,
victims
Mis. 123–11   a religion that demands *h·* victims
view
Mis. 282– 3   brings to *h·* view an
views
My. 221– 5   with certain purely *h·* views.
wants
Peo. 12–23   application of . . . to *h·* wants.
weakness
Mis. 292–13   energy that brings to *h·* weakness
     358–14   Human pride is *h·* weakness.
Un. 39–12   divine Science removes *h·* weakness
My. 287– 7   giving to *h·* weakness strength,
weal
Mis. 65– 9   subject of *h·* weal and woe?
My. 36–27   * affection for the cause of *h·* weal,
     213– 9   lurking foe to *h·* weal,
will
Mis. 59– 6   using the power of *h·* will,
     74– 4   the *h·* will, and the unnatural
     118– 1   *H·* will must be subjugated.
     141–21   impulses of *h·* will and pride ;
     181–32   born not of the *h·* will
     201– 5   its original sin, or *h·* will ;
     212–22   *h·* will is lost in the divine ;
     243–22   the basis of matter, or *h·* will,
     254–25   laurels of headlong *h·* will.
Rud. 9–10   malpractice is in erring *h·* will,
No. 11– 1   whereas matter and *h·* will,
'01. 2– 9   magnetic element of *h·* will.
     19–26   unbridled individual *h·* will.
My. 5–31   *H·* will may mesmerize and mislead
     159–26   could not control *h·* will,
     349–26   *h·* will divorced from Science.
wills
Mis. 224–12   different *h·* wills, opinions,
wisdom
Mis. 73–14   *H·* wisdom therefore can get no
     204–17   in *h·* wisdom, human policy,
Un. 44–18   *H·* wisdom says of evil,
     54–22   addition to *h·* wisdom,
Peo. 1– 3   is not born of *h·* wisdom ;
My. 224– 2   when *h·* wisdom is inadequate
woe
Mis. 361–22   speculative wisdom and *h·* woe.
Ret. 31–13   relief from *h·* woe.
Un. 58–16   the full compass of *h·* woe,
No. 33–23   physical suffering and *h·* woe.
'02. 6–13   all *h·* woe is seen to obtain in
My. 190– 2   bring the recompense of *h·* woe,
wrong
Mis. 340–32   *H·* wrong, sickness, sin, and death

Mis. 16–11   these claims are divine, not *h·* ;
     58–23   All Science is divine, not *h·*,

human
Mis. 63–26   Jesus as the son of man was *h·* :
     63–28   through the crucifixion of the *h·*,
     64–22   for science is not *h·*.
     100–22   of the divine with the *h·*,
     102–18   expressed in modes above the *h·*.
     103–22   Any inference . . . derived from the *h·*,
     121– 9   *h·* struggles against the divine,
     161–16   both *h·* and divinely endowed,
     163–16   less *h·* and more divine
     184–31   purged of the animal and *h·*,
     187–19   our *h·* and divine Master,
     199–24   but the actor was *h·*.
     246– 7   both *h·* and divine rights,
     247– 2   both *h·* and divine rights ;
     258–29   differs essentially from the *h·*.
     286–22   states of the *h·* erring mind :
     291– 1   Mistaken or transient views are *h·* :
Ret. 28–26   Its Principle is divine, not *h·*,
     50–20   subordination of the *h·* to the
     56–10   is of *h·* instead of divine origin.
     67– 4   sin constitutes the *h·* or physical
     68– 9   *h·* material concept is *unreal*,
     89–29   and selfish influence is *h·*,
Un. 18–18   through divine law, not through *h·*.
No. 18–18   Thus falsely may the *h·* conceive of
     21–16   wherein the *h·* and divine mingle
     30–14   not by becoming *h·*, and knowing sin,
     30–18   His sympathy is divine, not *h·*,
Pan. 4–11   But reason and will are *h·* ;
     8– 8   the other a *h·* finite personality?
'01. 1–16   *h·* in communion with the Divine,
     10–12   The Christ was not *h·*.
     10–12   Jesus was *h·*.
     10–14   both the divine and the *h·*,
     12– 9   But this is *h·* :
     31– 7   neither personal nor *h·*, but divine.
Peo. 10–16   divine as well as *h·*.
My. 27– 7   for the divine and not the *h·*
     139–22   from the *h·* to the divine.
     244–19   put off the *h·* for the divine.
     262– 7   commemorates the birth of a *h·*,
     265–22   coincidence of the *h·* and divine,
     275– 5   The *h·*, material, so-called senses

humane
Mis. 26– 5   more *h·* and spiritual.
     89–14   it is *h·*, and not unchristian,
     184–32   submerged in the *h·* and divine,
Peo. 10– 9   put her *h·* foot on a tyrannical
My. 175–14   academies, *h·* institutions,
     291–21   renew euphony, emphasize *h·* power,

Human Freedom League
Mis. 305– 6   * the *H· F· L·*,

humanhood
Un. 49– 8   The more I understand true *h·*,

humanitarian
Mis. 284– 6   *h·* at work in this field of
Man. 47– 1   A Christian Scientist is a *h·* ;

humanity (*see also* **humanity's**)
advancing
No. 19– 9   second thought of advancing *h·*.
all
Un. 51–14   Man is the generic term for all *h·*.
and divinity
Ret. 91–14   great lessons — on *h·* and divinity
and equality
Mis. 294–29   true ideas of *h·* and equality.
and sympathy
Mis. 379–18   his rare *h·* and sympathy
benefited
Ret. 85–14   glorified, or *h·* benefited,
brings to
Mis. 338– 3   brings to *h·* some great good,
candor and
Mis. 147–28   full of truth, candor, and *h·*.
consecrated to
Mis. 350–30   My life, consecrated to *h·*
death and
My. 258–24   love, grief, death, and *h·*.
divinity and
My. 179–23   practice of a true divinity and *h·*.
drop of
Pul. 5–15   bedew my hope with a drop of *h·*.
ear of
Peo. 13–12   On the startled ear of *h·*
faith in
Mis. 338–15   faith in *h·* will subject one to
forcing
Mis. 359–12   forcing *h·* out of the proper channels
forearm
My. 273–17   to forewarn and forearm *h·*.
God and
     (*see* **God**)

humanity
grander
  Pul. 85–16 * a better and grander *h·*,
growing wants of
  Mis. 365–25 never met the growing wants of *h·*.
heart of
  (*see* **heart**)
help
  No. 43–25 will never . . . help *h·*.
higher
  Pul. 15–20 cement of a higher *h·* will
highest
  Pan. 9–16 demonstrates the highest *h·*,
his
  My. 291–15 His *h·*, weighed in the scales of
imparting to
  Mis. 372–31 imparting to *h·* the true sense of
impress
  Mis. 207– 4 impress *h·* with the genuine
jaded
  Mis. 366–16 At this date, poor jaded *h·* needs
justice, and
  '00. 10–15 in the name of God, justice, and *h·*
leading
  My. 252–22 leading *h·* into paths of peace
lifts
  Mis. 290– 5 Science lifts *h·* higher in the
love for
  My. 24– 7 * your unmeasured love for *h·*,
lower order of
  Peo. 13– 2 hence a lower order of *h·*,
methods of
  Peo. 11–24 mistaken in their methods of *h·*.
models of
  Peo. 14–11 form our models of *h·*.
needs of
  My. 147–18 moral, and spiritual needs of *h·*,
origin of
  Pul. 39– 3 * proof of the divine origin of *h·*
outrages
  Mis. 274–19 mocks morality, outrages *h·*,
poor
  Mis. 107–15 before poor *h·* is regenerated
       359–17 for poor *h·* to step upon the
problem of
  My. 306–18 solves the problem of *h·*,
pure
  Mis. 100–22 Pure *h·*, friendship, home,
reaching
  Mis. 63–28 reaching *h·* through the crucifixion
rescue of
  Mis. 293– 8 will come, . . . to the rescue of *h·*.
reveals itself to
  Mis. 95–21 reveals itself to *h·* through
sake of
  Pul. 51–30 * something good for the sake of *h·*.
should share
  My. 220–30 *h·* should share alike
sorrow-worn
  My. 40–18 * pain-racked and sorrow-worn *h·*.
spirit of
  My. 129– 5 But the spirit of *h·*, ethics,
suffering
  My. 190– 4 sympathy for suffering *h·*
sufferings of
  Ret. 30– 8 relieve the sufferings of *h·*
tendency of
  '02. 10–15 upward tendency of *h·*
universal
  Mis. 29– 6 touches universal *h·*.
  My. 37–16 * before the gaze of universal *h·*.
uplifted
  No. 34–25 over the steps of uplifted *h·*,
upon
  '00. 12– 2 projected from divinity upon *h·*,
verdict of
  Pan. 10– 7 the honest verdict of *h·*
victorious
  Un. 30–19 made *h·* victorious over death
vitals of
  Mis. 131– 4 gnawing at the vitals of *h·*.
wants of
  Ret. 52–10 the broader wants of *h·*,
  No. 19– 7 the growing wants of *h·*.
was misled
  Un. 44–10 *h·* was misled by a false

  My. 269– 5 Then shall *h·* have learned
humanity's
  Mis. 370–13 according to *h·* needs.
  Po. 22–15 To heal *h·* sore heart ;
humanized
  Ret. 54– 8 a *h·* conception of His power.
humankind
  Un. 59– 3 from what evils . . . to save *h·*?

humanly
  Mis. 71–21 Whatever is *h·* conceived is a
       81–25 his voice be heard divinely and *h·*.
  Un. 58–11 through what is *h·* called *agony.*
  No. 9–26 *h·* construed, and according to
humble
  Mis. 99–32 by the wayside, in *h·* homes.
       127–13 If this heart, *h·* and trustful,
       163–10 by the wayside, in *h·* homes :
       204– 3 *h·* before God, he cries,
       331– 5 did it make them *h·*, loving,
       337–14 *h·* himself as this little — *Matt.* 18 : 4.
       337–26 by the wayside, in *h·* homes,
  Pul. 87– 5 * with our *h·* benediction.
  '01. 14– 4 Publican's wail won his *h·* desire,
  Po. 33– 2 make this my *h·* request :
  My. 18–10 If this heart, *h·* and trustful,
       134– 6 cannot be too grateful nor too *h·*
       188–31 gains admittance to a *h·* heart,
       334–22 Publican's wail won his *h·* desire,
humbles
  Ret. 71– 2 *h·* him with the tax it raises on
  My. 131– 4 *h·*, exalts, and commands a man,
humbly
  Mis. 313–25 *H·*, and, . . . divinely directed,
  Po. 28– 6 Help us to *h·* bow
  My. 174–28 *h·* pray to serve Him better.
       182–19 *H·*, gratefully, trustingly.
       257–18 our hearts are kneeling *h·*.
       283–24 and to walk *h·*" — *Mic.* 6 : 8.
humbugs
  Ret. 33– 9 and from various *h·*,
Hume, David
  Ret. 37–12 David *H·*, Ralph Waldo Emerson, or
humiliates
  No. 39–15 Such prayer *h·*, purifies, and
humility
  Mis. 1–15 *H·* is the stepping-stone to
       7– 7 *h·* is necessary in this work
       158–17 test your *h·* and obedience
       316–28 patterns of *h·*, wisdom, and
       328– 7 that the valley is *h·*,
       341–13 comes of honesty and *h·*.
       354–23 *h·* is the first step in C. S.,
       356–22 The second stage of . . . is *h·*.
       356–25 *H·* is lens and prism to the
       356–30 Cherish *h·*, "watch," —*Matt.* 26 : 41.
       356–31 *H·* is no busybody :
       358–14 Self-knowledge, *h·*, and love
  Ret. 31–25 and a tint of *h·*,
       91–30 His holy *h·*, unworldliness, and
  Un. 45–10 come down and learn, in *h·*,
  No. 35– 5 through deep *h·* and adoration
  My. 36–18 * we are come, in *h·*, to pour out our
       37– 5 * Naught else than the grandeur of *h·*
       262–27 *h·*, benevolence, charity,
       303–29 We need much *h·*, wisdom,
hummed
  Pan. 1– 8 shrieked and *h·* their hymns ;
humor
  Mis. 117–11 * *h·*, and enduring vivacity
  My. 121–19 gentility and good *h·*
       338–23 his comparisons and ready *h·*.
hundred
  My. 112–14 ninety-nine out of every *h·*
  (*see also* **dates, numbers, values**)
hundredfold
  Mis. 12–17 temptations to sin are increased a *h·*.
       50–27 advance Christianity a *h·*.
hundreds
  Mis. 54–15 is curing *h·* at this very time ;
  Pul. 36– 7 * To this College came *h·* and *h·*
       41–14 * New York sent its *h·*,
       68– 6 * Students came to it in *h·*
  My. 30– 8 * many *h·* of other faiths,
       30–28 * *h·* had to be turned away,
       53– 2 * *h·* of dollars were sunk
       54– 2 * *h·* going away who could not
       59–10 * by the *h·* of thousands
       80–27 * there were many *h·* waiting
       85– 5 * churches have risen by *h·*,
       90– 1 * *h·* of great buildings
       92–17 * number to *h·* of thousands,
       93–31 * number *h·* of thousands,
       99–23 * there are *h·* of such churches.
       112–32 in *h·* of pulpits and
       293– 8 *H·*, thousands of others believed
       293– 9 *h·* of thousands who prayed
  (*see also* **numbers**)
hundredth
  (*see* **numbers**)

hung

Mis.	333–30	Chaldee *h·* his destiny out upon
Pul.	42–21	* a huge seven-pointed star was *h·*
	49– 5	* *h·* its walls with reproductions
My.	161– 1	*h·* around the necks of the wicked.

hunger

Ret.	31– 9	*h·* and thirst after divine things,
My.	40– 4	* to those who *h·* and thirst

hungered

Pul.	6–16	* for which I had *h·* since girlhood,

hungering

Mis.	235–18	*H·* and thirsting after a better life,
My.	15–28	* Seem *h·* and thirsting

hungry

Mis.	16– 2	These nourish the *h·* hope,
	127–11	When a *h·* heart petitions the
	225–28	he awoke, and was *h·*.
	322–20	it is God that feedeth the *h·* heart,
	324–28	Naked, *h·*, athirst, this time he
	369–20	We are *h·* for Love,
	391– 3	I hope the heart that's *h·*
	398–17	Feed the *h·*, heal the heart,
Ret.	46–23	Feed the *h·*, heal the heart,
	90– 8	he there taught a few *h·* ones,
Pul.	17–22	Feed the *h·*, heal the heart,
'02.	17–25	worth satisfies the *h·* heart,
Po.	14–21	Feed the *h·*, heal the heart,
	38– 2	I hope the heart that's *h·*
My.	18– 8	When a *h·* heart petitions the
	133 13	crumbs and monads will feed the *h·*,
	147–29	heavenly homesick or *h·* hearts

Hunt, Mrs.

My.	31–25	* soloist for the services, Mrs. *H·*,

hunters

Pan.	3–26	god of shepherds and *h·*,

Huntington and Massachusetts Avenues

My.	73–19	* corner of *H·* and *M· A·*.

Huntington Avenue

Pul.	57–24	* on Back Bay, just off *H· A·*,

Huntoon

Mehitable

Ret.	8–13	when my cousin, Mehitable *H·*,
	8–16	so loud that Mehitable heard it,
	8–19	Mehitable then said sharply,
	9– 4	Mother told Mehitable all about this

hurling

Mis.	254 22	*h·* its so-called healing at random,

hurls

Hea.	2– 6	*h·* the thunderbolt of truth,

hurried

My.	224– 8	*H·* conclusions as to the public thought

hurrying

Pul.	39–24	* *h·* throng before me pass,
My.	66–20	* are *h·* on with their work

hurt

Mis.	28–32	it shall not *h·* them ; — *Mark* 16 : 18.
	115–25	every effort to *h·* one will only
	224– 4	our egotism that feels *h·* by
	224–10	* I don't feel *h·* in the least.''
	249– 6	it shall not *h·* them.'' — *Mark* 16 : 18.
	280– 7	*h·* not the holy things of Truth.
'01.	20–15	or that they are *h·*.
Hea.	1– 4	*it shall not h· them;— Mark* 16 : 18.
	7–26	it shall not *h·* them.'' — *Mark* 16 : 18.
	15–12	it shall not *h·* them.'' — *Mark* 16 : 18.
Peo.	12– 4	it shall not *h·* them ; — *Mark* 16 : 18.
My.	33–24	sweareth to his own *h·*, — *Psal.* 15 : 4.
	48– 2	* it shall not *h·* them ; — *Mark* 16 : 18.
	146– 5	it shall not *h·* them.'' — *Mark* 16 : 18.
	233–16	healed also the *h·* of — *Jer.* 6 : 14.

hurting

'01.	20–14	not knowing what is *h·* them

husband (*see also* **husband's**)

Mis.	35–10	the following words of her *h·*,
	90– 8	to have a *h· treated for sin,*
	143–21	*h·* and wife reckoned as one,
	236–15	solicitations of *h·* or wife
	275–10	where the bereft wife or *h·*,
	287–22	When asked by a wife or a *h·*
	287–29	Please your *h·*, and he will be apt to
	339–20	Art thou a *h·*, and hast
	339–23	the o'erburdened head of thy *h·*?
	385– 9	poem
Man.	46– 3	spiritually adopted *h·* or wife.
	92–12	If both *h·* and wife are
Ret.	19– 1	I was united to my first *h·*,
	19–11	My *h·* was a freemason,
	43– 9	My *h·*, Asa G. Eddy,
Pul.	6–19	* I went with my *h·*,
	83– 3	* as *h·* and office-holder

husband

'02.	15–16	My *h·*, Colonel Glover,
Po.	page 48	poem
My.	189–26	There my *h·* died,
	290–19	Thy tender *h·*, our nation's chief
	312– 5	tragic death of my *h·*,
	312–18	My first *h·*, Major . . . Glover,
	314– 2	Dr. . . . Patterson, my second *h·*,
	314–19	that a *h·* was about to
	314–23	letter from me to this self-same *h·*,
	314–24	When this *h·* recovered these facts
	314–27	wife of this *h·* related these facts
	326–14	my *h·*, Major George W. Glover,
	329– 9	* reference to the death of her *h·*,
	330–16	* relating to her *h·*
	330–23	''My *h·* was a Free Mason,
	335–29	* save the life of her *h·*.

husbanding

My.	182–28	this vine of His *h·*,

husbandman

Mis.	154–15	vine whereof our Father is *h·*.
Hea.	8–24	by the parable of the *h·*.
Po.	47–17	Watching the *h·* fled ;

husbandmen

Mis.	253–18	and the *h·* that said,
	254–27	come and destroy the *h·*, — *Mark* 12 : 9.

husband's

Man.	111– 6	Christian name, not her *h·*,
Ret.	20– 1	I lost all my *h·* property,
Po.	9– 1	glance of her *h·* watchful eye
My.	329–14	* notice of her *h·* death
	334–10	* account of her *h·* demise
	335–23	* third day of her *h·* illness,
	395 30	* prayed incessantly for her *h·*
	336– 5	* come to her after her *h·* death,
	336– 8	* her *h·* Masonic brethren,
	336–12	I lost all my *h·* property,

husbands

Pul.	82–26	* the welfare of their *h·*,
'02.	5–10	*divine Love*, that heaven *h·*

hush

Pan.	3–10	silent as the storm's sudden *h·* ;

hushed

Mis.	246–14	has scarcely been heard and *h·*,
	395–13	*H·* is the heart.
Hea.	17–17	were *h·* by material sense
Po.	35–11	*H·* in the heart
	57–20	*H·* is the heart.

hushing

Mis.	323–19	*h·* the hissing serpents,

husks

Mis.	369–22	tired of theoretic *h·*,

Huxley

'01.	24–19	Berkeley, Darwin, or *H·*.

hyacinth

Po.	67–19	like the blue *h·*,

hydra

Mis.	246–16	lifts its *h·* head to forge anew

hydra-headed

No.	2– 3	spurious and *h·* mind-healing

hydraulics

No.	6–25	optics, acoustics, and *h·*

hydrology

Mis.	203–14	*h·* handles it with so-called

hydropathy

Ret.	33– 8	homœopathy, *h·*, electricity,

Hygeia

My.	205–17	spiritual Æsculapius and *H·*,

hygiene

Mis.	3–17	*H·*, manipulation, and mesmerism
	3–26	*materia medica, h·,* and
	6–23	faith in drugs and material *h·* ;
	17–11	put off your *materia medica* and *h·*
	80–27	pathology, *h·*, and therapeutics,
	138– 7	time and attention to *h·*
	240– 5	fattened by metaphysical *h·*.
Pan.	4–26	what need have we of drugs, *h·*, and
Hea.	3– 1	requires neither *h·* nor drugs
	14– 6	physiology, *h·*, or physics
	15– 6	It places no faith in *h·* or drugs ;
Peo.	4– 3	more faith in *h·* and drugs than in
My.	260–27	It leaves *h·*, medicine, ethics, and
	348– 3	drugs, surgery, *h·*, electricity,

hygienic

Mis.	40– 5	mingle *h·* rules, drugs, and prayers
Ret.	26– 2	neither obedience to *h·* laws, nor
No.	10–14	My *h·* system rests on Mind,
Peo.	12–23	faith in drugs and *h·* drills,

idea

and demonstration
Ret. 59–16 both in *i·* and demonstration.
and purpose
Mis. 303–23 *i·* and purpose of a Liberty Bell
any
My. 324– 5 * any *i·* for your book,
Christian
'02. 12– 9 Christian *i·* that God is come,
Christian Science
My. 84–18 * growth of the C. S. *i·*
compound
Mis. 167– 8 even the compound *i·* of
My. 269– 2 in the intelligent compound *i·*,
conceivable
'01. 6–27 lose all conceivable *i·* of Him
concept or
Ret. 68–10 divine concept or *i·* is spiritually
concise
Pul. 73–28 * concise *i·* of her belief
conclusive
Mis. 96–26 give to you any conclusive *i·*
divine
(*see* **divine**)
eternal
Mis. 79–12 man is the eternal *i·* of Truth,
Un. 61– 7 even the eternal *i·* of God,
No. 25–14 eternal *i·* of his divine Principle,
full
My. 205–26 full *i·* of its divine Principle,
fundamental
Pul. 69–17 * fundamental *i·* is that God is Mind,
God's
Mis. 261–25 Man as God's *i·* is already saved
336–14 dislike and hatred of God's *i·*,
Pul. 75– 3 the Principle of God's *i·*,
Po. 70–23 Give God's *i·* sway,
highest
Mis. 336– 9 His highest *i·* as seen to-day?
My. 283–17 a man's highest *i·* of right
His
Mis. 4– 8 of the universe as His *i·*,
13–24 that is, of God and His *i·*.
332–29 supposition is, that God and His *i·*
Ret. 23–23 were God and His *i·*.
60–11 C. S. reveals God and His *i·*
63– 1 God and His *i·* are the only
Un. 47– 6 is God and His *i·*.
62–28 and that of His *i·*, man ;
My. 5– 9 His *i·*, coexistent with Him
119– 6 His *i·*, image, and likeness.
239–16 *His i· or image and likeness*
239–17 His *i·*, image, or likeness, man,
his
My. 139–11 his *i·* is nearing the Way,
His own
Mis. 361–29 He elucidates His own *i·*,
immortal
My. 241–21 * immortal *i·* of the one divine Mind.
incorporeal
Mis. 164– 1 interprets the incorporeal *i·*,
166–16 the incorporeal *i·* of God,
My. 218–11 the incorporeal *i·*, came with the
individualized
No. 19–16 man is His individualized *i·*.
infant
Mis. 320–12 infant *i·* of divine perfection
infinite
Mis. 165– 9 This infinite *i·* of infinity will be,
No. 25–11 even as the infinite *i·* of Truth
its
Mis. 104–25 and its *i·* represents Love.
336–17 and not love its *i·* :
its own
Mis. 41–20 architect that builds its own *i·*,
man, as the
My. 239–19 Man, as the *i·* or image
Mind's
No. 27–16 divine Mind and that Mind's *i·*.
"Mother" of the
Pul. 63– 4 * "MOTHER" OF THE *I·*
My
Un. 62–22 My *i·*, never in matter,
new
Mis. 1–12 the new *i·* that comes welling up
No. 1–10 when thrilled by a new *i·*,
'02. 11–10 him who, having a new *i·*
Hea. 18–14 willingly adopt the new *i·*,
My. 92– 2 * the new *i·* will never have
of being
Mis. 166– 2 and spiritual *i·* of being,
188–10 divine Principle and *i·* of being,
of divine Mind
No. 24– 1 immeasurable *i·* of divine Mind.
of divine Principle
No. 4–20 not the *i·* of divine Principle,

idea

offspring and
Mis. 82–15 Man is the offspring and *i·* of
of God
(*see* **God**)
of infinite Mind
Mis. 5–26 man is the *i·* of infinite Mind,
247–22 man is the *i·* of infinite Mind,
of man
Mis. 62– 1 Holding the *right i·* of man
166–17 the *i·* of man was not understood.
of matter
Mis. 75– 2 of Jesus' *i·* of matter.
of sound
Mis. 46–27 even as the *i·* of sound, in tones,
of Spirit
Mis. 60–27 every creation or *i·* of Spirit
No. 16–14 Spirit and the *i·* of Spirit.
of the size
My. 69–26 * chapter sub-title
69–27 * an *i·* of the size of this building
of Truth
Mis. 79–12 man is the eternal *i·* of Truth,
No. 25–11 even as the infinite *i·* of Truth
Hea. 3–15 Christ is the *i·* of Truth ;
10– 4 ready to devour the *i·* of Truth.
Peo. 8– 2 to present the right *i·* of Truth ;
or likeness
My. 239–21 *i·* or likeness of the infinite *one*,
262– 2 *i·*, or likeness of perfection
perfect
Peo. 2–26 This more perfect *i·*,
perpetual
Mis. 83– 3 perpetual *i·* of inexhaustible good.
prevails
My. 329– 4 * The *i·* prevails that the last
Principle and
Mis. 82– 3 Principle and *i·* of all good.
104–26 Principle and *i·* are demonstrated,
182–27 of existence as Principle and *i·*,
188–10 divine Principle and *i·* of being,
218–15 Science of Principle and *i·* ;
361–29 Principle and *i·*, God and man,
374–16 announce their Principle and *i·*.
No. 13– 6 Principle and *i·* to be divine.
quite an
Mis. 375–13 * so got quite an *i·* of
repudiated the
Mis. 97– 9 repudiated the *i·* of casting out
ridicule the
My. 97– 5 * physicians, however, ridicule the *i·*
right
Mis. 62– 1 Holding the *right i·* of man
Hea. 4–22 gain a right *i·* of the Principle
Peo. 8– 1 to present the right *i·* of Truth ;
spiritual
(*see* **spiritual**)
that
Hea. 18–14 if that *i·* could be reconciled
My. 344–19 harbored that *i·* about a disease,
this
Mis. 78–27 this *i·* cannot fail to express
163–30 This *i·* or divine essence was,
360–30 and this *i·* is understood,
Ret. 93– 6 Science has elevated this *i·*
No. 10–24 this *i·* . . . turns like the needle
Peo. 8– 2 then will this *i·* cast out error
true
Mis. 101–11 a contest for the true *i·*,
111–13 higher sense of the true *i·*.
176–18 the true *i·* of God — the supremacy of
258–28 only suitable or true *i·* of Him ;
309–16 Son of God, the true *i·*
360–27 Jesus, as the true *i·* of Him,
No. 1–14 silent cultivation of the true *i·*
10–22 C. S. unveil the true *i·*,
21–25 the true *i·* of the Christ,
'00. 6– 9 in the true *i·* of God.
'02. 7– 9 give man the true *i·* of God
My. 181–11 through the true *i·* of Life,
Truth's
Mis. 320– 5 the history of Truth's *i·*,
321– 8 the steady gain of Truth's *i·*
vast
Mis. 77–20 In adopting all this vast *i·*

Mis. 186–20 an *i·* cannot be torn apart from its
Pul. 71– 4 * The *i·* that C. S. has declined in
No. 3– 3 the *i·* which claims only its

ideal

affection and
Mis. 276–23 a purer, higher affection and *i·*.
divine
(*see* **divine**)

ideal

his
Mis. 105–21 the individual and his *i·*
human
'02. 2– 7 this is . . . my human *i·*.
My. 271–12 * chapter sub-title
its
Mis. 217– 8 its *i·* or phenomenon must
its own
Mis. 223–10 that mind reaches its own *i·*,
my
Mis. 293– 1 and carried out my *i·*.
374–21 I never looked on my *i·* of
374–31 my *i·* of an angel is a woman
my only
Mis. 105–20 C. S. is my only *i·* ;
no higher
Mis. 270– 8 mankind hath no higher *i·*
of Christianity
My. 40–25 * the *i·* of Christianity,
of God
Ret. 93–10 *i·* of God is no longer impersonated as
'02. 12– 6 this *i·* of God is *now* and *forever*,
Peo. 5–16 our *i·* of God has risen above
of Love
Hea. 10– 8 presented the highest *i·* of Love.
one's
Mis. 374–27 Pictures are portions of one's *i·*,
perfect
My. 179–21 Christianity as the perfect *i·*.
right
Peo. 5–12 The right *i·* is not buried,
My. 166– 7 so long as we have the right *i·*,
spiritual
(*see* **spiritual**)
that
Hea. 6–17 whether that *i·* is a flower or
this
Mis. 374–27 this *i·* is not one's personality.
'02. 12– 6 this *i·* of God is *now* and *forever*,
true
Mis. 79–21 true *i·* of immortal man's
104–29 or would not gain the true *i·* of
Un. 62–12 true *i·* of omnipotent and
Peo. 6–18 more spiritual and true *i·* of Deity

Mis. 74–15 immortal sense of the *i·* world.
77–15 to support their *i·* man.
102– 2 stature of Christ, the *i·* man.
166– 7 *i·* Christ — or impersonal infancy,
205–21 in Christian metaphysics the *i·* man
217– 7 *i·* world whose cause is the
235–20 and know something of the *i·* man,
Ret. 68– 7 Even the spiritual idea, or *i·* man,
Un. 62–13 an *i·* . . . wherefor there is no evil.
No. 36–28 while the divine and *i·* Christ was
My. 64–21 * the realization of *i·* manhood
174– 5 proved an *i·* meeting place.
192– 7 The *i·* robe of Christ is seamless.
195–21 no miserable piece of *i·* legerdemain,
262– 3 an *i·* which cannot fall from its

idealism

Mis. 216–23 Was this . . . a happy hit at *i·*,
217– 1 True *i·* is a divine Science,
Pul. 23–11 * wave of *i·* that has swept over
38–27 * phases of *i·* and manifestations of
No. 38– 6 He established the only true *i·*
My. 5–16 spiritual *i·* and realism
205–19 This *i·* connects itself with
272–14 demonstration of this *i·*.
307–31 My *i·*, however, limped,

ideals

Ret. 75–10 Life and its *i·* are inseparable,
Hea. 6–15 I saw how the mind's *i·*
Peo. 3– 1 our *i·* form our characters,
3– 3 crudest *i·* of speculative theology
3– 4 the *i·* of *materia medica*
4–26 grown out of such false *i·*
5–10 The *i·* of primitive Christianity
7– 1 their highest or their lowest *i·*,
7– 2 working out our own *i·*,
7– 5 to rot and ruin the mind's *i·*.

ideas

advanced
Mis. 295–25 most advanced *i·* are inscribed
akin to mine
Un. 9–21 *i·* akin to mine have been held by
and principles
'01. 27– 7 * interpret their *i·* and principles
any
Mis. 306– 6 * any *i·* on that subject
author's
Ret. 76– 1 an author's *i·* and their words.
Christian Science
Pul. 80–21 * the spirit of C. S. *i·* has caused

ideas

conveying
Mis. 133– 5 conveying *i·* more opposite to the
different
Pul. 51–14 * and with them bring different *i·*.
God's
Mis. 164–30 The limited view of God's *i·*
His
Un. 24–19 God and His *i·* — that is,
individualized
Mis. 103–14 individualized *i·*, which dwell
its
Mis. 218–10 immortality of Mind and its *i·*.
language and
Ret. 75– 8 appropriating my language and *i·*,
Mind's
Mis. 23–30 All must be Mind and Mind's *i·* ;
my
Mis. 263–28 to appropriate my *i·* and discovery,
new
'02. 10– 3 uncovers new *i·*, unfolds spiritual
of Deity
Ret. 56– 1 The following *i·* of Deity,
Peo. 12–17 As our *i·* of Deity advance
14– 1 As our *i·* of Deity become more
of divinity
Peo. 14–10 our *i·* of divinity form our models
of God
No. 20–12 fully conveys the *i·* of God,
Peo. 4–16 mysterious *i·* of God and man
of Life
Peo. 14– 7 our *i·* of Life have grown
of primitive Christianity
Pul. 69–15 * the *i·* of primitive Christianity.
patchwork
No. 3– 1 not spread abroad patchwork *i·*
pre-Christian
Pul. 66–25 * pre-Christian *i·* of the Asiatics
spiritual
Mis. 82– 1 the mind with spiritual *i·*,
307– 1 gives you His spiritual *i·*,
'00. 3–17 the pioneer of spiritual *i·*,
these
Pul. 80–29 * all these *i·* are Christian.
true
Mis. 294–28 with the true *i·* of humanity
your
My. 324– 6 * you and your *i·* were too much alike

'01. 21– 9 * *i·* about the spiritual world

identical

Mis. 9– 9 *i·* with "Thou hast no enemies."
66–15 sin is *i·* with suffering,
296–16 they are by no means *i·*
375–21 * an almost *i·* resemblance,
Ret. 93–19 in substance *i·* with my own :
Un. 33– 2 which prove matter to be *i·*
33–13 not the Mind that is *i·* with Truth.
46–23 equally *i·* and self-conscious
No. 26– 1 believe that mortal man is *i·* with
26– 6 no more *i·* with C. S. than
26– 7 than the babe is *i·* with the adult,
'02. 16– 4 pointed out that *i·* phrase,
My. 78– 3 * six services, *i·* in character,
80–17 * introductory services were *i·*,
86–29 * At each of the *i·* services,

identification

Mis. 363– 7 its greatest flatterer, *i·*,
Un. 64–18 nor escape from *i·* with

identified

Mis. 375–29 * *i·* with the old masters,
Pul. 46–14 * *i·* with good and great names
My. 239–24 a kind of man who is *i·* by sex
323– 8 * so *i·* yourself with the truth

identifies

Mis. 14–32 *i·* himself with it,
My. 107–19 it *i·* this system with mind,
165–17 *i·* man with universal good.

identify

My. 119–19 could not *i·* Christ spiritually,

identities

Mis. 60–25 as many *i·* as mortal bodies ?

identity

Mis. 42– 4 nor does he lose his *i·*,
47–23 substantiates man's *i·*,
60–24 *connection between them and real i·*,
185–10 spiritual *i·* as the child of God,
205–17 man's *i·* or consciousness
362– 7 form, individuality, *i·*.
364–16 constituting and governing all *i·*,
Un. 34–23 so-called mind would have no *i·*.
46–14 In his *i·* there is no evil.
Pul. 23–13 * common *i·* of spiritual demand.

identity
No. 21–11 all phenomena, *i*·, individuality,
  25–22 is not man's eternal *i*·.
'01. 6– 3 and have no separate *i*·
My. 239–15 *and see their apparent i*·
  239–23 real and eternal in infinite *i*·.

idiocy
Mis. 107–25 this . . . mental state is moral *i*·.
  112–15 in extreme cases, moral *i*·.
  112–17 mental state called moral *i*·.
  113–23 insanity, dementia, or moral *i*·.
My. 249–10 Hate is a moral *i*·

idiot
Mis. 222–11 in other words, a moral *i*·.
  354– 4 moral *i*·, sanguine of success in

idle
Mis. 357– 2 no time for *i*· words,
Man. 81–23 No *i*· gossip, no slander,
Pul. 67– 6 * This is no *i*· word,
My. 74–23 * would be *i*· to attempt to

idleness
Mis. 206–12 *i*· is the foe of progress.
  230–17 They spend no time in sheer *i*·,
Man. 60–10 Amusement or *i*· is weariness.
'00. 8–16 mental *i*· or apathy is

idler
'00. 2–10 the *i*·, and the intermediate.
  2–16 *i*· earns little and is stingy ;

idlers
'00. 2–21 your *i*· are my busiest workers ;

idol (see also idol's)
Mis. 28–23 does not signify a graven *i*·,
'00. 3–10 One's *i*· is by no means his servant,

idolaters
Mis. 324–14 adulterers, fornicators, *i*· ;
Peo. 9–12 we shall not be *i*·,

idolatrous
Un. 31–11 *first i*· claim of sin is,
  38–17 This *i*· and false sense of life
'00. 13– 7 orgies of their *i*· feasts
Peo. 4–28 materialistic and *i*· theory
My. 151–30 discerned its *i*· tendencies,

idolatry
Mis. 45–27 This error of belief is *i*·,
  123– 6 it is the spirit of *i*·,
  174– 4 *i*·, having other gods ;
  196– 4 *I*·, the supposition of the
  307–22 *I*· is an easily-besetting sin
  340–11 This belief is a species of *i*·,
No. 20–20 common *i*· of man worship.
  35–17 because of the shocking human *i*·
'00. 3–25 sanctioned *i*·, — other gods.
  5– 4 leaves no opportunity for *i*·
  5–18 escape from *i*· of every kind,
  13–23 Æsculapius, *i*· and medicine.
Pan. 7–24 sequence of this error is *i*·
  8–16 *i*·, pantheism, and polytheism.
Peo. 4– 3 *I*· sprang from the belief
Po. 9– 2 Turned to his star of *i*·.
My. 151–29 was *i*· then and is *i*· now.
  152– 2 turned to another form of *i*·,
  220–16 I pray . . . for the end of *i*·
  248–18 No fatal circumstance of *i*·
  303–18 no *i*·, no human propaganda

idolizing
Mis. 123– 5 it is either *i*· something

idol's
My. 199– 1 Ye sit not in the *i*· temple.

idols
Mis. 307–24 keep yourselves from *i*·.'' — *I John* 5 : 21.
  394–13 No place for earth's *i*·,
Po. 45–17 No place for earth's *i*·,

ignoble
'02. 18–25 *i*· conduct of his disciples

ignorance
and charlatanism
Hea. 14–14 *i*· and charlatanism are miserable
and pride
Mis. 92–27 arrogant *i*· and pride,
  354–21 self-conceit, *i*·, and pride
and quackery
No. 19– 6 infidelity, *i*·, and quackery
and self-conceit
Mis. 78–17 *et cetera* of *i*· and self-conceit
and superstition
'02. 9–30 counteracts *i*· and superstition?
and vice
Mis. 81–28 the depths of *i*· and vice.
cave of
Mis. 370–8 tradition and the cave of *i*·.

ignorance
common
Mis. 365–28 held back by the common *i*·
No. 11–12 held back by the common *i*·
culpable
Mis. 115– 5 culpable *i*· of the workings
  283–17 mistaken kindness, a culpable *i*·,
fatal
Ret. 71–23 false convictions and a fatal *i*·.
helpless
Mis. 115–11 helpless *i*· of the community
his
Mis. 53–19 his *i*· of the meaning of the term
  367–30 His *i*· of that which is not,
No. 18–17 child, in his *i*·, may imagine
  44– 1 substantiates his *i*· of its
malice or
Mis. 353–12 through malice or *i*·.
manifested in
My. 245–14 manifested in *i*·, persecution,
man's
Ret. 61– 1 from mortal man's *i*·,
mortal
My. 162– 1 for mortal *i*· and need
mortals'
Mis. 108–16 would remove mortals' *i*·
of American society
Mis. 296– 6 Was it *i*· of American society
of Christian Science
'01. 21–17 a startling *i*· of C. S.,
My. 104–20 A person's *i*· of C. S.
  151– 4 sympathize with their *i*· of C. S. :
of Life
Un. 40–22 comes through our *i*· of Life,
of Science
Ret. 60–16 asks, in its *i*· of Science,
of self
My. 233–19 *I*· of self is the most stubborn
of sin
Un. 6–19 blindness to error and *i*· of sin.
of the cause
Mis. 66–29 *I*· of the cause of disease
or envy
Mis. 383– 8 preeminent over *i*· or envy,
or fanaticism
Mis. 48– 9 whether of *i*· or fanaticism,
present
No. 2–26 present *i*· in relation to C. S.
pride is
Mis. 2– 3 Pride is *i*· ;
sheer
No. 43–26 through the sheer *i*· of people,
spiritual
Mis. 298–10 spiritual *i*· and power of passion,
their
Mis. 171–26 their *i*· or false knowledge
My. 151– 4 sympathize with their *i*· of C. S. :
this
Un. 40–24 is the punishment of this *i*·.
torrents of
My. 316–20 the foaming torrents of *i*·,

Mis. 40–31 *i*· by which one unintentionally
  109–16 *I*· is only blest by reason of its
  109–18 *I*· was the first condition of sin in the
  293–19 brings greater torment than *i*·.
  374–12 *i*·, envy, and hatred
My. 108–20 *I*·, slang, and malice touch not

ignorant
Mis. 51– 8 the *i*·, the fraudulent, or the
  134– 1 and the sinful and *i*· who
  295–23 Nor is the world *i*· of the
  300– 8 it is an *i*· wrong.
  335–20 its supposed power, or *i*· of it.
  363–28 the *i*· man's dictionary,
  365– 8 and is *i*· thereof,
  367–15 to claim that He is *i*· of
Ret. 54–19 this same channel of *i*· belief.
  70– 3 *I*· of the origin and operations
  70– 4 that is, *i*· of itself,
  71– 7 an *i*· or an unprincipled mind-practice
  74– 3 He who does this is *i*· of the
Un. 49– 9 as *i*· of sin as is the perfect
No. 28– 8 Of his intermediate . . . I am *i*·.
Peo. 11–20 but *i*· of the law of belief,
My. 211– 4 they are too cowardly, too *i*·,
  224–22 to those *i*· of this Science
  305–12 * referred to as ''an *i*· woman
  309– 1 * characterizes as ''*i*·, dominating,
  313–11 various stories . . . I am *i*· of.

ignorantly
Mis. 87– 4 *i*· to caricature God's creation,
  261–10 whether intentionally or *i*· ;
Ret. 26–14 uninspired interpreters *i*· pronounce

ignorantly
No. 32–12 *i·* or maliciously misconstrued.
'02. 18– 6 mortals looked *i·*, as now,
Hea. 6–14 produces the manifestations *i·*
My. 146–28 do it *i·* or maliciously.
153–21 therefore ye *i·* worship." — *Acts* 17 : 23.

ignore
Pul. 79– 9 * not to *i·* a movement which,
Hea. 5–18 hypotheses *i·* Biblical authority,
My. 99–27 * *i·* them as we may

ignores
My. 153–19 *i·* the power of God,

Ill. (State)
(*see* **Bloomington, Chicago, Peoria**)

ill
Mis. 48– 2 avoid all that works *i·*.
190–23 evil, or whatever worketh *i·*.
225–14 was taken violently *i·*.
265–25 If others, . . . do *i·*,
389–17 No *i·*, — since God is good,
Ret. 61– 7 as when you awaken . . . and feel *i·*,
95– 9 * For heavy is the weight of *i·*
Un. 51–11 whose place is *i·* supplied by
Rud. 10–24 and make you *i·*, is an error
Po. 4–16 No *i·*, — since God is good,
25–19 Wreaths for the triumphs o'er *i·* !
My. 275–12 chapter sub-title
313–15 to help me when I was *i·*.
325– 4 * (he had been *i·*)
348–31 nothing that worketh *i·* can enter

ill-attuned
Mis. 287– 8 To an *i·* ear, discord is harmony ;

ill-concealed
Ret. 75– 2 *i·* question in mortal mind,

ill-done
Mis. 393– 9 Work *i·* within the misty Mine of
Po. 51–14 Work *i·* within the misty Mine of

illegal
Man. 46– 1 *I·* Adoption.

illegitimate
My. 167–28 marred by the *i·* claims of envy,

ill-humor
Mis. 313–14 without *i·* or hyperbolic tumor.

ill-humored
Mis. 116–27 never off guard, never *i·*,

illiberal
My. 167–30 day of heathenism, *i·* views,

illimitable
Pul. 4–24 Wait patiently on *i·* Love,
My. 41–30 * to understand how *i·* is the Love
107–28 nothing beyond *i·* divinity.

illness
Man. 49–25 without previous injury or *i·*,
Ret. 7– 3 after a short *i·*,
My. 307–29 might have caused my *i·*.
331–30 * during his late *i·*,
333–23 * attended him during his *i·*
335–11 * facts regarding . . . his *i·* and
335–23 * third day of her husband's *i·*,
336–16 * no will previous to his last *i·*,

illogical
'01. 3–27 therefore it is *i·* and
My. 111–10 swept away their *i·* syllogisms
225–24 by no *i·* conclusion,

ills
Mis. 22–15 of transmitting human *i·*,
33–27 * "the *i·* that flesh is heir to,"
37–18 Its antidote for all *i·* is God,
209–18 *i·* of indigestion tend to rebuke
334–27 remedies the *i·* of material beliefs.
Ret. 34–14 all the *i·* which befall mortals.
Un. 48–10 He heals all my *i·*,
Rud. 3– 3 to heal them of bodily *i·*,
10–12 Mortal *i·* are but errors of thought,
No. 42–10 * "the *i·* that flesh is heir to."
'01. 24– 7 the cause of all the *i·* of mortals
Hea. 15– 5 all *i·* that flesh is heir to.
My. 81–18 * debts of gratitude for *i·* cured,
99– 4 * above the suffering of petty *i·* ;
166–15 Life's *i·* are its chief recompense ;
268–21 solace the sore *i·* of mankind

ill-starred
Pul. 48–29 * hero who killed the *i·* Paugus.

ill-success
Rud. 14–23 *i·* of itself leaves them unprepared

illumed
Mis. 396–23 angel throng Of thoughts, *i·*
Pul. 18– 7 angel throng Of thoughts, *i·*
Po. 12– 7 angel throng Of thoughts, *i·*

illumes
Mis. 20– 1 *i·* our pathway with the radiance

illuminated
Mis. 75–26 It was evidently an *i·* sense
Ret. 23–16 character of the Christ was *i·*
Pul. 25–27 * *i·* texts from the Bible
My. 258– 6 seems *i·* for woman's hope

illuminates
Pul. 25–18 * seven-pointed star, which *i·* it.

illumination
Mis. 234–30 Christ is clad with a richer *i·*
290–17 * it produced a wonderful *i·*,
342–16 no spiritual *i·* to look upon him
Pul. 34–11 * became aware of a divine *i·*
Rud. 11–22 *i·* of spiritual understanding,
'00. 13– 9 their so-called prophetic *i·*.

illumine
Mis. 276–17 light will *i·* the darkness.
356– 3 *i·* its own atmosphere
Un. 41–16 can *i·* our present being
My. 187– 7 *i·* your faith and understanding,
197–17 *i·* the midnight of the latter,

illumined
Mis. 213–15 chastened and *i·* another's way
338– 9 Faith *i·* by works ;
Ret. 10–14 Learning was so *i·*,

illumines
Mis. 117–28 and He *i·* one's way
196–18 *i·* our present existence with
Po. 32–11 *i·* my spiritual eye,

illusion
and delusion
My. 5– 7 this *i·* and delusion of sense,
and error
Mis. 68–17 *i·* and error which Truth casts out.
declare an
Un. 25–14 this lie I declare an *i·*.
delusion and
Pan. 5–19 liar and lie, a delusion and *i·*.
effects of
My. 301–22 baneful effects of *i·* on mortal
evil is
'00. 10– 4 Evil is *i·*, that after a fight
growth of
Mis. 83– 8 "*Sickness is a growth of i·*,
its own
Mis. 259–27 must have produced its own *i·*,
mere
Ret. 32–14 * What is life? A mere *i·*,
mortal sense is
Mis. 24–22 gained from mortal sense is *i·*,
of matter
Mis. 28–19 he arose above the *i·* of matter.
of mortals
Mis. 50– 2 error is an *i·* of mortals ;
of sin
Ret. 62– 4 *i·* of sin, sickness, and death
of the senses
Mis. 368– 5 dispel this *i·* of the senses,
of time
Mis. 93–13 *i·* of time and mortality.
sick man's
Mis. 70– 4 cast out the sick man's *i·*,
termed sin
Ret. 64–20 in belief an *i·* termed sin,
that death
Un. 59–23 *i·* that death is as real as Life.
undisturbed in the
Ret. 23– 2 undisturbed in the *i·* that this
which calls
Un. 59–20 *i·* which calls sin real,
59–22 *i·* which calls sickness real,

Mis. 36–27 Mortal mind is an *i·* ;
70– 1 must have been an *i·*,
123– 3 Evil was, and is, the *i·* of
Ret. 64–27 in order that the *i·*, error,
Un. 34– 9 material sight is an *i·*, a lie.
'01. 13– 7 a lie from the beginning, — an *i·*,
14–14 We regard evil as a lie, an *i·*,
Hea. 10– 1 he saw it pass away, — an *i·*.

illusions
Mis. 8– 1 is given to material *i·*
24–31 all subtle falsities or *i·*,
68–10 * *maintained that* . . . *are not i·*
68–11 * *to believe they are i·*.
68–13 pain and sickness are . . . *i·*.
112– 5 look the *i·* in the face.
Ret. 64–22 classify sin, . . . and death as *i·*.
Un. 59–19 to rescue men from these very *i·*
Rud. 11–12 *i·* of the physical senses.
11–13 *i·* are not real, but unreal.

llusions
No. 23–21 not as realities, but as *i* ;
My. 278–20 civilization destroys such *i·*

illusive
Mis. 206–14 no emasculation, no *i·* vision,
Ret. 64–26 *i·* forms, methods, and subtlety of
Un. 8–13 That which is not so is *i·*
37–19 physical personality is *i·* and
No. 6– 1 If disease is real it is not *i·*,
Pan. 6– 6 *i·* claim that God is not supreme,
Hea. 19–10 The *i·* origin of disease is not

illustrate
Mis. 199–14 *i·* the life of Jesus
203–17 to rebuke the senses and *i·* C. S.
216–23 to *i·* the author's following point
218–27 What can *i·* Dr. ——'s views better
286–12 serve to *i·* the superiority of
286–23 *i·* mortal mind and body as *one*,
292–12 partly *i·* the divine energy
322–13 Life these give, the Truth they *i·*,
341–21 serves to *i·* the evil of inaction
373– 1 *i·* the simple nature of art.
Ret. 21–26 unless they *i·* the ethics of Truth.
No. 32–23 To *i·* : It seems a great evil to
'01. 3–24 last proposition does not *i·* the
My. 176– 7 *i·* the past by your present love.
221–11 and *i·* the Science of Mind.
308–19 To *i·* : One time when my father
349–18 *i·* "the way, the truth, — *John* 14: 6.

illustrated
Mis. 30–16 Way-shower *i·* Life unconfined,
33– 1 comments on my *i·* poem,
260– 1 *i·* by the life of Jesus,
346– 5 God is understood and *i·*.
371–27 An I· Poem
Man. 111–15 instructions *i·* in Form 1
Ret. 94–26 affection *i·* in Jesus' career,
'01. 19–10 he *i·* his saying by a parable.
Hea. 8–24 Jesus *i·* this by the parable of the
My. 40–26 * She has *i·* what the poet perceived
347–11 *i·* by Keats' touching couplet,

illustrates
Mis. 201–32 *i·* through the flesh the divine
337–11 Listen, and *he i·* the rule :
Man 47–16 *i·* the demonstration of Christ,
'02. 8– 2 *i·* God, and man as His likeness,
My. 179 22 *i·* the Principle and practice of a
230– 5 *i·* the digestion of spiritual nutriment
339–16 *i·* the joy, grace, and glory of

illustrating
Mis. 374–22 one *i·* my poem approximates it.

illustration
Mis. 375–20 * study each *i·* thoroughly,
Ret. 6– 5 a living *i·* of Christian faith,
No. 34–14 torture affords but a slight *i·* of
My. 107– 6 As a pertinent *i·* of the

illustrations
Mis. 33– 7 *i·* in "Christ and Christmas ; "
307–25 *i·* were not intended for a
309–27 My Christmas poem and its *i·*
371–28 This poem and its *i·*
372–16 * *i·* of your poem are truly
375– 9 *i·* of "Christ and Christmas" :
375–17 * impressed me in your *i·*

illustrative
Pul. 60–10 * with *i·* Scripture parallels,
My. 69– 8 * inscriptions *i·* of the faith of
311– 2 as *i·* of my disposition :

illustrious
'00. 12– 8 records Ephesus as an *i·* city,
Po. 27–24 I· year, farewell !
My. 85–21 * *i·* list for future generations to
294–26 religious energy of this *i·* pontiff

image
and likeness
Mis. 21–21 man is His *i·* and likeness.
23–23 man is His *i·* and likeness.
47–21 His *i·* and likeness, is spiritual,
61–21 man is the *i·* and likeness of God.
79–21 God's *i·* and likeness,
82–18 *i·* and likeness of infinite Life,
97–22 in the *i·* and likeness of God.
97–23 *i·* and likeness of Mind,
97–24 *i·* and likeness of Mind
97–27 *i·* and likeness of the infinite.
182–20 ever was the *i·* and likeness of God,
183–12 Man is God's *i·* and likeness ;
185–14 demonstrating the true *i·* and likeness.
186– 3 in His own *i·* and likeness.
186– 8 in the *i·* and likeness of God ;
235– 5 as *i·* and likeness, to reflect Him
308–30 in the *i·* and likeness of God.

image
and likeness
Mis. 330–17 in God's own *i·* and likeness,
368– 1 in his own *i·* and likeness.
Man. 15– 9 man in God's *i·* and likeness.
Ret. 59–24 made in His own *i·* and likeness ;
64– 8 "*i·* and likeness." — *see Gen.* 1 : 26.
67–20 was the *i·* and likeness of evil,
70–25 "*i·* and likeness," — *see Gen.* 1 : 26.
Un. 3–17 in the *i·* and likeness of good,
62– 6 forever His *i·* and likeness.
No. 17–11 God's *i·* and likeness can never
19–22 man is in His *i·* and likeness.
23–28 is God's own *i·* and likeness,
25–17 is the *i·* and likeness of God,
26–20 to be His *i·* and likeness ;
'00. 5–16 man in His *i·* and likeness,
'01. 5–21 man is His *i·* and likeness :
5–27 is His eternal *i·* and likeness.
7–10 in His own *i·* and likeness,
8–17 Then is man His *i·* and likeness,
'02. 6–21 the *i·* and likeness of divine Love.
Hea. 9–17 man, His own *i·* and likeness.
17– 5 present the *i·* and likeness of God.
Peo. 14–18 man in God's own *i·* and likeness,
My. 15–14 into His own *i·* and likeness.
36–24 * in the *i·* and likeness of God.
117–21 of man in His *i·* and likeness,
119– 6 His idea, *i·*, and likeness.
119–31 the true *i·* and likeness of God.
150–19 to become His own *i·* and likeness,
235–23 Man is but His *i·* and likeness.
239–16 *by His idea or i· and likeness*
239–20 *i·* and likeness of the infinite God,
244–16 in God's own *i·* and likeness,
261–15 man in His *i·* and likeness.
272–12 that is, God's *i·* and likeness ;
273–30 man in God's *i·* and likeness.
287 17 still rise to His *i·* and likeness,
319– 3 real man in His *i·* and likeness."
347– 4 man in the *i·* and likeness of the

child and
Un. 15–10 Man is God's child and *i·*.

express
Mis. 26–25 phrase, "express *i·*," — *Heb.* 1 : 3.

God's
Mis. 79–21 and never can be, God's *i·*
183–12 Man is God's *i·* and likeness ;
189–13 man as God's *i·*, or
Man. 15 0 man in God's *i·* and likeness.
Ret. 64– 8 even God's "*i·* and — *see Gen.* 1 : 20.
No. 17–11 God's *i·* and likeness can never
My. 5– 9 to reveal man as God's *i·*,
272–12 that is, God's *i·* and likeness ;
273–30 does not awaken man in God's *i·*

graven
Mis. 346–14 *i·* graven on wood or stone

His
Mis. 21–21 man is His *i·* and likeness.
23–23 man is His *i·* and likeness.
47–21 His *i·* and likeness, is spiritual,
Un. 62– 6 forever His *i·* and likeness.
Pul. 30–18 * man is made in His *i·*.
No. 19–22 man is in His *i·* and likeness.
26–20 to be His *i·* and likeness ;
'00. 5–16 man is His *i·* and likeness,
'01. 5–21 man is His *i·* and likeness :
8–17 Then is man His *i·* and likeness,
My. 117–21 man in His *i·* and likeness,
170–17 His *i·* and superscription.
235–23 Man is but His *i·* and likeness.
261–15 man in His *i·* and likeness.
287–17 rise to His *i·* and likeness,
319– 3 real man in His *i·* and likeness."

His own
My. 262– 1 perfect and eternal in His own *i·*.

is the reflection
My. 239–22 whose *i·* is the reflection of all

likeness and
Mis. 16–13 being His likeness and *i·*,

lost
Mis. 97–30 the lost *i·* is not this personality,
97–31 corporeal man is this lost *i·* ;
Pan. 11–25 obliterates the lost *i·* that

man in the
Mis. 294– 1 man in the *i·* of his Maker ;
308–30 man in the *i·* and likeness of God.
My. 347– 4 man in the *i·* and likeness of

man is the
Mis. 61–21 man is the *i·* and likeness of God.
No. 25–17 Man is the *i·* and likeness of God,
My. 262– 2 Hence man is the *i·*, idea, or

marred
Un. 15–11 is incomplete, the *i·* marred.

Mind's
Un. 14–24 reflected in man, Mind's *i·*.

image

molten
Peo. 2–23 no longer . . . a molten *i*·,
no inverted
No. 17–18 therein is no inverted *i*· of God,
of God
  (*see* **God**)
of Him
Pan. 11– 6 after the *i*· of Him that — *Col.* 3 : 10.
of his Maker
Mis. 98– 5 which is the *i*· of his Maker.
  294– 1 man in the *i*· of his Maker ;
of Spirit
Rud. 5– 8 made in the *i*· of Spirit, or God.
'01. 8–20 The reflex *i*· of Spirit is not unlike
of their Father
Mis. 278–18 reflect the *i*· of their Father.
of the soul
Po. 23– 8 An *i*· of the soul,
opposite
Mis. 62– 3 opposite *i*· of man, a sinner,
or likeness
My. 239–17 His idea, *i*·, or likeness,
  269– 2 *i*· or likeness, called man,
our
Mis. 69–11 make man in our *i*·, — *Gen.* 1 : 26.
spiritual
Rud. 13– 9 divine and spiritual *i*· of God.

Mis. 15–24 the *i*· of the infinite good

imagery
Mis. 142–20 *i*· of thought gave place to
Pan. 2–26 Pan in *i*· is preferable to

images
Mis. 96–29 not the transference of human *i*·
  335– 2 shall you turn . . . to graven *i*·?
Ret. 79– 6 false *i*· are effaced from
Un. 34– 5 it sees only material *i*·,
Peo. 10–22 the *i*· that thought reflects
My. 109–21 reflex *i*· of this divine Life,

imaginary
Mis. 65– 5 and her motions *i*·.
  129– 8 an *i*· or an actual wrong,
  268– 6 *i*· victories of rivalry
Un. 38–13 another power, an *i*· life,
  45–20 *i*· sphere of its own creation
Hea. 13–19 we resigned the *i*· medicine
Peo. 12– 8 *i*· laws of matter
My. 106–12 limited to *i*· diseases !
  118– 5 any *i*· benefit they receive

imagination
Mis. xi–17 be found to surpass *i*·,
  86–10 *exist only in i*·?
  86–24 It is more than *i*·.
  203–13 served the *i*· for centuries.
Ret. 70–12 chimerical wings to his *i*·,
Pul. 32–11 * fascinated the *i*·.
No. 4– 6 Disease is more than *i*·;
  20– 4 human reason, *i*·, and
My. 29–22 * appealed to and fired the *i*·.
  206– 8 Schisms, *i*·, and human beliefs

imaginations
Mis. 139–12 *casting down i*·, — *II Cor.* 10 : 5.

imagine
Mis. 87–30 *i*· they can help anybody
  280–14 we *i*· all is well if
Pul. 2–16 *I*· yourselves in a poorly
No. 18–17 may *i*· the face of Dante
My. 26–11 *i*· my gratitude and emotion
  103–16 *i*· a vain thing?" — *Psal.* 2 : 1.
  200– 5 *i*· a vain thing;" — *Psal.* 2 : 1.
  270–14 rage and *i*· a vain thing.

imagined
My. 303–10 and not *i*· to be unscientific

imagining
My. 59–32 * marvellous beyond all *i*·

imbecile
'01. 16–10 hatred gone mad becomes *i*·

imbedded
Pul. 63–25 * a tablet *i*· in its wall

imbibe
Mis. 303–18 *i*· the spirit of Christ's
My. 239– 8 *i*· the spirit and prove the

imbued
Mis. 4– 1 Thought *i*· with purity,
  194–24 and become *i*· with divine Love
  260–28 Mind, *i*· with this Science
Ret. 47–16 richly *i*· with the spirit of Christ,
Rud. 9–24 should be *i*· with a clear conviction
'01. 30– 8 consciousness which is most *i*·
Hea. 11–26 requires mind *i*· with Truth

imbued
Peo. 12–15 when *i*· with the spirit
My. 87–26 * it is certainly *i*· with the
  153–13 *i*· and associated with no int.

imitate
Un. 16– 2 which he is bidden to *i*·.
My. 310–28 for her other children to *i*·,

imitative
Mis. 106–31 organ, in *i*· tones

immaculate
Mis. 337– 9 *i*· Son of the Blessed
'01. 8–26 Jesus, the only *i*·, was born of
'02. 18– 5 the pure sense of the *i*· Jesus

immanent
Ret. 35–21 claim too *i*· to fall to the

Immanuel
Mis. 103–27 individuality that reflected the *I*·,
  374– 1 was so great a proof of *I*·

immaterial
No. 12–26 *i*·, though still individual.

immature
Mis. 87– 6 our *i*· sense of spiritual things,
  263–25 hampered by *i*· demonstrations,

immeasurable
Mis. 369– 8 surveying the *i*· universe of Mind,
No. 24– 1 *i*· idea of divine Mind.
Hea. 16–12 *i*· Life and Love will occupy your

immeasurably
Ret. 31– 6 *i*· paramount to rubric and dogma

immediate
Mis. 24– 8 it wrought my *i*· recovery from
  29– 5 only to his *i*· disciples.
  44– 7 *necessity for i*· relief,
  146–16 will give them *i*· attention,
  148–15 *i*· demand for them as a help
  257–16 and lead to *i*· or ultimate death.
  380–19 save the *i*· recovery of the sick,
Man. 3–12 *i*· demand for them as a help
  51–18 provides for *i*· action.
  78–19 Church bills of *i*· necessity
Ret. 24–12 My *i*· recovery from the effects of
  91–16 spake primarily to his *i*· disciples.
My. 113– 8 follower but not an *i*· disciple
  224–13 Avoid for the *i*· present
  343–12 * Mrs. Eddy's *i*· successor

immediately
Mis. 134– 4 an act which you have *i*· repeated,
  215–21 would fall *i*· if he knew where he
  379– 5 He *i*· presented them.
Man. 28–19 shall *i*· call a meeting
  52–17 the Clerk . . . shall *i*· so inform him.
  53– 4 duty of the Board of Directors *i*· to
  54–22 said member shall *i*· be disciplined,
  68– 1 shall *i*· notify a person who
  69–16 the Board shall *i*· appoint a proper
  69–17 the appointee shall go *i*·
  89– 5 a meeting of . . . shall *i*· be called,
  98– 9 Committee shall *i*· apply for aid to
  100–14 duty of the Directors *i*· to act
Ret. 44–27 was *i*· followed by a great revival of
  52–14 This was *i*· done,
Rud. 15– 4 to *i*· enter upon its practice.
'01. 19– 9 and if not *i*·, continue to ask,
My. 8–15 * something done, and done *i*·,
  22–28 * to get *i*· into the proper
  81– 1 * *i*· struck with the air of
  105–24 On seeing her *i*· restored by
  105–27 he urged me *i*· to write a book
  152– 1 *i*· turned to another form of
  340–17 courts *i*· annulling such bills
  360– 2 Answer this letter *i*·.

immense
Mis. 98–21 This purpose is *i*·,
  223–25 There is *i*· wisdom in the
Un. 43–10 time and *i*· spiritual growth.
Pul. 63– 5 * SHE HAS AN *I*· FOLLOWING
My. 28–15 * has been of *i*· value to them.
  61–30 * in such an *i*· undertaking,
  91– 1 * *i*· membership of the body

immersion
Mis. 205–13 *i*· of human consciousness

imminent
Mis. 113–10 Revelator's vision, . . . is *i*·.
My. 223–27 The hour is *i*·.
  266– 3 *i*· dangers confronting

immobility
No. 10–21 feasibility and *i*· of C. S.

immoral
Mis. 257– 8 a moral or an *i*· force.
  257–11 *i*· force of erring mortal mind,

al dose

...y College for *i*,
... to all *i*,
...g, and *i*·, which,

...d mortal are . . . opposites

...–18   heightens *i*· attributes

Hea. 1– 9   builds on less than an *i*· basis,
being
  Mis. 213– 1   could not behold his *i*· being
  Un. 57–26   forward the birth of *i*· being ;
  No. 27–28   the definition of *i*· being ;
  '02. 16–20   man's *i*· being.
courage
  My. 191–24   *I*· courage fills the human breast
cravings
  Mis. 287–13   can satisfy *i*· cravings.
  My. 189–20   satisfies the *i*· cravings
demands
  Mis. 201– 2   the *i*· demands of Truth.
facts
  Mis. 14– 4   take in only the *i*· facts
fruition
  My. 19–21   *i*· fruition of her unselfed love,
fruits
  My. 182–14   *i*· fruits through God's blessing
good
  Mis. 82–29   Immortal Mind is God, *i*· good ;
goodness is
  Mis. 70–17   too good to die ; for goodness is *i*·.
harmonious and
  Mis. 308– 3   be found harmonious and *i*·.
harmony
  Mis. 97– 4   *i*· harmony,— the grand verities of
hour
  My. 257–19   At this *i*· hour, all human hate,
idea
  My. 241–20   * *i*· idea of the one divine Mind.
immutable and
  Mis. 79–19   in Science are immutable and *i*·.
lexicographer
  Mis. 226–13   Shakespeare, the *i*· lexicographer
Life
  Mis. 56–12   direct opposite of *i*· Life,
life
  Mis. 170– 2   resurrection and life *i*·
  Pul. 23–24   * intimations of man's *i*· life.
Love
  Mis. 292–18   unlike the risen, *i*· Love ;
man
  (*see* **man**)
man is
  Mis. 34–22   Man is *i*·,
    61–25   A mortal ; but man is *i*·.
    89–24   Man is *i*·.
Mind
  (*see* **Mind**)
Mind is
  (*see* **Mind**)
mode
  No. 25–16   an *i*· mode of the divine Mind.
model
  My. 261–14   in unfolding the *i*· model,
modes
  Mis. 363–11   *i*· modes of Mind are spiritual,
parapets
  Mis. 383–11   the *i*· parapets of this Science.
part
  No. 29–14   the *i*· part of man a sinner?
power
  Po. 31–17   solemn splendor of *i*· power,
Principle
  Mis. 117– 2   Life that unfolds its *i*· Principle.
saying
  Mis. 76– 7   but this *i*· saying can never
Science
  Mis. 73– 7   testimony of *i*· Science
sense
  Mis. 74–15   *i*· sense of the ideal world.
  Un. 52–13   Christ's *i*· sense of Truth,
Soul
  Un. 51– 4   false . . . that *i*· Soul is sinful,
  No. 11– 3   Man has an *i*· Soul,
    29– 4   Immortal man has *i*· Soul
Soul is
  '01. 13–26   Soul is *i*·, but sin is mortal.
  My. 273–25   body is mortal, but Soul is *i*· ;
souls
  Mis. 76–12   belief . . . they contain *i*· souls !

immortal
Spirit, and
  Mis. 201–15   which is of Spirit, and *i*·.
status
  Un. 39–21   declare the *i*· status of man,
strains
  Mis. 345– 5   in *i*· strains of eloquence.
superstructure
  Hea. 11– 9   The only *i*· superstructure
teaching
  Ret. 91–22   his *i*· teaching was the bread of
Truth
  Mis. 21–18   Spirit is *i*· Truth ;
  Ret. 94–16   *i*· Truth be found true,
  No. 40– 6   sense of spiritual and *i*· Truth.
  Po. 70–17   *I*· Truth, — since heaven rang,
truths
  My. vii– 8   * *i*· truths testified to by Jesus
    203–25   buried *i*· truths in the bosom of
words
  Mis. 100– 2   *i*· words were articulated
  My. 146–16   his *i*· words and my poor prophecy,
    277–19   *i*· words and deeds of men
work
  Mis. 237–27   *i*· work, of loosing the fetters

  Mis. 2–28   and into good that is *i*· ;
    24–21   Mind and man are *i*· ;
    36– 5   or the Mind which is *i*·.''
    42–25   good, not evil, lives and is *i*·,
    65–14   God's universe and man are *i*·.
    72–28   Mind is not mortal, it is *i*·.
    76–14   to escape and be *i*·.
    79–21   ideal of *i*· man's divine Principle.
    111–20   prove its power to be *i*·.
    186–27   *i*· and true sense of being.
    190– 7   the mortal evolves not the *i*·,
    257– 9   force of *i*· and divine Mind.
    325– 8   few cravings for the *i*·,
  Ret. 59–20   as harmonious, *i*·, and spiritual :
    59–23   Science defines man as *i*·,
  Un. 30–18   man as *i*· instead of mortal
    37–18   physically mortal, but spiritually *i*·.
    37–20   spiritual individuality is *i*·.
    42–13   Man, . . . is as perfect and *i*· now,
    42–27   mortal does not develop the *i*·,
    52– 1   Hence Soul is sinless and *i*·,
    52– 3   supposition that . . . . *i*· sinners.
    53–24   *i*· and unerring Mind, God,
    61– 6   to *i*· and spiritual vision he
  Pul. 10–23   your plant is *i*·.
  No. 26– 2   believe . . . that the *i*· is inside
  My. 178–28   contents of "S. and H. . . . remain *i*·.
    179–11   mind and matter, mortal and *i*·,
    194– 6   but the spirit of it is *i*·.
    242– 4   declare yourself to be *i*·
    269–30   Truth is *i*·.

immortality (*see also* **immortality's**)
against
  Ret. 67–11   the mortal against *i*·,
and harmony
  Mis. 85–28   *i*· and harmony of Soul.
certainty of
  My. 295– 5   safe in the certainty of *i*·.
clad in
  My. 191–18   come forth . . . clad in *i*·.
concept of
  Un. 41– 2   a feeble concept of *i*·.
cravings for
  Mis. 16– 2   satisfy more the cravings for *i*·,
exists
  Mis. 42–25   that *i*· exists only in
glad
  Po. 70– 5   Like to the soul's glad *i*·,
glory of
  Peo. 9– 9   is the true glory of *i*·.
harmony and
  Un. 22– 4   in a sense of harmony and *i*·,
  Peo. 10– 1   man's harmony and *i*·.
health and
  My. 182–23   giving grace, health, and *i*·
his
  Mis. 2–22   the necessity of his *i*· ;
    47–24   his *i*· and preexistence,
holiness and
  (*see* **holiness**)
Life and
  Un. 38–20   brings to light Life and *i*·.
life and
  My. 207–14   * life and *i*· brought to light.
majesty, and
  Mis. 185–16   might, majesty, and *i*·.
manifests
  Un. 38– 2   which manifests *i*·,

immortality
of his words
Mis. 99–20 his faith in the *i·* of his words.
120–30 *i·* of his words and works.
of his works
My. 246–27 and the *i·* of his works
of man
Mis. 172–27 health, holiness, and *i·* of man.
My. 226–19 evidence of the *i·* of man
of Mind
Mis. 218–10 *i·* of Mind and its ideas.
of Truth
Mis. 163–17 faith in the *i·* of Truth.
proof of
Mis. 186–22 affords self-evident proof of *i·* ;
reason and
Mis. 218–17 comes to the rescue of reason and *i·*,
substance, and
Un. 60–23 space, substance, and *i·*
time, and
'00. 1– 6 filling all space, time, and *i·*
to demonstrate
Ret. 88–15 its power to demonstrate *i·*.
understand
Un. 3– 3 not ready to understand *i·*.

Mis. 364–15 all time, space, *i·*,
380– 6 universe, time, space, *i·*,
Ret. 58– 9 and brought to light *i·*,
Un. 29–27 and my God [my Soul, *i·*]." — *Psal.* 42 : 11.
No. 21– 9 all time, space, *i·*, thought,
'01. 2– 2 demonstrated— health, holiness, *i·*.
Hea. 18– 5 and *i·* be brought to light.
Peo. 8–23 to light our sepulchres with *i·*.
My. 110–26 *i·* will have been brought to light.
119–24 evidence of Soul, *i·*, eternal Life
154–22 * he have light, ... freedom, *i·* ?"
205–28 Hence health, holiness, *i·*,
349– 4 health, holiness, *i·*

immortality's
Un 58–14 sublime triumph . . . was *i·* goal.
My. 275–25 is *i·* self.

immortalized
Mis. 131–31 last year's records *i·*,

immortelles
Pul. 42–22 * with a centre of white *i·*,
Peo. 14– 9 * are wreaths of *i·*,

immovable
Ret. 89– 1 eternal stillness and *i·* Love.

immovably
Ret. 93–12 *i·* fixed in Principle.

immunity
Mis. 298–28 than *i·* from evil.
320–15 the sweet *i·* these bring

immutable
Mis. 71–30 *i·* and just law of Science,
72–11 The *i·* Word saith,
79–18 cause and effect in Science are *i·*
118–15 this *i·* decree of Love :
172–26 on the side of *i·* right,
Ret. 56–15 of Spirit in *i·* harmony.
Un. 29–13 absolutely *i·* and eternal,
51– 2 the reflection of *i·* good.
No. 4–21 of the *i·* laws of God ;
10–28 *i·* and eternal laws of God ;
26–23 *i·* harmony of divine law.
My. 106– 9 *i·* laws of omnipotent Mind

impanelled
Pul. 25–29 * illuminated texts . . . . *i·*.

impart
Mis. 72– 9 God is supposed to *i·* to man
292–11 Could I *i·* to the student
293– 9 should *i·* to his students
Ret. 48–19 to *i·* a thorough understanding of
72– 1 cannot *i·* a mental influence that
Pul. 14–23 ready for the blessing you *i·*
No. 12–11 duty for her to *i·* to others
Peo. 1–12 *i·* grandeur to the intellectual
Po. 23– 3 A look that years *i·* ?
My. 165–20 *i·* truth, health, and happiness,
244–11 designed to *i·* a fresh impulse

impartation
Ret. 48–28 scientific *i·* of Truth,
50– 3 an *i·* of a knowledge of
'01. 8–12 not God, but an *i·* of Him.

imparted
My. 238–12 has *i·* little power to practise

impartial
Mis. 77–19 *i·*, and unquenchable Love.
285–12 *i·* and impersonal in its tenor
Un. 7– 3 in the *i·* grace of God,
Pul. 21– 4 unambitious, *i·*, universal,

impartial
Po. 77– 8 *i·*, blessings spreadst abroad,
My. 218–27 Such labor is *i·*,
230– 9 This church is *i·*.
265–21 divine Love, *i·* and universal,

impartially
Pul. 8– 3 spoken out historically, *i·*.
My. 357–20 open the way, widely and *i·*,

imparting
Mis. 3– 6 *i·* the only power to heal
12–31 *i·*, so far as we reflect them,
372–30 *i·* to humanity the true sense of
Ret. 93–14 and *i·* divine Truth,
Pul. 58– 3 * *i·* this faith to her fellow-beings.

imparts
Mis. 3–21 and *i·* these states to the body ;
38– 3 When teaching *i·* the ability to
74– 6 *i·* a new apprehension of the
No. 46– 8 life-giving understanding C. S. *i·*,
'00. 8– 4 The good man *i·* . . . goodness ;

impassioned
Pul. 32– 4 * she was magnetic, earnest, *i·*.

impatient
Mis. 265–30 If *i·* of the loving rebuke,
No. 1–10 So men, . . . are sometimes *i·* ;
Hea. 19–21 he is *i·* perhaps, or doubts the
My. 203–29 will not be *i·* if you have

impecunious
Rud. 14–22 If the Primary students are still *i·*,

impede
Mis. 115–27 whatever tends to *i·* progress.
Man. 44–25 *i·* their progress in C. S.

impedes
Mis. 308–25 *i·* spiritual growth ;

impediment
Mis. 47–16 accompanies thought with less *i·*
256–16 the old *i·*, lack of time,

impel
Man. 40– 6 *i·* the motives or acts of the

impelled
Mis. 148–12 *i·* by a power not one's own,
380–11 call for help *i·* me to begin this
Man. 3– 9 *i·* by a power not one's own,
Ret. 31– 9 From my very childhood I was *i·*,
50– 1 When God *i·* me to set a price on my
My. 24– 1 * those who pass by are *i·* to ask,

impels
Mis. 80–19 promotes and *i·* all true reform ;
358– 1 Love *i·* good works.
No. 12–20 *i·* a spiritualization of thought
My. 9– 7 * *i·* the Christian to turn
211–15 it *i·* mortal mind into error of
224–12 forward footsteps it *i·*
308– 9 *i·* the impulse of Soul.

impending
Un. 57– 6 it foresees the *i·* doom

impenetrable
Mis. 204– 2 dark, *i·* cloud of error ;

imperative
Mis. 91–13 It is *i·*, at all times
273–32 *i·* call is for my exclusive teaching.
288– 6 Positive and *i·* thoughts
316–18 *I·*, accumulative, sweet demands
380–11 *i·* call for help impelled me
Un. 40–10 *i·* in the divine order
My. 134–12 *i·* demand not yet met.
235– 7 *i·* rules of Science,
245– 4 demand for this . . . . is *i·*,
264–18 the Decalogue more *i·*,
268– 5 *i·* nature of the marriage relation
291– 2 *I·*, accumulative, holy demands
308– 8 higher, nobler, more *i·*

imperatively
Mis. 277– 5 more *i·* than ever.
Pul. 20–16 *i·* propelling the greatest moral,

imperfect
Mis. 85–19 infantile and more or less *i·*.
86– 1 material and physical are *i·*.
353– 8 human concept is always *i·* ;
363–16 to make himself *i·*,
Ret. 21–22 The awakening . . . . is as yet *i·* ;
Rud. 9– 7 The pupil's *i·* knowledge
16– 8 an *i·* sense of the spiritual
My. 11– 2 * as yet but *i·* followers of the
103– 1 In the midst of the *i·*,

imperfection
Mis. 14– 9 into the *i·* that requires
79–11 by no means the medium of *i·*.
101–20 on mortality, on *i·* ;
320–13 dawning upon human *i·*,

imperfection
Mis. 363–17 God is not chargeable with i·.
Un. 4–11 destroys our sense of i·,
40–15 by believing in i· and
No. 7–13 every i· in the land of Sodom,
20– 3 nor discerned through i· ;
'00. 6– 1 There is no i·, no lack
My. 41–17 * with evil, sin, wrong, or i·,

imperfectly
Un. 40–15 believing in . . . and living i·.

imperial
Mis. 330–29 crown i· unveils its regal splendor
My. 290– 5 Queen's royal and i· honors

imperialism
My. 129– 4 i·, monopoly, and a lax system

imperious
Mis. 177– 1 a more solemn and i· call

imperishable
Pul. 10–12 rights of conscience, i· glory.
My. 122– 5 That glory only is i· which

impersonal
Mis. 161–17 personal and the i· Jesus.
166– 8 i· infancy, manhood, and
178–31 new, living, i· Christ-thought
180–10 Truth . . . the i· Saviour."
190–22 i· evil, or whatever worketh ill.
285–12 i· in its tenor and tenets.
310– 5 Christ, or the i· form of Truth,
322–10 dual and i· pastor, the Bible,
Ret. 76–26 sees each mortal in an i· depict.
Peo. 13– 6 i· Life, Truth, and Love,
My. 139–21 the personal to the i·,
256–14 i· presents, pleasures, achievements,

impersonality
My. 117–20 great truth of God's i·

impersonalize
Mis. 310–17 i· scientifically the material sense

impersonated
Ret. 93–10 no longer i· as a waif

impertinent
Man. 48– 9 uncharitable or i· towards religion,

impervious
My. 210– 8 Good thoughts are an i· armor ;

impetuosity
Mis. 359–19 Peter's i· was rebuked.

impetus
Mis. 245–11 giving it new i· and energy ;
Pul. vii–16 i· thereby given to Christianity;
My. 2–16 persuasive animus, an unerring i·,
205–16 their philosophical i·,
230–29 Its i·, accelerated by
248–21 for lack of the divine i·.
252–28 the i· comes from above
283– 9 leading i· of my life.

impious
Mis. 122–17 Such an inference were i·.
My. 160– 3 laws which it were i· to transgress,

implanted
Peo. 3–24 i· in our religions

implements
Pul. 51–18 * i· of theological warfare,

implication
My. 12– 2 * carried the i· that work should be

implicit
Mis. 105– 1 i· faith engendered by C. S.,
341–20 i· treason to divine decree.
Ret. 87–12 demands i· adherence to fixed rules,
My. 46–24 * more i· obedience to the sacred
137–27 i· confidence in each one of them

implicitly
Mis. 120– 4 they must obey i·
My. 284–25 believe i· in the full efficacy of

implied
Mis. 298–17 i· that the period demanded it.
'02. 9–14 condition i· by the great Master,
My. 88–29 * i· in the building of a great

implies
Mis. 56–29 Your question i· that Spirit,
193–32 Hebrew of which i· understanding.
367–13 i· the necessity of knowing evil,
Ret. 88–11 It i· such an elevation of
Un. 27– 7 Egotism i· vanity and self-conceit.
41–28 i· perpetual disagreement with
45–14 conscious matter i· pantheism.
50– 1 i· the possibility of its
Pan. 7–23 intelligence and law, which i· Mind,
12–25 includes all that the term i·,
Hea. 8– 1 it i· no necessity beyond the

implies
My. 233–31 i· that one is not thinking of
300–28 If, as he i·, C. S. is

implorations
My. 340–28 their i· for peace and plenty

implore
Mis. 141–19 Do not, I i· you,

imploring
No. 39– 3 silent intercession and unvoiced i·
Pan. 14– 7 if daily adoring, i·, and living
My. 314–23 i· him not to do it.

imply
Mis. 45–25 what the Scriptures i· Him to be,
49–28 as the Scriptures i· Him to be,
72–21 i· that Spirit takes note of matter
Rud. 5– 4 If, as the Scriptures i·,
Pan. 8– 7 Does not the belief . . . i· two Gods,
9– 6 in spiritualism they i· men and
My. 40– 8 * i· the subsidence of criticism
40– 9 * It may even i· that some who
222–24 rather does it i· that religion

import
Mis. 38–24 for questions of practical i·.
106–22 long been a question of earnest i·,
146–15 These are matters of grave i· ;
162– 4 wonderful spiritual i· to mankind !
197– 6 full i· . . . is not yet recognized.
275–13 words of strange i·.
280–28 topic of great i· to the student of
317–21 on subjects of such earnest i·.
No. v– 6 the i· of this edition is,
'00. 12– 3 the spiritual i· whereof
14–11 divine i· of the Revelator's vision
'01. 25–12 because of their more spiritual i·
My. 46–27 * Church Manual in its spiritual i·,
208– 5 whole i· of C. S.
270– 4 magnitude of their spiritual i·,

importance
Mis. 98– 1 making this . . . of any i·,
192– 6 It is of infinite i· to man's
Hea. 10–15 gather the i· of this saying,
16–25 it is of the utmost i· that we
My. 10–24 * they recognize the i· of
93–21 * attaching meanwhile no i· to
160– 9 It is of less i· that we receive
224– 1 understand the i· of that demand
236–28 i· at this stage of the workings
271– 8 of comparatively little i·
282–23 It is of paramount i·

important
Mis. 4–14 questions i· to be disposed of
35–21 Only because both are i·,
65–19 and this i· fact must be,
76–19 on other topics less i·.
92– 1 To omit these i· points is
92–18 i· to point out the lesson
157–10 all questions i· for your case,
170–20 no more i· to our well-being
232–20 most i· of all arts, — healing.
233– 3 i· to know that a malpractice
272–13 * with the following i· restrictions :
287–22 i· questions concerning their
Man. 47–14 Testimony . . . is highly i·.
78 11 Also i· movements of the manager
100–14 to act upon this i· matter
110– 5 It is i· that these seemingly
Ret. 6–27 Among other i· bills
37– 1 edition of my most i· work,
83–25 It is also highly i·
Un. 1– 8 reason together on this i·
22–17 be i· to our knowledge.
Pul. 4–12 that one is as i· a factor
No. 23–16 Which of the two is the more i·
Hea. 7–24 i· to progress and Christianity.
My. 20–27 * i· that the building fund
45 8 * most i· gatherings
53– 1 * i· missives of inquiry
91–31 * congregations in every i· town
142–13 most i· events are criticized.
170– 7 the i· sentiments uttered
216–30 Contemplating these i· wants,
231–20 i· demands on her time
241– 2 * to perform this i· work.
241–14 * issue raised is an i· one
243–11 i·, responsible offices,
249–25 perform this i· function.
289– 1 The thing most i· is
319–27 * an i· one in my experience,
355–10 i· factors in our field

imported
Mis. 88–24 * i· ice was miraculous to

importunate
Peo. 9–22 a desire, fervent, i· :

importunately
    Mis. 127–10 mentally, meekly, and *i*·.
    My. 18– 7 mentally, meekly, and *i*·.
importunity
    My. 10–21 * as the result of *i*·
impose
    Mis. 148–12 one person might *i*· on another.
    Man. 3– 8 one person might *i*· on another.
imposed
    Mis. 351– 3 burdens *i*· by students.
imposes
    Mis. 256–11 *i*· on me the severe task
imposing
    Mis. 143–15 with quiet, *i*· ceremony,
    My. 68–24 * *i*· effect of the interior.
    70– 2 * it certainly looks *i*·.
    71–16 * one of the most *i*· church edifices
    77–29 * to build the *i*· edifice
    78– 5 * *i*· structure of gray stone
imposition
    Mis. 366–17 *i*· in the field of medicine
impositions
    Man. 97–17 *i*· on the public in regard to
impossibility
    Mis. 22–15 the *i*· of transmitting
    43–26 *i*· for those unacquainted
    60–17 reveals the *i*· of two
    95–15 *i*· of intercommunion between
    182– 2 *i*· of putting him to death,
    380–24 Experience, . . . taught me the *i*·
    Un. 64– 8 To build the . . . is a moral *i*·
    Rud. 5–17 Matter without Mind is a moral *i*·.
    Hea.· 6–11 I saw the *i*·, in Science,
    My. 179–12 Science shows to be an *i*·.
impossible
    Mis. 24–24 knowledge of both good and . . . is *i*·.
    33–15 has not proved *i*· to heal those who,
    48–25 Such an occurrence would be *i*·,
    59–22 copartnership with that Mind is *i*· ;
    75–10 or it is *i*· to demonstrate the
    191–27 which would be *i*· if he were
    195–28 abstractions, impractical and *i*·
    237–12 how *i*· it is to sin and not suffer.
    261–26 *i*· to be a Christian Scientist without
    288–19 before it is understood is *i*·,
    364–25 *i*· partnership is dissolved.
    375–31 * *i*· of reproduction.
    Ret. 40–16 that it was *i*· for her to
    Un. 18–26 aught beside Myself is *i*·.
    Pul. 45– 8 * seems *i*· to mortal senses.
    Rud. 13– 5 renders it *i*· to demonstrate the
    15–21 *i*· to teach thorough C. S. to
    No. 17– 8 it is *i*· for the true man
    17–13 for man to be more . . . is *i*·.
    22–22 is not stated, and is *i*·.
    26– 8 Hence it is *i*· for those
    36– 3 for that would be *i*·.
    40– 5 they expect also what is *i*·,
    '01. 11–16 that does not make it *i*· for
    24– 1 * is an *i*· and unreal concept."
    '02 6– 1 *i*· to have aught unlike the infinite.
    6–14 an untrue consciousness, an *i*·
    Hea. 16–24 those senses through which it is *i*· to
    My. 61– 7 * seemed *i*· for the building to be
    81–29 * *i*· to convey a conception of
    106–14 *i*· for the surgeon or *materia medica*
    118–22 *i*· in the Science of God
    119– 2 *i*· in Science to believe this,
    178–17 But this is *i*· in reality,
    212–20 *i*· under other conditions,
    235– 3 as *i*· as to define truth
    344– 2 to my understanding . . . that is *i*·.
impostors
    Mis. 365–30 *i*· that come in its name.
    Rud. 16–12 some *i*· are committing this error.
impotence
    Mis. 121–10 namely, the *i*· of evil,
impotent
    Mis. 3–26 hygiene, and animal magnetism are *i*· ;
    90– 2 hence, that sin is *i*·.
    119–10 Evil is *i*· to turn the righteous
    134–22 nostrums, and knives, are *i*·
    252–11 evil thoughts are *i*·,
    No. 15–17 presuppose an *i*· God
    Hea. 10–10 therefore evil is *i*·.
impracticable
    Mis. 263–21 *i*· without a full knowledge of
    Rud. 15–10 systematic thinking is *i*· until
    '01. 6–20 regarded as *i*· for human use,
    My. 128–23 without . . . the latter were *i*·.

impractical
    Mis. 195–27 *i*· and impossible to us ;
    311–13 *i*·, unfruitful, Soul-less.
    Pul. 52– 6 * "*i*" Christian Scientists.
    '02. 4–27 liable to turn from them as *i*·,
    My. 58– 2 * *i*· Christian Scientists."
impregnable
    Mis. 10–10 furnished them defenses *i*·.
    103– 4 far more *i*· and solid than matter ;
impregnated
    Rud. 8–26 mortal mind should not be falsely *i*·.
impress
    Mis. 207– 4 *i*· humanity with the genuine
    Peo. 7– 3 and leaving the *i*· of mind
    My. 84–21 * *i*· even the man who cannot
    98– 1 * *i*· the most determined skeptic.
impressed
    Mis. 274– 3 This point, however, had not *i*· me
    313–15 *i*· by the articles entitled
    375–17 * "The first thing that *i*· me
    Ret. 54–24 *i*· with the true sense of
    Pul. 29–11 * earnestness *i*· the observer.
    31–25 * *i*· me as singularly graceful
    50–16 * has *i*· itself upon a
    My. 6–15 Greatly *i*· and encouraged thereby,
    31–21 * should have *i*· them as one
    59– 1 * *i*· with the grandeur
    271–25 * *i*· by the personality of
impressing
    My. 68– 2 * *i*· the audiences with the beauty
impression
    Mis. 142–15 My first *i*· was to indite a poem ;
    Pul. 49–27 * first *i*· given to the visitor
    '01. 24– 5 matter is only an *i*· produced
    My. 31–13 * first *i*· was of vastness,
    87–12 * The *i*· created is that of
    92–19 * statistics give a feeble *i*·
    322–31 * the *i*· he left with me was
    323–11 * nor willingly leave any false *i*·.
    324–20 * never gave us the *i*· that
    324–24 * conveyed this *i*· to us
    334– 1 * forthwith strives to give the *i*·
impressions
    Mis. 133–10 voices my *i*· of prayer :
    264–21 the bias of their first *i*·,
    Ret. 6– 1 * *i*· of that sainted spirit,
    Pul. 51– 3 * produce the same *i*· upon all.
    My. 188–28 convey all *i*· to man,
    261–13 the first *i*· of innocence,
impressive
    Pul. 12– 3 *i*· stillness of the audience
    30–28 * its present *i*· proportions,
    My. 38–23 * no more *i*· feature of the
    63–26 * even more *i*· than this
    78–12 * peculiarly rich and *i*·.
    92– 4 * its beginning has been *i*·,
impressively
    My. 203–25 laid the corner-stone . . . *i*·,
impressiveness
    My. 29–16 * the *i*· of this lay in its
    78–27 * can convey the peculiar *i*· of
    90–26 * *i*· and momentous significance.
imprisonment
    Ret. 6–29 abolition of *i*· for debt.
improve
    Mis. 62– 2 *i*· my own, and other people's
    62– 5 no more *i*· health or morals, than
    98– 3 whereby to *i*· his present condition ;
    112– 8 given new opportunities, will *i*·
    176–27 prepared to meet and *i*· them,
    230– 1 chapter sub-title
    253– 9 may *i*· our platforms ;
    267–11 and failed to *i*· it ;
    Ret. 34–20 renovated to *i*· the body.
    Un. 14– 9 *i*· upon His own previous work,
    No. 22– 9 fail to *i*· the conditions of mortals,
    Peo. 7–25 appeal to mind to *i*· its subjects
    My. 10– 3 * C. S. should *i*· the thought,
    42–14 * I desire to *i*· this opportunity to
    249– 3 *I*· every opportunity to correct sin
    294– 3 *i*· the morals and the lives of men,
improved
    Mis. 34– 5 not only healed . . . but is *i*· morally.
    34– 7 and mortal mind must be *i*·,
    137–12 such opportunity might have been *i*· ;
    147– 9 Have you *i*· past hours,
    220–20 and he is *i*· morally and physically.
    256– 3 they are at the same time *i*· morally.
    287– 2 The offspring of an *i*· generation,
    Un. 3– 1 having rightly *i*· the lessons of this
    36–19 *i*· physically, mentally, morally,

improved
Pul.	1–10	time *i·* is eloquent in God's praise.
'00.	3–27	*i·* on his work of
'01.	21–13	*i·* in its teaching and authorship
'02.	3–14	self-government under *i·* laws.
	3–15	so *i·* her public school system that
Peo.	2– 3	*i·* theory and practice of religion
	2– 4	due to the people's *i·* views
My.	107– 2	Has Christianity *i·* upon its
	175–18	greatly needs *i·* streets.
	217–24	"An *i·* belief is one step out of
	220–28	have greatly *i·* human nature
	307–25	At first my case *i·* wonderfully

improvement
Mis.	230– 3	upon the *i·* of moments
	243– 3	decided *i·* in health.
	370–23	has discovered an *i·* on

improves
Ret.	55– 8	and *i·* the race of Adam.
'00.	3– 6	*i·* moments ; to him time is money,
Peo.	6–18	*i·* the race physically and

improving
Mis.	230–15	*i·* moments before they pass into
My.	265–17	*i·* the morals and increasing the

improvise
My.	256– 3	allow me to *i·* some new notes,

impulse
Mis.	272–30	intuition and *i·* of love.
	274–20	gives *i·* to violence, envy, and
	288–26	temperance receives a strong *i·* from
Rud.	3–20	all true volition, *i·*, and action ;
	15–11	until this *i·* subsides.
No.	12–14	and given *i·* to goodness,
	13–24	given *i·* to reason and revelation,
'01.	32–30	governing *i·* of every action ;
My.	10– 5	* this mighty *i·* for good
	244–11	Is designed to impart a fresh *i·* to
	252–31	cold *i·* of a lesser gain !
	308– 9	impels the *i·* of Soul.
	316– 4	renews the heavenward *i·* ;

impulses
Mis.	141–21	*i·* of human will and pride ;
My.	213–17	for the *i·* of our own thought,

impulsion
Ret.	89–30	incorporeal *i·* is divine,
My.	10– 8	* inevitable that this same *i·*
	250–25	*i·* of this action in The

impure
Mis.	80– 1	sellers of *i·* literature,
	223– 7	*i·* streams flow from corrupt sources.

impurities
Pul.	6– 2	and *i·* are passing off.
'00.	13– 8	their *i·* were part of a system

impurity
Mis.	37–21	Intemperance, *i·*, sin of every sort,

impute
No.	29–16	*i·* such doctrines to mortal opinion

imputed
Hea.	6–15	manifestations ignorantly *i·* to
My.	177–11	(already *i·* to me),
	178–32	*Logia*, or *i·* sayings of Jesus

inability
Mis.	112–26	*i·* to see one's own faults,
No.	43–28	A man's *i·* to heal,

inaccuracy
My.	260– 8	*i·* of material sense would disappear.

inaccurate
Mis.	100–16	Human reason is *i·* ;

inaction
Mis.	341–22	illustrate the evil of *i·* and delay.

inactive
Pul.	10– 3	paralyzed by *i·* faith,

inadequate
Mis.	65–27	*i·* to compensate for the
	100–17	*i·* to grasp the word of Truth,
	317–20	Human desire is *i·* to
Man.	30– 6	be found at any time *i·*
Ret.	25–26	therefore *i·* to form any
No.	11–23	*i·* to grasp the Principle
	33–18	human blood was *i·* to
'01.	24–29	*i·* to prove the doctrine
My.	54– 1	* were *i·* for the occasion,
	56– 8	* was *i·* to meet the need,
	197–10	Words are *i·* to express
	224– 2	*i·* to meet the exigencies

inadmissible
Mis.	147–11	learned that sin is *i·*,
My.	130–24	Borrowing from my . . . is *i·*.
	364– 6	departure from . . . is *i·*.

inalienable
Mis.	140– 6	morally and spiritually *i·*,
	251–14	*i·* rights and radiant reality
No.	45–18	the right of woman . . . is *i·*,
My.	128–11	man's *i·* birthright
	200–16	receives his rights *i·*
	247– 2	*i·*, universal rights of men.
	254–23	It stands for the *i·*,

inanimate
Mis.	256–24	inert, *i·*, and non-intelligent.
Rud.	5– 9	inert, *i·*, and sensationless,
'01.	19–22	from the use of *i·* drugs

inapt
'01.	29–12	sometimes are *i·* or selfish

inasmuch
Mis.	186–20	*i·* as an idea cannot
	205–19	*i·* as it is the disembodied
	228–22	*i·* as perception, sensation, and
	293–18	*i·* as wilful transgression
Man.	42–21	*i·* as C. S. can only be
No.	28– 9	*I·* as these momentous facts
'00.	4–14	*i·* as these are progressive
'01.	14– 7	Yes, *i·* as we do know that
'02.	18–14	"*I·* as ye have done it — *Matt. 25 : 40.*
My.	134– 7	*i·* as our daily lives serve to

inaudible
Mis.	267– 2	audible and *i·* wail of evil
No.	40–13	the *i·* is more effectual.
'01.	20–13	suggestion of the *i·* falsehood,
Hea.	15–27	Prayer will be *i·*.
My.	139–24	from the audible to the *i·* prayer ;

inaugurated
Mis.	102–27	*i·* the irrepressible conflict
	382–28	*i·* our denominational form of
Pul.	31–11	* which that meeting *i·* for me.
My.	42–26	* *i·* by our beloved Leader,

inauguration
Mis.	305–29	* anniversary of the *i·* of
'02.	3–11	*i·* of home rule in Cuba,
My.	56– 6	* *i·* of two Sunday services

incantations
'00.	13–20	included charms and *i·*.

incapable
Mis.	14–15	*i·* of knowing the facts of
	14–27	a lie that is *i·* of proof
	71–25	man is *i·* of originating :
	209–32	Love, as unconscious as *i·* of error,
	371–10	*i·* of helping themselves thus?
Ret.	85–19	*i·* alike of abusing the practice of
Pul.	41–18	* *i·* of receiving this vast throng,
Pan.	1–14	God is *i·* of evil ;

incapacitates
Mis.	43–24	*i·* one to practise or teach C. S.
No.	44– 2	*i·* him for correct comment.

incarnated
Mis.	111–32	or is an *i·* babe,

incarnation
Mis.	77–10	should not only acknowledge the *i·*
My.	303– 3	I believe in but one *i·*,

incense
Pul.	83–22	* as if we would pour *i·* upon the
Hea.	2–28	altar of Love with perpetual *i·*.
My.	37– 5	* *i·* of gratitude and compassionate

incensed
Un.	46–16	This *i·* the rabbins against Jesus,

incentive
Mis.	238– 8	in defense of his own life's *i·*,
	279– 5	that is the *i·* in Science.
'00.	3–29	was not the *i·* of the devout Jew
My.	217– 4	your early, generous *i·* for action,
	229–13	But this should not be the *i·*
	278– 1	proper *i·* to the action of all
	288– 5	his life's *i·* and sacrifice need no
	357– 8	The only *i·* of a mistaken sense

incentives
Ret.	71–22	selfish motives . . . are dangerous *i·* ;
'02.	13– 3	Christ and our Cause my only *i·*,

inception
My.	47–17	* since the *i·* of this great Cause,
	243– 6	should be silenced at its *i·*.

incessant
Ret.	7– 9	* intense and almost *i·* study
My.	163–19	many years of *i·* labor

incessantly
Mis.	114– 7	need to watch *i·* the trend of
My.	335–30	* the young wife prayed *i·*

inch
Pul.	78– 5	* an eighth of an *i·* thick.

inches
Pul. 26– 3 * which is twenty-one *i·*
    78– 4 * twenty-six *i·* long,
    78– 5 * gold scroll, . . . nine *i·* wide,
    86– 2 * six *i·* in each dimension,
incident
Mis. 373– 1 One *i·* serves to illustrate
My. 29– 7 * *i·* of the dedicatory services
    311– 1 I will relate the following *i·*,
incidental
Mis. 253– 7 the *i·* platform is not broad enough
Man. 48–25 or give *i·* narratives.
incidents
Ret. 21–25 historic *i·* and personal events
My. 97–30 * *i·* witnessed during the week
    329–27 * some *i·* of her life in
incipient
Pul. 54–29 *i·* pulmonary consumption.
'01. 21–27 the *i·* touch of divine Love
Hea. 13–14 the *i·* stage of fever.
incision
Peo. 7–13 * With many a sharp *i·*.
    7–21 * With many a sharp *i·*,
incisions
Mis. 244– 7 closing the *i·* of the flesh.
incisors
Mis. 231–17 two *i·*, in a big pippin,
incited
Mis. 122–32 was *i·* by the same spirit
    296–27 or are they *i·* thereto by
inclement
Mis. 198–30 suffered from *i·* weather,
inclination
Mis. 240–18 with form and *i·* fixed,
Ret. 38–10 contrary to my *i·*,
Pul. vii– 7 *i·* given their own thoughts
'00. 9– 3 obedience is contrary to their *i·*.
My. 130–14 neither the time nor the *i·*
inclinations
Mis. 362–31 the influence of bad *i·*
'00. 8–29 to follow your own *i·*,
My. 211–17 foreign to the natural *i·*.
incline
Mis. 240–19 easier to *i·* the early thought
My. 125– 7 to *i·* the vine towards the parent
inclined
Mis. xi–21 *vox populi* is *i·* to grant us peace,
    117–24 *i·* to be too fast or too slow :
    129– 3 is *i·* to be uncharitable,
    264–18 * "As the twig is bent, the tree's *i·*."
Ret. 78– 2 He is *i·* to do either too much or
My. 97– 1 * almost every one is *i·* to admit.
    116– 7 *i·* to cling to the personality of
    226– 8 principle of the *i·* plane
    322–23 * She and Mrs. Wiggin seemed *i·* to
    338–28 *i·* to be, and is instructed to be,
inclining
Mis. 111–28 false beliefs *i·* mortal mind
My. 261–12 germinating and *i·* thought of
include
Mis. 11–25 *i·* them in his general effort to
    14– 5 immortal facts which *i·* these,
    68– 5 *i·* also man's changed appearance
    190–18 these terms will be found to *i·* the
    309–21 *i·* all obstacles to health,
    358– 8 They *i·* for him at present
Man. 47–18 not *i·* a description of symptoms or
    73– 4 *i·* at least one active practitioner
    93–11 *i·* in each lecture a true and just
Ret. 30– 9 *i·* all moral and religious reform.
Un. 31–19 *i·* all that denies and defies Spirit,
No. 39–18 *i·* all mankind in one affection.
'01. 7–12 *i·* within this Mind the thoughts
My. 26–18 *i·* enough of their own.
    30– 6 * *i·* Scientists from all over the
    106– 6 *i·* hopeless organic diseases
    129–30 *i·* the spirit and the letter of the
    329– 1 * was construed to *i·* the healers of
included
Mis. 24–15 *i·* a glimpse of the great fact
    34–10 *Is spiritualism . . . i· in C. S.?*
    349– 4 instructions *i·* about twelve lessons,
Un. 11–27 is *i·* in Mind ;
'00. 13–20 Its medical practice *i·* charms
Hea. 14–24 it *i·* more than they understood.
Po. vi–22 * are *i·* in this collection,
My. 16– 7 * *i·* the purchase price of the land
    95– 1 * C. S. would soon be *i·* among
    122–30 *i·* the very hearts that rejected it
    269– 1 universe *i·* in one infinite Mind

includes
Mis. 36–21 Mortal mind *i·* all evil,
    75– 9 *i·* a rule that must be understood,
    96–10 or what the infinite *i·* ;
    96–19 *i·* man's redemption from sickness
    96–25 This answer *i·* too much to
    113– 5 that which it *i·* is all
    152– 5 oneness of God *i·* also His presence
    193–30 *i·* the understanding of man's
    243–15 *i·* of necessity the Principle,
    257– 2 or *i·* Him in every mode and
    293–22 *i·* the whole duty of man :
Pul. 26–17 * chime of bells *i·* fifteen,
    28–17 * *i·* the use of Mrs. Eddy's book,
    30–10 * *i·* those all over the country.
    30–15 * The "confession of faith" *i·*
No. 9–24 excludes all error and *i·* all Truth.
    38–20 *i·* only His own nature,
Pan. 12– 7 for the universe *i·*man
    12–25 *i·* all that the term implies,
'00. 4–28 divine Love *i·* and reflects all
'02. 6–17 mortal concept and all it *i·*
Hea. 14–15 healing *i·* infinitely more than
My. 141–24 membership *i·* forty-eight thousand
    225–30 The divine Principle *i·* them all.
    239–18 God is *infinite* and so *i· all*
    364– 7 *i·* and inculcates the commandment,
including
Mis. 23–20 The universe, *i·* man,
    27–11 *i·* all inharmony, sin,
    41–27 governs the universe, *i·* man,
    56–30 created the universe, *i·* man,
    101–24 destroys matter and evil, *i·* sin
    272– 3 * (*i· the right to grant degrees*)
    333–21 relate to the universe, *i·* man
    361–25 spiritual universe, *i·* man
Un. 32– 6 man, *i·* the universe, is His
Pul. 37–27 * by seven persons, *i·* Mrs. Eddy.
Rud. 3–27 *i·* in itself all Mind,
'02. 6–30 *i·* nothing unlovely,
My. 16– 5 * up to and *i·* May 31, 1904,
    349–30 the infinite nature, *i·* all law
inclusive
Mis. 104– 8 substance of God, the one *i·* good.
income
Ret. 49– 1 which yields a large *i·*,
'02. 13–10 yield this church a liberal *i·*.
    15–10 *i·* from the sale of S. and H.,
    15–14 my *i·* from literary sources was
My. 135– 9 my *i·*, investments, deposits,
    137–12 my *i·*, investments, deposits,
incoming
My. 39–18 * introduce the *i·* President,
incommunicable
My. 133–25 then my sacred secret is *i·*,
incomparable
Mis. 250– 1 the *i·*, the infinite All
incompetence
My. 236– 8 notwithstanding "*i·*"
incompetency
Peo. 8– 5 *i·* that cannot heal the sick,
incompetent
Mis. 22–26 is *i·* to condemn it ;
Un. 23–17 whereof they are confessedly *i·*
No. 19–20 sinful sense is *i·* to understand
incomplete
Man. 69– 5 *I·* Term of Service.
Un. 15–11 so must man, or the likeness is *i·*,
incompleteness
Pul. 39– 6 * God's greatness flows around our *i·*,
inconceivable
Mis. 102– 5 a theory to me *i·*.
    217– 3 effect without a cause is *i·* ;
    218–16 they make Deity unreal and *i·*,
    234–27 seems to them still more *i·*.
No. 20– 2 Limitless personality is *i·*.
'01. 6–29 That God is either *i·*, or
inconsistency
My. 110–29 to convict the Scriptures of *i·*
    235– 1 chapter sub-title
inconsistent
Mis. 349–14 ground that it was *i·* with C. S.,
Hea. 4–28 consistent with our *i·* statement
My. 112–13 is not *i·* in a single instance
incontestable
Un. 7–22 *i·* point in divine Science
No. 21–22 Jesus, whose philosophy is *i·*,
inconvenience
My. 54– 3 * *i·* that comes from crowding,

inconveniences
　　My. 29–30 * the *i·* of an oppressive day.
inconvenient
　　Mis. 132–21 I find it *i·* to accept
　　My. 289–23 It being *i·* for me to attend
incorporated
　　Mis. 272–11 * *i·* in Public Statutes, Chapter 115,
　　　　272–20 * have simply an *i·* grant,
　　Man. 102–18 shall be *i·* in all such deeds
incorporates
　　Mis. 197– 1 *i·* their lessons into our lives
incorporation
　　Man. 25–17 See under "Deed of Trust" for *i·*
incorporeal
　　Mis. 102–16 Infinite personality must be *i·*.
　　　　161– 4 *The Corporeal and I· Saviour.*
　　　　162–22 There was no *i·* Jesus of Nazareth.
　　　　163–26 the *i·* Saviour— the Christ
　　　　164– 1 interprets the *i·* idea, or
　　　　164– 2 hence the *i·* and corporeal are
　　　　164– 7 reveals the *i·* Christ ;
　　　　166–15 Christ, the *i·* idea of God,
　　　　205– 4 the *i·* Truth and Love,
　　Ret. 70–24 individual, *i·*, and infinite,
　　　　89–30 *i·* impulsion is divine,
　　　　93– 5 the *i·* divine Principle of man,
　　'01. 12–26 *I·* evil embodies itself in the
　　My. 200–13 upward to the realms of *i·* Life
　　　　218–11 The *spiritual* body, the *i·* idea,
　　　　260–31 Christ is *i·*.
incorrect
　　Mis. 39– 8 grossly *i·* and false teachers
　　　　118–10 make *i·* your entire problem,
　　　　203–20 hampered . . . by *i·* teaching ;
　　　　264–22 whether those be correct or *i·*.
　　　　372– 2 *i·*, contradictory, unscientific,
　　Man. 43–21 No *I·* Literature.
　　No. 23– 1 *i·* concept of the nature of evil
　　My. 221–25 correct or *i·* state of thought,
incorrectly
　　My. 226– 2 To avoid using this word *i·*,
incorruptible
　　My. 41–26 * "*i·* and undefiled" — *I Pet.* 1 : 4.
increase
　　Mis. 21–14 except by *i·* of spirituality.
　　　　110–24 *i·* rapidly as years glide on.
　　　　175–12 shall *i·* by every spiritual touch,
　　　　229–23 faith in the power of God . . . *i·*,
　　Ret. 62– 2 and human suffering will *i·*.
　　Un. 5– 6 *i·* their apprehension of God,
　　No. 19– 4 and the demand to *i·*,
　　　　42– 9 * manifestations of God's power *i·*
　　'02. 1– 5 constantly *i·* in number, unity,
　　Po. 33– 3 *I·* Thou my faith
　　My. 36–22 * *i·* the measure of our devotion
　　　　55–30 * a steady *i·* in attendance,
　　　　87– 5 * temporary *i·* of the population
　　　　91–26 * even stranger is its *i·* in wealth.
　　　　162–27 May He *i·* its members,
　　　　230–12 *i·* the spirituality of him who obeys
　　　　240– 1 will *i·* till all men shall know Him
increased
　　Mis. 12–15 means for sinning . . . have so *i·*
　　　　12–16 one's temptations to sin are *i·*
　　　　29–20 shows that longevity has *i·*.
　　　　42–20 will be proportionately *i·*.
　　　　137–28 heal and teach with *i·* confidence.
　　　　204–24 permeates with *i·* harmony all the
　　　　262– 3 and to confer *i·* power
　　　　289–25 exalted and *i·* affections.
　　　　327– 3 When I went back . . . my misery *i·* ;
　　Ret. 15–17 The congregation so *i·* in number
　　　　39– 1 demand for this book *i·*,
　　　　44–11 church *i·* in members,
　　No. 8–27 and with *i·* power, patience,
　　'00. 7– 4 religious sentiment has *i·* ;
　　My. 53–20 * attendants steadily *i·*.
　　　　56– 3 * *i·*, until every seat was filled
　　　　56–18 * number of attendants *i·*
　　　　92–16 * its following had *i·*
　　　　132–19 blessings continue and be *i·* !
　　　　164– 3 But the demand *i·*,
　　　　266–22 have *i·* year by year.
increases
　　Mis. 204–18 *i·* the intellectual activities,
　　　　365–22 it continues, and *i·*,
　　Ret. 27–27 *i·* in power and perfection
　　　　28–19 which divides, subdivides, *i·*,
　　　　74– 1 *i·* one's sense of spirituality.
　　No. 42– 1 * as the faith of the Church *i·*,
　　'00. 2– 2 and this interest *i·*.

increases
　　'02. 10–22 *i·* the speed of mortals' transit
　　My. 12–25 *i·* our indebtedness to God.
　　　　305–17 demand for this book constantly *i·*.
increasing
　　Mis. 115–22 *i·* necessity for relying on God
　　　　300–21 and *i·* the record of theft
　　　　302– 2 the reformation begun and *i·*
　　　　307–15 *i·* inquiry of mankind as to
　　Man. 18– 9 went steadily on, *i·* in numbers,
　　Ret. 44–12 kept pace with its *i·* popularity ;
　　　　47– 8 applicants were rapidly *i·*.
　　Pul. 31–18 * by a new and *i·* interest
　　　　37– 4 * *i·* demands of the public
　　　　50–16 * upon a large and *i·* number
　　'00. 1–13 with rapidly *i·* numbers,
　　'01. 3– 2 *i·* virtue, fervor, and fidelity.
　　　　29–16 parents' *i·* years and needs,
　　My. 22– 5 * constantly *i·* attendance
　　　　53–28 * *i·* interest in C. S.
　　　　88–22 * all that *i·* host who have found
　　　　135–11 *i·* demands upon my time
　　　　137–17 *i·* demands upon my time,
　　　　139– 7 *i·*, advancing footsteps
　　　　174–25 An *i·* sense of God's love,
　　　　245–10 *i·* popularity of C. S.,
　　　　265–17 *i·* the longevity of mankind,
　　　　325–16 * With *i·* love and gratitude,
incredible
　　No. 15–17 and an *i·* Satan.
incredulity
　　Mis. 4–29 with an expression of *i·*.
　　　　7–11 skepticism and *i·* prevail
incriminating
　　Mis. 283–23 without *i·* the person
incubus
　　Un. 15– 4 May men rid themselves of an *i·*
inculcates
　　Mis. 288–17 Human knowledge *i·* that it is,
　　My. 364– 7 includes and *i·* the commandment,
incumbents
　　Man. 26– 5 *I·* who have served one year
　　　　80–26 *I·* who have served one year
　　My. 243–13 or more of the present *i·*.
incumbrance
　　No. 38–19 and material *i·* disappears.
incur
　　Mis. 126–29 to deride her is to *i·* the penalty
incurable
　　Mis. 6–10 cases that are pronounced *i·*
　　　　05– 6 pronounced by the physicians *i·*,
　　　　378– 3 A patient considered *i·*
　　Pul. 69– 9 * had pronounced his case *i·*.
　　My. 105–10 declared *i·* because the lungs
incurred
　　'02. 13– 3 *i·* a sharper fire from enmity.
incurring
　　Mis. 300–20 *i·* the penalty of the law,
incurs
　　My. 231– 5 *i·* the liability of working in
Ind. (State)
　　(*see* **Indianapolis, Lebanon, Terre Haute**)
indebted
　　Mis. 228– 3 deemed at least *i·* friends
　　Pul. 36–27 * to whose courtesy I am much *i·*
　　My. 74–14 * Boston is *i·* to them for
indebtedness
　　Man. 76–13 the amount of its *i·*
　　My. 12–25 increases our *i·* to God.
　　　　52– 8 * acknowledge our *i·* to her,
　　　　99–17 * was not a cent of *i·* left.
indecision
　　Mis. 230– 5 *i·* as to what one should do.
indeed
　　Mis. 9– 5 Sweet, *i·*, are these uses of His rod !
　　　　16–10 Principle of Christianity . . . is *i·* God ;
　　　　32– 1 if *i·* he desires success in this
　　　　36–26 neither *i·* can be." — *Rom.* 8 : 7.
　　　　125– 1 he will *i·* drink of our Master's cup,
　　　　126–27 God hath *i·* smiled on my church,
　　　　131–27 if, *i·*, it could be estimated.
　　　　147–27 is *i·* what he appears to be,
　　　　203–19 repentance is *i·* a stricken state
　　　　211–26 drink *i·* of my cup." — *Matt.* 20 : 23.
　　　　299–10 glad, *i·*, that this query has
　　　　354–13 are *i·* losing the knowledge of
　　　　374–19 To him . . . homage is *i·* due,
　　Ret. 37– 7 "This book is *i·* wholly original,
　　　　68– 6 neither *i·* can be, the father of
　　　　91–10 *I·*, this title really indicates

indeed
Un.	1– 3	*I·*, this may be set down as
	45– 7	"Yes ! you are *i·* yourself,
	59– 3	How, *i·*, is he a Saviour, if
Pul.	3–12	*i·* dwellers in Truth and Love,
	45–18	* This is *i·*, then, a scientific
	50– 5	* *I·*, one of her motives in buying
	57–12	* and, *i·*, in all New England.
	79–24	* *i·*, the breath of his soul is a
	80– 9	* socially, *i·* every way.
Rud.	11–25	healer who is *i·* a Christian Scientist,
No.	5–20	Disease becomes *i·* a
Pan.	4–20	is *i·* the preserver of man.
'00.	1– 4	If, *i·*, we may be absent from
'01.	25–27	which, if *i·* Spirit and infinite,
	28–22	is *i·* the way of salvation from
'02.	3–27	*i·*, right is the only real
	10–23	This is *i·* our sole proof
My.	9–11	* this would be scant *i·* if it
	10–27	* *i·*, they know that it is the
	17–10	disallowed *i·* of men, — I Pet. 2 : 4.
	46–27	* that we may *i·* reach
	50–25	* This was *i·* the little church
	61– 4	* has been very interesting *i·*,
	103– 9	that C. S. is *i·* Science,
	161–10	should drink *i·* of my — Matt. 20 : 23.
	165–31	that it has *i·* found and felt the
	175–16	if, *i·*, such must remain with us
	179–29	We are *i·* privileged in having
	192–22	It would *i·* give me pleasure
	244–22	students of my books are *i·* my
	315–25	If *I·* it be I, allow me to
	332– 6	* words are *i·* but a meagre tribute
	351–11	is *i·* a divine command,

indefinable
Pan.	3– 9	find an *i·* pleasure in stillness,

indefinite
Mis.	86–12	*i·* and vague human opinions,
Pul.	58–24	* but for an *i·* time
Hea.	4–16	for an *i·* period,

indelibly
My.	48–26	* burned *i·* upon the mind of

Independent
Pul.	88–15	* *I·*, Rockland, Mass.
	88–32	* *I·*, Harrisburg, Pa.
	89– 1	* *I·*, New York City.

independent
Mis.	43– 2	to act of itself, and *i·* of matter,
	289–13	voluntarily surrenders *i·* action
Pul.	55–27	* though each is entirely *i·*
No.	5–13	that life and health are *i·* of
'01.	27– 1	quite *i·* of all other authors except
Hea.	12– 5	to learn what matter is doing *i·* of

independently
Man.	55– 6	*i·* discipline its own members,
Hea.	19– 6	*i·* of material conditions.

indestructibility
Mis.	206– 9	scientific *i·* of the universe

indestructible
Mis.	64– 7	man's *i·* eternal life in God.
My.	127–27	staunch and *i·* on land or sea ;

India
Pul.	5–25	Greece, Japan, *I·*, and China ;
My.	30–15	* from *I·*, from England,
	289–16	Victoria, . . . Empress of *I·*,
	289–29	Victoria, . . . Empress of *I·*.

Indian
Ret.	3– 6	in the *I·* troubles of 1722–1725,

Indianapolis
Ind.
Pul.	90– 5	* *Sentinel*, *I·*, Ind.
My.	81–15	* "*I·* !" "Des Moines !" "Glasgow !"

indicate
Mis.	245–15	Their movements *i·* fear
Ret.	59–13	*Life* is a term used to *i·* Diety ;
No.	11–10	which must be used to *i·* thoughts
'00.	4–12	*i·* a renaissance greater than
My.	36– 5	* rose as one to *i·* their approval
	187– 2	*i·* that, spiritually as well as
	245–28	They *i·*, respectively, the degrees of
	319–14	* *i·* what he himself thought of

indicated
Mis.	70–20	poor thief's prayer for help *i·*.
	76–22	will find the right meaning *i·*.
	258–22	I AM, *i·* no personality
	314–12	*i·* in the Sunday School Lesson
Man.	47–20	name of the disease may be *i·*.
Ret.	23–11	were *i·* by no floral dial.
Pul.	12– 4	stillness . . . *i·* close attention.
No.	22–26	*i·* his ability to cast it out.

indicated
My.	8– 6	* The necessity here *i·* is
	114–32	steps either written or *i·*
	284–21	Veterans *i·* their desire

indicates
Mis.	100–30	our Father *i·* the different stages of
	147–11	and *i·* a small mind?
	182–22	apostle *i·* no personal plan
	288–18	while Science *i·* that it *is not*.
	290–12	*i·* misapprehension of the divine
Man.	76– 5	*i·* the proper management
Ret.	91–11	*i·* more the Master's mood,
No.	6–13	If, as the error *i·*,
	45–10	Such an attempt *i·* weakness,
Pan.	7–19	*i·*, . . . a lapse in the Mosaic religion,
My.	86–18	* *i·* plainly enough the generosity
	216–19	*i·* another field of work
	231– 3	to bestow . . . only as God *i·*.
	331– 8	* *i·* her irreproachable standing

indicating
Mis.	191–14	*i·* the existence of more than
Pul.	vii–13	*i·* the gain of intellectual

indication
Mis.	56–11	Every *i·* of matter's constituting

indications
Mis.	46–12	no such *i·* in the premises
Ret.	71–12	the *i·* of mental treatment,
My.	82–21	* to-day [June 14] the *i·* were

indifference
My.	195–12	hidden under an appearance of *i·*.
	233–14	can you demonstrate over . . . by *i·*
	248–28	to challenge universal *i·*,

indifferent
Mis.	146–16	you cannot be *i·* to this,
Pul.	21–19	they are not *i·* to the welfare of

indigenous
Mis.	211–11	are not *i·* to her soil.

indigent
Mis.	ix– 8	Christian Scientists are not *i·* ;
	11– 8	I taught *i·* students gratuitously,
Ret.	50–15	my list of *i·* charity scholars
'02.	15– 7	rooming and boarding *i·* students
My.	214–24	C. S. home for *i·* students,

indigestion
Mis.	209–18	ills of *i·* tend to rebuke

indignation
Mis.	345–21	turn the popular *i·* against
	374– 7	Keen and alert was their *i·*
Pul.	14– 6	shocked . . . into human *i·* ;

indignity
Un.	11–23	neither red tape nor *i·* hindered
	46–17	an *i·* to their personality ;
My.	165– 6	There is scarcely an *i·* which

indirectly
Mis.	381–23	from directly or *i·* printing,
Hea.	12–13	that God, directly or *i·*,
My.	223–20	coming directly or *i·* from

indiscretion
Mis.	129–16	of another man's *i·*,

indiscretions
Mis.	236– 5	*i·*, and errors of others ;

indiscriminately
Man.	59– 1	revelations of C. S. *i·*,

indispensable
Mis.	v– 5	PRACTICAL TEACHINGS *i·* TO
	38–21	divine metaphysics needful, *i·*.
	67–16	*i·* to health, happiness,
	87–27	*i·* to the demonstration of
	91– 4	It is not *i·* to organize
	91– 8	not as a perpetual or *i·* ceremonial
	108–20	the proper knowledge . . . is *i·* ;
	118– 7	the *i·* rule of obedience.
	122– 6	spoken of what was *i·*
	317–18	*i·* to the progress of every Christian
	318–23	*i·* demands on all those who
	356–27	it is *i·* to personal growth,
No.	6– 9	This refutation is *i·* to the
'00.	14–23	toiled for the spiritually *i·*.
'01.	2– 4	*i·* to the acquiring of
My.	8–27	* the natural and *i·* Leader
	196–26	even the spiritually *i·*,

indisputable
Un.	38– 3	the *i·* realities of being.

indisputably
Mis.	113– 4	If, as is *i·* true,

indissoluble
Mis.	77–12	which is the *i·* bond of union,

indistinct
Mis.	347–12	theirs grows *i·* and ends.

indite
  Mis. 142–15 impression was to *i·* a poem ;
indited
  Mis. 379– 3 if he *i·* anything pathological
  My. 271– 5 I little understood all that I *i·* ;
indites
  Mis. 311–27 transcribing what God *i·*,
individual (*see also* **individual's**)
 another
  Mis. 191–19 cast out of another *i·*
 any other
  My. 363–26 any other *i·* but the patient
 being is
  Mis. 104– 9 In Science all being is *i·* ;
 complexion of the
  Mis. 379– 8 height, and complexion of the *i·*,
 each
  Mis. 119– 8 Each *i·* is responsible for himself.
  Ret. 70–18 Each *i·* must fill his own niche
 good in an
  Mis. 338– 1 the appearing of good in an *i·*
 has met
  '02. 9–28 that an *i·* has met the need of
 hide from an
  Mis. 337–32 tends to hide from an *i·* this grand
 His being is
  Mis. 102–11 His being is *i·*, but not physical.
 interest of the
  '01. 31–16 except in the interest of the *i·*
 knew
  '01. 20–17 if the *i·* knew what was at work
 knowledge of the
  Ret. 71–10 or knowledge of the *i·* treated,
 leaves the
  Mis. 31–17 leaves the *i·* no alternative but to
 mind of the
  Hea. 6–21 mind of the *i·* only can produce a
 misguided
  Mis. 291–31 misguided *i·* who keeps not watch
 nature of the
  Mis. 119–11 nature of the *i·*, more stubborn than
 one
  Mis. 22–16 from one *i·* to another ;
  59–24 success that one *i·* has with another
  My. 267–20 One *i·* may first awaken from
 responsible
  My. 313–18 accompanied by some responsible *i·*
 rights of the
  Ret. 72– 3 nor interfere with the rights of the *i·*.
 single
  Pul. 20–15 * It is the gift of a single *i·*
 that
  Mis. 59–26 That *i·* is the best healer who
  Pan. 10–25 in that *i·* who finds the highest joy,
  My. 188–32 that *i·* ascends the scale of miracles
 this
  Mis. 223–14 This *i·* disbelieves in Mind-healing,
  266–11 this *i·* is doing the work
 unknown
  Mis. 296–29 What manner of man *is* this unknown *i·*
 unknown to the
  Hea. 6–23 may be wholly unknown to the *i·*,

  Mis. 32–26 at present necessary for the *i·*,
  35–14 * I never knew so unselfish an *i·*."
  42– 7 *i·* has but passed through a
  43– 4 without even having seen the *i·*,
  86– 1 The *i·* and spiritual are perfect ;
  105–20 the *i·* and his ideal can never
  107–23 the *i·* may become morally blind,
  108–32 an *i·* believing in that which is
  190–14 Its definition as an *i·* is too
  226– 9 What has an *i·* gained by
  310–27 I as an *i·* would cordially invite
  315–26 except the *i·* needing it asks
  348–28 an *i·* in a proper state of mind.
  Man. 74– 8 no *i·*, and no other church shall
  94– 9 *i·* who goes to hear and deride truth,
  Rud. 2– 4 * an *i·* of the human race."
  No. 23–19 Evil is a quality, not an *i·*.
  '00. 10– 7 greatness of a cause or of an *i·*,
  '01. 16–19 ought not to proceed from the *i·*,
  29–23 *i·* who loves most, does most,
  29–25 is the *i·* who soonest will
  Hea. 8–15 no longer quarrels with the *i·*.
  My. 4–17 such an *i·* subserves the
  206–13 believing that you see an *i·* who has
  218–23 belief that an *i·* can either
  218–28 an *i·* should not enter the
  219–30 I recommend, . . . that an *i·* submit
  249–25 *i·* best fitted to perform this
  303–15 If the *i·* governed
  359–11 can be read by the *i·* who desires
  (*see also* **Eddy**)

individual (adj.)
  Mis. 60–17 *i·* sleepers, in different phases of
  81–22 Every *i·* character,
  81–22 like the *i·* John the Baptist,
  85–17 perpetual, spiritual, *i·* existence.
  98–14 *i·* growth of Christian Scientists,
  98–22 must begin with *i·* growth,
  101–31 God is *i·* Mind.
  104– 1 his *i·* being, the Christ,
  105– 5 our Master's *i·* demonstrations
  105–10 resumed his *i·* spiritual being,
  118–14 can neither . . . advance *i·* growth,
  122– 8 or of the *i·* instrument in
  165–15 *i·* spirituality, perfect and eternal,
  204–18 It develops *i·* capacity,
  205–19 disembodied *i·* Spirit-substance
  267–18 loss from *i·* conceit,
  279– 3 *i·* punishment for sin
  290–27 *i·* blessedness and blessing
  290–28 not so much from *i·* as from
  309–22 Man's *i·* life is infinitely
  350–21 An *i·* state of mind sometimes
  364– 6 In return for *i·* sacrifice,
  Man. 64–17 *i·*, endearing term of Mother.
  70–19 *i·* unity and action of the churches
  72–17 branch churches shall be *i·*,
  Ret. 25–15 God I characterized as *i·* entity.
  67–22 collective as well as *i·*.
  70–14 No person can take the *i·* place
  70–15 fulfil the *i·* mission of Jesus
  70–24 will be, forever *i·*, incorporeal,
  73– 1 man being spiritual, *i·*,
  73–13 fail to appreciate *i·* character.
  74– 5 fails to distinguish the *i·*,
  Un. 5–11 following upward *i·* convictions,
  5–18 or enlighten the *i·* thought.
  25 22 is not *i·*, not actual.
  49– 2 I believe in the *i·* man,
  64– 5 build the *i·* spiritual sense,
  Pul. 4–21 His is an *i·* kingdom,
  74–25 "Christ is *i·*, and one with God,
  Rud. 2– 7 God is definitely *i·*,
  2–15 the phrase *an i·* God,
  2–16 but one infinite *i·* Spirit,
  15–28 to fill anew the *i·* mind.
  No. 1–21 correcting the *i·* thought,
  7–25 the distinctions of *i·* character
  12–26 immaterial, though still *i·*.
  17– 9 a spiritual and *i·* being,
  19–15 God is *i·*,
  19–19 essence of the *i·* infinite.
  23–27 He is definite and *i·*,
  25–19 for he is forever *i·* ;
  26–19 Man's *i·* being must reflect
  26–19 reflect the supreme *i·* Being,
  26–25 *i·* and forever harmonious.
  '01. 2– 9 Christianity in *i·* lives
  7–16 needs of the *i·* mind
  19–25 the unbridled *i·* human will.
  Hea. 8–12 to perceive *i·* advancement ;
  My. 10–30 * *i·* welfare is closely interwoven
  12–11 * his *i·* desires, both as to the
  14– 8 and something from the *i·*,
  111–31 with their *i·* demonstrations.
  117–21 *i·*, but not personal,
  119– 9 and is *i·* in consciousness
  223– 7 to any class of *i·* discords.
  236–30 in their *i·* experiences.
  249– 7 raging element of *i·* hate
  (*see also* **consciousness, rights**)

individualities
  Mis. 102– 1 elements of all forms and *i·*,
  Un. 51–16 not one of all these *i·*
individuality
 all
  Un. 24– 3 all *i·*, all being.
 and Life
  Un. 46–15 *I·* and Life were real to him
 and personality
  My. 344–11 God preserving *i·* and personality.
 and reality
  Un. 46– 7 *i·* and reality of man ;
 constitutes the
  '01. 7– 6 constitutes the *i·* of the infinite
 dwarf
  My. 118–30 dwarf *i·* in personality
 eternal
  Mis. 361–25 man and all eternal *i·*.
 everlasting
  No. 25–20 what this everlasting *i·* is,
 form and
  Mis. 103–13 form and *i·* are never lost,
 His
  Mis. 101–32 This one Mind and His *i·*
  102–15 In His *i·* I recognize

individuality
his
Mis. 104–17 feeble fight with his *i*,
No. 11– 6 constitute his *i*· in the
his own
Mis. 104–29 and recover his own *i*·
human
Un. 25–16 It honors conscious human *i*·
infinite
'00. 5–14 of eternal, infinite *i*·.
is endless
Mis. 104– 9 *i*· is endless in the calculus of
largest
Pul. 80–10 * Here they have the largest *i*·,
man's
Mis. 104–15 man's *i*· is sinless, deathless,
    104–22 man's *i*· reflects the divine law
Un. 53–21 Man's *i*· is not a mortal mind or
No. 23–28 man's *i*· is God's own image and
    26–17 If man's *i*· were evil,
Pan. 10– 9 notion that C. S. lessens man's *i*·.
material
Un. 24–10 *Evil.* I am . . . a material *i*·,
mighty
Mis. 258–23 declare a mighty *i*·,
my
Un. 48– 8 He sustains my *i*·.
    48– 8 He *is* my *i*· and my Life.
of God
Mis. 103–23 power, presence, and *i*· of God.
Rud. 2–18 Science defines the *i*· of God as
    3–24 *By the i· of God, do you mean*
of man
Un. 53– 8 reality and *i*· of man are good
Rud. 13– 8 not the actual *i*· of man
other people's
Mis. 62– 2 other people's *i*·, health, and
perpetual
No. 11– 5 Man has perpetual *i*· ;
personality and
'00. 4–29 all personality and *i*·.
spiritual
Mis. 103–27 his spiritual *i*· that reflected the
Ret. 73–15 man's spiritual *i*· in God,
Un. 37–20 spiritual *i*· is immortal.
    38– 1 take no cognizance of spiritual *i*·,
their
My. 211–18 The victims lose their *i*·,
this
Mis. 104– 6 this *i*· was safe in the substance of
No. 26–21 this *i*· never originated in molecule,
true
Un. 21–21 consciousness belonging to true *i*·,
    53–22 his true *i*· as a perfect child of
unseen
Mis. 104– 3 His unseen *i*·, so superior to
Un. 37–21 this unseen *i*· is real and

Mis. 22–14 absorption, or annihilation of *i*·.
    103–30 The *i*· is embraced in Mind,
    105– 2 of man's spirituality, *i*·,
    145– 6 *i*· to express Soul and substance.
    191–11 if devil is an *i*·,
    362– 6 reflects all real mode, form, *i*·,
    364–16 governing all identity, *i*·, law,
No. 21–11 all phenomena, identity, *i*·, law ;
My. 117–20 God's impersonality and *i*·
    344–14 The *i*· of him must make gradual
individualize
My. 160– 7 is to *i*· infinite power :
individualized
Mis. 103–13 *i*· ideas, which dwell forever in
Rud. 3– 9 this trinity of good — was *i*·,
No. 19–16 man is His *i*· idea.
individually
Mis. 137–21 to work out *i*· and alone,
    164–28 reveal man collectively, as *i*·,
Man. 76–25 *i*· responsible for said funds.
    77–14 Treasurer to be *i*· responsible
Rud. 15–24 persons who cannot be addressed *i*·,
My. 109–20 *i*· but specks in His universe,
    134– 9 keep the faith *i*· and collectively,
    259–24 either collectively or *i*·
individual's
My. 211–25 spoiling that *i*· disposition,
individuals
Mis. 9–12 those unfortunate *i*· are virtually thy
    191–19 can this passage mean several *i*·
    230–14 successful *i*· have become such
    237– 8 Not a few *i*· serve God
    314– 7 One of these *i*· shall open the
    347–14 Two *i*·, with all the goodness of
Man. 28– 8 nations, *i*·, and religion
    38– 1 *i*· who are known to them to be

individuals
Man. 38–18 *I*· who have heretofore been
    63–19 *i*· who take charge of the
    68–19 only those *i*· whom she engages
    78– 8 not . . . responsible for the debts of *i*·
Pul. 21–22 and close the door on church or *i*·
'00. 8–10 a bane upon *i*· and society.
    10–20 sceptre of self and pelf over *i*·,
    14–29 they are distinguished *i*·,
'01. 25–10 certain *i*· call aids to
Hea. 3–17 Josephus alludes to several *i*·
Peo. 2–28 nations as well as *i*·,
My. 110– 4 *i*· buried above-ground
    116– 6 certain *i*· are inclined to
    157–23 a deed of trust to three *i*·
    210–19 Certain *i*· entertain the notion
    211– 3 unseen wrong to *i*· and society
    223–11 Letters and despatches from *i*·
    243–11 two *i*· would meet meagrely
    265–12 sacred rights of *i*·, peoples,
    277– 7 settling difficulties between *i*·
    283–21 *I*·, as nations, unite harmoniously
    314–16 *I*· are here to-day who were
    359– 3 their difficulties with *i*·
indoor
My. 123–21 are bigger than the *i*·.
indorsement
My. 272–32 * gives no editorial *i*· to the
induce
Mis. 243–29 *i*· ulceration, bleeding,
Ret. 6– 3 * can hardly fail to *i*· them
My. 211–20 would *i*· their self-destruction.
induced
My. 40–32 * our Leader has *i*· a multitude
    211–32 *i*· by this secret evil influence
    348– 3 *i*· a deep research, which
    349–28 *i*· by love and deduced from God,
induces
Rud. 12–19 and *i*· rest in God,
My. 9– 9 * *i*· him to glory in every good deed
inductive
My. 349–27 *I*· or deductive reasoning
    349–31 *i*· reasoning reckons creation as
indulge
Mis. 93–29 Nothing is more fatal than to *i*·
    115–29 if you in any way *i*· in sin ;
    348–21 *i*· in homœopathic doses of
    369–14 leaders of materialistic schools *i*·
'01. 13–30 So long as we *i*· the presence
indulged
Mis. 12– 3 If *i*·, it masters us ;
    94– 3 a person who knowingly *i*· evil,
My. 334–18 * *i*· in while being called unreal.
indulgence
Mis. 354– 1 pleasure seeking, and sense *i*·,
    356– 7 rivalry, hate need no temporary *i*·
My. 64–20 * against the *i*· of the sins
indulgences
Mis. 119–13 its habits, tastes, and *i*·.
indulging
My. 5–28 *i*· sin, men cannot serve God ;
    5–32 *I*· deceit is like the
industrial
My. 266– 6 human power, *i*· slavery, and
    285– 8 *i*·, civic, and national peace.
Industrial Peace Conference
My. 285– 4 to attend the *I*· *P*· *C*·,
industries
My. 287–13 *i*·, human rights, liberty, life.
industrious
Mis. 339–10 good is made more *i*·
Pul. 50– 2 * the welfare of *i*· workmen,
industry
My. 216–16 your sweet *i*· and love
    265–29 governed by honesty, *i*·,
inebriate
Po. 71– 2 When earth, *i*· with crime,
ineffable
Mis. 184–25 Oh, for that light and love *i*·,
    337–29 The *i*· Life and light
Ret. 13–21 and a soft glow of *i*· joy
    25–29 I beheld with *i*· awe
My. 37–28 * its *i*· loving-kindness,
    257–11 humanity with *i*· tenderness.
ineligible
Man. 39–16 *I*· for Probation.

inert
  Mis. 3–16   Drugs, *i·* matter, never are needed
     256–24 matter in and of itself, is *i·*,
  Rud. 5– 9   Matter is *i·*, inanimate,

inestimable
  Mis. 114– 2 of *i·* value to all seekers

inevitable
  Mis. 127–21 The *i·* condition whereby to
  Un. 38–25 *i·* conclusion that Life is not in
  Pul. 79–18 * The first is that a revolt was *i·*
     80– 5 * *i·* in the nature of the case.
  Pan. 7–28 makes sin, disease, and death *i·*,
  '00. 13– 2 * ''a controversy was *i·* when the
  My. 10– 2 * *i·* that the transforming influence
     10– 5 * *i·* that this mighty impulse
     10– 7 * *i·* that this same impulsion
     178–18 Hence the *i·* revelation of C. S.
     248–14 the needed and the *i·* sponsors

inevitably
  Mis. 2–25 he would be *i·* self-annihilated.
     70–21 *i·* separated through Mind.
  Ret. 88–17 leads *i·* to a consideration of
  Pul. 21– 2 Scientists, . . . *i·* love one another
  '02. 10–19 is correct, and *i·* spiritual.
     11– 5 *i·* subject to sin, disease, and
  My. 100– 1 * *i·* brought out in connection with

inexhaustible
  Mis. 83– 3 perpetual idea of *i·* good.
     92– 4 *i·* topics of that book
  Ret. 84– 1 *i·* topics of S. and H.
     84–13 assimilate this *i·* subject — C. S.

inexpedient
  Mis. 00–12 sometimes, . . . *i·* to attack evil.

inexplicable
  Mis. 222–26 Principle, whose power seems *i·*,
  My. 97–10 * audacious, stupendous, *i·* faith

in extremis
  My. 45–18 * sense declared you to be *i· e·*.

infallible
  Mis. 66– 1 this law is not *i·* in wisdom ;
     84–12 The spiritual Christ was *i·* ;
  Ret. 89–30 incorporeal impulsion is divine, *i·*,
  Un. 57–15 and rendered this *i·* verdict ;
  My. 190–14 regard his sayings as *i·*.
     348–29 law of God — *i·*, eternal.
     364– 1 No mortal is *i·*,

infamous
  Hea. 1–18 * At fifty, chides his *i·* delay,

infancy
  Mis. 16– 4 In mine *i·*, this is enough of heaven
     166– 8 impersonal *i·*, manhood, and
     231– 3 *i·*, exuberant with joy,
     263–25 by the *i·* of its discovery,

infant
  Mis. 15–29 developed into an *i·* Christianity ;
     293– 2 the *i·* thought in C. S.
     320–12 *i·* idea of divine perfection
  My. 174–21 offered me to Christ in *i·* baptism.
     312–30 I did open an *i·* school,
     343–28 dangerous in an *i·* church.

infantile
  Mis. 85–18 *i·* and more or less imperfect.
     167– 2 *i·* thought of God's man,
     215–17 not according to the *i·* conception
  No. 26– 5 This *i·* talk about Mind-healing

infantry
  '00. 10–27 lieutenant of the United States *i·*

infants
  Mis. 345–23 took their *i·* to a place of worship

infect
  Mis. 257–31 may *i·* you with smallpox,

infection
  My. 344–29 more dangerous than any material *i·*,

infectious
  Mis. 228–30 People believe in *i·* and contagious
  My. 219–27 so-called *i·* and contagious diseases
     226–30 decline to doctor *i·* or contagious
     344–21 * heading
     344–23 * of *i·* and contagious diseases.

infer
  Mis. 32– 6 I *i·* that some of my students
  My. 334– 2 * to *i·* from newspaper reports

inference
  Mis. 103–21 Any *i·* of the divine derived from
     122–16 Such an *i·* were impious.
     195–18 in our text, contradicts this *i·*,
     216– 1 and *i·* from his acts,
  Ret. 59– 8 Such an *i·* is unscientific.
  Pul. 46– 7 * no such *i·* is to be drawn
  Rud. 6– 2 equal *i·* that there is no matter.

inference
  No. 16–18 *i·* of some other existence
     16–21 He can have no knowledge or *i·* but
  '01. 28–27 hence the *i·* that he who would

inferior
  Mis. 226–25 Perfidy of an *i·* quality,

inferred
  Mis. 379–10 from his remarks I *i·* that

infidel
  Mis. 63– 1 is *i·* in the one case,
     248–16 that I am an *i·*, a mesmerist,
     345–14 Methinks the *i·* was blind who said,
  No. 43–15 * convicting the *i·*, alarming the
  Peo. 13–22 The *i·* was blind who said,

infidelity
  Mis. 4–21 confounded with isms, and even *i·*,
     257– 1 that Mind can be in matter is rank *i·*,
     365–24 *i·*, bigotry, or sham has never
  Rud. 12–11 fosters *i·*, and is mental quackery,
  No. 19– 5 Even doctors will agree that *i·*,
     21–18 This is rank *i·* ;
  My. 220–17 the end of idolatry and *i·*,

infidels
  Mis. 345–15 but even *i·* may disagree.
  '01. 32–12 When *i·* assailed them,
  Peo. 13–24 *i·* disagree ; for Bonaparte said :

infinite (noun)
  against the
  Ret. 67–10 self-arrayed against the *i·*,
  apprehend the
  Peo. 3–21 wrongly to apprehend the *i·*,
  blessings of the
  My. 118–21 to supply the blessings of the *i·*,
  body of the
  Hea. 3–27 person of Truth, the body of the *i·*,
  cannot contain the
  Hea. 4– 1 finite cannot contain the *i·*,
  demonstrated the
  No. 36– 1 demonstrated the *i·* as one,
  includes
  Mis. 96–10 or what the *i·* includes ;
  is one
  My. 356–25 The *i·* is one, and this one is
  likeness of the
  Mis. 97–27 image and likeness of the *i·*.
  measures the
  My. 229–31 measures the *i·* against the finite.
  radiation of the
  No. 17–19 the focal radiation of the *i·*.
  scorner of the
  My. 107–21 O petty scorner of the *i·*,
  sense of the
  '01. 26– 8 only a finite sense of the *i·* :
  Spirit and
  '01. 25–28 which, if indeed Spirit and *i·*,
  unlike the
  '02. 6– 2 to have aught unlike the *i·*.
  voices the
  No. 13–19 voices the *i·*, and governs the

  Mis. 75–12 the *i·* is not within the finite ;
     102– 8 and the *i·* forever finite.
     136– 8 The eternal and *i·*,
     153–29 * Far-off, *i·*, Bliss !
     173–15 Can the *i·* be within the finite?
     322–28 from the infinitesimal to the *i·*.
  Un. 7– 9 the *i·* recognizes no disease,
  No. 1– 2 spiritual idea emanating from the *i·*,
     19–13 person of the *i·* is, we know not ;
     19–20 nature and essence of the individual *i·*.
  '01. 6– 7 reckons . . . the *i·* in a finite form,
     23– 6 and that the *i·* is not all ;
     23– 9 or exist outside of the *i·*,
  Hea. 4– 2 *i·* can neither go forth from,
  My. 159–14 *i·* will not be buried in the finite ;
     159–19 God, the *i·* and eternal
     186–12 Word welling up from the *i·*
     195–26 an edifice in which to worship the *i·*,
     226–14 from the infinitesimal to the *i·*,
     239–21 the infinite *one*, or one *i·*,
     248–17 into the transcendental, the *i·*
     272–10 is not the altitude of the *i·*.
     291– 9 from the infinitesimal to the *i·*.

infinite (adj.)
  All
  Mis. 250– 1 the *i·* All of good,
  Un. 24– 2 I am the *i·* All.
  ascent
  My. 117– 8 to pursue the *i·* ascent,
  Being
  Un. 19– 2 must be one, in an *i·* Being.
  being
  My. 262–17 with the glory of *i·* being.

infinite (adj.)

blessings
    (*see* **blessings**)
calculus
  Mis. 22–11 *i·* calculus defining the line,
  '01. 22–20 *i·* calculus of the infinite God.
calm
  '00. 11–25 * With a touch of *i·* calm.
care
  Mis. 370–17 *i·* care from His loving heart.
claims
  Mis. 16–10 hath *i·* claims on man,
consciousness
  Mis. 258–24 *i·* consciousness, ever-presence,
  No. 37– 6 eternal God and *i·* consciousness
Deity
  Un. 10–14 toward aught but *i·* Deity.
demand
  Mis. 77– 7 *i·* demand made upon the eunuch
energies
  Ret. 30–14 *i·* energies of Truth and Love,
essence
  Mis. 394– 4 *i·* essence from tropic to pole,
  Po. 45– 5 *i·* essence from tropic to pole,
faculties
  My. 154–19 * deep *i·* faculties of man.''
finite and
  Mis. 217–29 or to become both finite and *i·* ;
God
  (*see* **God**)
God is
  (*see* **God**)
good
  (*see* **good**)
good is
  Mis. 108– 5 good is *i·*, All.
goodness
  Rud. 2–25 higher range of *i·* goodness.
harmony
  No. 17–23 *i·* harmony would be fathomed.
idea
  Mis. 165– 9 This *i·* idea of infinity will be,
  No. 25–11 *i·* idea of Truth is beyond a finite
identity
  My. 239–23 real and eternal in *i·* identity.
importance
  Mis. 192– 6 of *i·* importance to man's spiritual
individuality
  '00. 5–14 of eternal, *i·* individuality.
inquiry
  Un. 1–14 to defer this *i·* inquiry,
instructions
  Ret. 83–10 *i·* instructions afforded by
law
  Mis. 172–19 feeble sense of the *i·* law of God ;
Life
  (*see* **Life**)
light
  No. 16–15 This infinite logic is the *i·* light,
logic
  No. 16–15 This *i·* logic is the infinite light,
Love
  (*see* **Love**)
manifestation
  Mis. 21–17 Mind and its *i·* manifestation,
manifestations
  '02. 7– 3 His *i·* manifestations of love
meaning
  (*see* **meaning**)
meanings
  Mis. 125–18 learn forever the *i·* meanings of
  '02. 4–23 *i·* meanings, applicable to all
  My. 202–16 *i·* meanings, endless hopes, and
  221– 8 in His more *i·* meanings,
  231–13 of its highest and *i·* meanings,
  262–31 reveals *i·* meanings and gives
mercy
  Pul. 74–16 for God to declare in His *i·* mercy.
Mind
  (*see* **Mind**)
mind
  Pan. 3–18 *i·* mind of one supreme, holy,
model
  Un. 14–22 Our *i·* model would be taken away.
nature
  Mis. 284– 6 Its *i·* nature and uses
  My. 349–29 makes manifest the *i·* nature,
ocean
  Mis. 205–14 in the *i·* ocean of Love,
One
  Pul. 4–15 reflects the *i·* One,
  '01. 4–22 understand that God is the *i·* One
one
  My. 239–21 idea or likeness of the *i·* one,
patience
  Hea. 2–17 Jesus, the model of *i·* patience,

infinite (adj.)

penetration
  Un. 2–15 in the *i·* penetration of Truth,
perfect and
  Mis. 82–16 whose law is perfect and *i·*.
perfection
  Un. 16– 1 man bows to the *i·* perfection
  My. 103–12 *I·* perfection is unfolded
Person
  Pan. 8– 7 one the divine, *i·* Person,
  '01. 3– 7 chapter sub-title
  4–19 He is the *i·* Person,
  6–10 a finite or an *i·* Person?
  6–27 We believe in God as the *i·* **Person** ;
  7– 6 individuality of the *i·* Person
  7–19 as well as *i·* Person,
  My. 109–15 This *i·* Person we know not of by
  192–13 the *i·* Person whom we worship,
  225–22 Principle, Love, the *i·* Person.
personality
  Mis. 102–16 *I·* personality must be incorporeal.
power
  Un. 13–13 His *i·* power would straightway
  My. 160– 7 is to individualize *i·* power ;
Principle
  (*see* **Principle**)
progression
  Mis. 82–13 *Is there i· progression with man*
  82–20 *I·* progression is concrete being,
query
  Mis. 337– 8 *I·* query ! Wonder in heaven
reality
  Un. 43– 5 cannot bring out the *i·* reality
remedy
  Mis. 63– 9 divine trinity is one *i·* remedy
results
  Ret. 92– 1 self-abandonment wrought *i·* results.
scope
  My. 259–25 give the activity of man *i·* scope ;
sinner
  Un. 15–19 precedence as the *i·* sinner,
  16– 2 such terms as *divine sin* and *i· sinner*
Soul
  Un. 48–18 Ego is God Himself, the *i·* Soul.
  Pul. 2–24 the eternal harmony of *i·* Soul.
source
  Mis. 287–12 Soul is the *i·* source of bliss :
  My. 165–31 *i·* source where is *all,*
Spirit
  (*see* **Spirit**)
Spirit is
  Pan. 13–19 great truth that Spirit is *i·*,
  My. 271– 2 God, Spirit, is *i·*,
  357–22 Spirit is *i·* ; therefore *Spirit is all.*
Truth
  (*see* **Truth**)
Unseen
  Un. 7–21 perfection of the *i·* Unseen
uses
  My. 182–32 *i·* uses of Christ's creed,
value
  Mis. 232–23 its *i·* value and firm basis.
wisdom
  Mis. 18–11 These commands of *i·* wisdom,
  Hea. 4–10 We ask *i·* wisdom to possess our

  Mis. 16– 9 Principle of Christianity is *i·* :
  102– 4 is only an *i·* finite being,
  189–20 declare Life to be the *i·* I AM,
  252– 2 not necessarily infinitesimal but *i·*.
  309–12 *i·* spiritual substance and
  330–12 since man's possibilities are *i·*,
  367–19 if . . . He would not be *i·*.
  386– 2 *i·* appear Life, Love divine,
  Ret. 57–11 but one Soul, and that one is *i·*.
  70–24 individual, incorporeal, and *i·*,
  Un. 19–13 this would be the end of *i·* moral
  24–13 an *i·*, and not a finite consciousness.
  29–12 Soul, or Mind, and that one is *i·*,
  41– 9 the *i·* and only Life.
  48–13 as *i·* and conscious Life,
  Rud. 1– 6 *i·* and immortal Mind,
  2–13 if we think of Him as less than *i·*.
  2–16 but one *i·* individual Spirit,
  3–26 *i·* and divine Principle of all being,
  7– 5 The *i·* and subtler conceptions
  No. 36– 2 one *i·* and the other finite ;
  36– 4 He knew God as *i·*,
  '01. 4–25 One because He is *i·* ;
  5– 7 one divine *i·* triune Principle,
  6– 8 reckons one as one and this one *i·*.
  6–22 in the *i·* scientific sense of Him,
  6–23 can neither be one nor *i·* in
  6–26 God's personality must be as *i·* as
  22–13 Spirit is true and *i·*,
  23– 5 God is Spirit and *i·*,

infinite (adj.)

'01.	23– 7	God is good and i·,
'02.	5–25	Since God is Love, and i·,
Hea.	4–17	to show itself i· again.
Peo.	2–25	Love universal, i·, eternal.
	4– 5	more than an i· and divine Mind ;
	4– 9	Life, which is i· and eternal,
Po.	49– 4	i· appear Life, Love divine,
My.	36–10	* with our i· heavenly Father
	108–16	only lawgiver, omnipotent, i·, All.
	116–12	God is Person, then Person is i· ;
	135–30	Love, omnipotent, omnipresent, i· ;
	235–21	Because Spirit is God and i·;
	267–10	supreme, i·, the great forever,
	267–16	Heaven is harmony,— i·, boundless
	269– 3	i· divine Principle, Love,
	279–16	God is Father, i·,
	296–20	God, good, omnipotent and i·.
	339– 6	one God, supreme, i·,
	350–19	Thou all, Thou i·
	356–28	God being i·, He is the only basis of

infinitely

Mis.	8–15	blesses i· one and all
	16–19	God is i· more than a person,
	121–28	I· greater than human pity,
	185–21	reveals man i· blessed,
	309–20	life is i· above a bodily form
	321–30	i· beyond all earthly
	332– 4	I· just, merciful, and wise,
Pul.	62–17	* with i· less expense.
No.	34–19	i· beyond the heathen conception
Hea.	14–15	Metaphysical healing includes i· more
My.	114–24	Truth and Love, i· above me,
	128– 8	i· less than God's benign
	146–13	C. S. contains i· more than

infinites

'01.	6–12	Who can conceive . . . of three i·?

infinitesimal

Mis.	252– 2	Mind is not necessarily i·
	322–27	from the i· to the infinite.
Hea.	12–19	made the i· dose effectual.
My.	226–13	from the i· to the infinite,
	291– 8	from the i· to the infinite.

infinitesimals

Mis.	26–15	Whence came the i·,

infinitude

Mis.	95–23	C. S. reveals the i· of divinity
	181–13	if we recognize i· as personality,
	259– 7	this i· and oneness of good
Un.	20–20	as you realize the divine i·
No.	26–16	into something below i·,
	30–19	Truth's knowledge of its own i·

infinity

Mis.	15–20	progress is the law of i·.
	27– 1	What can there be besides i·?
	72–30	aught material, or outside of i·.
	79–15	out of the focal distance of i·.
	102–10	His i· precludes the possibility of
	165– 9	This infinite idea of i· will be
	181–15	who can tell what is the form of i·?
	333– 4	every ray of Truth, of i·,
Ret.	58– 4	to work out the problem of i·
	59–12	in demonstration of i·.
	68– 9	though he reflects the i· of good.
	70– 7	an attempted infringement on i·"
Un.	5– 2	a theme involving the All of i·.
	25–16	from finiteness into i·.
No.	38–16	the i· and unity of good.
Pan.	7–16	absolute oneness and i· of God,
Peo.	4– 7	belief that . . . i· became finity,
My.	132–10	they embark for i· and anchor in

infirm

Pul.	4– 2	* "weak and i· of purpose."

infirmities

Mis.	162–18	The corporeal Jesus bore our i·,
	199–11	I take pleasure in i·,— II Cor. 12 : 10.
	200–22	"I take pleasure in i·,"— II Cor. 12 : 10.
	201–16	Paul took pleasure in i·,
	201–31	good that has pleasure in i· ;
Un.	55– 4	In his real self he bore no i·.

infirmity

Mis.	294– 2	last i· of evil is so-called man,
Un.	57–16	by affinity nor by i·,
'02.	10–25	is the i· of evil,
Po.	35– 6	binds to earth— i· of woe !

inflames

Mis.	222– 3	i· envy, passion, evil-speaking,

inflammation

Mis.	41–22	action of fear, manifests i·
	45– 7	power to allay fear, prevent i·,
	69–25	exciting cause of the i·
My.	301–27	Drugs cannot remove i·,

inflammatory

My.	107–30	stages of organic and i· diseases,

inflate

Mis.	129–17	i· it, and send it into the atmosphere of
	301–29	All error tends to . . . i· self ;

inflated

Mis.	354–29	genius i· with worldly desire.

inflection

My.	344–18	* with a prolonged i·,

inflictions

Mis.	312– 7	bears all burdens, suffers all i·,

inflow

Pul.	64–13	* the continued i· of money

influence

adverse

My.	213–26	adverse i· of animal magnetism.

benign

Mis.	63– 5	to hinder his benign i·

counteracting

Mis.	223–22	no counteracting i· can hinder

counteract the

Mis.	291–30	counteract the i· of envious minds

divine

No.	40–27	made better only by divine i·.

elevating

Peo.	2–27	a benign and elevating i·

evil

My.	211–32	induced by this secret evil i·
	212– 9	effects of this evil i·,

felt the

Mis.	290–16	* "I felt the i· of your thought
Un.	57–12	he must have felt the i· of

harmonious

Pul.	54–21	* environment and harmonious i·

her

Pul.	23– 7	* MRS. EDDY'S WORK AND HER I·
	50– 7	* thus add her i· toward the

hidden

Mis.	114–25	stop their hidden i· upon the

its

My.	28–14	* its i· upon the lives of
	47–12	* touched by its i· for good,
	295– 3	its i· remains in the minds

mental

Mis.	264–23	mental i· of their former teacher.
Ret.	72– 2	cannot impart a mental i· that

money and

Mis.	80– 7	its members to give money and i·

much

My.	272–31	* much i· on this generation.

no

No.	9– 9	use no i· to prevent their

of this Mind

Mis.	279–29	feel the i· of this Mind ;

originating

'01.	33–10	* was never the originating i·

salutary

Rud.	10– 4	its salutary i· on yourself

selfish

Ret.	89–29	Corporeal and selfish i· is human,

silent

No.	1– 6	changed by its silent i·.

strengthens the

Mis.	362–31	except when it strengthens the i· of

such an

Ret.	71–15	to be subjected to such an i·?

their

Peo.	8–10	extend their i· to others.

transforming

My.	10– 2	* transforming i· of C. S.

unite the

Un.	43–20	unite the i· of their own thoughts

uplifting

Mis.	245–13	its uplifting i· upon . . . mankind.

Man.	52–26	or shall i· others thus to act,
Ret.	44–30	Adding to its ranks and i·,
	89–27	endeavoring to i· other minds to any
'00.	12–21	Under the i· of St. Paul's preaching
My.	175–28	must fail to i· the minds of
	281–24	i· which President Roosevelt

influenced

Mis.	113–15	i· by any but the divine Mind,
	246– 6	pulpit and press that i· the people
Man.	40–14	influencing or being i· erroneously.
My.	137–21	i· me to select a Board of Trustees
	137–29	No person i· me to make this
	227–14	i· by their own judgment

influences

Mis.	71–12	good or bad i· on the unborn child?
	229–14	faith in Mind over all other i·
Ret.	52– 6	contaminating i· of those who

influences
Rud.   4–12   sweet *i·* of the Pleiades," — *Job* 38 : 31.
No.   7– 3   evil *i·* waver the scales of justice
       39– 8   no dishonesty or vanity *i·* the
influencing
Man. 40–14   *i·* or being influenced erroneously.
  '01. 20– 3   no authority in C. S. for *i·* the
influenza
Mis. 239–21   pride at sharing in a popular *i·*
influx
My. 114–21   *i·* of divine interpretation
     206– 4   hinder the divine *i·* and lose
     212–20   they would receive a spiritual *i·*
inform
Mis. 29–21   Daily letters *i·* me that a
     67–21   you shall, *Deo volente, i·* them
     87–15   *i· us, through your Journal,*
     88– 9   I am pleased to *i·* this inquirer,
     97–21   Scriptures *i·* us that man
   240–28   Likewise soberly *i·* them that
   322–10   Clerk of the church can *i·*
Man. 26–14   shall *i·* the Pastor Emeritus
     29– 1   to *i·* the Board of Directors
     52–17   shall immediately so *i·* him.
     57–11   Clerk to *i·* the Board of Directors
     66– 2   he shall *i·* her of this fact
No. 23–24   is not sufficient to *i·* us as to
     28–25   The Scriptures *i·* us that
My. 135–18   I *i·* you of this,
   359–12   to *i·* himself of the facts.
informally
Ret. 89–12   he did so *i·*,
My. 352– 4   * *I·* assembled, we, the ushers
informant
My. 14–13   * *i·* claimed to have good authority
information
Mis. 69–28   wish to apply to him for *i·*
     89–21   *I ask for i·, not for controversy,*
   132–22   for *i·* as to what I believe
   157–11   that they furnish all *i·* possible.
Man. 46–15   such *i·* as may come to them
     53–12   without her having requested the *i·*,
Pul. 37– 1   * "It is a pleasure to give any *i·*
My. 54–11   * the *i·*, 'No more standing-room.' "
     73–21   * all *i·* concerning rooms and board,
   236–27   I consider the *i·* there given
   242–17   *i·* relating to C. S. practice,
   319–20   * advised that I have this *i·*.
informed
Mis. 48–15   *i·* his audience that he could
     49– 4   *i·* that, before entering the College,
     91–24   I never dreamed, until *i·* thereof,
   195–32   *i·* by divine Science, the Comforter,
   378– 5   as he *i·* the patients,
Man. 76–22   *i·* as to the real estate
Ret. 15–28   agreeably *i·* the congregation
     21– 4   *i·* that my son was lost.
     38– 2   when the printer *i·* me that
     47–13   being *i·* of my intentions,
No. 3–17   to keep himself well *i·*.
  '01. 27–15   I shall rejoice in being *i·*
  '02. 15– 3   neither *i·* the police of these
My. 11–23   * *i·* of the purchase of the land
     14–12   * saying that he had just been *i·*
   166–27   I am for the first time *i·* of
   330– 7   * calumniator who *i·* you
   358–12   You have been duly *i·*
informer
Pul. 15–12   Is the *i·* one who sees the foe?
informing
Mis. 332– 3   governing, *i·* the universe,
Ret. 21– 2   *i·* him that his mother was dead
My. 198– 4   *i·* me of the dedication
   244– 1   before *i·* you of my purpose
   259–30   eternal *i·* Soul recognized only
informs
Mis. 339– 3   that which St. John *i·* us
infraction
Mis. 29–27   Miracles are no *i·* of God's laws ;
infrequently
Ret. 80–29   not *i·* met by envy, ingratitude,
Pul. 33–15   * which history not *i·* emphasizes,
My. 355– 8   not *i·* hinted at this.
infringe
Mis. 348– 5   *i·* neither the books nor the business
Pan. 8–11   *i·* the sacredness of one
My. 154– 8   if they can be made to *i·* the
infringed
Ret. 39– 2   the copyright was *i·*.
Un. 13–10   are not *i·* in ethics

infringement
Mis. 300–10   liable to arrest for *i·* of
   302– 4   encourages *i·* of my copyright,
Ret. 70– 6   attempted *i·* on infinity"
Peo. 12– 6   *i·* on the merciful and just
My. 167–25   *i·* of rights and privileges
infringes
Mis. 56–12   *i·* the rights of Spirit.
infringing
Mis. 80–17   *i·* individual rights,
   380–30   use of an *i·* pamphlet
   381–27   *i·* books, to the number of
infused
Mis. 190– 3   nor the outcome of life *i·* into
Ret. 58–13   it was not *i·* into matter ;
infusion
Un. 42–22   or of an *i·* of power into matter.
ingenuity
Mis. 286–16   put *i·* to ludicrous shifts ;
ingenuously
Pul. 23–15   * *i·* calling out a closer inquiry
Ingersoll's
  Robert
My. 110–28   Robert *I·* attempt to convict the
                     ———
Ret. 77– 3   *I·* repartee has its moral :
inglorious
Ret. 10–18   no earthly or *i·* theme.
ingrafting
Ret. 57–26   *i·* upon one First Cause
ingrained
My. 81– 5   * So *i·* is this good nature,
ingratitude
Mis. 13– 5   falsehood, *i·*, misjudgment,
   294–16   hides it in his cell of *i·*.
   389–15   hope deferred, *i·*, disdain !
Ret. 81– 1   envy, *i·*, and enmity,
Un. 56–27   *i·*, lust, malice, hate,
Pul. 84– 4   * bitterness and *i·* of her sting,
  '01. 15–16   mortals, and their *i·* and hate,
  '02. 19– 1   injustice, *i·*, treachery, and
Po. 4–14   For hope deferred, *i·*, disdain !
ingress
Mis. 325–28   sees robbers finding ready *i·* to
inhabit
Pul. 21– 9   praying for it to *i·* my own heart
  '01. 6– 9   infinite Mind *i·* a finite form?
My. 133– 6   *i·* His holy hill,
inhabitants
Mis. 334– 2   among the *i·* of the earth ; — *Dan.* 4 : 35.
My. 181–24   to the number of 1,650,000 *i·*.
   280–19   He will bless all the *i·*
inhabiters
Pul. 12–12   Woe to the *i·* of the earth — *Rev.* 12 : 12.
inhabiting
Mis. 330–30   modest grass, *i·* the whole earth,
My. 344–10   not the spirit of God, *i·* clay
inhabits
Mis. 189–30   extends to all time, *i·* eternity,
inharmonious
Mis. 58–24   If God does not govern . . . it is *i·* :
inharmony
Mis. 27–12   all *i·*, sin, disease, death
     98– 4   turn away from *i·*, sickness, and
Un. 13–11   To Him there is no moral *i·* ;
     18–19   My knowledge of harmony (not *i·*)
     60–10   and *i·* is its opposite,
inherent
Pul. 51– 7   * liberty which is their *i·* right
  '02. 2–22   It was an *i·* characteristic
My. 227–22   *I·* justice, constitutional
   262– 3   *i·* unity with divine Love,
   326– 6   * their *i·* rights are recognized
inherit
Mis. 145–13   "*i·* the earth." — *Psal.* 37 : 11.
   340–22   by patience, they *i·* the promise.
Ret. 92– 7   *i·* his legacy of love,
Un. 37– 4   in order to *i·* eternal life
  '01. 26–19   the meek that *i·* the earth ;
My. 228–18   Who shall *i·* the earth?
   228–21   they shall *i·* the earth,
inheritance
Mis. 153– 3   God will confirm His *i·*.
   251–20   Think of this *i·* !
   253–19   that the *i·* may be ours," — *Luke* 20 : 14.
   254–14   that the *i·* may be ours," — *Luke* 20 : 14.
   307– 5   What a glorious *i·* is given to us

inheritance
No. 3– 3 idea which claims only its *i·*,
My. 41–26 * and disregard his lawful *i·*,
206–27 partakers of the *i·* — *Col. 1 : 12.*

inherited
Ret. 1–13 was no sign that she *i·* a
4– 3 Mark Baker, who *i·* the homestead,
4– 4 he *i·* my grandfather's farm
My. 309–18 *i·* his father's real estate,

inhospitable
My. 89– 4 * all facts *i·* to it

inhuman
Mis. 121–15 That the innocent shall . . . is *i·*.
211–10 *I·* medical bills, class legislation,
246– 5 to blot out all *i·* codes.
Peo. 11– 8 not by *i·* warfare, but in divine
12–11 as with an *i·* State law ;

inhumanity
Mis. 246–15 *i·* lifts its hydra head

iniquities
Mis. 102–21 which blots out all our *i·*
174– 7 Him who removeth all *i·*,
Un. 48–10 destroys my *i·*, deprives death of
55– 7 bruised for *our i· ;— Isa. 53 : 5.*
Pul. 10– 6 forgiveth all thine *i· ;— Psal.* 103 : 3.
Pan. 4–25 forgiveth all thine *i· ;— Psal.* 103 : 3.
Peo. 12–13 forgiveth all thine *i· ;— Psal.* 103 : 3.
My. 13–20 forgiveth all thine *i· ;— Psal.* 103 : 3.
126–17 hath remembered her *i·* — *Rev. 18 : 5.*

iniquitous
Ret. 67– 9 *i·* manifestation of sin

iniquity
Mis. 19–19 wherewith to cover *i·*,
123–17 and is too pure to behold *i·*.
209–31 egotism and false charity say, . . . cover *i·*
210–29 foolhardiness to cover *i·*.
259–11 while *i·*, too evil to conceive of
259–13 declares that God knows *i·* !
335–21 notion that one is covering *i·* by
348– 8 When God bids one uncover *i·*,
367–30 God is too pure to behold *i·* ;
Ret. 63–19 Whosoever covers *i·* becomes accessory
Un. 2– 2 too pure to behold *i·* — *see Hab.* 1 : 13.
18– 8 God says, I am too pure to behold *i·*,
Pul. 15– 4 expose evil's . . . ways of accomplishing *i·*.
Rud. 10– 7 He is too pure to behold *i·*,
'01. 14– 3 that clings fast to *i·*.
My. 124–30 and the mystery of *i·*
126–10 kills this mystery of *i·*
161–10 all ye workers of *i·*. — *Luke* 13 : 27.
252–10 reward righteousness and punish *i·*.
334–21 that clings fast to *i·*.

initial
Mis. xi– 3 caused me to retain the *i·* "G"

initials
Man. 46– 7 Use of *I·* "C. S."
46– 8 shall not place the *i·* "C. S."
110–13 *I·* only of first names
111– 4 *I·* alone will not be received.

injunction
Mis. 120– 5 each and every *i·* of the
128– 6 with the apostle's *i·* :
191–31 Let us obey St. Paul's *i·*
302–25 This *i·* did not curtail the
381–21 A writ of *i·* was issued
Ret. 87–19 to obey the celestial *i·*,
Pul. 66–12 * under the *i·* to
My. 227–23 and the gospel *i·*,
282– 7 and the Scriptural *i·*,

injunctions
Pul. 29–20 * while all these *i·* could,
No. 14–21 the *i·* are not confined to

injure
Mis. 12– 8 him who has striven to *i·* you.
32–29 slander, hate, or try to *i·*,
48–30 offered solely to *i·* her
224–29 wilfully attempt to *i·* another,
260–31 whereby it may *i·* the race,
267– 7 whose chief aim is to *i·* me,
267–13 secretly striving to *i·* me.
My. 298– 5 nothing . . . could *i·* me ;
353–17 to *i·* no man, but to bless

injures
My. 210–12 *i·* him when he would harm

injuries
My. 204–26 the resenting of *i·*,
348– 2 healed of so-called disease and *i·*

injuring
Mis. 222– 6 *i·* himself and others.

injurious
Man. 53–26 false or unjust, hence *i·*, to C. S.
My. 128–26 but the result is as *i·*.

injury
Mis. 24– 9 an *i·* caused by an accident,
43–22 does a vast amount of *i·*
Man. 49–25 without previous *i·* or illness,
Ret. 24–12 an *i·* caused by an accident,
24–13 an *i·* that neither medicine nor
40–14 *i·* received from a surgical operation
My. 138– 8 not for my benefit . . . but for my *i·*,

injustice
Mis. 66– 8 No possible *i·* lurks in this
72– 4 were sore *i·*.
80–20 redress wrongs and rectify *i·*.
122–22 nor reconciles justice to *i·* ;
216–17 a big protest against *i·* ;
235–26 chapter sub-title
247–17 *i·* of their interpretations.
301–24 This method is an unseen form of *i·*
317–29 My soul abhors *i·*, and loves mercy.
Pul. 83–15 * wield the ruthless sword of *i·*.
'02. 19– 1 *i·*, ingratitude, treachery, and
Peo. 10–14 *i·* and error enslave him.
Po. 71–12 *I·* to the combat sprang ;
My. 116–23 from *i·* and personal contagion.
151–12 *i·* done by press and pulpit
191– 4 *I·* has not a tithe of the power of
220–14 *I·* denotes the absence of law.
252–14 clouds of wrong, *i·*, envy, hate ;
277–17 whereby wrong and *i·* are righted
283–19 When pride, self, . . . *i·* is rampant.

injustices
Man. 97–18 *i·* done Mrs. Eddy or members

inkling
'02. 16– 6 my first *i·* of Wyclif's use of

inlaid
Mis. 30–13 gates thereof . . . *i·* with pearl,

inmate
Mis. 324–20 this mortal *i·* withdraws ;

inmates
Mis. 283–11 rouse the slumbering *i·*,
325–14 find its *i·* asleep at noontide !

in memoriam
My. 289–28 *i· m·* of the late lamented Victoria,

inmost
My. 133–26 this *i·* something becomes articulate,

innate
Un. 26– 2 having its own *i·* selfhood
My. 341 1 I have one *i·* joy,

inner
Pul. 92–15 * may translate those *i·* experiences
'01. 30–19 kindles the *i·* genial life
My. 188–19 I enter your *i·* sanctuary,
244–17 *i·* sanctuary of divine Science,

innocence
Mis. 110– 6 it needs your *i·*, unselfishness,
121–20 this sentence passed upon *i·*
Ret. 80–25 while *i·* strayeth yearningly.
My. 261–13 the first impressions of *i·*,
269– 4 pledged to *i·*, purity,

innocent
Mis. 66– 3 may cause the *i·* to suffer
72– 2 For the *i·* babe to be born a
112– 9 can neither defend the *i·* nor
121–15 That the *i·* shall suffer for
121–17 the guilt of *i·* blood — *Deut.* 19 : 13.
121–31 punishes the guilty, not the *i·*.
210–23 *i·* enjoyment, and a medical
227– 6 to offer to the *i·*, security
257–14 It punishes the *i·*,
275–19 console the *i·*, and throw wide the
354– 5 and lead the *i·* to doom?
My. 33–26 reward against the *i·*. — *Psal.* 15 : 5.
220–29 That the *i·* should suffer for the

innocently
Mis. 357–28 sought the true fold . . . and strayed *i·* ;

innocents
Mis. 123– 2 same spirit that . . . slaughters *i·*.

innovations
Mis. 265–16 presume to make *i·* upon

innumerable
Mis. 137–26 one of the *i·* errors that
My. 46–29 * *i·* company of angels, — *Heb.* 12 : 22.

inordinate
Mis. 274–21 reign of *i·*, unprincipled clans.

inorganic
Mis. 56– 4 Life is *i·*, infinite Spirit ;

in propria persona
Pul. 1–19 that I should be present *i· p· p·?*
My. 5–23 I am not with you *i· p· p·*
25–19 I cannot be present *i· p· p·*
143– 1 I will attend . . . but not *i· p· p·*.

inquest
My. 128– 6 A coroner's *i·*, a board of health,

inquire
Mis. 381–10 requested her lawyer to *i·*
Man. 66–19 *i·* if all of the letter has been read,
My. 325– 3 * to *i·* of his welfare

inquired
Pul. 73– 1 * *i·* the speaker.
Peo. 4–24 *i·* of these heathen deities
My. 24–18 * *i·* about the progress of the work

inquirer
Mis. 88– 9 pleased to inform this *i·*,
Un. 20–15 Try this process, dear *i·*,

Inquirer
Pul. 88–32 * *I·*, Philadelphia, Pa.

inquiries
Mis. 132–18 *i·* from all quarters,
193– 1 entertaining the startling *i·*,
My. 223–20 *i·*, coming directly or indirectly
242–17 *i·* . . . relating to C. S. practice,
242–22 not to make *i·* on these subjects,
245–26 *I·* have been made as to the precise
356–13 In reply to *i·*, will you please state

inquiring
'01. 31–14 no vague, fruitless, *i·* wonder.

inquiry
Mis. 28–21 suggests the *i·*, What meaneth
237–19 This is a period of doubt, *i·*,
268–15 His whole *i·* and demonstration
307–16 *i·* of mankind as to Christianity
Man. 52– 9 shall address a letter of *i·* to
Un. 1–14 to defer this infinite *i·*,
27– 1 *i·* as to the meaning of a word
Pul. 23–16 * a closer *i·* into Oriental
33–21 * All *i·* in the neighborhood
No. 46– 9 must answer the constant *i·* :
'01. 17–18 interviews, that started the *i·*,
My. 53– 2 * important missives of *i·*
157–19 * In response to an *i·* from
165–19 oft-repeated *i·*, What am I?
245–10 The growth of human *i·*
292–13 My answer to the *i·*,

Inquisition
Mis. 274–28 car of the modern *I·*

inquisitive
Rud. 15– 9 renders the mind less *i·*, plastic,

inrush
My. 74– 3 * until Saturday night the *i·* will

insane
Mis. 48–23 *Was ever a person made i· by*
48–26 Mind-healing would cure the *i·*.
48–28 * "made *i·* . . . is a baseless fabrication
My. 301–21 committed to *i·* asylums
302–11 insanity is that brain, matter, is *i·*.

insanity
Mis. 49–10 had not produced *i·*."
49–11 into the claim of *i·*
49–13 notable cases of *i·* have been
113–22 if persisted in, will end in *i·*,
My. 222–16 executed (for "*i·*") because of
301–16 Is faith in divine metaphysics *i·*?
301–17 All sin is *i·*,
301–18 a universal *i·* which mistakes
301–23 supposition that we can correct *i·* by
301–24 is in itself a species of *i·*.
302–11 *i·* is that brain, matter, is insane.

inscribed
Mis. 121– 2 *i·* upon the hearts of men:
295–25 advanced ideas are *i·* on tablets
Ret. 2–12 on which was *i·* the name of
5–12 *i·* on the stone memorials
Pul. 46–20 * upon which had been *i·* the name
Po. 73– 1 *i·* to my friends in Lynn.

inscribes
Mis. 294– 7 he *i·* on the heart of humanity
Peo. 3–17 *i·* on the thoughts of men

inscription
Pul. 24–13 * *i·* carved in bold relief :
77– 8 * The *i·* reads thus :
78– 6 * *i·*, cut in script letters :
86– 3 * upon the cover of which is this *i·* :
My. 60–18 * It has this *i·* on the fly-leaf

inscriptions
My. 69– 8 * *i·* illustrative of the faith

inscrutable
Ret. 79–15 the *i·* problem of being

insects
My. 178–12 * "counting the legs of *i·*" ?

insensible
Un. 54–10 *i·* to every claim of error.

inseparability
Mis. 189– 9 *i·* of God and man,

inseparable
Mis. 182–28 man and his Maker are *i·*
266–16 *i·* from the unity of God.
361–30 are *i·* as cause and effect.
Ret. 75–10 Life and its ideals are *i·*,
Un. 21–18 man is *i·* from good.
38–10 and is *i·* from it.
My. 23–25 * Spirit, with its *i·* accompaniment,
185–16 spontaneity of Love, *i·* from Love,
300–20 these things, *i·* from C. S.,

insert
Ret. 38– 8 *i·* in my last chapter a partial

inserted
Man. 49–14 may be *i·* in *The C. S. Journal*

inside
Mis. 344–17 would place Soul wholly *i·* of body,
Pul. 58–13 * *I·* is a basement room, capable of
No. 26– 2 believe . . . the immortal is *i·* the
My. 145– 9 details outside and *i·*
346–13 * She was *i·*, and as she passed me

insidious
Ret. 19– 9 attacked by this *i·* disease,
My. 334– 3 * some *i·* disease was raging

insight
Mis. 169– 5 spiritual *i·* had been darkened
189–10 Spiritual *i·* of Truth and Love
Ret. 32– 4 spiritual *i·*, knowledge, and being.
My. 11–18 * needs no special *i·* to predict
296– 3 his flash of flight and *i·*,

insignia
Ret. 80– 2 and the *i·* of heaven.
No. 9–23 cabalistic *i·* of philosophy ;
My. 83– 9 * no flaunting of badges or *i·*
216–23 drop the *i·* of "Busy Bees,"

insignificance
Po. 1–15 On *i·* that peoples earth,
My. 77– 7 * pales into *i·*,

insignificant
My. 91–13 * no *i·* element in true Christianity.
92–16 * increased from an *i·* number
93–30 * faith had but an *i·* following.

insincerity
My. 166– 3 *i·* and a half-persuaded faith

insinuate
Ret. 36–10 which the evil-minded would *i·*

insist
Mis. 75– 6 *i·* that there is but one Soul,
283–19 I *i·* on the etiquette of C. S.,
336–12 *i·* on the rule and demonstration of
Ret. 63– 2 *i·* on the need of healing sickness
76–28 *i·* upon the strictest observance of
Un. 24– 7 Your assumptions *i·* that there is
43–13 I *i·* only upon the fact,
Pul. 27–11 * members strongly *i·* upon.
No. 10– 3 I *i·* that C. S. is demonstrably as
31–13 I *i·* on the destruction of sin
'01. 22–25 *i·* that the public receive their
My. 13– 1 they *i·* upon doing now.
180–23 *i·* on what we know is right,

insisted
Mis. 88–20 * *i·* that this Science is natural,
158– 6 When I *i·* on your speaking
193–31 The condition *i·* upon is,
327–13 and *i·* upon taking all of it
373– 3 I *i·* upon placing the serpent behind
No. 3– 9 some irresponsible people *i·*
My. 48–10 * *i·* that her students make,

insistence
Un. 8–13 My *i·* upon a proper understanding
My. 48–18 * *i·* upon the constant daily reading

insists
Mis. 200–11 The apostle Paul *i·* on the
241–21 Truth destroys the error that *i·*
346– 3 *i·* on the demonstration of
366–20 evil *i·* on the unity of good and
Ret. 69– 8 serpent, *i·* still upon the

insomnia
Mis. 209–15 *I·* compels mortals to learn

insomuch
Mis. 8–29 *i·* as the consciousness of good,
10–19 *i·* as they thereby have tried
10–20 *i·* as they have found their strength
189–26 *i·* that St. Matthew wrote,
359–15 *i·* as he was able to do this ;
Ret. 58– 9 sense of power . . . . *i·* that the people
My. 271–29 *i·* as I know myself, what is

inspected

My.	24–25	* have recently *i·* the work,
	145– 8	I *i·* the work every day,

inspiration

Mis.	124–28	it gives to suffering, *i·* ;
	144–27	exudes the *i·* of the wine
Ret.	30–23	neither can its *i·* be gained without
Un.	46– 3	All Truth is from *i·*
Pul.	56–18	* Welding . . . was a happy *i·*.
	83–11	* with the certainty of *i·* she works,
'02.	8–18	except we possess this *i·*,
Peo.	7–27	Scientific discovery and the *i·* of
My.	14–21	* endowed with genius and *i·*,
	48– 5	* one ready to receive the *i·*,
	55–17	* was an *i·* to Christian Scientists,
	131–11	restitution, redemption, and *i·*.
	156–23	the *i·* which giveth victory
	248–29	Your highest *i·* is found
	260–18	its fruits are *i·* and
	297–19	an *i·* to the whole field,
	303–26	I have not the *i·* nor the

inspire

Mis.	132–30	*i·* me with the hope that you wish
My.	58–21	* May her example *i·* us to
	134–19	beautify, bless, and *i·* man's power.

inspired

Mis.	58–13	I read the *i·* page through a higher
	101– 1	how hearts are *i·*,
	169– 6	God-driven back to the *i·* pages.
	169–21	to read what the *i·* writers left
	187–15	*i·* sense of the spiritual man,
	190–19	found to include the *i·* meaning.
	193– 1	Are the Scriptures *i·*?
	312–24	He spake *i·* ;
Man.	15– 3	we take the *i·* Word of the Bible
Pul.	72– 1	* *i·* in her great task by
No.	22–12	Compared with the *i·* wisdom and
Pan.	12–11	the *i·* Scriptural commands
'00.	14–12	his *i·* rebuke to all the churches
'01.	21–28	divine Love which *i·* it.
'02.	8–15	The spiritually minded are *i·* with
Po.	v–12	* I *by the grandeur of this*
My.	47–21	* so many of different races
	238–17	law, or *morale* of the *i·* Word
	362–20	* rejoice in your *i·* leadership,

inspires

Mis.	252–26	*i·* the teacher and preacher ;
	360– 1	*i·* wisdom and procures divine power.
Po.	32–12	*i·* my pen as I write ;
My.	24– 8	* *i·* you to welcome all mankind

inspiring

Mis.	169 29	* beautiful and *i·* are the thoughts
	213–21	*i·* tones from the lips of our Master,
	369 27	We thirst for *i·* wine from the
My.	50–24	* a very *i·* season to us all,
	363–15	This proof . . . . is soul *i·*.

installed

My.	70–23	* organ which has been *i·*.

instalments

My.	73–28	* bearing the first *i·* of the crowds

instance

Mis.	45–19	when Science in a single *i·* decides
	61–14	* For *i·*, the man is held responsible for
	93–31	if you suffer for it in the first *i·*,
	116–29	If in one *i·* obedience be lacking,
	183–16	fulfil the Scriptures in every *i·* ;
	221–19	denial of this fact in one *i·*
	247–10	to furnish a single *i·* of
	247–31	must be met, in every *i·*,
	248– 3	For *i·* : the literal meaning of the
	362– 2	for *i·*, intelligent matter, or
Ret.	59– 9	means subtraction in one *i·* and
Pul.	45– 3	* Sacrifices were made in many an *i·*
'01.	14–25	control it in the first *i·*, or
Peo.	10–27	in a single *i·* when African slavery
Po.	v– 9	* *"Old Man of the Mountain," for i·*,
My.	97– 4	* on the part of a sick person, for *i·*,
	112–13	not inconsistent in a single *i·*
	330– 7	* informed you in this *i·*

instances

Mis.	40–13	In some *i·* the students of
	107–28	in certain morbid *i·*
	301–10	startling *i·* of the above-named
	317–25	already seen in many *i·*
Ret.	41– 5	in most *i·* without even an
Pul.	79–15	* in most *i·* they are held at
My.	28–10	* in many *i·* the loving self-sacrifice,
	67–23	* were spent in other *i·*.
	137–15	except in one or two *i·*,
	301–21	only so many well-defined *i·*

instant

Pul.	44– 8	* willingly pause for an *i·*
My.	11–16	* the response was *i·*,
	360–29	Your favor of the 10th *i·*

instantaneous

Mis.	40–11	why do not its students perform as *i·*
	40–24	or they cannot be *i·* healers.
	200– 2	made his healing easy and *i·*.
	355– 8	not guesswork, . . . but *i·* cure.
Un.	7–14	raise the dying to *i·* health.

instantaneously

Mis.	359– 7	until you can cure without it *i·*,
Un.	7–11	*i·* to heal a cancer
Pul.	6–16	* was healed *i·* of an ailment

instantly

Ret.	41– 4	desperate cases I *i·* healed,
My.	178–24	I *i·* the table sank a charred mass.

instead

Mis.	16–25	from Soul *i·* of body,
	53–18	below *i·* of above the standard
	54–10	I *i·* of losing her power to heal,
	59– 6	*i·* of the divine power understood,
	119– 4	*i·* of aiding other people's
	135– 4	Principle, *i·* of person, is
	175– 8	matter, *i·* of Mind.
	182– 1	began spiritually *i·* of materially
	231–22	*i·* of a real set-to at crying,
	237– 4	thing of mortal mind *i·* of body :
	271– 4	a thought, *i·* of a thing.
	281–20	*i·*, of our poverty and
	300–15	the pulpit, *i·* of the press,
	303–13	Let us serve *i·* of rule,
	303–13	knock *i·* of push at the door
	340–13	agriculture *i·* of litigation,
	340–14	dug into soils *i·* of delving into
	340 15	raised potatoes *i·* of pleas,
	340 16	and drew up logs *i·* of leases.
	351–23	wherefore it is hate *i·* of Love ;
	354–20	I *i·* of relying on the Principle
Ret.	26–15	*i·* of seeing therein the operation of
	33– 3	mortal belief, *i·* of the drug,
	49– 9	more of the spirit *i·* of the letter,
	56–10	is of human *i·* of divine origin.
Un.	9–16	but have built *i·* upon the sand of
	29–23	by reading *sense i·* of *soul,*
	30–18	man as immortal *i·* of mortal
	35– 9	mortally mental, *i·* of material.
	36–18	(*i·* of acquiescence therein)
Rud.	12– 7	strengthen . . . disease, *i·* of cure it ;
No.	3–27	*i·* of possessing the essentials of
	4–13	error . . . becomes fable *i·* of fact.
	12–28	God must be found all *i·* of a part of
	44–17	and *i·* of healing,
'01.	4–22	the infinite One *i·* of three,
Hea.	3 19	*i·* of the divine Principle that
	7– 8	language of Soul *i·* of the senses ;
	7–10	gives the spiritual *i·* of the
	7–11	It begins with motive, *i·* of act,
	8–21	through Principle *i·* of a pardon ;
Peo.	2–13	of Soul *i·* of the senses,
My.	4–17	will be found that, *i·* of opposing,
	119–14	looked for the person, *i·* of
	120– 3	lose me *i·* of find me.
	152– 2	worshipping person *i·* of Principle,
	233– 8	*i·* of *putting out your watch*
		(*see also* **matter**)

instils

My.	224–12	or the prejudice it *i·*.

instinct

Ret.	69– 1	His origin is not, . . . in brute *i·*,
Pul.	9–11	Woman, true to her *i·*,

instinctive

My.	9– 7	* *i·* gratitude which not only

instinctively

Mis.	307–30	human thought must turn *i·* to

instincts

My.	235– 6	guided by love, faithful to her *i·*,

institute

Ret.	48– 3	Who else could sustain this *i·*,
	84–30	avoid leaving his own regular *i·*
'02.	15– 7	keeping a free *i·*,

instituted

'02.	13–20	legal proceedings were *i·* by
My.	252–24	*i·* in England on New Year's Day,

institutes

Mis.	273–17	Their *i·* have not yet
	303– 7	should have their own *i·*
No.	2–19	I *i·* furnished with such teachers

instituting

Mis.	175–20	*i·* matter and its methods

institution

Mis.	145– 1	more than any other *i·*,
	274– 2	no Biblical authority for a public *i·*.
	295–27	*i·* which names itself after
	378– 4	A patient . . . left that *i·*,
Ret.	6–18	ever connected with that *i·*.
	43–19	judged it best to close the *i·*,
	48–26	in the beginning in this *i·*,
	49– 1	height of prosperity in the *i·*,
My.	84– 4	* all the resources of the *i·*.

institutional

My.	8– 4	* outgrowing the *i·* end thereof.

institutions

Mis.	38–14	*other i· find little interest in*
	98–18	perpetuate our organizations and *i·* ;
	272–24	* Hence to name these *i·*,
Ret.	49– 4	Other *i·* for instruction in
'02.	12–29	When founding the *i·*
My.	104– 5	all sorts of *i·* flourish
	175–14	up-to-date academies, humane *i·*,
	340–31	*I·* of learning and progressive

instruct

Mis.	38–13	*college to i· in metaphysics,*
	114–31	specially *i·* his pupils
	130– 9	Does not the latter *i·* you
	331– 1	construct the stalk, *i·* the ear,
Man.	59–10	shall also *i·* their pupils
	84– 2	Teachers shall *i·* their pupils
	86–23	shall *i·* their pupils from the
Ret.	89–19	Jesus' method was to *i·* his
No.	40–14	I *i·* my students to pursue their
My.	49–23	* proceeded to *i·* those present
	49–30	* it was voted to *i·* the Clerk
	51–16	* It was moved to *i·* the Clerk
	60– 4	* wise to *i·* them on the subject
	142– 1	that he may *i·* him — *I Cor.* 2 : 16.

instructed

Mis.	4– 1	*i·* in the Science of metaphysical
	60–30	if mortals are *i·* in spiritual
	242–17	they shall be *i·* in the Principle
	333–31	Christians, *i·* in divine Science,
Man.	62–20	*i·* according to their understanding
	91–20	Students of C. S., duly *i·*
Ret.	48–22	students *i·* in C. S. Mind-healing,
	68–13	Our Master *i·* his students
My.	221–21	*i·* his followers, saying,
	314–21	the court *i·* the clerk
	338–29	is *i·* to be, charitable

instructing

Mis.	317–10	would have great pleasure in *i·*,
My.	223–16	*i·* persons in regard to that

instruction

Mis.	35–17	*student under your personal i·*
	37–26	Her time is wholly devoted to *i·*,
	39– 2	to take a course of *i·* in C. S.
	61– 4	*i·*, in spiritual Science,
	64–19	philosophy and religion that afford *i·*
	169–21	writers left for our spiritual *i·*.
	256– 9	that protest against receiving *i·*
	265–25	others, who receive the same *i·*,
	273–28	waiting for the same class *i·* ;
	278–24	perpetual *i·* of my students might
	292–23	serves as admonition and *i·*,
	293–10	gained from *i·*, observation, and
	350–13	Christian, and like my public *i·*.
Man.	63– 8	*i·* given by the children's teachers
	85–20	receiving *i·* as above, shall not
	86– 6	personal *i·* of Mrs. Eddy,
	87–13	No . . . shall advise against class *i·*.
	89–20	may apply to . . . for *i·* ;
	90–17	Special *I·*.
	91– 8	Tuition of class *i·* . . . shall be $100.00.
Ret.	48–18	give *i·* in scientific methods of
	49– 4	institutions for *i·* in C. S.,
	50– 1	my *i·* in C. S. Mind-healing,
	50–13	any real equivalent for my *i·*
	89–10	*i·* in the Mosaic law.
	90–11	he gave personal *i·*,
Pul.	69– 4	* *i·* of Mrs. Mary Baker Eddy,
Rud.	14–21	their tuition in the higher *i·*,
	14–27	regular course of *i·* from me,
	16– 7	class *i·* in any branch
No.	8–23	who is too blind for *i·*,
My.	62–24	* your wise counsel, timely *i·*,
	218–30	expectation of receiving *i·* from me,
	241–10	* chapter sub-title
	241–16	* fortunate to receive *i·* from
	251– 8	* Primary and Normal class *i·*
	251–17	*i·* in the Board of Education.
	287– 8	serving as admonition, *i·*,
	322–22	* a few days' *i·* by Mrs. Eddy
	361– 4	to give you personal *i·*

instructions

Mis.	11–12	if my *i·* had healed them
	65–17	*Have you changed your i·*
	65–20	those who understand my *i·*
	66–31	I endeavor to accommodate my *i·*
	213– 6	in the proportion that their *i·*
	264–20	Some students leave my *i·*
	292–29	my *i·* on this point of
	293–15	not understand all your *i·* ;
	302– 3	through the *i·* of "S. and H.
	318–14	Any student, having received *i·* in
	349– 4	*i·* included about twelve lessons,
Man.	92–16	No person shall receive *i·* . . . who is not
	109– 1	heading
	111–15	*i·* illustrated in Form 1 and
Ret.	47–19	received *i·* in a Primary class
	83–11	*i·* afforded by the Bible and my
Rud.	14–25	healed by means of my *i·*,
My.	46–26	* all-inclusive *i·* and admonitions
	49–17	* Clerk, by *i·* received
	51–32	* successful *i·* to heal the sick,
	52– 6	* example, as well as her *i·*,
	220–25	*i·* and example of the great

instructive

Pul.	vii–11	*i·* to turn backward the telescope

instructor (see also instructor's)
(see Eddy)

instructor's

Mis.	264–28	*i·* mind must take its hue from

instructors

Mis.	38– 9	*i·* and philanthropists in our land
Man.	73– 9	members of the faculty, *i·*, or

instructs

My.	140–23	This *i·* us how to be abased

instrument

Mis.	39–25	*i· by which God reaches others to heal*
	122– 8	*i·* in this holy (?) alliance
My.	70–24	* more musical, or more capable *i·*.

instrumentality

Mis.	260–10	divine Mind was his only *i·*
My.	288–16	divine Mind was his only *i·*

instruments

Mis.	107– 1	in imitative tones of many *i·*,
	244– 6	before surgical *i·* were invented,
Un.	23– 4	* Make *i·* to scourge us.
My.	105–13	*i·* were lying on the table ready
	287– 6	as *i·* of divine Love.

insubordination

Mis.	119–22	*I·* to the law of Love
	206–15	no *i·* to the laws that be,

insufficient

Mis.	95–11	time so kindly allotted me is *i·*
Man.	36–17	for *i·* cause, refuse to endorse
Ret.	33–24	were *i·* to satisfy my doubts
No.	33–16	would have been *i·* to insure the
My.	266– 2	chapter sub-title
	266– 6	*i·* freedom of honest competition ;
	292–15	*I·* faith or spiritual understanding,

insult

Mis.	121–24	shameless *i·* to divine royalty,
Un.	25– 3	*i·* my conscience,
'01.	30–29	* well-bred man will not *i·* me,

insurance

Man.	30–18	the Board shall attend to the *i·*

insure

No.	33–16	insufficient to *i·* the glory
My.	10–26	* in order to *i·* the prosperity of
	52–28	* to *i·* the moral rightness of

insures

Peo.	2– 1	which *i·* man's continuance and
My.	90–12	* *i·* fidelity in pain or death
	287–23	systematizes action, and *i·* success ;

intact

Mis.	173–25	The perfection of man is *i·* ;
	290– 5	the contract is preserved *i·*.
'02.	7– 1	true nature of Love *i·*

intangible

'01.	12– 1	mode of worship may be *i·*,

integrity

Mis.	147–14	The man of *i·* is one who
	270– 4	such as barter *i·* and peace

intellect

Ret.	5–14	father possessed a strong *i·*
	5–23	* She possessed a strong *i·*,
Un.	21–11	your *i·* will be circumscribed
	22–21	*human i·* and *will-power*,
	25– 3	stultify my *i·*, insult my conscience,
	25–14	enlarges the human *i·* by

intellect
No. 11– 2 *i*·, desire, and fear, are not
11–27 subdue the sophistry of *i*·,
Pan. 4– 3 to the reason, *i*·, and will
intellects
Mis. 345–17 * the loftiest *i*· have had
356–10 students, with cultured *i*·,
Peo. 13–26 * the loftiest *i*· have had
My. 48–27 * The *i*· of these people are not
intellectual
Mis. 88–12 *i*· culture, reading, writing,
112–29 *i*·, and spiritual discernment,
113–31 *i*·, moral, and spiritual
204–18 increases the *i*· activities,
339–13 the strain of *i*· wrestlings,
Ret. 7– 8 * highest order of *i*· powers,
Un. 8–16 physical, moral, and *i*·,
Pul. vii–13 gain of *i*· momentum,
80– 6 * the most *i*· city
No. 45–21 Drifting into *i*· wrestlings,
Peo. 1–12 *i*· wrestling and collisions
My. 87– 9 * happy, well-to-do, *i*·,
211–31 admits of no *i*· culture
294–25 *i*·, moral, and religious
309– 2 a well-informed, *i*· man,
309–31 * practically all the *i*· life.''
intellectuality
My. 274–13 success, *i*·, and happiness
intelligence
all-pervading
Mis. 16–21 all-pervading *i*· and Love,
and existence
Ret. 59–22 for *i*· and existence.
and law
Pan. 7–23 reality and power, *i*· and law,
and wisdom
My. 79–18 * the *i*· and wisdom of the country
another
Mis. 198–27 supposition of another *i*· than God ;
belief that
Mis. 36–28 belief that *i*·, Truth, and Love, are
centre and
Mis. 308– 1 Mind as its sole centre and *i*·.
divine
Mis. 23– 8 demonstrated a divine *i*·
83– 1 divine *i*·, or Principle,
336–27 Science is the fiat of divine *i*·,
'01. 7– 6 divine *i*· called God.
governed by
Mis. 206 17 Growth is governed by *i* ;
highest order of
My. 96 5 * of the highest order of *i*·,
his
Mis. 173–23 obstructing his *i*· — pains, fetters,
law, or
Mis. 101–27 no other power, law, or *i*·
Life and
Mis. 199–26 substance, Life, and *i*· are God.
200–10 substance, Life, and *i*· of man.
life and
(see life)
Life, or
Un. 32–13 as substance, Life, or *i*·,
life, substance, and
Mis. 175– 7 sense of life, substance, and *i*·,
218– 9 life, substance, and *i*·,
Ret. 67– 7 life, substance, and *i*·
manifestations of
Ret. 57–20 supply all manifestations of *i*·.
material
Rud. 4–15 if . . . you mean material *i*·.
matter has no
Mis. 44–28 matter has no *i*· of its own.
Ret. 69–20 matter has no *i*·, life, nor
Mind and
Un. 29–11 only Mind and *i*· in the universe.
no
Mis. 28–25 no *i*· nor life in matter ;
334– 7 has no foundation, — in fact, no *i*· ;
'01. 34–27 no *i*·, health, hope, nor
nor Life
Mis. 74–31 neither substance, *i*·, nor Life,
nor power
Mis. 355–19 neither *i*· nor power,
nor substance
Mis. 21–16 no . . . *i*·, nor substance in matter.
not
'01. 12–28 it is not *i*·, a person or a
obey this
Mis. 23–10 winds, and waves, obey this *i*·.
one
Ret. 30–11 as one *i*·, analyzing,
opposite
Mis. 45–26 an opposite *i*· or mind
346–13 belief . . . opposite *i*· to God.

intelligence
or power
Mis. 260–20 seemeth to be *i*· or power
people of
My. 96–30 * And they were people of *i*·.
personal
Rud. 7–19 neither sensation nor personal *i*·.
power or
Mis. 197–24 believes there is another power or *i*·
reaching
Ret. 69– 2 conditions prior to reaching *i*·.
real
'00. 8–11 wicked man has little real *i*· ;
Soul, and
No. 35–18 Life, substance, Soul, and *i*·
substance and
Mis. 309–13 infinite spiritual substance and *i*·.
Hea. 16– 5 no other Life, substance, and *i*·
substance, nor
Ret. 93–20 no life, truth, substance, nor *i*· in
substance or
My. 235–19 Matter as substance or *i*·

———

Mis. 23– 4 the *i*· that manifests power
49–25 belief, . . . *i*· in non-intelligence,
68– 1 divine substance, *i*·, Life,
333–11 Where do we hold *i*· to be?
344–18 They would place . . . *i*· in matter ;
Un. 31–13 claim . . . that matter has *i*· ;
Rud. 5–14 or *i*· in non-intelligence?
My. 88– 8 * above the average in *i*·.
95– 6 * *i*· of many communities
intelligences
Mis. 344–10 a fit habitation for the *i*·?''
intelligent
Mis. 23–16 for matter . . . is not *i*·,
26–17 Matter is not *i*·,
26–19 *i*·, self-creative, and infinite
36–30 there is no *i*· evil,
74–24 supposition that matter is *i*·,
103– 3 I' Spirit, Soul, is substance,
260– 1 *i*· Christ-idea illustrated by
267–23 governed by Spirit, *i*· good.
333– 1 that this something is *i*· matter;
362– 2 for instance, *i*· matter, or
Un. 22–21 will-power, — alias *i*· matter.
26– 1 Evil. I am *i*· matter ;
42– 8 a divine and *i*· — reality.
Pul. 56– 9 * and, as a rule, are the most *i*·.
60– 7 * manly, and *i*· tones,
63–17 * hundred thousand *i*· people
69–26 * have not done so in an *i*· manner,
No. 11– 6 *i*· and harmonious action,
38– 8 there is no *i*· sin,
Pan. 6–17 how can matter be an *i*· creator
7– 3 plurality of minds, or *i*· matter,
'01. 3–18 fundamental, *i*·, divine Being,
Peo. 4–10 and matter become *i*·
My. vii–12 * *i*· thinking untainted by the
45– 1 * strict and *i*· recognition of
74–21 * an *i*· and a happy appearing body,
92– 5 * numbers of *i*· men and women
93– 9 * the *i*·, and the well-behaved,
96–14 * *i*· and unbiased study
100–15 * a class who are reputable, *i*·,
108– 4 is mind or matter the *i*· cause
112–15 honest, *i*·, and scholarly
175–13 *i*· medical faculty,
226– 4 an *i*· usage of the word
226–10 the one divine *i*· Principle
226–20 *i*· divine Principle, Love.
269– 2 reflected in the *i*· compound idea,
intelligently
Mis. 105– 2 appeals *i*· to the facts
115–18 till you *i*· know and demonstrate,
370–14 more *i*· than ever before,
Un. 6–15 are not prepared to answer *i*·
'02. 5–13 God must be *i*· considered
My. 153–25 Principle of which works *i*·
intelligible
Man. 30– 2 shall select *i*· Readers
intemperance
Mis. 37–16 Can your Science cure *i*·?
37–21 I'·, impurity, sin of every sort,
210–19 I'· begets a belief of
210–21 kill this lurking serpent, *i*·,
296–18 C. S., antagonistic to *i*·,
Pan. 10–20 reform desperate cases of *i*·.
intend
Mis. 39–19 they *i*· to fill the human mind with
intended
Mis. 302–28 *i*· to forestall the possible evil
307–25 were not *i*· for a golden calf,

intended
Un. 13– 6 fulfil the i· harmony of being.
19– 9 He must virtually have i· it,
Pul. 42–13 * i· for the sole use of Mrs. Eddy.
56–27 * is i· to be a testimonial
84–25 * as God i· it should be.
My. 353–12 i· to hold guard over Truth,

intense
Ret. 7– 9 * i· and almost incessant study
Pul. 23–20 * are years of more i· life,

intensely
Mis. 308–24 i· contemplating personality
309–28 sometimes take things too i·.
386– 1 "I· grand and glorious
Po. 49– 3 "I· grand and glorious

intent
Mis. 11– 1 to suffer for his evil i· ;
117– 7 the God-given i· and volition
227–10 to extend their evil i·,
310– 2 neither the i· of my works nor
Ret. 21–17 heavenly i· of earth's shadows
My. 291–17 His public i· was uniform,

intention
Man. 57–12 Clerk to inform . . . of his i·,
Pul. 74–21 i· to be thus understood,
My. 340–25 his i· to rule righteously
362–22 * i· to take such action

intentional
My. 161– 5 The i· destroyer of others

intentionally
Mis. 261–10 whether i· or ignorantly ;
264–32 i· offers his own thought,
Man. 42–20 will not i· or knowingly
Ret. 89–26 trespass not i· upon

intentions
Mis. 236–25 notwithstanding one's good i·,
Ret. 47–14 informed of my i·,
Pul. 87–15 appreciate your kind i·.

intents
Pul. 11– 6 your hearts' holy i·.

intercedeth
My. 136– 2 and i· for us.

intercession
No. 39– 3 i· and unvoiced imploring

intercessory
No. 38–24 chapter sub-title
38–25 prayer that is desire is i· ;

interchange
Mis. 100–23 home, the i· of love,
No. 14– 6 no i· of consciousness,

intercommunion
Mis. 95–16 the impossibility of i·
Hea. 6–12 impossibility, in Science, of i·

intercourse
Ret. 88– 2 in the professional i· of

interest
Mis. 4–19 Much i· is awakened and expressed
12–18 mutely works in the i· of
38–14 other institutions find little i· in
98–13 and extend the i· already felt
139–29 As with all former efforts in the i· of
238–13 utilized in the i· of somebody.
273–21 growing i· in C. S. Mind-healing.
305–20 * articles of historic i· will
306–17 * We would add, as being of i·,
Ret. 37–24 may have an i· for the reader,
42–11 listened to him with deep i·.
83– 6 rather than try to centre their i· on
Pul. 27–30 * windows are of still more unique i·.
31–18 * new and increasing i· in the
50– 2 * in whom she takes a vital i·.
50–20 * will awaken some sort of i·.
68–21 * adds i· to the Baltimore
'00. 2– 2 and this i· increases.
'01. 31–16 except in the i· of the individual
'02. 13–18 the sum of $4,963.50 and i·,
14– 3 only i· I retain in this property
My. 25– 7 * great i· exhibited by the children
51–12 * such an i· manifested
51–22 * for the i· of the Cause,
52–25 * i· of the world to hear her word
53–28 * increasing i· in C. S.
84– 3 * heavy debt, the i· on which
89–23 * not a matter of i· to
92–10 * worthy of perhaps even more i·
217–10 This sum is to remain on i· till
217–14 will receive his dividend with i·
271–23 * reply will be read with deep i·
282–22 i· you manifest in the success of
297–27 not had sufficient i· in the matter
315– 2 is of i· in this connection :

interest
My. 319–19 * may i· you to be advised that
322–28 * my great i· in the subject,
329–10 * gives especial i· to the
329–23 * admitting its i· in the movement,
334–26 * Of further i· in this matter
336–19 * of absorbing i· to . . . Scientists
339– 2 subserve the i· of mankind,
341–21 * public i· centres in the
353–24 nothing . . . of any special i·.

interested
Mis. 353–28 being too much i· in themselves
Pul. 80–13 * sent us by i· friends,
'00. 1–24 my books and those i· in them,
2– 1 already i· in Christian Science ;
2– 4 i· in this old-new theme of
My. 12–10 * Each person i· must remember,
49–12 * meeting of those who were i·
51– 5 * all others now i· in said church,
61–21 * One feature about the work i· me.
245– 2 they became deeply i· in it.
272–24 * will be i· in this communication
272–29 * our readers will be i· in
289–27 i· in a meeting to be held
313–21 never was especially i· in

interesting
Mis. 155–17 all of her i· correspondence,
178–10 * delivered an i· discourse
320– 4 This i· day, crowned with
Pul. vii– 6 it will be i· to have not only
31– 6 * a most i· personality.
42– 9 * rendered particularly i·
65– 8 * undoubtedly an i· faith
72– 6 * very i· conversations
88– 5 * kind and i· articles
My. 13– 8 scanning its i· pages,
47–14 * i·, and epoch-marking stages
49–21 * i· record of this meeting
51–25 * i· record relative to this
53–27 * some very i· statements,
60–27 * i· part I had to perform
61– 3 * has been very i· indeed,
74–10 * chapter sub-title
74–12 * i· and agreeable visitors,
74–30 * each is i·, one for its
86–23 * proved one of the most i·
175– 1 this deeply i· anniversary,
177– 5 on so i· an occasion
231–29 thanks for your i· report
273– 3 * i· and remarkable proof
329–26 * some i· facts concerning
332–21 * in a most i· way.
351– 5 * especially i· on account of
(see also **letter**)

interests
Mis. 18–26 separate one man's i· from
237–20 a period . . . of divided i·,
246– 8 subserve the i· of wealth,
289–29 Mutual i· and affections
Man. 52–22 working against the i· of
52–23 i· of our Pastor Emeritus
80– 3 promotion of the i· of C. S.
Ret. 6–26 he served the public i·
Pul. 15–20 will unite all i· in the one
68– 9 * the i· of her religious work
My. 4–18 subserves the i· of both
291–11 uniting the i· of all

interfere
Mis. 89–11 or i· with materia medica.
Man. 74– 8 no other church shall i·
Ret. 72– 3 nor i· with the rights of
Un. 36–25 must i· with its practical
My. 359– 7 not to i· in cases of discipline,

interference
Mis. 87–31 this i· prolongs the struggle
Man. 73–26 No I·.

interferes
Ret. 82–18 This fact i· in no way with

interfering
My. 212–24 i· with the rights of Mind,

interim
Mis. 241–15 during which i·, by constant combat

interior
Pul. 36–24 * i· is one of the utmost taste
My. 31–21 * its i· should have impressed them
68– 1 * i· of this church is carried out
68–20 * enters . . . into the i· finish.
68–24 * imposing effect of the i·.
68–25 * stone and marble form the i·
69–15 * the rich beauty of the i·.
71–13 * chapter sub-title
71–17 * For in its i· architecture
71–19 * traditions of church i· architecture

interior
My. 72– 3   * traditions of *i·* church architecture.
    78–10   * They looked upon an *i·*
    78–23   * in spite of its vast *i·*,
    147–28   From the *i·* of Africa

interluding
Mis. xii– 4   meantime *i·* with loving thought

intermediate
Mis. 188–20   in the *i·* line of thought,
    206– 4   from extremes to *i·*.
    215– 4   Truth comes into the *i·* space,
No. 28– 6   Of his *i·* conditions
'00. 2–10   the idler, and the *i·*.
    2–25   *i·* worker works at times.
My. 181–18   the *i·* line of justice

intermission
Pul. 42– 5   * Then there was an *i·*,

internal
Mis. 347– 4   *i·* action of pent-up gas.
My. 121–20   to disguise *i·* vulgarity
    160–22   *i·* fires of our earth
    160–24   unpunished sin is this *i·* fire,

international
My. 85– 2   * in its widely *i·* range,
    89–31   * religious movement of *i·* sway ;
    290– 3   this sudden *i·* bereavement,

International Conciliation Committee
My. 282–19   I· C· C·,

Inter-Ocean, *The* (see also *Daily Inter-Ocean*)
Pul. 37– 1   * any information for The I·,"

interpolate
'02. 12–21   *i·* some matters of business
My. 7– 4   *i·* some matters of business

interpolation
Mis. 194–11   Divine Science is not an *i·* of
'01. 12–17   Divine Science is not an *i·* of

interpolations
Ret. 35–11   truths of C. S. are not *i·* of

interposition
Mis. 312–13   * *i·* of divine Providence

interpret
Mis. 58–18   I must . . . understand them to *i·*
    71–15   actual causation must *i·* omnipotence,
    100– 4   C. S. was to *i·* them ;
    166–21   than the senses could *i·*.
    206– 8   *i·* man's eternal existence,
Un. 43–22   This will *i·* the divine power
Pul. 69–18   * we *i·* the Scriptures wholly from
'01. 27– 6   * *i·* their ideas and principles
My. 112– 8   *i·* the Scriptures to fit a doctrine,

Interpretation
    (see **Spiritual Interpretation**)

interpretation
spiritual
    (see **spiritual**)
——
Mis. 158–10   But now, . . . comes the *i·* thereof.
    163–12   ripened into *i·* through Science.
    169–10   Truth dawned . . . through right *i·*.
    189– 5   *i·* therein will be found to be
    191–18   By no possible *i·* can this passage
    258–27   God's *i·* of Himself furnishes
Ret. 37 16   Scriptures gave no direct *i·* of
    83–20   leave S. and H. to God's daily *i·*.
Un. 30–17   *i·* of God and His creation
Pul. 29–25   * helpful in its suggestive *i·*.
    59–14   * with its parallel *i·* by Mrs. Eddy.
No. 44– 6   Truth, having its best *i·* in
My. 94–13   * in the *i·* of its tenets,
    114–20   in the line of Scriptural *i·*
    114–21   influx of divine *i·* would pour in

interpretations
Mis. 190–17   contradict the *i·* that the senses
    247–17   hence the injustice of their *i·*.
Ret. 35–12   but the spiritual *i·* thereof.
'02. 5– 6   stills all distress over doubtful *i·*
My. 178– 4   cloud not the . . . by material *i·*,
    340–18   through constitutional *i·*.

interpreted
Mis. 73– 6   I· materially, these passages
    169–15   cannot properly be *i·* in a literal
    170–15   Jesus *i·* all spiritually :
Un. 63– 1   *i·* this appearing as a risen Christ.
Pul. 29–21   * *i·* and fulfilled literally,
No. 27–12   this vision of Truth is fully *i·*
My. vi– 2   * does not need to be *i·* to those
    220– 5   This statement should be so *i·*

interpreter
No. 38–16   the *i·* of one God,

interpreters
Ret. 26–14   though uninspired *i·* ignorantly

interpreting
Mis. 302–16   mistake in *i·* revealed Truth,
    364– 3   I· the Word in the
Man. 66– 6   I· Communications.
Rud. 1– 2   *i·* and demonstrating the

interprets
Mis. 164– 1   *i·* the incorporeal idea,
    208–20   *i·* to mortals the gospel
    258–30   It *i·* the law of Spirit,
Pul. 12–24   This rule clearly *i·* God
No. 10– 8   the latter reveals and *i·* God
    21– 7   Science that . . . S. and H. *i·*.
'00. 6–12   *i·* the healing Christ.
My. 126–10   *i·* the mystery of godliness,

interred
My. 333–13   * where the body was *i·*
    333–26   * *i·* with Masonic honors.

interrogatory
Pul. 74–11   * a written answer to the *i·*,

interrupt
Mis. 353–30   *i·* the home-harmony,

interruption
My. 14–27   * will be carried on without *i·*

interrupts
Ret. 56– 8   *i·* the meaning of the omnipotence,
My. 69–18   * not a single pillar . . . *i·* the view

intersection
Pul. 24– 8   * *i·* of Norway and Falmouth Streets,
    77–10   * *i·* of Falmouth and Norway Streets,
    78– 9   * *i·* of Falmouth and Norway Streets,

interval
'01. 27–18   and in this *i·* number one million,
    34– 5   *i·* that detains the patient

intervale
Pul. 48–11   * *i·* of beautiful meadows and pastures

intervals
Mis. 256–17   irregular *i·* between my class terms,
Hea. 13–14   at *i·* of half an hour
My. 86–30   * services, repeated at *i·*
    105–22   breathing at *i·* in agony.
    181– 5   are aided only at long *i·* with

intervene
Mis. 02– 4   Centuries will *i·* before the
    319–28   No doubt must *i·* between the
Ret. 84– 1   Centuries will *i·* before the

intervened
My. 343–27   I *i·* . Dissensions are dangerous

intervenes
'02. 12– 3   Here C. S. *i·*, explains

intervening
Mis. 124– 1   *i·* between God and man,
Pul. 85– 3   * during the *i·* years

intervention
My. 278– 4   by the *i·* of the United States,

interview
Pul. 31–21   * begging the favor of an *i·*
    74–13   calling for an *i·*
My. 346–19   * recent *i·* which appeared

interviewing
My. 332–24   * much *i·* with Masonic authorities,

interviews
Mis. 276– 5   I did not hold *i·* with all
'01. 17–17   in from one to three *i·*,
    27–14   in one to three *i·*
My. 341–23   * granting of *i·* is not usual,

interwoven
My. 10–30   * *i·* with the general welfare of

intimate
Mis. 249–14   as well as my *i·* acquaintances.

intimately
Ret. 88–19   a part which concerns us *i·*,

intimates
No. 6–27   *i·* that the laws of Science are

intimations
Pul. 23–24   * *i·* of man's immortal life.

intolerance
Mis. xi–19   The shuttlecock of religious *i·*
    246–26   Shall religious *i·*, arrayed against
Hea. 11–14   he who has suffered from *i·*

intolerant
'01. 34–15   material religion, proscriptive, *i·*,
Hea. 11–14   is the first to be *i·*.

intoxicated
  Mis. 9–20 become *i·* ; become lethargic,
      100– 6 *i·* with pleasure or pain,
      277–30 on the cloud of the *i·* senses.
intoxicates
  Mis. 288–32 Whatever *i·* a man,
intoxicating
  Mis. 288–31 abstinence from *i·* beverages.
intoxication
  My. 212– 1 state induced . . . is a species of *i·*,
      212– 7 sins, and other forms of *i·*.
intrenching
  Pul. 2–28 *i·* ourselves in the knowledge
intrepid
  Mis. 172– 6 *I·*, self-oblivious Protestants
  Hea. 2– 9 Said the *i·* reformer, Martin Luther :
  My. 275–25 *I·*, self-oblivious love fulfils
intricate
  '00. 11–14 besieges you with tones *i·*,
  My. 61–29 * the many *i·* problems which
      71– 2 * some of the most *i·* discoveries
      212– 4 *i·* method of animal magnetism
intrinsic
  Mis. 108–31 they have no *i·* quality
  My. 153–14 with no *i·* healing qualities
      172–12 gift that has no *i·* value
introduce
  Mis. 247–14 statement of the Science I *i·*,
  My. 39–18 * *i·* the incoming President,
      42– 5 * It is my pleasure to *i·*
introduced
  Mis. 177–26 * The pastor *i·* Mr. Easton
      365–32 conscientiously understood and *i·*.
  Ret. 43– 1 *i·* the first purely metaphysical
      86– 7 Then be *i·* to this self.
  Pul. 5–17 *i·* himself to its author
  No. 9– 6 must not be *i·* or established
      11–15 understood and conscientiously *i·*.
introduces
  Rud. 2–21 *i·* us to higher definitions.
      11–26 never *i·* the subject of human
  Pan. 6–11 Mosaic theism *i·* evil,
introducing
  My. 39–17 * In *i·* the new President,
      234–19 question of *i·* C. S. into
introduction
  My. 218–15 *i·* of pure abstractions into C. S.,
introductory
  My. 80–16 * the *i·* services were identical,
intruding
  My. 221–29 wide open to the *i·* disease,
intrusted
  Mis. 284–30 if one is *i·* with the rules of
intuition
  Mis. 152–28 right *i·* which guides you safely
      272–30 *i·* and impulse of love.
invaded
  Ret. 61–10 man's harmony is no more to be *i·* than
      79–29 nor its golden streets *i·*.
  My. 87–10 * multitude that has *i·* the town.
invaders
  Peo. 13–13 iron tread of merciless *i·*,
invalid (*see also* **invalid's**)
  Mis. 27– 7 and prove themselves *i·*.
      83– 7 *every i· the cause of his*
  Un. 59–22 calls sickness real, and man an *i·*,
  Rud. 8–24 *i·* whom he is supposed to cure.
  '01. 13–28 hold it *i·*, give it the lie,
  Hea. 9– 9 sinner and the most hopeless *i·*
  My. 144– 6 that I am sick, helpless, or an *i·*.
invalidism
  Mis. 169– 8 *i·* she endured before Truth dawned
invalid's
  Ret. 40– 8 I went to the *i·* house.
invalids
  Un. 61–28 *I·* say, "I have recovered from
  Pul. 80–25 * into the homes of unnumbered *i·*.
  Rud. 3–16 manipulate *i·*, prescribe drugs, or
      12–16 erases from the minds of *i·*
      14–28 have been *i·* and were healed
      15–13 Few were taken besides *i·*
  Peo. 3– 5 made helpless *i·* and cripples.
  My. 231– 1 chapter sub-title
      231–15 letters from *i·* demanding her help
invaluable
  Mis. 45–10 *i·* in the practice of dentistry.
  '02. 16– 8 copy of Wyclif, the *i·* gift of

invariable
  '01. 24– 6 by means of *i·* rules
invariably
  Mis. 45–16 supply *i·* meets demand,
  My. 59–26 * My answer has *i·* been,
invective
  Mis. 335–13 charge upon me with full-fledged *i·*
  Man. 41–12 in return employ no violent *i·*,
invent
  Pul. 79–21 * we should be obliged to *i·* one."
invented
  Mis. 244– 7 before surgical instruments were *i·*,
  My. 14–22 * could not have *i·* a more subtle lie
invention
  Mis. 232– 7 perfection in art, *i·*, and
inventions
  Mis. 78–14 the *i·* of animal magnetism,
  Un. 60– 1 mortal *i·*, one and all
  Pan. 12–28 philosophy, or by man's *i·*.
  My. 345–25 * pursuit of modern material *i·*?"
inventor
  Pul. 71– 7 * Mrs. Eddy, the *i·* of this cure.
  '02. 9–27 the *i·* of a steam engine?
invert
  Mis. 109– 5 to reverse, *i·*, or controvert,
inverted
  Un. 53– 3 evil and all its forms are *i·* good.
  Rud. 7–11 be lost if *i·* or perverted.
  No. 17–18 therein is no *i·* image of God,
  Pan. 11–29 image of God, not fallen or *i·*,
inverts
  Ret. 70– 1 "Mortal mind *i·* the true likeness,
invested
  My. 217– 8 *i·* in safe municipal bonds
      349–17 Way-shower, *i·* with glory,
investigate
  Mis. 44– 4 ready to *i·* this subject,
investigated
  Pul. 64–17 * *i·* allopathy, homœopathy,
  My. 330–13 * carefully *i·* the points
investigating
  Mis. 222–29 cost of *i·*, for this age,
  Ret. 7–10 * He was fond of *i·* abstruse
investigation
  Mis. 87–20 in the *i·* of C. S.
      247– 9 challenge the world, upon fair *i·*,
  Pul. 14– 1 honest *i·* will bring the hour
investigations
  Hea. 6– 7 From my earliest *i·*
investigator
  '02. 2– 1 the earnest, honest *i·* sees
investments
  My. 135–10 *i·*, deposits, expenditures,
      137–13 *i·*, deposits, expenditures,
      137–14 selected all my *i·*, except
      231–11 uncertain, unfortunate *i·*.
invests
  My. 265– 7 *i·* less in trusts,
inveterate
  Rud. 9–23 oftentimes healed *i·* diseases.
  No. 22– 8 Hegel was an *i·* snuff-taker.
  Hea. 13–17 an *i·* case of dropsy.
  My. 300–13 heals the most *i·* diseases.
invigorate
  My. 230–12 *i·* his capacity to heal the sick,
invigoration
  '01. 1–16 refreshment and *i·* of the human
invincible
  Mis. 171–30 to keep bright their *i·* armor ;
  Ret. 30–14 *i·* and infinite energies of Truth
  My. 178– 5 nor lose the *i·* process and purity of
      189– 1 Clad in *i·* armor,
invincibles
  Pul. 83–17 * Amazons who conquered the *i·*,
inviolate
  Mis. 91–12 bond is wholly spiritual and *i·*.
invisibility
  Ret. 79– 8 pigment beneath fade into *i·*.
invisible
  Mis. 22–31 Mind-force, *i·* to material sense,
      205–18 good, whose visible being is *i·* to
      218– 5 declares the *i·* only by reversion,
      308–29 which is *i·* to corporeal sense.
      329–27 the cuckoo sounds her *i·* lute,
  Pul. 80–26 * that the *i·* is the only real world,
  '01. 13– 5 The visible sin should be *i·* :

invitation

Mis.	132–21	inconvenient to accept your *i·*
	137– 3	my thanks for your card of *i·*,
	148–28	Let the *i·* to this sweet converse
	296– 2	and, by special *i·*,
	311– 6	I would extend a tender *i·* to
Man.	45–22	not entitled . . . except by *i·*.
	85– 3	by *i·* attend each other's
Ret.	15–15	I accepted the *i·*
Pul.	36–10	* by Mrs. Eddy's kind *i·*,
	76–27	* an *i·* formally to accept the
	77– 3	* The *i·* itself is one of the most
	86–26	* *i·* to become the permanent pastor
My.	49–11	* unanimous *i·* to Mrs. Eddy
	49–18	* *i·* to Mrs. Eddy to become pastor
	51–19	* *i·* was extended to Mrs. Eddy
	53–18	* which *i·* she accepted.
	142–26	I thank you for your kind *i·*
	169– 1	chapter sub-title
	174–18	thanking you for your kind *i·*
	177– 4	comply with your cordial *i·*
	183–24	Thanks for *i·* to your dedication.
	191–28	card of *i·* to this feast of soul
	195– 4	acknowledging your card of *i·*
	285– 3	accept my thanks for your kind *i·*,
	324–26	* why he accepted your *i·*

invitations

Mis.	321–24	In reply to all *i·* from Chicago

invite

Mis.	149– 4	*I·* all cordially and freely
	246–18	to *i·* its prey, then turn and
	310–27	would cordially *i·* all persons
	322– 2	*i·* you to its contemplation
Man.	94– 1	The lecturer can *i·* churches
Pul.	87– 1	* cordially *i·* you to be present
Po.	32–10	A loftier life to *i·*
My.	169– 2	I *i·* you, one and all,
	171–11	Therefore I hereby *i·* all my
	173–16	Why not *i·* those who attend

invited

Pul.	77–15	* most lovingly *i·* to visit
	78–13	* most lovingly *i·* to visit
'00.	14–28	When *i·* to a feast you naturally
My.	96–20	* Members were *i·* to contribute
	244– 7	You have been *i·* hither to
	270– 7	*i·* me to its . . . anniversary ;
	304–14	*i·* to lecture in London,
	318–16	I *i·* Mr. Wiggin to visit one of
	322 15	* *i·* to dine with the Wiggin family.

inviting

Pul.	65– 4	* In *i·* the Eastern churches
My.	184–11	*i·* me to be present
	186–26	card *i·* me to be with you
	192–20	*i·* me to be present

invocation

Po.	page 28	poem

invoke

Peo.	9–18	*i·* the divine aid of Spirit

involuntarily

Mis.	290–20	my affections *i·* flow out
My.	210–13	Goodness *i·* resists evil.

involuntary

No.	v– 4	*i·* as well as voluntary error.
Hea.	12–21	without the *i·* thought,

involve

No.	33–10	because they *i·* divine Science,
My.	164– 2	such an effort would *i·* a

involved

Mis.	200–28	*i·* in its divine Principle, God :
Man.	47– 7	on the anatomy *i·*.
Ret.	22–15	*i·* errors are vanquished by
Pul.	35– 3	law *i·* in spiritual Science
'02.	13– 1	to meet the expensos *i·*.
My.	359– 9	not personally *i·* in the affairs

involves

Mis.	76–30	Soul, Spirit, *i·* this appearing,
	338– 2	*i·* the disappearing of evil.
Man.	44– 5	*i·* schisms in our Church
Ret.	47–10	shuns whatever *i·* material means
Un.	5–15	*mystery i·* the unknown.
	41– 7	*i·* a loss of the true sense of good,
	41– 9	*i·* a temporary loss of God,
No.	44– 4	C. S. *i·* a new language,
My.	139–14	*i·* Life, — calm, irresistible,
	261–23	Christmas *i·* an open secret,

involving

Mis.	54–30	to solve a problem *i·* logarithms ;
Man.	52– 1	*i·* The Mother Church discipline.
Un.	5– 1	a theme *i·* the All of infinity.
My.	309– 6	lawsuit *i·* a question of pauperism

inward

My.	159–16	from the *i·* to the outward,

inwardly

Mis.	232– 1	God comfort them all ! we *i·* prayed

iota

'02.	16–26	they never destroy one *i·* of
My.	107–11	have not an *i·* of the drug left
	321–19	* to change my opinion one *i·*

Iowa

(see **Burlington**)

ipecacuanha

Mis.	369–16	rhubarb tincture or an *i·* pill.

ipse dixit

Mis.	65– 6	man's *i· d·* as to the stellar system

ire

Po.	30–17	a patient love above earth's *i·*,

Ireland

Man.	94–19	in Canada, in Great Britain and *I·*.
	97– 9	Canada, Great Britain and *I·*.
	99– 6	Each county of Great Britain and *I·*,
	99–23	for Great Britain and *I·*.

iris

Mis.	355–28	to the light, and the *i·* of faith,

irksome

My.	166–21	sport would be more *i·* than work.

iron

Ret.	5–14	a strong intellect and an *i·* will.
Pul.	25– 6	* The partitions are of *i·* ;
	25–12	* girders are all of *i·*,
	25–14	* window frames are of *i·*,
	25–14	* staircases are of *i·*,
	82–30	* fear has ceased to kiss the *i·* heel
Peo.	13–12	*i·* tread of merciless invaders,
My.	4–21	*i·* in human nature rusts away ;
	68–29	* framed of *i·* and finished with
	160 15	cuts its way through *i·* and sod,

irony

Mis.	291–18	perversion of C. S. is the *i·*
Ret.	23– 4	ultimately yield to the *i·* of fate,

irrefutable

My.	179–27	are, *i·* and eternal.

irregular

Mis.	256–17	has occasioned the *i·* intervals

irreparable

Rud.	16–17	an *i·* loss of Science.
My.	333–29	" to lament this *i·* loss."

irrepressible

Mis.	102–27	the *i·* conflict between

irreproachable

My.	331– 8	* indicates her *i·* standing

irresistible

Mis.	16–31	the *i·* conflict between
	100–15	leads on *i·* forces, and will
	208–28	*i·*, permanent, eternal.
My.	49– 4	* as by an *i·* attraction.
	139–15	Life, — calm, *i·*, eternal.

irrespective

Mis.	357–21	love that is *i·* of self,

irresponsible

No.	3– 9	some *i·* people insisted
My.	316–12	*I·* Attacks on C. S.

irreverent

Man.	41– 3	*i·* reference to Christ Jesus

irrevocable

Pan.	12–26	C. S. is *i·* — unpierced by

irrevocably

Mis.	177–16	give yourselves wholly and *i·* to

irritate

My.	111–27	may *i·* a certain class of

Isaac

My.	161–12	Abraham, and *I·*, — *Luke* 13 : 28.

Isaiah

XI

Po.	43– 1	*picture depictive of I· xi.*
28: 16, 17		
My.	16–23	* Scripture reading, *I·* 28 : 16, 17,

Mis.	145–22	memorial such as *I·* prophesied :
	148–29	in the words of the prophet *I· ·*
	164–17	In our text *I·* foretold,
	301–31	to whom *I·* alluded thus :
Un.	55– 5	as *I·* says of him,
My.	140– 2	* Of this . . . the prophet *I·* said,
	171– 3	is fulfilled the prophecy of *I·* :
	177–22	this prophecy of *I·* is fulfilled
	184–26	*I·* said : "How beautiful — *Isa.* 52 : 7.
	193–26	may the prophecy of *I·* be fulfilled :

Isis

My. 92–12 * new temple to I· and Osiris would be

islands

My. 279–26 and those i· of the sea
286– 6 on earth and the i· of the sea

Isle

Mis. 392–18 poem
392–19 on receiving a painting of the I·
392–20 I· of beauty, thou art singing
393–21 I· of beauty, thou art teaching
Po. page 51 poem
51– 1 On receiving a painting of the I·.
51– 2 I· of beauty, thou art singing
52– 5 I· of beauty, thou art teaching

Isle of Patmos

Pul. 27–28 * representing John on the I· of P·,

isles

Mis. 153–10 green i· of refreshment.
227–24 on i· of sweet refreshment.

ism

Mis. 175–24 i· of to-day has nothing to do with
Ret. 28–18 I believe in no i·.
My. 119–11 towards Buddhism or any other "i·."

isms

Mis. 4–21 it is confounded with i·,
295– 7 * a gamut of i· and ists,
No. 43–25 reconstruct the wrecks of "i·"'

isolate

Pul. 21–16 shun whatever would i· us from

isolation

My. 50–13 * felt a peculiar sense of i·,

Israel (see also Israel's)

Mis. 9– 6 Well is it that the Shepherd of I·
72–13 concerning the land of I·,— Ezek. 18 : 2.
72–17 to use this proverb in I·." — Ezek. 18 : 3.
73–26 the twelve tribes of I·." — Matt. 19 : 28.
121–17 innocent blood from I·." — Deut. 19 : 13.
150– 3 you have the great Shepherd of I·
153–13 God is good to I·,
153–14 good to His I·
162– 2 Jacob was called I· ;
308–16 "Hear, O I·:— Deut. 6 : 4.
360–19 "I· after the flesh," — I Cor. 10 : 18.
360–21 "the I· according to Spirit"
Man. 17–18 heals the sick, and restores the lost I· :
Ret. 79–25 the children of I· were saved by
90–23 Thus must the Mother in I· give all
Pul. 44–12 * yet the mother in I·, alone
Peo. 11–17 children of I· still in bondage.
My. 42–31 * were the children of I· delivered
43–19 * I· came over this Jordan
44– 5 * I· is going up to possess the
108– 5 Christ, the Holy One of I·,
182–20 house of worship to the God of I·,
183–14 light upon the mountain of I·.
280–15 chapter sub-title — Deut. 6 : 4.
296– 9 chapter sub-title — Deut. 6 : 4.

Israelites

'00. 3–22 I· in Babylon hesitated not

Israel's

My. 125– 9 with the sling of I· chosen one

issue

Mis. xi– 2 copyrighted at the date of its i·,
4–11 chapter sub-title
7–23 price at which we shall i· it,
80– 4 on the single i· of opposition to
105–26 The senses join i· with error,
220–14 control . . . on the point at i·.
246–28 The question at i· with mankind is :
294–29 In an i· of January 17,
350–26 I i· no arguments, . . . in mental
Un. 46–26 Pharisees fought Jesus on this i·.
No. 46– 3 The question now at i· is :
My. 27–23 * in this i· of the Sentinel
73– 2 * to i· a similar notice or order,
98–14 * i· of the C. S. Sentinel
122– 3 i· from the brain of a dreamer.
241–14 * i· raised is an important one
284–12 In the i· of your good paper,
284–17 In your next i· please correct

issue

My. 330–18 * as claimed in your i·
334– 9 * i· of the C. S. Sentinel,
352–28 i· of The C. S. Monitor.
360–11 momentous question at i· in

issued

Mis. 372– 1 When the latter was first i·,
380–30 pamphlet printed and i· by
381–21 A writ of injunction was i·
Man. 91– 6 shall be on all certificates i·.
Pul. 38– 6 * S. and H., was i· in 1875.
Po. vii– 9 * a popular edition to be i·,
My. 236–26 which will be i· February 29
328–18 * Sheriff Wooten i· licenses
328–20 * first to be i· to the healers
356–16 nor consent to have my picture i·,

issues

Mis. 221–32 holds the i· of death
235–15 touches mind to more spiritual i·,
No. 27– 2 It i· a false claim ;
40–16 never . . . save to i· of Truth ;
Hea. 5–26 lead our lives to higher i· ;
My. 170– 9 not be confused with other i·,
221–24 All i· of morality, of Christianity,
287–23 it touches thought to spiritual i·,
329–16 * paper in the i· of July 3

isthmus-lordling

Mis. 393–17 Art hath bathed this i·
Po. 52– 1 Art hath bathed this i·

ists

Mis. 295– 7 * a gamut of isms and i·,

Italian

Mis. 376– 3 * authentic I· school, revived.
Pul. 25–22 * floor is in white I· mosaic,
26–21 * by an entrance of I· marble,
76– 4 * superb archway of I· marble
Rud. 1–13 In Spanish, I·, and Latin,

Italian Renaissance

My. 68– 1 * Built in the I· R· style,

Italy

Mis. 372–15 masters in France and I·.
375–12 * Years ago, while in I·.
Pul. 5–25 I·, Greece, Japan, India,

itching

Mis. 337–27 to i· ears and to dull disciples

Item

Mis. 391– 2 Written to the Editor of the I·,
Po. 38– 1 To the editor of the I·,

item

Mis. 391– 1 poem
391– 6 An i· rich in store ;
391–14 As i·, of our life ;
391–22 'T will be an i· more.
Po. page 38 poem
38– 5 An i· rich in store ;
38–13 As i·, of our life ;
38–21 'Twill be an i· more.
My. 54– 6 * Traveler contained the following i· :
145– 3 acquainted with the small i·

itemize

Mis. 131–13 prepared to i· a report
131–25 i· a bill of this church's gifts
131–29 to i· or audit their accounts,

itemized

Mis. 131–30 these will be found already i·,

items

Mis. 157–20 i· relative to Mrs. Stebbin's case.
391–10 Have many i· more ;
391–18 Find i· at our door.
'00. 12–11 St. Paul's life furnished i·
Po. 38– 9 Have many i· more ;
38–17 Find i· at our door.

iterated

'02. 5–20 i· in the law of God,

itinerancy

Ret. 88–27 I· should not be allowed to

itinerant

My. 314– 2 * "an i· dentist."

J

jacket

Mis. 233– 9 monkey in harlequin j·

Jackson, Mich.

Pul. 52– 8 * Jackson Patriot, J·, M·.,

Jackson Patriot

Pul. 52– 8 * J· P·, Jackson, Mich.,

Jacob (see also Jacob's)

Mis. 162– 2 J· was called Israel ;
My. 34– 9 seek thy face, O J·.— Psal. 24 : 6.
161–12 J·, and all the prophets,— Luke 13 : 28.

Jacob's

'02. 10–15 gain the scope of J· vision,

jaded
Mis. 366–16 poor *j·* humanity needs to get

jagged
Mis. 327–30 plunge headlong over the *j·* rocks.

Jahr
Ret. 33–11 remedies enumerated by *J·*,
Hea. 12–15 remedies of the *J·*,

jail
Po. vi–18 *nowhere but in the walls of a j·.*
My. 175–15 well-conducted *j·* and state prison,

jailer
Mis. 112–21 The *j·* thanked me, and said,

Jairus (see also Jairus')
Pul. 27–17 * raising of the daughter of *J·*.

Jairus'
Pul. 54–22 * In the case of *J·* daughter

James (see also St. James)
Mis. 51–30 The apostle *J·* said,
Pul. 54–25 * Peter, *J·*, and John,
No. 40– 1 The apostle *J·* said :

jammed
My. 99–21 * stuffed and *j·* with money.

January
(see **months**)

Japan
Pul. 2–16 war between China and *J·*.
5–25 Italy, Greece, *J·*, India,
6–22 * leading us to return to *J·*."
My. 279–25 war between Russia and *J·*;
281–19 * peace between Russia and *J·*

Japanese
My. 278–18 A *J·* may believe in a heaven

jarring
'00. 11– 6 *j·* elements among musicians

jaws
Mis. 106–11 Into the *j·* of hate,
294–21 their stings, and *j·*, and claws ;
Pan. 14–25 through the *j·* of death

jealous
Mis. 129–15 If a man is *j·*, envious, or

jealousy
Mis. 123– 6 spirit of idolatry, envy, *j·*,
250–12 which . . . become *j·* and hate.
281– 4 rivalry, *j·*, envy, revenge.
My. 167–20 claims of envy, *j·*, or persecution.
245–13 beasts, superstition and *j·*.

Jeanne d'Arc
Pul. 33– 3 * like *J· d'A·*, to hear "voices,"

jeers
My. 98–11 * must have done with scoffs and *j·*

Jehovah
Mis. 123–15 Babylonian Yawa, or *J·*,
182–23 no personal plan of a personal *J·*,
Ret. 13–15 and in a *J·* merciless
Un. 14–15 The *J·* of limited Hebrew faith
Pan. 7–11 character and sovereignty of *J·*
'00. 3–23 Yahwah, afterwards transcribed *J·* ;
3–26 Yahwah, misnamed *J·*,

Jericho
Mis. 279–16 before the walls of *J·*.

Jerusalem
Mis. 133–23 toward the *J·* of Love and Truth,
326–25 "O *J·*, *J·*, thou that — *Matt.* 23 : 37.
Ret. 89– 7 assembled in the one temple (at *J·*)
Pul. 7–12 as he wept over *J·* !
My. 13– 9 * "The church at *J·*, like a sun
13–13 church of *J·* seems to prefigure The
46–28 * the heavenly *J·*, — *Heb.* 12 : 22.

jest
Mis. 353–23 folly of tending it is no mere *j·*.

jester
Mis. 353–17 he said to the *j·*, "You must pay

Jesus (see also Jesus')
accepted
Un. 55– 1 *J·* accepted the one fact whereby
according to
Ret. 36– 4 expound the gospel according to *J·*.
achieved
Ret. 88–15 This end *J·* achieved,
action of
Mis. 214–11 This action of *J·* was stimulated by
admonished
Mis. 366–20 even as *J·* admonished.
adult
Mis. 159–20 risen Christ, and the adult *J·*.
against
Un. 46–17 incensed the rabbins against *J·*,

Jesus
and his apostles
Un. 10– 6 *J·* and his apostles, who have thus
and his disciples
Mis. 54–26 as *J·* and his disciples did,
Pul. 52–19 * practised by *J·* and his disciples.
'00. 10–16 and of *J·* and his disciples.
'01. 18–17 *J·* and his disciples would have
and Paul
Mis. 364–32 divine philosophy of *J·* and Paul.
No. 21– 1 life and teachings of *J·* and Paul,
and the apostles
Mis. 23– 7 *J·*, and the apostles, demonstrated
40–10 method . . . *J·* and the apostles used
Pul. 85–13 * of *J·* and the apostles,
Angelico's
Mis. 375–25 * hands and feet in Angelico's '*J·*,'
appeared
Un. 59–14 To mortal thought *J·* appeared as
as a man
Mis. 197–14 concerning *J·* as a man,
ascension of
Mis. 165– 4 because of the ascension of *J·*,
asserted by
Pul. 31– 6 * principles asserted by *J·*,
assumed
Mis. 63–30 *J·* assumed for mortals the
Un. 46–28 *J·* assumed the burden of disproof
as the Son
Mis. 180–30 speak of *J·* as the Son of God
'01. 10–16 and of *J·* as the Son of God
as the son
Mis. 63–26 *J·* as the son of man was human :
atonement of
No. 37–12 vicarious atonement of *J·*,
authority of
'01. 8–11 we have the authority of *J·* for
Peo. 9–21 despite the authority of *J·*
babe
Mis. 164–13 the babe *J·* seemed small to mortals ;
My. 262–10 homely origin of the babe *J·*
baptism of
Ret. 48–26 baptism of *J·*, of which he said,
'02. 5– 8 with the baptism of *J·*.
belief that
Pan. 8– 6 Does not the belief that *J·*,
blood of
No. 35– 1 This blood of *J·* is everything
called
Mis. 337–12 "*J·* called a little child — *Matt.* 18 : 2.
came
Mis. 60– 4 *J· came healing the sick*
63–15 *J·* came to seek and to save
Un. 50– 5 *J·* came to earth ;
59–19 *J·* came to rescue men from
No. 35–24 *J·* came announcing Truth,
'01. 12– 5 *J·* came neither eating nor drinking,
cast out
Mis. 6– 4 *J·* cast out disease as evil.
68–15 *J·* cast out a devil,
No. 23–13 the diseases *J·* cast out.
31–17 *J·* cast out evils,
My. 288–21 *J·* cast out evil, disease, death,
character of
Mis. 360–11 and the character of *J·*, by his
Ret. 22– 8 summarized the character of *J·*
child
Mis. 166–20 birth to the corporeal child *J·*,
commanded
'02. 9– 5 *J·* commanded, "Follow me ; — *Matt.* 8 : 22.
commands of
My. 47–27 * founded on the commands of *J·* :
concept of
Mis. 103–26 exchanges this human concept of *J·*
No. 36–27 Mankind's concept of *J·* was
condemned
No. 23– 3 personality that *J·* condemned
corporeal
Mis. 162–18 The corporeal *J·* bore our
crucified
'01. 9–12 the rabbis, who crucified *J·*
14– 5 self-righteousness crucified *J·*
My. 334–25 self-righteousness crucified *J·*."
crucifixion of
Man. 16– 5 the crucifixion of *J·* and his
declared
Mis. 259– 4 but is what *J·* declared it,
No. 12–17 the Christ, as *J·* declared himself,
32–15 *J·* declared that the devil
My. 122–26 is Truth, even as *J·* declared ;
190–27 *J·* declared that his teaching
declares
Un. 40–12 *J·* declares that they who
defined
No. 22–24 *J·* defined devil as a mortal who

Jesus

defined by
Ret. 58–12 Life, as defined by J·, had no
Un. 42–21 As defined by J·, Life had no

demonstrated
Mis. 90– 4 J· demonstrated sin and death to be
165– 1 that the personal J· demonstrated,
187– 3 J· demonstrated over sin, sickness,
189–25 This, J· demonstrated ;
No. 21– 5 The Science that J· demonstrated,
My. 218–13 J· demonstrated the divine Principle

demonstrated by
Pul. 70–22 * way of salvation demonstrated by J·
No. 28–18 Has Truth, as demonstrated by J·,

demonstration of
Mis. 244–26 teachings and demonstration of J·

demonstrations of
Un. 31– 8 demonstrations of J· annulled the

denounced
Ret. 65–15 hence J· denounced it.
My. 218–19 ultimates in what J· denounced,

dictum of
Mis. 133–19 following the dictum of J· ;

did
Un. 50– 9 We should subjugate it as J· did,
My. 111–21 Did J· mistake his mission

died, and lived
Un. 62–18 In material sense J· died, and lived.

directed
My. 156–11 When J· directed his disciples to

disciples of
My. 222– 2 even the disciples of J· once failed

distinctly taught
Un. 17–13 J· distinctly taught the arrogant

doctrine of
'01. 24–29 inadequate to prove the doctrine of J·,

drapery of
Mis. 376– 5 * face, figure, and drapery of J·,

enunciated
Pul. 54– 9 * J· enunciated and exemplified the

example of
Ret. 55– 3 Let us follow the example of J·,
No. 14–24 demand and example of J·

face of
Mis. 309– 9 The face of J· has uniformly
No. 18–18 the rapt face of J·.

fainting form of
Mis. 212–31 the fainting form of J·,

feet of
(see **feet**)

fleshly
Un. 62–19 The fleshly J· seemed to die,

foretold
Mis. 214–30 J· foretold the harvest hour

forgave
'02. 19–10 even as J· forgave, forgive thou.

formed
Hea. 7–11 where J· formed his estimate ;

fought
Un. 46–26 Pharisees fought J· on this issue.

gave
My. 190–22 J· gave his disciples (students)

had fulfilled
'01. 10–30 After J· had fulfilled his mission

hatred of
My. 104–10 they vented their hatred of J· in

head of
Pul. 27–22 * Mary anointing the head of J·,

healed
Mis. 63– 3 said . . . J· healed through Beelzebub ;

history of
Mis. 274– 1 history of J· and of his disciples,

human
Mis. 199–19 through the human J·.
No. 36–15 the human J· had a resort to his

illustrated this
Hea. 8–23 J· illustrated this by the parable of

immaculate
'02. 18– 5 pure sense of the immaculate J·

impersonal
Mis. 161–17 the personal and the impersonal J·.

interpreted
Mis. 170–15 J· interpreted all spiritually :

is recorded
Mis. 170–27 J· is recorded as having expressed

is the name
Hea. 3–16 J· is the name of a man born in a

knew
Mis. 260–14 J· knew that erring mortal thought
Hea. 7–22 J· knew that adultery is a crime,

life of
(see **life**)

looking unto
Mis. 361–20 looking unto J· the author— Heb. 12 : 2.
My. 258–13 "Looking unto J· the author— Heb. 12 : 2.
349–16 "looking unto J· the author— Heb. 12 : 2.

Jesus

loved
Mis. 110–10 maintain in yourselves what J· loved,
'02. 8– 3 commands man to love as J· loved.
18–18 heart that loves as J· loved.

loves you
Po. 43– 2 J· loves you ! so does mother :

made
Mis. 361– 1 No advancing modes . . . made J· ;
No. 34– 8 sacrifice that J· made for us,

man
(see **man**)

marked out
Mis. 197–10 in the way which J· marked out
358–17 in the way which J· marked out,

medicine of
No. 1 –18 theology and medicine of J· were one,

method of
Mis. 170–22 The method of J· was purely

mind of
Mis. 200– 2 Truth in the mind of J·,

miracles of
Mis. 77–31 where the miracles of J· had

mother of
Pul. 27–21 * great window . . . the mother of J·.

name of
Hea. 3–18 individuals by the name of J·.

nativity of
Mis. 374–18 memorize the nativity of J·.

nature of
'02. 18–30 nature of J· made him keenly

never thanked
Un. 11–22 never thanked J· for restoring his

obeyed
My. 220–26 J· obeyed human laws

of Nazareth
(see **Nazareth**)

oneness of
My. 338–24 recognize the oneness of J·

operated
Pul. 54– 6 * J· operated in perfect harmony with

our
Mis. 376–14 * You have given us back our J·,

patience of
Mis. 7– 8 The loving patience of J·,

Paul and
Mis. 360– 8 colossal characters, Paul and J·.

personal
Mis. 165– 1 the personal J· demonstrated,
166–30 the life of the personal J·.
My. 113–17 not a disciple of the personal J· ?

personality of
Mis. 309–14 the finite personality of J·,

phraseology of
Un. 59– 8 phraseology of J·, who spoke of

picture of
My. 206–13 seeing a person in the picture of J·,

portrayed
Mis. 376– 6 * drapery of that J· portrayed by

practice of
Ret. 65– 4 teaching and practice of J·,

practised by
Mis. 193–12 defined and practised by J·,
Pul. 52–19 * taught and practised by J·

prescribed by
Ret. 87–18 divine order as prescribed by J·,

presented
Mis. 197–18 divinity which J· presented

prior to
'01. 8–25 Christ existed prior to J·,

prophecy of
No. 13– 8 the prophecy of J· fulfilled,

proved
No. 37–28 J· proved to perfection,

rebuked
My. 222– 4 J· rebuked them, saying :

received
Mis. 298–16 J· received the material rite

recognized
Mis. 37– 8 J· recognized this relation

recognizes
Pul. 30–19 * it recognizes J· as the teacher

regard
'01. 8– 6 our brethren, who regard J· as God

regarded
Mis. 200– 3 J· regarded good as the normal

rendered
No. 37–25 J· rendered null and void

represented
Hea. 10– 6 manhood of God, that J· represented ;

required
Un. 11–24 J· required neither cycles of

said
Mis. 8–22 J· said : "Blessed are ye, — Matt. 5 : 11.
13–10 J· said, "If ye love them — Luke 6 : 32.
57–11 J· said of error,

Jesus

said

Mis.	58–13	J· said, "Having eyes, see ye — *Mark* 8 : 18.
	73–22	"*And J· said unto them,* — *Matt.* 19 : 28.
	76– 4	J· said, "If a man keep — *John* 8 : 51.
	118–31	J· said, "Not that which — *Matt.* 15 : 11.
	174–24	J· said it is within you,
	181– 1	J· said to call no man father ;
	219– 6	J· said, "Ye do err, — *Matt.* 22 : 29.
	220–29	J· said it would be according to
	261–18	J· said, "I came not to — *see Matt.* 5 : 17.
	374– 9	J· said, "Wisdom is justified — *Luke* 7 : 35.
Ret.	35–16	J· said, "*They* shall lay hands — *Mark* 16 : 18.
	75–13	J· said, "For there is no man — *Mark* 9 : 39.
	79–27	take it by force !" said J·. — *Matt.* 11 : 12.
	81–21	Said J· : "If the light — *see Matt.* 6 : 23.
Un.	46–13	J· said, "I and my Father — *John* 10 : 30.
Pul.	4– 2	J· said, "Be not afraid" ! — *Mark* 6 : 50.
	53–12	* J· said to him : "Arise, — *Luke* 17 : 19.
Rud.	7–17	J· said of personal evil,
	12–23	J· said : "Take no thought — *Matt.* 6 : 25.
No.	23– 7	J· said to Peter,
	24–22	J· said, "a murderer — *John* 8 : 44.
	31–25	but J· said to disease :
	34– 9	J· said : "The hour cometh, — *John* 4 : 23.
	37– 4	J· said, "Ye do err, — *Matt.* 22 : 29.
	41– 5	J· said, "For which of — *John* 10 : 32.
	42– 8	J· said to the sick,
	44–28	J· said : "I thank Thee, — *Luke* 10 : 21.
Pan.	8–20	J· said, "My Father is — *John* 14 : 28.
'00.	5– 7	J· said the opposite of God
'01.	7–27	J· said, "Thomas, because — *John* 20 : 29.
	8– 7	J· said, "I and my Father — *John* 10 : 30.
	8–15	J· said, "Be ye therefore — *Matt.* 5 : 48.
	10– 3	J· said, "For all these — *see Matt.* 10 : 17.
	19– 8	J· said, "Ask, and ye — *John* 16 : 24.
	28–23	J· said : "It is enough — *Matt.* 10 : 25.
	31 9	J· said, "I came not to — *Matt.* 10 : 34.
'02.	6–11	J· said a lie fathers itself,
	16–15	J· said : "I am the way." — *John* 14 : 6.
	17– 3	J· said, "If ye love me, — *John* 14 : 15.
Hea.	16–27	J· said, "I am the way, — *John* 14 : 6.
My.	28–20	* doing the works which J· said
	150–23	J· said : "If ye abide in me, — *John* 15 : 7.
	161–19	said J·, "Ye shall drink — *Matt.* 20 : 23.
	162– 3	J· said : "Suffer it to be — *Matt.* 3 : 15.
	253–11	J· said : "The world hath — *John* 17 : 25.
	339–24	J· said to his disciples,

saith

'02.	19–16	J· saith : "Come unto me." — *Matt.* 11 : 28.

saw

Mis.	370– 4	saw J· do such deeds of mercy,

saying of

Un.	53–26	hence that saying of J·,

sayings of

My.	178–32	*Logia,* or imputed sayings of J·

second appearing of

Ret.	70–20	The second appearing of J· is,

spake

Mis.	83–28	"These words spake J·, — *John* 17 : 1.

Spirit of

Mis.	70–24	holy Spirit of J· was eternal.

spoke

My.	146– 3	J· spoke the truth.
	266–15	of which J· spoke.

stooped not

Un.	11–14	J· stooped not to human

suffered

Un.	56– 3	If J· suffered, . . . it must have
No.	33–24	J· suffered for all mortals
	35–13	to show the allness . . . . J· suffered.

syllogism of

Mis.	195–20	That perfect syllogism of J·

taught

Mis.	3–10	J· taught them for this very
	25– 6	religion that J· taught and
	29–32	which J· taught and proved.
	59–21	If *C. S. is the same as J· taught,*
	99–32	J· taught by the wayside,
Un.	11– 3	J· taught us to walk *over,*
No.	35–28	J· taught and demonstrated the
My.	103–14	the Science which J· taught and
	303–20	J· taught and proved that

taught by

'01.	33–22	after the manner taught by J·,

teaching of

Pul.	35– 2	meaning of the teaching of J· and

teachings of

(*see* teachings)

the man

(*see* man)

turned

Un.	57–11	When J· turned and said,

unreal to

Mis.	200–29	were alike unreal to J· ;

Jesus

walked

Un.	58– 5	J· walked with bleeding **feet**

was compassionate

'02.	18–12	J· was compassionate, true,

was human

'01.	10–12	J· was human, but the

was questioned

My.	220– 8	When J· was questioned concerning

was the Messiah

Mis.	77– 4	fact that J· was the Messiah.

was the son

Mis.	161– 9	To the senses, J· was the son of man :
'01.	10– 9	J· was the son of Mary,

went about

Ret.	93– 1	J· went about doing good.

we see

Ret.	91–17	we see J· ministering to the

words of

Mis.	37–14	meaning of those words of J·,
	198–11	silences . . . with the words of J· :
My.	253–16	my love and these words of J· :

work of

No.	37–19	work of J· would lose its

would hate

Mis.	336–10	Then you would hate J· if you saw **him**

Mis.	25–30	why did not J· employ them
	55– 6	demonstrate to the extent that J· did,
	63–11	*why did J· come to save sinners?*
	63–22	*why did J· cry out,*
	70–10	*What did J· mean when he said*
	70–15	paradise of Spirit would come to J·,
	70–25	the thief would be with J· only in
	74–11	*If God does not . . . how did J·,*
	83–20	*Why did J· call himself*
	84–13	J·, as material manhood, was not
	88–21	* that J· was the highest type of
	96– 2	as wrought out by J·,
	111–24	his doctrines and those of J·,
	122– 6	Would J· thus have spoken
	158–28	J· was not ordained as our
	165–17	truth uttered and lived by J·,
	171– 6	To suppose that J· did actually
	189–14	plainly declared, through J·,
	193– 2	Did J· mean what he said?
	193– 4	J· did mean all, and even more
	201– 9	When J· reproduced his body
	211–27	J· stormed sin in its citadels
	212– 0	J· did his work, and left his
	215–28	the words, that J· used
	292– 6	J·, who so loved the world
	359–15	For J· to walk the water was
	300–27	J·, as the true idea of Him,
	366–32	sophistry and what J· had not,
Ret.	89–15	J· was once asked to exhort,
	90– 5	no evidence to show that J·
	91–13	Where did J· deliver this great
Un.	9– 8	J· has made the way plain,
	37– 1	J· not only declared himself
	61– 5	J· first appeared as a
No.	22–21	That J· cast several persons out of
	23–10	Out of . . . J· cast seven devils ;
	36–22	J· could not have resisted them ;
	41– 4	warned the people to beware of J·,
Pan.	5–26	J· treated the lie summarily.
'00.	14–20	cites J· as "he that — *Rev.* 3 : 7.
'01.	8–26	J·, the only immaculate, was born of
	25–28	J· likened such self-contradictions
'02.	18–19	J· laid down his life
Hea.	2–17	J·, the model of infinite patience,
	2–21	why should the world hate J·,
My.	vii– 8	* truths testified to by J·
	15–20	* Of J· and his glory,
	15–21	* Of J· and his love.
	125–32	of the martyrs of J·," — *Rev.* 17 : 6.
	222– 8	J·, the master Metaphysician,
	222–15	Even in those dark days J· was not
	261–27	J·, the Galilean Prophet,
	307–15	* and that you are J·."
	340– 1	J· attended feasts,

(*see also* **Beloved, Christ Jesus, Ensample, Galilean Prophet, Lamb, Master, Nazarene, Nazarene Prophet, Nazarite, Priest, Prince of Peace, Prophet, Son, Teacher, Watcher, Way, Way-shower**)

Jesus'

Mis.	12–13	law of loyalty to J· Sermon
	20– 3	aroma of J· own words,
	25–22	J· only medicine was omnipotent
	30– 3	according to J· example
	75– 2	hem of the garment of J· idea
	76–16	void by J· divine declaration,
	83–27	J· wisdom ofttimes was shown by
	91–16	J· character and example.

Jesus'

Mis.	103–24	J· personality in the flesh,
	108–25	J· definition of sin
	111–18	J· faith in Truth must not
	161–11	it was J· approximation to
	162–11	emblem of J· history ;
	170–24	J· proceedings with the blind man
	171– 3	J· first effort to realize Truth
	214– 2	J· life was full of Love,
	214–21	the personal J· labor in the flesh
	260– 7	line of J· thought or action.
	373–26	is followed by J· declaration,
	388–25	The right to sit at J· feet ;
Man.	15–14	We acknowledge J· atonement as
Chr.	53–30	that doom Was J· part ;
Ret.	25– 7	J· teaching and demonstration,
	35–24	perpetuity of J· command,
	45–20	in following J· command,
	54– 9	drinking J· cup,
	75– 4	J· Sermon on the Mount,
	89–19	J· method was to instruct
	94–26	illustrated in J· career,
	94–28	J· teachings bore much fruit,
Pul.	41–27	* the power of J· name,"
	60– 9	* J· miracle of loaves and fishes.
	72–30	* "Did you ever hear of J· taking
	81– 2	* the power of J· name,"
Rud.	3–17	J· healing was spiritual
No.	14–22	not confined to J· students
	33–22	J· sacrifice stands preeminently
	36– 6	J· true and conscious being
	36–11	popular view of J· nature.
Pan.	5– 7	chapter sub-title
	5–18	J· definition of devil (evil)
'01.	2–21	What J· disciples of old experienced,
	8–24	Christ was J· spiritual selfhood ;
	11– 3	because of J· great work on earth,
	19–15	a flat departure from J· practice
	24–25	necessary to follow J· teachings,
	26– 1	consistency of J· theory and practice
Hea.	18–19	J· mission extended to the sick
Po.	21–14	The right to sit at J· feet ;
My.	28–24	* J· gospel was for all time
	149– 2	divine Principle of J· life-work,
	152– 4	the touch of J· robe
	190–14	J· students, failing to cure a
	190–31	fulfilling J· prophecy and verifying
	211–10	even as in J· time
	214–11	J· three days' work in the sepulchre
	221– 3	J· doctrine, now as then,
	232–28	does that . . . accord with J· saying?
	340–26	J· example in this, as in all else,
		(see also **words**)

Jesus Christ

Mis.	77– 2	J· C· was the Son of God?
	161–24	new name, Messiah, or J· C·,
	196–28	Believe on the Lord J· C·,— Acts 16 : 31.
Chr.	55–18	In the name of J· C·— Acts 3 : 6.
Ret.	15– 6	"J· C· himself being the— Eph. 2 : 20.
Un.	4–24	J· C·, whom He has sent.
Pul.	85–19	* prayer and teachings of J· C·.
No.	21–24	which is J· C·."— I Cor. 3 : 11.
'02.	12–12	J· C· is not God,
My.	8–10	* of the religion of J· C·,
	17–13	acceptable to God by J· C·.— I Pet. 2 : 5.
	19– 9	grace of the Lord J· C·,— II Cor. 13 : 14.
	260–30	but one J· C· on record.

jet

Po.	74– 5	O blue eyes and j·,

Jew (see also **Jew's**)

'00.	3–30	not the incentive of the devout J·
'02.	11–29	J· and Christian can unite in doctrine
	11–30	The J· believes that the Messiah
	12– 7	The J· who believes in
	12– 9	J· unites with the Christian idea

jewel

No.	5–25	a lost j· in this misconception of
My.	121–15	plain dealing is a j· as beautiful
	357–12	C. S., which is its j·.

jewelry

Pul.	78–26	* window of J. C. Derby's j· store.

jewels

Mis.	159–29	embroidery, silver, gold, and j·,
	201–26	our j· have been stolen ;
	201–27	losing those j· of character,
	313–13	their j· of thought, so adapted to
	395–16	Quickly earth's j· disappear ;
Ret.	79–23	j· of Love, set in wisdom.
Po.	58– 1	Quickly earth's j· disappear ;

Jewish

Mis.	65–30	The J· religion demands that
	123–16	was the J· tribal deity.
	161–20	J· law that none should teach or

Jewish

Mis.	260– 6	J· religion, never entered into
Ret.	65–15	J· religion was not spiritual ;
Un.	29– 3	J· law condemned the sinner
No.	29– 1	this passage refers to the J· law,
My.	104– 3	J· pagans thought that the
	262– 8	herds of a J· village.

Jew's

Mis.	124–10	J· or Moslem's misconception of
'02.	12–12	J· belief in one God,

Jews (see also **Jews'**)

Mis.	186– 6	self-constituted belief of the J·
Pul.	82–12	* J· claimed to be the conservators
	82–15	* J· who never called Abraham "Father,"
	82–16	* J· themselves have long acknowledged
Rud.	17– 2	Like certain J· whom St. Paul
'02.	11–27	the J· put to death the Galilean

Jews'

Mis.	121– 4	Master partook of the J· feast

J. H. W.

Pul.	61–18	* signature

Job (see also **Job's**)

Mis.	278–14	J· sinned not in all he said,
Un.	5–28	Thy ways," says J· ;— see Job 26 : 14.
Pul.	3–19	with J· of old we exclaim,
My.	109–17	we may sometimes say with J·,
	218– 4	J· said, "In my flesh— Job 19 : 26.

Job's

Un.	55–17	J· faith and hope gained him

John (see also **John's, Revelator, St. John**)

I : 3

Mis.	45–28	In J· i. 3 we read,

II : 6

Pul.	27–15	* water-pots referred to in J· ii. 6.

IV : 24

Rud.	13–15	In J· (iv. 24) we may read :

XVII

Mis.	83–22	In J· xvii. he declared his sonship

Mis.	191– 8	The Scripture in J·, sixth chapter
Pul.	27–27	* J· on the Isle of Patmos,
	54–25	* followers, Peter, James, and J·,
	83–26	* to know what J· on Patmos meant
My.	307–14	* and I see that I am J·,

I John 3 : 1 – 3

My.	33– 6	* correlative Scripture, 1 J· 3 : 1–3.

John

the Baptist

Mis.	81–11	teachings of J· the Baptist?
	81–22	like the individual J· the Baptist,
	121–23	christened by J· the Baptist,
	181–31	J· the Baptist had a clear
My.	228–12	Referring to J· the Baptist,

Mis.	81–13	being baptized of J·,
	81–20	why does not J· hear this voice,
	82– 9	Such Christians as J· cognize the
	184–29	J·, came baptizing with water.

John (McNeil)

Ret.	1–15	J· and Marion Moor McNeil

John Bull's

Pul.	67–12	* enumeration of J· B· creeds.

Johnism

'01.	12– 8	That is J·,

Johnites

'01.	12– 8	only J· would be seen in such

John's

Un.	4–23	J· Gospel declares

Johnson

Dr. James

Peo.	6– 5	Dr. James J·, Surgeon Extraordinary

William B.

Pul.	43– 9	* Stephen A. Chase, and William B. J
	86–10	* Ira O. Knapp, William B. J·,
	87– 8	* signature
My.	21–30	* signature
	38– 7	* signature
	46–31	* signature
	63– 8	* signature
	280–12	* signature

William Lyman

My.	32–25	* music by William Lyman J·.

Johnson C.S.B.

Mr. William B.

My.	289– 7	Mr. William B. J·, C.S.B., Clerk.

Johnson, C.S.D.

William B.

My.	39–16	* Clerk, William B. J·, C.S.D.

join
Mis.	80–11	Anybody . . . can *j·* this league.
	105–26	The senses *j·* issue with error,
	281–30	"Though hand *j·* in hand, — *Prov.* 11 : 21.
	330– 7	should *j·* in nature's grand harmony,
'02.	20–16	brethren, are you ready to *j·* me in
Po.	66– 9	To *j·* with the neighboring choir ;
My.	197–27	*j·* with you in song and sermon.

joined
Mis.	94– 8	which God hath not *j·* together.
	188– 4	creation *j·* in the grand chorus
Pul.	58– 9	* *j·* The Mother Church in Boston,
My.	31–32	* *j·* in the song of praise.
	39–12	* Prayer, in which all *j·*.
	89– 8	* has *j·* lightness and grace
	268– 9	What God hath *j·* together,
	311–13	clerk's book shows that I *j·* the

joining
Mis.	79–29	*j·* any medical league which
Man.	45– 4	*J·* Another Society.
No.	46–11	*j·* the overture of angels.
My.	78–31	* *j·* with their shrill voices
	148–19	*j·* in your rejoicing,

joins
Mis.	396–13	My heart unbidden *j·* rehearse ;
Po.	59– 5	My heart unbidden *j·* rehearse,

joint
My.	199–13	The *j·* resolutions contained
	310–10	*j·* partner with Alexander Tilton,

joint-heirs
Mis.	46–24	*j·* with Christ." — *Rom.* 8 : 17.
	255–16	*j·* with Christ." — *Rom.* 8 : 17.

joints
Un.	7–14	able to replace dislocated *j·*

joker
Mis.	353–14	a practical *j·*, set a man who

Jones (see also **Jones'**)
Elizabeth Earl
My.	326–14	letter from Elizabeth Earl *J·*
	328– 4	* signature

Jones'
Miss
My.	328– 8	* referred to in Miss *J·* letter :

Miss Elizabeth Earl
My.	327–10	* heading

Jonson, Ben
Mis.	vii– 3	BEN *J·* : *Epigram I.*
	vii– 8	BEN *J·* : *Epigram 86.*

Jordan
Mis.	81–19	*the people from beyond J·?*
	206– 5	Above the waves of *J·*,
My.	43–12	* The crossing of the *J·* brought
	43–19	* Israel came over this *J·*

Jordan Hall
My.	80–14	* *J· H·*, Potter Hall,
	80–23	* crowded . . . *J· H·*,

Josephus
Hea.	3–17	*J·* alludes to several individuals

Joshua
Mis.	279–16	The first is that of *J·*
	279–24	In the case of *J·* and his band
My.	43–16	* In obedience to the command of *J·*,

jottings
Ret.	27–14	my first *j·* were but

Journal
Christian Science
Mis.	x– 7	writings published in *The C. S. J·*,
	113–30	Our churches, *The C. S. J·*, and
	126–18	able editors of *The C. S. J·*,
	155–22	editors of *The C. S. J·*
	155–27	and by way of *The C. S. J·* ;
	158–24	April number of *The C. S. J·*
	168–24	* *The C. S. J·* reported as follows :
	177–22	* editor of *The C. S. J·* said
	262– 6	patronage of *The C. S. J·*,
	285–10	*The C. S. J·* will hold high the
	303–21	*Editor of C. S. J·* :
	313– 2	*Editor of The C. S. J·* :
	313–13	contributors to *The C. S. J·*
	347–29	*The C. S. J·* was the oldest
	372–21	*The C. S. J·* gives no uncertain
	382–28	and gave it *The C. S. J·* ;
Man.	27–14	publication of *The C. S. J·*,
	49–15	inserted in *The C. S. J·*
	65–11	editors of the *C. S. J·*,
	72–16	advertised in *The C. S. J·*,
	73– 6	practitioners in *The C. S. J·*.
	74–16	a card in *The C. S. J·*
	81–10	editing or publishing *The C. S. J·*,
	81–19	relating to *The C. S. J·*.

Journal
Christian Science
Ret.	53– 2	*The C. S. J·*, as it was now called,
Pul.	9–18	editor of *The C. S. J·*
	36–26	* the editors of *The C. S. J·*,
	43– 7	* editor of *The C. S. J·*,
	84– 9	* [*The C. S. J·*, January, 1895]
My.	vi–18	* founded *The C. S. J·*
	vii– 1	* together with *The C. S. J·*,
	vii–15	* *The C. S. J·*, May, 1906
	19– 3	* current numbers of *The C. S. J·*,
	57–23	* advertised in *The C. S. J·*
	215–20	give my church *The C. S. J·*,
	223–10	cards are in *The C. S. J·*.
	286– 1	[*The C. S. J·*, May, 1908]
	304–16	I started *The C. S. J·*,
	304–19	editor of *The C. S. J·*,
page 326		* heading
	353–10	The first was *The C. S. J·*,
	363–17	*The C. S. J·*, July, 1895.

C. S.
Mis.	157– 9	find their card in *The C. S. J·*),

of Christian Science
Mis.	139–15	I started the *J·* of C. S.,
Ret.	52–20	was called *J· of C. S.*
Pul.	47– 6	* was called the *J· of C. S.*,

of 1904, page 184
My.	254–20	* in the June *J·* of 1904, page 184 :

Mis.	61–11	* In the October *J·* I read
	87–15	*inform us, through your J·*,
	88– 6	*Please give us, through your J·*,
	156– 8	contributions as usual to our *J·*.
	216– 8	In the May number of our *J·*,
	256–14	October number of the *J·*,
	262– 1	our *J·* is designed to bring health
	262–23	this white winged messenger, our *J·*.
	303–22	by giving place in your *J·* to
Man.	74 10	and societies advertised in said *J·*,
Pul.	65–10	* *J·*, Kansas City, Mo., January 10,
	89– 2	* *J·*, Lockport, N. Y.
	89–18	* *J·*, Atlanta, Ga.
	89–33	* *J·*, Columbus, Ohio.
	89–34	* *J·*, Topeka, Kans.
My.	57–26	* societies advertised in the *J·*
	97– 9	* The *J·* has kept no books on the
	226–27	*C. S. Sentinel* and *J·*

journalism
Mis.	297–10	Smart *j·* is allowable,
Pul.	31–16	* editorial work in daily *j·*

Journal of Christian Science
(see **Journal**)

journey
Mis.	206–32	As you *j·*, and betimes sigh for
	304–20	* it will *j·* from place to place,
	311– 5	as we *j·* to the celestial city.
	327–15	The *j·* commences.
Ret.	19–22	on her sad *j·* to the North.
Un.	17– 6	will aid your *j·*,
My.	215–24	take no scrip for their *j·*,
	331– 1	on her sad *j·* to the North.

journeying
Mis.	135– 9	sweet sense of *j·* on together,
My.	322–20	* my *j·* from the far South,

journeyings
Mis.	177–30	In my long *j·* I have met

joy
and crown
My.	150– 9	Strive thou for the *j·* and crown

and gladness
My.	171– 6	obtain *j·* and gladness, — *Isa.* 35 : 10.
	194– 3	songs of *j·* and gladness.

and gratitude
My.	45– 6	* witnessing with *j·* and gratitude

and power
Mis.	331–18	peace and *j·* and power ;
	389– 6	peace and *j·* and power ;
Po.	4– 1	peace and *j·* and power ;

and rejoicing
My.	260–18	understanding of *j·* and rejoicing,

and tears
Po.	77–12	giveth *j·* and tears, conflict and

a trembler
Mis.	341–14	is *j·* a trembler?

cause for
'02.	3– 4	It is cause for *j·* that among the

cometh
Hea.	10–18	and *j·* cometh with the light.

distant
Po.	31– 8	tear-filled tones of distant *j·*,

divinely fair
Mis.	387– 2	With *j·* divinely fair,
Po.	50–20	With *j·* divinely fair,

joy

eager
Mis. 98–14 to watch with eager *j·* the

earthly
Mis. 81–24 cry in the desert of earthly *j·* ;

eternity of
Mis. 135–18 an eternity of *j·* that outweighs

everlasting
My. 171– 5 songs and everlasting *j·* — *Isa.* 35 : 10.

express the
Mis. 149–19 Lips nor pen can ever express the *j·*

exuberant
Rud. 15– 8 with exuberant *j·*.

exuberant with
Mis. 231– 3 infancy, exuberant with *j·*,

filled with
Mis. 321– 7 My heart is filled with *j·*,

fills me with
Mis. 281– 7 that fills me with *j·*.

for the captive
Po. 71–15 *J·* for the captive !   Sound it long !

fresh
My. 155–19 a pure peace, a fresh *j·*,

giving
Mis. 262–16 giving *j·* to the suffering

gladdened
Po. 30–10 Thou gildest gladdened *j·*,

grateful
My. 229–29 my disappointed hope and grateful *j·*.

great
Mis. 133–28 affords me great *j·* to be able to
    278– 8 great *j·* in this consciousness,
'02. 20–21 gives me great *j·* to look into the

greets with
Mis. 177–29 greets with *j·* a familiar face.

grief and
Po. 9– 5 fountains of grief and *j·*

hail with
Mis. 141–10 hail with *j·* this proposed type

harbinger of
Un. 57–25 Sorrow is the harbinger of *j·*.

heartfelt
Mis. 231–29 such tones of heartfelt *j·*

heavenly
My. 38– 2 * the balm of heavenly *j·*,

highest
Pan. 10–25 who finds the highest *j·*,

holy
Mis. 287–13 only high and holy *j·*

illustrates the
My. 339–16 illustrates the *j·*, grace, and glory

in attesting
My. 96–12 * take *j·* in attesting their faith

ineffable
Ret. 13–21 a soft glow of ineffable *j·*

innate
My. 341– 1 I have one innate *j·*,

is real
'02. 17–16 wherein *j·* is real and fadeless.

is self-sustained
Mis. 209–26 *J·* is self-sustained ;

juvenile
My. 261– 7 full supply of juvenile *j·*.

know the
My. 220–22 know the *j·* and the peace of love.''

leap for
Mis. 126– 6 in tones that leap for *j·*,

legitimate
My. 41–25 * postpone his legitimate *j·*,

liberty and
Mis. 240–10 whereas forecasting liberty and *j·*

light and
Po. 23– 9 in truth, in light and *j·*,

meet with
Mis. 326–23 to meet with *j·* his own,

much
My. 21–23 * who have anticipated much *j·*
    27–21 * much *j·* and thanksgiving

my
Po. 16–25 waken my *j·*, as in earliest prime.
My. 253–25 and my *j·* therewith.

occasion for
My. 89–17 * Here is an occasion for *j·*

of acquiescence
My. 292– 7 *j·* of acquiescence consummated.

of angels
Pul. 11– 5 mingle with the *j·* of angels

of divine Science
Mis. 342– 1 *j·* of divine Science demonstrated.

of knowing
Mis. 263– 3 unselfish *j·* of knowing that the
    382– 9 *j·* of knowing that the sinner and
My. 236–13 *j·* of knowing that Christian Scientists

of Love
No. 8– 7 beauty of holiness, the *j·* of Love

joy

of repentance
My. 36–16 * the *j·* of repentance and the

of thy Lord
Mis. 122–26 into the *j·* of thy Lord.''—*Matt.* 25 : 23.

of thy lord
My. 62– 3 * into the joy of thy lord.''—*Matt.* 25 : 23.
    207–22 into the joy of thy lord''—*Matt.* 25 : 21.

one
Mis. 281– 9 I have now one ambition and one *j·*.

or woe
Po. 28– 8 Whate'er the gift of *j·* or woe,

our
Mis. 386–10 Our *j·* is gathered from
Po. 49–15 Our *j·* is gathered from
My. 63–20 * in some degree sharing in our *j·*.

peace and
Mis. 303–10 peace and *j·*, the fruits of Spirit,
    331–18 peace and *j·* and power ;
    389– 6 peace and *j·* and power ;
Po. 4– 1 peace and *j·* and power ;

perquisite of
My. 189– 7 affords even me a perquisite of *j·*.

phantom of
Po. 65– 7 A phantom of *j·*, it fled with

pride and
'02. 3–10 the old national family pride and *j·*

privileged
Mis. 143–29 breathing the donor's privileged *j·*.
Pul. 8–12 privileged *j·* at helping to build

profound
My. 157– 4 * profound *j·* and deep gratitude

promised
'02. 18– 1 light with promised *j·*.

real
Ret. 18–15 of real *j·* and of visions divine ;
Po. 64– 6 of real *j·* and of visions divine ;

refinement of
Mis. 101– 6 blesses . . . by the refinement of *j·*

return in
My. 170–30 return in *j·*, bearing your sheaves

righteousness and
My. 41–18 * truth and righteousness and *j·*.

rise with
Pul. 7–16 They will rise with *j·*,

run in
My. 155–13 run in *j·*, health, holiness,

secret
Ret. 15–27 who divulged their secret *j·*

short-lived
Ret. 32–16 * Short-lived *j·*, that ends in

shouted for
Mis. 259–21 sons of God shouted for *j·*.''—*Job* 38 : 7.
Un. 42–15 sons of God shouted for *j·*.''—*Job* 38 : 7.

smile of
Peo. 7–10 * face lit up with a smile of *j·*

special
Mis. 160–10 special *j·* in knowing that one is

spiritual
Ret. 21–20 spiritual *j·* and true estimate of

sublunary
Hea. 11– 3 survey the cost of sublunary *j·*,

tears of
Ret. 16– 5 tears of *j·* flooding her eyes
My. 161– 4 with tears of *j·*.

their
Mis. 150–12 hearts to-day are repeating their *j·*

this
Po. 68– 7 Earth held but this *j·*,

thrill of
Mis. 375–27 * thrill of *j·* as no words can

time and
My. 166–23 let our measure of time and *j·*

tired
Mis. 397–13 From tired *j·* and grief afar,
Pul. 18–22 From tired *j·* and grief afar,
Po. 13– 1 From tired *j·* and grief afar,

to know
My. 230–22 It is a *j·* to know that

trifle with
Mis. 257–16 a code whose modes trifle with *j·*,

unprecarious
My. 201–19 tenure of unprecarious *j·*.

unspeakable
Mis. 279– 8 sunshine and *j·* unspeakable.

was eagle-plumed
Mis. 385–22 and *j·* was eagle-plumed,
Po. 48–16 and *j·* was eagle-plumed,

well-earned
My. 47–20 * well-earned *j·* that is with us now.

which finds
Mis. 127–19 *j·* which finds one's own in another's
My. 18–16 *j·* which finds one's own in another's

wings of
My. 192–26 My love can fly on wings of *j·*

joy
your
Mis. 155–12 and peace will crown your j·.

Mis. ix–12 Where j·, sorrow, hope,
204– 8 hope, sorrow, j·, defeat, and
351–25 j· that becomes sorrow.
385–10 "J· for thee, happy friend !
389– 2 The hoary head with j· to crown ;
395–22 For j·, to shun my weary way,
Ret. 22–11 "Who for the j· that — Heb. 12 : 2.
'00. 14–15 to remind you of the j· you have
'02. 3–24 the j· of the sainted Queen,
19–11 I say it with j·,
Hea. 10–23 to argue stronger for sorrow than for j·.
Po. vii–14 * prove a j· to the heavy laden
21–16 The hoary head with j· to crown ;
31– 2 J· — not of time, nor yet by nature
48– 1 J· for thee, happy friend !
58– 7 For j·, to shun my weary way,
71–14 J· is in every belfry bell
My. 47–12 * it is with j· that those who have
62–13 * with the j· of Love's victory.
134–10 J· over good achievements
164–14 Is it not a j· to compare the
177–21 j· of many generations awaits it,
258–14 j· that was set before him— Heb. 12 : 2.
273–20 j·, sorrow, life, and death.
355–28 His reflection of peace, love, j·.

joyful
Mis. 15–15 j· adoption of good ;
394– 9 bless, and make j· again.
Po. 45–12 bless, and make j· again.

joyfully
'02. 20– 6 hues of heaven, ... j· whisper,

joy-giving
Mis. 19–20 spiritual, j·, and eternal?

joy-inspiring
Mis. 19–32 health-giving and j·.

joyous
Pul. 16– 6 J·, risen, we depart
Pan. 1– 9 j· June is here and ours.
Po. 54– 2 Since j· spring was there.
My. 131–20 this meeting is very j· to me.

joys
and sorrows
Mis. 84–26 material j· and sorrows,
celestial
Mis. 100–25 terrestrial and celestial j·,
consummate the
Mis. 213– 8 consummate the j· of acquiescence
departed
Po. 34–22 j· departed, unforgotten love.
earthly
My. 290–17 earthly j· seem most afar.
eternal
Mis. xi–16 become footsteps to j· eternal.
fleeting
Mis. 360–18 blighted flowers of fleeting j·,
higher
Mis. 287–25 they lead to higher j· :
330–21 higher j·, holier aims,
life's
Mis. 10– 2 wherewith to obstruct life's j·
man of
Mis. 84–14 knew that the man of j·,
misnamed
Mis. 327– 1 turned my misnamed j· to sorrow.
mortal
Mis. 385–16 travelled . . . far from mortal j·,
Po. 48–10 traveled . . . far from mortal j·,
of heaven
Po. 24– 1 Come to me, j· of heaven !
supernal
Mis. 387–23 Whence j· supernal flow,
Po. 6–18 Whence j· supernal flow,

Mis. 42–19 our j· and means of advancing
351–27 punishes the j· of this false sense
My. 158–14 and j· in the present

jubilant
Po. 27–17 Wrong j· and right with

jubilee
Mis. 135–15 to the j· of Spirit?
310–26 receding year of religious j·,
My. 177– 9 presence at your religious j·.

Judæo-Christian
'00. 13–27 * authorities of the J· church."

Judah's
Po. 10–15 To J· sceptered race,
My. 337–16 To J· sceptred race,

Judaism
Mis. 162–15 to stem the tide of J·,
No. 14– 8 Theosophy is a corruption of J·.
'00. 4– 9 purged by a purer J·
Peo. 8–11 J·, enjoining the limited and

Judas
Mis. 212– 3 a caressing J· that betrays

Judea
Mis. 81–18 all the cities and towns of J·,
Hea. 3–17 born in a remote province of J·,
My. 28–27 * preached . . . to the multitudes of J·

Judean and **Judæan**
Mis. 82– 1 reconstructs the J· religion,
166–18 J· religion even required the

judge
Mis. 90–19 then j· them by their fruits.
195–24 unfit to j· in the case ;
239– 2 j· for yourself whether I can talk
290– 8 chapter sub-title
290–2i cease to j· of causes from a personal
Pul. 46– 6 * words of the j· speak to the point,
57–11 * From the description we j· that
Hea. 7–16 and through which to j· of it.
My. 148– 5 to j· our doctrine by its fruits.
296– 2 * able discourse of our "learned j·,"
314–17 decision was given by the j·
344– 1 then you can j· for yourself.
364– 2 "J· no man." — John 8 : 15.

judged
Man. 42– 9 By his works he shall be j·,
Ret. 43–18 j· it best to close the institution.
Pan. 10– 7 if the effects . . . be thus j·,
'01. 33–13 not to be j· on a doctrinal
33–18 j· (if at all) by their works.
My. 127– 5 j· according to their works,
270– 5 to be criticized or j· by

judges
Mis. 74– 9 j·, . . . all human systems of etiology
130–21 He who j· others should know well
Hea. 7–21 as our j· would not have done

judgeth
My. 126–22 Lord God who j· her." — Rev. 18 : 8.
196–19 that j· righteously." — I Pet. 2 : 23.

judging
Mis. 73–25 j· the twelve tribes — Matt. 19 : 28.
Man. 40–13 prophesying, j·, condemning,
Pan. 11– 7 Was our Master mistaken in j· a
'00. 1–23 J· from the number of the

judgment
Mis. 140–11 to form a proper j·.
157–24 thy j· as the noonday." Psal. 37 : 6.
211– 9 by the good j· of people in
277–20 divine justice and j· are enthroned.
323 24 the justice of His j·,
372–14 I sought the j· of sound critics
381–16 stipulation for a j· and a decree
'00. 9–13 Strong desires bias human j·
10–21 justice and j· are the habitation of
'01. 35– 3 thy j· as the noonday." — Psal. 37 : 6.
My. 16–28 "J· also will I lay to the — Isa. 28 : 17.
41–10 * and so receive j· without mercy ;
104–18 suspend j· and sentence on the
170–25 thy j· as the noonday." — Psal. 37 : 6.
222–32 await the end — justice and j·.
227–15 influenced by their own j·
316–23 manifesting its unbiased j· by

judgment-day
Ret. 13–14 belief in a final j·,

judiciary
Pan. 14–16 and our national j· ;

jugular
Un. 7–12 had eaten its way to the j· vein.
My. 105–15 and exposed the j· vein

juice
Mis. 243–29 secretions of the gastric j·,

July
(see **months**)

juncture
Mis. 161–22 natural to conclude that at this j·
Ret. 44–15 At this j· I recommended that
My. 26–14 quite unexpected at this j·,

June
(see **months**)

juniors
Mis. 316–17 My j· can tell others

jurisdiction
Mis. 227– 8 their crime comes within its j·.
349–17 I claim no j· over any students.
Man. 18–15 reorganized, under her j·,
86– 7 under the j· of his former teacher.

just

Mis.	2– 9	When we remember that God is *j·*,
	11– 4	I used to think it sufficiently *j·*
	13– 2	*j·* so far as one and all permit
	26–23	this is *j·* what I call matter,
	32–28	should be *j·*, merciful ;
	61– 3	priceless, eternal, and *j·* at hand.
	71–31	immutable and *j·* law of Science,
	112– 9	The most *j·* man can neither
	112–10	unless he knows *how* to be *j·* ;
	121–13	would make this fatal doctrine *j·*
	121–29	Human tribunals, if *j·*,
	122–19	whose damnation is *j·*." — *Rom.* 3 : 8.
	122–32	The murder of the *j·* Nazarite
	123–22	whereby the *j·* obtain a pardon
	128– 8	whatsoever things are *j·*, — *Phil.* 4 : 8.
	131–19	It is but *j·* to consider the
	132–29	Even the desire to be *j·* is
	132–30	with the hope that you wish to be *j·*.
	170–30	he had *j·* told them.
	188–20	*J·* there, . . . the present writer found
	211–14	drowning man *j·* rescued
	228– 7	*j·* amid lawlessness,
	228–16	a kind, true, and *j·* person,
	239–17	*J·* then a tiny, sweet face appeared
	247– 7	I found health in *j·* what I teach.
	248– 9	The Greeks showed a *j·* estimate of
	262–13	I *j·* want to say, I thank you,
	275–15	*j·* comfort, encourage, and bless
	277–28	one can be *j·* amid lawlessness,
	280–32	*j·* at the moment when you are ready
	292–30	as to *j·* how this should be done,
	293– 2	*j·* breathing new Life and Love
	294–19	*j·* enough to reform and
	298– 6	whose damnation is *j·*." — *Rom.* 3 : 8.
	332– 4	Infinitely *j·*, merciful, and wise,
	334–20	*j·* reduce this falsity to its proper
	335–30	"whose damnation is *j·* ;" — *Rom.* 3 : 8.
	367– 3	requires man to be honest, *j·*,
Man.	16–12	to be merciful, *j·*, and pure.
	93–12	*j·* reply to public topics
Chr.	53–55	*J·* take Me in !
Ret.	5– 1	*j·* across the bridge,
	76–19	This *j·* affection serves to
Un.	15– 3	more *j·* than God?" — *Job* 4 : 17.
	23– 3	* The gods are *j·*,
	54–12	any claim whatever, *j·* or unjust,
Pul.	7– 9	remember also that God is *j·*,
	36–21	* *j·* beyond Massachusetts Avenue,
	37– 3	* *j·* in its attitude toward all questions."
	48– 9	* *j·* then, in the gorgeous October
	56–20	* And of the *j·* effect complain ;
	57–23	* *j·* off Huntington Avenue,
	64–24	* Boston has *j·* dedicated the first
	77– 2	* which the church has *j·* erected.
	86– 1	* *j·* completed, being of granite,
Rud.	11–16	*j·* so you can awake from
No.	27–13	but it is *j·* as veritable now
'01.	4– 7	*j·* as a departure from the
	33–25	*j·* what it was in the first centuries
Peo.	12– 7	merciful and *j·* government of God
Po.	23–18	Than *j·* to please mankind.
	41–19	the harpstring, *j·* breaking,
	43–21	*J·* the way Thou hast ;
	72– 4	Quench liberty that's *j·*.
My.	6– 4	Are we honest, *j·*, faithful?
	14–12	* saying that he had *j·* been informed
	31– 4	* "*J·* as I am, without one plea ;"
	41–21	* love which is *j·* and kind to all
	66–11	* *J·* what use the society will make
	71–21	* *j·* one vast auditorium
	74– 7	* *j·* about in time for the first
	83–23	* announcement, which has *j·* been
	91–27	* *j·* been dedicated at Boston
	96–31	* C. S. *j·* goes a little beyond
	97–27	* new temple, *j·* built at a cost of
	103–19	*j·* as I have discovered them.
	112– 5	did *j·* what he enjoined
	114– 4	be honest, *j·*, and pure ;
	132– 3	begin with the law as *j·* announced,
	141– 4	* has *j·* given out to the press,
	163–12	I always try to be *j·*,
	184– 3	Have *j·* received your despatch.
	208–15	expectation of *j·* such blessedness,
	215– 4	*J·* then God stretched forth His hand.
	223–28	*J·* now divine Love and wisdom
	224–30	Beloved students, *j·* now let us
	234–26	is *j·* what is needed.
	283–18	It is always safe to be *j·*.
	305–29	"Who shall be *j·*?"
	308–10	It becomes my duty to be *j·*
	314–28	*j·* as I have stated them.
	318–19	*j·* so long as he refrained from
	322– 9	* I have *j·* read your statement
	345–17	they acted *j·* the same
	355– 4	* on which we have *j·* entered.

just

My.	357–28	I have *j·* finished reading your

Justice

Po.	26– 8	While *J·* grasped the sword

justice

and being
'02.	15–12	connection between *j·* and being

and Christianity
Mis.	134– 6	characterize *j·* and Christianity.

and gratitude
Mis.	291–28	station *j·* and gratitude as sentinels

and humanity
'00.	10–14	in the name of God, *j·*, and humanity !

and judgment
Mis.	277–25	*j·* and judgment are enthroned.
'00.	10–21	*j·* and judgment are the habitation
My.	222–31	await the end — *j·* and judgment.

and Love
Ret.	80–17	permeate *j·* and Love,

and mercy
Mis.	146–25	understanding of *j·* and mercy.
	266–15	hold *j·* and mercy as inseparable
No.	7– 4	scales of *j·* and mercy.
My.	288– 1	revelation, *j·*, and mercy ;

and truth
Peo.	10–13	*J·* and truth make man free,
My.	316–17	in behalf of common *j·* and truth

basis of
My.	283–22	unite . . . on the basis of *j·*,

chariot-paths of
Pul.	7– 1	from the chariot-paths of *j·*,

common
My.	220– 3	safely submit . . . to common *j·*,
	316–17	in behalf of common *j·* and truth

divine
(see **divine***)*

eternal
Ret.	80– 3	though eternal *j·* be graciously

His
No.	34–21	to propitiate His *j·*

honesty and
My.	4–22	honesty and *j·* characterize the

human
Mis.	11–14	Love metes not out human *j·*,
	11–21	To mete out human *j·* to
	275– 3	Oh, tardy human *j·* !

industry, and
My.	265–30	honesty, industry, and *j·*,

inherent
My.	227–22	Inherent *j·*, constitutional

is the handmaid
Mis.	261–17	*J·* is the handmaid of mercy.

lack of
Mis.	7–31	not so much from a lack of *j·*,

law of
Mis.	123–23	through the eternal law of *j·* ;
	261–16	In this law of *j·*, the atonement

line of
My.	181–18	the intermediate line of *j·*

mercy, and
Mis.	11– 4	it is grace, mercy, and *j·*.

of civil codes
My.	268–13	the *j·* of civil codes,

of the peace
My.	136–22	Josiah E. Fernald, *j·* of the peace
	309–14	*j·* of the peace at one time.

plea for
My.	305–26	chapter sub-title

power of
My.	191– 5	not a tithe of the power of *j·*.

recompensed by
Mis.	2–12	subdued and recompensed by *j·*,

sense of
Mis.	121–30	borrow their sense of *j·* from

simple
Mis.	112–19	his act as one of simple *j·*,

steadfast
Ret.	50–21	steadfast *j·*, and strict adherence

tardy
Mis.	358– 9	at present naught but tardy *j·*,

the least
Pul.	32– 5	* can do the least *j·* to Mrs. Eddy,

the only
Mis.	13– 1	The only *j·* of which

thrones of
My.	200–22	on crumbling thrones of *j·*

waits
Mis.	277–10	*J·* waits, and is used to waiting ;

Mis.	67–19	*J·* uncovers sin of every sort ;
	119–24	*J·*, a prominent statute in
	122–22	nor reconciles *j·* to injustice ;
	154–28	*j·*, meekness, mercy, purity, love.
	322–24	the *j·* of His judgment,
Ret.	5–16	to which the pen can never do *j·*.

justice

Ret.	19–23	it is but *j·* to record,
Pul.	9– 8	but *j·*, mercy, and love kindle
Pan.	14–12	that *j·*, mercy, and peace continue
My.	139–13	*J·*, honesty, cannot be abjured ;
	160–10	that we receive from mankind *j·*,
	175–24	*j·*, fraternity, and Christian charity.
	180–20	in *j·*, as well as in mercy,
	220 13	*j·* is the moral signification of law.
	250– 6	quiets mad ambition, satisfies *j·*,
	265–11	and *j·* plead not vainly in behalf of
	272– 3	leavens the loaf of life with *j·*,
	282–12	nations are helped onward towards *j·*,
	331– 2	Here it is but *j·* to record,

Justice of the Peace

My.	138–31	* Allen Hollis, *J· of the P·*.
	315–20	* H. M. Morse, *J· of the P·*.

justifiable

My.	74–20	* pride and satisfaction . . . is *j·*.

justification

Mis.	243–31	in *j·* of material methods,
My.	22–19	* the *j·* of her labors

justified

Mis.	136–10	I cannot feel *j·* in turning
	300–17	you will then be *j·* in it.
	322–17	senses satisfied, or self be *j·*.
	354– 9	"*j·* of her children." — *Matt.* 11 : 19.
	374– 9	*j·* of all her children." — *Luke* 7 : 35.

justified

Man.	42– 9	and *j·* or condemned.
My.	12– 3	* *j·* the letting of contracts.
	228–22	*j·* of her children." — *Matt.* 11 : 19.

justifies

Mis.	216–15	*j·* one in the conclusion
	282–24	and the end *j·* the means ;
Pul.	61–17	* and *j·* the name given

justify

Mis.	299–32	does it *j·* you in appropriating
	374– 3	even the publicans to *j·* God.
My.	12– 9	* sufficient to *j·* the decision

Justin Martyr (see also Justin's)

Mis.	344– 2	It is related of *J· M·* that,

Justin's

Mis.	344–10	On *J·* confessing that he had

justly

Mis.	119–27	which one *j·* reserves to one's self,
Man.	85– 8	has so strayed as *j·* to be deemed,
Ret.	71–19	is not dealing *j·* and loving mercy,
Un.	1– 9	may *j·* be characterized as
Pul.	75– 7	they can *j·* declare it.
'00.	13–10	the apostle *j·* regards as heathen,
My.	264– 6	speak *j·* of my living.
	283–23	"To do *j·*, and to love— *Mic.* 6 : 8.

juvenile

Man.	63– 6	adapted to a *j·* class,
Pul.	8–30	By *j·* aid, . . . have come $4,460.
My.	261– 7	to the full supply of *j·* joy.

K

Kansas and Kans.

Pul.	59–22	* Joseph Armstrong, formerly of *K·*,
		(*see also* **Topeka**)

Kansas City, Mo.

Pul.	65–10	* *Journal*, *K· C·*, *M·*,
	90– 7	* *Star*, *K· C·*, *M·*.

Kant

Mis.	361–15	*K·*, Locke, Berkeley, Tyndall,
No.	22– 9	cold categories of *K·* fail
My.	349–9	*K·*, Locke, Berkeley, Tyndall,

Karma

Pul.	38–23	* opposed to the philosophy of *K·*

Keats'

My.	347–11	*K·* touching couplet,

keen

Mis.	224–18	with a *k·* relish for
	374– 6	*K·* and alert was their indignation

keener

Mis.	235–16	gives a *k·* sense of Truth

keenly

Mis.	118–12	However *k·* the human affections
	319– 9	seeing too *k·* their neighbor's.
'02.	18–30	made him *k·* alive to the
My.	139– 4	*k·* alive to the reality of
	275–15	I am well and *k·* alive

Keen's, Dr. W. W.

Ret.	49–13	certificate from Dr. W. W. *K·*

keep

Mis.	38–26	be healed by it and *k·* well?
	41–13	by those who *k·* the faith
	54–17	to *k·* well all my life?
	76– 4	"If a man *k·* my saying, — *John* 8 : 51.
	107–18	cannot *k·* pace with eternity.
	118–15	"*K·* My commandments." — *John* 15 : 10.
	123–25	love God, and *k·* His commandments.
	171–30	*k·* bright their invincible armor ;
	171–30	*k·* their demonstrations modest,
	175–14	shall *k·* the feast of Life,
	271– 6	*k·* out of their heads the notion
	278– 7	fight the good fight, and *k·* the faith.
	294–17	*k·* back thy offerings from asps
	307–23	*k·* yourselves from idols." — *I John* 5 : 21.
	311– 1	love God and *k·* His commandments,
	318–11	love God and *k·* His commandments.
	331–21	*K·* Thou my child on upward wing
	341–32	tended to *k·* aglow the flame
	389– 9	*K·* Thou my child on upward wing
	394–19	* I fain would *k·* the gates ajar,
Man.	30–20	*k·* the property in good repair,
	31–10	*k·* themselves unspotted from the
	76–21	*k·* themselves thoroughly informed
	78–20	*k·* on deposit the sum of
	104–15	shall each *k·* a copy of the
Ret.	31–19	"Whosoever shall *k·*— *Jas.* 2 : 10.
Un.	55–10	must *k·* close to his path,
Pul.	49–29	* a number of men to *k·* the grounds

keep

No.	3–17	to *k·* himself well informed.
	31–27	"If a man *k·* my saying, — *John* 8 : 51.
'01.	32–20	love God and *k·* His commandments
'02.	17– 3	"If ye love me, *k·* my — *John* 14 : 15.
	17–12	Many sleep who should *k·* . . . awake
Hea.	18–16	prevent its effervescing and *k·* it
Po.	4– 7	*K·* Thou my child on upward wing
	57– 5	* I fain would *k·* the gates ajar,
My.	8– 5	* We need to *k·* pace with
	14–30	* *k·* pace with the disbursements.
	51– 1	* so as to *k·* her with us,
	106– 3	or to *k·* silent,
	130– 8	effort . . . to *k·* my works from
	134– 8	*k·* the faith individually and
	145–12	* I do not feel able to *k·* about.
	158– 9	"able to *k·* that which I *II Tim.* 1 : 19.
	160– 5	to *k·* human consciousness in constant
	191–11	*K·* in mind the foundations of C. S.
	191–12	*K·* personality out of sight,
	210– 2	*k·* your minds so filled with Truth
	215–20	to *k·* . . . from clogging the wheels
	228–29	able to *k·* that which I — *II Tim.* 1 : 12.
	252– 3	*K·* yourselves busy with divine Love.
	253–16	*k·* through Thine own — *John* 17 : 11.
	290–14	*k·* him in perfect peace, — *Isa.* 26 : 3.
	300–19	"If a man *k·* my saying, — *John* 8 : 51.
	324–28	* one . . . who could *k·* to her text.

keepers

My.	83–16	* hotel and restaurant *k·*,

keepeth

Chr.	57– 1	*k·* my works— *Rev.* 2 : 26.
My.	285–18	*k·* my works— *Rev.* 2 : 26.

keeping

Mis.	6–30	in *k·* them clothed and fed,
	339–21	its all of happiness to thy *k·*
	368– 9	* *k·* watch above His own."
Ret.	20–27	A plot . . . for *k·* us apart.
	65–24	*k·* man unspotted from the world,
	69–30	and *k·* His commandment?'"
	81– 6	*k·* them in accord with Christ,
'01.	2–20	and *k·* peace with God.
'02.	15– 6	*k·* a free institute,
My.	223–22	the *k·* or the breaking of

keeps

Mis.	92–11	*k·* his own lamp trimmed
	268–14	*k·* straight to the course.
	291–31	individual who *k·* not watch
Ret.	84– 8	*k·* his own lamp trimmed
Pul.	50–24	* opposition . . . *k·* up a while,
Rud.	12– 3	*k·* unbroken the Ten Commandments,
'01.	15–23	* God's mere pleasure that *k·* you
My.	130–25	him who *k·* the commandments.
	145–20	*k·* the wheels revolving.
	153–16	it *k·* steadfastly the great
	159–28	and *k·* Mind much out of sight.

ken
'02.   4–27   or beyond the *k·* of mortals,
Po.   1– 5   Beyond the *k·* of mortal
My.   14– 4   beyond the *k·* of mortals
    45–22   * marvellous beyond human *k·*.

Kennebec Journal
Pul.   88–16   * *K· J·*, Augusta, Me.

kept
Mis.   62– 4   *k·* constantly in mind,
    110–18   Our hearts have *k·* time together,
    208–23   have I *k·* Thy word." — *Psal.* 119 : 67.
    211–27   and *k·* peace with God.
    238–27   *k·* constantly before the public.
Man.   44–21   *k·* abreast of the times.
Ret.   10– 2   *k·* me much out of school,
    44–12   *k·* pace with its increasing popularity ;
    90–14   whom he *k·* near himself
Pul.   26–28   * which will be *k·* always burning
    44–26   * it *k·* coming until the
    54–23   * He *k·* the unbelievers away,
    59– 1   * *k·* perpetually burning in her honor ;
'00.   14– 2   and hast *k·* my word, — *Rev.* 3 : 8.
Hea.   2–16   I have *k·* the faith." — *II Tim.* 4 : 7.
My.   97–10   * *k·* no books on the subject,
    314–24   he *k·* her a prisoner
    335–14   * were *k·* by his widow

Key
Mis.   92–30   C. S. textbook is the *K·*.
Ret.   84–18   S. and H. is the *K·*.

key
Mis.   330– 8   if on minor *k·*, make music in
Pul.   47–19   * *k·* words respectively used
    53–24   * the *k·* to health and heaven,
    77– 7   * golden *k·* of the church structure.
    78–21   * gold *k·* to the church door.
'00.   14–21   hath the *k·* of David ; — *Rev.* 3 : 7.
My.   256– 4   adapted to the *k·* of my feeling

keyboard
Pul.   62–11   * rung from an electric *k·*,

keynote
Mis.   366– 9   Scriptures give the *k·* of C. S.
Pul.   24– 2   * strikes a *k·* of definite attention.
Peo.   11– 4   struck the *k·* of higher claims,

keys
No.   23– 8   he to whom our Lord gave the *k·*

Keystone State (*see also* Pa.)
My.   196– 4   our denomination in the *K· S·*,

Key to the Scriptures
     (*see* **Scriptures**)

kid
Mis.   145–24   lie down with the *k·* ; — *Isa.* 11 : 6.

kill
Mis.   11– 6   by firing first could *k·* him
    40–28   is holding the purpose to *k·*
    58– 8   consumption did not *k·* him.
    67–10   "Thou shalt not *k·*;" — *Exod.* 20 : 13.
    210–21   and *k·* this lurking serpent,
    238– 1   * helped 'niggers' *k·* the white folks !"
    249–22   combined efforts . . . to *k·* me :
    253–19   come, let us *k·* him, — *Luke* 20 : 14.
    254–14   come, let us *k·* him, — *Luke* 20 : 14.
    254–16   he must at last *k·* this evil
    257–27   Cyclones *k·* and destroy,
    302– 2   a purpose to *k·* the reformation
    325–12   and afterwards try to *k·* him.
    336– 7   *k·* the serpent of a material mind.
    345–29   to *k·* and eat a human being.
'01.   33–19   not *k·* people with poisonous drugs,
    33–30   citizens that do not *k·* people
My.   268–16   "Thou shalt not *k·*," — *Exod.* 20 : 13.

killed
Mis.   69–24   had not quite *k·* him.
Pul.   48–29   * *k·* the ill-starred Paugus.
Hea.   18–27   *k·* a man by no other means than
My.   302– 3   can he be helped or be *k·* by a drug ;

killest
Mis.   326–26   thou that *k·* the prophets, — *Matt.* 23 : 37.

killeth
Ret.   65– 8   Pharisaism *k·* ; Spirit giveth Life.

killing
'01.   33–20   Is it for not *k·* them thus,
My.   277–15   *K·* men is not consonant with

kills
Mis.   12– 3   spreads its virus and *k·* at last.
    210– 7   the remaining third *k·* itself.
My.   126–10   uncovers and *k·* this mystery
    203–17   a mental malady which *k·* its

Kimball
    Edward A.
    My.   297–18   My beloved Edward A. *K·*,

Kimball
    Mr.
    My.   8– 3   * Mr. *K·* said in part :
    Mr. Edward A.
    My.   36– 4   * Mr. Edward A. *K·* of Chicago,

Kimball, C.S.D.
    Edward A.
    My.   7–14   * Edward A. *K·*, C.S.D., offered
    Mr. E. A.
    Mis.   157–19   Mr. E. A. *K·*, C. S. D., of Chicago,

kind
    after its
    Un.   6– 3   fruit after its *k·*." — *see Gen.* 1 : 11.
    any
    Pul.   72–17   * medicine or drugs of any *k·*,
    My.   83– 9   * badges or insignia of any *k·*.
    305–21   no special merit of any *k·*.
    every
    No.   20–24   when specimens of every *k·*
    '00.   5–19   from idolatry of every *k·*,
    My.   106– 7   diseases of almost every *k·*.
    just and
    My.   41–21   * love which is just and *k·* to all
    of man
    My.   239–24   in other words, a *k·* of man
    of men
    Mis.   261–24   I mean mortals, or a *k·* of men
    '02.   14–19   (not by mankind, but by a *k·* of men)
    right
    No.   40–13   audible prayer of the right *k·* ;
    this
    Mis.   156–20   "this *k·* goeth not — *Matt.* 17 : 21.
    My.   190–16   "This *k·* goeth not — *Matt.* 17 : 21.
    222–13   "This *k·* goeth not — *Matt.* 17 : 21.
    339–24   "This *k·* goeth not — *Matt.* 17 : 21.
    unutterably
    Mis.   312– 5   self-sacrificing, unutterably *k·* ;

    Mis.   88–28   depends upon what *k·* of a doctor
    127–29   a *k·* word spoken, at the right moment,
    137–15   It was *k·* of you to part so gently with
    143– 4   *k·* participants in beautifying this
    227–14   responsible for *k·* (?) endeavors.
    228–16   a *k·*, true, and just person,
    262– 5   *k·* patronage of *The C. S. Journal*,
    294–14   with sting ready for each *k·* touch,
    330–24   Nature's . . . lessons teach man to be *k·*,
    338–12   charity that suffereth long and is *k·*,
    Pul.   36– 9   * by Mrs. Eddy's *k·* invitation,
    44–22   * the first of its *k·* ;
    87–12   *k·* call to the pastorate of
    87–15   fully appreciate your *k·* intentions.
    88– 5   *k·* and interesting articles
    No.   45– 5   and is *k·* ; — *I Cor.* 13 : 4.
    '02.   2–23   *k·* of birthmark, to love the Church ;
    Po.   25–17   Flowers for the *k·*
    My.   142–26   I thank you for your *k·* invitation
    153– 4   if these *k·* hearts will only do this in
    172–19   your *k·*, expert call on me."
    174–18   thanking you for your *k·* invitation
    184–11   Your *k·* card, inviting me to
    192–20   Your *k·* letter, inviting me
    231–17   and is *k·*," — *I Cor.* 13 : 4.
    234–11   God will reward their *k·* motives,
    236– 3   for them and their *k·* thoughts.
    239–23   Gender means a *k·*.
    254–10   Responding to your *k·* letter,
    260–23   and is *k·*." — *I Cor.* 13 : 4.
    264– 3   *k·* enough to speak well of me
    285– 3   my thanks for your *k·* invitation,
    295–15   It was *k·* of you to give it to me.
    300–20   if, as this *k·* priest claims,
    314–29   he was *k·* to me up to the time of
    319– 7   he wrote a *k·* little pamphlet,
    331–29   * recounting the *k·* attention paid to
    332–11   * or remit his *k·* attention until he
    351– 2   With our Leader's *k·* permission,

kindergarten
My.   147–10   as a sort of C. S. *k·*

kindle
Mis.   1–11   To *k·* all minds with a gleam of
Ret.   17– 6   Muses' soft echoes to *k·* the grot.
Pul.   5– 7   we *k·* in place thereof the glow of
    9– 8   and love *k·* perpetually its fires.
No.   1– 1   *k·* in all minds a common sentiment of
'02.   16–15   *K·* the watch-fires of unselfed love,
Po.   62– 6   Muses' soft echoes to *k·* the grot.
My.   125– 1   no longer *k·* altars for

kindled
Mis.   376–26   lower lines of light *k·* into gold,

kindles
Mis.   356– 2   dilates and *k·* into rest.
'01.   30–19   *k·* the inner genial life of a man,

kindling

Mis.	313–10	k· its glories in the east,
	332– 1	k· the stars, rolling the worlds,
No.	22–14	as Stygian night to the k· dawn.
	38–25	k· desire loses a part of its
My.	164–21	k·, guiding, and guarding your way
	350–24	Love divine, whose k· mighty rays

kindly

Mis.	95–11	time so k· allotted me
	303– 5	k· shepherd has his own fold
	327–31	and k· binds up their wounds,
	378–16	He answered k· and squarely,
	388–12	Speaks k· when we meet and part.
Ret.	80–22	The k· shepherd of the East
Pul.	6–25	signalled me k· as my lone bark
	31–21	* she most k· replied,
Po.	7–12	Speaks k· when we meet and part.
	33–10	k· pass over a wound,
	74– 2	Think k· of me,
My.	29–25	* Even the sun smiled k· upon
	147– 7	flung its foliage in k· shelter
	163–10	who have so k· come
	163–16	chapter sub-title
	173–31	k· foresight in granting
	270– 7	k· invited me to its
	299– 4	k· referring to my address
	322–24	* Mr. Wiggin k· helped me
	331–23	* k· attended him during his
	342 5	* after a k· greeting

kindness

Mis.	117–16	reciprocate k· and work wisely,
	283–17	mistaken k·, a culpable ignorance,
	322– 1	In return for your k·,
Ret.	19–15	whose k· and sympathy
My.	42– 4	* the law of k·."— *Prov.* 31 : 26.
	121–21	no vulgarity in k·,
	281–21	* Will you do us the k·
	295–14	k· in its largest, profoundest
	330 27	whose k· and sympathy

kindnesses

My.	325– 1	* many k· you had shown them,

kindred

Mis.	305– 6	* and k· organizations.
	317– 4	we are all of one k·.
Ret.	6–12	the very dearest of my k·.
Pul.	66–23	* and others of k· meaning,
Po.	2– 2	Though k· rocks,

kinds

Mis.	51– 7	mesmerism is of one of three k· ;
	305–18	* They are to be of two k· :
Hea.	5– 4	by certain k· of food,

kine

Po.	43– 9	Leading k· with love.

King

My.	34–11	the K· of glory.— *Psal.* 24 : 9.
	34–12	this K· of glory? — *Psal.* 24 : 10.
	34–13	the K· of glory. — *Psal.* 24 : 10.

King David

My.	273–10	K· D·, the Hebrew bard,

kingdom

Christ's

Ret.	94–27	establishment of Christ's k·
My.	225–17	The coming of Christ's k·

divided

Mis.	56–17	a k· divided against itself,
	89– 2	k· divided against itself — *Matt.* 12 : 25.
	217–26	a k· divided against itself,
Un.	60– 4	Mortal man is a k· divided against
No.	5–21	"k· divided against itself — *Luke* 11 : 17.
'01.	25–29	a k· divided against itself,

floral

'00.	8– 7	As in the floral k· odors emit

give you the

Mis.	150– 2	to give you the k·."— *Luke* 12 : 32.
	321–18	to give you the k·."— *Luke* 12 : 32.
Pul.	9–23	to give you the k·."— *Luke* 12 : 32.

God's

No.	35–26	God's k· is everywhere

human

No.	35–28	the human k· is nowhere,

individual

Pul.	4–21	His is an individual k·,

its

Un.	63– 5	Its k·, not apparent to material

keys of the

No.	23– 8	our Lord gave the keys of the k·

of Christ

No.	33– 7	by advancing the k· of Christ.

of God

Mis.	21–10	k· of God is within you."— *Luke* 17 : 21.
	125–10	k· of God — the reign of righteousness
	154–17	k· of God, the reign of harmony
	251–16	"The k· of God cometh — *Luke* 17 : 20.

kingdom

of God

Mis.	251–18	k· of God is within you,"— *Luke* 17 : 21.
	254–16	in order to gain the k· of God.
	270–14	"Seek ye first the k· of God,— *Matt.* 6 : 33.
	344–25	receive the k· of God — *Luke* 18 : 17.
Chr.	55– 4	seek ye first the k· of God,— *Matt.* 6 : 33.
Pul.	3– 6	k· of God is within you."— *Luke* 17 : 21.
	10–30	k· of God within you,— with you alway,
No.	35–25	k· of God is at hand,"— *Mark* 1 : 15.
	35–25	k· of God is within you."— *Luke* 17 : 21.
Pan.	13– 7	k· of God is within you"— *Luke* 17 : 21.
My.	63–30	* had found the k· of God.
	161–12	in the k· of God, — *Luke* 13 : 28.
	265–23	k· of God is within you ;"— *Luke* 17 : 21.
	267–29	k· of God is within you"— *Luke* 17 : 21.

of heaven

Mis.	143– 9	May the k· of heaven come
	171–23	The k· of heaven is like unto — *Matt.* 13 : 33.
	174–16	What is the k· of heaven?
	174–23	The k· of heaven is the reign of
	325– 3	for theirs is the k· of heaven."— *Matt.* 5 : 3.
	337–15	greatest in the k· of heaven."— *Matt.* 18 : 4.
Ret.	79–26	"The k· of heaven suffereth — *Matt.* 11 : 12.
Un.	11–26	said that the k· of heaven is here,
	37– 6	k· of heaven is at hand."— *Matt.* 10 : 7.
	52– 6	It is the k· of heaven,
Pul.	85–17	* establish the k· of heaven upon earth
'01.	28– 5	working for the k· of heaven
	35– 9	the k· of heaven within us
'02.	8–27	having the k· of heaven within him.
My.	4–27	enter into the k· of heaven,"— *Matt.* 18 : 3.
	58–22	* k· of heaven is at hand,"— *Matt.* 3 : 2.
	161–14	the k· of heaven within himself,
	197–21	is the k· of heaven."— *Matt.* 19 : 14.
	228–14	least in the k· of heaven — *Matt.* 11 : 11.
	228 16	k· of heaven, the reign of holiness,

of its own

Mis.	197–25	rules over a k· of its own,

of our God

Pul.	12– 6	and the k· of our God, — *Rev.* 12 : 10.

of Spirit

'02.	20– 4	desired haven, the k· of Spirit ;

this

Mis.	174–19	Is this k· afar off?
	174–20	first to declare against this k· is
Ret.	79–30	We recognize this k·,

Thy

Mis.	174–25	"Thy k· come ;"— *Matt.* 6 : 10.
	211–31	"Thy k· come."— *Matt.* 6 : 10.
Man.	41–21	"Thy k· come ;"— *Matt.* 6 : 10.
Pul.	22– 7	"Thy k· come. — *Matt.* 6 : 10.
My.	281– 4	"Thy k· come. — *Matt.* 6 : 10.

universal

Mis.	213–28	God's universal k· will appear,

Mis.	143– 7	Across lakes, into a k·,
	312– 8	and for the k· of heaven's sake.
My.	206–30	k· of His dear Son."— *Col.* 1 : 13.

kingdoms

Mis.	217–14	mineral, vegetable, and animal k·,
Un.	38–24	mineral, vegetable, or animal k·.
	38–25	Life is not in these k·,
Rud.	8– 1	confusing . . . the three great k·.

King Edward

'02.	3–22	on the brow of good K· E·,

King Lear

Un.	22–23	In Shakespeare's tragedy of K· L·,

kings

My.	112–29	palaces of emperors and k·,
	258–18	greater than those of Magian k·,

kings'

Mis.	373–18	living feebly, in k· courts.

kinsman

Ret.	2–13	inscribed the name of a k·
Pul.	40–20	* inscribed the name of the k·

Kinston

My.	328–16	* how this came about in K·

Kinston Free Press

My.	328–16	* told in the K· F· P·

Kipling's

My.	v– 3	* K· Recessional

kiss

Mis.	124–21	to k· the feet of Jesus,
	387–21	For faith to k·, and know ;
	397– 3	I k· the cross, and wake to know
Ret.	17– 7	chords of my lyre, with musical k·,
Pul.	18–12	I k· the cross, and wake to know
	82–30	* has ceased to k· the iron heel
Pan.	9–19	k· the feet of such a messenger,
Po.	2–18	waves k· the murmuring rill
	6–16	For faith to k·, and know ;

kiss
Po. 8–19 ringlets to *k·* my cheek
12–12 I *k·* the cross, and wake to know
62– 7 chords of my lyre, with musical *k·*,

kissed
Mis. 386–22 *k·* my cold brow,
Ret. 15– 1 they came and *k·* me.
Pul. 1– 5 *k·* — and encumbered with greetings
Po. 50– 7 *k·* my cold brow,

kisses
Mis. 204– 9 *k·* the feet of Love,
Pul. 8–18 gave *k·* to earn a few pence

Knapp, Ira O.
Ret. 51– 2 Ira O. *K·* of Roslindale,
Pul. 43– 8 * On the platform . . . Ira O. *K·*,
59–24 * Ira O. *K·*, Edward P. Bates,
86– 9 * Ira O. *K·*, William B. Johnson,
87– 7 * signature
My. 21–29 * signature
65–22 * being taken by Ira O. *K·*

knee
Mis. 127–10 not verbally, nor on bended *k·*,
204– 3 the bended *k·* of prayer,
My. 18– 7 not verbally, nor on bended *k·*,

kneel
Mis. 369–19 we *k·* at our Master's feet,
'00. 15–19 and you *k·* at its altar.
Po. 32–18 *k·* at the altar of mercy
My. 170–27 *k·* with us in sacred silence

kneeling
Peo. 13–15 Galileo *k·* at the feet of priestcraft,
My. 29– 4 * *k·* in silent communion ;
79– 2 * *k·* for silent communion
257–18 our hearts are *k·* humbly.

kneels
Mis. 131– 7 *k·* on a stool in church,

knees
Po. 10– 5 With our hand, though not our *k·*.
My. 337– 6 With our hand, though not our *k·*.

knells
'02. 17– 2 *k·* tolling the burial of Christ,

knelt
Ret. 20–13 I *k·* by his side throughout the
Po. 71– 5 *K·* worshiping at mammon's shrine.
My. 78–19 * *k·* in silent communion,
302–29 *k·* in thanks upon the steps of its
311–26 *k·* in silent prayer

knew
Mis. 35–14 * I never *k·* so unselfish an individual."
82– 6 He who *k·* the foretelling Truth,
84–14 *k·* that the man of joys,
94– 3 I never *k·* a person who knowingly
140– 1 *k·* that to God's gift,
158– 7 I little *k·* that so soon another
166–16 *k·* not how to declare its
188–29 she *k·* that the last Adam,
215–21 if he *k·* where he was
231–20 papa *k·* that he could walk,
232–23 she *k·* its infinite value
260–14 *k·* that erring mortal thought
267–12 I *k·* they were secretly striving
290–19 I *k·* that this person was doing well,
292–28 I never *k·* a student who fully
296–31 If he but *k·* whereof he speaks,
336–11 and *k·* your right obligations
Man. 28–11 which *k·* his lord's will, — *Luke* 12 : 47.
Chr. 53–13 What the Beloved *k·* and taught,
Ret. 5–19 and *k·* my sainted mother
23–17 My heart *k·* its Redeemer.
25–20 I *k·* the human conception of God
Un. 54–24 *k·* and admitted the dignity of
No. 36– 4 He *k·* God as infinite,
'01. 20–17 *k·* what was at work
'02. 9–22 and *k·* not whence it came
17– 4 He *k·* that obedience is the test
Hea. 2–24 they *k·* it was not in the power of
6– 8 I *k·* it was misinterpreted,
7–22 Jesus *k·* that adultery is a crime,
My. 11–15 * She *k·* that we were ready ;
50– 9 * *k·* not the trials before them,
50–26 * and few *k·* of its teachings,
59–32 * *k·* of your early struggles.
137–25 before I *k·* aught about them,
140– 3 a way that they *k·* not ; — *Isa.* 42 : 16.
215– 3 *k·* well the priceless worth
290–25 *k·* that Thou hearest — *John* 11 : 42.
304–20 *k·* my ability as an editor.
307–28 drifting whither I *k·* not.
321– 7 * *k·* who and what you are,
321–31 * with people who *k·* you
322– 2 * she told me she *k·* you

Knickerbocker (see also *Albany* (N. Y.) *Knickerbocker*)
Pul. 89– 3 * *K·*, Albany, N. Y.

knife
Mis. 231–13 dexterous use of *k·* and fork,
381–29 under the edge of the *k·*,
My. 294–17 use of the *k·* or the drug,

knight
Ret. 3– 1 Sir John Macneill, a Scotch *k·*,

knives
Mis. 134–22 poisons, nostrums, and *k·*,

knock
Mis. 303–13 *k·* instead of push
328–13 Christ *k·* at the door of thine
Chr. 55–26 stand at the door, and *k·* : — *Rev.* 3 : 20.

knocked
My. 311– 4 a girl, totally blind, *k·* at the

knocks
Mis. 83–14 error which *k·* at the door
324– 5 Pausing . . . he *k·* and waits.
326– 6 Once more . . . *k·* loudly.
My. 265– 3 *k·* more loudly than ever

knots
Pul. 67–22 * *k·* of them are to be found.

know
Mis. vii– 4 * WHEN I would *k·* thee
18–30 Not to *k·* what is blessing you,
27–31 can *k·* a stone as substance,
29–24 the people of the Occident *k·*
32– 7 seem not to *k·* in what manner they
48–11 enough for me to *k·* that
52– 5 not so difficult to *k·* that
57–18 "God doth *k·* — *Gen.* 3 : 5.
58–10 *How does Mrs. Eddy k· that*
64–25 *Is it possible to k· why we are*
64–27 It is quite as possible to *k·*
66–25 The beginner in sin-healing must *k·*
67–12 shalt *k·* that by doing thus
68–16 *k·* that the works of Satan are
68–18 *k·* the meaning of divine metaphysics,
73–19 *k·* that the so-called pleasures
77–21 *k·* in whom he believed.
78–10 I *k·* not how to teach either
79– 4 will *k·* them no more forever,
79– 8 reflects all whereby we can *k·* God.
87– 8 *k·*, some time, the spiritual reality
90– 1 *k·* that God is omnipotent ;
90– 2 *k·* that the power of sin is the
96– 8 I *k·* not what the person of
97–17 *k·* that omnipotence has all power.
103–19 Neither does the temporal *k·* the
108–11 Not to *k·* that a false claim is false,
108–22 what we need to *k·* of evil,
108–28 that which we *k·* to be untrue.
110–11 to *k·* that your example,
112– 4 before they *k·* it,
115–19 till you intelligently *k·*
115–27 *K·* this : that you cannot
117– 9 We always *k·* where to look for
117–15 and *k·* as we are known,
120– 7 " *K·* ye not, that — *Rom.* 6 : 16.
125– 5 to *k·* that there is no sin,
125–15 "to *k·* aright is Life
127–22 you must so *k·* yourself,
130– 4 to those who *k·* her.
130–21 should *k·* well whereof he speaks.
130–27 *K·* ye not that he who exercises
138–18 *k·* that human strength is weakness,
140–17 to *k·* who owned God's temple,
146– 9 need to *k·* the circumstances
157–25 This I *k·*, for God is for us.
170– 4 Those who *k·* not this,
170–16 that ye *k·* not of," — *John* 4 : 32.
171–26 Few people at present *k·* aught of
179– 5 to *k·* where He is laid.
183– 3 that *k·* no death.
185–24 or to *k·* how much of a man
189–21 For man to *k·* Life as it is,
194– 6 that we may *k·* Him better,
194–27 you *k·* that God is the only Life.
196–10 and make you *k·* evil,
198–13 *k·* that evil proceedeth not from
198–19 We *k·* that man's body,
208– 8 whom the legislators *k·* not,
212–29 before letting another *k·* it.
213–22 and I *k·* them, — *John* 10 : 27.
220– 7 "You are well, and you *k·* it ;"
220–15 "I am well, and I *k·* it."
228– 2 To *k·* that a deception dark
233– 3 It is important to *k·* that a
235–20 *k·* something of the ideal man,

know

Mis.	247– 7	those who $k\cdot$ me, $k\cdot$ that I
	273– 1	will $k\cdot$ the value of these rebukes.
	282–17	you should $k\cdot$ that the person
	292–20	who $k\cdot$ not what he is doing
	299– 2	To $k\cdot$ the what, when, and how
	302–10	are expected to $k\cdot$ the teaching of
	306–25	we $k\cdot$ their presence by the love
	308–14	even they $k\cdot$ its practicality
	316–17	can tell others what they $k\cdot$,
	317–10	$k\cdot$ that the door to my teaching
	317–23	shalt $k\cdot$ hereafter." — *John* 13 : 7.
	333–32	$k\cdot$ that the prophet better understood
	335–27	and $k\cdot$ that you are out ;
	341–17	you may $k\cdot$ you are parting with
	347–26	Those who $k\cdot$ no will but His
	348– 3	They $k\cdot$ that whatsoever a man
	352–15	To $k\cdot$ the supposed bodily belief
	355–12	The physician must $k\cdot$ himself
	367–19	if He did $k\cdot$ aught else,
	367–29	would say that . . . must $k\cdot$ sin.
	371–12	They $k\cdot$ far more of C. S.
	379– 3	I had a curiosity to $k\cdot$ if he
	384– 9	Thy will to $k\cdot$, and do.
	386–14	and could not $k\cdot$ the strife
	386–26	I only $k\cdot$ my wife, Thy child, shall
	387–21	For faith to kiss, and $k\cdot$;
	397– 3	I kiss the cross, and wake to $k\cdot$
Man.	49– 6	ye shall $k\cdot$ them." — *Matt.* 7 : 20.
Ret.	9–23	have learned at last to $k\cdot$
	14–26	and $k\cdot$ my heart : — *Psal.* 139 : 23.
	14–26	and $k\cdot$ my thoughts : — *Psal.* 139 : 23.
	21–13	It is well to $k\cdot$, dear reader,
	26–27	$k\cdot$ yet more of the nothingness of
	34– 2	I must $k\cdot$ more of the
	54–16	"I $k\cdot$ whom I have— *II Tim.* 1 : 12.
	60–18	"$K\cdot$ that God is all-power
	71–12	$k\cdot$ not what is affecting them,
	86– 8	* "$K\cdot$ thyself !" as said the
Un.	1–11	*Does God $k\cdot$ or behold sin,*
	4–17	God has not forbidden man to $k\cdot$ Him ;
	15– 5	Do mortals $k\cdot$ more than God,
	17–20	Error says God must $k\cdot$ evil
	18– 3	saying, . . . therefore I $k\cdot$ not evil.
	18–13	Error says you must $k\cdot$ grief
	18–22	Error says God must $k\cdot$ death
	19–17	which Truth can $k\cdot$.
	22– 8	*Evil.* But I would taste and $k\cdot$
	22–10	something to $k\cdot$ or be known,
	41– 8	to $k\cdot$ death, or to believe in it,
	44– 4	$k\cdot$ not what they do." *Luke* 23 : 34.
	54–20	God forbade man to $k\cdot$ evil
Pul.	3– 7	$K\cdot$, then, that you possess
	13– 9	we $k\cdot$ the nothingness of
	11–27	they should $k\cdot$ the great benefit
	14–28	should also $k\cdot$ the great delusion
	15–17	$K\cdot$ thyself, and God will supply
	18–12	I kiss the cross, and wake to $k\cdot$
	40– 1	* Ah, love ! I only $k\cdot$
	81–10	* We all $k\cdot$ her — she is simply
	83–26	* $k\cdot$ what John on Patmos meant
	84–23	* enough for us now to $k\cdot$
Rud.	10– 5	$k\cdot$ that God alone governs man ;
	10–20	and $k\cdot$ that He afflicteth not
No.	14– 4	would $k\cdot$ that between those who have
	15– 2	ye shall $k\cdot$ them." — *Matt.* 7 : 20.
	16– 1	For God to $k\cdot$, is to be ;
	17–24	If God could $k\cdot$ a false claim,
	19–13	person of the infinite is, we $k\cdot$ not ;
	28–20	$k\cdot$ that Truth has reappeared.
	30– 9	He need not $k\cdot$ the evil He destroys,
	30–10	any more than the legislator need $k\cdot$ the
	36– 5	and we shall $k\cdot$ this truth
	37– 7	to $k\cdot$ both evil and good ;
	37– 9	He cannot $k\cdot$ beginning or end.
Pan.	1–19	$k\cdot$ and acknowledge one God
	2– 4	those who $k\cdot$ whereof they speak
	2– 4	who $k\cdot$ that C. S. *is* Science,
	7–14	$k\cdot$ of but three theistic religions,
	10– 5	ye shall $k\cdot$ them :'' — *Matt.* 7 : 20.
	11–23	God enables us to $k\cdot$ that
	13–18	Sooner or later all shall $k\cdot$ Him,
'00.	7–20	"I $k\cdot$ not where they have — *John* 20 : 13.
	8– 1	shall $k\cdot$ and behold more nearly
	9– 1	$k\cdot$ it were best not to do,
	14– 4	$k\cdot$ that I have loved thee. — *Rev.* 3 : 9.
	15–24	I $k\cdot$ thy works, — *Rev.* 2 : 19.
'01.	2– 6	We $k\cdot$ the healing standard of C. S.
	7–16	$k\cdot$ and supply the differing needs of
	7–20	$k\cdot$ not where they have laid Him.
	9–21	I $k\cdot$ thee who thou art ; — *Mark* 1 : 24.
	13– 6	we must $k\cdot$ it is not,
	14– 7	inasmuch as we do $k\cdot$
	14–27	$k\cdot$ that wrong has no divine authority ;
	18–10	$k\cdot$ the danger of questioning
	19– 5	I $k\cdot$ that prayer brings the

know

'01.	19–28	The whole world needs to $k\cdot$
	21–23	Does this critic $k\cdot$ of a better way
	21–25	did He not $k\cdot$ all things
	28–24	well to $k\cdot$ that even Christ Jesus,
'02.	12–24	so far as I $k\cdot$ them,
	18– 2	wilt $k\cdot$ when the thief cometh.
Hea.	3–27	we $k\cdot$ that the Principle is
	9–16	$k\cdot$ that God never cursed man,
	14–16	to $k\cdot$ that mind governs the body
Peo.	5– 5	$k\cdot$ not where they have laid him ;
	12–14	$k\cdot$ what a power mind is to heal
Po.	6–16	For faith to kiss, and $k\cdot$;
	12–12	I kiss the cross, and wake to $k\cdot$
	33–13	a prayer that His love I may $k\cdot$,
	36– 8	Thy will to $k\cdot$, and do.
	49–21	and could not $k\cdot$ the strife
	50–12	I only $k\cdot$ my wife, Thy child, shall
My.	7– 7	so far as I $k\cdot$ them,
	10–27	* $k\cdot$ that it is the prosperous growth
	10–29	* They $k\cdot$ that their own individual
	11– 4	* we $k\cdot$ that the Leader of
	11– 8	* We $k\cdot$, too, that during these years
	11–11	* we $k\cdot$ that in all this time she
	11–19	* cheered and encouraged to $k\cdot$
	15–23	* Because I $k\cdot$ 'tis true ;
	15–27	* For those who $k\cdot$ it best
	21– 3	* $k\cdot$ of the loving self-sacrifices
	24–11	* we $k\cdot$ that you rejoice in
	33–10	and $k\cdot$ my heart : — *Psal.* 139 : 23.
	33–10	and $k\cdot$ my thoughts : — *Psal.* 139 : 23.
	43– 4	* law was given that they might $k\cdot$
	43– 8	* and they learned to $k\cdot$ Him.
	46– 5	* for we $k\cdot$ that without this
	51–13	* we $k\cdot$ of no one who is so able
	87–13	* of people we like to $k\cdot$
	104 19	till they $k\cdot$ of what and of whom
	106–16	This infinite Person we $k\cdot$ not of by
	120– 5	meet in truth and $k\cdot$ each other
	120– 5	$k\cdot$ as we are known of God.
	122–17	Has it enabled us to $k\cdot$ more of the
	122–20	are we satisfied to $k\cdot$ that our
	133–23	Do you $k\cdot$ how much I love you
	133–27	is not all you $k\cdot$ of me.
	135– 8	Perhaps you already $k\cdot$ that I have
	136– 1	enough for you and me to $k\cdot$
	138– 9	I $k\cdot$ it was not needed to
	143–25	"And we $k\cdot$ that all things — *Rom.* 8 : 28.
	147–27	work . . . "ye $k\cdot$ not of." — *John* 4 : 32.
	149– 1	men must $k\cdot$ somewhat of the divine
	149– 5	We $k\cdot$ Principle only through
	149–19	may $k\cdot$ too much of human law
	151– 6	Because I $k\cdot$ that no Christian can
	151–14	I $k\cdot$; for God is for me" *Psal.* 56 : 9.
	156– 4	"I $k\cdot$ whom I have — *II Tim.* 1 : 12.
	174–27	Each day I $k\cdot$ Him nearer,
	179–17	Christian Scientists $k\cdot$ that if the
	180–23	insist on what we $k\cdot$ is right,
	180–29	$k\cdot$ not what they do." — *Luke* 23 : 34.
	186–27	It gives me great pleasure to $k\cdot$
	193– 2	unto Him whom to $k\cdot$ aright is life
	200–19	for you $k\cdot$ the way in C. S.
	203– 5	$K\cdot$ that religion should be distinct
	220–22	the joy and the peace of love."
	223–17	that of which I $k\cdot$ nothing.
	223–29	$k\cdot$ that I am God." — *Psal.* 46 : 10.
	228– 8	I fail to $k\cdot$ how one can be
	228–28	I $k\cdot$ whom I have — *II Tim.* 1 : 12.
	230–22	It is a joy to $k\cdot$ that they who
	233– 4	ye shall $k\cdot$ them," — *Matt.* 7 : 20.
	233–21	to $k\cdot$ what his errors are ;
	234– 7	$k\cdot$ how much I love them,
	235–10	should $k\cdot$ that it cannot be done
	237–10	teachings that I $k\cdot$ to be correct
	240– 1	till all men shall $k\cdot$ Him
	241–27	* not to $k\cdot$ as real the beliefs of
	241–29	* so that all may $k\cdot$ it."
	246–20	shalt $k\cdot$ hereafter ," — *John* 13 : 7.
	248–22	$k\cdot$ that to conceive God aright
	249–19	may $k\cdot$ that I am the Founder
	249–20	I alone $k\cdot$ what that means.
	251– 3	shalt $k\cdot$ hereafter." — *John* 13 : 7.
	253– 1	rejoices me to $k\cdot$ that you $k\cdot$ that
	258–12	to $k\cdot$ and to do God's will,
	270–20	$k\cdot$ not what they do." — *Luke* 23 : 34.
	271–30	insomuch as I $k\cdot$ myself,
	275– 8	$k\cdot$ that I am God." — *Psal.* 46 : 10.
	281– 2	even to $k\cdot$ how to pray
	282–14	we already $k\cdot$ of the Golden Rule,
	288–30	We can $k\cdot$ that all is good
	300– 8	Does he who believes in sickness $k\cdot$
	303– 2	$k\cdot$ of but one Christ.
	303– 4	I $k\cdot$ that I am not that one,
	305–11	People do not $k\cdot$ who is referred to
	306–20	ye shall $k\cdot$ them." — *Matt.* 7 : 20.
	313–13	I only $k\cdot$ that my father and

know
My. 314–18 and who *k·* the following facts :
318–25 * "How do you *k·* that there ever was
319– 2 I should still *k·* that God's
321–27 * *k·* of my own personal knowledge
327–11 * I *k·* the enclosed article will make
352–10 * we *k·* that the real gratitude is
356– 1 When will mankind awake to *k·*
357–30 I *k·* that every true follower of
360–22 This I *k·*, for He has proved it
(*see also* **truth**)

knowable
My. 238–21 God is understandable, *k·*,

knowest (*see also* **know'st**)
Mis. 151–18 *k·* thou thyself,
317–23 thou *k·* not now ;— *John* 13 : 7.
Po. 28– 9 Knowing Thou *k·* best.
77– 6 Thou *k·* best !
77–13 of Thee, who *k·* best !
77–19 Thou *k·* best !
78– 6 Thou *k·* best !
78–12 Thou *k·* best !
My. 229–28 Thou *k·* best what we need
246–25 thou *k·* not now ;— *John* 13 : 7.
251– 3 thou *k·* not now ;— *John* 13 : 7.

knoweth
Mis. 72–20 *heavenly Father k·— Matt.* 6 : 32.
73–15 He *k·* that we have need of
103–12 *k·* the substance of good?"
253– 4 what man *k·* as did our Master
367–31 He *k·* that which *is,*
Un. 64–18 can never turn back what Deity *k·,*
Pul. 12–14 because he *k·* that— *Rev.* 12 : 12.
13–22 devil *k·* his time is short.
No. 28– 3 How long this . . . no mortal *k·* ;
'01. 34–19 yea, which *k·* *no evil.*
Po. 78–16 benediction which *k·* best !
My. 160–28 but of the time no man *k·.*

knowing
Mis. 14–16 *k·* the facts of existence
79– 3 the places once *k·* them will
87–11 *k·* this, I shall be satisfied.
93–30 *K·* this, obey Christ's Sermon on the
103–10 lack of *k·* what substance is,
108–12 hence the utility of *k·* evil aright,
112– 3 Even honest thinkers, not *k·*
160–10 joy in *k·* that one is gaining
168–22 *Ye do err, not k· the— Matt.* 22 : 29.
192–14 *k·* the omnipotence of Truth.
219– 6 "Ye do err, not *k·* the— *Matt.* 22 : 29.
221–13 or, *k·* that he is a sinner,
233– 1 without *k·* its fundamental
263– 3 *k·* that the wrong motives are not yours,
265– 3 or, *k·* it, makes the venture from
269–27 well *k·* the willingness of
282–22 to treat him without his *k·* it,
367–13 Error says that *k·* all things
367–14 implies the necessity of *k·*
367–22 but against *k·* evil,
372–13 *K·* that this book would produce a
382– 9 *k·* that the sinner and the sick
Un. 3–13 by *k·* Him in whom they
4–26 such an understanding . . . such *k·,*
9–28 *k· the unreality of disease,*
23–24 *k·* both evil and good ;
27–14 *k·* only His own all-presence,
44–22 *k·* good and evil
No. 8–13 *k·* that God will make the
9–11 *k·*, as you should, that God
30–15 not by . . . *k·* sin, or naught,
37– 4 "Ye do err, not *k·* the— *Matt.* 22 : 29.
38– 5 by *k·* their claim.
Pan. 5–24 *K·* that evil is a lie,
'01. 20–14 not *k·* what is hurting them
'02. 10– 1 facilities for *k·* and doing good,
Hea. 8– 6 *k·* that Mind can master sickness
8–22 *k·* that we shall receive only what
Po. 28– 9 *K·* Thou knowest best.
28–17 In *k·* what Thou art !
My. 38– 2 * *k·* that every perfect gift
47– 6 * not had the means of *k·* the steps
164– 1 *k·* that such an effort would
213–19 wrong direction without *k·* it.
224– 5 *k·* a little, . . . the human need,
235– 9 *K·* that she cannot do this
236–13 joy of *k·* that Christian Scientists
243–14 not yet had the privilege of *k·*
244–20 *K·* this, our Master said :
250–25 in *k·* that the impulsion of this
295– 2 *k·* our dear God comforts such
297– 5 *k·* that she can bear the blows
344–28 *k·* it is not, and that the fear
356– 5 waken to the privilege of *k·* God,

knowingly
Mis. 11–32 and would not *k·* harm you."
94– 3 a person who *k·* indulged evil,
Man. 42–20 or *k·* mentally malpractise,
Ret. 71–17 then he is *k·* transgressing
'00. 8– 4 The good man imparts *k·*

knowledge
and being
Ret. 32– 4 spiritual insight, *k·*, and being.
and power
No. 37–17 His . . . presence, *k·*, and power,
any
No. 30–17 if He possessed any *k·* of them.
demonstrable
Man. 49–10 demonstrable *k·* of C. S. practice,
divine
Un. 4–22 evil is no part of the divine *k·.*
empirical
Mis. 234–16 Empirical *k·* is worse than useless :
false
Mis. 171–28 false *k·* in the name of Science,
No. 17–25 If . . . false *k·* would be a part of
'02. 6– 5 false *k·*, the fruits of the flesh
My. 345– 6 C. S. will overthrow false *k·*
fountain of
My. 79–10 * the supposed fountain of *k·*
full
Mis. 263–22 a full *k·* of the environments.
gained
Mis. 24–21 *k·* gained from mortal sense
general
Mis. 293– 9 general *k·* that he has gained
her
Man. 82– 8 without her *k·* or written consent.
his
Mis. 269–16 he who has fairly proven his *k·*
283– 6 without his *k·* or consent,
283–15 to treat another . . . without his *k·,*
historical
My. 318–28 his ample fund of historical *k·,*
human
Mis. 22– 8 so far in advance of human *k·*
288–17 Human *k·* inculcates that it is,
imperfect
Rud. 9– 7 imperfect *k·* will lead to weakness
I sought
Ret. 33– 7 I sought *k·* from the different
losing the
Mis. 354–13 losing the *k·* of the divine
Un. 20–19 will find yourself losing the *k·* and
man's
Mis. 181– 5 Man's *k·* of this grand verity
mine of
Pul. 51–12 * have worked in the mine of *k·*
My
Un. 18–18 and My *k·* of harmony
my
Mis. 249–17 to my *k·*, not one has been sent
Ret. 21– 3 Without my *k·* a guardian was
My. 138– 6 suit was brought without my *k·*
my own
Pul. 31– 8 * my own *k·* of Mrs. Eddy,
no
Mis. 47–30 I have no *k·* of mesmerism,
208– 8 God has no *k·* of evil,
Un. 2–16 God, has no *k·* of sin.
No. 16–20 He can have no *k·* or inference but
17–22 God who has no *k·* of sin
20– 5 and revelation give us no *k·.*
My. 223–14 and of whom I have no *k·,*
315–11 * At that time I had no *k·* of
obtained
Mis. 251–17 *k·* obtained from the senses),
of arithmetic
My. 8–18 * with my faint *k·* of arithmetic
of aught
Un. 18–25 A *k·* of aught beside Myself
of both
Mis. 24–23 A *k·* of both good and evil
198–22 tree of the *k·* of *both*
367–16 tree of *k·* of *both* good and
of Christ
Mis. 360–15 with the true *k·* of Christ
360–31 filled with the true *k·* of Christ.
My. 113–15 to aspire to this *k·* of Christ
239–13 *comes into the k· of Christ*
of Christian Science
Man. 49–10 demonstrable *k·* of C. S.
Rud. 16– 3 a thorough *k·* of C. S.,
of divine law
My. 190–26 power (*k·* of divine law)
of error
Ret. 55– 4 gain sufficient *k·* of error to
My. 232–21 *k·* of error and of its operations

knowledge

of evil
Mis. 107–22 k· of evil as evil, so-called.
108–19 proper k· of evil and its subtle
109–10 k· of evil that brings on repentance
208– 8 God has no k· of evil,
259– 9 no consciousness or k· of evil ;
Un. 15–12 destroyed by the k· of evil,
18 27 If such k· of evil were possible
41– 7 K· of evil, or belief in it,
53– 6 by calling the k· of evil good,
54–23 k· of evil would make man a
'02. 6– 6 k· of evil, of something besides

of God
Mis. 3– 6 understanding — the true k· of God
139–13 against the k· of God, — II Cor. 10 : 5.
183–26 As many as do receive a k· of God
Ret. 31–12 seek diligently for the k· of God
Un. 36– 8 and gains a k· of God from
39–16 as many as receive the k· of God
No. 12–12 this new-old k· of God.
My. 47–23 * demonstration of the k· of God,
294–12 spiritual k· of God.

of good
Mis. 109–23 third stage, — the k· of good ;

of his sins
Mis. 107–29 Without a k· of his sins,

of life
'02. 6– 3 k· of life, substance, or law,

of Mind-healing
Mis. 264–24 Their k· of Mind-healing may be

of one's self
Mis. 108–18 namely, the k· of one's self,

of philosophy
'01. 25– 8 k· of philosophy and of medicine,

of salvation
'02. 11–16 k· of salvation from sin,
16– 5 "S. and H.," . . . "k· of salvation."

of self-support
My. 216–26 in the k· of self-support,

of sin
Mis. 109–20 k· of sin and its consequences,
Un. 2–16 God, has no k· of sin,
13–15 If God has any real k· of sin,
16– 5 if God has, . . . a real k· of sin?
54–25 condemned the k· of sin
No. 17–22 God who has no k· of sin

of Soul
No. 29– 8 so slight a k· of Soul that they

of the individual
Ret. 71–10 consent of k· of the individual

of the true God
Ret. 49–25 to a k· of the true God,

of this Science
Mis. 261–29 even a k· of this Science,

of this something
Un. 22–14 a k· of this something is

of Truth
Mis. 160–11 k· of Truth and divine Love,
Ret. 86–17 growth in the k· of Truth,
Un. 2–22 a k· of Truth and Love

or consent
Mis. 282– 8 without their k· or consent?
283– 6 without his k· or consent,

or understanding
My. 107–26 k· or understanding of God,

our
Un. 22–17 and be important to our k·.
No. 30–15 removing our k· of what is not.

peculiar
My. 52–31 * out of his own peculiar k·

personal
My. 321–24 * personal k· of the authorship
321–28 * know of my own personal k·

practical
Mis. 28–26 The Master's practical k· of

priceless
Mis. 270–13 priceless k· of his Principle

real
Un. 13–15 If God has any real k· of sin,
16– 5 if God has, . . . a real k· of sin?

renewed in
Pan. 11– 5 which is renewed in k·

scientific
Mis. 186–22 This scientific k· affords
My. 273–21 scientific k· that is portentous ;

sequence of
Mis. 109–24 the valuable sequence of k·

sought
Pul. 47–10 * she states that she sought k·

stores of
My. 149–11 its radiant stores of k·

their
Mis. 264–24 Their k· of Mind-healing may
282– 8 without their k· or consent?

knowledge

their
My. 149– 3 prove their k· by doing
321–32 * told me of their k· of your work

the very
Un. 15–13 the very k· caught from God,

this
Mis. 24– 4 This k· came to me in
24– 7 This k· is practical,
39– 6 this k· can be obtained
112–10 this k· demands our time
125– 7 This k· enables him to overcome
188–31 This k· did become to her
Un. 3–14 This k· is not the forbidden
15– 1 that by this k·, ... came
54–19 and this k· would not be
No. 16– 7 this k· would manifest evil in
30–20 This k· is light wherein
'02. 6– 9 Love and Truth destroy this k·,
My. 113–15 for St. Paul to aspire to this k·

thought and
Mis. 68–23 * necessary to thought and k· ;

tree of
Mis. 235–13 at the root of the tree of k·,
367–16 this fruit of the tree of k·

true
Mis. 3– 5 the true k· of God
189– 8 and true k· of preexistence,
360–15 with the true k· of Christ
360–31 with the true k· of Christ.
Un. 41– 3 the true k· and consciousness
My. 177–13 the true k· and proof of life

Truth's
No. 30–18 Truth's k· of its own infinitude

uninspired
My. 238–11 Uninspired k· of the translations

vain
Mis. 168–13 emptied of vainglory and vain k·,

without
Mis. 284– 8 may possess a zeal without k·,

your
My. 133–27 your k· with its magnitude of meaning

Mis. 24– 2 k· of them makes man spiritually
61– 6 All the k· and vain strivings of
308–23 The k· that I have gleaned from
Ret. 10–12 most of the k· I had gleaned
11–11 Where k· plants the foot of power
50– 3 k· of that divine power which heals ;
Un. 4 24 in the k· of the only true God,
14–25 a k· which is everlasting
19– 1 With God, k· is necessarily
Pul. 2–28 intrenching ourselves in the k· that
No. 0 07 * it is "k·, duly arranged and
23–22 K· of a man's physical personality
Po. 60– 8 Where k· plants the foot of power
My. 293– 1 k· that all things are possible to

Knowles, Frederick Lawrence
My. 48–17 * the late Frederick Lawrence K· :

known

Mis. 26– 3 will be k· as self-evident truth,
29–16 Since that date I have k· of
108–24 to be k· for what it is not ;
117–16 and know as we are k·,
143–19 well k· physicians, teachers, editors,
171–19 true disciples of the Master k· :
222–24 for it is not yet k·.
223– 9 the tree is k· by its fruit ;
249–11 k· that I am not a spiritualist,
259–10 not a quality to be k· or
296– 1 system of religion, — widely k· ;
312–16 * k· as Christian Scientists,
350– 3 society k· as the P. M.,
350–12 would hesitate to have k·.
371–21 * "men are k· by their enemies."
Man. 17– 7 were k· as "Christian Scientists."
18–21 were k· as "First Members."
29– 5 shall not make k· the name of
38– 2 k· to them to be Christians,
69–26 k· as "Mother's Room"
Ret. 3– 7 k· historically as Lovewell's War.
44–25 No sooner were my views made k·,
57–12 If that pagan philosopher had k·
80–26 no greater miracles k·
89–28 not first made k· to them
91– 7 k· as the Sermon on the Mount,
Un. 5–20 "moderation be k· — Phil. 4 : 5.
22–10 something to know or be k·,
Pul. 8–14 only the need made k·,
20–18 reform ever k· on earth.
32–26 * was k· as a "godly man,"
42–14 * are k· in the church as the
45– 3 * instance which will never be k·
47– 4 * k· to her circle of pupils
51–19 * is very well k·.

known
Pul. 62– 3 * favorably *k·* in the Old Country,
68– 2 * *k·* as the Rev. Mary Baker Eddy.
68–15 * It is not generally *k·*
71–19 * It is well *k·* that Mrs. Eddy,
76– 3 * *k·* as the "Mother's Room,"
No. 7–16 loving sacrifice . . . is *k·* to God,
37–15 *k·* to the divine Mind,
'01. 20–26 flagrance will finally be *k·*,
21–26 should not have *k·* C. S.,
29– 3 or even *k·* of his sore necessities?
33–17 to be *k·* by their works,
'02. 13–29 trustees, who were to be *k·* as
Po. vii– 7 * *became k· to her friends,*
My. 37–22 * He has made *k·* through
64– 8 * *k·* as Christian Scientists,
66– 1 * *k·* as the Hotel Brookline,
91–19 * any other country has ever *k·*.
96–27 * *k·* as The Mother Church
108–24 to make *k·* the best work of
111–21 Is not the tree *k·* by its fruit?
112–24 The tree is *k·* by its fruit.
120– 6 know as we are *k·* of God.
136–26 that is *k·* by its fruits,
140– 4 that they have not *k·* : — *Isa.* 42 : 16.
142– 1 hath *k·* the mind of — *I Cor.* 2 : 16.
148– 4 faith be *k·* by your works.
157–17 * made *k·* in her original deed
221–11 not *k·* another so great
227– 7 it is *k·* by its patience
232–15 had *k·* what hour — *Luke* 12 : 39.
235–28 *k·* what was being done
240– 3 shall be *k·* and acknowledged
253–12 world hath not *k·* — *John* 17 : 25.
253–12 but I have *k·* Thee, — *John* 17 : 25.
253–13 and these have *k·* that — *John* 17 : 25.
274–27 thy way may be *k·* — *Psal.* 67 : 2.
289–10 first church of C. S. *k·* on earth,
299– 8 * let them make it *k·* to the world,
299–11 widely made *k·* to the world,
300–22 make *k·* his doctrine to the world,
300–28 tree is *k·* by its fruit.
305– 6 "I have always *k·* it."
329–29 * might not have been *k·* but for
333–20 * *k·* as Major George W. Glover,
338– 7 * are *k·* to us to be those uniformly
338–12 "The Unknown God Made *K·*,"
353–22 formerly *k·* as "Mother's Room"
359–23 * were *k·* as "the practitioners."

knows
Mis. 41–30 the Principle that he *k·* to be true.
55–24 Man *k·* that he can have
77–18 Truth that *k·* no error,
85– 7 all that he *k·* of Life,
88–14 *k·* whereof he speaks.
90– 9 *when she k· he is sinning,*
100–32 Who *k·* how the feeble lips
101– 3 He alone *k·* these wonders
103–17 and *k·* not the temporal.
112–10 unless he *k· how* to be just ;
122–27 Divine Love *k·* no hate ;
147–28 he *k·* no path but the fair, open,
179–32 this Life that *k·* no death,
194–27 sense of Life that *k·* no death,
201–12 omnipotence of the Mind that *k·* this :
208–23 He who *k·* the end from the
212– 4 never *k·* what happiness is,

knows
Mis. 219–16 A third person *k·* that if he
219–27 *k·* that if he can change this
220–25 believe that a man is sick and *k·* it,
220–31 he *k·* that an error of belief
221–13 and *k·* he is a sinner ;
265– 2 diverges from Science and *k·* it not,
367–18 He *k·* nothing but good ;
367–20 *k·* nothing beyond Himself
384–21 * But *k·* no ebb and flow.
Ret. 76–18 and *k·* no material limitations.
Un. 13– 8 *k·* nothing of discord.
13–19 He *k·* something which He must
17–20 because He *k·* all things ;
18– 1 must perish, if He *k·* evil
18– 7 if He *k·* and sees it not ;
20– 8 *Second :* The Lord *k·* it.
20–13 *Second :* He *k·* it not.
23– 8 and Truth *k·* only such.
39– 8 Life which *k·* no death,
43–26 Life which *k·* no death,
43–27 Spirit which *k·* no matter.
44–19 says of evil, "The Lord *k·* it !"
49–26 something which God sees and *k·*,
Pul. 82–10 * and to-day she *k·* many things
Rud. 12–28 A Christian Scientist *k·* that,
13– 3 *k·* that pantheism and theosophy
No. 13–12 Life that *k·* no death,
16– 2 what He *k·* must truly and eternally
16– 3 If He *k·* matter, and matter can exist
16– 5 whatever He *k·* is made manifest,
18–20 gets things wrong, and *k·* it not ;
43– 8 * "Only He who *k·* all things
'02. 19– 9 *k·* that that would harm him more
Hea. 1–17 * *K·* it at forty, and reforms his plan ;
4–11 what He *k·* deserves to be punished,
Po. 36–20 * But *k·* no ebb and flow.
My. vi– 7 * *k·* anything about C. S.
6– 2 decision which the defendant *k·* will be
93– 1 * so far as the writer *k·* them,
104–23 of which a man *k·* absolutely nothing
112–18 *k·* that it contains a Science which
132– 8 Scientist *k·* that spiritual faith
132–10 he also *k·* they embark for infinity
155–22 a dawn that *k·* no twilight
160–29 psychist *k·* that this hell is mental,
180– 3 Whosoever understands C. S. *k·*
180–20 for he *k·* not that . . . God is Love.
271– 9 what a man thinks or believes he *k·* ;
(*see also* **God**)

know'st
Mis. 398–12 And Thou *k·* Thine own ;
Ret. 46–18 And Thou *k·* Thine own.
Pul. 17–17 And Thou *k·* Thine own.
Po. 14–16 And Thou *k·* Thine own.
My. 350–15 *k·* Thou not the pathway glad

Know Thyself
My. 351–10 " *K· T·*," the title of your gem

Knox
General
Ret. 2–29 stories about General *K·*,
Pul. 48–28 * the McNeils and General *K·*
General Henry
Ret. 2–27 General Henry *K·* of Revolutionary

Ky. (State)
(*see* **Louisville**)

L

La. (State)
(*see* **New Orleans**)

label
Mis. 87– 4 and *l·* beauty nothing,

labelled
Mis. 248–12 the mixture would be *l·* thus :
My. 83– 3 * never going about *l·*.

labor
Mis. 2–13 the outlook demands *l·*,
20– 4 all ye that *l·* — *Matt.* 11 : 28.
37–29 the *l·* that C. S. demands.
120–25 away from their own fields of *l·*,
133–27 depressing care and *l·*
137–21 return to his place of *l·*,
214–21 the personal Jesus' *l·* in the flesh
230–25 * Learn to *l·* and to wait."
236– 4 the *l·* of uplifting the race,
238–14 *l·* for the establishment of
273–17 in their present line of *l·*
303– 1 within their own fields of *l·*,
338–10 which cannot choose but to *l·*.
340– 5 no excellence without *l·* ;

labor
Ret. 10– 3 less *l·* than is usually requisite.
79–24 * "Learn to *l·* and to wait."
84–30 regular institute or place of *l·*,
84–30 or expending his *l·* where
No. 43– 4 all ye that *l·* — *Matt.* 11 : 28.
46–22 continue to *l·* and wait.
'00. 3–13 * to awake the slumbering
Hea. 2–18 all ye that *l·* — *Matt.* 11 : 28.
My. v–20 * nine years of arduous preliminary *l·*,
50–28 * were willing to *l·* for the Cause.
52–16 * must use more energy and unselfish *l·*
57–11 * The *l·* of clearing the land
58–18 * *l·* and sacrifice of our revered Leader
135–12 demands upon my time and *l·*,
136–25 the *l·* that is known by its fruits,
149–17 richest blessings are obtained by *l·*.
163–19 from many years of incessant *l·*
182–15 faithful *l·* of loyal students,
185– 7 * Learn to *l·* and to wait."
193–24 you have grasped time and *l·*,
197–11 appreciation of your *l·* and success
218–27 Such *l·* is impartial,

labor
My. 231–18   else love's *l·* is lost
    234– 8   to express this love in *l·*
    243–17   remain in their own fields of *l·*
    248–27   philosophy of *l·*, duty, liberty,
    358–17   to relieve me of so much *l·*.
    (*see also* **field**)

laboratory
My. 178– 9   distilled in the *l·* of infinite Love

labored
'*00.* 12–25   he *l·* in the synagogue,
My. 22–16   * *l·* for the regeneration of mankind ;
    47–13   * *l·* unceasingly for the work
    50– 5   * in which they had *l·* faithfully
    194–25   sacrificed so much and *l·* so long.
    231– 7   whom she has *l·* much to benefit
    283–10   Many years have I prayed and *l·*

laborer
Pul. 50– 3   * *l·* is worthy of his — *Luke* 10 : 7.
My. 214–15   chapter sub-title
    215–25   *l·* is worthy of his — *Luke* 10 : 7.

laborers
Mis. 2–14   and the *l·* seem few.
    7–15   if faithful *l·* in His vineyard.
    120–11   loyal *l·* are ye that have wrought
    313–22   *l·* of the excellent sort,
    323– 8   where a few *l·* in a valley
Un. 12– 3   *l·* are few in this vineyard
No. v– 8   *l·* in the realm of Mind-healing.
My. 226–25   *l·* in the field of Science
    291–29   God of harvests send her more *l·*,

laboring
Mis. 155– 7   Forget self in *l·* for mankind ;
    283–30   Whoever is honestly *l·* to learn
    322–26   *l·* in its widening grooves

laborious
Hea. 8–22   this will make us honest and *l·*,

labors
Mis. 7–27   denied the results of our *l·*
    100–11   Love's *l·* are not lost.
    273– 9   so grateful a sense of my *l·*
    278– 9   throughout my *l·*,
    278–19   have shared less of my *l·* than many
    281– 1   to enter on the fruition of your *l·*,
    311–15   My deepest desires and daily *l·*
    322–23   my past poor *l·* and love.
Ret. 30– 7   The motive of my earliest *l·*
    66 21   and *l·* with her love,
Pul. 70–14   * a testimonial to her *l·*,
    72–26   * In our *l·* we take Christ as
    85–26   * the appreciation of her *l·*
    86–22   * love and gratitude for your *l·*
Rud. 14–11   The only pay taken for her *l·*
'*00.* 2–28   what of the fruits of your *l·*?
My. 22–19   * justification of her *l·* is the
    28–28   * speaks for the successful *l·*
    37–24   * unbroken activity of your *l·*,
    49–28   * their devoted *l·* in the cause
    50–11   * starting out on their *l·*
    51–27   * of Mrs. Eddy's tireless *l·*,
    51–31   * *l·*, and successful instructions
    137–17   my time, *l·*, and thought,
    163–15   time and attention for *l·*
    203–28   You whose *l·* are doing so much
    214–17   taking pay for their *l·*,
    214–20   no remuneration for my *l·*,
    291– 3   rested on the life and *l·*
    295–28   he still lives, loves, *l·*.
    296–12   his *l·* in divine Science ;
    298– 9   *l·* in placing this book

lab'ring
Mis. 398–10   *L·* long and lone,
Ret. 46–16   *L·* long and lone,
Pul. 17–15   *L·* long and lone
Po. 14–14   *L·* long and lone,

lace
My. 259– 4   on either side *l·* and flowers.

laces
My. 83–11   * *l·* of the women's frocks,

lack
Mis. 7–31   not so much from a *l·* of justice,
    31–12   consequently to the *l·* of faith
    53–25   because of their great *l·* of
    103–10   For *l·* of knowing what substance is,
    107–25   The *l·* of seeing one's
    158–16   to rebuke a *l·* of faith in divine help,
    195– 8   held back by reason of the *l·* of
    206–15   nor *l·* of what constitutes true manhood.
    256–16   the old impediment, *l·* of time,
    268–27   From *l·* of moral strength empires fall.
    344–16   are spoiled by *l·* of Science.
    356– 8   from *l·* of air and freedom.

lack
Mis. 365–27   hampered by *l·* of proper terms
Ret. 67–17   finally lost for *l·* of witness.
Rud. 10–27   It is only a *l·* of understanding
No. 3– 1   in some vital points *l·* Science.
    37–20   lose its efficacy and *l·* the
    45–11   arise from a spiritual *l·*,
'*00.* 6– 1   no *l·* in the Principle
'*01.* 1– 5   never *l·* God's outstretched arm
    25–11   regret their *l·* in my books,
Peo. 8– 6   or *l·* of love that will not ;
My. 128–23   A *l·* of wisdom betrays Truth
    213–25   will not rust for *l·* of use
    222– 9   unbelief'' (*l·* of *faith*) ; — *Matt.* 17 : 20.
    248–21   fall for *l·* of the divine impetus.
    293–14   a *l·* of the absolute understanding
    307–30   its *l·* of science, and the want of

lacked
Mis. 365–10   If C. S. *l·* the proof of its
No. 18– 6   If Science *l·* the proof of its
My. 307–32   for then it *l·* Science.

lacking
Mis. 16– 7   one finds so much *l·*,
    109–25   sequence of knowledge would be *l·*;
    116–30   If in one instance obedience be *l·*,
    291–19   if the spirit thereof be *l·*.
    365–21   effects of divine Science were *l·*,
Un. 40–25   and *l·* the spiritual sense of it,
No. 19– 3   If the . . . effects of C. S. were *l·*,
'*00.* 11–20   if the divine tone be *l·*,
Hea. 3– 2   *l·* these, to show its helplessness
My. 299–16   and *l·* in the creeds.

lacks
Mis. 263–23   *l·* the aid and protection of
Un. 45–25   It *l·* the substance of Spirit
Pan. 3 6   loneness *l·* but one charm

lad
Mis. 225–21   beside the sofa whereon lay the *l·*
Pul. 33–17   * when he was a *l·*, at work in a

Ladd, Dr.
My. 310 25   were diagnosed by Dr. *L·*
    310–30   Dr. *L·* said to Alexander Tilton :

ladder
Ret. 85–10   *l·* let down from the heaven of Truth
Un. 57–19   the *l·* which reaches heaven.

laden
Mis. 20– 4   labor and are heavy *l·*. — *Matt.* 11 : 28.
Man. 60 11   rest the weary and heavy *l·*.
No. 43– 5   labor and are heavy *l·*, — *Matt.* 11 : 28.
Hea. 2–18   labor and are heavy *l·*, — *Matt.* 11 : 28.
Po. vii–14   * *a joy to the heavy l· and a balm to*

ladened
Mis. 147– 9   *l·* them with records worthy to be

ladies
Ret. 16– 3   When the meeting was over, two *l·*
My. 72–10   * lords and *l·* who come to attend

lady
Mis. 49– 1   young *l·* entered the College class
    49– 5   this young *l·* had manifested
    180– 7   A dear old *l·* asked me,
Ret. 90–10   like ''the elect *l·*'' — *II John* 1 : 1.
Pul. 57–27   * a *l·* born of an old New Hampshire
    72–10   * very pleasant and agreeable *l·*,
No. 43– 8   A *l·* said : ''Only He who
My. 322– 1   * not long since I met a *l·*
    (*see also* **Eddy**)

Lafayette (Ind.) *Journal*
My. 91–15   * [*L·* (*I·*.) *J·*]

lagging
Po. 35– 2   Beguile the *l·* hours

laid
Mis. 120–15   with armor on, not *l·* down.
    143–15   is *l·* the corner-stone of
    144– 8   there are *l·* away a copy of
    144–14   *l·* away as a sacred secret
    163–23   yet the foundations me *l·*
    179– 6   to know where He is *l·*.
    250–15   and *l·* on a rose-leaf.
    285– 4   I ordered to be *l·* away
    343– 3   others before us have *l·* upon the
    365– 3   than that is *l·*,'' — *I Cor.* 3 : 11.
Man. 52– 7   shall be *l·* before this Board,
Ret. 18–13   but *l·* on the bier.
    27– 3   so *l·* the foundation of my work
    35– 5   basis it *l·* down for physical and
    45–10   and should be *l·* off,
    45–12   mortal existence is finally *l·* off,
    73–18   false personality is *l·* off.
    83– 9   are already *l·* in their minds
Un. 44–13   fable of error, is *l·* bare in C. S.
    64– 9   than that is *l·*.'' — *I Cor.* 3 : 11.

laid

Pul.	45–24	* l· down his responsibilities
Rud.	15–25	l· bare for anatomical examination.
	16–19	Principle and practice l· down in
No.	21–24	than that is l·, — I Cor. 3 : 11.
	46–11	l· on the rack, for joining the
'00.	7–21	where they have l· him." — John 20 : 13.
'01.	7–20	know not where they have l· Him.
	23–17	l· the axe at the root of all error,
'02.	18–19	Jesus l· down his life for mankind ;
Hea.	11–17	l· the foundation stone of mental
Peo.	5– 6	we know not where they have l· him ;
	14– 3	flowers l· upon the bier,
Po.	64– 3	but l· on the bier.
My.	16–10	* chapter sub-title
	16–12	* was l· Saturday, July 16, 1904,
	18–27	* The corner-stone was then l·
	23–29	* and stone is l· upon stone,
	44– 4	* heavy burdens are being l· down,
	55–32	* corner-stone of The . . . was l·,
	57–13	* corner-stone was l· July 16, 1904.
	67–16	* Corner-stone of cathedral l· . . . 1904
	122–24	place where they l· him" — Mark 16 : 6.
	127–28	nor l· down at the feet of
	158– 6	chapter sub-title
	158–25	has l· the chief corner-stone
	187–30	l· its foundations on the rock
	191–17	With grave-clothes l· aside,
	191–21	Behold the place where they l· me ;
	203–24	You have l· the corner-stone
	241– 7	* beware the net that is craftily l·
	326–17	l· on his bier the emblems

lain

Mis.	110–20	while leagues have l· between us.

lake

My.	150–15	Stand by the limpid l·,

Lake of Galilee

Ret.	91–15	shores of the L· of G·,

lakes

Mis.	143– 7	Across l·, into a kingdom,

Lamb

Mis.	358–17	the blood of the L· ;" — Rev. 7 : 14.
Pul.	12–10	the blood of the L·, — Rev. 12 : 11.
Hea.	10– 5	beast bowed before the L· ;
Peo.	9–10	white in the blood of the L· ;
My.	185–17	"L· slain from the — Rev. 13 : 8.
	206–22	L· is the light thereof." — Rev. 21 : 23.
	269– 4	man wedded to the L·,

lamb

Mis.	36–13	lion that lieth down with the l·.
	145–23	shall dwell with the l·, — Isa. 11 : 6.
	162–16	lay himself as a l· upon the altar
	250– 7	a butcher fattening the l·
	275–14	* "tempers the wind to the shorn l·,"

lambkin

Po.	41– 3	that fold for the l·

lambkins

Mis.	398–15	Lead Thy l· to the fold,
Ret.	46–21	Lead Thy l· to the fold,
Pul.	17–20	Lead Thy l· to the fold,
Po.	14–19	Lead Thy l· to the fold,

Lamb of God

Mis.	121–23	"the L· of G·." — John 1 : 29.

lambs

Mis.	357–27	They are as l· that have sought
Ret.	80–22	carries his l· in his arms
	90– 4	Does . . . shepherd forsake the l·,
Pul.	8–20	l· my prayers had christened,

lame

Mis.	22–24	the l·, the deaf, and the blind,
	168– 5	the l·, those halting between two
	244–21	the deaf to hear, the l· to walk,
	362–10	ears to these deaf, feet to these l·,
'01.	17–16	the blind, the dumb, the l·,
Peo.	11–12	The l·, the blind, the sick,
My.	105–18	and have made the l· walk.

lament

My.	295–26	have cause to l· the demise of
	333–28	* to l· this irreparable loss."

lamented

Ret.	19–14	l· by a large circle of friends
Pul.	9–16	loss of our late l· pastor,
My.	289–15	the late l· Victoria,
	289–28	in memoriam of the late l· Victoria,
	293– 7	Our l· President, in his loving
	296–10	The late l· Christian Scientist
	330–25	l· by a large circle of friends

lamp

Mis.	92–11	keeps his own l· trimmed and
	117–26	he would replenish his l· at the
	151–24	may the l· of your life continually

lamp

Mis.	341–25	if the l· she tends is
Ret.	84– 8	keeps his own l· trimmed and
Pul.	26–10	* l· stand of the Renaissance period
	26–27	* l· over two hundred years old,
	59– 1	* behind an antique l·,
My.	69– 3	* each l· of thirty-two candle-power.

lamps

Mis.	276–17	The wise will have their l· aglow,
	276–24	shall have their l· trimmed
	342– 3	had no oil in their l·
	342– 8	better-tended l· of the faithful.
	342–15	With no oil in them l·,
	342–19	our l· have gone out, — see Matt. 25 : 8.
Pul.	25–26	* silver l· of Roman design,
	26–12	* oxidized silver l·,
	27–18	* with l·, typical of S. and H.
My.	69– 3	* each suspending seventy-two l·,
	125–27	Are our l· trimmed and burning?

Lancaster Gate, West

My.	295–24	55 L· G·, W·, London, England.

lance

'01.	33–19	with poisonous drugs, with the l·,

Land

Deed Conveying

Man.	136– 1	heading

land

and building

Mis.	139–30	provisions for the l· and building

and sea

My.	291–24	waves over l· and sea,

and the church

Mis.	140– 3	l·, and the church standing on it,

bright

Mis.	386–20	beckoned me to this bright l·,
Po.	50– 5	beckoned me to this bright l·,

clearing the

My.	57–11	* The labor of clearing the l·

dwell in the

Chr.	55– 9	dwell in the l· of — Isa. 9 : 2.
My.	170–21	dwell in the l·, — Psal. 37 : 3.

entire

Mis.	150–17	churches are dotting the entire l·.

every

Mis.	v– 3	IN THIS AND EVERY l·
My.	341– 9	our land and in every l·,

exclusive of the

Pul.	28–12	* exclusive of the l·

fair

Pul.	82–29	* and in this fair l· at least

favored

My.	278–13	Congress of our favored l·

for the site

My.	16– 8	* price of the l· for the site of

gave back the

Pul.	20– 5	gave back the l· to the church.

is reached

'01.	26–15	then when l· is reached

laud the

Ret.	11–17	laud the l· whose talents
Po.	60–14	laud the l· whose talents

laws of the

My.	128–20	abide by . . . the laws of the l· ;
	219–22	make void the laws of the l·,
	220–12	obeying the laws of the l·.

lot of

Mis.	139–18	I gave a lot of l· — in Boston,
	140–20	The lot of l· which I donated
Ret.	51– 1	I gave a lot of l· in Boston

more

'02.	12–25	effort to purchase more l·
My.	7– 9	effort to purchase more l·
	9–23	towards the purchase of more l·

native

Mis.	295–16	to honor his native l·

of Israel

Mis.	72–13	concerning the l· of Israel, — Ezek. 18 : 2.

of promise

Mis.	153–10	and the l· of promise,

of Sodom

No.	7–14	imperfection in the l· of Sodom,

of the shadow

Chr.	55– 9	l· of the shadow — Isa. 9 : 2.

or sea

My.	127–27	indestructible on l· or sea ;

our

Mis.	38– 9	philanthropists in our l·
	141–16	law of God and the laws of our l·.
	141–24	law of Love and the laws of our l·.
	314– 1	throughout our l· and in other lands.
	329–25	is heard in our l·." — Song 2 : 12.
Man.	46– 6	according to the laws of our l·.
	48–10	or the laws of our l·.
Pul.	8– 2	throughout our l· the press has

land

our
Pul.	10– 9	Our *l·*, more favored, had its
	22–11	every Christian church in our *l·*,
No.	2–27	many are flooding our *l·* with
'01.	20–26	laws of our *l·* will handle
My.	341– 9	Beloved brethren all over our *l·*

over
My.	204– 9	Over sea and over *l·*, C. S. unites
	291–24	waves over *l·* and sea,

over the
My.	55–11	* was spreading over the *l·*.

parcel of
My.	12– 7	* to secure the large parcel of *l·*

promised
My.	43– 2	* possession of the promised *l·*.
	43–13	* into the promised *l·*,
	44– 5	* going up to possess the promised *l·*

purchased
Man.	102–16	shall not apply to *l·* purchased for

purchases of
Man.	102–11	deeds of further purchases of *l·*

recover the
Pul.	20– 6	recover the *l·* from the trustees,

redeem the
'02.	13–23	to redeem the *l·* by paying the

regive the
Pul.	20–10	regive the *l·* to the church.

their
'01.	33–17	constitutional laws of their *l·* ;

this
'02.	13–27	This *l·*, now valued at
My.	11–25	* this *l·* has been paid for.

throughout the
Mis.	113–32	is felt throughout the *l·*.

weary
Mis.	144–18	great rock in a weary *l· :"— Isa. 32 : 2.*
	203–10	great rock in a weary *l ,"— Isa. 32 : 2.*
Pul.	20–20	great rock in a weary *l·."— Psal. 32 : 2,*

Mis.	382–19	I donated to this church the *l·*
Man.	75–17	with the *l·* whereon they stand,
Pul.	20– 1	*l·* whereon stands The First Church
'02.	10–30	walking every step over the *l·* route,
	13–13	*l·* on which to build The First Church
	13–26	*l·* legally conveyed to me,
	14– 2	had been paid on the *l·*
	14– 5	nor the *l·* whereon it stands.
My.	11–24	* purchase of the *l·* upon which
	99–23	* was not a C. S. church in the *l·*.

landlord
My.	231–22	a *l·* who has not an empty

landmark
My.	47–18	* each *l·* of progress
	77– 7	* the leading *l·* of Boston,
	85–20	* another "*l·*" set in the

landmarks
Mis.	x– 9	and reliable as old *l·*.
	119–28	should tear up your *l·*,
No.	12–23	departed from the old *l·*.
My.	282–12	the *l·* of prosperity.

lands
Mis.	177–28	homesick traveller in foreign *l·*
	314– 2	our land and in other *l·*,
	373–24	rich . . . with houses and *l·*.
Ret.	4–12	undulating *l·* of three townships.
	48–22	our country, and into foreign *l·*,
Pul.	5–30	literature of our and other *l·*.
	22–11	and a few in far-off *l·*,
	41– 6	* from many *l·*, the love-offerings
	57– 5	* the Union, and from many *l·*.
My.	47–21	* in so many distant *l·*,
	112–32	our own and in foreign *l·*,
	129– 8	beloved country and in foreign *l·*,
	200– 1	in this and in other *l·*.

landscape
Mis.	62– 7	an artist in painting a *l·*.
	313–11	dawn, . . . lightens earth's *l·*.
Pul.	48–10	* coloring of the whole *l·*

Langley, Prof. S. P.
Rud.	6–13	met a response from Prof. S. P. L·,

language

and ideas
Ret.	75– 7	appropriating my *l·* and ideas,

and meaning
My.	238–10	His *l·* and meaning are wholly

any
Mis.	263– 6	to be found in any *l·*

appropriate
Mis.	280–24	in appropriate *l·* and metaphor

decaying
Mis.	100– 3	articulated in a decaying *l·*,
	121– 1	written in a decaying *l·*,

language
expressive
Pul.	2– 2	In the expressive *l·* of Holy Writ,

figurative
Pul.	66–16	* poetical and highly figurative *l·*.

gentleman's
Mis.	296–22	in this unknown gentleman's *l·*,

human
Un.	30– 3	Human *l·* constantly uses the

Longfellow's
Ret.	27–16	In Longfellow's *l·*,

modification of the
No.	v– 6	By a modification of the *l·*,

new
No.	44– 4	C. S. involves a new *l·*,

new style of
My.	318– 2	constituted a new style of *l·*.

no
Mis.	160– 5	But a mother's love . . . has no *l·* ;

of Soul
Hea.	7– 8	*l·* of Soul instead of the senses ;

of Spirit
My.	180–10	original tongue in the *l·* of Spirit,

one
Mis.	67–26	the sense of words in one *l·* by

original
Hea.	7– 9	into its original *l·*, which is Mind,
Peo.	1– 6	of law back to its original *l·*,

power of
My.	332– 2	* the power of *l·* would be

refers to
Mis.	67–25	If your question refers to *l·*,

speech nor
Ret.	61–18	no speech nor *l·*, — *Psal. 19 : 3.*

unmistakable
Mis.	297–16	I hereby state, in unmistakable *l·*,

Mis.	163–14	in the *l·* of a declining race,
	248– 1	"new tongue," the *l·* of — *see Mark 16 : 17.*
	262–11	its *l·* is always acceptable to
My.	308–27	attributes to my father *l·* unseemly,

languages
Mis.	64–11	the study of literature and *l·*
	64–23	*l·*, to a limited extent, are aids to
Ret.	80– 7	As the poets in different *l·* have
Pul.	46–26	* ancient *l·*, Hebrew, Greek, and

languid
Mis.	395–24	The *l·* brooklets yield their sighs,
Po.	58– 9	The *l·* brooklets yield their sighs,

lap
Ret.	18– 7	In *l·* of the pear-tree,
Po.	68–16	In *l·* of the pear-tree,

lapse
Mis.	79–13	cannot *l·* into a mortal belief
Un.	10–15	they cannot collapse, or *l·* into
Pan.	7–20	a *l·* in the Mosaic religion,
Hea.	4–19	after a temporary *l·*, to begin anew
Peo.	2–25	Truth without a *l·* or error,
My.	273–26	*l·* and relapse, come and go, until

lapses
Pan.	7–27	The hypothesis . . . *l·* into evil

large
Mis.	6–29	*l·* family of children where the
	168–27	* drew a *l·* audience.
	177– 8	*L·* numbers, in desperate malice,
	239– 6	to commence a *l·* class in C. S.
	249– 2	some *l·* doses of morphine,
	276– 1	the *l·* book of rare flowers,
	305–17	* *l·* contributions from a few.
	318– 5	a *l·* affection, not alone for
	318–27	either too *l·* or too little :
	318–27	if too *l·*, we are in the darkness
	371– 3	*l·* flocks of metaphysicians
Man.	60–22	No *l·* gathering of people
	98–14	shall circulate in *l·* quantities
Ret.	1–20	and flecked with *l·* flocks
	7–16	* practice of a very *l·* business.
	10– 2	too *l·* for my body
	19–14	lamented by a *l·* circle of friends
	49– 1	which yields a *l·* income,
	50–15	my list of . . . scholars is very *l·*,
	82–14	should locate in *l·* cities,
Pul.	1–12	by reason of its *l·* lessons,
	25– 4	* *l·* boilers in the basement
	26–21	* in *l·* golden letters on a
	27– 7	* three *l·* class-rooms and the
	27–30	* A *l·* bay window,
	32–10	* *l·* and enthusiastic following
	41–16	* The *l·* auditorium, with its
	42– 1	* had closed the *l·* vestry room
	42–28	* *l·* basket of white carnations
	50– 6	* in buying so *l·* an estate
	50–16	* a *l·* and increasing number
	56– 5	* a *l·* and growing number

large

Pul.	63–11	* pointed to a number of *l*· elms
	64–10	* others donating *l*· sums.
	73–26	* *l*· volume which Mrs. Eddy had
	76–15	* *l*· rug composed entirely of
Rud.	1–11	affords a *l*· margin for
	15–23	promiscuous and *l*· assemblies,
No.	2–22	and many . . . have *l*· practices
Pan.	6–13	social prestige, a *l*· following,
'01.	31–13	communicants of my *l*· church,
My.	9– 1	* *l*· accessions to their membership.
	12– 6	* to secure the *l*· parcel of land
	14–29	* necessitates *l*· payments of money,
	20–26	* expenditure of a *l*· amount of money,
	20–29	* the usual *l*· gathering in Boston
	22– 6	* *l*· gatherings at the annual
	30– 1	* held *l*· crowds of people,
	30–19	* The six collections were *l*·,
	54–26	* a *l*· congregation was present.
	54–30	* decided that this hall was too *l*·,
	69–10	* Two *l*· marble plates with
	74– 2	* from the far West to a *l*· degree
	83–17	* public at *l*· will scarcely realize
	88–14	* its proportions are so *l*·,
	92– 5	* *l*· numbers of intelligent men
	123–26	small beginnings have *l*· endings.
	132–18	every member of this *l*· church.
	148–17	To-day, with the *l*· membership
	156–16	show you a *l*· upper room— *Luke* 22 : 12.
	169–17	and of the world at *l*·,
	173–10	*l*· gathering at this annual meeting
	182–18	*l*· membership and majestic cathedral.
	231– 8	she has given *l*· sums of money,
	243– 8	The Empire City is *l*·,
	294– 2	are yet in a *l*· minority
	304–12	I have lectured in *l*· and crowded
	310–12	*l*· manufacturing establishment
	310–15	carried on a *l*· business in
	330–26	lamented by a *l*· circle of friends
	342– 2	* Seated in the *l*· parlor,
		(*see also* **number**)

large-eyed

My.	343– 3	* looking *l*· into space,

largely

Mis.	47–29	That *l*· depends upon what one
Man.	31– 9	prosperity of C. S. *l*· depends.
Pul.	31–17	* atmosphere was *l*· thrilled and
	48–28	* figure *l*· in her genealogy,
	66–20	* and which is *l*· Oriental
My.	vii–13	* which is *l*· self-glorification
	68–20	* enters so *l*· into the interior finish.
	248–25	I have *l*· committed to you,

largeness

Mis.	276– 5	in its cordiality and *l*·.

larger

Mis.	239– 9	substance is taking *l*· proportions.
	273–27	a *l*· number would be in waiting
Ret.	33–18	not affected by a *l*· dose.
My.	22– 3	* saw the need of a *l*· edifice
	56–32	* proved the need of a *l*· edifice.
	57– 8	* need of a *l*· church edifice,
	64– 3	* took on a *l*· and truer meaning.
	97– 8	* yet to be shown . . . a *l*· proportion
	190– 4	to evolve that *l*· sympathy
	227–31	cures a *l*· per cent of malignant
	244– 5	if a *l*· class were advantageous

largess

My.	188–18	a benediction for God's *l*·.
	349–12	a divine *l*·, a gift of God

largest

Mis.	130–27	he who exercises the *l*· charity,
	224–18	but with the *l*· patience ;
	252– 5	its *l*· dose is never dangerous
	305–14	* *l*· number of persons possible
Man.	98–25	three *l*· branch churches in each
	99– 8	its three *l*· branch churches,
Ret.	7– 2	it was the *l*· vote of the State ;
Pul.	80–10	* they have the *l*· individuality,
No.	10– 6	two *l*· words in the vocabulary of
My.	26–12	Your beneficent gift is the *l*· sum
	30–29	* by far the *l*· crowd of the day
	57–18	* *l*· in the history of the church
	57–20	* the hitherto *l*· admission,
	65– 3	* *l*· church business meeting
	65– 4	* perhaps the *l*· ever held in the
	70–29	* *l*· of which is thirty-two feet
	76– 3	* the *l*· of them all.
	77– 3	* one of the *l*· in the world.
	80–30	* where the *l*· meeting was held,
	89– 1	* This church is one of the *l*·
	89– 7	* one of the *l*· organs in the world.
	91–29	* it is the *l*· in New England.
	295–14	kindness in its *l*·, . . . sense is
	309–20	paid the *l*· tax in the colony.

lark (*see also* **lark's**)

Mis.	354–31	gaze on the *l*· in her emerald bower
Pul.	81–18	* as the *l*· who soars and sings
Po.	18– 9	gaze on the *l*· in her emerald bower?
	24–18	With song of morning *l*· ;

lark's

Mis.	390– 6	*l*· shrill song doth wake the dawn :
Po.	55– 7	*l*· shrill song doth wake the dawn :

last

Mis.	42–14	destroyed this *l*· enemy,
	57–26	*the sixth and l· day,*
	59– 9	the *l*· state of patients
	76–32	who overcame the *l*· enemy,
	81–12	*the l· eighteen centuries*
	85–16	The *l*· degree of regeneration
	90–26	the Passover, or *l*· supper,
	110–16	years, since *l*· we met ;
	124–24	The *l*· act of the tragedy
	131–31	*l*· year's records immortalized,
	132– 1	at our *l*· meeting,
	136–19	in my *l*· revised edition
	137–15	within the *l*· few years.
	138–15	the first and *l*· lesson of C. S.
	165– 7	The *l*· appearing of Truth will be
	170– 1	*l*· enemy to be overthrown ;
	185–28	*the l· Adam was made a— I Cor.* 15 : 45.
	186–29	undoubtedly refers to the *l*· Adam
	188– 8	and as *l*·, that which is primal,
	188–29	she knew that the *l*· Adam,
	189– 1	"The *l*· shall be first,— *Matt.* 20 : 16.
	189– 2	and the first *l*·."— *Matt.* 20 : 16.
	192–25	the *l*· chapter of Mark
	205–15	*l*· scene in corporeal sense.
	270–28	*l*· link in material medicine.
	293–17	the *l*· error will be worse than
	294– 2	the *l*· infirmity of evil is
	330–23	Nature's first and *l*· lessons
	350–17	proved to be our *l*· meeting.
	355–14	the *l*· third pierces itself,
	366–20	From first to *l*·, evil insists on
	375–10	* "In my *l*· letter,
Man.	76–14	expenditures for the *l*· year.
	98–12	shall read the *l*· *proof sheet*
Ret.	15–21	Our *l*· vestry meeting was
	28–12	The first must become *l*·.
	38– 8	insert in my *l*· chapter
	40–15	at the birth of her *l*· babe,
	42– 1	My *l*· marriage was with
	49–12	first, *l*·, and always,
	82–28	my *l*· revision, in 1890,
Un.	30–14	the *l*· Adam was made a— *I Cor.* 15 : 45.
	30–23	I discerned the *l*· Adam as a
	30–25	first shall be *l*·,"— *Matt.* 19 : 30.
Pul.	20–14	From first to *l*· The Mother Church
	23–10	* during the *l*· decade,
	23–18	* *l*· quarter of the nineteenth
	29– 8	* *L*· Sunday I gave myself the pleasure
	35–16	The first must become *l*·.
	42– 6	* repeated for the *l*· time.
	43–15	* the corner-stone laying *l*· spring,
	46–27	* Her *l*· marriage was in the spring
	55– 6	* *l*· quarter of preceding centuries.
	56–14	* *l*· quarter of the century.
	66–20	* during the *l*· decade,
	68–19	* dedication in Boston *l*· Sunday
	75–19	* ceremonies at Boston *l*· Sunday
Rud.	6–16	* within the *l*· *few years,*
	9– 1	*l*· state of that man— *Matt.* 12 : 45.
No.	5–28	*l*· state of one's patients
Pan.	1– 5	since *l*· you gathered
'00.	1– 9	in the *l*· year of the
	10–23	Only *l*· week I received a
	15–25	the *l*· to be more than— *Rev.* 2 : 19.
'01.	3– 1	added since *l*· November
	3–24	the *l*· proposition does not
	17–16	the *l*· stages of consumption,
	28– 2	approaching the *l*· stage of the
	33–13	Christian Scientists first and *l*· ask
'02.	2–12	Within the *l*· decade religion
	13– 5	During the *l*· seven years I have
Po.	27–12	heal her wounds too tenderly to *l*·?
My.	8–29	* "Since the *l*· report, in 1900,
	9–20	at our *l*· annual meeting
	11–27	* The size . . . was decided *l*· June,
	55–21	* during the *l*· year the hall was
	55–31	* the twenty-first of *l*· month,
	57–21	* number admitted during the *l*· year
	58– 4	* *C. S. Sentinel* of *l*· Saturday
	58–30	* at the C. S. church *l*· Sunday
	60–29	* On the twenty-fifth of *l*· March
	65–19	* The *l*· parcel in the block
	66– 8	* *l*· parcel on St. Paul Street
	79– 2	* then, at the *l*·, kneeling
	82– 8	* crowding Boston the *l*· week
	85–25	* *L*· Sunday it was entirely credible

last
My. 89–28   * marvels of the *l·* quarter century.
97–26   * forty thousand *l·* week to dedicate
98–14   * *l·* issue of the *C. S. Sentinel*
105– 8   consumption in its *l·* stages,
122–11   On the fifth of July *l·*,
125–21   The students in my *l·* class in 1898
137–20   I have designated by my *l·* will,
141– 7   * services attended *l·* Sunday
141– 8   * were thus the *l·* to be held.
141–13   * announcement . . . made *l·* night
170– 8   Message to the church *l·* Sunday
173–12   a note, sent at the *l·* moment,
174–10   And *l·* but not least, I thank the
185–21   destroys the *l·* enemy, death.
190–31   and verifying his *l·* promise,
193–25   and the *l·* by love.
217–17   In the *l· Sentinel* [Oct. 12, 1899]
217–29   does not require the *l·* step to be
241–19   * "*L·* evening I was catechized by
264–12   * *l·* Thanksgiving Day of the
264–15   New England's *l·* Thanksgiving
300–15   "the *l·* enemy" — *I Cor.* 15 : 26.
311–25   When I was *l·* in Washington,
320–29   * *l·* conversation I had with him
326–19   to their *l·* resting-place.
327–14   * *l·* winter's term of our Legislature,
327–19   * on the field until the *l·*.
328–11   * passed by the *l·* Legislature,
329– 4   * *l·* General Assembly of North Carolina
331–23   * attended him during his *l·* sickness,
333– 7   * paying the *l·* tribute
335– 1   * on the 27th June *l·*,
336–16   * previous to his *l·* illness,
338–11   The contents of the *l·* lecture of
345–21   the *l·* healing that will be vouchsafed
350–14   within the *l·* five years
    (*see also* **cross**)

last at-
Mis. 9– 8   giving them refuge at *l·*
10–28   mortals learn at *l·* the lesson,
12– 3   spreads its virus and kills at *l·*.
254–15   must at *l·* kill this evil
385–11   and safely moored at *l·*
Ret. 9–23   * learned at *l·* to know His voice
Pul. 13–21   comes back to him at *l·*
13–24   at *l·* stung to death
44– 3   * At *l·* you begin to see the
83–12   * At *l·* she is becoming
83–25   * at *l·* we begin to know
No. 8–16   at *l·* struggle into freedom
'00. 8–23   Then, at *l·*, the right will
Po. 43–19   Till they gain at *l·*
48– 4   and safely moored at *l·*
My. 133– 5   at *l·* come to acknowledge God,
155–14   at *l·*, it finds the full fruition of
230–26   realize at *l·* their Master's promise,

last-drawn
My. 189–22   *l·* sigh of a glory gone,

lasted
Pul. 36– 3   * The work . . . *l·* nine years,

lasting
Ret. 50– 7   tuition *l·* barely three weeks.
Rud. 8–27   the restoration is not *l·*,
'00. 2–24   more sudden, severe, and *l·*

lastly
Un. 2–10   *l·*, it removes the pain
'01. 27–30   * *L·*, they say they had always
My. 304–27   * *L·*, they say they have always
305– 5   *L·*, the defamer will declare

lasts
Mis. 85–24   so long as this temptation *l·*,
261– 3   and *l·* as long as the evil.
Man. 15–13   punished so long as the belief *l·*.

latchet
Mis. 341–15   unloose the *l·* of thy sandals ;

latchets
Ret. 92– 7   unloose the *l·* of his Christliness,

late
Mis. 10–32   Soon or *l·*, your enemy will wake
35–10   the *l·* Dr. Asa G. Eddy,
71– 3   The *l·* John B. Gough is said to have
117–30   or make them too *l·* to follow
306–19   * request of the *l·* Mrs. Harrison,
339–30   the wisdom . . . may come too *l·*.
351–11   The *l·* much-ado-about-nothing
379–33   pp. 152, 153 in late editions.
Ret. 3– 1   the *l·* Sir John Macneill,
Pul. 5–12   the *l·* A. Bronson Alcott.
9–16   loss of our *l·* lamented pastor,
My. 48–16   * the *l·* Frederick Lawrence Knowles :
105–20   the *l·* Dr. Davis of Manchester,

late
My. 141– 8   * Of *l·* years members of the church
195– 8   never too *l·* to repent,
287– 3   the *l·* Baron and Baroness de Hirsch
289–15   the *l·* lamented Victoria,
289–28   the *l·* lamented Victoria,
291– 3   labors of our *l·* beloved President,
296–10   The *l·* lamented Christian Scientist
308–12   my *l·* father and his family
311–27   her *l·* father, General John McNeil,
319– 8   hold the *l·* Mr. Wiggin in . . . memory
319–24   * the *l·* J. Henry Wiggin
323–29   * the *l·* Rev. J. Henry Wiggin
331–19   * of the *l·* Major George W. Glover
331–30   * during his *l·* illness.
334–29   * by the *l·* Charles W. Moore,
341–20   * has been so much to the fore of *l·*

late-comers
Pul. 29–12   * There was no straggling of *l·*.

latent
Mis. 201–24   tested and developed *l·* power.
237–10   belch forth their *l·* fires.
Ret. 61– 4   a belief, a *l·* fear,
Hea. 6–24   *l·* cause producing the effect we see.

later
Mis. 57– 2   all was *l·* made which
115–30   sooner or *l·*, you will
187–18   *l·* teachings and demonstrations
381– 9   *L·*, Mrs. Eddy requested
Ret. 6–20   *l·* Albert spent a year in
19–16   A month *l·* I returned to
24–20   a miracle which *l·* I found to be
35– 8   I did not venture . . . until *l·*,
Un. 6– 4   Sooner or *l·* the whole human race
41–12   must come to all sooner or *l·* ;
Pul. 29– 1   * and *l·* in Copley Hall,
29– 7   * venture to speak, a little *l·*,
29–27   * *L·* I was told that almost the
34–23   *l·* I found it to be in perfect
46–30   * *l·* he attracted the attention of
67–28   * charter was obtained two months *l·*.
83–21   * When we try to praise her *l·* works
No. 7–10   Sooner or *l·* the eyes of sinful
28– 4   mists of error, sooner or *l·*, will
Pan. 13–18   Sooner or *l·* all shall know Him,
'01. 20–20   agony . . . it must sooner or *l·* cause
23–27   In *l·* publications he declared
Po. vii– 4   * in her *l·* productions.
My. 11–16   * *L·* on she expressed
43–23   * A few years *l·* she gave us our
45–24   * fulfilment of the *l·* prophecy,
48–14   * twenty-six years *l·* the following
63– 4   * advisory capacity in the *l·* days :
169– 7   to visit me at a *l·* date,
311– 1   incident, which occurred *l·*
315–12   * *L·* on I learned that
319–22   * A few days *l·*,
330–28   A month *l·* I returned to

latest
Mis. 318–20   *l·* editions of my works,
Ret. 47–24   *l·* editions of my works,
Pul. 21– 2   grandchildren to the *l·* generations,

Lathrop
Mrs.
Pul. 72–21   * nor did she believe that Mrs. *L·*
74–20   "I think Mrs. *L·* was not understood.
Mrs. Laura
Pul. 74– 6   * statement made by Mrs. Laura *L·*,

Latin
Mis. 25–23   from the *L·* word meaning *all*,
Ret. 10–10   tongues, Hebrew, Greek, and *L·*.
Pul. 46–26   * Hebrew, Greek, and *L·*.
Rud. 1–13   In Spanish, Italian, and *L·*,
1–14   The *L·* verb *personare* is
'02. 7–11   *L·* omni, which signifies *all*,

latitude
Man. 99– 5   the 36th parallel of *l·*.

latitudes
Ret. 73–11   into more spiritual *l·*
No. 45–23   in more spiritual *l·*,
Peo. 1–14   into more spiritual *l·*.

Latour
Ret. 82– 3   dealing with a simple *L·*

latter (*see also* **latter's**)
Mis. 42–23   the *l·* is real and eternal.
53–17   not equal to the *l·*.
84–22   so far extinguished the *l·*
104–18   The *l·* move in God's grooves
112–13   belong to the *l·* days,
117– 8   arrest the former, and obey the *l·*.
130– 9   Does not the *l·* instruct you
164– 4   and the *l·* is the human

latter

Mis. 206– 3 being servant to the *l·*,
285–15 the *l·* fell *hors de combat;*
372– 1 When the *l·* was first issued,
382–12 In the *l·* half of the
Ret. 10– 6 the *l·* I had to repeat
24– 9 in the *l·* part of 1866
Pul. vii– 8 *l·* half of the nineteenth
23–23 * *l·* part of the present century,
Rud. 5–28 *l·* conclusion is the simple
No. 10– 8 *l·* reveals and interprets God
'00. 5–13 essence and source of the two *l·*,
'01. 25–24 and the *l·* superior,
My. 56– 5 * the *l·* a repetition of the
68–29 * *l·* framed of iron and finished
75– 1 * of the value of the *l·*,
108–13 and the *l·* couples faith with
127–21 *l·* days of the nineteenth century.
128–23 the *l·* were impracticable.
130– 2 leave the *l·* to propagate.
131–22 this hour of the *l·* days
180–31 *l·* solves the whence and why
190–11 shows the *l·* not only equalling
197–18 illumine the midnight of the *l·*,
215–30 That he preferred the *l·* is evident,
224–24 not safe to accept the *l·*

latter-day

Mis. 113–18 *l·* ultimatum of evil,
My. 98–24 * any of the *l·* methods

latter's

My. 359–24 * with the *l·* unqualified approval.

lattice

Mis. 376–18 morning burst through the *l·*

laud

Ret. 11–17 *l·* the land whose talents rock
Po. 60–14 *l·* the land whose talents rock

laudable

Mis. 281– 1 with *l·* ambition are about to chant

lauded

My. 302–21 but I am less *l·*, pampered,

laugh

Mis. 126–31 heavens shall *l·* :— *Psal.* 2: 4.
239– 3 whether I can talk — and *l·*
338–18 very heavens shall *l·* at them,
Pan. 1– 9 smile of April, the *l·* of May,
'01. 18– 9 Those who *l·* at or pray against
'02. 9–25 Did the age's thinkers *l·* long

laughed

Po. 71– 3 *L·* right to scorn,

laughing

Mis. 390–12 Looks love unto the *l·* hours,
Ret. 18–11 And ope . . . to the bright, *l·* day;
Po. 55–13 Looks love unto the *l·* hours,
63–23 And ope . . . to the bright, *l·* day;

laughingly

My. 81– 9 * *l·* give precedence to another
324–26 * He told us *l·* why he accepted

laughter

Mis. 324–10 the footfalls abate, the *l·* ceases.

launch

Mis. 111–11 they *l·* into the depths,

launched

My. 182–21 *l·* the earth in its orbit,

launching

My. 29–23 * religion *l·* upon a new era,

laureate's

Po. 10– 9 That wakes thy *l·* lay.
My. 337–10 That wakes thy *l·* lay.

laurel

Mis. 340– 2 torn the *l·* from many
Ret. 17–17 bay, and *l·*, in classical glee,
Po. 63– 1 bay, and *l·*, in classical glee,

laurels

Mis. 254–25 *l·* of headlong human will.
358– 9 hounded footsteps, false *l·*.
My. 125–14 they earn their *l·*.
155–12 the low *l·* of vainglory,

Laus Deo

Mis. 399–16 poem
399–18 *L· D·*, it is done !
399–23 *L· D·*,— on this rock
400– 1 *L· D·*, night star-lit
400–11 It has none, *L· D·* !
Pul. 16– 3 *L· D·*, it is done !
16– 8 *L· D·*,— on this rock
16–13 *L· D·*, night starlit
16–23 It has none, *L· D·* !
43–14 * "*L· D·*, it is done !"
44– 2 * '*L· D·*, it is done !'

Laus Deo

Po. page 76 poem
76– 2 *L· D·*, it is done !
76– 7 *L· D·*,— on this rock
76–12 *L· D·*, night star-lit
76–22 It has none, *L· D·* !

lavatory

Pul. 76–19 * a *l·* in which the plumbing

lavender-kid

Mis. 177–14 doff your *l·* zeal,

laving

Po. 73–11 *L·* with surges thy silv'ry beach !

law

absence of

My. 220–14 denotes the absence of *l·*.

all

Mis. 258–12 all *l·* was vested in the Lawgiver,
258–25 all *l·*, Life, Truth, and Love.
'02. 9– 4 All-science— all *l·* and gospel.
My. 349–30 infinite nature, including all *l·*

all's

My. 40–27 * "All's love, but all's *l·*."

and gospel

Mis. 18– 6 the *l·* and gospel of Christ,
65–22 demands both *l·* and gospel,
66–14 The *l·* and gospel of Truth
67– 3 the *l·* and gospel of healing.
121–32 Teacher of both *l·* and gospel
'02. 9– 4 All-science— all *l·* and gospel.
My. 247– 7 its *l·* and gospel are according to
252– 2 obey the *l·* and gospel.
254–28 its *l·* and gospel are according to
268–12 Principle of *l·* and gospel,
282–25 sunlight of the *l·* and gospel.
350– 1 of Deity and man, *l·* and gospel,

and order

Mis. 104–23 divine *l·* and order of being.
Ret. 76–29 observance of moral *l·* and order
Un. 11–14 sense of physical *l·* and order.
23– 7 are born of *l·* and order,
My. 222–30 will maintain *l·* and order,
245– 7 *L·* and order characterize its work

and power

Mis. 364–16 individuality, *l·*, and power.

and the gospel

Mis. 348– 3 claims of the *l·* and the gospel.
'02. 6–29 fulfils the *l·* and the gospel,
8– 4 The *l·* and the gospel concur,
8–13 between the *l·* and the gospel,
My. 131–23 of the divine *l·* and the gospel.
216– 6 The *l·* and the gospel,

another

No. 30–13 to rebuke any claim of another *l·*.

appears to be

Mis. 259– 3 Whatever appears to be *l·*,

authority and

Un. 26–10 is not your authority and *l·*.

begin with the

My. 132– 2 begin with the *l·* as just announced,

ceremonial

No. 34– 4 We shall leave the ceremonial *l·*

common

Mis. 11–16 in accordance with common *l·*,
274–20 breaks common *l·*, gives impulse to
285–27 in the face and eyes of common *l·*,
Ret. 75–25 no warrant in common *l·*

conceive of a

'02. 5–26 why should mortals conceive of a *l·*,

construes

Mis. 301– 9 what the *l·* construes as crime.

criminal

Un. 29– 4 as does all criminal *l·*,

defines

Mis. 300–11 *l·* defines and punishes as theft.

deific

Mis. 45–16 deific *l·* that supply invariably meets

delivered from the

No. 25– 5 delivered from the *l·*,— *Rom.* 7: 6.

demands of the

My. 43– 7 * Obedience to the demands of the *l·*

divine

(*see* **divine**)

doers of the

My. 125– 3 not only sayers but doers of the *l·* ?

enacted

No. 30–11 is punished by the *l·* enacted.

eternal

Mis. 123–23 through the eternal *l·* of justice ;
No. 30–22 is like the eternal *l·* of God,

evade the

Mis. 226–26 such as manages to evade the *l·*,
300–16 thus evade the *l·*, *but not the gospel.*

fabulous

Peo. 12–11 Deal, then, with this fabulous *l·*

law

first
Ret. 87– 3 * "Order is heaven's first *l·*,"

force or
Mis. 257–12 This so-called force, or *l·*,
Pan. 6–24 how can matter be force or *l·* ;

fulfilled the
My. 202–12 hath fulfilled the *l·*." — Rom. 13 : 8.

fulfilling of the
Mis. 11– 3 Love is the fulfilling of the *l·* :
258– 3 love is the fulfilling of the *l·*.
285– 9 Love is the fulfilling of the *l·*.

fulfilling the
Mis. 12–30 fulfilling the *l·* of Love,
Ret. 65–24 Love, fulfilling the *l·*

fulfils the
Mis. 66– 4 fulfils the *l·* in righteousness,
117–15 Love . . . fulfils the *l·*.
209–10 human belief fulfils the *l·* of belief,
Ret. 76–16 This affection, . . . fulfils the *l·*
'02. 6–18 fulfils the *l·* in righteousness,
6–29 Divine Science fulfils the *l·*
My. 275–26 self-oblivious love fulfils the *l·*

fulfil the
Mis. 39–24 fulfil the *l·* of Christ." — Gal. 6 : 2.
Ret. 45–23 fulfil the *l·* of Christ
My. 153– 6 fulfil the *l·* in righteousness.

God's
Mis. 360 3 God's *l·*, as in divine Science,
Ret. 76– 4 if mortals obeyed God's *l·*
Un. 4– 5 Truth is God, and in God's *l·*.
4– 8 consciousness of God's *l·* is
No. 30– 7 God's *l·* reaches and destroys evil
30–11 God's *l·* is in three words,

governing
My. 299–21 understand it and the *l·* governing it,

hard is the
My. 40–30 * Dura lex, sed lex (Hard is the *l·*,

has found
Mis. 227– 6 *L·* has found it necessary to

Hebrew
Mis. 8–27 The Hebrew *l·* with its

he read
Ret. 6–18 he read *l·* at Hillsborough,

higher
Mis. 28–30 superiority of the higher *l·* ;
244–19 by the higher *l·* of Spirit,
Peo. 12– 1 hearken to the higher *l·* of God,
My. 277–16 not consonant with the higher *l·*

His
Mis. 277–29 I thunder His *l·* to the sinner,
Un. 38– 5 not in accordance with His *l·*,
Rud. 10–22 His *l·* of Truth, when obeyed,

household
My. 308–27 his household *l·*, constantly

human
My. 149–19 may know too much of human *l·*
220– 9 obedience to human *l·*,
283–26 Human *l·* is right only as it

infinite
Mis. 172–20 the infinite *l·* of God ;

in righteousness
Mis. 66– 4 fulfils the *l·* in righteousness,
'02. 6–18 fulfils the *l·* in righteousness,
My. 153– 6 fulfil the *l·* in righteousness.

intelligence and
Pan. 7–23 power, intelligence and *l·*,

involved
Pul. 35– 3 Principle and the *l·* involved

is perfect
Mis. 82–16 whose *l·* is perfect and infinite.

is written
Mis. 172–20 which *l·* is written on the heart,

Jewish
Mis. 161–20 Jewish *l·* that none should teach
Un. 29– 3 Jewish *l·* condemned the sinner
No. 29– 1 passage refers to the Jewish *l·*,

lawless
Mis. 257–32 according to this lawless *l·*

material
Mis. 17– 3 as opposed to the material *l·*
198–24 based on physical material *l·*,
200–20 every supposed material *l·*.
Rud. 12–27 divine Mind, not material *l·*,

mental
Mis. 199– 6 his own erring mental *l·*,

moral
Mis. 73–14 The foolish disobey moral *l·*,
261–28 without apprehending the moral *l·*
Ret. 76–29 observance of moral *l·*

Mosaic
Ret. 89–11 instruction in the Mosaic *l·*.

name of
Mis. 199– 5 dignify . . . with the name of *l·* :

law

natural
Pul. 54– 7 * harmony with natural *l·*,
No. 45–15 In natural *l·* and in religion

never averts
Mis. 71–14 Science never averts *l·*,

not without the
Mis. 286– 3 marriage is not without the *l·*,

obedient to
My. 41– 2 * to become gladly obedient to *l·*,

obey the
My. 219–31 that he obey the *l·*,
252– 2 obey the *l·* and gospel.

of being
Mis. 181– 9 blind obedience to the *l·* of being,
259–18 the only *l·* of being.
No. 2– 8 which is natural and a *l·* of being.
My. 217–31 not to destroy the *l·* of being,

of belief
Mis. 209–10 fulfils the *l·* of belief,
Peo. 11–21 ignorant of the *l·* of belief,

of Christ
Mis. 39–24 fulfil the *l·* of Christ." — Gal. 6 : 2.
Ret. 45–23 fulfil the *l·* of Christ
No. 30– 2 Truth is the *l·* of Christ,

of creation
Mis. 258–15 This is the *l·* of creation :
259–14 was the only *l·* of creation,

of death
My. 154– 6 transcending the *l·* of death.

of divine Love
Mis. 208–13 the *l·* of divine Love gives,

of divine Mind
Mis. 269–22 Science is a *l·* of divine Mind.
My. 3 15 Science is a *l·* of divine Mind,
108–14 based on the *l·* of divine Mind.
240 11 Science is a *l·* of divine Mind,

of God
Mis. 22– 4 manifesto of Mind, the *l·* of God,
36–26 not subject to the *l·* of God, — Rom. 8 : 7.
141–15 I vindicate both the *l·* of God and
172–20 the infinite *l·* of God ;
172–23 This *l·* of God is the Science of
208– 8 *l·* of God has no knowledge of evil,
208–11 only to submit to the *l·* of God,
211–24 risks nothing who obeys the *l·* of God,
257– 8 The *l·* of God is the law of Spirit,
315–28 unerring wisdom and *l·* of God,
Ret. 28–20 according to the *l·* of God.
72– 4 is contrary to the *l·* of God ;
81– 8 The letter of the *l·* of God,
Rud. 1– 2 As the *l·* of God, the law of good,
No. 30–22 is like the eternal *l·* of God,
'02. 5–20 it is iterated in the *l·* of God,
Peo. 12– 1 hearken to the higher *l·* of God,
My. 187–10 and the perfect *l·* of God.
270– 2 not sanctioned by the *l·* of God,
347–24 Science is the *l·* of God ;
348–28 Science remains the *l·* of God

of good
Rud. 1– 2 As the law of God, the *l·* of good,

of health
Un. 6–13 Until the heavenly *l·* of health,

of his being
Ret. 69– 4 Life is the *l·* of his being"

of infinity
Mis. 15–19 progress is the *l·* of infinity.

of justice
Mis. 123–23 through the eternal *l·* of justice ;
261–16 In this *l·* of justice,

of kindness
My. 42– 4 * the *l·* of kindness." — Prov. 31 : 26.

of Life
Mis. 17– 2 of the spiritual *l·* of Life,
30–19 to demonstrate the *l·* of Life,
258–10 supremacy of the *l·* of Life
259– 5 God is the *l·* of Life,
No. 30– 2 *l·* of Life and Truth is the
My. 154– 4 it is the *l·* of Life understood

of Love
Mis. 12–25 the *l·* of Love rejoices the heart ;
12–30 fulfilling the *l·* of Love,
17– 3 the spiritual *l·* of Love.
67–18 demonstrates the *l·* of Love.
119–22 Insubordination to the *l·* of Love
121–14 a divine decree, a *l·* of Love !
141–14 even the annihilating *l·* of Love.
141–23 in obedience to the *l·* of Love
212–20 The *l·* of Love saith,
Ret. 76–16 fulfils the *l·* of Love.
My. 153–23 unmindful of the divine *l·* of Love,
154– 8 to infringe the divine *l·* of Love
279– 2 not sanctioned by . . . the *l·* of Love.

of love
My. 41– 9 * thoughts adverse to the *l·* of love.

law

of loving
 Mis. 13– 8 the *l·* of loving mine enemies.
of loyalty
 Mis. 12–13 *l·* of loyalty to Jesus' Sermon on
of matter
 Mis. 22– 3 Science is neither a *l·* of matter nor
  173– 4 sees nothing but a *l·* of matter.
  198–31 or violated a *l·* of matter
  256–23 gravitation as a *l·* of matter ;
  257–10 The so-called *l·* of matter is an
 My. 3–14 it is not a *l·* of matter,
of metaphysics
 My. 41–11 * *l·* of metaphysics says,
of Mind
 Mis. 173– 9 Science is the *l·* of Mind
of mortal belief
 Peo. 12– 6 is a *l·* of mortal belief,
of Moses
 Mis. 261–20 typified in the *l·* of Moses,
of nature
 Pul. 54–12 * no *l·* of nature violated
 Peo. 10–18 and not a *l·* of nature,
of omnipotent harmony
 Mis. 17– 4 the *l·* of omnipotent harmony
of opposites
 Mis. 14–22 proven by the *l·* of opposites
  57–12 By the *l·* of opposites.
 Un. 52–23 By the *l·* of opposites.
of our God
 Mis. 129– 9 The *l·* of our God and the rule of
of right thinking
 My. 41– 5 * the *l·* of right thinking,
of Science
 Mis. 71–31 immutable and just *l·* of Science,
of sin
 Mis. 17– 6 any supposititious *l·* of sin,
  30–21 the *l·* of sin and death.'' — *Rom.* 8 : 2.
  36–23 and the *l·* of sin and death.
  201–19 the *l·* of sin and death ;'' — *Rom.* 8 : 2.
  321–16 the *l·* of sin and death.'' — *Rom.* 8 : 2.
  326– 3 the *l·* of sin and death.'' — *Rom.* 8 : 2.
 Un. 56–17 freeth him from the *l·* of sin
 '02. 9–13 the *l·* of sin and death.'' — *Rom.* 8 : 2.
 My. 113–14 the *l·* of sin and death.'' — *Rom.* 8 : 2.
  272– 7 the *l·* of sin and death.'' — *Rom.* 8 : 2.
  293–29 the *l·* of sin and death.'' — *Rom.* 8 : 2.
of Spirit
 Mis. 244–19 by the higher *l·* of Spirit,
  257– 9 law of God is the *l·* of Spirit,
  258–30 It interprets the *l·* of Spirit,
 Un. 56–15 opposes the *l·* of Spirit ;
 Rud. 11– 2 contrary to the *l·* of Spirit.
 My. 293–25 *l·* of Spirit to control matter,
of Spirit's supremacy
 Un. 58–10 the *l·* of Spirit's supremacy ;
of the chord
 Ret. 82– 2 the *l·* of the chord remains
of the Spirit
 Mis. 201–18 *l·* of the Spirit of life — *Rom.* 8 : 2.
  321–15 *l·* of the Spirit of life — *Rom.* 8 : 2.
  326– 2 *l·* of the Spirit of life — *Rom.* 8 : 2.
 '02. 9–11 *l·* of the Spirit of life — *Rom.* 8 : 2.
 My. 41–23 * *l·* of the Spirit of life — *Rom.* 8 : 2.
  113–13 *l·* of the Spirit of life — *Rom.* 8 : 2.
  272– 5 *l·* of the Spirit of life — *Rom.* 8 : 2.
  293–28 *l·* of the Spirit of life — *Rom.* 8 : 2.
of "the survival
 No. 25–13 *l·* of "the survival of the fittest.''
of transmission
 Mis. 71–11 *set aside the l· of transmission,*
of Truth
 Mis. 208– 2 This is the *l·* of Truth to error,
 Un. 4– 6 *l·* of Truth destroys every
 Rud. 10–22 His *l·* of Truth, when obeyed,
old
 My. 327–19 * an old *l·*, or rather a section of an act
one
 Pan. 8–17 had one God and one *l·*,
or intelligence
 Mis. 101–27 no other power, *l·*, or intelligence
penalty of
 Mis. 227– 9 to evade the penalty of *l·*,
penalty of the
 Mis. 300–21 incurring the penalty of the *l·*,
perfect
 No. 30–12 this perfect *l·* is ever present
 My. 187–10 and the perfect *l·* of God.
physical
 Mis. 28–29 of physique and of physical *l·*,
  101–17 of mortality, of physical *l·*,
 Un. 11–14 sense of physical *l·* and order.
power and
 My. 36–31 * through His power and *l·*,
prohibitory
 Peo. 10– 9 on a tyrannical prohibitory *l·*

law

protected by
 My. 227–20 *are not specially protected by l·.*
rebels against
 My. 40–29 * Human sense often rebels against *l·*,
recognizes
 My. 328–12 * *l·* recognizes them as healers,
sacred
 Mis. 151– 9 Through the sacred *l·*, He speaketh
Science is the
 My. 267– 5 Science is the *l·* of the Mind
  347–24 Science is the *l·* of God ;
signification of
 My. 220–14 the moral signification of *l·*.
so-called
 Mis. 198–24 physical material *l·*, so-called
  257–10 The so-called *l·* of matter is
  257–22 governed by this so-called *l·*,
Spirit and
 Mis. 256–21 chapter sub-title
spiritual
 (*see* **spiritual**)
State
 Peo. 12–11 as with an inhuman State *l·* ;
substance, or
 '02. 6– 3 knowledge of life, substance, or *l·*,
suit at
 Ret. 39– 3 I entered a suit at *l·*,
 My. 136–16 won a suit at *l·* in Washington,
this
 Mis. 13– 9 This *l·* I now urge upon the
  66– 1 But this *l·* is not infallible
  82–17 In obedience to this *l·*,
  173–10 this *l·* has no relation to,
  208– 3 This *l·* is a divine energy.
  208– 4 the fulfilment of this *l·* ;
  257–31 is not exempt from this *l·*.
 Un. 4– 5 This *l·* declares that Truth is All,
  4– 6 This *l·* of Truth destroys every
 My. 221–21 Our Master conformed to this *l·*,
to destroy the
 Mis. 261–19 to destroy the *l·*,'' — *Matt.* 5 : 17.
 '02. 5–23 to destroy the *l·*, — *Matt.* 5 : 17.
 My. 219–24 to destroy the *l·*, — *Matt.* 5 : 17.
to Himself
 Mis. 258–13 Lawgiver, who was a *l·* to Himself.
translation of
 Peo. 1– 6 translation of *l·* back to its
understood the
 Pul. 54–15 * He understood the *l·* perfectly,
unto itself
 Mis. 260–29 Mind, . . . is a *l·* unto itself,
unto themselves
 Ret. 87–23 become a *l·* unto themselves.
violates the
 Ret. 75– 4 violates the *l·* given by Moses,
whole
 Ret. 31–20 shall keep the whole *l·*, — *Jas.* 2 : 10.
 Pul. 53–16 * the whole *l·* of human felicity
 My. 153– 8 have come to fulfil the whole *l·*.
without
 Mis. 367– 1 letter without *l·*, gospel, or

 Mis. 12–12 should be to-day a *l·* to himself,
  67– 4 First is the *l·*, which saith :
  71–16 *L·* brings out Truth, not error ;
  73–12 *L·* is never material ;
  244–15 * "Has the *l·* been abrogated
  256–25 assertion that matter is a *l·*,
  256–26 Wherever *l·* is, Mind is ;
  257– 7 that which is not *l·*,
  257– 7 *L·* ie either a moral or an
  259– 4 not of the nature of God, is not *l·*,
  316– 3 *l·* not unto others, but themselves.
 Man. 28– 3 *L·* constitutes government,
  84– 5 a *l·*, not unto others, but to
 Ret. 30–17 St. Paul declared that the *l·*
 Pul. 35– 8 * a *l·* as operative in the world to-day
 Rud. 1–16 In *l·*, Blackstone applies the word
  4–18 *L·* is not in matter, but in Mind
 No. 21–11 identity, individuality, *l·* ;
 '02. 4–20 a *l·* never to be abrogated
 Peo. 12– 5 only *l·* of sickness or death is
 My. 40–31 * nevertheless it is the *l·*).
  41– 4 * *l·* of Christian metaphysics,
  43– 4 * The *l·* was given that they might
  219–30 I recommend, if the *l·* demand,
  220– 8 when the *l·* so requires.
  238–17 man rises above the letter, *l·*, or
  285–27 which are written in the *l·* — *Acts* 24 : 14.
  328–11 * greatly pleased at the *l·*

law-abiding

 Mis. 206–18 *l·* Principle, God.
 Ret. 87–11 systematic and *l·* people

law-breaking
  Mis. 301–10   *l·* and gospel-opposing
law-creating
  Mis. 206–18   active, all-wise, *l·*,
law-disciplining
  Mis. 206–18   all-wise, law-creating, *l·*,
lawful
  Un. 23– 5   His *l·* son, Edgar, was to his
  Pul. 48–24   * The natural and *l·* pride
     82–18   * women had few *l·* claims
  My. 41–26   * disregard his *l·* inheritance,
Lawgiver
  Mis. 258–13   all law was vested in the *L·*,
     259–14   When the *L·* was the only
lawgiver
  Mis. 256–25   is a law, or a *l·*,
     364–26   If Spirit is the *l·*
  Peo. 12– 9   matter is not a *l·*
  My. 108–16   this Mind is the only *l·*,
lawless
  Mis. 257–32   according to this *l·* law
     260–30   *l·* mind, with unseen motives,
  My. 349–25   evil, which is *l·* and traceable to
lawlessness
  Mis. 228– 7   just amid *l·*, and pure amid
     277–28   one can be just amid *l·*,
  Ret. 77– 1   and *l·* in literature.
  '00. 11–29   His . . . ethics bravely rebuke *l·*.
  My. 41–14   * whatsoever *l·* of hatred he may
law-maker
  My. 347–25   that matter is not a *l·* ;
lawn
  My. 171–22   * *l·* of the Unitarian church
     174– 1   beautiful *l·* surrounding their
lawns
  Pul. 48– 3   * green stretches of *l·*,
law-office
  Ret. 6–24   he succeeded to the *l·*
Law of Psychic Phenomena
  Pul. 53–14   * book title
Lawrence
  Mis. 154– 2   chapter sub-title
laws
  abortive
    Un. 11–10   this mind and its abortive *l·*.
  broken
    Pul. 56–21   * We tread upon life's broken *l·*,
  church
    My. 200– 7   Church *l·* . . . are God's laws.
  constitutional
    '01. 33–16   constitutional *l·* of their land ;
  divine
    My. 190–19   certainty of the divine *l·* of Mind
  enforce the
    Pul. 82–25   * at least to help enforce the *l·*
  equitable
    My. 277– 9   wholesome tribunals, equitable *l·*,
  forces and
    Pan. 2–17   * forces and *l·* which are manifested
  God's
    Mis. 20–27   are no infraction of God's *l·* ;
    Ret. 26– 9   in his obedience to God's *l·*,
    No. 11– 5   God's *l·*, and their intelligent and
    My. 203– 8   Church laws . . . are God's *l·*.
  health
    My. 344–22   * the health *l·* of the States
  her
    Mis. 219– 4   nor teaches that nature and her *l·*
    Pul. 7– 5   her *l·* have befriended progress.
  His
    Mis. 29–28   on the contrary, they fulfil His *l·* ;
     175–27   perfect Mind and His *l·*
    No. 5–24   realities of God and His *l·*.
    Hea. 12–14   His providence or His *l·*,
    My. 277–14   shall be according to His *l·*.
  human
    My. 220–27   Jesus obeyed human *l·*
  hygienic
    Ret. 26– 2   neither obedience to hygienic *l·*,
  immutable
    No. 4–21   of the immutable *l·* of God ;
    My. 106– 9   immutable *l·* of omnipotent Mind
  improved
    '02. 3–14   self-government under improved *l·*.
  its
    Mis. 55–27   its *l·* are mortal beliefs.
  legislation and
    Mis. 80–17   coercive legislation and *l·*,
  make
    My. 222–23   shall make *l·* to regulate

laws
  make the
    Pul. 82–25   * right to help make the *l·*,
    Peo. 11–18   make the *l·* that govern their
  making
    My. 340–15   making *l·* for the State
  material
     (*see* **material**)
  medical
    Mis. 80– 5   opposition to unjust medical *l·*.
  obey the
    My. 345– 3   Christian Scientists obey the *l·*,
  of every State
    My. 327–29   * when the *l·* of every State
  of God
    Man. 83–20   with the unerring *l·* of God,
    Un. 11–12   through the higher *l·* of God.
    Pul. 80–28   * harmony with the *l·* of God,
    No. 4–21   of the immutable *l·* of God ;
     11– 1   immutable and eternal *l·* of God ;
    My. 128–19   abide by the *l·* of God
     282– 4   I believe . . . in the *l·* of God.
     349–23   The *l·* of God, or divine Mind,
  of health
    Mis. 6–25   where *l·* of health are
  of infinite Spirit
    Mis. 16–30   with the *l·* of infinite Spirit,
  of limitation
    My. 229–26   namely, *l·* of limitation for a
  of man
    My. 348–23   *l·* of man and the universe,
  of matter
    Mis. 173–30   are these forces *l·* of matter,
     244–18   so-called *l·* of matter
     332– 4   Mind is Truth,— not *l·* of matter.
    Un. 11– 8   He annulled the *l·* of matter,
    Pan. 8–16   annulled the so-called *l·* of matter,
     12–13   high above the so-called *l·* of matter,
    Peo. 11–21   calls its own . . . "*l·* of matter."
     12– 8   spurious, imaginary *l·* of matter
    My. 288–17   so-called *l·* of matter he eschewed ;
  of Mind
    Mis. 173–30   laws of matter, or *l·* of Mind?
    My. 190–19   certainty of the divine *l·* of Mind
  of mortal mind
    Un. 11– 9   *l·* of mortal mind, not of God.
  of my country
    '02. 15– 4   protection of the *l·* of my country.
  of nations
    '00. 10–12   *l·* of nations and peoples,
  of nature
    Mis. 216–26   * neither *l·* of nature nor the
    Pul. 54–14   * obedience to the *l·* of nature.
    '01. 24– 6   rules styled the *l·* of nature.
  of our land
    Mis. 141–15   and the *l·* of our land.
     141–24   law of Love and the *l·* of our land.
    Man. 46– 6   according to the *l·* of our land.
     48–10   the courts, or the *l·* of our land.
    '01. 20–20   *l·* of our land will handle
  of reason
    Mis. 216–26   * neither . . . nor the *l·* of reason
  of Science
    No. 6–27   the *l·* of Science are mental,
  of Spirit
    Mis. 260–11   *l·* of Spirit, not of matter ;
  of the land
    My. 128–28   abide by . . . the *l·* of the land,
     219–22   nor make void the *l·* of the land,
     220–12   obeying the *l·* of the land.
  of the State
    Man. 45–26   under the *l·* of the *State.*
    Pul. 7– 4   especially the *l·* of the State
  of the universe
    My. 340–30   beneficence of the *l·* of the universe
  other
    Mis. 260–13   these laws annulled all other *l·*.
  our
    Mis. 119– 7   our *l·* punish the dupe as accessory
    My. 222–25   religion shall permeate our *l·*.
  physical
    Po. 32–15   Such physical *l·* to obey,
  prominent
    Mis. 18– 8   The prominent *l·* which forward
  scientific
    Mis. 31– 7   subverts the scientific *l·* of being.
    Pul. 69–22   * certain Christian and scientific *l·*,
  so-called
    Mis. 198– 6   denying material so-called *l·*
     244–18   who annulled the so-called *l·*
    Pan. 8–16   virtually annulled the so-called *l·*
     12–13   high above the so-called *l·*
    My. 288–17   The so-called *l·* of matter
  spiritual
    Mis. 198–26   Principle, and its spiritual *l·*.
    My. 159–23   spiritual *l·* enforcing obedience

laws

State
Mis. 263–24 and protection of State *l*·.
My. 204–16 COMPLIANCE WITH THE STATE *L*·

supposed
Mis. 74–21 matter and its supposed *l*·.

these
Mis. 260–12 these *l*· annulled all other laws.
Pul. 69–23 * understand these *l*· aright.

those
My. 220–27 and fell a victim to those *l*·.

United States
My. 227–10 State or United States *l*·,

universal
Un. 13– 9 universal *l*·, His unchangeableness,

your
Po. 39–17 Since temperance makes your *l*·.

Mis. 56–14 constituted *l*· to that effect,
206–15 no insubordination to the *l*·
Man. 28– 5 disobedience to the *l*· of The
Pan. 3–20 whose *l*· are not reckoned as science.
'01. 34–24 obey strictly the *l*· that be,
My. 160– 2 *l*· which it were impious to
167–26 by the *l*· of my native State.
234–29 and when the *l*· are against it,
344–22 * "Then as to the *l*·

law-school
Mis. 340–11 That *l*· is not at fault

lawsuit
My. 309– 5 acting as counsel in a *l*·

lawyer
Mis. 157– 9 that you or your *l*· will ask
381–10 requested her *l*· to inquire
Ret. 7–15 * As a *l*· he was able
Pul. 32–29 * achieved eminence as a *l*·.
60– 6 * who was a Colorado *l*·
My. 310– 4 Albert was a distinguished *l*·.

lawyers
My. 111–10 by many doctors and *l*·,
149–18 *L*· may know too much of

lax
My. 129– 4 and a *l*· system of religion.

laxity
Ret. 77– 1 *l*· in discipline and lawlessness in

lay
Mis. 15–23 *l*· off the "old man," — Col. 3 : 9.
17– 8 *l*· aside your material appendages,
22–31 *l*· concealed in the treasure-troves
29– 1 *l*· hands on the sick, — Mark 16 : 18.
63–17 might *l*· hold of eternal Life,
162–16 *l*· himself as a lamb upon the altar
179–28 *l*· aside material consciousness,
192–29 *l*· hands on the sick, — Mark 16 : 18.
225–21 the sofa whereon *l*· the lad
248– 2 "*l*· hands on the sick," — Mark 16 : 18.
248– 4 "*l*· hands on the sick" — Mark 16 : 18.
319–23 *l*· them in the outstretched hand
327–20 *l*· down a few of the heavy weights,
335–16 I *l*· bare the ability,
348– 9 one should *l*· it bare ;
361–17 *l*· aside every weight, — Heb. 12 : 1.
365– 3 *l*· than that is laid," — I Cor. 3 : 11.
384– 2 Come, in the minstrel's *l*· ;
388– 2 Which swelled creation's *l*· :
Ret. 17– 4 I bend to thy *l*·,
18–24 they darken my *l*· :
35–17 *l*· hands on the sick, — Mark 16 : 18.
Un. 43–23 apprehend, or *l*· hold upon,
56–24 *l*· hold of him ere he can change
64– 9 *l*· than that is laid." — I Cor. 3 : 11.
Pul. 12–22 by which we *l*· down all for
85– 1 * began to *l*· the foundation
No. 21–24 *l*· than that is laid, — I Cor. 3 : 11.
'00. 11–24 * And it *l*· on my fevered spirit
14–27 *l*· not this sin to their — Acts 7 : 60.
'01. 35– 6 and *l*· ourselves upon the altar?
'02. 3–24 and the *l*· of angels
20–11 Which swelled creation's *l*·,
Hea. 1– 4 *l*· hands on the sick, — Mark 16 : 18.
8–10 *l*· hands on the sick, — Mark 16 : 18.
19–27 *l*· hands on the sick, — Mark 16 : 18.
Peo. 12– 4 *l*· hands on the sick, — Mark 16 : 18.
Po. 7– 2 Which swelled creation's *l*· :
8– 9 Till vestal pearls that on leaflets *l*·,
10– 9 That wakes thy laureate's *l*·.
26–11 Great willing heart did *l*·.
36– 1 in the minstrel's *l*· ;
41– 6 *l*· down their woes,
43–14 *l*· their pure hearts' off'ring,
53– 5 And soft thy shading *l*·
62– 4 I bend to thy *l*·,
64–21 they darken my *l*· :

lay
Po. 70– 2 In the dim distance, *l*·
My. 16–24 Behold, I *l*· in Zion — Isa. 28 : 16.
16–28 will I *l*· to the line, — Isa. 28 : 17.
17–15 Behold, I *l*· in Sion — I Pet. 2 : 6.
29–16 * *l*· in its very simplicity ;
48– 2 * *l*· hands on the sick, — Mark 16 : 18.
155–11 *l*· down the low laurels of vainglory,
178–21 textbook *l*· on a table
184–21 *l*· upon its altars a sacrifice
337–10 That wakes thy laureate's *l*·.
341–12 A lightsome *l*·, a cooing call,

laying
Mis. 2–29 thus *l*· off the material beliefs
143–13 chapter sub-title
216–13 "*l*· on of hands," — Heb. 6 : 2.
285–19 *l*· the axe at the root of error.
399–17 Written on *l*· the corner-stone
Man. 60–22 *L*· a Corner Stone.
60–24 when *l*· the Corner Stone of
Pul. 16– 2 poem
43–15 * corner-stone *l*· last spring,
Po. 76– 1 *l*· of the corner-stone of The
My. 17– 4 *l*· aside all malice, — I Pet. 2 : 1.
128– 3 *l*· again the foundation of — Heb. 6 : 1.

lays
Mis. 37–17 *l*· the axe at the root of the tree
235–12 *l*· the axe at the root of the tree
287–19 This *l*· the foundations of
312– 6 that which *l*· all upon the altar,
Rud. 12– 1 never *l*· his hands on the patient,
'01. 13–15 C. S. *l*· the axe at the root of sin,
Po. 30–22 heaven's lyres and angels' loving *l*·,
My. 146–30 *l*· his whole weight of thought,
268–24 *l*· the axe at the root of all evil,
287–21 *l*· the axe at the root of the tree
296– 3 *l*· the axe "unto the root — Matt. 3 : 10.

lazar-houses
Mis. 296–20 patronize tap-rooms and *l*·,

Lazarus
Pul. 27–26 * represents the raising of *L*·.
My. 218–11 even the self-same *L*·.

lazy
Mis. 342–15 over earth's *l*· sleepers.

lead
Mis. 51–18 they will *l*· him aright :
61– 7 that *l*· to death,
130–30 appoints to *l*· the line of
145–25 child shall *l*· them." — Isa. 11 : 6.
196– 1 purity, and . . . *l*· to the one God:
210–16 special adaptability to *l*· on C. S.,
211– 7 else the blind will *l*· the blind
257–16 *l*· to immediate or ultimate death.
287–25 they *l*· to higher joys :
314– 9 *l*· in silent prayer,
354– 5 and *l*· the innocent to doom?
389– 4 * "To point to heaven and *l*· the way."
398–15 *L*· Thy lambkins to the fold,
Man. 85–10 not ready to *l*· his pupils.
Ret. 14–27 *l*· me in the way — Psal. 139 : 24.
46–21 *L*· Thy lambkins to the fold,
65– 6 *l*· to self-righteousness and
76–14 stairs which *l*· up to spiritual love.
Pul. 17–20 *L*· Thy lambkins to the fold,
32– 8 * to dominate, to *l*·, to control,
Rud. 9– 8 will *l*· to weakness in practice,
No. 33– 3 *l*· us to bless those who curse,
Hea. 5–25 would *l*· our lives to higher issues ;
Po. 14–19 *L*· Thy lambkins to the fold,
21–18 * point to heaven and *l*· the way."
My. 33–12 and *l*· me in the way — Psal. 139 : 24.
45–20 * to *l*· you in the way,
51–14 * who is so able as she to *l*· us
59–23 * feeble attempts to *l*· the singing.
140– 3 I will *l*· them — Isa. 42 : 16.
162–25 *l*· it gently into
213–20 see whether they *l*· you to God
347– 3 What remains to *l*· on the centuries

leaden
No. 34–16 falls with its *l*· weight

Leader
Man. 33– 5 A Reader not a *L*·.
33– 6 Church Reader shall not be a *L*·,
65– 3 A Member not a *L*·.
65– 6 shall not be called *L*· by members
(see also **Eddy**)

Leader
Pul. 89–35 * *L*·, Bloomington, Ill.
89–36 * *L*·, Cleveland, Ohio.

leader
Mis. 266– 9 The true *l*· of a true cause
295– 4 noted English *l*·, whom he quotes
371– 4 wandering about without a *l*·,

leader

Pul. 59–13   * *l·* responding with its parallel
Pan. 3–26   *l·* of the nymphs,
'00. 9–27   *l·* of this mighty movement.
My. 31–31   * trained carefully under one *l·*,
43–12   * obedient to the voice of their *l·*.
291–27   loss of her renowned *l·* !
(*see also* **Eddy**)

Leader's
(*see* **Eddy**)

leaders

Mis. 369–14   *l·* of materialistic schools
370–19   chapter sub-title
Pul. 79–27   * thought of the world's scientific *l·*
'01. 30–14   *l·* of a reform in religion
32–18   old-fashioned *l·* of religion
Peo. 11–23   *l·* of public thought
My. 40–14   * Through rivalries among *l·*
116–24   Had the ages helped their *l·*
340–20   *l·* of our rock-ribbed State.

leadership

Mis. 371– 7   to help them by his own *l·*?
Ret. 3– 6   gallant *l·* and death,
My. 28–19   * consecrated *l·* of Mrs. Eddy,
44–30   * unerring wisdom of your *l·*,
64–15   * all the years of her *l·*,
356– 4   His reflection of love and *l·*
362–20   * we rejoice in your inspired *l·*,

leadeth

Mis. 163–27   which *l·* into all Truth
174–32   Holy Ghost that *l·* into all Truth ;
189– 6   Comforter that *l·* into all truth.
322–14   feedeth my flock, and *l·* them
397–20   Love, whereto God *l·* me.
Pul. 19– 4   Love, whereto God *l·* me.
Po. 13– 8   Love, whereto God *l·* me.
My. 119–30   Truth that *l·* away from person

leading

Mis. 46– 4   The *l·* self-evident proposition of
59–24   *l·* his thoughts away from
66–28   blind *l·* the blind." — see *Matt.* 15 : 14.
85– 9   every thought and act *l·* to good.
85–12   regeneration *l·* thereto is
292–22   *l·* them, if *possible*, to Christ,
346–19   This *l·*, self-evident proposition of
Man. 98–18   in a *l·* Boston newspaper
Ret. 91–19   *l·* them into the divine order,
Un. 6–15   *l·* questions about God
42–25   *l·* man into the true sense of
Pul. 6–21   * I feel the truth is *l·* us
25–19   * *l·* to the auditorium,
26–28   * *l·* off the "Mother's Room" are
72– 5   * a few of the *l·* members
88– 1   chapter sub-title
88– 4   received *l·* newspapers with
Rud. 11– 3   schoolmaster, *l·* you to Christ ;
No. 12– 4   *l·* us to see spirituality
32– 7   a crime nor the motives *l·* to it.
34– 2   *l·* up to health, harmony, and
'01. 21– 5   a demonstrable Science *l·* the ages.
Hea. 5–10   One of our *l·* clergymen
Po. 43– 9   *L·* kine with love.
My. 45–23   * we see the earlier *l·*,
77– 7   * *l·* landmark of Boston,
77–19   * filled the streets *l·* to the
79–16   * in the *l·* newspapers of
82–30   * streets *l·* directly to
140–19   God is *l·* you onward
152–19   the blind is *l·* the blind,
163–24   *l·* people of this pleasant city
225–15   the *l·* of our Lord's Prayer.
252–22   *l·* humanity into paths of peace
270– 8   *l·* editors and newspapers of
283– 9   *l·* impetus of my life.
304–10   writing for the *l·* newspapers,
312– 2   supply the place of his *l·* teacher
353– 6   Extract from the *l·* Editorial

leadings

Mis. 49–22   opposes the *l·* of the divine Spirit

leads

Mis. 37–20   *l·* to moral or physical death.
49–19   spirit of Truth *l·* into all truth,
100–15   *l·* on irresistible forces,
295– 6   power which in America *l·* women
344– 7   aught of that which *l·* to bliss,
347–27   from the night He *l·* to light.
351–25   life that *l·* unto death,
Ret. 73– 9   great fact *l·* into profound depths.
88–17   *l·* inevitably to a consideration
Un. 18– 2   necessarily *l·* to extinction
26–11   belief in which *l·* to such teaching
55–12   suffering which *l·* out of the flesh.
Rud. 6– 1   *l·* to the equal inference that

leads

Rud. 10–28   *l·* you to believe in the existence
My. 77– 5   * *l·* the Auditorium of Chicago.
272–26   * *l·* with such conspicuous success
339– 3   whose every link *l·* upward

leaf

Po. 22–12   'Tis writ on earth, on *l·* and
53– 3   The bud, the *l·* and wing
My. 149–30   solicit every root and every *l·*
192–27   and leave a *l·* of olive ;

leaflet (*see also* **leaflet's**)

Po. 41– 7   fountain and *l·* are frozen

leaflet's

Po. 31–11   veils the *l·* wondrous birth

leaflets

Man. 46–10   cards, or *l·*, which advertise
Po. 8– 9   vestal pearls that on *l·* lay,

leafy

Po. 34– 8   In what dark *l·* grove

league

Mis. 79–29   Beware of joining any medical *l·*
80– 6   *l·* which obligates its members
80–11   everybody, . . . can join this *l·*.
My. 200–24   relinquish its *l·* with evil.

leagued

Mis. 177– 6   *l·* together in secret conspiracy

leagues

Mis. 110–20   *l·* have lain between us.

lean

Mis. 298– 1   *l·* not unto thine own — *Prov.* 3 : 5.
Ret. 13–19   bade me *l·* on God's love,
'01. 34–30   *l·* not unto thine own — *Prov.* 3 : 5.
Peo. 8–17   and *l·* upon it for health and life.
My. 129–28   *L·* not too much on your Leader.
245–15   persecution, and *l·* glory,

leaned

'02. 15– 5   I *l·* on God, and was safe.

leaner

Mis. 131– 8   let the *l·* sort console this brother's

leaning

Ret. 16–13   went into the church *l·* on crutches

leap

Mis. 126– 6   in tones that *l·* for joy,
Un. 64–15   *l·* the dark fissures,
No. 44–11   no hobby, . . . that can *l·* into the
'02. 3–30   the first lie and *l·* into perdition
My. 129–18   ye who *l·* disdainfully from

leaped

My. 81–13   * up *l·* half a dozen Scientists.
104–20   has *l·* into living love.

learn

Mis. xii– 6   "*l·* war no more," — see *Isa.* 2 : 4.
3– 9   we *l·* in divine Science
10–28   mortals *l·* at last the lesson,
14–12   in order to *l·* Science,
16–19   We must *l·* that God is
37–13   *l·* the meaning of those words
42–24   *l·* that good, not evil, lives
77–23   there *l·*, in divine Science,
85–31   and to *l·* their way out of both
125–18   *l·* forever the infinite meanings
128– 4   to *l·* or to teach briefly ;
129– 6   first lesson is to *l·* one's self ;
176–11   It is then that we *l·*
183–14   we *l·* this, and receive it :
183–15   *l·* which man can fulfil the
185–23   to *l·* his origin and age,
186–13   We *l·* in the Scriptures,
199–18   *l·* somewhat of the qualities
205–31   who on the shores of time *l·*
205–32   and live what they *l·*,
207– 1   *L·* its purpose ;
200–15   compels mortals to *l·* that
230–25   * *L·* to labor and to wait."
233–31   *l·* that sensation is not in matter,
235–19   *l·* God aright, and know
251–25   *l·* a parable of the period,
252–12   *l·* that sick thoughts are
254–15   *l·* that he must at last
278–26   *l·* by the things they suffer,
279–15   from which we *l·* without study.
283–30   *l·* the principle of music
317–13   *l·* by spiritual growth
328– 2   *l·* from the things they suffer.
330–19   *l·* what report they bear,
341–18   O *l·* to lose with God !
341–29   We *l·* from this parable
355–21   *L·* what in thine own mentality
359–19   He had to *l·* from experience ;
366– 5   to *l·* the doctrine of theology,
378–15   to *l·* his practice,

learn

Mis.	387–20	*L·,* too, that wisdom's rod is given
	391– 9	And *l·* that Truth and wisdom
Man.	53–15	Not to *L·* Hypnotism.
	53–16	shall not *l·* hypnotism
Ret.	38–18	to *l·* that he had printed all
	49–14	Mortals must *l·* to lose their
	54– 9	and *l·* the divine way,
	79–24	* "*L·* to labor and to wait."
Un.	6– 4	whole human race will *l·* that,
	10–23	to *l·* the principle of
	10–26	Mortals must *l·* this ;
	13–12	*l·,* proportionately as we gain
	13–19	He must *l·* to *unknow,*
	28–17	*l·* Soul only as we *l·* God,
	41– 4	we must *l·* it of good.
	41– 5	Of evil we can never *l·* it,
	45–10	egotist must come down and *l·,*
	55–19	*l·* how false are the pleasures
	62–11	*l·* that there is no Life in evil.
Pul.	49–30	* to *l·* that this rich woman
	81– 3	* *l·* that the name of Christ
Rud.	2– 7	In C. S. we *l·* that God
	4–22	we can only *l·* and love Him
	10–26	must *l·* to acknowledge God
	11– 6	you *l·* that God is good,
No.	11–20	than to *l·* theology, physiology,
	27–28	they may *l·* the definition of
	42– 1	* more and more *l·* their duty
	43–22	to *l·* a system which they
'00.	8–26	*L·* to obey ;
	8–26	*l·* first what obedience is.
'01.	31– 8	*l·* and love the truths of C. S.
'02.	8– 7	When loving, we *l·* that
	17– 7	When mortals *l·* to love aright ;
	17– 7	when they *l·* that man's highest
Hea.	8–21	*l·* to reach heaven through
	9–27	*l·* this grand truth
	12– 5	to *l·* what matter is doing
	14–22	teach them how to *l·,*
	14–22	together with what they *l·.*
	17–12	*l·* this as we awake to behold
Peo.	2– 1	*l·* our capabilities for good,
	2– 7	we shall *l·* what God is,
	2–10	*l·* that God, good, is universal,
	6–16	when we *l·* God aright, we love Him,
	9–25	whereby we *l·* the great fact
Po.	6–15	*L·,* too, that wisdom's rod is
	38– 8	And *l·* that Truth and wisdom
My.	24– 1	* *l·* that the truth which Christ
	104–28	to *l·* of her who, thirty years ago,
	119– 7	In Science, we *l·* that man is
	121– 7	In metaphysics we *l·* that the
	142–18	*l·* this and rejoice with me,
	151–23	We *l·* from the Scriptures that
	181–17	all nations shall speedily *l·*
	185– 7	* *L·* to labor and to wait."
	197–16	*l·* that the translucent atmosphere of
	226–21	in this you *l·* to hallow His name,
	264– 5	until mankind *l·* more of my meaning
	278– 5	may *l·* to make war no more,
	303– 5	It suffices me to *l·* the Science of
	305–23	to *l·* definitely more from my
	346– 8	* *l·* authoritatively from the *Herald*

learned (adj.)

Mis.	363–28	Bible is the *l·* man's masterpiece,
Ret.	7–16	* As a lawyer he was able and *l·,*
Hea.	14–11	be sure he is a *l·* man and skilful ;
Peo.	6– 2	* "I am sick of *l·* quackery."
	11–25	The *l·* quacks of this period
My.	104– 3	thought that the *l·* St. Paul,
	296– 2	* able discourse of our "*l·* judge,"

learned (verb)

Mis.	3–20	We have *l·* that the erring
	14–12	could never be *l·* ;
	23– 1	having *l·* so much ;
	24–18	I *l·* that mortal thought
	41– 3	having *l·* the power of
	55–11	having *l·* the power of the
	110–27	*l·* how fleeting is that
	126– 8	Who hath not *l·* that when
	126–11	have *l·* that trials lift us
	128–12	both *l·,* and received, — *Phil.* 4 : 9.
	147–10	*l·* that sin is inadmissible,
	173– 5	*l·* of the schools that there is
	173– 8	has ever *l·* from the schools,
	190–14	needs yet to be *l·.*
	192–19	*l·* its adaptability to
	234– 7	not *l·* of the material senses,
	276–29	quickly *l·* when the door is shut.
	278–15	*l·* that a curse on sin is always a
	281– 7	I *l·* long ago that the world
	309–31	more than they have yet *l·.*
Ret.	9–23	* *l·* at last to know His voice
	21– 8	had *l·* that his mother still lived,

learned (verb)

Ret.	25–24	I *l·* that these material senses
	28– 9	I had *l·* that thought must be
	28–22	I had *l·* that Mind reconstructed
	32– 5	*l·* that whatever is loved materially,
	35– 8	having *l·* that the merits of C. S.
	45– 5	it was *l·* that material
	61–28	that however little be taught or *l·,*
	79– 3	spiritual truth *l·* and loved ;
Un.	57–21	he *l·* that spiritual grace was
Pul.	35–13	"I had *l·* that thought must
	35–21	I had *l·* that Mind reconstructed
	82–10	* She has long *l·* with patience,
No.	25–21	remains to be *l·.*
	28–10	Science of being must be *l·*
Pan.	12– 2	*l·* that good is not educed from evil,
'00.	7–15	having suffered, lived, and *l·,*
	10–25	I have *l·* it was a private soldier
'01.	17–24	*l·* that the dynamics of medicine
	22–25	*l·* its numeration table,
Hea.	6–13	When I *l·* how mind produces
	6–14	I *l·* how it produces the
	9–10	having *l·* that this method
	11–21	reached this high goal you have *l·*
	12–12	we *l·* from the Scripture
Peo.	2–12	this Principle is *l·* through goodness,
Po.	77–15	When we have *l·* of Truth
My.	vi– 8	* except as he has *l·* it from her
	21–14	* Christian Scientists have *l·*
	43– 8	* they *l·* to know Him.
	43–10	* but they *l·* from experience
	43–26	* We have *l·* from experience,
	61– 4	* lessons I have *l·* of the power of
	124–27	Now what have you *l·* ?
	125– 1	Have you *l·* to conquer sin,
	188–26	When it is *l·* that spiritual sense
	195–20	C. S. is at length *l·* to be
	269– 6	Then shall humanity have *l·*
	271– 7	I *l·* the truth of what I
	315–12	* I *l·* that Mary Baker G. Eddy,
	332–25	* it was *l·* that the lodge was
	343–15	I have simply taught as I *l·*

learner

Mis.	43–15	to the sick and to the *l·*
	43–30	on the practice of the *l·,*
	66–32	to the present capability of the *l·,*
	243–15	Principle, which the *l·* can

learning (*see also* learning's)

Mis.	47– 4	By *l·* that matter is but
	178–20	'Much *l·*'— or something else
	183–17	not by reason of the schools, or *l·,*
Ret.	10–14	*L·* was so illumined, that grammar
Un.	14–27	would become better by *l·* to
Pul.	72– 3	* *l·* the feeling of Scientists
No.	4– 2	task of *l·* thoroughly the Science
	11–16	the place in schools of *l·*
	33– 6	rightful place in schools of *l·,*
	39–17	True prayer . . . is *l·* to love,
'02.	2–11	religions, ethics, and *l·,*
	3–16	her dusky children are *l·* to read
My.	4–19	*l·* that Mind-power is good will
	65–13	* *L·* that a big church was required,
	79–11	* seat of *l·* of America ;
	114–26	*l·* the higher meaning of this book
	228– 4	by *l·* that so-called disease is a
	340–31	Institutions of *l·* and . . . religion

learning's

Ret.	11– 7	On *l·* lore and wisdom's might,
Po.	60– 3	On *l·* lore and wisdom's might,

learns

Mis.	58– 4	Waking . . . one *l·* its *unreality ;*
	58– 7	*l·* that consumption did not kill
	85– 6	*l·* spiritually all that he
	184–21	*l·* that all power is good
	195– 5	*l·* the letter of C. S.
	221– 6	*l·* more of its divine Principle.
Ret.	38–28	*l·* the letter of this book,
Hea.	14–20	*l·* the metaphysical treatment
Po.	1–17	to meditate on what it *l·*
My.	161–29	*l·* through meekness and love

leases

Mis.	340–16	drew up logs instead of *l·.*

least

Mis.	2– 4	who have the *l·* wisdom or
	7–12	where one would *l·* expect it,
	12–18	in a manner *l·* understood ;
	30– 2	we prove it, in at *l·* some
	37–28	is in reality the *l·* difficult
	43–10	is the one *l·* likely to
	55– 3	and the *l·* understanding . . . thereof
	59–27	who asserts himself the *l·,*
	80–30	at *l·* not until it shall come to
	119–22	Insubordination . . . even in the *l·,*
	126– 4	for once, at *l·,* to hear the soft

least

Mis.	224–10	* I don't feel hurt in the *l*.''
	228– 3	by those deemed at *l*· indebted
	291–12	or at *l*· it so appears in results.
	356–17	"the *l*· of all seeds,"— *Matt.* 13 : 32.
Man.	68– 2	member of this Church at *l*· three
	73– 4	at *l*· one active practitioner
	110–12	one, at *l*·, of the given names
Ret.	28–11	in order to have the *l*· understanding
Un.	56–21	he suffers *l*· from sin who is
Pul.	32– 4	* No photographs can do the *l*· justice
	35–15	in order to have the *l*· understanding
	55– 7	* not the *l*· eventful circumstance is
	80– 8	* sought the line of *l*· resistance.
	82–25	* at *l*· to help enforce the laws
	82–29	* and in this fair land at *l*·
	87–16	If it will comfort you in the *l*·,
No.	21–28	and is, to say the *l*·,
Pan.	6–23	religion has at *l*· two Gods.
'02.	2–25	or at *l*· agree to disagree,
	18–15	unto one of the *l*·— *Matt.* 25 : 40.
My.	88– 2	* at *l*· an æsthetic debt to
	91–29	* at *l*· it is the largest in
	174–10	And last but not *l*·,
	182–14	seemed the *l*· among seeds,
	197– 3	*l*· distinct to conscience.
	228–14	"He that is *l*·— *Matt.* 11 : 11.
	228–16	reign of holiness, in the *l*·
	240– 2	from the *l*· to the greatest,

leave

Mis.	37–12	*l*· the animal for the spiritual,
	43–30	the damaging effects these *l*·
	80–13	who *l*· C. S. to rise or fall
	194–22	how to *l*· self, the sense material,
	215– 5	peace I *l*· with thee :— *see John* 14 : 27.
	235–24	*l*· Christianity unbiased by
	249–24	will never *l*· me comfortless,
	264–20	Some students *l*· my instructions
	270–21	we cannot *l*· Christ for the
	274–10	therefore I *l*· all for Christ.
	293– 4	*l*· the righteous unfolding of error
	301–16	must not *l*· persistent plagiarists
	302–17	not to *l*· the Word unspoken
	324–21	seeks to *l*· the odious company
Ret.	23– 1	to *l*· me undisturbed in the
	63–24	and *l*· the subject there.
	79–15	*l*· the inscrutable problem
	83–20	*l*· S. and H. to God's
	90–29	*l*· with God the government
Un.	1–15	better *l*· the subject untouched,
Pul.	69–12	*l*· no room there for the bad,
No.	v–11	*l*· the meat and take the
	7–25	*L*· the distinctions of individual
	34– 4	shall *l*· the ceremonial law
	45–25	*l*· cradle and swaddling-clothes.
'00.	2–21	*l*· a lucrative business to
'01.	5–17	*l*· all sin to God's fiat
'02.	11– 1	to *l*· on a foreign shore.
Hea.	13–16	*l*· the drug out of the question,
	16–16	we will *l*· our abstract subjects
Peo.	6–26	for which we are to *l*· all else.
Po.	27–15	Though thou must *l*· the tear,
My.	56–27	* were obliged to *l*· the church
	114–20	would *l*· me until the rising of the
	117– 6	motive gratified by sense will *l*·
	130– 1	*l*· the latter to propagate.
	138–18	except I *l*· all for Christ.
	155–11	*l*· behind those things that
	167–12	*l*· their loving benedictions upon
	192–27	and *l*· a leaf of olive ;
	242–23	these duties to the Clerk
	311– 9	* I shall have to *l*· ;
	323–10	* nor willingly *l*· any false impression.
	325– 4	* to *l*· luscious hothouse fruit.

leaven

Mis.	39–20	enough of the *l*· of Truth
	39–20	to *l*· the whole lump,
	149– 6	to help *l*· your loaf
	166–22	*l*· that a certain woman hid
	171–23	is like unto *l*·,— *Matt.* 13 : 33.
	174–30	The *l*· which a woman took
	175– 8	spiritual *l*· of divine Science
	175–13	the *l*· expands the loaf.
	175–14	the old *l*· of the scribes
	175–15	"the *l*· of malice— *I Cor.* 5 : 8.
	366–18	the *l*· of the scribes — *see Matt.* 16 : 6.
Pul.	5–28	This book is the *l*· fermenting
'02.	2–16	*l*· hid in three measures
Po.	24– 3	A balm — the long-lost *l*·
My.	4–12	with the *l*· of divine Love
	59– 5	* the little *l*· that should *l*·

leavened

Mis.	166–26	until the whole shall be *l*·
	171–24	till the whole was *l*·.— *Matt.* 13 : 33.
	175– 5	the whole sense of being is *l*·

leavening

Mis.	166–24	C. S., is *l*· the lump
My.	114–28	this book is *l*· the whole lump

leavens

No.	43–11	* "Your book *l*· my sermons.''
My.	272– 2	*l*· the loaf of life with justice,

leaves

Mis.	6– 3	*l*· mortals but little time
	31–17	*l*· the individual no alternative
	130– 4	She readily *l*· the answer
	142–18	shaded as autumn *l*·
	165–13	*l*· nothing that is material ;
	188–19	right there he *l*· the subject.
	251–25	falling *l*· of old-time faiths
	251–28	even as dry *l*· fall
	330– 1	the *l*· clap their hands,
	331–22	falling *l*· of old-time faiths,
	341– 3	*l*· the unreal material basis
	390–17	The timid, trembling *l*·.
Man.	68– 6	member who *l*· her in less time
	69– 8	*l*· her before the expiration of
Ret.	18– 5	colored softly by blossom and *l*· ;
	75–23	when he *l*· the University,
	94–12	*l*· no flesh, no matter,
	95– 2	and its *l*· will be
Pul.	8– 4	the *l*· of an ancient oak,
	26–24	* with sprays of fig *l*·
Rud.	14–23	*l*· them unprepared to
No.	2– 7	*l*· you to work against that
'00.	4–18	*l*· the beaten path of human
	5– 4	*l*· no opportunity for idolatry
'02.	9–16	that *l*· the minor tones
Peo.	14– 4	evergreen *l*·, fragrant recesses,
Po.	9– 9	*l*· all faded, the fruitage shed,
	16–18	To the heart of the *l*·
	46– 6	its *l*· have shed
	55–18	The timid, trembling *l*·
	63–11	softly by blossom and *l*· ;
My.	3–10	*l*· of faith without works,
	89–11	* sect that *l*· such a monument
	99–29	* *l*· no choice but the acceptance
	218–17	*l*· the divine Principle of
	260–27	It *l*· hygiene, medicine,
	347–13	* that cannot shed Your *l*·,

leaving

Mis.	11–22	not *l*· all retribution to God
	34– 1	*l*· none of the harmful "after effects"
	37–27	*l*· to her students the work of
	58–27	*l*· it a human "mind-cure,"
	111–15	*L*· the seed of Truth to its
	240–30	or, *l*· these on,
	242–24	*l*· the patient well,
	242–29	before *l*· the class he took a
	358–31	*l*· the material forms thereof
Ret.	84–29	he should avoid *l*· his own
No.	19–24	*l*· sin, sense rises to the fulness
'01.	26–25	Before *l*· this subject of the
'02.	3–13	*l*· her in the enjoyment of
Peo.	7– 2	*l*· the impress of mind
	7– 4	*l*· to rot and ruin the mind's ideals.
	9– 5	love *l*· self for God.
My.	196–16	*l*· us an example,— *I Pet.* 2 : 21.
	263– 2	*l*· one alone and without His glory.
	301– 7	*l*· a solid Christianity at the
	350– 2	*l*· science at the beck of
	350– 3	*l*· it out of the question.

Lebanon, Ind.

Pul.	70– 1	* *The Reporter, L*·, *I*·.,

Lebanon, Pa.

Pul.	88–29	* *Evening Reporter, L*·, *P*·.

lecture

Mis.	280–19	at close of the *l*· on the fourth
Man.	73–20	may *l*· for said university
	93– 8	The *l*· year shall begin July 1
	93–12	to include in each *l*· a true
	94– 3	unite in their attendance on his *l*·,
	94– 4	for their churches a less *l*· fee ;
	94– 7	after a *l*· on C. S.,
	94–18	shall *l*· in the United States,
	95– 7	to *l*· at such places
	95–15	a member of the Board may *l*·
	95–20	No *l*· shall be given by a
	96– 3	shall not appoint a *l*· for
	96– 4	*L*· Fee.
	96– 4	The *l*· fee shall be left to
	96–10	If a lecturer receive a call to *l*·
Ret.	40–22	my notices for a second *l*·
No.	27–19	Bishop Foster said, in a *l*·
Peo.	5–26	Wendell Holmes said, in a *l*·
My.	296– 1	chapter sub-title
	304–15	invited to *l*· in London,
	304–21	In a *l*· in Chicago,

lecture

My. 338–11 The contents of the last *l·*
338–13 till after the *l·* was delivered
338–19 talented author of this *l·*

lectured

Ret. 42– 9 *l·* so ably on Scriptural topics
My. 304–12 I have *l·* in large and crowded

lecturer (see also lecturer's)

Man. 94– 1 The *l·* can invite churches
96– 5 the discretion of the *l·*.
96– 9 If a *l·* receive a call
Rud. 11–25 The *l·*, teacher, or healer

lecturer's

Man. 96– 6 The *l·* traveling expenses

lecturers

Man. 93–10 Duty of *L·*.

lectures

Mis. 48–13 at one of his recent *l·*
Man. 93–16 shall mail . . . copies of his *l·*
95– 2 CALLS FOR *l·*.
95–16 Annual *L·*.
95–19 for one or more *l·*.
95–20 No *L·* by Readers.
96– 1 No Wednesday Evening *L·*.
Pul. 36– 9 * I was present at the class *l·*
47– 2 * *l·* upon Scriptural topics.
Rud. 15–26 Public *l·* cannot be such
16– 2 public *l·* can take the place of
16– 5 *L·* in public are needed,
My. 125–16 When reading their *l·*,

Lectureship

(see **Board of Lectureship**)

lectureship

Mis. 95– 2 * platform of the Monday *l·*

lecturing

Mis. 239– 6 *L·*, writing, preaching,
266–25 in teaching or *l·* on C. S.,

led

Mis. 85–30 are thereby *l·* to Christ,
225–18 * I may be *l·* to believe.''
278–32 *l·* to some startling departures
296– 8 which I the unknown author
301–16 to be long *l·* into temptation ;
326–19 if they would be *l·* to the valley
Ret. 9– 2 *l·* my cousin into an adjoining
24–14 *l·* me to the discovery
27–29 *l·* me into a new world of light
30–19 Even so was I *l·* into
48–29 has *l·* to higher ways, means, and
50– 4 *l·* to name three hundred dollars
50– 8 *l·*, by a strange providence,
81–29 *l·* me to the feet of C. S.,
Pul. 43– 3 * *l·* the singing, under the
Pan. 14–23 *l·* by the dauntless Dewey,
'00. 12–13 *l·* northward and southward.
'02. 15–28 had *l·* me to write that book,
Po. 2– 9 Guided and *l·*, can never reach
My. 110–26 ''*l·* captivity captive,'' — *Psal.* 68 : 18.
212– 1 victim is *l·* to believe
314– 5 * *l·* a roving existence.

lees

My. 301– 6 the *l·* of religion will be lost,

left

Mis. 14– 2 neither place nor power *l·* for evil.
34–18 no more come to those they have *l·*,
65–11 *L·* to the decision of Science,
69–16 and then had *l·* him to die.
75– 1 may have all that is *l·* of it ;
89–18 *l·* this precaution for others.
90–29 *l·* their nets to follow him,
100– 3 *l·* to the providence of God.
106– 8 M. D.'s to *l·* of them,
165–18 *l·* to mortals the rich legacy
169–21 *l·* for our spiritual instruction.
178– 4 He has *l·* his old church,
179–16 Have we *l·* the consciousness of
180– 9 ''Christ never *l·*,'' I replied ;
188–22 And she has *not l·* it,
212– 6 *l·* his glorious career for our
267–19 while the *l·* beats its way downward,
274– 8 if *l·* undone might hinder the
310–28 all persons who have *l·* our fold,
326–27 is *l·* unto you desolate.'' — *Matt.* 23 : 38.
340– 6 neither to the right nor to the *l·*,
343–24 until no seedling be *l·* to propagate
348–13 Error, *l·* to itself, accumulates.
355–17 To strike out right and *l·*
378– 4 *l·* that institution,
378–10 *l·* the water-cure,
Man. 86–10 whose teacher has *l·* them,
87– 6 Choice of patients is *l·* to the
91–16 Any surplus funds *l·* in the

left

Man. 96– 5 *l·* to the discretion of the
Ret. 5– 2 *l·* bank of the Merrimac River.
8–21 I then *l·* the room,
14–18 *l·* me outside the doors.
16– 7 since she *l·* the choir
38–16 afternoon that he *l·* Boston
90– 9 and then *l·* them to starve
Un. 5–26 *l·* to the supernal guidance.
42– 2 there is no place *l·* for it.
Pul. 42–29 * on its *l·* a vase filled with
47–29 * nothing is *l·* excepting the
59–29 * *l·* by the rear doors,
81–25 * all that the twelve have *l·* undone.
83–30 * and he, departing, *l·* his scepter
Rud. 13–27 out *l·* to be fed, clothed, and
15– 3 *l·* it understanding sufficiently the
No. 30– 6 until nothing is *l·* to be forgiven,
36– 6 never *l·* heaven for earth.
'00. 12–18 *l·* thy first love — *Rev.* 2 : 4.
15–23 *l·* thy first love, — *Rev.* 2 : 4.
'01. 10–26 shall be nothing *l·* to perish
23– 3 little *l·* that the sects and
26–18 *l·* to such as see God
26–19 *l·* to them of a sound faith
27–24 and *l·* C. S. as it is,
29– 8 should not be *l·* to the mercy of
'02. 2–26 I never *l·* the Church,
2–27 I but began where the Church *l·* off.
7–14 nothing is *l·* to consciousness but
Po. 41–11 forsaken, and *l·* them to stray
65– 8 And *l·* but a parting in air.
68– 1 So one heart is *l·* me
My. 50– 4 * *l·* their former church homes,
92–18 * would soon be *l·* behind.
94– 2 * every other sect will be *l·* behind
99–17 * not a cent of indebtedness *l·*.
107–12 have not an iota of the drug *l·*
117–28 I *l·* Boston in the height of
126– 8 his *l·* foot on the earth,'' — *Rev.* 10 : 2.
130–18 A lie *l·* to itself is not
214–22 I had no monetary means *l·*
232–12 Our Lord and Master *l·* to us the
246–13 closed my College . . . . *l·* Boston,
257– 7 the Bethlehem babe has *l·* his
303–22 he *l·* his legacy of truth
312– 8 * He *l·* his young wife in a
317–17 *l·* my diction quite out of the
322–31 * the impression he *l·* with me was
323– 2 * Before we *l·* that evening,
333–27 * He has *l·* an amiable wife,

legacies

My. 201–11 repeat my *l·* in blossom.

legacy

Mis. 2–11 Adam *l·* must first be seen,
124–25 Love's great *l·* to mortals :
165–18 left to mortals the rich *l·* of
Ret. 92– 7 inherit his *l·* of love,
Pul. 87–25 a *l·* to our race.
My. 303–22 he left his *l·* of truth

legal

Mis. 140–10 over matter or merely *l·* titles.
140–13 I supposed the trustee-deed was *l·* ;
140–22 rescued from the grasp of *l·* power,
141–18 concerned about the *l·* quibble,
141–28 no *l·* authority for obtaining,
Man. 45–23 *L·* Titles.
46– 4, 5 *l·* adoption and *l·* marriage,
49–19 A *L·* Ceremony.
67–10 Unauthorized *L·* Action.
67–12 nor take *l·* action on a case
70–22 the *l·* title of The Mother Church.
Ret. 49–20 granted to a *l·* *college* for teaching
'02. 13–19 through my *l·* counsel.
13–20 *l·* proceedings were instituted by
My. 217–13 shall have arrived at *l·* age,
327– 6 made it *l·* to practise C. S.
327–28 * *l·* protection and recognition,

legalized

My. 5– 5 synonymous with *l·* lust,

legally

Mis. 226–27 cannot stoop to notice, except *l·*,
249–10 has been met and answered *l·*.
272–25 * but one *l·* chartered college
297– 6 by *l·* coercive measures,
297–23 or this contract is *l·* dissolved.
Man. 49–21 clergyman who is *l·* authorized.
75–17 land whereon they stand, *l·* ;
78– 7 shall not be made *l·* responsible
'02. 13–26 land *l·* conveyed to me,
My. 327– 1 *l·* to protect the practice

legendary

Ret. 22– 7 *l·* and traditional history

legends
Pul. 28– 7 * emblematic designs, with the l·,
legerdemain
My. 195–21 no miserable piece of ideal l·,
legibly
Man. 109–16 see that names are l· written,
legion
Mis. 366–31 false theories whose names are l·,
Pul. 81–20 * and their name is l·.
legislation
Mis. 80–16 unjust coercive l·
211–10 medical bills, class l·,
274–24 news-dealers shout for class l·,
Peo. 11–20 obedient to the l· of mind,
My. 128– 6 board of health, or class l·
340–12 and her frown on class l·.
legislative
Mis. 208– 6 Like a l· bill that governs
Peo. 11–19 as men pass l· acts
My. 167–24 disposal of the l· question
legislator
No. 30–10 any more than the l· need know
legislators
Mis. 208– 7 mortals whom the l· know not,
Peo. 11–22 l· who are greatly responsible
Legislature
Ret. 6–25 was soon elected to the L·
6–28 were carried through the L·
My. 310– 7 member of the New Hampshire L·,
327– 4 in the L· of North Carolina,
327–14 * last winter's term of our L·,
327–20 * section of an act in the L·,
328–11 * passed by the last L·,
328–23 * machinery act of the L·
legislatures
My. 320– 3 * l· and courts are thus
legitimate
Mis. 287– 9 the l· affection of Soul,
Un. 22–16 though not so l· a child of
54–18 becomes l· to mortals,
No. 9–10 to prevent their l· action
44–18 l· to the human race,
'02. 14–14 are its l· fruit.
My. 37–21 * the activities of l· existence,
41–25 * postpone his l· joy,
159–22 l· and eternal demands
legs
My. 178–12 * "counting the l· of insects"?
Leibnitz
No. 99 4 L·, Descartes, Fichte,
'01. 24–18 L·, Berkeley, Darwin,
lend
Mis. 146– 6 I cannot conscientiously l· my
342–19 "Oh, l· us your oil! — see Matt. 25:8.
My. 211–18 l· themselves as willing tools
lends
Mis. 320–10 l· its resplendent light
Pul. 53–27 * healing gift he l· to them
My. 158–14 to-day l· a new-born beauty
length
Mis. x– 4 has at l· offered itself for
xi–17 at l· be found to surpass
29–26 health and l· of days.
67–16 happiness, and l· of days.
120–17 will at l· be heard above the din
223– 4 at l· took up the research
227– 4 must at l· be given up
286–32 stop at l· at the spiritual ultimate:
291–23 at l· dissolve into thin air.
324–29 at l· reaches the pleasant path
326– 9 the flesh at l· did feel them;
My. 195–20 C. S. is at l· learned to be
273–27 at l· they are consigned to dust.
lengthen
Mis. 352–12 shadows of thought l·
lengthened
My. 52–32 * weeks l· into months;
lengthens
My. 146–10 "If wisdom l· my sum of years
177–10 if wisdom l· my sum of years
length'ning
Po. 3– 4 noonday's l· shadows flee,
leniency
No. 9–15 too great l·, on my part,
lens
Mis. 129–20 to magnify under the l· that
164–27 by means of the l· of Science,
194–16 The l· of Science magnifies the

lens
Mis. 299– 6 look through the l· of C. S.,
356–25 Humility is l· and prism to
Ret. 87–25 only through the l· of their
'01. 12–22 The l· of Science magnifies the
My. 129–15 seen through the l· of Spirit,
lenses
Pul. vii–12 its l· of more spiritual mentality,
lent
Pul. 45– 1 * l· a helping hand,
leopard
Mis. 145–23 l· shall lie down with— Isa. 11:6.
leper
Mis. 124–18 healing the sick, cleansing the l·,
lepers
Mis. 168– 7 physical and moral l· are cleansed;
Pul. 29–18 * cleanse the l·,— Matt. 10:8.
53–11 * When the ten l· were cleansed
66–12 * cleanse the l·,— Matt. 10:8.
My. 300–26 cleanse the l·,— Matt. 10:8.
leprosy
Pul. 29–23 * to cleanse the l· of sin,
53–11 * Can drugs suddenly cure l·?
less
Mis. 17–23 birth is more or l· prolonged
36– 8 they manifest l· of Mind.
38–29 be of l· practical value.
47–16 with l· impediment than when
58–27 "mind-cure," nothing more nor l·,
60– 6 regard sin, . . . with l· deference,
62–13 by that much, l· available.
76–19 on other topics l· important.
85–19 infantile and more or l· imperfect.
88– 4 but the l· this is required,
108–26 This cognomen makes it l· dangerous;
126–24 even gold is l· current.
145–12 l· than man to whom God gave
145–13 l· the meek who
155–18 and l· wherein to answer it
163–10 l· human and more divine
186–24 cannot produce a l· perfect man
217– 5 Spirit cannot become l· than Spirit;
229–21 would thus become beautifully l·;
231–12 turkey grew beautifully l·.
239– 8 my shadow is not growing l·;
243–11 effected the cure in l· than one
250–10 no sentiment l· understood,
264–22 students are more or l· subject to
271–12 books which are l· than the best.
272–17 * fine not l· than five hundred
278–19 shared l· of my labors than many
282–12 much l· would we have our minds
283–16 nothing l· than a mistaken
289– 9 and of two evils choose the l·;
302–17 of two evils the l· would be
316–12 Until minds become l· worldly-minded,
318– 8 who are l· lovable or Christly.
319–12 l· or more to them than to other
321– 4 whose birth is l· of a miracle than
327–17 those who, having l· baggage,
355– 6 L· teaching and good healing
366–23 To a greater or l· extent,
370–20 What figure is l· favorable than
370–22 braying donkey . . . is l· troublesome.
374–32 l· artistic or less natural
Man. 44–14 tax of not l· than one dollar,
54– 4 for not l· than three years
68– 6 leaves her in l· time without
73– 1 not be organized with l· than sixteen
79– 4 not l· than three loyal members
87–18 "The l· the teacher personally
90–17 Not l· than two thorough lessons
94– 4 so make . . . a l· lecture fee;
94–17 shall not be l· than three years.
97–14 not l· than four thousand dollars.
102– 5 not l· than three members,
Ret. 10– 3 l· labor than is usually requisite.
22– 5 Writers l· wise than the apostles
33–12 the l· material medicine we have,
34– 4 Nothing l· could solve the
45–24 withstood l· the temptation
47–18 who partakes l· of God's love.
52– 7 its letter and l· of its spirit.
54– 5 It demands l· cross-bearing,
73–10 human concept grew beautifully l·
73–12 personal corporeality became l·
84–24 The l· the teacher personally controls
87–23 They feel their own burdens l·,
Un. 6–28 l· than another fifty years
28–14 and have l· basis;
49– 7 I believe l· in the sinner,
50–19 The l· consciousness of evil
Pul. 3– 4 Can Love be l· than boundless?

less

Pul.	10–20	If you are *l·* appreciated to-day
	51–11	* Every truth is more or *l·*
	62–18	* with infinitely *l·* expense.
	87–20	more of earth now, ... and *l·* of heaven ;
Rud.	2–13	if we think of Him as *l·* than
	9– 6	more or *l·* blended with error ;
	15– 9	renders the mind *l·* inquisitive,
No.	17–11	can never be *l·* than a good man ;
	24–15	become both *l·* and more in C. S.,
	24–18	and *l·*, because evil, being thus
	37–18	would make the atonement to be *l·*
Pan.	10– 2	and makes man *l·* than man.
	10–15	With twelve lessons or *l·*,
	11–20	content with something *l·* than
'01.	5– 6	become *l·* coherent than the
	8–19	can man be . . . *l·* than spiritual?
	18– 2	one thousand degrees *l·*
	18– 5	*l·* now than were the sneers
	23– 1	neither more nor *l·* than three ;
	27–22	*l·* of my own personality
'02.	9– 7	pride, and ease concern you *l·*,
	18–24	effective healers and *l·* theorizing ;
Hea.	1– 9	*l·* than an immortal basis,
	1–14	*l·* need of publishing the
	9– 6	The *l·* said or thought of sin,
	11–19	"The *l·* medicine the better,"
	13– 3	accomplish *l·* on either side.
Peo.	6–10	* *l·* sickness and *l·* mortality
	7–29	become more or *l·* perfect as
	7–30	more or *l·* spiritual.
Po.	35– 4	love thee as I love life *l·* !
My.	21–24	* to make no *l·* sacrifice than
	22–22	* nothing *l·* than God-bestowed.
	24–22	* no *l·* than fifteen different trades
	26–14	but not the *l·* appreciated.
	59– 8	* in *l·* than forty years
	66– 6	* no *l·* than ten estates having been
	77–14	* not *l·* than twenty-five thousand
	98– 5	* growth of *l·* than a score of years.
	98–20	* little *l·* than three years.
	99–22	* *L·* than a generation ago
	107–15	administers half a dozen or *l·*
	113– 3	not *l·* the evangel of C. S.
	123–22	is *l·* sufficient to receive a
	128– 7	class legislation is *l·* than the
	128– 8	and infinitely *l·* than God's benign
	147–31	You have *l·* need of me
	160– 9	It is of *l·* importance that we
	178–11	*l·* profitable or scientific
	220–30	seems *l·* divine.
	224–20	more fashionable but *l·* correct.
	224–23	books *l·* correct and therefore *l·*
	259–15	require *l·* attention than packages
	259–20	nothing *l·* is man or woman.
	265– 6	*l·* subordinate to material sight
	265– 7	evil flourishes *l·*, invests *l·*
	265–27	*l·* thunderbolts, tornadoes, and
	302–21	*l·* lauded, pampered, provided for,
	363–28	this . . . is more or *l·* dangerous.

lessen

'01.	15– 7	Scientist has enlisted to *l·* sin,
My.	200–27	spare this plunge, *l·* its depths,

lessened

Mis.	60–21	Mind's possibilities are not *l·* by
My.	296–17	mortal dream . . . has been *l·*,

lessening

Mis.	86– 7	though in *l·* degrees
My.	164– 2	would involve a *l·* of the

lessens

Mis.	122–21	*l·* not the hater's hatred
	362–31	*l·* the activities of virtue.
Pan.	10– 9	opposite notion that C. S. *l·*
My.	134–17	Life *l·* all pride — its pomp and

lesser

Un.	33– 1	There are *l·* arguments which prove
Hea.	14– 2	the bigger animal beats the *l·* ;
My.	252–31	cold impulse of a *l·* gain !

Lesson

Mis.	314–30	this *L·* shall be such as is

lesson

Mis.	10–17	The best *l·* of their lives
	10–28	mortals learn at last the *l·*,
	92–19	point out the *l·* to the class,
	125–17	press on to Life's long *l·*,
	126–20	silent *l·* of a good example.
	129– 6	first *l·* is to learn one's self ;
	138–15	first and last *l·* of C. S.
	207– 1	ponder this *l·* of love.
	278–27	the sooner this *l·* is gained
	310– 9	is the *l·* of to-day.
	336– 2	Hath not Science voiced this *l·*

lesson

Mis.	392–12	A *l·* grave, of life, that teacheth
Man.	31– 8	reading of the Sunday *l·*,
	31– 8	a *l·* on which the prosperity
	32–16	made but once during the *l·*.
Ret.	83–26	study each *l·* before the recitation.
	91–13	Where did Jesus deliver this great *l·*
Pul.	29–22	* *l·* was to be taken spiritually
No.	28–11	time for beginning the *l·*.
Po.	20–16	A *l·* grave, of life,
My.	34–29	* S. and H. references in this *l·*
	109–12	teaching them the same heavenly *l·*.
	150– 2	where its tender *l·* is not awaiting
	244–25	may not require more than one *l·*.

lessons

Mis.	3– 9	The *l·* we learn in
	81–30	It gives *l·* to human life,
	84–28	teaches Life's *l·* aright.
	91–31	study the *l·* before recitations.
	128– 3	*l·* of this so-called life
	180–20	chapter sub-title
	197– 1	incorporates their *l·* into our
	264–15	They are taught their first *l·*
	330–24	Nature's first and last *l·*
	349– 2	*l·* outside of my College,
	349– 3	provided he received these *l·* of
	349– 4	included about twelve *l·*,
	371– 1	this is among the first *l·*
	393–22	*L·* long and grand,
Man.	62–24	Subject for *L·*.
	62–25	The first *l·* of the children
	63– 4	The next *l·* consist of
	90–18	Not less than two thorough *l·*
Ret.	10– 9	received *l·* in the ancient tongues,
	21–23	lucid and enduring *l·* of Love
	23– 6	As these pungent *l·* became
	50– 6	course of *l·* at my College,
	50–14	even in half as many *l·*.
	81–30	Though our first *l·* are changed,
	91–14	this series of great *l·*
Un.	3– 1	*l·* of this primary school
Pul.	1–12	by reason of its large *l·*,
Rud.	15–27	cannot be such *l·* in C. S. as
	16– 3	take the place of private *l·* ;
Pan.	10–15	With twelve *l·* or less,
Po.	52– 6	*L·* long and grand,
My.	61– 4	* and the *l·* I have learned
	186– 4	writes in living characters their *l·*
	231–25	chapter sub-title
	231–30	the By-law, "Subject for *L·*"
	244– 8	one or more *l·* on C. S.,
	244–26	*l·* will certainly not exceed three

Lesson-Sermon

Man.	32–21	no remarks explanatory of the *L·*
	58–11	The *L·*.
	58–12	The subject of the *L·*
	58–16	texts in the *L·* shall extend from
My.	32–28	* the specially prepared *L·*.
	32–29	* After the reading of the *L·*,
	33– 8	* subject of the special *L·*
	34–14	* *L·* consisted of the following
	78–17	* At the close of the *L·*,

Lesson-Sermon on Dedication Sunday, June, 1906

My. pages 34, 35 references from Bible and S. and H.

lest

Mis.	109–29	*l·* thereby it master you ;
	210–31	*l·* it should suffer from
	211–19	afraid to do this *l·* he suffer,
	347– 2	*l·* thou also be like — *Prov.* 26 : 4.
	348–15	*l·* he be wise in — *Prov.* 26 : 5.
	398– 2	*L·* my footsteps stray ;
Ret.	46– 8	*L·* my footsteps stray ;
Un.	22– 7	not touch it, *l·* ye die.
	49–27	*l·* it destroy them.
Pul.	17– 7	*L·* my footsteps stray ;
No.	8–24	*l·* it turn and rend you ;
	40– 9	*l·* your pearls be trampled upon.
'01.	11–27	*l·* thou also be like — *Prov.* 26 : 4.
Po.	14– 6	*L·* my footsteps stray ;
My.	v– 2	* *L·* we forget — *l·* we forget !
	161–23	*L·* human reason becloud
	196–21	*l·* ye be wearied and faint — *Heb.* 12 : 3.
	201–22	*L·* my footsteps stray ;
	227–24	*l·* they trample them — *Matt.* 7 : 6.
	288–26	*l·* a worse thing come — *John* 5 : 14.

let

Mis.	3–30	"Satan *l·* loose." — *see Rev.* 20 : 7.
	10–11	God will not *l·* them be lost ;
	47–14	*l·* loose from its own beliefs.
	59–20	*l·* us reason together." — *Isa.* 1 : 18.
	69–10	"*L·* us make man — *Gen.* 1 : 26.
	69–11	*l·* them have dominion — *Gen.* 1 : 26.

let

Mis.	81– 6	l· each society of practitioners,
	87– 7	l· us say of the beauties of
	91– 7	l· it be in concession to the
	111–27	L· me specially call the attention
	120–15	L· us rejoice, however, that
	121–27	nor l· me go."— *Luke* 22: 68.
	122–17	"L· us do evil, that— *Rom.* 3: 8.
	129– 4	l· him put his finger to his lips,
	129–13	"l· the dead bury their— *Matt.* 8: 22.
	129–13	l· silence prevail over his remains.
	131– 8	l· the leaner sort console this
	131–15	l· it do so;
	131–26	l· her state the value thereof,
	134–17	L· no consideration bend or
	141–19	L· this be speedily done.
	141–21	l· the divine will and the
	141–29	and l· them, not you, say
	142–13	L· me write to the donors,
	145– 9	l· him ask himself, and answer
	145–16	l· not mortal thought resuscitate too
	145–32	l· me say, 'T is sweet to
	148–28	L· the invitation to this sweet
	154–28	L· your light reflect Light.
	156–11	L· the reign of peace and harmony
	158–22	L· us be faithful and obedient,
	169–30	"L· the dead bury their— *Matt.* 8: 22.
	172– 4	l· us declare the positive
	172– 7	l· us meet and defeat the claims of
	174– 6	L· us have a clearing up of
	174– 6	L· us come into the presence
	174– 8	L· us attach our sense of Science to
	174–10	L· us open our affections to
	180–18	L· us do our work;
	186–18	l· us not lose this Science of man,
	191–31	L· us obey St. Paul's injunction
	194– 5	L· us, then, seek this Science;
	197–12	l· us see what it is to believe.
	197–20	"l· this Mind be in you,— *Phil.* 2: 5.
	197–29	L· man abjure a theory that is
	208–12	and to l· His will be done.
	208–15	to do His will or to l· it be done?
	211–22	When one protects . . . l· him remember,
	211–29	drink it all, and l· all drink of it.
	215– 7	Arise, l· us go hence;— *John* 14: 31.
	215– 7	l· us depart from the material
	215–10	l· us not seek to climb up some other
	220– 4	L· us suppose that there is a
	230– 6	l· him make the most of the
	230–22	* "L· us, then, be up and doing,
	238–19	L· one's life answer
	239– 1	l· me say to you, dear reader:
	240–14	l· it remain as harmlessly,
	253–10	come, l· us kill him, *Luke* 20: 14.
	254–14	come, l· us kill him,— *Luke* 20: 14.
	267– 9	l· them remember that there never
	268–24	l· us not adulterate His
	270– 1	l· us take the side of him who
	270–26	l· him glory in the Lord."— *I Cor* 1: 31.
	277–22	l· the earth rejoice."— *Psal.* 97: 1.
	284–25	Evil l· alone grows more real,
	289– 5	Drunkenness is sensuality l· loose,
	290– 2	L· other people's marriage relations
	298– 5	L· us do evil, that good may— *Rom.* 3: 8.
	299– 6	L· us look through the lens of C. S.,
	303–13	L· us serve instead of rule,
	309–29	L· them soberly adhere to the
	310–16	"L· all things be done— *I Cor.* 14: 40.
	319–20	l· the present season pass without
	328– 2	"L· them alone; they must learn
	330–15	l· mortals bow before the creator,
	343– 1	L· us watch and pray
	343– 3	l· us not forget that others
	345– 9	* "L· them come;
	346–26	lift the curtain, l· in the light,
	355–26	L· no clouds of sin gather
	356–19	Now l· my faithful students
	357– 4	L· Christian Scientists minister to
	357– 5	L· them seek the lost sheep
	358–26	L· Scientists who have grown
	361–17	"L· us lay aside— *Heb.* 12; 1.
	361–19	l· us run with patience— *Heb.* 12: 1.
	363–14	"L· us [Spirit] make man perfect;"
	368– 3	Even so, Father, l· the light
	368–27	l· us not forget that the
	370– 9	L· the sentinels of Zion's
	388– 3	"L· there be light,— *Gen.* 1: 3.
Man.	41–21	l· the reign of divine Truth,
	60–18	"L· the dead bury their— *Matt.* 8: 22.
	60–25	L· the ceremony be devout.
Ret.	55– 3	L· us follow the example of Jesus,
	61–29	L· there be milk for babes,
	61–29	l· not the milk be adulterated.
	85–10	l· down from the heaven of Truth
	87– 1	l· the dead bury their— *Matt.* 8: 22.
	87–14	L· some of these rules be

let

Un.	1– 8	L· us then reason together
	5–19	L· us respect the rights of
	5–21	L· no enmity, no untempered
	5–25	l· the stately goings of this
	8– 1	L· another query now be
	12– 4	but l· them apply to the
	18– 2	l· us think of God as saying,
	35– 2	L· mortal mind change,
	39–20	l· Science declare the immortal
	60–19	then l· them serve Him,
Pul.	10–23	L· us rejoice that chill vicissitudes
	21–11	L· this be our Christian endeavor
Rud.	5– 3	"L· God be true,— *Rom.* 3: 4.
No.	8– 4	l· us add one more privilege
	8–26	l· the unwise pass by,
	9– 8	l· your opponents alone,
	30– 5	will not l· sin go until it is
	45–13	L· it not be heard in Boston
	45–24	L· the Word have free course
	46–17	l· us lift their standard higher,
Pan.	6– 5	l· us continue to denounce evil
'00.	14– 9	Beloved, l· him that hath an ear
	14–17	L· no root of bitterness spring up
'01.	3– 9	L· us examine this.
	9–20	"L· us alone;— *Mark* 1: 24.
	16–11	l· the dead bury its dead,
	19–16	L· us remember that the
	26–17	l· it be left to such as
'02.	2– 4	To live and l· live,
	4– 7	L· us all pray at this Communion
	9– 5	l· the dead bury their— *Matt.* 8: 22.
	9– 6	L· the world, popularity, pride,
	10– 8	mortals cry out, . . . L· me alone.
	20–12	"L· there be light,— *Gen.* 1: 3.
Hea.	10– 8	L· us remember that God
	19–22	l· us work more earnestly in
Peo.	3–14	L· us rejoice that the bow
	5–21	L· us then heed this heavenly
	11– 9	l· us build another staging
	12– 2	L· them have "dominion— *Gen.* 1: 26.
	13–18	to l· loose the wild beasts upon him,
	13–19	* he replied: "L· them come;
Po.	1–10	"L· there be light"— *Gen.* 1: 3.
	7– 3	"L· there be light,— *Gen.* 1: 3.
	27–13	l· today grow difficult and vast
My.	8–11	* l· us have the best material symbol
	20–15	l· this suffice for her rich portion
	22–10	* l· us not be unconsciously blind
	01–25	* should be willing to l· God work.
	110–17	luxury of thought l· loose,
	116–24	l· them alone in, God's glory,
	123–31	l· us say with St. Paul
	128– 3	l· us go on unto perfection;— *Heb.* 6: 1.
	134–15	And here l· me add:
	145–11	* "I want to be l· off for a
	147–14	L· the Bible and the C. S. textbook
	148– 4	l· your faith be known by your works.
	150–31	"l· your peace *Matt.* 10: 13.
	163–22	Here l· me add that,
	166–22	l· us together sing the
	166–23	l· our measure of time and joy
	175–26	L· brotherly love continue.
	185– 4	* "L· us, then, be up and doing,
	186–21	l· His promise be verified—
	101–10	L· your light shine.
	196– 9	"L· every man be swift— *Jas.* 1: 19.
	200– 4	L· "the heathen rage,— *Psal.* 2: 1.
	201–15	So l· us meekly meet,
	211– 9	All that error asks is to be l· alone;
	211–10	"L· us alone;— *Mark* 1: 24.
	224–30	l· us adopt the classic saying,
	233–30	L· us examine it for ourselves.
	236– 1	L· us have no more of
	245–16	l· Christian Scientists be charitable.
	245–16	L· the voice of Truth
	248– 3	L· your watchword always be:
	249– 5	l· the "still small— *I Kings* 19: 12.
	249–10	a moral idiocy l· loose
	253–28	L· the creature become
	254–11	to your kind letter, l· me say:
	258–25	To the dear children l· me say:
	261– 7	l· it continue thus with one
	267– 8	Here l· us remember that God
	270–14	L· error rage and imagine a
	275–28	l· us unite in one *Te Deum*
	278–10	L· us have the molecule of faith
	284–23	But here l· me say that I am
	299– 8	* l· them make it known to the world,
	309–32	L· us see what were the fruits
	342–14	* l· it not be understood that
	344–30	l· your children be vaccinated,
	353–25	"L· the dead bury— *Luke* 9: 60.

lethargic

Mis.	9–20	become l·, dreamy objects of

lets

  Ret. 90– 2   God's window which *l·* in light,
  '02.   6–17   *l·* in the divine sense of being,

letter

above-mentioned
  My. 323– 2   * in the above-mentioned *l·*.
above the
  My. 238–17   man rises above the *l·*,
all of the
  Man. 66–19   inquire if all of the *l·* has
annexed
  My. 138–28   * the annexed *l·* directed to
another
  Peo.   2– 8   Hebrew term that gives another *l·*
appointment by
  My. 223– 3   without previous appointment by *l·*.
by Mrs. Eddy
  My. 357–26   chapter sub-title
       360– 7   chapter sub-title
       360–28   chapter sub-title
Christmas
  Mis. 159–10   chapter sub-title
comment on
  My. 209– 1   chapter sub-title
commonplace
  Mis. 142–24   answer in a commonplace *l·*.
composite
  My. 359–19   * quotations from a composite *l·*,
dear
  My. 156– 3   my gratitude for your dear *l·*,
       208–14   comes your dear *l·* to my
dedicatory
  My. 146– 1   In explanation of my dedicatory *l·*
duplicate
  Mis. 306–14   * a duplicate *l·* written,
Edward P. Bates'
  My. 322–12   * Edward P. Bates' *l·* to you
Elizabeth Earl Jones'
  My. 327–10   * heading
entire
  My. 137– 7   * entire *l·* is in Mrs. Eddy's own
excellent
  My. 118–10   thank you for your most excellent *l·*.
       120– 8   to answer your excellent *l·*
extract from a
  Mis. 148– 7   chapter sub-title
       375– 8   extract from a *l·* reverting to
  Man.   3– 1   heading
  No. 43–12   following extract from a *l·*
  My. 241–12   * extract from a *l·* to Mrs. Eddy,
first
  Mis. 191–16   and by omitting the first *l·*,
following
  Pul. 43–30   * following *l·* from a former pastor
  My. 134–24   * following *l·* from Mrs. Eddy.
       144– 1   * Mrs. Eddy also sent the following *l·*
       173– 2   * The following *l·* appeared in the
       329–11   * following *l·* from Newbern, N. C.,
       331–10   * The following *l·* of thanks,
form of a
  My. 137– 2   * affidavit, in the form of a *l·*
from a student
  My. 355– 6   A *l·* from a student in the field
from Mrs. Eddy
  My. 359–16   * chapter sub-title
from our Leader
  My. 351– 1   * chapter sub-title
getting the
  No. 28–21   getting the *l·* and omitting the
her
  My. 351– 3   * publish her *l·* of recent date,
her brother's
  My. 329–15   * and of her brother's *l·*,
in his hand
  '02. 11– 1   with a *l·* in his hand
instead of the
  Ret. 49– 9   of the spirit instead of the *l·*,
interesting
  My. 208– 4   your highly interesting *l·*.
       326– 2   * the following interesting *l·*
       326–13   following deeply interesting *l·*
       351– 7   Your interesting *l·* was
       357–29   reading your interesting *l·*.
I sent a
  Ret. 52–23   June, 1889, I sent a *l·*,
is gained
  Mis. 43–17   *l·* is gained sooner than the spirit
its
  Ret. 52– 7   have a small portion of its *l·*
kind
  My. 192–20   Your kind *l·*, inviting me
last
  Mis. 375–10   * "In my last *l·*, I did not utter
learns the
  Ret. 38–28   learns the *l·* of this book,

letter

limits of a
  Mis. 128– 5   within the limits of a *l·*.
Mary Hatch Harrison's
  My. 329–20   * heading
Miss Jones'
  My. 328– 9   * referred to in Miss Jones' *l·* :
Mrs. Eddy's
  My. 140–17   * following is Mrs. Eddy's *l·* :
       326–11   chapter sub-title
my
  My. 146– 8   The statement in my *l·* to
not the
  Mis. 260–27   The spirit, and not the *l·*,
of Christianity
  My. 246–15   teaching and *l·* of Christianity
of Christian Science
  Mis. 195– 5   learns the *l·* of C. S.
of dismissal
  My. 182– 5   *l·* of dismissal and recommendation
of inquiry
  Man. 52– 9   shall address a *l·* of inquiry to
of thanks
  My. 295– 9   L· of Thanks for the Gift
       331–10   * The following *l·* of thanks,
of the law
  Ret. 81– 8   The *l·* of the law of God,
of your work
  My. 194– 5   The *l·* of your work dies,
oldness of the
  No. 25– 7   oldness of the *l·*." — *Rom.* 7 : 6.
or a message
  Man. 66–15   When a *l·* or a message from
public
  Mis. 95– 6   * to reply to his public *l·*
received a
  My. 14–11   * received a *l·* from a friend
reply to a
  My. 204–14   Reply to a L· Announcing
spirit and the
  Mis. 146–18   the spirit and the *l·* of this
       195– 9   the spirit and the *l·* are requisite ;
  My. 129–30   include the spirit and the *l·*
spirit or
  Man. 44– 5   departure from the spirit or *l·*
tender
  My. 352–20   for your tender *l·* to me,
this
  Mis. 159– 5   read this *l·* to your church,
       303–26   will respond to this *l·*
  Pul. 74–11   * this *l·*, addressed to the editor
  My. 134–24   * In announcing this *l·*, he said :
       134–27   * This *l·* is in Mrs. Eddy's own
       351– 4   * This *l·* is especially interesting
       359–23   * This *l·* was forwarded to Mrs. Eddy
       359–25   * Upon receipt of this *l·*
       360– 2   Answer this *l·* immediately.
touching
  Mis. 143–29   accompanied with a touching *l·*
without law
  Mis. 367– 1   *l·* without law, gospel, or
without the
  Mis. 195– 7   hath the spirit without the *l·*,
without the spirit
  My. 158–19   The *l·* without the spirit
your
  Mis. 158– 2   to your *l·* I will say :
  My. 202–22   cheer and love in your *l·*.
       202–25   From the dear tone of your *l·*,
       252–19   Your *l·* and dottings are
       253–22   thanks for your *l·* and telegram.
your kind
  My. 254–10   Responding to your kind *l·*,

  Mis. 135–24   L· read at the meeting of
       142–16   my third, a *l·*. Why the *l·* alone?
       355– 4   need, however, is not of the *l·*,
  Man. 98–19   *l·* sent to the Pastor Emeritus
  Ret. 21– 1   *l·* was read to my little son,
  My. 118– 8   chapter sub-title
       133–21   chapter sub-title
       134–20   chapter sub-title
       134–27   * to read you a *l·* from her
       135– 1   heading
       135–24   chapter sub-title
       140–12   * *l·* addressed to Christian Scientists
       290–11   chapter sub-title
       299– 1   L· to the *New York Commercial*
       301–14   [L· to the *New York World*]
       302–12   [L· to the *New York Herald*]
       314–22   *l·* from me to this self-same husband.
       362– 9   * chapter sub-title

letterly

  Mis. 315– 9   who are *l·* fit

letters
Mis. 29–20 Daily *l·* inform me that a
132–18 *l·* and inquiries from all quarters,
155–20 write such excellent *l·* to her,
155–26 forward their *l·* to Him
256– 8 in daily *l·* that protest against
310–11 My answer to manifold *l·*
364– 5 from the world of *l·*.
372– 9 *l·* extolling it were pouring in
Man. 66–14 Reading and Attesting *L·*.
67–20 congratulatory despatches or *l·*
Pul. 26–21 * in large golden *l·* on a
42–17 * words, "Mother's Room," in gilt *l·*.
42–23 * in *l·* of red were the words :
78– 7 * inscription, cut in script *l·* :
'02. 15– 1 anonymous *l·* mailed to me
15– 4 neither informed . . . of these *l·* nor
My. 58–25 * chapter sub-title
124–20 is written in luminous *l·*,
175–27 counterfeit *l·* in circulation,
198– 3 Your *l·* of May 1 and June 19,
214–16 In reply to *l·* questioning the
215–13 *l·* begging me to accept it,
223– 4 I neither listen . . . read *l·*, nor
223– 5 *l·* which pertain to church
223– 7 *L·* from the sick are not read by me
223–11 *L·* and despatches from individuals
225– 7 A correct use of capital *l·*
225–10 where capital *l·* should be
231–14 *l·* from invalids demanding
245–27 *l·* of degrees that follow
305– 9 *l·* in my possession,
319–11 * heading
319–12 * following *l·* from students
336–19 * These *l·* and extracts are

letting
Mis. 176– 1 *l·* the harmony of Science
212–29 before *l·* another know it.
Un. 5–20 *l·* our "moderation be— *Phil.* 4 : 5.
My. 12– 3 * justified the *l·* of contracts.
195–10 *l·* the deep love which I cherished
262–28 *l·* good will towards man,

level
Mis. 143– 2 friendship's "*l·*" and the "square"
Pul. 53–19 * above the *l·* of the brute,
My. 306–18 will find its proper *l·*.

lever
My. 130–13 the *l·* which elevates mankind.

levity
My. 93–19 * approach it in a spirit of *l·*,

lexicographer
Mis. 216–12 *l·*, given to the Anglo-Saxon
226–13 Shakespeare, the immortal *l·*

lexicographers
Mis. 102– 3 often defined by *l·*
Rud. 3– 9 if our *l·* are right in

lexicography
Mis. 219– 1 According to *l·*, teleology is

lexicons
'01. 3–15 with the literal sense of the *l·* :

Lexington
Pul. 33–18 * on his father's farm at *L·*,

liability
Mis. 92– 3 *l·* of deviating from C. S.
Man. 46–22 *l·* to have his name removed
Ret. 83–29 present *l·* of deviating from
My. 231– 5 *l·* of working in wrong directions.

liable
Mis. 54–21 no reason why you should be *l·* to
229– 1 that any one is *l·* to have them
300–10 *l·* to arrest for infringement of
300–19 Your manuscript copy is *l·*,
Man. 41–16 renders this member *l·* to discipline
Rud. 9– 1 and the patient is *l·* to a relapse,
No. 1–11 are *l·* to be borne on by the
'02. 4–26 we are *l·* to turn from them as

liar
Mis. 24–26 a *l·*, and the father of it."— *John* 8 : 44.
83–18 "a *l·*, and the father of it— *John* 8 : 44.
108– 6 his definition of Satan as a *l·*
190–29 serpent, *l·*, the god of this world,
192– 4 so, when referring to a *l·*,
192– 5 defines devil as a "*l·*."— *John* 8 : 44.
196–14 a *l·*, and the father of it ;"— *John* 8 : 44.
224–32 of a flatterer, a fool, or a *l·*,
226–21 character of a *l·* and hypocrite is
259– 5 "a *l·*, and the father of it."— *John* 8 : 44.
Ret. 67–24 a *l·*, and the father of it."— *John* 8 : 44.
Un. 32–22 a *l·*, and the father of it."— *John* 8 : 44.
32–23 Here it appears that a *l·* was
Rud. 5– 4 every man a *l·*."— *Rom.* 3 : 4.
No. 32–16 "a *l·*, and the father of it."— *John* 8 : 44.

liar
Pan. 5–16 a *l·*, and the father of it— *John* 8 : 44.
5–19 It shows that evil is both *l·* and lie,
'00. 5– 8 a *l·*, and the father of it"— *John* 8 : 44.
'01. 16–13 *devil* is named *serpent— l·— the god of*
My. 269–30 lie and the *l·* are self-destroyed.

liberal
Mis. 242– 6 *l·* sum of one thousand dollars
274–13 to the public for its *l·* patronage,
308–19 your *l·* patronage and scholarly,
Ret. 49–22 the public for its *l·* patronage.
'02. 13–10 yield this church a *l·* income.
Hea. 14–13 as a physician is enlightened and *l·*
My. 11–17 * because of prompt and *l·* action,
12– 5 * spontaneous and *l·* donations
245– 7 on a broad and *l·* basis.
304–23 * sound education and *l·* culture."
309–27 * received a *l·* education.
361–22 * democratic and *l·* government.

liberalism
'02. 2–13 Protestantism to doubtful *l·*.

liberality
Mis. 242–19 to reward his *l·*, I offer him
My. 12–13 * by the *l·* and promptness of

liberally
My. 21–12 * in order to contribute more *l·*

liberals
Mis. 88–11 appreciated by many *l·*.

liberated
Mis. 41– 3 power of *l·* thought to do good,
67– 1 to support the *l·* thought
Ret. 82–21 Their *l·* capacities of mind

liberator
My. 268–23 Love is the *l·* and gives man the

liberties
My. 320– 3 * courts are thus declaring the *l·* of

liberty
against the
Peo. 11–28 against the *l·* and lives of men.
and glory
My. 356– 5 *l·* and glory of His presence,
and joy
Mis. 240–10 whereas forecasting *l·* and joy does ;
and light
Ret. 81–10 diviner sense of *l·* and light.
and love
My. 236–18 amplitude of *l·* and love
248–27 labor, duty, *l·*, and love,
and peace
Mis. 304– 5 * by the lovers of *l·* and peace
buoyant with
My. 110–17 buoyant with *l·* and the luxury of
careening in
Po. 18– 5 Careening in *l·* higher and higher
creators of
Mis. 304–27 * birthdays of the "creators of *l·* ;"
divine
Mis. 163–21 are the basis of divine *l·*,
forecasting
Mis. 240–10 whereas forecasting *l·* and joy does ;
full
Peo. 11– 1 full *l·* of the sons of God
giveth
Mis. 167–29 he giveth *l·* to the captive,
giveth him
'01. 10– 1 for the spirit giveth him *l·* :
glorious
Mis. 199– 9 "into the glorious *l·* of— *Rom.* 8 : 21.
glory of
My. 339–16 joy, grace, and glory of *l·*.
higher
Mis. 354–28 As rising he rests in a *l·* higher
human
Mis. 101–11 for human *l·* and rights.
is besieged
Mis. 274–17 press is gagged, *l·* is besieged ;
life and
My. 266– 5 the robbing of people of life and *l·*
light and
Mis. xii– 8 into light and *l·*.
My. 187–25 light and *l·* of His children,
loving
My. 20–10 loving *l·* of their license.
of conscience
My. 220–31 should share alike *l·* of conscience,
222–27 *l·* of conscience held sacred.
of Cuba
Pan. 14–29 for the *l·* of Cuba.
outlet to
My. 128– 2 can find no other outlet to *l·*.
progress toward
Mis. 304–25 * the world's progress toward *l·* ;

liberty

Protestant
Ret. 2– 3 devotion to Protestant *l·*
regain his
Mis. 269– 3 using falsehood to regain his *l·*,
regard the
My. 291–30 shall sacredly regard the *l·* of
religious
Mis. 145– 2 bulwark of civil and religious *l·*.
My. 148–14 beheld the omen, — religious *l·*,
181–15 religious *l·* and human rights.
200– 1 Religious *l·* and individual rights
341– 6 the ensign of religious *l·*
spring into
Mis. 251–22 burdened for an hour, spring into *l·*,
standard of
Peo. 10–15 grasps the standard of *l·*,
striking at
'00. 10–13 striking at *l·*, human rights,
that
Pul. 51– 7 * they are enjoying that *l·* which
that's just
Po. 72– 4 ne'er again Quench *l·* that's just.
to lie
Mis. 274–18 when the press assumes the *l·* to lie,

Mis. 176–13 for the *l·* of the sons of God.
251–13 the *l·* of the sons of God,
Man. 96–12 he is at *l·* to supply that need
Un. 5–19 *l·* of the sons of God,
Po. vi– 8 * poem
page 71 poem
71–13 God to the rescue— *L·*, peal !
My. 128–11 man's inalienable birthright — *L·*.
128–12 there is *l·.*" — *II Cor.* 3 : 17.
205– 4 *l·* wherewith Christ hath — *Gal.* 5 : 1.
287–14 human rights, *l·*, life.
317–23 The *l·* that I have taken

Liberty and West Streets
Mis. 306–13 * corner *L· and W· S·*, New York,

Liberty Bell
Mis. 303–23 idea and purpose of a *L· B·*

Liberty Island
Mis. 304–11 * it will go to Bunker Hill or *L· I·*,

Liberty National Bank
Mis. 306–12 * sent to the *L· N· B·*,

Librarian
Man. 63–19 *L·*.

libraries
Pul. 5–22 It is in the public *l·*

library
My. 342–17 * the hall, which serves as a *l·*,

license
Mis. 257–13 as a power, prohibition, or *l·*,
260–29 needing neither *l·* nor prohibition ;
No. 37– 6 the *l·* of a short-lived sinner,
'01. 16–23 if now it is permitted *l·*,
My. 20–10 loving liberty of their *l·*.
328–13 * it gives them a *l·* to heal.
328–14 * This *l·* of five dollars annually,
328–24 * application for *l·* was made
328–27 * a *l·* must be obtained
328–29 * a *l·* fee of five dollars."
329– 2 * *l·* was accordingly taken

licensed
My. 211– 7 has *l·* evil, allowing it

licenses
My. 328–18 * Sheriff Wooten issued *l·*

licentious
'00. 6–20 is profane, *l·*, and

licentiousness
Mis. 210–25 shameless brow of *l·*,

licking
Mis. 326–13 *l·* up the blood of martyrs

lids
Mis. 132– 4 token that heavy *l·* are opening,

lie (noun)
and the liar
My. 269–30 *l·* and the liar are self-destroyed.
basis of a
'02. 6– 8 on the basis of a *l·*,
beautiful
Un. 53– 1 which make a beautiful *l·*.
being a
Un. 53– 5 Being a *l·*, it would be truthful to
believe a
Mis. 238– 3 sometimes made to believe a *l·*,
Un. 45– 1 you shall believe a *l·*,
believe the
Pan. 5–20 we should neither believe the *l·*,

lie

bigger
Hea. 14– 1 bigger *l·* occupying the field
biggest
Mis. 123– 9 the serpent's biggest *l·* !
call itself a
Un. 53– 5 would be truthful to call itself a *l·* ;
constitutes the
Un. 53– 7 it constitutes the *l·* an evil.
evil as a
'01. 14–14 We regard evil as a *l·*,
evil is a
Pan. 5–25 Knowing that evil is a *l·*,
exposes the
Mis. 367– 7 exposes the *l·* of suppositional evil,
fathers itself
'02. 6–11 Jesus said a *l·* fathers itself,
first
'02. 3–30 the first *l·* and leap into perdition
give it the
'01. 13–28 hold it invalid, give it the *l·*,
gives the
Mis. 334–15 only as one gives the *l·* to a lie ;
No. 32–14 It gives the *l·* to sin,
giving the
Peo. 13–16 giving the *l·* to science.
godless
No. 18– 4 godless *l·* that denies Him
is never true
Mis. 336– 3 that a *l·* is never true
liar and
Pan. 5–19 that evil is both liar and *l·*,
maketh a
Mis. 137–27 that worketh or maketh a *l·*.
366–14 that worketh or maketh a *l·*
No. 15–26 "worketh or maketh a *l·*" — *see Rev.* 21 : 27.
'01. 28–23 that worketh or maketh a *l·*.
matter is a
Rud. 7–20 matter is a *l·*,
must say
Un. 53– 4 the *l·* must say He made them,
no sculptured
Po. 73–18 No sculptured *l·*, Or hypocrite sigh,
of evil
No. 42–19 The *l·* of evil holds its own by
one
Hea. 13–28 one *l·* getting the better of another,
pursuing a
My. 130–14 to be continually pursuing a *l·*
sin is a
'01. 13– 7 sin is a *l·* from the beginning,
13–14 evil, *alias* devil, sin, is a *l·*
speaketh a
Mis. 24–26 "When he speaketh a *l·*, — *John* 8 : 44.
198–11 "When he speaketh a *l·*, — *John* 8 : 44.
Pan. 5–16 When he speaketh a *l·*, — *John* 8 : 44.
subtle
Mis. 335–12 for opposing the subtle *l·*,
My. 14–22 * subtle *l·* with which to ensnare
takes its pattern
Un. 53– 1 a *l·* takes its pattern from Truth,
this
Un. 25–11 This *l·*, that Mind can be in matter,
25–13 this *l·* I declare an illusion.
36– 4 this *l·* was the false witness
45– 1 this *l·* shall seem truth]."
throttle the
My. 26–21 the time to *throttle the l·*
use of a
Un. 36– 6 The use of a *l·* is that it unwittingly
utter a
Mis. 67–14 thou shalt not utter a *l·*,
veils the truth
Mis. 62– 9 Believing a *l·* veils the truth
victor over a
Mis. 336– 2 Truth, the victor over a *l·*.
worketh a
Mis. 174–18 that maketh or worketh a *l·*.

Mis. 14–27 a *l·* that is incapable of proof
83–19 the father of it [the *l·*]." — *John* 8 : 44.
108– 8 a *l·*, being without foundation
108–26 Jesus' definition of sin as a *l·*.
174– 3 it is a *l·*, claiming to talk
334– 9 does this as a *l·* declaring itself,
334–11 fabrication is found to be a *l·*,
334–15 only as one gives the lie to a *l·* ;
334–16 a *l·*, without one word of Truth in it.
334–19 is a *l·* of the highest degree of
351–21 though it is a *l·* ;
Ret. 67–21 the *l·* was, and *is*, collective
Un. 17– 1 A *l·* has only one chance of
17– 3 and so make the *l·* seem part of
22–12 would be to admit the truth of a *l·*.
22–15 *Evil. . . .* A *l·* is as genuine as Truth,
25–11 whatever it appears to say . . . is a *l·*.

lie

Un.	33– 2	mortal mind, and this mind a *l*·.
	34– 9	is an illusion, a *l*·.
	36– 1	only as it adds *l*· to *l*·.
	44– 9	Of *Satan* and his *l*·.
	44–20	[when you, *l*·, get the floor],
No.	32–16	A *l*· is negation,
	42–24	would make a *l*· the author of
	42–24	and so make Truth itself a *l*·.
Pan.	5–17	the father of it [a *l*·]." — *John* 8 : 44.
	5–22	we should not believe that a *l*·,
	5–27	Jesus treated the *l*· summarily.
	6– 9	putteth his foot upon a *l*·.
'00.	5– 9	its origin is a myth, a *l*·.
'02.	6– 5	The curse . . . was pronounced upon a *l*·,
My.	130–18	A *l*· left to itself is not so soon

lie (verb)

Mis.	34–24	*l*· within the realm of mortal thought
	67– 3	Above physical wants, *l*· the
	145–23	leopard shall *l*· down with— *Isa.* 11 : 6.
	268–15	*l*· in the line of Truth ;
	274–18	assumes the liberty to *l*·,
	325–17	*l*· stretched on the floor,
	354–4, 5	can steal, and *l*· and *l*·,
Ret.	44–22	*l*· in Christian warfare.
	79– 9	*l*· in meekness, in unselfish
Pul.	10– 9	pomp and power *l*· low in dust.
	48–15	* does it *l*· on the brow of
Pan.	11– 3	"*L*· not one to another,— *Col.* 3 : 9.
Po.	65–12	'neath thy drap'ry still *l*·.
My.	166–18	the virtues that *l*· concealed
	223–27	*l*· burdens that time will remove.
	323–10	* not going to *l*· about anything

lied

Mis.	23–18	first talker in its behalf, *l*·.
Un.	32–25	it was not man . . . who *l*·,

lies

Mis.	266–28	The spirit of *l*· is abroad.
	365–14	the secret of its success *l*· in
Un.	10– 8	it *l*· in this utter reliance upon
	29–18	herein *l*· the discrepancy
Pul.	41–10	* territory that *l*· between,
	48–10	* landscape that *l*· below,
Rud.	7–21	"the father of *l*· ;" — *see John* 8 : 44.
No.	18–11	*l*· in the universal need of
My.	17– 1	the refuge of *l*·,— *Isa.* 28 : 17.
	112–32	book which *l*· beside the Bible
	122–19	where the young child *l*·,
	126–15	(hearken not to her *l*·),
	144– 5	*l*· afloat that I am sick,
	188–24	man's head *l*· at another's feet.
	204– 5	*l*· concealed in the calm
	211–24	miserable *l*·, poured constantly
	249–24	My preference *l*· with the

lieth

Mis.	36–12	*l*· down with the lamb.

lieu

Mis.	314– 4	Readers in *l*· of pastors.
My.	201–27	in *l*· of my presence

lieutenant

'00.	10–26	the name of a first *l*·

Life (see also Life's)

abides

Un.	40–16	Hence *L*· abides in man,

all

Pul.	4–20	in all *L*·, through all space.

and being

Ret.	68–24	*L*· and being are of God.

and God

Un.	37–16	not testify of *L*· and God.

and good

Un.	62–16	false sense of *L*· and good.

and goodness

Ret.	63–17	against man's *L*· and goodness.

and happiness

Un.	37– 8	stepping-stone to *L*· and happiness.

and immortality

Un.	38–20	brings to light *L*· and immortality.

and intelligence

Mis.	199–26	all substance, *L*·, and intelligence
	200– 9	substance, *L*·, and intelligence of

and its ideals

Ret.	75–10	*L*· and its ideals are inseparable,

and its manifestation

My.	261–28	thoughts of *L*· and its manifestation.

and light

Mis.	337–29	The ineffable *L*· and light which

and Love

Mis.	16– 1	more spiritual *L*· and Love.
	46–26	the *L*· and Love that are God,
	68– 2	intelligence, *L*·, and Love.
	151–28	everlasting *L*· and Love.
	190–10	infinite *L*· and Love.

Life

and Love

Mis.	258–11	the law of *L*· and Love.
	293– 3	breathing new *L*· and Love
	342–10	the bridal of *L*· and Love,
No.	15–24	from divine *L*· and Love.
	18–14	demonstration of divine *L*· and Love ;
	33–21	efficacy of divine *L*· and Love
Hea.	16–13	immeasurable *L*· and Love
Peo.	5–19	diviner sense of *L*· and Love,
	14–17	power of divine *L*· and Love
My.	52–13	* Mind, Truth, *L*·, and Love,
	153–32	one source, divine *L*· and Love,
	191–16	higher human sense of *L*· and Love,

and Mind

Un.	3–22	He is all the *L*· and Mind there is
	3–23	embodiment of *L*· and Mind.

and substance

Mis.	55–25	only Mind, *L*·, and substance.

and Truth

Mis.	12–26	and Love is *L*· and Truth.
	75– 3	*L*· and Truth were the way
No.	30– 2	The law of *L*· and Truth
Peo.	6–21	grand realities of *L*· and Truth
My.	149– 6	Love, resistless *L*· and Truth.

as defined

Ret.	58–12	*L*·, as defined by Jesus,

as God

Mis.	189–19	Life in God and *L*· *as* God.
Un.	38–23	*L*· as God, moral and spiritual
My.	273–22	spiritual understanding of *L*· as God,

as it is

Mis.	189–21	For man to know *L*· as it is,

attempt to separate

Mis.	18–28	attempt to separate *L*· from God.

at war with

Mis.	217–23	that death is at war with *L*·,

belief that

Mis.	78– 1	belief that *L*·, God, is not

better views of

Mis.	175–10	giving better views of *L*· ;

Book of

My.	258– 1	Wherever . . . the Book of *L*· is loved,

bread of

Ret.	91–23	his . . . teaching was the bread of *L*·.

conscious

Un.	48–13	as infinite and conscious *L*·,

consciousness of

Un.	41– 4	knowledge and consciousness of *L*·,

conscious of

Un.	18–24	for to be ever conscious of *L*· is

death into

Un.	41–18	portal from death into *L*· ;

deathless

Po.	29–16	living Love, And deathless *L*· !

demonstrated in

No.	13–19	that saying is demonstrated in *L*·

demonstrates

Mis.	189–31	demonstrates *L*· without beginning or
Un.	40–10	demonstrates *L*· as imperative
My.	238–23	it demonstrates *L*·, not death ;

demonstrating

Mis.	270–12	in demonstrating *L*· scientifically,

divine

(see **divine**)

endless

Mis.	77–17	it holds man in endless *L*·

eternal

Mis.	63–17	might lay hold of eternal *L*·,
	83–27	proof of his eternal *L*·
	85– 2	*L*· eternal brings blessings.
	103–29	He was eternal *L*·,
	125–15	"to know aright is *L*· eternal,"
	170– 6	with him is *L*· eternal,
	183– 3	omnipotent Love, and eternal *L*·,
	341–19	you find *L*· eternal :
Man.	15– 5	sufficient guide to eternal *L*·.
	16– 7	to understand eternal *L*·.
Un.	38–22	or to deny that He is *L*· eternal.
	39– 3	Eternal *L*· is partially understood ;
Pul.	30–16	* the guide to eternal *L*· ;
Rud.	11–24	health, harmony, and *L*· eternal.
No.	36–14	of eternal *L*·, and harmony.
My.	119–24	eternal *L*· without beginning

ever-conscious

Un.	18–23	God saith, I am ever-conscious *L*·,

everlasting

Mis.	28–13	true sense of reality, everlasting *L*·
	151–28	the ascending scale of everlasting *L*·
Pul.	3–23	and flow into everlasting *L*·.
'01.	10–27	emerge gently into *L*· everlasting.
My.	260– 1	and bounty of *L*· everlasting,
	267–28	environed with everlasting *L*·.

ever-present

Un.	43–26	ever-present *L*· which knows no death,

Life

evidence of
Un. 61– 1 to the true evidence of L·,
evidences of
Hea. 16–27 gain our evidences of L· from
feast of
Mis. 175–14 Man shall keep the feast of L·,
find the
Mis. 211–24 shall find the L· that cannot be lost.
giver of
Pul. 4–24 the lord and giver of L·.
giveth
Ret. 65– 8 Spirit giveth L·.
God is
Un. 37– 2 God is L· ;
37–13 because God is L·, all Life is
37–15 God is L· and All-in-all.
God is our
Mis. 50–24 understanding that God is our L·,
God or
Mis. 25– 3 there is but one God or L·,
Un. 39–23 As the image of God, or L·,
had no beginning
Un. 42–21 L· had no beginning ;
harmony, and
Un. 32–19 of holiness, harmony, and L·."
He alone is
Un. 38–15 declaring that not He alone is L·,
health, and
Un. 39– 4 yield to holiness, health, and L·,
higher rules of
Mis. 29–32 higher rules of L· which Jesus taught
holds
Un. 40–18 God, who holds L· by a spiritual
holiness, and
Un. 42– 4 Spirit, holiness, and L·.
ideal of
Mis. 104–29 would not gain the true ideal of L·
ideas of
Peo. 14– 7 ideas of L· have grown more spiritual ;
ignorance of
Un. 40–22 comes through our ignorance of L·,
illustrated
Mis. 30–16 great Way-shower illustrated L·
immortal
Mis. 56–12 direct opposite of immortal L·,
incorporeal
My. 200–13 to the realms of incorporeal L·
individuality and
Un. 46–15 Individuality and L· were real
infinite
Mis. 82–18 image and likeness of infinite L·,
190– 9 recognized reflection of infinite L·
Hea. 4– 6 the compass of infinite L·,
4–17 We expect infinite L· to become
4–19 as infinite L·, without beginning
in God
Mis. 189–19 released sense of L· in God
in harmony with
Mis. 105–14 in harmony with L· and its glorious
intelligence, nor
Mis. 74–31 substance, intelligence, nor L·,
involves
My. 139–14 their vitality involves L·,
is a term
Ret. 59–12 L· is a term used to indicate Deity ;
is Christ
My. 185–19 L· is Christ, and Christ, . . . heals
is eternal
Un. 37–13 all L· is eternal.
is God
Mis. 56– 9 L· is God, the only creator,
175–10 saying, Man's L· is God ;
209–17 man, whose L· is God,
Un. 10–11 L· is God, or Spirit,
40–16 L· is God, and God is good.
Rud. 13– 1 that L· is God, good ;
No. 19–21 realities of being,— that L· is God,
Peo. 5–16 saying unto us, "L· is God ;
8–14 L· is God ; but we say that Life is
is immortal Mind
Mis. 56– 9 L· is immortal Mind, not matter.
is inorganic
Mis. 56– 4 L· is inorganic, infinite Spirit ;
is light
Po. 79–16 L· is light, and wisdom might,
is not functional
Rud. 13– 2 hence L· is not functional,
is not temporal
Ret. 59– 5 L· is not temporal, but eternal,
is real
Un. 38– 9 L· is real ; and all is real which
is Spirit
Un. 41–22 All L· is Spirit, and Spirit can never
Hea. 9–26 L· is Spirit ; and when we waken from

Life

is the Principle
'01. 21–19 L· is the Principle of C. S.
its
No. 28–23 nor the practice of its L·.
law of
(see **law**)
lessens all pride
My. 134–17 L· lessens all pride — its pomp and
life in
Pan. 13–21 life in L·, all in All.
light and
Ret. 27–30 new world of light and L·,
living way to
My. 192–12 lights the living way to L·,
Love alone is
Mis. 388–10 For Love alone is L· ;
Po. 7–10 For Love alone is L· ;
Love, and
My. 185–17 inseparable from Love, and L·
Love that is
My. 275–16 Love that is L· — is sure
man and
No. 12–26 sense and Soul, man and L·,
manifestation of
Ret. 88– 9 a higher manifestation of L·.
man's
Mis. 174–29 man's L· here and now.
175–10 saying, Man's L· is God ;
measure of
Mis. 175–12 The measure of L· shall increase
Mind, or
Ret. 57–21 notion of more than one Mind, or L·,
Mind which is
Un. 38– 8 that Mind which is L·.
my
Un. 48– 9 my individuality and my L·.
never fled
Mis. 385–19 thy ever-self ; L· never fled ;
Po. 48–13 thy ever-self ; L· never fled ;
no conflict with
Mis. 105–12 would have no conflict with L·
no groundwork in
Un. 25–23 has no groundwork in L·,
no other
Hea. 16– 4 teaches us there is no other L·,
no quality of
Un. 38–20 Death has no quality of L· ;
not death
Un. 39–24 reflects and embodies L·, not death.
My. 238–23 demonstrates L·, not death ;
not in matter
My. 181–12 L· not in matter but in Mind.
not of death
Un. 3–18 image . . . of L·, not of death.
of all being
Mis. 399–12 L· of all being divine :
Po. 75–19 L· of all being divine :
office of
Un. 40–28 the nature and office of L·.
of good
Un. 62–11 only as they reach the L· of good,
of man
Mis. 76–26 admit that Soul is the L· of man.
Ret. 63–15 represents God, the L· of man.
of Spirit
No. 34–22 The real blood or L· of Spirit
omniscience of
My. 274– 8 omnipresence, and omniscience of L·,
one
Un. 37– 3 there can be but one L·.
Rud. 13–13 saith . . . there is more than one L·
only
Mis. 16–17 great fact that God is the only L· ;
28–14 will be found to be the only L·.
194–28 you know that God is the only L·.
367–32 the only L·, Truth, and Love,
Ret. 69–13 God, Spirit, who is the only L·.'
Un. 41–10 the infinite and only L·.
43– 6 there is no death, but only L·.
or God
Ret. 59–16 antipodes of L·, or God,
Un. 38– 4 contradiction of L·, or God ;
or intelligence
Un. 32–13 as substance, L·, or intelligence,
or Principle
Ret. 28– 2 the L·, or Principle, of all being ;
or Spirit
Mis. 56– 4 if L·, or Spirit, were organic,
over death
Mis. 61–10 and of L· over death.
321–12 triumphs . . . of L· over death,
permanence of
My. 177–15 possibilities and permanence of L·.
pinnacled in
Pul. 3– 1 and pinnacled in L·.

Life

presupposes
No. 35–18 idolatry that presupposes *L·*,
proceeds from
Un. 38–10 all is real which proceeds from *L·*
real as
Un. 60– 1 illusion that death is as real as *L·*.
No. 17–27 Then . . . death as real as *L·* ;
reality of
Mis. 117– 2 progressive life is the reality of *L·*
Un. 43– 5 the infinite reality of *L·*,
reflect the
Un. 30–27 reflect the *L·* of the divine Arbiter.
righteousness and
Ret. 62– 6 health, righteousness, and *L·*,
rule of
Un. 55– 2 rule of *L·* can be demonstrated,
Science of
(*see* **Science**)
Science reveals
Ret. 60– 3 Science reveals *L·* as a complete
sense of
(*see* **sense**)
signification of
Ret. 59–15 has the signification of *L·*.
solution of
Mis. 65–15 to gain the true solution of *L·*
Soul is
Un. 30– 7 Soul is *L·*, and . . . never sins.
space and
Mis. 332– 2 reflecting all space and *L·*,
spiritual
Mis. 16– 1 more spiritual *L·* and Love.
361– 7 spiritual *L·*, whose myriad forms
Un. 30– 7 and being spiritual *L·*, never sins.
30–11 Soul, or spiritual *L·*.
spiritual fact of
Mis. 42–22 and the spiritual fact of *L·* is,
spiritual idea of
My. 139– 6 even the spiritual idea of *L·*,
standard of
Un. 38–27 up to the Christian standard of *L·*,
substance, or
Mis. 367– 9 not Mind, substance, or *L·*.
such
No. 35– 5 demonstrate the Principle of such *L·* ;
supersensible
Mis. 86–31 the glory of supersensible *L·* ;
swallowed up in
Mis. 361– 7 death itself is swallowed up in *L·*,
No. 13– 7 death must be swallowed up in *L·*,
that heals
My. 260– 2 the *L·* that heals and saves
that is God
Mis. 194–29 naturalness of the *L·* that is God,
196–21 When the *L·* that is God, good,
that is Soul
My. 274– 2 even the *L·* that is Soul
that is Truth
My. 214– 8 demonstrating the *L·* that is Truth,
that lives
Po. 24–11 The *L·* that lives in Thee !
the word
Ret. 59– 6 The word *L·* never means that
this
Mis. 24–17 this *L·* being the sole reality
179–32 this *L·* that knows no death,
Un. 41–18 when this *L·* shall appear
Pul. 4–25 *Reflect this L·*, and with it cometh
Rud. 3– 8 This *L·*, Truth, and Love
through
Un. 41–20 not through death, but through *L·* ;
true idea of
My. 181–12 through the true idea of *L·*,
Truth and
(*see* **Truth**)
Truth, and Love
Mis. 2–17 *L·*, Truth, and Love will be found
6–19 conceptions of *L·*, Truth, and Love
77–14 presence, . . . of *L·*, Truth, and Love,
79–16 perpetual in *L·*, Truth, and Love.
82–18 of infinite *L·*, Truth, and Love,
150–27 as divine *L·*, Truth, and Love ;
167–17 divine *L·*, Truth, and Love,
234–31 fatherliness as *L·*, Truth, and Love,
258–25 all law, *L·*, Truth, and Love,
358–11 He . . . loseth in *L·*, Truth, and Love.
367–32 the only *L·*, Truth, and Love,
Un. 34–27 Spirit, *L·*, Truth, and Love,
51–24 see God as *L·*, Truth, and Love.
55–13 *L·*, Truth, and Love, redeeming us
Pul. 85–11 * God as *L·*, Truth, and Love,
Rud. 1– 8 Spirit, *L·*, Truth, and Love,
3– 8 *L·*, Truth, and Love — this trinity
4– 1 *L·*, Truth, and Love are this trinity
No. 1–19 the trinity, *L·*, Truth, and Love,

Life

Truth, and Love
Hea. 8–20 namely, *L·*, Truth, and Love,
Peo. 2–23 the divine *L·*, Truth, and Love,
4–18 Godhead is *L·*, Truth, and Love,
13– 7 impersonal *L·*, Truth, and Love,
My. 109–22 this divine *L·*, Truth, and Love,
116– 4 omnipotence of *L·*, Truth, and Love,
150–14 the divine *L·*, Truth, and Love.
180–14 Principle, or *L·*, Truth, and Love,
Truth, . . . and Love
(*see* **Truth**)
Truth and the
(*see* **Truth**)
Truth of
Un. 39– 2 Truth of *L·* is rendered practical
truth of
Peo. 9–11 life of Truth and the truth of *L·*.
Truth or
Un. 62–20 Truth or *L·* in divine Science
Truth, or Love
Mis. 67– 6 not adulterate *L·* Truth, or Love,
Truth that is
My. 214– 9 and the Truth that is *L·*.
truth that is
My. 260– 2 in the truth that is *L·*,
understanding
My. 248–23 Christ mode of understanding *L·*
understanding of
My. 273–22 understanding of *L·* as God,
understands
Un. 40–21 who fully understands *L·*.
victory for
Mis. 74–26 an everlasting victory for *L·* ;
volume of
My. 256–13 and open the volume of *L·*
was Spirit
Un. 42–23 To him, *L·* was Spirit.
way of
No. 35–10 He who pointed the way of *L·*
My. 191–25 lights the living way of *L·*.
which is infinite
Peo. 4– 9 *L·*, which is infinite and eternal,
without beginning
Mis. 189–31 demonstrates *L·* without beginning
Hea. 4–19 *L·*, without beginning and without end.
Peo. 2–24 *L·* without beginning or ending,
My. 119–24 *L·* without beginning or end of days.
without birth
Chr. 53–39 *L·*, without birth and without end,
woke to
Mis. 386–13 I woke to *L·*,
Po. 49–20 I woke to *L·*,
words of
Mis. 337–28 him who taught . . . the words of *L·*.

Mis. 23–26 reflects good, *L·*, Truth, Love
24–17 *L·* in and of Spirit ;
63– 7 *L·*, Truth, Love are the triune
85– 7 all that he knows of *L·*,
124–14 ever-living *L·*, Truth, Love :
180–16 it speaks to me of *L·*,
187–22 God, — *L·*, Truth, Love.
189–20 declare *L·* to be the infinite
190– 4 infinite Spirit, Truth, *L·*,
196–27 not through death, but *L·*,
322–12 and the *L·* these give,
352– 4 regarding *L·*, Truth, Love as
386– 3 infinite appear *L·*, Love divine,
Chr. 53–41 The Way, the Truth, the *L·*
Ret. 60–29 one Truth, *L·*, Love,
69– 4 *L·* is the law of his being"
69–14 is found to be not *L·*,
Un. 25–25 eternal All, — *L·*, Truth, Love,
29–14 eternal, — Truth, *L·*, Love.
37– 7 God and heaven, or *L·*, are present,
38–25 conclusion that *L·* is not in these
39– 7 that *L·* which knows no death.
41–23 *L·*, therefore, is deathless.
42– 1 *L·*, God, being everywhere,
42–16 With Christ, *L·* was not merely
43– 8 believe in the possibility that *L·*
45–25 Spirit, — Mind, *L·*, Soul.
51– 1 false premises, — that *L·* is
62–11 learn that there is no *L·* in evil.
Pul. 3– 3 Can *L·* die?
13– 1 *L·*, represented by the Father ;
Rud. 2–19 supreme good, *L·*, Truth, Love.
No. 20–10 substance, *L·*, Truth, Love ;
35–21 Mind, *L·*, substance, Soul
Pan. 12–24 self-existent *L·*, Truth, Love,
'01. 4–26 because He is *L·*, Truth, Love,
5– 8 named in the Bible *L·*, Truth, Love?
7– 5 *L·*, Truth, Love, constitutes the
Hea. 8– 4 but the *L·*, Love, and Truth that
Peo. 2–11 divine Principle, — *L·*, Truth, Love ;

Life

Peo.	8–14	but we say that *L·* is carried on
Po.	49– 5	infinite appear *L·*, Love divine,
	70–13	the *L·*, the Principle of man.
My.	180–17	C. S. meets death with *L.*,
	185–15	this trinity, Truth, *L·*, Love,
	185–16	*L·* is the spontaneity of Love,
	206–17	fact that portrays *L·*, Truth, Love.
	214–12	He proved *L·* to be deathless
	225–28	His synonyms are Love, Truth, *L·*,

life (*see also* **life's**)

abiding
Mis. 26– 2 hath *l·* abiding in it,

all
My. 186–14 in whom dwelleth all *l·*, health, and

and bliss
Un. 57–17 This gospel . . . brought *l·* and bliss.

and death
Mis. 286–21 *l·*, and death are subjective states of
  333– 3 good and evil, *l·* and death,
Ret. 57–28 health and sickness, *l·* and death ;
Un. 31–14 produces *l·* and death.
Pan. 8–26 sickness and sin, *l·* and death.
'00. 4– 2 health and sickness, *l·* and death,
My. 273–20 joy, sorrow, *l·*, and death.

and happiness
Mis. 209–25 *l·* and happiness should still attend
  341–17 material sense of *l·* and happiness
Ret. 21–19 false sense of *l·* and happiness,
Un. 58– 1 false sense of *l·* and happiness.

and health
Mis. 200– 4 holiness, *l·*, and health
Ret. 7–13 * Had *l·* and health been spared
No. 5–13 namely, that *l·* and health are
My. 218– 7 its restoration to *l·* and health
  219–16 the giving of *l·* and health to man

and hope
Peo. 11–13 gnawing away *l·* and hope ;

and immortality
My. 207–14 * *l·* and immortality brought to light.

and intelligence
Mis. 53– 5 supposed *l·* and intelligence in
  76– 9 belief . . . *l·* and intelligence are in
Ret. 69– 7 delusion that *l·* and intelligence
Hea. 17–23 supposition of *l·* and intelligence in
My. 161–30 supposititious *l·* and intelligence in

and labors
My. 291– 3 rested on the *l·* and labors of our

and liberty
My. 266– 4 *l·* and liberty under the warrant of

and love
My. 88– 8 * *l·*, and love which finds its temple
  113–28 a more spiritual *l·* and love?
  159–21 Truth, *l·*, and love are the only
  268–24 Truth, canonized by *l·* and love,

and peace
Mis. 24– 4 is *l·* and peace." — *Rom.* 8 : 6.
'02. 6–28 is *l·* and peace." — *Rom.* 8 : 6.

and religion
Mis. 374– 8 Christianity in *l·* and religion.

and sacrifice
My. 323–18 * your wonderful *l·* and sacrifice

and teachings
Mis. 244–17 *l·* and teachings of Jesus?
No. 21– 1 *l·* and teachings of Jesus

and the love
Mis. 398–26 In the *l·* and the love of our Lord.
Po. 75– 6 In the *l·* and the love of our Lord.

and understanding
Pan. 15– 9 *l·* and understanding of God,

appreciate a
'00. 3–13 workers who appreciate a *l·*,

battle of
Mis. 339–10 In the battle of *l·*, good is

belief of
Un. 40– 6 belief of *l·* in matter, must perish,
My. 132–25 destroy the belief of *l·* in matter.

better
Mis. 235–18 thirsting after a better *l·*,

brim of
'00. 8–23 will boil over the brim of *l·*

brought back to
Mis. 211–19 pitied and brought back to *l·*?

busy
My. 338–17 owing to my busy *l·*,

Christian
'01. 28–10 a more devout Christian *l·*
My. 200–18 holds us to the Christian *l·*

Christ Jesus'
No. 34–27 currents of Christ Jesus' *l·*,

claim to
Mis. 198–10 claim to *l·*, . . . in matter,

coming to
Mis. 211–16 cause him to suffer in coming to *l·*?

life

common
Mis. 202– 6 * beyond the walks of common *l·*,
  357–10 beyond the walks of common *l·*,

common walks of
My. 189– 6 in the common walks of *l·*,

consciousness and
Un. 36– 1 evidence of consciousness and *l·*
My. 203– 6 in our consciousness and *l·*,

consecrated
Mis. x– 2 grandeur of a consecrated *l·*
  354–17 character subdued, a *l·* consecrated,

constituting
Mis. 56–11 indication of matter's constituting *l·*

corrected
Mis. 356– 3 a *l·* corrected illumine its own

country
Pan. 3–27 patron of country *l·*,

crown of
'00. 13–15 give thee a crown of *l·*." — *Rev.* 2 : 10.

daily
My. 36–23 * to the daily *l·* and purpose
  43– 6 * order aright the affairs of daily *l·*.
  233– 4 to watch . . . in your daily *l·*,

defines
Ret. 60– 1 defines *l·* as something apart from
  60– 4 material sense defines *l·* as a

destroy
Un. 25–19 *Evil.* . . . I can destroy *l·*.

destroyers of
No. 11– 3 nor destroyers of *l·* or its

divine
Po. 70– 6 Making this *l·* divine,

does not dignify
Mis. 240– 9 Predicting danger does not dignify *l·*,

does not understand
Mis. 197–23 does not understand *l·* in, Christ.

dream of
(*see* **dream**)

earth
My. 158–11 natal hour of my lone earth *l·* ;

earthly
Mis. 166– 4 the earthly *l·* of a martyr ;

end of
Chr. 55–21 nor end of *l·* ; — *Heb.* 7 : 3.

eternal
Mis. 64– 8 indestructible eternal *l·* in God.
  170–22 bears upon our eternal *l·*.
  205–22 forever permeated with eternal *l·*,
  213–23 give unto them eternal *l·* ; — *John* 10 : 28.
Un. 4–23 "*l·* eternal" consists in — *John* 17 : 3.
  37– 4 in order to inherit eternal *l·*
Pul. vii–20 vast problem of eternal *l·*,
My. 273–23 good, and therefore *l·* eternal.
  274– 2 the Principle of *l·* eternal ;

everlasting
Un. 40–14 no more receive everlasting *l·* by
My. 129–23 health and *l·* everlasting
  193– 3 to know aright is *l·* everlasting.

every-day
'02. 17–26 Consult thy every-day *l·* ;

fatal to
Mis. 380–14 an accident, called fatal to *l·*,

fulfilled
'02. 4– 8 a more fulfilled *l·* and spiritual

give
Un. 25–19 *Evil.* . . . I give *l·*, and I can

giving
'02. 9– 3 the All-power — giving *l·*,

go forth into
Mis. 224–17 Then, we should go forth into *l·*

good
Mis. 233–18 good words for a good *l·*,

happifies
Mis. 394– 6 Hope happifies *l·*, at the altar
Po. 45– 8 Hope happifies *l·*, at the altar
My. 134–16 Truth happifies *l·* in the hamlet

happiness and
Mis. 212–19 happiness, and *l·* flow not into
Un. 22–15 essential to happiness and *l·*.

happy
My. 40–31 * her own blameless and happy *l·*,

hath its music
Po. 65–22 *l·* hath its music in low minor

health and
(*see* **health**)

healthful
Mis. 170–10 understanding is healthful *l·*.

her
Mis. 35–13 * the outgrowths of her *l·*.
  130– 2 her *l·* exemplified long-suffering,
Ret. 6– 4 * Her *l·* was a living illustration
Pul. 31–11 * with the work of her *l·* which
  32–14 * She told me the story of her *l·*,
My. 270–16 Her *l·* is proven under trial,
  329–28 * some incidents of her *l·*

life

here is
 Ret. 18– 1   Here is *l*· !   Here is youth !
 Po. 63– 8   Here is *l*· !   Here is youth !
higher
 Mis. 228–13   capacity for a higher *l*·.
 My. 112–25   his higher *l*· is the result of
his
 Mis. 211–23   will save his *l*· — *Matt.* 16 : 25.
  292– 6   so loved the world that he gave his *l*·
  327–26   "He that loseth his *l*· — *Matt.* 10 : 39.
 Ret. 32– 7   will save his *l*· — *Matt.* 16 : 25.
 '02. 18–19   Jesus laid down his *l*· for mankind ;
  19–29   our Saviour in his *l*· of love.
 My. 3–21   good which has come into his *l*·,
  110–29   made his *l*· an abject failure.
  216–11   Either his *l*· must be a miracle
  233–26   he that loseth his *l*· — *Matt.* 10 : 39.
  277–11   the question of his *l*·.
home
 Pul. 50– 8   * better home *l*· and citizenship.
honest
 Mis. 227–26   summary of an honest *l*·
hourly
 Mis. 248–17   or that my hourly *l*· is
human
  (*see* **human**)
imaginary
 Un. 38–13   another power, an imaginary *l*·,
immortal
 Mis. 170– 2   resurrection and *l*· immortal
 Pul. 23–24   * intimations of man's immortal *l*·.
individual
 Mis. 309–22   Man's individual *l*· is infinitely
in God
 Mis. 64– 8   indestructible eternal *l*· in God.
 My. 150–22   raising the . . . to *l*· in God.
in Him
 Pan. 13–19   and find *l*· in Him in whom
in Him was
 My. 295– 6   "In Him was *l*· ; — *John* 1 : 4.
in Life
 Pan. 13–20   *l*· in Life, all in All.
intellectual
 My. 309–31   * practically all the intellectual *l*·."
intelligence nor
 Mis. 28–25   no intelligence nor *l*· in matter ;
intense
 Pul. 23–20   * years of more intense *l*·,
into the world
 '01. 21–22   not . . . death but *l*· into the world.
in truth
 My. 273–20   The truth of life, or *l*· in truth,
is dead
 Ret. 20–19   Oh, *l*· is dead, bereft of all,
is not lost
 My. 295– 3   assurance that *l*· is not lost ;
its
 Ret. 69–14   Its *l*· is found to be not Life,
 '02. 18–24   faith without proof loses its *l*·,
 Peo. 1– 4   draws not its *l*· from human
Jesus'
 Mis. 214– 2   Jesus' *l*· was full of Love,
knowledge of
 '02. 6– 3   knowledge of *l*·, substance, or
later in
 My. 311– 2   which occurred later in *l*·,
line of
 Mis. 38– 5   elevate man in every line of *l*·,
lines of
 Mis. 81– 6   into more spiritual lines of *l*·
loaf of
 My. 272– 3   leavens the loaf of *l*· with justice,
loftier
 Po. 32–10   A loftier *l*· to invite
love for
 My. 90–10   * All the passionate love for *l*·
loyal
 Mis. 386–25   remembrance of her loyal *l*·,
 Po. 50–11   remembrance of her loyal *l*·,
made honest
 Mis. 227–17   wider aims of a *l*· made honest :
man's
 My. 277–12   sublime question as to man's *l*·
Master's
 My. 219–19   our great Master's *l*· of healing,
material
  (*see* **material**)
miscalled
 Mis. 361– 6   its miscalled *l*· ends in death,
mortal
 Mis. 28–10   the phenomena of mortal *l*·
most sweet
 Mis. 388–11   *l*· most sweet, as heart to heart
 Po. 7–11   *l*· most sweet, as heart to heart

life

my
 Mis. 54–18   *to keep well all my l*·
  350–30   My *l*·, consecrated to humanity
  392–14   Faithful and patient be my *l*·.
 Pul. 21–10   to be made manifest in my *l*·.
 '01. 24–12   * I owe my *l*· to it."
 Po. 20–18   Faithful and patient be my *l*·
 My. 42–17   * blessings which have come into my *l*·
  133–28   your knowledge . . . uncovers my *l*·,
  283–10   leading impetus of my *l*·.
  306– 3   to narrow my *l*· into a conflict for
my own
 Mis. 11– 7   and save my own *l*·,
no
 Mis. 21–16   "There is no *l*·, . . . in matter.
 Ret. 93–19   "There is no *l*·, . . . in matter."
 Un. 38– 8   Error has no *l*·,
  38–12   matter has no *l*·,
nor death
 My. 302– 6   *l*· nor death, health nor disease,
nor sensation
 Ret. 69–20   matter has no . . . *l*·, nor sensation,
not death
 Mis. 346– 1   *L*·, not death, was and is
of a Christian Scientist
 Man. 50–16   the *l*· of a Christian Scientist,
of a man
 '01. 30–19   the inner genial *l*· of a man,
of Christ
 No. 10–10   *l*· of Christ is the predicate and
  41–13   *l*· of Christ is the perfect example ;
of Christianity
 Mis. 199–30   outflowing *l*· of Christianity,
of Christ Jesus
 '02. 8–16   *l*· of Christ Jesus, his words and
of Godlikeness
 '02. 16–23   express the *l*· of Godlikeness.
of Jesus
 Mis. 199–15   illustrate the *l*· of Jesus
  199–16   The rulers sought the *l*· of Jesus ;
  260– 1   illustrated by the *l*· of Jesus,
  337–22   the *l*· of Jesus was belittled
 Ret. 22– 7   history of the early *l*· of Jesus.
 Un. 9–17   simple teaching and *l*· of Jesus
of Love
 My. 301–11   teach us the *l*· of Love.
of love
 '02. 19–29   our Saviour in his *l*· of love.
 Peo. 5– 6   a deathless *l*· of love ;
of man
 Mis. 187–21   substance, and *l*· of man
  200–16   recuperate the *l*· of man,
 My. 181–10   scientific, sinless *l*· of man
of nations
 My. 277–15   prosperity, and *l*· of nations.
of our Lord
 Mis. 25–15   teachings and *l*· of our Lord.
  83–21   In the *l*· of our Lord,
 '01. 1–10   commemorate . . . the *l*· of our Lord,
 '02. 16–17   agony in the *l*· of our Lord ;
 My. 136– 5   and by the *l*· of our Lord
  179–19   depicted in the *l*· of our Lord,
of spirituality
 My. 352– 9   * for your *l*· of spirituality,
of sympathy
 Ret. 95– 8   * Unto a *l*· of sympathy.
of the author
 Po. v– 2   * in the *l*· of the author,
of the personal Jesus
 Mis. 166–30   of the *l*· of the personal Jesus.
of Truth
 Peo. 9–11   bathes us in the *l*· of Truth
one's
 Mis. 11–15   If one's *l*· were attacked,
  109–27   and consecrate one's *l*· anew.
  238–20   Let one's *l*· answer well
opposite of
 My. 235– 3   suppositional opposite of *l*·,
organic
 Mis. 56– 3   *What is organic l*· ?
  56–21   Organic *l*· is an error of statement
 No. 28–26   soul means sense and organic *l*· ;
our
 Mis. 76–28   Christ, who is our *l*·, — *Col.* 3 : 4.
  391–14   As item, of our *l*· ;
 Po. 38–13   As item, of our *l*· ;
 My. 166– 8   and God takes care of our *l*·.
outcome of
 Mis. 190– 3   nor the outcome of *l*· infused into
perfect
 My. 111–13   spiritual status of a perfect *l*·
perfected
 '02. 17–15   on duty done and *l*· perfected,
 Po. 22–17   A *l*· perfected, strong and calm.

life

perpetuate
   No.   5–16   restore health and perpetuate *l·*,
physical
   Un.   39– 6   and the pride of physical *l·*
pride of
   Mis. 116–18   pleasures and pains and pride of *l·* :
       183– 1   pride of *l·* will then be quenched
   Hea.   17– 2   the pride of *l·*, envy, hypocrisy,
private
   My. 218–25   My private *l·* is given to a servitude
progressive
   Mis. 117– 2   progressive *l·* is the reality of Life
proof of
   My. 177–13   true knowledge and proof of *l·*
public
   Mis. 249–10   Both in private and public *l·*,
purpose in
   My. 306–11   quite another purpose in *l·*
purposes of
   My. 285– 9   crowns the great purposes of *l·*
rainbowy
   Mis. 231–27   yes, and his little rainbowy *l·*
real
   Mis. 105–14   Man's real *l·* or existence
realities of
   Hea.   17–12   they are not the realities of *l·* ;
religious
   My.   93–25   * our social and religious *l·*.
resurrection and
   Mis. 170– 2   resurrection and *l·* immortal
ruined for
   My.   60– 9   * you will be ruined for *l·* ;
rush into
   Po.   16–10   rush into *l·*, and roll on with
satisfaction with
   My.   81– 4   * healthy satisfaction with *l·*.
save the
   My. 292–15   prayers to save the *l·* of
      335–28   * nothing could save the *l·* of
scale of
   My. 268–27   harmoniously ascends the scale of *l·*.
science of
   Mis. 344–13   such a material science of *l·* !
sculptors of
   Peo.   7–16   * "Sculptors of *l·* are we
sensation and
   Mis.   53– 1   claim of sensation and *l·* in matter,
sense of
       (*see* **sense**)
short
   Ret.   7–10   * throughout his short *l·*.
so-called
   Mis.   28–11   this so-called *l·* is a dream
      128– 3   this so-called *l·* in matter
   Ret.   23– 2   illusion that this so-called *l·*
   My. 274– 3   apart from the so-called *l·* of matter
soul and
   Ret.   59– 3   mortal mind and soul and *l·*,
Spirit of
       (*see* **Spirit**)
spiritual
   Mis. 351–30   the antipode of spiritual *l·* ;
   My. 113–28   a more spiritual *l·* and love
St. Paul's
   '00. 12–10   St. Paul's *l·* furnished items
substance, and
   Mis. 187–21   substance, and *l·* of man are one,
substance, and intelligence
   Mis. 175– 6   *l·*, substance, and intelligence,
      218– 9   *l·*, substance, and intelligence
   Ret.   67– 7   *l·*, substance, and intelligence
substance of
   Mis. 103–11   senses say . . . "The substance of *l·* is
success in
   Mis. 230– 2   Success in *l·* depends upon
supposed
   Mis.   53– 5   supposed *l·* and intelligence in
      201–13   nothingness of supposed *l·* in matter,
sustains
   Mis.   50–23   belief that . . . sustains *l·*,
that
   Mis.   19–16   never change the current of that *l·*
   My. 154–13   that *l·* "was the light of — *John* 1 : 4.
this
   Mis.   52–18   *If this l· is a dream not dispelled,*
   Ret.   18–25   This *l·* is a shadow,
   Po.   41–16   And this *l·* but one given to suffer
       64–22   This *l·* is a shadow,
       70– 6   Making this *l·* divine,
thy
   Mis. 338–30   * Live truly, and thy *l·* shall be
   Po.   46–16   Be all thy *l·* in music given,
   My.   13–21   redeemeth thy *l·* from— *Psal.* 103 : 4.

life

tree of
   Ret.   95– 1   this "tree of *l·*" — *Rev.* 22 : 2.
   Un.   3–16   the "tree of *l·*." — *Gen.* 2 : 9.
   My.   3– 9   right to the tree of *l·*, — *Rev.* 22 : 14.
true
   No. 12–18   Living a true *l·*, casting out evil,
truth, and the
       (*see* **truth**)
truth of
   My. 235– 2   To teach the truth of *l·*
      273–20   The truth of *l·*, or life in truth,
ultimatum of
   My. 273–18   The ultimatum of *l·* here
vision of
   Hea.   9–28   St. John saw the vision of *l·*
walks of
   Ret.   5–20   in all the walks of *l·*.
   '00.   7–11   those in all the walks of *l·*,
was the light
   My. 295– 6   *l·* was the light of men." — *John* 1 : 4.
webs of
   My. 232– 5   webs of *l·* in looms of love
what is
   Ret.   32–13   * What is *l·*?   'T is but a madness.
       32–14   * What is *l·*?   A mere illusion,
wondrous
   Mis. 214–12   closed . . . that wondrous *l·*,
your
   Mis. 151–25   may the lamp of your *l·*
   My. 139–29   redeem . . . your *l·* from death.
      352– 9   * gratitude to you for your *l·*

   Mis.   42– 2   *does l· continue in thought only*
       51–13   *teach him l· in matter?*
       95–17   always attended my *l·* phenomena
      227–18   a *l·* in which the fresh flowers of
      227–21   a *l·* wherein calm, self-respected
      227–23   a *l·* wherein the mind can rest
      332– 2   but not *l·* in matter.
      351–24   five senses give . . . *l·* that leads unto
      392–12   A lesson grave, of *l·*,
   Man.   55–19   by uniform maintenance of the *l·* of
       93–14   *l·* of the Pastor Emeritus.
   Chr.   55–17   Spirit . . . is *l·* — *Rom.* 8: 10.
   Ret.   22– 4   *l·* of our great Master.
       58– 7   With our Master, *l·* was not merely
       69–12   and matter shall seem to have *l·*
       69–17   believing that there is *l·* in matter,
   Un.   37– 2   also "the *l·*." — *John* 14 : 6.
       38–16   but that something else also is *l·*,
       61–20   *l·* which I now live — *Gal.* 2 : 20.
   Pul.   33–26   * whose *l·* has been destined to more than
       54–27   * he raised the daughter to *l·*.
   '02.   18– 9   helped crown with thorns the *l·* of
   Hea.   9–25   *L·* in matter is a dream :
   Po.   20–16   A lesson grave, of *l·*,
       23–17   *L·* hath a higher recompense
       31–14   Not *l·*, the vassal of the
       35– 4   love thee as I love *l·* less!
   My.   77–11   * in the *l·* of their cult.
      131– 8   for the *l·* that we commemorate
      154–12   "in Him was *l·*," — *John* 1 : 4.
      165–16   goodness makes *l·* a blessing.
      166– 7   *l·* is worth living
      229–31   it takes *l·* profoundly ;
      287–14   human rights, liberty, *l·*.

life (adj.)
   Peo.   7–19   * Our *l·* dream passes o'er us.

life-battle
   Ret.   22–14   It may be that the mortal *l·*

life-bestowing
   Ret.   88–14   health-giving and *l·* qualities,

Life-encrowned
   Po.   29–11   Thou God-idea, *L·*,

life-experience
   Mis.   3–12   his stripes" — his *l·* — *Isa.* 53 : 5.

life-giving
   Mis. 113–28   are *l·* fountains of truth.
      144–29   the *l·* Principle of Christianity,
      233–10   onward march of *l·* Science,
   Un.   55–16   and the *l·* way of Truth.
   Pul.   10– 1   Master's self-immolation, his *l·*
   No.   v– 9   *l·* waters of a true divinity,
       46– 8   *l·* understanding C. S. imparts,
   '01.   26–11   he endows it with a *l·* quality
   '02.   9–21   When first I heard the *l·* sound
       14– 7   living and *l·* spiritual shield
   My. 180– 4   its *l·* truths were preached

life-lease
   My. 139–11   his is a *l·* of hope, home,

lifelessness
   Mis.   74–27   demonstrated the *l·* of matter,

lifelong
  Mis. 72– 3   to be born a *l·* sufferer
life-member
  Mis. 296– 3   *l·* of the Victoria Institute
life-preservers
  Pan. 14–21   be unto them *l·* !
Life-problem
  Un. 5–13   to solve every *L·* in a day.
life-purpose
  Mis. 207– 4   of the spirit of my *l·*,
Life's
  Mis. 84–27   teaches *L·* lessons aright.
      125–17   press on to *L·* long lesson,
      397–10   the rock, Upon *L·* shore,
  Pul. 18–19   the rock, Upon *L·* shore;
  Po. 12–19   the rock, Upon *L·* shore,
  My. 290–20   into *L·* substance.
life's
  Mis. 9–16   friends seem to sweeten *l·* cup
      10– 2   wherewith to obstruct *l·* joys
     116–13   filling the measures of *l·* music
     116–17   human chords express *l·* loss or
     120– 5   Principle of *l·* long problem,
     238– 8   in defense of his own *l·* incentive,
     316–19   on my retirement from *l·* bustle.
     386– 1   grand and glorious *l·* sphere,
     393–12   Crowns *l·* Cliff for such as we.
     397– 2   sweet mercies show *L·* burdens light.
  Pul. 18–11   sweet mercies show *L·* burdens light.
     54– 4   * We touch him in *l·* throng and press,
     56–21   * We tread upon *l·* broken laws,
  '02. 19–19   heaving surf of *l·* troubled sea
  Po. 12–11   sweet mercies show *L·* burdens light.
     24– 9   From out *l·* billowy sea,
     46– 3   Within *l·* summer bowers !
     49– 3   grand and glorious *l·* sphere,
     51–17   Crowns *l·* Cliff for such as we.
     65– 3   *L·* pulses move fitful and slow ;
     65– 9   enchained to *l·* dreary night,
     65–15   We waken to *l·* dreary sigh.
     67– 1   brief bliss of *l·* little day
     73–17   afar from *l·* turmoil its goal.
  My. 166–15   *L·* ills are its chief recompense ;
     288– 5   his *l·* incentive and sacrifice
     298– 4   occurred in my *l·* experience
lifetime
  No. 12– 9   After a *l·* of orthodoxy
  My. 88– 6   * development of a short *l·*.
     00– 1   * thousands during her *l·* ;
     346– 3   * lived with her subject for a *l·*,
     340– 3   * an ordinary *l·* ;
life-work
  Mis. 29– 6   The purpose of his *l·*
     42–18   our *l·* proves to have been
  '02. 15–14   Before entering upon my great *l·*,
  My. 149– 2   Principle of Jesus' *l·*,
     303–21   His *l·* subordinated the material
lift
  Mis. xii– 7   *l·* my readers above the smoke of
     9–17   We *l·* this cup to our lips ;
     19–10   *l·* the affections and motives of men
     52–16   that tends to *l·* mortals higher.
     126–11   learned that trials *l·* us to
     202– 3   *l·* man's being into the sunlight of
     275– 7   it were well to *l·* the veil on
     338– 4   to be able to *l·* others toward it.
     346–26   *l·* the curtain, let in the light,
     351– 2   so as to *l·* the burdens imposed by
     355–17   but to *l·* your head above it,
     360–19   *l·* every thought-leaflet Spiritward ;
     399– 3   And will *l·* the shade of gloom,
  Ret. 73–14   *l·* thought above physical personality,
  Pul. 13–17   struggling to *l·* their heads above
  No. 46–17   let us *l·* their standard higher,
  Peo. 3– 1   will *l·* man ultimately to
  Po. 30–17   *L·* Thou a patient love
     75–10   will *l·* the shade of gloom,
  My. 32– 9   * did not have to *l·* their voices
     34–10   *L·* up your heads,— *Psal.* 24 : 9.
     34–10   even *l·* them up,— *Psal.* 24 : 9.
     200–21   to *l·* itself on crumbling thrones of
     305–31   my purpose was to *l·* the curtain on
     350–13   *L·* from despair the struggler
lifted
  Mis. 83–23   *l·* up his eyes to heaven,— *John* 17 : 1.
     165–21   until *l·* to these by their
     187–15   were not *l·* to the inspired sense of
     224– 8   *l·* his hands to his head,
     234– 8   what we have not *l·* ourselves to *be*,
     255– 9   to be thus *l·* up.
     399–21   *L·* higher, we depart,
  Ret. 27–20   * are *l·* up and strengthened.

lifted
  Ret. 88– 6   *l·* his own body from the sepulchre.
     93– 8   "And I, if I be *l·* up — *John* 12 : 32.
  '02. 17–14   curtain . . . should be *l·* on reality,
  Po. 76– 5   *L·* higher, we depart,
  My. 34– 4   not *l·* up his soul unto — *Psal.* 24 : 4.
     81–19   * for ills cured, for hearts *l·* up,
     247–13   and you will be *l·* up
     341– 5   *l·* to her giant hills the ensign of
lifteth
  Pan. 6– 8   *l·* his head above it
     12–15   it *l·* the burden of sharp experience
  Po. 79–14   *l·* me, Ayont hate's thrall :
lifting
  Mis. 262–17   *l·* the fallen and strengthening the
  '02. 19– 6   *l·* up his hands and blessing them,
  Hea. 11–16   before *l·* its foot against its
  My. 296–27   *l·* the curtains of mortal mind,
lifts
  Mis. 246–16   inhumanity *l·* its hydra head
     287–15   until progress *l·* mortals to
     290– 5   Science *l·* humanity higher
     330–28   violet *l·* its blue eye to heaven,
  No. 32–13   Mind-healing *l·* with a steady arm,
  '00. 6–22   *l·* him from the stubborn thrall of
  Peo. 12–15   *l·* man above the demands of matter.
  My. 258– 3   What is it that *l·* a system of
     268–25   *l·* the curtain on the Science of
Light
  Mis. 154–29   Let your light reflect *L·*.
     384–15   *L·*, Love divine Is here,
  Po. 36–14   *L·*, Love divine Is here,
  My. 301– 2   rays — from *L·* emitting light.
light (noun)
  all
    '01. 15–17   wickedness against all *l·*.
  all is
    '02. 16–20   there is no darkness, but all is *l·*,
  and cheerfulness
    My. 31–14   * then of *l·* and cheerfulness,
  and color
    Mis. 87– 9   substance of form, *l·*, and color,
  and darkness
    Mis. 34–26   direct opposites as *l·* and darkness.
  and joy
    Po. 23– 9   Mirrored in truth, in *l·* and joy,
  and liberty
    Mis. xii– 8   lift my readers . . . into *l·* and liberty.
    My. 187–25   *l·* and liberty of His children,
  and Life
    Ret. 27–29   new world of *l·* and Life,
  and love
    Mis. 184–25   Oh, for that *l·* and love ineffable,
    235–10   through the *l·* and love of Truth.
    My. 355–23   the reflection of *l·* and love ;
  and might
    My. 246–20   the *l·* and might of the divine
  and song
    Po. 54– 4   With *l·* and song and prayer !
  and truth
    My. 154–24   *l·* and truth, emanating from the
  approach the
    Mis. 352–12   lengthen as they approach the *l·*,
  borrowed
    Ret. 57–15   Man shines by borrowed *l·*.
  brings the
    Mis. 205– 9   brings the *l·* which dispels darkness.
  brings to
    Mis. 189–12   brings to *l·* the true reflection :
    Ret. 64– 7   brings to *l·*, makes apparent,
    Un. 38–19   brings to *l·* Life and
    My. 253– 4   brings to *l·* the perfect original
  brought to
    Mis. 1–21   brought to *l·* by the evolutions of
    82–24   being is brought to *l·*.
    222–23   when brought to *l·*, will make
    Ret. 58– 9   brought to *l·* immortality,
    No. 33–21   brought to *l·* the efficacy
    Hea. 18– 5   immortality be brought to *l·*.
    My. 93–27   * certain statistics brought to *l·*
    110–27   will have been brought to *l·*.
    207–14   * immortality brought to *l·*.
    332–20   * The facts . . . were brought to *l·*
  cheerful
    Ret. 5–24   * gentle dew and cheerful *l·*,
  children of
    Mis. 342–29   children of *l·* ;" — *Luke* 16 : 8.
    Ret. 90–29   one of the children of *l·*.
    My. 191–10   Children of *l·*, you are
    206–32   as children of *l·*." — *Eph.* 5 : 8.
  consciousness of
    No. 30–22   The consciousness of *l·* is like
  darkness for
    Mis. 174–27   We do not look into darkness for *l·*.

light

deliberation and
   Ret. 85–18 due deliberation and *l·*,
divine
   (see **divine**)
dwelleth in
   Mis. 367–23 He dwelleth in *l·* ;
       367–25 that darkness dwelleth in *l·*,
dwelling in
   Un. 18– 4 Dwelling in *l·*, I can see
electric
   Pul. 58–30 * electric *l·*, behind an antique
emits
   Mis. 290–29 it emits *l·* because it reflects ;
emitting
   Chr. 53–40 Life, . . . Emitting *l·* !
   My. 282–15 to all mankind a *l·* emitting *l·*.
       301– 2 rays — from Light emitting *l·*.
eternal
   Mis. 134–14 dwelleth in eternal *l·*
   Po. 70–10 Truth is eternal *l·*,
everlasting
   My. 206–19 an everlasting *l·*, — *Isa.* 60 : 19.
fled with the
   Po. 65– 7 it fled with the *l·*,
focusing
   My. 164–12 a thing focusing *l·*
fountain of
   Mis. 117–28 God is the fountain of *l·*,
fringed with
   Ret. 23– 9 not even fringed with *l·*.
God is
   '01. 3–21 * God is *l·*, but light is not God."
golden
   Pul. 39–16 * its flood of golden *l·*.
great
   Mis. 374–18 brought a great *l·* to all ages,
   Chr. 55– 8 have seen a great *l·* : — *Isa.* 9 : 2.
   My. 133– 3 in the great *l·* of the present,
heat and
   No. 14–15 are to solar heat and *l·*.
heaven of
   Po. 71– 9 Spans our broad heaven of *l·*.
heaven's own
   Peo. 7–14 * With heaven's own *l·* the sculptor
He sees
   Mis. 367–24 and in the light He sees *l·*,
his own
   Ret. 83–17 difficult to rekindle his own *l·*
infinite
   No. 16–15 infinite logic is the infinite *l·*,
in the Lord
   My. 206–31 *l·* in the Lord : — *Eph.* 5 : 8.
into
   Mis. 130–32 out of darkness into *l·*.
is not God
   '01. 3–21 * God is light, but *l·* is not God."
knowledge is
   No. 30–20 This knowledge is *l·* wherein
leads to
   Mis. 347–27 from the night He leads to *l·*.
let in the
   Mis. 346–26 Then lift the curtain, let in the *l·*,
lets in
   Ret. 90– 2 God's window which lets in *l·*,
let there be
   Mis. 388– 3 "Let there be *l·*, — *Gen.* 1 : 3.
   '02. 20–12 "Let there be *l·*, — *Gen.* 1 : 3.
   Po. 1–10 "Let there be *l·*" — *Gen.* 1 : 3.
       7– 3 "Let there be *l·*, — *Gen.* 1 : 3.
liberty and
   Ret. 81–10 diviner sense of liberty and *l·*.
Life and
   Mis. 337–29 The ineffable Life and *l·*
Life is
   Po. 79–16 Life is *l·*, and wisdom might,
line of
   Mis. 105–19 follow this line of *l·* and battle.
   Ret. 42– 7 to follow in this line of *l·*.
lines of
   Mis. 376–26 the lower lines of *l·* kindled
   My. 155–21 lines of *l·* span the horizon
lost in
   Mis. 352–13 until they are lost in *l·*
love and
   Mis. 149– 6 what they possess of love and *l·*
manifest
   My. 164–13 love, . . . is present to manifest *l·*.
marvellous
   Un. 17–18 into a home of marvellous *l·*,
   Rud. 4–25 by His marvellous *l·*.
   My. 206–26 into His marvellous *l·*." — *I Pet.* 2 : 9.
material
   Pul. 2–10 Material *l·* and shade are temporal,
might and
   My. 133– 4 might and *l·* of the present

light

more
   No. 16–16 forever giving forth more *l·*,
morning
   Mis. 222–32 as easily as dawns the morning *l·*
   My. 31– 3 * '"The morning *l·* is breaking ;"'
never a
   Un. 28–10 never a *l·* or form was discerned
never see
   Ret. 64–16 they shall never see *l·*. — *Psal.* 49 : 19.
new
   Ret. 14–23 when the new *l·* dawned
       45– 2 A new *l·* broke in upon it,
no
   Mis. 276–30 Error giveth no *l·*,
       342–20 no *l·*·l earth's fables flee,
of a home
   Po. 8–21 The *l·* of a home of love and pride ;
of all ages
   Mis. 320–27 is the *l·* of all ages ;
of a single candle
   Pul. 28– 3 * by the *l·* of a single candle,
of Christian Science
   Mis. 165–11 this appearing is the *l·* of C. S.
       253–29 opened their eyes to the *l·* of C. S.
   My. 187– 6 May the divine *l·* of C. S.
of divine Science
   Mis. 192–17 with the *l·* of divine Science,
of Love
   Mis. 132– 5 to the *l·* of Love — and By-laws.
       320–28 is the *l·* of Love,
of men
   My. 154–13 "was the *l·* of men." — *John* 1 : 4.
       295– 6 was the *l·* of men." — *John* 1 : 4.
of modern science
   Pul. 54–19 * in the *l·* of modern science,
of one friendship
   Pul. 5– 6 *l·* of one friendship after another
of penetration
   Mis. 313– 9 throw the *l·* of penetration on
of revelation
   Hea. 8–18 becloud the *l·* of revelation,
   My. 114–18 *l·* of revelation and solar light.
of Science
   Mis. 254–19 would obscure the *l·* of Science,
of the city
   No. 27–10 Spirit will be the *l·* of the city,
of the moon
   My. 313– 6 * By the *l·* of the moon
of the Science
   My. 343–16 the *l·* of the Science came first
of this revelation
   Mis. 165–12 The *l·* of this revelation
of Truth
   Mis. 320–11 the *l·* of Truth, to cheer,
   My. 241–25 * coming to the *l·* of Truth,
one with
   '01. 8–10 and it is one with *l·*,
perceived a
   Ret. 76–12 which perceived a *l·* beyond
pinions of
   Ret. 85–12 on their pinions of *l·*
proper
   Un. 20– 2 seeing it in its proper *l·*,
pure white
   Pul. 26– 4 * being of pure white *l·*,
ray of
   '01. 8– 9 one ray of *l·* is light,
   '02. 12–17 a ray of *l·* one with the sun,
rays of
   Mis. 333– 9 absorbs all the rays of *l·*.
reflect
   Mis. 131– 6 to discern darkness or to reflect *l·*.
       154–29 Let your *l·* reflect Light.
reflected
   Mis. 340–29 shine with the reflected *l·* of God.
   My. 202–23 My work is reflected *l·*,
resplendent
   Mis. 320–10 lends its resplendent *l·* to this
seeking
   Mis. 276–26 seeking *l·* from matter instead of
seek the
   My. 98–11 * critics who seek the *l·*
sends forth
   Ret. 56–22 The sun sends forth *l·*,
shined
   Chr. 55– 9 hath the *l·* shined. — *Isa.* 9 : 2.
sketching in
   Po. 8–13 sketching in *l·* the heaven
solar
   No. 39–26 photography grasps the solar *l·*
   My. 114–18 light of revelation and solar *l·*.
sons of
   Mis. 321–19 Press on, press on! ye sons of *l·*,
spheres of
   Po. 30–21 Echo amid the hymning spheres of *l·*,

light

spiritual
Mis. 113– 2 God's presence gives spiritual l·,
276–28 thus shutting out spiritual l·.
341–10 the neglect of spiritual l·,
342– 6 steady decline of spiritual l·,
susceptible of
'02. 17–30 cheer the heart susceptible of l·
that illumines
Po. 32–11 l· that illumines my spiritual eye,
that is in thee
Ret. 81–21 l· that is in thee — Matt. 6 : 23.
that shineth
Mis. 368– 3 l· that shineth in darkness,
their
My. 269–21 have healing in their l·.
355–25 and their l· shines.
thereof
My. 206–22 Lamb is the l· thereof." — Rev. 21 : 23.
there was
Mis. 388–11 and there was l·." — Gen. 1 : 3.
'02. 20–12 and there was l·," — Gen. 1 : 3.
Po. 7– 3 and there was l·." — Gen. 1 : 3.
this
No. 39–24 Advancing in this l·, we reflect it ;
39–25 this l· reveals the pure
throw a
'02. 16–16 and they throw a l· upon the
Thy
Mis. 275–17 we thank Thee that Thy l·
thy
Po. 29– 4 Thy l· was born where storm
My. 183–14 Love be thy l· upon the mountain
183–27 thy l· is come, — Isa. 60 : 1.
to Love
My. 234–13 from l· to Love, from sense to Soul.
unconceived
'02. 5– 9 this almost unconceived l· of
untrue to the
Ret. 81–19 consciously untrue to the l·,
waves of
Pul. 39–18 * I watch the flow Of waves of l·.
which shineth
Un. 63–10 l· which shineth in darkness,
will illumine
Mis. 276–17 l· will illumine the darkness.
wisdom's
Po. 27– 9 dawn with wisdom's l·
with darkness
Mis. 333–22 hath l· with darkness? — II Cor. 6 : 14.
your
Mis. 154–29 Let your l· reflect Light.
My. 191–10 Let your l· shine.

Mis. 149–26 a l· that cannot be hid.
157–24 righteousness as the l·, — Psal. 37 : 6.
355–28 Hold thy gaze to the l·,
367–24 and in the l· He sees light,
Ret. 18– 5 l· colored softly by blossom
Un. 19–14 the l· that is in thee — Matt. 6 : 23.
Pul. 52–16 * believers receive l·, health, and
No. 30–21 not l· holding darkness within
'00. 6–24 is not darkness but l·.
'01. 3–25 l·, being matter, loses the nature of
8– 9 one ray of light is l·.
35– 3 righteousness as the l·, — Psal. 37 : 6.
Hea. 10–18 and joy cometh with the l·.
Peo. 3–15 spans the moral heavens with l·,
Po. 22– 7 lo, the l·! far heaven is nigh!
43–15 L· with wisdom's ray
53– 8 L· o'er the rugged steep.
63–13 l· colored softly by blossom
My. 45–21 * pillar of fire to give you l·,
140– 5 I will make darkness l· — Isa. 42 : 16.
154–22 * he have l·, . . .freedom, immortality?''
170–25 righteousness as the l·, — Psal. 37 : 6.
199– 5 l· hath sprung up,
206–28 of the saints in l· : — Col. 1 : 12

light (adj.)

Mis. 133–29 Love makes all burdens l·,
262–26 Christ-love that makes them l·
374–19 and named his burdens l·,
397– 2 Life's burdens l·.
Pul. 18–11 Life's burdens l·.
24–22 * Concord granite in l· gray,
Po. 12–11 Life's burdens l·.
My. 89– 5 * The building is of l· stone,
161–29 "My burden is l·." — Matt. 11 : 30.
342– 5 * uprightly and with l· step,

light (verb)

Peo. 8–23 to l· our sepulchres with
My. 340–32 l· their fires in every home.
345–28 They l· the way to the Church

lighted

Pul. 32– 1 * l· by luminous blue eyes,
My. 69– 1 * church is unusually well l·,

lighten

Mis. 277–29 sharply l· on the cloud
323– 6 for God doth l· it.
My. 206–22 glory of God did l· it, — Rev. 21 : 23.

lightens

Mis. 313–10 l· earth's landscape.

lighter

Mis. 19– 8 healing the sick is far l· than
66–16 suffering is the l· affliction.

lighteth

Pan. 12–16 and so l· the path that he who
My. 187– 6 light of C. S. that l· every
257–15 l· every man that — John 1 : 9.

lighting

Mis. 250–28 l· the dark places of earth.
393– 8 L· up this mortal dream.
Put. 25– 1 * l· and cooling of the church
Po. 51–13 L· up this mortal dream.
My. 68–31 * used in the l· fixtures,
110–10 daystar will appear, l· the
252–22 l· and leading humanity

lightly

Mis. 251–21 as men, clothed more l·,
329–19 her little feet trip l· on,
Ret. 75–15 that can l· speak — Mark 9 : 39.
No. 27–26 take off thy shoes and tread l·,

lightness

My. 89– 8 * joined l· and grace

lightning

Ret. 17–16 brave breast to the l· and storm,
'00. 9–15 l·, thunder, and sunshine
Po. 62–20 brave breast to the l· and storm,

lightnings

Un. 52–20 l·, earthquakes, poisons,
Po. 18–17 Though l· be lurid

lights

Mis. 303– 1 they are l· that cannot be hid,
306–28 spiritual idea that l· your path !
324–25 only to find the l· all wasted
Un. 14–17 "the Father of l·, — Jas. 1 : 17.
Pul. 26– 2 * electric l· in the form of a star,
48– 8 * l· and shades of spring
76–10 * in certain l· has a shimmer
'02. 5– 7 l· the fires of the Holy Ghost,
My. 101 31 l· the living way of Life.
192–11 l· the living way to Life,
232–13 living l· in our darkness :

lightsome

Mis. 142–20 my Muse lost her l· lyre,
My. 341–12 A l· lay, a cooing call,

like

Mis. 5–11 "I should l· to study,
17– 7 l· the patriarch of old,
21– 6 in the flesh, l· ourselves,
29–30 l· students in mathematics,
48–29 l· a hundred other stories,
51–23 * Shall, l· a whirlwind, scatter
51–28 * transparent l· some holy thing.''
66–24 l· the more physical ailment.
81–22 l· the individual John
84–24 l· a weary traveller,
88–16 l· a midnight sun.
88–17 l· a benediction after prayer,
102–12 l· Himself and l· nothing else.
103–25 was l· that of other men ;
111–11 l· Peter, they launch into the depths,
127–32 human heart, l· a feather bed, needs
132–14 would "l· to hear from Dr. Cullis ;
134–23 L· Elisha, look up, and behold :
139–25 l· all true wisdom,
162–30 l· him he went forth,
166–22 L· the leaven that a certain woman
171–23 is l· unto leaven, — Matt. 13 : 33.
196–22 "we shall be l· Him ;" — I John 3 : 2.
208– 6 L· a legislative bill
221–25 l· saying that five times ten are
227–19 l· the camomile, the more trampled
241–24 Then, l· blind Bartimeus,
264– 8 l· camera shadows thrown upon the
266–12 is l· the comet's course,
275– 2 in scenes l· these,
275– 7 In times l· these
276– 4 l· all else, was purely Western
329– 6 nature l· a thrifty housewife
331– 5 downtrodden l· the grass,
335–22 zealots, who, l· Peter, sleep when
340–28 l· the stars, comes out in the
343–21 reappear, l· devastating witch-grass,
346–23 l· apples of gold — Prov. 25 : 11.

like

Mis.	347– 2	lest thou also be *l·* — *Prov.* 26 : 4.
	347– 6	hanging *l·* a horoscope
	350–13	*l·* my public instruction.
	353– 3	*l·* the action of sickness.
	355–25	*l·* the dove from the deluge.
	369–25	*L·* him, we would find our
	384–19	* Love, *l·* the sea,
	387–10	*L·* brother birds, that soar
	390–24	*l·* things of earth,
	394– 3	*l·* the dew on the flower,
	400– 4	*L·* this stone, be in thy place :
Chr.	55–21	*l·* unto the Son of God. — *Heb.* 7 : 3.
Ret.	5–24	* *l·* the gentle dew and
	10–13	vanished *l·* a dream.
	25–21	personal being, *l·* unto man ;
	27– 8	*l·* all great truths,
	27–21	*l·* the brooklet in its
	48–26	*l·* the baptism of Jesus,
	57– 7	This would be *l·* correcting the
	58– 4	*l·* trying to compensate for
	59– 8	*l·* saying that addition means
	64–17	is *l·* the beasts — *Psal.* 49 : 20.
	68–29	His origin is not, *l·* that of
	73–23	is *l·* the sick talking sickness.
	78– 1	acts *l·* a diseased physique,
	90– 9	*l·* "the elect lady" — *II John* 1 : 1.
	90–19	*l·* the ardent mother?
Un.	4– 4	and become *l·* Him.
	10–23	*l·* commencing with the minus sign,
	19– 4	and, *l·* ourselves, He foresees
	21– 7	In *l·* manner good and evil talk
	23–23	conceive of God only as *l·* itself,
	27–13	fleeing *l·* a shadow at daybreak ;
	41–19	"we shall be *l·* Him," — *I John* 3 : 2.
	44– 5	*l·* the structure raised thereupon,
	50–18	*L·* evil, it is destitute of Mind,
	58–17	*l·* as we are, — *Heb.* 4 : 15.
Pul.	2– 1	*l·* the Queen of Sheba,
	8– 3	*L·* the winds telling tales
	10–25	descended *l·* day-spring
	15– 6	people *l·* you better when
	16–16	*L·* this stone, be in thy place ;
	23–21	* *l·* Prof. Max Muller,
	32–13	* *l·* any abbess of old.
	33– 3	* began, *l·* Jeanne d'Arc, to hear
	46–23	* applied herself, *l·* other girls,
	51– 6	* to a matter *l·* C. S.,
	82– 3	* comes *l·* the south wind
Rud.	17– 1	*L·* certain Jews whom
No.	10–25	*l·* the needle to the pole
	13–25	and sparkle *l·* a diamond,
	21–28	*l·* a cloud without rain,
	30–22	*l·* the eternal law of God,
'00.	7–22	*l·* Peter we believe in
	11–23	* *L·* the close of an angel's psalm,
'01.	11–27	lest thou also be *l·* — *Prov.* 26 : 4.
	19–24	hypnotism, and the *l·*,
	29–13	They are *l·* children that
	30–23	no emperor is obeyed *l·*
	30–24	*l·* the clear, far-seeing vision,
'02.	4–15	ringing *l·* soft vesper chimes
	10–28	is *l·* sentencing a man for
	14– 9	* "Great not *l·* Cæsar,
	17–29	*l·* the sun beneath the horizon,
	18–18	*l·* the summer brook,
Hea.	9–14	*l·* furnishing fuel for the flames.
	11–11	*l·* the great pyramid of Egypt,
Peo.	3–17	*l·* a promise upon the cloud,
Po.	2– 8	*L·* a trained falcon in the
	6– 4	*L·* brother birds, that soar
	10–11	Our eagle, *l·* the dove,
	16– 6	*L·* thee, it endureth
	18– 6	*L·* genius unfolding a quenchless
	19– 1	My course, *l·* the eagle's,
	34– 4	*L·* thee, my voice had stirred
	36–18	* Love, *l·* the sea,
	45– 3	*l·* the dew on the flower,
	47–14	sobbing, *l·* some tired child
	56– 3	Ne'er perish young, *l·* things of
	65–18	darkness and death *l·* mist melt away,
	66– 4	*l·* the thrill of that mountain rill,
	67–19	*l·* the blue hyacinth, change not
	70– 5	*L·* to the soul's glad immortality,
	76–15	*L·* this stone, be in thy place :
My.	5–32	Indulging deceit is *l·* the
	13–10	* *l·* a sun in the centre of its
	13–11	* *l·* so many planets,
	13–24	renewed *l·* the eagle's," — *Psal.* 103 : 5.
	15–29	* To hear it *l·* the rest.
	82–18	* in something *l·* ten minutes.
	87–13	* we *l·* to know and *l·* to have here.
	94– 1	* growth continues in *l·* proportion
	95– 2	* *l·* a green bay-tree,
	99– 5	* doeth good *l·* a medicine,
	105–16	so that it stood out *l·* a cord.

like

My.	121–10	This strength is *l·* the ocean,
	121–14	Peace, *l·* plain dealing,
	122– 7	Sin is *l·* a dock root.
	134–18	*l·* a soft summer shower,
	139– 9	*L·* the verdure and evergreen
	147– 3	past comes forth *l·* a pageant
	149–25	predicament quite *l·* that of
	186– 5	*l·* tender nestlings in the crannies
	188–23	in which, *l·* beds in hospitals,
	208–12	*L·* the gentle dews of heaven
	212–18	Being *l·* the disciples of old,
	221–26	*l·* a watchman forsaking his post,
	248– 5	* not *l·* Cæsar, stained with blood,
	252– 4	Then you will be toilers *l·* the bee,
	252– 6	you will not be *l·* the spider.
	302–17	use of the word spread *l·* wildfire.
	307– 1	certainly read *l·* words that I
	337–12	Our eagle, *l·* the dove,
	343–12	* would, *l·* herself, be the ruler.
	345–16	came *l·* blessed relief to me,

likely

Mis.	43–10	least *l·* to pour into other minds
Pul.	50–26	* *l·* to show even some one side
My.	61– 8	* would *l·* be postponed until

likened

Mis.	175– 6	*l·* to the false sense of life,
'01.	25–28	Jesus *l·* such self-contradictions to

likeness

after our

Mis.	69–11	after our *l·* : — *Gen.* 1 : 26.

and image

Mis.	16–13	being His *l·* and image,

divine

Ret.	60– 2	very far from the divine *l·*.
Un.	39–27	losing the divine *l·*.
No.	36– 6	when we awake in the divine *l·*.
My.	121–23	reflects the divine *l·*.

eternal

Un.	22– 2	made after God's eternal *l·*,

God's

Mis.	61–29	logic that man is God's *l·*.
	89–28	Immortal man, in God's *l·*,
	186–32	real man in God's *l·*,
Un.	45– 9	very far from God's *l·*."
Pul.	21–25	a clear expression of God's *l·*,
No.	17–12	more than God's *l·* is impossible.
	25–23	immortal man alone is God's *l·*,

God's essential

Mis.	61–22	Does God's essential *l·* sin,

God's own

Mis.	77–27	man, made in God's own *l·*,

harmless

Rud.	8– 6	sends forth its own harmless *l·*.

His

Mis.	15–22	man awake in His *l·*.
	16–13	being His *l·* and image,
	17–20	and of man as His *l·*,
	30–32	and awake in His *l·*,
	79–15	man as His *l·* is erect
	358–13	"awake in His *l·*," — see *Psal.* 17 : 15.
Rud.	7–11	His *l·* would be lost if inverted
	11– 7	in Science man is His *l·*,
'02.	8– 2	God, and man as His *l·*,
Hea.	17–13	awake to behold His *l·*.
Po.	79–20	doth His will — His *l·* still
My.	194–15	melted into the radiance of His *l·*.
	205–21	makes . . . man more His *l·*,

his

Un.	15–15	for his *l·* to his creator.
'00.	8– 3	till we awake in his *l·*.

His own

Mis.	173–28	made man in His own *l·*.

human

Mis.	23–28	human *l·* thrown upon the
	308–30	human *l·* is the antipode of

idea or

My.	239–21	idea or *l·* of the infinite
	262– 2	idea, or *l·* of perfection

image and

   (see **image**)

image or

My.	239–17	His idea, image, or *l·*,
	269– 2	compound idea, image or *l·*,

is incomplete

Un.	15–10	or the *l·* is incomplete,

lost

Mis.	184–24	gives back the lost *l·*
'02.	8–29	Adam, . . . or His lost *l·*,

of error

Rud.	13–11	*l·* of error — the human belief

of God

   (see **God**)

likeness
of his Maker
Mis. 62– 8   the true *l·* of his Maker.
    164–23   actual *l·* of his Maker.
My. 232–26   the true *l·* of his Maker"?
of Love
'02.   8– 6   the *l·* of Love is loving
of Spirit
Mis. 61–30   man in the *l·* of Spirit
Rud. 13–10   body is not the *l·* of Spirit ;
original
Mis. 18– 2   original *l·* of perfect man,
perfect
Mis. 79– 8   God's perfect *l·*, that reflects all
this
Un. 22– 3   this *l·* consists in a sense of
to his creator
Un. 15–15   for his *l·* to his creator.
to the portraits
My. 342– 8   * The *l·* to the portraits
true
Mis. 62– 8   the true *l·* of his Maker.
    97–29   of him who is the true *l·* :
    188–30   the true *l·* of God,
Ret. 70– 1   "Mortal mind inverts the true *l·*,
No. 16–19   God and His true *l·*,
My. 232–26   as the true *l·* of his Maker"
unfallen
Mis. 79–23   that perfect and unfallen *l·*,
likening
Mis. 30–13   *l·* them to the priceless understanding
likewise
Mis. 131– 9   leaner sort console . . . by doing *l·*.
    240–28   *L·* soberly inform them that
    241–12   and try to make others do *l·*,
    338– 8   All must go and do *l·*.
Ret.   3– 4   were *l·* connected with
Pul.   2–21   *L·* should we do as
'00.   7– 4   *L·* the religious sentiment has
'01.   0–15   taught his followers to do *l·*.
    23–20   taught his disciples . . . to do *l·* ;
My. 106–31   commanded his followers to do *l·*.
    149– 4   "Go, and do thou *l·*." — *Luke* 10 : 37.
lilies
Pul. 42–22   * a star of *l·* resting on palms,
    42–26   * palms and ferns and Easter *l·*.
My. 155–27   gathering Easter *l·* of love
limb
Mis. 230–11   travel of *l·* more than mind.
limbs
Peo. 10–19   they alone have fettered free *l·*,
My. 105–12   saving the *l·* when the
lime
My. 108– 2   carbonate and sulphate of *l·* ;
limit
Mis. 60–12   *Does it not l· the power of Mind*
    60 15   Does it *l·* the power of Mind
    282– 2   a sense that does not *l·* God,
Pul. 62–19   * practically no *l·* to the uses
Hea.   4– 7   Clothing Deity with personality, we *l·*
My. 327–15   * to *l·* or stop the practice of C. S.
limitation
Un. 45–21   sphere of its own creation and *l·*,
My. 229–26   namely, laws of *l·* for a
limitations
Ret. 73– 6   *L·* are put off in proportion as the
    76–18   and knows no material *l·*.
My. 118–29   holiness, entirely apart from *l·*,
    119– 1   convenient for history to record *l·*
    177–14   putting off the *l·*
limited
Mis. 64–23   to a *l·* extent, are aids
    85–10   his power is temporarily *l·*.
    102– 7   originate in a *l·* body,
    102– 9   In this *l·* and lower sense
    164 30   The *l·* view of God's ideas
    190–14   too *l·* and contradictory.
Un. 14–15   Jehovah of *l·* Hebrew faith
Pul.   6– 4   engendering the *l·* forms of a
    30– 9   * not *l·* to the Boston adherents,
Rud. 15–19   a very *l·* number of students
No. 19–11   He is neither a *l·* mind nor
    19–12   nor a *l·* body.
Hea.   4– 2   cannot start from a *l·* body.
Peo.   3–22   This *l·* sense of God as good
    8–11   the *l·* and definite form of a
My. 106–12   *l·* to imaginary diseases !
limiting
Hea.   5– 3   we shall be *l·* His power
limitless
Mis. 284– 7   in this field of *l·* power
No. 20– 1   *L·* personality is inconceivable.

limits
Mis. 42–30   Mind is not confined to *l·* ;
    128– 5   within the *l·* of a letter.
    282– 5   sense of personality . . . that *l·* man.
No. 12–27   It removes all *l·* from divine power.
Hea.   4– 3   nor remain for a moment within *l·*.
Peo.   3–23   *l·* human thought and action
My. 106–21   Mind calms and *l·* with a word.
limner's
Mis. 393– 6   Paints the *l·* work, I ween,
Po. 51–11   Paints the *l·* work, I ween,
limp
Mis. 112–20   sank back in his chair, *l·* and pale ;
limped
My. 307–32   My idealism, however, *l·*,
limpid
My. 150–15   Stand by the *l·* lake,
Lincoln, Miss Elsie
Pul. 37–18   * Mrs. Hanna, Miss Elsie *L·*,
    43– 5   * Mr. . . . Case and Miss Elsie *L·*.
    59–21   * a Scientist, Miss Elsie *L·* ;
Lincoln, Neb.
My. 97–14   * [*Nebraska State Journal, L·, N·.*]
Lincoln's
Po. 26–10   *L·* own Great willing heart
Linden Avenue
1414
Pul. 68–18   * services . . . at 1414 *L· A·*.
Lindley Murray's Grammar
Ret. 10– 5   familiar with *L· M· G·*
line
another
Un. 26–22   as sings another *l·* of this hymn,
defining the
Mis. 22 11   infinite calculus defining the *l·*,
direct
Mis. 212–15   One step away from the direct *l·*
'01.   2–23   a departure from the direct *l·*
dividing
Man. 99– 5   dividing *l·* being the 36th parallel
every
Mis. 38– 4   elevate man in every *l·* of life,
    220– 2   in every *l·* of mental healing,
intermediate
Mis. 188–20   in the intermediate *l·* of thought,
My. 181–18   practise the intermediate *l·* of
lead the
Mis. 130–30   and appoints to lead the *l·* of
of Jesus' thought
Mis. 260– 7   *l·* of Jesus' thought or action.
of least resistance
Pul. 80– 8   * sought the *l·* of least resistance.
of life
Mis. 38 4   elevate man in every *l·* of life,
of light
Mis. 105–19   I must ever follow this *l·* of light
Ret. 42– 7   to follow in this *l·* of light.
of liquids
My. 260–14   the *l·* of liquids, the lure of gold,
of occupation
Mis. 296–25   Do they enter this *l·* of occupation
of the syllogism
Un. 34– 6   What then is the *l·* of the syllogism?
of thought
Mis.   3–16   enter this *l·* of thought or action.
    186–28   proceeds in this *l·* of thought,
    188–20   in the intermediate *l·* of thought,
of Truth
Mis. 268–15   inquiry . . . in the *l·* of Truth ;
one
'01. 24–21   I had not read one *l·* of
orderly
My. 247–16   came out in orderly *l·*
poet's
Ret. 87– 3   poet's *l·*, "Order is heaven's first
present
Mis. 273–17   in their present *l·* of labor
upon line
Mis. 32–11   *l·* upon line" — *Isa.* 28 : 10.
    278–21   *l·* upon line and precept upon precept.
whole
Mis. 265–19   whole *l·* of reciprocal thought.
with progress
Mis. 287–20   human affection in *l·* with progress,

      —

Mis. 264– 2   random thought in *l·* with mine.
Ret.   2–30   In the *l·* of my Grandmother Baker's
My. 16–28   will I lay to the *l·*, — *Isa.* 28 : 17.
    114–19   *l·* of Scriptural interpretation
    201–27   Please accept a *l·* from me
    232– 5   that *l·* the sacred shores.
    (*see also* **Science and Health**)

lineage
Mis. 162–30   Of the *l·* of David,
No.   13–15   chapter sub-title

lines
Mis.   81– 6   into more spiritual *l·* of life
   291–29   sentinels along the *l·* of thought,
   376–26   lower *l·* of light kindled into
Ret.   20–15   The following *l·* are taken from
   46– 1   L· penned when I was pastor of the
Un.   23– 2   which makes true the *l·* :
Pul.   66–18   * mystical which, along many *l·*, has
   87–25   luminous *l·* from your lives linger,
No.   7–21   recommend that Scientists draw no *l·*
Po. page 41   poem
   page 67   poem
My. 124–19   between these *l·* of thought
   155–21   May long *l·* of light span the
   177–19   succeeding years show in livid *l·*
   339–12   *l·* of progressive Christendom,
   342–10   * no mistaking certain *l·*
   354–26   * The above *l·* were written
   (*see also* **Science and Health**)

linger
Mis. 218–24   this nature may *l·* in memory :
Pul.   87–25   luminous lines from your lives *l·*,

lingering
Mis. 230– 9   making *l·* calls,
'02.   3– 8   any *l·* sense of the North's

lining
Ret.   23– 8   seemed to have a silver *l·* ;

linings
Pul.   77– 6   * plush casket with white silk *l·*.

link
Mis. 143– 7   a closer *l·* hath bound us.
   270–28   Homœopathy is the last *l·* in
My. 339– 3   whose every *l·* leads upward

links
My. 206– 1   Philosophical *l·*, which would

lion
Mis.   36–12   *l·* that lieth down with the lamb.
   145–24   calf and the young *l·* — *Isa.* 11 : 6.
Rud.   8– 4   the *l·* of to-day is the *l·* of
Po.   43– 8   Fondling e'en the *l·* furious,

lions
Un.   11– 5   beard the *l·* in their dens.

lip
My. 258–31   a child with finger on her *l·*

lips
Mis.   9–18   We lift this cup to our *l·* ;
   51–22   * "When from the *l·* of Truth
   100–32   Who knows how the feeble *l·*
   129– 4   let him put his finger to his *l·*.
   135– 4   on our *l·*, and in our lives.
   149– 9   opened his *l·* to discourse
   149–18   L· nor pen can ever express
   213–21   from the *l·* of our Master,
   275–13   repeat with quivering *l·*
   311–31   never escaped from my *l·*,
   331–16   words from a mother's *l·*
   338–25   * To give the *l·* full speech.
Ret.   31–27   the tearful *l·* of a babe.
Rud.   9–16   answer of the *l·* from the Lord.
No.   38–26   if the *l·* try to express it.
   39– 8   the heart prays, and not the *l·*,
Peo.   13–14   forcing from the *l·* of manhood

liquidate
Mis.   xi– 8   While no offering can *l·*
   302–31   to subvert or to *l·*.

liquids
My. 260–14   the line of *l·*, the lure of gold,

liquor
'01.   33–20   with the lance, or with *l·*,

lisping
No.   44–16   the mouth *l·* God's praise ;

lispings
'02.   19–14   listens to the *l·* of repentance

list
Mis. 144– 9   subscription *l·* on which appear
Man.   54–15   branch church's *l·* of membership
   73– 5   published in the *l·* of practitioners
Ret.   50–15   my *l·* of indigent charity scholars
Pul.   48–27   * long *l·* of worthy ancestors
   88– 1   chapter sub-title
'01.   31–20   Among the *l·* of blessings infinite
Po.   10–14   L·, brother ! angels whisper
   73– 9   *l·* the moan Of the billows' foam,
My.   39–13   * following *l·* of officers for the
   85–21   * illustrious *l·* for future generations
   106– 6   The *l·* of cases healed by me

list
My. 305–19   eighth in a *l·* of twenty-two
   337–15   L·, brother ! angels whisper

listen
Mis. 222–13   ready to *l·* complacently to
   328– 3   *l·* for the mountain-horn,
   337–11   L·, and *he* illustrates the rule :
   398– 1   I will *l·* for Thy voice,
Man.   59–18   to *l·* to the Sunday sermon
Ret.   46– 7   I will *l·* for Thy voice,
Pul.   15–12   If so, *l·* and be wise.
   17– 6   I will *l·* for Thy voice,
   41–11   * to *l·* to the Message sent them by
   61–22   * to *l·* to the first peal of the chimes
'01.   20–13   People may *l·* complacently to
Po.   14– 5   I will *l·* for Thy voice,
My. 152–21   *l·* to His Word and serve no other
   201–21   I will *l·* for Thy voice,
   223– 4   I neither *l·* to complaints,
   331–28   * yet when we *l·* to Mrs. Glover

listened
Mis. 332–18   supposed to have . . . been *l·* to,
Ret.   9– 3   I *l·* with bated breath.
   42–11   *l·* to him with deep interest.
Pul.   61–26   * who *l·* with delight.

listeners
Mis. 100– 1   artless *l·* and dull disciples.
   357–14   fall by the wayside, on artless *l·*.
Man.   58–21   To pour into the ears of *l·*
Pul.   46– 2   * that he was attracting *l·*

listening
Mis. 156–24   *l·* to each other amicably,
Man.   56–15   These assemblies shall be for *l·* to
Ret.   2–27   I was fond of *l·*,
Pul.   5– 3   *l·* to an address on C. S.
My.   59–15   * *l·* again to your words

listens
'02.   19–14   *l·* to the lispings of repentance

lit
Peo.   7–10   * face *l·* up with a smile of joy

literal
Mis. 169–15   interpreted in a *l·* way.
   169–22   The *l·* rendering of the Scriptures
   169–25   The *l·* or material reading
   171–12   in *l·* or physical terms,
   248– 4   the *l·* meaning of the passage
Pul.   38–25   * the *l·* teachings of Christ.
   66–14   * *l·* teachings of the Bible
No.   23–15   a *l·* and a moral meaning.
   23–17   the *l·* or the moral sense of
'01.   3–15   the *l·* sense of the lexicons :

literally
Mis.   28–28   He *l·* annulled the claims
   108– 9   spiritually, *l·*, it *is nothing.*
   133–18   *l·* following the dictum
   175–30   is *l·* saying,
   204–29   *l·* governs the aims, ambition,
   258– 8   *l·* spat upon matter ;
   300–15   You *l·* publish my works
   333–13   is *l·* fulfilled, when we
Pul.   13– 7   is *l·* fulfilled, when we
   25– 7   * *l·* fire-proof as is conceivable.
   29–21   * interpreted and fulfilled *l·*,
My.   99–20   * *l·* stuffed and jammed with money.
   142–14   *l·* a communion of branch church
   187– 2   spiritually as well as *l·*,

literary
No.   11– 8   In its *l·* expression, my system
   29–23   *l·* driftwood on the ocean
'02.   15–14   my income from *l·* sources
   15–26   I showed it to my *l·* friends,
My. 319–30   * that he had done some *l·* work
   320– 1   * that he was a fine *l·* student
   324–22   * as quite his *l·* equal,
   324–23   * among his *l·* friends.

Literary Digest
My. 305–28   scandal in the *L· D·*

literature
Mis.   xi–18   to suit and savor all *l·*.
   64–10   *the study of l· and languages*
   64–22   L· and languages, . . . are aids to
   80– 1   sellers of impure *l·*,
   365–26   As a *l·*, Christian metaphysics is
Man.   27–17   and all other C. S. *l·*
   27–24   other *l·* connected therewith.
   43–21   No Incorrect *L·*.
   43–23   C. S. *l·* which is not correct
   44– 1   in which the writer has written his *l·*
   44– 3   his *l·* shall not be adjudged C. S.
   64– 3   L· in Reading Rooms.
   64– 4   *l·* sold or exhibited in the
   64– 8   also the *l·* published or sold by

literature

Man.	82– 1	books and l· it sends forth.
	82– 3	disapproves of certain books or l·,
	97–20	by periodicals or circulated l·
Ret.	77– 2	lawlessness in l·.
Pul.	5–30	l· of our and other lands.
'01.	21–18	to criticise it or·to compare its l·.
	27– 4	* made to the l· of C. S.
My.	224–28	to recommend any l· as wholly

literatures

Mis.	169– 4	ancient philosophies or pagan l·,

litigation

Mis.	340–13	followed agriculture instead of l·,

little

Mis.	2– 5	they have so l· of their own.
	4–15	but l· time has been devoted to
	6– 3	often leaves mortals but l· time
	38–14	*other institutions find l· interest in*
	107–32	thinks either too much or too l·
	108– 3	Christian asleep, thinks too l· of sin.
	127– 2	His "l· ones," — Matt. 18 : 6.
	130–25	God's "l· ones." — Matt. 18 : 6.
	142– 8	the l· pond at Pleasant View.
	144– 6	a l· band called Busy Bees,
	145–25	l· child shall lead them." — Isa. 11 : 6.
	150– 1	"Fear not, l· flock ; — Luke 12 : 32.
	158– 5	I l· thought of the changes
	158– 7	I l· knew that so soon
	176–11	we learn a l· more of the
	221–11	The evil-doer can do l· at
	231–18	poked into the l· mouth
	231–24	soft l· palms patting together,
	231–27	and his l· rainbow life
	236– 5	l· else than the troubles,
	240– 3	through the cold air the l· one
	243–24	"Take a l· wine — see I Tim. 5 : 23.
	250–26	l· feet tripping along the sidewalk ;
	255– 1	chapter sub-title
	262–27	l· need of words of approval
	275–12	the motherless l· ones, wondering,
	291– 9	Too much and too l· is attached
	308–20	This l· messenger has done its work,
	318–27	either too large or too l· :
	319– 7	If the sense of sin is too l·,
	321–16	"Fear not, l· flock ; — Luke 12 : 32.
	324– 8	But a l· while, and the music
	329–18	her l· feet trip lightly on,
	337–12	called a l· child — Matt. 18 : 2.
	337–14	as this l· child, — Matt. 18 : 4.
	341–23	a l· girl of eight years,
	344–26	as a l· child, — Luke 18 : 17.
	354–15	A l· more grace, a motive made pure,
	376–21, 22	L· by l· this topmost pall,
	400–17	Guide my l· feet
Man.	17– 1	l· band of earnest seekers
	18– 8	the l· Church went steadily on,
Ret.	6–14	than this l· book can afford.
	8–14	I sat in a l· chair by her side,
	9– 9	Scriptural narrative of l· Samuel,
	20– 7	my l· son, about four years of age,
	21– 1	letter was read to my l· son,
	27–30	new to His "l· one." — see Matt. 10 : 42.
	35– 3	This l· book is converted into
	40–19	never before suffered so l·
	61–28	that however l· be taught or learned,
	61–29	that l· shall be right.
	78– 3	either too much or too l·.
Un.	1–12	l· apprehended and demonstrated
Pul.	4– 3	"What if the l· rain should say,
	4–15	Each of Christ's l· ones reflects
	8–17	L· hands, never before devoted to
	29– 7	* a l· later, in this article.
	33– 9	* the l· maid was afraid
	39– 9	a l· poem that I consider
	42–11	* the l· contributors to the
	48–13	* valley of the l· truant river,
	50–25	* after a l· skirmishing,
	62–12	* require but l· muscular power
	62–22	* l· sets of silver bells
	67–22	* l· knots of them are to be found.
Rud.	v– 1	THIS l· BOOK IS . . . DEDICATED
No.	9–18	first edition of this l· work
	21–27	has l· resemblance to Science,
	26–27	O ye of l· faith?" — Matt. 6 : 30.
'00.	2–11	gives l· time to society
	2–16	earns l· and is stingy ;
	8–10	wicked man has l· real intelligence ;
	8–27	through one of His l· ones,
	14– 1	"Thou hast a l· strength, — Rev. 3 : 8.
'01.	15–17	I can conceive of l· short of
	23– 3	they have l· left that the
	26–26	I have read l· of their writings.
'02.	2–16	l· leaven hid in three measures
Hea.	15–25	that you have l· or no faith in
Po.	v– 1	* garnered up in this l· volume

little

Po.	vii–11	* this l· volume is presented
	24– 5	O l· heart, To me thou art
	53–16	Their downy l· breasts.
	67– 2	bliss of life's l· day
	69– 5	Guide my l· feet
My.	17–30	His "l· ones," — Matt. 18 : 6.
	38–19	* l· ones were not a whit behind
	50– 6	* l· band of prayerful workers.
	50– 9	* so this l· band of pioneers,
	52–23	* L· cares she, if only
	59– 5	* the l· leaven that should leaven
	59–17	* l· hall on Market Street, Lynn,
	59–21	* I thought of the l· melodeon
	60–15	* I have yet the l· Bible
	60–27	* may I ask a l· of your time
	60–30	* care to do a l· watching
	68–23	* and contributes not a l· to the
	79– 3	* l· faces turned upward.
	79– 8	* it must stagger their faith not a l·
	93– 4	* have l· of the spirit of bigotry.
	96–31	* C. S. just goes a l· beyond
	97–12	* Scientists have a l· the advantage
	98–20	* in a l· less than three years.
	107–13	lower attenuations have so l·
	123–21	My l· hall, which holds
	123–30	"the l· foxes — Song 2 : 15.
	130–31	that you borrow l· else from it,
	131–12	given to me in a l· symbol,
	147–13	May this l· sanctum be preserved
	147–23	work-rooms and a l· hall,
	148–21	singing of this dear l· flock,
	154– 7	to send flowers to this l· hall
	172–12	to present to you a l· gift
	175–16	must remain with us a l· longer,
	186– 4	May God's l· ones
	224– 6	knowing a l·, . . . the human need,
	238–12	has imparted l· power to practise
	247–14	l· fishes in my fountain
	247–17	these sweet l· thoughts
	247–24	Do you come to your l· flock
	247–28	The l· that I have accomplished
	262–19	afford l· divine effulgence.
	271– 5	I l· understood all that I indited ;
	271– 8	of comparatively l· importance
	288– 4	reformer gives l· thought to
	298– 5	not a l· is already reported
	313–31	my l· boy was not welcome in
	319– 7	l· pamphlet, signed "Phare Pleigh."
	323– 7	* I have his l· book yet.
	340–13	clad in a l· brief authority,
	349–10	Tyndall, and Spencer afford l· aid
		(see also **children, church**)

Littleton

New Hampshire

My.	315– 4	* with me in L·, New Hampshire.

N. H.

My.	314–31	R. D. Rounsevel of L·, N. H.,

liturgical

Ret.	89–10	they went for l· worship,

live

Mis.	7–18	reflects that it is dangerous to l·,
	8– 6	we l·, and move, — Acts 17 : 28.
	44– 2	speak the truth . . . and l· it :
	50–25	we exist in Mind, l· thereby,
	72–15	As I l·, saith the Lord — Ezek. 18 : 3.
	79– 9	we l·, move, and have being.
	82–29	"we l·, and move, — Acts 17 : 28.
	84–20	to l· is Christ, — Phil. 1 : 21.
	84–25	is to l· in Christ, Truth.
	99–24	still l·, and to-morrow speak
	106–26	"So l·, that your lives attest your
	115–15	practise, teach, and l· C. S. !
	140–31	the spiritual idea would l·,
	163–20	they still l· ; and are the basis of
	180– 1	he lives, I l·," — see John 14 : 19.
	205–32	and l· what they learn,
	210–12	A l· lexicographer,
	237–17	few feel and l· now as when
	296–13	l· on the plan of heaven?
	338–30	* L· truly, and thy life shall be
	388– 9	Fed by Thy love divine we l·,
Man.	39– 1	l· according to its requirements
	51–10	does not l· in Christian fellowship
Chr.		they that hear shall l·. — John 5 : 25.
Ret.	11– 8	l· to bless mankind.
	93–17	we l·, and move, — Acts 17 : 28.
Un.	10–16	They l·, because He lives ;
	41–26	appears to both l· and die,
	48– 9	Because He lives, I l·.
	61–20	life which I now l· — Gal. 2 : 20.
	61–21	I l· by the faith of — Gal. 2 : 20.
Pul.	2–23	"we l·, and move, — Acts 17 : 28.
	21– 7	I long, and l·, to see this
	50–27	* l· down any attempted repression.

live

Pul.	83–24	* *l·* in the reflected royalty
Rud.	12–17	mistaken belief that they *l·* in
No.	17– 7	we *l·*, and move,— *Acts* 17 : 28.
	25– 2	We must *l·* it, until
	35–13	He lived that we also might *l·*.
Pan.	13–20	"*l·*, and move,— *Acts* 17 : 28.
'01.	6– 2	that *l·* in the Father
	34–27	man cannot *l·* without it ;
'02.	2– 4	To *l·* and let *l·*,
	12–19	we *l·*, and move,— *Acts* 17 : 28.
Po.	7– 9	Fed by Thy love divine we *l·*,
	11– 3	Victorious, all who *l·* it,
	15–14	I would *l·* in their empire,
	60– 5	And *l·* to bless mankind.
My.	105–23	declared that she could not *l·*.
	109–22	"we *l·*, and move,— *Acts* 17 : 28.
	126–31	We have it only as we *l·* it.
	127– 5	Happy are the . . . who *l·* to love.
	128–15	to *l·* or to die according to the
	131–10	"he shall *l·* forever,"— *John* 6 : 51.
	132–20	where we may see God and *l·*,
	133–25	then . . . we *l·* apart.
	158– 9	We *l·* in an age of Love's divine
	160– 5	To *l·* so as to keep human
	160–12	a *l·* truth, even though it be a sapling
	164–30	man must *l·*, he cannot die ;
	166–14	will *l·* on and never drift apart.
	195–22	mortals expect to *l·* and die,
	213–11	to *l·* pure and Christian lives,
	216– 2	Till . . . *l·* without eating,
	241–23	* I did not *l·* in my flesh,
	252–12	not only know the truth but *l·* it
	290– 7	Those *l·* on in the affection of .
	338– 3	Victorious, all who *l·* it,
	345–14	doctors said I would *l·* if the

lived

Mis.	70–16	Christ Jesus *l·* and reappeared.
	165–17	truth uttered and *l·* by Jesus,
	211–30	He *l·* the spirit of his prayer,
	213– 3	All that I have written, . . . or *l·*,
	229–24	holier, happier, and longer *l·*.
	293–27	Truth talked and not *l·*,
	312– 3	so *l·*, that when weighed in the
	337–24	*l·* according to his precepts,
Ret.	21– 8	learned that his mother still *l·*,
Un.	62–19	Jesus died, and *l·*.
Pul.	34– 2	* who *l·* only a year.
	49–10	* "You have *l·* here only four years,
	58– 6	* she has *l·* in Concord, N. H.,
No.	35–13	He *l·* that we also might live.
'00.	7–14	reward for having suffered, *l·*,
'01.	28– 9	perhaps none *l·* a more devout
	32–16	were honest, and they *l·* them ;
'02.	18– 6	*l·* when mortals looked ignorantly,
Po.	26–19	chain and charter I have *l·* to see
My.	81–14	* the places where they *l·*.
	89–12	* sect that . . . has not *l·* in vain.
	150– 8	* better for having *l·* in it."
	241–22	* because I still *l·* in my flesh.
	241–24	* my flesh *l·* or died according to
	241–26	* I *l·* and moved and had my being
	287–11	Love talked and not *l·*
	287–12	Love *l·* in a court or cot
	291–15	not talked but felt and *l·*.
	314– 3	* "*l·* for a short time at Tilton,
	314–28	I *l·* with Dr. Patterson peaceably,
	322– 1	* I met a lady who *l·* in Lynn,
	325–10	* old part of Boston in which he *l·*
	327–31	* as *l·* by our dear, dear Leader,
	346– 2	* as one who has *l·* with her subject

lively

Ret.	5–29	* *l·* sense of the parental obligation,
My.	17–11	"Ye also, as *l·* stones,— *I Pet.* 2 : 5.
	268–22	a *l·* battle with "the world,

livery

Mis.	19–18	taking the *l·* of heaven wherewith to

lives (noun)

affections and

My.	156–23	receive into their affections and *l·*

against the

Mis.	177–11	have sworn enmity against the *l·* of

are the embodiment

Peo.	5– 4	whose *l·* are the embodiment of a

better

My.	352–11	* is proved in better *l·*.

characters and

Mis.	357–23	whose Christian characters and *l·*

children's

Mis.	240– 7	out of the children's *l·*

Christian

My.	213–11	to live pure and Christian *l·*,

cleanse our

Mis.	30–30	cleanse our *l·* in Christ's

lives

crown the

Po.	44– 2	Crown the *l·* thus blest

daily

My.	134– 7	our daily *l·* serve to enhance or to

hearts and

Mis.	291–24	fall gently on the hearts and *l·* of

human

Mis.	19–11	bring them out in human *l·*.
	360– 2	Human *l·* are yet uncarved,

individual

'01.	2– 4	Christianity in individual *l·*

mortal

No.	41–15	compare mortal *l·* with this model

noble

My.	112–22	pure morals and noble *l·*,

of Christian Scientists

Pul.	22– 9	*l·* of Christian Scientists attest
My.	114– 9	to the *l·* of Christian Scientists

of great men

Mis.	340–26	The *l·* of great men and women

of his followers

My.	28–21	* mark the *l·* of his followers.

of its professors

My.	107– 3	Compare the *l·* of its professors

of men

Pan.	10– 6	effects of C. S. on the *l·* of men
Peo.	11–28	the liberty and *l·* of men.
My.	277–14	The characters and *l·* of men
	294– 4	the morals and the *l·* of men,

of mortals

Mis.	114–26	influence upon the *l·* of mortals.

of prophets

My.	103–24	the *l·* of prophets and apostles.

of saints

My.	249–15	patience, silence, and *l·* of saints.

our

Mis.	3– 7	demonstrate in our *l·* the power of
	135– 5	on our lips, and in our *l·*.
	160– 8	Thus may our *l·* flow on
	172–22	demonstrated in our *l·*.
	197– 2	incorporates their lessons into our *l·*
'02.	4–28	thoughts of the Bible utter our *l·*.
Hea.	5–25	would lead our *l·* to higher issues ;
Peo.	7– 7	to beautify and exalt our *l·*.
	7–17	* With our *l·* uncarved before us,
	7–23	* Our *l·* that angel-vision."
My.	132– 1	fulfilment of divine Love in our *l·*
	186– 4	writes . . . their lessons on our *l·*
	215–27	a better example for our *l·*

our own

Peo.	8–10	qualities of character in our own *l·*

their

Mis.	10–17	The best lesson of their *l·*
	84– 8	This cost them their *l·*,
Un.	1–17	able to testify, by their *l·*,
	2–24	because their *l·* have grown so far
Pul.	12–11	loved not their *l·*— *Rev.* 12 : 11.
'01.	32–17	the sermons their *l·* preached
Hea.	9–13	to bring out in their *l·* ?
My.	31–22	* one of the events of their *l·*.
	114–10	book which has moulded their *l·*

their own

Mis.	176–15	counted not their own *l·* dear
	213–16	may perfect their own *l·*

uncontaminated

Mis.	110– 7	it needs . . . uncontaminated *l·*.

visible

Mis.	144–25	our visible *l·* are rising to God.

your

Mis.	106–27	that your *l·* attest your sincerity
Pul.	87–25	luminous lines from your *l·*
My.	143– 2	directs your meetings and your *l·*,
	167–13	loving benedictions upon your *l·*.

Mis.	54– 9	*l·* are worthy testimonials,
	98–23	The *l·* of all reformers
	172– 1	their claims and *l·* steadfast in
'01.	32–18	*l·* of those old-fashioned leaders
My.	28–15	* its influence upon the *l·* of
	28–18	* but in the *l·* of those who,

lives (verb)

Mis.	42–25	learn that good, not evil, *l·*
	86–25	It *l·* with our earth-life,
	115–25	If one *l·* rightly,
	160– 6	*l·* steadily on, through time and
	166– 6	Truth he has taught and spoken *l·*,
	180– 1	"Because he *l·*, I live,"— *see John* 14 : 19.
	205–30	man born of the great Forever, *l·* on,
	269–10	*L·* there a man who can
	294–10	He *l·* for all mankind,
Man.	97– 6	Scientist who *l·* in Boston,
Ret.	70–26	*l·* the truth he teaches.
Un.	10–17	They live, because He *l·* ;
	40–17	*l·* in God, who holds Life by

lives

Un.	41–25	hence matter neither *l·* nor dies.
	48– 9	Because He *l·*, I live.
	63– 4	This trinity of Love *l·* and reigns
Pul.	4–20	Who *l·* in good, *l·* also in God,
	4–20	*l·* in all Life, through all space.
	47–25	* she *l·* very much retired,
	68–11	* She now *l·* in a beautiful
Rud.	3–11	it *l·* more because of his spiritual
	5–10	*L·* there a man who has ever
Po.	24–11	The Life that *l·* in Thee !
My.	39–26	* and the memory *l·* with us.
	164–29	Man *l·*, moves, and has his being
	165– 9	by this spirit man *l·* and thrives,
	195–23	in whom man *l·*, moves, and has
	271–14	* *l·* at eighty-six years of age
	275– 5	it explains love, it *l·* love,
	289–18	*l·* on in the heart of millions.
	295–28	he still *l·*, loves, labors.

liveth

Chr.	55–28	*l·* and believeth in me— *John* 11 : 26.
No.	13– 8	*l·* and believeth in me— *John* 11 : 26.
Pan.	9–13	*l·* and believeth in me— *John* 11 : 26.
'01.	9–27	*l·* most the things of Spirit,
Po.	16– 6	it endureth and *l·* in love.
My.	136– 2	our "Redeemer *l·*"— *Job* 19 : 25.

livid

My.	177–19	succeeding years show in *l·* lines

living (noun)

Mis.	95–17	between the so-called dead and *l·*.
	325–25	charnel-house of the so-called *l·*,
Man.	60–20	daily Christian endeavors for the *l·*
Chr.	53– 7	rouse the *l·*, wake the dead,
Ret.	81– 3	both for the *l·* and the dead.
Un.	62–23	"Why seek ye the *l·* — *Luke* 24 : 5.
'02.	2– 7	sanity and perfection of *l·*,
Hea.	6–13	between the so-called dead and the *l·*.
Po.	25–13	And breath of the *l·* above.
My.	36–17	* peace of a more righteous *l·*,
	46– 5	* more spiritual plane of *l·*,
	46–19	* fulfil the pledge in righteous *l·*,
	264– 6	can speak justly of my *l·*.
	292– 9	His staff comfort the *l·*
	345–27	more etherealized ways of *l·*.
	352–14	* that our daily *l·* may be a

living (adj.)

Mis.	72– 5	only *l·* and true origin, God.
	83– 3	*l·* witness to and perpetual idea of
	114–32	through Christ, the *l·* Truth,
	150–23	peopled with *l·* witnesses
	178–31	new, *l·*, impersonal Christ-thought
	185–27	made a *l·* soul ; — *I Cor.* 15 : 45.
	307– 3	drink with me the *l·* waters
	294– 9	the *l·*, palpable presence
	323–21	drink from its *l·* fountains?
	333–15	away from the only *l·* and true God,
	357– 7	yearn to find *l·* pastures
	372–28	character of the *l·* God,
	376 11	* handed down from the *l·* reality.
	376–13	* *l·* Saviour engraven on the heart.
Chr.	53–19	this *l·* Vine Ye demonstrate.
Ret.	6– 5	* *l·* illustration of Christian faith.
	59–18	only *l·* and true God,
	88–13	apprehend the *l·* beauty of Love,
Un.	14–20	the corner-stone of *l·* rock,
	30–14	made a *l·* soul ; — *I Cor.* 15 : 45.
	30–25	*l·* Soul shall be found a
	38–14	above the *l·* and true God.
	42– 8	because it is not a *l·* . . . reality.
	49–13	*l·* God and the genuine man.
	62–22	"I am the *l·* God,
Pul.	3–21	*l·* waters have their source in God,
Rud.	2– 2	* "a *l·* soul ; a self-conscious being ;
	2– 3	* a *l·* human being,
No.	27–19	* "No man *l·* hath yet seen man."
	27–24	Who *l·* hath seen God
'02.	14– 7	*l·* and life-giving spiritual shield
Po.	29–15	Thou gentle beam of *l·* Love,
My.	12–27	"act in the *l·* present."
	17– 9	unto a *l·* stone, — *I Pet.* 2 : 4.
	46–28	* city of the *l·* God, — *Heb.* 12 : 22.
	64–25	* to be "*l·* stones" — see *I Pet.* 2 : 5.
	70–16	* "Angelus" had *l·* reproductions
	126– 7	such as drink of the *l·* water.
	164–20	has leaped into *l·* love.
	186– 3	that writes in *l·* characters
	191–25	lights the *l·* way of Life.
	192– 5	raise the *l·* dead,
	192–11	lights the *l·* way to Life,
	232–13	as *l·* lights in our darkness :
	268–19	without a *l·* Divina.
	305–19	* of the foremost *l·* authors."
	323–12	* *l·* witness to Truth and Love,
	(see also **faith**)	

living (ppr.)

Mis.	69–27	The man is *l·* yet ;
	344–24	His words, *l·* in our hearts,
	373–18	as *l·* feebly, in kings' courts.
Ret.	40– 3	*l·* on a small annuity.
Un.	7–15	now *l·* who can bear witness to
	40–15	and *l·* imperfectly.
	43–19	more faith in *l·* than in dying.
Pul.	34– 5	* while *l·* in Lynn, Mass.,
	58–28	* with all conveniences for *l·*,
	84– 7	* all that is worth *l·* for,
No.	12–18	*L·* a true life, casting out evil,
Pan.	8–27	*l·* by reason of it,
	14– 7	*l·* the divine Life, Truth, Love,
Po.	68– 3	"I'm *l·* to bless thee ;
My.	82–30	* those *l·* in the streets leading
	139– 3	*l·*, loving, acting, enjoying.
	139– 5	alive to the reality of *l·*,
	166– 7	life is worth *l·*
	268–26	of wedlock, of *l·* and of loving,
	311– 3	While I was *l·* with Dr. Patterson
	323– 9	* by loving it and *l·* it

loaded

Mis.	7– 4	*l·* down with coverings
	7–18	so *l·* with disease seems the
	327–19	gaining the summit, *l·* as they are,

loaf

Mis.	149– 7	to help leaven your *l·*
	175–13	as the leaven expands the *l·*.
My.	272– 2	one who leavens the *l·* of life

loam

Mis.	26–11	from the seedling and the *l·* ;

loan

Mis.	299–25	did he sell them or *l·* them to you?
Pul.	8–11	nor a *l·* solicited,

loathed

Mis.	222–14	would have resisted and *l·* ;

loathes

Ret.	81–18	The enlightened heart *l·* error,

loathing

Mis.	277–31	*l·* the phenomena of drunkenness
My.	249–14	only to satiate its *l·* of

loathsome

Mis.	240–27	nothing but a *l·* worm
Pan.	10–26	no pleasure in *l·* habits

loaves

Pul.	60– 9	* Jesus' miracle of *l·* and fishes.
My.	123–23	"five *l·* and two fishes" — *Matt.* 14 : 17.

lobbies

Pul.	42– 2	* the spacious *l·* and the sidewalks

local

Man.	55– 4	the members of their *l·* church ;
	59–20	The *L·* Members' Welcome
	59–21	privilege of the *l·* members
	70–10	*L·* Self-government.
	96–11	and the *l·* church is unable to meet the
Pul.	41–19	* nearly a thousand *l·* believers.
My.	19–14	* their *l·* church building funds
	21–20	* *l·* members, who have always
	30– 7	* nearly all the *l·* Scientists,
	83– 6	* members of the *l·* arrangement
	330–10	* *l·* Christian Scientist of your city,

localities

Man.	99– 2	to serve in their *l·*.
My.	123–11	one of the finest *l·* in the city,
	216–24	work in your own several *l·*,
	237–18	physicians in their respective *l·*.

locality

Man.	49– 3	healing work in any church or *l·*,
	99–10	to serve in its *l·*.
Ret.	91–12	more . . . than the material *l·*.
My.	83–15	* fewer questions as to *l·*

locate

Man.	68–18	or allows to visit or to *l·* therein
Ret.	82–11	who *l·* permanently in one section,
	82–14	students should *l·* in large cities,

located

Man.	27–21	*l·* in the same building,
	63–18	provided these rooms are well *l·*.
	70–17	churches, *l·* in the same State,
Pul.	24– 8	* It is *l·* at the intersection of
	56–26	* *l·* at Norway and Falmouth Streets,
Pan.	4– 9	*l·* in the brain ;
My.	79– 9	* vast temple *l·* in the heart of
	314– 8	was *l·* in Franklin, N. H.

locates

My.	330– 7	* *l·* Mrs. Eddy in Wilmington in 1843,

location
Man.	68–17	L·.
Pul.	68–26	* meeting held at the present l·
My.	11–25	* The l· is, therefore, determined.
	55– 5	* or church, in a suitable l·.

Locke
Mis.	361–15	L·, Berkeley, Tyndall, Darwin,
My.	349–9	Kant, L·, Berkeley, Tyndall,

Lockport, N. Y.
Pul.	89– 2	* Journal, L·, N.Y.

locks
Mis.	282–12	or our l· picked?
Hea.	18–25	no blind Samson shorn of his l·.

Lodge
My.	334–30	* Grand Secretary of the Grand L·
	335– 9	* a member and officer of the L·

lodge
My.	332–22	* to look up the records of this l·,
	332–26	* the l· was no longer in existence,
	333–15	* procession then returned to the l·,

lodged
Mis.	356–19	have l· in its branches.

lodging-houses
My.	75–11	* assigned rooms in hotels or l·,

loftier
Mis.	235–11	It gives to the race l· desires
Po.	32–10	A l· life to invite
My.	45–30	* l· than the Bunker Hill monument,

loftiest
Mis.	345–17	* the l· intellects have had
Peo.	13–26	* the l· intellects have had

lofty
Mis.	297–12	ventilating his l· scorn of
	392– 8	from thy l· summit, pouring down
Peo.	13–16	l· faith of the pious Polycarp
Po.	v–11	* this l· New Hampshire crag,
	vii– 3	* by the same l· trend of thought
	20–11	from thy l· summit, pouring down
	39– 2	Gifts, l·, pure, and free,
My.	193–25	l· temple, dedicated to God
	287–20	it wakens l· desires,

log
My.	124–24	thy records, time-table, l·,

logarithms
Mis.	54–30	solve a problem involving l· ;

Logia
My.	178–30	L· of Papias, written in A.D.
	178–32	L·, or imputed sayings of Jesus

logic
Mis.	27– 9	abandon their own l·.
	61–29	the l· that man is God's likeness.
	148–15	from necessity, the l· of events,
	195–17	The Master's divine l·,
	209–29	scientific l· and the l· of events,
	223– 8	l·, and revelation coincide.
	360–26	regenerates philosophy and l· ;
	367–26	nor foundation in nature, in l·,
Man.	3–11	from necessity, the l· of events,
Ret.	10– 8	philosophy, l·, and moral science.
Un.	36–24	This error stultifies the l· of
	54–28	diabolical and sinuous l· ?
Pul.	46–25	* philosophy, l·, and moral science,
No.	16–15	infinite l· is the infinite light,
	17– 3	From this l· there is no escape.
'01.	4– 3	In l· the major premise must be
	5–25	God and man . . . or the l· of Truth,
	6–18	l· of divine Science being faultless,
	8–21	l· of divine metaphysics
	23– 2	the numeration table and the l· of
My.	224– 4	should wait on the l· of events?
	272– 4	the l· of events pushes onward
	350– 5	is minus divine l· and plus human

logical
Mis.	26– 5	The only l· conclusion is
	26–30	the l· conclusion that God is
	93–11	the l· conclusion drawn from
	217– 2	which combines in l· sequence,
Un.	33–17	Hence the l· sequence,
	53–17	no more l·, philosophical, or
Pul.	67– 8	* the hub of the l· universe,
Pan.	7–24	the l· sequence of this error
'01.	3–28	l· that because God is Love,
'02.	7–19	No other l· conclusion can be
My.	111–17	l· in premise and in conclusion.
	111–24	his conclusion was l· and divine
	112–13	its l· premise and conclusion,

logically
Mis.	182– 2	to reckon himself l· ;
My.	8–27	* whom we recognize as l· the
	45–26	* l· followed the preceding one.

logos
Mis.	362– 8	Christ's l· gives sight to

logs
Mis.	340–16	drew up l· instead of leases.

loiter
My.	11– 3	* may falter or stumble or l·

London
Can.
Pul.	90–13	* Free Press, L·, Can.

England
Man.	99–19	in which L·, England, is situated
'02.	16–10	Mrs. F. L. Miller, of L·, England.
My.	13– 5	published in L·, England,
	183–10	chapter sub-title
	198– 2	chapter sub-title
	200–10	chapter sub-title
	203–23	chapter sub-title
	205–14	chapter sub-title
	259–10	* from members L·, England,
	295–24	Lancaster Gate, West, L·, England.
	304–15	invited to lecture in L·, England,

Mis.	295– 3	Mr. Wakeman writes from L·,
'00.	1–22	Montreal, L·, Edinburgh,
My.	149–26	could not see L· for its houses.
	252–18	chapter sub-title
	259– 5	First Church of Christ, . . . in L·,

Londonderry, Vermont
Pul.	35–28	* Dr. Asa Gilbert Eddy, of L·, V·,

lone
Mis.	159–22	and to their l· Leader.
	385–18	Brave wrestler, l·.
	386–24	Rears the sad marble . . . In l· retreat.
	392–11	To my l· heart thou art a power
	398–10	Lab'ring long and l·,
Chr.	53– 4	One l·, brave star.
Ret.	4–16	now the l· night-bird cries,
	46–16	Lab'ring long and l·,
Pul.	6–25	as my l· bark rose and fell
	17–15	Lab'ring long and l·,
Po.	2–12	still art thou drear and l· !
	14–14	Lab'ring long and l·,
	20–15	To my l· heart thou art a power
	48–12	Brave wrestler, l·
	50–10	to our memory now, In l· retreat.
	68– 5	sweet pledge to my l· heart
	73–13	The sea-mew's l· cry,
My.	158–11	natal hour of my l· earth life ;
	331–25	* l·, feeble, and bereaved widow

lonely
Mis.	324–27	rushes again into the l· streets,
Po.	53–12	Poor robin's l· mass.
My.	41– 8	* proud are l· and uncomforted,
	309–29	* l· and unstimulating existence.
	309–32	* "l· and unstimulating existence."
	313–16	* long and l· wanderings,

loneness
Pan.	3– 6	that l· lacks but one charm
Po.	31– 8	Deep l·, tear-filled tones of

long
Mis.	ix–15	To preserve a l· course of years
	x–23	the name would be too l·.
	2– 6	a l· and strong determination
	13– 7	which I have l· endured
	99–17	to stand a l· siege,
	106–22	It has l· been a question
	120– 5	Principle of life's l· problem,
	120–21	l· distance from Massachusetts,
	125–17	press on to Life's l· lesson,
	126–26	in the l· race, honesty always
	169– 8	the l· years of invalidism
	177–30	In my l· journeyings I have met
	192–16	as l· as the sun." — Psal. 72 : 17.
	210–28	it may suffer l·,
	215–24	a l· warfare with error
	241–31	discomforted, and who l· for relief !
	261– 3	lasts as l· as the evil.
	281– 7	I learned l· ago that the world
	301–15	to be l· led into temptation ;
	332– 7	* l· winter of our discontent,"
	338–12	suffereth l· and is kind,
	357– 8	These l· for the Christlikeness
	385–16	"You've travelled l·, and far
	393–22	teaching Lessons l· and grand,
	398–10	Lab'ring l· and lone,
Ret.	46–16	Lab'ring l· and lone,
	76–27	I have l· remained silent
Un.	14– 5	l· after God made the universe,
Pul.	17–15	Lab'ring l· and lone
	21– 7	I l·, and live, to see this
	46–16	* not l· before the Revolution.

long

Pul. 48–27 * a l· list of worthy ancestors
49–20 * l· wished to get away from
66–21 * departure from l· respected views
78– 4 * gold scroll, twenty-six inches l·,
79–28 * condition can never l· continue.
82–10 * has l· learned with patience,
82–17 * have l· acknowledged woman as
83– 7 * sunlight cannot l· be delayed.
84–26 * the result of l· years of untiring,
No. 28– 2 How l· this false sense remains
41–19 Through l· ages people have
45– 5 "Charity suffereth l·,— I Cor. 13 : 4.
'01. 1– 5 so l· as you are in His service.
19–22 From . . . to C. S. is a l· ascent,
31–12 After a l· acquaintance with the
'02. 9–25 Did the age's thinkers laugh l·
9–26 Did they quarrel l· with the
Hea. 4–13 to drop divinity l· enough to
Peo. 6– 7 * founded on l· observation
8–26 that man will ere l· stop trusting
Po. 14–14 Lab'ring l· and lone,
48– 9 "You've traveled l·, and far from
52– 6 Lessons l· and grand,
65–17 claspeth earth's raptures not l·,
71–15 Sound it l· !
My. 15–33 * That I have loved so l·.
38– 1 * recompense your l· sacrifice
41–28 * through l· years of consecration
45–13 * have l· prophetically seen
70–30 * which is thirty-two feet l·.
80–31 * l· before seven the auditorium
123–19 Ere I· I will see you in this hall,
130– 6 will ere l· be unearthed and punished
142– 5 * communicants who come l· distances
155–21 May l· lines of light span the
163– 1 l· call the worshipper
169– 4 if you would enjoy so l· a trip
170–27 have come l· distances to kneel
176– 5 L· ago you of the dear South
181– 5 are aided only at l· intervals
189–18 senses wake from their l· slumber
194–25 sacrificed so much and labored so l·.
204– 1 nor will you be l· in doing more.
204–23 too l· treatment of a disease,
222– 5 how l· shall I be with you?— Matt. 17 : 17.
222– 6 how l· shall I suffer you?— Matt. 17 : 17.
231–17 "Charity suffereth l·— I Cor. 13 : 4.
260–23 love that "suffereth l·,— I Cor. 13 : 4.
268–29 Look l· enough, and you see
289–16 Empress of India,— l· honored,
306–30 holding l· conversations with him
311–31 * reached l· division in arithmetic,"
312–26 l· procession, followed the remains
313–16 * l· and lonely wanderings.
318–27 continued with a l· argument.
320 25 * were at times somewhat l·
322– 1 * It is not l· since I met a lady
323– 7 * How l· must it be before the
324–12 * explained how l· you had waited
326–18 in l· procession with tender dirge
(see also **night**)

long so — as

Mis. 85–24 so l· as this temptation lasts,
100–10 so l· as there remains a claim
130– 1 so l· as a hope remained
290– 4 vow is never annulled so l· as the
Man. 15–13 so l· as the belief lasts.
30–21 so l· as Mrs. Eddy does not occupy
37–18 so l· as both are loyal to
Ret. 68–21 so l· as it bases creation on
Un. 49–13 So l· as I hold evil
Pul. 7–27 so l· as this church is satisfied
59– 7 * so l· as there were attendants ;
'01. 13–30 So l· as we indulge the presence
My. 23– 7 * so l· as we follow His commands.
166– 7 so l· as we have the right ideal,
175–25 must remain so l· as I remain.
268– 3 should never be annulled so l· as
318–19 so l· as he refrained from questioning
345– 3 So l· as Christian Scientists obey

long-buried

Po. 67– 5 at work with the l· hours,

longed

Mis. 142–28 I l· to say to the masonic brothers :

longer

Mis. 9–25 wherefore our failure l· to relish
141–26 Delay not l· to commence
229–24 holier, happier, and l· lived.
Pul. 82–27 * l· remain deaf to their cry?
No. 13–11 and though the hiatus be l· still
My. 175–16 must remain with us a little l·,

longer no-

Mis. 5–17 There is no l· any reason for
136– 1 this you must no l· expect.
234– 2 then shall matter remain no l· to
235– 2 He is no l· obliged to sin,
354– 8 can no l· promote peace
Man. 86– 7 no l· under the jurisdiction
Ret. 23– 9 no l· spanned with its rainbow
66– 4 no l· buried in materiality.
93–10 no l· impersonated as a waif
Pul. 3–18 No l· are we of the church militant,
82–28 * The date is no l· B. C.
82–29 * Might no l· makes right,
No. 8–23 no l· cast your pearls before
32–20 no l· be the servants of sin,
34– 6 no l· venture to materialize the
'01. 11– 6 he is no l· a material man,
11– 7 and mind is no l· in matter.
Hea. 8–14 no l· quarrels with the individual.
13–11 until it was no l· aconite,
Peo. 2–22 no l· a personal tyrant
6–19 God is no l· a mystery
6–23 it should no l· be deemed treason
Po. 72– 3 Till God is God no l·
My. 90–28 * can no l· be questioned,
124–31 no l· kindle altars for
126–12 no l· a mystery or a miracle,
132–14 no l· to appeal to human strength,
151–14 when it no l· blesses
216–24 and no l· contribute to
226–16 and the universe would no l· exist.
265–20 no l· tyrannical and proscriptive ;
306– 9 question that is no l· a question.
318–23 until he could control himself no l·
332–26 * the lodge was no l· in existence,

longevity

Mis. 29–20 shows that l· has increased.
My. 103–21 health, l·, and morals of men ;
265–17 increasing the l· of mankind,

Longfellow

Mis. 271–17 and L· is right.

Longfellow's

Ret. 27–15 In L· language,

long-hushed

Mis. 390–20 Ask of its June, the l· heart,
Po. 55–21 Ask of its June, the l· heart,

longingly

Mis. 1– 2 ancient Greek looked l· for
231 30 tear-filled eyes looking l

longings

My. 15–24 * It satisfies my l·,

long-kept

My. 134– 2 tell my l· secret — evidence a heart

long-lost

Po. 24– 3 A balm — the l· leaven

long-suffering

Mis. 130– 2 l·, meekness, charity,
Man. 47– 2 benevolent, forgiving, l·,
Ret. 45–22 l· and temperance, fulfil the
No. 8– 3 We should endeavor to be l·,
Pan. 9–17 l·, self-surrender, and spiritual

look

Mis. 8–12 l· upon the object of your own
66–20 "we l· not at the things — II Cor. 4 : 18.
87–16 to l· after the students ;
112– 5 l· the illusions in the face.
117– 9 We always know where to l· for
134–23 Like Elisha, l· up, and behold :
159–28 I l· at the rich devices in
174–27 We do not l· into darkness for light.
179–26 yet we l· into matter and the
203– 6 as I l· on this smile of C. S.
228– 6 new standpoint whence to l· upward ;
228–13 We should l· with pitying eye on
228–15 This will bring us also to l· on
231–23 a l· of cheer and a toy
239–18 and tired l·, told the story ;
286– 7 We l· to future generations for
292–15 and l· no more into them
294–21 then, l· out for their stings,
299– 6 l· through the lens of C. S.,
307–26 at which the sick may l· and
315–16 l· after the welfare of his students,
324–30 whence he may hopefully l· for
342–16 to l· upon him whom they had
369– 2 l· up with shouts and thanksgiving,
Un. 11–28 I say, L· up, not down,
Pul. 49–15 "L· at those big elms !
83–17 * l· now to their daughters to
Rud. 10–19 l· up to the loving God,
No. 41–12 to l· for perfection in churches

look

'01.	27– 5	* I l· to see some St. Paul arise
	34–10	where shall we l· for the standard
'02.	20–21	great joy to l· into the faces
Hea.	10–16	l· on the bright side ;
	16–26	that we l· into these subjects,
Peo.	5– 8	we l· in vain for their more
	14–15	and l· upon this dream of life
Po.	1–14	from yon cloud-crowned height to l·
	23– 3	A l· that years impart?
My.	47–13	* l· back to the picturesque,
	47–16	* we l· back over the years
	119–29	l· and wait and watch and pray
	120– 1	We l· for the sainted Revelator
	120– 2	Those who l· for me in person,
	151–25	sun-worshippers failed to l·
	151–27	to l· no higher than the symbol.
	234–18	but to l· at both sides of the
	247–20	loving l· which brings forth
	248–26	to face the foe with loving l·
	259– 1	l· again at your gift,
	268–27	L· high enough, and you see
	268–29	L· long enough, and you see
	282– 7	"L· unto me, and be — Isa. 45 : 22.
	327–28	* l· forward to the day, not far
	332–22	* requested to l· up the records

looked

Mis.	1– 2	ancient Greek l· longingly
	320– 9	star that l· lovingly down
	374–20	I never l· on my ideal of
	380– 8	it l· as if centuries of spiritual
Pul.	43–23	* which was l· forward to as the
	71–23	* l· upon as having a divine mission
'01.	29– 2	Have we l· after or even known
'02.	18– 6	when mortals l· ignorantly,
My.	50–16	* and l· towards the spiritual,
	78–10	* They l· upon an interior done
	82– 6	* this morning it l· as though
	119–13	stooped down and l· into the
	119–14	l· for the person, instead of
	221– 5	The prophets of old l· for

looketh

Mis.	320–24	l· down on the long night
	335– 8	he l· not for him, — Matt. 24 : 50.

looking

Mis.	7–17	L· over the newspapers of
	130– 9	l· continually for a fault in
	135–28	You may be l· to see me
	225–23	L· away from all material aid,
	231–30	l· longingly at the portal
	239–19	l· up quaintly, the poor child
	330– 5	l· upward, does it patiently pray
	330–16	l· through Love's transparency,
	331– 2	l· up, waiting on God,
	361–20	l· unto Jesus — Heb. 12 : 2.
	372–11	* "L· at the pictures in your
	374–28	L· behind the veil,
Pul.	46–25	* l· into the ancient languages,
	49– 8	* L· down from the windows
Po.	v–14	* l· "up through nature,
My.	87–20	* cheerful l· groups of people
	124– 6	L· on this annual assemblage
	125–24	l· into the subject of C. S.,
	154–28	whereby we are l· heavenward,
	154–29	not l· nor gravitating earthward,
	204– 7	only by l· heavenward
	258–13	"L· unto Jesus — Heb. 12 : 2.
	343– 3	* l· large-eyed into space,
	346–14	* same expression of l· forward,
	349–16	"l· unto Jesus — Heb. 12 : 2.

look-out

Pul.	48– 5	* straight to her beloved "l·"

looks

Mis.	vii– 4	* my thought l· Upon thy
	23–29	mirror repeats precisely the l· and
	241–24	doubting heart l· up through faith,
	275–10	l· in dull despair at the
	308– 4	Whosoever l· to me personally
	324–11	a face l· out, anxiously surveying
	324–16	he alone who l· from that dwelling,
	325–19	and l· at the Stranger,
	336–25	l· in upon the heart,
	386–11	This hour l· on her heart
	390–12	L· love unto the laughing hours,
Un.	11–16	"That withered hand l· very real
Po.	2– 1	no soul those l· betray ;
	2–13	The moon l· down upon
	49–16	This hour l· on her heart
	55–13	L· love unto the laughing hours,
My.	43–29	* The world l· with wonder upon
	70– 1	* and it certainly l· imposing.
	110– 5	l· down upon the long night of
	119–15	Mary of to-day l· up for Christ,
	257–30	child l· up in prayer,

looms

Mis.	99– 6	through the l· of time,
Pan.	2– 7	l· above the mists of pantheism
My.	232– 5	webs of life in l· of love

loose

Mis.	3–30	"Satan let l·." — see Rev. 20 : 7.
	47–14	let l· from its own beliefs.
	147–18	a l· and unstable character.
	289– 5	Drunkenness is sensuality let l·,
Rud.	4–13	"l· the bands of Orion." — Job 38 : 31.
Peo.	13–18	to let l· the wild beasts upon him,
My.	110–17	luxury of thought let l·,
	249–10	Hate is a moral idiocy let l·

loosed

Ret.	12– 4	Are l·, and not effete ;
Po.	61– 2	Are l·, and not effete ;

loosening

'02.	3– 3	l· cords of non-Christian religions

loosens

Mis.	394– 7	And l· the fetters of pride
Po.	45– 9	And l· the fetters of pride

looseth

Mis.	262–20	divine Love which l· the chains
Po.	79–14	Love l· thee, and lifteth me,

loosing

Mis.	237–28	l· the fetters of one form of

lopsided

Pul.	79–28	* become materialistically "l·,"

loquacious

'01.	16–21	in its origin evil was l·,

Lord (see also Lord's)

and Master

My.	161–17	the cup of their L· and Master
	232–12	Our L· and Master left to us the
	256–19	nativity of our L· and Master.

arm of the

Mis.	183–21	He to whom the arm of the L·
Un.	39–10	He to whom the arm of the L·

beloved in the

Mis.	151–18	Brother, sister, beloved in the L·,
	157– 5	Reign then, my beloved in the L·.

blessing from the

My.	34– 6	the blessing from the L·, — Psal. 24 : 5.

created it

Un.	20– 7	First: The L· created it.

crucified the

Un.	56– 7	"crucified the L· — I Cor. 2 : 8.

fear the

My.	33–23	them that fear the L·. — Psal. 15 : 4.

gave the word

Mis.	153–11	"the L· gave the word : — Psal. 68 : 11.

glory in the

Mis.	270–26	let him glory in the L·." — I Cor. 1 : 31.

glory of the

My.	183–27	glory of the L· is risen — Isa. 60 : 1.

hill of the

My.	34– 1	into the hill of the L· — Psal. 24 : 3.

is God

Un.	21–15	Good. The L· is God.

is gracious

My.	17– 8	that the L· is gracious. — I Pet. 2 : 3.

knows it

Un.	20– 8	Second: The L· knows it.
	44–19	"The L· knows it !"

light in the

My.	206–31	now are ye light in the L· : — Eph. 5 : 8.

loveth

Mis.	18– 3	"Whom the L· loveth — Heb. 12 : 6.
	73– 4	"whom the L· loveth — Heb. 12 : 6.
	125– 4	"whom the L· loveth — Heb. 12 : 6.
	208–19	"whom the L· loveth — Heb. 12 : 6.
Ret.	80– 5	whom the L· loveth — Heb. 12 : 6.

magnify the

Mis.	75–22	doth magnify the L·," — Luke 1 : 46.
	75–23	spiritual sense doth magnify the L· ;"
Un.	30– 2	doth magnify the L· — Luke 1 : 46.
Pul.	12–17	magnify the L· of Hosts.

mind of the

My.	142– 1	known the mind of the L·, — I Cor. 2 : 16.

of heaven

Mis.	167–23	L· of heaven and earth, — Luke 10 : 21.
No.	44–28	L· of heaven and earth, — Luke 10 : 21.

of hosts

My.	34–12	The L· of hosts, — Psal. 24 : 10.
	131–26	the L· of hosts, — Mal. 3 : 10.
	269–26	the L· of hosts, — Mal. 3 : 10.

of the vineyard

Mis.	254–26	the L· of the vineyard — Mark 12 : 9.

one

Mis.	308–17	our Lord is one L·." — Deut. 6 : 4.
Peo.	1– 1	One L·, one faith, — Eph. 4 : 5.
	5– 3	"one L·, one faith, — Eph. 4 : 5.

Lord

one
Peo.	9– 1	one faith, one L·, one baptism ;
	9–11	Having one L·, we shall not be
	14–19	"one L·, one faith, — *Eph.* 4 : 5.
My.	280–15	chapter sub-title — *Deut.* 6 : 4.

our
Mis.	25–15	teachings and life of our L·
	70–21	dying malefactor and our L· were
	70–26	while our L· would soon be rising to
	83–21	In the life of our L·, meekness was
	120–13	in the vineyard of our L· ;
	123–19	from the sepulchre of our L· ;
	193–24	who follow the commands of our L·
	244–31	especially the children of our L·
	276–14	the full coming of our L· and Christ.
	276–19	comes the glory of our L·,
	311– 8	ready for the table of our L· :
	320–10	on the manger of our L·,
	398–26	In the life and the love of our L·.
Ret.	65–19	follows the example of our L·
No.	23– 8	our L· gave the keys of the kingdom
Pan.	14– 5	commune at the table of our L·
'01.	1–11	in unity the love of our L·,
	33– 5	admitted to the vineyard of our L·,
'02.	16–17	agony in the life of our L· ;
Peo.	3–28	way that our L· has appointed ;
	5– 5	have not taken away our L·,
Po.	75– 6	In the life and the love of our L·.
My.	113– 9	immediate disciple of our L·,
	136– 6	and by the life of our L·
	179–20	as depicted in the life of our L·,
	232–12	Our L· and Master left to us the
	250–11	in this vast vineyard of our L·.
	256–19	advent and nativity of our L·
	330– 4	* noteworthy follower of our L·

our blessed
No.	33–14	sacrifice of our blessed L·
My.	201–14	bleeding brow of our blessed L·,

our loved
My.	159– 5	those words of our loved L·,

our loving
Pan.	13–10	the love of our loving L·
My.	18–18	the love of our loving L·

our risen
Man.	60–21	whereby to exemplify our risen L·.

peace of the
Pul.	39– 4	* it finds the peace of the L·

present with the
Mis.	344–22	and present with the L·." — *II Cor.* 5 : 8.

ransomed of the
My.	171– 4	ransomed of the L· — *Isa.* 35 : 10.

redeemed of the
'01.	11–11	and are the redeemed of the L·,

reigneth
Mis.	277–22	"The L· reigneth ; — *Psal.* 97 : 1

reigns
Mis.	368–28	let us not forget that the L· reigns,

rejoice in the
Mis.	330–11	"Rejoice in the L· — *Phil.* 4 : 4.

saith the
Mis.	103–32	saith the L·." — *Jer.* 23 : 23.
	130–16	will repay, saith the L·." — *Rom.* 12 : 19.
	136–16	saith the L·." — *I Cor.* 6 : 17.
My.	131–26	saith the L· of hosts, — *Mal.* 3 : 10.
	154–12	"my Spirit, saith the L·;" — *Zech.* 4 : 6.
	268–18	"Thus saith the L·," — *Exod.* 4 : 22.
	269 26	saith the L· of hosts, — *Mal.* 3 : 10.

shall see the
'02.	16–13	shall see the L·." — *Heb.* 12 : 14.

Spirit of the
My.	128–12	"Where the Spirit of the L· — *II Cor.* 3 : 17.

their
'00.	15– 6	To sit at this table of their L·
'01.	7–20	they have not taken away their L·,
My.	161–17	cup of their L· and Master

thy
Mis.	122–26	into the joy of thy L·." — *Matt.* 25 : 23.

trust in the
Mis.	298– 1	"Trust in the L· — *Prov.* 3 : 5.
'01.	34–29	"Trust in the L· — *Prov.* 3 : 5.
My.	170–20	"Trust in the L·, — *Psal.* 37 : 3.

unto the
Mis.	157–22	thy way unto the L· ; — *Psal.* 37 : 5.
	269– 1	thy way unto the L· ; — *Psal.* 37 : 5.
My.	170–23	thy way unto the L· ; — *Psal.* 37 : 5.
	229– 6	abomination unto the L· : — *Deut.* 18 : 12.

way of the
Mis.	246–24	the way of the L·, — *Matt.* 3 : 3.

word of the
Pul.	7–23	word of the L· endureth — *I Pet.* 1 : 25.

work of the
Chr.	55–13	the work of the L·, — *Isa.* 5 : 12.

Mis.	63–19	the L· He is God ; — *Deut.* 4 : 35.

Lord

Mis.	97–18	"I am the L·, — *Isa.* 45 : 5.
	126–31	the L· shall have them — *Psal.* 2 : 4.
	177– 7	secret conspiracy against the L·
	209–30	and false charity say, "'Not so, L·;'
	229–16	L·, which is my refuge, — *Psal.* 91 : 9.
	245– 5	sought not to the L·, — *II Chron.* 16 : 12.
	268–19	"help is from the L·," — see *Psal.* 121 : 2.
	308–16	The L· our God — *Deut.* 6 : 4.
	364– 5	"Wait . . . on the L·, — see *Isa.* 40 : 31.
	366–11	the L· He is God, — *Deut.* 4 : 35.
	388–20	Last at the cross to mourn her L·,
Man.	18–11	the L· helped us." — *I Sam.* 7 : 12.
Ret.	9–11	"Speak, L· ; — *I Sam.* 3 : 9.
	68– 3	in the name of "the L·," or good,
Un.	2–21	if they die in the L·
	3– 7	which die in the L·." — *Rev.* 14 : 13.
	6–28	"Wait . . . on the L· ;" — see *Psal.* 40 : 1.
Pul.	33– 8	* "Speak, L·, — *I Sam.* 3 : 9.
Rud.	9–16	an answer of the lips from the L·.
	13–14	"The L·, He is God ; — *Deut.* 4 : 35.
'00.	14–27	"L·, lay not this sin — *Acts* 7 : 60.
Po.	21– 9	Last at the cross to mourn her L·,
My.	24–15	* temple in the L·." — *Eph.* 2 : 21.
	33–15	L·, who shall abide in — *Psal.* 15 : 1.
	170–22	also in the L· ; — *Psal.* 37 : 4.
	183– 2	love the L· thy God — *Luke* 10 : 27.
	206–19	"The L· shall be unto thee — *Isa.* 60 : 19.
	229– 7	the L· thy God doth — *Deut.* 18 : 12.
	280–15	chapter sub-title — *Deut.* 6 : 4.
	324–13	* how long you had waited on the L·

lord (*see also* **lord's**)
Mis.	335– 4	l· delayeth his coming ; — *Matt.* 24 : 48.
	335– 7	l· of that servant — *Matt.* 24 : 50.
Pul.	4–24	the l· and giver of Life.
Po.	10– 6	L· of the main and manor !
My.	62– 4	* joy of thy l·." — *Matt.* 25 : 23.
	207–22	joy of thy l·" — *Matt.* 25 : 21.
	337– 7	L· of the main and manor !

Lord God
Mis.	57–20	and the L· G· never said it.
	72–15	saith the L· G·, — *Ezek.* 18 : 3.
	172–14	"the L· G· omnipotent — *Rev.* 19 : 6.
Ret.	15– 8	the strength of the L· G· :— *Psal.* 71 : 16.
My.	v– 1	* L· G· of Hosts, be with us yet ;
	16–24	* thus saith the L· G·, — *Isa.* 28 : 16.
	126–22	L· G· who judgeth her." — *Rev.* 18 : 8.

Lord Jesus Christ
Mis.	196–28	Believe on the L· J· C·, *Acts* 16 : 31,
My.	19– 9	grace of the L· J· C·, — *II Cor.* 13 : 14.

Lord of Hosts
Pul.	12 17	and magnify the L· of H·.

Lord's
Mis.	170– 8	drinking of wine at the L· supper,
Ret.	88–24	The L· command means this,
'02.	11–21	this is thy L· benediction
My.	33–28	earth is the L·, — *Psal.* 24 : 1.
	258–26	hallowed by our L· blessing.

lord's
Man.	28–11	which knew his l· will, — *Luke* 12 : 47.

lords
Mis.	333–15	"l· many and gods — see *I Cor.* 8 : 5.
My.	72–10	* l· and ladies who come to attend

Lord's Prayer
Mis.	211–31	Shall we repeat our L· P· when
	314–10	repeat in concert . . . the L· P·.
	314–18	interpretation of the L· P· ;
	331–17	which taught them the L· P· ?
Man.	63– 1	the L· P· . . . and its Spiritual
Pul.	22– 4	one prayer, — the L· P·.
	43–20	* the L· P·, with its spiritual
'01.	31–23	my cradle hymn and the L· P·,
Hea.	15–24	The L· P·, understood in its
My.	17–25	* audible repetition of the L· P·
	29– 6	* the words of the L· P· !
	32– 4	* began to repeat the L· P·,
	32–18	* the L· P· with its spiritual
	32–31	* audible repetition of the L· P·.
	39–12	* audible repetition of the L· P·,
	78–20	* audible repetition of the L· P·.
	225–16	the leading of our L· P·.
	233– 6	Otherwise, wherefore the L· P·,

lore
Mis.	125–18	the eternal l· of Love ;
Ret.	11– 7	learning's l· and wisdom's might,
Po.	60– 3	learning's l· and wisdom's might,

Los Angeles, Cal.
My.	192–19	chapter sub-title

lose
Mis.	10–13	The good cannot l· their God,
	42– 4	nor does he l· his identity,

lose

Mis.	80– 3	you *l·* much more than can be gained
	84–25	To *l·* error thus, is to live in Christ,
	100–13	may *l·* sight thereof ;
	110– 8	*l·* them not through contact with
	116–30	you *l·* the scientific rule and its
	181–25	Mortals will *l·* their sense of
	182– 9	*l·* their false sense of existence,
	184–16	yield to material sense, and *l·*
	186–18	let us not *l·* this Science of man,
	211– 1	or you will not *l·* them ;
	211–23	save his life shall *l·* it.” — *Matt.* 16 : 25.
	221– 2	may *l·* his power to harm
	242–12	he would *l·* his money.
	265– 8	make mistakes and *l·* their way.
	270–12	to *l·* the priceless knowledge of
	287–10	and thereby *l·* it.
	296–31	*his* shame would not *l·* its blush !
	311–22	I should *l·* my hope of heaven.
	319–14	they must not *l·* sight of sin ;
	327–28	and *l·* sight of their guide ;
	341–19	O learn to *l·* with God !
	354–30	nor his pinions *l·* power
Man.	59– 5	is to *l·* some weight in the scale
Ret.	32– 7	save his life shall *l·* it,” — *Mark.* 8 : 35.
	49–14	Mortals must learn to *l·* their
	80–28	*l·* them in proportion to our
Un.	1–19	they *l·* all sense of error.
	2–17	the sick *l·* their sense of sickness,
	4–14	*l·* our own consciousness of error.
	4–16	how could we *l·* all consciousness of
	49–19	should appear real . . . or we *l·* the
	54– 5	one must *l·* sight of a false claim.
No.	9–13	err in effort, and *l·* your fruition.
	21–18	because by it we *l·* God’s ways
	37–19	*l·* its efficacy and lack the
Pan.	7–11	*l·* the character and sovereignty of
’00.	8–18	We *l·* a percentage due to
’01.	4–10	you *l·* its susceptibility of
	5– 5	*l·* the nature of one God,
	5– 5	*l·* monotheism, and become less
	6–27	*l·* all conceivable idea of
	13–27	To *l·* the sense of sin we must first
Hea.	10–24	win or *l·* according to your plea.
Peo.	10– 4	refinements that *l·* some materiality ;
	12–24	*l·* faith in omnipotence.
Po.	18– 7	tear dim his eye, or pinion *l·* power
My.	120– 3	*l·* me instead of find me.
	134–14	will never *l·* their claim on us.
	142–16	might in time *l·* its sacredness
	149–24	*l·* the Science of Christianity,
	178– 4	nor *l·* the invincible process
	206– 4	*l·* Science, — *l·* the Principle of
	211–17	The victims *l·* their individuality,
	229–14	*l·* all selfishness, as she has
	290– 6	*l·* their lustre in the tomb,

loser

’02.	20–20	I shall be the *l·* by this change,

loses

Mis.	17–31	by which one *l·* himself as matter,
	226–11	he *l·* the homage of fools,
	261–16	atonement of Christ *l·* no efficacy.
	308– 7	*l·* the path to health, happiness,
Un.	2–12	The sinner *l·* his sense of sin,
No.	24– 2	evil *l·* all place, person, and power.
	33– 1	slander *l·* its power to harm ;
	38–26	*l·* a part of its purest spirituality if
’00.	3– 3	he *l·* self in love,
	3– 4	unless he *l·* the chord.
’01.	3–25	*l·* the nature of God, Spirit,
’02.	18–24	faith without proof *l·* its life,
Hea.	13–10	so-called drug *l·* its power.
My.	132–29	and never *l·* a case.
	212–26	*l·* his own power to heal.
	265– 8	*l·* capital, and is bought at par

loseth

Mis.	327–25	*l·* his life for my sake, — *Matt.* 10 : 39.
	358–11	*l·* in Life, Truth, and Love.
My.	233–26	*l·* his life . . . for my sake — *Matt.* 10 : 39.

losing

Mis.	54–11	Instead of *l·* her power
	111– 8	*l·* hold of divine Love,
	113–12	is *l·* in the scale of moral and
	201–26	*l·* those jewels of character,
	226– 9	by *l·* his own self-respect?
	354–13	*l·* the knowledge of the divine
Un.	20–19	You will find yourself *l·* the
	39–26	*l·* the divine likeness.
	47– 4	is *l·* its false claim to existence
No.	41–23	sin is *l·* prestige and power.
’01.	23– 2	*l·* the numeration table
My.	4– 1	*l·* his faith in matter and sin,
	149–22	*L·* the comprehensive in the
	268– 6	marriage relation is *l·* ground,

loss

compensate

Mis.	111–12	compensate *l·*, and gain a higher

error and

Mis.	276–28	error and *l·* will be quickly learned

every

My.	116–22	Every *l·* in grace and growth

gain is

Mis.	358– 7	and their gain is *l·* to the

heavy

Pul.	20– 3	Owing to a heavy *l·*,

his own

My.	212–27	compensate himself for his own *l·*

hour of

Mis.	179– 4	rightful desire in the hour of *l·*,

irreparable

Rud.	16–17	an irreparable *l·* of Science.
My.	333–29	* to lament this irreparable *l·*.”

is gain

Mis.	389–17	God is good, and *l·* is gain.
Po.	4–16	God is good, and *l·* is gain.

its

My.	289–14	its *l·* and the world’s loss,

marked

Mis.	204–16	marked *l·* of faith in evil,

mourn the

My.	291–26	called to mourn the *l·* of

of funds

’02.	13–15	when a *l·* of funds occurred,

of help

My.	195– 5	Adverse circumstances, *l·* of help,

of material objects

Ret.	31– 1	*l·* of material objects of affection

of self-knowledge

Mis.	112–25	then, in a *l·* of self-knowledge

of suffering

Mis.	219–19	ease and *l·* of suffering ;

of the Golden Rule

My.	224–16	blind to his *l·* of the Golden Rule,

of the true sense

Un.	41– 7	a *l·* of the true sense of good,

or gain

Mis.	116–17	express life’s *l·* or gain,

possible

Man.	44– 6	possible *l·*, for a time, of C. S.

shame and

Mis.	267–15	suffered temporary shame and *l·*

sorrow and

Ret.	7–23	* too much of sorrow and *l·*.

temporary

Mis.	99– 8	temporary *l·* of his self-respect.
Un.	41– 9	involves a temporary *l·* of God,

total

Mis.	112–29	total *l·* of moral, intellectual, and

world’s

My.	289–14	its loss and the world’s *l·*,

Mis.	116–17	*l·* of the pleasures and pains
	206–15	no *l·* nor lack of what constitutes
	209–18	The *l·* of gustatory enjoyment
Pul.	9–16	*l·* of our late lamented pastor,
My.	290– 1	a *l·* felt by the strong hearts of

losses

Mis.	xi–27	sadly to survey . . . the enemy’s *l·*.
Ret.	79– 6	from our own material *l·*.
My.	12–19	is the greatest of *l·*.

lost

Mis.	9–22	human enjoyment having *l·* its flavor,
	10–11	God will not let *l·* be *l·* ;
	14–14	if man has *l·* his Principle
	33– 5	and thereby they *l·*, and he won,
	54– 3	*Has Mrs. Eddy l· her power to heal?*
	54– 8	understand . . . what cannot be *l·*.
	59–16	to admit that it has been *l·*
	97–29	the *l·* image is not this
	97–31	corporeal man is this *l·* image ;
	100–11	Love’s labors are not *l·*.
	103–13	form and individuality are never *l·*,
	111– 8	*l·* your fishes, and . . . blamed others
	111–13	Nothing is *l·* that God gives :
	113– 8	free moral agency is *l·* ;
	142–19	my Muse *l·* her lightsome lyre,
	149–13	and see that nothing has been *l·*.
	179– 5	believing we have *l·* sight of Truth,
	182–19	man was never *l·* in Adam,
	184–24	gives back the *l·* likeness and
	185– 1	giving back the *l·* sense of
	186–31	the *l·* sense of man’s perfection,
	190–26	the wrong power, or the *l·* sense,
	195–12	save that which was *l·*.” — *Matt.* 18 : 11.
	211–25	the Life that cannot be *l·*.
	212–12	human will is *l·* in the divine ;
	212–32	*l·* sight of him ;
	221–14	if he denies it, the good effect is *l·*.
	226–10	or what has he *l·* when,

lost

Mis.	226–22	those who have *l·* their honor
	252–25	and restores its *l·* element,
	269– 4	Galileo virtually *l·* it.
	287–12	and restores *l·* Eden.
	295–14	*l·* these sentiments from his
	319– 2	the unreality of evil is *l·*.
	348–25	had *l·* all faith in them.
	352–13	until they are *l·* in light
	357– 5	Let them seek the *l·* sheep
	357– 6	*l·* their great Shepherd
Man.	17–12	and its *l·* element of healing.
	17–18	and restores the *l·* Israel :
Ret.	14– 2	forever *l·* its power over me.
	14– 7	unbelievers in these dogmas *l·*,
	20– 1	*l·* all my husband's property,
	21– 4	informed that my son was *l·*.
	21–30	the *nexus* is *l·*,
	32– 6	whatever is . . . is eventually *l·*.
	54–18	not understood, it may be *l·*,
	62– 1	Unless . . . healing will again be *l·*,
	67–16	false claim called sin is finally *l·*
	73–17	evil is *l·* in supersensible good.
Un.	51–17	They have none of them *l·* their
	53–22	or else he has *l·* his true
	60–24	Without Him, . . . immortality be *l·*.
Rud.	7–11	His likeness would be *l·* if inverted
No.	3–13	not having *l·* the Spirit which
	5–25	*l·* jewel in this misconception of
	10–17	a so-called material sense is *l·*,
	10–17	and Truth restores that *l·* sense,
	43– 1	had *l·* its efficacy for him,
Pan.	5– 1	monotheism is *l·* and
	10–25	never *l·*, in that individual who
	11–25	obliterates the *l·* image
'01.	3–22	is not *l·* by the conclusion,
	13–26	not a sinful soul, that is *l·*.
	34–16	the *l·* chord of Christ ;
'02.	8–29	or His *l·* likeness,
	15– 3	never *l·* my faith in God,
Hea.	3–11	*l·* Christianity and the power to
Peo.	5–11	Truth is not *l·* in the mists
	8– 4	to be saved and others to be *l·*,
Po.	22–20	peace is won, and *l·* is vice :
	77–17	some dear *l·* guest
My.	12–18	*l·* opportunity is the greatest of
	12–21	carelessly *l·* in speaking
	40–11	* Nothing will be *l·*, however,
	46–12	its *l·* element of healing."
	117– 1	the world would not have *l·* the
	117–23	philosophy *l·* to the centuries
	134–12	eclipsed by some *l·* opportunity,
	165–27	*l·* the power of being magnanimous.
	178–14	true sense of life is *l·* to those
	179–14	truths that cannot be *l·*,
	185–19	was *l·*, and is found ;" *Luke* 15 : 32.
	187– 9	hath not *l·* its saltness.
	191–23	Death has *l·* its sting,
	194–14	human self *l·* in divine light,
	220–15	lose all . . . as she has *l·* it,
	231–18	else love's labor is *l·*
	243– 6	cannot have *l·* sight of the rules
	267–23	bitter sense of *l·* opportunities
	278–22	Nothing is gained . . . but much is *l·*.
	283–22	when self is *l·* in Love
	290– 7	her personal virtues can never be *l·*.
	294–31	the loved and *l·* of many millions.
	295– 3	assurance that life is not *l·* ;
	301– 7	loes of religion will be *l·*,
	311–11	and so I *l·* my housekeeper.
	336–12	*l·* all my husband's property,
	339– 5	C. S. cannot be *l·* sight of,

lot

Mis.	80–24	we should commiserate the *l·* of
	139–18	I gave a *l·* of land
	140–20	The *l·* of land which I donated
Ret.	51– 1	I gave a *l·* of land in Boston
'02.	13–16	purchased the mortgage on the *l·*
Po.	79– 1	matters not what be thy *l·*,

lots

Mis.	302– 5	"cast *l·* for his vesture,"— *see Psal.* 22 : 18.
'01.	26–17	and they cast *l·* for it
My.	206–11	divide Truth's garment and cast *l·*

loud

Mis.	238–26	* unable to speak a *l·* word,"
Ret.	8–16	so *l·* that Mehitable heard it,
	16– 9	she could not speak a *l·* word,
Pul.	12– 5	I heard a *l·* voice saying — *Rev.* 12 : 10.
No.	39– 7	*l·* enough to be heard ;
My.	186–12	swelling the *l·* anthem of

louder

Mis.	99–25	speak *l·* than to-day.
	277– 4	Truth is speaking *l·*, clearer,
Pul.	12–18	A *l·* song, sweeter than has

loudest

Mis.	277– 8	Whosoever proclaims Truth *l·*,
Po.	30–19	sacred song and *l·* breath of praise

loudly

Mis.	292–16	It calls *l·* on them to
	326– 6	Once more he . . . knocks *l·*.
'01.	35– 7	appeals *l·* to those asleep
My.	265– 3	knocks more *l·* than ever

Loudon

My.	309– 7	towns of *L·* and Bow,
	309– 9	the counsel for *L·*

Louisville, Ky.

Pul.	89–17	* *Commercial, L·, K·.*

lovable

Mis.	318– 8	less *l·* or Christly.

Love (*see also* **Love's**)

  abiding in

Mis.	135– 8	Abiding in *L·*, not one of you

  aflame with

Po.	22– 5	hundred years, aflame with *L·*,

  allness of

No.	35–12	but to show the allness of *L·*

  alone

Mis.	388–10	For *L·* alone is Life ;
Man.	40– 7	divine *L·* alone governs man ;
Po.	7–10	For *L·* alone is Life ;
My.	247–22	it is *L·* alone that feeds them.

  altar of

Hea.	2–27	sprinkled the altar of *L·*

  amenities of

Man.	40– 9	reflects the sweet amenities of *L·*,

  and Truth

Mis.	133–24	the Jerusalem of *L·* and Truth,
No.	39–14	false sense of Life, *L·*, and Truth,
'02.	6– 4	curse of *L·* and Truth was
	6– 8	*L·* and Truth destroy this knowledge,
Hea.	8– 4	*L·*, and Truth that destroy error
	16–10	and abound in *L·* and Truth,
Po.	77–10	Thou wisdom, *L·*, and Truth,

  and wisdom

Po.	44– 1	O tender *L·* and wisdom,
My.	223–28	divine *L·* and wisdom saith,

  antipode of

Mis.	351–27	declares itself the antipode of *L·* ;

  arms of

Mis.	140–23	put back into the arms of *L·*,

  as God

Mis.	234–10	true sense of *L·* as God ;

  atones

My.	288–26	*L·* atones for sin

  based on

My.	005–27	It is forever based on *L·*,

  beauty of

Ret.	88–13	apprehend the living beauty of *L·*,

  becomes

Mis.	391–13	*L·* becomes the substance,
Po.	38–12	*L·* becomes the substance,

  bonds of

Mis.	135–20	and so cement the bonds of *L·*.

  charity is

Mis.	210–29	Charity is *L·* ;

  chastisements of

My.	282–11	wholesome chastisements of *L·*,

  comes

My.	134–18	*L·* comes to our tears

  decree of

Mis.	118–15	this immutable decree of *L·* :

  define

'01.	3–16	to define *L·* in divine Science

  demands of

Peo.	9– 8	or meet the demands of *L·*.

  demonstrate

'01.	4– 9	demonstrate *L·* according to
'02.	8–17	his deeds, demonstrate *L·*.

  demonstrates

Mis.	209– 9	this Principle demonstrates *L·*,

  demonstration of

Mis.	214– 3	and a demonstration of *L·*,

  divine

    (*see* **divine**)

  door of

Mis.	106–12	Out through the door of *L·*,

  doth enter

Po.	22–19	*L·* doth enter in,

  doth guide

Po.	79– 2	So *L·* doth guide ;

  efficacious

Man.	15–15	of divine, efficacious *L·*,

  eternal

Mis.	206–31	baptismal font of eternal *L·*.
	286–10	the unity of eternal *L·*.

  eternal lore of

Mis.	125–18	the eternal lore of *L·* ;

Love

ever-present
No. 20–18 Ever-present *L·* must seem
'00. 1– 6 ever-present *L·* filling all space,
expresses
'01. 3–23 *L·* expresses the nature of God ;
faith, and
Mis. 152–25 tower of hope, faith, and *L·*,
feast of
'01. 2–18 death's-head at the feast of *L·*,
feet of
Mis. 204– 9 and kisses the feet of *L·*,
flood-gates of
'01. 32–29 through the flood-gates of *L·* ;
forgiving
Mis. 124–26 *L· forgiving its enemies.*
foundation of
Pul. 2–30 reared on the foundation of *L·*,
fruits of
Mis. 100–16 finally show the fruits of *L·*.
Un. 40– 8 and bears the fruits of *L·*,
full of
Mis. 214– 2 Jesus' life was full of *L·*,
gems of
Mis. 343–17 burnishing anew the hidden gems of *L·*,
gives
My. 193–15 *L·* gives nothing to take away.
God and
'02. 8–14 fact that God and *L·* are *one.*
God as
'02. 4–18 chapter sub-title
9– 1 consciousness of God as *L·*
My. 152–16 Do I understand God as *L·*,
God is
(see **God**)
God who is
Mis. 337–11 its Principle, God who is *L·*.
gospel of
Mis. 135–18 spreading the gospel of *L·*,
great
Mis. 77–15 This is the Father's great *L·*
hath one race
Po. 22–13 *L·* hath one race, one realm,
heart of
Po. 24–20 Dear heart of *L·*,
heavenly dews of
Mis. 343–11 by the heavenly dews of *L·*,
heaven of
Mis. 156–10 heaven of *L·* within your hearts.
hieroglyphics of
Mis. 331–31 hieroglyphics of *L·*, are understood ;
home of
Mis. 84–25 traveller, to the home of *L·*.
hungry for
Mis. 369–20 We are hungry for *L·*,
ideal of
Hea. 10– 8 presented the highest ideal of *L·*.
illimitable
Pul. 4–24 Wait patiently on illimitable *L·*,
immortal
Mis. 292–18 unlike the risen, immortal *L·* ;
immovable
Ret. 89– 1 stillness and immovable *L·*.
impels
Mis. 358– 1 *L·* impels good works.
infinite
Mis. 59–14 pleading with infinite *L·* to love us,
123– 8 the forever-law of infinite *L·*,
292– 9 rare revelation of infinite *L·*,
Ret. 14–10 the good pleasure of infinite *L·*.
23– 5 merged into the one infinite *L·*.
'01. 7– 1 as the personality of infinite *L·*,
'02. 5–28 an antipode of *infinite L·*
6–29 wherein God is infinite *L·*,
14–26 outstretched arm of infinite *L·*
Hea. 4– 6 the effects of infinite *L·*,
4–13 We expect infinite *L·* to
My. 178– 9 in the laboratory of infinite *L·*
inseparable from
My. 185–17 Life is . . . inseparable from *L·*,
instead of
Mis. 351–23 wherefore it is hate instead of *L·* ;
intelligence and
Mis. 16–22 an all-pervading intelligence and *L·*,
is at the helm
Mis. 113–25 when *L·* is at the helm of thought,
is divine Principle
'01. 3–28 God is Love, *L·* is divine Principle ;
is God
'01. 3–21 * no argument that *L·* is God ;
is Life
Mis. 12–26 and *L·* is Life and Truth.
is my God
Mis. 206–22 *L·* is my God, and my God is Love."

Love

is our refuge
Mis. 389–10 *L·* is our refuge ;
Po. 4– 9 *L·* is our refuge ;
is Principle
No. 19–12 *L·* is Principle, not person.
is spiritual
Mis. 351–21 *L·* is spiritual,
is the liberator
My. 268–23 in which *L·* is the liberator
is the master
Mis. 336– 1 *L·* is the master of hate ;
is the Principle
Mis. 117–13 *L·* is the Principle of unity,
234– 6 *L·* is the Principle of divine
'02. 8–20 and *L·* is the Principle thereof.
is the way
'01. 35–10 *L·* is the way alway.
is triumphant
Mis. 153– 4 and *L·* is triumphant.
jewels of
Ret. 79–23 jewels of *L·*, set in wisdom.
joy of
No. 8– 7 beauty of holiness, the joy of *L·*
justice and
Ret. 80–17 permeate justice and *L·*,
law of
(see **law**)
lessons of
Ret. 21–23 lucid and enduring lessons of *L·*
Life and
(see **Life**)
life of
My. 301–11 Father, teach us the life of *L·*.
Life, Truth, and
(see **Life**)
Life, Truth, or
Mis. 67– 6 not adulterate Life, Truth, or *L·*,
light of
Mis. 132– 5 to the light of *L·*— and By-laws.
320–28 is the light of *L·*,
light to
My. 234–14 from light to *L·*, from sense to Soul.
likeness of
'02. 8– 6 the likeness of *L·* is loving
living
Po. 29–15 Thou gentle beam of living *L·*,
looseth
Po. 79–14 *L·* looseth thee, and lifteth me,
lost in
My. 283–23 when self is lost in *L·*
loved of
Hea. 2–21 loved of the Father, the loved of *L·*
makes
Mis. 133–29 *L·* makes all burdens light,
Hea. 17– 7 *L·* makes the spiritual man,
manifestations of
Mis. 102–19 are the manifestations of *L·*.
Mind is
Mis. 332– 5 merciful, and wise, this Mind is *L·*,
Mother
Mis. 159–24 "O glorious Truth ! O Mother *L·* !
nature of
'02. 7– 1 the true nature of *L·* intact
not hate
My. 239– 1 Truth, not error ; *L·*, not hate.
ocean of
Mis. 205–14 in the infinite ocean of *L·*,
offspring of
Mis. 117–13 Obedience is the offspring of *L·* ,
omnipotent
Mis. 183– 3 omnipotent *L·*, and eternal Life,
Un. 39– 7 omnipotent *L·* which annihilates hate,
omnipresent
Mis. 307– 7 understanding of omnipresent *L·* !
opens the eyes
Mis. 210–29 *L·* opens the eyes of the blind,
opposed to
My. 279– 1 an element opposed to *L·*,
panoply of
Pul. 15–19 Clad in the panoply of *L·*,
peace in
'02. 19–18 a rest in Christ, a peace in *L·*.
peace of
My. 185– 8 The peace of *L·* is published,
perfect
Mis. 229–27 the "perfect *L·*"— *I John* 4: 18.
334–32 the might of perfect *L·*
Ret. 61–17 for 'perfect *L·*— *I John* 4: 18.
Un. 20–16 and so reach that perfect *L·*
Peo. 6–16 whereas "perfect *L·*— *I John* 4: 18.
power of
No. 9–21 and show the power of *L·*.
prevailing
My. 50–18 * of *L·* prevailing over the

Love

purpose of
Mis. 214–15 accomplishing its purpose of *L*·,
purposes of
Mis. 292–24 works out the purposes of *L*·.
realm of
Pul. 10–15 hope's reality — the realm of *L*·.
redeeming
'00. 2– 5 old-new theme of redeeming *L*·
reflect
Mis. 150–29 that reflect Him — that reflect *L*·.
reflected
Mis. 293–21 sum total of *L*· reflected is
represents
Mis. 104–26 and its idea represents *L*·.
righteousness of
My. 182–31 abound in the righteousness of *L*·,
rules
My. 278– 7 *L*· rules the universe,
same
Mis. 214–11 Jesus was stimulated by the same *L*·
sends forth
Pul. 12–21 *L*· sends forth her primal . . . strain.
significance of
Mis. 250–11 The divine significance of *L*·
spirit of
Mis. 288–29 spirit of *L*· that nerves the
No. v– 4 self-sacrificing spirit of *L*·
spiritual
Mis. 288– 7 weighed by spiritual *L*·,
spontaneity of
My. 185–16 Life is the spontaneity of *L*·,
steadfast in
Mis. 12–16 watchful and steadfast in *L*·,
sunshine of
My. 252–22 eternal sunshine of *L*·,
that guards
Mis. 331–20 Thou *L*· that guards the nestling's
389– 8 Thou *L*· that guards the nestling's
Po. 4– 5 Thou *L*· that guards the nestling's
that is Life
My. 275–16 truth of being — the *L*· that is Life
the word
Pul. 26–22 * over the door, . . . the word "*L*·."
this
Un. 20–17 then see if this *L*· does not
touch of
My. 256–21 springs aside at the touch of *L*·.
trespass on
Pul. 3– 9 nothing can . . . trespass on *L*·.
trinity of
Un. 63– 4 trinity of *L*· lives and reigns
triumphant
Mis. 124–29 to understanding, *L*· triumphant !
Truth and
(*see* Truth)
Truth, Life, and
(*see* Truth)
truth of
Mis. 287–11 corrects . . . with the truth of *L*·,
337– 2 that which reveals the truth of *L*·,
unction of
'00. 11–18 I want . . . the unction of *L*·.
understanding and
Pul. 22–18 spiritual understanding and *L*·,
understanding of
My. 278–12 armed with the understanding of *L*·,
unfolds
My. 288– 2 *L*· unfolds marvellous good
universal
Mis. 141–11 proposed type of universal *L*· ;
Peo. 2–25 *L*· universal, infinite, eternal.
unquenchable
Mis. 77–19 impartial, and unquenchable *L*·
328–12 unchanging, unquenchable *L*·
unveiled
Ret. 31–29 *L*· unveiled the healing promise
which is faithful
My. 167– 9 in that *L*· which is faithful,
will reign
Mis. 213–29 *L*· will reign in every heart,
wisdom and
Mis. 321–29 a world of wisdom and *L*·

Mis. ix–20 a *L*· that is a boy,
8–15 *L*· that is omnipresent good,
11–14 *L*· metes not out human justice,
12–27 demonstrably is not *L*·.
23–26 reflects good, Life, Truth, *L*·.
63– 7 Life, Truth, *L*· are the triune
100–27 He understands this Principle, — *L*·.
104–24 How shall we . . . Through *L*·.
104–25 The Principle of C. S. is *L*·,
124–15 ever-living Life, Truth, *L*· :
130–29 *L*· is not puffed up ;
186– 2 who originates in God, *L*·,

Love

Mis. 187–22 God, — Life, Truth, *L*·.
209– 8 Principle of divine Science being *L*·,
212–22 and *L*·, the white Christ,
215–15 *L*·, peace, and good will toward
234– 6 *L*· is not learned of the material
249–27 chapter sub-title
277–26 *L*· is especially near in times of
290–11 divine Principle, which is *L*·,
292– 7 *L*· had a new commandment
292–12 higher sense I entertain of *L*·,
322–13 the *L*· they demonstrate,
351–21 it says, "I am *L*·,"
352– 4 regarding Life, Truth, *L*· as
358– 1 *L*· is greatly needed,
384–13 And *L*·, the evermore.
384–19 * *L*·, like the sea,
387– 7 poem
387–24 from that *L*·, divinely near,
388– 5 'T was *L*· whose finger traced
397–19 An offering pure of *L*·,
399– 2 *L*· wipes your tears all away,
Ret. 60–29 one Truth, Life, *L*·,
61–20 *L*· that casts out fear.
65–23 *L*·, fulfilling the law and
Un. 25–25 the eternal All, — Life, Truth, *L*·,
29–14 eternal, — Truth, Life, *L*·.
56–25 *L*· which is without dissimulation
Pul. 3– 4 Can *L*· be less than boundless?
13– 2 as *L*·, represented by the Mother.
19– 3 An offering pure of *L*·,
21– 5 loves only because it *is L*·.
Rud. 2–19 supreme good, Life, Truth, *L*·.
10–18 *L*· punishes nothing but sin,
No. 20–10 substance, Life, Truth, *L*·.
Pan. 12–24 self-existent Life, Truth, *L*·,
14– 7 living the divine Life, Truth, *L*·,
'01. 3–19 called in Scripture, Spirit, *L*·.
4– 1 *L*· as either divine Principle or
4–26 because this *L*· is divine Principle,
5– 8 named in the Bible Life, Truth, *L*·
7– 5 in C. S. being Life, Truth, *L*·,
8– 4 idea of the divine Principle, *L*·.
18–26 The divine Life, Truth, *L*·
32–30 *L*· was the governing impulse of
'02. 7–14 *L*·, without beginning and without
20–14 'T was *L*· whose finger traced
Hea. 19–16 Heaven's signet is *L*·.
Peo. 2–11 divine Principle, — Life, Truth, *L*· ;
Po. page 6 poem
6–19 from that *L*·, divinely near,
7– 5 'Twas *L*· whose finger traced
13– 7 An offering pure of *L*·,
36–12 And *L*·, the evermore.
36–18 * *L*·, like the sea,
47– 9 Ever to Truth and to *L*·
75– 9 *L*· wipes your tears all away,
My. 40–28 * obeyed the divine Principle, *L*·,
41–31 * how illimitable is the *L*· which
110–14 God is divine Principle, *L*·,
150– 1 where *L*· has not been before thee
164–30 has his being in God, *L*·.
164–30 *L*· must necessarily promote and
180–17 C. S. meets . . . hate with *L*·,
185–14 *L*· is the generic term for God.
185–14 *L*· formed this trinity,
185–15 this trinity, Truth, Life, *L*·,
200–29 with its divine Principle, *L*·.
206–17 fact that portrays Life, Truth, *L*·.
214–13 and *L*· to be the master of hate.
225–22 names God as divine Principle, *L*·,
225–28 His synonyms are *L*·, Truth, Life,
226–20 the intelligent divine Principle, *L*·.
267–26 man's divine Principle, *L*·,
269– 3 infinite divine Principle, *L*·,
281–10 the Father-Mother *L*·, is ours
303–10 divine Principle — God, *L*·
348–29 *L*· is the basic Principle

love (*see also* love's)

abounding in
My. 155– 6 always abounding in *l*·
affection or
Ret. 80– 1 an unselfish affection or *l*·,
alight with
My. 160– 5 is seldom alight with *l*·.
all-conquering
My. 258–11 Christ's all-conquering *l*·.
all's
My. 40–27 * "All's *l*·, but all's law."
alone
Mis. 32–14 *l*· alone is admissible
and God
Mis. 395– 4 Is out of tune With *l*· and God ;
Po. 57–11 Is out of tune With *l*· and God ;

love

and good will
'02. 8–12 *l·* and good will towards men.
My. 201– 6 *l·* and good will to man,

and gratitude
Man. 75– 9 this Church's *l·* and gratitude,
Pul. 86–22 * testimonial of *l·* and gratitude
My. 58–16 * *l·* and gratitude of a great multitude
325–16 increasing *l·* and gratitude,

and hate
'00. 4– 1 misnomer couples *l·* and hate,

and leadership
My. 356– 3 His reflection of *l·* and leadership

and light
Mis. 149– 6 what they possess of *l·* and light

and loyalty
Mis. 275–24 expressions of *l·* and loyalty

and pride
Po. 8–21 light of a home of *l·* and pride ;

and respect
My. 331–11 * *l·* and respect entertained for

and righteousness
My. 292– 1 *l·* and righteousness achieve

and thanks
My. 257–27 two words enwrapped, — *l·* and *thanks.*

and unity
My. 39–28 * our own growth in *l·* and unity
205–15 *L·* and unity are hieroglyphs

anthems of
Pul. 81–23 * the unwritten anthems of *l·*.

apart from
My. 189–17 no loyalty apart from *l·*.

apostles of
Po. 25–10 Fair floral apostles of *l·*,

benevolence and
Mis. 199– 1 not reward benevolence and *l·* with

betokens a
My. 290– 1 It betokens a *l·* and a loss felt by

bonds of
Mis. 273–14 bonds of *l·* and perfectness,

brotherly
Mis. 149–22 of Christianity, brotherly *l·*,
Man. 77–19 wisdom, economy, and brotherly *l·*
'00. 14–14 signifies "brotherly *l·*." — *Heb.* 13 : 1.
My. 41–20 * brotherly *l·* which is just and kind
153– 9 the church of brotherly *l·*,
175–26 Let brotherly *l·* continue.
196– 6 called the "city of brotherly *l·*."
213– 2 brotherly *l·*, spiritual growth and

bruised
No. 34–23 *L·* bruised and bleeding,

Christian
My. 362–24 * in the bonds of Christian *l·*

circle of
'02. 2–29 in the circle of *l·*, we shall meet

claspeth
Po. 65–17 *l·* claspeth earth's raptures

compassionate
My. 37– 6 * gratitude and compassionate *l·*

constant as
Po. 15–20 constant as *l·* that outliveth

core of
My. 350–17 bitter searing to the core of *l·*,

dear
Mis. 81– 5 by right of God's dear *l·*,
330–10 springtide of Christ's dear *l·*.
My. 257– 3 more of His dear *l·*
258–28 consciousness of God's dear *l·*

deep
My. 44–27 * greetings and their deep *l·*.
195–11 letting the deep *l·* which I cherished

demands on
Mis. 250–16 I make strong demands on *l·*,

demonstrated
Pul. 21– 8 to see this *l·* demonstrated.

demonstrates
My. 275– 5 it demonstrates *l·*.

depths of
My. 258–24 him who sounded all depths of *l·*,

devoted
My. 328– 3 * With devoted *l·*,

diadems of
My. 258–20 coronals of meekness, diadems of *l·*.

divine
Mis. 388– 9 Fed by Thy *l·* divine we live,
'00. 11–13 compensated by divine *l·*.
Po. 7– 9 Fed by Thy *l·* divine we live,

early
My. 182– 7 my early *l·* for this church

earthly
Mis. 395–21 Is every earthly *l·* ;
Po. 58– 6 Is every earthly *l·* ;

enfolds thee
My. 290–14 Him whose *l·* enfolds thee.

everlasting
My. 131–13 the covenant of everlasting *l·*.

love

explains
My. 275– 5 it explains *l·*, it lives love,

faith and
Mis. 176–17 steadfast in faith and *l·*,
My. 64–23 * with renewed faith and *l·*
152–25 God, demands all our faith and *l·* ;
156–20 with hope, faith, and *l·* ready

fallible
Mis. 332– 5 Mind is Love, — but not fallible *l·*.

fire of
Mis. 176–22 melted away in the fire of *l·*

first
'00. 12–19 left thy first *l·* — *Rev.* 2 : 4.
15–24 left thy first *l·*, — *Rev.* 2 : 4.
My. 131–14 praise return to its first *l·*,

for all
My. 341–14 in her heart is beating A *l·* for all

for God
Mis. 12–28 should measure our *l·* for God by
50–28 and *l·* for God and man ;
126– 6 with *l·* for God and man.
348– 6 hearts overflowing with *l·* for God,
Peo. 14–13 holier *l·* for God and man ;
Po. 11– 4 The *l·* for God and man.
My. 158–17 manifests *l·* for God and man.
287–15 only and true sense of *l·* for God,
338– 4 The *l·* for God and man.

for his enemies
My. 270–19 breathing *l·* for his enemies,

for life
My. 90–10 * All the passionate *l·* for life

for man
Mis. 12–28 our love for God by our *l·* for man ;
234– 9 In *l·* for man, we gain a
Pan. 8–23 rest on the basis of . . . *l·* for man.
My. 287–15 In *l·* for man we gain the

for mankind
My. 288– 8 *L·* for mankind is the elevator of

for one another
Mis. 91–11 compact is *l·* for one another.

for the sake of
Pul. 81–15 * scorn self for the sake of *l·*

fulfils
My. 106– 4 *l·* fulfils divine law
275–25 self-oblivious *l·* fulfils the law

full of
My. 167–17 full of *l·*, peace, and good will
338–19 heart full of *l·* towards God

God is
Un. 26–16 * God is wisdom, God is *l·*.

God's
Mis. 154– 6 God's *l·* for His flock is
307–17 God's *l·* opening the eyes of
Ret. 13–19 bade me lean on God's *l·*,
47–18 partakes less of God's *l·*.
My. 174–26 increasing sense of God's *l·*,
180– 2 man can prove God's *l·*,

goodness and
Po. 67–23 fragrance of goodness and *l·* ;

gratitude and
Mis. 160– 3 gratitude and *l·* unite more
Man. 60–16 Gratitude and *l·* should abide
Pul. 85–15 * is entitled to the gratitude and *l·*
My. 64– 7 * tender gratitude and *l·* for all
194–22 token of your gratitude and *l·*.

great
Mis. 182–25 their place in God's great *l·*,

growth in
My. 39–28 * our own growth in *l·* and unity

guided by
My. 235– 6 tender mother, guided by *l·*,

habitual
Mis. 18–24 habitual *l·* for his fellow-man.

hand of
'01. 33– 6 hand of *l·* must sow the seed.

heart's
My. 236– 3 accept my full heart's *l·*

hearts all
Po. 9–11 reason made right and hearts all *l·*.

heel of
'00. 10– 2 Hatred bites the heel of *l·*

her
Mis. 127– 4 that in the ratio of her *l·*
Ret. 90–21 labors with her *l·*, to promote
Pul. 82– 7 * whom her *l·* had glorified
My. 18– 1 that in the ratio of her *l·*

His
Mis. 127– 5 hath His *l·* been bestowed upon her ;
138–27 under the banner of His *l·*,
154–24 Continue in His *l·*.
208–20 His rod brings to view His *l·*,
249–25 in the amplitude of His *l·* ;
322–25 the omnipotence of His *l·* ;
Po. 33–12 that His *l·* I may know,
My. 18– 2 hath His *l·* been bestowed upon her ;

love

His
My. 187–29 of the riches of His *l·*
292–10 O may His *l·* shield, support,
his
Mis. 84–23 to quench his *l·* for it.
238– 9 silent endurance of his *l·*.
'02. 19– 2 Yet behold his *l·* !
My. 15–21 * Of Jesus and his *l·*.
His rod is
My. 288–28 His rod is *l·*.
holiness and
'01. 12–19 with health, holiness, and *l·*.
My. 274– 6 goodness, holiness, and *l·* do this,
hospitable
My. 40– 2 * evidence to us of her hospitable *l·*.
human
Mis. 107–13 should swell the lyre of human *l·*.
290–11 human *l·*, guided by the divine
308– 5 by reason of human *l·* or hatred
humility and
Mis. 358–15 humility, and *l·* are divine strength.
impulse of
Mis. 272–30 with the intuition and impulse of *l·*.
induced by
My. 349–28 induced by *l·* and deduced from God,
interchange of
Mis. 100–23 home, the interchange of *l·*,
is allegiant
My. 189–16 for *l·* is allegiant,
is consistent
Mis. 312– 4 *L·* is consistent, uniform,
is the fulfilling
Mis. 11– 3 *L·* is the fulfilling of the law :
258– 2 *l·* is the fulfilling of the law.
285– 9 *L·* is the fulfilling of the law.
is universal
No. 8– 1 Father, . . . whose *l·* is universal.
it lives
My. 275– 5 It explains love, it lives *l·*,
labors and
Mis. 322–23 my past poor labors and *l·*.
lack of
Peo. 8– 6 or lack of *l·* that will not ;
law of
My. 41– 9 * thoughts adverse to the law of *l·*.
leaving self
Peo. 9– 5 *l·* leaving self for God.
legacy of
Ret. 92– 7 inherit his legacy of *l·*,
lesson of
Mis. 207– 1 ponder this lesson of *l·*.
liberty and
My. 236–18 amplitude of liberty and *l·*
248–27 labor, duty, liberty, and *l·*,
life and
My. 88–21 * serenity of faith, life, and *l·*
113–29 a more spiritual life and *l·*
159–21 Truth, life, and *l·* are the only
268–24 Truth, canonized by life and *l·*,
life and the
Mis. 398–26 life and the *l·* of our Lord.
Po. 75– 6 life and the *l·* of our Lord.
life-giving
Pul. 10– 2 self-immolation, his life-giving *l·*,
life of
'02. 19–29 our Saviour in his life of *l·*.
Peo. 5– 7 a deathless life of *l·* ;
light and
Mis. 184–25 that light and *l·* ineffable,
235–11 the light and *l·* of Truth.
My. 355–23 the reflection of light and *l·* ;
lilies of
My. 155–27 gathering Easter lilies of *l·*
lived
My. 287–12 *L·* lived in a court or cot
liveth in
Po. 16– 6 endureth and liveth in *l·*.
living
My. 164–20 has leaped into living *l·*.
loathing of
My. 249–15 satiate its loathing of *l·*
looks
Mis. 390–12 Looks *l·* unto the laughing hours,
Po. 55–13 Looks *l·* unto the laughing hours,
looms of
My. 232– 5 webs of life in looms of *l·*
made perfect
Mis. 138–16 *l·* made perfect through the cross.
manifest
Mis. 147–12 manifest *l·* for those that hate
manifestations of
'02. 7– 4 His infinite manifestations of *l·*
manifested in
Mis. 357–19 mental growth is manifested in *l·*,

love

meekness and
My. 161–30 learns through meekness and *l·*
mercy, and
Mis. 152–16 May meekness, mercy, and *l·* dwell
Pul. 9– 8 mercy, and *l·* kindle perpetually its fires.
might of
My. 258–28 give you the might of *l·*,
more
Mis. 107–11 More *l·* is the great need of
Mother's
Mis. 354– 8 When the Mother's *l·* can no longer
mother's
Mis. 160– 4 But a mother's *l·* behind words
253–22 mother's *l·* touches the heart of God,
Po. 8–18 Of a mother's *l·*, that no words
mutual
Ret. 44–28 a great revival of mutual *l·*,
my
My. 163–13 cannot show my *l·* for them in social
167–19 Give to all the dear ones my *l·*,
192–26 My *l·* can fly on wings of joy
253–15 Accept my *l·* and these words
obedience, and
Mis. 127–13 more grace, obedience, and *l·*.
My. 18–10 more grace, obedience, and *l·*.
ocean of
My. 202–24 a drop from His ocean of *l·*,
of a Father
No. 30–13 *l·* of a Father for His child,
of Christ
Mis. 246–10 when the *l·* of Christ would have
Rud. 17– 3 to convert . . . to the *l·* of Christ,
of God
(see **God**)
of good
Mis. 232–26 sought from the *l·* of good,
of pictures
Mis. 365– 7 what a child's *l·* of pictures is to
No. 18–16 what a child's *l·* of pictures is to
of self
Un. 27– 9 passionate *l·* of self,
of the Scriptures
'00. 7– 6 greater *l·* of the Scriptures
on a false basis
Mis. 287–10 may place *l·* on a false basis
one in
Mis. 387–19 make men one in *l·* remain.
Po. 6–14 make men one in *l·* remain.
our
Mis. 12–28 measure our *l·* for God by our *l·* for
My. 37–32 * our rejoicing, and our *l·*
38– 5 * renew the story of our *l·* for you
outpouring
No. 33–19 outpouring *l·* that sustains man's
overflowing
Peo. 9– 4 an overflowing *l·*, washing away the
patient
Po. 30–17 a patient *l·* above earth's ire,
peace and
Mis. 152– 8 thoughts winged with peace and *l·*
Ret. 42–14 with a smile of peace and *l·*
'00. 11–12 The human sigh for peace and *l·*
peace of
My. 220–23 to know the joy and the peace of *l·*."
perfect
Mis. 138–16 perfect *l·*, and love made perfect
176– 3 healing, and peace, and perfect *l·*.
My. 159–14 perfect *l·* of God and man.
perfumed
Mis. 396–25 in raptured song, With *l·* perfumed.
Pul. 18– 9 in raptured song, With *l·* perfumed.
Po. 12–11 in raptured song, With *l·* perfumed.
power, and
Un. 2– 8 God's presence, power, and *l·*,
present
My. 176– 7 the past by your present *l·*.
prize
My. 123– 4 must continue to prize *l·* even more
proof of
My. 106– 4 and without this proof of *l·*
purity, and
Mis. 195–32 meekness, purity, and *l·*,
Pul. 9–25 purity, and *l·* are treasures
recompense of
No. 3–24 trust Love's recompense of *l·*.
redolent with
Mis. 194–12 redolent with *l·*, health, and
remembrance and
Mis. 91–16 conditions,— remembrance and *l·* ;
My. 166–13 proof of your remembrance and *l·*.
result of the
My. 62– 6 * To me it is the result of the *l·*
sanctuary of
Mis. 159–14 into this sanctuary of *l·*,

love

selfless
Mis. 294– 7 With selfless *l·*, he inscribes on the

selflessness, and
Rud. 17–16 selflessness, and *l·* are the paths of

self-renunciation, and
Ret. 30– 6 toil, self-renunciation, and *l·*,

sense of
Mis. 17– 4 opposed to the material sense of *l·* ;
351–28 this false sense of *l·*,
'02. 18–18 It is a false sense of *l·*
My. 287–15 the only and true sense of *l·*

sensuous
Mis. 351–22 sensuous *l·* is material,

shall dwell
Pul. 84– 5 * *l·* shall dwell in the tents of hate ;

shout of
My. 289–18 this shout of *l·* lives on

soil of
Mis. 392–16 deeply rooted in a soil of *l·* ;
Po. 20–20 deeply rooted in a soil of *l·* ;

spirit of
Po. 66– 6 spirit of *l·*, at soft eventide

spiritual
(*see* **spiritual**)

talked
My. 287–11 *L·* talked and not lived is a poor

test of
'02. 17– 4 obedience is the test of *l·* ;
My. vii–10 * the sound test of *l·* ;

that
Mis. 254– 5 all that *l·* which brooded tireless
254– 6 all that *l·* that hath fed them
Pul. 21– 3 that *l·* wherewith Christ loveth

that destroys sin
My. 288–27 through *l·* that destroys sin.

that foresees
Mis. 238–18 the *l·* that foresees more to do,

that heals
My. 52– 7 * or the *l·* that heals.

that is talked
Mis. 312– 2 may the *l·* that is talked, be *felt!*

that rebukes
My. 162–18 the *l·* that rebukes praises also,

their
Mis. 203– 8 mirror their *l·*, loyalty, and
277– 1 is wedded to their *l·*,
Pan. 14–20 Oh, may their *l·* of country,
'01. 29–13 selfish in showing their *l·*.
My. 85–25 * Mecca of their *l·* and duty.

their Leader's
My. 155–29 their Leader's *l·*, which she sends

this
Pul. 21– 8 live, to see this *l·* demonstrated.
Pan. 9–23 this *l·* benefits its enemies
'00. 11– 7 weaned me from this *l·*
My. 133–24 and the nature of this *l·*
234– 8 to express this *l·* in labor for them,

Thy
Mis. 275–17 that Thy light and Thy *l·* reach earth,
388– 9 Fed by Thy *l·* divine we live,
Po. 7– 9 Fed by Thy *l·* divine we live,
77– 6 Yet wherefore this Thy *l·*?

to God
Pul. 39– 2 * great essentials of *l·* to God
My. 274–24 and *l·* to God and man ;

token of
My. 172–29 as a simple token of *l·*."

to man
Pul. 39– 2 * love to God and *l·* to man

translates
Mis. 124–28 This grand act . . . translates *l·* ;

truth, and
(*see* **truth**)

unforgotten
Po. 34–22 O'er joys departed, unforgotten *l·*.

union and
My. 343–30 brought all back to union and *l·*

unite in
Pul. 22– 5 rejoicing that we unite in *l·*,

unity, and
My. 6–17 your progress, unity, and *l·*.

universal
Mis. 290–28 from individual as from universal *l·* :

unknown
My. 189– 9 nor talk of unknown *l·*.

unmeasured
My. 24– 7 * your unmeasured *l·* for humanity,

unselfed
Mis. 238– 9 What has not unselfed *l·* achieved
'02. 16–16 watch-fires of unselfed *l·*,
My. 19–22 fruition of her unselfed *l·*,
62–11 * enough for your unselfed *l·*.
195–27 unselfed *l·* that builds without
200–19 seven-fold shield of . . . unselfed *l·*.

love

unselfed
My. 265– 3 It signifies that *l·*, unselfed,
306–16 unselfed *l·*, waits on God.

unselfish
Mis. 100–14 but Science voices unselfish *l·*,
Pul. 21– 3 a *l·* unselfish, unambitious,
My. 157–13 * evidence of your unselfish *l·*."

unutterable in
My. 134– 4 in protest and unutterable in *l·*.

wealth of
'02. 17–21 and the wealth of *l·*.

wireless
My. 259–13 my heart's wireless *l·*.

wisdom and
Mis. 316–22 pounding wisdom and *l·* into sounding
My. 303–30 wisdom, and *l·* to perform

wishes and
My. 358–23 Give my best wishes and *l·* to

with
Mis. 128–14 With *l·*, Mother,
135–21 With *l·*,
142– 4 With *l·*,
143–11 With *l·*,
149–14 With *l·*,
156– 4 With *l·*,
156–29 With *l·*,
157–29 Ever with *l·*,
159– 8 With *l·*,
395– 4 Is out of tune With *l·* and God ;
Man. 48– 5 with *l·* and without fear.
Po. 57–11 Is out of tune With *l·* and God ;
My. 144– 8 With *l·*, ever yours,
169– 9 With *l·*, Mother,
215–13 I returned this money with *l·* ;
289–19 With *l·*,
290–28 With *l·*,

woman's
Pul. 83– 1 * woman's *l·* and woman's help

words of
My. 360–15 subscribe these words of *l·* :

your
Mis. 149–12 full of accessions to your *l·*,
My. 135–26 Your *l·* and fidelity cheer my

Mis. 52–13 occasionally a *l·* affair.
38–15 lesson of C. S. is *l·*,
152– 4 and in *l·* continents clasp hands,
154–28 meekness, mercy, purity, *l·*.
162–13 good will, *l·*, teaching, and healing.
215– 5 I do it all in *l·* ;
250–14 *L·* is not something put upon a shelf,
250–20 *L·* cannot be a mere abstraction,
306–25 *l·* they create in our hearts.
330– 4 Has *l·* ceased to moan over the
351–25 *L·* that is not the procurator of
357–20 *l·* that is irrespective of self,
386–16 a *l·* that steady turns To God ;
Pul. 40– 1 * Ah, *l·* ! I only know
81– 7 * the express image of God for *l·*.
No. 8–10 to rebuke each other always in *l·*,
39–17 prayer is not asking God for *l·* ;
39–19 the *l·* wherewith He uses us.
Pan. 13–10 the *l·* of our loving Lord
'00. 3– 3 he loses self in *l·*,
3–27 a god of hate and of *l·*,
15–30 And *l·*, the evermore.
'01. 13–19 destroy the fear and the *l·* of it ;
'02. 2–25 or at least agree to disagree, in *l·*,
8–24 *L·*, purity, meekness, co-exist in
Po. 43– 9 Leading kine with *l·*.
49–24 a *l·* that steady turns To God ;
My. 6–28 *l·* catching a glimpse of glory.
14– 5 two millions of *l·* currency
18–18 the *l·* of our loving Lord
123– 3 *l·* is the greater marvel,
139– 8 primeval faith, hope, *l·*.
158–15 holiness, patience, charity, *l·*.
164–12 focusing light where *l·*, memory, and
184–18 a *l·* which stays the shadows of
189–16 *l·* it creates in the heart of man ;
191– 8 and *l·* will cast it out.
191– 9 steadfast in *l·* and good works.
193–25 and the last by *l·*.
202–22 words of cheer and *l·*
216–16 your sweet industry and *l·*
247–29 has all been done through *l·*,
258– 5 save one lowly offering — *l·*.
260–22 basis of Christmas is *l·* loving its
260–23 *l·* that "suffereth long, — *I Cor.* 13 : 4.
290–23 where no partings are for *l·*,
355–28 His reflection of peace, *l·*, joy.

love (verb)
Mis. vii– 6 * Then do I *l·* thee, and behold
8– 8 chapter sub-title

love (verb)

Mis.	8– 9	that thou shouldst *l·* him?
	9– 9	"*L·* thine enemies"— *see Matt.* 5 : 44.
	11–17	We must *l·* our enemies
	11–19	whereby we *l·* our friends ;
	11–31	all who *l·* me not,
	11–32	"I *l·* you, and would not knowingly
	13–11	*l·* them which *l·* you,— *Luke* 6 : 32.
	13–12	*l·* those that *l·* them."— *Luke* 6 : 32.
	18–13	Thou shalt *l·* Spirit only,
	33– 5	I *l·* all ministers and ministries of
	51–18	and cause him to *l·* them,
	51–20	he will *l·* and obey you
	59–13	all things to those who *l·* Him ;
	59–14	pleading with infinite Love to *l·* us,
	87– 8	"I *l·* your promise ;
	94– 6	must repent, and *l·* good
	104–30	I will *l·*, if another hates.
	111–25	I *l·* the orthodox church ;
	111–26	in time, that church will *l·* C. S.
	116–26	you profess to understand and *l·*,
	117–17	in proportion as we *l·*.
	120–23	*l·* to be with you on Sunday,
	124– 6	neither do we *l·* and obey Him by
	125–16	not having seen, we *l·*.
	127–20	To *l·*, and to be loved,
	129– 8	forgive his brother and *l·* his
	133–12	they *l·* to pray standing in— *Matt.* 6 : 5.
	180–16	I *l·* the Easter service :
	183– 5	*l·* his neighbor as himself,
	194– 6	know Him better, and *l·* Him
	206–27	if you *l·* good supremely,
	210–32	*L·* your enemies,
	211– 1	if you *l·* them, you will help
	236–11	"*L·* and honor thy parents,
	238–23	Are you faithful? Do you *l·*?
	266–21	cannot find it in my heart not to *l·*
	267– 9	* as "*hating* those whom I do not *l·*,"
	260 7	and *l·* the other ;— *Matt.* 6 : 24.
	292– 5	That ye *l·* one another."— *John* 13 : 34.
	294–10	*L·* such specimens of mortality
	311–16	I *l·* my enemies and would help all to
	311–18, 19	*l·* others more than they can *l·* me.
	318– 7	*l·* some of those devoted students
	336– 8	Do you *l·* that which represents
	336–17	and not *l·* its idea :
	338–10	choose but to labor and *l·* ;
	353–29	They do not *l·* Mother,
	367– 3	*l·* his neighbor as himself,
	387–13	from those who watch and *l·*.
	389–16	*l·* more for every hate,
	392–13	To *l·* the Hebrew figure of a tree.
	394–13	but hope thou, and *l·*.
	397–16	Thine own children are, I *l·* to be.
Ret.	18–23	those we most *l·* find a happiness
	29– 3	*l·* them, and hold to loving our
	80–27	We *l·* our friends, but ofttimes
Pul.	7– 4	I *l·* Boston, and especially the
	18–25	Thine own children are, I *l·* to be.
	21– 2	inevitably *l·* one another
	21– 5	Moreover, they *l·* their enemies,
	56–19	* "And still we *l·* the evil cause,
Rud.	3– 1	while mortals *l·* to sin,
	3– 2	they do not *l·* to be sick.
	4–22	we can only learn and *l·* Him
No.	7– 7	We must *l·* our enemies,
	32–21	and shall cease to *l·* it,
	30–18	prayer . . . is learning to *l·*,
Pan.	9–24	*l·* them which *l·* you,— *Matt.* 5 : 46.
	13–13	*L·* all Christian churches
	14– 5	*l·* one another ;
'00.	3–11	they who *l·* a good work
	11–11	them that love God,"— *l·* good.— *Rom.* 8 : 28.
'01.	14–13	make us *l·* it and so hinder our
	19– 5	I *l·* this doctrine, for I know
	28–19	I *l·* Christ more than all the
	31– 8	and *l·* the truths of C. S.
	32–17	caused me to *l·* their doctrines.
'02.	2–23	birthmark, to *l·* the Church ;
	7 22	chapter sub-title
	7–25	That ye *l·* one another ;— *John* 13 : 34.
	8– 3	commands man to love as Jesus loved.
	9– 7	concern you less, and *l·* thou.
	17– 3	"If ye *l·* me,— *John* 14 : 15.
	17– 6	seek and obey what they *l·*.
	17– 7	When mortals learn to *l·* aright ;
	17–18	to *l·* one's enemies,
	18–16	"*L·* one another,— *John* 13 : 34.
Peo.	6–15	fear God more than we *l·* Him ;
	6–17	we *l·* Him, because He is
Po.	4–15	Wait, and *l·* more for every hate,
	6– 8	not from those who watch and *l·*.
	13– 4	Thine own children are, I *l·* to be.
	20–17	To *l·* the Hebrew figure of a tree.
	35– 4	make me *l·* thee as I *l·* life less !
	45–18	but hope thou, and *l·*.

love (verb)

Po.	64–18	And those we most *l·*
My.	5–21	he continues to *l·* more
	15–18	* I *l·* to tell the story,
	15–22	* I *l·* to tell the story,
	15–26	* I *l·* to tell the story ;
	18–21	*L·* all Christian churches
	52–19	* *l·* our neighbor as ourselves."
	105–30	noble men and women, and I *l·* them ;
	127– 6	the people . . . who live to *l·*.
	132–22	may *l·* our neighbor as ourselves,
	133–23	Do you know how much I *l·* you
	151– 7	no Christian can . . . and not *l·* it :
	163–25	I *l·* its people
	163–26	*l·* their scholarship, friendship,
	174–27	know Him nearer, *l·* Him more,
	175– 1	I would *l·* to be with you at
	175–24	the friendship of those we *l·*,
	183– 1	"Thou shalt *l·* the Lord — *Luke* 10 : 27.
	187–15	should *l·* one another."— *I John* 3 : 11.
	187–28	"that ye *l·* one another."— *John* 15 : 12.
	195– 8	to *l·* more, to work more,
	195–16	To do good to all because we *l·* all,
	200–15	to *l·* our neighbor as ourself,
	202–10	but to *l·* one another :— *Rom.* 13 : 8.
	233–20	as much as they *l·* mankind?
	234– 7	know how much I *l·* them,
	262–27	*l·* to observe Christmas in quietude,
	270–24	What we *l·* determines what we are.
	270–24	I *l·* the prosperity of Zion,
	283–24	and to *l·* mercy,— *Mic.* 6 : 8.
	286– 7	*l·* their neighbor as themselves.
	313– 5	Tell her I *l·* her ;
	316– 2	those who *l·* Truth ;
	316– 6	causing man to *l·* his enemies ;
	341– 1	*l·* to breathe it to the breeze
	356– 2	*l·* the spot where God dwells
	350–23	and *l·* the other ;— *Matt.* 6 : 24.

(*see also* **God, neighbor**)

Love-Children's Offering

Pul.	42–23	* "*L· O·* — 1894."

loved

Mis.	110–10	maintain in yourselves what Jesus *l·*,
	127–20	To love, and to be *l·*,
	231–31	through which the *l·* one comes not,
	245–23	*l·* the Church and followed it,
	292– 6	Jesus, who so *l·* the world
	306–27	nor a *l·* person present ;
	334–31	you have not *l·* sufficiently
	386– 7	tidings from our *l·* on earth,
	387–17	Who *l·* and healed mankind :
Ret.	33 5	whatever is *l·* materially,
	75–16	is comprehended and *l·*
	79– 4	is spiritual truth learned and *l·* ;
Pul.	12–11	*l·* not their lives
'00.	7–12	*l·* the Bible and appreciated its
	14– 4	that I have *l·* thee.— *Rev.* 3 : 9.
'01.	29–11	not because reformers are not *l·*,
	32– 7	*l·* Christians of the old sort
'02.	2–24	and the Church once *l·* me.
	7–26	as I have *l·* you."— *John* 13 : 34.
	8– 3	commands man to love as Jesus *l·*.
	18–16	as I have *l·* you."— *John* 13 : 34.
	18–18	the heart that loves as Jesus *l·*.
Hea.	2–21	*l·* of the Father, the *l·* of Love?
Po.	6–12	Who *l·* and healed mankind :
	17– 4	My *l·* ones in glory
	26–10	on her altar our *l·* Lincoln's own
	49–11	from our *l·* on earth,
	65– 4	A meeting with *l·* ones
My.	15–33	* That I have *l·* so long.
	86– 4	* *l·* its golden State House
	159– 5	those words of our *l·* Lord,
	189–31	Dead is the who *l·* me dearly :
	256–17	Again *l·* Christmas is here,
	256–23	Parents call home their *l·* ones,
	258– 1	or the Book of Life is *l·*,
	294–31	the *l·* and lost of many millions.
	302–21	I may be more *l·*,
	313–27	My oldest sister dearly *l·* me,

loveliness

My.	152–32	my skilful florist has coaxed into *l·*

love-linked

My.	206– 6	*l·* holiness which heals and saves.

love-lorn

Po.	34–11	Or sing thy *l·* note

lovely

Mis.	128– 9	whatsoever things are *l·*,— *Phil.* 4 : 8.
	142–17	expressed in their *l·* gift
	167– 6	the one altogether *l·*
	342–13	One "altogether *l·*."— *Song* 5 : 16.
Ret.	23–19	One "altogether *l·*,"— *Song* 5 : 16.

lovely
'01. 6–30 He is "altogether *l*·,"— *Song* 5 : 16.
Peo. 6–17 He is found altogether *l*·.
Po. 53– 7 With sunshine's *l*· ray

love-offerings
Pul. 41– 6 * *l*· of the disciples of C. S.
52–13 * *l*· of the disciples of

lover
Pul. 83– 2 * promise as *l*· and candidate
'01. 32– 6 an eager *l*· and student of

lovers
Mis. 304– 5 * *l*· of liberty and peace
'02. 17–16 Who of the world's *l*· ever found
My. 199–16 loyal *l*· of God and man.

Love's
Mis. 100–11 *L*· labors are not lost.
124–25 unveiled *L*· great legacy to mortals :
125– 3 then hath he part in *L*· atonement,
330–16 looking through *L*· transparency,
387– 1 "When *L*· rapt sense
Ret. 47– 3 wars with *L*· spiritual compact,
No. 3–24 trust *L*· recompense of love.
'00. 15–18 To-day you have come to *L*· feast,
Po. 31– 3 dropped from *L*· throne.
31–11 *L*· verdure veils the leaflet's
50–18 "When *L*· rapt sense
My. 62–13 * with the joy of *L*· victory.
129–13 They come at *L*· call.
158– 9 We live in an age of *L*· divine

love's
My. 231–18 else *l*· labor is lost

loves
Mis. 100–26 Christian Scientist *l*· man more
100–27 because he *l*· God most.
224–13 ambitions, tastes, and *l*· ;
317–29 abhors injustice, and *l*· mercy.
395– 2 Who *l*· not June
Un. 39–11 He *l*· them from whom
Pul. 21– 4 *l*· only because it *is* Love.
No. 39–19 the love wherewith He *l*· us.
Pan. 9–21 It *l*· one's neighbor as one's self ;
9–22 it *l*· its enemies
'00. 3–18 good man *l*· the right thinker
'01. 13–18 because he fears it or *l*· it.
17– 6 *l*· even the repentant prodigal
21–15 individual who *l*· God
29–23 The individual who *l*· most,
'02. 18–18 the heart that *l*· as Jesus loved.
Po. 43– 2 Jesus *l*· you ! so does mother :
57– 9 Who *l*· not June
My. 4–14 *l*· Protestant and Catholic,
4–15 *l*· all who love God,
4–16 and he *l*· his enemies.
295–28 he still lives, *l*·, labors.

loveth
Mis. 18– 4 "Whom the Lord *l*·— *Heb.* 12 : 6.
73– 5 "Whom the Lord *l*·— *Heb.* 12 : 6.
125– 4 "whom the Lord *l*·— *Heb.* 12 : 6.
150–13 and *l*· the gates of Zion.
208–19 "whom the Lord *l*·— *Heb.* 12 : 6.
Man. 69–18 "He that *l*· father or— *Matt.* 10 : 37.
Ret. 80– 5 whom the Lord *l*·— *Heb.* 12 : 6.
Pul. 21– 3 love wherewith Christ *l*· us ;
'01. 9–27 He of God's household who *l*·
My. 202–11 he that *l*· another— *Rom.* 13 : 8.

love-token
My. 171–26 * as a *l*· for the church

Lovewell, Capt. John
Ret. 3– 5 Capt. John *L*· of Dunstable,

Lovewell's War
Ret. 3– 8 known historically as *L*· *W*·.

loving (adj.)
Mis. xii– 4 interluding with *l*· thought
7– 8 The *l*· patience of Jesus,
96–11 as a *l*· Father and Mother ;
102–15 *l*·, divine Father-Mother God.
131–22 that *l*· sense of gratitude
138–30 Your *l*· teacher,
151– 2 In the words of the *l*· disciple,
238– 2 Even the *l*· children are
254– 3 Should not the *l*· warning,
265–30 If impatient of the *l*· rebuke,
292–22 by *l*· words and deeds.
370–16 that twines its *l*· arms
Un. 53–25 man's origin and *l*· Father,
Pul. 49– 7 * gifts of her *l*· pupils.
76–18 * tribute of *l*· friends.
77–12 * *l*· hands of four thousand
78–10 * *l*· hands of four thousand
86–20 * In behalf of your *l*· students
86–23 * your labors and *l*· sacrifice,

loving (adj.)
Rud. 10–19 look up to the *l*· God,
No. 7–16 Every *l*· sacrifice for the good of
Pan. 13–10 the love of our *l*· Lord
'00. 6–23 a meek and *l*· disciple of Christ,
7–27 the tender, *l*· Christ is found near,
'01. 31–17 would bear *l*· testimony.
'02. 1– 1 God's *l*· providence for His
8– 6 the likeness of Love is *l*·?
9–13 *L*· chords set discords in harmony.
9–15 was *l*· and spiritual,
Po. 8– 5 seek the *l*· rose,
30–22 heaven's lyres and angels' *l*· lays,
My. 9– 8 * to turn in *l*· thankfulness
13–30 their *l*· giving has been blessed.
18–18 the love of our *l*· Lord
20–10 the *l*· liberty of their license.
21– 3 * all know of the *l*· self-sacrifices
23–20 * loyal and *l*· greetings to you,
28–10 * in many instances the *l*·
44– 9 * obedient to the *l*· counsel
62–20 * *l*· greetings and congratulations
131–10 cup red with *l*· restitution,
162–25 *l*· Shepherd of this feeble flock
167–13 *l*· benedictions upon your lives.
197–26 I send *l*· congratulations,
207– 9 * unite in *l*· greetings to you,
207–15 * Yours in *l*· obedience,
224–27 speak in *l*· terms of their efforts,
247–20 not a stern but a *l*· look
248–26 to face the foe with *l*· look
259– 9 * *L*·, grateful Christmas greetings
261– 2 *l*· parents and guardians
280– 6 * *l*· solicitude for the welfare of
280– 9 * a universal, *l*· brotherhood
287–19 Philanthropy is *l*·, ameliorative,
293– 7 President, in his *l*· acquiescence,
319– 8 in *l*·, grateful memory
323–12 * In *l*· gratitude for your
338–22 his broad views and *l*· nature
362–18 * send you their *l*· greetings.
(*see also* **heart, hearts**)

loving (ppr.)
Mis. 13– 9 law of *l*· mine enemies.
50–30 *one* God and *l*· Him supremely,
87–26 honest, earnest, *l*·, and truthful,
130–29 the meek and *l*·, God anoints
258– 1 for *l*· his neighbor as himself,
311– 9 *l*· one another, go forth to
328–30 *l*· God supremely
331– 5 make them humble, *l*·, obedient,
400–15 Father-Mother God, *L*· me,
Ret. 29– 3 *l*· our enemies and doing good
49–16 attain the bliss of *l*· unselfishly,
71–20 not dealing justly and *l*· mercy,
Pul. 85–27 * her labors and *l*· generosity
No. 38–21 *l*· your neighbor as yourself,
'00. 5–16 *l*· another as himself.
'01. 14–21 following it, or *l*· it,
32– 8 I could not help *l*· them.
'02. 8– 7 When *l*·, we learn that
Po. 43– 4 *L*· God and one another,
69– 3 Father-Mother God, *L*· me,
My. 52– 5 * *l*· them that despitefully use her,
139– 3 living, *l*·, acting, enjoying.
204–27 good for evil, *l*· one's enemies,
260–22 love *l*· its enemies,
268–27 Science of . . . living and of *l*·,
323– 9 * by *l*· it and living it

loving-cup
My. 347– 6 chapter sub-title
347– 9 their beautiful gift to me, a *l*·,
347–20 I shall treasure my *l*·

lovingkindness
My. 13–22 *l*· and tender mercies ;— *Psal.* 103 : 4.
37–29 * its ineffable *l*·, its wise counsel

lovingly
Mis. v– 4 I *l*· DEDICATE THESE PRACTICAL
148– 4 *L*· yours,
155–13 *L*· yours,
160–16 *L*· yours,
320– 9 star that looked *l*· down on the
400–20 Father-Mother good, *l*· Thee I seek,
Pul. 44–13 * "Yours *l*·,
77–15 * You are hereby most *l*· invited
78–13 * You are hereby most *l*· invited
87– 6 * *L*· yours,
No. 19–14 gratefully and *l*· conscious of
35– 8 yield *l*· to the purpose of
Po. 69– 8 Father-Mother good, *l*· Thee I seek,
My. 5–25 *l*· thanking your generosity
26–25 *L*· yours,
63– 6 * *L*· and gratefully your students,
135–20 *L*· yours in Christ,

lovingly

My. 143– 5   L· yours,
168– 7   L· yours,
171–15   L· yours,
201–16   forgive, wisely ponder, and l·
263– 8   L· thine,
284– 6   L· yours,
351–18   L· yours in Christ,
358–25   L· your teacher and Leader,
360– 3   As ever, l· your teacher,
360–24   L· yours,

low

Mis. 228–15   mad ambition and l· revenge.
242–21   where the patient is very l·
396–20   L·, sad, and sweet, whose measures
400– 7   Dirge and song and shoutings l·
Ret. 4–18   winds sigh l· requiems
18– 6   alder is whispering l·,
31–24   My heart bent l· before the
Pul. 10– 9   her pomp and power lie l·
16–19   Dirge and song and shoutings l·,
18– 4   L·, sad, and sweet, whose measures
39–15   * The sunset, burning l·,
Hea. 6– 7   fly too high or too l·.
Po. 12– 3   L·, sad, and sweet, whose measures
16–15   when the day-god is l·;
63–15   nestling alder is whispering l·,
65–22   its music in l· minor tones,
76–18   Dirge and song and shoutings l·
My. 155–12   the l· laurels of vainglory,

Lowell

Mis. 368–10   signature
Pul. 28–25   * selections from Whittier and L·,

lower

Mis. 36–15   express the l· qualities of the
84–28   transition from our l· sense of
102– 9   In this limited and l· sense
250– 8   What the l· propensities express,
287–19   higher nature of man governs the l·.
376–20   l· lines of light kindled into
Un. 18–28   it would l· His rank.
30– 8   this l· sense sins and suffers,
32–15   This l·, misnamed mind is a
Pul. 49– 9   * tree-tops on the l· terrace.
Rud. 8–15   from a l· to a higher condition
8–26   If by such l· means the health
No. 24– 7   through the l· orders of matter
'01. 30–19   destroying all l· considerations.
Peo. 13– 2   hence a l· order of humanity,
13– 4   a l· order of Christianity than
My. 107–12   l· attenuations have so little
152– 7   far l· in the scale of thought,
253– 2   brightening this l· sphere

lowest

Mis. 57–28   beginning with the l· form
No. 32–26   reduce this evil to its l· terms,
Peo. 7– 1   by their highest or their l· ideals,

lowly

Mis. 167–29   he exalteth the l·;
168–11   the poor — the l· in Christ,
My. 41– 6   * the meek and l· in heart
258– 5   save one l· offering — love.
258–29   l· in its majesty.
259–18   a l·, triumphant trust,

loyal

Mis. v– 2   L· CHRISTIAN SCIENTISTS
91–24   informed thereof, that a l· student
120–11   l· laborers are ye that have
141–10   All l· Christian Scientists
213–27   L· Christian Scientists, be of
251–10   l· to the heart's core to
264– 3   who are l· to Christ, Truth,
273–16   L· Christian Scientists should
275–20   chapter sub-title
276–11   active, earnest, and l·,
277–10   a heart l· to God is patient
318–15   from a l· student of C. S.,
347–31   L· Scientists are targets for envy,
354– 6   l·, self-forgetful, faithful
386–25   remembrance of her l· life,
Man. 35–21   l· to the teachings of the
36–14   L· Christian Scientists whose
37–19   l· to their Leader and to the
38– 5   not a l· student of Mrs. Eddy,
55–16   shall not be counted l· till
64–15   l· Christian Scientists had given
71–16   shall be considered l·
72– 6   l· exemplary Christian Scientist
73– 1   sixteen l· Christian Scientists,
79– 4   not less than three l· members
84–17   the pupils of l· teachers shall
84–23   A l· teacher of C. S.
84–25   another l· teacher's pupil,
85– 5   A l· teacher of C. S. may
85–19   active and l· Christian Scientists

loyal

Man. 89–11   L· students who have been taught
89–18   L· Christian Scientists' pupils
92–25   deemed l· teachers of C. S.
97– 6   one l· Christian Scientist who
109– 3   L· members of The Mother Church
109– 7   l· students of Mrs. Eddy,
Chr. 53– 6   Spirit sped A l· ray
Ret. 47–20   from me, or a l· student,
53– 1   presenting to its l· members
85–19   The l· Christian Scientist is
Un. 23– 5   was to his father ever l·.
'01. 3–10   The l· Christian Scientists
'02. 3– 1   ten thousand l· Christian Scientists
Po. 31– 1   l· struggler for the right,
50–11   remembrance of her l· life,
My. v–11   * earnest and l· Christian Scientists
14–23   * a generous and l· people.
23–20   * their l· and loving greetings
118– 1   the l·, royal natures of the
125–13   L· to the divine Principle
130–25   I need not say this to the l·
199–16   all l· lovers of God and man.
225– 3   l· at heart and the worker
229– 9   that l· Christian Scientists,
251–11   not if you and they are l·
(see also **students**)

loyalty

Mis. 12–13   law of l· to Jesus' Sermon
99– 9   His fear overcame his l·;
203– 8   love, l·, and good works.
275–24   expressions of love and l·
Man. 35–15   the l· of the applicants.
55–18   if his l· has been proved
Ret. 50–19   By l· in students I mean this,
My. 19–12   * chapter sub-title
21–16   * trial and deprivation in our l·
44–28   * continued l· to your teachings,
76–15   * show the earnestness and l·
189–17   no l· apart from love.

lucid

Mis. 50–11   as l· in presentation as can be
Ret. 21–22   l· and enduring lessons

lucidly

No. 39– 1   that we can think more l·

lucky

Mis. 123–14   god of sin, was the "l· god;"

lucrative

'00. 2–22   will leave a l· business

ludicrous

Mis. 286–17   put ingenuity to l· shifts;

luminary

Mis. 340–27   Every l· in the constellation

luminous

Mis. 192–16   L· with the light of
335–15   made l· by divine Love.
Pul. 32– 2   * lighted by l· blue eyes,
87 25   l· lines from your lives
My. 124–20   is written in l· letters,

lump

Mis. 39–20   to leaven the whole l·.
166–25   leavening the l· of human thought,
My. 59– 5   * should leaven the whole l·,
114–20   is leavening the whole l·

lunacy

Pan. 8– 4   find expression in sun worship, l·,
My. 190–15   to cure a severe case of l·,
192– 6   cast out fashionable l·.
222– 4   a violent case of l·.

Lundy Lane

My. 311–28   McNeil, the hero of L· L·.

Lundy's Lane

Ret. 3–10   general who fought at L· L·,

lungs

Pul. 79–24   * much as his l· call for breath;
My. 105–10   l· were mostly consumed.

lure

My. 260–15   the l· of gold,

lured

My. 283–29   L· by fame, pride, or gold,

lures

My. 93–14   * rare l· for weary hearts,

lurid

Po. 18–17   Though lightnings be l·

lurking

Mis. 210–21   uncover and kill this l· serpent,
My. 213– 9   l· foe to human weal,

lurks

Mis. 66– 8   l· in this mandate,
302– 1   Behind the scenes l· an evil

luscious

My. 325– 4 * to leave *l·* hothouse fruit.

lust

Mis. 19– 2 covetousness, *l·*, hatred, malice,
118–21 self-will, self-righteousness, *l·*,
123– 7 *l·*, hypocrisy, *witchcraft.*
297–27 unmercifulness, tyranny, or *l·*.
337–19 evil-speaking, *l·*, envy, hate.
366–27 self-will, envy, and *l·*.
Un. 39– 5 *l·* of the flesh and the pride
56–27 ingratitude, *l·*, malice, hate,
Rud. 9–20 envy, *l·*, and all fleshly vices.
'02. 8–25 *L·*, hatred, revenge, coincide
17– 1 worldliness, hatred, and *l·*,
Hea. 7– 1 which is good for nothing, *l·*,"
17– 7 *l·* makes the material so-called
My. 4– 5 *L·*, dishonesty, sin, disable the
5– 5 synonymous with legalized *l·*,
126–25 over the widowhood of *l·*,
205–25 *l·* of the flesh and the pride
257–20 pride, greed, *l·* should bow

lustre

No. 13–26 other parts of it have no *l·*.
My. 290– 6 lose their *l·* in the tomb,

lusts

Mis. 52– 1 consume it upon your *l·*." — *Jas.* 4 : 3.
182–32 *l·* of the flesh and the pride of
Ret. 79–13 "*l·* of the flesh," — *see I John* 2 : 16.
No. 40– 3 consume it on your *l·*." — *see Jas.* 4 : 3.
Pan. 5–13 the *l·* of your father — *John* 8 : 44.
'01. 16– 8 the demon of this world, its *l·*,
Hea. 17– 2 *l·* of the flesh, the pride of life,

lute

Mis. 329–27 cuckoo sounds her invisible *l·*,

Luther (*see also* Luther's)

Martin
Hea. 2–10 intrepid reformer, Martin *L·* :

Luther's

Martin
My. 295– 9 COPY OF MARTIN *L·* TRANSLATION

luxury

Mis. 326– 8 caught in the dwelling of *l·*,
326–30 from the dwelling of *l·*,
Pul. 36–24 * of the utmost taste and *l·*,
My. 110–17 *l·* of thought let loose,

Lyceum Club

Ret. 40– 4 speak before the *L· C·*,

Lyceum League of America

Mis. 305– 5 * *L· L· of A·*, the Society of

lying

Mis. 273–23 applications *l·* on the desk
Ret. 4– 5 *l·* in the adjoining towns
67– 7 the *l·* supposition that
'00. 2–19 "By cheating, *l·*, and crime ;
Hea. 6–24 *l·* back in the unconscious thought,
My. 105–13 instruments were *l·* on the table
227–18 *l·* in wait to catch them

Lynn

Mass.
Mis. 391– 2 Editor of the *Item*, *L·*, Mass.
Pul. 34– 5 * In 1866, while living in *L·*, Mass.,
46–28 * at *L·*, Mass., she became
58– 1 * found herself in *L·*, Mass.,
Po. vi– 6 * in *L·*, Mass., in 1866,
vi– 9 * in a *L·*, Mass., newspaper,
vi–25 * she resided in *L·*, Mass.,
9–12 *L·*, Mass., *September* 3, 1866.
21–19 *L·*, Mass., *May* 6, 1876.
23–23 *L·*, Mass., *November* 8, 1866.
27–25 *L·*, Mass., *January* 1, 1866.
38– 1 the editor of the *Item*, *L·*, Mass.
40– 5 *L·*, Mass., *August* 4, 1866.
42– 8 *L·*, Mass., *February* 19, 1868.
46–18 *L·*, Mass., *December* 8, 1866.
47–23 *L·*, Mass., *September* 3, 1871.
66–15 *L·*, Mass., *August* 25, 1866.
68–24 *L·*, Mass., *August* 24, 1865.
70–26 *L·*, Mass., *April*, 1871.
72– 5 *L·*, Mass., *February* 3, 1865.
78–17 *L·*, Mass., *December* 7, 1865.
My. 59– 3 * your *first* class in *L·*, Mass.,
Massachusetts
Ret. 42– 3 solemnized at *L·*, Massachusetts,

Ret. 38–15 started for *L·* to see me.
38–16 he left Boston for *L·*,
38–18 at the Eastern depot in *L·*,
'02. 16– 2 Miss Dorcas Rawson of *L·*
Po. 73– 1 inscribed to my friends in *L·*.
My. 59–17 * little hall on Market Street, *L·*,
60– 8 * First Congregational Church of *L·*,
322– 1 * I met a lady who lived in *L·*,

lyre

Mis. 107–13 swell the *l·* of human love.
142–20 my Muse lost her lightsome *l·*,
329–24 sweep in soft strains her Orphean *l·*.
Ret. 17– 7 Wake chords of my *l·*,
Pul. 9– 6 no Delphian *l·* could break the
Pan. 3–12 and *l·* of bird and brooklet.
Po. 62– 7 Wake chords of my *l·*,
66– 7 Wake gently the chords of her *l·*,

lyres

Po. 30–22 heaven's *l·* and angels' loving lays,

M

macadamize

My. 175–19 to *m·* a portion of Warren Street
175–20 to *m·* North State Street

machinery

Mis. 353–22 makes the *m·* work rightly ;
My. 145–19 at home attending to the *m·*
328–23 * *m·* act of the Legislature

Macneil, John

Ret. 3– 9 John *M·*, the New Hampshire general
(*see also* McNeil)

Macneill, Sir John

Ret. 3– 1 Sir John *M·*, a Scotch knight,

mad

Mis. 178–21 learning' . . . 'hath made thee *m·*.'
228–14 *m·* ambition and low revenge.
254–13 victim of *m·* ambition
263–27 whose *m·* ambition drives them to
351–15 repeated attempts of *m·* ambition
363–27 and drives diviners *m·*.
369–14 indulge in *m·* antics.
Ret. 79–13 Dishonesty, envy, and *m·* ambition
'01. 16–10 hatred gone *m·* becomes imbecile
My. 129– 9 counteract the trend of *m·* ambition.
250– 5 promotes wisdom, quiets *m·* ambition,
262–23 merriment, *m·* ambition, rivalry,

made

Mis. vii– 5 * thy well *m·* choice of friends
x–25 *m·* out to Mary Baker Eddy,
10–21 *m·* perfect in weakness,
26–11 the Scripture declares He *m·*
26–13 and what *m·* the soil?
30–20 "hath *m·* me free — *Rom.* 8 : 2.
34– 9 is simply thought *m·* manifest.

made

Mis. 37– 4 this Mind is *m·* manifest
43– 4 *m·* acquainted with the mental
44–19 thought *m·* manifest in the flesh.
45–21 *If God made all that was m·*,
45–28 "All things were *m·* by Him ; — *John* 1 : 3.
45–29 anything *m·* that was *m·*." — *John* 1 : 3.
48–14 *m·* a man drunk on water,
48–20 *m·* in season to open the eyes
48–23 *Was ever a person m· insane by*
48–28 * "*m·* insane by Mrs. Eddy's teachings,"
50– 1 God made all that was *m·*,
57– 2 later *m·* which *He* had *m·*.
57– 6 The creative "Us" *m·* all,
64– 3 way he *m·* for mortals' escape.
77– 8 demand *m·* upon the eunuch
77–10 God *m·* manifest through
77–27 *m·* in God's own likeness,
78– 3 *m·* manifest in the flesh,
79–25 all be *m·* alive." — *I Cor.* 15 : 22.
91–19 that can be *m·* visible.
93– 4 history shall be *m·* glad !
97–21 *m·* in the image and likeness
101– 1 lips are *m·* eloquent,
114–10 and so *m·* to misteach others.
117– 1 *m·* "ruler over many — *Matt.* 25 : 23.
122–28 God never *m·* it,
122–28, 29 He *m·* all that was *m·*.
132– 1 A motion was *m·*, and a vote
134– 1 sorrowful who are *m·* hopeful,
138–16 *m·* perfect through the cross.
142– 2 *m·* her wildernesses to bud
152–19 *m·* ready for the pure in affection.
154–19 Through the word . . . are you *m·* free.
154–21 be *m·* manifest in the flesh

made

Mis.	158– 6	changes about to be *m*.
	161–12	that *m*˙ him the Christ-Jesus,
	166–30	It *m*˙ him an honest man,
	178–21	'hath *m*˙ thee mad.' — *see Acts* 26 : 24.
	179–25	He *m*˙ every flower in Mind
	182–29	When the Word is *m*˙ flesh,
	184– 6	The Word will be *m*˙ flesh
	185– 5	is *m*˙ manifest as Truth,
	185–27	*m*˙ *a living soul;* — *I Cor.* 15 : 45.
	185–28	*m*˙ *a quickening spirit.* — *I Cor.* 15 : 45.
	186– 8	the spiritual man *m*˙ in the image
	189–10	knowledge of . . . *m*˙ him mighty.
	191–30	sin or disease *m*˙ manifest.
	200– 2	that *m*˙ his healing easy and
	201–19	*m*˙ me free from the law — *Rom.* 8 : 2.
	219–25	*m*˙ manifest on the body,
	227–17	wider aims of a life *m*˙ honest :
	229–16	thou hast *m*˙ the Lord, — *Psal.* 91 : 9.
	231– 7	*m*˙ busy many appetites ;
	231–16	Why, he *m*˙ a big hole,
	234–23	she has *m*˙ some progress,
	236– 4	been *m*˙ the repository of
	238– 2	sometimes *m*˙ to believe a lie,
	239–24	*m*˙ them more serious over it.
	241–19	"God never *m*˙ you sick :
	243– 5	not yet *m*˙ surgery one of the
	247–30	He never *m*˙ sickness.
	248–10	*m*˙ the word synonymous with devil.
	248–27	saved me . . . and *m*˙ me well,
	257– 7	must be *m*˙ by Mind
	259– 1	were *m*˙ by Him ; — *John* 1 : 3.
	259– 2	was not any thing *m*˙." — *John* 1 : 3.
	262–19	*m*˙ glad by the divine Love
	266–24	correct mistakes which may be *m*˙
	269–17	*m*˙ his choice between matter and
	280–22	The presentation was *m*˙
	280–30	by which so many wrecks are *m*˙.
	287– 5	He that hath *m*˙ us, — *Psal.* 100 : 3.
	289– 5	in whatever form it is *m*˙ manifest.
	289–16	marriage contract two are *m*˙ one,
	301– 8	whose substance is *m*˙ up of my
	303–24	*m*˙ profitable to the heart of our
	305–19	* can be *m*˙ a part of the bell ;
	306–18	* having been *m*˙ such by the
	321–15	hath *m*˙ me free from — *Rom.* 8 : 2.
	324– 3	streets of a city *m*˙ with hands.
	326– 3	hath *m*˙ you free from — *see Rom.* 8 : 2.
	335–15	path *m*˙ luminous by divine Love.
	339–10	good is *m*˙ more industrious and
	340–18	Is a musician *m*˙ by his teacher?
	341– 9	and be *m*˙ ruler over many things.
	343– 7	Thought must be *m*˙ better,
	354–15	more grace, a motive *m*˙ pure,
	360–32	No advancing modes . . . *m*˙ Jesus ;
	362– 8	Scholastic dogma has *m*˙ men blind.
	362–12	God, having *m*˙ *all*,
	362–12	believing that God, . . . *m*˙ evil ;
	362–13	all that He *m*˙ was good.
	364– 8	*m*˙ the public your friend,
	364–18	He *m*˙ all that was *m*˙,
	396–14	I hope it's better *m*˙,
	398–24	'T was the Truth that *m*˙ us free,
Man.	32–15	announcement shall be *m*˙ but once
	42– 7	not be *m*˙ to forget nor to neglect
	46–14	private communications *m*˙ to them
	50– 1	an autopsy shall be *m*˙ by
	67– 8	shall not be *m*˙ public without
	72–13	application, *m*˙ in accordance with
	78– 7	not be *m*˙ legally responsible for
	78–10	Donations . . . shall not be *m*˙ without
	110– 2	that are not correctly *m*˙ out.
Chr.	55–21	*m*˙ like unto the Son — *Heb.* 7 : 3.
Ret.	7–14	* he would have *m*˙ himself one of the
	14–17	*m*˙ any profession of religion,
	15–21	*m*˙ memorable by eloquent addresses
	18–18	all His spirit hath *m*˙,
	44–24	No sooner were my views *m*˙ known,
	53– 3	This monthly magazine had been *m*˙
	59–19	and all that is *m*˙ by Him,
	59–24	*m*˙ in His own image and likeness ;
	61– 4	*m*˙ manifest on the body
	64–12	the fact is *m*˙ obvious that the
	67–19	error *m*˙ its man mortal,
	69–22	*m*˙ all perfect and eternal.
	80–29	sacrifices *m*˙ for others are not
	89–28	not first *m*˙ known to them
	93–16	spiritual ideal is *m*˙ our own,
Un.	9– 8	Jesus has *m*˙ the way plain,
	20–12	God never *m*˙ evil.
	22– 2	*m*˙ after God's eternal likeness,
	30–14	was *m*˙ a living soul ; — *I Cor.* 15 : 45.
	30–15	*m*˙ a quickening spirit." — *I Cor.* 15 : 45.
	30–19	*m*˙ humanity victorious over
	39– 1	"the Word" is "*m*˙ flesh" — *John* 1 : 14.

made

Un.	44– 1	Many misrepresentations are *m*˙
	45–11	that God never *m*˙ evil.
	53– 3	God never *m*˙ them ;
	53– 4	the lie must say He *m*˙ them,
	56– 1	chaos of mortal mind is *m*˙ the
	56–23	*m*˙ to fret in their chains ;
	59– 6	which *m*˙ heaven and earth
	60–14	*m*˙ after the similitude — *Jas.* 3 : 9.
Pul.	2–14	not *m*˙ with hands, — *II Cor.* 5 : 1.
	6–11	*m*˙ the mistake of thinking she
	7–15	*m*˙ morals for mankind.
	8–14	only the need *m*˙ known,
	13–20	*m*˙ his bosom companion,
	21– 9	be *m*˙ manifest in my life.
	30–18	* man is *m*˙ in His image.
	34– 4	* no special record is to be *m*˙.
	36–16	* *m*˙ me feel I could have walked
	45– 3	* Sacrifices were *m*˙ in many an
	45–28	* result of rules *m*˙ by Mrs. Eddy.
	53–13	* hath *m*˙ thee whole." — *Luke* 17 : 19.
	60–16	* organ, *m*˙ by Farrand & Votey
	61–27	* The chimes were *m*˙ by the
	63–10	* *m*˙ recently as she pointed to
	63–15	* *m*˙ by a remarkable woman,
	65–14	* progress which has been *m*˙
	65–20	* *m*˙ it to be called the Bible of
	73–20	* *m*˙ a careful and searching study
	74– 6	* *m*˙ by Mrs. Laura Lathrop,
	80–23	* It has *m*˙ a myriad of
	85– 3	* *m*˙ its erection possible.
Rud.	3–21	error *m*˙ manifest physically,
	5– 8	*m*˙ in the image of Spirit,
	12–10	first *m*˙ sick by matter,
	13– 9	*m*˙ in the divine and spiritual image
	14–18	No discount on tuition was *m*˙
No.	2–12	should be *m*˙ to test the
	3–11	should not be *m*˙ public ;
	4–10	never *m*˙ sickness a stubborn
	9–24	More mistakes are *m*˙ in its name
	16– 5	whatever He knows is *m*˙ manifest,
	29–20	pardoned by God . . . he is *m*˙ whole.
	34– 8	sacrifice that Jesus *m*˙ for us,
	40–27	*m*˙ better only by divine influence.
Pan.	5– 5	were *m*˙ by Him," — *John* 1 : 3.
	5–10	who or what hath *m*˙ evil?
	6–17	Spirit *m*˙ all that was *m*˙,
'00.	6–27	*m*˙ better physically, morally, and
'01.	7–10	and *m*˙ them male and female
	9– 9	a sense so pure it *m*˙ seers of men,
	9–16	*m*˙ manifest in the flesh, healing and
	11–13	*m*˙ the Bible, and "S. and H.
	13– 2	and God never *m*˙ it.
	14–12	evil cannot be *m*˙ so real as to
	27– 4	* contributions that have been *m*˙
'02.	1–11	is *m*˙ to glorify God.
	9–12	hath *m*˙ me free from — *Rom.* 8 : 2.
	18– 5	*m*˙ him a man of sorrows.
	18–30	*m*˙ him keenly alive to the
Hea.	6–16	evolved and *m*˙ tangible ;
	8–14	it is willing to be *m*˙ whole,
	9–18	God never *m*˙ a wicked man ;
	9–23	God made all that was *m*˙,
	9–24	He never *m*˙ sin or sickness.
	12–14	God, . . . never *m*˙ a man sick.
	12–19	*m*˙ the infinitesimal dose effectual.
	17– 9	God made all that was *m*˙ ;
	19–14	He *m*˙ "every plant — *Gen.* 2 : 5.
Peo.	3– 4	have *m*˙ monsters of men ;
	3– 5	have *m*˙ helpless invalids
	10–18	have *m*˙ men sinning and sick,
	11–11	*m*˙ subject to his Maker.
Po.	v–18	* *who m*˙ *her acquaintance,*
	9–11	Our reason *m*˙ right
	59– 6	I hope it's better *m*˙,
	64– 9	all His spirit hath *m*˙,
	75– 1	the Truth that *m*˙ us free,
My.	vi–22	* she *m*˙ over to trustees
	vii– 5	* *m*˙ to deprive their Leader of
	10–16	* No appeal has ever been *m*˙
	10–17	* probable that none will be *m*˙
	11–20	* we have also *m*˙ good the pledge.
	16– 3	* *m*˙ to the annual meeting,
	21– 4	* self-sacrifices which have been *m*˙
	27–22	* announcement *m*˙ by Mr. Chase
	37–21	* He has *m*˙ known through your
	48– 7	* and which Mrs. Eddy *m*˙
	52–27	* she has *m*˙ sacrifices from which
	55– 4	* efforts were *m*˙ to obtain
	55–18	* were *m*˙ for a church home.
	56–26	* further provision must be *m*˙,
	58– 9	* statements that have been *m*˙
	64– 9	* *m*˙ the name an honored one
	66–13	* a number of changes will be *m*˙
	76– 9	* formal announcement was *m*˙

made
My.	80– 8	* they had been *m·* whole,
	81–26	* If an attempt were *m·* to give
	83–23	* announcement, which has just been *m·*,
	83–29	* *m·* steady gains in recent years.
	92–15	* astonishing revelation was *m·*
	100–12	* C. S. sect *m·* its appearance
	105–18	and have *m·* the lame walk.
	106– 6	could be *m·* to include
	107–24	God made all that was *m·*,
	110–29	*m·* his life an abject failure.
	113–14	hath *m·* me free from— *Rom.* 8 : 2.
	130–11	has been *m·* too many times
	138–20	statements herein *m·* by me,
	138–27	* *m·* oath that the statements
	141–12	* was *m·* last night [June 21]
	149–15	Epictetus *m·* answer,
	152– 6	hath *m·* thee whole."— *Matt.* 9 : 22.
	154– 8	if they can be *m·* to infringe
	157–17	* *m·* known in her original deed of
	157–20	* *m·* the following statement :
	173–10	no preparations would be *m·* for
	178–17, 18	He *m·* all "that was *m·*."— *John* 1 : 3.
	188– 2	you have *m·* the head of the corner.
	188– 7	that is *m·* in this place."— *II Chron.* 7 : 15.
	188–13	"house not *m·* with hands,— *II Cor.* 5 : 1.
	194– 7	"house not *m·* with hands,— *II Cor.* 5 : 1.
	204–18	on the decision you have *m·*
	205– 4	Christ hath *m·* us free."— *Gal.* 5 : 1.
	205–18	* as the thing *m·* is good or bad,
	206–27	hath *m·* us meet to be— *Col.* 1 : 12.
	211–29	Other minds are *m·* dormant by it,
	224–15	or *m·* blind to his loss of
	233–10	are you not *m·* better by watching?
	235–16	Did God make all that was *m·*?
	235–18	Who or what *m·* matter?
	235–19	Matter as substance . . . never was *m·*.
	239–27	God, Spirit, who *m·* all that was *m·*.
	244–27	No charge will be *m·* for my services.
	245–26	Inquiries have been *m·* as to the
	264–17	Truth and Love *m·* more practical ;
	267– 7	"All things were *m·* by Him ;— *John* 1 : 3.
	267– 8	any thing *m·* that was *m·*."— *John* 1 : 3.
	271–18	* has *m·* her famous.
	272– 6	hath *m·* me [man] free— *Rom.* 8 : 2.
	287–17	are *m·* partakers of that Mind
	288–30	can make the best of what God has *m·*.
	293–29	hath *m·* me free from— *Rom.* 8 : 2.
	299–10	C. S. has been widely *m·*
	302– 9	all effect *m·* manifest through
	305–22	All that I am in reality, God has *m·*
	312–16	* Mrs. Glover *m·* only one effort at
	315–17	* *m·* oath that the within statement
	315–28	*m·* me the beloved Leader
	317– 4	* *m·* by Mrs. Eddy in refutation
	321–19	* the statements have been *m·*,
	326–10	* in which Mrs. Eddy has *m·* her home.
	327– 5	*m·* it legal to practise C. S.
	327–12	* *m·* glad the hearts of all
	328–25	* application for license was *m·*
	334– 7	* efforts are being *m·* to buy them
	335– 4	* and was *m·* a Mason
	336–15	* Mr. Glover had *m·* no will
	338–12	"The Unknown God *M·* Known,"
	343–23	I *m·* a code of by-laws,
	345–15	could be *m·* to act on me.
	346–11	* *m·* several turns about the
	346–24	* when the statement was *m·*,
	348– 7	God *m·* manifest in the flesh,
	348–20	demonstration thereof was *m·*,
	361–20	* promptly *m·* its demonstration
		(*see also* **God, man**)

Madison
Pul.	56– 3	* Toledo, Milwaukee, *M·*,

madness
Mis.	369–11	"method" in the "*m·*"
	369–12	*m·* it seems to many onlookers.
Ret.	32–13	* What is life? 'T is but a *m·*.
'00.	5–29	Not *m·*, but might and majesty
My.	14– 7	not a *m·* and nothing,

Madonna
Mis.	375–26	* in . . . Botticelli's '*M·*' !

maëlstrom
Mis.	294– 3	the *m·* of human passions,

magazine
Mis.	132–19	editing a *m·*,
	271–10	They should take our *m·*,
Ret.	53– 3	This monthly *m·* had been
My.	215–18	to plant our first *m·*,
	316–11	January number of *The Arena m·*,

magazines
Mis.	271–11	They should eschew all *m·* . . . which
My.	304–11	I wrote for the best *m·*

Magdalen
No.	23–10	Out of the *M·*, Jesus cast

Magian
My.	258–18	greater than those of *M·* kings,

magic
Mis.	29–25	*m·* and Oriental barbarisms
	78–13	occultism, *m·*, alchemy,
Ret.	18–21	communion with home's *m·* spell !
Pul.	81–23	* plays upon *m·* strings
No.	14–11	with its *m·* and enchantments.
Po.	64–14	communion with home's *m·* spell !
My.	61–23	* seemed to move as by *m·* ;

magical
'00.	12–16	*M·* arts prevailed at Ephesus ;
	12–22	*m·* books in that city were

magicians
My.	127–15	rods of the *m·* of Egypt.

magistrate (*see also* **magistrate's**)
Mis.	289–28	fairly stated by a *m·*,
Pan.	14–15	guide and bless our chief *m·*,
My.	290–19	our nation's chief *m·*,

magistrate's
No.	32– 4	A *m·* pardon may encourage a

Magna Charta
My.	246–30	The *M· C·* of C. S. means much,
	254–21	"The *M· C·* of C. S. means much,

magnanimous
My.	165–27	lost the power of being *m·*.

magnetic
Mis.	233–15	*m·* force of mortal mind,
	378–11	proved to be a *m·* practitioner.
Ret.	24– 2	*m·* doctor, Mr. P. P. Quimby,
Pul.	32– 3	* *m·*, earnest, impassioned.
	46– 2	* so eloquent and *m·* that
'01.	2– 9	*m·* element of human will
My.	90– 4	* no eloquence of orator or *m·* ritual,
	307– 6	back of his *m·* treatment and

Magnetism
(*see* **Animal Magnetism**)

magnetism
animal
Mis.	3–26	hygiene, and animal *m·* are
	48–11	animal *m·* is neither of God nor
	48–18	as to the animus of animal *m·*
	78–15	are the inventions of animal *m·*,
	97–13	human control is animal *m·*,
	175–29	both animal *m·* and divine power,
	280–31	doors of animal *m·* open wide for
	284–14	treat malicious animal *m·*?
	366–22	drugs, electricity, and animal *m·*
'01.	20– 1	animal *m·* and hypnotism are
My.	180–13	hypnotism or animal *m·*.
	211–12	Animal *m·*, in its ascending steps
	211–20	Animal *m·* fosters suspicious
	212– 4	This intricate method of animal *m·*
	212–12	animal *m·* is the highest form of
	212–22	resist the animal *m·* by which
	212–29	saying that animal *m·* never
	212–30	saying that . . . teaches animal *m·* ;
	213– 4	perverted mind-power, or animal *m·*,
	213–26	adverse influence of animal *m·*.
	236–29	of the workings of animal *m·*,
	357– 9	animal *m·*,— the name of all evil,
	358– 6	animal *m·* is the opposite of divine
	359–28	temptation produced by animal *m·*
	364– 9	Animal *m·*, hypnotism, *etc.*,

My.	348– 3	electricity, *m·*, or will-power,

magnetizer
Mis.	156–22	through which the animal *m·* **preys,**

magnificence
My.	70–19	* chapter sub-title

magnificent
Mis.	275–27	Palmer House, . . . is *m·*
Pul.	25–16	* entrance to this *m·* temple.
	30–29	* its own *m·* church building,
	77– 1	* *m·* new edifice of worship
	77–24	* chapter sub-title
	78– 2	* probably one of the most *m·*
My.	6–14	*m·* temple wherein to enter and
	43–30	* dedication of our *m·* temple,
	45–14	* The *m·* edifice stands a
	58– 7	* *m·* growth of this Cause,
	58–15	* This *m·* structure,
	59–13	* the gallery of that *m·* temple,
	62– 5	* But what of this *m·* structure?
	62–21	* completion of the *m·* extension
	69–14	* sculptor added *m·* carvings to
	77–19	* streets leading to the *m·* temple
	94–18	* *m·* new temple of the cult.

magnificent
My. 95– 9   * *m·* C. S. church in Boston
    98– 6   * *m·* church, holding five thousand
  194–20   princely gift of your *m·* church
  198– 5   dedication of your *m·* church
  274–21   my thanks for their *m·* gifts,

magnified
Mis. 164–26   will become so *m·* to human sense,
Un.   7– 1   His name will be *m·* in the

magnifies
Mis. 194–16   *m·* the divine power to human sight ;
'01. 12–22   *m·* the divine power to human sight ;
Hea. 2–26   *m·* his name who built, on Truth,

magnify
Mis. 75–22   doth *m·* the Lord," — *Luke* 1 : 46.
   75–23   "My *spiritual sense* doth *m·*
  129–20   faults to *m·* under the lens
Un.   30– 2   doth *m·* the Lord." — *Luke* 1 : 46.
Pul. 12–16   give thanks and *m·* the Lord

magnitude
Mis. 61– 8   when aping the wisdom and *m·* of
  100–13   the *m·* of self-abnegation,
  360–13   these stars of the first *m·*
  380– 7   majesty and *m·* of this query,
Ret. 65–28   *m·* and distance of the stars,
   71–11   an error of much *m·*.
'01. 30– 7   The *m·* of its meaning forbids
My. 47–11   * has grown to great *m·*,
   59– 1   * grandeur and *m·* of your work
   63–22   * new sense of the *m·* of C. S.,
   84–20   * Its very *m·* and the cheerful
  133–28   your knowledge with its *m·* of
  270– 4   *m·* of their spiritual import,

magnolia
Ret. 17–18   *m·*, and fragrant fringe-tree ;
Po. 63– 3   *m·*, and fragrant fringe-tree ;

mahogany
Pul. 76–11   * frames are of white *m·*
My. 68–32   * pews and . . . woodwork are of *m·*.
   78–13   * semi-circular sweep of *m·* pews

maid
Pul. 33– 9   * but the little *m·* was afraid
Pan.   3–17   * fair wisdom, that celestial *m·*."

maiden
Mis. x–22   to retain my *m·* name,
  390–16   Gives back some *m·* melody,
Po. 55– 9   Gives back some *m·* melody,

mail
Mis. 171–30   all clad in the shining *m·*
Man. 93–15   *m·* to the Clerk of this Church
Pul. 44–28   * checks by *m·* or otherwise.
My. 73–33   * to which all *m·* may be directed,

mailed
'02. 15– 1   anonymous letters *m·* to me
Po. v 22   * *was subsequently m· to them.*
My. 215–13   but it was again *m·* to me

main
Pul. 58–15   * *m·* auditorium has wide galleries,
Po. 10– 6   Lord of the *m·* and manor !
My. 80–30   * in the *m·* body of the church,
   81–11   * announced at the *m·* meeting
  137– 6   * "in the *m·*, an example of
  337– 7   Lord of the *m·* and manor !

Maine and **Me.** (*see also* **Pine Tree State**)
     (*see* **Augusta, Calais, Eastport, Portland**)

mainly
Mis. 38–22   *m·*, elaborating a man-made
Un. 25– 1   thus affirms is *m·* correct.
Peo. 2– 4   *m·* due to the people's improved
My. 3–20   its effect on man is *m·* this

maintain
Mis. 27–15   the Scriptures *m·* this fact
   38– 3   ability to gain and *m·* health,
  110–10   *m·* in yourselves what Jesus loved,
  146–13   and still *m·* this position,
  148–17   *m·* the dignity and defense
  205–23   *m·* their obvious correspondence,
  286–16   *m·* morality and generation,
Man. 3–13   *m·* the dignity and defense
   33– 6   he shall *m·* the Tenets,
   74–20   *m·* toward them an attitude
   93– 5   *m·* a Board of Lectureship,
Ret. 44–15   able to *m·* the church
Un. 46– 7   I *m·*, the individuality and reality
Pul. 3–10   If you *m·* this position,
   74–23   *m·* but one conclusion and statement
'01. 13– 9   not well to *m·* the position that
My. 86–20   * *m·* towards their church.
  165–25   They *m·* themselves and others
  211– 7   in order to *m·* harmony,
  222–30   will *m·* law and order,

maintain
My. 230– 2   will *m·* its rank as in the past,
  294– 1   Human governments *m·* the right of
  358–31   to *m·* them and sustain them.

maintained
Mis. 68– 9   * *m· that pain and disease are not*
   93–19   neither *m·* by Science nor
Ret. 14–14   *m·* that I was willing to trust God,
Pul. 6– 5   *m·* on the spiritual foundation of
   9–17   the church services were *m·* by
My. 37–17   * has been organized and *m·*,
  216–10   by which each is provided for and *m·*.

maintaining
My. 279– 9   *m·* its obvious correspondence with

maintains
Rud. 12–27   *m·* human health and life.
My. 41–17   * *m·* the perfect standard of truth
  111–15   C. S. *m·* primitive Christianity,

maintenance
Man. 55–19   by uniform *m·* of the life of a
My. 220– 4   *m·* of individual rights,
  268–12   *m·* of individual rights,

majestic
Mis. 123–20   *m·* atonement of divine Love.
  385–26   shed *M·* forms ;
  392– 6   *m·* oak, from yon high place
Po. 18– 3   eagle's proud wing, His soaring *m·*,
   20– 8   *m·* oak, from yon high place
   49– 1   shed *M·* forms ;
My. 182–18   large membership and *m·* cathedral.
  245–18   *m·* march of C. S. go on *ad infinitum*,

majestically
Mis. 145–28   float *m·* heaven's heraldry,
  338–18   move *m·* to your defense

majesty
Mis. 141–13   freedom, might, and *m·* of Spirit,
  185–16   man be clothed with might, *m·*, and
  191–16   name of his satanic *m·* is found to be
  292–14   to human weakness might and *m·*.
  294–10   might and *m·* ! — of goodness.
  380– 7   *m·* and magnitude of this query,
'00. 2–18   his satanic *m·* is supposed to
   5–30   might and *m·* attend every footstep
'01. 33–22   might and *m·* of divine power
My. 58–11   * *m·* and the dignity of this church
  149– 8   More than regal is the *m·* of
  187–29   the *m·* of His might
  188–25   the *m·* of C. S.
  188–26   teaches the *m·* of man.
  258–29   lowly in its *m·*.

Major
    (*see* **Glover**)

major
'01. 4– 9   In logic the *m·* premise must be

majority
Mis. 6– 8   the *m·* of the acute cases
  102–31   "one on God's side is a *m·*."
  130–23   *m·* of one's acts are right,
  245–29   * "one with God is a *m·*."
Man. 26–23   A *m·* vote or the request of
   30– 8   removed from office by a *m·*
   38–11   elected by *m·* vote
   65–21   supplied by a *m·* vote
   82–12   except by a *m·* vote
  102– 9   supply a vacancy . . . by a *m·* vote.
Ret. 7– 1   *m·* vote of seven thousand,
Pul. 4–17   "one on God's side is a *m·*."
   56– 8   * In some churches a *m·* of the
   67–18   * the *m·* of whom are in the
Rud. 8–17   error has the *m·*.
No. 46– 1   "One on God's side is a *m·* ;"
Peo. 3– 7   minority to be saved and the *m·* to be
My. 182– 2   To-day it is said to have a *m·*
  294– 1   the right of the *m·* to rule.

make
Mis. 4–26   to *m·* your demonstrations."
   24–16   tried to *m·* plain to others,
   38–27   to *m·* each patient a student
   39–10   risen up in a day to *m·* this claim ;
   43–11   *m·* safe and successful practitioners.
   48–31   trying to *m·* capital out of
   51–16   *m·* clear to the child's thought
   52–23   What progress would a student . . . *m·*,
   53–24   to *m·* the rulers understand,
   60–10   The Nazarene Prophet could *m·* the
   61–28   can neither *m·* them so nor
   69–10   *m·* man in our image, — *Gen.* 1 : 26.
   75–17   used and *m·* complete sense.
   99–26   "*M·* straight God's paths ;
   99–27   *m·* way for health, holiness,
  117–29   *m·* their moves before God
  117–30   or *m·* them too late to follow

make

Mis.	118–10	*m·* incorrect your entire problem,
	121–13	would *m·* this fatal doctrine just
	130–13	same power to *m·* you a sinner
	130–14	to *m·* a man sick?
	133– 2	the statement you *m·* at the close
	151–20	*m·* Him thy first acquaintance.
	166–31	it could *m·* the glorified.
	170–13	we *m·* our own heavens
	196– 7	will *m·* you as gods ;" — *see Gen.* 3 : 5.
	196–10	and *m·* you know evil,
	203– 3	I *m·* no distinction between
	218–15	they *m·* Deity unreal
	222–23	will *m·* stout hearts quail.
	223–28	* should *m·* him hate somebody."
	230– 7	*m·* the most of the present.
	241–12	try to *m·* others do likewise,
	241–23	shall *m·* you free.' " — *John* 8 : 32.
	244–20	*m·* the blind to see,
	246–24	*m·* His paths straight." — *Matt.* 3 : 3.
	250– 5	they *m·* it what it is not,
	250–16	I *m·* strong demands on love,
	253–10	and *m·* amends for the
	256– 5	to *m·* the body harmonious.
	261–30	or else *m·* the claim valid.
	265– 7	*m·* mistakes and lose their way.
	265–16	presume to *m·* innovations
	267– 1	screaming, to *m·* itself heard
	271–22	To *m·* this plain,
	284–10	adhere to the right, and *m·*
	299–20	can I *m·* this right by saying,
	319–12	tends to *m·* sin less or more
	328– 3	*M·* thine own way ;
	330– 2	the winds *m·* melody
	330– 8	*m·* music in the heart.
	331– 5	did it *m·* them humble, loving,
	343– 1	*m·* us wise unto salvation !
	354–18	*m·* manifest the movement of
	362–11	Theologians *m·* the mortal mistake **of**
	363–16	to *m·* himself imperfect,
	387–19	*m·* men one in love remain.
	389–14	O *m·* me glad for every
	394– 9	bless, and *m·* joyful again.
	398– 7	*M·* self-righteousness be still,
	399– 4	for you *m·* radiant room
Man.	28–15	to watch and *m·* sure that the
	29– 5	shall not *m·* known the name
	32–20	They shall *m·* no remarks
	39– 2	*m·* application for membership
	48–14	or *m·* a summer resort near
	50–18	from Christian motives *m·* this
	70– 2	shall not *m·* a church By-Law,
	94– 4	*m· . . .* a less lecture fee ;
Chr.	53–23	*M·* merriment on Christmas eves,
Ret.	15– 8	I will *m·* mention — *Psal.* 71 : 16.
	24–15	and how to *m·* others so.
	46–13	*M·* self-righteousness be still,
	69–10	saying, . . . I will *m·* error as real
Un.	7– 8	*m·* also the following statement :
	8– 5	Everything is as real as you *m·* it,
	17– 3	and so *m·* the lie seem part of
	23– 4	* *M·* instruments to scourge us.
	45–18	Anatomy and physiology *m·*
	49–20	Standing in no basic Truth, we *m·*
	51– 7	human reason can never *m·*
	53– 1	which *m·* a beautiful lie.
	61–19	*m·* the earthly acme of
Pul.	1– 2	*m· them drink of the* — *Psal.* 36 : 8.
	3–17	*m·* them drink of the — *Psal.* 36 : 8.
	7–30	*m·* them drink of the — *Psal.* 36 : 8.
	13– 7	I will *m·* thee ruler — *Matt.* 25 : 23.
	17–12	*M·* self-righteousness be still,
	58–29	* to *m·* it a home by day or night.
	82– 1	* *m·* the body not the prison,
	82–24	* to help *m·* the laws,
	87–16	*m·* me your *Pastor Emeritus,* nominally.
Rud.	10–24	belief that matter can . . . *m·* you ill,
No.	5– 9	would be to *m·* it Truth.
	8–13	*m·* the wrath of man to praise Him,
	23– 5	nor *m·* evil omnipotent
	32–15	other theories *m·* sin true.
	37–18	would *m·* the atonement to be
	42–23	would *m·* a lie the author of Truth,
	42–24	and so *m·* Truth itself a lie.
	44– 3	failure should *m·* him modest.
Pan.	3– 7	to *m·* it half divine
	12–10	will *m·* strong claims on religion,
'00.	14– 3	Behold, I will *m·* — *Rev.* 3 : 9.
'01.	10– 2	shall *m·* you free." — *John* 8 : 32.
	11–16	that does not *m·* it impossible
	14–13	*m·* us love it and so hinder our
'02.	6–21	*M·* me the image and likeness
Hea.	3– 4	to *m·* men better, to cast out error,
	8–22	and this will *m·* us honest
	9–20	wherewith to *m·* himself wicked.

make

Peo.	2–15	*m·* a Christian only in theory,
	3–13	that *m·* a mysterious God
	4–22	can *m·* a spiritual mind out of
	8–16	and yet we *m·* more of matter,
	10–21	*m·* it harmonious or discordant
	11–18	*m·* the laws that govern their
Po.	4–13	O *m·* me glad for every
	6–14	*m·* men one in love remain.
	14–11	*M·* self-righteousness be still,
	33– 2	*m·* this my humble request :
	35– 4	To *m·* me love thee as I
	45–12	bless, and *m·* joyful again.
	75–11	for you *m·* radiant room
My.	8–15	* *m·* reasonable accommodation for
	16–27	shall not *m·* haste. — *Isa.* 28 : 16.
	21–24	* have been called upon to *m·*
	28– 1	* to *m·* this announcement
	40–21	* them that *m·* peace." — *Jas.* 3 : 18.
	48–11	* insisted that her students *m·*,
	48–25	* forces that *m·* for righteousness.
	52– 9	* will *m·* greater efforts
	66–11	* what use the society will *m·*
	66–20	* their work to *m·* the spacious
	75–16	* it would not *m·* much difference,
	87–22	* Their happy faces would *m·* sunshine
	98– 2	* *m·* up a mighty host,
	108–24	*m·* known the best work of a
	117–11	*m·* one a Christian Scientist.
	123–29	* "trifles *m·* perfection,"
	124–15	enough to *m·* this hour glad.
	137–29	No person influenced me to *m·*
	140– 4	*m·* darkness light — *Isa.* 42 : 16.
	149–13	*m·* their treasures yours.
	156– 6	*m·* all grace abound — *II Cor.* 9 : 8.
	156–17	there *m·* ready." — *Luke* 22 : 12.
	172– 4	* to *m·* room for Vanderbilt Hall.
	173–23	vied with each other to *m·*
	177–24	will *m·* an everlasting — *Isa.* 61 : 8.
	179–32	as *m·* even God demonstrable,
	186–19	*m·* this church the fold of flocks,
	192– 5	*m·* spotless the blemished,
	203–16	they *m·* us what we are.
	219–22	cannot annul nor *m·* void the
	220–21	*m·* them Thy friends ;
	222–23	*m·* laws to regulate man's
	226– 3	only where you can . . . *m·* sense.
	235–16	Did God *m·* all that was made?
	235–17	Infinite Spirit *m·* that
	236– 7	to *m·* the *amende honorable*
	237–16	*m·* their charges for treatment
	242–20	not to *m·* inquiries on these subjects,
	252–11	*m·* one not only know the truth
	252–12	*m·* one enjoy doing right,
	252–12	*m·* one . . . work midst clouds of wrong,
	257–22	*m·* man's being pure and blest.
	260– 3	would *m·* matter an alien
	260– 6	to *m·* room for substance,
	278– 5	may learn to *m·* war no more,
	280– 8	* *m·* for the establishment of a
	288–29	*m·* the best of what God has made.
	299– 8	* *m·* it known to the world,
	300–22	that he *m·* known his doctrine
	319– 2	would *m·* no difference to me.
	327–11	* will *m·* your heart glad,
	336–18	* he was unable to *m·* a will.
	344–15	must *m·* gradual approaches to
	345–29	*m·* them our figures of speech.

(*see also* **man**)

Maker

his

Mis.	46–15	Man is not equal with his *M·* ;
	47–25	coexistence with his *M·*.
	62– 8	the true likeness of his *M·*.
	65–26	man's account with his *M·*
	98– 5	which is the image of his *M·*.
	164–23	actual likeness of his *M·*.
	182–27	man and his *M·* are inseparable
	183–32	Scriptures declare reflects his *M·*,
	185– 1	and reflecting, his *M·*.
	196–18	man's unity with his *M·*,
	217–24	a rebel against his *M·*.
	255– 5	Man is not equal to his *M·*.
	294– 2	man in the image of his *M·* ;
Un.	41–16	man's unity with his *M·*
	46–10	man and his *M·* are here ;
	52–11	of man separated from his *M·*.
Hea.	9–19	power underived from his *M·*
Peo.	6–14	the victim of his *M·*,
	11–12	is made subject to his *M·*.
My.	232–26	the true likeness of his *M·* "?
Mis.	103–20	neither the pattern nor *M·* of
	184– 1	very opposite of that *M·*,
	363–15	and there is no other *M·* :
Un.	23– 6	turn again and rend their *M·*.

Maker

Un. 49– 9 as is the perfect *M·*.
50–23 is without Mind or *M·*.
My. 219–14 believe that man's *M·* is not equal to

maker

Ret. 48– 9 one builder and *m·*, God,
My. 205–18 * is good or bad, so is its *m·*."
282– 2 its peace *m·* or breaker.

makers

My. 160–30 *m·* of hell burn in their fire.

makes

Mis. 14–32 he *m·* a great reality of evil,
21–11 *m·* practical all his words
28– 9 what mortal mind *m·* them ;
38–20 *m·* divine metaphysics needful,
108–26 This cognomen *m·* it less dangerous ;
110–11 *m·* morals for mankind !
117–30 make their moves before God *m·* His,
133–29 Love *m·* all burdens light,
147–14 *m·* it his constant rule
160–14 *m·* us stronger and firmer
165–19 *m·* his followers the heirs to
169–22 *m·* them nothing valuable,
219–22 that mortal mind *m·* sick,
219–23 immortal Mind *m·* well ;
219–24 mortal mind *m·* sinners,
219–24 immortal Mind *m·* saints ;
224– 2 *m·* another's criticism rankle,
221 3 *m·* another's deed offensive,
228–28 and it *m·* disease catching.
234–32 *m·* His sovereignty glorious.
262–25 Christ-love that *m·* them light
265– 3 *m·* the venture from vanity,
287–27 *m·* one ruler over one's self
293–25 *m·* mortals either saints or sinners.
294–14 *m·* honey out of the flowers
316– 3 know the truth that *m·* free,
324– 2 *m·* his way into the streets
340–18 *m·* himself a musician by
353–21 that *m·* the machinery work rightly ;
355–24 the error . . . that *m·* his body sick,
363– 7 is mind and *m·* men,
399– 8 'T is the Spirit that *m·* pure,
Man. 84– 5 know the truth that *m·* free,
Chr. 53–36 For health *m·* room.
Ret. 63– 8 which *m·* him a sinner,
64– 7 *m·* apparent, the real man,
78– 7 scientific practice *m·* perfect,
82–29 *m·* the subject-matter clearer
Un. 23– 2 which *m·* true the lines :
Pul. 14–29 when it *m·* them sick or sinful.
56–16 * It *m·* people better and happier.
82–29 * Might no longer *m·* right,
Rud. 9–23 he *m·* morally worse the invalid
No. 5–28 *m·* the last state of one's patients
12–25 it *m·* both sense and Soul,
13– 3 *m·* disease unreal, and this heals it.
39–20 It *m·* new and scientific discoveries
Pan. 7–28 *m·* sin, disease, and death
'00. 4– 3 misnomer . . . *m·* His opposites as real
11–19 Mind, not matter, *m·* music ;
'02. 2– 9 Truth *m·* haste to meet and to
Hea. 7–14 *m·* pure the fountain,
13–26 Mesmerism *m·* one disease while
17– 7 Love *m·* the spiritual man,
17– 8 *m·* the material so-called man,
19–19 *m·* a more spiritual demand,
Peo. 2– 9 and *m·* it *good,*
5–24 *m·* a pure Christianity
9– 9 *m·* them white in the blood of the
Po. 39–17 Since temperance *m·* your laws.
75–15 'Tis the Spirit that *m·* pure,
My. 24– 3 * the truth which *m·* free
41–16 * C. S. *m·* no compromise with evil,
52–31 * statement "Phare Pleigh" . . . *m·*
92– 6 * *m·* it appear that Science cannot
99– 5 * a religion that *m·* the merry heart
110–20 if bodily sensation *m·* us captives
112– 6 what C. S. *m·* practical to-day
145–21 *m·* me the servant of the race
154–25 it *m·* the church militant,
155– 1 *m·* healing the sick and reforming
157–10 * *m·* necessary the commodious
158–21 *m·* the heart tender, faithful, true.
165–16 goodness *m·* life a blessing.
204–11 which *m·* them one in Christ.
212– 5 evil, which *m·* mankind drunken.
336– 9 * She *m·* grateful acknowledgment
346–29 "S. and H. *m·* it plain to us
349–29 *m·* manifest the infinite nature,
(*see also* **God, man**)

maketh

Mis. 137–26 that worketh or *m·* a lie.
174–18 nothing that *m·* or worketh a lie.

maketh

Mis. 366–14 nothing that worketh or *m·* a lie
393–13 Students wise, he *m·* now
No. 15–26 "worketh or *m·* a lie"—*see Rev.* 21 : 27.
'01. 28–23 all that worketh or *m·* a lie.
Po. 51–18 Students wise, he *m·* now

make-up

My. 122– 6 in one's own moral *m·*.

making

Mis. vii– 7 * In *m·* thy friends books,
62–12 *m·* the aggregate positive,
97–32 The only cause for *m·* this
133–20 *m·* the following statement :
192–26 *m·* healing a condition of salvation,
230– 9 *m·* lingering calls,
261–25 a kind of men after man's own *m·*.
294– 4 *m·* place for himself and
302–26 derived from *m·* his copy,
305–13 * *m·* the undertaking successful.
318–26 namely, *m·* sin seem
Ret. 57–28 *m·* mortality the status
Pul. 11– 2 *m·* melody more real,
Pan. 4–16 a creator, *m·* two creators ;
'01. 24–12 *M·* matter more potent than Mind,
'02. 1– 8 *m·* total twenty-four thousand
2–11 *m·* the children our teachers.
12–25 *m·* another united effort
Hea. 12–22 *m·* you more powerful,"
18–28 *m·* him believe he was bleeding
19–25 *m·* our words golden rays
Po. v– 5 * with a view of *m·* a book,
70– 6 *M·* this life divine,
70– 7 *M·* its waters wine,
My. 7– 8 before *m·* another united effort
25– 2 * propriety in *m·* a special effort
79–25 * *m·* their remarkable statements
97– 4 * towards *m·* the patient well.
306–10 purpose of *m·* the true apparent.
309– 4 *m·* out deeds, settling quarrels,
340–15 *m·* laws for the State

malady

Mis. 241–17 Truth heals him of the moral *m·*.
My. 116– 9 mental *m·*, which must be met
116–20 not a symptom of this contagious *m·*,
203–17 Dishonesty is a mental *m·*

male

Mis. 18–16 "*m·* and female," — *Gen.* 1 : 27.
199– 8 *m·* and female come into their
314– 6 two Readers : a *m·*, and a female.
'01. 7–10 made them *m·* and female
10–11 term for both *m·* and female.
My. 268–29 you see *m·* and female one
355–11 *m·* element is a strong

malefactor

Mis. 70–21 dying *m·* and our Lord

malice

Mis. 19– 2 hatred, *m·*, are always wrong,
48–10 prompted by money-making or *m·*.
54–13 *m·* would fling in her path.
175–15 "the leaven of *m·* — *I Cor.* 5 : 8.
177– 9 Large numbers, in desperate *m·*,
227– 9 yet with *m·* aforethought
228–11 the buffetings of envy or *m·*
248–15 *m·* aforethought of sinners."
277–17 purposes of envy and *m·*
343–14 weeds of passion, *m·*, envy,
353–12 through *m·* or ignorance.
368–14 Charlatanism, fraud, and *m·*
368–25 Others, from *m·* and envy, are
Un. 56–27 ingratitude, lust, *m·*,
Pul. 13–25 stung to death by his own *m·* ;
No. 36–24 conquered the *m·* of his foes,
45–10 indicates weakness, fear, or *m·* ;
'02. 19– 9 more than all the *m·* of his foes.
Hea. 2–20 beneath the *m·* of the world.
10– 4 vision of envy, sensuality, and *m·*,
17– 3 envy, hypocrisy, or *m·*,
18–22 appetites, passions, envy, and *m·*
My. 17– 4 laying aside all *m·*, — *I Pet.* 2 : 1.
108–20 slang, and *m·* touch not the hem of
164–28 against which envy, enmity, or *m·*
316–20 torrents of ignorance, envy, and *m·*.

malicious

Mis. 51– 8 *m·* workings of error or mortal mind.
67–11 shalt not strike . . . with a *m·* aim
119– 1 If *m·* suggestions whisper evil
222–15 *m·* mental argument and its action
274–15 chapter sub-title
284–14 How shall I treat *m·* animal magnetism ?
351–12 solely from mental *m·* practice,
352–19 the *m·* mental operation must

malicious
My. 130– 3 against *m·* mental malpractice,
213– 3 *m·* aim of perverted mind-power,
357– 9 is *m·* animal magnetism,

maliciously
No. 32–12 ignorantly or *m·* misconstrued.
My. 146–28 do it ignorantly or *m·*.

malignant
Mis. 249–21 efforts of some *m·* students,
My. 105–11 I healed *m·* diphtheria
227–15 in taking a case of *m·* disease.
227–31 a larger per cent of *m·* diseases

maligned
Mis. 94– 1 are misjudged and *m·* ;
105–22 If either is misunderstood or *m·*,
'01. 33–24 Is it for . . . that they are *m·* ?
My. 103–12 has been persecuted and *m·*.
330– 4 * not be surprised that . . . be *m·*,

malpractice
mental
    (*see* **mental**)
————
Mis. 233– 3 a *m·* of the best system
249– 1 to test that *m·* I experimented
Man. 42–19 No *M·*.
84– 1 Defense against *M·*.
90–20 of mental practice and *m·*.
Rud. 9–10 *m·* is in erring human will,

malpractise
Man. 42–20 or knowingly mentally *m·*,
My. 363–24 was not to *m·* unwittingly.

malpractises
Man. 42–26 *m·* upon or treats our Leader

malpractitioner
Mis. 19–24 hypocrite or mental *m·*.
115– 9 his own guilt as a mental *m·*,
221– 2 a mental *m·* may lose his
284–17 gone personally to the *m·*
316– 2 never to attack the *m·*,
368–19 address of a mental *m·*
Rud. 9– 9 poor practitioner, if not a *m·*.
'01. 20–10 The mental *m·* is not,
My. 212–24 *m·*, interfering with the

mamma
Mis. 231–23 a toy from *m·*
239–28 and which *m·* thought must be

mammal
Rud. 8– 2 no pine-tree produces a *m·*

mammon (*see also* **mammon's**)
Mis. 269– 9 cannot serve God and *m·*.''— *Matt.* 6 : 24.
Un. 49–15 serve the *m·* of materiality
Pul. 21–17 we cannot serve *m·*.
My. 356–24 cannot serve God and *m·*.— *Matt.* 6 : 24.

mammon's
Po. 71– 5 worshiping at *m·* shrine.

mammoth
Mis. 231–12 *m·* turkey grew beautifully less.

man (*see also* **man's**)
abides in
Un. 40–17 Hence Life abides in *m·*,
40–17 if *m·* abides in good,
action of
Mis. 58–24 does not govern the action of *m·*,
activity of
My. 259–25 give the activity of *m·* infinite scope ;
advanced
Mis. 234–17 it never has advanced *m·*
agency of
My. 14– 9 Godlike agency of *m·*.
a kind of
My. 239–24 in other words, a kind of *m·*
allotted years of
My. 273– 7 * far beyond the allotted years of *m·*,
ambitious
Po. 2– 7 Ambitious *m·*, Like a trained falcon
and divine Science
'00. 5–12 God, *m·*, and divine Science.
and God
Mis. 77–11 eternal unity of *m·* and God,
332–17 pondered the things of *m·* and God.
Ret. 60–27 or of the real *m·* and God.
Peo. 1– 7 final unity between *m·* and God.
and his Maker
Mis. 182–27 *m·* and his Maker are inseparable
Un. 46– 9 scientific *m·* and his Maker are here ;
and Life
No. 12–26 both sense and Soul, *m·* and Life,
and the universe
    (*see* **universe**)

man
and universe
'01. 5–19 real spiritual *m·* and universe.
My. 253– 4 perfect original *m·* and universe.
and woman
Mis. 12–12 Every *m·* and woman should be
Un. 52–14 spiritual idea, *m·* and *woman.*
Pan. 10–12 were the average *m·* and woman.
'01. 7–14 mentalities of *m·* and woman,
My. 239–13 *until every m· and woman comes into*
animal
Mis. 36–16 qualities of the so-called animal *m·* ;
animus of
Pan. 11– 9 gauge the animus of *m·* ?
annihilate
Mis. 56– 6 would destroy Spirit and annihilate *m·*.
Ret. 64– 6 does not annihilate *m·*,
any
Mis. 151– 4 neither shall any *m·* — *John* 10 : 28.
213–24 neither shall any *m·* — *John* 10 : 28.
226–17 * canst not then be false to any *m·*.
252–15 any *m·* can satisfy himself
Chr. 55–26 if any *m·* hear my — *Rev.* 3 : 20.
Ret. 81–26 * canst not then be false to any *m·*.
'01. 21–25 God knows more than any *m·*
My. 196–12 ''If any *m·* offend not — *Jas.* 3 : 2.
285–22 disputing with any *m·*, — *Acts* 24 : 12.
346–28 did not mean any *m·* to-day on earth.
appeals to
Mis. 252–19 It appeals to *m·* as man ;
applied to
Mis. 180–28 This term, as applied to *m·*,
as God's idea
Mis. 261–25 *M·* as God's idea is already saved
as God's offspring
Un. 24–20 *M·*, as God's offspring, must be
as His likeness
Mis. 17–20 Spirit, and of *m·* as His likeness,
79–15 *m·* as His likeness is erect
'02. 8– 2 God, and *m·* as His likeness,
as the idea
My. 239–19 *M·*, as the idea or image
attains
My. 103–13 as *m·* attains the stature of man
at variance
Mis. 214– 6 set a *m·* at variance — *Matt.* 10 : 35.
average
Pan. 10–12 the average *m·* and woman.
My. 106–24 more than does the average *m·*,
awake
Mis. 15–21 and *m·* awake in His likeness.
awakes
My. 273–28 ''*M·* awakes from the dream of death
became a
Mis. 359–10 when I became a *m·*, — *I Cor.* 13 : 11.
My. 135– 4 when I became a *m·*, — *I Cor.* 13 : 11.
261–17 when I became a *m·*, — *I Cor.* 13 : 11.
becomes
Mis. 235– 6 *m·* becomes the partaker of
'02. 6–25 In the degree that *m·* becomes
10–17 that *m·* becomes finally spiritual.
My. 179– 9 and *m·* becomes both good and
before
Mis. 165–30 before *m·* can truthfully conclude
Un. 54–21 when Satan held it up before *m·*
be found
Mis. 164–22 until *m·* be found in the
No. 28– 6 *m·* be found perfect and eternal.
begins
'00. 8–20 When a *m·* begins to quarrel with
behold
Mis. 330–17 behold *m·* in God's own image
belief that
Mis. 77–26 mortal belief that *m·* has fallen
believe in
Un. 49– 1 *Do you believe in m· ?*
believing that
Peo. 6–14 Believing that *m·* is the victim of his
beneath
My. 350–23 Sunk from beneath *m·*,
better
Mis. 336–26 behold a better *m·*, woman, or
bidding
Hea. 19–20 bidding *m·* go up higher,
bless
Mis. 320–11 to cheer, guide, and bless *m·*
blind
Mis. 170–25 Jesus' proceedings with the blind *m·*
body of
Mis. 25– 1 on the mind and body of *m·*,
born of Spirit
Mis. 184– 9 *m·* born of Spirit is spiritual,
bows
Un. 16– 1 *m·* bows to the infinite perfection
brother
Mis. 50–30 helping our brother *m·*.

man

brotherhood of
Mis. 56–20 one God, and the brotherhood of *m·*.
318– 4 brotherhood of *m·* is stated and
Peo. 13–10 brotherhood of *m·* in unity of Mind
My. 220–16 I pray for . . . the brotherhood of *m·*,
240– 3 brotherhood of *m·* shall be known
265–11 brotherhood of *m·* should be
279–18 establish the brotherhood of *m·*,
business
Mis. 252–28 and empowers the business *m·*
My. 106–26 politician or business *m·*
call
Pan. 11–26 that mortals are content to call *m·*,
called
Mis. 205–28 mortal molecules, called *m·*,
My. 269– 3 image or likeness, called *m·*,
called a
Mis. 294–13 sometimes called a *m·*,
can do no
Ret. 68–25 In C. S., *m·* can do no harm,
can fulfil
Mis. 183–15 *m·* can fulfil the Scriptures
cannot be separated
Mis. 186–19 see that *m·* cannot be separated from
cannot punish a
My. 128–17 Men cannot punish a *m·* for suicide ;
can prove
My. 180– 1 whereby *m·* can prove God's love,
capability of
'00. 3–14 slumbering capability of *m·*.
causes a
Pan. 8– 2 causes a *m·* to be mentally deranged ;
character of
Peo. 7–29 the health and character of *m·*
claims on
Mis. 16–11 Principle hath infinite claims on *m·*,
colored
Peo. 11– 3 the rights of the colored *m·*
commands
'02. 8– 3 commands *m·* to love as Jesus loved.
commands a
My. 131– 4 exalts, and commands a *m·*,
conception of
Mis. 186–10 separates its conception of *m·*
concerns
Mis. 63–18 great reality that concerns *m·*,
condition of
No. 5–23 normal and real condition of *m·*,
consciousness in
Un. 21 17 Individual consciousness in *m·*
consecrate
Hea. 5–27 elevate, and consecrate *m·* ;
constitute
My. 259–19 true heart, and . . . constitute *m·*,
constitution of
Pul. 79–23 * something in the constitution of *m·*
cooperates
Peo. 11–11 *m·* cooperates with and is made
corporeal
Mis. 97–30 corporeal *m·* is this lost image ;
163–26 crucifixion of the corporeal *m·*,
Rud. 2– 3 * a corporeal *m·*, woman, or child ;
created
Mis. 50–30 implies that Spirit, . . . created *m·*
57–12 with *m·* created spiritually.
97–23 "He created *m·* in the image and
186– 2 created *m·* in His own image
My. 232–25 *m·* created by and of Spirit,
created after
Pul. 82–14 * because she was created after *m·*,
creator of
Pan. 4–16 that He is the creator of *m·*,
defileth a
Mis. 118–32 "Not that . . . defileth a *m·* ;— *Matt.* 15 : 11.
119– 1 this defileth a *m·*." — *Matt.* 15 : 11.
defines
Ret. 59–23 Science defines *m·* as immortal,
Deity and
My. 350– 1 draws its conclusions of Deity and *m·*,
deliver
Mis. 50–26 would deliver *m·* from heart-disease,
demanded of
My. 103– 5 faith and works demanded of *m·*
demand for
Mis. 247– 1 demand for *m·* his God-given heritage,
demands upon
My. 159–22 eternal demands upon *m·* ;
deny
Hea. 15–14 why should *m·* deny all might to the
dies not
Un. 43–14 I insist only . . . that *m·* dies not
does
My. 271– 9 good that a *m·* does is the one thing
does not absolve
My. 274– 5 Death alone does not absolve *m·*

man

dooms
Mis. 258– 1 lawless law which dooms *m·*
drowning
Mis. 211–14 drowning *m·* just rescued from
dying
Mis. 187–25 create a sick, sinning, dying *m·* ?
each
Ret. 86–22 God will help each *m·*
effect on
My. 3–20 its effect on *m·* is mainly this
elevate
Mis. 38– 4 elevate *m·* in every line of life,
elevates
Pul. 53–18 * elevates *m·* above the level of the
emerges
My. 200–15 *m·* emerges from mortality
enable a
Mis. ix– 5 * enable a *m·* to dispense with
enabled
Mis. 30–19 enabled *m·* to demonstrate the law
enables
Mis. 49–20 enables *m·* to discern between the
enrobe
Mis. 332– 9 enrobe *m·* in righteousness ;
equips
Mis. 183–23 equips *m·* with divine power
every
Mis. 12–12 Every *m·* and woman should be
232–22 Every *m·* and every woman would
Ret. 86–24 every *m·* cared for and blessed.
Rud. 5– 4 every *m·* a liar." — *Rom.* 3 : 4.
My. 9–10 * thought on the part of every *m·*
196– 9 every *m·* be swift to hear, — *Jas.* 1 : 19.
239–13 *until every m· and woman comes into*
257–15 "which lighteth every *m·* — *John* 1 : 9.
evil
'00. 8– 5 evil *m·* also exhales . . . his evil
faculties of
My. 154–20 * deep infinite faculties of *m·*."
faith in
My. 152– 9 faith in *m·* and in matter,
fallen
Mis. 78–25 *Has m· fallen from a state of*
181–30 evil, or a fallen *m·*.
Father bids
Un. 4–18 the Father bids *m·* have the same
Father of
Mis. 164–32 God is the Father of *m·*,
father of
Mis. 77–20 or, that man is the father of *m·*.
Ret. 68– 6 never was, . . . the father of *m·*.
findeth
Mis. 252–32 if a *m·* findeth, he goeth and
finite
Peo. 4– 9 could enter finite *m·* through his
first
Mis. 185–27 *The first m· Adam* — *I Cor.* 15 : 45.
187–14 presuppose . . . to be the first *m·*,
189–13 "the first *m·*." — *I Cor.* 15 : 45.
Un. 30–14 "The first *m·* Adam — *I Cor.* 15 : 45.
forbade
Un. 54–20 God forbade *m·* to know evil
forbids
Mis. 145–14 vanity forbids *m·* to be vain ;
forever in
'02. 9–21 should abide forever in *m·*.
forever reflects
Un. 39–23 *m·* forever reflects and embodies Life,
furnishes
Mis. 258–27 furnishes *m·* with the only
gains the power
Mis. 182–11 *m·* gains the power to become
gave
Mis. 373–24 God gave *m·* dominion
genuine
Un. 49–13 only living God and the genuine *m·*.
gift to
Mis. 181– 3 sonship a personal gift to *m·*,
give
'02. 7– 9 give *m·* the true idea of God
gives
Mis. 97– 2 gives *m·* ability to rise above
'02. 9– 1 gives *m·* power with untold
My. 268–23 gives *m·* the victory over himself.
gives to
My. 129–22 divine law gives to *m·* health
giveth
Un. 39–18 gave and giveth *m·* dominion
God and
(*see* **God**)
Godlike
Mis. 178– 7 wanted to become a Godlike *m·*.
No. 20– 7 Truth is moulding a Godlike *m·*.
'01. 7– 4 C. S. makes *m·* Godlike.
My. 161–28 the Godlike *m·* said,

man

godly
Pul. 32–26   * was known as a "godly *m·*,"
God or
No. 23–25   we cannot understand God or *m·*,
    27–24   personality of God or *m·*
God's
Mis. 36– 2   mortal man, is neither God's *m·* nor
    167– 2   infantile thought of God's *m·*,
Un. 46– 6   for he is God's *m·* ;
God to
Ret. 31– 5   "the ways of God" to *m·*.— *Job* 40 : 19.
    68–27   thoughts, passing from God to *m·*"
My. 208–17   ministrations of God to *m·*.
God warned
Mis. 24–27   God warned *m·* not to believe the
good
Mis. 122– 1   substitution of a good *m·* to
    166–31   a good carpenter, and a good *m·*,
    192– 1   When we speak of a good *m·*,
    202– 5   * where the good *m·* meets his fate
    257–30   Even the chamber where the good *m·*
No. 17–12   can never be less than a good *m·* ;
'00. 3–18   good *m·* loves the right thinker
    8– 4   good *m·* imparts knowingly and
'01. 32–19   explain in a few words a good *m·*.
Hea. 3–19   it signified a "good *m·*," — *John* 7 : 12.
My. 306– 6   philosophy of a great and good *m·*,
    333–20   * records that this good *m·*,
goodness in
Mis. 164– 5   presentation of goodness in *m·*.
good will to
My. 201– 6   love and good will to *m·*,
govern
Mis. 59–21   should and does govern *m·*.
governed
My. 247– 5   *m·* governed by his creator is
    254–26   *m·* governed by his creator is
governing
Mis. 37– 3   governing *m·* or the universe.
government of
Ret. 90–30   leave with God the government of *m·*.
governs
Man. 40– 8   divine Love alone governs *m·* ;
Rud. 10– 5   know that God alone governs *m·* ;
gray-haired
My. 310–24   * a gray-haired *m·* of fifty,
great
Mis. 312–10   chapter sub-title
guides
Mis. 118– 6   scientific understanding guides *m·*.
half
Pan. 3– 4   animal, half goat and half *m·*,
half a
No. 29–13   * a sick body is not half a *m·*."
has power
Mis. 180–25   assures us that *m·* has power
having all
My. 5–10   *m·* having all that God gives.
heals
Mis. 20– 2   heals *m·* spontaneously,
health to
Peo. 12–26   if He would, give health to *m·* ;
My. 219–17   giving of life and health to *m·*
heart of
Mis. 203–10   so the heart of *m·* — *Prov.* 27 : 19.
My. 189–16   creates in the heart of *m·* ;
helping
Mis. 49–23   that are helping *m·* Godward :
heritage of
Mis. 259–15   and was the heritage of *m·* ;
highest style of
No. 10– 8   is the highest style of *m·* ;
His power in
'02. 10–27   to God and His power in *m·*.
history of
Un. 50–27   as the history of *m·*, disappears,
holding
Mis. 83– 2   holding *m·* forever in the
holds
Mis. 77–16   it holds *m·* in endless Life
No. 26–22   God holds *m·* in the eternal
honest
Mis. 166–30   It made him an honest *m·*,
My. 272– 1   is an honest *m·* or woman
    321–11   * Mr. Wiggin was an honest *m·*
ideal
Mis. 77–15   to support their ideal *m·*.
    102– 2   stature of Christ, the ideal *m·*.
    205–21   in Christian metaphysics the ideal *m·*
    235–20   know something of the ideal *m·*,
Ret. 68– 7   spiritual idea, or ideal *m·*,
idea of
Mis. 62– 1   Holding the *right* idea of *m·*
    166–17   the idea of *m·* was not understood

man

identifies
My. 165–17   goodness identifies *m·* with
image of
Mis. 62– 4   the opposite image of *m·*,
immortal
Mis. 17–23   a mortal, not the immortal *m·*.
    79–12   Immortal *m·* is the eternal idea of
    79–20   A mortal . . . is not immortal *m·* ;
    89–28   Immortal *m·*, in God's likeness,
    103–21   neither the . . . Maker of immortal *m·*.
    186–11   the opposite of immortal *m·*,
    332–27   the antipode of immortal *m·*.
Ret. 73– 1   immortal *m·* being spiritual,
No. 25–23   immortal *m·* alone is God's likeness,
    25–26   the counterfeit of immortal *m·*.
    26– 2   believe . . . identical with immortal *m·*,
    27–17   the antipode of immortal *m·*,
    29– 3   Immortal *m·* has immortal Soul
immortality of
Mis. 172–28   holiness, and immortality of *m·*.
My. 226–19   evidence of the immortality of *m·*
immortal part of
No. 29–14   the immortal part of *m·* a sinner?
impart to
Mis. 72– 9   God is supposed to impart to *m·*
in Christ
Mis. 15–25   stature of *m·* in Christ appears.
No. 19–25   the stature of *m·* in Christ.
My. 103–13   attains the stature of *m·* in Christ
includes
Pan. 12– 8   for the universe includes *m·*
including
Mis. 23–20   The universe, including *m·*,
    41–28   governs the universe, including *m·*,
    56–30   created the universe, including *m·*,
    333–21   to the universe, including *m·*
    361–25   spiritual universe, including *m·*
Un. 32– 6   *m·*, including the universe,
individual
Un. 49– 2   I believe in the individual *m·*,
individuality of
Un. 53– 8   reality and individuality of *m·*
Rud. 13– 9   not the actual individuality of *m·*
in God's image
Man. 15– 8   *m·* in God's image and likeness.
My. 273–30   *m·* in God's image and likeness.
in His image
'00. 5–16   *m·* in His image and likeness,
My. 117–21   *m·* in His image and likeness,
    261–14   *m·* in His image and likeness.
in Science
Mis. 41–26   manifestation of *m·* in Science.
Un. 40– 5   *m·* in Science never dies.
    42–13   *M·*, in Science, is as perfect and
'02. 8–26   Christ Jesus reckoned *m·* in Science,
intellectual
My. 309– 2   a well-informed, intellectual *m·*,
intelligence of
Mis. 200–10   Life, and intelligence of *m·*.
in the image
Mis. 294– 1   *m·* in the image of his Maker ;
    308–30   *m·* in the image and likeness of God.
My. 347– 4   *m·* in the image and likeness of the
in the likeness
Mis. 61–30   *m·* in the likeness of Spirit
in the moon
My. 206–12   Seeing a *m·* in the moon,
intoxicates a
Mis. 288–32   Whatever intoxicates a *m·*,
is a celestial
No. 26–24   *M·* is a celestial ;
is aroused
My. 308– 6   to say that *m·* is aroused to thought or
is as definite
Un. 49– 3   *m·* is as definite and eternal as God,
is coexistent
Mis. 190– 8   *m·* is coexistent with Mind,
Un. 49– 3   *m·* is coexistent with God,
is dominant
Mis. 297–23   *m·* is dominant over the animal,
is eternal
Mis. 287– 3   forever fact that *m·* is eternal
is foremost
Mis. 57–31   wherein *m·* is foremost.
is forever
Mis. 82–17   *m·* is forever unfolding the
Un. 62– 5   *m·* is forever His image
is found
Mis. 15–23   until *m·* is found to be the image of
Ret. 73– 7   *m·* is found in the reflection of
Un. 3–17   *m·* is found in the image and likeness
is free
My. 119– 8   *M·* is free from the flesh
is free born
Mis. 183–10   *M·* is free born :

man

is Godlike
  '02. 8–24 whereby *m· is* Godlike.
is God's child
  Un. 15– 9 *M·* is God's child and image.
is God's image
  Mis. 183–12 *M·* is God's image and likeness ;
is God's likeness
  Mis. 61–29 the logic that *m·* is God's likeness.
is healed
  Hea. 14– 5 *m·* is healed morally and physically.
is His image
  Mis. 21–21 *m·* is His image and likeness.
      23–23 *m·* is His image and likeness.
  '01. 5–21 *m·* is His image and likeness :
is His likeness
  Rud. 11– 7 in Science *m·* is His likeness,
is immortal
  Mis. 34–21 *M·* is *im*-mortal, and there is not a
      61–25 but *m·* is *immortal.*
      89–24 *M·* is immortal.
is improved
  Un. 36–19 *m·* is improved physically,
is its master
  '01. 14–28 therefore *m·* is its master.
is made
  Un. 22– 2 Because *m·* is made after God's
  Pul. 30–18 * *m·* is made in His image.
is more
  No. 25– 9 *M·* is more than physical personality,
is mortal
  No. 5–21 then . . . *m·* is mortal.
is My idea
  Un. 62–22 *m·* is My idea, never in matter,
is not absorbed
  No. 25–10 *M·* is not absorbed in Deity ;
  My. 119– 7 we learn that *m·* is not absorbed
is not annihilated
  Mis. 42– 4 *M·* is not annihilated,
is not equal
  Mis. 46–14 *M·* is not equal with his Maker ;
    255– 5 *M·* is not equal to his Maker.
is not fallen
  Mis. 259–19 In this . . . *m·* is not fallen :
is not material
  Mis. 21–21 Therefore *m·* is not material ;
is not met
  Mis. 173–22 *m·* is not met by another
is not mortal
  Mis. 385–20 *M·* is not mortal, never of the dead :
  Po. 48–14 *M·* is not mortal, never of the dead :
is perfect
  Mis. 46–29 *m·* is perfect even as the Father,
    280–30 *m·* is perfect even as the Father
  Pan. 11–11 Governed by . . . *m·* is perfect.
is person
  '01. 5–11 *M·* is person ;
is reflected
  Un. 51–25 *m·* is reflected not as human
is saved
  Man. 16– 1 that *m·* is saved through Christ,
is seen
  Mis. 62– 8 *M·* is seen only in the true
  Hea. 11– 5 *m·* is seen wholly apart from
is spiritual
  Rud. 5– 7 *m·* is spiritual and eternal,
is the cause
  Po. 65–23 *m·* is the cause of its tear.
is the climax
  No. 17–13 *M·* is the climax of creation ;
is the idea
  Mis. 5–26 *m·* is the idea of infinite Mind,
    78–26 *m·* is the idea of God ;
    247–20 *m·* is the idea of infinite Mind,
is the image
  Mis. 61–21 *m·* is the image and likeness of God.
  No. 25–17 *M·* is the image and likeness of God,
  My. 262– 2 *m·* is the image, idea, or likeness
is the offspring
  Mis. 82–15 *M·* is the offspring and idea of
    181–17 *m·* is the offspring of Spirit,
  Ret. 68–28 "*M·* is the offspring of Spirit.
is the reflection
  Un. 51– 1 wherein *m·* is the reflection of immutable
is the true image
  Pan. 11–28 *m·* is the true image of God,
is the ultimatum
  Mis. 79–10 *m·* is the ultimatum of perfection.
Jesus
  Mis. 164–24 human concept of the *m·* Jesus.
    187– 3 The *m·* Jesus demonstrated over sin,
  Ret. 93– 4 appeared . . . as the *m·* Jesus.
  Rud. 3–10 individualized, . . . in the *m·* Jesus.
  My. 348–12 the belief that the *m·* Jesus,
Jesus as a
  Mis. 197–14 concerning Jesus as a *m·*,

man

just
  Mis. 112– 9 most just *m·* can neither defend the
keeping
  Ret. 65–24 keeping *m·* unspotted from the
killed a
  Hea. 18–27 killed a *m·* by no other means than
knows
  Mis. 55–24 *M·* knows that he can have
  My. 104–23 of which a *m·* knows absolutely
laws of
  My. 348–23 laws of *m·* and the universe,
leading
  Un. 42–25 leading *m·* into the true sense
learned
  Hea. 14–11 he is a learned *m·* and skilful ;
less than
  Mis. 145–12 then is he less than *m·*
  Pan. 10– 2 and makes man less than *m·*.
let us make
  Mis. 69–10 "Let us make *m·* — *Gen.* 1 : 26.
Life of
  Mis. 76–26 Soul is the Life of *m·*.
  Ret. 63–15 represents God, the Life of *m·*.
life of
  Mis. 187–21 substance, and life of *m·* are one,
    209–16 neither . . . recuperate the life of *m·*,
  My. 181–10 scientific, sinless life of *m·*
life of a
  '01. 30–19 the inner genial life of a *m·*,
lifts
  Peo. 12–15 lifts *m·* above the demands of matter.
like unto
  Ret. 25–21 personal being, like unto *m·* ;
limits
  Mis. 282– 5 personality, . . . that limits *m·*.
lives
  My. 164–29 *M·* lives, moves, and has his being
    165– 9 by this spirit *m·* lives and thrives,
    195–23 in whom *m·* lives, moves, and has
love for
  Mis. 12–28 our love for God by our love for *m·* ;
    234– 9 In love for *m·*, we gain a
  Pan. 8–23 on the basis of . . . love for *m·*.
  My. 287–15 In love for *m·* we gain the only
loves
  Mis. 100–26 Christian Scientist loves *m·* more
  '00. 3–18 good *m·* loves the right thinker
love to
  Pul. 39– 2 * love to God and love to *m·*
made
  Mis. 77–27 *m·*, made in God's own likeness,
    173–27 made *m·* in His own likeness.
  '01. 7– 9 God made *m·* in his own image
    0–19 As God made *m·*, is he not wholly
  Hea. 9–18 *m·* made by God had not a
  My. 179– 6 allegory, of . . . *m·* made of dust.
majesty of
  My. 188–26 teaches the majesty of *m·*.
make
  Mis. 57–25 *Why does the record make m· a*
    183–32 material senses would make *m·*,
    363–14 "Let us [Spirit] make *m·* perfect ;"
  Un. 32– 4 make *m·* and the material universe."
    54–23 knowledge of evil would make *m·* a
  Pan. 8–26 They make *m·* the servant of
  Peo. 10–14 Justice and truth make *m·* free,
  My. 235–15 Did God make *m·* ? Yes.
makes
  Mis. 24– 2 makes *m·* spiritually minded.
  Pan. 10– 2 makes *m·* less than man.
  '01. 7– 4 C. S. makes *m·* Godlike.
    8–21 makes *m·* none too transcendental,
    13–17 When *m·* makes something of sin
  '02. 8–22 it makes *m·* active,
    8–30 makes *m·* conscious that God is his
manner of
  Mis. 370–22 What manner of *m·* is it that
man's
  Un. 46– 6 while ours is man's *m·*.
material
  (*see* **material**)
material sense of
  Mis. 15–28 mortal and material sense of *m·*,
matter and
  My. 153–32 pointing away from matter and *m·*
meaning woman
  My. 268–31 *m·* meaning woman as well,
measures
  Mis. 172–12 unerring Mind measures *m·*,
meekest
  Mis. 163– 9 the meekest *m·* on earth.
Mind and
  Mis. 24–20 Mind and *m·* are immortal ;
Mind governs
  Mis. 51–16 and Mind governs *m·*.

man

mislead
My. 5–31 may mesmerize and mislead *m·* ;
misname
No. 27–20 personality, which we misname *m·*,
misnamed
Un. 38– 1 mortal mind which is misnamed *m·*,
model of
Peo. 10–20 marred in mind the model of *m·*.
moral status of the
Mis. 45–14 moral status of the *m·* demands
mortal
(*see* **mortal**)
must live
My. 164–30 *m·* must live, he cannot die ;
must reflect
Mis. 16–13 *m·* must reflect the full dominion
named
Mis. 186–16 the divine idea named *m·* ;
Un. 49– 7 sinner, wrongly named *m·*.
name of a
Hea. 3–16 Jesus is the name of a *m·*
nature and
Mis. 258–32 and shows that nature and *m·* are
My. 152–28 Principle of nature and *m·*,
nature of
Mis. 287–18 higher nature of *m·* governs
need of
My. 260–27 supplies every need of *m·*.
needs of
Mis. 3–10 applicable to all the needs of *m·*.
259–29 applicable to all the needs of *m·*.
My. 349–30 supplying all the needs of *m·*.
never cursed
Hea. 9–17 God never cursed *m·*,
new
Pul. 84– 7 * shall stand the new *m·*
Pan. 11– 5 put on the new *m·*,— *Col.* 3 : 10.
no
Mis. 76–17 no *m·* can rationally reject his
89– 1 "No *m·* can serve two— *Matt.* 6 : 24.
113– 8 "no *m·* might buy or sell,— *Rev.* 13 : 17.
153–19 no *m·* who honors Him not
181– 1 Jesus said to call no *m·* father ;
197– 9 unless this be so, no *m·* can be
269– 6 "No *m·* can serve two— *Matt.* 6 : 24.
269–30 "no *m·* might buy or sell,— *Rev.* 13 : 17.
287– 6 "Call no *m·* your father— *Matt.* 23 : 9.
365– 3 can no *m·* lay than that— *I Cor.* 3 : 11.
Ret. 68–13 "call no *m·* your father— *Matt.* 23 : 9.
75–14 no *m·* which shall do— *Mark* 9 : 39.
Un. 53–26 "Call no *m·* your father— *Matt.* 23 : 9.
64– 9 can no *m·* lay than that— *I Cor.* 3 : 11.
Rud. 14– 4 "owe no *m·*."— *Rom.* 13 : 8.
No. 21–24 can no *m·* lay than that— *I Cor.* 3 : 11.
22–16 No *m·* hath seen the person of
27–19 * "No *m·* living hath yet seen man."
Pan. 8–18 "Call no *m·* your father— *Matt.* 23 : 9.
12–14 a door that no *m·* can shut ;
'00. 14– 5 no *m·* take thy crown."— *Rev.* 3 : 11.
14–22 and no *m·* shutteth,— *Rev.* 3 : 7.
14–22 and no *m·* openeth ;"— *Rev.* 3 : 7.
'01. 30–20 No *m·* or woman is roused to
'02. 16–13 without which no *m·* shall— *Heb.* 12 : 14.
17–18 to be willing . . . to hate no *m·*,
Hea. 16–28 No *m·* cometh unto the— *John* 14 : 6.
My. 41– 1 * how great no *m·* can number
114– 3 Owe no *m·* ; be temperate ;
160–28 but of the time no *m·* knoweth.
185–15 the trinity no *m·* can sunder.
191– 2 "No *m·* can do these— *John* 3 : 2.
202–10 Owe no *m·*— *Rom.* 13 : 8.
324–30 no *m·* could have done so any better.
353–17 to injure no *m·*, but to bless all
356–22 No *m·* can serve two— *Matt.* 6 : 24.
364– 2 "Judge no *m·*."— *John* 8 : 15.
no part of
Pan. 10–30 constitute no part of *m·*,
normal state of
Mis. 200– 3 good as the normal state of *m·*,
nor matter
'01. 4–12 neither *m·* nor matter can
not
Mis. 332–26 Not *m·*, but a mortal
Un. 32–25 not *m·* (the image of God)
No. 25–24 that which is mortal is not *m·*
My. 231–14 as God, not *m·*, directs.
obscure
Pan. 10–30 no part of man, but obscure *m·*.
of business
Mis. 147–23 the conscientious *m·* of business,
of Galilee
Pan. 8– 6 Jesus, the *m·* of Galilee,
of God
Mis. 159–19 the *m·* of God, the risen Christ,

man

of himself
Pul. 73–22 * *m·* of himself has no power,
of integrity
Mis. 147–14 The *m·* of integrity is one who
of joys
Mis. 84–14 *m·* of joys, his spiritual self,
of sorrows
Mis. 84–14 "*m·* of sorrows"— *Isa.* 53 : 3.
Un. 55– 4 "a *m·* of sorrows,— *Isa.* 53 : 3.
'02. 18– 5 made him a *m·* of sorrows.
old
Mis. 15–23 lay off the "old *m·*,"— *Col.* 3 : 9.
Pul. 33–18 * an old *m·* with a snowy beard
No. 27–21 old *m·* and his deeds,"— *see Col.* 3 : 9.
Pan. 11– 4 old *m·* with his deeds ;— *Col.* 3 : 9.
Hea. 18– 4 "the old *m·*"— *Col.* 3 : 9.
Po. v– 9 * poem
page 1 poem
My. 308–16 * old *m·* tramping doggedly
one
Mis. 295–22 wholly represented by one *m·*.
My. 239–15 one *m·* and one woman
opposite of
Mis. 187– 9 was to him the opposite of *m·*,
or a woman
'01. 13– 1 a *m·* or a woman, a place or a thing,
or beast
'01. 20– 8 to harm either *m·* or beast.
or God
Ret. 71–19 without the permission of *m·* or God,
originated
Mis. 57– 6 *M·* originated not from dust,
origin of
Mis. 75–27 the spiritual origin of *m·*.
165–32 virgin origin of *m·* according to
Un. 30– 1 Spirit as the sole origin of *m·*,
or the universe
Mis. 37– 3 governing *m·* or the universe.
164–12 Principle of *m·* or the universe,
or woman
Mis. 123–13 or a miscalled *m·* or woman !
228– 9 To be a great *m·* or woman,
297–18 A *m·* or woman, having
'01. 30–20 No *m·* or woman is roused to
My. 152–26 matter, *m·*, or woman can never
159–12 greatest *m·* or woman on earth
165–28 The best *m·* or woman is the most
194– 9 a silent, grand *m·* or woman,
259–20 and nothing less is *m·* or woman.
272– 1 is an honest *m·* or woman
outlives
No. 25–12 *M·* outlives finite mortal definitions
perfect
Mis. 18– 2 original likeness of perfect *m·*,
97–28 I have not seen a perfect *m·*
186–24 cannot produce a less perfect *m·*
363–14 "Let us [Spirit] make *m·* perfect ;"
363–15 a perfect *m·* would not desire to
Ret. 42–15 "Mark the perfect *m·*,— *Psal.* 37 : 37.
No. 20–13 a perfect *m·*, and divine Science.
27–24 hath seen God or a perfect *m·*?
My. 187–10 to demonstrate the perfect *m·*
196–13 the same is a perfect *m·*,— *Jas.* 3 : 2.
262– 1 God creates *m·* perfect
perfectibility of
Mis. 98–21 the perfectibility of *m·*.
perfecting of
My. 342–23 and the perfecting of *m·*
perfection of
Mis. 173–24 The perfection of *m·* is intact ;
personal
Mis. 97–20 Is there a personal *m·*?
personality of
Mis. 97–32 the real personality of *m·*.
person of
No. 29–15 a disparagement of the person of *m·*
Hea. 5–23 relying not on the . . . person of *m·*
physical
Ret. 88– 7 Truth called the physical *m·* from
physically
Mis. 252–20 to *m·* physically, as well as
popular
My. 314– 9 was a popular *m·*, and considered a
possible to
Mis. 183–13 possible to *m·* as God's reflection.
predicating
My. 207–24 predicating *m·* upon divine Science.
preserver of
Pan. 4– 6 creator and preserver of *m·*.
4–19 chapter sub-title
4–20 is indeed the preserver of *m·*.
7–10 God, the preserver of *m·*,
prevent a
Mis. ix– 3 * noblest charity is to prevent a *m·*

man

Principle of
    (*see* **Principle**)
profane
  Mis. 45–12 *Can an atheist or a profane m·*
prove
  Un. 40– 7 in order to prove *m·* deathless.
punish
  Mis. 198–29 seems to punish *m·* for doing good,
punishes
  Peo. 8– 8 punishes *m·* eternally,
puzzles the
  '00. 6–15 spiritual sense that puzzles the *m·*.
quarrel with a
  My. 270–28 I would no more quarrel with a *m·*
quibbled
  Pul. 9–12 so, when *m·* quibbled over an
real
  Mis. 61–12 real *m·*, who was created in the
     104–27 to be God and the real *m·*.
     186–32 real *m·* in God's likeness,
     235–21 real *m·*, harmonious and
  Ret. 22–18 The real *m·* is not of the dust,
     60–27 or of the real *m·* and God.
     64– 7 makes apparent, the real *m·*,
     74– 6 the individual, or real *m·*
     86–14 that you may behold the real *m·*,
  Un. 46– 5 We do not see much of the real *m·*
  Pan. 11– 2 to perceive the real *m·*,
  My. 272–11 real *m·* was, is, and ever shall be
     319– 3 spiritual ideal is the only real *m·*
reality of
  Mis. 187– 8 as the reality of *m·* ;
  Un. 46– 8 individuality and reality of *m·* ;
recognize
  Mis. 198–16 recognize *m·* as governed by God,
redeems
  Mis. 17–16 redeems *m·* from under the curse
reflected in
  Un. 14–24 Mind must be reflected in *m·*,
reflects
  Mis. 17–20 *m·* reflects the divine power
     184– 7 only when *m·* reflects God in body
  '01. 5–21 *m·* reflects Spirit, not matter.
  My. 124–18 Nature reflects *m·*
reinstate
  Peo. 14–18 reinstate *m·* in God's own image
relative to
  Mis. 187–12 accepted as true relative to *m·*.
religious
  Ret. 5– 3 was a very religious *m·*,
remarkable
  My. 307–22 he was a remarkable *m·*.
represents
  Mis. 46–25 *m·* represents his divine Principle,
requires
  Mis. 367– 3 Science requires *m·* to be honest,
reveal
  Mis. 164–28 reveal *m·* collectively, as individually,
  My. 5– 8 to reveal *m·* as God's image,
     124–19 remains for Science to reveal *m·*
reveals
  Mis. 5– 4 Science reveals *m·* as spiritual,
     185–21 reveals *m·* infinitely blessed,
righteous
  Mis. 119–10 impotent to turn the righteous *m·*
rights of
    (*see* **rights**)
rises
  My. 238–16 *m·* rises above the letter, law, or
save
  Ret. 63–18 and so to save *m·* from it?
  Un. 18– 6 may say that God can never save *m·*
saved
  Mis. 197– 8 *m·* saved from sin, sickness, and
saves
  My. 348–13 divine Principle, God, saves *m·*,
Saviour of
  My. 293–00 And the Saviour of *m·* saith :
Science of
  Mis. 14–11 the Science of *m·* could never
     186–18 let us not lose this Science of *m·*,
  '02. 2– 8 The Science of *m·* and the universe,
  My. 350–10 the cosmos and Science of *m·*.
Science saith to
  Mis. 101–21 but Science saith to *m·*,
scientific
  Un. 46– 9 scientific *m·* and his Maker
seen
  No. 27–19 * "No man living hath yet seen *m·*."
seen in
  '01. 5–26 nature of God must be seen in *m·*,
sees
  Mis. 228–21 Whatever *m·* sees, feels, or
seeth
  Pan. 1–15 what a *m·* seeth he hopeth not for,

man

sense of
    (*see* **sense**)
sentencing a
  '02. 10–28 is like sentencing a *m·* for
separated
  Un. 52–11 *m·* separated from his Maker.
shall keep
  Mis. 175–13 *M·* shall keep the feast of Life,
shall utilize
  Mis. 69– 8 *m·* shall utilize the divine power.
shines
  Ret. 57–15 *M·* shines by borrowed light.
showed
  No. 21–11 showed *m·* as reflecting God
shows
  My. 41–24 * shows *m·* that his real estate is
sick
  Mis. 69–14 called to visit a sick *m·*
     69–30 Had that sick *m·* dominion over the
     130–14 has to make a *m·* sick?
  Hea. 12–14 never made a *m·* sick.
  My. 339–29 The fact that he healed the sick *m·*
so-called
  Mis. 294– 2 infirmity of evil is so-called *m·*,
  Hea. 17– 8 the material so-called *m·*,
  My. 239–25 so-called *m·* born of the flesh,
Son of
    (*see* **Son**)
son of
    (*see* **son**)
Soul of
  Rud. 1– 7 the Soul of *m·* and the universe.
soul of
  My. 344– 9 * "And the soul of *m·*?"
soweth
  Mis. 66– 7 "Whatsoever a *m·* soweth, — *Gal.* 6 : 7.
     105–29 "Whatsoever a *m·* soweth, — *Gal.* 6 : 7.
     348– 4 whatsoever a *m·* soweth, that shall he
  No. 32– 9 "Whatsoever a *m·* soweth, — *Gal.* 6 : 7.
  Hea. 5–27 "whatsoever a *m·* soweth, — *Gal.* 6 : 7.
  My. 6– 6 whatsoever a *m·* soweth, — *Gal.* 6 : 7.
spake
  Mis. 76–17 who spake as never *m·* spake,
     269–12 as never *m·* spake," — *see John* 7 : 46.
  Un. 17–16 as never *m·* spake," — *see John* 7 : 46.
spake of
  '02. 8–28 He spake of *m·* not as the
species of
  Un. 51–15 the highest species of *m·*,
spiritual
    (*see* **spiritual**)
spiritualizes
  My. 4– 4 obedience . . . spiritualizes *m·*,
standard of
  Pan. 11–21 original standard of *m·*
stature of
  Mis. 15–25 stature of *m·* in Christ appears.
  No. 19–25 of the stature of *m·* in Christ.
  My. 103–13 attains the stature of *m·* in Christ
status of
  Mis. 183–31 arrive at the true status of *m·*
  Un. 39–21 declare the immortal status of *m·*,
strength is in
  My. 162– 6 Strength is in *m·*, not in muscles ;
strong
  Pul. 62–10 * required a strong *m·* to ring them,
subject of
  Mis. 185–29 reasoning on this subject of *m·*
such a
  My. 318–25 * was such a *m·* as Christ Jesus?"
suitable
  Man. 100–26 If a suitable *m·* is not obtainable
suspects
  Hea. 1–16 * *m·* suspects himself a fool :
teach
  Mis. 229–15 would teach *m·* as David taught :
     330–24 lessons teach *m·* to be kind,
tell a
  Pul. 15– 9 to tell a *m·* his faults,
testify that
  Un. 39–22 which testify that *m·* dies.
that
  Mis. 122– 4 but woe to that *m·* — *Matt.* 18 : 7.
     123– 8 That *m·* can break the forever-law
     187–28 That *m·* must be evil before he
     353–18 "You must pay that *m·*."
  Ret. 36– 3 that *m·* would not expound the
     42–15 end of *that m· is* — *Psal.* 37 : 37.
  Un. 42– 9 That *m·* must be vicious before
  Rud. 9– 1 last state of that *m·* — *Matt.* 12 : 45.
  Pan. 4–16 but that *m·* also is a creator,
  '01. 12– 4 If St. John should tell that *m·* that
the generic term
  My. 347– 5 *m·* the generic term for mankind."

man

the only
Mis. 188–30 was the first, the only *m·*.
the supposer
Mis. 332–25 Is *m·* the supposer, false believer,
thinks
Hea. 6–18 *M·* thinks he is a medium of
My. 271– 9 what a *m·* thinks or believes
this
Mis. 61–18 * This '*m·*' was held responsible
294–12 The *vice versa* of this *m·*
312–21 this *m·* must have risen above
Un. 46–11 none other than this *m·*,
My. 162–16 "This *m·* began to build, — *Luke* 14 : 30.
through
Mis. 77–11 God made manifest through *m·*,
'02. 18– 7 power manifested through *m·* ;
thus weds
Un. 17– 8 *m·* thus weds himself with God,
to be Christlike
My. 148–29 summons . . . for *m·* to be Christlike
to God
Un. 51–25 scientific relation of *m·* to God,
to man
Mis. 203–10 so the heart of *m·* to man." — *Prov.* 27 : 19.
My. 124–19 for Science to reveal *m·* to man ;
to show
'02. 17–21 to show *m·* the beauty of holiness
towards
My. 262–28 letting good will towards *m·*,
tributary to
Un. 13– 3 theology makes God tributary to *m·*,
true
Mis. 18–15 true *m·* and true woman,
Un. 2–14 The true *m·*, really *saved*,
No. 17– 8 impossible for the true *m·*
truth of
Mis. 57–12 truth of *m·* had been demonstrated,
uneducated
My. 305– 1 (an obscure, uneducated *m·*),
unfit for
Mis. 25–29 are bad and unfit for *m·* ;
universe and
Mis. 65–13 God's universe and *m·* are immortal.
Un. 10–12 The universe and *m·* are the spiritual
unlimited
Mis. 102– 5 finite being, an unlimited *m·*,
unwary
Mis. 119– 7 If a criminal coax the unwary *m·*
upright
Mis. 147–19 The upright *m·* is guided by a fixed
wake in
Mis. 23– 6 * "sleep in the . . . and wake in *m·*"?
wakes in
Pan. 9– 2 * "sleeps in the . . . and wakes in *m·*."
was made
Mis. 97–21 *m·* was made in the image and likeness
was never lost
Mis. 182–19 *m·* was never lost in Adam,
wedded
My. 269– 4 *m·* wedded to the Lamb,
well-being of
Rud. 12–21 requisite for the well-being of *m·*.
well-bred
'01. 30–29 * honest, sensible, and well-bred *m·*
were begirt
'01. 12–13 Though a *m·* were begirt with the
what manner of
Mis. 296–29 What manner of *m· is* this unknown
who applied
Mis. 353–14 a *m·* who applied for work,
who falls
Pan. 11–19 as the *m·* who falls physically needs
whole
Pul. 9–19 is a very whole *m·*
whole duty of
Mis. 293–22 includes the whole duty of *m·* :
'01. 32–21 is the whole duty of *m·*.
wicked
Mis. 191– 9 refers to a wicked *m·* as the devil :
257– 5 and wakes in a wicked *m·*.
'00. 8–10 A wicked *m·* has little real
Hea. 9–18 God never made a wicked *m·* ;
will ere long
Peo. 8–26 and that *m·* will ere long stop
will lift
Peo. 3– 1 will lift *m·* ultimately to the
will naturally
My. 188–28 *m·* will naturally seek the Science of
will of
Mis. 180–23 nor of the will of *m·*, — *John* 1 : 13.
181–17 nor of the will of *m·*, — *John* 1 : 13.
182–17 "Nor of the will of *m·*." — *John* 1 : 13.
will receive
Un. 6– 6 *m·* will receive a higher selfhood,

man

will then claim
Mis. 196– 3 *m·* will then claim no mind apart from
wise
Man. 41– 9 The wise *m·* saith,
My. 135– 2 The wise *m·* has said,
with God
Un. 5–24 marvellous unity of *m·* with God
with the smallpox
Mis. 344–15 or to a *m·* with the smallpox?
woman or a
My. 343– 8 a woman or a *m·*.
work of
Ret. 77– 5 * the noblest work of *m·*."
would enable
'00. 5–18 it would enable *m·* to escape from
wrath of
Mis. 41– 6 "the wrath of *m·*" — *Psal.* 76 : 10.
No. 7–17 wrath of *m·* cannot hide it from Him.
8–13 make the wrath of *m·* to praise Him,
33– 1 wrath of *m·* shall praise Him.
'02. 1–12 "The wrath of *m·* — *Psal.* 76 : 10.
My. 111– 2 "the wrath of *m·* — *Psal.* 76 : 10.
151–10 "The wrath of *m·* — *Psal.* 76 : 10.
wrench from
Mis. 246– 7 influenced the people to wrench from *m·*
young
Mis. 201–28 the young *m·* is awakened to
Ret. 7– 7 * young *m·* of uncommon promise.
My. 149–14 a young *m·* vainly boasted,

Mis. 2–24 If *m·* should not progress after
3–14 is *m·* healed and saved,
6– 2 bring *m·* nearer to God,
11– 5 if a *m·* should aim a ball at
14– 9 It is urged that, . . . *m·* has fallen
14–14 if *m·* has lost his Principle
18–22 *m·* could never separate himself from
22– 3 neither a law of matter nor of *m·*.
47–21 *m·*, His image and likeness,
48–14 made a *m·* drunk on water,
51–27 * *M·* in the sunshine of the world's
57–29 the scale of being up to *m·*.
61–15 * the *m·* is held responsible for
61–16 * where a *m·* was said to be 'hanged
61–24 a sinner, — anything but a *m·* !
64–27 wherefore *m·* is thus conditioned,
65–31 by *m·* shall his blood be — *Gen.* 9 : 6.
67– 8 thou shalt not rob *m·* of money,
69–26 The *m·* is living yet ;
70– 7 As a *m·* "thinketh in his — *Prov.* 23 : 7.
70– 9 the *m·* was well.
71–25 *m·* is incapable of originating :
72– 4 Science sets aside *m·* as a creator,
76– 4 "If a *m·* keep my saying, — *John* 8 : 51.
77–28 or, that *m·* is the father of man.
79– 7 *m·* was, and is, God's perfect
82–13 *Is there infinite progression with m·*
97–25 we have not seen all of *m·* ;
123–27 not through the *death* of a *m·*,
129–15 If a *m·* is jealous, envious, or
131– 7 *m·* of more than average avoirdupois
144–15 *m·* shall be as an — *Isa.* 32 : 2.
153– 1 than in *m·* and his material ways
161–10 in Science, *m·* is the son of God.
165– 8 *m·*, without the fetters of the flesh,
173–14 says that *m·* is both matter and
173–16 must not *m·* have preexisted
173–19 to pretend that it is *m·*?
174–10 religious sentiment within *m·*.
183– 5 *M·* must love his neighbor as himself,
184– 2 by claiming that . . . *m·* is matter ;
184– 2 claiming that . . . *m·* is evil ;
184– 3 by claiming that . . . *m·* dies.
184–14 If *m·* should say of the power
185–15 and *m·* be clothed with might,
185–24 how much of a *m·* he ever has been :
186–15 universal Father and Mother of *m·* ;
187–23 *m·* is their reflection and glory.
188– 3 *M·* is as perfect now,
189–12 *m·* as God's image, or
189–21 For *m·* to know Life as it is,
192– 2 we do not mean that *m·* is God
194– 7 Though a *m·* were begirt with
197–29 Let *m·* abjure a theory that is
198– 2 *m·* has no sinful thoughts
205–29 *m·* born of the great Forever,
217–24 and *m·* a rebel against his Maker.
220–25 people believe that *m·* is sick
232–28 of God, and not of *m·* ;
235– 1 *m·* has a changed recognition of
241– 4 *m·* will no more enter heaven sick
245–18 rights that *m·* is bound to respect.
252–19 It appeals to man as *m·* ;
253– 4 what *m·* knoweth as did our Master

man

Mis.	255–10	M· should be found not claiming
	269–10	Lives there a m· who can better
	269–20	m· can only be Christianized through
	282– 5	personality in God or in m·,
	292–19	Christ enjoins it upon m· to help
	308– 2	Until this be done, m· will never
	330– 9	And m·, more friendly, should
	354–24	not by m· or laws material,
	363– 5	molecule and monkey up to m·,
	380– 6	time, space, immortality, m·
Man.	29–21	shall be a m· and a woman,
Chr.	53–48	Mind, mother, m·.
	55–14	M· that is born of a — Job 14 : 1.
Ret.	35–23	Though a m· were girt with the
	48–20	health, hope, and harmony to m·,
	59– 2	to believe m· has a finite and
	60– 2	as very far from the
	64–16	M· that is in honor, — Psal. 49 : 20.
Un.	4–17	God has not forbidden m· to know Him ;
	14– 6	earth, m·, animals, plants,
	14–24	How then could m· escape,
	14–27	God never said that m· would
	15–10	If God knows evil, so must m·,
	15–12	If m· must be destroyed by
	15–16	called . . . m· the sinful;
	24–14	m·, whose source is infinite Mind.
	26–14	* M· decays and ages move ;
	26–19	can it be also true . . . that m· decays?
	28– 8	define Soul as something within m·?
	37– 4	Must m· die, then, in order to
	39–14	M· has no underived power.
	39–25	They presuppose . . . that m· is evil,
	39–26	that Deity is deathless, but that m·
	51–14	M· is the generic term for
	59–21	calls sin real, and m· a sinner,
	59–22	calls sickness real, and m· an invalid,
	62–28	and that of His idea, m· ;
Pul.	4– 7	Is not a m· metaphysically and
	13–29	brought forth the m· child. — Rev. 12 : 13.
	16–15	Then, O m· ! Like this stone,
	82–15	* was created solely for m·.
Rud.	5–11	Lives there a m· who has ever
	7– 9	m· is the manifest reflection of God.
	7–13	According to . . . m· is material,
	8–18	The m· who calls himself a
No.	3– 7	hands of God, than of m·.
	11– 3	M· has an immortal Soul,
	11– 5	M· has perpetual individuality ;
	12–28	m· the reflection of His power
	17–12	and for m· to be more than
	19–15	m· is His individualized idea.
	19–21	m· is in His image and likeness.
	24– 6	according to Spinoza, m· is
	25– 8	chapter sub-title
	25–13	M· is the eternal idea of
	26–14	m· can no more relapse or collapse
	28–24	chapter sub-title
	31–27	"If a m· keep my saying, — John 8 : 51.
	45–14	rights which m· is bound to respect.
	46–19	M· has a noble destiny ;
Pan.	7–10	declared that m· should die,
	9–26	chapter sub-title
	10– 3	"If a m· think himself to be — Gal. 6 : 3.
	11–14	will demonstrate m· to be superior
	11–16	If m· is spiritually fallen,
'00.	3– 1	"When a m· is right,
	4– 3	couples . . . life and death, with m·
	6–19	a m· who uses tobacco,
'01.	8–13	Is m·, according to C. S.,
	8–17	is m· His image and likeness,
	8–18	can m· be . . . less than spiritual?
	10–11	m· is the generic term for
	20– 5	M· is properly self-governed,
	27–26	Mind of God and not of m·
	30–23	like the m· "clouting his own cloak"
	34–27	m· cannot live without it ;
'02.	5–12	For m· to be thoroughly subordinated
Hea.	5– 8	if a m· has taken cold by
	17– 4	Not by the senses . . . does m· get nearer
Peo.	3– 2	as a m· "thinketh in his — Prov. 23 : 7.
	4– 7	became finity, or m·,
	13–13	putting m· to the rack for his
My.	5– 3	m· is supposed to start from dust
	84–22	* m· who cannot reconcile himself to
	104–11	what would be thought to-day of a m·
	124–20	O m·, what art thou?
	129–15	m·, seen through the lens of Spirit,
	131– 9	bread of heaven whereof if a m· eat
	149–25	m· who could not see London for its
	182–24	health, and immortality to m·.
	188–28	convey all impressions to m·,
	205–20	m· more His likeness,
	216–10	What, then, can a m· do with
	235–22	M· is but His image and likeness.

man

My.	239–17	His idea, image, or likeness, m·,
	239–18	M· is the generic term for
	248–17	reality of God, m·, nature,
	249–22	a m·, rather than a woman,
	268–10	God hath joined . . . m· cannot sunder.
	272– 6	hath made me [m·] free — Rom. 8 : 2.
	272– 9	no claim that m· is equal to God,
	300–18	"If a m· keep my saying, — John 8 : 51.
	308–31	The m· whom McClure's Magazine
	316– 6	causing m· to love his enemies ;
	341–16	* 'Tis meet that m· be meek."
	343– 8	It will be a m·."
	343– 9	* "Can you name the m·?"
	344–13	absurd to say that when a m· dies,
	344–13	m· will be at once better than
	346–22	* her successor would be a m·.
	346–27	"I did say that a m· would be
	347–25	m· is not the author of Science,
	348–15	neither m· nor materia medica,

manage

Man.	79–22	shall hold and m· the property

managed

Man.	77–12	have not been properly m·,

management

Mis.	283– 8	m· of another man's property.
Man.	76– 5	indicates the proper m· of
Pul.	55–28	* m· of its own affairs.

manager

Man.	26– 1	for the editors and the m·
	26– 3	m· of the general Committee
	27– 4	m· of the general Committee
	78–12	the m· of the Committee
	80–22	Editors and M·.
	80–23	for the editors and the m·
	97– 7	m· of the Committees
	101– 2	m· of the general Committee
	101– 5	appoint an assistant m·,
Pul.	59–22	* m· of the Publishing Society,

managers

Mis.	296– 4	its constituents and m·

manages

Mis.	226–25	m· to evade the law,

Manchester, N. H.

Po.	vi– 3	* published in M·, N. H.,
My.	105–20	Dr. Davis of M·, N. H.

mandate

Mis.	66– 8	No . . . lurks in this m·,
	74– 9	the stern m· of Science,
	283–28	Science is the m· of Truth
	304–12	m· that speaks from above,
'00.	8–28	you obey the m· but retain a
Po.	45–15	m· that speaks from above,
My.	302– 2	Through the m· of mind

man-face

Pan.	3–31	his m·, the celestial world.

manfully

Mis.	118–23	they must be met m·

manger

Mis.	320– 9	on the m· of our Lord,
No.	36–27	Jesus was a babe born in a m·,
My.	262– 8	born in a m· amidst the flocks

manhood (see also **manhood's**)

Mis.	16– 6	m· or womanhood of Christianity,
	33–10	m· of God, our divine Father
	84–13	Jesus, as material m·, was not
	166– 8	m·, and womanhood of Truth
	185–23	no need . . . to measure his m·,
	206–16	of what constitutes true m·.
	257–25	childhood, age, and m·
	324– 6	youth, m·, and age gayly tread
Un.	2–25	stature of m· in Christ Jesus,
	42–28	wherein true m· and womanhood
	51– 9	gained through Christ as perfect m·,
	59–14	Jesus appeared . . . and grew to m·,
No.	37– 3	in Science his divine nature and m·
Pan.	10–24	A higher m· is manifest,
'00.	10–24	touching token of unselfed m·
'01.	9– 3	referring to . . . his temporal m·.
Hea.	10– 6	supposed to have fought the m· of
Peo.	13–14	forcing from the lips of m· shameful
My.	12–30	gems in the settings of m·
	64–21	* realization of ideal m·
	272–19	* chapter sub-title
	273–17	presented to youth and to m·
	274–12	intellectuality, and happiness in m·.
	346–30	m· and womanhood of God

manhood's
My. 253– 9 * manhood's glorious crown to gain."

manifest
Mis. 34– 9 simply thought made m·.
26– 8 but they m· less of Mind.
37– 5 m· in all thoughts and desires
44–20 made m· in the flesh.
47– 4 matter is but m· mortal mind.
72–25 Matter is m· mortal mind,
77–10 God made m· through man,
78– 3 God is made m· in the flesh,
86– 7 m· growth at every experience.
145– 6 seems as requisite to m· its
147–12 Do you m· love for those that
154– 7 is m· in His care.
154–21 be made m· in the flesh
185– 5 is made m· as Truth,
191–30 sin or disease made m·.
199–20 his transcendent goodness is m·
219–25 made m· on the body,
289– 6 in whatever form it is made m·.
354–18 make m· the movement of
Chr. 53–61 "God was m· in the flesh."— I Tim. 3 : 16.
Ret. 61– 4 latent fear, made m· on the body
Pul. 21– 9 to be made m· in my life.
52–25 * belief in what he taught is m·,
Rud. 3–21 mental error made m· physically,
7– 9 man is the m· reflection of God,
No. 16– 5 whatever He knows is made m·,
16– 8 this knowledge would m· evil
Pan. 10–24 A higher manhood is m·,
13–11 never more m· than in
'01. 9–16 God is made m· in the flesh,
12–27 and thus is m· in the flesh.
21–18 m· unfitness to criticise it
Hea. 6–18 strong enough to m· it.
12–11 before they can become m·
My. 10– 8 * should now m· itself
18–19 never more m· than in its
48–32 * is already m· in their faces,
76–16 * m· in the support of their
85–14 * it is conspicuously m·.
109–24 "m· in the flesh,"— I Tim. 3 : 16.
124–28 "m· in the flesh,"— I Tim. 3 : 16.
150–30 if the wisdom you m· causes
164–13 is present to m· light.
282–22 interest you m· in the success
302– 9 m· through so-called matter.
348– 7 made m· in the flesh,
349–29 makes m· the infinite nature,

manifestation
Mis. 21–18 Mind and its infinite m·,
26– 6 all is Mind and its m·,
27–24 Creation, evolution, or m·,
27–29 it is a small m· of Mind,
41–26 m· of man in Science.
84–17 m· of the Son of God
150–30 with its universal m·,
164–16 m· of Truth and Love.
271– 3 as matter and its m· in effect
312–13 * "No more striking m· of
361–24 His m· is the spiritual universe,
Ret. 27–26 Its natural m· is beautiful
67– 9 The first iniquitous m·
88– 8 a higher m· of Life.
94–22 its m· must be
Rud. 3–22 m· of Truth upon the body
'00. 10– 3 some m· of God asserting
'01. 5–18 m· of the real spiritual man
'02. 2–21 to a more spiritual m·,
5–28 Love and the m· thereof?
Hea. 6–20 to whatever m· we see.
My. 124– 7 by m· of the truth
207–12 * more perfect m· of the truth
261–29 thoughts of Life and its m·.
267–31 expression, and m· of goodness
347–27 the m· of a fixed Principle
357– 7 opposite of spiritual means, m·,

manifestations
Mis. 11–18 m· wherein and whereby we love our
61– 1 material belief, in all its m·,
102–19 His chastisements are the m· of Love.
362– 1 divine modes and m· are not those of
362–19 material m· of evil,
374– 5 in most of its varied m·.
65–25 practical m· of Christianity
Ret. 57–20 supply all m· of intelligence.
Un. 26– 8 and for my varying m·.
Pul. 38–27 * m· of a higher spirituality
No. 42– 3 * such m· of God's power
'02. 7– 3 His infinite m· of love
Hea. 6–14 m· ignorantly imputed to spirits.
7– 2 m· of the power of Truth
My. 88–16 * remarkable external m·
349–20 Divine modes or m· are natural,

manifested
Mis. 49– 5 m· some mental unsoundness,
176–10 supreme devotion to Principle . . . m·.
256– 8 public confidence m· in daily
357–19 third stage . . . is m· in love,
Pul. 23–20 * years of more intense life, m· in
Rud. 4– 8 Science is Mind m·.
10–15 Disease is a thing of thought m·
No. 31–14 Son of God was m·,— I John 3 : 8.
Pan. 2–17 * m· in the existing universe."
'00. 7– 6 greater love of the Scriptures m·.
'02. 18– 7 divine power m· through man ;
My. 51–13 * interest m· on the part of the people,
85–16 * m· in the building of a church
245–14 animal elements m· in ignorance,
318–22 m· more and more agitation,

manifesting
Pul. 23–11 * m· itself under several different
My. 316–23 m· its unbiased judgment by

manifestly
Mis. 187–10 a chord is m· the reality of music,

manifesto
Mis. 22– 4 unerring m· of Mind,

manifests
Mis. 12–26 Whatever m· aught else in its effects
23– 4 intelligence that m· power
23–27 m· all His attributes and power,
25–20 m· the spirit of Christ.
41–22 m· inflammation and a belief of
206–13 scientific growth m· no weakness,
Un. 38– 2 m· immortality, whose Principle is
My. 158–17 m· love for God and man.

manifold
Mis. x– 9 m· demands on my time
132–18 m· letters and inquiries
310–11 My answer to m· letters
343–26 Among the m· soft chimes
363–18 His m· wisdom shines through
Rud. 6– 4 assuming m· forms and colors,
My. 257–24 m· Christmas memorials,
262–32 and gives m· blessings.

Manila
Pan. 14–23 succor and protect them, as at M·,

manipulate
Mis. 119–28 Would you consent that others . . . m·
Pul. 62–13 * little muscular power to m·
Rud. 3–16 no more . . . than they will m·

manipulates
Ret. 71–18 He who secretly m· mind
Rud. 12– 2 nor m· the parts of the body

manipulating
Mis. 113–11 mentally m· human mind,

manipulation
Mis. 3–17 Hygiene, m·, and mesmerism
248– 5 literal meaning . . . would be m· ;
378–16 she did ask him how m· could benefit
My. 307– 6 treatment and m· of patients,

mankind (see also **mankind's**)
advantage for
No. 41–10 to the best advantage for m·
aid of
Mis. 57– 1 and, by the aid of m·, all was
all
Mis. 114–27 will test all m· on all questions ;
252–21 spiritually, and to all m·.
294–10 He lives for all m·,
Man. 41–24 enrich the affections of all m·,
45–12 promote the welfare of all m·
Rud. 10– 2 the controller of all m·.
No. 39–18 include all m· in one affection.
Pan. 9–21 Christianity blesses all m·.
My. 24– 8 * inspires you to welcome all m·
106– 3 to speak charitably of all m·
122–30 mission of our Master was to all m·,
158–11 all m· to-day hath its gloom
170–16 God hath given it to all m·.
218–26 which all m· may share.
264–13 * should signify to all m· ?
282–15 which is to all m· a light
351–16 May you and I and all m· meet
353–18 but to bless all m·.
allegiance of
My. 299– 9 * claim the allegiance of m·."
appetites of
'01. 27–20 appetites of m· corrected,
application to
My. 146–20 their present application to m·,
are better
No. 40–24 m· are better because of this.

mankind

awake
My. 356– 1 When will *m·* awake to know their
benedictions for
Mis. 320– 8 with divine benedictions for *m·*.
beneficial to
Ret. 85– 8 and beneficial to *m·*.
benefit
Mis. 227–20 send forth to benefit *m·* ;
      351–18 nor benefit *m·* by such endeavors.
'01. 20– 4 to serve God and benefit *m·*.
My. 203–28 doing so much to benefit *m·*
benefits
'02. 1–19 honors God and benefits *m·*
beset
Mis. 318–26 Two points of danger beset *m·* ;
better for
Hea. 9– 7 better for *m·*, morally and
Peo. 6– 1 * all the better for *m·*
better part of
Mis. 273–13 as well as the better part of *m·*,
bless
Ret. 11– 8 And live to bless *m·*.
Pul. 87–23 states of mind, to bless *m·*.
Po. 60– 5 And live to bless *m·*.
blessed
My. 232– 7 *m·* blessed, and God glorified.
brings forth
My. 247–20 brings forth *m·* to receive your
common walks of
Mis. 125–24 Apart from the common walks of *m·*,
comprehension of
Mis. 200–15 general comprehension of *m·*
Pul. 84–22 * to the comprehension of *m·*.
concerns
Ret. 88–11 The spiritual . . . most concerns *m·*.
confidence of
Mis. 229–20 The confidence of *m·* in
consecrating
Mis. 291–27 refreshing, and consecrating *m·*,
convictions of
'02. 14–17 common convictions of *m·*
coworkers for
'01. 29–15 grand coworkers for *m·*,
delivering
Mis. 235–10 delivering *m·* from all error
determination of
Mis. 2– 7 strong determination of *m·*
dormant in
Pul. 72–24 * dormant in *m·* for ages,"
effects upon
Mis. 12–27 in its effects upon *m·*,
elevates
My. 130–13 lever which elevates *m·*.
enlightened
Mis. 040–31 have not sufficiently enlightened *m·*.
existence of
Rud. 12–19 health or existence of *m·*,
friends of
My. 213–10 truest friends of *m·*,
gave to
Pul. 53–23 * gave to *m·* the key to health
governs
No. 35–20 and yet governs *m·*.
great need of
Mis. 107–11 More love is the great need of *m·*.
growth of
Mis. 237–23 push on the growth of *m·*.
healed
Mis. 387–17 loved and healed *m·* :
Po. 6–12 loved and healed *m·* :
healing
Mis. ix– 9 healing *m·* morally, physically,
helped
'02. 11–14 each in turn has helped *m·*,
ills of
My. 268–21 solace the sore ills of *m·*
inquiry of
Mis. 307–16 inquiry of *m·* as to Christianity
interest of
My. 339– 2 subserve the interest of *m·*,
laboring for
Mis. 155– 7 Forget self in laboring for *m·* ;
longevity of
My. 265–18 increasing the longevity of *m·*,
love
My. 233–30 as much as they love *m·* ?
love for
My. 288– 8 Love for *m·* is the elevator of the
masses of
My. 181–19 classes and masses of *m·*,
message to
'01. 31–11 entrusted me with a message to *m·*
morals for
Mis. 110–12 makes morals for *m·* !
Pul. 7–15 made morals for *m·*.

mankind

morals of
My. 249–14 fatal to . . . the morals of *m·*,
multiplication of
Mis. 244–11 in the multiplication of *m·* ?
must gravitate
Mis. 267–22 *M·* must gravitate from sense to Soul,
need of
'02. 9–29 has met the need of *m·* with
open to
'00. 9– 9 The secret . . . is open to *m·*,
passing out of
Pan. 12– 7 constantly passing out of *m·*
possibilities of
Mis. 251–19 present possibilities of *m·*.
prevent
Mis. 232–28 prevent *m·* from striking out
receive from
My. 160– 9 that we receive from *m·* justice,
reform
'02. 8–11 No person can . . . reform *m·* unless
reforming
'01. 27–13 healing and reforming *m·*.
regenerating
'02. 9–10 regenerating *m·* and fulfilling
regeneration of
My. 22–17 * for the regeneration of *m·* ;
      352–15 * in the regeneration of *m·*.
regulator of
Mis. 353–19 steer the regulator of *m·*.
saves
Mis. 261–24 has saved, and still saves *m·* ;
My. 260– 2 Life that heals and saves *m·*.
      348–16 God, heals and saves *m·*.
saving
Pul. 6–10 healing and saving *m·*.
servant of
Mis. 266–10 unacknowledged servant of *m·*.
spirituality of
Mis. 245–14 morals, and spirituality of *m·*.
struggling with
Mis. 126– 9 when struggling with *m·* his temper,
taught
My. 163– 4 taught *m·* to win through
teach
Un. 59–16 could reach and teach *m·*
telling
Pul. 15–11 telling *m·* of the foe in
term for
My. 347– 5 man the generic term for *m·*."
to help
My. 216– 4 in order to help *m·* with it.
to please
Po. 23–18 Than just to please *m·*.
to save
Mis. 229–23 to heal and to save *m·*
'02. 11– 6 waits and pleads to save *m·*
unprofitable to
My. 113– 7 such a book be . . . unprofitable to *m·* ?
unwarned
'01. 19–24 subject *m·* unwarned and undefended
uplift
Mis. 3–29 The tendency . . . is to uplift *m·* ;
uplifts
Mis. 260–22 truth of Mind-healing uplifts *m·*,
No. 45– 9 whatever uplifts *m·*,
war with
'00. 8–22 before we can . . . war with *m·*.
woes of
Peo. 11–23 responsible for all the woes of *m·*
wrongs of
No. 40–18 only the wrongs of *m·*.

────

Mis. vii–10 And *m·* from the dust ;
      25–17 gives God's infinite meaning to *m·*,
      37– 5 draw *m·* toward purity,
      106–23 How shall *m·* worship the
      107–32 *M·* thinks either too much or
      162– 4 wonderful spiritual import to *m·* !
      246–28 question at issue with *m·* is :
      261–24 by *m·* I mean mortals,
      270– 8 than whom *m·* hath no higher ideal
Man. 42– 8 to God, to his Leader, and to *m·*.
Ret. 72– 6 to benefit himself and *m·*.
Pul. 74–18 the blessing it has been to *m·*
'01. 1– 3 through the mental avenues of *m·*
'02. (not by *m·*, but by a kind of men)
      18–20 Jesus laid down his life for *m·* ;
My. 45– 5 * of its adherents and of *m·*.
      117–32 is all that I ask of *m·*.
      212– 5 which makes *m·* drunken.
      215–30 effect of both methods on *m·*.
      222–25 *M·* will be God-governed
      225–20 *M·* almost universally gives to
      239– 8 *m·* will, as aforetime,

mankind

My.	239–12	*Must m· wait for the ultimate of*
	239–23	m· . . . is the material, so-called man
	264– 5	until m· learn more of my meaning
	295–26	You, I, and m· have cause to
	303–22	his legacy of truth to m·.
	344–27	Were . . . I should tremble for m· ;
	348– 1	My discovery that m· is absolutely
	350–18	m· . . . dost doom above.

mankind's

Mis.	130–30	m· triumphal march out of the
No.	36–27	M· concept of Jesus was a babe

manlike

Mis.	178– 6	not satisfied with a m· God,
No.	20– 6	would fashion Deity in a m· mould,
'01.	6–29	That God is . . . m·, is not my sense of
	7– 3	Scholastic theology makes God m· ;

manly

Mis.	88–17	Its m· honesty follows like a
	296–19	Do m· Britons patronize taprooms
	325–15	Robust forms, with m· brow
Pul.	60– 7	* clear, m·, and intelligent tones,

man-made

Mis.	38–22	elaborating a m· theory,
	64–15	M· theories are narrow,
	168–11	not the m· rabbi

man-midwife

Peo.	6– 9	* m·, chemist, druggist, or drug

manna

Mis.	153– 7	they were fed with m· :
My.	31– 6	* "Day by day the m· fell ;''

manner

after the

Mis.	96–15	"after the m· of my — see Acts 24 : 14.
	140– 7	even after the m· that all
	167– 2	after the m· of a mother
	315– 3	after the m· of the Sunday service.
Un.	58– 9	saving himself after the m· that
No.	19–26	after the m· of mortal man,
'01.	33–22	after the m· taught by Jesus,

after this

Mis.	126–30	bard spake after this m· :
Ret.	86–23	After this m· and in no other
Pan.	5–23	After this m· our Master cast out

all

Mis.	8–24	all m· of evil — Matt. 5 : 11.
	196– 5	in all m· of subtleties
Ret.	60–18	saith to all m· of disease,
'01.	2– 5	healing all m· of diseases.
	3– 5	all m· of evil — Matt. 5 : 11.
	24–27	healing all m· of diseases.
	34– 3	healing of all m· of diseases.
'02.	11–23	all m· of evil — Matt. 5 : 11.
	15– 6	Healing all m· of diseases
My.	104–31	all m· of evil — Matt. 5 : 11.
	190–22	power over all m· of diseases ;
	214–21	healing all m· of diseases,
	219–17	all m· of diseases.
	239–10	healing all m· of disease,
	245– 1	healing all m· of disease,
	316– 8	all m· of evil — Matt. 5 : 11.
	364–16	heals all m· of sickness

animated

My.	320–32	* spoke in a very animated m·

any

Mis.	351–10	method of Mind-healing, or in any m·.
Pul.	75– 8	or speak of me in any m· as a
My.	223–22	which relate in any m· to the
	301–26	in any m· whatever.

authoritative

My.	326– 7	* official and authoritative m·.

bearing and

Pul.	31–26	* winning in bearing and m·,

best possible

Rud.	15–15	to fill in the best possible m· the

Christian

Man.	97–17	to correct in a Christian m·

Christian spirit and

Man.	77–26	in a Christian spirit and m·,

intelligent

Pul.	69–26	* not done so in an intelligent m·,

like

Un.	21– 7	In like m· good and evil talk to

material

Pul.	63–20	* in a very tangible and material m·

no

Man.	81– 8	shall in no m· be connected with
	82– 5	are in no m· connected with these

of man

Mis.	296–28	What m· of man is this unknown
	370–22	What m· of man is it that has

of Science

No.	35– 3	What m· of Science were C. S. without

manner

same

Un.	2–17	In the same m· the sick lose their

some

Mis.	295–11	* for some m· of notoriety.''

striking

Pul.	45–20	* proved, in most striking m·,

suitable

Man.	61–22	dignified and suitable m·.

way or

Mis.	381–24	in any way or m· disposing of,

wicked

'01.	15–29	* wicked m· of attending

Mis.	12–18	in a m· least understood ;
	31– 4	To mentally argue in a m· that
	32– 7	seem not to know in what m· they
	171–14	and see what m· they are of.
My.	69–28	* m· in which the dome seems to
	280–28	In no way nor m· did I request
	321–18	* m· in which the statements have

manners

Mis.	283–16	breach of good m· and morals ;
	313– 5	It is a digest of good m·
'00.	2–12	he gives little time to society m·
My.	309– 3	cultivated in mind and m·.

manor

Po.	10– 6	Lord of the main and m·!
My.	337– 7	Lord of the main and m·!

manright

Ret.	76– 4	God's law of m·.

man's

Mis.	2–19	God, m· saving Principle,
	2–21	M· probation after death is the
	16–12	m· ability to meet them is from God ;
	17–27	m· primitive, sinless, spiritual
	18–26	can we . . . separate one m· interests
	30–14	understanding of m· real existence,
	46–17	It is possible, and it is m· duty,
	47–23	substantiates m· identity,
	52–21	M· existence is a problem to be
	64– 7	m· indestructible eternal life in God.
	65– 6	m· ipse dixit as to the stellar system
	65–25	balancing m· account with his Maker.
	65–31	"whoso sheddeth m· blood, — Gen. 9 : 6.
	68– 5	include also m· changed appearance
	70– 2	else the Scriptures misstate m· power.
	70– 4	cast out the sick m· illusion,
	75– 4	m· possible earthly development.
	79– 9	M· origin and existence being in Him,
	79–22	immortal m· divine Principle.
	96– 1	m· salvation from sickness and
	96–19	m· redemption from sickness
	98– 2	m· perfect model should be
	100–31	stages of m· recovery from sin
	105– 2	facts of m· spirituality,
	105–13	M· real life or existence
	119–17	against m· high destiny.
	124–19	m· true sense is filled with peace,
	124–32	In proportion to a m· spiritual
	129–16	an atom of another m· indiscretion,
	151–14	He is m· only real relative
	154–10	God only waits for m· worthiness
	171– 6	annoint the blind m· eyes
	173– 2	human reason, or m· theorems,
	173–26	the counterfeit of m· creator
	174–29	spiritual facts of m· Life here
	175–10	M· Life is God ;
	181– 3	m· spiritual sonship
	181– 4	M· knowledge of this grand verity
	181–15	understand m· true birthright,
	181–27	gain the sense of m· spiritual
	182– 6	perceive m· actual existence
	182–15	m· primal, spiritual existence,
	183–25	is a denial of m· spiritual sonship ;
	183–28	m· "dominion over all the — see Gen. 1 : 26.
	184–25	as the seal of m· adoption.
	186– 7	far below m· original standard,
	186–31	lost sense of m· perfection,
	192– 6	infinite importance to m· spiritual
	192–20	m· ability to prove the truth of
	193–30	the understanding of m· capabilities
	196–17	m· unity with his Maker,
	198–19	We know that m· body, as matter,
	199– 5	m· ability to annul his own erring
	205–17	m· identity or consciousness
	205–25	Mortal m· repentance and
	206– 8	interpret m· eternal existence,
	214– 9	m· foes shall be they of — Matt. 10 : 36.
	220– 9	to refute the sick m· thoughts,
	222– 1	takes away a m· proper sense of

man's

Mis. 229– 8 than he does the sick *m*.
234–12 What hinders *m*· progress is
241– 4 are correlated in *m*· salvation ;
241–21 *m*· bondage to sin and sickness.
244–22 And he did this for *m*· example ;
252–30 wise *m*· spiritual dictionary ;
252–31 the poor *m*· money ;
261–25 men after *m*· own making.
267–28 spiritualizes *m*· motives and
283– 9 management of another *m*· property.
286– 9 *m*· oneness with God,
309–16 true idea of *m*· divine Principle.
309–22 *M*· individual life is infinitely
320–13 that calms *m*· fears,
330–11 *m*· possibilities are infinite,
331– 7 for *m*· rich heritage,
362– 5 *m*· reason is at rest in God's
363–28 the learned *m*· masterpiece,
363–28 the ignorant *m*· dictionary,
363–29 the wise *m*· directory.
Man. 15–15 unfolding *m*· unity with God
Ret. 9–24 * to know His voice From *m*·
10–16 *m*· origin and signification.
21–14 dreams, not of *m*· real existence,
61– 1 arises . . . from mortal *m*· ignorance,
61–10 *m*· harmony is no more to be invaded
63–16 conspiracy against *m*· Life
73–15 *m*· spiritual individuality in God,
77– 3 * honest *m*· the noblest work of
Un. 2– 9 takes away *m*· fondness for sin
4–20 forbid *m*· acquaintance with evil.
15– 1 by *m*· first disobedience,
41–15 *m*· unity with his Maker
46– 6 while ours is *m*· man.
53–23 *M*· Father is not a mortal mind
53–25 *m*· origin and loving Father,
57– 7 *M*· refuge is in spirituality,
Pul. vii–21 the actual bliss of *m*· existence
3–12 *m*· eternal mansion.
23–24 * Intimations of *m*· immortal life.
82–17 * woman as *m*· proper helpmeet.
No. 23–23 Knowledge of a *m*· physical
25–22 is not *m*· eternal identity.
26–16 *M*· real ego, or selfhood,
26–19 *M*· individual being must reflect
33–19 *m*· at-one-ment with God ;
43–28 A *m*· inability to heal,
Pan. 4–27 if these are not *m*· preservers?
10– 1 takes away *m*· personality
10–29 does not degrade *m*· personality.
11–23 belittles *m*· personality.
11–20 *m*· unfallen spiritual perfectibility.
12–28 unpierced . . . by *m*· inventions.
'00. 3–20 would destroy this *m*· goodness.
'01. 1–21 better side of *m*· nature
10–19 *m*· salvation comes through
13–20 *m*· fear, unconquered, conquers him,
'02. 9–30 enlarges *m*· facilities for
10–18 If such is *m*· ultimate,
16–20 and *m*· immortal being.
17– 8 learn that *m*· highest happiness,
Hea. 5– 7 bias a *m*· character.
19–18 Tireless Being, patient of *m*·
Peo. 2– 1 insures *m*· continuance
9–28 *m*· harmony and immortality.
10–16 battles for *m*· whole rights,
12–19 *m*· salvation from sickness
My. 5– 4 the outcome of *m*· rib,
105– 3 *m*· only medicine for mind and body.
124– 4 to every *m*· conscience." — II Cor. 4 : 2.
128–10 *m*· inalienable birthright — Liberty.
128–14 *m*· right to adopt a religion,
129–24 good *m*· heart takes hold on heaven,
134–19 bless, and inspire *m*· power.
188–24 one *m*· head lies at another's feet.
200–15 *m*· soul is safe ;
219–14 to believe that *m*· Maker is
222–23 make laws to regulate *m*· religion ;
244–16 is unquestionably *m*· spiritual state
267–26 *m*· divine Principle, Love,
267–29 *m*· spiritual understanding of
277–10 A bullet in a *m*· heart never
277–12 sublime question as to *m*· life
283–17 Wrong may be a *m*· highest idea
302– 3 according to a *m*· belief,
340–11 which *m*· diligence has utilized.
350–14 the scalding tear *m*· shedding.
(see also being, individuality)

mansion

Mis. 239–12 before a stately *m*· ;
324–13 Within this mortal *m*· are
325– 1 a massive carved stone *m*·,
Un. 52–25 the most beautiful *m*· is sometimes
Pul. 3–12 Truth and Love, man's eternal *m*·.

mansions

Mis. 140–28 title clear" to heavenly *m*·.
My. 133– 1 house in which are many *m*·,

manslaughter

My. 227–10 citizens are arrested for *m*·

mantel

Pul. 26–26 * *m*· is of onyx and gold.
48–20 * photograph . . . adorned the *m*·.
76–13 * superb *m*· of Mexican onyx

mantle

Pul. 65–23 * Roman soldier parted his *m*·

mantled

Ret. 31–25 tint of humility, . . . *m*· the earth.

Manual (see also Church Manual)

Mis. 148– 8 Rules and By-laws in the *M*·
Man. 3– 3 Rules and By-Laws in the *M*·
27– 7 named in the *M*· of this Church
45–10 specified in The Mother Church *M*·,
71–19 allowed and named in this *M*·.
72– 1 *M*·.
72– 2 nor publish the *M*· of
72–24 with The Mother Church *M*·.
80–11 By-Laws contained in this *M*·.
104–10 *M*· shall not be revised without the
My. 230–11 Rule and By-law in this *M*·
252– 1 S. and H., and our *M*·,

manual

Un. 6–27 drilled in the plainer *m*·
No. 3–10 people insisted that my *m*· of

manuals

(see organ)

manufacture

Mis. 232– 8 art, invention, and *m*·.
My. 216– 7 *m*·, agriculture, tariff,
265–28 agriculture, *m*·, commerce,

manufactured

Mis. 299–21 he *m*· them and owns them,

manufacturer

Mis. 353–13 My brother was a *m*· ;

manufacturing

My. 310–12 *m*· establishment in Tilton, N. H.

manumits

Mis. 124–27 it *m*· mortals ;

manuscript

Mis. 300–19 Your *m*· copy is liable.
My. 59–28 * I read it in *m*· before it was
272–22 * with the corrections on the *m*·
273– 2 * This *m*· is presented simply as
322– 3 * that she had seen the *m*·.

manuscripts

Mis. 249– 9 appropriated other people's *m*·
315– 7 written, and read from *m*·,
381– 3 *m*· originally composed by
382– 5 *m*· of mine were in circulation.
Man. 32– 8 not read from copies or *m*·,
Ret. 1– 8 *m*· containing Scriptural sonnets,
36– 7 writing out my *m*· for students
36– 9 unpublished *m*· extant,
My. 179– 4 were in two distinct *m*·.
305– 9 *m*· and letters in my possession,
306–24 these comprised the *m*· which

man-worship

No. 20–20 the common idolatry of *m*·.

many

Mis. 4–13 *M*· questions important to be
5–11 *M*· say, "I should like to study,
6– 7 and *m*· more are needed for the
6–13 it surely does, to *m*· thinkers,
7–15 to *m*·, if faithful laborers in His
7–24 able to reach *m*· homes with healing,
39– 1 *M*· who apply for help are
52–14 susceptible of *m*· definitions.
60–25 as *m*· identities as mortal bodies?
71– 5 saved *m*· a drunkard from this
81–18 *m*· of the people from beyond Jordan?
88–11 whose thought is appreciated by *m*·
99–15 How *m*· are there ready to suffer for
106–31 imitative tones of *m*· instruments,
112–14 *m*· features and forms of
117– 1 "ruler over *m*· things." — Matt. 25 : 23.
120–21 *m*· of its members reside a long
150–16 salvation of *m*· people by means of
159–11 My heart has *m*· rooms :
159–26 *m*· weary wings sprung upward !
168–28 * and *m*· had to go away
171–27 so *m*· are obtruding upon the
175–31 done *m*· wonderful works?
180–21 But as *m*· as received him, — John 1 : 12.
181–24 "But as *m*· as received him, — John 1 : 12.

many

Mis.	182– 5	"As *m·* as received him ;" — *John* 1 : 12.
	182– 5	as *m·* as perceive man's actual
	183–26	As *m·* as do receive a knowledge of
	185–17	"As *m·* as received him," — *John* 1 : 12.
	185–25	"as *m·* as received him, — *John* 1 : 12.
	194– 1	How *m·* to-day believe that the
	201–21	they were so *m·* proofs that he had
	221–16	This accounts for *m·* helpless
	222– 7	state of false consciousness in *m·*
	231– 7	rich viands made busy *m·* appetites ;
	231–28	How *m·* homes echo such tones of
	244–28	as *m·* as should believe in him.
	247–18	To *m·*, the healing force developed by
	255– 3	on pedestals, as so *m·* petty deities ;
	264–13	*M·* students enter the Normal class
	269–25	*M·* are bidding for it,
	271– 5	(and *m·* who are not students)
	276– 6	so *m·* people and circumstances
	280–30	by which so *m·* wrecks are made.
	299–11	conviction to the minds of *m·*
	303–25	that *m·* Christian Scientists will respond
	305–16	* small contributions from *m·* persons
	307–13	and *m·* orders on hand,
	309–10	that it has turned *m·* from the
	312–18	* to restore the waning faith of *m·*
	317–25	having already seen in *m·* instances
	327–10	*M·* there were who had entered the
	333–16	"lords *m·* — *I Cor.* 8 : 5.
	340– 2	has torn the laurel from *m·* a brow
	340– 3	and repose from *m·* a heart.
	341– 9	and be made ruler over *m·* things.
	369–12	madness it seems to *m·* onlookers.
	375–22	* resemblance, in *m·* things, to
	375–24	* how *m·* times have I seen these
	391–10	Have *m·* items more ;
Man.	28–13	beaten with *m·* stripes." — *Luke* 12 : 47.
Ret.	7–22	* It blights too *m·* hopes ;
	8– 1	*M·* peculiar circumstances
	15– 1	To the astonishment of *m·*,
	16–12	*M·* pale cripples went into
	25–22	senses are so *m·* witnesses to
	41– 4	*M·* were the desperate cases
	50–14	or even in half as *m·* lessons.
	50–16	as *m·* as seventeen in one class.
	52– 1	For *m·* successive years I have
	82–17	ample to supply *m·* practitioners,
Un.	8– 2	trouble to *m·* earnest thinkers
	18–10	*M·* fancy that our heavenly Father
	26–19	*M·* ordinary Christians protest
	39–16	as *m·* as receive the knowledge of God
	44– 1	*M·* misrepresentations are made
Pul.	11– 4	as the sound of *m·* waters,
	13– 7	ruler over *m·*," — *Matt.* 25 : 23.
	13–25	how *m·* periods of torture it may
	14–29	*M·* are willing to open the eyes of
	20–22	one of the *m·* dates selected and
	33–25	* certainly true that *m·* and *m·* persons,
	36–18	* met Mrs. Eddy *m·* times since then,
	41– 6	* from *m·* lands, the love-offerings of the
	45– 3	* Sacrifices were made in *m·* an instance
	46–17	* the *m·* souvenirs that Mrs. Eddy
	47– 1	* the attention of *m·* clergymen
	48–26	* *m·* another well-born woman's.
	49– 3	* speaking of her *m·* followers
	50–20	* *m·* who have worn off the novelty
	51– 9	* *m·* pioneers who are searching
	51–12	* *m·* who have worked in the
	51–20	* *m·* a new project in religious
	55–10	* emancipation from *m·* of the
	55–15	* she has revised it *m·* times,
	56–15	* comfort to *m·* weary souls.
	57– 5	* contributions . . . from *m·* lands.
	58– 1	* who, after *m·* vicissitudes,
	60–13	* *m·* having remained over a week
	66–18	* the mystical which, along *m·* lines,
	67–21	* while in *m·* towns and villages
	68– 7	* *m·* are now pastors or in practice.
	68–22	* There are *m·* other church edifices in
	71–21	* faith to which *m·* thousands
	75–17	* *M·* Toronto Scientists Present
	80–12	* her book has *m·* a time been sent
	82–11	* *m·* things dear to the soul
	82–15	* *m·* still are Jews who never
	83–22	* It is the proudest boast of *m·*
Rud.	14–26	*M·* students, who have passed through
No.	2–21	and *m·* who are not teachers have
	2–27	*m·* are flooding our land with
	14–23	to as *m·* as shall believe on him.
Pan.	3–25	* are so *m·* members."
	4–15	that there are *m·* so-called minds;
'00.	7– 8	*M·* of our best . . . men and women,
'01.	21– 9	* may be traced *m·* of the ideas
'02.	17–12	*M·* sleep who should keep . . . awake
Peo.	7–13	* With *m·* a sharp incision,
	7–21	* With *m·* a sharp incision,

many

Po.	vi–23	* *m· poems written in girlhood*
	38– 9	Have *m·* items more ;
My.	4– 9	how *m·* are following the
	13–11	* like so *m·* planets, revolving
	13–30	returns it unto them after *m·* days,
	19–13	* To one of the *m·* branch churches
	21– 4	* by *m·* of the branch churches
	21– 9	* the erection of *m·* branch churches.
	21–23	* in meeting very *m·* of them
	24–25	* remarked by the *m·* visitors
	28– 6	* *m·* who have contributed
	28–10	* in *m·* instances the loving
	29–13	* *M·* more gorgeous church pageantries
	30– 8	* *m·* hundreds of other faiths,
	38–13	* *m·* of the visitors showed a
	43–31	* and *m·* are asking,
	47– 5	* *m·* of whom have not had the means
	47–21	* in so *m·* distant lands,
	47–22	* inspired so *m·* of different races
	52– 2	* *m·* obstacles to overcome,
	52– 3	* *m·* mental hardships to endure,
	53–31	* *m·* different ones address them
	56– 4	* *m·* stood in the aisles,
	56–26	* *m·* were obliged to leave
	58–28	* *m·* thousands who attended the
	60– 1	* I have been solicited by *m·*
	61–29	* the *m·* intricate problems which
	62–26	* We acknowledge with *m·* thanks
	66–29	* *m·* beautiful houses of worship
	80–27	* there were *m·* hundreds waiting
	84– 4	* *M·* a clergyman can testify
	84– 9	* experience of *m·* generations
	84–28	* is notable in *m·* ways.
	90– 1	* should number *m·* thousands
	90– 9	* diseases *m·* and diverse.
	90–14	* the door to this gospel for *m·*,
	93–22	* underlie *m·* of the practices
	93–23	* *m·* of us have missed entirely
	94–23	* from *m·* foreign countries
	95– 6	* intelligence of *m·* communities
	96– 5	* *m·* of them prominent figures
	104–25	*m·* professional men and women
	111– 9	by *m·* doctors and lawyers,
	114–12	uncovered to the gaze of *m·* men,
	130–11	has been made too *m·* times
	133– 1	*m·* mansions, *m·* welcomes,
	133– 2	* pardons for the penitent.
	149–15	* have conversed with *m·* wise men,"
	149–16	* "And I with *m·* rich men,
	164– 4	to give to *m·* in this city
	173–13	but as *m·* gifts had come from
	177–21	joy of *m·* generations awaits it,
	198– 5	received with *m·* thanks to you
	236–11	Too *m·* centres may become
	244–20	"*M·* are called, — *Matt.* 22 : 14.
	247–26	after *m·* or a few days it will
	266–25	that *m·* points in theology
	294– 7	"did not *m·* mighty — *Matt.* 13 : 58.
	295– 1	loved and lost of *m·* millions.
	301–21	so *m·* well-defined instances
	305–13	*M·* of the nation's best and
	319–18	* observation of *m·* of your students,
	321–24	* my *m·* conversations with you,
	322–25	* *m·* good points in the Science,
	325– 1	* *m·* kindnesses you had shown
	332– 9	* *M·* thanks are due Mr. Cooke,
	332–27	* *m·* Masonic records were transferred
	340–12	In *m·* of the States
	345–31	* We talked on *m·* subjects,
	360–14	as *m·* students think I can,
		(*see also* **gods, minds, others, years**)

many-hued

Mis.	332–15	stately palms, *m·* blossoms,

many-throated

Mis.	106–31	*m·* organ, in imitative tones

maple (*see also* **maple's**)

Mis.	395–15	Written in childhood, in a *m·* grove
Po.	vi–28	* (*written in a m· grove*),
	59– 9	Written in girlhood, in a *m·* grove.

maple's

Mis.	396–16	Beneath the *m·* shade.
Po.	59– 8	Beneath the *m·* shade.

marble

Mis.	316–23	warming *m·* and quenching volcanoes !
	360– 3	rough *m·*, encumbered with
	386–23	Rears the sad *m·* to our memory
Pul.	24–12	* On the front is a *m·* tablet,
	24–27	* The entrances are of *m·*,
	25– 6	* floors of *m·* in mosaic work,
	25–15	* *m·* stairs of rose pink,
	25–15	* and *m·* approaches.
	25–25	* are of pink Tennessee *m·*.

marble

Pul.	26–21	* an entrance of Italian *m·*,
	26–22	* golden letters on a *m·* tablet,
	26–23	* the mosaic *m·* floor of white
	27– 3	* in *m·* approaches and rich carving,
	58–19	* the steps *m·*, and the walls stone.
	76– 5	* superb archway of Italian *m·*
Peo.	7– 4	as well as on history and *m·*,
	7– 6	turn often from *m·* to model,
	7– 9	* With his *m·* block before him ;
Po.	50– 9	Rears the sad *m·*
My.	68–17	* is of a beautiful foreign *m·*,
	68–25	* Bedford stone and *m·*
	68–27	* floors of the first story are of *m·*.
	68–28	* seven broad *m·* stairways,
	68–30	* bronze, *m·*, and Bedford stone.
	69–10	* Two large *m·* plates
	69–13	* pure white *m·* was used,
	291– 9	warming the *m·* of politics

March
(see **months**)

march

Mis.	xii– 3	With armor on, I continue the *m·*,
	130–31	mankind's triumphal *m·* out of the
	138–25	equal to the *m·* triumphant,
	138–28	for the music of our *m·*,
	138 20	*m·* on in spiritual organization.
	233–10	onward *m·* of life-giving Science,
Pul.	14– 1	The *m·* of mind and of honest
	83–14	* *m·* under the black flag of
My.	155–13	in the onward *m·* of Truth,
	245–18	majestic *m·* of C. S.

marched

Mis.	106–14	*M·* the one hundred.
	153– 7	they *m·* through the wilderness :

marches

Mis.	136– 6	taking forward *m·*,
My.	11–10	* not . . . by means of forced *m·*,

marching

Mis.	135– 1	*m·* under whatsoever ensign,
Po.	10–20	Is *m·* under orders ;
My.	337–21	Is *m·* under orders ;

margin

Rud.	1–11	large *m·* for misapprehension,

Mark (see also **St. Mark**)

Mis.	32–13	In *M·*, ninth chapter,
	191–12	In *M·*, ninth chapter
	192–25	last chapter of *M·* is emphatic

Mark (Baker)
(see **Baker**)

mark

Mis.	18– 3	efface the *m·* of the beast.
	113– 9	save he that had the *m·*,— *Rev.* 13 : 17.
	269–31	save he that had the *m·*, *Rev.* 13 : 17.
	271–26	* more strongly *m·* the difference
	277– 8	becomes the *m·* for error's shafts.
	279–23	*M·*, that in the case of Joshua
	347–32	whoever hits this *m·* is well paid
	348– 2	towards the *m·* of a high calling.
	358– 2	*m·* the way in divine Science,
Ret.	42–14	"*M·* the perfect *man,*— *Psal.* 37 : 37.
'00.	6– 7	I press toward the *m·*— *Phil.* 3 : 14.
My.	28–14	* qualities which *m·* the true Christian,
	28–21	* *m·* the lives of his followers.
	66–27	* *m·* an epoch in the history of
	203–13	A spiritual hero is a *m·* for

marked

Mis.	4– 4	*m·* tendency of mortal mind to
	160–12	Your progress, . . . has been *m·*.
	197–10	the way which Jesus *m·* out
	204–16	*m·* loss of faith in evil,
	358 17	way which Jesus *m·* out,
	363–32	show their *m·* consonance with
Pul.	23–23	* *m·* by peculiar intimations of
	43–13	* simplicity *m·* the exercises.
	50–11	* *m·* by the erection of a visible
	66–22	* *m·* by the dedication of
No.	2–22	some *m·* success in healing
'02.	1– 3	*m·* the history of C. S.
My.	79–29	* *m·* the close of their visit
	181–30	It is a *m·* coincidence that
	239–30	is *m·*, and will increase till
	339–13	New Hampshire's advancement is *m·*.

market

Mis.	342–29	they watch the *m·*,

marketh

Mis.	157– 5	He that *m·* the sparrow's fall

Market Street

My.	59–17	* little hall on *M· S·*, Lynn,

marking

Mis.	124–16	*m·* the unwinged bird,
	304–25	* *m·* the world's progress

marks

Pul.	44– 9	* Surely it *m·* an era in the
	49– 4	* air of hospitality that *m·* its
My.	89–17	* that *m·* it as different from
	226–12	that *m·* the sparrow's fall,

marred

Un.	15–11	likeness is incomplete, the image *m·*.
Rud.	6– 9	the beauty is *m·*, through a
Peo.	10–19	*m·* in mind the model of man.
My.	167–28	will, I trust, never be *m·*

Marriage

Pul.	38–12	"*M·*," "Animal Magnetism,"

marriage

Mis.	x–20	first *m·*, to Colonel Glover
	52–11	*What do you think of m·?*
	52–13	*M·* is susceptible of many
	285–20	to write briefly on *m·*,
	285–24	severs the *m·* covenant,
	286– 3	*m·* is not without the law,
	286– 6	*m·* and progeny will continue
	286– 9	when *m·* shall be found to be
	286–14	neither marry nor are given in *m·*,
	286–15	To abolish *m·* at this period,
	288–16	Is *m·* nearer right than celibacy?
	289–15	by the *m·* contract two are made one,
	290– 2	Let other people's *m·* relations *alone:*
	297–19	claims of the *m·* covenant,
Man.	46– 5	legal adoption and legal *m·*,
	49–18	*m·* AND DECEASE.
Ret.	20– 5	before my father's second *m·*,
	20–21	*m·* was very unfortunate,
	20–25	after our *m·* his stepfather
	42– 1	last *m·* was with Asa Gilbert Eddy,
Pul.	46–27	* Her last *m·* was in the spring
My.	5– 4	*m·* synonymous with legalized lust,
	268– 4	*morale* of *m·* is preserved.
	268– 5	imperative nature of the *m·* relation
	269– 8	nor are given in *m·* :— *Luke* 20 : 35.
	312– 4	Regarding my first *m·*
	312– 7	* six months after his *m·*,
	313–30	after my father's second *m·*
	314– 3	It says that after my *m·*

Marriage of the Lamb

Pul.	6–11	book title

married

Man.	49–20	If a Christian Scientist is to be *m·*,
	111– 5	If the applicant is a *m·* woman
Ret.	1–17	was *m·* to an Englishman,
	20– 9	our family nurse, who had *m·*,
Pul.	34– 1	* Miss Baker was *m·* to Colonel Glover,
	35–27	* Mrs. Glover *m·* Dr. Asa Gilbert Eddy,
My.	290– 9	born in 1819, *m·* in 1840,
	314– 7	When I was *m·* to him,

marrow

My.	48–22	* the *m·* of their characters.

marry

Mis.	286–14	wherein they neither *m·* nor
	298–14	"It is not good to *m·*."— *Matt.* 19 : 10.
My.	269– 8	neither *m·*, nor are given— *Luke* 20 : 35.

marrying

Ret.	20–24	dominant thought in *m·* again

Mars', **Gerhardt C.**

My.	351–23	have not read Gerhardt C. *M·* book,

marshal

My.	174– 8	courtesy of the efficient city *m·*

Mars' Hill and **Mars' hill**

Mis.	344–29	St. Paul, when he stood on *M· h·*
My.	104– 4	St. Paul, the *M· H·* orator,
	125–17	the spirit of the *M· H·* orator,

martyr

Mis.	166– 4	the earthly life of a *m·* ;
	288–23	The selfish *rôle* of a *m·*

martyrdom

Mis.	121– 7	even the cup of *m·* :
'02.	10–25	*m·* of God's best witnesses
My.	293– 8	believed that his *m·* was God's way.

martyrs

Mis.	121–12	blood of *m·* was believed to be the
	326–14	licking up the blood of *m·*
No.	44–25	* are *m·* to-day.
My.	125–31	with the blood of the *m·*— *Rev.* 17: 6.
	177–17	* "The blood of the *m·* is the seed of

marvel

Mis.	160– 1	*m·* at the power and permanence of
	163– 5	mission was a *m·* of glory :
	294– 6	A real Christian Scientist is a *m·*,
Pul.	55– 4	* Nature's *m·* in thy thought."

marvel
My. 67–21 * *m·* of architectural beauty.
85– 4 * growth of this cult is the *m·* of
123– 3 love is the greater *m·*,
126–12 a *m·*, casting out evil and
249–16 The *m·* is, that at this enlightened

marvelled
Ret. 13–24 The physician *m·* ;

marvellous
Mis. 199–23 The Principle of these *m·* works
199–29 The *m·* healing-power of goodness
237–20 *m·* good, and mysterious evil.
354– 3 Sin in its very nature is *m·* !
Ret. 26– 1 his *m·* skill in demanding
Un. 5–24 *m·* unity of man with God
17–18 into a home of *m·* light,
Rud. 4–24 extinguishes . . . by His *m·* light.
No. 37–14 this most *m·* demonstration,
My. 43–14 * this experience was almost as *m·*
45–22 * *m·* beyond human ken.
59–32 * *m·* beyond all imagining
81–27 * account of the *m·* cures
88–23 * a *m·* revelation given to this
99– 2 * one of the *m·*, great, and
127– 6 *m·* speed of the chariot-wheels of
206–26 into His *m·* light." — *I Pet.* 2 : 9.
288– 3 Love unfolds *m·* good

marvels
Mis. 376–24 glided into a glory of mottled *m·*.
My. 89–28 * one of the *m·* of the

Mary (see also **Mary's**)
Mis. 166–16 and a *M·* knew not how to declare its
179–29 say with *M·*, "Rabboni !" — *John* 20 : 16.
Un. 59–12 divine idea . . . in the son of *M·*.
62–27 *M·* had risen to discern faintly God's
Pul. 27–21 * *M·* anointing the head of Jesus,
27–22 * *M·* washing the feet of Jesus,
27–22 * *M·* at the resurrection ;
Pan. 8– 9 belief that *M·* was the mother of God
'00. 7–20 we say as did *M·* of old :
'01. 10–10 Jesus was the son of *M·*,
My. 119–12 *M·* of old wept because she
258–10 one word, "*M·*," — *John* 20 : 16.
303– 4 one incarnation, one Mother *M·*.
(see also **Baker, Eddy**)

Mary's
Mis. 75–21 *M·* exclamation, . . . is rendered
84–18 the Son of man, or *M·* son.
(see also **Baker**)

Marys
Mis. 337–24 Only the devout *M·*,
Pul. 27–21 * pictorial story of the four *M·*

masculine
Un. 32–24 neither *m·* nor feminine.

mask
Mis. 147–26 He seeks no *m·* to cover him,
210–24 tears the black *m·* from the
371–24 What is under the *m·*,

masked
Mis. 332–20 *m·* with deformity the glories

Mason
My. 326–18 emblems of a master *M·*,
330–12 * assisted by a *M·* of good
333– 5 * one of your own citizens, a *M·*,
334–25 * heading
335– 4 * a *M·* in "St. Andrew's Lodge,
351–15 as the widow of a *M·*.
(see also **Free Mason, Royal Arch Mason**)

Masonic and **masonic**
Mis. 142–10 a number of *m·* symbols.
142–28 say to the *m·* brothers :
My. 330–19 * sustained by *M·* records
332–25 * interviewing with *M·* authorities,
332–27 * *M·* records were transferred
333–26 * interred with *M·* honors.
336– 8 * her husband's *M·* brethren,
351–14 It was truly *M·*, tender, grand

Masonry
My. 335– 8 * devotedly attached to *M·*,

Masons and **masons**
Ret. 19–13 Number 3, of Royal Arch *m·*.
19–21 directions to his brother *m·*
My. 312–11 * *M·* also paid Mrs. Glover's fare
330–25 of Royal Arch *M·*.
331– 1 directions to his brother *M·*

masquerades
Un. 49–21 the unreal *m·* as the real,

mass
Mis. 331– 4 tosses earth's *m·* of wonders
Chr. 53–56 No *m·* for Me !

mass
Po. 53–12 Poor robin's lonely *m·*.
My. 178–25 the table sank a charred *m·*.

Massachusetts and **Mass.** (see also **Bay State**)
Mis. 120–22 reside a long distance from *M·*,
Man. 99–15 applies to all States except *M·*,
Ret. 6–23 two States, *M·* and New Hampshire.
21– 9 and came to see me in *M·*.
24– 1 in *M·*, in February, 1866
Peo. 10– 8 *M·* succored a fugitive slave
My. 275–18 twice since I came to *M·*.
334–30 * of the Grand Lodge of *M·* :
339–13 *M·* has exchanged Fast Day,
(see also **Arlington, Athol, Attleboro, Boston, Brookline, Cambridge, Charlestown, Chestnut Hill, Lynn, Methuen, Rockland, Salem, Springfield, Swampscott**)

Massachusetts Avenue
Pul. 36–21 * just beyond *M· A·*,

Massachusetts Metaphysical College
Mis. 38–16 taught by me at the *M· M· C·*,
39– 7 genuineness at the *M· M· C·*.
48–27 gone away from the *M· M· C·*
64–12 a course at the *M· M· C·*,
110–13 chapter sub-title
116– 8 chapter sub-title
132– 9 *M· M· C·*, 571 COLUMBUS AVENUE,
135–27 ASSOCIATION OF THE *M· M· C·*.
239– 2 Call at the *M· M· C·*, in 1889,
256– 9 instruction in the *M· M· C·*
271–18 chapter sub-title
271–21 about Mrs. Eddy's *M· M· C·*
272–27 * and that is the *M· M· C·*),
273–24 Primary class in the *M· M· C·*,
279–10 PRIMARY CLASS OF THE *M· M· C·*,
316–24 Before entering the *M· M· C·*,
348–29 students of the *M· M· C·*
358–23 *M· M· C·*, the first and only
Man. 35–12 students of the *M· M· C·*
36– 7 Normal Course at the *M· M· C·*
68–15 the degree of the *M· M· C·*.
85–15 Normal Course at the *M· M· C·*
88– 6 President of the *M· M· C·*
89– 3 President of the *M· M· C·*,
90– 9 The term of the *M· M· C·*
92– 1 *M· M· C·* Board of Education.
92–17 any class in the *M· M· C·*,
Ret. 43– 4 the *M· M· C·* in Boston,
48– 1 *M· M· C·* drew its
48–16 *M· M· C·*, chartered in
52–15 Association of the *M· M· C·*,
Pul. 24–18 * president of the *M· M· C·*,
64– 3 * president of the *M· M· C·*,
68– 4 * *M· M· C·* was founded
70– 8 * president of the *M· M· C·*,
No. 12– 7 *M· M· C·* and Church
Pan. 10–11 students at the *M· M· C·*,
My. 125–20 auspices of the *M· M· C·*,
218–29 not enter the *M· M· C·*
240–28 * certificates from the *M· M· C·*
244–10 degree of C.S.D., of the *M· M· C·*.
244–28 chapter sub-title
244–29 The *M· M· C·* of Boston,
245–22 students of the *M· M· C·*,
245–31 or Vice-President of the *M· M· C·*.
246– 5 Students who enter the *M· M· C·*.
318–17 one of my classes in the *M· M· C·*,
(see also **Metaphysical College**)

Massachusetts Metaphysical College Association
Mis. 135–24 meeting of the *M· M· C· A·*,

Massachusetts State House
My. 77– 6 * Beside it the dome of the *M· S· H·*,
95–14 * famous old *M· S· H·*.

massacres
Mis. 123– 1 in our time *m·* our missionaries,

masses
My. 181–18 classes and *m·* of mankind,

massive
Mis. 325– 1 a *m·* carved stone mansion,
Pul. 52–11 * erection of a *m·* temple in Boston
My. 45–28 * *m·* pile of New Hampshire granite
78– 6 * of gray stone with a *m·* dome

massiveness
My. 67–28 * its *m·* is unnoticed

Master (see also **Master's**)
beloved
Man. 60–18 sacred words of our beloved *M·*,
buried
Mis. 393–15 When the buried *M·* hails us
Po. 51–20 When the buried *M·* hails us

Master

commanded
Ret. 87–16 as the M· commanded.
command of the
My. 128–21 following the command of the M·,
disciples of the
Mis. 171–19 true disciples of the M·
divine
Mis. 187–19 our human and divine M·,
example of the
Mis. 270– 7 example of the M· in C. S.,
followers of the
My. 112– 5 followers of the M· in the early
glorified
'02. 11–18 gave our glorified M· a bitter cup
great
Mis. 17–14 idea that our great M· gave
33– 4 crucifixion of even the great M· ;
90–25 Our great M· administered
121–25 drew from the great M· this answer
150–20 as taught by our great M·.
190–20 that our great M· cast out
195–11 those words of the great M·,
371– 2 taught by our great M·.
Ret. 22– 4 to the life of our great M·.
27–28 guidance of the great M·.
Pan. 8–15 as taught . . . by our great M·,
'00. 4–17 as taught by our great M· ;
'02. 9–14 implied by the great M·,
19–26 great M· triumphed in furnace fires.
My. 4–25 Our great M· said
103–24 demonstrations of our great M·
148–30 and the works of our great M·.
153–11 To-day our great M· would say
172–16 In the words of our great M·,
178–30 the sayings of the great M·
215–23 When the great M· first sent forth
227 · 1 The great M· said,
251– 2 The great M· saith :
265–23 fulfils the saying of our great M·,
305–23 more from my great M·,
330– 5 * great M· himself was scandalized,
339–18 said to the great M·,
hear the
Mis. 269– 5 Hear the M· on this subject :
Lord and
My. 161–17 cup of their Lord and M·
232–12 Our Lord and M· left to us
256–20 nativity of our Lord and M·.
my
Mis. 180–12 said, in the words of my M·,
of metaphysics
Hea. 7–17 M· of metaphysics, reading the mind
our
Mis. 21– 9 Our M· said, "The works— John 14 : 12.
28–15 our M· proved to his doubting
63– 7 Our M· understood that Life,
64– 4 Our M· bore the cross
76– 5 This statement of our M· is true,
83–18 In the words of our M·,
89–17 caused our M· to refuse help to
97– 8 Our M· said of one of his students,
108– 6 Our M·, in his definition of Satan
111–16 Our M· said, "Heaven— Matt. 24 : 35.
121– 4 our M· partook of the Jews' feast
158–28 the example of our M·.
161–18 The only record of our M·
165–28 example, and suffering of our M·.
187–32 such as crucified our M·,
189– 1 those words of our M·,
192–31 This declaration of our M·
196–14 hence the words of our M· :
200–16 so-called miracles of our M·,
211–26 Our M· said, "Ye shall drink— Matt. 20 : 23.
213–21 from the lips of our M·,
245– 1 no record showing that our M·
251–15 whereof our M· said :
252–32 whereof our M· said,
253– 4 knoweth as did our M·
257–20 Our M· called it "a murderer— John 8 : 44.
275– 1 Would not our M· say to the
282–14 Our M· said, "When ye— Matt. 10 : 12.
317–22 These words of our M· explain
359–21 The methods of our M· were in advance
370– 2 in the spirit of our M·,
380–23 for thus saith our M·.
Man. 17–11 word and works of our M·,
17–17 demonstrated by our M·,
Ret. 44– 2 words and works of our M·,
58– 7 With our M·, life was not merely
67–24 In the words of our M·,
68–13 Our M· instructed his students
87– 1 our M· said, "Follow me ;— Matt. 8 : 22.
93– 8 Hear this saying of our M·,
Un. 32–21 even as did our M· :
37– 6 Our M· said, "The kingdom— Matt. 10 : 7.

Master

our
Pul. 3– 5 our M· said : "Destroy this— John 2 : 19.
10–19 our M· said : "The stone— Matt. 21 : 42.
No. 2–10 Our M· taught his students to
14–18 Hear the words of our M· :
43– 4 Our M· said, "Come unto— Matt. 11 : 28.
Pan. 5–10 Our M· gave the proper answer
5–23 our M· cast out evil,
11– 1 required the divinity of our M·
11– 7 Was our M· mistaken in judging
'00. 5– 6 Here note the words of our M·
8–14 Our M· saith to his followers :
14– 1 approval of this church by our M·
'01. 28– 6 narrow way, whereof our M· said,
Hea. 3–21 wonderful works of our M·
My. 28–23 * our M· healed and reformed them.
46–11 word and works of our M·,
108–23 which our M· designated as
122–30 The mission of our M· was
147–27 in the words of our M·,
150–26 what our M· said unto his
152– 5 and our M· declared,
190–13 accept our M· as authority,
190–18 This declaration of our M·,
215–27 better . . . than that of our M·?
221–21 Our M· conformed to this law,
225– 5 spoken by our M·.
228–14 Referring to . . . our M· declared :
233–24 Our M· said, "He that— Matt. 10 : 38.
244–20 Knowing this, our M· said :
246–25 Our M· said : "What I do— John 13 : 7.
our blessed
Un. 30–17 the Messiah, our blessed M·,
Pul. 15– 9 the spirit of our blessed M·
Peo. 12–20 Our blessed M· demonstrated this
our dear
Pul. 7–10 were our dear M· in our
pledge of the
No. 46– 2 is the pledge of the M·.
predicted
My. 63–27 * as the M· predicted,
saith
My. 156–14 "The M· saith unto thee,— Luke 22 : 11.
saying of the
'01. 8–28 that mystic saying of the M·
their
Mis. 212–10 reiterated warning of their M·
'02. 18–26 ignoble conduct . . . towards their M·,
used
Mis. 270–11 other means than those the M· used
words of the
Un. 43–15 words of the M· in support of this
My. 114– 1 in the words of the M·,

Mis. 24–25 of the origin of evil, the M· said :
179–30 "Rabboni !"— M· !— John 20 : 16.
191–13 "M·, we saw one— Mark 9 : 38.
393–11 Soon abandoned when the M·
Ret. 32– 7 lose it," saith the M·.— Mark 8 : 35.
91– 9 and not by the M· himself
Pul. 52–20 * The M· was the great healer.
'01. 26– 4 The great teacher, . . . is the M·,
Po. 51–16 Soon abandoned when the M·
My. 165– 4 in doing this the M· became
294– 7 M· "did not many mighty— Matt. 13 : 58.

master (see also master's)

great
Mis. 373–15 One great m· clearly delineates
'01. 18–22 great m· Metaphysician's precept
My. 104– 7 great m· of metaphysics,
his
'00. 3–11 One's idol is . . . his m·.
'01. 28–24 that he be as his m·."— Matt. 10 : 25.
its
Mis. 47–18 servant of Mind, not its m· :
108–25 then we are its m·, not servant.
'01. 14–28 therefore man is its m·.
Mason
My. 326–17 the emblems of a m· Mason,
Metaphysician
Mis. 76–31 prophecy of the m· Metaphysician,
200– 6 The m· Metaphysician understood
270–10 is the m· Metaphysician.
Ret. 55– 3 Jesus, the m· Metaphysician,
Pul. 20–23 baptism of our m· Metaphysician,
No. 31–22 with this m· Metaphysician.
My. 111– 6 Our m· Metaphysician, the Galilean
222– 8 Jesus, the m· Metaphysician,
of evil
Mis. 209–27 good is the m· of evil.
of hate
Mis. 336– 1 Love is the m· of hate ;
My. 214–13 Love to be the m· of hate.

master

of metaphysics
Mis. 252–23 healer and m· of metaphysics,
My. 104– 7 said of the great m· of metaphysics,
of mind
Un. 34– 3 declares that matter is the m· of mind,
of the gods
My. 159–26 Zeus, the m· of the gods,
of the house
'01. 10– 4 the m· of the house— Matt. 10 : 25.
one
Mis. 52– 6 if he were to serve one m·,

Mis. 40–27 has to m· those elements of evil
45–18 Sin is not the m· of divine Science,
53– 6 only as we m· error with Truth.
109–29 fear not sin, lest thereby it m· you ;
265–13 is m· of the situation.
No. 37–18 power, to meet and m· it
Rud. 10–24 The belief that matter can m· Mind,
'01. 14–13 as to frighten us and so m· us,
Hea. 8– 6 knowing that Mind can m· sickness

mastered

Mis. 208–18 m· by divine Truth's negativing error
284–27 will be m· by Science.
344– 8 without having m· the sciences
Ret. 55– 5 Evil is not m· by evil ;
64–21 which must be met and m·,
My. 134–10 conflicting elements must be m·.

mastering

Mis. 221– 5 m· it one gains in the rules of
My. 207–23 m· evil and defending good,

masterpiece

Mis. 363–28 the learned man's m·,
Po. v–13 * this m· of nature's handiwork,

masterpieces

Mis. 372–27 having seen the painter's m· ;
Pul. 49– 6 * reproductions of some of Europe's m·.

Master's

Mis. 28–26 The M· practical knowledge
105– 5 our M· individual demonstrations
110– 2 poured on our M· feet,
125– 1 indeed drink of our M· cup,
144–18 whisper our M· promise,
195–17 The M· divine logic,
287– 5 and the M· demand,
300–14 spare you our M· condemnation?
369–19 we kneel at our M· feet,
Ret. 25–29 our great M· purpose in not
91– 4 our M· greatest utterance
91–11 indicates more the M· mood,
Un. 44– 3 I can only repeat the M· words :
58–13 The M· sublime triumph
Pul. 10– 1 It was our M· self-immolation,
'01. 23–16 according to the M· teaching
32– 9 busy about their M· business,
35–13 the M· glory won thus,
'02. 5–22 Hence our M· saying,
My. 52–17 * establish these our M· commands
108– 9 Hence our M· saying,
179–16 verification of our M· sayings.
219–19 our great M· life of healing,
222–21 the sandals of thy M· feet.
230–26 realize at last their M· promise,
233– 2 spirit of our M· command?
234–21 M· sayings are practical
258–21 they who drink their M· cup
347–17 our great M· first disciples,

master's

Mis. 373–19 This m· thought presents a sketch

masters

Mis. 12– 3 If indulged, it m· us ;
89– 2 "No man can serve two m· ;"— Matt. 6 : 24.
269– 6 "No man can serve two m· :— Matt. 6 : 24.
270– 5 the skill of the m· in sculpture,
323–14 m· their secret and open attacks
350–28 I cannot serve two m· ;
372–15 m· in France and Italy.
372–18 * delineations from the old m·."
375–12 * I studied the old m·
375–22 * resemblance, . . . to the old m· !
375–29 * identified with the old m·,
376– 7 * by the oldest of the old m·,
Pul. 13–11 and m· his mortal beliefs,
Rud. 3–13 m· in music and painting
14– 1 Neither can they serve two m·,
Peo. 9–21 cannot serve two m·."— see Matt. 6 : 24.
My. 6– 3 We cannot serve two m·,
70–21 * both ancient and modern m·,
138–17 cannot "serve two m·."— Matt. 6 : 24.
302–10 craze is that matter m· mind ;
356–22 No man can serve two m· : — Matt. 6 : 24.

mat

Pul. 42–29 * resting on a m· of palms,

matchless

Hea. 20– 2 * "Oh, could we speak the m· worth,

material (noun)

Mis. 190– 7 nor does the m· ultimate in the
305–19 * M· that can be made a part of
306– 1 * m· to be melted into the bell,
Un. 42–27 nor the m· the spiritual,
Pul. 76– 1 * m· used in its construction
My. 10–10 * design, m·, and situation.

material (adj.)

age
My. 221– 2 medicine in a m· age
aid
Mis. 225–23 Looking away from all m· aid,
My. 105–24 restored by me without m· aid,
appendages
Mis. 17– 9 lay aside your m· appendages,
approach
Mis. 180–13 shuddered at her m· approach ;
atom
Un. 35–26 The m· atom is an outlined falsity
atoms
Mis. 26–14 Was it molecules, or m· atoms?
attraction
Un. 36– 2 This process it names m· attraction,
basis
Mis. 254–22 mental healing on a m· basis
341– 4 leaves the unreal m· basis of things,
Ret. 85–21 of healing on a m· basis.
No. 6–16 trying to heal on a m· basis.
belief
Mis. 60–28 Every m· belief hints the
60–30 it will be seen that m· belief,
186– 7 m· belief has fallen far below
Un. 30– 9 suffers, according to m· belief,
beliefs
Mis. 2–29 m· beliefs that war against Spirit,
5–28 mortal thought with m· beliefs.
334–27 remedies the ills of m· beliefs.
birth
Mis. 362– 2 m· birth, growth, and decay :
bloodgiving
No. 37–14 as a personal and m· bloodgiving
body
Mis. 73– 2 m· body is said to suffer,
105–11 way to escape from the m· body.
Rud. 12– 1 structure of the m· body.
13– 8 A mortal and m· body is not the
13–10 The m· body is not the likeness of
My. 217–19 * deny . . . disease in the m· body
218–14 m· body absolved from death
273–24 the m· body is mortal,
brains
Un. 22–20 physical senses and m· brains,
cause
My. 181– 4 human hypotheses, or m· cause
changes
Un. 26–10 the m· changes, the phantasma,
Christ
My. 122–26 not the m· Christ of creeds,
Christ Jesus
'01. 9– 1 spiritual and m· Christ Jesus,
concept
Ret. 68– 1 m· concept was never a creator,
68– 9 m· concept is unreal,
conceptions
Mis. 375– 1 disordered phases of m· conceptions
Peo. 2– 6 m· conceptions of spiritual being,
8–13 m· conceptions of Deity.
conditions
Mis. 17–25 m· conditions attending it.
Ret. 69– 2 m· conditions prior to reaching
Un. 42–17 ability to subdue m· conditions.
No. 5–14 dependent on m· conditions.
5–16 but that m· conditions can and do
Hea. 19– 7 independently of m· conditions.
conjectures
Un. 28–14 ordinary m· conjectures,
consciousness
Mis. 179–28 must lay aside m· consciousness,
Un. 42– 6 the results of m· consciousness,
42– 6 m· consciousness can have no
control
Rud. 16– 1 If publicity and m· control
corporeality
Mis. 165–14 The m· corporeality disappears ;
creation
Pan. 7– 9 a m· creation took place,
curative
Ret. 34– 1 using a m· curative.
death
Un. 38–11 transition called m· death,

material

deity
Peo. 13– 1 a more *m·* deity,
development
My. 88–20 * a slight and *m·* development
disease
Rud. 10–12 *m·* disease and mortality.
dream
Mis. 28–12 this mortal and *m·* dream,
ear
Rud. 5–13 hearing in the *m·* ear,
earth
My. 181–30 *m·* earth or antipode of heaven.
ego
Mis. 375– 3 What is the *m·* ego, but the
element
Hea. 3–10 *m·* element stole into religion,
elements
Mis. 3–24 *m·* elements of sin and death.
Ret. 60–17 raging of the *m·* elements cease
Peo. 1– 5 crumbling away of *m·* elements
environments
My. 257– 8 swaddling-clothes (*m·* environments)
error
My. 232–24 *m·* error finally disappears,
evidence
Mis. 380–20 a *m·* evidence wherewith to
Un. 11–18 taking away the *m·* evidence.
Rud. 7–10 *m·* evidence being wholly false.
My. 93– 5 * *m·* evidence of their prosperity ;
existence
Mis. 42–21 a belief of *m·* existence
Ret. 30–15 fables of . . . *m·* existence.
32–10 termed mortal and *m·* existence
eyes
Mis. 170–28 belief of *m·* eyes as having any
falsity
Mis. 201– 7 element of matter, or *m·* falsity,
201–10 myth or *m·* falsity of evil ;
fast
My. 339–30 observance of a *m·* fast
finesse
Mis. 373–12 Neither *m·* finesse, standpoint, nor
flames
Mis. 237– 5 so, in place of *m·* flames
force
Mis. 23–21 not a result of . . . *m·* force or
forces
Peo. 8–16 speculate concerning *m·* forces.
form
Ret. 45– 8 *m·* form of cohesion and fellowship
My. 140–19 a *m·* form of communion
140–21 The *m·* form is a
formation
Mis. 71–18 based on a mortal or *m·* formation ;
forms
Mis. 358–32 by leaving the *m·* forms
No. 42– 7 *m·* forms to meet a mental want.
gifts
My. 262–32 *M·* gifts and pastimes tend to
gods
Mis. 198– 5 turning away from *m·* gods ;
history
No. 45–27 *m·* history is drawing to a close.
hygiene
Mis. 6–22 faith in drugs and *m·* hygiene;
illusions
Mis. 8– 1 thought is given to *m·* illusions
images
Un. 34– 4 it sees only *m·* images,
incumbrance
No. 38–19 *m·* incumbrance disappears.
individuality
Un. 24–10 a *m·* individuality,— a mind in
infection
My. 344–29 more dangerous than any *m·* infection,
intelligence
Rud. 4 15 if . . . you mean *m·* intelligence.
interpretations
My. 178– 4 cloud not the . . . *m·* interpretations,
inventions
My. 345–25 * pursuit of modern *m·* inventions
joys
Mis. 84–26 falsity of *m·* joys and sorrows,
law
Mis. 17– 3 opposed to the *m·* law of death ;
198–24 based on physical *m·* law,
200–19 every supposed *m·* law.
Rud. 12–26 divine Mind, not *m·* law,
laws
Mis. 23– 9 subordinates so-called *m·* laws ;
36–22 relative to the so-called *m·* laws,
104– 5 to laws *m·*, to death, or
181–19 spiritual, and not *m·* laws ;
198–17 governed . . . not by *m·* laws,
354–25 not by man or laws *m·*,

material

laws
Un. 31– 9 and overruled laws *m·*
Rud. 7–25 science, so-called, or *m·* laws,
10– 8 *m·* laws are only human beliefs,
life
Mis. 205–26 dissolves all supposed *m·* life
351–30 *M·* life is the antipode of
Un. 30– 8 sense is the so-called *m·* life.
'02. 9–17 minor tones of so-called *m·* life
Hea. 17–15 explains this dream of *m·* life,
light
Pul. 2–10 *M·* light and shade are
limitations
Ret. 76–18 knows no *m·* limitations.
locality
Ret. 91–11 more . . . than the *m·* locality.
losses
Ret. 79– 6 from our own *m·* losses.
man
Mis. 15–26 In mortal and *m·* man,
185– 8 constitutes a so-called *m·* man,
187–14 presuppose a *m·* man to be
205–16 drops the curtain on *m·* man
Rud. 7– 8 Is man *m·* or spiritual?
No. 19–16 *m·* man and the physical senses
'01. 11– 7 he is no longer a *m·* man,
Hea. 17– 6 *m·* man and the personal senses
17– 9 therefore the so-called *m·* man
Peo. 4–15 a third person, called *m·* man,
manhood
Mis. 84–13 Jesus, as *m·* manhood, was not
manifestations
Mis. 362–19 *m·* manifestations of evil,
manner
Pul. 63–20 * very tangible and *m·* manner
means
Mis. 268–25 not adulterate . . . with *m·* means.
Ret. 47–11 C. S. shuns . . . *m·* means
My. 206– 2 with matter and *m·* means,
medicine
Mis. 96– 6 no remedies in drugs, no *m·* medicine.
255–22 It does away with *m·* medicine,
270–28 the last link in *m·* medicine.
Ret. 33– 4 governed the action of *m·* medicine.
33–12 the less *m·* medicine we have,
No. 46– 5 *m·* medicine and superficial religion
'01. 23–18 He used no *m·* medicine,
My. 110– 7 material religion, *m·* medicine,
medicines
Mis. 33–25 does away with all *m·* medicines,
Ret. 34 11 does away with all *m·* medicines,
method
Ret. 43–15 renounced his *m·* method of practice
My. 106– 2 more certain . . . than any *m·* method.
methods
Mis. 6–24 uselessness of such *m·* methods,
40– 4 if one were to mix *m·* methods with
124– 6 cannot find God in . . . *m·* methods ;
182– 4 through violent means or *m·* methods.
243–31 in justification of *m·* methods,
Ret. 33–23 *m·* methods of medicine,
mind
Mis. 336– 7 to kill the serpent of a *m·* mind.
Un. 23–22 An evil *m·* mind, so-called,
mode
Mis. 363–10 *m·* mode of a suppositional mind ;
modes
Mis. 112– 6 The ages are burdened with *m·* modes.
136– 3 such *m·* modes as society
No. 21–16 *m·* modes, wherein the human
motion
Ret. 89– 3 opposed to it by *m·* motion,
music
'00. 11– 6 passionately fond of *m·* music,
nature
Mis. 119–14 This *m·* nature strives
nerves
Un. 34–16 and the nerves, *m·* nerves,
objects
Mis. 36–23 and all *m·* objects,
86– 9 Is it correct to say of *m·* objects,
Ret. 31– 1 *m·* objects of affection
obliquity
Ret. 31–22 mortal mind's *m·* obliquity
observation
'02. 1–17 wrestling only with *m·* observation,
offering
Pul. 87–21 refusal of that as a *m·* offering.
organism
Rud. 12–18 or that a so-called *m·* organism
organization
Mis. 359– 2 *M·* organization is requisite in
Ret. 45– 6 *m·* organization has its value
47– 2 final outcome of *m·* organization,

material

organization
Ret. 48–25 Whereas, The m· organization was,
49–13 m· organization is first ;

origin
Mis. 361– 3 When the belief in m· origin,
Un. 50–26 m· origin, growth, maturity,

passover
My. 156–12 to prepare for the m· passover,

personality
Mis. 105– 4 discords of this m· personality.
308– 6 clings to my m· personality,
309– 4 m· personality is an error in premise,

phenomena
My. 349–24 obtain not in m· phenomena,
350– 2 at the beck of m· phenomena,

philosophy
Mis. 340–30 M· philosophy, human ethics,

pigment
Ret. 79– 8 the m· pigment beneath

portraiture
Mis. 309– 6 m· portraiture often fails

power
Un. 35–14 says gravitation is a m· power,

prescription
'01. 34– 9 the M. D.'s m· prescription.

presents
My. 274–22 an abundance of m· presents ;

processes
Un. 12– 2 by mental, not m· processes.

questions
Mis. 167– 1 m· questions at this age

race
'01. 5–17 the m· race of Adam,

reading
Mis. 169–25 The literal or m· reading is

record
Mis. 170–19 The m· record of the Bible,
Ret. 22– 2 the m· record expunged.

religion
Mis. 17–10 m· religion with its rites
'01. 34–14 a m· religion, proscriptive,
My. 110– 6 m· religion, material medicine,

rite
Mis. 298–16 m· rite of water baptism,
No. 34– 9 commemorating . . . with a m· rite

science
Mis. 344–13 such a m· science of life !
Rud. 4–14 There is no m· science,

sensation
Mis. 198– 6 so-called laws and m· sensation,
331–29 their dream of m· sensation,
No. 4– 8 m· sensation and mental delusion.

sense
Mis. 15–28 mortal and m· sense of man,
17– 4 as opposed to the m· sense of love ;
22–31 Mind-force, invisible to m· sense,
24– 7 dawned on the night of m· sense.
27–28 To erring m· sense, No !
37–10 as we oppose the belief in m· sense,
42–27 in sin or sense m·,
47–19 reverses the evidence of m· sense
66–18 the m· sense must be controlled by
70–26 finite and m· sense of relief ;
72–26 it exists only to m· sense.
75–28 mortal man (alias m· sense)
76–23 misnamed human soul is m· sense,
82–22 m· sense of life, is put off,
103–24 so far as m· sense could discern it,
120– 3 unclasp the m· sense of things
183–29 refute the evidence of m· sense
184–16 yield to m· sense, and lose his power ;
186–25 m· sense of existence is not the
190–24 an error of m· sense,
194–23 how to leave self, the sense m·,
215– 7 m· sense of God's ways and means,
217–30 To the m· sense, everything is matter ;
218– 6 testimony of m· sense in relation to
310– 8 the m· sense of existence
341–17 parting with a m· sense of life and
341–30 pleasures or pains of m· sense
Ret. 59–24 m· sense defines life as something
60– 4 m· sense defines life as a broken
60– 7 m· sense says that matter,
60– 8 M· sense adds that the divine
60–16 M· sense asks, in its ignorance
60–20 M· sense saith, "Oh, when will
60–25 M· sense contradicts Science,
66– 4 It raises men from a m· sense
79–16 Through the channels of m· sense,
Un. 29–17 C. S. defines as m· sense ;
29–19 that m· sense of a soul which
30– 7 M· sense is the so-called
38–14 A m· sense of life robs God,
39–28 Science and m· sense conflict
40– 4 this dark shadow of m· sense,

material

sense
Un. 40– 6 M· sense, or the belief of
40–18 not by a m· sense of being.
40–25 Holding a m· sense of Life,
40–27 A sense m· apprehends nothing
55–19 pleasures and pains of m· sense,
60–26 m· sense, which sees not God.
61– 5 To m· sense, Jesus first
62–18 In m· sense Jesus died, and lived.
63– 5 not apparent to m· sense,
Pul. 45–12 * every evidence of m· sense
Rud. 5– 9 There is no m· sense.
7–18 because there is no m· sense.
No. 5– 9 from a false and m· sense,
5–11 this m· sense, which is untrue,
5–15 M· sense also avers that Spirit,
6–20 To m· sense it is plain also
6–24 to m· sense and feeling,
10–16 When a so-called m· sense is lost,
20–19 ever-present selfishness or m· sense.
29–10 not even a m· sense.
40– 4 a m· sense of approval ;
'00. 6–18 but in the m· sense which
'01. 12– 3 and it corrects the m· sense
'02. 8–26 coincide in m· sense.
Hea. 17–17 were hushed by m· sense
My. 110– 4 buried . . . in m· sense.
119–21 discharged evidence of m· sense
260– 5 The despotism of m· sense
260– 8 the inaccuracy of m· sense
262– 6 Observed by m· sense,
271– 2 matter and m· sense are null,
274– 5 a false m· sense of life,

senses
Mis. 47– 8 the m· senses cannot take in.
73–31 testimony of the so-called m· senses.
99– 3 saith to the five m· senses,
102–25 thus only to the m· senses,
118– 2 m· senses, false suggestions,
161–10 m· senses could not cognize the
183–31 The m· senses would make
185–20 so-called m· senses would close,
187–31 declaration of the m· senses
188–17 effects of Truth on the m· senses ;
204–21 they rebuke the m· senses,
218–11 evidence of the m· senses
234– 7 not learned of the m· senses,
277–23 No evidence before the m· senses
299–15 which the m· senses see not
362– 1 are not those of the m· senses :
Ret. 9–16 never again to the m· senses
25–24 m· senses testify falsely,
59–20 the five m· senses define
Un. 10–22 evidence before the m· senses,
28–16 evidence of the m· senses.
29– 9 testimony of the m· senses,
30– 6 testimony of the m· senses.
35– 8 so-called m· senses are found,
37–22 The so-called m· senses,
39–22 evidence of the m· senses,
39–24 The m· senses testify falsely.
57– 3 the design of the m· senses
Rud. 4–26 The five m· senses testify
5– 2 testimony of the m· senses.
5–24 verdict of the m· senses,
6–10 to the m· senses, evil takes
6–19 evidence of the m· senses,
No. 25–10 cognize through the m· senses.
38– 3 the evidence of the m· senses
42–16 m· senses would enthrone error
'01. 7–22 to the personal m· senses
7–26 through the m· senses,
Peo. 2–15 evidences gained from the m· senses,
My. 114–23 as the sunlight on the m· senses.
188–27 spiritual sense and not the m· senses
217–23 all that the m· senses affirm.
274– 4 of matter or the m· senses.
301–19 testimony of the m· senses.

side
Mis. 140–18 m· side of this question.

sight
Un. 34– 9 m· sight is an illusion, a lie.
My. 265– 6 subordinate to m· sight and sound

signification
Hea. 7–10 instead of the m· signification.

standpoint
Pan. 9–27 From a m· standpoint,

state
Mis. 64–30 of a m· state and universe,

states
Un. 50–16 In reality there are no m· states

structure
Un. 34– 1 the so-called m· structure,
My. 28–18 * not to be found in the m· structure,

material

substance
Un. 24–16 There is no *m·* substance,
superstructure
Mis. 140–29 though the *m·* superstructure should crumble
symbol
My. 8–11 * let us have the best *m·* symbol
172–13 *m·* symbol of my spiritual call
systems
Mis. 232–14 part with *m·* systems and theories,
Peo. 8–25 uncremated fossils of *m·* systems,
tendencies
Mis. 10–25 worldly or *m·* tendencies
terms
No. 11– 9 is hampered by *m·* terms,
theology
'01. 26– 2 my tired sense of . . . *m·* theology
theories
Un. 28–15 *m·* theories are built on the
My. 159–18 *M·* theories tend to check spiritual
things
Mis. 72–18 *Are m· things real when they*
Ret. 28–13 Our reliance upon *m·* things must
31–16 error of faith in things *m·* ;
Pul. 35–17 Our reliance upon *m·* things must
My. 159–28 thought chiefly regards *m·* things,
194– 5 dies, as do all things *m·*,
thought
Mis. 102–26 state of mortal and *m·* thought.
Peo. 3–16 Truth meets the old *m·* thought
My. 267–24 *M·* thought tends to obscure
title
Mis. 140– 3 no one could hold a wholly *m·* title.
token
Mis. 160– 5 it may give no *m·* token,
tonic
My. 152– 8 said, "My *m·* tonic has
type
My. 45–31 * *m·* type of Truth's permanence.
universe
Mis. 72–23 as well as the *m·* universe,
219– 5 nor teaches that . . . are the *m·* universe,
Un. 10–26 not the blind force of a *m·* universe.
32– 5 man and the *m·* universe."
Rud. 4– 4 our *m·* universe and men are
10–11 beliefs of a mortal *m·* universe,
My. 179– 6 allegory, of a *m·* universe
view
Mis. 14– 3 the mortal and *m·* view which
ways
Mis. 153– 1 in man and his *m·* ways
world
Mis. 167–11 substance outweighs the *m·* world.
Ret. 20–18 before the *m·* world saw him.
Un. 52–17 tho *m·* world, the flesh, and
Rud. 3– 7 the flesh, — the *m·* world and evil.
'01. 23–26 of an external *m·* world.
My. 71 33 * bondage of the *m·* world,
110– 7 material medicine, a *m·* world ;

Mis. 13–18 basis of *m·* and mortal evidence
17–22 A *m·* or human birth is
19–26 *m·* and spiritual gravitations,
19–29 the sinful, *m·*, and perishable,
21–22 man is not *m·* ; he is spiritual."
30–10 They were spiritual, not *m·* ;
30– 1 termed *m·* or mortal man,
42–10 to awaken with . . . as *m·* as before.
47–22 man, . . . is spiritual, not *m·*.
52– 1 to such as seek the *m·* to aid the
55–31 either a godless and *m·* Mind, or
61– 5 *m·* symbolic counterfeit sciences.
61–30 Mortals seem very *m·* ;
64–22 It is spiritual, and not *m·*.
72–24 nothing which is *m·* is in
72–27 Real sensation is not *m·* ;
72–29 cannot cognize aught *m·*,
73–12 Law is never *m·* :
80– 1 The *m·* and physical are imperfect.
89– 9 under *m·* medical treatment,
102–24 Whatever seems *m·*,
165–13 leaves nothing that is *m·* ;
180–11 another person, more *m·*, met me,
180–29 in both a *m·* and a spiritual sense.
181–20 regard him as spiritual, and not *m·*.
184– 9 man . . . is spiritual, not *m·*.
185–31 namely, that creation is *m·* :
186– 5 *m·* self-constituted belief of
187–29 *m·*, before spiritual ;
188– 7 that which appears second, *m·*, and
196–11 thus become *m·*, sensual, evil.
198– 6 denying *m·* so-called laws
217–17 Sensuous and *m·* realistic views
218–20 things spiritual, and not *m·*.
219– 6 or that . . . is finite or *m·*.
308–29 *m·* human likeness is the antipode of

material

Mis. 342– 4 their way was *m·* ;
351–22 sensuous love is *m·*,
352– 5 error of regarding . . . Love as *m·*
352– 5 or as both *m·* and spiritual,
361– 8 are neither *m·* nor mortal.
Ret. 21–13 our *m·*, mortal history is but
21–19 from a *m·*, false sense of life
67– 8 supposition that . . . are both *m·* and
67–15 testimony of *m·* personal sense
73– 2 his mortal opposite must, be *m·*
73– 9 *m·* human concept grew . . . less
Un. 9– 5 *M·* and sensual consciousness are
25–18 a *m·*, not a spiritual basis.
32–17 mortal mind declares itself *m·*,
33– 6 Now these senses, being *m·*,
35– 9 mortally mental, instead of *m·*.
42–10 *m·* before he can be spiritual,
43– 3 This generation seems too *m·* for
46–16 as spiritual and good, not as *m·* or
51– 3 false premises, — that Life is *m·*,
53–12 To say that Mind is *m·*,
Rud. 4– 8 It is not *m·* ;
5– 6 there is no *m·* mortal man,
6– 5 *are they not tangible and m·?*
7–13 According to . . . man is *m·*,
10– 8 with nothing evil or *m·* ;
No. 6–28 laws of Science are mental, not *m·* ;
10–19 former position, that sense is . . . *m·*,
17– 2 something unreal, *m·*, and mortal.
25–25 A *m·*, sinful mortal is but
26– 9 holding such *m·* and mortal views
27–20 This *m·* sinful personality,
29– 8 believe *m·* and sinning sense to be
31– 2 *M·* and mortal mind-healing
36–19 from *m·* to spiritual selfhood
40– 6 a *m·* and mortal sense of
'01. 8–18 Then can man be *m·*,
10– 9 Christ must be spiritual, not *m·*.
19–12 mixing *m·* and spiritual means,
22– 4 Is Science *m·*? No!
22– 5 Is Truth *m·*? No!
Hea. 6– 2 and we grow more *m·*,
7– 7 is the spiritual . . . as opposed to the *m·*.
17– 8 lust makes the *m·* so-called man,
Peo. 1–16 from *m·* to spiritual standpoints.
2–16 shockingly *m·* in practice,
4–22 out of beliefs that are as *m·* as
My. 6–25 giving to the *m·* a spiritual
48–23 * subordination of merely *m·* to
74–29 * the *m·* and the mental,
94–29 giving to the *m·* a spiritual
118–23 by a *m·* and not by the spiritual
139–20 from the *m·* to the spiritual,
139–24 *m·* to the spiritual communion ;
160–29 this hell is mental, not *m·*,
166–24 time and joy be spiritual, not *m·*.
178–15 those who regard being as *m·*.
239–25 is the *m·*, so-called man
260–13 Nothing conditional or *m·* belongs
262– 7 human, *m·*, mortal babe
262–22 which so transcends mortal, *m·*,
273–19 apart from a *m·* or personal sense
275– 6 The human, *m·*, so-called senses
303–21 subordinated the *m·* to the spiritual,
345–11 * are these too *m·* for C. S.?"

materialism

Mis. 17–17 from under the curse of *m·*,
19–27 we go out of *m·* or sin,
30–29 mist of *m·* will vanish
144–31 wake the long night of *m·*,
156–21 It is *m·* through which the
162–17 lamb upon the altar of *m·*,
166–26 and all *m·* disappear.
Pul. 52–21 * wave of *m·* and bigotry
79–19 * cross *m·* of the cruder science
'01. 25–21 metaphysics based on *m·* ?
Hea. 8–18 suffocate reason by *m·*.
Peo. 4– 2 *materia medica* nothing but *m·*,
My. 110– 6 upon the long night of *m·*,
221– 3 distance between Christianity and *m·*
254– 7 Released from *m·*,

materialisms

Peo. 5– 7 cold *m·* of dogma and doctrine

materialistic

Mis. 64–16 Man-made theories are . . . always *m·*.
245– 8 *m·* portion of the pulpit
246–29 a *m·* religion and a *materia medica*
369–14 the leaders of *m·* schools
Ret. 78–13 which advocate *m·* systems ;
Peo. 4–28 a *m·* and idolatrous theory

materialistically

Pul. 79–27 * had become *m·* "lopsided,"

materiality
Mis. 28–17 can overbear m· and mortality ;
73–11 and the unreality of m·.
103– 7 m·, and destructive forces,
104–16 His m·, clad in a false
156–19 It is their m· that clogs
162–25 M·, worldliness, human pride,
205– 5 shining through the mists of m·
Ret. 66– 4 no longer buried in m·.
68–21 bases creation on m·'''
73– 4 He is without m·, without finiteness
Un. 49–16 serve the mammon of m·
No. 26–21 corpuscle, m·, or mortality.
'02. 5– 5 religion parting with its m·.
Peo. 10– 4 refinements that lose some m· ;
My. 122–22 idea unenvironed by m·
357– 1 m· is wholly apart from C. S.,

materialization
Mis. 349– 8 m· of a student's thought,

materialize
No. 34– 6 no longer venture to m· the

materialized
Peo. 4– 6 belief that Spirit m· into

materializes
Mis. 268– 1 m· human modes and consciousness,

materially
Mis. 57– 1 created man over again m· ;
57– 7 not from dust, m·, but from Spirit,
57–24 the universe created m·.
73– 6 Interpreted m·, these passages
91– 4 to organize m· Christ's church.
140– 6 but m· questionable
182– 2 began spiritually instead of m·
Ret. 32– 5 whatever is loved m·,
Rud. 5–22 and we could not see m· ;
'01. 5–16 defined spiritually, not m·
My. 119–19 not . . . spiritually, but he could m·.
181– 1 defines . . . spiritually, not m·.

materia medica
Mis. 3–25 m· m·, hygiene, and
5–15 M· m· says, "I can do no more.
17–11 put off your m· m· and hygiene
81– 2 this is not the basis of m· m·,
89–11 or interfere with m· m·.
134–21 The reeling ranks of m· m·,
246–30 materialistic religion and a m· m·?
379–21 beyond the basis of m· m·,
Ret. 33– 5 dim mazes of m· m·,
'01. 24–28 m· m·, and scholastic theology
30–18 in theology and m· m·,
Peo. 3– 4 and the ideals of m· m·
4– 2 given to all systems of m· m·
5– 9 whose m· m· and theology were one.
5–27 * if the whole m· m· could be sunk
My. 106–14 impossible for the surgeon or m· m·
127–13 Comparing . . . with m· m·,
127–14 overwhelms m· m·, even as
127–18 ninety-nine to the ten of m· m·.
190– 8 Does C. S. equal m· m·
190–10 both practices— m· m· and
222–23 does not provide that m· m·
227–32 larger per cent . . . than does m· m·.
265–19 that religion and m· m· should
266–26 points in theology and m· m·,
288–15 creed, dogma, or m· m·.
292–23 In the practice of m· m·,
307–27 emerging from m· m·,
307–29 The fallacy of m· m·,
348–13 and that m· m· heals him.
348–15 neither man nor m· m·,

maternal
Pul. 32–25 * her m· grandfather, was known as

mathematical
Mis. 57–27 is stated in m· order,
210– 5 proving with m· certainty

mathematically
Pul. 4– 7 metaphysically and m· number one,

mathematician
My. 237– 7 The best m· has not attained

mathematics
Mis. 26– 4 truth, as demonstrable as m·.
29–31 Christians, like students in m·,
52–23 if, when tired of m· or failing to
60–16 addition is not subtraction in m·
62–10 even as in m·,
118– 8 To obey the principle of m·
233–23 scientist in m· who finds fault
Ret. 87– 6 as in astronomy or m·.
Un. 10–24 principle of positive m·.
'01. 4– 5 In m· four times three is twelve,
4– 6 To depart from the rule of m·
4– 7 destroys the proof of m· ;

mathematics
'01. 23–14 a change of the denominations of m· ;
Hea. 8–27 as we do to the rule of m·,
My. 235–10 she cannot do this in m·,

matin
Mis. 396–11 songsters' m· hymns to God
Po. 59– 3 songsters' m· hymns to God

matter (see also **matter's**)
above
Ret. 18–17 May soar above m·,
Po. 64– 8 May soar above m·,
My. 106–10 above m· in every mode and form,
190–20 over the human mind and *above* m·
all
'01. 27–24 taken out of its metaphysics all m·
My. 217–18 * "If all m· is unreal, why do we
an alien
My. 260– 3 would make m· an alien
and evil
Mis. 27–11 m· and evil . . . are *unreal*.
101–24 virtually destroys m· and evil,
367– 5 M· and evil are subjective states of
Ret. 60–10 and that m· and evil are as real as
Un. 8–14 the unreality of m· and evil
50–24 M· and evil cannot be conscious,
53–11 M· and evil are anti-Christian,
No. 21–13 would . . . substitute m· and evil for
24–10 denies . . . both m· and evil.
Pan. 7–22 It certainly gives to m· and evil
My. 262–16 the gloom of m· and evil
and human will
No. 11– 1 whereas m· and human will,
and its methods
Mis. 175–21 instituting m· and its methods
and man
My. 153–31 pointing away from m· and man
and Mind
Mis. 175–28 The attempt to mix m· and Mind,
269–18 his choice between m· and Mind,
and mind
Mis. 173–14 says that man is both m· and mind,
'01. 25–10 which mix m· and mind,
Hea. 13– 1 and divide . . . between m· and mind,
and mortal mind
Un. 35–20 m· and mortal mind are one ;
No. 15–22 m· and mortal mind have neither
24– 7 lower orders of m· and mortal mind.
and Spirit
Mis. 217–11 fallacy . . . m· and Spirit are one
No. 26– 3 believe . . . m· and Spirit are one ;
Pan. 8–25 admixtures of m· and Spirit,
'01. 22– 6 do not try to mix m· and Spirit,
Peo. 9–13 between m· and Spirit ;
and the earth
Mis. 179–27 yet we look into m· and the earth
annihilate
My. 226–16 But annihilate m·, and man . . . would
any compromise with
Mis. 53–15 by any compromise with m· ;
apart from
'01. 24– 1 * M· apart from conscious mind
My. 108– 8 to act apart from m·.
167– 6 which is apart from m·,
appears
Un. 41–26 m· appears to both live and die,
as its effect
Mis. 218–22 with m· as its effect,
as substance
Un. 32–12 all sense of m· as substance,
My. 235–18 M· as substance or intelligence
as useful
'01. 25–26 to be as real, and m· as useful,
basis of
Mis. 243–21 who practise on the basis of m·,
because of
Rud. 12–17 that they live in or because of m·,
belief in
Mis. 56–19 this false belief in m·
Un. 50– 8 pantheistic belief in m·
belief of pain in
Mis. 44–18 a belief of pain in m· ;
belief that
Rud. 10–24 belief that m· can master Mind,
No. 5–10 belief that m· has sensation.
believe in
Un. 50– 3 *Do you believe in m· ?*
50– 4 I believe in m· only as
belongs to
Mis. 51–15 that sensation belongs to m·.
better than
Ret. 31–11 higher and better than m·,
brain is
Pan. 4–14 that brain is m·,
buried in
Mis. 78– 1 Life, God, is not buried in m·.

matter

called
Mis. 173–29 atom or molecule called m·?
Un. 33– 5 of a substance called m·.
Rud. 5–16 mind which is called m·,
'01. 24– 5 which is generally called m·
calling on
Mis. 333–18 calling on m· to work out the
cannot be, in
Un. 25– 8 Mind is not, cannot be, in m·.
cannot cure
Hea. 12– 9 when m· cannot cure it,
cannot even talk
Mis. 23–16 M· cannot even talk ;
cannot feel
Un. 34–15 that m· cannot feel m· ;
Rud. 10–14 m· cannot feel, see, or report
cannot talk
Un. 25– 9 M· cannot talk ;
character of
Un. 31–18 nature and character of m·,
claim of
Mis. 258– 5 unrelenting false claim of m·
Un. 32– 3 the claim of m· usurps the
claims
Mis. 27–22 m· claims something besides God,
claims of
Un. 31– 9 annulled the claims of m·,
36–18 rejection of the claims of m·
conditions of
Pan. 4–10 conditions of m·, or brain,
confining itself to
Un. 62–25 Mortal sense, confining itself to m·,
conscious
Un. 44–22 [you shall be conscious m·],
45–14 conscious m· implies pantheism.
control
My. 293–25 law of Spirit to control m·,
cords of
Un. 30–22 to break the cords of m·,
created
Ret. 60– 9 adds . . . divine Spirit created m·,
currents of
Un. 11– 4 currents of m·, or mortal mind.
dead
My. 206– 1 would unite dead m· with animate,
declaims against
'01. 26–10 he declaims against m·,
demands of
No. 18–26 against the so-called demands of m·,
Peo. 12–16 lifts man above the demands of m·.
denial of
Un. 31–16 position, in the denial of m·,
disappearance as
Mis. 271– 3 the point of its disappearance as m·
disarrangement of
Pan. 8– 2 the disarrangement of m· causes
discovered in
Pan. 5– 3 Can . . . be discovered in m·?
does not express
Mis. 218–24 m· does not express the nature of
does not recognize
Mis. 74–11 If God does not recognize m·,
dream of life in
Mis. 16–17 from the dream of life in m·,
Hea. 9–27 from the dream of life in m·,
Peo. 14–16 look upon this dream of life in m·,
My. 267–21 from his dream of life in m·
dweller in
Mis. 189–21 not a dweller in m·.
element of
Mis. 201– 7 and death is an element of m·,
error or
Mis. 190– 4 Life, defiant of error or m·.
Un. 42–24 Truth, defiant of error or m·,
evil and
Mis. 27–20 evil and m· are negation :
'01. 25–28 excludes evil and m·.
evil or
Un. 50–19 consciousness of evil or m·
evolve
Mis. 23–32 could not change . . . and evolve m·.
evolving
Rud. 7–24 by evolving m· from Spirit,
existent in
Un. 46–14 no selfhood as existent in m·.
faith in
Mis. 334– 9 mortals' faith in m· may have
Peo. 9–20 showing our greater faith in m·,
My. 4– 1 losing his faith in m· and sin,
finite
Ret. 58– 3 taking the rule of finite m·,
forces of
Un. 35–18 the merciless forces of m·.
35–19 What then are the . . . forces of m·?

matter

formed by
Mis. vii– 9 If worlds were formed by m·,
form of
Un. 33–16 that form of m· called brains,
forms of
My. 212–11 use of higher forms of m·,
for rejoicing
Pul. 22– 5 m· for rejoicing that we unite
My. 285–13 m· for rejoicing that the best,
God is not in
Mis. 75–14 God is not in m· or the mortal
has no
Mis. 76–25 m· has no sense.
198– 8 understanding that m· has no sense ;
Un. 38–12 since m· has no life,
My. 109– 2 M· has no . . . substance and reality
has no intelligence
Mis. 44–27 m· has no intelligence of its own.
Ret. 69–20 m· has no intelligence, life, nor
has no sensation
Mis. 44–18 for m· has no sensation.
Ret. 61–22 for m· has no sensation
hypothesis of
My. 349–15 putting off the hypothesis of m·
I challenge
My. 108– 5 I challenge m· to act apart from mind ;
idea of
Mis. 75– 2 Jesus' idea of m·.
if He knows
No. 16– 3 If He knows m·,
illusion of
Mis. 28–19 he arose above the illusion of m·.
important
Man. 100–15 to act upon this important m·
in and out of
Hea. 4–16 in and out of m· for an indefinite
independent of
Mis. 43– 2 act of itself, and independent of m·,
inert
Mis. 3–16 Drugs, inert m·, never are needed
infused into
Mis. 190– 3 It is neither . . . infused into m· :
Ret. 58–13 it was not . . . infused into m· ;
instead of
Mis. 35– 3 fact that Mind, instead of m·,
190–25 belongs to Mind instead of m·,
276–27 from m· instead of Spirit,
Hea. 12– 2 Mind instead of m· heals
Peo. 2–12 of Mind instead of m·,
12–25 to m· instead of Spirit.
is a frail conception
Mis. 87–11 M· is a frail conception of
is a lie
Rud. 7–20 m· is a lie,
is a misstatement
Mis. 174– 2 M· is a misstatement of Mind ;
is a phase
Mis. 25– 7 m· is a phase of error,
is egoistic
Un. 26– 1 Evil. . . . m· is egoistic,
is erroneous
Un. 36–14 m· is erroneous, transitory,
is inert
Rud. 5– 9 M· is inert, inanimate,
is mortal error
Mis. 21–19 m· is mortal error.
is mortal mind
Un. 35–10 m· is mortal mind ;
is mythology
Mis. 55–27 m· is mythology,
is not a lawgiver
Peo. 12– 9 when m· is not a lawgiver
is not conscious
My. 221–26 since m· is not conscious ;
is not intelligent
Mis. 26–17 M· is not intelligent,
is not Mind
No. 27– 4 M· is not Mind, to claim aught ;
is not seen
Un. 34– 7 That m· is not seen ;
is not sensible
My. 349– 9 and m· is not sensible.
is nowhere
Mis. 173–20 m· is nowhere and sin is obsolete.
is obsolete
Ret. 34– 4 in which m· is obsolete.
is proven powerless
Mis. 29–29 whereby m· is proven powerless
is the opposite
Un. 36–12 m· is the opposite of Spirit,
is the substratum
No. 16–25 m· is the substratum of evil,
is the unreal
Mis. 21–20 m· is the unreal and temporal.

matter

is unconscious
Un. 25– 2 If you say that *m·* is unconscious,
lawgiver to
Mis. 364–26 If Spirit is the lawgiver to *m·*,
law of
(*see* **law**)
laws of
(*see* **laws**)
lifelessness of
Mis. 74–27 demonstrated the lifelessness of *m·*,
Life not in
My. 181–12 Life not in *m·* but in Mind.
light, being
'01. 3–25 light, being *m·*, loses the nature of
manifest as
Hea. 12–12 before they can become manifest as *m·* ;
man nor
'01. 4–12 neither man nor *m·* can be.
medicine of
'01. 18– 8 the old-time medicine of *m·*.
Mind and
Mis. 56–16 Mind and *m·* mingling in perpetual
280–12 not two,— Mind *and m·*.
Ret. 59–21 define Mind and *m·* as distinct,
mind and
(*see* **mind**)
mind in
(*see* **mind**)
Mind is not in
Rud. 7–21 Mind is not in *m·*,
13– 1 that Mind is not in *m·* ;
Mind, not
Mis. 56–10 Life is immortal Mind, not *m·*.
190– 1 Atomic action is Mind, not *m·*.
'00. 11–19 Mind, not *m·*, makes music ;
mind, not
My. 107–20 identifies . . . with mind, not *m·*,
302– 4 mind, not *m·*, produces the result
Mind or
Mis. 23–10 Was it Mind or *m·* that spake
mind or
Mis. 103–20 Mortal man, as mind or *m·*,
218–16 inconceivable, either as mind or *m·* ;
No. 38– 8 no intelligent sin, evil *mind* or *m·*
My. 108– 4 is mind or *m·* the intelligent cause
Mind over
Mis. 35– 5 supremacy of Mind over *m·*,
Hea. 7– 6 the power of Mind over *m·*.
mind over
Pul. 31–19 * dominance of mind over *m·*,
Hea. 15– 9 the power of mind over *m·*,
My. 74–14 * triumph of mind over *m·*.
97– 2 * the power of mind over *m·*.
Mind to
Mis. 268–11 who departs from Mind to *m·*,
Rud. 6– 9 when we change . . . from Mind to *m·*,
misnamed
Mis. 201– 4 resolves the element misnamed *m·*
mists of
No. 16–23 mists of *m·* — sin, sickness,
molecule, as
Un. 35–23 molecule, as *m·*, is not formed by
more than
Mis. 47– 6 substance means more than *m·* :
Un. 24–23 My mind is more than *m·*.
No. 25–10 Mind is more than *m·*,
mortal mind or
No. 16–12 evil, called mortal mind or *m·*,
must be understood
Mis. 233–30 *M·* must be understood as a false
must disappear
Mis. 217–29 and *m·* must *disappear*,
mythical nature of
Mis. 47–14 the mythical nature of *m·*,
named
Mis. 27– 6 its opposite, named *m·*,
361–28 named *m·*, or mortal mind.
Rud. 7–22 its opposite, named *m·*.
namely
Mis. 217–12 antipode of Spirit, namely, *m·*.
name of
Mis. 258–20 and call Mind by the name of *m·*,
names
Mis. 24–19 subjective state which it names *m·*,
neither in
No. 15–21 finds Spirit neither in *m·* nor in
neither lives
Un. 41–25 hence *m·* neither lives nor dies.
neither sees
Ret. 25–25 *m·* neither sees, hears, nor feels
never appealed to
My. 288–19 He never appealed to *m·*
never escaped from
Hea. 18– 9 never escaped from *m·* ;

matter

never in
Un. 62–22 man is My idea, never in *m·*,
never produced
Mis. 218– 3 *m·* never produced Mind, and *vice versa.*
no
Mis. 108–31 and that there is no *m·*
174–17 No *m·* is there,
183– 8 there is no *m·* to cope with.
357–25 no *m·* who has taught them.
Ret. 94–12 leaves no flesh, no *m·*,
Un. 31– 6 surely there can be no *m·* ;
34–13 consequently there is no *m·*.
41–25 In C. S. there is no *m·* ;
43–27 Spirit which knows no *m·*.
Rud. 4–19 *Is there no m·?*
6– 2 inference that there is no *m·*.
My. 75–21 * no *m·* how far they had travelled
357–23 "There is no *m·*"
no easy
No. 15–14 It is no easy *m·* to believe
no longer in
'01. 11– 7 and mind is no longer in *m·*.
nor mortal mind
Un. 33–18 neither *m·* nor mortal mind,
Rud. 13– 2 neither *m·* nor mortal mind ;
no sense in
Un. 21–19 no sense in *m·* ;
not by
Pul. vii–18 not by *m·*, but by Mind ;
'01. 5–16 by Mind, not by *m·*.
not conscious of
Un. 36–24 yet is not conscious of *m·*,
not contingent on
No. 43– 3 Truth is not contingent on *m·*.
nothingness of
(*see* **nothingness**)
of fact
My. 14–24 * As a *m·* of fact, the building fund
310–10 As a *m·* of fact, he was
of interest
My. 89–23 * *m·* of interest to that city
of the brain
Mis. 247–21 believe it . . . in *m·* of the brain ;
of wonder
My. 82–11 * it was a *m·* of wonder
or evil
Mis. 363–13 changes of *m·*, or evil.
No. 17– 4 *M·*, or evil, is the absence of Spirit
organizations of
Un. 33–27 through the organizations of *m·*,
organized
Ret. 60– 5 as a broken sphere, as organized *m·*,
Rud. 5–27 the five senses as organized *m·*,
or Mind
Mis. 334–23 by means of *m·*, or Mind?
or mortals
Mis. 22– 5 that *m·* or mortals can evolve Science?
or power
Un. 35–15 Which was first, *m·* or power?
or spirit
My. 235–20 is he *m·* or spirit?
or the body
My. 349– 7 *m·*, or the body, cannot cause disease,
or the flesh
Mis. 124– 7 by means of *m·*, or the flesh,
pains of
Mis. 73–20 so-called pleasures and pains of *m·*
209–13 so-called pains of *m·*
passed into
Ret. 69– 8 delusion that life . . . passed into *m·*.
plane of
Mis. 143– 6 above the plane of *m·*.
pleasures of
Mis. 200–29 so-called pains and pleasures of *m·*
points away from
Peo. 5–18 points away from *m·* and doctrine,
power over
'01. 23–21 demonstrated his power over *m·*,
'02. 10– 4 power over *m·*, molecule, space,
predicate
Mis. 364–22 Human hypotheses predicate *m·* of
problem of
My. 110–22 solve the blind problem of *m·*.
produce
Mis. 217–20 and that these . . . produce *m·*,
prove
Un. 33– 1 which prove *m·* to be identical
qualities of
Un. 35– 4 the qualities of *m·* are but
quality of
Mis. 256–23 every quality of *m·*, in and of
recognition of
Mis. 173–11 no relation to, or recognition of, *m·*
regarded
Mis. 200–30 regarded *m·* as only a vagary of

matter

saying unto
My. 191–20 Spirit is saying unto *m·* :
schools and
'01. 26–13 to the schools and *m·* for help
self and
Mis. 343–13 the sordid soil of self and *m·*.
self-conscious
Mis. 183–12 and pains of self-conscious *m·*.
Un. 53– 1 supposed modes of self-conscious *m·*,
self-existent
Peo. 5–23 ego is not self-existent *m·*
selfhood in
Ret. 73–15 personality, or selfhood in *m·*,
sense of
Mis. 74–13 Christ Jesus' sense of *m·* was the
187– 5 above every sense of *m·*,
Un. 32–12 destroys all sense of *m·*
sensible
Un. 21–18 There is no sensible *m·*,
sepulchre of
Mis. 180–15 door from this sepulchre of *m·*.
servant of
Pan. 8–27 They make man the servant of *m·*,
shall seem
Ret. 69–12 *m·* shall seem to have life
shows that
No. 16– 9 C. S. shows that *m·*, evil, sin,
so-called
My. 302– 9 manifest through so-called *m·*.
so-called facts of
Mis. 55–20 the so-called facts of *m·* ;
so-called life in
Mis. 128– 3 lessons of this so-called life in *m·*
so-called life of
My. 274– 3 apart from the so-called life of *m·*
so-called power of
My. 293– 4 the so-called power of *m·*,
so great a
Un. 5–10 personal opinion on so great a *m·*,
spat upon
Mis. 258– 8 literally spat upon *m·* ;
Spirit and
(*see* **Spirit**)
Spirit, not
Mis. 5–19 power of Spirit, not *m·*,
'01. 5–22 man reflects Spirit, not *m·*.
Peo. 9– 2 builds on Spirit, not *m·* ;
Spirit, or
Mis. 28–22 What meaneth this Me, — Spirit, or *m·* ?
Spirit over
Mis. 140–10 superiority of . . . Spirit over *m·*
Ret. 26–11 superiority of Spirit over *m·*.
Spirit with
My. 206– 2 would unite . . . Spirit with *m·*
strips
Mis. 185– 0 it strips *m·* of all claims,
subdued
Ret. 58– 9 sense of power that subdued *m·*
subduing
'02. 10–13 subjugating the body, subduing *m·*,
subjugates
'02. 10– 2 and subjugates *m·*,
submerged in
My. 179– 8 In this . . . are submerged in *m·*.
subordinates
Mis. 189–24 spiritual power that subordinates *m·*
suffering
My. 132–27 dreaming of suffering *m·* ;
summary of the
Mis. 35–12 complete, summary of the *m·* :
superiority over
Mis. 379–29 Mind and its superiority over *m·*,
supposed life in
Mis. 201–13 nothingness of supposed life in *m·*,
supposed power of
Mis. 199– 3 deny the supposed power of *m·*
supposition that
Mis. 74–24 supposition that *m·* is intelligent,
supremacy over
Mis. 63–30 Spirit proved its supremacy over *m·*.
take away
Un. 34–21 Take away *m·*, and mortal mind
takes no cognizance
Mis. 28– 8 *M·* takes no cognizance of matter.
teaching that
Un. 45–13 teaching that *m·* can be conscious ;
termed
No. 10–15 What is termed *m·*, or relates to its
testifies
Un. 33–10 *m·* testifies of itself, "I am matter ;"
theory that
Mis. 74–22 theory that *m·* is substance ;
this
Mis. 146–24 you will act, relative to this *m·*,
299– 9 detailed report of this *m·*,

matter

this
My. 130–16 I ask the help of others in this *m·*,
334–26 * Of further interest in this *m·*
through
Mis. 185– 6 not as or through *m·*,
333–26 that God wrought through *m·*
thus affirms
Un. 24–25 Whatever *m·* thus affirms is
to be matter
Mis. 173–32 For *m·* to be matter, it must
to create
Mis. 174– 1 to evolve or to create *m·*
to govern
Hea. 15– 9 it enables mind to govern *m·*,
to Mind
Peo. 7– 6 turn often . . . from *m·* to Mind,
to Spirit
Mis. 194–22 how to turn from *m·* to Spirit
'02. 10–22 transit from *m·* to Spirit
My. 163– 6 from *m·* to Spirit.
181–10 departure from *m·* to Spirit,
translates
Mis. 25–12 translates *m·* into Mind,
Hea. 7– 9 translates *m·* into its original
Truth is not in
Mis. 179–14 Truth is not in *m·* ;
unconscious of
No. 36–12 unconscious of *m·*, of sin,
usurpation, by
Un. 51–12 pretentious usurpation, by *m·*,
usurps
Un. 31–17 rests on the fact that *m·* usurps
32– 3 *m·* usurps the prerogative of
vanquished
Mis. 74–21 virtually vanquished *m·* and its
veil of
Mis. 124–25 rent the veil of *m·*,
weary of
Hea. 11– 8 weary of *m·*, it would catch
we name
Mis. 267–24 which we name *m·*, or *non-intelligent*
went out
Hea. 11–22 proportionately as *m·* went out
what made
My. 235–18 Who or what made *m·* ?
whole
Un. 34–10 summary of the whole *m·*,
will become vague
Peo. 10– 6 *m·* will become vague,
will be proved
No. 27–11 *m·* will be proved a myth.
within the skull
Un. 33–14 Brain, . . . only *m·* within the skull,
without
Un. 34– 8 mortal mind cannot see without *m·* ;
without Mind
Rud. 5–16 it must be . . . or *m·* without Mind.
5–17 *M·* without Mind is a
with Spirit
'01. 26– 9 combines *m·* with Spirit.
worshipping of
My. 151–28 worshipping of *m·* in the name of

Mis. 5–25 but believe it to be brain *m·*.
17–31 by which one loses himself as *m·*,
21–17 "There is no life, . . . in *m·*.
23–15 for *m·* is not the Christian's God,
26–16 from infinite Mind, or from *m·* ?
26–16 If from *m·*, how did *m·* originate?
26–23 just what I call *m·*, *nothing*.
28– 2 *M·* can neither see, hear, feel,
28– 8 Matter takes no cognizance of *m·*.
28–25 no intelligence nor life in *m·* ;
30–17 Life . . . untrammelled, by *m·*.
30–28 mist from the earth [*m·*] ;"— *Gen.* 2 : 6.
36–29 in *m·* and separate from God,
44–20 You call this body *m·*,
44–21 That *m·* can report pain,
44–22 or that mind is *in m·*,
45– 3 *m·* is but a belief,
47– 1 *there is no such thing as m·*,
47– 4 *m·* is but manifest mortal mind.
49–25 belief, that Mind is in *m·*,
50–23 the belief that the heart is *m·*
51–13 *teach him life in m· ?*
53– 2 false claim of . . . life in *m·*,
53– 6 error of supposed life . . . in *m·*,
55–22 over their opposite, or *m·*,
55–29 If Mind is in *m·*
55–31 or it is God in *m·*,
58–15 As *m·*, the eye cannot see ;
60–28 has its counterfeit in some *m·* belief.
63– 1 and the *sickness of m·*,
68–25 * as distinguished from that of *m·* ;
70–22 The thief's body, as *m·*

matter

Mis.	71–17	neither human hypothesis nor *m·*.
	72–22	*that Spirit takes note of m·?*
	72–25	*M·* is manifest mortal mind,
	73– 1	no evidence of the reality of *m·*,
	74–30	*m·* is neither substance, . . . nor Life,
	76–10	belief that . . . are in *m·*.
	76–24	false sense of mentality in *m·*,
	84–22	Paul's sense of life in *m·*,
	85–22	mortal mind which seems to be *m·*
	85–23	suggests pleasure and pain in *m·* ;
	93–19	Fear is a belief of sensation in *m·* :
	101–23	not *m·*, but Mind.
	103– 4	more impregnable and solid than *m·* ;
	113– 2	Mind that is God is not in *m·* ;
	124– 5	cannot find God in *m·*,
	173–10	law of Mind and not of *m·*,
	173–15	that Mind is in *m·*?
	174–20	first to declare against . . . is *m·*.
	175– 8	says, I am sustained by bread, *m·*,
	179– 8	Is our consciousness in *m·* or in God?
	184– 2	by claiming that . . . man is *m·* ;
	189–16	supposition . . . is breathed into *m·*,
	190– 2	It is neither the energy of *m·*,
	196– 2	ego is found not in *m·* but in Mind,
	198–19	man's body, as *m·*, has no power to
	199–22	which mortals name *m·*.
	200– 8	*m·* was palpably an error of premise
	217–18	presuppose that nature is *m·*,
	217–21	that *m·* is both cause and
	217–29	must change in order to become *m·*,
	217–31	To . . . sense, everything is *m·* ;
	218– 7	*m·* can neither see, hear, nor feel,
	219– 3	neither reveals God in *m·*,
	228–24	belong to mind and not to *m·*.
	233–32	sensation is not in *m·*,
	234– 2	then shall *m·* remain no longer to
	234–22	is *m·* of grave wonderment to
	256–25	The assertion that *m·* is a law,
	257– 1	the notion that Mind can be in *m·*
	258–30	the law of Spirit, not of *m·*.
	260– 8	His faith partook not of drugs, *m·*,
	260–12	in the laws of Spirit, not of *m·* ;
	280–16	not put into the scales with *m·* ;
	332– 2	but not life in *m·*.
	333– 1	that this . . . is intelligent *m·* ;
	333–12	in *m·* as well as Spirit.
	334– 8	simulates power and Truth in *m·*
	334–23	Is *m·* Truth? No!
	336– 7	resort to stones and clubs,— yea, to *m·*,
	344–18	would place . . . intelligence in *m·* ;
	362– 2	for instance, intelligent *m·*,
	362–18	mortal mind, with its phenomenon *m·*,
	379–13	*m·* was not as real as Mind,
	379–25	Is it *m·*, or is it Mind,
Man.	66– 4	a clear understanding of the *m·*,
Ret.	23– 9	*M·* was no longer spanned with
	25–19	and *m·*, the *unreality*.
	25–23	witnesses to the . . . existence of *m·* ;
	33–19	and *m·* is thereby rarefied
	57–17	*M·* is substance in error,
	60– 8	material sense says that *m·*,
	60–25	*m·* and its so-called organizations
	68–19	"How can *m·* originate or transmit
	69–11	into what I call *m·*,
	69–18	believing that there is life in *m·*,
	69–28	belief that mind is in *m·*,
	93–20	no life, . . . nor intelligence in *m·*."
Un.	22–22	*will-power,— alias intelligent m·*.
	24–24	In my mortal mind, *m·* becomes
	25– 9	as Mind, and not as *m·*.
	25–11	This lie, that Mind can be in *m·*,
	26– 1	*Evil.* I am intelligent *m·* ;
	26– 3	is in *m·*, and *m·* reproduces
	31–12	claim of sin is, that *m·* exists ;
	31–12	*second*, that *m·* is substance ;
	31–13	that *m·* has intelligence ;
	31–14	that *m·*, being so endowed,
	32– 1	according to belief, obtain in *m·* ;
	32– 7	By *m·* is commonly meant mind,
	33– 3	(*m·* really having no sense)
	33–10	testifies of itself, "I am *m·* ;"
	33–11	but unless *m·* is mind,
	33–26	Mortal mind declares that *m·* sees
	34– 1	or that mind sees by means of *m·*,
	34– 3	and declares that *m·* is the master of
	34–17	says . . . nerves, *do feel m·*.
	34–19	that *m·* is substantial, is hot or
	34–20	Take away . . . and *m·* could not feel
	35–12	is not *m·*, but Spirit.
	36–21	deny the existence or reality of *m·*,
	40– 6	or the belief of life in *m·*,
	41–23	Spirit can never dwell in . . . *m·*.
	42– 3	*M·*, sin, and death are not
	42– 5	What then are *m·*, sin, and death?
	42–23	nor . . . power into *m·*.

matter

Un.	45–24	the visionary substance of *m·*.
	45–28	*M·* is not truly conscious ;
	50–11	*m·* is only a phenomenon of
	50–17	*m·* has neither Mind nor sensation.
	56– 5	comes from mind, not from *m·*,
Pul.	6– 8	not *m·*, but Mind ;
	51– 6	* to a *m·* like C. S.,
Rud.	4–17	Spirit is not in *m·*,
	4–18	Law is not in *m·*, but in Mind
	5– 1	testify to the existence of *m·*.
	5–12	who has ever found Soul in . . . *m·*,
	5–13	who has found sight in *m·*,
	5–15	If there is any such thing as *m·*,
	5–18	Mind in *m·* is pantheism.
	6– 6	they are real, but not as *m·*.
	7–18, 19	*M·*, as *m·*, has neither sensation nor
	10–13	of mortal mind, and not of *m·* ;
	10–28	to believe in the existence of *m·*,
	11– 1	or that *m·* can frame its own
	12–10	belief . . . made sick by *m·*,
No.	16– 3	If . . . *m·* can exist in Mind,
	17–15	*M·*, or any mode of mortal mind,
	25–15	neither *m·* nor a mode of mortal mind,
	29– 6	believes that Spirit, . . . exists in *m·*.
	29–14	statement . . . that Soul is in *m·*,
	31–20	not as in or of *m·*, but as . . . beliefs
	35–19	*m·*,— which is the antipode of God,
Pan.	5– 5	What, then, can *m·* create,
	6–17	can *m·* be an intelligent creator or
	6–24	can *m·* be force or law ;
	7– 4	intelligent *m·*, signifies more than
	7–27	hypothesis of . . . *m·* governing Mind,
'01.	22–13	therefore *m·* cannot be a reality.
	24– 3	He denies the existence of *m·*,
	24– 3	and argues that *m·* is not *without*
	24–12	Making *m·* more potent than
	25–15	*m·* minus, and God all,
	25–23	Had he taught the . . . power of *m·*,
	27–26	born of the Spirit and not *m·*.
'02.	7– 5	*m·*, sin, . . . and death enter not into
Hea.	9–25	Life in *m·* is a dream :
	10– 1	the vision of life in *m·* ;
	12– 5	to learn what *m·* is doing
	17–24	false supposition of life . . . in *m·*.
Peo.	4–10	said . . . and *m·* become intelligent
	8–17	and yet we make more of *m·*,
My.	5–11	Whence, then, came the creation of *m·*,
	75–15	* *m·* of securing accommodations.
	108– 5	If *m·*, I challenge matter to
	109– 1	*M·* is but the subjective state of
	119–10	in Mind, not in *m·*.
	132–25	destroy the belief of life in *m·*.
	151–22	"NOT *M·*, BUT SPIRIT"
	152– 9	By reposing faith . . . in *m·*,
	152–26	*m·*, man, or woman can never heal
	153–25	as the divine Mind, not as *m·*,
	161–31	supposititious life . . . in *m·*,
	205–24	human hypotheses, *m·*, creed and
	228– 5	sensation of mind, not of *m·*.
	260– 4	*m·* would reverentially withdraw
	260–10	the things of Spirit, not of *m·*.
	261–27	born of Spirit and not of *m·*.
	271– 2	*m·* and material sense are null,
	288–18	*m·* was not the auxiliary of Spirit.
	297–27	not had sufficient interest in the *m·*
	302–10	The general craze is that *m·* masters
	302–11	specific insanity is that brain, nor *m·*,
	307– 8	which had nothing to do with *m·*,
	320– 3	* presented my *m·* for a theme
	345– 5	will be thought to *m·* much.
	347–25	*m·* is not a law-maker ;
	350– 5	with the phenomenon, *m·*,
	357– 6	wherein *m·* has neither part nor
	357– 6	*m·* is the absolute opposite of

matter-agencies

Mis.	244–22	to be raised without *m·*.

matter-cure

Mis.	62–20	A "mind-cure" is a *m·*.

matter-physician

Hea.	12– 4	*m·* feels the pulse,

matter-physicians

Mis.	81– 6	the *m·* and the metaphysicians,

matter's

Mis.	56–11	indication of *m·* constituting
	218–25	*m·* graven grins are neither
Un.	3– 2	and still believe in *m·* reality,

matters

Mis.	146–15	These are *m·* of grave import ;
	376– 1	* no mean attention to such *m·*,
Pan.	11–16	it *m·* not what he believes ;
'00.	2–12	society manners or *m·*,
'02.	12–21	to interpolate some *m·* of business
Hea.	6–16	*m·* not whether that ideal is a

matters
Po. 79– 1   *m·* not what be thy lot,
My. v– 7   * *m·* of general wonderment
7– 4   to interpolate some *m·* of business
276–19   * in such *m·* no one should seek to
320–25   * and went into *m·* of detail

Matthew and **Matt.** (*see also* **St. Matthew**)
5: 3–12
Man. 63– 4   Sermon on the Mount (*M·*. 5 : 3–12)
6: 9–13
Man. 63– 2   Lord's Prayer (*M·*. 6 : 9–13),
ix. 2
Mis. 24–11   and opened it at *M·* ix. 2.
xii. 31, 32
Mis. 55–14   spoken of in *M·*. xii. 31, 32.
18: 15–17
Man. 51– 3   demand in *M·* 18 : 15–17 ;
51–16   the requirements . . . in *M·* 18 : 15–17,

mature
Mis. 85–20   new-born Christian Scientist must *m·*,
Un. 11–25   to *m:* fitness for perfection
No. 2–19   to *m·* what he has been taught.
'02. 3–26   that power must *m·* into

matures
Mis. 286– 6   Until time *m·* human growth,

maturing
My. 181– 8   Progress is the *m·* conception of

maturity
Un. 50–26   material origin, growth, *m·*,

maximum
Mis. 232–16   *m·* of perfection in all things.
My. 114– 7   *m·* of these teachings
165–29   rapidly nearing the *m·* of might,
181–26   the death-rate was at its *m·*.

May
(*see* **months**)

mayhap
Mis. 109– 5   *m·* never have thought of,
308–22   and *m·* taught me more than

Mayor
My. 173–26   Special thanks are due . . . the *M·*,

mazes
Ret. 30–19   *m·* of divine metaphysics
33– 5   dim *m·* of *materia medica*,

McClure
My. 315–21   the *M·* "history," so called,

McClure's Magazine
My. 308– 5   chapter sub-title
308–12   *M· M·*, January, 1907,
308 15   *M· M·* refers to my father's
308–26   Although *M· M·* attributes
308–28   *M· M·* also declares
308–31   The man whom *M· M·* characterizes as
309–21   *M· M·* says, describing the
309–26   *M· M·* states : "Alone of the
310– 8   *M· M·* calls my youngest brother,
310–17   Regarding the allegation by *M· M·*
310–22   *M· M·* says that "the quarrels
311–29   Notwithstanding that *M· M·* says,
312– 5   of my husband, *M· M·* says :
312–32   rhyme attributed to me by *M· M·*
313– 8   various stories told by *M· M·*
313–17   as stated by *M· M·*.
313–25   as *M· M·* says.
314– 1   *M· M·* calls Dr. Daniel Patterson,
314–13   Although, as *M· M·* claims,

McCrackan
Mr.
My. 32– 8   * Mr. *M·* and Mrs. Conant
34–17   * read by Mr. *M·* and Mrs. Conant :
81–11   * Mr. *M·* announced at the
Mr. William D.
My. 134–23   * First Reader, Mr. William D. *M·*,
William D.
My. 31–23   * First Reader William D. *M·*,
35–28   * First Reader William D. *M·*

McKenzie
Mr.
My. 39–17   * In introducing . . . Mr. *M·* said :
Rev. William P.
My. 39– 4   * the President, Rev. William P. *M·*,

McKinley (*see also* **McKinley's**)
Mrs.
My. 290–11   chapter sub-title
290–12   *My Dear Mrs. M·* :
President
My. 291– 1   chapter sub-title
292–15   to save the life of President *M·*,"
President, William
My. 291– 4   beloved President, William *M·*.

McKinley's
President
My. 293–22   and President *M·* recovery

McLellan
Archibald
My. 21–31   * signature
136–19   Archibald *M·*, editor-in-chief
Mr. Archibald
My. 135–15   Trustees . . . Mr. Archibald *M·*,
137–23   Trustees . . . Mr. Archibald *M·*,

McNeil
Fanny
My. 311–20   Fanny *M·*, President Pierce's niece,
General John
My. 311–27   General John *M·*, the hero of
John
Ret. 1– 3   John *M·* of Edinburgh.
Marion
Ret. 1–17   This second Marion *M·*
2– 7   Marion *M·*, came to America
Marion Moor
Ret. 1–15   Marion Moor *M·* had a daughter,

My. 311–18   regarding the *M·* coat-of-arms
(*see also* **Macneil, Macneill**)

McNeils
Pul. 48–28   * *M·* and General Knox

McRee, Dr.
My. 335–26   * (Dr. *M·* we think it was),

M. D.
Mis. 349– 6   students with the degree of *M. D.*
Man. 47– 7   he may consult with an *M. D.*
47– 9   to confer with an *M. D.* on Ontology,
'01. 34– 1   the early employment of an *M. D.*,
34– 6   from the attendance of an *M. D.*,
My. 4–15   loves . . . D.D. and *M. D.*
105–20   patient of a distinguished *M. D.*,
294–16   surgeon or the faithful *M. D.*

M. D.'s
Mis. 6– 9   cases are given to the *M. D.'s*,
39–16   Unlike the *M. D.'s*,
106– 8   *M. D.'s* to left of them,
Pan. 10–19   *M. D.'s* have failed to heal ;
'00. 14–25   the better class of *M. D.'s*
'01. 34– 9   the *M. D.'s* material prescription.
My. 105– 8   *M. D.'s*, by verdict of the stethoscope
105–29   In the ranks of the *M. D.'s* are

Me and **me**
Mis. 18–10   no other gods before *m·* ;" — *Exod.* 20 : 3.
21– 3   no other gods before *m·*." — *Exod.* 20 : 3.
23–13   no other gods before *m·*." — *Exod.* 20 : 3.
23–14   It is plain that the *M·* spoken of
28–21   no other gods before *m·*;" — *Exod.* 20 : 3.
28–22   What meaneth this *M·*,
45–27   "other gods before *m·*." — *Exod.* 20 : 3.
97–19   no God beside *m·*." — *Isa.* 45 : 5.
123– 4   no other gods before *m·* :" — *Exod.* 20 : 3.
209–22   "other gods before *m·*," — *Exod.* 20 : 3.
Chr. 53–55   Just take *M·* in !
53–56   No mass for *M·* !
Un. 18–19   which alone enable *M·* to rebuke,
24– 3   From *m·* proceedeth all Mind,
Pan. 9–10   no other gods before *m·* ;" — *Exod.* 20 : 3.
'00. 5–20   no other gods before *m·* ;" — *Exod.* 20 : 3.
'02. 4–20   no other gods before *m·* ," — *Exod.* 20 : 3.
5–30   no other gods before *m·* ," — *Exod.* 20 : 3.
6–20   no other gods before *m·* ," — *Exod.* 20 : 3.
My. 5–14   no other gods before *m·* ," — *Exod.* 20 : 3.
64–13   no other gods before *m·* ," — *Exod.* 20 : 3.
131–26   prove *m·* now herewith, — *Mal.* 3 : 10.
132– 3   "Prove *m·* now herewith, — *Mal.* 3 : 10.
153–17   no other gods before *m·*" — *Exod.* 20 : 3.
221–19   no other gods before *m·*." — *Exod.* 20 : 3.
278– 9   no other gods before *m·*" — *Exod.* 20 : 3.
279–12   no other gods before *m·*" — *Exod.* 20 : 3.
282– 7   "Look unto *m·*, — *Isa.* 45 : 22.
364– 8   no other gods before *m·*." — *Exod.* 20 : 3.

meadow
Mis. 329–14   passes over mountain and *m·*,
Pul. 39–26   * Under the *m·* grass.

meadows
Mis. 330– 1   melting murmurs to merry *m·* ;
Pul. 48–12   * an intervale of beautiful *m·*
My. 186– 1   rocks, rills, mountains, *m·*,

meagre
Mis. 137– 5   I gave you a *m·* reception
My. 284– 2   honest efforts (however *m·*)
332– 6   * *m·* tribute for so noble an effort

meagrely
My. 243–12   meet *m·* the duties of half a dozen

meal
Mis. 166–23 hid in three measures of *m·*,
    171–24 *three measures of m·,— Matt.* 13 : 33.
    174–31 hid in three measures of *m·*,
    175– 5 The three measures of *m·*
  '02. 2–16 hid in three measures of *m·*,

mean
Mis. 26–32 to *m·* that good is evil,
    28–23 and must *m·* Spirit.
    38–29 if this is what you *m·*.
    70–10 *What did Jesus m· when he said*
    72–12 "What *m·* ye,— *Ezek.* 18 : 2.
    86–12 They either *m·* formations of
   171–14 This does not *m·* communing with
   191–19 By no . . . can this passage *m·*
   192– 2 we do not *m·* that man is God
   192– 4 we *m·* not that he is a personal devil,
   193– 2 Did Jesus *m·* what he said?
   193– 4 Jesus did *m·* all, and even more
   197–17 But it does *m·* so to understand the
   261–24 by mankind I *m·* mortals,
   375–32 * no *m·* attention to such matters,
  Ret. 8– 8 What do you *m·*?"
    50–19 By loyalty in students I *m·* this,
  Un. 21– 3 "the *m·* while accusing— *Rom.* 2 : 15.
  Rud. 1–10 *Do you m· by this that God is a*
    3–24 *do you m· that God has a finite*
    3–26 I *m·* the infinite and divine
    4–14 if by that term you *m·*
    8–25 By this I *m·* that mortal mind
  '00. 5–12 *m·* God, man, and divine Science.
  '01. 3–18 By this we *m·* Mind,
  My. 30–13 * sacrifices on *m·* order ;
    43–18 * "What *m·* ye by these— *Josh.* 4 : 6.
    43–31 * "What *m·* ye by these— *Josh.* 4 : 6.
    55– 8 * In the *m·* time,
    55–19 * In the *m·* time Sunday services
   232–31 Then should not "watching out" *m·*,
   233– 2 It must *m·* that.
   242–11 I do not *m·* that mortals are
   255– 7 I do not *m·* that minor officers
   307–14 * "I see now what you *m·*,
   323–25 * should *m·* to your older students much
   342–15 * not be understood that I *m·* weak,
   346–28 did not *m·* any man to-day on earth.

meandering
Ret. 27–22 *m·* midst pebbles and rocks,

meaneth
Mis. 28–21 What *m·* this Me,— Spirit, or matter?

meaning
clears the
  Mis. 75–20 clears the *m·*, and assists one to
dual
  Mis. 169–18 dual *m·* to every Biblical passage,
fullest
  Mis. 169–32 In their fullest *m·*,
her
  My. 334–17 * Nothing could be further from her *m·*
higher
  Hea. 16– 9 name of Christ with a higher *m·*,
  My. 114–26 learning the higher *m·* of this book
    241– 5 * higher *m·* of the Scriptures.
holy
  Po. 71–17 holy *m·* of their song.
infinite
  Mis. 25–17 gives God's infinite *m·* to mankind,
    100– 6 infinite *m·* of those words.
    188–23 up to its infinite *m·*,
  No. 22–12 infinite *m·* of the Word of Truth,
    34– 7 infinite *m·* and efficacy of Truth
inspired
  Mis. 190–19 found to include the inspired *m·*.
interrupts the
  Ret. 56– 9 interrupts the *m·* of the
its
  My. 226– 5 convey its *m·* in C. S.
kindred
  Pul. 66–23 * and others of kindred *m·*,
language and
  My. 238–10 His language and *m·* are wholly
magnitude of
  My. 133–28 knowledge with its magnitude of *m·*
magnitude of its
  '01. 30– 7 The magnitude of its *m·* forbids
mighty
  Pul. 84–21 * tell the story of its mighty *m·*
moral
  Mis. 248– 5 its moral *m·*, found in the
  No. 23–16 a literal and a moral *m·*.
my
  Mis. 66–22 Cynical critics misjudge my *m·*
  Rud. 13–17 elucidate my *m·*.
  No. 32–11 when I touch this subject my *m·* is
  My. 251–16 misapprehension of my *m·*
    264– 6 until mankind learn more of my *m·*

meaning
new
  Ret. 25– 5 a new *m·*, a new tongue.
  Pul. 35– 1 it came to me with a new *m·*,
of a word
  Un. 27– 1 inquiry as to the *m·* of a word
of divine metaphysics
  Mis. 68–19 *m·* of divine metaphysics,
of it all
  Mis. 158–13 The *m·* of it all, as now shown,
of pantheism
  Pan. 2–14 gives the *m·* of pantheism as a
of Spirit
  Hea. 11– 8 it would catch the *m·* of Spirit.
of the context
  Hea. 8– 9 perceive the *m·* of the context,
of the declaration
  Un. 30–24 understood the *m·* of the declaration
of the passage
  Mis. 75–25 bring out the *m·* of the passage.
   248– 4 the literal *m·* of the passage
of the Scriptures
  Mis. 25–14 original *m·* of the Scriptures,
  Man. 87–17 the higher *m·* of the Scriptures.
  Un. 29–22 the deep *m·* of the Scriptures
  My. 241– 5 * higher *m·* of the Scriptures.
of the term
  Mis. 53–19 *m·* of the term and of C. S.
   190–13 The *m·* of the term
   191– 6 changed the *m·* of the term,
of the text
  Mis. 197–12 comprehend the *m·* of the text,
of the word
  Ret. 74– 3 ignorant of the *m·* of the word
of those words
  Mis. 37–13 learn the *m·* of those words
   188–32 beheld the *m·* of those words
original
  Mis. 25–14 original *m·* of the Scriptures,
   74–16 into its original *m·*, Mind.
   77– 5 verb *believe* took its original *m·*,
Paul's
  Mis. 84–19 *Please explain Paul's m·*
right
  Mis. 76–22 you will find the right *m·*
spiritual
    (see **spiritual**)
their
  My. 99–28 * their existence points out their *m·*
true
  Mis. 171– 2 be wrested from its true *m·*
truer
  My. 64– 4 * took on a larger and truer *m·*.

  Mis. 25–23 from the Latin word *m·* all,
   100–12 that grasp neither the *m·* nor
   236–22 *m·* by this, Be not estranged from
  Pan. 2–11 Greek words *m·* "all" and "god."
  '01. 4–28 "divine Principle," *m·* divine Love,
  My. 22–29 * proper perspective of the *m·* of
   268–31 designation *man m·* woman as well,

meaningless
  Pan. 7–21 wherein theism seems *m·*,
  My. 235–26 *m·* commemoration of birthdays,

meanings
  Mis. 125–18 learn forever the infinite *m·*,
  Man. 62–22 to grasp the simpler *m·*
  '02. 4–23 in a few of their infinite *m·*,
  My. 202–16 infinite *m·*, endless hopes,
   221– 9 in His more infinite *m·*,
   231–14 its highest and infinite *m·*,
   262–32 reveals infinite *m·* and gives

means (noun)
and end
  My. 278– 5 this *m·* and end will be
and ends
  No. 21–14 for divine *m·* and ends.
  My. 259–29 merely temporary *m·* and ends.
   260–11 with human *m·* and ends,
and measure
  Mis. 154–11 *m·* and measure of His grace.
and methods
  Mis. 52– 9 beyond all human *m·* and methods.
   152–30 His spiritual *m·* and methods,
  Rud. 13–23 *m·* and methods of trustworthy
  My. 154–23 I welcome the *m·* and methods,
and understanding
  Ret. 48–29 ways, *m·*, and understanding,
better
  Mis. 268–12 better *m·* for healing the sick
by no
  Mis. 6–32 is by no *m·* the exception.
   43– 8 By no *m·* : C. S. is not
   79–11 by no *m·* the medium of imperfection,
   97–10 human mind is by no *m·* a desirable

means

by no
Mis.	296–16	they are by no *m·* identical
	296–18	is by no *m·* associated therewith.
	348–29	I have by no *m·* encouraged
	361–27	is by no *m·* a creative partner
Un.	43–12	by no *m·* spoken of myself,
Rud.	11–18	by no *m·* rests on the strength of
'*00.*	3–10	One's idol is by no *m·* his servant,
My.	213– 6	is by no *m·* a right of evil
	219– 7	I by no *m·* would pluck their plumes.

comprehensive
My. 45– 2 * comprehensive *m·* by you provided

earned the
My. 215–16 thus that I earned the *m·*

every
Ret. 21– 4 Every *m·* within my power
Pul. 2–20 by every *m·* in your power,

for sinning
Mis. 12–14 *m·* for sinning unseen

heaven-appointed
My. 221–19 no other heaven-appointed *m·*

human
Mis. 52– 9 beyond all human *m·* and methods.
My. 260–12 no partnership with human *m·*

justifies the
Mis. 282–24 and the end justifies the *m·* ;

lower
Rud. 8–26 If by such lower *m·* the health

material
Mis. 268–26 not adulterate . . . with material *m·*.
Ret. 47–11 shuns whatever involves material *m·*
My. 206– 3 with matter and material *m·*,

members and
Mis. 349–25 had sufficient members and *m·*

mental
Mis. 40–29 to kill his patient by mental *m·*,

methods, and
Mis. 135–17 God's methods and *m·* of healing,
313– 6 manners, morals, methods, and *m·*.

mistaken
My. 234–10 task themselves with mistaken *m·*.

monetary
My. 214–22 no monetary *m·* left wherewith to

no other
'*02.* 3– 1 used no other *m·* myself ;
Hea. 18–28 killed a man by no other *m·* than

of advancing
Mis. 42–19 our joys and *m·* of advancing

of Christianity
Mis. 269–23 proper *m·* of Christianity,

of Christian Science
Mis. 150–16 by *m·* of C. S.

of grace
Mis. 115–24 thus becomes a *m·* of grace.
127–25 Ofttimes the rod is His *m·* of grace ;
'*01.* 19– 2 a divinely appointed *m·* of grace

of healing
Mis. 135–17 God's methods and *m·* of healing,
'*01.* 34– 7 Christ's mode and *m·* of healing,

of knowing
My. 47– 6 * not had the *m·* of knowing the

of matter
Un. 33–27 or that mind sees by *m·* of matter.

of paying
Rud. 14–20 *m·* of paying for their tuition

of reconciling
My. 314–25 the *m·* of reconciling the couple.

of support
My. 312–15 * without *m·* of support.

of travel
My. 124–26 the rate of speed, the *m·* of travel,

other
Mis. 60– 9 after all other *m·* have failed.
270–11 other *m·* than those the Master used
282–25 when other *m·* have failed.
Pan. 6– 2 more effectual than all other *m·* ;

our only
My. 195–17 our only *m·* of adding to that talent

plenty of
'*00.* 2–17 he has plenty of *m·*,

provided the
'*01.* 29– 4 God has provided the *m·* for him

purchased the
Mis. 165–23 purchased the *m·* of mortals'

reproachable
Mis. 147–30 than attain it by reproachable *m·*.

some
Mis. 96–27 some *m·* by which it is not done.

spiritual
Mis. 152–30 faith in God and His spiritual *m·*
'*01.* 19–12 mixing material and spiritual *m·*,
26–12 from Christ's purely spiritual *m·*,
My. 357– 7 absolute opposite of spiritual *m·*,

such
Rud. 16– 5 will never undertake . . . by such *m·*.

means

supplied the
My. 23– 5 * and supplied the *m·* to consummate the

that build
My. 165–30 the *m·* that build to the heavens,

their
My. 30–18 * gave generously of their *m·*

to devise
My. 51– 1 * to devise *m·* to pay our pastor,

to promote
Mis. 288–30 *m·* to promote the ends of temperance ;

used
Mis. 69–22 with the *m·* used in their effort

violent
Mis. 182– 4 violent *m·* or material methods.

ways and
(*see* **ways**)

your
Mis. 90–18 be sure that your *m·* for doing good
115–15 Your *m·* of protection and defense

Mis.	45– 5	C. S., by *m·* of its Principle
	124– 7	by *m·* of matter, or the flesh,
	140–25	The diviner claim and *m·* for
	164–27	by *m·* of the lens of Science,
	175–29	by *m·* of both animal magnetism and
	222–30	ways, *m·*, and potency of Truth
	333–27	by *m·* of that which does not
	334–22	by *m·* of matter, or Mind?
Pul.	11– 7	whose *m·*, energies, and prayers
	20– 9	by *m·* of a statute of the State,
Rud.	7– 2	Not that all healing is . . . by any *m·* ;
	14–25	healed by *m·* of my instructions,
'*01.*	24– 6	by *m·* of invariable rules
My.	11– 9	* not tried to guide us by *m·* of
	38– 8	* By *m·* of a carefully trained corps of
	48–20	* a *m·* of spiritual development
	71– 4	* beautiful effects by *m·* of the bells.
	103–14	by *m·* of the Science which Jesus
	112– 1	by *m·* of the Principle of C. S.
	214–28	where were the *m·* with which to
	216– 7	civil, and educational *m·*,
	267–30	all the divine modes, *m·*, forms,
	277– 8	by *m·* of their wholesome tribunals,
	358– 8	is the *m·* whereby the conflict

means (verb)

Mis.	23–25	what C. S. *m·* by the word
	25–24	omniscience *m·* as well, all-science.
	28–24	the commandment *m·*,
	38–22	metaphysics at other colleges *m·*,
	47– 6	substance *m·* more than matter:
	68– 3	It *m·* more than mere disappearance
	75–28	*m·* that mortal man shall die;
	76–21	word *m·* the so-called soul
	89–27	This salvation *m·*:
	170–32	often *m·* spiritual power.
	197– 7	It *m·* a *full* salvation,
	197–13	It *m·* more than an opinion
	216–11	*m·* more than "hands off."
	216–15	Whatever his *nom de plume m·*,
	365–27	terms in which to express what it *m·*.
Ret.	59– 6	The word *Life* never *m·*
	59– 9	saying that addition *m·* subtraction
	88–25	The Lord's command *m·* this,
Pul.	84–20	* understanding of what it *m·*.
No.	28–26	soul *m·* sense and organic life;
Pan.	8–13	chapter sub-title
	9– 3	"Infinite Spirit" *m·* one God
	9– 4	term "spirits" *m·* more than
My.	24– 1	* What *m·* this edifice?
	72–24	* This *m·* that nearly two million
	239–23	Gender *m·* a kind.
	246–30	Magna Charta of C. S. *m·* much,
	249–20	I alone know what that *m·*.
	254–21	"The Magna Charta of C. S. *m·* much,
	261–22	chapter sub-title
	323–19	* all that your wonderful life . . . *m·*

meant

Mis.	46–22	significance of what the apostle *m·*
	73–26	*What is m· by regeneration?*
	77– 7	it *m·* to discern and consent to
	214–15	*m·*, all the way through,
	224–26	offended when no wrong is *m·*,
	255–13	what the apostle *m·* when he said :
Man.	64–20	*m·* nothing more than a tender term
Un.	32– 8	By matter is commonly *m·* mind,
Pul.	83–26	* to know what John on Patmos *m·*
Rud.	2–11	if by *person* is *m·* infinite Spirit.
My.	291– 5	*m·* more to him than a mere

meantime

Mis. xii– 4 *m·* interluding with loving thought
354– 1 *m·* declaring they "never disobey

meanwhile and **mean while**

Mis. 283–25   conscious, *m*·, that God worketh
     379–23   *m*·, assiduously pondering the
Ret.   21–10   *M*· he had served as a volunteer
Un.   21– 3   *m*· *w*· accusing — *Rom.* 2 : 15.
My.   55– 5   * *M*· it was felt that the church
     93–21   * attaching *m*· no importance to
     222–28   *M*·, they who name the name of

measurably

'00.   6–12   can *m*· understand C. S.,
     7–25   this attempt *m*· fails,

measure

Mis.   12–28   We should *m*· our love for God by
     48– 1   save as I *m*· its demonstrations as
     154–11   the means and *m*· of His grace.
     175–12   The *m*· of Life shall increase
     185–23   or to *m*· his manhood,
     222–20   the *m*· it has meted must be
     261–13   *m*· he has meted is measured to him
     298– 8   "With what *m*· ye mete, — *Matt.* 7 : 2.
     317–31   not the Spirit by *m*· — *John* 3 : 34
     324–19   Startled beyond *m*· at beholding
     325–21   amazed beyond *m*· that anybody
Ret.   44–27   This *m*· was immediately followed
Pul.   28–19   * equal *m*· to its use of the Bible.
     84–20   * have some *m*· of understanding
     85– 8   * In the *m*· in which she has
No.   45–16   woman to fill the highest *m*·
'01.   15–16   filling up the *m*· of wickedness
     32–20   They fill the ecclesiastic *m*·,
My.   21–19   * "good *m*·, pressed down, — *Luke* 6 : 38.
     36–22   * increase the *m*· of our devotion
     166–23   let our *m*· of time and joy be
     320–17   * but was in a *m*· in sympathy with

measured

Mis.   12–29   *m*· by our obedience to God,
     261–13   measure he has meted is *m*· to him
     298– 8   *m*· to you again." — *Matt.* 7 : 2.
Un.   29–20   can never be seen or *m*·
My.   85– 6   * handful of members *m*· its
     291– 7   heavy strokes, *m*· movements,

measureless

'02.   4–17   the *m*· rounds of eternity.

measures

Mis.   90–16   in your *m*·, obey the Scriptures,
     116–13   the *m*· of life's music
     166–23   hid in three *m*· of meal,
     171–24   *three m*· *of meal,* — *Matt.* 13 : 33.
     172–12   unerring Mind *m*· man,
     172–13   until the three *m*· be
     174–31   hid in three *m*· of meal,
     175– 5   The three *m*· of meal may
     297– 7   by legally coercive *m*·,
     396–20   Low, sad, and sweet, whose *m*· bind
Ret.   44–25   proper *m*· were adopted
Pul.   18– 4   Low, sad, and sweet, whose *m*· bind
'00.   11–16   for he *m*· himself against
'02.   2–16   hid in three *m*· of meal,
Po.   12– 3   Low, sad, and sweet, whose *m*· bind
My. 229–31   it *m*· the infinite against the

measuring

Mis.   x–14   mile-stones *m*· the distance,

meat

No.   v–11   leave the *m*· and take the
     43– 2   power of daily *m*· and drink.
My. 131–25   may be *m*· in mine house, — *Mal.* 3 : 10.

Mecca

My.   84–12   * Boston is the *M*· for . . . Scientists
     85–25   * *M*· of their love and duty.
     96– 9   * *M*· and the Hindu shrines,

mechanical accessories

(*see* **organ**)

mechanics

My. 226– 9   the inclined plane in *m*·,

Mechanics Building

Pul.   57–24   * not far from the big *M*· *B*·
My.   57– 3   * and in the *M*· *B*·,

mechanism

Mis. 354–18   right action of the mental *m*·,

meddle

Man.   93–20   not allowed in anywise to *m*·
No.   5–20   If . . . God, does not *m*· with it.
     40–21   is it right for one mind to *m*· with

meddlesomeness

Mis. 288– 1   which is virtually *m*·.

mediæval

'00.   4–13   greater than in the *m*· period ;

mediating

No.   31–17   *m*· between what is and is not,

mediation

Pul.   73– 7   * through the *m*· of her God.
My.   91– 5   * that spiritual and mystic *m*·

medical

aids
  Hea.   14–15   ignorance . . . are miserable *m*· aids.
attendant
  Mis.   89–13   *m*· attendant and friends
bill
  My. 327–15   * when a *m*· bill was proposed
bills
  Mis. 211–10   *m*· bills, class legislation,
charlatans
  Mis.   80– 7   *m*· charlatans in general,
college
  Mis. 382–22   charter for a metaphysical *m*· college,
discoveries
  Mis. 244–31   because of their *m*· discoveries?
examination
  My. 329– 7   * *m*· examination before a board
examiners
  My. 329– 7   * before a board of *m*· examiners.
faculty
  Mis.   80–11   will fight the *m*· faculty,
     243–26   *m*· faculty will tell you
  No.   2– 4   ostracized by the *m*· faculty,
  My.   4–18   both *m*· faculty and Christianity,
     175–13   intelligent *m*· faculty,
laws
  Mis.   80– 5   opposition to unjust *m*· laws.
league
  Mis.   79–29   joining any *m*· league
men
  Mis.   80–13   conscientious *m*· men,
practice
  '00.   13–19   Its *m*· practice included charms
  '01.   17–24   From my *m*· practice I had learned
  My. 107– 7   modern phase of *m*· practice,
practitioner
  Hea.   14–10   If you employ a *m*· practitioner,
prescription
  Mis. 210–23   and a *m*· prescription.
profession
  Mis. 378–19   taught her of his *m*· profession.
purposes
  Ret.   48–17   chartered . . . for *m*· purposes,
school
  Mis. 349–13   feasibility of entering a *m*· school ;
     349–18   He entered the *m*· school,
schools
  Mis. 348–30   to enter *m*· schools,
  Ret.   34– 5   an answer from the *m*· schools,
skill
  Mis.   29–22   that had defied *m*· skill.
statutes
  Mis.   79–28   *for violation of m*· *statutes*
system
  Mis.   80–31   to understand the *m*· system
systems
  Mis. 252– 3   *m*· systems of allopathy
therapeutics
  Pan.   4–27   drugs, hygiene, and *m*· therapeutics,
treatment
  Mis.   89– 9   under material *m*· treatment,
use
  '01.   18–17   If God created drugs for *m*· use,

medically

My.   97– 9   * those who were *m*· treated.

medication

My. 345–17   pellets without any *m*·

medicinal

Hea.   12– 1   contain no *m*· properties,

medicine

abjure
  My.   97– 8   * of the sick who abjure *m*·
and religion
  No.   44– 5   demonstration of *m*· and religion.
  '02.   2–17   ethics, *m*·, and religion,
  Peo.   5– 1   practice of *m*· and religion,
and theology
  My.   28–32   * aspect of *m*· and theology.
applies it
  Mis. 203–14   *m*· applies it physically,
art of
  Peo.   6–11   * "The art of *m*· consists in
Christendom and
  My.   4–13   put into Christendom and *m*·.
doses of
  Mis. 348–16   I tried several doses of *m*·,
dynamics of
  '01.   17–25   the dynamics of *m*· is Mind.
elevates
  My. 260–24   elevates *m*· to Mind :

medicine

experimented in
 Mis. 379–20 I had already experimented in *m·*
field of
 Mis. 366–18 imposition in the field of *m·*
god of
 '00. 13–18 Æsculapius, the god of *m·*,
gods of
 Peo. 4–24 Apollo and . . . the gods of *m·*,
grain of
 Hea. 13– 5 one hundredth part of a grain of *m·*
his
 Mis. 268–17 His *m·* is Mind
 '01. 18–10 Scientist's religion or his *m·*,
idolatry and
 '00. 13–23 school of . . . idolatry and *m·*.
imaginary
 Hea. 13–19 we resigned the imaginary *m·*
Jesus' only
 Mis. 25–22 Jesus' only *m·* was . . . Mind.
less
 Hea. 11–19 "The less *m·* the better,"
man's only
 My. 105– 3 man's only *m·* for mind and body
material
  (*see* **material**)
mental
 Mis. 252– 3 mental *m·* of divine metaphysics
 252– 4 Mental *m·* gains no potency by
methods of
 Ret. 33–23 material methods of *m·*,
Mind's
 Mis. 3–18 are not Mind's *m·*.
mode of
 Mis. 98–14 in a higher mode of *m·* ;
modes of
 Mis. 88–30 are opposite modes of *m·*.
 300–23 on drugs, . . . as modes of *m·*.
morals, or
 Mis. 284– 5 religion, morals, or *m·*,
new *régime* of
 Mis. 348–23 under this new *régime* of *m·*,
no
 Hea. 11–20 "until you arrive at no *m·*."
 13– 9 they have taken no *m·*,
nor surgery
 Ret. 24–13 neither *m·* nor surgery could reach,
of homœopathy
 '01. 18– 6 sneers . . . at the *m·* of homœopathy ;
of matter
 '01. 18– 8 the old-time *m·* of matter.
of Mind
 Mis. 252– 1 this *m·* of Mind is not necessarily
 348–24 found myself under . . . the *m·* of Mind,
 '01. 18– 7 *m·* of Mind is more honored
or drugs
 Pul. 72–17 * *m·* or drugs of any kind,
or religion
 Mis. 25–32 in philosophy, *m·*, or religion,
practice of
 Peo. 5– 1 theory and practice of *m·*
 10–10 regulating the practice of *m·*
 My. 190–11 metaphysical practice of *m·*
 340–15 on the practice of *m·* !
religion and
 Peo. 8– 1 Religion and *m·* must be dematerialized
 My. 221– 1 spirituality in religion and *m·*
 340–10 progress of religion and *m·*
religion or
 Mis. 260–10 potency, in religion or *m·*.
 My. 288–16 instrumentality in religion or *m·*
schools of
 Ret. 15–26 the popular schools of *m·*,
 Pul. 70–21 * philosophy and schools of *m·*,
 '01. 22–23 the differing schools of *m·*
 My. 245– 2 the approved schools of *m·*,
Science in
 My. 127– 2 Science in *m·*, in physics, and
Science of
 My. 221–14 natural, and divine Science of *m·*,
sure
 Mis. 252–27 with safe and sure *m·* ;
system of
 Mis. 81– 9 is the true system of *m·*.
 243–13 every system of *m·* claims more
 243–19 my system of *m·* is not generally
 My. 105–31 misrepresenting a system of *m·* which
systems of
 No. 4–18 beyond other systems of *m·*,
taking
 Pul. 72–30 * ever hear of Jesus' taking *m·*
their own
 Mis. 39–17 not afraid to take their own *m·*,
theology and
 No. 1–18 theology and *m·* of Jesus were one.

medicine

this
 Mis. 25–24 this *m·* is all-power ;
 39–18 for this *m·* is divine Mind ;
 252– 1 and this *m·* of Mind is
 '01. 24–10 * my having taken this *m·*
 Hea. 13– 7 There is a moral to this *m·* ;
to prepare the
 Hea. 12–20 To prepare the *m·* requires time and
triturations of
 My. 107–11 the same triturations of *m·*
true
 Mis. 233–20 for the practice of true *m·*,
use of
 My. 97– 6 * getting well without the use of *m·*.
worst form of
 Mis. 233– 4 will result in the worst form of *m·*.
your
 Mis. 241– 9 Use as your *m·* the great alterative,

 Mis. 53–11 Do you sometimes . . . use *m·*
 Man. 48– 9 towards religion, *m·*, the courts, or
 '01. 17–10 chapter sub-title
 19–13 either in *m·* or in religion,
 25– 8 A knowledge of philosophy and of *m·*,
 30–14 reform in religion and in *m·*,
 Hea. 14– 3 *M·* will not arrive at the science of
 15–21 He cannot reach, but *m·* can?
 Peo. 2– 4 practice of religion and of *m·*
 4–26 Systems of religion and of *m·*
 6– 4 * "*M·* is the science of guessing."
 My. 99– 6 * what doeth good like a *m·*,
 260–27 leaves hygiene, *m·*, ethics, . . . to God

medicine-man
 My. 152– 7 The *m·*, far lower in the scale of

medicines
 Mis. 33 25 It does away with all material *m·*,
 Ret. 34–11 It does away with all material *m·*,
 Pul. 69– 9 * He says they use no *m·*,

meditate
 Pul. 34–25 * withdrew from the world to *m·*,
 Po. 1–17 to *m·* on what it learns.

meditated
 Pul. 73– 9 * *m·* over His divine Word.

meditates
 Mis. 148– 1 *m·* evil against us in his heart.
 309–12 *m·* most on . . . spiritual substance

meditation
 Pul. 28– 3 * in solitude and *m·*,
 33–16 * certainly offer food for *m·*.

medium
 Mis. 70 11 by no means the *m·* of imperfection.
 132–22 through the *m·* of a newspaper ;
 163–21 *m·* of Mind, the hope of the race.
 248–17 that I am an infidel, . . . a *m·*
 No. 14– 3 If a spiritualist *m·* understood the
 Pan. 11–24 evil is not the *m·* of good,
 Hea. 6– 4 * "People say you are a *m·*,"
 6–11 they take pleasure in calling me a *m·*.
 6–18 Man thinks he is a *m·* of disease ;
 My. 313–20 I was not a *m·* for spirits.

mediumship
 Mis. 95–19 which spiritualists have miscalled *m·* ;
 No. 13–23 on the subject of *m·*,
 Hea. 6– 8 mental phenomenon named *m·*,

meek
 Mis. 1– 6 The *m·* Nazarene,
 130–29 the *m·* and loving, God anoints
 145–13 *m·* who "inherit the earth." — *Psal.* 37 : 11.
 152–20 pure in affection, the *m·* in spirit,
 189– 8 The *m·* Nazarene's steadfast and true
 393–18 In a beauty strong and *m·*
 400–22 Thee I seek,— Patient, *m·*,
 '00. 6–22 *m·* and loving disciple of Christ,
 '01. 26–19 the *m·* that inherit the earth ;
 '02. 16–21 The *m·* might, sublime patience,
 Po. 52– 2 In a beauty strong and *m·*
 69–10 Thee I seek,— Patient, *m·*,
 My. 41– 6 * It is a forever fact that the *m·* and lowly
 228–18 The *m·*, who sit at the feet of
 341–16 * 'Tis meet that man be *m·*."

meekest
 Mis. 163– 9 the *m·* man on earth.
 Po. 78–14 O *m·* of mourners,

meekly
 Mis. 17–13 *m·* bow before the Christ,
 111– 4 Faithfully, as *m·*, you have toiled
 127–10 mentally, *m·*, and importunately.
 155–10 While pressing *m·* on,
 232–15 *m·* to ascend the hill of Science,
 330–31 stoops *m·* before the blast ;
 369–19 *M·* we kneel at our Master's feet.

meekly

Hea.	19–23	bearing the cross *m·*
Po.	77–14	to Thee we'll *m·* bow,
My.	4–11	only as we follow truly, *m·*,
	18– 7	mentally, *m·*, and importunately.
	201–15	*m·* meet, mercifully forgive,

meekness

Mis.	1–18	*M·* heightens immortal attributes
	83–21	*m·* was as conspicuous as might.
	126–16	*m·*, honesty, and obedience of the
	130– 2	long-suffering, *m·*, charity, purity
	141–22	nobility of human *m·* rule this
	152–16	May *m·*, mercy, and love dwell
	154–28	justice, *m·*, mercy, purity, love.
	195–31	*m·*, purity, and love, informed by
	360– 1	*M·*, moderating human desire,
	372–31	true sense of *m·* and might.
Ret.	79– 9	in *m·*, in unselfish motives
	79–22	*M·* and temperance are the jewels of
Un.	5– 6	This *m·* will increase their
Rud.	17–15	*M·*, selflessness, and love
'02.	8–24	Love, purity, *m·*, coexist
	19–12	*M·* is the armor of a Christian,
My.	149– 9	*m·* of the Christ-principle ;
	161–30	Only he who learns through *m·*
	163– 4	to win through *m·* to might,
	194–15	It stands for *m·* and might,
	202– 4	faith, *m·*, and might of
	247–11	Christ is *m·* and Truth
	258–20	coronals of *m·*, diadems of love.

meet

Mis.	3–31	to *m·* sin, and uncover it ;
	4–18	adequate to *m·* the requirement.
	4–28	we *m·* with an expression of
	16–12	ability to *m·* them is from God ;
	39–22	who has more to *m·* than others
	42– 1	*do we m· those gone before?*
	42–17	If, before the change whereby we *m·*
	91– 9	it is to *m·* the demand,
	115–13	and *m·* the pressing need of a
	120–20	Association hereafter *m·* triennially :
	130–11	thinking it over, and how to *m·* it,
	134–10	*M·* together and *m· en masse,*
	139– 3	to *m·* again in three years.
	147– 7	*m·* in unity, preferring one another,
	160– 9	*m·* and mingle in bliss supernal.
	172– 7	let us *m·* and defeat the claims of
	176–27	prepared to *m·* and improve them,
	256–16	To *m·* the old impediment,
	263–10	power, and peace *m·* all human needs
	281–18	So, whatever we *m·* that is hard
	320–20	It doth *m·* the antagonism of error ;
	324–24	to go on and to *m·* the Stranger.
	326–23	first, to *m·* with joy his own,
	351– 2	and *m·* the mental malpractice,
	384– 3	When two hearts *m·*,
	386–21	With thee to *m·*.
	388–12	Speaks kindly when we *m·* and part.
Man.	96–12	is unable to *m·* the expense,
Ret.	48–23	to *m·* the demand of the age
	52–10	To *m·* the broader wants of humanity,
	76–14	*m·* on the stairs which lead up to
Pul.	8–16	vied with their parents to *m·* the
	39– 1	* that all *m·* on common ground
No.	37–17	to *m·* and master it
	39–28	What but silent prayer can *m·* the
	42– 7	to *m·* a mental want.
'00.	12–13	elders travelled to *m·* St. Paul,
'01.	1–10	To-day you *m·* to commemorate
	17– 8	*m·* the sad sinner on his way
'02.	2– 9	Truth makes haste to *m·* and to
	2–29	we shall *m·* again, never to part.
	13– 1	to *m·* the expenses involved.
Hea.	5–21	to *m·* the responsibility of our own
Peo.	9– 8	or *m·* the demands of Love.
Po.	7–12	Speaks kindly when we *m·* and part.
	36– 2	When two hearts *m·*,
	50– 6	With thee to *m·*.
My.	24–27	* *m·* the needs of The Mother Church
	28– 5	will *m·* every human need,"
	47– 3	* It seems *m·* at this time,
	56– 8	* inadequate to *m·* the need,
	73–10	will *m·* every human need."
	85– 9	* its congregations *m·* in Europe
	120– 5	that you and I may *m·* in truth
	125–10	chosen one to *m·* the Goliaths.
	131–20	Where God is we can *m·*,
	201–16	So let us meekly *m·*,
	206–27	*m·* to be partakers— *Col.* 1 : 12.
	214– 5	will *m·* every human need.
	214–25	*m·* my own current expenses.
	217–22	*m·* this negation more readily
	224– 3	*m·* the exigencies of the hour
	243–12	*m·* meagerly the duties of
	249– 6	*M·* dispassionately the raging

meet

My.	285– 6	time requisite to *m·* with you ;
	290–24	holy call you again to *m·*.
	339–26	not sufficient to *m·* his demand.
	341–16	* 'Tis *m·* that man be meek."
	351–16	*m·* in that hour of Soul

meeting

adjourned

Mis.	156–13	merge the adjourned *m·*

after the

Ret.	14–30	After the *m·* was over they came

annual

Mis.	147– 4	annual *m·* has convened,
Man.	25–11	annual *m·* of the Church.
	26– 8	annual *m·* held for this purpose,
	56–18	annual *m·* of the C. S. Board
	56–21	annual *m·* of the Church.
	98–20	in annual *m·* assembled.
My.	9–21	who at our last annual *m·*
	11–30	* pledge of the annual *m·*
	16– 4	* report . . . made to the annual *m·*,
	20–25	* the communion and annual *m·*
	22– 7	* gatherings at the annual *m·* ;
	22– 7	* the annual *m·* in June, 1902,
	23–15	* pledged at the annual *m·*, 1902,
	27– 6	our annual *m·* and communion
	38–28	* annual *m·* of The First Church
	39–22	* to preside at an annual *m·*
	42–21	* our first annual *m·* held in the
	44–25	* members . . . in annual *m·* assembled,
	49–29	* at the annual *m·*, December 1
	57– 9	* annual *m·* of the same year
	57–14	* first annual *m·* of the church
	82–16	* sessions of the annual *m·*,
	125– 4	annual *m·* is a grave guardian.
	142–27	annual *m·* of The Mother Church
	154–16	At this, your first annual *m·*,
	172–24	* annual *m·* of The Mother Church
	173–11	annual *m·* of The Mother Church,
	361–21	* by action at its annual *m·*

business

My.	8–25	* in annual business *m·* in Boston,
	23–19	* in annual business *m·* assembled,
	49–15	* business *m·* of the church
	65– 3	* largest church business *m·*

call a

Man.	28–20	shall immediately call a *m·*
	53– 4	immediately to call a *m·*,

calling a

Man.	57– 9	calling a *m·* of the members

Church

Man.	76–11	report at the annual Church *m·*

church

My.	76–20	* annual church *m·* in Boston,

dispersed a

Po.	vi–14	* *dispersed a m· of the*

evening

Man.	47–23	at the Wednesday evening *m·*.
My.	134–21	* At the Wednesday evening *m·*

every

My.	90– 2	* should be filled at every *m·*

first

Pul.	30–26	* first *m·* held on April 12, 1879.
	31– 9	* my first *m·* with her
My.	49–32	* first *m·* of this little church

for greetings

My.	142–17	merge into a *m·* for greetings.

grand

Mis.	275–22	at the grand *m·* in Chicago

largest

My.	80–30	* where the largest *m·* was held,

last

Mis.	132– 2	vote passed, at your last *m·*,
	350–17	This proved to be our last *m·*.

main

My.	81–11	* announced at the main *m·*

members

My.	139–18	the Executive Members' *m·*,

memorial

My.	289–24	to attend the memorial *m·*

of the Board

Man.	50–18	a *m·* of the Board of Directors
Ret.	48–12	At a special *m·* of the Board

of the church

(see **church**)

of this Church

Man.	66– 7	If at a *m·* of this Church
	66–16	brought before a *m·* of this Church,

one

Man.	60– 5	One *m·* on Sunday during the

open the

Mis.	314– 7	open the *m·* by reading the hymns

places for

My.	54–29	* consideration of places for *m·*

meeting

previous
My. 49–18 * received at the previous *m*,
49–22 * "The minutes of the previous *m*

public
My. 59–16 * first public *m* in the little hall

said
Man. 57–16 before he can call said *m*.

special
Ret. 48–12 At a special *m* of the Board
My. 289–11 special *m* of its First Members
333– 7 * a special *m* was convened

that
Mis. 350–15 subject given out at that *m* was,
Pul. 31–11 * which that *m* inaugurated

their
My. 54– 7 * had their *m* Easter Sunday

this
Man. 18–18 At this *m* twenty others of
My. 49–21 * An interesting record of this *m*
49–31 * at this *m* Mrs. Eddy
50–13 * "The tone of this *m*
131–19 this *m* is very joyous to me.
148–23 what is being recorded of this *m*

vestry
Ret. 15–21 Our last vestry *m* was

Mis. 135–24 Letter read at the *m* of
310–22 upon a *m* being called,
385– 9 poem
Man. 17– 8 At a *m* of the . . . Association,
82–14 a *m* held for this purpose
89– 4 *m* of the C. S. Board of Directors
Ret. 14– 3 *m* was held for the examination of
16– 3 When the *m* was over, two ladies
43–23 At a *m* of the . . . Association,
47–12 In view of all this, a *m* was called
52–23 at its *m* in Cleveland, Ohio,
Pul. 68–25 * *m* held at the present location
'02. 20–23 *m* you all *occasionally*
Po. page 48 poem
65– 4 A *m* with loved ones
My. 21–23 * joy in *m* very many of them
39– 3 * *m* was opened by the President,
49–12 * *m* of those who were interested
49–20 * *m*, with Mrs. Eddy in the chair.
49–26 * At a *m* held October 19, 1879,
53–15 * At a *m* October 22, 1883,
83–21 * *m* of the Christian Scientists
124–11 heart *m* heart across continents
143– 1 I will attend the *m*,
174– 5 proved an ideal *m* place.
207–20 *m* and mastering evil
289–27 *m* to be held in the capital

Meetings and meetings

Mis. 136–23 close your *m* for the summer ;
148–25 at your Friday evening *m*.
350–11 no transactions at those *m* which
Man. 31–18 and the Wednesday evening *m*.
38–13 semi-annual *m* held for this
51–25 shall be present at *m* for the
56– 7 heading
56– 9 REGULAR AND SPECIAL *m*.
56–10 Annual *M*.
56–11 *m* of The Mother Church
56–17 *M* of Board of Directors.
56–22 *m* for electing candidates
57– 3 properly come before these *m*,
57– 6 Special *m* may be held
61– 3 Overflow *M*.
76–21 shall hold quarterly *m*
84–22 for more frequent *m*.
86–14 *m* of their association.
Pul. 28–28 * held its *m* in Chickering Hall,
79–14 * notices of C. S. *m*,
My. 53–10 * voted that the church hold its *m*
57– 1 * *m* were overcrowded
69– 6 * *m* presenting an oval . . . appearance
73–16 * June *m* of The Mother Church
79–24 * chapter sub-title
79–29 * testimony *m* that marked the
80–10 * *M* were held in the extension
80–16 * At each of the *m* the introductory
80–25 * it took ten *m* to
81–27 * at the *m* of the Scientists,
121– 4 holding our semi-annual church *m*,
143– 2 pray that God directs your *m*

meets

Mis. 45–16 supply invariably *m* demand,
201– 2 *m* the immortal demands of Truth.
202– 5 * where the good man *m* his fate
207– 2 heart *m* heart reciprocally blest,
323–14 *m* and masters their . . . attacks
Pul. 74– 7 * *m* every Sunday in Hodgson Hall,
Peo. 3–16 Truth *m* the old material thought

meets

My. 180–16 C. S. *m* error with Truth,
188–32 and *m* the warmest wish of men

Mehitable (Huntoon)
(*see* **Huntoon**)

melancholy
Mis. 391– 7 That *m* mortals Will count their
Po. 38– 6 That *m* mortals Will count their

Melanchthon
Hea. 2–12 Said the more gentle *M* :
2–13 * Adam is too strong for young *M*."

mellow
Ret. 4–16 in the *m* hues of autumn,
Pul. 62–15 * tone . . . being rich and *m*.

mellower
Ret. 18– 4 While cactus a *m* glory receives
Po. 63–12 While cactus a *m* glory receives

melodeon
My. 59–21 * *m* on which my wife played,

melody
Mis. 330– 2 make *m* through dark pine groves.
390– 8 Gives back some maiden *m*,
Pul. 11– 3 making *m* more real,
'00. 11–20 human tone has no *m* for me.
Po. 34– 2 soul of *m* by being blest
55– 9 Gives back some maiden *m*,
66–11 No *m* sweeps o'er its strings !

melt
Mis. 145–19 names may *m* into one,
156– 9 when the mist shall *m* away
264– 9 they *m* into darkness.
320–26 to pierce the darkness and *m* into dawn.
No. 28– 4 *m* in the fervent heat of suffering,
Peo. 10– 6 and *m* into nothing under the
Po. 23–22 Bid error *m* away !
65–18 and death like mist *m* away,

melted
Mis. 176–21 *m* away in the fire of love
306– 1 * material to be *m* into the bell,
360–16 *m* away the cloud of false
Ret. 15– 2 clergyman's heart also *m*,
31–29 philosophy and religion *m*,
My. 194–14 *m* into the radiance of His

melting
Mis. 205– 5 *m* away the shadows called sin,
329–30 The brooklet sings *m* murmurs
300–16 To *m* murmurs ye have stirred
Po. 55–17 To *m* murmurs ye have stirred

melts
Un. 58–12 hypocrite *m* in fervent heat,

member (*see also* **member's**)

another
Man. 50–17 another *m* in good standing
51– 9 Pastor Emeritus or another *m*,
52–23 against the interests of another *m*,
54– 1 upon complaint by another *m*,
85– 7 pupils of another *m*

any
Man. 28–25 duty of any *m* of this Church,
51– 8 Any *m* who shall unjustly
95– 6 may call on any *m* of this

calls a
Man. 48– 3 calls a *m* to bear testimony

complaint of a
Man. 53– 2 complaint of a *m* for her

dismiss a
Man. 26–24 majority vote . . . shall dismiss a *m*.
52–18 dismiss a *m* from the Church.

disqualifies a
Man. 41–14 disqualifies a *m* for office

each
Mis. 92–22 require each *m* to own a copy
305–24 * Each *m* of the society
Man. 78– 1 demand that each *m* thereof
92– 7 I recommend that each *m*
93–15 Each *m* shall mail to the Clerk
Ret. 84–11 each *m* should own a copy
My. 165–18 Thus may each *m* of this church

every
Mis. 305–12 * circular is sent to every *m*
Man. 33– 1 every *m* of The Mother Church,
41–20 every *m* of this Church
42– 5 duty of every *m* of this Church
44–12 Every *m* of The Mother Church
44–17 privilege and duty of every *m*,
59– 6 duty of every *m* of this Church,
'01. 31–17 every *m* of my church
My. 132–17 every *m* of this large church.
279–22 I request that every *m* of

full
Man. 39– 8 A full *m* or a probationary

member

name of the
Man. 53– 5   drop forever the name of the *m·*
no
Man. 43– 5   No *m·* shall use written formulas,
    53–18   No *m·* shall enter a complaint
    87–12   No *m·* of this Church shall
My. 98–21   * no *m·* of the church anywhere,
of a branch
Man. 54– 9   *m·* of a branch of this Church
    112– 8   not a *m·* of a branch church,
of another Church
Man. 34–18   receive a *m·* of another Church
of any church
Man. 45–16   not be a *m·* of any church whose
of both
Man. 54–26   *m·* of both The Mother Church and
    74– 3   shall not be a *m·* of both
offending
Man. 65–19   removal of the offending *m·*
of her Church
Man. 67– 8   to a *m·* of her Church
of one branch
Man. 73–27   may be a *m·* of one branch
of the Board
Man. 73–19   *m·* of the Board of Lectureship may
    95–15   *m·* of the Board may lecture for a
of the church
Mis. 129– 2   If a *m·* of the church is inclined
Pul. 73–17   * prominent *m·* of the church.
My. 98–21   * no *m·* of the church anywhere,
of the family
Mis. 89– 4   to care for a *m·* of the family,
of The First Church
Man. 45–14   A *m·* of The First Church
    65– 4   A *m·* of The First Church
    92–19   not a *m·* of The First Church
of The Mother Church
Man. 33– 1   every *m·* of The Mother Church,
    34– 5   become a *m·* of The Mother Church,
    37– 1   *m·* of The Mother Church shall not
    42–25   *m·* of The Mother Church who
    44–12   *m·* of The Mother Church shall pay
    45–19   *m·* of The Mother Church is not
    46– 7   *m·* of The Mother Church shall not
    46–19   *m·* of The Mother Church shall not,
    48–11   *m·* of The Mother Church shall not
    49– 7   *m·* of The Mother Church who
    49–23   If a *m·* of The Mother Church shall
    52– 4   against a *m·* of The Mother Church,
    53–23   If a *m·* of The Mother Church
    54– 8   If a *m·* of The Mother Church
    73–26   *m·* of The Mother Church may be a
My. 223–21   from a *m·* of The Mother Church
    279–22   every *m·* of The Mother Church
of this Board
Man. 95– 6   any *m·* of this Board
    95–11   a *m·* of this Board of Lectureship
of this Church
Man. 28–25   duty of any *m·* of this Church,
    29– 9   a *m·* of this Church
    41–20   duty of every *m·* of this Church
    42– 5   duty of every *m·* of this Church
    43–14   A *m·* of this Church shall not
    43–21   A *m·* of this Church shall neither
    44– 8   A *m·* of this Church shall not
    46– 2   *m·* of this Church who claims
    47– 4   If a *m·* of this Church has a patient
    48– 7   A *m·* of this Church shall not
    50– 8   A *m·* of this Church shall not
    50–14   If a *m·* of this Church shall
    52–21   If a *m·* of this Church shall,
    53– 8   If a *m·* of this Church were
    54–19   If a *m·* of this Church,
    55–21   If a *m·* of this Church is found
    59– 6   duty of every *m·* of this Church,
    67–11   A *m·* of this Church shall not
    68– 2   *m·* of this Church at least three years
    69–16   appoint a proper *m·* of this Church
    72– 4   A *m·* of this Church who obeys its
    85– 7   pupils of another *m·* of this Church
    85–12   A *m·* of this Church shall not
    87– 2   nor a *m·* of this Church
    87–12   No *m·* of this Church shall advise
    92– 7   recommend that each *m·* of this Church
one
My. 230–10   Its rules apply not to one *m·* only,
probationary
Man. 39– 8   A full member or a probationary *m·*,
said
Man. 43– 3   name of said *m·* to be dropped
    50–20   and said *m·* exonerated, . . . or
    52– 5   *if said m· belongs to no branch*
    54–22   said *m·* shall immediately be
    56– 4   if said *m·* persists in this offense,

member

that
Man. 53–10   that *m·* should be excommunicated.
    56– 3   admonish that *m·* according to
this
Man. 41–16   renders this *m·* liable to discipline
weak
Man. 55–15   this weak *m·* shall not be
who leaves her
Man. 68– 5   A *m·* who leaves her in less time

Mis. 306–18   * *m·* of the above organization,
Man. 37– 5   A *m·* who violates this By-Law
    39–17   If a *m·* has been twice notified
    50–22   A *m·* who is found violating any
    52–10   letter of inquiry to the *m·*
    52–11   If a *m·* is found guilty
    53–11   If a *m·*, . . . shall trouble her
    65– 3   A *M·* not a Leader.
    68– 4   shall be the duty of the *m·*
    94–20   A *m·* shall neither resign nor
Ret. 19–11   being a *m·* in Saint Andrew's Lodge,
    89–14   or to a *m·* who had been away
My. 59– 2   * *m·* of your *first* class in Lynn,
    174–23   *m·* of the Congregational Church
    310– 6   *m·* of the New Hampshire Legislature,
    330–23   being a *m·* in St. Andrew's Lodge,
    335– 8   * faithful as a *m·* and officer

member's

Mis. 129–12   drop this *m·* name from the
Man. 46–21   payment for said *m·* practice,

members *(see also members')*

active
Man. 73–17   vote of, the active *m·* present,
actual
Pul. 55–29   * actual *m·* of different congregations
all
Man. 90– 1   All *m·* of this class must
among the
Man. 66– 8   shall arise among the *m·*
Pul. 56– 6   * among the *m·* of all the churches
assembled
My. 76–20   * pledged by the *m·* assembled
become
Mis. 310–20   and to become *m·* of it,
Man. 45– 9   shall not hereafter become *m·* of
    73–15   become *m·* of the organization
beloved
My. 118– 2   beloved *m·* of my church
Church
Man. 18–14   students and Church *m·* met
    75–18   Church *m·* own the aforesaid
    98–20   Church *m·* in annual meeting
Pul. 29–26   * heading
church
Man. 51–26   complaints against church *m·* ;
My. 74– 6   * numbers of belated church *m·*
    76–11   * church *m·* and their friends
    170– 4   in the request of my church *m·*
dear
My. 122–12   The deportment of its dear *m·*
    171– 1   these dear *m·* of my church :
    254–15   this class and its dear *m·*.
    302–27   dear *m·* wanted to greet me
devout
Mis. 249–13   devout *m·* of evangelical churches
distant
My. 140–15   * need not debar distant *m·*
    140–26   not prevent its distant *m·* from
distinguished
'00.   7–10   distinguished *m·* of the bar
duties of
Man. 64–10   heading
errors of the
Man. 55– 3   errors of the *m·* of their local church ;
five
Man. 26–20   Directors shall consist of five *m·*.
following
My. 136–13   following *m·* constitute the Board
forty thousand
My. 135–18   about forty thousand *m·*,
four thousand
Pul. 30– 8   * numbers now four thousand *m·* ;
    55–25   * now over four thousand *m·*.
    77–12   * loving hands of four thousand *m·*.
    78–11   * loving hands of four thousand *m·*.
greetings from
My. 259– 9   * Christmas greetings from *m·*
handful of
My. 85– 6   * and a mere handful of *m·*
in Mother Church
Man. 52– 3   *M·* in Mother Church Only.
its
Mis. 80– 6   obligates its *m·* to give
    120–21   many of its *m·* reside a long

members

its
Man.	45– 3	occupation for all its *m*.
	76–18	Its *m*. shall be appointed
	102– 8	supply a vacancy of its *m*.
Ret.	44–22	from the danger to its *m*.
My.	vii– 5	* its *m*. can so protect their
	100–14	* its *m*. are numbered by thousands
	162–27	May He increase its *m*.,
	195–27	in the hearts of its *m*.
	339– 1	The purpose of its *m*. is to

its own
Man.	55– 7	discipline its own *m*.,
	99–11	not . . . confined to its own *m*.

leading
Pul.	72– 5	* a few of the leading *m*.

local
Man.	59–21	local *m*. of The Mother Church
My.	21–20	* The local *m*., who have always

loyal
Man.	79– 4	not less than three loyal *m*.
	109– 3	Loyal *m*. of The Mother Church are
Ret.	53– 1	presenting to its loyal members

majority of the
Pul.	56– 8	* a majority of the *m*. are

many
Pan.	3–25	* are so many members."

new
My.	50–25	* two new *m*. were added

number of
Pul.	67–20	* there is a large number of *m*.

of a church
Mis.	90–23	*m*. of a church not organized

of branch churches
Man.	54–25	*M*. of Branch Churches.
My.	359– 4	with the *m*. of branch churches.

officious
Man.	45–19	Officious *M*.

of her church
My.	144– 1	* letter to the *m*. of her church
	172– 9	* to the *m*. of her church,

of her household
My.	354–27	* *m*. of her household were with her

of my Church
My.	27– 2	To the beloved *M*. of my Church,

of my church
My.	118– 2	beloved *m*. of my church
	171 1	these dear *m*. of my church :
	173– 7	to the *m*. of my church,
	280–16	request that the *m*. of my church

of my household
My.	143 11	by the *m*. of my household

of our Board
My.	125–12	All honor to the *m*. of our Board

of that body
Ret.	13– 3	*m*. of that body for a half-century.

of that faith
Pul.	75–20	* by which the *m*. of that faith

of the Board
Man.	29–15	salary of the *m*. of the Board of
My.	125–19	*m*. of the Board of Education,
	338–15	*m*. of the Board of Lectureship

of the Church
Man.	38–19	*m*. of the Church of Christ,
My.	51– 5	* *m*. of the Church of Christ,
	51–28	* *m*. of The Church of Christ,

of the church
(see **church**)

of the College
Man.	90–13	teacher and *m*. of the College class

of the Committees
Man.	65–12	*m*. of the Committees on Publication,

of the community
No.	3–21	to be safe *m*. of the community.

of the faculty
Man.	73– 9	*m*. of the faculty, instructors, or

of The Mother Church
Mis.	120–22	they are *m*. of The Mother Church
	251– 2	chapter sub-title
Man.	30– 4	must be *m*. of The Mother Church.
	32–18	shall be *m*. of The Mother Church.
	36– 1	or from *m*. of The Mother Church,
	37–22	*M*. of The Mother Church.
	37–23	Only *m*. of The Mother Church are
	40– 6	acts of the *m*. of The Mother Church.
	45– 5	duty of the *m*. of The Mother Church
	45– 7	*m*. of The Mother Church shall not
	45–18	*m*. of The Mother Church.
	48–18	*m*. of The Mother Church, nor
	51–23	excommunicate *m*. of The Mother Church.
	59–21	local *m*. of The Mother Church
	60–15	*m*. of The Mother Church.
	73– 2	four . . . are *m*. of The Mother Church.
	77–20	of the *m*. of The Mother Church,
	79– 4	loyal *m*. of The Mother Church,
	87– 8	*M*. of The Mother Church who are

members

of The Mother Church
Man.	92–15	Not *M*. of The Mother Church.
	109– 3	Loyal *m*. of The Mother Church
	109– 9	and are *m*. of The Mother Church.
	110– 7	*m*. of The Mother Church will be
My.	9–19	To the *M*. of The Mother Church :
	13–16	that the *m*. of The Mother Church,
	19–28	of the *m*. of The Mother Church,
	20–24	* *m*. of The Mother Church at the
	44–23	* The *m*. of The Mother Church,
	64–26	* *m*. of The Mother Church before men.

of this Board
Man.	51–24	Only the *m*. of this Board shall

of this Church
Man.	18–20	were elected *m*. of this Church,
	29–14	suitable *m*. of this Church to fill
	38–18	been *m*. of this Church,
	40–11	*m*. of this Church should daily
	42–15	*m*. of this Church shall neither
	44–24	*M*. of this Church shall not
	46–12	*M*. of this Church shall hold
	47–24	While *m*. of this Church do not
	53–15	*M*. of this Church shall not
	57– 9	meeting of the *m*. of this Church
	65– 6	by *m*. of this Church,
	66–23	*M*. of this Church shall not report
	67–17	*M*. of this Church who turn their
	76–17	consist of three *m*. of this Church
	82–16	*M*. of this Church who practise
	92–22	persons who are *m*. of this Church
	97–19	injustices done . . . *m*. of this Church

of this Committee
Man.	79– 8	While the *m*. of this Committee

of your church
My.	23–17	* The *m*. of your church,
	36– 8	* The *m*. of your church

older
Mis.	311–11	some of the older *m*. are not

other
Pul.	59–23	* other *m*. of the C. S. Board

privilege of
Man.	73– 7	Privilege of *M*.

return of
Mis.	310–12	letters relative to the return of *m*.

strayed
Man.	85– 4	Caring for Pupils of Strayed *M*.

such
Man.	85–18	Such *m*. who have not been

sufficient
Mis.	349–25	When the church had sufficient *m*.

ten thousand
My.	125–23	a church of ten thousand *m*.

thirty thousand
My.	172–15	church of over thirty thousand *m*. ;

those
Man.	68–13	Those *m*. whom she teaches
	82–18	excepting those *m*. who are

three
Man.	36–21	recommendation signed by three *m*.
	76–17	consist of three *m*. of this Church
	88– 7	consisting of three *m*.,
	102– 5	of not less than three *m*.,

twenty-four thousand
My.	8–10	* church of twenty-four thousand *m*.

twenty-six
Man.	18– 4	the *m*., twenty-six in number,
Ret.	16–17	the *m*., twenty-six in number,
	44– 6	*m*., twenty-six in number,
Pul.	30–27	* It opened with twenty-six *m*.,
	38– 1	* was founded with twenty-six *m*.,
	67–28	* founded . . . with twenty-six *m*.,

were asked
My.	96–25	* *m*. were asked to quit giving.

were invited
My.	96–19	* *M*. were invited to contribute

women
My.	30–14	* devoted women *m*.,

Mis.	131–28	*m*. of the C. S. Board of Directors
	135–26	*M*. OF THE CHRISTIAN SCIENTISTS'
	136–26	*m*. coming from a distance will
	138–21	*m*. of the National . . . Association,
	138–22	*m*. of students' organizations.
Man.	17– 4	*m*. of evangelical churches,
	18–19	*m*. of her former Church were
	26–24	*M*. shall neither report the
	38–17	*M*. who once Withdrew.
	39– 7	*M*. once Dismissed.
	40– 3	GUIDANCE of *m*.
	42–19	*M*. will not intentionally or
	51–11	*m*. who are in good . . . standing
	57–14	for which the *m*. are to convene.
	59–10	*M*. shall also instruct their pupils
	68–10	*M*. thus serving the Leader shall
	73– 7	*M*. in good standing

members
Man.	73–13	*m·* in good standing
	93– 5	*m·* of which shall be elected annually
Ret.	44–11	my church increased in *m·*,
Pul.	27–10	* that the *m·* strongly insist upon.
	30– 1	* *m·* of their own families,
	41–13	* *m·* of the denomination
	47– 7	* *m·* of this fast-increasing faith.
	71– 2	* eight hundred of the *m·* are
	76–26	* *m·* of The First Church of Christ,
	77–25	* *M·* of The First Church of Christ,
'02.	1– 6	Two thousand . . . *m·*
	1– 9	twenty-four thousand . . . *m·* ;
My.	16–13	* *m·* of the C. S. Board
	18–27	* by the *m·* of the C. S. Board
	20–30	* ask the *m·* to contribute
	30–10	* devotion of the *m·* to their faith,
	49–10	* *m·* extended a unanimous invitation
	56–25	* *m·* of which had formerly been
	62–27	* *m·* of the business committee,
	65– 5	* *m·* of The First Church of Christ,
	72– 8	* *m·* of the titled aristocracy
	83– 6	* *m·* of the local . . . committee
	83–30	* the readiness of the *m·* to
	95– 6	* by *m·* who represent the
	155–18	the *m·* of this dear church
	157– 3	* *m·* of the Concord church
	164–16	*m·* of which not only possess a
	363–19	chapter sub-title

members'
Man.	59–20	The Local *M·* Welcome.

Membership
(see **Church Membership**)

membership
Mis.	x–25	a certificate of *m·* made out to
	278–30	gradually withdrawing from active *m·*
Man.	34– 3	QUALIFICATIONS FOR *m·*.
	34–21	until that *m·* is dissolved.
	35– 6	may be admitted to *m·* with The
	35– 9	APPLICATIONS FOR *m·*.
	35–11	Applications for *m·* with The
	35–18	Applicants for *m·* who have not
	36– 5	Applications for *m·* with The
	36–18	endorse their applications for *m·*
	36–23	admit said applicant to *m·*.
	36–25	All applications for *m·*
	37– 3	countersign an application for *m·*
	37– 8	If an application for *m·*
	38– 1	to approve for *m·* individuals who
	38– 9	Applicants for *m·* in this Church,
	38–16	PROBATIONARY *m·*.
	39– 2	make application for *m·*
	39– 5	shall be received into full *m·*,
	39–13	eligible to probationary *m·*
	45–14	Forbidden *M·*.
	46–23	to have his name removed from *m·*.
	51– 6	dropped from the roll of Church *m·*.
	51–22	has power to . . . remove from *m·*,
	53– 6	from the roll of Church *m·*.
	54– 6	suspended . . . from Church *m·*.
	54–15	branch church's list of *m·*
	54–24	from *m·* in The Mother Church.
	55–15	repentant . . . and retaining his *m·*,
	56–22	for electing candidates to *m·*
	71– 7	nor written on applications for *m·*
	73– 3	This *m·* shall include
	73–24	shall not confine their *m·* to
Ret.	14– 4	examination of candidates for *m·*,
Pul.	30–23	* entire *m·* of Christian Scientists
	66– 5	* with a *m·* of only twenty-six,
	71– 1	* *m·* of four thousand,
'00.	1–12	a *m·* of over sixteen thousand
My.	9– 2	* large accessions to their *m·*.
	23– 3	* total *m·* of The Mother Church
	49– 7	* the reading of its *m·*,
	56–20	* the *m·* and the attendance
	57–15	* *m·* at that date was 1,545.
	57–16	* *m·* of this church to-day is
	57–24	* show a *m·* of 41,944.
	76–29	* a *m·* of twenty-six persons.
	85– 1	* character of the assembling *m·*,
	91– 1	* immense *m·* of the body
	97–23	* and the zeal of its *m·*.
	141–24	*m·* includes forty-eight thousand
	148–17	*m·* of seventy-four communicants,
	182– 7	a *m·* of thirty years
	182–18	large *m·* and majestic cathedral.
	242–19	relating to . . . Mother Church *m·*,
	311–17	date of my first church *m·*,
	332–19	* facts regarding Major Glover's *m·*
	335– 6	* retained his *m·* in both till

membranes
Mis.	210–20	a belief of disordered brains, *m·*,

membranous
Mis.	44– 7	*for immediate relief. as in m· croup*

Memento
Po.	page 73	poem

memorable
Mis.	144– 8	On this *m·* day there are laid away
Ret.	15–21	last vestry meeting was made *m·* by
	16– 1	One *m·* Sunday afternoon,
My.	5–24	*m·* dedication and communion season,
	55– 1	* This date is *m·* as the one
	81–25	* a fitting close to a *m·* week.
	148–13	*M·* date, all unthought of till
	327– 3	Is it not a *m·* coincidence

memorial
Mis.	145–22	*m·* such as Isaiah prophesied :
Pul.	27– 9	* There are no "*m·*'' windows ;
	27–10	* a testimonial, not a *m·*
	71– 6	* a *m·* church for Mrs. Eddy,
My.	20– 2	for a *m·* of her."— *Mark* 14 : 9.
	43–17	* on the other side for a *m·*.
	194–13	tender *m·* engraven on your
	289–23	to attend the *m·* meeting

memorialized
Pul.	65–24	* and so was *m·* in art
	76–23	* REV. MARY BAKER EDDY *M·* BY A

memorials
Ret.	5–12	inscribed on the stone *m·* in
Pul.	77– 4	* one of the most chastely elegant *m·*
'01.	28–13	choicest *m·* of devotion
My.	257–24	your manifold Christmas *m·*,

Memorial service
My.	284–13	*M· s·* of the E. E. Sturtevant Post
	284–19	*M· s·* has been held annually

memories
Po.	3– 7	With evening, *m·* reappear
My.	47–15	* recall *m·* of trials, progress, and
	256–18	dearest *m·* in human history
	258–23	beautiful are the Christmas *m·*

memorize
Mis.	374–17	Scientists *m·* the nativity of Jesus.

memory (see *also* **memory's, mem'ry**)
Mis.	xi–24	thought sometimes walks in *m·*,
	142–27	The symbols . . . wakened *m·*,
	159–12	the *m·* of my students.
	218–24	this nature may linger in *m·* :
	232– 2	but the *m·* was too much ;
	290–25	hold a place in one's *m·*,
	329–11	restoring in *m·* the sweet rhythm
	339–27	will some time flood thy *m·*,
	343–27	fill the haunted chambers of *m·*,
	386–23	Rears the sad marble to our *m·*
	394–16	* The gates of *m·* unbar :
Ret.	5–15	*m·* recalls qualities to which
	6–10	the *m·* of my second brother,
	8– 2	throng the chambers of *m·*.
Pul.	1–12	garner the *m·* of 1894,
	5– 8	*M·*, faithful to goodness,
Po.	25– 7	Around you in *m·* rise !
	34–18	Bearing no bitter *m·* at heart ;
	50– 9	Rears the sad marble to our *m·*
	57– 2	* The gates of *m·* unbar :
	67– 9	*m·* of dear ones deemed dead
	74– 3	those moments to *m·* bestowed?
My.	19–27	fill the *m·* and swell the hearts
	26–12	emotion at the touch of *m·*.
	38–26	* carry with them the *m·* of it.
	39–26	* and the *m·* lives with us.
	125– 5	to report progress, to refresh *m·*,
	147– 3	when at the touch of *m·*
	147–14	sacred to the *m·* of this pure
	164–12	*m·*, and all within the human heart
	258–17	The *m·* of the Bethlehem
	319– 8	in loving, grateful *m·*
	319–27	* very well fixed in my *m·*,
	326–16	so signally honored his *m·*,

memory's
Mis.	159–16	In this chamber is *m·* wardrobe,
Po.	66– 5	songs float in *m·* dream.
	68–15	o'er the heartstrings in *m·* hour.

mem'ry
Mis.	392–22	To my busy *m·* bringing
Po.	33–11	(And *m·* but part us awhile),
	51– 4	To my busy *m·* bringing

men (see *also* **men's**)
actions of
Mis.	237– 7	a change in the actions of *m·*.
	280– 6	the thoughts and actions of *m·* ;

a kind of
Mis.	261–25	I mean mortals, or a kind of *m·*
'02.	14–19	not by mankind, but by a kind of *m·*

all
Mis.	358–12	All *m·* shall be satisfied when they
Ret.	49–24	bring all *m·* to a knowledge of
	93– 9	draw all *m·* unto me."— *John* 12 : 32.

men

all

Un.	5–21	known to all *m·*." — *see Phil.* 4 : 5.
No.	8– 9	recommending to all *m·* fellowship
'02.	16–12	"Follow peace with all *m·*, — *Heb.* 12 : 14.
My.	28–25	* for all time and for all *m·* ;
	37– 2	* salvation of all *m·* from all evil.
	127–31	adapted to all *m·*, all nations,
	240– 1	till all *m·* shall know Him
	247–13	will draw all *m·* unto you.
	295–20	enriches the being of all *m·*.

among

Ret.	70–27	Preeminent among *m·*, he virtually
'00.	5–15	under heaven and among *m·*

and angels

My.	189– 1	warmest wish of *m·* and angels.

and women

Mis.	99–12	*M·* and women of the nineteenth
	110– 5	as children than as *m·* and women :
	158–19	God's servants are minute *m·* and women.
	340–26	lives of great *m·* and women
Pul.	36–11	* the *m·* and women present
Pan.	9– 6	they imply *m·* and women ;
'00.	7– 9	most scholarly *m·* and women,
My.	54–10	* tide of *m·* and women was turned
	80– 3	* prosperous, contented *m·* and women,
	92– 5	* numbers of intelligent *m·* and women
	104–25	many professional *m·* and women
	105–29	are noble *m·* and women,
	113–32	*m·* and women of this age.
	158–22	Most *m·* and women talk well,
	194–10	*m·* and women gain greatness
	239–19	generic term for *m·* and women.
	285–14	*m·* and women of this period
	305–13	most distinguished *m·* and women
	315–29	millions of the good *m·* and women
	344– 5	each separate ray for *m·* and women.

appetites of

Mis.	296–28	and the bad appetites of *m·*?

are known

Mis.	371–20	* "*m·* are known by their enemies."

as angels

Mis.	251–21	and *m·* as angels who,

assembled

Ret.	89– 7	*M·* assembled in the one temple

before

My.	04–27	* worthy members . . . before *m·*.

best

My.	331–13	* by Wilmington's best *m·*,

better

Mis.	365–15	better health and better *m·*.

blind

Mis.	362– 8	dogma has made *m·* blind.

brave

Pan.	14–23	at Manila, where brave *m·*,

brotherhood of

Mis.	348– 7	on the brotherhood of *m·*.

business

My.	30–12	* were business *m·* come from far
	82– 1	* hard-headed shrewd business *m·*.

call God

'01.	18–26	whom *m·* call God

cannot punish

My.	128–17	*M·* cannot punish a man for suicide ;

children of

Rud.	10–21	not willingly the children of *m·*,
My.	90–11	* endows the children of *m·*,
	103–10	the children of *m·*." — *Psal.* 107 : 8.

consist of

Man.	99–25	shall consist of *m·* generally.

count cost

My.	127–26	not costly as *m·* count cost,

covereth

Mis.	153–16	covereth *m·* as a garment,

curse we

Un.	60–14	therewith curse we *m·*, — *Jas.* 3 : 9.

damning

My.	211– 1	error that is damning *m·*.

deeds of

My.	277–20	immortal words and deeds of *m·*

dispraise of

Mis.	245–22	praise or the dispraise of *m·*.

distinguished

Ret.	7–15	* one of the most distinguished *m·*
My.	305–13	most distinguished *m·* and women

doctrines of

Mis.	366–19	doctrines of *m·*, even as

dogmas of

Pan.	11– 9	doctrines, and dogmas of *m·*

draw

Ret.	88–27	spiritual attitude as will draw *m·*

fisher of

My.	247–19	called you to be a fisher of *m·*.

fishers of

Mis.	111–10	"fishers of *m·*" — *Mark* 1 : 17.
My.	295–17	Scientists are fishers of *m·*.

men

give counsel

Mis.	359–28	*M·* give counsel ; but they give not the

have not heard

My.	184– 4	*m·* have not heard with the ear,

healer of

My.	104–15	the healer of *m·*, the Christ,

heard of

No.	39– 5	offered to be heard of *m·*,

hearts of

Mis.	121– 2	inscribed upon the hearts of *m·* :
My.	123– 6	moves the hearts of *m·* to goodness

in our ranks

My.	355– 5	chapter sub-title

killing

My.	277–15	Killing *m·* is not consonant with

learn

Mis.	251–25	*m·* learn a parable of the

light of

My.	154–13	"was the light of *m·*." — *John* 1 : 4.
	295– 6	was the light of *m·*." — *John* 1 : 4.

lives of

Pan.	10– 6	effects of C. S. on the lives of *m·*
Peo.	11–28	liberty and lives of *m·*.
My.	277–14	characters and lives of *m·* determine
	294– 4	morals and the lives of *m·*,

made

Peo.	10–18	mortal beliefs, . . . made *m·* sinning

made monsters of

Peo.	3– 4	have made monsters of *m·* ;

made seers of

'01.	9– 9	a sense so pure it made seers of *m·*,

make

Mis.	387–10	make *m·* one in love remain.
Hea.	3– 4	Christianity was to make *m·* better,
Po.	6–14	make *m·* one in love remain.

makes

Mis.	363– 7	supposition . . . is mind and makes *m·*,

many

My.	114–12	to the gaze of many *m·*,

may revile

My.	6–10	*m·* may revile us and despitefully

medical

Mis.	80–13	cultured and conscientious medical *m·*,

minds of

My.	225–18	begins in the minds of *m·*
	264–16	signifies to the minds of *m·*
	295– 4	remains in the minds of *m·*,

morals of

My.	103–21	longevity, and morals of *m·* ;

more

My.	355– 7	need for more *m·* in C. S.

most

My.	160–15	trenchant truth . . . most *m·* avoid

motives of

Mis.	19–10	the affections and motives of *m·*
My.	268–14	uplifting the motives of *m·*.

must approach

Un.	13– 4	*M·* must approach God reverently,

must know

My.	149– 1	*m·* must know somewhat of

number of

Pul.	49–29	* She employs a number of *m·*

of science

My.	95–23	* higher critics and the *m·* of science

opinions of

Mis.	x–16	opinions of *m·* and the progress of
	92–25	opinions of *m·* cannot be substituted
Ret.	84–14	opinions of *m·* cannot be substituted

or women

Un.	4–28	no wise *m·* or women will rudely

other

Mis.	103–25	was like that of other *m·* ;

professional

My.	30–14	* professional *m·*, devoted women
	81–32	* professional *m·*, hard-headed
	104–25	many professional *m·* and women

raises

Ret.	66– 4	It raises *m·* from a material sense

rejected of

'01.	9–18	and yet Christ is rejected of *m·* !

representative

My.	327–22	* representative *m·* of our dear State

rescue

Un.	59–19	Jesus came to rescue *m·*

rich

My.	149–16	* "And I with many rich *m·*,

rights of

My.	247– 2	inalienable, universal rights of *m·*.
	254–23	inalienable, universal rights of *m·*.

save

Un.	60– 2	Christ Jesus came to save *m·*,

saving

'01.	9–17	healing and saving *m·*,

Saviour of

My.	104–15	says that the Saviour of *m·*,

men

seen of
Mis. 133–13 may be seen of *m*.— *Matt.* 6 : 5.
My. 124–29 seen of *m*, and spiritually understood ;

sentence
No. 44–14 sentence *m* to the dungeon

shall revile
Mis. 8–22 when *m* shall revile— *Matt.* 5 : 11.
'01. 3– 4 when *m* shall revile— *Matt.* 5 : 11.
'02. 11–22 when *m* shall revile— *Matt.* 5 : 11.
My. 104–30 when *m* shall revile— *Matt.* 5 : 11.
316– 7 when *m* shall revile— *Matt.* 5 : 11.

should do
Mis. 90–14 would that *m* should do— *Matt.* 7 : 12.
119–32 would that *m* should do— *Matt.* 7 : 12.
146–18 would that *m* should do— *Matt.* 7 : 12.
235–28 would that *m* should do— *Matt.* 7 : 12.
282–10 would that *m* should do— *Luke* 6 : 31.
Man. 42–23 would that *m* should do— *Matt.* 7 : 12.
Ret. 87–20 would that *m* should do— *Matt.* 7 : 12.
'00. 14–17 would that *m* should do— *Luke* 6 : 31.
My. 266– 9 would that *m* should do— *Matt.* 7 : 12.

street-car
My. 83–13 * street-car *m* and policemen,

thoughts of
Peo. 3–18 inscribes on the thoughts of *m*

tongues of
'01. 26–22 with the tongues of *m* — *I Cor.* 13 : 1.

toward
Mis. 145–30 good will toward *m*." — *Luke* 2 : 14.
215–15 peace, and good will toward *m*.
369– 5 good will toward *m*." — *Luke* 2 : 14.
Man. 45– 7 and good will toward *m* ;
Pul. 41–26 * good will toward *m*." — *Luke* 2 : 14.
No. 44–27 good will toward *m*" — *Luke* 2 : 14.
My. 90–20 * good will toward *m*." — *Luke* 2 : 14.
127–30 good will toward *m*,." — *Luke* 2 : 14.
167–12 good will toward *m*,," — *Luke* 2 : 14.
279–19 good will toward *m*,." — *Luke* 2 : 14.
281–10 good will toward *m*,." — *Luke* 2 : 14.
283–12 good will toward *m*." — *Luke* 2 : 14.

towards
Pul. 22– 2 peace and good will towards *m*.
Pan. 15–10 and good will toward *m*.
'02. 8–12 love and good will towards *m*.
My. 4–20 is good will towards *m*.
210–17 reflect peace, good will towards *m*,
282– 1 purpose is good will towards *m*.

turned
Mis. 345–31 Christianity turned *m* away from

universe and
Rud. 4– 4 our material universe and *m*

unselfs
My. 288– 2 unselfs *m* and pushes on the ages.

warring
Pul. 83–30 * She brought to warring *m*

weak
Mis. 345–15 * fit only for women and weak *m* ;"

weak-minded
Peo. 13–24 * only for women and weak-minded *m*."

wise
Mis. 321– 1 wise *m* follow this guiding star ;
Un. 4–28 no wise *m* or women will
My. 149–15 * conversed with many wise *m*,"

wrath of
My. 207– 4 The wrath of *m* shall praise God,

Mis. 27–16 "Do *m* gather grapes of— *Matt.* 7 : 16.
36– 7 Beasts, as well as *m*, express Mind
56–26 *if all minds (m) have existed*
110–28 how fleeting is that which *m* call great ;
210– 7 Do *m* whine over a nest of serpents,
251–21 where angels are as *m*,
Ret. 35– 6 *m* were so unfamiliar with the subject
Un. 15– 4 *m* rid themselves of an incubus
Pul. 45– 1 * *M*, women, and children
64– 8 * *M*, women, and children contributed,
No. 1– 9 So *m*, when thrilled by a new idea,
'01. 16–25 *m* go to mock, and go away to pray
Peo. 11–19 as *m* pass legislative acts
My. 5–28 indulging sin, *m* cannot serve God ;
17–10 disallowed indeed of *m*,— *I Pet.* 2 : 4.
83–11 * and the *m* go entirely unadorned.
94–31 a few years ago, *m* there were who
104–17 that *m* suspend judgment
113–26 *m* are found casting out the evils
355– 9 *m* are very important factors

menacing
Mis. 67–20 if you see the danger *m* others,

mendicant
Mis. 330–26 mere *m* that boasts and begs,

menial
Pul. 8–17 never before devoted to *m* services,
My. 165– 5 The grand must stoop to the *m*.

men's
Mis. 240–29 takes off *m* heads ;
Pul. 79–20 * taken possession of *m* minds,
My. 6–24 above the work of *m* hands,
94–28 above the work of *m* hands,

mens populi
Mis. 7–31 *m p* is not sufficiently enlightened

mental

advancement
My. 239–28 and stage of *m* advancement,

agencies
Pul. 14– 5 active yet unseen *m* agencies

and moral
Mis. 73–12 it is always *m* and moral,

anguish
Mis. 237– 5 *m* anguish is generally accepted as

animus
My. 277–11 The *m* animus goes on,

argument
Mis. 220– 5 healer begins by *m* argument.
221– 3 by a false *m* argument ;
222–15 malicious *m* argument and its action
359– 5 you continue the *m* argument
Rud. 9–22 an audible or even a *m* argument,

arrow
Mis. 223–30 *m* arrow shot from another's

atmosphere
Mis. 355–27 from thine own *m* atmosphere.
Man. 31–11 the *m* atmosphere they exhale
'00. 9–15 till the *m* atmosphere is clear.

avenues
'01. 1– 3 the *m* avenues of mankind

bane
'01. 20–15 *m* bane could not bewilder,

branches
Mis. 243– 5 one of the *m* branches taught

cause
Ret. 24– 9 physical effects to a *m* cause ;

collisions
Mis. 339–13 In the *m* collisions of mortals

condition
Mis. 43– 5 the *m* condition of the patient.
112–28 Unless this *m* condition be overcome,
204–15 *m* condition settles into strength,
281– 6 I find also another *m* condition
Hea. 17–21 Sin is a supposed *m* condition ;

conditions
Mis. 91–15 types of these *m* conditions,
Un. 56–27 Such *m* conditions as ingratitude,

consciousness
Ret. 94–12 no matter, to the *m* consciousness.

conviction
My. 121– 8 a true, tried *m* conviction

darkness
Mis. 355–18 *M* darkness is senseless error,

deformity
Mis. 203–22 the veil that hides *m* deformity.

delusion
No. 4– 8 material sensation and *m* delusion.

denomination
Ret. 28–18 to their own *m* denomination,

depression
Mis. 51– 5 *accompanied by great m depression,*

design
Mis. 249–22 of their *m* design to do this

development
Mis. 264–27 to aid the *m* development of
356–22 second stage of *m* development is

digestion
My. 229–19 chapter sub-title

disease
Mis. 112–24 This *m* disease at first shows

dose
Mis. 241–10 give to the immoralist a *m* dose

efforts
Ret. 71–27 Secret *m* efforts to obtain help

error
Rud. 3–20 *m* error made manifest physically,

evil
My. 212–12 highest form of *m* evil,

force
Mis. 220– 7 supports this silent *m* force

forces
Mis. 19–25 centripetal and centrifugal *m* forces

formation
Mis. 287–16 discern the Science of *m* formation

growth
Mis. 357–19 The third stage of *m* growth

hardships
My. 52– 3 * many *m* hardships to endure,

haziness
My. 211–30 a *m* haziness which admits of no

healers
Pul. 57–23 * There are several sects of *m* healers,
No. 2–11 *M* healers who admit that disease is

mental

healing
Mis.   3–29 The tendency of m· healing is to
       4– 5 to plant m· healing on the basis
      34–28 *Who is the Founder of m· healing?*
      58–26 the theology of m· healing
      80– 2 spurious works on m· healing.
     171–27 the Science of m· healing ;
     172–23 the Science of m· healing,
     174–14 the Science of m· healing.
     175–18 m· healing must be understood.
     175–25 m· healing which acquaints us with
     220– 2 in every line of m· healing,
     223–16 believing in m· healing,
     254–22 m· healing on a material basis
     271–27 * false teachers of m· healing,
     282– 6 chapter sub-title
Ret. 48–18 scientific methods of m· healing
No.   31–21 Physical and m· healing
Hea. 11–18 foundation stone of m· healing ;
idleness
'00.   8–16 m· idleness or apathy is always
influence
Mis. 264–23 m· influence of their former teacher.
Ret. 72– 2 m· influence that hazards another's
law
Mis. 199– 6 to annul his own erring m· law,
malady
My. 116– 9 a m· malady, which must be met
     203–17 Dishonesty is a m· malady
malpractice
Mis. 31– 1 *consider to be m· malpractice?*
      31– 2 M· malpractice is a bland denial
      31– 9 and is m· malpractice.
      41– 5 m· malpractice would disgrace
     113–21 m· malpractice, if persisted in,
     115– 4 sin and m· malpractice,
     222–17 the effects of m· malpractice,
     233– 7 the breath of m· malpractice,
     233 19 Substituting m· malpractice for
     248 29 m· malpractice of poisoning people
     316– 1 I defend . . . against m· malpractice,
     351– 2 and meet the m· malpractice.
     351– 7 the silent m· malpractice.
Man. 52– 6 complaint is not for m· *malpractice*,
      53–19 enter a complaint of m· malpractice
      53–21 the offense of m· malpractice,
      84– 3 against m· malpractice,
Ret. 38– 9 partial history . . . of m· malpractice.
'01. 19–20 chapter sub-title
My. 110– 3 against malicious m· malpractice,
     212–31 to cover his crime of m· malpractice,
     213–15 to the modes of m· malpractice,
malpractitioner
Mis. 19–23 hypocrite or m· malpractitioner.
     115 9 guilt as a m· malpractitioner,
     221– 2 a m· malpractitioner may lose his
     368–19 silent address of a m· malpractitioner
'01. 20 9 The m· malpractitioner is not,
My. 212–24 m· malpractitioner, interfering with
means
Mis. 40–29 to kill his patient by m· means,
mechanism
Mis. 354–18 right action of the m· mechanism,
medicine
Mis. 252– 2 m· medicine of divine metaphysics
     252– 4 M· medicine gains no potency by
method
Mis. 220–21 this m· method has power
     351– 9 m· method of Mind-healing,
methods
Mis. 260–31 silent m· methods whereby
miasma
My. 249–13 m· miasma fatal to health,
millstone
Mis. 362–23 to remove this m· millstone
ministrations
No.   40–14 pursue their m· ministrations
monument
My.   0–23 rises to a m· monument,
      94–27 "rises to a m· monument,
mood
Ret. 75–17 the author's own m· mood,
mortally
Un.   35– 9 to be mortally m·,
operation
Mis. 352–19 m· operation must be understood
origin
Hea. 17–26 Then was not sin of m· origin,
perfection
Mis. 234–25 physical and m· perfection,
period
Mis. 204– 6 m· period is sometimes chronic,
phenomenon
Ret. 24–11 every effect a m· phenomenon.
Pul. 70–18 every effect a m· phenomenon."

mental

phenomenon
Hea.   6– 8 m· phenomenon named mediumship,
power
Mis. 115–31 Using m· power in the right direction
practice
Mis. 219–11 chapter sub-title
     282–20 the above rule of m· practice.
     283– 1 m· practice where there is no
     293–10 observation, and m· practice.
     350–27 none to be used in m· practice,
Man. 90–20 m· practice and *malpractice*.
Ret. 71–21 motives entering into m· practice
'01. 19–21 From ordinary m· practice to
Hea. 14–17 the method of a m· practice.
My. 106– 5 without . . . m· practice were profitless.
     364– 3 rule of m· practice in C. S.
     364– 7 m· practice includes and inculcates
practitioner
Mis. 220–16 m· practitioner has changed his
     220–19 m· practitioner undertook to
practitioners
Mis. 221–16 many helpless m· practitioners
My. 212–15 dissension among m· practitioners
problem
Ret. 34– 5 solve the m· problem.
process
Mis. 220–24 if this m· process and power
processes
Un.   21– 2 description of m· processes
      21– 4 If we observe our m· processes,
purgation
Mis. 41–13 M· purgation must go on :
quackery
Rud. 12–11 m· quackery, that denies the
remedy
Mis. 44–28 applying this m· remedy
reservations
My. 345– 4 their m· reservations will be
Science
Mis. 172–25 M· Science, and the five personal
     173– 2 misstate m· Science,
Peo. 10–15 M· Science alone grasps the
science
Mis.   4– 6 calling this method "m· science."
      58–21 Without . . . there is no m· science,
seal
Mis. 269–29 opening of this silent m· seal,
sense
Un.   9– 2 Destroy the m· sense of the disease,
signs
Mis. 347–10 the m· signs of these times,
stages
Mis. 112–12 The m· stages of crime,
standpoint
Mis. 379–22 m· standpoint not understood,
state
      (*see* state)
struggle
My. 307–28 m· struggle might have caused my
struggles
Un.   5– 7 their m· struggles and pride
suggestion
Man. 42– 6 against aggressive m· suggestion,
system
Mis. 35– 8 blessings of this m· system
Hea. 13–25 this m· system of healing is the
teeth
Pul. 80–14 * fairly broken our m· teeth
therapeutics
Pul. 54–20 * practice of m· therapeutics,
My. 306–31 my views of m· therapeutics.
treatment
Mis. 31– 8 the abuse of m· treatment,
     315–26 needing it asks for m· treatment.
Ret. 71– 9 Promiscuous m· treatment,
      71–12 indications of m· treatment,
My. 363–26 avoid naming, in his m· treatment,
unsoundness
Mis. 49– 5 manifested some m· unsoundness,
vigor
My. 355– 3 * spiritualized thought and m· vigor
virtues
Ret. 33–23 m· virtues of the material methods
want
No.   42– 7 material forms to meet a m· want.
ways
Pul. 15– 3 evil's hidden m· ways
work
Mis. 350–10 no advice given, no m· work,

———

Mis. 27–26 must be spiritual and m·.
      28– 5 Perception by the . . . senses is m·,
      72–27 Real sensation . . . must be, m· :
     220– 9 His m· and oral arguments aim to

mental

Mis. 244–12 are the conditions of salvation m,
269–17 on a Christian, m, scientific basis ;
319–11 m and audible protest against the
351–12 solely from m malicious practice,
Un. 12– 2 by m, not material processes.
Rud. 16–22 a pathological Science purely m.
No. 6–27 the laws of Science are m,
'01. 1–14 constitute m and physical perfection.
My. 74–29 * the material and the m,
79–29 * from diseases, physical and m,
114–30 each step of m and spiritual progress,
134–29 * her usual m and physical vigor.''
160–29 this hell is m, not material,
294– 9 m counteracting elements,

mentalities

'01. 7–13 express the different m of

mentality

Mis. 76–24 false sense of m in matter,
104–16 His materiality, clad in a false m,
107–26 lack of seeing one's deformed m,
109–12 most hopeful stage of mortal m.
355–22 what in thine own m is unlike
Un. 56– 4 from the m of others ;
56–10 suffering from m in opposition to
56–15 m which opposes the law of Spirit ;
58–14 sublime triumph over all mortal m
Pul. vii–13 its lenses of more spiritual m,
My. 106–19 Human m, expressed in disease,
364– 4 strictly to handle no other m

mentally

Mis. 31– 4 To m argue in a manner
67– 6 m, morally, or physically.
67–14 either m or audibly,
113–11 Whoever is m manipulating
127–10 m, meekly, and importunately.
206–20 accentuating harmony . . . m and orally,
220– 5 person whom another would heal m.
220– 6 He m says, ''You are well,
221–15 stultify the power to heal m.
221–24 we must m struggle against both
282– 8 treated m without their knowledge
282–16 When you enter m the personal
293–24 To affirm m and audibly
297– 8 m destroys the appetite for
315–24 shall not silently m address
380–18 Although I could heal m,
Man. 42–20 will not . . . knowingly m malpractise,
42–25 who m malpractises upon
52–21 m or otherwise, persist in
Ret. 38–23 Not a word . . . audibly or m,
Un. 36–19 m, morally, spiritually.
Pul. 32–12 * I m questioned this modern
No. 2–24 destroys one's ability to heal m.
40–16 never to trespass m on individual
Pan. 8– 3 causes a man to be m deranged ;
Hea. 14– 5 until disease is treated m
14–19 You must first m educate
My. 18– 7 m, meekly, and importunately.
146–26 never m or audibly takes
222– 2 once failed m to cure by their faith

mention

Ret. 15– 9 I will make m of — Psal. 71 : 16.

mentioned

Mis. 68–18 Does the gentleman above m know
170–31 The putting on of hands m,
Man. 69– 9 expiration of the time therein m
102–13 m in the deeds given by
My. 106– 8 I name those m above
294–20 hindrances previously m,
324–32 * m many kindnesses

mercantile

My. 53– 2 * inquiry and m reproach ;

mercenary

Mis. 283– 2 or the motive is m,
No. 43–18 take it up from m motives,

mercies

Mis. 391– 8 Will count their m o'er,
391–17 Share God's most tender m,
397– 1 Then His unveiled, sweet m
Pul. 18–10 Then His unveiled, sweet m
Po. 12–10 Then His unveiled, sweet m
33–14 Whose m my sorrows beguile,
38– 7 Will count their m o'er,
38–16 Share God's most tender m,
My. 13–22 and tender m ; — Psal. 103 : 4.

merciful

Mis. 32–28 and should be just, m ;
332– 4 Infinitely just, m, and wise,
Man. 16–12 and to be m, just, and pure.
Peo. 12– 7 m and just government of God.
My. 41–12 * ''Blessed are the m,'' — Matt. 5 : 7.
190– 3 m design of divine Love,

mercifully

My. 201–16 m forgive, wisely ponder,

merciless

Mis. 211–14 rescued from the m wave
257–13 so-called force, . . . is cruel and m.
Ret. 13–15 m towards unbelievers ;
Un. 35–18 not the m forces of matter.
Peo. 13–13 iron tread of m invaders,

mercilessly

Mis. 335–12 m assails me for opposing

mercury

Pul. vii– 9 rise of the m in the glass

mercy

acme of
Mis. 122–14 divine order is the acme of m :
altar of
Po. 32–18 To kneel at the altar of m
and charity
Mis. 13– 2 m and charity toward every one,
and justice
Mis. 11– 3 it is grace, m, and justice.
and love
Mis. 152–16 May meekness, m, and love
Pul. 9– 8 justice, m, and love kindle
and might
Mis. 69– 4 His goodness, m, and might.
and peace
Pan. 14–12 justice, m, and peace continue
and truth
Mis. 151–24 m and truth go before you :
deeds of
Mis. 370– 4 saw Jesus do such deeds of m,
demands
Mis. 67–19 m demands that if you see the
divine
Mis. 11–14 Love metes . . . divine m.
Ret. 94–11 this purgation of divine m.
My. 89–20 * constant as petitions for divine m.
equity and
My. 277–19 equity and m tips the beam
errand of
Mis. 250–25 stealing on an errand of m,
God's
My. 162– 1 God's m for mortal ignorance
handmaid of
Mis. 261–17 Justice is the handmaid of m,
His
Mis. 322–24 the amplitude of His m,
Un. 26–15 * But His m waneth never,
No. 34–21 and bring His m
infinite
Pul. 74–16 to declare in His infinite m.
justice and
Mis. 146–25 understanding of justice and m.
266–15 hold justice and m as inseparable
No. 7– 4 scales of justice and m.
My. 288– 2 revelation, justice, and m ;
love
My. 283–24 do justly, and to love m, — Mic. 6 : 8.
loves
Mis. 317–30 abhors injustice, and loves m,
loving
Ret. 71–20 not dealing justly and loving m,
showeth
Mis. 261–18 showeth m by punishing sin.
tender
Chr. 53– 5 In tender m, Spirit sped
upon us
Un. 3–28 He has m upon us,
without
My. 41–11 * and so receive judgment without m ;

Mis. 154–28 meekness, m, purity, love.
'01. 29– 8 should not be left to the m of
My. 180–21 in justice, as well as in m,
272– 3 with justice, m, truth, and love.

mere

Mis. 34–14 is a m speculative opinion
67– 2 the m alphabet of Mind-healing.
68– 4 more than m disappearance
80– 4 by m unity on the single issue
230–10 and m motion when at work,
250–20 Love cannot be a m abstraction,
330–26 A m mendicant that boasts
353–23 the folly of tending it is no m jest.
366–32 m book-learning, — letter without law,
368–23 the m puppets of the hour
Man. 40– 5 nor m personal attachment
47–14 a m rehearsal of blessings,
Ret. 21–25 M historic incidents and
32– 6 as m corporeal personality.
32–14 * What is life? A m illusion,
Pul. 9–27 understanding, not m belief,
55–12 * not, . . . as a m coincidence

mere

Rud.	17– 2	m· motives of self-aggrandizement
No.	13–17	of being held as a m· theory.
'01.	15–23	* nothing but God's m· pleasure
'02.	16–27	The m· form of godliness,
My.	78–27	* No m· words can convey the
	84– 1	* more plainly than m· assertion
	85– 6	* a m· handful of members
	92–18	* But m· statistics give a feeble
	92–22	* ridiculed . . . as m· guesswork,
	94– 4	* ridiculed . . . as m· guesswork,
	259–25	m· merry-making or needless
	291– 5	a m· rehearsal of aphorisms,

merely

Mis.	77– 1	depend m· on his believing
	108– 9	a lie, . . . is m· a falsity ;
	111–21	Christianity that is m· of sects,
	116–21	it is not m· saying, but doing,
	140–10	over matter or m· legal titles.
	147–17	not guided m· by affections
	170– 8	m· symbolize the spiritual
	189–23	not m· a sense of existence,
	253– 2	Christianity is not m· a gift,
Ret.	58– 7	not m· a sense of existence,
Un.	42–16	not m· a sense of existence,
No.	14– 7	are m· subjective states of mortal mind.
'02.	16–24	m· outside forms of religion,
Hea.	14–16	m· to know that mind governs
My.	48–23	* subordination of m· material
	85–23	* not m· for its thousands of
	231– 3	Giving m· in compliance with
	236–17	M· this appellative seals the
	259–29	in m· temporary means and ends.
	339–26	M· to abstain from eating was not

merge

Mis.	156–13	to m· the adjourned meeting
My.	142–16	and m· into a meeting for greetings.

merged

Ret.	23– 4	m· into the one infinite Love.

Meribah

Mis.	153–14	washed in the waters of M·,
My.	132– 9	pass through the waters of M· here

meridian

My.	177–12	nearer the eternal m· than now,
	254– 6	you must reach its m·.

merit

Mis.	80–14	on its own m· or demerit,
	237–24	Honor to faithful m· is delayed,
No.	34–13	who discern his true m·,
'01.	4–29	If . . . we m· the epithet "godless,"
My.	305–21	I claim no special m·
	306–17	Human m· or demerit will find its

merited

Hea.	3–21	works of our Master more than m·.
My.	49–27	* m· the thanks of the society

meritorious

Mis.	118–16	guerdon of m· faith

merits

Ret.	35– 8	m· of C. S. must be proven
My.	333–25	* m· of a crucified Redeemer.

Merkel

My.	32–12	* Fantasie in E minor, M·

Merodach

Mis.	123–14	Assyrian M·, or the god of sin,

Merrimack, ss.

My.	138–25	* STATE OF NEW HAMPSHIRE, M·, ss.

Merrimac River

Ret.	4–11	picturesque view of the M· R·
	5– 2	left bank of the M· R·.

merriment

Chr.	53–23	Make m· on Christmas eves,
My.	262–23	m·, mad ambition, rivalry,

merry

Mis.	329–30	melting murmurs to m· meadows ;
My.	99– 5	* m· heart that doeth good

merry-making

My.	259–25	mere m· or needless gift-giving

meshes

Mis.	111– 7	human pride, creeping into its m·,

Mesmerism

Mis.	277–19	French Commissioners on M· :

mesmerism

Mis.	3–18	Hygiene, manipulation, and m·
	34–10	Is spiritualism or m· included in
	45– 2	that is not Science but m·.
	47–28	exhibitions of m·
	47–30	I have no knowledge of m·,
	48– 3	If m· has the power
	51– 6	Is a belief of nervousness, . . . m·?

mesmerism

Mis.	51– 7	All m· is of one of three kinds ;
	59– 5	produces the effect of m·.
'01.	19–23	m·, hypnotism, and the like,
Hea.	13–25	is the antipode of m·,
	13–26	M· makes one disease while it
	13–28	m· is one lie getting the better of
My.	v–12	* m· of personal pride
	218–22	A fad of belief is the fool of m·.
	313–22	* never "dabbled in m·,"

mesmerist

Mis.	248–16	that I am an infidel, a m·,
	249– 1	first undertaken by a m·,
My.	229– 2	No m· . . . is fit to come hither.

mesmerists

Mis.	79–31	vendors of patent pills, m·,

mesmerize

My.	5–31	Human will may m· and mislead

Message

Mis.	125–21	chapter sub-title
	322– 4	chapter sub-title
Pul.	41–11	* to listen to the M· sent them
Pan.	1– 1	heading
'02.	12–22	ordinarily find no place in my M·.
My.	3– 1	chapter sub-title
	7– 1	chapter sub title
	7– 5	ordinarily find no place in my M·.
	26–15	My M· for June 10 is ready
	32–26	* M· from the Pastor Emeritus,
	36– 1	* dedicatory M· from their teacher
	37–27	* We have read your annual M·
	57– 7	* M· to the church in 1902
	64–11	* M· to The Mother Church,
	133–10	will not receive a M· from me
	133–11	M· is swallowed up in sundries
	151–21	chapter sub-title
	155–16	chapter sub-title
	159– 1	chapter sub-title
	170– 8	M· to the church last Sunday
	240–10	M· to The Mother Church,
	263– 3	chapter sub-title
	292–19	M· to my church in Boston,
	334–19	* She declares in her M·

message

Mis.	158– 9	obeyed the m· of divine Love,
	169–16	before their m· can be borne fully to
Man.	66–15	When a letter or a m· from
Pul.	41–25	* chimes . . . rung out their m·
	44– 8	* brief m· of congratulation.
'01.	31–11	Has God entrusted me with a m·
'02.	11–16	helped onward by a new-old m·
Po.	15– 7	unless thou canst bear A m· from
My.	187–14	the m· that ye heard— I John 3 : 11.
	259– 6	I received the following cabled m· :
	280– 4	the receipt of your m·,

messages

Mis.	171–11	spiritual translations of God's m·,
	277–13	have never silenced the m· of
Ret.	91–25	was peopled with holy m·
'00.	12– 6	his m· to the churches
My.	167–11	I pray that heaven's m·
	229–23	their swift m· of rejoicing

messenger

Mis.	262–23	white-winged m·, our Journal.
	308–21	m· has done its work,
	326–25	Well might this heavenly m· exclaim,
Pan.	9–19	kiss the feet of such a m·,
		(see also Eddy)

messengers

Mis.	280–16	m· of pure and holy thoughts

Messiah (see also Messiah's)

Mis.	22– 2	one God, one Christ or M·.
	77– 4	fact that Jesus was the M·.
	77– 6	great truths asserted of the M· :
	78– 2	spiritual dawn of the M·,
	161–24	new name, M·, or Jesus Christ,
Un.	30–16	M·, our blessed Master,
	39–13	M·, whose name is Wonderful.
	55–15	This threefold M· reveals the
	59– 1	why did the M· come to the world,
No.	37–23	M· and prophet saved the sinner
'01.	9– 7	glorious glimpses of the M·
'02.	12– 1	believes that the M· or the Christ
	12– 5	on the basis that Christ is the M·,

Messiah's

Ret.	91–26	were the M· university.

Messiahship

Hea.	18–21	established his M· on the basis that

Messianic

Mis.	162–12	point of his M· mission was peace,
Ret.	70–10	M· mission of Christ Jesus ;

Messias
  Mis. 186–30   last Adam represented by the *M·*,

met
  Mis. 44–25   this demand . . . once *m·*,
    66–27   Error in premise is *m·* with
    74–28   He *m·* and conquered the
    110–16   years, since last we *m·* ;
    118–23   they must be *m·* manfully
    173–22   man is not *m·* by another power
    177–30   In my long journeyings I have *m·*
    180–11   another person, more material, *m·* me,
    200–26   *m·* no obstacle or circumstances
    208–17   are *m·* and mastered by divine
    247–31   must be *m·*, in every instance,
    249– 9   has been *m·* and answered *legally*.
    258– 4   *m·* and abolished this
    263–19   *m·* in the most effectual way.
    276– 9   my heart's desire *m·* the demand.
    279–22   *m·* together in an upper chamber ;
    280–26   *m·* the class to answer some questions
    284–27   *m·* with Science, it can and will be
    345–26   Christians *m·* in midnight feasts
    350– 7   The P. M. . . . Society *m·* only twice.
    350–18   and we have not *m·* since.
    365–24   has never *m·* the growing wants of
    383– 4   *m·* with the universal approval
  Man. 18–14   Church members *m·* and reorganized,
  Ret. 21– 6   We never *m·* again until he had
    38–17   We *m·* at the Eastern depot in Lynn,
    52–17   *m·* in general convention at New York
    64–21   which must be *m·* and mastered,
    80–29   not infrequently *m·* by envy,
    94– 5   the conclusion must be *m·*
  Un. 36–10   *m·* and solved by C. S.
  Pul. 32–19   * At the time I *m·* her she must have
    34– 6   * *m·* with a severe accident,
    36–14   * evening that I first *m·* Mrs. Eddy
    36–18   * *m·* Mrs. Eddy many times since then,
    84–24   * all obstacles . . . *m·* and overcome,
  Rud. 6–12   truth in C. S. *m·* a response
  No. 19– 6   have never *m·* the growing wants of
  '02. 1–17   *m·* with opposition and detraction ;
    9–28   *m·* the need of mankind with
    14–19   every forward step has been *m·*
  Po. 3–11   Since first we *m·*, in weal or woe
    68–18   when *we three m·*,
  My. 28– 4   "Divine Love always has *m·*
    43–10   * and *m·* with disappointments,
    50–31   * The business committee *m·*
    51– 8   * she has not *m·* with the support
    55–14   * the members of the church *m·*,
    63–16   * exultation as friend *m·* friend
    73– 9   "Divine Love always has *m·*
    81–28   * two or more of them are *m·* together,
    87–21   * *m·* in Boston during the
    104–28   was *m·* with the anathema
    112– 2   first *m·* with denunciations.
    116– 9   must be *m·* and overcome.
    134–13   imperative demand not yet *m·*.
    148–18   you have *m·* to praise God.
    187–22   You have *m·* to consecrate
    214– 5   Divine Love always has *m·*
    245– 4   it should be *m·* as heretofore,
    312–13   * *m·* and taken to her father's home
    320–31   * I *m·* him in the vestibule
    322– 1   * not long since I *m·* a lady

metal
  Mis. 250–20   having no ring of the true *m·*.
  My. 4–20   unfolding the true *m·* in character,

metaphor
  Mis. 280–24   appropriate language and *m·*
    353–25   turn from the *m·* of the mill
  '01. 3–26   expresses God only in *m·*,

metaphorically
  Mis. 75–18   word *Soul* may sometimes be used *m·* ;

metaphors
  Mis. 253–16   The Scriptural *m·*,

metaphysical
  Mis. 5–22   *M·* therapeutics can seem a miracle
    50–11   *m·* method of healing is as lucid
    50–13   necessity to express the *m·*
    68–19   or of *m·* theology?
    169–20   to get at the highest, or *m·*,
    169–24   The *m·* rendering is health and
    170–22   The method of Jesus was purely *m·* ;
    172– 5   the negative of *m·* Science ;
    182–26   text is a *m·* statement of existence
    184–30   to foreshadow *m·* purity,
    223– 1   the *m·* mystery of error
    237– 3   yielded somewhat to the *m·* fact
    240– 5   painted and fattened by *m·* hygiene.
    272– 6   * a college, for *m·* purposes *only*,
    282–15   Prolonging the *m·* tone
    349– 9   the *m·* mode of obstetrics

metaphysical
  Mis. 378–20   to see that *m·* therapeutics,
    379– 9   not at all *m·* or scientific ;
    379–31   adjusting . . . a *m·* practice,
    382–22   for a *m·* medical college,
  Ret. 7–11   * abstruse and *m·* principles,
    43– 1   purely *m·* system of healing
    57–30   demonstration of *m·*, or C. S.
    78–14   right sense of *m·* Science.
    79– 1   *honest m·* theory and practice.
  Un. 9–27   difference in my *m·* system?
  Pul. 6–27   * in Mrs. Eddy's *m·* teachings
    69–19   * spiritual or *m·* standpoint.
  Rud. 6–15   * this is not "any *m·* subtlety,"
  No. 22– 6   Berkeley ended his *m·* theory with
    22–10   Such miscalled *m·* systems are reeds
  Hea. 14–18   preparation for a *m·* practitioner
    14–21   learns the *m·* treatment of disease ;
    14–25   *M·* or divine Science reveals the
    16– 4   *M·* Science teaches us there is no
  Peo. 3–18   more *m·* religion founded upon C. S.
  My. 52– 1   * by *m·* truth or C. S.,
    127–12   system of *m·* therapeutics
    190–10   *m·* practice of medicine
    (*see also* **healing**)

Metaphysical College
  Mis. 242– 5   as President of the *M· C·*
  Pul. 36– 1   * after her founding of the *M· C·*
    36– 3   * *M· C·* lasted nine years,
  My. 215–18   to establish a *M· C·*,
    322–17   * the day before at the *M· C·*
    (*see also* **Massachusetts Metaphysical College**)

Metaphysical College Corporation
  Ret. 48–12   Board of the *M· C· C·*,

metaphysically
  Mis. 51–12   *How can I govern a child m·?*
    169–31   one of the passages explained *m·*.
    203–16   *M·*, baptism serves to rebuke
  Pul. 4– 7   Is not a man *m·* and
  No. 11–10   that are to be understood *m·*.

Metaphysician (*see also* **Metaphysician's**)
  Mis. 76–31   prophecy of the master *M·*,
    187– 4   great *M·* wrought, over and
    200– 6   The master *M·* understood
    270–10   He . . . is the master *M·*.
  Ret. 55– 3   example of Jesus, the master *M·*,
  Pul. 20–23   baptism of our master *M·*,
  No. 31–22   the same with this master *M·*.
  '01. 19–16   great *M·* healed the sick,
    25–17   The great *M·*, Christ Jesus,
  My. 111– 6   master *M·*, the Galilean Prophet,
    222– 8   Jesus, the master *M·*, answered,

metaphysician
  Mis. 308–32   is not the model for a *m·*.
    379–12   neither a scholar nor a *m·*.
  '01. 26– 8   *m·* is sensual that combines
  Hea. 12– 7   *m·* goes to the fount
  My. 40–25   * because she is an exact *m·*.

Metaphysician's
  '01. 18–22   great master *M·* precept

metaphysicians
  Mis. 81– 7   the *m·*, agree to disagree,
    233– 6   those who call themselves *m·*
    368–12   to say that all are not *m·*,
    371– 4   large flocks of *m·*
  Pul. 2–22   *m·* and Christian Scientists.
  '01. 26–25   this subject of the old *m·*,

metaphysics
  adds
    Hea. 11–19   *m·* adds, "until you arrive at
  Bishop Berkeley's
    '01. 24–14   Bishop Berkeley's *m·* and personality
  Christian
    Mis. 205–21   in Christian *m·* the ideal man
    365–26   Christian *m·* is hampered by
    No. 11– 8   my system of Christian *m·*
    My. 41– 4   * the law of Christian *m·*,
  classified in
    Mis. 112–13   are strictly classified in *m·*
  college of
    Mis. 272–26   * legally chartered college of *m·*,
  cured by
    Mis. 45–12   *Can an atheist . . . be cured by m·*,
  divine
    (*see* **divine**)
  faith in
    My. 301–15   chapter sub-title
  his
    My. 303–23   His *m·* is not the sport of philosophy,
  in Christian Science
    My. 108–11   *m·* in C. S. consists in
  in homœopathy
    My. 108–10   difference between *m·* in homœopathy

metaphysics

instruct in
Mis. 38–14   college to instruct in *m*,

is seen
Peo. 9–23   *m*· is seen to rise above physics,

is understood
Hea. 18–23   when *m*· is understood ;

its
'01. 27–24   taken out of its *m*· all matter

law of
My. 41–11   * but the law of *m*· says,

Master of
Hea. 7–17   The Master of *m*·, reading the mind of

master of
Mis. 252–23   great healer and master of *m*·,
My. 104– 8   said of the great master of *m*·,

mistake in
Mis. 264–30   A single mistake in *m*·,

modes of
My. 111– 6   crude theories or modes of *m*·.

my
No. 26–10   to demonstrate my *m*·.

my system of
No. 24– 8   at variance with my system of *m*·,

not physics
Mis. 369– 7   *M*·, not physics, enables us to

of Christ
'01. 24–26   Christianity — the *m*· of Christ

physics and
Mis. 126– 3   in physics and *m*·.

power of
Mis. 6–12   power of *m*· over physics ;
     7–28   nature and power of *m*·,

questionable
'01. 21– 6   chapter sub-title

requires
Hea. 11–25   *M*· requires mind imbued with Truth

rules of
Mis. 221– 5   one gains in the rules of *m*·,

sneer at
Mis. 69– 3   A sneer at *m*· is a scoff at Deity ;

so-called
Mis. 271– 7   compounded *m*· (so-called)
'01. 25– 9   and the *m*· (so called)

standard of
Mis. 53–18   above the standard of *m*· ;

studying
Mis. 48–23   made insane by studying *m*·?

such
'01. 25–14   alluded to or required in such *m*·,

superiority of
Ret. 34–16   superiority of *m*· over physics.

system of
'01. 26– 5   who founded his system of *m*·
My. 105–28   my curative system of *m*·.

teaching
Mis. 38–21   Teaching *m*· at other colleges

true
Mis. 69– 5   is the unfolding of true *m*· ;

understanding of
Ret. 48–19   a thorough understanding of *m*·,

vulgar
My. 305– 9   * on the subject of "vulgar *m*·,"

Mis. 5–18   *m*· comes in, armed with the power of
     34– 2   proving that *m*· is above physics.
     38–14   *M*·, as taught by me at the
     68–21   According to Webster, *m*· is defined
     68–27   calls *m*· "the science which
     203–15   *m*· appropriates it topically as
     209–11   *M*· also demonstrates this Principle
     233–14   the new cloth of *m*· ;
     233–18   terming it *m*· !
     234–28   In this new departure of *m*·,
     255–27   and *m*· is above physics.
'01. 25–20   *m*· based on materialism?
Hea. 6–21   But the fact remains, in *m*·,
     11– 7   physics are yielding slowly to *m*· ;
     11–16   against its neighbor, *m*·,
     11–23   *M*· places all cause and cure as
My. 121– 7   In *m*· we learn that the strength
     127– 3   in medicine, in physics, and in *m*·.
     235–11   it cannot be done in *m*·,

Metcalf, Albert
Man. 102–14   the deeds given by Albert *M*·

mete
Mis. 11–21   To *m*· out human justice
     298– 8   "With what measure ye *m*·, — Matt. 7 : 2.

meted
Mis. 222–21   the measure it has *m*·
     261–13   the measure he has *m*·
My. 218–27   *m*· out to one no more than

metes
Mis. 11–14   Love *m*· not out human justice,

methinks
Mis. 106–25   *m*· I hear the soft, sweet sigh
     155–29   *M*·, were they to contemplate
     345–14   *M*· the infidel was blind
Pul. 1–19   *m*· I should be much like the
'00. 1– 1   *m*· even I am touched with
My. 6–27   *M*· this church is the one edifice
     110–20   night thought, *m*·, should unfold
     162–18   *m*· the same wisdom which spake
     261– 2   *M*· the loving parents and

method

aforenamed
Man. 59–11   aforenamed *m*· for the benefit of

and design
Rud. 3–18   in its nature, *m*·, and design.

best
Mis. 2–32   best *m*· for elevating the race

Christly
Mis. 359– 3   Christly *m*· of teaching and
Ret. 93–13   best spiritual type of Christly *m*·

divine
My. 103–15   Alluding to this divine *m*·,

entire
Mis. 50– 6   entire *m*· of metaphysical healing,

Hebrew
Mis. 170–26   Hebrew *m*· of expressing the

hidden
My. 130– 5   hidden *m*· of committing crime

intricate
My. 212– 4   intricate *m*· of animal magnetism

Jesus'
Ret. 89–19   Jesus' *m*· was to instruct his

material
Ret. 43–15   his material *m*· of practice
My. 106– 2   than any material *m*·.

mental
Mis. 220–21   this mental *m*· has power
     351– 9   mental *m*· of Mind healing,

metaphysical
Mis. 50–11   its metaphysical *m*· of healing

no other
Mis. 170–23   and no other *m*· is C. S.

novel
Pul. 40–11   * NOVEL *M*· OF ENABLING

of his religion
Ret. 92– 1   *m*· of his religion was not too simple

of Jesus
Mis. 170–22   The *m*· of Jesus was purely

of perfection
Hea. 14–26   Principle and *m*· of perfection,

operative
Ret. 85– 6   any other organic operative *m*·

same
Mis. 40–10   C. S. is the same *m*· of healing

sanative
Mis. 220–27   any other possible sanative *m*· ;

scientific
Mis. 5–10   by studying this scientific *m*·

this
Mis. 3–30   but this *m*· perverted, is
     4– 6   calling this *m*· "mental science."
     62–21   An adherent to this *m*·
     301–24   This *m*· is an unseen form of
     369–12   This *m*· sits serene at the portals of
     360–17   This *m*· is devout enough to trust
Ret. 61–30   Unless this *m*· be pursued,
Hea. 9–10   this *m*· has not saved them from either,

thought and
No. 12–21   spiritualization of thought and *m*·,

your
Mis. 41–18   be healed by your *m*·
     89–14   no faith in your *m*·,

Mis. 369–11   "*m*·" in the "madness" of this system,
Pan. 13–15   united in purpose, if not in *m*·,
Hea. 14–17   the *m*· of a mental practice.
My. 18–23   united in purpose, if not in *m*·,
     137–26   consulted Lawyer . . . about the *m*·.

Methodist Conference Seminary
My. 312– 1   *M*· *C*· *S*· at Sanbornton Bridge,

Methodist Elder
'01. 32– 5   Father Hines, *M*· *E*·.

Methodist Episcopal Church
Pul. 6–21   * under the auspices of the *M*· *E*· *C*·.

Methodist Review
My. 48–16   * appeared in the *M*· *R*·

methods

and means
Mis. 135–16   God's *m*· and means of healing,
     313– 5   morals, *m*·, and means.

and power
Mis. 222–30   *m*· and power of error.

and subtlety
Ret. 64–27   *m*·, and subtlety of error,

methods

and tenets
My. 84–23 * *m·* and tenets of the sect.
both
My. 215–30 to test the effect of both *m·*
different
Pul. 51–13 * others who have different *m·*,
its
Mis. 175–21 instituting matter and its *m·*
latter-day
My. 98–24 * latter-day *m·* of raising money.
material
(*see* **material**)
means and
Mis. 52–10 beyond all human means and *m·*.
153– 1 His spiritual means and *m·*,
Rud. 13–23 *What are the means and m· of*
My. 154–24 I welcome the means and *m·*,
mental
Mis. 260–31 silent mental *m·* whereby it may
motives and
Mis. 267–28 spiritualizes man's motives and *m·*,
of divine Love
Mis. 213– 8 in the *m·* of divine Love.
of God
Mis. 270–25 through the modes and *m·* of God.
of medicine
Ret. 33–23 material *m·* of medicine,
of our Master
Mis. 359–20 The *m·* of our Master were
of Truth
Mis. 141–12 hates the bonds and *m·* of Truth,
orderly
Ret. 82–13 orderly *m·* herein delineated.
ordinary
Mis. 33–22 *ordinary m· of healing disease?*
other
Mis. 97–14 other *m·* of treating disease.
'01. 17–12 exceeded that of other *m·*,
our
Peo. 7–31 and our *m·* grow more spiritual
scientific
Ret. 48–18 give instruction in scientific *m·*
such
Ret. 57–29 such *m·* can never reach the
their
Mis. 114–25 uncover their *m·*, and stop their
Peo. 11–24 mistaken in their *m·* of humanity.
thoughts and
Rud. 12– 6 Wrong thoughts and *m·* strengthen the
well-established
Pul. 51–16 * affect the well-established *m·*.

Methuen, Mass.
Pul. 62– 1 * Bell Company, of *M·*, *M·*.,

metropolis
Pul. 7–10 Master in our New England *m·*
'02. 20–24 in the *m·* of my native State,
My. 196– 5 a State whose *m·* is called

Mexican
Pul. 76–13 * superb mantel of *M·* onyx

Mexican Herald
My. 95– 8 * *M· H·*, City of Mexico,

miasma
Un. 56–28 constitute the *m·* of earth.
My. 249–13 sends forth a mental *m·*

Mich. (State)
(*see* **Detroit, Grand Rapids, Jackson**)

Mickley, Miss Minnie F.
Mis. 306–16 * Miss Minnie F. *M·*, Mickleys, Pa.

Mickleys, Pa.
Mis. 306–16 * Miss Minnie F. Mickley, *M·*, *P·*.

microbe
Mis. 131– 3 a moral nuisance, a fungus, a *m·*,

microbes
Mis. 112– 6 Hypnotism, *m·*, X-rays,

microscope
Peo. 10– 7 under the *m·* of Mind.

'mid
Mis. 393– 5 Soul, sublime *'m·* human *débris*,
Pul. 39–25 * *'m·* them all I only see *one* face,
Po. 16–20 *'M·* graves do I hear the glad voices
34– 9 chant thy vespers *'m·* rich glooms?
51–10 Soul, sublime *'m·* human *débris*,

middle
Mis. 231– 2 *m·* age, in smiles

Middle States
Pul. 88–24 * heading

midnight
Mis. 88–16 like a *m·* sun.
117–26 replenish his lamp at the *m·* hour
226–29 Slander is a *m·* robber;

midnight
Mis. 276–15 In C. S. the *m·* hour will
342– 7 the *m·* gloom upon them,
342–14 It was *m·* : darkness profound brooded
345–27 *m·* feasts in the early days,
Ret. 23–17 the *m·* torches of Spirit.
Un. 58–20 *m·* sun shines over the Polar Sea.
Po. 26– 7 Chill was thy *m·* day,
My. 82–23 * and more . . . by *m·* to-night.
190– 1 Did that *m·* shadow,
197–18 illumine the *m·* of the latter,

midst
Mis. 133–26 In the *m·* of depressing care
141–32 God is in the *m·* of her :
152–11 I, as . . . am not in your *m·* :
166– 6 lives, and moves in our *m·*
234–26 in the *m·* of an age so sunken in sin
264– 4 *m·* of this seething sea of sin.
325–29 in the *m·* of murderous hordes,
331–22 *M·* the falling leaves of old-time
332–14 *m·* the stately palms,
337–13 in the *m·* of them, — *Matt.* 18 : 2.
338–11 steadfastly to good in the *m·* of
399– 5 *M·* the glories of one endless day."
Ret. 17– 3 *m·* the zephyrs at play
18– 9 *M·* grotto and songlet and streamlet
27–22 meandering *m·* pebbles and rocks,
Pul. 48– 2 * in the *m·* of green stretches
Pan. 15– 6 *m·* of our enemies," — *see Psal.* 23 : 5.
'00. 12– 4 walketh in the *m·* of — *Rev.* 2 : 1.
Hea. 11– 6 in the *m·* of a revolution ;
Po. 30–14 and *m·* the rod, . . . Lift Thou a
62– 1 *m·* the zephyrs at play
63–18 *M·* grotto and songlet and streamlet
75–12 *M·* the glories of one endless day."
My. 43–16 * taken from the *m·* of the river
99– 9 * is welcomed within our *m·*
103– 1 In the *m·* of the imperfect,
185–25 in the *m·* of the mountains,
246–12 in the *m·* of unprecedented
252–14 work *m·* clouds of wrong,

midwifery
Mis. 349– 5 the surgical part of *m·*.

might

all
Hea. 15–14 why should man deny all *m·* to the
and ability
Un. 42–17 a sense of *m·* and ability to subdue
and light
My. 133– 4 *m·* and light of the present
and majesty
Mis. 141–13 *m·*, and majesty of Spirit,
292–13 to human weakness *m·* and majesty.
294– 9 *m·* and majesty ! — of goodness.
'00. 5–30 *m·* and majesty attend every
'01. 33–21 *m·* and majesty of divine power
clothed with
Mis. 185–16 man be clothed with *m·*,
divine
Mis. 138–19 unity is divine *m·*, giving to
162–14 Clad with divine *m·*, he was ready
My. 3– 4 divine *m·* of Truth demands
His
My. 187–29 and the majesty of His *m·*
its
My. 149– 9 its *m·* is the ever-flowing tides
light and
My. 246–20 the light and *m·* of the divine
maximum of
My. 165–30 rapidly nearing the maximum of *m·*,
meek
'02. 16–21 The meek *m·*, sublime patience,
meekness and
Mis. 372–32 true sense of meekness and *m·*.
My. 194–16 It stands for meekness and *m·*,
202– 4 to the faith, meekness, and *m·* of
mercy and
Mis. 69– 4 His goodness, mercy, and *m·*.
of divine Love
My. 61–19 * before the *m·* of divine Love,
of divine power
'02. 18– 6 *m·* of divine power manifested through
of empires
My. 162– 9 stronger than the *m·* of empires.
of love
My. 258–28 give you the *m·* of love,
of perfect Love
Mis. 334–32 demonstrate the *m·* of perfect Love
of Truth
Mis. 52– 8 even the *m·* of Truth,
100– 8 show the word and *m·* of Truth
My. 3– 4 *m·* of Truth demands well-doing
right nor
'01. 20– 7 gives neither moral right nor *m·* to harm

might

through meekness to
My. 163– 5 to win through meekness to *m·*,
wisdom, and
Mis. 316–28 patterns of humility, wisdom, and *m·*
wisdom's
Ret. 11– 7 On learning's lore and wisdom's *m·*,
Po. 60– 4 On learning's lore and wisdom's *m·*,
word of
Mis. 388– 1 God, who gave that word of *m·*
'02. 20–10 God who gave that word of *m·*
Po. 7– 1 God, who gave that word of *m·*

Mis. 83–22 meekness was as conspicuous as *m·*.
Pul. 82–29 * *M·* no longer makes right,
Po. 30–14 fan Thou the flame Of right with *m·* ;
79–16 Life is light, and wisdom *m·*,

mightily

Mis. 119–16 weighs *m·* in the scale against
My. 294–13 He would *m·* rebuke a single doubt

mighty

Mis. 43–27 unacquainted with the *m·* Truth
51–22 * the lips of Truth one *m·* breath
103–29 He was too *m·* for that.
120–13 a *m·* victory is yet to be won,
139–10 *m· through God — II Cor.* 10 : 4.
161– 7 The *m·* God, — *Isa.* 9 : 6.
164–18 The *m·* God, — *Isa.* 9 : 6.
189–10 true knowledge . . . made him *m·*.
223–26 better than the *m·*." — *Prov.* 16 : 32.
234–20 to establish this *m·* system
258–23 did declare a *m·* individuality,
321– 5 The *m·* God, — *Isa.* 9 : 6.
344–23 the *m·* Nazarene Prophet.
389–18 shadow of His *m·* wing ;
Ret. 11–16 Science the *m·* source,
57– 1 *m·* wrestlings with mortal beliefs,
Un. 10–21 the calculation of His *m·* ways,
Pul. 12–17 *m·* conquest over all sin?
46–21 * Wallace of *m·* Scottish fame.
84–21 * tell the story of its *m·* meaning
'00. 9–27 as leader of this *m·* movement.
Po. 2–17 the sun's more genial, *m·* ray ;
4–17 Beneath the shadow of His *m·* wing ;
60–13 Science the *m·* source,
My. 10– 5 * inevitable that this *m·* impulse
42–30 * "With a *m·* hand, — *Deut.* 26 : 8.
58–14 * the erection of these *m·* walls.
59–20 * *m·* chorus of five thousand voices,
98– 2 * truly make up a *m·* host,
115– 1 *m·* chariot of divine Love,
140 29 a *m·* rush, which waken the
164–18 A great sanity, a *m·* something
196–11 better than the *m·* ; — *Prov.* 16 : 32.
294– 7 "did not many *m·* works — *Matt.* 13 : 58.
350–24 Love divine, whose kindling *m·* rays

mild

Mis. 109–12 Even a *m·* mistake must be seen as a
My. 150–17 moon ablaze with her *m·* glory.

milder

'01. 19–28 *m·* forms of animal magnetism

mile

Pul. 47–22 * one *m·* from the State House
49–25 * within one *m·* of the "Eton of
My. 68– 6 * one *m·* and a half of pews.

miles

Ret. 5–10 eighteen *m·* from Concord,
Pul. 44– 5 * Across two thousand *m·* of space,
My. 69–30 * in Cambridge, some four *m·* away.
332– 2 * of more than a thousand *m·*,

mile-stones

Mis. x–14 to serve as *m·* measuring the

militant

Pul. 3–18 No longer are we of the church *m·*,
My. 125–23 grateful that the church *m·* is
133– 7 church *m·* rioc to the
154–25 it makes the church *m·*,
196– 6 May this dear church *m·* accept

military

'02. 3–12 our *m·* forces withdrawing,
My. 310–13 His *m·* title of Colonel came from

militates

Rud. 9–28 whatever *m·* against health,
No. 18–25 *m·* against the so-called demands of

milk

Mis. 15–30 on the *m·* of the Word,
149– 2 come, buy wine and *m·* — *Isa.* 55 : 1.
Ret. 61–29 Let there be *m·* for babes,
61–30 let not the *m·* be adulterated.
No. v–12 unadulterated *m·* of the Word,
Hea. 13–17 using only the sugar of *m·* ;
My. 17– 6 the sincere *m·* of the word, — *I Pet.* 2 : 2.

mill

Mis. 353–25 turn from the metaphor of the *m·*
My. 310–10 * "a workman in a Tilton woolen *m·*."

millenial

My. 265–15 full-orbed in *m·* glory ;

millennium

My. 239–12 *ultimate of the m·*
239–27 The *m·* is a state and

Miller, Mrs. F. L.

'02. 16–10 Mrs. F. L. *M·*, of London,

Miller, K.C., Mr. W. Nicholas

'02. 16– 9 Mr. W. Nicholas *M·*, *K.C.*,

Millet's "Angelus"

My. 70–15 * *M· "A·"* had living reproductions

million

(*see* **numbers, values**)

millions

Mis. 208– 7 bill that governs *m·* of mortals
Ret. 54–12 *M·* are believing in God,
Pul. 14–14 *M·* of unprejudiced minds
Pan. 15– 2 destroying *m·* of her money,
'00. 11– 2 gave me more pleasure than *m·*
My. 160–27 may take *m·* of cycles,
249–19 *M·* may know that I am the
289–18 lives on in the heart of *m·*.
294–25 will move the pen of *m·*.
295– 1 the loved and lost of many *m·*.
315–29 the beloved Leader of *m·*
(*see also* **values**)

mills

Mis. 353–14 a workman in his *m·*,
Ret. 80– 8 * *m·* of God grind slowly,

millstone

Mis. 122–11 better for him that a *m·* — *Matt.* 18 : 6.
362–23 to remove this mental *m·*

millstones

My. 160–32 wrongs done to others, are *m·*

Milwaukee

Wis.
Pul. 90– 6 * *Sentinel, M·*, Wis.
My. 207– 2 chapter sub-title

Pul. 56– 3 * *Detroit, Toledo, M·*, Madison,

mimicry

My. 262–25 a human mockery in *m·* of the

Mind (*see also* **Mind's**)

action of
Mis. 70– 6 healing action of *M·* upon the body
all
Ret. 56 20 supplying all *M·* by the reflection,
Un. 24– 3 From me proceedeth all *M·*,
Rud. 4– 1 including in itself all *M·*,
all is
Mis. 26– 6 all is *M·* and its manifestation,
105–32 all is good and all is *M·*.
200–32 statement that all is *M·*,
286–21 All is *M·*.
Rud. 4–20 All is *M·*.
all-knowing
Mis. 71–16 omnipotence, the all-knowing *M·*.
71–26 God, good, the all-knowing *M·*.
all must be
Rud. 5– 5 all must be *M·*, since God is Mind.
allness of
Mis. 253–11 with the allness of *M·*.
alone
Mis. 244– 5 *M·* alone constructing the
No. 18–25 asks for what *M·* alone can supply.
altitude of
Mis. 255–11 that altitude of *M·* which was in
and body
No. 40–20 obstruct the harmony of *M·* and body,
and man
Mis. 24–20 *M·* and man are immortal ;
and matter
Mis. 56–16 *M·* and matter mingling in
280–12 There are not two, — *M· and* matter.
Ret. 59–21 *M·* and matter as distinct,
apart from
Rud. 5–10 considered apart from *M·*.
'01. 18–12 administered no remedy apart from *M·*,
based on
My. 154– 2 Science of all healing is based on *M·*
before
My. 260– 5 withdraw itself before *M·*.
belief, that
Mis. 49–25 belief, that *M·* is in matter,
body and
Mis. 86–21 the harmony of body and *M·*.
call
Mis. 258–20 call *M·* by the name of matter,

Mind

came in
  Hea. 11–22   *M·* came in as the remedy,
came not from
  Mis. 196–12   that saying came not from *M·*,
can master
  Hea. 8– 6   *M·* can master sickness as well as
capabilities of
  Mis. 43– 2   recognizing the capabilities of *M·*
casts out
  Mis. 73– 3   when *M·* casts out the suffering.
causation is of
  Pul. 55–20   * all causation is of *M·*,
causation was
  Ret. 24–10   certainty that all causation was *M·*,
  Pul. 70–18   "all causation was *M·*,
coexistent with
  Mis. 190– 9   man is coexistent with *M·*,
conscientious
  Un. 25–21   Evil is not . . . conscientious *M·* ;
consciousness is
  Ret. 56–18   All consciousness is *M·*, and Mind is
  Un. 24–12   *Good.* All consciousness is *M·* ;
  No. 10–18   all consciousness is *M·* and eternal,
consciousness of
  My. 131–31   say with the consciousness of *M·*
consent of
  Pan. 8– 1   or by the consent of *M·* !
controls
  Mis. 5–24   reality that *M·* controls the body.
demonstrates
  Mis. 190– 5   Divine Science demonstrates *M·* as
  Ret. 88–28   *M·* demonstrates omnipresence and
departs from
  Mis. 268–11   who departs from *M·* to matter,
despite of
  Pan. 8– 1   despite of *M·*, or by the consent of
destitute of
  Un. 50–18   Like evil, it is destitute of *M·*,
discredit
  Mis. 223–13   to say, if it must, "I discredit *M·*
divine
  (*see* **divine**)
embraced in
  Mis. 103–30   individuality is embraced in *M·*,
employed
  Hea. 13–20   employed *M·* as the only curative
error is not
  Mis. 367– 8   showing that error is not *M·*,
  Ret. 57–19   Evil, or error, is not *M·* ;
eternal
  Mis. 36– 9   eternal *M·*, which is God,
    102–20   The sympathy of His eternal *M·*
    103–17   the eternal *M·* is free, unlimited,
  Un. 14–23   eternal *M·* must be reflected in man,
    64– 7   on the foundations of an eternal *M·*
    64–19   dwelleth in the eternal *M·*.
  No. 15–23   existence in the eternal *M·*.
  My. 267–11   eternal *M·* that hath no beginning
every flower in
  Mis. 179–26   He made every flower in *M·*
evil is not
  Rud. 4–16   Good is Mind, but evil is not *M·*.
exist in
  Mis. 190–27   the right sense, and exist in *M·*.
  Rud. 5–28   or exist in *M·* only ;
  No. 16– 3   If matter can exist in *M·*,
express
  Mis. 36– 7   express *M·* as their origin;
fact that
  Mis. 35– 2   fact that *M·*, . . . is the Principle
faculties of
  Mis. 332–28   are not faculties of *M·*,
faith in
  Mis. 229–14   faith in *M·* over all other influences
forever
  Mis. 218– 3   the fact that Deity was forever *M·*,
God is
  (*see* **God**)
good is
  Rud. 4–16   Good is *M·*, but evil is not Mind.
  Pan. 6–22   For if God, good, is *M·*,
governed by
  Mis. 256– 4   The body is governed by *M·*,
governs all
  Mis. 6–18   *M·* governs all.
governs man
  Mis. 51–16   and *M·* governs man.
has no
  Mis. 174– 1   *M·* has no more power to
heal through
  Mis. 53–14   your power to heal through *M·*,
He is
  No. 16– 4   He is *M·* ; and whatever He knows is
highest
  Un. 32– 8   not the highest *M·*, but a false form

Mind

his
  Ret. 57–16   He reflects God as his *M·*,
his medicine is
  Mis. 268–17   His medicine is *M·* — the omnipotent
imbued with
  Mis. 260–28   *M·*, imbued with this Science
immortal
  Mis. 3–19   unerring and immortal *M·*.
    35–27   *What is immortal M·?*
    36–18   of mortal mind, — not immortal *M·*.
    36–20   *mortal mind and immortal M·?*
    37– 4   Immortal *M·* is God ;
    37–12   spiritual and immortal *M·*,
    56–10   Life is immortal *M·*, not matter.
    61– 8   magnitude of immortal *M·*,
    82–28   Immortal *M·* is God, immortal good ;
    84–16   mortal mind, not the immortal *M·*,
    87–14   glory of the immortal *M·*."
    102– 6   the unlimited and immortal *M·*
    219–23   and immortal *M·* makes well ;
    219–24   while immortal *M·* makes saints ;
    365–19   immortal *M·* alone can supply.
  Ret. 25–11   God I called *immortal M·*.
    33–20   immortal *M·*, the curative Principle,
    34–13   antidote . . . in the immortal *M·* ;
  Un. 24– 1   the opposite of immortal *M·*,
    34–26   Immortal *M·* is the real substance,
    35–16   immortal *M·*, the Parent of *all.*
    45–28   Spirit, immortal *M·*, or good.
    56– 2   the cosmos of immortal *M·*.
  Rud. 1– 7   infinite and immortal *M·*,
    7–10   perfect and immortal *M·*,
    9–14   immortal *M·*, the divine Principle
  Hea. 18– 3   government of God, immortal *M·?*
immortality of
  Mis. 218–10   immortality of *M·* and its ideas.
implies
  Pan. 7–23   which implies *M·*, Spirit, God ;
in behalf of
  My. 190–21   a divine decision in behalf of *M·*.
included in
  Un. 11–27   heaven is here, and is included in *M·* ;
individual
  Mis. 101–31   God is individual *M·*.
infinite
  Mis. 5–26   man is the idea of infinite *M·*,
    21–17   All is infinite *M·* and its infinite
    26–15   from infinite *M·*, or from matter?
    26–19   self-creative, and infinite *M·*.
    217–19   containing infinite *M·* ;
    247–22   man is the idea of infinite *M·*,
    258–17   infinite *M·* governs all things.
    331–31   and infinite *M·* is seen
    367–20   Infinite *M·* knows nothing beyond
    373–13   infinite *M·* and spiritual vision
  Ret. 25–27   proper conception of the infinite *M·*.
    57–19   infinite *M·* is sufficient to supply all
  Un. 10–13   phenomena of this one infinite *M·*.
    24–15   whose source is infinite *M·*.
    50– 2   how can infinite *M·* be defiled?
  Rud. 4–15   God is infinite *M·*,
  No. 20–16   or of an infinite *M·* starting from a
  '01. 6– 9   Can the infinite *M·* inhabit a
    6–28   with an infinite *M·*.
    7– 8   God being infinite *M·*, He is
  My. 64– 4   * the realm of infinite *M·*,
    269– 1   included in one infinite *M·*
    293– 3   power and purpose of infinite *M·*,
infinite as
  '01. 6–26   must be as infinite as *M·* is.
instead of
  Mis. 175– 8   by bread, matter, instead of *M·*.
    190–25   belongs to *M·* instead of matter,
  Hea. 12– 2   *M·* instead of matter heals
  Peo. 2–12   and of *M·* instead of matter,
is All-in-all
  Mis. 183– 8   found that *M·* is All-in-all,
is God
  Mis. 37– 4   Immortal *M·* is God ;
    82–28   Immortal *M·* is God,
    173–12   *M·* is God, omnipotent and
  Ret. 56–18   consciousness is Mind, and *M·* is God.
  Un. 24–12   consciousness is Mind ; and *M·* is God,
    24–18   because *M·* is God.
    50–18   destitute of Mind, for *M·* is God.
  No. 27– 5   *M·* is God, and evil finds no place
is immortal
  Mis. 82–25   the one *M·* is immortal.
    367– 6   But *M·* is immortal ;
  Un. 32–17   True *M·* is immortal.
    35–11   no mortal mind, for *M·* is immortal,
  No. 16–28   *M·* is immortal.
is Love
  Mis. 332– 5   *M·* is Love, — but not fallible love.

Mind

is made manifest
  Mis. 37– 4   this *M·* is made manifest in
is more
  No. 25–10   *M·* is more than matter,
is not confined
  Mis. 42–30   *M·* is not confined to limits ;
is not in matter
  Rud. 7–21   *M·* is not in matter,
       13– 1   that *M·* is not in matter ;
is not mortal
  Mis. 72–27   *M·* is not mortal, it is immortal.
is supreme
  Mis. 45– 1   prove the fact that *M·* is supreme.
       47–18   *M·* is supreme.
     336– 1   *M·* is supreme :
  Peo. 8–16   *M·* is supreme ; and yet we
is the architect
  Mis. 41–19   *M·* is the architect that builds
is Truth
  Mis. 332– 3   *M·* is Truth, — not laws of matter.
law of
  Mis. 173–10   law of *M·* and not of matter,
laws of
  Mis. 173–31   laws of matter, or laws of *M·*?
  My. 190–19   laws of *M·* over the human mind
Life and
  Un. 3–22   He is all the Life and *M·* there is
      3–23   embodiment of Life and *M·*.
likeness of
  Mis. 97–24   in the image and likeness of *M·*,
      97–24   in the image and likeness of *M·*
made by
  Mis. 257– 7   must be made by *M·* and as Mind.
manifestation of
  Mis. 27–20   it is a small manifestation of *M·*,
manifested
  Rud. 4– 8   Science is *M·* manifested.
manifest less of
  Mis. 36– 8   but they manifest less of *M·*.
manifesto of
  Mis. 22– 4   the unerring manifesto of *M·*,
man nor
  Mis. 36– 2   is neither God's man nor *M·* ;
matter and
  Mis. 175–28   The attempt to mix matter and *M·*,
     269–18   choice between matter and *M·*,
matter is not
  No. 27– 4   Matter is not *M·*, to claim aught ;
matter, or
  Mis. 334–23   by means of matter, or *M·*?
matter to
  Peo. 7– 7   shall turn often . . . from matter to *M·*,
medicine of
  Mis. 252– 1   this medicine of *M·* is . . . infinite.
     348–24   new *régime* . . . the medicine of *M·*,
  '01. 18– 7   the medicine of *M·* is more honored
medium of
  Mis. 163–21   medium of *M·*, the hope of the race.
microscope of
  Peo. 10– 7   under the microscope of *M·*.
misstatement of
  Mis. 174– 3   Matter is a misstatement of *M·* ;
  Un. 35–21   this one is a misstatement of *M·*,
mode of
  Ret. 89– 2   potency of this spiritual mode of *M·*,
modes of
  Mis. 303–12   modes of *M·* are spiritual,
more
  Ret. 33–12   the more *M·*, the better the work is
My
  Un. 24– 4   My *M·* is divine good,
never produced
  Mis. 218– 4   that matter never produced *M·*,
no other
  Mis. 182– 8   no other *M·*, no other origin ;
  Rud. 4–16   hence there is no other *M·*.
nor sensation
  Un. 50–17   matter has neither *M·* nor sensation.
notion that
  Mis. 257– 1   the notion that *M·* can be in matter
not matter
  Mis. 56–10   Life is immortal *M·*, not matter.
     190– 1   Atomic action is *M·*, not matter.
  '00. 11–19   *M·*, not matter, makes music ;
of Christ
  Un. 33–12   it is certainly not the *M·* of Christ,
of God
  No. 37–27   if . . . sin existed in the *M·* of God.
  '01. 22– 4   It is the *M·* of God
     27–25   the *M·* of God and not of man
of Spirit
  Un. 32–11   It is not the *M·* of Spirit ;
omnipotence of the
  Mis. 201–12   omnipotence of the *M·* that knows

Mind

omnipotent
  My. 106– 9   immutable laws of omnipotent *M·*
omniscient
  Mis. 25–23   omnipotent and omniscient *M·*.
  No. 23–27   omnipresent and omniscient *M·* ;
one
  Mis. 82–25   the one *M·* is immortal.
     101–31   This one *M·* and His individuality
     173– 6   that there is but one *M·*,
     196– 3   there is but one God, one *M·* ;
     279–28   enough . . . if we are of one *M·* ;
  Ret. 56–19   Hence there is but one *M·* ;
     57–21   The notion of more than one *M·*,
  Un. 24– 7   assumptions . . . more than the one *M·*,
  Rud. 13–13   one Life and one *M·*.
  No. 20–12   one *M·*, a perfect man, and
     27– 2   supposition . . . more than one *M·*.
     38–20   one *M·*, one consciousness,
  Pan. 6–18   Did one *M·*, or two minds,
     7–27   hypothesis of . . . more than one *M·*,
  My. 109– 8   we shall have one *M·*, one God,
     132–21   one *M·* and that divine ;
     279–14   Had all peoples one *M·*, peace would
     281–11   namely, one God, one *M·*,
     286– 6   have one God, one *M·* ;
only
  Rud. 4–18   not in matter, but in *M·* only.
     5–28   or exist in *M·* only ;
or God
  Mis. 69– 6   *M·*, or God, and His attributes.
  Ret. 56– 5   the one divine *M·*, or God,
  No. 5–19   *M·*, or God, does not meddle with it.
or good
  Ret. 56–24   does not subdivide *M·*, or good,
  Un. 45–28   immortal *M·*, or good.
or Life
  Ret. 57–21   notion of more than one *M·*, or Life,
or matter
  Mis. 23–10   Was it *M·* or matter that spake
over matter
  Hea. 7– 6   the power of *M·* over matter.
perfect
  Mis. 3–22   the supreme and perfect *M·*,
     37–18   God, the perfect *M·*,
     175–26   and reveals the one perfect *M·*
     198– 1   governed by the one perfect *M·*,
  Ret. 28– 7   Science of the perfect *M·*
power of
  Mis. 60–12   *Does it not limit the power of M·*
     60–15   Does it limit the power of *M·* to say
  Hea. 7– 6   power of *M·* over matter.
pretension to be
  Rud. 7–20   As a pretension to be *M·*, matter is
Principle is
  No. 20–10   This Principle is *M·*, substance,
problem of
  Mis. 333–19   to work out the problem of *M·*,
pure
  Mis. 260–16   pure *M·* is the truth of being
     260–23   acknowledging pure *M·* as absolute
     260–25   Pure *M·* gives out an atmosphere that
realities of
  Mis. 333–28   the grand realities of *M·*,
  No. 6– 3   to attempt to destroy the realities of *M·*
reality of
  No. 10–23   discords have not the reality of *M·*
reconstructed
  Ret. 28–22   *M·* reconstructed the body,
  Pul. 35–21   *M·* reconstructed the body,
reign of
  Mis. 51–25   * reign of *M·* commence on earth,
relating to
  Mis. 379–28   momentous facts relating to *M·*
rely on
  Pul. 69–10   * rely on *M·* for cure,
rests on
  No. 10–14   My hygienic system rests on *M·*,
reveals
  Ret. 59–18   reveals *M·*, the only living and true
revolves
  Ret. 88–29   *M·* revolves on a spiritual axis,
right
  Mis. 59–20   There is but one right *M·*,
     104–14   Clothed, and in its right *M·*,
rights of
  My. 212–25   interfering with the rights of *M·*,
same
  Un. 4–19   bids man have the same *M·*
scale of
  Mis. 280–15   into the scale of *M·*,
Science of
     (see **Science**)
self-existent
  Ret. 60– 4   as eternal, self-existent *M·* ;

Mind

servant of
Mis. 47–18   body is the servant of *M·*,

sin is not
No. 27– 1   Sin is not *M·* ; it is but the

Soul, or
Mis. 189–15   supposition that Soul, or *M·* is
Un. 29–12   one God, one Soul, or *M·*,

spake
Mis. 280– 1   *M·* spake and form appeared.

sphere of
No. 37– 9   and when, as a sphere of *M·*,

subordinate to
Mis. 29–30   powerless and subordinate to *M·*.

such a
Un. 64–10   approximate to such a *M·*,

superiority of
Mis. 30–18   superiority of *M·* over the flesh,

supremacy of
Mis. 35– 5   supremacy of *M·* over matter,

that
Mis. 59–22   Any copartnership with that *M·*
    235– 7   becomes the partaker of that *M·*
Man. 16–10   pray for that *M·* to be in us
Un. 38– 7   of that *M·* which is Life.
Pul. 75– 3   that *M·* which was in Christ Jesus.
My. 287–17   are made partakers of that *M·*

that governs
Peo. 8–17   *M·*, that governs the universe,

that is God
Mis. 4– 7   Science of the *M·* that is God,
    57–30   in and of the *M·* that is God,
   113– 1   *M·* that is God is not in matter ;
My. 267– 5   the law of the *M·* that is God,

that is identical
Un. 33–13   not the *M·* that is identical with

theology of
Mis. 59– 2   the healing theology of *M·*,

the only
Mis. 55–25   regards God as the only *M·*,
   361–24   God is the only *M·*,
Un. 25– 8   the only substance, the only *M·*.
   29–11   the only *M·* and intelligence
No. 35–21   God is the only *M·*,

this
Mis. 82–30   This *M·*, then, is not subject to
   105–31   God is Mind, and this *M·* is good,
   197–21   "let this *M·* be in you,— *Phil.* 2 : 5.
   279–29   will feel the influence of this *M·* ;
   332– 3   this *M·* is Truth,
   332– 5   this *M·* is Love,
   364–20   nothing apart from this *M·*,
Un. 14–21   if this *M·* is familiar with evil,
'01. 7–13   include within this *M·* the thoughts
Hea. 15–16   perpetually at war with this *M·*,
My. 108–15   this *M·* is the only lawgiver,
   108–18   The more of this *M·* the better

through
Mis. 70–22   inevitably separated through *M·*.
   74–23   through *M·*, he removed any
   258– 7   through *M·*, he restored sight
   269–20   can only be Christianized through *M·* ;
   368–19   treating disease through *M·*.
Chr. 53–48   gleaming through *M·*, mother, man.
Ret. 69–22   God created all through *M·*,
My. 103–20   demonstrated through *M·* the effects
   106–31   Nazarene Prophet, healed through *M·*,

to matter
Rud. 6– 9   when we change . . . from *M·* to matter,

translates
Mis. 22–10   C. S. translates *M·*, God,

true
Ret. 73–16   in God,— in the true *M·*,
Un. 32–17   True *M·* is immortal.

unerring
Mis. 172–12   unerring *M·* measures man,
Un. 53–24   the immortal and unerring *M·*,

unfathomable
Un. 28–22   must be the unfathomable *M·*,

unity of
Peo. 13–11   unity of *M·* and oneness of Principle.

universe of
Mis. 369– 9   immeasurable universe of *M·*,

unlimited
Hea. 4– 1   unlimited *M·* cannot start from

was the creator
Mis. 57– 6   and *M·* was the creator.

we exist in
Mis. 50–25   we exist in *M·*, live thereby,

which is God
Un. 44–18   not expressive of the *M·* which is God.
   56– 6   no sin . . . in the *M·* which is God.

which is good
Un. 2–16   the *M·* which is good, or God,

which is immortal
Mis. 36– 5   Truth, or the *M·* which is immortal."

Mind

without
Mis. 269–21   without *M·* the body is without action ;
Un. 50–23   a consciousness which is without *M·*
Rud. 5–16   must be . . . or matter without *M·*.
   5–17   Matter without *M·* is . . . impossibility.
My. 106–15   Without *M·*, man . . . would collapse ;

would be chained
Mis. 102– 7   If . . . *M·* would be chained to finity,

Mis. 8– 6   "in Him [*M·*] we live,— *Acts* 17 : 28.
   23–15   must be *M·* ; for matter is not the
   23–22   Spirit, *M·*, are terms synonymous
   23–30   All must be *M·* and Mind's ideas ;
   25–12   translates matter into *M·*,
   27–25   being in and of Spirit, *M·*,
   55–29   If *M·* is in matter
   55–31   either a godless and material *M·*, or
   56– 7   If *M·* is not substance,
   74–17   into its original meaning, *M·*.
  101–24   not matter, but *M·*.
  173–12   *M·* is its own great cause
  173–15   that *M·* is in matter?
  173–21   *M·*, God, is all-power
  175–21   and its methods in place of God, *M·*.
  196– 2   found not in matter but in *M·*,
  243–22   or human will, not *M·*.
  256–26   Wherever law is, *M·* is ;
  257– 7   must be made by Mind and as *M·*.
  280–15   *M·* is not put into the scales with
  379–13   matter was not as real as *M·*,
  379–25   Is it matter, or is it *M·*,
Ret. 28–19   *M·*, which divides, subdivides,
   56– 6   Whatever . . . divides *M·* into minds,
   56–23   God reflects Himself, or *M·*,
   59–19   and all that is made by Him, *M·*,
   60–29   but one Spirit, *M·*, Soul.
   73– 5   without finiteness of form or *M·*.
   76–17   *M·* "which was also in— *Phil.* 2 : 5.
Un. 25– 8   *M·* is not, cannot be, in matter.
   25– 9   as *M·*, and not as matter.
   25–11   This lie, that *M·* can be in matter,
   45–25   substance of Spirit,— *M·*, Life, Soul.
   50– 1   notion of the destructibility of *M·*
   53–12   To say that *M·* is material,
   53–13   or that evil is *M·*,
Pul. vii–19   not by matter, but by *M·* ;
   6– 9   not matter, but *M·* ;
   14–27   benefit which *M·* has wrought.
Rud. 5–17   *M·* in matter is pantheism.
   6– 6   As *M·* they are real,
   6– 7   beauty and goodness are in . . . *M·*,
   10–24   belief that matter can master *M·*,
Pan. 7–28   hypothesis of . . . matter governing *M·*,
   12–24   Truth, Love, substance, Spirit, *M·*,
'00. 4–25   must proceed from God, from *M·*,
'01. 3–18   By this we mean *M·*,
   5–16   by *M·*, not by matter.
   17–25   dynamics of medicine is *M·*.
   24–13   Making matter more potent than *M·*,
Hea. 7– 9   its original language, which is *M·*,
   13–23   *M·*, divine Science, the truth of
Peo. 1– 7   back to its original language,— *M·*,
   9–25   of any other power than *M·*
My. 52–13   * *M·*, Truth, Life, and Love,
  119– 9   in *M·*, not in matter.
  159–27   * "What is the essence of God?   *M·*."
  160– 1   and keeps *M·* much out of sight.
  181–12   and Life not in matter but in *M·*.
  225–29   *M·*, Soul, which combine as *one*.
  260–24   elevates medicine to *M·* ;
  350– 4   with the divine noumenon, *M·*,

mind (*see also* **mind's**)

action of
   (*see* **action**)

affects
Mis. 247–26   believe that the body affects *m·*,

affects the
Mis. 5–31   believe that the body affects the *m·*,

affects the body
Mis. 5–32   that the *m·* affects the body.

aid of
My. 301–28   cannot . . . without the aid of *m·*.

already full
My. 210– 5   added to the *m·* already full.

altitude of
Pan. 6–26   elevating evil to the altitude of *m·*

and body
Mis. 25– 1   supposed power on the *m·* and body of
   60–23   *If mortal m· and body are myths*,
   62–29   over the human *m·* and body ;
   65–25   the equipoise of *m·* and body,
  187– 1   regeneration of both *m·* and body,
  187– 7   the perfection of *m·* and body,
  268–24   ailments of mortal *m·* and body.

mind

and body
Mis. 286–24   mortal *m·* and body as *one,*
Pul. 10– 2   healing both *m·* and body,
No. 40–26   *m·* and body are made better only by
Hea. 3– 2   to heal both *m·* and body ;
    8– 3   that heals both *m·* and body ;
    8– 6   the truth regarding *m·* and body,
Peo. 5–25   and a healthy *m·* and body.
My. 105– 3   only medicine for *m·* and body.
and character
Mis. 67– 9   his rights of *m·* and character.
and manners
My. 309– 3   cultivated in *m·* and manners.
and matter
Un. 32– 9   so-called *m·* and matter cannot
    45– 6   saying, . . . Am I not *m·* and matter,
Hea. 11–25   supposed to be both *m·* and matter.
My. 179–10   good and evil, both *m·* and matter,
    293– 6   this compound of *m·* and matter
animated by
Peo. 5–23   is not . . . matter animated by *m·,*
another
Mis. 37– 2   if there were in reality another *m·*
    96–28   not one mind acting upon another *m·* ;
No. 40–21   to meddle with another *m·,*
Hea. 15–15   claim another *m·* perpetually at war
another's
Mis. 83–15   If . . . originated in another's *m·,*
apart from
My. 108– 6   challenge matter to act apart from *m·* ;
appeal to
Peo. 7–25   appeal to *m·* to improve its subjects
assent of
Mis. 240–14   without the assent of *m·,*
as something separate
Ret. 60– 5   *m·* as something separate from God.
athletic
Pul. 5–14   his athletic *m·,* scholarly and serene,
attitude of
My. 290–27   Hold this attitude of *m·,* and it will
attribute of
Pul. 53–18   * attribute of *m·* which elevates man
bear in
Mis. 93–24   Bear in *m·,* however, that human
    126–25   bear in *m·* that, in the long race,
    196–11   bear in *m·* that a serpent said that ;
    263–12   bear in *m·* that His presence,
My. 148–24   Bear in *m·* always that Christianity
begins in
Hea. 7 15   begins in *m·* to heal the body,
belief that
Ret. 69–28   belief that *m·* is in matter,
believed to be
Un. 33–15   believed to be *m·* only through error
belong to
Mis. 228–24   belong to *m·* and not to matter.
benefit the
Mis. 241– 3   God . . . to benefit the *m·.*
biased
Mis. 240–20   easier . . . than the biased *m·.*
body and
Mis. 163–29   spiritual healing of body and *m·.*
    241– 3   Body and *m·* are correlated
    268–19   heals body and *m·,* head and heart ;
called
Un. 46– 1   mortal error, called *m·,*
call to
My. 347–17   call to *m·* the number of
came through
Hea. 17–27   If sickness and . . . came through *m·,*
can rest
Mis. 227–23   a life wherein the *m·* can rest
capacities of
Ret. 82–21   Their liberated capacities of *m·*
carnal
Mis. 36–24   says, "The carnal *m· — Rom.* 8 : 7.
    54– 1   carnal *m·* cannot discern spiritual
    169–26   carnal *m·,* which is enmity
    214– 3   it appeared hate to the carnal *m·,*
change the
Un. 35– 5   Change the *m·,* and the quality
child's
Mis. 51–15   a declaration to the child's *m·*
claims to be
Ret. 56–21   Whatever else claims to be *m·,*
classified as
Pan. 4– 9   are properly classified as *m·,*
comes from
Un. 56– 5   since all suffering comes from *m·,*
connecting
Mis. 393– 3   Nature, with the *m·* connecting,
Po. 51– 8   Nature, with the *m·* connecting,
conscious
'01. 24– 1   * Matter apart from conscious *m·*
constantly in
Mis. 62– 4   opposite image . . . constantly in *m·,*

mind

disease as
Hea. 12– 8   he diagnoses disease as *m·,*
dishonest
Mis. 288–24   the shift of a dishonest *m·,*
dominance of
Pul. 31–18   * the dominance of *m·* over matter,
enables
Hea. 15– 9   it enables *m·* to govern matter,
erring
Mis. 63– 4   claim that one erring *m·* cures
    199– 4   erring *m·* can claim to do thus,
    286–22   states of the human erring *m·* ;
Ret. 59– 2   a finite and erring *m·,*
error of
Hea. 9–24   an error of *m·* or of body.
evil
Mis. 173–17   Does an evil *m·* exist without space
    362–18   an evil *m·* already doomed,
Un. 24–18   There is, can be, no evil *m·,*
No. 38– 8   no intelligent sin, evil *m·* or matter :
My. 228– 7   The evil *m·* calls it "skulking,"
evil, as
Mis. 261– 1   evil, as *m·,* is doomed,
expression of
Mis. 247–27   body is an expression of *m·,*
faith in
Hea. 15– 7   it reposes all faith in *m·,*
feeblest
Peo. 11– 5   it was found that the feeblest *m·,*
ferocious
Mis. 36–10   ferocious *m·* seen in the beast
fill the
Pul. 69–12   * fill the *m·* with good thoughts
finite
Mis. 162–24   without corporeality or finite *m·.*
Ret. 30–15   finite *m·* and material existence.
Un. 24–15   There is no really finite *m·,*
form of
Un. 32– 9   not . . . but a false form of *m·.*
governed by
Mis. 34– 6   The body is governed by *m·* ;
    291– 3   *m·* governed by Principle
governs
Hea. 14–16   to know that *m·* governs the body
harpstrings of the
Mis. 396–18   O'er waiting harpstrings of the *m·*
Pul. 18– 2   O'er waiting harpstrings of the *m·*
Po. 12– 1   O'er waiting harpstrings of the *m·*
My. 31– 8   * "O'er waiting harpstrings of the *m·* ; "
has departed
My. 302– 7   a corpse, whence *m·* has departed.
his
Peo. 9– 8   but it cannot purify his *m·,*
My. 211–25   poured constantly into his *m·,*
his own
Mis. 266– 8   the subjective state of his own *m·*
human
    (*see* **human**)
if it is
Un. 33–12   if it is *m·,* it is certainly not
impress of
Peo. 7– 3   leaving the impress of *m·* on the
independent of
Hea. 12– 6   what . . . is doing independent of *m·,*
individual
Rud. 15–28   to fill anew the individual *m·.*
'01. 7–17   differing needs of the individual *m·*
infinite
Pan. 3–18   infinite *m·* of one supreme, holy,
in harmony
Hea. 14–26   a *m·* in harmony with God,
in matter
Mis. 26–20   belief of *m·* in matter is pantheism.
    113– 1   result of sensuous *m·* in matter.
    179–21   It is the belief of *m·* in matter.
    198 6   denying . . . *m·* in matter,
    198–10   mortal claim to . . . *m·* in matter,
Ret. 21–22   false sense of . . . *m·* in matter,
Un. 24–11   *Evil.* I am . . . a *m·* in matter,
    54– 2   the doctrine of *m·* in matter.
Pan. 2–15   human opinion of . . . *m·* in matter.
    7–26   hypothesis of *m·* in matter,
'01. 17– 3   mortal sense of . . . *m·* in matter
My. 109– 4   Adam-dream of *m·* in matter,
    296–16   mortal dream of . . . *m·* in matter,
instructor's
Mis. 264–28   instructor's *m·* must take its hue from
is stayed
My. 290–15   *m·* is stayed on Thee :— *Isa.* 26 : 3.
is the cause
My. 302– 8   proof that *m·* is the cause of
is the criminal
Hea. 7–22   a crime, and *m·* is the criminal.
keep in
My. 191–11   Keep in *m·* the foundations of

mind

lawless
  Mis. 260–30   lawless *m·*, with unseen motives,
legislation of
  Peo. 11–20   obedient to the legislation of *m·*,
limited
  No. 19–11   He is neither a limited *m·* nor a
mandate of
  My. 302– 2   Through the mandate of *m·*
manipulates
  Ret. 71–18   He who secretly manipulates *m·*
march of
  Pul. 14– 1   march of *m·* and of honest
marred in
  Peo. 10–20   fettered free limbs, and marred in *m·*
master of
  Un. 34– 3   declares . . . is the master of *m·*,
material
  Mis. 336– 7   to kill the serpent of a material *m·*.
  Un. 23–22   An evil material *m·*, so-called,
matter and
  Mis. 173–15   says that man is both matter and *m·*,
  '01. 25–10   which mix matter and *m·*,
  Hea. 13– 1   and divide . . . between matter and *m·*,
mind over
  Mis. 59–18   *Is not all argument mind over m·?*
      220–28   in this action of mind over *m·*,
misnamed
  Un. 32–15   misnamed *m·* is a false claim,
modes of
  Mis. 360– 8   Theirs were modes of *m·*
moods of
  Pan. 3– 9   Certain moods of *m·* find an
mortal
      (see **mortal**)
motive, and
  Mis. 195– 3   all action, motive, and *m·*,
moved by
  Mis. 106–30   Moved by *m·*, your many-throated
My
  Un. 18–11   If pain . . . were not in My *m·*,
my
  Mis. 62– 2   the *right* idea of man in my *m·*,
      224–31   it is a question in my *m·*,
      290–16   * influence of your thought on my *m·*,
  Un. 24–23   My *m·* is more than matter.
  My. 59–16   * my *m·* was carried back to
New England
  Pul. 65– 3   * what is called the New England *m·*
no
  Mis. 196– 3   will then claim no *m·* apart from
  Un. 33–17   and you find no *m·* therein.
no other
  '01. 20– 6   guided by no other *m·* than Truth,
not matter
  My. 107–20   identifies . . . with *m·*, not matter,
      302– 4   *m·*, not matter, produces the result
obtrude upon the
  Mis. 10– 1   obtrude upon the *m·* or engraft upon
of a person
  Mis. 283– 5   to enter the *m·* of a person,
of Christ
  My. 142– 2   * we have the *m·* of Christ.' — *I Cor.* 2 : 16.
of his pupil
  Rud. 9– 7   spring up in the *m·* of his pupil.
of Jesus
  Mis. 200– 2   Truth in the *m·* of Jesus,
of the individual
  Hea. 6–21   the *m·* of the individual only
of the Lord
  My. 142– 1   the *m·* of the Lord, — *I Cor.* 2 : 16.
of the neophyte
  My. 48–26   * upon the *m·* of the neophyte
of the perpetrator
  Mis. 222–16   action on the *m·* of the perpetrator,
of the pupil
  Rud. 15–24   *m·* of the pupil may be dissected
of the reader
  My. 218–18   tends to confuse the *m·* of the reader,
of your patient
  My. 364– 4   but the *m·* of your patient,
one
  Mis. 96–28   not one *m·* acting upon another
      134–12   Be "of one *m·*," — *II Cor.* 13 : 11.
      175–23   that one *m·* controls another ;
      279–23   and they were of one *m·*.
      279–26   disciples, too, were of one *m·*.
  No. 40–21   is it right for one *m·* to meddle
or body
  Mis. 59–25   away from the human *m·* or body,
      97–28   perfect man in *m·* or body,
      103–22   inference . . . either as *m·* or body,
      341– 2   the right action of *m·* or body.
originate
  Hea. 17–26   did not *m·* originate the delusion?

mind

originate in
  Hea. 12–11   all physical effects originate in *m·*
or matter
  Mis. 103–20   Mortal man, as *m·* or matter,
      218–16   inconceivable, either as *m·* or matter ;
  No. 38– 8   no intelligent sin, evil *m·* or matter :
  My. 108– 4   is *m·* or matter the intelligent cause
over matter
  Hea. 15– 8   the power of *m·* over matter,
  My. 74–13   * triumph of *m·* over matter.
      97– 2   * admit the power of *m·* over matter.
patient's
  Mis. 220–12   until the patient's *m·* yields,
      355–24   discern the error in thy patient's *m·*
people's
  Peo. 2–27   constantly before the people's *m·*,
peoples the
  Mis. 82– 1   peoples the *m·* with spiritual ideas,
personality of
  Ret. 25–23   physical personality of *m·*
philosophy of
  Mis. 68–24   * defines it as "the philosophy of *m·*,
possibilities of
  Mis. 47–14   and the possibilities of *m·* when
power of
  Hea. 15– 8   the power of *m·* over matter,
      19– 2   test the power of *m·* over body ;
  My. 97– 2   * admit the power of *m·* over matter.
produces disease
  Hea. 6–13   I learned how *m·* produces disease
public
  Mis. 78–19   Misguiding the public *m·* and
purification of
  Peo. 9– 3   this baptism is the purification of *m·*,
reaches
  Mis. 223–10   that *m·* reaches its own ideal,
reading the
  Hea. 7–17   reading the *m·* of the poor woman
reassuring the
  My. 293–17   reassuring the *m·* and through the
renders the
  Rud. 15– 9   This renders the *m·* less inquisitive,
repeal it in
  Peo. 12–12   repeal it in *m·*, and acknowledge only
requires
  Hea. 11–26   requires *m·* imbued with Truth
restless
  Ret. 11– 6   Go fix thy restless *m·*
  Po. 60– 2   Go fix thy restless *m·*
right
  '00. 6–23   clothed and in his right *m·*,
satisfies the
  Mis. 227–26   honest life satisfies the *m·*
science of
  My. 307– 7   and it was the science of *m·*,
science of the
  Mis. 68–24   * defined . . . science of the *m·*."
self-satisfied
  My. 180–25   the disguised or the self-satisfied *m·*,
sensation of
  My. 228– 4   so-called disease is a sensation of *m·*,
sensible
  Un. 50– 8   belief in matter as sensible *m·*.
sensuous
  Mis. 113– 1   the result of sensuous *m·* in matter.
separate
  Mis. 196– 8   a separate *m·* from God (good),
shock to the
  Rud. 15– 7   glad surprise . . . is a shock to the *m·* ;
small
  Mis. 147–11   and indicates a small *m·* ?
so-called
  Mis. 41–24   the cause in that so-called *m·*
      196– 9   so-called *m·* shall open your eyes
      233–32   sensation . . . in this so-called *m·* ;
      363– 1   more nearly an erring so-called *m·*
  Ret. 70– 4   so-called *m·* puts forth its own
  Un. 23–22   An evil material *m·*, so-called,
      32– 9   so-called *m·* and matter cannot be
      34–23   so-called *m·* would have no identity.
spiritual
  Peo. 4–22   No . . . can make a spiritual *m·*
state of
      (see **state**)
states of
  Mis. 221–15   these states of *m·* will stultify
  Pul. 87–22   states of *m·*, to bless mankind.
stopped by
  Hea. 19– 6   could not have been stopped by *m·*
substance, or
  Mis. 198–10   claim to life, substance, or *m·*
  My. 296–16   dream of life, substance, or *m·*
suppositional
  Mis. 363–11   material mode of a suppositional *m·*
  Un. 32–16   a false claim, a suppositional *m·*,

mind

teacher's
Mis. 264–26 teacher's *m·* must be pure, grand,
this
Mis. 42– 7 this *m·* is still in a
    220–13 has the full control over this *m·*
Ret. 34–20 this *m·* must be renovated
Un. 11–10 showed the need of changing this *m·*
    32–11 What is this *m·*?
    33– 2 which prove . . . this *m·* a lie.
Hea. 14–28 a body governed by this *m·*.
My. 364– 5 and treat this *m·* to be Christly.
thy
My. 183– 3 and with all thy *m·* ; — *Luke* 10 : 27.
to meditate
Po. 1–17 turns The *m·* to meditate on
touches
Mis. 235–15 touches *m·* to more spiritual issues,
transmit
Ret. 68–19 can matter originate or transmit *m·* ?
triumph of
Peo. 13–17 triumph of *m·* over the body,
My. 74–13 * triumph of *m·* over matter.
Truth-filled
Peo. 5–24 therefore a Truth-filled *m·* makes
universal
'01. 23–30 * operations of the universal *m·*,
with mind
My. 154–27 *m·* with mind, soul with soul,
without
Mis. 28– 7 muscles cannot move without *m·*.
without the
'01. 24– 3 not *without* the *m·*, but within it,
your
Mis. 271–14 Cleanse your *m·* of the cobwebs
My. 345– 1 see that your *m·* is in such a state

Mis. 23– 5 Does *m·* "sleep in the mineral,
    36– 6 *Do animals and beasts have a m·?*
    44–15 has the *m·*, or extracting, or both,
    44–22 or that *m·* is *in* matter,
    45–26 intelligence or *m·* termed evil.
    98– 2 perfect model should be held in *m·*,
    184– 7 reflects God in body as well as in *m·*.
    228–22 must be caught through *m·* ;
    230–12 travel of limb more than *m·*.
    261– 3 As *m·*, evil finds no escape from
    308–26 holding in *m·* the consciousness of
    350–20 in the *m·* that handled them.
    363– 6 supposition that . . . is *m·*
Ret. 27–23 *m·* can duly express it to the ear,
    09–28 belief . . . that evil is *m·*,
    76–11 *m·* to which this Science was revealed
Un. 26– 3 and the capacity to evolve *m·*,
    32– 8 By matter is commonly meant *m·*,
    33–11 but unless matter is *m·*,
    33– 2 or that *m·* sees by means of
Pul. 6–30 whose *m·* never swerved from
    53– 9 * in the *m·* of both reader and patient,
    80– 1 * must be a righting-up of the *m·*
Rud. 5–15 either *m·* which is called matter, or
No. 5–22 *m·* that attacks a normal and real
Pan. 6–22 if . . . evil also is *m·*,
    9– 1 that *m·* "sleeps in the mineral,
'01. 11– 7 and *m·* is no longer in matter.
    17–25 must be *m·* that controls the effect ;
    24– 0 produced by divine power on the *m·*
Hea. 7–20 he charged home a crime to *m·*,
    11–24 places all cause and cure as *m·* ;
    18– 1 in ruling them out of *m·*
    19– 5 governed . . . entirely by *m·*,
Peo. 5–24 but in itself is *m·* ;
    12–14 know what a power *m·* is to heal
My. 48–30 * higher nature through the *m·*,
    108– 6 and if *m·*, I have proved beyond cavil
    210– 7 in a *m·* filled with goodness.
    256–13 close the door of *m·* on this
    272–30 * a *m·* that has had so much influence
    293–17 through the *m·* resuscitating the
    301–29 If *m·* be absent from the body,
    301–30 *m·* must be, is, the vehicle of
    302–10 craze is that matter masters *m·* ;
    334–14 * the woman whom he had in *m·*
    346–23 * had in *m·* any particular person

mind (verb)
Mis. 13– 4 special care to *m·* my own business.
    283–14 * "*M·* your own business,"

mind-cure
Mis. 58–27 "*m·*," nothing more nor less,
    59– 5 This is the mortal "*m·*"
    59– 8 there had better be no "*m·*,"
    62–15 *when the m· claims to heal*
    62–20 A "*m·*" is a matter-cure.
    62–30 "*m·*" rests on the notion that

mind-cure
Mis. 233–16 and naming that "*m·*,"
    243–21 There are charlatans in "*m·*,"

Mind-cure on a Material Basis
Mis. 62–22 book title

mind-curists
'01. 21– 1 mortal *m·*, nor faith-curists ;

minded
Mis. 24– 2 makes man spiritually *m·*.
    24– 3 to be carnally *m·* is death ; — *Rom.* 8 : 6.
    24– 4 to be spiritually *m·* is — *Rom.* 8 : 6.
Ret. 76–14 The spiritually *m·* meet on the
'02. 6–26 degree that man becomes spiritually *m·*
    6–27 to be carnally *m·* is death ; — *Rom.* 8 : 6.
    6–28 to be spiritually *m·* is — *Rom.* 8 : 6.
    8–15 The spiritually *m·* are inspired with

Mind-force
Mis. 22–31 *M·*, invisible to material sense,
    331–23 divine *M·*, filling all space

Mind-healer
Ret. 76–20 serves to constitute the *M·*

Mind-healers
No. 3–20 sense which *M·* specially need ;

Mind-healing

Christian Science
Mis. 78– 7 *Can C. S. M· be taught to*
    80–32 C. S. *M·* rests demonstrably on
    273–22 interest in C. S. *M·*
    358–24 teaching C. S. *M·*,
    364– 1 the textbook of C. S. *M·*,
    382–15 first student in C. S. *M·* ;
Ret. 43– 3 teaching one student C. S. *M·*.
    48–23 instructed in C. S. *M·*,
    50– 2 instruction in C. S. *M·*,
Rud. 7– 1 how much you understand of C. S. *M·*.
    17– 8 understanding of C. S. *M·*
No. 2–27 in relation to C. S. *M·*,
    3–10 the practice of C. S. *M·*
    12– 1 C. S. *M·* can only be gained by
    32–13 C. S. *M·* lifts with a steady arm,
    43–17 C. S. *M·* is dishonored by
My. 210–20 notion that C. S. *M·* should be
    212–17 the teaching of C. S. *M·*.
    213– 1 natural fruits of C. S. *M·*

Science of
    (*see* **Science**)

Mis. 41 5 malpractice would disgrace *M·*,
    48–26 study of *M·* would cure the
    66–11 verified in all directions in *M·*,
    67– 2 mere alphabet of *M·*.
    67–22 right practice of *M·* achieved,
    88–38 *M·*, and healing with drugs,
    221–22 baffles the student of *M·*,
    223–14 This individual disbelieves in *M·*,
    255–17 chapter sub-title
    260–22 The truth of *M·* uplifts
    264–24 Their knowledge of *M·* may be
    269–23 *M·* is the proper means of
    282–23 believe in the efficacy of *M·*,
    351–10 through the mental method of *M·*,
    356–26 to the understanding of *M·* ;
Ret. 33–14 to prove the Principle of *M·*.
    35– 2 spiritual, scientific *M·*,
    42–12 remarkably successful in *M·*,
    44– 2 a *M·* church, without a creed,
    52– 3 expansion of scientific *M·*,
    78–15 rules of *M·* are wholly Christlike
    85–20 abusing the practice of *M·*
    89– 4 proven . . . in the practice of *M·*.
Pul. 35–24 * convinced of the Principle of *M·*,
Rud. 6–18 basis of *M·* a destruction of
    6–22 this predicate and postulate of *M·* ;
    8–18 not otherwise in the field of *M·*.
    9– 3 The teacher of *M·* who is not
    12–12 denies the Principle of *M·*,
    16– 9 its scientific relation to *M·*,
    16–23 shades of difference in *M·*
No. v– 8 laborers in the realm of *M·*.
    1–21 the only *M·* I vindicate ;
    3–18 The Nemesis of the history of *M·*
    5– 3 this grand verity of *M·*.
    15–14 far more mystic than *M·*.
    19– 1 high premium on *M·*,
    26– 5 This infantile talk about *M·*
    44– 7 My system of *M·* swerves not

mind-healing
Mis. 272–19 * "All the *m·* colleges . . . have simply
No. 2– 3 A spurious and hydra-headed *m·*
    31– 3 Material and mortal *m·*

minding
My. 276–11 she is *m·* her own business,

mind-manipulator
  Ret. 71–16 Ask the unbridled *m·* if he
mind-matter
  Un. 45–18 make *m·* a habitant of the
Mind-medicine
  Mis. 270–29 The next step is *M·*.
mind-method
  Mis. 277–16 falsehoods, and a secret *m·*,
mind-models
  Peo.   7–29 as his *m·* are more or less spiritual.
Mind-pictures
  No. 39–25 this light reveals the pure *M·*,
mind-pictures
  Un. 64–11 more real those *m·* would become
Mind-power
  My.   4–19 *M·* is good will towards men.
mind-power
  Mis. 222–22 under this new *régime* of *m·*,
  My. 213– 3 malicious aim of perverted *m·*,
Mind-practice
  Ret. 78– 5 achieved the entire wisdom of *M·*.
mind-practice
  Ret. 71– 8 ignorant or an unprincipled *m·*
mind-quacks
  No. 26– 1 *m·* believe that mortal man is
  29– 7 *m·* have so slight a knowledge of
Mind's
  Mis.   3–18 Hygiene, . . . not *M·* medicine.
  23–30 All must be Mind and *M·* ideas ;
  60–20 *M·* possibilities are not lessened by
  Un. 12– 5 curving sickle of *M·* eternal circle,
  14–24 reflected in man, *M·* image.
  No. 27–16 divine Mind and that *M·* idea.
mind's
  Mis. 33–28 found in mortal *m·* opposite,
  119– 2 through the *m·* tympanum,
  139–28 in advance of the erring *m·* apprehension.
  Ret. 31–22 Into mortal *m·* material obliquity
  Pul.   2–15 With the *m·* eye glance at the
  Hea.   6–15 I saw how the *m·* ideals were
  Peo.   7– 5 leaving to rot and ruin the *m·* ideals.
  10–24 follow the *m·* freedom from sin ;
minds
  all
  Mis.   1–11 kindle all *m·* with a gleam of
  6–12 prove to all *m·* the power of
  56–26 *if all m· (men) have existed from the*
  307–18 is fast fitting all *m·* for the
  No.   1– 1 kindle in all *m·* a common sentiment of
  become
  Mis. 316–12 Until *m·* become less worldly-minded,
  class of
  My. 111– 7 same class of *m·* to deal with
  envious
  Mis. 291–30 counteract the influence of envious *m·*
  evil
  My. 228– 5 Evil *m·* signally blunder in divine
  influence the
  My. 175–29 must fail to influence the *m·* of
  many
  Mis.   4–21 in many *m·* it is confounded with
  7–20 descriptions carry fears to many *m·*,
  196– 4 the supposition of . . . many *m·*
  Un. 24– 5 To believe in *m·* many is to
  '00.   4– 4 so unwittingly consents to many *m·*
  men's
  Pul. 79–20 * had taken possession of men's *m·*,
  mortal
  Peo. 11–18 Mortals, *alias* mortal *m·*,
  My. 301–22 effects of illusion on mortal *m·*
  of all present
  My. 170– 9 in the *m·* of all present
  of invalids
  Rud. 12–16 erases from the *m·* of invalids their
  of men
  My. 225–18 begins in the *m·* of men
  264–16 signifies to the *m·* of men
  295– 4 remains in the *m·* of men,
  of mortals
  Mis. 257–11 *alias* the *m·* of mortals.
  My.   5– 1 originates in the *m·* of mortals.
  294–10 contradicting *m·* of mortals.
  of others
  Mis. 220–26 put it into the *m·* of others
  of the healthy
  Rud. 12–24 to free the *m·* of the healthy
  of the people
  My. 234–28 *m·* of the people are prepared
  of thinkers
  No. 13–23 a revolution in the *m·* of thinkers

minds
  other
  Mis. 40–28 evil too common to other *m·*.
  43–11 least likely to pour into other *m·*
  92–10 enlightens other *m·* most readily,
  96–30 not the transference . . . to other *m·* ;
  175–22 that there are other *m·*
  Man. 87–19 personally controls other *m·*,
  Ret. 84– 7 enlightens other *m·* most readily,
  84–24 personally controls other *m·*,
  89–27 endeavoring to influence other *m·*
  My. 211–29 Other *m·* are made dormant by it,
  our
  Mis. 169–17 borne fully to our *m·* and hearts.
  282–12 would we have our *m·* tampered with.
  plurality of
  Pan.   7– 3 shows that a plurality of *m·*,
  so-called
  Pan.   4–15 there are many so-called *m·* ;
  students'
  Mis. 93– 2 able to empty his students' *m·*,
  Ret. 84–21 able to empty his students' *m·*
  their
  Ret. 83– 9 foundations are already laid in their *m·*
  Pul. 66– 2 * to their *m·*, exists as much to-day
  two
  Mis. 289–20 *divorced* two *m·* in one.
  Pan.   6–19 Did one Mind, or two *m·*, enter
  6–21 if two *m·*, what becomes of theism
  unprejudiced
  Pul. 14–14 Millions of unprejudiced *m·*
  unprepared
  Mis. 84– 8 on *m·* unprepared for them.
  your
  My. 196–22 and faint in your *m·*." — *Heb.* 12 : 3.
  210– 2 keep your *m·* so filled with Truth

  Mis. 265–17 whose *m·* are, . . . disturbed by this
  299–11 conviction to the *m·* of many
  Ret. 56– 6 or divides Mind into *m·*,
  56–24 does not subdivide Mind, . . . into *m·*,
  My. 106–23 Is it because he *m·* his own business
Mind-science
  No. 43–24 garbling my statements of *M·*
Mind-sowing
  Un. 12– 3 few in this vineyard of *M·*
mine (noun)
  Mis. 393–10 Work ill-done within the misty *M·*
  Pul. 51–12 * worked in the *m·* of knowledge
  Po. 51–15 Work ill-done within the misty *M·*
mine (pronoun)
  Mis. 130–15 "Vengeance is *m·* ; — *Rom.* 12 : 19.
  My. 131–25 meat in *m·* house, — *Mal.* 3 : 10.
  188– 4, 5 *m·* eyes and *m·* heart — *I Kings* 9 : 3.
  188– 5 *m·* eyes shall be open, — *II Chron.* 7 : 15.
  188– 6 *m·* ears attent unto — *II Chron.* 7 : 15.
  193–28 thou art *m·*." — *Isa.* 43 : 1.
mineral
  Mis. 23– 5 * Does mind "sleep in the *m·*,
  217–13 *m·*, vegetable, and animal kingdoms,
  257– 4 sleeps in the *m·*, dreams in the
  Un. 38–24 *m·*, vegetable, or animal kingdoms.
  Pan.   9– 2 * "sleeps in the *m·*, dreams in the
minerals
  Rud.   7–26 transforming *m·* into vegetables
Minerva's
  Ret. 12– 3 *M·* silver sandals still
  Po. 61– 1 *M·* silver sandals still
mingle
  Mis. 40– 4 *m·* hygienic rules, drugs, and
  73– 7 they *m·* the testimony of
  160– 9 meet and *m·* in bliss supernal.
  Pul. 11– 5 *m·* with the joy of angels
  No. 21–17 *m·* in the same realm and consciousness.
mingled
  Mis. 81–11 *m· with the teachings of John*
  Ret. 80–16 *m·* sternness and gentleness
  My. 310–26 * *m·* with bad temper."
mingling
  Mis. 56–16 *m·* in perpetual warfare
  396–15 When *m·* with the universe,
  Ret.   1–19 thus *m·* in her children.
  Po. 59– 7 When *m·* with the universe,
minifying
  My. 227– 5 *m·* of his own goodness by another.
Minister
  Mis. 151–13 our *M·* and the great Physician :
minister
  Mis. 98–10 to *m·* and to be ministered unto ;
  289–29 by a magistrate, or by a *m·*
  296–11 noble women who *m·* in the sick-room

minister
Mis. 357– 4 Christian Scientists m· to the sick ;
Ret. 14–19 The m· then wished me to tell him
My. 323– 6 * by some m· in the far West.

ministered
Mis. 98–10 to minister and to be m· unto ;

ministering
Mis. 257–29 Samaritan m· to his neighbor's need.
Ret. 91–18 m· to the spiritual needs of all who

ministers
Mis. 5– 9 and m·, to heal the sick
33– 5 all m· and ministries of Christ,
158–29 as our churches ordain m·.
Pul. 45–25 * succeeded by the grandest of m·

ministration
Ret. 92– 5 His order of m· was
Pul. 34 12 * divine illumination and m·.

ministrations
No. 40–14 pursue their mental m· very sacredly,
My. 130–29 in all your public m·,
208–17 m· of God to man.

ministries
Mis. 33– 6 all ministers and m· of Christ,
My. 230– 3 amid m· aggressive and active,

ministry
Mis. 138– 8 in your m· and healing.
195–14 the m· of healing at this period.
Ret. 88–26 adopt the spirit of the Saviour's m·,
Pul. 20–11 my original system of m·
53– 8 * three years of his m· on earth,
My. 24– 4 * all who accept its divine m·.
28–30 * whose m· has revealed the one true
123–27 to attain to the m· of righteousness
147 17 This m·, reaching the physical,
153– 6 The healing and the gospel m·
327–30 * will dignify the m· of Christ
352– 9 * with its years of tender m·,

Ministry of Healing, The
No. 29–11 Dr. Gordon's sermon on The M· of H·,

Minn. (State)
(see Duluth, Minneapolis, St. Paul)

Minneapolis, Minn.
Pul. 90–10 * Times, M·, M·.
90–11 * Tribune, M·, M·.
My. 193–14 chapter sub-title

Minneapolis (**Minn.**) *News*
My. 275– 1 [M· (M·.) N·]

minor
Mis. 330 8 and, if on m· key,
Pul. 42– 7 * scarcely even a m· variation
Rud. 16–23 M· shades of difference in
'01. 4– 4 must be convertible to the m·.
'02. 9–16 m· tones of so-called material life
Po. 65–22 hath its music in low m· tones,
My. 255– 7 I do not mean that m· officers

minority
Mis. 308–13 those are a m· of its readers,
Rud. 8–16 Truth is in the m·
Peo. 3– 7 election of the m· to be saved
My. 294– 2 a large m· on the subject

minstrel (see also minstrel's)
Mis. 394–10 The harp of the m·,
Po. 45–13 The harp of the m·,

minstrel's
Mis. 384– 2 Come, in the m· lay ;
Po. 36– 1 Come, in the m· lay ;

minus
Un. 10–23 like commencing with the m· sign,
'01. 25–15 demonstration of matter m·,
'02. 7– 7 M· this spiritual understanding
My. 350– 5 is m· divine logic

minute
Mis. 158–19 God's servants are m· men

minutes
Mis. 95– 6 * ten m· in which to reply
353–16 bucket of water every ten m·
Man. 61–24 about eight or nine m·
62– 1 six or seven m· for the
Ret. 40–10 stood by her side about fifteen m·
Pul. 43–19 * A few m· of silent prayer came next,
My. 32– 3 * five m· of silent communion
38–12 * filled . . . in about twenty m·,
49–21 * "The m· of the previous meeting
82–18 * in something like ten m·.
333– 9 * m· record this further proceeding :

minutiæ
Mis. 166–29 entered into the m· of the
204–24 all the m· of human affairs.

miracle
Mis. 5–22 seem a m· and a mystery
77–30 the m· of grace appears,
98–16 Chicago, — the m· of the Occident.
99– 6 To weave . . . is a m· in itself.
294– 6 m· in the universe of mortal mind.
321– 4 whose birth is less of a m·
Ret. 24–20 Spirit had wrought the m·
24–20 a m· which later I found
75–14 do a m· in my name, — Mark 9 : 39.
Pul. 8–15 erect this "m· in stone."
34–21 Spirit had wrought a m·,"
60– 9 * m· of loaves and fishes.
Hea. 11–11 is the m· of the hour,
11–12 great pyramid . . . a m· in stone.
Peo. 4–21 No m· of grace can make a
My. 109–25 not alone by m· and parable,
126–12 no longer a mystery or a m·,
216–12 a m· that frightens people,

miracles
Mis. 29–27 M· are no infraction of
54–26 as great m· in healing as
77–30 m· of Jesus had their birth,
199–14 m· recorded in the Scriptures
199–27 The so-called m· contained in
200–16 the so-called m· of our Master,
202– 1 basis of all supposed m· ;
340–26 m· of patience and perseverance.
Ret. 26–12 The m· recorded in the Bible,
80–26 no greater m· known to earth
Hea. 15–13 so-called m· recorded in
My. 80– 2 * back to the age of m·.
95–20 * telling of m· performed in this
107–22 wouldst thou mock God's m·
123–25 Scientist is not frightened at m·,
188–32 ascends the scale of m·
191– 2 m· that thou doest, John 3 : 2.

miraculous
Mis. 88–25 * as imported ice was m· to
104–11 sin is m· and supernatural ;
104–14 perfection is normal, — not m·.
Ret. 26–15 pronounce Christ's healing m·,
Pul. 35– 7 * Christ's healing was not m·,
Rud. 17–12 she needed m· vision to
My. 95–22 * their disbelief in the m·.

miraculously
Pul. 66–11 * rescued from death m·

mirage
'01. 14–15 unreal as a m· that misleads

Miriam
Pul. 82–19 * True, there were M· and Esther,

Miriams
Pul. 82–22 * and M· by the million,

mirror
Mis. 23–28 likeness thrown upon the m·
203– 8 it will always m· their love,

mirrored
Po. 23– 9 M· in truth, in light and joy,
My. 150–16 See therein the m· sky
208– 5 m· forth by your loving hearts,

mirrors
Pul. 27– 2 * with full-length French m·
Po. 25– 1 M· of morn

mirth
Mis. 324– 6 the sounds of festivity and m· ;

misapprehending
Mis. 345–25 distorting or m· the purpose

misapprehension
Mis. 290–12 m· of the divine Principle
Un. 53–13 is a m· of being,
Rud. 1–11 affords a large margin for m·,
No. 7– 6 m· as to the motives of others.
My. 251–16 some m· of my meaning

misapprehensive
Mis. 290–22 conjectural and m· !

misbelief
Un. 38–12 m· must enthrone another power,

miscall
Mis. 250– 5 misrepresent and m· affection ;
Un. 29–17 What the physical senses m· soul,
44–15 Human theories call, or m·,

miscalled
Mis. 95–18 which spiritualists have m·
123–13 or a m· man or woman !
361– 6 its m· life ends in death,
No. 22–10 Such m· metaphysical systems

miscellaneous
Mis. x– 6 to collect my m· writings

Miscellaneous Writings
p. 127
  My. 18–16 (*M· W·*, p. 127.)

  Man. 3– 1 heading
  My. 318– 6 proofreader for my book "*M· W·*,"
mischief
  Mis. 230– 9 gossiping *m·*, making lingering calls,
    287–31 Great *m·* comes from attempts to
  Un. 15–24 who seeks to do them *m·*,
  My. 211–27 unless the cause of the *m·* is found
mischief-making
  Man. 81–23 No idle gossip, no slander, no *m·*,
mischievous
  Mis. 245–21 most *m·* to the human heart,
misconceived
  No. 14– 1 It is neither warped nor *m·*,
misconception
  Mis. 46–13 such a *m·* of Truth is not scientific,
    108–21 *m·* of what we need to know of evil,
    124–11 Moslem's *m·* of Deity,
    188– 9 *m·* of God and man,
    350–20 because of the *m·* of those subjects
  Ret. 83–16 communicates, . . . his *m·* of Truth,
  No. 5–25 a lost jewel in this *m·* of reality.
misconceptions
  Ret. 70– 2 names and natures upon its own *m·*.
  No. 8–20 over the *m·* of C. S.,
misconduct
  Mis. 265–23 misstatements or *m·* of this student.
misconstrued
  Mis. 250– 9 No word is more *m·* ;
  No. 32–12 ignorantly or maliciously *m·*.
misconstrues
  My. 180–25 rebels, *m·* our best motives,
misdeeds
  Mis. 264– 6 others stumble over *m·*,
misemployed
  Mis. 312–23 reason too supine or *m·*
miserable
  Mis. 224– 6 to be *m·* for the faults of others.
  Hea. 14–14 ignorance and . . . are *m·* medical aids.
  My. 195–20 no *m·* piece of ideal legerdemain,
    211–24 *m·* lies, poured . . . into his mind,
    312– 8 * in a *m·* plight.
misery
  Mis. 327– 2 my *m·* increased ;
misfortune
  Mis. 119– 5 then whining over *m·*,
  Pul. 37–22 * the *m·* of a church depending on
misguide
  '00. 9–13 bias human judgment and *m·* action,
  '01. 20–16 could not bewilder, darken, or *m·*
  My. 111–22 and unwittingly *m·* his followers?
misguided
  Mis. 114– 9 *m·*, and so made to misteach others.
    268–20 enlightening the *m·* senses,
    291–30 *m·* individual who keeps not watch over
    353–11 attention of the *m·*, fallible sort,
  Ret. 79–17 If beset with *m·* emotions,
misguides
  Mis. 363–23 *m·* reason and affection,
  My. 153–19 *m·* the understanding,
misguiding
  Mis. 78–19 *M·* the public mind and
misinterpret
  Mis. 194–10 *m·* evangelical religion.
  '01. 12–16 *m·* evangelical religion.
misinterpretation
  Mis. 169– 7 through the *m·* of the Word,
  No. 32– 1 The *m·* of such passages has
  My. 238–20 no possibility of *m·*.
misinterpreted
  Hea. 6– 9 I knew it was *m·*,
  My. 213–31 *m·* by the adverse influence
misinterprets
  Ret. 83–15 if he *m·* the text to his pupils,
  My. 304–29 first attack . . . Mrs. Eddy *m·* the
misjudge
  Mis. 66–22 Cynical critics *m·* my meaning
  '01. 4–21 Those who *m·* us because we
misjudged
  Mis. 94– 1 if you . . . are *m·* and maligned ;
    236– 2 human passions . . . have *m·* motives
misjudgment
  Mis. 13– 5 falsehood, ingratitude, *m·*,
    66– 8 no human *m·* can pervert it ;

mislead
  Ret. 83–12 which *m·* no one and are
  '01. 20–12 opportunity to *m·* the human mind,
  My. 5–31 may mesmerize and *m·* man ;
    178– 2 do not *m·* the seeker after Truth.
misleading
  No. 3–28 Plagiarism . . . are tempting and *m·*.
  My. 318–10 as ungrammatical as it was *m·*.
misleads
  '01. 14–15 mirage that *m·* the traveller
misled
  Mis. 222–12 In this state of *m·* consciousness,
    302–13 the temptation to be *m·*.
  Un. 44–10 was *m·* by a false personality,
  My. 212–23 they are being deceived and *m·*.
misname
  No. 27–20 personality, which we *m·* man,
misnamed
  Mis. 76–22 *m·* human soul is material sense,
    201– 4 resolves the element *m·* matter
    327– 1 turned my *m·* joys to sorrow.
  Un. 32–15 *m·* mind is a false claim,
    37–22 mortal mind which is *m·* man,
  '00. 3–26 Yahwah, *m·* Jehovah, was a god of
misnomer
  '00. 4– 1 This seedling *m·* couples love and
misquoting
  My. 110–30 *m·* of "S. and H. with Key to the
misread
  '01. 34–11 Have we *m·* the evangelical precepts
misrepresent
  Mis. 109– 2 Beware of those who *m·* facts ;
    250– 5 Mortals *m·* and miscall affection ;
  Ret. 75–13 misunderstand or *m·* the author.
misrepresentation
  Mis. 245– 9 efforts . . . to retard by *m·*
misrepresentations
  Un. 44– 1 *m·* are made concerning my doctrines,
  My. 354– 3 because of alleged *m·* by persons
misrepresented
  Mis. 132–27 * "If we have in any way *m·*
  Man. 41–10 *m·* by the churches or the press,
  My. 139–12 *m·*, belied, and trodden upon.
    363–22 My address . . . has been *m·*
misrepresenting
  My. 105–31 must refrain from persecuting and *m·*
misrepresents
  Mis. 353–12 *m·* one through malice or ignorance.
  My. 306– 1 persistently *m·* my character,
misrule
  Ret. 11–10 No despot bears *m·*,
  Po. 60– 7 No despot bears *m·*,
Miss
  Man. 110–14 Women must sign "*M·*" or " Mrs."
    111– 8 unmarried women must sign "*M·*."
miss
  Mis. 356–31 or you will *m·* the way of Truth
  Po. 3– 3 I *m·* thee as the flower the dew !
missed
  My. 93–23 * many of us have *m·* entirely its
missing
  My. 151–25 thus *m·* the discovery of all cause
mission
divine
  Pul. 71–23 * having a divine *m·* to fulfil,
earthly
  Mis. 74–15 His earthly *m·* was to translate
her
  Pul. 73–12 * Her *m·* was then the mission of a
    85– 5 * who now, in part, understand her *m·*,
his
  '01. 10–30 After Jesus had fulfilled his *m·*
  My. 111–22 Did Jesus mistake his *m·*
    246–27 spirit of his *m·*, the wisdom of his
holy
  Pan. 9–19 aided, not hindered, in his holy *m·*.
human
  Ret. 32– 2 on its divinely appointed human *m·*,
its
  Mis. 304–20 * fulfilling its *m·* throughout the
    308–21 fulfilled its *m·*, retired with honor
Jesus'
  Hea. 18–19 Jesus' *m·* extended to the sick
Messianic
  Mis. 162–12 point of his Messianic *m·* was peace,
  Ret. 70–10 Messianic *m·* of Christ Jesus ;
Mrs. Eddy's
  Pul. 72–25 * it was Mrs. Eddy's *m·* to revive it.

mission

my
Mis. 278– 6 I shall fulfil my m',
Ret. 24–23 to ponder my m', to search the
of a Christian
Pul. 73–12 * m' of a Christian, to do good
of Christian Science
Mis.   4–29 m' of C. S. to heal the sick,
of Jesus
Ret. 70–16 m' of Jesus of Nazareth.
of missions
Pul. 81–26 * Hers is the m' of missions
of our Master
My. 122–29 m' of our Master was to all mankind,
spirit and
Mis. 372–22 concerning the spirit and m' of
such a
My. 150–10 the service of such a m'.
their
Mis. 98–24 attest the authenticity of their m',
three-years
Mis. 163– 5 his three-years m' was a marvel
thy
Mis. 392–10 Whate'er thy m', mountain sentinel,
Po.   20–14 Whate'er thy m', mountain sentinel,

Mis. 347–25 m' of those whom He has anointed.
My.   90–16 * has a m' that can be readily

missionaries
Mis. 123– 1 massacres our m',

missionary
Mis. 304– 9 * as a m' of freedom,
Pul.   6–19 * a m' to China, in 1884.

missions
Pul. 81–26 * Hers is the mission of m'

missives
My.   53– 1 * important m' of inquiry

Missouri and Mo.
My. 207– 8 * societies of C. S. in M',
     207–17 * signature
     (see also Kansas City, St. Joseph, St. Louis)

misstate
Mis. 70– 1 or else the Scriptures m'
     173– 2 man's theorems, m' mental Science,

misstatement
Mis. 174– 2 Matter is a m' of Mind ;
     188   0 m' and misconception of God
Ret. 56– 7 m' of the unerring divine Principle
Un.   35–21 this one is a m' of Mind,
My. 304– 2 chapter sub-title

misstatements
Mis. 265–22 not morally responsible for the m'
Un.   20– 5 these three statements, or m'.

mist
Mis. 30–28 "There went up a m' — Gen. 2 : 6.
      30–29 the m' of materialism will vanish
      85–21 Temptation, that m' of mortal mind
     156– 9 when the m' shall melt away
     355–17 To strike out . . . against the m',
     355–27 fall in m' and showers
Pan.   6– 8 not as one that beateth the m',
'02.   2– 2 through the m' of mortal strife,
Po.   65–18 darkness and death like m' melt away,
My. 290–21 Through a momentary m' he beheld

mistake
following
Mis. 299– 7 look . . . at the following m',
forgive a
Mis. 118–13 yearn to forgive a m',
grave
Mis. 291– 5 notion that . . . is a grave m' ;
great
My. 317– 9 It is a great m' to say that I
his
Mis. 265–16 his m' is visited upon himself
in physics
Mis. 264–30 more fatal than a m' in physics.
made the
Pul.   6–12 made the m' of thinking she
may have occurred
My. 311–15 a m' may have occurred as to the
mild
Mis. 109–12 Even a mild m' must be seen as a
mortal
Mis. 339–16 it points to every mortal m' ;
     362–11 Theologians make the mortal m' of
of believing
Mis. 223–15 alas ! for the m' of believing in
one single
Mis. 130–20 accomplished, without one single m',
seen as a
Mis. 109–12 must be seen as a m', in order to

mistake
single
Mis. 264–29 A single m' in metaphysics,
this
My. 284–17 next issue please correct this m'.
to be rectified
Un.   20– 1 How is a m' to be rectified?
which will die
Un.   53–13 a m' which will die of its own delusion ;

Mis. 10–14 If they m' the divine command,
      18–28 This is the m' that causes
      87–18 which is certainly a m',
     284– 8 thus m' the sphere of his
     298–27 I say, You m' ;
     298–29 When unconscious of a m',
     300– 7 We answer, It is a m' ;
     302–16 If . . . Scientists occasionally m'
Ret. 83–13 student may m' in his conception of
Un.   26– 9 Good. You m', O evil !
'00.   6– 3 Only the demonstrator can m'
My. 111–21 Did Jesus m' his mission
     213–16 working so subtly that we m' its
     229– 2 unless I m' their calling.
     348–28 demonstrator of this Science may m',

mistaken
Mis. 66– 2 false testimony or m' evidence
     107– 3 m' for the oracles of God.
     216–18 the best may be m'.
     248–13 m' views of Mrs. Eddy's book,
     283–17 nothing less than a m' kindness,
     285– 7 m' for the corrected edition,
     288– 3 convictions . . . may be m' ;
     290– 9 M' views ought to be dissolving
     291– 1 M' or transient views are human :
     298–29 one thinks he is not m',
Rud. 12–13 aided in this m' fashion,
      12–17 m' belief that they live in
No.   6–15 the m' healer is not successful,
Pan. 11– 7 Was our Master m' in judging a
Hea.   8–17 m' views entertained of Deity
Peo. 11–24 m' in their methods of humanity.
My. 211– 6 This m' way, of hiding sin
     234–10 not task themselves with m' means.
     357– 8 only incentive of a m' sense

mistakenly
Pul.   7–17 m' committed in the name of religion.

mistakes
Mis. 72– 3 because of his parents' m'
     130–24 should avoid referring to past m'.
     265– 7 make m' and lose their way.
     266   7 but ho m' mo,
     266–24 If I correct m' which may be made
     299– 1 suffering and m' recur until
     308   5 Whosoever looks to . . . m'.
No.   9– 5 It is true that the m', prejudices,
       9–24 More m' are made in its name
      28– 1 their present m' would extinguish
My. 301–18 m' fable for fact
     322–10 * correcting m' widely published

mistaking
Mis. 284–12 are in no danger of m' their way.
Ret. 57–25 M' divine Principle for corporeal
My.   81–21 * in a way there was no m'.
     342– 6 * There was no m' that.
     342–10 * There is no m' certain lines
     342–11 * there is no m' the eyes

mistaught
Mis. 240–20 Children not m', naturally love

misteach
Mis. 114–10 and so made to m' others.

misteaching
Man. 55–21 M'.

mistiness
No.   20–23 Adam's m' and Satan's reasoning,

mists
Mis. 107– 9 above the seeming m' of sense,
     205– 4 through the m' of materiality
     251–30 as the mountain m' before the sun.
     264– 8 shadows thrown upon the m' of time,
     363–20 Even through the m' of mortality
No.   16–23 m' of matter — sin, sickness, and
      28– 3 the m' of error, sooner or later,
Pan.   2– 7 above the m' of pantheism
Peo.   5–11 not lost in the m' of remoteness

misty
Mis. 393– 9 within the m' Mine of human thoughts,
Po.   51–14 within the m' Mine of human thoughts,
My. 341–27 * change from the m' air outside

misunderstand
Ret. 75–12 m' or misrepresent the author.

misunderstanding
Man. 64–23 the public m· of this name,

misunderstood
Mis. 105–21 If either is m· or maligned,
My. 363–22 evidently m· by some students.

misuse
'01. 19–23 susceptible m· of the human mind,

misused
Mis. 310– 4 teachings of Jesus would be m· by

mite
Pul. 45– 2 * some giving a m· and some
Hea. 7–18 dropped her m· into the treasury,

mitigating
My. 265–18 are m· and destroying sin,

mix
Mis. 40– 4 to m· material methods with the
175–28 The attempt to m· matter and Mind,
'01. 22– 6 I do not try to m· matter and Spirit,
22– 7 and they will not m·.
25–10 which m· matter and mind,
Hea. 4–14 We expect infinite Truth to m· with

mixed
Ret. 33–16 m· with the faith of ages,
My. 292–23 croton oil is not m· with morphine

mixing
Mis. 371–15 m· all grades of persons is not
371–17 he who has self-interest in this m·
'01. 19–12 The notion that m· material and

mixture
Mis. 248–12 the m· would be labelled thus :

moan
Mis. 330– 4 to m· over the new-made grave,
396– 1 The wild winds mutter, howl, and m·,
Chr. 53–57 no broken wing, no m·,
Po. 58–13 The wild winds mutter, howl, and m·,
73– 9 list the m· Of the billows' foam,

moaning
Mis. 225–22 sofa whereon lay the lad . . . m·

moans
Po. 15– 3 m· from the footsteps of time!

mob
Mis. 224– 7 m· had broken the head of his
Po. vi–12 In 1835 a m· in Boston

mock
'01. 16–26 go to m·, and go away to pray
'02. 18– 7 only to m·, wonder, and perish.
Po. 73–20 E'er to m· the bright truth
My. 107–22 wouldst thou m· God's miracles
258–22 blossoms that m· their hope

mocked
Pul. 7–22 "God is not m·,"— Gal. 6 : 7.
My. 6– 5 "God is not m· :— Gal. 6 : 7.
201–14 thorns, which m· the bleeding brow

mockeries
Mis. 51–24 * whole dark pile of human m· ;

mockery
'02. 14–19 m·, envy, rivalry, and
My. 262–24 seem a human m·

mocking
Un. 33–23 find them . . . m· the Scripture

mockingly
Un. 58– 7 His persecutors said m·,

mocks
Mis. 274–19 m· morality, outrages humanity,
351–30 m· the bliss of spiritual being ;

mode
Mis. 98–13 felt in a higher m· of medicine ;
165–32 found in the order, m·, and
211– 3 His m· is not cowardly,
257– 3 in every m· and form of evil.
277–14 present m· of attempting this
349– 9 metaphysical m· of obstetrics
361– 9 When every form and m· of evil
362– 6 and reflects all real m·, form,
363–11 material m· of a suppositional
366–29 according to His m· of C. S. ;
Ret. 89– 2 divine potency of this spiritual m·
Un. 8– 6 is a m· of consciousness,
No. 17–15 Matter, or any m· of mortal mind,
25–15 neither matter nor a m· of mortal
25–16 immortal m· of the divine Mind.
'01. 12– 1 m· of worship may be intangible,
34– 7 Christ's m· and means of healing,
My. 49–25 * m· of conducting the church."
106–10 above matter in every m· and form,
248–23 Christ m· of understanding Life
251–17 as to the m· of instruction

Model
Mis. 159–27 how has our M·, Christ, been unveiled

model
Mis. 98– 2 perfect m· should be held in mind,
308–31 is not the m· for a metaphysician.
Ret. 22– 9 as the m· of Christianity,
93–16 it becomes the m· for human action.
Un. 14–11 shortcomings of the Puritan's m·
14–22 Our infinite m· would be taken away.
No. 41–15 to compare mortal lives with this m·
Pan. 11–13 to turn from clay to Soul for the m·
'01. 6–17 because He is not after this m·
Hea. 2–17 Jesus, the m· of infinite patience,
4–24 God must be our m·, or we have none ;
4–25 if this m· is one thing at one time,
4–26 can we rely on our m· ?
19–23 according to the m· on the mount,
Peo. 7– 6 turn often from marble to m·,
9–14 after the m· of our Father,
10–20 marred in mind the m· of man.
My. 123– 8 continue to urge the perfect m·
261–14 unfolding the immortal m·,
361– 6 stated in C. S. to be used as a m·.

models
Mis. 353– 6 they are neither standards nor m·.
Rud. 3–12 m· of the masters in music
Peo. 14–11 form our m· of humanity.
My. 111–19 healers and m· of good morals,

moderately
My. 93– 8 * any class save the m· well-to-do,

moderating
Mis. 360– 1 Meekness, m· human desire,

moderation
Un. 5–20 letting our "m· be known— Phil. 4 : 5.

modern
Mis. 173– 1 Ancient and m· philosophy,
225– 9 the seventh m· wonder, C. S. ;
274–28 the car of the m· Inquisition
333–31 ancient or m· Christians,
344–16 Ancient and m· philosophies
Ret. 34– 7 Neither ancient nor m· philosophy
57– 4 Neither ancient nor m· philosophy
89– 6 in the m· sense of the term.
Pul. 32– 1 * questioned this m· St. Catherine,
47–13 * No ancient or m· philosophy gave
54–19 * in the light of m· science,
64–18 * m· philosophy gave her no
No. 11–23 Ancient and m· human philosophy
'00. 6–28 Some m· exegesis on the
'01. 16– 7 scarcely equal the m· nondescripts,
27–16 Or if a m· St. Paul could
Peo. 11–16 m· Pharaohs that hold the
My. 70–21 * both ancient and m· masters,
98–10 * hardly parallel in m· times,
103–22 * in ancient or in m· systems
107– 7 a m· phase of medical practice,
345–25 * pursuit of m· material inventions

modernized
Pul. 47–28 * delightfully remodelled and m·

modes
Mis. 71–19 suppositional m·, not the factors of
88–24 * or understand its m·
88–29 are opposite m· of medicine.
102–18 expressed in m· above the human.
112– 6 ages are burdened with material m·.
114–32 to guard against evil and its silent m·,
136– 3 routine of such material m· as
257–15 a code whose m· trifle with joy,
268– 1 materializes human m· and
270–25 through the m· and methods of God.
293– 3 all the claims and m· of evil ;
293– 6 unerring m· of divine wisdom.
360– 8 m· of mind cast in the moulds of
360–32 No advancing m· of human mind
361–32 The divine m· and manifestations
362–19 whose m· are material manifestations
363–12 immortal m· of Mind are spiritual,
363–17 His m· declare the beauty of holiness,
364–27 has the same power or m·
364–29 would either extinguish . . . His m·, or
366–22 as m· of medicine.
Un. 52–27 supposed m· of self-conscious matter,
No. 15–21 nor in the m· of mortal mind.
21–16 material m·, wherein the human
39–12 nor bring His designs into mortal m· ;
39–13 it can and does change our m·
My. 111– 5 crude theories or m· of metaphysics.
211–14 m· of good, in their silent
213–15 m· of mental malpractice,
221–16 Then m· of healing, other than
266–17 all codes, m·, hypotheses, of man
266–27 spiritual m· and significations

modes
My. 267–30 of all the divine *m*·, means, forms,
302– 1 all *m*· of healing disease
349–20 Divine *m*· or manifestations are

modest
Mis. 145–20 their *m*· sign be nothingness.
172– 1 to keep their demonstrations *m*·,
243–18 students are proverbially *m*· :
330–30 the *m*· grass, inhabiting the
372–24 the *m*· glory of divine Science.
395–12 Veiled is the *m*· moon
Ret. 17–10 and the *m*· Moss-rose ;
No. 2–17 is *m*· in his claims
3– 4 *m*·, generous, and sincere !
44– 3 failure should make him *m*·.
Hea. 11–10 her *m*· tower rises slowly,
Po. 57–19 Veiled is the *m*· moon
62–11 and the *m*· Moss-rose ;
My. 6–17 *m*· edifice of The Mother Church
39–18 * my *m*· task will be ended.
123–10 in Concord, N. H., we have a *m*· hall
147– 9 have provided for you a *m*· hall,
271–13 * In a *m*·, pleasantly situated home

modestly
My. 9–15 * we *m*· renew the hope

modesty
Ret. 94–25 *m*· and distinguishing affection
My. 357–12 spiritual *m*· of C. S.,

modification
Mis. 193–18 a *m*· of silence on this subject,
No. v– 6 By a *m*· of the language,

modifications
Mis. 68–29 * from its phenomenal *m*·."
'02. 2–19 present *m*· in ecclesiasticism

modified
Ret. 83– 1 changed, *m*·, broadened,
My. 266–27 agitated, *m*·, and disappearing,

modify
Mis. 67–29 I *m*· my affirmative answer.

modus
Mis. 380– 3 human *m*· for demonstrating this,
Ret. 24–19 explain the *m*· of my relief.
'01. 20–25 its hidden *m*· and flagrance

modus operandi
Mis. 117–19 movements, or *m*· *o*·, of other folks.
150–15 student's opinions or *m*· *o*·
Pan. 12– 3 rejection of evil and its *m*· *o*·.
'02. 10–26 *m*· *o*· of human error,
My. 292–18 against the *m*· *o*· of another,

Mohammed
Pan. 8–10 doctrine that *M*· is the only prophet

Mohammedan
Pan. 7–15 the Christian, and the *M*·.

moiety
Mis. 317–15 Scarcely a *m*·, . . . is yet assimilated

molds
Po. 78– 6 Till *m*· the hero form?

molecule
Mis. 173–28 Whence, then, is the atom or *m*·
313– 6 the scientific spiritual *m*·,
363– 5 from *m*· and monkey up to man,
Un. 35–23 *m*·, as matter, is not formed by
No. 26–21 never originated in *m*·, corpuscle,
'02. 10– 5 and their power over matter, *m*·,
My. 110–11 progress from *m*· and mortals
278–10 Let us have the *m*· of faith

molecules
Mis. 26–14 Was it *m*·, or material atoms?
205–28 The encumbering mortal *m*·,

molestation
Ret. 11–21 envy and *m*· of other churches,

mollusca
My. 271– 3 no vertebrata, *m*·, or radiata.

mollusk
Mis. 361–10 *m*· and radiate are spiritual concepts

molten
Peo. 2–23 a personal tyrant or a *m*· image,
My. 269–18 This hour is *m*· in the furnace
303–31 This glory is *m*· in the furnace of

moment (*see also* moment's)
Mis. 15–13 not the work of a *m*·.
16–27 pause for a *m*· with me,
34–22 not a *m*· when he ceases to
42– 8 a *m*· of extreme mortal fear,
60–11 apparent in a *m*·.
85–12 is not won in a *m*· ;
93–30 to indulge . . . for even one *m*·.
127–29 word spoken, at the right *m*·,
154–30 Forget not for a *m*·, that

moment
Mis. 188–28 At the *m*· of her discovery,
280–32 just at the *m*· when you are
307– 5 have all you need every *m*·.
375–15 * devoting every *m*· to the study
Ret. 21–26 are frivolous and of no *m*·,
23–13 Thus it was when the *m*· arrived
72– 9 desolation, as in a *m*· ! *Psal.* 73 : 19.
89–13 bidden . . . at that particular *m*·.
Un. 63– 4 were never absent for a *m*·.
Pul. 2–12 think for a *m*· with me of the
30–22 * need of living faith at the *m*·
Rud. 11–16 In a *m*· you may awake from
No. 24–25 There was never a *m*· in which
'01. 15–24 * from being this *m*· swallowed up
16– 1 * reason why you do not at this *m*·
Hea. 4– 3 nor remain for a *m*· within limits.
Peo. 12– 2 we should think for one *m*·
My. 173–12 a note, sent at the last *m*·,
224– 2 that demand at the *m*·,
250–23 can wait for the favored *m*·
351– 8 earliest *m*· in which to answer it.

momentarily
Mis. 283–21 may *m*· be forgotten ;

momentary
Mis. 42– 6 After the *m*· belief of dying
228–14 *m*· success of all villainies,
My. 290–21 Through a *m*· mist he beheld

momentous
Mis. 63–29 that *m*· demonstration of God,
337– 4 how can you be certain of so *m*· an
379–28 *m*· facts relating to Mind
No. 28– 9 these *m*· facts in the Science of
My. 42–23 * significance of this *m*· occasion.
45–17 * revealed to you in that *m*· hour
90–26 * an event of . . . *m*· significance.
360–11 present *m*· question at issue

moment's
Mis. 342–11 Each *m*· fair expectancy
My. 144– 5 spare not a *m*· thought to lies

moments
Mis. 15–14 begins with *m*·, and goes on with years ;
15–14 *m*· of surrender to God,
15–16 *m*· of self-abnegation,
32–21 I have not *m*· enough in which to
36–27 as much in our waking *m*· as
68– 2 This translation is not the work of *m*· ;
230– 3 upon the improvement of *m*·
230–15 improving *m*· before they pass
356–32 it has no *m*· for trafficking
'00. 8– 7 He improves *m*· ; to him time is money.
Po. 65–16 *m*· most sweet are fleetest alway,
74– 3 those *m*· to memory bestowed
My. 17–24 * a few *m*· of silent prayer
147– 2 *m*· when at the touch of memory

momentum
Mis. 110–24 and the *m*· of C. S.,
Pul. vii–14 the gain of intellectual *m*·,

monads
My. 133–13 crumbs and *m*· will feed the hungry,

monarch (*see also* monarch's)
Mis. 392– 2 mountain *m*·, at whose feet I stand,
Po. 20– 1 mountain *m*·, at whose feet I stand,
25–15 Be he *m*· or slave,

monarch's
My. 257–29 have their record in the *m*· palace,

Monday
Mis. 95– 2 * *M*· lectureship in Tremont Temple,
95– 3 * on *M*·, March 16, 1885,
Man. 25–10 *M*· preceding the annual meeting
56–12 *M*· following the first Sunday in June.
56–20 *M*· preceding the annual meeting
93– 6 *M*· preceding the Annual Meeting,
My. 171–14 *M*·, June 13, 1904.

monetary
My. 214–22 no *m*· means left wherewith to

money
Mis. 67– 8 thou shalt not rob man of *m*·,
78–20 taking its *m*· in exchange for
80– 6 to give *m*· and influence
141–30 what shall be done with their *m*·.
144– 2 *m*· for building "Mother's Room,"
149– 1 he that hath no *m*· ;— *Isa.* 55 : 1.
149– 3 milk without *m*·— *Isa.* 55 : 1.
242–12 he would lose his *m*·
252–31 the poor man's *m*· ;
270– 4 such as barter integrity . . . for *m*·
274–26 for *m*·, place, and power,
305–23 * *m*· with which to pay for the bell.
315–21 shall be no question of *m*·,
368–24 are playing only for *m*·,

money

Man.	80– 7	*m·* subject to the order of
	83– 6	not be a question of *m·*,
Ret.	5– 4	gave the *m·* for erecting the first
	20– 2	except what *m·* I had brought
	41– 5	"without *m·* and without— *Isa.* 55 : 1.
Pul.	8– 8	unemployed in our *m·* centres,
	8–14	and forth came the *m·*,
	41– 3	* an appeal, not for more *m·*,
	42–12	* whose *m·* was devoted to the
	44–25	* *m·* has flowed in from all parts
	50– 1	* using her *m·* to promote the welfare
	59–27	* the *m·* for the Mother's Room,
	64– 7	* *M·* came freely from all parts
	64–13	* stop the continued inflow of *m·*
	71– 7	* *m·* comes from C. S. believers
	79– 6	* for which the *m·* was all paid
Pan.	15– 2	destroying millions of her *m·*,
'00.	2–14	earns his *m·* and gives it
	2–18	Ask how he gets his *m·*,
	3– 7	to him time is *m·*, and he hoards
	10–30	some of his hard-earned *m·*
	11– 2	more pleasure than millions of *m·*
'02.	12–30	I furnished the *m·* from my own
	15– 8	"without *m·* and without— *Isa.* 55 : 1.
My.	v–17	* "without *m·* and without— *Isa.* 55 : 1.
	10–11	* Some *m·* has been paid in
	10–21	* not expected to contribute *m·*
	10–23	* the *m·* necessary to this end,
	12– 3	* as soon as the *m·* in hand
	13–18	any part of two millions of *m·*
	14–29	* necessitates large payments of *m·*,
	20–26	* of a large amount of *m·*,
	21– 5	* *m·* which had been collected
	22– 8	* *m·* adequate to erect such a
	26–12	gift is the largest sum of *m·*
	27–16	* requested to send no more *m·*
	33–25	his *m·* to usury,— *Psal.* 15 : 5.
	65–14	* *m·* to provide it was pledged
	67–20	* *m·* was used in giving Boston
	67–23	* vaster sums of *m·* were spent
	72–14	* chapter sub-title
	72–15	* do not send us any more *m·*
	76– 4	* notices that more *m·* was needed
	76– 7	* enough *m·* was on hand
	86–16	* to give no more *m·*,
	89–19	* petitions for *m·* are almost as
	96–21	* *m·* was sent in such quantities that
	98–16	* requested to send no more *m·*
	98–25	* methods of raising *m·*.
	99–21	* stuffed and jammed with *m·*.
	123–15	furnished him the *m·* to pay for it.
	215– 4	bestowed without *m·* or price.
	215–12	sent me the full tuition *m·*.
	215–12	However, I returned this *m·*
	215–15	* more to me than *m·* can be."
	216– 3	obtain their *m·* from a fish's mouth,
	216–29	will want *m·* for your own uses.
	217– 1	*m·* that you expend for flowers.
	231– 8	to whom she has given large sums of *m·*,
	231–10	spend no more time or *m·*
	312–10	* entirely without *m·* or friends.
	312–22	amount of *m·* he would need
	336–13	except what *m·* I had brought
	358–18	I thank you for the *m·*

money-bag

Un.	15–26	criminal appeases, with a *m·*,

moneychangers

Mis.	270– 2	the tables of the *m·*,— *Matt.* 21 : 12.

moneyed

Mis.	148–26	collect no *m·* contributions from

money-making

Mis.	48–10	prompted by *m·* or malice.

Monitor

Christian Science, The

My.	352–29	first issue of *The C. S. M·*.
	353– 7	*The C. S. M·*, November 25, 1908
My.	353–15	the next I named *M·*,
	353–17	The object of the *M·* is to

monitor

Mis.	100–20	The spiritual *m·* understood

monkey

Mis.	233– 9	*m·* in harlequin jacket
	363– 5	from molecule and *m·* up to man,

monomania

Mis.	49– 2	had a tendency to *m·*,

monopolize

Man.	49– 2	shall not endeavor to *m·*
Un.	9–21	Sometimes it is said, . . . that I *m·*;

monopoly

Man.	49– 1	No *M·*.
Un.	10– 8	If there be any *m·* in my teaching,
My.	129– 4	imperialism, *m·*, and a lax system of

monotheism

Pan.	4– 1	It is opposed to atheism and *m·*,
	5– 1	*m·* is lost and pantheism is found in
	12–21	Christianity is strictly *m·*,
'00.	4– 9	nearer approach to *m·*
'01.	5– 5	lose *m·*, and become less coherent
My.	127–20	purer Protestantism and *m·*
	303–17	demonstrate Science and its pure *m·*

monotheist

'02.	12– 8	The Jew who . . . is a *m·*,
	12–11	The Christian who . . . is a *m·* :

monotheists

'01.	4–21	Scientists are theists and *m·*.

Monroe doctrine

My.	282– 3	believe strictly in the *M· d·*,

monster

Mis.	204– 2	and a mortal seems a *m·*,

monsters

Peo.	3– 4	ideals of . . . have made *m·* of men ;

monstrous

Mis.	122– 9	accomplishing such a *m·* work

Mont Blanc

Un.	64–17	stand on the summit of *M· B·* ;

month (see also month's)

Mis.	180–27	a *m·* is called the son of a year.
	314–32	On the first Sunday of each *m·*,
Man.	18– 4	and the same *m·* the members,
	40–19	first Sunday of each *m·*.
	78–24	on the first of the following *m·*,
Ret.	16–17	and the same *m·* the members,
	19–16	A *m·* later I returned to
	44– 6	during the same *m·* the members,
Pul.	45–11	* one *m·* before the close of the year
My.	49–10	* in the same *m·* the members
	55–31	* the twenty-first of last *m·*,
	272–20	* The *Cosmopolitan* presents this *m·*
	290–10	first *m·* of the new century.
	319–26	* the twentieth of the above-named *m·*.
	330–28	A *m·* later I returned to

monthly

Ret.	53– 3	This *m·* magazine had been made
Pul.	36–26	* *The C. S. Journal*, a *m·*

month's

Mis.	54–18	*after one m· treatment*

months

January

Man.	61–13	on the second Sunday in *J·*
My.	316–11	article in the *J·* number
		(see also dates, dates — affidavits, dates — chapter
		sub-titles, dates — newspaper articles)

January 6

Pul.	20–21	church was dedicated on *J·* 6,
	31– 1	* service on *J·* 6 shall be
		(see also dates — chapter sub-titles, dates —
		headings, dates — letters to Mrs. Eddy, dates —
		newspaper articles, dates — telegrams)

January, 6th of

Pul.	56–12	* taking place on the 6th of *J·*,

January ninth

Mis.	242– 4	came not to my notice until *J· n·*.

January 17

Mis.	294–13	In an issue of *J·* 17,

January 29

Pul.	74– 5	* in the *Herald* on *J·* 29,

February 3

My.	289–25	on Sunday evening, *F·* 3,
		(see also dates — poems by Mrs. Eddy)

February 22

My.	148–12	completed its organization *F·* 22
		(see also dates)

March

Mis.	279– 9	chapter sub-title
Pan.	1– 7	rushing winds of *M·* have shrieked
My.	55–22	* In *M·*, however, the church was
		(see also dates, dates — newspaper articles)

March, fifth of

Mis.	280–19	dismissed the *f·* of *M·*,

March 18

Mis.	132–13	*Zion's Herald*, *M·* 18,
		(see also dates)

March, twenty-fifth of last

My.	60–29	* On the *t·* of *l· M·*

April

Mis.	158–24	*A·* number of *The C. S. Journal*
Pul.	45–16	* could not be completed before *A·*
Pan.	1– 8	the frown and smile of *A·*,
		(see also dates, dates — newspaper articles)

months

April's
  Po. 46– 5 Nor *A·* changeful showers,
April 5
  My. 338–14 was delivered in Boston, *A·* 5.
April 30th
  Mis. 305–29 * bell shall be cast *A·* 30th,
    (*see also* **dates — interview**)
May
  Mis. 216– 8 In the *M·* number of our *Journal*,
    384– 5 And all is morn and *M·*.
  Pul. 45–16 * before April or *M·* of 1895.
  Pan. 1– 9 smile of April, the laugh of *M·*,
  Po. 36– 4 And all is morn and *M·*.
  My. 254– 4 chapter sub-title
    (*see also* **dates, dates — chapter sub-titles, dates — newspaper articles**)
May 1
  My. 198– 3 *Brethren:—* Your letters of *M·* 1
    (*see also* **dates — newspaper articles**)
May first
  Man. 77– 4 books are to be audited on *M· f·*.
May 18
  My. 137– 5 * was filed . . . *M·* 18.
May 21
  My. 284–13 In the issue of . . . the *Patriot, M·* 21,
    (*see also* **dates — poems by Mrs. Eddy**)
May 26
  My. 51– 3 * *M·* 26 of the same year,
    (*see also* **dates — chapter sub-titles**)
June
  Mis. 136–22 I recommend that the *J·* session
    390– 1 poem
    390– 2 Whence are thy wooings, gentle *J·*?
    390–20 Ask of its *J·*,
    394–15 * "The flowers of *J·*
    394–17 * The flowers of *J·*
    394–21 * The flowers of *J·*."
    395– 2 Who loves not *J·*
    395–11 The curtain drops on *J·* ;
  Man. 56–13 following the first Sunday in *J·*.
    57– 4 preceding the first Sunday in *J·*,
  Pul. 38– 1 * charter obtained the following *J·*.
  Pan. 1– 3 heading
    1–10 roseate blush of joyous *J·* is here
  Po. page 55 poem
    55– 2 Whence are thy wooings, gentle *J·*?
    55–21 Ask of its *J·*,
    57– 1 * THE flowers of *J·*
    57– 3 * The flowers of *J·*
    57– 7 * The flowers of *J·*.
    57– 9 Who loves not *J·*
    57–18 The curtain drops on *J·* ;
  My 11–27 * building was decided last *J·*,
    25–20 and the dedication in *J·* next
    57–24 * *C. S. Journal* of this *J·*
    73–16 * *J·* meetings of The Mother Church
    254–20 * in the *J· Journal* of 1904,
    (*see also* **dates, dates — addresses, dates — chapter sub-titles**)
June 2
  My. 76– 6 * *J·* 2 it became evident to the Board
    (*see also* **dates — notices**)
June 5
  My. 57–18 *candidates admitted *J·* 5
    (*see also* **dates — letters from Mrs. Eddy**)
June 10
  My. 26–15 My Message for *J·* 10 is ready
    61–11 * in the new extension on *J·* 10.
    61–18 * ready for the service, *J·* 10."
    (*see also* **dates — chapter sub-titles**)
June 12
  My. 38–30 * Tuesday, *J·* 12, at ten o'clock in the
    (*see also* **dates — chapter sub-titles, dates — letters to Mrs. Eddy, dates — telegrams**)
June 13
  Mis. 134–18 to be in Chicago on *J·* 13.
    (*see also* **dates — addresses, dates — chapter sub-titles, dates — letters from Mrs. Eddy, dates — letters to Mrs. Eddy**)
June 14
  My. 82–21 * at noon to-day [*J·* 14]
    141– 7 * attended last Sunday [*J·* 14]
    (*see also* **dates — chapter sub-titles**)
June 19
  My. 198– 4 Your letters of May 1 and *J·* 19,
    (*see also* **dates — newspaper articles**)
June 21
  My. 141–13 * was made last night [*J·* 21]
    (*see also* **dates — letters from Mrs. Eddy**)
June, 27th
  My. 335– 1 * Died . . . on the 27th *J·* last,
June, twenty-seventh of
  My. 333–21 * Thursday night, the *t· of J·*.
    (*see also* **dates — letters from Mrs. Eddy**)

months

July
  Man. 60– 6 during the months of *J·* and August
    61–14 in January and *J·* of each year,
    (*see also* **dates, dates — newspaper articles**)
July 1
  Man. 93– 9 shall begin *J·* 1 of each year.
    (*see also* **dates — newspaper articles**)
July 3
  My. 329–16 * appear . . . in the issues of *J·* 3
July Fourth
  Mis. 176– 4 chapter sub-title
July, Fourth of
  Mis. 251– 1 chapter sub-title
    (*see also* **dates, dates — chapter sub-titles**)
July 5
  My. 169– 3 I invite you, . . . on *J·* 5,
July, fifth of
  My. 122–11 On the *f· of J·* last, my church
July 19
  My. 359–19 * a composite letter, dated *J·* 19,
    (*see also* **dates**)
August
  Mis. 313– 3 your editorial in the *A·* number
  Man. 60– 7 during the months of July and *A·*
    (*see also* **dates, dates — newspaper articles**)
August 22
  My. 49–17 * *A·* 22 the Clerk, by instructions
August 27
  My. 49–19 * *A·* 27 the church held a meeting,
    (*see also* **dates**)
September
  Mis. 88– 7 *critique in the S·* number,
    (*see also* **dates**)
September, first of
  My. 54–23 * from the *f· of S·* to our opening,
October
  Mis. 61–11 * In the *O· Journal* I read
    256–14 *O·* number of the *Journal*,
  Pul. 48– 9 * in the gorgeous *O·* coloring
    (*see also* **dates**)
October 11th
  Mis. 304–29 * ring at nine o'clock on *O·* 11th,
    (*see also* **dates — letters to Mrs. Eddy**)
October 26
  Mis. 168–27 * on the afternoon of *O·* 26,
    (*see also* **dates**)
November
  Mis. 376–17 brave splendor of a *N·* sky
  Man. 57– 5 first Friday in *N·* of each year.
  '01. 3– 1 added since last *N·*
  My. 243–19 chapter sub-title
    (*see also* **dates, dates — newspaper articles**)
December
  Man. 90–11 first Wednesday of *D·*.
  My. 254– 9 chapter sub-title
    (*see also* **dates, dates — chapter sub-titles, dates — newspaper articles**)
December 1
  My. 49–29 * *D·* 1 of the same year,
December third
  Mis. 242– 3 in *Zion's Herald, D· t·*,
December 28
  Pul. 23– 8 * Boston, Mass., *D·* 28.
    (*see also* **dates — letters from Mrs. Eddy**)

———

  Mis. 110–16 Weeks have passed into *m·*,
    110–16 and *m·* into years,
    136–25 convening once in four *m·* ;
    143–23 within about three *m·*,
    315–23 as often as once in three *m·*.
  Man. 60– 5 continued twelve *m·* each year.
    60– 6 *m·* of July and August
  Ret. 8– 3 For some twelve *m·*,
    19–18 at the end of four *m·*,
    20– 5 A few *m·* before my father's
    38– 7 After *m·* had passed,
  Un. 11–28 There are yet four *m·*,
  Pul. 6–13 * "Six *m·* ago your book,
    8– 9 Scientists, within fourteen *m·*,
    67–28 * charter was obtained two *m·* later.
    69– 3 * about eighteen *m·* ago.
  Rud. 14–12 often those were put off for *m·*,
  '02. 16– 1 Six *m·* thereafter Miss Dorcas Rawson
  Po. 54– 1 It may be *m·* or years
  My. 52–27 * Within a few *m·* she has
    53– 1 * weeks lengthened into *m·* ;
    55–28 * During the *m·* that
    77– 1 * has for *m·* been the cynosure of
    145–17 Within the past year and two *m·*,
    312– 7 * six *m·* after his marriage,
    322–21 * waiting *m·* in Boston
    330–29 at the end of four *m·*,
    333–28 * brief space of six *m·*,

Montreal
Pul. 67– 4   * The M· Branch
      67–20   * Toronto and M· have strong churches,
'00.   1–22   M·, London, Edinburgh, Dublin,
Montreal (Can.) Gazette
My. 88– 2   * [M· (C·.) G·]
Montreal Daily Herald
Pul. 67– 1   * M· D· H·, Saturday, February 2, 1895

monument
Mis. 141– 2   prophecy fulfilled, the m· upreared,
      166– 3   m· whose finger points upward,
Po.   1–12   Ye rose, a m· of Deity,
My.   6–23   rises to a mental m·,
       36–29   * to stand as an enduring m·,
       45–15   * fitting m· of your obedience
       45–31   * loftier than the Bunker Hill m·,
       74–17   * m· to the sincerity
       76–26   * first great m· to C. S.,
       89–11   * A sect that leaves such a m·
       94–27   "rises to a mental m·,
      287– 2   chapter sub-title
      287– 3   movement to erect a m·
      289– 5   for the De Hirsch m· fund.

monumental
Mis. 388–14   Grave on her m· pile :
Po.   21– 1   Grave on her m· pile :

monuments
Ret. 71– 1   m· which weigh dust,
Peo. 14– 6   smiling fountains, and white m·.

mood
Ret. 75–18   author's own mental m·,
       91–11   indicates how the Master's m·,
Pul. 14– 6   another extreme mortal m·,

moods
Mis. 329– 3   nature in all her m· and forms,
Pan.   3– 8   Certain m· of mind find an

moon
Mis. 323– 6   neither of the m·, for God doth
      395–12   Veiled is the modest m·
Un.   14– 7   m·, and "the stars also," — Gen. 1 : 16.
Pul. 83–28   * the m· under her feet, — Rev. 12 : 1.
Po.   2–13   The m· looks down below,
        8–12   O'er the silv'ry m· and ocean flow ;
       57–19   Veiled is the modest m·
My. 150–17   m· ablaze with her mild glory.
      206–12   Seeing a man in the m·,
      206–21   neither of the m·, — Rev. 21 : 23.
      313– 6   By the light of the m·

moonbeam
Ret. 31–25   soft as the heart of a m·,

moonbeams
No.   22–13   they are as m· to the sun,

moon god
Pan.   8– 3   Babylonian sun god, m· g·,

moonlit
Po.   73– 3   I come to thee O'er the m· sea,

Moor, Marion
Ret.   1– 4   my great-grandmother, was Marion M·,

Moore
Charles W.
My. 334–29   * published by the late Charles W. M·,
Mr. George H.
My. 145–15   Mr. George H. M· of Concord,

Po.   41– 2   signature

moored
Mis. 385–11   m· at last — Beyond rough foam.
Po.   48– 4   m· at last — Beyond rough foam.

moral
Mis. 10–23   a m· chemicalization, wherein
       35–22   Why do we read m· science, and then
       37–20   leads to m· or physical death.
       45–14   m· status of the man demands
       45–17   effectual in treating m· ailments.
       73–12   it is always mental and m·,
       73–14   The foolish disobey m· law,
       83–15   you are a free m· agent to reject or
      107–25   this . . . mental state is m· idiocy.
      109– 7   a sure pretext of m· defilement.
      112–15   in extreme cases, m· idiocy.
      112–17   mental state called m· idiocy.
      112–29   total loss of m·, . . . discernment,
      113– 7   free m· agency is lost ;
      113–13   scale of m· and spiritual being,
      113–22   insanity, dementia, or m· idiocy.
      113–32   m·, and spiritual animus is felt
      119–19   a plea for free m· agency,
      131– 3   he will be called a m· nuisance,
      143– 3   the "square" of m· sentiments.
      155–27   fulfilling their m· obligation
      168– 6   m· lepers are cleansed ;

moral
Mis. 199– 7   only to m· and spiritual law,
      204–19   so quickens m· sensibility
      222–11   in other words, a m· idiot.
      240–12   to m· and physical strength
      241–17   Truth heals him of the m· malady.
      241–28   the physical than the m· ailment.
      248– 5   its m· meaning, found in the
      251–26   all error, physical, m·, or
      257– 8   Law is either a m· or an
      257– 9   a m· and spiritual force of
      259–16   m· power of good, not of evil :
      261–28   apprehending the m· law so clearly
      261–32   produced physical and m· harmony.
      264–25   m· and spiritual status of thought
      266– 4   when these sides are m· opposites,
      268–27   From lack of m· strength empires fall.
      284–32   thus it is with all m· obligations.
      297– 4   physical and m· reformation.
      303– 4   as healers physical and m·.
      339–14   m· tension is tested,
      341–27   The m· of the parable is pointed,
      346– 3   m· and spiritual healing
      352–19   in healing the m· sickness ;
      354– 4   m· idiot, sanguine of success in sin,
      365–13   physical and m· harmony ;
      365–17   this want has worked out a m· result ;
      365–19   If the uniform m· and spiritual,
      393– 2   Is the m· that it brings ;
Man. 31– 4   M· Obligations.
       87–15   m· and spiritual qualifications
       91–21   and with good m· records,
Ret. 10– 8   philosophy, logic, and m· science.
       30– 9   include all m· and religious reform.
       35– 5   for physical and m· health
       70–28   civil, m·, and religious reform.
       76–29   strictest observance of m· law
       77– 4   Ingersoll's repartee has its m· :
Un.   8–15   physical, m·, and intellectual,
       13–11   To Him there is no m· inharmony ;
       19–13   would be the end of . . . m· unity.
       35–17   forces of Truth are m· and spiritual,
       36–22   yet admit the reality of m·
       38–23   Life as God, m· and spiritual good,
       60–18   Mortals are free m· agents,
       64– 8   is a m· impossibility.
Pul. 20–17   greatest m·, physical, civil, and
       46–25   * philosophy, logic, and m· science,
       83– 6   * the m· strength and courage
Rud.   2– 2   * person, . . . a m· agent ;
        4–10   a m· and spiritual force,
        5–17   is a m· impossibility.
        8–15   In all m· revolutions,
       17– 6   m· power, and its divine efficacy
No.   13– 4   m· and physical growth,
       18–10   physical and m· harmony,
       18–23   have wrought this m· result,
       19– 1   m· and spiritual, as well as
       23–15   a literal and a m· meaning.
       45–20   its m· and religious reforms.
       46–12   upon free m· agency ;
'01.   20– 2   no m· right and no authority
       20– 7   neither m· right nor might to harm
Hea.   9–11   their m· advisers talk for them
       12–16   the general and m· symptoms
       13– 7   There is a m· to this medicine ;
Peo.   3–15   spans the m· heavens with light,
Po.   51– 7   Is the m· that it brings ;
My.   22–23   * the m· and the physical effects
       52–28   * the m· rightness of her book."
       91–11   * his m· standards debased
      104– 7   That epithet points a m·.
      122– 6   fixed in one's own m· make-up.
      147–18   physical, m·, and spiritual needs
      220–13   the m· signification of law.
      221– 2   and the m· distance between
      221–13   find a better m· philosophy,
      241– 1   * m· and spiritual qualifications
      249– 9   The m· abandon of hating
      249–10   Hate is a m· idiocy let loose
      252–29   it is m·, spiritual, divine.
      294–25   m·, and religious upon
      318–13   m· and spiritual effect upon the age
      364–17   disease, m· or physical.
      (see also **sense**)

morale
Mis. 297–17   statute in the m· of C. S. :
      298–20   the m· of absolute C. S.,
My. 238–17   rises above the letter, law, or m·
      268– 4   the m· of marriage is preserved.
      351–11   m· of Free Masonry is above ethics

moralist
Mis. 265–15   theorist or shallow m· may
Pan. 11–15   the best church-member or m·
My. 297– 2   patriot, philanthropist, m·,

morality

Mis.	274–19	mocks *m·*, outrages humanity,
	286–16	maintain *m·* and generation,
My.	221–24	issues of *m·*, of Christianity,

morally

Mis.	ix– 9	acquired by healing mankind *m·*,
	3– 1	elevating the race physically, *m·*,
	20– 2	heals man . . . *m·* and physically,
	31– 6	harm him *m·*, physically,
	34– 6	but is improved *m·*.
	45–20	better both *m·* and physically.
	67– 7	mentally, *m·*, or physically.
	107–24	may become *m·* blind,
	140– 5	*m·* and spiritually inalienable,
	214–24	mortal mind in being healed *m·*,
	220–20	improved *m·* and physically.
	222–10	he becomes *m·* paralyzed
	222–16	is fatal, *m·* and physically.
	256– 3	at the same time improved *m·*.
	259–24	physically, *m·*, and Christianly,
	265–22	not *m·* responsible for the
	289– 1	degenerate physically and *m·*.
	297–20	*m·* bound to fulfil all the claims
	300–32	Healing *m·* and physically
	301– 9	*m·* responsible for what the
	301–15	too sincere and *m·* statuesque
	315–15	hold himself *m·* obligated to
	357–26	not *m·* responsible for this,
	362–10	physically, *m·*, spiritually.
Man.	83–14	*m·* obligated to promote their
Ret.	34–18	advanced *m·* and spiritually.
Un.	36–19	physically, mentally, *m·*,
Rud.	3–14	will no more deviate *m·*
	8–24	he makes *m·* worse the invalid
No.	13–20	physically, *m·*, and spiritually,
	18–21	the teacher is *m·* responsible.
	22–10	*m·*, spiritually, or physically.
'00.	6–27	are made better physically, *m·*,
'01.	20–16	physically, *m·*, or spiritually,
Hea.	9– 7	the better for mankind, *m·*
	11– 5	is healed *m·* and physically.
My.	130– 6	socially, physically, and *m·*
	130–11	and striven to uplift *m·*
	146–24	tip the scale . . . *m·* and physically,

morals

Mis.	5– 8	perfect *m·* in their children
	62– 3	individuality, health, and *m·* ;
	62– 5	can no more improve health or *m·*,
	110–11	makes *m·* for mankind !
	241– 8	one having *m·* to be healed,
	245–13	influence upon the health, *m·*,
	249–15	whose *m·* are not unquestionable,
	283–10	breach of good manners and *m·* ;
	283–20	its *m·* and Christianity.
	284– 5	of religion, *m·*, or medicine,
	313– 5	of good manners, *m·*, methods,
	315–21	no question of money, but of *m·*
Man.	83– 6	not be a question of money, but of *m·*
Ret.	71–30	end in destroying health and *m·*.
Pul.	7–15	made *m·* for mankind.
	82–13	* conservators of the world's *m·*
No.	18–12	need of better health and *m·*.
My.	103–21	health, longevity, and *m·* of men ;
	111–20	healers and models of good *m·*,
	112–21	pure *m·* and noble lives,
	249–13	fatal to health, happiness, and the *m·*
	265–17	improving the *m·* . . . of mankind,
	294– 3	improve the *m·* and the lives of men,

morbid

Mis.	107–27	in certain *m·* instances stopping,

More, Hannah

Mis.	223–27	Hannah *M·* said, "If I wished to
Ret.	1– 6	in some way related to Hannah *M·*,
	1–13	inherited a spark from Hannah *M·*,
Pul.	32–24	* Hannah *M·* was a relative of

more

Mis.	vii–11	Till time shall end *m·* timely,
	vii–19	Whereof, I've *m·* to glory,
	xii– 6	"learn war no *m·*," — see *Isa.* 2 : 4.
	2–15	of a *m·* spiritual Christianity,
	2–16	a *m·* rational and divine healing.
	3– 4	If we regard good as *m·* natural
	4–28	*m·* than faith is necessary,
	5–15	says, "I can do no *m·*.
	6– 7	many *m·* are needed for the
	7–32	*M·* thought is given to material
	8– 7	we shall have done *m·*.
	9–31	*m·* disastrous to human progress
	10–16	*m·* assured to press on safely.
	12– 7	*m·* severely than you could,
	16– 1	*m·* spiritual Life and Love.
	16– 2	satisfy *m·* the cravings for
	16–20	infinitely *m·* than a person,

more

Mis.	17–10	your *m·* material religion
	17–23	birth is *m·* or less prolonged
	22–28	*m·* than the simple fact
	23– 2	but Science, demanding *m·*,
	25–25	are *m·* deplorably situated
	26– 5	*m·* humane and spiritual.
	26–22	What can be *m·* than All?
	32–16	*m·* than to many others.
	33–30	It is *m·* effectual than drugs ;
	34–17	they can no *m·* come to those
	39–22	who has *m·* to meet than others
	39–28	assumes no *m·* when claiming to
	40–29	it requires *m·* divine understanding
	43–14	far *m·* advantageous to the
	44–26	There is no *m·* pain.
	45– 6	do *m·* than to heal a toothache ;
	45–15	*m·* in this than in most cases ;
	47– 6	substance means *m·* than matter :
	50–19	understand — which is *m·*
	52– 7	he could do vastly *m·*.
	52–25	farther on and *m·* difficult
	53–22	*why is it not m· simple,*
	58– 3	*does that disease have any m· power*
	59– 1	you admit that there is *m·* than
	62– 4	can no *m·* improve health or
	65– 3	no *m·* proof of human discord,
	66–24	like the *m·* physical ailment.
	68– 3	*m·* than mere disappearance
	72–16	have occasion any *m·* — *Ezek.* 18 : 3.
	77– 3	this believing was *m·* than faith
	78– 9	can no *m·* be taught thus,
	78–28	any *m·* than goodness,
	79– 4	know them no *m·* forever,
	80– 3	lose much *m·* than can be gained
	81– 5	into *m·* spiritual lines of life
	84–11	and *m·* spiritual understanding,
	85–19	and *m·* or less imperfect.
	85–26	The pleasures — *m·* than the pains
	85–29	Disease in error, *m·* than ease in it,
	86–16	Earth is *m·* spiritually beautiful
	86–17	*m·* earthly to the eyes of Eve.
	86–23	It is *m·* than imagination.
	93–28	Nothing is *m·* fatal than to
	96–18	atonement becomes *m·* to me
	97–13	*m·* despicable than all other
	97–26	*m·* than personal sense can cognize,
	99–19	Jesus of Nazareth *m·* divine
	100–26	loves man *m·* because he
	103– 4	*m·* impregnable and solid than
	107– 9	we behold *m·* clearly that all
	107–11	*M·* love is the great need
	109–13	how much *m·*, then, should one's sins
	110– 5	*m·* as children than as men and
	111– 9	blamed others *m·* than yourself.
	111–29	inclining mortal mind *m·* deviously :
	115–23	turns us *m·* unreservedly to Him
	117–27	the *m·* provident watcher.
	119–11	*m·* stubborn than the circumstance,
	120–17	come *m·* sweetly to our ear
	124–17	with *m·* than a father's pity ;
	127–13	*m·* grace, obedience, and love.
	131– 7	*m·* than average avoirdupois
	133– 5	ideas *m·* opposite to the fact.
	134–24	*m·* than they that be — *II Kings* 6 : 16.
	135–19	Add one *m·* noble offering to the
	138–24	growth of these at first is *m·*
	142–22	A boat song seemed *m·* Olympian
	144–32	The Church, *m·* than any other
	150–26	Not *m·* to one than to all,
	151– 9	that they may bear *m·* fruit.
	160– 3	unite *m·* honestly in uttering the
	163–16	less human and *m·* divine
	164– 8	continue to be seen *m·* clearly
	165– 2	*m·* than eighteen centuries ago,
	166–13	has evolved a *m·* ready ear
	166–21	Jesus, whose origin was *m·* spiritual
	170–19	no *m·* important to our well-being
	174– 1	has no *m·* power to evolve or to
	176–11	learn a little *m·* of the nothingness of
	176–11	and *m·* of the divine energies of good,
	177– 1	a *m·* solemn and imperious call
	179–15	Truth has become *m·* to us,
	179–15	*m·* true, *m·* spiritual."
	180–11	another person, *m·* material, met me,
	182–21	*m·* than he hath seen the Father.
	182–32	*m·* than eighteen centuries ago.
	188–28	but that we can discern *m·* of them.
	191– 4	"*m·* subtle than — *Gen.* 3 : 1.
	191–11	if . . . there is *m·* than one devil.
	191–15	the existence of *m·* than one
	191–32	*m·* spiritual and practical sense.
	192–28	Nothing can be *m·* conclusive
	193– 4	Jesus did mean all, and even *m·*
	194– 6	know Him better, and love Him *m·*.
	195–29	practice *m·* than theory,

more

Mis. 196– 5 of many minds and *m·* than one God,
196–30 require *m·* than a simple admission
197– 4 *m·* frequently used than many others,
197–13 It means *m·* than an opinion
197–15 would be of no *m·* help to save from
199–29 goodness is *m·* natural than evil.
201–25 protect our dwellings *m·* securely
209–13 destroy its *m·* dangerous pleasures.
216–11 means *m·* than "hands off."
218–22 its effect, is *m·* ridiculous than the
221– 6 learns *m·* of its divine Principle.
222–25 Error is *m·* abstract than Truth.
222–27 good should seem *m·* natural than
226–27 disgraces human nature *m·* than
227–19 like the camomile, the *m·* trampled
229– 9 good is *m·* contagious than evil,
229–11 how much *m·* certain would be the
230– 3 *m·* than upon any other one thing.
230–11 travel of limb *m·* than mind.
232– 9 a *m·* perfect and practical Christianity
232–18 hence a *m·* spiritual Christianity
232–19 will be one having *m·* power,
233–16 into a *m·* fashionable cut
234–27 seems to them still *m·* inconceivable.
234–29 God is regarded *m·* as absolute,
235–15 It touches mind to *m·* spiritual
238–11 *m·* than history has yet recorded.
238–18 love that foresees *m·* to do,
239–25 made them *m·* serious over it.
239–29 saying even *m·* bravely,
241– 4 will no *m·* enter heaven sick than
241–29 how much *m·* should we heal,
242–14 I performed *m·* difficult tasks
243–14 claims *m·* than it practises.
245–12 directing *m·* critical observation to
246–20 A conflict *m·* terrible than the
247– 6 Those familiar . . . are *m·* tolerant ;
248–19 ·not *m·* true than that I am dead,
248–25 when he could do no *m·* for me.
249–25 *m·* tenderly to save and bless.
250– 9 No word is *m·* misconstrued ;
251–21 as men, clothed *m·* lightly,
252– 6 the *m·* the better in every case.
255–25 It is *m·* effectual than drugs,
262–22 we should be *m·* grateful
264–22 *m·* or less subject to the
264–30 *m·* fatal than a mistake in physics.
271–26 * *m·* strongly mark the difference
272–18 * not *m·* than one thousand dollars.
273–31 The work is *m·* than one person can
274– 9 *m·* than my teaching would
277– 5 *m·* imperatively than ever.
277–20 * one *m·* fact to be recorded
278– 5 will hate *m·* as it realizes *m·*
281–26 but it came to me *m·* clearly
281–32 *practice m·* than theory.
283– 4 no *m·* right to enter the mind
284– 4 *m·* than any other system
284–25 or that becomes *m·* real
284–26 Evil let alone grows *m·* real,
286–11 *m·* spiritual conception and
292–15 look no *m·* into them as realities.
297– 6 it has achieved far *m·* than
298–27 one no *m·* gains freedom from
300–30 is *m·* apt to recover than
306–27 it is *m·* than this :
307– 7 *M·* we cannot ask :
307– 7 *m·* we do not want :
307– 8 *m·* we cannot have.
308–22 and mayhap taught me *m·* than
309–30 *m·* than they have yet learned.
311–18 love others *m·* than they can
312–13 * "No *m·* striking manifestation
313–21 to send forth *m·* laborers
319–13 tends to make sin less or *m·*
321– 9 adjusted *m·* on the side of God,
324–20 growing *m·* and *m·* troubled,
326– 5 Once *m·* he seeks the dwelling-place
327–21 *m·* than ever determined not to
330– 9 man, *m·* friendly, should call
330–20 reported *m·* spiritual growth.
339–10 good is made *m·* industrious
339–12 plants our feet *m·* firmly.
342–31 How much *m·* should we be faithful
343– 8 and human life *m·* fruitful,
346–14 is not *m·* true or real than
349–28 I never received *m·* than this ;
352–17 to act *m·* understandingly
354–15 *m·* grace, a motive made pure,
354–33 No vision *m·* bright than the
355–29 *m·* beautiful than the rainbow
360–21 shall be no *m·*,
362–32 The *m·* nearly an erring so-called mind
363– 1 the *m·* conscious it becomes of its
363–31 a *m·* spiritual apprehension of the
365–16 and a *m·* spiritual religion

more

Mis. 365–29 and *m·* than all else,
366– 4 True, it requires *m·* study
368–16 *m·* deadly than the upas-tree
369–17 devout enough to trust Christ *m·*
370–14 *m·* intelligently than ever before,
371–12 They know far *m·* of C. S. than
371–15 *m·* and *m·* of Truth and Love ;
373–30 C. S. is *m·* than a prophet
375– 6 demands *m·* than a Raphael to
382– 7 *m·* than thirty years of
389–16 love *m·* for every hate,
391–10 Have many items *m·* ;
391–22 'T will be an item *m·*.
396– 7 *M·* sorrowful it scarce could seem ;
397– 4 A world *m·* bright.
Man. 26– 6 have served one year or *m·*,
42–17 a belief in *m·* than one Christ,
43–18 calls *m·* serious attention to the
47–14 *M·* than a mere rehearsal of
61– 4 two or *m·* Sunday services
61– 8 No *m·* Communion.
61–10 observe no *m·* Communion seasons.
63–16 two or *m·* churches may unite
69–19 *m·* than me— *Matt.* 10 : 37.
71– 4 where *m·* than one church
72–17 not *m·* than two small churches
81– 1 served one year or *m·*
84– 9 consist of not *m·* than thirty pupils.
84–22 or assemble . . . for *m·* frequent meetings.
87–19 the *m·* he trusts them to the divine
95–19 for one or *m·* lectures.
Ret. 2– 9 *m·* than a score of years prior to
6–13 *m·* space than this little book can
7–20 * who expected no *m·* than they
8–22 and once *m·* asked her if she had
23–14 heart's bridal to *m·* spiritual
26–27 know yet *m·* of the nothingness of
33–12 the *m·* Mind, the better the work
33–21 found to be even *m·* active.
34– 2 I must know *m·* of the unmixed,
34–14 It is *m·* effectual than drugs,
38–20 come to tell me he wanted *m·*,
45– 2 *m·* beautiful became the garments
49– 9 need is for *m·* of the spirit
54– 1 sometimes *m·* speedy than
57–21 The notion of *m·* than one Mind,
61–10 no *m·* to be invaded than
63–20 *m·* dangerous than sickness,
63–20 *m·* subtle, *m·* difficult to heal.
73–11 into *m·* spiritual latitudes and purer
83–17 *m·* difficult to rekindle his own
84–25 the *m·* he trusts them to the divine
87– 8 *m·* thoroughly and readily acquired
91– 5 No purer and *m·* exalted teachings
91–11 indicates *m·* the Master's mood,
Un. 6–22 Not much *m·* than a half-century ago
8– 5 as real as you make it, and no *m·* so.
13–10 not infringed in ethics any *m·* than
15– 3 *m·* just than God?"— *Job* 4 : 17.
15– 5 Do mortals know *m·* than God,
24– 7 insist that there is *m·* than the one
24– 7 assumptions . . . *m·* than the one God ;
24–23 *Evil*. . . . My mind is *m·* than matter.
27– 8 *Egoism* is a *m·* philosophical word,
28–13 even *m·* vague than ordinary
31– 1 *m·* accurately translated,
38–17 rulership of *m·* gods than
40–13 therefore mortals can no *m·*
46–20 To them evil was even *m·* the
48– 6 I believe *m·* in Him than do most
48– 8 Nay, *m·* — He *is* my individuality
48–15 no *m·* enters into His creation than
49– 8 The *m·* I understand true humanhood,
49– 8 the *m·* I see it to be sinless,
53–16 which are no *m·* logical,
56–28 *M·* obnoxious than Chinese stenchpots
64– 3 for God can no *m·* behold it,
64–11 the *m·* real those mind-pictures
Pul. vii–12 lenses of *m·* spiritual mentality,
2– 3 no *m·* spirit in her ;"— *I Kings* 10 : 5.
6–27 * *m·* than is dreamt of in your
10– 9 Our land, *m·* favored, had its
10–22 devout as they, and *m·* scientific,
11– 3 making melody *m·* real,
18–13 A world *m·* bright.
23–20 * years of *m·* intense life,
27–25 * One *m·* window in the auditorium
27–29 * of still *m·* unique interest.
31–24 * I was hardly *m·* than seated
33–26 * to *m·* than ordinary achievement,
35–25 * the *m·* attenuated the drug,
35–25 * the *m·* potent was its effects.
41– 2 * not for *m·* money, but for
41– 8 * *m·* than four thousand of these
51–11 * Every truth is *m·* or less in a
53–15 * "That word, *m·* than any other.

more

Pul.
- 56– 1   * One or *m·* organized societies
- 62– 8   * not *m·* than five by eight feet.
- 66– 9   * *m·* from the graveyards than
- 73–27   * no *m·* complete and yet concise
- 75–10   would savor *m·* of heathenism
- 80–24   * *m·* thoughtful and devout ;
- 81– 4   * with *m·* reverence than it was
- 82– 8   * you could no *m·* turn her from
- 87–20   *m·* of earth now, than I desire,
- 87–21   *M·* effectual than the forum

Rud.
- 3–11   it lives *m·* because of his
- 3–14   will no *m·* deviate morally
- 7–23   Spirit no *m·* changes its species,
- 9– 5   *m·* or less blended with error ;
- 12–14   will return, and be *m·* stubborn
- 13–12   saith there is *m·* than one God,
- 13–13   saith . . . there is *m·* than one Life
- 13–25   not be expected, *m·* than others,
- 15–25   may be dissected *m·* critically
- 16–14   *Is there m· than one school of*

No.
- 1–17   we can read *m·* clearly the
- 2–15   I have healed *m·* disease by the
- 4– 6   Disease is *m·* than *imagination ;*
- 6–22   *m·* apparent than the adverse
- 8– 5   let us add one *m·* privilege
- 9– 7   clearer and *m·* conscientious
- 9–24   *M·* mistakes are made in its name
- 11–19   it requires *m·* study
- 14–11   Theosophy is no *m·* allied to
- 14–20   perhaps *m·* than any other
- 15–13   *m·* mystic than Mind-healing.
- 16–16   forever giving forth *m·* light,
- 16–22   can take in no *m·* than all.
- 17–12   and for man to be *m·* than
- 18–22   a *m·* spiritual religion
- 12–20   follows that there is *m·* than one
- 23–16   Which of the two is the *m·* important
- 24–13   but much *m·* real,
- 24–15   become both less and *m·* in C. S.,
- 24–16   *m·*, because the evil that is hidden
- 24–27   another and *m·* glorious truth,
- 25– 9   *m·* than physical personality,
- 25–10   Mind is *m·* than matter,
- 26– 6   no *m·* identical with C. S. than
- 26–14   no *m·* relapse or collapse
- 26–27   much *m·* clothe you, — *Matt. 6 : 30.*
- 27– 2   supposition that there is *m·* than
- 27– 9   there will be no *m·* sea.
- 29–21   *m·* than a fraction of himself.
- 30– 3   It does *m·* than forgive
- 30– 9   any *m·* than the legislator
- 31–26   enter no *m·* into him." — *Mark 9 : 25.*
- 35– 0   there will be no *m·* sickness,
- 39– 1   we can think *m·* lucidly
- 39–22   It shows us *m·* clearly than
- 40–13   the inaudible is *m·* effectual.
- 42– 1   * *m·* and *m·* learn their duty
- 45–23   in *m·* spiritual latitudes,

Pan.
- 6– 2   because it was *m·* effectual
- 6–27   belief in *m·* than one spirit,
- 7– 4   signifies *m·* than one God,
- 7–26   hypothesis . . . *m·* than one Mind,
- 9– 4   means *m·* than one Spirit ;
- 13– 1   will witness *m·* steadfastly to its
- 13–11   never *m·* manifest than in its
- 14– 4   Once *m·* I write, Set your affections

'00.
- 2–23   and it will be *m·* sudden,
- 6–15   accepts C. S. *m·* readily
- 7– 8   there had been *m·* Bibles sold
- 7–17   Is there *m·* than one Christ,
- 7–23   walk *m·* closely with Christ ;
- 8– 1   know and behold *m·* nearly
- 9–10   a *m·* convenient season ;
- 9–18   Sincerity is *m·* successful than
- 11– 1   it gave me *m·* pleasure than
- 11–13   Music is *m·* than sound in unison.
- 14–16   following the *m·* perfect way,
- 15–25   *m·* than the first." — *Rev. 2 : 19.*

'01.
- 1– 7   *m·* extended, *m·* rapidly advancing,
- 4–29   meaning divine Love, *m·* frequently
- 6– 1   *m·* transcendental than theology's
- 8– 5   *m·* transcendental than the belief
- 8–13   Is man, . . . *m·* transcendental than
- 10– 5   how much *m·* shall they — *Matt. 10 : 25.*
- 17–22   *m·* difficult stage of action
- 18– 7   *m·* honored and respected to-day
- 21–24   God knows *m·* than any man
- 23– 1   neither *m·* or less than three ;
- 24–13   Making matter *m·* potent than
- 24–17   *m·* than two hundred years old.
- 25–12   because of their *m·* spiritual import
- 27– 7   * will interpret . . . *m·* clearly,
- 27– 8   * apply them *m·* rationally to
- 28– 9   perhaps none lived a *m·* devout
- 28–19   I love Christ *m·* than all the world,
- 33– 8   * in the *m·* advanced decaying stages

more

'01.
- 34– 8   is proven to be *m·* pathological

'02.
- 2–21   gives place to a *m·* spiritual
- 3– 6   regarded now *m·* as a philosophy
- 4– 8   for *m·* grace, a *m·* fulfilled life
- 10–20   reformer who finds the *m·* spiritual way,
- 11–10   *m·* spiritual understanding of God,
- 11–15   how much *m·* is accomplished
- 12–25   united effort to purchase *m·* land
- 18–20   what *m·* could he do?
- 18–23   *m·* effective healers and less theorizing;
- 19– 9   *m·* than all the malice of his foes.

Hea.
- 1–11   *m·* practical and spiritual religion
- 1–21   *m·* spiritual basis and tendency
- 2–11   Said the *m·* gentle Melanchthon :
- 3– 5   proof, *m·* than a profession thereof ;
- 3– 6   demonstration, *m·* than a doctrine.
- 3–21   works of our Master *m·* than merited.
- 5–28   The *m·* spiritual we become here,
- 6– 1   the *m·* are we separated from
- 6– 2   and we grow *m·* material,
- 7–19   *m·* than they all." — *see Mark 12 : 43.*
- 8–28   and do *m·* than we are now doing,
- 9– 4   employed our thoughts *m·* in
- 12–22   making you *m·* powerful,"
- 14–16   includes infinitely *m·* than
- 14–24   included *m·* than they understood.
- 19–20   makes a *m·* spiritual demand,
- 19–22   But let us work *m·* earnestly

Peo.
- 1– 2   is a step *m·* spiritual.
- 1–13   into *m·* spiritual latitudes.
- 2–26   This *m·* perfect idea,
- 3–15   and *m·* spiritual idea of good
- 3–18   a *m·* metaphysical religion
- 4– 4   *m·* than an infinite and divine
- 5– 2   the *m·* spiritual Christianity,
- 5– 8   for their *m·* spiritual ideal,
- 6–15   fear God *m·* than we love Him ;
- 6–18   a *m·* spiritual and true ideal
- 7–29   become *m·* or less perfect
- 7–30   mind-models are *m·* or less spiritual.
- 7–32   our methods grow *m·* spiritual
- 8–12   was not *m·* the antithesis of
- 8–16   and yet we make *m·* of matter,
- 9–28   *m·* potent evidences in C. S.
- 10– 3   steam is *m·* powerful than water,
- 10– 3   because it is *m·* ethereal.
- 12–27   bestows heaven not *m·* willingly
- 13– 1   have a *m·* material deity,
- 13– 5   the Divine Being is *m·* than a
- 14– 1   As our ideas . . . become *m·* spiritual,
- 14– 2   express them by objects *m·* beautiful.
- 14– 8   ideas of Life have grown *m·* spiritual ;

Po.
- 2–17   sun's *m·* genial, mighty ray ;
- 4–15   love *m·* for every hate,
- 9–10   wishing this earth *m·* gifts
- 12–13   A world *m·* bright.
- 15–12   as the vision *m·* vain
- 31– 7   annoy No *m·* the peace of
- 35–15   Written *m·* than sixty years ago
- 38– 9   Have many items *m·* ;
- 38–21   'Twill be an item *m·*.
- 41– 9   the mountains *m·* friendless,
- 53– 9   *M·* softly warm and weave
- 58–19   *M·* sorrowful it scarce could seem ;
- 73– 8   with thee in spirit once *m·*.

My.
- vi– 4   * a simpler or *m·* pleasing form.
- 5–21   to love *m·* and to serve better.
- 7– 9   effort to purchase *m·* land
- 8–20   * *m·* than nine hundred,
- 9–23   the purchase of *m·* land
- 14–22   * invented a *m·* subtle lie
- 18– 9   *m·* grace, obedience, and love.
- 18–19   never *m·* manifest than in its
- 19–20   but I ask for *m·*, even this :
- 21–12   * contribute *m·* liberally to the
- 21–15   * *m·* than compensates for every
- 24–30   * no *m·* appropriate time for
- 27–16   * send no *m·* money to this fund.
- 28– 9   * can give no *m·* than a hint of
- 29–13   * *m·* gorgeous church pageantries
- 29–15   * appealed *m·* to the eye,
- 30– 4   * nobody attended *m·* than one,
- 36–17   * peace of a *m·* righteous living,
- 38–10   * no *m·* were admitted until
- 38–23   * no *m·* impressive feature of
- 39–26   * *m·* distinctly may we realize
- 40– 4   * *m·* adequate reception to those
- 40–17   * may *m·* widely reassert its
- 46– 5   * *m·* spiritual plane of living,
- 46–23   * *m·* sincere and Christly love
- 46–24   * a *m·* implicit obedience to the
- 50–29   * *m·* than twenty-six years ago,
- 52–10   * *m·* faithfully to sustain her in
- 52–16   * *m·* energy and unselfish labor
- 52–24   * *M·* than once, in her earnestness,
- 54–12   * 'No *m·* standing-room.' "

more

My. 56–22 * and *m·* branch churches were
57–20 * which is 2,194 *m·* than the
58– 4 * no *m·* funds are needed
61–19 * never *m·* did I have any doubt.
63–26 * even *m·* impressive than this
67–24 * never was a *m·* artistic effect
68– 7 * is *m·* than twice the size
70– 5 * has *m·* fine church edifices
70–23 * Nowhere in the world is there a *m·*
70–24 * *m·* musical, or *m·* capable instrument.
71–24 * And what is *m·*, every person
72– 7 * *m·* frequented by members of
72–15 * do not send us any *m·* money
72–19 * to the thirty thousand or *m·*
73– 3 * *m·* than ten thousand dollars
76– 4 * that *m·* money was needed
76– 9 * no *m·* contributions to the
79–20 * must be something *m·* than a **fad**
81–16 * No *m·* cosmopolitan audience
81–28 * wherever two or *m·* of them are met
82–22 * twenty thousand and *m·* visitors
84– 1 * facts speak *m·* plainly than mere
84– 2 * *m·* of a drag on a church
86–16 * brethren to give no *m·* money,
87–20 * *m·* cheerful looking groups of people
88–12 * ceremonial of far *m·* than usual
92–10 * even *m·* interest than it has evoked
92–12 * hardly *m·* than a day's wonder.
98–16 * requested to send no *m·* money
105– 1 *m·* than the words of Christ,
105–32 *m·* certain and curative in
106–23 minds his own business *m·* than
108–18 The *m·* of this Mind the better
109– 2 no *m·* substance and reality
113–28 *m·* spiritual life and love?
122– 3 a destiny *m·* grand than can issue
122–17 know *m·* of the healing Christ
123– 4 prize love even *m·* than the gifts
124–15 What *m·* abounds and abides in
127–10 *m·* of Christ's teachings and
133–16 one *m·* round of old Sol give birth
135–12 my yearning for *m·* peace
136–27 that I may have *m·* peace,
137–18 and yearning for *m·* peace
141–27 no *m·* communion season in
146–13 *m·* than has been demonstrated,
148– 2 *m·* than ever persistently,
149– 8 *M·* than regal is the majesty **of**
159– 3 Never *m·* sweet than to-day,
163–15 which I think do them *m·* good.
163–25 all and *m* than I anticipated.
166–21 would be *m·* irksome than work.
174–28 love Him *m·*, and humbly pray
183–13 With you be there no *m·* sea,
191– 1 *m·* of the wisdom of Nicodemus
195– 8 to love *m·*, to work *m·*,
195–14 cannot do *m·* than we are
204– 1 nor will you be long in doing *m·*.
205–20 God *m·* supreme in consciousness,
205–21 man *m·* His likeness,
205–21 friends *m·* faithful,
207–10 * strive *m·* earnestly, day by day,
207–11 * *m·* perfect manifestation of the truth
212– 6 older and *m·* open sins,
213–12 be *m·* zealous to do good,
213–12 *m·* watchful and vigilant.
213–22 strengthen your own citadel *m·*
215–15 * are worth much *m·* to me
216–28 you will feel *m·* than at present
217–22 meet this negation *m·* readily
218–27 to one no *m·* than to another.
219–13 would not be *m·* preposterous than
220–31 seems *m·* divine to-day than
221– 8 in His *m·* infinite meanings,
221–13 *m·* complete, natural, and divine
224–19 *m·* fashionable but less correct
231–10 spend no *m·* time or money in
231–19 *m·* important demands on her time
231–24 to receive *m·* tenants.
234–25 *m·* fatal than the Boxers' rebellion.
236– 1 no *m·* of echoing dreams.
236–20 we can say, the *m·* the better.
240– 7 * to explain *m·* fully why you
243– 9 should be *m·* than one church in it.
243–12 the duties of half a dozen or *m·*
243–15 take charge of three or *m·* churches.
244– 8 one or *m·* lessons on C. S.,
244–24 may not require *m·* than one lesson.
248– 2 I am *m·* than satisfied with your
257– 2 *m·* of His dear love that heals
257–14 Christ is, *m·* than ever before,
259–16 *m·* time to think and work for others.
264– 5 learn of my meaning
264–17 Truth and Love made *m·* practical ;
264–18 the Decalogue *m·* imperative,
265– 1 *m·* possible and pleasurable.

more

My. 265– 3 knocks *m·* loudly than ever
265– 6 and *m·* apparent to reason ;
266–27 and the *m·* spiritual modes
269– 9 die any *m·* : — *Luke* 20 : 36.
270–28 I would no *m·* quarrel with a **man**
278– 5 may learn to make war no *m·*,
282–13 In order to apprehend *m·*,
284– 4 may have accorded me *m·* than
286– 4 no *m·* war, no *m·* barbarous
288–26 "Sin no *m·*, — *John* 5 : 14.
289–17 is heard no *m·* in England,
291– 5 *m·* to him than a mere rehearsal
291–29 God of harvests send her *m·* laborers,
292– 2 *m·* than history has yet recorded.
302–21 I may be *m·* loved,
305–23 to learn definitely *m·* from
308– 8 higher, nobler, *m·* imperative
316–22 once *m·* under Mr. Flower's able
317–14 to explain *m·* clearly the points
318–22 manifested *m·* and *m·* agitation,
325– 5 * One thing *m·*, . . . will amuse you :
332– 1 * *m·* than a thousand miles,
344–29 fear of . . . smallpox is *m·* dangerous
345–27 *m·* etherealized ways of living.
355– 7 need for *m·* men in C. S. practice.
363–28 deviation . . . is *m·* or less dangerous.
(see also **faith, nothing, words**)

moreover

Mis. 233– 4 *M·*, the feverish, disgusting
Pul. 21– 5 *M·*, they love their enemies,
50– 4 * *m·*, that he deserves to have **a**
No. 5–12 *M·*, this unreal sense substitutes
My. 40– 1 * *M·*, this completed extension **of**

morn

Mis. 144–24 fresh as a summer *m·*,
384– 5 And all is *m·* and May.
Chr. 53–28 glorious worth Of his high *m·*
Pul. 83–12 * "as fair as the *m·*, — *see Song* 6 : 10.
Pan. 3–12 the gentle murmur of early *m·*,
'02. 5– 1 foretells the dawn and din of *m·* ;
Po. 17– 2 their radiant home and its *m·* !
23–16 In brighter *m·* will find
25– 1 Mirrors of *m·*
page 29 poem
29– 1 Blest Christmas *m·*, though murky **clouds**
page 30 poem
36– 4 And all is *m·* and May.
70–19 To hail creation's glorious *m·*
My. 31– 5 "Blest Christmas *m·* ;"
155–17 May this glad Easter *m·*
155–30 she sends to them this glad *m·*
202– 1 springs exultant on this blest *m·*.
202– 5 him who hallowed this Easter *m·*,
202–15 the glory of the resurrection *m·*
208–13 the refreshing breeze of *m·*,

morning (*see also* **morning's**)

Mis. 179–20 between us and the resurrection *m·*
222–32 as easily as dawns the *m·* light
239–11 upon the sidewalk one winter *m·*,
259–20 *m·* stars sang together, — *Job* 38 : 7.
280–26 On the *m·* of the fifth,
281–26 it came to me more clearly this *m·*
304–23 * at nine o'clock in the *m·*
376–18 a November sky that this *m·*
Man. 58–12 *m·* service of The Mother Church,
59–24 come to attend the *m·* services.
Chr. 55– 4 bright and *m·* star. — *Rev.* 22 : 16.
57– 4 give him the *M· STAR.* — *Rev. 2 : 28.*
Ret. 17– 9 Here *m·* peers out, from her
Un. 42–14 *m·* stars sang together, — *Job* 38 : 7.
61–10 evening and the *m·* of human thought.
Pul. 34– 8 * a Sunday *m·* when her pastor came
34– 9 * proceeding to his *m·* service,
36–11 * as was given to her *m·* talks
81– 2 * on the *m·* of the dedication.
'00. 7–30 *m·* dawns on eternal day.
Po. 2–16 On wings of *m·* gladly flit away,
24–18 With song of *m·* lark ;
32– 1 rise in the *m·* and drink in the view
62– 9 Here *m·* peers out, from her
My. 29–10 * closing incident . . . yesterday *m·*.
29–28 * half past five in the *m·*
31– 3 * "The *m·* light is breaking ;"
56– 5 * two services were held, *m·* **and**
56– 6 * repetition of the *m·* service.
56–25 * condition of the *m·* service
77–22 * at six o'clock this *m·*.
78– 4 * *m·*, afternoon, and evening.
82– 6 * For a while this *m·* it looked
82–25 * taxed to the utmost from early *m·*,
86–30 * at intervals from early *m·*
145–14 and the next *m·* said
147– 5 the *m·* and afternoon services
190– 5 *m·* beams and noonday glory

morning

My. 191–15 glad Easter *m·* witnesseth
354–27 by Mrs. Eddy on New Year's *m·*.

morning's

Mis. 398–18 Till the *m·* beam ;
Ret. 46–24 Till the *m·* beam ;
Pul. 17–23 Till the *m·* beam ;
Po. 3– 1 blends with *m·* hue,
14–22 Till the *m·* beam ;

morphine

Mis. 242–21 is very low and taking *m·*
248–24 physician prescribed *m·*,
249– 2 taking some large doses of *m·*,
My. 292–24 croton oil is not mixed with *m·*

Morrison, Henry K.

My. 174–16 William P. Ballard, Henry K. *M·*,

morrow

Ret. 85–26 *m·* will crown the effort of
My. 13– 3 taking no thought for the *m·*,

Morse (see also Baker)

Mis. x–22 I dropped the name of *M·*

Morse, H. M.

My. 315–19 * signature

morsel

Mis. 130–12 sweet *m·* under your tongue,"

Morse's

'02. 9-25 *M·* discovery of telegraphy

mortal (see also mortal's)

appearing of a
Mis. 17–22 birth is the appearing of a *m·*,
counsel of a
Mis. 236–20 "Take no counsel of a *m·*,
each
Ret. 76–26 each *m·* in an impersonal depict.
Un. 21– 5 each *m·* is not two personalities,
earthly
My. 241–28 * the beliefs of an earthly *m·*.
every
Pul. 13– 3 Every *m·* at some period, here or
exalts a
Ret. 70–29 exalts a *m·* beyond human praise,
ken of
Po. 1– 5 Beyond the ken of *m·* e'er to tell
no
Mis. 182–21 no *m·* hath seen the spiritual man,
No. 28– 3 no *m·* knoweth ;
My. 304– 1 No *m·* is infallible,
ordinary
My 65–15 * ordinary *m·* passing out a nickel
pardoned
No. 29–19 A *m·* pardoned by God is not sick,
reformed
Mis. 146–21 every reformed *m·* that desired to
sinful
No. 25–25 sinful *m·* is but the counterfeit of
sinning
Mis. 186–12 in a sick and sinning *m·*.
this
Ret. 67–20 this *m·* was the image and likeness of
vain
Mis. 209– 3 vain *m·*, that usurpest the

Mis. 34–20 the immortal and *m·* are . . . opposites
61–25 A *m·* ; but man is *immortal.*
79–19 A *m·* who is sinning, sick, and
85–25 and the *m·* is not regenerated.
190– 7 the *m·* evolves not the immortal,
204– 1 and a *m·* seems a monster,
332–26 Not man, but a *m·*
333–17 Where art thou, O *m·* !
Ret. 67–11 the *m·* against immortality,
Un. 42–26 *m·* does not develop the immortal,
No. 22–24 devil as a *m·* who is full of evil.
29– 1 that a *m·* should be put to death
Pan. 9–14 What *m·* to-day is wise enough to

mortal (adj.)

admission
Mis. 346–16 *m·* admission of the reality of
anticipations
Ret. 81–28 frailty of *m·* anticipations,
as unreal
No. 36–18 holding the *m·* as unreal,
babe
My. 262– 7 a human, material, *m·* babe
belief
Mis. 59–17 prayer of doubt and *m·* belief
76– 9 *m·* belief that soul is in body,
77–25 sternly to rebuke the *m·* belief
79–13 cannot lapse into a *m·* belief
200–30 only a vagary of *m·* belief,
341– 1 still appear in *m·* belief,
Ret. 33– 3 *m·* belief, instead of the drug,

mortal (adj.)

belief
Pul. 13– 4 *m·* belief in a power opposed to
Peo. 12– 6 death is a law of *m·* belief,
beliefs
Mis. 55–27 its laws are *m·* beliefs.
79– 2 *m·* beliefs will be purged and
Ret. 57– 1 mighty wrestlings with *m·* beliefs,
Pul. 13–12 masters his *m·* beliefs,
No. 31–20 as *m·* beliefs to be exterminated.
Peo. 10–17 *m·* beliefs, and not a law of nature,
My. 182–25 wilderness of *m·* beliefs and fears
bodies
Mis. 60–25 *as many identities as m· bodies?*
body
Mis. 75–14 God is not in matter or the *m·* body.
Ret. 34–19 The *m·* body being but
Un. 28– 3 a reality within the *m·* body?
Hea. 18– 2 mortal mind and *m·* body shall yield to
claim
Mis. 198– 9 the *m·* claim to life, . . . in matter,
clay
Po. 2– 2 to sport at *m·* clay
concept
'02. 6–16 *m·* concept and all it includes
conclusions
Mis. 366–23 *m·* conclusions start from this false
conditions
Un. 59–16 this conformity to *m·* conditions ;
consciousness
Un. 61– 3 belong to *m·* consciousness.
Po. 35– 5 *m·* consciousness Which binds to earth
definitions
No. 25–12 Man outlives finite *m·* definitions
discord
Mis. 97– 4 destroy *m·* discord with immortal
dream
Mis. 393– 8 Lighting up this *m·* dream.
Po. 51 13 Lighting up this *m·* dream.
My. 5 7 Wholly apart from this *m·* dream,
296–16 The *m·* dream of life, substance, or
element
Mis. 2–28 out of evil, their *m·* element,
environment
Mis. 86–27 constitutes our *m·* environment.
error
Mis. 21–19 matter is *m·* error.
56–14 a *m·* error, a human conception
77–28 could fall into *m·* error ;
Un. 46– 1 *m·* error, called *mind*, is not
evidence
Mis. 13–19 basis of material and *m·* evidence
existence
Mis. 53– 9 wickedness of *m·* existence,
?88 11 If the premise of *m·* existence
Ret. 45–12 the first stages of *m·* existence
Un. 3– 2 primary school of *m·* existence,
No. 4– 7 comprise the whole of *m·* existence,
experience
Mis. 205– 7 In *m·* experience, the fire of
fear
Mis. 42– 9 a moment of extreme *m·* fear,
fetters
Peo. 3–24 and assigns them *m·* fetters
history
Ret. 21–13 *m·* history is but the record of
hypotheses
No. 20–27 continued series of *m·* hypotheses,
ignorance
My. 162– 1 God's mercy for *m·* ignorance
ills
Rud. 10–12 *M·* ills are but errors of thought,
inmate
Mis. 324–19 this *m·* inmate withdraws ;
inventions
Un. 60– 1 From such thoughts— *m·* inventions.
joys
Mis. 385–16 and far from *m·* joys,
Po. 48– 9 and far from *m·* joys,
life
Mis. 28–10 and the phenomena of *m·* life
life-battle
Ret. 22–14 the *m·* life-battle still wages,
lives
No. 41–14 compare *m·* lives with this model
man
Mis. 36– 2 termed material or *m·* man,
64–29 the existence of a *m·* man,
74– 5 enmity of *m·* man toward God.
75–28 *m·* man (*alias* material sense)
89–20 If *m· man is unreal, how can he be*
89–24 *M·* man is a false concept
89–29 *M·* man is saved on this divine
103–19 *M·* man, as mind or matter,
140–17 till *m·* man sought to know who
197–23 *M·* man believes in, but does not

mortal (adj.)

man
Mis. 205–27 corporeal or *m·* man disappears
309– 7 fails to express even *m·* man,
Ret. 67–19 error made its man *m·*,
Un. 15– 3 "Shall *m·* man be— *Job* 4 : 17.
60– 4 *M·* man is a kingdom divided
Rud. 5– 7 there is no material *m·* man,
No. 19–26 after the manner of *m·* man,
26– 1 believe that *m·* man is identical with
27–17 *M·* man is the antipode of
29– 4 *M·* man has but a false sense
My. 235–19 Is *m·* man a creator,

man is
No. 5–21 If . . . and man is *m·*.

man's
Mis. 205–25 *M·* man's repentance and
Ret. 61– 1 arises . . . from *m·* man's ignorance,

mansion
Mis. 324–13 Within this *m·* mansion are

mentality
Mis. 109–11 hopeful stage of *m·* mentality.
Un. 58–14 triumph over all *m·* mentality

mind
Mis. 2–10 mortals, *alias m·* mind,
4– 4 marked tendency of *m·* mind
5–25 an erring or *m·* mind,
10– 5 motives that govern *m·* mind
12–17 *M·* mind at this period mutely works
15–20 through the sore travail of *m·* mind
17–29 through the travail of *m·* mind,
28– 9 only what *m·* mind makes them ;
33–26 as *m·* mind is the cause of
34– 6 *m·* mind must be improved,
36– 3 classify evil and error as *m·* mind,
36–11 *m·* mind, which is harmful
36–17 nature and quality of *m·* mind,
36–19 *distinction between m· mind and*
36–21 *M·* mind includes all evil,
36–25 *m·* mind] is enmity— *Rom.* 8 : 7.
36–26 *M·* mind is an illusion ?
41–21 *m·* mind, through the action of fear,
42– 6 belief of dying passes from *m·* mind,
47– 4 matter is but manifest *m·* mind.
51– 9 workings of error or *m·* mind.
58–15 as *m·* mind, it is a belief that sees.
60–23 If *m· mind and body are myths*,
61– 6 vain strivings of *m·* mind,
72–25 Matter is manifest *m·* mind,
82–14 *after the destruction of m· mind?*
82–22 *m·* mind, or the material sense of
82–25 *M·* mind is a myth ;
84–15 *m·* mind, not the immortal Mind,
85–22 *m·* mind which seems to be matter
86–27 The atmosphere of *m·* mind
87–12 frail conception of *m·* mind ;
87–12 *m·* mind is a poorer representative of
103–16 *m·* mind, which must be ever in
111–29 false beliefs inclining *m·* mind
127–30 *M·* mind presents phases of
129–17 into the atmosphere of *m·* mind
184–31 *m·* mind purged of the animal and
204–32 and *m·* mind, thus purged,
214–24 *m·* mind in being healed morally,
215– 2 The tendency of *m·* mind is
218– 8 *m·* mind must change all its
219–22 that *m·* mind makes sick,
219–23 that *m·* mind makes sinners,
233–15 *m·* mind, termed hypnotism,
233–31 belief of product of *m·* mind :
237– 4 of *m·* mind instead of body :
247–21 They acknowledge . . . *m·* mind,
247–31 an evil belief of *m·* mind,
254–21 it is the *m·* mind sense
256– 4 *m·* mind must be corrected
257–11 immoral force of erring *m·* mind,
260– 9 the travesties of *m·* mind.
264–18 As *m·* mind is directed, it acts
268–24 ailments of *m·* mind and body.
286–24 *m·* mind and body as *one,*
294– 7 miracle in the universe of *m·* mind.
343– 6 to find disease in the *m·* mind,
343–20 The weeds of *m·* mind
355–10 *m·* mind must pass through
356– 5 The pent-up elements of *m·* mind
360–25 When *m·* mind is silenced by the
361– 3 belief in material origin, *m·* mind,
361–28 error, named matter, or *m·* mind.
362– 2 *m·* mind, material birth,
362–17 whose noumenon is *m·* mind,
365–18 *m·* mind is calling for what
367– 5 states of error or *m·* mind.
367– 7 there being no *m·* mind,
Ret. 23– 7 the cloud of *m·* mind seemed
25–12 That which sins, . . . I named *m· mind.*
33–20 its fatal essence, *m·* mind ;

mortal (adj.)

mind
Ret. 34–13 *m·* mind as the source of all the ills
34–20 objective state of the *m·* mind,
59– 3 consequently a *m·* mind
61–22 it is in the *m·* mind only,
61–25 suffering from *m·* mind,
68–23 "In reality there is no *m·* mind,
70– 1 "*M·* mind inverts the true likeness,
70– 3 origin and operations of *m·* mind,
75– 2 ill-concealed question in *m·* mind,
79– 7 effaced from the canvas of *m·* mind ;
Un. 9– 1 *m·* mind is the cause of all disease.
11– 4 currents of matter, or *m·* mind.
11– 9 laws of *m·* mind, not of God.
23–19 *Evil.* But *m·* mind and sin really
24– 1 *M·* mind is the opposite of
24–24 In my *m·* mind, matter becomes
28–20 cannot be taken in by *m·* mind
32–16 which I prefer to call *m· mind.*
32–17 *m·* mind declares itself material,
32–26 which I call *m· mind ;*
33– 2 identical with *m·* mind,
33–18 neither matter nor *m·* mind,
33–26 *M·* mind declares that matter sees
34– 2 *m·* mind says, "I cannot see ;"
34– 4 *M·* mind admits that it sees only
34– 7 that *m·* mind cannot see
34–14 *M·* mind says that matter cannot
34–18 What evidence does *m·* mind afford
34–20 Take away *m·* mind,
34–21 *m·* mind could not cognize its
35– 1 *M·* mind says, "I taste ;
35– 2 Let *m·* mind change, and say
35– 3 If every *m·* mind believed
35– 5 are but qualities of *m·* mind.
35–10 matter is *m·* mind ;
35–11 there is no *m·* mind,
35–13 *M·* mind says gravitation
35–20 the phenomena of *m·* mind,
35–20 matter and *m·* mind are one ;
37–22 *m·* mind which is misnamed **man,**
38– 7 even the unreality of *m·* mind,
45–25 *M·* mind is self-creative
50–11 a phenomenon of *m·* mind,
50–13 no such thing as *m· mind,*
53–21 is not a *m·* mind or sinner ;
53–23 Man's Father is not a *m·* mind
56– 1 The chaos of *m·* mind is made
Pul. 14–28 the great delusion of *m·* mind,
Rud. 8–25 that *m·* mind should not be
9–11 outcome of what I call *m· mind,*
10–13 diseases of *m·* mind,
13– 3 is neither matter nor *m·* mind ;
No. 8–24 before this state of *m·* mind,
14– 7 subjective states of *m·* mind.
15–21 nor in the modes of *m·* mind.
15–22 matter and *m·* mind have neither
16–12 called *m·* mind or matter,
16–27 its highest attenuation is *m·* mind ;
16–27 strictly speaking, *no m·* mind.
17–15 Matter, or any mode of *m·* mind,
18–24 the so-called *m·* mind asks for
24– 7 lower orders of matter and *m·* mind.
25–15 matter nor a mode of *m·* mind.
Pan. 5–27 denied it, cast it out of *m·* mind,
Hea. 11– 7 *m·* mind rebels at its own boundaries ;
18– 2 *m·* mind and mortal body shall yield to
My. 109– 1 the subjective state of *m·* mind.
110–15 *m·* mind pressing to the front,
201–17 scan the convulsions of *m·* mind,
211–15 it impels *m·* mind into error of
296–28 lifting the curtains of *m·* mind,
349–25 lawless and traceable to *m·* mind

mind-cure
Mis. 59– 5 *m·* "mind-cure" that produces the effect

mind-curists
'01. 21– 1 *m·* mind-curists, nor faith-curists ;

mind-healing
No. 31– 3 Material and *m·* mind-healing

mind's
Mis. 33–28 found in *m·* mind's opposite,
Ret. 31–22 Into *m·* mind's material obliquity

minds
Peo. 11–17 Mortals, *alias m·* minds,
My. 301–22 effects of illusion on *m·* minds

mistake
Mis. 339–16 it points to every *m·* mistake ;
362–11 Theologians make the *m·* mistake of

modes
No. 39–12 nor bring His designs into *m·* modes ;

molecules
Mis. 205–28 The encumbering *m·* molecules,

mood
Pul. 14– 6 another extreme *m·* mood,

mortal (adj.)

nothingness
My. 245–18   dire din of m· nothingness,
opinion
Mis.   7–13   of what can m· opinion avail?
No.   29–17   impute such doctrines to m· opinion
opposite
Ret.   73– 2   his m· opposite must be material,
plane
Mis. 368–26   on the m· plane may become the
pride
My.   5–11   m· pride and power,
purpose
Mis. 204–26   it unselfs the m· purpose,
scoff
Mis. 201– 2   receives the m· scoff only because it
self
Ret.   86– 9   Note well the falsity of this m· self !
sense
Mis.   24–21   knowledge gained from m· sense
  27–32   Take away the m· sense of substance,
  58–14   through a higher than m· sense.
  73– 8   immortal Science with m· sense ;
  81–17   in order to overcome m· sense,
  82–26   m· sense of existence
  163– 6   a grave to m· sense dishonored
  188–26   the unreal or m· sense of things ;
  396– 6   Fills m· sense with dread ;
Un.   30–22   through a change in the m· sense
  43– 6   The present m· sense of being
  52–12   redemption of soul, as m· sense,
  58–19   revelation that beams on m· sense
  61– 9   The mutations of m· sense are the
  62–25   M· sense, confining itself to matter,
  62–28   her m· sense, reversing Science
Pul.   44– 5   * as m· sense puts it,
Rud.   3– 9   to the perception of m· sense,
No.   29– 3   m· sense, sins and dies.
  40– 6   a material and m· sense of
'01.   17– 3   sufferer from the m· sense of sin
Peo.   5–13   risen higher to our m· sense,
Po.   58–18   Fills m· sense with dread ;
  70–14   Away, then, m· sense !
My.   45–17   * purblind m· sense declared
  61–12   * with the evidence of m· sense
  293–20   to m· sense the flesh prevailed.
  350–20   Oft m· sense is darkened unto death
senses
Mis.   13–20   what the shifting m· senses confirm
Pul.   45– 8   * seems impossible to m· senses.
  45–21   * the evidence of the m· senses
shadows
Mis.   71–28   m· shadows flitting across the dial
side
My.   50–15   * turned steadfastly from the m· side,
sigh
Po.   30– 7   dayspring ! 'reft of m· sigh
sin is
'01.   13–27   Soul is immortal, but sin is m·.
sinner
Mis. 268–31   the sin and the m· sinner.
sphere
Un.   61–17   infinite good in this m· sphere
strife
'02.   2– 2   through the mist of m· strife
Po.   29–18   so far above All m· strife,
things
Hea.   19–12   origin of all m· things.
thought
Mis.   3–20   the erring or m· thought
  4–30   to destroy sin in m· thought.
  5–28   weighed down as is m· thought
  24–18   I learned that m· thought evolves
  34–24   within the realm of m· thought
  37–19   which corrects m· thought,
  44–19   It was a state of m· thought
  44–25   this demand of m· thought
  70– 8   When the m· thought, or belief,
  97– 5   It is not one m· thought transmitted
  102–28   M· thought wars with this sense
  145–16   m· thought resuscitate too soon.
  198–21   the product of m· thought
  214– 4   the carnal mind, or m· thought,
  228–25   popular current of m· thought
  260–14   knew that erring m· thought
Ret.   68–24   no transference of m· thought
Un.   59–13   To m· thought Jesus appeared as a
No.   5– 4   In erring m· thought
  37– 5   M· thought gives the eternal God
My. 113–27   casting out the evils of m· thought,
throes
Un.   57–25   M· throes of anguish
views
No.   26– 9   such material and m· views
vision
My.   59– 7   * beyond our m· vision.

mortal (adj.)

will-power
Mis. 281– 5   the self-asserting m· will-power
woes
Po.   8– 6   Her bosom to fill with m· woes.
yearnings
Mis. 386– 4   Where m· yearnings come not,
Po.   49– 6   Where m· yearnings come not,

Mis.   2–23   therefore evil must be m·
  14– 3   the m· and material view which
  15–26   In m· and material man,
  15–28   m· and material sense of man,
  28–12   from this m· and material dream,
  49–15   If all that is m· is a dream
  56–11   Every indication of . . . is m·,
  71–18   on a m· or material formation ;
  72–28   Mind is not m·, it is immortal.
  76–12   the bodies of mortals are m·,
  102–26   state of m· and material thought.
  104–28   Who wants to be m·,
  188– 7   appears second, material, and m· ;
  199– 4   only m·, erring mind can claim to
  361– 8   neither material nor m·.
  385–20   Man is not m·, never of the dead :
Ret.   32–10   What is termed m· and material
  59–15   Whatever errs is m·,
  68– 1   This m· material concept was never
Un.   4– 2   our m·, finite sense of sin,
  9– 5   Material and sensual . . . are m·.
  30–19   man as immortal instead of m·
  37–17   Human beings are physically m·,
  37–19   personality is illusive and m· ;
  60–26   to m· and material sense,
Rud.   7–13   fallen, sick, depraved, m·.
  10–11   beliefs of a m· material universe,
  13– 8   A m· and material body is not the
No.   17– 2   unreal, material, and m·.
  25–24   that which is m· is not man
  26– 3   and that . . . is inside the m· ;
Po.   48–14   Man is not m·, never of the dead :
My. 109– 5   dream which is m· and God-condemned
  110–25   mortals will cease to be m·.
  179–10   mind and matter, m· and immortal,
  203–18   that its possessor is m·.
  232–23   until the entire m·, material error
  262–22   m·, material, sensual giving
  273–24   that the material body is m·,

mortality (see also mortality's)

and discord
No.   16– 1   then m· and discord must be
condition of
Mis.   64–20   put into this condition of m· ?
current of
Mis. 234–22   even the entire current of m·,
disease and
Rud.   10–13   and of material disease and m·.
emerges from
My. 200–16   man emerges from m·
evil and
Mis. 363–10   mythology of evil and m·
foundations of
Mis. 101–10   undermines the foundations of m·,
less
Peo.   6–10   * less sickness and less m·
man and
Mis. 205–16   on material man and m·.
materiality and
Mis.   28–17   can overbear materiality and m· ;
materiality, or
No.   26–22   corpuscle, materiality, or m·.
mists of
Mis. 363–20   through the mists of m·
nothing but
Un.   41– 1   beholds nothing but m·,
only
Un.   40– 2   It is m· only that dies.
phenomena of
Mis. 286–23   phenomena of m·, nothingness,
sense of
Mis. 181–26   will lose their sense of m·
shall disappear
Hea.   18– 4   m· shall disappear
sin and
Pan.   8– 5   lunacy, sin, and m·.
My. 192–11   conquest over sin and m·,
sorrow and
Mis. 103–11   is sorrow and m· ;
specimens of
Mis. 294–19   Love such specimens of m·
state of
Mis.   64–29   as . . . that he is in a state of m·.
statistics of
My. 181–25   The statistics of m· show
time and
Mis.   93–14   illusion of time and m·.

mortality

unself
My. 161–18 to unself *m·* and to destroy its
vice, and
Rud. 11–12 disease, vice, and *m·*

Mis. 101–20 bases his conclusions on *m·*,
103– 7 *M·*, materiality, and destructive
Ret. 57–28 making *m·* the status and rule
No. 28– 5 *m·* will burst the barriers of sense,
'02. 10– 5 molecule, space, time, *m·* ;

mortality's
My. 191–22 *M·* thick gloom is pierced.

mortally
Un. 35– 9 *m·* mental, instead of material.

mortal's
Mis. 243–17 a *m·* poor performances.
Pul. 10– 4 sense of *m·* necessities,
My. 181–10 *m·* painless departure from

mortals (*see also* **mortals'**)

all
Mis. 326–16 all *m·*, under every hue of
No. 33–25 Jesus suffered for all *m·*
allow
Pan. 11–12 allow *m·* to turn from clay
among
Un. 39– 1 "made flesh" among *m·*,— *John* 1 : 14.
My. 197–19 will disappear from among *m·*.
appears to
Mis. 14–21 What appears to *m·* from their
apply
Ret. 59–11 even as *m·* apply finite terms
approach Spirit
No. 16–24 in proportion as *m·* approach Spirit,
approximate
No. 38–17 In proportion as *m·* approximate
are content
Pan. 11–26 image that *m·* are content to call
are experiencing
My. 109– 4 *m·* are experiencing the Adam-dream
are hoping
Pan. 1–11 *m·* are hoping and working,
are not compelled
No. 42– 5 *m·* are not compelled to have
are the embodiments
Mis. 61–26 *m·* are the embodiments (or bodies,
assumed for
Mis. 63–30 Jesus assumed for *m·* the
awake
Mis. 331–29 As *m·* awake from their dream
bears to
My. 258–17 Bethlehem babe bears to *m·* gifts
becloud
Ret. 78–22 To becloud *m·*, or for yourself to
become educated
Mis. 9–27 wherewith *m·* become educated to
befall
Ret. 34–14 all the ills which befall *m·*.
beliefs of
My. 146–24 the beliefs of *m·* tip the scale
beliefs that
Mis. 28– 5 on the beliefs that *m·* entertain.
believed
No. 36– 8 while *m·* believed it was here.
bestows on
'01. 15–15 that divine Love bestows on *m·*,
blesses
Mis. 109–18 seeing the need of . . . blesses *m·*.
bodies of
Mis. 76–12 bodies of *m·* are mortal,
cannot prevent
Mis. 208– 3 *M·* cannot prevent the fulfilment of
can understand
Un. 62–10 *M·* can understand this only as
causes
Mis. 292–14 causes *m·* to turn away from
Christianization of
'02. 6–16 The Christianization of *m·*, whereby
cleansing
Mis. 185–12 cleansing *m·* of all uncleanness,
collisions of
Mis. 339–13 In the mental collisions of *m·*
commands
Un. 49–26 commands *m·* to shun
compels
Mis. 209–15 Insomnia compels *m·* to learn that
conceive
'02. 5–25 why should *m·* conceive of a law,
conditions of
No. 22– 9 fail to improve the conditions of *m·*,
cry out
'02. 10– 5 *m·* cry out, "Art thou come— *Matt.* 8 : 29.
dawn on
No. 20–15 omnipresence will dawn on *m·*.

mortals

deification of
Pul. 74–24 the Christ and the deification of *m·*.
deliver
Mis. 81–28 deliver *m·* out of the depths of
My. 233–12 better adapted to deliver *m·* from
demands on
No. 45–26 urging its highest demands on *m·*,
demonstrated by
Un. 1–13 apprehended and demonstrated by *m·*,
demoralize
Ret. 81– 9 tends to demoralize *m·*,
depravity of
Mis. 2–10 depravity of *m·*, *alias* mortal mind,
die
Un. 40–26 lacking . . . *m·* die, in belief,
do not understand
No. 16–17 *M·* do not understand the All ;
dwell among
Mis. 184– 6 made flesh and dwell among *m·*,
dwelling-place of
Mis. 326– 5 he seeks the dwelling-place of *m·*
dying
Peo. 4–21 sinning, sick, and dying *m·*.
earth and
Un. 52–22 Why are earth and *m·* so elaborate in
entertain
Mis. 74–14 opposite of that which *m·* entertain :
environment of
Mis. 85–23 seems to be . . . the environment of *m·*,
estranges
No. 15–24 estranges *m·* from divine Life
even
My. 110–23 show us that even *m·* can mount higher
face of
Mis. 332–21 and shamed the face of *m·*.
finite
Mis. 82–21 finite *m·* see . . . only as abstract
flutterings of
Mis. 85–18 feeble flutterings of *m·* Christward
freedom of
No. 34–28 freedom of *m·* from sin and death.
gain
Mis. 203–20 *m·* gain severe views of themselves ;
give to
Mis. 351–23 five senses give to *m·* pain,
giving
Mis. 204–13 giving *m·* new motives,
govern
Rud. 10– 9 which govern *m·* wrongfully.
great legacy to
Mis. 124–25 Love's great legacy to *m·* :
hating
'02. 8– 7 *m·* hating, or unloving, are
healed
No. 31– 4 but has not healed *m·* ;
hear
Mis. 86–28 What *m·* hear, see, feel, taste,
ills of
'01. 24– 8 all the ills of *m·*
illusion of
Mis. 50– 3 error is an illusion of *m·* ;
ken of
'02. 4–27 or beyond the ken of *m·*,
My. 14– 5 beyond the ken of *m·*
learn
Mis. 10–28 *m·* learn at last the lesson,
'02. 17– 7 When *m·* learn to love aright ;
legitimate to
Un. 54–19 becomes legitimate to *m·*,
lexicographer of
Mis. 226–13 immortal lexicographer of *m·*,
lift
Mis. 52–17 that tends to lift *m·* higher.
lifts
Mis. 287–16 until progress lifts *m·* to
lives of
Mis. 114–26 influence upon the lives of *m·*.
looked
'02. 18– 6 when *m·* looked ignorantly,
love to sin
Rud. 3– 1 while *m·* love to sin,
makes
Mis. 293–25 makes *m·* either saints or
manumits
Mis. 124–27 it manumits *m·* ;
matter or
Mis. 22– 6 Who dare say that matter or *m·*
may climb
Un. 64–15 *M·* may climb the smooth glaciers,
melancholy
Mis. 391– 7 melancholy *m·* Will count their
Po. 38– 6 melancholy *m·* Will count their
millions of
Mis. 208– 7 that governs millions of *m·*

mortals

minds of
Mis. 257–12 alias the minds of m·.
My.   5– 1 originates in the minds of m·.
294–10 contradicting minds of m·.
misrepresent
Mis. 250– 4 M· misrepresent and miscall affection ;
must learn
Ret. 49–14 M· must learn to lose their
Un. 10–26 M· must learn this ;
must take up
Ret. 65–12 M· must take up the cross
must work
Mis. 22– 9 m· must work for the discovery of
no opinions of
Mis. 3–15 No opinions of m· nor
now believe
Un. 43– 7 m· now believe in the possibility
obey
Mis. 208–15 M· obey their own wills,
obeyed
Ret. 76– 3 if m· obeyed God's law
poor
My. 195–21 by which we poor m· expect
purify
Mis. 298–18 Trials purify m· and deliver them
redeem
Mis. 82– 9 to enlighten and redeem m·.
redemption of
Un. 6– 8 redemption of m· from sin,
remember
Mis. 331–14 do m· remember their cradle hymns,
rescue of
Mis. 107– 7 these come to the rescue of m·,
362–22 must come to the rescue of m·,
restored to
Mis. 186–30 restored to m· the lost sense of
rights of
Mis. 283–18 trespass on the rights of m·.
seek
No. 40– 4 m· seek, and expect to receive,
seem
Mis. 61–30 M· seem very material ;
sensual
Mis. 328–11 acquaint sensual m· with the
showing
Mis. 162–20 showing m· how to escape from
sinful
Mis. 380– 4 how can sinful m· prove that a
No. 7–10 eyes of sinful m· must be opened
sinning
Mis. 36–14 animal qualities of sinning m· ;
some
'01. 15–20 Some m· may even need to hear the
spiritualizing
No. 10–24 dematerializing and spiritualizing m·
suffer
Mis. 261– 9 m· suffer from the wrong they commit,
suffering
Ret. 92– 3 for the needs of suffering m·,
sufferings of
'01. 17– 1 self-inflicted sufferings of m·
teaches
Mis. 211– 4 it teaches m· to handle serpents
think
Mis. 219–12 admitted that m· think wickedly
219–14 m· think also after a sickly fashion.
to show
No. 35–14 to show m· the awful price paid by
turn from
Mis. 28–11 In proportion as m· turn from
turns
'00. 11– 9 turns m· away from earth to heaven ;
two
Mis. 332–14 two m·, walking in the cool of
understanding of
Mis. 260– 4 reduced to the understanding of m·,
vain
Mis. 362–27 O vain m· ! which shall it be?
warn
Un. 57– 4 warn m· of the approach of danger
who seek
'02. 11– 2 m· who seek for a better country
wicked
Mis. 187–32 wicked m· such as crucified our
will become
Ret. 64–28 m· will become the victims of error.
willingness of
Mis. 269–28 willingness of m· to buy error at par
will lose
Mis. 181–25 M· will lose their sense of mortality
yield
No. 35– 7 m· yield lovingly to the purpose of

Mis. 6– 3 leaves m· but little time
15–23 that m· can lay off the

mortals

Mis. 19–19 most fearful sin that m· can commit.
22–11 C. S. translates Mind, God, to m·.
27–12 M· accept natural science,
27–31 M· can know a stone as
52–29 M· have the sum of being to work out,
60–29 if m· are instructed in spiritual
84–12 which dawns by degrees on m·.
103– 8 m· virtually name substance ;
109–22 m· must hasten through the
164–13 babe Jesus seemed small to m· ;
165–18 left to m· the rich legacy of
199–21 which m· name matter.
205–31 M· who on the shores of time
208–11 M· have only to submit to the law of
208–21 interprets to m· the gospel of
209–31 then shall m· have peace."
257–26 churches, schools, and m·.
261–24 by mankind I mean m·,
289– 8 m· must first choose between
292–27 m·, with the penetration of Soul,
319– 7 m· are in danger of not
328–24 m· who are striving to enter the
330–15 let m· bow before the creator,
331– 2 then, are m· looking up,
358–16 put on only when m· are
361–21 So shall m· soar to final freedom,
Ret. 64–26 m· must first open their eyes to
69– 1 His origin is not, like that of m·,
Un. 15– 5 Do m· know more than God,
40– 3 To say that you and I, as m·,
40–13 therefore m· can no more
50–19 less consciousness of . . . m· have,
52–21 beasts, fatal reptiles, and m·,
58– 2 M·, if at ease in so-called existence,
60–17 M· are free moral agents,
Rud. 2 17 whom m· have named God.
12–22 why should m· concern themselves
No. 17–21 If m· could grasp these two words
23–20 As m·, we need to discern
25–21 M· have not seen it.
27–27 probation of m· must go on
35– 5 what hope have m· but through
Pan. 11–20 M·, content with something less than
'01. 29– 5 m· in the advancing stages of
Peo. 11–17 M·, alias mortal minds,
My. 110–11 progress from molecule and m·
110–25 m· will cease to be mortal.
161–16 M· must drink . . . of the cup
242–11 I do not mean that m· are
244–18 m· do not enter without a struggle

mortals'

Mis. 61 3 way he made for m· escape.
107 19 M· false senses pass through
108–15 would remove m· ignorance
117–23 God's time and m· differ.
165–23 of m· redemption from sin ;
334– 9 that m· faith in matter may
'02. 10–22 increases the speed of m· transit

mortgage

Mis. 140–11 No one could buy, sell, or m·
140 21 I redeemed from under m·.
Pul. 8–10 Not a m· was given nor a
20 4 were unable to pay the m· ;
'02. 13–16 purchased the m· on the lot
13–19 After the m· had expired
13–24 amount due on the m·.
13–26 the m· was foreclosed,
14– 4 can neither rent, m·, nor sell

mortgages

My. 89–15 * not blanketed with debts and m·.

Mosaic

Ret. 89–10 instruction in the M· law.
Pan. 6–11 M· theism introduces evil,
7–14 the M·, the Christian, and the
7–20 a lapse in the M· religion,

mosaic

Pul. 2– 7 from its m· flooring to the
25– 6 * floors of marble in m· work,
25–23 * floor is in white Italian m·,
26– 9 * m· work, with richly carved seats
26–23 * the m· marble floor of white
58–18 * The floors are all m·,
76– 8 * The floor is of m·

Mosaic Decalogue

Mis. 248–18 obedience to the M· D·,

Moses

Mis. 261–20 typified in the law of M·,
Ret. 75– 4 the law given by M·,

Moslem's

Mis. 124–11 M· misconception of Deity,

Moss-rose

Ret.	17–10	Prairie Queen and the modest *M·* ;
Po.	62–12	Prairie Queen and the modest *M·* ;

most

Mis.	x–10	*m·* of these articles were
	x–14	where these are *m·* requisite,
	2– 3	those assume *m·* who have the
	4– 3	the *m·* potent and desirable
	6– 6	The *m·* of our C. S. practitioners
	6–28	there is the *m·* sickness.
	10– 5	the *m·* remorseless motives
	13– 8	*m·* happily wrought out for me
	19–19	is the *m·* fearful sin that
	26– 7	in the *m·* subtle ether,
	35–11	*m·* concise, yet complete, summary
	39–26	*what m· obstructs the way?*
	45–15	more in this than in *m·* cases ;
	52–14	the *m·* wretched condition
	81– 2	some of the *m·* skilful and
	87–21	who is *m·* reliant on himself
	89–10	advisable in *m·* cases that Scientists
	91–18	should represent the *m·* spiritual
	92–10	He who sees *m·* clearly and
	92–11	enlightens other minds *m·* readily,
	92–31	does *m·* for his students
	92–31	who *m·* divests himself of pride
	100–27	because he loves God *m·*.
	106–23	*m·* adorable, but *m·* unadored,
	108–27	*m·* of us would not be seen
	109–11	*m·* hopeful stage of mortal mentality.
	112– 9	The *m·* just man can neither
	126–22	*M·* people condemn evil-doing,
	157–16	helps us *m·* when help is *m·* needed,
	169–18	the *m·* eminent divines of the
	173– 3	The *m·* enlightened sense herein
	226–28	disgraces . . . more than do *m·* vices.
	229–17	even the *m·* High — *Psal.* 91 : 9.
	230– 7	make the *m·* of the present.
	232–11	behind . . . in things *m·* essential,
	232–20	that *m·* important of all arts,
	232–26	*m·* spiritual and unselfish motives.
	234–12	things *m·* essential and divine.
	242–22	in its *m·* concentrated form,
	245–21	which may be *m·* mischievous
	246–19	this *m·* unprecedented warfare.
	249–12	The *m·* devout members of
	250– 3	the best become the *m·* abused,
	251– 9	welcomed you . . . *m·* graciously,
	257–19	where there is *m·* danger.
	263–19	be met in the *m·* effectual way.
	267– 6	sacrificed the *m·* time,
	267– 8	caused me to exercise *m·* patience.
	273– 6	where I now seem to be *m·* needed,
	281–24	the *m·* beautiful and the *m·* costly,
	282–19	exceptions to *m·* given rules :
	287– 1	the *m·* exalted divine conception.
	295–24	The *m·* advanced ideas are inscribed
	304– 6	* in the *m·* appropriate place
	309–11	He advances *m·* in divine Science
	309–12	who meditates *m·* on infinite
	316–26	could have derived *m·* benefit from
	317–17	by the *m·* faithful seekers ;
	319–11	Scientists must be *m·* watchful.
	336– 8	that which represents God *m·*,
	341–24	the *m·* solemn vow of celibacy
	353–26	four thousand children, *m·* of whom,
	372–20	and *m·* distinguished artists.
	374– 4	in *m·* of its varied manifestations.
	374–17	*m·* fitting that Christian Scientists
	376– 2	* *m·* revered, *m·* authentic
	376– 3	* I use the words *m· authentic*
	388–11	And life *m·* sweet, as heart to heart
	391–17	Share God's *m·* tender mercies,
Ret.	6–16	one of the *m·* talented,
	7–14	* one of the *m·* distinguished men
	7–19	* with the *m·* poignant grief,
	10–12	*m·* of the knowledge I had
	18–23	those we *m·* love find a happiness
	19–24	obligations *m·* faithfully.
	32–17	* Whose *m·* constant substance
	37– 1	edition of my *m·* important work,
	41– 5	in *m·* instances without even
	54–22	the *m·* sacred and salutary
	84– 7	enlightens other minds *m·* readily,
	84–19	does *m·* for his students
	84–20	divests himself *m·* of pride
	87–11	*m·* systematic and law-abiding
	88–11	*m·* concerns mankind.
	90– 1	student should be *m·* careful
Un.	7– 8	When I have *m·* clearly seen
	7– 9	and *m·* sensibly felt that the
	45– 8	need *m·* of all to be rid of
	48– 6	more . . . than do *m·* Christians,
	52–24	The *m·* beautiful blossom is often
	52–25	*m·* beautiful mansion is sometimes
	54–16	*m·* potent and deadly enemy.

most

Pul.	22–20	her *m·* beautiful garments,
	23– 4	* THE *M·* UNIQUE STRUCTURE
	23–17	* one of the *m·* potent factors
	24– 5	* one of the *m·* beautiful,
	24– 5	* the *m·* unique structure
	28–22	* its songs are for the *m·* part
	31– 6	* a *m·* interesting personality.
	31–21	* she *m·* kindly replied,
	36–23	* one of the *m·* beautiful residences
	37–14	* it is her *m·* earnest aim to
	44–10	* It is a *m·* auspicious hour
	45–10	* grandest and *m·* helpful
	45–19	* proved, in *m·* striking manner,
	47–25	* But for the *m·* part she
	49–11	* of *m·* unpromising ground
	54–26	* *m·* perfect obtainable environment,
	56– 9	* as a rule, are the *m·* intelligent.
	56–13	* one of the *m·* remarkable,
	57–11	* one of the *m·* beautiful
	65–16	* a *m·* beautiful structure
	66–10	* *m·* of those who embrace the faith
	70–11	* *m·* remarkable women in America.
	75– 2	Whoever in any age expresses *m·*
	75– 3	has *m·* of the spirit of Christ,
	75–25	* the *m·* nearly fire-proof church
	77– 3	* one of the *m·* chastely elegant
	77–15	* *m·* lovingly invited to visit
	78– 2	* one of the *m·* magnificent
	78–13	* hereby *m·* lovingly invited
	79–15	* in *m·* instances they are held at
	80– 6	* in the *m·* intellectual city
	80–11	* *m·* recognition, the widest outlook.
	82–23	* singing *m·* for their own sex.
	87– 1	* *m·* cordially invite you to be present
Rud.	7– 3	*m·* difficult case so treated.
No.	1– 3	is a *m·* needful work ;
	2–23	the *m·* defiant forms of disease.
	23–14	The *m·* eminent divines,
	28–10	the *m·* acceptable time
	37–14	*m·* marvellous demonstration,
	39–23	*m·* of all, it shows us what God is.
	41– 7	work *m·* derided and envied
	41– 7	that is *m·* acceptable to God?
Pan.	2–13	word "pantheism" is *m·* suggestive.
	15– 7	establish us in the *m·* holy faith,
'00.	1–18	in *m·* of the principal cities,
	2– 4	the people *m·* interested
	7– 9	*m·* scholarly men and women,
	15–10	which of all . . . is the *m·* divine ;
'01.	1–12	*m·* essential to your growth
	9–27	who loveth and liveth *m·*
	9–28	receiveth them *m·* ;
	15–14	The *m·* deplorable sight is to
	16–22	to carry a *m·* vital point.
	29–24	loves *m·*, does *m·*, and sacrifices *m·*
	30– 8	consciousness which is *m·* imbued
	33–24	The richest and *m·* positive proof
'02.	17– 8	has *m·* of heaven in it,
Hea.	9– 8	the *m·* hopeless invalid
	9– 9	think *m·* of sickness and of sin ;
	12–26	attenuations are the *m·* powerful.
	14–18	*m·* arduous task I ever performed.
	16– 7	hath the *m·* actual substance,
Po.	7–11	life *m·* sweet, as heart to heart
	38–16	God's *m·* tender mercies,
	64–18	Those we *m·* love find a
	65–16	Those moments *m·* sweet
My.	4–30	Thou God *m·* high and nigh.
	6–28	*m·* prefigures self-abnegation,
	25–11	* and are *m·* gratifying :
	27–26	* to *m·* of them the fact that he
	32– 2	* two of the *m·* striking features
	36–13	* *M·* of us are here because we
	42–13	* *M·* unexpectedly to me came the
	45– 7	* *m·* important gatherings
	50– 4	* *M·* of those present had left their
	51– 6	* *m·* sincerely regret that our
	52–28	* *m·* authors would have shrunk,
	71– 2	* *m·* intricate discoveries
	71– 3	* the *m·* beautiful effects
	71–16	* *m·* imposing church edifices
	75– 9	* *m·* of them headed straight for
	77–10	* the *m·* notable feature
	84–24	* Its hold and . . . are *m·* notable.
	86–23	* one of the *m·* interesting
	86–24	* the *m·* notable of such occasions.
	87– 6	* to the *m·* casual observer
	91– 2	* *m·* of whom were already
	91–17	* one of the *m·* remarkable
	96–16	* perhaps the *m·* remarkable,
	98– 1	* the *m·* determined skeptic.
	107–30	heals the *m·* violent stages of
	118– 9	your *m·* excellent letter.
	138–21	*m·* respectfully yours,
	142–13	*m·* important events are criticized.

most
My.	142–21	*M·* truly yours,
	158–22	*M·* men and women talk well,
	160–10	*M·* of us willingly accept
	160–15	*m·* men avoid until compelled
	164–25	unfolds the thought *m·* within
	165–28	is the *m·* unselfed.
	177– 3	*M·* happily would I comply with
	188–10	of the *m·* High," — *Psal.* 91 : 1.
	197– 3	That error is *m·* forcible which is
	211–24	where there is *m·* danger ;
	219– 8	Human power is *m·* properly used in
	229–28	Thou knowest best what we need *m·*,
	231– 6	suffered *m·* from those whom she
	233–20	*m·* stubborn belief to overcome,
	240–26	* She *m·* assuredly does,
	249– 7	counteract its *m·* gigantic falsities.
	249–28	student who is *m·* spiritually-minded.
	259–14	*m·* pleasing Christmas presents,
	259–27	*m·* appropriate and proper exercise.
	266– 3	the *m·* imminent dangers
	271–14	* the *m·* discussed woman in
	282–27	*M·* truly yours,
	283– 8	Your appointment . . . is *m·* gracious.
	285–13	*m·* cultured men and women
	285–29	*M·* sincerely yours,
	289– 1	The thing *m·* important is what we do,
	290–18	when all earthly joys seem *m·* afar.
	300–13	heals the *m·* inveterate diseases.
	305–13	*m·* distinguished men and women
	312–25	in my behalf were *m·* tender.
	326– 4	* is *m·* gratifying to our people ;
	331– 3	performed their . . . *m·* faithfully."
	332–21	* in a *m·* interesting way.
	347–24	*M·* thinkers concede that Science is
	356– 3	where God dwells *m·* conspicuously

Most High and **most High**
Mis.	229–17	even the *m· H·* — *Psal.* 91 : 9.
	277–14	the messages of the *M· H·*.
My.	188–10	of the *m· H·*," — *Psalm* 91 : 1.

mostly
Mis.	379– 7	composition was . . . *m·* descriptive of
My.	97–28	* have *m·* departed,
	105–10	the lungs were *m·* consumed.
	160– 4	The heart that beats *m·* for self

mote
Mis.	336–15	*m·* of evil out of other eyes.

moth
Mis.	82–27	is consumed as a *m·*,
Ret.	32– 9	is crushed as the *m·*.
Pul.	81–17	* not as the *m·* to be destroyed
My.	230– 1	the sacrilegious *m·* of time,

Mother (see also **mother's**)
Mis.	18–19	Father, *M·*, and child are the
	33–11	God, our divine Father and *M·*.
	96–12	first, as a loving Father and *M·* ;
	113– 5	Spirit is our Father and *M·*,
	151–13	God is our Father and our *M·*,
	154–23	Honor thy Father and *M·*, God.
	159–24	"O glorious Truth ! O *M·* Love !
	167–17	His Father and *M·* are divine Life,
	186–14	He is the universal Father and *M·*
Pul.	13– 3	as Love, represented by the *M·*.
Un.	48–14	Father and *M·* of all He creates ;
'00.	5–10	Father and *M·* are synonymous terms ;
'01.	10–18	nature of God as both Father and *M·*.
		(see also **Eddy**)

mother (see also **mother's**)
and husband
Mis.	385– 9	poem
Po.	page 48	poem

ardent
Ret.	90–19	Who can feel . . . like the ardent *m·*?

become a
Mis.	253–26	until she herself is become a *m·*
	289–24	the right to become a *m·* ;

father and
		(see **father**)

father or
Man.	69–19	loveth father or *m·* more — *Matt.* 10 : 37.

her
Mis.	214– 8	daughter against her *m·*, — *Matt.* 10 : 35.
Pul.	32–27	* her *m·* was a religious enthusiast,
	33– 5	* would often run to her *m·*
	33–12	* answered as her *m·* had bidden her,

his
Mis.	225– 4	eighty-second birthday of his *m·*
My.	257–12	for himself and for his *m·*,

my
Ret.	5–15	Of my *m·* I cannot speak as
	6–12	next to my *m·*, the very dearest
	8–11	my *m·* was perplexed and
	8–21	left the room, went to my *m·*,
	9– 8	my *m·* read to me

mother
my
Ret.	9–14	as my *m·* had bidden me.
	13–18	My *m·*, as she bathed my
My.	145–13	* an old ailment my *m·* had."
	310–26	My *m·* often presented my

my sainted
Ret.	5–19	and knew my sainted *m·*

of eight
Mis.	7– 6	often busier than the *m·* of eight.

of Jesus
Pul.	27–21	* the *m·* of Jesus,

of one child
Mis.	7– 5	and the *m·* of one child

related
Pul.	33– 6	* One night the *m·* related to her

saw this
Ret.	13–23	*M·* saw this, and was glad.

sister, and
Chr.	55–24	and sister, and *m·*. — *Matt.* 12 : 50.

stricken
Mis.	275– 9	the faithful, stricken *m·*,

tender
My.	235– 6	tender *m·*, guided by love,

to help
'01.	29–18	go not to help *m·* but to recruit

true
Ret.	90–16	The true *m·* never willingly

virgin
'01.	8–27	was born of a virgin *m·*,

wise
Un.	6–20	No wise *m·*, though a graduate of

without
Chr.	55–20	Without father, without *m·*, — *Heb.* 7 : 3.

worked
'01.	29–21	*m·* worked and won for them

wrote
Mis.	372–10	A *m·* wrote, "Looking at the pictures

your
Ret.	8–18	"Your *m·* is calling you !"
	8–20	your *m·* is calling you !"

Mis.	6–29	where the *m·* has all that she can
	152–13	but I, as a *m·* whose heart
	167– 3	after the manner of a *m·*
	225–10	whereupon the *m·*, Mrs. Rawson,
	253–23	Can a *m·* tell her child one tithe of
	317– 2	"May I call you *m·*?"
Ret.	5–28	* As a *m·*, she was untiring in
	8– 9	"*M·*, who *did* call me?
	8–24	and said that *m·* wanted me.
	9– 4	*M·* told Mehitable all about this
	16– 5	for she was a *m·*
	40–18	The *m·* afterwards wrote to me,
Pan.	8– 9	belief that Mary was the *m·* of God
My.	13–12	* a *m·* and a ruling church."
		(see also **Eddy**)

mother-bird
Mis.	137–16	protecting wings of the *m·*,
	254– 8	as the *m·* tendeth her young

Mother Church
Man.	52– 3	Members in *M· C·* Only.
	71– 9	*M· C·* Unique.
My.	11–15	* need of our *M· C·*.
	88–10	* *M· C·* of the C. S. faith
	89–22	* dedication of the new *M· C·*
	91–29	* *M· C·* is absolutely free from debt.
	97–20	* *M· C·* of the C. S. faith
	242–19	relating to . . . *M· C·* membership,
	320–30	* dedication of the first *M· C·*

Mother Church, The
Building and **building**
Man.	103– 3	The *M· C·* Building.
My.	15– 5	THE *M· C·* BUILDING.
	357–11	have crowned The *M· C·* building

Directors
My.	360–19	supporting The *M· C·* Directors.

Manual
Man.	45–10	specified in The *M· C·* Manual,
	72–23	consonance with The *M· C·* Manual.

member of
		(see **member**)

members of
		(see **members**)

Mis.	106–15	chapter sub-title
	125–21	chapter sub-title
	127– 3	connection with The *M· C·*,
	129– 1	chapter sub-title
	143–24	toward building The *M· C·*.
	148–22	chapter sub-title
	311– 2	come and unite with The *M· C·*
	316– 9	The *M· C·* must be self-sustained
	322– 4	chapter sub-title
	322– 6	to hear me speak in The *M· C·*,

Mother Church, The

Mis. 399–17	corner-stone of The *M· C·*
Man. 17–15	draft the Tenets of The *M· C·*
26–13	shall be elected in The *M· C·*
27– 2	business of The *M· C·*
27– 9	Directors of The *M· C·*
28– 1	may be formed by The *M· C·*,
28– 5	laws of The *M· C·*
29–19	READERS OF THE *M· C·*.
29–21	Readers for The *M· C·*
30– 6	If a Reader in The *M· C·*
30–13	the First Reader of The *M· C·*
31– 2	DUTIES OF READERS OF THE *M· C·*
31– 5	The Readers of The *M· C·*
35– 7	membership with The *M· C·*.
35–11	membership with The *M· C·*
36– 5	membership with The *M· C·*
36–18	membership with The *M· C·*,
40–17	shall be read in The *M· C·*
41–17	dismissal from The *M· C·*.
43– 4	dropped forever from The *M· C·*.
45– 2	the wide channels of The *M· C·*
52– 1	involving The *M· C·* discipline.
54–14	shall be erased from The *M· C·*
54–17	not be received into The *M· C·*
54–24	membership in The *M· C·*.
54–26	The *M· C·* and a branch
55– 2	send notices to The *M· C·*,
56–11	meetings of The *M· C·*
57– 1	membership with The *M· C·*,
58– 7	Pastor over The *M· C·*,
58–13	morning service of The *M· C·*,
60– 4	services of The *M· C·*
61–15	Tenets of The *M· C·*
61–19	The music in The *M· C·* shall not
63–21	Reading Rooms of The *M· C·*
68– 9	excommunicated from The *M· C·*.
68–21	Directors of The *M· C·*.
69–26	room in The *M· C·* formerly known as
70– 2	The *M· C·* shall not make a
70– 7	heading
70–22	legal title of The *M· C·*.
71– 1	Branch churches of The *M· C·*
71–11	The *M· C·* stands alone ;
71–22	not write the Tenets of The *M· C·* in
71–25	publish them as Tenets of The *M· C·*
72– 3	nor publish the Manual of The *M· C·*.
73– 8	in good standing with The *M· C·*,
73–13	in good standing with The *M· C·*,
73–23	The *M· C·* and the branch churches
76–24	by the Treasurer of The *M· C·*,
78– 6	The *M· C·* shall not
80– 6	the Treasurer of The *M· C·*.
81–26	Publishing Society of The *M· C·*
91–18	the Treasurer of The *M· C·*.
94–15	The *M· C·* shall appoint a
95– 5	Board of Directors of The *M· C·*
95–16	The *M· C·* and the branch churches
97– 3	In The *M· C·*.
97– 4	shall be appointed by The *M· C·*
101– 7	an adequate salary from The *M· C·*.
103– 1	The *M· C·* or The First Church of
104– 3	For The *M· C·* Only.
104– 7	adapted to The *M· C·* only.
120– 2	heading
127– 2	heading
Ret. 16–16	The charter for The *M· C·*
Pul. 2– 7	spirit of beauty dominates The *M· C·*,
8–12	helping to build The *M· C·*.
11– 8	helped erect The *M· C·*,
20–14	The *M· C·* seemed type and shadow of
40–10	* chapter sub-title
58– 9	* joined The *M· C·* in Boston,
68–20	* C. S. church, called The *M· C·*,
84–11	* chapter sub-title
84–12	* The *M· C·* edifice . . . . is erected.
88– 6	on the dedication of The *M· C·*.
Pan. 1– 1	heading
'00. 1– 4	storied walls of The *M· C·*.
15–22	may the angel of The *M· C·*
'02. 13– 6	I have transferred to The *M· C·*,
Po. 76– 1	corner-stone of The *M· C·*.
My. 7– 1	chapter sub-title
7–12	chapter sub-title
7–17	* auditorium for The *M· C·*
9– 3	* audience-room in The *M· C·*
10– 7	* in an edifice of The *M· C·*.
10–24	* importance of The *M· C·*
12– 7	land adjoining The *M· C·*,
14–15	* The *M· C·* building fund
16– 3	* building fund of The *M· C·*,
16–11	* auditorium for The *M· C·*
16–16	* President of The *M· C·* ;
17–31	connection with The *M· C·*,
19– 2	* "The *M· C·* ."
19–14	* building funds to The *M· C·*
20–15	The *M· C·* building fund,

Mother Church, The

My. 20–27	* building fund of The *M· C·*
21– 8	* completion of The *M· C·*,
22– 4	* for the home of The *M· C·*,
22–24	* produced by The *M· C·*,
23– 3	* total membership of The *M· C·*
23–18	* your church, The *M· C·*,
24–13	* showing that The *M· C·*
24–19	* extension to The *M· C·*,
24–28	* will meet the needs of The *M· C·*
25– 8	* Sunday School of The *M· C·*
26– 4	* extension of The *M· C·*
27– 2	my Church, The *M· C·*,
27–12	* extension of The *M· C·*,
27–26	* extension of The *M· C·*,
29– 8	* extension of The *M· C·*
29–26	* extension of The *M· C·*.
32–22	* Tenets of The *M· C·*.
38–30	* extension of The *M· C·*
40– 1	* extension of The *M· C·*
40– 6	* branch churches of The *M· C·*
42–21	* extension of The *M· C·*
55–12	* ground on which The *M· C·*
55–27	* until The *M· C·* edifice was ready
55–32	* corner-stone of The *M· C·*
56–11	* overcrowded condition of The *M· C·* ;
56–16	* attendance in The *M· C·*,
56–21	* The *M· C·* steadily grew,
56–24	* attendants at The *M· C·*,
57– 2	* overcrowded in The *M· C·*,
57–27	* dedication of The *M· C·*
58– 5	* extension of The *M· C·*,
63–12	* extension of The *M· C·*
64–11	* Message to The *M· C·*,
65– 6	* The *M· C·* of the denomination,
67– 5	*Extension of The M· C·*
73– 1	* erected . . . . The *M· C·*.
73–16	* June meetings of The *M· C·*
75–26	* big addition to The *M· C·*
76–14	* dedication of The *M· C·* in 1895,
76–19	* cost of the extension of The *M· C·*
80–10	* in the extension of The *M· C·*,
80–12	* old auditorium of The *M· C·*,
80–12	* in The *M· C·* vestry,
80–22	* extension of The *M· C·*,
81– 1	* Upon entering The *M· C·*
82–14	* dedicatory services of The *M· C·*
90–22	* dedication of The *M· C·*
96– 3	* The *M· C·* of that denomination.
96–27	* known as The *M· C·* extension
125–13	connected with The *M· C·*.
135–24	chapter sub-title
140–16	* attending occasionally The *M· C·*
140–25	Dropping the communion of The *M· C·*
141–23	The *M· C·* seats only five thousand
141–28	communion season in The *M· C·*
142– 6	* find no seats in The *M· C·*.
142– 9	* First Reader, The *M· C·*,
142–12	communion season of The *M· C·*.
142–14	The *M· C·* communion season
142–28	annual meeting of The *M· C·*
166– 9	heading
166–17	Had I never suffered for The *M· C·*,
172– 1	* President of The *M· C·*.
173–11	this annual meeting of The *M· C·*,
216–24	The *M· C·* flower fund.
230–17	TEACHERS OF THE *M· C·* SUNDAY SCHOOL
240–10	dedicatory Message to The *M· C·*,
242–21	C. S. Board of Directors of The *M· C·* ;
242–24	to leave these duties to the Clerk of The *M·C·*,
250–26	impulsion of this action in The *M· C·*
302–25	My first visit to The *M· C·*
334–19	* in her Message to The *M· C·*
353–22	room in The *M· C·* formerly known as
358–30	I approve the By-laws of The *M· C·*,
360–18	support the Directors of The *M· C·*,
360–21	obedience to The *M· C·*,

Mother Church of Christ, Scientist, The

extension of

My. 3– 3	chapter sub-title
62–22	* extension of The *M· C· of C·, S·,*

Man. 54– 7	The *M· C· of C·, S·,* Tenets.
54– 8	member of The *M· C· of C·, S·,*
61– 9	The *M· C· of C·, S·,* shall
70–11	The *M· C· of C·, S·,* shall
72–21	of The *M· C· of C·, S·,* Leader
My. 6–14	provided for The *M· C· of C·, S·,*
6–18	edifice of The *M· C· of C·, S·,*
13–14	prefigure The *M· C· of C·, S·,*
25–20	* of The *M· C· of C·, S·,*.
172–24	* meeting of The *M· C· of C·, S·,*
173– 8	The *M· C· of C·, S·,* in Boston.
217– 6	in trust to The *M· C· of C·, S·,*
223– 6	outside of The *M· C· of C·, S·,*
223–21	member of The *M· C· of C·, S·,*
246–23	The *M· C· of C·, S·,* in Boston.

Mother Church of Christ, Scientist, The

My.	250– 2	By-law of The *M· C· of C·, S·*,
	250–15	By-law of The *M· C· of C·, S·*,
	279–23	member of The *M· C· of C·, S·*,
	289– 8	proper that The *M· C· of C·, S·*,
	347– 7	Members of The *M· C· of C·, S·*,
	352–19	*Ushers of The M· C· of C·, S·* :

Mother Church's, The

Man.	71–17	The *M· C·* form of government,

Mother in Israel

(*see* **Eddy**)

mother-in-law

Mis.	214– 8	against her *m·*.— *Matt.* 10 : 35.

motherless

Mis.	275–11	and the *m·* little ones,

Mother Mary

My.	303– 3	one incarnation, one *M· M·*.

Mother's

Mis.	206– 6	heard the Father and *M·* welcome,

(*see also* **Eddy**)

mother's

Mis.	160– 4	a *m·* love behind words
	253–22	*m·* love touches the heart of
	331–16	words from a *m·* lips
Ret.	1–16	perpetuated her *m·* name.
	8– 6	thought this was my *m·* voice,
	20– 3	until after my *m·* decease.
Po.	8–18	Of a *m·* love, that no words
	29– 9	No natal hour and *m·* tear,
My.	311–24	which is of my *m·* ancestry.
	336–15	until after my *m·* decease.''

(*see also* **Eddy**)

mothers

Mis.	5– 7	*M·* should be able to

Mother's Darling

Ret.	20–15	taken from my poem, ''*M· D·*,''

Mother's Evening Prayer

(*see* **Appendix A**)

Mother's Room and room

Mis.	144– 3	The money for building ''*M· R·*,''
Man.	69–26	formerly known as ''*M· R·*''
Pul.	v– 5	*M· R·* IN THE FIRST CHURCH OF
	8–27	*M· R·* in The First Church of
	25–10	* the ''*M· R·*,'' designed for
	25–19	* the auditorium, the ''*M· R·*,''
	26–19	* leading
	26–20	* The ''*M· R·*'' is approached by
	27– 1	* Leading off the ''*M· R·*'' are
	27–20	* In the ''*M· R·*'' the windows are
	42–12	* money was devoted to the ''*M· R·*,''
	42–17	* words, ''*M· R·*,'' in gilt letters.
	40– 3	* or sometimes ''*M· r·*,''
	58–27	* a room . . . called ''*M· R·*,''
	59–27	* the money for the *M· R·*,
	76– 3	* apartment known as the '' *M· R·*,''
	76– 5	* The furnishing of the ''*M· R·*''
My.	353–22	formerly known as ''*M· R·*''

mother tincture

'01.	18– 1	''*m· t·*'' of one grain of the drug

motion

Mis.	132– 1	A *m·* was made, and a vote passed,
	208–13	unbroken *m·* of the law of divine Love
	230–10	and mere *m·* when at work,
Man.	17– 9	on *m·* of Mrs. Eddy, it was voted,
Ret.	31–14	spontaneous *m·* of Truth and Love,
	89– 3	opposed to it by material *m·*,
My.	7–15	* offered the following *m·* :
	8– 3	* In support of the *m·*, Mr. Kimball
	8– 8	* in seconding the *m·*, said :
	8–22	* The *m·* was carried unanimously.
	22–19	* every purpose she has set in *m·*,
	44–18	* The *m·* was carried unanimously
	65– 2	* chapter sub-title
	65–10	* This astonishing *m·* was passed

motionless

No.	6–17	evidence that the earth is *m·*

motions

Mis.	65– 5	and her *m·* imaginary.

motive

Mis.	117– 6	discern between the thought, *m·*, and
	117– 6	superinduced by the wrong *m·* or
	130–22	Where the *m·* to do right exists,
	135– 7	one in *m·*, purpose, pursuit.
	195– 3	all action, *m·*, and mind,
	283– 2	or the *m·* is mercenary,
	354–15	more grace, a *m·* made pure,
Man.	83– 4	*M·* in Teaching.
Ret.	28–30	no *m·* can cause a surrender of
	30– 7	The *m·* of my earliest labors
Hea.	7–11	begins with *m·*, instead of act,

motive

Hea.	7–12	and there correcting the *m·*,
	7–13	act that results from the *m·*.
	7–16	begins in *m·* to correct the act,
	19–17	to spiritualize thought, *m·*, and
My.	117– 5	personal *m·* gratified by sense
	128–25	the *m·* is not as wicked,
	181–13	the *m·* of true religion,
	236–10	far-reaching *m·* and success,

motive-power

Mis.	197– 2	become the *m·* of every act.

motives

affections and

Mis.	19–10	lift the affections and *m·* of men

and acts

Man.	40– 4	A Rule for *M·* and Acts.
Ret.	79–10	in unselfish *m·* and acts,

and aims

My.	125– 2	false affections, *m·*, and aims,

and circumstances

Ret.	38–25	*m·* and circumstances unknown to me.

and methods

Mis.	267–28	spiritualizes man's *m·* and methods,

and object

My.	296–27	traced its emotions, *m·*, and object.

best

My.	180–26	misconstrues our best *m·*,

Christian

Man.	50–18	from Christian *m·* make this evident,

desire, and

No.	12–13	The same affection, desire, and *m·*

for sin

Peo.	9– 5	washing away the *m·* for sin ;

for teaching

Rud.	16 1	If . . . are the *m·* for teaching,

govern acts

Mis.	51–15	*M·* govern acts, and Mind governs man.

her

Pul.	50– 5	* Indeed, one of her *m·*

his

Mis.	162–26	his *m·* and Christlikeness,

kind

My.	234–11	God will reward their kind *m·*,

leading

No.	32– 7	nor the *m·* leading to it.

mercenary

No.	43–18	take it up from mercenary *m·*,

mere

Rud.	17 3	from mere *m·* of self-aggrandizement to

misjudged

Mis.	236– 2	human passions . . . have misjudged *m·* ?

my

Mis.	263– 1	if my *m·* are sinister, they will harm
	278–11	when my *m·* and acts are understood

new

Mis.	204–14	giving mortals new *m·*,

of human affection

My.	268– 8	If the *m·* of human affection are

of men

Mis.	19–10	lift the affections and *m·* of men
My.	268–14	uplifting the *m·* of men.

of others

No.	7– 7	as to the *m·* of others.

or acts

Man.	40– 6	should impel the *m·* or acts

personal

Mis.	291– 7	demonstrates above personal *m·*,

remorseless

Mis.	10– 5	the most remorseless *m·* that

right

Mis.	51–17	the right *m·* for action,

same

'01.	33–27	the same *m·* which actuate

selfish

Mis.	118– 3	self-will, selfish *m·*, and
Ret.	71–21	selfish *m·* entering into

sinister

Ret.	78– 9	but carnal and sinister *m·*,

their

Mis.	84–10	their *m·* were rewarded
	214–23	their *m·*, aims, and tendency.

unseen

Mis.	260–30	lawless mind, with unseen *m·*,

unselfish

Mis.	232–27	spiritual and unselfish *m·*.
Ret.	79–10	in unselfish *m·* and acts,

wrong

Mis.	215–12	or start from wrong *m·*.
	263– 3	knowing that the wrong *m·* are not
My.	223–18	superinduced by wrong *m·*

your

Mis.	90–19	are equal to your *m·* ;

'02.	17–26	take its answer as to thy aims, *m·*,

motor
  Pul. 25– 5   * with *m·* electric power.
mottled
  Mis. 376–24   into a glory of *m·* marvels.
motto
  Mis. 139–17   the above Scripture for its *m·*.
       306– 5   * *m·* has not yet been decided upon,
  Ret. 86– 9   as said the classic Grecian *m:*
  '02. 14– 6   a *m·* for every Christian Scientist,
  My. 170–18   it is my sacred *m·*,
mould
  No. 20– 6   would fashion Deity in a manlike *m·*,
  My. 261–12   To *m·* aright the first impressions
moulded
  My. 114–10   book which has *m·* their lives
moulder
  Mis. 293–29   there to *m·* and rot.
moulding
  No. 20– 6   Truth is *m·* a Godlike man.
moulds
  Mis. 360– 8   cast in the *m·* of C. S. :
Moulton, Edward A.
  My. 174–15   Edward A. *M·*, John C. Thorne,
mound
  My. 311–27   knelt in silent prayer on the *m·*
Mount
       (*see* **Sermon on the Mount**)
mount
  Mis. 17– 7   on this *m·* of revelation,
       44– 2   showed to thee in the *m·*,"— *Heb.* 8 : 5.
     164–14   from the *m·* of revelation,
     206–29   upon the *m·* of holiness,
     234– 4   attempt to *m·* above error
     326–20   to the valley and up the *m·*.
     328–16   been driven . . . to the foot of the *m·*,
     356–14   from the *m·* of revelation,
     369– 2   foot of the *m·* of holiness,
     387– 4   *m·* upward unto purer skies ;
  No. 1–16   on the *m·* of revelation,
  '01. 10–24   after the pattern of the *m·*.
  Hea. 19–23   to the model on the *m·*,
  Po. 50–22   *m·* upward unto purer skies ;
  My. 110–24   *m·* higher in the altitude of being.
     189– 3   should reach the *m·* of revelation ;
mountain (*see also* **mountain's**)
  Mis. 41–15   the *m·* of human endeavor,
     251–30   *m·* mists before the sun.
     323– 8   at the foot of the *m·*
     323–17   at the foot of the *m·*.
     323–18   Would ye ascend the *m·*,
     324–30   at the foot of the *m·*,
     326–24   and take them up the *m·*.
     327– 6   "Wilt thou climb the *m·*,
     328– 7   *m·* is heaven-crowned Christianity,
     329–16   over *m·* and meadow,
     392– 2   Oh, *m·* monarch, at whose feet
     392–10   Whate'er thy mission, *m·* sentinel,
  No. 7–12   as a bird to your *m·*,"— *Psal.* 11 : 1.
  Hea. 10–26   As the *m·* hart panteth for
  Po. v– 9   * poem
     page 1   poem
     20– 1   *m·* monarch, at whose feet
     20–14   Whate'er thy mission, *m·* sentinel,
     66– 4   the thrill of that *m·* rill,
  My. 183–14   upon the *m·* of Israel.
     186–10   up the *m·*, and on to the
     222–11   say unto this *m·*,— *Matt.* 17 : 20.
mountain-horn
  Mis. 328– 4   listen for the *m·*,
mountain's
  Mis. 392– 1   poem
  Po. page 20   poem
mountains
  Un. 11– 1   the *m·* of unholiness
  Pul. 73–16   * If you have faith, you can move *m·*."
  Pan. 3–27   president of the *m·*,
  Po. 41– 9   And the *m·* more friendless,
  My. 184–26   beautiful upon the *m·* — *Isa.* 52 : 7.
     185–22   In 1888 I visited these *m·*
     185–25   to be in the midst of the *m·*,
     185–30   refuge in *m·*, and good universal.
     186– 1   The rocks, rills, *m·*,
     194– 3   fell forests and remove *m·*,
     278–11   molecule of faith that removes *m·*,
mounted
  My. 115– 1   *m·* thought on the swift
     259– 2   *m·* on its pedestal
mounting
  Mis. 1–16   *m·* sense gathers fresh forms
  No. 34–23   *m·* to the throne of glory

mounting
  '02. 20– 1   *m·* the billow or going down into
  My. 110–24   *M·* higher, mortals will cease to
mounts
  My. 129–27   where faith *m·* upward,
mourn
  Mis. 124–15   comforting such as *m·*,
     275–16   encourage, and bless all who *m·*.
     353– 1   it has nothing to *m·* over,
     388–20   Last at the cross to *m·* her Lord,
  Pul. 56–22   * And *m·* our self-inflicted pain."
  Po. 21– 9   Last at the cross to *m·* her Lord,
     67–17   The cypress may *m·* with her
  My. 126–24   and who should *m·* over the
     132–31   comforts such as *m·*,
     230–13   to comfort such as *m·*,
     291–26   called to *m·* the loss of
     291–28   stops to think, to *m·*, yea, to pray,
     295– 1   I sympathize with those who *m·*,
     335–10   * companions, who *m·* his early death.
     339–22   rejoice . . . and have no cause to *m·* ;
mourned
  Mis. 375–30   * true art — that we have . . . *m·*
  My. 12–19   *m·* it as what "might have been."
mourner
  Mis. 399– 1   *M·*, it calls you, — "Come to my bosom,
  Po. 75– 7   *M·*, it calls you, — "Come to my bosom,
  My. 292–11   support, and comfort the chief *m·*
mourners
  Po. 78–14   meekest of *m·*, while yet the chief,
mourning
  My. 126–21   death, and *m·*, and famine ;— *Rev.* 18 : 8 .
mourns
  My. 294–30   The court of the Vatican *m·* him ;
mouse
  Mis. 131– 3   a *m·* gnawing at the vitals of
mouth
  Mis. 118–31   which goeth into the *m·* — *Matt.* 15 : 11.
     118–32   which cometh out of the *m·*, — *Matt.* 15 : 11.
     183–16   if he open his *m·* it shall be filled
     209– 5   wouldst shut the *m·* of His prophets,
     231–18   poked into the little *m·*
     231–25   pucker the rosebud *m·* into saying,
     240–26   with a cigarette in his *m·*
     373–10   the serpent cast out of his *m·*,
  Ret. 81–23   puts this pious counsel into a father's *m·* :
  Un. 33–24   "In the *m·* of two or three — *Matt.* 18 : 16.
     60–15   Out of the same *m·* — *Jas.* 3 : 10.
  Pul. 14– 9   cast out of his *m·* water — *Rev.* 12 : 15.
     14–11   the earth opened her *m·*, — *Rev.* 12 : 16.
     14–13   dragon cast out of his *m·*. — *Rev.* 12 : 16.
  No. 44–16   the *m·* lisping God's praise ;
  '02. 16–22   opening not his *m·* in self-defense
  My. 6–22   proceedeth out of the *m·* of God.
     13–23   satisfieth thy *m·* with — *Psal.* 103 : 5.
     42– 3   * openeth her *m·* with — *Prov.* 31 : 26.
     216– 3   obtain their money from a fish's *m·*,
mouthpiece
  Mis. 277– 9   archers aim at Truth's *m·* ;
  My. 247– 6   The church is the *m·* of C. S.,
     254–27   The church is the *m·* of C. S.,
mouths
  Pul. 8–21   "Out of the *m·* of babes — *Matt.* 21 : 16.
movable
  Pul. 58–15   * by the use of *m·* partitions.
move
  Mis. 8– 6   we live, and *m·*, — *Acts* 17 : 28.
     28– 7   muscles cannot *m·* without mind.
     69–21   even to *m·* his bowels,
     79– 9   we live, *m·*, and have being.
     82–30   "we live, and *m·*, — *Acts* 17 : 28.
     104–18   The latter *m·* in God's grooves
     227–13   may give it a forward *m·*,
     338–18   *m·* majestically to your defense
     342–31   and are ready for the next *m·*.
     343– 8   to *m·* it onward and upward.
     377– 1   should *m·* our brush or pen
  Ret. 93–18   we live, and *m·*, — *Acts* 17 : 28.
  Un. 26–14   * Man decays and ages *m·* ;
  Pul. 2–23   "we live, and *m·*, — *Acts* 17 : 28.
     73–16   * have faith, you can *m·* mountains."
  No. 17– 7   we live, and *m·*, — *Acts* 17 : 28.
  Pan. 13–20   we do "live, and *m·*, — *Acts* 17 : 28.
  '02. 12–20   we live, and *m·*, — *Acts* 17 : 28.
  Po. 65– 3   Life's pulses *m·* fitful
  My. 9–11   * *m·* us to utter our gratitude
     61–23   * seemed to *m·* as by magic ;
     69–21   * where . . . people can freely *m·*.
     109–22   "we live, and *m·*, — *Acts* 17 : 28.
     258–29   may you *m·* onward and upward,
     294–24   and will *m·* the pen of millions.

moved

Mis.	106–30	M⋅ by mind, your many-throated organ,
	275–25	m⋅ me to speechless thanks.
Ret.	5–26	* in the circles in which she m⋅,
	48–10	m⋅ me to close my flourishing
Un.	11–13	The palsied hand m⋅,
My.	33–27	shall never be m⋅. — *Psal.* 15 : 5.
	44–17	* m⋅ that it be forwarded at once
	51–16	* m⋅ to instruct the Clerk
	129–25	whose feet can never be m⋅.
	241–26	* found that I lived and m⋅
	314– 4	* then m⋅ to Franklin.
	333–11	* m⋅ to the residence of the

movement

Mis.	235–21	This m⋅ of thought must push on
	354–18	the m⋅ of body and soul
Pul.	23–14	* This m⋅, under the guise of C. S.,
	31–28	* as flexible in m⋅ as that of
	50–19	* Any new m⋅ will awaken some
	51–15	* predict where this m⋅ will go,
	52–17	* rapid growth of the new m⋅.
	59–26	* connected with the m⋅.
	69– 2	* to organize this m⋅.
	69– 5	* the Founder of the m⋅.
	79–10	* not to ignore a m⋅ which,
'00.	9–27	leader of this mighty m⋅.
My.	10–28	* prosperous growth of this m⋅
	11– 4	* the Leader of this m⋅,
	45–12	* animus and spirit of our m⋅.
	89–30	* should found a religious m⋅
	163–28	m⋅ of establishing in this city
	282–17	chapter sub-title
	287– 3	m⋅ to erect a monument
	316–14	Survey of the C. S. M⋅,"
	320–17	* in sympathy with the m⋅,
	329–23	* admitting its interest in the m⋅,

movements

Mis.	117–19	participating in the m⋅,
	245–15	Their m⋅ indicate fear
Man.	78–11	important m⋅ of the manager
Ret.	82– 6	not allow their m⋅ to be
Pul.	38–26	* Yet each and all these m⋅,
	56–13	* helpful, and powerful m⋅
	67–14	* one of those m⋅ which seek to
'02.	12–29	institutions and early m⋅ of
My.	91–18	* religious m⋅ that this country
	291– 8	heavy strokes, measured m⋅,

moves

Mis.	117–29	The disobedient make their m⋅
	166– 6	lives, and m⋅ in our midst
	174–11	Principle that m⋅ all in harmony,
	335–14	neither m⋅ me from the path
Peo.	8–19	as directly as it m⋅ a planet
My.	123– 6	which m⋅ the hearts of men
	164–29	m⋅, and has his being in God,
	195–23	m⋅, and has deathless being.
	205– 9	* m⋅ in a mysterious way

moving

Mis.	47–10	when m⋅ your body,

Mozart

'00.	11–15	M⋅ rests you.

Mrs.

Man.	110–15	Women must sign " Miss" or "M⋅."
	111– 7	prefix her signature with "M⋅ ;"

Mrs. ——

Mis.	87–16	*if you sent M⋅ —— to ——.*

Mt. Ararat

Pan.	2– 7	higher than *Mt. A⋅* above the deluge.

Mt. Auburn

My.	69–30	* *Mt. A⋅* cemetery in Cambridge,

much

Mis.	vii–10	Wherefor, have m⋅ to pay.
	4–19	M⋅ interest is awakened
	5–30	It is m⋅ easier for people to
	7–30	not so m⋅ from a lack of justice,
	8– 3	we shall have accomplished m⋅ ;
	8–20	however m⋅ we suffer in
	11–26	Because I can do m⋅ general good
	16– 7	one finds so m⋅ lacking,
	16– 8	and so very m⋅ requisite
	17–19	m⋅ higher and holier conception
	18–29	m⋅ that must be repented of
	23– 1	having learned so m⋅ ;
	36–21	as m⋅ in our waking moments
	52– 3	how m⋅ one can do for himself,
	55– 7	as m⋅ of the divine Spirit
	62–13	by that m⋅, less available.
	80– 3	m⋅ more than can be gained
	96–25	This answer includes too m⋅
	107–32	either too m⋅ or too little
	108– 1	sorrowing saint thinks too m⋅
	108–23	the misconception . . . costs m⋅.

much

Mis.	109– 8	how m⋅, sin claims of you ;
	109– 9	how m⋅ of this claim you admit
	109–13	how m⋅ more, then, should
	111– 5	at break of day caught m⋅.
	114– 3	cannot give too m⋅ time
	130– 6	how m⋅ better it is to be wronged,
	137–23	you must give m⋅ time to
	143–28	sometimes at m⋅ self-sacrifice,
	147–29	would m⋅ rather fail of success
	155–18	(however m⋅ she desires thus to do),
	159–19	not so m⋅ the Bethlehem babe,
	167–10	How m⋅ does he weigh?
	178–20	'M⋅ learning' — or something else
	185–24	how m⋅ of a man he ever has been :
	198–20	a belief of disease is as m⋅
	229–11	how m⋅ more certain would be
	230–13	is no proof of accomplishing m⋅.
	232– 2	but the memory was too m⋅ ;
	241–29	how m⋅ more should these heal,
	247–25	It is m⋅ easier for people to
	253–15	portends m⋅ for the future.
	262–29	because I take so m⋅ pleasure in
	271–20	M⋅ is said at this date,
	273– 4	although it will cost him m⋅,
	282–12	m⋅ less would we have our minds
	287–26	it will spare you m⋅ bitterness.
	290–28	not so m⋅ from individual as
	291– 9	Too m⋅ and too little is attached
	302–14	M⋅ good has been accomplished
	309–30	which contain all and m⋅ more
	335–14	having too m⋅ charity ;
	341– 7	m⋅ slipping and clambering,
	342–31	How m⋅ more should we
	353–11	People give me too m⋅ attention
	353–28	too m⋅ interested in themselves
	357–15	M⋅ of what has been sown
	376–14	* and in a m⋅ better form."
	378– 8	After m⋅ consultation among
Ret.	6– 9	my m⋅ respected parents,
	7–23	* too m⋅ of sorrow and loss.
	9–18	* Is it not m⋅ that I may
	10– 2	kept me m⋅ out of school,
	44–19	m⋅ time and attention
	69–12	seem to have life as m⋅ as God,
	71–11	an error of m⋅ magnitude.
	78– 3	either too m⋅ or too little.
	82–22	m⋅ good or else evil ;
	94–29	Jesus' teachings bore m⋅ fruit,
	95–11	* comforters are needed m⋅
Un.	1– 2	rouses so m⋅ natural doubt
	6–22	Not m⋅ more than a half-century
	8– 2	gives m⋅ trouble to many
	27– 6	who talks m⋅ of himself.
	46– 5	We do not see m⋅ of the real man
Pul.	2– 1	m⋅ like the Queen of Sheba,
	21–22	however m⋅ this is done to us
	36–27	* I am m⋅ indebted for some of the
	45–16	* M⋅ was the ridicule heaped upon
	46–10	* m⋅ is told of herself in detail
	47–25	* she lives very m⋅ retired,
	58–20	* too m⋅ so for comfortable reading,
	61–21	* M⋅ admiration was expressed
	66– 2	* exists as m⋅ to-day as it did
	72–10	* m⋅ absorbed in the work
	72–11	* given so m⋅ of her attention.
	79–23	* as m⋅ as his lungs call for breath ;
	80–20	* but this m⋅ is true :
	81–12	* she thinks so m⋅ of herself
	81–19	* those who have so m⋅ to give
	87–15	You ask too m⋅ when asking me to
Rud.	6–26	how m⋅ you understand of C. S.
No.	3–22	not so m⋅ thine own as another's good,
	24–13	but m⋅ more real,
	26–27	m⋅ more clothe you, — *Matt.* 6 : 30.
	41– 6	as m⋅ as to ask, Is it the
'01.	10– 5	how m⋅ more shall they — *Matt.* 10 : 25.
'02.	11–15	how m⋅ more is accomplished
	15–18	m⋅ of his property in slaves,
	18–20	how m⋅ of what he did are we
Hea.	14– 3	in fine, m⋅ ado about nothing.
	16– 5	How m⋅ are you demonstrating
	18–20	as m⋅ as to the sinner :
Po.	2– 4	M⋅ as the chisel of the sculptor's art
My.	11–17	* expressed m⋅ gratification
	21–21	* experienced m⋅ pleasure
	21–23	* have anticipated m⋅ joy
	23– 2	* how m⋅ our neighbor has given,
	27–21	* will read with m⋅ joy
	30–10	* It spoke m⋅ for the devotion
	53–30	* must have been very m⋅ broken
	62–25	* when they were so m⋅ needed.
	75–16	* it would not make m⋅ difference,
	89– 3	* that faith which is so m⋅
	91–23	* the objects of m⋅ ridicule,
	94–14	* m⋅ to convince the skeptic.

much

My. 111– 7   m· the same class of minds
114–28   Is it too m· to say that this book
129–28   Lean not too m· on your Leader.
131–23   fulfilling m· of the divine law
133–23   Do you know how m· I love you
149–19   may know too m· of human law
160– 1   and keeps Mind m· out of sight.
163–23   retirement I so m· coveted,
164– 3   retirement I so m· desired.
193– 4   will bring to your hearts so m·
194–25   you have sacrificed so m·
202–29   that ye bear m· fruit." — John 15 : 8.
203–28   You whose labors are doing so m·
212–14   Why is there so m· dissension
215–14   * "Your teachings are worth m·
216–20   work by which you can do m· good
231– 7   labored m· to benefit
233–29   as m· as they love mankind?
234– 7   know how m· I love them,
236–11   Too m· of one thing spoils the
240– 7   * "Would it be asking too m·
246–30   Magna Charta of C. S. means m·,
247–21   not so m· eloquence as
254–22   Magna Charta of C· S. means m·,
259–28   respects the Christ too m· to submerge
261–10   Too m· cannot be done towards
272–30   * m· influence on this generation.
278–22   Nothing is gained . . . but m· is lost.
280–11   * righteous prayer which availeth m·.
303–29   We need m· humility, wisdom,
309– 4   called upon to do m· business
311– 9   * she troubles me so m·."
320– 5   * He also seemed very m· pleased
323–26   * should mean to your older students m·
324– 7   * ideas were too m· alike for
324– 9   * no one could be of m· service to
325– 6   * Mr. Wiggin was very m· troubled
331–26   * M· has often been said of the
332–24   * m· interviewing with Masonic
341–20   * C. S. has been so m· to the fore
345– 5   will be thought to matter m·.
358–13   however m· I desire to read all that
358–17   to relieve me of so m· labor.

much-ado-about-nothing

Mis. 351–11   late m· arose solely from

muffled

'02. 3–22   m· fear of death and triumph

Muller, Prof. Max

Pul. 23–22   * and scholars . . . like Prof. Max M·,

multiplicand

Mis. 221–29   might serve as the m·.

multiplication

Mis. 221–27   m· of the same two numbers
244–11   in the m· of mankind?

multiplied

My. 236– 7   this name continues to be m·,

multiply

Mis. 56–25   m·, and replenish — Gen. 1 : 28.
57–15   m· thy sorrow." — Gen. 3 : 16.
Un. 44–16   would m· and subdivide
No. 31– 7   They progress and will m·
My. 183–15   God will m· thee.
214– 2   as our churches m·,

multiplying

'02. 1–10   churches are m· everywhere
My. 93– 2   * They are m· without efforts

multitude

Mis. 227– 4   to the hisses of the m·,
Pul. 42– 3   * filled with a waiting m·.
My. 41– 1   * our Leader has induced a m·
58–17   * love and gratitude of a great m·
77–18   * m· which began to gather
78– 8   * m· passed through the
85–24   * m· of strangers to whom
87– 9   * cheerfully contented m·
123–24   to feed the m· ;

multitudes

Un. 7– 4   in m· of other religious folds.
My. v–24   * healed m· of disease
28–26   * to the m· of Judea
87– 4   * the m· going and coming.
141–19   * vast m· of Christian Scientists

multitudinous

Ret. 50–10   shown me, in m· ways,

multum in parvo

Mis. 25– 4   the m· in p· of C. S.,
My. 247– 1   m· in p·, — all-in-one and one-in-all.
254–22   m· in p·, — all-in-one and one-in-all.

municipal

My. 217– 8   invested in safe m· bonds

munificent

Mis. 143–23   m· sum of forty-two thousand dollars
Man. 75–11   declined to receive this m· gift,
My. 13–29   pledged this m· sum
164– 9   my thanks for your m· gift
166–10   m· gift of ten thousand dollars,

murder

Mis. 61–14   * Or who does m·?
61–16   * was said to be 'hanged for m·'
122–32   The m· of the just Nazarite
324–15   emulation, hatred, wrath, m·.
335–17   to m·, steal, commit adultery,

murderer

Mis. 257–20   "a m· from the beginning." — John 8 : 44.
Un. 17–15   was the would-be m· of Truth.
32–21   a m· from the beginning. — John 8 : 44.
No. 24–23   "a m· from the beginning, — John 8 : 44.
Pan. 5–13   a m· from the beginning, — John 8 : 44.

murderers

My. 5– 5   m· of their brothers !

murdering

Pan. 15– 1   m· her peaceful seamen

murderous

Mis. 325–29   in the midst of m· hordes,

murders

No. 3– 5   error m· either friend or foe
'01. 20–27   its thefts, adulteries, and m·,

murky

Po. 29– 2   Blest Christmas morn, though m· clouds

murmur

Pan. 3–11   the gentle m· of early morn,
Po. 41–23   to welcome the m· it gave
My. 150– 3   Therefore despair not nor m·,

murmuring

Mis. 237–18   m· winds of their forest home.
Po. 2–18   white waves kiss the m· rill
66– 3   When we walk by that m· stream ;

murmurings

No. 9–14   repeated complaints and m·

murmurs

Mis. 329–30   The brooklet sings melting m·
390–16   To melting m· ye have stirred
Po. 30– 5   wakening m· from the drowsy rills
55–17   To melting m· ye have stirred

muscles

Mis. 28– 7   m· cannot move without mind.
Peo. 8–19   controls the m· of the arm.
My. 162– 6   Strength is in man, not in m· ;

muscular

Pul. 62–12   * require but little m· power
Rud. 11–27   m·, vascular, or nervous operations

Muse

Mis. 142–19   my M· lost her lightsome lyre,

muse

Mis. 124–21   silence wherein to m· His praise,

Muses'

Ret. 17– 6   M· soft echoes to kindle the grot.
Po. 62– 6   M· soft echoes to kindle the grot.

music

Mis. 106–28   M· is the harmony of being ;
106–28   the m· of Soul affords the only
116–13   filling the measures of life's m·
116–16   crescendo and diminuendo accent m·,
126– 5   m· of our Sabbath chimes
138–28   for the m· of our march,
153–28   * Hear the first m· of this
187–10   manifestly the reality of m·,
270– 6   sculpture, m·, or painting?
283–31   learn the principle of m·
324– 9   a little while, and the m· is dull,
324–25   all wasted and the m· fled.
330– 8   make m· in the heart.
344– 5   * have you studied m·,
375–15   * study of m· and art.
385–13   gales celestial, in sweet m· bore
Man. 61–17   m· IN THE CHURCH.
61–18   The m· in The Mother Church
61–23   M· from the organ alone
Ret. 27–21   As sweet m· ripples in one's
57– 8   correcting the principle of m·
Un. 13– 8   principle of m· knows nothing of
13–11   any more than in m·
Pul. 29–14   * The m· was spirited,
Rud. 3–13   masters in m· and painting
'00. 11– 3   have no discord over m·.
11– 6   passionately fond of material m·,
11– 8   spiritual m·, the m· of Soul.
11–13   M· is more than sound in unison.
11–18   M· is divine.
11–19   Mind, not matter, makes m· ;

music

'02. 4– 9 *m·* to the ear, rapture to the heart
Po. 41–15 Where the *m·* of waters had fled
46–16 Be all thy life in *m·* given,
48– 6 gales celestial, in sweet *m·* bore
65–22 life hath its *m·* in low minor tones,
My. 32–25 * *m·* by William Lyman Johnson.
155–23 May those who discourse *m·* to-day,
267–21 awaken . . . with a sense of *m·* ;

musical

Man. 61–21 standard of *m·* excellence ;
Ret. 17– 7 chords of my lyre, with *m·* kiss,
18– 7 the pear-tree, with *m·* flow.
Pul. 61–25 * sweet, *m·* tones attracted
Po. 62– 7 chords of my lyre, with *m·* kiss,
63–16 the pear-tree, with *m·* flow.
My. 70–24 * more beautiful, more *m·*,
256– 3 not specially *m·* to be sure,

Music Hall

Pul. 57–25 * proposed site of the new *M· H·*,

musician

Mis. 283–31 *m·* to practise for him.
340–18 Is a *m·* made by his teacher?
340–19 He makes himself a *m·*

musicians

'00. 11– 7 jarring elements among *m·*

music-tone

Chr. 53–59 Eternal swells Christ's *m·*,

mustard

My. 222–10 grain of *m·* seed, — *Matt.* 17 : 20.

mustard-seed

Pul. 52– 4 * a faith of the *m·* variety.
My. 57–32 * a faith of the *m·* variety.

mutations

Un. 61– 9 *m·* of mortal sense are the

mute

Mis. 390– 9 Too pure for aught so *m·*.
Po. 55–10 Too pure for aught so *m·*.

mutely

Mis. 12–17 Mortal mind at this period *m·* works

mutiny

My. 203– 8 obeyed without *m·* are God's laws.

mutter

Mis. 396– 1 wild winds *m·*, howl, and moan,
Po. 58–13 wild winds *m·*, howl, and moan,

mutual

Mis. 289–22 except by *m·* consent.
289–25 by *m·* consent,
289 29 *M·* interests and affections are
297–22 relinquished by *m·* consent
Ret. 44–28 revival of *m·* love, prosperity, and
My. 155– 2 *m·* aid society, which is effective
204– 7 *m·* friendships such as ours

mutually

Mis. 98–11 *m·* to aid one another in finding
266–26 thus we *m·* aid each other,
Ret. 59–21 distinct, but *m·* dependent,

muzzled

No. 44–16 Ecclesiastical tyranny *m·* the

My

Mis. 118 16 "Keep *M·* commandments." — *John* 15 : 10.
268– 8 to *M·* commandments ! — *Isa.* 48 : 18.
Un. 18– 4 brightness of *M·* own glory.
18–11 were not in *M·* mind,
18–12 tears from the eyes of *M·* children.
18–17 show *M·* pity through divine law,
18–18 It is *M·* sympathy with
18–18 and *M·* knowledge of harmony
24– 4 *M·* Mind is divine good,
62–22 man is *M·* idea, never in matter,

myriad

Mis. 114–19 sin, appearing in its *m·* forms :
325–27 sensualism in its *m·* forms.
361– 7 spiritual Life, whose *m·* forms
Pul. 80–23 * *m·* of women more thoughtful

Myself

Un. 18– 9 everything that is unlike *M·*.
18–26 aught beside *M·* is impossible.

mysteries

My. 149–12 *m·* of exhaustless being.

mysterious

Mis. 221–17 mental practitioners and *m·* diseases.
237–21 marvellous good, and *m·* evil.
Ret. 9– 4 all about this *m·* voice,
9–16 never again . . . was that *m·* call
Peo. 3–13 a *m·* God and a natural devil.
4–16 *m·* ideas of God and man
My. 50– 8 * vast gloom of the *m·* forests,
205– 9 * "God moves in a *m·* way

mysteriously

My. 303– 1 fell *m·* upon my spirit.

mystery

of godliness

Mis. 53–29 is the *m·* of godliness ;
328–11 with the *m·* of godliness,
Ret. 37–20 this "*m·* of godliness." — *I Tim.* 3 : 16.
Un. 5–14 the *m·* of godliness," — *I Tim.* 3 : 16.
62– 8 This is the *m·* of godliness
No. 38– 9 This divine *m·* of godliness
'01. 24–30 the spirit or *m·* of godliness.
My. 124–27 The *m·* of godliness
126–11 interprets the *m·* of godliness,

Mis. 5–23 seem a miracle and a *m·*
222–24 Its *m·* protects it now,
223– 1 metaphysical *m·* of error
247–19 the healing force . . . seems a *m·*,
Ret. 28–24 It was a *m·* to me then,
Un. 5–15 *m·* involves the unknown.
No. 17–22 this *m·* of a God who has no
'00. 6– 9 Any *m·* in C. S. departs
'01. 20–25 At present its *m·* protects it,
Peo. 6–20 God is no longer a *m·*
My. 124–29 and the *m·* of iniquity
126–10 kills this *m·* of iniquity
126–12 the second is no longer a *m·*
192– 9 *m·* and gloom of his glory
344– 7 *m·* is scientifically explained.

mystic

Un. 9–11 human philosophy, or *m·* psychology.
Pul. 53–25 * Whittier, grandest of *m·* poets,
No. 15–13 far more *m·* than Mind-healing.
'01. 8–27 C. S. explains that *m·* saying
Po. 34–13 Has wooed some *m·* spot,
My. 91– 5 * spiritual and *m·* mediation

mystical

Pul. 66–18 * satisfy a taste for the *m·*

mysticism

Mis. 30–26 any seeming *m·* surrounding realism
260– 6 Pagan *m·*, Grecian philosophy,
Pan. 13–25 with the *m·* of opposites
'01. 9 11 * complained of by the rabbis,
10 15 removes the *m·* that used to enthrall
25– 1 *m·*, so called, of my writings
My. 167– 3 *m·* of good is unknown to the flesh,
254– 1 *m·* departs, heaven opens,

mysticisms

My. 288–14 pagan *m·*, tribal religion,

mystify

Pan. 7–16 Does not each of these religions *m·*

myth

Mis. 82–25 Mortal mind is a *m·* ;
201–10 *m·* or material falsity of evil ;
No. 27–11 matter will be proved a *m·*.
'00. 5– 9 its origin is a *m·*, a lie.
Peo. 4– 8 Mythology, or the *m·* of ologies,

mythical

Mis. 47–13 *m·* nature of matter,
71–22 hence its *m·* origin and certain end.
82–26 *m·* or mortal sense of existence
Pan. 3– 1 *m·* deity may please the fancy,
'02. 15–13 being approached the *m·*.

mythological

Pan. 2–24 *m·* deity of that name ;

mythology

Mis. 55–27 matter is *m·*, and its laws are
363–10 *m·* of evil and mortality is but
Pan. 3–23 *m·* (one of my girlhood studies),
Peo. 4– 8 *M·*, or the myth of ologies,

myths

Mis. 60–23 If mortal mind and body are *m·*,

N

naiad

Po. 8– 8 *n·* from woodland bower ;

Naiad's and naiad's

Mis. 390– 3 Thou hast a *N·* charm ;
Po. 55– 3 Thou hast a *n·* charm ;

nails

My. 119–20 to the prints of the *n·*,

naked

Mis. 324–28 *N·*, hungry, athirst,
Pul. 65–24 * gave half . . . to a *n·* beggar ;
My. 117–14 or *n·*, and clothed thee? — *Matt.* 25 : 38.

name (noun)
another
Mis. 336–21 What is it but another n· for C. S.,
any
Ret. 78–18 any n· given to it other than
author's
Mis. 300– 5 announcing the author's n·,
Man. 32–14 and give the author's n·.
58–20 Announcing Author's N·.
My. 130–22 must have the author's n· added
blest
Po. 30–16 cast on Thy blest n·,
Christian
Mis. x–18 changed from my Christian n·,
Man. 111– 6 must sign her own Christian n·,
Christian Science
Pul. 52–18 * The n· C. S. alone is new.
55–17 * she selected the n· C. S.
Christ's
Pul. 14–17 cup of cold water in Christ's n·,
My. 153– 5 will only do this in Christ's n·,
300–17 raise the dying . . . in Christ's n·,
divine
'00. 3–23 to call the divine n· Yahwah,
excellent
Pul. 57–20 * Such is the excellent n· given to
first
My. 236–16 they accepted the first n·.
generic
Man. 47–20 generic n· of the disease
having the
Man. 50–15 having the n· without the life
her
Man. 54–14 her n· shall be erased from The
54–24 remove his or her n· from membership
56– 5 his or her n· shall be dropped
Pul. 33– 4 * heard her n· called distinctly,
His
Un. 7– 1 His n· will be magnified
My. 225–19 sacredly holding His n· apart from
226–21 in this you learn to hallow His n·,
his
Mis. 113–10 number of his n·,"— Rev. 13 : 17.
145–10 answer to his n· in this
161– 6 his n· shall be called— Isa. 9 : 6.
164–17 "His n· shall be called— Isa. 9 : 6.
167–14 What is his n·?
180–22 believe on his n· :— John 1 : 12.
192–15 "His n· shall endure— Psal. 72 : 17.
192–15 His n· shall be continued— Psal. 72 : 17.
269–32 number of his n·."— Rev. 13 : 17.
321– 5 "his n· shall be called— Isa. 9 : 6.
Man. 46– 9 after his n· on circulars,
46–23 to have his n· removed
51– 5 his n· shall be dropped
Pul. 22–13 to heal the sick in his n·.
53–28 * Who use it in his n· ;
Hea. 2–26 Past, present, future magnifies his n·
holy
My. 225–13 giving unto His holy n· due
I AM
Mis. 258–21 The n·, I AM, indicated
in the
Mis. 57–21 told in the n· of Truth,
59– 4 in the n· of Truth.
171–29 in the n· of Science,
233– 1 practising in the n· of Science
334–19 evil at work in the n· of good,
Chr. 55–18 In the n· of Jesus Christ— Acts 3 : 6.
Ret. 68– 2 claimed to originate in the n· of
68– 3 in the n· of human concept,
Pul. 7–18 in the n· of religion.
No. 42–14 in the n· and for the sake of Christ,
'00. 10–14 in the n· of God, justice, and
10–26 in the n· of a first lieutenant
My. 147–19 in the n· of Almighty God,
151–28 worshiping . . . in the n· of nature,
190–30 in the n· of God, wherefore vilify
is legion
Pul. 81–20 * and their n· is legion.
is Wonderful
Un. 39–13 Messiah, whose n· is Wonderful.
its
Mis. 365–30 impostors that come in its n·.
No. 9–24 More mistakes are made in its n·
11–13 by those who come falsely in its n·.
My. 93–23 * many of the practices in its n·.
228– 1 I call disease by its n·
Jesus'
Pul. 41–28 * "All hail the power of Jesus' n·,"
81– 2 * "All hail the power of Jesus' n·,"
justifies the
Pul. 61–17 * justifies the n· given by Mrs. Eddy,
maiden
Mis. x–22 to retain my maiden n·,

name (noun)
Mary's
Ret. 9– 5 if she really did hear Mary's n·
member's
Mis. 129–12 drop this member's n· from the
mother's
Ret. 1–16 perpetuated her mother's n·.
my
Mis. xi– 2 in my n· of Glover,
Ret. 75– 7 Why withhold my n·,
75–14 do a miracle in my n·,— Mark 9 : 39.
'00. 14– 3 hast not denied my n·.— Rev. 3 : 8.
Hea. 1– 1 In my n· shall they— Mark 16 : 17.
6–27 In my n· shall they— Mark 16 : 17.
My. 47–30 * In my n· shall they— Mark 16 : 17.
153– 3 send these floral offerings in my n·
188– 4 put my n· there forever ;— I Kings 9 : 3.
new
Mis. 153–19 giveth this "new n·"— Rev. 3 : 12.
161–24 was given the new n·, Messiah,
320–29 giving to it a new n·,
Pul. 8–21 with his own new n·,
22–14 give to Christianity his new n·,
of a candidate
Man. 100– 4 the n· of a candidate for its
of a kinsman
Ret. 2–13 inscribed the n· of a kinsman
of all evil
My. 357– 9 magnetism,— the n· of all evil,
of Almighty God
My. 147–19 in the n· of Almighty God,
of a man
Hea. 3–16 Jesus is the n· of a man
of Christ
Mis. 19–12 has named the n· of Christ,
223–21 have named the n· of Christ
Pul. 81– 4 * we learn that the n· of Christ
Hea. 16– 9 have named the n· of Christ
of Christian Science
My. 182–31 honor the n· of C. S.,
222–28 name the n· of C. S.
of Deity
Mis. 75–24 n· of Deity used in that place
of God
'00. 10–14 this, too, in the n· of God,
My. 190–30 in the n· of God, wherefore vilify
233–19 taking the n· of God in vain.
of its author
Mis. 314–25 this book, with the n· of its author,
of Jesus
Hea. 3–18 individuals by the n· of Jesus.
of law
Mis. 199– 5 dignify the result with the n· of law :
of matter
Mis. 258–20 and call Mind by the n· of matter,
of Morse
Mis. x–21 I dropped the n· of Morse
of religion
Pul. 7–18 in the n· of religion.
My. 258– 4 worthy the n· of religion
of said member
Man. 43– 3 n· of said member to be dropped
of Science
Mis. 171–29 false knowledge in the n· of Science,
233– 1 practising in the n· of Science
of the author
Mis. 88– 6 the n· of the author of
Man. 59– 9 announce the n· of the author.
of the beast
Mis. 113– 9 n· of the beast,— Rev. 13 : 17.
269–31 n· of the beast,— Rev. 13 : 17.
of the complainant
Man. 29– 5 the n· of the complainant.
of their author
Man. 71–23 give the n· of their author
of the kinsman
Pul. 46–20 * inscribed the n· of the kinsman
of the member
Man. 53– 5 n· of the member guilty of this
of Truth
Mis. 57–21 told in the n· of Truth.
59– 4 in the n· of Truth.
only a
Po. 42– 7 were only a n· !
other
Ret. 59–13 every other n· for the Supreme Being,
present
My. 236–14 will exchange the present n· for
something in a
My. 353– 8 chapter sub-title
suggest a
'02. 15–21 waited on God to suggest a n· for
suggested the
My. 236– 6 Because I suggested the n· for

name (noun)
that
Pan. 2–24 mythological deity of that *n·* ;
'02. 15–29 whispered that *n·* to my waiting hope
Thine own
My. 253–16 keep through Thine own *n·* — *John* 17 : 11.
this
Man. 64–24 public misunderstanding of this *n·*,
Ret. 91– 8 this *n·* has been given it by compilers
My. 236– 6 this *n·* continues to be multiplied,
Thy
My. 225–26 "Hallowed be Thy *n·*." — *Matt.* 6 : 9.
thy
Mis. 175–30 Have we not in thy *n·* cast out devils,
191–14 devils in thy *n·*." — *Mark* 9 : 38.
My. 193–28 called thee by thy *n·* ; — *Isa.* 43 : 1.
whereof
'00. 14–13 Philadelphia — the *n·* whereof signifies
without the Spirit
Mis. 302– 7 teaching the *n·* without the Spirit,
your
My. 236– 9 adopt generally for your *n·*,

Mis. x–23 the *n·* would be too long.
144– 5 and the *n·* thereof,
157–19 I enclose you the *n·* of
191–16 *n·* of his satanic majesty is found
228– 9 a *n·* whose odor fills the world with
233– 7 but are such in *n·* only,
305–28 * the *n·* of each contributor.
Man. 100–22 *n·* the Committee if it so desires,
Ret. 8– 5 calling me distinctly by *n·*,
My. 64–10 * made the *n·* an honored one
104– 6 flourish under the *n·* of
187–27 Him whose *n·* they would glorify
225–21 to the divine Spirit the *n·* God.
302–18 *n·* is not applicable to me.
318–10 I availed myself of the *n·* of
353– 9 I have given the *n·* to all
name (verb)
Mis. 15–24 infinite good that we *n·* God,
26–28 Scriptures *n·* God as good,
96–26 I can *n·* some means by which
103– 8 mortals virtually *n·* *substance* ;
199–22 which mortals *n·* matter.
258–21 error could neither *n·* nor
267–24 The antipode . . . which we *n·* *matter*,
272–23 * to *n·* these institutions,
314–21 shall *n·*, at each reading,
Ret. 50– 4 to *n·* three hundred dollars
Un. 10– 5 to *n·* any previous teachers,
My. 20–11 and *n·* your gifts to her,
81–14 * They had been told to *n·*,
106– 7 I *n·* those mentioned above
169– 8 date, which I hope soon to *n·*
222–28 *n·* the name of C. S.
225– 4 not *n·* its opposite, error.
235– 9 and never *n·* a cipher?
235–12 definitely *n·* the error,
257–25 memorials, too numerous to *n·*,
302–16 not to *n·* me thus.
343– 9 * "Can you *n·* the man?"
named
Mis. 19–12 has *n·* the name of Christ,
23– 1 Newton *n·* it gravitation,
27– 6 its opposite, *n·* matter,
84–30 through the door *n·* death,
166–24 *n·* in this century C. S.,
186–16 the divine idea *n·* man ;
196– 9 separate mind . . . *n·* evil ;
223–21 *n·* the name of Christ
244–10 conditions *n·* in Genesis
258–18 God *n·* Himself, I am.
329– 4 what shall this be *n·*,
361–28 *n·* matter, or mortal mind.
374–19 and *n·* his burdens light,
379–29 *n·* my discovery C. S.
Man. 18–16 and *n·* it, The First Church
27– 7 not *n·* in the Manual
71–19 and *n·* in this Manual.
92–23 qualifications *n·* in Sect. 9
100–23 any Committee so *n·*
102–13 *n·* in them all the trusts
Ret. 1–18 Englishman, *n·* Joseph Baker,
24– 6 which I afterward *n·* C. S.
25–10 I *n·* it *Christian*,
25–12 I *n·* mortal mind.
63–16 Its opposite, nothing, *n·* evil,
Un. 49– 7 the sinner, wrongly *n·* man.
60– 9 presence *n·* evil.
Pul. 31–23 * At the hour *n·* I rang the bell
Rud. 2–17 whom mortals have *n·* God.
7–22 its opposite, *n·* matter.
No. 4–10 error of belief, *n·* disease,
23–11 but not one person was *n·*

named
No. 30– 4 the false sense *n·* sin,
32–18 its opposite, *n·* evil,
'00. 5– 8 good — *n·* devil — evil
14– 7 full number of days *n·*
'01. 5– 7 triune Principle, *n·* in the Bible
6–21 its theory even seldom *n·*.
16–13 *devil is n· serpent*
18–18 used them and *n·* them
Hea. 6– 8 phenomenon *n·* mediumship,
16– 9 *n·* the name of Christ
Peo. 4–12 When . . . God, was *n·* a person,
My. 55–15 * *n·* it The First Church of Christ,
56–13 * in each of the following *n·* places :
56–20 * three foregoing *n·* churches
217–15 my request as above *n·*.
259– 4 I have *n·* it my *white student.*
353–15 the next I *n·* *Monitor*,
nameless
Mis. 166–16 incorporeal idea of God, was *n·*,
350–31 through *n·* suffering and sacrifice,
No. 34–26 *N·* woe, everlasting victories,
namely
Mis. x– 5 *n·*, to collect my miscellaneous
24–16 *n·*, Life in and of Spirit ;
31–15 *n·*, that God, good, has *all* power.
40–16 *n·*, the action of the divine
48– 6 *n·*, that its so-called power
51– 7 *n·*, the ignorant,
77– 5 original meaning, *n·*, to be *firm*,
108–18 *n·*, the knowledge of one's self,
116–30 *n·*, to be made "ruler — *Matt.* 25 : 23.
121–10 *n·*, the impotence of evil,
127– 8 *n·*, that Christian Scientists,
172–30 *n·*, the oft-repeated declaration
185–31 *n·*, that creation is material :
186–11 *n·*, in a sick and sinning mortal.
188–29 *n·*, the true likeness of God,
189–22 *n·* God, the eternal good,
190–25 *n·*, that speech belongs to Mind
194–31 set forth in the text, *n·*, believe ;
217–12 antipode of Spirit, *n·*, matter.
221– 8 *n·*, that error and sickness
234– 9 to be, *n·*, a Christian.
240–31 belongs to nature, — *n·*, pure odors.
247– 2 *n·*, that his honest convictions
252–25 *n·*, healing the sick.
261– 9 *n·*, that mortals suffer from
277–15 *n·*, by slanderous falsehoods,
298–13 *n·*, "It is not good — *Matt.* 19 : 10.
299–27 *n·*, What right have I to do this?
307–21 *n·*, Cast not pearls before
318–26 *n·*, making sin seem either
365–18 *n·*, that mortal mind is calling
366–32 *n·* mere book-learning,
Ret. 33–11 *n·*, that the less material medicine
61– 9 *n·*, that man's harmony is
Un. 8–18 *n·*, by the establishment,
43– 5 *n·*, that there is no death,
55– 2 *n·*, that there is no death.
Pul. 55–19 * *n·*, — that all causation is
Rud. 11–10 *n·*, that there are no sickness, sin, and
No. 4– 8 *n·*, material sensation and
5–13 *n·*, that life and health are
8– 5 *n·*, silence whenever it can
10–22 *n·*, that earth's discords have not
12–17 *n·*, "the way, the truth, — *John* 14 : 6.
24–21 *n·*, that evil has no claims
35–20 *n·*, that God is the only Mind,
Pan. 8–17 one law, *n·*, divine Science.
9– 9 rules pertaining thereto, *n·*,
'01. 2–22 *n·*, that a departure from the
11–23 *n·*, that God is a Person,
21– 4 *n·*, students of a demonstrable
'02. 20–17 *n·*, in 1902 to begin omitting our
Hea. 8–20 *n·*, Life, Truth, and Love,
Peo. 3–28 *n·*, by working out our own
12–19 *n·*, man's salvation from sickness
My. 18– 5 *n·*, that Christian Scientists,
46–10 * *n·*, "To organize a church
52–18 * *n·*, heal the sick, and preach the
107– 8 *n·*, the homœopathic system,
135–14 *n·*, the Hon. Henry M. Baker.
137–22 *n·*, the Hon. Henry M. Baker.
165– 2 *n·*, of choosing the best,
172–13 *n·*, a material symbol of my
175–19 *n·*, to macadamize a portion of
183– 1 uses of Christ's creed, *n·*,
218–19 *n·*, straining at gnats and
226–14 the infinite, — *n·*, grants and
229–26 *n·*, laws of limitation
240–15 *n·*, that C. S. is the
251–28 *n·*, the unity in C. S.
281–11 *n·*, one God, one Mind,

namely
My. 299–21 *n*, that God, the divine Principle
339– 5 *n* — one God, supreme, infinite,

names
Mis. 24–19 state which it *n* matter,
144–10 *n* in your own handwriting,
145–19 our *n* may melt into one,
145–27 their *n* in the web of history,
258–19 Error, . . . might give *n* to itself,
281–25 because you have signed your *n*.
295–27 which *n* itself after her
306– 8 * *n* to be commemorated.
366–31 theories whose *n* are legion,
Man. 25– 3 *n*, ELECTION, AND DUTIES.
25– 4 *N*.
26–15 the *n* of its candidates
79–12 *n* of the persons nominated
109–15 see that *n* are legibly written,
110– 6 the *n* of the members
110–10 *n*, whether of applicants,
110–12 one, at least, of the given *n*
110–13 Initials only of first *n*
110–15 "Miss" or "Mrs." before their *n*
110–16 *n* must be written the same in
111– 3 *n* must be written in full.
Ret. 5–11 *n* of both father and mother
70– 2 confers animal *n* and natures
Un. 36– 2 it *n* material attraction,
Pul. 23–13 * and under various *n*,
46–14 * identified with good and great *n*
88– 8 append only a few of the *n*
'00. 3–24 also that women's *n* contained
My. 225–15 distinguishes it from all other *n*,
225–19 *n* of that which He creates.
225–21 C. S. *n* God as divine Principle,
228– 3 My book S. and H. *n* disease,
245–27 letters of degrees that follow the *n*

naming
Mis. 61–28 *N* these His embodiment,
233–16 and *n* that "mind-cure,"
290–15 *n* the time of the occurrence,
295– 4 whom he quotes without *n*,
Man. 32–10 *N* Book and Author.
71– 8 in *n* such churches.
Pul. 31–22 * *n* an evening on which
72–28 * *n* as one great essential that
My. 363–25 avoid *n*, in his mental treatment,

napping
Mis. 231–21 but grandpa was taken *n*.
295–12 *awake*, and caught *n*?

narrated
My. 81–27 * cures *n* at the meetings of
298– 4 if correctly *n* and understood,

narrations
Ret. 21–27 such *n* may be admissible

narrative
Ret. 9– 9 Scriptural *n* of little Samuel,
70– 9 Scriptural *n* of the Virgin-mother

narratives
Man. 48–26 they may . . . give incidental *n*.
Ret. 22– 3 Gospel *n* bear brief testimony
My. 179–18 Old Testament and gospel *n*

narrow
Mis. 32–21 from the straight and *n* path.
64–15 Man-made theories are *n*,
245–28 the straight and *n* way ;
323–23 up the hill it is straight and *n*,
347–22 it is always straight and *n* ;
389–19 sweet secret of the *n* way,
Ret. 55– 1 enter this strait and *n* path,
71– 8 straight and *n* path of C. S.
'01. 28– 6 enter the strait and *n* way,
Po. 4–18 sweet secret of the *n* way,
My. 104– 2 strait and *n* way of Truth.
202–27 The way is *n* at first,
306– 3 attempts to *n* my life

natal
Po. 29– 9 No *n* hour and mother's tear,
My. 129–14 The nod of Spirit is nature's *n*.
158–10 This day is the *n* hour of

nation (*see also* **nation's**)
Mis. 101–10 have had two in this *n* ;
159–30 from all parts of our *n*,
176–23 Pilgrims came to establish a *n*
237–17 live now as when this *n* began,
297–13 sects, or societies, of a *n*
304–10 * the capital of the *n*
Pan. 14–17 and uphold our *n* with the
14–27 our *n*, which fed her starving foe,
'02. 3–18 rejoices with our sister *n*
My. 89–24 * interest . . . but to the *n* ;
89–24 * not to the *n* alone, but to the

nation
My. 129– 3 danger threatening our *n*,
148–15 and the father of our *n*
183–11 To-day a *n* is born.
200– 2 under the Constitution of our *n*
206–24 an holy *n*, — *I Pet.* 2 : 9.
234–20 introducing C. S. into a heathen *n*
234–23 If the . . . Empress could hold her *n*,
234–26 Silent prayer in and for a heathen *n*
279–26 pray that God bless that great *n*
282– 2 government of a *n* is its peace maker
289–13 sympathy with the bereaved *n*,
291– 4 Presiding over the destinies of a *n*

national
Mis. 138– 3 to prepare for this *n* convention
295–13 Scotchman's *n* pride and affection,
370–25 into a "*n* convention"
Pul. 6– 4 forms of a *n* or tyrannical religion,
Pan. 14–16 associated with . . . our *n* judiciary ;
'02. 3– 9 the old *n* family pride and joy
Peo. 8–12 definite form of a *n* religion,
Po. page 77 poem
My. 220–15 pacification of all *n* difficulties,
285– 8 industrial, civic, and *n* peace.
286– 8 *N* disagreements can

National Association
Mis. 276–12 convention of our *N A*,

National Board of Management
Mis. 305– 8 * *N B of M* has placed

National Christian Science Association
Mis. 382–27 by-laws of the *N C S A* ;
Mis. 98– 9 *N C S A* has brought us together
134– 9 chapter sub-title
134–11 annual session of the *N C S A*.
137– 1 chapter sub-title
137– 6 convention of the *N C S A*,
137–19 Disorganize the *N C S A* !
138–21 members of the *N C S A*,
275–22 meeting in Chicago of the *N C S A*
Ret. 52–13 forming a *N C S A*.
52–22 *N C S A*, at its meeting in
(*see also* **Christian Scientist Association**)

National Convention
Mis. 98– 7 Address at the *N C* in Chicago,

National Library Building
My. 157–15 * *N L B* in Washington

National Magazine
My. 305–18 I am rated in the *N M* (1903) as

National Society
Mis. 305– 9 * representing the *N S* of

National State Capital Bank
My. 136–23 *N S C B*, Concord, N. H.

nation's
Mis. 251–12 our *n* civil and religious freedom,
Ret. 43–23 Centennial Day of our *n* freedom.
Pul. 8– 6 condition of our *n* finances,
10–11 they planted a *n* heart,
'02. 3–11 Our *n* forward step was
Po. 77– 3 A *n* holiest hymn in grateful
My. 277–21 But if our *n* rights or honor
290–19 our *n* chief magistrate,
291–23 our *n* ensign of peace
292– 8 May God sanctify our *n* sorrow
305–13 Many of the *n* best and

nations (*see also* **nations'**)
affection of
My. 290– 7 Those live on in the affection of *n*.
all
Pan. 13–21 Then shall all *n*, peoples,
14–14 and that they shall rule all *n*.
My. 127–31 adapted to all men, all *n*,
181–17 that all *n* shall speedily learn
274–28 health among all *n*." — *Psal.* 67 : 2.
278– 2 the action of all *n*.
282– 6 in and for all *n*,
282–24 all *n* under the sunlight of
among
My. 286–12 preserving peace among *n*.
and peoples
My. 284–26 quarrels between *n* and peoples.
are helped
My. 282–11 *n* are helped onward
awakening the
My. 316– 5 the Redeemer awakening the *n*,
both
My. 277– 6 satisfactory to both *n*?"
character of
Peo. 2–28 the character of *n* as well as
crises of
Mis. 176– 8 chiefly in the great crises of *n*
foreign
'02. 10–29 communicating with foreign *n*

nations

healing for the
Ret. 49–24 will prove a healing for the *n·*,
healing of the
Ret. 95– 3 the healing of the *n·."* — *Rev.* 22 : 2.
individuals and
My. 277– 8 between individuals and *n·*
laws of
'00. 10–12 religious rights and laws of *n·*
life of
My. 277–15 prosperity, and life of *n·*.
peace between
My. 265–10 civilization, peace between *n·*,
peace of
My. 280–17 prayer for the peace of *n·*,
280–29 praying for the peace of *n·*,
peoples and
My. 265–13 rights of individuals, peoples, and *n·*.
power over the
Chr. 57– 3 power over the *n·* : — *Rev.* 2 : 26.
My. 285–19 power over the *n·."* — *Rev.* 2 : 26.
welfare of the
My. 280– 6 * solicitude for the welfare of the *n·*

Man. 28– 8 *n·*, individuals, and religion
'02. 4– 2 deceit in councils, dishonor in *n·*,
My. 281–28 when *n·* are ripe for progress.
283–21 *n·*, unite harmoniously on the basis of

nations'

Po. 10–17 Allied by *n·* grace,
My. 281– 1 spiritual foresight of the *n·* drama
337–18 Allied by *n·* grace,

native

Mis. 64– 7 and rose to his *n·* estate,
70–23 dissolve into its *n·* nothingness ;
109–15 reduced to their *n·* nothingness !
144– 2 New Hampshire, my *n·* State.
251–10 of this city and of my *n·* State
295–16 to honor his *n·* land
343–24 away from their *n·* soil,
Ret. 6–25 Legislature of his *n·* State,
Un. 58– 3 in their *n·* element of error,
Pul. 6–30 the *n·* course of whose mind
24–24 * New Hampshire, Mrs. Eddy's *n·* State.
43–11 * *n·* of Concord, New Hampshire.
49–21 * return to her *n·* granite hills,
68–11 * residence in her *n·* State.
Pan. 11–17 regain his *n·* spiritual stature
'01. 26–27 a *n·* or an acquired taste
'02. 20–24 metropolis of my *n·* State,
Mis. 120–12 gives to soul its *n·* freedom.
136–17 by a *n·* of New Hampshire.
155– 5 so near my heart and *n·* hills,
157– 8 * capital city of your *n·* State.
167–26 by the laws of my *n·* State.
184– 9 Christian Scientists of my *n·* State
186– 2 forests of our *n·* State
270– 9 newspapers of my *n·* State
289–28 held in the capital of my *n·* State
327– 4 New Hampshire, my *n·* State,
341– 2 A *n·* of New Hampshire,

natives

My. 305–14 *n·* of the Granite State.

nativity

Mis. 74–14 his *n·* was a spiritual and immortal
162–17 rise to his *n·* in Spirit.
320– 5 its earthly advent and *n·*,
374–18 Scientists memorize the *n·* of Jesus.
My. 162–29 This church, born in my *n·*,
256–19 earthly advent and *n·* of our Lord
262–31 splendor of this *n·* of Christ

Natrum muriaticum

Mis. 348–21 doses of *N· m·* (common salt).
Ret. 33–15 thirtieth attenuation of *N· m·*,

natural

Mis. 3– 4 If we regard good as more *n·*
20–20 *N·* history shows that neither
72–19 *disappear only to the n· sense?*
88–20, 21 * this Science is *n·*, spiritually *n·* ;
161–22 it is *n·* to conclude that
183–18 but by the *n·* ability,
199–29 goodness is more *n·* than evil.
206– 2 *n·*, civil, or religious,
222–28 more *n·* than evil.
247–12 charges . . . are false, but *n·*,
259–25 demonstrates good, and is *n·* ;
318– 9 *n·* affection for goodness
360– 9 *n·* transforming power
374–32 less artistic or less *n·*?
Ret. 10– 7 *n·* philosophy, logic, and
26–13 divinely *n·* and apprehensible ;
26–17 a *n·* and divine Scientist.
27–26 Its *n·* manifestation is beautiful
Un. 1– 2 *n·* doubt and questioning

natural

Un. 11–20 professor of *n·* philosophy,
Pul. 35– 7 * *n·* fulfilment of divine law
48–24 * The *n·* and lawful pride
54– 6 * harmony with *n·* law,
54– 8 * The perfectly *n·* is the
55– 9 * the *n·* outcome of a period
No. 2– 8 against that which is *n·*
45–15 In *n·* law and in religion
Pan. 2–20 deification of *n·* causes,
Peo. 3–11 would affirm that these are *n·*,
3–13 mysterious God and a *n·* devil.
My. 4–31 Whatever is not divinely *n·*
8–27 * the *n·* and indispensable Leader
36–31 * *n·* healer of all our diseases
178–11 is this *n·* Science less profitable
205–29 health, holiness, . . . are its *n·* effects.
211–17 foreign to the *n·* inclinations.
213– 1 *n·* fruits of C. S. Mind-healing
221–14 *n·*, and divine Science of medicine,
288–10 Good is divinely *n·*.
349–13 *n·* to him who sits at the feet of
349–20 Divine . . . manifestations are *n·*,
349–21 the so-called *n·* sciences
(*see also* **science**)

naturalist (*see also* naturalist's)

My. 304–24 Agassiz, the celebrated *n·*

naturalist's

'01. 28– 2 last stage of the great *n·* prophecy.

naturally

Mis. 7–17 *n·* reflects that it is dangerous
7–29 would have returned *n·*
26–30 *n·* and divinely infinite good.
33–18 Patients *n·* gain confidence
129– 7 having done this, one will *n·*,
240–20 Children not mistaught, *n·* love
240–28 nothing but a . . . worm *n·* chews tobacco.
364 4 *n·* evokes new paraphrase
Ret. 27–14 *N·*, my first jottings were
76–10 gravitate *n·* toward Truth.
No. 2– 3 *n·* glared at by the pulpit,
3– 3 *n·* modest, generous, and sincere !
Pan. 12– 6 Then, we *n·* ask, how can Spirit
'00. 14–28 you *n·* ask who are to be
'01. 4–30 *n·* conclude that he breaks faith
12– 6 he would *n·* reply,
Peo. 6–14 Believing that . . . we *n·* fear God
My. 83–22 * *n·* takes on a tone of deserved
178 10 because Science is *n·* divine,
188–28 man will *n·* seek the Science of
227–13 we *n·* turn to divine justice

naturalness

Mis. 194–29 *n·* of the Life that is God,
200– 1 consummate *n·* of Truth

nature (*see also* nature's)

all
Mis. 329–16 rippling all *n·* in ceaseless flow,
and character
Un. 1–12 *n·* and character of God is
3–21 in His own *n·* and character,
6–18 the divine *n·* and character
31–18 the *n·* and character of matter,
and essence
Mis. 121–18 the *n·* and essence of Deity,
No. 19–19 drinking in the *n·* and essence of
and government
'00. 5– 2 *n·*, and government of all things
and her laws
Mis. 219– 4 nor teaches that *n·* and her laws
and man
Mis. 258–31 *n·* and man are as harmonious
My. 152–27 divine Principle of *n·* and man,
and office
Un. 40–28 the *n·* and office of Life.
and power
Mis. 7–28 *n·* and power of metaphysics,
and quality
Mis. 36–17 *n·* and quality of mortal mind,
and stature
Mis. 102– 1 the *n·* and stature of Christ,
and truth
My. 111– 4 The *n·* and truth of C. S.
anticipating
My. 346– 7 * Those who have been anticipating *n·*
as thought
Mis. 331–25 divine Science evolved *n·* as thought,
at work in
Mis. 257–12 so-called force, . . . at work in *n·*
becomes Spirit
Mis. 218– 1 in which *n·* becomes Spirit ;
belongs to
Mis. 240–31 sweet something which belongs to *n·*,
cures the disease
Peo. 6–12 * while *n·* cures the disease."

nature

declares
Mis. 217–13 *N·* declares, throughout the mineral,
divine
   (*see* **divine**)
dual
Mis. 161–15 the appearing of this dual *n·*,
endows
My. 90–11 * *n·* endows the children of men,
essential
Mis. 264–10 Unity is the essential *n·* of C. S.
evil
'00. 8– 6 evil man also exhales . . . his evil *n·*
exact
Mis. 78–28 exact *n·* of its Principle,
fleshly
Ret. 73– 7 as the fleshly *n·* disappears
foundation in
Mis. 367–26 neither . . . nor foundation in *n·*,
God of
My. 349–23 and coexist with the God of *n·*
good
My. 81– 4 * Scientists fairly radiate good *n·*
   81– 5 * So ingrained is this good *n·*,
had reproduced
My. 347–14 suggest that *n·* had reproduced
hidden
Mis. 48–21 hidden *n·* of some tragic events
higher
Mis. 287–18 the higher *n·* of man governs
My. 48–30 * feed the higher *n·* through the mind,
   159–18 whereby we reach our higher *n·*.
His
Un. 23–22 unlike Himself and foreign to His *n·*
His own
No. 38–21 includes only His own *n·*,
human
   (*see* **human**)
imperative
My. 268– 5 imperative *n·* of the marriage relation
infinite
Mis. 284– 6 Its infinite *n·* and uses
My. 349–29 makes manifest the infinite *n·*,
in the name of
My. 151–28 matter in the name of *n·*,
is constituted
Mis. 217–15 and that *n·* is constituted of
its
Pul. 3– 1 Such being its *n·*,
Rud. 3–18 spiritual in its *n·*, method,
Jesus'
No. 36–11 the popular view of Jesus' *n·*.
law of
Peo. 10–18 mortal beliefs, and not a law of *n·*,
laws of
Mis. 216–26 in which neither laws of *n·* nor
Pul. 54–15 * obedience to the laws of *n·*.
'01. 24– 7 rules styled the laws of *n·*.
loving
My. 338–22 his broad views and loving *n·*
man's
'01. 1–21 it is the better side of man's *n·*
material
Mis. 119–14 material *n·* strives to tip the beam
my
'02. 2–23 inherent characteristic of my *n·*,
mythical
Mis. 47–13 or the mythical *n·* of matter,
no fleshly
Mis. 86– 3 these have no fleshly *n·*.
no law of
Pul. 54–13 * "There was no law of *n·* violated
nor grace
'02. 7– 8 neither philosophy, *n·*, nor grace
of a cat
Mis. 218–23 grin expresses the *n·* of a cat,
of all
'01. 5– 9 possesses the *n·* of all,
of a revelation
My. 93–29 * will come in the *n·* of a revelation.
of beauty
Rud. 6– 8 when we change the *n·* of beauty
of Christianity
My. 179–19 *n·* of Christianity, as depicted in
of Deity
Mis. 79– 1 divine order and the *n·* of Deity.
   192– 9 *n·* of Deity and devil
of dreams
Mis. 252–10 possessing the *n·* of dreams.
of evil
No. 23– 1 incorrect concept of the *n·* of evil
of God
   (*see* **God**)
of Jesus
'02. 18–30 *n·* of Jesus made him keenly alive to

nature

of man
Mis. 287–18 higher *n·* of man governs the lower,
of occultism
Mis. 78–13 partook of the *n·* of occultism,
of one God
'01. 5– 5 lose the *n·* of one God,
of sin
Un. 5–24 differ from them as to the *n·* of sin
of Spirit
Mis. 218–25 does not express the *n·* of Spirit,
of the case
Mis. 379– 9 and the *n·* of the case :
Pul. 80– 6 * inevitable in the *n·* of the case.
of the individual
Mis. 119–11 The *n·* of the individual,
of their source
Mis. 354–14 prove the *n·* of their source.
of this love
My. 133–24 and the *n·* of this love?
penchant for
Mis. 329– 2 an obstinate *penchant* for *n·*
person and
'01. 5–29 to explain both His person and *n·*,
personified
Pan. 2–21 conceived as one personified *n·*,
poetic
Po. v– 6 * *outpouring of a deeply poetic n·*
presuppose that
Mis. 217–18 presuppose that *n·* is matter,
real
Mis. 88–22 * highest type of real *n·* ;
   218–18 unfolds the real *n·* of God
reflects man
My. 124–18 *N·* reflects man and art pencils him,
sensuous
Ret. 25–13 physical senses, or sensuous *n·*,
simple
Mis. 373– 1 to illustrate the simple *n·* of art.
specific
Mis. 217–14 specific *n·* of all things
spiritual
Mis. 119–15 tip the beam against the spiritual *n·* ;
My. 188–29 seek the Science of his spiritual *n·*,
this
Mis. 208– 5 by virtue of this *n·* and allness
   218–24 this *n·* may linger in memory :
through
Po. v–14 * *through n·, unto nature's God,"*
My. 151–25 "through *n·* up to nature's God,"
true
Mis. 140– 5 the true *n·* of the gift ;
'02. 7– 1 the true *n·* of Love intact
unison with
Pan. 1–11 In unctuous unison with *n·*,
universal
Pan. 3–24 * "universal *n·* proceeding from
   12– 5 * Spirit, is ever in universal *n·*."
unsubstantial
Pan. 14– 1 unsubstantial *n·* of whatever
very
Mis. 99– 2 revolutionary in its very *n·* ;
   354– 3 Sin in its very *n·* is marvellous !
'01. 31– 6 from the very *n·* of Truth,

Mis. 189– 9 *n·* and the inseparability of God and
   217– 2 *n·*, reason, and revelation.
   218–30 * recognition of teleology in *n·*
   240–14 *n·* would take it out as gently,
   259–27 belongs not to *n·* nor to God.
   329– 6 *n·* like a thrifty housewife
   393– 3 *N·*, with the mind connecting,
No. 9–18 wrongs of the *n·* referred to.
'01. 1–23 *n·* and practical possibilities of
   23–30 * *n·* being nothing more than
Po. 31– 2 nor yet by *n·* sown,
   51– 8 *N·*, with the mind connecting,
My. 248–17 reality of God, man, *n·*,
   269–13 * Whose body *n·* is, and God the Soul.

nature's
Mis. 330– 7 join in *n·* grand harmony,
   330–23 *N·* first and last lessons
Ret. 91–26 *n·* haunts were the Messiah's
Pul. 55– 4 * *N·* marvel in thy thought."
Pan. 3– 6 My sense of *n·* rich glooms
   3–10 *n·* stillness is voiced with a
Po. v–13 * *masterpiece of n· handiwork,*
   v–14 * *through nature, unto n· God,"*
My. 129–14 The nod of Spirit is *n·* natal.
   151–25 * through nature up to *n·* God,"

natures
Mis. 226–26 dignified *n·* cannot stoop to
   228–12 seeking to raise those barren *n·*
   272–31 If certain *n·* have not profited
   330–25 sanction what our *n·* need.

natures
Mis.	347–14	all the goodness of generous n·,
Ret.	70– 2	confers animal names and· n·
No.	1– 5	only as our n· are changed
'01.	19–14	That animal n· give force to
Hea.	13– 7	higher n· are reached soonest by
My.	118– 1	royal n· of the beloved members

naught
Mis.	260–24	evil is n·, although it seems to be.
	279–20	evil is n· and good is all.
	358– 8	n· but tardy justice,
Ret.	9–19	* n· my spirit's breathings to control,
Un.	21– 8	evil is n·, and good only is reality.
	26–24	there is in God n· fantastic.
Pul.	4– 1	my strength is n·
Rud.	4–21	all is God, and there is n· beside
No.	30–15	not by . . . knowing sin, nor n·,
'02.	7–16	All, than which there is n· else.
My.	37– 4	* N· else than the grandeur of
	199– 7	I have n· against thee.

nave
My.	71–21	* neither n·, aisles, nor transept

navies
My.	121–10	like the ocean, able to carry n·,
	286–11	armament of n· is necessary,

navigation
My.	110–14	wireless telegraphy, n· of the air ;

Nazarene (see also Nazarene's)
Mis.	1– 6	meek N·, the scoffed of all scoffers,
	15– 7	The great N· Prophet said,
	24–29	The N· Prophet declared that
	60–10	The N· Prophet could make
	120–28	Biblical record of the great N·,
	121–22	His beloved Son, the righteous N·,
	162– 6	the N· stepped suddenly before the
	344–23	far from the rules of the mighty N·
Pul.	6– 5	church established by the N· Prophet
Pan.	10– 4	The great N· Prophet said,
My.	106–30	Our great Exemplar, the N· Prophet,
	179–22	character of the N· Prophet

Nazarene's
Mis.	189– 8	N· steadfast and true knowledge of
My.	146–15	heights of the great N· sayings

Nazareth
Jesus of
Mis.	99–19	seemed Jesus of N· more divine
	162–22	no incorporeal Jesus of N·.
	252–24	master of metaphysics, Jesus of N·.
	258– 4	Our great Ensample, Jesus of N·,
	270– 8	Master in C. S., Jesus of N·,
Ret.	20–17	Jesus of N· was a natural and divine
	70–16	individual mission of Jesus of N· .
Pul.	20–24	master Metaphysician, Jesus of N·.
	34–20	* when Jesus of N· walked the earth,
	53– 7	* condition which Jesus of N·,
	53–22	* Jesus of N· proclaimed its potency
	75– 1	one Christ, one Jesus of N·.
My.	217–28	our great Exemplar, Jesus of N·,

Chr.	55–18	name of Jesus Christ of N· — Acts 3: 6.
Ret.	89–17	been some time absent from N·

Nazarite
Mis.	122–32	murder of the just N· was incited by
	374–21	the face of the N· Prophet ;

near
Mis.	139–19	n· the beautiful Back Bay Park,
	277–26	especially n· in times of hate,
	277–27	and never so n· as when
	282–28	and no other aid is n·.
	377– 4	so n· and full of radiant relief
	387–24	that Love, divinely n·,
Man.	48–14	make a summer resort n·
Ret.	5– 1	town situated n· Concord,
	90–14	whom he kept n· himself
	91–15	n· the sloping shores of the
Un.	4– 1	n· to them who adore Him.
	26– 4	my forms, n· or remote.
Pul.	58– 6	* Concord, N. H., n· her birthplace,
	84– 2	* "The time of times" is n·
No.	27– 6	When we get n· enough
'00.	7–27	loving Christ is found n·,
'01.	31– 7	Every true Christian in the n· future
Po.	6–19	that Love, divinely n·,
	29– 7	forever here and n·,
	68–23	whether n· or afar.
	70–11	A help forever n· ;
My.	14– 6	discerned in the n· future
	21–22	* brethren from far and n·,
	82– 3	* one n· and dear to them.
	84–17	* Boston is n· to another great
	155–41	nestled so n· my heart
	166–20	divine aid is n·.
	187– 4	I may at some n· future

near
My.	202– 6	may his salvation draw n·,
	290– 3	the n· seems afar, the distant nigh,
	290–17	Divine Love is never so n· as when
	345–23	n· a state of spiritual perfection.

nearer
Mis.	6– 2	bring man n· to God,
	84–31	a clearer and n· sense of Life
	249–25	coming n· in my need,
	288–16	Is marriage n· right than
	397–14	And n· Thee,
Un.	1–16	until they draw n· to the
	4–14	as we get still n· Him,
	7–24	and brings us n· to God,
	64–10	The n· we approximate
Pul.	12–20	n· to the great heart of Christ ;
	18–23	And n· Thee,
'00.	4– 9	n· approach to monotheism
'01.	1– 8	n· the whole world's acceptance.
Hea.	16–13	come n· your hearts
	17– 4	get n· his divine nature
Po.	13– 2	tired joy and grief afar, And n· Thee,
My.	107–20	n· the grooves of omnipotence.
	174–27	Each day I know Him n·,
	177–12	n· the eternal meridian
	270–11	n· my consciousness than before,
	342–32	will advance n· perfection."

nearest
Mis.	116–11	This question, ever n· to my heart,
	288–13	begins with what is n· right
Pan.	13– 4	and n· my heart, is this :
Hea.	2– 1	religion n· right is that one.
My.	178–29	n· approach to the sayings of
	248 29	n· the divine Principle
	248–30	n· the scientific expression of
	271 23	* "What is n· and dearest to your
	271–30	"n· and dearest" to my heart

nearing
My.	139–12	his idea is n· the Way,
	165–29	n· the maximum of might,

nearly
Mis.	362–32	The more n· an erring so-called
	381– 8	The time . . . having n· expired,
Ret.	90–27	* follow, as n· as we can,
Pul.	40–18	* n· six thousand persons,
	41–19	* n· a thousand local believers.
	52–23	* n· obliterated all vital belief in
	56– 4	* n· every other centre of
	75–25	* the most n· fire-proof church
	85– 1	* n· thirty years ago.
'00.	8– 1	know and behold more n·
My.	30– 7	* n· all the local Scientists,
	59– 3	* n· forty years ago.
	59–11	* in part by n· every religious
	67–25	* begun n· two years ago,
	71–19	* In fact, n· all the traditions of
	72–24	* n· two million dollars
	77–25	* n· forty thousand believers
	100– 8	* n· all, parts of the country,
	171–10	Concord church is so n· completed
	174–22	For n· forty years
	272–25	* n· eighty-seven years of age,

'neath
Mis.	387– 9	'N· which our spirits blend
Po.	6– 3	'N· which our spirits blend
	65–12	'n· thy drap'ry still lie.
My.	151–19	* 'n· the temple of uplifted sky

Neb. (State)
(see Lincoln, Norfolk, Omaha)

Nebraska State Journal
My.	97–14	* [N· S· J·, Lincoln, Neb.]

nebulous
Mis.	378–22	than the n· system is from

necessarily
Mis.	18–23	n· entertain habitual love
	218–31	* is n· the recognition of
	223– 6	n· have pure fountains ;
	252– 2	not n· infinitestimal but infinite.
	346–20	its opposite is n· unreal,
	366–24	n· culminate in sickness, sin,
Man.	99–11	Each church is not n· confined to
Ret.	50–26	my necessity is not n· theirs ;
Un.	18– 1	evil n· leads to extinction
	19– 1	knowledge is n· foreknowledge ;
No.	3–19	Dishonesty n· stultifies the
My.	61–30	* intricate problems which must n·
	165– 1	n· promote and pervade all his

necessary
Mis.	4–17	Further enlightenment is n·
	4–28	more than faith is n·,
	7– 7	charity and humility is n·
	14– 6	or find its existence n·

necessary

Mis.	32–26	*n·* for the individual,
	38–25	*Is it n· to study your Science*
	38–27	It is not *n·* to make
	39–30	Divine help is as *n·* in the
	51–29	*Are both prayer and drugs n·*
	68–23	* *n·* to thought and knowledge ;
	91– 5	It is not absolutely *n·*
	169–20	it is *n·* rightly to read
	177–18	*n·* to the salvation of
	227– 6	*n·* to offer to the innocent,
	362–29	except when it is *n·* to
Man.	41– 6	When it is *n·* to show
	49–12	wisdom *n·* in a sick room,
	59–23	give their seats, if *n·*,
	87–15	must have the *n·* moral and
Ret.	30–13	Why was this conviction *n·*
Un.	14–13	Was it *n·* for God to
Pul.	15– 5	since exposure is *n·*
	54–11	* *n·* in apostolic times.
	64–10	* When the *n·* amount was raised,
	68– 9	* *n·* for the interests of her
No.	28– 8	*n·* to effect this end
'01.	24–24	I found it *n·* to follow
'02.	8– 5	Is it *n·* to say that the
My.	8– 1	* *n·* for this purpose."
	10–23	* money *n·* to this end,
	12– 1	* for this purpose,"
	23– 1	not *n·* for us to delay
	23–14	* *n·* to complete the sum
	56– 9	* it was found *n·* to organize
	66–14	* *n·* to have this property.
	72– 2	* it was *n·* to set aside
	73– 1	* it was found *n·* to issue a
	83–31	* the *n·* expense of church work,
	110–32	torn from their *n·* contexts,
	123–17	and other *n·* expenses
	157–11	* makes *n·* the commodious
	161– 8	the sentence *n·* to reclaim
	212– 8	A harder fight will be *n·*
	241– 1	* *n·* moral and spiritual qualifications
	286–11	armament of navies is *n·*,
	343–23	authority," . . . "became *n·*.
	343–23	Rules were *n·*,

necessitate

Mis.	349– 8	not *n·* essential materialization

necessitates

Mis.	256–15	*n·* receiving but a select number
'01.	5–28	God as a Person *n·* a creed
My.	10–29	* now *n·* this onward step.
	14–28	* *n·* large payments of money,

necessities

Mis.	199–11	in reproaches, in *n·*, — *II Cor.* 12 : 10.
	201–23	took pleasure in "*n·*," — *II Cor.* 12 : 10.
	278–23	*n·* and God's providence
Pul.	10– 4	quickened sense of mortal's *n·*,
'01.	29– 3	or even known of his sore *n·* ?

necessity

absolute
My.	22–13	* shown the absolute *n·* of giving.

all
Mis.	119–20	exemption from all *n·* to obey a

brother's
Mis.	131– 9	console this brother's *n·*

case of
Man.	100–25	Case of *N·*.

consider the
Ret.	83–28	when we consider the *n·* of

destroy the
Mis.	45– 8	destroy the *n·* for ether

for understanding
Mis.	92– 2	*n·* for understanding Science,

halted from
My.	214–26	I therefore halted from *n·*.

human
'01.	34–26	Christianity is a human *n·* :

immediate
Man.	78–19	Church bills of immediate *n·*

implies the
Mis.	367–13	implies the *n·* of knowing evil,

increasing
Mis.	115–22	increasing *n·* for relying on God

my
Mis.	311–24	and my *n·* was to tell it ;
Ret.	50–26	my *n·* is not necessarily theirs ;

never a
My.	279– 1	never requisite, never a *n·*,

no
Mis.	241–20	there is no *n·* for pain ;
	283– 1	there is no *n·* for it.
Pan.	10–27	no *n·* for disease and death.
Hea.	8– 1	no *n·* beyond the understanding of

of his immortality
Mis.	2–21	the *n·* of his immortality ;

necessity

of this By-Law
Man.	28– 9	hence the *n·* of this By-Law

recognition of the
My.	9– 2	* In recognition of the *n·* for

recognizing the
My.	7–16	* "Recognizing the *n·* for providing

sad
Man.	55– 7	if this sad *n·* occurs.

sort of
'01.	1–18	All that is true is a sort of *n·*,

sprang from
Mis.	148–15	They sprang from *n·*,
Man.	3–11	They sprang from *n·*,

submitted to
My.	195–10	and so have submitted to *n·*,

that
Mis.	248–27	saved me from that *n·*

understand the
Mis.	136–13	you will understand the *n·* for my

without
Mis.	14–23	for evil, is . . . without *n·*.

Mis.	4–13	has become a *n·*.
	14–22	appears to mortals . . . to be the *n·*
	44– 7	*n·* for immediate relief,
	50–12	under the *n·* to express
	241–21	error that insists on the *n·* of
	243–15	it includes of *n·* the Principle,
	256–11	of *n·* this imposes on me the
Ret.	69–23	Where then is the *n·* for recreation
Un.	15–18	of *n·* take precedence as
Rud.	14–16	must of *n·* do better
No.	5–11	which is untrue, is of *n·* unreal.
My.	8– 6	* *n·* here indicated is beyond cavil ;
	99– 6	* not a *n·*, but a pleasure

neck

Mis.	122–12	hanged about his *n·*, — *Matt.* 18 : 6.
	370–17	about the *n·* of omnipotence,
My.	105–15	eaten the flesh of the *n·*

necks

My.	161– 1	around the *n·* of the wicked.

necromancy

Mis.	78–13	magic, alchemy, or *n·*.
	334– 6	*N·* has no foundation,
'01.	20–24	this new-old *régime* of *n·*

nectar

Mis.	9–17	fill it with the *n·* of the gods.
Pul.	8–25	deft fingers distilled the *n·*
Po.	66– 1	pure *n·* our brimming cup fill,

need (noun)

any
Un.	5–13	frightened sense of any *n·* of

church's
Ret.	44–18	carefully, noting the church's *n·*,

grave
My.	355– 7	a grave *n·* for more men

great
Mis.	24– 5	came to me in an hour of great *n·* ;
	107–11	love is the great *n·* of mankind.
Ret.	49– 8	great *n·* is for more of the spirit
My.	244–12	great *n·* of which I daily discern.

have
Mis.	73–19	we have *n·* to know that the

human
		(*see* **human**)

ignorance and
My.	162– 1	mercy for mortal ignorance and *n·*

is apparent
Man.	95– 4	When the *n·* is apparent,

less
Hea.	1–14	less *n·* of publishing the good news."
My.	147–31	You have less *n·* of me

little
Mis.	262–27	little *n·* of words of approval

made known
Pul.	8–14	only the *n·* made known,

meet the
My.	56– 9	* inadequate to meet the *n·*,

my
Mis.	249–25	coming nearer in my *n·*,

neighbor's
Mis.	257–29	ministering to his neighbor's *n·*.

no
Mis.	185–22	no *n·* of statistics by which to
No.	27–10	no *n·* of the sun,
My.	71– 8	* no *n·* of fussing about the
	206–20	no *n·* of the sun, — *Rev.* 21 : 23.

nor
Mis.	323– 5	nor *n·* of the sun

of changing
Un.	11–10	showed the *n·* of changing this mind

of experience
Mis.	73–16	we have *n·* of experience.

need (noun)

of living faith
Pul. 30–21   * n· of living faith at the moment

of man
My. 260–26   supplies every n· of man.

of mankind
Mis. 107–11   love is the great n· of mankind.
'02. 9–29   has met the n· of mankind

of our Mother Church
My. 11–14   * the n· of our Mother Church.

of physical help
Mis. 88– 2   feel the n· of physical help,

of these things
Mis. 73–18   We have n· of *these* things ;

of watching
Mis. 12–19   hence the n· of watching,

present
My. 281– 6   I cited, as our present n·,

pressing
Mis. 115–14   and meet the pressing n· of a

saw the
My. 22– 3   * saw the n· of a larger edifice

seeing the
Mis. 109–17   seeing the n· of somethingness

see the
Mis. 371– 5   opened his eyes to see the n·
My. 216–27   and see the n· of self-culture,

special
Man. 96–11   where he sees there is special n·,
My. 177– 8   there seems to be no special n·

spiritual
Mis. 245–16   a physical and spiritual n·

suggested the
My. 57– 8   * suggested the n· of a larger church

supply that
Man. 96–13   he is at liberty to supply that n·

times of
'01. 26–13   matter for help in times of n .

universal
Mis. 365–14   universal n· of better health
No. 18–11   universal n· of better health

urgent
My. 62–31   * when there was urgent n· of both.

was felt
My. 57– 4   * n· was felt of an auditorium

what
Pul. 1–18   what n· that I should be present
Pan. 4–26   what n· have we of drugs, hygiene,

world has
Mis. 110– 4   the world has n· of you,

Mis. 72–21   n· of all these things," — *Matt.* 6 : 32.
263–16   The n· of their teacher's counsel,
355– 4   n·, however, is not of the letter,
Ret. 63– 3   then insist on the n· of healing
Un. 53– 8   n· that human consciousness should
'02. 19–23   n· of all these things." — *Matt.* 6 : 32.
My. 26–20   as I foresee, the n· of it.
56–32   * proved the n· of a larger edifice.
217– 2   or, if n· be, to help your parents,

need (verb)
Mis. 32–23   time and attention that they n·,
50–28   n· to be changed from self
86–11   which n· correct definition.
87–23   What they n· thereafter is to
89–21   *why does he n· to be saved?*
108–21   what we n· to know of evil,
110– 7   You n· also to watch,
114– 7   teachers of C. S. n· to watch
127–31   which n· close attention and
145– 4   n· no organization to express it.
146– 8   I should n· to be with you.
146– 9   n· to know the circumstances
157–26   Write me when you n· me.
214–19   n· to search the Scriptures
214–22   they n· to do this even to
270–17   Then you will n· no other aid,
281–32   You will n·, in future,
303– 2   and n· only to shine from
307– 5   you will have all you n·
330–25   sanction what our natures n·.
344–29   We n· the spirit of St. Paul.
345– 7   We n· the spirit of the pious
356– 5   n· no terrible detonation
356– 6   n· no temporary indulgence
357–27   and n· special help.
Ret. 64– 8   N· it be said that any
65–26   and they n· no creed.
Un. 14–15   might n· repentance,
20–14   We therefore n· not fear it.
45– 8   n· most of all to be rid of
45–12   These falsities n· a denial.
No. 3–20   which Mind-healers specially n· ;
23–20   As mortals, we n· to discern
30– 9   He n· not know the evil
30–10   than the legislator n· know

need (verb)
'01. 15–21   even n· to hear the following
29– 6   n· the watchful and tender care
30–16   religion and therapeutics n·
Hea. 19–16   n· it to stamp our religions
Po. 24–14   all I n· to comfort mine.
My. vi– 2   * does not n· to be interpreted to
8– 5   * We n· to keep pace with
31– 4   * " I n· Thee every hour ;"
85–11   * One does not n· to accept the
126–29   We n· it in our homes,
130–24   I n· not say this to the loyal
134–10   Defeat n· not follow victory.
137–30   able to select the Trustees I n·
140–15   * n· not debar distant members
200–19   I n· not say this to you,
229–28   Thou knowest best what we n·
234– 8   and how I n· every hour wherein
249–29   What our churches n· is that
288– 5   life's incentive and sacrifice n· no
303– 8   Scientists n· to be understood
303–29   We n· much humility,
312–23   amount of money he would n·
351–27   divine Science is all they n·,
355–12   we n· in our ranks . . . the strong,
358– 9   Beloved ! you n· to watch and pray

needed
Mis. 3–17   never are n· to aid
6– 7   and many more are n·
157–16   when help is most n·,
273– 6   now seem to be most n·,
358– 2   Love is greatly n·,
Man. 31–14   *animus* so universally n·.
Ret. 26–20   who n· no discovery of the
95–11   * comforters are n· much
Pul. 41– 4   * amount n· was received.
Rud. 16– 6   Lectures in public are n·,
17–12   she n· miraculous vision
My. 9– 0   * may be n· for that purpose.
10–17   * none will be made or ever be n·.
55– 3   * n· a place of its own,
58– 5   * no more funds are n·
59–29   * Now my testimony is not n·.
62–25   * when they were so much n·.
65– 8   * that might be n· to build
65–13   * why the building was n·.
72–14   * chapter sub-title
76– 4   * notices that more money was n·
76–10   * no more contributions . . . were n·.
83 24   * two million dollars n· for the
138– 9   not n· to protect my person or
229–26   which I said . . . would never be n·,
234–27   Silent prayer . . . is just what is n·.
848 11   the n· and the inevitable sponsors
324–20   * that he thought you n· help,

needful
Mis. 38–20   makes divine metaphysics n·,
No. 1– 3   is a most n· work ;
My. 120–32   that n· one thing — divine Science,
271–10   is the one thing n·

needing
Mis. 230–27   n· but canvas and the touch of an
260–29   n· neither license nor prohibition ;
315–26   except the individual n· it asks
Un. 50 91   man a sinner, n· a Saviour ;
59–23   an invalid, n· a physician ;

needle
No. 10–25   turns like the n· to the pole

needless
Mis. 31– 9   It is n· to say that such a
My. 259–26   merry-making or n· gift-giving

needs (noun)

differing
'01. 7–16   supply the differing n· of the

further
My. 22 11   * further n· of the building fund,

human
   (see **human**)

humanity's
Mis. 370–13   according to humanity's n·.

of man
Mis. 3–10   applicable to all the n· of man.
259–29   applicable to all the n· of man.
My. 349–30   supplying all the n· of man.

of the present
My. 22–21   * discernment of the n· of the present

spiritual
Ret. 91–18   ministering to the spiritual n· of
My. 147–18   physical, moral, and spiritual n·

your
My. 186–15   will supply all your n·

Ret. 90–19   comprehend the n· of her babe
92– 3   for the n· of suffering mortals,

needs (noun)
 '01. 29–16 increasing years and *n*·,
 My. 24–27 * that it will meet the *n*· of
needs (verb)
 Mis. 1–12 *n*· to be understood.
  13–25 only *n*· to be conceded,
  39–22 *n*· support at times ;
  46– 6 truism *n*· only to be tested
  56–22 *n*· only to be understood ;
  92– 7 *n*· continually to study this
  108–24 *n*· only to be known for what
  110– 5 it *n*· your innocence.
  122– 3 it must *n*· be that — *Matt.* 18 : 7.
  127–32 *n*· often to be *stirred*,
  163–28 must *n*· come in C. S.,
  190–13 *n*· yet to be learned.
  194–13 It only *n*· the prism of
  274– 7 The work that *n*· to be done,
  283–26 that he *n*· no personal aid.
  313– 7 pinnacle, that everybody *n*·.
  338–24 * It *n*· the overflow of heart,
  346–21 *n*· to be grasped in all its
  354– 5 History *n*· it,
  366–16 jaded humanity *n*· to get
 Man. 101– 3 Committee on Publication *n*· an
 Ret. 22– 1 history *n*· to be revised,
 No. 34–21 atonement . . . *n*· to be understood.
  35–21 *n*· no reconciliation with God,
  43– 6 theology *n*· Truth to stimulate
 Pan. 11–19 who falls physically *n*· to rise
 '01. 12–19 It only *n*· the prism of
  19–28 The whole world *n*· to know that
  29– 3 Gifts he *n*· not.
 My. 11–18 * *n*· no special insight to predict
  12–23 Whatever *n*· to be done
  89– 9 * edifice *n*· only an open space
  120– 8 Forgive, if it *n*· forgiveness,
  175–18· greatly *n*· improved streets.

needy
 Ret. 6– 7 The *n*· were ever welcome,

ne'er
 Mis. 390–24 *N*· perish young, like things of earth,
  391–20 Some good *n*· told before,
 Chr. 53–26 signalize the birth Of him *n*· born
 Ret. 18–19 radiance and glory *n*· fade.
 Pul. 4– 5 Can *n*· refresh a drooping earth,
 Po. 38–19 Some good *n*· told before,
  56– 3 *N*· perish young, like things of earth,
  64–10 radiance and glory *n*· fade.
  70–16 Thy discord *n*· in harmony began !
  71–10 Righteousness *n*· — awestruck or dumb
  72– 3 *n*· again Quench liberty that's just.
 My. 194–30 * *N*· in a sunny hour fall off.''

negation
 Mis. 27–21 evil and matter are *n*· :
  107–17 Evil is a *n*· :
  334–22 How shall we treat a *n*·,
 Un. 49–24 clearer right to call evil a *n*·,
 No. 32–17 A lie is *n*·, — *alias* nothing,
 My. 217–22 we can meet this *n*· more readily

negations
 No. 16–10 *n*· of Spirit, Truth, and Life,

negative
 Mis. 62–10 positive and *n*· quantities,
  62–11 the *n*· quantity offsets an
  65–12 a *n*· which the positive Truth destroys ;
  172– 5 the *n*· of metaphysical Science ;
 Un. 45–17 error's affirmative to Truth's *n*·.
 My. 105–26 When answered in the *n*·,
  217–22 *n*· all that the material senses affirm.
  232–31 watching against a *n*· watch,

negatives
 No. 16–12 *n*· destitute of time and space ;

negativing
 Mis. 208–18 by divine Truth's *n*· error

neglect
 Mis. 213–10 to *n*· opportunities which God giveth,
  341–31 the *n*· of spiritual light,
  351– 5 for want of time, . . . I *n*· myself.
 Man. 42– 7 nor to *n*· his duty to God,
  51– 3 if he *n*· to accept such admonition,
  62– 4 not *n*· to sing any special hymn
 Hea. 5– 5 the *n*· of a bath, and so on.

neglecting
 Ret. 89–24 for *n*· their own students,
 My. 163–14 without *n*· the sacred demands

neglects
 Man. 100–10 *n*· to fulfil the obligations
 Ret. 90–16 never willingly *n*· her children

negotiated
 '02. 13–14 The land . . . had been *n*· for,
  13–23 previously *n*· for the property

neighbor (*see also* **neighbor's**)
his
 Mis. 183– 5 Man must love his *n*· as himself,
  258– 1 loving his *n*· as himself,
  367– 3 to love his *n*· as himself,
 Hea. 5– 8 by doing good to his *n*·,
 My. 33–20 doeth evil to his *n*·, — *Psal.* 15 : 3.
  33–21 reproach against his *n*·. — *Psal.* 15 : 3.
its
 Hea. 11–16 lifting its foot against its *n*·,
 My. 166– 1 from which it can help its *n*·.
love thy
 Mis. 7– 9 love thy *n*· as thyself" — *Matt.* 19 : 19.
  18–10 "Love thy *n*· as thyself." — *Matt.* 19 : 19.
  311–21 love thy *n*· as thyself," — *Matt.* 19 : 19.
 Pan. 9–11 "Love thy *n*· as thyself ;" — *Matt.* 19 : 19.
 '00. 5–21 "Love thy *n*· as thyself." — *Matt.* 19 : 19.
 My. 109– 9 "Love thy *n*· as thyself." — *Matt.* 19 : 19.
  196–15 "Love thy *n*· as thyself." — *Matt.* 19 : 19.
  265– 1 "Love thy *n*· as thyself" — *Matt.* 19 : 19.
  278– 9 "Love thy *n*· as thyself." — *Matt.* 19 : 19.
  281–12 "Love thy *n*· as thyself," — *Matt.* 19 : 19.
my
 My. 276–25 love God supremely, and my *n*·
next-door
 Ret. 40– 6 her next-door *n*· was dying.
one's
 Pan. 9–22 It loves one's *n*· as one's self ;
our
 My. 23– 2 * how much our *n*· has given,
  52–19 * love our *n*· as ourselves."
  132–22 love our *n*· as ourselves,
  200–15 to love our *n*· as ourself,
their
 Mis. 2– 5 they steal from their *n*·,
 My. 286– 7 love their *n*· as themselves.
thy
 Mis. 328–30 loving God supremely and thy *n*·
 My. 183– 4 and thy *n*· as thyself." — *Luke* 10 : 27.
  (*see also* **love thy**)
your
 No. 38–21 loving your *n*· as yourself,

neighborhood
 Ret. 89–15 had been away from the *n*· ;
 Pul. 33–21 * All inquiry in the *n*·
  48–18 * born and bred in that same *n*·.
 My. 70–17 * on every corner in the *n*·.

neighboring
 Ret. 3–11 *n*· battle of Chippewa,
 Po. 66– 9 To join with the *n*· choir ;

neighbor's
 Mis. 211–22 protects himself at his *n*· cost,
  257–29 ministering to his *n*· need.
  319– 9 seeing too keenly their *n*·.

neighbors
 Ret. 87–19 the rights of their *n*·,

neither
 Mis. 14– 1 *n*· place nor power left for evil.
  14–26 evil is *n*· a primitive nor
  22– 3 *n*· a law of matter nor of man.
  25– 8 *n*· one really exists,
  26–21 *n*· a genus nor a species
  28– 3 *n*· see, hear, feel, taste,
  28–25 find *n*· pleasure nor pain therein.
  29–25 *n*· flavor Christianity nor
  30–22 * "is *n*· Christian nor science !"
  36– 2 is *n*· God's man nor Mind ;
  36–26 *n*· indeed can be." — *Rom.* 8 : 7.
  48– 4 should *n*· be taught nor practised,
  48–11 animal magnetism is *n*· of God nor
  59– 2 you can *n*· understand nor
  61–28 can *n*· make them so nor
  66–29 can *n*· remove that cause nor
  71–17 *n*· human hypothesis nor matter.
  74–30 *n*· substance, intelligence, nor
  93–19 *n*· maintained by Science nor
  93–21 *n*· fear nor sin can bring on
  99– 5 *n*· can you understand." — *see Mark* 8 : 17.
  100–12 that grasp *n*· the meaning nor
  103–19 *N*· does the temporal know the
  103–20 *n*· the pattern nor Maker
  109–20 *n*· is a knowledge of sin and its
  112– 9 can *n*· defend the innocent nor
  115–19 evil has *n*· prestige, power, nor
  118–10 is *n*· Science nor obedience.
  118–14 sympathy can *n*· atone for error,
  122–14 it is *n*· questionable nor assailable :
  122–24 *N*· spiritual bankruptcy nor a
  123–16 The *Christian's* God is *n*·,
  124– 6 *n*· do we love and obey Him by
  131– 2 can *n*· help himself nor others ;
  134–26 *n*· silence nor disarm God's voice.
  151– 4 *n*· shall any man — *John* 10 : 28.
  165–13 *n*· darkness, doubt, disease, nor

neither

Mis. 165–20	can *n·* appreciate nor appropriate
172–16	it is *n·* of human origin nor
175–15	*n·* with "the leaven of — *I Cor.* 5 : 8.
182–16	created *n·* from dust nor carnal
183–10	he is *n·* the slave of sense, nor
190– 1	It is *n·* the energy of matter,
192–18	*N·* can we question the
197–32	*n·* be sick nor forever a sinner.
199–28	*n·* supernatural nor preternatural ;
209–15	compels mortals to learn that *n·*
209–17	for God *n·* slumbers nor sleeps.
210–28	but has *n·* the cowardice nor the
213–24	*n·* shall any man — *John* 10 : 28.
216–25	* in which *n·* laws of nature nor
217– 3	*n·* philosophy nor reason attempts to
217–24	This is *n·* Science nor theism.
218– 8	matter can *n·* see, hear, nor
218–26	*n·* eliminated nor retained by Spirit.
219– 3	*n·* reveals God in matter,
229–18	*n·* shall any plague — *Psal.* 91 : 10.
249–16	*n·* purchased nor ordered a drug
258–21	error could *n·* name nor
260–29	*n·* license nor prohibition ;
266– 5	is *n·* politic nor scientific ;
281– 8	*n·* deprive me of something nor
284–21	*n·* an evil claim nor
284–22	*n·* to be *feared* nor
286– 5	*n·* be obscured nor throttled.
286–14	wherein they *n·* marry nor
286–24	*n·* real nor eternal.
289–19	*N·* divine justice nor human
310– 2	*n·* the intent of my works nor
319– 4	can *n·* be coeval nor coequal,
323– 5	nor need of the sun, *n·* of the
335–14	but *n·* the cares of this world nor
340– 7	turning *n·* to the right nor to
341–20	*n·* the cares of this world nor
348– 5	infringe *n·* the books nor the business
353– 5	they are *n·* standards nor models.
355–19	*n·* intelligence nor power,
359–16	*n·* wisdom nor Science
361– 8	whose myriad forms are *n·* material
367–26	has *n·* precedent nor foundation in
373–11	*N·* material finesse, standpoint, nor
379–12	*n·* a scholar nor a metaphysician.
Man. 26–25	*n·* report the discussions of this
28–12	*n·* did according to — *Luke* 12 : 47.
37–11	*n·* the Clerk nor the Church shall be
40– 5	*N·* animosity nor mere
42–16	shall *n·* entertain a belief nor
43–22	shall *n·* buy, sell, nor circulate
74– 4	*n·* shall he exercise supervision
87– 1	*N·* the Pastor Emeritus nor
94–20	shall *n·* resign nor transfer
103– 5	shall *n·* be demolished, nor
Chr. 55–13	*n·* consider the — *Isa.* 5 : 12.
55–20	*n·* beginning of days, — *Heb.* 7 : 3.
Ret. 24–13	that *n·* medicine nor surgery could
25–26	matter *n·* sees, hears, nor feels Spirit,
26– 2	*n·* obedience to hygienic laws,
30–23	*n·* can its inspiration be gained
34– 6	*N·* ancient nor modern philosophy
57– 4	*N·* ancient nor modern philosophy
63– 6	in reality no evil, *n·* sickness nor
67–18	The sinner created *n·* himself nor
68– 6	*n·* indeed can be, the father of man.
Un. 2–19	contains *n·* discord nor disease.
5–17	*n·* will it promote the Cause of
11–23	*n·* red tape nor indignity
11–24	Jesus required *n·* cycles of time nor
14–18	*n·* shadow of turning." — *Jas.* 1 : 17.
26–10	*N·* is He the author of the material
32–24	*n·* masculine nor feminine.
33–18	*n·* matter nor mortal mind,
41–25	hence matter *n·* lives nor dies.
46– 2	which *n·* think nor speak.
50–17	matter has *n·* Mind nor sensation.
51– 5	reality of being is *n·* seen, felt,
57–10	*n·* temptation nor glory.
57–15	but he *n·* held her error by
60–21	He is *n·* absent from Himself
61– 8	*n·* young nor old, *n·* dead nor risen.
61–15	*n·* advancing, retreating, nor
62– 5	ever presence that *n·* comes nor goes,
63– 2	The I AM was *n·* buried nor
Pul. 14–19	*n·* drown your voice with its roar,
51– 2	* *N·* does the Christian faith
Rud. 4– 8	*n·* is it of human origin.
7–19	matter, has *n·* sensation nor
13– 2	*n·* matter nor mortal mind ;
14– 1	*N·* can they serve two masters,
No. 14– 1	*n·* warped nor misconceived,
15–20	finds Spirit *n·* in matter nor in
15–22	*n·* origin nor existence in the
17–15	*n·* part nor parcel of divine

neither

No. 19–11	He is *n·* a limited mind nor a
20– 3	*n·* self-created, nor discerned through
23– 5	Evil can *n·* grasp the prerogative
25–15	*n·* matter nor a mode of mortal mind,
28–22	*n·* the comprehension of its Principle
32– 6	*n·* extinguish a crime nor the
39–11	Prayer can *n·* change God, nor
Pan. 2– 5	*n·* hypothetical nor dogmatical,
5–20	should *n·* believe the lie, nor
13– 6	"*N·* shall they say, — *Luke* 17 : 21.
'01. 4–12	*n·* man nor matter can be.
6–23	He can *n·* be one nor infinite in the
12– 5	*n·* eating nor drinking,
12–27	Evil is *n·* quality nor quantity :
13–12	Sin can have *n·* entity, verity,
20– 7	*n·* moral right nor might to harm
21–21	*n·* the predicate nor postulate
23– 1	*n·* more nor less than three ;
31– 6	*n·* personal nor human,
'02. 6–12	God made *n·* evil nor its
7– 8	*n·* philosophy, nature, nor
8– 8	*n·* Christians nor Scientists.
11–12	*n·* Christian nor Science.
14– 4	*n·* rent, mortgage, nor sell
14–23	*n·* favor nor protection in the
15– 3	*n·* informed the police of these
Hea. 3– 1	*n·* hygiene nor drugs
4– 2	The infinite can *n·* go forth
16–20	They can *n·* see, hear, feel,
My. 13– 1	They speculate *n·* on the past,
15– 7	shall *n·* be demolished nor
71–21	* *n·* nave, aisles, nor transept
94– 9	* *N·* can we overlook the
113–18	*N·* is it presumptuous
121– 9	*n·* tremulous nor relapsing.
130–13	*n·* the time nor the inclination
139– 3	*n·* dead nor plucked up by
166–17	*n·* she nor I would be practising
184– 5	*n·* hath the eye seen, what God
186– 8	*n·* dome nor turret tells the tale
206–20	*n·* of the moon, — *Rev.* 21 : 23.
218– 5	*N·* the Old nor the New
223– 4	I *n·* listen to complaints,
227–19	*n·* should they forget that
227–23	"*N·* cast ye your pearls — *Matt.* 7 : 6.
235–20	is he matter or spirit? *N·* one.
242– 5	it is *n·* behind the point
250–17	*n·* binds nor compels the
252–30	*n·* slumbers nor is stilled
260–31	*N·* the you nor the I in the flesh
269– 8	*n·* marry, nor are given — *Luke* 20 : 35.
269– 8	*n·* can they die — *Luke* 20 : 36.
276– 5	she begs to say, . . . that she is *n·* ;
285–21	they *n·* found me — *Acts* 24 : 12.
285–22	*n·* raising up the people, — *Acts* 24 : 12.
285–22	*n·* in the synagogues, — *Acts* 24 : 12.
285–23	*n·* can they prove — *Acts* 24 : 13.
296–12	*n·* does he sleep nor rest from
302– 6	*N·* life nor death, health nor
323–19	* *N·* do I now feel at all equal
324–15	* sure that *n·* Mr. Wiggin nor
348–15	*n·* man nor *materia medica*.
357– 6	matter has *n·* part nor portion,
359– 2	*n·* do they trouble me with

Nemesis

No. 3–18	*N·* of the history of Mind-healing

neophyte

Mis. 117–23	*n·* is inclined to be too fast or
273– 2	the *n·* will be benefited
Ret. 78– 1	*n·* in C. S. acts like
My. 48–27	* upon the mind of the *n·*

Neoplatonic

No. 14– 9	renewal in the *N·* philosophy ;
'00. 4– 8	Babylonian and *N·* religion,

nerve

Mis. 44–17	thought was pain in the bone or *n·*,
My. 253– 6	what greater glory can *n·* your

nerved

Pul. 9–10	and *n·* its grand fulfilment.
No. 12–15	*n·* her purpose to build on the

nerves

Mis. 210–20	membranes, stomach, and *n·* ·
288–29	Love that *n·* the struggle.
Un. 34–16	and the *n·*, material *n·*, do

nervous

Rud. 11–27	the muscular, vascular, or *n·*
No. 42–26	* suffering from *n·* prostration,

nervousness

Mis. 51– 5	*Is a belief of n·*, . . . *mesmerism?*

nest

Mis. 210– 7 Do men whine over a *n·* of serpents,
254– 8 *n·* of the raven's callow brood !
354–32 Whenever he soareth to fashion his *n·*,

nestled

My. 155– 4 little church, *n·* so near my heart

nestles

Mis. 331–13 *n·* them under her wings,

nestling

Ret. 18– 6 *n·* alder is whispering low,
Po. 63–15 *n·* alder is whispering low,

nestling's

Mis. 331–20 guards the *n·* faltering flight !
389– 8 guards the *n·* faltering flight !
Po. 4– 5 guards the *n·* faltering flight !

nestlings

Mis. 152–25 hope, faith, and Love, are God's *n·* ;
My. 186– 5 like tender *n·* in the crannies

nests

Mis. 356–20 *n·* of the raven's callow brood.
Po. 53–14 And build their cozy *n·*,

net

Mis. 111– 5 At times, your *n·* has been so full
111–14 had He filled the *n·*, it would
Man. 80– 4 The *n·* profits of the business shall
'02. 13– 8 *n·* profits from the business of The
My. 224–15 not caught in some author's *n·*,
241– 7 * beware the *n·* that is craftily laid

nets

Mis. 90–29 left their *n·* to follow him,
111–11 cast their *n·* on the right side,
212–11 cast their *n·* on the right side.

neuter

Un. 32–24 a *liar* was in the *n·* gender,

neutralize

Mis. 224–25 to *n·* what is bitter in it,
241–14 big enough apparently to *n·* your

neutralized

Mis. 69–20 and *n·* the bad effects of the

neutralizes

Mis. 204– 5 *n·* and destroys error.
My. 293– 6 mind and matter *n·* itself.

neutralizing

Pul. 6– 1 when Truth is *n·* error
My. 292–21 one . . . belief unwittingly *n·* another,

never (*see also* ne'er)

Mis. ix–19 youth that *n·* grows old ;
3–16 Drugs, inert matter, *n·* are needed
5–29 That which *n·* existed, can seem
12– 8 *N·* return evil for evil ;
14–12 could *n·* be learned :
18–22 *n·* separate himself from good,
19– 6, 7 *n·* unmerciful, *n·* unwise.
19–15 can *n·* change the current
32–28 *n·* envy, elbow, slander, hate,
35–14 * I *n·* knew so unselfish an
45–23 It *n·* originated or existed
47– 9 Have you *n·* been so preoccupied
47–11 If *n·* in your waking hours,
49–31 Truth *n·* created error,
57–20 the Lord God *n·* said it.
66–26 or he *n·* can reach the Science
71–14 Science *n·* averts law,
73–12 Law is *n·* material :
76– 5 shall *n·* see death."— *John* 8 : 51.
76– 8 can *n·* be tested or proven true
76–17 spake as *n·* man spake,
78–12 *n·* dreamed that either of these
79–20 *n·* was, and *n·* can be,
87–19 I *n·* commission any one to
88–25 * had *n·* seen water freeze."
91–24 I *n·* dreamed, . . . that a loyal
94– 3 *n·* knew a person who knowingly
95–15 I am not, and *n·* was.
96–20 adore Christ as *n·* before.
99–24 *n·* bear into oblivion his words.
103–13 form and individuality are *n·* lost,
105–21 individual and his ideal can *n·*
106–25 praise that shall *n·* end?
107–18 it *n·* started with time,
107–27 deep, *n·* to be repented of,
109– 5 mayhap *n·* have thought of,
116–26 *N·* absent from your post,
116–27 *n·* off guard, *n·* ill-humored,
116–27 *n·* unready to work for God,
121– 1 his words can *n·* pass away :
122–28 God *n·* made it,
127–30 a kind word . . . is *n·* wasted.
129–21 lens that he *n·* turns on himself.
134–13 such as you *n·* before received.
148– 1 *n·* shows us a smiling countenance

never

Mis. 148– 2 We shall *n·* find one part of
154–26 *n·* desert the post of spiritual
160– 2 *N·* did gratitude and love
165–16 appears— *n·* to disappear.
165–24 *n·* paid the price of sin.
170– 6 which *n·* changes to death.
171– 2 can *n·* be wrested from its
174–27 Death can *n·* usher in the dawn
177– 1 *N·* was there a more solemn and
180– 9 "Christ *n·* left," I replied ;
182–19 understanding that man was *n·* lost
187–26 *n·* extinguished in a night of discord.
195–22 He who *n·* unsheathed his blade
201– 8 element of matter, . . . *n·* of Spirit.
210– 4 C. S. *n·* healed a patient without
210–31 Charity *n·* flees before error,
212– 4 *n·* knows what happiness is,
213–24 they shall *n·* perish,— *John* 10 : 28.
218– 3 that matter *n·* produced Mind,
232–10 It will *n·* do to be behind the times
234–15 can *n·* find a place in Science.
234–16 it *n·* has advanced man a single step
237–10 Some people *n·* repent until
239– 4 I *n·* was in better health.
241–19 "God *n·* made you sick :
247–30 He *n·* made sickness.
249–24 will *n·* leave me comfortless,
252– 6 its largest dose is *n·* dangerous,
260– 7 *n·* entered into the line of Jesus'
265–20 can *n·* bring forth the real fruits of
267– 2 wail of evil *n·* harms Scientists,
267–10 remember that there *n·* was a time
269–12 *n·* man spake,"— *John* 7 : 46.
273– 8 My students have *n·* expressed so
273–10 *n·* have been so capable of
275–21 Pen can *n·* portray the satisfaction
277–13 The stake and scaffold have *n·*
277–17 silence Truth? *N·*.
277–27 and *n·* so near as when
278–11 I have *n·* given occasion
284– 2 *n·* try to hinder others
290– 4 nuptial vow is *n·* annulled
292–28 I *n·* knew a student who
297–14 perhaps he has *n·* visited.
299– 4 but *n·* until then.
307– 2 *N·* ask for tomorrow :
307– 4 if you wait, *n·* doubting,
308– 2 Until . . . man will *n·* be found
310–28 together with those who *n·*
311–30 *n·* escaped from my lips,
316– 1 but *n·* to return evil for evil ;
316– 2 *n·* to attack the malpractitioner,
336– 3 that a lie is *n·* true?
339– 6 victor, *n·* the vanquished ;
340– 3 Good is *n·* the reward of evil,
340–12 who *n·* brings out a brief.
341– 1 they *n·* bring out the right action
341–27 so that the flame *n·* expires.
344–19 Such philosophy can *n·* demonstrate
346–11 Evil *n·* did exist as an entity.
346–24 *n·* to repeat error unless it
349–28 I *n·* received more than this ;
350– 2 was *n·* receipted for.
351– 5 I *n·* have practised by arguments
351–16 *n·* can place it in the wrong hands
353–10 and *n·* until then.
354– 1 they "*n·* disobey Mother" !
355–17 *n·* clears the vision ;
356–24 One can *n·* go up, until
358–13 they *n·* should be until then.
360–12 Philosophy *n·* has produced,
365–24 *n·* met the growing wants
366–26 *n·* have abated and *n·* will
367–21 To good, evil is *n·* present ;
372–26 *n·* having seen the painter's
373– 9 I had *n·* before seen it :
374–20 I *n·* looked on my ideal of
378–14 *n·* occurred to the author to learn his
379–13 I *n·* heard him say that matter was
385–19 Now see thy ever-self ; Life *n·* fled ;
385–20 Man is not mortal, *n·* of the dead :
Man. 84– 4 *n·* to return evil for evil,
Chr. 55–28 shall *n·* die.— *John* 11 : 26.
Ret. 5–16 to which the pen can *n·* do justice.
6– 3 * impressions . . . can *n·* be effaced,
7–11 * and he *n·* forsook them until
9–15 but *n·* again to the material senses
14–12 declaring that *n·* could I unite with
21– 6 We *n·* met again until he had
27– 5 been read by any one but myself,
30– 7 The motive of . . . has *n·* changed.
37– 8 * but it will *n·* be read."
40– 4 * "I *n·* before suffered so little
57–29 such methods can *n·* reach
59– 6 The word *Life n·* means that

never

Ret.
64–16 shall *n·* see light. — *Psal.* 49 : 19.
64–18 and thoughts have *n·* changed,
68– 1 material concept was *n·* a creator,
68– 6 human concept *n·* was. . . . the father
74– 9 I desire *n·* to think of it,
76–24 *n·* abuses the corporeal personality,
85–17 *N·* forsake your post without
87–18 *n·*, in any way, to trespass
90–16 The true mother *n·* willingly

Un.
10–13 Spiritual phenomena *n·* converge
11–22 he *n·* thanked Jesus for restoring
14–27 *n·* said that man would become
15– 5 which God *n·* can throw off?
17–16 *n·* man spake," — *John* 7 : 46.
18– 6 Error may say that God can *n·*
18–25 to be *n·* conscious of death.
20–12 God *n·* made evil.
24– 9 you can *n·* be outside of His
25–25 evil can *n·* take away.
26–15 * His mercy waneth *n·*,
26–17 God's power *n·* waneth,
28– 5 It was *n·* touched by the
28–10 *n·* a light or form was discerned
29– 6 Spirit *n·* sins,
29–20 can *n·* be seen or measured
30– 7 Soul is Life, and . . . *n·* sins.
40– 5 man in Science *n·* dies.
40–13 his sayings will *n·* die ;
40–20 Death can *n·* alarm or even
41– 4 Of evil we can *n·* learn it,
41–22 Spirit can *n·* dwell in its
43–16 can *n·* "pass away — *see Matt.* 5 : 18.
45–11 that God *n·* made evil.
45–22 But Truth *n·* dies,
51– 7 human reason can *n·* make
53– 3 God *n·* made them ;
59– 7 was *n·* absent from the earth
59–17 *n·* saw the Saviour come and go,
62– 2 that they *n·* were sick.
62– 9 good, is *n·* absent.
62–18 In Science, Christ *n·* died.
62–22 *n·* in matter, nor resurrected
63– 4 *n·* absent for a moment.
63– 6 *n·* disappeared to spiritual sense,
64–17 but they can *n·* turn back

Pul.
6–30 whose mind *n·* swerved
8–17 Little hands, *n·* before devoted to
9– 7 *n·* be shattered in our hearts,
14–17 *n·* fear the consequences.
36–12 * I *n·* saw equalled.
45– 3 * will *n·* be known in this world.
52– 1 * Wonders will *n·* cease.
72–20 * that she had *n·* claimed,
74–27 *n·* can be but one God,
79– 8 * are not, and *n·* have been,
79–28 * condition can *n·* long continue.
80–12 * Mrs. Eddy we have *n·* seen ;
82–16 * *n·* called Abraham "Father,"
83– 3 * what we *n·* fulfil as husband

Rud.
11–26 *n·* introduces the subject of
11–27 *n·* depicts the muscular,
11–28 *n·* talks about the structure of
12– 1 *n·* lays his hands on the patient,
14– 8 *n·* sought charitable support,
14–12 *n·* taught a Primary class without
16– 3 can *n·* give a thorough knowledge
16– 4 will *n·* undertake to fit students
17– 9 Mind-healing *n·* originated in pride,

No.
4–10 *n·* made sickness a stubborn reality.
13– 9 shall *n·* die." — *John* 11 : 26.
17–11 can *n·* be less than a good man ;
18– 2 has *n·* diminished sin
19– 6 have *n·* met the growing wants
24–22 and was *n·* a claimant ;
24–25 There was *n·* a moment in which
26–21 *n·* originated in molecule,
28–17 Truth is *n·* understood too soon,
31– 9 *n·* actual persons or real facts.
31–27 shall *n·* see death ;" — *John* 8 : 51.
36– 6 *n·* left heaven for earth.
40–15 *n·* to touch the human thought
40–16 *n·* to trespass mentally on
40–17 *n·* to take away the rights,
41–18 *n·* admit such as come to steal
43–21 can *n·* engraft Truth into error.
43–24 will *n·* prevent or reconstruct

Pan.
6– 3 *n·* disappear in any other way.
9–13 shall *n·* die." — *John* 11 : 26.
10–24 is manifest, and *n·* lost,
13–10 was *n·* more manifest than in

'00.
7–11 they *n·* loved the Bible
7–19 this Christ is *n·* absent.
10– 8 Such conflict *n·* ends till
10–24 from a person I *n·* saw.

'01.
1– 5 rest assured you can *n·* lack

never

'01.
11– 2 *n·* suffered and *n·* died.
13– 2 and God *n·* made it.
13–23 *n·* punishes it only as it
13–24 and *n·* afterwards ;
15–13 or he would *n·* quit sinning.
20–19 This unseen evil . . . is *n·* forgiven.
25–19 *n·* recommended drugs, he *n·* used them.
33– 9 * *n·* the originating influence

'02.
2–26 I *n·* left the Church,
2–29 we shall meet again, *n·* to part.
4–20 a law *n·* to be abrogated
5–15 can *n·* be answered satisfactorily
11– 2 Our heavenly Father *n·* destined
14–15 could *n·* have been compassed
15– 3 I *n·* lost my faith in God,
15–19 I could *n·* believe that a human being
16–26 they *n·* destroy one iota of

Hea.
2– 8 *n·* seen amid the smoke
6– 6 The pioneer . . . is *n·* hit :
9–17 God *n·* cursed man,
9–18 God *n·* made a wicked man ;
9–24 *n·* made sin or sickness,
12–14 *n·* made a man sick.
14–11 *n·* trust yourself in the hands of
16– 2 can *n·* be repeated too often
17–19 *n·* proceeded from Truth,
18– 9 *n·* entered and it *n·* escaped
18–10 good and evil *n·* dwelt together.
18–18 *n·* did anything for sickness

Peo.
9–14 who *n·* pardons the sin that

Po.
2– 9 can *n·* reach to thee
24– 7 A sign that *n·* can depart.
35– 8 Whose streams will *n·* dry
42– 1 Oh, there's *n·* a shadow where
42– 3 And *n·* the sunshine without a
47– 6 to gladness and *n·* to tears,
47– 8 *N·* to toiling and *n·* to fears,
48–13 Now see thy ever-self ; Life *n·* fled ;
48–14 *n·* of the dead :

My.
vii– 4 * can *n·* do for its Leader what
5–32 divine wisdom, *n·*.
9–24 I *n·* before felt poor in thanks,
11–12 * *n·* urged upon us a step that
18–19 *n·* more manifest than in its
33–27 shall *n·* be moved. — *Psal.* 15 : 5.
57–29 * "Wonders will *n·* cease.
61–19 * *n·* more did I have any doubt.
61–31 * I appreciated as *n·* before
66–30 * *n·* before has such a grand church
67–23 * *n·* was a more artistic effect
72– 7 *N·* before has the city been
83– 2 * of *n·* going about labelled.
92– 2 * Of course tho now idea will *n·*
117–28 There was *n·* a religion or
121–12 *n·* selfish, stony, nor stormy,
127–24 can *n·* surrender.
129–17 *n·* severed from Spirit !
129–25 whose feet can *n·* be moved.
130–19 Truth *n·* falters nor fails ;
131–21 where God is we can *n·* part.
132–29 Divine Love . . . *n·* loses a case.
134–14 will *n·* lose their claim on us.
146–26 *n·* mentally or audibly takes
147–25 *n·* stop ceremoniously to
150–13 *n·* weary of struggling to
152–26 can *n·* heal you nor pardon a
159– 3 *N·* more sweet than to-day,
161– 7 which *n·* remits the sentence
162–27 may their faith *n·* falter
165–15 Goodness *n·* fails to receive its
165–25 Goodness and benevolence *n·* tire.
165–26 and *n·* stop from exhaustion.
166– 2 will *n·* end in anarchy
166–15 we will live on and *n·* drift apart.
166–16 Had I *n·* suffered for
167–10 that Love . . . which *n·* deserts us.
167–28 will, I trust, *n·* be marred by
179–18 narratives had *n·* been written,
185–13 the victors *n·* to be vanquished.
195– 7 it is *n·* too late to repent,
203– 9 begin with work and *n·* stop
204– 8 can begin and *n·* end.
205–30 The . . . may fail, but the Science *n·*.
212– 2 would *n·*, otherwise, think or do
212–29 saying that animal magnetism *n·*
214–29 To desert . . . *n·* occurred to me,
227– 4 as one who *n·* weakened
228–31 such a one was *n·* called to
229–26 said in my heart would *n·* be needed,
235– 9 and *n·* name a cipher ?
235–19 Matter as substance . . . *n·* was made.
235–30 would *n·* have entered into the
242– 3 can *n·* demonstrate spirituality until
261–10 deceit or falsehood is *n·* wise.
262–11, 12 *n·* born and *n·* dying.

never

My.	268– 3	*n·* be annulled so long as
	277–10	*n·* settles the question of
	279– 1	*n·* requisite, *n·* a necessity,
	283–30	*n·* fastens on the good
	288–18	He *n·* appealed to matter
	290– 7	virtues can *n·* be lost.
	290–17	Divine Love is *n·* so near as when
	297–23	realize that he *n·* died ;
	300–19	shall *n·* see death." — *John* 8 : 51.
	303– 4	I have *n·* claimed to be.
	308– 2	powers of earth . . . can *n·* prevent
	308–19	He *n·* used a walking-stick.
	308–24	* "I *n·* use a cane."
	310–19	that there was *n·* a death in my
	311–23	I *n·* doubted the veracity of
	313–16	I was *n·* "given to long and
	313–21	I *n·* was especially interested
	313–22	*n·* "dabbled in mesmerism,"
	313–22	*n·* was "an amateur clairvoyant,"
	313–24	I *n·* went into a trance
	318–32	If there had *n·* existed such a
	324–19	* *n·* gave us the impression that
	325– 8	* would *n·* be worth what you
	325–13	* my desire has *n·* changed.
	333–16	* It has *n·* been claimed by Mrs. Eddy
	348–24	*n·* producing an opposite effect,

never-ending

My.	357–20	the way, . . . to their *n·* success,

nevermore

Mis.	397–12	waves can shock, Oh, *n·* !
Pul.	18–21	waves can shock, Oh, *n·* !
Po.	12–22	waves can shock, Oh, *n·* !
page 47		poem
	47– 5	Oh, ever and *n·* ?
	47–18	*N·* reaping the harvest

nevertheless

Ret.	14–21	*N·*, he persisted in the assertion
	50–14	*N·*, my list of indigent
	93–22	but it is *n·* true.
Un.	4–28	*N·*, at the present crude hour,
	7– 6	*N·*, though I thus speak,
Pul.	2– 9	*N·*, there is a thought higher
No.	13–13	the declaration is *n·* true,
My.	40–30	* *n·* it is the law).
	314–15	the cause *n·* was adultery.

New

Mis.	187–20	as spiritual as the *N·*.
	292– 1	chapter sub-title
Pan.	7–18	study of the Old and *N·* Testaments
'02.	page 1	heading
My.	179–13	The Old and the *N·* Testaments

new

Mis.	10–24	and all things become *n·*.
	15– 4	chapter sub-title
	16– 1	a *n·* and more spiritual Life
	21– 7	*n·* heaven and a *n·* earth," — *Rev.* 21 : 1.
	44–26	your belief assumed a *n·* form,
	51–27	* sunshine of the world's *n·* spring,
	74– 6	imparts a *n·* apprehension of
	80–28	now elbowed by a *n·* school
	80–30	will not patronize the *n·* school,
	80–31	the medical system of the *n·*.
	84–29	a *n·* and higher sense thereof,
	86–20	the *n·* heaven and earth,
	112– 8	error, given *n·* opportunities,
	171–17	by which the *n·* teacher would
	178–22	* found C. S. a *n·* gospel,
	178–29	between the old and the *n·* ;
	178–31	the *n·*, living, impersonal
	179–13	In the *n·* religion the teaching
	204–13	giving mortals *n·* motives,
	204–14	*n·* purposes, *n·* affections,
	218– 1	spiritual sense takes in *n·* views,
	222–22	committed under this *n· régime*
	228– 6	is to take a *n·* standpoint
	233–13	the *n·* cloth of metaphysics,
	234–28	this *n·* departure of metaphysics,
	235–11	loftier desires and *n·* possibilities.
	239–23	her dividend, . . . was *n·* ;
	245–11	giving it *n·* impetus and energy ;
	262– 7	*n·* and costly spring dress.
	292– 4	"A *n·* commandment — *John* 13 : 34.
	292– 7	a *n·* commandment even for him.
	292–10	*n·* tone on the scale ascending,
	293– 2	breathing *n·* Life and Love
	299–29	*n·* patterns which are useful to them ;
	348–23	under this *n· régime* of medicine,
	364– 4	naturally evokes *n·* paraphrase
	366–17	to a *n·* style of imposition
	375–11	* *n·* book you have given us.
Man.	26– 7	or *n·* officers elected,
	81– 1	or *n·* officers elected,
	102– 6	until the *n·* church edifice is

new

Man.	105– 1	No *n·* Tenet or By-Law shall be
	109–18	*n·* applications will be required,
Ret.	14–23	when the *n·* light dawned within me.
	20–18	Awoke *n·* beauty in the surge's roll !
	25– 5	Scriptures had to me a *n·* meaning,
	26–19	a *n·* date in the Christian era,
	27–29	led me into a *n·* world of light
	27–30	old to God, but *n·* to His
	35– 4	It was so *n·*
	45– 2	A *n·* light broke in upon it,
	50–27	a *n·* rule of order in divine Science,
	52– 2	endeavored to find *n·* ways
Un.	7– 2	in the apprehension of this *n·* subject,
Pul.	1– 4	A *n·* year is a nursling,
	14–18	send forth a *n·* flood to drown the
	29– 1	* in the *n·* Grundmann Studio Building
	31–18	* a *n·* and increasing interest
	35– 1	it came to me with a *n·* meaning,
	45– 9	* publication of the *n·* denomination :
	46– 4	* *n·* rules were formulated.
	50–19	* Any *n·* movement will awaken
	51–20	* Ere this many a *n·* project
	52–17	* growth of the *n·* movement.
	52–17	* We call it *n·*. It is not.
	52–18	* The name C. S. alone is *n·*.
	52–26	* No *n·* doctrine is proclaimed,
	53– 6	* no *n·* thing under the — *Eccl.* 1 : 9.
	57–20	* given to a *n·* Boston church.
	57–25	* site of the *n·* Music Hall,
	60– 3	* the *n·* order of service
	63–15	* a *n·* phase of religious belief,
	65– 7	* which is rather small and *n·*
	67– 5	* "If you would found a *n·* faith:
	84– 7	* the *n·* man with the new woman.
No.	8–28	This counsel is not *n·*,
	39–21	*n·* and scientific discoveries
	41–22	by *n·* discoveries of Truth
	44– 4	C. S. involves a *n·* language,
Pan.	11– 5	put on the *n·* man, — *Col.* 3 : 10.
'00.	4–11	*n·* and forward steps in religion,
	8–15	things *n·* and old." — *Matt.* 13 : 52.
	15– 2	a *n·* one that is up to date.
	15–20	a wedding garment *n·* and old,
'01.	1– 6	Our first communion in the *n·* century
	21– 3	or *n·* editions of old errors ;
	34–12	or must we have a *n·* Bible
	34–13	a *n·* system of Christianity,
'02.	4–14	*n·* commandment in the gospel of peace,
	7–25	"A *n·* commandment — *John* 13 : 34.
	7–27	attention to his *n· commandment.*
	8– 8	The *n·* commandment of Christ Jesus
	8–13	the old and the *n·* commandment,
	10– 3	uncovers a *n·* ideas, unfolds spiritual
	17–10	both the old and the *n·* commandment,
Hea.	1– 2	speak with *n·* tongues ; — *Mark* 16 : 17.
	6– 5	pioneer of something *n·* under the sun
Peo.	11– 4	a *n·* abolitionist struck the keynote
	11–15	enforce *n·* forms of oppression,
Po.	page 22	poem
	22– 8	*N·* themes seraphic,
	32– 6	fragrance and charms ever *n·*
	65–19	rise to a seraph's *n·* song.
My.	8–30	* one hundred and five *n·* churches
	11–24	* *n·* building will be erected,
	15–31	* I sing the *N·*, *N·* SONG,
	16– 8	* site of the *n·* building.
	16–11	* corner-stone of the *n·* auditorium
	29–22, 23	* *n·* religion launching upon a *n·* era,
	31–17	* The *n·* home for worship
	32– 7	* acoustic properties of the *n·*
	39–17	* In introducing the *n·* President,
	47–31	* with *n·* tongues ; — *Mark* 16 : 17.
	50– 8	* strangeness of their *n·* home,
	50–24	* two *n·* members were added
	51–23	* *n·* fields to teach and preach."
	59– 8	* *n·* system of faith and worship,
	60–26	* dedication of our *n·* church
	61–10	* held in the *n·* extension
	63–22	* *n·* sense of the magnitude
	70–11	* chimes for the *n·* C. S. temple
	71–14	* this *n·* cathedral or temple
	72–18	* fund of the *n·* C. S. temple,
	72–25	* subscribed for the *n·* building,
	76– 2	* *n·* two-million-dollar edifice,
	76– 5	* *n·* contributions were constantly
	76–26	* *n·* two-million-dollar cathedral
	76–31	* The *n·* structure, which is now
	86– 5	* pleasure in this *n·* symbol,
	86– 7	* the hosts of a *n·* religion.
	86–11	* *n·* two-million-dollar church,
	87–25	* turned to the *n·* religion.
	88–10	* Mother Church of the C. S. faith
	89–22	* dedication of the *n·* Mother Church
	90– 5	* these things are *n·*, utterly *n·*,
	92–13	* swift growth of the *n·* faith
	97–20	* opening of the *n·* Mother Church

new

My.	167–16	in our *n·* church edifice,
	171– 9	The *n·* Concord church is
	173–15	*n·* church building in Concord,
	187–27	in a *n·* commandment
	187–28	In this *n·* recognition of the
	195– 6	*n·* problems to be worked out
	201–29	opening of your *n·* church
	203– 3	nothing *n·* to communicate ;
	221– 7	*n·* dispensation of Truth
	228– 2	nothing *n·* on this score.
	231–22	for her to undertake *n·* tasks,
	256– 3	improvise some *n·* notes,
	257– 5	the *n·* cradle of an old truth.
	280– 8	* this *n·* reminder from you
	287–20	lofty desires, *n·* possibilities,
	290–10	first month of the *n·* century.
	307–11	that seemed at first *n·* to him.
	318– 2	constituted a *n·* style of language.
	325–10	* greater future than the *n·* Back Bay.

(*see also* **birth, church, edifice, idea, name, temple, tongue, wine, woman**)

Newark, N. J.

Pul.	89– 5	* *News,* *N·,* *N. J.*

Newbern, N. C.

My.	329–11	* letter from *N·,* *N. C.,*

new-born

Mis.	16–28	this *n·* spiritual altitude ;
	74– 3	This *n·* sense subdues not only the
	85–19	*n·* Christian Scientist must mature,
	254– 1	Cherish these *n·* children
Pul.	10–28	This is the *n·* of Spirit,
No.	12–16	*n·* conception of the Christ,
	38–11	built his Church of the *n·,*
Peo.	14–12	thou of the church of the *n·* ;
Po.	30– 3	*n·* beauty in the emerald sky,
My.	17– 6	"As *n·* babes, — *I Pet.* 2 : 2.
	158–14	lends a *n·* beauty to holiness,

new-built

Pul.	41–10	* to view the *n·* temple

New Commandment

Mis.	292– 1	chapter sub-title
'02.	page 1	heading

New England (*see also* **New England's**)

Mis.	176–16	sought the *N· E·* shores,
Ret.	2–11	brought to *N· E·* a heavy sword,
Pul.	7–10	In our *N· E·* metropolis
	32– 3	* of tint so often seen in *N· E·,*
	41–13	* From all *N· E·* the members
	57–12	* and, indeed, in all *N· E·*
	65– 5	* what is called the *N· E·* mind
	75–22	* in the great *N· E·* capital
My.	91–29	* it is the largest in *N· E·.*
	204–10	* to the people of *N· E·,*
	290– 2	by the strong hearts of *N· E·*

New England's

My.	264–15	*N· E·* last Thanksgiving Day of this

newer

Pul.	81–11	* an added grace — a *n·* charm.
My.	345–26	*n·,* finer, more etherealized ways of

New Hampshire and **N. H.** (*see also* **Granite State, New Hampshire's**)

Mis.	144– 2	the quarries in *N· H·,*
	378– 2	Hydropathic Institute in *N· H·,*
Ret.	3– 5	John Lovewell of Dunstable, *N· H·,*
	3–10	the *N· H·* general who fought at
	4– 6	Bow, in the State of *N· H·.*
	6–23	Massachusetts and *N· H·,*
	19–17	later I returned to *N· H·,*
	20–10	northern part of *N· H·.*
Pul.	24–23	* pink granite of *N· H·,*
	48–17	* Congressman Baker from *N· H·,*
	57–27	* born of an old *N· H·* family,
No.	46–15	among the first settlers of *N· H·.*
Po.	v–11	* *this lofty* *N· H·* crag,
My.	45–28	* massive pile of *N· H·* granite
	136–18	received by a native of *N· H·.*
	138–25	* STATE OF *N· H·,* Merrimack, ss.
	167–27	religious rights in *N· H·*
	168– 6	people of my dear old *N· H·.*
	304– 4	Sanbornton Academy, *N· H·,*
	305–12	* "an ignorant woman in *N· H·.*"
	310– 6	member of the *N· H·* Legislature,
	310–14	staff of the Governor of *N· H·.*
	312–31	educational system in *N· H·.*
	327– 4	in the Court of *N· H·,*
	330–29	later I returned to *N· H·,*
	339–11	chapter sub-title
	340–10	religion and medicine in *N· H·,*
	340–22	the Governor of *N· H·* has

New Hampshire and **N. H.**

My.	341– 2	A native of *N· H·,*

(*see also* **Bow, Concord, Fabyans, Franklin, Littleton, Manchester, North Groton, Sanbornton Bridge, Tilton**)

New Hampshire Patriot

Po.	35–15	Written . . . for the *N· H· P·.*

New Hampshire's

Pul.	47–22	* State House of *N· H·* quiet capital,
My.	339–12	*N· H·* advancement is marked.

New Hampshire State Militia

My.	309–12	chaplain of the *N· H· S· M·,*

New Haven, Conn.

Pul.	88–17	* *News,* *N· H·,* *C·.*

New Jerusalem

Ret.	85–27	diadem of gems from the *N· J·.*

New London, Conn.

My.	166–26	heading

newly

Mis.	16–23	This *n·* awakened consciousness

new-made

Mis.	330– 4	to moan over the *n·* grave,

newness

No.	25– 6	serve in *n·* of spirit, *Rom.* 7 : 0.

new-old

No.	12–12	this *n·* knowledge of God.
'00.	10–15	*n·* doctrines of the prophets
'01.	2– 8	*n·* cloth of Christian healing.
	20–23	*n·* *régime* of necromancy
	30–21	establishment of a *n·* religion
'02.	9–29	some *n·* truth that counteracts
	11–16	by a *n·* message from God,
My.	154–17	weaving the *n·* vesture
	182– 8	by establishing a *n·* church,
	248–10	*n·* birthright is to put an end to
	301– 3	C. S. is the *n·* Christianity,

New Orleans La.

Pul.	89–20	* *Telegram,* *N· O·,* La.
	89–21	* *Times,* *N· O·,* La.

Mis.	304–12	* to the battle-field of *N· O·*
Pul.	88– 3	From Canada to *N· O·,*
'00.	1–20	Atlanta, *N· O·,* Chicago,

Newport, R. I.

Pul.	88–18	* *News,* *N·,* R. I.

News

Pul.	88–17	* *N·,* New Haven, Conn.
	88–18	* *N·,* Newport, R. I.
	89– 4	* *N·,* Buffalo, N. Y.
	89– 5	* *N·,* Newark, N. J.
	89–37	* *N·,* St. Joseph, Mo.

news

Pul.	71–11	* SURPRISED AT THE *N·*
Hea.	1–14	of publishing the good *n·.*"

news-dealers

Mis.	274–23	*n·* shout for class legislation,

newspaper

Mis.	4–12	*n·* edited and published by
	132–22	through the medium of a *n·* ;
Man.	98– 3	corrected a false *n·* article
	98–19	in a leading Boston *n·*
Po.	vi– 9	* *in a Lynn, Mass.,* *n·,*
My.	151– 1	patient with the *n·* wares
	249–17	that . . . *n·* should countenance
	306– 8	*n·* controversy over a question
	334– 2	* to infer from *n·* reports
	353– 2	and read our daily *n·.*

newspapers

Mis.	7–17	Looking over the *n·* of the day,
	220–27	publish it in the *n·* that he
Ret.	2–21	some *n·,* yellow with age.
	2–24	for they were American *n·,*
Pul.	88– 1	chapter sub-title
	88– 4	author has received leading *n·*
	88– 9	prominent *n·* whose articles
'02.	13–21	advertising . . . in the Boston *n·,*
My.	79–16	* in the leading *n·* of the world.
	95–17	* described in the *n·* of the Hub
	173– 3	* in the Concord (N. H.) *n·*
	270– 9	the leading editors and *n·*
	304–10	writing for the leading *n·,*
	330–20	* Wilmington *n·* of that year.

News-Tribune

Pul.	90– 1	* *N·,* Duluth, Minn.

new-style

Mis.	285–23	a *n·* conjugality,

New Testament
Mis. 66– 6 these words of the N· T·:
195–13 said that the N· T· does not
373– 8 translation of the N· T·
Un. 14–17 but the N· T· tells us of
36–13 referred to in the N· T· as the
Pul. 52–15 * with the N· T· at the foundation,
'00. 4– 6 gospel of the N· T· and the
'02. 16– 3 translation of the N· T·,
My. 218– 5 Neither the Old nor the N· T·
(see also **Apocryphal New Testament**)

Newton
Benjamin Wills
My. 13– 4 book by Benjamin Wills N·,

Mis. 22–28 falling apple suggested to N·
23– 1 N· named it gravitation,

New Year (see also **New Year's**)
Mis. 400–13 MOTHER'S N· Y· GIFT
Man. 67–21 Thanksgiving, Christmas, N· Y·,
Po. 69– 1 Mother's N· Y· Gift
My. 252–26 gave to the "happy N· Y·"
354–17 O glad N· Y·!
355– 3 * symbol of the glad N· Y·

New Year's
My. 354–27 written . . . on N· Y· morning.

New Year's Day
My. 252–25 in England on N· Y· D·,

New Year's Sunday
Pul. 59– 3 * was dedicated on N· Y· S·

New York and **N. Y.** (State)
(see **Albany, Auburn, Bridgeport, Brooklyn, Buffalo, Lockport, New York, Rochester, Saratoga Springs, Syracuse, Troy**)

New York (see also **Empire City, Greater New York, New York City**)
N. Y.
My. 193–21 chapter sub-title
201– 9 chapter sub-title
201–26 chapter sub-title
325–19 * N· Y·, N. Y., December 7, 1906.
361–25 FIRST CHURCH . . . N· Y·, N. Y.,
361–28 * N· Y·, N. Y., Januray 19, 1910.
363–11 * N· Y·, N. Y., February 5, 1910.

Mis. 266–19 students in Chicago, N· Y·,
306–13 * Liberty and West Streets, N· Y·,
Ret. 20– 7 George W. Patterson of N· Y·,
Pul. 41–14 * N· Y· sent its hundreds,
43– 2 * First Church . . . of N· Y·,
56– 2 * have sprung up in N· Y·,
56–23 * The Outlook, N· Y·,
57–18 * American Art Journal, N· Y·,
71–15 * announcements in N· Y· papers
73–24 * in the reports from N· Y·
74– 8 * in Hodgson Hall, N· Y·,
'00. 1–19 Boston, N· Y·, Philadelphia,
My. 74– 6 * church members from N· Y·
108–27 the words of the N· Y· press
165–11 heading
231–27 SECOND CHURCH OF CHRIST, . . . N· Y·
243– 1 chapter sub-title
243–15 students in N· Y· and elsewhere
332–10 * to accompany her only to N· Y·,
357–13 When my dear brethren in N· Y·
359–22 * First Church of Christ, . . . of N· Y·,

New York American
My. 267–13 [N· Y· A·, February, 1905]
296–25 N· Y· A·, January 6, 1908,

New York City
Ret. 52–17 in general convention at N· Y· C·,
Pul. 88–25 * Advertiser, N· Y· C·.
89– 1 * Independent, N· Y· C·.
89– 6 * Once A Week, N· Y· C·.
89– 9 * Press, N· Y· C·.
89–12 * Sun, N· Y· C·.
My. 169–16 Christian Scientists of N· Y· C·
194–21 church edifice in N· Y· C·,
243– 4 the several churches in N· Y· C·
282–20 542 Fifth Avenue, N· Y· C·,
283– 4 FIRST CHURCH OF . . . N· Y· C·,
304–13 crowded halls in N· Y· C·,
312–12 * Mrs. Glover's fare to N· Y· C·,
357–27 MRS. AUGUSTA E. STETSON, N· Y· C·.
360– 9 FIRST CHURCH OF . . . N· Y· C·,
360–12 First Church of . . . N· Y· C·,
360–17 First Church of . . . N· Y· C·,
362– 3 FIRST CHURCH OF . . . N· Y· C·.

New York Commercial Advertiser
My. 299– 1 [Letter to the N· Y· C· A·]

New York Herald
Pul. 74– 1 * [N· Y· H·, February 6, 1895]
My. 76–23 * [N· Y· H·]
275–11 [N· Y· H·]
302–12 [Letter to the N· Y· H·]
341–17 * [N· Y· H·, May 1, 1901]
346–20 * in the columns of the N· Y· H·,

New York Journal
'01. 21– 7 published in the N· Y· J·,
My. 169–13 [N· Y· J·]
169–15 Please say through the N· Y· J·,

New York Mail and Express
My. 287– 1 [N· Y· M· and E·]

New York Tribune
Pul. 64–22 * [N· Y· T·, February 7, 1895]

New York World
My. 77–16 * [N· Y· W·]
259–21 [N· Y· W·]
266– 1 [N· Y· W·, December, 1900]
301–14 [Letter to the N· Y· W·]
315–23 whom the N· Y· W· declared dying

next
Mis. 69–18 n· day he attended to his business.
86–24 It is n· to divine beauty
129–11 take the n· Scriptural step :
135– 4 n· to our hearts, on our lips,
193–22 The n· step for ecclesiasticism
232–13 foreshadows what is n· to appear
270–29 The n· step is Mind-medicine.
304–14 * sent to the n· World's Exhibition,
316–22 breaches widened the n· hour ;
325–31 N· he enters a place of worship,
326–12 they consumed the n· dwelling;
342–31 and are ready for the n· move.
Man. 63– 4 The n· lessons consist of
Ret. 6–11 n· to my mother, the very dearest
9–13 resolving to do, n· time, as my
Pul. 43–19 * silent prayer came n·,
60– 3 * n· Sunday the new order of
Rud. 11– 4 n· to belief in God as omnipotent ;
11– 9 n· proposition in C. S.,
Pan. 8– 1 N·, it follows that the disarrangement
'01. 17–22 n· more difficult stage of action
26–10 in the n· he endows it with
27–29 * N·, they say it has been discovered
My. 25–20 the dedication in June n·
38–11 * admitted until the n· service.
141–11 * n· of which would have been held n·
145–14 and the n· morning said to
184–17 and I treasure it n· to your
215–25 N·, on the contrary, he bade them
217–26 and aids in taking the n· step
240–19 In the n· edition of S. and H.
284–17 In your n· issue please correct
304–27 * N·, they say it has been discovered
322–18 * to enter the n· Primary class
353–15 the n· I named Monitor,

next-door
Ret. 40– 6 that her n· neighbor was dying.

nexus
Ret. 21–29 but if . . . the n· is lost,

nice
Mis. 227–10 n· distinction by which they endeavor
240–27 habit of smoking is not n·,

nicely
My. 71–30 * n· adjusted acoustic properties

niche
Ret. 70–19 must fill his own n· in time

nickel
Mis. 305–21 * silver, bronze, copper, and n·
My. 65–16 * passing out a n· for carfare.

Nicodemus
My. 191– 1 the wisdom of N· of old,

Nicolaitan
'00. 12–29 N· church presents the phase of
13–11 so he denounces the N· church.

Nicolaitanes
'00. 13– 5 hatest the deeds of the N·, — Rev. 2 : 6.

niece
My. 311–20 Fanny McNeil, President Pierce's n·,

niggers
Mis. 238– 1 * story that "he helped 'n·'

nigh
Mis. 229–19 n· thy dwelling." — Psal. 91 : 10.
389–12 His habitation high is here, and n·,
Peo. 5–10 are n·, even at our door.
Po. 4–11 His habitation high is here, and n·,
22– 3 Eternity Draws n·
22– 7 lo, the light ! far heaven is n· !

nigh
　My.　4–30　Thou God most high and *n*·.
　　290– 4　the near seems afar, the distant *n*·,
night (*see also* **night's**)
all
　Mis. 111– 4　meekly, you have toiled all *n*· ;
and day
　My.　66–19　* artists are working *n*· and day
day and
　Mis. 177– 9　engaged day and *n*· in organizing
　　341–26　not replenished with oil day and *n*·,
　Pul.　12– 9　our God day and *n*·.— *Rev.* 12 : 10.
　　26–28　* always burning day and *n*·.
day or
　Pul.　58–29　* make it a home by day or *n*·.
dreary
　Po.　65– 9　enchained to life's dreary *n*·,
every
　My.　61– 2　* every *n*· since that time.
from the
　Mis. 347–27　from the *n*· He leads to light.
is far spent
　Mis. 213–27　the *n*· is far spent, the day dawns ;
　Pan.　1–17　*n*· is far spent, and day is
　My. 202– 6　*n*· is far spent and the day is
last
　My. 141–13　* announcement . . . was made last *n*·
long
　Mis. 144–30　wake the long *n*· of materialism,
　　253–28　through the long *n*·,
　　320–25　long *n*· of human beliefs,
　'00.　7–29　till the long *n*· is past
　Peo.　1–10　a long *n*· to the traveller ;
　My. 110– 6　upon the long *n*· of materialism,
no
　Mis. 174–17　No matter is there, no *n*·
　　276–16　"no *n*· is there."— *see Rev.* 21 : 25.
　　352–18　and no *n*· is there !
　　389–23　No *n*· drops down upon the
　No.　27– 8　No *n*· will be there,
　Po.　5– 2　No *n*· drops down upon the
　　70– 9　In God there is no *n*·,
　My. 129–10　There is no *n*· but in God's frown ;
　　155–23　knows no twilight and no *n*·.
　　183–13　no ebbing faith, no *n*·.
noon of
　Mis. 276–25　burning at the noon of *n*·,
of chaos
　Chr.　53– 3　O'er the grim *n*· of chaos
of discord
　Mis. 187–27　never extinguished in a *n*· of discord.
of materialism
　Mis. 144–30　wake the long *n*· of materialism,
　My. 110– 6　upon the long *n*· of materialism,
of material sense
　Mis. 24– 7　dawned on the *n*· of material sense.
of physics
　Peo.　10– 5　through the cold *n*· of physics,
old
　Pul. 14–21　deep waters of chaos and old *n*·,
one
　Pul. 33– 6　* One *n*· the mother related to her
Saturday
　My.　74– 3　* From now until Saturday *n*·
shadowy
　Po.　27– 7　tremulous with shadowy *n*· !
silence of
　'02.　15–23　came to me in the silence of *n*·,
silent
　'02.　5– 1　As silent *n*· foretells the dawn
starless
　Mis. 268–16　no shipwreck in a starless *n*·
star-lit
　Mis. 400– 1　*Laus Deo, n*· star-lit
　Pul. 16–13　*Laus Deo, n*· starlit
　Po. 76–12　*Laus Deo, n*· star-lit
stillness of the
　My.　61–27　* dark stillness of the *n*·,
Stygian
　No.　22–14　as Stygian *n*· to the kindling dawn.
tear-dews of
　Po.　8– 4　Where tear-dews of *n*· seek the
that
　Ret.　9– 8　That *n*·, before going to rest,
Thursday
　My. 333–21　* died on Thursday *n*·,
traversed
　Mis. 320–19　it hath traversed *n*·,
　My. 257– 6　This truth has traversed *n*·,

　Mis. 226–16　* must follow, as the *n*· the day,
　Ret. 20–12　The *n*· before my child was taken
　　81–25　* must follow, as the *n*· the day,
　'00.　12–15　temple was burned on the *n*· that
　'01.　31–24　Lord's Prayer, repeated at *n*· ;

night
　Hea. 10–17　sorrow endureth but for the *n*·,
　Po.　24–16　And *n*· grows deeply dark ;
　　65–11　twin sister of death and of *n*· !
　My.　45–20　* by *n*· in a pillar of fire
　　45–26　* pillar of fire by *n*·,"— *Exod.* 13 : 22
　　61–13　* but after a while, in the *n*·,
　　74– 5　* *n*· trains of Saturday will bring
　　110–20　The *n*· thought, methinks, should
　　110–23　The *n*· thought should show us
　　313–17　* wanderings, especially at *n*·,"
　　333– 9　* on the *n*· of the twenty-seventh.
night-bird
　Ret.　4–16　now the lone *n*· cries,
　Po. 16–16　voice of the *n*· must here send a
night-dream
　Rud. 11–16　In a moment you may awake from a *n*· ;
night-dreams
　Mis. 47–12　you have been in your *n*· ;
　My. 109– 3　than it has in our *n*·.
nightless
　Un. 61–11　*n*· radiance of divine Life.
night's
　Mis. 392– 7　the earth, asleep in *n*· embrace,
　Po. 20– 9　the earth, asleep in *n*· embrace,
　　73–12　N· dewy eye, The sea-mew's lone cry,
nights
　My. 335–29　* nine days and *n*· of agony
nine
　Mis. 304–23　* at *n*· o'clock in the morning
　　304–28　* ring at *n*· o'clock on October 11th,
　Man. 61–24　about eight or *n*· minutes
　Pul. 36– 3　* The work . . . lasted *n*· years,
　　59– 6　* services were held from *n*· to four o'clock,
　　68– 6　* here she taught . . . for *n*· years.
　　78– 4　* *n*· inches wide,
　No. 24–19　exposure is *n*· points of destruction.
　My.　v–19　* in 1875, after *n*· years of arduous
　　123–12　a reading-room and *n*· other rooms
　　312–21　died in about *n*· days.
　　314– 4　* During the following *n*· years
　　335–17　* end of *n*· days he passed away.
　　335–29　* *n*· days and nights of agony
　　(*see also* **numbers**)
nineteen
　My.　48– 4　* *n*· centuries had passed
　　70–26　* seventy-two stops, *n*· couplers,
　　70–26　* *n*· adjustable combination pistons,
　　220–27　*n*· centuries have greatly
　　(*see also* **dates, numbers**)
nineteenth
　Mis. 99–12　Men and women of the *n*· century,
　　382–12　latter half of the *n*· century
　Pul. vii– 8　latter half of the *n*· century,
　　23–18　* last quarter of the *n*· century.
　　55– 7　* our remarkable *n*· century
　'00.　1– 9　last year of the *n*· century
　My. 127–21　latter days of the *n*· century.
　　131–22　latter days of the *n*· century,
　　257–18　the close of the *n*· century,
　　264–13　* Thanksgiving Day of the *n*· century
nineteenth-century
　Mis. 168–17　The *n*· prophets repeat,
ninety-first
　Pul.　5–21　*n*· edition of one thousand copies.
　　38– 8　* it is now in its *n*· edition.
　　55–15　* the *n*· edition is announced.
Ninety-first Psalm
　'01.　32–23　N· P·, . . . educated my thought
ninety-five
　　(*see* **dates**)
ninety-four
　　(*see* **dates**)
ninety-nine
　Mis. 118– 8　*n*· times in one hundred
　No. 21– 3　has *n*· parts of error to the
　My. 112–14　*n*· out of every hundred
　　127–17　*n*· to the ten of *materia medica.*
ninety-six
　Mis. 231– 5　fall upon *n*· years.
　　(*see also* **numbers**)
ninth
　Mis. 32–13　In Mark, *n*· chapter,
　　191–16　In Mark, *n*· chapter,
　　242– 4　not to my notice until January *n*·.
　　332–13　Genesis, third chapter and *n*· verse,
Nirvana
　My. 118–26　a heathen basis for its *N*·,

N. J. (State)
(see **Newark, Trenton**)

nobility
Mis. 141–22 the *n·* of human meekness
Pul. 81–14 * beauty, sweetness, and *n·*
My. 72– 7 * in welcome to *n·*.

noble
Mis. 135–19 Add one more *n·* offering to
250–17 *n·* sacrifices and grand achievements
264– 3 My *n·* students, who are loyal
296–11 *n·* women who minister in the
338–31 * A great and *n·* creed."
Ret. 7– 4 His *n·* political antagonist,
45–16 *n·*, unprecedented action
48–21 fulfilled its high and *n·* destiny,
49–23 for her great and *n·* work,
No. 46–19 Man has a *n·* destiny ;
My. 22–10 * for this grand and *n·* purpose,
61–32 * work of our *n·* Board of Directors.
85–30 *n·* dome of pure gray tint,
88–24 * a *n·* and devoted woman,
105–29 In the ranks of the M.D.'s are *n·* men
112–21 pure morals and *n·* lives,
167–24 praise for the *n·* disposal of the
290– 9 beloved as this *n·* woman,
326–20 *n·* Southrons of North Carolina
331–27 * the *n·* generosity of heart
332– 6 * meagre tribute for so *n·* an effort

nobler
Mis. 227–17 *n·* purposes and wider aims
Ret. 12– 1 Strains *n·* far than clarion call
Po. 60–21 Strains *n·* far than clarion call
My. 253– 5 What *n·* achievement,
308– 8 higher, *n·*, more imperative

noblest
Mis. ix– 3 * "The *n·* charity is to
294– 1 The *n·* work of God is man
Ret. 77– 3 * man's the *n·* work of God ;"
77– 4 * the *n·* work of man."
No. 45–19 vindicated by the *n·* of both sexes.

nobly
Peo. 10–11 and sustained as *n·* our
My. 125–21 have acquitted themselves *n·*.

nobody
Mis. 108–14 proper denominator, — *n·* and nothing.
265–14 *N·* can gainsay this.
266–11 work that *n·* else can or will do.
381–31 * that "*n·* can be both founder and
My. 30– 4 * *n·* attended more than one,
214–29 *n·* then wanted C. S.,

nod
My. 129–14 The *n·* of Spirit is nature's natal.

nodding
Mis. 325–15 *n·* on cushioned chairs,

noise
No. 1–15 *n·* and stir of contending sentiments

noisy
No. 1– 7 Small streams are *n·*

nolens volens
My. 4– 4 world's *n· v·* cannot enthrall it.

nom de plume
Mis. 216–14 Whatever his *n· de p·* means,
My. 52–30 * *n· de p·* of the Rev. . . . Wiggin

nomenclature
My. 324–11 * thought he could give a clearer *n·*

nominal
My. 91– 3 * were already *n·* Christians,

nominally
Pul. 87–17 make me your *Pastor Emeritus, n·*.

nominated
Man. 79–13 persons *n·* for said office
My. 310– 7 and was *n·* for Congress,

nomination
Ret. 7– 1 *n·* to Congress on a majority

noms de plume
Mis. x–19 to assume various *n· de p·*.

non-Christian
'02. 3– 3 loosening cords of *n·* religions

non-church-going
Pul. 56– 7 * churches and *n·* people.

nondescript
Mis. 285–26 this *n·* phœnix, . . . may appear

nondescripts
'01. 16– 7 scarcely equal the modern *n·*,

none
Mis. 22–21 "there is *n·* other." — *Mark* 12 : 32.
34– 1 *n·* of the harmful "after effects"
54–25 *n· of your students have been*

none
Mis. 63–20 *n·* else beside Him," — *Deut.* 4 : 35.
70–29 *n·* could equal his glory.
93–12 *n·* besides the eternal,
97–19 there is *n·* else, — *Isa.* 45 : 5.
151–16 *n·* upon earth that I — *Psal.* 73 : 25.
161–20 Jewish law that *n·* should teach or
165–24 This cost, *n·* but the sinner can pay ;
185– 2 *N·* but the pure in heart shall
249–14 *N·* are permitted to remain
273– 6 *n·* other can do the work.
301–32 there was *n·* with me." — *Isa.* 63 : 3.
324–27 seeking peace but finding *n·*.
334– 3 *n·* can stay His hand, — *Dan.* 4 : 35.
347–27 *N·* can say unto Him,
350–16 *n·* beside Him." — see *Deut.* 4 : 35.
350–26 *n·* to be used in mental practice,
363–12 *n·* of the changes of matter,
366–12 *n· beside Him.*" — see *Deut.* 4 : 35.
400–10 No, It has *n·*,
Man. 62–15 *N·* except the officers, teachers, and
70–13 it shall be controlled by *n·* other.
90–12 *N·* but the teacher and members
110– 1 *n·* will be returned that are
Ret. 26–24 *n·* but the pure in heart can see God,
26–26 *n·* but . . . could first state this
63– 5 and there is *n·* beside Him,
Un. 46–10 *n·* other than this man,
51–17 They have *n·* of them lost their
60– 6 and there is *n·* beside Him,
62– 9 and there is *n·* beside good.
Pul. 16–22 No, It has *n·*,
Rud. 9–26 there can be *n·* beside Him ;
13–15 *n·* else beside Him." — *Deut.* 4 : 35.
16– 8 *N·* with an imperfect sense of
No. 16–13 for there is *n·* beside God
17–20 "*n·* beside Him." — see *Deut.* 4 : 35.
24–28 As there is *n·* beside Him,
28–13 then to-day is *n·* too soon for
37–22 God, and *n·* beside Him ;
'01. 7– 2 than whom there is *n·* other.
8–21 makes man *n·* too transcendental,
18–13 and taught his disciples *n·* other.
24–25 Jesus' teachings, and *n·* other,
28– 9 perhaps *n·* lived a more devout
'02. 13–12 and desire *n·* other.
Hea. 4–24 God must be our model, or we have *n·* ;
Po. 2–11 and paralleled by *n·*,
35–11 whereunto *n·* reply,
76–21 No, It has *n·*,
78– 9 whose destiny *n·* may outrun ;
My. 10–16 * probable that *n·* will be made
78–16 * and *n·* proffering small change.
96– 6 * *n·* of them afflicted with
152–17 good, than which there is *n·* else
200– 7 and *n·* can stay His hand or say,
228–13 *n·* greater had been born of women,
229– 1 call *n·* but genuine . . . Scientists,
235–27 of birthdays, since there are *n·*
261–24 understood by few — or by *n·*
276–23 politics?" I have *n·*, in reality,
280–20 *n·* can stay His hand nor say
338–27 whose sandals *n·* may unloose.
339– 1 charitable towards all, and hating *n·*.

None good but one
My. 359–18 * under the heading "*N· g· b· o·*,"

nonentities
Un. 59– 4 if the evils . . . are *n·*

nonentity
'01. 13– 3 sin, is another *n·*

non-existent
Mis. 259–26 error, or evil, is really *n·*,
Un. 45–27 until it becomes *n·*.
Rud. 5–27 must either become *n·*, or
My. 346– 8 * and declaring Mrs. Eddy *n·*

non-intelligence
Mis. 49–25 *n·*, sin, and death.
Un. 34– 3 declares . . . that *n·* governs.
Rud. 5–14 or intelligence in *n·*?

non-intelligent
Mis. 256–24 is inert, inanimate, and *n·*.
267–24 *matter, or n· evil,*
My. 179– 9 enters *n·* dust

non-resistants
'01. 30–10 Scientists are practically *n·* ;

nonsense
Mis. 230–20 into the ditch of *n·*,
Un. 16– 4 *would* they be sheer *n·*, if
'01. 19–15 egregious *n·* — a flat departure

nook
Ret. 7–12 * explored their every *n·* and corner,

noon
Mis. 276–25   burning at the *n·* of night,
   385– 4   * And one eternal *n·*.''
Pul. 42– 4   * and at *n·* still another.
   77–17   * twentieth day of . . . at high *n·*.
   78–15   * 20th day of . . . at high *n·*.
Po. 37– 4   * And one eternal *n·*.''
My. 38–16   * It was ''children's day'' at *n·*,
   82–21   * for at *n·* to-day [June 14]

noonday (*see also* **noonday's**)
Mis. 157–25   judgment as the *n·*.''— *Psal.* 37 : 6.
   392– 9   her *n·* glories crown?
'01. 35– 3   judgment as the *n·*.''— *Psal.* 37 : 6.
Po. 20–12   her *n·* glories crown
My. 170–26   judgment as the *n·*.''— *Psal.* 37 : 6.
   190– 5   morning beams and *n·* glory

noonday's
Po. 3– 4   *n·* length'ning shadows flee,

noons
My. 147– 8   my childhood's Sunday *n·*.

noontide
Mis. 325–14   its inmates asleep at *n·* !

Norcross
Lanson P.
Pul. 44–14   * signature
Rev. Lanson P.
Mis. 313–16   New Pastor,'' by Rev. Lanson P. *N·*,
Rev. L. P.
Pul. 29– 3   * Rev. D. A. Easton and Rev. L. P. *N·*,
Rev. Mr.
Mis. 149–20   your beloved pastor, Rev. Mr. *N·*,
   150– 6   and then send it to Rev. Mr. *N·*,

Norfolk **(Neb.)** *Tribune*
My. 79– 5   *[N· (N·.) T·]*

Normal
Mis. 143–19   the *N·* class graduates of my
   264–13   Many students enter the *N·* class
   273–30   one Primary and two *N·*
Man. 37–16   Pupils of *N·* Students.
   37–17   One *N·* student cannot recommend
   37–18   the pupil of another *N·* student,
   84–11   *N·* class not exceeding thirty
   86–17   teachers of the *N·* class
   89–11   *N·* Teachers.
   90– 1   eligible to enter the *N·* class.
   90–19   given to each *N·* class
   91–22   may enter the *N·* class
Ret. 43–16   taught the Primary, *N·*, and
   47–17   a *N·* class student who partakes
My. 251– 8   * Primary and *N·* class instruction
   251–13   eligible to enter the *N·* class,
   323–31   * *N·* class in the fall of 1887

normal
Mis. 17–25   *n·* or abnormal material conditions
   41–26   *n·* manifestation of man in Science.
   52–15   To be *n·*, it must be a union of
   104–13   According to C. S., perfection is *n·*,
   200– 3   Jesus regarded good as the *n·* state
   350–24   Hence it prevents the *n·* action,
Ret. 13–23   in a *n·* condition of health.
No. 2– 6   To aver that disease is *n·*,
   5–23   a *n·* and real condition of man,
'00. 4– 3   as real and *n·* as the one
My. 218– 1   its *n·* action, functions, and

Normal Course
Man. 36– 7   the Primary or *N· C·*
   85–15   or has taken a *N· C·* at the

North (*see also* **North's**)
Ret. 19–22   on her sad journey to the *N·*.
My. 304–12   best magazines in the South and *N·*.
   329–28   * her life in *N·* and South Carolina
   331– 2   on her sad journey to the *N·*.
   333–18   * never . . . were carried *N·*.
   336– 6   * to take her back to the *N·*.

north
My. 63–28   * from the *n·*, and from the— *Psal.* 107 : 3.

North America
Pul. 75–21   * members . . . all over *N· A·*

North Carolina and **N. C.**
My. 327– 1   noble Southrons of *N· C·*
   327– 5   in the Legislature of *N· C·*,
   327–13   * Christian Scientists in *N· C·*.
   329– 5   * General Assembly of *N· C·*
   (*see also* **Asheville, Newbern, Raleigh, Wilmington**)

northeast
Mis. 144– 4   tower on the *n·* corner

Northern
My. 326– 9   * in the Southern and *N·* States

northern
Ret. 20–10   *n·* part of New Hampshire.
No. 14–14   coruscations of the *n·* sky

North Groton
N. H.
My. 311– 4   at his country home in *N· G·*, N. H.,

—

My. 314– 6   * from Tilton to *N· G·*
   314–10   He bought a place in *N· G·*,

North's
'02. 3– 8   the *N·* half-hostility to the South,

North State Street
My. 147– 6   grand old elm on *N· S· S·*
   171–24   * came to a standstill on *N· S· S·*,
   175–20   to macadamize *N· S· S·*

northward
'00. 12–13   its gates, . . . led *n·* and southward.

Norway
'02. 13–17   Falmouth and Caledonia (now *N·*)

Norway and Falmouth Streets
Pul. 24– 8   * intersection of *N· and F· S·*,
   40–19   * in Boston at *N· and F· S·*
   56–26   * located at *N· and F· S·*,

Norway, and St. Paul Streets
My. 65–20   * Falmouth, *N·, and St. P· S·*,

nose
Mis. 239–18   red *n·*, suffused eyes, cough, and

nostrils
Peo. 4–10   enter finite man through his *n·*,

nostrums
Mis. 134–21   with poisons, *n·*, and knives,

Nota Bene
My. 139– 1   chapter sub-title
   236– 4   chapter sub-title

notable
Mis. 49–13   *n·* cases of insanity
Pul. 1– 9   *n·* for good and evil.
   55–10   * *n·* for her emancipation from many
   79– 7   * dedication day, is a *n·* event.
'00. 6–16   This *n·* fact proves that the
My. 67–12   * *N· Dates in C. S.*
   77–10   * *n·* feature in the life of their cult.
   84–24   * Its hold and . . . are most *n·*.
   84–28   * is *n·* in many ways.
   86–24   * the most *n·* of such occasions.

notary public
My. 329–18   * by the certificate of a *n· p·*

note
Mis. 72–21   *imply that Spirit takes n· of*
   130–14   *N·* the Scripture on this
   158–27   It is satisfactory to *n·*,
   100–19   *N·* this, only such as are pure
   253– 1   *N·* the scope of that saying,
   296–20   *n·* or foster a feminine ambition
Ret. 80– 9   *N·* well the falsity of this mortal
Pul. vii–15   *n·* the impetus thereby given
   31–20   * To a *n·* which I wrote her,
   54–28   *N·* :— About 1868, the author
Rud. 10– 2   *N·* this, that if you have power in
'00. 5– 6   *n·* the words of our Master
   14–12   *N·* his inspired rebuke to all the
'02. 13–19   the *n·* therewith became due,
Po. vi–10   * *A n· from the author*,
   34–11   Or sing thy love-lorn *n·*
My. 172–25   * enclosed *n·* from Mrs. Eddy was read :
   173–12   a *n·*, sent at the last moment,
   256– 6   strict observance or *n·* well.
   266–25   *N·*, if you please, that many
   272–20   * EDITOR'S *N·*.
   297–28   to read or to *n·* from others' reading

noted
Mis. 295– 3   *n·* English leader, whom he quotes
   299–31   the property of a *n·* firm,
Ret. 7–17   * *n·* for his boldness and firmness,
Mv. 94–17   * were *n·* in the recent dedication

notes
Mis. 158– 7   insisted on your speaking without *n·*,
   158–16   command, to drop the use of *n·*,
   158–30   no record that he used *n·* when
Ret. 27– 5   If these *n·* and comments,
Pul. 60–22   * C. C. C. to C. 4, 61 *n·* ;
No. 3–18   Nemesis of the . . . *n·* this hour.
Hea. 20– 7   * In *n·* almost divine.''
My. 114–14   began with *n·* on the Scriptures.
   114–19   not write these *n·* after sunset.
   256– 3   to improvise some new *n·*,

noteworthy
Ret. 13– 4   some circumstances are *n·*.
My. 330– 3   * a *n·* follower of our Lord

nothing
absolutely
My. 104–23   of which a man knows absolutely *n·* ?

nothing

alias
  No. 32–17 A lie is negation, — *alias n·*,
and something
  Mis. 86–11 *N·* and *something* are words which
antagonistic
  My. 87–28 * *n·* antagonistic to it in this
apart
  Mis. 364–19 *n·* apart from this Mind,
appears
  Mis. 105–24 *N·* appears to the physical senses but
apprehends
  Un. 40–27 apprehends *n·* strictly belonging to
beholds
  Un. 41– 1 beholds *n·* but mortality,
beside
  Ret. 60– 7 that there is *n·* beside God ;
     60–19 there is *n·* beside Him ;"
  Un. 21–16 because there is *n·* beside Him
beyond Himself
  Mis. 367–20 knows *n·* beyond Himself
but a conspiracy
  Ret. 63–16 *evil*, is *n·* but a conspiracy against
but an outline
  Rud. 8–10 *n·* but an outline of the practice.
but good
  Mis. 367–18 He knows *n·* but good ;
but materialism
  Peo. 4– 2 has given . . . *n·* but materialism,
but sin
  Rud. 10–18 Love punishes *n·* but sin,
but Spirit
  Un. 34–12 there is *n·* but Spirit ;
can be added
  My. 210– 4 *n·* can be added to the
can be clearer
  Un. 25– 4 *n·* can be clearer than the
can compete
  Ret. 31– 2 *N·* can compete with C. S.,
can dispossess you
  Pul. 3– 8 *n·* can dispossess you of this
can do
  Hea. 12– 6 self-evident it can do *n·*,
can exceed
  My. 208–16 than which *n·* can exceed
can substitute
  Man. 92– 6 and *n·* can substitute this
circulates
  Mis. 126–23 yet *n·* circulates so rapidly :
conditional
  My. 260–12 *N·* conditional or material
contrary
  Man. 86–22 shall teach *n·* contrary thereto.
could save
  My. 335–28 * *n·* could save the life of
count as
  Mis. 281–20 we must count as *n·*,
covered
  '01. 10– 7 *n·* covered, that shall not — *Matt.* 10 : 26.
dethrones
  My. 193–16 *N·* dethrones His house.
doing
  Mis. 230– 5 doing *n·*, and indecision as to
else
  Mis. 102–12 like Himself and like *n·* else.
     199–15 illustrate . . . as *n·* else can ;
  Ret. 28–23 and that *n·* else could.
  Un. 7–21 confers a power *n·* else can.
     49–11 are *good*, and *n·* else.
  Pul. 35–22 and that *n·* else could.
  Rud. 11–15 of harmony and of *n·* else.
  No. 12–22 in *n·* else has she departed
     30–23 revealing Him and *n·* else.
  '00. 4–27 they reflect God and *n·* else.
  '01. 15–30 * *n·* else that is to be given as
  '02. 17–25 satisfies . . . and *n·* else can.
  My. 15–25 * As *n·* else can do.
     146–30 eternal, and *n·* else.
evil
  Mis. 72– 1 *n·* evil, or unlike Himself.
  Rud. 10– 7 divides His power with *n·* evil
except sin
  Ret. 81– 4 *N·* except sin, in the students
found
  My. 103–22 have found *n·* in ancient or
further
  My. 319– 5 I heard *n·* further from him
gain
  Mis. 227– 1 by which he can gain *n·*.
giving birth to
  '01. 30–13 giving birth to *n·* and death to
good for
  Hea. 7– 1 "that which is good for *n·*,
has been lost
  Mis. 149–12 and see that *n·* has been lost.

nothing

has occurred
  My. 298– 3 *n·* has occurred in my life's
have to pray
  Mis. vii–16 And *n·* have to pray :
have we gained
  Mis. vii–15 *N·* have we gained therefrom,
here
  Mis. vii–12 There's *n·* here to trust.
in Christ
  Mis. 155– 4 this world that has *n·* in Christ.
  My. 4–25 this world that hath *n·* in Christ.
in this room
  My. 353–24 *n·* in this room now of any
is gained
  Mis. 298– 2 *N·* is gained by wrong-doing.
  My. 278–22 *N·* is gained by fighting,
is hid
  Mis. 348–11 "*N·* is hid — *Matt.* 10 : 26.
is left
  Pul. 47–29 * *n·* is left excepting the angles
  No. 30– 5 until *n·* is left to be forgiven,
  '02. 7–14 *n·* is left to consciousness but
is lost
  Mis. 111–13 *N·* is lost that God gives :
is more fatal
  Mis. 93–28 *N·* is more fatal than to indulge a
is worthy
  My. 258– 4 *N·* is worthy the name of
left
  '01. 10–26 shall be *n·* left to perish
less
  Mis. 283–16 *n·* less than a mistaken kindness,
  Ret. 34– 4 *N·* less could solve the
  My. 22–22 * *n·* less than God-bestowed.
     259–20 *n·* less is man or woman.
madness and
  My. 14– 7 not a madness and *n·*,
melt into
  Peo. 10– 6 become vague, and melt into *n·*
more
  Mis. 58–27 "mind-cure," *n·* more nor less,
     136– 4 Rumors are rumors, — *n·* more.
  Man. 64–20 meant *n·* more than a tender term
  Pul. 74–16 I claim *n·* more than what
  '01. 23–30 * nature being *n·* more than
  My. 70–22 * *n·* more wonderful than the organ
much ado about
  Hea. 14– 3 in fine, much ado about *n·*.
new
  My. 203– 3 I have *n·* new to communicate ;
     228– 2 there is *n·* new on this score.
nobody and
  Mis. 108–14 proper denominator, — nobody and *n·*.
out of
  Mis. 362–16 out of *n·* would create something,
outside
  Un. 3–26 can be *n·* outside of Himself.
     20–21 He can see *n·* outside of
profiteth
  My. 108– 9 flesh profiteth *n·*." — *John* 6 : 63.
promises
  My. 93–12 * promises *n·* in the way of
receive
  Mis. 342–26 and receive *n·* in return ;
risks
  Mis. 211–23 He risks *n·* who obeys the law of God,
saying
  My. 210–21 saying *n·*, in particular,
sees
  Mis. 173– 4 sees *n·* but a law of matter.
settled
  Pul. 51–10 * There is really *n·* settled.
short
  Mis. 224–28 *N·* short of our own errors should
     288–24 *n·* short of self-seeking ;
sin can do
  Mis. 93–18 Sin can do *n·* :
stops it
  Mis. 44–13 *and n· stops it until*
take
  Mis. 327– 6 take *n·* of thine own with thee?"
talking
  Mis. 230– 5 time is consumed in talking *n·*,
that is material
  Mis. 165–13 leaves *n·* that is material ;
that is wrong
  Mis. 240–25 teach them *n·* that is wrong.
that worketh
  Mis. 366–13 *n·* that worketh or maketh a lie
  No. 15–26 *N·* that "worketh — *Rev.* 21 : 27.
  My. 348–31 *n·* that worketh ill can enter
thinking of
  Mis. 230–10 thinking of *n·* or planning for

nothing

to do
Mis. 147-20 to do n· but what is honorable,
175-24 has n· to do with the Science of
My. 307- 8 had n· to do with matter,
to fear
Mis. 113-25 n· to fear when Love is at the helm
to mourn
Mis. 353- 1 in the sense that it has n· to mourn
to say
Mis. 230-18 talking when they have n· to say,
Pul. 41-18 * to say n· of . . . local believers.
79-13 * to say n· of cities
unlike
Mis. 366-13 He is in n· unlike Himself ;
Un. 35-25 can form n· unlike itself, Spirit,
'02. 6-30 producing n· unlike Himself,
unlovely
'02. 6-30 Love, including n· unlovely,
will be lost
My. 40-11 * N· will be lost, however,
would remain
Un. 34-23 N· would remain to be seen
written
My. 179-26 being contingent on n· written
you pay
Mis. 301- 2 sermon for which you pay n·,

———

Mis. 5-16 There is n· to build upon.
15- 8 N· aside from the spiritualization
26-22 What can be more than All? N· :
26-23 just what I call matter, n·.
27- 1 What . . . besides infinity? N· !
27- 2 Science of good calls evil n·.
42-30 n· but our own false admissions
71-25 n· can be formed apart from God,
72-24 shows that n· which is material is
86- 9 n· and exist only in imagination
87- 4 and label beauty n·,
108-10 spiritually, literally, it is n·.
122-28 for hate, or the hater, is n· :
169-22 makes them n· valuable,
174-18 n· that maketh or worketh a lie.
192-27 N· can be more conclusive
240-27 that n· but a loathsome worm
280-11 there is n· in the opposite scale.
334-17 You must find error to be n· :
Ret. 8- 8 " N·, child ! What do you mean?"
63-15 Its opposite, n·, named evil,
Un. 13- 8 principle of music knows n· of
42- 5 can be n· except the results of
54 4 it is n· but a false claim.
No. 15-25 in n· is He unlike Himself.
17-22 these two words all and n·,
32-26 evil to its lowest terms, n·,
Pan. 5-22 not believe that a lie, n·, can
10- 4 when he is n·.— Gal. 6 · 3.
'01. 13- 8 an illusion, n·,
13- 8 assumption that n· is something.
13-14 sin, is a lie— therefore is n·
15-23 * "It is n· but God's mere pleasure
27-10 n· has since appeared that is
My. 84- 2 * N· is more of a drag on a church
92-28 * due apparently to n· save
93- 7 * n· in them to attract
107-27 n· beyond illimitable divinity.
108-17 n· in the divine Mind to attenuate.
193-16 Love gives n· to take away.
197- 4 Attempt n· without God's help.
223-17 of which I know n·.
267- 3 N· can be correct . . . which
321-17 * n· in the circumstances which
334-17 * N· could be further from her meaning
354- 5 n· but what is published or sold by

nothingness

abyss of
Un. 60- 9 from the dark abyss of n·,
basis of
'01. 13-16 on the very basis of n·.
error and
Mis. 201-13 error and n· of supposed life
fact of its
Mis. 93-25 not test sin and the fact of its n·,
father of
'01. 13-15 and the father of n·.
highest degree of
Mis. 334-20 lie of the highest degree of n· :
is thus proven
No. 17- 5 Their n· is thus proven ;
its
Mis. 109-16 blest by reason of its n· ;
335-22 by asserting its n·,
Un. 61-13 the apprehension of its n·,
its own
No. 13- 2 rebukes sin with its own n·,

nothingness

mortal
My. 245-18 dire din of mortal n·,
native
Mis. 70-23 dissolve into its native n· ;
109-15 reduced to their native n· !
of any other
No. 38-22 n· of any other state or stage
of error
Pul. 13- 9 by which the n· of error is seen ;
13-10 n· of error is in proportion to
of every claim
Un. 8-20 n· of every claim of error,
of evil
Mis. 108- 8 powerlessness— yea, n· — of evil :
109-27 must discern the n· of evil,
176-11 a little more of the n· of evil,
Ret. 55- 6 brings out the n· of evil
of hate
No. 35-12 allness of Love and the n· of hate.
of matter
Mis. 176-19 and the n· of matter.
194-18 and the n· of matter.
253-10 amends for the n· of matter
279-19 to find out the n· of matter ;
Man. 16- 8 and the n· of matter.
Ret. 26-27 yet more of the n· of matter
'01. 12-24 therefore the n· of matter.
of sickness
Mis. 64- 6 n· of sickness, sin, and death,
of the dream
Mis. 49-24 recognition of the n· of the dream,
of wrong
Mis. 267- 3 consciousness of the n· of wrong
simply
Ret. 64-13 sinner and . . . are alike simply n· ;
to nothingness
No. 26-28 dust . . . to dust, n· to nothingness.
utter
Mis. 114-29 evil, — even its utter n·.

Mis. 145-20 their modest sign be n·.
286-23 phenomena of mortality, n·,
333- 7 a palpable falsity, yea, n· ;
363- 9 vanity with n·, dust with dust !
Ret. 61-15 you are darkness, n·.

notice

Mis. 226-27 cannot stoop to n·, except legally,
242- 4 came not to my n· until January
256-18 send to each applicant a n·
302-23 no elect and give suitable n·,
303-20 chapter sub-title
303-22 giving place . . . to the following n·
331- 8 gave n· through his counsel
Man. 37- 7 N· of Rejection.
37-11 shall send to the applicant a n· of
Ret. 8-17 though I had ceased to n· it.
Po. 18-15 n· the frail fledgling hath.
My. 36 19 The enclosed n· I submit to you,
26-23 and this n· is requisite
27- 1 chapter sub-title
27-10 * chapter sub-title
58- 3 * The fact that a n· was published
72-17 * the n· which Stephen A. Chase,
73- 2 * to issue a similar n· or order,
87-11 * one does not n· these unless
173- 9 given n· that no preparations would be
236-23 chapter sub-title
237- 4 chapter sub-title
237-12 chapter sub-title
237-20 chapter sub-title
242-15 chapter sub-title
250-13 please send . . . n· of their action.
329-14 * the n· of her husband's death
351-22 chapter sub-title
358-29 chapter sub-title

noticeable

Mis. 6-25 n· fact, that in families where
My. 82-29 * not be n· to the residents of

noticed

My. 61-21 * I n· that as soon as the workmen
307-10 I n· he used that word,

notices

Mis. 308-20 scientific n· of my book.
314-11 give out any n· from the pulpit,
Man. 32-22 shall read all n· and remarks
55- 2 shall not report nor send n·
Ret. 40-22 n· for a second lecture pulled down,
Pul. 60- 5 * no address of any sort, no n·,
79-14 * n· of C. S. meetings.
My. 32-21 * Reading of n·.
76- 3 * n· that more money was needed

noticing

Mis. 169- 2 n·, all along the way

notification
　　Mis. 306-14 　* as a *n·* of the same,
notified
　　Man. 39-17 　twice *n·* of his excommunication,
　　　68- 4 　duty of the member thus *n·*
　　　109-18 　the applicant will be *n·,*
　　My. 27-13 　* *n·* that sufficient funds
notifies
　　Mis. 285-25 　coolly *n·* the public
notify
　　Mis. 322- 8 　*n·* the Directors when I shall be
　　Man. 28-20 　call a meeting and *n·* this officer
　　　68- 1 　*n·* a person who has been
　　　100-17 　may *n·* any Church of Christ,
　　My. 223- 2 　I hereby *n·* the public that
noting
　　Ret. 44-17 　*n·* the church's need,
notion
　　Mis. 62-30 　"mind-cure" rests on the *n·* that
　　　218-21 　the *n·* . . . is more ridiculous than
　　　256-26 　*n·* that Mind can be in matter
　　　271- 7 　keep out of their heads the *n·*
　　　280-13 　We must get rid of that *n·.*
　　　291- 3 　*n·* that a mind governed by
　　　335-21 　*n·* that one is covering iniquity
　　Ret. 57-20 　*n·* of more than one Mind,
　　Un. 49-27 　This *n·* of the destructibility of
　　No. 20-15 　*n·* of an everywhere-present body
　　Pan. 10- 9 　*n·* that C. S. lessens man's
　　'01. 19-12 　*n·* that mixing material and
　　My. 91- 5 　* It affords refutation of the *n·*
　　　210-19 　individuals entertain the *n·*
notions
　　Pul. 6-12 　thinking she caught her *n·* from
　　No. 15-12 　*n·* of personality to be found in
notoriety
　　Mis. 295-11 　* passion for some manner of *n·."*
　　　296-26 　from a desire for *n·*
　　My. 130-10 　students seeking only public *n·,*
notwithstanding
　　Mis. 236-25 　*n·* one's good intentions,
　　　307-12 　*N·* the rapid sale already
　　　349-16 　*n·* my objection, he should do as
　　Pul. 8- 6 　*N·* the perplexed condition
　　　84-16 　* prognostications to the contrary *n·.*
　　My. 11- 1 　* *N·* the fact that as Christian
　　　56-16 　* *n·* the relief that the
　　　67-27 　* *N·* its enormous size,
　　　230- 1 　*N·* the sacrilegious moth of time,
　　　236- 8 　*amende honorable* — *n·* "incompetence"
　　　311-29 　*N·* that *McClure's Magazine* says,
noumenon
　　Mis. 23-19 　God is both *n·* and phenomena,
　　　74- 2 　*n·* and phenomenon understood,
　　　216-28 　* *phenomenon without a n·*
　　　362-17 　whose *n·* is mortal mind,
　　Ret. 22- 4 　spiritual *n·* and phenomenon
　　No. 19-23 　*n·* or the phenomena of Spirit ;
　　Pan. 12-23 　Principle, *n·* and phenomena,
　　My. 180-32 　defines *n·* and phenomena
　　　287- 9 　Love is the *n·* and phenomenon,
　　　347-26 　Principle whose *n·* is God
　　　350- 4 　To begin with the divine *n·,* Mind,
noun
　　My. 226- 1 　not be written or used as a common *n·*
nourish
　　Mis. 16- 1 　These *n·* the hungry hope,
　　Pul. 63- 8 　has the strength to *n·* trees
nourished
　　My. 177-20 　nurtured and *n·* this church
novel
　　Mis. 139-24 　in a circuitous, *n·* way,
　　　252-15 　My proof of these *n·* propositions
　　Pul. 40-11 　* *N·* METHOD OF ENABLING
　　　59- 3 　* in a somewhat *n·* way.
novelty
　　Pul. 50-21 　* who have worn off the *n·*
　　　62- 2 　* something of a *n·* in this country,
　　My. 74-31 　* and the other for its *n·.*
　　　77- 2 　* and the *n·* of the cult
November
　　(*see* **months**)
novices
　　Rud. 16-12 　some *n·,* in the truth of Science,
now
　　Mis. ix- 7 　*N·,* Christian Scientists are not indigent ;
　　　ix-11 　*n·* rejuvenated by the touch
　　　ix-13 　*n·* hope sits dove-like.
　　　x-15 　difference between then and *n·,*
　　　13- 9 　This law I *n·* urge upon the

now
　　Mis. 16-27 　*N·,* dear reader, pause for a moment
　　　21- 8 　C. S. *n·* bears testimony.
　　　30-15 　recognized here and *n·.*
　　　37-26 　She *n·* does not.
　　　59-19 　"Come *n·,* and let us — *Isa.* 1 : 18.
　　　69-30 　*N·* comes the question :
　　　76-20 　*N·,* exchange the term *soul* for *sense*
　　　76-26 　*N·* if Soul sinned, it would die ;
　　　80-28 　*n·* elbowed by a new school
　　　81-19 　*N·, if all this be a fair*
　　　86- 7 　beautiful to my gaze *n·*
　　　87-10 　I *n·* through you discern dimly ;
　　　91-10 　"Suffer it to be so *n·."* — *Matt.* 3 : 15.
　　　101-11 　*N·* cometh a third struggle ;
　　　134- 3 　And *n·,* dear sir, as you have
　　　137-17 　*N·,* dear ones, if you take my advice
　　　137-29 　can *n·* organize their students
　　　139-19 　*n·* valued at $20,000
　　　140-23 　*n·* it must be put back into
　　　150-18 　houses and halls can *n·* be obtained
　　　158- 9 　But *n·,* after His messenger
　　　158-13 　meaning of it all, as *n·* shown,
　　　158-25 　you will find . . . (as I *n·* think)
　　　174-29 　facts of man's Life here and *n·.*
　　　186-18 　*N·* let us not lose this Science
　　　188- 3 　Man is as perfect *n·,*
　　　188-13 　*n·* no condemnation — *Rom.* 8 : 1.
　　　193-21 　which the people are *n·* adopting.
　　　208-22 　but *n·* have I kept — *Psal.* 119 : 67.
　　　216-11 　*N·,* Phare Pleigh evidently means
　　　219- 7 　*N·,* what saith the Scripture?
　　　220- 1 　*N·,* demonstrate this rule,
　　　220-18 　is *n·* the diametrical opposite
　　　222-24 　Its mystery protects it *n·,*
　　　231-21 　*N· !* baby has tumbled,
　　　237-17 　few feel and live *n·* as when
　　　238- 4 　It is pleasant, *n·,* to contrast
　　　245-17 　The conclusion cannot *n·* be pushed,
　　　247- 9 　*n·* I calmly challenge the world,
　　　253- 8 　speakers that will *n·* address you
　　　262- 6 　*n·* entering upon its fifth volume,
　　　273- 6 　I *n·* seem to be most needed,
　　　273- 9 　my labors with them as *n·,*
　　　281- 9 　I have *n·* one ambition
　　　284-20 　must *n·* be dealt with as evil,
　　　286-19 　The time cometh, and *n·* is,
　　　295-32 　*N·,* I am a Christian Scientist,
　　　311-19 　As I *n·* understand C. S.
　　　317-23 　thou knowest not *n·* ; — *John* 13 : 7.
　　　321-13 　cometh, and *n·* is, — *John* 4 : 23.
　　　329-26 　*n·* chirps to the breeze ;
　　　330-13 　consciousness thereof is here and *n·*
　　　340- 6 　the time to work, is *n·.*
　　　347-20 　I see the way *n·.*
　　　353-25 　*N·* turn from the metaphor of the
　　　356-19 　*N·* let my faithful students
　　　359-11 　*n·* we see through a — *I Cor.* 13 : 12.
　　　380-23 　"Suffer it to be so *n·."* — *Matt.* 3 : 15.
　　　384- 6 　Come Thou ! and *n·,* anew,
　　　385-19 　*N·* see thy ever-self ;
　　　386-23 　sad marble to our memory *n·,*
　　　393-13 　Students wise, he maketh *n·*
　　Man. 75-11 　she *n·* understands the financial
　　Chr. 53-37 　faith's pale star *n·* blends
　　　53-42 　Are here, and *n·*
　　　55- 6 　coming, and *n·* is, — *John* 5 : 25.
　　Ret. 4-16 　*n·* the lone night-bird cries,
　　　4-21 　*n·* the scrub-oak, poplar, and fern
　　　9-25 　* *N·* hath redeemed her birthright
　　　13-16 　of these things he *n·* spoke,
　　　16- 9 　*n·,* oh, thank God, she is healed !"
　　　23- 8 　*n·* it was not even fringed with light.
　　　37-12 　*n·* declare Bishop Berkeley, David Hume,
　　　48-27 　"Suffer it to be so *n·,"* — *Matt.* 3 : 15.
　　　53- 2 　The C. S. *Journal,* as it was *n·* called,
　　Un. 3-27 　*N·* this self-same God is our
　　　6-10 　as *n·* presented to the people
　　　7-15 　People are *n·* living who can
　　　8- 1 　another query *n·* be considered,
　　　23- 5 　*N·* God has no bastards
　　　26-17 　*N·* if it be true that
　　　33- 5 　*N·* these senses, being material,
　　　37- 9 　They are *n·* and here ;
　　　37-20 　Existing here and *n·,*
　　　42-13 　is as perfect and immortal *n·,* as
　　　43- 8 　*n·* believe in the possibility that **Life**
　　　53- 1 　*N·* a lie takes its pattern from
　　　55-22 　*N·* and here shall I behold God,
　　　61-20 　life which I *n·* live — *Gal.* 2 : 20.
　　Pul. 7-14 　God has *n·* unsealed their
　　　12- 6 　*N·* is come salvation, — *Rev.* 12 : 10.
　　　12-19 　*n·* rises clearer and nearer to the
　　　30- 8 　* church numbers *n·* four thousand
　　　30-24 　* *n·* exceeds two hundred thousand
　　　30-28 　* has *n·* its own magnificent church

now

Pul. 36– 9 * at the class lectures n· and then,
36–25 * n· occupied by Judge and Mrs. Hanna,
38– 8 * n· in its ninety-first edition.
49–17 almost as big as they are n·,
55–25 * n· over four thousand members.
58– 9 * have n· erected this edifice
59–22 * and n· the business manager
63–13 almost as big as they are n·,
66– 7 * n· there are societies in every
68– 2 * n· known as the Rev. Mary Baker Eddy.
68– 7 * and many are n· pastors
68–10 * She n· lives in a beautiful
68–17 * n· holds regular services in the
71–21 * are n· so entirely devoted.
83–17 * look n· to their daughters to
84–23 * It is enough for us n· to know
85– 5 * Those who n·, in part, understand
87–20 more of earth n·, than I desire,

No. 7–20 must n· fight their own battles.
9–19 I n· point steadfastly to the power
25– 4 n· we are delivered — Rom. 7 : 6.
27–14 it is just as veritable n· as it
28–10 n· is the most acceptable time
34–10 hour cometh, and n· is,— John 4 : 23
35–22 one with Him n· and forever.
41–21 n· the Church seems almost
46– 3 The question n· at issue is:

'00. 3– 1 N·, what saith C. S.?
12–26 The entire city is n· in ruins.

'01. 2– 1 is n· what Christ Jesus taught
7–24 n· claim to believe in and worship
9–26 n·, as aforetime — they cast out evils
13–18 N·, destroy the conception of sin
16–22 if n· it is permitted license,
18– 5 less n· than were the sneers
21–10 * are n· taught in C. S."
31– 9 truths . . . that n· seem troublesome.
33 27 the same reviling . . . it receives n·,

'02. 3– 6 regarded n· more as a philosophy
3–19 n·, British and Boer may prosper
12– 6 n· and forever, here and everywhere.
13–17 Caledonia (n· Norway)
13–27 n· valued at twenty thousand
18– 6 mortals looked ignorantly, as n·,

Hea. 5– 9 saying, . . . God will punish him n·
9– 1 more than we are n· doing,
9– 1 faster than we are n· progressing.

Peo. 6–11 * less mortality than n· obtains."
6–24 "acquaint n· thyself — Job 22 : 21.

Po. 30– 5 Come Thou ! and n·, anew,
48–13 N· see thy ever-self ;
50– 9 sad marble to our memory n·,
51–19 Students wise, he maketh n·
77–16 what Thou doest n·
78– 8 the Union n· is one,

My. vi–15 * always has been and is n· its guide,
8–13 * "N· I am sure that I have but
9–25 I never before felt . . . but I do n·,
10– 8 * should n· manifest itself in a
10–13 * but the time is at hand, n·,
10–29 * n· necessitates this onward step.
12–16 chapter sub-title
12–17 n· is the accepted time."— II Cor. 6 : 2.
12–21 we possess only n·.
12–21 If the reliable n· is carelessly lost
12–23 which cannot be done n·,
12 25 while that which can be done n·,
12–27 supplies the ever-present help and n·,
13– 1 good . . . they insist upon doing n·.
14– 1 In the n· they brought their
15–15 all that you are able to bear n·,
26–20 N· is the time to throttle the lie
36–17 * and n· with blessed accord
40– 5 * sure that n· the branch churches
45–23 * we n· discern the fulfilment
47–20 * well-earned joy that is with us n·.
51– 5 * n· interested in said church,
53– 6 * This book has n· reached its
55–12 * The Mother Church n· stands.
59–29 * N· my testimony is not needed.
60–25 * N· that the . . . dedication of
64–22 * and n· it is ours to address
66– 8 * n· comes the purchase of the
72– 9 * more frequented by . . . than it is n·.
74– 3 * From n· until Saturday night
76–31 * structure, which is n· completed,
86– 5 * so will it n· find pleasure in
88– 5 * C. S., as n· before this continent,
93–28 * n· being held in Boston
97– 2 * The best physicians n· admit
109–17 "But n· mine eye — Job 42 : 5.
110– 2 a dispensation n· ended,
111– 9 n· assumed by many doctors
113–11 n· no condemnation — Rom. 8 : 1.
122– 9 N· I am done with homilies

now

My. 123–18 n· about twenty thousand dollars.
124–27 N· what have you learned?
131–26 prove me n· herewith,— Mal. 3 : 10.
132– 3 "Prove me n· herewith,— Mal. 3 : 10.
140–21 "Suffer it to be so n·,"— Matt. 3 : 15.
146–11 may then be even younger than n·."
147– 8 And n·, at this distant day,
148– 2 n·, through the providence of God,
151–29 idolatry then and is idolatry n·.
153– 4 N·, if these kind hearts will only
155– 3 is effective here and n·.
162– 4 "Suffer it to be so n· :— Matt. 3 : 15.
164–15 N· [1904] six dear churches
176– 6 and n· illustrate the past by your
177–13 even younger and nearer . . . than n·,
187–11 "N· the end of the— I Tim. 1 : 5.
188– 5 "N· mine eyes shall be open,— II Chron. 7 : 15.
201– 7 are enthroned n· and forever.
202– 6 N· may his salvation draw near,
205– 1 n· no condemnation— Rom. 8 : 1.
206–31 but n· are ye light— Eph. 5 : 8.
216–31 you should begin n· to earn
218– 3 "Suffer it to be so n· :— Matt. 3 : 15.
221– 4 precludes Jesus' doctrine, n· as then,
223–28 Just n· divine Love and wisdom
224–30 n· let us adopt the classic saying,
240–15 I n· repeat another proof,
245– 3 N· the wide demand for this
246–25 thou knowest not n· ;— John 13 : 7.
250–22 But if n· is not the time,
251– 3 thou knowest not n· ;— John 13 : 7.
266–26 are n· agitated, modified, and
269–26 "Prove me n· herewith,— Mal. 3 : 10.
273–11 and n· am old ;— Psal. 37 : 25.
280–16 I n· request that the members
285–24 whereof they n· accuse me.
294–28 has n· passed through the shadow of
297– 1 N· if Miss Barton were not
297–20 is here n· as veritably as when
307–13 * "I see n· what you mean,
318–30 "N·, Mr. Wiggin," I said,
323–19 * Neither do I n· feel at all equal to
329–21 * At no better time than n·,
332–17 * paper containing this card is n· in
333– 2 * is n· in the possession of the chairman
335–24 * Mrs. Glover (n· Mrs. Eddy)
342–25 * all n· concerned in its government
343–10 "I cannot answer that n·."
353–24 nothing . . . n· of any special
356–17 ones n· and heretofore presented in
357– 3 "Suffer it to be so n·"— Matt. 3 : 15.

nowhere

Mis. 173–21 matter is n· and sin is obsolete.
Ret. 89–21 N· in the four Gospels
Un. 42– 2 it must follow that death can be n· ;
47– 3 N· in Scripture is evil connected with
Pul. 81– 4 * n· spoken with more reverence
No. 35–28 the human kingdom is n·
Po. vi–17 n· but in the walls of a jail.
My. 70–23 * N· in the world is there a

noxious

Mis. 343–14 n· weeds of passion, malice, envy,
Peo. 3– 6 eternal roasting amidst n· vapors ;

nucleus

Pul. 22– 4 one n· or point of convergence,

nuisance

Mis. 7–22 counteract . . . this public n· ;
131– 3 a moral n·, a fungus, a microbe,

null

Mis. 22–19 therefore these are n· and void.
No. 37–25 Jesus rendered n· and void whatever
My. 271– 2 matter and material sense are n·,

nullified

'01. 15– 4 Error uncondemned is not n·

nullify

Mis. 40–30 than to n· either the disease itself or
119–29 n· or reverse your rules,

nullity

'01. 13–11 with such a sense of its n·
18–29 does it and so proves their n·.

numb

Po. 53–15 Where wind nor storm can n·

number (noun)

April
Mis. 158–24 April n· of The C. S. Journal

August
Mis. 313– 3 your editorial in the August n·

en route
My. 124–26 means of travel, and the n· en route.

equal
'01. 27–18 an equal n· of sick healed,

number (noun)
full
  '00. 14– 6 full *n·* of days named
great
  My. 75–14 * a great *n·* of visitors
greater
  Pul. 67–10 * would probably show a greater *n·*
greatest
  Mis. 288– 5 greatest good to the greatest *n·*,
  Ret. 82–15 greatest good to the greatest *n·*,
growing
  Pul. 56– 5 * a large and growing *n·*
increased in
  Ret. 15–17 congregation so increased in *n·*
increase in
  '02. 1– 5 constantly increase in *n·*,
increasing
  Pul. 50–17 * a large and increasing *n·*
insignificant
  My. 92–16 * increased from an insignificant *n·*
January
  My. 316–11 article in the January *n·*
large
  Ret. 7–19 * by a large *n·* of friends,
  Pul. 29–13 * and a large *n·* of chairs
  67–19 * there is a large *n·* of members.
  '02. 12–26 so as to seat the large *n·*
  My. 7–10 so as to seat the large *n·*
larger
  Mis. 273–27 a larger *n·* would be in waiting
largest
  Mis. 305–14 * largest *n·* of persons possible
May
  Mis. 216– 8 In the May *n·* of our *Journal,*
October
  Mis. 256–14 October *n·* of the *Journal,*
of attendants
  My. 53–19 * *n·* of attendants steadily increased.
  56–18 * the *n·* of attendants increased
of believers
  Pul. 66– 6 * *n·* of believers has grown
of candidates
  My. 57–17 * *n·* of candidates admitted June 5
of changes
  My. 66–12 * *n·* of changes will be made
of his name
  Mis. 113–10 or the *n·* of his name,"— *Rev.* 13 : 17.
  269–32 or the *n·* of his name."— *Rev.* 13 : 17.
of large elms
  Pul. 63–11 * pointed to a *n·* of large elms
of men
  Pul. 49–29 * She employs a *n·* of men
of Pupils
  Man. 84– 7 *N·* of Pupils.
of quotations
  My. 359–18 * a *n·* of quotations from a
of requests
  My. 276–21 * In reply to a *n·* of requests
of societies
  My. 57–25 * *n·* of societies advertised in the
of students
  Mis. 256–15 a select *n·* of students.
  Rud. 15–19 very limited *n·* of students
of the members
  Man. 48–18 *n·* of the members of The
of the readers
  '00. 1–23 Judging from the *n·* of the readers
of thirty
  Pul. 75–18 * Scientists . . . to the *n·* of thirty,
of visitors
  My. 75–14 * a great *n·* of visitors
  173–19 The *n·* of visitors, . . . exceeded
of years
  Pul. 72–13 * healed a *n·* of years ago
  My. 335–12 * was for a *n·* of years a resident
one
  Pul. 4– 7 Is not a man . . . *n·* one,
plural
  Mis. 191–21 here employed in its plural *n·*,
  No. 22–19 being used in the plural *n·*.
  My. 226– 1 or in the plural *n·*.
selected
  Man. 84–21 or assemble a selected *n·* of them,
September
  Mis. 88– 8 *genuine critique in the September n·,*
that
  Mis. 273–26 class which contains that *n·*.
their
  Chr. 55– 2 verses, whereto their *n·* corresponds.
three in
  My. 244–26 certainly not exceed three in *n·*.
time or
  '00. 14– 8 signifies a complete time or *n·*
total
  My. 57–21 * total *n·* admitted during the
  57–22 * total *n·* of branch churches

number (noun)
twenty-six in
  Man. 18– 5 the members, twenty-six in *n·*,
  Ret. 16–18 the members, twenty-six in *n·*,
  44– 6 the members, twenty-six in *n·*,
vast
  Mis. 156– 3 vast *n·* of earnest readers,
  My. 100– 9 * vast *n·* of the followers
whole
  Pul. 4– 8 a unit, and therefore whole *n·*,
  ———
  Mis. 142– 9 a *n·* of masonic symbols.
  381–27 to the *n·* of thirty-eight hundred
  Man. 112– 2 churches are designated by *n·*,
  112– 3 *n·* must be written First, Second,
  Pul. 51– 5 * *n·* of conscientious followers
  72– 6 * *n·* of very interesting
  72–14 * *n·* of well-known physicians.
  My. 97–26 * to the *n·* of forty thousand
  181–24 *n·* of 1,650,000 inhabitants.
  226– 7 conservation of *n·* in geometry,
  347–17 call to mind the *n·* of

number (verb)
  '01. 27–18 in this interval *n·* one million,
  My. 41– 1 * how great no man can *n·*
  59– 9 * *n·* its adherents by the
  85– 7 * adherents *n·* probably a million,
  89–31 * *n·* many thousands
  93–31 * adherents *n·* hundreds of thousands,

numbered
  Ret. 13– 8 *n·* among those who were doomed to
  37– 9 edition *n·* one thousand copies.
  Pul. 51– 9 * *n·* among the many pioneers
  My. 100–14 * members are *n·* by thousands

numbering
  Mis. 9– 7 *n·* them, and giving them refuge
  Man. 48–16 *N·* the People.
  48–21 shall turn away from personality and *n·*
  Pul. 43– 3 * *n·* thirty-five singers in all
  My. 38– 8 * corps of ushers, *n·* two hundred,
  324–23 * *n·* you among his literary friends.

numbers
one thousandth
  My. 107–10 the *o· t·* attenuations
one hundredth
  No. 21– 3 *o· h·* part of Truth,
  Hea. 13– 4 *o· h·* part of a grain
one quarter
  My. 294–27 for *o· q·* of a century.
two and a half
  Pul. 49–13 she ejaculated ; *"t· and a h·,*
  49–14 only *t· and a h·* years."
twenty-one and one half
  Pul. 24–26 * *t· and o· h·* feet square.
36th
  Man. 99– 5 the 36th parallel of latitude.
a hundred
  Mis. 48–29 like *a h·* other stories,
  Un. 48– 3 already told *a h·* times,
one hundred
  Mis. 106–14 Marched the *o· h·*.
  118– 9 ninety-nine times in *o· h·*
  Ret. 4– 7 *O· h·* acres of the old farm
  Pul. 67–23 * *o· h·* years from the date
  '01. 16–27 *o· h·* falsehoods told about it?
  Po. 22– 5 *O· h·* years, aflame with Love,
  My. 127–17 out of *o· h·* cases I healed
one hundred and five
  My. 8–29 * *o· h· and f·* new churches
one hundred and twenty
  Pul. 24–25 * tower is *o· h· and t·* feet
one hundred and twenty-six
  Pul. 41–24 * rises *o· h· and t·* feet
one hundred and forty-four
  Pul. 26– 1 * *o· h· and f·* electric lights
one hundred and fifty
  My. 83– 5 * *o· h· and f·* members of the
one hundred and sixty
  Mis. 273–23 *o· h· and s·* applications
one hundred and seventy-fifth
  My. 174–18 *o· h· and s·* anniversary
  270– 7 *o· h· and s·* anniversary ;
two hundred
  Mis. 47– 2 *weigh over t· h· pounds*
  Pul. 26–27 * lamp over *t· h·* years old,
  '01. 24–17 more than *t· h·* years old.
  My. 38– 9 * ushers, numbering *t· h·*,
  123–21 holds a trifle over *t· h·*
two hundred and twenty
  My. 89– 6 * *t· h· and t·* feet high,
220x220x236 ft.
  My. 67– 7 * Shape, triangular . . . 220x220x236 ft.

numbers

two hundred and twenty-four
  My. 45–30   * height of *t· h· and t·* feet,
       68–10   * dome is *t· h· and t·* feet
       78– 6   * *t· h· and t·* feet
224 ft.
  My. 67– 8   * Height . . . 224 ft.
two hundred and twenty-five
  My. 53–14   * about *t· h· and t·*.
two hundred and sixty
  Hea. 12–15   *t· h· and s·* remedies
two hundred and sixty-two
  Ret. 33–10   *t· h· and s·* remedies
267
  My. 57–26   * societies advertised . . . is 267.
three hundred
  Ret. 47– 6   over *t· h* applications
four hundred
  Mis. 345– 3   had stood *f· h·* years before,
four hundredth
  My. 53– 7   * reached its *f· h·* edition,
four hundred and sixty-four
  My. 54–30   * seated *f· h· and s·*.
five hundred
  Ret. 4– 4   farm of about *f· h·* acres,
614
  My. 57–24   * 614 of which show a membership
six hundred and twenty-five
  My. 55–25   * capacity of *s· h· and t·*,
682
  My. 57–24   * number of branch churches . . . is 682,
eight hundred
  Pul. 27– 6   * vestry seats *e· h·* people,
       71– 1   * *e· h·* of the members
  My. 54–14   * present about *e· h·* people.
nine hundred
  My. 8–20   * capacity of more than *n· h·*,
several hundred
  Pul. 42 10   * *s· h·* children in the central pews.
a thousand
  Pul. 41–19   * nearly *a t·* local believers.
       58–16   * will seat over *a t·*
       83– 9   * by *a t·* denials
one thousand
  Mis. 276–10   *o· t·* Christian Scientists,
       285– 3   edition of *o· t·* pamphlets
  Ret. 37– 9   numbered *o· t·* copies.
  Pul. 5–21   edition of *o· t·* copies.
  '01. 18– 2   attenuated *o· t·* degrees
  My. 53– 7   * each of *o· t·* copies.
eleven hundred
  Pul. 25– 8   * seating *o· h·* people
twelve hundred
  My. 68–14   * seating capacity of *t· h·*,
fourteen hundred
  Pul. 41–17   * holding from *f· h·* to
fourteen and fifteen hundred
  Pul. 57– 6   * *f· and f· h·*,
fifteen hundred
  Pul. 25– 0   * capable of holding *f· h·* ;
       41–17   * to *f· h·* persons,
1,545
  My. 57–16   * membership at that date was 1,545.
1893
  '00. 7– 8   in all the other 1893 years.
nineteen hundred
  Pul. 35– 9   * *n· h·* years ago.
       53– 2   * *n· h·* years ago,
  My. 109–10   If *n· h·* years ago
two thousand
  Pul. 44– 5   *t· t·* miles of space,
  Hea. 13– 5   reducing the . . . *t· t·* times,
2,194
  My. 57–19   * which is 2,194 more than
two thousand four hundred and ninety-six
  '01. 2–29   *t· t· f· h· and n·*
2,500
  Mis. 251– 2   chapter sub-title
two thousand and six hundred
  Pul. v– 2   *t· t· and s· h·* CHILDREN
two thousand seven hundred and eighty-four
  '02. 1– 5   *T· t· s· h· and e·*
3,000
  My. 67–11   * 3,000 garments
three thousand
  My. 69–23   * *t· t·* wraps.
       169–18   *t· t·* believers
thirty-eight hundred
  Mis. 381–27   number of *t· h·*
four thousand
  Mis. 353–26   *f· t·* children,
  Pul. 30– 8   * numbers now *f· t·* members·
       41– 8   * *f· t·* of these contributors
       55–25   * now over *f· t·* members.
       71– 1   * membership of *f· t·*,
       77–12   * *f· t·* members.

numbers

four thousand
  Pul. 78–11   * *f· t·* members.
  My. 173–19   about *f· t·*,
four and five thousand
  My. 65–10   * *f· and f· t·* persons.
four or five thousand
  My. 7–17   * *f· or f· t·* persons,
       9– 4   * *f· or f· t·* persons,
forty-five hundred and thirty-eight
  My. 70–29   * *f· h· and t·* pipes,
4,889
  My. 57–19   * and numbers 4,889,
5,000
  My. 67–10   * Seating capacity . . . 5,000
five thousand
  Mis. 29–17   about *f· t·* students.
  My. 24–29   * seating capacity of *f· t·*.
       29– 4   * *F· t·* people kneeling
       36– 4   * the *f· t·* present
       59–21   * chorus of *f· t·* voices,
       69–20   * *f· t·* people
       71–29   * seat *f· t·* people,
       77– 4   * capacity of over *f· t·*.
       78– 1   * capacity . . . is *f· t·*,
       98– 7   * holding *f· t·* people,
       99–15   * seating *f· t·* people,
       141–23   seats only *f· t·* people,
five thousand and twelve
  My. 71–22   * *f· t· and t·* people
six thousand
  Rud. 8– 4   lion of *s· t·* years ago ;
  Pul. 40–11   * ENABLING S· T· BELIEVERS TO
       40–18   * nearly *s· t·* persons,
       64–26   * *s· t·* people
6,181
  My. 57–22   * number admitted . . . is 6,181.
seven thousand
  Ret. 7– 1   majority vote of *s· t·*,
ten thousand
  Ret. 23–20   "among *t· t·*." — *Song* 5 : 10.
  Pul. 82–22   * *t· t·* Esthers.
  '02. 3– 1   *t· t·* . . . Scientists
  My. 8–24   * "T· t·* Christian Scientists
       123–22   a church of *t· t·* members
       141– 7   * *t· t·* persons
fifteen thousand
  My. 80–21   * *F· t·* Scientists
sixteen thousand
  '00. 1–12   over *s· t·* communicants
twenty thousand
  My. 82–22   * *t· t·* and more visitors
       88– 3   * *T· t·* Christian Scientists
twenty-one thousand six hundred and thirty-one
  '01. 2–28   *t· t· s· h· and t·*
twenty-four thousand
  My. 8–19   * *t· t·* members
twenty-four thousand two hundred and seventy-eight
  '02. 1– 8   *t· t· t· h· and s·*
twenty-five thousand
  My. 77–14   * *t· t·* visitors
thirty thousand
  My. 30– 5   * over *t· t·* people
       45– 9   * upwards of *t· t·*
       72–10   * *t· t·* or more
       79–11   * *t· t·* people
       83–27   * The *t· t·* visitors
       92–23   * *t· t·* worshippers
       94– 7   * *t· t·* worshippers
       99–17   * *T· t·* of the faith,
       100– 7   * *t· t·* worshippers
       172–14   * *t· t·* members ;
thirty-six thousand
  My. 175– 3   *t· t·* communicants,
forty thousand
  My. 77–25   * nearly *f· t·* believers
       04 21   * *f· t·* Christian Scientists
       95–15   * *f· t·* . . . Scientists
       96– 1   * *f· t·* . . . Scientists
       97–26   * to the number of *f· t·*
       98– 1   * *F· t·* people
       135–18   about *f· t·* members,
40,000 sq. ft.
  My. 67– 9   * Area of site . . . 40,000 sq. ft.
40,011
  My. 57–17   * membership is 40,011.
41,944
  My. 57–25   * a membership of 41,944.
forty-eight thousand
  My. 141–24   *f· t·* communicants,
one hundred thousand
  Pul. 55–30   * between *o· h· t·* and
       63–16   * numbers over *o· h· t·*
       70– 5   * *O· H· T·* FOLLOWERS
       70–12   * *o· h· t·* converts,

numbers

hundreds of thousands
(*see* **hundreds**)
two hundred thousand
Pul. 30–24 * exceeds t· h· t· people.
55–30 * between . . . and t· h· t·.
238,000
My. 181–23 a population of 238,000
quarter of a million
Pul. 67–17 * over a q· of a m·
four hundred thousand
My. v–22 * f· h· t· copies
a million
Mis. 35– 7 a m· of people acknowledge
Pul. 83– 9 * a m· of broken pledges.
No. 33–14 it was a m· times greater
'00. 1–24 over a m· of people
Peo. 8–28 proved a m· times unskilful.
My. 85– 7 * adherents number probably a m·,
one million
'01. 27–18 o· m·, and an equal number
the million
Pul. 82–23 * Miriams by the m·,
1,650,000
My. 181–24 number of 1,650,000 inhabitants.
two millions
My. 14– 5 t· m· of love currency
two hundred and fifty million
My. 294–28 t· h· and f· m· human beings
a thousand million
Mis. 224–12 a t· m· different human

Mis. 55– 2 pupil and the science of n·.
104–10 calculus of forms and n·.
177– 8 Large n·, in desperate malice,
221–27 multiplication of the same two n·
296– 3 n· among its constituents and
Man. 18– 9 went steadily on, increasing in n·,
Ret. 59–11 demonstration of the science of n· ;
Pul. 30– 8 * church n· now four thousand
63–16 * n· over one hundred thousand
67–17 * n· over a quarter of a million
'00. 1–13 with rapidly increasing n·,
My. vi– 1 * to well-nigh countless n·
19– 2 * current n· of *The C. S. Journal,*
57–19 * n· 4,889, which is 2,194 more
74– 6 * n· of belated church members
82–27 * came to Boston in such n·
84–18 * growth of the C. S. idea in n·,
86–27 * unprecedented, as regards n·.
91–25 * growth in n· is remarkable,
92– 5 * n· of intelligent men and women
235– 9 correct numeration of n·

numeral
Mis. 118– 9 and then allow one n· to
numeration
'01. 22–15 n· table of C. S.
22–20 n· table of C. S.,
22–25 have learned its n· table,
22–28 n· table of C. S.
23– 2 losing the n· table
My. 235– 8 the correct n· of numbers
numerical
My. 94– 3 * the race for n· supremacy.
numerically
Pul. 80– 9 * women's paradise, — n·, socially,
numerous
Ret. 5–22 * distinguished for n· excellences.
My. 31– 9 * n· doors of the church
257–25 memorials, too n· to name,
nuptial
Mis. 290– 4 The n· vow is never annulled
My. 268– 3 n· vow should never be annulled
Nuremberg
My. 295–10 PRINTED IN N· IN 1733
nurse
Mis. 388–24 To n· the Bethlehem babe
Man. 49– 7 C. S. N·.
49– 9 C. S. n· shall be one who
Ret. 20– 9 under the care of our family n·,
90–18 to the care of n· or stranger.
Po. 21–13 To n· the Bethlehem babe
nursing
Mis. 329–15 n· the timid spray,
nursling
Pul. 1– 4 A new year is a n·,
nurtured
'01. 29–14 the parents who n· them,
My. 177–19 n· and nourished this church
nutriment
My. 230– 6 digestion of spiritual n·
N. Y. Commercial Advertiser
Pul. 71– 3 * [N. Y. C· A·, January 9, 1895]
nymph
Po. 8– 8 n· and naiad from woodland
34–12 solitude, where n· or saint
nymphs
Pan. 3–27 leader of the n·,

O

oak
Mis. 240–17 sturdy o·, . . . breasts the tornado.
392– 1 poem
392– 6 majestic o·, from yon high place
Pul. 8– 4 leaves of an ancient o·,
24–27 * doors of antique o· richly carved.
Po. page 20 poem
20– 8 majestic o·, from yon high place
Oakland, Cal.
Pul. 89–28 * Enquirer, O·, C·.
My. 202–20 chapter sub-title
Oak on the Mountain's Summit, The
Mis. 392– 1 poem
Po. page 20 poem
oasis
My. 252–20 o· in my wilderness.
oath
My. 138–27 * made o· that the statements
315–17 * made o· that the within statement
obduracy
Pul. 13–26 must depend upon sin's o·.
obdurate
My. 36–15 * redeemed from o· sin.
obedience
and love
Mis. 127–13 more grace, o·, and love.
My. 18–10 more grace, o·, and love.
crowns
Mis. 118–27 o· crowns persistent effort
demanded
Mis. 19– 5 o· demanded of His servants
enforcing
My. 159–23 spiritual laws enforcing o·
filial
Mis. 254– 1 that filial o· to which the

obedience
final
Mis. 116–19 final o· to spiritual law.
follows
My. 224– 7 blessing which follows o·
gives
'02. 17– 5 when o· gives him happiness.
My. 131– 4 o· gives him courage,
homage and
Peo. 9–12 dividing our homage and o·
honesty, and
Mis. 126–16 meekness, honesty, and o·
humility and
Mis. 158–17 to test your humility and o·
implicit
My. 46–24 * and a more implicit o·
is the test
'02. 17– 4 o· is the test of love ;
loving
My. 207–15 * Yours in loving o·,
of Christ
Mis. 139–14 to the o· of Christ. — II Cor. 10 : 5.
patience and
Ret. 80–20 Patience and o· win the
perfect
Pul. 54–14 * perfect o· to the laws of nature.
required
Man. 65– 9 O· Required.
reward of
'02. 17–11 receive the reward of o·.
rule of
Mis. 118– 8 the indispensable rule of o·.
spiritual
'01. 34– 6 in prayer and in spiritual o·
strict
Mis. 119–23 or strict o· thereto,
248–18 not in strict o· to the Mosaic

obedience

this
'00.   9– 2   I discern that this *o·* is
My. 220–13   I practise and teach this *o·*,
to divine law
Un.   13– 6   in *o·* to divine law,
to God
Mis.   12–29   measured by our *o·* to God,
    267–27   action, in *o·* to God,
to God's laws
Ret.   26– 8   in his *o·* to God's laws,
to His government
Hea.   8– 2   and *o·* to His government,
to human law
My. 220– 9   concerning *o·* to human law,
to hygienic laws
Ret.   26– 2   neither *o·* to hygienic laws,
to the call
Man.   69–18   go immediately in *o·* to the call.
to the command
My.   43–15   * In *o·* to the command of Joshua,
to the demands
My.   43– 7   * *O·* to the demands of the law
to the law
Mis. 141–23   in *o·* to the law of Love
    181– 8   blind *o·* to the law of being,
to the teachings
My.   43–24   * *O·* to the teachings of this book
to this rule
My.   4– 3   *o·* to this rule spiritualizes man,
understanding and
Mis. 160–15   firmer in understanding and *o·*.
unto righteousness
Mis. 120– 9   *o·* unto righteousness — *Rom.* 6: 16.
yield
Mis. 236–11   and yield *o·* to them
your
My.   37 14   * your *o·* during forty years
    45–15   * fitting monument of your *o·*
    358– 4   you will be blessed in your *o·*.

Mis.   66– 1   *o·* thereto may be found faulty,
    67–15   *O·* to these commandments is
    82–16   In *o·* to this law, man is
    104–22   In *o·* to the divine nature,
    116–10   Subject: *O·*.
    116–28   to work for God, — is *o·*;
    116–29   If in one instance *o·* be lacking,
    117–13   *O·* is the offspring of Love;
    118–11   is neither Science nor *o·*.
    156–27   Experience and, above all, *o·*,
'00.   8–26   learn first what *o·* is.
    8–29   that is not *o·*.
Peo.   3–27   *o·* to our Father's demands,
My.   45– 1   * recognition of and *o·* to
    156–18   In *o·* to this command
    189– 5   so due, to God is *o·*,
    360–20   *o·* to The Mother Church,

obedient
Mis. 117–29   when one is *o·*.
    158–22   Let us be faithful and *o·*,
    331– 5   make them humble, loving, *o·*,
Ret.   71– 4   *o·* to the divine command,
Peo.   11–20   *o·* to the legislation of mind,
My.   41– 2   * to become gladly *o·* to law.
    43–11   * *o·* to the voice of their leader.
    44– 8   * *o·* to the loving counsel of our
    46–20   * faithful, *o·*, deserving disciples.
    209– 3   bless this willing and *o·* church
    332–13   * Your friend and *o·* servant,

obediently
Ret.   80–14   *o·* receptive of the heavenly

obelisk
My. 203–12   Be great not as a grand *o·*,

obey
Mis.   23–10   winds, and waves, *o·* this
    46– 3   servants to *o·*, — *Rom.* 6: 10.
    51–19   and *o·* the Golden Rule,
    51–20   he will love and *o·* you without
    90–16   *o·* the Scriptures,
    93–20   *o·* Christ's Sermon on the Mount,
    99–13   Then *o·* this call.
    117– 8   arrest the former, and *o·* the latter.
    118– 1   cannot *o·* both God, good, and evil,
    118– 8   To *o·* the principle of mathematics
    119–20   to *o·* a power that should be
    120– 4   they must *o·* implicitly each
    120– 8   servants to *o·*, — *Rom.* 6: 16.
    120– 9   to whom ye *o·*; — *Rom.* 6: 16.
    124– 7   neither do we love and *o·* Him **by**
    158–11   we both had first to *o·*,
    191–31   *o·* St. Paul's injunction
    206–27   and *o·* the Way-shower,
    208–15   Mortals *o·* their own wills,
    266–27   and *o·* the Golden Rule.

obey
Mis. 287–25   *o·* the Golden Rule for human life,
    303–17   to *o·* the Ten Commandments
    346–18   servants to *o·*, — *Rom.* 6: 16.
Man.   68– 7   or who declines to *o·* this call
Ret.   87–19   to *o·* the celestial injunction
'00.   5–19   to *o·* the First Commandment
    8–26   Learn to *o·*;
    8–28   and you *o·* the mandate
    9– 7   therefore, not ready — to *o·*.
'01.   30–28   to *o·* the Golden Rule,
    31–12   I cannot choose but *o·*.
    34–24   *o·* strictly the laws that be,
'02.   17– 6   seek and *o·* what they love.
    17–10   *o·* both the old and the new
Po.   32–15   Such physical laws to *o·*,
My.   37–31   * give heed and ponder and *o·*.
    64–17   * how to *o·* this commandment
    109– 8   we shall *o·* the commandment,
    118– 2   who cheerfully *o·* God and
    219–31   that he *o·* the law,
    241–27   * and to *o·* Christ was not to
    252– 1   and you will *o·* the law and gospel.
    345– 3   Christian Scientists *o·* the laws,

obeyed
Mis. 158– 9   after His messenger has *o·*
    172–24   discerned, understood, and *o·*.
Man.   51–17   have been strictly *o·*,
Ret.   76– 3   if mortals *o·* God's law
Un.   3–10   those who have *o·* God's commands,
Rud.   10–22   His law of Truth, when *o·*,
No.   3–11   I *o·* a diviner rule.
Pan.   11–13   Science . . . understood and *o·*,
'01.   11–18   and *o·* throughout the week,
    19–18   winds and waves, which *o·* him
    30–23   And no emperor is *o·* like
My.   40–27   * She has *o·* the divine Principle,
    41–29   * has *o·* its every demand,
    203– 8   which are *o·* without mutiny
    220–26   Jesus *o·* human laws
    268–16   *o·*, will eliminate divorce and **war.**
    279–12   The First Commandment . . . . *o·*,

obeying
Mis. 116–25   *O·* the divine Principle
    119– 5   instead of aiding . . . by *o·* them,
No.   14–21   *o·* these commands;
My. 220–12   *o·* the laws of the land.
    225–15   *o·* the leading of our Lord's Prayer.

obeys
Mis. 211–23   He risks nothing who *o·* the law of
Man.   72– 5   member . . . who *o·* its By-Laws
'02.   17– 5   that one gladly *o·* when
My. 230–12   spirituality of him who *o·* it,

obituary
My. 334–27   * extract from an editorial *o·*

object
Mis.   8–12   *o·* of your own conception
    23–29   actions of the *o·* in front of it.
    68–26   * a science of which the *o·* is
    215–14   Principle and *o·* of our work,
    224–29   an *o·* of pity rather than of
    319–24   The *o·* to be won affords ample.
Ret.   5– 7   *o·* of their tender solicitude.
Pan.   9–28   the best of people sometimes *o·* to
'01.   23–25   Its *o·* was to deny,
    30– 4   We err in thinking the *o·* of
My.   71–28   * aim and *o·* of the architect:
    285–15   grand *o·* embodied in the
    296–27   its emotions, motives, and *o·*.
    353–17   The *o·* of the *Monitor* is to

objected
Mis. 348–31   and *o·* to their entering
    349–13   to this I *o·* on the ground that
    373– 5   My artist at the easel *o·*,
Man.   64–18   Mrs. Eddy *o·* to being called thus,

objection
Mis. 349–16   notwithstanding my *o·*,
No.   40–12   I have no *o·* to audible prayer
Hea.   12–27   only *o·* to giving the

objectionable
Mis.   64–11   *Do you regard the study . . . as o·?*
Man.   81–20   No *o·* pictures shall be exhibited
'01.   16–18   these qualities are *o·*,

objective
Ret.   34–19   *o·* state of the mortal mind,

object-lesson
Mis. 110–20   wrought steadfastly at the same *o·*,
    372– 8   voices C. S. through song and *o·*.

objects
Mis.   9–21   dreamy *o·* of self-satisfaction;
    36–23   material laws, and all material *o·*,
    86– 9   *Is it correct to say of material o·*,

objects
Mis. 227–16 these weak, pitifully poor o·
344– 9 disengage the soul from o· of sense,
Man. 26–16 if she o·, said candidates shall not
Ret. 31– 1 The loss of material o·
Peo. 7–24 To remove those o· of sense
7–26 its subjects and o· of thought,
14– 2 express them by o· more beautiful.
My. 91–23 * the o· of much ridicule,

obligated
Mis. 315–16 morally o· to look after
Man. 83–14 morally o· to promote their

obligates
Mis. 79–30 which in any way o· you
80– 6 o· its members to give

obligation
Mis. 155–28 thus fulfilling their moral o·
Ret. 5–30 * lively sense of the parental o·,
My. 336– 9 * performed their o· to her.
354– 8 under no o· to buy

obligations
Mis. 176–25 ourselves, and our times and o·?
264– 4 loyal to . . . human o·,
284–32 thus it is with all moral o·.
291– 4 affinities, self-interests, or o·,
336–11 right o· towards him.
Man. 28–18 all the o· of his office,
31– 4 Moral O·.
100–10 neglects to fulfil the o· of his
Ret. 19–23 they performed their o·
My. 331– 3 they performed their o·

oblige
Mis. 303–21 You will o· me by giving place

obliged
Mis. 35–17 is one o· to become a student
35–18 if one is o· to study under you,
52–27 he would be o· to turn back
235– 2 He is no longer o· to sin,
368–12 We regret to be o· to say
Man. 37–12 o· to report the cause
Ret. 44–12 o·, . . . to preach only occasionally,
Pul. 79–21 * should be o· to invent one.''
My. 55–22 * o· to seek other quarters,
56–26 * o· to leave the church
251– 7 * o· to take both Primary and Normal
313–29 o· to be parted from my son,

obliquity
Ret. 31–22 mortal mind's material o·

obliterate
My. 263– 1 tend to o· the spiritual idea

obliterated
Pul. 52–23 * nearly o· all vital belief
'02. 6–17 all it includes is o·,

obliterates
Pan. 11–25 o· the lost image
My. 270– 3 o· the epicycle of evil.

oblivion (see also oblivion's)
Mis. 99–24 never bear into o· his words.
209–15 to learn that neither o· nor dreams
Rud. 5–26 and sinking into o·.
No. 42–16 engulfing error in bottomless o·,
My. 285–12 shall be relegated to o·.

oblivion's
Po. 15–22 cannot quench in o· wave.

oblivious
Mis. 162–28 he must be o· of human self.

obnoxious
Man. 44– 8 O· Books.
44–10 has for sale o· books.
Un. 56–28 More o· than Chinese stenchpots

obscuration
Mis. 2– 8 causing great o· of Spirit.

obscure
Mis. 181– 9 tend to o· the order of Science,
222–26 healing Principle, . . . is not so o· ;
254–18 would o· the light of Science,
337–21 they o· its divine element,
Ret. 22– 1 becomes correspondingly o·.
Un. 53–10 evil belief that renders them o·.
Pan. 10–30 appetites, and passions, . . . o· man.
Hea. 5–18 the one grand truth
14– 7 o· the divine Principle of healing
My. 267–25 Material thought tends to o·
305– 1 P. P. Quimby (an o·, uneducated

obscured
Mis. 113– 7 and divine light to be o·,
286– 5 can neither be o· nor throttled.
333– 6 God cannot be o·,
Ret. 84–16 o· even the power and glory
'01. 12–20 scholastic theology has o·,

obscurity
My. 183–21 the blind see out of o·.

obsequious
Mis. 87–29 If they are haunted by o· helpers,

observance
Ret. 76–28 strictest o· of moral law
My. 256– 5 emphatically phrasing strict o·
339–15 o· of the holiday illustrates the
339–30 without the o· of a material fast
340–23 to recur to a religious o· which

observances
Man. 60–12 Easter O·.
60–13 there shall be no special o·,
My. 66–22 * elaborate o· of Sunday,
340– 5 religious o· and precedents

observation
Mis. 88–11 Patience, o·, intellectual culture,
154–26 never desert the post of spiritual o·
245–12 directing more critical o· to its
251–17 cometh not with o·'' — Luke 17 : 20.
293–10 gained from instruction, o·, and
308–33 to remove from their o·
Ret. 45–14 From careful o· and experience
'01. 26–30 C. S. is the result of my own o·,
'02. 1–17 wrestling only with material o·,
Peo. 6– 7 * founded on long o· and reflection,
My. 319–17 * o· of many of your students,

observe
Mis. 328–27 o· the apostle's admonition,
Man. 61– 9 shall o· no more Communion seasons.
Un. 21– 4 If we o· our mental processes,
33–22 o· the foundations of their testimony,
My. 29–21 * opening they had gathered to o·,
173–21 sweet to o· with what unanimity my
262–27 I love to o· Christmas in quietude,

observed
Mis. 6–26 caution is o· in regard to diet,
91– 3 it should be o· at present
127– 1 Hitherto, I have o· that
239–11 I o· a carriage draw up
314–27 This form shall also be o·
Man. 61–12 Communion shall be o·
Ret. 38– 9 of what I had already o·
88– 1 courtesy should be o·
Pul. 20–22 selected and o· in the East
54–19 * shows that he o·, in his
My. 17–29 "Hitherto, I have o· that
226– 4 This rule strictly o·
244–31 As the people o· the success
259–24 Certain occasions, . . . o· properly,
262– 6 O· by material sense, Christmas

observer
Mis. 220–23 Christian Scientist and the o·.
Pul. 29–11 * earnestness impressed the o·.
'00. 2– 8 o· reports three types
My. 48–31 * I am bound as an o· of them
87– 6 * to the most casual o·.

observers
Ret. 19–20 was remarked by all o·.
My. 330–31 was remarked by all o·.

observing
'01. 30–11 o· the Golden Rule,
My. 340– 2 we have no record of his o·

obsolete
Mis. 173–21 matter is nowhere and sin is o·.
318– 2 o· terms in absolute C. S.,
Ret. 34– 4 in which matter is o·.
No. 26–28 Sin must be o·,

obstacle
Mis. 200–26 met no o· or circumstances

obstacles
Mis. 54–12 power of C. S. over all o·
135–11 surmounts all o·,
309–21 include all o· to health,
Ret. 50–29 such o· as were encountered
Pul. 84–23 * all o· to its completion
My. 52– 3 * had many o· to overcome,
91–24 * despite the o· put in the way

Obstetric
Ret. 43–17 Primary, Normal, and O·

obstetricians
Mis. 349– 7 students . . . who are skilful o·.

obstetrics
Mis. 349–10 o· taught in my College.
349–12 above-named course in o·
Man. 88– 9 O· will not be taught.

obstinate
Mis. 329– 2 Mine is an o· penchant
Rud. 3– 4 o· resistance to all efforts
My. 180–19 o· sinner, however, refuses

obstinately
 Mis. 327–27 *O·* holding themselves back,
obstruct
 Mis. 10– 2 wherewith to *o·* life's joys
 No. 40–20 *o·* the harmony of Mind
obstructing
 Mis. 173–23 *o·* his intelligence
obstructions
 My. 61– 5 * to remove human *o·*
obstructs
 Mis. 39–27 *and what most o· the way?*
   328–23 Whatever *o·* the way,
obtain
 Mis. 123–22 whereby the just *o·* a pardon
  168–29 * had to go away unable to *o·* seats.
  232– 9 and we not *o·* a more perfect
  270–20 if we would *o·* that promise.
  272–21 * may *o·* for any secular purposes ;
 Man. 66– 4 *o·* a clear understanding of
 Ret. 65–28 to *o·* health, harmony, and
  71–27 Secret mental efforts to *o·* help
  86–18 *o·* it by taking up his cross
 Un. 31–22 evil does not *o·* in Spirit,
  32– 1 evil *does*, . . . *o·* in matter ;
 '02. 6–13 human woe is seen to *o·* in
 My. 48–12 * *o·* the spiritual understanding
  54– 2 * could not *o·* entrance ;
  55– 4 * to *o·* by purchase some building,
  171– 6 they shall *o·* joy — *Isa.* 35 : 10.
  216– 3 *o·* their money from a fish's mouth,
  269– 7 worthy to *o·* that world, — *Luke* 20 : 35.
  349–24 *o·* not in material phenomena,
obtainable
 Man. 100–26 If a suitable man is not *o·*
 Pul. 54–27 * the most perfect *o·* environment,
obtained
 Mis. 39– 6 this knowledge can be *o·*
  150–18 halls can now be *o·* wherein,
  212– 5 what happiness is, and how it is *o·*.
  251–17 with knowledge *o·* from the senses
  272– 1 * *o·* a college charter
  382–17 *o·* the first charter for the first
  382–21 *o·* the first and only charter for a
 Man. 18– 3 charter for the Church was *o·*
 Ret. 16–16 was *o·* June, 1879,
  44– 5 charter for this church was *o·* in June,
 Pul. 38– 1 * charter *o·* the following June.
  67–28 * charter was *o·* two months later.
  73–28 * concise idea of her belief could be *o·*
 Peo. 4–15 the error . . . *o·* expression.
 My. 49– 9 * charter . . . was *o·* August 23, 1879,
  54–20 * that some place would be *o·*,
  149–17 blessings are *o·* by labor.
  327–17 * *o·* by Miss Mary Hatch Harrison
  328–25 * application . . . was made and *o·*,
  328–27 * for which a license must be *o·*
obtaining
 Mis. 141–28 no legal authority for *o·*,
 Pan. 6–13 thereby *o·* social prestige,
 My. 55– 7 * thought of *o·* a church edifice,
obtains
 Mis. 205– 1 mind, thus purged, *o·* peace
  220– 1 rule, which *o·* in every line
  368–17 This evil *o·* in the present
 '00. 6–17 *o·* not in the Science,
 Peo. 6–11 * less mortality than now *o·*.''
obtrude
 Mis. 9–32 all that an enemy or enmity can *o·*
obtruding
 Mis. 171–27 *o·* upon the public attention
obtrusive
 Mis. 282– 6 chapter sub-title
obviate
 Mis. 249– 3 to see if C. S. could not *o·* its
obvious
 Mis. 110–23 *o·* that the world's acceptance
  205–23 maintain their *o·* correspondence
 Ret. 64–12 In C. S. the fact is made *o·* that
  87– 5 its wisdom is as *o·* in religion
 '02. 7–26 It is *o·* that he called his
 My. 279– 9 its *o·* correspondence with the Scriptures
obviously
 Pul. 54–10 * *o·*, the conditions requisite in
occasion
 Mis. 72–16 not have *o·* any more — *Ezek.* 18 : 3.
  91–27 as *o·* required, read from the book
  129–16 he will seek *o·* to
  148–14 written . . . as the *o·* required.
  171– 4 he rose to the *o·* with the second
  274–11 disappointment this will *o·*,

occasion
 Mis. 278–11 never given *o·* for a single censure,
  282–25 *o·* which may call for aid unsought,
  284– 6 Its infinite nature and uses *o·* this.
  315– 3 especially adapted to the *o·*,
  321–28 offered upon this approaching *o·*.
 Man. 3–10 written . . . as the *o·* required.
  76– 4 as the right *o·* may call for it.
 Un. 57– 5 by the pain they feel and *o·* ;
 Pul. 15–18 *o·* for a victory over evil.
  16– 1 and Sung on This *O·*
  43–22 * sermon prepared for the *o·*
  56–11 * *o·* of the erection of the temple,
  60–15 * come to Boston for this . . . *o·*
 Pan. 1– 2 heading
  14–27 Great *o·* have we to rejoice
 Po. vi– 7 * *was written for that o·*,
 My. 3– 1 chapter sub-title
  16–16 * there were present on this *o·* :
  26–17 better to be brief on this rare *o·*.
  39–21 * My thoughts revert to a former *o·*,
  42–23 * significance of this momentous *o·*.
  46–21 * On this solemn *o·*,
  54– 1 * were inadequate for the *o·*,
  64– 1 * the significance of the *o·*,
  77–24 * present to participate in the *o·*.
  79–14 * anywhere in the world on any *o·* ;
  85– 3 * in the significance of the *o·*,
  80 17 * an *o·* for joy that marks it as
  141–18 * Boston church has offered an *o·* for
  159– 1 chapter sub-title
  170– 2 this was no festal *o·*, no formal
  174– 8 club-house to them on this *o·* ;
  174–11 their reports of the happy *o·*.
  177– 5 on so interesting an *o·*
  201–28 my presence on the auspicious *o·* of
  219– 9 preventing the *o·* for its use ;
  281–19 * to offer an appropriate *o·*
  289–11 should upon this solemn *o·*
  289–26 may be read on that tender *o·*.
  321–12 * with whom he had *o·* to talk,
  355– 9 if the *o·* demands it,
occasional
 Mis. 43–25 The *o·* temporary success
 Ret. 1–12 stray sonnet and an *o·* riddle,
occasionally
 Mis. 52–13 *o·* a love affair.
  88– 3 *o·* receive it from others ;
  302–15 If Christian Scientists *o·*
 Ret. 44–14 to preach only *o·*,
  83–23 *o·* reading aloud from the
 No. 9–16 have opposed *o·* and strongly
 '02. 20–24 privilege of meeting you all *o·*
 My. 81–20 * *o·* the voices would ring out
  140–16 * attending *o·* The Mother Church.
  140 26 *o·* attending this church.
occasioned
 Mis. 256–16 that has *o·* the irregular
 My. 244– 3 the stir that might be *o·*
occasions
 Mis. 148–27 people present on these *o·*.
  250–15 to be taken down on rare *o·*
  261– 4 sin and suffering it *o·*
  350–22 *o·* effects on patients which
 Pul. 53– 8 * on various *o·* during the
 My. 86–25 * the most notable of such *o·*.
  259–23 Certain *o·*, considered either
Occident
 Mis. 29–24 Surely the people of the *O·*
  98–16 the miracle of the *O·*.
 My. 193– 8 dazzling glory in the *O·*,
occultism
 Mis. 78–13 *o·*, magic, alchemy,
  351– 8 I have no skill in *o·* ;
 Pul. 14– 3 growing *o·* of this period.
occultists
 Mis. 80– 1 *o·*, sellers of impure literature,
occupancy
 My. 55–27 * until The . . . was ready for *o·*,
occupant
 Ret. 88–24 stated *o·* of that pulpit.
occupants
 Man. 30–22 *o·* are satisfactory to her.
occupation
 Mis. 296–25 Do they enter this line of *o·*
 Man. 45– 2 sufficient *o·* for all its members.
 '02. 3–15 brief *o·* of that pearl of the ocean,
occupied
 Ret. 6–24 law-office which Mr. Pierce had *o·*,
 Pul. 36–25 * now *o·* by Judge and Mrs. Hanna,
  44– 6 * You are fully *o·*,
 '01. 30–11 too *o·* with doing good,

occupied
'01. 34– 6 o· in prayer and in spiritual
My. vi–25 * then o· by the Publishing Society
79–22 * than it ever o· before.
184–12 so o· that I omitted to wire
359–21 * who then o· offices in the building

occupies
Man. 71–12 o· a position that no other church
85– 1 o· only his own field of labor.
No. 11–16 schools . . . that physiology o·,

occupy
Mis. 112– 7 o· time and thought ;
173–18 Does . . . exist without space to o·,
230–16 hours that other people may o· in
Man. 30–13 o·, during his term of Readership
30–21 does not o· the house herself
Ret. 85–16 Seek to o· no position whereto you
Hea. 16–13 Life and Love will o· your affections,

occupying
Pul. 62– 8 * o· a space not more than
Hea. 14– 1 o· the field for a period ;

occur
Mis. 11–24 If special opportunity . . . o· not,
76–15 theory that death must o·,
Man. 80–17 Whenever a vacancy shall o·,
94– 8 there may o· exceptions,
My. 143–24 cease to bless they will cease to o·.

occurred
Mis. 49–12 o· in a class of Mrs. Eddy's ;
304–25 * days on which great events have o·
378– 3 About the year 1862, . . . this o· :
378–14 never o· to the author to learn his
'02. 13–15 when a loss of funds o·,
My. 79–15 * this o· in staid old Boston,
214–29 To desert . . . never o· to me,
284–16 * that such an event has o·.''
298– 3 o· in my life's experience
311– 1 incident, which o· later
311–16 Hence a mistake may have o·

occurrence
Mis. 48–25 Such an o· would be impossible,
290–15 naming the time of the o·,
Ret. 16–11 It was not an uncommon o·

occurring
Man. 26–21 a vacancy o· on that Board
My. 266–13 consequent vacancies o·

occurs
Mis. 11–21 whenever opportunity o·.
Man. 41–13 when the opportunity o·.
55– 7 if this sad necessity o·.
My. 24–30 * It therefore o· to us that

ocean
Mis. 205–14 in the infinite o· of Love,
339–26 sent along the o· of events a wave
Ret. 2–23 nor had they crossed the o· ;
Pul. 88– 4 from the Atlantic to the Pacific o·,
No. 29–23 driftwood on the o· of thought ;
'02. 3–15 occupation of that pearl of the o·,
11– 1 swimming the o· with a letter
12–17 drop of water is one with the o·,
20– 1 o· of events, mounting the billow
Po. 8–12 the silv'ry moon and o· flow ;
65–20 O'er o· or Alps,
My. 121–10 This strength is like the o·,
202–24 a drop from His o· of love,

oceans
My. 124–12 across continents and o·,

o'clock
(see time)

Oconto
Mis. 149–17 chapter sub-title

octagonal
Pul. 24–11 * circular front and an o· form,

October
(see months)

Odd Fellows Hall
My. 54–13 * communion was held at O· F· H·,

odds
Mis. 234–21 to establish . . . against such o·,

odious
Mis. 324–21 seeks to leave the o· company
No. 3–26 becoming o· to honest people ;

odor
Mis. 227–20 the sweeter the o· they send forth
228–10 name whose o· fills the world
237– 5 in place of material flames and o·,
329–17 "breath all o· and cheek all bloom."
331– 6 obedient, full of good o·,
No. 14–12 the o· of the upas-tree
My. 184–18 the o· of my childhood,

odorous
Mis. 267–15 * Comparisons are o·.
Ret. 17–12 the pink — in its o· bed ;
Po. 62–15 the pink — in its o· bed ;

odors
Mis. 240–32 belongs to nature, — namely, pure o·.
Ret. 65– 8 The o· of persecution,
'00. 8– 7 o· emit characteristics of tree

o'er
Mis. 152–10 o· the work of His hand.
384–10 Stay ! till the storms are o·
386–19 o· thy broken household band,
386–22 She that has wept o· thee,
386–28 cloud not o· our ransomed rest
387– 8 Brood o· us with Thy shelt'ring wing,
388–23 And hover o· the couch of woe ;
391– 8 Will count their mercies o·,
395–25 A requiem o· the tomb
396–18 O· waiting harpstrings of the mind
397– 5 And o· earth's troubled, angry sea
397–23 O· the hillside steep,
Chr. 53– 3 O· the grim night of chaos shone
53–24 O· babe and crib.
Ret. 20–17 as sunshine o· the sea,
46– 4 O· the hillside steep,
Pul. 17– 3 O· the hillside steep,
18– 2 O· waiting harpstrings of the mind
18–14 And o· earth's troubled, angry sea
39–16 * o· the Charles its flood of
'00. 15–27 Watch ! till the storms are o·
Peo. 7–11 * As an angel dream passed o· him.
7–19 * Our life dream passes o· us.
Po. 6– 1 Brood o· us with Thy shelt'ring wing,
8–11 I'm watching alone o· the starlit
8–12 O· the silv'ry moon and ocean flow ;
12– 1 O· waiting harpstrings of the mind
12–14 And o· earth's troubled, angry sea
14– 2 O· the hillside steep,
19– 2 breezes that waft o· its sky !
21–12 And hover o· the couch of woe ;
23– 6 Come ever o· thy heart?
25–19 Wreaths for the triumphs o· ill !
27–10 To brighten o· thy bier?
32– 7 Are scattered o· hillside and dale ;
34–22 O· joys departed, unforgotten love.
36– 9 Stay! till the storms are o·
38– 7 Will count their mercies o·,
50– 3 o· thy broken household band,
50– 7 She that has wept o· thee,
50–14 cloud not o· our ransomed rest
53– 8 Light o· the rugged steep.
58–10 A requiem o· the tomb
65–20 O· ocean or Alps,
66–11 No melody sweeps o· its strings !
67–15 o· the dark wavy grass.
68–15 To sweep o· the heartstrings
73– 3 O· the moonlit sea,
My. 31– 7 * "O· waiting harpstrings of the mind ;"
186–13 o· all victorious !

o'erarching
Mis. 394–11 rainbow of rapture, o·, divine ;
Po. 45–14 rainbow of rapture, o·, divine ;

o'erburdened
Mis. 339–22 hast bowed the o· head

offal
Un. 17–10 evil ties its wagon load of o· to the

offence (see also offense)
My. 313–29 to a Baker that was a sorry o·.

offend
Mis. 224–28 our own errors should o· us.
224–32 to o· a whole-souled woman.
Ret. 31–20 yet o· in one point, — Jas. 2 : 10.
Un. 57– 1 which o· the spiritual sense.
My. 196–12 "If any man o· not — Jas. 3 : 2.

offended
Mis. 224–26 determined not to be o·
235–14 shall not be o· in me." — Matt. 11 : 6.
My. 307–17 my theological belief was o·

offender (see also offender's)
Mis. 66– 9 for the o· alone suffers,
212–28 speaks plainly to the o·
Man. 46–18 subject the o· to Church discipline.
54– 3 the o· shall be suspended
54–16 o· shall not be received into

offender's
Man. 50–19 o· case shall be tried

offending
Man. 65–19 removal of the o· member

offense (see also offence)
Mis. 115– 2 o· against God and humanity.
122– 4 by whom the o· cometh!" — Matt. 18 : 7.
223–24 chapter sub-title

offense
Mis. 224–27 unless the o· be against God.
Man. 43– 2 a second o· as aforesaid shall
51– 5 or if he repeat the o·,
52–18 second o· shall dismiss a member
53– 5 member guilty of this o·
53–14 it shall be considered an o·.
53–21 the o· of mental malpractice,
54– 2 that the o· has been committed,
54–19 Special O·.
54–23 second similar o· shall remove
56– 4 if said member persists in this o·,
No. 32– 5 a criminal to repeat the o· ;
'02. 19–11 no person can commit an o· against

offenses
Mis. 122– 3 because of o· !— Matt. 18 : 7.
122– 4 that o· come ;— Matt. 18 : 7.
279– 1 "O· will come :— Luke 17 : 1.

offensive
Mis. 224– 3 makes another's deed o·,

offer
Mis. 35–15 o· for sale at three dollars,
159–21 o· at the shrine of C. S.,
227– 6 necessary to o· to the innocent,
242–19 o· him three thousand dollars if he
345–24 to o· them in sacrifice,
349– 1 o· of pecuniary assistance
366– 7 o· Science, with fixed Principle,
Ret. 86–16 when we o· our gift upon the altar.
Pul. 33–16 * o· food for meditation.
My. 17–12 to o· up spiritual sacrifices,
281–19 * to o· an appropriate occasion

offered
Mis. x– 4 opportunity has at length o· itself
48–30 o· solely to injure her
242– 5 the Professor o· me,
321–28 to hear what is to be o·
Man. 42– 2 o· for the congregations
Pul. 5– 2 o· his audible adoration
No. 39– 5 o· to be heard of men,
My. 7–14 * o· the following motion :
141–18 * o· an occasion for the gathering
174–21 o· me to Christ in infant baptism.
293–21 prayer so fervently o·
325–12 * Years ago I o· my services

offering (see also off'ring)
Mis. xi– 8 While no o· can liquidate
135–19 Add one more noble o·
141– 4 of your hearts' o· to her
397–19 An o· pure of Love,
Pul. 19– 3 An o· pure of Love,
26–15 * A votive o· of gratitude
30– 4 * rather than o· their strength to
87– 4 * to accept this o·, with our
87–11 For your costly o·,
87–21 refusal of that as a material o·.
'02. 13–24 But no one o· the price
Po. 7– 2 An o· pure of Love,
39– 5 An o· bring to Thee !
46–13 An o· pure to God.
My. 258– 5 save one lowly o· — love.
354– 3 by persons o· Bibles

offerings
Mis. 51– 3 Burnt o· and drugs,
149– 8 presenting the various o·,
275–29 floral o· sent to my apartments
294–17 keep back thy o· from asps
319–23 Take thither thy saintly o·,
My. 24–10 * builded by the prayers and o· of
153– 3 floral o· in my name

offers
Mis. 265– 1 o· his own thought,

offertory
Man. 62– 2 o· conforming to the time
My. 78–14 * The o· taken at the beginning

office
Mis. 194– 8 Urim and Thummim of priestly o·,
194–10 this denial would dishonor that o·
366–28 is the o· of Christ, Truth,
Man. 25–12 President shall hold o· for one year,
25–16 term of o· for the Clerk
26– 5 from the time of election to o·.
28–19 fulfil all the obligations of his o·,
28–21 to perform his o· faithfully ;
29–12 shall resign their o· or
30– 8 he or she shall be removed from o·
41–15 disqualifies a member for o·
45–20 hold o· or read in branch churches
54– 5 his or her o· in this Church
65–20 cause for the removal . . . from o·.
78– 4 he may be dismissed from o·
79–12 Before being eligible for o·
79–13 persons nominated for said o·

office
Man. 80–23 term of o· for the editors
80–26 from the time of election to the o·.
89– 3 or vacate her o· of President
94–16 His term of o·, if approved,
94–21 resign nor transfer this sacred o·.
100– 9 Removal from O·.
100–11 to fulfil the obligations of his o·
Ret. 6–19 in the o· of Franklin Pierce,
6–21 Albert spent a year in the o· of
35–24 Urim and Thummim of priestly o·,
42– 6 symbolic words on his o· sign.
Un. 40–28 the nature and o· of Life.
Pul. 28–27 * has filled the o· of pastor
'00. 5–14 and their o· is that of
'01. 4–27 one in essence and in o·.
12–14 Urim and Thummim of priestly o·,
12–16 he would dishonor that o· and
My. 42–12 * Mr. Gross, on assuming o·, said :
137– 4 * in the o· of the Clerk of the Court,
172–22 * and my successors in o·."
247– 9 rotation in o·.
250– 5 Rotation in o· promotes wisdom,
250–29 filled this sacred o· many years,
254–16 * chapter sub-title
255– 3 rotation in o·."
255– 6 By "rotation in o·" I do not mean

office-holder
Pul. 83– 3 * never fulfil as husband and o·?

officer
Mis. 272–14 * any o·, agent, or servant
Man. 28–18 If an o· fails to fulfil
28–20 call a meeting and notify this o·
28–22 said o· shall be dismissed
29– 3 of any other o· in this Church
Un. 15–27 appeases, . . . the venal o·.
My. 335– 8 * o· of the Lodge and Chapter,

Officers and officers
Man. 21– 1 Church O·.
25– 1 heading
25– 4 The Church o· shall consist of
26– 7 re-elected, or new o· elected,
28– 3 Duties of Church O·,
28–15 make sure that the o· of this Church
56–13 o· are required to be present.
56–19 for electing o· and other business,
62–15 o·, teachers, and pupils
65–10 duty of the o· of this Church,
81– 1 re-elected, or new o· elected,
88– 4 O·.
100– 2 for the election of o·,
My. 39–13 * o· for the ensuing year
49–17 * for the purpose of electing o·.
231–26 To THE O· OF THE SUNDAY SCHOOL
255– 7 minor o· who are filling their

offices
Man. 28–17 functions of their several o·
74–10 Teachers' and Practitioners' O·.
74–12 shall not have their o· or rooms in
77–15 performance of their several o·
My. 69–22 * and the administration o·,
243–11 important, responsible o·,
255– 9 or be elevated to o·
359–21 * occupied o· in the building

official
Man. 29– 4 to perform his o· duties.
65–17 applies to their o· functions.
70–12 assume no general o· control
Ret. 52–19 The first o· organ of the
Pul. 47– 5 * first o· organ of this sect.
'00. 7– 2 United States o· statistics
My. 281–18 * "O· announcement of peace
326– 6 * o· and authoritative manner.

officially
Mis. 271–28 * statistics are o· submitted :
Man. 82–19 o· engaged in the work
Pul. 24– 7 * as it is o· called,
59–25 * gentlemen o· connected with

officials
My. 230–21 fidelity . . . in the o· of my church

officious
Man. 45–19 O· Members.

off'ring
Po. 43–14 lay their pure hearts' o·,

offset
Ret. 86– 2 to o· boastful emptiness,

offsets
Mis. 62–11 o· an equal positive quantity,

offspring
Mis. 72– 9 to their helpless o·,
82–15 Man is the o· and idea of
117–13 Obedience is the o· of Love ;

offspring

Mis.	181–18	man is the *o·* of Spirit,
	181–28	as the *o·* of good, and not of
	286–30	in the *o·* of divine Mind,
	287– 2	*o·* of an improved generation,
Chr.	55– 4	the *o·* of David, — *Rev.* 22 : 16.
Ret.	68– 4	it claimed to beget the *o·* of evil,
	68– 5	*alias* an evil *o·*.
	68–28	"Man is the *o·* of Spirit.
Un.	22–18	*Evil.* . . . Error, even, is His *o·*.
	24–20	Man, as God's *o·*, must be spiritual,
No.	37– 1	In human conception God's *o·* had to
'02.	8–28	not as the *o·* of Adam,
My.	5– 5	*o·* of sense the murderers of
	348– 5	the *o·* of a universal cause.
	357– 5	born of God, the *o·* of Spirit,

oft

Mis.	125–25	revolving *o·* the hitherto untouched
	248–19	that I am dead, as is *o·* reported.
Chr.	53–53	To-day, as *o·*, away from sin
Ret.	18–13	*O·* plucked for the banquet,
'01.	35– 4	The question *o·* presents itself,
Po.	1–16	Recalling *o·* the bitter draft
	64– 3	*O·* plucked for the banquet,
My.	280–19	only because of *o·* speaking,
	339–19	the Pharisees fast *o·*, — *Matt.* 9 : 14.
	350–20	*O·* mortal sense is darkened

often

Mis.	4–24	It is *o·* said, "You must
	6– 3	*o·* leaves mortals but little time
	7– 5	mother of one child is *o·* busier
	40– 9	It is *o·* asked, "If C. S.
	52–12	*o·* convenient, sometimes pleasant,
	59–23	speaking *o·* one to another,
	85–30	the sick *o·* are thereby led to Christ,
	102– 3	A corporeal God, as *o·* defined by
	102–22	Human pity *o·* brings pain.
	120–24	as *o·* as they can afford to
	127–32	needs *o·* to be *stirred*,
	159–14	I *o·* retreat, sit silently,
	169–23	*o·* is the foundation of unbelief
	170–32	*o·* means spiritual power.
	284–13	This question is *o·* proposed,
	291–11	*o·* construed as direct orders,
	309– 7	portraiture *o·* fails to express
	311–30	Being *o·* reported as saying
	315–23	as *o·* as once in three months.
	316– 7	When will you . . . is *o·* asked.
	346– 9	The question is *o·* asked,
	373– 5	objected, as he *o·* did,
Ret.	30–10	It is *o·* asked why C. S.
	54– 1	*o·* asked, Why are faith-cures
	82–27	It is *o·* asked which revision
Un.	26–12	hymn-verse so *o·* sung in church :
	27– 3	two English words, *o·* used as if
	29–22	*O·* we can elucidate the
	52–24	beautiful blossom is *o·* poisonous,
Pul.	32– 3	* tint so *o·* seen in New England,
	33– 5	* would *o·* run to her mother
	43–28	* religious teachers so *o·* receive.
	58–19	* rather dark, *o·* too much so
Rud.	14–11	and *o·* those were put off for
No.	43–26	Science *o·* suffers blame through
'01.	19– 9	because of your *o·* coming
	31–27	was my fair fortune to be *o·*
Hea.	16– 2	can never be repeated too *o·*
Peo.	7– 6	turn *o·* from marble to model,
My.	40–29	* Human sense *o·* rebels against law,
	61–25	* *o·* stood under the great dome,
	86– 2	* *o·* unaccustomed to fine architectural
	93–19	* too *o·* disposed to touch upon it
	93–20	* Too *o·* we see only its ridiculous
	130–12	failed too *o·* for me to fear it.
	138–14	other students *o·* ask me
	142–19	as they so *o·* have done,
	212–14	The question is *o·* asked,
	310–27	My mother *o·* presented my
	317–19	He *o·* dissented from what I
	324– 1	* He *o·* spoke his thoughts
	324– 8	* *o·* said you were so original
	324–10	* *o·* hinted that he thought he
	331–26	* Much has *o·* been said of the
	342– 9	* so *o·* seen in reproductions,
	343– 4	* reaching an answer *o·* unexpectedly

often-coming

Mis.	322–18	my *o·* is unnecessary ;

oftener

Mis.	125–26	*o·*, perhaps, the controversies
	136–25	*o·* is not requisite,
	156– 1	would contribute *o·* to the pages
	204– 6	sometimes chronic, but *o·* acute.

oftenest

Un.	18–14	you *o·* console others

oftentimes

Mis.	7–26	*O·* we are denied the results of
Rud.	9–23	has *o·* healed inveterate diseases.

oft-repeated

Mis.	x– 5	comply with an *o·* request ;
	107–23	*o·* violations of divine law,
	172–30	the *o·* declaration in Scripture
Ret.	6– 1	* The *o·* impressions of
Pul.	45–20	* *o·* declarations of our textbooks,
My.	165–19	the *o·* inquiry, What am I?

ofttimes

Mis.	84– 1	Jesus' wisdom *o·* was shown by his
	117–22	experiments *o·* are costly.
	127–24	*O·* the rod is His means of grace ;
Ret.	80–28	*o·* we lose them in proportion to
'00.	3–17	*o·* to shun him as their tormentor.
	7–25	*o·* this attempt measurably fails,
My.	123–25	*o·* small beginnings have large
	128–32	*O·* examine yourselves,
	133– 3	*O·* I think of this in the
	261– 3	guardians of youth *o·* query :

Ohio

(*see* **Cleveland, Columbus, Sandusky**)

oil

Mis.	69–16	three doses of Croton *o·*,
	69–21	bad effects of the poisonous *o·*.
	117–27	borrow *o·* of the more provident
	151–25	continually be full of *o·*,
	276–26	not . . . be found borrowing *o·*,
	341–26	replenished with *o·* day and night,
	342– 3	The foolish virgins had no *o·*
	342–15	With no *o·* in their lamps,
	342–19	lend us your *o·* ! — *see Matt.* 25 : 8.
	342–22	wise virgins had no *o·* to spare,
My.	292–23	croton *o·* is not mixed with morphine

Old

'02.	page 1	heading
My.	218– 5	Neither the *O·* nor the New Testament

old

Mis.	ix–19	There is an *o·* age of the heart,
	ix–20	a youth that never grows *o·* ;
	x– 9	and reliable as *o·* landmarks.
	xi–25	on to *o·* battlegrounds,
	10–24	wherein *o·* things pass away
	80–29	outdoing the healing of the *o·*.
	80–29	The *o·* will not patronize the new
	93– 6	*Can fear or sin bring back o· beliefs*
	167–12	How *o·* is he?
	175–14	not with the *o·* leaven of the scribes
	178– 4	left his *o·* church, as I did,
	178– 8	could not be put into *o·* bottles
	178–29	wall between the *o·* and the new ;
	178–30	the *o·* religion in which we have
	179– 1	The *o·* churches are saying,
	179–12	This is the *o·* consciousness.
	179–22	*o·* consciousness of Soul in sense.
	180– 7	A dear *o·* lady asked me,
	211–10	people in the *o·* Bay State.
	223–25	wisdom in the *o·* proverb,
	233–13	into the *o·* garment of drugging
	246–16	to forge anew the *o·* fetters ;
	256–16	To meet the *o·* impediment,
	283–13	Any exception to the *o·* wholesome
	329–28	*O·* robin, though stricken to the
	372–18	* delineations from the *o·* masters."
	375–12	* in Italy, I studied the *o·* masters
	375–22	* resemblance, . . . to the *o·* masters !
	375–29	* identified with the *o·* masters,
	376– 7	* oldest of the *o·* masters,
	390– 5	*O·* Time gives them her palm.
Man.	35– 1	Children when Twelve Years *O·*.
Ret.	4– 7	One hundred acres of the *o·* farm
	8– 4	when I was about eight years *o·*,
	27–30	*o·* to God, but new to His
Un.	23– 1	treatment received by *o·* Gloster
	28– 9	declare some *o·* castle to be peopled
	44– 8	The *o·*, *o·* story,
	61– 8	and is — neither young nor *o·*,
Pul.	1– 8	An *o·* year is time's adult,
	14–18	What if the *o·* dragon should send
	14–21	waters of chaos and *o·* night.
	26–27	* lamp over two hundred years *o·*,
	41–27	* *O·* familiar hymns
	49–24	* She chose the stubbly *o·* farm
	57–27	* born of an *o·* New Hampshire family,
No.	12–22	departed from the *o·* landmarks.
	15– 9	to explain and prop *o·* creeds,
	43–21	"new wine into *o·* bottles ;" — *Matt.* 9 : 17.
'00.	8–15	things new and *o·*." — *Matt.* 13 : 52.
	15– 1	Putting aside the *o·* garment,
	15–20	wedding garment new and *o·*,
'01.	2– 7	trying to put into the *o·* garment
	15–18	little short of the *o·* orthodox hell
	21– 4	new editions of *o·* errors ;

old

'01. 24–17 more than two hundred years o'.
24–19 It is as o' as God,
26–25 subject of the o' metaphysicians,
29–17 whenever they return to the o' home
31–28 taught by some grand o' divines,
32– 7 I loved Christians of the o' sort
'02. 3– 9 the o' national family pride and joy
8 13 the o' and the new commandment,
10–24 The o' and recurring martyrdom
17–10 the o' and the new commandment,
Hea. 2–12 * "O' Adam is too strong for young
18– 6 to put new wine into o' bottles ;
18–12 new wine into o' bottles.
18–15 reconciled with the o' belief ;
18–16 new wine into the o' bottle
Peo. 3–16 Truth meets the o' material thought
Po. 22– 6 shall bid o' earth good-by
page 26 poem
39–14 Sons of the o' Bay State,
55– 6 O' Time gives thee her palm.
My. 15–32 * 'Twill be the O', O' STORY
60– 7 * my uncle, the good o' deacon of
68–13 * The o' church at the corner of
72– 9 * titled aristocracy of the o' world
79–15 * this occurred in staid o' Boston,
80–11 * o' auditorium of The Mother Church,
80–22 * into the o' church,
90–19 * reincarnation of the o', o' gospel
95–14 * o' Massachusetts State House.
107– 8 to which the o' school has become
117–13 Is not the o' question still rampant?
133–16 one more round of o' Sol
135– 6 may be applied to o' age,
145–13 * an o' ailment my mother had."
147– 6 o' elm on North State Street
168– 6 people of my dear o' New Hampshire,
172– 2 * o' Yale College Athenæum,
225– 8 of the o' "new tongue."— see Mark 16 : 17.
236–10 An o' axiom says :
257– 5 the new cradle of an o' truth.
273– 3 * Mrs. Eddy's ability in o' age
273–11 and now am o' ;— Psal. 37 : 25.
310–23 * Mary, a child ten years o',
325– 9 * o' part of Boston in which he
327–19 * an o' law, or rather a section of an
350–22 o' foundations of an early faith
(see also man)

old of-

Mis. 17– 8 like the patriarch of o',
33– 3 The high priests of o'
63– 2 said of o' by Truth-traducers.
158–20 As of o', I stand with sandals on
Ret. 65–17 of o' ruled Christ out of the
76–21 as of o', on the Pentecost Day,
79–25 Of o' the children of Israel were
Pul. 8 10 with Job of o' we exclaim,
32–14 * like any abbess of o'.
No. 41– 3 Pharisees of o' warned the people
'00. 7–20 we say as did Mary of o' :
9–11 or as of o' cry out :
'01. 2–21 disciples of o' experienced,
'02. 11–27 Of o' the Jews put to death the
Hea. 2– 5 synagogues as of o' closed upon it,
My. 104– 7 Of o' the Pharisees said of the
119–12 Mary of o' wept because she
191– 2 Nicodemus of o', who said,
212–19 Being like the disciples of o',
221– 5 prophets of o' looked for

Old and New Testaments

Pan. 7–18 study of the O' and N· T·

Old and the New Testaments

My. 179–13 The O' and the N· T· contain

Old Country

Pul. 62– 3 * favorably known in the O· C',

olden

Mis. 237– 2 o' opinion that hell is fire
Chr. 53–37 Thus o' faith's pale star
Ret. 2–18 books, printed in o' type
Pul. 82–12 * In o' times the Jews claimed
83–16 * In o' times it was the Amazons
Po. 47– 3 the o' and dainty refrain,
My. 147–20 truth that to-day, as in o' time,
162–19 wisdom which spake thus in o' time
177–17 was allied to that o' axiom :

older

Mis. 187–13 translators of the o' Scriptures
311–11 some of the o' members are not
Ret. 80–23 the o' sheep pass into the fold
My. 29–14 * and in an o' civilization ;
212– 6 o' and more open sins,
216–26 As you grow o', advance in the
323–26 * should mean to your o' students
342– 7 * O' in years, white-haired

oldest

Mis. 347–29 C. S. Journal was the o'
376– 2 * true art of the o', most revered,
376– 7 * the o' of the old masters,
Ret. 14–29 even the o' church-members wept.
My. 310–14 My o' brother, Samuel D. Baker,
313–27 My o' sister dearly loved me,

old-fashioned

Pul. 62– 6 * cast bells of o' chimes.
62–10 * the o' chimes required
'01. 32–18 lives of those o' leaders

Old Man of the Mountain

Po. v– 9 * poem
page 1 poem

oldness

No. 25– 7 the o' of the letter."— Rom. 7 : 6.

old-new

'00. 2– 5 o' theme of redeeming Love
My. 166–22 the o' song of salvation,

old rose

Pul. 25–22 * upholstered in o' r' plush.
25–23 * with frieze of the o' r',
26–25 * pale green with relief in o' r'.

old-school

Ret. 14– 5 pastor was an o' expounder

Old Testament

Mis. 187–19 the O· T· might have been as
My. 179–17 if the O· T· and gospel

old-time

Mis. 251–25 falling leaves of o' faiths
331–22 falling leaves of o' faiths,
394–18 * Such o' harmonies retune,
'01. 18– 8 the o' medicine of matter.
Peo. 1 13 collisions with o' faiths,
Po. 57– 4 * Such o' harmonies retune,

old-wives'

My. 340– 7 o' fables, and endless genealogies.

olive

My. 192–27 and leave a leaf of o' ;

ologies

Peo. 4– 8 Mythology, or the myth of o',

Olympiad

Mis. 1– 2 looked longingly for the O'.

Olympian

Mis. 142–22 A boat song seemed more O'

Omaha, Neb.

Pul. 89–24 * Bee, O', N'.

Omega

Mis. 333–10 "Alpha and O'" — Rev. 1 : 8.
Un. 10–19 God is the Alpha and O',
'02. 2–22 Christ is Alpha and O'.
My. 267– 9 Alpha and O' of man
267–27 no Alpha and no O'.

omen

Mis. 132– 4 a favorable o', a fair token
My. 148–14 Then we beheld the o',

ominous

Mis. 239–13 and take . . . the o' hand-trunk.

omit

Mis. 92– 1 To o' these important points
My. 20–29 * been decided to o' this year the

omits

My. 276– 8 because of . . . she o' her drive,

omitted

Ret. 83 27 That these . . . are ever o',
Pul. 59–10 * hymns and psalms being o'.
88– 2 chapter sub-title
88–10 articles are reluctantly o'.
My. 184–13 I o' to wire an acknowledgment
275–17 have o' my drive but twice

omitting

Mis. 191–15 and by o' the first letter,
No. 28–21 o' the spirit of this Science
'02. 20–17 begin o' our annual gathering

omni

Mis. 25–23 As o' is from the Latin word
'02. 7–11 Latin o', which signifies all,

omnipotence

absence of
Ret. 58– 5 for the absence of o'
anchor in
My. 132–11 and anchor in o'.
and omnipresence
Mis. 96– 9 person of o' and omnipresence
Ret. 56–16 o' and omnipresence of God,
Rud. 9–25 o' and omnipresence of God ;
No. 10–26 His o' and omnipresence.
20–14 God's o' and omnipresence

omnipotence

bow of
Peo. 3–14 bow of *o·* already spans
definition of
My. 221–10 establish the definition of *o·*,
faith in
Peo. 12–24 Having . . . we lose faith in *o·*,
God's
No. 20–14 God's *o·* and omnipresence
My. 293–15 understanding of God's *o·*,
good is
Mis. 13–30 you will find that good is *o·*,
grooves of
My. 107–21 nearer the grooves of *o·*.
hands of
My. 127–29 through the hands of *o·*.
has all power
Mis. 97–17 and know that *o·* has all power.
His
No. 10–26 His *o·* and omnipresence.
Peo. 5–17 to declare His *o·*."
its
My. 189–15 Love derives its *o·* from
meaning of the
Ret. 56– 9 meaning of the *o·*, omniscience,
must interpret
Mis. 71–15 causation must interpret *o·*,
neck of
Mis. 370–17 arms about the neck of *o·*,
of God
Mis. 31–20 he has no faith in the *o·* of God,
of good
Mis. 121–10 the *o·* of good, as divinely
200–27 faith in the *o·* of good,
of His love
Mis. 322–25 the *o·* of His love ;
of Life
My. 116– 4 *o·* of Life, Truth, and Love,
of Spirit
Ret. 31–24 bent low before the *o·* of Spirit,
of Truth
Mis. 61– 9 *o·* of Truth over error,
192–14 knowing the *o·* of Truth.
omnipresence and
Ret. 88–29 demonstrates omnipresence and *o·*,
My. 174–26 omnipresence, and *o·* enfolds me.
omniscience of
My. 188–12 even the omniscience of *o·* ;
proof of the
Pan. 7– 6 gives in proof of the *o·* of
right hand of
Pul. 9–28 ear and right hand of *o·*,
Science of
Mis. 101–22 Science of *o·* demonstrates
sense of
Peo. 14–16 girt with a higher sense of *o·* ;
supremacy and
No. 18– 8 God's supremacy and *o·*.
understanding of
My. 294–19 conscious understanding of *o·*,
understood
Mis. 200– 6 understood *o·* to be All-power :
unfolds
Mis. 183–22 Science unfolds *o·*,
vindicates the
Hea. 15– 3 vindicates the *o·* of the Supreme

———

Mis. 174– 5 presence and power over *o·* !
201–11 *o·* of the Mind that knows this :
258–25 as infinite consciousness, . . . *o·* ;
333– 5 *o·*, omnipresence, goodness,
Ret. 58– 1 Stating the divine Principle, *o·*
Peo. 9–26 no *o·*, unless *o·* is the *All*-power.
My. 5–29 demonstrate the *o·* of divine Mind
274– 8 *o·*, omnipresence, and omniscience

omnipotent

Mis. 3–25 God is supreme and *o·*,
17– 4 the law of *o·* harmony
25–22 *o·* and omniscient Mind.
37– 1 God would not be *o·* if
63–19 God is *o·* and omnipresent ;
90– 1 He must know that God is *o·* ;
134–23 when at war with the *o·* !
172–14 "the Lord God *o·* — *Rev. 19 : 6.*
172–31 good is *o·* and omnipresent.
173–13 Mind is God, *o·*
183– 2 ever-present good, *o·* Love,
197–30 recognize God as *o·*,
205–15 This *o·* act drops the curtain
232–18 Spirit is *o·* ;
260–19 Truth is supreme and *o·*.
268–18 *o·* and ever-present good.
Un. 19– 4 else He is not *o·*,
39– 6 *o·* Love which annihilates hate,
60– 7 We call God *o·* and

Un. 62–12 *o·* and ever-present good
Rud. 11– 4 next to belief in God as *o·* ;
No. 23– 5 nor make evil *o·* and omnipresent.
42–16 senses would enthrone error as *o·*
Pan. 6–24 if God, good, is *o·*,
'01. 5– 9 and God *o·*, omnipresent,
25– 4 eternal in the heavens, *o·* on earth,
Hea. 5– 3 admitting that God is *o·*,
10– 9 God — good — is *o·* ;
My. 106– 9 immutable laws of *o·* Mind
108–16 lawgiver, *o·*, infinite, All.
135–30 divine Love, *o·*, omnipresent,
294– 5 God has all power, is *o·*,
296–20 God, good, *o·* and infinite.

omnipresence

Mis. 96– 9 person of omnipotence and *o·*
102–32 defines *o·* as universality,
174–22 the All of God, and His *o·* ?
229–10 since God is *o·*,
333– 5 omnipotence, *o·*, goodness,
Ret. 28– 6 understand the *o·* of good
56–10 omniscience, and *o·* of Spirit,
56–17 omnipotence and *o·* of God,
88–29 demonstrates *o·* and omnipotence,
Rud. 9–25 omnipotence and *o·* of God ;
No. 10–26 His omnipotence and *o·*.
20–14 God's omnipotence and *o·*
My. 174–26 *o·*, and omnipotence enfolds me.
274– 8 *o·*, and omniscience of Life,

omnipresent

Mis. 8–15 Love that is *o·* good,
14– 1 it fills all space, being *o·* ;
63–19 God is omnipotent and *o·* ;
105–18 unknown to the *o·* Truth.
172–32 good is omnipotent and *o·*.
173–13 Mind is God, omnipotent and *o·*.
307– 6 understanding of *o·* Love !
Un. 3–25 because, if He is *o·*,
43–27 *o·* Spirit which knows no matter.
60– 8 We call God omnipotent and *o·*,
No. 23– 6 nor make evil omnipotent and *o·*.
23–27 *o·* and omniscient Mind ;
42–17 would enthrone error as . . . *o·*,
'01. 5– 9 and God omnipotent, *o·*,
'02. 12– 8 he has one *o·* God :
Po. 23–19 Supreme and *o·* God,
My. 135–30 divine Love, omnipotent, *o·*,
294– 5 omnipotent, omniscient, *o·*,

omniscience

Mis. 25–24 *o·* means as well, all-science.
Ret. 56– 9 *o·*, and omnipresence of Spirit,
My. 188–11 even the *o·* of omnipotence ;
274– 8 omnipresence, and *o·* of Life,

omniscient

Mis. 25–22 omnipotent and *o·* Mind.
Chr. 53–47 *O·* power, — gleaming through Mind,
No. 23–27 omnipresent and *o·* Mind ;
'01. 5–10 omnipotent, omnipresent, *o·*.
Po. 18–15 *o·* notice the frail fledgling hath.
My. 294– 5 *o·*, omnipresent, supreme

omnis potens

Ret. 58– 1 Principle, omnipotence (*o· p·*),

once

Mis. ix–10 *o·* fragmentary and faint
6–23 *o·* convinced of the uselessness
44–25 demand of mortal thought *o·* met,
54–20 When *o·* you are healed by Science,
61–15 * I went *o·* to a place
69–14 I was *o·* called to visit a sick man
73– 8 *o·* discern their spiritual meaning,
79– 3 and the places *o·* knowing them
120–24 *o·* in three years is perhaps as often
126– 4 *o·*, at least, to hear the soft music
136–25 convening *o·* in four months ;
138–17 I *o·* thought that in unity
159–17 grand collections *o·* in each year.
159–23 Here I talk *o·* a year,
195–25 I *o·* believed that the practice
222–13 that *o·* he would have resisted
278–13 I *o·* wondered at the Scriptural
315–23 as often as *o·* in three months.
326– 5 *O·* more he seeks the dwelling-place
339– 4 took place *o·* in Heaven,
348–17 *o·* in about seven years
370– 9 watch-towers shout *o·* again,
Man. 25–14 but *o·* in three years.
32–15 but *o·* during the lesson.
38–17 Members who *o·* Withdrew.
39– 7 Members *o·* Dismissed.
39– 9 who has been excommunicated *o·*,
52–16 sufficient . . . for forgiveness for *o·*,
91–23 will be held *o·* in three years
Ret. 4–13 Where *o·* stretched broad fields

once

Ret.	8–22	o· more asked her if she had
	63–22	St. Augustine o· said,
	89–16	Jesus was o· asked to exhort,
	89–17	o· again entered the synagogue
Pul.	30– 2	* o· when a Boston clergyman
	32– 6	* At o· one would perceive
	49–26	* O· bought, the will of the
	82– 7	* and as one . . . o· said
No.	22– 5	o· clothed with a "brief authority;"
	36– 8	He o· spoke of himself
Pan.	14– 4	O· more I write, Set your affections
'00.	11– 5	O· I was passionately fond of
'01.	16–20	o· refer to an evil spirit as *dumb,*
'02.	2–24	and the Church o· loved me.
Peo.	14–17	o· again the power of divine Life
Po.	73– 8	with thee in spirit o· more.
My.	44–17	* forwarded at o· to our Leader,
	52–24	* More than o·, in her earnestness,
	108–21	for if they did o· touch it,
	189–26	the sunny South — o· my home.
	222– 2	the disciples of Jesus o· failed
	316–22	o· more under Mr. Flower's able
	338–20	For o· he may have overlooked

once at-

Mis.	177–19	Answer at o· and practically,
	302–22	destroyed the copies at o·
	305–32	* we ask every one . . . *to act at* o·.
	380–12	to begin this stupendous work at o·,
Ret.	5–27	* at o· pleasing and profitable.
	31–15	banished at o· and forever
Hea.	12–17	saw at o· the concentrated power
Peo.	13–19	* I cannot change at o·
My.	61–11	* I saw at o· that somebody had
	157– 6	* to be used at o· to build a
	344 13	will be at o· better than he was

Once A Week

Pul.	89– 6	* O· A W·, New York City.

oncoming

Ret.	23–10	o· hours were indicated by

One

Mis.	18–21	one in good, and good in O·.
	258–14	In divine Science, God is O·
	264–11	Its Principle is O·,
	264–11	to demonstrate the divine O·,
	268– 8	The Holy O· saith,
	342–12	O· "altogether lovely." — *Song* 5 : 16.
Ret.	23–19	O· "altogether lovely," — *Song* 5 : 16.
Pul.	4–15	reflects the infinite O·,
No.	24– 9	rests on God as O· and All,
Pan.	12–22	monotheism, — it has O· GOD.
'00.	4–24	believe that God is O· and *All?*
'01.	4–22	that God is the infinite O·
	4–25	conceive of God as O·
	5– 3	by the word Person, or as O· ;
	6 14	yet God must be O·
	8– 1	chapter sub-title
	9–22	the Holy O· of God." — *Mark* 1 : 24.

one *(see also one's)*

Mis.	6–32	families of o· or two children,
	7– 5	mother of o· child is often busier
	7–12	where o· would least expect it,
	7–17	o· naturally reflects that
	8–16	that blesses infinitely o· and all?
	10–29	Even in belief you have but o·
	10–30	and this o· enemy is your self
	11–15	and o· could save it only in
	11–17	would o· sooner give up his own?
	11–22	persecute and despitefully use o·,
	11–25	o· can include them in his
	11–29	When smitten on o· cheek,
	12– 2	Hate no o· ; for hatred is
	12–15	unless o· be watchful and steadfast
	13– 2	mercy and charity toward every o·,
	13– 3	just so far as o· and all permit me
	16– 3	so comfort, cheer, and bless o·,
	16– 6	as o· grows into the manhood or
	16– 7	o· finds so much lacking,
	16– 8	o· saith : The Principle . . . is infinite :
	17–31	by which o· loses himself as matter,
	18–18	children of o· common Parent,
	18–20	o· in good, and good in One.
	18–26	can we in belief separate o· man's
	19–21	o· who abides by his statements
	22–15	from o· individual to another ;
25– 3, 4		o· cause and o· effect,
	25– 8	neither o· really exists,
	34– 4	O· who has been healed by C. S.
	35–17	*is o· obliged to become a student*
	35–18	*if o· is obliged to study under you,*
	37– 9	"I and my Father are o·." — *John* 10 : 30.
	39–14	God giveth to every o· this
	39–21	o· Christian Scientist who has
	39–23	"o· another's burdens, — *Gal.* 6 : 2.

one

Mis.	40– 1	is as necessary in the o· case as
	40– 3	its power would be arrested if o·
	40–31	or the ignorance by which o·
	41– 2	in the diabolical practice of o· who,
	43– 3	enables o· to heal cases without even
	43–10	is the o· least likely to pour into
	43–12	The simple sense o· gains
	43–21	If o· student tries to undermine
	43–24	incapacitates o· to practise or
	43–26	temporary success of such an o· is
	44–10	when conducted by o· who
	47–27	*What should o· conclude as to*
	47–29	That largely depends upon what o·
	48–13	alleged that at o· of his recent lectures
	50–15	that gives o· the power to heal ;
	51– 7	mesmerism is of o· of three kinds ;
	51–22	* from the lips of Truth o· mighty breath
	52– 4	how much o· can do for himself,
	52– 6	if he were to serve o· master,
	52–19	*if o· gets tired of it, why not*
	52–24	or failing to demonstrate o· rule
	54–18	*after o· month's treatment*
	54–19	*treatment by o· of your students.*
	58– 1	*If o· has died of consumption,*
	58– 4	o· learns its *unreality ;*
	58– 5	then it has no power over o·.
	58–11	*if o· must deny the evidences of*
	58–28	o· human mind governing another ;
	59– 1	o· government and God.
	59–20	There is but o· right Mind,
	59–21	that o· should and does govern man.
	59–23	speaking often o· to another,
	59–24	success that o· individual has with
	60–19	or for o· who sleeps to
	63– 1	which is infidel in the o· case, and
	63– 4	claim that o· erring mind cures
	63– 4	claim that . . . cures another o·
	63– 9	divine trinity is o· infinite remedy
	64–18	must benefit every o· ;
	65–27	proves that strict adherence to o·
	67–25	whereby o· expresses the sense
	67–26	sense of words in o· language by
	69–17	In o· hour he was well,
	69–27	I will send his address to any o·
	71– 6	o· writer thinks that he was
	75– 6	*insist that there is but o· Soul,*
	75–13	hence Soul is o·, and is God ;
	75–20	assists o· to understand C. S.
	77–17	o· eternal round of harmonious being.
	84–24	turn o·, like a weary traveller,
	87– 3	into o· gulp of vacuity
	87 17	*that no o· there was working in*
	87–19	I never commission any o· to
	88–30	As a rule, drop o· of these doctors when
	91–11	Christian compact is love for o· another.
	93–29	for even o· moment.
	94– 7	the twain that are o· flesh,
	97– 5	It is not o· mortal thought
	97– 8	Our Master said of o· of his students,
	98–11	to aid o· another in finding ways
	99– 5	To weave o· thread of Science
	99–26	voice of o· crying in the wilderness,
	101–22	demonstrates but o· power,
	102–29	as o· that beateth the air,
	102–30	"o· on God's side is a majority."
	103– 5	o· is temporal, while the other is
	104– 8	God, the o· inclusive good.
	109–26	To understand good, o· must discern
	112– 1	in other words, the o· evil
	112–18	regarded his act as o· of simple
	115–25	If o· lives rightly,
	115–25	every effort to hurt o·
	115–26	will only help that o· ;
	116–29	If in o· instance obedience be
	117–28	He illumines one's way when o·
	118– 9	allow o· numeral to make incorrect
	118–25	it gives o· plenty of employment,
	119–26	rights which o· justly reserves to
	126– 2	to o· eternal sermon ;
	127–20	o· must do good to others.
	129– 6	having done this, o· will naturally,
	130–20	without o· single mistake,
	130–24	The greatest sin that o· can commit
	130–25	o· of God's "little ones." — *Matt.* 18 : 6.
	131–12	o· faith, . . . o· baptism.
	131–24	I, for o·, would be pleased to have
	134–12	"in o· place," — *Acts* 2 : 1.
	135– 7	o· in heart, — o· in motive,
	135– 8	not o· of you can be separated from me ;
	135–14	Is it a cross to give o· week's time
	135–19	Add o· more noble offering to
	136–10	in turning aside for o·
	137–20	each o· return to his place of labor,
	137–26	each o· of the innumerable errors
	140– 2	no o· could hold a wholly material

one

Mis. 140–11	No o· could buy, sell, or mortgage
141– 6	no o· can suffer from it,
141– 7	for no o· can resist the power
143–22	husband and wife reckoned as o·,
143–26	"with o· accord — *Acts* 2 : 1.
143–27	in o· place." — *Acts* 2 : 1.
145–19	our names may melt into o·,
147– 7	in unity, preferring o· another,
147–14	The man of integrity is o· who
147–29	the fair, open, and direct o·,
148– 2	We shall never find o· part of
148–29	every o· that thirsteth, — *Isa.* 55 : 1.
149– 8	o· after another has opened his lips
150–26	Not more to o· than to all,
155– 1	but o· cause and effect.
155– 6	Sacrifice self to bless o· another,
156–13	in the o· held at Chicago,
156–15	in o· student's opinions
159–11	o· of these is sacred to
160–10	joy in knowing that o· is gaining
167– 6	the o· altogether lovely.
169–31	was o· of the passages explained
171–10	When o· comes to the age with
175–23	o· belief takes the place of another.
175–26	reveals the o· perfect Mind
178– 1	have met o· who comes from the
178–18	* If any o· had said to me that
181– 1	"for o· is your Father," — *Matt.* 23 : 9.
181–12	and infinite Spirit must be o·.
187–21	substance, and life of man are o·,
187–22	and that o· is God,
189–28	as o· having authority, — *Matt.* 7 : 29.
191–10	o· of you is a devil?" — *John* 6 : 70.
191–12	if . . . there is more than o· devil.
191–13	"Master, we saw o· — *Mark* 9 : 38.
191–15	assertion . . . of more than o· devil ;
191–22	supposition of the existence of o·
193–25	no o· is following . . . without
195–10	every o· can prove, in some degree,
195–20	o· correct premise and conclusion,
197– 4	o· more frequently used than many
198– 1	wholly governed by the o· perfect Mind,
198– 4	o· must commence by turning away from
209–27	goodness and blessedness are o· :
211–21	When o· protects himself
212– 4	O· step away from the direct line
212–19	flow not into o· of their channels.
212–24	If, . . . o· is at work in a wrong
215– 3	go from o· extreme to another :
216–15	justifies o· in the conclusion
216–19	O· of these extracts is the story of
217– 4	nor reason attempts to find o· ;
217–11	fallacy . . . matter and Spirit are o·
219–17	in the o· he must change his patient's
220– 3	a good rule works o· way,
221– 4	gives o· opportunity to handle the
221– 5	o· gains in the rules of metaphysics,
221– 9	error and sickness are o·,
221–19	denial of this fact in o· instance
222–12	In this state . . . o· is ready to
225–28	In about o· hour he awoke,
227–12	Some uncharitable o· may give it a
227–13	ere that o· himself become aware,
229– 1	believe . . . that any o· is liable to
229– 3	This mental state prepares o· to
230– 5	indecision as to what o· should do.
230– 6	If o· would be successful in the future,
230– 8	o· of which is contemptible,
231– 9	walking ! o·, two, three steps,
231–31	through which the loved o· comes not,
232–19	will be o· having more power,
236–16	to give, to o· or the other, advice
236–27	as a general rule, o· will be blamed
237–16	is not essentially o· of conscience :
237–28	fetters of o· form of human slavery.
239–11	upon the sidewalk o· winter morning,
240– 3	through the cold air the little o·
241– 8	o· having morals to be healed,
242– 6	offered me, . . . or o· of my students,
242– 9	give sight to o· born blind.
242–20	if he will heal o· single case of
242–22	at the rate of o· ounce in two weeks,
243– 5	I have not yet made surgery o· of the
243–11	effected the cure in less than o· week.
245–27	a thing to be thankful for that o· can
245–29	* "o· with God is a majority."
247–10	in o· of my works
249–18	not o· has been sent to my house,
253– 9	o· a congressman
253–24	o· tithe of the agonies that gave that
256–19	notice from o· to two weeks previous to
261–29	o· will either abandon his claim
265– 9	All must have o· Principle
265–11	have but o· opinion of it.
269– 7	either he will hate the o·, — *Matt.* 6 : 24.
Mis. 269– 8	will hold to the o·, — *Matt.* 6 : 24.
270–18, 19	o· fold, and o· shepherd ;" — *John* 10 : 16.
271– 9	o· cause and o· effect.
272–25	* but o· legally chartered college of
273–14	o· grand family of Christ's followers.
273–30	o· Primary and two Normal
276–25	not o· . . . be found borrowing oil,
277–20	* o· more fact to be recorded
277–27	never so near as when o· can be just
280– 4	o· of the angels presented himself
281– 9	o· ambition and o· joy.
281–10	if o· cherishes ambition unwisely,
281–10	o· will be chastened for it.
281–23	yours is o· of the most beautiful
282–25	O· other occasion which may call for
283– 2	or o· can to advantage speak the
283– 4	As a rule, o· has no more right to
283– 6	than o· has to enter a house,
284– 1	each o· to do his own work well,
284–30	if o· is intrusted with the rules of
285– 4	and not o· of them circulated,
286–24	mortal mind and body as o·,
287– 6	for o· is your Father, — *Matt.* 23 : 9.
287–27	it makes o· ruler over one's self
289–16	marriage contract two are made o·,
289–17	"they twain shall be o· — *Matt.* 19 : 5.
289–20	*divorced* two minds in o·.
290–24	o· must benefit those who
291–14	every o· has equal opportunity
292– 5	That ye love o· another." — *John* 13 : 34.
295–22	not wholly represented by o· man.
297– 2	o· readily sees that this Science
298–25	O· says, "I find relief from pain in
298–27	through unconsciousness o· no more
298–29	o· thinks he is not mistaken,
299– 1	mistakes recur until o· is awake to
300–32	Healing morally and physically are o·.
303–15	every o· the same rights and
305– 2	* o· representative from each Republic
305–24	* asked to contribute o· cent to be fused
305–31	* ask every o· receiving this circular
309– 1	the personal sense of any o·,
310–14	plead for all and every o·,
310–19	o· must comply with the church rules.
311– 9	so, loving o· another,
311–18	I hate no o· ;
311–28	ought not that o· to take the cup,
314– 6	O· of these individuals shall open
317– 4	we are all of o· kindred.
319–20	season pass without o· gift to me.
325–18	Balancing on o· foot,
326–29	Discerning in his path the penitent o·
334–15	only as o· gives the lie to a lie ;
334–16	without o· word of Truth in it.
335–12	O· mercilessly assails me
335–21	The notion that o· is covering iniquity
336–25	wherever o· ray of its effulgence
338–16	will subject o· to deception ;
339–19	o· furrow to the brow of care?
339–30	O· backward step,
340– 1	o· relinquishment of right
340– 2	o· faithless tarrying,
344– 4	expressed the wish to become o· of
347–15	O· says, Go this way ;
347–17	premonition of o· of them,
348– 8	When God bids o· uncover iniquity,
348– 9	o· should lay it bare ;
348–25	o· who had lost all faith in them.
350–14	convened in about o· week
351– 9	would not if I could, harm any o·
352–20	in order to enable o· to
352–23	Through the divine energies alone o·
353– 7	If o· asks me, Is my concept of
353– 9	concept of me, or of any o·,
353–10	you have gained the right o·
353–12	this misrepresents o· through
356–24	O· can never go up, until o·
361–11	testifying to o· creator,
361–30	are not o·, but are inseparable as
361–31	If o·, who could say which
361–31	who could say which that "o·" was?
372– 3	had not o· feather's weight
373– 1	O· incident serves to illustrate
373–15	O· great master clearly delineates
374–21	the o· illustrating my poem
374–24	o· renders not unto Cæsar
375–32	* as o· who gives no mean attention
376–20	there rose o· rod of rainbow hues,
378– 6	o· Mr. P. P. Quimby of Portland,
379–18	o· could write a sonnet.
385– 4	* And o· eternal noon."
387–19	That make men o· in love remain.
399– 5	Midst the glories of o· endless day."
399–22	Lifted higher, we depart, Having o·.
Man. 15– 6	adore o· supreme and infinite God.

one

Man.
28–26 especially of *o·* who has been
29–22 *o·* to read the BIBLE,
29–22 *o·* to read S. AND H.
35– 4 *o·* of Mrs. Eddy's loyal students,
37–17 *O·* Normal student cannot recommend
38– 8 must be countersigned by *o·* of these.
38–22 on *o·* year's probation,
43–12 by a written text as no *o·* else can.
49–10 C. S. nurse shall be *o·* who
50– 4 by *o· of her own sex.*
60– 5 *O·* meeting on Sunday during
72–18 under *o·* church government.
73– 4 include at least *o·* active practitioner
73–25 the pupils of *o·* teacher.
73–27 member of *o·* branch Church
74– 1 or of of *o·* C. S. society
78–20 $200 for any *o·* transaction,
84– 8 shall teach but *o·* class yearly,
84–11 shall have *o·* class triennially,
90–12 will continue not over *o·* week.
90–20 *O·* student in the class shall prepare
92–13 either *o·*, not both,
92–14 should teach yearly *o·* class.
95–12 *o·* shall be assigned them by the Board.
95–18 for *o·* or more lectures.
97– 5 consist of *o·* loyal Christian Scientist
110–12 *o·*, at least, of the given names
111– 2 *o·* of the Christian names must be
Chr.
53– 4 *O·* lone, brave star.
55–25 *o·* fold, and *o·* shepherd.— *John* 10 : 16.
Ret.
2–17 *o·* of my Grandmother Baker's
2–24 *o·* of which contained a full account
3– 2 at *o·* time held the position of
6– 6 *o·* with the open hand.
6–16 *o·* of the most talented,
6–29 was *o·* for the abolition of
7–14 * *o·* of the most distinguished men in
11– 3 *o·* of my girlhood productions.
14–16 not *o·* of whom had had then made
16– 1 *O·* memorable Sunday afternoon,
16– 6 *o·* of them said, "Did you hear
16– 8 *o·* hour ago she could not speak a
19– 6 spared to me for only *o·* brief year.
22–19 father and mother are the *o·* Spirit,
22–20 *o·* parent, the eternal good.
23– 5 merged into the *o·* infinite Love.
26–22 To *o·* "born of the flesh," — *John* 3 : 6.
27– 6 never been read by any *o·* but myself,
28– 1 "little *o·*." — *see Matt.* 10 : 42.
28– 3 *o·* must acquaint himself with God,
30–11 revealed to me as *o·* intelligence,
30–21 No *o·* else can drain the cup
31–13 *o·* great and ever-present relief
31–20 yet offend in *o·* point, — *Jas.* 2 : 10.
33–11 *o·* pervading secret :
33–14 *O·* drop of the thirtieth attenuation
33–16 *o·* teaspoonful of the water
34– 8 give me *o·* distinct statement of
40– 4 *o·* time I was called to speak before
43– 3 I began by teaching *o·* student
43–17 taught the . . . . class *o·* term.
43–18 taught *o·* Primary class, in 1889,
48– 7 every *o·* should build on his own
48– 9 subject to the *o·* builder and maker,
49–20 only *o·* ever granted to a *legal college* for
49–25 in *o·* common brotherhood.
50– 5 *o·* course of lessons at my College,
50–16 as many as seventeen in *o·* class.
56– 5 diverges from the *o·* divine Mind,
56–19 and that *o·* is the infinite good,
57–11 but *o·* Soul, and that *o·* is infinite.
57–26 ingrafting upon *o·* First Cause
58–11 as *o·* having authority, — *Matt.* 7 : 29.
59– 9 means subtraction in *o·* instance and
60–28 *o·* Truth, Life, Love,
60–29 but *o·* Spirit, Mind, Soul.
64– 1 in this sense they are *o·*.
64–10 good is equally *o·* and *all,*
64–11 opposite claim of evil is *o·*.
68–11 *O·* is false, while the other is true.
68–11 *O·* is temporal, but the other is
68–14 *o·* is your Father, — *Matt.* 23 : 9.
71–27 efforts to obtain help from *o·* who
72– 1 In the practice of C. S. *o·* cannot
76–22 when the disciples were of *o·* accord.
76–25 He thinks of every *o·* in his real
82–12 who locate permanently in *o·* section,
83–12 mislead no *o·* and are their best guides.
86– 4 is but *o·* way of *doing* good,
86– 5 but *o·* way of *being* good,
86–19 and another *o·* undertakes to
86–21 No *o·* can save himself without God's
88– 3 C. S. healers with *o·* another.
88–22 *O·* would, . . . blush to enter unasked
89– 6 preaching and teaching were . . . . *o·*.

Ret.
89– 7 Men assembled in the *o·* temple
89–11 If *o·* worshipper preached to the others,
90–10 to whom St. John addressed *o·* of his
90–14 even though *o·* of the twelve
90–26 *O·* of my students wrote to me :
90–29 *o·* of the children of light.
94–17 and practice be essentially *o·*.
94–23 since Science is eternally *o·*,
Un.
1– 4 this may be set down as *o·* of the
5– 9 Every *o·* should be encouraged not to
7–20 here is *o·* such conviction :
10–12 phenomena of this *o·* infinite Mind.
17– 1 has only *o·* chance of successful
19– 2 must be *o·*, in an infinite Being.
21– 3 excusing *o·* another." — *Rom.* 2 : 15.
21– 6 not two personalities, but *o·*.
21– 7 good and evil talk to *o·* another ;
21– 8 not two but *o·*, for evil is naught,
27– 6 An *egotist* is *o·* who talks much of
27–10 is *o·* uncertain of everything except
29–12 *o·* Soul, or Mind, and that *o·* is
35–21 matter and mortal mind are *o·* ;
35–21 this *o·* is a misstatement of Mind,
37– 3 there can be but *o·* Life.
38–17 rulership of more gods than *o·*.
42–19 as *o·* having authority, — *Matt.* 7 : 29.
46–13 "I and my Father are *o·*." — *John* 10 : 30.
48– 1 fair to ask of every *o·* a reason for
49–18 *O·* should appear real to us,
51– 7 never make *o·* hair white or black,
51–16 not *o·* of all these individualities
53–19 would have *o·* question.
53–27 for *o·* is your Father, — *Matt.* 23 : 9.
54– 5 *o·* must lose sight of a false claim.
55– 1 Jesus accepted the *o·* fact whereby
59– 8 as *o·* who came down from heaven,
60– 1 mortal inventions, *o·* and all
61– 7 he was *o·* with the Father,
Pul.
3–26 Perchance some *o·* of you may say,
4– 8 mathematically number *o·*,
4–12 will find that *o·* is as important
4–16 "*o·* on God's side is a majority."
5– 1 *o·* of the very clergymen who had
5– 6 light of *o·* friendship after another
13–20 The sin, which *o·* has made his
14– 7 *o·* extreme follows another.
15–12 Is the informer *o·* who sees the foe?
15–21 unite all interests in the *o·* divinity.
16– 7 Joyous, risen, we depart Having *o·*.
20–21 *o·* of the many dates selected
21– 2 inevitably love *o·* another
21–20 to the welfare of any *o·*.
22– 3 Christian churches have *o·* bond
22– 3 *o·* nucleus or point of convergence,
22– 4 Christian churches have . . . *o·* prayer,
23–17 * *o·* of the most potent factors in
24– 4 * It is *o·* of the most beautiful,
26–13 * It is *o·* of vast compass,
27–12 * *o·* representing the heavenly city
27–25 * *O·* more window in the auditorium
32– 7 * At once *o·* would perceive that
32–28 * *O·* of her brothers, Albert Baker,
33– 6 * *O·* night the mother related to her
33–22 * no *o·* else had seen him,
30–23 * *o·* of the most beautiful residences
36–24 * *o·* of the utmost taste and luxury,
37– 5 * *o·* factor in her removal to Concord,
37–19 * and *o·* or two other friends
37–22 * depending on any *o·* personality.
38–30 * in *o·* form of belief or another
39– 5 * all teach that *o·* great truth,
39–25 * 'mid them all I only see *o·* face,
42– 8 * at any *o·* of these services.
45–10 * "*O·* of the grandest and most helpful
45–11 * *o·* month before the close of the
47–22 * *o·* mile from the State House
48–25 * *o·* of her characteristics,
49–17 and not *o·* died."
49–25 * within *o·* mile of the "Eton of
50– 5 * *o·* of her motives in buying
50– 9 * No *o·* religious body holds the
52–26 * and C. S. is *o·* result.
53–10 * is contained in the *o·* word — *faith.*
53–12 * and *o·* returned to give thanks
54–15 * as no *o·* before him understood it ;
54–29 healed Mr. Whittier with *o·* visit,
56– 1 * *O·* or more organized societies
56–12 * *o·* of the most remarkable,
57–11 * *o·* of the most beautiful buildings
59–13 * congregation repeating *o·* sentence
59–29 * Before *o·* service was over
63–14 and not *o·* died."
65–22 * *o·* bitter winter day,
67–14 * *o·* of those movements which seek
70–10 * *o·* of the most remarkable women in

one

Pul.
72– 8 * o· of the first to be seen.
72–28 * naming as o· great essential
73–11 * o· of the greatest Biblical scholars
74–23 maintain but o· conclusion
74–25 "Christ is individual, and o· with
75– 1 o· Jesus of Nazareth.
76–18 * O· of the two alcoves is
77– 3 * o· of the most chastely elegant
78– 2 * o· of the most magnificent examples
79–12 * o· cannot take up a daily paper
79–22 * we should be obliged to invent o·."
80– 3 * pendulum that has swung to o· extreme
81– 9 * chapter sub-title
82– 7 * o· whom her love had glorified
82–19 * and no o· to urge them.
85–14 * as the o· chosen of God

Rud.
2– 5 o· of the three subjects, or agents,
2–16 but o· infinite individual Spirit,
4– 1 the o· Father-Mother God.
9–18 If o· is untruthful,
11– 8 Therefore good is o· and All.
13–13 o· Life and one Mind.
16–14 Is there more than o· school of
16–15 but o· school of the Science of

No.
1–18 theology and medicine of Jesus were o·,
2–13 by healing o· case audibly,
5– 5 o· of the severe realities of
5–27 prevents o· from healing
7–20 strict performance of each o·
8– 4 let us add o· more privilege
8–23 If o· be found who is too blind for
9– 5 prejudices, and errors of o· class
10–11 but o· standard statement,
10–12 o· rule, and o· Principle
15– 6 would enable any o· to prove
22–20 it follows that there is more than o·
22–25 o· of you is a devil?" — John 6 : 70.
26– 4 believe . . . matter and Spirit are o· ;
31–21 Physical and mental healing were o·
34–15 o· upon whom the world of sense
35–22 o· with Him now and forever.
36– 1 demonstrated the infinite as o·,
36– 2 o· infinite and the other finite ;
38–20 o· consciousness, — which includes only
39–18 include all mankind in o· affection.
45–28 "O· on God's side is a majority ;"

Pan.
1–19 one God and o· Christianity.
2–21 conceived as o· personified nature,
3– 7 lacks but o· charm to make it
3–19 o· supreme, holy, self-existent God,
3–23 (o· of my girlhood studies),
4–17 but God is Mind and o·.
6– 7 but not as o· that beateth the mist,
6–27 the belief in more than o· spirit,
7– 6 o· divine, infinite Principle.
8– 7 o· the divine, infinite Person,
8–11 sacredness of o· Christ Jesus?
8–17 one God and o· law,
8–19 for o· is your Father, — Matt. 23 : 9.
9– 5 term "spirits" means more than o·
9–20 to help such a o· is to help one's
11– 3 "Lie not o· to another, — Col. 3 : 9.
13–12 rebuke and exhort o· another,
14– 5 love o· another ;
14– 5 at the table of our Lord in o· spirit ;

'00.
5–28 enables o· to utilize the power of
8–27 When God speaks to you through o·
9–23 no o· can fight against God, and win.
9–26 have some o· take my place
9–29 But no o· else has seemed equal to
15– 2 a new o· that is up to date.
15– 3 o· that for many years has been

'01.
3–12 * "The o· Supreme Being,
4–26 these three are o· in essence
5– 7 o· divine infinite triune Principle,
5–13 by calling o· the divine Principle
6– 7 which reckons three as o·
6– 8 reckons o· as o· and this o· infinite.
6–10 o· Person, or three persons?
6–23 neither be o· nor infinite in the
8– 8 "I and my Father are o·," — John 10 : 30.
8– 9 in the sense that o· ray of light is
8–10 it is o· with light, but it is not
12– 1 to such a o· our mode of worship
14–21 o· must watch and pray
14–22 even as o· guards his door against
15–11 in proportion as o· understands it
15–18 to waken such a o· from his
16–27 commence with o· truth told
17–17 in from o· to three interviews,
18– 1 "mother tincture" of o· grain
22–11 so if o· is true, the other is false.
22–16, 17 I do not say that o· added to o· is
22–17 or o· and a half,
22–19 that o· and o· are two all the way

one

'01.
23– 1 o· and two are neither more nor less
24–21 I had not read o· line of Berkeley's
26– 9 In o· sentence he declaims against
27–13 If any o· as yet has healed
27–14 as I have in o· to three interviews
33–28 motives which actuate o· sect

'02.
3– 2 thousand loyal . . . to o· disloyal,
7–22 chapter sub-title
7–25 love o· another ; — John 13 : 34.
8–15 God and Love are o·.
12– 8 he has o· omnipresent God :
12–16 "I and my Father are o·," — John 10 : 30.
12–16 o· in quality, not in quantity.
12–17 drop of water is o· with the ocean,
12–17 a ray of light o· with the sun,
12–18 Father and son, are o· in being.
13–14 about o· half the price paid,
13–24 no o· offering the price I had paid
16–26 they never destroy o· iota of
17– 4 o· gladly obeys when obedience gives
18–14 unto o· of the least — Matt. 25 : 40.
18–16 "Love o· another, — John 13 : 34.
18–29 all his disciples save o·.
19– 6 called o· a "fool" — see Luke 24 : 25.

Hea.
1–20 o· religion has a more spiritual basis
2– 1 the religion nearest right is that o·.
3–25 not three persons in o·,
3–26 three statements of o· Principle.
4–25 if this model is one thing at o· time,
5–10 O· of our leading clergymen
5–14 Does any o· think the departed are not
5–19 obscure the o· grand truth
5–19 covered, in o· way or another,
9–15 Is it a duty for any o· to believe
13–13 o· teaspoonful of this water
13–26 Mesmerism makes o· disease while it
13–27 that o· is worse than the first ;
13–28 o· lie getting the better of another,
14–20 perceptive faculty by which o· learns

Peo.
1– 1 one faith, o· baptism. — Eph. 4 : 5.
4–19 three terms for o· divine Principle
4–20 three in o· that can be understood,
5– 3 one faith, o· baptism." — Eph. 4 : 5.
5– 9 whose . . . and theology were o·.
8– 5 answers the prayer of o· and not of
9– 1 one faith, one Lord, o· baptism ;
11–26 " with o· of their fingers." — Matt. 23 : 4.
12– 1 we should think for o· moment of
14–19 one faith, o· baptism." — Eph. 4 : 5.

Po.
6–14 That make men o· in love remain.
22–11 And bask in o· eternal day.
22–13 hath o· race, o· realm, o· power.
27– 5 O· word, receding year,
37– 4 And o· eternal noon."
40– 1 "Good Templars" o· and all,
41–16 but o· given to suffer and be?
42– 4 Yet there's o· will be victor,
43– 4 Loving God and o· another,
66– 8 whisper of o· who sat by her side
68– 1 So o· heart is left me
75–12 Midst the glories of o· endless day."
76– 6 Lifted higher, we depart, Having o·.
78– 8 the Union now is o·

My.
vi– 6 * no o· on earth to-day,
4– 1 o· finds the spirit of Truth,
6–27 is the o· edifice on earth which
10–22 * entreaty on the part of some o· else.
11– 7 * She has been the o· of all the world who
14–19 * a fabrication of the evil o·,
18–21 rebuke and exhort o· another.
19–13 * To o· of the many branch churches
22– 4 * o· that would accommodate me
25–16 o· and all of my dear correspondents
28–28 * divinely guided woman,
28–31 * revealed the o· true Science
29–12 * sight which no o· who saw it will ever
30– 3 * awaiting admission to o·.
30– 4 * nobody attended more than o·,
31– 4 * "Just as I am, without o· plea ;"
31–22 * o· of the events of their lives.
31–31 * trained carefully under o· leader,
32– 6 * their voices rose as o·
36– 5 * rose as o· to indicate their approval
41– 4 * No o· can change the law of
41–12 * no o· to escape that blessedness,
41–24 * that his real estate is o· of blessedness.
41–25 * Why should any o· postpone his
42– 7 * o· who has for many years
42– 9 * o· of the helpful contributors
45– 7 * o· of the greatest and most
45–27 * logically followed the preceding o·.
45–30 * o· foot loftier than the Bunker Hill
49– 4 * half-persuaded o· is wholly
51– 2 * no o· in the world who could take
51–14 * no o· who is so able as she to lead

one

My. 54– 8 * o· hour before the service
55– 2 * date is memorable as the o·
56–12 * o· in each of the following named
57– 5 * o· that would have the sacred
58–30 * doubtful if there was o· so deeply
59–32 * to o· who knew of your early
60–29 * I was asked by o· of the Directors
61–21 * O· feature about the work
62– 7 * love that trembled in o· human heart
64– 1 * As o· thought upon the significance
64–10 * an honored o· before the world.
66–15 * is so well situated . . . as this o·,
68– 6 * about o· mile and a half of pews.
69– 1 * o· of the extraordinary features
69–27 * If o· would get an idea of the size
71– 1 * stationed in o· of the towers,
71–16 * o· of the most imposing church
71–21 * o· vast auditorium
74–14 * Boston is indebted to them for o· of
74–30 * o· for its hopefulness
77– 3 * o· of the largest in the world.
78–20 * O· of the remarkable features
80– 1 * cures that carried o· back to the
81– 1 * Upon entering The Mother Church o· was
81– 8 * o· of them without pause and
81–23 * swelling as o· voice.
82– 3 * o· near and dear to them.
83– 4 * is patent to every o· residing in
85–11 * O· does not need to accept the
85–30 * o· of the few perfect sky-lines
86–18 * o· which indicates plainly enough
86–23 * o· of the most interesting
87–11 * o· does not notice these unless
89– 1 * This church is o· of the largest
89– 7 * o· of the largest organs in the world.
89–10 * o· finds in the English cathedrals,
89–27 * has been o· of the marvels of the
91–17 * serves to call attention to o· of the
91–28 * o· of the finest places of worship
92–22 * but o· cannot sneer away the
94– 6 * "O· cannot sneer away the
96– 8 * in no sense, save o·, be compared
96–10 * The o· point of resemblance is
97– 1 * almost every o· is inclined to
98–25 * record is one of which any church
99– 1 * o· of the marvellous, great, and
105–14 I have healed at o· visit a cancer
107–23 or scatter the shade of o· who
109–19 God is o· because God is All.
114– 7 Has o· Christian Scientist yet
116–12 If God is o· and God is Person,
117 6 A personal motive . . . will leave o·
117–11 make o· a Christian Scientist.
117–29 to seek the o· divine Person,
119– 5 based on o· infinite God, and man,
121–25 If o· would follow the advice
122– 1 advice that o· gratuitously bestows
123–10 o· of the finest localities in
125–10 sling of Israel's chosen o·
130–15 the o· evil or the evil o·.
132–21 God all, o·,— one Mind
133– 6 acknowledge God, and be o· ;
143–16 o· more round of old Sol
137–15 except in o· or two instances,
137–28 implicit confidence in each o·
143–10 o· and all of my beloved friends
145– 4 o· of Concord's best builders
150–11 hallowed by o· chord of C. S.,
153–32 up to the o· source, divine Life
155– 8 and that o· the God and Saviour
165–17 portion of o· stupendous whole,
167– 6 and unites us to o· another.
167–17 be o· acceptable in His sight,
169– 2 I invite you, o· and all,
178–26 not o· word in the book was effaced.
181–27 o· expositor of Daniel's dates
186–12 o· Father-Mother God,
187–15 love o· another." — I John 3 : 11.
187–28 "that ye love o· another." — John 15 : 12.
188–24 o· man's head lies at another's feet.
189–11 vibrating from o· pulpit to another
189–12 and from o· heart to another,
189–13 commingling in o· righteous prayer,
195–17 to use . . . the o· talent that we all
198– 6 great gratitude to our o· Father.
202–10 but to love o· another :— Rom. 13 : 8.
204–10 in o· Principle, divine Love,
204–11 which makes them o· in Christ.
212–19 "with o· accord in o· place," — Acts 2 : 1.
213– 8 o· rancorous and lurking foe
213–27 chapter sub-title
214– 1 select o· only to place on the walls
215–10 dozen or upward in o· class.
217–25 "An improved belief is o· step
218–27 to o· no more than to another.

one

My. 223–23 of o· of the Church By-laws,
224–18 words, and classification of o· author
225–29 Mind, Soul, which combine as o·.
226– 9 are but an effect of o· universal cause,
226–10 the o· divine intelligent Principle
227– 3 as o· who never weakened
227–11 o· out of three of their patients,
228– 9 I fail to know how o· can be
228–31 such a o· was never called to
229– 5 cannot be found at Pleasant View o· of
230–10 apply not to o· member only,
230–10 but to o· and all equally.
231–20 o· woman is sufficient to
233–21 O· should watch to know
233–23 should o· watch against such a result?
233–31 Thinking of person implies that o·
235– 5 Straining at gnats, o· may swallow
235–20 is he matter or spirit? Neither o·.
236– 6 name for o· central Reading Room,
236–14 exchange the present name for the o·
239–15 identity as o· man and o· woman
239–17 God is o·, and His idea, image, or
239–17 image, or likeness, man, is o·.
239–18 and so includes all in o·.
239–21 the infinite o·, or o· infinite,
241–14 * issue raised is an important o·
241–14 * and o· upon which there should be
241–21 * idea of the o· divine Mind.
244– 7 o· or more lessons on C. S.,
244–24 may not require more than o· lesson.
249– 2 without harming any o·
252–11 to make o· not only know the truth
252–12 make o· enjoy doing right,
252–12 make o· not . . . run away in the storm,
253–17 that they may be o·,— John 17 : 11.
254– 1 become o· with his creator,
257–25 I group you in o· benison
258– 5 save o· lowly offering love.
258–10 o· word, . . . broke the gloom
260–30 but o· Jesus Christ on record.
261– 7 continue thus with o· exception :
263– 2 leaving o· alone and without His glory.
266–15 This flux and flow in o· direction,
266–16 tends in o· ultimate
267– 1 the o· and the only religion
267–20 O· individual may first awaken
268–30 and you see male and female o·
269– 1 universe included in o· infinite Mind
269–12 * parts of o· stupendous whole,
272– 1 o· who steadfastly and actively
272– 2 o· who leavens the loaf of life
273–13 I for o· accept his wise deduction,
274–12 To begin rightly enables o· to end rightly,
274–14 that o· achieves the Science of Life,
275–28 unite in o· Te Deum of praise.
276 3 as o· watches a criminal
276–19 * no o· should seek to dictate
292–19 prayers in which o· earnest, tender
292–20 effect of o· human desire
293– 5 o· against the other
301–10 unite as brethren in o· prayer :
303– 3 o· incarnation, o· Mother Mary.
303– 4 I know that I am not that o·,
305– 1 from o· P. P. Quimby
307–22 For o· so unlearned, he was
308–20 O· time when my father was visiting
309–14 justice of the peace at o· time.
312–14 * Her position was an embarrassing o·.
312–16 * only o· effort at self-support.
312–27 the remains of my beloved o·
313–19 evening walk, but I seldom took o·.
315–10 * happy home as o· could wish for.
316– 2 uniting in o· body those who
318–16 to visit o· of my classes
319–27 * considered the time an important o·
321– 6 * of your devoted and faithful
321– 7 * o· who knew who and what you are,
321–12 * told the same story to every o·
321–19 * to change my opinion o· iota
324– 7 * from any o· but yourself.
324– 9 * no o· could be of much service
324–28 * to see if there was o· woman
325– 2 * spoke of o· especial day
328– 8 * o· referred to in Miss Jones' letter :
333– 5 * found by o· of your own citizens,
334–14 * the woman . . . is some other o·?
335–27 * the case was o· of yellow fever
339– 6 and o· Christ Jesus.
341– 1 I have o· innate joy,
342–21, 22 all the churches, o· by o·,
343–24 each o· was the fruit of experience
343–26 I found at o· time that they had
344– 6 Christ is 'o· with the Father,'
356–22 either he will hate the o·,— Matt. 6 : 24.
356–23 else he will hold to the o·,— Matt. 6 : 24.

one

My.	356–25 infinite is *o·*, and this *o·* is Spirit ;
	362–15 * in *o·* place with *o·* accord,
	363–25 be sure that *o·* is not doing this,

(see *also* **Christ, church, day, Eddy, faith, God, Lord, Mind, mind, numbers, person, side, thing, values, year**)

one-hundredth
(see **numbers**)

one-in-all

My.	247– 1 all-in-one and *o·*.
	254–22 all-in-one and *o·*.

oneness

Mis.	93– 8 allness and *o·* of God
	131–12 upon the rock of divine *o·*,
	152– 5 the *o·* of God includes also
	259– 7 It is this infinitude and *o·*
	264–12 demands *o·* of thought and action.
	271– 8 C. S., — that rests on *o·* ;
	286– 9 man's *o·* with God,
	289–17 *O·* in spirit is Science,
Un.	24– 9 can never be outside of His *o·*.
	54–15 *at-one-ment*, or *o·* with God,
No.	1–19 in the divine *o·* of the trinity,
Pan.	7–16 absolute *o·* and infinity of God,
Peo.	13–11 unity of Mind and *o·* of Principle.
My.	338–24 recognize the *o·* of Jesus
	342–22 simplicity of the *o·* of God ;
	342–23 the *o·* of Christ and the perfecting
	356–27 This simple statement of *o·*

one's

Mis.	xi– 8 *o·* debt of gratitude to God,
	11–15 If *o·* life were attacked,
	12–16 *o·* temptations to sin are increased
	43–23 To fill *o·* pocket at the expense of
	107–23 *o·* oft-repeated violations of
	107–25 lack of seeing *o·* deformed mentality,
	109–14 *o·* sins be seen and repented of,
	109–27 consecrate *o·* life anew.
	112–26 inability to see *o·* own faults,
	117–28 He illumines *o·* way when one
	118–13 *o·* sympathy can neither atone **for**
	127–19 finds *o·* own in another's good.
	129– 5 *O·* first lesson is to learn
	130–23 Where . . . *o·* acts are right,
	148–13 impelled by a power not *o·* own,
	221–20 saps *o·* understanding of the
	236–25 notwithstanding *o·* good intentions,
	236–26 in *o·* efforts to help another,
	238–19 Let *o·* life answer well
	290–25 hold a place in *o·* memory,
	310–18 *o·* connection with this church,
	374–27 Pictures are portions of *o·* ideal,
	374–28 this ideal is not *o·* personality.
Man.	3– 9 a power not *o·* own,
Ret.	27–21 ripples of *o·* first thoughts of it
	67– 2 hence *o·* concept of error is
	72– 5 *o·* ability to do good,
	74– 1 *o·* sense of corporeality,
	75–10 *o·* writings on ethics,
	75–16 If *o·* spiritual ideal is comprehended
Rud.	1–17 in distinction from *o·* appearance
No.	2–24 destroys *o·* ability to heal
	5–28 the last state of *o·* patients
Pan.	9–21 It loves *o·* neighbor as
'00.	3–10 *O·* idol is by no means his servant,
'02.	2– 6 on the tablet of *o·* own heart,
Hea.	12–28 dishonest and divide *o·* faith
	15–12 any *o·* perfect satisfaction
Peo.	9– 7 may declare *o·* belief ;
My.	18–16 finds *o·* own in another's good."
	87–27 * whatever *o·* special creed may be,
	105– 6 prove *o·* faith by his works.
	117–10 will break *o·* own dream
	118–19 *O·* voluntary withdrawal from society
	122– 5 in *o·* own moral make-up.
	161–25 because *o·* thought and conduct
	213–15 Unless *o·* eyes are opened to
	234– 3 absorbing *o·* time writing or reading
	249–11 for *o·* own destruction.

(see *also* **enemies, self**)

ones

Mis.	11–10 teaching the wayward *o·*
	127– 2 His "little *o·*," — *Matt.* 18 : 6.
	130–26 God's "little *o·*." — *Matt.* 18 : 6.
	137–17 dear *o·*, if you take my advice
	231–10 groan for the unfeasted *o·*.
	275–12 the motherless little *o·*,
	317– 9 The dear *o·* whom I would
	329– 8 putting down the green *o·*,
Ret.	90– 8 there taught a few hungry *o·*,
	90– 9 To these selected *o·* . . . he gave
Pul.	4–15 Each of Christ's little *o·*
	45–17 * upon the hopeful, trustful *o·*,

ones

Pul.	81–12 * Some of her dearest *o·*
'00.	8–27 through one of His little *o·*,
Hea.	17–22 are supposed physical *o·*,
Po.	17– 4 My loved *o·* in glory
	65– 4 A meeting with loved *o·*
	67– 9 memory of dear *o·* deemed dead
My.	17–30 His 'little *o·*,' — *Matt.* 18 : 6.
	38–19 * the little *o·* were not a whit behind
	53–31 * by having so many different *o·*
	90–13 * in pain or death for self or dear *o·*.
	127–24 garrisoned by God's chosen *o·*,
	163– 9 beloved *o·* who have so kindly
	166–22 my dear *o·*, let us together sing
	167–19 Give to all the dear *o·* my love,
	186– 4 May God's little *o·*
	256–23 Parents call home their loved *o·*,
	356–16 *o·* . . . presented in S. and H.

onlooker

Pul.	45–15 * predictions of workman and *o·* alike

onlookers

Mis.	369–12 madness it seems to many *o·*.

Only

Mis.	173–17 preexisted in the All and *O·*
Ret.	60–12 God and His idea as the All and *O·*.
No.	25– 2 the All and *O·* of our being.

only

Mis.	1–19 *o·* by removing the dust
	3– 6 imparting the *o·* power to heal
	3–27 their *o·* supposed efficacy is in
	4– 9 Its *o·* power to heal is its power to
	5–23 those *o·* who do not understand
	6– 9 *o·* those cases that are pronounced
	8–28 can *o·* be fulfilled through the gospel's
	9–29 great and *o·* danger in the path
	11–15 and one could save it *o·* in
	13– 1 The *o·* justice of which I feel
	13–19 *o·* upon what the shifting mortal
	13–23 the existence of good *o·* ;
	13–25 Science *o·* needs to be conceded,
	14– 4 take in *o·* the immortal facts
	15–20 *O·* through the sore travail of
	18–13 Thou shalt love Spirit *o·*,
	18–15 as God's spiritual child *o·*,
	18–24 *O·* by admitting evil as a
	23–19 the first and *o·* cause.
	23–26 God is seen *o·* in that which
	25–19 Christianity is Christlike *o·* as it
	25–22 Jesus' *o·* medicine was omnipotent
	26– 5 *o·* logical conclusion is
	27–31 *o·* by first admitting that it is
	28– 1 *o·* to reappear in the spiritual
	28– 9 *o·* what mortal mind makes them ;
	29– 4 Had it been applicable *o·* to his
	29– 8 he prayed, not for the twelve *o·*,
	34– 5 is not *o·* healed of the disease, but
	35–21 *O·* because both are important.
	36– 8 *o·* cause is the eternal Mind,
	41– 1 brute-force that *o·* the cruel and
	42– 2 *does life continue in thought o·*
	42–23 *O·* as we understand God,
	42–25 exists *o·* in spiritual perfection,
	44–18 could *o·* have been a belief of pain
	46– 6 needs *o·* to be tested scientifically
	49–10 *o·* case that could be distorted into
	49–27 This belief presupposes not *o·* a
	52–18 *dream not dispelled, but o· changed,*
	53– 6 *o·* as we master error with Truth.
	53–14 You *o·* weaken your power to heal
	53–26 *o·* the thought educated away from
	55–24 knows that he can have one God *o·*,
	55–25 when he regards God as the *o·* Mind,
	56– 9 Life is God, the *o·* creator,
	56–22 Life needs *o·* to be understood ;
	59–22 *o·* benefit in speaking often
	59–28 divine Mind, who is the *o·* physician ;
	60– 7 *o·* as the woeful unrealities of being,
	60– 7 is the *o·* way to destroy them ;
	60–13 *departed friends — dead o· in belief?*
	62– 8 Man is seen *o·* in the true likeness
	64– 8 the *o·* philosophy and religion
	64–29 The *o·* evidence of the existence of
	67–21 *O·* thus is the right practice of
	70– 3 I believe, not *o·*, but I *demonstrated*
	70– 6 *o·* explanation in divine metaphysics.
	70–25 *o·* in a finite and material sense
	71–31 law of Science, that God is good *o·*,
	72– 5 *o·* living and true origin, God.
	72–19 *disappear o· to the natural sense?*
	72–26 it exists *o·* to material sense.
	74– 3 new-born sense subdues not *o·* the
	77– 9 not *o·* acknowledge the incarnation,
	82–21 mortals see and comprehend *o·* as
	86–10 *exist o· in imagination?*

only

Mis. 88–23	* o· to those who do not enter into
89–30	o· avail himself of the efficacy of
93–16	sanctions o· what is supported by
93–20	exists o· as fable.
97–32	o· cause for making this question
102– 4	is o· an infinite finite being,
102–25	seems thus o· to the material senses,
105–20	C. S. is my o· ideal ;
106–20	I can o· bring crumbs fallen from
106–29	affords the o· strains that thrill
108–14	be conceived of o· as a delusion.
108–24	needs o· to be known for what
109–16	Ignorance is o· blest by reason of
109–30	fear not sin, . . . but o· *fear to sin.*
115– 8	o· as the result of sin ;
115–26	every effort to hurt one will o· help
115–32	mental power in the right direction o·,
134–25	Error is o· fermenting,
140–18	urged o· the material side
151–14	He is man's o· real relative
154–10	God o· waits for man's worthiness
161–18	The o· record of our Master as a
163–22	O· three years a personal Saviour !
164–25	portrayed him as the o· Son of God,
164–25	the o· begotten of the Father,
168–12	o· such as are pure in spirit,
172–26	peace can o· be declared on the
179–21	o· come into the spiritual
182– 3	putting him to death, o· in belief,
184– 7	o· when man reflects God in body
188–30	was the first, the o· man.
191–29	could o· be possible as evil beliefs,
194–13	o· needs the prism of this Science
199– 3	o· mortal, erring mind can claim
199– 7	amenable o· to moral and spiritual
200–30	o· a vagary of mortal belief,
201– 2	receives the mortal scoff o· because
205–17	consciousness reflects o· Spirit,
208– 6	He is cognizant o· of good.
208–11	o· to submit to the law of God,
218– 5	declares the invisible o· by
222–20	cancelled o· through human agony :
228–17	as the o· suitable fabric
229– 9	If o· the people would believe
229–12	if o· the pulpit would
233– 7	but are such in name o·,
233–28	they o· who adhere to that standard.
234– 1	o· by reason of our belief in it
237–21	o· work out its own destruction ;
243 16	o· in proportion as he understands
247–30	o· an evil belief of mortal mind,
248–23	The opium falsehood has o· this to it :
251–12	commemorate not o· our nation's
252–17	C. S. is not o· the acme of Science
256– 2	not o· cured of their belief in disease,
258–28	o· suitable or true idea of Him ;
259–14	the o· law of creation,
259–18	the o· law of being.
260–10	The divine Mind was his o·
260–14	mortal thought holds o· in itself
261– 5	can o· be removed by reformation.
261– 8	C. S. not o· elucidates but
262– 2	they will harm myself o·,
269–19	Mind to be the o· physician.
260 20	man can o· be Christianized through
270–23	the o· passport to his power ;
271–21	o· chartered College of Metaphysics.
272– 7	* for metaphysical purposes o·,
278–17	Those o· who are tried in the furnace
280–16	then o· are we working on one side
283–32	o· personal help required
285– 1	in favor of combating evil o·,
286–26	Spirit, God, is the o· creator :
287–12	o· high and holy joy can satisfy
288– 9	rash conclusion that regards o· one
289– 4	o· temperance is total abstinence.
289 32	whence they can choose o· good.
290– 3	two persons o·, should be found
295–20	should not o· be queried, but flatly
299–15	is the o· absolute good ;
299–17	is the o· absolute evil.
301–14	require o· a word to be wise ;
303– 2	need o· to shine from their home
308–14	know its practicality o· by healing
308–23	o· to reappear in due season.
313–27	hereafter the o· pastor of
315–11	can teach annually three classes o·.
315–14	o· of such as have promising
315–17	not o· through class term, but
324–25	o· to find the lights all wasted
325–14	o· to find its inmates asleep
327–21	o· to take them up again,
333–15	away from the o· living and true God,
334–15	o· as one gives the lie to a lie ;
334–17	o· then, do you handle it in Science.

only

Mis. 336–28	touches time o· to take away its
337–24	O· the devout Marys,
338–13	afford the o· rule I have found
340– 6	O· by persistent, unremitting,
345–15	* fit o· for women and weak men ; "
346– 9	God created o· the good,
347–30	o· authenticated organ of C. S.
348–12	o· a question of time when God
350– 8	The P. M. . . . Society met o· twice.
350–29	teach the use of such arguments o·
352–28	o· difference between the healing of
355–15	o· stimulates and gives scope to
358– 6	o· appropriate seals for C. S.
358–16	Christ's vestures are put on o· when
358–24	o· College for teaching C. S.
359–26	o· as we rise in the scale of being.
360– 6	Great o· as good,
361–24	God is the o· Mind,
368–20	can o· be portrayed in these words
368–24	o· for money, and at a fearful stake.
375–28	* the o· true art
382–21	obtained the first and o· charter
382–23	was its first and o· president ;
386–26	I o· know my wife, Thy child,
389–10	Love is our refuge ; o· with mine eye
Man. 34–14	o· textbooks for self-instruction in
35–20	can unite with this Church o· by
37–23	O· members of The Mother Church
42–21	C. S. can o· be practised according to
43–18	This By-Law not o· calls more
51–24	O· the members of this Board
52– 3	Members in Mother Church O·.
57– 8	Called o· by the Clerk.
64– 5	literature sold or . . . shall consist o· of
68–19	calls to her home . . . o· those
80– 9	o· in accordance with the By-Laws
81–25	O· the Publishing Society
83 10	such o· as have good past records
83–16	not o· during the class term but
85– 1	occupies o· his own field of labor.
86–24	chapter on "Recapitulation" o·.
91–13	O· the President gives free
92–22	O· those persons who are members
99–17	elected o· by the C. S. Board
104– 3	For The Mother Church O·.
104– 7	is adapted to The Mother Church o·.
110–13	Initials o· of first names will not
Ret. 14–24	I could o· answer him in the words of
15 9	even of Thine o·.— *Psal.* 71 : 10.
19– 6	spared to me for o· one brief year.
21–27	To this end, but o· to this end,
23–20	o·, "among ten thousand."— *Song* 5 : 10.
24 10	I could o· assure him that the divine
34–15	cures when they fail, or o· relieve ;
34–17	A person healed by C. S. is not o·
43– 6	It is the o· College, hitherto,
43–20	the o· assistant teachers in the
44–14	to preach o· occasionally,
45– 7	requisite o· in the earliest periods
49–20	o· ever granted to a *legal college*
55– 5	can o· be overcome with good.
59–18	the o· living and true God,
60–24	C. S. is the o· sure basis
61–22	it is in the mortal mind o·,
63– 2	God and His idea are the o· realities,
65–26	constitute the o· evangelism,
69–14	o· a transient, false sense of
73–17	This is the o· way whereby
83–19	should explain o· Recapitulation,
84–27	take charge o· of his own pupils
85–22	awaiting o· an opportunity
87–25	it is o· through the lens of
94–25	I am persuaded that o· by the
Un. 3– 4	they awake o· to another sphere of
3–20	Hence He is in Himself o·,
4–24	knowledge of the o· true God,
9–18	as the o· true solution of
15–20	become o· an echo of the divine?
17– 1	has o· one chance of successful
18– 4	o· the brightness of My own glory.
19–16	evil is o· a delusive deception,
21– 8	and good o· is reality.
21–20	this is the o· consciousness
23– 8	Truth knows o· such.
23–23	conceive of God o· as like itself,
25– 7	only substance, the o· Mind.
25–20	God, good, is the o· creator.
25–23	Life, whose o· source is Spirit.
27–14	knowing o· His own all-presence,
28–17	we learn Soul o· as we learn God,
29–10	the o· Mind and intelligence
32– 6	Spirit is the o· creator,
33– 4	give the o· pretended testimony
33– 6	can o· testify from their own
33–14	is o· matter within the skull,

only

Un.	33–15	believed to be mind o· through error
	34– 4	Mortal mind admits that it sees o·
	35–26	Spirit is the o· creator.
	36– 1	o· as it adds lie to lie.
	37– 1	Jesus not o· declared himself
	40– 2	It is mortality o· that dies.
	43–13	I insist o· upon the fact,
	44– 3	I can o· repeat the Master's words :
	46–15	o· as spiritual and good,
	49–12	the o· living God
	50– 4	o· as I believe in evil,
	50–11	matter is o· a phenomenon of
	51–23	full Truth is found o· in
	53–10	o· the evil belief that renders them
	57–28	o· conscious existence in the flesh
	59–16	o· through this conformity to mortal
	61–19	O· faith and a feeble understanding
	62–10	Mortals can understand this o· as
	62–14	Sin exists o· as a sense,
	64– 6	conscious of o· health, holiness, and
Pul.	vii– 7	to have not o· a record of
	8–13	o· the need made known,
	21– 4	that loves o· because it is Love.
	21–18	to o· that which is Christlike,
	21–30	O· what feeds and fills the sentiment
	34– 2	* who lived o· a year.
	34–27	"the Bible was my o· textbook.
	35–10	o· the 'pure in heart' — Matt. 5 : 8.
	39–25	* 'mid them all I o· see one face,
	40– 1	* Ah, love ! I o· know
	45– 5	* Christian Scientists not o· say
	46–10	* can o· be touched upon in this
	49–10	* "You have lived here o· four years,
	49–13	o· two and a half years."
	51–28	* o· aspire to take its place alongside
	54–24	* permitting o· the father and mother,
	58–25	* o· pastor shall be the Bible,
	66– 5	* with a membership of o· twenty-six,
	75– 9	statement would not o· be false,
	75–26	* o· combustible material used in
	80–27	* the invisible is the o· real world,
	84–20	* o· the future will tell the story
	88– 8	append o· a few of the names
Rud.	2–24	It is o· the bugle-call to thought and
	4– 6	o· of Divine or C. S.?
	4–17	Good is not in evil, but in God o·.
	4–18	not in matter, but in Spirit o·.
	4–18	not in matter, but in Mind o·.
	4–22	we can o· learn and love Him through
	5–18	Soul is the o· real consciousness
	5–28	exist in Mind o·.
	7–15	o· true evidence of the being
	8– 9	o· an epitome of the Principle,
	9–27	the producer o· of good ;
	10– 8	material laws are o· human beliefs,
	10–27	o· a lack of understanding
	14– 2	giving o· a portion of their time
	14–10	The o· pay taken for her labors
	14–15	o· from those who were able to pay.
	15–19	O· a very limited number of students
No.	1– 5	o· as our natures are changed by its
	1–21	the o· Mind-healing I vindicate ;
	3– 3	at the idea which claims o· its
	4–26	disease must be — and can o· be
	6– 6	that God is the o· creator,
	12– 1	C. S. Mind-healing can o· be
	20–11	Principle is found to be the o· term
	20–22	o· power, presence, and glory.
	24–12	not o· as real as good, but
	31–13	as the o· full proof of its pardon.
	35–21	God is the o· Mind,
	35–24	announcing Truth, and saying not o·
	36–13	was conscious o· of God,
	38– 6	He established the o· true idealism
	38– 8	o· true philosophy and realism.
	38–20	includes o· His own nature,
	40–17	o· the wrongs of mankind.
	40–19	O· when sickness, sin, and fear
	40–27	made better o· by divine influence.
	43– 8	* "O· He who knows all things
Pan.	8–11	the o· prophet of God
	13–26	o· traversed my subject that you may
'00.	3–18	O· the good man loves the right
	4–16	the o· perfect religion is divine Science,
	6– 2	O· the demonstrator can mistake
	6–15	The child not o· accepts C. S.
	10–23	O· last week I received a touching token
	11–17	I want not o· quality, quantity, and
	14–19	charity that seeketh not o· her own,
'01.	2–25	O· a firm foundation in Truth
	3–26	and expresses God o· in metaphor,
	8–26	Jesus, the o· immaculate,
	9– 5	o· generating or regenerating power.
	10–10	son of man o· in the sense that
	12– 8	That is Johnism, and o· Johnites

only

'01.	12–19	o· needs the prism of divine Science,
	13– 4	this is the o· annihilation.
	13– 8	o· an assumption that nothing is
	13–23	o· as the sin is removed
	13–24	o· as it is destroyed
	14–10	o· departure from ecclesiasticism
	18–15	discerned o· through divine Science.
	23– 4	If Christian Scientists o· would admit
	23–28	* "o· the constant relation between
	24– 5	matter is o· an impression produced
	26– 5	o· on Christ, Truth,
	26– 7	five personal senses can have o· a
	28– 4	It is o· by praying, watching, and
	28–18	my o· apology for trying to follow
	30– 4	o· the bequeathing of itself
	31– 3	The o· opposing element
	34–25	o· so far as she follows Christ.
'02.	1–17	o· with material observation,
	2– 1	o· the earnest, honest investigator
	3–27	right is the o· real potency ;
	3–27	o· true ambition is to serve God
	4– 4	o· so far as she follows Christ.
	13– 3	Christ and our Cause my o· incentives,
	14– 2	o· interest I retain in this property
	14–10	* But o· great as I am good."
	14–11	The o· genuine success possible for any
	14–12	the o· success I have ever achieved
	17–22	o· what God gives,
	18– 7	o· to mock, wonder, and perish.
Hea.	6–21	mind of the individual o· can
	8–23	we shall receive o· what we have
	9–21	o· correct answer to the question,
	11– 9	o· immortal superstructure is built on
	12–27	o· objection to giving the
	13–16	using o· the sugar of milk ;
	13–20	Mind as the o· curative Principle.
	16–17	The o· evidence we have of sin,
Peo.	2–16	make a Christian o· in theory,
	9–16	destroyed o· through suffering.
	12– 5	The o· law of sickness or death
	12–12	acknowledge o· God in all thy ways,
	13–23	* "Christianity is fit o· for women
Po.	4– 9	Love is our refuge ; o· with mine eye
	42– 6	were o· a name !
	50–12	I o· know my wife, Thy child,
My.	vi– 9	* Christian Scientists are honest o· as
	vi–27	* o· a place for the publishing of
	3–15	nor a . . . that heals o· the sick.
	4–10	follow Truth o· as we follow truly,
	9– 7	* gratitude which not o· impels
	12–21	we possess o· now.
	13–29	not o· to my church but to Him who
	20–12	o· what God gives to His church.
	21– 7	* course suggested will not o· hasten the
	23–24	* rising, not o· to faith but also to
	30– 6	* Not o· did these include Scientists
	36–21	* dedicated to the o· true God,
	41–27	* not o· discovered C. S., but
	42–23	* o· as infinite good unfolds in each
	45–10	* represent o· a small part of the
	46–18	* O· as we pledge ourselves anew to
	52–23	* if o· through her work Truth may be
	55– 9	* not o· was the attendance rapidly
	58–12	* not o· shows the growth of this Cause,
	60–10	* o· expressed the thought of all the
	70– 4	* been organized o· thirty years,
	70– 5	* its first church o· twelve years ago,
	74–19	* satisfaction that is not o· evident
	76–11	* o· feebly expresses the gratification.
	77– 8	* as its dimensions are o· half as great.
	86–13	* Not o· was every cent of the
	88–19	* o· a slight and material development
	89– 9	* needs o· an open space about it,
	90–14	* it is not the o· source of appeal.
	93–20	* Too often we see o· its
	96–14	* reached o· through intelligent and
	100–11	* It is o· twenty-five years,
	103–25	Bible has been my o· authority.
	105– 3	man's o· medicine for mind and body
	108–15	Mind is the o· lawgiver,
	112–10	founded . . . o· on the Scriptures.
	115– 7	I was o· a scribe echoing the
	117–26	o· in the right direction !
	118– 4	O· the disobedient
	118–23	credited o· by human belief,
	121–24	not o· polite to all but is
	122– 5	glory o· is imperishable which
	124–14	waiting o· your swift hands,
	125– 3	not o· sayers but doers of the law?
	125–11	I have o· to dip my pen in my heart
	126–31	We have it o· as we live it.
	127– 5	ask o· to be judged according to
	129–29	o· as they include the spirit
	130– 9	seeking o· public notoriety,
	132–28	Divine Love is our o· physician,

only

My. 141–23 seats o· five thousand people,
142– 4 * o· abolished the disappointment
149– 5 We know Principle o· through Science.
152–14 worship o· Spirit and spiritually,
153– 4 if these kind hearts will o· do this in
159–16 this is the o· right activity,
159–21 o· legitimate and eternal demands
160–30 O· the makers of hell burn in
161–29 O· he who learns through meekness
164–17 not o· possess a sound faith, but
170–15 o· that this gift is already yours.
173–31 not o· to use the beautiful lawn
174–25 To-day my soul can o· sing and soar.
180–18 o· thus, does it overcome evil
181– 5 are aided o· at long intervals with
187–23 the worship of the o· true God.
190–11 not o· equalling but vastly excelling
194– 1 o· that which Christianity writes in
194–10 O· those men and women
195–17 is our o· means of adding to
198– 7 not o· the continuance of His favors,
201– 5 Satan is unchained o· for a season,
203–13 Be great o· as good.
204– 7 It is o· by looking heavenward
210–10 not o· yourselves are safe, but
210–16 His thoughts can o· reflect peace,
210–20 and o· denounce error in general,
213–27 chapter sub-title
214– 1 select one o· to place on the walls of
224–10 helpful or dangerous o· in proportion to
224–31 * "They also serve who o· stand and
226– 2 o· where you can substitute the
230– 8 digested o· when Soul silences the
230–10 Its rules apply not to one member o·,
231– 3 for such purposes o· as God indicates.
234– 5 they o· cloud the clear sky,
234–18 when regarded on one side o·,
237–10 wise to accept o· my teachings
238– 7 o· be determined by personal proof.
248– 6 * But o· great as I am good."
248–20 You soar o· as uplifted by God's
249–14 all this o· to satiate its loathing of
250–19 applies o· to C. S. churches
251–15 taught in the Board of Education o·.
251–27 o· to convince yourselves of this grand
252–11 not o· know the truth but live it
259–17 churches will remember me o· thus.
259–30 Soul recognized o· in harmony,
267– 1 one and the o· religion
268–21 I can o· solace the sore ills of
272–23 * Not o· Mrs. Eddy's own devoted
273–22 o· by the spiritual understanding
280–18 o· because of oft speaking,
283–26 Human law is right o· as it
284–22 o· as other churches had done.
287–15 In love for man we gain the o·
288–16 Mind was his o· instrumentality
301–21 o· so many well-defined instances
303–12 of which I have seen o· extracts,
306–10 false should be antagonized o· for
307–19 I concluded that he o· referred to
308– 7 o· by ease, pleasure, or recompense.
308–29 Bible was the o· book in his house.
309–30 * supplied the o· social diversions,
312–16 * made o· one effort at self-support.
313–13 I o· know that my father
318– 6 for o· two of my books.
319– 3 o· real man in His image
329– 6 * The board o· excused them from
332–10 * accompany her o· to New York,
339–22 o· those who have not the Christ,
345–12 o· false science — healing by drugs.
345–31 * some o· of which are
349–27 o· as it is spiritual,
349–29 o· as it makes manifest the infinite
352–20 I thank you not o· for your tender
354–21 Give us not o· angels' songs,
356–27 o· . . . . correct version of C. S.
357– 1 He is the o· basis of Science ;
357– 2 apart from C. S., and is o·
357– 8 o· incentive of a mistaken sense
357–18 o· as they build upon the rock
357–23 not o· the axiom of true C. S.,
357–24 o· basis upon which this Science
363–27 practise o· to heal.
(see also **Life, substance**)

Ontario
(see **Ottawa**)

Ontology
Man. 47– 9 O·, or the Science of being.

onward
Mis. 233– 9 o· march of life-giving Science,
343– 9 move it o· and upward.
Pul. 7–21 stumble o· to their doom ;

onward
Pul. 44– 9 * blessed o· work of C. S.
'02. 11–15 helped o· by a new-old message
Po. 19– 4 o· and upward and heavenward borne.
My. 10–29 * now necessitates this o· step.
140–19 God is leading you o· and upward.
155–12 o· march of Truth,
202–17 o· and upward chain of being.
258–29 may you move o· and upward,
272– 5 pushes o· the centuries ;
282–11 nations are helped o· towards
355–24 their way is o·, and their light

onyx
Pul. 26–26 * mantel is of o· and gold.
76–14 * superb mantel of Mexican o·

opal
Mis. 376–28 diamond, topaz, o·, garnet,

opaque
Mis. 347–11 peer through the o· error.

ope
Ret. 18–11 And o· their closed cells
Po. 63–22 And o· their closed cells

open
Mis. 92– 9 o· fount of Truth and Love.
147–29 no path but the fair, o·, and direct
174–10 o· our affections to the Principle
180–14 o· door from this sepulchre
183–16 if he o· his mouth it shall be filled
196– 9 so-called mind shall o· your eyes
212–25 o· his eyes to see this error?
275–18 o· the prison to them that are bound,
280–31 doors of animal magnetism o· wide
281– 3 this animal element flings o·
282–11 our houses broken o· or our locks
283–11 wrong to burst o· doors
292–15 away from the o· sepulchres of sin,
314– 7 o· the meeting by reading the hymns,
317–28 divine Love will o· the way
323–14 masters their secret and o· attacks
325–18 with eyes half o·, the porter starts
326– 6 The door is burst o·,
332– 7 doors that closed . . . are o· flung.
347– 6 escape from their houses to the o·
366–17 humanity needs to get her eyes o·
Man. 90– 9 Metaphysical College will o·
Chr. 55–26 o· the door, — Rev. 3 : 20.
Ret. 6– 6 one with the o· hand.
64–26 mortals must first o· their eyes to
71– 2 o· the gates of heaven.
84– 6 o· fount of Truth and Love.
Un. 56– 8 "put him to an o· shame." — Heb. 6 : 6.
'00. 9– 9 secret of C. S. , . . . is o· to mankind,
'02. 14–29 afford an o· field and fair play.
16–17 they o· the enigmatical seals
My. 31–10 * doors of the church were thrown o·
36–14 * withheld from o· graves or
72– 5 * chapter sub-title
72– 6 * gates of Boston are o· wide
73–18 * o· to visitors this forenoon
77–27 * o· its doors absolutely free of
89– 9 * needs only an o· space about it,
110–21 o· the prison doors
126– 9 has in his hand a book o·
131–27 o· you the windows — Mal. 3 : 10.
132– 4 o· you the windows — Mal. 3 : 10.
160–16 o· their hearts to it for actual
174– 2 throwing o· their doors
188– 6 mine eyes shall be o·, — II Chron. 7 : 15.
212– 6 older and more o· sins,
221–29 wide o· to the intruding disease,
256–13 o· the volume of Life
261–23 Christmas involves an o· secret,
269–27 o· you the windows — Mal. 3 : 10.
289– 2 God's o· secret is seen through grace,
312–30 I did o· an infant school,
357–19 This will o· the way,
(see also **eyes**)

opened
Mis. 24–11 o· it at Matthew ix. 2.
30–18 o· the door to the captive,
57–19 your eyes shall be o·, — Gen. 3 : 5.
149– 9 one after another has o· his lips
253–29 o· their eyes to the light of C. S.?
274– 3 when I o· my College.
371– 5 o· his eyes to see the need of
Ret. 23–14 When the door o·, I was waiting
Un. 44–21 your eyes shall be o· — Gen. 3 : 5.
Pul. 14–11 earth o· her mouth, — Rev. 12 : 16.
30–26 * o· with twenty-six members,
No. 7–10 eyes of sinful mortals must be o·
'02. 9–24 o· my closed eyes.
Hea. 19–10 a vein had not been opened,
My. 31–18 * o· by the Scientists in Boston
39– 3 * meeting was o· by the President.

opened

My.   47–26   * o· an era of Christian worship
       54–26   * October 18, . . . the rooms were o·
       94–19   * doors were o· to the public,
       97–21   * o· the eyes of the country
     132–19   Divine Love hath o· the gate
     172–23   * was o· the following day
     213–15   Unless one's eyes are o· to

openeth

Pan.   12–12   The altitude of Christianity o·,
'00.   14–21   o· and no man shutteth, — Rev. 3 : 7.
      14–22   shutteth and no man o· ; " — Rev. 3 : 7.
My.   42– 3   * "she o· her mouth — Prov. 31 : 26.

opening

Mis. 101–18   o· the doors for them that are
     124–15   o· the prison doors
     132– 4   token that heavy lids are o·,
     250–27   gentle hand o· the door
     256–19   notice . . . previous to the o· term.
     262–20   o· the prison doors
     269–29   o· of this silent mental seal,
     280– 4   o· of the seals,
     307–17   God's love o· the eyes of
Un.   41–17   o· wide the portal from death
Pul.   27– 6   * o· from it are three large
     60–19   * was not ready for the o·.
'02.   16–22   o· not his mouth in self-defense
My.   29–20   * edifice whose formal o·
     29–29   * for the o· of the doors
     30– 6   * people who witnessed the o·.
     31–29   * o· of the dedicatory service.
     54–24   * from the first . . . to our o·,
     88– 4   * o· of their great new temple.
     97–19   * o· of the new Mother Church
    174– 7   o· their spacious club-house
    201–28   o· of your new church
    270–27   o· the eyes of the blind
    300–31   Are the churches o· fire on

openly

Mis.   81– 3   scholarly physicians o· admit.
    133–17   reward thee o·." — Matt. 6 : 6.
    133–26   He will reward "o·." — Matt. 6 : 6.
    349–21   students have o· acknowledged this.
No.   39–11   He has rewarded them o·.

opens

Mis.   17–18   o· to the enraptured understanding
    161–19   record . . . o· when he was thirty
    185–11   o· the very flood-gates of heaven ;
    185– 9   o· the gates of paradise
    196–20   o· wide the portals of salvation
    210–29   Love o· the eyes of the blind,
Rud.   8–21   o· a way whereby, through
My. 236–18   o· wide on the amplitude of liberty
    254– 2   heaven o·, right reigns,

operated

Pul.   54– 6   * Jesus o· in perfect harmony with

operates

My. 353–16   Science that o· unspent.

operatic

Man.   61–19   The music . . . shall not be o·,

operation

Mis. 205– 9   o· of the spirit of Truth
    244– 4   even a "surgical o·"
    347–13   diversities of o· by the same spirit.
    352–19   malicious mental o· must be understood
Chr.   55–13   the o· of His hands. — Isa. 5 : 12.
Ret.   26–16   o· of the divine law.
    40–15   injury received from a surgical o·
Un.   20–19   the knowledge and the o· of sin,
Pul.   60– 4   * new order of service went into o·.

operations

Ret.   70– 3   origin and o· of mortal mind,
Rud.   11–27   nervous o· of the human frame.
'01.   23–29   * by the o· of the universal mind,
My.   11–29   * date for commencing building o·.
    14–25   * building o· have been commenced,
   232–22   "A knowledge of error and of its o·

operative

Mis. 177– 7   Christ, as expressed and o· in C. S.
    207– 5   recognition of practical, o· C. S.
Ret.   85– 6   any other organic o· method
Pul.   35– 8   * a law as o· in the world to-day

opinion

Mis.   7–13   of what can mortal o· avail?
    34–14   speculative o· and human belief.
    49– 9   o· given to her friends,
   197–13   It means more than an o·
   237– 2   olden o· that hell is fire
   265–11   have but one o· of it.
Un.   5– 7   mental struggles and pride of o·
    5–10   not to accept any personal o·
Pul. vii–10   in the glass of the world's o·.

opinion

Pul.   57–15   * whatever difference of o·
    80–17   * we have no o· to pronounce,
No.   29–17   impute such doctrines to mortal o·
Pan.   2–14   pantheism as a human o·
'01.   21–12   clergyman gives it as his o·
    22–18   to accommodate popular o·
My.   88– 1   * chapter sub-title
   219–26   I have expressed my o· publicly
   316–22   * "twentieth-century review of o·"
   320–26   * I am of the o· that he
   321–19   * to change my o· one iota

opinions

Mis.   x–16   o· of men and the progress
    3–15   No o· of mortals nor
    17– 9   human o· and doctrines,
    64–20   speculative o· and fables.
    86–13   indefinite and vague human o·,
    92–25   The o· of men cannot be
   148–11   They were not arbitrary o·
   156–15   student's o· or modus operandi
   168– 5   halting between two o·
   224–12   o·, ambitions, tastes,
   265– 8   Diverse o· in Science are
   288–30   People will differ in their o·
   372– 3   those human o· had not one
Man.   3– 7   They were not arbitrary o·
Ret.   65– 2   they must rest their o·
    78– 8   and not by human o·;
    84–14   The o· of men cannot be
Pan.   11– 8   the o·, systems, doctrines,
'02.   1–16   systems of religious beliefs and o·
Hea.   6– 6   o· of people fly too high
My.   74–31   * Whatever o· we may entertain
    93– 7   * if their o· seem visionary,
   148–26   nor the o· of a sect
   273– 1   * it has no religious o·
   288–14   the travesties of human o·,

opium

Mis. 242–30   addicted to the use of o·
   248–16   That I take o· ; . . . is not more true
   248–23   The o· falsehood has only this

opium-eating

Mis. 242–20   will heal one single case of o·

opponent

My. 358– 8   this o· is the means whereby

opponents

No.   9– 9   let your o· alone,

opportunities

Mis. 112– 8   given new o·, will improve them.
   176–26   Are we duly aware of our own great o·
   213–10   to neglect o· which God giveth,
Hea.   19–19   affords him fresh o· every hour ;
My. 267–23   bitter sense of lost o·

opportunity

Mis.   x– 4   The o· has at length offered itself
    11–20   but to do them good whenever o· occurs.
    11–24   If special o· for doing good
    13–26   afford o· for proof of its
   131–23   delights in the o· to
   137–12   such o· might have been improved ;
   221– 4   o· to handle the error,
   225–15   Then was the clergyman's o·
   267–10   when I saw an o· really to help
   291–15   each and every one has equal o·
   319–24   o· for the grandest achievement
Man.   41–13   do good unto . . . when the o· occurs.
    67–24   O· for Serving the Leader.
    94–12   o· to depart in quiet thought
Ret.   50–27   o· for furnishing a new rule of
    85–22   awaiting only an o·
'00.   5– 4   leaves no o· for idolatry
'01.   20–11   o· to mislead the human mind,
'02.   13–22   giving o· for those who had
My.   11–20   * seized upon this privilege and o·,
    12–18   A lost o· is the greatest of losses.
    42–15   * I desire to improve this o· to
   117–31   this o· is all that I ask of mankind.
   119–27   give you the o· of seeing
   134–12   not be eclipsed by some lost o·,
   148– 6   good folk of Concord have this o·,
   151– 8   o· for explaining C. S.:
   163–20   o· in Concord's quiet to revise our
   190–24   o· to become students of the Christ,
   204– 3   o· to use their hidden virtues,
   244– 4   those who wish to share this o·
   244–10   This o· is designed to impart a
   249– 3   Improve every o· to correct sin
   346– 5   * welcomes it as another o· for

oppose

Mis.   37– 9   In proportion as we o· the belief
   201– 5   o· bringing the qualities of Spirit

oppose

My. 345– 8 * Do you *o·* it?''
345–26 "Oh, we cannot *o·* them.

opposed

Mis. 17– 2 spiritual law of Life, as *o·* to
17– 4 as *o·* to the material sense of love ;
17– 5 *o·* to any supposititious law
48– 8 *o·* to it, as to every form of error,
49–27 presupposes not only a power *o·* to
56–15 human conception *o·* to the divine
62–17 *o·* to which is the error of sickness,
188– 1 teachings *o·* the doctrines of Christ
198–25 material law, . . . as *o·* to good,
198–28 belief in self-existent evil, *o·* to
199–21 over the qualities *o·* to Spirit
284–32 I am *o·* to all personal attacks,
Ret. 89– 3 *o·* to it by material motion,
Un. 22– 6 ungodliness, which is *o·* to Truth,
38– 6 Death, then, is error, *o·* to Truth,
Pul. 13– 5 mortal belief in a power *o·* to God.
38–22 * *o·* to the philosophy of Karma
No. 9–16 I have *o·* . . . strongly
36–10 as wholly *o·* to the popular view
Pan. 3–22 It is *o·* to atheism and monotheism,
'01. 31– 4 Truth *o·* to all error,
Hea. 7– 7 spiritual meaning as *o·* to the
14–27 *o·* to all that is wrong,
My. 279– 1 an element *o·* to Love,
284–24 religiously *o·* to war,

opposes

Mis. 49–22 *o·* the leadings of the divine Spirit
119–16 whatever or whoever *o·* evil,
Un. 39–15 which *o·* itself to God,
56–15 which *o·* the law of Spirit ;

opposing

Mis. 335–12 for *o·* the subtle lie,
Rud. 16–24 certain *o·* factions, springing up
'01. 31– 3 The only *o·* element that
My. 4–17 found that, instead of *o·*,
293–22 possessed no *o·* element,

opposite (noun)

absolute
My. 357– 7 absolute *o·* of spiritual means,
always the
Mis. 374– 6 always the *o·* of what it was.
diametrical
Mis. 220–18 diametrical *o·* of what it was
direct
Mis. 56–12 direct *o·* of immortal Life,
elementary
Mis. 260–18 elementary *o·* to Him
God has no
No. 5– 6 God has no *o·* in Science.
God's
Mis. 181–29 not of God's *o·*, — evil,
good's
Mis. 14–24 good's *o·*, has no Principle,
46– 5 good's *o·*, is unreal.
His
Un. 51–22 and not of His *o·*, evil.
its
Mis. 18–13 love Spirit only, not its *o·*,
26–21 neither . . . produces its *o·*.
27– 5 its *o·*, named matter,
27–14 no species ever produces its *o·*.
122–20 not educed from its *o·* :
346–20 its *o·* is necessarily unreal,
Ret. 63–15 Its *o·*, nothing, named *evil*,
Un. 60–10 inharmony is its *o·*,
Rud. 7–22 cannot originate its *o·*,
No. 32–18 Hence its *o·*, named *evil*,
'01. 22–12 If Truth is true, its *o·*, error,
My. 235– 4 and not name its *o·*, error.
mortal
Ret. 73– 2 his mortal *o·* must be material,
no
'01. 22–13 Spirit is true . . . it hath no *o·* ;
of divine Science
My. 358– 7 is the *o·* of divine Science,
of goodness
Mis. 49–21 belief in the *o·* of goodness,
Un. 24– 2 sin the *o·* of goodness.
of Himself
Un. 41–24 God cannot be the *o·* of Himself.
of immortal man
Mis. 186–10 ultimates in the *o·* of *immortal* man,
of life
My. 235– 2 the suppositional *o·* of life,
of man
Mis. 187– 9 *o·* of man, hence the unreality ;
of something
No. 32–17 nothing, or the *o·* of something.

opposite (noun)

of Spirit
Mis. 26–18 it is the very *o·* of Spirit,
Un. 32–19 saying, "I am the *o·* of Spirit,
36–12 matter is the *o·* of Spirit,
of Truth
Mis. 24–22 error, the *o·* of Truth ;
Ret. 69– 9 insists still upon the *o·* of Truth,
Un. 44–12 pretender taught the *o·* of Truth.
to the fact
Mis. 133– 5 ideas more *o·* to the fact.
very
Mis. 26–18 it is the very *o·* of Spirit,
184– 1 the very *o·* of that Maker,
Un. 42–11 very *o·* of this error
My. 175–29 very *o·* of my real sentiments.

Mis. 33–29 mortal mind's *o·*, — the divine Mind.
55–22 over their *o·*, or matter,
188– 2 demonstrated the *o·*, Truth.
Un. 24– 1 is the *o·* of immortal Mind,
'00. 5– 7 *o·* of God — good — named devil — evil
'01. 23– 5 yet that God has an *o·*
Hea. 4–25 and the *o·* of it at another,

opposite (adj.)

Mis. 45 26 *o·* intelligence or mind termed evil.
55– 9 *O·* to good, is the universal claim of
57–17 The *o·* error said, "I am true,"
62– 3 *o·* image of man, a sinner,
63– 9 *o·* triad, sickness, sin, and death.
74–13 *o·* of that which mortals entertain :
88–29 are *o·* modes of medicine.
173–13 an *o·* so-called science,
191–28 *o·* characters ascribed to him
220– 3 and a false rule the *o·* way.
280–11 nothing in the *o·* scale.
292–18 to shut out all *o·* sense,
295–13 against the *o·* claims of error.
346–13 belief that there is an *o·* . . . to God.
347–16 Take the *o·* direction !
351–29 turns it into the *o·* channels.
355– 3 presents two *o·* aspects,
367–25 *o·* conclusion, that darkness
Ret. 57–27 such *o·* effects as good and evil,
64– 9 any *o·* theory is heterodox
64–10 even as the *o·* claim of evil is one.
69–21 *o·* belief is the prolific source
Un. 36– 8 a knowledge of God from *o·* facts,
38–19 The *o·* understanding of God
49–17 two *o·* states of existence.
Rud. 3–21 establishes the *o·* manifestation
Pan. 10– 9 prevail over the *o·* notion
Hea. 14– 8 faith in an *o·* direction?
My. 159–20 by an *o·* attraction towards the
170– 5 the second was an *o·* story,
292–25 supposed to possess *o·* qualities
292–26 and so to produce *o·* effects.
348 24 never producing an *o·* effect,

oppositely

Hea. 15–19 acting *o·* to your prayer,

opposites

compounds and
'01. 22–11 are compounds and *o·* ;
direct
Mis. 34–26 direct *o·* as light and darkness.
excludes
Ret. 75–19 Science of Mind excludes *o·*,
fraught with
My. 258– 6 This period, so fraught with *o·*,
God's
'00. 5–29 in casting out God's *o·*,
His
'00. 4– 3 makes His *o·* as real and
its
Mis. 105–16 common sense of its *o·*
law of
Mis. 14–22 proven by the law of *o·*
57–12 By the law of *o·*,
Un. 52–24 By the law of *o·*.
moral
Mis. 266– 4 when these sides are moral *o·*,
mysticism of
Pan. 13–25 with the mysticism of *o·* ?
no greater
No. 13–19 No greater *o·* can be conceived
their
Un. 10–15 cannot . . . lapse into their *o·*,
these
Mis. 217–19 these *o·*, in suppositional unity
364–23 these *o·* must either cooperate or
Ret. 68– 9 difference between these *o·*

Hea. 13– 3 work at *o·* and accomplish less

opposition
Mis. 80– 4 o· to unjust medical laws.
135–11 conquers all o·, surmounts all
197–29 a theory that is in o· to God,
Ret. 40–24 o· which C. S. encountered
71– 8 in o· to the straight and narrow path
Un. 11– 7 in direct o· to human philosophy
56–10 suffering from mentality in o· to
Pul. 50–23 * The o· against it from
'01. 31– 5 o· springs from the very nature of
'02. 1–18 met with o· and detraction ;
10–27 o· to God and His power

oppressed
My. 215– 2 Though sorely o·, I was above

oppression
Mis. 246–15 another sharp cry of o·.
Pul. 83–14 * under the black flag of o·
'02. 3–26 mature into o· ;
Peo. 11–15 fears, that enforce new forms of o·,
Po. 27– 3 Bloated o· in its awful hour,
My. 285–10 Bloodshed, war, and o·

oppressions
Pul. 55–11 * prejudices, and o· of the past.

oppressive
Pul. 7–19 unmerciful, and o· priesthood
My. 29–30 * the inconveniences of an o· day.

opprobrious
My. 104–10 vented their hatred . . . in o· terms.

opprobrium
'01. 12–10 word Christian was anciently an o· ;

optics
No. 6–25 Astronomy, o·, acoustics, and

optimism
Mis. 119–18 either for pessimism or for o·,
My. 84–21 * o· and energy of its followers

optimistic
My. 99–11 * remarkably o· body of people,

oracle
'02. 17–27 this o· of years will put to flight
My. 188–14 your o·, under the wings of

oracles
Mis. 107– 3 not be mistaken for the o· of God.

oracular
My. 129–11 The o· skies, the verdant earth

oral
Mis. 220– 9 His mental and o· arguments

orally
Mis. 206–21 in word and deed, mentally and o·,

orange
Mis. 376–27 gold, o·, pink, crimson, violet ;

orator
My. 90– 4 * wooed by no eloquence of o·
104– 4 St. Paul, the Mars' Hill o·,
125–17 spirit of the Mars' Hill o·,

oratories
'01. 28–14 Catholic and Protestant o·.

orbit
Rud. 4–11 which holds the earth in its o·.
My. 182–22 launched the earth in its o·,
226–11 holds the earth in its o·

orbits
Mis. 22–17 true thoughts revolve in God's o·:
104–19 revolve in their own o·,

orchards
Ret. 4–15 o· of apples, peaches, pears,

ordain
Mis. 91– 5 to o· pastors and to dedicate
158–29 as our churches o· ministers.
313–26 I hereby o· the Bible, and
Man. 58– 5 o· the BIBLE, and S. AND H.

ordained
Mis. 90–21 If not o·, shall the pastor
90–27 organization and o· priesthood.
158– 5 requested you to be o·,
158–14 you were bidden to be o·,
158–29 Jesus was not o· as our
244– 9 compliance to o· conditions.
382–32 In 1895 I o· that the Bible,
Man. 18– 7 and was o· A. D. 1881.
Ret. 16–20 and was o· A. D. 1881.
44– 8 and was o· in 1881,
44– 9 five years before being o·.
49–15 powers that are not o· of God,
Pul. 7–24 I have o· the Bible and the
38– 3 * before being o· in this church,
58–24 * their prime instructor has o·

ordained
Pul. 68– 2 * Mrs. Eddy . . . in 1881 was o·,
86–29 * have already o· as our pastor.
My. 37– 1 * o· the way of salvation

ordains
Ret. 85–17 whereto you do not feel that God o· you.

ordeal
Mis. 1– 9 the o· of a perfect Christianity,
42–13 passed the o· called death,
43–19 the great o· of this century.
126–13 o· refines while it chastens.

order
adherent of the
Pul. 59–19 * not an adherent of the o·,
and harmony
Pan. 6–14 o· and harmony of God's creation.
and truth
Mis. 215–12 C. S. demands o· and truth.
decree and
Mis. 380–29 by decree and o· of the Court,
divine
(*see* divine)
from Mrs. Eddy
Man. 66–25 an o· from Mrs. Eddy
highest
Ret. 7– 8 * highest o· of intellectual powers,
My. 96– 5 * highest o· of intelligence,
law and
(*see* law)
lower
Peo. 13– 2 hence a lower o· of humanity,
13– 4 a lower o· of Christianity
mathematical
Mis. 57–28 stated in mathematical o·,
no mean
My. 30–13 * at personal sacrifices of no mean o· ;
notice or
My. 73– 2 * to issue a similar notice or o·,
of being
Mis. 104–23 divine law and o· of being.
Un. 40–11 in the divine o· of being.
of divine Science
Mis. 181–22 the o· of divine Science.
of ministration
Ret. 92– 5 His o· of ministration was
of reading
Man. 32– 1 O· of Reading.
of Science
Mis. 99–13 voice a higher o· of Science
181– 9 tend to obscure the o· of Science,
205–22 This o· of Science is the chain of
Un. 56–13 In the divine o· of Science
of service
Pul. 28–14 * heading
28–15 * o· of service in the C. S. Church
60– 3 * the new o· of service
My. 32–12 * o· of service was as follows :
of the services
My. 16–21 * The o· of the services,
of wisdom
Mis. 287–18 In the o· of wisdom,
perfect
Pul. 49–30 * grounds and farm in perfect o·,
prescribed
Ret. 85–15 by any deviation from the o· prescribed
rule of
Ret. 50–27 new rule of o· in divine Science,
spiritual
Ret. 10–16 Syntax was spiritual o· and unity.
their
Mis. 10–15 countermand their o·, retrace their
uncommon
Mis. 95–18 phenomena of an uncommon o·,
written
Man. 65–16 any written o·, signed by

———

Mis. 21–23 The o· of this sentence has been
58–22 no o· that proceeds from
131– 5 in o· rightly to discern darkness
137– 3 your badge, and o· of exercise,
158–27 o· therein given corresponds to
165–32 o·, mode, and virgin origin of man
276– 8 not big enough to fill the o· ;
310–17 decently and in o·." — I Cor. 14 : 40.
329– 7 sets the earth in o· ;
Man. 27– 5 shall o· no special action to be
80– 7 hold this money subject to the o· of
80– 9 authorized to o· its disposition
Ret. 87– 3 * "O· is heaven's first law,"
Pul. 75–16 * TO THE FOUNDER OF THE O·
Po. vi–10 by o· of Governor Andrew,
My. 43– 6 * o· aright the affairs of daily life.
141– 6 * by o· of Mrs. Mary Baker Eddy.

order in — that
Mis. 279–25   in o· that the walls might fall ;
    305–28   * In o· that the bell
Ret. 64–27   in o· that the illusion, error,
'01.   7–22   in o· that belief may attend their
My.   78– 2   * in o· that all might participate
    190–23   Bible was written in o· that

order in — to
Mis. 14–12   in o· to learn Science, we begin with
    31–12   in o· to retain his faith in evil
    33–12   *in o· to be healed by it*
    38–25   *in o· to be healed by it*
    38–28   in o· to cure his present disease,
    50–17   it is essential . . . in o· to heal.
    54–17   *in o· to keep well all my life?*
    65–15   in o· to gain the true solution of
    65–22   in o· to demonstrate healing,
    81–16   *in o· to overcome mortal sense,*
    94– 6   love good in o· to understand God.
    109–13   in o· to be corrected ;
    181– 7   in o· to understand his sonship,
    187–25   Did . . . Spirit, become a clod, in o· to
    187–30   in o· to be healed and saved,
    197–12   In o· to comprehend the
    217–28   in o· to become matter,
    246– 8   in o· to subserve the interests of
    254–16   in o· to gain the kingdom
    256– 5   in o· to make the body harmonious.
    265– 3   in o· to be thought original,
    273– 5   I close my College in o· to work in
    274– 5   in o· to do this I must
    345–24   in o· to offer them in sacrifice,
    348– 8   in o· to exterminate it,
    352–20   in o· to enable one to destroy
Man. 74–15   In o· to be eligible to
Ret. 26–21   In o· to rebuke the evidence.
    28–10   in o· to apprehend Spirit.
    28–11   in o· to have the least understanding
    34– 2   in o· to gain the Science of Mind,
    38–29   in o· to demonstrate C. S.
    45–13   in o· to gain spiritual freedom
    57– 6   in o· to heal his body.
    63– 9   in o· to destroy this belief
    63–11   in o· to heal them.
    82–15   in o· to do the greatest good
    89–25   in o· to enlarge their sphere of
Un.   2– 8   in o· to be saved from sin.
    11–25   in o· to mature fitness for
    18–13   in o· to console it.
    18–22   in o· to strike at its root ;
    32–27   in o· to demonstrate the falsity
    37– 4   in o· to inherit eternal life
    40– 7   in o· to prove man deathless.
    41 3   In o· to reach the true knowledge
    45 21   dies in o· to better itself.
    54– 9   In o· to be whole,
Pul. 35–14   in o· to apprehend Spirit.
    35–15   in o· to have the least understanding
    64–12   * in o· to stop the continued inflow
Rud. 14–12   in o· to do gratuitous work.
No.   3–21   in o· to be safe members of the
    6– 3   in o· to heal the sick.
    23–18   in o· to cast out this devil?
Pan. 11–18   in o· to be in proper shape,
'01. 15– 3   in o· to understand and demonstrate
    15– 5   In o· to prove it false,
    24–25   in o· to demonstrate the divine
    33–20   in o· to heal them.
Hea.   7–14   in o· to purify the stream.
My.   3– 5   in o· to demonstrate truth,
    10–26   * in o· to insure the prosperity of
    21–11   * in o· to contribute more liberally
    22–12   * in o· to complete this great work,
    23– 2   * in o· to find out how much
    39– 1   * in o· to accommodate those who
    121– 4   in o· to separate these sessions
    211– 7   in o· to maintain harmony,
    216– 4   in o· to help mankind with it.
    231–12   in o· to help God's work
    244– 2   in o· to avoid the stir
    251– 9   * in o· to become teachers of
    273–17   in o· to forewarn and forearm
    282–13   in o· to apprehend more,
    318– 1   in o· to express the
    363–24   In o· to be sure that one is

ordered
Mis. 249–16   neither purchased nor o· a drug
    285– 3   pamphlets I o· to be laid away
    381–18   It was o· that the complainant
Un. 19– 9   intended it, or o· it aforetime,
No. 46–10   Woman should not be o· to the rear,

orderly
Mis. 275–28   is magnificent and o·.
Ret. 82–12   o· methods herein delineated.
    87–13   in the o· demonstration thereof.

orderly
Ret. 87–22   In this o·, scientific dispensation
My. 247–15   came out in o· line

Order of Communion Services etc.
Present
Man. 125– 1   heading

Order of Exercises
for the Sunday School
Man. 127– 1   heading

Order of Services
Present
Man. 120– 1   heading

orders
Mis. 10–16   reinstate His o·, more assured to
    119–30   countermand your o·, steal your
    285– 6   gentleman who fills o· for my books,
    291–12   often construed as direct o·,
    307–13   and many o· on hand,
    311–26   I was a scribe under o· ;
No. 24– 7   lower o· of matter and mortal mind.
Po. 10–20   Is marching under o· ;
My. 337–21   Is marching under o· ;

ordinance
Mis. 91– 2   This o· is significant as a type of
    383– 3   This o· took effect the same year,

ordinarily
'02. 12–22   o· find no place in my Message.
My.   7– 5   o· find no place in my Message.
    83– 3   * O· the holding of a great convention

ordinary
Mis. 33–22   o· methods of healing disease
Un. 26–19   Many o· Christians protest against
    28–14   o· material conjectures,
Pul. 33–26   * more than o· achievement,
'01. 19–21   From o· mental practice to C. S.
'02.   1–16   o· systems of religious beliefs
My. 65–15   * o· mortal passing out a nickel
    346– 3   * an o· lifetime ;

ordination
Man. 58 4   O·.
Pul.   7–28   This is my first o·.

Ore. (State)
      (see **Portland**)

O'Rell's, Max
Pul. 67–11   * Max O· famous enumeration of

organ (see also **organ's**)
 choir
Pul. 60–30   * The choir o·, enclosed
 couplers
Pul. 61– 5   * swell to great ;
    61– 6   * choir to great ;
    61– 6   * swell to choir ;
    61– 6   * swell to great octaves,
    61– 7   * swell to great sub-octaves ;
    61– 7   * choir to great sub-octaves ;
    61– 8   * swell octaves ;
    61– 8   * swell to pedal ;
    61– 8   * great to pedal ;
    61– 9   * choir to pedal.
 every
Rud. 13–10   to treat every o· in the body.
Hea. 19– 4   every o· of the system,
 forty-five hundred and thirty-eight pipes
My. 70–29   * forty-five hundred and thirty-eight pipes,
 four manuals
My. 70–25   * four manuals, seventy-two stops,
 grand crescendo pedal
My. 70–28   * a grand crescendo pedal,
 great
Pul. 26–12   * The great o· comes from Detroit.
    60–23   * great o· has double open diapason
My. 68–21   * The great o· is placed back of
    71–27   * in front of the great o·,
 manual compass
Pul. 60–22   * three-manual compass, C. C. C. to C.
 mechanical accessories
Pul. 61– 9   * swell tremulant,
    61–10   * choir tremulant,
    61–10   * bellows signal ;
    61–10   * wind indicator.
 nineteen adjustable combination pistons
My. 70–26   * nineteen adjustable combination pistons,
 nineteen couplers
My. 70–26   * seventy-two stops, nineteen couplers,
 pedal
Pul. 61– 3   * The pedal o· has open diapason,
 pedal compass
Pul. 60–23   * pedal compass, C. C. C. to F. 30.
 pedal movements
Pul. 61–11   * three affecting great and pedal stops,
    61–11   * three affecting swell and pedal stops
    61–12   * great to pedal reversing pedal ;

organ

pedal movements
Pul. 61–13   * crescendo and full organ pedal ;
     61–13   * balanced great and choir pedal ;
     61–14   * balanced swell pedal.
powerful
My. 59–20   * sonorous tones of the powerful *o·*
seven combination pedals
My. 70–28   * seven combination pedals,
seventy-two stops
My. 70–26   * seventy-two stops, nineteen couplers,
solo
My. 71– 4   * There is also a solo *o·* attached.
swell
Pul. 60–27   * swell *o·* has bourdon, open diapason,
swell-box
Pul. 61– 1   * enclosed in separate swell-box,
three balanced swells
My. 70–27   * three balanced swells,

    —

Mis. 106–31   your many-throated *o·*,
     155–29   for our denominational *o·*.
     243–28   and the *o·* to contract ;
     347–30   only authenticated *o·* of C. S.
Man. 61–23   Music from the *o·* alone should
Ret. 52–19   The first official *o·* of
Pul. 26– 6   * *o·* and choir gallery is spacious
     42–20   * where the *o·* is to be hereafter
     43–14   * After an *o·* voluntary,
     47– 5   * first official *o·* of this sect.
     60–16   * The *o·*, made by Farrand & Votey
My. 32–11   * Following the *o·* voluntary
     38–20   * with the roll of the *o·*
     69–11   * placed on the two sides of the *o·*.
     70–19   * chapter sub-title
     70–22   * *o·* which has been installed.
     70–30   * Attached to the *o·* is a set of
     71– 2   * discoveries of *o·* builders
     166–12   with which to furnish . . . with an *o·*,
     (*see also* **organ stops**)

organic

Mis. 56– 3   *What is o· life?*
     56– 5   if Life, or Spirit, were *o·*,
     56–21   *O·* life is an error of statement
Ret. 85– 6   any other *o·* operative method
No. 10–19   that sense is *o·* and material,
     28–26   Here *soul* means sense and *o·* life ;
Pan. 10–18   *o·*, chronic, and acute diseases
My. 106– 1   in functional and *o·* diseases
     106– 7   *o·* diseases of almost every kind.
     107–30   *o·* and inflammatory diseases,
     190– 9   contagious and *o·* diseases

organism

Rud. 12–18   a so-called material *o·*

organist

Man. 61–18   Soloist and *O·*.
My. 71– 3   * enable the *o·* to produce

organization

above
Mis. 306–18   * a member of the above *o·*,
abuses of
Ret. 45–15   uses and abuses of *o·*.
and duties
Man. 93– 3   *O·* AND DUTIES.
Baltimore
Pul. 68–21   * adds interest to the Baltimore *o·*.
Christian Science
Man. 73–11   form and conduct a C. S. *o·*
church
Pul. 66– 4   * first church *o·* of this faith
college
Man. 73–21   for said university or college *o·*.
concerning the
Pul. 57–15   * concerning the *o·* of
continued
Ret. 45– 9   continued *o·* retards spiritual growth,
corporeal
Ret. 45–11   corporeal *o·* deemed requisite
disrupt the
Man. 93–20   to disrupt the *o·* of branch churches.
distinctive
My. 100–13   * its appearance as a distinctive *o·*
functions, and
My. 218– 2   normal action, functions, and *o·*,
good ends of
Mis. 358–31   fulfilled all the good ends of *o·*,
great
My. 273– 9   * a very great *o·*
its
My. 148–12   completed its *o·* February 22
material
     (*see* **material**)
members of the
Man. 73–15   may become members of the *o·*

organization

no
Mis. 145– 5   need no *o·* to express it.
of branch churches
Man. 93–20   to disrupt the *o·* of branch churches.
My. 56–17   * the *o·* of branch churches
of churches
Ret. 85– 5   to continue the *o·* of churches,
original
My. 46– 9   * this church in its orginal *o·* ;
parent
Pul. 55–26   * It is regarded as the parent *o·*,
periods of
Ret. 49– 5   working out their periods of *o·*,
result of
Mis. 190– 2   result of *o·*, nor the
Ret. 58–13   not the result of *o·*,
Un. 42–22   nor was it the result of *o·*,
spiritual
Mis. 138–29   march on in spiritual *o·*.
such an
Mis. 295–25   on tablets of such an *o·*
tenets of the
Pul. 58–22   * symbolic of the tenets of the *o·*.
that
Ret. 45–18   when dissolving that *o·*,
their
My. 83–28   * growth of their *o·*,
visible
Mis. 90–27   conferred by a visible *o·*

    —

Mis. 304–29   * in recognition of the *o·*
Man. 88– 3   *O·*.
Ret. 45– 7   *o·* is requisite only in the

organizations

Mis. 32–25   social *o·* and societies
     98–17   and perpetuate our *o·*
     137–30   hold these *o·* of their own,
     138–23   members of students' *o·*.
     305– 7   * Freedom League, and kindred *o·*.
     358–21   to dissolve their *o·*, or to
Man. 44–23   Church *O·* Ample.
     44–25   shall not unite with *o·* which
Ret. 60–26   matter and its so-called *o·*
Un. 33–27   through the *o·* of matter,
Peo. 1– 4   draws not its life from human *o·* ;
My. 10–12   * other *o·* have taken steps
     175– 4   with the *o·* connected therewith,

organize

Mis. 91– 4   It is not indispensable to *o·*
     137–29   can *now o·* their students into
Man. 17–10   To *o·* a church designed to
Ret. 44– 1   voted to *o·* a church
     50–24   continue to *o·* churches, schools,
Pul. 69– 2   * came . . . to *o·* this movement.
My. 46–10   "To *o·* a church designed to
     56– 9   * necessary to *o·* branch churches

organized

Mis. 23–21   it is not *o·* dust.
     90–23   *members of a church not o·*
     91– 9   If our church is *o·*,
     144– 7   *o·* by Miss Maurine R. Campbell.
     300–24   which I had *o·* and of which
     350– 3   *o·* a secret society
     382–24   *o·* the first Christian Scientist
Man. 38–20   *o·* in 1879 by Mary Baker Eddy,
     73– 1   shall not be *o·* with less than
Ret. 43–21   Association was *o·* by myself
     44– 4   first such church ever *o·*.
     44–30   spiritually *o·* Church of Christ,
     49– 8   purpose for which they were *o·*,
     60– 5   defines life . . . as *o·* matter,
Pul. 30–25   * was *o·* by Mrs. Eddy,
     37–26   * was *o·* on July 4, 1876,
     55–24   * was *o·* April 12, 1879,
     56– 1   * One or more *o·* societies
     58– 5   * she . . . *o·* a church.
     67–25   * was *o·* by seven persons,
     68–16   * *o·* in this city about a year ago.
     68–25   * *o·* at a meeting held at
Rud. 5–27   the five senses as *o·* matter,
My. vi–11   * Mrs. Eddy *o·* The First Church
     vi–19   * *o·* . . . The C. S. Publishing Society,
     37–17   * Cause of C. S. has been *o·*
     56–12   * three branch churches were *o·*,
     67–14   * First church *o·* . . . 1879
     70– 4   * has been *o·* only thirty years,

organizer

Ret. 42– 7   He was the first *o·* of a
Pul. 46–29   * He was the first *o·* of a
     (*see also* **Eddy**)

organizes

Pul. 21–12   which Christ *o·* and blesses.

organizing
Mis. 177– 9 in *o·* action against us.
    358–22 *o·* churches and associations.
Man. 72– 4 *O·* Churches.
    72–25 Requirements for *O·* Branch
My. 343–20 followed it up, teaching and *o·*,

organ's
Pul. 11– 3 *o·* voice, as the sound of many waters,

organs
Man. 44–19 periodicals which are the *o·* of
My. 70–25 * it is a combination of six *o·*,
    89– 7 * one of the largest *o·* in the world.

organ stops
great organ
Pul. 60–24 * double open diapason (stopped bass),
    60–24 * open diapason,
    60–25 * dulciana,
    60–25 * viola di gamba,
    60–25 * doppel flute,
    60–25 * hohl flute,
    60–25 * octave,
    60–26 * octave quint,
    60–26 * superoctave,
    60–26 * trumpet,
swell organ
Pul. 60–27 * bourdon,
    60–27 * open diapason,
    60–27 * salicional,
    60–28 * æoline,
    60–28 * stopped diapason,
    60–28 * gemshorn,
    60–28 * flute harmonique,
    60–29 * flageolet,
    60–29 * cornet — 3 ranks, 183,
    60–29 * cornopean,
    60–29 * oboe,
    60–29 * vox humana
choir organ
Pul. 61– 1 * geigen principal,
    61– 1 * dolce,
    61– 1 * concert flute,
    61– 2 * quintadena,
    61– 2 * fugara,
    61– 2 * flute d'amour,
    61– 2 * piccolo harmonique,
    61– 3 * clarinet,
pedal organ
Pul. 61– 4 * open diapason,
    61– 4 * bourdon,
    61 4 * lieblich gedeckt (from stop 10),
    61– 5 * violoncello-wood,

orgies
'00. 13 7 *o·* of their idolatrous feasts

Orient
Mis. 332 16 crystal streams of the *O·*,
'02. 3– 4 non-Christian religions in the *O·*
My. 193– 7 gorgeous skies of the *O·*

Oriental
Mis. 29–25 esoteric magic and *O·* barbarisms
    341–28 and the diction purely *O·*.
Pul. 8–29 which will eclipse *O·* dreams.
    23–16 * inquiry into *O·* philosophy,
    53–12 * to give thanks in *O·* phrase,
    66 20 * largely *O·* in its choice.
No. 14–10 *O·* philosophy of Brahmanism,

origin
and action
Un. 32–10 cannot be separated in *o·* and action.
and aim
My. 257–13 Christ's heavenly *o·* and aim.
and demonstration
Mis. 58–23 not human, in *o·* and demonstration.
and operations
Ret. 70– 3 *o·* and operations of mortal mind,
divine
    (*see* **divine**)
his
Mis. 79–14 concerning himself and his *o·* :
    167–23 in admiration of his *o·*,
    185–23 by which to learn his *o·* and age,
Ret. 68–29 His *o·* is not, like that of mortals,
My. 129–16 counterpoised his *o·* from dust,
homely
My. 262–10 homely *o·* of the babe Jesus
human
    (*see* **human**)
its
Un. 22–20 has its *o·* in the physical senses
Pul. 55–20 * every effect has its *o·* in desire
    67– 4 * Sketch of Its *O·* and Growth
No. 18– 7 proof of its *o·* in God,
Pan. 4– 3 owes its *o·* and continuity to the
'00. 5– 9 its *o·* is a myth, a lie.
'01. 16–20 in its *o·* evil was loquacious,

origin
man's
Mis. 79– 9 Man's *o·* and existence being in Him,
Ret. 10–16 in man's *o·* and signification.
Un. 53–25 God *is* man's *o·*
material
Mis. 361– 3 belief in material *o·*, mortal mind,
Un. 50–26 material *o·*, growth, maturity,
mental
Hea. 17–26 Then was not sin of mental *o·*,
mythical
Mis. 71–22 its mythical *o·* and certain end.
no
Un. 45–27 has no *o·* or existence in Spirit,
'00. 5– 5 It gives evil no *o·*, no reality.
'02. 7– 2 concedes no *o·* or causation apart from
My. 288–10 it has no *o·* in the nature of God,
no other
Mis. 182– 8 no other Mind, no other *o·* ;
nor existence
No. 15–22 neither *o·* nor existence in the
of all
My. 266–19 *o·* of all that really is,
of disease
Hea. 19–11 The illusive *o·* of disease
of evil
Mis. 24–25 Speaking of the *o·* of evil,
    346– 6 chapter sub-title
    346– 7 *o·* of evil is the problem of ages.
of man
Mis. 75–27 the spiritual *o·* of man.
    165–32 virgin *o·* of man according to
Un. 30– 1 Spirit as the sole *o·* of man,
or existence
Un. 45–27 has no *o·* or existence in Spirit,
or ultimate
Mis. 14– 6 either to the *o·* or ultimate of good
our
Ret. 22 17 He alone is our *o·*, aim, and being.
spiritual
Mis. 18–17 spiritual *o·*, God's reflection,
    75–27 discovered the spiritual *o·* of man.
    166–17 how to declare its spiritual *o·*,
statement of the
'00. 5– 2 This scientific statement of the *o·*,
their
Mis. 36– 7 express Mind as their *o·* ;
Man. 59– 2 without characterizing their *o·*
true
Mis. 72– 6 the only living and true *o·*,

Mis. 166–21 whose *o·* was more spiritual
    187–21 *o·*, substance, and life of man
Hea. 19–11 *o·* of all mortal things.

original
Mis. 14– 8 his *o·* state of perfection,
    18– 2 *o·* likeness of perfect man,
    25–14 *o·* meaning of the Scriptures,
    74–16 into its *o·* meaning, Mind.
    77– 5 *o·* meaning, namely, to be *firm*,
    114–19 arm . . . against *o·* sin,
    186– 7 far below man's *o·* standard,
    187–16 set forth in *o·* Holy Writ.
    188– 6 the translator, not the *o·* Word,
    191–23 *o·* devil was a great talker,
    191–26 the *o·* texts define him as
    192– 5 *o·* text defines devil as a
    201– 4 its *o·* sin, or human will ;
    263–29 or a single *o·* conception,
    265– 4 in order to be thought *o·*,
    295–10 * cause of this "same *o·* evil"
    300–20 printed as your *o·* writings,
    360–11 his *o·* scientific sonship with God.
    371–28 are as hopelessly *o·* as
    381– 1 alleging that . . . were not *o·*
Ret. 35– 6 was so hopelessly *o·*
    37– 7 book is indeed wholly *o·*,
    68– 3 claimed to originate . . . *o·* evil ;
Pul. 20–11 my *o·* system of ministry
    65– 2 * *o·* apostles and promulgators,
Pan. 7–19 in connection with the *o·* text
    11–21 the *o·* standard of man
'01. 16–16 *o·* text defines *devil* as
'01. 33– 2 the *o·* beauty of holiness
Hea. 3–14 In the *o·* text the term *God*
    7– 9 translates matter into its *o·* language,
    13–17 and with this *o·* dose we cured
Peo. 1– 6 back to its *o·* language,
My. 46– 9 * church in its *o·* organization ;
    123–16 The *o·* cost of the estate
    129–17 how he presses to his *o·*,
    157–17 * in her *o·* deed of trust,
    180– 9 restores their *o·* tongue
    253– 4 perfect *o·* man and universe.
    262– 4 spotless purity and *o·* perfection.
    315– 1 *o·* of which is in my possession,

original

My. 317–23   My diction, . . . has been called o·.
    324– 8   * often said you were so o·.
    324–25   * as entirely unique and o·.
    334–10   * o· account of her husband's demise

originally

Mis.   x–11   were o· written in haste,
    381– 3   manuscripts o· composed by
No.   13–10   after those words were o· uttered,

originate

Mis.   26–16   how did matter o·?
    45–22   *where did evil o·?*
   102– 6   o· in a limited body,
Ret.   36–10   would insinuate did not o· with me.
    68– 2   it claimed to o· in the name of
    68–19   "How can matter o·
Rud.   7–22   Spirit cannot o· its opposite,
Hea.   12–11   physical effects o· in mind
    17–26   did not mind o· the delusion?

originated

Mis.   45–23   It never o· or existed
    57– 6   Man o· not from dust,
    83–14   o· in another's mind
   148– 9   o· not in solemn conclave
  382–18   o· its form of government,
Man.   3– 5   o· not in solemn conclave
Ret.   69– 6   sleep, in which o· the delusion
Pul.   32–12   * What had she o·?
    63–15   * woman, who has o· a
    70–24   * Thus o· the divine or spiritual
Rud.   16–23   o· with certain opposing factions,
    17– 9   never o· in pride, rivalry, or
No.   26–21   individuality never o· in molecule
Peo.   4– 5   sickness, and death o· in the
My.   vi–13   * o· its form of public worship,

originates

Mis. 186– 2   spiritual man who o· in God,
Rud.   16–18   o· from the Principle and practice
My.   5– 1   o· in the minds of mortals.

originating

Mis.   71–25   man is incapable of o· :
'01.   33–10   * quackery was never the o· influence
    34–13   o· not in God, but

originator

My. 267– 6   the o· of all that really is.

originators

Ret.   37–14   declare . . . to have been the o·

oriole's

Mis. 329–20   rocking the o· cradle,

Orion

Rud.   4–13   "loose the bands of O·." — *Job* 38 : 31.

orison

My. 281– 8   spirit of this o· is the fruit of

orphan

Mis. 388–19   To bless the o·, feed the poor ;
Po.   21– 8   To bless the o·, feed the poor ;

Orphean

Mis. 329–24   sweep in soft strains her O· lyre.

orthodox

Mis. 111–26   I love the o· church ;
   225– 6   o· clergyman, his wife and child.
Pul.   50–24   * so-called o· religious bodies
'01.   15–18   little short of the old o· hell
    31–21   Devout o· parents ;
My. 307–16   At that date I was a staunch o·

orthodoxy

No.   12– 9   After a lifetime of o·

Osiris

My.   92–12   * new temple to Isis and O·

osseous

My. 342–11   * depend upon the o· structure ;

ossification

My. 107–32   pneumonia, diphtheria, and o·

ostensibly

No.   39– 5   o· to catch God's ear,

ostentation

My.   30–23   * Without o· and quite voluntarily

ostracize

No.   45– 8   to o· whatever uplifts mankind.
'00.   9–22   Whosoever attempts to o· C. S.

ostracized

No.   2– 4   o· by the medical faculty,

other (see also other's)

Mis.   8–14   or any o· creature separate you from
   11–30   I have turned the o· :
   21–13   seen to depart from the trend of o·
   22–21   "there is none o·." — *Mark* 12 : 32.
   25–13   rejects all o· theories of causation,

other

Mis.   27– 8   o· systems of religion abandon
   33–17   o· than to place themselves under my
   38–14   *o· institutions find little interest in*
   38–21   metaphysics at o· colleges means,
   40– 1   in the one case as in the o·.
   41–21   There is no o· healer in the case.
   48–29   like a hundred o· stories,
   57– 5   what evidence . . . of any o· creation?
   60– 9   after all o· means have failed.
   62– 2   o· people's individuality,
   63– 2   and anomalous in the o·.
   65–28   for the absence of the o·,
   76–18   on o· topics less important.
   78–10   than can science in any o· direction.
   89– 1   when you employ the o·.
   91–29   my example, and that of o· teachers,
   97–14   all o· methods of treating disease.
   99–19   In no o· one thing seemed
  101–27   no o· power, law, or intelligence
  103– 5   while the o· is eternal,
  103–25   was like that of o· men ;
  105–22   or maligned, it eclipses the o·
  112–21   * " O· visitors have brought to him
  112–27   exaggerating sense of o· people's.
  117–20   *modus operandi*, of o· folks.
  119– 4   instead of aiding o· people's devices
  129–18   for o· green eyes to gaze on :
  142– 9   among o· beautiful decorations,
  144–12   o· works written by the same author,
  145– 1   more than any o· institution,
  170–23   and no o· method is C. S.
  179– 9   any o· consciousness than that of
  182– 8   no o· God, no o· Mind, no o· origin ;
  193–10   can be established on no o· claim
  195– 1   in any o· remedy than Christ,
  197–32   working from no o· Principle,
  219–19   while in the o· he must
  229–14   faith in Mind over all o·
  229–26   any o· possible sanative method ;
  230– 3   more than upon any o· one thing.
  230–16   hours that o· people may occupy in
  236–16   to give, to one or the o·, advice
  241– 8   the o· having a physical ailment.
  241–18   On the o· hand,
  244–24   "And o· sheep I have, — *John* 10 : 16.
  249– 8   o· people's manuscripts
  256–10   from any o· than Mrs. Eddy,
  260–12   these laws annulled all o· laws.
  264– 1   quote from o· authors
  266–19   Chicago, New York, or any o· place,
  269– 7   and love the o· ; — *Matt.* 6 : 24.
  269– 8   despise the o·. — *Matt.* 6 : 24.
  270–11   To seek or employ o· means than
  270–17   Then you will need no o· aid,
  273– 5   in order to work in o· directions,
  273– 7   where none o· can do the work.
  273–29   the o· three classes
  279– 1   startling departures on the o· hand.
  282–25   when o· means have failed.
  282–25   One o· occasion which may
  282–27   and no o· aid is near.
  284– 4   C. S., more than any o· system
  286–28   shut out all sense of o· claims.
  287–31   attempts to steady o· people's altars,
  290– 2   Let o· people's marriage relations
  291–10   o· people's thoughts and actions.
  297– 3   this Science has distanced all o·
  304–17   * When not in use in o· places,
  308– 6   human love or hatred or any o· cause
  314– 2   throughout our land and in o· lands.
  317–28   penalty for o· people's faults ;
  319–13   more to them than to o· people.
  336–16   the mote of evil out of o· eyes.
  340– 8   seeking no o· pursuit or pleasure
  347–15   the o· says, Take the opposite
  357– 1   trafficking in o· people's business,
  363–15   and there is no o· Maker;
  364–12   and there is no o· philosophy.
  365– 2   "o· foundation can no man — *I Cor.* 3 : 11.
  374–25   the o· sees "Helen's beauty in a
  378– 9   in company with several o· patients,
Man.   27–16   all o· C. S. literature
   27–24   o· literature connected therewith.
   29– 3   any o· officer in this Church
   34–13   with S. AND H. and o· works by
   34–17   Free from O· Denominations.
   45– 9   become members of o· societies
   48–25   they may quote from o· periodicals
   56–13   No o· than its officers are required
   56–20   for electing officers and o· business,
   57– 2   such o· business as may properly
   58–14   shall be repeated at the o· services
   64– 7   o· writings by this author ;
   69–23   o· affairs outside of her house.
   70–13   it shall be controlled by none o·.

other

Man. 71–10   In its relation to *o·* C. S. churches,
     71–13   position that no *o·* church can fill.
     74– 5   or control over any *o·* church.
     74– 8   and no *o·* church shall interfere
     74–18   all *o·* C. S. churches
     82–16   who practise *o·* professions or
     82–17   pursue *o·* vocations,
     98– 4   not been replied to by *o·* Scientists,
     99–21   he shall, in addition to his *o·* duties,
     102–17   *o·* than the erection of a church edifice.
Ret.   1– 9   besides *o·* verses and enigmas
     6–27   Among *o·* important bills
     15–23   Among *o·* diseases cured they specified
     32–18   * But the dream of *o·* dreams.
     42–10   clergymen of *o·* denominations
     45–21   turn to him the *o·* also."— *Matt.* 5 : 39.
     49– 4   *O·* institutions for instruction in
     52–16   branch associations in *o·* States,
     59–13   *o·* name for the Supreme Being,
     59–22   dependent, each on the *o·*,
     68–11   One is false, while the *o·* is true.
     68–12   One is temporal, but the *o·* is
     71–29   same as *o·* forms of stealing,
     75– 9   from the works of *o·* authors?
     78–18   any name given to it *o·* than C. S.,
     78–20   *o·* than is stated in S. and H.
     82–24   either excel or fall short of *o·*
     83–22   same as *o·* teachers;
     85– 1   *o·* teachers who should be specially
     85– 6   any *o·* organic operative method
     88–21   *o·* vineyards than our own.
     89–26   trespass not . . . upon *o·* people's
     90–19   What *o·* heart yearns with
Un.   7– 5   multitudes of *o·* religious folds.
     8– 7   can have no *o·* reality than
     8–21   heredity and *o·* physical causes.
     36– 5   beside which there is no *o·*
     40–10   none *o·* than this man,
     48– 7   I have no faith in any *o·* thing
     49–18   and the *o·* unreal,
     64– 8   "*o·* foundation can no man— *I Cor.* 3 : 11.
Pul.   5 30   literature of our and *o·* lands.
     21–21   our denomination and *o·* sects,
     21–26   Our unity with churches of *o·*
     21–28   It cannot come from any *o·* source.
     27–16   * The *o·* rose window represents
     28– 6   * *o·* panels are decorated with
     28–16   * not differ widely from that of any *o·*
     28–23   * *o·* recognized devotional poets,
     37–29   * one or two *o·* friends
     38– 2   * Mrs. Eddy had preached in *o·*
     46–23   * applied herself, like *o·* girls,
     47– 1   * many clergymen of *o·*
     51–19   * it may, on the *o·* hand,
     51–28   * alongside *o·* great demonstrations
     53– 3   * practised in *o·* countries
     53–16   * "That word, more than any *o·*
     56– 4   * nearly every *o·* centre of
     59–23   * *o·* members of the C. S. Board
     68–22   * Many *o·* church edifices in
     72–29   * any power *o·* than that which
     76–19   * the *o·* a lavatory in which
     80– 4   * one extreme will surely find the *o·*.
     88– 8   *o·* prominent newspapers
Rud.   2– 1   *O·* definitions of *person,*
     4–16   there is no *o·* Mind.
     8–13   there is no *o·* healer.
No.   4–17   beyond *o·* systems of medicine,
     13–26   *o·* parts of it have no lustre.
     14–20   more than any *o·* religious sect,
     16–18   hence their inference of some *o·*
     21–23   *o·* foundation can no man— *I Cor.* 3 : 11.
     32–15   *o·* theories make sin true.
     36– 3   one infinite and the *o·* finite ;
     38–23   nothingness of any *o·* state
Pan.   6– 2   more effectual than all *o·* means ;
     8– 8   the *o·* a human finite personality?
     10–22   *o·* religious teachers are unable to
'00.   7– 8   more Bibles sold than in all the *o·*
     8–11   steal *o·* people's good thoughts,
     14–12   seek thou the divine . . . and no *o·*
'01.   7– 2   than whom there is none *o·*.
     15–26   * no *o·* reason to be given
     17–12   exceeded that of *o·* methods,
     18–13   taught his disciples none *o·*.
     20– 6   guided by no *o·* mind than Truth,
     22–11   if one is true, the *o·* is false.
     23–21   as no *o·* person has ever
     24–25   Jesus' teachings, and none *o·*,
     27– 2   all *o·* authors except the Bible.
     30– 1   are persecuted even as all *o·*
     30–30   * will not insult me, and no *o·* can."
'02.   3– 1   used no *o·* means myself ;
     6– 1   forbids the thought of any *o·* reality,
     6– 3   law, apart or *o·* than God

other

'02.   7–18   No *o·* logical conclusion
     7–20   no *o·* scientific proposition
     10–29   in *o·* ways than by walking
     13–12   and desire none *o·*.
     14–16   on any *o·* foundation,
Hea.   1–21   more spiritual basis . . . than the *o·* ;
     6– 3   When I was told the *o·* day,
     11–28   this excellence above *o·* systems.
     15– 4   by employing no *o·* remedy
     16– 4   no *o·* Life, substance, and
     18–27   killed a man by no *o·* means than
Peo.   9–24   remove all evidence of any *o·* power
My.   v– 9   * by *o·* Christian denominations
     10–12   * churches and *o·* organizations
     18–30   * all *o·* published writings of
     30– 8   * many hundreds of *o·* faiths,
     43–17   * on the *o·* side for a memorial.
     55–22   * obliged to seek *o·* quarters,
     56–22   * were established in *o·* suburbs,
     62–29   * services of *o·* members of the church,
     67–23   * vaster sums . . . in *o·* instances,
     70– 7   * any *o·* denomination in the world,
     70–15   * chimes were being tested the *o·* day.
     71–18   * different from any *o·* church
     73– 5   * in *o·* countries since that time,
     74–15   * achievements in this or any *o·* city,
     74–16   * *o·* denominations might profit by
     74–31   * and the *o·* for its novelty.
     83–27   * *o·* evidences of the strength and
     84–14   * *o·* architectural efforts
     85–29   * Aside from every *o·* consideration,
     89–18   * all *o·* of the Christian churches,
     91– 4   * did not find in *o·* communions.
     91– 7   * good example to *o·* denominations
     91–18   * that this country or any *o·* country
     93 17   * every *o·* sect in the country
     94– 2   * every *o·* sect will be left behind
     95–21   * clergymen of *o·* denominations
     96–15   * comparison with *o·* creeds.
     96–28   * dedication . . . the *o·* day,
     104– 1   I have had no *o·* guide
     104–26   in this or any *o·* country.
     114–15   I consulted no *o·* authors
     114–16   read no *o·* book but the Bible
     119–11   Buddhism or any *o·* "ism."
     123–12   a reading-room and nine *o·* rooms
     123–17   repairs and *o·* necessary expenses
     127–11   *o·* religions since the first century.
     128– 2   no *o·* outlet to liberty.
     153 18   no *o·* than the spiritual help
     170– 9   not to be confused with *o·* issues,
     171– 2   *and have no o· trusts.*
     182– 3   any *o·* city in the United States.
     199–21   in this and in *o·* lands.
     212– 7   *o·* forms of intoxication.
     212–20   impossible under *o·* conditions,
     218–30   *o·* than that which my books afford,
     221 16   modes of healing, *o·* than the
     221–19   no *o·* heaven-appointed means
     225–15   distinguishes it from all *o·* names,
     227–28   turn to him the *o·* also."— *Matt.* 5 : 39.
     231–13   in *o·* of its highest . . . meanings,
     233–14   effects of *o·* people's sins
     235–22   no *o·* creator and no *o·* creation.
     276–24   *o·* than to help support a
     277– 2   chapter sub-title
     281– 3   *o·* than the daily prayer of my
     291–30   liberty of *o·* peoples
     293– 5   one against the *o·*
     303– 8   Catholics, or any *o·* sect.
     307–10   *o·* terms which I employed
     310–27   for her *o·* children to imitate,
     315–30   in our own and in *o·* countries,
     324–16   * any *o·* thought but that you were
     327–18   * *o·* Scientists who stayed on
     327–25   * "All *o·* professionals who practise
     328–28   * all *o·* professionals who practise
     334–14   * whom he had in mind is some *o·* one?
     340–11   in excess of *o·* States,
     342–16   * *o·* and smaller parlor
     348– 2   healed . . . by *o·* than drugs,
     354– 3   offering Bibles and *o·* books
     356–16   *o·* than the ones presented in
     356–23   love the *o·* ;— *Matt.* 6 : 24.
     356–24   despise the *o·*.— *Matt.* 6 : 24.
     357–17   than which there is no *o·*,
     363–26   any *o·* individual but the patient
     364– 4   handle no *o·* mentality
     364–12   any *o·* cause or effect

(*see also* **churches, each, gods, minds, students
way, words**)

other's

Man. 85– 2   Pupils may visit each *o·* churches,
     85– 3   attend each *o·* associations.

others (*see also* **others'**)

actions of
  My. 276–20 * to dictate the actions of *o·.*
advance of
  Ret. 94– 2 perceived, in advance of *o·,*
all
  Un. 10– 2 separates my system from all *o·.*
  Pul. 55–26 * all *o·* being branches,
  My. 51– 5 * and all *o·* now interested in
basis for
  Mis. 156–16 becoming the basis for *o·* :
before us
  Mis. 343– 3 not forget that *o·* before us have
believe
  Mis. 228–27 believe what *o·* believe,
best for
  Mis. 288– 3 regarding what is best for *o·*
bestowed upon
  Mis. 227–30 happiness it has bestowed upon *o·.*
bestows on
  My. 122– 2 gratuitously bestows on *o·,*
blamed
  Mis. 111– 9 blamed *o·* more than yourself.
bless
  Mis. 127–22 to become blessed, is to bless *o·* :
  Pan. 9–18 endeavor to bless *o·,*
blessing
  '02. 17– 9 blessing *o·,* and self-immolation
business of
  Mis. 348– 5 the books nor the business of *o·* ;
concerning
  Mis. 311–31 rehearsing facts concerning *o·*
conquer
  '00. 9–18 before he can conquer *o·.*
console
  Un. 18–14 you oftenest console *o·* in
crowded with
  Pul. 60– 1 * crowded with *o·,* waiting for
destroyer of
  My. 161– 5 intentional destroyer of *o·*
doing to
  Mis. 115–32 doing to *o·* as you would have
doing unto
  Mis. 135–10 doing unto *o·* as ye would they should
  223–18 while doing unto *o·* what we
  My. 275–24 Doing unto *o·* as we would that
do unto
  Mis. 301– 6 as you would have *o·* do unto you?
  Man. 16–11 do unto *o·* as we would have
  My. 114– 6 Do unto *o·* as ye would have
  252– 8 the good you do unto *o·*
downfall of
  Mis. 43–24 to build on the downfall of *o·,*
errors of
  Mis. 131– 1 challenges the errors of *o·*
  236– 6 indiscretions, and errors of *o·* ;
experiences of
  Ret. 79– 5 from the experiences of *o·.*
eyes of
  Mis. 211– 6 to open the eyes of *o·,*
faults of
  Mis. 224– 6 miserable for the faults of *o·.*
forgive
  Mis. 129– 5 forgive *o·* as he would *be* forgiven.
forsook
  Ret. 90–15 betrayed him, and *o·* forsook him.
giving it to
  Pul. 73– 1 * taking . . . or giving it to *o·*?"
God reaches
  Mis. 39–26 *God reaches o· to heal them,*
goodness in
  Pul. 21–17 true sense of goodness in *o·,*
good of
  No. 7–16 sacrifice for the good of *o·*
hands of
  Mis. 13– 8 endured at the hands of *o·*
healed
  Mis. 71– 8 he healed *o·* who were sick.
  My. 112– 1 healed *o·* by means of the Principle
help
  Mis. 90–15 Then help *o·* to be free ;
helping
  Mis. 353–29 to think of helping *o·,*
  Pul. 81–13 * spends her whole time helping *o·.*
  My. 165– 3 helping *o·* thus to choose.
help of
  My. 130–16 Therefore I ask the help of *o·*
  138– 1 without the help of *o·.*
impart to
  No. 12–11 duty for her to impart to *o·*
I say to
  Mis. 12– 1 *Because* I thus feel, I say to *o·* :
judges
  Mis. 130–21 He who judges *o·* should know
lift
  Mis. 338– 4 able to lift *o·* toward it.

others

love
  Mis. 311–18 and love *o·* more than they
love for
  Mis. 127– 5 in the ratio of her love for *o·,*
  My. 18– 2 in the ratio of her love for *o·,*
many
  Mis. 32–17 more than to many *o·.*
  197– 5 more frequently used than many *o·,*
  278–20 shared less of my labors than many *o·,*
  Ret. 15–29 many *o·* present had been healed
  My. 353– 1 and as many *o·* as possible,
means for
  '01. 29– 5 providing ways and means for *o·.*
menacing
  Mis. 67–20 if you see the danger menacing *o·,*
mentality of
  Un. 56– 4 from the mentality of *o·* ;
minds of
  Mis. 220–26 put it into the minds of *o·*
misteach
  Mis. 114–10 and so made to misteach *o·.*
more than
  Rud. 13–25 not be expected, more than *o·,*
motives of
  No. 7– 7 as to the motives of *o·.*
ourselves and
  '02. 17–23 and what we give ourselves and *o·*
preached to the
  Ret. 89–11 If one worshipper preached to the *o·,*
precaution for
  Mis. 89–19 he left this precaution for *o·.*
quarrelling with
  '00. 8–21 stops quarrelling with *o·.*
recommended
  Mis. 245– 2 or recommended *o·* to use, drugs ;
recover
  My. 227–12 dies while the *o·* recover,
sacrificed for
  '01. 29–10 even as he has sacrificed for *o·*
sake of
  Mis. 312– 8 endures all . . . for the sake of *o·,*
saw
  Ret. 76–12 a light beyond what *o·* saw.
say
  Mis. 228–27 and say what *o·* say.
show
  My. 117–30 show *o·* the footsteps from sense to
some
  My. 307–21 understood . . . better than some *o·*
success of
  My. 212–28 hindering . . . the success of *o·.*
teach
  Mis. 114–14 and teach *o·* to practise,
tell
  Mis. 316–17 My juniors can tell *o·*
thoughts of
  Un. 56–19 suffered from the thoughts of *o·.*
  '01. 20– 4 influencing the thoughts of *o·,*
thousands of
  My. 293– 9 thousands of *o·* believed the same,
to be lost
  Peo. 8– 4 that elects . . . and *o·* to be lost,
to fit
  '00. 9–28 to fit *o·* for this great
to hinder
  Mis. 284– 2 and never try to hinder *o·*
treat
  Mis. 71– 1 *Is it right for me to treat o·, when*
true to
  Rud. 8–11 true to thyself, and true to *o·* ;
twenty
  Man. 18–18 twenty *o·* of Mrs. Eddy's students
welcome
  Pul. 51–13 * are glad to welcome *o·*
welfare of
  Ret. 72– 4 To disregard the welfare of *o·*
will approach
  Mis. 233–27 *o·* will approach it :
will attain
  '01. 2–16 *o·* will attain it,
work for
  Mis. 138– 2 sustain themselves and work for *o·.*
  My. 259–16 time to think and work for *o·.*
would harm
  My. 210–13 when he would harm *o·.*
yourself and
  Rud. 10– 4 influence on yourself and *o·.*
  '00. 8–18 doing rightly by yourself and *o·.*

  Mis. 24–16 tried to make plain to *o·,*
  39–22 who has more to meet than *o·*
  88– 3 occasionally receive it from *o·* ;
  119–28 Would you consent that *o·* should
  127–20 one must do good to *o·.*
  131– 2 can neither help himself nor *o·* ;

others

Mis.	137–22	for himself and for o˙,
	215–25	error in themselves and in o˙
	222– 6	injuring himself and o˙.
	226–12	false to themselves as to o˙?
	228–26	we do what o˙ do,
	234–14	his effort to steal from o˙
	241–12	try to make o˙ do likewise,
	244–23	not to teach himself, but o˙,
	254–28	vineyard unto o˙.'' — *Mark* 12 : 9
	264– 6	o˙ stumble over misdeeds,
	265–25	o˙, who receive the same instruction,
	291–20	to bestow it upon o˙,
	298– 7	causing o˙ to go astray,
	305–27	* collect two dollars from o˙,
	308–23	taught me more than it has o˙
	316– 4	law not unto o˙, but themselves.
	335–13	o˙ charge upon me
	368–24	O˙, from malice and envy,
	391–19	Then if we've done to o˙
Man.	18–20	o˙ that have since been elected
	49– 3	to the exclusion of o˙,
	53– 1	influence o˙ thus to act,
	84– 6	law, not unto o˙, but to themselves.
	87–11	or permit o˙ to solicit,
Ret.	24–16	to be well . . . and how to make o˙ so.
	50–18	for o˙ through them.
	80–29	sacrifices made for o˙
	81–20	faithless to itself and to o˙,
	91–21	His power over o˙ was spiritual,
Pul.	27–18	* o˙ with lamps, typical of S. and H.
	27–28	* o˙ of pictorial significance.
	41–28	* and o˙ such — were chimed
	64–10	* o˙ donating large sums.
	66–22	* o˙ of kindred meaning,
	75– 6	of this spirit than in o˙,
Rud.	14–18	require o˙ to pay him.
No.	7– 9	and blot it out of o˙.
	34–13	glory of suffering for o˙.
'01.	27–23	than o˙ do in proportion,
Peo.	8–10	extend their influence to o˙.
Po.	38–18	Then if we've done to o˙
My.	21–25	* no less sacrifice than have o˙ ;
	38–22	* service was the same as all the o˙.
	93–13	* attaining dominion over o˙,
	114– 6	would have o˙ do to you.
	146–27	O˙ who take the side of error
	160–32	wrongs done to o˙,
	165–25	maintain themselves and o˙
	302–22	am less lauded, . . . than o˙
	343–25	Entrusting their enforcement to o˙,

others'

Mis.	115–31	your own as well as of o˙ sins.
	223–29	To punish ourselves for o˙ faults,
	291–11	tacit acquiescence with o˙ views
	309– 2	upon their own or o˙ corporeality,
Ret.	71– 3	not the forager on o˙ wisdom
	87–24	bear the weight of o˙ burdens,
My.	297–28	to read or to note from o˙ reading

otherwise

Mis.	x–22	o˙ the name would be too long.
	25–28	if He could create them o˙,
	41–16	that o˙ could not be reached,
	115– 8	o˙, his own guilt as a
	131–15	o˙, I recommend that you
	288–20	believing o˙ would prevent
	350–25	benefit that would o˙ accrue.
Man.	30–12	Unless Mrs. Eddy requests o˙,
	52–21	If a member . . . mentally or o˙,
	59–19	and are not o˙ provided with seats.
Ret.	78–23	the blessings o˙ conferred,
Pul.	44–28	* refused . . . checks by mail or o˙.
	80–16	* to the credit of the book than o˙.
Rud.	8–17	not o˙ in the field of Mind-healing.
No.	15–23	Thinking o˙ is what estranges mortals
	40–18	O˙ they forfeit their ability
'02.	17– 6	Selfishly, or o˙, all are ready
My.	83– 8	* o˙ there has been no flaunting of
	84– 7	* work that would o˙ be done.
	111– 1	thus reveal truths which o˙
	212– 2	would never, o˙, think or do
	214– 2	O˙, as our churches multiply,
	219– 9	o˙ its use is abuse.
	229–11	o˙ might cost them a half century.
	233– 5	O˙, wherefore the Lord's Prayer,
	266–19	How can it be o˙, since

Ottawa, Ontario

My.	209– 2	chapter sub-title

ought

Mis.	89– 7	o˙ the patient to follow the
	130–18	it o˙ not to be expected that they
	212–14	sense of ways and means o˙ to
	239–27	something that she o˙ not to have,
	290– 9	Mistaken views o˙ to be

ought

Mis.	311–27	o˙ not that one to take the cup,
Ret.	83– 9	which o˙ not to be tampered with.
Un.	60–17	things o˙ not so to be.'' — *Jas.* 3 : 10.
Pan.	9–18	o˙ to be aided, not hindered,
'00.	4–13	o˙ not this to be an agreeable
'01.	13– 5	o˙ not to be seen, felt, or acted :
	13– 6	because it o˙ not, we must know
	15–13	A sinner o˙ not to be at ease,
	16–18	o˙ not to proceed from the individual,
'02.	1–18	this o˙ not so to be,
Peo.	7– 5	Recognizing this as we o˙,
My.	213– 7	they o˙ not to be encouraged in it.
	224– 6	knowing . . . as I o˙, the human need,
	315– 9	* if he had done as he o˙,

ounce

Mis.	242–22	at the rate of one o˙ in two weeks,

outcome

Mis.	190– 2	nor the o˙ of life infused into matter :
Ret.	47– 2	final o˙ of material organization,
Un.	9–15	its combinations, phenomena, and o˙,
	42– 4	not the o˙ of Spirit, holiness, and
Pul.	55– 9	* natural o˙ of a period notable for
Rud.	9–11	o˙ of what I call *mortal mind*,
'01.	13– 2	The o˙ of evil, called sin,
'02.	2–19	an o˙ of progress ;
My.	5– 4	supposed . . . woman to be the o˙ of
	6–24	even the o˙ of their hearts,
	94–28	even the o˙ of their hearts,

outcomes

Mis.	267–16	the vital o˙ of Truth

outdoes

'01.	16–11	o˙ itself and commits suicide,

outdoing

Mis.	80–29	o˙ the healing of the old.

outdoor

Mis.	253– 7	not enough . . . for o˙ speaking,
My.	123–19	o˙ accommodations at Pleasant View

outflowing

Mis.	199–30	the o˙ life of Christianity,

outgrowing

My.	8– 4	* o˙ the institutional end thereof.

outgrown

Mis.	309–20	whatever is . . . must be o˙.
Pan.	1–12	o˙, wornout, or soiled garments
My.	54–16	* Hawthorne Rooms, . . . were o˙.
	181– 6	and o˙, proofless positions.

outgrowth

No.	12– 8	o˙ of the author's religious experience.

outgrowths

Mis.	35–13	* works are the o˙ of her life.

outlet

My.	128– 2	find no other o˙ to liberty.

outline

Rud.	8–10	give you here nothing but an o˙

outlined

Mis.	103–13	thoughts are o˙, individualized
	103–28	This God was not o˙.
Un.	35–26	an o˙ falsity of consciousness,

outlines

Po.	v–11	* *whose rugged o˙ resemble*
My.	67–29	* unnoticed in the graceful o˙.

outlives

No.	25–12	o˙ finite mortal definitions of
'02.	17–20	Then thy gain o˙ the sun,

outliveth

Po.	15–20	love that o˙ the grave,

Outlook, The

Pul.	56–23	* The O˙, New York,

outlook

Mis.	2–13	the o˙ demands labor,
	150–15	The o˙ is cheering.
Pul.	80–11	* most recognition, the widest o˙.
My.	50–19	* the apparently discouraging o˙

outmasters

Mis.	102–29	o˙ it, and ends the warfare.

outpouring

No.	33–19	the o˙ love that sustains
Po.	v– 6	* o˙ of a deeply poetic nature
My.	90–24	* o˙ of eager communicants
	118–10	It is an o˙ of goodness

outrages

Mis.	274–19	mocks morality, o˙ humanity,

outrun

Po.	78– 9	star whose destiny none may o˙ ;

outset

Mis.	284–16	so dealt with at the o˙.
Peo.	3–24	assigns them mortal fetters in the o˙.

outside

Mis.	8–10	thing o· thine own creation?
	50–14	no . . . secret o· of its teachings,
	72–30	aught material, or o· of infinity,
	205– 1	obtains peace and power o· of itself.
	274– 7	work . . . o· of College work,
	349– 2	lessons o· of my College,
	352– 9	facts of Truth o· of the error ;
Man.	69–24	other affairs o· of her house.
	84–26	O· of this Board each student
Ret.	14–18	even if my creedal doubts left me o·
Un.	3–26	can be nothing o· of Himself.
	18–16	from o· and above ourselves?
	20–21	o· of His own focal distance.
	21–17	nothing beside Him or o· of Him.
	24– 9	never be o· of His oneness?
Pul.	50–14	* no additional sums o· of the
	57–21	* Few people o· its own circles
'01.	23– 8	or exist o· of the
'02.	16–24	merely o· forms of religion,
Po.	47–11	O· this ever of pain?
My.	74–22	* even if those o· are unable to
	141– 9	* members of the church o· of Boston
	145– 9	details o· and inside
	223– 6	o· of The Mother Church of Christ,
	272–28	* o· of the C. S. periodicals,
	341–27	* change from the misty air o·

outstretched

Mis.	319–23	in the o· hand of God.
Un.	26– 6	proud to be in His o· hands,
Pul.	7–14	with His o· arm.
No.	44–18	weak hand o· to God.
'01.	1– 5	never lack God's o· arm
'02.	14–25	o· arm of infinite Love
My.	42–30	* with an o· arm" — *Deut.* 26 : 8.
	124–11	the world's arms o· to us,

outtalk

'01.	16–21	was supposed to o· Truth

outtalked

Mis.	191–24	was supposed to have o· even Truth,

outward

Mis.	380– 1	o· sign of such a practice :
	380–25	any o· form of practice.
Pul.	11– 1	o·, upward, heavenward.
	30–13	* not celebrated by o· symbols
	32–14	* so far as o· events may translate
'02.	10–14	taking steps o· and upwards.
Hea.	7–20	regardless of any o· act,
My.	110–11	o· and upward in the scale of being.
	127– 1	reaching o· and upward to Science
	159–16	from the inward to the o·,

outweigh

Mis.	134–17	bend or o· your purpose

outweighs

Mis.	135–18	joy that o· an hour.
	167–11	o· the material world.
'02.	17–15	on that which o· time ;

outworn

Un.	13–21	an o· theological platform,

oval

My.	69– 6	* presenting an o· and dome

over (*see also* **o'er**)

Mis.	6–10	passed o· to the Scientist.
	6–12	power of metaphysics o· physics;
	7–17	Looking o· the newspapers
	16–14	its supremacy o· sin, sickness,
	30–18	superiority of Mind o· the flesh,
	33–21	o· the ordinary methods of healing
	35– 5	supremacy of Mind o· matter,
	40–24	power o· sin in themselves,
	47– 2	weigh o· two hundred pounds
	54–12	power of C. S. o· all obstacles
	55–21	assert themselves o· their opposite,
	57– 1	created man o· again
	58– 3	have any more power o· him?
	58– 5	then it has no power o· one.
	59–18	Is not all argument mind o· mind?
	61– 9	omnipotence of Truth o· error,
	61–10	and of Life o· death.
	62–29	divine Mind o· the human mind
	63–30	proved its supremacy o· matter.
	64– 4	to show his power o· death ;
	69–12	dominion o· the fish — *Gen.* 1 : 26.
	69–12	o· the fowl of the air." — *Gen.* 1 : 26.
	69–31	Had that sick man dominion o·
	69–32	His want of control o·
	70– 4	exercised my power o· the fish,
	74–25	His triumph o· the grave
	97– 1	it is Truth o· error ;
	105– 5	individual demonstrations o· sin,
	105– 9	His physical sufferings, . . . were o·
	107– 4	Art must not prevail o· Science.
	116–29	"faithful o· a few things." — *Matt.* 25 : 21.

over

Mis.	117– 1	"ruler o· many things." — *Matt.* 25 : 23.
	118–13	pass a friend o· it smoothly,
	119– 5	then whining o· misfortune,
	125– 8	dominion o· his own sinful sense
	129–14	let silence prevail o· his remains.
	130–11	talking about it, thinking it o·,
	137–14	rejoice o· the growth of my students
	140–10	o· matter or merely legal titles.
	145–13	o· all the earth," — *Gen.* 1 : 26.
	145–15	O· a wounded sense of its own error,
	150– 4	Shepherd of Israel watching o· you
	152– 8	benediction o· all the earth,
	162– 9	o· their fretted, foaming billows.
	167–22	dominion o· the whole earth ;
	170– 5	weep o· the graves of their beloved ;
	172–10	white-winged charity, brooding o· all,
	174– 5	having presence and power o·
	181–12	What avail, then, to quarrel o·
	183–28	o· all the earth." — *Gen.* 1 : 26.
	187– 3	Jesus demonstrated o· sin,
	187– 4	o· and above every sense of matter,
	197–25	rules o· a kingdom of its own,
	199–21	o· the qualities opposed to Spirit
	201–17	enabled him to triumph o· them,
	204–21	holding sway o· human consciousness.
	210– 7	Do men whine o· a nest of serpents,
	220–13	full control o· this mind
	220–28	this action of mind o· mind,
	221– 1	it has no power o· him.
	225–27	a cool perspiration spread o·
	229–14	faith in Mind o· all other
	239–25	made them more serious o· it.
	240–23	o· the fresh, unbiased thought.
	249–28	O· what worlds on worlds it hath
	254– 5	love which brooded tireless o· their
	261–14	full, pressed down, and running o·.
	264– 6	others stumble o· misdeeds,
	270– 9	He who demonstrated his power o· sin,
	279– 7	but o· and above it all
	286–12	superiority of spiritual power o·
	287–14	should preponderate o· the evil,
	287–15	the spiritual o· the animal,
	287–24	Be faithful o· home relations ;
	287–28	it makes one ruler o· one's self
	291–31	keeps not watch o· his emotions
	297–24	If the man is dominant o· the
	307– 1	charge o· thee." — *Psal.* 91 : 11.
	315– 9	Scientists, all o· the world,
	315–13	consist of not o· thirty-three students,
	317– 8	o· all sin, disease, and death.
	321– 2	o· the cradle of a great truth,
	321–11	triumphs of Truth o· error,
	321–11	of health o· sickness,
	321–12	Life o· death,
	321–12	Soul o· sense.
	327–30	plunge headlong o· the jagged rocks.
	329–14	o· mountain and meadow,
	330– 4	o· the new-made grave,
	330–14	alders bend o· the streams
	331– 7	o· all the earth" — *Gen.* 1 : 26.
	336– 2	Truth, the victor o· a lie.
	339–17	faithful o· a few things." — *Matt.* 25 : 23.
	340–16	not been faithful o· a few things.
	340–24	thou hast been faithful o· a few things.
	341– 9	be made ruler o· many things.
	342–14	o· earth's lazy sleepers.
	342–32	faithful o· the few things of Spirit,
	349–17	I claim no jurisdiction o· any
	353– 2	it has nothing to mourn o·,
	356–23	This virtue triumphs o· the flesh ;
	373–25	God gave man dominion o· all
	374–15	hold charge o· both,
	376–22	o· a deeply dazzling sunlight,
	379–29	Mind and its superiority o·
	383– 8	preeminence o· ignorance or
Man.	17– 2	deliberations o· forming a church
	58– 7	Pastor o· The Mother Church,
	74– 5	control o· any other church.
	80– 5	shall be paid o· semi-annually
	89– 2	resign o· her own signature
	90–12	continue not o· one week.
	91–17	shall be paid o· annually to
Chr.	57– 3	power o· the nations :— *Rev.* 2 : 26.
Ret.	13–22	ineffable joy came o· me.
	14– 2	forever lost its power o· me.
	14–30	After the meeting was o·
	15–25	treated and given o· by physicians
	16– 3	When the meeting was o·,
	22–17	God is o· all.
	26–10	supremacy of good o· evil,
	26–11	superiority of Spirit o· matter.
	34–16	metaphysics o· physics.
	47– 5	Students from all o· our continent,
	47– 6	o· three hundred applications
	57– 2	o· the unfathomable sea of

over

Ret.
73–20 or terrifies people *o·* it,
79–21 victory *o·* self and sin.
85–26 rapidly spreading *o·* the globe ;
91–21 His power *o·* others was spiritual,

Un.
11– 3 taught us to walk *o·*, not *into*
14– 3 do His work *o·* again,
30–19 made humanity victorious *o·*
39–18 giveth man dominion *o·* all the
43– 4 any strong demonstration *o·*
43–10 complete triumph *o·* death,
45–19 telegraphs and telephones *o·* its
58–14 triumph *o·* all mortal mentality
58–20 midnight sun shines *o·* the Polar Sea.

Pul.
3–14 good fight we have waged is *o·*,
3–28 so far from victory *o·* the flesh
7–11 would not weep *o·* it, as he wept *o·*
9–13 quibbled *o·* an architectural exigency,
12–16 For victory *o·* a single sin,
12–18 mighty conquest *o·* all sin?
13– 6 faithful *o·* a few things, — *Matt.* 25 : 23.
13– 7 make thee ruler *o·* many," *Matt.* 25 : 23.
15–18 occasion for a victory *o·* evil.
23–11 * has swept the country,
26–21 * *o·* the door, in large golden letters
26–27 * lamp *o·* two hundred years old,
30–10 * includes those all *o·* the country.
30–21 * power of Truth *o·* error,
30–29 ✦ *o·* two hundred thousand dollars,
31–18 * dominance of mind *o·* matter,
43– 7 * presided *o·* the exercises.
44–20 * shown its power *o·* its students,
52–12 * *o·* two hundred thousand dollars,
52–21 * bigotry that swept *o·* the world
53 10 * dominion *o·* the physical world.
55–25 ✦ now *o·* four thousand members.
57– 3 * *o·* two hundred thousand dollars.
58–10 * *o·* two hundred thousand dollars,
58–16 * will seat *o·* a thousand
59–29 * Before one service was *o·*
60–13 * many having remained *o·* a week
63–16 * numbers *o·* one hundred thousand
63–25 * Christian Scientists all *o·* the country,
67–17 * numbers *o·* a quarter of a million
68–20 * *o·* two hundred thousand dollars,
70– 5 * O· One Hundred Thousand Followers
70–12 * *o·* one hundred thousand converts,
70–16 * Christian Scientists all *o·* the country.
70–23 * *o·* all error, sin, sickness, and
71–13 * in fact all *o·* the country,
71–14 ✲ discomfited *o·* the announcements
73– 9 * meditated *o·* His divine Word.
75–21 * members . . . all *o·* North America
79– 5 ✲ *o·* two hundred thousand dollars,
80–14 * *o·* its granitic pebbles.

No.
3–17 Every teacher must pore *o·* it
8 20 enmity *o·* doctrines and traditions,
8–20 *o·* the misconceptions of C. S.,
29–24 *o·* the waves of sin, sickness, and
33–22 Love and its power *o·* death.
34–24 *o·* the steps of uplifted humanity,
36–20 recuperated him for triumph *o·* sin,
41–19 slumbered *o·* Christ's commands,

Pan.
3– 3 supposed to preside *o·* sylvan
10– 8 prevail *o·* the opposite notion

'00.
1–12 *o·* sixteen thousand communicants
1–24 *o·* a million of people
8–23 will boil *o·* the brim of life
10–20 *o·* individuals, weak provinces, or
11– 3 have no discord *o·* music.
12–24 *o·* two years — he labored
15– 9 passage *o·* a tear-filled sea

'01.
2–28 my church of *o·* twenty-one thousand
10–23 victory *o·* self, sin, disease,
11– 4 his demonstration *o·* sin, disease,
14– 1 it sticks to us and has power *o·* us.
20–18 and his power *o·* it.
23–21 demonstrated his power *o·* matter.

'02.
3–18 *o·* the close of the conflict in
5– 6 *o·* doubtful interpretations of
6–24 the struggle *o·*, and victory
9–25 *o·* Morse's discovery of telegraphy?
10– 4 power *o·* matter, molecule, space,
10–30 walking every step *o·* the land route,
15–24 steadfast stars watched *o·* the world,
20– 1 Christ walketh *o·* the wave ;

Hea.
7– 6 power of Mind *o·* matter.
8– 7 carrying out this government *o·*
10–20 even the triumph of Soul *o·* sense.
15– 9 power of mind *o·* matter,
19– 2 to test the power of mind *o·* body ;

Peo.
2–20 demoniacal contests *o·* religion.
11–11 supremacy of Soul *o·* sense,
12– 3 *o·* all the earth." — *Gen.* 1 : 26.
13–17 triumph of mind *o·* the body,

Po.
33–10 To kindly pass *o·* a wound,

over

Po.
47–15 *O·* the tears it has shed ;
78– 3 Peace her white wings will spread *o·*

My.
v–22 * *o·* four hundred thousand copies
vi–22 * she made *o·* to trustees
21–20 * and running *o·*." — *Luke* 6 : 38.
30– 5 * *o·* thirty thousand people
30– 7 * Scientists from all *o·* the world,
31–12 * from *o·* the entire world.
43–19 * Israel came *o·* this Jordan
47–11 * people the world *o·* have been
47–16 * we look back *o·* the years
49– 4 * one is wholly drawn *o·*,
50–18 * Love prevailing *o·* the apparently
55–10 * the Cause itself was spreading *o·*
60–26 * Now that the great event, . . . is *o·*,
61–14 * I was climbing *o·* stones and
63–12 * annual communion and . . . are *o·*,
65–12 * It was not even talked *o·*.
72–22 * members of the church all *o·* the
73– 5 * churches all *o·* this country
73–13 * from all *o·* the world
74–14 * their triumph of mind *o·* matter.
75–18 * They do not get excited *o·* trifles.
77– 4 * seating capacity of *o·* five thousand.
77– 9 * From all *o·* the world
77–18 * *O·* the heads of a multitude
82–19 * when the entertainment is *o·*
84–12 * Christian Scientists all *o·* the world.
89– 6 * *o·* two hundred and twenty feet high,
90–25 * from all *o·* the civilized world,
93–13 * or attaining dominion *o·*
97– 2 * power of mind *o·* matter.
106–10 power *o·* and above matter
119–18 gives dominion *o·* all the earth.
123–21 *o·* two hundred people,
126–25 *o·* the widowhood of lust,
134–10 Joy *o·* good achievements
137–11 It is *o·* forty years that I have
142–19 *o·* a step higher in their passage
147– 4 *O·* a half century ago,
147– 7 *o·* my childhood's Sunday noons.
148–27 to gain power *o·* contending
154– 3 power of Truth *o·* error.
156–23 which giveth victory *o·* sin, disease,
158–13 heaven here, the struggle *o·* ;
161–31 can triumph *o·* their ultimatum,
162–11 Christian Scientists all *o·* the field,
172–14 church of *o·* thirty thousand
182– 3 *o·* any other city in the
184–25 unwearied watch *o·* a world.
185–10 reign triumphant *o·* all the earth.
190–19 Mind *o·* the human mind
100 22 power *o·* all manner of diseases ;
192–11 conquest *o·* sin and mortality,
194– 2 in broad facts *o·* great continents
196 28 *O·* the glaciers of winter
204– 8, 9 *O·* sea and *o·* land, C. S. unites
208– 6 its heavenly rays *o·* all the earth.
219–29 "Rather than quarrel *o·* vaccination,
229–23 messages of rejoicing *o·* the
230–23 faithful *o·* foundational trusts,
232– 3 sailing *o·* rough seas
233–14 *o·* the effects of other people's
245– 1 *o·* and above the approved schools
257– 4 *o·* the new cradle of an old truth.
258–21 repine *o·* blossoms that mock
268–24 gives man the victory *o·* himself.
275–27 white-winged charity brooding *o·* all,
276– 9 or swallow camels *o·* it,
285–19 power *o·* the nations." — *Rev.* 2 : 26.
291– 4 *o·* the destinies of a nation
291–24 prosperity waves *o·* land and sea,
294– 6 omnipresent, supreme *o·* all.
299– 3 *O·* the signature "A Priest of
306– 8 newspaper controversy *o·* a question
323–22 * Your crowning triumph *o·* error
341– 9 Beloved brethren all *o·* our land
353–13 intended to hold guard *o·* Truth,
361– 9 not seen Mrs. Stetson for *o·* a year,
362– 5 right *o·* wrong, of Truth *o·* error.

overbalance
Mis. 354– 7 to *o·* this foul stuff.

overbear
Mis. 28–16 Science alone can *o·* materiality

overcame
Mis. 76–32 *o·* the last enemy, death.
99– 9 His fear *o·* his loyalty ;
Pul. 12– 9 they *o·* him by the — *Rev.* 12 : 11.

overcome
Mis. 6–22 *o·* the patient's faith in drugs
18–29 must be repented of and *o·*.
55– 8 utilizes its power to *o·* sin.
66–27 "*o·* evil with good." — *Rom.* 12 : 21.

overcome

Mis.	81–16	in order to o· mortal sense,
	89–27	saved from error, or error o·.
	104–32	wherewith to o· all error.
	112–28	Unless this mental condition be o·,
	115–27	God will give the ability to o·
	115–28	o· the baneful effects of sin
	116– 1	will o· evil with good,
	118–23	must be met manfully and o·,
	125– 7	enables him to o· the world,
	131–22	which they have o·.
	236–17	the best way to o· them,
	334–29	"Be not o· of evil,— Rom. 12 : 21.
	334–30	o· evil with good,"— Rom. 12 : 21.
	352–27	through argument . . . o· evil.
Man.	47– 2	seeks to o· evil with good.
	55– 5	strive to o· these errors.
Ret.	55– 6	it can only be o· with good.
Pul.	13– 4	o· the mortal belief in a
	15–16	o· evil with good.
	83–18	* o· our own allied armies of evil
	84–24	* all obstacles . . . met and o·,
No.	9–20	power of grace to o· evil
	33– 4	thus we may o· evil with good.
'01.	14–25	To o· all wrong,
	15– 9	teaching him that they cannot o· us.
	17–19	o· a difficult stage of the work,
	34–21	be not o· of evil,
	34–21	but o· evil with good ;
'02.	2–30	to o· evil with good,
Peo.	5–14	having o· death and the grave,
My.	6–10	When we have o· sin
	52– 3	* she had many obstacles to o·,
	116– 9	must be met and o·.
	128–27	"o· evil with good."— Rom. 12 : 21.
	132– 7	I have o· the world."— John 16 : 33.
	180–18.	o· evil and heal disease.
	228– 8	"o· evil with good."— Rom. 12 : 21.
	233–20	most stubborn belief to o·,
	278–21	should o· evil with good.
	300– 3	o· sin according to the Scripture,
	300–15	o· "the last enemy"— I Cor. 15 : 26.

overcomes

'01.	15– 8	he o· them through Christ,
My.	106–18	o· the evidence of diseased sensation.

overcometh

Mis.	168– 2	and o· the world !
Chr.	57– 1	he that o·,— Rev. 2 : 26.
My.	285–18	he that o·,— Rev. 2 : 26.

overcoming

Mis.	53– 7	by o· temptation and sin
	319–14	o· sin in themselves,
Man.	16– 3	healing the sick and o· sin
No.	33–24	o· sickness, sin, and death.
My.	64–24	* o· all that is unlike God,
	204–28	o· evil with good,
	239–10	by o· sin and death.
	291–12	universal good o· evil.

overcrowded

My.	56–11	* relieve the o· condition of
	56–24	* o· condition of
	57– 1	* annual meetings were o·
	57– 2	* o· in Tremont Temple,

overcrowding

My.	56–31	* continued o·, proved the need of

overcrowned

My.	201–14	was o· with a diadem of duties done.

overflow

Mis.	98–28	* Thy heart must o·, if thou
	296– 9	o· in shallow sarcasm,
	338–22	* Thy soul must o·, if thou
	338–24	* It needs the o· of heart,
Man.	61– 3	O· Meetings.
My.	17– 1	o· the hiding place."— Isa. 28 : 17.

overflowing

Mis.	310–25	chapter sub-title
	348– 6	hearts o· with love for God,
Pul.	29–14	* chairs . . . for the o· throng.
Peo.	9– 4	tears of repentance, an o· love,
My.	55–21	* hall was crowded to o·.
	96–22	* the fund was full to o·

overflows

Mis.	250–24	self-forgetful heart that o· ;

overlook

Pul.	65– 6	* should not o· the Boston sect of
My.	94– 9	* Neither can we o· the
	123–28	we must not o· small things
	227–17	they should not o· the fact that

overlooked

My.	93–26	* have o· these essentials of
	338–20	For once he may have o· the

overmuch

Rud.	16–10	attempt o· in their translation of

overrule

My.	293–24	to o· the purposes of hate

overruled

Un.	31– 9	and o· laws material

overrules

Mis.	41– 6	were it not that God o· it,

overseer's

Mis.	353–15	in the o· absence,

overshadow

My.	202– 1	May its white wings o· this

overshadowed

Mis.	361–12	C. S. has o· all human philosophy,

overshadowing

Mis.	84–21	o· Paul's sense of life in matter,
My.	46– 3	* in towering, o· dome,

overshadows

My.	127–14	o· and overwhelms materia medica,

oversubscribed

My.	73– 3	* which had been o·.

overthrew

Mis.	270– 2	"o· the tables of the— Matt. 21 : 12.

overthrow

Mis.	61–29	nor o· the logic that man is
	119– 6	rise and o· both.
Pul.	2–25	would o· this sublime fortress,
My.	345– 6	Science will o· false knowledge

overthrown

Mis.	170– 1	the last enemy to be o· ;

overture

Mis.	78– 2	o· of the angels.
	166–14	ready ear for the o· of angels
No.	46–11	joining the o· of angels.

overtures

Mis.	374–14	Angels, with o·, hold charge over
My.	13–25	reach the stars with divine o·,

overturn

Mis.	80–22	"turn and o·'"— see Ezek. 21 : 27.
My.	220–20	o· until He whose right it is shall

overturned

Peo.	2–19	Such a theory has o· empires

overturning

My.	220–20	He who is o· will overturn

overturns

Mis.	13–21	o· the testimony of the

overwhelming

Mis.	273– 7	I withdraw from an o· prosperity.
	292– 2	o· tides of revelation,
Ret.	81–16	o· sense of error's vacuity,
No.	1– 9	demolishing bridges and o· cities.

overwhelms

My.	127–14	overshadows and o· materia medica,

overworked

Mis.	198–30	by saying he has o·,

owe

Mis.	126–16	sensible of what we o· to the
Ret.	94– 2	we o· to ourselves and to the world
Rud.	14– 4	"o· no man."— Rom. 13 : 8.
'01.	24–12	* under Providence I o· my life to it."
My.	9–26	draw on God for the amount I o· you,
	73– 6	* very few of them o· a cent.
	114– 3	O· no man ; be temperate ;
	202–10	O· no man any thing,— Rom. 13 : 8.
	331–22	* express the feeling of gratitude we o·

owes

Pan.	4– 2	o· its origin and continuity to
My.	37–23	* this church o· itself and its prosperity to

owing

Mis.	x– 9	O· to the manifold demands on my
	43–26	success of such an one is o·, in part,
	161–20	o· in part, perhaps, to the Jewish law
Man.	64–23	o· to the public misunderstanding
Pul.	20– 3	O· to a heavy loss, they were unable
My.	25–17	O· to the time consumed
	338–17	o· to my busy life,

owl

Peo.	14– 8	* "bat and o· on the bending stones,

own

Mis.	2– 5	they have so little of their o·.
	7–21	A periodical of our o· will
	8–10	thing outside thine o· creation?
	8–12	object of your o· conception?
	10– 9	Because He has called His o·,
	11– 7	and save my o· life,
	11–17	would one sooner give up his o· ?
	13– 4	special care to mind my o· business.

own

Mis.	20– 3	aroma of Jesus' *o·* words,
	22–30	by reason of its *o·* ponderosity,
	24–26	he speaketh of his *o·* : — *John* 8 : 44.
	27– 9	abandon their *o·* logic.
	28– 4	having no sensation of its *o·*.
	31–18	argue against his *o·* convictions
	32–22	give to my *o·* flock all the
	33– 3	wrong will receive its *o·* reward.
	39–17	to take their *o·* medicine,
	41– 8	destroys their *o·* possibility of
	41–20	architect that builds its *o·* idea,
	42–31	our *o·* false admissions prevent us
	44–28	matter has no intelligence of its *o·*.
	47–15	loose from its *o·* beliefs.
	62– 2	improve my *o·*, and other people's
	62–31	can cure its *o·* disease,
	67–12	by doing thus thine *o·* sense of Life
	74–20	stone from the door of his *o·* tomb.
	77–27	made in God's *o·* likeness,
	80–14	rise or fall on its *o·* merit or
	82–27	treacherous glare of its *o·* flame
	83– 7	*cause of his o· sufferings.*"
	83– 9	*your o· thought or another's.*"
	83–13	with the consent of his *o·* belief.
	83–14	at the door of your *o·* thought
	83–17	arbiter of your *o·* fate,
	85–20	work out his *o·* salvation.
	92–11	his *o·* lamp trimmed and burning.
	92–22	*o·* a copy of the above-named book
	92–32	spiritualizes his *o·* thought,
	104–19	revolve in their *o·* orbits,
	104–29	recover his *o·* individuality?
	105–25	*o·* subjective state of thought.
	111–15	seed of Truth to its *o·* vitality,
	112–27	inability to see one's *o·* faults,
	113–14	depths of perdition by his *o·*
	114– 8	trend of their *o·* thoughts ;
	115– 6	even the teacher's *o·* deficiency
	115– 8	his *o·* guilt as a mental
	115–30	your *o·* as well as of others' sins.
	116– 2	destroy your *o·* sensitiveness to
	120–25	away from their *o·* fields of labor.
	122– 2	foretelling his *o·* crucifixion,
	123–24	sinners suffer for their *o·* sins,
	125– 8	dominion over his *o·* sinful sense
	126– 9	has his *o·* thoughts to guard,
	127–19	finds one's *o·* in another's good.
	131– 2	and cherishes his *o·*,
	134–16	guard and guide His *o·*.
	134–28	blind to its *o·* fate,
	137–17	spread your *o·* so bravely.
	138 1	organizations of their *o·*,
	144 10	names in your *o·* handwriting,
	145 16	wounded sense of its *o·* error,
	148–13	impelled by a power not one's *o·*,
	154–13	beneath your *o·* vine and fig-tree
	155–24	If my *o·* students cannot spare time
	165–21	lifted to these by their *o·* growth
	170–13	make our *o·* heavens and our *o·* hells,
	173–12	Mind is its *o·* great cause and
	173–27	made man in His *o·* likeness.
	176–15	counted not their *o·* lives dear
	176–26	our *o·* great opportunities
	178– 1	place of my *o·* sojourning
	182– 1	antedated his *o·* existence,
	184–27	not her *o·*, but another's good ;
	186– 3	in His *o·* image and likeness.
	197–25	rules over a kingdom of its *o·*,
	198–12	he speaketh of his *o·*." — *John* 8 : 44.
	199– 6	annul his *o·* erring mental law,
	208–15	Mortals obey their *o·* wills,
	209–10	and dies of its *o·* physics.
	209–23	Evil passions die in their *o·* flames
	211– 5	Our *o·* vision must be clear
	212–27	cast the beam out of his *o·* eye,
	213–16	may perfect their *o·* lives by
	214– 0	his *o·* household." — *Matt.* 10 : 30.
	216– 2	your *o·* state of combat with error.
	223–10	that mind reaches its *o·* ideal,
	224– 1	unless our *o·* thought barbs it.
	224– 5	wounded by our *o·* faults ;
	224–28	Nothing short of our *o·* errors should
	226– 9	by losing his *o·* self-respect?
	226–10	retaining his *o·*, he loses the
	226–15	* To thine *o·* self be true,
	227–22	abide in tabernacles of their *o·*,
	227–29	reckoning its *o·* by the
	237–22	work out its *o·* destruction ;
	238– 8	his *o·* life's incentive,
	242–18	C. S. that furnishes its *o·* proof.
	259–26	produced its *o·* illusion,
	261–25	kind of men after man's *o·* making.
	264– 6	their *o·* unsubstantiality,
	265– 1	offers his *o·* thought,
	266– 8	subjective state of his *o·* mind

own

Mis.	266–23	in unison with my *o·* endeavors
	268–23	potions of His *o·* qualities.
	268–30	error dies of its *o·* elements.
	278–25	substitute my *o·* for their growth,
	283–14	* "Mind your *o·* business,"
	283–24	work out his *o·* problem
	284– 1	each one to do his *o·* work well,
	288–22	as well as thine *o·*,
	294– 4	elbowing the concepts of his *o·*
	295–15	sentiments from his *o·* breast?
	296–28	by their *o·* poverty
	297–25	consequences of his *o·* conduct ;
	298– 2	thine *o·* understanding." — *Prov.* 3 : 5.
	300– 6	reading it publicly as your *o·*
	302– 6	preserves in his *o·* consciousness
	302–32	within their *o·* fields of labor,
	303– 5	kindly shepherd has his *o·* fold
	303– 6	and tends his *o·* flock.
	303– 6	should have their *o·* institutes
	308– 7	stops his *o·* progress,
	309– 2	their *o·* or others' corporeality,
	312–20	his *o·* spiritual discernment,
	317– 6	Scientists to do their *o·* work ;
	319– 8	not seeing their *o·* belief in sin,
	324–17	his *o·* heart tired of sin,
	326–23	to meet with joy his *o·*,
	327– 6	take nothing of thine *o·* with thee?"
	327–13	heavy baggage of their *o·*,
	327–18	burden them with their *o·*.
	328– 3	Make thine *o·* way
	328–13	door of thine *o·* heart,
	330–17	God's *o·* image and likeness,
	336–13	first cast out your *o·* dislike and
	336–14	beam in your *o·* eye that hinders
	348–16	wise in his *o·* conceit." — *Prov.* 26 : 5.
	350– 1	of my *o·* contributions.
	350–32	its *o·* proof of my practice.
	354–21	to govern His *o·* creation,
	355–21	out of thine *o·* eye." — *Matt.* 7 : 5.
	355–22	in thine *o·* mentality
	355–27	thine *o·* mental atmosphere.
	356– 3	life corrected illumine its *o·*
	356–25	gone down in his *o·* esteem.
	360–20	who partaketh of its *o·* altars,
	361–29	He elucidates His *o·* idea,
	362–15	regards creation as its *o·* creator,
	363– 2	of its *o·* unreality,
	368– 1	His *o·* image and likeness.
	368 9	* keeping watch above His *o·*."
	371– 7	help them by his *o·* leadership?
	379–16	had advanced views of his *o·*,
	387– 6	Our spirits' *o·* !"
	397 15	where Thine *o·* children are,
	398–12	And Thou know'st Thine *o·* ;
Man.	3– 9	impelled by a power not one's *o·*,
	20–11	given in her *o·* handwriting,
	50– 4	by *one* of her *o·* sex.
	55– 6	discipline its *o·* members,
	70–15	its *o·* form of government.
	75–18	*o·* the aforesaid premises
	81– 4	given in her *o·* handwriting.
	85– 1	occupies only his *o·* field of labor.
	89– 2	resign over her *o·* signature
	97–12	given in her *o·* handwriting,
	99–11	not . . . confined to its *o·* members
	111– 6	sign her *o·* Christian name,
Ret.	9–26	* her *o·* unfettered way !
	14– 2	rightly called his *o·* tenet
	15– 5	till I founded a church of my *o·*,
	16–11	occurrence in my *o·* church
	28–18	their *o·* mental denomination,
	46–18	And Thou know'st Thine *o·*.
	48– 8	every one should build on his *o·*
	57–22	must be of God, and not our *o·*,
	59–24	in His *o·* image and likeness ;
	70– 2	upon its *o·* misconceptions,
	70– 5	puts forth its *o·* qualities,
	70–19	his *o·* niche in time and eternity.
	73–21	victim of his *o·* corporeality.
	74– 4	by his *o· corpus sine pectore*
	74– 8	My *o·* corporeal personality
	75–17	author's *o·* mental mood,
	75–24	write out as his *o·* the substance of
	78–24	your *o·* success and final happiness,
	79– 6	from our *o·* material losses.
	81–24	* To thine *o·* self be true ;
	83–17	more difficult to rekindle his *o·*
	84– 5	spiritualize his *o·* thoughts
	84– 8	keeps his *o·* lamp trimmed
	84–11	should *o·* a copy of S. and H.,
	84–27	take charge only of his *o·* pupils
	84–29	avoid leaving his *o·* regular
	85– 2	doing their *o·* work well.
	86–22	each man who performs his *o·* part.
	87–23	They feel their *o·* burdens less,

own

Ret.	88– 6	his o· body from the sepulchre.
	88–22	other vineyards than our o·.
	89–19	to instruct his o· students ;
	89–24	neglecting their o· students,
	91–20	his o· perfect understanding.
	93–16	spiritual ideal is made our o·,
	93–19	identical with my o· :
Un.	1– 7	their o· destruction.'' — *II Pet.* 3 : 16.
	3–21	in His o· nature and character,
	4–14	lose our o· consciousness of error.
	10–28	under their o· falsities,
	13– 5	doing their o· work in obedience to
	14– 9	improve upon His o· previous work,
	18– 5	only the brightness of My o· glory.
	20–22	outside of His o· focal distance.
	26– 2	having its o· innate selfhood
	27–10	doubts all existence except its o·.
	27–11	everything except his o· existence.
	27–15	knowing only His o· all-presence,
	29–16	any standpoint of their o·.
	33– 6	only testify from their o· evidence,
	34–22	its o· so-called substance,
	43–21	influence of their o· thoughts
	45–19	telephones over its o· body,
	45–20	imaginary sphere of its o· creation
	53–14	will die of its o· delusion ;
	55– 6	''in his o· body — *I Pet.* 2 : 24.
	56– 7	Not his o· sins, but the sins of the
Pul.	vii– 7	inclination given their o· thoughts
	3–30	Because of my o· unfitness
	5–20	with a beauty all its o·
	8–21	rechristen them with his o· new name.
	13–24	stung to death by his o· malice ;
	17–17	And Thou know'st Thine o·
	18–24	where Thine o· children are,
	21– 9	to inhabit my o· heart
	30– 1	* members of their o· families,
	30–28	* its o· magnificent church
	31– 8	* my o· knowledge of Mrs. Eddy.
	35–29	* sympathy with her o· views,
	48–14	* pleased her to point out her o·
	50– 5	* home and family of his o·.
	55–28	* management of its o· affairs.
	57–21	* Few people outside its o· circles realize
	81–22	* her o· soul plays upon magic strings
	82–24	* by singing most for their o· sex.
	83–18	* our o· allied armies of evil
Rud.	8– 5	in Science, Spirit sends forth its o·
	11– 1	can frame its o· conditions,
	13–21	according to their o· belief
	14–22	it is their o· fault,
No.	3–23	seek not so much thine o·
	6– 8	take cognizance of their o· phenomena,
	7– 9	cancel error in our o· hearts,
	7–21	must now fight their o· battles.
	8–12	work out his o· salvation,
	9–10	their o· standpoint of experience,
	13– 2	rebukes sin with its o· nothingness,
	16–21	His o· consciousness,
	23–28	is God's o· image and likeness,
	26–11	brings forth its o· sensuous conception.
	29– 2	put to death for his o· sin,
	30–18	Truth's knowledge of its o·
	38–20	includes only His o· nature,
	42–19	The lie of evil holds its o· by
	42–22	cleaving to their o· vices.
	43–19	build a baseless fabric of their o·
Pan.	5–16	he speaketh of his o· : — *John* 8 : 44.
'00.	8–12	purloined garment as his o·,
	8–29	desire to follow your o·
	14–19	not only her o·, but another's good.
'01.	1–23	you seek to define God to your o·
	7–10	God made man in His o· image
	10–25	working out our o· salvation,
	13– 3	annihilates its o· embodiment :
	20– 9	alone with his o· being
	26–30	result of my o· observation,
	27–22	less of my o· personality
	29–26	a tithe of my o· difficulties,
	30–24	* man ''clouting his o· cloak''
	34–19	not her o· but another's good,
	34–30	thine o· understanding. — *Prov.* 3 : 5.
'02.	2– 6	on the tablet of one's o· heart,
	13– 1	from my o· private earnings
Hea.	5– 1	our o· erring finite sense of God,
	5–21	work out our o· salvation,
	5–22	responsibility of our o· thought
	9–17	His o· image and likeness.
	11– 7	rebels at its o· boundaries ;
Peo.	4– 1	by working out our o· salvation.
	7– 2	working out our o· ideals,
	7–14	* With heaven's o· light the sculptor
	7–22	* Its heavenly beauty shall be our o·,
	8–10	these qualities . . . in our o· lives
	9–13	work out our o· salvation,

own

Peo.	10–21	We possess our o· body,
	11–21	calls its o· enactments ''laws
	14–18	reinstate man in God's o· image
Po.	13– 3	where Thine o· children are,
	14–16	Thou know'st Thine o· ;
	26–10	on her altar our loved Lincoln's o·
	41– 1	* my o· stricken deer.
	50–24	Our spirits' o· !''
My.	vii– 6	* can so protect their o· thoughts
	8– 5	* our o· growth and progress.
	10–30	* their o· individual welfare
	12–13	* promptness of his o· contribution.
	12–20	We o· no past, no future,
	15–14	transform you into His o· image
	18–16	finds one's o· in another's good.''
	19–23	''seeketh not her o·'' — *I Cor.* 13 : 5.
	21– 6	* building church homes of their o·,
	26–18	include enough of their o·.
	33–24	sweareth to his o· hurt, — *Psal.* 15 : 4.
	39–28	* our o· growth in love and unity
	40–31	* her o· blameless and happy life,
	41–30	* for our sakes as well as for her o· ;
	48–19	* Bible and her o· writings,
	52–31	* his o· peculiar knowledge of the
	55– 4	* needed a place of its o·,
	59–22	* my o· feeble attempts
	83– 7	* for their o· self-identification,
	84– 5	* testify from his o· experience
	103–23	on which to found my o·,
	106–23	because he minds his o· business
	108–29	will close with his o· words :
	112–31	our o· and in foreign lands,
	117–10	one's o· dream of personal sense,
	122– 6	fixed in one's o· moral make-up.
	124–31	they consume in their o· fires
	128–16	his o· rational conscience
	130– 2	Watch and guard your o· thoughts
	132–15	''Of His o· will — *Jas.* 1 : 18.
	134–28	* Mrs. Eddy's o· handwriting,
	136–14	Trustees who o· my property :
	137– 8	* in Mrs. Eddy's o· handwriting
	150–19	become His o· image and likeness.
	161–15	within his o· consciousness,
	174–23	until I had a church of my o·,
	212–26	loses his o· power to heal.
	212–27	compensate himself for his o· loss
	213–17	impulses of our o· thought,
	213–22	strengthen your o· citadel
	214–25	even to meet my o· current expenses.
	216–23	work in your o· several localities,
	216–29	will want money for your o· uses.
	217– 2	for your o· school education,
	227– 4	in his o· personal sense of
	227– 6	minifying of his o· goodness by
	227–15	influenced by their o· judgment
	243–17	remain in their o· fields of labor
	243–18	caring for their o· flocks.
	244–16	God's o· image and likeness,
	249– 2	or your o· moral sense,
	249– 4	through your o· perfectness.
	249–11	let loose for one's o· destruction.
	253–16	through Thine o· name — *John* 17 : 11.
	257–19	We o· his grace,
	262– 1	perfect and eternal in His o· image.
	272–22	* reproduced in her o· handwriting.
	272–23	* Mrs. Eddy's o· devoted followers,
	273– 4	* to vindicate in her o· person
	275–12	chapter sub-title
	276– 4	begs to say, in her o· behalf,
	276–11	is minding her o· business,
	278–28	pierced by its o· sword.
	280–22	with His o· truth and love.
	283–15	Sin is its o· enemy.
	283–23	God's o· plan of salvation.
	291–30	work for their o· country,
	300– 4	your o· salvation — *Phil.* 2 : 12.
	300–31	fire on their o· religious ranks,
	306–19	and that in God's o· time.
	306–29	purporting to be Dr. Quimby's o·
	311–22	her o· family coat-of-arms.
	315–30	in our o· and in other countries,
	321–28	* my o· personal knowledge
	330– 8	* contradicting his o· statement,
	333– 5	* found by one of your o· citizens,
	334–16	* quote her o· words.
	343– 2	* in Mrs. Eddy's o· spirit.
	343– 4	* in her o· way,
	349–32	reckons creation as its o·
	359– 4	individuals in their o· church
	364–10	excludes from his o· consciousness,

owned

Mis.	140–17	to know who o· God's temple,
Man.	76–22	real estate o· by this Church
Ret.	4– 8	o· by Uncle James Baker's grandson,
Pul.	68–23	* o· by Christian Scientists.

owned
My. 310–11 and together they *o·* a large
314–12 *o·* a house in Franklin, N. H.
ownership
My. 65–21 * has passed to the *o·* of the
66– 3 * the *o·* of the entire block.
66–10 * the *o·* of the entire block.
356– 1 their present *o·* of all good,
owning
Pul. 58– 7 * *o·* a beautiful estate
owns
Mis. 299–22 manufactured them and *o·* them,

owns
Mis. 331–19 that *o·* each waiting hour ;
389– 7 that *o·* each waiting hour,
Man. 75–16 *o·* the church edifices,
Po. 4– 3 that *o·* each waiting hour,
Oxford
Hea. 18–27 The *O·* students proved this :
Oxford University
Pul. 5–25 *O· U·* and the Victoria Institute,
oxidized
Pul. 25–25 * *o·* silver lamps of Roman design,
26–11 * six richly wrought *o·* silver lamps,

P

Pa. (*see also* **Keystone State**)
(*see* **Harrisburg, Lebanon, Mickleys, Philadelphia, Pittsburg, York**)
pace
Mis. 107–18 cannot keep *p·* with eternity.
Ret. 44–12 spiritual growth kept *p·* with
My. 8– 5 * We need to keep *p·* with our
14–30 * keep *p·* with the disbursements.
Pacific
Mis. 251– 5 from the *P·* to the Atlantic
Pul. 41– 9 * from the far-off *P·* coast
88– 4 from the Atlantic to the *P·*
My. 85–10 * from the Atlantic to the *P·*
pacification
My. 220–15 *p·* of all national difficulties,
pacified
Pul. 14–24 The waters will be *p·*,
pacify
No. 9–14 Hoping to *p·* repeated complaints
packages
My. 259–15 they require less attention than *p·*
packed
Mis. 168–28 * Hawthorne Hall was densely *p·*,
paddling
Mis. 329–19 *p·* the watercresses,
pæan
My. 167–23 send forth a *p·* of praise
355–18 chapter sub-title
pagan
Mis. 111–23 Plato was a *p·* ;
123–10 *p·* priests bloated with crime ;
194–10 *p·* Jew's or Moslem's misconception
169– 4 philosophies or *p·* literatures,
173– 8 *p·* philosophy, or scholastic
187–31 transcribed by *p·* religionists,
260– 6 *P·* mysticism, Grecian philosophy,
345–22 *p·* slanderers affirmed that Christians
Ret. 57–12 If that *p·* philosopher had known
Pul. 65–22 * the spot where, in *p·* times,
'00. 13–26 * amalgamation of different *p·* religions
'02. 5– 3 *p·* philosophies and tribal religions
Peo. 4–23 The *p·* priests appointed Apollo
My. 288–14 *p·* mysticisms, tribal religion,
paganism
Pan. 7–12 and hint the gods of *p·* ?
8–25 pantheism, polytheism, and *p·*
9– 5 in *p·* they stand for gods ;
pagans
My. 104– 3 Jewish *p·* thought that the
page
Mis. 58–14 I read the inspired *p·* through a
280–22 hand-painted flowers on each *p·*,
294– 8 transcribes on the *p·* of reality
313– 9 light of penetration on the *p·* ;
314–27 unnecessary to repeat the title or *p·*.
318–12 the paragraph on *p·* 47
Man. 87–22 Retrospection . . . *p·* 84.
112– 4 as shown on *p·* 118.
112–11 according to the form on *p·* 114.
Chr. 53–52 And writes the *p·*.
Pul. 39– 9 on the following *p·* a little poem
'00. 10–25 since publishing this *p·* I have
Po. 28– 4 Help us to write a deathless *p·*
My. 146– 2 dedicatory letter . . . *p·* 177
254–20 * *Journal* of 1904, *p·* 184 :
(*see also* **Science and Health**)
pageant
My. 147– 3 the past comes forth like a *p·*
pageantries
My. 29–13 Many more gorgeous church *p·*
pageantry
My. 189–22 twilight of the world's *p·*,

pages
Mis. xi– 5 These *p·*, although a reproduction
156– 2 contribute oftener to the *p·*
169– 1 Within Bible *p·* she had found all
169– 6 God-driven back to the inspired *p·*.
Man. 111–16 on *p·* 114 and 118.
Ret. 2– 5 in the *p·* of Sir Walter Scott
Pul. 6–15 * I had not read three *p·* before I
88– 7 too voluminous for these *p·*.
My. 13– 8 When scanning its interesting *p·*,
47– 8 * from the *p·* of its history.
256–14 pure *p·* of impersonal presents,
(*see also* **Science and Health**)
paid
Mis. 165–24 they never *p·* the price of sin.
239–24 familiarity with what the stock *p·*,
253– 5 the price that he *p·* for it?
347–32 is well *p·* by the umpire.
350– 1 $1,480.50 *p·* in,
Man. 68–10 shall be *p·* semi-annually
76– 2 spared after the debts are *p·*,
79–11 be *p·* from the Church funds.
80– 5 shall be *p·* over semi-annually
91–17 shall be *p·* over annually to the
96– 7 cost of hall shall be *p·* by
97–13 an annual salary, *p·* quarterly,
Ret. 38– 3 *p·* him seven hundred dollars,
49–29 debts of the corporation have been *p·*,
Pul. 20– 4 therefore I *p·* it,
30–30 * and entirely *p·* for when its
41– 2 * with every stone *p·* for
57– 4 * It is entirely *p·* for,
58–11 * every bill being *p·*.
63–23 * was *p·* for before it was begun,
70–16 * *p·* for by Christian Scientists
79– 6 * for which the money was all *p·* in
No. 35–14 the awful price *p·* by sin,
'02. 13–15 about one half the price *p·*,
13–25 no one offering the price I had *p·*
14– 2 five thousand dollars had been *p·*
15–11 *p·* me not one dollar of royalty
My. 10–11 * Some money has been *p·* in
11–25 * this land has been *p·* for.
14–15 * entire amount . . . had been *p·* in ;
70– 8 * and they are all *p·* for.
72–26 * every cent of it was *p·* in
75–24 * chapter sub-title
87–16 * their costly church fully *p·* for,
89–16 * Everything, . . . is *p·* for,
91– 8 * church edifices to be fully *p·* for
136–17 *p·* the highest fee ever received by
137–15 and have *p·* for the same.
161– 2 Christ Jesus *p·* our debt
232– 7 whereby all our debts are *p·*,
309–20 *p·* the largest tax in the colony.
312–11 * *p·* Mrs. Glover's fare to New York
325– 9 * what you then *p·* for it.
331–29 * kind attention *p·* to the
paid-up
My. 90–23 * *p·* cost of two million dollars
pain
all
Po. 41–18 call them to banish all *p·*,
and disease
Mis. 68– 9 * *maintained that p· and disease*
68–14 penalty . . . the very *p·* and disease.
Rud. 11–14 unreality of *p·* and disease ;
and pleasure
Mis. 74–25 recognize or express *p·* and pleasure.
and sickness
Mis. 68–12 *p·* and sickness are . . . illusions.
and sin
Po. 22–18 dark domain of *p·* and sin
and sorrow
Un. 18–11 *p·* and sorrow were not in My mind,

pain

bedside of
Mis. 201–30 Go to the bedside of *p·*,
beds of
Pul. 54– 3 * Is by our beds of *p·* ;
belief in
Mis. 44–27 When your belief in *p·* ceases,
belief of
Mis. 44–18 a belief of *p·* in matter ;
brings
Mis. 102–22 Human pity often brings *p·*.
caused the
Mis. 44–15 *caused the p· to cease?*
ceases
Mis. 44–14 *and then the p· ceases,*
compels
Mis. 85–27 *p·* compels human consciousness to
ease or
My. 253– 8 * art not here for ease or *p·*,
ever of
Po. 47–11 Outside this ever of *p·*?
foretells the
Un. 57– 7 foresees . . . and foretells the *p·*.
freedom from
Mis. 298–28 no more gains freedom from *p·* than
in the bone
Mis. 44–17 What you thought was *p·* in the bone
moaning in
Mis. 225–22 the lad . . . moaning in *p·*.
no
'02. 20– 7 "No drunkards . . no sorrow, no *p·* ;
My. 80– 6 * felt no *p·* when having
351–17 where are no partings, no *p·*.
no more
Mis. 44–26 There is no more *p·*.
no necessity for
Mis. 241–20 there is no necessity for *p·* ;
or death
My. 90–12 * insures fidelity in *p·* or death
or disease
Rud. 10–14 cannot . . . report *p·* or disease.
or power
No. 32– 8 its pleasure, *p·*, or power
pestilence or
Mis. 389–22 no fowler, pestilence or *p·* ;
Po. 5– 1 no fowler, pestilence or *p·* ;
pillow of
Mis. 257–31 Smoothing the pillow of *p·*
pleasure and
Mis. 85–23 suggests pleasure and *p·* in matter ;
198– 7 varied forms of pleasure and *p·*.
333– 2 pleasure and *p·*, good and evil,
Un. 3– 3 matter's reality, pleasure, and *p·*,
pleasure nor
Mis. 28–26 neither pleasure nor *p·* therein.
pleasure or
Mis. 100– 6 intoxicated with pleasure or *p·*,
relief from
Mis. 262–16 giving to the sick relief from *p·* ;
298–26 "I find relief from *p·* in
removes the
Un. 2–10 and, lastly, it removes the *p·*
self-inflicted
Pul. 56–22 * And mourn our self-inflicted *p·*."
to control
Mis. 45– 4 enables you to control *p·*.
without
Mis. 30–11 without *p·*, sin, or death.
would cease
Mis. 44–24 extracted, the *p·* would cease:

Mis. 44–22 That matter can report *p·*,
44–27 belief . . . ceases, the *p·* stops ;
200–22 the touch of weakness, *p·*,
351–23 five senses give to mortals *p·*,
396–21 whose measures bind The power of *p·*,
Un. 57– 5 by the *p·* they feel and occasion ;
58– 1 sin, *p·*, death,— a false sense of
Pul. 1–10 Time past . . . may *p·* us,
18– 5 whose measures bind The power of *p·*.
Po. 12– 5 whose measures bind The power of *p·*,
31–22 sting of death — sin, *p·*.
My. 221–25 of pleasure, or of *p·*
273–19 personal sense of pleasure, *p·*,

painful

Mis. 17–24 more or less prolonged and *p·*,
Ret. 38–11 to fulfil this *p·* task,

painless

Po. 70–21 A *p·* heraldry of Soul,
My. 181–10 mortal's *p·* departure from matter

pain-racked

My. 40–18 * *p·* and sorrow-worn humanity.

pains

pleasures and
(*see* **pleasures**)

pains

Mis. 17–30 accumulating *p·* of sense,
85–26 The pleasures — more than the *p·*
173–24 *p·*, fetters, and befools him.
185– 7 disabilities, *p·* or pleasures.
200–28 so-called *p·* and pleasures of matter
209–13 admits the so-called *p·* of matter
341–30 pleasures or *p·* of material sense
395– 6 The stars reject his *p·*,
Hea. 17– 3 *p·* of the personal senses
Po. 57–13 The stars reject his *p·*,

paint

Mis. 329–23 *p·* in pink the petals of arbutus,
377– 2 brush or pen to *p·* frail fairness
Po. 34–14 Divinely desolate the shrine to *p·*
53– 2 And *p·* the gray, stark trees,

painted

Mis. 240– 5 ruby cheeks *p·* and fattened by
Pul. 8–25 *p·* the finest flowers in the

painter's

Mis. 372–27 the *p·* masterpieces ;

painting

Mis. 62– 6 an artist in *p·* a landscape.
270– 6 in sculpture, music, or *p·*.
392–19 on receiving a *p·* of the Isle
Rud. 3–13 models . . . in music and *p·*
Po. 51– 1 On receiving a *p·* of the Isle.

paintings

Pul. 65–20 * arrangement of statuary and *p·*

paints

Mis. 393– 6 *P·* the limner's work, I ween,
Po. 51–11 *P·* the limner's work, I ween,

palace

Pul. 82– 1 * but the *p·* of the soul,
My. 257–29 their record in the monarch's *p·*,

palaces

My. 112–29 *p·* of emperors and kings,

palatial

Mis. 324– 4 at the threshold of a *p·* dwelling,
Pul. 70–26 * She has a *p·* home in Boston

pale

Mis. 112–20 sank back in his chair, limp and *p·* ;
Chr. 53–37 Thus olden faith's *p·* star
53–44 Crowns the *p·* brow.
Ret. 16–12 *p·* cripples went into the church
Pul. 26–25 * The room is toned in *p·* green
76– 7 * *p·* green and gold decoration
My. 200–21 *P·*, sinful sense, at work to

pales

My. 77– 7 * *p·* into insignificance,

Palestina's

Chr. 53–49 As in blest *P·* hour,

Palestine

Pul. 53–23 * from the hilltops of *P·*,

pall

Mis. 376–22 Little by little this topmost *p·*,

palm

Mis. 390– 5 Old Time gives thee her *p·*.
Ret. 17–17 *p·*, bay, and laurel, in classical glee,
Po. 10– 7 Thy *p·*, in ancient day,
55– 6 Old Time gives thee her *p·*.
63– 1 *p·*, bay, and laurel, in classical glee,
My. 337– 8 Thy *p·*, in ancient day,

Palmer House

Mis. 275–27 The *P· II·*, where we stopped,
276– 3 spacious rooms of the *P· H·*,

Palmetto

Mis. 251– 5 from the *P·* to the Pine Tree
My. 176– 9 hallow your *P·* home

palms

Mis. 231–24 soft little *p·* patting together,
332–15 stately *p·*, many-hued blossoms,
Pul. 27–17 * windows bearing *p·* of victory,
42–22 * a star of lilies resting on *p·*,
42–26 * *p·* and ferns and Easter lilies.
42–29 * resting on a mat of *p·*,
My. 176– 9 *p·* of victory and songs of glory.

palpable

Mis. 294– 9 the living, *p·* presence
333– 7 renders error a *p·* falsity,

palpably

Mis. 200– 8 *p·* an error of premise
Pul. 5–29 *p·* working in the sermons,
My. 8– 4 * denomination is *p·* outgrowing

palpitating

Mis. 376–13 * a *p·*, living Saviour

palsied

Un. 11–13 The *p·* hand moved,
No. 44–17 it *p·* the weak hand

palsy
  Mis. 238–26 or that I died of *p·*,
paltering
  My. 340–19 *p·*, timid, or dastardly policy,
pampered
  My. 302–21 but I am less lauded, *p·*,
pamphlet
  Mis. 380–30 use of an infringing *p·*
    381–25 disposing of, the enjoined *p·*,
  No. v– 1 each edition of this *p·*
  My. 319– 7 *p·*, signed "Phare Pleigh."
    323– 3 * Mr. Wiggin gave me a *p·*
pamphlets
  Mis. 285– 3 edition of one thousand *p·*
    285– 7 some of these *p·* were mistaken for
    301– 7 authors and editors of *p·*
Pan
  Pan. 2–26 *P·* in imagery is preferable to
    3– 2 *P·*, as a deity, is supposed to
    3–23 *P·* stood for "universal nature
    3–26 *P·* was the god of shepherds
pan
  Pan. 2–23 *P·* is a Greek prefix,
panacea
  Mis. 355–18 is a sovereign *p·*.
pane
  Mis. 324–17 clearer *p·* of his own heart
panel
  Pul. 28– 2 * The central *p·* represents
    28– 5 * *p·* containing the C. S. seal,
panelled
  Pul. 26– 5 * The galleries are richly *p·*
  My. 69– 8 * curved and *p·* surface,
panels
  Pul. 28– 1 * composed of three separate *p·*,
    28– 6 * other *p·* are decorated with
pang
  Po. 15–18 Flowers fresh as the *p·* in the bosom
pangs
  Un. 56–23 *p·* of hell must lay hold of him
  No. 34–15 *p·* which come to one upon whom
  Peo. 1–17 Even the *p·* of death disappear,
panoplied
  Mis. 162–31 *P·* in the strength of
panoply
  Mis. 374– 3 clad in *p·* of power,
  Pul. 15–19 Clad in the *p·* of Love,
panteth
  Hea. 10–20 hart *p·* for the water brooks,
    10–27 so *p·* my heart for the true fount
pantheism
  Mis. 23– 4 Is *p·* true?
    26–20 belief of mind in matter is *p·*.
    56– 1 theories of agnosticism and *p·*,
    76–11 is not theism, but *p·*.
    257– 3 *P·* presupposes that God
  Ret. 23–21 *p·*, and theosophy were void.
  Un. 45–14 conscious matter implies *p·*.
    45–14 This *p·* I unveil.
    51–10 In *p·* the world is bereft of
  Rud. 5–18 Mind in matter is *p·*
    13– 3 *p·* and theosophy are not
  No. 15–20 C. S. refutes *p·*,
    29– 6 This is *p·*, and is not the
  Pan. 1– 4 Subject : *Not P·*, *but C. S.*
    2– 1 chapter sub-title
    2– 3 that C. S. is *p·* is anomalous
    2– 7 looms above the mists of *p·*
    2– 9 chapter sub-title
    2–10 the word "*p·*" is derived from
    2–12 word "*p·*" is most suggestive.
    2–14 gives the meaning of *p·*
    2–19 *p·* is the doctrine of
    2–24 might stand, in the term *p·*,
    2–26 preferable to *p·* in theology.
    3– 1 *p·* suits not at all the
    4– 1 agrees with certain forms of *p·*
    5– 1 is found in scholastic theology.
    8–16 idolatry, *p·*, and polytheism.
    8–24 *p·*, polytheism, and paganism
    9– 1 reiterate the belief of *p·*,
    13– 2 And Science is not *p·*,
pantheist
  Mis. 133– 6 In refutation . . . that I am a *p·*,
    248–17 a mesmerist, a medium, a "*p·*;"
    249–12 I am not a spiritualist, a *p·*,
pantheistic
  Mis. 133– 3 * "the *p·* and prayerless Mrs. Eddy,
    189–16 *p·* doctrine that presents a

pantheistic
  Ret. 69– 8 *p·* error, or so-called *serpent*,
  Un. 50– 7 the temptation of *p·* belief
  No. 15–19 chapter sub-title
    29–13 Is this *p·* statement sound theology,
pantheon
  No. 21–20 in the *p·* of many gods,
papa
  Mis. 231–20 *p·* knew that he could walk,
paper
  Mis. 7–22 through our *p·*, . . . we shall be able
    294–26 I have read the daily *p·*,
  Man. 90–21 prepare a *p·* on said subject
    90–23 this *p·* shall be given to the teacher,
    91– 3 but shall destroy this *p·*.
  Pul. 36–28 * for some of the data of this *p·*.
    79–13 * a daily *p·* in town or village
  My. 60–16 * a reward for the best *p·*
    157–20 * inquiry from the editor of that *p·*,
    173– 5 Allow me through your *p·*
    284–12 In the issue of your good *p·*,
    329–16 * as they appear in that *p·*
    330– 1 * was published in your *p·*
    331–18 * Through the columns of your *p·*,
    332–17 * The *p·* containing this card
papers
  Man. 98–15 *p·* containing such an article,
  Pul. 27– 5 * safe preservation of *p·*.
    71–15 * announcements in New York *p·*
  My. 332–29 * roll of *p·* recording the death
Papias
  My. 178–30 *Logia* of *P·*, written in A.D. 145,
    179– 1 ancient *Logia*, . . . by *P·*,
par at
  Mis. 269–28 to buy error at *p·* value.
  My. 265– 8 and is bought at *p·* value ;
parable
  Mis. 27–16 maintain this fact by *p·*
    251–26 learn a *p·* of the period,
    341–21 *p·* of "the ten virgins" — *see* Matt. 25 : 1
    341–22 This *p·* is drawn from the
    341–27 moral of the *p·* is pointed,
    341–29 We learn from this *p·* that
  Ret. 91– 3 *p·* of "the prodigal son"
  '01. 19–11 illustrated his saying by a *p·*.
  Hea. 8–24 the *p·* of the husbandman,
  My. 109–25 not alone by miracle and *p·*,
    347–18 *P·* of the priceless pearl
parables
  Ret. 91– 4 rightly called "the pearl of *p·*,"
  '01. 25–13 No Christly axioms, practises, or *p·*
paradisaical
  Mis. 70–12 *P·* rest from physical agony
paradise
  Mis. 70–11 *shalt thou be with me in p·*" — *Luke* 23 : 43.
    70–14 *p·* of Spirit would come
    185–20 opens the gates of *p·*
  Pul. 80– 9 * emphatically the women's *p·*,
  My. 118–27 finds its *p·* in Spirit,
paragons
  Mis. 316–27 there would be on earth *p·*
paragraph
  Mis. 88–15 following *p·*, glows in the shadow
    318–12 an amendment of the *p·*
  Pul. 60–10 * Each *p·* he supplemented
  My. 236–25 universally to read the *p·*
    305– 7 S. and H., page 68, third *p·*,
paragraphs
  Mis. 309–25 page 229, third and fourth *p·*,
  Pul. 59–15 * Antiphonal *p·* were read
  My. 110–31 quoting sentences or *p·*
parallel
36th
  Man. 99– 5 being the 36th *p·* of latitude.

  Mis. 66–12 supported in the Scripture by *p·* proof.
  Pul. 59–14 * *p·* interpretation by Mrs. Eddy.
  My. 98– 9 * such as religious annals hardly *p·*
paralleled
  Mis. 258–22 no personality that could be *p·*
  Pul. 23–10 * during the last decade
  Po. 2–11 Great as thou art, and *p·* by none,
parallels
  Pul. 60–11 * illustrative Scripture *p·*,
paralyze
  Ret. 81– 2 threaten to *p·* its beneficence.
  My. 213– 4 malicious aim of . . . is to *p·* good

paralyzed

Mis. 222–10 he becomes morally *p·*
Pul. 10– 3 *p·* by inactive faith,
My. 48–29 * *p·* by sentimental fiction.

paramount

Mis. 160– 7 as part and *p·* portion of her being.
200–26 no obstacle or circumstances *p·* to
Ret. 31– 7 *p·* to rubric and dogma
My. 282–23 It is of *p·* importance

parapets

Mis. 383–11 beat in vain against the immortal *p·*

paraphrase

Mis. 364– 4 naturally evokes new *p·*
My. 313– 1 a *p·* of a silly song

paraphrased

Un. 44– 7 popular couplet may be so *p·*

paraphrases

'00. 12– 2 *p·* projected from divinity

paraphrasing

Pul. 5–18 Then eloquently *p·* it.

parcel

Mis. 336–24 Part and *p·* of Truth and Love,
362–13 was evil part and *p·* of His creation?
No. 17–16 is neither part nor *p·* of divine
My. 12– 7 * to secure the large *p·* of land
65–19 * The last *p·* in the block
66– 1 * The purchase of this *p·*,
66– 9 * purchase of the last *p·*

pardon

Mis. xi–22 *p·* for the preliminary battles
123–22 whereby the just obtain a *p·* for
261– 7 cancelled by repentance or *p·*.
Pul. 87–21 *p·* my refusal of that as a material
No. 31–11 To me *divine p·* is that
31–14 as the only full proof of its *p·*.
32– 4 A magistrate's *p·* may encourage
42– 9 God's *p·* is the destruction of
Hea. 6– 4 *p·* me if I smiled.
8–21 through Principle instead of a *p·* ;
Peo. 3–26 dependence on personal *p·*
Po. 32–19 *p·* and grace, through His Son,
My. 152–26 nor *p·* a single sin ;
195– 3 You will *p·* my delay
299–18 those who claim to *p·* sin,

pardonable

Man. 46–20 shall not, under *p·* circumstances,
My. 64– 8 * If to-day we feel a *p·* pride

pardoned

Mis. 93–26 believing that sin is *p·* without
No. 29–19 A mortal *p·* by God is not sick,
Hea. 2– 8 afterwards *p·* and adopted,

pardons

Peo. 9–14 who never *p·* the sin that
My. 133– 2 many *p·* for the penitent.

Parent

Mis. 18–18 as children of one common *P·*,
155–26 to Him as our common *P·*,
Un. 35–16 immortal Mind, the *P·* of *all*.
48–15 *P·* no more enters into His creation
'01. 7–12 then does not our heavenly *P·*
7–16 does not this heavenly *P·* know

parent

Mis. 254–10 what of the hope of that *p·*
Ret. 22–20 are all the children of one *p·*,
68– 7 is not a *p·*, though he reflects
69– 5 "The *p·* of all human discord
Pul. 55–26 * regarded as the *p·* organization,
My. 10–26 * must be a prosperous *p·* church,
125– 8 vine towards the *p·* trunk.

parental

Ret. 5–30 * lively sense of the *p·* obligation,

parents (see also parents')

Mis. 72– 8 good and bad traits of the *p·*
167–16 his *p·*, brothers, and sisters.
184– 9 has the formation of his *p·* ;
225–29 The *p·* said :— "Wait until we
236–10 child complaining of his *p·*
236–11 "Love and honor thy *p·*,
240– 6 *P·* and doctors must not take
Ret. 5– 9 my *p·* removed to Tilton,
6–10 *p·*, brothers, and sisters,
13– 2 my *p·* having been members
20– 3 remained with my *p·* until after
Un. 17–21 God told our first *p·*
Pul. 8–16 children vied with their *p·* to
'01. 29–14 *p·* who nurtured them,
29–19 if they attempt to help their *p·*,
31–21 Devout orthodox *p·* ;
My. 174–21 where my *p·* first offered
217– 3 your *p·*, brothers, or sisters.

parents

My. 256–23 *P·* call home their loved ones,
261– 2 loving *p·* and guardians of youth
336–14 remained with my *p·* until

parents'

Mis. 72– 3 because of his *p·* mistakes or sins,
Ret. 5– 7 youngest of my *p·* six children
'01. 29–16 forget their *p·* increasing years

par excellence

Mis. 313– 3 your editorial . . . is *p· e·*.

Paris

France

Mis. 304–15 * takes place at *P·*, France.

Mis. 375–15 * I spent two years in *P·*,
'00. 1–22 London, Edinburgh, Dublin, *P·*,

parishes

Pul. 38– 2 * preached in other *p·* for five years

Park Cemetery

Ret. 5–12 stone memorials in the *P· C·*

Parker

Mr.

Pul. 33–23 * and Mr. *P·* always believed,

Theodore

Pul. 33–16 * Theodore *P·* related that when

Park Street, No. 3

My. 53–13 * Hawthorne Rooms, at No. 3 *P· S·*,

parlance

Mis. 219–15 In common *p·*, one person feels sick,
300– 7 in common *p·*, it is an *ignorant*

parlor

Pul. 68–17 * holds regular services in the *p·* of
My. 342– 2 * Seated in the large *p·*,
342–17 * smaller *p·* across the hall,

parlors

Mis. 324– 7 the gorgeously tapestried *p·*,
My. 53–10 * in the *p·* of Mrs. Eddy's home,

parody

Mis. 62–25 and ends in a *p·* on this Science
106– 5 *p·* on Tennyson's grand verse,
122–30 his existence is a *p·*,

parsimonious

My. 149–27 Clouds *p·* of rain,

part (noun)

and parcel

Mis. 336–24 *P·* and parcel of Truth and Love,
362–13 was evil *p·* and parcel of His creation?

another

Ret. 88–18 another *p·* of C. S. work,

any

My. 9–22 any *p·* of two millions of dollars
13–18 any *p·* of two millions of money
57–10 * any *p·* of two millions of dollars
65– 7 * any *p·* of two millions dollars
75–28 * with any *p·* of the expense

better

Mis. 273–12 as well as the better *p·* of mankind,

constituent

No. 4– 7 error, a constituent *p·* of what

demonstrate in

Peo. 13– 6 can demonstrate in *p·* this great

early

Mis. 373–20 early *p·* of the Christian era,

even in

Ret. 28– 7 to demonstrate, even in *p·*,
My. 5–21 understanding even in *p·*,

every

Pul. 61–16 * in every *p·* of this unique church,
66– 8 * in every *p·* of the country.
79–11 * adherents in every *p·* of
No. 14– 1 is sound in every *p·*.
My. 32– 9 * heard perfectly in every *p·*

good

Mis. 327– 9 "thou hast chosen the good *p·* ;

his

My. 315– 8 * being wholly on his *p·* ;

his own

Ret. 86–23 man who performs his own *p·*.

immortal

No. 29–14 the immortal *p·* of man a sinner?

interesting

My. 60–28 * to tell you of the interesting *p·*

in this resurrection

Un. 41–13 have *p·* in this resurrection

Jesus'

Chr. 53–30 that doom Was Jesus' *p·* ;

latter

Ret. 24– 9 and in the latter *p·* of 1866
Pul. 23–23 * as is the latter *p·* of

loses a

No. 38–26 loses a *p·* of its purest spirituality

part

most
Pul. 28–22 * its songs are for the most p·
    47–25 * for the most p· she lives very
my
No. 9–15 too great leniency, on my p·,
My. 170– 7 due to a desire on my p·
    244–14 to contribute my p· towards
no
Un. 4–21 evil is no p· of the divine
    52–23 if God has no p· in them
Pan. 10–30 constitute no p· of man,
My. 160–30 that the Christian has no p· in it.
nor parcel
No. 17–15 neither p· nor parcel of divine
nor portion
My. 357– 6 matter has neither p· nor portion,
northern
Ret. 20–10 northern p· of New Hampshire.
no studied
Mis. 147–26 for he acts no studied p· ;
of a grain
Hea. 13– 5 one hundredth p· of a grain of
of a system
'00. 13– 8 p· of a system supported by their
of being
No. 12–28 all instead of a p· of being,
of Christian worship
Mis. 345–29 a p· of Christian worship
of eternal Truth
Un. 17– 3 the lie seem p· of eternal Truth.
of every night
My. 61– 2 * p· of every night since that time.
of His consciousness
No. 17–25 would be a p· of His consciousness.
of the bell
Mis. 305–10 * that can be made a p· of the bell ;
of the city
My. 66–16 * being in a fine p· of the city.
of their duties
My. 358–16 It is p· of their duties
of the preamble
My. 254–18 * p· of the preamble to our By-laws,
of this transfer
'02. 13– 9 (which was a p· of this transfer)
of true followers
Mis. 278–31 on the p· of true followers,
of Truth
Un. 5–26 this wonderful p· of Truth
No. 21– 4 to the one-hundredth p· of Truth,
old
My. 325– 9 * old p· of Boston in which he lived
one
Mis. 148– 2 one p· of his character at variance
our
My. 234–26 not against us is on our p·." — Mark 9 : 40.
principal
Man. 31–17 principal p· of the Sunday services,
shall have
Mis. 180–18 shall have p· in his resurrection.
small
My. 45–11 * small p· of the entire body
smallest
Rud. 2–23 the smallest p· of C. S.
Soul hath
Mis. 300–32 In which the Soul hath p·,
Po. 56– 2 In which the Soul hath p·,
surgical
Mis. 349– 5 the surgical p· of midwifery.
take
My. 86–12 * take p· in the subsequent ceremonies
third
Mis. 254–19 take away a third p· of the stars
took
Pul. 75–19 * took p· in the ceremonies at Boston
understood in
Peo. 6–21 divine Principle, understood in p·,
your
My. 148– 3 called to do your p· wisely

Mis. 43–26 is owing, in p·, to the
  102–14 God is not p·, but the whole.
  125– 3 hath he p· in Love's atonement,
  132–17 consisting in p· of dictating
  160– 7 as p· and paramount portion of
  161–20 owing in p·, perhaps, to the Jewish
  305–15 * shall have a p· in it.
  381– 5 taken on the p· of Mrs. Eddy,
  381– 7 on the p· of the defendant
  395–10 When sweet rondeau Doth play a p·,
Man. 31–20 as a p· of the Wednesday evening
  110– 8 and become a p· thereof.
Ret. 88–18 a p· which concerns us intimately,
Pul. 84–27 * on the p· of our beloved teacher
  85– 5 * who now, in p·, understand
Hea. 3–22 we must understand in p· this divine

part

Hea. 3–23 or we cannot demonstrate it in p·.
  19– 3 not in p·, but as a whole ;
Po. 57–17 When sweet rondeau Doth play a p·,
My. 8– 3 * Mr. Kimball said in p· :
  9–10 * on the p· of every man
  10–19 * sacrifice on the p· of its people.
  10–22 * on the p· of some one else.
  51–13 * on the p· of the people,
  59–11 * accepted wholly or in p· by
  63–13 * has become a p· of our expanding
  93–24 * p· it has come to play in the
  97– 3 * faith on the p· of a sick person,
  110–21 unfold in p· the facts of day,
  219– 4 such an anticipation on the p· of
  272–26 * plays so great a p· in the world

part (verb)

Mis. 137–15 kind of you to p· so gently with
  232–14 as we p· with material systems
  286– 4 * "until death do us p· ;"
  291–19 would p· with a blessing myself to
  327–22 determined not to p· with their
  339–29 Change and the grave may p· us ;
  384–17 You therefore cannot p·.
  388–12 Speaks kindly when we meet and p·.
'00. 10–29 to p· with his soap,
'02. 2–25 remains friends, or . . . p· fair foes.
  2–29 shall meet again, never to p·.
Po. 3–13 Till bursting bonds our spirits p·
  7–12 Speaks kindly when we meet and p·.
  33–11 (And mem'ry but p· us awhile),
  36–16 You therefore cannot p·.
My. 131–21 where God is we can never p·.

partake

Mis. 170–18 strength, we also may all p· of.
  387–10 Pray that his spirit you p·,
Un. 17–22 p· of the fruit of evil,
Pan. 14– 8 p· of the bread that cometh down
'00. 15– 6 p· of what divine Love hath prepared
Po. 6–11 Pray that his spirit you p·,
My. 156–21 p· of the bread that cometh down
  267–19 to p· of the quality . . . of heaven.

partaker

Mis. 235– 6 man becomes the p· of that Mind

partakers

Mis. 291–16 If any are not p· thereof,
Un. 23–13 whereof all are p·, — Heb. 12 : 8.
My. 206–27 p· of the inheritance of — Col. 1 : 12.
  287–17 p· of that Mind whence springs the

partakes

Mis. 280– 3 p· not of the nature of God,
Ret. 47–18 p· less of God's love.

partaketh

Mis. 360–20 p· of its own altars,

parted

Ret. 15–19 we p· in Christian fellowship,
Pul. 65–22 * p· his mantle with his sword
My. 313–29 I was obliged to be p· from my son,

partial

Mis. 182–23 a personal Jehovah, p· and finite ;
  290–12 p·, unmerciful, or unjust,
Ret. 38– 8 in my last chapter a p· history of

partiality

Peo. 8– 3 p· that elects some to be saved

partially

Un. 5–23 Christians who wholly or p· differ
  9– 7 That time has p· come,
  39– 3 Eternal Life is p· understood ;

participants

Mis. 143– 4 explained to the kind p·
  335–19 either willing p· . . . or ignorant
My. 86–29 * accommodate the throng of p·.

participate

Pul. 64–27 * to p· in the ceremonies,
My. 77–10 * to p· in the most notable
  77–15 * will p· in the dedication.
  77–24 * present to p· in the occasion
  78– 2 * that all might p· in the dedication,
  96– 2 * to p· in the dedication

participating

Mis. 117–19 while p· in the movements,
My. 23–27 * p· in the work of its erection.

particular

Ret. 89–13 duty at that p· moment.
Pul. 50–15 * p· phase of religious belief
My. 10–18 * could prosper, in any p·,
  83–29 * But of this p· example
  210–21 saying nothing, in p·, of error
  346–23 * whether she had in mind any p·

particularly
Mis. 305–14   * *p·* desired that the largest number
     305–20   * will be *p·* appreciated
Pul. 42– 9   * was rendered *p·* interesting
     47–18   * dwelling *p·* upon the terms
     76– 6   * is described as "*p·* beautiful,

particulars
Mis. 51– 9   We have not the *p·* of the case

parties
Mis. 141–17   spirit of Christ actuating all the *p·*
     297–23   by mutual consent of both *p·*,
Pul. 41–15   * came *p·* of forty and fifty.
My. 281–23   * effect on the two *p·* to the treaty

parting
Mis. 149–19   *p·* so promptly with your beloved pastor,
     341–17   *p·* with a material sense of life
     386–10   gathered from her *p·* sigh :
     386–26   her loyal life, And *p·* prayer,
Ret. 19– 5   *p·* with the dear home circle
     19–20   With his *p·* breath he gave
'02. 5– 5   religion *p·* with its materiality.
Hea. 2–11   * the *p·* will be easy."
Po. 8–19   *p·* the ringlets to kiss my cheek.
     49–15   gathered from her *p·* sigh :
     50–12   her loyal life, And *p·* prayer,
     65– 8   And left but a *p·* in air.
     74– 6   blue eyes and jet, Soft as when *p·*
My. 170–30   In *p·* I repeat to these
     330–32   With his *p·* breath he gave

partings
Po. 15– 7   "No *p·* are there."
My. 290–23   where no *p·* are for love,
     351–16   where are no *p·*, no pain.

partition
Mis. 178–29   we are as a *p·* wall

partitions
Pul. 25– 5   * The *p·* are of iron ;
     58–15   * by the use of movable *p·*.

partizanship
My. 291–11   quenching the volcanoes of *p·*,

partly
Mis. 292–12   *p·* illustrate the divine energy

partner
Mis. 242–26   formerly *p·* of George T. Brown,
     361–27   *p·* in the firm of error,
My. 310–11   joint *p·* with Alexander Tilton,

partners
Pul. 84– 6   * equal *p·* in all that is worth

partnership
Mis. 364–25   this impossible *p·* is dissolved.
Peo. 4–14   error that . . . entered into *p·*
My. 260–11   hath no *p·* with human means

partnerships
Mis. 289–12   All *p·* are formed on agreements

partook
Mis. 78–12   *p·* of the nature of occultism,
     121– 4   our Master *p·* of the Jews' feast
     260– 8   His faith *p·* not of drugs,
My. 288–13   His piety *p·* not of the travesties of

parts
Mis. 31–21   He *p·* with his understanding of good,
     159–30   Scientists from all *p·* of our nation,
Ret. 48–21   sent to all *p·* of our country,
Un. 5–18   but *p·* of Thy ways," — see *Job* 26 : 14.
     6– 1   the whole is greater than its *p·*.
Pul. 44–25   * money has flowed in from all *p·* of
     60–15   * from all *p·* of the country.
     64– 8   * from all *p·* of the United States.
     68– 7   * from all *p·* of the world,
Rud. 12– 2   *p·* of the body supposed to be ailing.
No. 13–26   other *p·* of it have no lustre.
     21– 3   has ninety-nine *p·* of error to the
My. 47– 5   * from all *p·* of the world,
     88– 7   * It shows strength in all *p·*,
     95– 7   * in different *p·* of the world.
     96– 2   * Scientists from all *p·* of the world
     96–29   * from all *p·* of the United States.
     99–18   * coming from all *p·* of the world,
     100– 9   * nearly all, *p·* of the country,
     141–19   * Scientists from all *p·* of the world.
     147–28   to the utmost *p·* of the earth,
     206– 9   human beliefs are not *p·* of C. S. ;
     269–12   * *p·* of one stupendous whole,

party
Mis. 289–13   each *p·* voluntarily surrenders
     290– 1   is not a *p·* to the compact of
My. 300–32   attacking a peaceable *p·*

pass
Mis. 10–24   wherein old things *p·* away
     34–20   *p·* on to their state of existence,

pass
Mis. 99–21   earth shall *p·* away, — *Matt.* 24 : 35.
     99–22   my words shall not *p·* — *Matt.* 24 : 35.
     107–19   Mortals' false senses *p·* through
     111–17   earth shall *p·* away, — *Matt.* 24 : 35.
     111–18   my words shall not *p·* — *Matt.* 24 : 35.
     118–13   yearn to . . . *p·* a friend over it
     121– 1   his words can never *p·* away :
     157–23   shall bring it to *p·*. — *Psal.* 37 : 5.
     163–19   earth shall *p·* away, — *Matt.* 24 : 35.
     163–19   my words shall not *p·* — *Matt.* 24 : 35.
     190–12   it came to *p·*, — *Luke* 11 : 14.
     213–18   *p·* through a baptism of fire.
     230–15   improving moments before they *p·*
     269– 2   shall bring it to *p·*." — *Psal.* 37 : 5.
     304– 8   * bell will *p·* from place to place
     319–20   season *p·* without one gift to me.
     355–10   mortal mind must *p·* through
     363–12   *p·* through none of the changes of
     385–24   To *p·* away.
Ret. 24– 7   discovery came to *p·* in this way.
     69– 1   *p·* through material conditions
     80–23   older sheep *p·* into the fold
Un. 3– 5   *p·* through another probationary
     43–16   words which can never "*p·* — *Matt.* 5 : 18.
Pul. 1–14   *P·* on, returnless year !
     1–17   *P·* proudly to thy bier !
     39–24   * hurrying throng before me *p·*,
No. 8–26   let the unwise *p·* by,
     27–11   Until centuries *p·*,
Pan. 12–18   *p·* gently on without
'01. 20–28   *p·* sentence on the darkest and
Hea. 10– 1   saw it *p·* away, — an illusion.
Peo. 1– 8   footsteps of thought, as they *p·*
     11–19   directly as men *p·* legislative acts
Po. 26– 1   *P·* on, returnless year !
     26– 6   *P·* proudly to thy bier !
     33–10   To kindly *p·* over a wound,
     48–20   To *p·* away.
     67–14   *p·* From your sight as the
My. 23–29   * those who *p·* by are impelled to
     132– 9   *p·* through the waters of Meribah here
     151–17   * "*P·* ye the proud fane by,
     170–24   shall bring it to *p·*. — *Psal.* 37 : 5.
     225– 2   come to the surface to *p·* off,
     301– 7   dogma and creed will *p·* off

passage
Mis. 72–31   *p·* quoted affords no evidence of
     75–25   bring out the meaning of the *p·*.
     169–18   dual meaning to every Biblical *p·*,
     170–24   *p·* recording Jesus' proceedings
     182–15   This *p·* refers to man's primal,
     191–18   By no . . . interpretation can this *p·*
     248– 4   literal meaning of the *p·*
No. 22–22   *p·* must refer to the *evils* which
     29– 1   this *p·* refers to the Jewish law,
'00. 15– 9   *p·* over a tear-filled sea
'01. 10–21   Love spans the dark *p·* of sin,
'02. 7–23   *p·* which serves to confirm C. S.
My. 43–14   * *p·* of the Red Sea
     135– 5   this *p·* of Scripture
     142–19   in their *p·* from sense to Soul.
     170–18   This gift is a *p·* of Scripture ;
     182–27   May the birds of *p·* rest their

passages
Mis. 73– 6   materially, these *p·* conflict ;
     169–28   * Taking several Bible *p·*,
     169–31   was one of the *p·* explained
     300–26   *p·* giving the spiritual meaning
Pul. 45–29   * *p·* read from the two books
     60–11   * and then by *p·* selected for him
     73–10   * She delved deep into the Biblical *p·*.
No. 32– 1   misinterpretation of such *p·*

passed
Mis. 6–10   are *p·* over to the Scientist.
     42– 8   individual has but *p·* through
     42–13   *p·* the ordeal called death,
     110–15   Weeks have *p·* into months,
     121–20   sentence *p·* upon innocence?
     132– 1   vote *p·*, at your last meeting,
     137–13   but that time has *p·*.
     152–26   till the storm has *p·*.
     153– 8   *p·* through the Red Sea, untouched
     165–17   *p·* on and left to mortals the rich
     284–14   hour has *p·* for this evil to be
     343– 4   have *p·* to their reward.
     356–12   remember that the seedtime is *p·*,
     386–19   "Years had *p·* o'er thy
Man. 36–10   *p·* an examination by the Board of
Ret. 7– 3   *p·* away at the age of thirty-one,
     38– 7   After months had *p·*,
     38–22   Not a word had *p·* between us,
     42–13   In 1882 he *p·* away,
     48–11   following resolutions were *p·* :
     48–14   presented and *p·* unanimously :

passed

Ret. 69– 7   and *p·* into matter.
Pul. 38–18   * *p·* the change of death
Rud. 14–27   *p·* through a regular course
No. 13– 9   centuries *p·* after those words were
    14– 5   not *p·* the transition called death,
'01. 26–14   I have *p·* through deep waters to
    28– !   *p·* through the first two stages,
'02. 2–13   *p·* from stern Protestantism to
Hea. 2–14   ere he *p·* from his execution to
    11– 5   when the dream has *p·*,
Peo. 7–11   * As an angel dream *p·* o'er him.
Po. 50– 3   "Years had *p·* o'er thy
My. 47–17   * back over the years that have *p·*
    47–23   * years that have *p·* since
    48– 4   * Not until nineteen centuries had *p·*
    51– 4   * following resolutions were *p·* :
    65–11   * This astonishing motion was *p·*
    65–21   * *p·* to the ownership of the
    78– 8   * *p·* through the twelve entrances
    99–20   * contribution baskets when *p·*
    148–13   unthought of till the day had *p·* !
    168– 1   uncultivated understanding has *p·*.
    206–14   *p·* through the shadow called death,
    230– 4   when those have *p·* to rest.
    257– 9   *p·* from a corporeal to the
    290–20   has *p·* earth's shadow
    294–29   *p·* through the shadow of death
    309–28   * Mary Baker *p·* her first fifteen years
    326–15   George W. Glover, *p·* on
    327–19   * amendment had been *p·*,
    328–11   * *p·* by the last Legislature,
    335–18   * at the end of nine days he *p·* away.
    340–29   The dark days of . . . have *p·*,
    342–26   * all now concerned . . . have *p·* on?"
    346–13   * and as she *p·* me

passes

Mis. 9– 6   *p·* all His flock under His rod
    42– 6   momentary belief of dying *p·*
    329–14   Spring *p·* over mountain
    363– 4   *p·* from molecule and monkey
Pul. 5– 6   *p·* from earth to heaven,
Peo. 7–19   * Our life dream *p·* o'er us.

passeth

Mis. 125–14   Love that *p·* all understanding ;
    133–30   peace that *p·* understanding,
No. 8– 8   *p·* all understanding,"— *Phil.* 4 : 7.

passing

Mis. 42– 5   *p·* through the belief called death.
    78–21   froth of error *p·* off ;
    224–22   so settled that no *p·* breath
Ret. 44–26   *p·* without a dissenting voice.
    68–26   thoughts, *p·* from God to man"
Un. 47– 1   with every *p·* hour
Pul. 6– 2   and impurities are *p·* off.
Pan. 12– 6   how can Spirit be constantly *p·*
'02. 17–19   square accounts with each *p·* hour.
Po. v–18   * *Some tourists who were p·*,
    vi–19   *p· of a resolution in Congress*
My. 46– 6   * it were but a *p·* dream.
    65–15   * *p·* out a nickel for carfare.

passion

Mis. 114–19   *p·*, appetites, hatred, revenge,
    137–25   *p·*, pride, envy, evil-speaking,
    222– 3   It inflames envy, *p·*, evil-speaking,
    295–10   * *p·* for some manner of notoriety."
    298–14   spiritual ignorance and power of *p·*,
    343–14   noxious weeds of *p·*, malice,
    374–11   fogs of sense and storms of *p·*,
Ret. 65–11   gratification of appetite and *p·*,
My. 339–28   appetites, *p·*, and all that wars

passionate

Un. 27– 9   signifying a *p·* love of self,
My. 90–10   * All the *p·* love for life
    309– 1   * dominating, *p·*, fearless,"

passionately

'00. 11– 5   *p·* fond of material music,

passionless

Po. 2– 1   Stern, *p·*, no soul those looks betray ;

passions

Mis. 36–13   Appetites, *p·*, anger, revenge,
    123–12   human *p·* and human gods,
    209–22   Evil *p·* die in their own flames,
    236– 1   human *p·* in their reaction
    237– 9   the worst of human *p·*
    240–22   *P·*, appetites, pride, selfishness,
    294– 3   by the maëlstrom of human *p·*,
    324–15   *p·* have so dimmed their sight
Pan. 10–29   Sin, sickness, appetites, and *p·*,
'01. 30–22   stress of the appetites and *p·*.
Hea. 18–22   Pride, appetites, *p·*, envy, and malice
My. 93–13   * gratifying the *p·* or

Passover

Mis. 90–26   *P·*, or last supper,
    121– 5   partook of the Jews' feast of the *P·*,
Pan. 1– 6   gathered at the feast of our *P·*,
'00. 15– 5   and this feast is a *P·*.
    15– 8   *P·*, spiritually discerned, is a
    15–11   after this *P·* cometh victory,

passover

My. 156–12   to prepare for the material *p·*,
    156–12   *p·* from sense to Soul,
    156–15   eat the *p·* — *Luke* 22 : 11.

passport

Mis. 270–23   the only *p·* to his power ;

past (noun)

Mis. 100– 8   *P·*, present, future, will show the
    253–15   it repeats the *p·* and portends much
    285–29   having no Truth, it will have no *p·*,
    311– 9   so, bury the dead *p·* ;
    339–15   The *p·* admonishes us :
    339–30   wisdom that might have blessed the *p·*
    375–31   * a thing of the *p·*, impossible of
Un. 46–27   furnished the battle-ground of the *p·*,
Pul. 7– 7   Yet when I recall the *p·*,
    7–20   prophets in the present as in the *p·*
    55–11   * and oppressions of the *p·*.
    69–25   * than the Church has had in the *p·*.
    81–10   * woman of the *p·* with an added grace
'02. 2–20   dogmatism, relegated to the *p·*,
    4–23   all periods -- *p·*, present, and future.
Hea. 2–25   *P·*, present, future magnifies his
Po. 27–11   Or we the *p·* forget,
    68–17   Of the *p·* 'tis the talisman,
My. 12–20   We own no *p·*, no future,
    13– 2   on the *p·*, present, nor future,
    147– 3   *p·* comes forth like a pageant
    153–22   in the *p·* as in the present,
    158–14   it profits by the *p·*
    170– 7   illustrate the *p·* by your present
    191–18   come forth from the tomb of the *p·*,
    230– 3   will maintain its rank as in the *p·*,
    340–24   virtually belongs to the *p·*,

past (adj., adv., etc.)

Mis. 125–29   within the *p·* few years :
    130–24   avoid referring to *p·* mistakes.
    131–31   perils *p·* and victories won.
    147– 9   Have you improved *p·* hours,
    295– 7   * leads . . . *p·* a score of reforms,
    322–23   my *p·* poor labors and love,
    330–19   good to talk with our *p·* hours,
    385–10   happy friend ! thy bark is *p·*
Man. 83–10   such only as have good *p·* records
Un. 14– 8   power from *p·* experience
Pul. 1– 9   Time *p·* and time present,
    58– 6   * For several years *p·* she has
    72–16   * "And for the *p·* eleven years,"
'00. 7– 7   that during the *p·* three years
    7–29   till the long night is *p·*
'02. 4–27   and *p·* finding out.
Po. 48– 2   happy friend ! thy bark is *p·*
My. 29–28   * half *p·* five in the morning
    30–28   * service at half *p·* seven,
    30–32   * Before half *p·* seven the chimes
    31– 9   * Promptly at half *p·* six
    38–17   * the service at half *p·* twelve
    66– 5   * During the *p·* two weeks
    73–15   * have been for several days *p·*
    78–28   * of the half *p·* twelve service ;
    86–10   * into Boston in the *p·* few days
    87–22   * in Boston during the *p·* few days.
    220–24   *P·*, present, or future philosophy
    270–21   for the *p·* forty years I have
    321–29   during the *p·* twenty years.
    (*see also* **times, year**)

pastime

My. 119–26   pleasant *p·* of seeing your
    261– 9   aught to do with this *p·*.

pastimes

Mis. xi–16   *p·* become footsteps to joys
My. 263– 1   *p·* tend to obliterate the spiritual

Pastor and pastor (see also pastor's)

Mis. 90–21   shall the *p·* of the Church
    149–20   *p·*, Rev. Mr. Norcross,
    150– 2   May He soon give you a *p·* ;
    152– 3   *Beloved P· and Brethren :*
    313–27   to be hereafter the only *p·*
    322–11   dual and impersonal *p·*,
    383– 2   C. S. textbook, be the *p·*,
    383– 7   *p·* is the Bible and my book.
Man. 58– 3   THE CHRISTIAN SCIENCE *p·*.
    58– 6   *P·* over The Mother Church,
Ret. 14– 5   *p·* was an old-school expounder of
    15–15   by the *p·* of this church.
Pul. 7–26   *p·* of The First Church of Christ,

Pastor and pastor
Pul. 7–28 is satisfied with this *p*.
  9–16 loss of our late lamented *p*,
  28–27 * *p* to the church in this city,
  34– 8 * her *p* came to bid her goodby
  43–30 * letter from a former *p*
  58–25 * only *p* shall be the Bible, with
  68–18 * parlor of the residence of the *p*,
  69– 1 * Dr. Hammond, the *p*,
  74– 6 * *p* of the C. S. congregation
  86–29 * already ordained as our *p*.
'01. 11–12 chapter sub-title
  11–14 *p* for all the churches of the
  11–16 not make it impossible for this *p*
My. 174–14 *P* of the First Congregational Church,
  178– 1 *p* and ethical tenets,
  (see also **Eddy**)

pastorate
Pul. 45–23 * withdrew from the *p* of the church,
  87–12 kind call to the *p* of
My. 49–31 * call Mrs. Eddy to the *p*
  51–20 * the *p* for the ensuing year ;

Pastor Emeritus
My. 174–13 Rev. Franklin D. Ayer, D.D., *P E* ;
  (see also **Eddy**)

pastor's
Pul. 27– 7 * class-rooms and the *p* study.
  58–23 * Adjoining the chancel is a *p* study ;
  (see also **Eddy**)

pastors
Mis. 91– 5 not absolutely necessary to ordain *p*
  143–20 editors, and *p* of churches,
  314– 4 by Readers in lieu of *p*.
Pul. 68– 7 * many are now *p* or in practice.

pastorship
Pul. 68– 1 * Mrs. Eddy assumed the *p*

pasture
Mis. 151– 1 folds the sheep of His *p* ;

pastures
Mis. 227–24 mind can rest in green *p*,
  357– 7 yearn to find living *p*
Ret. 4–19 green *p* bright with berries,
Pul. 48–12 * beautiful meadows and *p*
My. 129–26 These are His green *p*
  162–26 into "green *p* — *Psal.* 23 : 2.
  252–20 They point to verdant *p*,

patching
Mis. 316–21 *p* breaches widened the next hour ;

patchwork
No. 3– 1 should not spread abroad *p* ideas

patent
Mis. 79–31 vendors of *p* pills,
  220–22 is *p* both to the conscientious
Pan. 4–12 it is *p* that will is capable of
My. 83– 4 * holding of a great convention is *p* to

paternal
Ret. 1–18 so became my *p* grandmother,
  19– 3 under the *p* roof in Tilton.
  20– 1 After returning to the *p* roof
My. 336–12 "After returning to the *p* roof

Pater Noster
Pul. 59–11 * The *P N* was repeated

path
back to the
Mis. 328– 5 will call thee back to the *p*
beaten
'00. 4–18 beaten *p* of human doctrines
behind thee
Pul. 1–15 *p* behind thee is with glory crowned ;
entered the
Mis. 206–24 you have entered the *p*.
enter the
Mis. 328–25 are striving to enter the *p*,
  347–21 I enter the *p*.
her
Mis. 54–13 malice would fling in her *p*.
his
Mis. 326–29 Discerning in his *p* the penitent
Un. 55–11 must keep close to his *p*,
Po. 18–14 He penciled his *p*
lighteth the
Pan. 12–17 and so lighteth the *p*
made luminous
Mis. 335–15 *p* made luminous by divine Love.
narrow
Mis. 32–21 from the straight and narrow *p*.
Ret. 55– 1 enter this strait and narrow *p*,
  71– 9 straight and narrow *p* of C. S.
no
Mis. 147–28 he knows no *p* but the fair, open,

path
of Christian Science
Ret. 71– 9 narrow *p* of C. S.
No. 42–20 *p* of C. S. is beset with
perfect
My. 187– 9 perfect *p* wherein to walk,
pleasant
Mis. 324–29 reaches the pleasant *p* of the valley
pointing the
Mis. xi–12 guide-book, pointing the *p*,
My. 176– 8 pointing the *p* to heaven within you,
  202– 2 pointing the *p* from earth to heaven
points the
Pan. 12–20 way-seeker gains and points the *p*.
point the
'02. 11– 8 find and point the *p* to heaven.
My. 186–10 point the *p* above the valley,
prowl in the
Mis. 323–12 beasts of prey prowl in the *p*,
this
No. 28–14 none too soon for entering this *p*.
thy
'02. 19–24 A danger besets thy *p* ?
to health
Mis. 308– 8 loses the *p* to health,
to heaven
'02. 11– 8 find and point the *p* to heaven.
My. 176– 8 pointing the *p* to heaven within you,
your
Mis. 306–28 spiritual idea that lights your *p* !

Mis. 9–29 in the *p* that winds upward.
Ret. 90–28 * in the *p* you have pursued !"
Un. 9–10 this way is not the *p* of physical

pathetic
Mis. 230–28 to render it *p*, tender, gorgeous.
Ret. 19–21 gave *p* directions to his
My. 330–32 gave *p* directions to his

pathological
Mis. 297– 4 other religious and *p* systems
  379– 3 if he indited anything *p*
Rud. 16–21 elucidates a *p* Science
'01. 34– 8 proven to be more *p* than

pathology
Mis. 35– 3 the Principle of *p* ;
  80–27 what they deem *p*, hygiene,
Ret. 43– 7 the *p* of spiritual power,
My. 108– 5 the intelligent cause in *p* ?
  230– 5 Scientific *p* illustrates the

pathos
Mis. 295–17 with his ready pen and *p*

paths
Mis. 99–27 "Make straight God's *p* ;
  223– 1 its hidden *p*, purpose, and fruits
  246–24 make His *p* straight." — *Matt.* 3 : 3.
Rud. 17–16 are the *p* of His testimony
'01. 35– 2 shall direct thy *p* ;" — *Prov.* 3 : 6.
My. 140– 4 I will lead them in *p* — *Isa.* 42 : 16.
  161–27 "He shall direct thy *p*." — *Prov.* 3 : 6.
  252–22 into *p* of peace and holiness.
  260–14 philosophy may pursue *p* devious,
  361– 3 will direct you into the *p* of peace.

pathway
Mis. 20– 1 illumes our *p* with the radiance
  270–24 *p* of goodness and greatness
Ret. 30– 6 have cleared its *p*.
Pul. vii–15 the *p* of this generation ;
My. 62–12 * brightest beams on your *p*,
  350–15 the *p* glad and free?

patience
Mis. 7– 8 The loving *p* of Jesus,
  88–11 *P*, observation, intellectual culture,
  100–29 *p*, forgiveness, abiding faith,
  124–29 gives . . . to *p*, experience ,
  224–18 but with the largest *p* ;
  228–11 bear with *p* the buffetings
  267– 8 caused me to exercise most *p*.
  268–31 Through *p* we must possess
  340–22 by *p*, they inherit the promise.
  340–26 miracles of *p* and perseverance.
  361–19 run with *p* the race — *Heb.* 12 : 1.
Ret. 80–10 * Though with *p* He stands
  80–20 *P* and obedience win the
  90–20 endures with her *p*,
Pul. 82–10 * has long learned with *p*,
  83–11 * with the *p* of genius
No. 8–27 power, *p*, and understanding,
'00. 15–25 thy *p*, and thy works ;" — *Rev.* 2 : 19.
'02. 16–21 meek might, sublime *p*,
  17–28 *P* and resignation are the
Hea. 2–17 Jesus, the model of infinite *p*,
My. 158–15 holiness, *p*, charity, love.
  209– 7 fidelity, courage, *p*, and grace.

patience

My.	227– 8	known by its *p·* and endurance.
	249–15	*p·*, silence, and lives of saints.
	306–16	Age, with experience-acquired *p·*

patient (*see also* patient's)

amusing the
Peo.	6–12	* amusing the *p·* while nature cures

attend the
My.	105–19	I was wired to attend the *p·*

belief of the
Mis.	352–16	supposed bodily belief of the *p·*

condition of the
Mis.	43– 5	mental condition of the *p·*.

each
Mis.	38–27	to make each *p·* a student

first
Mis.	382–14	first *p·* healed in this age by C. S.

friends of a
Mis.	282–21	If the friends of a *p·* desire you to

healer and
Pul.	53–10	* in the mind of both healer and *p·*,

his
Mis.	40–29	to kill his *p·* by mental means,
	355–13	the mental state of his *p·*.
Man.	46–20	shall not, ... sue his *p·* for
Un.	11–19	If his *p·* was a theologian of
Rud.	13–22	it will free his *p·*.
My.	306–30	while I was his *p·* in Portland

is better
Mis.	45–20	*p·* is better both morally and

is liable
Rud.	8–27	and the *p·* is liable to a relapse,

may gain
Pul.	69–24	* *p·* may gain a better understanding

physician and
My.	108–19	better for both physician and *p·*.

practitioner to
Man.	46–17	relation of practitioner to *p·*.

receive a
Ret.	87–29	not receive a *p·* who is under the

says
Mis.	220–14	*p·* says and feels, "I am well,

this
Mis.	89– 6	*would it be right to treat this p·*

treating a
Rud.	13–18	When treating a *p·*,

who pays
Mis.	300–29	*p·* who pays whatever he is able

would have died
My.	336– 1	* but for . . . the *p·* would have died

your
Mis.	241–25	your *p·* rejoices in the gospel of
My.	364– 5	the mind of your *p·*,

Mis.	89– 7	*ought the p· to follow the*
	89–11	If tho *p·* is in peril,
	210– 4	C. S. never healed a *p·* without
	242–21	where the *p·* is very low
	242 24	leaving the *p·* well.
	242–29	*p·* . . . addicted to the use of opium
	378– 3	A *p·* considered incurable
Man.	47– 5	a *p·* whom he does not heal,
Rud.	10–19	the *p·* can then look up to
	12– 2	He never lays his hands on the *p·*,
No.	40–25	religious views of the *p·*
'01.	34– 5	interval that detains the *p·* from
	34– 8	cannot be fatal to the *p·*,
Po.	47–22	Or to the *p·* who sow?
My.	97– 4	* go far towards making the *p·* well.
	97– 6	* *p·* getting well without the use of
	105–21	The *p·* was pronounced dying
	293–18	resuscitating the body of the *p·*.
	293–26	and the *p·* would have recovered.
	363–27	*p·* whom he is treating,

patient (adj.)

Mis.	277–10	heart loyal to God is *p·* and strong.
	020–17	He saith unto the *p·* toilers
	330–31	when the *p·* corn waits
	384–14	Be *p·*, waiting heart :
	392–14	Faithful and *p·* be my life
	400–22	Thee I seek, *P·*, meek,
Ret.	79–25	were saved by *p·* waiting.
	86– 3	to crown *p·* toil,
'01.	35–18	do we walk in *P·* faith
Hea.	19–18	*p·* of man's procrastination,
Peo.	14–14	be *p·* in tribulation,
Po.	20–18	Faithful and *p·* be my life
	22– 1	God-crowned, *p·* century,
	30–17	*p·* love above earth's ire,
	36–13	Be *p·*, waiting heart :
	53–10	The *p·*, timid grass,
	69–10	Thee I seek, *P·*, meek,
My.	75–18	* very *p·* and good-natured.
	151– 1	*p·* with the newspaper wares
	191– 4	Be *p·* towards persecution.

patient (adj.)

My.	222–19	Be *p·*, O Christian Scientist !
	247–29	*p·*, unfaltering tenderness.

patiently

Mis.	81– 8	*p·* wait on God to decide,
	118–18	suffer *p·* for error until
	206–25	Press *p·* on ;
	315–27	*p·* strive to educate their
	325–13	*p·* seeks another dwelling,
	330– 5	does it *p·* pray for the
	331– 6	cause them to wait *p·*
	364– 5	"Wait *p·* on the Lord — *see Isa.* 40 : 31.
Man.	83–19	and *p·* counsel his pupils
Ret.	49–16	loving unselfishly, working *p·*,
Un.	6–28	"Wait *p·* on the Lord ;" — *see Psal.* 37 : 7.
Pul.	4–23	Wait *p·* on illimitable Love,
Pan.	1–16	waiteth *p·* the appearing
'01.	34–20	brethren, wait *p·* on God ;
My.	4–11	meekly, *p·*, spiritually.
	29–29	* were able to wait *p·* for the
	185– 2	waited *p·* for the appearing

patient's

Mis.	6–22	the *p·* faith in drugs
	53–13	*to start the p· recovery?*
	219–17	must change his *p·* consciousness
	219–20	*p·* sense of sinning at ease
	220–12	until the *p·* mind yields,
	220–16	changed his *p·* consciousness
	220–17	The *p·* mental state is now
	355–23	discern the error in thy *p·* mind

patients

Mis.	33–18	*P·* naturally gain confidence
	37–25	*Does Mrs. Eddy take p·?*
	59– 9	in which the last state of *p·*
	89– 9	When *p·* are under material
	171– 9	seances with their *p·*,
	241– 7	metaphysical healing on two *p·* :
	350–22	sometimes occasions effects on *p·*
	378– 6	as he informed the *p·*,
	378–10	with several other *p·*,
	379– 1	After treating his *p·*,
	379– 4	relative to his *p·*,
	380–20	my students' *p·*,
Man.	43– 6	nor permit his *p·* or pupils to use
	46–12	Practitioners and *P·*.
	46–15	made to them by their *p·* ;
	47– 4	Duty to *P·*.
	87– 5	Choice of *p·* is left to the wisdom of
Ret.	33–17	would cure *p·* not affected by a
	83– 4	commend . . . *p·* to the teachings of
	84–28	only of his own pupils and *p·*,
No.	3–15	in the hands of their *n·*.
	5–28	makes the last state of one's *p·*
'01.	17–17	restored the *p·* in from one to three
	17–20	put *p·* into the hands of my students
	27–15	interviews with the *p·*,
My.	219– 2	Nor should *p·* anticipate
	227–11	one out of three of their *p·*,
	306–23	were descriptions of his *p·*,
	307– 6	treatment and manipulation of *p·*,
	364–11	his own . . . and that of his *p·*,

Patmos

Pul.	83–26	* to know what John on *P·* meant

patriarch

Mis.	17– 8	like the *p·* of old,

Patriot

My.	284–13	your good paper, the *P·*,

patriot

My.	297– 2	*p·*, philanthropist, moralist,

patriotic

Mis.	304–13	* any great *p·* celebration
	305– 3	* from the *p·* societies,

patriotism

Ret.	2–14	from whose *p·* and bravery

Patriots' Day

My.	339–15	exchanged Fast Day, . . . for *P· D·*,

patron

Pan.	3–27	Pan was the . . . *p·* of country life,

patronage

Mis.	262– 6	*p·* of *The C. S. Journal*,
	274–13	to the public for its liberal *p·*,
	296–23	Why fall into such *p·*,
	308–19	I thank you, . . . for your liberal *p·*
Ret.	49–22	we thank the public for its liberal *p·*.

patronize

Mis.	80–29	The old will not *p·* the new school,
	296–19	Do manly Britons *p·* tap-rooms
Man.	44– 9	member of this Church shall not *p·* a

Pat's

Mis.	218–27	better than *P·* echo,

pattern
  Mis. 44– 2 "according to the *p·* — *Heb.* 8 : 5.
    103–20 is neither the *p·* nor Maker
    197–20 compel us to *p·* after both;
  Un. 53– 2 lie takes its *p·* from Truth,
  '01. 10–24 after the *p·* of the mount.
patterns
  Mis. 299–29 gives to the public new *p·*
    316–28 *p·* of humility, wisdom,
  My. 283–26 only as it *p·* the divine.
Patterson (*see also* **Patterson's**)
  Dr.
  My. 311– 3 living with Dr. *P·* at his
    313–12 Dr. *P·* driving into Franklin,
    314–14 my divorce from Dr. *P·*
    314–20 about to have Dr. *P·* arrested
    314–29 lived with Dr. *P·* peaceably,
    315– 3 * About the year 1874, Dr. *P·*,
  Dr. Daniel
  My. 314– 1 Dr. Daniel *P·*, my second husband,
    314– 8 Dr. Daniel *P·* was located
  Lieutenant-Governor George W.
  Ret. 20– 7 Lieutenant-Governor George W. *P·*
Patterson's
  Dr.
  My. 314–22 prevented Dr. *P·* arrest
Pattersons
  My. 314– 5 * the following nine years the *P·*
patting
  Mis. 231–24 little palms *p·* together,
Paugus
  Pul. 48–30 * killed the ill-starred *P·*.
Paul (*see also* **Paul's, St. Paul**)
  admonished
  Mis. 361–17 To this great end, *P·* admonished,
  and Jesus
  Mis. 360– 7 characters, *P·* and Jesus.
  apostle
  Mis. 200–11 The apostle *P·* insists on
  asked
  Mis. 333–22 *P·* asked: "What communion— *II Cor.* 6 :14.
  declares
  My. 113– 9 *P·* declares the truth of the
  enjoined
  Ret. 76–16 fulfils the law of Love which *P·* enjoined
  Jesus and
  Mis. 364–32 divine philosophy of Jesus and *P·*.
  No. 21– 2 life and teachings of Jesus and *P·*,
  refers
  Mis. 184–10 *P·* refers to this when speaking of
    190–30 *P·* refers to this personality
  said
  Mis. 157– 3 *P·* said, "If we suffer,— *II Tim.* 2 : 12.
  Peo. 10–13 *P·* said, "I was free born."— *Acts* 22 : 28.
  says
  Un. 5–14 of godliness," says *P·* ;— *I Tim.* 3 : 16.
    43–24 as *P·* says in the third chapter of
  termed
  My. 41–22 * what *P·* termed "the law of— *Rom.* 8 : 2.
  understood
  Mis. 344–21 Science which *P·* understood when he
  words of
  Hea. 18– 3 In the words of *P·*,
  writes
  Un. 30–13 *P·* writes : "The first man— *I Cor.* 15 : 45.

  Mis. 71– 5 *P·* had a thorn in the flesh :
    162– 2 was called Israel ; and Saul, *P·*.
    201–16 *P·* took pleasure in infirmities,
  Un. 1– 6 were taught by his fellow-apostle *P·*,
  No. 46–17 rejoicing, as *P·* did, that we
Paul's
  Mis. 84–19 Please explain *P·* meaning
    84–21 overshadowing *P·* sense of life in
    200–25 The holy calm of *P·* well-tried hope
    201– 3 The Science of *P·* declaration
    243–23 alludes to *P·* advice to Timothy.
    360– 9 *P·*, by the supremely natural
  Un. 57–20 confirmation of *P·* faith.
pauperism
  My. 309– 6 involving a question of *p·*
pause
  Mis. 16–27 dear reader, *p·* for a moment
  Pul. 44– 7 * willingly *p·* for an instant to
  My. 81– 8 * *p·* and laughingly give precedence to
    280–29 simply to *p·* in special prayer for
paused
  Pul. 48–16 * she *p·* and reminded the reporter
pausing
  Mis. 324– 4 *P·* at the threshold of a
paved
  My. 176– 6 *p·* the way to my forever gratitude,

pay
  Mis. vii–20 Wherefor, have much to *p·*.
    165–25 cost, none but the sinner can *p·* ;
    269–26 but are not willing to *p·* the price.
    299–22 *p·* me, not him, for this exhibit
    300–30 pays whatever he is able to *p·*
    301– 2 sermon for which you *p·* nothing,
    301– 3 and receive *p·* therefor,
    305–23 * money with which to *p·* for the bell.
    305–26 * twenty-five cents to *p·* for it.
    317–27 should not *p·* the penalty for
    342–25 you are willing to *p·* for error
    342–26 if you *p·* the price of Truth,
    349–26 and means to *p·* a salary,
    349–30 accepted no *p·* from my church
    353–18 "You must *p·* that man."
    353–20 God makes *us p·* for
  Man. 30–16 Board of Directors shall *p·* from
    44–13 *p·* annually a per capita tax
    69–10 student shall *p·* to Mrs. Eddy
    78–18 may *p·* from the funds of the
  Ret. 40– 3 refusing to take any *p·*
    89–13 It was the custom to *p·* this
  Pul. 20– 4 were unable to *p·* the mortgage ;
  Rud. 14–10 The only *p·* taken for her labors
    14–16 from those who were able to *p·*.
    14–17 better than he who does not *p·*,
    14–18 expect and require others to *p·* him.
  My. vi–22 * *p·* all future profits to her church ;
    27–25 * *p·* all bills in connection with the
    51– 1 * to devise means to *p·* our pastor,
    96–20 * what they could to *p·* for it.
    123–15 the money to *p·* for it.
    161– 2 by enabling us to *p·* it ;
    214–17 taking *p·* for their labors,
    306–25 I would *p·* for having published.
    328–29 * practise the art of healing for *p·*,
    328–29 * shall *p·* a license fee
payable
  Man. 77–10 shall render them *p·*.
paying
  Man. 77– 5 Prior to *p·* bills against the
  Rud. 14–20 means of *p·* for their tuition
  No. 35–15 how to avoid *p·* it.
  '02. 13–18 *p·* for it the sum of $4,963.50
    13–23 to redeem the land by *p·*
  My. 16– 7 * *p·* out the sum of $199,607.93,
    74–17 * *p·* for their church before dedicating
    329– 5 * relieved . . . from *p·* this fee,
    333– 7 * *p·* the last tribute of respect
payment
  Man. 46–21 recovery of *p·* for said
    78–22 for the *p·* of such bills.
  My. 10–15 * amount and date of *p·*.
    204–25 the suing for *p·*, hypnotism,
payments
  Man. 78–23 Such *p·* shall be reported,
  My. 14–16 * further *p·* or subscriptions
    14–29 * necessitates large *p·* of money,
pays
  Mis. 261–12 *p·* his full debt to divine law,
    300–30 *p·* whatever he is able to pay
  Rud. 14–16 student who *p·* must of necessity
Peabody, D.D., Rev. A. P.
  My. 53–23 * Rev. A. P. *P·*, D.D., of Cambridge,
peace
  and good will
  Mis. 215–15 *p·*, and good will toward men.
  Pul. 22– 1 *p·* and good will towards men.
  My. 167–18 full of love, *p·*, and good will
  and harmony
  Mis. 156–11 Let the reign of *p·* and harmony
  and holiness
  Mis. 167–28 He giveth power, *p·*, and holiness ;
  '02. 16–14 To attain *p·* and holiness
  My. 252–22 into paths of *p·* and holiness.
  and joy
  Mis. 303–10 *p·* and joy, the fruits of Spirit,
    331–18 O gentle presence, *p·* and joy
    389– 6 O gentle presence, *p·* and joy
  Po. 4– 1 O gentle presence, *p·* and joy
  and love
  Mis. 152– 7 thoughts winged with *p·* and love
  Ret. 42–13 with a smile of *p·* and love
  '00. 11–12 human sigh for *p·* and love
  and perfect love
  Mis. 176– 3 healing, and *p·*, and perfect love.
  and plenty
  Mis. 232– 3 *p·*, and plenty, and happy households.
  My. 340–28 their implorations for *p·* and plenty
  and power
  Mis. 124–19 is filled with *p·*, and power;
    205– 1 obtains *p·* and power outside of

peace

and progress
Mis. 118–22 foes to grace, *p*, and progress ;
and prosperity
My. 279–26 God bless . . . with *p* and prosperity.
291–23 ensign of *p* and prosperity
and understanding
Mis. 290–17 * *p*, and understanding ;"
announcement of
My. 281–18 * "Official announcement of *p*
armaments of
Mis. xii– 2 privileged armaments of *p*.
at
Mis. 209–21 it has no right to be at *p*.
211–18 if a criminal is at *p*,
Ret. 28– 4 if he would be at *p*.
Peo. 6–25 and be at *p* ;" — *Job* 22 : 21.
be declared
Ret. 56–14 must go on until *p* be declared
be still
Mis. 307– 9 "*P*, be still" — *Mark* 4 : 39.
between nations
My. 265–10 civilization, *p* between nations,
bonds of
Pul. 22–17 bonds of *p* are cemented by
break his
Mis. 211–16 Why, then, do you break his *p*
bring
Mis. 7–15 if you cannot bring *p* to all,
brings the
Mis. 82– 5 brings the *p* symbolized by
call of
Mis. 120–16 clarion call of *p* will at length
compassionate in
Pan. 15– 4 has been compassionate in *p*.
consolation and
My. 283–27 Consolation and *p* are based on
convenient
My. 211– 2 a false, convenient *p*,
curtailed in
My. 127–27 it is not curtailed in *p*,
demonstrates
My. 279– 7 C. S. demonstrates *p*.
destroy the
Mis. 209–19 destroy the *p* of a false sense.
divine
Peo. 11– 8 victory is achieved, . . . in divine *p*.
dove of
My. 192–16 the dove of *p* sits smilingly
dwelleth
Mis. x– 2 life wherein dwelleth *p*,
fathomless
'02. 4–10 fathomless *p* between Soul and
follow
'02. 16–12 "Follow *p* with all men, — *Heb.* 12 : 14.
giveth a
Mis. 133–30 it giveth a *p* that passeth
give you
Mis. 159– 7 May the God of all grace give you *p*.
God of
Mis. 128–13 God of *p* shall be with you." — *Phil.* 4 : 9.
153–30 God of *p* be and abide with
gospel of
'02. 4–15 commandment in the gospel of *p*,
grace, and
Mis. 9– 1 grace, and *p*, comes through affliction
grant us
Mis. xi–21 *vox populi* is inclined to grant us *p*,
have
Mis. 209–32 then shall mortals have *p*."
health and
Mis. 169–25 health and *p* and hope for all.
My. 350–18 * crushing out of health and *p*,
home and
Mis. 386– 5 home and *p* and hearts are found
Po. 49– 8 home and *p* and hearts are found
in error
My. 233–22 destroys his *p* in error,
in God
Mis. 385– 3 * Find *p* in God,
Po. 37– 3 * Find *p* in God,
in goodness
Mis. 219–21 discomfort in sin and *p* in goodness.
in Love
'02. 19–18 a rest in Christ, a *p* in Love.
integrity and
Mis. 270– 4 such as barter integrity and *p* for
is desirable
My. 121–15 *p* is desirable, and plain dealing is
is the promise
My. 278–23 *P* is the promise and reward of
is won
Po. 22–20 Love doth enter in, And *p* is won,
justice of the
My. 136–22 Josiah E. Fernald, justice of the *p*
309–14 justice of the *p* at one time.

peace

liberty and
Mis. 304– 5 * by the lovers of liberty and *p*
life and
Mis. 24– 4 is life and *p*." — *Rom.* 8 : 6.
'02. 6–28 is life and *p*." — *Rom.* 8 : 6.
make
My. 40–21 * them that make *p*." — *Jas.* 3 : 18.
mercy, and
Pan. 14–12 justice, mercy, and *p*
more
My. 135–12 my yearning for more *p*
136–27 that I may have more *p*,
137–18 yearning for more *p*
my
Mis. 215– 5 my *p* I leave with thee :
278– 4 my *p* returns unto me.
My. 279– 4 "My *p* I give unto you : — *John* 14 : 27.
national
My. 285– 8 industrial, civic, and national *p*.
no
Mis. 209– 6 when there is no *p*," — *Jer.* 6 : 14.
My. 233–18 when there is no *p*." — *Jer.* 6 : 14.
not power
My. 341–15 * "'Tis *p* not power I seek,
of a desert
Mis. 246–22 yield its prey the *p* of a desert,
of God
No. 8– 8 "the *p* of God, — *Phil.* 4 : 7.
of Love
My. 185– 8 The *p* of Love is published,
of love
My. 220–23 the joy and the *p* of love."
of nations
My. 280–17 special prayer for the *p* of nations,
280–29 praying for the *p* of nations,
of the Lord
Pul. 39– 4 * until it finds the *p* of the Lord
on earth
Mis. 145–30 on earth *p*, — *Luke* 2 : 14.
153–26 * *P* on earth and Good-will !
214– 5 to send *p* on earth : — *Matt.* 10 : 34.
227–27 cool waters of *p* on earth ;
369– 5 "on earth *p*, — *Luke* 2 : 14.
Man. 45– 6 to promote *p* on earth
Pul. 41–25 * "On earth *p*, — *Luke* 2 : 14.
No. 44 26 "On earth *p*, — *Luke* 2 : 14.
Po. 24– 8 Come to me, *p* on earth !
My. 90–19 * "on earth *p*, — *Luke* 2 : 14.
127–30 "on earth *p*, — *Luke* 2 : 14.
167–11 "on earth *p*, — *Luke* 2 : 14.
279–19 "on earth *p*, — *Luke* 2 : 14.
281– 9 "on earth *p*, — *Luke* 2 : 14.
283–11 "on earth *p*, — *Luke* 2 : 14.
paths of
My. 301– 3 direct you into the paths of *p*.
perfect
My. 290–15 keep him in perfect peace, — *Isa.* 26 : 3.
permanence and
Mis. 352– 2 bereft of permanence and *p*.
pillars of
'02. 17–29 are the pillars of *p*
plenty and
Po. 77– 5 Plenty and *p* abound
power, and
Mis. 263–13 power, and *p* meet all human
prayer for
My. 279–21 chapter sub-title
280–30 to pause in special prayer for *p*.
pregnant with
My. 283–13 Association, pregnant with *p*,
preserving
My. 286–12 preserving *p* among nations.
promote
Mis. 354– 8 can no longer promote *p*
Man. 45– 6 its branches to promote *p*
prosper in
'02. 3–20 British and Boer may prosper in *p*,
publisheth
Ret. 45– 4 that publisheth *p*." — *Isa.* 52 : 7.
pure
Po. 79– 3 storm or shine, pure *p* is thine,
My. 155–18 this dear church having a pure *p*,
purer
Mis. 330–22 holier aims, a purer *p*
purity and
No. 34–24 throne of glory in purity and *p*,
reflect
My. 210–16 His thoughts can only reflect *p*,
reflection of
My. 355–28 His reflection of *p*, love, joy.
righteousness, and
My. 282–12 justice, righteousness, and *p*,
sacrificed
'02. 13– 2 self was forgotten, *p* sacrificed,

peace

seeking
Mis. 324–27 seeking *p·* but finding none.
silly
Mis. 254–24 resting in silly *p·* upon the
sown in
My. 40–21 * is sown in *p·* — *Jas.* 3 : 18.
spiritual
My. 93–15 * physical health and spiritual *p·*.
strength of
My. 121– 7 we learn that the strength of *p·*
this
Mis. 82– 5 this *p·* floweth as a river
My. 121–11 This *p·* is spiritual ;
thy
Mis. 268– 9 thy *p·* been as a river." — *Isa.* 48 : 18.
to send
Mis. 214– 6 I came not to send *p·*, — *Matt.* 10 : 34.
'01. 31–10 "I came not to send *p·* — *Matt.* 10 : 34.
treacherous
Mis. 9–28 trained in treacherous *p·*
weapons of
Pul. 84– 3 * with the weapons of *p·*.
white-winged
Mis. 204–10 white-winged *p·* sings to the heart
with God
Mis. 211–27 and kept *p·* with God.
'01. 2–20 keeping *p·* with God.
would reign
My. 279–14 one Mind, *p·* would reign.
your
My. 150–31 your *p·* return to you." — *Matt.* 10 : 13.

Mis. 124–11 turn, with sickened sense, . . . for *p·* ;
133–31 As to the *p·*, it is unutterable ;
138–19 divine might, giving . . . *p·*.
155–11 and *p·* will crown your joy.
162–12 *p·*, good will, love, teaching, and
172–26 *p·* can only be . . . on the side of
209– 6 and cry, "*P·*, *p·* ; — *Jer.* 6 : 14.
209–23 *P·* has no foothold on the false
Ret. 42–16 end of *that* man *is p·*." — *Psal.* 37 : 37.
'01. 23– 9 be in *p·* with the schools.
Po. 31– 7 *p·* of Soul's sweet solitude !
78– 3 *P·* her white wings will spread
My. 36–17 * *p·* of a more righteous living,
121–14 *P·*, like plain dealing,
153–30 will give thee rest, *p·*, health,
233–17, 18 saying, *P·*, *p·* ; — *Jer.* 6 : 14.
277–15 *p·*, prosperity, and life of nations.
278– 3 If His purpose for *p·* is to be
281–25 * influence . . . exerted for *p·*,
282– 2 is its *p·* maker or breaker.
282–17 chapter sub-title

peaceable
My. 40–20 * first pure, then *p·*, — *Jas.* 3 : 17.
300–32 are they attacking a *p·* party

peaceably
My. 314–29 I lived with Dr. Patterson *p·*,

peacebreakers
My. 40–10 * some who have been *p·*

peaceful
Mis. 392– 5 With *p·* presence hath begirt
Pan. 14–19 In your *p·* homes remember
15– 1 murdering her *p·* seamen
Po. 20– 6 With *p·* presence hath begirt
23–21 Give *p·* triumph to the
My. 280– 7 * *p·* tranquillity of the race.
333–22 * "His end was calm and *p·*,

peacefully
My. 250–25 I rest *p·* in knowing that the
277– 4 settled *p·* by statesmanship

peacemakers
My. 40–11 * into the blessedness of *p·*.
40–22 * "Blessed are the *p·* : — *Matt.* 5 : 9.

peacemaking
My. 40–16 * demand of this age is for *p·*,

peaches
Ret. 4–15 orchards of apples, *p·*,

peal
Pul. 61–22 * the first *p·* of the chimes
Po. 71–13 God to the rescue — Liberty, *p·* !

pealed
My. 77–21 * *p·* from the chimes a first hymn

pearl
Mis. 30–13 he declared were inlaid with *p·*,
252–31 yea, it is the *p·* priceless
313– 7 spiritual molecule, *p·*, and pinnacle,
Ret. 91– 4 "the *p·* of parables,"
'02. 3–15 occupation of that *p·* of the ocean,
My. 347–18 parable of the priceless *p·*

pearls
Mis. 7–14 Cast not your *p·* before swine ;
89–16 "*p·* before swine" — *Matt.* 7 : 6.
127–24 though your *p·* be downtrodden.
211–20 trample on your *p·* of thought,
247– 4 not as *p·* trampled upon.
307–21 Cast not *p·* before the unprepared
325–11 seize his *p·*, throw them away,
No. 8–24 no longer cast your *p·* before
40– 9 *p·* of awakened consciousness,
40– 9 lest your *p·* be trampled upon.
Po. 8– 9 vestal *p·* that on leaflets lay,
My. 215–21 preying upon my *p·*,
227–24 *p·* before swine — *Matt.* 7 : 6.
347–16 *p·* that crown this cup

pears
Ret. 4–15 orchards of apples, peaches, *p·*,

Pears' soap
'00. 10–28 gold pieces snuggled in *P· s·*.

pear-tree
Ret. 18– 7 In lap of the *p·*, with musical flow.
18–26 from the bent branch of a *p·*.
Po. 63–16 In lap of the *p·*, with musical flow.
63–24 from the bent branch of a *p·*.

pebbles
Mis. 343–15 cold, hard *p·* of selfishness,
Ret. 27–22 meandering midst *p·* and rocks,
Pul. 80–14 * over its granitic *p·*.

peculiar
Ret. 8– 1 *p·* circumstances and events
Pul. 23–23 * marked by *p·* intimations of
57–13 * *p·* tenets of the . . . Scientists,
59–12 * way *p·* to Christian Scientists,
My. 50–12 * felt a *p·* sense of isolation,
52–31 * *p·* knowledge of the circumstances.
78–27 * convey the *p·* impressiveness
90–30 * *p·* department of healing,
123–31 *p·* people whose God is All-in-all,
206–24 holy nation, a *p·* people ; — *I Pet.* 2 : 9.
352– 6 * *p·* privileges we enjoy

peculiarities
Hea. 12–16 characteristic *p·* and . . . symptoms

peculiarly
Pul. 36–15 * I went to her *p·* fatigued.
My. 78–11 * carvings *p·* rich and impressive.

pecuniarily
Mis. 11– 9 afterwards assisting them *p·*,
My. 130–10 whom I have assisted *p·*

pecuniary
Mis. 349– 1 even the offer of *p·* assistance

pedal
Pul. 60–23 * *p·* compass, C. C. C. to F. 30.
(*see also* **organ**)

pedal movements
(*see* **organ**)

pedal organ
(*see* **organ**)

pedals
(*see* **organ**)

pedestal
My. 79– 6 * chapter sub-title
79–21 * placed upon a far higher *p·*
259– 3 mounted on its *p·*

pedestals
Mis. 255– 3 set themselves on *p·*,

peel
Mis. 231–18 to arrest the *p·* !

peep
Po. 73– 7 And the stars *p·* out,
My. 173–17 to take a *p·* at this church
258–32 take a *p·* into my studio ;

peer
Mis. 22–19 It hath no *p·*, no competitor,
347–10 *p·* through the opaque error.

peering
Mis. 369– 9 *p·* into the cause which

peers
Ret. 17– 9 morning *p·* out, from her
Po. 62– 9 morning *p·* out, from her

Pekin
'00. 1–23 Paris, Berlin, Rome, *P·*.

pelf
Mis. 325–10 they have plenty of *p·*,
'00. 10–20 the sceptre of self and *p·*

pellets
My. 107–13 that a vial full of the *p·* can
107–17 tells you, . . . with these *p·* he heals
345–17 *p·* without any medication

Pembroke

Ret.   4–24   Nathaniel Ambrose of *P·*,
      5– 5   Congregational Church in *P·*.
'01. 32– 1   Abraham Burnham of *P·*,

pen

Mis. xii– 6   take my *p·* and pruning-hook,
    149–18   lips nor *p·* can ever express
    227–15   Would that my *p·* or pity could
    275–21   *P·* can never portray the satisfaction
    295–17   with his ready *p·* and pathos?
    377– 2   *p·* to paint frail fairness
Ret.   5–16   the *p·* can never do justice.
Pul.   5– 4   address on C. S. from my *p·*,
    87–23   This wish stops not with my *p·*
'00. 12– 1   beyond the power of the *p·*.
Po.   32–12   inspires my *p·* as I write ;
My. 48–16   * *Methodist Review* from the *p·* of
    124–17   *p·* may not tell.
    125–11   to dip my *p·* in my heart
    136–25   hard earnings of my *p·*,
    146–31   weight of thought, tongue, and *p·*
    148–23   as with the *p·* of an angel
    294–24   will move the *p·* of millions.
    296–26   dipped her *p·* in my heart,

penal

Peo. 11–19   and enact *p·* codes ;

penalties

Mis. 199– 1   God does not reward . . . love with *p·* ;
    209– 1   attaches to sin due *p·*

penalty

Mis. 08–14   *p·* for believing in their reality
    119–31   and escape the *p·* therefor?
    126–29   *p·* of which the Hebrew bard spake
    222–19   suffer its full *p·* after death.
    227– 9   Thus, to evade the *p·* of law,
    237– 6   accepted as the *p* for sin.
    300–20   incurring the *p·* of the law,
    317–21   Such students should not pay the *p·*
    381–25   on *p·* of ten thousand dollars.
Man. 46–22   on *p·* of discipline and liability to
    53–17   on *p·* of being excommunicated
Un. 11– 2   from the *p·* of error.
My. 248–24   sin and suffering and their *p·*, death

penance

Mis. 244–12   are they bodily *p·* and torture, or
'02. 16–24   Fasting, feasting, or *p·*,
My. 228–31   for *p·* or for reformation ;

pence

Pul.   8–10   to earn a few *p·* toward

penchant

Mis. 329– 2   Mine is an obstinate *p·* for nature

penciled

Po. 18–13   He *p·* his path

pencils

My. 124–18   Nature reflects man and art *p·* him,

pendulum

Pul. 80– 3   * *p·* that has swung to one extreme

penetrated

Pul. 65– 2   * it has *p·* what is called the

penetration

Mis. 202–27   with the *p·* of Soul,
    313– 9   throw the light of *p·* on the page ;
Un.   2–15   in the infinite *p·* of Truth,

penitent

Mis. 326–29   *p·* one who had groped his way
'01. 17– 4   cause him to return . . . *p·* and saved ;
My. 133– 2   many pardons for the *p·*.

penmanship

My. 137– 9   * in both substance and *p·* :

Penna. Ave., 1505

Mis. 304– 2   * 1505 *P· A·*, WASHINGTON, D. C.
    306 15   * 1505 *P· A·*, Washington, D. C.,

penned

Ret. 46– 1   Lines *p·* when I was pastor of

pennies

Mis. 305–27   * in *p·*, if possible,

pennings

Mis. 379– 4   asked if I could see his *p·*

penny

My. 77–28   * every *p·* of the two million dollars

Pentecost Day

Ret. 76–21   as of old, on the *P· D·*,

pent-up

Mis. 347– 4   the internal action of *p·* gas.
    356– 5   *p·* elements of mortal mind

people (*see also* people's)
accuse
Ret. 73–22   or accuse *p·* of being unduly personal,

people
all
Mis. 32–27   all *p·* can and should be just,
Pan.   1–18   day when all *p·* shall know
among the
My. 53–29   * C. S. among the *p·*,
any
My. 148– 5   All that we ask of any *p·*
are being healed
Rud. 14–25   *P·* are being healed by means of
are surprised
'00. 4–11   *p·* are surprised at the new
attended by
My. 96–29   * attended by *p·* from all parts
before the
Mis. 162– 7   before the *p·* and their schools
'01. 22–22   rules, are before the *p·*,
My. 323– 8   * before the *p·* find out
believe
Mis. 220–25   *p·* believe that a man is sick
    228–30   *P·* believe in infectious and
best
'00. 2– 5   best *p·* on earth and in heaven.
blinding the
Rud. 17– 5   blinding the *p·* to the true
body of
Mis. 312–16   * body of *p·* known as . . . Scientists,
My. 95–18   * well-dressed body of *p·*.
    99–12   * optimistic body of *p·*,
chosen
Mis. 151–23   Ye are a chosen *p·*,
Christian
Pul. 50–17   * number of Christian *p·*,
Christian(?)
My. 60–11   * all the Christian (?) *p·* at that time.
Christian Science
My. 328–10   * The C. S. *p·*, greatly pleased at
clamor
No. 45–25   The *p* clamor to leave cradle and
coming
Mis. 322– 5   *P·* coming from a distance
consign
Mis. 350–27   which consign *p·* to suffering.
crowds of
My. 30– 1   * held large crowds of *p·*,
dear
My. 175–29   influence the minds of this dear *p·*
    197– 5   be upon this dear *p·*,
dependent
No. 3–12   *P·* dependent on the rules of this
devourer of the
'00. 12–29   as the devourer of the *p·*.
diseased
Rud. 15–19   advising diseased *p·* not to enter
disinterested
Ret. 50–11   I beg disinterested *p·* to ask
do not kill
'01. 33–19   We admit that they do not kill *p·*
    33–30   citizens that do not kill *p·*
do not know
My. 305–11   *P·* do not know who is referred to as
do not understand
Mis. 7–27   because *p·* do not understand
easier for
Mis. 5–30   It is much easier for *p·* to believe
    247–25   It is much easier for *p·* to believe
eight hundred
Pul. 27– 6   * The vestry seats eight hundred *p·*,
My. 54–15   * about eight hundred *p·*.
eleven hundred
Pul. 25– 9   * seating eleven hundred *p·*
exhort
Mis. 197– 5   exhort *p·* to turn from sin
eyes of the
Mis. 48–20   to open the eyes of the *p·*
Pul. 15– 1   to open the eyes of the *p·*
few
Mis. 171–26   Few *p·* at present know aught of
Pul. 57–21   * Few *p·* outside its own circles
five thousand
My. 29– 4   * Five thousand *p·* kneeling
    69–21   * where five thousand *p·* can
    71–29   * would seat five thousand *p·*,
    98– 7   * holding five thousand *p·*,
    99–15   * seating five thousand *p·*,
    141–24   seats only five thousand *p·*,
five thousand and twelve
My. 71–23   * five thousand and twelve *p·*
forty thousand
My. 98– 2   * Forty thousand *p·* truly make
frightens
My. 160–14   a live truth, . . . frightens *p·*.
    216–12   a miracle that frightens *p·*,
gathering of
Man. 60–23   No large gathering of *p·*
My. 87–13   * a great gathering of *p·*

people

generally
   Mis. 380–20 *p·* generally, called for a sign
God's
   Mis. 117–12 * vivacity among God's *p·*."
good
   '02. 20–25 whose good *p·* welcome
groups of
   My. 87–21 * cheerful looking groups of *p·*
handful of
   My. 59–18 * preached to a handful of *p·*
have slumbered
   No. 41–19 long ages *p·* have slumbered
healthy
   Mis. 229– 6 contact with healthy *p·*,
His
   Mis. 144–22 the assembling of His *p·*
       150–28 His *p·* are they that reflect Him
       152–19 God has prepared for His *p·*,
       153– 6 went forth before His *p·*,
   '02. 1– 2 loving providence for His *p·*
honest
   Ret. 29– 3 I esteem all honest *p·*,
   No. 3–26 odious to honest *p·* ;
ignorance of
   No. 43–27 sheer ignorance of *p·*,
imagine
   My. 103–16 *p·* imagine a vain— *Psal.* 2 : 1.
       200– 5 *p·* imagine a vain— *Psal.* 2 : 1.
influenced the
   Mis. 246– 7 press that influenced the *p·* to
intelligent
   Pul. 63–17 * intelligent *p·* among her devoted
irresponsible
   No. 3– 9 irresponsible *p·* insisted
its
   My. 10–20 * sacrifice on the part of its *p·*.
       163–25 I love its *p·*
law-abiding
   Ret. 87–12 most systematic and law-abiding *p·*
leading
   My. 163–24 the leading *p·* of this pleasant city
loyal
   My. 14–23 * to ensnare a generous and loyal *p·*.
many
   Mis. 150–16 seen the salvation of many *p·*
       276– 6 solely because so many *p·*
many of the
   Mis. 81–18 *many of the p· from beyond Jordan*
may listen
   '01. 20–12 *P·* may listen complacently to
million of
   Mis. 35– 7 a million of *p·* acknowledge and
   '00. 2– 1 over a million of *p·*
minds of the
   My. 234–28 before the minds of the *p·* are
most
   Mis. 126–22 Most *p·* condemn evil-doing,
my
   Mis. 209– 7 the wounds of my *p·*
   My. 126–14 "Come out of her, my *p·*"— *Rev.* 18 : 4.
       233–17 the daughter of my *p·*— *Jer.* 6 : 14.
       270–13 shall be my *p·*"— *Ruth* 1 : 16.
non-church-going
   Pul. 56– 7 * churches and non-church-going *p·*.
numbering the
   Man. 48–16 Numbering the *P·*.
       48–21 turn away from . . . numbering the *p·*.
observed
   My. 244–30 As the *p·* observed the success
of common sense
   No. 2– 5 scorned by *p·* of common sense.
of God
   Mis. 216– 4 rest for the *p·* of God ;
of intelligence
   My. 96–30 * And they were *p·* of intelligence.
of New England
   My. 264–10 * to the *p·* of New England,
of standing
   My. 81–31 * *p·* of standing and of substance,
of substance
   My. 80– 3 * *p·* of substance and of standing,
of the Occident
   Mis. 29–24 the *p·* of the Occident know
of the South
   My. 331–28 * characterized the *p·* of the South,
opinions of
   Hea. 6– 6 opinions of *p·* fly too high or
other
   Mis. 230–16 hours that other *p·* may occupy in
       319–13 or more to them than to other *p·*.
our
   My. 326– 4 * is most gratifying to our *p·* ;
peculiar
   My. 123–31 peculiar *p·* whose God is All-in-all,
       206–24 a peculiar *p·* ;— *I Pet.* 2 : 9.

people

poisoning
   Mis. 248–29 mental malpractice of poisoning *p·*
prepare
   Mis. 347– 8 *p·* prepare shelter in caves of the
present
   Mis. 148–26 contributions from the *p·* present
presented to the
   Un. 6–11 presented to the *p·* in divine light,
privileges of the
   My. 168– 5 forever the privileges of the *p·*
raising up the
   My. 285–22 raising up the *p·*,— *Acts* 24 : 12.
robbing of
   My. 266–4 the robbing of *p·* of life and
say
   Mis. 335–25 Such *p·* say, "Would you
   '01. 27–28 * First, *p·* say it conflicts with
   Hea. 6– 4 * "P· say you are a medium,"
   My. 49– 2 * when these smiling *p·* say,
       304–26 * First, *p·* say it conflicts with
six thousand
   Pul. 64–27 * six thousand *p·* to participate in
some
   Mis. 78–17 some *p·* employ the *et cetera* of
       237–10 Some *p·* never repent until
       317–12 not absolutely requisite for some *p·*
       353–18 Some *p·* try to tend folks,
   Pul. 59– 8 * some *p·* heard these exercises four
sometimes object
   Pan. 9–27 the best of *p·* sometimes object to
stirred the
   My. 105– 2 stirred the *p·* to search the
stirreth up the
   My. 104– 8 stirreth up the *p·*."— *Luke* 23 : 5.
       104–16 "stirreth up the *p·*"— *Luke* 23 : 5.
       222–19 stirreth up the *p·*."— *Luke* 23 : 5.
teach
   Mis. 44– 4 may profitably teach *p·*,
terrifies
   Ret. 73–20 wrongs it, or terrifies *p·* over it,
that walked
   Chr. 55– 8 *p·* that walked in darkness— *Isa.* 9 : 2.
their
   Pul. 82–20 * sang and sacrificed for their *p·*,
these
   Rud. 13–25 These *p·* should not be expected,
   My. 48–28 * The intellects of these *p·*
       71–14 * When these *p·* enter this new
       75–17 * these *p·* would take it
       95–19 * The faith of these *p·* is certainly
       96– 4 * These *p·* were of the highest
thirty thousand
   My. 30– 5 * well over thirty thousand *p·*
       79–12 * thirty thousand *p·* assembling
this
   My. v– 9 * extended to this *p·* by
       187–26 in the hearts of this *p·*
       202–16 the spiritual sense of this *p·*
those
   My. 81–21 * In those *p·* was the depth of
throng of
   Pul. 61–25 * attracted quite a throng of *p·*,
thy
   My. 270–12 "thy *p·* shall be— *Ruth* 1 : 16.
two hundred
   My. 123–22 a trifle over two hundred *p·*,
two hundred thousand
   Pul. 30–24 * exceeds two hundred thousand *p·*.
unaware
   Ret. 71–11 *P·* unaware of the indications
unfamiliar
   My. 338–21 that *p·* unfamiliar with his
unfortunate
   My. 301–20 Those unfortunate *p·* who are
warned the
   No. 41– 4 warned the *p·* to beware of Jesus,
warning
   Mis. 210– 8 warning *p·* not to stir up
well-meaning
   Pul. 80–22 * an army of well-meaning *p·*
   '01. 29–12 well-meaning *p·* sometimes are
were astonished
   Mis. 189–26 "The *p·* were astonished— *Matt.* 7 : 28.
   Ret. 58–10 the *p·* "were astonished — *Matt.* 7 : 28.
   Un. 42–18 "*p·* were astonished— *Matt.* 7 : 28.
were healed
   Ret. 39– 1 *p·* were healed simply by reading
what sort of
   Mis. 178–16 * wondered what sort of *p·* you were,
whose God
   My. 127– 4 the *p·* whose God is All-in-all,
will chain
   Pul. 14– 2 the hour when the *p·* will chain,
will differ
   Mis. 288–29 *P·* will differ in their opinions

people

wrong class of
Mis. 80–15   with a wrong class of *p·*.

Mis. 193–20   which the *p·* are now adopting.
    211– 9   by the good judgment of *p·* in
    229– 9   If only the *p·* would believe
    245–24   allows the *p·* to go no further
    282– 7   Shall *p·* be treated mentally
    301–32   of the *p·* there was none — *Isa.* 63 : 3.
    339– 2   If *p·* would confine their talk to
    347– 5   *p·* have to escape from their houses
    353–10   *P·* give me too much attention
Ret. 73–13   less to me than it is to *p·* who
Un. 7–15   *P·* are now living who can
Pul. 15– 6   *p·* like you better when you
    56–16   * It makes *p·* better and happier.
’00. 2– 4   *p·* most interested in this old-new
Hea. 18– 5   *P·* are willing to put new wine into
My. 47–11   * *p·* the world over have been
    51–13   * on the part of the *p·*,
    114– 9   why point the *p·* to the lives of
    171–21   * *p·* who were assembled on the lawn
    321–31   * *p·* who knew you years before

People and Patriot
Pul. 77–23   * *P·* and *P·*, Concord, N. H.,

peopled
Mis. 150–23   *p·* with living witnesses
Ret. 91–24   *p·* with holy messages from the
Un. 28– 9   *p·* with demons or angels,
Rud. 4– 3   *p·* with perfect beings,

people's
Mis. 62– 2   other *p·* individuality, health,
    112–27   exaggerating sense of other *p·*.
    119– 4   aiding other *p·* devices
    249– 8   appropriated other *p·* manuscripts
    287–32   attempts to steady other *p·* altars,
    290– 2   Let other *p·* marriage relations *alone:*
    291–10   other *p·* thoughts and actions.
    317–28   penalty for other *p·* faults ;
    357– 1   trafficking in other *p·* business,
Ret. 89–26   upon other *p·* thoughts,
’00. 8–11   he may steal other *p·* good
Peo. 2– 4   due to the *p·* improved views
    2–20   Proportionately as the *p·* belief
    2–26   constantly before the *p·* mind,
My. 147–16   the *p·* sense of C. S.
    233–14   the effects of other *p·* sins

peoples
Mis. 81–30   *p·* the mind with spiritual
    244–27   for all *p·* and for all time ;
    307–22   easily-besetting sin of all *p·*.
Ret. 26– 9   demonstrated for all time and *p·*
Pan. 12–14   it showeth to all *p·* the way
    13–21   Then shall all nations, *p·*,
’00. 10–13   laws of nations and *p·*,
    10–20   weak provinces, or *p·*.
’02. 2–10   It is purifying all *p·*.
Peo. 6–28   *p·* are characterized by
Po. 1 –15   insignificance that *p·* earth,
My. 178–10   and prepared for all *p·*.
    190–24   in order that all *p·*, in all ages,
    265–12   individuals, *p·*, and nations.
    265–30   reaching out to all classes and *p·*
    279–14   Had all *p·* one Mind,
    281–10   brotherhood of all *p·*
    284– 3   to help human purpose and *p·*,
    284–27   quarrels between nations and *p·*.
    286– 5   prayed that all the *p·* on earth
    291–12   uniting the interests of all *p·* ;
    291–31   liberty of other *p·*

Peoria
Pul. 56– 4   * Scranton, *P·*, Atlanta, Toronto,
My. 81–16   * “Dresden !” “*P·* !” they cried.

Peoria (Ill.) *Journal*
My. 96–24   * [*P·* (*I·*.) *J·*]

pepper
Mis. 348–20   capsicum (red *p·*) ;

per
Rud. 1–15   *p·* (through) and *sonare* (to sound).
My. 234– 1   fifty telegrams *p·* holiday

Per Capita Tax
Man. 44–12   *P· C· T·*.
    44–13   shall pay annually a *p· c· t·*

perceive
Mis. 53–28   abstract or difficult to *p·*.
    179–29   then we can *p·* Truth,
    182– 5   as many as *p·* man's actual existence
Pul. 32– 7   * *p·* that she had the temperament
    35– 6   * Mrs. Eddy came to *p·* that Christ's
Rud. 6–21   so far as you *p·* and understand
Pan. 11– 1   to *p·* the real man,

perceive
Hea. 8– 9   *p·* the meaning of the context,
    8–12   slow to *p·* individual advancement ;
    13–24   You can readily *p·* this
My. 242– 8   Unless you fully *p·* that you are
    275– 6   so-called senses do not *p·* this fact

perceived
Ret. 76–12   *p·* a light beyond what others saw.
    94– 1   Having *p·*, in advance of others,
My. 40–26   * She has illustrated what the poet *p·*

perceives
Mis. 374–29   *p·* a semblance between the thinker

per cent
My. 227–31   C. S. cures a larger *p· c·* of

percentage
No. 32–25   diminishing the *p·* of sin.
’00. 8–18   We lose a *p·* due to our activity
’01. 29–28   * “With this *p·*,” students wrote me,

perception
Mis. 15–10   give the true *p·* of God
    28– 4   *P·* by the five personal senses
    139–25   but to my spiritual *p·*,
    228–23   *p·*, sensation, and consciousness
Ret. 28–14   a *p·* of and dependence on
Un. 20–18   awake to the *p·* of God
    61–12   Human *p·*, advancing toward
Pul. 35–18   a *p·* of and dependence on
Rud. 3– 9   to the *p·* of mortal sense,
My. 37–22   * through your spiritual *p·*
    113–22   and have a clear *p·* of it.
    149–19   to have a clear *p·* of divine justice,

perceptions
Un. 46–11   subordinate the fleshly *p·*

perceptive
Hea. 14–20   the spiritual sense or *p·* faculty

perchance
Mis. 9–19   *P·*, having tasted its tempting wine,
Pul. 3–26   *P·* some one of you may say,
Po. 66–14   Might cheer it, *p·*, when she sings.

per contra
Mis. 24–20   *P· c·*, Mind and man are immortal ;
    254–21   *P· c·*, it is the mortal mind sense
My. 119–11   *P· c·*, C. S. destroys such tendency.

perdition
Mis. 113–14   carried to the depths of *p·*
Ret. 14– 8   converted and rescued from *p·* ;
’02. 3–30   the first lie and leap into *p·*

perfect
Mis. 1– 9   ordeal of a *p·* Christianity,
    5– 8   produce *p·* health and *p·* morals
    5–26   always *p·* in God, in Truth,
    6–18   we exist in God, *p·*,
    6–20   Truth, and Love must be *p·* ;
    10–21   strength made *p·* in weakness,
    21– 4   *p·* unity with Christ's Sermon
    46–29   man is *p·* even as the Father,
    46–30   his divine Principle, is *p·*.
    50–22   “Be ye therefore *p·* ;” — *Matt.* 5 : 48.
    66–17   to discern God's *p·* ways
    79– 7   man was, and is, God's *p·* likeness,
    79–17   If the great cause is *p·*,
    79–17   its effect is *p·* also ;
    79–22   *p·* and unfallen likeness,
    82–16   whose law is *p·* and infinite.
    85–14   “Be ye therefore *p·*,— *Matt.* 5 : 48.
    85–15   which is in heaven is *p·*.” — *Matt.* 5 : 48.
    86– 2   individual and spiritual are *p·* ;
    98– 2   *p·* model should be held in mind,
    138–15   lesson of C. S. is love, *p·* love,
    138–16   love made *p·* through the cross.
    176– 3   healing, and peace, and *p·* love.
    184–14   power to be *p·* which he possesses,
    186–20   his *p·* Principle, God,
    188– 3   Man is as *p·* now,
    195–19   That *p·* syllogism of Jesus
    213–16   may *p·* their own lives
    232– 6   *p·* Principle of things ;
    232– 9   *p·* and practical Christianity
    286–30, 31   man is *p·* even as the Father is *p·*,
    362– 5   wherein God and man are *p·*,
    375–23   * In other words, the art is *p·*.
    376– 1   * the art is *p·*.
Ret. 24–21   in *p·* scientific accord with divine
    78– 7   scientific practice makes *p·*,
    91–20   his own *p·* understanding.
Un. 3–21   is *p·* being, or consciousness.
    5– 5   toward the *p·* thought divine.
    10–17, 18   eternally *p·*, because He is *p·*,
    24–21   must be spiritual, *p·*, eternal.
    40–15   than they can become *p·* by
    42–13   is as *p·* and immortal now,
    49– 9   ignorant of sin as is the *p·* Maker.

perfect

Un.	51– 9	gained through Christ as *p·* manhood.
	53–22	as a *p·* child of God.
Pul.	26–18	* of fine range and *p·* tone.
	34–23	in *p·* scientific accord with the divine
	49–30	* grounds and farm in *p·* order,
	54– 6	* *p·* harmony with natural law,
	54–14	* *p·* obedience to the laws of .
	54–26	* most *p·* obtainable environment,
	62–16	* so that the harmony is *p·*.
	81–21	* as a *p·* harp,
Rud.	4– 3	peopled with *p·* beings,
	7– 9	*p·* and immortal Mind.
No.	30–12	this *p·* law is ever present
	31–18	*p·* consciousness is attained.
	41–14	life of Christ is the *p·* example ;
Pan.	9–11	'' Be ye therefore *p·*,— *Matt. 5 : 48.*
	9–12	which is in heaven is *p·* ;''— *Matt. 5 : 48.*
	11–11	Governed by . . . man is *p·*.
	12– 1	''Be ye therefore *p·*,''— *Matt. 5 : 48.*
'00.	4–10	*p·* worship of one God.
	4–16	only *p·* religion is divine Science,
	14–16	following the more *p·* way,
'01.	8–15	''Be ye therefore *p·*,— *Matt. 5 : 48.*
	8–16	which is in heaven is *p·*''— *Matt. 5 : 48.*
Hea.	15–12	to any one's *p·* satisfaction
Peo.	2–26	This more *p·* idea,
	7–29	become more or less *p·* as
My.	11– 2	* followers of the *p·* Christ,
	38– 2	* every *p·* gift cometh from above,
	38–21	* in almost *p·* time.
	41–18	* maintains the *p·* standard of truth
	75–12	* So *p·* have been all the
	78–22	* congregation singing in *p·* unison.
	78–24	* were found to be *p·*.
	85–31	* one of the few *p·* sky-lines
	111–13	spiritual status of a *p·* life
	113–19	to *p·* His praise.
	123– 8	continue to urge the *p·* model
	150–14	never weary of struggling to be *p·*
	159–14	*p·* love of God and man.
	179–21	Christianity as the *p·* ideal.
	187– 9	*p·* path wherein to walk,
	187– 9	the *p·* Principle whereby
	187–10	*p·* law of God.
	205–27	demonstrated by *p·* rules ;
	207–11	* more *p·* manifestation of the truth
	242– 9	you are the child of God, hence *p·*,
	253– 4	brings to light the *p·* original man
	290–14	keep him in perfect peace,— *Isa. 26 : 3.*

(*see also* **eternal, Love, man, Mind**)

perfected

Mis.	232–19	having *p·* in Science that
Pul.	8–22	Thou has *p·* praise.''— *Matt. 21 : 16.*
'01.	2– 5	the *p·* Science of healing
'02.	17–15	duty done and life *p·*,
Po.	22–17	A life *p·*, strong and calm.

perfectibility

Mis.	98–21	God and the *p·* of man.
Pan.	11–27	man's unfallen spiritual *p·*.
'00.	7–15	the Science of *p·*

perfecting

My.	342–23	*p·* of man stated scientifically.''

perfection

and demonstration
Ret.	57–29	*p·* and demonstration of metaphysical,

cannot force
My.	344–26	cannot force *p·* on the world.

collapse from
No.	26–15	no more relapse or collapse from *p·*,

divine
Mis.	320–12	infant idea of divine *p·*

fitness for
Un.	11–25	in order to mature fitness for *p·*

in art
Mis.	232– 7	pushing towards *p·* in art,

in churches
No.	41–13	to look for *p·* in churches

infinite
Un.	16– 1	man bows to the infinite *p·*
My.	103–12	Infinite *p·* is unfolded

is normal
Mis.	104–13	According to C. S., *p·* is normal,

less than
Pan.	11–20	with something less than *p·*

likeness of
My.	262– 2	image, idea, or likeness of *p·*

man's
Mis.	186–31	the lost sense of man's *p·*,

maximum of
Mis.	232–17	maximum of *p·* in all things.

mental
Mis.	234–25	physical and mental *p·*,

perfection

method of
Hea.	14–26	Principle and method of *p·*,

nearer
My.	342–32	will advance nearer *p·*.''

of all things
My.	52–15	* does bring out the *p·* of all things,

of living
'02.	2– 7	sanity and *p·* of living,

of man
Mis.	173–24	The *p·* of man is intact ;

of the rule
Mis.	233–25	*p·* of the rule of C. S.

original
My.	262– 5	its spotless purity and original *p·*.

person and
No.	20– 2	His person and *p·* are

physical
'01.	1–15	mental and physical *p·*.

point of
My.	242– 6	neither behind the point of *p·* nor

power and
Mis.	189–18	power and *p·* of a released sense of
Ret.	27–27	increases in power and *p·*

practicality of
My.	182–32	prove the practicality of *p·*,

proved to
No.	38– 1	Jesus proved to *p·*,

pure
Mis.	343–17	their pure *p·* shall appear

Soul's
My.	344–15	gradual approaches to Soul's *p·*.''

spiritual
Mis.	42–26	exists only in spiritual *p·*,
My.	345–23	near a state of spiritual *p·*.

state of
Mis.	14– 8	his original state of *p·*,
	78–25	*Has man fallen from a state of p·?*

strives for
My.	272– 2	actively strives for *p·*,

trifles make
My.	123–29	* ''trifles make *p·*,''

ultimatum of
Mis.	79–10	man is the ultimatum of *p·*,

unto
My.	128–3	let us go on unto *p·* ;— *Heb. 6 : 1.*

would dethrone
No.	21–13	philosophy would dethrone *p·*,

Mis.	85–11	*P·*, the goal of existence,
	187– 7	the *p·* of mind and body,
Ret.	80–26	*p·* and an unbroken friendship.
Un.	7–20	an acknowledgment of the *p·* of
No.	10–27	harmony, perpetuity, and *p·*,
My.	103– 1	*p·* is reluctantly seen
	269– 5	pledged to innocence, purity, *p·*.

perfections

Ret.	52– 5	should shelter its *p·* from the
Un.	43– 1	eternal being and its *p·*,

perfectly

Mis.	243– 2	cured her *p·* of this habit,
Pul.	54– 8	* The *p·* natural is the *p·* spiritual.
	54–15	* He understood the law *p·*,
	72–18	* and yet have been *p·* well.''
	73–21	* *p·* versed in all their beliefs
My.	32– 9	* Mrs. Conant could be heard *p·*

perfectness

Mis.	273–14	in the bonds of love and *p·*,
Ret.	76–19	unity of good and bond of *p·*.
My.	164–23	It is *unity*, the bond of *p·*,
	249– 4	correct sin through your own *p·*.

perfidy

Mis.	226– 8	chapter sub-title
	226–25	*P·* of an inferior quality,

perform

Mis.	40–11	*p·* as instantaneous cures
	54–25	to *p·* as great miracles
Man.	28–16	*p·* the functions of their
	28–21	to *p·* his office faithfully ;
	29– 4	to *p·* his official duties.
	29–12	or *p·* their functions faithfully.
My.	42–18	* endeavor to *p·* this service
	60–28	* the interesting part I had to *p·*
	205–10	* His wonders to *p·* ;
	241– 1	* to *p·* this important work.
	249–25	to *p·* this important function.
	288–19	to *p·* the functions of Spirit,
	303–30	*p·* the functions of foreshadowing

performance

Man.	77–14	*p·* of their several offices
No.	7–19	strict *p·* of each one of them.
My.	42–28	* in the *p·* of her daily tasks.

performances
Mis. 243–17 unbecoming a mortal's poor *p·*.
performed
Mis. 242–14 I *p·* more difficult tasks
244– 5 *p·* by divine power,
Man. 49–21 ceremony shall be *p·* by a clergyman
Ret. 19–23 *p·* their obligations most faithfully.
Pul. 73–14 * and this duty she faithfully *p·*.
Hea. 14–19 the most arduous task I ever *p·*.
My. 95–20 * telling of miracles *p·*
331– 2 *p·* their obligations
336– 9 * faithfully *p·* their obligation
performs
Mis. 260–27 *p·* the vital functions of Truth
Ret. 86–22 each man who *p·* his own part.
perfume
Ret. 18–10 beauty and *p·* from buds burst away,
'00. 8– 8 a *p·* or a poison,
Po. 46–12 And yield its beauty and *p·*
63–20 beauty and *p·* from buds burst away,
perfumed
Mis. 396–25 in raptured song, With love *p·*.
Pul. 18– 9 in raptured song, With love *p·*.
Po. 12– 9 in raptured song, With love *p·*.
perfume-laden
Mis. 332–15 many-hued blossoms, *p·* breezes,
Pergamene
'00. 13–22 The *P·* church consisted of the
Pergamos
'00. 13–17 city of *P·* was devoted to a sensual
perhaps
Mis. 35– 9 *P·* the following words
120–24 once in three years is *p·* as often as
125–26 oftener, *p·*, the controversies
126–15 *P·* our church is not yet quite
161–20 owing in part, *p·*, to the Jewish law
197– 5 than many others, *p·*,
262–28 *P·* it is even selfish in me
207–13 that *p·* he has never visited.
Un. 1– 1 *P·* no doctrine of C. S.
Pul. 28–18 * in *p·* equal measure to its use of
46–24 * though *p·* with an unusual zest,
48–25 * is *p·* one of her characteristics,
No. 14–20 *p·* more than any other religious sect,
'01. 28– 9 *p·* none lived a more devout
Hea. 19–21 he is impatient *p·*, or doubts
My. 65– 4 * *p·* the largest ever held in the
82–30 * except *p·* those living in the
92–10 * worthy of *p·* even more interest
96–16 * *p·* the most remarkable,
135– 8 *P·* you already know that I have
319–17 some facts which *p·* have
343– 7 You would ask, *p·*, whether my
peril
Mis. 80–12 If the patient is in *p·*,
323–10 descent and ascent are beset with *p·*,
Ret. 45– 6 organization has its value and *p·*,
periled
Po. 71– 7 *p·* right, Rescued by the
perilous
Mis. 110–26 dared the *p·* defense of Truth,
perils
Mis. 131–31 with *p·* past and victories won.
period
advance of the
Mis. 359–21 were in advance of the *p·*
concession to the
Mis. 91– 7 let it be in concession to the *p·*,
demanded it
Mis. 298–18 implied that the *p·* demanded it.
end of the
Pul. 73–10 * at the end of the *p·* came from
enlightened
My. 249–16 that at this enlightened *p·*
eventful
Mis. 162– 3 third event of this eventful *p·*,
every
Mis. 192–23 belongs to every *p·* ;
Ret. 35–16 his true followers in every *p·*,
indefinite
Hea. 4–16 for an indefinite *p·*,
mediæval
'00. 4–13 greater than in the mediæval *p·* ;
mental
Mis. 204– 6 This mental *p·* is sometimes chronic,
notable
Pul. 55–10 * *p·* notable for her emancipation
of captivity
'00. 3–21 during the *p·* of captivity
of doubt
Mis. 237–19 This is a *p·* of doubt, inquiry,

period
parable of the
Mis. 251–26 learn a parable of the *p·*,
religious
Mis. 307–15 this revolutionary religious *p·*,
Renaissance
Pul. 26–10 * lamp stand of the Renaissance *p·*
restricted
Mis. 244–28 a privileged class or a restricted *p·*,
Revolutionary
Ret. 2–10 prior to the Revolutionary *p·*.
senior
Mis. 235–25 superstitions of a senior *p·*.
some
Ret. 94– 4 At some *p·* and in some way
Pul. 13–3 Every mortal at some *p·*,
successive
Mis. 26– 4 Each successive *p·* of progress
that
My. 152– 3 At that *p·*, the touch of Jesus'
this
Mis. 4– 4 At this *p·* there is a marked
12–17 Mortal mind at this *p·* mutely works
48–22 sudden deaths at this *p·*.
195–14 ministry of healing at this *p·*.
237–16 This *p·* is not essentially one of
253–14 This *p·* is big with events.
253–27 Do the children of this *p·* dream of
274–22 At this *p·*, 1888, those quill-drivers
286–15 To abolish marriage at this *p·*,
317– 8 to demonstrate, as this *p·* demands,
337– 1 I discovered and founded at this *p·*
Ret. 27– 1 I wrote also, at this *p·*,
82–14 At this *p·* my students should
94–30 In this *p·* and the forthcoming
Pul. 14– 3 growing occultism of this *p·*.
No. 9–25 More . . . than this *p·* comprehends.
Pun. 2– 2 At this *p·* of enlightenment,
Peo. 3–18 on the thoughts of men at this *p·*
11–25 learned quacks of this *p·*
My. 54–22 * A record of this *p·* reads,
131– 6 For this hour, for this *p·*,
136– 3 At this *p·* my demonstration of
159–12 At this *p·*, the greatest man or
258– 6 This *p·*, so fraught with opposites,
285–14 men and women of this *p·*
woman of the
Mis. 253– 6 not enough the new woman of the *p·*

Mis. 26– 5 is a *p·* more humane and spiritual,
162– 9 a *p·* of such wonderful spiritual
Hea. 14– 1 occupying the field for a *p·* ;
periodical
Mis. 4–17 a *p·* devoted to this work
7–21 A *p·* of our own will counteract
302–24 proprietor of the first C. S. *p·* ;
Man. 98– 8 promptly published by the *p·*
My. 304–18 sole editor of that *p·*.
333–32 * This *p·* then forthwith strives to
periodicals
Mis. 301– 7 editors of pamphlets and *p·*
Man. 44–16 Church *P·*.
44–18 *p·* which are the organs of this
44–20 these *p·* are ably edited
47–22 testimonials which appear in the *p·*
48–22 The *p·* of our denomination
48–25 they may quote from other *p·*
65– 2 already used in our *p·*.
81–14 *P·*.
81–14 *P·* which shall at any time be
82–11 removed from our *p·*
97–20 by *p·* or circulated literature
My. 42–10 * helpful contributors to our *p·*,
136–20 editor-in-chief of the C. S. *p·*,
173– 9 C. S. *p·* had given notice
250–13 send to the Editor of our *p·* notice of
272–29 * outside of the C. S. *p·*,
326–12 I send for publication in our *p·*
353–10 given the name to all the C. S. *p·*.
periods
Mis. 12–21 at former *p·* in human history
205–24 unites all *p·* in the divine
Ret. 45– 7 requisite only in the earliest *p·*
49– 5 working out their *p·* of organization,
Pul. 13–25 but how many *p·* of torture
'02. 4–23 applicable to all *p·*
Peo. 6–28 *P·* and peoples are characterized
Po. v– 2 * *were written at different p·*
My. 279–10 uniting all *p·* in the design of
perish
Mis. 204– 4 cries, "Save, or I *p·*."— *see Matt.* 8 : 25.
213–24 they shall never *p·*,— *John* 10 : 28.
358– 7 State honors *p·*,
390–24 Ne'er *p·* young, like things of earth,

perish
Ret. 64–17 like the beasts that *p*.''— *Psal.* 49 : 20.
Un. 18– 1 God must *p*·, if He knows evil
40– 6 belief of life in matter, must *p*·,
Pul. 7–20 oppressive priesthood must *p*·,
'00. 7–26 we cry, ''Save, or I *p*·!''— *see Matt.* 8 : 25.
'01. 10–26 shall be nothing left to *p*·
'02. 18– 8 only to mock, wonder, and *p*·.
Po. 56– 3 Ne'er *p*· young, like things of earth,

perishable
Mis. 19–29 sinful, material, and *p*·,
103– 3 which say that . . . substance is *p*·.
My. 273–26 five personal senses are *p*· :

perishing
Mis. 17–29 *p*· pleasure and accumulating pains

perishless
Pul. 9–10 warmed also our *p*· hope,

permanence
Mis. 47– 7 glory and *p*· of Spirit :
74–27 power and *p*· of Spirit.
126– 1 from unsettled questions to *p*·,
160– 1 power and *p*· of affection
194– 9 *p*· of Christ's command
196–17 sweet, sacred sense and *p*·
206– 3 from flux to *p*·, from foul to pure,
287–21 giving them strength and *p*·.
320–30 in token of purity and *p*·.
352– 1 it is bereft of *p*· and peace.
Un. 41–15 sacred sense of the *p*· of
'01. 12–15 *p*· of Christ's command
My. 45–32 * material type of Truth's *p*·.
177–15 possibilities and *p*· of Life.

permanency
My. 94–16 * the apparent *p*· of C. S.

permanent
Mis. 110–28 how *p*· that which God calls good.
268–28 Right alone is irresistible, *p*·,
Un. 8–12 All that is beautiful . . . is *p*·.
13–18 that which is not *p*·,
Pul. 86–27 * the *p*· pastor of this church,
'01. 3–18 Mind, a *p*·, fundamental,

permanently
Ret. 82–12 locate *p*· in one section,
My. 51–18 * for a few Sundays if not *p*·.''

permeate
Mis. 223–20 May divine Love so *p*· the
Ret. 80–17 *p*· justice and Love,
My. 222–24 religion shall *p*· our laws.

permeated
Mis. 205–21 *p*· with eternal life, holiness, heaven.
My. 265–25 *p*· with divine Love,

permeates
Mis. 204–23 *p*· with increased harmony all the

permission
Mis. 299–24 Did he give you *p*· to do this,
300–25 I gave *p*· to cite, . . . from my work
302–18 till this *p*· was *withdrawn*,
Man. 43–16 quotations . . . without her *p*·,
71–24 her *p*· to publish them as
Ret. 40– 7 I asked *p*· to see her.
71–19 without the *p*· of man or God,
75–25 no *p*· in the gospel for
Po. vii–10 * *acknowledgment*, . . . *of this p*·,
My. 134–26 * ''*P*·'' has been secured from
173–31 foresight in granting *p*·,
254–17 * May we have *p*· to print,
298–10 my *p*· to publish . . . this work.
322–18 * *p*· to enter the next Primary class
335–21 * refused *p*· to take the remains to
351– 2 * With our Leader's kind *p*·,

permit
Mis. 11–28 since they *p*· me no other way,
13– 3 *p*· me to exercise these sentiments
84– 6 thereby hasten or *p*· it.
313– 2 *P*· me to say that your editorial
Man. 43– 6 nor *p*· his patients . . . to use them,
73–12 provided its rules so *p*·,
73–18 if the rules . . . so *p*·.
87–11 or cause or *p*· others to solicit,
Pul. 87–14 *p*· me, respectfully, to decline their
My. 154–16 *p*· me to congratulate this little
172–11 *P*· me to present to you
236– 7 *p*· me to make the *amende honorable*
271–29 to your question *p*· me to say
275–13 *P*· me to say, the report . . . is dead,
331–18 * will you *p*· me, in behalf of

permitted
Mis. 249–14 None are *p*· to remain in my
262– 2 wherein it is *p*· to enter,
Pul. 58–12 * pictures we are *p*· to publish,
'01. 16–22 if now it is *p*· license,

permitted
My. 69–12 * within . . . where conditions *p*· it
256– 8 that I be *p*· total exemption

permitting
Pul. 54–24 * *p*· only the father and mother,

permits
'02. 19–30 cup that our Father *p*· us.

perpetrator
Mis. 222–16 action on the mind of the *p*·,
'01. 20–21 sooner or later cause the *p*·,

perpetual
Mis. x– 1 coloring glory of *p*· bloom ;
29– 4 that his promise is *p*·.
56–16 mingling in *p*· warfare
72–25 is in *p*· harmony.
79–16 *p*· in Life, Truth, and Love.
83– 3 *p*· idea of inexhaustible good.
85–17 *p*·, spiritual, individual existence.
91– 7 not as a *p*· or indispensable
140–31 a *p*· type of the divine
269–13 *p*· freshness in relation to
278–24 *p*· instruction of my students might
330– 5 *p*· springtide wherein no arrow
Ret. 13– 8 *p*· banishment from God.
Un. 41–28 *p*· disagreement with Spirit.
No. 11– 5 Man has a *p*· individuality ;
'02. 8–22 it prompts *p*· goodness,
Hea. 2–28 sprinkled . . . with *p*· incense.

perpetually
Mis. 206–21 *p*· repeating this diapason
Ret. 73–19 *p*· warns you of ''personality,''
74– 2 *p*· egotistical sensibility.
Un. 21– 5 *p*· arguing with ourselves ;
Pul. 9– 8 kindle *p*· its fires.
59– 1 * lamp, kept *p*· burning
Hea. 15–15 *p*· at war with this Mind,
My. 188– 5 shall be there *p*·.''— *I Kings* 9 : 3.

perpetuate
Mis. 91–14 *p*· no ceremonials except
98–17 We come to strengthen and *p*· our
Pul. 21–20 To *p*· a cold distance between
No. 5–16 restore health and *p*· life,
21–19 *p*· the supposed power and reality of

perpetuated
Mis. 244–10 have those conditions . . . been *p*·
Ret. 1–16 who *p*· her mother's name.

perpetuates
Mis. 46– 1 *p*· the belief or faith in evil.
346–16 *p*· faith in evil ;

perpetuating
My. 261–13 aids in *p*· purity

perpetuity
Ret. 35–24 *p*· of Jesus' command,
No. 10–27 Eternal harmony, *p*·, and
My. 45– 3 * will result in its *p*·

perplexed
Ret. 8–11 my mother was *p*· and anxious.
Pul. 8– 6 *p*· condition of our nation's

perplexing
Un. 9–18 true solution of the *p*· problem

perplexities
Mis. 131–20 *p*· and difficulties which the

perplexity
My. 214–18 relieving the questioners' *p*·,

perquisite
My. 189– 7 affords even me a *p*· of joy.

per se
Mis. 109–21 Their mental state . . . *p*· *s*·;

persecute
Mis. 8–23 revile you, and *p*· you,— *Matt.* 5 : 11.
11–21 who *p*· and despitefully use one,
Ret. 29– 5 and *p*· you.''— *Matt.* 5 : 44.
No. 32–24 great evil to . . . *p*· a Cause
'01. 3– 4 revile you, and *p*· you,— *Matt.* 5 : 11.
33–28 to *p*· another in advance of it.
'02. 11–22 revile you, and *p*· you,— *Matt.* 5 : 11.
My. 104–30 revile you, and *p*· you,— *Matt.* 5 : 11.
300–30 why *p*· it?
316– 7 revile you, and *p*· you,— *Matt.* 5 : 11.

persecuted
Mis. 8–25 so *p*· they the prophets— *Matt.* 5 : 12.
Pul. 7– 8 praised and *p*· in Boston,
13–28 *p*· the woman— *Rev.* 12 : 13.
'01. 9–13 healing power . . . that is *p*· to-day,
28–17 *p*· from city to city.
30– 1 Christian Scientists are *p*· even as
'02. 11–25 so *p*· they the prophets— *Matt.* 5 : 12.
My. 103–12 Science, until understood, has been *p*·
270– 2 so *p*· they the prophets— *Matt.* 5 : 12.

persecuting
'02. 10–28   P· a reformer is like sentencing a
My. 105–30   but they must refrain from p·

persecution
Ret. 45–25   Christianity has withstood . . . p·.
    54–11   gaining the end through p·
    65– 8   p·, tobacco, and alcohol
No. 14–25   frozen dogmas, persistent p·,
    34–12   baptized in the purification of p·
    41– 9   on account of p·,
    44–23   the horrors of religious p·.
'00. 10– 5   Conflict and p· are the truest signs
'02. 1– 2   for His people in times of p·
My. v–10   * threatens to supersede p·,
    127–19   should thank God for p·
    167–29   claims of envy, jealousy, or p·.
    191– 4   Be patient towards p·.
    191– 7   P· is the weakness of tyrants
    221– 2   price . . . in a material age is p·,
    224–32   under the present p·
    245–14   manifested in ignorance, p·,

persecutions
Mis. 199–12   in necessities, in p·,— II Cor. 12 : 10.
    201–20   "reproaches" and "p·,"— II Cor. 12 : 10.

persecutors
Un. 58– 6   His p· said mockingly,

perseverance
Mis. 340–27   are miracles of patience and p·.

Persia
Ret. 3– 3   position of ambassador to P·.

persist
Mis. 220–28   and p· in this action of mind
Man. 52–22   If a member . . . p· in working against
My. 160–20   a hell for all who p· in

persisted
Mis. 113–22   mental malpractice, if p· in,
Ret. 14–22   he p· in the assertion that I

persistent
Mis. 118–27   obedience crowns p· effort
    230– 2   depends upon p· effort,
    301–16   must not leave p· plagiarists
    339–11   made more industrious and p
    340– 6   Only by p·, unremitting,
Ret. 6–28   by his p· energy
No. 14–25   frozen dogmas, p· persecution,
My. 116–20   p· pursuit of his or her person

persistently
Mis. 326–22   those who p· rejected him,
Man. 83 18   p· and patiently counsel
Ret. 75–12   those who p· misunderstand
My. 148– 2   Faithfully and more than ever p·,
    306– 1   p· misrepresents my character,

persisting
Mis. 184–18   p· in believing that he is sick

persists
Mis. 184–20   yet p· in evil,
    220–11   He p· in this course until
Man. 56– 4   if said member p· in this offense,

Person
Pan. 8– 7   one the divine, infinite P·,
'01. 3– 7   chapter sub-title
    4– 1   Principle or P· stands for God
    4–19   He is the infinite P·,
    4–29   Love, more frequently than P·,
    5– 3   defined strictly by the word P·,
    5– 3   for if P· is God,
    5– 4   does not P· here lose the nature of
    5– 7   Christian Scientist's sense of P·
    5–20   God is infinite Spirit or P·,
    5–28   The theological God as a P·
    6– 4   Who says the God of theology is a P·,
    6–10   a finite or an infinite P·?
    6–11   Is He one P·, or three
    6–13   except He be a P·,
    6–14   this P· contains three persons :
    6–22   God is P· in the . . . scientific sense
    6–27   God as the infinite P· ;
    6–28   idea of Him as a finite P·
    7– 6   individuality of the infinite P·
    7–19   as well as infinite P·,
    11–24   namely, that God is a P·,
My. 109–14   operative divine Principle (or P·,
    109–15   This infinite P· we know not of by
    116–12   If God is one and God is P·,
    116–12   then P· is infinite ;
    117–29   to seek the one divine P·,
    192–13   the infinite P· whom
    225–22   Principle, Love, the infinite P·.

person (see also person's)
and power
No. 24– 2   evil loses all place, p·, and power.

person
and thing
    Un. 45– 6   mind and matter, p· and thing?"
another
    Mis. 180–11   another p·, more material,
    190–21   cast out of another p· ;
    No. 15–16   cast out of another p·.
    22–21   out of another p·,
    Peo. 4–12   and evil another p·,
    My. 123–14   by the courtesy of another p·
any particular
    My. 346–24   * had in mind any particular p·
assailed the
    Po. vi–15   and assailed the p· of
away from
    My. 119–30   Truth that leadeth away from p·
corporeal
    Mis. 152–11   I, as a corporeal p·, am not in
defining
    Rud. 2–10   right in defining p· as
definitions of
    Rud. 2– 1   definitions of p·, as given by
demoralizes the
    Ret. 71–28   demoralizes the p· who does this,
each
    Mis. 224–13   each p· has a different history,
    My. 12–10   * Each p· interested must remember,
    72– 1   * each p· could hear what was said.
event or
    Mis. 197–17   any historical event or p·.
every
    My. 71–24   * every p· seated in the auditorium,
evil
    Mis. 284–22   neither an evil claim nor an evil p·
finite
    Mis. 217–18   and that Deity is a finite p·
    308–31   a finite p· is not the model
God as a
    No. 20– 4   and of God as a p·,
    Hea. 3–12   the qualities of God as a p·,
God is not a
    '01. 3– 9   their God is not a p·.
healed
    Ret. 34–17   A p· healed by C. S. is
her own
    My. 273– 4   * vindicate in her own p· the value
His
    No. 20– 2   His p· and perfection are
    '01. 5–29   explain both His p· and nature,
his or her
    My. 116–21   pursuit of his or her p· is.
human
    Mis. 78– 4   gave us, through a human p·,
    Rud. 2–13   The human p· is finite ;
    '01. 5–30   Is the human p·, as defined by
incriminating the
    Mis. 283–23   without incriminating the p·
instead of
    Mis. 135– 4   Principle, instead of p·,
    My. 119–14   p·, instead of the Principle
    152– 2   p· instead of Principle,
is defined
    '01. 6– 5   P· is defined differently
is formed
    No. 19–26   P· is formed after the manner of
is man a
    No. 25– 8   chapter sub-title
is meant
    Rud. 2–11   if by p· is meant infinite Spirit.
is not corporeal
    My. 109–15   whose p· is not corporeal,
just
    Mis. 228–16   a kind, true, and just p·,
loved
    Mis. 306–27   it is not . . . a loved p· present ;
man is
    '01. 5–11   Man is p· ;
mind of a
    Mis. 283– 5   to enter the mind of a p·,
more than a
    Mis. 16–20   God is infinitely more than a p·,
    Peo. 13– 6   Divine Being is more than a p·,
my
    My. 118–12   In a call upon my p·,
    138– 9   not needed to protect my p·
my father's
    My. 308–18   My father's p· was erect
no
    Mis. 83–12   No p· can accept another's belief,
    107–30   no p· is or can be a
    Man. 46– 1   No p· shall be a member . . . who
    92–16   No p· shall receive instructions in
    Ret. 70–14   No p· can take the individual place of
    70–15   No p· can compass or fulfil the
    70–16   No p· can take the place of

person
no
'02.   8–11   No *p·* can heal or reform mankind
    19–11   no *p·* can commit an offense against
My. 137–29   No *p·* influenced me to make this
no other
'01.   23–22   no other *p·* has ever
notify a
Man. 68– 1   notify a *p·* who has been a
not the
Hea.   3–28   the Principle is not the *p·*,
    9– 3   is not the *p·* of God,
My. 154– 3   not the *p·* who gives the drug
of either
No. 23–26   through the *p·* of either.
of God
Hea.   5–23   relying not on the *p·* of God
    9– 3   is not the *p·* of God,
of good
No. 22–16   No man hath seen the *p·* of good
of man
No. 29–15   a disparagement of the *p·* of man
Hea.   5–23   relying not on . . . the *p·* of man
of omnipotence
Mis. 96– 9   *p·* of omnipotence and omnipresence
of Spirit
Mis. 181–13   over what is the *p·* of Spirit,
of the infinite
No. 19–13   What the *p·* of the infinite is,
of Truth
Hea.   3–27   cannot tell what is the *p·* of Truth,
one
Mis. 148–12   such as one *p·* might impose on
    219–15   one *p·* feels sick, another feels
    219–26   while one *p·* feels wickedly
    273–31   The work is more than one *p·* can
Man.   3– 8   such as one *p·* might impose on
No.   7–22   between one *p·* and another,
    15–15   three persons in one *p·*,
    15–15   that one *p·* is cast out of
    23–11   not one *p·* was named among them.
    24–12   three persons in one *p·*.
'01.   4–20   not three persons in one *p·*,
    6–12   of three persons as one *p·*,
or a Principle
My. 117– 3   A *p·*, or a Principle?
or a principle
'01. 12–28   a *p·* or a principle,
Principle, not
No. 19–13   Love is Principle, not *p·*.
Principle or
My. 233–28   chapter sub-title
removal of a
Mis. 67–28   the removal of a *p·* to heaven,
same
Man. 25–13   same *p·* is eligible for election
seeing a
My. 206–12   seeing a *p·* in the picture of Jesus,
sick
Mis. 220– 4   suppose that there is a sick *p·*
My. 97– 3   *faith on the part of a sick *p·*,
    276– 4   watches a criminal or a sick *p·*,
such a
My. 319– 1   such a *p·* as the Galilean Prophet,
that
Mis. 145– 9   when that *p·* shall possess these,
the word
Rud.   1–11   The word *p·* affords a large margin
thinking of
My. 233–31   Thinking of *p·* implies that
    234– 2   signalize the thinking of *p·*.
third
Mis. 219–16   A third *p·* knows that if he would
    290– 1   A third *p·* is not a party to the
'01.   8– 7   as the third *p·* in the Godhead?
Peo.   4–14   a third *p·*, called material man,
this
Mis. 290–19   knew that this *p·* was doing well,
turned to the
My. 119–20   He turned to the *p·*, . . . to prove
vile
My. 33–22   vile *p·* is contemned ;— *Psal.* 15 : 4.
worshippers of a
Peo. 13– 4   worshippers of a *p·* have a lower

Mis. 48–23   *Was ever a p· made insane by*
    94– 3   a *p·* who knowingly indulged evil,
    135– 2   *p·* is not in the question of C. S.
    190–20   It could not have been a *p·*
    226–18   was asked what a *p·* could gain by
    248– 9   of the *p·* they called slanderer,
    282–17   the *p·* with whom you hold communion
    285– 2   combating evil only, rather than *p·*.
    290–15   A *p·* wrote to me,
Man. 67–14   if said case relates to the *p·* or
    81– 5   A *p·* who is not accepted by

person
Rud.   1–10   *Do you mean by this that God is a p·?*
    2– 8   we learn that God is . . . not a *p·*,
'00. 10–24   from a *p·* I never saw.
'01.   6– 5   God of C. S. is not a *p·*,
Hea.   4– 9   even as we ask a *p·*
    8– 3   not a *p·* to whom we should pray
Peo.   4–12   God, was named a *p·*,
My. 118–18   A saving faith comes not of a *p·*,
    120– 3   Those who look for me in *p·*,

persona
Rud.   1–14   In Spanish, . . . it is *p·*.

personal
Mis.   9–28   gratification in *p·* pleasure
    35–17   *under your p· instruction?*
    97–20   Is there a *p·* man?
    102– 9   God is not *p·*.
    161–16   the *p·* and the impersonal Jesus.
    161–19   public benefactor, or *p·* Saviour,
    163–22   Only three years a *p·* Saviour !
    165– 1   idea that the *p·* Jesus demonstrated.
    166–30   minutiæ of the life of the *p·* Jesus.
    181– 3   Is man's spiritual sonship a *p·* gift
    181– 8   *p·* requirement of blind obedience
    181–22   it is not, then, a *p·* gift,
    182–23   no *p·* plan of a *p·* Jehovah,
    191–22   supposition of one *p·* devil.
    192– 4   we mean not that he is a *p·* devil,
    214–21   *p·* Jesus' labor in the flesh for
    232–15   *p·* doctrines and dogmas,
    236– 8   giving advice on *p·* topics.
    268– 3   Two *p·* queries give point to
    282–16   *p·* precincts of human thought,
    283–26   he needs no *p·* aid.
    283–32   only *p·* help required
    284–29   I deprecate *p·* animosities
    284–32   I am opposed to all *p·* attacks,
    285– 5   had been *p·* in condemnation.
    291– 4   into *p·* channels, affinities,
    291– 7   demonstrates above *p·* motives,
    305–12   * asking for her *p·* cooperation
    308– 9   *p·* revelators will take their
    322–15   *p·* presence, or word of mine,
    356–28   indispensable to *p·* growth,
Man. 40– 5   animosity nor mere *p·* attachment
    83–12   shall not assume *p·* control of,
    84–20   not by their teachers' *p·* views.
    86– 6   *p·* instruction of Mrs. Eddy,
Ret.   21–25   historic incidents and *p·* events
    25–21   physically *p·* being, like unto man ;
    73–12   *p·* corporeality became less to me
    73–23   or accuse people of being unduly *p·*,
    76–15   so far from being *p·* worship,
    90–11   he gave *p·* instruction,
Un.   5– 9   not to accept any *p·* opinion
Pul. 31–27   * with great claim to *p·* beauty.
    43–28   * that sort of *p·* worship which
    46– 8   * In Mrs. Eddy's *p·* reminiscences,
Rud.   1–16   Blackstone applies the word *p·* to
    2–11   God is *p·*, if by *person* is meant
    7–17   Jesus said of *p·* evil,
    7–19   sensation nor *p·* intelligence.
No.   7– 4   No *p·* considerations should
    19–10   chapter sub-title
    22–15   chapter sub-title
    37–14   as a *p·* and material
'00. 12–28   symbolic, rather than *p·*
'01.   4–17   God is *p·* in a scientific sense,
    7–22   tangible to the *p·* material senses
    11–22   no sermon without *p·* preaching,
    11–25   his personal God !
    31– 6   neither *p·* nor human, but divine.
'02.   9–28   Is it cause for . . . *p·* abuse
    13– 6   of my *p·* property and funds,
    13–10   I receive no *p·* benefit
    3–10   proportion as the *p·* and material
Hea.   3–10   proportion as the *p·* and material
Peo.   2–22   no longer a *p·* tyrant
    3–26   such as dependence on *p·* pardon
    4–13   error that . . . a *p·* devil entered
    13– 3   who believe that God is a *p·* Spirit.
My.   v–12   * mesmerism of *p·* pride
    30–13   * *p·* sacrifices of no mean order ;
    105–32   from *p·* experience I have proved
    113–17   not a disciple of the *p·* Jesus ?
    116– 1   chapter sub-title
    116–13   there is no *p·* worship,
    116–15   darkness of *p·* contagion.
    116–17   based upon *p·* sight or sense.
    116–23   from injustice and *p·* contagion.
    117– 5   A *p·* motive gratified by sense
    117–22   individual, but not *p·*,
    118– 4   the disobedient spread *p·* contagion,
    119–27   of seeing your *p·* self,
    138–11   My *p·* reputation is assailed
    138–12   my students and trusted *p·* friends
    139–20   the *p·* to the impersonal,

personal

My 177– 8 no special need of my p· presence
234– 6 p· worship which C. S. annuls.
238– 7 be determined by p· proof.
290– 6 her p· virtues can never be lost.
321–24 * my p· knowledge of the authorship
321–28 * know of my own p· knowledge
361– 4 to give you p· instruction as to your
301– 7 do not bring . . . into a p· conflict.
(see also God, sense, senses)

personalities

Mis. 337–23 belittled and belied by p·
Un. 21– 6 is not two p·, but one.

personality

absolute
No. 27–23 the absolute p· of God
all
'00. 4–29 all p· and individuality.
My. 205–23 C. S., shorn of all p·,
and presence
My. 143–15 p· and presence of Mary Baker Eddy,
belief in the
Pan. 3–18 Theism is the belief in the p· and
believe in
'01. 5–14 Do Christian Scientists believe in p·?
blind
Mis. 375– 2 p· blind with animality,
centres in the
My. 341–21 * public interest centres in the p· of
claim to
Un. 32–26 the false claim to p·,
clings to
Ret. 73–19 He who clings to p·, or
cling to
Mis. 310– 8 rather than cling to p·
cling to the
My. 116– 7 inclined to cling to the p· of
conceive of
No. 20– 1 so far as he can conceive of p·.
contemplating
Mis. 308–25 contemplating p· impedes spiritual
corporeal
Mis. 102–10 precludes . . . corporeal p·.
Ret. 32– 6 as mere corporeal p·,
57–26 Mistaking . . . for corporeal p·,
67–13 rising above corporeal p·,
74– 8 My own corporeal p· afflicteth me not
76–24 never abuses the corporeal p·,
dual
'01. 8–28 his dual p·, or the spiritual
egotistical
Ret. 73–24 violent and egotistical p·,
element of
Pul. 37–15 * to eliminate the element of p·
evil-doer or
Mis. 284–20 not as an evil-doer or p·.
false
Ret. 73–18 whereby the false p· is laid off.
Un. 44–11 humanity was misled by a false p·,
finite
Mis. 307–29 against the deification of finite p·.
309–14 finite p· of Jesus,
Pan. 8– 8 a human finite p·?
gifted
Pul. 37–24 * a highly gifted p·."
God's
'01. 4–23 should be able to explain God's p·
6–26 God's p· must be as infinite as
his
Mis. 104– 1 Even while his p· was on earth
infinite
Mis. 102–16 Infinite p· must be incorporeal.
interesting
Pul. 31– 6 * is a most interesting p·.
Jesus'
Mis. 103–24 Jesus' p· in the flesh.
limitless
No. 20– 1 Limitless p· is inconceivable.
man's
Pan. 10– 1 takes away man's p·,
10–29 does not degrade man's p·.
11–23 belittles man's p·.
material
Mis. 105– 4 discords of this material p·.
308– 6 clings to my material p·,
309– 4 material p· is an error in premise,
model
'01. 6–17 not after this model of p·
Mrs. Eddy's
Pul. 36–13 * heading
my
Mis. 276– 7 my p· was not big enough to
My. 307–23 Had his remark related to my p·,
my own
'01. 27–22 I have put less of my own p· into

personality

no
Mis. 258–22 indicated no p· that could
notions of
No. 15–12 notions of p· to be found in creeds
of infinite Love
'01. 7– 1 as the p· of infinite Love,
of infinite Spirit
Mis. 219– 5 the p· of infinite Spirit
one
Pul. 37–23 * depending on any one p·.
one's
Mis. 374–28 this ideal is not one's p·.
or form
No. 23– 2 in p·, or form
physical
(see physical)
poor
My. 153–15 from my poor p·.
question of
Mis. 98– 1 making this question of p· a point,
real
Mis. 97–32 the real p· of man.
seeks
My. 153–23 seeks p· for support,
sense of
Mis. 282– 4 sense of p· in God or in man,
sinful
No. 27–20 sinful p·, which we misname man,
spiritual
Mis. 218–31 * recognition of purely spiritual p·
subdivide
Un. 44–16 would multiply and subdivide p·
substituting
Mis. 310– 5 misused by substituting p·
such a
Pul. 32– 9 * such a p·, . . . fascinated the
their
Un. 46–18 an indignity to their p·;
'01. 5–15 their p· is defined spiritually,
theological
'01. 6–25 departure from theological p·
the word
Ret. 74– 4 meaning of the word p·,
this
Mis. 97–30 lost image is not this p·,
190–30 Paul refers to this p· of evil
Un. 46–18 this p· they regarded as
turn away from
Man. 48–20 they shall turn away from p·
unity and
Mis. 217–20 suppositional unity and p·,
warns you of
Ret. 73–20 perpetually warns you of "p·,"
wrong
No. 7–24 reference to right or wrong p·
your
My. 117–17 to get some good out of your p·?

Mis. 33– 9 or that these refer not to p·,
97–29 such must be the p· of him who
181–14 if we recognize infinitude as p·,
282– 4 it is p·, . . . that limits man.
307–11 chapter sub-title
Ret. 73– chapter sub-title
Man. 67–10 from the divine Principle . . . to p·,
No. 23– 3 p· that Jesus condemned as devilish,
24–14 since evil subordinates good in p·.
'01. 24–14 Bishop Berkeley's metaphysics and p·
Hea. 4– 7 Clothing Deity with p·, we limit
My. 117–24 except by sinking . . . in p·.
118–30 would dwarf individuality in p·
191–12 Keep p· out of sight,
271–25 * p· of this remarkable woman.
344–12 preserving individuality and p·

personally

Mis. 132–18 answering p· manifold letters
284–15 for this evil to be treated p·,
284–17 gone p· to the malpractitioner
308– 4 Whosoever looks to me p· for
336–10 if you saw him p·,
359–21 period in which he p· appeared;
381– 6 defendant being present p·
Man. 67–15 p· conferred with her
78–16 p·, or through the Clerk of
87–18 "The less the teacher p· controls
Ret. 84–24 The less the teacher p· controls
Pul. 37–10 * She p· attends to a vast
My. 135– 8 p· attended to my secular affairs,
137–12 attended p· to my secular affairs,
137–14 p· selected all my investments,
138–26 * p· appeared Mary Baker Eddy
147–26 I shall be with you p· very seldom.
219– 1 unless I am p· present.
294–11 if he were p· with us to-day,
315–16 * p· appeared R. D. Rounsevel

personally

My.	325– 2	* you *p·* called to inquire of
	359– 9	not *p·* involved in the affairs of the

personare
Rud.	1–14	Latin verb *p·* is compounded of

personified
Pan.	2–21	conceived as one *p·* nature,
	6–10	chapter sub-title

personne
Rud.	1–13	In French the equivalent word is *p·*.

person's
My.	91–10	* no *p·* spiritual aspirations were
	104–20	A *p·* ignorance of C. S.

persons
actual
No.	31– 9	never actual *p·* or real facts.

all
Mis.	310–27	would cordially invite all *p·*

all grades of
Mis.	371–16	mixing all grades of *p·* is not

and purposes
My.	137–20	*p·* and purposes I have designated

applications from
Ret	47– 7	applications from *p·* desiring to

composed of
Pul.	29–28	* composed of *p·* who had either been

divine
'01.	6– 2	theology's three divine *p·*,

few
Mis.	139–24	wisdom whereof a few *p·* have since

few thousand
My.	91–21	* The few thousand *p·* who followed

fifteen hundred
Pul.	41–17	* to fifteen hundred *p·*,

five thousand
My.	7–18	* will seat four or five thousand *p* ,
	9– 4	* will seat four or five thousand *p·*,
	65–10	* between four and five thousand *p·*.

instructing
My.	223–16	capable of instructing *p·*

many
Mis.	305–16	* contributions from many *p·*
Pul.	33–25	* true that many and many *p·*,

nominated
Man.	79–13	*p·* nominated for said office

no respecter of
'01.	27–21	God is no respecter of *p·*.
My.	128– 9	"no respecter of *p·*." — *Acts* 10 : 34.

number of
Mis.	305–15	* largest number of *p·* possible

of all sects
Man.	59–17	*p·* of all sects and denominations

representative
My.	281–21	views by representative *p·*.

seven
Pul.	37–27	* seven *p·*, including Mrs. Eddy.
	67–26	* was organized by seven *p·*,

several
No.	22–21	That Jesus cast several *p·* out of

six thousand
Pul.	40–18	* aggregating nearly six thousand *p·*,

such
Man.	49–14	The cards of such *p·* may be

ten thousand
My.	141– 7	* attended . . . by ten thousand *p·*

these
My.	91– 2	* that it supplies these *p·*,

three
No.	15–15	believe there are three *p·* in one
	24–12	three *p·* in one person.
'01.	4–20	not three *p·* in one person.
	5– 2	who believes that three *p·* are
	5– 4	he believes three *p·* constitute the
	6–11	Is He one Person, or three *p·*?
	6–12	of three *p·* as one person,
	6–14	and this Person contains three *p·* :
Hea.	3–25	not three *p·* in one,

to receive
My.	138–15	ask me to receive *p·* whom I

twenty-six
My.	76–30	* a membership of twenty-six *p·*.

two
Mis.	290– 3	two *p·* only, should be found within

who are members
Man.	92–22	Only those *p·* who are members

Mis.	48–27	That *p·* have gone away from
	64–12	*P·* contemplating a course at
	79–27	*p· brought before the courts*
	256– 1	*P·* who have been healed by C. S.
Man.	109– 6	No *p·* are eligible to countersign
Ret.	15–22	from *p·* who feelingly testified
	15–27	*p·* who divulged their secret joy
Rud.	15–23	or to *p·* who cannot be addressed

persons
My.	249– 2	but condemn *p·* seldom, if ever.
	313–10	and about *p·* being hired to
	354– 3	alleged misrepresentations by *p·*

perspective
Mis.	373–12	Neither . . . standpoint, nor *p·*
My.	22–26	* appear in their proper *p·*.
	22–29	* proper *p·* of the meaning

perspiration
Mis.	225–26	a cool *p·* spread over it,

perspire
Mis.	7– 3	when they *p·*, they must be

persuade
Ret.	38– 5	All efforts to *p·* him to finish

persuaded
Ret.	94–25	*p·* that only by the modesty
My.	156– 4	*p·* that He is able" — *II Tim.* 1 : 12.
	228–28	*p·* that he is able — *II Tim.* 1 : 12.

persuasion
My.	247–22	not so much eloquence as *tender p·*

persuasive
My.	3–16	*p·* animus, an unerring impetus,

pertain
Mis.	167– 3	*p·* to the spiritual idea,
My.	223– 5	which *p·* to church difficulties

pertaining
Mis.	272– 2	* privileges *p·* thereunto
Man.	18–26	*p·* to "Executive Members"
	93–14	the facts *p·* to the life of
Pan.	9– 9	four first rules *p·* thereto,
My.	199–13	Christian canon *p·* to the hour.

pertinent
My.	107– 6	As a *p·* illustration of the

perturbed
Ret.	13– 9	So *p·* was I by the thoughts

perusal
Mis.	29–21	a *p·* of my volume is healing
Pul.	73–28	* than by a *p·* of it.

pervade
My.	165– 1	promote and *p·* all his success.

pervaded
Pul.	31–17	* was largely thrilled and *p·* by

pervading
Ret.	33–11	I found, in . . . one *p·* secret ;

perverse
My.	222– 5	"O faithless and *p·* — *Matt.* 17 : 17.

perversion
Mis.	291–17	the possible *p·* of C. S.

perversity
Mis.	250– 3	By what strange *p·* is the

pervert
Mis.	66– 9	no human misjudgment can *p·* it ;
	293–16	he will *p·* the rules of C. S.,

perverted
Mis.	3–30	but this method *p·*, is
	293–22	Truth *p·*, in belief, becomes the
	351– 6	arguments which, *p·*, are the
	368–26	*p·*, . . . may become the worst,
Rud.	7–11	would be lost if inverted or *p·*.
My.	213– 3	malicious aim of *p·* mind-power,

perverter
Mis.	302– 6	*p·* preserves in his own consciousness

perverts
Mis.	41– 3	*p·* it, and uses it to accomplish an

pessimism
Mis.	119–18	not an argument either for *p·* or

pessimistic
My.	81– 4	* No *p·* faces there !

pest
My.	104–12	call St. Paul a "*p·*," — see *Acts* 24 : 5.
	104–13	Scientist a "*p·*"? — see *Acts* 24 : 5.
	106–22	Scientist a "*p·*"? — see *Acts* 24 : 5.

pestilence
Mis.	389–12	no fowler, *p·* or pain ;
Po.	5– 1	no fowler, *p·* or pain ;

pestilent
My.	104– 4	a "*p·* fellow," — *Acts* 24 : 5.
	104– 6	this "*p·* fellow." — *Acts* 24 : 5.

pests
Mis.	227– 7	slanderers — those *p·* of society

petals
Mis.	329–23	paint in pink the *p·* of arbutus,

Peter (see also **Peter's**)
Mis.	111–11	like *P·*, they launch into the depths,
	335–22	zealots, who, like *P·*, sleep when the
Un.	1– 5	such as the apostle *P·* declared

Peter
Un. 57–23   P· rejoiced that he was found worthy
Pul. 54–25   * followers, P·, James, and John,
No. 23– 7   Jesus said to P·,
'00.   7–22   like P· we believe in the

I Peter 2: 1–6
My. 17– 3   * Also, 1 P· 2 : 1–6,

Peter's
Mis. 359–19   P· impetuosity was rebuked.

petition
Mis. 212– 1   fulfil the conditions of our p·?
Pul. 22– 6   and in this sacred p· with every
No. 39– 9   vanity influences the p·.
'02.   6–21   all devout desire, virtually p·,

petitions
Mis 127–11   When a hungry heart p· the divine
263–18   constant p· for the same,
310–21   send in their p· to this effect
'01.   7–23   attend their p· to divine Love.
My. 18– 8   When a hungry heart p· the divine
89–19   * where p· for money are
89–20   * p· for divine mercy.
231– 4   solicitations or p· from strangers,

petty
Mis. 255– 3   on pedestals, as so many p· deities ;
Man. 78–21   p· cash fund, to be used by him for
My. 99– 4   * above the suffering of p· ills ;
107 21   O p· scorner of the infinite,

pews
Ret. 15–17   p· were not sufficient to seat the
16– 2   floating up from the p·,
Pul. 25–21   * with p· of curly birch,
42–11   * children in the central p·.
58–17   * its exceedingly comfortable p·.
70– 2   * used in the doors and p·.
My. 59–19   * that would scarce fill a couple of p·
68 6   * about one mile and a half of p·.
68 31   * p· and principal woodwork are of
78–13   * semi-circular sweep of mahogany p·
79– 2   * before the p·, in absolute stillness,

phantasm
My. 148–26   a philosophical p·,

phantasma
Un. 26–11   p·, a belief in which leads to

phantasmagoria
Un. 26–24   p· is a product of human dreams.

phantom
Po. 20–13   thy p· finger, grim and cold,
65– 7   A p· of joy,

Pharaohs
Peo. 11–16   are the modern P·

Phare Pleigh
Mis. 216–10   "Scientific Theism," by P· P·
216–11   P· P· evidently means more than
My. 52–29   * "P· P·" [the nom de plume of
319– 7   little pamphlet, signed "P· P·."
323– 4   * "C. S. and the Bible," by "P· P·,"

Pharisaism
Ret. 65– 7   P· killeth ; Spirit giveth Life.

Phariseeism
Mis. 234–13   the P· of the times,

Pharisee's
'01. 14– 4   P· self-righteousness crucified Jesus.
My. 334–22   P· self-righteousness crucified Jesus."

Pharisees
Mis. 175–15   old leaven of the scribes and P·,
366–19   scribes and P·," — see Matt. 16 : 6.
370– 4   P· saw Jesus do such deeds of mercy,
374– 4   P· scorned the spirit of Christ
Un. 17–13   distinctly taught the arrogant P·
46–26   P· fought Jesus on this issue.
No. 41– 3   P· of old warned the people to
My. 104– 7   P· said of the great master
339–19   we and the P· fast oft, — Matt. 9 : 14.

pharmacist
Mis. 242–27   partner of George T. Brown, p·,

pharmacy
Mis. 271– 2   exclusion of compounds from its p·,
Hea. 12–18   on the p· of homœopathy,
13– 4   p· of homœopathy is reducing the
My. 108–12   faith in the p· of the human mind,

phase
Mis. 25– 7   matter is a p· of error,
Un. 4– 7   Truth destroys every p· of error.
Pul. 50–15   * particular p· of religious belief
63–16   * a new p· of religious belief,
Pan. 3– 5   poetical p· of the genii of forests.
'00. 12–30   the p· of a great controversy,
'01. 15– 5   condemn the claim of error in every p·

phase
My. 107– 7   a modern p· of medical practice,
281–22   * on some p· of the subject,

phases
Mis. 60–18   in different p· of thought,
127–30   Mortal mind presents p· of character
191–30   p· of sin or disease made manifest.
237–13   p· of error in human nature
375– 1   p· of material conceptions
Pul. 38–27   * p· of idealism and manifestations of
My. 93–21   * we see only its ridiculous p·,

phenomena
Mis. 23–19   God is both noumenon and p·,
28– 9   the p· of mortal life are as
73–31   The p· of Spirit in C. S.,
95–17   p· of an uncommon order,
105–15   Life and its glorious p·.
218–14   cognizance of Spirit or of its p·.
277–31   the p· of drunkenness produced by
286–23   p· of mortality, nothingness,
Un. 7–25   bringing out the highest p·
9–15   combinations, p·, and outcome,
10–12   p· of this one infinite Mind.
10–13   Spiritual p· never converge toward
35–20   They are the p· of mortal mind,
36– 9   from opposite facts, or p·.
41–27   p· appear to go on ad infinitum ;
No. 4 20   not the p· of the immutable laws
6– 8   take cognizance of their own p·,
10–28   constitute the p· of being,
14– 6   all sensible p· are merely
19–23   noumenon or the p· of Spirit ;
21–10   the Principle of all p·, identity,
Pan. 12–23   noumenon and p·, is demonstrably
'01. 23–28   * constant relation between p·
My. 180–32   defines noumenon and p·
249– 6   let the . . . produce God's p·.
349–24   obtain not in material p·,
350– 2   at the beck of material p·,

phenomenal
Mis. 68–29   * from its p· modifications."
My. 349–24   p· evil, which is lawless

phenomenally
Mis. 379–23   with p· good results ;

phenomenism
Mis. 216–27   * attempt of p· to conceive the

phenomenon
Mis. 74– 2   noumenon and p· understood,
216–28   * a p· without a noumenon
217– 8   p· must correspond in quality
317–11   p· of Spirit is the antipode of
362–18   mortal mind, with its p·
Ret. 22– 5   His spiritual noumenon and p·
24–11   every effect a mental p·.
Un. 50–11   only a p· of mortal mind,
Pul. 70–18   every effect a mental p·."
Hea. 6– 8   p· named mediumship,
My. 89–29   * greatest religious p· of all
98–12   * if they would deal with the p·
260– 4   matter an alien save as p·,
287–10   Love is the noumenon and p·,
347–26   and that a p· is chimerical,
347–28   and whose p· is Science.
350– 4   to end with the p·, matter,

Philadelphia
Pa.
Pul. 88–32   * Inquirer, P·, Pa.
89–10   * Press, P·, Pa.
89–13   * Telegram, P·, Pa.
My. 199– 2   chapter sub-title

Ret. 43–12   Hahnemann Medical College of P·.
Pul. 56– 3   * P·, Detroit, Toledo, Milwaukee,
'00. 1–19   Boston, New York, P·,
13–30   angel of the church in P·
14–13   except the church in P·
My. 153– 8   angel of the church in P·," — Rev. 3 : 7.
199– 7   May God say this of the church in P· :

Philadelphia School of Anatomy and Surgery
Ret. 43–13   P· S· of A· and S·,

philanthropist
Mis. 166– 5   p·, hero, and Christian.
My. 288– 4   p· . . . gives little thought to
297– 2   soldier, patriot, p·, moralist,

philanthropists
Mis. 38– 9   instructors and p· in our land
'01. 30–17   P·, and the higher class of critics

philanthropy
Mis. 238–19   stimulate p· and are an ever-present
'00. 14–24   p· of the better class of M.D.'s

philanthropy
My. 203– 9 Goodness and p· begin with work
287–19 P· is loving, ameliorative,
Philip (see also **Philip's**)
Pul. 83– 5 * appeals from P· drunk to P· sober,
Philippians
Un. 43–25 in the third chapter of P·,
Philippine Islands
'00. 1–18 P· I·, Hawaiian Islands;
10–27 in the P· I·,
Philip's
Mis. 77– 9 P· requirement was, that he should
Phillips, Wendell
Mis. 245–29 in the words of Wendell P·,
Pul. 6–30 apostle of anti-slavery, Wendell P·,
philosopher
Mis. ix– 1 apothegm of a Talmudical p·
363–26 This Word corrects the p·,
Ret. 57–12 If that pagan p· had known
'02. 1–21 engaging the attention of p· and
My. 159–25 Even Epictetus, a heathen p·
philosophers
Mis. 296– 5 profound p·, brilliant scholars.
Ret. 37–13 Emerson, or certain German p·,
philosophical
Un. 27– 8 Egoism is a more p· word,
53–17 no more logical, p·, or
My. 148–26 it is not . . . a p· phantasm,
205–16 and their p· impetus,
206– 1 P· links, which would unite
Philosophical Society of Great Britain
Mis. 295–26 P· S· of G· B·, an institution which
philosophies
Mis. 169– 4 the bypaths of ancient p·
344–16 Ancient and modern p· are
No. 24–16 than in human p· or creeds:
'02. 5– 3 pagan p· and tribal religions
14–22 popular p· and religions
philosophy
and logic
Mis. 360–26 regenerates p· and logic;
and religion
Mis. 64–18 the only p· and religion that
Ret. 31–29 systems of p· and religion
57–24 Human systems of p· and religion
and schools
Pul. 70–21 * p· and schools of medicine,
bald
Pan. 12–27 by bald p·, or by man's inventions.
broader
Mis. 2–16 embraces a deeper and broader p·
concerned with
My. 351–26 are not concerned with p·;
delighting in
Pul. 46–24 * delighting in p·, logic, and
divine
Mis. 364–12 It is the soul of divine p·,
364–32 reproduces the divine p· of Jesus
No. 21–25 Divine p· is demonstrably the
dogma and
No. 42–12 vain power of dogma and p·
Emerson's
My. 305– 4 resorted to Ralph Waldo Emerson's p·
false
No. 24–11 false p· and scholastic theology,
'01. 26– 2 my tired sense of false p·
My. 112– 3 false p· flourishes for a time
Grecian
Mis. 260– 6 Pagan mysticism, Grecian p·,
Greek
My. 288–14 tribal religion, Greek p·,
his
Ret. 57–13 his p· would have yielded to Science.
human
(see **human**)
hypotheses or
'02. 5–16 human hypotheses or p·.
insignia of
No. 9–23 cabalistic insignia of p·;
knowledge of
'01. 25– 8 A knowledge of p· and of medicine,
material
Mis. 340–30 Material p·, human ethics,
modern
Mis. 173– 1 Ancient and modern p·,
Ret. 34– 7 Neither ancient nor modern p· could
57– 4 Neither ancient nor modern p·
Pul. 47–14 * No ancient or modern p· gave her any
64–18 * and modern p· gave her no
moral
My. 221–13 can we find a better moral p·,

philosophy
natural
Ret. 10– 7 natural p·, logic, and moral science.
Un. 11–20 or a professor of natural p·,
Neoplatonic
No. 14– 9 a renewal in the Neoplatonic p·;
no other
Mis. 364–12 and there is no other p·.
nor reason
Mis. 217– 3 neither p· nor reason attempts
of Christian Science
Pan. 9–28 sometimes object to the p· of C. S.,
of Karma
Pul. 38–22 * opposed to the p· of Karma
of mind
Mis. 68–24 * defines it as "the p· of mind,
of the ages
My. 37–18 * p· of the ages transformed.
Oriental
Pul. 23–16 * inquiry into Oriental p·,
No. 14–10 Oriental p· of Brahmanism,
or physics
Mis. 366– 6 theology, p·, or physics,
or religion
My. 4–32 in ethics, p·, or religion,
220–24 present, or future p· or religion,
pagan
Mis. 173– 8 pagan p·, or scholastic theology,
principles of
'01. 23–26 on received principles of p·,
reason and
My. 260–13 Human reason and p· may
religion and
My. 248–27 religion and p· of labor, duty,
religion or
Mis. 363–23 shoals of a sensual religion or p·
My. 117–23 never a religion or p· lost
schools of
Mis. 162– 8 people and their schools of p·;
Science and
Mis. 359–27 chapter sub-title
Spinoza's
No. 24– 3 According to Spinoza's p·
sport of
My. 303–23 metaphysics is not the sport of p·,
such
Mis. 344–19 Such p· can never demonstrate
344–23 Such p· is far from the rules of
No. 22– 1 Such p· has certainly not
theology and
Un. 45–16 forms of theology and p·,
this
Mis. 365– 1 This p· alone will bear the strain
true
Mis. 344– 1 chapter sub-title
No. 38– 9 true p· and realism.
which cannot heal
No. 21–26 A p· which cannot heal the sick
your
Pul. 6–28 * more than is dreamt of in your p·."

Mis. 25–32 in p·, medicine, or religion,
216–25 * "When p· becomes fairy-land,
360–11 P· never has produced,
362–15 P· hypothetically regards creation
Un. 44–16 P· would multiply and subdivide
No. 21–22 whose p· is incontestable,
'01. 24–27 P·, materia medica, and
'02. 3– 6 more as a p· than as a religion.
7– 8 neither p·, nature, nor grace
My. 181– 3 p· and so-called natural science,
306– 6 p· of a great and good man,
phœnix
Mis. 285–26 nondescript p·, . . . may appear
My. 164–21 this p· fire, this pillar by day,
photograph
Pul. 48–19 * p· of Hon. Hoke Smith,
photographed
My. 329–13 * has in her possession p· copies
photographs
Pul. 32– 4 * No p· can do the least justice
My. 329–17 * The p· are verified by the
photography
No. 39–26 as p· grasps the solar light
phrase
Mis. 26–25 The p·, "express image," — Heb. 1: 3.
Man. 102–19 p·, "Mary Baker Eddy's Church,
Un. 50–14 we are compelled to use the p·
Pul. 53–12 * to give thanks in Oriental p·,
Rud. 2–15 the p· an individual God,
'01. 3–17 we use this p· for God
'02. 16– 4 that identical p·, "S. and H.,"

phraseology
Ret. 2–19 replete with the *p·* current in the
Un. 59– 8 hence the *p·* of Jesus,
No. 31–11 Our *p·* varies.

phrases
My. 308–28 no profanity and no slang *p·*.

phrasing
My. 256– 5 emphatically *p·* strict observance

phrenology
Hea. 5– 6 *P·* will be saying the developments of

phylacteries
My. 357–14 to enlarge their *p·* and

physic
Ret. 48–24 higher than *p·* or drugging ;

physical
agony
Mis. 70–12 Paradisaical rest from *p·* agony
ailment
Mis. 66–24 like the more *p·* ailment.
241– 8 the other having a *p·* ailment.
Pul. 69– 7 * cured by Mrs. Eddy of a *p·* ailment
ailments
Mis. 168–10 buried in dogmas and *p·* ailments,
causes
Un. 8–21 heredity and other *p·* causes.
cleanliness
Mis. 184–30 a type of *p·* cleanliness
concept
Ret. 67– 5 the human or *p·* concept.
death
Mis. 37–21 leads to moral or *p·* death.
effects
Mis. 365–20 spiritual, as well as *p·*, effects of
Ret. 24– 8 all *p·* effects to a mental cause ;
No. 19– 2 spiritual, as well as *p·*, effects of
Hea. 12–10 all *p·* effects originate in mind
My. 22–23 * *p·* effects produced by The
growth
No. 13– 4 demonstration of moral and *p·* growth,
harmony
Un. 6–10 The Science of *p·* harmony,
healing
Rud. 3–11 more . . . than his *p·* healing.
health
My. 93–14 * *p·* health and spiritual peace.
help
Mis. 88– 3 feel the need of *p·* help,
law
Mis. 28–29 claims of physique and of *p·* law,
101–17 it undermines . . . *p·* law,
Un. 11–14 boastful sense of *p·* law
laws
I'o. 89–15 Such *p·* laws to obey,
life
Un. 39– 5 pride of *p·* life must be quenched
man
Ret. 88– 7 called the *p·* man from the tomb
moral or
My. 364–17 sickness and disease, moral or *p·*.
ones
Hea. 17–22 are supposed *p·* ones,
perfection
'01. 1–14 constitute mental and *p·* perfection.
personality
Ret. 25–22 the *p·* personality of mind
73– 3 *P·* personality is finite ;
73–14 lift thought above *p·* personality,
73–22 to scrutinize *p·* personality,
Un. 37–18 evil accompanying *p·* personality
No. 23–23 Knowledge of a man's *p·* personality
25– 9 Man is more than *p·* personality,
rejuvenation
Mis. 169–11 With . . . had come *p·* rejuvenation.
results
My. 220– 1 save him from bad *p·* results.
science
Un. 9–10 is not the path of *p·* science,
My. 160–21 *P·* science has sometimes argued
sensation
Mis. 123–31 far apart from *p·* sensation
205–26 material life or *p·* sensation,
sense
Ret. 57–12 *p·* sense, not Soul, causes
senses
Mis. 104–17 his *p·* senses with his spiritual
105–24 Nothing appears to the *p·* senses but
205–18 invisible to the *p·* senses :
Ret. 25–13 *p·* senses, or sensuous nature,
25–22 *p·* senses are so many witnesses to
30–12 false testimony of the *p·* senses.
56–13 evidences of the five *p·* senses ;
65– 3 evidences of the *p·* senses,
Un. 8– 4 *of which the p· senses are cognizant*
22–20 has its origin in the *p·* senses

physical
senses
Un. 28– 6 five *p·* senses do not cognize it.
29–16 What the *p·* senses miscall soul,
33– 3 The *p·* senses . . . give the only
33–19 self-testimony of the *p·* senses
Rud. 5–22 with each of the *p·* senses.
7–12 evidence of the so-called *p·* senses,
11–12 illusions of the *p·* senses.
No. 6–26 testimony of the *p·* senses,
19–17 *p·* senses receive no spiritual idea,
sickness
Rud. 2–23 Healing *p·* sickness is the smallest
side
Ret. 33– 1 *p·* side of this research was aided by
Pul. 47–11 * knowledge concerning the *p·* side
strength
Mis. 240–12 contribute to moral and *p·* strength
substance
'01. 23–27 declared *p·* substance to be "only
suffering
Mis. 222– 7 causes the victim great *p·* suffering ;
No. 33–23 amidst *p·* suffering and human woe.
sufferings
Mis. 105– 8 His *p·* sufferings, which came from
221– 7 Error produces *p·* sufferings,
terms
Mis. 50–13 the metaphysical in *p·* terms.
171–12 expressed in literal or *p·* terms,
torture
No. 34–14 *P·* torture affords but a slight
vigor
My. 134–30 * her usual mental and *p·* vigor."
wants
Mis. 67– 2 Above *p·* wants, lie the higher claims
world
Pul. 53–20 * dominion over the *p·* world.

Mis. 86– 1 The material and *p·* are imperfect.
102–11 His being is individual, but not *p·*.
168– 6 *p·* and moral lepers are cleansed ;
198–24 bad deed, based on *p·* material law,
234–25 *p·* and mental perfection.
241–27 easier to heal the *p·* than the
244–12 are the conditions . . . mental, or *p·*;
245–15 a *p·* and spiritual need
251–26 all error, *p·*, moral, or religious.
261–31 must produce *p·* and moral harmony.
297– 4 for *p·* and moral reformation.
303– 3 as healers *p·* and moral.
365–13 *p·* and moral harmony ;
Ret. 35– 5 for *p·* and moral health
58– 5 *p·*, false, and finite substitute.
Un. 8–15 deleterious effects, *p·*, moral, and
35–17 moral and spiritual, not *p·*.
Pul. 20–17 *p·*, civil, and religious reform
Rud. 10–23 erroneous *p·* and mental state.
No. 18– 9 *p·* and moral harmony,
31–21 *P·* and mental healing were one
My. 79–28 * from diseases, *p·* and mental,
111–13 *p·* and spiritual status of a perfect
147–18 *p·*, moral, and spiritual needs

physicality
Un. 29–21 can never be . . . touched by *p·*.
56–20 *p·* and the sense of sin.

physically
Mis. ix– 9 healing mankind morally, *p·*,
3– 1 elevating the race *p·*, morally,
20– 3 heals man . . . morally and *p·*,
31– 6 morally, *p·*, or spiritually
45–20 is better both morally and *p·*.
51– 2 *p·* as well as spiritually,
67– 7 mentally, morally, or *p·*.
138–14 ethically, *p·*, and spiritually,
168– 4 the blind, spiritually and *p·*,
203–14 medicine applies it *p·*,
214–25 is the same as its attitude *p·*.
220–20 he is improved morally and *p·*.
222–17 is fatal, morally and *p·*.
252–20 to man *p·*, as well as spiritually,
259–23 *p·*, morally, and Christianly,
289– 1 degenerate *p·* and morally.
300–32 Healing morally and *p·* are one.
362–10 *p·*, morally, spiritually.
Ret. 25–21 a *p·* personal being, like unto
Un. 36–19 man is improved *p·*, morally,
37–17 Human beings are *p·* mortal,
Rud. 3–21 mental error made manifest *p·*,
No. 13–20 *p·*, morally, and spiritually,
22–10 morally, spiritually, or *p·*.
Pan. 11–19 man who falls *p·* needs to rise again.
'00. 6–27 better *p·*, morally, and spiritually.
'01. 20–16 *p·*, morally, or spiritually,
Hea. 9– 8 better for mankind, morally and *p·*.
14– 5 man is healed morally and *p·*.

physically
Peo. 6–19 improves the race *p·* and spiritually.
My. 45–10 * *p·* present at the dedication
105–16 *p·* restored sight to the blind,
130– 6 socially, *p·*, and morally
146–24 scale of being, morally and *p·*,

Physician
Mis. 151–14 our Minister and the great *P·*:
Pul. 6–19 * and turned to the 'great *P·*.'

physician
Mis. 59–28 divine Mind, who is the only *p·* ;
89– 6 *employing a regular p·*,
248–24 my regular *p·* prescribed morphine,
269–19 divine Mind to be the only *p·*.
349– 3 a certain regular-school *p·*,
355–12 *p·* must know himself and understand
355–26 "*P·*, heal thyself." — *Luke 4 : 23.*
Ret. 13–24 The *p·* marvelled ;
24–17 homœopathic *p·* who attended me,
87–30 under the care of a regular *p·*,
Un. 11–20 a *p·*, or a professor of natural
59–23 and man an invalid, needing a *p·* ;
Pul. 35–28 * a *p·* who had come into sympathy with
Hea. 14–12 In proportion as a *p·* is enlightened
Peo. 6– 8 * *p·*, surgeon, apothecary,
My. 105–23 Her *p·*, who stood by her bedside,
108– 2 homœopathic *p·* succeeds as well
108–19 better for both *p·* and patient.
128–15 man's right . . . to employ a *p·*,
132–28 Divine Love is our only *p·*,
310–20 by *p·* or post-mortem examination
335–24 * sent for the distinguished *p·* who
335–31 * told by the expert *p·* that

physicians
Mis. 24–10 pronounced fatal by the *p·*.
35– 6 pronounced by the *p·* incurable,
69–15 *p·* had given three doses
69–21 *p·* had failed even to move his
81– 3 scholarly *p·* openly admit.
143–20 well known *p·*, teachers,
245– 5 but to the *p·*. — *II Chron. 16 : 12.*
Ret. 15–25 by *p·* of the popular schools
40– 9 The *p·* had given up the case
40–13 told me that her *p·* had said
Pul. 34– 7 * pronounced hopeless by the *p·*.
72–15 * by a number of well-known *p·*.
Hea. 14–10 exercised in the choice of *p·*.
My. 97– 2 * best *p·* now admit the
97– 5 * *p·*, however, ridicule the idea of
237–17 equal to those of reputable *p·*
293–11 Even the *p·* may have feared this.
328–15 * license . . . required of *p·*,

physicists
Rud. 6–17 * universally accepted, . . . by *p·*."

physics
Mis. 6–13 power of metaphysics over *p·* ;
34– 3 metaphysics is above *p·*.
53–17 He that resorts to *p·*,
126– 3 from darkness to daylight, in *p·*
209–11 and dies of its own *p·*.
209–12 Short-sighted *p·* admits the so-called
255–27 metaphysics is above *p·*.
264–31 more fatal than a mistake in *p·*.
340–31 theology, and *p·* have not
366– 6 theology, philosophy, or *p·*,
369– 7 Metaphysics, not *p·*, enables us
Ret. 34–16 superiority of metaphysics over *p·*.
No. 11–20 theology, physiology, or *p·* ;
Pan. 4– 7 may agree with *p·* and anatomy
Hea. 11– 6 *p·* are yielding slowly to
14– 6 physiology, hygiene, or *p·*
Peo. 9–23 metaphysics is seen to rise above *p·*,
10– 5 through the cold night of *p·*,
My. 127– 2 in *p·*, and in metaphysics.
307– 9 matter, electricity, or *p·*.

Physiology
Pul. 38–10 "*P·*," "Footsteps of Truth,"

physiology
Un. 45–17 Anatomy and *p·* make mind-matter a
No. 11–16 place . . . that *p·* occupies,
11–20 learn theology, *p·*, or physics ;
Hea. 5– 7 *P·* will be saying,
14– 6 *p·*, hygiene, or physics

physique
Mis. 28–29 claims of *p·* and of physical
34– 8 since the *p·* is simply
Ret. 78– 2 acts like a diseased *p·*,

piazza
Pul. 48– 6 * broad *p·* on the south side
48–15 * Straight . . . from her *p·*,

pick
Mis. 357–15 fowls of the air *p·* them up.

picked
Mis. 282–12 houses broken open or our locks *p·*?

picking
Mis. 343–15 *p·* away the cold, hard pebbles

pictorial
Pul. 25– 1 * are very rich in *p·* effect.
27–20 * great window tells its *p·* story
27–28 * and others of *p·* significance.

picture
Mis. 279–22 second *p·* is of the disciples
323– 2 *P·* to yourself "a city — *Matt. 5 : 14.*
373– 4 in the *p·* "Seeking and Finding."
Po. 43– 1 *p· depictive of Isaiah xi.*
My. 58–16 * speaks more than words can *p·*
206–13 seeing a person in the *p·* of Jesus,
356–16 nor consent to have my *p·* issued,

pictured
Un. 34– 5 images, *p·* on the eye's retina.

picture-lesson
Mis. 280– 3 third *p·* is from Revelation,

pictures
Mis. ix–10 easel of time presents *p·*
279–14 *p·* from which we learn
346–23 in *p·* of silver." — *Prov. 25 : 11.*
365– 7 what a child's love of *p·* is
372–11 * *p·* in your wonderful book
374–27 *P·* are portions of one's ideal,
375– 1 *P·* which present disordered
Man. 81–21 No objectionable *p·* shall be
Pul. 58–12 * appearance is shown in the *p·*
58–21 * *p·* symbolic of the tenets
76–16 * *P·* and bric-a-brac everywhere
No. 18–16 what a child's love of *p·* is
27– 8 similitude of the Apocalyptic *p·*.
My. 308–16 *p·* "the old man tramping

picturesque
Ret. 4–11 *p·* view of the Merrimac River
Pul. 47–26 * is so *p·* all about Concord
My. 47–13 * look back to the *p·*, interesting,
175–17 Our *p·* city, however,

picturesqueness
Ret. 2– 4 poetic daring and pious *p·*

picture-stories
Mis. 279–13 three *p·* from the Bible

picturing
Po. 9– 3 I'm *p·* alone a glad young face,

pie
Mis. 231–14 delicious *p·*, pudding, and fruit

piece
My. 71–10 * a stunning *p·* of architecture
195–21 no miserable *p·* of ideal legerdemain,

pieces
'00. 10–28 ten five-dollar gold *p·*

Pierce (*see also* **Pierce's**)
Franklin
Ret. 6–19 in the office of Franklin *P·*,
My. 309– 7 Franklin *P·*, afterwards President of
Governor
My. 308–20 my father was visiting Governor *P·*,
Mr.
Ret. 6–24 law-office which Mr. *P·* had occupied,
My. 309–11 Mr. *P·* bowed to my father

pierce
Mis. 320–25 *p·* the darkness and melt into dawn.
'00. 12– 1 His types of purity *p·* corruption

pierced
Mis. 339–20 hast *p·* the heart venturing its all
342–17 him whom they had *p·*,
My. 191–22 Mortality's thick gloom is *p·*.
278–28 *p·* by its own sword.

Pierce's
President
My. 311–20 Fanny McNeil, President *P·* niece,
President Franklin
My. 308–21 President Franklin *P·* father,

pierces
Mis. 355–15 and the last third *p·* itself,

piercing
Mis. 312– 8 endures all *p·* for the sake of others,
Po. 30–18 *P·* the clouds with its triumphal

piers
My. 68– 6 * tops of great stone *p·*,

piety
Mis. 111– 1 proven that the greatest *p·* is
'01. 33– 1 their *p·* was the all-important
My. 288–13 His *p·* partook not of the

pigment
Ret. 79– 8 *p·* beneath fade into invisibility.

Pilate
Un. 59–15 to suffer before *P·* and on Calvary,

pile
Mis. 51–24 * dark *p·* of human mockeries ;
388–14 Grave on her monumental *p·* :
Po. 21– 1 Grave on her monumental *p·* :
My. 45–28 * massive *p·* of New Hampshire granite

piled
My. 78–15 * basket *p·* high with bank-notes,

pilgrim
Mis. 155– 9 win the *p·* and stranger
341–15 weary *p·*, unloose the latchet

pilgrimage
'02. 20–20 sacrament in our church and a *p·* to
My. 150– 9 joy and crown of such a *p·*

pilgrimages
Ret. 90–13 depart on their united *p·*.

Pilgrim Fathers
Pul. 10–10 Our land, . . . had its *P· F·*.
My. 183– 6 wrote in 1620 to our *P· F·* :

Pilgrims
Mis. 176–20 When first the *P·* planted their
176–23 *P·* came to establish a nation
My. 50– 7 * *P·* felt the strangeness of

pilgrims
Pul. 51–24 * *P·* from everywhere will go there
My. 77–13 * *p·* are pouring into Boston,

pill
Mis. 369–16 tincture or an ipecacuanha *p·*.

pillar
Mis. 149–28 Guided by the *p·* and the cloud,
My. 45–19 * by day in a *p·* of cloud
45–20 * by night in a *p·* of fire
45–25 * *p·* of cloud by day,— *see Exod.* 13 : 22.
45–25 * *p·* of fire by night," – *Exod.* 13 : 22.
69–17 * not a single *p·* or post anywhere
164–21 this phœnix fire, this *p·* by day,

pillars
'02. 17–29 Patience and resignation are the *p·* of

pillow
Mis. 257–31 Smoothing the *p·* of pain
Un. 57–18 earth's Bethel in stone,— its *p·*,
Po. 27–23 *P·* thy head on time's untired

pillows
Mis. 144–25 from earth's *p·* of stone,

pills
Mis. 79–31 vendors of patent *p·*, mesmerists,

pin
My. 83–10 * Scientists frequently wear a small *p·*,
192–25 demands . . . *p·* me to my post.

pine
Mis. 330– 2 make melody through dark *p·* groves.
Ret. 4–18 requiems through dark *p·* groves.
Po. 68–10 the sea and the tall waving *p·*

Pine Grove Cemetery
Po. page 67 poem

pinest
Po. 34–21 Nor *p·* thou in vain

pine-tree
Rud. 8– 2 no *p·* produces a mammal

Pine Tree State (*see also* **Maine**)
Mis. 251– 6 from the Palmetto to the *P· T· S·*,

pining
Po. 35– 7 Or *p·* tenderness

pinion
Po. 18– 7 or *p·* lose power

pinions
Mis. 354–30 nor his *p·* lose power
385–23 "When . . . Thy *p·* drooped ;
Ret. 85–12 bearing on their *p·* of light
Po. 33–16 faith spreads her *p·* abroad,
48–18 "When . . . Thy *p·* drooped ;
My. 238–16 swift *p·* of spiritual thought

pink
Mis. 329–23 paint in *p·* the petals of arbutus,
376–27 orange, *p·*, crimson, violet ;
Ret. 17–12 On the heart of the *p·*
Pul. 24–23 * with trimmings of the *p·* granite
25–15 * with marble stairs of rose *p·*,
25–24 * of *p·* Tennessee marble.
42–30 * filled with beautiful *p·* roses.
Po. 62–15 On the heart of the *p·*

pinnacle
Mis. 313– 7 molecule, pearl, and *p·*,
358–26 at the *p·* of prosperity,
Man. 47–15 scales the *p·* of praise

pinnacled
Pul. 2–30 *p·* in Life.

pinnacles
Ret. 47–10 being placed on earthly *p·*,

pinned
'01. 26–16 shall the word popularity be *p·* to

pioneer
Mis. x–10 in the early *p·* days,
xii– 1 *p·* signs and ensigns of war,
213–17 In every age, the *p·* reformer
Ret. 30– 1 As the *p·* of C. S. I stood alone
50–30 in the beginning of *p·* work.
Pul. 47– 9 * her experiences as the *p·* of C. S.,
'00. 3–16 not apt to worship the *p·* of
Hea. 6– 5 *p·* of something new under the sun
Po. vi–13 *Boston has since been the p· of*
My. 148– 1 to do your *p·* work in this city.

Pioneer-Press
Pul. 90– 2 * *P·*, St. Paul, Minn.

pioneers
Pul. 51– 9 * many *p·* who are searching after
My. 50–10 * so this little band of *p·*,
104–18 on the *p·* of Christianity
104–20 of whom these *p·* speak.

pious
Mis. 147–24 *p·* worker, the public-spirited citizen.
345– 7 need the spirit of the *p·* Polycarp,
Ret. 1– 6 the *p·* and popular English authoress
2– 4 the poetic daring and *p·*
81 22 Shakespeare puts this *p·* counsel
Peo. 13–17 lofty faith of the *p·* Polycarp

pipe
Chr. 55–12 tabret, and *p·*, and wine, — *Isa.* 5 : 12.
Pan. 3–28 His *p·* of seven reeds denotes the

pipes
Pul. 60 26 * 61 *p·* each.
60–30 * 61 *p·* each.
61– 3 * 61 *p·* each.
61– 5 * 30 *p·* each.
(*see also* **organ**)

pippin
Mis. 231–17 made a big hole, . . . in a big *p·*,

piqued
Mis. 363– 8 flatterer, identification, is *p·*

pistons
(*see* **organ**)

pit
Mis. 389–11 the snare, the *p·*, the fall :
Po. 4 10 the snare, the *p·*, the fall :

pitch
Pul. 47 30 * angles and *p·* of the roof,

pith
Mis. 27–10 *p·* of the basal statement,
My. 303 24 *p·* and finale of them all.

pitiable
Mis. 115–12 ignorance . . . on this subject is *p·*,

pitied
Mis. 105–27 has no right either to be *p·* or to
211–18 is he not to be *p·* and brought back

pities
Un. 3–27 God is our helper. He *p·* us.
4– 9 that God comes to us and *p·* us ;
No. 30–13 God *p·* our woes with the love of a

pitieth
Un. 2– 3 God *p·* them who fear Him ;

pitifully
Mis. 227–16 these weak, *p·* poor objects from

pitiless
Mis. 257–28 This *p·* power smites with disease

pittance
Pul. 64– 9 * some giving a *p·*,

Pittsburgh, Pa.
Pul. 89– 7 * *Post, P·, P·*.
My. 196– 2 chapter sub-title

pity
Mis. 102–17 His *p·* is expressed in modes above
102–22 Human *p·* often brings pain.
105–26 and *p·* what has no right either to
121–28 Infinitely greater than human *p·*,
124–17 with more than a father's *p·* ;
224–30 is an object of *p·* rather than of
227–15 Would that my pen or *p·* could
Un. 18–17 show My *p·* through divine law,
Pul. 52– 5 * What a *p·* some of our practical
84– 5 * revenge shall clasp hands with *p·*,
'01. 16–12 surviving defamers share our *p·*.
'02. 18–12 nor spared through false *p·*

pity
   My. 57–32   * What a *p·* some of our practical
       189–29   why throng in *p·* round me?

pitying
   Mis. 124–16   *p·* with more than a father's pity ;
       212–30   *P·* friends took down from the cross
       228–13   We should look with *p·* eye
       386–11   looks on her heart with *p·* eye,
   Po. 49–16   looks on her heart with *p·* eye,

placards
   Mis. 210– 8   *p·* warning people not to stir up

place (noun)
accustomed
   Mis. 135–29   to see me in my accustomed *p·*
all
   No. 24– 2   evil loses all *p·*, person, and
   My. 353–26   and the spiritual have all *p·*
and power
   Mis. 274–26   exchange for money, *p·*, and power,
       351–15   aspirants for *p·* and power.
   My. 353–26   the spiritual have all *p·* and power.
appropriate
   Mis. 304– 6   * in the most appropriate *p·*
behold the
   My. 122–24   behold the *p·* where— *Mark* 16 : 6.
       191–21   Behold the *p·* where they laid me ;
each
   My. 330–19   * Masonic records in each *p·*
for himself
   Mis. 294– 4   making *p·* for himself
from the
   Mis. 178– 1   from the *p·* of my own sojourning
gave
   Mis. 142–20   gave *p·* to chords of feeling
gives
   '02.   2–21   gives *p·* to a more spiritual
giving
   Mis. 303–22   giving *p·* in your *Journal* to the
her
   Man. 72–20   her *p·* as the head or Leader
   My. 51– 2   * no one . . . who could take her *p·*
hiding
   Mis. 144–16   an hiding *p·* from the— *Isa.* 32 : 2.
   My. 17– 2   overflow the hiding *p·.*"— *Isa.* 28 : 17.
high
   Mis. 392– 6   majestic oak, from yon high *p·*
   Po. 20– 8   majestic oak, from yon high *p·*
his
   Mis. 137–20   each one return to his *p·*
   Man. 28–21   either to resign his *p·* or
   '00. 12–20   candlestick out of his *p·,* — *Rev.* 2 : 5.
historic
   My. 90–27   * The historic *p·* of Mrs. Eddy as the
hold a
   Mis. 290–25   hold a *p·* in one's memory,
holy
   Mis. 301–25   injustice standing in a holy *p·.*
   My. 34– 2   stand in his holy *p·*? — *Psal.* 24 : 3.
individual
   Ret. 70–14   the individual *p·* of the Virgin
in North Groton
   My. 314–10   bought a *p·* in North Groton,
in schools
   No. 11–16   the *p·* in schools of learning
in Science
   Mis. 234–15   can never find a *p·* in Science.
its
   Mis. 334– 5   Astrology is well in its *p·*,
   Pul. 51–28   * aspire to take its *p·* alongside
meeting
   My. 174– 5   proved an ideal meeting *p·*.
my
   '00. 9–27   to have some one take my *p·*
needed a
   My. 55– 3   * church needed a *p·* of its own,
no
   Mis. 31–13   Such false faith finds no *p·* in,
       357– 1   no *p·* for envy, no time for
       367– 2   have no *p·* in C. S.
       394–13   No *p·* for earth's idols,
   Ret. 21–15   dream has no *p·* in the Science of being.
   Un. 2– 3   no *p·* where His voice is not heard ;
       42– 2   because there is no *p·* left for it.
   No. 27– 5   evil finds no *p·* in good.
   '02. 12–22   ordinarily find no *p·* in my Message.
   Po. 45–17   No *p·* for earth's idols,
   My. 7– 5   ordinarily find no *p·* in my Message.
       54–18   * no *p·* suitable could be found
nor power
   Mis. 14– 1   neither *p·* nor power left for evil.
of a virtue
   Mis. 227– 3   may stand in the *p·* of a virtue ;
of darkness
   My. 199– 4   In *p·* of darkness, light hath

place
of good
   Rud. 6–11   takes the *p·* of good.
of labor
   Mis. 137–20   return to his *p·* of labor,
   Ret. 84–30   regular institute or *p·* of labor,
of the author
   Ret. 70–17   No person can take the *p·* of the author of
of the Golden Rule
   My. 266– 8   in *p·* of the Golden Rule,
of worship
   Mis. 325–31   Next he enters a *p·* of worship,
       345–23   took their infants to a *p·* of worship
one
   Mis. 134–12   "in one *p·*," — *Acts* 2 : 1.
       143–27   in one *p·*," — *Acts* 2 : 1.
   My. 212–19   in one *p·*," — *Acts* 2 : 1.
       362–15   * in one *p·* with one accord,
or a thing
   '01. 13– 1   a man or a woman, a *p·* or a thing,
or power
   My. 4–24   The pride of *p·* or power
other
   Mis. 266–19   Chicago, New York, or any other *p·*,
pleasant
   My. 147–22   I have purchased a pleasant *p·*
proper
   Mis. 308–10   take their proper *p·* in history,
rightful
   No. 33– 6   rightful *p·* in schools of learning,
   My. vii– 7   * her rightful *p·* as the revelator
same
   Mis. 27–18   send forth at the same *p·* — *Jas.* 3 : 11.
   Man. 71– 5   established in the same *p·* ;
secret
   My. 188–10   secret *p·* of the most High," — *Psal.* 91 : 1.
       244–15   "secret *p·*," whereof — *Psal.* 91 : 1.
some
   My. 54–20   * expectation that some *p·* would
supply the
   My. 312– 2   supply the *p·* of his leading teacher
take
   My. 84–28   * to take *p·* on Sunday,
       217–12   This disbursal will take *p·* when
take a
   My. 31–19   * take a *p·* in the front rank of
takes
   Mis. 42– 1   *change called death takes p·,*
       304–15   * takes *p·* at Paris, France.
takes the
   Mis. 175–24   one belief takes the *p·* of another.
   Pul. 25–30   * takes the *p·* of chandeliers.
take the
   Rud. 16– 2   take the *p·* of private lessons ;
taking
   Ret. 19– 3   taking *p·* under the paternal roof
   Pul. 56–12   * taking *p·* on the 6th of January,
taking the
   My. 212– 6   In this era it is taking the *p·* of
that
   Mis. 75–24   name of Deity used in that *p·*
   My. 55–26   * in that *p·* Sunday services were held
their
   Mis. 182–24   finding their *p·* in God's great love,
thereof
   Mis. 189–18   revealing, in *p·* thereof, the power
this
   Mis. 334– 5   but this *p·* is secondary.
   My. 188– 7   made in this *p·*." — *II Chron.* 7 : 15.
thy
   Mis. 400– 4   Like this stone, be in thy *p·* :
   Pul. 16–16   Like this stone, be in thy *p·* ;
   Po. 76–15   Like this stone, be in thy *p·* :
time and
   My. 169–20   beauty of time and *p·*
took
   Mis. 339– 3   took *p·* once in heaven,
   Pul. 38– 4   * which ceremony took *p·* in 1881.
   Pan. 7–10   belief, . . . a material creation took *p·*,
to place
   Mis. 304– 8   * will pass from *p·* to place
       304–20   * journey from *p·* to place,
where Demosthenes
   Mis. 345– 4   in the *p·* where Demosthenes had
will hold
   My. 85–17   * structure which will hold *p·* among
yonder
   My. 222–12   Remove hence to yonder *p·* ; — *Matt.* 17 : 20.

   Mis. 61–16   * a *p·* where a man was said to
       175–21   and its methods in *p·* of God,
       237– 4   in *p·* of material flames and odor,
       304–13   * *p·* where any great patriotic
       341–16   *p·* whereon thou standest is sacred.
   Man. 96–10   a *p·* where he sees there is
   Un. 26–22   what *p·* has *chance* in the divine

place
Un.	51–11	whose *p·* is ill supplied by
Pul.	5– 7	we kindle in *p·* thereof the glow of
	60–12	* The *p·* was again crowded,
Peo.	14– 8	in *p·* of "bat and owl on the
My.	vi–27	* *p·* for the publishing of her works ;
	37– 3	* no pride of circumstances has *p·*
	53–14	* seating capacity of which *p·* was
	188–23	C. S. has a *p·* in its court,

place (verb)
Mis.	33–17	*p·* themselves under my care,
	117– 8	will *p·* him on the safe side
	287–10	may *p·* love on a false basis
	296–10	*p·* the barmaids of English alehouses
	344–17	would *p·* Soul wholly inside of body,
	351–16	never can *p·* it in the wrong hands
Man.	46– 8	shall not *p·* the initials "C. S."
	51–21	to discipline, *p·* on probation,
Ret.	42– 5	and *p·* these symbolic words on
	84–28	*p·* themselves under his direction ;
Pul.	35–30	* *p·* "Christian Scientist" on the sign
My.	214– 1	one only to *p·* on the walls
	321– 6	* *p·* him as one of your devoted and

placed
Mis.	134– 5	you are *p·* in this dilemma :
	304– 5	* *p·* by the lovers of liberty
	304–32	* *p·* in the hands of a committee
	305– 8	* *p·* upon me the responsibility
Man.	51– 4	he shall be *p·* on probation,
Ret.	47– 9	being *p·* on earthly pinnacles,
	91–18	*p·* themselves under his care,
Pul.	42–21	* where the organ is to be . . . *p·*,
	48– 1	* well *p·* upon a terrace
	02–23	* *p·* on a small centre table.
	73–23	* She *p·* no credit whatever in the
My.	68–21	* *p·* back of the Readers' platform
	69– 8	* whereon are *p·* inscriptions
	69–11	* *p·* on the two sides of the organ.
	79–21	* *p·* upon a far higher pedestal
	166–29	cabinet, . . . *p·* in my room

places
Mis.	7–11	*p·* where one would least expect it,
	79– 3	the *p·* once knowing them
	116– 4	wickedness in high *p·*."— *Eph.* 6 : 12.
	126–28	she sitteth in high *p·* ;
	127– 6	watering her waste *p·*,
	134–28	wickedness is standing in high *p·* ;
	250–29	lighting the dark *p·* of earth.
	304–17	* When not in use in other *p·*,
Man.	05 7	at such *p·* and at such times
	110–17	*p·* where they are required.
Pul.	22–21	her waste *p·* budded
No.	45 17	highest *p·* in government,
Hea.	11–23	*p·* all cause and cure as mind ;
	15– 6	*p·* no faith in hygiene or drugs ;
My.	3–11	scattered abroad in Zion's waste *p·*,
	18– 3	watering her waste *p·*,
	54–17	* different *p·* were considered,
	54–29	* consideration of *p·* for meeting
	55– 5	* Several *p·* were considered,
	56–13	* each of the following named *p·* :
	80–27	* when these *p·* had all been filled,
	81–14	* the *p·* where they lived.
	91–28	* one of the finest *p·* of worship
	107–20	*p·* it nearer the grooves of
	310– 4	at various times and *p·*.
	334–12	* *p·* certain circumstances in 1843,

placid
Ret.	5–23	* sympathizing heart, and a *p·* spirit.

placing
Mis.	197–31	*p·* his trust in this grand Truth,
	351–14	*p·* C. S. in the hands of
	373– 3	*p·* the serpent behind the woman
My.	298– 9	*p·* this book before the public,

plagiarism
Ret.	76–27	a growing evil in *p·* ;
No.	3–25	*P·* from my writings is so common

plagiarists
Mis.	301–17	must not leave persistent *p·*

plagiarize
Man.	43–17	shall not *p·* her writings.

plagiarizing
Ret.	76– 1	for *p·* an author's ideas

plague
Mis.	229–18	neither shall any *p·*— *Psal.* 91 : 10.

plagues
My.	126–15	receive not of her *p·*.— *Rev.* 18 : 4.
	126–20	*p·* come in one day,— *Rev.* 18 : 8.

plague-spot
Mis.	12– 2	hatred is a *p·* that spreads

plain
Mis.	23–14	It is *p·* that the Me spoken of
	24–16	since tried to make *p·* to others,
	115–12	is pitiable, and *p·* to be seen.
	121–17	This is *p·* : that whatever belittles,
	124– 1	*p·* that aught unspiritual,
	124– 4	It is also *p·*, that we should not
	271–22	To make this *p·*,
Ret.	30–17	The answer is *p·*.
	90–11	and gave in *p·* words,
Un.	9– 8	Jesus has made the way *p·*,
	9– 9	so *p·* that all are without excuse who
No.	6–20	To material sense it is *p·* also that
Pan.	6–26	It is *p·* that elevating evil to the
'01.	13–22	In C. S. it is *p·* that God removes the
My.	121–14	Peace, like *p·* dealing,
	121–15	and *p·* dealing is a jewel
	210– 4	*p·* that nothing can be added to
	343– 1	* *p·* that the answers to questions
	346–29	"S. and H. makes it *p·* to all

plainer
Un.	6–27	drilled in the *p·* manual

plainly
Mis.	93– 8	The Scriptures *p·* declare the allness
	189–13	Christ *p·* declared, through Jesus,
	192–23	as the above Scripture *p·* declares,
	212–27	speaks *p·* to the offender
Man.	110–11	must be *p·* written,
Pan.	5– 3	The Scriptures *p·* declare,
My.	84– 1	* facts speak more *p·* than mere
	86–18	* one which indicates *p·* enough
	216– 1	is *p·* set forth in the Scriptures.
	319–29	* I also recall very *p·* the

plain-speaking
My.	137– 7	* crisp, clear, *p·* English."

plaintiff
My.	6– 1	arguing for the *p·* in favor of

plan
Mis.	182–23	apostle indicates no personal *p·* of
	296–14	live on the *p·* of heaven
	348–23	show the *p·* of battle.
Hea.	1–17	* Knows it at forty, and reforms his *p·* ;
Peo.	12–18	God's *p·* of redemption,
	12–22	as God's whole *p·*,
My.	145– 4	*p·* for C. S. Hall in Concord,
	145– 6	He drew the *p·*, showed it to me,
	269–11	Christ's *p·* of salvation from divorce.
	278– 3	to be subserved by the battle's *p·*
	283–23	or God's own *p·* of salvation.

plane
Mis.	22–19	defining the line, *p·*, space,
	34–24	on this present *p·* of existence,
	42–14	same *p·* of conscious existence
	143– 0	above the *p·* of matter,
	368–27	perverted, on the mortal *p·*
	393–20	Points the *p·* of power to seek.
Pul.	38–19	* different a *p·* of consciousness
Po.	52– 4	Points the *p·* of power to seek.
My.	46– 5	* more spiritual *p·* of living,
	226– 8	inclined *p·* in mechanics,

planet
Mis.	174–14	the atmosphere of our *p·*,
	383– 2	textbook, be the pastor, on this *p·*,
No.	6 18	revolves around our *p·*,
Peo.	8–19	as directly as it moves a *p·*
My.	160–23	will eventually consume this *p·*.
	267– 2	the only . . . therapeutics on this *p·*.

planets
Mis.	54– 4	and the *p·* to revolve around it?
Pan.	3–29	celestial harmony of the seven *p·* ;
My.	13–11	* other churches, like so many *p·*,

plank
Mis.	21–15	My first *p·* in the platform of

planks
Un.	14– 1	such *p·* as the divine repentance,
My.	61–14	* over stones and *p·* and plaster,

planning
Mis.	230–11	or *p·* for some amusement,

plans
My.	55–17	* *p·* were made for a church home.
	352–28	thanks for your successful *p·*

plant
Mis.	4– 5	to *p·* mental healing on the
	26–12	"every *p·* of the field— *Gen.* 2 : 5.
	107– 7	*p·* the feet steadfastly in Christ.
Pul.	10–23	your *p·* is immortal.
Pan.	15– 7	*p·* our feet firmly on Truth,
'01.	33– 4	To *p·* for eternity,
Hea.	19–14	"every *p·* of the field— *Gen.* 2 : 5.
My.	122– 7	To cut off the top of a *p·*
	122– 8	or the *p·* will continue to grow.
	129–19	*p·* thy steps in Christ,

plant
My. 154–19   * "Wouldst thou p· for eternity,
    154–19   * p· into the deep infinite faculties
    186–20   those that p· the vineyard
    215–18   to p· our first magazine,

planted
Mis. 80–26   have p· and sown and reaped
    176–20   p· their feet on Plymouth Rock,
Pul. vii–15   C. S. as p· in the pathway of
    10–11   they p· a nation's heart,
    10–16   you have p· your standard

planting
My. 202–30   God bless this vine of His p·.

plants
Mis. 339–12   p· our feet more firmly.
Ret. 11–11   knowledge p· the foot of power
Un. 14– 6   earth, man, animals, p·,
Rud. 7–27   or p· into animals,
Po. 60– 8   knowledge p· the foot of power
My. 205–11   * He p· His footsteps in the sea
    356– 7   * "He p· His footsteps in the sea

plaster
Pul. 25–13   * galleries are in p· relief,
    25–14   * iron, coated with p· ;
My. 61–14   * stones and planks and p·,
    68–26   * p· work for the great arches

plastic
Rud. 15– 9   renders the mind less inquisitive, p·,

plated
Pul. 76–20   * heavily p· with gold."

plates
My. 30–20   * when the p· were returned
    69–10   * Two large marble p·

Platform
    (see **Christian Science Platform**)

platform
Mis. 21–15   plank in the p· of C. S.
    95– 2   * p· of the Monday lectureship
    177–26   * came on the p·.
    244– 3   on the p· of C. S. !
    253– 7   p· is not broad enough for me,
    364–17   It stands on this Scriptural p· :
Man. 34– 9   according to the p· and teaching
Ret. 16– 4   two ladies . . . reached the p·.
Un. 14– 1   an outworn theological p·,
Pul. 12– 3   were read from the p·.
    26– 7   * p· — corresponding to the chancel of
    42–20   * choir gallery above the p·,
    42–25   * choir and the steps of the p·
    43– 7   * On the p· with him were
    59–21   * on the p· sat Joseph Armstrong,
    60–20   * recess behind the spacious p·,
No. 12–10   on the p· of doctrines, rites, and
'01. 33–14   not to be judged on a doctrinal p·,
Peo. 11– 9   Above the p· of human rights
My. 31–26   * was on the Readers' p·.
    31–26   * Stepping to the front of the p·,
    32–10   * above the usual p· tone.
    44–16   * advanced to the front of the p·,
    68–17   * p· is of a beautiful foreign marble,
    68–21   * placed back of the Readers' p·
    69–19   * view of the p· from any seat.
    71–26   * p· in front of the great organ.
    145–18   I cannot go upon the p·

platforms
Mis. 253–10   may improve our p· ;

Plato
Mis. 111–23   P· was a pagan ;
    361–14   Socrates, P·, Kant, Locke,
Ret. 57– 5   P· believed he had a soul,
No. 21– 6   Confucius and P· but dimly discerned,
Hea. 8–15   P· did better ; he said,

platoons
Un. 6–25   while the p· of C. S. are not

play
Mis. 224–15   human life is the work, the p·,
    395–10   Doth p· a part,
Ret. 17– 3   midst the zephyrs at p·
    18– 3   Cool waters at p· with the
'02. 14–29   an open field and fair p·.
Hea. 11– 1   fountains p· in borrowed sunbeams,
Po. 57–17   Doth p· a part,
    62– 2   midst the zephyrs at p·
    63–10   Cool waters at p· with the
My. 31– 1   * chimes . . . began to p·,
    93–25   * and the part it has come to p·

played
Man. 61–22   shall be p· in a dignified and
Pul. 81– 2   * p· "All hail the power of
My. 59–22   * melodeon on which my wife p·,

playful
Po. 9– 4   Upturned . . . in p· grace ;

playing
Mis. 368–23   puppets of the hour are p·

plays
Pul. 81–23   * her own soul p· upon magic strings
Po. 2– 5   * "P· round the head,
My. 272–25   * p· so great a part

plea
Mis. 119–19   a p· for free moral agency,
Hea. 10–25   win or lose according to your p·
My. 31– 4   * "Just as I am, without one p· ;"
    305–26   chapter sub-title

plead
Mis. 310–14   my affections p· for all
    341–31   nor . . . adequate to p· for the
My. 265–11   p· not vainly in behalf of the

pleaded
Mis. 345– 5   p· for freedom in immortal strains

pleading
Mis. 59–14   p· with infinite Love to love us,
Po. 78–15   Give to the p· hearts comfort

pleads
Mis. 174–21   p· for Spirit — the All of God,
    371–14   my heart p· for them to
Chr. 53–55   Truth p· to-night :
'02. 11– 6   Love waits and p· to save mankind

pleas
Mis. 340–15   raised potatoes instead of p·,
My. 309–10   Both entered their p·,

pleasant
Mis. 52–12   often convenient, sometimes p·,
    86–18   p· sensations of human belief,
    238– 3   It is p·, now, to contrast with
    324–29   reaches the p· path of the valley
Un. 23– 3   * and of our p· vices
Pul. 72– 9   * very p· and agreeable lady,
No. 3–22   How good and p· a thing it is
    39–27   portray the face of p· thought.
Po. 73–15   P· a grave By the "Rock" or
My. 39–22   * my p· duty to preside at an
    87– 8   * p·, congenial, quietly happy,
    119–26   p· pastime of seeing your
    121–25   p· to those who practise it.
    147–22   I have purchased a p· place
    163–24   leading people of this p· city
    173–24   Scientists' short stay so p·.
    315– 9   * as p· and happy home
    341–27   * p· warmth within the

pleasanter
Mis. 287–27   p· to do right than wrong ;

pleasantly
Man. 27–20   p· located in the same building,
No. 46–12   descant p· upon free moral agency ;
My. 271–13   * In a modest, p· situated home

Pleasant View
Mis. 116– 5   P· V·, Concord, N. H.,
    142– 8   for the little pond at P· V·.
    203– 2   pretty pond contributed to P· V·,
    251– 1   chapter sub-title
    376–16   chapter sub-title
Pul. 37– 6   * beautiful residence, called P· V·.
    49–28   * as he approaches P· V·.
    58– 7   * beautiful estate called P· V· ;
'02. 20–18   our *annual* gathering at P· V·,
Po. 22–22   P· V·, Concord, N. H.,
    24–22   P· V·, Concord, N. H.,
    25–20   P· V·, Concord, N. H.,
    31–23   P· V·, Concord, N. H.,
    44– 5   P· V·, Concord, N. H.,
    79–22   P· V·, Concord, N. H.,
My. 9–29   P· V·, Concord, N. H.,
    20– 5   P· V·, Concord, N. H.,
    20–20   P· V·, Concord, N. H.,
    25–29   P· V·, Concord, N. H.,
    26–27   P· V·, Concord, N. H.,
    44–22   * P· V·, Concord, N. H.
    58–27   * P· V·, Concord, N. H.
    60–24   * P· V·, Concord, N. H.
    62–18   * P· V·, Concord, N. H.
    66–24   * P· V·, in Concord, N. H.,
    123–20   accommodations at P· V·
    133–19   P· V·, Concord, N. H.,
    135–22   P· V·, Concord, N. H.,
    136–10   P· V·, Concord, N. H.,
    136–30   P· V·, Concord, N. H.,
    138–23   P· V·, Concord, N. H.,
    155–31   flowers and the cross from P· V·,
    169– 3   P· V·, Concord, N. H.,
    169–11   P· V·, Concord, N. H.,
    170–11   chapter sub-title
    170–13   Welcome to P· V·,

Pleasant View

My.	171–17	*P· V·*, Concord, N. H.,
	175– 8	*P· V·*, Concord, N. H.,
	187–18	*P· V·*, Concord, N. H.,
	193–11	*P· V·*, Concord, N. H.,
	197–29	*P· V·*, Concord, N. H.,
	223– 3	received at *P· V·*
	228–26	Who shall be called to *P· V·*?
	228–31	never called to *P· V·* for penance
	229– 4	there cannot be found at *P· V·* one
	230–28	*P· V·*, Concord, N. H.,
	236–21	*P· V·*, Concord, N. H.,
	259– 7	* *P· V·*, Concord, N. H.
	261–19	*P· V·*, Concord, N. H.,
	272–17	*P· V·*, Concord, N. H.,
	279–29	*P· V·*, Concord, N. H.,
	280– 2	* *P· V·*, Concord, N. H.
	280–24	*P· V·*, Concord, N. H.,
	282–29	*P· V·*, Concord, N. H.,
	284– 8	*P· V·*, Concord, N. H.,
	284–29	*P· V·*, Concord, N. H.,
	285–31	*P· V·*, Concord, N. H.
	289–21	*P· V·*, Concord, N. H.,
	290–30	*P· V·*, Concord, N. H.,
	295–30	*P· V·*, Concord, N. H.,
	296– 7	*P· V·*, Concord, N. H.,
	296–22	*P· V·*, Concord, N. H.,
	297– 9	*P· V·*, Concord, N. H.,
	301–12	*P· V·*, Concord, N. H.,
	327– 8	*P· V·*, Concord, N. H.,
	346–10	* on my return from *P· V·*,
	351–20	*P· V·*, Concord, N. H.,

please

Mis.	61–27	(or bodies, if you *p·*)
	83–10	*Will you p· explain this seeming*
	81 19	*I· explain Paul's meaning*
	87–15	*P· inform us, through your Journal,*
	88– 6	*P· give us, through your Journal,*
	156– 7	*P· send in your contributions*
	287–20	*P· your husband,*
	287–29	and he will be apt to *p·* you ;
	306– 1	* *p·* send fullest historical
Pan.	3– 1	mythical deity may *p·* the fancy,
Po.	23–18	Than just to *p·* mankind.
My.	20–14	*p·* add to your givings to The
	72–15	* "*P·* do not send us any more
	109–14	Principle (or Person, if you *p·*)
	169–15	*P·* say through the *New York Journal,*
	172–18	You will *p·* accept my thanks
	172–27	You will *p·* accept from me
	175– 6	*P·* accept the enclosed check
	199–11	will *p·* accept my grateful
	201–27	*P·* accept a line from me
	236– 9	and to say, *p·* adopt generally
	241–28	* *P·* give the truth in the *Sentinel,*
	250–12	will *p·* send to the Editor
	264–10	* *p·* send through the *Globe*
	266–25	Note, if you *p·*, that many points
	284 17	In your next issue *p·* correct this
	285– 2	*P·* accept my thanks
	347– 8	will *p·* accept my heartfelt
	356–14	will you *p·* state that within the
	361– 6	*P·* find it there,

pleased

Mis.	88– 9	am *p·* to inform this inquirer,
	131–24	I, for one, would be *p·* to have the
	328–19	hast thou tarried . . . *p·* and stupefied,
Pul.	48–14	* It *p·* her to point out her
Po.	v–20	* *They were so p· with it*
My.	136–13	I am *p·* to say that the
	184–15	The beautiful birch bark . . . *p·* me ;
	302–26	My first visit to . . . *p·* me,
	316–21	I am *p·* to find this
	320– 5	* He also seemed very much *p·*
	321–30	* I am also *p·* to have had
	324–23	* *p·* in numbering you among
	328–10	* greatly *p·* at the law
	328–12	* *p·* with the fact that the law

pleasing

Mis.	86–30	even this *p·* thraldom,
	303–23	purpose of a Liberty Bell, is *p·*,
Ret.	5–27	* themes at once *p·* and profitable.
Pul.	3–24	what is *p·* to the divine Mind.
	49–30	* it was *p·* to learn that this
My.	vi– 4	* in a simpler or more *p·* form.
	259–14	most *p·* Christmas presents,

pleasurable

My.	265– 2	more possible and *p·*.

pleasure

and pain

Mis.	85–23	suggests *p·* and pain in matter ;
	198– 7	its varied forms of *p·* and pain.
	333– 2	*p·* and pain, good and evil,
Un.	3– 3	believe in matter's . . . *p·*, and pain,

pleasure

childish

Mis.	310– 1	prohibit ourselves the childish *p·* of

false

Mis.	209–20	False *p·* will be, is, chastened ;

find

My.	86– 5	* find *p·* in this new symbol,

fleeting

Ret.	32–15	* Fleeting *p·*, fond delusion,

give me

My.	192–22	It would indeed give me *p·* to

good

Mis.	150– 1	your Father's good *p·* — *Luke* 12 : 32.
	321–17	your Father's good *p·* — *Luke* 12 : 32.
Ret.	14–10	good *p·* of infinite Love.
Pul.	9–22	your Father's good *p·* — *Luke* 12 : 32.
My.	300– 7	to do of His good *p·*." — *Phil.* 2 : 13.

great

Mis.	143–18	It gives me great *p·* to say
	317–10	would have great *p·* in instructing,
My.	42–20	* affords me great *p·* to welcome you
	186–27	It gives me great *p·* to know

he finds

Mis.	15– 1	fancies he finds *p·* in it,

His

Mis.	127–17	"river of His *p·*," — *see Psal.* 36 : 8.
My.	18–14	'river of His *p·*,' — *see Psal.* 36 : 8.

his

Un.	2–10	sin and his *p·* in it ;

indefinable

Pan.	3– 9	indefinable *p·* in stillness,

in infirmities

Mis.	201–16	Paul took *p·* in infirmities,
	201–31	good that has *p·* in infirmities ;

in sin

Mis.	90– 3	power of sin is the *p·* in sin.
	241–11	"You have no *p·* in sin,"
My.	133 26	sinner, dreaming of *p·* in sin ;

is no crime

Mis.	362–30	*p·* is no crime except when it

its

No.	32– 7	belief in sin — its *p·*, pain, or power

mere

'01.	15–23	* nothing but God's mere *p·*

more

'00.	11– 1	and it gave me more *p·* than

much

Mis.	263– 1	because I take so much *p·* in
My.	21–21	* always experienced much *p·* in

my

My.	42– 5	* It is my *p·* to introduce to you

no

Pan.	10–26	no *p·* in loathsome habits

nor pain

Mis.	28–25	neither *p·* nor pain therein.

of attending

Pul.	29– 8	* *p·* of attending the service

of hearing

Mis.	155–23	the *p·* of hearing from you.

of sin

Ret.	63– 7	sinner's belief in the *p·* of sin,

of thanking

My.	174–17	I have the *p·* of thanking you

or pain

Mis.	100– 6	intoxicated with *p·* or pain,

or recompense

'01.	30–21	the hope of ease, *p·*, or recompense,
My.	308– 7	by ease, *p·*, or recompense.

pain and

Mis.	74–25	or express pain and *p·*.

perishing

Mis.	17–30	perishing *p·* and accumulating pains

personal

Mis.	9–28	gratification in personal *p·*

pursuit of

Mis.	230–17	occupy in the pursuit of *p·*.

pursuit or

Mis.	340– 8	seeking no other pursuit or *p·*

read with

My.	230–18	read with *p·* your approval

sense of

My.	273–19	personal sense of *p·*, pain, joy,

slaves to

My.	197– 2	but becoming slaves to *p·*

take

Mis.	199–11	*take p· in infirmities,* — *II Cor.* 12 : 10.
	200–21	take *p·* in infirmities," — *II Cor.* 12 : 10.
Hea.	6–10	they take *p·* in calling me a medium.

takes

My.	26– 3	* takes *p·* in announcing

that is false

Mis.	351–24	senses give . . . *p·* that is false,

this

Mis.	90– 4	Take away this *p·*, and you

thrill of

Mis.	132–26	It was with a thrill of *p·* that

pleasure

took
Mis. 201–20 he took *p·* in
201–23 he took *p·* in
Ret. 37– 6 critics took *p·* in saying,

Mis. 353–32 world worship, *p·* seeking, and
Pul. 36–28 * a *p·* to give any information
My. 99– 6 * but a *p·* and an essential ;
143– 9 I have the *p·* to report
163–11 must not allow myself the *p·* of
221–24 All issues of morality, . . . of *p·*,

pleasures

and pains
Mis. 73–19 so-called *p·* and pains of matter
84–27 joys and sorrows, *p·* and pains,
116–17 loss of the *p·* and pains
183–11 the so-called *p·* and pains of
Un. 55–19 how false are the *p·* and pains of
Pan. 1–13 the *p·* and pains of sensation
corporeal
My. 260–20 tradition, usage, or corporeal *p·*,
dangerous
Mis. 209–14 destroy its more dangerous *p·*.
deny
Po. 32–16 with appetite, *p·* deny,
earth's
'02. 19–21 Are earth's *p·*, its ties and
hater's
Mis. 122–29 The hater's *p·* are unreal ;
His
Pul. 3–21 The river of His *p·*
9–21 river of His *p·*."— see Psal. 36 : 8.
or pains
Mis. 341–30 nor the so-called *p·* or pains of
or the pains
Hea. 17– 3 *p·* or the pains of the personal
pains and
Mis. 200–29 so-called pains and *p·* of matter
pains or
Mis. 185– 7 abilities or disabilities, pains or *p·*.
Thy
Pul. 1– 2 river of Thy *p·*.— Psal. 36 : 8.
3–18 river of Thy *p·*."— Psal. 36 : 8.
7–30 river of Thy *p·*."— Psal. 36 : 8.

Mis. 85–25 The *p·* — more than the pains
My. 256–14 *p·*, achievements, and *aid*.

pledge

Ret. 80– 2 this is the *p·* of divine good
No. 46– 2 the *p·* of the Master.
Po. 68– 5 sweet *p·* to my lone heart
My. 11–21 * we have also made good the *p·*.
11–29 * The *p·* of the annual meeting was
46–18 * Only as we *p·* ourselves anew
46–19 * fulfil the *p·* in righteous living,
46–22 * we do hereby *p·* ourselves to
207–10 * *p·* themselves to strive more

pledged

My. 7–13 chapter sub-title
9–21 *p·* yourselves with startling grace
13–17 *p·* to this church in Boston
13–28 virtually *p·* this munificent sum
22– 9 * sum of money adequate . . . was *p·*.
23–15 * $2,000,000 *p·* at the annual meeting,
65–14 * money to provide it was *p·*
76–19 * was *p·* by the members assembled
269– 4 *p·* to innocence, purity, perfection.

pledges

Pul. 83– 9 * or a million of broken *p·*.
My. 93–10 * prospers according to the *p·*

Pleiades

Rud. 4–12 influences of the *P·*,"— Job 38 : 31.

plenitude

Pul. 54–16 * and in the *p·* of his power

plenty

Mis. 6– 7 C. S. practitioners have *p·* to do,
118–25 it gives one *p·* of employment,
232– 3 drank to peace, and *p·*,
325–10 they have *p·* of pelf,
'00. 2–17 he has *p·* of means,
Po. 77– 5 *P·* and peace abound at Thy behest,
My. 340–28 their implorations for peace and *p·*

plight

My. 312– 9 * in a miserable *p·*.

Pliny

My. 150– 5 *P·* gives the following description of

plot

Ret. 20–26 A *p·* was consummated for
Pul. 24– 9 * on a triangular *p·* of ground,
My. 55–11 * Mrs. Eddy gave the *p·* of ground

pluck

Mis. 151– 4 neither shall any man *p·* — John 10 : 28.
213–24 neither shall any man *p·* — John 10 : 28.
374–13 *p·* not their heaven-born wings.
My. 219– 7 I by no means would *p·* their plumes.

plucked

Ret. 18–13 Oft *p·* for the banquet,
Hea. 11– 1 *p·* from the wings of vanity.
Po. 64– 3 Oft *p·* for the banquet,
My. 139– 4 neither dead nor *p·* up by the roots,

plucking

My. 340–17 annulling such bills and *p·* their

plucks

'01. 35–11 Love divine that *p·* us From the

plumbing

Pul. 76–19 * *p·* is all heavily plated

plumed

Mis. 267–21 *p·* for rarefied atmospheres

plumes

Mis. 371–25 error in borrowed *p·*?
Ret. 11– 5 If fancy *p·* aerial flight,
Un. 17–17 despoil error of its borrowed *p·*,
Hea. 11– 1 *p·* are plucked from the wings
Po. 34– 7 airy wing, and fold thy *p·*?
60– 1 If fancy *p·* aerial flight,
My. 219– 8 I by no means would pluck their *p·*.
340–18 and plucking their *p·* through

plummet

My. 16–29 righteousness to the *p·* :— Isa. 28 : 17.

plunge

Mis. 327–30 they *p·* headlong over the
My. 200–27 God spare this *p·*,

plural

Mis. 191–21 employed in its *p·* number,
No. 22–19 used in the *p·* number.
My. 226– 1 not be written . . . in the *p·* number.

plurality

Pan. 7– 3 Science shows that a *p·* of minds,

plus

My. 350– 5 and *p·* human hypothesis,

plush

Pul. 25–22 * upholstered in old rose *p·*.
76–10 * hangings of deep green *p·*,
77– 5 * in a handsome *p·* casket
86–12 * encased in an elegant *p·* box.

Plymouth Rock

Mis. 176–20 planted their feet on *P· R·*,
Ret. 11–19 wreaths are twined round *P· R·*,
Pul. 10–11 shores of solitude, at *P· R·*,
Po. 60–16 wreaths are twined round *P· R·*,

P. M.

Mis. 350– 4 secret society known as the *P. M.*,
350– 7 The *P. M.* (Private Meeting) Society met
350–14 The second *P. M.* convened in

pneumatic

Pul. 60–20 * *p·* wind-chests throughout,

pneumonia

'01. 17–16 last stages of consumption, *p·*,
My. 105–21 pronounced dying of *p·*,
107–32 gastritis, hyperæmia, *p·*,

pocket

Mis. 43–23 fill one's *p·* at the expense of

pockets

Mis. 274–23 whose consciences are in their *p·*

poem

Mis. 33– 1 comments on my illustrated *p·*,
142–12 beautiful boat and presentation *p·*.
142–15 first impression was to indite a *p·* ;
309–27 Christmas *p·* and its illustrations
313–17 "The Temptation," a *p·* by J. J. Rome,
371–27 An illustrated *P·*
371–28 This *p·* and its illustrations
372–16 * "The illustrations of your *p·* are
374–22 the one illustrating my *p·*
Ret. 20–15 my *p·*, "Mother's Darling,"
Pul. 39– 9 *p·* that I consider superbly sweet
54– 1 * in a *p·* entitled "The Master,"
Po. v– 5 * each *p·* being the spontaneous
v–15 * the *p·* began to take form
v–20 * she replied by reading the *p·*
vi– 1 * *p·* finally found its way into print,
vi– 5 * *p·* on the "Dedication of a
vi–11 * was published with the *p·*,
My. 189–28 a *p·* written in 1844,

poems

Man. 59– 8 books or *p·* of our Pastor Emeritus,
Po. v– 1 * *p·* garnered up in this little volume
vi–23 * many *p·* written in girlhood
vi–26 * Among her earliest *p·*

poems
Po. vii– 6   * *bound volumes of her p'*,
My. 358–16   shall publish your *p'*.

poet (*see also* poet's)
Ret. 32–11   Calderon, the famous Spanish *p'*,
My. 40–26   * illustrated what the *p'* perceived

poetic
Mis. 294–27   terse, graphic, and *p'* style
Ret. 2– 4   *p'* daring and pious picturesqueness
Pul. 61–16   * is practical as well as *p'*,
Po. v– 6   * *outpouring of a deeply p' nature*

poetical
Pul. 66–15   * *p'* and highly figurative language.
Pan. 3– 5   *p'* phase of the genii of forests.

poet-patriarch
Un. 15– 4   more just . . . asks the *p'.—Job* 4 : 17.

poetry
Ret. 11– 1   *P'* suited my emotions better
Po. 46–14   Sweet as the *p'* of heaven,

poet's
Ret. 18– 1   Here the *p'* world-wish,
87– 3   *p'* line, "Order is heaven's first
Po. 63– 8   Here the *p'* world-wish,

poets
Mis. 372–10   letters . . . from artists and *p'*.
Ret. 80– 7   *p'* in different languages have
Pul. 28–24   * other recognized devotional *p'*,
53–26   * Whittier, grandest of mystic *p'*,

poignant
Ret. 7–19   * deplored, with the most *p'* grief,
'01. 16– 5   *p'* present sense of sin

point (noun)
achieved the
Mis. 316–25   had my students achieved the *p'*
at issue
Mis. 320–12   over this mind on the *p'* at issue.
cardinal
Mis. 27–10   cardinal *p'* in C. S.,
Un. 9 –27   cardinal *p'* of the difference
No. 25– 4   this cardinal *p'* of divine Science,
'01. 8– 2   I reiterate this cardinal *p'* :
central
Mis. 162–12   central *p'* of his Messianic mission
every
Mis. 46–20   but comprehending at every *p'*,
Hea. 5– 4   His power at every *p'*,
My. 304–22   * "Mrs. Eddy is from every *p'* of view
following
Mis. 216–24   illustrate the author's following *p'*
give
Mis. 268– 3   Two personal queries give *p'* to
incontestable
Un. 7 23   incontestable *p'* in divine Science
of convergence
Pul. 22– 4   one nucleus or *p'* of convergence,
of departure
Pul. 31– 9   * and take, as the *p'* of departure,
of discovery
Mis. 121– 9   up to a *p'* of discovery ;
of its disappearance
Mis. 271– 3   up to the *p'* of its disappearance
of perfection
My. 242– 6   is neither behind the *p'* of perfection
of view
Mis. 241– 1   From a religious *p'* of view,
Pul. 81– 9   * chapter sub-title
My. 69–29   * best *p'* of view is on top of the
304–22   * "Mrs. Eddy is from every *p'* of view
one
Ret. 31–20   and yet offend in one *p',— Jas.* 2 : 10.
Pul. 81– 9   * chapter sub-title
My. 96–10   * The one *p'* of resemblance is
sharp
Pan. 12–27   bold conjecture's sharp *p'*,
sneering
My. 96–27   * will soon be beyond the sneering *p'*.
speak to the
Pul. 46– 6   * words of the judge speak to the *p'*,
this
Mis. 186– 1   he was not at this *p'* giving the
198– 4   To arrive at this *p'* of unity
274– 3   This *p'*, however, had not impressed
292–29   my instructions on this *p'*
Pul. 37–15   * "On this *p'*, Mrs. Eddy feels
My. 69–31   * From this *p'* the building
241–17   * receive instruction . . . on this *p'*.
242– 7   it is at this *p'* and must be
to point
Pul. 26– 3   * twenty-one inches from *p'* to point,
vital
'01. 16–22   and to carry a most vital *p'*.
My. 146–23   Scientists hold as a vital *p'*

point
Mis. 98– 1   question of personality a *p'*,
Pul. 27–10   * a *p'* that the members

point (verb)
Mis. 92–18   *p'* out the lesson to the class,
117–20   To *p'* out every step to a student
147–16   voice of his conscience *p'* it out
213– 7   *p'* the way, shorten the process,
344–27   *p'* out the way to heaven
357–30   help them and *p'* the way.
389– 4   * *p'* to heaven and lead the way."
Chr. 53– 8   wake the dead, And *p'* the Way
Ret. 85–19   wait for God's finger to *p'* the way.
Pul. 15– 2   *p'* out the evil in human thought,
48–14   * *p'* out her own birthplace.
No. 9–19   *p'* steadfastly to the power of grace
'02. 11– 8   *p'* to the path to heaven.
Po. 21–18   * "To *p'* to heaven and lead the way."
My. 114– 8   why *p'* the people to the lives of
186–10   *p'* the path above the valley,
252–20   They *p'* to verdant pastures,
273– 6   * fortunate in being able to *p'* to

pointed
Mis. 341–27   The moral of the parable is *p'*,
Pul. 63–11   * *p'* to a number of large elms
No. 35– 9   He who *p'* the way of Life
'02. 16– 3   *p'* out that identical phrase,
My. 87–12   * unless they are *p'* out.
292– 6   the way *p'* out, the process shortened,

pointing
Mis. xi–12   guide-book, *p'* the path,
204–14   new affections, all *p'* upward.
268– 5   *p'* the way to heaven,
327–23   the Stranger is *p'* the way,
Pul. 49–15   * touching my sleeve and *p'*,
No. 28–11   If Science is *p'* the way,
Peo. 14 10   * white fingers *p'* upward."
My. 124–23   with finger *p'* upward,
153–31   *p'* away from matter and man
162–32   towering top . . . *p'* to the heavens,
176– 8   *p'* the path to heaven
202– 2   *p'* the path from earth to heaven

points
all
Un. 39–28   Science and . . . conflict at all *p'*,
58–16   "in all *p'* tempted like— *Heb.* 4 : 15.
'00. 9–17   reformer must be a hero at all *p'*,
My. 181– 2   to settle all *p'* beyond cavil,
cardinal
Mis. 107–14   Three cardinal *p'* must be gained
My. 339– 4   cardinal *p'* of C. S.
chief
Man. 111–14   chief *p'* of these instructions
disputed
Mis. 84– 7   prophets thrust disputed *p'* on
distant
My. 30–13   * come from far distant *p'*
doctrinal
'02. 12– 4   explains these doctrinal *p'*,
essential
Ret. 83–27   That these essential *p'* are ever
good
My. 322–25   * advancing many good *p'*
important
Mis. 92– 1   To omit these important *p'* is
many
My. 266–25   that many *p'* in theology
nine
No. 24–19   exposure is nine *p'* of destruction.
of action
Hea. 13– 1   so weaken both *p'* of action ;
spiritual
Mis. 143– 5   spiritual *p'*, above the plane of
two
Mis. 318–26   Two *p'* of danger beset mankind ;
vital
No. 3– 1   in some vital *p'* lack Science.

Mis. 166– 3   whose finger *p'* upward,
211– 3   Christ *p'* the way of salvation.
254– 2   *p'* with promise of prosperity
313– 6   *p'* to the scientific spiritual
339–16   it *p'* to every mortal mistake ;
356–28   *p'* out the chart of its divine
393–20   *P'* the plane of power to seek.
Ret. 31– 2   and *p'* to heaven.
Pan. 12–20   way-seeker gains and *p'* the path.
'02. 6–23   divine metaphysics *p'* the way,
Peo. 5–18   thought *p'* away from matter
Po. 52– 4   *P'* the plane of power to seek.
My. 99–28   * *p'* out their meaning
104– 6   That epithet *p'* a moral.
140–23   Christ, *p'* the advanced step.
158–12   it *p'* to the new birth,

points

My. 266–14 *p·* unmistakably to the
317–14 *p·* that might seem ambiguous
330–13 * *p·* concerning Major Glover's

point'st

Po. 26–13 Thou *p·* thy phantom finger,

poise

Mis. 263–20 *p·* the wavering balance

poises

Mis. 296–22 * which, "*p·* and poses,

poison

Mis. 248–21 have said that I died of *p·*,
368–15 sending forth a *p·* more deadly
368–21 "the *p·* of asps— *Rom.* 3 : 13.
'00. 8– 8 emit . . . a perfume or a *p·*,
My. 126– 6 to *p·* such as drink of the

poisoning

Mis. 248–29 mental malpractice of *p·* people

poisonous

Mis. 69–20 effects of the *p·* oil.
Un. 52–24 beautiful blossom is often *p·*,
'01. 33–19 with *p·* drugs, with the lance,
My. 90–15 * that discord is *p·*,
245–12 *p·* reptiles and devouring beasts,

poisons

Mis. 134–21 with *p·*, nostrums, and knives,
Un. 52–20 lightnings, earthquakes, *p·*,

poked

Mis. 231–18 finger . . . *p·* into the little mouth

polar

Mis. 320–17 *p·* star, fixed in the heavens

Polar Sea

Un. 58–20 sun shines over the *P· S·*.

pole

Mis. 394– 4 An infinite essence from tropic to *p·*,
No. 10–25 turns like the needle to the *p·*
Po. 45– 5 An infinite essence from tropic to *p·*,

poles

My. 74–29 * representatives of the two *p·*

police

'02. 15– 3 neither informed the *p·*
My. 174– 9 marshal and his staff of *p·*

policemen

My. 83–14 * street-car men and *p·*,

policy

Mis. 118– 4 selfish motives, and human *p·*.
204–17 human wisdom, human *p·*,
212– 1 Human *p·* is a fool
212– 4 This godless *p·* never knows
212– 8 reminded . . . of their worldly *p·*.
327–11 worldly *p·*, religion, politics,
Ret. 78–16 adoption of a worldly *p·*
79–16 worldly *p·*, pomp, and pride,
My. 340–20 timid, or dastardly *p·*,

polite

My. 121–24 not only *p·* to all but is

politic

Mis. 266– 5 is neither *p·* nor scientific ;

political

Mis. 246– 9 religious caste, civil and *p·* power.
Ret. 6–30 received further *p·* preferment,
7– 4 His noble *p·* antagonist,
My. 276–22 * an expression of her *p·* views,

politician

My. 106–26 nor a dishonest *p·*

politics

Mis. 327–11 religion, *p·*, finance,
Ret. 3– 2 prominent in British *p·*,
My. 266– 6 claims of *p·* and of human power,
276–16 * chapter sub-title
276–23 I am asked, "What are your *p·*?"
291– 9 warming the marble of *p·*
355–12 to religion as well as to *p·*,

Polycarp

Mis. 345– 7 need the spirit of the pious *P·*,
Peo. 13–17 *P·* proved the triumph of mind over

polytheism

Pan. 4– 2 forms of pantheism and *p·*.
8–16 idolatry, pantheism, and *p·*.
8–24 doctrines that embrace pantheism, *p·*,

pomp

Mis. 144–14 without *p·* or pride,
Ret. 79–16 worldly policy, *p·*, and pride,
Pul. 10– 9 her *p·* and power lie low in dust.
Po. 16–11 toil for its *p·* and its pride.
27– 2 *p·* and tinsel of unrighteous power ;
My. 134–17 pride—its *p·* and its frown

pond

Mis. 142– 8 little *p·* at Pleasant View.
203 chapter title
203– 2 your gift of the pretty *p·*

ponder

Mis. 159–15 sit silently, and *p·*.
207– 1 *p·* this lesson of love.
Ret. 24–23 to *p·* my mission,
Po. 33–17 I *p·* the days may be few
My. 37–31 * give heed and *p·* and obey.
117–25 Christian Scientists *p·* this fact,
201–16 mercifully forgive, wisely *p·*,

pondered

Mis. 332–16 *p·* the things of man and God.

pondering

Mis. 309–14 *P·* on the finite personality of
379–24 assiduously *p·* the solution of

ponderosity

Mis. 22–30 by reason of its own *p·* ;

ponderous

My. 188–20 *p·* walls of your grand cathedral

ponders

Mis. 26– 9 *p·* the history of a seed,

pontiff

My. 294–26 energy of this illustrious *p·*

poor

Mis. 70–20 *p·* thief's prayer for help
106– 4 *p·* parody on Tennyson's grand verse,
107–14 before *p·* humanity is regenerated
137– 8 the privilege, *p·* as it was,
142–24 *P·* return, is it not?
168–10 *p·*— the lowly in Christ,
171–19 to the *p·* the gospel is preached.
227–16 these weak, pitifully *p·* objects
231– 8 but, what of the *p·* !
233–20 a *p·* shift for the weak and worldly
239–19 the *p·* child said,
243–17 a mortal's *p·* performances.
252–31 the *p·* man's money ;
322–23 my past *p·* labors and love.
325– 3 "Blessed are the *p·*— *Matt.* 5 : 3.
344–14 *p·* sinner struggling with temptation,
359–17 nor Science for *p·* humanity to
366–16 *p·* jaded humanity needs to
388–19 bless the orphan, feed the *p·* ;
Ret. 26–26 "*p·* in spirit"— *Matt.* 5 : 3.
Rud. 9– 9 and he will be a *p·* practitioner,
No. 35– 2 Without it, how *p·* the precedents of
'01. 2–19 blessing the *p·* in spirit
'02. 15–16 I became *p·* for Christ's sake.
Hea. 7–17 reading the mind of the *p·* woman
12–21 cannot shake the *p·* drug without the
Po. 21– 8 bless the orphan, feed the *p·* ;
28–10 Aid our *p·* soul to sing
53–12 *P·* robin's lonely mass.
My. 9–24 I never before felt *p·* in thanks,
132–30 heals the *p·* body,
146–17 and my *p·* prophecy,
153–15 from my *p·* personality.
154–20 *" If the *p·* . . . toil that we have food,
195–21 by which we *p·* mortals expect to
196–27 The *p·* toil for our bread,
215–17 home for the *p·* worthy student,
231– 8 undeserving *p·* to whom she has given
287–11 a *p·* shift for the weak and worldly.
293–19 divine power and *p·* human sense

poorer

Mis. 87–12 mortal mind is a *p·* representative

poorly

Pul. 2–17 in a *p·* barricaded fort,
Pan. 3– 5 *p·* presents the poetical phase of

Pope (*see also* Pope's)

Ret. 77– 2 *P·* was right in saying,
My. 269–14 * signature

pope

My. 343–13 * heading
343–14 "I have been called a *p·*,
343–21 term *p·* is used figuratively.
343–30 If that is to be a *p·*,

Pope Leo XIII

My. 294–22 chapter sub-title
294–23 decease of *P· L·* XIII,

Pope's

'01. 30–28 and to adopt *P·* axiom :

poplar

Ret. 4–22 scrub-oak, *p·*, and fern flourish.

popping

Hea. 18–17 keep it from *p·* out

poppy

Ret. 26– 6 a preparation of *p·*, or aconite,

popular

Mis.	228–24	p· current of mortal thought
	239–21	sharing in a p· influenza
	345–21	To turn the p· indignation
Ret.	1– 6	pious and p· English authoress
	15–25	physicians of the p· schools
Un.	13– 3	P· theology makes God tributary
	38–26	p· views to this effect
	44– 7	p· couplet may be so paraphrased
No.	32– 5	*forgiveness,* in the p· sense of
	36–10	p· view of Jesus' nature.
'01.	18–28	destroys the p· triad
	22–18	to accommodate p· opinion as to
	28–25	Jesus, who was not p· among the
	28–26	not p· with them in this age ;
	28–27	he who would be p· if he could,
'02.	14–22	p· philosophies and religions
Hea.	18–17	until it became p·.
Po.	vii– 8	* *to allow a p· edition to be issued,*
My.	302–23	Because C. S. is not yet p·,
	314– 9	He . . . was a p· man,

popularity

Mis.	295–19	for whose ability and p·
	330–25	P·,— what is it?
Ret.	44–12	kept pace with its increasing p· ;
	45–24	withstood less the temptation of p·
	47– 4	unprecedented p· of my College.
Pul.	21–28	P·, self-aggrandizement,
	71– 4	* idea that C. S. has declined in p·
'01.	26–16	shall the word p· be pinned to the
'02.	9– 6	Let the world, p·, pride, and
My.	v– 9	* when p· threatens to supersede
	245–10	the increasing p· of C. S.,

population

Ret.	82–16	The p· of our principal cities
Pul.	56– 5	* nearly every other centre of p·,
My.	87– 5	* temporary increase of the p·
	181–23	Chicago has gained from a p· of

pore

No.	3–17	teacher must p· over it in secret,

portal

Mis.	180– 5	dark shadow and p· of death,
	231–31	looking longingly at the p·
Un.	41–18	opening wide a p· from death

portals

Mis.	196–20	opens wide the p· of salvation
	369–13	p· of the temple of thought,
	391– 5	Will find within its p·
Po.	38– 4	Will find within its p·
My.	92–24	* who entered its p· Sunday.
	94– 8	* who entered its p· Sunday,"

portend

Mis.	2– 6	signs of these times p· a

portending

Peo.	1–10	p· a long night to the traveller ;

portends

Mis.	253–15	p· much for the future.

portent

My.	92–10	* p· worthy of perhaps even more

portentous

My.	273–21	scientific knowledge that is p· ;

porter

Mis.	325–19	p· starts up in blank amazement

porticos

Pul.	24–11	* accented by stone p·

portion

Mis.	22–10	discovery of even a p· of it
	139–16	p· of the above Scripture for its
	160– 7	paramount p· of her being.
	245– 8	materialistic p· of the pulpit
	252–19	to the whole and not to a p· ;
	314– 8	chapter (or p· of the chapter)
	335–10	appoint him his p· — *Matt.* 24 : 51.
Man.	31– 6	devote a suitable p· of their time
Ret.	52– 6	have a small p· of its letter
Rud.	14– 2	giving only a p· of their time
'01.	1–18	p· of the primal reality of things.
My.	8– 1	* any p· of two million dollars
	9– 5	* any p· of two million dollars
	11–30	* "any p· of two million dollars
	20–16	let this suffice for her rich p·
	151– 2	attacks of a p· of Christendom :
	165–16	active p· of one stupendous whole,
	175–20	macadamize a p· of Warren Street
	357– 6	matter has neither part nor p·,

portions

Mis.	374–27	Pictures are p· of one's ideal,
My.	209–12	also whatever p· of truth

Portland

Maine

Mis.	378– 6	Mr. P. P. Quimby of P·, Maine.

Portland

Me.

My.	306–22	Dr. Quimby of P·, Me.,

Mis.	378–11	*en route* for the aforesaid doctor in P·.
My.	304–13	Chicago, Boston, P·,
	306–30	while I was his patient in P·

Portland (**Me.**) *Advertiser*

My.	98–27	* [P· (M·.) A·]

Portland, Ore.

Pul.	90– 8	* *Telegram,* P·, O·.

Portland (**Ore.**) *Telegram*

My.	98–13	* [P· (O·.) T·]

portly

Mis.	239–12	a p· gentleman alight,

portrait

Pul.	58–30	* Therein is a p· of

portraits

My.	342– 8	* p· of twenty years ago,

portraiture

Mis.	309– 6	material p· often fails to express
Ret.	22– 5	noumenon and phenomenon silenced p·.

portray

Mis.	275–21	Pen can never p· the satisfaction
No.	39–26	to p· the face of pleasant thought.
'00.	14– 0	He goes on to p· seven churches,

portrayed

Mis.	164–24	p· him as the only Son of God,
	368–20	p· in these words of the apostle,
	376– 6	* p· by the oldest of the

portrays

Ret.	72– 7	p· the result of secret faults,
My.	206–16	fact that p· Life, Truth, Love.

Portsmouth

My.	281–23	* two parties to the treaty of P·,
	281–29	treaty of P· is not an executive

poses

Mis.	296–22	* "poises and p·, higgles and wriggles"

position

Mis.	146–14	and still maintain this p·.
Man.	71–12	a p· that no other church can fill.
	71–14	such p· would be disastrous
Ret.	3– 2	p· of ambassador to Persia.
	85–16	Seek to occupy no p· whereto
Un.	31–16	Hence my conscientious p·,
Pul.	3–10	If you maintain this p·,
No.	10–19	former p·, that sense is organic
'01.	13– 9	It is not well to maintain the p·
My.	22–25	* p· taken by our Pastor Emeritus
	92– 2	* its real p· in the doctrines of
	120– 9	Forgive, . . . my honest p·.
	206– 3	power and pride of p·,
	312–14	* Her p· was an embarrassing one.
	321– 8	* also your p· as regards your
	321–10	* he always gave you that p·
	343–22	"A p· of authority," she went on,

positions

My.	181– 7	and outgrown, proofless p·.
	255– 8	filling their p· satisfactorily

positive

Mis.	44– 8	power of C. S. is p·,
	62–10	p· and negative quantities,
	62–11	offsets an equal p· quantity,
	62–12	making the aggregate p·, . . . less
	65–12	which the p· Truth destroys ;
	153–20	by p· proof of trustworthiness.
	172– 4	let us declare the p·
	288– 6	P· and imperative thoughts
Un.	10–24	principle of p· mathematics.
Pul.	4–10	scientific, p· sense of unity
'01.	33–24	richest and most p· proof
My.	91– 2	* proof p· that it supplies these
	166–13	p· proof of your remembrance

positives

No.	16–11	p· that cannot be gainsaid.

possess

Mis.	40–20	does not in every case p·
	40–22	p· the spirit of Truth and Love,
	145– 9	when that person shall p· these,
	149– 6	what they p· of love and light
	201–14	somethingness of the good we p·,
	268–31	we must p· the sense of Truth ;
	284– 8	may p· a zeal without knowledge,
	371–14	to p· more and more of Truth
Pul.	3– 7	you p· sovereign power to
No.	3–20	which they must p·, in order to
	7–11	to see every error they p·,
'02.	8–18	except we p· this inspiration,
Hea.	4–11	We ask infinite wisdom to p·
Peo.	10–21	We p· our own body,

possess
My. 12–20 we p· only now.
    44– 5 * going up to p· the promised land
    164–17 not only p· a sound faith, but
    292–25 supposed to p· opposite qualities

possessed
Man. 92–23 p· of the qualifications named
Ret. 5–14 My father p· a strong intellect
    5–22 * She p· a strong intellect,
Un. 2–23 Love beyond what they p· before ;
No. 30–17 if He p· any knowledge of them.
Pan. 5– 9 p· of the nature of God,
'01. 9–14 and Christ Jesus p· it,
My. 181–13 p· the motive of true religion,
    293–21 Had prayer so fervently offered p· no

possesses
Mis. 55– 6 when the student p· as much of the
    184–15 power to be perfect which he p·,
    195– 6 but p· not its spirit,
No. 23–24 amount of good or evil he p·.
Pan. 4– 4 p· all wisdom, goodness, and
'01. 5– 8 each of these p· the nature of all,
My. 127–10 C. S. p· more of Christ's teachings
    164–17 but that faith also p· them.

possessing
Mis. 252–10 p· the nature of dreams.
    337–23 personalities p· these defacing
No. 3–27 p· the essentials of C. S.,

possession
Mis. 373–23 it has rich p· here,
Pul. 79–19 * that had taken p· of men's minds,
'01. 13–10 can take p· of us and
    13–11 take p· of sin with such a sense of
My. 43– 2 * in p· of the promised land.
    192– 4 unto the p· of unburdened bliss.
    273–28 in p· of the five personal senses,
    305–10 manuscripts and letters in my p·,
    315– 1 original of which is in my p·,
    329–13 * has in her p· photographed copies
    333– 2 * now in the p· of the chairman

possessions
Mis. 119–30 that others should . . . steal your p·,

possessor
Mis. 12– 4 brings suffering . . . to its p·,
Pan. 9–24 and rewards its p· ;
'02. 16– 8 happy p· of a copy of Wyclif,
My. 203–17 malady which kills its p· ;
    203–18 precursor that its p· is mortal

possibilities
Mis. 30– 7 all the p· of Christianity?
    44–12 demonstrate its highest p·.
    47–14 p· of mind when let loose
    55– 5 prove all its p·.
    60–20 Mind's p· are not lessened by
    187– 6 proper sense of the p· of Spirit.
    235–12 loftier desires and new p·.
    251–19 the present p· of mankind.
    330–12 man's p· are infinite,
Ret. 32– 3 p· of spiritual insight,
    57– 3 unfathomable sea of p·.
Un. 11–25 fitness for perfection and its p·.
Pul. 30–22 * p· of the divine Life.
    81–20 * She is as full of beautiful p· as
'01. 1–24 practical p· of divine Love :
My. 177–14 the p· and permanence of Life.
    287–20 lofty desires, new p·,

possibility
Mis. 41– 8 destroys their own p· of progressing.
    54–27 does it not suggest the p·
    60–12 deny the p· of communion with
    102–10 His infinity precludes the p· of
    182–24 but the p· of all finding
    214–28 p· of destroying the tares :
Un. 43– 8 mortals now believe in the p·
    50– 1 the p· of its defilement ;
Pul. 38–21 * no p· of communication.
    45–14 * transcended human p·.
My. 238–20 no p· of misinterpretation.

possible
Mis. 46–16 It is p·, and it is man's duty,
    48–18 p· purpose to which it can be
    50–12 as can be p·, under the
    64–25 Is it p· to know why we are
    64–27 p· to know wherefore man
    66– 7 No p· injustice lurks in this
    67–30 believe in this removal being p·
    75– 4 man's p· earthly development.
    78–15 deceive, if p·, the very elect.
    157–11 furnish all information p·.
    175–20 if it were p·, — Matt. 24 : 24.
    183–13 whatever is p· to God,
    183–13 p· to man as God's reflection.
    191–18 By no p· interpretation can this

possible
Mis. 191–29 could only be p· as evil beliefs,
    229–26 any other p· sanative method ;
    247–11 the highest p· ethics.
    255– 7 it is p·, and dutiful,
    286–17 yet this is p· in Science,
    291–17 p· perversion of C. S.
    292–22 leading them, if p·, to Christ,
    294–20 transform them, — if it be p·,
    302–28 intended to forestall the p· evil of
    305–15 * largest number of persons p·
    305–27 * in pennies, if p·,
    310– 2 neither the intent of my works nor p·
    344– 6 do you think it p· for you to
Man. 44– 6 p· loss, for a time, of C. S.
    50– 2 When it is p· the body
    77–24 any p· future deviation from duty,
Ret. 52– 4 if p·, to build a hedge round about
Un. 15–17 if the thought of sin could be p· in
    18–27 If such knowledge of evil were p·
Pul. 85– 4 * made its erection p·.
    85–17 * who believe it to be p· to
Rud. 15–15 to fill in the best p· manner
No. 2–14 if this is p·.
Pan. 12– 1 it will be found p· to fulfil it.
'01. 5– 1 has no p· conception of ours,
'02. 14–11 The only genuine success p·
My. vi– 3 * not p· to state . . . in a simpler
    20–28 be completed as early as p·,
    62–29 * to assist us in every way p· ;
    63–16 * scarcely p· to repress a feeling of
    126– 6 and if p·, to poison such as drink
    161–25 Sickness is p· because one's
    180–15 to whom all things are p· ;
    243–17 give all p· time and attention to
    265– 1 more p· and pleasurable.
    293– 1 all things are p· to God
    349– 3 to whom all things are p·.
    353– 1 and as many others as p·,
    356–27 only p· correct version of C. S.

possibly
Mis. 80– 8 and p· to aid individual rights
    111– 8 p· blamed others more than
Man. 41–17 discipline and, p·, dismissal
Un. 22– 4 in which no evil can p· dwell.
Pul. 3– 2 how can our godly temple p· be
My. 60– 6 * P· you may remember the words
    93–18 * p· too prone to approach it

Post
Pul. 72– 4 * a P· reporter called upon
    88–19 * P·, Boston, Mass.
    88–20 * P·, Hartford, Conn.
    89– 7 * P·, Pittsburgh, Pa.
    89–19 * P·, Washington, D. C.

Post, The
Pul. 71– 9 * The P·, Syracuse, New York,

post
Mis. 116–27 Never absent from your p·,
    154–26 never desert the p· of spiritual
    210– 8 p· around it placards warning people
Ret. 70–29 p· of duty, unpierced by vanity,
    85–17 Never forsake your p· without due
My. 11– 5 * constantly at her p· during all the
    69–17 * not a single pillar or p· anywhere
    192–25 pin me to my p·.
    221–27 like a watchman forsaking his p·,

postal
'02. 11–13 If a p· service, a steam engine,

posterity
Mis. 93– 3 so teach that p· shall
    364– 9 and p· your familiar !
Ret. 61–26 P· will have the right to demand
    84–22 p· will call him blessed,

posterns
Mis. 383–13 down the dim p· of time unharmed,

Post-Intelligencer
Pul. 90– 3 * P·, Seattle, Wash.

postlude
Man. 62– 1 six or seven minutes for the p·,

post mortem
Rud. 16–27 or else p· m· evidence.

post-mortem
My. 310–20 by physician or p· examination

post-office
My. 73–23 * There is here also a p·

postpone
My. 41–25 * Why should any one p·

postponed
My. 54–19 * Sunday services were p·.
    61– 9 * communion would likely be p·

postulate
Mis. 13–25 This *p·* of divine Science only needs to
57–13 the *p·* of error must
364–11 not a *p·* of the divine Principle,
Rud. 6–22 predicate and *p·* of Mind-healing ;
No. 10–10 predicate and *p·* of all that I teach,
'01. 21–21 neither the predicate nor *p·* of Truth,
My. 224–17 C. S. is the predicate and *p·*,

potatoes
Mis. 340–15 raised *p·* instead of pleas,

potato-patch
Mis. 26– 7 from the rolling of . . . to a *p·*.

potence
'02, 7–12 words *p·*, *presence, science.*

potency
Mis. 222–31 ways, means, and *p·* of Truth
252– 5 gains no *p·* by attenuation,
260–10 his only instrumentality and *p·*,
Ret. 31–30 the healing promise and *p·*
89– 2 divine *p·* of this spiritual mode
Pul. 53–23 * proclaimed its *p·* from the hilltops
'02. 3–27 right is the only real *p·* ;
Hea. 11–23 as matter went out and . . . was its *p·*.

potent
Mis. 4– 3 is the most *p·* and desirable
126–20 No reproof is so *p·* as the silent
252–11 Good thoughts are *p·* ;
Un. 54–16 most *p·* and deadly enemy.
Pul. 23–17 * as one of the most *p·* factors
35–25 * the more *p·* was its effects.
No. 39– 3 an honest and *p·* prayer
'01. 24–13 Making matter more *p·* than
Peo. 9–28 more *p·* evidences in C. S.
My. 108– 8 *p·* in proportion as it is seen to act

potential
Mis. 331–20 supreme *p·* Principle reigns
379–14 not as *p·* or remedial,

potentially
My. 349– 2 is first *p·*, and is the healer

potion
Mis. 239–16 and what may the *p·* be?''

potions
Mis. 268–22 are *p·* of His own qualities.

potted
Pul. 42–25 * *p·* palms and ferns

Potter, Mrs. Judge
My. 311–21 Mrs. Judge *P·*, presented me my
311 26 Mrs. Judge *P·* and myself knelt

Potter Hall
My. 80–14 * held in *P· H·*,
80–23 * Jordan Hall, *P· H·*,

pounding
Mis. 316–22 *p·* wisdom and love into

pounds
Mis. 47– 2 *weigh over two hundred p·*
Ret. 40–18 babe . . . weighed twelve *p·*.

pour
Mis. 43–10 least likely to *p·* into other minds
134–13 God will *p·* you out a blessing
139– 5 God will *p·* you out a blessing
330 28 *p·* forth the unavailing tear.
353–15 to *p·* a bucket of water
Man. 58–21 *p·* into the ears of listeners
Un. 7–18 *p·* into my waiting thought
Pul. 83–21 * *p·* incense upon the rose.
No. 40–10 and *p·* forth a hypocrite's prayer ;
Po. 22–16 probe the wound, then *p·* the balm
My. 14– 3 God will *p·* them out a blessing
36–18 * *p·* out our gratitude to God
114–21 would *p·* in upon my spiritual sense
126– 3 *p·* wormwood into the waters
131–27 *p·* you out a blessing,— *Mal.* 3 : 10.
132 4 *p·* you out a blessing,'' *Mal.* 3 : 10.
269–27 *p·* you out a blessing,— *Mal.* 3 : 10.

poured
Mis. 110– 2 *p·* on our Master's feet,
140–16 generously *p·* into the treasury.
144–28 *p·* into the cup of Christ.
396–12 Are *p·* in strains so sweet,
Po. 31–19 *P·* on the sense which deems no
59– 4 Are *p·* in strains so sweet,
78–10 Tears of the bleeding slave *p·* on
My. 75– 8 * They *p·* into the city
81–18 * *p·* out their debts of gratitude
211–24 lies, *p·* constantly into his mind,

pouring
Mis. 172– 9 clans *p·* in their fire upon us ;
372–10 letters extolling it were *p·* in
392– 8 from thy lofty summit, *p·* down
Po. 20–11 from thy lofty summit, *p·* down

pouring
My. 77–13 * pilgrims are *p·* into Boston,
86– 9 * have been *p·* into Boston
269–23 *p·* out blessing for cursing,

pours
No. 44–19 *p·* the healing balm of Truth

poverty
Mis. 281–20 our *p·* and helplessness without this
296–28 incited thereto by their own *p·*
'00. 8–13 takes it off for his *p·* to appear.

poverty-stricken
Ret. 86–10 this *p·* "stranger— *Deut.* 5 : 14.
My. 100– 6 * property of no *p·* sect.

powder
Mis. 242–21 and taking morphine *p·*

power
accumulation of
Ret. 82–20 an accumulation of *p·* on his side
activity and
Mis. 250–21 goodness without activity and *p·*.
actual
Mis. 103–23 hides the actual *p·*, presence, and
all
Mis. 13–30 omnipotence, has all *p·* ;
14–30 deprives evil of all *p·*,
31–16 God, good, has *all p·*.
97–18 omnipotence has all *p·*.
155– 4 All *p·* and happiness are spiritual,
184–21 learns that all *p·* is good
331–24 filling all space and having all *p·*,
333–14 good, is supreme, *all p·*
373–26 "All *p·* is given unto— *Matt.* 28 : 18.
No. 42–11 All *p·* belongs to God ;
My. 278–29 The Principle of all *p·* is God,
204– 5 basis that God has all *p·*,
and glory
Mis. 92–28 *p·* and glory of the Scriptures,
Ret. 84–16 *p·* and glory of the Scriptures,
No. 18– 5 all presence, *p·*, and glory.
and good
Mis. 284– 7 field of limitless *p·* and good
and goodness
No. 13– 1 reflection of His *p·* and goodness.
and love
Un. 2– 8 God's presence, *p·*, and love,
and peace
Mis. 263–13 His presence, *p·*, and peace
and perfection
Mis. 189 18 the *p·* and perfection of a
Ret. 27–27 increases in *p·* and perfection
and permanence
Mis. 74–27 the *p·* and permanence of Spirit.
160– 1 *p·* and permanence of affection
and prerogative
My. 179– 7 *p·* and prerogative of Spirit
218– 9 *p·* and prerogative of Truth
and presence
Mis. 77–13 *p·* and presence, in divine Science,
173–22 not met by another *p·* and presence,
333–14 is supreme, *all p·* and presence,
and pride
My. 206– 3 with *p·* and pride of position,
and purpose
Pul. 10– 5 God's *p·* and purpose to supply them.
My. 293– 3 *p·* and purpose of infinite Mind,
and spell
Mis. 392–11 thou art a *p·* and spell ;
Po. 20–15 thou art a *p·* and spell ;
and Truth
Mis. 334– 8 Whatever simulates *p·* and Truth
another
Un. 38–13 must enthrone another *p·*,
any
Mis. 170–29 eyes as having any *p·* to see.
Pul. 72–22 * that Mrs. Eddy had any *p·* other than
any more
Mis. 58– 3 *have any more p· over him?*
any other
Peo. 9–24 remove all evidence of any other *p·*
armed with
My. 277–23 armed with *p·* girt for the hour.
assumed
Un. 45–12 An evil ego, and his assumed *p·*,
attributed
Mis. 48– 3 If mesmerism has the *p·* attributed
attributes and
Mis. 23–27 manifests all His attributes and *p·*,
authority and
Mis. 333–25 believed that . . . had authority and *p·*,
belief in the
Mis. 58– 8 belief in the *p·* of disease
Christ's
My. 257–21 should bow and declare Christ's *p·*,

power

circumstance or
Mis. 155- 3   pride of circumstance or p·
claimed the
Mis. 60—26   Evil in the beginning claimed the p·,
claim to
Mis. 31—11   Its claim to p· is in proportion to
confers a
Un. 7—21   confers a p· nothing else can.
deific
Un. 17- 5   Be allied to the deific p·,
destroy the
Mis. 97- 1   to destroy the p· of the flesh ;
divine
   (see **divine**)
effect of
Mis. 334—10   may have the effect of p· ;
electric
Pul. 25- 5   * with motor electric p·.
embodiment or
Pan. 5—21   that it hath embodiment or p· ;
energy and
Pul. 37- 8   * retains . . . her energy and p· ;
ever-present
My. 294—14   ever-present p· of divine Spirit
evil
Mis. 103- 2   which say that sin is an evil p·,
executive
My. 281—29   is not an executive p·,
faculty or
Hea. 9—19   not a faculty or p· underived from
fame and
Mis. 145- 8   burn for fame and p·?
fatal
Mis. 72—10   supposed to impart . . . this fatal p·.
foot of
Ret. 11—11   knowledge plants the foot of p·
Po. 60- 8   knowledge plants the foot of p·
gives it
Pan. 6—27   altitude of mind gives it p·,
gives man
'02. 9- 1   God as Love gives man p·
giveth
Mis. 167—28   He giveth p·, peace,
God-endued with
My. 190—26   thus become God-endued with p·
God's
Mis. 52- 3   to support God's p· to heal
52- 8   has no doubt of God's p·,
194—24   how to accept God's p·
Un. 26—17   true that God's p· never waneth,
Pul. 10- 5   God's p· and purpose to supply them.
No. 29—16   a denial of God's p·?
42- 3   * manifestations of God's p· increase
My. 248—21   only as uplifted by God's p·,
goodness and
No. 39—22   of His goodness and p·.
Pan. 4- 5   possesses all wisdom, goodness, and p·,
greater
'01. 2- 4   to the acquiring of greater p·
healing
Mis. 5—13   healing p· is Truth and Love,
258—10   he demonstrated the healing p·
373—16   and his healing p·,
Pul. 22—19   healing p· of Christ will prevail.
Rud. 9—19   weighs against his healing p· ;
No. 42—13   to dispossess the . . . of healing p·,
46- 4   Christianity, with its healing p·,
'01. 9—13   it is the healing p· of Truth
'02. 9—13   its divine origin, and healing p·,
Peo. 12—24   and give the healing p· to matter
My. 81- 8   * healing p· of the faith,
her
Ret. 11—18   The cradle of her p·,
Po. 60—15   The cradle of her p·,
My. 90—28   * and the sources of her p·
His
Mis. 183—27   have power to reflect His p·,
Chr. 53—51   same hand unfolds His p·,
Ret. 54- 8   humanized conception of His p·,
Rud. 10- 7   divides His p· with nothing evil
No. 13- 1   reflection of His p· and goodness.
'02. 10—27   God and His p· in man.
Hea. 5- 3   we shall be limiting His p·
My. 36—31   * God, through His p· and law,
his
Mis. 31—19   destroy his p· to be or to do good,
64- 4   to show his p· over death ;
85—10   his p· is temporarily limited.
162—15   prove his p·, derived from Spirit,
162—27   would have dethroned his p·
184—16   he would . . . lose his p· ;
197—19   his p· to heal and to save,
221- 3   may lose his p· to harm
270- 9   demonstrated his p· over sin,
270—24   the only passport to his p· ;

power

his
Ret. 91—21   His p· over others was spiritual,
92- 2   nor was his p· so exalted as to
Pul. 54—16   * in the plenitude of his p·
'01. 20—17   if the individual knew . . . his p·
23—21   demonstrated his p· over matter,
human
Mis. 138—19   giving to human p·, peace.
My. 219- 8   Human p· is most properly
266- 6   claims of politics and of human p·,
humane
My. 291- 21   emphasize humane p·,
immortal
Po. 31—17   splendor of immortal p·,
increased
Mis. 262- 3   increased p· to be good
No. 8—27   in equanimity, and with increased p·,
in criticism
Mis. 216—16   he is a p· in criticism,
infinite
Un. 13—14   His infinite p· would straightway
My. 160- 7   to individualize infinite p· ;
infusion of
Un. 42—22   infusion of p· into matter.
intelligence nor
Mis. 355—19   error, neither intelligence nor p·,
intelligence or
Mis. 260—20   seemeth to be intelligence or p·
in this world
Pul. 53—17   * human felicity and p· in this world,
is good
Mis. 101—23   this p· is good, not evil ;
184—21   learns that all p· is good
its
Mis. 4- 9   its p· to do good, not evil.
40- 3   its p· would be arrested if one
40—21   Christ-spirit and its p·
45- 7   its p· to allay fear,
48- 8   If such be its p·, I am opposed
55- 8   utilizes its p· to overcome sin.
90- 4   all reality from its p·.
111—19   prove its p· to be immortal.
Ret. 14- 2   forever lost its p· over me.
88—15   its p· to demonstrate immortality.
88—30   and its p· is displayed
Pul. 44—20   * C. S. has shown its p·
No. 33- 1   slander loses its p· to harm ;
33—21   Love and its p· over death.
'00. 6- 3   in proving its p· and divinity.
'02. 8—19   its p· to heal and to save.
Hea. 13—10   so-called drug loses its p·.
joy and
Mis. 331—18   peace and joy and p· ;
389- 6   peace and joy and p· ;
Po. 4- 2   peace and joy and p· ;
knowledge, and
No. 37—17   presence, knowledge, and p·,
latent
Mis. 201—24   tested and developed latent p·.
law, and
Mis. 364—17   individuality, law, and p·.
learned the
Mis. 41- 3   having learned the p· of liberated
55—11   having learned the p· of the
legal
Mis. 140—22   rescued from the grasp of legal p·,
Life and
Mis. 70—16   spiritual sense of Life and p·.
little
My. 238—12   has imparted little p· to practise
lose
Mis. 354—30   nor his pinions lose p·
Po. 18- 8   or pinion lose p·
lost the
My. 165—27   lost the p· of being magnanimous.
manifests
Mis. 23- 4   intelligence that manifests p· ?
man's
Mis. 70- 2   else the Scriptures misstate man's p·.
My. 134—19   bless, and inspire man's p·.
material
Un. 35—14   says gravitation is a material p·,
matter or
Un. 35—15   Which was first, matter or p· ?
mental
Mis. 115—31   Using mental p· in the right direction
methods and
Mis. 222—30   the methods and p· of error.
moral
Mis. 259—16   freedom was the moral p· of good,
Rud. 17- 6   its moral p·, and its divine efficacy
more
Mis. 232—19   will be one having more p·,
muscular
Pul. 62—13   * require but little muscular p·

power

my
Mis. 70– 4   exercised my *p·* over the fish,
Ret. 21– 5   Every means within my *p·*
no
Mis. 2–26   second death hath no *p·*" — *Rev.* 20 : 6.
36–30   and no *p·* besides God, good.
46–16   has no *p·* underived from
58– 5   then it has no *p·* over one.
93–15   This being true, sin has no *p·* ;
157–26   Error has no *p·* but to destroy itself.
198–19   has no *p·* to govern itself ;
221– 1   it has no *p·* over him.
Un. 3– 9   second death, . . . hath no *p·*,
41–14   the second death has no *p·*.
Pul. 73–14   * She of herself had no *p·*.
73–22   * man of himself has no *p·*,
My. 296–14   Evil has no *p·* to harm,
no more
Mis. 174– 1   no more *p·* to evolve or to create
no other
Mis. 101–27   no other *p·*, law, or intelligence
nor existence
Mis. 115–20   neither prestige, *p·*, nor existence,
no underived
Mis. 255– 6   and has no underived *p·*.
Un. 39–14   Man has no underived *p·*.
of absolute Truth
My. 293–16   the *p·* of absolute Truth
of a drug
Mis. 194– 2   equals even the *p·* of a drug
of any doctrine
Mis. 46– 8   beyond the *p·* of any doctrine
of being
Pul. 4–25   cometh the full *p·* of being.
of Christ
Mis. 225–11   testimony to the *p·* of Christ,
Ret. 65–22   demonstrates the *p·* of Christ
Pul. 22–19   healing *p·* of Christ will prevail.
72–24   * *p·* of Christ has been dormant in
No. 11–18   through the *p·* of Christ.
of Christianity
Mis. 193–26   the spirit and *p·* of Christianity.
193–29   *p·* of Christianity to heal ;
No. 44– 7   *p·* of Christianity to heal.
My. 239– 9   redemptive *p·* of Christianity
of Christian Science
Mis. 44– 8   remedial *p·* of C. S.
54–12   *p·* of C. S. over all
Ret. 86– 3   spirit and *p·* of C. S.,
of civilization
My. 278–20   elevating *p·* of civilization
of darkness
My. 206–29   the *p·* of darkness, — *Col.* 1 : 13.
of divine Life
Peo. 14–17   *p·* of divine Life and Love
of divine Love
'00. 5–28   utilize the *p·* of divine Love
My. 293–24   *p·* of divine Love to overrule
of divine Mind
Pul. 58– 2   * healed by the *p·* of divine Mind,
My. 61– 5   * learned of the *p·* of divine Mind
of eloquence
Hea. 2–24   knew it was not in the *p·* of eloquence
of faith
Pul. 80–22   * believe in God and the *p·* of faith,
of God
Mis. 17–14   *p·* of God to heal and to save.
168–22   *p·* of God. — *Matt.* 22 : 29.
184–24   *p·* of God as the seal of man's
194– 1   believe that the *p·* of God equals
196–19   ever-presence and *p·* of God, good.
219– 7   *p·* of God." — *Matt.* 22 : 29.
222–27   for this is the *p·* of God,
229–22   faith in the *p·* of God to heal
259–28   Truth is the *p·* of God
Pul. 81– 6   * set forth as the *p·* of
No. 37– 5   *p·* of God." — *Matt.* 22 : 29.
'01. 19– 7   *p·* of God to heal and to save.
My. 153–19   ignores the *p·* of God,
293–23   contingent on the *p·* of God,
of good
Mis. 259–16   freedom was the moral *p·* of good,
Un. 41–17   presence and *p·* of good,
Pul. 15– 1   *p·* of good resident in divine Mind,
of grace
No. 9–19   point steadfastly to the *p·* of grace
of Him
Un. 39–18   reflect, . . . the *p·* of Him
of His Christ
Pul. 12– 7   *p·* of His Christ : — *Rev.* 12 : 10.
of his teachings
Un. 43–21   with the *p·* of his teachings,
of infinite Truth
Hea. 4– 6   the *p·* of infinite Truth.

power

of Jesus' name
Pul. 41–27   * "All hail the *p·* of Jesus' name,"
81– 2   * "All hail the *p·* of Jesus' name,"
of justice
My. 191– 5   has not a tithe of the *p·* of justice.
of language
My. 332– 2   * *p·* of language would be but beggared
of Love
No. 9–21   and show the *p·* of Love.
of metaphysics
Mis. 6–12   *p·* of metaphysics over physics ;
7–28   nature and *p·* of metaphysics,
of Mind
Mis. 60–12   *Does it not limit the p· of Mind*
60–15   Does it limit the *p·* of Mind to say
Hea. 7– 6   the *p·* of Mind over matter.
of mind
Hea. 15– 8   the *p·* of mind over matter,
19– 2   *p·* of mind over body ;
My. 97– 2   * admit the *p·* of mind over matter.
of passion
Mis. 298–10   ignorance and *p·* of passion,
of prayer
My. 292–12   chapter-sub-title
of Spirit
Mis. 5–18   armed with the *p·* of Spirit,
52– 7   understands the *p·* of Spirit,
185– 4   The will of God, or *p·* of Spirit,
188–23   explanation of the *p·* of Spirit
201–32   the divine *p·* of Spirit,
258– 6   righteous scorn and *p·* of Spirit.
Un. 30–21   I discovered the *p·* of Spirit to
'01. 25–22   he taught the *p·* of Spirit,
of the human soul
Pul. 53–21   * It constitutes the *p·* of the human soul.
of the pen
'00. 12– 1   beyond the *p·* of the pen.
of the Word
Mis. 398–23   Felt ye the *p·* of the Word?
Po. 75– 3   Felt ye the *p·* of the Word?
of thought
Hea. 12–18   the concentrated *p·* of thought
of Truth
Mis. 2– 1   whereby we discern the *p·* of Truth
3– 8   in our lives the *p·* of Truth
40–17   *p·* of Truth to destroy error,
99–29   *p·* of Truth, . . . casting out evils
183– 6   *p·* of Truth must be seen and felt
184–20   he has denied the *p·* of Truth,
220–32   belief has not the *p·* of Truth,
293–13   *p·* of Truth against the opposite
333–29   exemplify the *p·* of Truth and Love.
360–10   transforming *p·* of Truth ;
Pul. vii 21   absolute *p·* of Truth
30–20   * affirms the *p·* of Truth over error,
70–23   * *p·* of Truth over all error, sin,
No. 43– 9   *p·* of Truth is not contingent on
'01. 9–13   *p·* of Truth that is persecuted
Hea. 7– 2   manifestations of the *p·* of Truth
My. 114–23   divine *p·* of Truth and Love,
122–31   *p·* of Truth in healing.
153– 5   the *p·* of Truth and Love
154– 2   *p·* of Truth over error.
268–13   *p·* of Truth uplifting the motives of
of words
Pul. 26– 7   * beyond the *p·* of words to depict.
omniscient
Chr. 53–47   The great I Am, — Omniscient *p·*,
one
Mis. 101–23   demonstrates but one *p·*,
Po. 22–13   one race, one realm, one *p·*.
only
Mis. 3– 6   imparting the only *p·* to heal
4– 9   Its only *p·* to heal is
No. 20–22   the only *p·*, presence, and glory.
opposed to God
Mis. 49–27   presupposes . . . *p·* opposed to God,
Pul. 13– 5   belief in a *p·* opposed to God.
or good
Mis. 335–31   seeking *p·* or good aside from God,
or intelligence
Mis. 197–24   another *p·* or intelligence
over death
Mis. 64– 4   to show his *p·* over death ;
No. 33–21   Love and its *p·* over death.
over matter
'01. 23–21   demonstrated his *p·* over matter,
'02. 10– 4   *p·* over matter, molecule, space,
over sin
Mis. 40–23   must gain the *p·* over sin
270– 9   demonstrated his *p·* over sin,
over the nations
Chr. 57– 3   *p·* over the nations : — *Rev.* 2 : 26.
My. 285–19   *p·* over the nations." — *Rev.* 2 : 26.

power

pain, or
No. 32– 8 its pleasure, pain, or p·

panoply of
Mis. 374– 3 Although clad in panoply of p·,

peace and
Mis. 124–19 is filled with peace, and p· ;
205– 1 peace and p· outside of itself.

peace not
My. 341–15 * "'Tis peace not p· I seek,

person, and
No. 24– 2 evil loses all place, person, and p·.

pitiless
Mis. 257–28 This pitiless p· smites with disease

place and
Mis. 274–27 exchange for money, place, and p·,
351–15 aspirants for place and p·.
My. 353–26 the spiritual have all place and p·.

place nor
Mis. 14– 2 neither place nor p· left for evil.

place or
My. 4–24 pride of place or p· is the prince of

political
Mis. 246– 9 civil and political p·.

pomp and
Pul. 10– 9 her pomp and p· lie low

presence and
(see presence)

presence or
My. 262–20 deific presence or p·.

prestige and
No. 41–23 sin is losing prestige and p·.

pride and
My. 5–12 mortal pride and p·, prestige or

pride and of
Mis. 394– 7 fetters of pride and of p· ;
Po. 45– 9 fetters of pride and of p· ;

pride of
My. 205–25 of the flesh and the pride of p·.

pride, or
My. 252–28 allurements of wealth, pride, or p· ;

pristine
My. 40–17 * its pristine p· to bring health

process and
Mis. 220–24 mental process and p· be reversed,

reality and
Mis. 252– 9 Right thoughts are reality and p· ;
364–30 or give reality and p· to evil
Pan. 7–23 reality and p·, intelligence and

redemptive
Mis. 107– 5 Its redemptive p· is seen in
My. 239– 9 redemptive p· of Christianity

regenerating
'01. 9– 5 only generating or regenerating p·.

remains
Hea. 12–25 drug disappears . . . the p· remains,

remedial
Mis. 44– 8 remedial p· of C. S.

right and
Mis. 193–29 the right and p· of Christianity

salutary
Ret. 54–23 most sacred and salutary p·

same
Mis. 130–12 has the same p· to make you a
295– 6 same p· which in America
364–26 If . . . good has the same p· or modes

saving
Mis. 374– 1 Its healing and saving p·

seeming
Mis. 298–22 delivers you from the seeming p· of

sense of
Mis. 184–23 destroys his self-deceived sense of p·
Ret. 58– 8 sense of p· that subdued matter

sequel of
Po. 16– 9 sequel of p·, of glory, or gold ;

show of
Pul. 55– 3 * Not for show of p·,

so-called
Mis. 48– 6 its so-called p· is despotic,
My. 293– 4 so-called p· of matter,

sovereign
Pul. 3– 8 sovereign p· to think and act rightly,

spirit and
Mis. 193–26 spirit and p· of Christianity.
Ret. 86– 3 rejoice in the spirit and p· of C. S.,

spiritual
(see spiritual)

stationary
Ret. 93–15 stationary p·, stillness, and

strange
Po. 35– 3 strain which hath strange p·

supernatural
Mis. 3– 4 shall claim . . . no supernatural p·.
Pul. 72– 2 * inspired . . . by supernatural p·.

power

supposed
Mis. 24–32 claims exercising their supposed p·
199– 3 to deny the supposed p· of matter
334–11 away goes all its supposed p·
335–20 afraid of its supposed p·,
No. 21–19 supposed p· and reality of evil

sustains
Po. 1– 6 What p· sustains thee

that
Mis. 55–13 and who are using that p· against

that saved
Pan. 14–24 shielded by the p· that saved them,

that Truth bestows
Rud. 10– 3 you forfeit the p· that Truth bestows,

this
Mis. 101–23 this p· is good, not evil ;
188–24 recognition of this p· came to her
194– 3 reveals the Principle of this p·,

to act
Mis. 173–18 without space to occupy, p· to act,
My. 12–27 p· to "act in the living present."

to become
Mis. 180–21 p· to become the sons of— John 1 : 12.
180–25 p· to become the son of God.
181–24 p· to become the sons of — John 1 : 12.
182–12 p· to become the son of God,
185–18 p· to become the sons of — John 1 : 12.
185–25 p· to become the sons of — John 1 : 12.

to be perfect
Mis. 184–14 say of the p· to be perfect

to declare vacancies
Man. 80–14 have the p· to declare vacancies

to demonstrate
Mis. 181– 5 p· to demonstrate his divine Principle,
Ret. 88–15 its p· to demonstrate immortality.
No. 35– 4 without the p· to demonstrate

to determine
No. 42–17 with p· to determine the fact

to discipline
Man. 51–21 Board of Directors has p· to discipline,

to escape
Mis. 109–25 even the p· to escape from the

to gain
My. 148–27 sect struggling to gain p·

to heal
Mis. 4– 9 Its only p· to heal is
5–12 faith that I have the p· to heal."
41– 8 deprives those . . . of the p· to heal,
50–15 that gives one the p· to heal ;
52– 3 God's p· to heal them.
53–14 your p· to heal through Mind,
54– 3 Has Mrs. Eddy lost her p· to heal?
54–11 Instead of losing her p· to heal,
197–19 his p· to heal and to save,
221–15 stultify the p· to heal mentally.
223–13 having the p· to heal."
No. 43– 1 if Christ's p· to heal was not
'02. 8–19 its p· to heal and to save.
Hea. 3–11 Christianity and the p· to heal ;
My. 212–26 loses his own p· to heal.

to prayer
Po. 30–12 Give risen p· to prayer ;

to reflect
Mis. 183–27 will have p· to reflect His power,

to sin
Mis. 184–17 saying, "I have the p· to sin

to wash away
Pul. 7–16 with p· to wash away, . . . every crime,

unity and
My. 162– 6 unity and p· are not in atom

unknown
My. 153–21 appeals to an unknown p·

unrighteous
Po. 27– 2 pomp and tinsel of unrighteous p· ;

uplifting
Pan. 10– 8 humanity will attest its uplifting p·,

use the
'01. 31–15 I can use the p· that God gives

using the
Mis. 59– 6 It is using the p· of human will,

vain
No. 42–12 vain p· of dogma and philosophy

verity, nor
'01. 13–12 neither entity, verity, nor p·

war weakens
My. 278–27 war weakens p· and must finally fall,

was the thought
Hea. 12–24 prove that the p· was the thought,

widest
Ret. 82– 9 widest p· and strongest growth

wisdom and
Mis. 204–26 foresight, wisdom, and p· ;
Un. 14– 8 He should so gain wisdom and p·

world
My. 85–13 * this wonderful woman is a world p·.

power
wrong
Mis. 190–26 the wrong *p·*, or the lost sense,
your
Pul. 2–20 by every means in your *p·*,

Mis. 23– 3 *p·* back of gravitation,
90– 3 *p·* of sin is the pleasure in sin.
116– 2 sensitiveness to the *p·* of evil.
119–20 to obey a *p·* that should be
141– 7 the *p·* that is behind it ;
148–13 impelled by a *p·* not one's own,
170–31 explained as the putting forth of *p·*.
184–15 If man should say . . . "I am the *p·*,"
199–19 *p·* of his transcendent goodness
220–21 That this mental method has *p·*
222–26 whose *p·* seems inexplicable,
257–13 as a *p·*, prohibition, or license,
388– 7 Thou to whose *p·* our hope we give,
393–20 Points the plane of *p·* to seek.
396–21 whose measures bind The *p·* of pain,
Man. 3– 9 impelled by a *p·* not one's own,
Pul. 18– 5 whose measures bind The *p·* of pain.
53–29 * *p·* that filled his garment's hem
69–20 * *p·* fully developed to heal
Rud. 10– 3 if you have *p·* in error, you forfeit
No. v– 4 *p·* and self-sacrificing spirit of
43– 2 equal to the *p·* of daily meat and
Pan. 6–25 what *p·* hath evil?
'01. 14– 1 or believe in the *p·* of sin,
14– 1 sticks to us and has *p·* over us.
25–23 Had he taught . . . *p·* of matter,
'02. 3–26 not follow that *p·* must mature into
Peo. 12–14 who know what a *p·* mind is
Po. 7– 7 Thou to whose *p·* our hope we give,
12– 5 whose measures bind The *p·* of pain,
52– 4 Points the plane of *p·* to seek.
68–14 is the spell that hath *p·*
My. 106–10 *p·* over and above matter
190–22 *p·* over all manner of diseases ;
204– 4 *p·* which lies concealed in the calm

powerful
Ret. 7–17 * and for his *p·* advocacy of the
Un. 60– 9 and then conjure up, . . . a *p·* presence
Pul. 56–13 * helpful, and *p·* movements of
'01. 11–20 Word of God is a *p·* preacher,
Hea. 12–22 "I am making you more *p·*,"
12–26 higher attenuations are the most *p·*.
Peo. 10– 3 steam is more *p·* than water,
My. 59–20 * sonorous tones of the *p·* organ
164–11 a *p· camera obscura,*

powerless
Mis. 29–29 matter is proven *p·*
90– 5 sin and death to be *p·*.
119–21 and is found *p·* in C. S.
134–20 earth and hell are proven *p·*.
252–10 wrong thoughts are . . . *p·*,
336– 3 that evil is *p·*,
My. 128–29 shaft aimed at you . . . will fall *p·*,
296–19 will end in harmony, — evil *p·*,

powerlessness
Mis. 108– 7 attested the absolute *p·*
114–29 show us the *p·* of evil,
201–10 its *p·* to destroy good,

powers
Mis. 134–20 *p·* of earth and hell
177– 5 *p·* of evil are leagued together
272–26 * with *p·* to confer diplomas
Ret. 7– 8 * highest order of intellectual *p·*,
49–15 *p·* that are not ordained of
'02. 14– 7 against the *p·* of darkness,
My. 308– 1 all the *p·* of earth combined

practicability
Mis. 192–18 *p·* of the divine Word.

practical
Mis. v– 4 DEDICATE THESE *p·* TEACHINGS
21–11 makes *p·* all his words and works.
24– 8 This knowledge is *p·*,
28–26 Master's *p·* knowledge of this
35– 1 Years of *p·* proof,
38–18 *p·* application to benefit the race,
38–24 questions of *p·* import.
39– 1 would be of less *p·* value.
90– 6 This *p·* Truth saves from sin,
182–30 rendered *p·*, — this eternal Truth
192– 1 more spiritual and *p·* sense.
205– 3 *p·* C. S. is the divine Mind,
207– 5 *p·*, operative C. S.
232– 9 more perfect and *p·* Christianity?
246–32 earnest seeking after *p·* truth
315–19 health, and *p·* C. S.
345–18 * had a *p·* faith in God."
353–14 workman in his mills, a *p·* joker,
Man. 49–12 *p·* wisdom necessary in a sick room,

practical
Man. 83–18 sound in sentiment and *p·* in C. S.
Ret. 35–20 was and is demonstrated as *p·*,
48–19 mental healing on a purely *p·* basis,
65–25 *p·* manifestations of Christianity
Un. 36–25 interfere with its *p·* demonstration.
39– 2 is rendered *p·* on the body.
Pul. 52– 5 * some of our *p·* Christian folk
61–16 * which is *p·* as well as poetic,
Rud. 6–23 best understood in *p·* demonstration.
No. 46– 3 a *p·*, spiritual Christianity,
Pan. 13– 2 will witness . . . to its *p·* truth.
'01. 1–24 *p·* possibilities of divine Love :
11–20 not too spiritual to be *p·*,
Hea. 1–11 more *p·* and spiritual religion
Peo. 13–26 * had a *p·* faith in God ;"
My. 40– 5 * thirst after *p·* righteousness ;
58– 1 * some of our *p·* Christian folk
81–24 * It was a *p·* demonstration of
112– 6 what C. S. makes *p·* to-day
121–24 Self-denial is *p·*,
168– 3 *p·* religion in agreement with
180– 1 make . . . the divine Love *p·*,
234–21 our great Master's sayings are *p·*
237–22 is *p·* and scientific,
264–17 Truth and Love made more *p·* ;
287–16 love for God, *p·* good,
306–14 to be transfused into the *p·*
362–24 * demonstrating *p·* Christianity.

practicality
Mis. 193– 8 *p·* of all Christ's teachings
308–14 know its *p·* only by healing
Ret. 88–13 living beauty of Love, its *p·*,
My. 103– 7 proof of the *p·* of this faith
180– 6 by him who proved their *p·*,
182–32 prove the *p·* of perfection,
239– 9 *p·*, validity, and redemptive power

practically
Mis. 48– 1 *p·* or theoretically,
177–19 Answer at once and *p·*,
224– 1 *p·* harmless, unless our own thought
333–13 literally and *p·* denying that God,
Ret. 28– 4 He must be ours *p·*,
79–19 and *p·* come short of the
Un. 1–17 *p·* able to testify, by their lives,
Pul. 62–19 * *p·* no limit to the uses to which
67–16 * *p·* unknown a decade since,
72–14 * *p·* been given up by a number of
'01. 10–19 Theoretically and *p·* man's
30 10 Christian Scientists are *p·*
My. 77–12 * *p·* every civilized country,
84– 3 * calls for *p·* all the resources
111– 9 on *p·* the same grounds as are
273– 9 * covers *p·* the civilized world.
309 31 * *p·* all the intellectual life."

practice
and proof
'01. 19–16 departure from Jesus' *p·* and proof.
and teachings
Mis. 195–26 the *p·* and teachings of Jesus
ceased
My. 231–12 has ceased *p·* herself in order to
character and
Ret. 28–30 character and *p·* of the anointed ;
Christian
Ret. 54–20 whose Christian *p·* is far in advance of
'01. 11–19 would be enough for Christian *p·*.
Christian Science
Man. 49–11 knowledge of C. S. *p·*,
My. 242–18 information relating to C. S. *p·*,
355– 7 need for more men in C. S. *p·*.
diabolical
Mis. 41– 2 given vent in the diabolical *p·* of
error in
Mis. 66–28 is met with error in *p·* ;
faithful
Man. 82–21 devote ample time for faithful *p·*.
false
Mis. 368–18 false teaching and false *p·* of
fit students for
Rud. 16– 5 undertake to fit students for *p·*
form of
Mis. 380–26 by any outward form of *p·*.
genuine
No. 3–14 sustains the genuine *p·*,
good
My. 251–20 and after three years of good *p·*,
her
Man. 92– 8 to demonstrate by his or her *p·*,
his
Mis. 378–15 to learn his *p·*,
Pul. 54–20 * in his *p·* of mental therapeutics,
My. 107–29 homœopathist handles in his *p·*
its
Rud. 15– 5 to immediately enter upon its *p·*.

practice

malicious
  Mis. 351–12   solely from mental malicious *p·*,
material in
  Peo.   2–16   shockingly material in *p·*,
medical
  '00.   13–20   Its medical *p·* included charms
  '01.   17–24   From my medical *p·* I had learned
  My. 107– 7   a modern phase of medical *p·*,
member's
  Man. 46–22   payment for said member's *p·*,
mental
  (*see* **mental**)
metaphysical
  Mis. 379–31   adjusting . . . a metaphysical *p·*,
  My. 190–11   metaphysical *p·* of medicine
method of
  Ret. 43–15   his material method of *p·*
more than theory
  Mis. 195–28   and *p·* more than theory,
    281–32   will need, . . . *p·* more than theory.
my
  Mis. 350–32   its own proof of my *p·*.
not profession
  Pul.   9–26   *P·*, not profession, — goodness, not
of Christian healing
  Mis. 359– 5   in the *p·* of Christian healing
of Christian Science
  Mis. 282– 9   direct rule for *p·* of C. S.
  Ret. 72– 1   In the *p·* of C. S. one cannot
  No.   3–10   manual of the *p·* of C. S.
  My. 42– 8   * in the *p·* of C. S.
    204–18   *p·* of C. S. in your State,
    251–18   can teach pupils the *p·* of C. S.,
    327– 1   protect the *p·* of C. S.
    327–16   * or stop the *p·* of C. S.
of dentistry
  Mis. 45–10   invaluable in the *p·* of dentistry.
of divine metaphysics
  '01.   2–13   certainty in the *p·* of divine metaphysics
of its Life
  No. 28–23   its Principle nor the *p·* of its Life.
of *materia medica*
  My. 292–23   In the *p·* of *materia medica*,
of medicine
  Peo. 10–10   regulating the *p·* of medicine in 1880.
  My. 190–11   metaphysical *p·* of medicine
    340–15   laws . . . on the *p·* of medicine !
of Mind-healing
  Mis. 67–22   right *p·* of Mind-healing achieved,
  Ret. 85–20   of abusing the *p·* of Mind-healing
    89– 4   in the *p·* of Mind-healing.
of the learner
  Mis. 43–30   on the *p·* of the learner,
outline of the
  Rud.   8–10   nothing but an outline of the *p·*.
preaching, and
  Ret. 94–17   teaching, preaching, and *p·*
precepts and
  Mis. 270–23   Fidelity to his precepts and *p·*
Principle and
  (*see* **Principle**)
Principle or
  Ret. 64–19   either in Principle or *p·*.
put into
  Pul. 53– 2   * a Principle that was put into *p·* by
  My. 204– 4   to put into *p·* the power which
quiet
  No.   1–14   the quiet *p·* of its virtues.
right
  Mis. 67–22   right *p·* of Mind-healing achieved,
rule of
  Mis. 356–29   Principle and rule of *p·*.
rules and
  Mis. 252–23   rules and *p·* of the great healer
  My. 239– 5   rules, and *p·* of Christianity
safe side of
  Mis. 117– 9   place him on the safe side of *p·*.
same
  My. 76– 1   * same *p·* would be followed
scientific
  Ret. 78– 7   scientific *p·* makes perfect,
successful
  Ret.   7–16   * in the successful *p·* of
such
  My. 219– 3   Such *p·* would be erroneous,
such a
  Mis. 380– 2   outward sign of such a *p·*:
teaching and
  Ret. 65– 4   teaching and *p·* of Jesus,
  My. 190–28   Jesus declared that his teaching and *p·*
teachings and
  Pul. 10– 1   Christ's teachings and *p·*.

practice

their
  '01.   33–30   by their *p·* or by preventing the
  My. 111–18   establish their *p·* of healing
    227–19   in their *p·*, whether successful **or**
theories and
  No.   2–28   conflicting theories and *p·*.
theory and
  (*see* **theory**)
this
  Ret. 78– 6   textual explanation of this *p·*
    78– 9   entering into this *p·*,
  No.   3–12   dependent on the rules of this **p·**
weakness in
  Rud.   9– 8   will lead to weakness in *p·*,
wrong
  Mis. 67–22   and the wrong *p·* discerned,
your
  Rud.   9–13   base your *p·* on immortal Mind,
  My. 128–28   shaft aimed at you or your *p·*

  Mis. 233–20   for the *p·* of true medicine,
  Ret. 57– 9   it is *p·* that is wrong.
  Pul. 68– 8   * many are now pastors or in *p·*.
  '02. 11–30   unite in doctrine and in *p·*
  My.   4– 6   they preclude the *p·* . . . of C. S.,
    127–16   declare that when I was in *p·*,
    245– 9   preparation of the student for *p·*.

practices
  No.   2–22   many . . . have large *p·*
  '01. 25–13   No Christly axioms, *p·*, or
  My. 93–23   * many of the *p·* in its name.
    190–10   My experience in both *p·*
    221– 6   systems and *p·* of their times.

practise
  Mis. 41– 7   It deprives those who *p·* it of
    43–25   incapacitates one to *p·* or
    59– 3   *p·* your belief of it
    114–13   They must themselves *p·*,
    114–14   and teach others to *p·*,
    115–14   *p·*, teach, and live C. S. !
    233–25   to work hard enough to *p·* it?
    243–21   who *p·* on the basis of matter,
    283–31   learn the principle . . . and *p·* it,
    283–32   teacher or musician to *p·* for him.
  Man. 55–22   trying to *p·* or to teach
    82–16   Members . . . who *p·* other professions
  No.   6–12   as all understand who *p·* the
    28–19   Study C. S. and *p·* it,
  '00.   6–27   accept it, understand and *p·* it,
  '01. 33–23   enjoined his students to teach and *p·*,
  My. 41–14   * whatsoever lawlessness . . . he may *p·*
    121–25   pleasant to those who *p·* it.
    158–22   and some *p·* what they say.
    181–17   nations shall speedily learn and *p·*
    204–15   ᴛᴏ *P·* ᴡɪᴛʜᴏᴜᴛ Fᴇᴇs
    212–16   Because they do not *p·* in strict
    220–12   I *p·* and teach this obedience,
    238– 8   to read and to *p·* the Scriptures,
    238–12   has imparted little power to *p·*
    281–16   * chapter sub-title
    282–14   we must *p·* what we already know
    327– 6   made it legal to *p·* C. S.
    327–25   * who *p·* the art of healing,"
    328–29   * who *p·* the art of healing for pay,
    363–27   and *p·* only to heal.

practised
  Mis. 29–10   Christ-healing was *p·* even before
    48– 4   should neither be taught nor *p·*,
    193–12   as defined and *p·* by Jesus,
    228– 3   has been *p·* upon thee,
    351– 6   never have *p·* by arguments which,
    378–14   Having *p·* homœopathy,
    380–17   My students at first *p·* in
  Man. 42–21   *p·* according to the Golden Rule :
    89–13   *p·* C. S. healing acceptably
    89–21   *p·* C. S. healing successfully
  Un.   9–25   not been *p·* since the days of Christ.
  Pul. 52–19   * *p·* by Jesus and his disciples.
    53– 3   * though *p·* in other countries
  '01.   9–14   Christ Jesus possessed it, *p·* it,
  My. 103–15   which Jesus taught and *p·*.
    180– 5   truths were preached and *p·*
    204–20   *p·* gratuitously when starting
    238– 2   *the Bible, if read and p·*,
    238–20   When the Bible is thus read and *p·*,
    242– 7   and must be *p·* therefrom.
    246– 8   *p·* C. S. three years
    271– 6   when I *p·* its precepts,
    314– 6   * *p·* in several towns,
    327–30   * as taught and *p·* in C. S.,

practises
  Mis. 243–14   medicine claims more than it *p·*.
  Rud. 12– 4   *p·* Christ's Sermon on the Mount.

practises
'00. 6–16 not only accepts . . . but he *p·* it.
My. 4– 2 then he *p·* the Golden Rule
113– 4 *p·* the teachings of this book

practising
Mis. 4–15 and to the *p·* students,
5–10 scientific method of *p·* Christianity.
62–27 she is *p·* this Science.
232–29 *p·* in the *name* of Science
340–19 by *p·* what he was taught,
349–15 which he claimed to be *p·* ;
382–30 teaching and *p·* C. S.
Man. 34–15 teaching and *p·* metaphysical healing.
Rud. 14– 6 strictly *p·* Divine Science,
'01. 20–22 till he . . . stops *p·* it.
My. 166–17 neither she nor I would be *p·*
242–12 In *p·* C. S. you must state its

practitioner
Mis. 40–26 *p·* has to master those elements
41–29 *p·* may not always prove equal to
220–16 *p·* has changed his patient's
220–19 *p·* undertook to transform it,
352–17 enables the *p·* to act
378–11 He proved to be a magnetic *p·*.
Man. 46–11 except as a C. S. *p·*.
46–16 relation of *p·* to patient.
73– 4 include at least one active *p·*
87– 6 left to the wisdom of the *p·*,
Pul. 69–23 * *p·* must understand these laws
Rud. 8–23 sense may say the unchristian *p·*
9– 9 he will be a poor *p·*,
9–24 thoughts of the *p·* should be imbued
12–24 *p·* should also endeavor to
Hea. 14–10 If you employ a medical *p·*,
14–18 preparation for a metaphysical *p·*
My. 154 5 Life understood by the *p·*
205–29 *p·* may fail, but the Science never.
212–28 You will find this *p·* saying
241–20 * catechized by a C. S. *p·*
241–21 * *p·* said that my statement was wrong,
364–10 are disarmed by the *p·* who

practitioners (*see also* **practitioners'**)
Mis. 6– 6 C. S. *p·* have plenty to do,
43–12 make safe and successful *p·*.
80–28 by a new school of *p·*,
81– 6 let each society of *p·*,
221–16 accounts for many helpless mental *p·*
Man. 46–12 *P·* and Patients.
73– 5 list of *p·* in *The C. S. Journal,*
74–11 Teachers and *p·* of C. S.
Ret. 82– 7 *p·* of the same blessed faith.
82–17 to supply many *p·*, teachers, and
Rud. 15–14 until there were enough *p·* to
'02. 9– 9 we shall have better *p·*,
My. 212–15 dissension among mental *p·* ?
223– 9 should be sent to the C. S. *p·*
237–16 C. S. *p·* should make their
246– 3 continue for three years as *p·*
359–23 * were known as "the *p·*."

practitioners'
Man. 74–10 Teachers' and *P·* Offices.
My. 237–15 chapter sub-title

Prairie Queen
Ret. 17–10 *P· Q·* and the modest Moss-rose ;
Po. 62–11 *P· Q·* and the modest Moss-rose ;

praise (noun)
Mis. 48– 7 Mr. Carpenter deserves *p·* for his
106–24 begin that *p·* that shall never end?
106–27 and resound His *p·*."
124–21 silence wherein to muse His *p·*,
128–11 if there be any *p·*, — *Phil.* 4 : 8.
146– 3 and her gates with *p·* !
226–11 pretentious *p·* of hypocrites,
245–22 *p·* or the dispraise of men.
331– 9 sunlight of prayer and *p·*
Man. 47–16 it scales the pinnacle of *p·*
Ret. 71– 1 exalts a mortal beyond human *p·*,
Pul. 1–11 eloquent in God's *p·*.
8– 1 All *p·* to the press of America's
8–22 Thou hast perfected *p·*." — *Matt.* 21 : 16.
No. 44–17 mouth lisping God's *p·* ;
Po. 30–20 sacred song and loudest breath of *p·*
77– 4 nation's holiest hymn in grateful *p·* !
My. 6–21 evidencing the *p·* of babes
27– 8 sacred season of prayer and *p·*.
31–32 * joined in the song of *p·*.
113–20 to perfect His *p·*.
116–19 rendering *p·* to whom *p·* is due,
131–14 apostate *p·* return to its first love,
167–24 send forth a pæan of *p·*
170–29 faith, understanding, prayer, and *p·*
208–19 wherein to gather in *p·*
229–24 heaps of *p·* confront me,
262–29 eloquent silence, prayer, and *p·*

praise (noun)
My. 275–28 unite in one *Te Deum* of *p·*.
297– 3 shrink from such salient *p·*.
323–20 * gratitude and *p·* to God
355–18 chapter sub-title

praise (verb)
Mis. 41– 7 wrath of man" to *p·* Him. — *Psal.* 76 : 10.
107– 2 sweetness and beauty . . . that *p·* Him,
Un. 29–26 I shall yet *p·* Him. — *Psal.* 42 : 11.
Pul. 80–20 * either to *p·* or blame,
83–21 * When we try to *p·* her
No. 8–14 make the wrath of man to *p·* Him,
33– 2 wrath of man shall *p·* Him.
Pan. 4–23 I shall yet *p·* Him, — *Psal.* 42 : 11.
'02. 1–13 wrath of man shall *p·* — *Psal.* 76 : 10.
My. 111– 3 wrath of man shall *p·* — *Psal.* 76 : 10.
148–18 you have met to *p·* God.
151–11 wrath of man shall *p·* — *Psal.* 76 : 10.
163– 3 to *p·* him who won the way
207– 4 The wrath of men shall *p·* God,
356– 2 and *p·* and love the spot

praised
Pul. 7– 8 *p·* and persecuted in Boston,
My. 200– 4 Heaven be *p·* for the signs of

praises
Mis. 107– 1 organ, . . . *p·* Him;
My. 162 18 love that rebukes *p·* also,
206–25 show forth the *p·* — *I Pet.* 2 : 9.
332–30 *p·* to his honorable record

praiseworthy
My. 195–24 *p·* success of this church,

praising
Mis. 295–13 *p·* the Scotchman's national pride
My. 149–31 while those . . . ask no *p·*.
245–19 go on *ad infinitum*, *p·* God,

pray
Mis. vii– 1 * *P·* thee, take care, that tak'st my book
vii–16 And nothing have to *p·* :
59–11 to *p·* for the recovery of the sick ?
59–12 Not if we *p·* Scripturally,
87–26 To watch and *p·*, to be honest,
109–30 Watch and *p·* for self-knowledge ;
110– 7 *p·* that you preserve these virtues
114–22 cannot . . . *p·* to God too fervently,
127– 9 *p·* daily for themselves ;
133–12 love to *p·* standing in — *Matt.* 6 : 5.
133–15 *p·* to thy Father which — *Matt.* 6 : 6.
144 29 To-day I *p·* that divine Love,
151–20 I *p·* thee as a Christian Scientist,
154 25 *P·* without ceasing.
174–25 and taught us to *p·*,
174–26 did not teach us to *p·* for death
276–24 I *p·* that all my students
313–20 *p·* ye therefore the God of harvest
330– 5 *p·* for the perpetual springtide
343– 1 Let us watch and *p·* that we
356–30 "*p·* without ceasing," — *I Thess.* 5 : 17.
387–16 *P·* that his spirit you partake,
389– 3 the right to work and *p·*,
389–21 watch and *p·*.
Man. 16– 9 promise to watch, and *p·*
40–12 watch and *p·* to be delivered from
41 20 every member of this Church to *p·*
Un. 50– 7 We should watch and *p·* that we
Pul. 34–25 * to *p·*, to search the Scriptures.
No. 8–22 *p·* for the amelioration of sin,
39–28 "*P·* without ceasing" — *I Thess.* 5 : 17.
Pan. 14–11 *P·* for the prosperity of our country,
14–14 *P·* that the divine presence may
'00. 2– 8 work — work — watch and *p·*."
'01. 14–21 one must watch and *p·* that he
16–26 men go to mock, and go away to *p·*
18– 9 Those who laugh at or *p·* against
18–30 clergymen *p·* for sinners ;
'02. 4– 7 *p·* at this Communion season
Hea. 4– 8 We *p·* for God to remember us,
8– 4 not a person to whom we should *p·*
15–17 You *p·* for God to heal you,
15–24 is it not asking amiss to *p·* for
Po. 4–21 watch and *p·*.
6–11 *P·* that his spirit you partake,
21–17 the right to work and *p·*,
32–18 kneel at the altar of mercy and *p·*
My. 6–15 temple wherein to enter and *p·*.
18– 6 *p·* daily for themselves ;
37–30 * With sacred resolution do we *p·*
119–29 watch and *p·* for the spirit of Truth
128–30 Watch, and *p·* daily
143– 1 *p·* that God directs your meetings
167–11 I *p·* that heaven's messages of
174–28 humbly *p·* to serve Him better.
180–28 in the spirit of our great Exemplar *p·* :
189–30 Wherefore, *p·*, the bell did toll?
195– 9 to work more, to watch and *p·* ;

pray

My.	196–27	Work and *p·* for it.
	200–30	For this I shall continue to *p·*.
	203– 4	*P·* aright and demonstrate your
	220–15	Each day I *p·* for the pacification of
	220–21	I *p·*: "God bless my enemies;
	234– 4	I cannot watch and *p·* while
	254– 6	Watch, *p·*, demonstrate.
	279–23	*p·* each day for the amicable
	279–25	*p·* that God bless that great nation
	281– 3	even to know how to *p·*
	291–28	to think, to mourn, yea, to *p·*,
	293–31	when ye *p·*, believe."— *Mark* 11 : 24.
	340– 4	"*P·* without ceasing."— *I Thess.* 5 : 17.
	358– 5	"Watch and *p·*,— *Matt.* 26 : 41.
	358–10	Beloved! you need to watch and *p·*

prayed

Mis.	29– 7	At another time he *p·*,
	232– 1	God comfort them all! we inwardly *p·*
Ret.	9–13	*p·* that God would forgive me,
	13–21	I *p·*; and a soft glow of
Pul.	33–11	* she *p·* for forgiveness,
	44– 4	* worked, toiled, *p·* for.
	69–25	* have *p·* for the cure of disease,
My.	283–10	Many years have I *p·* and labored
	286– 3	*p·* daily that there be no more war,
	286– 5	*p·* that all the peoples on earth
	293–10	thousands who *p·* for him
	335–30	* the young wife *p·* incessantly

Prayer

Lord's

(*see* **Lord's Prayer**)

Pul.	38–13	"*P·*," "Atonement and Eucharist,"

prayer

after

Mis.	88–18	like a benediction after *p·*,

all

No.	38–25	All *p·* that is desire is intercessory;

and drugs

Mis.	51–29	*Are both p· and drugs necessary*

and fasting

Mis.	156–21	but by *p·* and fasting."— *Matt.* 17 : 21.
My.	190–17	but by *p·* and fasting."— *Matt.* 17 : 21.
	222–13	but by *p·* and fasting"— *Matt.* 17 : 21.
	339–25	but by *p·* and fasting,"— *Matt.* 17 : 21.

and praise

Mis.	331– 9	sunlight of *p·* and praise
My.	27– 8	sacred season of *p·* and praise.
	170–29	understanding, *p·*, and praise
	262–29	eloquent silence, *p·*, and praise

and teachings

Pul.	85–18	* *p·* and teachings of Jesus Christ.

and watchfulness

No.	33– 8	struggle, *p·*, and watchfulness

audible

No.	39– 4	audible *p·* may be offered to
	40–12	I have no objection to audible *p·*

bended knee of

Mis.	204– 3	on the bended knee of *p·*,

brings

'01.	19– 5	*p·* brings the seeker into

cannon's

Po.	26–20	Purged by the cannon's *p·*;

ceaseless

Mis.	250–24	the silent, ceaseless *p·*;

daily

Man.	41–19	Daily *P·*.
My.	281– 3	daily *p·* of my church,

days for

My.	340– 3	St. Paul's days for *p·* were

earnest

My.	352–12	* It is our earnest *p·* that we

effect of

'01.	34– 2	effect of *p·*, whereby Christendom

evening

Mis.	389– 5	poem
Po.	page 4	poem

family

'01.	31–23	Bible reading and family *p·*;

for peace

My.	279–21	chapter sub-title
	280–30	to pause in special *p·* for peace.

hope and

'02.	6–20	Christian faith, hope, and *p·*,
	15–30	my waiting hope and *p·*.
My.	155–15	its faith, hope, and *p·*.

hour of

Po.	65–10	"Sweet hour of *p·*"!

hypocrite's

No.	40–11	and pour forth a hypocrite's *p·*;

inaudible

My.	139–24	from the audible to the inaudible *p·*;

in church

Man.	42– 1	*P·* in Church.

in stone

Mis.	141– 1	The First Church . . . our *p·* in stone,
	320– 1	push upward our *p·* in stone,
Pul.	23– 4	* "OUR *P·* IN STONE"
	24– 8	* is termed . . . "Our *p·* in stone."
	44– 4	* The '*p·* in stone' is accomplished.
	57–19	* chapter sub-title
	65–17	* call it their "*p·* in stone,"
	84–15	* completion of "our *p·* in stone,"

intercessory

No.	38–24	chapter sub-title

is the utilization

No.	39–18	*P·* is the utilization of the love

looks up in

My.	258– 1	Wherever the child looks up in *p·*,

my

Mis.	385– 5	Oh, Thou hast heard my *p·*;
	397–17	My *p·*, some daily good to do
Pul.	19– 1	My *p·*, some daily good to do
Po.	13– 5	My *p·*, some daily good to do
	37– 5	Oh, Thou hast heard my *p·*;
My.	167–20	my *p·* for their health, happiness,
	183–26	blending with thine my *p·*
	220–19	faith that my *p·* availeth,

my form of

Pul.	4–29	used, . . . my form of *p·*

my impressions of

Mis.	133–10	voices my impressions of *p·*:

not fatigued by

Man.	60– 8	Scientist is not fatigued by *p·*,

occupied in

'01.	34– 6	The interval . . . occupied in *p·*

of doubt

Mis.	59–16	*p·* of doubt and mortal belief

of faith

No.	41–25	* *p·* of faith shall save— *Jas.* 5 : 15.
My.	221–32	*p·* of faith shall save— *Jas.* 5 : 15.

of one

Peo.	8– 5	or that answers the *p·* of one

one

Pul.	22– 4	Christian churches have . . . one *p·*,
My.	301–10	unite as brethren in one *p·*:

parting

Mis.	386–26	her loyal life, And parting *p·*,
Po.	50–12	her loyal life, And parting *p·*,

potent

No.	39– 4	an honest and potent *p·*

power of

My.	292–12	chapter sub-title

power to

Po.	30–12	Give risen power to *p·*;

praise and

My.	208–19	to gather in praise and *p·*

result of

My.	343–25	each one was . . . the result of *p·*.

righteous

Mis.	33– 2	righteous *p·* that avails with God.
My.	189–13	commingling in one righteous *p·*,
	280–10	* righteous *p·* which availeth much.

ripe in

My.	350–27	Science ripe in *p·*, in word, and

secret

No.	39–10	glorified God in secret *p·*,

sentence or

Pul.	59– 5	* sentence or *p·* of consecration,

silent

Mis.	133–24	in silent *p·* to the Father
	314– 9	lead in silent *p·*,
Pul.	30–14	* by uniting in silent *p·*.
	43–19	* A few minutes of silent *p·*
No.	39–26	pure Mind-pictures, in silent *p·*,
	39–28	silent *p·* can meet the demand,
Peo.	9–22	Silent *p·* is a desire,
My.	17–24	* a few moments of silent *p·*
	32–17	* Silent *p·*, followed by the audible
	39–11	* Then followed a short silent *p·*
	234–26	Silent *p·* in and for a heathen nation
	311–26	knelt in silent *p·* on the mound

song and

Po.	54– 4	With light and song and *p·*!

special

My.	280–17	special *p·* for the peace of nations,
	280–30	to pause in special *p·* for peace.

speechless

My.	150–18	in speechless *p·*, ask God to

spirit of his

Mis.	211–30	He lived the spirit of his *p·*,

spirit of the

My.	292–26	spirit of the *p·* of the righteous

such

No.	39–14	Such *p·* humiliates, purifies,

their

My.	225–25	to forget their *p·*,

thief's

Mis.	70–20	poor thief's *p·* for help

prayer
true
No. 39–17 True *p·* is not asking God for love ;
unto the
My. 188– 6 attent unto the *p·* — *II Chron.* 7 : 15.
watchfulness and
Mis. 115–17 constant watchfulness and *p·*
your
Hea. 15–19 acting oppositely to your *p·*,
My. 203– 5 Pray aright and demonstrate your *p·* ;

Mis. 116–23 fruits of watchfulness, *p·*,
132– 8 chapter sub-title
242– 1 chapter sub-title
Ret. 13–20 if I went to Him in *p·*,
No. 39–11 *P·* can neither change God, nor
39–19 *P·* begets an awakened desire to
Pan. 14–10 chapter sub-title
'01. 19– 1 *p·* is a divinely appointed means of
Hea. 15–27 *P·* will be inaudible,
Po. 33–12 a *p·* that His love I may know,
My. 205– 7 won through faith, *p·*, experience ;
206– 3 *p·* with power and pride of
293–21 *p·* so fervently offered

"Prayer and Healing ; supplemental"
Mis. 132–13 the heading, "*P·* and *H·* ; *s·*,"
prayerful
My. 48–11 * a *p·* study of the Bible,
50– 6 * a little band of *p·* workers.
prayerfully
Ret. 44–17 Examining the situation *p·*
prayerless
Mis. 133– 3 * "the pantheistic and *p·* Mrs. Eddy,
133– 8 As to being "*p·*," I call your
248–17 or that my hourly life is *p·*,
249–12 well known that I am not . . . *p·*.
Pul. 5– 2 * "the *p·* Mrs. Eddy,"
prayers
Mis. 40– 5 hygienic rules, drugs, and *p·*
154–25 that your *p·* be not hindered,
237–18 forefathers' *p·* blended with the
266–23 my own endeavors and *p·*.
Man. 42– 1 *p·* in C. S. churches
Un. 15–25 they wish to bribe with *p·*
Pul. 8–20 lambs my *p·* had christened,
9–25 constant *p·*, prophecies,
11– 7 means, energies, and *p·*
'01. 19– 1 God answers their *p·*,
My. 24–10 * builded by the *p·* and offerings
37–32 * We would be glad if our *p·*,
189– 9 silent *p·* of our churches,
192–28 ever-presence, answering your *p·*,
290–19 does not hear our *p·* only because
292–14 fail in their *p·* to save the life of
292–17 a compound of *p·* in which
336– 1 but for her *p·* the patient
345– 2 that by your *p·* vaccination will
prayest
Mis. 133–11 "When thou *p·*, — *Matt.* 6 : 5.
133–14 when thou *p·*, — *Matt.* 6 : 6.
praying
Pul. 21– 8 I am seeking and *p·* for it
22– 6 every *p·* assembly on earth,
'01. 28– 4 It is only by *p·*, watching,
My. 254–12 sure reward . . . of watching and *p·*,
275–21 Working and *p·* for my dear
280–29 *p·* for the peace of nations,
prays
Pul. 83–10 * With the assurance of faith she *p·*,
No. 30– 8 but when the heart *p·*,
preach
Mis. 151–27 heal, and teach, and *p·*,
161–21 that none should teach or *p·* in
177–25 * was announced to *p·* the sermon,
178–19 * to *p·* a sermon on C. S.,
178–24 * could not have stood up again to *p·*,
325–32 *p·* the gospel, — *Mark* 16 : 15.
Man. 58– 9 continue to *p·* for this Church
Ret. 15–13 I was called to *p·* in Boston
44–13 to *p·* only occasionally,
88–23 and *p·* without the consent of the
Pul. 46– 3 * came to hear him *p·*,
No. 41–20 * *p·* the gospel ;" — *Mark* 16 : 15.
'01. 11–16 for this pastor of ours to *p·* !
My. 46–16 * To *p·* the gospel and heal the
47–28 * *p·* the gospel — *Mark* 16 : 15.
51–24 * go into new fields to teach and *p·*."
52–18 * heal the sick, and *p·* the gospel,
53–17 * to ascertain if she would *p·*
53–21 * when she could give the time to *p·*,
147–15 *p·* the gospel which heals
150–28 heal the sick and *p·* the gospel,
300–25 *p·* the gospel — *Mark* 16 : 15.

preached
Mis. 168–12 to the poor . . . the gospel is *p·*.
171–20 to the poor the gospel is *p·*.
315– 1 shall be *p·* to the children,
349–23 state that I *p·* four years,
349–28 each Sunday when I *p·*.
349–29 the contributions, when I *p·*,
Ret. 40– 1 I healed, *p·*, and taught
44– 8 *p·* five years before
89–11 If one worshipper *p·* to the
Pul. 38– 2 * had *p·* in other parishes
'01. 32–17 sermons their lives *p·*
'02. 15– 2 the hall where I *p·* ;
My. 19–31 gospel shall be *p·* — *Mark* 14 : 9.
28–26 * he *p·* the Word of God
50–30 * *p·* her farewell sermon
53–32 * When our pastor *p·* for us
54–32 * Mrs. Eddy *p·* at this service
59–17 * *p·* to a handful of people
180– 4 its life-giving truths were *p·*
preacher
Mis. 176– 7 solemnly expounded by the *p·*,
252–26 inspires the teacher and *p·* ;
'01. 11–20 The Word of God is a powerful *p·*,
26– 3 great teacher, *p·*, and demonstrator
preachers
Ret. 82–17 many practitioners, teachers, and *p·*
My. 178– 3 These unpretentious *p·* cloud not the
preaches
Mis. 169– 2 the divine Science she *p·* ;
preaching
Mis. 158–30 no record that he used notes when *p·*.
239– 7 Lecturing, writing, *p·*, teaching,
301– 4 the *precedent* for *p·* C. S.,
359– 4 Christly method of teaching and *p·*
Ret. 15–23 healed through my *p·*,
15–30 healed under my *p·*,
88–16 *p·* the gospel.
89– 5 In those days *p·* and teaching were
89– 6 no church *p·*, in the modern sense
94–17 scientific teaching, *p·*, and practice
No. 12–19 *p·* the gospel of Truth,
43–14 * *p·* deliverance to the captive,
'00. 12–21 Under the influence of St. Paul's *p·*
'01. 11–23 sermon without personal *p·*,
My. 58–12 * inspire us to follow her in *p·*,
91–23 * during the first years of her *p·*
128–21 *p·* the gospel and healing the sick.
preamble
My. 254–18 * part of the *p·* to our By-laws,
precaution
Mis. 89–18 he left this *p·* for others.
285–20 We have taken the *p·* to
precautions
My. 219–26 *p·* against the spread of
precede
Man. 32– 6 The readings from the SCRIPTURES shall *p·*
Ret. 63–12 denunciation must *p·* its destruction.
My. 232–22 must *p·* that understanding of Truth
precedence
Un. 15–19 Would God not of necessity take *p·*
My. 81– 9 laughingly give *p·* to another
precedent
Mis. 220– 8 explanation, attestation, and *p·*,
301– 3 *p·* for preaching C. S.,
367–26 neither *p·* nor foundation in nature,
Ret. 89–22 Nowhere . . . find any *p·* for
'00. 4– 5 *p·* that would commingle Christianity,
My. 237– 6 I do not consider a *p·* for
precedents
No. 35– 2 Without it, how poor the *p·* of
My. 340– 6 religious observances and *p·*
precedes
My. 297–13 dark hour that *p·* the dawn.
precedeth
Un. 61–11 *p·* the nightless radiance
preceding
Man. 25–11 *p·* the annual meeting of the
56–20 *p·* the annual meeting of the
57– 4 *p·* the first Sunday in June,
93– 6 Monday *p·* the Annual Meeting,
Pul. 29– 2 * *P·* Judge Hanna were
55– 6 * last quarter of *p·* centuries.
My. 45–27 * logically followed the *p·* one.
precept
Mis. 11–11 followed them with *p·* upon *p·* ;
32–10 "*p·* upon *p·* ; line upon — *Isa.* 28 : 10.
66–11 This sacred, solid *p·* is
235–27 tried to follow the divine *p·*,
278–22 line upon line and *p·* upon *p·*.
289–17 according to the divine *p·*,

precept
Ret. 88–16 both by example and p'.
'01. 18–22 Metaphysician's p' and example,
My. 64–16 * teaching . . . both by p' and example
precepts
Mis. 129–22 your Leader's p' and example!
269–12 whose p' and example have a
270–23 Fidelity to his p' and practice
337–25 lived according to his p',
'01. 34–11 misread the evangelical p'
My. 271– 6 when I practised its p',
pre-Christian
Pul. 66–25 * p' ideas of the Asiatics
precinct
Pul. 49–23 * do honor to that p' of Concord.
precincts
Mis. 282–16 personal p' of human thought,
290– 3 found within their p'.
precious
Mis. 144–21 p' in God's sight
320– 7 Christ's appearing . . . is so p',
Ret. 20–12 I regarded as very p'.
37– chapter sub-title
Un. 52–12 p' redemption of soul,
Pul. 8–24 p' children, your loving hearts
My. 16–25 a p' corner stone, — Isa. 28 : 16.
17–10 chosen of God, and p', — I Pet. 2 : 4.
17–15 corner stone, elect, p' : — I Pet. 2 : 6.
47–16 * victories that are p' each and all.
61– 6 * the lessons . . . have been very p'.
62– 8 * may I not take this p' truth
169– 6 My p' Busy Bees,
184–24 p' in the sight of divine Love,
precipitately
No. 1– 7 Small streams are noisy and rush p';
precise
Ret. 14–21 I could not designate any p' time.
My. 245–26 p' signification of the letters of
precisely
Mis. 23–29 mirror repeats p' the looks and
242–25 I cured p' such a case in 1869.
My. 30– 3 * all the services were p' the same
preclude
My. 4– 5 p' the practice or efficient teaching of
precludes
Mis. 102–10 His infinity p' the possibility of
103– 1 p' the presence of evil.
My. 221– 3 materialism p' Jesus' doctrine,
precursor
'01. 33–11 * p' that they were about to die."
My. 203–18 sure p' that its possessor is mortal.
predestinates
No. 37–28 What God knows, He also p';
predestination
Ret. 13– 6 doctrine of . . . election, or p',
14– 1 "horrible decree" of p'
predestine
Un. 19–12 if . . . could p' or foreknow evil,
predestined
Mis. 122–10 whom God foreordained and p'
Un. 17– 9 union p' from all eternity;
predicament
My. 149–25 a p' quite like that of the man who
predicate
Mis. 103– 6 the ultimate and p' of being.
364–22 Human hypotheses p' matter of Spirit
Rud. 6–21 this p' and postulate of Mind-healing;
No. 10–10 life of Christ is the p' and postulate of
'01. 21–21 Death is neither the p' nor postulate
'02. 10–18 his p' tending thereto is correct,
My. 224–17 of which C. S. is the p' and
272– 8 p' and ultimate of scientific being
predicated
'01. 4–13 p' of Principle and demonstrated as
My. 219–20 p' of what Christ Jesus taught
predicating
My. 207–24 p' man upon divine Science.
predict
Pul. 22–10 I p' that in the twentieth century
51–15 * It is too early to p'
My. 11–18 * to p' that she will be cheered
predicted
My. 63–27 * had come, as the Master p',
94–31 * men there were who p'
predicting
Mis. 240– 9 P' danger does not dignify life,

predictions
Pul. 45–14 * p' of workman and onlooker
84–15 * all p' and prognostications
My. 95– 3 * Those p' have not been verified.
predilections
My. 273– 1 * has no religious opinions or p'
predisposes
Mis. 265– 7 p' his students to make mistakes
predisposing
Mis. 229– 2 certain p' or exciting causes.
267–25 p' and exciting cause of all
Ret. 44–18 p' and exciting cause of its
My. 152–29 remote, p', and present cause
predominate
Mis. 113– 6 evil seems to p'
preeminent
Mis. 383– 8 p' over ignorance or envy,
Ret. 70–27 P' among men, he virtually
My. 161–28 his p' goodness, the Godlike man
preeminently
No. 33–22 Jesus' sacrifice stands p'
'02. 14–25 prospered p' our great Cause,
preen
My. 186– 6 p' their thoughts for upward flight.
preexisted
Mis. 173–16 And must not man have p'
preexistence
Mis. 47–24 with his immortality and p',
181–28 man's spiritual p' as God's child ;
189– 9 true knowledge of p',
prefaced
Mis. 178–13 * which he p' by saying :
prefer
Un. 32–16 which I p' to call mortal mind.
Rud. 2–14 I p' to retain the proper sense of
My. 233–11 Which should we p', ease or
249–22 report that I p' to have a
249–27 I should p' that student who
preferable
Pan. 2–26 Pan in imagery is p' to pantheism
preference
My. 249–24 My p' lies with the individual
276– 8 a p' to remain within doors
preferment
Ret. 6–30 received further political p',
preferred
Mis. 354–10 When depraved reason is p' to
Man. 99–12 if p', can appoint a Committee on
Pul. 74–10 * Mrs. Eddy p' to prepare a
My. 215–30 That he p' the latter is evident,
preferring
Mis. 147– 7 meet in unity, p' one another,
prefers
Ret. 65–19 and p' Christ to creed.
prefigure
My. 13–13 seems to p' The Mother Church
prefigures
Pul. 23–16 * p' itself to us as one of the
My. 6–28 p' self-abnegation, hope, faith ;
prefix
Man. 111– 7 p' her signature with "Mrs ;"
Rud. 1–15 p' per (through) and sonare
Pan. 2–23 Pan is a Greek p',
'02. 7–12 English p' to the words potence,
pregnant
'02. 14–26 This p' question, answered frankly
My. 283–12 grand Association, p' with peace,
prejudice
No. 15– 4 Reading my books, without p',
My. 224–12 or the p' it instils.
224–12 This p' the future must disclose
prejudices
Pul. 55–11 * p', and oppressions of the past.
No. 9– 5 p', and errors of one class of
Hea. 2– 4 factions and p' arrayed against it,
preliminary
Mis. xi–22 p' battles that purchased it.
64–10 take for p' studies ?
Man. 51–14 P' Requirement.
My. v–19 * nine years of arduous p' labor,
75–13 * So perfect have been all the p'
prematurely
Mis. 293– 1 It is safe not to teach p' the
Un. 5– 1 rudely or p' agitate a theme

premise
Mis. 26–29 From this *p·* comes the logical
27– 7 conclusions that destroy their *p·*
66–27 Error in *p·* is met
76– 8 never be tested . . . upon a false *p·*,
101–28 On this proof rest *p·* and
195–20 but one correct *p·* and conclusion,
200– 8 an error of *p·* and conclusion,
265–20 An error in *p·* can never
288–11 If the *p·* of mortal existence
309– 5 personality is an error in *p·*,
344–18 and from error of *p·* would seek a
366–24 start from this false *p·*,
'01. 3–26 deserts its *p·*,
4– 3 In logic the major *p·* must be
My. 111–17 is logical in *p·* and in conclusion.
111–24 in adhering to his *p·*
112–13 with its logical *p·* and conclusion,

premises
Mis. 46–12 in the *p·* or conclusions of C. S.,
93– 9 to be the *p·* of Truth,
195–16 *p·* whereof are not to be found
Man. 75–19 aforesaid *p·* and buildings,
Ret. 21–29 are separated from their *p·*,
51– 5 the *p·* thereby conveyed,
Un. 51– 3 Reasoning from false *p·*,
'02. 7–19 can be drawn from the *p·*,
Peo. 3–20 personal God is based on finite *p·*,

premium
No. 19– 1 present high *p·* on Mind-healing.
19– 3 the *p·* would go down.

premonition
Mis. 347–17 accepting the *p·* of one of them,

prenatal
Mis. 71–12 *law of transmission, p· desires,*

preoccupied
Mis. 47– 9 Have you never been so *p·*

preparation
Mis. x–11 written in haste, without due *p·*.
84– 3 a *p·* of the human heart
114– 5 in the *p·* of the *Quarterly*
115–14 a proper *p·* of heart
322– 3 and to *p·* to behold it.
Man. 31– 7 *p·* for the reading of the
Ret. 26– 6 a *p·* of poppy, or aconite,
Rud. 9–15 requires a *p·* of the heart
'01. 32–25 all the way up to its *p·*
Hea. 13– 6 shaking the *p·* thirty times
14–17 *p·* for a metaphysical practitioner is
My. 245 8 thorough *p·* of the student
319–23 * about the *p·* of a theme,

preparations
Mis. 268–22 God's *p·* for the sick are potions of
268–25 let us not adulterate His *p·* for
My. 173 10 notice that no *p·* would be made for

prepare
Mis. 64–13 *p·* for it through no books except
138– 3 to *p·* for this national convention
246–24 "*P·* ye the way of — *Matt.* 3:3.
347– 8 *p·* shelter in caves of the earth.
Man. 90–21 *p·* a paper on said subject
Pul. 74–10 * Mrs. Eddy preferred to *p·* a
'00. 14–30 *p·* accordingly for the festivity.
Hea. 12–20 To *p·* the medicine requires time and
Po. vii– 6 * to *p·* a few bound volumes of
My. 156–11 to *p·* for the material passover,

prepared
Mis. 39– 2 *p·* to take a course of instruction
90–28 His spiritually *p·* breakfast,
131–13 If our Board of Directors is *p·* to
152–18 receive the heritage that God has *p·*
176–27 Are we *p·* to meet and improve them,
Man. 18–23 By-Laws, as *p·* by Mrs Eddy,
28–11 and *p·* not himself, — *Luke* 12:47.
38–11 whose applications are correctly *p·*,
50– 3 shall be *p·* for burial by
Ret. 40–12 clothes already *p·* for her burial ;
83–10 Also, they are *p·* to receive the
Un. 6–15 not *p·* to answer intelligently
Pul. 43–22 * sermon *p·* for the occasion by
57– 8 * The sermon, *p·* by Mrs. Eddy,
59–17 * The sermon, *p·* by Mrs. Eddy,
77– 4 * elegant memorials ever *p·*,
'00. 15– 6 partake of what divine Love hath *p·*
My. 32–28 * the specially *p·* Lesson-Sermon.
147–22 and *p·* for your use work-rooms
156–19 *p·* for the reception of Truth
178– 9 and *p·* for all peoples.
184– 5 what God hath *p·* for them that wait
234–28 before the minds . . . are *p·* for it,

prepares
Mis. 229– 2 This mental state *p·* one to
My. 12–24 God *p·* the way for doing ;

preparing
Mis. 163– 4 *p·* to heal and teach divinely ;
'00. 15–17 Love has been *p·* a feast for
My. 345–30 They are *p·* the way for us."

preponderate
Mis. 287–14 should *p·* over the evil,

preposterous
My. 219–13 not be more *p·* than to believe

prerogative
Mis. 90–26 without this *p·* being conferred by
209– 3 usurpest the *p·* of divine wisdom,
Un. 32– 3 usurps the *p·* of God, saying,
No. 23– 5 neither grasp the *p·* of God nor
My. 179– 7 power and *p·* of Spirit
218– 9 The power and *p·* of Truth
340–14 the *p·* of making laws for the State

prerogatives
Ret. 70– 6 usurps the deific *p·*

presage
Ret. 18–24 clouds are a *p·*, — they darken my lay :
Po. 64–20 clouds are a *p·*, — they darken my lay :

Presbyterian
Ret. 14– 5 of the strictest *P·* doctrines.

prescribe
Rud. 3–16 *p·* drugs, or deny God.
Peo. 4–25 inquired of . . . what drugs to *p·*.

prescribed
Mis. 248–24 my regular physician *p·* morphine,
Ret. 85–15 order *p·* by supernal grace.
87–17 divine order as *p·* by Jesus,
My. 345–16 *p·* pellets without any medication

prescribing
Ret. 26– 2 nor *p·* drugs to support the

prescription
Mis. 210–23 and a medical *p·*.
243–26 Even doctors disagree on that *p·* :
'01. 34– 9 the M. D.'s material *p·*.

presence
all
No. 18– 5 all *p·*, power, and glory.
all-pervading
Un. 45–15 I try to show its all-pervading *p·*
and glory
No. 20–22 only power, *p·*, and glory.
and power
Mis. 71–19 factors of divine *p·* and power.
174– 4 claiming *p·* and power over
175– 1 breathes His *p·* and power,
Un. 41–17 continual *p·* and power of good,
My. 118 18 of Truth's *p·* and power.
bodily
Rud. 1–17 the word *personal* to *bodily p·*,
continual
No. 37–17 His continual *p·*, knowledge, and
divine
(see **divine**)
dread
Un. 64–13 hope of ever eluding their dread *p·*
eternal
Un. 60–28 must yield to His eternal *p·*,
gentle
Mis. 331–18 O gentle *p·*, peace and joy
389– 6 O gentle *p·*, peace and joy
Po. 4– 1 O gentle *p·*, peace and joy
God's
Mis. 113– 2 God's *p·* gives spiritual light,
345– 2 God's *p·* and providence.
Un. 2– 7 realize God's *p·*, power, and
My. 354–19 sign and substance Of God's *p·*
her
Ret. 5–24 * Her *p·*, like the gentle dew
My. 39–27 * realize her *p·* with us to-day.
His
Mis. 152– 5 includes also His *p·*
175– 1 breathes His *p·* and power,
263–13 His *p·*, power, and peace
347–20 guardians of His *p·* go before me.
Ret. 9–20 * feel His *p·* in the vast and dim
Un. 4–10 the understanding of His *p·*,
10–28 to hide from His *p·* under their
37–12 and the heaven of His *p·* ;
'01. 7–27 any evidence of His *p·* thereby.
Peo. 1–11 the angels of His *p·*
My. 177–21 glory of His *p·* rests upon it,
188– 1 but in recognition of His *p·* ;
193– 3 His *p·* with you will bring
356– 5 liberty and glory of His *p·*,
his
Mis. 379– 6 I read the copy in his *p·*,
its
Ret. 88–30 and its *p·* felt in eternal stillness
No. 18–11 the secret of its *p·* lies in the

presence

its
My.   3–17   Its *p·* is felt, for it acts
    240–12   Its *p·* is felt, for it acts
my
Po. 73–14   Witness my *p·* and utter my
My. 201–28   a line from me in lieu of my *p·*
  321–16   * talked so freely in my *p·*.
of evil
Mis. 103– 1   precludes the *p·* of evil.
of Him
Mis. 174– 7   come into the *p·* of Him
of its tormentor
Mis. 278– 5   the *p·* of its tormentor.
of Mary Baker Eddy
My. 143–15   personality and *p·* of Mary Baker Eddy,
of the thousands
My. 63–26   * *p·* of the thousands who had come,
or power
My. 262–19   effulgence, deific *p·* or power.
palpable
Mis. 294– 9   transcribes . . . the living, palpable *p·*
peaceful
Mis. 392– 5   With peaceful *p·* hath begirt thee
Po. 20– 6   With peaceful *p·* hath begirt thee
personal
Mis. 322–15   By any personal *p·*, or word
My. 177– 8   no special need of my personal *p·*
power and
Mis. 77–13   bond of union, the power and *p·*,
  173–23   not met by another power and *p·*,
  333–14   good, is supreme, *all* power and *p·*,
powerful
Un. 60– 9   then conjure up, . . . a powerful *p·*
primal
My. 347–15   had reproduced her primal *p·*,
prompt
My. 243–20   Your prompt *p·* in Concord
spiritual
Mis. 328–22   spiritual *p·* and idea of God.
supposititious
Mis. 355–20   responsible for its supposititious *p·*.
their
Mis. 306–25   we know their *p·* by the love
'02. 12–27   annually favor us with their *p·*
My. 7–11   annually favor us with their *p·*
  63–29   * to tell by their *p·* that they
your
My. 188–19   will not shut me out from your *p·*.

Mis. 103–23   *p·*, and individuality of God.
Pul. 40–17   * *p·* of four different congregations,
  42–10   * *p·* of several hundred children
No. 27–25   In *p·* of such thoughts
'01. 13–30   So long as we indulge the *p·*
'02. 7–12   prefix to the words *potence, p·*,
My. 46–21   * in the *p·* of this assembled host,

present (noun)

Mis. 12–11   The *p·* is ours ;
  84–31   those who have utilized the *p·*,
  100– 8   Past, *p·*, future, will show
  230– 7   make the most of the *p·*.
  285–22   In the *p·* or future,
  285–30   will have no past, *p·*, or future.
Un. 46–27   as it does of the *p·*.
Pul. 7–20   false prophets in the *p·*
No. 28–16   *p·*, as well as the future,
Pan. 10–15   *p·* and future of those students
Hea. 2– 5   Past, *p·*, future magnifies his name
My. 12–28   power to "act in the living *p·*.''
  13– 2   on the past, *p·*, nor future,
  22–21   * needs of the *p·* and of the future
  133– 3   in the great light of the *p·*,
  147– 4   the *p·* is prophetic.
  153–22   in the past as in the *p·*,
  158–14   and joys in the *p·*
  224–14   Avoid for the . . . *p·* public debating

present (adj., adv.)

Mis. 9–14   good far beyond the *p·* sense
  34–18   in our *p·* state of existence,
  34–24   mortal thought on this *p·* plane
  38–28   in order to cure his *p·* disease,
  42–29   *Can I be treated without being p·*
  56–28   *of existence to the p· time?*
  66–32   *p·* capability of the learner,
  86–29   constitutes their *p·* earth and
  92– 3   *p·* liability of deviating from
  95– 8   * shorthand reporter who was *p·*,
  98– 3   to improve his *p·* condition ;
  146–12   This is not my *p·* province ;
  148–26   contributions from the people *p·*
  152–12   I, as a dictator, . . . am not *p·* ;
  152–14   am *p·*, and rejoice with them
  160–13   It satisfies my *p·* hope.
  188–21   where the *p·* writer found it,
  196–18   illumines our *p·* existence

present (adj., adv.)

Mis. 251–19   *p·* possibilities of mankind.
  273–16   in their *p·* line of labor
  277–14   Then can the *p·* mode
  284– 9   sphere of his *p·* usefulness.
  299– 8   which demands our *p·* attention.
  306–27   nor a loved person *p·* ;
  316–14   profited up to their *p·* capacity
  319–20   let the *p·* season pass without
  322– 8   *p·* to address this congregation,
  322–19   though I be *p·* or absent,
  344–22   *p·* with the Lord.'' — *II Cor.* 5 : 8.
  352– 7   error of its *p·* erroneous course,
  355– 2   *p·* stage of progress in C. S.
  357– 9   is above the *p·* status of religion
  358–28   Let Scientists . . . do their *p·* work,
  367–21   To good, evil is never *p·* ;
  368–17   This evil obtains in the *p·* false
  381– 6   defendant being *p·* personally
Man. 51–24   shall be *p·* at meetings
  56–14   its officers are required to be *p·*.
  72–22   continue its *p·* form of government
  73–17   vote of, the active members *p·*,
  90–14   shall be *p·* at the sessions,
Chr. 53–33   Forever *p·*, bounteous, free,
Ret. 14– 4   I was of course *p·*.
  15–29   many others *p·* had been healed
  31–30   potency of a *p·* spiritual *afflatus.*
  41– 2   as contrasted with its *p·* welcome
  83–29   *p·* liability of deviating
  93– 4   At the *p·* epoch
Un. 2– 4   "a very *p·* help — *Psal.* 46 : 1.
  4–28   at the *p·* crude hour,
  6– 1   Our *p·* understanding is
  37– 7   God and heaven, or Life, are *p·*,
  41–16   illumine our *p·* being with
  43– 6   The *p·* mortal sense of being
  54– 6   If the claim be *p·* to the thought,
  59–18   divine idea is always *p·*.
Pul. 1–10   Time past and time *p·*,
  1–19   be *p· in propria persona ?*
  1–19   Were I *p·*, methinks I should
  3–29   to reach out for a *p·* realization
  14– 4   *p·* apathy as to the tendency of
  23–23   * latter part of the *p·* century,
  30–28   * grown to its *p·* impressive
  31– 5   * *p·* application of the principles
  36– 9   * I was *p·* at the class lectures
  36–11   * by the men and women *p·*
  55–24   * The *p·* Boston congregation
  68–25   * meeting held at the *p·* location
  75–17   * MANY TORONTO SCIENTISTS *P·*
  87– 1   * cordially invite you to be *p·*
  87– 3   * We especially desire you to be *p·*
No. 2–26   *p·* ignorance in relation to C. S.
  18–26   regulates the *p·* high premium on
  28– 1   else their *p·* mistakes would
'00. 1– 5   *p·* with the ever-present Love
'01. 16– 5   poignant *p·* sense of sin
  17– 1   The *p·* self-inflicted sufferings of
'02. 2–19   *p·* modifications in ecclesiasticism
  4–23   all periods — past, *p·*, and future.
My. 16–15   * there were *p·* on this occasion :
  23– 6   * erection of the *p·* edifice in 1894,
  24–21   * *p·* time there are no less than
  25– 1   * the *p·* Thanksgiving season ;
  25–18   I cannot be *p· in propria persona*
  36– 5   * five thousand *p·* rose as one
  39–23   * Mrs. Eddy, was *p·*.
  41–22   * into *p·* and hourly application
  45–10   * physically *p·* at the dedication
  47– 7   * church has reached its *p·* growth,
  49–23   * instruct those *p·* as to their duties
  50– 4   * Most of those *p·* had left their
  54– 3   * those *p·* enduring the
  54–14   * there were *p·* about eight hundred
  54–27   * large congregation was *p·*.
  63–24   * has come to the *p·* age.
  74–25   * Our *p·* relations with them are
  77–24   * *p·* to participate in the occasion.
  86–10   * to be *p·* at the dedication
  100– 8   * were *p·* in the building,
  110– 5   At the *p·* time this Bethlehem star
  129–23   *p·* harmony wherein the good man's
  133– 4   light of the *p·* fulfilment.
  137–24   before the *p·* proceedings were
  138–10   *p·* proceedings test my trust
  142–27   your kind invitation to be *p·*
  146–19   their *p·* application to mankind,
  151– 2   *p·* schoolboy epithets and attacks
  152–29   remote, predisposing, and *p·* cause
  162– 3   "very *p·* help — *Psal.* 46 : 1.
  164–13   is *p·* to manifest God.
  164–15   with its *p·* prosperity?
  170–10   all *p·* here in Concord.
  176– 7   illustrate the past by your *p·* love.

present (adj., adv.)
My. 184–12 inviting me to be *p·*
192–21 to be *p·* at the dedication
204–18 *p·* practice of C. S. in your State,
216–21 adapted to your *p·* unfolding
219– 1 unless I am personally *p·.*
220–24 Past, *p·,* or future philosophy
224–32 under the *p·* persecution
236–14 exchange the *p·* name for
237– 6 for a *p·* student of this Science.
237–11 adapted to the *p·* demand.
243–13 dozen or more of the *p·* incumbents.
281– 6 I cited, as our *p·* need,
301– 5 *p·* flux in religious faith
314–17 *p·* in court when the decision was
339–21 rejoice in their *p·* Christianity
342–31 *p·* rules of service and *p·* rulership
343– 6 "No *p·* change is contemplated
350– 1 know their *p·* ownership of all good,
360–10 *p·* momentous question at issue

present at —
Mis. 6– 8 At *p·* the majority of the acute
13– 1 of which I feel at *p·* capable,
32–26 at *p·* necessary for the individual,
43– 6 *Do all who at p· claim to be*
91– 3 it should be observed at *p·*
145– 1 at *p·* is the cement of society,
171–20 Few people at *p·* know aught of
242–15 At *p·*, I am in another department
256–12 remaining at *p·* a public servant :
272–11 * this Act is at *p·* incorporated
273–11 of relieving my tasks as at *p·.*
273–20 should continue, as at *p·,*
274– 6 I must stop teaching at *p·.*
286–10 At *p·*, more spiritual conception
289–10 at *p·* the application of scientific
358– 8 They include for him at *p·*
Man. 29–16 salary . . . shall be at *p·*
Ret. 50–24 at *p·,* continue to organize
85– 5 at *p·* they can employ any other
Rud. 14– 4 must at *p·* ask a suitable price
'01. 20–25 At *p·* its mystery protects it,
My. 187– 5 too busy to think of doing so at *p·.*
216–28 you will feel more than at *p·*
251–14 which at *p·* is taught in the
345–23 At *p·* I am conservative about

present ever —
Mis. 27–22 though God is ever *p·* ;
Un. 37–11 Because God is ever *p·*,
60–21 If God is ever *p·*,
No. 30–12 this perfect law is ever *p·*
'02. 12–10 that God is come, and is ever *v·*,
My. 110– 2 is ever *p·*, casting out evils,

present (verb)
Mis. 11–30 I have but two to *p·.*
33– 9 *p·* the type and shadow of Truth's
46–11 would not *p·* this question.
78–29 to *p·* the quality of good.
164–15 *p·* a wonderful manifestation of
196–31 acceptance of the truths they *p·* ;
279–13 *p·* themselves to my thought ;
282– 7 The question will *p·* itself :
375– 1 Pictures which *p·* disordered phases
381–11 why he did not *p·* evidence to
381–15 "There is no evidence to *p·.*"
Man. 36–20 *p·* to him a recommendation
89–14 *p·* such credentials as are required
Pul. 86–21 * we hereby *p·* this church to you
'02. 14–17 truths . . . to *p·* to the world.
Hea. 17– 5 *p·* the image and likeness of God.
Peo. 8– 1 to *p·* the right idea of Truth ;
My. 47– 7 * *p·* in this report a few
61–30 * problems which . . . *p·* themselves
170–14 I would *p·* a gift to you to-day,
172–11 Permit me to *p·* to you
194–19 you *p·* to me the princely gift
216–19 which I *p·* to your thought,

presentation
Mis. 50–11 as lucid in *p·* as can be possible,
142–12 beautiful boat and *p·* poem.
164– 5 human *p·* of goodness in man.
280–22 *p·* was made in a brief address by
Man. 91–12 on *p·* of the card to the teacher.
Pul. 56–10 * does not admit of an elaborate *p·*
My. 238–13 discovery, and *p·* of C. S.
272–30 * interested in this *p·* of the

presented
Mis. 95– 5 * was *p·* to Mr. Cook's audience,
142– 7 boat *p·* by Christian Scientists
148–24 *p·* at your Friday evening meetings.
153–23 to whom I *p·* a copy of . . . "S. and H.
197–19 divinity which Jesus *p·*

presented
Mis. 261–22 No greater type of . . . Love can be *p·*
280– 4 one of the angels *p·* himself
280–19 *p·* their teacher with an elegant
379– 5 He immediately *p·* them.
379–11 vein of thought *p·* by these.
Man. 75– 7 *p·* to Rev. Mary Baker Eddy
79–13 names . . . shall be *p·* to Mrs. Eddy
Ret. 48–14 *p·* and passed unanimously :
Un. 6–10 as now *p·* to the people
Pul. 28– 9 * crown and the star are *p·* in
Hea. 10– 8 *p·* the highest ideal of Love.
Po. vii–11 * *volume is p· to the public,*
My. vi–24 * *p·* to her church the property
13– 6 was *p·* to me in 1903 by
40–24 * Mrs. Eddy, has *p·* to the world
95– 5 * built upon the tenets first *p·* by
121–16 Christmas ring *p·* to me
165–13 *p·* to me for First Church
171–26 * *p·* as a love-token for the church
218–14 *p·* his *material* body absolved from
273– 2 * This manuscript is *p·* simply as an
273–16 should be early *p·* to youth
281– 1 *p·* itself and awakened a wiser want,
310–27 *p·* my disposition as exemplary
311–21 *p·* me my coat-of-arms,
320– 3 * I *p·* my matter for a theme
329–18 * *p·* to Mrs Eddy by Miss Harrison.
347– 9 a loving-cup, *p·* July 16, 1903.
356–17 now and heretofore *p·* in S. and H.

presenting
Mis. 149– 8 after *p·* the various offerings,
184–10 *p·* our bodies holy and acceptable,
Man. 66– 3 before *p·* it to the Church
Ret. 53– 1 *p·* to its loyal members
Pul. 43–29 * Before *p·* the sermon,
My. 69– 6 * *p·* an oval and dome appearance
172– 8 * In *p·* this gavel to President Bates,
315–21 what is the *McClure* "history," . . . *p·* ?
346– 5 * *p·* another view of her religion.

Present Order of Communion Services
in Branch Churches
Man. 125– 1 heading

Present Order of Services, etc.
Man. 120– 1 heading

presents
Mis. ix–10 easel of time *p·* pictures
52–14 sometimes *p·* the most wretched
127–30 Mortal mind *p·* phases of character
172–19 *p·* but a finite, feeble sense of
188– 6 *p·* as being first that which
189–10 *p·* a false sense of existence,
355– 2 stage of progress in C. S. *p·*
373–19 This master's thought *p·* a sketch
373–31 It *p·* not words alone, but works,
Un. 52–13 *p·* Truth's spiritual idea,
Pul. 6– 8 It *p·* to the understanding,
No. 27–14 *p·* the grand and eternal verities
Pan. 3– 5 poorly *p·* the poetical phase of
'00. 12–30 Nicolaitan church *p·* the phase of
'01. 35– 4 The question oft *p·* itself,
My. 20–14 what you would expend for *p·* to her,
256–14 the pure pages of impersonal *p·*,
259–14 most pleasing Christmas *p·*,
272– 8 *p·*, . . . no claim that man is equal to
272–20 * The *Cosmopolitan p·* this month
274–22 an abundance of material *p·* ;
299–14 *p·* the demonstrable divine Principle

preservation
Pul. 27– 5 * vault for the safe *p·* of papers.

preserve
Mis. ix–15 To *p·* a long course of years
110– 8 pray that you *p·* these virtues
131– 9 Christian Scientists *p·* unity,
287–30 *p·* affection on both sides.
Pul. 4–10 to *p·* a scientific, positive sense of
'01. 26–14 to *p·* Christ's vesture unrent ;
My. 226– 4 *p·* an intelligent usage of the word

preserved
Mis. 290– 5 animus of the contract is *p·* intact.
My. 147–13 May this little sanctum be *p·* sacred
268– 4 so long as the *morale* . . . is *p·.*

preserver
Pan. 4– 5 the creator and *p·* of man.
4–18 chapter sub-title
4–20 Spirit, is indeed the *p·* of man.
7–10 God, the *p·* of man, declared

preservers
Pan. 4–27 if these are not man's *p·* ?

preserves
Mis. 302– 6 *p·* in his own consciousness

preserving
My. 286–12   p· peace among nations.
    344–11   p· individuality and personality

preside
Pan.   3– 3   supposed to p· over sylvan
My.   39–22   * pleasant duty to p· at an annual

presided
Pul.   43– 7   * p· over the exercises.
    60– 7   * Judge Hanna, . . . p·, reading in clear,

presidency
Man.   89– 1   P· of College.

President
Mis. 305–30   * first P· of the United States,
    306–20   * who was at that time the P·
    312–11   P· of the World's Congress
Man.   25– 6   P·, a Clerk, a Treasurer, and
    25– 8   P·.
    25– 8   P· shall be elected, subject to
    25–12   P· shall hold office for one year,
    33– 8   A Reader shall not be a P·
Ret.   6–19   afterwards P· of the United States ;
'02.   3– 7   I rejoice that the P· of
My.   16–16   * P· of The Mother Church ;
    39– 4   * meeting was opened by the P·,
    39–15   * P·, Willis F. Gross, C.S.B. ;
    39–17   * In introducing the new P·,
    39–18   * When I introduce the incoming P·,
    42– 6   * P· for the coming year,
    112–30   home of the P· of the United States,
    171–25   * by the P·, Mr. E. P. Bates,
    172– 1   * P· of The Mother Church.
    278–13   The revered P· and Congress
    293– 7   Our lamented P·, in his loving
    309– 8   afterwards P· of the United States,
    (see also Eddy, Garfield, McKinley, Pierce's, Roosevelt)

president
Pan.   3–27   p· of the mountains,
My. 136–22   justice of the peace and p· of
    (see also Eddy)

presiding
My. 291– 4   P· over the destinies of

Press
Pul.   89– 8   * P·, Albany, N. Y.
    89– 9   * P·, New York City.
    89–10   * P·, Philadelphia, Pa.

press
Mis.   10–16   more assured to p· on safely.
    125–17   p· on to Life's long lesson,
    206–24   P· patiently on ; God is good,
    245– 9   combined efforts of . . . pulpit and p·
    246– 1   It is the pulpit and p·,
    246– 6   It was the Southern pulpit and p·
    274–17   p· is gagged, liberty is besieged ;
    274–18   when the p· assumes the liberty to
    300–16   the pulpit, instead of the p·,
    321–19   P· on, p· on ! ye sons of light,
    338–19   armies of earth p· hard upon you.
    348– 1   They p· forward towards the mark
Man.   41–11   by the churches or the p·,
    97–19   by the daily p·, by periodicals or
Pul.   vii– 1   scintillations from p· and pulpit
    5–16   p· and pulpit cannonaded this book,
    8– 1   All praise to the p· of
    8– 2   the p· has spoken out historically,
    8– 5   chimes repeat my thanks to the p·.
    31–21   * favor of an interview for p· use,
    54– 4   * touch him in life's throng and p·,
'00.   6– 7   I p· toward the mark — Phil. 3 : 14.
    7–10   bar and bench, p· and pulpit,
'01.   16–19   individual, the pulpit, or the p·.
Po.   39– 9   May we p· on and up !
My.   95–11   * p· gallery of commentators.
    99–19   * p· reports state that the
    108–27   words of the New York p·
    114–31   from pulpit and p·,
    141–21   * has just given out to the p·,
    151–12   injustice done by p· and pulpit
    154–25   emanating from the pulpit and p·.
    182–32   p· on to the infinite uses of
    192– 3   p· on unto the possession of
    195–14   p· on with what we are,
    201– 2   p· on towards the high calling
    202–27   P· on. The way is narrow at first,
    207– 4   P· on ! The wrath of men shall
    253– 6   P· on ! My heart and hope
    297– 1   gave her discovery to the p·.
    316–17   eloquent appeal to the p·
    317– 5   * allegations in the public p·
    329–24   * fair attitude of the p·

pressed
Mis. 261–14   full, p· down, and running over.
Pul.   29–13   * number of chairs p· into service
My.   21–19   * "good measure, p· down, — Luke 6 : 38.

presses
My. 129–17   he p· to his original,

pressing
Mis. 115–14   p· need of a proper preparation of
    155–10   p· meekly on, be faithful,
My. 110–15   mortal mind p· to the front,
    155–12   p· forward in the onward march of

prestige
Mis. 115–20   evil has neither p·, power, nor
    334–12   all its supposed power and p·.
No.   41–23   sin is losing p· and power.
Pan.   6–13   social p·, a large following,
My.   5–12   mortal pride and power, p· or

presume
Mis. 265–15   shallow moralist may p· to
My. 330– 3   * I p· we should not be surprised
    361– 4   I do not p· to give you

presumption
My. 228–27   who has the divine p· to say :

presumptuous
Ret.   72– 8   result of secret faults, p· sins,
My. 113–18   Neither is it p· or unscriptural

presumptuously
Mis. 231–17   finger p· poked into the little mouth

presuppose
Mis. 187–13   p· a material man to be the first
    217–17   p· that nature is matter,
Un.   39–25   They p· that . . . man is evil,
No.   15–17   p· an impotent God and an incredible

presupposes
Mis.   49–26   p· . . . a power opposed to God,
    257– 3   Pantheism p· that God sleeps
No.   35–18   p· Life, substance, . . . in matter,

pretence
Mis. 210–22   under the false p· of human need,

pretend
Mis. 173–18   without . . . power to act, or vanity to p·
    353–30   They do not love Mother, but p· to ;

pretended
Un.   33– 4   give the only p· testimony
My. 327–24   * section formerly read, "p· healers,"

pretender
Un.   44–12   p· taught the opposite of Truth.
No.   31– 4   has for ages been a p·,

pretense
Un.   64– 1   If sin has any p· of existence,

pretension
Rud.   7–20   As a p· to be Mind,

pretentious
Mis. 226–11   p· praise of hypocrites,
Un.   51–11   supplied by the p· usurpation,

preternatural
Mis. 199–28   neither supernatural nor p· ;
Peo.   3–12   would affirm that . . . are p· ;

pretext
Mis. 109– 6   sure p· of moral defilement.
My.   37–25   * p· for our confident and favorable

pretty
Mis. 203– 2   your gift of the p· pond
    218–29   "P· well, I thank you !"
    231–25   into saying, "Oh, p· !"

prevail
Mis.   7–11   skepticism and incredulity p·
    107– 4   Art must not p· over Science.
    129–14   let silence p· over his remains.
    141– 9   gates of hell" cannot p·. — Matt. 16 : 18.
    144–20   gates of hell shall not p· — Matt. 16 : 18.
Pul.   22–19   healing power of Christ will p·.
No.   38–12   gates of hell cannot p·.
Pan.   10– 8   p· over the opposite notion

prevailed
Mis. 140–16   Unity p·, — till mortal man sought
'00.   12–16   Magical arts at Ephesus ;
My. 293–20   to mortal sense the flesh p·.

prevailing
Pul.   66–24   * encroachment upon p faiths,
My.   50–18   * Love p· over the apparently
    309–24   p· style of architecture

prevails
My. 329– 4   * idea p· that the last

prevalent
Un.   11–21   the ruder sort then p·,

prevent
Mis.	ix –3	* *p·* a man from accepting charity ;
	19– 4	and *p·* its demonstration ;
	42–31	our own false admissions *p·* us from
	45– 7	allay fear, *p·* inflammation, and
	81– 4	*p·* all unpleasant and unchristian
	208– 4	Mortals cannot *p·* the fulfilment of
	214–28	This would *p·* the possibility of
	232–28	this will *p·* mankind from
	236–19	restore harmony and *p·* dishonor.
	243–28	will *p·* the secretions of
	256–12	*p·* my classes from forming
	279– 4	*p·* the wrong action?
	288–20	would *p·* scientific demonstration.
	302– 1	an evil which you can *p·* :
	362–29	*p·* sin or reform the sinner.
Man.	43–19	*p·* C. S. from being *adulterated.*
	110– 3	*p·* applications being duplicated
Ret.	78– 9	will *p·* the demonstration of C. S.
No.	9– 9	to *p·* their legitimate action
	43–24	will never *p·* or reconstruct
Hea.	18–16	if it could *p·* its effervescing
My.	64–21	* sins which would *p·* the realization
	140–26	does not *p·* its distant members
	188–20	cannot *p·* me from entering
	241– 8	* concealed to *p·* their advancement
	292–19	would *p·* the result desired.
	308– 2	can never *p·* being accomplished

prevented
No.	9– 2	would have *p·*, to a great extent,
My.	195– 7	have hitherto *p·* my reply.
	235–29	in time to have *p·* it,
	293–15	and thus they *p·* the power of
	314–22	*p·* Dr. Patterson's arrest

preventing
'01.	33–30	by *p·* the early employment of an M.D.
My.	219– 9	*p·* the occasion for its use ;
	286–12	for the purpose of *p·* war

prevention
My.	268– 2	chapter sub-title

preventive
Mis.	229–25	a better *p·* of contagion

prevents
Mis.	49–23	it *p·* a recognition of the
	308–26	consciousness of disease *p·* the
	350–24	Hence it *p·* the normal action,
No.	5–27	*p·* one from healing scientifically,
Pan.	7– 4	and thus *p·* the demonstration
My.	233– 5	which *p·* an effective watch?
	275–20	all that *p·* my daily drive.

previous
Mis.	52–28	work out the *p·* example,
	256–19	*p·* to the opening term.
Man.	49–25	without *p·* injury or illness,
	52–12	his *p·* character has been good,
Ret.	44–15	*p·* harmony and prosperity.
	82–29	clearer than any *p·* edition,
Un.	10– 6	to name any *p·* teachers,
	14– 9	improve upon His own *p·* work,
Pul.	55– 5	* In a *p·* article we have referred
My.	49–18	* received at the *p·* meeting,
	49–22	* minutes of the *p·* meeting were
	54–28	* *p·* consideration of places for
	223– 3	without *p·* appointment
	336–10	* had made no will *p·* to his

previously
Mis.	46– 8	any doctrine *p·* entertained.
Ret.	23– 7	*P·* the cloud of mortal mind
'02.	13–22	*p·* negotiated for the property
My.	9– 1	* those *p·* established have had
	294–20	hindrances *p·* mentioned.

prey
Mis.	156–23	and in turn becomes a *p·*.
	246–18	to invite its *p·*, then turn and
	246–22	refused to yield its *p·*
	323–12	beasts of *p·* prowl in the path,
	323–20	taming the beasts of *p·*,

preying
My.	215–21	*p·* upon my pearls,

preys
Mis.	156–22	the animal magnetizer *p·*,

price
Mis.	7–23	*p·* at which we shall issue it,
	99– 8	awful *p·* : the temporary loss of his
	149– 3	and without *p·*." — *Isa.* 55 : 1.
	165–24	but, they never paid the *p·* of sin.
	253– 3, 4	bought with a *p·*, a great *p·* ;
	253– 5	the *p·* that he paid for it?
	269–26	not willing to pay the *p·*.
	342–26	if you pay the *p·* of Truth,
Man.	46–24	reduce his *p·* in chronic cases
	84–13	student's *p·* for teaching C. S.

price
Ret.	41– 5	and without *p·*," — *Isa.* 55 : 1.
	50– 1	God impelled me to set a *p·* on my
	50– 5	*p·* for each pupil in one course
Rud.	14– 5	suitable *p·* for their services,
	14–15	to take the full *p·* of tuition
No.	35–14	the awful *p·* paid by sin,
'00.	15– 1	you purchase, at whatever *p·*,
'02.	13–15	about one half the *p·* paid,
	13–25	the *p·* I had paid for it,
	15– 8	and without *p·*," — *Isa.* 55 : 1.
Po.	22–21	blood was not its *p·*.
My.	v–18	* and without *p·*." — *Isa.* 55 : 1.
	16– 8	* the purchase *p·* of the land
	127–26	but it is rich beyond *p·*,
	215– 4	bestowed without money or *p·*.
	221– 1	The earthly *p·* of spirituality

priceless
Mis.	30–13	*p·* understanding of man's real
	61– 2	*p·*, eternal, and just at hand.
	252–31	yea, it is the pearl *p·*
	270–13	*p·* knowledge of his Principle
My.	215– 3	knew well the *p·* worth of
	347–18	parable of the *p·* pearl

pride

all
My.	134–17	Life lessens all *p·*

and affection
Mis.	295–13	Scotchman's national *p·* and affection,

and ease
'02.	9– 7	*p·* and ease concern you less,

and joy
'02.	3–10	the old national family *p·* and joy

and satisfaction
My.	74–18	* *p·* and satisfaction that is

and self
Mis.	92–32	divests himself of *p·* and self,
Ret.	84–20	divests himself most of *p·* and self,

apparent
Mis.	239–21	Her apparent *p·* at sharing in

arrogant
Ret.	84–15	In times past, arrogant *p·*,

burdened by
Mis.	328–17	burdened by *p·*, sin, and self,

chastens
Mis.	387–25	chastens *p·* and earth-born fear,
Po.	6–20	chastens *p·* and earth-born fear,

cheek of
Ret.	31–23	Blanched was the cheek of *p·*.

come from
Rud.	9–19	similar effects come from *p·*,

disgusting
My.	233– 5	the feverish, disgusting *p·* of

fetters of
Mis.	394– 7	loosens the fetters of *p·*
Po.	45– 9	loosens the fetters of *p·*

her
My.	313–28	wounded her *p·* when I adopted C. S.,

human
(*see* **human**)

ignorance and
Mis.	92–27	arrogant ignorance and *p·*,
	354–22	self-conceit, ignorance, and *p·*

is ignorance
Mis.	2– 3	*P·* is ignorance ;

lawful
Pul.	48–24	* The natural and lawful *p·*

love and
Po.	8–21	a home of love and *p·* ;

mortal
My.	5–12	mortal *p·* and power, prestige or

of circumstance
Mis.	155– 3	*p·* of circumstance or power

of circumstances
My.	37– 3	* no *p·* of circumstances has place

of life
Mis.	116–18	pleasures and pains and *p·* of life :
	183– 1	*p·* of life will then be quenched
Hea.	17– 2	lusts of the flesh, the *p·* of life,

of opinion
Un.	5– 7	mental struggles and *p·* of opinion

of physical life
Un.	39– 5	and the *p·* of physical life

of place
My.	4–24	The *p·* of place or power

of power
My.	205–25	lust of the flesh and the *p·* of power

of sects
'01.	2–17	feverish *p·* of sects and systems

or gold
My.	283–29	Lured by fame, *p·*, or gold,

or power
My.	252–28	allurements of wealth, *p·*, or power ;

our
Mis.	224– 2	our *p·* that makes another's criticism

pride

pardonable
My. 64– 8 * If to-day we feel a pardonable *p·*
personal
My. v–12 * the mesmerism of personal *p·*
pomp and
Ret. 79–17 worldly policy, pomp, and *p·*,
pomp and its
Po. 16–11 toil for its pomp and its *p·*.
pomp or
Mis. 144–14 without pomp or *p·*,
power and
My. 206– 3 with power and *p·* of position,
rebels
Mis. 204– 1 agony struggles, *p·* rebels,
self-seeking
My. 210–12 self-seeking *p·* of the evil thinker
should sanction
Mis. 330–24 even *p·* should sanction
struggle with
Mis. 378– 9 After . . . a struggle with *p·*,
their
Mis. 226–24 should be restrained by their *p·*.
327–24 rebuking their *p·*, consoling their
will and
Mis. 141–21 impulses of human will and *p·* ;

Mis. 9– 3 *p·*, self-ignorance, self-will,
137–25 must control appetite, passion, *p·*,
145–15 *p·* is a hooded hawk which flies in
153–15 encompassed not with *p·*, hatred,
240–22 Passions, appetites, *p·*, selfishness,
Rud. 17– 9 never originated in *p·*, rivalry, or
'*02.* 16–26 *p·*, self-will, envy, or hate.
Hea. 18–22 *P·*, appetites, passions, envy, and
My. 41– 9 * *P·*, arrogance, and self-will are
82–16 * *p·* of the Church Directors that
257–20 all human hate, *p·*, greed, lust
283–19 When *p·*, self, and human reason

Priest and priest
Mis. 301–30 the commands of our hillside *P·*,
Ret. 91–28 this hillside *p·*, this seaside teacher,
My. 300–20 If, as this kind *p·* claims,

priestcraft
Mis. 106– 9 *P·* in front of them,
Peo. 13–15 Galileo kneeling at the feet of *p·*,

priesthood
Mis. 90–27 organization and ordained *p·*.
105– 6 rested the anathema of *p·*
Pul. 7–19 unmerciful, and oppressive *p·*
My. 17–12 an holy *p·*,— *I Pet.* 2 : 5.
206–23 a royal *p·*,— *I Pet.* 2 : 9.

priestly
Mis. 194– 8 Urim and Thummim of *p·* office,
Ret. 35–24 Urim and Thummim of *p·* office,
'*01.* 12–14 Urim and Thummim of *p·* office,

priests
Mis. 33– 3 high *p·* of old caused the crucifixion
123–10 pagan *p·* bloated with crime ;
Peo. 4–23 pagan *p·* appointed Apollo

primal
Mis. 22–30 the *p·* cause, or Mind-force,
182–15 man's *p·*, spiritual existence,
187–26 *p·* facts of being are eternal ;
188– 8 that which is *p·*, spiritual, and
Pul. 12–21 her *p·* and everlasting strain.
'*01.* 1–19 the *p·* reality of things.
My. 347–15 reproduced her *p·* presence,

primarily
Mis. 9–13 *P·* and ultimately,
Ret. 91–16 spake *p·* to his immediate

Primary
Mis. 264–14 not fitted for it by the *P·* course.
273–24 applications . . . for the *P·* class
273–29 if I should teach that *P·* class,
273–30 one *P·* and two Normal
280–18 students of this *P·* class,
318–14 received instructions in a *P·* class
Man. 36– 7 taken the *P·* or Normal Course
86–23 teachers of the *P·* class shall
89–12 taught in a *P·* class by Mrs. Eddy
90–14 no *P·* classes shall be taught under
91–19 *P·* Students.
Ret. 43–16 taught the *P·*, Normal, and
43–18 taught one *P·* class, in 1889,
47–16 *P·* class student, richly imbued with
47–19 received instructions in a *P·* class
Rud. 14–13 never taught a *P·* class without
14–22 If the *P·* students are
My. 245–32 given to students of the *P·* class ;
251– 8 * Normal class instruction
251– 9 * to become teachers of *P·* classes?''
251–18 A *P·* student of mine can teach

Primary
My. 251–20 my *P·* student can himself be
319–21 * I entered your *P·* class at Boston.
320–21 * while I was in your *P·* class
322–19 * to enter the next *P·* class

primary
Un. 3– 1 *p·* school of mortal existence,
My. 46– 9 * *p·* declaration of this church

Primary Class
Mis. 279– 9 chapter sub-title
279–10 To the *P· C·* of

prime
Ret. 88– 4 his *p·* command, was that his
Pul. 58–24 * their *p·* instructor has ordained
Po. 16–25 waken my joy, as in earliest *p·*.

primeval
Po. 1– 3 *P·* dweller where the wild winds rest,
My. 139– 8 *p·* faith, hope, love.

primitive
Mis. 14–23 Good is the *p·* Principle of man ;
14–26 evil is neither a *p·* nor a
17–27 man's *p·*, sinless, spiritual
102–13 He is universal and *p·*.
192–24 as *p·* Christianity confirms.
Man. 17–12 should reinstate *p·* Christianity
Ret. 69– 3 *p·* and ultimate source of being ;
Pul. 47–29 * modernized from a *p·* homestead
69–15 * ideas of *p·* Christianity.
'*01.* 30– 2 since ever the *p·* Christians,
Hea. 3– 3 *p·* privilege of Christianity
Peo. 5–10 ideals of *p·* Christianity are nigh,
My. 46–12 reinstate *p·* Christianity
95–28 * days of the *p·* Christians,
111–15 maintains *p·* Christianity,
239– 4 relegates Christianity to its *p·*
245–20 doing the works of *p·* Christianity,

primitives
Mis. 316–13 depart farther from the *p·* of the

primordial
My. 180–10 that *p·* standard of Truth.

prince
Mis. 155– 3 *p·* of this world that has nothing in
My. 4–24 *p·* of this world that hath nothing in

princely
My. 194–20 *p·* gift of your magnificent church

Prince of Peace
Mis. 161– 8 The *P·* of *P·*.— *Isa.* 9 : 6.
164–19 The *P·* of *P·*.'' — *Isa.* 9 : 6.
321– 6 The *P·* of *P·*.'' — *Isa.* 9 : 6.
Pul. 83–30 * brought to warring men the *P·* of *P·*,

Principal
My. 311–32 Rev. R. S. Rust, D.D., *P·* of the

principal
Man. 31–17 *p·* part of the Sunday services,
Ret. 82–16 population of our *p·* cities
Pul. 5–22 public libraries of the *p·* cities,
25– 8 * The *p·* features are
Rud. 15–12 This was the *p·* reason for
'*00.* 1–19 in most of the *p·* cities,
13–24 *p·* deity in the city of Thyatira
Peo. 8–15 carried on through *p·* processes,
My. vi–19 * *p·* contributor to its columns ;
68–32 * pews and *p·* woodwork are of
304– 4 *p·* of Sanbornton Academy,

principally
Mis. 143–18 *p·* the Normal class graduates

Principle

and demonstration
Mis. 69– 7 Science rests on *P·* and demonstration.
and idea
(*see* **idea**)
and practice
Mis. 173– 2 Science, its *P·* and practice.
270–13 knowledge of his *P·* and practice.
Rud. 16–18 *P·* and practice laid down in S. and H.,
No. 44– 1 ignorance of its *P·* and practice,
My. 179–22 illustrates the *P·* and practice of
287–10 *P·* and practice of divine metaphysics.
and rule
Mis. 265–10 all *who follow the P· and rule*
337– 7 *P·* and rule of C. S.
356–29 its divine *P·* and rule of practice.
Man. 87–16 *P·* and rule of C. S.,
Ret. 25– 8 *P·* and rule of spiritual Science
Rud. 1– 3 *P·* and rule of universal harmony.
'*01.* 2–15 demonstrable *P·* and rule
4– 8 *P·* and rule of divine Science
My. 113–25 in proportion as this *P·* and rule are
241– 4 * *P·* and rule of C. S.

Principle

and rules
Mis. 19– 9   *P·* and rules of C. S.
354–14   *P·* and rules of C. S.,
Man. 43–24   statement of the divine *P·* and rules
'00.   4–20   *P·* and rules of this Christianity
6– 2   no lack in the *P·* and rules
'01. 22–21   C. S., its divine *P·* and rules,
22–24   if they understood its *P·* and rules
My. 299–14   divine *P·* and rules of the Bible,

basic
My. 348–30   Love is the basic *P·* of all Science,

changing
Hea.   4–27   can we demonstrate a changing *P·*?

curative
Ret. 25– 2   reveal the great curative *P·*,
33–21   the curative *P·*, remains,
Pul. 64–16   * a search for the great curative *P·*.
64–21   * curative *P·* was the Deity.
70–20   * to find the great curative *P·*
Hea. 13–21   Mind as the only curative *P·*.

deific
Pul.   4–14   thus demonstrating deific *P·*.
Rud.   1– 9   these are the deific *P·*.

demonstrable
'01.   2–15   demonstrable *P·* and rule
My. 348–26   demonstrable *P·* and given rule.

demonstrate the
Mis. 215–16   Then we shall demonstrate the *P·*
266–14   demonstrate the *P·* of C. S.,
336–16   demonstrate the *P·* of C. S.
Rud. 13– 6   demonstrate the *P·* of this Science,
No. 35– 4   demonstrate the *P·* of such Life ;

destitute of
Un. 49–22   destitute of *P·*, it is devoid of

devotion to
Mis. 176– 9   supreme devotion to *P·*

discerned the
Ret. 26– 4   Adoringly I discerned the *P·*

divine
    (*see* divine)

epitome of the
Rud.   8– 9   only an epitome of the *P·*,

eternal
Mis. 369–26   perfect and eternal *P·* of man.
Pul.   4–23   ever unfolding its eternal *P·*.

exemplified the
Pul. 54– 9   * enunciated and exemplified the *P·* ;

fixed
Mis. 147–19   upright man is guided by a fixed *P·*,
232–24   fixed *P·* of all healing is God ;
366– 7   with fixed *P·*, given rule,
No. 11–21   divine Science, with fixed *P·*,
33–10   with fixed *P·*, a given rule,
'01. 23–15   its fixed *P·* and given rule,
My. 106–18   on the basis of fixed *P·*,
113 24   demonstrated on a fixed *P·*
347–27   manifestation of a fixed *P·*

fixed in
Ret. 03–12   immovably fixed in *P·*.

fundamental
Mis. 233– 2   without knowing its fundamental *P·*.

God is the
Mis. 78–26   If God is the *P·* of man
Hea.   3–21   God is the *P·* of Christian healing,

governed by
Mis. 291– 3   a mind governed by *P·*

great
Mis. 192–17   great *P·* of a full salvation.

healing
Mis. 222–25   healing *P·*, . . . is not so obscure ;

heals
No. 21–26   wherein *P·* heals and saves.
My. 180–15   and this *P·* heals sin,

his
Mis. 14–14   if man has lost his *P·*
270–13   priceless knowledge of his *P·*

immortal
Mis. 117– 2   unfolds its immortal *P·*.

infinite
Mis. 16–10   infinite *P·* hath infinite claims
16–22   Love, a divine, infinite *P·* ;
150–29   infinite *P·*, with its universal
181–11   Infinite *P·* and infinite Spirit
258–18   this infinite *P·* of freedom,
Pan.   7– 7   one divine, infinite *P·*.
12–22   infinite *P·*, noumenon and phenomena,
Hea.   4– 5   results of an infinite *P·*,

instead of
Mis. 135– 3   *P·*, instead of person,
Hea.   8–21   through *P·* instead of a pardon ;
My. 152– 2   worshipping person instead of *P·*,

intelligent
My. 226–10   the one divine intelligent *P·*

is found
No. 20–11   *P·* is found to be the only term

Principle

is God
Un. 38– 2   individuality, . . . whose *P·* is God.
38–28   being, whose *P·* is God.

is One
Mis. 264–11   Its *P·* is One,

is right
Ret. 57– 8   *P·* is right ;

its
Mis. 14–14   with harmony and its *P·* ;
45– 5   its *P·* of metaphysical healing,
78–28   exact nature of its *P·*,
173– 2   Science, its *P·* and practice.
264–11   Its *P·* is One,
265–13   demonstrates its *P·* according to
337–10   the Golden Rule and its *P·*,
338– 7   proved . . . that its *P·* is divine.
Ret. 28–26   Its *P·* is divine, not human,
78– 7   for it is governed by its *P·*,
No. 28–23   neither the comprehension of its *P·*
44– 1   substantiates his ignorance of its *P·*
'01. 22–24   understood its *P·* and rules
Peo. 12–22   proved the application of its *P·*
My. 242–13   state its *P·* correctly,

law-abiding
Mis. 206–18   law-abiding *P·*, God.

Life, or
Ret. 28– 2   Life, or *P·*, of all being ;

lose the
My. 206– 4   lose the *P·* of divine metaphysics

Love is
No. 19–12   God is Love ; and Love is *P·*,

Love is the
Mis. 117–14   Love is the *P·* of unity,
234– 6   Love is the *P·* of divine Science ;
'02.   8–21   and Love is the *P·* thereof.

Mind or
My. 246–17   divine Mind or *P·* of man's being

no
Mis. 14–24   evil, good's opposite, has no *P·*,
My. 242– 9   Unless . . . you have no *P·*

no other
Mis. 197–32   and working from no other *P·*,

of all
Mis. 354–20   relying on the *P·* of all
'01.   5–13   calling one the divine *P·* of all.
Hea.   4–22   *P·* of all that is right,
My. 152–16   divine *P·* of all that really is,

of all being
Ret. 28– 2   Life, or *P·*, of all being ;

of all cure
Mis.   3–18   The *P·* of all cure is God,

of all harmony
No. 13– 5   deduction from the *P·* of all harmony,

of all phenomena
No. 21–10   demonstrated the *P·* of all phenomena

of all power
My. 278–29   The *P·* of all power is God,

of all Science
My. 348–30   Love is the basic *P·* of all Science,

of all science
Rud.   4– 6   *Is God the P· of all science,*

of all things
Ret. 20–25   the *P·* of all things pure ;

of being
Mis. 93–17   the unerring *P·* of being.
269–11   elucidate the *P·* of being,
Man. 67–19   the divine *P·* of being

of Christ
My. 149– 5   The *P·* of Christ is divine Love,

of Christianity
Mis. 16– 9   *P·* of Christianity is infinite :
144–29   life-giving *P·* of Christianity,

of Christian Science
Mis. 69– 7   *P·* of C. S. is divine.
104–24   The *P·* of C. S. is Love,
147– 8   divine *P·* of C. S.
221– 8   fundamental *P·* of C. S. ;
242–17   instructed in the *P·* of C. S.
266–14   demonstrate the *P·* of C. S.,
336–16   demonstrate the *P·* of C. S.
363–24   hold fast to the *P·* of C. S.
Rud.   1– 5   *What is the P· of C. S.?*
No. 11–24   grasp the *P·* of C. S.,
43–28   on the *P·* of C. S.,
'01. 21–20   Life is the *P·* of C. S.
My. 112– 1   by means of the *P·* of C. S.
118– 3   promoting the true *P·* of C. S.
218–13   the divine *P·* of C. S.
270–29   *P·* of C. S. will ultimately
279– 7   *P·* of C. S. demonstrates peace.
299–22   God, the divine *P·* of C. S.,
300–12   *P·* of C. S., demonstrated,

Principle

of divine healing
  Pul. 34–17   * heading
      34–18   * the *P·* of divine healing,
      67–13   * C. S., or the *P·* of divine healing,
of divine Science
  Mis. 209– 8   *P·* of divine Science being Love,
     234– 6   Love is the *P·* of divine Science ;
     291– 2   by the *P·* of divine Science :
of God's idea
  Pul. 75– 2   Love, the *P·* of God's idea,
of good
  My. 152–22   Then the divine *P·* of good,
of healing
  Mis. 40– 1   *P·* of healing demands
  Ret. 37–17   the spiritual *P·* of healing,
  Hea. 14– 7   obscure the divine *P·* of healing
of health
  Mis. 163–31   heralding the *P·* of health,
of his cure
  Mis. 260–11   *P·* of his cure was God,
of law
  My. 268–12   the *P·* of law and gospel,
of life
  My. 274– 2   demonstrates the *P·* of life
of man
  Mis. 14–23   Good is the primitive *P·* of man ;
     78–26   If God is the *P·* of man
    164–12   *P·* of man or the universe,
    186–23   *P·* of man cannot produce a
    369–26   perfect and eternal *P·* of man.
  Ret. 93– 6   incorporeal divine *P·* of man,
  Un. 51–27   the divine *P·* of man.
  Po. 70–13   Life, the *P·* of man.
of Mind-healing
  Ret. 33–14   prove the *P·* of Mind-healing.
  Pul. 35–24   * convinced of the *P·* of Mind-healing,
  Rud. 12–12   denies the *P·* of Mind-healing.
of pathology
  Mis. 35– 3   is the *P·* of pathology ;
of Science
  Rud. 8–21   the Truth and the *P·* of Science,
of this proof
  Hea. 15–26   God, the *P·* of this proof?
of unity
  Mis. 117–14   Love is the *P·* of unity,
one
  Mis. 265– 9   All must have *one P·*
  No. 10–12   one *P·* for all scientific truth.
  Hea. 3–26   three statements of one *P·*.
  My. 204–10   unites its true followers in one *P·*,
oneness of
  Peo. 13–11   unity of Mind and oneness of *P·*.
or person
  My. 233–28   chapter sub-title
or practice
  Ret. 64–19   either in *P·* or practice.
perfect
  Mis. 186–20   his perfect *P·*, God,
    232– 6   towards the perfect *P·* of things ;
  My. 187– 9   perfect *P·* whereby to demonstrate
person, or a
  My. 117– 3   A person, or a *P·* ?
potential
  Mis. 331–26   This supreme potential *P·*
predicated of
  '01. 4–14   predicated of *P·* and demonstrated as
primitive
  Mis. 14–23   Good is the primitive *P·* of man ;
reveals the
  Mis. 194– 3   Divine Science reveals the *P·*
  Hea. 14–25   reveals the *P·* and method of
same
  Mis. 40–15   demonstrated on, the same *P·*
    352–14   sickness is healed upon the same *P·*
saving
  Mis. 2–19   God, man's saving *P·*,
Science of the
  My. 149– 7   Science of the *P·* must be
self-created
  Mis. 217– 7   whose cause is the self-created *P·*,
spiritual
  Mis. 186–17   spiritual *P·* of spiritual man.
  Ret. 37–17   demonstrating the spiritual *P·*
that is God
  Peo. 5–20   yea, to the *P·* that is God,
that moves
  Mis. 174–10   *P·* that moves all in harmony,
that reveals
  My. 119–14   the *P·* that reveals Christ.
their
  Ret. 93– 7   in consonance with their *P·*.
thinking of
  My. 234– 1   implies that one is not thinking of *P·*,

Principle

this
  Mis. 100–27   He understands this *P·*, — Love.
    194– 5   God is this *P·*.
    198–18   On this *P·*, disease also is treated
    209– 9   rule of this *P·* demonstrates Love,
    209–11   demonstrates this *P·* of cure
    232–25   this *P·* should be sought from
  Ret. 26–27   could first state this *P·*,
  No. 11–25   Revelation shows this *P·*,
    20–10   This *P·* is Mind, substance, Life,
    35– 7   to reach the understanding of this *P·* !
  Hea. 8–27   adhere to the rule of this *P·*
    15– 3   established upon this *P·*,
  Peo. 2–11   this *P·* is learned through goodness,
  My. 113–25   in proportion as this *P·* and rule are
    180–15   this *P·* heals sin, sickness,
triune
  Mis. 63– 8   triune *P·* of all pure theology ;
  '01. 5– 7   as one divine infinite triune *P·*,
understand the
  Mis. 215–14   understand the *P·* and object of
understood the
  Hea. 9– 4   if we understood the *P·* better
we know
  My. 149– 5   We know *P·* only through Science.
without
  Un. 49–22   Evil is without *P·*.
word
  My. 225–30   The word *P·*, when referring to God,

  Mis. 31–14   *P·* or the rules of C. S. ;
    41–30   the result of the *P·*
    83– 1   *P·*, of all real being ;
    199–23   *P·* of these marvellous works
    243–15   includes of necessity the *P·*,
  Ret. 94–24   unchanging, in *P·*, rule, and
  Pul. 35– 3   *P·* and the law involved in
    53– 1   * fresh development of a *P·* that
  No. 5– 2   *P·* of this grand verity
  Hea. 3–28   know that the *P·* is not the person,
  My. 149–23   Losing . . . the *P·* in its accessories,
    153–24   *P·* of which works intelligently as the

principle

  Mis. 118– 8   To obey the *p·* of mathematics
    283–30   laboring to learn the *p·* of music
    353–21   regulator is governed by the *p·*
    359– 5   On the same *p·*, you continue the
  Ret. 49–11   The fundamental *p·* for growth
    57– 7   like correcting the *p·* of music for
  Un. 10–23   *p·* of positive mathematics.
    13– 2   same *p·* that it does in astronomy.
    13– 8   The *p·* of music knows nothing of
  '01. 13– 1   not intelligence, a person or a *p·*,
  My. 226– 6   the *p·* of harmonious vibration,
    226– 7   the *p·* of conservation of
    226– 8   the *p·* of the inclined plane
    237– 8   the full understanding of the *p·*

principles

  Mis. 68–26   * *p·* and causes of all things existing,"
  Ret. 7–11   * abstruse and metaphysical *p·*,
  Pul. 31– 5   * *p·* asserted by Jesus,
    32–22   * due to the *p·* of C. S.
    50–18   * tempted to examine its *p·*,
    51–24   * help on the growth of its *p·*.
    68– 5   * taught the *p·* of the faith
  No. 9–28   * referred to general truths and *p·*
  '01. 23–25   on received *p·* of philosophy,
    27– 7   * interpret their ideas and *p·*

print

  Mis. x–12   those heretofore in *p·*,
    300– 9   If you should *p·* and publish
  Man. 72– 2   *p·*, nor publish the Manual
  Po. vi– 1   * *poem finally found its way into p·*,
  My. 254–17   * May we have permission to *p·*,

printed

  Mis. 300–20   *p·* as your original writings,
    380–30   *p·* and issued by a student of C. S.
  Man. 32–23   *p·* in the C. S. QUARTERLY.
  Ret. 2–18   *p·* in olden type and replete with
    37– 6   When it was first *p·*,
    38–19   he had *p·* all the copy on hand,
  Pul. 59– 9   * *p·* program was for some
  My. 26–16   too short to be *p·* in book form,
    59–29   * before it was ever *p·*."
    295–10   *p·* IN NUREMBERG IN 1733

printer (see also printer's)

  Ret. 38– 2   *p·* informed me that he could not
    38–13   my *p·* resumed his work
    38–24   I had grown disgusted with my *p·*,
  My. 53– 5   * would she allow *p·* and binder to

printer's

  Mis. 300–13   and spares you the *p·* bill,

printing
Mis. 381–23 p·, publishing, selling, giving
Ret. 38–14 finished p· the copy he had on hand,
prints
My. 119–20 to the person, to the p· of the nails,
prior
Mis. 382– 4 p· to my discovery of this Science.
Man. 77– 5 P· to paying bills against the
100– 1 If p· to the meeting of the church
Ret. 2–10 n· to the Revolutionary period.
24– 7 twenty years p· to my discovery
69– 2 p· to reaching intelligence.
'01. 8–25 Christ existed p· to Jesus,
My. 244– 8 p· to conferring . . . the degree of C.S.D.,
prism
Mis. 194–14 needs the p· of this Science
356–26 Humility is lens and p·
Ret. 35–13 Science is the p· of Truth,
'01. 12–19 needs the p· of divine Science,
prisms
Pul. 26– 4 * p· which reflect the rainbow tints.
prison
Mis. 124–15 opening the p· doors to the
262–21 opening the p· doors to such
275–18 open the p· to them that are bound,
Pul. 82– 1 * make the body not the p·,
My. 119–22 open the p· doors and solve
117–15 sick, or in p·, — Matt. 25 : 39.
175–15 well-conducted jail and state p·,
prisoner
My. 314–25 kept her a p· in her home,
pristine
My. 40–17 * widely reassert its p· power
private
Mis. 249–10 Both in p· and public life,
275–24 public and p· expressions of love
301–18 since my p· counsel they disregard.
315– 7 either in p· or in public assemblies,
Man. 46–14 all p· communications made to them
67– 6 P· Communications.
67– 7 strictly p· communication from
Rud. 16– 2 can take the place of p· lessons ;
'00. 10–25 I have learned it was a p· soldier
12–26 and also in p· houses.
'02. 13– 1 money from my own p· earnings
14–28 forever silence all p· criticisms,
Po. vii– 7 * her poems, for p· distribution.
My. 49– 1 ⁴ both in public and p·.
82– 9 * boarding-houses, and p· houses
218–25 My p· life is given to a servitude
privately
My. 310– 5 I was p· tutored by him.
Private Meeting
Mis. 350– 7 The P. M. (P· M·) Society
privation
Mis. 323–10 peril, p·, temptation,
privilege
Mis. 137– 7 simply to give you the p·,
266– 6 a single human right or p·
289–24 if the wife esteems not this p·,
300 28 this was a special p·,
302–20 p· of copying and reading my works
360–28 p· of saying to the sick,
Man. 44–17 p· and duty of every member,
47– 8 p· of a Christian Scientist
59–21 duty and p· of the local members
73– 7 P· of Members.
100–21 shall be the p· of this Board to
Pul. 51– 4 * Freedom to believe . . . is a great p·
No. 8– 5 let us add one more p·
'02. 12–22 It is a p· to acquaint communicants
13–11 p· of publishing my books
20 23 the p· of meeting you all
Hea. 3– 3 The primitive p· of Christianity
My. 5–12 pride and power, prestige or p·?
7– 6 p· to acquaint communicants with
11–20 * having seized upon this p·
23–27 * p· of participating in the work
39–20 * p· of saying a few words
193– 5 p· remains mine to watch
241–11 * p· of publishing an extract
243–13 p· of knowing two students
276–12 recommends this surprising p·
298– 1 request the p· of buying,
356– 4 the p· of knowing God,
privileged
Mis. xii– 2 p· armaments of peace.
143–29 breathing the donor's p· joy.
202– 6 * p· beyond the walks of common life,
244–27 not for a p· class
Man. 49– 5 p· to enter into this holy work,

privileged
Ret. 89–12 bidden to this p· duty
Pul. 8–12 p· joy at helping to build
My. 179–29 p· in having the untranslated
184– 8 To-day I am p· to congratulate
351– 3 * p· to publish her letter
privileges
Mis. 272– 2 * with all the rights and p·
303–15 p· that we claim for ourselves.
Ret. 6– 8 accorded special household p·.
My. 24– 8 * welcome all mankind to the p·
167–25 infringement of rights and p·
168– 5 forever the p· of the people
195– 9 p· I have not had time to express,
247– 9 its rules . . . equal rights and p·,
255– 2 its rules . . . equal rights and p·,
352– 6 * p· we enjoy in this church work.
prize
Un. 55–11 that they may win the p·.
'00. 6– 8 p· of the high calling — Phil. 3 : 14.
My. 123– 4 continue to p· love even more
probability
Pul. 34–10 * no p· that she would be alive
probable
My. 10–16 * p· that none will be made
probably
Pul. 67–10 * would p· show a greater number
78– 2 * p· one of the most magnificent
My. 85– 7 * adherents number p· a million,
86–27 * attendance . . . p· unprecedented,
328–19 * p· the first to be issued
probation
Mis. 2–21 Man's p· after death
Man. 38–23 received . . . on one year's p·,
39–16 Ineligible for P·.
50–21 exonerated, put on p·, or
51– 4 he shall be placed on p·, or
51–22 power to discipline, place on p·,
55–10 P·.
No. 27–26 P· of mortals must go on
probationary
Man. 38–16 p· MEMBERSHIP.
39– 8 A full member or a p· member,
39–13 eligible to p· membership
Un. 3– 5 pass through another p· state
probe
Po. 22–16 p· the wound, then pour the balm
problem
of being
Mis. 201–21 that he had wrought the p· of being
283–24 work out his own p· of being ;
Ret. 79–15 the inscrutable p· of being
Rud. 6– 1 solution of the p· of being,
My. 348–30 it solves the p· of being ;

Mis. 52–21 p· to be wrought in divine Science.
52–29 before solving the advanced p·
54–30 to solve a p· involving logarithms ;
55– 2 simplest p· in C. S. is
118–10 make incorrect your entire p·,
120– 6 divine Principle of life's long p·,
291–29 would aid the solution of this p·,
333–19 to work out the p· of Mind,
346– 7 The origin of evil is the p· of ages.
Ret. 34– 5 could solve the mental p·.
58– 4 work out the p· of infinity or
Un. 9–18 perplexing p· of human existence.
Pul. vii–20 vast p· of eternal life,
My. 110–22 solve the blind p· of matter.
181–15 the p· of religious liberty
306–18 alone solves the p· of humanity,
problematic
Mis. 286–18 although it is to-day p·.
'01. 20–28 p· and self-contradictory.
problematical
Mis. 14–28 therefore, wholly p·.
problems
Mis. 125–25 hitherto untouched p· of being,
Un. 6–21 about the p· of Euclid.
'02. 4–26 by abstruse p· of Scripture,
My. 12– 9 * decision of these remaining p·.
61–29 * As I discovered the many intricate p·
181– 6 and ultimate in unsolved p·
195– 6 p· to be worked out for the field,
348–32 solution of God's p·.
Probst, Arthur O.
My. 361–27 * signature
proceed
Mis. 76– 1 and must p· from God ;
155– 5 spiritual, and p· from goodness.
232–11 p· from the standard of right

proceed
Ret. 71–22　they *p·* from false convictions
'00. 4–25　whatever is real must *p·* from God,
'01. 16–18　ought not to *p·* from the individual,
'02. 7–23　*p·* to another Scriptural passage
My. 300–15　understand . . . and *p·* to overcome

proceeded
Ret. 69– 7　delusion that life . . . *p·* from
Hea. 17–19　never *p·* from Truth, Life, and Love.
My. 49–23　* Mrs. Eddy *p·* to instruct those
318–21　As I *p·*, Mr. Wiggin manifested more

proceedeth
Mis. 198–13　evil *p·* not from God,
Un. 24– 3　From me *p·* all Mind,
60–16　*p·* blessing and cursing.— *Jas.* 3 : 10.
My. 6–21　*p·* out of the mouth of God.

proceeding
Pul. 34– 9　* before *p·* to his morning service,
No. 16– 8　and *p·* from Him.
Pan. 3–24　* "universal nature *p·* from
My. 24–20　* erection of the building is *p·*
333–10　* minutes record this further *p·* :

proceedings
Mis. 170–24　Jesus' *p·* with the blind man
Man. 77–20　characterize all the *p·* of
'02. 13–20　legal *p·* were instituted by
My. 137–24　the present *p·* were brought
138–10　present *p·* test my trust in

proceeds
Mis. 36–11　is harmful and *p·* not from God ;
49–29　that the capacity to err *p·* from
58–22　no order that *p·* from
186–28　As the apostle *p·* in this line
Un. 38– 9　all is real which *p·* from Life
Pul. 66– 8　* *p·* more from the graveyards

process
Mis. 8–21　however much we suffer in the *p·*.
40– 5　mingle . . . in the same *p·*,
213– 7　point the way, shorten the *p·*,
215– 1　through this very *p·*,
220–24　if this mental *p·* and power be
221–32　belief in evil and in the *p·* of evil,
Un. 8–22　You demonstrate the *p·* of Science,
11–24　neither . . . hindered the divine *p·*.
20–10　By a reverse *p·* of argument
20–15　Try this *p·*, dear inquirer,
36– 2　*p·* it names material attraction,
Pul. 34–28　*p·* by which I was restored to health ;
Hea. 12–25　when the drug disappears by your *p·*
My. 71–15　* has been in *p·* of construction,
178– 5　nor lose the invincible *p·*
219–30　an individual submit to this *p·*,
292– 6　way pointed out, the *p·* shortened,

processes
Un. 12– 2　by mental, not material *p·*.
21– 2　description of mental *p·*
21– 4　If we observe our mental *p·*,
No. 28– 7　*p·* and terrible revolutions
Peo. 8–15　carried on through principal *p·*,

procession
My. 312–26　his staff, with a long *p·*,
326–18　long *p·* with tender dirge
333–11　* *p·* was formed, which moved to
333–14　* The *p·* then returned to the

proclaim
My. 248–11　*p·* Truth so winningly that
353–14　*p·* the universal activity

proclaimed
Pul. 5– 2　clergymen who had publicly *p·*
52–26　* No new doctrine is *p·*,
53–22　* When Jesus of Nazareth *p·*

proclaims
Mis. 277– 7　Whosoever *p·* Truth loudest,
My. 28–24　* *p·* to the world that Jesus' gospel
58–12　* *p·* the trust, the willingness

proclivities
Mis. 315–14　such as have promising *p·*
Man. 83–11　promising *p·* toward C. S.

proconsul
Mis. 345– 8　when the *p·* said to him,

procrastination
Hea. 19–18　patient of man's *p·*,

procreation
Mis. 286–21　Human *p·*, birth, life, and
Ret. 69–24　for recreation or *p·* ?"

Proctor, Adelaide A.
'00. 11–21　Adelaide A. *P·* breathes my thought :

procurator
Mis. 351–26　is not the *p·* of happiness,
Rud. 10–16　fear is the *p·* of the thought which

procures
Mis. 360– 2　and *p·* divine power.

prodigal
Mis. 369–22　as tired as was the *p·* son
Ret. 91– 3　The parable of "the *p·* son"
'01. 17– 7　who so loves even the repentant *p·*

prodigious
My. 92– 9　* *p·* convention of Christian Scientists

prodigy
Pul. 51– 2　* If it did, it would be a *p·*.

produce
Mis. 5– 8　able to *p·* perfect health and
8– 5　drugs do not, cannot, *p·* health
48–15　could *p·* the effect of alcohol,
174– 2　than has good to *p·* evil.
186–23　cannot *p·* a less perfect man
217–20　that these opposites, . . . *p·* matter,
221– 1　does not, *p·* the slightest effect,
229– 4　which he believes *p·* it.
261–31　must *p·* physical and moral harmony.
352–17　and what has claimed to *p·* it,
372–13　Knowing that this book would *p·* a
Pul. 51– 3　* Neither . . . *p·* the same impressions
No. 17– 3　He must *p·* its consequences.
Hea. 6–22　can *p·* a result upon his body.
My. 71– 3　* *p·* the most beautiful effects
124–23　Then *p·* thy records, time-table,
249– 5　*p·* God's phenomena.
275– 3　does *p·* universal fellowship.
292–25　to *p·* opposite effects.
301–29　drugs can *p·* no curative effect

produced
Mis. 49–10　had not *p·* insanity."
186–24　than it *p·* in the beginning.
218– 4　matter never *p·* Mind,
221–12　believes that sin has *p·* the effect
259–26　must have *p·* its own illusion,
277–31　drunkenness *p·* by animality.
290–17　* *p·* a wonderful illumination,
360–12　Philosophy never has *p·*,
375–18　* to see *p·* to-day that art
Pul. 6– 1　upheaval *p·* when Truth is
51–17　* *p·* a sensation in religious
'01. 24– 5　impression *p·* by divine power
Hea. 8–13　the thought that has *p·* this,
17–25　sickness and death were *p·* by sin.
18–26　death has been *p·* by a belief alone.
Peo. 3–10　beliefs that have *p·* sin, sickness,
My. 22–24　* moral and the physical effects *p·* by
97–29　* *p·* by that stupendous gathering.
238– 6　effects *p·* by reading the
302– 6　Neither life nor . . . can be *p·* on
359–28　temptation *p·* by animal magnetism

producer
Rud. 9–27　God is good, and the *p·* only of

produces
Mis. 26–21　neither . . . *p·* its opposite.
27–13　no species ever *p·* its opposite.
41–20　*p·* all harmony that appears.
59– 5　*p·* the effect of mesmerism.
221– 6　Error *p·* physical sufferings,
337–17　*p·* a growing affection for all good,
Un. 31–14　*fourth*, that matter, . . . *p·* life
Rud. 8– 2　no pine-tree *p·* a mammal
Hea. 6–13　When I learned how mind *p·* disease
6–14　I learned how it *p·* the
6–22　The belief that *p·* this result
7– 4　*p·* the harmonious effect on the body.
My. 232–27　If so-called watching *p·* fear
302– 4　mind, not matter, *p·* the result

producing
Mis. 53–12　to assist in *p·* a cure,
122–15　it is not evil *p·* good.
Rud. 10–10　*p·* the beliefs of a mortal material
'02. 6–30　*p·* nothing unlike Himself,
Hea. 6–25　a latent cause *p·* the effect we see.
My. 302– 2　of healing disease and of *p·* disease.
348–24　never *p·* an opposite effect,

product
Mis. 198–20　as much the *p·* of mortal thought
221–28　would not yield the same *p·*
233–30　belief or *p·* of mortal mind :
Un. 26–25　The phantasmagoria is a *p·* of

production
Mis. 304–31　* The responsibility of its *p·*,

productions
Mis. 376–11　* Their *p·* are expressionless copies of
Ret. 11– 3　following is one of my girlhood *p·*.
Po. vii– 4　* *reached its fulness in her later p·*.

productive
Mis. 371–16　is not *p·* of the better sort,

profane
- *Mis.* 45–12 *Can an atheist or a p· man*
- '00. 6–20 a man who . . . is *p·*, licentious,
- *My.* 106–25 a tobacco user, a *p·* swearer,
-   113–15 Was it *p·* for St. Paul to aspire to
-   307–24 I should still think that it was *p·*.

profanely
- *No.* 5–23 is *p·* tampering with the

profanity
- *My.* 308–28 no *p·* and no slang phrases.

profess
- *Mis.* 116–25 you *p·* to understand and love,
-   311–10 exemplifying what we *p·*.

professed
- *Mis.* 247– 8 *p·* Christianity a half-century ;
-   301–12 a few *p·* Christian Scientists.

profession
- *Mis.* 378–19 taught her of his medical *p·*.
- *Man.* 46–10 which advertise his business or *p·*,
- *Ret.* 14–17 made any *p·* of religion,
- *Pul.* 9–26 Practice, not *p·*, . . . gain the
- *Hea.* 3– 5 a proof, more than a *p·*

professional
- *Ret.* 88– 2 observed in the *p·* intercourse
- *Pul.* 59–18 * read by a *p·* elocutionist,
- *My.* 30–13 * *p·* men, devoted women
-   81–32 * *p·* men, hard-headed shrewd
-   104–25 *p·* men and women of the highest

professionally
- *Mis.* 51–11 cannot answer your question *p·*.

professionals
- *My.* 111–27 irritate a certain class of *p·*
-   327–25 * other *p·* who practise the art
-   328–28 * all other *p·* who practise the art

professions
- *Man.* 82–17 who practise other *p·*
- '01. 31– 3 sects or *p·* can encounter
- *My.* 328–26 * enumerating the different *p·*

Professor
- *Mis.* 47–27 *P· Carpenter's exhibitions of*
-   242– 2 The article of *P·* T——,
-   242– 4 In it the *P·* offered me,
-   243–13 I agree with the *P·*,
-   243–23 The *P·* alludes to Paul's advice
-   243–31 Again, the *P·* quotes,
-   244– 3 we have the *P·* on the platform
- '01. 27–27 *P·* Agassiz said :

professor
- *Mis.* 344– 3 a Pythagorean *p·* of ethics,
-   344–12 he was dismissed by the *p·*,
- *Un.* 11–20 a *p·* of natural philosophy,

professors
- *Mis.* 120– 1 The *p·* of C. S. must
- *My.* 89– 4 * deemed by its *p·* not to exist
-   107– 4 Compare the lives of its *p·* with

proffer
- *Po.* 10– 3 We *p·* thee warm welcome
- *My.* 337– 5 We *p·* thee warm welcome

proffering
- *My.* 78–16 * and none *p·* small change.

profile
- *Po.* v–12 * *resemble the p· of a human face.*

profit
- *Mis.* 213–14 May my friends and my enemies so *p·*
-   359–29 give not the wisdom to *p·* by it.
- *My.* 74–16 * might *p·* by their example
-   261– 4 How shall we . . . *p·* them withal?

profitable
- *Mis.* 64–21 Works on science are *p·* ;
-   303–24 *p·* to the heart of our country.
-   339– 3 subjects that are *p·*,
- *Ret.* 5–27 * themes at once pleasing and *p·*.
- *My.* 178–11 less *p·* or scientific

profitably
- *Mis.* 44– 3 and may *p·* teach people,
- *Ret.* 35–10 before . . . could be *p·* published.

profited
- *Mis.* 272–31 have not *p·* by my rebukes,
-   316–14 *p·* up to their present capacity

profiteth
- *My.* 108– 9 "The flesh *p·* nothing." — *John* 6 : 63.

profitless
- *My.* 106– 5 mental practice were *p·*.

profits
- *Man.* 80– 4 The net *p·* of the business
- '02. 13– 8 net *p·* from the business of
- *My.* vi–23 * to pay all future *p·* to her church ;
-   158–13 it *p·* by the past

profound
- *Mis.* 234–23 wonderment to *p·* thinkers.
-   296– 5 *p·* philosophers, brilliant scholars.
-   342–14 darkness *p·* brooded over
-   392– 4 Nature divine, in harmony *p·*,
- *Ret.* 73– 9 great fact leads into *p·* depths.
- *Un.* 43–18 Because of these *p·* reasons I
- *Pul.* 87–13 accept my *p·* thanks.
- *No.* 13–14 *p·* deduction from C. S.
- '00. 11–14 tones intricate, *p·*, commanding.
- *Po.* 20– 5 Nature divine, in harmony *p·*,
- *My.* 29– 5 * a stillness *p·* ;
-   157– 4 * with *p·* joy and deep gratitude
-   224–23 less correct and therefore less *p·*.
-   229–22 accept *p·* thanks for
-   250– 4 has received *p·* attention.
-   253–21 accept my *p·* thanks

profoundest
- *My.* 295–14 in its largest, *p·* sense

profoundly
- *No.* 39– 2 can think more lucidly and *p·*
- *My.* 194–22 *p·* thank you for it,
-   229–31 it takes life *p·* ;

profuse
- *Man.* 43–15 shall not publish *p·* quotations

progeny
- *Mis.* 286– 6 marriage and *p·* will continue
-   297–26 effects, on himself and his *p·*,

prognostications
- *Pul.* 84–15 * *p·* to the contrary

program
- *Pul.* 50– 9 * *p·* was for some reason

progress
  and Christianity
- *Hea.* 7–24 important to *p·* and Christianity.
  and victories
- *My.* 47–15 * trials, *p·*, and victories
  befriended
- *Pul.* 7– 6 her laws have befriended *p·*.
  continued
- *Mis.* 110–22 thanksgiving for the continued *p·*
  every step of
- *Peo.* 1– 2 Every step of *p·* is a step more
  feet of
- *My.* 127–29 nor laid down at the feet of *p·*
  foe of
- *Mis.* 206–13 idleness is the foe of *p·*.
  footsteps of
- *My.* 139– 8 advancing footsteps of *p·*,
  growth and
- *My.* 0– 0 * pace with our own growth and *p·*.
  hinder
- *Mis.* 290– 7 break all bonds that hinder *p·*,
  his own
- *Mis.* 308– 7 greatly errs, stops his own *p·*,
  human
- *Mis.* 9–31 more disastrous to human *p·*
  in Christian Science
- *Mis.* 355– 2 present stage of *p·* in C. S.
- *Man.* 44–25 which impede their *p·* in C. S.
  indispensable to the
- *Mis.* 317–18 indispensable to the *p·* of every
  is demonstration
- *Mis.* 235– 8 In C. S., *p·* is demonstration,
  is spiritual
- *My.* 181– 8 *P·* is spiritual.
  is the law
- *Mis.* 15–19 *p·* is the law of infinity.
  is the maturing
- *My.* 181– 8 *p·* is the maturing conception
  its
- *Pul.* vii– 3 its *p·* during the ensuing
- *My.* 47– 8 * a few of the stages of its *p·*,
  landmark of
- *My.* 47–19 * touched by each landmark of *p·*
  lifts mortals
- *Mis.* 287–15 *p·* lifts mortals to discern the
  line with
- *Mis.* 287–20 affection in line with *p·*,
  man's
- *Mis.* 234–13 What hinders man's *p·*
  of Christianity
- *No.* 32– 2 retarded the *p·* of Christianity
  of Christian Science
- *My.* 134– 5 unprecedented *p·* of C. S.
-   329–22 * recognizing the steady *p·* of C. S.
  of our Cause
- *Mis.* x–16 *p·* of our Cause.
-   274– 8 might hinder the *p·* of our Cause
- *My.* 21–13 * aid the *p·* of our Cause
  of religion
- *My.* 340– 9 the *p·* of religion and medicine
  of students
- *Mis.* 156–20 clogs the *p·* of students,
  of the human race
- *Ret.* 78–24 against the *p·* of the human race

progress

of the work
My. 24–18 * inquired about the *p·* of the work
our
My. 44– 7 * our *p·* may be fast or it
outcome of
'02. 2–20 are an outcome of *p·* ;
peace, and
Mis. 118–23 foes to grace, peace, and *p·* ;
period of
Mis. 26– 4 Each successive period of *p·*
promote their
Man. 83–14 obligated to promote their *p·*
report
My. 125– 5 It requires you to report *p·*,
ripe for
My. 281–28 when nations are ripe for *p·*.
rise and
Ret. 80–20 unceasing spiritual rise and *p·*.
some
Mis. 234–24 she has made some *p·*,
spiritual
Mis. 124–32 In proportion to a man's spiritual *p·*,
192– 6 importance to man's spiritual *p·*,
My. 114–30 each step of mental and spiritual *p·*,
stage of
Mis. 355– 2 stage of *p·* in C. S.
steps of
My. 110–11 guiding the steps of *p·*
their
Man. 44–25 impede their *p·* in C. S.
88–21 subjects essential to their *p·*.
My. 267–18 in proportion to their *p·*,
to impede
Mis. 115–27 whatever tends to impede *p·*.
unity and
My. 123– 1 Our unity and *p·* are proverbial,
waymarks of
Ret. 27–11 valuable to me as waymarks of *p·*,
wheels of
Mis. 234– 3 and clog the wheels of *p·*.
Rud. 17– 4 clogging the wheels of *p·* by
world's
Mis. 304–25 * marking the world's *p·* toward liberty ;
your
Mis. 160–12 Your *p·*, the past year,
My. 6–17 I thank you for this proof of your *p·*,

Mis. 2–24 If man should not *p·* after death,
2–27 those who *p·* here and hereafter
52–22 What *p·* would a student of science
98–15 *p·* of our common Cause in Chicago,
Pul. 10–22 as *p·* certainly demands,
65–13 * Attention is directed to the *p·*
No. 31– 7 They *p·* and will multiply into
44–18 *P·*, legitimate to the human race,
Hea. 9– 1 and *p·* faster than we are now
My. 35–27 * During the *p·* of each service,
181– 8 *P·* is the maturing conception of

progresses
My. 342–28 government will develop as it *p.*"

progressing
Mis. 41– 9 destroys their own possibility of *p·*.
Hea. 9– 1 faster than we are now *p·*.

progression
Mis. 82–13 *Is there infinite p· with man*
82–20 Infinite *p·* is concrete being,

progressive
Mis. 117– 1 A *p·* life is the reality of Life
Rud. 16–26 snatch at whatever is *p·*,
'00. 4–14 these are *p·* signs of the times
My. 65–18 * chapter sub-title
114–32 and find these *p·* steps
339–12 Along the lines of *p·* Christendom,
340–32 of learning and *p·* religion

prohibit
Mis. 309–31 *p·* ourselves the childish pleasure of

prohibited
Man. 41– 5 is abnormal . . . and is *p·*.

prohibiting
Mis. 246– 1 and the *p·* of free speech,
Po. vi–20 *p· slavery in the United States.*"

prohibition
Mis. 257–13 as a power, *p·*, or license,
260–30 needing neither license nor *p·* ;

prohibitory
Peo. 10– 9 *p·* law regulating the practice of

project
Pul. 51–20 * Ere this many a new *p·*

projected
'00. 12– 2 paraphrases *p·* from divinity

prolific
Mis. 113–31 *p·* sources of spiritual power
Ret. 69–21 opposite belief is the *p·* source of
My. 132–12 Oh, may this hour be *p·*,

prolong
Po. 31– 5 *P·* the strain "Christ risen !"

prolonged
Mis. 17–24 This birth is more or less *p·*
89–25 concept that is not spared or *p·*
366–10 and this is the *p·* tone :
Ret. 3– 7 caused that *p·* contest to be known
My. 343– 5 * unexpectedly after a *p·* exordium.
344–18 * "Oh," with a *p·* inflection,

prolonging
Mis. 282–15 *P·* the metaphysical tone of his

prolongs
Mis. 87–31 this interference *p·* the struggle
274–21 *p·* the reign of . . . unprincipled clans.

prominent
Mis. 18– 8 *p·* laws which forward birth in
119–25 a *p·* statute in the divine law,
Ret. 3– 1 *p·* in British politics,
15–28 *p·* churchman agreeably informed the
Pul. 73–17 * a very *p·* member of the church.
88– 9 names of other *p·* newspapers
My. 90–29 * *P·* among these is the
96– 5 * many of them *p·* figures in
328–22 * Upon the request of a *p·* healer

promiscuous
Mis. 282–29 *p·* and unannounced mental practice
Ret. 71– 9 *P·* mental treatment,
Rud. 15–22 to *p·* and large assemblies,
My. 214– 2 *p·* selections would write your

promiscuously
Mis. 232–29 prevent mankind from striking out *p·*,

promise
Mis. 29– 3 his *p·* is perpetual.
39–15 I have faith in His *p·*,
87– 8 "I love your *p·* ;
144–19 to whisper our Master's *p·*,
153–10 and the land of *p·*,
254– 2 points with *p·* of prosperity?
270–20 if we would obtain that *p·*.
319–28 between the *p·* and event :
340–22 by patience, they inherit the *p·*.
355– 3 a full-orbed *p·*, and a gaunt want.
356–11 give *p·* of grand careers.
373–27 his *p·* that the Christlike shall
388– 6 A bow of *p·* on the cloud.
394– 5 *p·*, the home, and the heaven of
Man. 16– 9 we solemnly *p·* to watch,
Ret. 7– 7 * young man of uncommon *p·*.
23–10 spanned with its rainbow of *p·*.
31–30 Love unveiled the healing *p·*
89–21 even according to his *p·*,
92– 8 reach the fruition of his *p·* :
Un. 43–20 I exhort them to accept Christ's *p·*,
Pul. 1– 5 *p·* clad in white raiment,
83– 2 * *p·* as lover and candidate
'00. 11–10 we have the *p·* that
13–16 A glad *p·* to such as wait
'02. 9–15 every *p·* fulfilled,
20–15 A bow of *p·* on the cloud.
Peo. 3–17 like a *p·* upon the cloud,
Po. 7– 6 A bow of *p·* on the cloud.
45– 6 The *p·*, the home, and the heaven
My. 12– 8 * *p·* of the speedy accumulation of
25–27 divinity appears in all its *p·*.
125– 9 your flocks, big with *p·* ;
186–21 Here let His *p·* be verified :
188– 3 This house is hallowed by His *p·* :
190–32 verifying his last *p·*,
230–26 realize at last their Master's *p·*,
278–23 the *p·* and reward of rightness.

promised
Pul. 33–11 * *p·* to reply if the call came
'02. 17–30 susceptible of light with *p·* joy.
Po. 33– 5 bless me with Christ's *p·* rest ;
My. 43– 2 * in possession of the *p·* land.
43–13 * brought them into the *p·* land,
44– 5 * going up to possess the *p·* land

promises
Pul. 73–15 * God has fulfilled His *p·* to her
My. 48–13 * spiritual understanding of its *p·*.
92–29 * for some such comfort as it *p·*.
93–12 * C. S. *p·* nothing in the way of
155– 7 *p·*, and proofs of Holy Writ.
201– 4 is fast fulfilling the *p·*.

promising
Mis. 315–14 *p·* proclivities toward C. S.
Man. 83–10 *p·* proclivities toward C. S.

promote
Mis. 273–21   *p·* the growing interest in C. S.
   288–30   to *p·* the ends of temperance ;
   296–26   wish to *p·* female suffrage?
   350–29   *p·* health and spiritual growth.
   354– 8   can no longer *p·* peace
Man. 31–12   shall *p·* health and holiness,
   45– 6   *p·* peace on earth and good will
   45–11   strive to *p·* the welfare of all
   83–14   obligated to *p·* their progress
Ret. 90–21   *p·* the welfare and happiness
Un. 5–17   neither will it *p·* the Cause of
   6–11   is radical enough to *p·*
Pul. 50– 1   * using her money to *p·* the welfare
My. 99– 7   * cult able to *p·* its faith with
   165– 1   *p·* and pervade all his success.

promoted
Mis. 228– 4   whose welfare thou hast *p·*,
My. 270–25   be it *p·* by Catholic, by Protestant,

promoters
Mis. 240–10   *p·* of health and happiness.

promotes
Mis. 41–14   it *p·* spiritual growth,
   80–19   *p·* and impels all true reform ;
Ret. 82–20   *p·* the ease and welfare of
Pan. 10–27   Whatever *p·* statuesque being,
My. 250– 5   *p·* wisdom, quiets mad ambition,

promoting
My. 118– 3   *p·* the true Principle of
   362–16   * *p·* and enlarging the activities

promotion
Man. 80– 2   *p·* of the interests of C. S.
Ret. 47–11   for the *p·* of spiritual ends.
   52– 2   *p·* and expansion of scientific

prompt
Mis. 317–19   These considerations *p·* my answers
My. 11–17   * because of *p·* and liberal action,
   243–20   Your *p·* presence in Concord

prompted
Mis. 48–10   *p·* by money-making or malice.
My. 23– 5   * Love that *p·* the desire,
   24–17   * We are *p·* to state,
   352– 7   * We are *p·* to acknowledge

promptings
Mis. 228– 1   the *p·* of human nature.

promptly
Mis. 143–27   Each donation came *p·* ;
   110 10   parting so *p·* with your
Man. 28–17   perform the functions of . . . *p·*
   65 15   *p·* to comply with any written
   79– 6   shall transact *p·* and efficiently
   98– 7   If the correction . . . is not *p·*
My. 14–18   * Our friend very *p·*
   31– 9   * *P·* at half past six
   361–20   * *p·* made its demonstration

promptness
My. 12–13   * *p·* of his own contribution.

prompts
'02. 8–22   it *p·* perpetual goodness,

promulgated
Un. 7–17   that the views here *p·*
My. 316– 1   the truth I have *p·* has

promulgators
Pul. 65– 2   * original apostles and *p·*,

prone
My. 93–18   * possibly too *p·* to approach it

pronoun
Mis. 29– 5   the *p·* would be *you*, not *them*.

pronounce
Mis. 314–13   shall *p·* the benediction.
Ret. 26–15   *p·* Christ's healing miraculous,
Pul. 80–17   * we have no opinion to *p·*,
My. 111–28   they may *p·* it absurd,

pronounced
Mis. 6–10   cases that are *p·* incurable
   24– 9   *p·* fatal by the physicians.
   35– 5   *p·* by the physicians incurable,
   247–29   Everything . . . He *p·* good.
Ret. 9– 5   *p·* in audible tones.
   13–11   *p·* me stricken with fever.
Un. 15– 8   and *p·* them good.
Pul. 34– 7   * *p·* hopeless by the physicians.
   69– 8   * *p·* his case incurable.
'02. 6– 5   The curse . . . was *p·* upon a lie,
My. 14–18   * *p·* the story a fabrication
   105–21   *p·* dying of pneumonia,

pronouncement
My. 46–14   * this early *p·* is the work of

pronounces
My. 178–15   Scripture *p·* all that God made

proof
absolute
Ret. 31– 6   absolute *p·* and self-evident
another
My. 240–15   I now repeat another *p·*,
any
No. 10– 4   as any *p·* that can be given
convincing
Ret. 93–24   convincing *p·* of the validity of
demand a
Mis. 225–15   opportunity to demand a *p·*
denies in
Hea. 15–17   admits . . . what he denies in *p·*?
eminent
Mis. 346– 4   spiritual healing as eminent *p·*
fair
Mis. 239– 7   give fair *p·* that my shadow is
full
No. 31–13   as the only full *p·* of its pardon.
further
Un. 36–16   A further *p·* of this is the
incapable of
Mis. 14–28   a lie that is incapable of *p·*
its own
Mis. 242–18   C. S. that furnishes its own *p·*.
   350–32   furnishes its own *p·* of my practice.
lacked the
Mis. 365–10   If C. S. lacked the *p·* of its
No. 18– 6   If Science lacked the *p·* of its
my
Mis. 68–13   My *p·* of this is, that the penalty
   252–14   My *p·* of these novel propositions
no
Mis. 230–12   Rushing around smartly is no *p·* of
   338– 6   these afford no *p·*,
of Christianity
Hea. 2–23   and gave this *p·* of Christianity
of divine power
Hea. 15–25   to pray for a *p·* of divine power,
of healing
Pul. 13–12   rejoices in the *p·* of healing,
of Immanuel
Mis. 374– 1   was so great a *p·* of Immanuel
of life
My. 177–13   true knowledge and *p·* of life
of mathematics
'01. 4– 7   destroys the *p·* of mathematics ;
of the omnipotence
Pan. 7– 6   *p·* of the omnipotence of one divine,
of the prosperity
Mis. 154–12   *p·* of the prosperity of His Zion.
opportunity for
Mis. 13–26   to afford opportunity for *p·* of its
parable and
Mis. 27–16   maintain this fact by parable and *p·*,
parallel
Mis. 66–13   supported . . . by parallel *p·*,
personal
My. 238– 7   be determined by personal *p·*.
positive
Mis. 153–20   by positive *p·* of trustworthiness.
'01. 33–25   richest and most positive *p·*
My. 91– 2   * *p·* positive that it supplies these
   166–13   positive *p·* of your remembrance
practical
Mis. 35– 1   Years of practical *p·*,
practice and
'01. 19–16   from Jesus' practice and *p·*.
primitive
My. 239– 4   relegates . . . to its primitive *p·*,
rational
My. 348–18   Science demanded a rational *p·*
real
My. 119–22   gave the real *p·* of his Saviour,
remarkable
My. 273– 3   * interesting and remarkable *p·* of
scientific
Mis. 277–24   the scientific *p·* that God,
'01. 4–11   its susceptibility of scientific *p·*.
My. 218– 8   restoration . . . as the scientific *p·*
sealed that
Mis. 35– 6   sealed that *p·* with the signet of
self-evident
Mis. 186–22   self-evident *p·* of immortality ;
signal
Pul. 39– 3   * a signal *p·* of the divine origin of
simple
Mis. 265–16   innovations upon simple *p·* ;
sole
'02. 10–24   This is indeed our sole *p·*
My. 271–10   and the sole *p·* of rightness.
susceptible of
Mis. 27–26   and is susceptible of *p·*.
   200–13   a rule that is susceptible of *p·*,
teaching and
'01. 23–16   to the Master's teaching and *p·*.

proof

that Christian Science
Mis. 193–11 p· that C. S.,. . . heals the sick,
No. 28–14 The p· that C. S. is the way
My. 158–18 burden of p· that C. S. is Science
238–22 p· that C. S. is Science,

this
Mis. 101–28 On this p· rest premise and
Hea. 2–23 gave this p· of Christianity
15–27 God, the Principle of this p·
My. 6–16 this p· of your progress, unity,
106– 4 and without this p· of love
363–14 This p· that sanity and Science

unmistakable
Mis. 366– 8 given rule, and unmistakable p·.
No. 11–22 given rule, and unmistakable p·.
33–11 a given rule, and unmistakable p·.

without
Un. 49–24 Hence it is undemonstrable, without p·.
'02. 18–24 faith without p· loses its life,

Mis. 65– 3 We have no more p· of
83–27 p· of his eternal Life and sonship.
183–27 in p· of man's "dominion— Gen. 1: 26.
186–23 p·, also, that the Principle of man
249–23 of their mental design . . . I have p·,
Man. 98–12 shall read the last p· sheet
Rud. 6–24 The p· of what you apprehend,
No. 37–15 or as a p· that sin is known to
'02. 9–23 was the p· of its divine origin,
Hea. 3– 5 a p·, more than a profession thereof ;
My. 36–30 * p· that our Supreme God, through
103– 7 p· of the practicality of this faith
109–25 not alone by miracle . . . but by p·,
302– 8 is p· that mind is the cause of all

proofless
My. 181– 7 outgrown, p· positions.

proofreader
My. 318– 5 Mr. Wiggin was not my p· for
318–11 name of the former p· for
320– 2 * student and a good p·.

proofs
Mis. 65– 2 by repeated p· of its falsity.
201–21 because they were so many p·
247– 3 convictions and p· of advancing truth
My. 155– 7 promises, and p· of Holy Writ.

prop
No. 15– 9 to explain and p· old creeds,

propaganda
My. 303–18 no idolatry, no human p·

propagate
Mis. 343–24 until no seedling be left to p·
My. 130– 2 then leave the latter to p·.

propagates
Mis. 111–15 Leaving the seed of . . . it p· :

propagation
'01. 30– 7 are essential to its p·.
My. 344–17 * theory of the p· of disease?"

propelling
Pul. 20–17 p· the greatest moral, physical,

propensities
Mis. 36–15 beasts that have these p·
250– 8 What the lower p· express,

proper
Mis. 48–26 p· study of Mind-healing would cure
89–23 p· answer to this question
107–16 (1) A p· sense of sin ;
108–13 reducing its claim to its p·
108–18 p· knowledge of evil
115–14 p· preparation of heart to practise,
138–26 God will give . . . the p· command,
146–11 to form a p· judgment.
177–23 * hour for the church service p·,
187– 5 p· sense of the possibilities of
222– 1 man's p· sense of good,
269–23 correct Mind-healing is the p· means
307–18 p· reception of C. S. healing.
308–10 take their p· place in history,
334–20 to its p· denomination,
348–28 individual in a p· state of mind.
359–13 p· channels for development,
365–27 lack of p· terms in which to express
373–18 forced out of its p· channel,
Man. 28– 7 p· system of government
49–13 who can take p· care of the sick.
69–16 appoint a p· member of this Church
72–12 Upon p· application,
76– 5 p· management of the Church funds ;
77–16 p· distribution of the funds
Ret. 25–26 any p· conception of the infinite
44–25 p· measures were adopted to
90–26 * p· thing for us to do is to follow,

proper
Un. 8–14 p· understanding of the unreality
20– 2 by seeing it in its p· light,
35–10 Reduced to its p· denomination,
40–19 p· or true sense of Life,
Pul. 82–17 * woman as man's p· helpmeet.
Rud. 2–14 retain the p· sense of Deity by
Pan. 4–11 for their p· exercise.
5–11 Our Master gave the p· answer
11–18 in order to be in p· shape,
Hea. 4–21 p· conception of the divine character,
My. 22–26 * appear in their p· perspective.
22–28 * p· perspective of the meaning of
162–21 Our p· reason for church edifices is,
220– 7 reporting . . . to the p· authorities
232– 1 recognizing the p· course,
259–27 appropriate and p· exercise.
278– 1 p· incentive to the action
289– 8 I deem it p· that The Mother
306–17 will find its p· level.

properly
Mis. 112–14 of what is p· denominated,
169–14 cannot p· be interpreted in a
193–23 p· called Scientists who follow the
Man. 37– 4 p· filled out by an applicant.
57– 2 such other business as may p·
77–12 have not been p· managed,
Ret. 59–14 p· employed, has the signification
Pul. 50–11 * p· marked by the erection of a
No. 14– 2 when p· demonstrated.
Pan. 4– 8 are p· classified as mind,
'01. 3–27 the conclusion is not p· drawn.
20– 5 Man is p· self-governed, and he
My. 219– 8 most p· used in preventing the
259–24 Certain occasions, . . . observed p·,

properties
No. 22– 7 treatise on the healing p· of
Hea. 12– 1 contain no medicinal p·,
My. 32– 7 * acoustic p· of the new structure
72– 1 * nicely adjusted acoustic p·
78–22 * acoustic p· of the temple,
293– 4 the different p· of drugs

property
Mis. 248–22 bequeathed my p· to
283– 9 management of another man's p·.
299–31 p· of a noted firm,
Man. 30–18 taxes and rent on this p· ;
30–20 keep the p· in good repair,
67–14 or to the p· of Mary Baker Eddy
79–22 shall hold and manage the p·
Ret. 20– 2 lost all my husband's p·,
'02. 13– 6 my personal p· and funds,
13–21 advertising the p· in the
13–23 previously negotiated for the p·
13–25 nor to take the p· off my hands,
14– 3 only interest I retain in this p·
15–18 much of his p· was in slaves,
15–20 never believe that . . . was my p·.
My. vi–24 * presented to her church the p·
vii– 2 * p· of the Publishing Society.
66– 6 * in p· on these streets,
66–11 * use the society will make of the p·
66–14 * it was necessary to have this p·.
100– 6 * p· of no poverty-stricken sect.
123–13 I had the p· bought by
135–14 to take the charge of my p· ;
136–14 Board of Trustees who own my p· :
137–19 have my p· . . . carefully taken care of
137–22 to take charge of my p· ;
138– 1 I gave them my p· to take care of
138– 4 agreed . . . to take care of my p·
138–10 to protect my person or p·.
325– 8 * Back Bay would never
336–13 lost all my husband's p·,

prophecies
Mis. 84– 9 the p· were fulfilled,
Pul. 9–25 prayers, p·, and anointings.
My. 155– 7 p·, promises, and proofs

prophecy
Mis. 76–31 glorious p· of the master
141– 2 will be the p· fulfilled,
144–15 there to typify the p·,
192–21 man's ability to prove the . . . p·.
270–18 have full faith in his p·,
286– 1 above p·, written years ago,
373–30 more than a prophet or a p· :
Pul. 1– 4 p· and promise clad in white
5–20 That p· is fulfilled.
No. 13– 8 p· of Jesus fulfilled,
27–13 this p· will be scoffed at ;
'00. 12–20 This p· has been fulfilled.
'01. 28– 3 great naturalist's p·.
'02. 18–22 p· of the great Teacher
Peo. 11– 1 that hour was a p· of

prophecy

My. 39–20   * words of reminder and *p·*.
    44–11   * rejoices in *p·* fulfilled,
    45–24   * fulfilment of the later *p·*,
  146–17   his immortal words and my poor *p·*,
  171– 3   fulfilled the *p·* of Isaiah :
  177–22   *p·* of Isaiah is fulfilled
  190–31   who are fulfilling Jesus' *p·*
  193–20   may the *p·* of Isaiah be fulfilled :
  258–19   hopes . . . that waken *p·*,

prophesied

Mis. 145–22   such as Isaiah *p·* :
  161–15   *p·* the appearing of this
My. 238–15   of which St. Mark *p·*
  330– 5   * he *p·* that his followers

prophesies

Mis. 329–29   *p·* of fair earth and sunny skies.
'02.   5– 2   *p·* renewed energy for to-morrow,
My. 147–12   of which St. Mark *p·*.

prophesy

Mis. 84– 5   did not *p·* his death,
  102– 1   *p·* the nature and stature
Ret. 23–12   could not *p·* sunrise

prophesying

Man. 40–13   from *p·*, judging, condemning,
Pul.   5–19   and *p·* its prosperity,

Prophet

Galilean
Man. 16– 3   demonstrated by the Galilean *P·*
'02. 11–27   put to death the Galilean *P·*,
My. 111– 7   Metaphysician, the Galilean *P·*,
  220–26   example of the great Galilean *P·*,
  261–27   Galilean *P·*, was born of the
  288–12   The great Galilean *P·* was, is,
  319– 1   such a person as the Galilean *P·*,
Nazarene
Mis. 15– 7   great Nazarene *P·* said,
  24–29   Nazarene *P·* declared that his
  60–10   Nazarene *P·* could make the
  344–24   rules of the mighty Nazarene *P·*.
Pul.   6– 5   established by the Nazarene *P·*
Pan. 10– 5   great Nazarene *P·* said,
My. 106–30   Nazarene *P·*, healed through Mind,
  179–22   character of the Nazarene *P·*

Mis. 374–21   face of the Nazarite *P·* ;

prophet (see also prophet's)

Mis. 79–12   saith, through the *p·* Ezekiel,
  121–16   The *p·* declared,
  148–29   in the words of the *p·* Isaiah :
  161–14   *p·* whose words we have chosen
  164–14   *p·* beheld it from the beginning
  308–16   In the words of the *p·*,
  333–32   the *p·* better understood Him
  373–30   C. S. is more than a *p·*
Pul. 20–19   In the words of the *p·* :
No. 37–23   Messiah and *p·* saved the sinner
  39–10   *P·* and apostle have glorified God
Pan.   8–11   doctrine that Mohammed is the only *p·*
My.   5–27   saying virtually what the *p·* said :
  140– 2   Of this . . . the *p·* Isaiah said,

prophetic

'00.   6–28   modern exegesis on the *p·* Scriptures
  13– 9   their so-called *p·* illumination.
My. 46– 8   * it stands in *p·* verity of the
  147– 4   and the present is *p·*.
  186– 3   should be *p·* of the finger divine

prophetically

My. 45–14   * which you have long *p·* seen

prophet's

Mis. 245– 3   we have his words, and the *p·*,

prophets

Mis.   8–25   persecuted they the *p·* — Matt. 5 : 12.
  23– 7   The *p·*, Jesus, and the apostles,
  40–14   equal the ancient *p·* as healers.
  84– 7   *p·* thrust disputed points on
  168–17   nineteenth-century *p·* repeat,
  209– 5   shut the mouth of His *p·*,
  326–26   thou that killest the *p·*, — Matt. 23 : 37.
Un. 56–18   *P·* . . . . suffered from the thoughts of
Pul.   7–20   false *p·* in the present
No. 39– 6   after the fashion of Baal's *p·*,
'00. 10–16   new-old doctrines of the *p·*
'02.   5–24   law, or the *p·* : — Matt. 5 : 17.
  11–26   persecuted they the *p·* — Matt. 5 : 12.
Peo.   5– 3   The *p·* and apostles,
My. vii– 9   * testified to by Jesus and the *p·*.
  103–25   the lives of *p·* and apostles.
  106–32   *p·* and apostles and the Christians
  161–12   Jacob, and all the *p·*, — Luke 13 : 28.
  190–30   wherefore vilify His *p·* to-day
  219–24   law, or the *p·* : — Matt. 5 :17.

prophets

My. 221– 5   *p·* of old looked for something higher
  248– 9   Spiritual heroes and *p·* are they
  270– 2   persecuted they the *p·* — Matt. 5 : 12.
  285–28   in the law and in the *p·*." — Acts 24 : 14.

propitiate

No. 34–21   to *p·* His justice

proportion

as a physician
Hea. 14–12   In *p·* as a physician is enlightened
as he understands
Mis. 243–16   only in *p·* as he understands it.
as mortals
Mis. 28–11   In *p·* as mortals turn from this
No. 16–24   in *p·* as mortals approach Spirit,
  38–17   In *p·* as mortals approximate
as one understands
'01. 15–10   in *p·* as one understands it
as this church
Mis. 127– 1   in *p·* as this church has
My. 17–29   in *p·* as this church has
as we love
Mis. 117–17   work wisely, in *p·* as we love.
as we oppose
Mis. 37– 9   In *p·* as we oppose the belief
larger
My. 97– 8   * a larger *p·* have died than
like
My. 94– 1   * growth continues in like *p·*
prospers in
Mis. 288–28   and their cause prospers in *p·*
same
Mis. 229–21   in the same *p·* would faith in
that Science
Mis. 367–10   in the *p·* that Science is understood,
that they gain
Mis. 181–27   in the *p·* that they gain the sense of
to its right
My. 224–10   only in *p·* to its right or its wrong concept,
to its wickedness
Pul. 13–10   in *p·* to its wickedness.
to its worth
Mis. 273– 4   and in *p·* to its worth.
to our affection
Ret. 80–28   lose them in *p·* to our affection.
to the faith
Mis. 31–11   in *p·* to the faith in evil,
to their fitness
My. 267–18   in *p·* to their fitness to partake of
to their progress
My. 267–18   enter heaven in *p·* to their progress,

Mis. 124–32   In *p·* to a man's spiritual progress,
  218– 6   in the *p·* that their instructions
Ret. 73– 6   Limitations are put off in *p·*
Un.   6– 5   in *p·* as the spotless selfhood
'01. 27–23   than others do in *p·*,
Hea. 3–10   In *p·* as the personal and
My. 108– 8   is salutary and potent in *p·* as
  113–25   in *p·* as this Principle and rule
  222–25   in *p·* as God's government becomes

proportionably

Un. 20–20   *p·* as you realize the divine
My. 357–17   *p·* estimate their success

proportionately

Mis. 42–20   joys . . . will be *p·* increased.
  232–14   *P·* as we part with material
Un.   5– 8   pride of opinion will *p·* diminish.
  13–12   *p·* as we gain the true understanding
Hea. 11–21   *p·* as matter went out
Peo.   2–20   *P·* as the people's belief of God,
My. 67–29   * it is so *p·* built
  213–13   Then they will be *p·* successful

proportions

Mis. 55–10   seeks the *p·* of good.
  239– 9   substance is taking larger *p·*.
Pul. 30–28   * its present impressive *p·*,
My. 88–14   * its *p·* are so large,

propose

Mis. 137–10   if you had any questions to *p·*,
  371–17   although he . . . . is apt to *p·* it.
My. 300–22   we *p·* that he make known

proposed

Mis. 141–10   *p·* type of universal Love ;
  156–13   I *p·* to merge the
  284–13   This question is often *p·*,
  304–22   * *p·* use of the bell :
Pul. 57–25   * *p·* site of the new Music Hall,
My. 145– 4   *p·* to one of Concord's best builders
  327–15   * when a medical bill was *p·*

proposition

Mis.	13–14	theology elaborates the *p·*
	13–21	Science of Soul reverses this *p·*,
	14–11	Were we to admit this vague *p·*,
	46– 4	The leading self-evident *p·*
	346–19	self-evident *p·* of C. S.,
Rud.	11– 9	next *p·* in C. S.,
No.	4–15	self-evident *p·*, in the Science
'01.	3–22	The first *p·* is correct,
	3–24	last *p·* does not illustrate
'02.	7–20	no other scientific *p·* can be
	20–16	ready to join me in this *p·*,

propositions

Mis.	193– 6	they form *p·* of self-evident
	252–15	My proof of these novel *p·*
	269–19	These are self-evident *p·* :
Ret.	31– 6	self-evident *p·* of Truth
Un.	7–18	Certain self-proved *p·*
Rud.	13–16	These *p·*, understood in their Science,
'01.	22– 3	demonstrates the truth of these *p·*
My.	146–14	altitude of its highest *p·*

propound

'02.	5–26	*p·* a question, formulate a doctrine,

proprietor

My.	314–32	*p·* of the White Mountain House,
		(*see also* **Eddy**)

propriety

Mis.	255– 4	no fairness or *p·* in the aspersion.
Ret.	52–12	the *p·* of forming a National
My.	25– 2	* *p·* in making a special effort
	138–19	not exceeded the bounds of *p·*
	225–13	God is All ; hence the *p·* of

prosaics

My.	122–10	Now I am done with . . . tedious *p·*.

proscription

Hea.	11–13	fires of ancient *p·* burn upon the

proscriptive

'01.	34–14	material religion, *p·*, intolerant,
My.	265–20	no longer tyrannical and *p·* ;

prose

Ret.	11– 2	suited my emotions better than *p·*.

prosecute

Pul.	83– 6	* courage to *p·* the appeal.

prosecution

My.	127–19	for persecution and for *p·*,

proselytizing

My.	93– 3	* without efforts at *p·* ;

prosody

Ret.	10–17	*P·*, the song of angels,

prospect

Mis.	262– 5	will aid our *p·* of fulfilling it
My.	208–18	I congratulate you on the *p·* of

prospective

Mis.	64– 9	*p· students of the College*

Prospectus

Mis.	1– 1	chapter sub-title

prosper

Mis.	213– 9	shall not *p·*." — *Prov.* 28 : 13.
Pul.	38–29	* It is good that each and all shall *p·*,
'02.	3–20	British and Boer may *p·* in peace,
My.	10–18	* It is doubtful if . . . could *p·*,
	13–32	"*p·* in the thing whereto — *Isa.* 55 : 11.
	282–26	May God guide and *p·*
	360–22	God will bless and *p·* you.

prospered

Mis.	140–14	church was *p·* by the right hand of
	140–26	diviner claim and means . . . were *p·*.
'02.	14–25	*p·* preeminently our great Cause,
My.	37–18	* its followers have been *p·*,
	215– 6	and it *p·* at every step.
	328– 2	* dignified, blessed, and *p·* it,

prospering

My.	143–20	The Cause of C. S. is *p·*

prosperity

Mis.	110–22	progress and unprecedented *p·* of
	154–12	proof of the *p·* of His Zion.
	254– 2	points with promise of *p·*?
	273– 8	I withdraw from an overwhelming *p·*.
	291–13	equal growth and *p·* of all
	358–26	at the pinnacle of *p·*,
Man.	31– 8	*p·* of C. S. largely depends.
Ret.	44–16	previous harmony and *p·*.
	44–28	love, *p·*, and spiritual power.
	45– 5	the *p·* of my church,
	48–30	at the height of *p·* in the institution,
	82–18	with the *p·* of each worker ;
Pul.	2– 5	thy wisdom and *p·* — *I Kings* 10 : 7.
	5–19	and prophesying its *p·*,
	20–13	*p·* of this church is unsurpassed.
	36– 4	* in the very zenith of its *p·*,

prosperity

Pan.	14–11	Pray for the *p·* of our country,
'00.	1–12	crowned with unprecedented *p·* ;
'02.	14–14	remarkable growth and *p·* of C. S.
My.	v– 6	* growth and *p·* of the Cause
	10–26	* *p·* of the branch churches ;
	37–24	* church owes itself and its *p·* to
	81– 2	* air of well-being and of *p·*
	93– 6	* material evidence of their *p·* ;
	116– 6	In time of religious or scientific *p·*,
	117–28	I left Boston in the height of *p·*
	157– 8	* rejoice that the *p·* of the Cause
	164–15	with its present *p·* ?
	175–12	growth and *p·* of our city
	184–24	The *p·* of Zion is very precious
	192–23	to visit you, to witness your *p·*,
	246–12	in the midst of unprecedented *p·*,
	270–25	I love the *p·* of Zion,
	277–15	peace, *p·*, and life of nations.
	279–27	with peace and *p·*.
	282–13	which are the landmarks of *p·*.
	291–23	ensign of peace and *p·* waves

prosperous

Ret.	53– 4	*p·* under difficult circumstances,
	85–25	The Cause, *our* Cause, is highly *p·*,
My.	10–26	* must be a *p·* parent church,
	10–28	* *p·* growth of this movement
	80– 2	* *p·*, contented men and women,
	95–10	* cheerful and *p·* body of believers

prospers

Mis.	288–28	and their cause *p·* in proportion
My.	93–10	* religion *p·* according to the pledges

prostration

No.	42–26	* suffering from nervous *p·*,

protect

Mis.	115– 1	to *p·* themselves therefrom,
	201–25	We *p·* our dwellings more securely
Pan.	14–22	May the divine Love succor and *p·*
Po.	vi–17	*authorities could p· him nowhere*
My.	vii– 5	* so *p·* their own thoughts
	138– 9	not needed to *p·* my person
	245–22	To *p·* the public,
	327– 1	to *p·* the practice of C. S.

protected

Ret.	39– 4	and my copyright was *p·*.
Pul.	4– 9	*p·* by his divine Principle, God
My.	138– 2	because I wanted it *p·*
	227–20	*they are not specially p· by law.*

protecting

Mis.	137–16	*p·* wings of the mother-bird,

protection

Mis.	115–16	means of *p·* and defense from sin
	263–12	by divine *p·* and affection.
	263–24	lacks the aid and *p·* of State laws.
Ret.	76– 2	nor would *p·* by copyright be
'01.	33–16	*p·* of the constitutional laws
'02.	14–23	afforded me neither favor nor *p·*
	15– 4	*p·* of the laws of my country.
My.	227– 9	*p·* of State or United States laws,
	327–28	* dignified legal *p·* and recognition,

protects

Mis.	211–21	*p·* himself at his neighbor's cost,
	222–24	Its mystery *p·* it now,
'01.	20–25	At present its mystery *p·* it,

protest

Mis.	68– 8	* *A true Christian would p· against*
	216–17	a big *p·* against injustice ;
	256– 8	in daily letters that *p·* against
	319–12	*p·* against the reality of sin,
Ret.	15– 3	and my *p·* along with me,
Un.	26–20	*p·* against this stanza of Bowring's,
My.	134– 3	evidence a heart wholly in *p·*

Protestant

Mis.	111–25	between the Catholic and *P·* sects.
Ret.	2– 3	Calvinistic devotion to *P·* liberty
'01.	28–13	in Catholic and *P·* oratories.
My.	4–14	loves *P·* and Catholic, D.D. and M.D.,
	270–25	be it promoted by Catholic, by *P·*, or

Protestantism

Mis.	281–13	was converted to *P·* through a
No.	44–13	In Queen Elizabeth's time *P·* could
'02.	2–13	from stern *P·* to doubtful liberalism.
My.	127–20	purer *P·* and monotheism

Protestants

Mis.	172– 6	*P·* in a higher sense than ever before,
My.	303– 7	Scientists have no quarrel with *P·*,

protestations

My.	358– 3	if you are sincere in your *p·*

protesting

My.	193–17	*P·* against error, you unite with

proud

Ret.	17–10	p· Prairie Queen and the modest
Un.	26– 6	p· to be in His outstretched hands,
Po.	1–13	P· from yon cloud-crowned height
	18– 2	the eagle's p· wing,
	62–11	On p· Prairie Queen
My.	41– 8	* If the p· are lonely
	84–13	* temple is something to be p· of.
	98–26	* any church might well be p·.
	122–12	tempted me tenderly to be p· !
	151–17	* "Pass ye the p· fane by,
	210–14	evil thinker is the p· talker
	320–13	* quite p· of his having had
	320–27	* p· of his acquaintance with you.
	321– 2	* He seemed very p· to think that

proudest

Pul.	83–22	* the p· boast of many

proudly

Un.	45– 5	rears its crest p·,
Pul.	1–17	Pass p· to thy bier !
Po.	26– 6	Pass p· to thy bier !

prove

Mis.	6–12	should certainly p· to all minds
	27– 7	p· themselves invalid.
	30– 2	understand . . . before we p· it,
	41–29	may not always p· equal to
	45– 1	p· the fact that Mind is supreme.
	55– 4	p· all its possibilities.
	111–19	who p· its power to be immortal.
	138–13	especially should he p· his faith by
	162–15	p· his power, derived from Spirit,
	167–28	His works thus p· him.
	171–17	p· his right to be heard.
	192–20	man's ability to p· the truth of
	195–10	every one can p·, in some degree,
	250–17	active witnesses to p· it,
	311–15	p· that I love my enemies
	315–18	p· sound in sentiment, health, and
	354–14	whose fruits p· the nature of their
	380– 4	p· that a divine Principle heals
	382– 2	contradict it and p· an exception.
Man.	83–17	p· sound in sentiment and practical
Ret.	33–13	p· the Principle of Mind-healing.
	49–24	p· a healing for the nations,
Un.	28– 4	Who can p· that?
	33– 1	arguments which p· matter to be
	40– 7	in order to p· man deathless.
No.	15– 6	would enable any one to p·
Pan.	5–23	deny it and p· its falsity.
	13–27	you may p· for yourselves the
'01.	2–23	his followers of to-day will p·,
	15– 6	p· it false, therefore unreal.
	81–20	to p· the doctrine of Jesus,
Hea.	12–23	p· that the power was the thought,
Po.	vii–13	* p· a joy to the heavy laden
My.	vi– 1	* p·, (1) that S. and H. does not
	64–24	* thus p· our worthiness
	98– 6	* anything that its foes try to p· it
	105– 6	p· one's faith by his works.
	119–21	He turned to . . . to p· Christ,
	124–25	p· fairly the facts
	131–26	p· me now herewith, — Mal. 3 : 10.
	132– 3	"P· me now herewith, — Mal. 3 : 10.
	149– 2	must p· their knowledge by
	180– 1	whereby man can p· God's love,
	182–31	p· the practicality of perfection,
	184–20	shall p· a historic gem
	239– 9	imbibe the spirit and p· the
	269–26	"P· me now herewith, — Mal. 3 : 10.
	285–24	neither can they p· — Acts 24 : 13.
	293–11	that the bullet would p· fatal.

proved

Mis.	28–15	Master p· to his doubting disciple,
	29–32	which Jesus taught and p·.
	30–17	He p· the superiority of Mind
	33–15	not p· impossible to heal those who,
	63–29	Spirit p· its supremacy over matter.
	74–22	he p· the fallacy of the theory
	338– 5	I first p· to myself,
	348–27	so p· to myself that drugs have no
	350–17	This p· to be our last meeting.
	378–11	p· to be a magnetic practitioner.
Man.	55–19	decide if his loyalty has been p·
Ret.	19–10	which in his case p· fatal.
	69–13	This error has p· itself to be error.
Un.	14–16	created children p· sinful ;
	40– 5	is to assert what we have not p· ;
Pul.	45–19	* p·, in most striking manner,
	57–17	* p· their faith by their works.
No.	27–11	matter will be p· a myth.
	38– 1	Jesus p· to perfection,
Hea.	18–27	Oxford students p· this :
	19– 2	they did test it, and p· it.
	19– 3	p· it not in part, but as a whole ;

proved

Hea.	19– 4	p· that every organ of the system,
Peo.	8–28	skill p· a million times unskilful.
	12–22	p· the application of its Principle
	13–17	p· the triumph of mind over
My.	28– 5	* this has been p· true
	56–32	* p· the need of a larger edifice.
	86–23	* p· one of the most interesting
	105–32	p· to be more certain
	106–17	p· that C. S. rests on the
	108– 6	I have p· beyond cavil
	174– 5	p· an ideal meeting place.
	180– 5	by him who p· their practicality,
	214–12	He p· Life to be deathless
	303–20	Jesus taught and p· that
	303–28	What I am remains to be p·
	348– 4	p· conclusively that all effect
	348–25	demonstrated Christianity and p·
	352–10	what is p· in better lives.
	360–22	He has p· it to me

proven

Mis.	10–20	tried their strength and p· it ;
	14–22	p· by the law of opposites to be
	22–25	have p· to a waiting world.
	29–29	whereby matter is p· powerless
	73– 3	this supposition is p· erroneous
	76– 8	or p· true upon a false premise,
	111– 1	p· that the greatest piety is
	134–20	powers of earth . . . are p· powerless.
	269–16	he who has fairly p· his knowledge
	269–18	p· the divine Mind to be
	278–10	it can be p· that I have never
Ret.	35– 9	merits of C. S. must be p·
	83– 2	already been p· that this volume is
	89– 3	p· beyond a doubt in the practice of
No.	10–19	the former position, . . . is p·
	17– 5	Their nothingness is thus p· ;
'00.	6–20	the Science of God is p· when,
'01.	13–30	and its unreality is p·.
	19–14	The notion . . . is p· false.
	28–21	p· to me beyond a doubt
	34– 8	and is p· to be more pathological
My.	24– 3	* is to-day being p· and is ready
	270–16	Her life is p· under trial,

proverb

Mis.	72–13	that ye use this p· — Ezek. 18 : 2.
	72–16	to use this p· — Ezek. 18 : 3.
	223–25	wisdom in the old p·,
My.	40–29	* often rebels . . . hence the p· :

proverbial

Ret.	75–20	p· that dishonesty retards
	80– 3	This also is p·,
My.	123– 1	Our unity and progress are p·,
	134– 5	progress of C. S. is p·,

proverbially

Mis.	243–18	students are p· modest :

proves

Mis.	42–18	life-work p· to have been well done,
	56–23	p· the correctness of my statements,
	58– 6	p· to him who thought he died that
	65–26	p· that strict adherence to one is
	102–30	p· daily that "one on God's side
	209– 9	p· that human belief fulfils the
	212–21	C. S. p· that human will is lost
	223– 9	Science p·, beyond cavil,
	309–13	Experience p· this true.
	336–30	the sequence p·.
Un.	8–22	it p· my view conclusively,
'00.	6–17	fact p· that the so-called fog of
'01.	18–29	and so p· their nullity.
Hea.	12–23	and the sequel p· it ;
My.	58– 6	* p· the truth of the axiom,

provide

Man.	27–13	to p· a suitable building for the
	27–20	to p· suitable rooms,
Ret.	52– 8	to p· a home for every true seeker
	52–10	p· folds for the sheep that were
My.	10–23	* They will p· the money necessary
	65–14	* money to p· it was pledged
	76– 7	* to p· for the entire cost of
	222–22	does not p· that *materia medica* shall

provided

Mis.	302–21	p·, they each and all
	349– 2	p· he received these lessons of
Man.	36– 2	as p· in Article VI, Sect. 2,
	36–12	except in such cases as are p· for
	37–20	except as p· for in Article V,
	38–23	p· they are willing and anxious to
	59–19	not otherwise p· with seats.
	63–17	p· these rooms are well located.
	67–12	on a case not p· for in its By-Laws
	73–12	p· its rules so permit.

provided

Man. 91–24   p· their diplomas are for
'00. 10– 7   p· this warfare is honest
'01. 28–30   usually are handsomely p· for.
    29– 4   God has p· the means for him
My. 6–13   wisely p· for The Mother Church
    45– 2   * p· for the furtherance of our Cause,
    75–12   * if they had not already been p· for.
  147– 9   have p· for you a modest hall,
  216– 9   by which each is p· for
  217–14   p· he has complied with my request
  261– 5   seems to have amply p· for this,
  302–21   less lauded, pampered, p· for,

Providence

Mis. 312–14   * divine P· in human affairs
  320– 1   trust the divine P·,
'01. 24–12   * under P· I owe my life to it."

providence

Mis. 80–18   through the p· of God,
  100– 3   left to the p· of God.
  163–15   committed to the p· of God.
  278–23   since necessities and God's p· are
  345– 2   God's presence and p·.
Ret. 21– 8   by a strange p· had learned
  30–20   p· of God, and the cross of Christ.
  50– 9   finally led, by a strange p·,
Pul. 20–12   Thus committed to the p· of God,
Pan. 3–24   * from the divine Mind and p·,
  3–30   care and p· by which he governs
'02. 1– 2   God's loving p· for His people
Hea. 12–13   through His p· or His laws,
My. 148– 3   through the p· of God,
  220– 3   submit to the p· of God,
  355–19   * "Behind a frowning p·

provident

Mis. 117–27   oil of the more p· watcher.

provides

Man. 51–18   p· for immediate action.
Rud. 8– 2   or p· breast-milk for babes.

providing

'01. 29– 4   p· ways and means for others.
My. 7–16   * necessity for p· an auditorium
  9– 3   * necessity for p· an audience-room

province

Mis. 146–12   This is not my present p· ;
  336– 4   your p· to wrestle with error,
Hea. 3–17   in a remote p· of Judea,
My. 359– 6   My p· as a Leader

provinces

'00. 10–20   sways . . . weak p·, or peoples.

proving

Mis. 34– 2   thus p· that metaphysics
  60– 8   is p· this by healing
  210– 4   never healed . . . without p·
  337– 5   By p· its effect on yourself
Man. 92–10   thus p· this Science to be
Ret. 31– 7   paramount . . . in p· the Christ.
  34–16   thus p· the superiority of
No. 38– 2   what C. S. is to-day p·
Pan. 10–17   thus p· the utility of what they
'00. 6– 3   p· its power and divinity.
My. 111–24   p· that his conclusion was

provision

Man. 77–23   P· for the Future.
My. 56– 8   * this p· was inadequate
  56–26   * still further p· must be made,
  215–28   p· for their expenses?

provisions

Mis. 139–30   that the p· for the land
Man. 81–17   conducted according to the p·
  85– 9   p· of Article XII,
My. 175–14   p· for the army,
  312–24   and their p· in my behalf

provoke

Mis. 325–23   "p· Him in the wilderness, — Psal. 78 : 40.

provoked

Un. 6–23   p· discussion and horror,

provoking

'01. 15–28   * p· His pure eyes by your sinful,

prowl

Mis. 323–12   beasts of prey p· in the path,

proximity

'01. 19– 6   closer p· with divine Love,

proxy

Rud. 1–18   one's appearance . . . by deputy or p·.
My. 218–23   either teach or heal by p·

prudence

Mis. 204–30   divine ruling gives p· and energy ;

prudent

Mis. 167–25   the wise and p·, — Luke 10 : 21.
No. 45– 2   the wise and p·, — Luke 10 : 21.
Pan. 3–15   * Choice of the p· ! envy of the great !
Hea. 1–19   * Pushes his p· purpose to resolve."

prudential

My. 173–29   chairman of the p· committee

prune

Mis. 154– 8   p· its encumbering branches,

pruning-hook

Mis. xii– 6   I take my pen and p·,

psalm

Mis. 142–16   my second, a p· ; my third, a letter.
  142–22   seemed more Olympian than the p·
'00. 11–23   * Like the close of an angel's p·,

Psalmist

Mis. 153–11   In the words of the P·,
  306–29   The P· saith :
Ret. 14–25   answer him in the words of the P· :
  64–14   where the P· saith :
  72– 7   The P· vividly portrays the result of
Pul. 10– 6   in the words of the P·,
My. 103–15   Alluding to this . . . the P· said :
  188–11   whereof the P· sang,
  274–27   The P· sang,

Psalms 15 : 1–5 ; 24 : 1–6, 9, 10

My. 33–13   * P· 15 : 1–5 ; 24 : 1–6, 9, 10.

psalms

Pul. 59–10   * hymns and p· being omitted.

Psyche

Mis. ix–20   a P· who is ever a girl.

psychic

Pul. 54–10   * conditions requisite in p· healing

psychics

My. 111– 5   cannot be destroyed by false p·,

psychist

My. 160–29   p· knows that this hell is mental,

psychology

Mis. 3–31   demand for the Science of p·
Un. 9–11   human philosophy, or mystic p·.

public (noun)

Mis. 161–21   teach or preach in p·
  238–28   kept constantly before the p·.
  274–12   grateful acknowledgments to the p·
  285–25   notifies the p· of broken vows.
  297–11   p· cannot swallow reports of
  299–29   gives to the p· new patterns
  301–17   without this word of warning in p·,
  364– 8   made the p· your friend,
Man. 50– 6   DEBATING IN p·.
  58–19   READING IN p·.
  97–17   impositions on the p·
Ret. 15–30   were too timid to testify in p·.
  37–21   My reluctance to give the p·,
  49–21   we thank the p· for its liberal
Pul. 37– 4   * increasing demands of the p·
Rud. 16– 6   Lectures in p· are needed,
'01. 22–26   and insist that the p· receive
Po. vii–11   * volume is presented to the p·,
My. 31–10   * p· had its first glimpse of the
  49– 1   * both in p· and private.
  83–16   * p· at large will scarcely realize
  92–13   * p· has in a general way
  93–27   * essentials of its hold upon the p·,
  94–19   * the doors were opened to the p·,
  175–18   May I ask in behalf of the p·
  223– 2   I hereby notify the p· that
  245–22   To protect the p·, students of the
  272–23   * the p· generally, will be interested
  298– 3   recommending it to the p·.
  298–10   placing this book before the p·,
  338– 5   * chapter sub-title

public (adj.)

Mis. 7–22   counteract . . . this p· nuisance ;
  48– 7   for his p· exposure of it.
  78–19   Misguiding the p· mind and
  78–23   purification of p· thought
  95– 6   * to reply to his p· letter
  161–18   our Master as a p· benefactor,
  171–28   obtruding upon the p· attention
  221–31   or call p· attention to that crime?
  238–25   The frequent p· allegement
  249–10   Both in private and p· life,
  256– 7   acknowledging the p· confidence
  256–12   at present a p· servant :
  274– 2   for a p· institution.
  275–23   p· and private expressions
  299–14   * read them for our p· services?"
  301–20   read them for our p· services?"
  315– 7   in private or in p· assemblies,
  335–16   In my p· works I lay bare the

public (adj.)
Mis. 350–13 and like my *p·* instruction.
Man. 50– 9 in *p·* debating assemblies,
64–23 owing to the *p·* misunderstanding
67– 9 shall not be made *p·* without
74– 2 C. S. society holding *p·* services,
93–12 reply to *p·* topics condemning C. S.,
Ret. 6–26 served the *p·* interests faithfully
7–23 * It is a *p·* calamity.
Pul. 4–29 used, in all its *p·* sessions,
5–22 It is in the *p·* libraries of the
31–15 * that close contact with *p·* feeling
62–21 * concert halls, and *p·* buildings,
79– 9 * as students of *p·* questions
Rud. 15–26 *P·* lectures cannot be such lessons in
16– 2 *p·* lectures can take the place of
No. 1–11 when *p·* sentiment is aroused,
3–11 should not be made *p·* ;
'01. 17–13 would not have arrested *p·* attention
17–19 when the *p·* sentiment would allow
'02. 3–16 so improved her *p·* school system
14–28 all unjust *p·* aspersions.
My. vi–13 * originated its form of *p·* worship,
51–11 * to have the *p·* services discontinued
59–16 * that first *p·* meeting in the little hall
88–17 * which must arrest *p·* attention.
129–32 Refrain from *p·* controversy ;
130– 9 to keep my works from *p·* recognition
130– 9 students seeking only *p·* notoriety,
130–29 in all your *p·* ministrations,
144– 6 The *p·* report that I am in
224–10 *p·* sentiment is helpful or dangerous
224–14 Avoid . . . *p·* debating clubs.
291–17 His *p·* intent was uniform,
316–18 demands *p·* attention.
317– 5 * allegations in the *p·* press
341–21 * unusual *p·* interest centres in
(*see also* **thought**)

Publican's
'01. 14– 4 *P·* wail won his humble desire,
My. 334–21 *P·* wail won his humble desire,

publicans
Mis. 374– 2 caused even the *p·* to justify God.

Publication
(*see* **Committee on Publication, Committees on Publication**)

publication
Mis. 29–18 date of the first *p·* of my work,
155–22 send them to the . . . *Journal* for *p·*,
307–14 thought best to stop its *p·*
372– 9 two weeks from the date of its *p·*
382– 4 Before the *p·* of my first work
Man. 27–14 suitable building for the *p·* of
27–21 *p·* and sale of the books of
48–17 not report for *p·* the number of
Ret. 35– 1 I copyrighted the first *p·* on
35– 7 not venture upon its *p·* until later,
Pul. 5–13 After the *p·* of "S. and H.
36–27 * C. S. *Journal*, a monthly *p·*,
45– 9 * from a *p·* of the new denomination :
My. 141–13 * Alfred Farlow of the *p·* committee
242–18 *p·* committee work, reading-room work,
326–12 for *p·* in our periodicals
333– 3 * the C. S. *p·* committee.

Publication Committee
'02. 4– 6 congratulate our . . . *P· C·*,

publications
Mis. 132–24 refer you . . . to my various *p·*,
133– 7 to read my sermons and *p·*.
300–12 from copies of my *p·*
301– 8 made up of my *p·*,
Man. 48– 6 Uncharitable *P·*.
53–23 *P·* Unjust.
'01. 23–27 In later *p·* he declared
Po. vi–26 * *in various p· of that day*,
My. 272–28 * for any *p·* outside of the

publicity
Mis. 296–23 wriggles" itself into *p·*?
Rud. 16– 1 If *p·* and material control

publicly
Mis. 136– 2 socially, *p·*, and finally,
300– 6 then reading it *p·* as your own
301–22 read it *p· without my consent.*
Man. 59– 7 when *p·* reading or quoting from
72–11 shall be acknowledged *p·* as a
Ret. 42– 4 first student *p·* to announce
Pul. 5– 1 clergymen who had *p·* proclaimed
'00. 12–22 in that city were *p·* burned.
My. 219–26 expressed my opinion *p·*
359– 8 I hereby *p·* declare that

public-spirited
Mis. 147–24 the pious worker, the *p·* citizen.

Public Statutes
Chapter 115, Section 2
Mis. 272–12 * in *P· S·*, Chapter 115, Section 2,

publish
Mis. 220–27 *p·* it in the newspapers
300– 9 If you should print and *p·* your copy
300–15 You literally *p·* my works through
Man. 43–14 shall not *p·* profuse quotations from
48– 7 member of this Church shall not *p·*,
48–23 do not *p·* descriptions of our
71–24 her permission to *p·* them
72– 2 not adopt, print, nor *p·* the Manual
82– 4 the Society will not *p·* them.
Pul. 58–13 * pictures we are permitted to *p·*.
My. 237– 3 I have since decided not to *p·*.
255– 5 my consent to *p·* the foregoing
298–11 my permission to *p·* . . . this work.
326– 1 * glad to *p·* the following
351– 3 * to *p·* her letter of recent date,
358–16 whether or not they shall *p·* your

published
Mis. x– 6 writings *p·* in *The C. S. Journal,*
x–27 in connection with my *p·* works.
4–12 *p·* by the Christian Scientists
80–24 proper answer . . . in my *p·* works.
153–12 those that *p·* it."— *Psal.* 68 : 11.
242– 3 *p·* in *Zion's Herald,*
271–24 *p·* in the *Boston Traveler*
300– 3 Copying my *p·* works *verbatim,*
Man. 27–17 *p·* by The C. S. Publishing Society.
48– 8 nor cause to be *p·*, an article that
53–25 publishes, or causes to be *p·*,
64– 8 also the literature *p·* or sold by
73– 5 *p·* in the list of practitioners
81–15 *p·* by The C. S. Publishing Society,
81–22 C. S. textbook is *p·* or sold,
81–25 Books to be *P·*.
82– 7 not be *p·* . . . without her knowledge
98– 7 not promptly *p·* by the periodical
98–13 see that it is *p·* according to copy ;
98–18 have *p·* each year in a leading
Ret. 27– 4 S. and H., *p·* in 1875.
27– 6 If these notes . . . were *p·*,
35–10 could be profitably *p·*.
36– 8 This will account for certain *p·*
37– 4 was *p·* in 1875.
Pul. 46– 8 * which are *p·* under the title of
55–14 * should have been *p·* in 1875.
74– 4 * article *p·* in the *Herald*
Rud. 16–20 a work which I *p·* in 1875.
'00. 7– 2 "S. and H. was . . . first *p·*.
'01. 21– 7 *p·* in the *New York Journal,*
23–23 Bishop Berkeley *p·* a book
24–22 when I *p·* my work S. and H.,
27– 9 first ever *p·* on C. S.,
'02. 13–30 is *p·* in our Church Manual.
Po. vi– 3 * *p·* in *Manchester, N. H.,*
vi–11 * *which was p· with the poem,*
My. v–20 * wrote and *p·* the C. S. textbook,
13– 5 *p·* in London, England, in 1853,
18–30 * all other *p·* writings of
58– 3 * was *p·* in the *C. S. Sentinel*
76–13 * *p·* at the time of the dedication
130–21 All *p·* quotations from my works
185– 8 peace of Love is *p·*,
218–24 My *p·* works are teachers
243– 7 as *p·* in our Church Manual.
266–24 "S. and H. . . . was *p·* in 1875.
306–25 that I would pay for having *p·*.
306–27 Dr. Quimby had tried to get them *p·*
306–28 Quotations have been *p·*,
310–30 first edition of S. and H. was *p·*,
317– 1 * which was *p·* in the *Sentinel*
321– 9 * as regards your *p·* works ;
321–14 * your relations to your *p·* works
322–10 * correcting mistakes widely *p·*
330– 1 * which was *p·* in your paper
334–28 * *p·* by the late Charles W. Moore,
354– 6 nothing but what is *p·* or sold by
359–10 through my written and *p·* rules,

publisher
'02. 15–10 my *p·* paid me not one dollar
Po. vii– 5 * *Mrs. Eddy requested her p· to prepare*
My. 296–11 the *p·* of my books,
(*see also* **Eddy**)

publishers
Man. 49–16 rules established by the *p·*.

publishes
Man. 53–24 *p·*, or causes to be published,
82– 1 *p·* the books and literature

publisheth
Ret. 45– 3 that *p·* peace." — *Isa.* 52 : 7.

publishing

Mis.	380–29	the unlawful *p·* and use of
	381–23	*p·*, selling, giving away,
Man.	44– 9	not patronize a *p·* house or
	81– 9	connected with *p·* her books,
	81– 9	nor with editing or *p· The*
'00.	10–24	since *p·* this page I have learned
'02.	13–11	privilege of *p·* my books in their
	13–12	*p·* my books in their *p·* house,
Hea.	1–14	less need of *p·* the good news."
My.	vi–27	* place for the *p·* of her works ;
	241–11	* *p·* an extract from a letter

Publishing Buildings

Man.	27–11	*P· B·*.

Publishing Committee

Mis.	271–23	*P· C·* of the . . . Association

Publishing Society

Christian Science, The

Man.	26– 2	manager of The C. S. *P· S·*,
	27–18	published by The C. S. *P· S·*.
	64– 9	sold by The C. S. *P· S·*,
	65–14	Trustees of The C. S. *P· S·*,
	72–14	rules of The C. S. *P· S·*,
	79–15	heading
	80– 1	business of "The C. S. *P· S·*"
	80–24	manager of The C. S. *P· S·*
	81–12	nor with The C. S. *P· S·*.
	81–16	published by The C. S. *P· S·*,
'02.	13– 9	business of The C. S. *P· S·*
My.	vi–20	* organized The C. S. *P· S·*.
	354– 7	sold by The C. S. *P· S·*.
	358–14	The C. S. *P· S·* will settle the
Mis.	114– 1	Our *P· S·*, and our Sunday Lessons,
	126–19	and to our efficient *P· S·*.
Man.	81–26	Only the *P· S·* . . . selects,
Pul.	59–23	* business manager of the *P· S·*,
My.	vi–25	* occupied by the *P· S·*
	vii– 2	* the property of the *P· S·*.
	321–23	* connection with . . . the *P· S·*,

pucker

Mis.	231–24	*p·* the rosebud mouth into saying,

pudding

Mis.	231–14	delicious pie, *p·*, and fruit

pudding-sauce

Mis.	232– 3	in a bumper of *p·*

puffed

Mis.	130–29	Love is not *p·* up ;
	325– 9	*p·* up with the applause

puissance

Mis.	39–14	God giveth to every one this *p·*;

pull

Mis.	111–10	will not *p·* for the shore ;

pulled

Ret.	40–22	notices for a second lecture *p·* down,
My.	82–25	* trains *p·* out of the city

pulling

Mis.	139–11	*p· down of strong holds ;— II Cor.* 10 : 4.
Ret.	80–12	*p·* down of sin's strongholds,
My.	200–22	*p·* down its benefactors,

pulmonary

Pul.	54–30	incipient *p·* consumption.

pulpit

Mis.	88–13	twenty years in the *p·*,
	111–21	is merely of sects, the *p·*, and
	158– 8	another change in your *p·*
	229–13	if only the *p·* would
	245– 9	materialistic portion of the *p·*
	245–24	but, if the *p·* allows the people
	246– 1	It is the *p·* and press,
	246– 6	It was the Southern *p·*,
	246– 9	the *p·* had to be purged of
	300– 5	taking this copy into the *p·*,
	300–12	Reading in the *p·* from
	300–15	publish my works through the *p·*,
	301–14	read copies of my works in the *p·*
	314–11	give out any notices from the *p·*,
	316– 5	chapter sub-title
Ret.	44–10	in the *p·* every Sunday,
	88–23	to enter unasked another's *p·*,
	88–24	the stated occupant of that *p·*.
Pul.	vii– 2	scintillations from press and *p·*
	5–16	press and *p·* cannonaded this book,
	42–18	* *p·* end of the auditorium
No.	2– 4	is naturally glared at by the *p·*,
Pan.	2– 3	declaration from the *p·*
'00.	7–10	bar and bench, press and *p·*,
	14–26	if you are stoned from the *p·*,
'01.	16–19	individual, the *p·*, or the press.
My.	53–20	* *p·* was supplied by Mrs. Eddy,
	114–31	from *p·* and press, in religion and

pulpit

My.	151–12	injustice done by press and *p·*
	154–24	emanating from the *p·* and press.
	185–12	in the *p·*, in the court-room,
	189–12	vibrating from one *p·* to another

pulpits

Mis.	6– 1	We hear from the *p·* that sickness is
My.	113– 1	in hundreds of *p·*
	266–14	vacancies occurring in the *p·*,

pulsates

Mis.	152–13	*p·* with every throb of theirs

pulse

Hea.	12– 4	matter-physician feels the *p·*,
My.	159– 8	the throbbing of every *p·*

pulses

Po.	65– 3	Life's *p·* move fitful and slow ;

pungent

Ret.	23– 6	As these *p·* lessons became clearer,

punish

Mis.	12– 7	*p·*, more severely than you could,
	119– 7	our laws *p·* the dupe as accessory
	198–29	seems to *p·* man for doing good,
	209– 4	wouldst teach God not to *p·* sin?
	209–31	to cover iniquity and *p·* it not,
	215– 5	"I wound to heal ; I *p·* to reform ;
	223–27	* "If I wished to *p·* my enemy,
	223–29	To *p·* ourselves for others' faults,
No.	8–17	sin will so *p·* itself that it will
Hea.	5– 9	saying, . . . God will *p·* him
My.	128–17	Men cannot *p·* a man for suicide ;
	252–16	reward righteousness and *p·* iniquity

punished

Mis.	73–14	disobey moral law, and are *p·*.
	209–23	are *p·* before extinguished.
	261– 2	evil, as *mind*, is . . . *p·* ;
	272–16	* shall be *p·* by a fine
Man.	15–13	*p·* so long as the belief lasts.
Un.	15–14	the creature is *p·* for his
Rud.	10–21	*p·* because of disobedience
No.	30– 6	to suffer, or to be *p·*.
	30–10	*p·* by the law enacted.
'01.	10–26	nothing left to perish or to be *p·*,
Hea.	4–12	He knows deserves to be *p·*,
Peo.	3– 7	majority to be eternally *p·* ;
	9–15	sin that deserves to be *p·*
My.	130– 7	unearthed and *p·*
	331–15	* as quickly as it would have *p·*

punishes

Mis.	93–27	Sin *p·* itself, because it cannot
	121–31	*p·* the guilty, not the innocent.
	257–14	It *p·* the innocent,
	300–11	defines and *p·* as theft.
	351–27	*p·* the joys of this false sense
Rud.	10–18	Love *p·* nothing but sin,
No.	30– 4	for it pursues and *p·* it,
'01.	13–24	never *p·* it only as it is destroyed,
Peo.	8– 8	if . . . *p·* man eternally,
My.	288–25	that sin *p·* itself ;

punishing

Mis.	261–18	showeth mercy by *p·* sin.
	293– 7	uncovering and *p·* of sin
'01.	16– 5	*p·* itself here and hereafter
My.	159–23	spiritual laws . . . *p·* disobedience.

punishment

Mis.	11– 2	thwarted, its *p·* is tenfold.
	51–21	having to resort to corporeal *p·*.
	118–29	fiery *p·* of the evil-doer.
	279– 3	certainty of individual *p·*
Ret.	13–14	the danger of endless *p·*,
Un.	40–24	the *p·* of this ignorance.
'01.	13–23	God removes the *p·* for sin only as
	16– 3	chapter sub-title
	16– 4	a future and eternal *p·*
My.	296–18	reward of good and *p·* of evil

pupil (*see also* **pupil's**)

Mis.	54–29	the *p·* in simple equations
	55– 1	the *p·* and the science of numbers.
Man.	37–17	cannot recommend the *p·* of another
	62–13	but no *p·* shall remain in the
	84–15	not exceed $100.00 per *p·*.
	84–25	another loyal teacher's *p·*,
	86– 4	After a student's *p·* has been
Ret.	50– 5	as the price for each *p·* in
Rud.	9– 7	spring up in the mind of his *p·*.
	15–24	so that the mind of the *p·* may be
		(*see also* **Eddy**)

pupilage

Mis.	316–27	derived most benefit from their *p·*,
Ret.	50–17	speak with delight of their *p·*,

pupil's

Man.	84–13	*P·* Tuition.
Rud.	9– 7	The *p·* imperfect knowledge

pupils

Mis. 91–30 require their *p·* to study the
114–31 specially instruct his *p·*
Man. 36– 4 Students' *P·*.
36– 6 from *p·* of loyal students
36– 9 or from *p·* of those who have
37–16 *P·* of Normal Students.
43– 7 nor permit his patients or *p·* to
59–10 instruct their *p·* to adopt the
62– 8 *P·* may be received in the
62–16 officers, teachers, and *p·* should
73–24 to the *p·* of one teacher.
83– 8 Care of *P·*.
83– 9 select for *p·* such only
83–13 or attempt to dominate his *p·*,
83–19 patiently counsel his *p·* in
84– 2 Teachers shall instruct their *p·*
84– 7 Number of *P·*.
84–10 consist of not more than thirty *p·*.
84–12 class not exceeding thirty *p·*.
84–17 associations of the *p·* of loyal
84–18 *p·* shall be guided by the Bible,
84–21 shall not call their *p·* together, or
85– 2 *P·* may visit each other's churches,
85– 4 *P·* of Strayed Members.
85– 7 the *p·* of another member of
85–10 not ready to lead his *p·*.
85–12 shall not teach *p·* C. S. unless
80– 2 *P·*.
86–23 shall instruct their *p·* from the
87–11 shall not solicit, . . . *p·* for their classes.
89–19 Loyal Christian Scientists' *p·*
Ret. 83–15 if he misinterprets the text to his *p·*,
83–25 highly important that their *p·* study
84–27 take charge only of his own *p·*
Pul. 47– 4 * her circle of *p·* and admirers
49– 7 * gifts of her loving *p·*,
My. 251–13 it, . . . your *p·* are found eligible
251–18 teach *p·* the practice of C. S.,

puppets

Mis. 368–23 Some of the mere *p·* of the hour

purblind

My. 45–17 * when *p·* mortal sense declared

purchase

'00. 15– 1 you *p·*, at whatever price,
'02. 12–25 united effort to *p·* more land
My. 7– 9 united effort to *p·* more land
9–23 *p·* of more land for its site,
11–23 * informed of the *p·* of the land
16– 8 * included the *p·* price of the land
55– 4 * *p·* some building, or church,
66– 1 * The *p·* of this parcel
66– 8 * now comes the *p·* of the last parcel
215–19 to *p·* the site for a church edifice,

purchased

Mis. xi–23 preliminary battles that *p·* it.
165–22 *p·* the means of mortals' redemption
249–16 I have neither *p·* nor ordered
Man. 102–16 rule shall not apply to land *p·* for
Pul. 20– 2 *p·* by the church and society.
'02. 13–16 *p·* the mortgage on the lot
My. 147–22 I have *p·* a pleasant place for you,

purchases

Man. 102–11 All deeds of further *p·* of land
My. 347–18 priceless pearl which *p·* our

purchasing

Mis. 299–28 saves your *p·* these garments,
300– 2 avoiding the cost of hiring or *p·*
No. 34–27 *p·* the freedom of mortals from sin
My. 123–15 responsibility of *p·* it,

pure

Mis. 63– 8 triune Principle of all *p·* theology ;
98–19 *p·* and undefiled religion
100–22 *P·* humanity, friendship, home,
107–11 A *p·* affection, concentric,
123–17 is too *p·* to behold iniquity,
128– 8 whatsoever things are *p·*, — *Phil.* 4 : 8.
152–19 made ready for the *p·* in affection,
159–13 where all things are *p·*
168–12 only such as are *p·* in spirit,
185–22 infinitely blessed, upright, *p·*, and free ;
206– 4 from foul to *p·*, from torpid to serene,
223– 6 necessarily have *p·* fountains ;
228– 7 and *p·* amid corruption.
240–31 namely, *p·* odors.
260–16 *p·* Mind is the truth of being
260–23 acknowledging *p·* Mind as absolute
260–25 *P·* Mind gives out an atmosphere that
262– 4 wish to brighten so *p·* a purpose,
264–16 to assimilate *p·* and abstract Science
264–27 teacher's mind must be *p·*, grand,
266– 3 unselfish and *p·* aims and
270–16 Gain a *p·* Christianity ;
280– 6 messengers of *p·* and holy thoughts

pure

Mis. 295–23 high and *p·* ethical tones
338–15 a *p·* faith in humanity will
343–17 their *p·* perfection shall appear?
345–12 his *p·* and strong faith rose higher
354–15 a motive made *p·*,
367– 3 requires man to be honest, just, *p·* ;
367–29 God is too *p·* to behold iniquity ;
368–15 the ranks of the good and *p·*,
388–18 The right to worship deep and *p·*,
390– 9 Too *p·* for aught so mute.
397–19 An offering *p·* of Love,
399– 8 'T is the Spirit that makes *p·*,
Man. 16–12 to be merciful, just, and *p·*.
Ret. 26–24 none but the pure in heart
26–25 Principle of all things *p·* ;
28–11 honest, unselfish, and *p·*,
65–20 C. S. is the *p·* evangelic truth.
68–29 The beautiful, good, and *p·*
71–20 *p·* and undefiled religion.
Un. 2– 1 God is too *p·* to — *see Hab.* 1 : 13.
18– 7 too *p·* to behold iniquity,
57–14 His *p·* consciousness was
Pul. 19– 3 An offering *p·* of Love,
21–10 unite with me in this *p·* purpose,
26– 3 * the centre being of *p·* white light,
35–15 become honest, unselfish, and *p·*,
42–27 * with ferns and *p·* white roses
Rud. 10– 6 He is too *p·* to behold iniquity,
No. v–13 the *p·* spirituality of Truth.
39–25 reveals the *p·* Mind-pictures,
40– 9 *p·* pearls of awakened consciousness,
Pan. 3–16 * By thy *p·* stream,
'01. 6–15 Is this *p·*, specific Christianity?
9– 8 submerged them in a sense so *p·*
15–28 * provoking His *p·* eyes by your
20–18 to the *p·* in spirit, and the meek
'02. 18– 4 *p·* sense of the immaculate Jesus
Hea. 7–14 makes *p·* the fountain,
Peo. 5–14 wrapped in a *p·* winding-sheet,
5–25 makes a *p·* Christianity
13–21 his *p·* faith went up through
Po. 13– 7 An offering *p·* of Love,
21– 7 right to worship deep and *p·*,
39– 2 Gifts, lofty, *p·*, and free,
43–14 their *p·* hearts' off'ring,
46–13 An offering *p·* to God.
55–10 Too *p·* for aught so mute.
66– 1 *p·* nectar our brimming cup fill,
68–21 *p·* as its rising, and bright
75–15 'Tis the Spirit that makes *p·*,
79– 3 *p·* peace is thine,
My. 40–30 * first *p·*, then peaceable, — *Jas.* 3 : 17
69–13 * *p·* white marble was used,
85–30 * noble dome of *p·* gray tint,
112–21 their uniformly *p·* morals
114– 5 be honest, just, and *p·* ;
147–14 memory of this *p·* purpose,
152–12 The restoration of *p·* Christianity
155–18 a *p·* peace, a fresh joy,
213–11 to live *p·* and Christian lives,
218–15 introduction of *p·* abstractions into
256–14 *p·* pages of impersonal presents,
257–22 make man's being *p·* and blest.
303–17 Science and its *p·* monotheism
315– 7 * a *p·* and Christian woman,
(*see also* **heart**)

purely

Mis. 170–22 method of Jesus was *p·* metaphysical ;
218–31 * *p·* spiritual personality in God."
276– 4 was *p·* Western in its cordiality
341–28 and the diction *p·* Oriental.
359– 3 *p·* Christly method of teaching
Ret. 43– 1 first *p·* metaphysical system of
48–18 on a *p·* practical basis,
48–27 *p·* spiritual and scientific impartation
Un. 23–24 *p·* good and spiritual consciousness
Rud. 16–22 pathological Science *p·* mental.
No. 12– 2 from a *p·* Christian standpoint.
'01. 26–12 from Christ's *p·* spiritual means
27–25 left C. S. as it is, *p·* spiritual,
My. 221– 5 with certain *p·* human views.

pure-minded

Mis. 240–21 *p·*, affectionate, and generally **brave.**

purer

Mis. 276–22 a *p·*, higher affection and ideal.
330–22 a *p·* peace and diviner energy,
387– 4 mount upward unto *p·* skies ;
Ret. 73–11 and *p·* realms of thought.
91– 5 No *p·* and more exalted teachings
'00. 4– 9 is being purged by a *p·* Judaism
'01. 15–25 * He is of *p·* eyes than to bear to
Po. 50–22 mount upward unto *p·* skies ;
My. 127–20 a *p·* Protestantism and monotheism
300– 1 "of *p·* eyes than to behold — *Hab.* 1 : 13.

purest
No. 38–26 loses a part of its p· spirituality
Po. vii–12 * these gems of p· thought

purgation
Mis. 41–14 Mental p· must go on :
Ret. 94–11 this p· of divine mercy,

purge
'00. 12–23 to p· our cities of charlatanism.

purged
Mis. 41–10 is p· through Christ, Truth,
79– 2 beliefs will be p· and dissolved
184–31 mortal mind p· of the animal
205– 1 mortal mind, thus p·, obtains peace
246–10 p· of that sin by human gore,
'00. 4– 8 p· by a purer Judaism
Po. 26–20 P· by the cannon's prayer ;

purgeth
Mis. 151– 8 Those who bear fruit He p·,

purification
Mis. 9– 3 p· it brings to the flesh,
18– 1 The p· or baptismals that come from
78–23 for the p· of the public thought
Ret. 79–12 p· of the affections and desires.
94–10 his p· through suffering,
No. 34–12 baptized in the p· of persecution
Peo. 9– 3 this baptism is the p· of mind,

purified
Mis. 125– 2 p· as by fire, — the fires of suffering ;
166–19 to go to the temple and be p·,
My. 58–18 * p· through the labor and sacrifice of
265–26 reflect this p· subjective state

purifies
Mis. 8–19 p·, sanctifies, and consecrates
151– 7 p· the human character,
351–28 chastens its affection, p· it,
No. 39–15 Such prayer humiliates, p·, and
'00. 8–24 fire that p· sense with Soul
My. 131– 1 that which p· the affections

purify
Mis. 5– 1 will elevate and p· the race.
223– 6 Streams which p·,
298–18 Trials p· mortals and deliver them
341– 6 First p· thought,
Hea. 5–26 p·, elevate, and consecrate man ;
7–14 in order to p· the stream.
Peo. 9– 8 p· his mind, or meet the demands of

purifying
Mis. 7–24 with healing, p· thought.
204–23 By p· human thought,
No. 28– 7 p· processes and terrible revolutions
'02. 2–10 p· all peoples, religions, ethics,

Puritan (see also **Puritan's**)
No. 46–15 P· standard of undefiled religion.

Puritan's
Un. 14–11 shortcomings of the P· model

Puritans
No. 46–16 As dutiful descendants of P·,
My. 181–13 The P· possessed the motive of

purity
and love
Mis. 195–31 when meekness, p·, and love,
Pul. 9–24 p·, and love are treasures
and peace
No. 34–24 yet mounting . . . in p· and peace,
and permanence
Mis. 320–30 in token of p· and permanence.
and sweetness
Pul. 62–13 * p· and sweetness of their tones.
approaches
Mis. 363– 1 The more nearly . . . approaches p·,
christened
Un. 17–11 its vileness may be christened p·,
faith and
'00. 6–14 through his simple faith and p·,
imbued with
Mis. 4– 1 Thought imbued with p·,
its
My. 63–25 * its p·, stateliness, and vastness ;
metaphysical
Mis. 184–30 to foreshadow metaphysical p·,
of Christianity
My. 178– 5 process and p· of Christianity
perpetuating
My. 261–14 aids in perpetuating p·
persecution and
Ret. 54–11 gaining . . . through persecution and p·.
self-abnegation and
Mis. 298–21 self-abnegation and p·;
spotless
My. 262– 4 spotless p· and original perfection.

purity
types of
'00. 11–29 His types of p· pierce corruption
unity and the
'00. 13– 1 to destroy the unity and the p· of

Mis. 37– 6 toward p·, health, holiness, and
130– 3 long-suffering, meekness, charity, p·
154–28 meekness, mercy, p·, love.
Ret. 28–17 P·, self-renunciation, faith, and
'02. 8–24 Love, p·, meekness, co-exist in
My. 200–18 seven-fold shield of honesty, p·, and
269– 5 pledged to innocence, p·,
274–11 honesty, p·, unselfishness

purloined
'00. 8–12 and wear the p· garment

purporting
My. 175–28 p· to have my signature,
306–28 p· to be Dr. Quimby's own words,

purpose
and fruits
Mis. 223– 2 its hidden paths, p·, and fruits
animated with a
Mis. 325–21 that anybody is animated with a p·,
another
My. 306–11 I have quite another p· in life
any
Man. 102–16 for any p· other than the
charitable
My. 358–20 a worthy and charitable p·.
definition of
Mis. 371–23 to unite, in a definition of p·,
divine
Ret. 37–23 divine p· that this should be done,
83– 3 accomplishing the divine p·
entire
My. 252–10 entire p· of true education
every
My. 22–18 * every p· she has set in motion,
evil
Mis. 41– 4 uses it to accomplish an evil p·.
exalted
Mis. 341–10 finds . . . its strength in exalted p·.
Pul. 10–13 No dream . . . broke their exalted p·,
feeling and
Mis. 177–10 Their feeling and p· are deadly,
her
No. 12–15 nerved her p· to build on the
His
My. 143–27 according to His p·.
278– 2 If His p· for peace is to be
his
Mis. 85– 9 His p· must be right,
Un. 59– 2 his p· to save humankind
No. 33–25 his p· was to show them that the
holy
Mis. 162–28 To carry out his holy p·,
My. 283– 9 To aid in this holy p· is
human
My. 284– 3 to help human p· and peoples,
idea and
Mis. 303–23 idea and p· of a Liberty Bell
infirm of
Pul. 4– 2 * "weak and infirm of p·."
its
Pul. 59–17 * was well adapted for its p·,
My. 282– 1 its p· is good will towards men.
learn its
Mis. 207– 1 Learn its p· ;
life and
My. 36–23 * devotion to the daily life and p·
Master's
Ret. 25–29 our great Master's p·
misapprehending the
Mis. 345–26 distorting or misapprehending the p·
mortal
Mis. 204–26 it unselfs the mortal p·,
my
My. 164– 1 my p·, when I came here,
244– 2 my p· in sending for you,
305–31 my p· was to lift the curtain
noble
My. 22–10 * for this grand and noble p·,
no such
My. 317–11 It was for no such p·.
of blessing
Mis. 351– 4 for the p· of blessing even my
of building
My. 21– 6 * for the p· of building church homes
57–10 * for the p· of building a suitable
of Christian Science
Rud. 2–26 The emphatic p· of C. S.
of divine Love
Mis. 154–16 It is the p· of divine Love
No. 35– 8 yield . . . to the p· of divine Love,

purpose

of electing
My. 49–16 * for the p· of electing officers.
of God
Mis. 366–21 as the p· of God ;
My. 216–18 The p· of God to youward
of its members
My. 339– 1 The p· of its members is to
of learning
Pul. 72– 3 * p· of learning the feeling of
of Love
Mis. 214–15 accomplishing its p· of Love,
of preventing
My. 286–11 for the p· of preventing war
possible
Mis. 48–19 possible p· to which it can be
power and
Pul. 10– 5 power and p· to supply them.
My. 293– 3 power and p· of infinite Mind,
prudent
Hea. 1–19 * Pushes his prudent p· to resolve."
pure
Pul. 21–10 unite with me in this pure p·,
My. 147–14 memory of this pure p·,
right
My. 160– 2 he abides in a right p·,
sacred
My. 289–12 convene for the sacred p· of
singleness of
Mis. 317–26 singleness of p· to uplift
sinister
Man. 53–19 a complaint . . . for a sinister p·.
strong of
Mis. 238– 6 honest . . . and strong of p·.
stubborn
Un. 5–15 No stubborn p· to force conclusions
such a
Man. 48–15 near her for such a p·.
that
Mis. 25–31 recommend them for that p·?
'01. 18–19 would have used them . . . for that p·,
29– 2 or visited a reformer for that p·?
My. 9– 6 * that may be needed for that p·.
their
No. 15– 5 convince all that their p· is right.
this
Mis. 98–21 This p· is immense,
315–22 form associations for this p· ;
Man. 26– 8 meeting held for this p·,
38–14 meetings held for this p·.
82–14 a meeting held for this p·
No. 31–14 "For this p· the Son — I John 3 : 8.
Mu. 8– 3 * may be necessary for this p·,"
12– 1 * may be necessary for this p·,"
this very
Mis. 3–11 Jesus taught them for this very p· ;
thought and
My. 24–12 * unity of thought and p·
thy
Po. 26–12 Thy p· hath been won !
to kill
Mis. 40–28 holding the p· to kill
302– 2 a p· to kill the reformation
to restore
Mis. 230–18 with the p· to restore harmony
vital
Ret. 48– 4 was aimed at its vital p·,
worthy
Ret. 49– 7 having accomplished the worthy p·
your
Mis. 134–17 your p· to be in Chicago

Mis. 29– 6 p· of his life-work touches
135– 7 one in motive, p·, pursuit.
139–20 for the p· of having erected thereon
203 chapter title
261–22 effecting so glorious a p·.
262– 4 If you wish to brighten so pure a p·,
351–13 for the p· of placing C. S. in
Man. 57–13 state definitely the p· for which
98– 5 for the p· of having him reply
Ret. 57– 8 for the p· of destroying discord.
No. v– 1 p· of each edition of this pamphlet
Pan. 13–15 united in p·, if not in method,
My. 18–23 united in p·, if not in method,
29–18 * unanimity of thought and of p·.
126– 2 p· of the destroying angel,
139–18 p· of my request was sacred.
169– 5 so long a trip for so small a p·
204–14 P· OF THE CHRISTIAN SCIENTISTS TO
216–31 for a p· even higher,
248– 8 p· of grasping and defining the
306–10 p· of making the true apparent.
312–30 for the p· of starting that
333– 7 * p· of paying the last tribute

purposes
Mis. 10– 1 or engraft upon its p·
152– 6 unite in the p· of goodness.
204–14 new p·, new affections,
227–17 nobler p· and wider aims
272– 7 * for metaphysical p· only,
272–22 * obtain for any secular p· ;
277–16 the p· of envy and malice
292–24 works out the p· of Love.
Man. 99– 2 For the p· of this By-Law, the
Ret. 43– 6 granted for similar p·
48–11 for medical p·,
'02. 17–27 aims, motives, fondest p·,
My. 63–15 * work out the p· of divine Love.
66–15 * well situated for church p·
137–20 persons and p· I have designated
231– 3 charities for such p·
285– 9 crowns the great p· of life
293–21 to overrule the p· of hate

pursue
Mis. 197–11 and bade his followers p·.
342–24 Seek Truth, and p· it.
Man. 82–17 or p· other vocations,
No. 40–14 I instruct my students to p· their
Po. 29– 3 though murky clouds P· thy way,
My. 117– 8 to p· the infinite ascent,
260–14 may p· paths devious,

pursued
Ret. 61–10 Unless this method be p·,
90–28 * in the path you have p· !"
Un. 10–27 unless, p· by their fears,
My. 19–20 shall be p· by her substance,
340–20 is p· by the leaders of our

pursues
Mis. 210– 1 p· the evil that hideth itself,
No. 30– 4 for it p· and punishes it,

pursuing
Mis. 230–24 * Still achieving, still p·,
250– 7 The so-called affection p· its
My. 130–14 to be continually p· a lie
185– 6 * Still achieving, still p·,

pursuit
Mis. 135– 7 one in motive, purpose, p·.
230–16 in the p· of pleasure.
268–12 in p· of better means
340– 8 no other p· or pleasure
My. 116–20 p· of his or her person
345–25 * the p· of modern material

pursuits
Mis. 10–26 human affections and p·
19–31 Life and its grand p·
147–28 In all his p·, he knows no

push
Mis. 129–19 and try to p· him aside ;
235–22 thought must p· on the ages :
237–22 p· on the growth of mankind.
303–14 knock instead of p· at the door of
320– 1 p· upward our prayer in stone,

pushed
Mis. 245–18 The conclusion cannot now be p·,
Un. 6–25 if hastily p· to the front
54–27 serpent, who p· that claim
My. 14–28 * the work will be p· forward
24–20 * being p· with the utmost energy,

pushes
Mis. 23– 2 p· the question :
Hea. 1–19 * P· his prudent purpose to resolve."
My. 272– 4 logic of events p· onward the
288– 2 it unselfs men and p· on the ages.

pushing
Mis. 232– 7 is p· towards perfection in art,
Ret. 16– 3 p· their way through the crowd

pussy-willow
Mis. 329–22 put the fur cap on p·,

put
Mis. 17–11 p· off your materia medica and
24–30 p· down all subtle falsities
64–25 p· into this condition of mortality?
82–22 material sense of life, is p· off,
121–16 "Thou shalt p· away — Deut. 19 : 13.
129– 4 let him p· his finger to his lips,
140–23 p· back into the arms of Love,
178– 8 could not be p· into old bottles
214– 1 chapter sub-title — John 18 : 11.
214–14 "P· up thy sword." — John 18 : 11.
214–16 "P· up thy sword ;" — John 18 : 11.
220–26 p· it into the minds of others
233–13 p· into the old garment of drugging
243– 8 doctor had p· on splints
250–14 Love is not something p· upon a shelf,
280–15 Mind is not p· into the scales with
286–16 p· ingenuity to ludicrous shifts ;

put

Mis.	288– 8	before being *p·* into action.
	299–19	*p·* myself and them on exhibition,
	329–22	*p·* the fur cap on pussy-willow,
	330–32	to *p·* forth its slender blade,
	341– 6	then *p·* thought into words,
	349–32	I have *p·* into the church-fund
	358–15	Christ's vestures are *p·* on only
	359–10	I *p·* away childish things. — *I Cor.* 13 : 11.
	381– 9	he should not *p·* in testimony.
	381–28	*p·* under the edge of the knife,
Man.	50–21	*p·* on probation, or
Ret.	20– 9	*p·* under the care of our family nurse,
	69–11	saying, . . . 'I will *p·* spirit into
	73– 6	Limitations are *p·* off in proportion
Un.	34–15	yet *p·* your finger on a burning
	56– 8	"*p·* him to an open shame." — *Heb.* 6 : 6.
Pul.	6–14	* S. and H., was *p·* into my hands.
	22–20	*p·* on her most beautiful garments,
	53– 1	* Principle that was *p·* into practice
	54–23	* "*p·* them all out," — *Luke* 8 : 54.
	62–20	* to which these bells may be *p·*.
Rud.	14–11	often those were *p·* off for months,
No.	3–14	will *p·* that book in the hands of
	27–22	to be "*p·* off." — *Col.* 3 : 9.
	29– 2	*p·* to death for his own sin,
	43–20	cannot *p·* the "new wine — *Matt.* 9 : 17.
Pan.	11– 4	*p·* off the old man with — *Col.* 3 : 9.
	11– 4	*p·* on the new man, — *Col.* 3 : 10.
'00.	8– 1	Then, if sin and flesh are *p·* off,
'01.	2– 7	by trying to *p·* into the *old* garment
	17–20	*p·* patients into the hands of my
	27–22	I have *p·* less of my own
'02.	3– 7	*p·* an end, at Charleston, to
	11–27	*p·* to death the Galilean Prophet,
	17–27	will *p·* to flight all care
Hea.	18– 4	shall be "*p·* off," — *Col.* 3 : 9.
	18– 6	to *p·* new wine into old bottles ;
	18–12	cannot *p·* the new wine into old bottles.
	18–15	it would *p·* the new wine into
Peo.	10– 8	and *p·* her humane foot on a
	14–13	*p·* on the whole armor of Truth ;
My.	4–12	woman has *p·* into Christendom
	22–17	* and time has *p·* its seal
	43– 1	* did not *p·* them in possession of
	91–24	* despite the obstacles *p·* in the way
	125–25	*p·* on her beautiful garments
	130–27	has an enormous strain *p·* upon it,
	135– 4	I *p·* away childish things." — *I Cor.* 13 : 11.
	188– 4	*p·* my name there forever ; — *I Kings* 9 : 3.

put

My.	204– 4	to *p·* into practice the power which
	212– 9	*p·* down the evil effects of alcohol.
	233– 8	should you not *p·* that out
	244–19	*p·* off the human for the divine.
	247–12	*P·* on the robes of Christ,
	248–10	*p·* an end to falsities in a wise way
	261–17	I *p·* away childish things." — *I Cor.* 13 : 11.
	273– 2	* to *p·* before its readers.
	329–26	* *p·* before them some interesting
	338–22	construction that people . . . might *p·*
	353–11	to *p·* on record the divine Science

puts

Mis.	120–29	*p·* to flight every doubt as to the
	210–17	*p·* her foot on the head of the
	240–16	or *p·* it into the ice-cream
	285–24	*p·* virtue in the shambles,
	362–16	Philosophy . . . *p·* cause into effect,
Ret.	70– 4	so-called mind *p·* forth its own
	81–22	Shakespeare *p·* this pious counsel
Pul.	44– 5	* as mortal sense *p·* it,

putteth

Pan.	6– 8	*p·* his foot upon a lie.
My.	33–25	*p·* not out his money to — *Psal.* 15 : 5.

putting

Mis.	2–30	*p·* on the spiritual elements
	170–30	The *p·* on of hands mentioned,
	170–31	explained as the *p·* forth of power.
	182– 3	impossibility of *p·* him to death,
	302–28	forestall the possible evil of *p·* the
	329– 8	and *p·* down the green ones,
Pan.	1–12	*p·* off outgrown, wornout, or soiled
'00.	14–30	*P·* aside the old garment,
Peo.	13–13	*p·* man to the rack for his conscience,
My.	177–14	*p·* off the limitations
	177–14	and *p·* on the possibilities
	233– 8	instead of *p·* *out your watch?*
	349–14	*p·* off the hypothesis of matter

puzzled

My.	346– 4	* far from being *p·* by any question,

puzzles

'00.	6–14	spiritual sense that *p·* the man.

pyramid

Hea.	11–12	like the great *p·* of Egypt,

Pythagorean

Mis.	344– 2	*P·* professor of ethics,

Q

quack

Hea.	14–12	in the hands of a *q·*.

quackery

Rud.	12–12	*q·*, that denies the Principle of
No.	19– 6	infidelity, ignorance, and *q·*
'01.	33– 7	* "*Q·* and dupery do abound
	33– 9	* *q·* was never the originating
Peo.	6– 3	* "I am sick of learned *q·*."

quacks

'01.	30–12	Christian Scientists . . . are not *q·*,
Peo.	11–25	The learned *q·* of this period

quail

Mis.	222–23	will make stout hearts *q·*.

quaintly

Mis.	239–19	looking up *q·*, the poor child

qualifications

Man.	34– 3	*q·* FOR MEMBERSHIP.
	87–15	moral and spiritual *q·*
	89–18	*Q·*.
	92–23	*q·* named in Sect. 9
My.	241– 1	* moral and spiritual *q·*

qualified

Man.	37–23	*q·* to approve for membership
	50– 2	made by *q·* experts.
	90– 5	if found *q·* to receive them.
	90–18	lessons by a well *q·* teacher
	92–12	found duly *q·* to teach C. S.,
My.	231–11	*q·* students for healing
	240–27	* by those who are duly *q·*,
	255–10	for which they are not *q·*.

qualify

Mis.	43–19	thoroughly to *q·* students

qualities

Mis.	36–14	animal *q·* of sinning mortals ;
	36–16	express the lower *q·* of
	199–18	*q·* of the divine Mind
	199–21	over the *q·* opposed to Spirit

qualities

Mis.	201– 6	bringing the *q·* of Spirit into
	250–11	distorted into human *q·*,
	268–23	are potions of His own *q·*.
	332–28	but are *q·* of error.
Ret.	5–16	*q·* to which the pen can never
	70– 5	puts forth its own *q·*,
	88–14	health-giving and life-bestowing *q·*,
Un.	32–14	the eternal *q·* of His being.
	35– 4	for the *q·* of matter
	35– 5	are but *q·* of mortal mind.
'01.	16–18	these *q·* are objectionable,
Hea.	3–12	*q·* of God as a person,
Peo.	2–17	out of the worst human *q·*,
	8– 9	we shall bring out these *q·*
My.	28–14	* stimulated those gentle *q·*
	153–14	with no intrinsic healing *q·*
	292–25	supposed to possess opposite *q·*

quality

and quantity

Mis.	217– 9	correspond in *q·* and quantity.

begets the

Hea.	3–13	Principle that begets the *q·*,

changes

Un.	35– 6	Change the mind, and the *q·* changes.

disappears

Un.	35– 6	and the *q·* disappears.

evil is a

No.	23–18	Evil is a *q·*, not an individual.

evil is not a

Mis.	259–10	evil is not a *q·* to be known

human

Mis.	75–19	warped to signify human *q·*,
	250–21	As a human *q·*, the glorious

inferior

Mis.	226–25	Perfidy of an inferior *q·*,

life-giving

'01.	26–11	endows it with a life-giving *q·*

nature and

Mis.	36–17	nature and *q·* of mortal mind,

quality

no
Un. 38–20 Death has no *q·* of Life ;
no intrinsic
Mis. 108–31 they have no intrinsic *q·*
nor quantity
'01. 12–28 Evil is neither *q·* nor quantity :
of God
Pan. 5– 2 Can a single *q·* of God,
of good
Mis. 78–29 to present the *q·* of good.
of matter
Mis. 256–23 while every *q·* of matter
of tone
Pul. 62–14 * The *q·* of tone is something superb,
one in
'02. 12–16 one in *q·*, not in quantity.
or quantity
Mis. 333–28 in a single *q·* or quantity !
or the quantity
Peo. 3–21 *q·* or the quantity of eternal good.
quantity or
Un. 31–20 defies Spirit, in quantity or *q·*.
real
Ret. 76–25 every one in his real *q·*,
third
Mis. 217–21 a third *q·* unlike God.
unselfed
My. 249–29 unselfed *q·* of thought

Mis. 250– 4 either as a *q·* or as an entity
'00. 11–17 *q·*, quantity, and variation in tone,
My. 267–19 *q·* and the quantity of heaven.

quantities

Mis. 62 11 positive and negative *q·*,
Man. 98–14 shall circulate in large *q·* the papers
My. 96–21 * money was sent in such *q·*

quantity

Mis. 62–11 the negative *q·* offsets an equal
62–12 offsets an equal positive *q·*,
62–12 aggregate positive, or true *q·*,
217– 9 must correspond in quality and *q·*.
333–28 in a single quality or *q·* !
Un. 31–20 in *q·* or quality.
'00. 11–17 quality, *q·*, and variation in tone,
'01. 12–28 Evil is neither quality nor *q·* :
'02. 12–16 one in quality, not in *q·*.
Peo. 3–22 quality or the *q·* of eternal good.
My. 267–19 quality and the *q·* of heaven.

quarrel

Mis. 181–12 What avail, then, to *q·* over
364–24 must either cooperate or *q·*
'00. 8 20 When a man begins to *q·* with himself
'02. 6 36 Did they *q·* long with the inventor
My. 219–29 "Rather than *q·* over vaccination,
270–28 would no more *q·* with a man because
303– 7 Scientists have no *q·* with

quarrelling

'00. 8–21 he stops *q·* with others.

quarrels

Mis. 284–29 personal animosities and *q·*.
Hea. 8–14 and no longer *q·* with the individual.
My. 284–26 *q·* between nations and peoples.
309– 5 making out deeds, settling *q·*,
310–22 * says that "the *q·* between

quarries

Mis. 144– 1 taken from the *q·* in New Hampshire,

quarter

Pul. 23–18 * last *q·* of the nineteenth century.
55– 6 * last *q·* of preceding centuries.
56–14 * the last *q·* of the century.
My. 53– 1 * from every *q·* came important
78– 8 * from every *q·* of the city.
89–28 * marvels of the last *q·* century.
(see also **numbers, values**)

quarter-century

Ret. 41– 1 which C. S. encountered a *q·* ago,
My. 89–28 marvels of the last *q·*.

Quarterly

Christian Science
Mis. 113–30 Journal, and the C. S. *Q·*,
300–26 permission to cite, in the C. S. *Q·*,
314–13 Lesson of the C. S. *Q·*,
Man. 32–23 printed in the C. S. *Q·*.
63– 7 found in the C. S. *Q·* Lessons,
My. 19– 5 current numbers of . . . C. S. *Q·*.

Mis. 114– 5 in the preparation of the *Q·*
314–30 shall be taken from the *Q·*
Pul. 60– 8 * reading . . . the *Q·* Bible Lesson,

quarterly

Man. 76–21 They shall hold *q·* meetings
97–13 an annual salary, paid *q·*,

quarters

Mis. 132–19 letters and inquiries from all *q·*,
Pul. vii– 4 Three *q·* of a century hence,
My. 55–23 * was obliged to seek other *q·*,
77–23 * Scientists from all *q·* of the globe

Queen (see also **Queen's**)

'02. 3–24 the joy of the sainted *Q·*,
My. 289–17 "God save the *Q·*"

queen

Mis. 295–28 unquestionably the best *q·* on earth ;

Queen Elizabeth's

No. 44–13 In *Q· E·* time Protestantism

Queen of Great Britain

My. 289–15 lamented Victoria, *Q· of G· B·*
289–29 lamented Victoria, *Q· of G· B·*

Queen of Sheba

Pul. 2– 1 I should be much like the *Q· of S·*,

Queen's

My. 290– 5 *Q·* royal and imperial honors

Queen Victoria (see also **Victoria**)

My. 289– 6 chapter sub-title

quench

Mis. 84–23 forever to *q·* his love for it.
348–17 To *q·* the growing flames of
Po. 15–22 cannot *q·* in oblivion's wave.
72– 4 *Q·* liberty that's just.
My. 127–32 cannot *q·* my desire to say
128–13 nor rulers rampant can *q·* the

quenched

Mis. 183– 1 pride of life will then be *q·*
Un. 39– 6 *q·* in the divine essence,
Pul. 3–24 all human desires are *q·*,
'02. 18–10 *q·* not the smoking flax,

quenching

Mis. 316–23 warming marble and *q·* volcanoes !
'02. 9– 3 the All-presence — *q·* sin ;
My. 291–10 *q·* the volcanoes of partizanship,

quenchless

Po. 18– 6 genius unfolding a *q·* desire.

queried

Mis. 295–20 should not only be *q·*, but

queries

Mis. 268– 3 Two personal *q·* give point to
303–12 therefore no *q·* should arise as to

query

Mis. 32 10 The *q·* is abnormal,
32–31 To the *q·* in regard to some
65–12 your *q·* concerns a negative
299–10 glad, indeed, that this *q·* has finally
337– 8 Infinite *q·* !
380– 8 majesty and magnitude of this *q·*,
Un. 8– 1 Let another *q·* now be considered
Pan. 5–11 proper answer . . . . to this hoary *q·*.
'01. 5–14 This suggests another *q·* :
My. 261– 3 guardians of youth ofttimes *q·* :
299–17 I *q·* : Do Christians, who believe

querying

Ret. 35–18 There is no authority for *q·* the

quest

My. 181– 1 The specific *q·* of C. S. is

question

ancient
Hea. 19–12 the ancient *q·*, Which is first,
answer to a
Mis. 349–22 In answer to a *q·* on the
answer to the
Hea. 9–21 only correct answer to the *q·*,
answer your
Mis. 51–11 cannot answer your *q·* professionally.
any
My. 346– 4 * far from being puzzled by any *q·*,
as to religion
'00. 4–22 The *q·* as to religion is :
at issue
Mis. 246–27 The *q·* at issue with mankind is :
My. 360–11 momentous *q·* at issue in First Church
brings up the
Mis. 350– 6 student who brings up the *q·* of
carried the
Mis. 191–25 and carried the *q·* with Eve.
conjugal
Mis. 289–26 Science touches the conjugal *q·*
dodge the
Mis. 53– 4 Committing suicide to dodge the *q·*
every
Mis. 65–10 Every *q·* between Truth and error,

question

fervid
My. 25–17 my answer to their fervid *q*˙ :
finishes the
Hea. 10–13 that finishes the *q*˙ of
following
Mis. 299– 9 simply answer the following *q*˙
My. 217–18 In the . . . was the following *q*˙ :
251– 5 I reply to the following *q*˙
great
Mis. 379–25 solution of this great *q*˙ :
'02. 5–17 have answered this great *q*˙
My. 234–19 both sides of the great *q*˙
human
'02. 5–14 ever-recurring human *q*˙
ill-concealed
Ret. 75– 2 spring from this ill-concealed *q*˙
legislative
My. 167–24 noble disposal of the legislative *q*˙
no
Mis. 315–20 shall be no *q*˙ of money,
Pul. 57–16 * there can be no *q*˙ but that the
now at issue
No. 46– 3 The *q*˙ now at issue is :
of applying
Man. 88–18 on the *q*˙ of applying for admission
of Christian Science
Mis. 135– 3 person is not in the *q*˙ of C. S.
of money
Mis. 315–20 shall be no *q*˙ of money,
Man. 83– 5 shall not be a *q*˙ of money,
of pauperism
My. 309– 6 involving a *q*˙ of pauperism
of time
Mis. 348–12 It is only a *q*˙ of time when
of unity
My. 236–17 seals the *q*˙ of unity,
old
My. 117–13 Is not the old *q*˙ still rampant?
one side of a
Mis. 288– 9 regards only one side of a *q*˙,
out of the
No. 45– 9 is of course out of the *q*˙.
Hea. 13–16 leave the drug out of the *q*˙,
My. 317–18 left my diction quite out of the *q*˙,
350– 3 or leaving it out of the *q*˙.
pregnant
'02. 14–26 This pregnant *q*˙, answered frankly
propound a
'02. 5–26 conceive of a law, propound a *q*˙,
pushes the
Mis. 23– 2 but Science, . . . pushes the *q*˙ :
settles the
Mis. 192–31 declaration of . . . settles the *q*˙ ;
My. 277–10 never settles the *q*˙ of his life.
settle the
My. 358–15 Publishing Society will settle the *q*˙
settling the
Mis. 380– 1 settling the *q*˙, What shall be the
shocks me
Pul. 74–15 "Even the *q*˙ shocks me.
sublime
My. 277–12 sublime *q*˙ as to man's life
this
Mis. 23– 7 Christianity answers this *q*˙.
32– 6 From this *q*˙, I infer that some
46–11 would not present this *q*˙.
65–21 my instructions on this *q*˙.
81–20 *fair or correct view of this q*˙,
89–23 answer to this *q*˙ in my . . . works.
98– 1 making this *q*˙ of personality
116–11 This *q*˙, ever nearest to my heart,
133–20 to set you right on this *q*˙,
140–19 material side of this *q*˙.
284–13 This *q*˙ is often proposed,
299–26 have you asked yourself this *q*˙
333–11 C. S. voices this *q*˙ :
346–11 To this *q*˙ C. S. replies :
381–14 asked the defendant's counsel this *q*˙,
Un. 5–11 divine Science of this *q*˙ of Truth
Rud. 6–26 this *q*˙ of how much you understand of
My. 190– 7 The age is fast answering this *q*˙ :
271–21 * addressed this *q*˙,
vexed
Man. 66–12 to report to her the vexed *q*˙
whole
'02. 12– 4 settles the whole *q*˙ on the basis
without
No. 41–16 Without *q*˙, the subtlest forms of sin
wrong side of the
Hea. 9– 6 talking on the wrong side of the *q*˙.
your
Mis. 56–29 Your *q*˙ implies that Spirit,
67–25 If your *q*˙ refers to language,
My. 271–29 to your *q*˙ permit me to say

question

your
My. 277– 3 In reply to your *q*˙,
———
Mis. 33–14 *q*˙ that is being asked every day.
69–30 Now comes the *q*˙ :
88–10 author of the article in *q*˙
106–22 long been a *q*˙ of earnest import,
192–18 Neither can we *q*˙ the
224–30 while it is a *q*˙ in my mind,
270– 5 What artist would *q*˙ the skill of
282– 7 The *q*˙ will present itself :
301–19 To the *q*˙ of my true-hearted
337– 3 Have I discovered . . . is the *q*˙.
346– 9 The *q*˙ is often asked,
Ret. 48– 3 The *q*˙ was, Who else could
70– 8 We do not *q*˙ the authenticity of
Pul. 47–16 * no . . . has been equal to the *q*˙.
'01. 35– 4 The *q*˙ oft presents itself,
Hea. 5–12 * the *q*˙ chiefly is concerning
My. 133– 9 chapter sub-title
133–23 secret to tell you and a *q*˙ to ask.
162– 2 *q*˙ our want of more faith
212–14 The *q*˙ is often asked,
218–21 chapter sub-title
233–30 Aye, that's the *q*˙.
240–24 * *q*˙, Does Mrs. Eddy approve of class
241–17 * The *q*˙ and Mrs. Eddy's reply follow.
305–28 My recent reply . . . was not a *q*˙ of
306– 8, 9 a *q*˙ that is no longer a *q*˙.
318–19 I agreed not to *q*˙ him
343– 4 * and works around a *q*˙
344–23 * *q*˙ of infectious and contagious

questionable

Mis. 122–15 is neither *q*˙ nor assailable :
140– 6 a type . . . materially *q*˙
243–24 Did he refer to that *q*˙ counsel,
'01. 21– 6 chapter sub-title

questioned

Pul. 32–12 * I mentally *q*˙ this modern
My. 90–28 * can no longer be *q*˙,
220– 8 When Jesus was *q*˙ concerning
330–14 * are *q*˙ by this critic,
342–18 * Mrs. Eddy sat back to be *q*˙.

questioners (see also questioners')

My. 251– 5 question from unknown *q*˙ :

questioners'

My. 214–18 relieving the *q*˙ perplexity,

questioning

Mis. 228–25 without *q*˙ the reliability of
Ret. 25–30 not *q*˙ those he healed as to
Un. 1– 2 much natural doubt and *q*˙
Pul. 33– 5 * often run to her mother *q*˙
'01. 18–11 *q*˙ Christ Jesus' healing,
My. 190–21 remains beyond *q*˙ a divine
214–16 letters *q*˙ the consistency of
318–20 so long as he refrained from *q*˙ me.

questions

Mis. 4–14 *q*˙ important to be disposed of
38–24 for *q*˙ of practical import.
91–26 take his textbook . . . ask *q*˙ from it,
92–13 repeat the *q*˙ in the chapter on
92–16 adhere to the *q*˙ and answers
95–13 I shall confine myself to *q*˙ and
114–27 will test all mankind on all *q*˙ ;
121–25 to the *q*˙ of the rabbinical rabble :
126– 1 from unsettled *q*˙ to permanence,
137–10 if you had any *q*˙ to propose,
157–10 all *q*˙ important for your case,
167– 1 The material *q*˙ at this age
179– 7 resolves itself into these *q*˙ :
238–20 Let one's life answer . . . these *q*˙,
265–27 constantly called to settle *q*˙
280–27 I met the class to answer some *q*˙
287–22 *q*˙ concerning their happiness,
317–20 prompt my answers to the above *q*˙.
Man. 63– 5 *q*˙ and answers as are adapted to
Ret. 14–11 I was ready for his doleful *q*˙,
25– 3 It answered my *q*˙
83–23 they should ask *q*˙ from it,
Un. 6–15 *q*˙ about God and sin,
Pul. 34–26 * in reply to my *q*˙,
34–27 It answered my *q*˙
37– 3 * just in its attitude toward all *q*˙."
79– 9 * as students of public *q*˙
Pan. 13– 4 Chief among the *q*˙ herein,
'02. 5–30 silences all *q*˙ on this subject,
My. 83–14 * fewer *q*˙ as to locality
223–13 *q*˙ about secular affairs,
223–17 such *q*˙ are superinduced by
228–11 chapter sub-title
238– 1 chapter sub-title
277–20 can settle all *q*˙ amicably

questions
My. 318–18   not ask him any *q·*.
     319–18   * *q·* which have recently appeared,
     343– 1   * plain that the answers to *q·* would
     348– 8   greatest of all *q·* was solved

quibble
Mis. 141–18   concerned about the legal *q·*,

quibbled
Pul. 9–13   *q·* over an architectural exigency,

Quibus
Mis. 88– 8   * "*What Q· Thinks.*"

quicken
Mis. 98–12   to *q·* and extend the interest
     145–21   to *q·* even dust into sweet memorial

quickened
Mis. 352– 3   When human sense is *q·*
Un. 56– 9   Holding a *q·* sense of
Pul. 10– 4   a *q·* sense of mortal's

quickening
Mis. 185–28   *was made a q· spirit.— I Cor.* 15 : 45.
     188–31   to her "a *q·* spirit ;"— *I Cor.* 15 : 45.
     189–17   *q·* spirit takes it away :
Un. 30–15   was made a *q·* spirit."— *I Cor.* 15 : 45.
     30–23   last Adam as a *q·* Spirit,
     30–26   shall be found a *q·* Spirit ;
No. 43–16   * and *q·* the Christian."

quickens
Mis. 204–19   so *q·* moral sensibility
     352–10   *q·* the true consciousness of
No. 39–15   purifies, and *q·* activity,

quickly
Mis. 49– 2   I *q·* saw, had a tendency to
     57–11   "That thou doest, do *q·*."— *John* 13 : 27.
     74– 5   It *q·* imparts a new
     276–29   *q·* learned when the door is shut.
     325–26   the Stranger turns *q·*,
     395–16   *Q·* earth's jewels disappear ;
Man. 92– 9   C. S. heals the sick *q·*
Ret. 9– 6   My cousin answered *q·*,
No. 13– 2   destroys sin *q·* and utterly.
'01. 9–30   he worketh well and healeth *q·*,
     17– 5   *q·* to return to divine Love,
     29–29   * "quite *q·* we have regained
     32–14   they armed *q·*, aimed deadly,
Po. 58– 1   *Q·* earth's jewels disappear ;
My. v 16   * and reforming the sinner *q·*
     331–15   * as *q·* as it would have punished

quicksands
Ret. 79–18   *q·* of worldly commotion,

quiescence
Un. 15–25   to bribe with prayers into *q·*,

quiet
Mis. 143–15   with *q·*, imposing ceremony,
     143–25   *q·* call from me for this extra
Man. 94–12   to depart in *q· thought*
Pul. 47–23   * of New Hampshire's *q·* capital,
Rud. 12– 7   or else *q·* the fear of the sick
No. 1–14   *q·* practice of its virtues.
My. 103–21   opportunity in Concord's *q·*
     291– 6   a *q·* assent or dissent.

quieted
My. 317–20   I *q·* him by quoting . . . texts

quietly
No. 8–25   *q·*, with benediction and hope,
My. 11–14   * *q·* alluded to the need
     79–25   * *Q·*, without a trace of fanaticism,
     87– 8   * congenial, *q·* happy, well-to-do,

quiets
My. 250– 5   promotes wisdom, *q·* mad ambition,

quietude
My. 262–27   I love to observe Christmas in *q·*,

quill-drivers
Mis. 274–22   *q·* whose consciences are in

Quimby (*see also* **Quimby's**)
Dr.
Mis. 381–12   claim that Dr. *Q·* was the author
My. 306–22   when I first visited Dr. *Q·*
     306–26   Dr. *Q·* had tried to get them published
Dr. P. P.
Mis. 381– 4   composed by Dr. P. P. *Q·*.
Mr.
Mis. 379– 1   Mr. *Q·* would retire to an anteroom
My. 324– 5   * scorned the suggestion that Mr. *Q·*
Mr. P. P.
Mis. 378– 6   one Mr. P. P. *Q·* of Portland,
Ret. 24– 2   magnetic doctor, Mr. P. P. *Q·*,

Quimby
P. P.
My. 305– 1   P. P. *Q·* (an obscure, uneducated
Quimby's
Dr.
My. 306–29   purporting to be Dr. *Q·* own words,
Mr.
Mis. 379–27   It was after Mr. *Q·* death

quinine
Mis. 244–30   discoverers of *q·*, cocaine, etc.,

quintessence
Mis. 336–22   the *q·* of Christianity,

quit
'01. 15–13   or he would never *q·* sinning.
My. 96–23   * members were asked to *q·* giving.

quite
Mis. 48– 6   One thing is *q·* apparent ;
     64–27   It is *q·* as possible to know
     69–24   had not *q·* killed him.
     126–15   church is not yet *q·* sensible of
     200–15   this rule is *q·* as remote from
     202– 7   * *Q·* on the verge of heaven."
     216–20   * which "vanished *q·* slowly,
     229– 7   *q·* as surely and with better effect
     264–20   before they are *q·* free from
     311–11   not *q·* ready to take this advanced
     357–10   *q·* on the verge of heaven.
     372–17   * artist seems *q·* familiar with
     375–13   * *q·* an idea of what constitutes
Ret. 93–20   It is *q·* clear that as yet
Pul. 61–25   * attracted *q·* a throng
'01. 27– 1   *q·* independent of all other
     29–29   * "*q·* quickly we have regained
     34– 2   *q·* as salutary in the healing of
My. 26–13   *q·* unexpected at this juncture,
     30–23   * *q·* voluntarily the Scientists
     70–13   * The effect . . . is *q·* remarkable.
     149–25   predicament *q·* like that of the man
     177– 9   I am *q·* able to take the trip
     184–23   success *q·* sacred in its results.
     227– 6   Charity is *q·* as rare as wisdom,
     234–20   gives the subject *q·* another aspect.
     300–32   peaceable party *q·* their antipode?
     306–11   I have *q·* another purpose in life
     307–20   in some respects he was *q·* a seer
     317–17   left my diction *q·* out of the
     320–12   * and seemed *q·* proud of his
     324–22   * as *q·* his literary equal,

quitting
Mis. 179–22   by *q·* the old consciousness of

quivering
Mis. 274–25   headless trunks, and *q·* hearts
     275–13   and repeat with *q·* lips
     347– 3   rumbling and *q·* of the earth

quotation
My. 73– 8   * in the form of a *q·* from S. and H.
     213–27   chapter sub-title
     227–21   above *q·* by the editor-in-chief

quotation-marks
My. 130–22   *Q·* are not sufficient.
     224–18   one author without *q·*,

quotations
Man. 43–15   shall not publish profuse *q·*
My. 69–10   * marble plates with Scripture *q·*
     130–21   published *q·* from my works
     213–28   three *q·* from "S. and H.
     306–28   *Q·* have been published,
     307– 1   these *q·* certainly read like
     359–18   * *q·* from a composite letter,

quote
Mis. 264– 1   while they *q·* from other authors
Man. 48–25   may *q·* from other periodicals
My. 334–16   * to *q·* her own words.

quoted
Mis. 72–31   The Scriptural passage *q·*
     83–28   * *Q·* from the sixteenth edition.
Ret. 76– 8   is cited, and *q·* deferentially.
My. 146– 9   has been *q·* and criticized :
     313– 2   Correctly *q·*, it is as follows,
     351–10   the title of your gem *q·*,

quotes
Mis. 243–31   Professor *q·*, in justification of
     295– 4   whom he *q·* without naming,

quotient
Un. 53–20   would have one *q·*.

quoting
Man. 59– 7   *q·* from the books or poems
My. 110–31   or *q·* sentences or paragraphs
     317–20   *q·* corroborative texts of Scripture.

R

rabbi
  Mis. 168–11 lowly in Christ, not the man-made r·
rabbinical
  Mis. 121–26 the questions of the r· rabble :
rabbins
  Un. 46–17 incensed the r· against Jesus,
rabbis
  Mis. 199–16 cost him the hatred of the r·.
  '01. 9–11 mysticism complained of by the r·,
rabble
  Mis. 121–26 questions of the rabbinical r· :
  274–26 are held up before the r·
Rabboni
  Mis. 179–29 "R· !"—Master!— *John* 20 : 16.
rabid
  Un. 52–20 r· beasts, fatal reptiles,
race
  achieved for the
  Mis. xi– 8 hitherto achieved for the r·.
  238–10 unselfed love achieved for the r·
  achieve for the
  My. 292– 2 righteousness achieve for the r·
  affection for the
  My. 248–12 honest, fervid affection for the r·
  benefit the
  Mis. 11–26 general effort to benefit the r·.
  38–19 application to benefit the r·,
  '01. 21–24 whereby to benefit the r·
  declining
  Mis. 163–15 language of a declining r·,
  elevating the
  Mis. 3– 1 elevating the r· physically, morally,
  emancipation of the
  My. 248–13 for the emancipation of the r·.
  exalts the
  No. 12– 3 heals the sick and exalts the r·.
  freedom for the
  Mis. 120–14 great freedom for the r· ;
  gives to the
  Mis. 235–11 It gives to the r· loftier desires
  help the
  '02. 3–28 to serve God and to help the r·.
  his
  Mis. 330– 9 should call his r· as gently
  hope for the
  My. 246–11 to gain a higher hope for the r·,
  hope of our
  Pul. 9– 3 the hope of our r· !
  hope of the
  Mis. 163–21 the basis . . . the hope of the r·.
  No. 46– 6 The advancing hope of the r·,
  human
      (*see* human)
  improves the
  Peo. 6–19 improves the r· physically
  injure the
  Mis. 260–32 it may injure the r·,
  is helped
  '02. 11–15 when the r· is helped onward
  long
  Mis. 126–26 in the long r·, honesty always
  of Adam
  Ret. 55– 8 improves the r· of Adam.
  '01. 5–17 the material r· of Adam,
  of the centuries
  My. 126–30 win we the r· of the centuries.
  one
  Po. 22–13 one r·, one realm, one power.
  our
  Un. 13–20 for the benefit of our r·.
  Pul. 15–11 doing right and benefiting our r·.
  87–26 a legacy to our r·.
  '01. 16–27 Shall the hope for our r·
  primitives of the
  Mis. 316–14 the primitives of the r·,
  purify the
  Mis. 5– 2 elevate and purify the r·.
  sceptered
  Po. 10–15 To Judah's sceptered r·,
  sceptred
  My. 337–16 To Judah's sceptred r·,
  servant of the
  My. 145–21 makes me the servant of the r·
  spiritualization of the
  No. 32– 3 and the spiritualization of the r·
  strong
  Mis. 126–24 have a strong r· to run,
  suffering
  Mis. 156– 1 in behalf of a suffering r·,

race
  this
  My. 37–11 * everlasting advantage of this r·.
  tranquillity of the
  My. 280– 7 * peaceful tranquillity of the r·.
  uplifting the
  Mis. 236– 4 labor of uplifting the r·,
  315–21 of morals and of uplifting the r·.
  Man. 83– 7 healing and uplifting the r·.
  uplift the
  Mis. 317–27 purpose to uplift the r·.
  upon the
  Un. 8–16 deleterious effects, . . . upon the r·.
  value to the
  No. 19– 5 shows its real value to the r·.
  My. 348–21 value to the r· firmly established.
  work for the
  Mis. 303– 1 to work for the r· ;
  ———
  Mis. 148–20 which will do for the r·
  329–21 streams to r· for the sea.
  361–19 r· that is set before us, — *Heb.* 12 : 1.
  365–23 value of C. S. to the-r·.
  382–11 this gift of God to the r·,
  Man. 3–17 which will do for the r· what
  No. 21– 5 an unsafe decoction for the r·.
  My. 94– 2 * r· for numerical supremacy.
  155–14 the r· set before it,
  167–19 your flock, and the r·.
races
  My. 47–22 * inspired so many of different r·
  127–32 all times, climes, and r·.
rack
  No. 46–11 or laid on the r·,
  Peo. 13–13 putting man to the r· for his
radiance
  Mis. 20– 1 with the r· of divine Love ;
  Ret. 18–19 r· and glory ne'er fade.
  Un. 42–28 go forth in the r· of eternal being
  61–11 nightless r· of divine Life.
  '00. 12– 5 the r· of glorified Being.
  Po. 64–10 r· and glory ne'er fade.
  My. 194–15 r· of His likeness.
radiant
  Mis. 251–14 r· reality of Christianity,
  356– 1 r· sunset, beautiful as blessings
  377– 4 so near and full of r· relief
  385–26 r· glory sped The dawning day.
  399– 4 for you make r· room
  Po. 17– 2 their r· home and its morn !
  49– 1 r· glory sped The dawning day.
  70– 4 At sunset's r· hour,
  75–11 for you make r· room
  My. 149–11 its r· stores of knowledge
  150–20 r· reflection of Christ's glory,
radiata
  My. 271– 3 no vertebrata, mollusca, or r·.
radiate
  Mis. 361–10 mollusk and r· are spiritual concepts
  My. 81– 3 * Scientists fairly r· good nature
radiating
  Un. 51–20 r· throughout all space
radiation
  Mis. 290–26 share the benefit of that r·.
  No. 17–19 focal r· of the infinite.
radical
  Mis. 193–28 r· and unmistakable declaration
  226–30 red-tongued assassin of r· worth ;
  Un. 6–11 is r· enough to promote as forcible
  Pul. 66–24 * wonder as to how r· is to be
radically
  Man. 39–12 and of being r· reformed,
radius
  Mis. 12–32 r· of our atmosphere of thought.
rage
  My. 103–16 "Why do the heathen r·,— *Psal.* 2 : 1.
  200– 5 Let "the heathen r·, — *Psal.* 2 : 1.
  270–14 Let error r· and imagine a
raged
  Ret. 19– 8 yellow-fever r· in that city,
ragged
  Mis. 391–15 That every r· urchin,
  Po. 38–14 That every r· urchin,

raging
Ret. 60–17 r· of the material elements
My. 249– 6 r· element of individual hate
334– 4 * disease was r· at that time.

railroads
My. 73–22 * rooms and board, hotels, r·,

railways
Mis. 296–10 English alehouses and r·

raiment
Mis. 373–17 soft r· or gorgeous apparel ;
Pul. 1– 5 clad in white r·,
No. 29–22 though clad in soft r·,

rain
Mis. 394– 8 as the soft summer r·,
Pul. 4– 3 "What if the little r· should say,
No. 21–28 like a cloud without r·,
Po. 45–11 as the soft summer r·,
My. 149–27 Clouds parsimonious of r·,
149–31 with the treasures of r·,

rainbow
Mis. 339– 9 robes the future with hope's r·
355–29 r· seen from my window
376–20 one rod of r· hues,
394–11 A r· of rapture, o'erarching,
Ret. 17–13 Flora has stolen the r· and sky,
23– 9 spanned with its r·
Pul. 26– 4 * which reflect the r· tints,
Po. 25– 3 Soft tints of the r·
45–14 A r· of rapture, o'erarching,
62–16 Flora has stolen the r· and sky,

rainbows
Po. 8–17 r· of rapture floated by !

rainbowy
Mis. 231–27 his little r· life

raining
My. 341–26 * It had been r· all day

raise
Mis. 227–15 that my pen or pity could r·
228–12 to r· those barren natures
326– 1 cast out devils, r· the dead ;
Ret. 88– 5 "r· the dead." — Matt. 10 : 8.
88–10 "R· the dead," — Matt. 10 : 8.
Un. 7–14 r· the dying to instantaneous
Pul. 3– 6 I will r· it up." — John 2 : 19.
29–18 * r· the dead, — Matt. 10 : 8.
66–12 * r· the dead, — Matt. 10 : 8.
Po. 77– 2 to Thee we r· A nation's
70 8 To r· up seed   in thought
My. 57–10 * to r· any part of two millions
65– 7 * to r· any part of two million
99– 3 * "A faith which is able to r·
192– 5 r· the living dead,
218–10 and to r· the dead
300–15 r· the dying to health?
300–16 Christian Scientists r· the dying
300–26 r· the dead, — Matt. 10 : 8.

raised
Mis. 28–28 healed the sick and r· the dead.
74–18 he r· the dead,
168–10 how the dead, . . . are r· ;
244–22 and the dead to be r·
340–15 r· potatoes instead of pleas,
Un. 44– 6 like the structure r· thereupon,
60–24 if Christ be not r·, — I Cor. 15 : 17.
Pul. 10– 2 r· the deadened conscience,
54–27 * he r· the daughter to life.
64–11 * necessary amount was r·,
No. 37–23 Messiah . . . r· the dead,
'01. 19–17 healed the sick, r· the dead,
My. 61–15 * I r· my eyes, and the
83–25 * the new temple has been r·
98–19 * r· in a little less than
241–14 * issue r· is an important one

raises
Ret. 66– 4 It r· men from a material sense
71– 2 tax it r· on calamity
My. 67– 1 * r· its dome above the city
219–16 Christ, . . . who r· the dead,
260–25 r· the dormant faculties,

Raise the Dead
Pul. 28– 7 * "R· the D·," — Matt. 10 : 8.

raising
Mis. 25–18 r· the spiritually dead.
124–18 r· the dead, saving sinners.
187– 2 *healing the sick*, and r· the dead.
312–15 * shown in the r· up of the
Ret. 66– 2 in casting out error, in r· the dead.
Pul. 27–16 * r· of the daughter of Jairus.
27–26 * represents the r· of Lazarus.
Peo. 12–21 healing the sick and r· the dead
My. 98–24 * latter-day methods of r· money.

raising
My. 110– 3 healing the sick, and r· the dead
150–22 r· the spiritually dead
285–22 neither r· up the people, — Acts 24 : 12.

Raleigh (N. C.) News and Observer
My. 328– 7 * copied from the R· (N. C.) N· and O·,

rampant
My. 117–13 Is not the old question still r· ?
128–13 nor rulers r· can quench the
283–20 When . . . injustice is r·.

ran
Mis. 379–11 usually r· in the vein of thought
Po. 1– 9 And far the universal fiat r·,

rancorous
My. 213– 8 one r· and lurking foe

random
Mis. 254–23 its so-called healing at r·,
264– 2 r· thought in line with mine.
Man. 59– 4 who think at r· on this subject,

rang
Pul. 31–23 * r· the bell at a spacious house
61–20 * chapter sub-title
Po. 70–17 Immortal Truth, — since heaven r·,

range
Mis. 249–29 it hath r· and is sovereign !
Pul. 26–17 * of fine r· and perfect tone.
62–21 * as they r· in all sizes,
Rud. 2–25 higher r· of infinite goodness.
My. 85– 2 * in its widely international r·,

ranged
Mis. 231– 3 r· side by side.

rank
Mis. 6–15 will r· far in advance of allopathy
99–17 take the front r·, face the foe,
257– 1 notion that Mind . . . is r· infidelity,
357 21 irrespective of self, r·, or
Un. 18–28 it would lower His r·.
No. 21–18 This is r· infidelity ;
My. 31–19 * take a place in the front r· of
230– 3 maintain its r· as in the past,

rankle
Mis. 224– 2 that makes another's criticism r·,

ranks
Mis. 29–17 but fourteen deaths in the r·
134–21 reeling r· of *materia medica*,
135– 2 come into the r· !
368–15 r· of the good and pure,
Ret. 44–30 Adding to its r· and influence,
85 23 to divide the r· of C. S.
My. 105–29 In the r· of the M. D.'s
127– 8 calm coherence in the r· of C. S.
300–32 on their own religious r·,
355– 5 chapter sub-title
355–12 in our r· of divine energy,

ransomed
Mis. 386–28 cloud not o'er our r· rest
Po. 50–14 cloud not o'er our r· rest
My. 171– 4 r· of the Lord shall — Isa. 35 : 10.
192– 3 thou r· of divine Love,

Raphael
Mis. 375– 6 it demands more than a R·

rapid
Mis. 6–14 r· growth of the work shows.
6–24 once convinced . . . the gain is r·.
125–30 r· transit from halls to churches,
205–32 take r· transit to heaven,
206–26 Your growth will be r·,
307–12 Notwithstanding the r· sale already
Pul. 52–16 * r· growth of the new movement.
66–21 * Such a r· departure
'01. 2–27 history of C. S. explains its r·
My. 52–11 * while we realize the r· growth,
92–27 * Its growth has been wonderfully r·,
113–30 in the r· and steady advancement of

rapidity
Pul. 66– 7 * has grown with remarkable r·.
My. 14–27 * The r· with which the work
99–25 * grown with a r· that is startling,

rapidly
Mis. 110–24 increase r· as years glide on.
126–23 yet nothing circulates so r· :
Ret. 47– 8 applicants were r· increasing.
85–25 r· spreading over the globe ;
Pul. 67–18 * and is r· growing.
No. 32–25 r· diminishing the percentage of sin.
'00. 1–13 with r· increasing numbers,
'01. 1– 7 more extended, more r· advancing,
'02. 2–17 little leaven . . . is r· fermenting,
My. 24–20 * building is proceeding r· ;
55– 9 * the attendance r· growing

rapidly
My. 77– 9 * are r· gathering in this city
165–29 r· nearing the maximum of might,
200– 2 individual rights . . . r· advancing,
336– 3 * The disease spread so r·

rapt
Mis. 387– 1 "When Love's r· sense
No. 18–17 to be the r· face of Jesus.
Po. 50–18 "When Love's r· sense
My. 343– 2 * She has a r· way of talking,

rapture
Mis. 394–11 A rainbow of r·, o'erarching,
Ret. 18–19 r· and radiance and glory
'02. 4–10 music to the ear, r· to the heart
Po. 8–17 What rainbows of r·
45–14 A rainbow of r·, o'erarching,
64–10 r· and radiance and glory
My. 163– 1 bursting into the r· of song

raptured
Mis. 396–24 breathed in r· song,
Pul. 18– 8 breathed in r· song,
Po. 12– 8 breathed in r· song,

raptures
Po. 65–17 claspeth earth's r· not long,

rare
Mis. 159–17 recollections and r· grand collections
200–11 Paul insists on the r· rule
250–15 to be taken down on r· occasions
276– 1 the large book of r· flowers,
283–14 Any exception to . . . is r·.
292– 9 It must have been a r· revelation
379–18 his r· humanity and sympathy
Ret. 18–23 And those . . . find a happiness r· ;
30– 3 r· bequests of C. S. are costly,
82– 8 exception to this rule should be very r·.
Po. 31–13 r· footprints on the dust of earth.
64–19 And those . . . find a happiness r· ;
My. 26–17 to be brief on this r· occasion.
70–20 * replete with r· bits of art,
93–14 * yet it has r· lures for weary hearts,
227– 7 Charity is quite as r· as wisdom,

rarefied
Mis. 267–21 plumed for r· atmospheres
Ret. 33–19 thereby r· to its fatal essence,

rarely
My. 272–28 * Mrs. Eddy writes very r· for
314–10 considered a r· skilful dentist.

rash
Mis. 288– 9 r· conclusion that regards only

rate
Mis. 242–22 r· of one ounce in two weeks,
Man. 68–11 r· of one thousand dollars yearly
My. 92–17 * a r· at which every other sect
124–26 r· of speed, the means of travel,

rated
My. 305–18 r· in the *National Magazine*

rather
Mis. 24–28 r· the allegory describing it.
55–12 to harm r· than to heal,
81–12 r·, *Are not the last eighteen*
127–28 r· than on the ear or heart
147–29 r· fail of success than
224–30 pity r· than of resentment ;
285– 1 evil only, r· than person.
305–17 * r· than large contributions
310– 8 r· than cling to personality
361– 1 r· was it their subjugation,
Ret. 65– 3 r· than on the teaching
82–19 r· does it represent an accumulation
83– 6 r· than try to centre their interest
91–13 r·, this series of great lessons
91–29 Ask, r·, what has he *not* done.
Un. 5– 3 R· will they rejoice in the
5–25 R· let the stately goings
17– 8 r· he ratifies a union predestined
18– 2 R· let us think of God as saying,
30–26 or, r·, shall reflect the Life of
Pul. 2–19 would you not r· strengthen
30– 4 * r· than offering their strength to
46– 3 * r· than in search of the truth
47–25 * driving r· into the country,
58–19 * It is r· dark, often too much so
65– 7 * which is r· small and new,
80–15 * r· to the credit of the book
Rud. 2–15 r· than *a personal* God ;
11–14 r·, the absolute consciousness
'00. 12–28 r· than personal or historical.
Peo. 1– 5 r· is it the crumbling away of
3–26 r· than obedience to
My. 50–14 * "The tone . . . was r· sorrowful ;"
97–15 * a r· bitter critic of Mrs. Eddy
98–15 * a r· remarkable announcement

rather
My. 219– 5 a hindrance r· than help.
219–29 "R· than quarrel over vaccination,
222–24 r· does it imply that religion
249–22 a man, r· than a woman,
303–24 r· is it the pith and finale
327–20 * an old law, or r· a section of
345–22 or r· attained by us, as we
348–12 r· than his divine Principle,

ratifies
Un. 17– 8 or rather he r· a union

ratio
Mis. 127– 4 in the r· of her love for others,
Ret. 67–14 In the r· that the testimony of
My. 18– 1 in the r· of her love for others,
239– 7 In the r· that C. S. is

rational
Mis. 2–16 a more r· and divine healing.
'00. 4–16 r· that the only perfect religion
My. 128–16 dictates of his own r· conscience
348–18 Science demanded a r· proof

rationally
Mis. 76–17 no man can r· reject his authority
'01. 4–23 to explain God's personality r·
27– 8 * apply them more r· to human needs."
My. 350– 8 calmly and r·, though faintly,

ravening
Mis. 294–18 from wolves . . . and all r· beasts.

raven's
Mis. 254– 9 nest of the r· callow brood !
356–21 nests of the r· callow brood.

ravished
Po. 8–10 R· with beauty the eye of day.

Rawson
Miss Dorcas
'02. 16– 2 Six months thereafter Miss Dorcas R·
Mr.
Mis. 225– 2 At the residence of Mr. R·,
Mrs.
Mis. 225–10 whereupon the mother, Mrs. R·,
225–20 Mrs. R· then rose from her seat,
226– 1 But Mrs. R· said :— " Give the child

ray
Mis. 333– 4 every r· of Truth, of infinity,
336–25 wherever one r· of its effulgence
Chr. 53– 6 Spirit sped A loyal r·
Pul. 26– 4 * each r· under prisms which reflect
'01. 8– 9 in the sense that one r· of light is
'02. 12–17 a r· of light one with the sun,
Po. 2–17 sun's more genial, mighty r· ;
43–15 Light with wisdom's r·
53– 7 With sunshine's lovely r·
My. 282–10 no uncertain r· of dawn.
344– 4 and each separate r· for men and

rays
Mis. 194–14 to divide the r· of Truth,
333– 8 it absorbs all the r· of light.
Ret. 35–13 prism of Truth, which divides its r·
'01. 12–21 to divide the r· of Truth,
Hea. 19–25 making our words golden r·
Po. 31–13 Rich r·, rare footprints
My. 208– 6 heavenly r· over all the earth.
252–21 r· from the eternal sunshine of Love,
269–22 sending forth their r· of reality
301– 2 it shines with borrowed r·
344– 4 all his r· collectively stand for
350–24 whose kindling mighty r·

razed
My. 172– 4 * built in 1761, and r· in 1893

reach
Mis. 7–24 r· many homes with healing,
66–16 To r· the summit of Science,
66–26 r· the Science of Mind-healing,
82–10 r· the sure foundations of time,
86–31 r· the glory of supersensible Life ;
98–29 * another's heart wouldst r·."
104–24 How shall we r· our true selves?
143– 8 I r· out my hand to clasp yours,
194–29 r· the consummate naturalness of
218–10 r· the immortality of Mind and
232–16 r· the maximum of perfection
234–11 r· this spiritual sense, and rise
235– 3 no longer . . . die to r· heaven,
275–18 Thy light and Thy love r· earth,
309–15 through which we r· the Christ,
338–23 * Another's soul wouldst r· ;
358–18 r· the heaven-crowned summit
Ret. 24–14 neither medicine nor . . . could r·,
57–29 such methods can never r· the
92– 8 r· the fruition of his promise :
Un. 2–28 Those who r· this transition,
20–15 r· that perfect Love which

reach

Un.	41– 3	In order to r˙ the true knowledge
	49–12	I r˙, in thought, a glorified
	59–15	r˙ and teach mankind only through
	62–10	only as they r˙ the Life of good,
Pul.	3–28	to r˙ out for a present realization
	15–19	human hatred cannot r˙ you.
No.	35– 6	r˙ the understanding of this
'02.	16–25	r˙ not the heart nor renovate it ;
Hea.	8–21	we shall learn to r˙ heaven
	14–23	student to r˙ the ability to teach ;
	15–21	cannot r˙, but medicine can?
	18–19	or claimed to r˙ that woe ;
Po.	v–23	* requests continued to r˙ the author
	2– 9	can never r˙ to thee
My.	13–25	r˙ the stars with divine overtures,
	46–27	* r˙ "unto the city of — *Heb.* 12 : 22.
	159–17	whereby we r˙ our higher nature.
	189– 3	r˙ the mount of revelation ;
	231–15	letters from . . . do not r˙ her.
	254– 6	you must r˙ its meridian.
	300–17	to r˙ the summit of Jesus' words,

reached

Mis.	41–16	that otherwise could not be r˙,
	81–21	has not Truth yet r˙ the shore?
Ret.	16– 4	two ladies . . . r˙ the platform.
	21– 6	he had r˙ the age of thirty-four,
	37–10	it had r˙ sixty-two editions.
	54–13	not having r˙ its Science.
Un.	3–12	Thus they have r˙ the goal
Pul.	12–19	ever before r˙ high heaven,
'01.	26–15	when land is r˙ and the world
Hea.	11–21	When you have r˙ this high goal
	13– 8	r˙ soonest by the higher
Po.	vii 2	* r˙ its fulness in her later
My.	47– 7	* church has r˙ its present growth,
	52 25	* has r˙ her bottom dollar,
	53– 7	* r˙ its four hundredth edition,
	67–24	* never was a more artistic effect r˙.
	76–13	* A similar decision was r˙
	96–14	* r˙ only through intelligent and
	114– 7	r˙ the maximum of these teachings?
	126–16	have r˙ unto heaven, — *Rev.* 18 : 5.
	146–15	altitude . . . has not yet been r˙.
	152–10	human race has not yet r˙ the
	238–18	whereby the Science is r˙
	311–31	* r˙ long division in arithmetic,"
	346–10	* Soon after I r˙ Concord

reaches

Mis.	39–26	by which God r˙ others to heal
	67– 1	until its altitude r˙ beyond
	156– 3	it r˙ a vast number of earnest
	202– 1	r˙ the basis of all supposed
	220–10	that mind r˙ its own ideal,
	320–12	r˙ forth for the infant idea of
	324–29	at length r˙ the pleasant path
	348–10	and those whom it r˙.
Un.	57–19	the ladder which r˙ heaven.
No.	30– 8	God's law r˙ and destroys evil
Hea.	8–13	but when it r˙ the thought that
My.	68–11	* r˙ an altitude twenty-nine feet
	189– 5	that it r˙ high heaven
	194–10	builds that which r˙ heaven.
	290–12	My soul r˙ out to God

reaching

Mis.	30– 6	or despair of ultimately r˙ them,
	63–24	r˙ toward a higher goal,
	63–27	r˙ humanity through the crucifixion
	154– 4	fast r˙ out their broad shelter
	232– 6	This age is r˙ out towards
	328–29	r˙ forth unto those — *Phil* 3 : 13.
Man.	62–14	after r˙ the age of twenty.
Ret.	28–26	r˙ higher than the stars of heaven.
	69– 2	conditions prior to r˙ intelligence.
'00.	6– 6	r˙ forth to those — *see Phil.* 3 : 13.
My.	127– 1	r˙ outward and upward to Science
	147–17	r˙ the physical, moral, and
	208–26	r˙ the very acme of C. S.
	248–15	r˙ deep down into the universal
	265–30	r˙ out to all classes and peoples.
	291– 8	r˙ from the infinitesimal
	343– 4	* r˙ an answer often unexpectedly

react

Mis.	263– 4	not yours, to r˙ on yourselves.

reaction

Mis.	224–16	action and r˙ upon each other
	236– 2	human passions in their r˙

read

Mis.	vii– 2	* r˙ it well ; that is, to understand.
	24–12	As I r˙, the healing Truth dawned
	35–20	Why do we r˙ the Bible, and then
	35–22	Why do we r˙ moral science,
	45–28	In John i. 3 we r˙,
	58–10	she has r˙ and studied correctly,

read

Mis.	58–12	She had to use her eyes to r˙.
	58–13	I r˙ the inspired page through
	58–16	I may r˙ the Scriptures through a
	61–11	* In the October *Journal* I r˙
	69–10	In Genesis i. 26, we r˙ :
	91–27	r˙ from the book as authority for
	106– 5	it would r˙ thus :
	132–26	I r˙ in your article these words :
	133– 7	I request you to r˙ my sermons
	135–24	Letter r˙ at the meeting of
	140–27	* when we can "r˙ our title clear"
	155–17	not the time even to r˙ all of
	156–16	r˙ "Retrospection" on this subject.
	159– 5	r˙ this letter to your church,
	169–20	it is necessary rightly to r˙.
	170– 9	having rightly r˙ His Word,
	271–11	write for it, and r˙ it.
	294–25	I have r˙ the daily paper,
	299–13	* r˙ them for our public services?"
	301–13	r˙ copies of my works in the pulpit
	301–20	r˙ them for our public services?"
	301–22	r˙ it publicly *without my consent*.
	314–12	shall r˙ the Scriptures indicated
	314–15	First Reader shall r˙ from my book,
	314–18	r˙ all the selections from S. and H.
	315– 3	r˙ after the manner of the Sunday
	315– 7	and r˙ from manuscripts,
	373 24	In Genesis we r˙ that God gave
	379– 5	I r˙ the copy in his presence,
Man.	29–22	one to r˙ the Bible,
	29–22	one to r˙ S. and H.
	31–20	The First Readers shall r˙,
	32– 2	r˙ the correlative texts in S. and H.
	32– 5	Second Readers shall r˙ the Bible texts.
	32– 8	Readers shall not r˙ from copies or
	32–12	before commencing to r˙ from
	32–19	They shall r˙ understandingly
	32–22	shall r˙ all notices and remarks
	40–16	To be R˙ in Church.
	40–17	above Church Rule shall be r˙
	40–21	Church Tenets are to be r˙.
	45–21	not entitled to hold office or r˙ in
	61–15	the Tenets . . . are to be r˙.
	63– 8	Lessons, r˙ in Church services.
	66–19	inquire if . . . letter has been r˙,
	66–20	require all of it to be r˙ ;
	90–22	shall be r˙ to the class,
	98–12	shall r˙ the *last proof sheet*
Ret.	6–18	he r˙ law at Hillsborough,
	9– 8	That night, . . . my mother r˙ to me
	21– 1	letter was r˙ to my little son,
	27– 6	never been r˙ by any one but myself,
	37 8	original, but it will never be r˙."
	78–11	not to r˙ so-called scientific
Un.	3– 8	second death, of which we r˙
	21– 1	we r˙ the apostle's description of
	28– 1	We r˙ in the Hebrew Scriptures,
Pul.	5– 4	r˙ by Judge S. J. Hanna,
	6–14	* I had not r˙ three pages before
	12– 2	were r˙ from the platform.
	29–16	* were finely r˙ by Judge Hanna.
	43–18	* r˙ by Judge Hanna and Dr. Eddy.
	43–24	* sermon . . . was then r˙ by Mrs. Bemis.
	43–29	* Mrs. Bemis r˙ the following letter
	45– 8	* R˙ the following,
	45–29	* passages r˙ from the two books by
	57– 8	* was r˙ by Mrs. Bemis.
	59–15	* r˙ from the book of Revelation
	59–18	* r˙ by a professional elocutionist,
Rud.	13–14	In Deuteronomy (iv. 35) we r˙ :
	13–16	In John (iv. 24) we may r˙ :
No.	1–17	r˙ more clearly the tablets of Truth.
'01.	11–17	r˙ each Sunday without comment
	18–23	should r˙ this Scripture :
	24–21	I had not r˙ one line of Berkeley's
	26–26	I have r˙ little of their writings.
'02.	3 17	learning to r˙ and write.
Po.	vi–11	* r˙ as follows :
My.	15– 4	* has been amended to r˙ as follows :
	17–28	* following extracts . . . were r˙ :
	27–21	Scientists will r˙ with much joy
	34–17	* r˙ by Mr. McCrackan and Mrs. Conant :
	35–28	* r˙ to the congregation the
	36– 3	* telegram . . . to Mrs. Eddy was r˙
	37–27	* We have r˙ your annual Message
	39– 4	* r˙ from the Bible and S. and H.
	39–13	* list of officers . . . was r˙ by
	44–16	* r˙ the following despatch,
	49–22	* minutes . . . were r˙ and approved.
	59–28	* I r˙ it in manuscript
	79– 8	* to r˙ the account of the dedication
	114–17	r˙ no other book but the Bible
	126– 9	a book open (ready to be r˙),
	134–23	* r˙ the following letter from
	134–27	* to r˙ you a letter from her

read

My.	149–20	deeply *r·* in scholastic theology
	150– 7	* writing what deserves to be *r·* ;
	162–16	We *r·* in Holy Writ :
	172–26	* note from Mrs. Eddy was *r·* :
	205– 1	We *r·* in the Scriptures :
	222– 2	we *r·* that even the disciples of Jesus
	223– 4	I neither . . . *r·* letters, nor
	223– 8	not *r·* by me or by my secretaries.
	230–18	I *r·* with pleasure your approval
	232–21	*r·* on page 252, "A knowledge of
	236–24	universally to *r·* the paragraph
	238– 2	*Bible, if r· and practised,*
	238– 7	Rightly to *r·* and to practise the
	238–19	When the Bible is thus *r·*
	271–23	* will be *r·* with deep interest
	284–15	it *r·*, "It is said to be the first
	289–26	*r·* on that tender occasion.
	297–27	*r·* or to note from others' reading
	297–30	have *r·* Sibyl Wilbur's book,
	307– 1	certainly *r·* like words that I
	310–31	* "*R·* it, for it will do you good.
	322– 9	* have just *r·* your statement
	327–24	* The section formerly *r·*,
	327–24	* changed to *r·* as follows :
	339–17	*r·* in Holy Writ that the disciples
	351–23	have not *r·* Gerhardt C. Mars' book,
	353– 2	*r·* our daily newspaper.
	358–13	however much I desire to *r·*
	359–11	can be *r·* by the individual

Reader (*see also* Reader's)

Mis.	314–21	The *R·* of the Scriptures
	314–22	The *R·* of "S. and H.
Man.	30– 5	If a *R·* in The Mother Church
	33– 4	the church in which he is *R·*.
	33– 5	A *R·* not a Leader.
	33– 6	Church *R·* shall not be a Leader,
	33– 8	A *R·* shall not be a President of
	55– 1	a *R·*, shall not report nor send
	55–12	not to be fit for the work of a *R·*
	95–21	No lecture shall be given by a *R·*
	95–22	The duties alone of a *R·* are ample.

(*see also* **First Reader, Second Reader**)

reader

Mis.	xi–11	May this volume be to the *r·*
	16–27	dear *r·*, pause for a moment
	30–26	Take courage, dear *r·*,
	46–11	A *r·* of my writings would not
	239– 1	let me say to you, dear *r·* :
	328– 6	Dear *r·*, dost thou suspect
Ret.	21–13	It is well to know, dear *r·*,
	37–24	may have an interest for the *r·*,
My.	111– 2	the *r·* would not have sought.
	218–18	confuse the mind of the *r·*,
	225– 9	the *r·* who does not comprehend
	274–10	Dear *r·*, right thinking,
	308–31	my father was a great *r·*.
	317–15	seem ambiguous to the *r·*.

Reader's

My.	81–10	* the first to catch the *R·* eye.

Readers (*see also* Readers')

Mis.	314– 4	conducted by *R·* in lieu of pastors.
	314– 6	shall elect two *R·* :
Man.	25– 7	Clerk, a Treasurer, and two *R·*.
	26–12	*R·*.
	26–12	Every third year *R·* shall be elected
	26–18	shall fix the salaries of the *R·*
	29–19	*r·* OF THE MOTHER CHURCH.
	29–20	The *R·* for The Mother Church
	30– 2	Directors shall select intelligible *R·*
	31– 2	DUTIES OF *r·* OF THE MOTHER CHURCH
	31– 4	The *R·* of The Mother Church
	32– 7	*R·* shall not read from copies or
	32–11	The *R·* of S. AND H.
	32–17	*R·* in Branch Churches.
	32–18	These *R·* shall be members of
	32–24	*R·* in all the branch churches.
	45–17	whose *R·* are not Christian Scientists
	95–20	No Lectures by *R·*.
	98–24	*R·* of the three largest branch
	99– 7	through the *R·* of its three largest
	100– 5	*R·* shall appoint said candidate.
Pul.	45–29	* read from the two books by *R·*,
My.	71–26	* see and hear the two *R·*
	71–30	* each of whom could see the *R·*,
	243–10	The *R·* of The Church of Christ,
	249–21	chapter sub-title
	250– 3	three years' term for church *R·*,
	250– 8	their *R·* will retire *ex officio,*
	250–10	acceptable service as church *R·*,
	250–17	three years as the term for its *R·*,
	250–28	*R·* who have filled this sacred office
	362–13	* The Trustees and *R·* of

readers

Mis.	xii– 7	lift my *r·* above the smoke of
	35–16	*teach its r· to heal the sick.*
	62–26	amusing to astute *r·*,
	156– 3	vast number of earnest *r·*,
	262– 1	Dear *r·*, our *Journal* is designed to
	308–13	but those are a minority of its *r·*,
	313– 8	May the . . . rest on the dear *r·*,
	378–20	*r·* of my books cannot fail to see
'00.	1–24	number of the *r·* of my books
My.	11–23	* Our *r·* have been informed of the
	25– 2	* it is suggested to our *r·* that
	112–15	its *r·* — honest, intelligent, and
	272–21	* presents this month to its *r·*
	272–29	our *r·* will be interested in this
	273– 2	* to put before its *r·*.
	329–25	* to give your *r·* the following

Readers'

My.	31–25	* Mrs. Hunt, was on the *R·* platform.
	68–17	* The *R·* platform is of a beautiful
	68–21	* placed back of the *R·* platform
	68–22	* above the *R·* special rooms.

Readership

Man.	30–14	shall occupy, during his term of *R·*,
	95–22	during his term of *R·*.

readily

Mis.	52–24	failing to demonstrate one rule *r·*,
	53–22	*so that all can r· understand it?*
	53–26	*r·* understood by the children ;
	92–11	enlightens other minds most *r·*,
	130– 4	She *r·* leaves the answer to
	297– 2	one *r·* sees that this Science has
Ret.	84– 8	enlightens other minds most *r·*,
	87– 8	more thoroughly and *r·* acquired by
'00.	6–16	accepts C. S. more *r·* than the
Hea.	13–24	You can *r·* perceive this
My.	75– 6	* chapter sub-title
	90–16	* can be *r·* grasped by sick or well.
	90–29	* can be *r·* apprehended.
	217–22	we can meet this negation more *r·*
	320– 4	* he *r·* consented to assist me,

readiness

My.	11–10	* grow into *r·* for each step,
	65–15	* *r·* and despatch of an ordinary mortal
	83–30	* example of the *r·* of the members

reading (noun)

Mis.	43–14	contemplative *r·* of my books,
	54–13	*r·* of her book, "S. and H.
	88–12	*r·*, writing, extensive travel, and
	169–25	The literal or material *r·* is
	169–26	*r·* of the carnal mind,
	302–27	his hearers received from his *r·*
	314–22	shall name, at each *r·*,
Man.	31– 7	*r·* of the Sunday lesson,
	32– 1	Order of *R·*.
Pul.	28–19	* *r·* is from the two alternately ;
	54–18	* careful *r·* of the accounts of
	58–20	* too much so for comfortable *r·*,
'01.	31–22	daily Bible *r·* and family prayer ;
My.	16–23	* Scripture *r·*, Isaiah 28 : 16, 17,
	17–17	* *r·* of selections from "S. and H.
	32–15	* *R·* from the Scriptures :
	32–21	* *R·* of notices.
	32–22	* *R·* of Tenets
	32–26	* *R·* of annual Message
	32–28	* *R·* the . . . Lesson-Sermon.
	32–29	* *r·* of the Lesson-Sermon,
	33– 2	* *R·* of a despatch from the members
	33– 4	* *R·* of "the scientific statement
	33–13	* responsive *r·* was from Psalms
	48– 9	* With the *r·* of her textbook,
	48–19	* constant daily *r·* of the Bible
	48–27	* every day through its *r·*.
	49– 7	* the *r·* of its membership,
	79– 1	* singing and responsive *r·*,
	80–17	* appropriate *r·* from the Bible,
	297–28	to note from others' *r·* what the

reading (ppr.)

Mis.	35–24	You are benefited by *r·* S. and H.,
	159– 1	*r·* the Scriptures and expounding
	300– 5	*r·* it publicly as your own
	300–11	*R·* in the pulpit from copies of
	302–20	*r·* my works for Sunday service ;
	314– 7	open the meeting by *r·* the hymns,
Man.	58–19	*r·* IN PUBLIC.
	59– 7	*r·* or quoting from the books or
	60– 8	not fatigued . . . by *r·* the Scriptures
	66–14	*R·* and Attesting Letters.
	72– 9	by *r·* the SCRIPTURES and the
Ret.	1– 8	I remember *r·*, in my childhood,
	39– 2	were healed simply by *r·* it,
	83–24	occasionally *r·* aloud from the book
Un.	29–23	by *r· sense* instead of *soul,*
Pul.	60– 7	* *r·* in clear, manly, and intelligent
No.	4– 1	*R·* S. and H. has restored the sick

reading (ppr.)

No.	15– 4	*R·* my books, without prejudice,
'00.	7–13	after *r·* "S. and H.
Hea.	7–17	*r·* the mind of the poor woman
Po.	v–20	* *by r· the poem to them.*
My.	125–16	When *r·* their lectures,
	234– 3	writing or *r·* congratulations?
	234– 4	while *r·* telegrams ;
	238– 6	*r·* the above-named books
	258–31	a child with finger on her lip *r·*
	357–28	*r·* your interesting letter.

reading-matter

Mis.	155–28	obligation to furnish some *r·*

Reading Room

Man.	63–16	church . . . shall have a *R· R·*,
My.	236– 6	name for one central *R· R·*,
	236–10	for your name, C. S. *R· R·*.

reading-room

My.	123–11	*r·* and nine other rooms
	242–18	publication committee work, *r·* work,

Reading Rooms

Man.	63–12	heading
	63–17	may unite in having *R· R·*,
	63–20	take charge of the *R· R·*
	64– 3	Literature in *R· R·*.
	64– 4	exhibited in the *R· R·*
	74–13	in the *R· R·*, nor in rooms connected

readings

Man.	32– 5	*r·* from the Scriptures shall
	32– 6	precede the *r·* from S. and H.

reads

Mis.	ix– 2	*r·* thus : "The noblest charity is
	191–13	it *r·* : "Master, we saw one— *Mark* 9 : 38.
Pul.	77– 8	* The inscription *r·* thus :
'02.	12–19	Scripture *r·* : "For in Him— *Acts* 17 : 28.
My.	4– 7	Scripture *r·* : "He that— *Matt.* 10 : 38.
	49–21	* record of this meeting *r·* :
	51–27	* interesting record . . . which *r·*,
	54–22	* A record of this period *r·*,
	118–16	Scripture *r·*: "Blessed are they— *John* 20 : 29.
	170–19	my sacred motto, and it *r·* thus :
	267– 6	Scripture *r·* : "All things— *John* 1 : 3.

ready

Mis.	41–11	*r·* for victory in the ennobling
	44– 4	*r·* to investigate this subject,
	99–16	*r·* to suffer for a righteous cause,
	152–19	made *r·* for the pure in affection,
	162–14	*r·* to stem the tide of Judaism,
	165–26	*r·* to avail himself of the rich
	166–13	has evolved a more *r·* ear
	222–12	In this state . . . one is *r·* to
	253–17	dragon that stood *r·* to devour the
	280–32	just at the moment when you are *r·*
	294–14	a hived bee, with sting *r·*
	296–17	with his *r·* pen and pathos?
	308–12	*r·* for "Christ and Christmas ;"
	311 7	*r·* for the table of our Lord :
	311–11	not quite *r·* to take this advanced
	313–20	the storehouse is *r·* :
	316–15	they are not *r·* for the word
	323–13	wolves . . . are *r·* to devour ;
	325–28	sees robbers finding *r·* ingress to
	342–31	are *r·* for the next move.
	357–29	we should be *r·* and glad to help
Man.	85– 9	not *r·* to lead his pupils.
	86–13	*r·* for this high calling,
Ret.	14–11	I was *r·* for his doleful questions,
Un.	2–14	is *r·* to testify of God
	2–25	*r·* for a spiritual transfiguration,
	3– 3	not *r·* to understand immortality.
	6–16	the world is far from *r·* to
Pul.	14–23	Those *r·* for the blessing you impart
	60–18	* was not *r·* for the opening.
	72–10	* *r·* to converse,
	80– 2	* under stress of storm it is *r·* to
'00.	9– 7	therefore, not *r·* — to obey.
	12–30	*r·* to destroy the unity
'02.	17– 6	*r·* to seek and obey what they love.
	18–13	faithful to rebuke, *r·* to forgive.
	20–16	are you *r·* to join me in this
Hea.	10– 2	wroth with the woman, and stood *r·*
	10– 4	*r·* to devour the idea of Truth.
My.	11–15	* She knew that we were *r·* ;
	24– 3	* *r·* to heal all who accept its
	26–15	My Message for June 10 is *r·*
	48– 5	* one *r·* to receive the inspiration,
	55–27	* The Mother Church edifice was *r·*
	61–17	* this house will be *r·*
	62–28	* ever *r·* to assist us in every way
	81–12	* *r·* to receive testimony,
	105–13	*r·* for their amputation.
	126– 9	book open (*r·* to be read),
	156–17	there make *r·*."— *Luke* 22 : 12.
	156–20	*r·* to partake of the bread

ready

My.	180–25	not *r·* to be uplifted, rebels,
	197–13	great hearts and *r·* hands of our
	203–21	if it is *r·* for the blessing.
	241– 6	* Students who are *r·* for this step
	244– 9	any or all of you who are *r·* for it,
	338–23	his comparisons and *r·* humor.

real

affection

Mis.	91–16	a *r·* affection for Jesus' character

all is

Un.	26–24	All is *r·*, all is serious.
	38– 9	all is *r·* which proceeds from Life

All that is

Mis.	125–20	All that is *r·* is divine,

and eternal

Mis.	14–17	to him evil is as *r·* and eternal as
	21–19	Spirit is the *r·* and eternal ;
	42–23	the latter is *r·* and eternal.
	113– 6	all that is *r·* and eternal,
	164–32	of all that is *r·* and eternal.
Ret.	69–10	as *r·* and eternal as Truth.
Un.	37–21	individuality is *r·* and eternal.
Pan.	12–25	is all that is *r·* and eternal.
My.	239–22	of all that is *r·* and eternal.

and normal

'00.	4– 3	makes . . . as *r·* and normal as

and the unreal

Mis.	49–20	discern between the *r·* and the unreal.
	119–24	the *r·* and the unreal Scientist.

appear

Un.	49–18	One should appear *r·* to us,

appears

No.	6–24	appears *r·*, to material sense

as good

Mis.	49–22	belief . . . that evil is as *r·* as good,
	108–20	wherein evil seems as *r·* as good,
No.	17–26	Then evil would be as *r·* as good,
	24–13	By the same token, . . . as *r·* as good,

as health

No.	5–18	If disease is as *r·* as health,
	17–26	would be . . . as *r·* as health,

as Life

Un.	59–23	illusion that death is as *r·* as Life.
No.	17–27	Then evil would be . . . as *r·* as Life ;

as Mind

Mis.	379–13	not as *r·* as Mind,

as Spirit

Ret.	60–10	as *r·* as Spirit and good.

atonement

No.	34–19	*r·* atonement — so infinitely beyond

being

Mis.	46– 5	good being *r·*, evil, . . . is unreal.
	60– 1	Principle, of all *r·* being ,
	340–20	good being *r·*, its opposite is
No.	26–13	All *r·* being represents God,

blood

No.	34–22	The *r·* blood or Life of Spirit

Christ

No.	36–12	*r·* Christ was unconscious of

Christian compact

Mis.	91–10	*r·* Christian compact is love for

Christian Scientist

Mis.	206–19	The *r·* Christian Scientist is
	294– 6	*r·* Christian Scientist is a marvel,
My.	122–24	*r·* Christian Scientist can say
	122–27	the *r·* Christian Scientist is

condition

No.	5–23	a normal and *r·* condition

consciousness

Rud.	5–18	Soul is the only *r·* consciousness

earth

Mis.	30– 9	He saw the *r·* earth and heaven.

ego

No.	26–17	Man's *r·* ego, or selfhood,

equivalent

Ret.	50–13	any *r·* equivalent for my instruction

estate

My.	41–24	* his *r·* estate is one of blessedness.

everything is as

Un.	8– 5	Everything is as *r·* as you make it,

existence

Mis.	30–14	understanding of man's *r·* existence,
Ret.	21–14	not of man's *r·* existence,
	25–23	many witnesses to . . . the *r·* existence of
Un.	42– 7	can have no *r·* existence,

facts

No.	31–10	never actual persons or *r·* facts.

fruits

Mis.	265–20	never . . . the *r·* fruits of Truth.

gratitude

My.	352–10	* we know that the *r·* gratitude

great and

No.	32–18	Good is great and *r·*.

harmony

Mis.	312–17	* to declare the *r·* harmony

real

harmony is
Un.   60–10   harmony is *r·*, . . . yet we descant upon
harmony is the
Rud.   13–19   To aver that harmony is the *r·*
house
Pul.   2–22   The *r·* house in which
identity
Mis.   60–24   *between them and r· identity,*
intelligence
'00.   8–10   wicked man has little *r·* intelligence;
joy
Ret.   18–15   of *r·* joy and of visions divine;
Po.   64– 6   of *r·* joy and of visions divine;
joy is
'02.   17–16   wherein joy is *r·* and fadeless.
knowledge
Un.   13–15   If God has any *r·* knowledge of sin,
        16– 5   a *r·* knowledge of sin?
life
Mis. 105–13   Man's *r·* life or existence
Life is
Un.   38– 9   Life is *r·*; and all is real which
man
        (*see* **man**)
mode
Mis. 362– 6   and reflects all *r·* mode,
more
Mis. 284–25   or that becomes more *r·* when
        284–26   Evil let alone grows more *r·*,
Un.   64–11   the more *r·* those mind-pictures
Pul.   11– 3   making melody more *r·*,
No.   24–13   but much more *r·*,
nature
Mis.   88–22   * highest type of *r·* nature;
        218–18   unfolds the *r·* nature of God
nor eternal
Mis. 286–24   and neither *r·* nor eternal.
personality
Mis.   97–31   *r·* personality of man.
position
My.   92– 2   * have determined its *r·* position
potency
'02.   3–27   right is the only *r·* potency;
proof
My.   119–22   gave the *r·* proof of his Saviour,
quality
Ret.   76–25   of every one in his *r·* quality,
realm of the
Mis. 174–17   the realm of the *r·*.
        331–27   reigns in the realm of the *r·*,
relative
Mis. 151–14   He is man's only *r·* relative
right or
'01.   14–19   as either right or *r·*
satisfaction
Pul.   47–13   * without receiving any *r·* satisfaction.
Scientist
Mis. 117–10   where to look for the *r·* Scientist,
self
Un.   55– 4   In his *r·* self he bore no infirmities.
sensation
Mis.   72–26   *R·* sensation is not material;
sense
Un.   41– 5   sin shuts out the *r·* sense of
sensible and
No.   6–18   is as sensible and *r·* as the
sentiments
My.   175–30   the very opposite of my *r·* sentiments.
set-to
Mis. 231–22   instead of a *r·* set-to at crying,
something
Mis. 108–23   conception of . . . as something *r·*,
spiritually
Ret.   68–11   concept or idea is spiritually *r·*.
stepping-stone
Un.   37– 8   not the *r·* stepping-stone to Life
substance
Un.   34–26   Immortal Mind is the *r·* substance,
suffering
Mis. 288–24   *r·* suffering would stop the farce.
this faith is
My.   90– 8   * Whatever else it is, this faith is *r·*
true or
Mis. 346–14   and is not more true or *r·* than
Truth is the
Hea. 10–14   Truth is the *r·*;
        18–11   Truth is the *r·*;
unreal and the
Mis.   86–14   of the unreal and the *r·*.
value
Mis. 365–22   shows the *r·* value of C. S.
No.   19– 5   shows its *r·* value to the race.
very
Un.   11–17   looks very *r·* and feels very *r·*;"
My.   90– 8   * and is given very *r·* tests.

real

whatever is
'00.   4–24   whatever is *r·* must proceed from God,
world
Pul.   80–27   * invisible is the only *r·* world,
worship
My.   262–25   in mimicry of the *r·* worship
wrongs
Mis.   13– 6   *r·* wrongs (if wrong can be real)
_____

Mis.   10–31   belief . . . that evil is *r·*;
        13– 7   (if wrong can be *r·*)
        49–16   *is not our capacity . . . r·;*
        50– 4   it cannot be *r·*.
        71–30   Whatever is *r·* is right
        72–18   *Are material things r· when they*
        125– 6   all that is *r·* is *right.*
        177–15   *r·* and consecrated warriors?
        188–25   through a spiritual sense of the *r·*,
        267–25   is no *r·* aid to being.
        284–22   neither an evil claim nor . . . is *r·*,
        341– 5   superstructure that is *r·*, right,
Ret.   23– 3   could be a *r·* and abiding rest.
        25–16   The *r·* I claimed as eternal;
        28–18   reduce all things *r·* to their own
        60–14   good is all that is *r·*.
Un.   8– 4   *Is anything r· of which the physical*
         8–10   not absolute, and therefore not *r·*,
        46–15   *r·* to him only as spiritual
        49–21   the unreal masquerades as the *r·*,
        59–21   illusion which calls sin *r·*,
        59–22   illusion which calls sickness *r·*,
        60– 7   talk of sin and sinners as *r·*.
Rud.   6– 6   As Mind they are *r·*,
        11–13   illusions are not *r·*, but unreal.
No.   2–12   healers who admit that disease is *r·*
         5– 8   As Truth alone is *r·*,
         5– 8   to declare error *r·* would be to
         6– 1   If disease is *r·* it is not illusive,
        24–25   never a moment in which evil was *r·*.
        36–18   and the divine as *r·*.
'01.   5–19   *r·* spiritual man and universe.
         5–24   anything that is *r·*, good, or true;
        14–10   enjoys, suffers, or is *r·*.
        14–12   evil cannot be made so *r·* as to
        23– 7   yet that evil exists and is *r·*,
        25–26   been avowed to be as *r·*,
My.   110–19   if waking to bodily sensation is *r·*
        111–30   C. S. is valid, simple, *r·*, and
        119– 2   and to regard evil as *r·*,
        119– 4   divine Principle of that which is *r·*,
        241–28   * not to know as *r·* the beliefs of
        260– 9   Christmas stands for the *r·*,
        296–14   or to destroy the *r·* spiritual man.

real estate

Man.   76–22   *r· e·* owned by this Church
My.   309–18   inherited his father's *r· e·*,

realism

Mis.   xi–17   *R·* will at length be found to
        30–27   seeming mysticism surrounding *r·*
        87– 6   unjust . . . to the divine *r·*.
        374– 2   a proof of Immanuel and the *r·* of
No.   38– 9   only true philosophy and *r·*.
Pan.   11–28   *r·* that man is the true image of God,
My.   5–16   the spiritual idealism and *r·*
        364–11   excludes . . . all sense of the *r·* of

realistic

Mis. 217–17   Sensuous and material *r·* views
        218–14   False *r·* views sap the Science of

realities

forever-existing
Mis. 362– 4   forever-existing *r·* of divine Science;
grand
Peo.   6–21   grand *r·* of Life and Truth
great
Mis.   65–16   solution of Life and its great *r·*.
'01.   1–14   the great *r·* of being,
not as
No.   23–21   not as *r·*, but as illusions;
of being
Mis. 188–27   in the *r·* of being,
Un.   38– 3   the indisputable *r·* of being.
        49–17   not two *r·* of being,
No.   19–21   to understand the *r·* of being,
'01.   1–14   the great *r·* of being,
of God
No.   5–24   tampering with the *r·* of God
of life
Hea.   17–11   they are not the *r·* of life;
of Mind
Mis. 333–28   the grand *r·* of Mind,
No.   6– 3   attempt to destroy the *r·* of Mind
severe
No.   5– 6   one of the severe *r·* of this error.

realities

spiritual
Mis. 53– 2   spiritual r· of existence,
the only
Ret. 63– 2   God and His idea are the only r·,

Mis. 68–10   * are not illusions but r·;
    292–16   look no more into them as r·.
Un. 60–12   yet we descant upon . . . as r·.

reality

admit the
Un. 36–22   yet admit the r· of moral evil,
all
Mis. 90– 4   and you remove all r· from its power.
No. 2– 9   scientific to rob disease of all r·;
My. 164–26   the sum of all r· and good.
and individuality
Un. 53– 8   The r· and individuality of man
and omnipotence
Mis. 61– 9   r· and omnipotence of Truth
and power
Mis. 252– 9   Right thoughts are r· and power;
    364–30   or give r· and power to evil
Pan. 7–22   r· and power, intelligence and
and Soul
Peo. 1– 9   r· and Soul of all things,
and strength
Mis. 252–14   healthy thoughts are r· and strength.
and substance
Un. 49–10   r· and substance of being are good,
any
Un. 54– 7   becomes as tangible as any r·.
any other
'02. 6– 1   forbids the thought of any other r·,
believe in the
Mis. 13–15   to believe in the r· of evil
    63–16   such as believe in the r· of the
My. 300–10   do not believe in the r· of disease,
conscious
No. 36–17   conscious r· and royalty of his
contending for the
Hea. 9–13   Contending for the r· of
deathless
Pul. 5– 8   glow of some deathless r·.
divine
Mis. 345–20   * Christianity must be a divine r·."
Peo. 13–28   * Christianity must be a divine r·."
establishes the
Mis. 73–10   establishes the r· of what is
eternal
Un. 36–12   Spirit is Truth and eternal r·;
    49–11   the eternal r· of existence
existence or
Un. 36–21   To deny the existence or r· of
gleam of
My. 14– 7   discerned . . . as a gleam of r·;
good only is
Un. 21– 9   good only is r·.
grand
Mis. 5–24   grand r· that Mind controls
great
Mis. 14–32   he makes a great r· of evil,
    63–17   the great r· that concerns man,
    363– 2   the great r· of divine Mind
hope's
Pul. 10–14   the wish to reign in hope's r·
impossible in
My. 178–17   But this is impossible in r·,
intelligent
Un. 42– 8   a divine and intelligent — r·.
its
No. 2–10   cannot begin by admitting its r·.
lifted on
'02. 17–14   the curtain . . . should be lifted on r·,
living
Mis. 376–11   * handed down from the living r·.
misconception of
No. 5–26   jewel in this misconception of r·.
no
Mis. 63–12   If there is no r· in sickness,
Un. 59– 1   If there is no r· in evil,
    64– 3   but there is no r· in sin,
Pan. 9– 4   no r· in aught else.
'00. 5– 6   It gives evil no origin, no r·.
'01. 12–25   chapter sub-title
    14– 2   To assume there is no r· in sin,
My. 334–20   "To assume there is no r· in sin,
no other
Un. 8– 7   can have no other r· than the
of being
Mis. 367–11   r· of being — goodness and harmony
Un. 38–27   r· of being, whose Principle is God.
    51– 5   r· of being is neither seen, felt,
No. 16–25   Spirit, which is the r· of being.

reality

of God
Un. 34–25   r· of God and the universe
My. 248–17   to the r· of God, man, nature,
of his being
Mis. 181– 4   r· of his being, in divine Science
of Life
Mis. 117– 2   A progressive life is the r· of Life
Un. 43– 5   the infinite r· of Life,
of living
My. 139– 5   keenly alive to the r· of living,
of man
Mis. 187– 7   health and harmony, . . . the r· of man;
Un. 46– 7   individuality and r· of man;
of Mind
No. 10–23   r· of Mind in the Science of being;
of music
Mis. 187–10   chord is manifestly the r· of music,
of sin
Ret. 63– 8   pleasure of sin, alias the r· of sin,
of that Mind
Un. 38– 7   r· of that Mind which is Life.
of things
'01. 1–19   portion of the primal r· of things.
    20– 9   and with the r· of things.
of Truth
No. 4–14   Science demonstrates the r· of Truth
    5– 4   the r· of Truth has an antipode,
one side to
Hea. 10–11   there is but one side to r·,
page of
Mis. 294– 9   transcribes on the page of r·
power and
No. 21–19   supposed power and r· of evil
radiant
Mis. 251–14   radiant r· of Christianity,
rays of
My. 269–22   sending forth their rays of r·
realm of
Mis. 30–30   spirituality, the realm of r·;
sole
Mis. 24–17   Life being the sole r· of existence.
spiritual
Mis. 60–29   hints the existence of spiritual r·;
    87– 9   spiritual r· and substance of form,
stubborn
No. 2– 6   a God-bestowed and stubborn r·,
    4–11   never made sickness a stubborn r·.
    5–21   becomes indeed a stubborn r·,
substance and
My. 109– 2   no more substance and r· in
such
My. 260– 6   flesh would flee before such r·,
tangible
My. 98–10   * magnificent church, . . . is a tangible r·,
their
Mis. 68–14   penalty for believing in their r·
Ret. 62– 6   better . . . than a belief in their r·
Hea. 5–14   * and not the doubt of their r·."
true sense of
Mis. 28–13   turn . . . to the true sense of r·,
within
Un. 28– 3   Is it a r· within the mortal body?

Mis. 10–29   (that, not in r),
    18–25   Only by admitting evil as a r·,
    37– 2   if there were in r· another mind
    37–28   in r· the least difficult of the
    46– 1   The admission of the r· of
    73– 1   no evidence of the r· of matter,
    93–12   is in r· none besides the eternal,
    93–23   since there is in r· no disease.
    155– 1   in r· there is but one cause
    170–11   This is the r· behind the symbol.
    319–12   protest against the r· of sin,
    346–16   mortal admission of the r· of
Ret. 25–18   Spirit I called the r·;
    63– 6   there is in r· no evil,
    63–10   belief of the sick in the r· of
    68–23   "In r· there is no mortal mind,
Un. 3– 2   still believe in matter's r·,
    10– 3   r· of these so-called existences
    33–18   in r· neither matter nor mortal mind,
    50–16   In r· there are no material states
Rud. 16–15   In r· there is, and can be, but one
No. 5– 5   antipode, — the r· of error;
    27– 3   is in r· no claim whatever.
Pan. 5–15   no truth [r·] in him — John 8: 44.
'01. 13–19   conception of sin as . . . a r·,
    22–14   therefore matter cannot be a r·.
    23–26   to deny, . . . the r· of an external
Hea. 10–19   and your waking the r·
    18–10   There is in r· but the good:
My. 70–25   * In r· it is a combination of six
    110–19   And what of r·, if waking
    276–24   I have none, in r·,

reality
My. 297–14 for there is in *r·* no evil,
    305–22 All that I am in *r·*, God has made me.
    351–27 all they need, or can have in *r·*.

realization
Ret. 81–27 A *r·* of the shifting scenes of
Un. 2– 9 *r·* takes away man's fondness for sin
    7–23 of this fact dispels even
    61–24 demonstration and *r·* of this Science !
Pul. 3–29 present *r·* of my hope
My. 64–21 * would prevent the *r·* of ideal
    297–17 and a higher *r·* of heaven.

realize
Mis. 171– 3 Jesus' first effort to *r·* Truth
    237–12 then they are brought to *r·*
    280–15 we must *r·* that Mind is not
Ret. 61– 8 whose existence you do not *r·* ;
Un. 2– 7 *r·* God's presence, power, and
    20–20 as you *r·* the divine infinitude
Pul. 30–22 * to *r·* the possibilities of the
    57–21 * *r·* how extensive is the belief in
My. 10–25 * *r·* that there must be a prosperous
    39–27 * *r·* her presence with us to-day.
    42–23 * I *r·* that only as infinite good
    52–11 * while we *r·* the rapid growth,
    52–16 * *r·* we must use more energy
    83–17 * scarcely *r·* that the Scientists
    230–26 *r·* at last their Master's promise,
    297–22 and *r·* that he never died ;

realized
Mis. 137–11 *r·* that such opportunity
    281–27 *r·* what a responsibility you
Ret. 7–20 * expected no more than they *r·*
Pul. 6–15 * *r·* I had found that for which
My. 5–18 idealism and realism which, when *r·*,
    116– 5 this great fact in C. S. *r·*

realizes
Mis. 278– 5 as it *r·* more the presence
Pul. 81–21 * *r·* that all the harmonies
Rud. 13–22 if the *healer r·* the truth,

really
Mis. 25– 8 neither one *r·* exists,
    27–23 when God is *r·* All.
    27–25 all that *r·* is, — must be spiritual
    30– 1 Do we *r·* understand
    57–29 all that *r·* is, always was
    112– 5 *r·* look the illusions in the face.
    150–30 is all that *r·* is or can be ;
    259–26 evil, is *r·* non-existent,
    267–11 when I saw an opportunity *r·* to help
    345–31 *R·*, Christianity turned men . . . from
    354–20 Principle of all that *r·* exists,
Ret. 9– 5 if she *r·* did hear Mary's name
    91–10 Indeed, this title *r·* indicates
    94– 8 and yet errs, . . . is *r·* evil.
Un. 2–14 true man, *r· saved*, is ready to
    23–19 *Evil* . . . mortal mind and sin *r·* exist !
    24–15 There is no *r·* finite mind,
    27– 4 *r·* have a shade of difference
    33– 3 (matter *r·* having no sense)
    50–12 *r·* there is no such thing as
    62– 1 fact *r·* remains, in divine Science,
Pul. 21–18 *r·* united to only that which is
    51–10 * There is *r·* nothing settled.
    69–15 * *r·* is a return to the ideas of
    85–12 * all things which *r·* exist,
'00. 4–28 reflects all that *r·* is,
My. 8–17 * and I believe *r·*,
    14–20 * If the devil were *r·* an entity,
    59–25 * "Did Mrs. Eddy *r·* write S. and H.?
    99– 2 * great, and *r·* good things
    152–17 divine Principle of all that *r·* is,
    266–20 origin of all that *r·* is,
    267– 6 originator of all that *r·* is.
    287– 9 governing all that *r·* is.
    297– 4 all that Miss Barton *r·* is,
    334–13 * which records show *r·* existed in 1844,
    345– 9 "Not," . . . "if it is *r·* science."

realm
Mis. 30–30 spirituality, the *r·* of reality ;
    34–24 lie within the *r·* of mortal thought
    174–17 abode of Spirit, the *r·* of the real.
    331–27 reigns in the *r·* of the real,
Pul. 10–14 hope's reality — the *r·* of Love.
No. v– 8 laborers in the *r·* of Mind-healing.
    21–17 in the same *r·* and consciousness.
Po. 22–13 Love hath one race, one *r·*,
My. 64– 4 * glories of the *r·* of infinite Mind,

realms
Ret. 73–41 and purer *r·* of thought.
My. 200–13 upward to the *r·* of incorporeal Life

realness
No. 17– 1 false assumption of the *r·* of

reap
Mis. 15– 2 will *r·* what he sows ;
    38–11 *r·* your carnal things?" — *I Cor.* 9 : 11.
    66– 7 that shall he also *r·*." — *Gal.* 6 : 7.
    105–30 that shall he also *r·*." — *Gal.* 6 : 7.
    348– 4 man soweth, that shall he *r·*.
    386–29 Hither to *r·*, with all the crowned
No. 32– 9 that shall he also *r·*." — *Gal.* 6 : 7.
Hea. 5–28 that shall he also *r·*." — *Gal.* 6 : 7.
Po. 50–16 Hither to *r·*, with all the crowned
My. 6– 6 that shall he also *r·*." — *Gal.* 6 : 7.
    19–23 *r·* richly the reward of goodness.
    185– 1 for he that soweth shall *r·*.
    230–24 will *r·* the reward of rightness,
    254–11 *r·* the sure reward of right thinking

reaped
Mis. 80–26 have planted and sown and *r·*

reapers
Mis. 313–19 *r·* are strong, the rich sheaves are
My. 291–24 while her *r·* are strong,

reaping
Un. 12– 4 vineyard of Mind-sowing and *r·* ;
Po. 47–18 Nevermore *r·* the harvest we deem,

reappear
Mis. 28– 2 only to *r·* in the spiritual sense
    308–23 only to *r·* in due season.
    343–21 *r·*, like devastating witch-grass,
Po. 3– 7 With evening, memories *r·*

reappearance
Mis. 324–31 look for the *r·* of the Stranger,

reappeared
Mis. 70–16 Christ Jesus lived and *r·*.
No. 28–18 Has Truth, . . . *r·*?
    28–20 you will know that Truth has *r·*.

reappearing
Mis. 167– 1 *r·* of the infantile thought
    343–23 stupid gardener ! watch their *r·*,
Un. 63– 8 so-called . . . *r·* of ever-presence,
No. 13–10 before this *r·* of Truth,
    46– 7 the *r·* Christ, whose life-giving
My. 279– 8 scientific being *r·* in all ages,

reappears
Peo. 1–18 as the understanding . . . *r·*,

rear
Pul. 59–30 * auditors left by the *r·* doors,
No. 46–10 Woman should not be ordered to the *r·*,

reared
Ret. 2– 1 Mrs. . . . Baker was *r·* among
Pul. 2–30 *r·* on the foundation of Love,
    65–21 * Frankish church was *r·* upon the
No. 46–15 *r·* there the Puritan standard
My. 59–14 * temple, which has been *r·* by you,

rears
Mis. 386–23 *R·* the sad marble to our memory
Ret. 17–15 hickory *r·* his bold form,
Un. 45– 5 *r·* its crest proudly,
Po. 50– 9 *R·* the sad marble to our memory
    62–18 hickory *r·* his bold form,

reascending
Pul. 11– 1 *r·*, bear you outward,

reason (noun)
   and affection
   Mis. 363–23 that misguides *r·* and affection,
   and immortality
   Mis. 218–17 to the rescue of *r·* and immortality,
   and philosophy
   My. 260–13 *r·* and philosophy may pursue
   and revelation
   Mis. 23–18 *R·* and revelation declare that
     27–20 According to *r·* and revelation,
     217– 2 nature, *r·*, and revelation.
   No. 13–24 impulse to *r·* and revelation,
   and will
   Pan. 4– 8 *r·* and will are properly classified
     4–11 But *r·* and will are human ;
   any
   Mis. 5–17 There is no longer any *r·* for
   based upon
   My. 96–13 * It is a faith based upon *r·*,
   better
   Un. 49–20 * "the worse appear the better *r·*,"
   deluding
   Mis. 3–28 apparently deluding *r·*,
     260–21 deluding *r·* and denying revelation,
   depraved
   Mis. 354–10 When depraved *r·* is preferred
   erring
   Mis. 362–24 refute erring *r·* with the
   eyes of
   Mis. 332–20 blinded the eyes of *r·*,

reason (noun)
for his faith
   My. 294–20 r· for his faith in what
for the faith
   Un. 48– 1 a r· for the faith within.
for the hope
   My. 348– 9 to give a r· for the hope
given as a
   '01. 15–30 * to be given as a r· why you
human
   (see **human***)*
laws of
   Mis. 216–26 * nor the laws of r· hold good,
man's
   Mis. 362– 5 man's r· is at rest in God's
my
   My. 165–21 this is . . . my r· for existing.
no
   Mis. 54–20 there is no r· why you should be
no other
   '01. 15–26 * no other r· to be given
or belief
   Un. 28–21 human reflection, r·, or belief
our
   Po. 9–11 Our r· made right
philosophy nor
   Mis. 217– 4 neither philosophy nor r·
principal
   Rud. 15–12 This was the principal r·
proper
   My. 162–22 proper r· for church edifices
right
   My. 288– 1 starts the wheels of right r·,
sole
   Mis. 200–17 sole r· that it is their basis.
some
   Pul. 50 0 * for some r· not followed,
sufficient
   My. 104–21 sufficient r· for his silence
suffocate
   Hea. 8–18 suffocate r· by materialism.
supporting
   Peo. 2–14 revelation supporting r·.
this
   Mis. 51–10 for this r· cannot answer
       305–15 * For this r· small contributions
to expect
   My. 51– 9 * should have r· to expect,
wheels of
   Mis. 235–22 it must start the wheels of r·
will rescue
   No. 11–26 will rescue r· from the thrall

   Mis. x1–20 It is r· for rejoicing.
      22–30 by r· of its own ponderosity ;
      40–18 r· that the same results follow not
      59–20 let us r· together.'' — *Isa.* 1 : 18.
      93– 1 by r· thereof is able to
     100 16 by r· of its nothingness ;
     183–17 not by r· of the schools,
     195– 8 by r· of the lack of understanding.
     234– 1 only by r· of our belief in it :
     308– 5 by r· of human love or hatred
     312–23 r· too supine or misemployed
   Man. 46–16 by r· of their relation of
   Ret. 84–20 by r· thereof is able to
   Un. 8–19 through r·, revelation, and Science,
   Pul. 1–12 wiser by r· of its large lessons,
   Pan. 4– 3 to the r·, intellect, and will of
      8–27 living by r· of it,
   Peo. 1– 6 of material elements from r·,
   Po. 32–16 As r· with appetite,
   My. 37–16 * By r· of your spiritual achievement
      56–27 * for the r· that there was not
     239– 5 proof, wherein r·, revelation,
     265– 7 more apparent to r· ;
     300–11 for the r· that the divine Principle

reason (verb)
   Mis. 218–12 whence to r· out God,
   Un. 1– 8 Let us then r· together

reasonable
   Mis. 184–11 which is our r· service ;
     200–27 triumph of a r· faith
   My. vii–13 * is a r· service which all
     8–15 * r· accommodation for
    130–32 request, . . . should seem r·.
    334– 2 * It is r· to infer

reasonably
   Man. 46–24 shall r· reduce his price
   Pul. 66–23 * may r· excite wonder

reasoning
   Mis. 185–29 When r· on this subject
   Un. 34–14 Take another train of r·.
     51– 3 R· from false premises.
   No. 20–23 Adam's mistiness and Satan's r·,

reasoning
   My. 349–27 r· is correct only as it
    349–31 inductive r· reckons creation
reasons
   Mis. 188–16 St. Paul first r· upon the basis of
     301–22 My r· are as follows :
   Man. 55–10 For sufficient r· it may be decided
    80–15 for such r· as to the Board may seem
   Un. 18–10 fancy that our . . . Father r· thus :
    43–18 Because of these profound r·
   Pul. 79–16 * believe there are two r· for this
   Hea. 2– 5 while it r· with the storm,
   My. 218– 6 furnishes r· or examples for the
reassert
   My. 40–17 * widely r· its pristine power
reassured
   Mis. 345–19 * r· me that Christianity must be
   Pul. 5–20 his conversation . . . r· me.
   Peo. 13–27 * r· me that Christianity must be
reassures
   No. 44–20 It r· us that no Reign of Terror
reassuring
   My. 293–16 r· the mind and through the mind
rebel
   Mis. 217–24 and man a r· against his Maker.
rebellion
   My. 234–25 more fatal than the Boxers' r·.
rebels
   Mis. 204– 1 agony struggles, pride r·,
   Hea. 11– 7 mortal mind r· at its own boundaries ;
   My. 40–29 * Human sense often r· against law,
    180–25 r·, misconstrues our best motives,
rebound
   My. 252–10 must, will, r· upon you.
rebuild
   My. 195–30 continue to build, r·, adorn,
rebuke
   Mis. 77–25 sternly to r· the mortal belief
    158–16 r· a lack of faith in divine help,
    203–17 baptism serves to r· the senses
    204–21 they r· the material senses,
    209–19 tend to r· appetite
    254– 4 gentle entreaty, the stern r·
    265–30 If impatient of the loving r·,
    277–32 I r· it wherever I see it.
   Ret. 21–18 to r· human consciousness
    26–21 in order to r· the evidence.
    80–12 divine r· is effectual
    88– 1 to r· vainglory,
   Un. 18–20 which alone enable Me to r·,
   No. v 3 "reprove, r·, exhort," — *II Tim.* 4 : 2.
    8–10 to r· each other always in love,
    30 12 to r· any claim of another law.
   Pan. 13–12 r· and exhort one another.
   '00. 11–29 bravely r· lawlessness.
    14–12 r· to all the churches
   '02. 18–13 faithful to r·, ready to forgive.
   Po. 23–14 A stern r· to wrong !
   My. 18–20 r· and exhort one another.
    130–17 reprove, r·, and exhort.
    132 24 Divine Love will also r·
    269–24 r· the devourer — *Mal.* 3 : 11.
    294–11 r· whatever accords not
    294–13 He would mightily r·
    343–29 in exhortation, and in r·,
rebuked
   Mis. 359–19 Peter's impetuosity was r·.
    374–1 whatever r· hypocrisy
   No. 8–11 as I have r· them.
   02. 19– 5 he r· them on the eve of his
   Hea. 2–22 r· their carnality,
   My. 222– 4 Jesus r· them, saying :
    307–18 demurrer which r· him.
rebukes
   Mis. 210–30 r· error, and casts it out.
    272–31 not profited by my r·,
    273– 2 the value of these r·.
   No. 13– 1 This Science r· sin
    18– 3 Blasphemy r· not the
    43– 5 Truth r· error ;
   My. 162–18 the love that r· praises
rebuking
   Mis. 327–24 r· their pride,
   Man. 40– 9 r· sin, in true brotherliness,
recall
   Ret. 14–14 Distinctly do I r· what followed.
   Pul. 7– 7 Yet when I r· the past,
   My. 39–24 * We r· the harmonious tones
    47–15 * and r· memories of trials,
    59– 2 * whom you will r· as a member

recall
My. 319–28 * r· very plainly the conversation
322–31 * The exact words I do not r·,

recalling
Po. 1–16 R· oft the bitter draft
My. v–13 * r· the following historical facts :

recalls
Ret. 5–16 for memory r· qualities

Recapitulation
Mis. 92–13 in the chapter on R·,
Man. 86–18 shall teach from the chapter "R·"
86–24 from the said chapter on "R·"
Ret. 35– 4 chapter on R· in S. and H.
83–19 should explain only R·,
84–10 in the chapter on R·.
Pul. 38–15 "R·." Key to the Scriptures,

recapitulation
Mis. 316–20 What, then, of continual r·

receding
Mis. 206– 5 dashing against the r· shore,
310–26 r· year of religious jubilee,
321– 7 each r· year sees the steady gain of
Po. 27– 5 One word, r· year,

receipt
Mis. 142– 7 Written on r· of a beautiful boat
My. 199–12 acknowledgment of the r· of their
280– 4 * the r· of your message,
295–12 grateful r· of your time-worn Bible
359–25 * Upon r· of this letter Mrs Eddy wrote

receipted
Mis. 350– 2 balance was never r· for.

receipts
Mis. 350– 1 I hold r· for $1,489.50 paid in,
My. 23–12 * total r· June 19, 1902 to June 1, 1905,

receive
Mis. 33– 3 wrong will r· its own reward.
51–30 "Ye ask, and r· not, — Jas. 4 : 3.
81–15 to r· the benediction of
84– 3 r· startling announcements.
88– 3 occasionally r· it from others ;
90–23 r· the communion?
123–26 r· the reward of righteousness :
127–16 a fitness to r· the answer
152–18 then will they r· the heritage
168– 4 spiritually and physically, r· sight ;
168–13 pure in spirit, . . . r· Truth.
182– 7 r· the Truth of existence ;
183–15 we learn this, and r· it :
183–26 r· a knowledge of God
194–26 r· the sense of Life that knows no
265–25 who r· the same instruction,
301– 3 and r· pay therefor,
324–31 r· his heavenly guidance.
342–26 and r· nothing in return ;
342–27 you shall r· all.
344–25 r· the kingdom of God — Luke 18 : 17.
349–26 or to r· my gratuitous services,
357–24 should r· full fellowship from us,
Man. 34–18 This Church will r· a member of
65–26 If the Clerk of this Church shall r·
68–15 r· the degree of the
75–10 declined to r· this munificent gift,
85– 6 teach and r· into his association
89–16 eligible to r· the degree of C.S.D.
90– 5 if found qualified to r· them.
92–16 No person shall r· instructions in
92–18 r· the degree of C.S.B. or C.S.D.,
96–10 If a lecturer r· a call to lecture
97–13 shall r· an annual salary,
101– 6 who shall r· an adequate salary
Ret. 83–10 r· the infinite instructions
87–29 not r· a patient who is under the
Un. 6– 6 man will r· a higher selfhood,
39–16 as many as r· the knowledge of God
40–13 therefore mortals can no more r·
Pul. 31–22 * evening on which she would r· me.
43–28 * which religious teachers so often r·.
44– 8 * to r· this brief message of
52–16 * r· light, health, and strength,
No. 19–17 physical senses r· no spiritual idea,
40– 2 "Ye ask, and r· not, — Jas. 4 : 3.
40– 4 mortals seek, and expect to r·,
'01. 19– 8 "Ask, and ye shall r· ;" — John 16 : 24.
22–26 public r· their sense of the Science,
22–26 r· no sense whatever of it.
'02. 13–10 I r· no personal benefit therefrom
17–10 r· the reward of obedience.
Hea. 8–23 r· only what we have earned.
15–23 "Ye ask, and r· not, — Jas. 4 : 3.
Peo. 9–17 We ask and r· not, because we
My. 18–13 a fitness to r· the answer to its
21–18 * will r· a greater blessing
34– 6 shall r· the blessing — Psal. 24 : 5.

receive
My. 41–10 * so r· judgment without mercy ;
48– 5 * one ready to r· the inspiration,
73–21 * visitors will r· all information
81–12 * ready to r· testimony,
118– 5 any imaginary benefit they r· is
123–22 is less sufficient to r· a church of
126–15 r· not of her plagues. — Rev. 18 : 4.
131–29 enough to r· it." — Mal. 3 : 10.
133–10 will not r· a Message from me
138–15 often ask me to r· persons whom
138–16 decline to r· solely because I
156–22 to r· into their affections and lives
160– 9 of less importance that we r·
163– 9 Not having the time to r· all
165–15 Goodness never fails to r· its
169–17 was happy to r· at Concord,
194–24 but I must decline to r· that
212–20 would r· a spiritual influx
217–13 each contributor will r· his
231–23 to r· more tenants.
241–16 * to r· instruction from their Leader
244– 7 to r· from me one or more lessons
247–21 brings forth mankind to r· your
251–21 r· a certificate of the degree C.S.D.
269–29 enough to r· it." — Mal. 3 : 10.
293–31 believe that ye r· them, — Mark 11 : 24.

received
Mis. x–24 I r· from the Daughters of the
128–12 both learned, and r·, — Phil. 4 : 9.
134–14 such as you never before r·.
137–11 I r· no reply.
139– 6 such as you even yet have not r·.
172–20 r· through the affections,
180–21 But as many as r· him, — John 1 : 12.
181–24 "But as many as r· him, — John 1 : 12.
182– 5 "As many as r· him ;" — John 1 : 12.
185–17 "As many as r· him," — John 1 : 12.
185–25 "as many as r· him, — John 1 : 12.
212–12 they r· the blessing.
298–16 Jesus r· the material life of
299– 4 error, has r· its death-blow ;
302–27 good that his hearers r· from his
306– 6 * will be gratefully r· ;
318–14 r· instructions in a Primary class
349– 1 r· my consent and even the offer of
349– 3 provided he r· these lessons of
349–28 I never r· more than this ;
Man. 38–22 may be r· into this Church
39– 4 r· into full membership,
39–18 not again be r· into this Church.
45–25 r· these titles under the laws
54–16 offender shall not be r· into
62– 9 r· in the Sunday School classes
76–23 amount of funds r· by the Treasurer
110–14 Initials only . . . will not be r·.
111– 4 Initials alone will not be r·.
Ret. 6–30 r· further political preferment,
10– 9 I r· lessons in the ancient tongues,
15– 2 r· me into their communion,
40–14 injury r· from a surgical operation
43–12 who also r· a certificate from
47–19 r· instructions in a Primary class
Un. 23– 1 cruel treatment r· by old Gloster
Pul. 41– 5 * amount needed was r·.
52– 3 * already subscribed can be r· !
76–26 * has r· from the members of
85–24 * Rev. Mary Baker Eddy r· Friday,
88– 4 author has r· leading newspapers
No. 43–13 specimen of those r· daily :
'00. 10–23 I r· a touching token of
'01. 23–25 on r· principles of philosophy,
33–26 the same reviling it r· then
'02. 19– 2 brutality that he r·.
My. 14–11 * we r· a letter from a friend in
16– 5 * total of $425,893.66 had been r·
26–10 Your generous check . . . is duly r·.
26–13 ever r· from my church,
27–14 sufficient funds have been r·
27–24 * sufficient funds have been r·
28– 9 * dollars and cents r· by him,
49–18 * r· at the previous meeting,
57–31 * those already subscribed can be r·.
76– 5 * were constantly being r· ;
76–10 * it was r· with rejoicing by
136–17 highest fee ever r· by a native of
163–24 also r· from the leading people of
172–17 'Freely ye have r·, — Matt. 10 : 8.
182– 4 I r· from the Congregational
184– 3 Have just r· your despatch.
191–30 card of invitation . . . was duly r·.
192–22 Your kind letter, . . . was duly r·.
198– 5 been r· with many thanks to you
207– 4 communication is gratefully r·.
223– 2 no comers are r· . . . without
240–27 * who have r· certificates from

received
My. 242–23 nor to reply to any r·,
245–23 students . . . have r· certificates,
250– 4 has r· profound attention.
259– 6 I r· the following cabled message :
309–27 * r· a liberal education.
312–11 * thus r· a decent burial.
322–18 * r· your permission to
326– 2 * enclosures r· from our Leader.
331– 4 * r· at the hands of
341–24 * r· the *Herald* correspondent.

receivers
Pul. 56– 6 * r· of the faith among the

receives
Mis. 31–13 and r· no aid from,
201– 1 r· the mortal scoff only because it
288–26 r· a strong impulse from the cause of
Ret. 28– 4 While cactus a mellower glory r·
'01. 14–30 evil-doer r· no encouragement from
33–27 same reviling . . . it r· now,
Po. 63–12 While cactus a mellower glory r·
My. 118–19 Soul, not sense, r· and gives it.
200–16 and r· his rights inalienable

receiveth
Mis. 18– 5 every son whom He r· ;" *Heb.* 12 : 6.
Ret. 80– 6 every son whom He r·.— *Heb.* 12 : 6.
'01. 9–28 who loveth . . . r· them most ;

receiving
Mis. 132–20 teaching C. S., r· calls, etc.,
146– 7 on r· or dismissing candidates.
256– 8 letters that protest against r·
256–15 r· but a select number of students.
305–31 * we ask every one r· this circular
392–19 on r· a painting of the Isle
Man. 27– 9 r· the written consent of
85–20 since r· instruction as above,
89– 7 found worthy, on r· her approval
Ret. 33– 9 but without r· satisfaction.
Pul. 41–18 * incapable of r· this vast throng,
47–13 * without r· any real satisfaction.
Rud. 13–26 r· no wages in return,
No. 20–20 asking amiss and r· not,
Po. 51– 1 On r· a painting of the Isle.
My. 163–11 the pleasure of r· any of them.
218–30 r· instruction from me,
231–19 Mrs. Eddy is constantly r·
246– 2 after r· the first degree,

recent
Mis. 48–13 at one of his r· lectures
312–15 * has come in r· years,
Ret. 48– 6 r· experience of the church
Po. v– 4 * *girlhood up to r· years.*
My. 83–29 * made steady gains in r· years.
94–17 * in the r· dedication in Boston
99–30 * r· dedication of a C. S. temple
305–27 My r· reply to the reprint
316–12 R· Reckless . . . Attacks on
346–19 * r· interview which appeared
351– 3 * to publish her letter of r· date,

recently
Mis. 148–23 Until r·, I was not aware
Pul. 52–24 * R· a revived belief in what he
63– 6 * R· BUILT IN HER HONOR
63–10 * remark . . . made r· as she
63–20 * tangible and material manner r·,
70–13 * r· saw completed in Boston,
My. 24–25 * have r· inspected the work,
98–17 * church which was r· dedicated
99–14 * r· built a splendid cathedral
100– 4 * temple r· dedicated
282– 9 Douma r· adopted in Russia
319–19 * which have r· appeared,
321–18 * which have arisen r·,
323–23 * which we have so r· witnessed,

receptacle
Pul. 7–14 now unsealed their r·

reception
Mis. 137– 5 gave you a meagre r·
276– 3 r· in the spacious rooms
307–18 proper r· of C. S.
'01. 32–25 r· of the Science of Christianity.
My. 15–16 for your gracious r· of it
40– 4 * able to give more adequate r·
156–20 prepared for the r· of Truth

receptions
Man. 94– 6 R·.
94– 7 no r· nor festivities

receptive
Mis. 189– 3 as little children, we are r·,
290–29 all who are r· share this
Ret. 80–14 becomes obediently r·

receptivity
Mis. 229–15 governing the r· of the body,

recess
Pul. 60–19 * r· behind the spacious platform,

recesses
Peo. 14– 5 fragrant r·, cool grottos,

Recessional
My. v– 3 * Kipling's R·

rechristen
Pul. 8–20 r· them with his own new name.

reciprocal
Mis. 265–19 whole line of r· thought.

reciprocally
Mis. 207– 3 where heart meets heart r· blest,

reciprocate
Mis. 117–16 r· kindness and work wisely,

recitation
Ret. 83–26 study each lesson before the r·.
Pul. 43–20 * followed by the r· of the Lord's Prayer,

recitations
Mis. 91–31 study the lessons before r·.
92–20 to study it before the r· ;

reckless
My. 316–12 R· and Irresponsible Attacks

recklessly
Pul. 83– 2 * r· promise as lover and candidate

reckon
Mis. 182– 2 to r· himself logically ;
288–21 To r· the universal cost and gain,

reckoned
Mis. 143–22 husband and wife r· as one,
Un. 9– 6 in some way, be r· unreal.
9–13 talent and genius . . . have wrongly r·.
Pan. 3–21 whose laws are not r· as science.
'01. 20–24 The crimes . . . are not easily r·.
'02. 8–26 Christ Jesus r· man in Science,

reckoning
Mis. 227–28 r· its own by the amount of
My. 203–10 All that is worth r· is what we do,

reckons
'01. 6– 6 by theology, which r· three as one
6– 8 C. S., which r· one as one
21–15 critic, who r· hopefully on the death
My. 349–31 r· creation as its own creator,

reclaim
My. 161– 8 necessary to r· the sinner.

reclaimed
My. 36–14 * withheld from open graves or r· from

reclaiming
Mis. 100– 9 Truth r· the sinner

reclaims
My. 113– 9 heals the sick and r· sinners

reclines
Ret. 17–11 vesper r· — when the dewdrop
Po. 62–13 vesper r· — when the dewdrop

recognition
Mis. 1–15 a higher r· of Deity.
18–22 With this r· man could
49–24 a r· of the nothingness of
173–11 no relation to, or r· of, matter?
188–24 The r· of this power
196–26 arise to spiritual r· of being,
207– 5 r· of practical, operative C. S.
214–27 r· or approbation of it.
218–30 * "The r· of teleology
218–31 * the r· of purely spiritual
235– 1 r· of his relation to God.
255–13 r· of what the apostle meant
304–29 * r· of the organization
Man. 74–15 R·.
Ret. 63– 4 establishing the r· that God *is All,*
Pul. 80–11 * most r·, the widest outlook.
No. 1– 5 which comes to our r·
'02. 2– 5 for distinction or r· ;
My. 9– 2 * In r· of the necessity for
45– 1 * r· of and obedience to
130– 9 to keep . . . from public r·
187–28 r· of the riches of His love
188– 8 in r· of His presence ;
297–22 If we would awaken to this r·,
326– 8 * declaration of this r·
327–28 * legal protection and r·,
352– 1 * chapter sub-title
352– 5 * r· of the blessings

recognize
Mis. 18–14 thou shalt r· thyself as
28–24 r· no intelligence nor life in
33–19 as they r· the help they derive
37–11 r· ourselves under the control
42–16 to communicate with and to r·
42–27 r· a better state of existence.

recognize

Mis.	43–28	to r·, as such, the barefaced errors
	60– 2	*God does not r· any,*
	74–11	*If God does not r· matter,*
	74–24	or can r· or express pain
	89–30	if he will . . . r· his Saviour.
	102–15	In His individuality I r·
	113–21	r· that mental malpractice,
	181–13	if we r· infinitude as personality,
	181–18	r· him through spiritual, . . . laws ;
	182–12	r· his perfect and eternal estate.
	197–30	r· God as omnipotent,
	198–16	r· man as governed by God,
	286–27	should r· this verity of being,
	348– 2	They r· the claims of the law
Ret.	79–30	We r· this kingdom,
	80–16	If the Christian Scientist r· the
Pul.	21–24	r· a clear expression of God's
Pan.	13–18	r· the great truth that Spirit is
'01.	30–18	r· that C. S. kindles the
'02.	16–14	r· the divine presence and allness.
My.	8–26	* whom we r· as logically the
	10–24	* r· the importance of The
	37–21	* we also r· that He has made
	85–12	* to r· the fact that this wonderful
	212–21	r· and resist the animal magnetism
	326–20	I r· the divine hand
	338–24	r· the oneness of Jesus

recognized

Mis.	30–14	to be r· here and now.
	37– 8	Jesus r· this relation so clearly
	85– 8	God is r· as the divine Principle
	190– 9	the r· reflection of infinite Life
	197– 7	full import . . . is not yet r·.
	204–20	demands of spiritual sense are r·,
	286–20	r· and understood in Science.
Man.	61–21	r· standard of musical excellence ;
Ret.	71–24	must be r·, and uprooted,
Pul.	25– 2	* cooling is a r· feature as well as
	28–23	* and other r· devotional poets,
	37–13	* r· head of the C. S. Church.
	55–28	* Truth is the sole r· authority.
No.	20–21	God is r· as the only power,
My.	232–25	r· as the true likeness of his Maker''
	259–30	Soul r· only in harmony,
	326– 6	* r· in an official and authoritative

recognizes

Mis.	33–26	r· the fact that, as mortal mind
	255–22	r· the fact that the antidote for
Ret.	34–12	r· the antidote for all sickness,
Un.	7– 9	the infinite r· no disease,
	54–16	sin r· as its most potent . . . enemy.
Pul.	30–19	* r· Jesus as the teacher and guide
My.	108–15	C. S. r· that this Mind is the
	328–12	* the law r· them as healers,

recognizing

Mis.	43– 1	C. S., r· the capabilities of Mind
Peo.	7– 5	R· this as we ought, we shall turn
My.	7–16	* "R· the necessity for providing an
	37–19	* R· the grand truth that God is the
	232– 1	It rejoices me that you are r· the
	329–22	* r· the steady progress of C. S.
	364–15	r· the supremacy and allness of good.

recollect

Ret.	63–23	r· that it encourages sin to say,
My.	309–13	as I r· it, he was justice of the

recollection

Pul.	65–18	* suggests to r· the story of

recollections

Mis.	159–16	where I deposit certain r·
My.	321– 6	* My r· of Mr. Wiggin

recommend

Mis.	25–31	and r· them for that purpose?
	120–20	I r· that this Association
	131–16	I r· that you waive the
	136–22	I r· that the June session
	139– 1	I r· this honorable body
	302–32	I r· that students stay within
	357–24	characters and lives r· them,
Man.	37–17	One Normal student cannot r· the
	92– 7	I r· that each member of this
Ret.	78–11	I r· students not to read so-called
No.	3–15	and r· it to their students,
	7–21	I r· that Scientists draw no
My.	204–19	r· it under the circumstances.
	219–29	I r·, if the law demand,
	224–28	we cannot afford to r·
	237–23	I r· its careful study
	354– 5	to state that I r· nothing but

recommendation

Man.	36–20	present to him a r·
	37–15	r· AND ELECTION.
My.	182– 5	r· to evangelical churches

recommended

Mis.	245– 2	or r· others to use, drugs ;
Ret.	44–23	I r· that the church be dissolved.
'01.	23–19	used no material medicine, nor r· it,
	25–19	He never r· drugs,

recommending

No.	8– 8	r· to all men fellowship
My.	298– 2	r· it to the public.

recommends

Peo.	5– 2	devoutly r· the more spiritual
My.	276–11	r· this surprising privilege to all

recompense

Mis.	12– 6	God will r· this wrong,
	364– 7	what a r· to have healed,
No.	3–24	trust Love's r· of love.
'01.	30–22	hope of ease, pleasure, or r·,
Po.	23–17	Life hath a higher r·
My.	37–32	* r· your long sacrifice
	166–15	Life's ills are its chief r· ;
	190– 2	bring the r· of human woe,
	283–16	Right has its r·,
	308– 8	by ease, pleasure, or r·.

recompensed

Mis.	2–12	subdued and r· by justice,
My.	139–26	and you have been greatly r·.

reconcile

My.	84–22	* cannot r· himself to the methods

reconciled

Mis.	124– 8	will not be r· thereto.
Hea.	18–14	if that idea could be r· with
My.	107– 9	old school has become r·.

reconciles

Mis.	122–22	nor r· justice to injustice ;

reconciliation

No.	35–22	needs no r· with God,

reconciling

My.	314–25	the means of r· the couple.

reconstruct

No.	43–24	will never prevent or r·

reconstructed

Ret.	28–22	I had learned that Mind r· the body,
Pul.	20–10	I r· my original system of ministry
	35–21	learned that Mind r· the body,

reconstructs

Mis.	82– 1	r· the Judean religion,

record

Bible

My.	219–19	Bible r· of our great Master's life

Biblical

Mis.	120–27	Biblical r· of the great Nazarene,

court

My.	314–14	the court r· may state that my divorce

dark

Po.	26–15	dark r· of our guilt unrolled,

first

Mis.	57– 2	If the first r· is true,

first on

Mis.	272– 7	* the first on r· in history,

honorable

My.	332–31	* his honorable r· and Christian

interesting

My.	49–21	* interesting r· of this meeting reads :
	51–25	* An interesting r· relative to this

Major Glover's

My.	334–25	* heading

material

Mis.	170–19	The material r· of the Bible,
Ret.	22– 2	and the material r· expunged.

no

Mis.	158–30	no r· that he used notes
	245– 1	no r· showing that our Master ever
My.	340– 1	no r· of his observing

of dreams

Ret.	21–14	history is but the r· of dreams,

of theft

Mis.	300–21	increasing the r· of theft

of this period

My.	54–22	* A r· of this period reads,

only

Mis.	161–18	The only r· of our Master

put on

My.	353–11	put on r· the divine Science of

said

My.	333– 1	* said r·, with the seal of the

special

Pul.	34– 4	* no special r· is to be made.

their

My.	257–28	Christian Scientists have their r·

this

No.	22–18	This r· shows that the term devil
Po.	26–17	"This r· I will bear

record

true
Ret. 44–29 that hour holds this true r·.
unparalleled
My. v–23 * unparalleled r· for a work of

Mis. 17– 1 r· the thunderings of the spiritual
57–25 Why does the r· make man a
390–21 What hath the r· been?
Ret. 19–23 Here it is but justice to r·,
Pul. vii– 7 to have not only a r· of
Po. 55–22 What hath the r· been?
My. 30–25 * some of the r· collections
50–29 * The r· of May 23, 1880,
98–25 * r· is one of which any church
119– 1 for history to r· limitations
125–15 History will r· their words,
260–30 but one Jesus Christ on r·.
309–19 on r· that Mark Baker's father
314–21 to r· the divorce in my favor.
331– 2 Here it is but justice to r·,
333–10 * The minutes r· this

recorded

Mis. 170–27 So Jesus is r· as having
199–14 miracles r· in the Scriptures
238–11 more than history has yet r·.
277–20 * "It is one more fact to be r·
Man. 110– 7 r· in the history of the Church
Ret. 26–12 miracles r· in the Bible,
Rud. 16–20 first book, r· in history, which
'02. 14–22 achievement has been . . . r· in heaven.
15–25 r· the hallowed suggestion.
Hea. 15–13 miracles r· in the Bible.
My. 148–22 and what is being r·
292– 3 more than history has yet r·.

recording

Mis. 141–31 O r· angel ! write :
170–24 passage r· Jesus' proceedings
My. 126– 7 the r· angel, standing with
332–29 * roll of papers r· the death of

records

Mis. 131–31 last year's r· immortalized,
147– 9 ladened them with r· worthy to be
390–25 In r· of the heart.
Man. 28–24 shall be written on the Church r·.
83–10 as have good past r·
91–21 with good moral r·,
Pul. 1–13 and r· deeply engraven,
'00. 12– 8 History r· Ephesus as an illustrious
Po. 56– 4 In r· of the heart.
My. 50–13 * for their r· state,
50–16 * as the r· further relate,
50–21 * the r· contain these simple
51–21 * but, as the r· state,
107– 3 improved upon its earlier r·,
124–24 produce thy r·, time-table, log,
184–21 glowing r· of Christianity,
270–10 r· of my ancestry attest honesty
330–19 * sustained by Masonic r·
332–22 * to look up the r· of this lodge,
332–27 * Masonic r· were transferred to
333– 4 * In the r· of St. John's Lodge,
333–19 * Chronicle of July 3, 1844, r· that
334–13 * r· show really existed in 1844,

recounting

Pul. 47– 9 * r· her experiences as the pioneer
My. 331–29 * r· the kind attention paid to

recover

Mis. 10–14 they will r· it, countermand their
29– 1 and they shall r·."— Mark 16 : 18.
104–29 and r· his own individuality
192–30 and they shall r·."— Mark 16 : 18.
248– 2 and they shall r·,"— Mark 16 : 18.
300–31 is more apt to r· than he who
381–19 r· of the defendant her cost of suit,
Ret. 35–18 and they shall r·."— Mark 16 : 18.
Pul. 20– 6 In 1892 I had to r· the land
Hea. 1– 4 and they shall r·.— Mark 16 : 18.
8–11 and they shall r·."— Mark 16 : 18.
11–15 may not r· from the heel of
19–28 and they shall r·."— Mark 16 : 18.
Peo. 12– 5 and they shall r·."— Mark 16 : 18.
My. 48– 3 * and they shall r·."— Mark 16 : 18.
200–28 to r· its connection with its divine
227–12 one . . . dies while the others r·,

recovered

Un. 62– 1 Invalids say, "I have r·
My. 97–28 * Boston has not yet r· from
293–27 and the patient would have r·.
314–24 When this husband r· his wife,

recovery

Mis. 24– 8 wrought my immediate r·
35– 4 and subsequently her r·,

recovery

Mis. 53–13 to start the patient's r·?
59–11 to pray for the r· of the sick ?
100–31 man's r· from sin and his
308–27 prevents the r· of the sick.
355– 8 chronic r· ebbing and flowing,
380–19 immediate r· of the sick,
Man. 46–21 for r· of payment
46 25 chronic cases of r·,
Ret. 24–12 My immediate r· from the effects
24–18 and rejoiced in my r·,
My. 293–22 President McKinley's r·
335–31 * for her husband's r·,

recreation

Ret. 69–23 for r· or procreation?''

recruit

Pul. 30– 7 * did not r· itself from other
'01. 29–18 but to r· themselves.

rectified

Un. 20– 1 How is a mistake to be r·?

rectify

Mis. 80–20 redress wrongs and r· injustice.
371–22 To sympathize . . . is not to r·
Un. 14–13 that He might r· His

recuperate

Mis. 209–16 can r· the life of man,

recuperated

No. 36–19 which r· him for triumph

recur

Mis. 299– 1 suffering and mistakes r· until
My. 340–23 to r· to a religious observance

recurrence

Ret. 70–13 the r· of such events.

recurring

Mis. xi–14 At each r· holiday the
321– 9 each r· year witnesses
'02. 10–25 old and r· martyrdom
My. 192–24 constant r· demands upon

red

Mis. 239–18 r· nose, suffused eyes, cough,
253–17 r· dragon that stood ready
254–18 the great r· dragon of this hour,
348–20 capsicum (r· pepper) ;
Un. 11–23 neither r· tape nor indignity
Pul. 42–23 * in letters of r· were the words :
My. 131–10 cup r· with loving restitution,

Red Dragon

Mis. 269–30 heard the great R· D·

redeem

Mis. 82– 9 to enlighten and r· mortals.
Rud. 3– 6 Truth and Love, which r· them,
'02. 13–23 r· the land by paying the amount
My. 139–27 so doth the divine Love r· your body

redeemed

Mis. 140–20 I r· from under mortgage.
310–15 my desire is that all shall be r·,
Ret. 9–25 * r· her birthright of the day,
Pul. 10–29 this is His ; this, His beloved.
'01. 11–11 and are the r· of the Lord.
'02. 14– 2 paid on the land when I r· it.
My. 36–15 * r· from obdurate sin.
229–29 The r· should be happier than

Redeemer

Mis. 123–28 divine Life, which is our R·.
164–15 from the beginning as the R·,
Ret. 23–17 My heart knew its R·.
My. 136– 2 know that our "R· liveth"— Job 19 : 25.
192–17 and sings of our R·.
316– 5 the harvest song of the R·
333–25 * on the merits of a crucified R·.

redeemeth

My. 13–21 r· thy life— Psal. 103 : 4.

redeeming

Un. 55–14 r· us from the false sense of
'00. 2– 5 this old-new theme of r· Love

redeems

Mis. 17–16 divine Principle that r· man

redemption

Mis. 15– 6 the r· of our body."— Rom. 8 : 23.
95–22 the r· of our body,"— Rom. 8 : 23.
96–19 includes man's r· from sickness
165–23 the means of mortals' r· from sin ;
182–10 to wit, the r· of the body.
Un. 6– 7 r· of mortals from sin, sickness, and
52–12 This is the precious r· of soul,
Peo. 10–26 the r· of our body."— Rom. 8 : 23.
12–19 of God's plan of r·,
My. 131–11 restitution, r·, and inspiration,

redemptive
Mis. 107– 5 Its *r·* power is seen in sore trials,
　　331–16 thank God for those *r·* words
'01. 11– 8 Through this *r·* Christ, Truth,
My. 239– 9 *r·* power of Christianity

rediscovery
My. 284– 1 Because of my *r·* of C. S.,

redolent
Mis. 194–12 *r·* with love, health, and holiness,
Pul. 1– 6 *r·* with grief and gratitude.
'01. 12–18 *r·* with health, holiness, and love.

redress
Mis. 80–20 *r·* wrongs and rectify injustice.
'01. 30–12 too occupied with . . . to seek *r·* ;

Red Sea
Mis. 153– 8 they passed through the *R· S·*,
My. 43–14 * the passage of the *R· S·*

red-tongued
Mis. 226–29 *r·* assassin of radical worth ;

reduce
Mis. 334–20 just *r·* this falsity to its
Man. 46–24 shall reasonably *r·* his price
Ret. 26–29 *r·* the demonstration of being,
　　28–18 must *r·* all things real to their
Un. 13–14 *r·* the universe to chaos.
No. 32–26 *r·* this evil to its lowest terms,

reduced
Mis. 109–15 *r·* to their native nothingness !
　　260– 4 C. S. has been *r·* to
Un. 35– 9 *R·* to its proper denomination,

reducing
Mis. 108–13 *r·* its claim to its proper
Hea. 13– 4 *r·* the one hundredth part of a grain

reduction
Un. 36–17 by the *r·* and the rejection of
No. 33– 2 The *r·* of evil, in Science,

redundant
'02. 19–29 no *r·* drop in the cup

reecho
Po. 41–19 harpstring, just breaking, *r·* again

reechoing
'02. 4–16 echoing and *r·* through

Reed, Rev. George H.
My. 174–14 Rev. George H. *R·*, Pastor of

reed
Mis. 387–14 If thou the bending *r·* wouldst break
'02. 18–10 broke not the bruised *r·*
Po. 6– 9 If thou the bending *r·* wouldst break
My. 117– 6 *r·* shaken with the— *Matt.* 11 : 7.

reeds
No. 22–11 are *r·* shaken by the wind.
Pan. 3–28 His pipe of seven *r·* denotes

re-elected
Man. 26– 6 *r·*, or new officers elected,
　　81– 1 can be *r·*, or new officers elected,

reeling
Mis. 134–21 The *r·* ranks of *materia medica*,

reenact
No. 44–21 or *r·*, . . . the horrors of

reenunciated
Pul. 57–10 * *r·* the truths which

reestablished
Hea. 3– 8 *r·* on its former basis.

refer
Mis. 33– 8 these *r·* not to personality,
　　35–28 we *r·* you to "S. and H.
　　51–10 the case to which you may *r·*,
　　52– 1 text may *r·* to such as seek
　　59–19 Scriptures *r·* to God as saying,
　　67–27 If you *r·* to the removal of a person
　　132–23 would *r·* you to the Holy Scriptures,
　　243–24 Did he *r·* to that questionable
No. 22–22 passage must *r·* to the *evils*
'01. 16–20 *r·* to an evil spirit as *dumb*,
My. 240–20 I shall *r·* to this.
　　292–20 I *r·* to the effect of one human

reference
Mis. x– 8 in book form,— accessible as *r·*,
　　243–11 *R·*, Mrs. M. A. F——,
Man. 41– 4 irreverent *r·* to Christ Jesus
Pul. 34–22 * in *r·* to this experience.
No. 7–24 without *r·* to right or wrong
My. 237– 1 contemplated *r·* in S. and H.
　　249–27 then without *r·* to sex
　　329– 9 * *r·* to the death of her husband,
　　338– 8 * A *r·* to her writings

references
Mis. 295– 1 certain *r·* to American women
My. 34–29 * S. and H. *r·* in this lesson

referred
Mis. 48– 4 by the gentleman *r·* to,
　　181–20 His sonship, *r·* to in the text,
　　186– 6 as *r·* to by St. Paul.
　　190–22 devil herein *r·* to
　　314–19 *r·* to in the Sunday Lessons.
Man. 66–17 or she is *r·* to as authority
Un. 36–13 *r·* to in the New Testament
Pul. 27–15 * six water-pots *r·* to in John
　　55– 5 * we have *r·* to cyclic changes
　　73–25 * She *r·* the reporter to the
No. 9–18 wrongs of the nature *r·* to.
　　9–28 * *r·* to general truths
Hea. 7– 2 signs *r·* to are the manifestations
My. 125–29 woman, *r·* to in Revelation,
　　241–20 * because I *r·* to myself
　　305–12 People do not know who is *r·* to
　　307–19 *r·* to the *coming* anew of Truth,
　　320–21 * at the time above *r·* to,
　　320–22 * *r·* to you as the author of
　　321– 4 * always *r·* to you as the one who
　　328– 8 * *r·* to in Miss Jones' letter :

referring
Mis. 130–24 we should avoid *r·* to past mistakes.
　　133– 2 *r·* to me, "the pantheistic and
　　163–18 *R·* to this, he said,
　　192– 3 so, when *r·* to a liar,
　　193–14 *R·* to The Church of Christ, Scientist,
Pul. 3– 4 *R·* to this temple, our Master said :
'01. 9– 2 *r·* to his eternal spiritual selfhood
My. 137– 5 * The *Boston Globe*, *r·* to this
　　225–31 The word Principle, when *r·* to God,
　　228–12 *R·* to John the Baptist,
　　284–13 *r·* to the Memorial service
　　299– 4 kindly *r·* to my address to

refers
Mis. 67–25 If your question *r·* to language,
　　182–15 *r·* to man's primal, spiritual
　　184–10 Paul *r·* to this when speaking of
　　186–29 undoubtedly *r·* to the last Adam
　　190–30 Paul *r·* to this personality of evil
　　191– 9 *r·* to a wicked man as the devil :
　　191–23 our text *r·* to the devil as dumb,
Un. 30–15 apostle *r·* to the second Adam as
No. 29– 1 this passage *r·* to the Jewish law,
Pan. 14–28 This *r·* to the war between
'00. 11–26 In Revelation St. John *r·* to
　　12–28 It *r·* to the Hebrew Balaam as the
　　13–21 The Revelator *r·* to the church in
My. 308–15 *McClure's Magazine r·* to my father's

refilled
My. 149–18 must be emptied before it can be *r·*.

refinement
Mis. 101– 6 blesses . . . by the *r·* of joy

refinements
Peo. 10– 4 *r·* that lose some materiality ;

refines
Mis. 126–13 the ordeal *r·* while it chastens
My. 131– 3 that which *r·* character

reflect
Mis. 8–19 Christ-image that you should *r·*.
　　12–31 imparting, so far as we *r·* them,
　　16–13 *r·* the full dominion of Spirit
　　127–26 it must be ours, . . . if we *r·* Him.
　　131– 6 to discern darkness or to *r·* light.
　　150–28 His people are they that *r·* Him
　　150–29 His people are they . . . that *r·* Love.
　　154–29 Let your light *r·* Light.
　　183–27 will have power to *r·* His power,
　　235– 5 *r·* Him who destroys death and hell.
　　263–14 meet all human needs and *r·* all bliss.
　　278–17 *r·* the image of their Father.
　　333–27 by means of that which does not *r·* Him
Man. 19– 5 to *r·* in some degree the Church
Un. 30–26 *r·* the Life of the divine Arbiter.
　　39–17 must *r·*, in some degree, the power of
Pul. 4–24 *R· this Life*,
　　26– 4 * prisms which *r·* the rainbow tints.
No. 26–19 Man's individual being must *r·* the
　　39–24 Advancing in this light, we *r·* it ;
'00. 4–27 they *r·* God and nothing else.
My. 150–14 *r·* the divine Life, Truth, and
　　150–19 ask God to enable you to *r·* God,
　　208– 6 to *r·* its heavenly rays over all
　　210–16 His thoughts can only *r·* peace,
　　265–26 *r·* this purified subjective state
　　352–12 * may so *r·* in our thoughts

reflected
Mis. 103–27 individuality that *r·* the Immanuel,
　　293–21 sum total of Love *r·*

reflected

Mis.	337–29	Life and light which he *r·*
	340–29	to shine with the *r·* light of God.
	368– 1	and is *r·* by a universe
Un.	14–23	must ·be *r·* in man, Mind's image.
	24–14	*r·* in individual consciousness,
	51–26	*r·* not as human soul,
Pul.	83–24	* we live in the *r·* royalty
My.	74–20	* *r·* in their faces,
	202–23	My work is *r·* light,
	269– 1	*r·* in the intelligent compound idea,
	301– 1	C. S. is a *r·* glory ;

reflecting

Mis.	77–27	in God's own likeness, and *r·* Truth,
	185– 1	in unity with, and *r·*, his Maker.
	332– 1	*r·* all space and Life,
	393– 1	Chief, the charm of thy *r·*,
No.	21–J1	showed man as *r·* God
Po.	51– 6	Chief, the charm of thy *r·*,

reflection

and glory

Mis.	187–23	man is their *r·* and glory.

divine

'00.	1– 8	in the glow of divine *r·*.
My.	129–13	richly fraught with divine *r·*.

forever

Rud.	11– 7	the forever *r·* of goodness.

God's

Mis.	18–17	of spiritual origin, God's *r·*,
	183–14	possible to man *as God's r·*.
	291– 6	dims the true sense of God's *r·*,

His

'00.	4–25	and is His *r·* and Science.
My.	355–27	God is glorified in His *r·*
	356– 3	in His *r·* of love and leadership

human

Un.	28–21	human *r·*, reason, or belief

image is the

My.	239–22	whose image is the *r·* of all

is creation

Mis.	23–23	God, whose *r·* is creation,

man is the

Un.	51– 1	man is the *r·* of immutable good.

no

Peo.	4–20	find no *r·* in sinning, sick, and

observation and

Peo.	6– 7	* founded on long observation and *r·*,

of God

Rud.	7– 9	man is the manifest *r·* of God,

of His power

No.	12–28	man the *r·* of His power and goodness.

of light

My.	355–23	the *r·* of light and love ;

of Spirit

Ret.	73– 7	man is found in the *r·* of Spirit.

of the divine

Mis.	352–25	his consciousness is the *r·* of the divine,

of the Ego

Un.	48–17	not the Ego, but the *r·* of the Ego.

radiant

My.	150–20	radiant *r·* of Christ's glory,

recognized

Mis.	190– 9	recognized *r·* of infinite Life

shocking

No.	29–18	such a statement is a shocking *r·*

this

Mis.	235– 6	By this *r·*, man becomes the
Ret.	57–16	and this *r·* is substance,

true

Mis.	189–12	brings to light the true *r·* :

Mis.	23–25	what C. S. means by the word *r·*.
	183–18	that *r·* already has bestowed
Ret.	56–20	supplying all Mind by the *r·*,
	70–25	the *r·*, . . . of the infinite God.

reflects

Mis.	7–18	*r·* that it is dangerous to live,
	17–20	man *r·* the divine power to heal
	23–26	*r·* good, Life, Truth, Love
	79– 8	*r·* all whereby we can know God.
	104–23	*r·* the divine law and order of being.
	140–32	type of the divine Principle it *r·*.
	183–32	Scriptures declare *r·* his Maker.
	184– 7	only when man *r·* God in body
	205–17	man's identity . . . *r·* only Spirit,
	247–27	*r·* harmony or discord according to
	290–29	it emits light because it *r·* ;
	313– 8	May the Christlikeness it *r·* rest on
	362– 6	comprehends and *r·* all real mode, form,
	364–18	*r·* the divine Mind,
Man.	40– 9	*r·* the sweet amenities of Love,
Ret.	56–23	God *r·* Himself, or Mind,
	57–15	He *r·* God as his Mind,
	68– 8	he *r·* the infinity of good.
Un.	39–23	man forever *r·* and embodies

reflects

Pul.	4–14	A dewdrop *r·* the sun.
	4–15	Each of Christ's little ones *r·*
'00.	4–28	divine Love includes and *r·*
'01.	5–21	man *r·* Spirit, not matter.
Peo.	10–22	the images that thought *r·*
My.	121–23	and *r·* the divine likeness.
	124–18	Nature *r·* man and art pencils him,
	288– 9	demonstrates Truth and *r·* divine **Love**.

reflex

'01.	8–20	The *r·* image of Spirit is not
My.	109–21	*r·* images of this divine Life,

reform

Mis.	38–20	enlighten and *r·* the sinner,
	80–19	promotes and impels all true *r·* ;
	211– 1	you will help to *r·* them.
	215– 5	saying, . . . I punish to *r·* ;
	222– 9	failing of conviction and *r·*,
	237–22	*r·* does and must push on
	244–13	repentance and *r·*, which are
	246– 5	through civil and religious *r·*,
	294–20	*r·* and transform them,
	362–29	prevent sin or *r·* the sinner.
Ret.	30– 9	all moral and religious *r·*.
	70–28	civil, moral, and religious *r·*.
Pul.	20–18	physical, civil, and religious *r·*
No.	11–17	revolutionize and *r·* the world,
Pan.	10–20	they *r·* desperate cases
'01.	30–14	they are leaders of a *r·*
'02.	8–11	No person can . . . *r·* mankind unless
Peo.	1– 3	The great element of *r·*
My.	5–17	heal the sick, *r·* the sinner,
	9–15	* the effort for righteous *r·*,
	26–23	date some special *r·*,
	51–16	* heal the sick and *r·* the sinner.
	51–32	* heal the sick, and *r·* the sinner,
	306–13	The greatest *r·*, . . . must wait

reformation

Mis.	93–26	without repentance and *r·*.
	205– 8	*r·* brings the light which
	261– 5	can only be removed by *r·*.
	297– 4	physical and moral *r·*.
	302– 2	it is a purpose to kill the *r·*
My.	229– 1	for penance or for *r·* ;

reformatory

'01.	9–25	they are revolutionary, *r·*,

reformed

Mis.	146–21	I would gather every *r·* mortal
	219–30	and he has *r·* the sinner.
Man.	39–12	and of being radically *r·*,
'01.	27–19	sick healed, also sinners *r·*
My.	28–23	* our Master healed and *r·* them.
	250– 2	there the sinner is *r·*
	348–26	healed the sick and *r·* the sinner

reformer

Mis.	213–17	pioneer *r·* must pass through a
	237–14	*r·* must encounter and help
	238– 7	The *r·* has no time to
	238–11	*r·* works on unmentioned,
'00.	9–14	*r·* continues his lightning,
	9–16	*r·* must be a hero
'01.	23–17	He was ultra ; he was a *r·* ;
	29– 2	visited a *r·* for that purpose?
	29– 8	aged *r·* should not be left to
	29–24	sacrifices most for the *r·*,
'02.	10– 9	footprints of a *r·* are
	10–20	Wherefore, then, smite the *r·*
	10–28	Persecuting a *r·* is like
Hea.	2– 9	intrepid *r·*, Martin Luther :
My.	288– 4	*r·* gives little thought to
	288–12	Galilean Prophet was, is, the *r·*

reformers

Mis.	98–23	lives of all *r·* attest the
	237– 1	chapter sub-title
	238– 3	to believe a lie, and to hate *r·*.
'01.	28–29	After a hard . . . *r·* usually are
	29–11	not because *r·* are not loved,
	30– 6	successive utterances of *r·*
My.	3–11	Zion's waste places, appeal to *r·*,
	288–12	was, is, the reformer of *r·*.

reforming

'01.	27–13	healing and *r·* mankind.
My.	v–16	* healing the sick and *r·* the sinner
	58–23	* healing the sick and *r·* the sinful,
	155– 1	healing the sick and *r·* the sinner
	182–16	the *r·* of the sinner,
	271– 6	healing the sick and *r·* the sinner,

reforms

Mis.	222– 8	*r·* him, and so heals him :
	245–20	charities, and *r·* of to-day.
	295– 8	* past a score of *r·*,
Ret.	67–14	*r·* the sinner and destroys sin.
No.	45–20	its moral and religious *r·*.

reforms

Hea.	1–17	* Knows it at forty, and r· his plan ;
My.	28–22	* heals the sick and r· the sinful
	161– 6	were it not that his suffering r· him,
	287– 7	Divine Love r·, regenerates,

refrain

Mis.	311–27	and who can r· from transcribing
	392–21	singing To my sense a sweet r· ;
Po.	47– 3	Singing the olden and dainty r·,
	51– 3	singing To my sense a sweet r· ;
My.	105–30	they must r· from persecuting
	129–32	R· from public controversy ;

refrained

My.	318–19	just so long as he r· from

refraining

My.	222–14	r· from admitting the claims of

refresh

Pul.	4– 5	Can ne'er r· a drooping earth,
Peo.	9– 6	The cool bath may r· the body,
My.	125– 5	to report progress, to r· memory,

refreshing

Mis.	149–21	a r· demonstration of Christianity,
	291–26	r·, and consecrating mankind.
My.	208–13	and the r· breeze of morn,
	259–14	r· and most pleasing . . . presents,

refreshment

Mis.	153–10	land of promise, green isles of r·.
	170– 8	spiritual r· of God's children
	170–17	was r· of divine strength,
	227–25	on isles of sweet r·.
Pul.	1–11	For due r· garner the memory of
'01.	1–15	r· and invigoration of the human

reft

Po.	30– 7	dayspring ! 'r· of mortal sigh

refuge

Mis.	9– 8	r· at last from the elements of earth.
	229–17	my r·, even the most High — Psal. 91 : 9.
	389–10	Love is our r· ;
	396–17	poem
Ret.	91– 2	God is their sure defense and r·.
Un.	2– 6	no r· from sin, except in God,
	57– 7	Man's r· is in spirituality,
Pul.	18– 1	poem
No.	7–14	rescue and r· in Truth and Love.
Po.	4– 9	Love is our r· ;
	page 12	poem
My.	17– 1	sweep away the r· of lies, — Isa. 28 : 17.
	185–30	sermons in stones, r· in mountains,

refusal

Pul.	87–21	r· of that as a material offering.

refuse

Mis.	89–17	caused our Master to r· help to some
	246–18	and r· the victim a solitary vindication
	248– 3	interpretation they r· to hear.
Man.	36–17	r· to endorse their applications
	111–18	r·, without sufficient cause, to sign
Ret.	64–30	If evangelical churches r· fellowship
Pul.	64–12	* to r· further contributions,
My.	302–24	and I r· adulation.
	311– 7	I could not r· her.

refused

Mis.	196–24	which the builders r· — Psal. 118 : 22.
	246–21	r· to yield its prey
	349–26	and r· to give me up
Ret.	26– 5	when he r· to drink the
	40–23	r· me a hearing in their halls
Pul.	20– 8	Commissioner, who r· to grant it,
	44–28	* r· to accept any further checks
My.	122–31	r· to see the power of Truth
	335–21	* but they r· permission

refuses

Mis.	113–15	r· to be influenced by any but
	211–32	r· to bear the cross
My.	180–19	r· to see this grand verity

refusing

Ret.	40– 2	r· to take any pay

refutation

Mis.	133– 6	In r· of your statement
No.	6– 9	This r· is indispensable to the
My.	58– 8	* r· of the statements
	91– 4	* affords r· of the notion that
	317– 4	* in r· of allegations

refute

Mis.	183–29	dares at this date r· the evidence
	220– 9	to r· the sick man's thoughts,
	362–24	r· erring reason with the

refutes

Mis.	22–13	absolutely r· the amalgamation,
	364–10	r· everything that is not a
No.	6– 7	C. S. r· the validity of
	15–20	C. S. r· pantheism,

regain

Mis.	265– 5	He grows dark, and cannot r·,
	269– 3	By using falsehood to r· his
	310–19	to r· it, one must comply with
Pan.	11–17	r· his native spiritual stature

regained

Rud.	15– 6	surprise of suddenly r· health
'01.	29–29	* we have r· our tuition

regal

Mis.	330–29	unveils its r· splendor
My.	149– 8	More than r· is the majesty

regard

Mis.	3– 4	If we r· good as more natural
	6–27	caution is observed in r· to
	32–31	To the query in r· to some
	60– 6	To r· sin, disease, and death
	64–10	Do you r· the study of literature
	79–26	in r· to aiding persons
	181–19	and r· him as spiritual,
Man.	47–13	Testimony in r· to the healing
	97–17	impositions on the public in r· to
Chr.	55–12	they r· not the work — Isa. 5 : 12.
Ret.	2–29	for whom she cherished a high r·.
	5–30	* in r· to the education of her
Un.	40–26	r· all things as temporal.
	54– 7	To r· sickness as a false claim,
Pul.	55–12	* r· it as a mere coincidence
	72–19	* In r· to Mrs. Eddy,
No.	1– 1	r· for the spiritual idea
	37–13	but to r· this wonder of glory,
'01.	8– 6	who r· Jesus as God
	14–14	We r· evil as a lie,
	31–13	they r· me with no vague, fruitless,
My.	119– 2	and to r· evil as real,
	141–12	* announcement in r· to the services
	143–22	I do not r· this attack upon
	157– 9	* without r· to class or creed,
	178–14	those who r· being as material.
	190–13	r· his sayings as infallible.
	223–16	in r· to that of which
	244–23	have come so to r· them.
	291–30	shall sacredly r· the liberty of
	302–20	I r· self-deification as blasphemous.
	320– 9	* as to his high r· for you

regarded

Mis.	112–18	r· his act as one of simple justice,
	139–26	will in future be r· as
	200– 3	Jesus r· good as the normal
	200–30	r· matter as only a vagary of
	234–28	God is r· more as absolute,
Ret.	20–11	my home I r· as very precious.
	20–29	was then r· as the Far West.
Un.	46–18	personality they r· as both good and
Pul.	55–26	* r· as the parent organization,
'01.	6–20	r· as impracticable for human use,
	13–13	Sin can have neither . . . thus r·,
'02.	3– 6	r· now more as a philosophy
My.	54–16	* had been r· as the church home,
	86–17	* r· as an extraordinary achievement,
	234–17	when r· on one side only,
	293–23	r· as wholly contingent on the
	309–15	slavery he r· as a great sin.
	324–21	* Mr. Wiggin r· you as quite
	324–25	* he r· you as entirely unique
	325– 9	* r· the old part of Boston

regarding

Mis.	98– 4	his contemplation r· himself
	130–13	acting thus r· disease
	146–10	facts r· both sides of the subject,
	288– 2	convictions r· what is best for
	352– 4	error of r· Life, Truth, Love as
Man.	109– 2	R· Applications for Church Membership.
Pul.	74– 5	* r· a statement made by
Hea.	8– 5	truth r· mind and body,
My.	116–18	truth r· an individual
	227– 2	r· that which he spake
	231–29	interesting report r· the By-law,
	297–29	are said to be circulating r· my
	310–17	R· the allegation by McClure's
	311–18	r· the McNeil coat-of-arms
	312– 4	R· my first marriage
	319–13	* confirm her statement r· the work
	320–26	* matters of detail r· your work,
	332–19	* r· Major Glover's membership
	335–11	* Additional facts r· Major Glover,

regardless

Mis.	172– 8	r· of the bans or clans
Hea.	7–20	r· of any outward act,

regards
Mis. 55–25   he r· God as the only Mind,
   68–28   * r· the ultimate grounds of being,
   288– 9   r· only one side of a question,
   362–15   r· creation as its own creator,
'00. 13–10   the apostle justly r· as heathen,
My. 86–27   * unprecedented, as r· numbers.
   159–28   thought chiefly r· material things,
   250–21   as r· its adaptability to their
   319–29   * as r· Mr. Wiggin.
   321– 8   * as r· your published works ;

regenerate
No.   9–12   that God will well r·

regenerated
Mis. 85– 5   has he who is sick been r·?
   85–25   and the mortal is not r·.
   107–15   before poor humanity is r·
Ret. 14–22   that I had been truly r·,

regenerates
Mis. 360–26   Truth that r· philosophy and logic ;
My. 287– 7   Divine Love reforms, r·,

regenerating
'01.   9– 5   only generating or r· power.
   30–16   religion and therapeutics need r·.
'02.   9–10   r· mankind and fulfilling the

regeneration
Mis. 73–23   in the r· when the Son — Matt. 19 : 28.
   73–27   What is meant by r·?
   85–12   r· leading thereto is gradual,
   85–16   last degree of r· rises into the
   85–26   pleasures . . . of sense, retard r· ;
   86– 3   This final degree of r· is saving,
   187– 1   spiritual r· of both mind and body,
My. 22–17   * has labored for the r· of mankind ;
   45– 4   * ultimate r· of its adherents
   352–15   * in the r· of mankind.

regenerative
Mis. 235– 9   This Science is ameliorative and r·,

régime
Mis. 160– 2   under the r· of C. S. !
   222–22   under this new r· of mind-power,
   348–23   this new r· of medicine,
'01. 20–23   this new-old r· of necromancy

regions
Pul. 76–16   * brought from the Arctic r·.

registered
Mis. 395–23   Is r· above.
Po. 58– 8   Is r· above.

registry
Pul. vii– 9   r· of the rise of the mercury

regive
Pul. 20–10   r· the land to the church.

regret
Mis. 137– 9   I remember my r·, when,
   368–12   We r· to be obliged to say
Pan. 10–21   immorality, which, we r· to say,
'01. 25–11   r· their lack in my books,
My. 51– 6   * sincerely r· that our pastor,
   245–11   The growth of . . . I r· to say,

regrets
My. 40–28   * without r· and without resistance.

regretting
Mis. 274–11   Deeply r· the disappointment

regular
Mis. 69–15   to whom the r· physicians
   80–25   the lot of r· doctors,
   89– 6   employing a r· physician,
   243– 8   r· doctor had put on splints
   248–24   r· physician prescribed morphine,
Man. 51–11   are in good and r· standing
   56– 9   r· AND SPECIAL MEETINGS.
   56–10   r· meetings of The Mother Church
   56–21   R· meetings for electing
   57–10   (excepting its r· sessions)
   111– 9   There are two r· forms
Ret. 84–29   r· institute or place of labor,
   87–29   under the care of a r· physician,
Pul. 68–17   * now holds r· services
Rud. 14–27   a r· course of instruction
My.   8–16   * accommodation for the r· business
   171–20   * on her r· afternoon drive
   246– 3   in good and r· standing.

regularly
Ret. 87– 9   r· settled and systematic
My. 308–17   * r· beating the ground

regular-school
Mis. 349– 3   a certain r· physician,

regulate
Mis. 354–22   would r· God's action.
My. 222–23   laws to r· man's religion ;

regulated
My. 216– 8   r· by a government currency,

regulates
Mis. 232–12   standard of right that r· human
No. 18–26   r· the present high premium on

regulating
Peo. 10– 9   law r· the practice of medicine
My. 327–20   * act in the Legislature r· taxes,

regulator
Mis. 353–16   pour a bucket of water . . . on the r·.
   353–19   should steer the r· of mankind.
   353–21   r· is governed by the principle
   354–12   the children are tending the r· ;

rehearsal
Man. 47–15   More than a mere r· of blessings,
My. 291– 5   more to him than a mere r· of

rehearse
Mis. 396–13   My heart unbidden joins r· ;
Chr. 53–27   What can r· the glorious worth
Pul. 11– 6   r· your hearts' holy intents.
Po. 59– 5   My heart unbidden joins r·,

rehearsed
Pul. 57– 9   * It r· the significance of the

rehearsing
Mis. 311–31   r· facts concerning others
My. 269–24   r· : "I will rebuke the— Mal. 3 : 11.

reign
of Christianity
Mis. 345–17   * since the r· of Christianity began
of difficulties
Mis. 212–16   return under the r· of difficulties,
of divine Science
Mis. 174–23   heaven is the r· of divine Science :
My. 267–24   Heaven is the r· of divine Science.
of divine Truth
Man. 41–21   r· of divine Truth, Life, and Love
of harmony
Mis. 154–17   r· of harmony already within us.
   344–28   way to heaven and the r· of harmony.
Ret. 79–30   r· of harmony within us,
Un. 52– 7   the ever-present r· of harmony,
of heaven
Mis. 384–12   The r· of heaven begun,
'00. 15–29   The r· of heaven begun,
Po. 36–11   The r· of heaven begun,
of holiness
My. 228–16   kingdom of heaven, the r· of holiness,
of Mind
Mis. 51–25   * r· of Mind commence on earth,
of peace
Mis. 156–11   r· of peace and harmony
of righteousness
Mis. 125–10   r· of righteousness— within him ;
'01. 35– 8   call to the r· of righteousness,
My.   4–27   r· of righteousness, the glory of
of the Christ
My. 64–22   * the r· of the Christ
of Truth
My. 257–21   the r· of Truth and Life
of universal harmony
Mis. 134–19   the r· of universal harmony,
peace would
My. 279–15   one Mind, peace would r·.
prolongs the
Mis. 274–21   prolongs the r· of inordinate,

―――――

Mis. 94– 2   in the second, you will r· with him.
   125– 4   Then shall he also r· with him :
   157– 4   shall also r· with him." — II Tim. 2 : 12.
   157– 4   R· then, my beloved in the Lord.
   213–29   Love will r· in every heart,
Un. 57–24   to suffer with him is to r· with him.
Pul. 10–14   the wish to r· in hope's reality
My. 185–10   till Truth shall r· triumphant
   220–21   He whose right it is shall r·.
   283–19   When pride, self, and . . . r·,

reigned
Mis. 259–15   freedom reigned, and was the heritage

reigneth
Mis. 172–15   God omnipotent r·." — Rev. 19 : 6.
   277–22   "The Lord r· ;— Psal. 97 : 1.
My. 184–28   Thy God r· !" — Isa. 52 : 7.
   278–12   divine Science, where right r·.

Reign of Terror
No. 44–20   It reassures us that no R· of T·

reigns
Mis.	80–22	God r·, and will
	331–27	r· in the realm of the real,
	368–28	not forget that the Lord r·,
	395– 5	The rose his rival r·,
Un.	63– 5	Love lives and r· forever.
'00.	10–21	hope anchors in God who r·,
Po.	22–21	Right r·, and blood was not
	57–12	The rose his rival r·,
My.	126–28	r· supreme to-day, to-morrow,
	182–21	Love that r· above the shadow,
	183– 7	* "When Christ r·, and not till then,
	254– 2	heaven opens, right r·,

reincarnation
Pul.	38–23	* philosophy of Karma and of r·,
My.	90–18	* r· of the old, old gospel

reinforces
My.	279– 6	C. S. r· Christ's sayings

reinstate
Mis.	10–16	and r· His orders,
Man.	17–12	should r· primitive Christianity
Peo.	14–18	r· man in God's own image
My.	46–12	should r· primitive Christianity

reinstated
My.	46–17	* requirement of a r· Christianity.

reinstating
'02.	3– 9	r· the old national family pride

reiterate
Mis.	134– 5	r· such words of apology
Pan.	9– 1	r· the belief of pantheism,
'01.	8– 2	I r· this cardinal point :
'02.	10– 8	and r·, Let me alone.'

reiterated
Mis.	212–10	remember the r· warning
'02.	5–20	r· in the gospel of Christ,

reiterates
Mis.	25–19	only as it r· the word,
Ret.	93–23	If C. S. r· St. Paul's teaching,

reject
Mis.	76–17	no man can rationally r·
	83–15	to r· or to accept this error ;
	191–31	St. Paul's injunction to r· fables,
	352–31	aroused to r· the sense of error ;
	395– 6	The stars r· his pains,
'00.	5–23	the builders r· for a season ;
'01.	25– 6	stone which the builders r·
	25– 6	The stone . . . which they r·
Po.	57–13	The stars r· his pains,
My.	344–16	* "Do you r· utterly the

rejected
Mis.	5–20	stone that the builders have r·,
	326–22	those who persistently r· him,
Man.	18– 1	which the builders r·, — *Matt.* 21 : 42.
	37– 9	If an application . . . is r·,
Pul.	10–19	which the builders r·, — *Matt.* 21 : 42.
No.	38–13	rock which the builders r· ;
'01.	9–18	yet Christ is r· of men !
Hea.	3– 9	stone which the builders r·
My.	48– 6	* the stone that had been r·,
	60–12	* which the builders r·" — *Matt.* 21 : 42.
	122–31	the very hearts that r· it
	129–20	which the builders r·" ! — *Matt.* 21 : 42.
	188– 1	stone which the builders r·

rejection
Man.	37– 7	Notice of R·.
	37–11	notice of such r· ;
	37–13	report the cause for r·.
Un.	36–17	r· of the claims of matter
Pan.	12– 3	comes from the r· of evil

rejects
Mis.	25–13	r· all other theories of causation,
	245–26	r· apostolic Christianity,

rejoice
Mis.	18– 5	therefore r· in tribulation,
	120–16	r·, however, that the clarion call
	137–14	r· over the growth of my students
	152–14, 15	and r· with them that r·.
	277–22	let the earth r·." — *Psal.* 97 : 1.
	279– 6	I r· with those who r·,
	330–11	"R· in the Lord — *Phil.* 4 : 4.
	353– 1	consciousness be allowed to r· in
	368–28	r· in His supreme rule,
	370– 1	We r· to say, in the spirit of our
	398– 3	I will follow and r·
Ret.	9–22	* Shall I not r· That I have learned
	9–24	* I will r· !
	46– 9	I will follow and r·
	86– 3	r· in the spirit and power of C. S.,
Un.	5– 3	Rather will they r· in the
Pul.	9–23	Christians r· in secret,
	10–23	Let us r· that chill vicissitude

rejoice
Pul.	12–11	Therefore r·, ye heavens, — *Rev.* 12 : 12.
	17– 8	I will follow and r·
	44–11	* we all r·, yet the mother in Israel,
	83–25	* We r· with her that at last
No.	8–15	r· that every germ of goodness
Pan.	14–27	Great occasion have we to r·
'01.	14–28	r· in the scientific apprehension of
	27–15	shall r· in being informed thereof.
	34–18	rejoicing with them that r· ;
'02.	3– 7	I r· that the President of the
	11–24	R·, and be exceeding glad : — *Matt.* 5 : 12.
Peo.	3–14	r· that the bow of omnipotence
	14–14	r· in hope ; be patient in tribulation,
Po.	14– 7	I will follow and r·
My.	6–11	r·, "for great is — *Matt.* 5 : 12.
	21–26	* r· in the glad reunion
	23–23	* We r· greatly that the walls of
	24–12	* r· in the unity of thought
	43–27	* r· that we have found in C. S.
	139–26	R· and be exceedingly glad,
	142–18	learn this and r· with me,
	157– 8	* r· that the prosperity of the Cause
	174–30	r· in the church triumphant
	183–18	*Brethren :* — I r· with you ;
	192–23, 24	"r· with them that do r·," — *Rom.* 12 : 15.
	190– 3	BRETHREN : — I r· with thee.
	201–23	I will follow and r·
	270– 1	"R·, and be exceeding glad : — *Matt.* 5 : 12.
	280– 7	* We r· also in this new reminder
	285– 7	I r· with you in all your wise
	295– 2	r· in knowing our dear God comforts
	339–21	r· in their present Christianity
	361–19	* We r· that our church has
	362– 4	I r· with you in the victory of
	362–19	* r· in your inspired leadership,

rejoiced
Ret.	24–18	and r· in my recovery,
Un.	57–23	r· that he was found worthy
My.	169–19	r· at the appropriate beauty

rejoices
Mis.	12–25	law of Love r· the heart ;
	241–25	r· in the gospel of health.
Pul.	13–12	r· in the proof of healing,
No.	7– 2	to be wise and true r· every
'02.	3–18	r· with our sister nation
My.	44–11	* r· in prophecy fulfilled,
	232– 1	r· me that you are recognizing
	253– 1	r· me to know that you

rejoiceth
No.	45– 6	r· in the truth." — *I Cor.* 13 : 6.
My.	159– 6	Christ r· and comforteth us.

rejoicing
Mis.	xi–21	reason for r· that the *vox populi*
	72–10	It is cause for r· that this belief
	213–19	But the faithful . . . have gone on r·.
Pul.	22– 5	It is matter for r· that we
No.	46–17	r·, as Paul did,
'01.	34–17	r· with them that rejoice ;
My.	37–32	* our r·, and our love
	63–17	* at every turn with words of r· ;
	76–10	* That it was received with r·
	125–22	stars in my crown of r·.
	148–20	joining in your r·,
	183–26	blending with thine my prayer and r·.
	229–23	their swift messages of r·
	260–19	understanding of joy and r·,
	274–25	this is my crown of r·,
	280– 3	* We acknowledge with r· the
	285–13	It is a matter for r· that the

rejuvenate
My.	125– 6	to r· the branches

rejuvenated
Mis.	ix–11	r· by the touch of God's

rejuvenation
Mis.	169–12	With . . . had come physical r·.

rekindle
Ret.	83–17	difficult to r· his own light

relapse
Rud.	9– 1	patient is liable to a r·,
No.	26–14	can no more r· or collapse
	30– 7	sickness and sin have no r·.
My.	165–24	a r· into the common hope
	273–26	they lapse and r·, come and go,

relapsed
My.	307–26	case improved . . . but it r·.

relapsing
My.	121– 9	is neither tremulous nor r·.

relate
Mis.	333–20	harmonies of Spirit that r· to the
	350– 5	* "terrible and too shocking to r·."

relate

My. 50–17 * as the records further *r*·,
223–22 which *r*· in any manner to the
311– 1 I will *r*· the following incident,

related

Mis. 344– 2 It is *r*· of Justin Martyr that,
Ret. 1– 5 in some way *r*· to Hannah More,
Pul. 33– 6 * *r*· to her the story of Samuel,
33–16 * Theodore Parker *r*· that when he was
My. 307–23 Had his remark *r*· to my personality,
314–27 *r*· these facts to her just as I have

relates

Man. 67–13 if said case *r*· to the person
No. 10–15 What is termed matter, or *r*· to its

relating

Mis. 131–17 By-law *r*· to finances
379–28 facts *r*· to Mind and its
Man. 81–18 *r*· to *The C. S. Journal.*
My. 124–25 facts *r*· to the thitherward,
242–17 information *r*· to C. S. practice,
330–15 * Mrs. Eddy's statements, *r*· to

relation

Mis. 4– 8 and their *r*· to each other.
37– 8 Jesus recognized this *r*· so clearly
173–10 this law has no *r*· to,
181–21 his spiritual *r*· to Deity :
218– 7 testimony of material sense in *r*· to
235– 2 recognition of his *r*· to God.
269–13 in *r*· to human events
285–21 showing its *r*· to C. S.
Man. 46–16 *r*· of practitioner to patient.
64–10 heading
71–10 In its *r*· to other C. S. churches,
Un. 29– 1 Soul stands in this *r*· to
51–25 scientific *r*· of man to God,
Rud. 16– 9 its scientific *r*· to Mind-healing,
No. 2–26 present ignorance in *r*· to C. S.
36–15 his higher self and *r*· to the Father,
'01. 23–28 * "only the constant *r*· between
My. 64– 2 * our beloved Leader and her *r*· to
70– 1 in their *r*· to the city itself,
160– 6 in constant *r*· with the divine,
268– 6 marriage *r*· is losing ground,
302–18 I stand in *r*· to this century as

relations

Mis. 68–22 * science of the conceptions and *r*·
69– 2 His essence, *r*·, and attributes.
287–24 Be faithful over home *r*·;
290– 2 Let other people's marriage *r*· alone:
My. 74–25 * Our present *r*· with them are
291–14 His home *r*· enfolded a wealth
317– 3 * exactly defining her *r*· with
321–14 * your *r*· to your published works
361– 5 your *r*· with other students.

relationship

My. 8–18 * arithmetic and the *r*· of figures,
114–17 strange coincidence or *r*· with

relative

Mis. 9–10 Wherein is this conclusion *r*· to
36–22 all beliefs *r*· to the so-called
146–24 will act, *r*· to this matter,
147–23 the trusty friend, the affectionate *r*·,
151–14 He is man's only real *r*·
157–20 *r*· to Mrs. Stebbin's case.
187–12 accepted as true *r*· to man.
195–26 teachings of Jesus *r*· to healing
291–21 *r*· to the true and unswerving
310–11 *r*· to the return of members
379– 3 anything pathological *r*· to
Ret. 1–14 no sign that she . . . was her *r*·.
2–26 *r*· of my Grandfather Baker
Pul. 32–25 * Hannah More was a *r*· of
48–20 * another distinguished *r*·,
No. 10– 4 *r*· to the unseen verities of being,
My. 51–25 * *r*· to this very early work
190–18 as to the *r*· value, skill, and
250– 3 *r*· to a three years' term
303– 6 Scriptures *r*· to this subject.
338–16 not allowed to consult me *r*· to

relatives

My. 294–30 his *r*· shed "the unavailing tear."
331–19 * in behalf of the *r*· and friends

release

No. 7–19 will not *r*· them from the strict

released

Mis. 189–19 a *r*· sense of Life in God
My. 254– 7 *R*· from materialism, you shall run

relegated

'02. 2–20 dogmatism, *r*· to the past,
My. 285–11 shall be *r*· to oblivion.

relegates

My. 239– 4 *r*· Christianity to its primitive

relentless

Ret. 13–13 My father's *r*· theology

reliability

Mis. 228–25 without questioning the *r*· of its

reliable

Mis. x– 8 and *r*· as old landmarks.
Hea. 16–21 shall we call that *r*· evidence
My. 12–21 If the *r*· now is carelessly lost
121–12 *r*·, helpful, and always at hand.
175–13 dear churches, *r*· editors,

reliance

Mis. 257–18 *r*· where there should be avoidance,
Ret. 28–13 Our *r*· upon material things
Un. 10– 9 utter *r*· upon the one God,
Pul. 35–17 Our *r*· upon material things
My. 211–22 *r*· where there should be avoidance,
333–25 * and of his full *r*· for salvation

reliant

Mis. 87–21 who is most *r*· on himself

relief

Mis. 44– 7 *necessity for immediate r*·,
70–26 and material sense of *r*· ;
241–31 and who long for *r*· !
262–16 giving to the sick *r*· from pain ;
298–26 One says, "I find *r*· from
377– 4 yet so near and full of radiant *r*·
Ret. 20–14 a vision of *r*· from this trial.
24–19 explain the *modus* of my *r*·.
31–13 ever-present *r*· from human woe.
54– 7 and appeal to God for *r*·
Pul. 24–13 * inscription carved in bold *r*· :
25–13 * galleries are in plaster *r*·,
26– 5 * richly panelled in *r*· work.
26–25 * pale green with *r*· in old rose.
Rud. 12–14 because the *r*· is unchristian
My. 56–17 * notwithstanding the *r*· that the
267–22 *r*· from fear or suffering,
345–16 homœopathy came like blessed *r*·

relieve

Mis. 262–29 *r*· my heart of its secrets,
378–12 seemed at first to *r*· her,
Ret. 30– 8 It was to *r*· the sufferings of
34–15 cures when they fail, or only *r*· ;
My. 20–10 May I *r*· you of selecting,
56–10 * would *r*· the overcrowded condition
358–16 to *r*· me of so much labor.

relieved

My. 138– 3 *r*· of the burden of doing this.
329– 5 * *r*· the healers of this sect from

relieving

Mis. 273–10 so capable of *r*· my tasks
My. 214–18 *r*· the questioners' perplexity,

religion (see also religion's)

abound in
'01. 33– 7 * "Quackery and dupery do abound in *r*· ;
adopt a
My. 128–14 man's right to adopt a *r*·,
and art
My. 270–31 *r*· and art in unity and harmony.
and ethics
My. 114–31 pulpit and press, in *r*· and ethics,
and *materia medica*
My. 265–19 *r*· and *materia medica* should be
and medicine
Peo. 7–32 *R*· and medicine must be dematerialized
My. 221– 1 spirituality in *r*· and medicine
340– 9 progress of *r*· and medicine
and philosophy
My. 248–27 *r*· and philosophy of labor, duty,
and scholarship
Ret. 87– 5 as obvious in *r*· and scholarship
and Science
Mis. 312–17 * harmony between *r*· and Science,
and therapeutics
'01. 30–16 Even *r*· and therapeutics need
My. 267– 1 the only *r*· and therapeutics
at the sick-bed
Hea. 18–24 and *r*· at the sick-bed will be
better
My. 221–15 or a better *r*· than his?
Christian
Pan. 6–23 if . . . the Christian *r*· has at least two
My. 220–18 Christian *r*· — Christ's Christianity.
Christian Scientist's
'01. 18–10 Christian Scientist's *r*· or his
claims on
Pan. 12–11 will make strong claims on *r*·,
contests over
Peo. 2–20 demoniacal contests over *r*·.
denominations of
Pul. 21–15 in all denominations of *r*·,

religion

devotees of a
  My. 76–28   * by the devotees of a *r·* which
essence of
  My. 178– 8   This Science is the essence of *r·*,
ethics, and
  My. 260–27   It leaves . . . ethics, and *r·* to God
evangelical
  Mis. 193– 9   evangelical *r·* can be established
  194–11   and misinterpret evangelical *r·*.
  Ret. 35–15   glow and grandeur of evangelical *r·*.
  '01. 12–17   and misinterpret evangelical *r·*.
form of
  Mis. 345–22   an advanced form of *r·*,
  My. 99–13   * whenever their form of *r·* is
forms of
  '02. 16–24   merely outside forms of *r·*,
forward steps in
  '00. 4–12   new and forward steps in *r·*,
heathen
  '00. 3–29   animus of heathen *r·* was not the
her
  My. 346– 6   * presenting another view of her *r·*.
his
  Ret. 92– 1   method of his *r·* was not too simple to
  My. 270–28   quarrel with a man because of his *r·*
in this century
  '01. 33–25   proof that a *r·* in this century is
Jewish
  Mis. 65–30   The Jewish *r·* demands that
  260– 6   Grecian philosophy, or Jewish *r·*,
  Ret. 65–15   Jewish *r·* was not spiritual ;
Judean
  Mis. 82– 2   reconstructs the Judean *r·*,
  166–18   The Judæan *r·* even required
leaders of
  '01. 32–18   those old-fashioned leaders of *r·*
lees of
  My. 301– 6   by which the lees of *r·* will
life and
  Mis. 374– 8   demanded Christianity in life and *r·*.
life of
  '01. 33–11   * not the health and life of *r·*,
man's
  My. 222–24   make laws to regulate man's *r·* ;
material
  Mis. 17–10   more material *r·* with its rites and
  '01. 34–14   material *r·*, proscriptive, intolerant,
  My. 110– 6   material *r·*, material medicine,
materialistic
  Mis. 246–29   spiritual . . . or a materialistic *r·*
medicine and
  No. 44– 5   demonstration of medicine and *r·*.
  '02. 2–17   ethics, medicine, and *r·*,
  Peo. 5– 1   practice of medicine and *r·*,
medicine, or
  Mis. 26– 1   philosophy, medicine, or *r·*,
metaphysical
  Peo. 3–19   metaphysical *r·* founded upon C. S.
morals and
  Man. 83– 6   of morals and *r·*, healing and
Mosaic
  Pan. 7–20   a lapse in the Mosaic *r·*,
name of
  Pul. 7–18   committed in the name of *r·*.
  My. 258– 4   Nothing is worthy the name of *r·* save
national
  Peo. 8–12   definite form of a national *r·*,
nearest right
  Hea. 2– 1   *r·* nearest right is that one.
Neoplatonic
  '00. 4– 8   Babylonian and Neoplatonic *r·*,
new
  Mis. 179–13   In the new *r·* the teaching is,
  My. 29–22   * A comparatively new *r·*
  86– 7   * the hosts of a new *r·*.
  87–25   * world turned to the new *r·*.
new-old
  '01. 30–21   establishment of a new-old *r·*
of growth
  My. 95–24   * no *r·* of growth and vitality
of Jesus Christ
  My. 8–10   * expression of the *r·* of Jesus Christ,
of pagan priests
  Mis. 123–10   ultimates in a *r·* of pagan priests
of to-day
  Ret. 65–16   If the *r·* of to-day is constituted
old
  Mis. 178–30   old *r·* in which we have been
one
  Hea. 1–20   one *r·* has a more spiritual basis
or medicine
  Mis. 260–10   potency, in *r·* or medicine.
  My. 288–16   instrumentality in *r·* or medicine.

religion

or philosophy
  Mis. 363–22   sensual *r·* or philosophy
  My. 117–23   never a *r·* or philosophy lost
or science
  My. 303–24   not the sport of . . . *r·*, or science ;
perfect
  '00. 4–16   rational that the only perfect *r·* is
philosophy and
  Mis. 64–18   the only philosophy and *r·* that
  Ret. 31–29   philosophy and *r·* melted,
  57–24   systems of philosophy and *r·*
philosophy, or
  My. 4–32   true, in ethics, philosophy, or *r·*,
  220–24   future philosophy or *r·*,
practical
  My. 168– 3   practical *r·* in agreement
practice of
  Peo. 2– 3   theory and practice of *r·*
profession of
  Ret. 14–17   made any profession of *r·*,
progressive
  My. 340–32   learning and progressive *r·*
prospers
  My. 93–10   * *r·* prospers according to
question as to
  '00. 4–22   The question as to *r·* is :
reform in
  '01. 30–14   reform in *r·* and in medicine,
scientific
  My. 265–16   that scientific *r·* and
sense of
  Pan. 3– 2   the Christian sense of *r·*.
shall permeate
  My. 222–24   *r·* shall permeate our laws.
spiritual
  Mis. 365–16   a more spiritual *r·*
  No. 18–22   a more spiritual *r·*
  Hea. 1–11   more practical and spiritual *r·*
spiritualizes
  Mis. 252–24   spiritualizes *r·* and restores its
stages of
  '01. 33– 8   * decaying stages of *r·*,
status of
  Mis. 357– 9   above the present status of *r·*
stole into
  Hea. 3–11   material element stole into *r·*,
such a
  My. 348–14   writer's departure from such a *r·*
superficial
  No. 46– 5   material medicine and superficial *r·* ?
system of
  Mis. 284– 5   than any other system of *r·*, morals,
  296– 1   Founder of this system of *r·*,
  My. 129– 4   and a lax system of *r·*.
  258– 3   lifts a system of *r·* to deserved fame
systems of
  Mis. 27– 9   other systems of *r·* abandon their
  '00. 5–26   foundation of all systems of *r·*.
  Peo. 4–26   Systems of *r·* and of medicine
  My. 216– 5   All systems of *r·* stand on
their
  Ret. 87–12   their *r·* demands implicit
  No. 44–14   dungeon or stake for their *r·*,
tribal
  My. 288–14   pagan mysticisms, tribal *r·*,
true
  Mis. 336–22   cognomen of all true *r·*,
  My. 181–13   possessed the motive of true *r·*,
tyrannical
  Pul. 6– 4   a national or tyrannical *r·*,
undefiled
  Mis. 98–20   pure and undefiled *r·*
  320–28   to-day christening *r·* undefiled,
  Ret. 71–20   according to pure and undefiled *r·*.
  No. 46–16   Puritan standard of undefiled *r·*.
unhealing
  Ret. 65–30   an unspiritual and unhealing *r·*.
vitality to
  Ret. 66– 3   C. S. gives vitality to *r·*,
war on
  My. 234–24   But a war on *r·* in China would be
which heals
  My. 28–22   * a *r·* which heals the sick
your
  Mis. 345– 9   * unless you yield your *r·*,''

  Mis. 25– 6   the *r·* that Jesus taught
  123–10   a *r·* that demands human victims
  232– 8   Why, then, should *r·* be stereotyped,
  251–11   loyal to the heart's core to *r·*,
  327–11   in worldly policy, *r·*, politics,
  366–18   in the field of medicine and of *r·*,
  Man. 28– 8   nations, individuals, and *r·* are
  48– 9   towards *r·*, medicine, the courts, or

religion
Pul. 5–28 is the leaven fermenting r· ;
No. 45–15 In natural law and in r·
Pan. 3–21 In r·, it is a belief in one God,
4–12 In academics and in r·
9– 8 Is there a·r· under the sun that
'01. 19–13 either in medicine or in r·,
'02. 2–12 r· in the United States has
3– 6 more as a philosophy than as a r·.
5– 5 r· parting with its materiality.
My. 70– 3 * a r· which has been organized only
99– 4 * a r· that makes the merry heart
203– 5 r· should be distinct in our
355–12 a strong supporting arm to r·

religionists (see also **religionists'**)
Mis. 187–31 transcribed by pagan r·,
Ret. 2– 4 gave those r· the poetic
82–24 fall short of other r· ;
'00. 4–23 Do r· believe that God

religionists'
Mis. 248–13 "R· mistaken views of

religion's
Mis. 25–15 It is r· "new tongue," — see Mark 16 : 17.

religions
Pan. 7–13 chapter sub-title
7–14 We know of but three theistic r·,
7–16 Does not each of these r·
'00. 13–26 * amalgamation of different pagan r·
'02. 2–10 purifying all peoples, r·, ethics,
3– 3 cords of non-Christian r·
5– 3 tribal r· of yesterday
10–17 R· in general admit that man
14–22 popular philosophies and r·
Hea. 1–20 difference between r· is,
2–23 this proof . . . that r· had not given.
19–17 We need it to stamp our r·
Peo. 3–25 It has implanted in our r·
My. 127–11 r· since the first century.
166– 6 R· may waste away,

religious
Mis. xi–19 shuttlecock of r· intolerance
4–22 so that its r· specialty
38– 8 education, secular and r·,
122–24 Neither . . . nor a r· chancery
145– 3 r· element, or Church of Christ,
174– 9 touches the r· sentiment
206– 2 revolutions, natural, civil, or r·,
241– 1 From a r· point of view,
246– 5 through civil and r· reform,
246– 8 interests of wealth, r· caste,
246–26 Shall r· intolerance,
251–13 civil and r· freedom,
251–27 all error, physical, moral, or r·,
297– 3 r· and pathological systems
307–15 In this revolutionary r· period,
310–26 receding year of r· jubilee,
Man. 61–20 of an appropriate r· character
Ret. 5– 3 was a very r· man,
15– 4 My connection with this r· body
30– 9 include all moral and r· reform.
70–28 civil, moral, and r· reform.
Un. 7– 5 in multitudes of other r· folds.
15–21 found in heathen r· history.
Pul. 20–18 moral, physical, civil, and r·
32–27 * her mother was a r· enthusiast,
36– 6 * deeper foundation of her r· work
43–28 * personal worship which r· teachers
50–16 * This particular phase of r· belief
50–24 * so-called orthodox r· bodies
50–25 * No one r· body holds the whole of
51–10 * searching after r· truth.
51–17 * produced a sensation in r· circles,
51–21 * many a new project in r· belief
51–29 * demonstrations of r· belief
63–16 * a new phase of r· belief,
67– 9 * census of the r· faiths
68– 9 * for the interests of her r· work
79–23 * that requires the r· sentiment
80– 4 * r· sentiment in women is so strong
No. 12– 9 the author's r· experience.
14–20 more than any other r· sect,
15–10 civil and r· arms in their defense ;
40–25 change in the r· views of the patient
44–23 horrors of r· persecution.
45–20 its moral and r· reforms.
Pan. 2–21 to which the r· sentiment is
10–22 other r· teachers are unable to
'00. 7– 4 Likewise the r· sentiment has
10–12 r· rights and laws of nations
'01. 22–22 the different r· sects
30– 2 even as all other r· denominations
'02. 1–16 systems of r· beliefs and opinions
Hea. 2– 3 r· factions and prejudices arrayed

religious
Peo. 9– 7 as compliance with a r· rite
My. 8–28 * Leader of our r· denomination
49– 5 * The r· body which can direct,
59–11 * nearly every r· and scientific body
89–27 * growth of this form of r· faith
89–29 * the greatest r· phenomenon
89–30 * r· movement of international sway ;
90– 5 * in the history of r· expression.
91–18 * most remarkable r· movements
93–25 * economy of our social and r· life.
95–30 * demonstration of r· faith
98– 9 * such as r· annals hardly parallel
100–13 * organization among r· bodies,
112– 8 Our r· denominations interpret
116– 6 In time of r· or scientific prosperity,
163–27 I respect their r· beliefs,
167–22 chapter sub-title
167–27 r· rights in New Hampshire
177– 9 presence at your r· jubilee.
270– 6 my first r· home in this capital
271–24 * who, whatever their r· beliefs,
273– 1 * it has no r· opinions
294–25 r· energy of this illustrious pontiff
300–31 opening fire on their own r· ranks,
301– 5 The present flux in r· faith
311–14 my r· experience seemed to
340– 5 seasons for r· observances
340–23 to recur to a r· observance
348–11 r· departure from divine Science
(see also **liberty**)

religiously
Mis. 203–13 Theology r· bathes in water,
My. 284–24 r· opposed to war,

relinquish
Mis. 31–17 to r· his faith in evil,
353– 8 r· your human concept of me,
Man. 72–20 If . . . Mrs. Eddy, should r· her
Un. 49–27 commands mortals to shun or r·,
My. 40–12 * r· their cherished resentments,
200–24 r· its league with evil.

relinquished
Mis. 64– 5 r· his earth-task of teaching
297–22 unless such claims are r· by
'01. 24–29 I r· the form to attain the

relinquishing
My. 140–19 R· a material form of

relinquishment
Mis. 340– 1 r· of right in an evil hour,

relish
Mis. 9–25 our failure longer to r· this
224–19 keen r· for and appreciation of

relishes
Mis. 226– 2 * "Give the child what he r·,

reluctance
Ret. 37–21 My r· to give the public,

reluctant
My. 10–19 * basis of fretful or r· sacrifice

reluctantly
Pul. 34–13 * and r· they did so,
88– 9 articles are r· omitted.
My. 103– 1 perfection is r· seen
129– 3 I r· foresee great danger

rely
Pul. 69–10 * r· on Mind for cure,
Hea. 4–26 can we r· on our model?
16–19 how can we r· on their testimony

relying
Mis. 115–22 necessity for r· on God
354–20 Instead of r· on the Principle
Hea. 5–22 r· not on the person of God

remain
Mis. 2–24 but should r· in error,
234– 2 r· no longer to blind us
240–14 let it r· as harmlessly,
243– 9 bandages to r· six weeks,
249–14 None are permitted to r·
265–32 r· until suffering compels the
387–19 make men one in love r·.
Man. 62–13 no pupil shall r· in the
68– 4 notified to r· with Mrs. Eddy
68–14 Those . . . who r· with her
69– 2 a signed agreement to r·
76– 2 should r· on safe deposit,
91– 2 not allow it or a copy of it to r·,
Un. 34–23 Nothing would r· to be seen
Pul. 2–20 r· within the walls
82–28 * r· deaf to their cry?
'02. 2–24 Then why not r· friends,
Hea. 4– 3 nor r· for a moment within limits.
Po. 6–14 make men one in love r·.

remain

My.	4–29	The height of my hope must r.
	51–10	* hope she will r with us.
	51–17	* r with us for a few Sundays
	68–15	* church . . . will r as it was,
	108–28	I r steadfast in St. Paul's faith,
	138–21	I r most respectfully
	175–16	r with us a little longer,
	175–25	must r so long as I r.
	178–28	would r immortal.
	190–28	would r, even as it did,
	195–29	grant that this unity r,
	217–10	This sum is to r on interest
	226–17	would r the forever fact,
	243–16	r in their own fields
	276– 8	a preference to r within doors
	311– 6	begged to be allowed to r

remained

Mis.	130– 1	so long as a hope r
	216–21	* which r some time after the
	379–30	there r the difficulty of
Man.	75–21	r in the hands of the Directors,
Ret.	5–10	and there the family r
	20– 3	r with my parents until
	76–27	I have long r silent
Un.	63– 6	r forever in the Science of being.
Pul.	43–25	* r at her home in Concord,
	60–13	* many having r over a week
My.	11–27	* still r for definite decision
	145–14	He r at work, and the next
	336–14	r with my parents until

remainder

Mis.	355–15	for the r only stimulates
No.	8–14	r thereof He will restrain.
'02.	1–13	r of wrath shalt Thou — Psal. 76 : 10.
My.	151–11	r of wrath shalt Thou — Psal. 76 : 10.
	207– 5	r thereof He will restrain.

remaineth

Mis.	144–23	rest that r for the righteous,
	216– 3	There r, it is true, a
	357–16	what r has fallen into the good and
'02.	19–17	r a rest for the righteous,

remaining

Mis.	210– 6	and the r third kills itself.
	256–11	r at present a public servant :
Man.	80–20	r trustees shall fill the vacancy,
Peo.	12–18	we shall take in the r two thirds
My.	12– 9	* decision of these r problems.
	75–29	* expense . . . r unprovided for,

remains

Mis.	7–26	greater work yet r to be done.
	23–12	and the command r,
	76– 6	and r to be demonstrated;
	100–10	so long as there r a claim of
	129–14	let silence prevail over his r.
	145–21	visible unity of spirit r,
	372– 4	fact r, that the textbook of
Ret.	33–21	Mind, the curative Principle, r,
	82– 2	law of the chord r unchanged,
Un.	62– 1	when the fact really r,
No.	13–13	r a clear and profound deduction
	25–20	r to be learned.
	28– 2	How long this false sense r
Hea.	6–20	But the fact r, in metaphysics,
	12–25	when the drug disappears . . . power r,
My.	6–20	The room of your Leader r
	124–18	but it r for Science to reveal
	190–20	r beyond questioning a divine
	193– 5	privilege r mine to watch
	295– 4	r in the minds of men,
	303–28	What I am r to be proved
	312–26	long procession, followed the r
	326–19	bore his r to their last
	333–17	* Major Glover's r were carried North.
	333–26	* r were interred with Masonic
	335–22	* to take the r to Charleston.
	347– 3	What r to lead on the centuries
	348–28	Science r the law of God

remake

My.	288–29	We cannot r ourselves,

remark

Pul.	63– 9	* r Rev. Mary Baker Eddy, . . . made
My.	307–23	Had his r related to my

remarkable

Mis.	125–28	r achievements that have been ours
Ret.	83– 3	accomplishing . . . to a r degree.
Pul.	27– 8	* windows are a r feature of
	29–10	* whose r earnestness impressed the
	31– 2	* certainly a very r retrospect.
	55– 7	* Of our r nineteenth century
	56–13	* one of the most r, helpful,
	63–14	* This is a r statement,
	63–15	* but it is made by a r woman,

remarkable

Pul.	66– 7	* has grown with r rapidity,
	70– 4	* R Career of Rev. Mary Baker Eddy,
	70–11	* most r women in America.
	79–16	* two reasons for this r development,
No.	36–10	r words, as wholly opposed to
'02.	14–13	r growth and prosperity of C. S.
My.	70–13	* The effect on all . . . is quite r.
	78–21	* One of the r features of the
	79–26	* making their r statements
	82–28	* departing with such r expedition,
	84–19	* It is a r story
	85– 1	* r in the character of the
	86–26	* The attendance . . . was r,
	88–16	* r external manifestations
	89–13	* A r thing in this building is
	91–17	* one of the most r religious
	91–25	* Its growth in numbers is r,
	94–16	* r growth and the apparent
	96–16	* A r feature, perhaps the most r,
	98–15	* a rather r announcement
	100– 3	* as r in their aggregate
	271–25	* personality of this r woman.
	273– 3	* r proof of Mrs. Eddy's ability
	273– 8	* guiding with r skill,
	287– 5	used in a r degree
	307–22	he was a r man.

remarkably

Ret.	42–11	r successful in Mind-healing,
Pul.	47–30	* r well placed upon a terrace
My.	99–11	* a r optimistic body of people,

remarked

Ret.	19–20	was r by all observers.
Pul.	37– 1	* r Mrs. Hanna,
My.	24–24	* have been r by the many visitors
	330–31	was r by all observers.

remarks

Mis.	32– 5	r on "Christ and Christmas"
	176– 5	Extempore R.
	312–12	in his r before that body,
	379–10	from his r I inferred that
Man.	32–20	shall make no r explanatory of
	32–22	shall read all notices and r
My.	170– 6	The brevity of my r was due to
	185–26	closing my r with the words of

remeasured

Mis.	222–21	measure . . . must be r to it.

remedial

Mis.	4– 3	potent and desirable r agent
	44– 8	r power of C. S.
	379–14	was not as potential or r,

remedies

Mis.	96– 6	no other gods, no r in drugs,
	209– 2	as its antidotes and r.
	334–27	Science r the ills of
Ret.	33–10	r enumerated by Jahr,
Un.	14–10	as Burgess, the boatbuilder, r
Hea.	12–15	two hundred and sixty r
My.	283–14	r for all earth's woe.

remedy

Mis.	2–18	found alone the r for sin,
	44–29	By applying this mental r
	45–14	demands the r of Truth
	63– 9	r for the opposite triad
	97–15	is not a r of faith alone,
	195– 1	any other r than Christ,
	200–24	to seek the r for it,
	221–10	Truth is their r.
	236–24	r for all human discord.
	371– 7	behold the r, to help them
Un.	18–12	I could not r them,
Pul.	6–18	* false r I had vainly used,
'01.	18–12	no r apart from Mind,
Hea.	11–22	Mind came in as the r,
	12–17	symptoms requiring the r,
	15– 4	no other r than Truth,
My.	118– 6	r is worse than the disease.
	292–24	not mixed with morphine to r

remember

Mis.	2– 9	r that God is just,
	108–25	R, and act on, Jesus' definition
	137– 9	I r my regret, when,
	138–14	R that the first and last
	146– 1	'T is sweet to r thee,
	175–32	r God in all thy ways,
	211–22	let him r,
	212–10	r the reiterated warning
	224–11	r that the world is wide ;
	237–29	I r, when a girl,
	267– 9	r that there never was a time
	268–28	R that human pride forfeits
	281–29	r the words of Solomon,
	282– 4	R, it is personality, and the

remember

Mis.	331–15	r· *their* cradle hymns,
	335– 2	R· the Scripture :
	335–28	r· the Scripture concerning
	338–15	r·, a pure faith in humanity
	339–24	R·, that for all this thou alone
	356–12	r· that the seedtime is passed,
	359–24	r· that Science is demonstrated by
Ret.	1– 8	I r· reading, in my childhood,
	6– 6	I r· as one with the open hand.
	86–10	Behold its vileness, and r·
Pul.	7– 9	r· also that God is just,
Pan.	14–19	r·our brave soldiers,
'00.	8–15	r· that sensitiveness is sometimes
'01.	18–28	r· it is He who does it
	19–16	r· that the great Metaphysician
	29–21	r· that mother worked and won
Hea.	4– 8	We pray for God to r· us,
	10– 8	r· that God — good — is omnipotent ;
Po.	33– 1	To daily r· my blessings
My.	12–10	* Each person interested must r·,
	39–23	* We r· her graciousness and dignity.
	60– 6	* Possibly you may r· the words of
	149–31	R·, thou canst be brought into no
	154–10	r· it is not he who gives the
	194– 6	R· that a temple but foreshadows the
	259–17	churches will r· me only thus.
	267– 8	Here let us r· that God is
	313–11	Nor do I r· any such stuff
	323–28	* I wonder if you will r·
	324–11	* I r· telling you of this,
	351–14	grand in you to r· me as the

remembered

Mis.	91 17	Be it r·, that all types employed
	284–21	It must also be r· that neither
My.	126–16	hath r· her iniquities — *Rev.* 18 : 5.
	284– 5	but 'tis sweet to be r·.

remembers

Mis.	100–28	Who r· that patience, forgiveness,
Pul.	46–18	* souvenirs that Mrs. Eddy r·
My.	331– 6	* she r· the Rev. Mr. Reperton,

remembrance

Mis.	58– 1	no r· of that disease or dream,
	91–15	mental conditions, — r· and love ;
	184–12	brings to r· the Hebrew strain,
	386–25	"By the r· of her loyal life,
Po.	34– 5	Some dear r· in a weary breast.
	50–11	"By the r· of her loyal life,
My.	166–13	proof of your r· and love.

remind

'00.	14–15	to r· you of the joy you have had
My.	110–15	r· me of my early dreams of flying

reminded

Mis.	212– 7	r· his students of their worldly
Pul.	48–16	* she paused and r· the reporter

reminder

My.	39–20	* a few words of r· and prophecy.
	262–20	Christmas to me is the r· of God's
	280– 8	* We rejoice also in this new r·

reminds

Mis.	176–14	r· us of the heroes and heroines
My.	322–13	* r· me of a conversation I had with

reminiscences

Ret.	6– 9	Among the treasured r·
Pul.	46– 8	* In Mrs. Eddy's personal r·,
My.	306–21	chapter sub-title

remit

My.	332–11	* or r· his kind attention until

remits

My.	161– 8	never r· the sentence necessary

remodelled

Pul.	47–28	* delightfully r· and modernized
My.	55–23	* Chickering Hall was to be r·.

remodelling

My.	145– 7	r· of the house was finished,

remonstrated

Pul.	30– 3	* when a Boston clergyman r·

remorse

Pul.	33–10	* This caused her tears of r·
My.	267–23	lost opportunities and r·.

remorseless

Mis.	10– 5	the most r· motives
	72–11	as false as it is r·.

remorselessly

Mis.	339–25	Carelessly or r· thou mayest

remote

Mis.	200–15	r· from the general comprehension
Ret.	7–13	* corner, however hidden and r·.
Un.	26– 4	my forms, near or r·.

remote

Hea.	3–16	a r· province of Judea,
My.	152–29	r·, predisposing, and present cause

remoteness

Peo.	5–11	not lost in the mists of r·

removal

Mis.	67–27	If you refer to the r· of a person
	67–30	this r· being possible
Man.	30– 5	R·.
	65–19	r· of the offending member
	82–10	R· of Cards.
	100– 9	R· from Office.
Ret.	21– 1	After his r· a letter was read
Pul.	37– 5	* factor in her r· to Concord,

remove

Mis.	xii– 1	to r· the pioneer signs
	66–30	can neither r· that cause nor
	90– 4	r· all reality from its power.
	108–15	would r· mortals' ignorance
	219–16	if he would r· this feeling
	237– 8	but r· that fear,
	245–16	should r· with glorious results.
	249–19	something to r· stains or vermin.
	308–33	to r· from their observation
	328–25	Whatever obstructs . . . Love will r· ;
	355–24	discern the error . . . and r· it,
	362–23	to r· this mental millstone
	370– 5	how they might r· him.
Man.	51–22	power to . . . r· from membership,
	54–23	shall r· his or her name
	100–17	to r· its Committee on Publication
Pul.	13–26	torture it may take to r· all sin,
Rud.	10–17	R· this fear by the true sense
'00.	12–19	r· thy candlestick — *Rev.* 2 : 5.
Peo.	7–24	To r· those objects of sense
	9–24	r· all evidence of any other
My.	61– 5	* to r· human obstructions
	194– 3	fell forests and r· mountains,
	222–11	R· hence — *Matt.* 17 : 20.
	222–12	and it shall r·." — *Matt.* 17 : 20.
	223–28	burdens that time will r·.
	290–27	will r· the sackcloth from thy home.
	301–27	Drugs cannot r· inflammation,

removed

Mis.	69–19	I r· the stoppage,
	70– 9	When the . . . belief, was r·,
	74–23	he r· any supposition that
	243–10	r· these appliances the same day
	261– 5	can only be r· by reformation.
	378–22	are farther r· from such thoughts
Man.	30– 7	he or she shall be r·
	46–23	liability to have his name r·
	82–11	r· from our periodicals
	103– 6	nor r· from the site
Ret.	5– 9	my parents r· to Tilton,
	20–28	The family . . . very soon r· to
	94–15	every spot and blemish . . . is r·,
Pul.	36–20	* Several years ago Mrs. Eddy r·
'01.	13–23	only as the sin is r·
Hea.	19– 8	r· the bandage from his eyes,
My.	15– 8	nor r· from the site
	55–24	* church r· to Copley Hall
	163–17	When I r· from Boston
	255– 8	I do not mean that . . . should be r·

removes

Un.	2–10	and, lastly, it r· the pain
	39–11	divine Science r· human weakness
Rud.	10–22	r· every erroneous physical and
No.	12–26	It r· all limits from divine power.
'01.	10–15	metaphysics r· the mysticism
	13–22	r· the punishment for sin only as
My.	107–31	stops decomposition, r· enteritis,
	131– 2	r· fear, subdues sin,
	278–11	faith that r· mountains,

removeth

Mis.	174– 7	Him who r· all iniquities,

removing

Mis.	1–19	by r· the dust that dims them.
	41–23	r· the cause in that so-called mind
	221–11	r· the effect of sin on himself,
Un.	25–15	r· its evidence from sense to Soul,
No.	30–15	r· our knowledge of what is not.

remuneration

Mis.	349–24	before I would accept the slightest r·.
Man.	91– 7	R· and Free Scholarship.
Rud.	14– 9	seven-eighths of her time without r·,
My.	214–20	taking no r· for my labors,

remunerator

Mis.	212–23	Love, the white Christ, is the r·.

Renaissance

Pul.	26–10	* lamp stand of the R· period
My.	68– 1	* Built in the Italian R· style,

renaissance
'00.   4–12   indicate a r· greater than

rend
Mis. 211–20   and turn on you and r· you?
Un. 23– 6   to turn again and r· their Maker.
No.   8–25   lest it turn and r· you ;
My. 227–25   turn again and r· you."— *Matt.* 7 : 6.

render
Mis. 45–10   r· this Science invaluable in the
      230–28   to r· it pathetic, tender, gorgeous.
      277–28   be just . . . and r· good for evil.
Man. 77– 9   shall r· them payable.
Ret. 71– 5   "*R*· to Cæsar the things— *Mark* 12 : 17.
My. vii–14   * service which all . . . can r·
      202– 8   "*R*· therefore to all their — *Rom.* 13 : 7.
      220– 9   '*R*· to Cæsar the things— *Mark* 12 : 17.
      220–11   r· 'to God the things that— *Mark* 12 : 17.
      344–25   '*R*· to Caesar the things— *Mark* 12 : 17.

rendered
Mis. 75–22   r· in Science, "My *spiritual sense*
       76–16   r· void by Jesus' divine declaration,
      182–29   made flesh,— that is, r· practical,
Un.   39– 2   Truth of Life is r· practical
       57–14   and r· this infallible verdict ;
Pul. 42– 9   * was r· particularly interesting
No.   37–25   Jesus r· null and void whatever
'02.   16– 4   r· in the Authorized Version
My. 62–27   * valuable services r· to this Board

rendering
Mis. 80– 2   By r· error such a service,
      169–22   The literal r· of the Scriptures
      169–24   The metaphysical r· is health and
      344– 9   so r· it a fit habitation for
'02.   16– 7   combination of words, or of their r·.
My. 116–19   r· praise to whom praise is due,
      150– 7   * r· the world happier and better

renderings
My. 179–24   different r· or translations

renders
Mis. 262–26   and r· the yoke easy.
      333– 6   r· error a palpable falsity,
      374–24   one r· not unto Cæsar
Man. 41–16   r· this member liable to
Un.   53–10   belief that r· them obscure.
Rud. 13– 5   r· it impossible to demonstrate
       15– 9   r· the mind less inquisitive,

rends
Mis. 165–12   Science which r· the veil
      203–21   state of mind which r· the veil
      364–31   C. S. r· this veil
No.   21–20   C. S. r· this veil

renew
Mis. 312–25   and r· its emphasis
      364– 6   will r· your strength."— see *Isa.* 40 : 31.
My.   9–15   * we modestly r· the hope
       38– 5   * r· the story of our love for you
      291–20   shall reverberate, r· euphony,

renewal
No.   14– 9   r· in the Neoplatonic philosophy ;

renewed
Mis. 34– 7   body is r· and harmonious,
Ret. 82– 2   yet their core is constantly r· ;
Pan. 11– 5   r· in knowledge— *Col.* 3 : 10.
'02.   5– 2   r· energy for to-morrow,
My. 13–23   r· like the eagle's,"— *Psal.* 103 : 5.
       64–23   * address ourselves with r· faith
      157–13   * r· evidence of your unselfish
      202–16   r· vision, infinite meanings,

renews
Mis. 130–28   r· his strength, and is exalted
My. 316– 4   r· the heavenward impulse ;

renounce
Pul.   5–10   firmest to suffer, soonest to r·.
'01.   32–12   willing to r· all for Him.

renounced
Mis. 238–22   Have you r· self?
Ret. 43–14   having r· his material method
My. 123–32   r· the hidden things— *II Cor.* 4 : 2.

renovate
'02.   16–25   they reach not the heart nor r· it ;

renovated
Ret. 34–20   this mind must be r·
Un.   6– 6   human nature will be r·,

renown
My. 271–20   * aged woman of world-wide r·

renowned
Pul.   6–29   r· apostle of anti-slavery,
My. 177–16   In your r· city, the genesis of
      291–26   mourn the loss of her r· leader !

rent
Mis. 124–24   r· the veil of matter,
Man. 30–17   taxes and r· on this property ;
       68–12   in addition to r· and board.
'02.   14– 4   can neither r·, mortgage, nor sell
Po.   72– 1   O not too soon is r· the chain

reobtain
Pul. 20– 7   and r· its charter

reorganize
Pul. 20– 6   r· the church, and

reorganized
Man. 18–14   Church members met and r·,
My. 55–15   * r· the church, and named it The

repair
Man. 30–20   keep the property in good r·,

repairing
My. 175– 7   to aid in r· your church

repairs
My. 123–17   r· and other necessary expenses

repartee
Ret. 77– 4   Ingersoll's r· has its moral :

repay
Mis. 130–15   will r·, saith the Lord."— *Rom.* 12 : 19.
Po.   32–17   That health may my efforts r· ;

repays
Mis. 257–14   r· our best deeds with sacrifice

repeal
Peo. 12–11   r· it in mind, and acknowledge only

repealed
Mis. 272– 5   * "This Act was r· from
Man. 18–27   By-Laws pertaining to . . . were r·

repealing
Mis. 272– 9   * r· of said Act in January, 1882.

repeat
Mis. 42–19   we shall not have to r· it ;
       92–13   r· the questions in the chapter on
      120– 6   or r· their work in tears.
      135– 2   Again I r·, person is not in the
      168–17   nineteenth-century prophets r·,
      211–31   Shall we r· our Lord's Prayer when
      275–12   r· with quivering lips words of
      314– 9   r· in concert with the congregation
      314–27   unnecessary to r· the title or page.
      346–24   rule in C. S. never to r· error
      348–18   r· this,— that I use no drugs
      391–21   When angels shall r· it,
Man. 51– 5   if he r· the offense,
Ret. 10– 6   latter I had to r· every Sunday.
Un.   44– 3   I can only r· the Master's words :
       48– 2   to r· my twice-told tale,
Pul.   8– 5   church chimes r· my thanks
No.   32– 5   pardon may encourage a criminal to r·
       41– 9   r· his work to the best advantage for
'02.   4– 3   I again r·, Follow your Leader,
Po.   38–20   When angels shall r· it,
My. 32– 4   * began to r· the Lord's Prayer,
      171– 1   In parting I r· to these
      201–11   r· my legacies in blossom.
      240–15   I now r· another proof,
      270– 5   we r· the signs of these times.
      285–20   In the words of St. Paul, I r· :
      355– 9   I will r· that men are very important

repeated
Mis. 65– 2   by r· proofs of its falsity.
      134– 4   an act which you have immediately r·,
      196– 5   has r· itself in all manner of
      351–15   r· attempts of mad ambition
Man. 58–14   r· at the other services on Sunday.
Ret.   8–19   the same call was thrice r·.
        9–17   never . . . was that mysterious call r·.
Pul. 36–19   * always with this experience r·.
       40–12   * THE SERVICE R· FOUR TIMES
       40–16   * simple ceremonies, four times r·,
       41–20   * Hence the service was r·
       42– 5   * service was r· for the last time.
       59– 8   * these exercises four times r·.
       59–12   * The *Pater Noster* was r·
No.   9–14   Hoping to pacify r· complaints
'01.   31–23   Lord's Prayer, r· at night ;
Hea. 16– 2   can never be r· too often
My. 29–11   * r· six times during the day.
       86–30   * services, r· at intervals
      332–28   * but on r· search a roll of papers
      333–24   * r· assurance of his willingness to

repeatedly
Ret.   8– 4   I r· heard a voice,
Pul. 45–18   * r· asseverated to the contrary.

repeating
Mis.	150–12	to-day are *r·* their joy
	206–21	*r·* this diapason of heaven :
Un.	44– 6	are vain shadows, *r·*
Pul.	59–13	* congregation *r·* one sentence
My.	148–22	what is each heart in this house *r·*,

repeats
Mis.	23–28	*r·* precisely the looks and actions of
	25–20	reiterates the word, *r·* the works,
	253–15	*r·* the past and portends much
Chr.	53–14	What the Beloved knew . . . Science *r·*,
Pul.	25–24	* wainscoting *r·* the same tints.
	39–20	* splendor of the sky *R·* its glory
No.	41– 3	History *r·* itself.
'00.	10–17	History shows that error *r·* itself
Hea.	1– 6	History *r·* itself ;
My.	58– 6	* "History *r·* itself."

repent
Mis.	94– 6	must *r·*, and love good
	123–24	*r·*, forsake sin, love God,
	237–10	Some people never *r·* until
'00.	12–20	except thou *r·*." — *Rev.* 2 : 5.
'01.	15– 2	*r·* and forsake it,
My.	195– 8	it is never too late to *r·*,

repentance
Mis.	93–26	without *r·* and reformation.
	107–16	(1) A proper sense of sin ; (2) *r·* ;
	107–26	and of *r·* therefor,
	107–29	*r·* so severe that it destroys them,
	108–17	advance the second stage . . . *r·*.
	109–11	*r·* is the most hopeful stage
	109–21	and its consequences, *r·*,
	109–31	and thus, cometh *r·*,
	110– 1	*R·* is better than sacrifice.
	203–19	The baptism of *r·* is
	205– 7	fire of *r·* first separates the dross
	205–25	*r·* and absolute abandonment
	244–13	bodily penance and torture, or *r·*
	261– 7	are not cancelled by *r·*
Un.	14– 1	such planks as the divine *r·*,
	14–16	might need *r·*, because
'00.	15– 9	over a tear-filled sea of *r·*
'02.	19–14	listens to the lispings of *r·*
Peo.	9– 4	tears of *r·*, an overflowing love,
My.	36–16	* joy of *r·* and the peace of
	128– 4	*r·* from dead works." — *Heb.* 6 : 1.
	150–21	bringing the sinner to *r·*,
	228–20	with tears of *r·*

repentant
Man.	55–14	Although *r·* and forgiven
'01.	17– 0	loves even the *r·* prodigal

repented
Mis.	18–20	causes much that must be *r·* of
	107–27	deep, never to be *r·* of,
	109–14	one's sins be seen and *r·* of,
Man.	39–12	evidence of having genuinely *r·*
'00.	3–27	*r·* himself, improved on his work

repenteth
Peo.	8– 3	If changeableness that *r·* itself ;

Reperton, Rev. Mr.
My.	331– 6	* Rev. Mr. *R·*, a Baptist clergyman,

repetition
My.	17–25	* audible *r·* of the Lord's Prayer
	19– 6	* *r·* of "the scientific statement of
	32– 1	* unanimity and *r·* in unison
	32–17	* audible *r·* of the Lord's Prayer
	32–30	* audible *r·* of the Lord's Prayer.
	39–12	* audible *r·* of the Lord's Prayer,
	56– 5	* a *r·* of the morning service.
	78–20	* audible *r·* of the Lord's Prayer.

repetitions
My.	56–30	* being *r·* of the first service.

repine
My.	258–21	*r·* over blossoms that mock

replace
Un.	7–13	able to *r·* dislocated joints and

replenish
Mis.	56–26	and *r·* the earth," — *Gen.* 1 : 28.
	92– 8	His work is to *r·* thought,
	117–26	*r·* his lamp at the midnight hour
	149– 7	and *r·* your scanty store.

replenished
Mis.	341–26	if the lamp she tends is not *r·*

replete
Ret.	2–18	printed in olden type and *r·* with
Po.	29–13	Beloved, by flesh embound
My.	70–20	* church is *r·* with rare bits of art,

repletion
Pul.	41–22	* filled the church to *r·*.

replied
Mis.	178–20	* I should have *r·*, 'Much learning'
	180– 9	"Christ never left," I *r·* ;
	226–19	he *r·*, "Not to be credited
	281–14	He *r·* to his wife, who urged him
	344– 5	"Very well," the teacher *r·* ;
	345– 9	*r·* : "Let them come ;
	381–14	and he *r·*, in substance,
Man.	98– 3	not been *r·* to by other Scientists,
Ret.	14–24	I *r·* that I could only answer
Pul.	30– 6	* he *r·* that the C. S. Church
	31–21	* she most kindly *r·*, naming an
Peo.	13–19	he *r·* : "Let them come ;
Po.	v–19	* she *r·* by reading the poem
My.	60– 3	* I have *r·* that if Mrs. Eddy
	220– 9	questioned . . . he *r·* :
	241–23	* I *r·* that I did not live in
	324–30	* When we asked him . . . he *r·*

replies
Mis.	317– 2	my heart *r·*, Yes,
	346–11	To this question C. S. *r·* :
	367–29	*r·* that God is too pure to
	372–16	such *r·* as the following :
My.	223– 5	*r·* to letters which pertain to
	240–23	* *r·*, through her student,

reply (noun)

in
Mis.	35–28	In *r·*, we refer you to "S. and H.
	158– 2	In *r·* to your letter I will say :
	321–24	In *r·* to all invitations
Pul.	34–26	* said, in *r·* to my questions,
My.	172–20	* In *r·* Mr. Bates said,
	204–14	In *R·* to a Letter Announcing
	214–16	In *r·* to letters questioning
	276–21	* In *r·* to a number of requests
	277– 3	In *r·* to your question,
	356–13	In *r·* to inquiries,

just
Man.	93–12	just *r·* to public topics

Mrs. Eddy's
Pul.	87–10	* heading
My.	142– 7	chapter sub-title
	207– 6	* chapter sub-title
	207–20	heading
	241–13	* and Mrs. Eddy's *r·* thereto.
	241–18	* The question and Mrs. Eddy's *r·*
	242– 1	heading
	255– 4	heading
	271–23	* Mrs. Eddy's *r·* will be read
	281–26	heading
	352–18	heading
	361–15	* chapter sub-title
	362– 1	heading
	362– 9	* chapter sub-title
	363–13	heading

my
Mis.	244–17	Will he accept my *r·*
	287–23	the substance of my *r·* is :
My.	195– 7	have hitherto prevented my *r·*.
	311–12	My *r·* to the statement that the

no
Mis.	137–11	I received no *r·*.

recent
My.	305–27	My recent *r·* to the reprint

to Mark Twain
My.	302–13	chapter sub-title

to McClure's
My.	308– 5	chapter sub-title

Mis.	95– 7	* which *r·* was taken in full by
Ret.	34– 6	the *r·* was dark and contradictory.
No.	46– 7	halts for a *r·* ;
My.	73– 8	* the *r·* will be in the form of
	271–21	* requesting the courtesy of a *r·* :

reply (verb)
Mis.	05– 6	* ten minutes in which to *r·*
	193– 3	we *r·* in the affirmative
	353– 7	I *r·*, The human concept
Man.	98– 6	purpose of having him *r·* to it.
Ret.	9–10	to *r·* as he did,
Pul.	33– 8	* to *r·* as he did :
	33–10	* was afraid and did not *r·*.
	33–11	* promised to *r·* if the call came
'01.	12– 7	he would naturally *r·*,
Po.	35–11	heart whereunto none *r·*,
My.	156– 3	to *r·* in words of the Scripture :
	242–22	nor to *r·* to any received,
	251– 5	I *r·* to the following question

report
Mis.	44–21	That matter can *r·* pain,
	128–10	things are of good *r·* : — *Phil.* 4 : 8.
	131–13	is prepared to itemize a *r·*
	159–14	are pure and of good *r·*,
	171– 7	according to the *r·* of some,

report

Mis.	183–20	hath believed our *r·*?" — *Isa.* 53 : 1.
	249– 8	false *r·* that I have appropriated
	249–20	The *r·* that I was dead
	267– 8	When they *r·* me as *"hating*
	277–19	truth of Benjamin Franklin's *r·*
	299– 8	I have no time for detailed *r·*
	330–19	learn what *r·* they bear,
	340–21	through evil or through good *r·*,
Man.	26–25	shall neither *r·* the discussions
	37–12	to *r·* the cause for rejection.
	48–17	shall not *r·* for publication
	55– 2	shall not *r·* nor send notices
	66–11	duty of the Clerk to *r·* to her
	66–24	shall not *r·* on authority
	76– 7	*R·* of Directors.
	76–10	*r·* at the annual Church meeting
Un.	39– 9	hath believed our *r·*?" — *Isa.* 53 : 1.
Rud.	10–14	cannot feel, see, or *r·* pain
My.	8–29	* "Since the last *r·*, in 1900,
	16– 1	* chapter sub-title
	16– 2	* *r·* of Mr. Stephen A. Chase,
	22– 2	* *Extract from the Clerk's R·*
	23– 9	* *Extract from the Treasurer's R·*
	25–10	* taken from the *r·* of the secretary
	47– 1	* heading
	47– 7	* to present in this *r·* a few of the
	53–25	* annual *r·* of the business committee
	125– 5	It requires you to *r·* progress,
	143–10	I have the pleasure to *r·* to
	144– 6	public *r·* that I am in either of the
	231–29	interesting *r·* regarding the By-law,
	234–16	The *r·* of the success of C. S. in
	249–22	The *r·* that I prefer to have a
	275–13	Permit me to say, the *r·*

reported

Mis.	168–24	* *The C. S. J. r·* as follows :
	248–19	that I am dead, as is oft *r·*.
	248–20	alleged to have *r·* my demise,
	298– 4	as we be slanderously *r·*,
	311–30	Being often *r·* as saying
	330–20	*r·* more spiritual growth.
Man.	78–23	Such payments shall be *r·*,
Pul.	72– 4	* *r·* deification of Mrs. Eddy,
My.	178–31	all else *r·* as his sayings are
	298– 5	not a little is already *r·* of the
	310–20	*r·* by physician or post-mortem

Reporter, The

Pul.	70– 1	* *The R·*, Lebanon, Ind.,

reporter

Mis.	95– 8	* shorthand *r·* who was present,
Pul.	48–16	* she paused and reminded the *r·*
	49– 9	* the *r·* exclaimed :
	72– 5	* a *Post r·* called upon a few of
	73–26	* She referred the *r·* to the

reporting

Mis.	44–22	or that mind is . . . *r·* sensations,
	311–32	others who were *r·* false charges,
My.	220– 7	*r·* of a contagious case to the

reports

Mis.	274–15	chapter sub-title
	297–11	the public cannot swallow *r·* of
Man.	56–15	*r·* of Treasurer, Clerk, and
	56–16	general *r·* from the Field.
	66–23	Unauthorized *R·*.
Pul.	73–24	* in the *r·* from New York
'00.	2– 8	close observer *r·* three types of
My.	99–19	* press *r·* state that the
	174–11	for their *r·* of the happy occasion.
	243– 2	According to *r·*, the belief is
	333–31	* "We are assured that *r·* of
	334– 3	* newspaper *r·* of that date

repose

Mis.	128– 2	uncomfortable whereon to *r·*.
	340– 3	*r·* from many a heart.
Ret.	17– 9	peers out, from her crimson *r·*,
	18– 8	sentinel hedgerow is guarding *r·*,
Po.	41– 4	the lambkin soft virtue's *r·*,
	62–10	peers out, from her crimson *r·*,
	63–17	sentinel hedgerow is guarding *r·*,

reposes

Hea.	15– 7	it *r·* all faith in mind,

reposing

My.	152– 8	By *r·* faith in man

repository

Mis.	236– 4	*r·* of little else than

repossess

My.	201–12	hope *r·* us of heaven.

represent

Mis.	91–30	*r·* the most spiritual forms
	266– 7	may *r·* me as doing it ;
Ret.	82–19	*r·* an accumulation of power

represent

No.	33–18	was inadequate to *r·* the
My.	45–10	* *r·* only a small part of the
	95– 6	* *r·* the intelligence of many

representation

Un.	54–23	a *r·* that God both knew

representations

Mis.	55–19	Spirit and its forms and *r·*,

representative

Mis.	61– 2	*r·* of verities priceless,
	87–13	mortal mind is a poorer *r·*
	305– 2	* *r·* from each Republic
	305– 3	* *r·* from the patriotic
My.	30–30	* *r·* of the entire body
	227– 3	he spake as God's *r·*
	281–20	* views by *r·* persons.
	327–21	* *r·* men of our dear State

representatives

Mis.	200– 5	the better *r·* of God
My.	74–28	* *r·* of the two poles of healing,
	112–22	better *r·* of C. S. than
	207– 7	* *r·* of churches and societies

represented

Mis.	186–29	Adam *r·* by the Messias,
	295–22	not wholly *r·* by one man.
Pul.	13– 1	Life, *r·* by the Father ;
	13– 2	Truth, *r·* by the Son ;
	13– 2	Love, *r·* by the Mother.
'01.	10–13	*r·* both the divine and the
Hea.	10– 7	manhood of God, that Jesus *r·* ;
My.	24–22	* fifteen different trades *r·*.
	239–16	*r· by His idea or image*

representing

Mis.	140– 5	*r·* the true nature of the gift ;
	305– 1	* women *r·* each State
	305– 9	* the National Society
Pul.	27–12	* *r·* the heavenly city
	27–27	* *r·* John on the Isle of Patmos,
My.	100– 9	* *r·* a vast number of the followers

represents

Mis.	46–25	man *r·* his divine Principle,
	46–27	sound, in tones, *r·* harmony ;
	104–25	and its idea *r·* Love.
	164– 4	idea that *r·* divine good,
	336– 8	Do you love that which *r·* God
Man.	49– 8	member of The Mother Church who *r·*
	54–20	*r·* falsely to or of the Leader
Ret.	63–14	*r·* God, the Life of man.
Pul.	27–16	* other rose window *r·* the
	27–25	* *r·* the raising of Lazarus.
	28– 2	* central panel *r·* her in solitude
	81–14	* She *r·* the composite beauty,
Rud.	4–10	All true Science *r·* a moral
No.	26–13	All real being *r·* God,
My.	23–25	* *r·* the worship of Spirit,
	24– 6	* vastness of the truth it *r·*,
	77– 3	* novelty of the cult which it *r·*.
	118–26	*r·* not the divinity of C. S.,
	172–13	save that which it *r·*
	259–29	*r·* the eternal informing Soul

repress

My.	63–16	* to *r·* a feeling of exultation

repressed

Mis.	250– 9	should be *r·* by the sentiments.

repression

Pul.	50–28	* and live down any attempted *r·*.

reprint

My.	305–27	My recent reply to the *r·*

reprinted

My.	29– 1	* *R·* from *Boston Herald*
	363–17	*R·* in *C. S. Sentinel,*

reproach

Mis.	228–17	and honest beyond *r·*,
My.	33–20	nor taketh up a *r·* — *Psal.* 15 : 3.
	53– 2	* inquiry and mercantile *r·* ;

reproachable

Mis.	147–30	than attain it by *r·* means.

reproaches

Mis.	199–11	in infirmities, in *r·*, — *II Cor.* 12 : 10.
	201–20	pleasure in "*r·*" — *II Cor.* 12 : 10.

reproduce

Mis.	360–12	nor can it *r·*, these stars of the
	372–24	to *r·*, with reverent touch,

reproduced

Mis.	165–30	treasures *r·* and given to the world,
	201– 9	Jesus *r·* his body after its burial,
	337–30	is again *r·* in the character which
Pul.	32– 6	* expression cannot thus be *r·*.
My.	272–22	* *r·* in her own handwriting.
	347–14	*r·* her primal presence,

reproduces
Mis. 364-32 r· the divine philosophy of Jesus
Un. 26- 3 Evil. . . . and matter r· God.
No. 21-21 r· the teachings of Jesus,
reproduction
Mis. xi- 5 r· of what has been written,
375-31 * thing of the past, impossible of r·.
reproductions
Pul. 49- 5 * has hung its walls with r· of
My. 70-16 * Millet's "Angelus" had living r·
342- 9 * so often seen in r·,
reproof
Mis. 126-20 No r· is so potent as the silent
Ret. 80-17 he will not scorn the timely r·,
reprove
No. v- 3 "r·, rebuke, exhort," — II Tim. 4 : 2.
My. 130-17 my students r·, rebuke, and
reptiles
Mis. 210- 9 warning people not to stir up these r·
Un. 52-21 rabid beasts, fatal r·, and
My. 245-12 poisonous r· and devouring beasts,
Republic
Mis. 305- 2 * one representative from each R·
My. 341- 3 child of the R·, a Daughter of
Republic, The
Pul. 63- 1 * The R·, Washington, D. C.,
Republican
Pul. 88-21 * R·, Springfield, Mass.
republish
Mis. x- 7 and r· them in book form,
republished
Man. 82- 8 published nor r· by this Society
repudiated
Mis. 97- 9 r· the idea of casting out
repudiates
Hea. 15- 1 r· the evidences of the senses
reputable
My. 100-15 * a class who are r·, intelligent,
237-17 equal to those of r· physicians
reputation
My. 52-22 * Mrs. Eddy's future r·,
138-11 My personal r· is assailed
reputations
Mis. 274-24 legislation, and decapitated r·,
reputed
Ret. 6-16 r· one of the most talented,
request
Mis. x 5 comply with an oft-repeated r· ;
127- 8 and again earnestly r·,
133- 7 I r· you to read my sermons
306-19 * r· of the late Mrs. Harrison,
319-20 and grant me this r·,
Man. 18-13 r· of Rev. Mary Baker Eddy,
26-23 A majority vote or the r· of
67-25 r· of the Pastor Emeritus,
82-11 without the r· of the advertiser,
94-15 written r· of Mrs. Eddy,
100- 6 If she shall send a special r·
100- 7 r· shall be carried out
100-21 to comply with this r·.
Ret. 45-16 in accord with my special r·,
Po. 33- 2 And make this my humble r· :
My. 18- 5 and again earnestly r·,
130-31 r·, that you borrow little else
139-19 purpose of my r· was sacred.
170- 3 r· of my church members
182- 4 at my r· I received from the
216-22 r· that from this date you disband
217-15 my r· as above named.
236-24 I r· the Christian Scientists
256- 8 my r· that I be permitted
279-22 I r· that every member of
280-16 I now r· that the members
280-28 In no way nor manner did I r·
298- 1 r· the privilege of buying,
307- 2 which I, at his r·, had added
328-22 * r· of a prominent healer
requested
Mis. 49- 2 r· her to withdraw
157-10 r· that they furnish
158- 5 r· you to be ordained,
381-10 r· her lawyer to inquire
Man. 53-11 without her having r· the
Pul. 34-12 * r· those with her to withdraw,
Po. v-21 * each r· a copy,
vii- 5 * r· her publisher to prepare a few
My. 27-15 * r· to send no more money
98-16 * r· to send no more money
169- 7 are r· to visit me at a later
242-21 I have r· my secretary not to

requested
My. 332-22 * r· to look up the records
339- 7 specially r· to be wise
requesting
My. 271-21 * r· the courtesy of a reply :
requests
Mis. 155-19 she hereby r· : First, that you,
Man. 30-12 Unless Mrs. Eddy r· otherwise,
Po. v-22 * Similar r· continued to reach the
My. 276-21 * In reply to a number of r·
requiem
Mis. 395-25 A r· o'er the tomb
Po. 58-10 A r· o'er the tomb
requiems
Ret. 4-18 wandering winds sigh low r·
require
Mis. 4-25 "It must r· a great deal of faith
39- 4 would r· the understanding of how you
51- 4 drugs, God does not r·.
54-23 r· an understanding of the Science
91-30 r· their pupils to study the lessons
92-19 r· the students thoroughly to study it
92-22 teacher should r· each member to
196-30 Scriptures r· more than a simple
197- 1 they r· a living faith,
301-14 r· only a word to be wise ;
358-20 Be it understood that I do not r·
Man. 66-20 r· all of it to be read ;
Ret. 6-13 would r· more space than
Pul. 62-12 * r· but little muscular power
Rud. 14-17 expect and r· others to pay him.
My. 177- 7 daily duties r· attention elsewhere,
217-29 not r· the last step to be . . . first.
244-24 may not r· more than one lesson.
259-15 r· less attention than packages
358-31 r· the C. S. Board of Directors
required
Mis. 4-27 there is no will-power r·,
43-18 time is r· thoroughly to qualify
88- 4 the less this is r·, the better
91-27 as occasion r·, read from the book
148-14 and as the occasion r·.
166-18 The Judæan religion even r·
235- 3 r· and empowered to conquer sin,
283-32 The only personal help r·
334-25 understanding is r· to do this.
Man. 3-10 and as the occasion r·.
56-13 its officers are r· to be present.
62- 2 offertory conforming to the time r·
65- 9 Obedience R·.
68-23 Agreement R·.
74-17 churches and societies are r· to
89-15 such credentials as are r·
109-13 as r· by Article V, Sect. 6,
110- 1 new applications will be r·,
110-17 in all places where they are r·.
Un. 11-24 Jesus r· neither cycles of time nor
Pul. 62-10 * r· a strong man to ring them,
Rud. 15-27 as are r· to empty and to fill anew the
Pan. 11- 1 r· the divinity of our Master
'01. 25-14 or r· in such metaphysics,
My. 14 14 * entire amount r· to complete
43- 5 * might know what was r· of them,
65-14 * Learning that a big church was r·,
77-28 * the two million dollars r·
98 19 * all of the funds r· to build it
212- 9 than has been r· to put down
245-24 these credentials are still r·
328-14 * license . . . r· of physicians,
328-15 * has been r· of them,
requirement
Mis. 4-19 adequate to meet the r·.
77- 9 Philip's r· was, that he should
181- 8 personal r· of blind obedience
181-10 unless that r· should express
Man. 51-14 Preliminary R·.
77-18 God's R·.
110- 2 This r· is to prevent
My. 46-17 * r· of a reinstated Christianity.
requirements
Mis. 261-19 divine r· typified in the law
346-21 grasped in all its divine r·.
Man. 29- 8 fulfil the r· of this By-Law,
39- 1 to live according to the r·
51-15 r· according to the Scriptures,
72-25 R· for Organizing Branch Churches.
Pul. 50-22 * thoroughly carried away with the r·,
requires
Mis. ix-17 r· strength from above,
6-21 r· time to overcome the patient's
14- 9 imperfection that r· evil
40-29 it r· more divine understanding
68- 3 it r· both time and eternity.

requires
Mis.	246– 4	r· the enlightenment of these
	366– 4	it r· more study to understand
	367– 2	This Science r· man to be honest,
Man.	44–26	God r· our whole heart,
	77–18	God r· wisdom, economy,
Un.	43–10	r· time and immense spiritual
Pul.	15– 8	r· the spirit of our blessed Master
	79–23	* r· the religious sentiment
Rud.	9–15	r· a preparation of the heart
No.	11–18	it r· more study to understand
	33– 8	r· sacrifice, struggle, prayer,
	34–20	heathen conception that God r·
Hea.	3– 1	Christianity r· neither hygiene nor
	11–26	r· mind imbued with Truth
	12–20	To prepare the medicine r· time
My.	125– 5	r· you to report progress,
	175– 4	r· my constant attention and time,
	220– 8	when the law so r·.
	276– 7	When accumulating work r· it,

requiring
Hea.	12–17	moral symptoms r· the remedy,
My.	91– 8	* r· their church edifices to be fully

requisite
Mis.	x–14	where these are most r·,
	16– 8	r· to become wholly Christlike,
	67–30	after all the footsteps r·
	136–25	oftener is not r·,
	145– 6	r· to manifest its spirit,
	148–18	r· to demonstrate genuine C. S.,
	181– 6	r· in order to understand
	195– 9	spirit and the letter are r· ;
	257–18	fear where courage is r·,
	270–16	r· for healing the sick.
	317–12	is not absolutely r·
	346–25	unless it becomes r·
	359– 2	is r· in the beginning ;
	380– 9	were r· to enable me
Man.	3–15	r· to demonstrate genuine C. S.,
	43– 9	Whatever is r· for either
Ret.	10– 4	less labor than is usually r·.
	45– 7	r· only in the earliest periods
	45–11	r· in the first stages
	76– 3	nor . . . copyright be r·,
	79–20	wisdom r· for teaching
	81–29	r· at every stage of advancement.
Un.	40–19	A sense of death is not r·
Pul.	54–10	* conditions r· in psychic healing
Rud.	12–20	r· for the well-being of man.
My.	26–23	this notice is r· to give
	238–15	became r· in the divine order.
	279– 1	never r·, never a necessity,
	285– 6	cannot spare the time r·

requisition
Pul.	62–20	* They can be called into r·

rescue
Mis.	107– 7	come to the r· of mortals,
	134–19	Firm in your . . . go to its r·.
	218–17	Truth comes to the r·
	293– 8	will come, . . . to the r·
	362–22	must come to the r· of mortals,
Un.	59–19	Jesus came to r· men from
Pul.	9–12	came to the r· as sunshine
No.	7–14	find r· and refuge in Truth
	11–25	r· reason from the thrall of
'02.	13–16	and I came to the r·,
Po.	71–13	God to the r·
My.	350– 8	came to the writer's r·,

rescued
Mis.	140–22	had to be r· from the grasp
	211–14	r· from the merciless wave
Ret.	14– 8	converted and r· from perdition ;
Pul.	66–11	* r· from death miraculously
Po.	71– 8	R· by the "fanatic" hand,

research
Mis.	114– 5	should spare no r·
	116–20	scientific r· and attainment
	223– 4	at length took up the r·
Ret.	33– 1	physical side of this r· was
Pul.	23–21	* scholars of special r·,
	47–11	* physical side in this r·
My.	348– 4	induced a deep r·,

researches
Mis.	169– 2	all along the way of her r·

resemblance
Mis.	375–21	* I find an almost identical r·,
No.	21–27	has little r· to Science,
My.	96–10	* The one point of r· is that the

resemble
Mis.	376– 5	* very closely r· in detail the
Po.	v–12	* r· the profile of a human face.

resembles
Mis.	167– 9	compound idea of all that r· God.
No.	26– 8	or the human belief r· the
My.	310–32	* it so r· the author."

resembling
No.	23– 2	To conceive of God as r·

resenting
My.	204–25	hypnotism, and the r· of injuries,

resentment
Mis.	137–25	pride, envy, evil-speaking, r·,
	224–30	an object of pity rather than of r· ;
'02.	19– 8	Christian Scientist cherishes no r· ;

resentments
My.	40–12	* relinquish their cherished r·,

reservations
My.	345– 4	do not suppose their mental r·

reserved
My.	38–17	* was specially r· for them.
	159–30	All rights r·.
	164–27	This unity is r· wisdom and strength.

reserves
Mis.	119–27	individual rights which one justly r·
Man.	80–18	Pastor Emeritus r· the right to

reserving
My.	vi–26	* r· for herself only a place for

reset
Mis.	242– 7	if either would r· certain dislocations

reside
Mis.	120–21	r· a long distance from Massachusetts,
	247–21	believe it to r· in matter of the brain ;

resided
Ret.	5–18	for many years had r· in Tilton
	20–10	r· in the northern part of
Po.	vi–24	* during the years she r· in Lynn,
My.	312–18	r· in Charleston, S. C.
	335– 3	* Brother Glover r· in Charleston,

residence
Mis.	225– 2	At the r· of Mr. Rawson,
	249–17	since my r· in Boston ;
	294–25	Since my r· in Concord,
Man.	30–11	First Reader's R·.
Pul.	37– 6	* where she has a beautiful r·,
	68–11	* r· in her native State.
	68–17	* the r· of the pastor,
My.	27– 4	Assemble not at the r· of
	284–18	Since my r· in Concord,
	333–11	* the r· of the deceased,

residences
Pul.	36–23	* one of the most beautiful r·

resident
Pul.	8–23	r· youthful workers were called
	15– 1	good r· in divine Mind,
My.	330– 9	* not then a r· of Wilmington.
	335–12	* a r· of Charleston, S. C.,

residents
My.	82–29	* not be noticeable to the r·

residing
My.	83– 4	* r· in the convention city.

resign
Man.	28–21	notify this officer either to r·
	29–11	Directors shall r· their office or
	89– 2	Should the President r·
	94–20	A member shall neither r· nor
My.	167– 7	teaches us to r· what we are not
	195–13	r· with good grace what we are denied,

resignation
'02.	17–28	Patience and r· are the pillars of
My.	51– 7	* feels it her duty to tender her r·,

resigned
Pul.	71–19	* Mrs. Eddy has r· herself
Hea.	13–19	we r· the imaginary medicine
My.	276–10	try to be composed and r·

resist
Mis.	64–20	r· speculative opinions and fables.
	114–17	r· the foe within and without.
	141– 7	for no one can r· the power
	223–18	what we would r· to the hilt
	278–20	seem stronger to r· temptation
Ret.	80–14	it may stir the human heart to r·
My.	212–21	r· the animal magnetism

resistance
Mis.	74–28	conquered the r· of the world.
Pul.	80– 8	* sought the line of least r·.
Rud.	3– 4	r· to all efforts to save them
'01.	15–10	r· to C. S. weakens in proportion
My.	8– 7	* beyond r· in your thought."
	40–28	* without regrets and without r·.

resisted
Mis. 113–23   evil can be r· by true Christianity.
222–14   would have r· and loathed ;
No. 36–23   could not have r· them ;

resistless
My. 149– 6   divine Love, r· Life and Truth.

resists
My. 210–14   Goodness involuntarily r· evil.

resolution
Po. vi–20   r· in Congress prohibiting
My. 37–30   * With sacred r· do we pray

resolutions
Ret. 48–11   following r· were passed :
48–14   r· which were presented
Po. vi–27   * poem
page 32   poem
32–13   form r·, with strength from on high,
33–15   If these r· are acted up to,
My. 51– 4   * the following r· were passed :
199–13   joint r· contained therein
364–23   preamble and r·

Resolutions for the Day
Po. vi–27   * poem
page 32   poem

resolve
Mis. 204–27   gives steadiness to r·, and success to
319–29   faith and r· are friends to Truth ;
Pul. 82– 6   * steel tempered with holy r·,
Hea. 1–19   * Pushes his prudent purpose to r·."
My. 36–28   * have fulfilled a high r·

resolved
Ret. 40–19   R·, That we thank the State
My. 52– 2   * R· : That while she had many
52–11   * R· : That while we realize the
231– 9   r· to spend no more time

resolves
Mis. 179– 6   r· itself into these questions :
201– 3   Science of Paul's declaration r· the

resolving
Ret. 9–13   r· to do, next time, as my mother

resort
Mis. 51–21   to r· to corporeal punishment.
336– 6   you cannot, . . . r· to stones and clubs,
Man. 48–14   or make a summer r· near
Ret. 78–17   or a r· to subterfuge in the
No. 36–15   Jesus had a r· to his higher self
My. 98–23   * No r· was had to any of the latter-day

resorted
My. 305– 3   the calumniator has r· to

resorts
Mis. 53–17   He that r· to physics,

resound
Mis. 106 27   and r· His praise."
295–24   r· from Albion's shores.

resounding
My. 189– 9   r· through the dim corridors of time,

resources
Mis. 235–23   educate the affections to higher r·,
Un. 9–14   source and r· of being,
My. 84– 4   * the r· of the institution.

respect
Mis. 223–11   I r· that moral sense which
245–19   rights that man is bound to r·.
Man. 112–10   fill out his application in this r·
Un. 5–19   Let us r· the rights of conscience
Pul. 21–14   entertain due r· and fellowship
80–13   * and out of r· to them we have
No. 45–15   rights which man is bound to r·.
'00. 14–24   r· the character and philanthropy of
'01. 17–14   commands the r· of our best thinkers.
My. 30– 4   * precisely the same in every r·
37 8   * tenderest gratitude, r·, and
38–21   * In every r· their service was
77– 5   * In this r· it leads the Auditorium
88–25   * to whom they rightfully turn with r·
122–13   such as to command r· everywhere.
163–27   I r· their religious beliefs,
321–20   * to change my opinion . . . in this r·.
331–12   * testifies to the love and r·
333– 8   * paying the last tribute of r·

respectable
My. 97–18   * r·, evidently wealthy congregation
249–17   that at this . . . period a r· newspaper

respected
Ret. 6– 9   reminiscences of my much r· parents,
Pul. 66–21   * departure from long r· views
'01. 18– 7   more honored and r· to-day
My. 137–11   R· Sir : — It is over forty years

respecter
'01. 27–21   God is no r· of persons.
My. 128– 9   "no r· of persons." — Acts 10 : 34.

respectful
My. 75– 2   * our r· acknowledgment of its

respectfully
Pul. 86–26   * r· extend to you the invitation
87–14   permit me, r·, to decline their
Rud. v– 3   TENDERLY AND r· DEDICATED
Po. 73– 1   R· inscribed to my friends in Lynn.
My. 60–20   * R· and faithfully yours,
138–21   I remain most r· yours,
224– 5   I r· call your attention to this

respective
My. 237–18   physicians in their r· localities.

respectively
Pul. 43– 4   * under the direction, r·, of
47–19   * key words r· used in the
59–16   * read from . . . and her work r·.
My. 16–19   * r· the architect and the builder
245–28   indicate, r·, the degrees of
329–17   * of July 3 and August 21, 1844, r·.

respects
My. 89–29   * in some r·, the greatest religious
259–28   Christmas r· the Christ too much to
307–20   in some r· he was quite a seer

resplendent
Mis. 320–10   lends its r· light to this hour :

respond
Mis. 303–25   r· to this letter by contributions.
Ret. 14–20   I had to r· that I could not

responded
Pul. 8– 9   r· to the call for this church
My. 171–20   * Mrs. Eddy r· graciously to the

responding
Mis. 95–10   * Mrs. Eddy r·, said :
Pul. 59–13   * r· with its parallel interpretation
My. 254–10   R· to your kind letter,

responds
Un. 32–20   To this declaration C. S. r·,

response
Mis. 314–17   in r· to the congregation.
Rud. 6–12   met a r· from Prof. S. P. Langley,
My. 11–15   * r· was instant, spontaneous.
157–19   * In r· to an inquiry from the
165–20   rise above . . . to the scientific r· :
264–14   heading

responsibilities
Mis. 176 27   our own great opportunities and r·
Pul. 45–24   * gladly laid down his r·

responsibility
Mis. 201 07   I realized what a r· you assume
304–31   * The r· of its production,
305– 9   * r· of representing the National
Un. 20– 7   I shirk all r· for myself as evil,
'00. 9–28   to fit others for this great r·.
Hea. 5–21   r· of our own thoughts and acts ;
My. 123–14   to be rid of the care and r· of

responsible
Mis. 61–15   * man is held r· for the crime :
61–18   * This 'man' was held r·
119– 3   r· for our thoughts and acts;
119– 8   Each individual is r· for himself.
227–14   r· for kind (?) endeavors.
263–20   r· for supplying this want,
265–22   I am not morally r· for
301– 9   are morally r· for what
347–25   God is r· for the mission
355–20   its victim is r· for its
357–26   not morally r· for this,
Man. 76–25   individually r· for said funds.
77–14   r· for the performance
78– 7   shall not be made legally r·
98– 1   shall be r· for correcting
Ret. 77– 1   I become r·, as a teacher,
85– 1   should be specially r·
Un. 64– 2   If . . . God is r· therefor ;
No. 18–21   the teacher is morally r·.
Peo. 11–22   legislators who are greatly r·
My. 243–11   hold important, r· offices,
313–15   accompanied by some r· individual

responsive
My. 33–13   * The r· reading was from
79– 1   * singing and r· reading,

rest (noun)
abiding
Ret. 23– 3   could be a real and abiding r·.
all the
Mis. 224–15   different . . . from all the r· ;
and drink
Pul. 14–16   watching for r· and drink.
at
Mis. 104– 2   at r· in the eternal harmony.
362– 5   reason is at r· in God's wisdom,

rest (noun)

calls for
My. 165–23   becomes tired and calls for *r*·.

comfort and
Po. 78–15   Give . . . comfort and *r*·,

compass his
Po. 18–10   he soareth to compass his *r*·,

conflict and
Po. 77–12   joy and tears, conflict and *r*·,

day of
Mis. 279–20   the seventh is the day of *r*·,

find
Mis. 124–12   find *r*· in the spiritual ideal,
     133–28   I turn . . . and find *r*·.
No. 36–16   could find *r*· from unreal trials

for the righteous
'02. 19–17   remaineth a *r*· for the righteous,

heavenly
Mis. 389–25   finds her home and heavenly *r*·.
Po. 5– 7   finds her home and heav'nly *r*·.

His
Pul. 39– 7   * Round our restlessness, His *r*·.

in Christ
'02. 19–18   a *r*· in Christ, a peace in Love,

in God
Rud. 12–19   induces *r*· in God, divine Love,
My. 282– 6   my hope must still *r*· in God,

kindles into
Mis. 356– 2   dilates and kindles into *r*·.

like the
My. 15–29   * To hear it like the *r*·.

no
Pul. 39– 3   * no *r*· until it finds the peace of the
Pan. 13–26   Truly there is no *r*· in them,

of righteousness
Pan. 14– 2   rise into the *r*· of righteousness

our
Mis. 216– 5   and entered into our *r*·,

paradisaical
Mis. 70–12   Paradisaical *r*· from physical agony

passed to
My. 230– 4   when those have passed to *r*·.

promised
Po. 33– 5   bless me with Christ's promised *r*· ;

ransomed
Mis. 386–28   cloud not o'er our ransomed *r*·
Po. 50–15   cloud not o'er our ransomed *r*·

Sabbath
Mis. 216– 3   a Sabbath *r*· for the people of God ;

sigh for
Mis. 206–32   journey, and betimes sigh for *r*·

stupid
Mis. 398– 8   Break earth's stupid *r*·.
Ret. 46–14   Break earth's stupid *r*·.
Pul. 17–13   Break earth's stupid *r*·.
Po. 14–12   Break earth's stupid *r*·.

such a
Pul. 9– 6   break the full chords of such a *r*·.

take thy
Po. 27–22   and may take thy *r*·,

that remaineth
Mis. 144–23   sweet as the *r*· that remaineth

triumph and
Po. 78– 5   waited their reward, triumph and *r*·,

will give thee
My. 153–30   will give thee *r*·, peace, health,

will give you
Mis. 20– 5   and I will give you *r*·."— *Matt.* 11 : 28.
No. 43– 5   and I will give you *r*·."— *Matt.* 11 : 28.
Hea. 2–19   and I will give you *r*·."— *Matt.* 11 : 28.

would give me
Ret. 13–19   God's love, which would give me *r*·,

Mis. 85–16   the *r*· of perpetual, . . . existence.
     158–23   and God will do the *r*·.
     208–14   to the weary and heavy-laden, *r*·.
     216–22   * after the *r*· of it had gone.''
     313– 8   reflects *r*· on the dear readers,
'01. 26– 3   give my tired sense . . . *r*·.
My. 183– 8   * will the world have *r*·.''

rest (verb)
Mis. 101–28   On this proof *r*· premise and
     114–26   *R*· assured that God in His wisdom
     125–12   *r*· on the bosom of God ;
     125–13   *r*·, in the understanding of divine
     125–14   *r*·, in that which "to know aright
     160–13   Of this we *r*· assured,
     227–24   a life wherein the mind can *r*·
     276– 8   *r*· assured my heart's desire met the
     289–11   seems to *r*· on this basis.
     303–10   fruits of Spirit, will *r*· upon us
     316–19   *r*· on my retirement from
     323–21   *r*· in its cool grottos,
     355–24   *r*· like the dove from the deluge.
     357– 8   *r*· beside still waters.

rest (verb)
Mis. 361–21   and *r*· from the subtlety of
     395–19   May *r*· above my head.
Man. 60–10   *r*· the weary and heavy laden.
Ret. 9– 8   That night, before going to *r*·,
     65– 2   *r*· their opinions of Truth . . . on
     82–10   *r*· on divine Principle for guidance,
     85– 9   Of this also *r*· assured,
Un. 8– 9   *r*· upon the evidence of the senses,
Pul. 21–27   must *r*· on the spirit of Christ
Pan. 8–22   must ever *r*· on the basis of the
'01. 1– 4   *r*· assured you can never lack
Peo. 9–23   and *r*· all faith in Spirit,
Po. 1– 4   where the wild winds *r*·,
     17– 3   I'll think of its glory, and *r*·
     41– 1   * Come, *r*· in this bosom,
     44– 4   Whereon they may *r*· !
     58– 4   May *r*· above my head.
My. 38– 4   * *r*· in this satisfying assurance,
     83–16   * who will have time to *r*·
     139– 2   *R*· assured that your Leader
     151–12   *R*· assured that the injustice
     182–27   *r*· their weary wings amid the
     186–13   *R*· assured that He in whom
     192–15   blessing of divine Love *r*· with you.
     202–14   *r*· worthily on the builders of
     210–10   all whom your thoughts *r*· upon
     250–25   I *r*· peacefully in knowing
     252– 8   *R*· assured that the good you do
     296–12   nor *r*· from his labors

restaurant
My. 83–15   * hotel and *r*· keepers,

rested
Mis. 105– 6   *r*· the anathema of priesthood
     140–12   Thus the case *r*·,
My. 85–27   * *r*· on this structure,
     291– 2   *r*· on the life and labors of

restful
Mis. 153– 4   Truth is *r*·, and Love is triumphant.

resting
Mis. 254–24   *r*· in silly peace upon the
     325–16   their feet *r*· on footstools,
Ret. 42–14   *r*· on his serene countenance.
Pul. 42–22   * a star of lilies *r*· on palms,
     42–29   * white carnations *r*· on a mat of palms,

resting-place
Mis. 118– 5   when faith finds a *r*·
     150–23   and the desert is *r*·
My. 257–30   the Christian traveller's *r*·.
     326–19   bore his remains to their last *r*·.

restitution
My. 131–10   loving *r*·, redemption, and inspiration,

restless
Ret. 11– 6   Go fix thy *r*· mind
Po. 60– 2   Go fix thy *r*· mind

restlessness
Pul. 39– 7   * Round our *r*·, His rest.

restoration
Rud. 6–19   *r*· *of the true evidence of*
     8–27   If by such . . . the *r*· is not lasting,
My. 152–12   The *r*· of pure Christianity
     218– 7   its *r*· to life and health

restore
Mis. 59–14   or to *r*· health and harmony,
     236–19   *r*· harmony and prevent dishonor,
     312–18   * to *r*· the waning faith of many
     354–17   *r*· the right action of the mental
Ret. 48–20   *r*· health, hope, and harmony to man,
No. 5–16   *r*· health and perpetuate life,
Pan. 6– 1   Science will *r*· and establish,
My. 48– 5   * to *r*· to human consciousness
     301–27   *r*· disordered functions, or
     332– 1   * to *r*· her to her friends

restored
Mis. 41–25   and health will be *r*· ;
     49– 6   *r*· by C. S. treatment.
     180– 6   beholding me *r*· to health.
     180– 8   * "How is it that you are *r*· to us ?
     186–30   *r*· to mortals the lost sense of
     186–32   *r*· this sense by the spiritual
     258– 7   he *r*· sight to the blind,
     282–24   he is *r*· through C. S.
     382–13   *r*· the first patient healed in this
Pul. 34–24   process by which I was *r*· to health ;
Rud. 8–27   the health is seemingly *r*·,
     12–10   and then *r*· through its agency.
No. 4– 1   Reading S. and H. has *r*· the sick to
'01. 17–17   *r*· the patients in from one to three
My. 105–16   I have physically *r*· sight to the blind,
     105–24   On seeing her immediately *r*· by me
     218– 1   He *r*· the diseased body to

restores
- *Mis.* 25–13   *r·* the spiritual . . . meaning
- 252–25   *r·* its lost element, namely,
- 287–11   and *r·* lost Eden.
- *Man.* 17–18   and *r·* the lost Israel :
- *Un.* 30–10   *r·* Soul, or spiritual Life.
- *No.* 10–17   Truth *r·* that lost sense,
- *My.* 180– 9   *r·* their original tongue

restoreth
- *Un.* 30–11   "He *r·* my soul,"— *Psal.* 23 : 3.

restoring
- *Mis.* 65–24   *r·* the equipoise of mind
- 329–11   *r·* in memory the sweet rhythm
- *Un.* 11–22   for *r·* his senseless hand ;
- 30–18   *r·* the spiritual sense of man

restrain
- *Mis.* 380–28   a bill in equity . . . to *r·*,
- *Ret.* 79–24   *R·* untempered zeal.
- *No.* 8–15   remainder thereof He will *r·*.
- '*02.* 1–14   wrath shalt Thou *r·*."— *Psal.* 76 : 10.
- *My.* 151–11   wrath shalt Thou *r·*."— *Psal.* 76 : 10.
- 207– 5   remainder thereof He will *r·*.

restrained
- *Mis.* 226–24   should be *r·* by their pride.

restraining
- *Mis.* 381–22   *r·* the defendant from directly

restricted
- *Mis.* 244–28   not for a . . . *r·* period,
- 359–12   Growth is *r·* by forcing

restriction
- *My.* 320–24   * without any hesitation or *r·*.
- 321–10   * position without any *r·*.

restrictions
- *Mis.* 272–13   * the following important *r·* :

rests
- *Mis.* 62–30   "mind-cure" *r·* on the notion that
- 69– 6   Science *r·* on Principle
- 80–32   Mind-healing *r·* demonstrably on
- 104–32   On this *r·* the implicit faith
- 118–17   trustworthiness *r·* on being willing
- 267–27   *r·* on this scientific basis :
- 271– 8   that *r·* on oneness ;
- 336–29   *r·* on everlasting foundations,
- 354–28   he *r·* in a liberty higher
- 365–11   it *r·* alone on demonstration.
- *Ret.* 75 10   and *r·* on unity.
- *Un.* 31–17   *r·* on the fact that matter usurps
- *Rud.* 11–19   Mind-healing by no means *r·* on
- *No.* 4–24   *r·* on the exclusive truth
- 10 14   My hygienic system *r·* on Mind,
- 18– 7   *r·* alone on the demonstration of
- 24– 9   *r·* on God as One and All,
- '*00.* 11–15   Mozart *r·* you.
- '*01.* 3– 3   benediction . . . *r·* upon this hour :
- *Hea.* 15– 2   *r·* upon the supremacy of God.
- *Po.* 18–19   rides on the whirlwind or *r·* on the
- 46– 1   thy rosebud heart *r·* warm
- *My.* 106–17   *r·* on the basis of fixed Principle,
- 118–25   *r·* on a heathen basis for its
- 152–12   *r·* solely on spiritual understanding,
- 158–18   *r·* on Christian Scientists.
- 177–21   glory of His presence *r·* upon it,
- 204– 2   *r·* in the fact that He is infinite
- 258–27   A transmitted charm *r·* on them.

result (noun)
- **await the**
  - *Mis.* 241–15   else he will doubtingly await the *r·* ;
- **bringing out the**
  - *Mis.* 41–30   bringing out the *r·* of the Principle
- **desired**
  - *My.* 292–19   would prevent the *r·* desired.
- **dignify the**
  - *Mis.* 199– 5   dignify the *r·* with the name of law :
- **moral**
  - *Mis.* 365–18   has worked out a moral *r·* ;
  - *No.* 18–24   have wrought this moral *r·*,
- **of importunity**
  - *My.* 10–21   * as the *r·* of importunity or entreaty
- **of organization**
  - *Mis.* 190– 2   neither . . . *r·* of organization, nor
  - *Ret.* 58–13   it was not the *r·* of organization,
  - *Un.* 42–22   nor was it the *r·* of organization,
- **of prayer**
  - *My.* 343–25   and the *r·* of prayer.
- **of rules**
  - *Pul.* 45–27   * *r·* of rules made by Mrs. Eddy.
- **of secret faults**
  - *Ret.* 72– 7   portrays the *r·* of secret faults,
- **of sin**
  - *Mis.* 115– 8   only as the *r·* of sin ;
- **of the love**
  - *My.* 62– 6   * To me it is the *r·* of the love that

result (noun)
- **of the work**
  - *My.* 327–13   * This is the *r·* of the work done
- **one**
  - *Pul.* 52–26   * and C. S. is one *r·*.
- **produce a**
  - *Hea.* 6–22   produce a *r·* upon his body.
- **produces the**
  - *My.* 302– 4   mind, not matter, produces the *r·*
- **scientific**
  - *Mis.* 172–28   To gain this scientific *r·*,
- **such a**
  - *Ret.* 38–13   I had not thought of such a *r·*,
  - *My.* 233–23   watch against such a *r·*
- **this**
  - *Mis.* 69–23   effort to accomplish this *r·*,
  - *Ret.* 21–23   which tend to this *r·*,
  - 49–10   adapted to work this *r·* ;
  - '*02.* 1– 4   effort to achieve this *r·*,
  - *Hea.* 6–23   The belief that produces this *r·*
  - *My.* 244–14   my part towards this *r·*.

- *Mis.* 23–20   not a *r·* of atomic action,
- 24–13   *r·* was that I rose, dressed myself,
- 112–32   *r·* of sensuous mind in matter.
- 210– 2   behold the *r·* : evil, uncovered.
- *Pul.* 84–26   * *r·* of long years of untiring,
- '*01.* 26–30   *r·* of my own observation,
- *My.* 48–32   * the *r·* is already manifest
- 112–25   *r·* of his conscientious study of
- 128–26   but the *r·* is as injurious.
- 246–22   *r·* is an auxiliary to the College
- 293–26   *r·* would have been scientific,

result (verb)
- *Mis.* 27– 5   or aught that can *r·* in evil,
- 233– 4   *r·* in the worst form of medicine.
- 309– 5   *r·* in erroneous conclusions.
- *Man.* 110– 4   confusion that might *r·*
- *My.* 11–12   * that did not *r·* in our welfare.
- 45– 3   * will *r·* in its perpetuity

resulting
- *Pul.* 31–15   * *r·* from editorial work

results
- **appears in**
  - *Mis.* 291–12   at least it so appears in *r·*.
- **bad**
  - *Mis.* 243– 3   with no bad *r·*,
- **calculating the**
  - *Hea.* 4– 5   before calculating the *r·* of an
- **denied the**
  - *Mis.* 7–27   denied the *r·* of our labors
- **depend on**
  - *My.* 244–25   This, however, must depend on *r·*.
- **fatal**
  - *Mis.* 45 9   avoiding the fatal *r·* that frequently
- **glorious**
  - *Mis.* 245–17   remove with glorious *r·*.
  - *My.* 213–14   and bring out glorious *r·*.
- **good**
  - *Mis.* 379–23   with phenomenally good *r·* ;
  - *My.* 232–28   exhaustion and no good *r·*,
- **infinite**
  - *Ret.* 92– 1   His . . . wrought infinite *r·*.
- **its**
  - *Mis.* 19–28   choose our course and its *r·*.
  - 250–18   grand achievements as its *r·*.
  - 299– 1   not change the fact, or its *r·* ;
  - '*01.* 21–20   Principle of C. S. and of its *r·*.
  - *My.* 184–24   quite sacred in its *r·*.
- **of error**
  - *Mis.* 288–10   works out the *r·* of error.
- **of Science**
  - *Mis.* 341–11   to arrive at the *r·* of Science :
- **physical**
  - *My.* 220– 1   save him from bad physical *r·*.
- **same**
  - *Mis.* 40–18   same *r·* follow not in every case,
- **their**
  - *My.* 143– 4   are blessed in their *r·*.
- **things and**
  - '*01.* 21–26   did He not know all things and *r·*
- **witness**
  - *Pul.* 8–29   are destined to witness *r·*

- *Un.* 42– 6   *r·* of material consciousness ;
- *Hea.* 8– 8   *r·* of this higher Christianity,
- *My.* 45–21   * *r·* of such following have been

results (verb)
- *Mis.* 15–11   *r·* in health, happiness, and
- '*01.* 23–13   *r·* as would a change of the
- *Hea.* 7–13   corrects the act that *r·* from

resumed
- *Mis.* 105–10   *r·* his individual spiritual being,
- *Ret.* 38–13   my printer *r·* his work

resurrect
 Mis. 154–16 to *r·* the understanding,
resurrected
 Un. 62–23 never in matter, nor *r·* from it."
   62–26 all that can be buried or *r·*.
   63– 3 neither buried nor *r·*.
 Peo. 5– 6 *r·* a deathless life of love ;
resurrecting
 Mis. 77–32 *r·* the human *sense*
 My. 110– 3 *r·* individuals buried
resurrection
 Mis. 90–29 breakfast, after his *r·*,
   170– 2 *r·* and life immortal are
   179–20 between us and the *r·* morning?
   179–22 come into the spiritual *r·*
   180–19 shall have part in his *r·*.
 Man. 16– 6 *r·* served to uplift faith
 Un. 41–11 *R·* from the dead
   41–13 have part in this *r·*
   61– 1 the *r·* that takes hold of
 Pul. 27–22 * window . . . Mary at the *r·* ;
 My. 164–19 has wrought a *r·* among you,
   202–15 the glory of the *r·* morn
   258–11 her *r·* and task of glory,
   269– 7 *r·* from the dead, — *Luke* 20 : 35.
resuscitate
 Mis. 145–17 let not mortal thought *r·* too soon.
resuscitated
 Hea. 19–10 he would have *r·*.
resuscitating
 My. 293–17 mind *r·* the body of the patient.
retain
 Mis. x–22 to *r·* my maiden name,
   xi– 3 caused me to *r·* the initial "G"
   xii– 2 to *r·* at this date the privileged
   31–22 in order to *r·* his faith in evil
 Rud. 2–14 I prefer to *r·* the proper sense of
 '00. 8–28 *r·* a desire to follow your own
 '02. 14– 3 only interest I *r·* in this property
retained
 Mis. 218–26 neither eliminated nor *r·* by Spirit.
 Ret. 15– 4 *r·* till I founded a church of my own,
 My. 335– 6 * *r·* his membership in both till
retaining
 Mis. 226–10 when, *r·* his own, he loses the
 Man. 55–15 *r·* his membership, this weak member
 Ret. 90– 4 *r·* his salary for tending the
 My. 126– 2 *r·* the heart of the harlot
retains
 Pul. 37– 8 * *r·* . . . her energy and power ;
retaken
 Mis. 289–21 must not be *r·* by the contractors,
retaliate
 '01. 30–12 to *r·* or to seek redress ;
retard
 Mis. 85–26 pleasures . . . of sense, *r·*
   233– 9 *r·* the onward march of life-giving
   245– 9 to *r·* by misrepresentation
   351–16 mad ambition may *r·* our Cause,
retarded
 No. 32– 2 *r·* the progress of Christianity
retarding
 Mis. 107–27 *r·*, and in . . . instances stopping,
retards
 Ret. 45–10 organization *r·* spiritual growth,
   75–20 dishonesty *r·* spiritual growth
 My. 84– 6 * *r·* and holds back work
retina
 Un. 34– 5 pictured on the eye's *r·*.
retire
 Mis. 133–22 I *r·* to seek the divine blessing
   227– 2 *r·* for forgiveness to no fraternity
   379– 1 Mr. Quimby would *r·* to an anteroom
 Pul. 36– 6 * to *r·* from active contact with
   68–10 * to *r·* from active contact with
 '01. 17–21 *r·* from the comparative ease of
 My. 250– 9 their Readers will *r·* *ex officio,*
retired
 Mis. 136– 1 When I *r·* from the field
   308–21 *r·* with honor
 Ret. 40– 9 given up the case and *r·*.
 Pul. 47–25 * she lives very much *r·*,
retirement
 Mis. 316–19 my *r·* from life's bustle.
 Ret. 48– 2 but I was yearning for *r·*.
 My. 117– 8 time and *r·* to pursue
   163–19 that I might find *r·*
   163–23 *r·* I so much coveted,
   164– 2 the *r·* I so much desired.

retiring-room
 Pul. 76–18 * One of the two alcoves is a *r·*
retrace
 Mis. 10–15 they will . . . *r·* their steps,
retreat
 Mis. 159–15 *r·*, sit silently, and ponder.
   386–24 In lone *r·*.
 No. 36–19 It was this *r·* from material
 Pan. 3–14 * sacred solitude ! divine *r·* !
 Po. 50–10 In lone *r·*.
 My. 117–28 to *r·* from the *world,*
retreating
 Un. 61–16 neither advancing, *r·*, nor
retreats
 Un. 61–13 *r·*, and again goes forward ;
retribution
 Mis. 11–22 is not leaving all *r·* to God
retrograded
 My. 107– 3 improved . . . or has it *r·* ?
retrospect
 Pul. 31– 2 * certainly a very remarkable *r·*.
 My. 45–23 * in *r·* we see the earlier leading,
   145– 1 chapter sub-title
"Retrospection"
 Mis. 156–16 read "*R·*" on this subject.
Retrospection and Introspection
 p. 19
  My. 330–20 * In "*R·* and I·'" (p. 19)
 p. 20
  My. 336–10 * "*R·* and I·*." . . . (p. 20)
 page 47
  Mis. 318–13 page 47 . . . "*R·* and I·*":
 page 84
  Man. 87–21 *R·* and I·*, page 84.

      ——
 Pul. 46– 9 * under the title of "*R·* and I·*,"
 My. 334– 5 * Mrs. Eddy's book, "*R·* and I·*,"
   336–21 * by Mrs. Eddy in "*R·* and I·*."
retune
 Mis. 394–18 * Such old-time harmonies *r·*,
 Po. 57– 4 * Such old-time harmonies *r·*,
return (noun)
 in
  Mis. 38– 6 expect in *r·* something to
   254– 4 in *r·* for all that love
   322– 1 In *r·* for your kindness,
   342–26 and receive nothing in *r·* ;
   364– 6 In *r·* for individual sacrifice,
  Man. 41–11 in *r·* employ no violent invective,
  Rud. 13–27 receiving no wages in *r·*,
  My. 154–21 * in *r·*, that he have light, . . . freedom,
 my
  My. 346–10 * on my *r·* from Pleasant View,
 of Christ
  My. 181–29 for the *r·* of Christ
 of members
  Mis. 310–11 relative to the *r·* of members
 of the disease
  Mis. 54–21 be liable to a *r·* of the disease
 sharp
  Mis. 13– 6 sharp *r·* of evil for good
 speedy
  Mis. 212–15 A speedy *r·* under the reign of
 under difficulties
  '01. 2–23 costs a *r·* under difficulties ;

  Mis. 142–24 Poor *r·*, is it not?
  Pul. 69–15 * C. S. really is a *r·* to
  My. 181–29 the *r·* of the spiritual idea
return (verb)
 Mis. 12– 8 Never *r·* evil for evil ;
   22–17 come from God and *r·* to Him,
   34–19 *r·* to his boyhood.
   34–21 they cannot *r·* to ours.
   58– 9 destroyed, disease cannot *r·*.
   137–20 *r·* to his place of labor,
   141–27 or else *r·* every dollar
   304–17 * will *r·* to Washington
   316– 1 never to *r·* evil for evil ;
   353–31 "*r·* to their vomit," — *see Prov.* 26 : 11.
 Man. 84– 4 never to *r·* evil for evil,
 Pul. 6–22 * leading us to *r·* to Japan."
   49–21 * *r·* to her native granite hills,
 Rud. 12–14 will *r·*, and be more stubborn
 '01. 17– 4 * *r·* to the Father's house
   17– 5 quickly to *r·* to divine Love,
   17– 8 and struggling to *r·*
   29–17 whenever they *r·* to the old home
   34–20 *r·* blessing for cursing;
 Hea. 4– 3 neither go forth from, *r·* to, nor
 My. 73– 2 * *r·* more than ten thousand dollars

return (verb)
My. 128–26   R· not evil for evil,
129–19   r· and plant thy steps in Christ,
131–14   r· to its first love,
150–32   "let your peace r·— *Matt.* 10 : 13.
170–29   r· in joy, bearing your sheaves
171– 4   r·, and come to Zion— *Isa.* 35 : 10.
184–14   and to r· my cordial thanks
247–26   it will r· to you.
259–12   I r· my heart's wireless love.
331–21   * to r· our thanks and express

returned
Mis. 7–29   r· naturally without any assistance.
214–17   r· into the scabbard.
226– 6   clergyman's son r· home— *well.*
326–22   the Stranger r· to the valley ;
353–17   When my brother r· and saw it,
378– 4   in a few weeks r· apparently well,
379– 6   I read the copy . . . and r· it to him.
Man. 109–12   should have applications r· to them
110– 1   as none will be r· that are
Ret. 9– 1   r· with me to grandmother's room,
19–17   I r· to New Hampshire,
Pul. 34– 3   * r· to her father's home— in 1844
53–12   * and one r· to give thanks
No. 31–24   r·, to be again forgiven ;
My. 30–20   * plates were r· after having been
165– 7   I r· blessing for cursing.
215–12   However, I r· this money
270–22   I have r· good for evil,
330–28   I r· to New Hampshire,
333–14   * procession then r· to the lodge,

returning
Mis. 11–23   r· blessing for cursing.
330–21   With each r· year, higher joys,
Ret. 20– 1   After r· to the paternal roof
45–19   forgiving enemies, r· good for evil,
No. 20–17   starting from . . . and r· to it
26–28   dust r· to dust, nothingness to
'01. 2–24   beset all their r· footsteps.
My. 204–27   while r· good for evil,
260–22   r· good for evil,
336–12   "After r· to the paternal roof
346–12   * made several turns . . . before r·.

returnless
Pul. 1–14   Pass on, r· year !
Po. 26– 1   Pass on, r· year !

returns
Mis. 278– 4   my peace r· unto me.
324–24   So he r· to the house,
Po. 10–12   R· to bless a bridal
Mu. 10–00   r· it unto them after many days,
337–13   It· to bless a bridal

reunion
My. 21–27   * rejoice in the glad r·

Rev. ——
Mis. 68– 7   *The R· said in a sermon :*
'01. 21– 8   R· writes : " To the famous Bishop

reveal
Mis. 164–28   r· man collectively, as individually,
192–17   his words r· the great Principle
308– 9   Scriptures and C. S. r·
348–12   God shall r· His rod,
Ret. 25– 1   r· the great curative Principle,
28–24   Science of Mind must r·.
Un. 37–10   would r· this wonder of being.
My. 5– 8   r· man as God's image,
111– 1   r· truths which otherwise the
124–19   for Science r· man to man ;
299– 6   * have any truth to r·
323–22   * to r· to us His way.
347– 3   and r· my successor,

revealed
Mis. 2–20   spiritual idea of God will be r·.
30– 8   spiritually discerned and r·
35– 2   r· to her the fact that Mind,
141– 5   r· to you God's all-power,
167–25   r· them unto babes !"— *Luke* 10 : 21.
179–31   when God r· to me this
183–21   arm of the Lord is r· ;— *Isa.* 53 : 1.
201–10   r· the myth or material falsity
210–13   wisdom of God, as r· in C. S.,
302–16   in interpreting r· Truth,
315–30   to study His r· Word,
348–11   that shall not be r·."— *Matt.* 10 : 26.
Ret. 46–10   asked why C. S. was r· to me
76–11   mind to which this Science was r·
Un. 39–10   arm of the Lord is r·.
51–22   Ego is r· as Father, Son,
58–19   unreality of sin, sickness, . . . was r·,
Pul. 77–13   * Truth, as r· by divine Love
78–12   * Truth, as r· by divine Love
No. 45– 2   r· them unto babes."— *Luke* 10 : 21.

revealed
'01. 10– 7   that shall not be r·."— *Matt.* 10 : 26.
My. v–25   * r· God to well-nigh countless numbers
24– 2   * truth which Christ Jesus r·
28–30   * has r· the one true Science
37–12   * r· the verity and rule of
43– 7   * r· the God of their fathers,
43–22   * r· to our beloved Leader,
44– 1   * The way . . . has been r·.
45–16   * divine Principle r· to you
58–20   * r· a demonstrable way of salvation.
64– 5   * realm of infinite Mind, r· to us
246–17   r· through the human character.
299– 7   * has not been r· by the church
324–14   * to have those very terms r·
347– 1   have already been r· in a degree

revealing
Mis. 189–18   r·, in place thereof,
No. 30–23   r· Him and nothing else.
Peo. 13– 9   r· the one God and His all-power

revealings
Mis. 15–30   it drinks in the sweet r· of

reveals
Mis. 1–20   Goodness r· another scene
5– 4   Science r· man as spiritual,
13–22   r· in clearer divinity the existence
60–17   Science . . . r· the impossibility of
82– 2   r· God and man as the Principle and
95–21   Mind r· itself to humanity
95–23   C. S. r· the infinitude of divinity
164– 6   r· the incorporeal Christ ;
174–28   Science that r· the spiritual facts of
175–26   r· the one perfect Mind and His laws.
185–21   r· man infinitely blessed, upright,
194– 3   Divine Science r· the Principle of
219 3   neither r· God in matter,
337– 2   that which r· the truth of Love,
Ret. 59– 1   C. S. r· the grand verity,
59–18   r· Mind, the only living and true
60– 3   Science r· Life as a complete sphere,
60– 6   Science r· Spirit as All,
60–11   C. S. r· God and His idea as
61–21   C. S. r· the fact that,
65–30   Christianity r· God as ever-present
Un. 29–15   Science r· Soul as that which the
52– 5   r· and sustains the unbroken
55–15   r· the self-destroying ways of error
Rud. 11–22   r· the all-power and ever-presence
No. 10– 8   the latter r· and interprets God
28 16   r· the fact that Truth is never
39–25   this light r· the pure Mind-pictures,
Pan. 3–19   self-existent God, who r· Himself
Hea. 14–23   Science r· the Principle and method
My. 119–15   Principle that r· Christ.
262–31   r· infinite meanings and gives
272–13   C. S. r· the divine Principle,

Revelation
Mis. 21– 5   culminates in the R· of St. John,
280– 3   third picture-lesson is from R·,
366–10   keynote of C. S. from Genesis to R·,
Man. 58–17   shall extend from Genesis to R·.
Pul. 59–16   * read from the book of R·
No. 20–27   antagonistic to R· and Science.
37–21   From Genesis to R· the Scriptures
'00. 11–26   In R· St. John refers to
12– 6   In R·, second chapter,
12–27   R· of St. John in the apostolic age
'01. 32–24   St. John's R·, educated my thought
My. 125–29   Babylonish woman, referred to in R·,
285–17   In R· 2 : 26, St. John says :

revelation
and Science
Un. 8–19   through reason, r·, and Science,
astonishing
My. 92–15   * astonishing r· was made that since
based upon
Un. 9–13   have not based upon r· their
denying
Mis. 3–28   denying r·, and dethroning Deity.
260–21   denying r·, and seeking to dethrone
glories of
Mis. 332–21   masked . . . the glories of r·,
God's
Mis. 92–26   cannot be substituted for God's r·.
Ret. 84–15   cannot be substituted for God's r·.
imagination and
No. 20– 5   human reason, imagination, and r·
inevitable
My. 178–18   Hence the inevitable r· of C. S.
inspiration and
Un. 46– 3   Truth is from inspiration and r·,
light of
Hea. 8–18   becloud the light of r·,
My. 114–18   light of r· and solar light.

revelation

logic, and
 Mis. 223– 8 divine light, logic, and *r*·
marvellous
 My. 88–23 * marvellous *r*· given to this
mount of
 Mis. 17– 7 died away on this mount of *r*·,
  164–14 but from the mount of *r*·,
  356–14 ascend from the mount of *r*·,
  369– 2 at the foot of the mount of *r*·,
 No. 1–16 die away on the mount of *r*·,
 My. 189– 3 should reach the mount of *r*· ;
must come
 Mis. 362–22 *r*· must come to the rescue
must subdue
 No. 11–26 *R*· must subdue the sophistry of
nature of a
 My. 93–29 * will come in the nature of a *r*·.
of divine Love
 My. 301– 4 was and is the *r*· of divine Love.
of divinity
 My. 63–23 * *r*· of divinity which has come to
of Spirit
 Mis. 56–19 at the full *r*· of Spirit,
rare
 Mis. 292– 9 a rare *r*· of infinite Love,
reason and
 Mis. 23–18 Reason and *r*· declare that God
  27–20 According to reason and *r*·,
  217– 2 nature, reason, and *r*·.
 No. 13–24 given impulse to reason and *r*·,
Science is a
 Ret. 28–26 All Science is a *r*·.
 Pul. 35–22 All Science is a *r*·.''
shows
 No. 11–25 *R*· shows this Principle,
spiritual
 Mis. 75– 4 spiritual *r*· of man's possible
this
 Mis. 165–13 light of this *r*· leaves
 My. 63–25 * Grandly . . . symbolize this *r*·,
tides of
 Mis. 292– 3 overwhelming tides of *r*·,

 Mis. 158–21 *r*· of what, how, whither.
  354–10 When . . . reason is preferred to *r*·,
 Un. 58–19 a *r*· that beams on mortal sense
 Peo. 2–13 by *r*· supporting reason.
 My. 238–13 *r*·, . . . and presentation of C. S.
  239– 5 primitive proof, wherein reason, *r*·,
  265– 5 *r*·, spiritual voice and vision,
  288– 1 reason, *r*·, justice, and mercy ;
  318–32 not . . . in history, but in *r*·.
  350– 7 *r*·, uplifting human reason,

revelations
 Mis. 248–26 glorious *r*· of C. S.
 Man. 59– 1 sacred *r*· of C. S.
 My. 179–30 untranslated *r*· of C. S.

Revelator (*see also* **John, Revelator's, St. John**)
 Mis. 269–28 *R*· beheld the opening of
  278– 1 vision of the *R*· is before me.
 '00. 13– 3 *R*· commends the church at Ephesus
  13–13 *R*· writes of this church
  13–20 *R*· refers to the church
  13–29 *R*· speaks of the angel
 My. 120– 1 We look for the sainted *R*·
  126–22 *R*· saw in spiritual vision
  201– 5 for a season, as the *R*· foresaw,

revelator
 (*see* **Eddy**)
Revelator's
 Mis. 113– 8 and the *R*· vision, that
 '00. 12–17 hence the *R*· saying :
  14–11 import of the *R*· vision
revelators
 Mis. 308–10 *r*· will take their proper place
revelling
 Pul. 48– 8 * *r*· in the lights and shades of
revenge
 Mis. 10– 4 Whatever envy, hatred, *r*·
  36–13 Appetites, passions, anger, *r*·,
  114–20 passion, appetites, hatred, *r*·,
  118–22 lust, covetousness, envy, *r*·,
  228–15 mad ambition and low *r*·.
  281– 4 rivalry, jealousy, envy, *r*·,
 Pul. 84– 5 * *r*· shall clasp hands with pity,
 '02. 8–25 Lust, hatred, *r*·, coincide in
 My. 249–15 its loathing of love and its *r*·
revenged
 '00. 3–28 and *r*· himself upon his enemies.
revengeful
 Mis. 129–15 If a man is jealous, envious, or *r*·,

revenue
 My. 216– 8 and *r*· subsist on demand and supply,
reverberate
 Mis. 312–25 *r*· and renew its emphasis
 My. 291–20 waken a tone of truth that shall *r*·,
reverberating
 My. 13–26 harmony, *r*· through all cycles of
revere
 Pul. 41–12 * sent them by the teacher they *r*·.
 My. 362–21 * *r*· and cherish your friendship,
revered
 Mis. 376– 2 * true art of the oldest, most *r*·,
 My. 58–18 * labor and sacrifice of our *r*· Leader
  278–13 The *r*· President and Congress
  289–16 long honored, *r*·, beloved
  290– 8 as venerable, *r*·, and beloved
  362–12 * *R*· Leader, Counsellor, and Friend:
reverence
 Mis. 96–20 I *r*· and adore Christ as never before.
  238– 4 *r*· of my riper years for all who
 Pul. 81– 5 * is nowhere spoken with more *r*·
 My. 63–21 * and of *r*· beyond words,
  85–21 * for future generations to *r*·
  98– 8 * an enthusiasm and *r*· of worship
Reverend
 Man. 45–24 drop the titles of *R*· and Doctor,
reverent
 Mis. 372–24 aimed to reproduce, with *r*· touch,
reverentially
 My. 260– 4 *r*· withdraw itself before Mind.
reverently
 Un. 13– 5 Men must approach God *r*·,
reversal
 Un. 20– 1 By *r*· or revision,
reverse
 Mis. 109– 5 and try to *r*·, invert, or controvert,
  119–29 nullify or *r*· your rules,
 Un. 13– 4 whereas the *r*· is true in Science.
  20–10 By a *r*· process of argument
  30– 5 delusion that the senses can *r*· the
reversed
 Mis. 61– 1 in all its manifestations, *r*·,
  220–24 if this mental process . . . be *r*·,
reverses
 Mis. 13–21 Science of Soul *r*· this
  47–19 Science *r*· the evidence of
  222– 4 It *r*· C. S. in all things.
 Un. 13– 1 Science *r*· the evidence of
  30– 5 Science *r*· the testimony of
  36– 7 Science, which *r*· false testimony
reversing
 Un. 20– 4 undo the statements of error by *r*·
  53– 2 lie takes its pattern . . . by *r*· Truth.
  62–28 mortal sense, *r*· Science
 My. 211–13 *R*· the modes of good,
reversion
 Mis. 218– 5 declares the invisible only by *r*·,
 '02. 19–24 a spiritual behest, in *r*·,
revert
 Mis. 261–11 wrong will *r*· to the wrong-doer,
 My. 39–21 * My thoughts *r*· to a former occasion,
  288–24 wrong will *r*· to the wrong-doer ;
reverting
 Mis. 375– 8 letter *r*· to the illustrations of
review
 Mis. 216– 9 there appeared a *r*· of,
 My. 316–21 * "twentieth-century *r*· of opinion"
revile
 Mis. 8–23 men shall *r*· you, — *Matt.* 5 : 11.
 '01. 3– 4 men shall *r*· you, — *Matt.* 5 : 11.
 '02. 11–22 men shall *r*· you, — *Matt.* 5 : 11.
 My. 6–10 men may *r*· us and despitefully
  104–30 men shall *r*· you, — *Matt.* 5 : 11.
  316– 7 men shall *r*· you, — *Matt.* 5 : 11.
reviled
 My. 196–18 was *r*·, *r*· not again ; — *I Pet.* 2 : 23.
reviling
 '01. 33–26 the same *r*· it received then
revise
 Mis. 274– 4 I desire to *r*· my book
 My. 163–21 in Concord's quiet to *r*· our textbook,
revised
 Mis. 136–19 my last *r*· edition of S. and H.
  309–32 See the *r*· edition of 1890,
  379–32 S. and H., p. 47, *r*· edition of 1890,
 Man. 86–21 page 330 of the *r*· editions
  104–10 This Manual shall not be *r*·

revised

Man.	104–17	appears in any *r·* edition,
Ret.	22– 2	human history needs to be *r·*,
Pul.	38– 7	* has been greatly *r·* and enlarged,
	55–14	* she has *r·* it many times,
No.	3– 8	When I *r·* "S. and H.
My.	15– 3	* Article XLI (XXXIV in *r·* edition)

revising

My.	246–19	While *r·* "S. and H. with Key to the

revision

Ret.	82–27	often asked which *r·* of S. and H.
	82–28	The arrangement of my last *r·*,
Un.	20– 1	By reversal or *r·*,

revisions

My.	318– 4	I have erased them in my *r·*.

revisits

Po.	73– 4	hoarse wave *r·* thy shore !

revival

Ret.	44–27	*r·* of mutual love, prosperity,

revive

Pul.	72–26	* it was Mrs. Eddy's mission to *r·* it.

revived

Mis.	355– 9	demonstration of Science must be *r·*.
	376– 3	* most authentic Italian school, *r·*.
Pul.	52–25	* *r·* belief in what he taught is manifest,

reviver

Pul.	52–13	* *r·* of the ancient faith and author of

reviving

My.	257–19	We own his grace, *r·* and healing.

revolt

Pul.	79–18	* a *r·* was inevitable
	80– 5	* the *r·* was headed by them ;

Revolution

Pul.	46–17	* not long before the *R·*.
My.	341– 3	a Daughter of the *R·*,

revolution

Un.	40– 1	from the *r·* of the earth to the
No.	6–21	error of the *r·* of the sun
	13–22	S. and H. has effected a *r·*
Hea.	11– 6	We are in the midst of a *r·* ;

Revolutionary

Ret.	2–10	score of years prior to the *R·* period.
	2–27	General Henry Knox of *R·* fame.
Pul.	48–27	* in Colonial and *R·* days,

revolutionary

Mis.	99– 1	It is *r·* in its very nature ;
	101– 9	It is a *r·* struggle.
	307–15	In this *r·* religious period,
'01.	9–25	they are *r·*, reformatory, and
My.	287–19	is loving, ameliorative, *r·* ;

revolutionize

No.	11–17	*r·* and reform the world,
	33– 6	they would *r·* the world

revolutions

Mis.	206– 1	*r·*, natural, civil, or religious,
Rud.	8–15	*r·*, from a lower to a higher
No.	28– 7	*r·* necessary to effect this end

revolve

Mis.	22–16	all true thoughts *r·* in
	54– 5	the planets to *r·* around it?
	104–19	*r·* in their own orbits,

revolves

Ret.	88–29	Mind *r·* on a spiritual axis,
No.	6–18	*r·* around our planet,

revolving

Mis.	125–24	*r·* oft the hitherto untouched
	184– 4	from the *r·* of worlds to the
My.	13–11	* like so many planets, *r·* around
	145–20	keeps the wheels *r·*.

reward

ever-present

Mis.	238–19	and are an ever-present *r·*.
My.	288– 7	are his ever-present *r·*.

good is the

Mis.	206–25	good is the *r·* of all who

great

Mis.	358–10	his shield and great *r·*.
'00.	7–14	great *r·* for having suffered,

in heaven

'02.	11–25	*r·* in heaven :— *Matt.* 5 : 12.
My.	6–12	*r·* in heaven." — *Matt.* 5 : 12.

its

Mis.	116–30	scientific rule and its *r·* :
	341–10	Fidelity finds its *r·*
My.	165–15	never fails to receive its *r·*,
	273–15	feeling, and acting, and its *r·*.

its own

Mis.	33– 3	wrong will receive its own *r·*.

reward

no

Mis.	362–28	suffering has no *r·*, except

of evil

Mis.	340– 4	Good is never the *r·* of evil,

of good

My.	296–17	*r·* of good and punishment of evil

of goodness

My.	19–23	reap richly the *r·* of goodness.

of obedience

'02.	17–11	receive the *r·* of obedience.

of righteousness

Mis.	123–26	receive the *r·* of righteousness :

of rightness

My.	230–25	will reap the *r·* of rightness,
	278–23	promise and *r·* of rightness.

of thy hands

My.	199– 5	*r·* of thy hands is given thee

rich

My.	209– 4	with the rich *r·* of those that

sure

'01.	2–26	a fearless wing and a sure *r·*.
My.	254–11	sure *r·* of right thinking

taketh

My.	33–26	nor taketh *r·* against — *Psal.* 15 : 5.

their

Mis.	343– 5	and have passed to their *r·*.
Po.	78– 5	Why waited their *r·*,

won the

My.	62– 2	* in the battle, and won the *r·*,

Mis.	133–17	*r·* thee openly." — *Matt.* 6 : 6.
	133–26	He will *r·* "openly." — *Matt.* 6 : 6.
	158–14	in *r·* for your faithful service,
	199– 1	does not *r·* . . . love with penalties ;
	242–19	to *r·* his liberality,
Pan.	9–25	what *r·* have ye?" — *Matt.* 5 : 46.
Hea.	5–10	the *r·* of his good deed
My.	60–10	* as a *r·* for the best paper on
	123– 7	will *r·* these givers,
	128–29	will *r·* your enemies according to
	194–26	*r·* you according to your works,
	217– 5	to *r·* your hitherto unselfish toil,
	234–11	God will *r·* their kind motives,
	252–15	who will *r·* righteousness

rewarded

Mis.	xi– 7	*r·* by what they have hitherto
	84–10	their motives were *r·*
No.	39–11	and He has *r·* them openly.

rewarding

'02.	20– 8	*r·*, satisfying, glorifying
My.	270–12	I am *r·* your waiting,

rewards

Pan.	9–24	and *r·* its possessor ;

rhetoric

Ret.	79–11	in shuffling off scholastic *r·*,

rheumatism

Mis.	71– 7	he was troubled with *r·*,

Rhine

Mis.	120–19	vintage bells to villagers on the *R·*.

Rhode Island and R. I.

(see **Newport, Westerly**)

rhubarb

Mis.	369–16	is higher than a *r·* tincture

rhyme

My.	312–32	The *r·* attributed to me by

rhythm

Mis.	160– 8	same sweet *r·* of head and heart,
	259–16	same *r·* that the Scripture describes,
	329–12	*r·* of unforgotten harmonies,
Ret.	61–10	no more to be invaded than the *r·* of

rhythmic

Mis.	89– 2	*r·* round of unfolding bliss,

rib

My.	5– 4	the outcome of man's *r·*,

ribbon

Pul.	42–28	* fastened with a broad *r·* bow.
	78–21	* Attached by a white *r·* to the scroll

rich

Mis.	149–22	and all the *r·* graces of the Spirit.
	159–28	*r·* devices in embroidery, silver,
	165–18	*r·* legacy of what he said and did,
	165–27	to avail himself of the *r·* blessings
	231– 4	grandmother, *r·* in experience,
	231– 7	*r·* viands made busy many appetites ;
	313–20	the *r·* sheaves are ripe,
	331– 7	wait . . . on God for man's *r·* heritage,
	373–23	it has *r·* possession here,
	391– 6	An item *r·* in store ;
Ret.	4–21	covered areas of *r·* acres,

rich

Pul. 24–28 * very r· in pictorial effect.
26– 6 * choir gallery is spacious and r·
27– 4 * marble approaches and r· carving,
42–18 * r· with the adornment of flowers.
50– 1 * r· woman is using her money to
62–15 * superb, being r· and mellow.
76– 9 * r· hangings of deep green plush,
78–24 * satin-lined box of r· green velvet.
Pan. 3– 6 My sense of nature's r· glooms is,
'00. 1–13 r· spiritual attainments,
Po. 31–13 R· rays, rare footprints on the
34– 9 chant thy vespers 'mid r· glooms
38– 5 An item r· in store ;
My. 20–16 suffice for her r· portion
69–15 * r· beauty of the interior.
78–11 * peculiarly r· and impressive.
88–13 * r· in the architectural symbolisms of
127–26 but it is r· beyond price,
132–18 may these r· blessings continue
149–16 * with many r· men, but I am not r·."
159– 9 r· fruit of this branch of his vine,
160–13 a sapling within r· soil
185–29 r· in signs and symbols,
201–19 R· hope have I in him who says
209– 4 r· reward of those that seek
252–21 r· rays from the eternal sunshine of
253–24 you have His r· blessing already
297–16 r· blessing of disbelief in death,

richer

Mis. 234–30 Christ is clad with a r· illumination
My. 90–18 * The world is enormously r· for this
175–22 r· than the diamonds of Golconda,

riches

Mis. 325– 8 small conceptions of spiritual r·,
'01. 10–20 "the r· of His grace" — Eph. 1 : 7.
My. 186–15 according to His r· in glory.
187–29 the r· of His love
203–11 but is economy and r·.

richest

Mis. 166–28 seen as diffusing r· blessings.
'01. 33–24 r· and most positive proof
My. 149–17 r· blessings are obtained by labor.

richly

Mis. xi– 7 r· rewarded by what they have hitherto
294–28 r· flavored with the true ideas
Ret. 4–16 pears, and cherries shone r·
47–16 r· imbued with the spirit
Pul. 24–27 * doors of antique oak r· carved.
26– 5 * r· panelled in relief work.
26– 9 * with r· carved seats
26–11 * wrought oxidized silver lamps,
My. 19–23 reap r· the reward of goodness.
129–12 r· fraught with divine reflection.
342– 1 * ample, r· furnished house

rid

Mis. 239–28 thought must be gotten r· of,
280–13 must get r· of that notion.
Un. 15– 4 May men r· themselves of an incubus
45– 8 to be r· of this self,
My. 123–14 r· of the care and responsibility of

ridden

No. 44–10 no hobby, however boldly r·

ridding

Ret. 79–11 r· the thought of effete doctrines,

riddle

Ret. 1–12 stray sonnet and an occasional r·,

ride

My. 74– 4 * within two or three days' r·,
219–12 To say that it is sin to r· to church

rides

Po. 18–19 He r· on the whirlwind
My. 205–12 * And r· upon the storm."
356– 8 * And r· upon the storm."

ridicule

Pul. 45–16 * r· heaped upon the hopeful,
My. 91–23 * were the objects of much r·,
92– 7 * cannot be brushed aside by r·
97– 5 * physicians, however, r· the idea

ridiculed

My. 92–21 * The statistics have been r·
94– 4 * The figures . . . have been r·

ridiculous

Mis. 218–22 is more r· than the "grin
My. 93–20 * we see only its r· phases,

right (noun)

adhere to the
Mis. 284–10 strictly adhere to the r·,
and power
Mis. 193–28 r· and power of Christianity

right (noun)

beams of
My. 269–21 beams of r· have healing in their
clearer
Un. 49–24 This gives me a clearer r·
determines the
My. 117– 4 determines the r· or the wrong
doing
Pul. 4–13 in being and doing r·,
15–10 for the sake of doing r·
My. 252–12 to make one enjoy doing r·,
faith in the
Mis. 213– 5 and my faith in the r·.
My. 292– 5 and human faith in the r·.
flame of
Po. 30–14 fan Thou the flame Of r·
God speed the
'02. 2–14 God speed the r· !
good
Mis. 371–19 * "good r·, and good wrong,"
groundwork of
Mis. 264– 7 without the groundwork of r·,
highest idea of
My. 283–17 a man's highest idea of r·
his
Mis. 171–18 prove his r· to be heard.
human
Mis. 266– 6 to abridge a single human r·
immutable
Mis. 172–27 on the side of immutable r·,
in dust
Po. 72– 2 charter, trampling r· in dust !
inherent
Pul. 51– 7 * which is their inherent r·
moral
'01. 20– 7 neither moral r· nor might
no
Mis. 105–26 no r· either to be pitied or
209–21 it has no r· to be at peace.
Ret. 61–17 and have no r· to exist,
My. 278–24 Governments have no r· to
no moral
'01. 20– 2 no moral r· and no authority
no more
Mis. 283– 4 one has no more r· to enter
of the majority
My. 294– 1 r· of the majority to rule.
of way
My. 232– 6 right way wins the r· of way,
of woman
No. 45–16 r· of woman to fill the highest
over wrong
My. 362– 5 victory of r· over wrong,
periled
Po. 71– 7 periled r·, Rescued by the
reigneth
My. 278–12 in divine Science, where r· reigneth.
reigns
Po. 22–21 R· reigns, and blood was not its
My. 254– 2 heaven opens, r· reigns,
relinquishment of
Mis. 340– 1 relinquishment of r· in an evil hour,
reserves the
Man. 80–18 reserves the r· to fill the same by
side of
Mis. 255– 8 thought and action on the side of r·,
standard of
Mis. 232–12 proceed from the standard of r·
struggler for the
Po. 31– 1 loyal struggler for the r·,
subversion of
Mis. 31–10 subversion of r· is not scientific.
supremacy of
Mis. 267– 4 and the supremacy of r·.
this
Man. 80–20 not elect to exercise this r·,
to adopt
My. 128–14 man's r· to adopt a religion,
to demand
Ret. 61–26 the r· to demand that C. S. be stated
to deny
Mis. 199– 2 the r· to deny the supposed power of
to expose error
Mis. 335–19 my wisdom or r· to expose error,
to grant
Mis. 272– 3 * (including the r· to grant degrees)
to help
Pul. 82–24 * They are demanding the r· to help
to sit
Mis. 388–25 The r· to sit at Jesus' feet ;
Po. 21–14 The r· to sit at Jesus' feet ;
to work
Mis. 389– 3 the r· to work and pray,
Po. 21–17 the r· to work and pray,

right (noun)

to worship
Mis. 388–18   The r· to worship deep and pure,
Po.   21– 7   The r· to worship deep and pure,
unconquerable
'00.   10– 9   unconquerable r· is begun anew,
wins
Mis. 277–11   r· wins the everlasting victory.

———

Mis.   71– 9   unquestionably right to do r· ;
  80–23   until r· is found supreme.
  81– 5   by r· of God's dear love,
  130–22   Where the motive to do r· exists,
  287–27   It is pleasanter to do r·
  289–23   the r· to become a mother ;
  299–27   What r· have I to do this?
Pul.   82–29   * Might no longer makes r·,
'00.   8–23   r· will boil over the brim of life
'01.   31– 2   of truth, of r·, and of wrong.
'02.   3–27   r· is the only real potency ;
Po.   23–13   Yielding a holy strength to r·,
  27–17   and r· with bright eye wet,
  71– 3   Laughed r· to scorn,
My.   3– 9   r· to the tree of life,— Rev. 22 : 14.
  213– 6   is by no means a r· of evil
  213–11   in their desire to do r·
  220–20   He whose r· it is shall reign.
  283–15   R· has its recompense,

right (adj.)
Mis.   11– 7   I used to think . . . this was r·.
  39–23   r· to bear "one another's — Gal. 6 : 2.
  51–17   r· motives for action,
  55– 1   failed to get the r· answer,
  59–20   There is but one r· Mind,
  62– 1   Holding the r· idea of man
  65–17   instructions as to the r· way
  67–21   Only thus is the r· practice of
  68–16   hence it is r· to know that the
  71– 1   Is it r· for me to treat others, when
  71– 9   It is unquestionably r· to do right ;
  71–10   is a very r· thing to do.
  71–30   Whatever is real is r·
  76–22   will find the r· meaning indicated.
  85–10   His purpose must be r·,
  88–27   Is it r· for a Scientist to treat
  89– 6   would it be r· to treat this patient
  90–11   It is always r· to act rightly ;
  104–14   Clothed, and in its r· Mind,
  106– 7   Traitors to r· of them,
  111–12   cast their nets on the r· side,
  115–31   mental power in the r· direction
  117–14   basis of all r· thinking and acting ;
  125– 6   all that is real is r·.
  127–29   kind word spoken, at the r· moment,
  130–23   and the majority of one's acts are r·,
  133–20   because of my desire to set you r·
  152–28   to silence the r· intuition
  153– 3   If r· yourself, God will confirm
  169–10   through r· interpretation.
  170–14   by r· and wise, . . . conceptions
  171–12   our r· action is not to condemn
  177– 2   makes to us all, r· here,
  188–19   and r· there he leaves the subject.
  190–27   must yield to the r· sense,
  212–11   cast their nets on the r· side.
  212–18   rush in against the r· course ;
  236–12   obedience to them in all that is r· ;
  236–27   blamed for all that is not r· :
  251–20   Heaven r· here, where angels
  252– 8   R· thoughts are reality and power ;
  263–21   balance on the r· side,
  264–24   may be r· theoretically,
  264–26   status of thought must be r·
  267–19   The bird whose r· wing
  268–27   R· alone is irresistible,
  271–17   and Longfellow is r·.
  283–10   It would be r· to break into a
  288– 4   be demonstratively r· yourself,
  288–12   is not absolutely r·.
  288–14   begins with what is nearest r·
  288–16   Is marriage nearer r· than celibacy?
  288–22   is r· in every state and stage
  299–13   * "Is it r· to copy your works
  299–20   can I make this r· by saying,
  301–20   "Is it r· to copy my works
  301–21   not r· to copy my book . . . without
  336–11   r· obligations towards him.
  340– 7   turning neither to the r· nor to
  341– 1   they never bring out the r· action
  341– 5   that is real, r·, and eternal?
  353– 7   Is my concept of you r·?
  353–10   you have gained the r· one
  354–17   would restore the r· action
  355–16   To strike out r· and left
  359–22   but his example was r·,

right (adj.)
Mis. 359–23   available at the r· time.
  365–12   r· thinking and r· acting,
Man.   59– 5   in the scale of r· thinking.
  76– 4   r· occasion may call for it.
Ret.   7–18   * the side he deemed r·.
  30–13   r· apprehension of the invincible
  45–21   on thy r· cheek, — Matt. 5 : 39.
  57– 9   Principle is r· ;
  57– 9   Soul is r· ;
  61–29   that little shall be r·.
  70–26   The r· teacher of C. S.
  77– 2   Pope was r· in saying,
  78–14   r· sense of metaphysical Science.
Un.   17–15   r· apprehension of the wonderful
  54–25   Which is r·,— God, . . . or
Pul.   42–28   * On its r· was a basket
  83–20   * and that r· early." — Psal. 46 : 5.
Rud.   2– 9   if our lexicographers are r·
  9–21   power of a scientific, r· thought,
No.   7–24   without reference to r· or wrong
  12– 4   r· thinking and r· acting
  15– 5   convince all that their purpose is r·.
  18– 9   R· thinking and r· acting,
  40–13   audible prayer of the r· kind;
  40–20   is it r· for one mind to meddle
Pan.   4–13   capable . . . of r· and wrong action,
  14–17   r· arm of His righteousness.
'00.   1–14   and r· convictions fast forming
  2– 9   the r· thinker and worker,
  2–11   The r· thinker works ;
  3– 2   "When a man is r·,
  3– 2   his thoughts are r·, active, and
  3– 4   r· thinker and worker does his best,
  3– 9   If the r· thinker and worker's
  3–18   good man loves the r· thinker
  6–23   clothed and in his r· mind,
  9– 8   secret of C. S. in r· thinking
'01.   2–11   a fair seeming for r· being,
  14–19   as either r· or real
Hea.   2– 1   religion nearest r· is that one.
  3– 7   foundation of r· thinking and r· acting,
  4–22   gain a r· idea of the Principle
  4–23   Principle of all that is r·,
  12–10   showing he was r·.
  14–27   in sympathy with all that is r·
  17–28   are we not r· in ruling them out
Peo.   5–12   The r· ideal is not buried,
  8– 1   to present the r· idea of Truth ;
Po.   9–11   reason made r· and hearts all love.
My. vii–11   * consistent and constant r· thinking
  14–20   * he was entirely r· in doing so.
  21–17   * but r· to expect that those who
  41– 5   * the law of r· thinking,
  117–27   free scope only in the r· direction !
  126– 8   "r· foot upon the sea,— Rev. 10 : 2.
  146–25   in the r· or in the wrong direction,
  159–17   this is the only r· thinking,
  160– 2   he abides in a r· purpose,
  166– 7   so long as we have the r· ideal,
  180–24   insist on what we know is r·,
  193–23   * if it succeeds, it is a r· thing."
  209–5, 6   in r· thinking and r· acting,
  210–15   The r· thinker abides under the shadow of
  224–11   to its r· or its wrong concept,
  225–23   In this, as in all that is r·,
  227–27   smite thee on thy r· cheek, — Matt. 5 : 39.
  232– 6   The r· way wins the right of way,
  244–13   I have awaited the r· hour,
  254–11   sure reward of r· thinking,
  268– 8   If the motives of . . . are r·,
  274–10   Dear reader, r· thinking,
  274–10   r· feeling, and r· acting
  277–19   mercy tips the beam on the r· side,
  283–14   R· thoughts and deeds are the
  283–26   Human law is r· only as it patterns
  288– 1   it starts the wheels of r· reason,
  292– 5   Through divine Love the r· government
  316–25   and of all that is r·.
  (see also **hand**)

righted
My. 277–17   whereby wrong and injustice are r·

righteous
Mis.   33– 1   r· prayer that avails with God.
  99–16   ready to suffer for a r· cause,
  119–10   Evil is impotent to turn the r· man
  121–22   His beloved Son, the r· Nazarene,
  144–24   rest that remaineth for the r·,
  258– 6   r· scorn and power of Spirit.
  281–31   seed of the r·— Prov. 11 : 21.
  293– 4   r· unfolding of error
'00.   4– 7   teaching of the r· Galilean.
'02.   19–17   there remaineth a rest for the r·,
My.   9–15   * forefront of the effort for r· reform,
  36–17   * the peace of a more r· living,

righteous

My. 46–19 * then fulfil the pledge in r· living,
165– 8 the r· suffer for the unrighteous;
189–13 commingling in one r· prayer,
273–11 not seen the r· forsaken,— *Psal.* 37 : 25.
276–24 to help support a r· government ;
280–10 * r· prayer which availeth much.
292–26 prayer of the r· heals the sick,

righteously

My. 41– 3 * they think rightly or r·.
196–19 Him that judgeth r·."— *I Pet.* 2 : 23.
340–25 rule r· the affairs of state.

righteousness

all
My. 162– 5 to fulfil all r·."— *Matt.* 3 : 15.
218– 4 to fulfil all r·."— *Matt.* 3 : 15.
and joy
My. 41–18 * standard of truth and r· and joy.
and Life
Ret. 62– 6 fruits of health, r·, and Life,
and peace
My. 282–12 towards justice, r·, and peace,
because of
Chr. 55–17 life because of r·.— *Rom.* 8 : 10.
Christ's
Mis. 30–31 cleanse our lives in Christ's r· ;
'01. 10–22 Love spans the . . . with Christ's r·,
fruit of
My. 40–20 * the fruit of r·— *Jas.* 3 : 18.
His
Mis. 140–15 by the right hand of His r·,
270–14 kingdom of God, and His r· ;— *Matt.* 6 : 33.
Chr. 55–10 kingdom of God, and His r· ;— *Matt.* 6 : 33.
Pan. 14–18 with the right arm of His r·.
My. 323–25 * by the right hand of His r·,
law in
Mis. 66– 4 gospel that fulfils the law in r·,
'02. 6–18 fulfils the law in r·,
My. 153– 6 Love will fulfil the law in r·.
love and
My. 292– 1 What cannot love and r· achieve
ministry of
My. 123–27 ministry of r· in all things,
of Love
My. 182–30 abound in the r· of Love,
practical
My. 40– 5 * thirst after practical r· ;
reign of
Mis. 125–10 in the . . . reign of r·
'01. 35– 8 call to the reign of r·,
My. 4–27 reign of r·, the glory of good,
rest of
Pan. 14– 2 rise into the rest of r·
reward
My. 252–15 reward r· and punish iniquity.
reward of
Mis. 123–26 receive the reward of r·:
sense of
My. 227– 4 personal sense of r·
suffer for
Mis. 291–25 worthy to suffer for r·,
Thy
Ret. 15– 9 make mention of Thy r·,— *Psal.* 71 : 16.
thy
Mis. 157–24 bring forth thy r·— *Psal.* 37 : 6.
'01. 35– 2 bring forth thy r·— *Psal.* 37 : 6.
My. 170–25 bring forth thy r·— *Psal.* 37 : 6.
vested in
Mis. 298–22 faith vested in r· triumphs !
work
My. 184– 6 wait upon Him and work r·.
worketh
My. 33–17 and worketh r·,— *Psal.* 15 : 2.
228–24 and worketh r·,— *Psal.* 15 : 2.

Mis. 120–10 *obedience* unto r·— *Rom.* 6 : 16.
185– 5 manifest as Truth, and through r·,
261–20 fulfil it" in r·,— *see Matt.* 5 : 17.
332– 9 and enrobe man in r· ;
Ret. 45–23 fulfil the law of Christ in r·.
Pul. 81– 6 * power of God for r·
Po. 71–10 *R·* ne'er — awestruck or dumb
My. 16–28 and r· to the plummet :— *Isa.* 28 : 17.
34– 7 r· from the God of his— *Psal.* 24 : 5.
48–25 * are all forces that make for r·.
217–31 but to fulfil it in r·.
274– 1 true sense of life and of r·,

rightful

Mis. 179– 4 r· desire in the hour of loss,
199– 9 come into their r· heritage,
Ret. 21–30 argument, with its r· conclusions,
No. 33– 6 r· place in schools of learning,
My. vii– 7 * r· place as the revelator

rightfully

My. 88–25 * r· turn with respect

righting-up

Pul. 80– 1 * must be a r· of the mind

rightly

Mis. 9– 2 through affliction r· understood,
90–11 It is always right to act r· ;
115–25 If one lives r·,
131– 5 r· to discern darkness or
169–20 it is necessary r· to read
169–29 * thoughts when r· understood.
170– 9 having r· read His Word,
240–19 incline the early thought r·,
353–22 makes the machinery work r· ;
Ret. 14– 1 as John Calvin r· called his own tenet
91– 3 r· called "the pearl of parables,"
Un. 3– 1 r· improved the lessons
Pul. 3– 8 power to think and act r·,
Rud. 2–12 We do not conceive r· of God,
'00. 8–18 doing r· by yourself and others.
Hea. 15– 8 r· understanding the power
My. 41– 2 * they think r· or righteously.
152–30 cause of all that is r· done.
238– 7 *R·* to read and to practise
274–13 begin r· enables one to end r·,

rightness

My. 52–29 * the moral r· of her book."
230–25 reap the reward of r·,
271–10 the sole proof of r·.
273–15 This sense of r· acquired by
278–23 promise and reward of r·.
281– 9 is the fruit of r·,

rights

all
My. 159–29 All r· reserved.
and privileges
Mis. 272– 2 * with all the r· and privileges
303–15 the same r· and privileges
My. 167–25 r· and privileges guaranteed
247– 8 equal r· and privileges,
255– 2 equal r· and privileges,
bill of
Mis. 289–27 on the basis of a bill of r·.
conjugal
Mis. 289–28 Can the bill of conjugal r· be
divine
Mis. 246– 1 both human and divine r·,
247– 2 both human and divine r· ;
My. 303–14 C. S. eschews divine r· in
human
  (*see* **human**)
inalienable
Mis. 251–14 inalienable r· and radiant reality
My. 200–16 and receives his r· inalienable
individual
Mis. 80– 8 individual r· in a wrong direction
80–17 laws, infringing individual r·,
119–26 individual r· which one justly reserves
274–27 individual r· are trodden under foot,
Ret. 71–14 robbed of their individual r·,
No. 40–17 never to trespass . . . on individual r· ;
46–13 begin by admitting individual r·.
My. 200– 1 Religious liberty and individual r·
220– 4 the maintenance of individual r·,
227–22 constitutional individual r·,
268–13 maintenance of individual r·,
inherent
My. 326– 6 * their inherent r· are recognized
liberty and
Mis. 101–11 for human liberty and r·.
nation's
My. 277–21 if our nation's r· or honor were
no
Mis. 245–18 no r· that man is bound to respect.
272–23 * bestow no r· to *confer degrees.*
No. 45–14 no r· which man is bound to respect.
of Christian Scientists
My. 316–24 the r· of Christian Scientists
of conscience
Mis. 176–24 freedom, in the r· of conscience.
236–12 you have the r· of conscience,
Un. 5–19 Let us respect the r· of conscience
Pul. 10–12 r· of conscience, imperishable glory.
No. 44–15 abrogate the r· of conscience
'01. 33–15 to be allowed the r· of conscience
of freedom
Mis. 297–29 belongs to the r· of freedom.
of individuals
My. 265–12 in behalf of the sacred r· of individuals,
of man
Mis. 246–26 arrayed against the r· of man,
Peo. 10–13 Discerning the God-given r· of man,
10–26 The r· of man were vindicated
My. 222–27 r· of man and the liberty of
291–31 sacredly regard . . . the r· of man.

rights

of men
My. 247– 2 inalienable, universal r· of men.
254–23 inalienable, universal r· of men.
of Mind
My. 212–25 interfering with the r· of Mind,
of mind
Mis. 67– 9 his r· of mind and character.
of mortals
Mis. 283–18 trespass on the r· of mortals.
of Spirit
Mis. 56–13 and infringes the r· of Spirit.
of the individual
Ret. 72– 3 with the r· of the individual.
of their neighbors
Ret. 87–19 the r· of their neighbors,
religious
'00. 10 12 religious r· and laws of nations
My. 167–27 religious r· in New Hampshire
States'
My. 309–15 strong believer in States' r·,
these
Mis. 289–30 the spirit of these r·,
No. 45–18 these r· are ably vindicated
universal
My. 247– 2 universal r· of men.
254–23 inalienable, universal r· of men.
whole
Peo. 10–16 battles for man's whole r·,
woman's
Mis. 388–13 poem
Po. page 21 poem

Mis. 289–21 R· that are bargained away
No. 40–17 never to take away the r·,
Peo. 11– 2 r· of the colored man were

rill
Po. 2 18 waves kiss the murmuring r·
66– 4 the thrill of that mountain r·,

rills
Po. 30– 6 murmurs from the drowsy r·
My. 180– 1 rocks, r·, mountains, meadows,

rim
My. 247–16 to the r· where I stood.

ring
Mis. 250–19 having no r· of the true metal.
304–23 * It shall r· at sunrise and sunset ;
304–28 * It will always r· at nine o'clock
Pul. 62–11 * required a strong man to r· them,
'02. 3–25 hallow the r· of state.
My. 81–20 * occasionally the voices would r· out
121–16 gems that adorn the Christmas r·
256– 2 Before the Christmas bells shall r·,

ringing
'02. 4–15 r· like soft vesper chimes
Po. vi–19 r· to celebrate the passing of a
My. 185– 3 and the harvest bells are r·.
302–28 with escort and the r· of bells,

ringlets
Po. 8–19 parting the r· to kiss my cheek.

rings
Peo. 13–12 r· out the iron tread of merciless

ripe
Mis. 85– 1 are r· for the harvest-home.
313–20 the rich sheaves are r·,
My. 281–28 when nations are r· for progress.
350–27 Science r· in prayer, in word, and

ripen
Mis. 331–10 understanding will r· the fruits of Spirit,
Po. 46–10 Thus may it r· into bloom,

ripened
Mis. 163–12 r· into interpretation through
332–10 r· sheaves, and harvest songs.
My. 198– 8 their abundant and r· fruit.

ripeness
Mis. 164– 6 has appeared in the r· of time,

ripening
My. 155–27 happy hearts and r· goodness.
159– 9 r· and rich fruit of this branch
195–15 nor understand what is not r·

riper
Mis. 238– 5 the reverence of my r· years

ripples
Ret. 27–21 As sweet music r· in one's first

rippling
Mis. 329–16 r· all nature in ceaseless flow,

rise
Mis. 10–12 if they fall they shall r· again,
80–13 to r· or fall on its own merit
97– 2 gives man ability to r· above the
107– 8 As we r· above the seeming mists of

rise
Mis. 119– 6 r· and overthrow both.
125– 5 r· to know that there is no sin,
162–17 r· to his nativity in Spirit.
234–11 reach this spiritual sense, and r·
234–11 r· — to things most essential
254–11 whose children r· up against her ;
289–31 r· to the spiritual altitude whence they
359–26 only as we r· in the scale of being.
370– 1 "R· and walk." — see John 5 : 8.
374–12 its art will r· triumphant ;
383–14 r· higher in the estimation of
Chr. 55–19 r· up and walk. — Acts 3 : 6.
Ret. 80–19 spiritual r· and progress.
Pul. vii– 9 a registry of the r· of the mercury
7–16 They will r· with joy,
No. 1– 8 fill the rivers till they r· in floods,
19– 4 it continues to r·, and the demand to
42– 9 r· up and walk !" — Luke 5 : 23.
Pan. 11–19 physically needs to r· again.
14– 2 r· into the rest of righteousness
'01. 1–11 to r· higher and still higher
'02. 10–16 r· from sense to Soul, from earth to
Peo. 9–23 metaphysics is seen to r· above physics,
Po. 25– 7 Around you in memory r· !
32– 1 r· in the morning and drink in
65–19 r· to a seraph's new song.
My. 41–19 * r· from sentimental affection
40–13 * r· to the demands of this
116– 3 r· in consciousness to the true
133– 7 r· to the church triumphant,
165–19 r· above the oft-repeated inquiry,
230–25 r· in the scale of being,
287–16 so r· and still r· to His image
359–30 get your students to help you r·

risen
Mis. 39–10 They have r· up in a day
123–19 r· to the awakened thought
178–11 r· with Christ, — Col 3 : 1.
179–14 he is r· ; — Matt. 28 : 6.
292–18 unlike the r·, immortal Love ;
312–21 this man must have r· above
370– 7 r· from the grave-clothes
Man. 60–21 to exemplify our r· Lord.
Ret. 76–11 r· to the altitude which
Un. 61– 9 neither dead nor r·.
62–24 not here, but is r·." — Luke 24 : 6.
62–27 Mary had r· to discern faintly
Pul. 16– 6 Joyous, r·, we depart
No. 36–25 r· from human sense
'01. 11– 5 r to human apprehension,
'02. 20– 7 glory of earth's woes is r·
Peo. 5–13 r· higher to our mortal sense,
5 17 r· above the sod to declare
Po. 30–12 Give r· power to prayer ;
My. 85– 8 * churches have r· by hundreds,
119–29 have r· to look and wait
122–21 r· to grasp the spiritual idea
122–23 "He is r· ; he is not here :— Mark 16 : 6.
122–25 can say his Christ is r·
183–28 is r· upon thee." — Isa. 60 : 1.
191–15 witnesseth a r· Saviour,
191–21 but human thought has r· !
(see also **Christ**)

rises
Mis. 85–16 r· into the rest of perpetual,
113–16 r· superior to suggestions from
359–25 r· only as we rise
Pul. 12–19 now r· clearer and nearer to
41–24 * r· one hundred and twenty-six feet
No. 19–24 r· to the fulness of the stature of
Hea. 11–10 her modest tower r· slowly,
15– 9 r· to that supreme sense
My. 6–23 r· to a mental monument,
94–27 "r· to a mental monument,
200–12 r· upward to the realms of
238–17 man r· above the letter,

rising
Mis. 70–27 r· to the supremacy of Spirit,
139–20 valued at $20,000 and r· in value
144–25 our visible lives are r· to God.
162– 9 stem these r· angry elements,
354–28 As r· he rests in a liberty higher
392–17 grandly r· to the heavens above.
Ret. 51– 3 twenty thousand dollars, and r· in value,
67–13 r· above corporeal personality,
Un. 60–28 R· above the false, to the true
Po. 20–21 grandly r· to the heavens above.
68–21 pure as its r·, and bright as the star,
My. 23–24 * walls of our new edifice are r·,
29– 5 * r· in unison from the
38–20 * r· with the roll of the organ
44–19 * carried unanimously by a r· vote.
45–29 * massive pile . . . r· to a height of
78– 6 * massive dome r· to a height of

rising

My. 110–17 r· higher and forever higher
114–20 would leave me until the r· of the sun.
225– 4 r· to the zenith of success,
248–16 r· above theorems into the

risk

Mis. 99– 7 The r· is stupendous.
213–10 No r· is so stupendous as to
Pul. 15– 9 and so r· human displeasure
31– 7 * At the r· of colloquialism,

risks

Mis. 211–23 He r· nothing who obeys the law of

rite

Mis. 298–16 material r· of water baptism,
No. 34– 9 commemorating . . . with a material r·.
Hea. 2–25 not in the power of . . . a dead r·
Peo. 9– 7 compliance with a religious r·

rites

Mis. 17–10 material religion with its r· and
No. 12–10 doctrines, r·, and ceremonies,

ritual

Mis. 176–21 frozen r· and creed
No. 12–22 beyond doctrine and r· ;
My. 90– 4 * eloquence of orator or magnetic r·,
262–24 r· of our common Christmas
266– 7 r·, creed, and trusts in place of

ritualism

Ret. 65– 6 R· and dogma lead to

ritualistic

Mis. 81–14 ceremonial (or r·) waters

rival

Mis. 395– 5 The rose his r· reigns,
Po. 57–12 The rose his r· reigns,

rivalries

My. 40–14 * Through r· among leaders

rivalry

Mis. 43–22 such sinister r· does . . . injury
204–31 all envy, r·, evil thinking,
268– 7 imaginary victories of r·
281– 4 r·, jealousy, envy, revenge.
347–31 targets for envy, r·, slander ;
356– 6 Envy, r·, hate need no temporary
Rud. 17– 9 never originated in pride, r·,
'02. 14–20 envy, r·, and falsehood
My. 40–14 * their strongholds of r·.
262–23 merriment, mad ambition, r·,

rivals

My. 95–14 * a dome which r· that of

river (see also river's)

Mis. 82– 6 peace floweth as a r·
127–17 "r· of His pleasure,"— see Psal. 36 : 8.
268– 9 peace been as a r·."— Isa. 48 : 18.
373–11 cast out . . . water as a r·,
Pul. 1– 2 r· of Thy pleasures.— Psal. 36 : 8.
3–17 r· of Thy pleasures."— Psal. 36 : 8.
3–20 The r· of His pleasures is a
3–23 We drink of this r· when all
7–30 r· of Thy pleasures."— Psal. 36 : 8.
9–21 r· of His pleasures."— see Psal. 36 : 8.
48–13 * r·, as it wanders eastward.
My. 18–14 'r· of His pleasure,'— see Psal. 36 : 8.
43–16 * taken from the midst of the r·

river-borne

Mis. 373–11 might cause her to be r·."

river's

Pul. 39–20 * Repeats its glory in the r· flow ;

rivers

No. 1– 8 fill the r· till they rise in floods,

road

Mis. 32– 2 broad r· to destruction.
147–15 to follow the r· of duty,
Pul. 49–24 * on the r· from Concord,
My. 313– 9 the r· in front of his house

roads

'00. 12–12 Corresponding to its r·, its gates,

roadside

Pan. 12–18 and walk, not wait by the r·,
Po. v–17 * seated herself by the r·

roam

Mis. 396– 3 to r· Where ghosts and goblins stalk.
Po. 58–15 to r· Where ghosts and goblins stalk.

roams

Po. 65–20 the stranger who r·

roar

Pul. 14–20 drown your voice with its r·,

roasting

Peo. 3– 6 eternal r· amidst noxious vapors ;

rob

Mis. 67– 8 thou shalt not r· man of money,
No. 2– 8 to r· disease of all reality ;
41–19 such as come to steal and to r·.
My. 5–18 r· the grave of its victory.
165– 2 Of two things fate cannot r· us ;

robbed

Mis. 96– 2 r· the grave of victory
114– 9 watch that these be not secretly r·,
Ret. 71–13 r· of their individual rights,
Pul. 84– 4 * wrong be r· of her bitterness

robber

Mis. 226–29 Slander is a midnight r· ;

robberies

Mis. 201–29 to bar his door against further r·.

robbers

Mis. 325–28 he sees r· finding ready ingress

robbery

Mis. 201–25 protect . . . more securely after a r·,

robbing

My. 266– 4 r· of people of life and liberty

robe

Pul. 13–11 He that touches the hem of Christ's r·
'01. 26–17 pinned to the seamless r·,
My. 152– 4 the touch of Jesus' r·
192– 7 The ideal r· of Christ is seamless.

Robertson

G. D.
My. 73–21 * It is in charge of G. D. R·,

Pul. 28–23 * Faber, R·, Wesley, Bowring,

robes

Mis. 246– 1 pulpit and press, clerical r· and
339– 8 r· the future with hope's rainbow
Un. 3–11 washed their r· white through
Peo. 9– 9 baptism of Spirit that washes our r·
Po. 65– 6 r· were as spotless as snow :
My. 125–25 beautiful garments — her bridal r·.
247–12 Put on the r· of Christ,

robin (see also robin's)

Mis. 329–28 Old r·, though stricken to the heart

robin's

Po. 53–12 Poor r· lonely mass.

Robinson, John

My. 183– 6 verify what John R· wrote

robs

Un. 38–14 A material sense of life r· God,
48–11 r· the grave of its victory.

robust

Mis. 325–15 R· forms, with manly brow
My. 308–19 My father's person was erect and r·.

Rochester, N. Y.

Pul. 88–31 * Herald, R·, N. Y.

Rochester (N. Y.) Post Express

My. 92–25 *[R· (N. Y.) P· E·]

Rock

Man. 19– 2 to be built on the R·, Christ;
Po. 73–16 By the "R·" or wave,

rock

and feathers
Mis. 263– 6 in any language— r· and feathers :
and the sea
Po. 68– 9 Here the r· and the sea
built on the
Mis. 140–28 Built on the r·, our church
great
Mis. 144–17 shadow of a great r· — Isa. 32 : 2.
263– 9 shadow of a great r· — Isa. 32 : 2.
Pul. 20–19 shadow of a great r· — Isa. 32 : 2.
heart of a
Mis. 144–15 in the heart of a r·,
living
Un. 14–20 corner-stone of living r·,
of Christ
Mis. 152–22 founded upon the r· of Christ,
176–18 to build upon the r· of Christ,
383–10 built upon the r· of Christ.
Pul. 10–17 your standard on the r· of Christ,
Pan. 15– 8 Truth, the r· of Christ,
My. 187–30 its foundations on the r· of Christ,
357–18 build upon the r· of Christ,
of Christ's teachings
'01. 25– 3 on the r· of Christ's teachings,
of divine oneness
Mis. 131–11 upon the r· of divine oneness,
of salvation
My. 165–21 this is my r· of salvation
of Truth
No. 38–10 r· of Truth, on which he built his

rock

rests on the
Po. 18–20   or rests on the r·.
sea-beaten
My. 295–18   The Bible is our sea-beaten r·.
this
Mis. 144–19   "Upon this r· I will build — Matt. 16 : 18.
263– 7   "Upon this r· I will build — Matt. 16 : 18.
399–23   Laus Deo, — on this r·
Pul. 16– 8   Laus Deo, — on this r·
'00.   5–22   On this r· C. S. is built.
Po. 76– 7   Laus Deo, — on this r·
My. 129–18   leap disdainfully from this r·
Truth is the
No. 38–13   Truth is the r· which the builders
upon the
My. 139– 6   soulfully founded upon the r·, Christ Jesus,
162–30   may it build upon the r· of ages
164–28   It builds upon the r·,

Mis. 153– 7   the r· became a fountain ;
393–19   As the r·, whose upward tending
397– 9   Truth engrounds me on the r·,
Ret. 11–17   r· The cradle of her power,
Pul. 18–18   Truth engrounds me on the r·,
Rud.   8– 1   No r· brings forth an apple ;
'00.   5–23   r· which the builders reject
Po. 10– 8   Didst r· the country's cradle
12–18   Truth engrounds me on the r·,
52– 3   r·, whose upward tending
60–14   r· The cradle of her power,
My. 260–17   basis of Christmas is the r·,
313–10   persons being hired to r· me,
337– 9   Didst r· the country's cradle

rock-bound
Mis. 145 18   In our r· friendship,
Po.   1– 6   sustains thee in thy r· cell.

Rockies
My. 77–11   * From beyond the R·,

rocking
Mis. 329–20   r· the oriole's cradle ;

Rockland, Mass.
Pul. 88–15   * Independent, R·, M·.

rock-ribbed
Mis. 254– 8   her young in the r· nest
356–20   r· nests of the raven's callow
My. 186– 5   cluster around this r· church
340–20   leaders of our r· State.

rocks
Mis. 280–20   r· and sirens in their course,
323–12   serpents hide among the r·,
327–30   plunge headlong over the jagged r·.
Ret. 27–22   meandering midst pebbles and r·,
Po.   2– 2   Though kindred r·, to sport at
My. 186– 1   r·, rills, mountains, meadows,
186– 6   nestlings in the crannies of the r·,
341– 5   engraven on her granite r·,

rod
Mis.   9– 5   these uses of His r· !
9– 6   passes all His flock under His r·
19– 4   but the r· of God, and the
51–13   Doesn't the use of the r· teach
51–14   The use of the r· is virtually
118–19   His r· and His staff comfort you.
127–24   Ofttimes the r· is His means of grace ;
208–20   His r· brings to view His love,
348–13   when God shall reveal His r·,
376–20   there rose one r· of rainbow hues,
387–20   Learn, too, that wisdom's r· is given
Ret. 80–24   under his compelling r·.
Po.   6–15   Learn, too, that wisdom's r·
30–14   and midst the r·,
My. 127–15   even as Aaron's r· swallowed up the
288–27   His r· is love.
292– 8   His r· and His staff comfort the

rode
Pul.   6–25   rose and fell and r· the rough sea.

rods
My. 127–15   r· of the magicians of Egypt.

rôle
Mis. 285–28   in the r· of a superfine conjugality ;
288–23   The selfish r· of a martyr

roll
Mis. 179– 2   r· away the stone?" — see Mark 16 : 3.
275– 4   r· away the stone from the door
Man. 51– 6   name shall be dropped from the r·
53– 6   the r· of Church membership.
56– 5   name shall be dropped from the r·
Ret.   9–21   * where dying thunders r·
20–18   Awoke new beauty in the surge's r· !
Po. 16–10   rush into life, and r· on with its tide.

roll
My. 38–20   * rising with the r· of the organ
332–29   r· of papers recording the death of

rolled
Mis.   1–20   and another self seemingly r· up in
74–19   r· away the stone from the door of
123–18   Divine Science has r· away the stone
147– 3   Another year has r· on,
179– 3   r· away by human suffering.
399–19   R· away from loving heart
Pul. 16– 4   R· away from loving heart
No. 36–24   r· away the stone from the sepulchre,
Po. 76– 3   R· away from loving heart
My. 191–22   The stone is r· away.

rolling
Mis. 26– 7   r· of worlds, in the most subtle
130–11   "r· sin as a sweet morsel
174–12   from . . . to the r· of a world.
332– 1   kindling the stars, r· the worlds,
Po. 28– 2   Of every r· sphere,
77– 1   God of the r· year !

rolls
Mis. 274–29   r· along the streets besmeared with
293–27   r· on the human heart a stone ;
384–20   * like the sea, R· on with thee,
Po. 36–19   * like the sea, R· on with thee,

Roman
Pul. 25–26   * silver lamps of R· design,
65–22   * a R· soldier parted his mantle
Pan.   3–23   R· mythology (one of my girlhood studies),
'00. 12–10   time of the R· Emperor Augustus.
My. 305–24   not of the Greek nor of the R·

Roman Catholics
Man. 87– 3   Neither . . . shall teach R· C·

Romanesque
Pul. 24–10   * the design a R· tower
24–24   * architecture is R· throughout.
26–23   * has a R· border

Romans
Un. 21– 1   In R· (ii. 15) we read

Rome (see also Rome's)
Pul.   5–27   and the Vatican at R·.
65– 5   * inviting . . . to unity with R·,
65– 9   * whatever attitude R· may assume
'00.   1–23   Paris, Berlin, R·, Pekin.

Rome
James J.
My. 62–15   * signature
J. J.
Mis. 313–18   "The Temptation," a poem by J. J. R·,

Rome's
Pul. 10– 8   R· fallen fanes and silent Aventine

rondeau
Mis. 395– 9   And yet I trow, When sweet r·
Po. 57–16   And yet I trow, When sweet r·

Rondelet
Mis. 394–14   * poem
Po. page 57   * poem

roof
Mis. 215–19   summit of the r· of the house
Ret. 19– 3   under the paternal r· in Tilton.
20– 1   After returning to the paternal r·
Pul. 25–12   * the r· is of terra cotta tiles,
47–30   * angles and pitch of the r·,
My. 69– 5   * ceiling or r· and side walls
309–24   father's house had a sloping r·,
336–12   "After returning to the paternal r·

room
Mis. 399– 4   And for you make radiant r·
Man. 49–13   wisdom necessary in a sick r·,
69–25   Mrs. Eddy's R·.
69–25   The r· in The Mother Church
Chr. 53–36   For health makes r·.
Ret.   8–15   in the same r· with grandmother,
8–21   I then left the r·,
9– 2   returned with me to grandmother's r·,
Pul. 25–11   * the "directors' r·," and the vestry.
25–20   * and the directors' r·.
26–22   * In this r· the mosaic marble
26–25   * The r· is toned in pale green
27– 3   * The directors' r· is very beautiful
31–25   * Mrs. Eddy entered the r·.
34–15   * walked into the adjoining r·,
40–14   * R· WHICH THE CHILDREN BUILT
42– 1   * had closed the large vestry r·
49– 1   * sunny r· which Mrs. Eddy
58–14   * Inside is a basement r·,
58–27   * a r· devoted to her,
69–12   * to leave no r· there for the bad,
Po. 75–11   And for you make radiant r·

room

My.	6–19	The *r·* of your Leader remains
	56–15	* *r·* for growth of attendance
	68–16	* famous *r·* will be undisturbed.
	78–29	* *r·* in which they were seated,
	131–28	shall not be *r·* enough — *Mal.* 3 : 10.
	156–16	upper *r·* furnished : — *Luke* 22 : 12.
	166–29	cabinet, . . . placed in my *r·*
	172– 4	* *r·* for Vanderbilt Hall.
	216–16	the *r·* of the Pastor Emeritus
	217– 9	the *r·* of the Pastor Emeritus.
	260– 7	to make *r·* for substance,
	269–28	shall not be *r·* enough — *Mal.* 3 : 10.
	353–21	Mrs. Eddy's *R·*.
	353–21	The *r·* in The Mother Church
	353–24	nothing in this *r·* now

rooming

'02.	15– 7	*r·* and boarding indigent students

rooms

Mis.	159–11	My heart has many *r·* :
	276– 3	*r·* of the Palmer House,
Man.	27–20	Directors to provide suitable *r·*,
	63–18	these *r·* are well located.
	74–12	not have their offices or *r·* in
	74–13	nor in *r·* connected therewith.
	81–21	*r·* where the C. S. textbook
My.	54–26	* the *r·* were opened and a large
	68–22	* the Readers' special *r·*.
	73–22	* information concerning *r*
	75–11	* were assigned *r·* in hotels
	123–12	*r·* in the same building.
	296–28	she depicted its *r·*,

Roosevelt, President

My.	281–24	* influence which President *R·* has

root

Mis.	37–17	the axe at the *r·* of the tree.
	235–12	the axe at the *r·* of the tree
	285–19	laying the axe at the *r·* of error.
Chr.	55– 4	I am the *r·* and the — *Rev.* 22 : 16.
Un.	18–23	in order to strike at its *r·* ;
No.	7– 5	any *r·* of bitterness to spring up
'00.	14–17	Let no *r·* of bitterness spring up
'01.	13–15	lays the axe at the *r·* of sin,
	23–17	axe at the *r·* of all error,
My.	122– 7	Sin is like a dock *r·*.
	128–31	take no *r·* in your thought
	149–30	solicit every *r·* and every leaf
	268–25	lays the axe at the *r·* of all evil,
	287–21	lays the axe at the *r·* of the tree
	296– 3	"unto the *r·* of the trees," — *Matt.* 3 : 10.

rooted

Mis.	392–16	deeply *r·* in a soil of love ;
Po.	20–20	deeply *r·* in a soil of love ;
My.	47–21	* *r·* itself in so many distant lands,

roots

Mis.	154– 9	enrich its *r·*, and enlarge its borders
My.	122– 8	the *r·* must be eradicated
	139– 4	nor plucked up by the *r·*,

rope

Mis.	61–18	* dangling at the end of a *r·*.
	61–23	or dangle at the end of a *r·*

rose (*see also* **rose's**)

Mis.	24–13	I *r·*, dressed myself,
	64– 7	and *r·* to his native estate,
	142– 3	to bud and blossom as the *r·* !
	171– 4	*r·* to the occasion with the second
	225–20	Mrs. Rawson then *r·* from her seat,
	345–12	his pure and strong faith *r·* higher
	376–20	there *r·* one rod of rainbow hues,
	395– 5	The *r·* his rival reigns,
Chr.	53–31	Sharon's *r·* must bud and bloom
Ret.	13–22	and I *r·* and dressed myself,
	40–11	sick woman *r·* from her bed,
Pul.	6–25	*r·* and fell and rode the rough sea.
	22–21	budded and blossomed as the *r·*.
	25–15	* marble stairs of *r·* pink,
	27–12	* In the auditorium are two *r·* windows
	27–16	* The other *r·* window represents
	83–22	* pour incense upon the *r·*.
Rud.	6–14	* "color is in *us*," not "in the *r·* ;"
'01.	11– 1	*r·* to the fulness of his stature in
'02.	1–10	and blossoming as the *r·*.
	15–24	I *r·* and recorded the hallowed
	19– 7	he *r·* from earth to heaven.
Po.	1–12	Ye *r·*, a monument of Deity,
	8– 5	seek the loving *r·*,
	39– 7	*R·* from a water-cup ;
	57–12	The *r·* his rival reigns,
My.	32– 5	* and their voices *r·* as one
	36– 5	* the five thousand present *r·* as one
	81–23	* *r·* tingling to the great dome,

roseate

Pan.	1– 9	*r·* blush of joyous June is here

rosebud

Mis.	231–24	pucker the *r·* mouth into saying,
Po.	46– 1	thy *r·* heart rests warm

rose-flush

Pul.	32– 2	* transparency and *r·* of tint

rose-leaf

Mis.	250–16	and laid on a *r·*.

rose's

Mis.	390– 4	Thy breezes scent the *r·* breath ;
Po.	55– 4	Thy breezes scent the *r·* breath ;

roses

Pul.	42–27	* with ferns and pure white *r·*
	42–30	* filled with beautiful pink *r·*.

rosewood

My.	171–27	* *r·* casket beautifully bound with

Roslindale

Ret.	51– 2	Mr. Ira O. Knapp of *R·*,

rosy

Pul.	83– 7	* But the east is *r·*,

rot

Mis.	293–30	there to moulder and *r·*.
	343–25	left to propagate — and *r·*.
Pul.	7–22	tabernacles crumble with dry *r·*.
Peo.	7– 4	to *r·* and ruin the mind's ideals.

rotation

My.	247– 9	equality of the sexes, *r·* in office.
	250– 4	*R·* in office promotes wisdom,
	254–16	* chapter sub-title
	255– 2	equality of the sexes, *r·* in office."
	255– 6	By "*r·* in office" I do not mean

Rotherham's

Mis.	373– 7	the following from *R·* translation

rough

Mis.	323–19	climbing its *r·* cliffs,
	360– 3	in the *r·* marble, encumbered .
	385–12	moored at last — Beyond *r·* foam.
Pul.	6–25	and rode the *r·* sea.
Po.	43–17	*R·* or treacherous way.
	48– 5	moored at last — Beyond *r·* foam.
My.	194–29	* stood the storm when seas were *r·*,
	232– 3	sailing over *r·* seas

roughly

Mis.	128– 1	needs often to be *stirred*, sometimes *r·*,

round

Mis.	77–17	eternal *r·* of harmonious being.
	83– 2	rhythmic *r·* of unfolding bliss,
	237–30	fear clustered *r·* his coming.
	277–25	Though clouds are *r·* about Him,
	385–25	triumphant *r·* thy death-couch
	392– 5	peaceful presence hath begirt thee *r·*.
Ret.	11–19	wreaths are twined *r·* Plymouth Rock,
	52– 4	to build a hedge *r·* about it
Pul.	39– 7	* *R·* our restlessness, His rest.
'02.	2–28	*r·* the gospel of grace,
Po.	2– 5	* "Plays *r·* the head,
	20– 7	peaceful presence hath begirt thee *r·*.
	25–12	Fragrance fresh *r·* the dead,
	48–21	faith triumphant *r·* thy
	60–16	wreaths are twined *r·* Plymouth Rock,
My.	133–16	one more *r·* of old Sol
	189–29	why throng in pity *r·* me?

rounded

Mis.	13–16	*r·* sense of the existence of good.

rounds

'02.	4–17	through the measureless *r·* of eternity.

Rounsevel, R. D.

My.	314–31	following affidavit by R. D. *R·*
	315–15	* signature
	315–17	* personally appeared R. D. *R·*

rouse

Mis.	283–11	*r·* the slumbering inmates,
Chr.	53– 7	*r·* the living, wake the dead,

roused

Ret.	31–15	acting . . . on my *r·* consciousness,
'01.	30–20	*r·* to the establishment of a new-old

rouses

Un.	1– 1	*r·* so much natural doubt

route

'02.	10–30	walking every step over the land *r·*,

routine

Mis.	136– 3	*r·* of such material modes

rove

Po.	34– 6	But whither wouldst thou *r·*,

roving

My.	314– 5	* the Pattersons led a *r·* existence.

Roxbury

My.	56–14	* Cambridge, Chelsea, and *R·*.

royal

My. 3–13 not a dweller apart in *r·* solitude ;
  118– 1 My soul thanks the loyal, *r·* natures
  206–23 a *r·* priesthood, — *I Pet.* 2 : 9.
  290– 5 Queen's *r·* and imperial honors

Royal Arch Mason

My. 335– 5 * degree of a *R· A· M·*

Royal Arch Masons and masons

Ret. 19–13 Number 3, of *R· A· m·*.
My. 330–25 No. 3, of *R· A· M·*.

Royal College of Physicians

Peo. 6– 3 Fellow of the *R· C· of P·*

royalty

Mis. 121–24 insult to divine *r·*,
Pul. 83–24 * we live in the reflected *r·*
No. 36–17 reality and *r·* of his being,
'02. 3–21 dazzling diadem of *r·*
  15–11 paid me not one dollar of *r·*

rubric

Ret. 31– 7 paramount to *r·* and dogma

rubs

Mis. 325–20 calls out, *r·* his eyes,

ruby

Mis. 240– 4 sparkling eyes, and *r·* cheeks

rude

Mis. 360– 4 with crude, *r·* fragments,

rudely

Un. 5– 1 will *r·* or prematurely agitate

ruder

Un. 11–21 the *r·* sort then prevalent,

rudimentary

My. 309–23 * building of *r·* architecture.''

rudiments

Mis. 44– 5 teach . . . the *r·* of C. S.,

ruffle

Mis. 224–23 no . . . shall agitate or *r·* it ;

rug

Pul. 76–15 * *r·* composed entirely of skins of

rugged

Mis. 347–21 may be smooth, or it may be *r·* ;
  398– 4 All the *r·* way.
Ret. 46–10 All the *r·* way.
Pul. 17 0 All the *r·* way.
Hea. 19–24 along the *r·* way, into the
Po. v –11 * *whose r· outlines resemble*
  14– 8 All the *r·* way.
  53– 8 Light o'er the *r·* steep.
My. 201–24 All the *r·* way.

ruin

Peo. 7– 5 leaving to rot and *r·* the

ruined

My. 60– 9 * you will be *r·* for life ;

ruins

Mis. 326–14 wrapping their altars in *r·*.
'00. 12–26 The entire city is now in *r·*.

Rule

My. 230–11 each *R·* and By-law in this Manual

rule (noun)

above
Mis. 282–20 above *r·* of mental practice.
according to
Mis. 265–13 demonstrates . . . according to *r·*,
and demonstration
Mis. 336–12 insist on the *r·* and demonstration
Ret. 94–24 Principle, *r·*, and demonstration.
apostle's
Hea. 5–24 but on the apostle's *r·*,
as a
Mis. 88–30 As a *r·*, drop one of these doctors
  283– 4 As a *r·*, one has no more right to
Man. 94– 6 As a *r·* there should be no receptions
Ret. 83–18 as a *r·*, the student should explain
Pul. 56– 9 * as a *r·* are the most intelligent.
'00. 3–16 As a *r·* the Adam-race are not apt to
My. 231– 6 As a *r·*, she has suffered most from
commandment and
My. 64–17 * obey this commandment and *r·*,
constant
Mis. 147–15 makes it his constant *r·*
definite
My. 43– 5 * they might have a definite *r·*
direct
Mis. 282– 9 direct *r·* for practice of C. S.
My. 363–28 this direct *r·* is more or less
divine
Mis. 85–13 this divine *r·* in Science :
  209– 9 the divine *r·* of this Principle
  301–26 divine *r·* for human conduct.

rule (noun)

diviner
No. 3–12 but I obeyed a diviner *r·*.
emphatic
My. 12–17 an emphatic *r·* of St. Paul :
false
Mis. 220– 3 a false *r·* the opposite way.
first
Mis. 52–26 because the first *r·* was not
for motives
Man. 40– 4 A *R·* for Motives and Acts.
general
Mis. 155–21 will hereafter, as a general *r·*,
  236–27 as a general *r·*, one will be
  293– 5 (as a general *r·*)
Ret. 82– 5 general *r·* is, that my students
given
Mis. 366– 7 fixed Principle, given *r·*,
No. 11–22 fixed Principle, given *r·*,
  33–11 fixed Principle, a given *r·*,
'01. 23–15 fixed Principle and given *r·*,
My. 113–25 fixed Principle and a given *r·*,
  348–27 demonstrable Principle and given *r·*.
golden
My. 364– 6 departure from this golden *r·*
good
Mis. 220– 2 you will find that a good *r·*
home
'02. 3–12 inauguration of home *r·* in Cuba,
illustrates the
Mis. 337–11 and he illustrates the *r·* :
in Christian Science
Mis. 200–11 Paul insists on the rare *r·* in C. S.
  346–24 It is a *r·* in C. S.
Pul. 12–23 Self-abnegation, . . . a *r·* in C. S.
includes a
Mis. 75– 9 includes a *r·* that must be understood,
indispensable
Mis. 118– 7 the indispensable *r·* of obedience.
in Science
Mis. 85–13 this divine *r·* in Science :
  265–12 understands a single *r·* in Science,
no
My. 242–10 and no *r·* for its demonstration.
of addition
Un. 53–18 assertion that the *r·* of addition
of being
Mis. 189– 4 divine Principle and *r·* of being,
of Christian Science
Mis. 10– 3 will break the *r·* of C. S.
  233–26 perfection of the *r·* of C. S.
  337– 7 Principle and *r·* of C. S.
Man. 87–16 Principle and *r·* of C. S.,
My. 241– 5 * Principle and *r·* of C. S.
of conduct
Man. 81–20 *R·* of Conduct.
of divinity
Ret. 57–28 the status and *r·* of divinity,
No. 7– 2 The *r·* of divinity is golden ;
of error
No. 44–21 no Reign of Terror or *r·* of error
of finite matter
Ret. 58– 3 taking the *r·* of finite matter,
of human mind
Mis. 62–24 to solve . . . by the *r·* of human mind,
of Life
Un. 55– 1 *r·* of Life can be demonstrated,
of mathematics
'01. 4– 6 To depart from the *r·* of mathematics
Hea. 8–27 as we do to the *r·* of mathematics,
of mental practice
My. 364– 3 *r·* of mental practice in C. S.
of order
Ret. 50–27 for furnishing a new *r·* of order
of our church
Mis. 129– 9 and the *r·* of our church
of Science
Mis. 172–29 first and fundamental *r·* of Science
Un. 50–25 Adopt this *r·* of Science,
of spiritual love
'02. 8–22 works out the *r·* of spiritual love ;
of subtraction
Un. 53–18 assertion that . . . is the *r·* of subtraction,
of this Church
Man. 67–22 break a *r·* of this Church and are
of this Principle
Hea. 8–26 adhere to the *r·* of this Principle
one
Mis. 52–24 or failing to demonstrate one *r·*
No. 10–12 one *r·*, and one Principle for all
or demonstration
'01. 23–12 *r·*, or demonstration of C. S.,
Principle and
  (see **Principle**)

rule (noun)

same
Mis. 265–10 one Principle and the same r˙ ;
352–15 by the same r˙ that sin is healed.
Un. 2–20 According to this same r˙,
scientific
Mis. 116–30 lose the scientific r˙ and its reward :
Scriptural
Mis. 283–20 The Scriptural r˙ of this Science
second
Mis. 341– 9 up the scale of Science to the second r˙,
supreme
Mis. 368–29 rejoice in His supreme r˙,
the only
Mis. 338–13 these afford the only r˙ I have found
this
Mis. 90–13 This r˙ is forever golden :
129–11 If this r˙ fails in effect,
187–11 This r˙ of harmony must be accepted
200–14 The divine Science of this r˙
220– 1 demonstrate this r˙, which obtains
Man. 41–14 departure from this r˙ disqualifies a
102–15 but this r˙ shall not apply to
Ret. 59–10 applying this r˙ to a demonstration of
82– 8 exception to this r˙ should be very rare.
Un. 50–25 Adopt this r˙ of Science,
Pul. 12–24 This r˙ clearly interprets God as
Hea. 6– 2 should this r˙ fail hereafter,
My. 4– 3 obedience to this r˙ spiritualizes
226– 3 This r˙ strictly observed will preserve
227–28 I abide by this r˙ and triumph by it.
verity and
My. 37–12 * verity and r˙ of the Christianity of
wholesome
Mis. 283–13 Any exception to the old wholesome r˙,

———

Mis. 6–31 health is generally the r˙ ;
52–25 r˙ farther on and more difficult
69– 8 Its r˙ is, that man shall utilize
194– 3 and the r˙ whereby sin, sickness,
200–12 a r˙ that is susceptible of proof,
233–24 with the exactness of the r˙
382– 1 were either a truism or a r˙,
My. 84– 7 * It is a r˙ in some denominations
272–13 the r˙, and the demonstration of

rule (verb)
Mis. 141–22 r˙ this business transaction,
303–13 Let us serve instead of r˙,
Man. 41–23 and r˙ out of me all sin ;
Ret. 61–24 r˙ out every sense of disease
Pan. 14–13 they shall r˙ all nations.
My. 192–10 gloom of his glory r˙ not
294– 1 right of the majority to r˙.
340–25 intention to r˙ righteously

ruled
Ret. 65–17 r˙ Christ out of the synagogues,

ruler
Mis. 117– 1 "r˙ over many things."— Matt. 25 : 23.
152–12 dictator, arbiter, or r˙,
287–28 makes one r˙ over one's self
341– 9 be made r˙ over many things.
Pul. 13– 7 r˙ over many,"— Matt. 25 : 23.
My. 294–27 r˙ . . . has now passed through
342–30 * directed by a single earthly r˙ ?"
343–12 * would, like herself, be the r˙.

rulers
Mis. 53–24 to make the r˙ understand,
199–16 The r˙ sought the life of Jesus ;
My. 128–13 No crown nor sceptre nor r˙

rulership
Un. 38–17 r˙ of more gods than one.
My. 342–31 present r˙ will advance
343– 6 * is contemplated in the r˙.

Ruler Supreme
Po. 77–14 R˙ S˙ ! to Thee we'll

Rules
Mis. 148– 8 R˙ and By-laws in the Manual
Man. 3– 3 R˙ and By-Laws in the Manual
18–22 Tenets, R˙, and By-Laws,
33– 7 maintain the Tenets, R˙,
51– 1 R˙ herein set forth,
52–15 compliance with our Church R˙

rules
and by-laws
My. 49–14 * formulate the r˙ and by-laws,
and divine Principle
Mis. 32– 9 r˙ and divine Principle of C. S.
195– 3 r˙ and divine Principle of
and practice
Mis. 252–23 divine Principle, r˙ and practice
My. 239– 5 divine Principle, r˙, and practice
both
Un. 53–19 sums done under both r˙

rules
church
Mis. 310–19 comply with the church r˙.
contrary to the
My. 359– 2 do not act contrary to the r˙
definite
My. 358– 1 C. S. abides by the definite r˙
demonstrated
My. 105– 5 r˙ demonstrated prove one's faith
divine Principle and
Mis. 19– 9 divine Principle and r˙ of C. S.
87–23 taught the divine Principle and r˙
307–28 adhere to the divine Principle and r˙
established
Man. 49–15 r˙ established by the publishers.
fixed
Ret. 87–13 implicit adherence to fixed r˙,
for branch churches
My. 243– 7 r˙ for branch churches as published
four first
Pan. 9– 9 four first r˙ pertaining thereto,
furnish
My. 180– 1 furnish r˙ whereby man can prove
given
Mis. 282–19 exceptions to most given r˙ :
higher
Mis. 29–32 working up to those higher r˙
30– 5 and doubt its higher r˙,
hygienic
Mis. 40– 5 to mingle hygienic r˙, drugs,
in Christian Science
Ret. 56– 3 demonstrable r˙ in C. S.,
invariable
'01. 24– 6 by means of invariable r˙
its
Man. 73–12 provided its r˙ so permit.
Ret. 93– 7 established its r˙ in consonance
My. 230– 9 Its r˙ apply not to one member only,
247– 7 its r˙ are health, holiness, and
255– 1 its r˙ are health, holiness, and
new
Pul. 46– 4 * new r˙ were formulated.
of Christian Science
Mis. 19– 9 Principle and r˙ of C. S.
31–14 Principle or the r˙ of C. S. ;
293–16 will pervert the r˙ of C. S.,
354–14 Principle and r˙ of C. S.,
Ret. 87– 7 the r˙ of C. S. can be
of church government
Mis. 284–30 the r˙ of church government,
of conduct
My. 223– 1 chapter sub-title
of divine Love
Man. 45–12 demonstrating the r˙ of divine Love.
of divine Science
Mis. 114–11 r˙ of divine Science announced in
of its divine Principle
Mis. 22–23 the r˙ of its divine Principle,
of its Tenets
Man. 54–10 break the r˙ of its Tenets
of metaphysics
Mis. 221– 5 one gains in the r˙ of metaphysics,
of Mind-healing
Ret. 78–15 r˙ of Mind-healing are wholly
of Science
My. 235– 7 imperative r˙ of Science,
of service
My. 342–31 "In time its present r˙ of service
of the university
Man. 73–17 if the r˙ of the university or
of this practice
No. 3–12 dependent on the r˙ of this practice
perfect
My. 205–28 demonstrated by perfect r˙ ;
Principle and
(see **Principle**)
published
My. 359–11 my written and published r˙,
result of
Pul. 45–27 * result of r˙ made by Mrs. Eddy.
scientific
Mis. 289–10 the application of scientific r˙
these
Ret. 87–14 Let some of these r˙ be here stated.
those
Mis. 284–31 those r˙ must be carried out ;
were necessary
My. 343–23 R˙ were necessary, and I made a code
your
Mis. 119–29 nullify or reverse your r˙,

———

Mis. 197–25 r˙ over a kingdom of its own,
344–23 r˙ of the mighty Nazarene Prophet.
Man. 72–13 r˙ of The C. S. Publishing Society,
My. 278– 7 Love r˙ the universe,

Rules and By-Laws
Mis. 148– 8 *R· and B·* in the Manual
Man.   3– 3 *R· and B·* in the Manual

ruleth
My. 196–11 he that *r·* his spirit — *Prov.* 16 : 32.
        200– 6 *r·* in heaven and upon earth,

ruling
Mis. 204–30 divine *r·* gives prudence and energy ;
Hea. 17–28 are we not right in *r·* them out
My.   13–12 * a *mother* and a *r·* church.''

rumbling
Mis. 347– 3 *r·* and quivering of the earth

Rumney
My. 314– 7 * to North Groton and then to *R·*.''

rumor
Mis. 266–17 chapter sub-title
        345–28 *r·* that it was a part of Christian
My. 334– 2 * impression that the *r·* is not true.

rumors
Mis. 136– 4 *R·* are *r·*, — nothing more.

run
Mis. 126–25 Scientists have a strong race to *r·*,
        203–11 waters that *r·* among the valleys,
        353– 3 Human concepts *r·* in extremes ;
        361–19 *r·* with patience the race — *Heb.* 12 : 1.
Pul.   33– 5 * would often *r·* to her mother
No.   20–25 *r·* through the veins of all human
Pan.   12–17 may *r·* and not weary,
My.   155–13 *r·* in joy, health, holiness,
        189– 4 if ye would *r·*, who shall hinder you?
        252–13 not . . . *r·* away in the storm,
        254– 7 you shall *r·* and not be weary,

rung
Pul.   41–25 * *r·* out their message of
        62–11 * *r·* from an electric keyboard,
        62–12 * and even when *r·* by hand

running
Mis. 261–14 pressed down, and *r·* over.
        266–29 *r·* to and fro in the earth,
My.   21–20 * and *r·* over.'' — *Luke* 6 : 38.

runs
Mis. 270–25 *r·* through the modes and methods of

rural
My. 184–23 Your *r·* chapel is a social success

rush
Mis. 212–18 currents of human nature *r·* in against
Pul.   2–18 Would you *r·* forth single-handed
No.   1– 7 are noisy and *r·* precipitately ;
Po.   16–10 *r·* into life, and roll on with its
My. 149–29 a mighty *r·*, which waken the

rushes
Mis. 324–26 he *r·* again into the lonely streets,

rushing
Mis. 230–12 *R·* around smartly is no proof of
Pan.   1– 7 *r·* winds of March have shrieked

Russia
Pul.   5–24 France, Germany, *R·*,
My. 279–25 war between *R·* and Japan ;
        281–18 * peace between *R·* and Japan
        282– 9 Douma recently adopted in *R·*

Russia's
My. 127–25 Unlike *R·* armament,

Rust, D.D.
Rev. Richard S.
Ret.   5–18 eulogy of the Rev. Richard S. *R·*, D.D.,
Rev. R. S.
My. 311–32 called by the Rev. R. S. *R·*, D.D.,

rust
My. 213–24 will not *r·* for lack of use

rustic
My. 184–17 *r·* scroll brought back to me

rustle
Mis. 306–23 we do not hear the *r·* of wings,

rusts
My.   4–21 iron in human nature *r·* away ;

ruthless
Pul. 83–15 * the *r·* sword of injustice.
Po.   46– 9 Unplucked by *r·* hands.

ruthlessly
My. 308–11 tread not *r·* on their ashes.

S

Sabbath
Mis. 126– 5 music of our *S·* chimes
        216– 3 *S·* rest for the people of God ;

Sabbath School
Man. 62–10 *S· S·* children shall be taught

sackcloth
Mis. 275– 8 veil on the *s·* of home,
Pan.   1–14 and the *s·* of waiting
'00.   15–15 it sits in *s·* — it waits in the
My. 290–27 it will remove the *s·* from thy
        339–23 only those . . . should wear *s·*.

sacked
'00. 13–13 it was taken and *s·*.

sacrament
'02. 20–19 the *s·* in our church
My. 131– 6 for spiritual *s·*, sacrifice,

sacraments
Mis. 345–26 purpose of Christian *s·*.

sacred
Mis.   x– 2 *s·* and sincere in trial
        66–10 *s·*, solid precept is verified
        144–14 laid away as a *s·* secret
        151– 9 Through the *s·* law, He speaketh
        150–12 *s·* to the memory of my students.
        196–17 *s·* sense and permanence of
        312–19 * verities of the *s·* Scriptures.''
        318–19 Before entering this *s·* field
        323– 6 Then from this *s·* summit
        331–25 In *s·* solitude divine Science
        341–16 whereon thou standest is *s·*.
Man. 46–13 shall hold in *s·* confidence
        58–21 the *s·* revelations of C. S.
        60–17 *s·* words of our beloved Master,
        94–21 nor transfer this *s·* office.
Ret. 18–21 In *s·* communion with home's
        54–23 most *s·* and salutary power
        90–17 in their early and *s·* hours,
        90–23 to those first *s·* tasks,
Un.   41–15 The sweet and *s·* sense of the
Pul.   7–13 Those *s·* drops were but
        11– 4 Word spoken in this *s·* temple
        22– 6 in this *s·* petition with every
No.   12–11 a *s·* duty for her to impart
Pan.   3–14 * ''O *s·* solitude ! divine retreat !

sacred
'01. 28–15 *S·* history shows that those who
'02.   5–29 *s·* command, ''Thou shalt — *Exod.* 20 : 3.
Po.   30–19 *s·* song and loudest breath of praise
        64–14 In *s·* communion with home's magic
My.   27– 7 *s·* season of prayer and praise.
        36– 9 * assembled at this *s·* time to
        37– 3 * *s·* confines of this sanctuary.
        27–30 * With *s·* resolution do we pray
        46–24 * obedience to the *s·* teachings of
        57– 6 * *s·* atmosphere of a church home.
        63–20 * within our *s·* edifice
        133–24 No : then my *s·* secret is
        139–19 purpose of my request was *s·*.
        147–13 *s·* to the memory of this pure
        163–14 *s·* demands on my time and
        170–18 it is my *s·* motto,
        170–28 to kneel with us in *s·* silence
        184–23 a social success quite *s·* in its
        193–28 Within its *s·* walls may song and
        204–10 that *s·* *ave* and essence of Soul
        222–28 liberty of conscience held *s·*.
        232– 5 looms of love that line the *s·* shores.
        250–29 filled this *s·* office many years,
        265–12 *s·* rights of individuals,
        289–12 convene for the *s·* purpose of

sacredly
No.   40–15 pursue their . . . ministrations very *s·*,
My.   19–29 gift which you so *s·* bestowed
        225–18 *s·* holding His name apart
        291–30 shall *s·* regard the liberty of

sacredness
Pan.   8–11 infringe the *s·* of one Christ Jesus ?
My. 142–16 lose its *s·* and merge into

sacrifice
and ascension
My. 131– 6 sacrament, *s·*, and ascension,
and suffering
Mis. 257–15 repays . . . with *s·* and suffering.
and torture
Peo.   3– 8 *s·* and torture of His favorite Son,
better than
Mis. 110– 1 Repentance is better than *s·*.
fleshly
Mis. 345–32 away from the thought of fleshly *s·*,

sacrifice
his
  No. 33–16 to insure the glory his s˙ brought
human
  My. 125– 1 kindle altars for human s˙.
incentive and
  My. 288– 5 his life's incentive and s˙
individual
  Mis. 364– 7 In return for individual s˙,
Jesus'
  No. 33–22 Jesus' s˙ stands preeminently
labor and
  My. 58–18 * through the labor and s˙ of our
life and
  My. 323–18 * your wonderful life and s˙
long
  My. 38– 1 * could recompense your long s˙
loving
  Pul. 86–23 * your labors and loving s˙,
  No. 7–16 Every loving s˙ for the good of
no
  Mis. 238– 8 since no s˙ is too great for
no less
  My. 21–25 * no less s˙ than have others ;
offer them in
  Mis. 345–24 in order to offer them in s˙,
reluctant
  My. 10–19 * fretful or reluctant s˙
requires
  No. 33– 8 requires s˙, struggle, prayer,
spirit of
  Mis. 261–23 spirit of s˙ always has saved,
suffering and
  Mis. 350–31 nameless suffering and s˙,
that Jesus made
  No. 34– 7 the s˙ that Jesus made for us,
this
  Mis. 149–23 May this s˙ bring to your

  Mis. 155– 6 S˙ self to bless one another,
  343– 4 all that we have to s˙,
  Ret. 49– 2 to s˙ all for the advancement of
  No. 33–13 The s˙ of our blessed Lord
  '01. 29– 9 s˙ for him even as he has sacrificed
  35– 4 Are we willing to s˙ self for
  My. 184–21 a s˙ and service acceptable in God's

sacrificed
  Mis. 123–11 human victims to be s˙ to
  267– 6 I have s˙ the most time,
  Pul. 82–20 * sang and s˙ for their people,
  '01. 29– 9 as he has s˙ for others
  '02. 13– 2 self was forgotten, peace s˙,
  My. 194–25 that for which you have s˙

sacrifices
  Mis. 250–17 s˙ and grand achievements
  Ret. 80–29 s˙ made for others are not
  Pul. 45– 2 * S˙ were made in many an instance
  '01. 29–24 does most, and s˙ most for
  My. 17–12 to offer up spiritual s˙,
  30–13 * personal s˙ of no mean order ;
  52–27 * she has made s˙ from which

sacrificial
  Ret. 89– 8 for s˙ ceremonies, not for sermons.
  No. 33–12 chapter sub-title

sacrilegious
  Pul. 75– 8 or speak of me . . . as a Christ, is s˙.
  '01. 16– 9 envy, and hate, supply s˙ gossip with
  My. 230– 1 Notwithstanding the s˙ moth of time,

sad
  Mis. 43–17 s˙ fact at this early writing is,
  329–10 whose voices are s˙ or glad,
  341–23 the s˙ history of Vesta,
  386–23 Rears the s˙ marble to our memory
  396–20 a strain, Low, s˙, and sweet,
  Man. 55– 7 if this s˙ necessity occurs.
  Ret. 7–21 * This s˙ event will not be
  19–22 her s˙ journey to the North.
  Pul. 18– 4 a strain, Low, s˙, and sweet,
  No. 3– 2 How s˙ it is that envy will
  '01. 17– 8 meet the s˙ sinner on his way
  '02. 18– 8 S˙ to say, the cowardice and
  Po. 12– 3 a strain, Low, s˙, and sweet,
  31– 5 S˙ sense, annoy No more the peace of
  50– 9 Rears the s˙ marble to our memory
  53–17 Come at the s˙ heart's call,
  65– 2 My spirit is s˙,
  66–10 that heart is silent and s˙,
  My. 294–23 The s˙, sudden announcement of
  331– 1 her s˙ journey to the North.

sadly
  Mis. xl–26 s˙ to survey the fields of the slain

sadness
  Ret. 32–16 * Short-lived joy, that ends in s˙,

safe
  Mis. 43–11 s˙ and successful practitioners.
  89–28 is s˙ in divine Science.
  104– 6 s˙ in the substance of Soul,
  111– 7 extended it beyond s˙ expansion ;
  117– 9 This will place him on the s˙ side of
  140–27 Our title to God's acres will be s˙
  157–14 s˙ under the shadow of His wing.
  193– 5 deemed it s˙ to say at that time.
  252–27 with s˙ and sure medicine ;
  263–10 s˙ in His strength,
  293– 1 s˙ not to teach prematurely the
  Man. 76– 2 should remain on s˙ deposit,
  Ret. 90–29 It is s˙ to leave with God the
  Pul. 27– 5 * s˙ preservation of papers.
  No. 3–21 s˙ members of the community.
  '02. 15– 5 I leaned on God, and was s˙.
  Po. 43–20 S˙ in Science, bright with glory
  My. 200–15 man's soul is s˙ ;
  203–26 in the bosom of earth s˙ from
  210–10 not only yourselves are s˙,
  217– 8 invested in s˙ municipal bonds
  224–24 not s˙ to accept the latter as
  283–18 It is always s˙ to be just.
  295– 5 divine Love holds its substance s˙

safely
  Mis. 10–16 more assured to press on s˙.
  152–24 s˙ sheltered in the strong tower of
  152–28 right intuition which guides you s˙
  328–31 wilt s˙ bear thy cross up to the
  385–11 s˙ moored at last — Beyond rough foam.
  Ret. 40–17 her babe was s˙ born,
  Po. 48– 3 s˙ moored at last — Beyond rough foam.
  My. 139– 5 s˙, soulfully founded upon
  220– 2 s˙ submit to the providence of God,

safer
  Mis. 228– 1 a s˙ guide than the promptings of

safety
  Mis. 257–19 a belief in s˙ where there is
  Ret. 14–16 and take my chance of spiritual s˙
  My. 211–23 a belief in s˙ where there is

sage
  Mis. 1–14 The seer of this age should be a s˙.
  Ret. 11–15 Hero and s˙ arise to show
  '02. 1–21 attention of philosopher and s˙,
  Po. 60–12 Hero and s˙ arise to show

said
  Mis. ix–18 Truly may it be s˙ :
  1– 7 the scoffed of all scoffers, s˙,
  4–24 often s˙, "You must have
  15– 7 The great Nazarene Prophet s˙,
  21– 9 Our Master s˙, "The works — *John* 14 : 12.
  24–25 s˙ : "When he speaketh — *John* 8 : 44.
  30–25 fool hath s˙ in his heart, — *Psal.* 14 : 1.
  37– 8 he s˙, "I and my Father — *John* 10 : 30.
  44–26 s˙, There is no more pain.
  51–30 The apostle James s˙,
  57–15 God, denounced it, and s˙ :
  57–17 error s˙, "I am true,"
  57–20 and the Lord God never s˙ it.
  61–16 * a man was s˙ to be 'hanged
  63– 2 It was s˙ of old by Truth-traducers,
  68– 7 *The Rev.* —— s˙ *in a sermon :*
  70–10 *What did Jesus mean when he s˙*
  71– 3 John B. Gough is s˙ to have
  73– 2 material body is s˙ to suffer,
  83–24 and s˙, Father, the hour is come ;
  87–16 *She s˙ that you sent her there*
  95–10 * Mrs. Eddy responding, s˙ :
  97– 8 Our Master s˙ of one of his students,
  99–21 He s˙, "Heaven and earth — *Matt.* 24 : 35.
  111–16 s˙, "Heaven and earth — *Matt.* 24 : 35.
  112–21 The jailer thanked me, and s˙,
  112–31 fool hath s˙ in his heart, — *Psal.* 14 : 1.
  122– 2 he s˙, "Woe unto the — *Matt.* 18 : 7.
  122– 9 s˙ of him whom God foreordained
  142–13 Each day since they arrived I have s˙,
  157– 3 Paul s˙, "If we suffer, — *II Tim.* 2 : 12.
  159–23 a bit of what I s˙ in 1890 ?
  163–18 he s˙, "Heaven and earth — *Matt.* 24 : 35.
  165–18 legacy of what he s˙ and did,
  170–17 ye know not of," he s˙. — *John* 4 : 32.
  170–19 record of the Bible, she s˙,
  170–25 he is s˙ to have spat upon the dust,
  177–22 * editor of *The C. S. Journal* s˙
  178–18 * If any one had s˙ to me
  180–12 I s˙, in the words of
  193– 2 Did Jesus mean what he s˙ ?
  193– 5 all, and even more than he s˙
  193–19 s˙ when critics attacked me for
  195–13 It has been s˙ that the New Testament
  196–12 bear in mind that a serpent s˙ that ;
  208–21 David s˙, "Before I was — *Psal.* 119 : 67,
  210– 9 Christ s˙, "They shall — *Mark* 16 : 18.

said

Mis.	211–26	Our Master *s*·, "Ye shall— *Matt.* 20 : 23.
	211–28	and he *s*· to his followers,
	214– 4	He *s*·, "Think not that I— *Matt.* 10 : 34.
	218–28	when he *s*· "How do you do?"
	223–27	Hannah More *s*·, "If I wished
	225–16	he *s*· to·this venerable Christian :
	225–29	The parents *s*· :— "Wait until we
	226– 1	*s*· :— "Give the child what he relishes,
	236–10	we have *s*·, "Love and honor thy
	236–20	In such cases we have *s*·,
	236–23	by anything that is *s*· to you,
	239–19	the poor child *s*·,— "I've got cold,
	244–24	He *s*·, "And other sheep— *John* 10 : 16.
	248–21	have *s*· that I died of poison,
	251–15	*s*· : "The works that I do— *John* 14 : 12.
	252–32	our Master *s*·, if a man findeth,
	253–18	and the husbandmen that *s*·,
	255– 2	It is sometimes *s*·, cynically,
	255–13	what the apostle meant when he *s*· :
	258– 2	Christ has *s*· that love is the
	266–18	assertion that I have *s*· hard things
	270–14	He *s*·, "Seek ye first the— *Matt.* 6 : 33.
	271–20	Much is *s*· at this date, 1889,
	272– 9	* till the repealing of *s*· Act
	278–14	that Job sinned not in all he *s*·,
	282–14	Our Master *s*·, "When ye— *Matt.* 10 : 12.
	302–22	at once after *s*· service.
	312–13	*s*·, "No more striking manifestation
	334– 1	*s*· : "He doeth according to— *Dan.* 4 : 35.
	337–13	in the midst of them, and *s*·,— *Matt.* 18 : 2, 3.
	342–23	and they *s*· to the foolish,
	345– 8	the proconsul *s*· to him,
	345–14	*s*·, "Christianity is fit only for
	345–18	Webster *s*·, "My heart has always
	349–15	I was willing, and *s*· so,
	353–17	he *s*· to the jester, "You must pay
	363–13	Truth *s*·, and *s*· from the beginning,
	376– 7	* and *s*· to have been authentic ;
	380–22	*s*·, "Suffer it to be so— *Matt.* 3 : 15.
	381–22	under the seal of the *s*· Court,
Man.	26–16	*s*· candidates shall not be chosen.
	27– 6	to be taken by *s*· Committee
	27–10	written consent of *s*· Board.
	28–22	*s*· officer shall be dismissed
	36–23	may admit *s*· applicant
	39– 3	expiration of *s*· one year,
	43– 3	name of *s*· member to be dropped
	46–21	for *s*· member's practice,
	50–20	and *s*· member exonerated,
	52– 5	*if s*· *member belongs to no*
	54–22	*s*· member shall immediately be
	56– 4	if *s*· member persists in this
	57–16	before he can call *s*· meeting.
	67–13	if *s*· case relates to the person
	67–16	conferred with her on *s*· subject.
	69– 1	*s*· student shall come under a
	70– 5	consulting her on *s*· subject
	70–18	confer on a statute of *s*· State,
	70–20	the churches in *s*· State.
	73–14	graduates of *s*· university
	73–20	may lecture for *s*· university
	74–19	advertised in *s*· *Journal*,
	75–13	situation between . . . and *s*· Church
	76–25	responsible for *s*· funds.
	77– 7	submit them all to *s*· committee
	79–13	persons nominated for *s*· office
	80–14	vacancies in *s*· trusteeship,
	86–24	instruct . . . from the *s*· chapter
	88–13	elected every third year by *s*· Board,
	90–22	prepare a paper on *s*· subject
	100– 1	employing *s*· Committee.
	100– 5	shall appoint *s*· candidate.
	100–15	in accordance with *s*· By-Laws.
Ret.	1– 5	her family is *s*· to have been
	1–10	my grandmother *s*· were written
	8–18	my cousin turned to me and *s*·,
	8–20	Mehitable then *s*· sharply,
	8–24	*s*· that mother wanted me.
	14–29	This was so earnestly *s*·,
	16– 6	*s*·, "Did you hear my daughter
	40–13	that her physicians had *s*·
	48–26	baptism of Jesus, of which he *s*·,
	63–22	St. Augustine once *s*·,
	64– 8	Need it be *s*· that any
	86– 8	*s*· the classic Grecian motto.
	87– 1	Master *s*·, "Follow me ; — *Matt.* 8 : 22.
	93–17	St. Paul *s*· to the Athenians,
Un.	3– 6	before it can be truly *s*·
	9–20	Sometimes it is *s*·, by those who
	9–21	and this is *s*· because ideas
	11–26	*s*· that the kingdom of heaven
	14–27	God never *s*· that man
	21–10	*Evil.* God hath *s*·,
	37– 6	Our Master *s*·, "The kingdom— *Matt.* 10 : 7.
	57–11	When Jesus turned and *s*·,

said

Un.	58– 6	His persecutors *s*· mockingly,
Pul.	2– 4	*s*·, "Behold, the half — *I Kings* 10 : 7.
	3– 5	Master *s*· : "Destroy this— *John* 2 : 19.
	3– 6	*s*· : "The kingdom of God— *Luke* 17 : 21.
	6–26	At a *conversazione* in Boston, he *s*·,
	7– 2	*s*· : "Had I young blood in my veins,
	10–19	Master *s*· : "The stone— *Matt.* 21 : 42.
	29–20	* Judge Hanna *s*· that while all these
	34–16	* that it was my apparition," she *s*·.
	34–21	* *s*·, in reference to this experience.
	34–26	* she *s*·, in reply to my questions,
	35–12	* Mrs. Eddy has *s*· :— "I had learned
	37–16	* *s*· a gentleman to me on Christmas eve,
	57– 6	* The auditorium is *s*· to seat
	66– 8	* This growth, it is *s*·, proceeds
	67– 6	* *s*· by a great American writer.
	72–16	* past eleven years," *s*· Mrs. Copeland,
	72–19	* Mrs. Copeland *s*· that she was the
	73–27	* and *s*· that no more complete
	74–20	If she *s*· aught with intention to
	79–21	* wicked but witty writer has *s*·,
	82– 7	* *s*·— she is soft and gentle,
	82–14	* *s*· that because she was created after
Rud.	16–17	Whatever is *s*· and written correctly
No.	25– 4	St. Paul *s*·, "But now we are— *Rom.* 7 : 6.
	27–18	Bishop Foster *s*·, in a lecture
	29–12	he *s*·, "The forgiven soul in a
	31–26	He *s*· also: "If a man— *John* 8 : 5·.
	40– 1	The apostle James *s*· :
	41–25	Baptist clergyman, in a sermon :
	42–18	It is *s*· that the devil is the ape
	42–25	He *s*· : "I am suffering from
	43– 4	Master *s*·, "Come unto me,— *Matt.* 11 : 28.
	43– 8	A lady *s*· : "Only He who knows
	43–10	distinguished Doctor of Divinity *s*· :
	45– 3	St. Paul *s*· that without charity
Pan.	5–12	He *s*· of evil :
	8–18	It *s*·, "Call no man your— *Matt.* 23 : 9.
	10– 5	The great Nazarene Prophet *s*·,
'00.	3–14	thinker and worker has *s*·
	13– 1	It is *s*· "a controversy was
	14–26	as the devout St. Stephen *s*· :
'01.	3– 8	We hear it *s*· the Christian Scientists
	3–20	It is sometimes *s*· : "God is Love,
	8– 9	was *s*· in the sense that one ray of
	8–25	Christ existed prior to Jesus, who *s*·,
	16–24	Shall it be *s*· of this century
	18–24	fool hath *s*· in his heart,— *Psal.* 14 : 1.
	26–21	St. Paul *s*· : "Though I speak— *I Cor.* 13 : 1.
	27–27	Agassiz *s*· : "Every great scientific
	28– 6	narrow way, whereof our Master *s*·,
'02.	3– 5	Buddhism and Shintoism are *s*· to
	11–28	for the truths he *s*· and did ;
	18–14	He *s*·, "Inasmuch as ye— *Matt.* 25 : 40.
	18–21	*s*·, "The works that I do— *John* 14 : 12.
Hea.	2– 9	*S*· the intrepid reformer,
	2–11	*S*· . . . gentle Melanchthon :
	2–17	model of infinite patience, *s*· :
	2–19	*s*· this when bending beneath
	6– 9	misinterpreted, and I *s*· it.
	7–18	the poor woman . . . *s*·,
	8–15	Plato did better ; he *s*·,
	9– 6	The less *s*· or thought of sin, sickness,
Peo.	4– 8	*s*· that Life, which is infinite
	4–11	because a serpent *s*· it.
	5–26	Oliver Wendell Holmes *s*·,
	10–13	Discerning the . . . Paul *s*·,
	13–23	The infidel was blind who *s*·,
	13–25	for Bonaparte *s*· :
	13–27	and Daniel Webster *s*· :
My.	4–25	Our great Master *s*· :
	5–27	virtually what the prophet *s*· :
	8– 3	* Mr. Kimball *s*· in part :
	8– 8	* in seconding the motion, *s*· :
	15–15	I have *s*· to you all
	28– 3	* Our Leader has *s*· in S. and H.
	38–24	* *s*· after the service that
	39–17	* Mr. McKenzie *s*· :
	40–27	* poet perceived when he *s*·,
	42–12	* on assuming office, *s*· :
	51– 6	* now interested in *s*· church,
	57–28	* *Transcript s*· :
	61–16	* so clearly, I *s*· aloud,
	66–12	* *s*· that a number of changes
	72– 2	* could hear what was *s*·.
	83–19	* chapter sub-title
	91– 9	* It is to be *s*· for C. S.
	92–26	* two things to be *s*· in favor of
	93– 6	* it may be *s*· that if their opinions
	93– 9	* It has been *s*· cynically
	99–12	* *s*· in their behalf that they
	103–16	the Psalmist *s*· :
	104– 7	Of old the Pharisees *s*·
	104–14	what shall be *s*· of him
	131–24	The divine law has *s*· to us :

said

My. 134–25	* In announcing this letter, he *s·* :
135– 2	The wise man has *s·*,
137–27	I selected *s·* Trustees
140– 2	the prophet Isaiah *s·*,
145–11	carpenters' foreman *s·* to me :
145–15	*s·* to Mr. George H. Moore
146– 3	*s·* : "They shall take up— *Mark* 16 : 18.
150–26	what our Master *s·*
152– 7	The medicine-man, . . . *s·*,
161–29	the Godlike man *s·*,
172–20	* In reply Mr. Bates *s·*,
173–30	his colaborers on *s·* committee
178–29	*s·* that the nearest approach
181–27	It is authentically *s·* that one
182– 2	To-day it is *s·* to have a majority
184–26	Isaiah *s·* : "How beautiful— *Isa.* 52 : 7.
191– 2	Nicodemus of old, who *s·*,
218– 3	*s·*, "Suffer it to be so— *Matt.* 3 : 15.
218– 4	Job *s·*, "In my flesh— *Job* 19 : 26.
219–23	*s·*, "Think not that I am— *Matt.* 5 : 17.
222–18	he was arrested because, as was *s·*,
227– 1	The great Master *s·*,
227– 2	He *s·* this to satisfy himself
227–30	fool hath *s·* in his heart,— *Psal.* 14 : 1.
228–13	John the Baptist, of whom he *s·*
229–25	That which I *s·* in my heart
233–24	Master *s·*, "He that taketh— *Matt.* 10 : 38.
240–11	I *s·*, "This Science is a law of
241–21	* *s·* that my statement was wrong,
244–20	Knowing this, our Master *s·* :
246–25	Master *s·* : "What I do— *John* 13 : 7.
267–28	Our great Teacher hath *s·* :
279– 3	The Founder of Christianity *s·* :
283–12	fruits of *s·* grand Association,
284–15	* "It is *s·* to be the first time
297– 6	*s·* description of her soul-visit,
297–29	what the enemies of C. S. are *s·* to
304–21	In a lecture in Chicago, he *s·* :
304–25	*s·* : "Every great scientific truth
307– 1	words that I *s·* to him,
307–21	understood what I *s·* better than
310–30	Dr. Ladd *s·* to Alexander Tilton :
311– 8	my good housekeeper *s·* to me :
318–30	"Now, Mr. Wiggin," I *s·*,
321–13	* cannot believe that he has ever *s·*
323– 5	* he *s·* he had written in answer to
324– 6	* as he *s·* you and your ideas
324– 8	* *s·* you were so original
324–24	* Everything he *s·* conveyed this
324–27	* He *s·* he wanted to see if
324–30	* and *s·* that no man could have
331–26	* Much has often been *s·* of the
333– 1	* *s·* record, with the seal of the
339–18	disciples of St. John the Baptist *s·*
340– 4	*s·*, "Pray without ceasing."— *I Thess.* 5 : 17.
342–20	* she *s·*, in her clear voice,
345–14	The doctors *s·* I would live if
	(*see also* **Jesus**)

sail

Ret. 57– 2	we *s·* into the eternal haven

sailed

Pan. 14–24	*s·* victoriously through the jaws of

sailing

My. 232– 2	*s·* over rough seas

saint

Mis. 108– 1	sorrowing *s·* thinks too much of it :
257–23	strikes down the hoary *s·*.
Pul. 65–26	* exemplar afterward became a *s·*.
Po. 29–21	be thou our *s·*, Our stay,
34–12	solitude, where nymph or *s·*
My. 4–11	spiritually, blessing *s·* and sinner
104– 4	Mars' Hill orator, the canonized *s·*,

Saint and **St. Andrew's Lodge, Number 10**

Ret. 19–11	member in *S· A· L·*, *N·* 10,
My. 330–23	member in *St. A· L·*, No. 10,
332–20	* membership in *St. A· L·*, No. 10,
335– 4	* Mason in "*St. A· L·*, No. 10."

sainted

Ret. 5–19	and knew my *s·* mother
6– 2	* impressions of that *s·* spirit,
'02. 3–24	the joy of the *s·* Queen,
My. 120– 1	We look for the *s·* Revelator

saintly

Mis. 319–23	Take thither thy *s·* offerings,
Pul. 32–27	* a *s·* and consecrated character.

saints

Mis. 149–26	fellowship with *s·* and angels.
219–24	immortal Mind makes *s·* ;
293–25	makes mortals either *s·* or
'00. 8– 2	with *s·* and angels shall be satisfied
My. 125–31	blood of the *s·*,— *Rev.* 17 : 6.

saints

My. 206–28	inheritance of the *s·* — *Col.* 1 : 12.
249–16	patience, silence, and lives of *s·*.

saith

Mis. 16– 3	*s·* : In mine infancy, this is enough of
16– 9	*s·* : The Principle of Christianity
67– 4	First is the law, which *s·* :
72–12	the immutable Word *s·*,
72–15	As I live, *s·* the Lord— *Ezek.* 18 : 3.
99– 3	*s·* to the five material senses,
101–20	but Science *s·* to man,
109–28	Christ, Truth, *s·* unto you,
151–11	He *s·* of the barren fig-tree,
179–32	Life that knows no death, that *s·*,
184–27	*s·* Abba, Father, and *is* born of
192–15	The Hebrew bard *s·*,
203– 9	Solomon *s·*, "As in water— *Prov.* 27 : 19.
212– 2	Human policy is a fool that *s·*
212–20	The law of Love *s·*,
219– 8	Now, what *s·* the Scripture?
254–13	victim of mad ambition that *s·*,
268– 8	The Holy One *s·*,
306–29	The Psalmist *s·* :
307–23	*s·*, "Little children,— *I John* 5 : 21.
321– 3	*s·*, "Unto us a child— *Isa.* 9 : 6.
323–17	He *s·* unto the patient toilers
325– 2	*s·* unto the dwellers therein,
325–31	enters a place of worship, and *s·*
326–30	the Stranger *s·* unto him,
327– 5	And the Stranger *s·* unto him,
327– 8	"Then," *s·* the Stranger,
334–29	divine Science, which *s·*,
339–17	*s·*, "Thou hast been faithful— *Matt.* 25 : 23.
380–23	for thus *s·* our Master.
Man. 41– 9	The wise man *s·*,
Ret. 32– 7	*s·* the Master.
60–14	C. S. *s·* to the wave
60–18	*s·* to all manner of disease,
60–20	Material sense *s·*,
61–13	Science *s·* to fear,
64–15	where the Psalmist *s·* :
Un. 18–23	*s·*, I am ever-conscious Life,
62– 3	The Christian *s·*,
62–21	Truth or Life . . . . *s·* forever,
Rud. 13–12	human belief which *s·*
No. v–10	*s·* tenderly, "Come and drink ;"
Pan. 10– 2	But what *s·* the apostle?
'00. 3– 1	Now, what *s·* C. S.?
8–14	*s·* to his followers :
11–26	"the Spirit *s·* — *Rev.* 2 : 7.
14– 1	The Revelator . . . *s·* :
14–10	hear what the Spirit *s·*
15–12	*s·* "there is no sin,"
'01. 11–22	Whosoever *s·* there is no
'02. 7–24	*s·*, "A new commandment— *John* 13 : 34.
19–16	*s·* : "Come unto me."— *Matt.* 11 : 28.
20– 3	him who stilled the tempest *s·*,
My. 16–24	thus *s·* the Lord God,— *Isa.* 28 : 16.
126–19	*s·* in her heart,— *Rev.* 18 : 7.
153– 9	*s·* He that is holy."— *Rev.* 3 : 7.
156–14	Master *s·* unto thee,— *Luke* 22 : 11.
184–28	that *s·* unto Zion,— *Isa.* 52 : 7.
205–17	Æsculapius and Hygeia, *s·*,
223–29	divine Love and wisdom *s·*,
251– 2	The great Master *s·* :
270–11	Divine Love, . . . *s·* :
293–30	the Saviour of man *s·* :
	(*see also* **Lord, Scripture**)

sake

Mis. 8–24	*falsely*, for my *s·* ;— *Matt.* 5 : 11.
199–12	*for Christ's s·*. — *II Cor.* 12 : 10.
243–25	*for thy stomach's s·*"?— *I Tim.* 5 : 23.
261–28	for conscience' *s·*, one will either
312– 8	endures all piercing for the *s·* of
312– 9	for the kingdom of heaven's *s·*.
327–26	loseth his life for my *s·*,— *Matt.* 10 : 39.
Pul. 15–10	for the *s·* of doing right
51–30	* for the *s·* of humanity.
81–15	* scorn self for the *s·* of love
No. 42–14	and for the *s·* of Christ,
Pan. 13–14	Love all . . . for the gospel's *s·* ;
'01. 3– 6	*falsely*, for my *s·*."— *Matt.* 5 : 11.
'02. 11–24	*falsely*, for my *s·*.— *Matt.* 5 : 11.
15–16	I became poor for Christ's *s·*.
My. 18–22	Love all . . . for the gospel's *s·* ;
54– 4	* for the *s·* of the eternal truth
104–31	*falsely*, for my *s·*"?— *Matt.* 5 : 11.
233–24	for my *s·* shall find— *Matt.* 10 : 39.
316– 8	*falsely*, for my *s·*."— *Matt.* 5 : 11.

sakes

My. 41–29	* for our *s·* as well as for her own ;
269–24	for your *s·*,— *Mal.* 3 : 11.

salaries

Man. 26–18	fix the *s·* of the Readers.

salary
- *Mis.* 300–13 gives you the clergyman's s·
- 349–26 church had . . . means to pay a s·,
- *Man.* 29–15 s· of the members of the Board
- 97–13 shall receive an annual s·,
- 101– 6 shall receive an adequate s·
- *Ret.* 90– 5 his s· for tending the home flock
- *My.* 312–29 My s· for writing gave me

sale
- *Mis.* 35–15 S· and H·, that you offer for s·
- 299–19 garments that are on s·,
- 307–12 rapid s· already of two editions
- *Man.* 27–22 publication and s· of the books of
- 44–10 that has for s· obnoxious books.
- *'02.* 15–10 income from the s· of S. and H.,
- *My.* 354– 4 Bibles and other books for s·

Salem
Massachusetts
- *Ret.* 20–23 in the city of S·, Massachusetts.

- *Mis.* 211–11 class legislation, and S· witchcraft,

salient
- *My.* 297– 3 shrink from such s· praise.

sallies
- *My.* 201–18 that its sudden s· may help us,

salt
- *Mis.* 348–22 Natrum muriaticum (common s·).

Salt Lake City
Utah
- *Pul.* 90– 4 * Salt Lake Herald, S· L·.C·, Utah.
- 90–12 * Tribune, S· L· C·, Utah.
- *My.* 186–24 chapter sub-title

- *'00.* 1–21 St. Louis, Denver, S· L· C·,
- *My.* 187– 3 church in S· L· C· hath not lost its

Salt Lake Herald
- *Pul.* 90– 4 * S· L· H·, Salt Lake City, Utah.

saltness
- *My.* 187– 3 hath not lost its s·.

salts
- *My.* 108– 1 the effects of calcareous s·

salutary
- *Ret.* 54–23 most sacred and s· power
- *Rud.* 10– 4 s· influence on yourself and others.
- *'01.* 34– 3 s· in the healing of all manner of
- *Hea.* 14–14 and his efforts are s·,
- *My.* 108– 7 the action of the divine Mind is s·
- 252– 5 will be s· as Soul ;

salute
- *Mis.* 282–14 enter a house, s· it."— see Matt. 10 : 12.
- *My.* 347–15 bough, bird, and song, to s· me.

saluting
- *Mis.* 126– 5 s· the ear in tones that leap for joy,

salvation
abundance of
- *My.* 36–19 * bear witness to the abundance of s·
and strength
- *Pul.* 12– 6 s·, and strength,— Rev. 12 : 10.
condition of
- *Mis.* 192–26 making healing a condition of s·,
conditions of
- *Mis.* 244–12 are the conditions of s· mental, or
cup of
- *Pan.* 14– 9 drink of the cup of s·,
everlasting
- *Mis.* 261–26 saved with an everlasting s·.
from divorce
- *My.* 269–11 Christ's plan of s· from divorce.
from sin
- *Mis.* 123–26 s· from sin, . . . through a divine
- 168– 1 s· from sin to the sinner
- 196–20 the portals of s· from sin,
- *'02.* 11–17 s· from sin, disease, and death.
- *My.* 154– 1 s· from sin, disease, and death.
full
- *Mis.* 192–18 great Principle of a full s·.
- 197– 7 It means a full s·,
grace and
- *'01.* 19– 2 means of grace and s·.
guide to
- *Pul.* 30–19 * as the teacher and guide to s· ;
healing and
- *Mis.* 244–24 the way of healing and s·.
his
- *Un.* 2– 7 except in God, who is his s·.
- *My.* 34– 7 from the God of his s·.— Psal. 24 : 5.
- 202– 6 Now may his s· draw near,
his own
- *Mis.* 85–20 and work out his own s·.
- *No.* 8–12 to work out his own s·,
is as eternal
- *Un.* 59–13 S· is as eternal as God.

salvation
knowledge of
- *'02.* 11–17 knowledge of s· from sin,
- 16– 5 Authorized Version "knowledge of s·."
man's
- *Mis.* 96– 1 man's s· from sickness and death,
- 241– 4 correlated in man's s· ;
- *'01.* 10–19 man's s· comes through
- *Peo.* 12–19 man's s· from sickness and death.
of a world
- *Mis.* 122– 7 s· of a world of sinners,
of many people
- *Mis.* 150–16 s· of many people by means of
of the eunuch
- *Mis.* 77– 1 Did the s· of the eunuch
of the world
- *Mis.* 177–18 necessary to the s· of the world
our own
- *'01.* 10–25 working out our own s·,
- *Hea.* 5–21 to work out our own s·,
- *Peo.* 4– 1 working out our own s·.
- 9–14 shall work out our own s·,
pardon for
- *Peo.* 3–26 personal pardon for s·,
plan of
- *My.* 283–23 God's own plan of s·.
rock of
- *My.* 165–21 and this is my rock of s·
song of
- *My.* 166–23 sing the old-new song of s·,
their
- *Mis.* 214–21 labor in the flesh for their s· :
this
- *Mis.* 89–26 This s· means : saved from error,
universal
- *Un.* 6–23 assertion of universal s·
- *'01.* 13–25 hence the hope of universal s·.
vocal with
- *Mis.* 146– 2 May her walls be vocal with s· ;
way of
- (see **way**)
whole
- *Mis.* 96–23 It brings . . . a whole s·.
wise unto
- *Mis.* 134– 2 "wise unto s·" !— II Tim. 3 : 15.
- 343– 1 to make us wise unto s· !
your own
- *My.* 300– 5 "Work out your own s· — Phil. 2 : 12.

- *Mis.* 160–32 s· from the belief of death,
- *Ret.* 14– 9 both s· and condemnation depended.
- *Pul.* 53–17 * s· in the world to come.
- *My.* 333–25 * reliance for s· on the merits of
- 357–21 to s· and eternal C. S.

Samaritan
- *Mis.* 257–28 smites with disease the good S·

same
- *Mis.* 27–18 send forth at the s· place— Jas. 3 : 11.
- 40– 5 in the s· process,
- 40– 9 asked, "If C. S. is the s· method
- 40–15 the s· Principle as theirs ;
- 40–18 s· results follow not in every case,
- 42–14 s· plane of conscious existence
- 53–21 If C· S· is the s· as Jesus taught,
- 54–28 they do not heal on the s· basis.
- 92–14 answer them from the s· source.
- 110–19 steadfastly at the s· object-lesson,
- 123– 1 incited by the s· spirit
- 130–12 s· power to make you a
- 144–12 written by the s· author,
- 147–22 hence we find him ever the s·,
- 160– 8 flow on in the s· sweet rhythm
- 214–11 was stimulated by the s· Love
- 214–25 s· as its attitude physically.
- 221–24 multiplication of the s· two numbers
- 221–28 would not yield the s· product
- 229–21 in the s· proportion would faith
- 243–10 removed these appliances the s· day
- 259–19 governed in the s· rhythm
- 263–19 constant petitions for the s·,
- 265– 9 one Principle and the s· rule ;
- 265–25 who receive the s· instruction,
- 273–28 waiting for the s· class instruction ;
- 295– 6 s· power which in America
- 295–10 * cause of this "s· original evil"
- 296–11 in the s· category with noble women
- 296–30 barmaid and . . . in the s· breath?
- 298– 9 Under the s· circumstances,
- 298–10 in the s· spiritual ignorance
- 303–15 the s· rights and privileges
- 306–14 * as a notification of the s·,
- 337–14 the s· is greatest — Matt. 18 : 4.
- 347–13 operation by the s· spirit.
- 349–20 the s· as the foregoing,
- 352–14 healed upon the s· Principle

same

Mis.	352–15	and by the s· rule
	359– 4	On the s· principle,
	364–26	s· power or modes
	364–27	the s· consciousness,
	381–32	* founder and discoverer of the s·
	387–11	And on the s· branch belief.
Man.	18– 1	s· is become the head — *Matt.* 21 : 42.
	18– 4	the s· month the members,
	25–13	s· person is eligible for election
	27–21	located in the s· building,
	61– 5	services at the s· hour.
	70–17	located in the s· State,
	71– 5	established in the s· place ;
	80–18	reserves the right to fill the s·
	110–16	names must be written the s·
Chr.	53–51	s· hand unfolds His power,
	55–23	the s· is my brother, — *Matt.* 12 : 50.
Ret.	8–15	in the s· room with grandmother,
	8–19	s· call was thrice repeated.
	16–17	the s· month the members,
	44– 5	during the s· month the members,
	49–30	and the s· is hereby dissolved.
	54–19	s· channel of ignorant belief.
	71–29	the s· as other forms of stealing,
	82– 7	practitioners of the s· blessed faith.
	83–22	the s· as other teachers ;
	88– 1	s· courtesy should be observed
	94–22	"the s· yesterday, — *Heb.* 13 : 8.
Un.	2–17	In the s· manner the sick lose
	2–20	According to this s· rule,
	4–19	bids man have the s· Mind
	7–13	In the s· spiritual condition
	8–17	s· basis whereby sickness is healed,
	13– 2	on the s· principle that it does in
	60– 5	With the s· breath he articulates
	60–15	Out of the s· mouth — *Jas.* 3 : 10.
	61– 3	"the s· yesterday, — *Heb.* 13 : 8.
Pul.	5–24	the s· in Great Britain, France,
	10–20	s· is become the head — *Matt.* 21 : 42.
	25–24	* repeats the s· tints.
	48–18	* bred in that s· neighborhood.
	51– 3	* the s· impressions upon all.
	53–30	* Is evermore the s·.
	54–11	* are the s· as were necessary
	73–19	* of the s· theory as Mrs. Copeland.
No.	12–13	s· affection, desire, and motives
	13–15	chapter sub-title
	21–17	in the s· realm and consciousness.
	24–12	By the s· token, evil is not only
	31–22	were one and the s· with this
	38–14	s· is become the head — *Matt.* 21 : 42.
'01.	33–26	the s· reviling it received
	33–27	and from the s· motives
Hea.	7–15	the s· as it begins in motive
Po.	vii– 3	* s· lofty trend of thought
	6– 6	And on the s· branch bend.
My.	10– 8	* this s· impulsion should now
	30– 3	* services were precisely the s·
	38–22	* the s· as all the others.
	49–10	* in the s· month the members
	76– 1	* the s· practice would be
	82– 1	* all have the s· stories
	97– 5	* These s· physicians, however,
	107–11	s· triturations of medicine
	107–15	dozen or less of these s· globules,
	109–12	the s· heavenly lesson.
	109–12	"the s· yesterday, — *Heb.* 13 : 8.
	111– 7	s· class of minds to deal with
	111– 9	on practically the s· grounds
	123–12	other rooms in the s· building.
	137–16	and have paid for the s·.
	149–28	seen and forgotten in the s· hour ;
	157–14	* s· beautiful Concord granite
	162–19	s· wisdom which spake thus in
	182– 9	foundations of which are the s·,
	190–24	s· opportunity to become students
	196–12	the s· is a perfect man, — *Jas.* 3 : 2.
	227–11	having a s· disease
	227–12	and in the s· family,
	246–28	his works are the s· to-day as
	292–28	Mind is the s· yesterday, to-day, and
	293– 9	thousands of others believed the s·,
	321–11	* told the s· story to every one
	322–13	* letter to you on the s· subject;
	345–18	they acted just the s·
	346–13	* s· expression of looking forward,
		(*see also* **time, year**)

Samson

Hea.	18–25	no blind S· shorn of his locks.

Samuel

Ret.	9– 9	Scriptural narrative of little S·,
	9–15	I did answer, in the words of S·,
Pul.	33– 7	* related to her the story of S·,

sanative

Mis.	229–26	any other possible s· method ;

Sanborn, Professor Dyer H.

My.	304– 6	studies under Professor Dyer H. S·,

Sanborn's Grammar

My.	304– 6	book title

Sanbornton Academy

My.	304– 4	principal of S· A·,

Sanbornton Bridge
N. H.

My.	332–15	* S· B·, N. H., August 12, 1844.
My.	312– 1	Seminary at S· B·,

sanctified

Mis.	9– 2	s· by the purification it brings
'01.	32–27	their s· souls would take in the

sanctifies

Mis.	8–19	purifies, s·, and consecrates

sanctify

My.	292– 8	s· our nation's sorrow

sanction

Mis.	330–25	s· what our natures need.
'01.	16–23	under s· of the gown,

sanctioned

Man.	78–13	s· by the Board of Directors
'00.	3–25	and so s· idolatry,
My.	279– 2	not s· by the law of God,

sanctions

Mis.	93–16	Science s· only what is

sanctuary

Mis.	77–22	to enter the spiritual s·
	150–22	the wayside is a s·,
	159–14	into this s· of love,
Ret.	91–24	a fishing-boat became a s·,
No.	41–18	s· will never admit such
My.	37– 4	* sacred confines of this s·.
	188–17	I enter your inner s·,
	244–17	inner s· of divine Science,

sanctum

No.	44–11	leap into the s· of C. S.
My.	147–13	May this little s· be preserved

sand

Mis.	135–13	you would build on s·.
	298–15	is to build on s·.
Un.	9–16	the s· of human reason.
Hea.	1– 9	whoso . . . hath built on s·.

sandals

Mis.	158–20	with s· on and staff in hand,
	341–15	unloose the latchet of thy s· ;
Ret.	12– 3	Minerva's silver s·
Po.	61– 1	Minerva's silver s·
My.	222–20	s· of thy Master's feet.
	338–27	whose s· none may unloose.

Sandusky (Ohio) Star-Journal

My.	95–27	* [S· (O·) S·]

sane

My.	49– 6	* direct, . . . through s· counsel,

saneness

My.	93–22	* s· and common sense which

San Francisco
Cal.

Pul.	89–25	* Bulletin, S· F·, Cal.
	89–26	* Chronicle, S· F·, Cal.
Mis.	304–12	* Then it will go to . . . S· F·,
'00.	1–21	S· F·, Montreal, London,
My.	285– 3	Civic League of S· F·,

sang

Mis.	151–15	David s·, "Whom have I — *Psal.* 73 : 25.
	188– 4	when the stars first s· together,
	259–21	stars s· together, — *Job* 38 : 7.
Un.	42–14	stars s· together, — *Job* 38 : 7.
Pul.	82–20	* s· and sacrificed for their people,
	83–19	* will succeed, for as David s·
Po.	70–18	while the glad stars s·
My.	81–22	* when they s·, the volume of
	188–11	whereof the Psalmist s·,
	244–15	whereof David s·,
	273–10	King David, the Hebrew bard, s·,
	274–27	s·, "That thy way may be — *Psal.* 67 : 2.

sanguine

Mis.	354– 4	s· of success in sin,

Sanhedrim

Mis.	148–10	as in ancient S·.
Man.	3– 6	as in ancient S·.

sanitary

Ret.	30– 8	a s· system that should include all
	70–28	s·, civil, moral, and religious

sanity
'02.   2– 6   s· and perfection of living,
My.   14– 7   a s· and something
164–18   A great s·, a mighty something
363–14   proof that s· and Science govern

San José, Cal.
My. 197– 9   chapter sub-title

sank
Mis. 112–20   s· back in his chair, limp and pale ;
My. 178–24   the table s· a charred mass.

Santa Claus
My. 261– 9   that S· C· has aught to do with

sap
Mis. 218–14   realistic views s· the Science of
Ret. 63–12   When we deny . . . we begin to s· it ;

sapling
Mis. 240–17   The s· bends to the breeze,
My. 160–12   even though it be a s·

sapphire
Mis. 376–28   opal, garnet, turquoise, and s·
Pul. 40– 4   * Beyond the s· sea?

saps
Mis. 221–20   s· one's understanding of the
Rud. 13– 4   Whatever s·, with human belief,

Saratoga Springs, N. Y.
Pul. 89–11   * Saratogian, S· S·, N. Y.

Saratogian
Pul. 89–11   * S·, Saratoga Springs, N. Y.

sarcasm
Mis. 296– 9   to overflow in shallow s·,

sat
Mis. 225–20   s· down beside the sofa
231– 6   s· at that dinner-table.
Ret.   8–14   s· in a little chair by her side,
Pul. 37–17   * s· in the beautiful drawing-room,
59–21   * on the platform s· Joseph Armstrong,
'01. 15–27   * since you have s· here in the house
Po.   66– 8   of one who s· by her side
My. 81–17   * audience ever s· in Boston.
342–18   * s· back to be questioned.

Satan (see also **Satan's**)
Mis.   3–30   is "S· let loose." — see Rev. 20 : 7.
23–17   S·, the first talker in its behalf,
68–16   the works of S· are the
108– 6   in his definition of S·
Un. 44– 9   Of S· and his lie.
54–21   S· held it up before man
No. 15–18   and an incredible S·.
20 7   "Got thee behind me, S· :" — Matt. 16 : 23.
'00. 14– 4   the synagogue of S· — Rev. 3 : 9.
'01. 25–25   S· demanded in the beginning,
My. 201– 5   S· is unchained only for a

satanic
Mis. 191–16   name of his s· majesty
'00.   2–18   his s· majesty is supposed

Satan's
No. 20–23   Adam's mistiness and S· reasoning,
'00. 13–22   "where S· seat is." — Rev. 2 : 13.

satiate
My. 249–14   only to s· its loathing

satin
Pul. 42–15   * wore a white s· badge

satin-lined
Pul. 78–23   * encased in a white s· box

satisfaction
Mis. 141–18   corrected to the s· of all.
240–16   to the s· of all.
275–21   Pen can never portray the s·
329– 3   a s· with whatever is hers.
Ret. 33– 9   but without receiving s·.
Pul. 47–13   * without receiving any real s·.
Hea. 15–13   explains to any one's perfect s·
My. 74–19   * pride and s· that is not only
74–24   * s· that springs from a belief in
81– 4   * and healthy s· with life.
83–22   * takes on a tone of deserved s·,
152–31   I have the sweet s· of
207–22   s· of meeting and mastering evil

satisfactorily
Man. 66–21   supposed to come . . . s· attested.
77–15   their several offices s·,
'02.   5–15   can never be answered s· by
My. 255– 8   filling their positions s·
277–21   settle all questions amicably and s·.

satisfactory
Mis. 158–27   It is s· to note, however,
Man. 30–22   occupants are s· to her.
My. 55– 6   * but were not s· :

satisfactory
My. 277– 6   honorable and s· to both nations
302–26   and the situation was s·.

satisfied
Mis. 15–21   shall soul as sense be s·,
87–11   knowing this, I shall be s·.
178– 5   not s· with a manlike God,
322–17   senses s·, or self be justified.
358–12   All men shall be s· when
Pul.   1– 1   shall be abundantly s· — Psal. 36 : 8.
2–13   shall be abundantly s·," — Psal. 36 : 8.
3–16   shall be abundantly s· — Psal. 36 : 8.
3–24   s· with what is pleasing to
4–26   shall be abundantly s· — Psal. 36 : 8.
7–27   so long as this church is s·
7–29   shall be abundantly s· — Psal. 36 : 8.
51–25   * some may be s· and some will not.
Pan.   6–15   is not s· with this theism,
'00.   8– 3   s· to go on till we awake in
Po. page 79   poem
79–21   Who doth His will . . . Is s·.
My.   9–26   s· with what my heart gives
40– 8   * seekers everywhere may be s·.
53– 4   * not until the authoress was s·
122–19   are we s· to know that our sense of
132–27   slothful, s· to sleep and dream.
182–26   fears turn hither with s· hope.
248– 2   I am more than s· with your work :

satisfies
Mis. 160–12   It s· my present hope.
227–26   s· the mind craving a
Rud. 15– 7   s· the thought with
'02. 17–24   s· the hungry heart,
My. 15–24   * It s· my longings,
189–20   s· the immortal cravings
250– 5   s· justice, and crowns

satisticth
My. 13–22   s· thy mouth with — Psal. 103 : 5.

satisfy
Mis. 16– 2   s· more the cravings for
252–16   can s· himself of their verity.
287–13   can s· immortal cravings.
348–24   I wanted to s· my curiosity
380–21   wherewith to s· the sick
Ret. 33–24   insufficient to s· my doubts
Pul. 66–18   * s· a taste for the mystical
My. 227– 2   to s· himself regarding

satisfying
'02. 20– 8   rewarding, s·, glorifying
My. 38– 4   * rest in this s· assurance,

Saturday
Pul. 61– 1   * 3 , February 2, 1805
My. 16–12   * S·, July 16, 1904,
58– 4   * Sentinel of last S·
74– 3   * From now until S· night
74– 5   * the night trains of S·
137– 5   * filed in the office . . . S·,

Saul
Mis. 162– 2   called . . . S·, Paul.

save
Mis. 11– 6   and s· my own life,
11–15   s· it only in accordance with
17–15   to heal and to s·.
48– 1   s· as I measure its demonstrations
60– 2   when He sent His Son to s·
63–11   why did Jesus come to s·
63–16   s· them from this false belief;
89–12   you s· him or alleviate his
90– 6   s· all who understand it.
113– 9   s· he that had the mark, — Rev. 13 : 17.
116– 3   be with you, and s· you from
129–23   Were they to s· the sinner,
171– 1   that it cannot s·," — Isa. 59 : 1.
195–12   s· that which was lost." Matt. 18 : 11.
197–16   of no more help to s· from sin,
197–19   to heal and to s·,
204– 4   "S·, or I perish." — see Matt. 8 : 25.
210–26   s· him from his destroyer.
211–17   wish to s· him from death.
211–23   "Whosoever will s· — Matt. 16 : 25.
229–22   to heal and to s· mankind
238–12   s· when he is abused
244– 8   states that God cannot s·
249–26   more tenderly to s· and bless.
269–31   s· he that had the mark, — Rev. 13 : 17.
380–19   s· the immediate recovery of
Ret. 32– 7   whosoever will s· — Matt. 16 : 25.
63– 9   in order to . . . s· him
63–18   and so to s· man from it?
86–21   No one can s· himself
Un. 10– 6   s· Jesus and his apostles,
18– 6   can never s· man from sin,

save

Un.	58– 7	"S· thyself, — *Mark* 15 : 30.
	59– 3	his purpose to s· humankind?
	60– 2	Christ Jesus came to s· men,
	62– 4	and came to s· me ;"
Pul.	28–16	* s· that its service includes
	83–18	* and to s· us from ourselves.
Rud.	3– 4	all efforts to s· them from sin
No.	39– 4	potent prayer to heal and s·.
	40–16	s· to issues of Truth ;
	41–25	* shall s· the sick, — *Jas.* 5 : 15.
'00.	7–26	"S·, or I perish !" — *see Matt.* 8 : 25.
'01.	19– 4	worketh with them to s· sinners.
	19– 8	to heal and to s·.
'02.	8–19	its power to heal and to s·.
	11– 6	waits and pleads to s· mankind
	14– 3	is to s· it for my church.
	18–28	of all his disciples s· one.
My.	92–28	* s· the desire in the human heart
	93– 8	* s· the moderately well-to-do,
	96– 8	* gathering can in no sense, s· one,
	150– 3	for that which seeketh to s·,
	159–11	to heal and to s·.
	172–12	s· that which it represents
	200–27	s· sinners and fit their being to
	220– 1	s· him from bad physical results.
	221–32	shall s· the sick"? — *Jas.* 5 : 15.
	258– 5	s· one lowly offering — love.
	260– 4	an alien s· as phenomenon,
	289–17	"God s· the Queen"
	292–14	fail in their prayers to s·
	335–28	* nothing could s· the life of
	364–12	s· that which cometh from God.

saved

Mis.	3–14	is man healed and s·.
	71– 5	yet he s· many a drunkard
	89–20	*how can he be s·,*
	89–21	*does he need to be s·?*
	89–26	being s· from itself,
	89–27	s· from error, or error overcome.
	89–29	s· on this divine Principle,
	185–15	whereby we can be s·,
	187–30	in order to be healed and s·,
	196–28	*and thou shalt be s·.* — *Acts.* 16 : 31.
	197– 8	man s· from sin, sickness, and
	248–26	s· me from that necessity
	261–23	spirit of sacrifice always has s·,
	261–26	s· with an everlasting salvation.
Man.	16– 1	man is s· through Christ,
Ret.	13– 7	unwilling to be s·, if my brothers
	79–25	were s· by patient waiting.
Un.	2– 8	in order to be s· from sin.
	2–14	The true man, really s·,
Pul.	vii–18	the sick are healed and sinners s·,
No.	37–23	s· the sinner and raised the dead,
Pan.	5–24	healed the sick, and s· sinners.
	14–24	shielded by the power that s· them,
'00.	7–27	we are s· from our fears.
'01.	11– 8	we are healed and s·,
	11–10	s· from the sins and sufferings
	17– 5	to return . . . penitent and s· ;
Hea.	9–10	this method has not s· them from
Peo.	3– 7	the election of the minority to be s·
	8– 4	partiality that elects some to be s·
My.	161–16	is s· through Christ, Truth.
	178– 6	the sick are healed and sinners s·.
	282– 7	and be ye s·, — *Isa.* 45 : 22.

saves

Mis.	90– 6	practical Truth s· from sin,
	260–26	an atmosphere that heals and s·.
	261–23	has saved, and still s· mankind ;
	299–28	s· your purchasing these garments,
	367–28	whatever s· from sin,
	369–21	charity that heals and s· ;
Un.	59– 4	evils from which he s·
No.	21–26	wherein Principle heals and s·.
'01.	34– 2	whereby Christendom s· sinners,
'02.	8–20	The energy that s· sinners
My.	43–28	* that which heals and s·.
	122–18	healing Christ that s· from sickness
	185–20	heals the sick, s· sinners,
	206– 7	holiness which heals and s·.
	260– 2	Life that heals and s· mankind.
	348–13	his divine Principle, God, s· man,
	348–16	God, heals and s· mankind.
	348–19	heals the sick and s· the sinner.

saveth

| Mis. | 258–16 | s· the upright in heart." — *Psal.* 7 : 10. |

saving

Mis.	2–19	God, man's s· Principle,
	39–18	this s·, exhaustless source
	86– 3	final degree of regeneration is s·,
	124–18	raising the dead, s· sinners.
	373–32	Its healing and s· power

saving

Man.	19– 4	healing and s· the world
Un.	58– 9	s· himself after the manner
Pul.	6–10	healing and s· mankind.
'01.	9–16	healing and s· men,
'02.	6–10	s· the sinner and healing
My.	4–28	healing the sick and s· the sinner.
	24– 9	* this healing and s· gospel.
	104–32	healing of the sick, the s· of sinners,
	105–12	s· the limbs when the surgeon's
	118–17	A s· faith comes not of
	122–29	healing the sick and s· sinners.
	153–15	healing faith is a s· faith ;
	274–28	thy s· health among — *Psal.* 67 : 2.

Saviour (see also Saviour's)

Mis.	90– 1	and recognize his S·.
	161– 4	*Corporeal and Incorporeal S·.*
	161–19	benefactor, or personal S·,
	163–22	three years a personal S· !
	163–26	the incorporeal S· — the Christ
	164– 9	the S·, which is Truth,
	180–11	always here, — the impersonal S·."
	234–30	as our S· from sickness, sin,
	345–28	talked of the crucified S· ;
	376–13	* *Yours* is a palpitating, living S·
	398–22	Saw ye my S· ?
Un.	59– 3	How, indeed, is he a S·,
	59–17	never saw the S· come and go,
	59–21	a sinner, needing a S· ;
Rud.	3– 6	and become their S·,
'02.	19–29	our S· in his life of love.
Hea.	20– 4	* Which in our S· shine,
Po.	75– 1	Saw ye my S· ?
My.	104–14	S· of men, the healer of men,
	119–22	gave the real proof of his S·,
	155– 9	S· whom the Scriptures declare.
	191–15	witnesseth a risen S·,
	270–18	words of our dear, departing S·,
	293–30	And the S· of man saith :

saviour

| My. | 108–30 | the s· of the body." — *Eph.* 5 : 23. |

Saviour of the World

| Pul. | 53–25 | * earned the title of S· *of the W·*." |

Saviour's

| Ret. | 88–26 | spirit of the S· ministry, |

savor

Mis.	xi–18	to suit all its literature.
Ret.	65– 9	sweet-smelling s· of Truth
Pul.	75–10	would s· more of heathenism

savors

| Pul. | 3–29 | present realization of my hope s· of |

saw

Mis.	30– 9	He s· the real earth and heaven.
	49– 2	I quickly s·, had a tendency to
	61–17	* certainly I s· him, or his effigy,
	156–14	because I s· no advantage,
	171– 5	and the blind s· clearly.
	191–13	s· one casting out devils — *Mark* 9 : 38.
	267–10	when I s· an opportunity
	292– 7	s· that Love had a new commandment
	326– 8	the blind s· them not,
	336–10	Then you would hate Jesus if you s· him
	353–17	When my brother returned and s· it,
	370– 4	Pharisees s· Jesus do such deeds of
	398–22	S· ye my Saviour?
Ret.	13–23	Mother s· this, and was glad.
	26–18	before the material world s· him.
	37–18	until our heavenly Father s· fit,
	44–19	I s· that the crisis had come
	45–23	I also s· that Christianity has
	76–13	a light beyond what others s·.
Un.	59–17	never s· the Saviour come and go,
Pul.	2– 1	s· the house Solomon had erected.
	13–27	when the dragon s· that — *Rev.* 12 : 13.
	33– 2	* As a child Mary Baker s· visions
	36–12	* I never s· equalled.
	53–26	* Whittier, . . . s· the truth :
	70–13	* very recently s· completed
No.	39–22	more clearly than we s· before,
'00.	10–24	from a person I never s·.
Hea.	6–11	I s· the impossibility, in Science, of
	6–15	I s· how the mind's ideals
	9–28	St. John s· the vision of life in
	10– 1	he s· it pass away, — an illusion.
	12–17	we s· at once the concentrated
Po.	75– 1	S· ye my Saviour?
My.	22– 3	* s· the need of a larger edifice
	29–12	* no one who s· it will ever
	50–27	* few s· the grandeur of its work
	61–11	* I s· at once that somebody had to
	78– 5	* worshippers s· an imposing structure
	117–13	"When s· we thee a — *Matt.* 25 : 38.

saw

My.	117–15	Or when s· we thee sick, — *Matt.* 25 : 39.
	126–23	That which the Revelator s·
	145–10	and s· them carried out.
	320–28	* s· Mr. Wiggin several times
	321–21	* twenty years since I first s· you
	332–11	* until he s· her in the fond

Saxon

Mis.	26 28	S· term for God is also good.

say

Mis.	vii–14	to evolution's Geology, we s·,
	5–11	Many s·, "I should like to study,
	8–23	shall s· all manner of evil — *Matt.* 5 : 11.
	12– 1	*Because* I thus feel, I s· to others :
	22– 5	Who dare s· that matter or
	27–27	But, s· you, is a stone spiritual?
	31–10	It is needless to s· that
	33– 1	I will s· : It is the righteous prayer
	50– 8	*is there a secret . . . as some s·?*
	52– 3	It is difficult to s· how much
	60–15	to s· that addition is not subtraction
	73–15	can get no farther than to s·,
	73–22	*Verily I s· unto you,* — *Matt.* 19 : 28.
	83– 6	*you s· : "Every sin is the*
	83– 8	*you s· : "Sickness is a growth of*
	86– 9	*Is it correct to s· of material objects,*
	87– 7	let us s· of the beauties of the
	103– 2	which s· that sin is an evil power,
	103–10	the senses s· vaguely :
	124–20	we s·, It is well that C. S. has
	141–29	let them, not you, s· what shall be
	142–28	to s· to the masonic brothers :
	143–18	gives me great pleasure to s·
	146– 1	let me s·, 'T is sweet to
	153–21	May you be able to s·,
	158– 3	In reply to your letter I will s· :
	108–10	voice from heaven seems to s·,
	179–16	Can we s· this to-day?
	170–20	perceive Truth, and s· with Mary,
	184–14	If man should s· of the power
	193– 5	deemed it safe to s· at that time.
	200–20	Christians to-day should be able to s·,
	209–30	egotism and false charity s·,
	223–12	and to s·, if it must,
	228–27	and s· what others say.
	230–18	when they have nothing to s·,
	238–17	It is enough, s· they, to
	239– 1	let me s· to you, dear reader :
	245–21	It is difficult to s· which
	240– 4	I s· with tearful thanks,
	249–13	members of . . . churches will s·
	262–13	I just want to s·,
	275– 1	Would not our Master s· to the
	280 7	pure and holy thoughts that s·,
	282–15	I s·, When you enter mentally
	298– 5	some affirm that we s·, — *Rom.* 3 : 8.
	299–17	not s· that it was God's command ;
	298–26	I s·, You mistake ;
	313– 3	Permit me to s· that
	321–26	I s·, Do not expect me.
	334– 3	or s· unto Him, — *Dan.* 4 : 35.
	335– 3	shall s· in his heart, — *Matt.* 24 : 48.
	335–14	they s·, having too much charity ;
	335–25	Such people s·, "Would you
	337– 9	who shall s·?
	347–28	None can s· unto Him,
	361–31	who could s· which that "one" was?
	367–28	The senses would s· that whatever
	368–12	We regret to be obliged to s·
	370– 2	to s·, in the spirit of our Master,
	371–12	I as their teacher can s·,
	371–19	to s·, "good right, and good wrong,"
	375–32	* "All that I can s· to you,
	379–13	I never heard him s· that matter
Chr.	55– 6	verily, I s· unto you, — *John* 5 : 25.
Ret.	8– 9	would s·, "Mother, who *did* call me?
	14–23	asked me to s· how I felt when
	15– 7	I could s· in David's words,
	54–15	Blind belief cannot s· with the
	63– 1	Scientists s· God and His idea
	63–24	it encourages sin to s·,
Un.	11–27	ye s·, There are yet four months,
	11–28	I s·, Look up, not down,
	17– 4	I s·, Be allied to the deific power,
	18– 6	Error may s· that God can never
	24– 8	I s· unto you, God is All-in-all ;
	25– 2	If you s· that matter is unconscious,
	25–10	hence, whatever it appears to s·
	35– 2	and s· that sour is sweet,
	36–22	or to s· that the divine Mind is
	40– 3	To s· that you and I, as mortals,
	42– 8	that is to s·, a divine and
	51–13	*What s· you of woman?*
	52–15	*What s· you of evil?*
	53– 4	the lie must s· He made them,

Un.	53–12	To s· that Mind is material,
	54– 3	s· there *is* a false claim,
	60– 5	We s· that God is All,
	60–10	We s· that harmony is real,
	61–28	Invalids s·, "I have recovered
Pul.	3–26	Perchance some one of you may s·,
	4– 3	"What if the little rain should s·,
	12–17	What shall we s· of the mighty
	41–18	* to s· nothing of nearly a thousand
	45– 5	* Christian Scientists not only s·
	69–17	* I may s· that the fundamental idea
	79–13	* to s· nothing of cities
	80– 7	* that is to s·, it sought the line of
Rud.	8–22	sense may s· the unchristian
No.	2–13	test the feasibility of what they s·
	16–25	not enough to s· that matter is the
	21–28	is, to s· the least, like a cloud
	27–23	Who can s· what the absolute
Pan.	10–21	immorality, which, we regret to s·,
	13– 7	"Neither shall they s·, — *Luke* 17 : 21.
'00.	1– 9	I am grateful to s· that in
	7–20	we s· as did Mary of old :
	9– 4	withdraw that advice and s· :
	9– 5	But I s· this not because it is
	14–26	s· in your heart as the devout St. Stephen
'01.	3– 5	shall s· all manner of evil — *Matt.* 5 : 11.
	7–14	whereby we may consistently s·,
	22 16	I do not s· that one added to
	22–17	nor s· this to accommodate
	27–28	* First, people s· it conflicts
	27–29	* they s· it has been discovered before.
	27–30	* they s· they had always believed
	29–11	I s· this not because reformers
'02.	8– 5	Is it necessary to s· that the
	11–23	shall s· all manner of evil — *Matt.* 5 : 11.
	18– 8	Sad to s·, the cowardice and
	19–11	I s· it with joy,
Hea.	6– 4	* "People s· you are a medium,"
	16–23	Again, shall we s· that God
Peo.	8–14	but we s· that Life is carried on
	8–22	I s· unto thee, arise." — *Mark* 5 : 41.
Po.	27– 8	S·, will the young year dawn
	47–20	S·, are the sheaves and the
My.	19–30	"Verily I s· unto you, — *Mark* 14 : 9.
	27– 4	Divine Love bids me s· :
	28–12	* Suffice it to s·, however,
	48–31	* bound as an observer of them to s·,
	49– 2	* when these smiling people s·,
	59–25	* Some s· she did not."
	59–26	* "Send those who s· she did not
	60– 2	* to s· something about the early
	63–19	* seemed to s· that all the world was
	70–13	* They s· that workingmen stopped
	104–30	shall s· all manner of evil — *Matt.* 5 : 11.
	109–17	may sometimes s· with Job,
	114–28	Is it too much to s· that this book
	122–22	Can we s· with the angels
	122–25	can s· his Christ is risen
	123–31	let us s· with St. Paul :
	124– 9	who would s· to-day,
	125–11	to s·, All honor to the members of our
	128– 1	cannot quench my desire to s·
	130–24	I need not s· this to the loyal
	131–19	but I wish to s· briefly that
	131–31	I s· with the consciousness of Mind
	136–13	I am pleased to s· that the
	143–27	What shall we then s·— *Rom.* 8 : 31.
	146– 2	I will s· : It is understood by all
	150–28	I s· unto you :
	153–11	To-day our great Master would s·
	156–13	he bade them s· to the goodman
	158–23	and some practise what they s·.
	161–24	s· not in thy heart :
	162–19	would s· to the builder of the
	169–15	s· through the *New York Journal,*
	175–11	Allow me to s· to the good folk
	177– 7	I am glad to s· that
	199– 6	May God s· this of the church
	200– 7	none can stay His hand or s·,
	200–19	I need not s· this to you,
	214–18	with the hope of . . . I will s· :
	216–18	on behalf of the . . . I s· :
	219–12	To s· that it is sin to ride to church
	219–21	but I do s· that C. S.
	222–11	s· unto this mountain, — *Matt.* 17 : 20.
	228–27	has the divine presumption to s· :
	232–13	"What I s· unto you — *Mark* 13 : 37.
	232–13	I s· unto all, — *Mark* 13 : 37.
	233–16	s·, "They have healed also — *Jer.* 6 : 14.
	236– 9	to s·, please adopt generally
	236–19	we can s·, the more the better.
	244–24	What I have to s·
	245–11	I regret to s·,
	251– 2	What these are I cannot yet s·.
	254–11	to your kind letter, let me s· :

say
My.	258–25	To the dear children let me *s·* :
	270–15	those who *s·* that she is
	271–29	permit me to *s·* that, insomuch as I
	273–27	But *s·* you, "Man awakes from
	274–21	allow me to *s·* that I am not fond of
	275–13	Permit me to *s·*, the report
	276– 4	to *s·*, in her own behalf,
	277– 6	I will *s·* I can see no other way
	280–20	none can stay His hand nor *s·*
	284–23	But here let me *s·* that I am
	289– 2	what we do, not what we *s·*.
	297– 6	I will *s·*, Amen, so be it.
	298–10	hereby *s·* that they have my
	304–26	* *s·* it conflicts with the Bible.
	304–27	* *s·* it has been discovered before.
	304–28	* *s·* they have always believed it."
	308– 6	It is calumny on C. S. to *s·*
	310–19	I will *s·* that there was never
	316– 8	shall *s·* all manner of evil— *Matt.* 5 : 11.
	317– 9	It is a great mistake to *s·* that I
	342–14	* And when I *s·* frail,
	344– 3	If we *s·* that the sun stands for God,
	344–12	I hold it absurd to *s·* that when
	344–25	"I *s·* : 'Render to Caesar— *Mark* 12 : 17.
	344–30	I *s·* : Where vaccination
	346–27	"I did *s·* that a man
	358– 4	doing as you *s·* you are,
	358– 5	*s·*, "Watch and pray,— *Matt.* 26 : 41.
	360–12	I am constrained to *s·*,
	361– 5	All I *s·* is stated in C. S.

sayers
My.	125– 3	not only *s·* but doers of the law

sayeth
'02.	19–23	Love that doeth it, and *s·*,

saying (noun)
apostle's
'02.	9–11	fulfilling the apostle's *s·* :

classic
My.	224–31	let us adopt the classic *s·*,

fulfils the
My.	265–23	fulfils the *s·* of our great Master,

his
Mis.	312–10	chapter sub-title
	325– 4	they understand not his *s·*.
'01.	19–11	and he illustrated his *s·*
My.	288–25	his *s·*, "Sin no more,— *John* 5 : 14.
	307–17	was offended by his *s·*
	339–27	animus of his *s·* was :

immortal
Mis.	76– 7	this immortal *s·* can never

Jesus'
My.	232–28	does that watch accord with Jesus' *s·*?

Master's
'02.	5–22	Hence our Master's *s·*,
My.	108– 9	Hence our Master's *s·*,

my
Mis.	76– 4	"If a man keep my *s·*,— *John* 8 : 51.
No.	31–27	"If a man keep my *s·*,— *John* 8 : 51.
My.	300–18	"If a man keep my *s·*,— *John* 8 : 51.
	319– 5	My *s·* touched him,

mystic
'01.	8–28	mystic *s·* of the Master

Revelator's
'00.	12–17	hence the Revelator's *s·* :

stale
Mis.	30–22	The stale *s·* that C. S.

that
Mis.	196–12	that *s·* came not from Mind,
	253– 2	Note the scope of that *s·*,
Un.	53–26	hence that *s·* of Jesus,
No.	13–12	before that *s·* is demonstrated

this
Ret.	93– 8	Hear this *s·* of our Master,
'02.	9– 8	the full significance of this *s·*
Hea.	10–16	gather the importance of this *s·*,
My.	146–- 5	I believe this *s·* because I
	146–12	Few believe this *s·*.
	229–16	according to this *s·* of Christ Jesus :

wise
Mis.	371–20	It is a wise *s·* that

Mis.	383– 8	In 1896 it goes without *s·*,
My.	76– 1	* it went without *s·* that the same
	228–30	It goes without *s·* that such a one

saying (verb)
Mis.	11–32	*s·* to them, "*I love you*,
	59–19	Scriptures refer to God as *s·*—
	72–13	*s·*, The fathers have eaten— *Ezek.* 18 : 2.
	116–21	it is not merely *s·*, but doing,
	168–30	* speaker began by *s·*
	170–13	*s·*, that we make our own heavens
	175–10	*s·*, Man's Life is God,
	175–30	*s·*, Have we not in thy name
	178–14	* which he prefaced by *s·* :

saying (verb)
Mis.	179– 1	The old churches are *s·*,
	179–10	He is *s·* to us to-day,
	184–17	*s·*, "I have the power to sin
	196– 6	*s·* as in the beginning,
	198–30	by *s·* he has overworked,
	206– 6	*s·* forever to the baptized
	215– 4	*s·*, "I wound to heal;
	221–25	*s·* that five times ten are fifty
	223– 2	I was *s·* all the time,
	223–17	*s·*, "I am a Christian Scientist,"
	224– 9	lifted his hands to his head, *s·* :
	231–25	*s·*, "Oh, pretty !"
	239–29	taught the value of *s·*
	245– 4	"Take no thought, *s·*,— *Matt.* 6 : 31.
	299–21	can I make this right by *s·*,
	311–30	often reported as *s·*
	327–25	and helping them on, *s·*,
	360–27	*s·* to sensitive ears
	369–28	privilege of *s·* to the sick,
Man.	18–10	at every epoch *s·*,
Ret.	37– 7	critics took pleasure in *s·*,
	59– 8	*s·* that addition means subtraction
	69– 9	*serpent*, insists . . . *s·*,
	77– 2	Pope was right in *s·*,
Un.	18– 3	let us think of God as *s·*,
	32– 3	*s·*, "I am a creator.
	32–18	*s·*, "I am the opposite of
	45– 5	*s·*, "Am I not myself?
Pul.	5–17	*s·*, "I have come to comfort you."
	12– 5	heard a loud voice *s·*— *Rev.* 12 : 10.
	45–24	* *s·* he gladly laid down his
No.	35–24	announcing Truth, and *s·*
'00.	3–15	not far from *s·* and doing.
	13– 4	commends the church . . . *s·* :
'01.	8–11	authority of Jesus for *s·*
Hea.	5– 4	*s·* He is beaten by certain
	5– 6	Phrenology will be *s·*
	5– 7	Physiology will be *s·*,
	5–11	startles us by *s·* that
Peo.	5–16	*s·* unto us, "Life is God ;
My.	5–26	*s·* virtually what the prophet
	14–12	* *s·* that he had just been
	39–20	* privilege of *s·* a few words
	108–23	designated as his best work, *s·*,
	126–14	And a voice was heard, *s·*,
	148–20	What are the angels *s·*
	191–19	Spirit is *s·* unto matter :
	210–21	*s·* nothing, in particular,
	212–29	*s·* that animal magnetism never
	215–14	begging me to accept it, *s·*,
	215–24	*s·*, "The laborer is— *Luke* 10 : 7.
	221–22	*s·*, "He that believeth— *John* 14 : 12.
	222– 4	Jesus rebuked them, *s·* :
	228– 6	always *s·* the unexpected
	233–17	*s·*, Peace, peace ; — *Jer.* 6 : 14.
	307–13	*s·* what I cannot forget
	308–24	*s·*, "I never use a cane."
	310–28	*s·*, "When do you ever see
	311–21	presented me my coat-of-arms, *s·*
	317–18	*s·*, "I wouldn't express it that way."

sayings
Mis.	84– 5	which characterized his *s·*,
	127–27	Wise *s·* and garrulous talk
	183–21	Who understands these *s·*?
Un.	39–10	Who understands these *s·*?
	40–12	they who believe his *s·*
'02.	12–15	with another of his *s·* :
My.	146–16	heights of the great Nazarene's *s·*
	146–19	absolute truth of his *s·*
	178–29	*s·* of the great Master
	178–31	all else reported as his *s·* are
	178–32	*Logia*, or imputed *s·* of Jesus
	179–16	verification of our Master's *s·*.
	190–14	regard his *s·* as infallible.
	227–18	to catch them in their *s·* ;
	232–12	left to us the following *s·*
	234–21	our great Master's *s·* are practical
	279– 6	C. S. reinforces Christ's *s·*

says
Mis.	5–15	*Materia medica s·*,
	36–24	*s·*, "The carnal mind— *Rom.* 8 : 7.
	173–14	so-called science, which *s·*
	175– 7	*s·*, I am sustained by bread,
	184–19	If he *s·*, "I am of God,
	188–12	but the apostle *s·*,
	218–30	Dr. —— *s·* : "The recognition of
	220– 6	He mentally *s·*, "You are well,
	220–14	patient *s·* and feels, "I am well,
	241–10	a mental dose that *s·*,
	244– 4	"surgical operation" that he *s·* was
	298–25	One *s·*, "I find relief from pain in
	347–15	One *s·*, Go this way ;
	347–16	the other *s·*, Take the opposite
	351–20	Evil counterfeits good : it *s·*,

says
Mis. 351–21   it s·, "I am Love,"
    359– 8   St. Paul s· : "When I was — I Cor. 13 : 11.
    367–13   Error s· that knowing all things
    367–15   God s· of this fruit of the tree
Ret. 31–19   As s· St. James:
    60– 7   material sense s· that matter,
Un.   5–14   of godliness," s· Paul ; — I Tim. 3 : 16.
    5–28   of Thy ways," s· Job ; — see Job 26 : 14.
    17– 4   Emerson s·, "Hitch your wagon to a
    17–20   Error s· God must know evil
    18– 7   God s·, I am too pure to
    18–13   Error s· you must know grief
    18–14   God, s· you oftenest console others
    18–17   God s·, I show My pity through
    18–22   Error s· God must know death
    30–11   restoreth my soul," s· David. — Psal. 23 : 3.
    34– 2   and then mortal mind s·,
    34–15   s· that matter cannot feel matter ;
    35– 1   Mortal mind s·, "I taste ;
    35–13   Mortal mind s· gravitation is a
    43–24   as Paul s· in the third chapter of
    44–18   Human wisdom s· of evil,
    55– 5   as Isaiah s· of him,
    60–24   St. Paul s·, "And if Christ — I Cor. 15 : 17.
Pul. 35–10   * is begotten of spirituality," she s·,
    46– 6   * Mrs. Eddy s· the words of the judge
    53–15   * Hudson s· : "That word, more than
    64–14   * Mrs. Eddy s· she discovered C. S.
    69– 6   * Dr. Hammond s· he was converted to
    69– 9   * He s· they use no medicines,
Rud.   5– 3   Bible s· : "Let God be true, — Rom. 3 : 4.
    5–20   Human belief s· that it does ;
    6–14   He s· that "color is in us,"
No. 44–25   s· : "Heretics of yesterday are
'00.   2–25   He s· : "It is my duty to take
'01.   6– 3   Who s· the God of theology is a
Hea. 15–23   Scripture s·, "Ye ask, and — Jas. 4 : 3.
Peo.   6– 6   s· : "I declare my conscientious belief,
    6–11   Voltaire s· : "The art of medicine
My. 41–11   * the law of metaphysics s·,
    64–12   * Mrs. Eddy s·, "The First Commandment
    94– 8   * s· the Springfield Republican.
    99– 3   * It s· : "A faith which is able to
    104–14   s· that the Saviour of men,
    153–29   s· : Come, and I will give thee rest,
    187–14   s· : "For this is the message — I John 3 : 11.
    201–19   in him who s· in his heart :
    210– 1   chapter sub-title
    212–31   he s· this to cover his crime
    236–10   An old axiom s· :
    285–17   In Revelation 2 : 26, St. John s· :
    309–21   McClure's Magazine s·, describing
    310–22   McClure's Magazine s· that
    311–29   McClure's Magazine s·, "Mary Baker
    312– 5   McClure's Magazine s· : "He
    313–26   as McClure's Magazine s·.
    314– 2   It s· that after my marriage
    328–28   * s·, "and all other professionals
    330–21   * Mrs. Eddy s· of this circumstance :
    355– 6   s· there is a grave need for

say'st
Po. 26–16   smiling, s·, "'Tis done !

scabbard
Mis. 214–18   could be returned into the s·.
Ret.   2–12   sword, encased in a brass s·,
Pul. 46–19   * sword, encased in a brass s·,

scaffold
Mis. 99–14   to the dungeon or the s·,
    277–13   stake and s· have never silenced
    368– 7   * "Truth forever on the s·,
    368– 8   * Yet that s· sways the future,

scalding
Mis. 389–14   O make me glad for every s· tear,
Po.   4–13   O make me glad for every s· tear,
My. 350–14   heed'st Thou not the s· tear

scale
of being
Mis. 57–29   ascending the s· of being
    96–12   as thought ascends the s· of being
    234–17   a single step in the s· of being.
    359–26   only as we rise in the s· of being.
My. 110–12   upward in the s· of being.
    146–24   tip the s· of being, morally and
    146–31   in the divine s· of being
    230–25   rise in the s· of being,

       —

Mis. 46–19   in the s· with his creator ;
    113–13   s· of moral and spiritual being,
    119–17   weighs mightily in the s· against
    151–27   ascending s· of everlasting Life
    280–12   nothing in the opposite s·.
    280–14   into the s· of Mind,
    290– 6   higher in the s· of harmony,

scale
Mis. 292–10   a new tone on the s· ascending,
    312– 3   weighed in the s· of God
    341– 8   you will go up the s· of Science
    379–31   adjusting in the s· of Science
Man. 59– 5   in the s· of right thinking.
Ret.   8– 5   three times, in an ascending s·.
Un. 64–16   s· the treacherous ice,
My. 150–12   can accomplish the full s· ;
    152– 7   far lower in the s· of thought,
    188–32   ascends the s· of miracles
    268–27   ascends the s· of life.
    277–18   weighs in the eternal s· of equity

scaled
Mis. 206–28   s· the steep ascent of C. S.,
My. 146–16   The heights . . . are not fully s·.

scales
Mis. 41–15   s· the mountain of human endeavor,
    280–16   Mind is not put into the s· with
    293–12   Experience weighs in the s· of God
    372– 4   weight in the s· of God.
Man. 47–15   it s· the pinnacle of praise
No.   7– 3   s· of justice and mercy.
My. 291–16   weighed in the s· of divinity,

scaling
My. 229–21   s· the steep ascent of Christ's Sermon

scalpel
Un. 28– 5   It was never touched by the s·

scan
Pul. vii–19   to s· further the features of
My. 201–17   s· the convulsions of mortal mind,

scandal
My. 48–28   * are not drugged by s·,
    305–27   s· in the Literary Digest

scandalized
My. 330   5   * great Master himself was s·,

scanning
My. 13– 8   s· its interesting pages,

scant
Mis. 274– 1   the s· history of Jesus
My.   9–10   * this would be s· indeed

scanty
Mis. 120–29   The Biblical record . . . is s· ;
    149– 7   replenish your s· store.

scarce
Mis. 396– 7   More sorrowful it s· could seem ;
Po. 58–19   More sorrowful it s· could seem ;
My. 59 18   * would s· fill a couple of pews

scarcely
Mis. 111– 1   s· sufficient to demonstrate
    222–18   s· awakes in time,
    246–10   s· been heard and hushed,
    317–14   s· a moiety, compared with
Pul. 42– 7   * s· even a minor variation
    58–17   * s· any woodwork is to be found.
'01. 16– 7   St. John's types of sin s· equal
Peo. 11– 3   done with their battles
My. 63–15   * s· possible to repress a
    83–17   * s· realize that the Scientists
    154– 7   s· venture to send flowers
    165– 5   s· an indignity which I have not
    173–11   I s· supposed that a note,

scare
Mis. 396– 2   To s· my woodland walk,
Po. 58–14   To s· my woodland walk,

scatter
Mis. 51–23   * s· in its breeze
Ret. 85–23   s· the sheep abroad ;
My. 107–22   or s· the shade of one who

scattered
Ret. 89– 9   s· about in cities
Po. 32– 7   s· o'er hillside and dale ;
My.   3–11   s· abroad in Zion's waste

scene
Mis.   1–20   Goodness reveals another s·
    205–15   last s· in corporeal sense.
Pul. 42– 9   * s· was rendered . . . interesting
My. 29–10   * s· repeated six times
    80–28   * A few were upon the s·

scenes
Mis. 275– 1   chief actors in s· like these,
    302– 1   Behind the s· lurks an evil
    392–23   s· that I would see again.
Ret. 81–27   shifting s· of human happiness,
Pul.   2–16   direful s· of the war
'02. 17–13   Earth's actors change earth's s· ;
Po. 51–13   s· that I would see again.
My. 15–30   * And when, in s· of glory,
    313–25   to describe s· far away,

scent
- *Mis.* 390– 4   Thy breezes *s·* the rose's breath ;
- *Po.* 55– 4   Thy breezes *s·* the rose's breath ;

scents
- *My.* 155–28   sweet *s·* and beautiful blossoms

scepter (*see also* **sceptre**)
- *Pul.* 83–30   * and he, departing, left his *s·*

sceptered (*see also* **sceptred**)
- *Po.* 10–15   To Judah's *s·* race,
- 21– 4   Her dazzling crown, her *s·* throne,

sceptre (*see also* **scepter**)
- *Mis.* 295–31   English crown and . . . English *s·*.
- '00. 10–19   sways the *s·* of self and pelf
- *My.* 128–13   No crown nor *s·* nor rulers
- 201– 7   good will to man, sweeter than a *s·*,

sceptred (*see also* **sceptered**)
- *Mis.* 388–16   Her dazzling crown, her *s·* throne,
- *My.* 337–16   To Judah's *s·* race,

scheme
- *My.* 68–18   * color *s·* for all the auditorium
- 200–23   will tumble from this *s·* into

schemes
- *Mis.* 312–22   risen above worldly *s·*,

schisms
- *Man.* 44– 6   involves *s·* in our Church
- *My.* 206– 8   *S·*, imagination, and human beliefs

scholar
- *Mis.* 318–21   and be a good Bible *s·*
- 379–12   neither a *s·* nor a metaphysician.
- *Ret.* 47–25   Bible *s·* and a consecrated Christian.
- *Rud.* 15– 1   has shown that this defrauds the *s·*,

scholarly
- *Mis.* 81– 3   skilful and *s·* physicians
- 308–19   *s·*, artistic, and scientific notices
- *Pul.* 5–14   his athletic mind, *s·* and serene,
- *Pan.* 12– 4   *s·* expositor of the Scriptures,
- '00. 7– 9   most *s·* men and women,
- *My.* 112–15   honest, intelligent, and *s·*
- 113–31   among the *s·* and titled,
- 316–15   *s·* editor, Mr. B. O. Flower,

scholars
- *Mis.* 296– 5   profound philosophers, brilliant *s·*.
- *Man.* 30– 3   Christians and good English *s·*.
- 90– 2   must be thorough English *s·*.
- *Ret.* 6–17   one of the most . . . thorough *s·*
- 50–15   my list of indigent charity *s·*,
- *Pul.* 23–21   * *s·* of special research,
- 73–11   * one of the greatest Biblical *s·*
- *My.* 215– 9   without having charity *s·*,

scholarship
- *Man.* 91– 7   Remuneration and Free *S·*.
- 91–10   bearer of a card of free *s·*
- *Ret.* 80–20   win the golden *s·* of
- 87– 5   is as obvious in religion and *s·*
- *My.* 104–26   talents, and character
- 163–26   love their *s·*, friendship,
- 319–10   and well-equipped *s·*.

scholastic
- *Mis.* 13–14   *S·* theology elaborates the
- 102– 4   lexicographers and *s·* theologians,
- 173– 9   pagan philosophy, or *s·* theology,
- 194–15   which *s·* theology has hidden.
- 340–30   human ethics, *s·* theology,
- 362– 8   *S·* dogma has made men blind.
- *Ret.* 79–10   in shuffling off *s·* rhetoric,
- *No.* 24–11   false philosophy and *s·* theology,
- *Pan.* 5– 2   pantheism is found in *s·* theology,
- '01. 7– 3   *S·* theology makes God manlike ;
- 12–20   which *s·* theology has obscured,
- 24–28   *materia medica,* and *s·* theology
- *My.* 149–21   too deeply read in *s·* theology
- 205–22   *S·* theology at its best
- 307–30   want of divinity in *s·* theology,

scholasticism
- '01. 25– 8   the *s·* of a bishop,

school
- **church and**
- *Mis.* 313–24   chapter sub-title
- **district**
- *My.* 309–30   * district *s·* practically all the
- **flooding the**
- *Ret.* 47– 6   Students . . . were flooding the *s·*.
- **flourishing**
- *Ret.* 48–10   to close my flourishing *s·*,
- **free**
- *Ret.* 11–12   In our God-blessed free *s·*.
- *Po.* 60– 9   In our God-blessed free *s·*.
- **her**
- *Mis.* 48–30   to injure her or her *s·*.

school
- **high**
- *My.* 171–23   * on the lawn . . . of the high *s·*.
- 173–28   green surrounding the high *s·* ;
- **infant**
- *My.* 312–30   I did open an infant *s·*,
- **Italian**
- *Mis.* 376– 3   * most authentic Italian *s·*,
- **medical**
- *Mis.* 349–15   of entering a medical *s·* ;
- 349–18   He entered the medical *s·*,
- **new**
- *Mis.* 80–28   a new *s·* of practitioners,
- 80–30   will not patronize the new *s·*,
- **of Balaam**
- '00. 13–23   *s·* of Balaam and Æsculapius,
- **of Tyrannus**
- '00. 12–25   labored . . . in the *s·* of Tyrannus,
- **old**
- *My.* 107– 8   old *s·* has become reconciled.
- **one**
- *Rud.* 16–14   *Is there more than one s· of*
- 16–15   but one *s·* of the Science of
- **out of**
- *Ret.* 10– 3   kept me much out of *s·*,
- **primary**
- *Un.* 3– 1   lessons of this primary *s·*
- **taught**
- *My.* 310– 3   all taught *s·* acceptably
- 312–17   * a brief season she taught *s·*."

- *Mis.* 365– 7   *s·* whose schoolmaster is not Christ,
- *Ret.* 47–14   voted that the *s·* be discontinued.
- *No.* 18–19   If . . . the *s·* gets things wrong,
- '02. 3–16   improved her public *s·* system
- *My.* 217– 2   for your own *s·* education,

schoolbooks
- *Ret.* 10–13   knowledge I had gleaned from *s·*

schoolboy
- *My.* 151– 2   the present *s·* epithets

schooled
- *Ret.* 7– 9   * trained and *s·* them

schoolmaster
- *Mis.* 365– 8   whose *s·* is not Christ,
- *Ret.* 30–18   the law was the *s·*,
- *Rud.* 11– 3   Sickness is the *s·*,
- *No.* 18–19   If the *s·* is not Christ,

schoolroom
- *Mis.* 91–23   have our textbook, . . . *in his s·*
- 357– 4   *s·* is the *dernier ressort.*
- *Ret.* 83–22   take their textbook into the *s·*

schools
- *Mis.* 162– 7   before the people and their *s·*
- 173– 5   learned of the *s·* that there is
- 173– 8   the *s·*, pagan philosophy, or
- 183–17   not by reason of the *s·*, or learning,
- 257–26   cities, churches, *s·*, and mortals.
- 270–22   we cannot leave Christ for the *s·*
- 348–30   to enter medical *s·*,
- 348–32   objected to their entering those *s·*.
- 366– 2   had in our *s·* the time or attention
- 369–14   leaders of materialistic *s·*
- *Ret.* 15–26   by physicians of the popular *s·*
- 33– 7   knowledge from the different *s·*,
- 34– 6   an answer from the medical *s·*,
- 50–24   churches, *s·*, and associations
- *Pul.* 47–12   * *s·* of allopathy, homœopathy,
- 70–21   * philosophy and *s·* of medicine,
- *Rud.* 17– 4   so-called *s·* are clogging the wheels of
- *No.* 11–16   had the place in *s·* of learning
- 33– 6   rightful place in *s·* of learning,
- *Pan.* 11–12   When will the *s·* allow mortals to
- '01. 22–23   the differing *s·* of medicine
- 23–10   would be in peace with the *s·*.
- 26–12   turns away . . . to the *s·* and matter
- 34–14   a creation of the *s·*
- *My.* 105– 9   of the stethoscope and the *s·*,
- 245– 2   the approved *s·* of medicine,
- 305–24   of the Greek nor of the Roman *s·*
- 340–11   as witness her *s·*, her churches,

Science
- **absolute**
- *Mis.* 286– 9   to comply with absolute *S·*,
- 286–29   Until this absolute *S·* of being is
- *Ret.* 27– 4   absolute *S·* of Mind-healing,
- *My.* 349–23   God of nature in absolute *S·*.
- **abstract**
- *Mis.* 264–16   to assimilate pure and abstract *S·*
- **acme of**
- *Mis.* 252–17   C. S. is not only the acme of *S·*
- **action is**
- *Mis.* 58–25   the action is *S·*.
- **affirmations of**
- *Mis.* 65– 9   submit to the affirmations of *S·*

Science

affords the evidence
Mis. 164–31 S· affords the evidence that God is the

all
Mis.   4– 6 All S· is C. S.;
     58–22 All S· is divine, not human,
   219– 3 (and all S· is divine)
   261–30 All S· is divine.
Ret.   28–25 All S· is a revelation.
Pul. 35–22 All S· is a revelation.''
My. 348–30 basic Principle of all S·,

and Christianity
Peo.   2– 9 unites S· and Christianity,

and material sense
Un. 39–28 S· and material sense conflict

and philosophy
Mis. 359–27 chapter sub-title

and sense
Mis. 184– 3 S· and sense conflict,

and spiritual sense
Rud.   7–14 S· and spiritual sense contradict this,

answers it
Un.   8– 2 before S· answers it.

antipodes of
Un. 53–12 anti-Christian, the antipodes of S·.

any departure from
Rud. 16–16 Any departure from S· is an

art and
Mis. 393– 7 Art and S·, all unweary,
Po. 51–12 Art and S·, all unweary,

author of
'01.   4–12 God is the author of S·
My. 347–26 man is not the author of S·,

basis of
My. 357– 1 He is the only basis of S·;

bonds of
No. 26–23 in the eternal bonds of S·,

brings out
Mis. 337–16 S· brings out harmony;

certainty of
Mis. 220–31 with the certainty of S· he knows

Christ
Mis. 167–15 What is his name? Christ S·.
My. 238–14 presentation of C. S. — the Christ S·,

Christian
Mis.   v– 8 DEMONSTRATE THE ETHICS OF C· S·
      4– 7 All Science is C· S·;
      4–30 the mission of C· S· to heal the sick,
      6– 6 The most of our C· S· practitioners
   12–25 In C· S·, the law of Love rejoices the
   16–26 the new birth begun in C· S·.
   21– 1 C· S· begins with the First Commandment
   21– 8 whereof C· S· now bears testimony.
   21–12 C· S· will be seen to depart from the
   21–15 My first plank in the platform of C· S·
   22–10 C· S· translates Mind, God, to mortals.
   22–22 That C· S· is Christian,
   23–25 what C· S· means by the word
   25– 4 is the multum in parvo of C· S·
   27– 8 Here is where C· S· sticks to its text,
   27–11 the cardinal point in C· S·,
   29–13 no analogy between C· S· and
   29–15 I taught the first student in C· S·.
   30– 5 adopt the "simple addition" in C· S·
   30–22 The stale saying that C· S· "is
   31– 3 and is the antipode of C· S·
   32– 9 rules and divine Principle of C· S·.
   33–12 Must I have faith in C· S· in order
   33–19 naturally gain confidence in C· S·
   33–23 Healing by C· S· has the following
   34– 4 One who has been healed by C· S·
   34–11 Is spiritualism . . . included in C· S·?
   34–12 C· S· is based on divine Principle;
   34–25 and are the antipodes of C· S·;
   35– 7 sealed that proof with the signet of C· S·
   37–17 C· S· lays the axe at the root of
   37–29 the labor that C· S· demands.
   38– 1 Why do you charge for teaching C· S·,
   39– 3 to take a course of instruction in C· S·.
   39– 9 false teachers of what they term C· S·;
   39–11 the Founder of genuine C· S·
   40– 9 It is often asked, "If C· S· is
   40–22 The Founder of C· S· teaches her
   41–10 The honest student of C· S· is
   43– 1 C· S·, recognizing the capabilities of
   43– 7 Do all who . . . claim to be teaching C· S·,
   43– 8 C· S· is not sufficiently understood for
   43–18 gained sooner than the spirit of C· S·:
   43–25 incapacitates one to practise . . . C· S·.
   43–28 the mighty Truth of C· S·
   44– 5 investigate . . . the rudiments of C· S·.
   44– 6 Can C· S· cure acute cases where
   44– 8 The remedial power of C· S· is
   45– 5 C· S·, by means of its Principle

Science

Christian
Mis. 45–13 be cured by metaphysics or C· S·?
   46– 4 self-evident proposition of C· S·
   46–13 in the premises or conclusions of C· S·,
   49– 7 been restored by C· S· treatment.
   53–20 the meaning of the term and of C· S·.
   53–21 If C· S· is the same as Jesus taught,
   53–25 C· S· is simple, and readily understood
   54– 6 demonstrated, and teaches C· S·?
   54–12 power of C· S· over all obstacles
   55– 3 The simplest problem in C· S·
   55–16 Is C· S· based on the facts of
   55–18 C· S· is based on the facts of Spirit
   56– 2 the very antipodes of C· S·.
   58–19 Does the theology of C· S· aid its
   59– 7 divine power understood, as in C· S·;
   60– 8 C· S· is proving this by healing
   62–17 The theology of C· S· is Truth;
   62–23 the author grapples with C· S·,
   62–28 The theology of C· S· is based on the
   64–24 a student of the Bible and of C· S·
   65–21 C· S· demands both law and gospel,
   68– 9 * metaphysical healing being called C· S·.
   69– 5 C· S· is the unfolding of true
   71–11 Does C· S· set aside the law of
   74– 1 The phenomena of Spirit in C· S·,
   75– 9 fact and grand verity of C· S·,
   75–21 assists one to understand C· S·.
   76– 7 it is the ultimatum of C· S·;
   78–22 and that C· S· will some time appear
   80– 9 A league . . . which C· S· eschews
   80–13 leave C· S· to rise or fall on its
   82– 4 Understanding this fact in C· S·,
   87–21 in the investigation of C· S·
   88–15 His allusion to C· S· in the
   91–18 employed in the service of C· S·
   92– 3 liability of deviating from C· S·.
   93– 7 that have been healed by C· S·
   93–10 C· S· authorizes the logical
   95– 1 chapter sub-title
   95–12 for even a synopsis of C· S·,
   95–23 C· S· reveals the infinitude of
   96–24 How is the healing done in C· S·?
   97–15 C· S· is not a remedy of faith alone,
  100– 4 C· S· was to interpret them;
  100–22 the acme of C· S·.
  101– 8 C· S· and the senses are at war.
  104–13 According to C· S·, perfection is
  105– 1 implicit faith engendered by C· S·,
  105– 8 is the foundation of C· S·.
  105–17 C· S· is an everlasting victor,
  105–20 C· S· is my only ideal;
  106– 3 C· S· and Christian Scientists will,
  107–15 before . . . C· S· is demonstrated:
  110–24 and the momentum of C· S·,
  111–27 in time, that church will love C· S·.
  113–17 C· S· shows that there is a way
  113–28 systematized centres of C· S·
  114–30 The teacher in C· S· who does not
  115–15 teach, and live C· S·!
  119–21 is found powerless in C· S·.
  120– 1 The professors of C· S· must
  120– 4 at the very threshold of C· S·:
  124–20 It is well that C· S· has taken
  127–18 growth in C· S· will follow,
  132–20 teaching C· S·, receiving calls,
  135– 3 is not in the question of C· S·.
  136–18 absolute demonstration of C· S·.
  138–15 first and last lesson of C· S· is love,
  139–30 in the interest of C· S·,
  141– 3 the monument upreared, of C· S·.
  142–30 nor you with me in C· S·,
  144–13 Discoverer and Founder of C· S·;
  148–19 demonstrate genuine C· S·,
  149– 5 to this banquet of C· S·,
  149–29 first temple for C· S· worship
  150–16 salvation . . . by means of C· S·.
  153– 2 establishing the Cause of C· S·.
  156–26 in acquiring solid C· S·.
  159–22 offer at the shrine of C· S·,
  160– 2 under the régime of C· S·!
  163–28 must needs come in C· S·,
  165–11 The daystar . . . is the light of C· S·
  166–24 idea, named in this century C· S·,
  167– 4 the spiritual idea, as in C· S·:
  170–23 and no other method is C· S·.
  177– 8 expressed and operative in C· S·.
  178–19 * to preach a sermon on C· S·
  178–22 * If I had not found C· S· a new gospel,
  185– 4 the divine Principle of C· S·
  188–22 when she discovered C· S·.
  193–12 C· S·, as defined and practised
  195– 5 Whosoever learns the letter of C· S·
  195–23 to try the edge of truth in C· S·,
  199–25 divine Principle is discerned in C· S·,

Science
Christian

Mis. 200–12	insists on the rare rule in *C· S·*
200–18	The foundational facts of *C· S·*
202– 2	the sweet harmonies of *C· S·*
203– 7	as I look on this smile of *C· S·*,
203–18	serves to . . . illustrate *C· S·*.
204–29	the divine Principle of *C· S·*,
205– 3	This practical *C· S·* is the
205–32	learn *C· S·*, and live what they learn,
206–11	The advancing stages of *C· S·* are
206–29	scaled the steep ascent of *C· S·*,
207– 6	practical, operative *C· S·*.
210– 4	*C· S·* never healed a patient without
210–13	as revealed in *C· S·*,
210–16	adaptability to lead on *C· S·*,
212–21	*C· S·* proves that human will is lost in
213–19	*C· S·* gives a fearless wing
215–12	*C· S·* demands order and truth.
219–22	This is *C· S·* :
222– 4	It reverses *C· S·* in all things.
225– 9	seventh modern wonder, *C· S·* ;
232– 5	chapter sub-title
232–21	Metaphysical healing, or *C· S·*.
233–22	who think the standard of *C· S·* too high
234–21	metaphysical healing, called *C· S·*,
235– 8	In *C· S·*, progress is demonstration,
239– 6	to commence a large class in *C· S·*.
244– 4	on the platform of *C· S·* !
245–10	the stately goings of *C· S·*,
245–16	spiritual need that *C· S·* should
246–12	washed it divinely away in *C· S·* !
247–19	healing force developed by *C· S·*
248–26	glorious revelations of *C· S·*
249– 3	to see if *C· S·* could not
252– 8	*C· S·* classifies thought thus :
252–17	*C· S·* is not only the acme
253–29	opened their eyes to the light of *C· S·* ?
255–20	I claim for healing by *C· S·*
256– 2	have been healed by *C· S·*
260– 3	*C· S·* has been reduced to the
261– 7	*C· S·* not only elucidates
263–23	educational system of *C· S·*
264–10	the essential nature of *C· S·*.
265–28	disaffections toward *C· S·*
266–25	in teaching or lecturing on *C· S·*,
269–25	*C· S·* may be sold in the shambles.
270– 7	example of the Master in *C· S·*,
271– 8	notion that . . . is, or can be, *C· S·*,
276–15	In *C· S·* the midnight hour will
278–10	connected with the Cause of *C· S·*,
281–28	assume when subscribing to *C· S·*.
282–25	he is restored through *C· S·*
283–19	I insist on the etiquette of *C· S·*,
283–27	It is the genius of *C· S·* to
284– 4	*C· S·*, more than any other system
285–21	showing its relation to *C· S·*.
286– 2	It is seen in *C· S·* that the
286– 7	will continue unprohibited in *C· S·*.
288–27	impulse from the cause of *C· S·* :
291–18	the possible perversion of *C· S·*
292–25	*C· S·*, full of grace and truth,
293– 2	the infant thought in *C· S·*
295– 8	* past a score of reforms, to *C· S·*."
296–15	This writer classes *C· S·* with
296–17	*C· S·*, antagonistic to intemperance,
297– 2	since the discovery of *C· S·*,
297–17	chapter sub-title
297–17	statute in the *morale* of *C· S·* :
297–20	held in *C· S·* as morally bound
298–20	the *morale* of absolute *C· S·*,
299– 6	look through the lens of *C· S·*,
300–29	*C· S·* demonstrates that the
301– 4	the *precedent* for preaching *C· S·*,
302–10	to know the teaching of *C· S·*
302–15	through *C· S·* Sunday services.
303– 9	these strongholds of *C· S·*,
307–21	absolute basis of *C· S·* ;
308– 9	The Scriptures and *C· S·*
308–28	*C· S·* is taught through its
309– 4	According to *C· S·*,
310– 7	by the discovery of *C· S·*.
311–19	As I now understand *C· S·*, I would
311–23	The works I have written on *C· S·*
315–15	proclivities toward *C· S·*.
315–19	health, and practical *C· S·*.
315–20	Teaching *C· S·* shall be no
316– 6	When will you take a class in *C· S·*
316–10	The date of a class in *C· S·* should
318– 3	obsolete terms in absolute *C· S·*,
318–18	gospel work of teaching *C· S·*,
321– 8	gain of Truth's idea in *C· S·* ;
322–22	He hath given you *C· S·*,
328–21	ascends the hill of *C· S·*
332– 7	doors that closed on *C· S·*
333–10	*C· S·* voices this question :

Science
Christian

Mis. 336–21	another name for *C· S·*,
337– 2	founded at this period *C· S·*,
337–20	Where these exist, *C· S·* has no
338–14	which demonstrates *C· S·*.
343–11	fruits of *C· S·* spring upward,
346– 2	*C· S·* carries this thought
346– 8	It confronts *C· S·*.
346–11	To this question *C· S·* replies :
346–20	self-evident proposition of *C· S·*,
346–24	It is a rule in *C· S·* never to
347–30	only authenticated organ of *C· S·*
349–14	it was inconsistent with *C· S·*,
351–14	placing *C· S·* in the hands of
354–24	humility is the first step in *C· S·*,
355– 2	present stage of progress in *C· S·*
356–16	The seed of *C· S·*, which
356–24	it is the genius of *C· S·*.
357–31	Divine Love is the substance of *C· S·*,
358– 6	the only appropriate seals for *C· S·*.
358–19	the heaven-crowned summit of *C· S·*.
360– 9	cast in the moulds of *C· S·* :
360–16	When *C· S·* has melted away the
361–12	and *C· S·* has overshadowed all
364–10	*C· S·* refutes everything that is not
364–31	*C· S·* rends this veil of the temple of
365–10	If *C· S·* lacked the proof of
365–23	the real value of *C· S·* to the race.
366– 9	give the keynote of *C· S·*
366–29	according to His mode of *C· S·* ;
367– 2	have no place in *C· S·*.
370–23	*C· S·* a "metaphysical healing"
371–13	They know far more of *C· S·* than
372– 7	voices *C· S·* through song and
372–28	the *art* of *C· S·*, with true hue
373–30	*C· S·* is more than a prophet
374–12	*C· S·* and its art will rise
375– 5	The truest art of *C· S·* is to be a
378–21	metaphysical therapeutics, as in *C· S·*,
379–30	and named my discovery *C· S·*.
380–13	the first student in *C· S·*.
382– 3	No works on the subject of *C· S·*
382– 7	discovery and founding of *C· S·*
382–14	patient healed in this age by *C· S·*.
382–24	the first *C· S·* periodical ;
382–31	teaching and practising *C· S·*
383– 3	churches of the *C· S·* denomination.
383– 6	a church of *C· S·* is established,
383– 9	*C· S· is founded by its discoverer,*
Man. 3–16	to demonstrate genuine *C· S·*,
17– 6	and students . . . in *C· S·*,
17–16	*C· S·*, as taught and demonstrated
27–16	and all other *C· S·* literature
31– 9	the prosperity of *C· S·*
34– 4	Believe in *C· S·*.
34– 8	believer in the doctrines of *C· S·*,
34–15	for self-instruction in *C· S·*,
35–18	who have not studied *C· S·*
41– 3	is the Ensample in *C· S·*.
41– 7	gulf between *C· S·* and theosophy,
42–12	In accordance with the *C· S·* textbooks,
42–21	inasmuch as *C· S·* can only
43– 8	auxiliaries to teaching *C· S·*
43–11	Discoverer and Founder of *C· S·*.
43–13	No Adulterating *C· S·*
43–20	tends to prevent *C· S·* from
43–23	nor circulate *C· S·* literature which
44– 4	shall not be adjudged *C· S·*.
44– 7	possible !oss, for a time, of *C· S·*.
44–26	impede their progress in *C· S·*.
46–11	except as a *C· S·* practitioner.
49– 7	*C· S·* Nurse.
49– 9	represents himself . . . as a *C· S·* nurse
49–11	demonstrable knowledge of *C· S·*
50– 9	shall not debate on *C· S·* in public
52–26	and to the Cause of *C· S·*,
53–26	hence injurious, to *C· S·*
55–23	trying to practise or to teach *C· S·*
58– 3	THE *C· S·* PASTOR.
59– 1	sacred revelations of *C· S·*
63–10	*C· S·* contained in their textbook.
63–15	church of the *C· S·* denomination
64–16	the Founder of *C· S·*,
65– 8	used in connection with *C· S·*.
71–15	would be disastrous to *C· S·*.
73–11	conduct a *C· S·* organization
74– 2	*C· S·* society holding public services,
74– 6	In *C· S·* each branch church
74–11	Teachers and practitioners of *C· S·*
80– 3	of the interests of *C· S·*.
82–20	engaged in the work of *C· S·*,
83– 1	heading
83– 5	Teaching *C· S·* shall not be a
83–11	proclivities toward *C· S·*.
83–18	and practical in *C· S·*.

Science
Christian

Man. 84–14 price for teaching *C· S·*
85–13 shall not teach pupils *C· S·* unless
85–21 shall not teach *C· S·* without
87– 3 Neither . . . teach Roman Catholics *C· S·*,
87–10 its By-Laws to teach *C· S·*,
92– 1 daily conversation on *C· S·*,
92– 5 demonstrates what we affirm of *C· S·*,
92– 9 that *C· S·* heals the sick quickly
92–13 duly qualified to teach *C· S·*,
92–17 receive instructions in *C· S·*
93–13 public topics condemning *C· S·*,
94– 8 after a lecture on *C· S·*,
95– 8 as the cause of *C· S·* demands.
97–18 impositions . . . in regard to *C· S·*,
111–11 For those who have studied *C· S·*
111–12 those who have not studied *C· S·*
Chr. 53–45 For *C· S·* brings to view
Ret. 10–12 After my discovery of *C· S·*,
15– 5 built on the basis of *C· S·*,
23–24 I had touched the hem of *C· S·*.
24– 6 which I afterwards named *C· S·*.
25– 9 metaphysical healing, — in a word, *C· S·*.
29– 2 spiritualism is the antipode of *C· S·*.
30– 1 the pioneer of *C· S·* I stood alone
30– 3 The rare bequests of *C· S·* are costly,
30–10 It is often asked why *C· S·* was
31– 3 Nothing can compete with *C· S·*,
31–15 acting through *C· S·* on my roused
34–17 A person healed by *C· S·* is not only
35– 9 the merits of *C· S·* must be proven
35–11 truths of *C· S·* are not interpolations
36– 6 Science of Mind-healing, *alias C· S·*,
37– 3 the complete statement of *C· S·*,
38–30 in order to demonstrate *C· S·*.
41– 1 opposition which *C· S·* encountered
42– 8 of a *C· S·* Sunday School,
47–10 *C· S·* shuns whatever involves
47–22 the gospel work of teaching *C· S·*
49– 5 institutions for instruction in *C· S·*,
49–12 principle for growth in *C· S·*
50–23 I see clearly that students in *C· S·*
51– 6 used as a temple for *C· S·* worship.
53– 6 the standard of genuine *C· S·*.
56– 3 demonstrable rules in *C· S·*,
57–25 are departures from *C· S·*.
57–30 and demonstration of . . . *C· S·*.
59– 1 *C· S·* reveals the grand verity,
59–18 *C· S·* reveals Mind, the only living
60–11 *C· S·* reveals God and His idea
60–14 *C· S·* saith to the wave and storm,
60–24 *C· S·* is the only sure basis of harmony.
60–28 *C· S·* declares that there is but one
61– 3 *C· S·* declares that sickness is a belief,
61– 9 conscious of the truth of *C· S·*,
61–21 *C· S·* reveals the fact that,
61–27 demand that *C· S·* be stated and
62– 3 Test *C· S·* by its effect on society,
63– 3 Because *C· S·* heals sin as it heals
64–12 In *C· S·* the fact is made obvious
65– 1 Church of Christ, Scientist, or with *C· S·*,
65–19 *C· S·* is the pure evangelic truth.
66– 3 *C· S·* gives vitality to religion.
68–25 In *C· S·*, man can do no harm,
70–18 the Discoverer and Founder of *C· S·*.
70–22 idea of God, as in *C· S·*.
71– 9 straight and narrow path of *C· S·*.
71–26 uprooted, . . . and *C· S·* demonstrated.
75– 6 violence to the ethics of *C· S·*.
76– 2 *C· S·* is not copyrighted ;
76– 7 cannot dishonestly compose *C· S·*.
76–10 the Spirit and Word of *C· S·*
76–24 God-crowned summit of *C· S·*
78– 1 The neophyte in *C· S·* acts like a
78–12 works, antagonistic to *C· S·*,
78–19 any name given to it other than *C· S·*,
81–29 first led me to the feet of *C· S·*,
83–30 deviating from absolute *C· S·*.
84–13 this inexhaustible subject — *C· S·*.
85–23 to divide the ranks of *C· S·* and
86– 4 in the spirit and power of *C· S·*
88– 2 professional intercourse of *C· S·*
88–18 another part of *C· S·* work,
93–22 If *C· S·* reiterates St. Paul's teaching,
Un. 1– 1 Perhaps no doctrine of *C· S·* rouses
1– 9 statement in *C· S·* may justly be
1–15 in their discussions of *C· S·*.
5–22 between *C· S·* students and
6–14 law of health, according to *C· S·*,
6–26 while the platoons of *C· S·* are not
7– 7 it is due both to *C· S·* and myself
17– 7 in *C· S·*, man thus weds himself with
25–13 Truth and its demonstration in *C· S·*,
26–21 its sentiment is foreign to *C· S·*.
29–17 *C· S·* defines as material sense :

Science
Christian

Un. 31–11 According to *C· S·*, the *first* . . . claim
32–20 To this declaration *C· S·* responds,
32–27 a claim which *C· S·* uncovers,
36– 7 when handled by *C· S·*, which
36–11 is met and solved by *C· S·*
36–17 demonstration, according to *C· S·*,
41–24 In *C· S·* there is no matter ;
44–14 fable of error, is laid bare in *C· S·*.
45– 4 as Truth and . . . are doing in *C· S·*,
51– 8 the demonstration of God, as in *C· S·*,
61–23 *C· S·* is both demonstration and
Pul. vii– 3 the story of the birth of *C· S·*,
vii–14 on the early footsteps of *C· S·*
5– 4 an address on *C· S·* from my pen,
12–24 Self-abnegation, . . . is a rule in *C· S·*.
21–23 To perpetuate a . . . is not *C· S·*.
23–15 * movement, under the guise of *C· S·*,
24–17 * Discoverer and Founder of *C· S·* ;
28– 5 * a panel containing the *C· S·* seal,
28–21 * called the "*C· S·* Hymnal,"
30– 2 * healed by *C· S·* treatment ;
31– 4 * and Discoverer of *C· S·*,
32–23 * due to the principles of *C· S·*.
35– 5 in a word — *C· S·*
37–12 * engaged on further writings on *C· S·*.
40–10 * chapter sub-title
40–22 * Discoverer and Founder of *C· S·*,
41– 7 * love-offerings of the disciples of *C· S·*
44–10 * the blessed onward work of *C· S·*.
44–20 * *C· S·* has shown its power over its
46– 5 * at *C· S·* headquarters this is denied ;
46–29 * first organizer of a *C· S·* Sunday School,
47–10 * experiences as the pioneer of *C· S·*,
47–18 * between faith-cure and *C· S·*,
50–11 * The growth of *C· S·* is properly
50–23 * simple and direct as they are, of *C· S·*.
51– 1 * *C· S·* does not strike all as a
51– 6 * apply themselves to a matter like *C· S·*,
51–26 * *C· S·* cannot absorb the world's thought.
52–10 * chapter sub-title
52–18 * The name *C· S·* alone is new.
52–26 * and *C· S·* is one result.
53–14 * That was *C· S·*.
55– 8 * advent of *C· S·*.
55–18 * Afterward she selected the name *C· S·*.
55–22 * *C· S·* is contained in the volume
56–14 * *C· S·* has brought hope and comfort
57– 1 * Discoverer and Founder of *C· S·*,
57–22 * how extensive is the belief in *C· S·*.
63– 3 * chapter sub-title
63–10 * Mary Baker Eddy, the "Mother" of *C· S·*,
64– 1 * Discoverer and Founder of *C· S·*,
64–14 * she discovered *C· S·* in 1866.
65–14 * made by what is called *C· S·*
67– 3 * chapter sub-title
67–13 * *C· S·*, or the Principle of divine healing,
68–15 * a *C· S·* congregation was organized
68–23 * *C· S·* was founded by Mrs. . . . Eddy.
69– 6 * converted to *C· S·* by being cured
69–14 * distinguishes *C· S·* from the faith-cure,
69–15 * This *C· S·* really is a return to
70– 3 * chapter sub-title
70– 7 * Discoverer and Founder of *C· S·*,
70–10 * pastor of the *C· S·* denomination,
70–25 * Mind-healing, which she termed *C· S·*.
71– 4 * The idea that *C· S·* has declined
71– 8 * The money comes from *C· S·* believers
71–16 * the acknowledged *C· S·* Leader,
74– 6 * pastor of the *C· S·* congregation
74– 9 * the *C· S·* "Discoverer,"
74–18 Discoverer and Founder of *C· S·*,
75–10 the absolute antipode of *C· S·*,
75–24 * Discoverer and Founder of *C· S·*,
76–25 * Discoverer of *C· S·*, has received
78– 1 * the Founder of *C· S·*,
70– 8 * never have been, devotees of *C· S·*,
79–14 * seeing notices of *C· S·* meetings,
79–26 * But when *C· S·* arose,
80–21 * the spirit of *C· S·* ideas has caused
84–29 * Discoverer and Founder of *C· S·*,
86– 5 * Discoverer and Founder of *C· S·*,
86–24 * Discoverer and Founder of *C· S·*,
Rud. 1– 1 *How would you define C· S·?*
2– 7 In *C· S·* we learn that God
2–24 is the smallest part of *C· S·*.
2–26 The emphatic purpose of *C· S·*
4– 7 *or only of Divine or C· S·?*
4–21 According to the Scriptures and *C· S·*,
6–12 Has not the truth in *C· S·* met a
7– 6 consistencies of *C· S·* are set forth
8– 7 *undertake to demonstrate C· S·*
9–13 To heal, in *C· S·*, is to base your
11– 6 *understanding* of God and man in *C· S·*,
11–10 the next proposition in *C· S·*,

Science

Christian

My. 315–13	* Discoverer and Founder of *C· S·*,
315–27	of the divine power of *C· S·*,
316–13	Attacks on *C· S·* and its Founder,
316–14	Survey of the *C· S·* Movement,''
317–13	criticisms of my statement of *C· S·*,
317–22	diction, as used in explaining *C· S·*,
318–32	find my authority for *C· S·*
322–22	* instruction by Mrs. Eddy in *C· S·*.
327– 6	made it legal to practise *C· S·*
327–31	* taught and practised in *C· S·*,
328–10	* *C· S·* people, greatly pleased
328–19	* two *C· S·* healers in this city.
329–23	* the steady progress of *C· S·*
333– 3	* *C· S·* publication committee.
339– 5	cardinal points of *C· S·*
339– 9	on the great subject of *C· S·*.
341–20	* *C· S·* has been so much to the fore
344–24	* How does *C· S·* stand as to them?''
345– 6	*C· S·* will overthrow false knowledge
345–11	* are these too material for *C· S·*?''
346– 1	* from the standpoint of *C· S·*.
346–21	* Discoverer and Founder of *C· S·*,
347– 2	* through Christ Jesus and *C· S·*,
347–23	chapter sub-title
349–12	*C· S·* is a divine largess,
352–29	first issue of *The C· S· Monitor.*
353– 7	*C· S· Monitor,* November 25, 1908
353– 9	given the name to all the *C· S·*
355– 7	need for more men in *C· S·* practice.
355–11	in our field of labor for *C· S·*.
356–28	correct version of *C· S·*.
357– 2	wholly apart from *C· S·*.
357– 4	even the divine idea of *C· S·*,
357–12	spiritual modesty of *C· S·*,
357–15	demonstrate *C· S·* to a higher extent,
357–21	to salvation and eternal *C· S·*.
357–23	the axiom of true *C· S·*,
358– 1	*C· S·* abides by the definite rules
359– 7	Discoverer and Founder of *C· S·*
361– 2	directions . . . as simplified in *C· S·*,
361– 6	stated in *C· S·* to be used as
362–17	* Cause of *C· S·* in this community,
364– 3	rule of mental practice in *C· S·*

(*see also* **Board of Directors, Church, church, Churches** and **churches, demonstration, healing,** *Herold,* **history,** *Journal,* **Mind-healing, practice, Principle, Publishing Society,** *Quarterly,* **rule, rules,** *Sentinel,* **student, students, teacher, teachers, teachings, temple, text-book, understanding**)

Christianity and

Pul. 56–17	* Welding Christianity and *S·*,
My. 179–25	Christianity and *S·*, being

come with

No. 18–10	Right thinking and . . . come with *S·*,

completeness of

No. 10– 5	proof . . . of the completeness of *S·*.

consciousness in

My. 117–10	order and consciousness in *S·*,

contains a

My. 112–18	contains a *S·* which is demonstrable

contradicts

Mis. 96–31	*S·* contradicts this evidence ;
Ret. 60–25	Material sense contradicts *S·*,

corrects

Mis. 287–10	*S·* corrects this error

dawn of

Mis. 174–28	the dawn of *S·* that reveals

decision of

Mis. 65–12	Left to the decision of *S·*,

declare

Un. 39–20	let *S·* declare the immortal

declares

Un. 29–10	*S·* declares God to be the Soul

defines

Mis. 102–32	*S·* defines *omnipresence* as
Rud. 2–18	*S·* defines the individuality

defines man

Ret. 59–22	*S·* defines man as immortal,

demanded

My. 348–17	*S·* demanded a rational proof

demonstrable

'01. 21– 5	demonstrable *S·* leading the ages.
My. 143–22	an eternal and demonstrable *S·*,

demonstrate

My. 303–17	demonstrate *S·* and its pure

demonstrate, in

Mis. 115–19	demonstrate, in *S·*, that evil has

demonstrate its

Mis. 59– 3	understand nor demonstrate its *S·*,

demonstrates

Mis. 98–20	religion whose *S·* demonstrates God
No. 4–14	*S·* demonstrates the reality of

Science

demonstrate the

Mis. 75–10	to demonstrate the *S·*.
344–20	demonstrate the *S·* of Life,

demonstration of

Mis. 355– 9	absolute demonstration of *S·*

departures from

Mis. 265–29	out of the departures from *S·*

devoid of

Un. 49–23	it is devoid of *S·*.

discernment of

My. 206–10	darken the discernment of *S·* ;

discern the

Mis. 287–16	lifts mortals to discern the *S·* of

discovered the

Ret. 24– 5	I discovered the *S·* of

diverges from

Mis. 265– 2	diverges from *S·* and knows it not,

Divine

Mis. 174–31	The leaven . . . is Divine *S·* ;
336–20	chapter sub-title
Rud. 14– 6	strictly practising Divine *S·*,

divine

Mis. 2–31	spiritual elements in divine *S·*.
3– 9	lessons we learn in divine *S·*
3–13	his life-experience — and divine *S·*,
13–25	This postulate of divine *S·*
15–11	divine *S·*, that results in health,
16–23	Christianity is a divine *S·*.
19–14	Truth and Love in divine *S·*,
25– 7	In divine *S·* it is found that
27– 3	In divine *S·* the terms God and good,
27–14	accept divine *S·* on this ground?
28–16	he demonstrated that divine *S·* alone
45–18	Sin is not the master of divine *S·*,
46–21	at every point, in divine *S·*,
52– 9	to heal, through divine *S·*,
52–22	problem to be wrought in divine *S·*.
59–17	belief that is unavailing in divine *S·*.
66–15	teach, through divine *S·*,
77–14	power and presence, in divine *S·*,
77–23	there learn, in divine *S·*,
89–28	God's likeness, is safe in divine *S·*.
102–20	fully expressed in divine *S·*,
114–11	rules of divine *S·* announced
116–21	divine *S·* is not an argument :
123–18	Divine *S·* has rolled away the stone
166– 1	according to divine *S·*,
169– 1	found all the divine *S·* she preaches ;
174–23	heaven is the reign of divine *S·* :
175– 9	divine *S·* changes this false sense,
181– 4	reality of his being, in divine *S·*?
181–22	but is the order of divine *S·*.
181–32	clear discernment of divine *S·* :
182–11	Through divine *S·* man gains
183– 2	in the divine *S·* of being ;
183–22	divine *S·* unfolds omnipotence,
184–16	he would trespass upon divine *S·*,
186–13	in the Scriptures, as in divine *S·*,
189– 5	as unfolded in divine *S·*,
190– 4	Divine *S·* demonstrates Mind
192–17	Luminous with the light of divine *S,*
194– 2	Divine *S·* reveals the Principle
194–11	Divine *S·* is not an interpolation
195–32	informed by divine *S·*,
200–14	The divine *S·* of this rule is quite as
206– 8	What but divine *S·* can interpret
209– 8	Principle of divine *S·* being Love
212–15	One step away from . . . divine *S·*
217– 1	True idealism is a divine *S·*,
219– 2	divine *S·* . . . neither reveals God in
222–19	This sin against divine *S·* is
234– 6	Love is the Principle of divine *S·* ;
255–12	He should comprehend, in divine *S·*,
258–14	In divine *S·*, God is One and All ;
259–17	divine *S·*, in which God is supreme,
291– 2	by the Principle of divine *S·*
309–12	He advances most in divine *S·* who
320–17	fixed in the heavens of divine *S·*,
320–29	religion undefiled, divine *S·* ;
331–25	divine *S·* evolved nature as thought,
333–32	Christians, instructed in divine *S·*,
334–29	dis-covered for you divine *S·*,
335–30	whoso departeth from divine *S·*,
336–12	rule and demonstration of divine *S·* :
337–30	which he reflected through divine *S·*
342– 1	joy of divine *S·* demonstrated.
358– 3	to mark the way in divine *S·*.
359–24	The *way* is absolute divine *S·* :
362– 4	realities of divine *S·* ;
365–20	If the uniform . . . effects of **divine** *S·*
369– 3	God's law, as in divine *S·*,
372–25	modest glory of divine *S·*,
Ret. 26–23	divine *S·* must be a discovery.
27–24	so the harmony of divine *S·*
28–12	understanding of God in divine *S·*.

Science

divine

Ret.
50–28 new rule of order in divine *S*,
54– 6 self-renunciation, and divine *S*
56–15 Divine *S* disclaims sin, sickness,
56–24 Divine *S* demands mighty wrestlings
61– 2 enmity to God and divine *S*.
64– 9 divine *S*, which teaches that good is
79– 9 signs for the wayfarer in divine *S*
88–28 the wings of divine *S*.
94– 6 whatsoever . . . contradicts divine *S*
94–21 There is no . . . in divine *S* ;
95– 1 watered by dews of divine *S*,

Un.
2–20 this same rule, in divine *S*,
3–13 reached the goal in divine *S*,
5–11 but to seek the divine *S*
6– 2 for it is divine *S*,
7–22 An incontestable point in divine *S*
10–19 in the Truth of divine *S*,
36–25 stultifies the logic of divine *S*,
39–11 divine *S* removes human weakness
43–14 the fact, as it exists in divine *S*,
51–24 full Truth is found only in divine *S*,
57–26 divine *S* wipes away all tears.
61–25 Truth, in divine *S*, is the
62– 2 fact really remains, in divine *S*,
62–20 The Truth or Life in divine *S*

Pul.
13–14 those who break faith with divine *S*
35– 9 "Divine *S* is begotten of spirituality,"
35–16 understanding of God in divine *S*.

Rud.
5– 6 in divine *S* there is no material
7–23 According to divine *S*, Spirit
11–21 understanding of God and divine *S*,

No.
11–21 because they teach divine *S*,
18–15 highest endeavors are, to divine *S*,
20–13 perfect man, and divine *S*.
20–21 In divine *S*, God is recognized as
25– 4 this cardinal point of divine *S*,
27–12 fully interpreted by divine *S*,
27–14 divine *S*, presents the grand and
33–10 divine *S*, with fixed Principle,

Pan.
8–18 one law, namely, divine *S*.

'00.
4–17 the only perfect religion is divine *S*,
4–28 In divine *S*, divine Love includes
5–12 God, man, and divine *S*.
5–17 the divine *S* of divine Love,

'01.
3–17 Then, to define Love in divine *S*
4– 8 Principle and rule of divine *S*
4–15 Christianity is divine *S*,
5–25 God and man in divine *S*,
6–18 logic of divine *S* being faultless,
6–30 In divine *S* He is
11– 6 we see the Son of man in divine *S* ;
12–17 Divine *S* is not an interpolation of
12–20 only needs the prism of divine *S*,
18–16 discerned only through divine *S*.
24–26 divine *S* of Christianity

'02.
6–28 Divine *S* fulfils the law and the
8–25 coexist in divine *S*.
19–28 divine *S* glorifies the cross

Hea.
13–23 divine *S*, the truth of being
14–25 divine *S* reveals the Principle and

My.
112–10 doctrines taught by divine *S*
126–32 that needful one thing — divine *S*,
133– 7 God-crowned summit of divine *S* ;
179–11 all of which divine *S* shows to be
207–24 thus predicating man upon divine *S*.
208–16 hope and hour of divine *S*,
221–14 natural, and divine *S* of medicine,
225–12 In divine *S* all belongs to God,
244–17 inner sanctuary of divine *S*,
265–21 as understood in divine *S*,
267– 3 demonstrated to be divine *S*
267–24 Heaven is the reign of divine *S*.
273–31 divine *S* of Life alone gives
278–12 in divine *S*, where right reigneth.
281–14 and we are His in divine *S*.
283–13 find their birthright in divine *S*.
306–13 nor rest from his labors in divine *S* ;
308– 4 divine healing and its divine *S*.
348– 8 understood through divine *S*.
348–11 religious departure from divine *S*
351–26 divine *S* is all they need,
353–11 put on record the divine *S*
358– 7 the opposite of divine *S*,

divine order of
Mis. 18– 9 in the divine order of *S*,

divine Principle of
Ret. 56– 8 unerring divine Principle of *S*,

divorced from
My. 349–26 human will divorced from *S*.

doors of
No. 41–17 to force the doors of *S*

entrance into
Mis. 100–32 man's . . . entrance into *S* ?

Science

evolve
Mis. 22– 6 that matter . . . can evolve *S* ?

exchanges
Mis. 103–25 *S* exchanges this human concept

existence in
Pul. vii–22 man's existence in *S*.

facts of
Mis. 183–30 refute . . . with the facts of *S*,
Un. 30– 5 reverse the spiritual facts of *S*,

fatal in
Rud. 17– 1 divergence is fatal in *S*.

field of
My. 226–25 laborers in the field of *S*

fields of
Mis. xi–14 hitherto unexplored fields of *S*.

finale in
Un. 2–12 this, as the *finale* in *S* :

foundation of
Mis. 81– 1 broad and sure foundation of *S* ;

grand verities of
Mis. 79– 5 grand verities of *S* will sift

grooves of
Mis. 104–19 move in God's grooves of *S* :

growth in
Ret. 79–14 uproot the germs of growth in *S*

handle it in
Mis. 334–18 do you handle it in *S*.

harmony of
Mis. 176– 2 harmony of *S* that declares
259–18 this eternal harmony of *S*,

has dethroned
Mis. 65– 2 delusive evidence, *S* has dethroned

has elevated
Ret. 93– 6 and *S* has elevated this idea

have
'01. 21– 2 they have *S*, understanding,

healed by
Mis. 54–20 When once you are healed by *S*,

healed in
Rud. 7– 2 the simplest case, healed in *S*,

higher order of
Mis. 99–13 voice a higher order of *S*

hill of
Mis. 232–16 meekly to ascend the hill of *S*,

ignorance of
Ret. 60–16 sense asks, in its ignorance of *S*,

immortal
Mis. 73– 8 testimony of immortal *S*

incentive in
Mis. 279– 5 that is the incentive in *S*.

in Christianity
My. 127– 1 upward to *S* in Christianity,

indicates
Mis. 288–17 while *S* indicates that it *is not*.

in medicine
My. 127– 2 *S* in medicine, in physics,

is absolute
Mis. 99– 1 *S* is absolute and final.
156–17 *S* is absolute,

is a law
Mis. 269–21 *S* is a law of divine Mind.

is demonstrated
Mis. 359–24 *S* is demonstrated by degrees,

is divine
(see **divine**)

is eternally one
Ret. 94–23 *S* is eternally one, and unchanging,

is Mind
Rud. 4– 8 *S* is Mind manifested.

is not pantheism
Pan. 13– 2 *S* is not pantheism, but *C* *S*

is pointing
No. 28–11 If *S* is pointing the way,

is reached
My. 238–18 whereby the *S* is reached

is Science
'01. 22– 1 Truth is true, and *S* is Science,

is the law
Mis. 173– 9 *S* is the law of Mind
My. 267– 5 *S* is the law of the Mind
347–24 concede that *S* is the law of God ;

is the mandate
Mis. 283–28 *S* is the mandate of Truth

is the prism
Ret. 35–13 *S* is the prism of Truth,

is true
Mis. 65– 7 this is because *S* is true,

is understood
Mis. 367–10 proportion that *S* is understood

is unimpeachable
My. 103– 2 Because *S* is unimpeachable,

its
Mis. 35–25 taught its *S* by the author of
372–29 the *art* . . . is akin to its *S* :
Ret. 54–13 not having reached its *S*.

Science

lack
No.   3– 1   in some vital points lack *S*·.
lacked
My. 307–32   for then it lacked *S*·.
lack of
Mis. 344–17   spoiled by lack of *S*·.
law of
Mis. 71–31   immutable and just law of *S*·,
laws of
No.   6–27   the laws of *S*· are mental,
lens of
Mis. 164–27   by means of the lens of *S*·,
     194–16   The lens of *S*· magnifies
    '01. 12–22   The lens of *S*· magnifies
life-giving
Mis. 233–10   onward march of life-giving *S*·,
lifts humanity
Mis. 290– 5   *S*· lifts humanity higher in the
light of
Mis. 254–19   would obscure the light of *S*·,
light of the
My. 343–17   It was in 1866 that the light of the *S*·
lose
My. 206– 4   and lose *S*·, — lose the Principle
loss of
Rud. 16–17   an irreparable loss of *S*·.
mandate of
Mis. 74– 9   through the stern mandate of *S*·,
man in
Mis. 41–26   manifestation of man in *S*·.
Un. 40– 5   but man in *S*· never dies.
     42–13   Man, in *S*·, is as perfect
    '02.   8–26   Jesus reckoned man in *S*·,
mastered by
Mis. 284–28   and will be mastered by *S*·.
mental
Mis. 172–25   Mental *S*·, and the five personal
     173– 2   theorems, misstate mental *S*·,
Peo. 10–15   Mental *S*· alone grasps the
metaphysical
Mis. 172– 5   the negative of metaphysical *S*· ;
Ret. 78–14   right sense of metaphysical *S*·.
Hea. 16– 4   Metaphysical *S*· teaches us
met with
Mis. 284–27   met with *S*·, it can . . . be mastered
must be understood
No. 11–14   *S*· must be understood
name of
Mis. 171–29   false knowledge in the name of *S*·,
     233– 1   practising in the *name* of *S*·
natural
My. 178–11   is this natural *S*· less profitable
no
    '01.   4–15   else there is no *S*· and no
no opposite in
No.   5– 7   God has no opposite in *S*·.
nor theism
Mis. 217–25   This is neither *S*· nor theism.
of all healing
My. 154– 2   *S*· of all healing is based on Mind
of being
Mis. 46–28   *S*· of being, wherein man is perfect
     60–22   conformed to the *S*· of being.
     82–23   *S*· of being is brought to light.
     183– 2   quenched in the divine *S*· of being ;
     184–23   *S*· of being gives back the
     286–29   Until this absolute *S*· of being
Man. 47–10   Ontology, or the *S*· of being.
Ret. 21–15   dream has no place in the *S*· of being.
     26–21   discovery of the *S*· of being
Un. 42–12   opposite . . . is the genuine *S*· of being.
     43–22   his teachings, in the *S*· of being.
     49–19   or we lose the *S*· of being.
     63– 7   forever in the *S*· of being.
No. 10–23   reality of Mind in the *S*· of being ;
     17–10   created in the eternal *S*· of being
     26–14   In this *S*· of being,
     28– 9   facts in the *S*· of being
Pan. 11–13   *S*· of being, understood and obeyed,
My. 268–26   lifts the curtain on the *S*· of being,
     285–10   demonstrates the *S*· of being.
     296– 4   whatever hinders the *S*· of being.
     (*see also* **Science of Being**)
of Christ
My. 103– 9   *S*· of Christ, the Science of God
of Christian healing
Ret. 62– 1   *S*· of Christian healing will again be
My. 43–21   * *S*· of Christian healing was revealed to
of Christianity
Mis. 164– 5   *S*· of Christianity, that has appeared
     382–13   I discovered the *S*· of Christianity,
Pan. 12–21   *S*· of Christianity is strictly monotheism,
    '01. 15–11   demonstrates the *S*· of Christianity.
     22–18   as to the *S*· of Christianity,
     24–26   demonstrate the divine *S*· of Christianity
     32–26   reception of the *S*· of Christianity.

Science

of Christianity
Hea.   7–13   *S*· of Christianity makes pure the
My. 117– 1   not have lost the *S*· of Christianity.
     149–24   lose the *S*· of Christianity,
     178– 6   *S*· of Christianity is not generally
     265–14   It signifies that the *S*· of Christianity
of creation
Mis. 57–22   *S*· of creation is the universe with
     57–27   In its genesis, the *S*· of creation is
of divine Love
    '00.   5–17   being the divine *S*· of divine Love,
offer
Mis. 366– 7   because they contain and offer *S*·,
of God
Mis. 96–22   understanding of the *S*· of God,
     166–23   *S*· of God and the spiritual idea,
Un.   4–11   through the *S*· of God,
     52– 4   This *S*· of God and man
    '00.   5–24   *S*· of God and His universe,
     6–25   C. S. is the *S*· of God
    '01.   4–13   *S*· of God must be, is, *divine*,
My. 103– 9   *S*· of God and man,
     118–22   impossible in the *S*· of God
of good
Mis. 27– 2   *S*· of good calls evil *nothing*.
     352– 6   to discern the *S*· of good.
No. 24– 2   In the *S*· of good,
of healing
Mis. 34–30   discovered the *S*· of healing
     260–28   Mind, imbued with this *S*· of healing,
Rud. 9–17   *S*· of healing is the Truth of
     15– 4   understanding . . . the *S*· of healing
    '01.   2– 5   in the perfected *S*· of healing
of Life
Mis. 56–22   *S*· of Life needs only to be
     84–21   *S*· of Life, overshadowing Paul's
     344–20   demonstrate the *S*· of Life,
     380–14   to discover the *S*· of Life,
My. 51– 3   * in teaching us the *S*· of Life.''
     273–31   *S*· of Life alone gives the true sense of
     274–14   one achieves the *S*· of Life,
of man
Mis. 14–11   the *S*· of man could never
     186–18   let us not lose this *S*· of man,
    '02.   2– 7   *S*· of man and the universe,
My. 350–10   the cosmos and *S*· of man.
of mental healing
Mis. 171–26   of the *S*· of mental healing ;
     172–23   is the *S*· of mental healing,
     174–14   is the *S*· of mental healing.
     175–18   *S*· of mental healing must be
     175–25   with the *S*· of mental healing
of metaphysical healing
Mis. 4– 2   in the *S*· of metaphysical healing,
     380–25   the *S*· of metaphysical healing
Hea. 16–12   the *S*· of metaphysical healing.
of Mind
Mis. 60–16   The *S*· of Mind reveals the
     72–23   The *S*· of Mind, . . . shows that
     78–11   either Euclid or the *S*·of Mind
Ret. 24–24   to find the *S*· of Mind
     28–24   *S*· of Mind must reveal.
     34– 3   in order to gain the *S*· of Mind,
     54–22   healing, in the *S*· of Mind,
     75–18   The *S*· of Mind excludes opposites,
My. 221–11   and illustrate the *S*· of Mind.
of Mind-healing
Mis. 66–26   reach the *S*· of Mind-healing,
     78– 9   *S*· of Mind-healing can no more be
     87–23   rules of the *S*· of Mind-healing.
     221–21   understanding of the *S*· of Mind-healing.
     269–15   the actual *S*· of Mind-healing
Ret. 27– 7   the absolute *S*· of Mind-healing,
     34– 8   the spiritual *S*· of Mind-healing.
     36– 6   I taught the *S*· of Mind-healing,
     37– 4   spiritual, *S*· of Mind-healing,
     37–14   originators of the *S*· of Mind-healing
     43– 8   *alias* the *S*· of Mind-healing.
     49–21   teaching the *S*· of Mind-healing ;
     57– 5   basis for the *S*· of Mind-healing.
     78–17   statement of the *S*· of Mind-healing,
     78–21   departure from the *S*· of Mind-healing.
Pul. 47–14   * statement of the *S*· of Mind-healing.
     64–19   * statement of the *S*· of Mind-healing.
     70–24   * spiritual *S*· of Mind-healing.
Rud. v– 7   OF THE *S*· OF MIND-HEALING
     6–22   *S*· of Mind-healing is best understood
     11–18   *S*· of Mind-healing by no means
     16–16   school of the *S*· of Mind-healing.
No.   4– 2   learning . . . the *S*· of Mind-healing
     4–12   *S*· of Mind-healing destroys the
     4–16   in the *S*· of Mind-healing
     6– 2   contradict the *S*· of Mind-healing
     6–12   the true *S*· of Mind-healing.
     7– 1   chapter sub-title
     14– 3   understood the *S*· of Mind-healing,

Science

of omnipotence
  Mis. 101–22 *S·* of omnipotence demonstrates
of perfectibility
  '00. 7–15 *S·* of perfectibility through Christ,
of physical harmony
  Un. 6–10 The *S·* of physical harmony,
of psychology
  Mis. 3–31 demand for the *S·* of psychology
of Soul
  Mis. 13–21 The *S·* of Soul reverses this
    76–29 *S·* of Soul, Spirit, involves this
    362–25 spiritual cosmos and *S·* of Soul.
  Un. 29–19 between the true *S·* of Soul and
  No. 11– 7 individuality in the *S·* of Soul.
    29– 7 and is not the *S·* of Soul.
of the Bible
  Ret. 27– 2 the *S·* of the Bible,
of the Principle
  My. 140 7 *S·* of the Principle must be
of the Scriptures
  My. 239– 2 *S·* of the Scriptures coexists with
    303– 5 to learn the *S·* of the Scriptures
of treating disease
  Mis. 368–18 *S·* of treating disease through Mind.
of Truth
  Mis. 14–29 *S·* of Truth annihilates error,
  My. 353–11 on record the divine *S·* of Truth ;
of wedlock
  My. 268 26 the *S·* of wedlock, of living
one thread of
  Mis. 99– 6 To weave one thread of *S·*
order of
  Mis. 181–10 to obscure the order of *S·*,
    205–22 order of *S·* is the chain of ages,
  Un. 56–13 In the divine order of *S·*
or suffering
  Mis. 362–27 is won through *S·* or suffering :
pathological
  Rud. 16–21 a pathological *S·* purely mental.
perfected in
  Mis. 232–20 perfected in *S·* that most important
phenomenon is
  My. 347–28 and whose phenomenon is *S·*.
place in
  Mis. 234–15 can never find a place in *S·*,
possible in
  Mis. 286–17 yet this is possible in *S·*,
    310– 3 is neither . . . nor possible in *S·*.
Principle of
  Rud. 8–21 Truth and the Principle of *S·*,
process of
  Un. 8–22 You demonstrate the process of *S·*,
proved itself
  My. 348–25 proved itself *S·*, for it healed
proves
  Mis. 223– 9 *S·* proves, beyond cavil, that the
religion and
  Mis. 312–18 * harmony between religion and *S·*,
remains
  My. 348–28 *S·* remains the law of God
remedies
  Mis. 334–27 *S·* remedies the ills of material
rendered in
  Mis. 75–22 is rendered in *S·*, "My *spiritual*
repeats
  Chr. 53–14 *S·* repeats, Through understanding,
rests on Principle
  Mis. 69– 6 *S·* rests on Principle and
results of
  Mis. 341–12 to arrive at the results of *S·* :
reveals
  Mis. 5– 4 *S·* reveals man as spiritual,
  Ret. 60– 3 *S·* reveals Life as a complete sphere,
    60– 6 *S·* reveals Spirit as All,
  Hea. 14–25 divine *S·* reveals the Principle
reveals Soul
  Un. 29–15 *S·* reveals Soul as that which the
Revelation and
  No. 20–27 antagonistic to Revelation and *S·*.
revelation, and
  Un. 8–19 through reason, revelation, and *S·*,
reverses
  Mis. 47–19 *S·* reverses the evidence of
  Un. 13– 1 *S·* reverses the evidence of
    30– 5 *S·* reverses the testimony of
reversing
  Un. 63– 1 mortal sense, reversing *S·*
rule in
  Mis. 85–14 fulfilment of this divine rule in *S·* :
    265–12 understands a single rule in *S·*,
rule of
  Mis. 172–29 first and fundamental rule of *S·*
  Un. 50–25 Adopt this rule of *S·*,
rules of
  My. 235– 7 the imperative rules of *S·*,

Science

safe in
  Po. 43–20 Safe in *S·*, bright with glory
saith
  Mis. 101–20 *S·* saith to man, "God hath all-power."
  Ret. 60–18 *S·* saith to all manner of disease,
    61–13 *S·* saith to fear, "You are the
sanctions
  Mis. 93–16 *S·* sanctions only what
sanity and
  My. 363–14 proof that sanity and *S·* govern
sap the
  Mis. 218–15 False realistic views sap the *S·* of
scale of
  Mis. 341– 8 you will go up the scale of *S·*
    379–31 adjusting in the scale of *S·*
sect and
  My. 316– 3 Truth divides between sect and *S*
seek the
  My. 188–28 seek the *S·* of his spiritual nature,
sense of
  Mis. 12–29 our sense of *S·* will be measured by
    174– 9 attach our sense of *S·* to
  My. 212–25 destroys the true sense of *S·*,
sense of the
  '01. 22–26 receive their sense of the *S·*,
sense without the
  Mis. 302– 9 the sense without the *S·*, of Christ's
shows
  Rud. 8–23 but *S·* shows that he makes
  Pan. 7– 3 *S·* shows that a plurality of minds,
speaks
  Mis. 100–19 *S·* speaks when the senses
spiritual
  (*see* **spiritual**)
statement of the
  Mis. 247–14 statement of the *S·* I introduce,
  Pul. 47 14 * distinct statement of the *S·*
suffering or
  Mis. 213– 5 Suffering or *S·*, or both,
summit in
  Mis. 41–16 and gains the summit in *S·*
summit of
  Mis. 66–17 To reach the summit of *S·*,
their
  Mis. 58–18 to interpret their *S·*.
  Rud. 13–17 understood in their *S·*,
this
  Mis. 31–15 the grand verity of this *S·*,
    43– 9 student of this *S·* who understands it
    43–13 The simple sense one gains of this *S·*
    44–11 who understands this *S·* sufficiently
    45–10 render this *S·* invaluable in
    45–17 this *S·* is effectual in treating
    59– 8 without this *S·* there had better be no
    62–25 and ends in a parody on this *S·*
    62–27 that she is practising this *S·*.
    88–20 * insisted that this *S·* is natural,
    186–18 let us not lose this *S·* of man,
    194– 5 Let us, then, seek this *S·* ;
    194–14 needs the prism of this *S·*
    195– 7 unable to demonstrate this *S·* ;
    235– 9 This *S·* is ameliorative and
    247–16 demonstrate this *S·* by healing the sick ;
    260–28 Mind, imbued with this *S·*
    261–30 even a knowledge of this *S·*,
    283 21 Scriptural rule of this *S·*
    284– 1 only personal help required in this *S·*
    297– 3 this *S·* has distanced all other
    297– 7 because this *S·* bases its work on
    367– 2 This *S·* requires man to be honest,
    382– 4 prior to my discovery of this *S·*.
    383–12 immortal parapets of this *S·*.
  Man. 92–10 proving this *S·* to be all that we
  Ret. 76–11 mind to which this *S·* was revealed
    78–20 demonstrate the facts of this *S·*
  Un. 52– 4 This *S·* of God and man
    61–25 realization of this *S·* !
  Rud. 13– 6 demonstrate the Principle of this *S·*,
    16–18 said and written correctly on this *S·*
    17–10 Discoverer of this *S·* could tell
    17–14 taking the first footsteps in this *S·*.
  No. 12– 4 essence of this *S·* is right thinking
    13– 1 This *S·* rebukes sin with its own
    21–10 This *S·* demonstrated the Principle
    26–14 In this *S·* of being, man can
    28–22 omitting the spirit of this *S·*.
  Pan. 11–16 who understands this *S·*.
  '00. 6–17 so-called fog of this *S·*
  My. 3–15 This *S·* is a law of divine Mind,
    37–15 * you have demonstrated this *S·*
    113–30 steady advancement of this *S·*
    151– 7 or does understand this *S·*
    178– 8 This *S·* is the essence of religion,
    224–22 to those ignorant of this *S·*
    237– 7 a present student of this *S·*.

Science

this
My. 240–11 "This *S·* is a law of divine Mind,
348–27 human demonstrator of this *S·*
357–24 basis upon which this *S·* can be
to learn
Mis. 14–12 for in order to learn *S·*, we
touches
Mis. 289–26 *S·* touches the conjugal question
transparency of
Mis. 183–14 Through the transparency of *S·*
treasure-troves of
Mis. 22–32 in the treasure-troves of *S·*.
true
Un. 29–19 between the true *S·* of Soul and
Rud. 4–10 All true *S·* represents a moral
No. 6–12 practise the true *S·* of Mind-healing.
6–22 true *S·* of the stellar universe.
My. 28–31 * has revealed the one true *S·*
true in
Un. 13– 4 whereas the reverse is true in *S·*.
truth of
Rud. 16–12 some novices, in the truth of *S·*,
ultimatum of
Un. 43– 9 achievement of this ultimatum of *S·*,
uncovered by
No. 24–18 human reason is uncovered by *S·* ;
understanding
Mis. 92– 2 necessity for understanding *S·*,
Ret. 83–29 thoroughly understanding *S·*,
understanding of
Un. 4–26 from such an understanding of *S·*,
understanding of the
Mis. 54–24 require an understanding of the *S·*
221–21 saps one's understanding of the *S·*
understood in
Mis. 286–20 recognized and understood in *S·*.
unfolds
Mis. 218– 2 *S·* unfolds the fact that Deity was
uprooted in
Un. 8–17 All forms of error are uprooted in *S·*,
vast
My. 354–22 *S·* vast, to which belongs
verity in
Mis. 338– 1 this grand verity in *S·*,
victory-bringing
Ret. 22–16 Vanquished by victory-bringing *S·* ;
voiced
Mis. 336– 2 Hath not *S·* voiced this lesson to you,
voices
Mis. 100–14 *S·* voices unselfish love,
Way in
Chr. 53–11 The Way in *S·* He appoints,
what manner of
No. 35– 3 What manner of *S·* were C. S. without
whole of
Rud. 2–22 * *Is healing the sick the whole of S·?*
will restore
Pan. 6– 1 *S·* will restore and establish,
wisdom nor
Mis. 359–17 but it is neither wisdom nor *S·*
working in
Mis. 87–18 *that no one there was working in S·*,
works on
Ret. 76– 5 voluminous works on *S·*
yielded to
Ret. 57–14 would have yielded to *S·*.
yields to
Mis. 37–23 appetite for alcohol yields to *S·*
your
Mis. 37–16 *Can your S· cure intemperance?*
38–25 *Is it necessary to study your S·*
54–17 *Must I study your S· in order to*

Mis. 4– 7 the *S·* of the Mind that is God,
10–32 that aught but good exists in *S·*.
22– 3 *S·* is neither a law of matter nor
23– 2 but *S·*, demanding more,
25–12 *S·*, understood, translates matter
27–26 is *S·*, and is susceptible of proof.
33–16 had no faith whatever in the *S·*,
38–18 *S·* that has the animus of Truth.
38–29 Were it so, the *S·* would be of
45– 2 for that is not *S·* but mesmerism.
45–19 and when *S·* in a single instance
46–25 In *S·*, man represents his divine
47–17 In *S·*, body is the servant of Mind,
48–12 magnetism is neither of God nor *S·*.
65–11 *S·* must and will decide.
71–14 *S·* never averts law, but supports it.
72– 4 *S·* sets aside man as a creator,
79–18 cause and effect in *S·* are immutable
93–20 is neither maintained by *S·* nor
98– 6 chapter sub-title
99–31 "This is *S·*."
101–29 premise and conclusion in *S·*,

Science

Mis. 102–23 *S·* supports harmony,
102–27 *S·* has inaugurated the
102–29 *S·* outmasters it, and ends the
103–12 In *S·*, form and individuality are
104– 9 In *S·* all being is individual ;
105–12 *S·* would have no conflict with Life
105–28 does not exist in *S·*.
107– 4 Art must not prevail over *S·*.
118–10 is neither *S·* nor obedience.
161– 9 in *S·*, man is the son of God.
163–13 interpretation through *S·*.
165–11 *S·* which rends the veil of the flesh
177–17 the truth, the gospel, and the *S·*
183–27 knowledge of God through *S·*,
185–10 *S·* that opens the very flood-gates
187–10 even as in *S·* a chord is manifestly
193–20 for supplying the word *S·* to
196–18 man's unity with his Maker, in *S·*,
198–26 which is corrected alone by *S·*,
201– 3 The *S·* of Paul's declaration
221–23 divorces his work from *S·*.
243–14 If the system is *S·*, it includes
254–21 This is not *S·*.
261–31 to be *S·*, it must produce
263–24 The *S·* is hampered by
265– 8 Diverse opinions in *S·* are
269–24 correct Mind-healing . . . is *S·*.
280–17 then only are we working . . . in *S·*.
289–18 Oneness in spirit is *S·*,
336–27 *S·* is the fiat of divine intelligence,
344–20 the *S·* which Paul understood
350–23 not in harmony with *S·*
352–14 In *S·*, sickness is healed
365– 6 their highest endeavors are to *S·*
365–28 As a *S·*, it is held back by the
379–17 and were not *S·*.
Man. 40– 7 In *S·*, divine Love alone governs
Ret. 11–16 *S·* the mighty source,
26–29 demonstration of being, in *S·*,
28– 7 *S·* of the perfect Mind
59– 5 In *S·*, Life is not temporal,
90– 2 careful not to thrust aside *S·*,
Un. 39–17 receive the knowledge of God in *S·*
42–24 *S·*, dispelling a false sense
62–18 In *S·*, Christ never died.
Pul. 6– 7 unites *S·* to Christianity.
Rud. 3–15 from that divine digest of *S·*
7– 1 Not that all healing is *S·*,
7– 9 In *S·*, man is the manifest
8– 5 in *S·*, Spirit sends forth its own
11– 7 in *S·* man is His likeness,
12–28 in *S·*, disease is unreal ;
13– 4 pantheism and theosophy are not *S·*.
13–18 not *S·* to treat every organ in the
No. 6–19 *S·* determines the evidence
9–22 *S·* is not the shibboleth of a sect
9–25 *S·* is the atmosphere of God ;
10– 7 "Christian" and "*S·*."
11–11 As a *S·*, this system is held back by
13–17 *S·* is not susceptible of being
17–17 In *S·* there is no fallen state
18– 6 If *S·* lacked the proof of its
21– 5 The *S·* that Jesus demonstrated,
21–27 has little resemblance to *S·*,
27–14 *S·*, . . . presents the grand and
30–26 In *S·*, the cure of the sick
33– 2 The reduction of evil, in *S·*,
37– 2 in *S·* his divine nature and
40–19 forfeit their ability to heal in *S·*.
42–15 While *S·* is engulfing error in
43–26 *S·* often suffers blame through the
Pan. 2– 5 who know that C. S. *is S·*,
'00. 4–26 is His reflection and *S·*.
4–27 coexist with God in *S·*,
6–18 obtains not in the *S·*, but in
8–25 not *S·* for the wicked to wallow
'01. 10–14 *S·* of divine metaphysics removes the
22– 4 Is *S·* material? No !
22– 7 I do not try . . . since *S·* does not
'02. 11–12 is neither Christian nor *S·*.
Hea. 6–11 I saw the impossibility, in *S·*, of
19–19 *S·* makes a more spiritual demand,
Po. 60–13 *S·* the mighty source,
My. 85–22 * *S·* church has become the great
92– 6 * *S·* cannot be brushed aside by
103– 9 C. S. is indeed *S·*,
103–11 *S·*, until . . . has been persecuted
103–14 *S·* which Jesus taught and practised.
112– 2 *S·* has always been first met with
112– 4 where *S·* gains no hearing.
119– 3 impossible in *S·* to believe this,
119– 7 In *S·*, we learn that man is
124–19 it remains for *S·* to reveal man
149– 5 We know Principle only through *S·*.
158–18 proof that C. S. is *S·*

Science

My.	178–10 because *S·* is naturally divine,
	205–30 The . . . may fail, but the *S·* never.
	229–11 *S·* that otherwise might cost them
	238–23 proof that C. S. is *S·*,
	322–25 * many good points in the *S·*,
	350–27 *S·* ripe in prayer, in word, and
	353–16 *S·* that operates unspent.

science

all
Rud. 4– 6 *Is God the Principle of all s·*,
cruder
Pul. 79–19 * materialism of the cruder *s·*
false
My. 345–12 false *s·* — healing by drugs.
in general
My. 345– 7 * attitude to *s·* in general?
lack of
My. 307–30 its lack of *s·*, and the want of
leaving
My. 350– 2 leaving *s·* at the beck of
material
Mis. 344–13 a material *s·* of life !
Rud. 4–14 There is no material *s·*,
men of
My. 95–23 * the men of *s·* may think
mental
Mis. 4– 6 calling this method "mental *s·*."
58–21 Without . . . there is no mental *s·*,
modern
Pul. 54–19 * in the light of modern *s·*,
moral
Mis. 35–22 Why do we read moral *s·*,
Ret. 10– 8 philosophy, logic, and moral *s·*.
Pul. 46–25 * philosophy, logic, and moral *s·*,
natural
Mis. 23–31 according to natural *s·*,
27–13 Mortals accept natural *s·*,
172–17 which is termed "natural *s·*,"
Un. 11– 8 so-called natural *s·*.
Rud. 7–25 no more . . . than natural *s·*,
My. 181– 4 and so-called natural *s·*,
not reckoned as
Pan. 3–21 laws are not reckoned as *s·*.
of guessing
Peo. 6– 5 * "Medicine is the *s·* of guessing."
of mind
My. 307– 7 it was the *s·* of mind,
of numbers
Mis. 55– 2 condemn . . . the *s·* of numbers.
Ret. 59–11 demonstration of the *s·* of numbers ;
of the mind
Mis. 68–23 * metaphysics . . . *s·* of the mind."
of treating disease
Hea. 14– 4 the *s·* of treating disease
physical
Un. 6–16 not the path of physical *s·*,
My. 160–21 Physical *s·* has sometimes
religion, or
My. 303–24 philosophy, religion, or *s·* ;
so-called
Mis. 173–14 an opposite so-called *s·*,
203–15 handles it with so-called *s·*,
Rud. 7–25 natural *s·*, so-called, or material
speculative
Mis. 68–30 * speculative *s·*, which soars
student of
Mis. 52–22 What progress would a student of *s·*
truth or
My. 107–26 classification as truth or *s·*
word
My. 307– 4 word *s·* was not used at all,
works on
Mis. 64–21 Works on *s·* are profitable ;

Mis. 30–23 * "is neither Christian nor *s·* !"
58–26 and you take away its *s·*,
64–21 for *s·* is not human.
68–22 * *s·* of the conceptions and relations
68–25 * a *s·* of which the object is to
68–28 * *s·* which regards the ultimate
78–10 than can *s·* in any other direction.
219– 1 *s·* of the final cause of things ;
'*02.* 7–12 to the words *potence, presence, s·*,
Peo. 13–16 and giving the lie to *s·*.
My. 307– 7 I declared . . . there was a *s·*,
345– 9 "Not," . . . "if it is really *s·*."
345–19 could I believe in a *s·* of drugs?"

Science and Health

page 35, lines 20-25
My. 17–23 " 35, " 20–25
p. 47, revised edition of 1890
Mis. 379–32 *S· and H·*, p. 47, revised edition of 1890,
p. 63
Ret. 69– 4 quotation from

Science and Health

page 68
My. 305– 7 In *S· and H·*, page 68,
pp. 103, 104
Ret. 68–27 quotation from
p. 135
My. 61–27 * (*S· and H·*, p. 135.)
page 136, lines 1-5, 9-14
My. 17–20 " 136, " 1–5, 9–14
page 137, lines 16-5
My. 17–21 " 137, "16–5
page 140
Man. 61– 2 (See *S· AND H·*, page 140.)
pp. 152, 153
Mis. 379–33 pp. 152, 153 in late editions.
page 181
Mis. 83– 5 *In your book, S· and H·, page* 181,
page 182
Mis. 83– 7 *On page* 182 *you say :*
p. 205
Ret. 69–24 quotation from
p. 227
My. 207–24 (See *S· and H·*, p. 227.)
page 229
Mis. 309–25 on page 229, third and fourth paragraphs,
page 241, lines 13-30
My. 17–19 Page 241, lines 13–30
page 252
My. 232–21 read on page 252, "A knowledge
p. 296
My. 217–27 (p. 296).
pp. 306, 307
Ret. 69–15 quotation from
pp. 307, 308
Ret. 69–30 quotation from
page 330
Man. 86–20 beginning on page 330
page 442, line 30
My. 237–13 *S· and H·*, page 442, line 30,
line 30 of page 442
My. 236–25 beginning at line 30 of page 442
page 468
My. 19– 7 * from *S· and H·* (p. 468),
33– 4 * (*S· and H·*, p. 468),
111–26 (*S· and H·*, p. 468)
(p. 494)
My. 28– 3 * has said in *S· and H·* (p. 494),
73– 8 * quotation from *S· and H·* (p. 494),
p. 495
My. 60–14 * (*S· and H·*, p. 495.)
pp. 512, 513
Ret. 70– 7 quotation from
p. 551
Ret. 68–22 quotation from
pages 568-571
Pul. 12– 2 pages 568–571, were read
page 583, lines 12-19
My. 17–22 "583, "12–19
Vol. I. page 14
Mis. 35–29 Vol. I. page 14:
(*see also* **Lesson-Sermon on Dedication Sunday,**
and **Selections read on June 12, 1906**)

Mis. xi– 1 The first edition of *S· and H·*
21–24 1908 edition of *S· and H·*.
29–19 publication of my work, "*S· and H·*
34–29 The author of "*S· and H·*
35–15 *Will the book S· and H·*, . . . *heal the sick,*
35–24 You are benefited by reading *S· and H·*,
35–28 In reply, we refer you to "*S· and H·*
42–10 *S· and H·* clearly states
50– 5 "*S· and H· with Key to the Scriptures*"
50– 9 "*S· and H·* with Key to the Scriptures"
54–14 "*S· and H·* with Key to the Scriptures,"
64–14 except the Bible, and "*S· and H·*
87–25 "*S· and H·* with Key to the Scriptures."
91–22 "*S· and H· with Key to the Scriptures*,"
92–17 contained in that chapter of "*S· and H·*
106–18 its correlative in "*S· and H·*
115– 2 With *S· and H·* for their textbook,
136–20 my last revised edition of *S· and H·*
153–24 copy of my first edition of "*S· and H·*
159– 2 God has given to this age "*S· and H·*
214–19 search the Scriptures and "*S· and H·*
248–19 views of Mrs. Eddy's book, '*S· and H·*
274– 4 I desire to revise my book "*S· and H·*
284–11 make the Bible and *S· and H·* a study,
285–14 about the year 1875 that *S· and H·*
285–17 *S· and H·*, the book that cast the first
300–26 from my work *S· and H·*,
302– 3 through the instructions of "*S· and H·*
302–29 divine teachings contained in "*S· and H·*
309–24 "*S· and H·* with Key to the Scriptures,"
309–29 adhere to the Bible and *S· and H·*,
313–26 ordain the Bible, and "*S· and H·*
314–15 shall read from my book, "*S· and H·*
314–19 read all the selections from *S· and H·*

Science and Health

Mis. 314–23   The Reader of "S· and H·
315– 2   taken from the Scriptures and S· and H·,
315–30   the Scriptures, and "S· and H·
318–16   studied thoroughly "S· and H·
322–11   the Bible, and "S· and H· with Key to
364– 2   "S· and H· with Key to the Scriptures."
366– 1   If the Bible and "S· and H· with
371–29   hopelessly original as is "S· and H·
372–29   S· and H· gives scopes and shades
382–32   ordained that the Bible, and "S· and H·
Man. 29–22   and one to read S· and H·
31–22   the SCRIPTURES, and from S· AND H·
32– 3   read the correlative texts in S· AND H·
32– 7   precede the readings from S· AND H·.
32–11   The Readers of S· AND H·
34–12   The BIBLE, together with S· AND H·
42–13   the BIBLE, and S· AND H·
53–20   If the author of S· AND H·
58– 5   ordain the BIBLE, and S· AND H·
64– 6   S· and H· with Key to the Scriptures,
71–25   copyrighted in S· AND H·
83–22   study the Scriptures and S· AND H·
84–19   guided by the BIBLE, and S· AND H·,
86–18   "Recapitulation" in S· AND H·
Ret. 27– 4   S· and H·, published in 1875.
27– 9   until S· and H· was written.
35– 4   Recapitulation in S· and H·.
37– 1   my most important work, S· and H·,
37–19   Key to the Scriptures, in S· and H·,
37–22   in my first edition of S· and H·,
38–21   of my first edition of S· and H·.
38–27   S· and H· is the textbook of C. S.
47–20   studied thoroughly S· and H·,
49– 9   S· and H· is adapted to work this result ;
68–16   S· and H·, the textbook of C. S.,
70–17   the place of the author of S· and H·,
78– 6   explanation is complete in S· and H· ;
78–20   other than is stated in S· and H·
82–27   often asked which revision of S· and H·
83–20   leave S· and H· to God's daily
84– 2   inexhaustible topics of S· and H·
84–12   should own a copy of S· and H·
84–17   to which S· and H· is the Key.
Pul. 5–13   After the publication of "S· and H·
6–13   * "Six months ago your book, S· and H·,
12– 1   following selections from "S· and H·
24–17   * author of "S· and H· with Key to the
25–28   * "S· and H· with Key to the Scriptures"
27–18   * with lamps, typical of S· and H·.
28–18   * Mrs. Eddy's book, entitled "S· and H·
29–15   * from the Bible and from S· and H·
38– 5   * Mrs. Eddy's book, S· and H·,
43–17   * from the Scriptures and from "S· and H·
45–26   * Bible and "S· and H· with Key to the
54–28   author of S· and H· healed Mr. Whittier
55–13   * first edition of Mrs. Eddy's S· and H·
55–22   * in the volume entitled "S· and H·
58–26   * "S· and H· with Key to the Scriptures."
Rud. 7– 6   set forth in my work S· and H·.
16–19   practice laid down in S· and H·.
No. 3– 8   When I revised "S· and H· with Key to
4– 1   Reading S· and H· has restored the sick
11–15   If the Bible and S· and H·
13–22   S· and H· has effected a revolution
21– 6   The Science . . . S· and H· interprets.
33– 5   Bible and my work S· and H· had their
42–22   Denial of the authorship of "S· and H·
43–13   * S· and H· is healing the sick,
'00. 7–13   as they did after reading "S· and H·
01. 11–13   the Bible, and "S· and H·
24–22   published my work S· and H·,
'02. 15–10   income from the sale of S· and H·,
15–22   Its title, S· and H·, came to me
16– 4   that identical phrase, "S· and H·,"
My. vi– 1   * S· and H· does not need to be
17–17   * reading of selections from "S· and H·
18–29   * The Holy Bible ; "S· and H·
34–15   * from the Bible and "S· and H·
34–29   * S· and H· references in this lesson
39– 5   * Bible and S· and H· as follows :
59–25   * "Did Mrs. Eddy really write S· and H·?
80–18   * Bible, and selections from "S· and H·
103– 6   our textbooks, the Bible and "S· and H·
110–30   the misquoting of "S· and H·
112–12   "S· and H· with Key to the Scriptures"
112–26   his conscientious study of S· and H·
114–25   divine power . . . dictated "S· and H·
115– 4   to write of "S· and H· . . . as I have,
130–26   "S· and H· with Key to the Scriptures"
136– 7   S· and H· with Key to the Scriptures."
178–27   "S· and H· . . . would remain immortal.
213–28   three quotations from S· and H·
215– 6   I wrote "S· and H· with Key to the
217–23   It is written in "S· and H·
228– 2   My book S· and H· names

Science and Health

My. 232–20   textbook of C. S., "S· and H·
236–26   the edition of S· and H· which will
237– 1   contemplated reference in S· and H·
238– 3   "S· and H· with Key to the Scriptures"
239– 3   "S· and H· with Key to the Scriptures"
240–19   In the next edition of S· and H·
246–19   While revising "S· and H·
252– 1   teachings of the Bible, S· and H·, and
266–23   My book, "S· and H· with Key to the
271– 4   When I wrote "S· and H·
304–31   "S· and H· with Key to the Scriptures,"
310–29   When the first edition of S· and H·
317– 6   * authorship of "S· and H·
318– 7   employed him on "S· and H·
318–14   "S· and H· with Key to the Scriptures."
320–11   * Mr. Wiggin spoke of "S· and H·
322– 3   * when you were writing S· and H·,
324– 2   * especially your book S· and H·.
324–11   * nomenclature for S· and H·.
346–29   "S· and H· makes it plain to all
356–17   heretofore presented in S· and H·.
(see also textbook)

Science of Being
Pul. 38–11   "Creation," "S· of B·,"

Science of Divine Metaphysical Healing, The
Pul. 55–16   * "The S· of D· M· H·."

sciences
Mis. 61– 6   material symbolic counterfeit s·.
344– 8   without having mastered the s·
Pul. 64–15   * studied the Scriptures and the s·,
My. 349–12   beyond the so-called natural s·

Science, Theology, Medicine
Pul. 38– 9   "S·, T·, M·," "Physiology,"

scientific
Mis. 5–10   by studying this s· method
31– 7   subverts the s· laws of being.
31–10   a subversion of right is not s·.
40– 1   The s· Principle of healing demands
46–14   misconception of Truth is not s·.
59–29   divine Mind is the s· healer.
66–22   s· treatment of the sick.
86–13   s· classifications of the unreal and
113–19   way of escape . . . through s· truth ;
116–20   The ultimate of s· research
116–30   you lose the s· rule and its reward :
118– 5   s· understanding guides man.
156– 2   swift vehicle of s· thought ;
166–14   s· understanding of Truth and Love.
172–28   To gain this s· result,
186–21   s· knowledge affords self-evident
186–25   is not the s· fact of being ;
206– 9   s· indestructibility of the universe
206–13   s· growth manifests no weakness,
209–29   s· logic and the logic of events,
216– 7   chapter sub-title
231–25   That was a s· baby ;
266– 5   is neither politic nor s· ;
277–24   s· proof that God, good, is supreme.
288–19   the consciousness of s· being
288–20   would prevent s· demonstration.
289–10   application of s· rules to human life
308–12   Advanced s· students are ready for
308–20   artistic, and s· notices of my book.
313– 6   points to the s· spiritual molecule,
353–27   at about three years of s· age,
359–15   For Jesus to walk the water was s·,
360–11   by his original s· sonship with God.
379–10   not at all metaphysical or s· ;
Ret. 24–10   s· certainty that all causation was
24–21   perfect s· accord with divine law.
33– 6   till I was weary of "s· guessing,"
35– 2   spiritual, s· Mind-healing,
40–21   This s· demonstration so stirred the
48–18   s· methods of mental healing
48–28   spiritual and s· impartation of Truth,
52– 3   expansion of s· Mind-healing,
59– 4   S· terms have no contradictory
64–24   It is s· to abide in conscious harmony,
66– 5   and s· demonstration of God.
68–26   s· thoughts are true thoughts,
70–23   the s· ultimate of this God-idea
78– 6   s· practice makes perfect,
78–11   not to read so-called s· works,
83– 1   elucidate s· healing and teaching.
83– 8   s· foundations are already laid
87–22   In this orderly, s· dispensation
94– 1   validity of this s· statement of being.
94– 2   Having perceived, . . . this s· fact,
94–16   s· teaching, preaching, and practice
shadowed forth in s· thought.
Un. 5–25
46– 9   The s· man and his Maker
51–25   s· relation of man to God,
53–17   are no more logical, . . . or s·

scientific

Pul.	2–27	How can we do this Christianly *s*
	4–10	a *s*, positive sense of unity
	10–22	are as devout as they, and more *s*,
	34–23	*s* accord with the divine law."
	45–19	* a *s* demonstration.
	55–19	* held to be a *s* certainty,
	69–22	* certain Christian and *s* laws,
	79–27	* the thought of the world's *s*
Rud.	7– 3	demonstrably *s*, in a small degree,
	9–21	power of a *s*, right thought,
	13–21	that harmony is the real . . . is scientific ;
	16– 9	*s* relation to Mind-healing,
	16–14	*more than one school of s* healing?*
No.	2– 8	*s* to rob disease of all reality,
	4–19	Sin and disease are not *s*,
	10–12	one Principle for all *s* truth.
	13– 5	*s* deduction from the Principle
	39–21	new and *s* discoveries of God,
Pan.	8–13	chapter sub-title
	9–15	attainment of *s* Christianity
'01.	4–11	lose its susceptibility of *s* proof.
	14–28	*s* apprehension of this grand verity.
	27–27	* "Every great *s* truth
	33–14	a diploma for *s* guessing.
'02.	7–20	no other *s* proposition
	8–21	*S* Christianity works out the rule
Peo.	7–27	*S* discovery and the inspiration
	11–27	*S* guessing conspires unwittingly
My.	59–12	* by nearly every . . . *s* body in the
	109– 7	When this *s* classification is
	116– 6	religious or scientific prosperity,
	127–12	*s* system of metaphysical
	153–15	*s*, healing faith is a saving faith ;
	165–20	rise . . . to the *s* response :
	178–11	is this natural Science less . . . *s*
	181– 9	demonstrates the *s*, sinless life
	190–10	metaphysical practice of
	218– 8	*s* proof of "God with us." — *Matt.* 1: 23.
	230– 5	*S* pathology illustrates the
	234–22	great Master's sayings are . . . *s*
	237–23	is practical and *s*,
	246–14	*s* unity which must exist
	248–30	the *s* expression of Truth.
	265–16	*s* religion and *s* therapeutics
	267– 4	Nothing . . . which is not divinely *s*,
	272– 8	predicate and ultimate of *s* being
	273–21	*s* knowledge that is portentous ;
	279– 8	*s* being reappearing in all ages,
	293–26	result would have been *s*,
	304–25	* "Every great *s* truth goes through
	349–14	A *s* state of health is a
		(see also basis, sense, statement)

scientifically

Mis.	44–29	you *s* prove the fact that Mind is
	46– 6	truism needs only to be tested *s*
	270–12	in demonstrating Life *s*,
	310– 7	impersonalize *s* the material sense
Ret.	34–10	I claim for healing *s* the following
No.	5–28	prevents one from healing *s*,
My.	105– 5	This Æsculapius, . . . demonstrated *s*,
	135–29	spiritually and *s* understand
	235–13	and teach truth *s*.
	242– 2	*s* correct in your statement
	245– 5	cautiously, systematically, *s*.
	342–24	the perfecting of man stated *s*."
	342–27	"It will evolve *s*.
	344– 7	so the mystery is *s* explained.

Scientific Theism

Mis.	216– 7	chapter sub-title
	216– 9	some extracts from, "*S T*,"

Scientist *(see also* Scientist's)

acts of the

Mis.	204–30	aims, ambition, and acts of the *S*.

Christian

Mis.	xi–15	the Christian *S* will find herein
	39–22	Christian *S* who has more to meet
	39–25	*In what way is a Christian S* an
	39–28	a Christian *S*, assumes no more when
	63–13	why does a Christian *S* go to the
	85– 4	*Is a Christian S* ever sick,
	85– 6	The Christian *S* learns spiritually
	85–20	The new-born Christian *S* must mature,
	86– 5	Until this be attained, the Christian *S*
	100–26	The Christian *S* loves man more
	107–31	is or can be a Christian *S*.
	108–29	What would be thought of a Christian *S*
	134– 9	chapter sub-title
	137– 1	chapter sub-title
	151–20	pray thee as a Christian *S*, delay not
	157–12	Every true Christian *S* will feel
	206–19	The real Christian *S* is constantly
	212–26	He who *is* a Christian *S*,
	214–26	The Christian *S* cannot
	220–22	to the conscientious Christian *S*

Scientist

Christian

Mis.	223–17	saying, "I am a Christian *S*,"
	225– 5	a friend of mine, and a Christian *S*.
	225–16	a proof of what the Christian *S* had
	261–27	impossible to be a Christian *S* without
	266–14	clear-headed and honest Christian *S*
	268–14	Christian *S* keeps straight to the
	291–22	unswerving course of a Christian *S*,
	294– 6	A real Christian *S* is a marvel,
	295–32	Now, I am a Christian *S*,
	296–30	bar-maid and Christian *S*
	317–18	progress of every Christian *S*.
	336– 6	but you cannot, as a Christian *S*,
	358– 8	gain is loss to the Christian *S*.
	369– 1	and the true Christian *S*
	375– 6	truest art . . . is to be a Christian *S* ;
Man.	40– 8	a Christian *S* reflects the sweet
	41– 5	is abnormal in a Christian *S*,
	46–26	A Christian *S* is a humanitarian ;
	47– 9	the privilege of a Christian *S*
	49–20	If a Christian *S* is to be married,
	50–16	the life of a Christian *S*,
	55–20	consistent, consecrated Christian *S*.
	60– 7	A Christian *S* is not fatigued by
	64– 2	and a devout Christian *S*.
	70– 4	Christian *S* in the employ of
	72– 6	loyal exemplary Christian *S*
	86–11	elect an experienced Christian *S*,
	97– 6	consist of one loyal Christian *S*
Ret.	26–20	a Christian *S*, who needed no
	42– 5	to announce himself a Christian *S*,
	70–11	in our time no Christian *S* will
	80–15	If the Christian *S* recognize the
	83– 4	wise Christian *S* will commend
	85–19	The loyal Christian *S* is
Pul.	35–30	* "Christian *S*" on the sign at his
Rud.	8–19	man who calls himself a Christian *S*,
	11–26	healer who is indeed a Christian *S*,
	12–28	Christian *S* knows that, in Science,
	16– 4	a Christian *S* will never undertake to
'01.	15– 7	Christian *S* has enlisted to lessen sin,
	20– 8	The Christian *S* is alone with his
	20–10	cannot be, a Christian *S* ;
	22– 4	is to some extent a Christian *S*.
	27–17	years ago without a Christian *S*
'02.	14– 6	a motto for every Christian *S*,
	19– 8	Christian *S* cherishes no resentment ;
Peo.	6–20	God is . . . to the Christian *S*,
	14–11	O Christian *S*, thou of the church
My.	3–22	A Christian *S* verifies his calling.
	4–14	Christian *S* loves Protestant and
	5–17	constitute a Christian *S*,
	52–21	* who was not a Christian *S*,
	73– 7	* If you ask a Christian *S*, how they
	97–11	* and is not a Christian *S*,
	104–13	who shall call a Christian *S* a
	106–22	In what sense is the Christian *S* a
	106–28	is the Christian *S* a charlatan?
	108–25	the best work of a Christian *S*.
	111–12	genuine Christian *S* will tell you
	114– 7	Has one Christian *S* yet reached
	117–12	make one a Christian *S*.
	122–25	the real Christian *S* can say
	122–28	of the real Christian *S*
	129–25	Christian *S* is not frightened at
	130–25	to the loyal Christian *S*
	132– 8	Christian *S* knows that spiritual
	138–17	cannot be a Christian *S* except
	139–10	Christian *S* thrives in adversity ;
	142–10	*Beloved Christian S* : — Accept my
	146–26	Christian *S* never mentally or
	146–29	The Christian *S* voices the harmonious
	178–22	A Christian *S* entered the house
	222–19	Be patient, O Christian *S* !
	229– 3	No mesmerist nor disloyal Christian *S*
	229–27	laws of limitation for a Christian *S*.
	235–24	Are you a Christian *S* ?
	241–12	* from a Christian *S* in the West,
	254– 3	have begun to be a Christian *S*.
	294–18	the Christian *S* with his conscious
	295–27	Christian *S*, the servant of God
	296–10	late lamented Christian *S* brother
	297–15	Christian *S* who believes that he dies,
	314–26	A Christian *S* has told me that
	320–16	* did not claim to be a Christian *S*,
	322–27	* told me he was not a Christian *S*.
	330–10	* A local Christian *S* of your city,
	330–12	* a Christian *S* of Charleston, S. C.,
	332–21	* A Christian *S* in Charleston
	353– 1	My desire is that every Christian *S*,

devout

My.	5–20	enables the devout *S* to worship,

divine

Ret.	26–17	a natural and divine *S*.

Scientist

real
Mis. 117–10   where to look for the real S·,
unreal
Mis. 119–24   the real and the unreal S·.

Mis.   6–11   are passed over to the S·.
   26–12   S· asks, Whence came the first seed,
   88–27   *Is it right for a S· to*
  168–26   * speak before the S· denomination
Man. 49– 1   A S· shall not endeavor to
Pul. 59–20   * The solo singer, however, was a S·,
My. 81–24   * demonstration of the S· claims,

scientist
Mis. 233–23   a s· in mathematics who

Scientist's
'01.   5– 6   Christian S· sense of Person
   18–10   the Christian S· religion

Scientists (see also **Scientists'**)
among
No.   9– 3   have sprung up among S·
beliefs of
Pul. 73–21   * study in the beliefs of S·,
called
Mis. 193–23   are properly called S·
Christian
Mis.   v– 2   TO LOYAL CHRISTIAN S·
  ix– 8   Now, Christian S· are not indigent ;
  4–13   published by the Christian S·
  13–10   consideration of all Christian S·.
  39–16   Unlike the M. D.'s, Christian S·
  55–13   using that power against Christian S·.
  62–14   *Why do Christian S· hold that*
  79–26   *What course should Christian S· take*
  91– 1   communion which Christian S· celebrate
  98–15   individual growth of Christian S·,
  106– 3   Christian S· will, *must*, have a history ;
  107–28   stopping, the growth of Christian S·.
  108– 5   is anomalous in Christian S·,
  110–26   As Christian S·, you have dared the
  111–19   Christian S· who prove its power
  114–21   Christian S· cannot watch too
  126–22   Works, . . . characterize Christian S·.
  126–24   Christian S· have a strong race to
  127– 8   Christian S·, here and elsewhere,
  131– 9   Christian S· preserve unity,
  140– 8   spiritual good comes to Christian S·,
  141–10   Christian S· hail with joy this
  142– 8   boat presented by Christian S·
  144– 6   dear children of Christian S· ;
  145–26   When the *hearts* of Christian S· are
  146–24   I feel sure that as Christian S·
  150–19   Christian S· may worship the Father
  153–18   Christian S· bring forth the fruits
  156– 7   *Beloved Christian S· :—* Please send
  159–29   all gifts of Christian S·
  171– 8   report . . . that Christian S·
  193–16   * "the so-called Christian S·."
  213–27   Christian S·, be of good cheer :
  235–19   and become Christian S· ;
  255– 2   sometimes said, . . . that Christian S·
  273– 1   as Christian S·, they will know
  273–16   Loyal Christian S· should
  275–20   chapter sub-title
  276–11   about one thousand Christian S·,
  276–31   In the dark hours, wise Christian S·
  284–16   Christian S· should have
  291–13   prosperity of all Christian S·,
  298–13   special application to Christian S· ;
  301–13   a few professed Christian S·.
  302–15   If Christian S· occasionally mistake
  303–25   that many Christian S· will respond
  307–27   Christian S· should beware of
  308–18   Friends, strangers, and Christian S·,
  308–33   I earnestly advise all Christian S·
  311– 3   true Christian S· will be welcomed,
  312–16   * body of people known as Christian S·,
  315– 9   Christian S·, all over the world,
  317– 5   hour has struck for Christian S·
  319–10   Christian S·, must be most watchful.
  319–18   Will all the dear Christian S·
  319–26   achievement to which Christian S·
  320– 6   dear to the heart of Christian S· ;
  325– 6   so-called Christian S· in sheep's
  334–13   Why do Christian S· treat disease *as*
  354– 7   faithful Christian S·
  357– 4   Christian S· minister to the sick ;
  358–21   I do not require Christian S·
  368–13   not metaphysicians, or Christian S·,
  371– 8   Is it that he can guide Christian S·
  374–17   It is most fitting that Christian S·
  383– 5   support of Christian S·.
Man. 17– 7   and were known as "Christian S·."
  36–15   Loyal Christian S· whose teachers
  45–17   whose Readers are not Christian S·

Scientists
Christian
Man. 48–17   Christian S· shall not report for
  64–15   Christian S· had given to the author
  64–21   it is the duty of Christian S· to
  73– 2   sixteen loyal Christian S·,
  83– 8   Christian S· who are teachers
  85–19   active and loyal Christian S·
Ret. 54– 3   cures wrought through Christian S·?
  63– 1   Why do Christian S· say
  76–29   moral law and order in Christian S·,
  82–22   enable Christian S· to
  83–21   Christian S· should take their textbook
  87–10   Genuine Christian S· are,
  87–15   Christian S· are to "heal the sick"
  87–28   understood that Christian S·
  89–22   Nowhere . . . will Christian S· find
  93–23   Christian S·, should give to the world
  94–27   Christian S· aid the establishment of
Un. 55– 9   Christian S· who would demonstrate
Pul. 2–22   metaphysicians and Christian S·.
  8– 8   Christian S·, within fourteen months,
  10–16   Christian S·, you have planted your
  21– 1   Christian S·, their children and
  21– 7   Christian S· in spirit and in truth.
  21–18   Christian S· are really united to only
  22– 9   If the lives of Christian S· attest
  22–15   will be classified as Christian S·.
  30–23   * entire membership of Christian S·
  38–17   * Christian S· do not accept the belief
  45– 5   * Christian S· not only say that they can
  52– 4   * Christian S· have a faith of the
  52– 7   * these "impractical" Christian S·.
  52–12   * erection of . . . by Christian S·,
  56– 8   * are Christian S·, and, as a rule,
  57–14   * peculiar tenets of the Christian S·,
  59–12   * way peculiar to Christian S·,
  63–25   * contributions of Christian S·
  64–13   * money from enthusiastic Christian S·.
  64–25   * the first church of the Christian S·,
  65– 6   * the Boston sect of Christian S·,
  68–23   * owned by Christian S·.
  70–16   * Christian S· all over the country.
  71–11   * CHRISTIAN S· OF SYRACUSE
  71–13   * Christian S· in this city,
  72–13   * healed . . . years ago by Christian S·,
  75– 5   "If Christian S· find in my writings,
  75–15   * chapter sub-title
  75–18   * The Christian S· of Toronto,
  86– 1   * new church of the Christian S·,
Rud. 3–12   His example is, to Christian S·,
  3–14   Genuine Christian S· will no more
  13–24   *methods of trustworthy Christian S·*
  14– 3   and still be Christian S·.
No. 5– 1   Christian S· are vindicating,
  7– 6   to spring up between Christian S·,
  7–18   God has appointed for Christian S·
  14–20   Christian S·, . . . are obeying these
Pan. 10–18   Christian S· heal functional,
'00. 15– 7   Christian S· start forward with
'01. 1–22   As Christian S· you seek to
  3– 8   We hear it said the Christian S·
  3–10   loyal Christian S· absolutely adopt
  4–20   Christian S· are theists and
  4–24   Christian S· consistently
  5–14   Christian S· believe in personality?
  7–18   Christian S· call their God "divine
  11–23   forgets what Christian S· do not,
  14– 6   Do Christian S· believe that evil
  20–30   Christian S· are not hypnotists,
  23– 4   If Christian S· only would admit
  27– 6   * Christian S· who will interpret their
  29– 1   Has the thought come to Christian S·,
  30– 1   Christian S· are persecuted even as
  30–10   Christian S· are practically
  30–27   I counsel Christian S· under all
  33–13   Christian S· first and last ask not
  33–29   Christian S· are harmless citizens
'02. 3– 2   ten thousand loyal Christian S·
  8–18   evidence of being Christian S·
  16– 9   invaluable gift of two Christian S·,
  19–27   Then, Christian S·, trust,
  20–25   people welcome Christian S·.
Hea. 8–28   shall be Christian S·, and do more
  16– 8   See to it, O Christian S·!
My. v–11   * earnest and loyal Christian S·
  vi– 9   * Christian S· are honest
  vii–14   * service which all Christian S· can
  7–19   * the Christian S· of the world,
  8–14   * universal voice of Christian S·,
  8–24   * "Ten thousand Christian S·
  10–20   * Christian S· are not expected to
  11– 1   * fact that as Christian S·
  13–28   Christian S· virtually pledged this
  18– 5   Christian S·, here and elsewhere,
  21–10   * feel sure that all Christian S· will

scope
  Mis. 100–16   the s· of the senses is inadequate to
      253– 2   Note the s· of that saying,
      355–16   gives s· to higher demonstration.
  '02. 10–15   gain the s· of Jacob's vision,
  My. 117–26   free s· only in the right direction !
      259–25   give the activity of man infinite s· ;

scopes
  Mis. 372–30   S. and H. gives s· and shades to

score
  Mis. 295– 8   * past a s· of reforms, to C. S.''
  Ret. 2–10   more than a s· of years prior to
  My. 98– 5   * growth of less than a s· of years.
     228– 2   there is nothing new on this s·.

scores
  My. 79–27   * s· of . . . Scientists told of cures

scorn
  Mis. 258– 6   righteous s· and power of Spirit.
     297–12   his lofty s· of the sects,
  Ret. 80–17   he will not s· the timely reproof,
  Pul. 81–15   * nobility of all those who s· self
  Po. 71– 3   Laughed right to s·,
  My. 48–22   * The s· of the gross and sensual,

scorned
  Mis. 374– 4   Pharisees s· the spirit of Christ
  No. 2– 5   s· by people of common sense.
  My. 324– 4   * and he s· the suggestion
     331–13   * Southern chivalry would have s·

scorner
  My. 107–21   O petty s· of the infinite,

Scotch
  Ret. 1–19   S· and English elements thus mingling
     3– 1   Sir John Macneill, a S· knight,
  Pul. 32–24   * S· and English ancestry,

Scotch Covenanters
  Ret. 2– 2   reared among the S· C·,

Scotchman's
  Mis. 295–13   S· national pride and affection,

Scotland
  Ret. 1– 2   were from both S· and England,
  Pul. 46–15   * both in S· and England.
     (*see also* **Edinburgh**)

Scots
  Ret. 2–15   "S· wha hae wi' Wallace bled.''

Scott, Sir Walter
  Ret. 2– 6   set forth in the pages of Sir Walter S·

Scottish
  Pul. 46–22   * Wallace of mighty S· fame.

scourge
  Un. 23– 4   * Make instruments to s· us.

scourged
  '01. 28–16   have been s· in the synagogues
  Hea. 2– 7   s· and condemned at every

scourgeth
  Mis. 18– 4   and s· every son— *Heb.* 12 : 6.
  Ret. 80– 6   And s· every son— *Heb.* 12 : 6.

scourging
  My. 148–28   s· the sect in advance of it.

Scranton
  Mis. 150– 9   chapter sub-title
  Pul. 56– 4   * S·, Peoria, Atlanta, Toronto,

scream
  Mis. 396– 5   cricket's sharp, discordant s·
  Po. 58–17   cricket's sharp, discordant s·

screaming
  Mis. 266–29   s·, to make itself heard

screen
  My. 68–23   * It has an architectural stone s·

scribblings
  My. 306–23   his s· were descriptions of
     307– 4   in his s·, the word science

scribe
     (*see* **Eddy**)

scribes
  Mis. 175–15   leaven of the s· and Pharisees,
     189–28   and not as the s·.''— *Matt.* 7 : 29.
     366–19   the s· and Pharisees,''— *see Matt.* 16 : 6.
  Ret. 58–11   and not as the s·.''— *Matt.* 7 : 29.
  Un. 42–20   and not as the s·.''— *Matt.* 7 : 29.

scrip
  My. 215–24   take no s· for their journey,
     215–26   he bade them take s·.

script
  Pul. 78– 7   * inscription, cut in s· letters :

Scriptural
  Mis. 50– 1   that God made all . . . is again S· ;
     72–31   The S· passage quoted
     129–11   then take the next S· step :
     194–19   the foregoing S· text
     253–16   S· metaphors, — of the woman
     278–13   S· declaration that Job sinned **not**
     283–20   S· rule of this Science
     364–17   stands on this S· platform :
  Man. 51– 2   the S· demand in Matthew
  Chr. 55– 1   These S· texts are the basis
  Ret. 1– 9   containing S· sonnets,
     9– 9   S· narrative of little Samuel,
     42–10   he lectured so ably on S· topics
     70– 8   authenticity of the S· narrative
  Pul. 47– 2   * lectures upon S· topics.
  Pan. 6–19   enter into the S· allegory,
     12–11   S· commands be fulfilled.
  '02. 7–17   we have S· authority for
     7–23   another S· passage which
  My. 5– 2   according to the S· allegory,
     114–19   in the line of S· interpretation
     240–18   on a S· basis,
     282– 6   and the S· injunction,

Scripturally
  Mis. 59–12   Not if we pray S·,

Scripture
above
  Mis. 139–16   with a portion of the above S·
     192–23   above S· plainly
according to
  Un. 36–11   solved by C. S. according to S·.
according to the
  Mis. 191–11   According to the S·, if devil is
  Man. 48–20   According to the S· they shall
  My. 300– 4   overcome sin according to the S·,
another
  Mis. 248– 6   as, in another S·,
answered by the
  Hea. 19–14   is answered by the S·,
believe the
  My. 221–31   Shall we not believe the S·,
called in
  '01. 3–19   called in S·, Spirit, Love.
     9– 1   called in S· the Son of God
composed of
  Mis. 106–18   Lesson, composed of S· and
correlative
  My. 33– 5   * and the correlative S·,
countermand the
  Mis. 124– 3   and countermand the S·
declaration in
  Mis. 172–30   oft-repeated declaration in S·
declares
  Mis. 26–11   even while the S· declares He made
  Pan. 5–25   and, as the S· declares,
  '02. 1–12   S· declares, "The wrath of— *Psal.* 76 : 10.
  My. 107–24   If, as S· declares, God made all
     178–12   The S· declares that God is All.
     224–25   since the S· declares,
declares the
  Un. 31– 2   declares the S· (*John* iv. 24),
describes
  Mis. 259–20   same rhythm that the S· describes,
explained in the
  Mis. 30–27   is explained in the S·,
following
  Mis. 133– 9   consideration to the following S·,
is true
  Mis. 193– 4   that the S· is true ;
learned from the
  Hea. 12–12   we learned from the S·
mocking the
  Un. 33–23   divided in evidence, mocking the S·
nowhere
  Un. 47– 3   Nowhere in S· is evil connected with
on this subject
  Mis. 130–14   Note the S· on this subject :
passage of
  My. 135– 5   this passage of S· and its
     170–18   This gift is a passage of S· ;
problems of
  '02. 4–26   abstruse problems of S·,
pronounces
  My. 178–15   S· pronounces all that God made
reads
  '02. 12–19   S· reads : "For in Him— *Acts* 17 : 28.
  My. 4– 7   S· reads : "He that taketh— *Matt.* 10 : 38.
     118–16   S· reads : "Blessed are they — *John* 20 : 29.
     267– 6   S· reads : "All things were— *John* 1 : 3.
remember the
  Mis. 335– 2   Remember the S· :
     335–28   remember the S· concerning those who

Scripture

saith

Mis. 73– 4 *S·* saith, "Whom the Lord — *Heb.* 12 : 6.
76–27 *S·* saith, "When Christ, — *Col.* 3 : 4.
82–29 in whom the *S·* saith
89– 1 *S·* saith, "No man can — *Matt.* 6 : 24.
213– 9 *S·* saith, "He that — *Prov.* 28 : 13.
326– 1 *S·* saith the law of the Spirit
'01. 11–26 *S·* saith "Answer not a — *Prov.* 26 : 4.

saith the

Mis. 219– 8 Now, what saith the *S·*?

says

Mis. 36–24 *S·* says, "The carnal mind — *Rom.* 8 : 7.
Hea. 15–23 *S·* says, "Ye ask, and — *Jas.* 4 : 3.

spoken of in

My. 104–29 anathema spoken of in *S·* :

supported by the

Ret. 64–14 this view is supported by the *S·*,

supported in the

Mis. 66–12 is supported in the *S·*

texts of

My. 317–21 corroborative texts of *S·*.

this

Mis. 72–20 *this S·,* " *Your heavenly* — *Matt.* 6 : 32.
112–30 is characterized in this *S·* :
146–18 and the letter of this *S·* :
'01. 18–24 should read this *S·* :

translations of

My. 179–24 renderings or translations of *S·*

truth of the

No. 17–20 and the truth of the *S·*,

understanding of

'02. 7– 7 spiritual understanding of *S·*,

understand the

My. 135–28 you understand the *S·*,

word of

Un. 23–10 agrees with the word of *S·*,

words of the

My. 150– 4 to reply in words of the *S·* :
196– 7 in these words of the *S·*,

Mis. 103–31 *S·,* "I am a God at hand, — *see Jer.* 23 : 23.
170–12 hades, or hell of *S·*,
190–15 When the *S·* is understood,
191– 8 The *S·* in John, sixth chapter
263– 5 These two words in *S·* suggest
287– 4 Hence the *S·* : "It is He — *Psal.* 100 : 3.
Man. 42–18 whereof the *S·* beareth testimony.
Ret. 91–10 or by the *S·* authors.
Pul. 13– 6 The *S·,* "Thou hast been — *Matt.* 25 : 23.
60–11 * with illustrative *S·* parallels,
'01. 12–11 the *S·,* "When the Son of — *Luke* 18 : 8.
My. 16–23 * *S·* reading, Isaiah 28 : 16, 17,
69–10 * marble plates with *S·* quotations
272– 5 the *S·,* "The law of — *Rom.* 6 : 2.
275– 7 hence the *S·,* "Be still, — *Psal.* 46 : 10.
364– 1 the *S·,* "Judge no man," — *John* 8 : 15.

scripture

My. 17–14 contained in the *s·,* — *I Pet.* 2 : 6.

Scripture-meanings

Mis. 169–11 With the understanding of *S·*,

Scriptures

accept the

Mis. 191–32 reject fables, and accept the *S·*

according to the

Mis. 71–23 According to the *S·*,
Man. 51–16 requirements according to the *S·*,
Rud. 4–20 According to the *S·* and C. S.,
'01. 5–20 We believe, according to the *S·*,
My. 130–17 I ask that according to the *S·*

apprehension of the

Mis. 363–32 spiritual apprehension of the *S·*,

are criticized

My. 179–15 the *S·* are criticized.

are the guide

Pul. 30–16 * *S·* are the guide to eternal Life ;

aver

Mis. 49–30 God is Truth, the *S·* aver ;

comments on the

Ret. 27– 1 wrote . . . comments on the *S·*,

declare

Mis. 46– 2 *S·* declare, "To whom ye — *Rom.* 6 : 16.
55–26 God is Spirit, as the *S·* declare,
63–20 as the *S·* declare.
183–32 *S·* declare reflects his Maker,
189–20 The *S·* declare Life to be
362–12 but the *S·* declare that
Un. 2– 1 The *S·* declare that God is
56– 3 suffered, as the *S·* declare,
Pul. 13–23 Here the *S·* declare that
'01. 7–11 made them . . . as the *S·* declare ;
7–17 even as the *S·* declare

declare

Hea. 3–24 The *S·* declare that
My. 155– 9 whom the *S·* declare.
271– 1 If, as the *S·* declare,

demand

'01. 10–28 This is what the *S·* demand

drawn from the

Mis. 93–11 conclusion drawn from the *S·*,

enjoin

Mis. 310–15 not unmindful that the *S·* enjoin,
Peo. 6–24 when the *S·* enjoin us to

explaining the

My. 59–15 * your words explaining the *S·*,

expositor of the

Pan. 12– 4 scholarly expositor of the *S·*,

found in the

Mis. 32–11 are to be found in the *S·*,
195–16 are not to be found in the *S·*.

fulfil the

Mis. 183–15 man can fulfil the *S·*

gave no

Ret. 37–16 *S·* gave no direct interpretation of

give the keynote

Mis. 366– 9 *S·* give the keynote of C. S.

glory of the

Mis. 92–29 power and glory of the *S·*,
Ret. 84–17 power and glory of the *S·*,

have declared

Hea. 8–19 God is what the *S·* have declared,

Hebrew

Un. 28– 1 We read in the Hebrew *S·*,

Holy

Mis. 132–24 refer you to the Holy *S·*,

imply

Mis. 45–25 what the *S·* imply Him to be,
49–28 as the *S·* imply Him to be,
Rud. 5– 4 If, as the *S·* imply,

inform us

Mis. 97–21 *S·* inform us that man
No. 28–25 The *S·* inform us that

inspired

Mis. 193– 1 Are the *S·* inspired?

interpolation of the

'01. 12–18 not an interpolation of the *S·*,

interpret the

Pul. 69–18 * we interpret the *S·* wholly from
My. 112– 9 denominations interpret the *S·*

Key to the

Mis. 20 19 "S. and H. with Key to the *S·*"
34–30 "S. and H. with Key to the *S·*,"
35–29 "S. and H. with Key to the *S·*,"
50– 5 "*S. and H. with Key to the S·*"
50 0 "S. and H. with Key to the *S·*"
54–14 "S. and H. with Key to the *S·*,"
64–15 "S. and H. with Key to the *S·*"
67–25 "S. and H. with Key to the *S·*,"
91–22 "*S. and H. with Key to the S·*,"
92–18 "S. and H. with Key to the *S·*,"
106–19 "S. and H. with Key to the *S·*,"
114–13 "S. and H. with Key to the *S·*,"
144–11 "S. and H. with Key to the *S·*,"
153–25 "S. and H. with Key to the *S·*,"
159– 3 "S. and H. with Key to the *S·*,"
214–20 "S. and H. with Key to the *S·*,"
248–14 'S. and H. with Key to the *S·*,'
274– 5 "S. and H. with Key to the *S·*,"
302– 4 "S. and H. with Key to the *S·*,"
302–30 "S. and H. with Key to the *S·*,"
309–25 "S. and H. with Key to the *S·*,"
313–27 "S. and H. with Key to the *S·*,"
314–16 "S. and H. with Key to the *S·*,"
314–23 "S. and H. with Key to the *S·*,"
315–31 "S. and H. with Key to the *S·*,"
318–17 "S. and H. with Key to the *S·*,"
322–12 "S. and H. with Key to the *S·*,"
364– 2 "S. and H. with Key to the *S·*,"
300– 2 "S. and H. with Key to the *S·*,"
371–29 "S. and H. with Key to the *S·*,"
383– 1 "S. and H. with Key to the *S·*,"
Man. 29–23 S. and H. with Key to the *S·*.
31–23 S. and H. with Key to the *S·*.
32– 4 S. and H. with Key to the *S·*.
32–12 S. and H. with Key to the *S·*,
34–11 S. and H. with Key to the *S·*,
36– 1 S. and H. with Key to the *S·*,
38– 4 S. and H. with Key to the *S·*,
42–14 S. and H. with Key to the *S·*,
56– 1 S. and H. with Key to the *S·*,
58– 6 S. and H. with Key to the *S·*,
64– 6 *S. and H. with Key to the S·*,
71–26 S. and H. with Key to the *S·*
83–23 S. and H. with Key to the *S·*
86–19 S. and H. with Key to the *S·*,
Ret. 37–19 Key to the *S·*, in S. and H.,

Scriptures

Key to the

Pul.	5–14	"S. and H. with Key to the S·,"
	7–25	"S. and H. with Key to the S·,"
	12– 2	"S. and H. with Key to the S·,"
	24–18	* "S. and H. with Key to the S· ;"
	25–28	* "S. and H. with Key to the S·''
	28–18	* "S. and H. with Key to the S·,"
	38–15	"Recapitulation." Key to the S·,
	43–18	* "S. and H. with Key to the S·,"
	45–26	* "S. and H. with Key to the S·."
	55–23	* "S. and H. with Key to the S·."
	58–26	* "S. and H. with Key to the S·."
	64– 2	* 'S. and H. with Key to the S·,'
	70– 8	* "S. and H. with Key to the S·,"
	86–25	* "S. and H. with Key to the S·,"
No.	3– 9	"S. and H. with Key to the S·,"
	42–23	"S. and H. with Key to the S·''
'00.	7– 1	"S. and H. with Key to the S·,"
	7–13	"S. and H. with Key to the S·."
'01.	11–14	"S. and H. with Key to the S·,"
My.	v–22	* "S. and H. with Key to the S· ;"
	17–18	* "S. and H. with Key to the S·"
	18–30	* "S. and H. with Key to the S·''
	34–16	* "S. and H. with Key to the S·."
	43–24	* "S. and H. with Key to the S·."
	48–10	* "S. and H. with Key to the S·."
	80–19	* "S. and H. with Key to the S·''
	103– 7	"S. and H. with Key to the S·,"
	110–31	"S. and H. with Key to the S·,"
	112–12	"S. and H. with Key to the S·"
	114–25	"S. and H. with Key to the S·."
	115– 5	"S. and H. with Key to the S·."
	130–27	"S. and H. with Key to the S·."
	136– 8	"S. and H. with Key to the S·."
	163–22	"S. and H. with Key to the S·."
	178–28	"S. and H. with Key to the S·."
	213–29	"S. and H. with Key to the S·''
	215– 7	"S. and H. with Key to the S·"
	217–24	"S. and H. with Key to the S·." :
	232–21	"S. and H. with Key to the S·,"
	238– 4	*"S. and H. with Key to the S·''
	239– 3	"S. and H. with Key to the S·"
	246–20	"S. and H. with Key to the S·,"
	266–24	"S. and H. with Key to the S·,"
	271– 5	"S. and H. with Key to the S·,"
	304–31	"S. and H. with Key to the S·,"
	305–16	"S. and H. with Key to the S·,"
	317– 7	* "S. and H. with Key to the S·."
	318– 8	"S. and H. with Key to the S·,"
	318–15	"S. and H. with Key to the S·,"
	320–11	* "S. and H. with Key to the S·''

learn from the
My. 151–23 We learn from the S· that the

love of the
'00. 7– 6 greater love of the S· manifested.

maintain
Mis. 27–15 since the S· maintain this fact

meaning of the
Mis. 25–14 original meaning of the S·,
Man. 87–17 higher meaning of the S·.
Un. 29–22 deep meaning of the S·
My. 241– 6 * higher meaning of the S·.

misinterprets the
My. 304–30 misinterprets the S· ;

notes on the
My. 114–15 began with notes on the S·.

not knowing the
Mis. 168–22 *not knowing the S·, — Matt.* 22 : 29.
219– 7 not knowing the S·, — Matt. 22 : 29.
No. 37– 5 not knowing the S·' — Matt. 22 : 29.

obey the
Mis. 90–16 in your measures, obey the S·,

older
Mis. 187–13 translators of the older S·

once refer
'01. 16–19 The S· once refer to an evil

plainly declare
Mis. 93– 8 S· plainly declare the allness
Pan. 5– 3 The S· plainly declare,

practise the
My. 238– 8 to read and to practise the S·,

prophetic
'00. 6–29 exegesis on the prophetic S·

Reader of the
Mis. 314–21 Reader of the S· shall name,

reading the
Mis. 159– 1 reading the S· and expounding
Man. 60– 8 reading the S· or the C. S. textbook.
72–10 reading the S· and the C. S. textbook

read the
Mis. 58–16 I may read the S· through a
314–12 shall read the S· indicated in

recorded in the
Mis. 199–14 miracles recorded in the S·

Scriptures

require
Mis. 196–30 The S· require more than a

sacred
Mis. 312–19 * verities of the sacred S·."

say
My. 233–16 S· say, "They have healed — *Jer.* 6 : 14.
358– 5 S· say, "Watch and pray, — *Matt.* 26 : 41.

Science of the
My. 239– 2 Science of the S· coexists with God ;
303– 6 Science of the S· relative to this

searching the
Pul. 28– 3 * searching the S· by the light of

search the
Mis. 214–19 My students need to search the S·
Ret. 24–23 to search the S·,
Pul. 34–25 * to pray, to search the S·.
My. 105– 2 stirred the people to search the S·

selections from the
Pul. 43–17 * Selections from the S· and from

sense of the
'00. 5–27 The spiritual sense of the S·
6–11 spiritual sense of the S·

speak
Mis. 180–29 S· speak of Jesus as the Son of God

studied the
Pul. 64–15 * studied the S· and the sciences,

study the
Man. 83–21 to study the S· and S. AND H.

synoptic
My. 179– 2 synoptic S·, as set forth in the

taught the
Man. 62–20 children shall be taught the S·,

teach
No. 37–21 S· teach an infinite God,

translation of the
Rud. 16–11 in their translation of the S·

translations of the
My. 238–11 the translations of the S·

truth in the
My. 179–20 and the truth in the S·,

truth of the
My. 299–12 the entire truth of the S·,

understanding of the
My. 28–30 * spiritual understanding of the S·,
180– 9 A spiritual understanding of the S·

warrant of the
My. 266– 5 under the warrant of the S· ;

whole of the
Mis. 317–15 compared with the whole of the S·

words of the
My. 206–18 words of the S· comfort you :

written in the
No. 42– 2 * all things written in the S·,

Mis.	26–28	The S· name God as good,
	59–19	The S· refer to God as saying,
	70– 1	else the S· misstate man's power.
	87–24	study thoroughly the S·
	169–14	She affirmed that the S·
	169–22	literal rendering of the S·
	186–13	in the S·, as in divine Science,
	194–12	not an interpolation of the S·,
	216– 5	as the S· give example.
	281–14	through a stray copy of the S·
	300– 4	in connection with the S·,
	308– 8	The S· and C. S. reveal
	315– 2	taken from the S· and S. and H.,
	315–30	study His revealed Word, the S·,
Man.	31–21	from the S·, and from S. AND H.
	32– 6	readings from the S· shall precede the
Ret.	25– 4	the S· had to me a new meaning,
	35–12	not interpolations of the S·,
No.	23–15	S· have both a literal and a moral
'00.	14– 8	of whatever is spoken of in the S·.
My.	32–15	* Reading from the S· :
	110–28	attempt to convict the S· of
	112–11	founded squarely . . . on the S·.
	112–24	not in accordance with the S·.
	205– 1	We read in the S· :
	216– 1	plainly set forth in the S·.
	279–10	obvious correspondence with the S·

scroll
Pul. 77– 4 s· of solid gold, suitably engraved,
77– 6 * Attached to the s· is a golden key
78– 4 * in the form of a gold s·,
78–21 * Attached . . . to the s· is a gold
78–25 * The s· is on exhibition in
My. 184–17 That rustic s· brought back to me

scrub-oak
Ret. 4–21 s·, poplar, and fern flourish.

scrupled
Mis. 139–25 whereof a few persons have since s· ;

scruples

Ret. 48– 6 conscientious *s·* about diplomas,

scrutinize

Ret. 73–22 to *s·* physical personality,

scrutiny

No. 41–15 is to subject them to severe *s·*.

sculptor (*see also* **sculptor's**)

Peo. 7–14 * With heaven's own light the *s·* shone,
My. 69–14 * hammer and chisel of the *s·*

sculptor-boy

Peo. 7– 8 * "Chisel in hand stood a *s·*,

sculptor's

Po. 2– 4 Much as the chisel of the *s·* art

sculptors

Peo. 7– 2 *s·*, working out our own ideals,
7–16 * "*S·* of life are we as we stand

sculpture

Mis. 270– 6 skill of the masters in *s·*, music,

sculptured

Pul. 39–21 * *s·* angels, on the gray church
Po. 73–18 No *s·* lie, Or hypocrite sigh,
My. 259– 2 sweetest *s·* face and form

scum

My. 301– 7 creed will pass off in *s·*,

sea

across the
My. 183–11 *Beloved Brethren across the S·* :
200–12 stretches across the *s·* and rises
259–12 To this church across the *s·*
angry
Mis. 397– 5 o'er earth's troubled, angry *s·*
Pul. 18–14 o'er earth's troubled, angry *s·*
Po. 12–14 o'er earth's troubled, angry *s·*
billowy
Po. 24– 9 From out life's billowy *s·*,
bottomless
My. 53– 3 * bottomless *s·* of corrections ;
bottom of the
Peo. 5–28 * sunk to the bottom of the *s·*,
dangerous
Mis. 385–11 is past The dangerous *s·*,
Po. 48– 3 is past The dangerous *s·*,
depth of the
Mis. 122–13 in the depth of the *s·*'' ? — *Matt.* 18 : 6.
fish of the
Mis. 69–12 over the fish of the *s·*, — *Gen.* 1 : 26.
69–32 over "the fish of the *s·*'' — *Gen.* 1 : 26.
fled to the
Po. 41–15 waters had fled to the *s·*,
islands of the
My. 279–26 and those islands of the *s·*
280– 6 and the islands of the *s·* have one
land and
My. 291–24 prosperity waves over land and *s·*,
land or
My. 127–27 indestructible on land or *s·* ;
like the
Mis. 384–19 * Love, like the *s·*,
Po. 36–18 * Love, like the *s·*,
moonlit
Po. 73– 3 O'er the moonlit *s·*,
no more
No. 27– 9 there will be no more *s·*.
My. 183–13 With you be there no more *s·*,
of heads
My. 59–14 * gazing across that *s·* of heads,
of repentance
'00. 15– 9 a tear-filled *s·* of repentance
of sin
Mis. 264– 5 of this seething *s·* of sin.
over
My. 204– 8 Over *s·* and over land,
race for the
Mis. 329–22 streams to race for the *s·*.
rock and the
Po. 68– 9 rock and the *s·* and the tall waving
rough
Pul. 6–26 and rode the rough *s·*.
sapphire
Pul. 40– 4 * Beyond the sapphire *s·*
surging
Pul. 13–17 They are in the surging *s·* of error,
troubled
'00. 7–22 the wave of earth's troubled *s·*,
'02. 19–19 heaving surf of life's troubled *s·*
unfathomable
Ret. 57– 3 unfathomable *s·* of possibilities.
upon the
My. 126– 8 "right foot upon the *s·*, — *Rev.* 10 : 2.

Ret. 20–17 as sunshine o'er the *s·*,
Pul. 12–13 earth and of the *s·* ! — *Rev.* 12 : 12.

sea

Pan. 3–25 * of which heaven, earth, *s·*,
My. 205–11 * He plants His footsteps in the *s·*
350–13 the struggler with the *s·*
356– 7 * "He plants His footsteps in the *s·*

sea-beaten

My. 295–18 The Bible is our *s·* rock.

seal

Mis. 184–24 as the *s·* of man's adoption.
269–29 opening of this silent mental *s·*,
381–21 under the *s·* of the said Court,
Pul. 28– 5 * panel containing the C. S. *s·*,
My. 22–18 * time has put its *s·* of affirmation
191–13 will *s·* your apostleship.
214–11 set the *s·* of eternity on time.
333– 1 * with the *s·* of the Grand Secretary,

sealed

Mis. 35– 6 *s·* that proof with the signet of
Pul. 52–24 * The Bible was a *s·* book.

sealing

My. 211–26 and *s·* his doom,

seals

Mis. 280– 4 at the opening of the *s·*,
358– 6 the only appropriate *s·* for C. S.
'02. 16–18 enigmatical *s·* of the angel,
My. 131–13 *s·* the covenant of everlasting love.
236–17 *s·* the question of unity,

seamen

Pan. 15– 2 murdering her peaceful *s·*

sea-mew's

Po. 73–13 The *s·* lone cry,

seamless

Pul. 54– 2 * healing of his *s·* dress
'01. 26–16 pinned to the *s·* robe,
My. 192– 7 ideal robe of Christ is *s·*.

seances

Mis. 171– 9 sit in back-to-back *s·*

sear

My. 3–10 *s·* leaves of faith without works,

search

Mis. 214–19 need to *s·* the Scriptures
327–12 *s·* for wealth and fame.
364–13 is not a *s·* after wisdom,
Ret. 14–25 "*S·* me, O God, — *Psal.* 139 : 23.
24–23 to *s·* the Scriptures, to find
Pul. 34–25 * to pray, to *s·* the Scriptures,
46– 3 * in *s·* of the truth as taught.
51–25 * will go there in *s·* of truth,
64–16 * a *s·* for the great curative
No. 21– 7 was not a *s·* after wisdom,
My. 60– 9 *S·* me, O God, — *Psal.* 139 : 23.
105– 2 the people to *s·* the Scriptures
332–20 * on repeated *s·* a roll of papers

searched

Mis. 292–27 *s·* the secret chambers of sense?

searching

Mis. 204– 4 Truth, *s·* the heart,
Pul. 28– 3 * *s·* the Scriptures by the light of
51– 9 * *s·* after religious truth.
73–20 * a careful and *s·* study
My. 122–18 Are we still *s·* diligently

searchings

My. 332–24 * After frequent *s·* and much

searing

My. 350–17 bitter *s·* to the core of love ;

seas

My. 33–30 founded it upon the *s·* — *Psal.* 24 : 2.
194–29 * stood the storm when *s·* were rough,
232– 3 sailing over rough *s·*

seaside

Ret. 91–28 hillside priest, this *s·* teacher,

season (*see also* **season's**)

Mis. 48–18 in *s·* to open the eyes of
117–25 and, sometimes out of *s·*,
160– 4 than ours at this *s·*.
264–19 directed, it acts for a *s·*.
308–23 only to reappear in due *s·*.
319–20 let the present *s·* pass
Man. 60–14 nor gifts at the Easter *s·*
'00. 5–23 the builders reject for a *s·* ;
9–11 a more convenient *s·* ;
'02. 4– 8 pray at this Communion *s·* for more
Hea. 4–15 become finite for a *s·* ;
My. 5–24 dedication and communion *s·*,
20–16 for her rich portion in due *s·*.
20–17 Send no gifts to her the ensuing *s·*,
25– 1 * the present Thanksgiving *s·* ;
27– 8 sacred *s·* of prayer and praise.
50–24 * a very inspiring *s·* to us all,

season
My. 141– 2 * chapter sub-title
141–17 * annual communion s· of the
141–27 no more communion s· in The
142–11 communion s· of The Mother Church.
142–14 The Mother Church communion s·
197–25 At this dedicatory s·
201– 5 Satan is unchained only for a s·,
256–20 At this happy s· the veil of time
312–17 * For a brief s· she taught school.''

season's
My. 121– 5 commotion of the s· holidays.

seasons
Mis. 384–18 * ''The s· come and go :
Man. 61–10 no more Communion s·.
Pul. 40– 3 * I wonder how the s· come and go
Po. 36–17 * ''The s· come and go :
My. 141–10 * to attend the communion s·
141–16 * its famous communion s·.
141–26 continue their communion s·,
166–18 lie concealed in the smooth s·
340– 5 usage of special days and s·

seat
Mis. 225–20 Mrs. Rawson then rose from her s·,
231–32 vacant s· at fireside and board
275–11 looks . . . at the vacant s·,
Ret. 15–18 not sufficient to s· the audience
Pul. 29–12 * every s· in the hall was filled
57– 6 * s· . . . fourteen and fifteen hundred,
58–16 * will s· over a thousand
'00. 13–22 ''where Satan's s· is.''— Rev. 2 : 13.
'02. 12–26 so as to s· the large number
My. 7–10 so as to s· the large number
7–17 * will s· four or five thousand
9– 4 * will s· four or five thousand
56– 3 * until every s· was filled
69–19 * view of the platform from any s·.
71–22 * s· . . . five thousand and twelve
71–23 * and s· them comfortably.
71–29 * auditorium that would s· five thousand
79–11 * s· of learning of America ;
342– 5 * after a kindly greeting took a s·

seated
Pul. 25–21 * s· with pews of curly birch,
31–24 * I was hardly more than s· before
Po. v–16 * she s· herself by the roadside
My. 31–15 * thousands had been s·,
54–30 * s· four hundred and sixty-four.
59–13 * S· in the gallery of that magnificent
71–24 * every person s· in the
78–29 * great room in which they were s·,
342– 2 * S· in the large parlor.
342–16 * When we were snugly s·

seating
Pul. 25– 8 * s· eleven hundred people
My. 8–20 * have a s· capacity of more than
24–29 * s· capacity of five thousand.
38–10 * when all s· space had been filled
53–13 * s· capacity of which place
55–25 * a s· capacity of six hundred
56– 1 * thought the s· capacity would be
57– 5 * would be of great s· capacity,
65– 9 * church edifice capable of s·
67–10 * S· capacity . . . 5,000
67–22 * exceeds it in s· capacity,
68–14 * s· capacity of twelve hundred,
77– 4 * s· capacity of over five thousand.
78– 1 * s· capacity of the temple
78–12 * The s· is accomplished in a
99–15 * s· five thousand people,
296–29 standing and s· capacity,

seats
Mis. 168–29 * go away unable to obtain s·.
270– 3 s· of them that sold — Matt. 21 : 12.
Man. 59–16 welcomes to her s· in the church,
59–19 not otherwise provided with s·.
59–22 give their s·, if necessary,
Pul. 26– 9 * with richly carved s·
27– 6 * vestry s· eight hundred people,
59–27 * s· were especially set apart
My. 31–27 * congregation had taken their s·,
38–10 * no confusion in finding s·,
38–18 * They filled all the s·
80–29 * s· in the main body of the church,
141–23 s· only five thousand people,
142– 6 * and then find no s· in

Seattle, Wash.
Pul. 90– 3 * Post-Intelligencer, S·, W·.

secluded
Pul. 73– 8 * s· herself from the world

seclusion
Mis. 136–14 necessity for my s·,
Pul. 73–11 * came from her s· one of the

Second
Man. 112– 3 must be written First, S·,

second
Mis. 2–26 s· death hath no power''— Rev. 20 : 6.
33–30 S· : It is more effectual than drugs ;
51–26 * starting fresh, as from a s· birth,
75–15 S· : Because Soul is a term for
94– 1 in the s·, you will reign
108–16 s· stage of human consciousness,
109–23 through the s· to the third stage,
142–15 my s·, a psalm ; my third, a letter.
144– 3 in the s· story of the tower
158–15 s· command, to drop the use of notes,
171– 4 rose to the occasion with the s·
188– 7 that which appears s·, material, and
204–12 S· : The baptism of the Holy Ghost
255–25 S· : It is more effectual than drugs,
279–22 s· picture is of the disciples
301–26 S· : It breaks the Golden Rule,
305–23 * S· : Of money with which to pay
318– 6 students of the s· generation.
332–23 s·, a false belief ;
341– 9 up the scale . . . to the s· rule,
350–14 s· P. M. convened in about one week
356–22 s· stage of mental development
Man. 43– 2 and a s· offense as aforesaid
52–18 s· offense shall dismiss a member
54–23 a s· similar offense shall remove
61–13 on the s· Sunday in January
Ret. 1–16 This s· Marion McNeil
6–11 my s· brother, Albert Baker,
20– 5 before my father's s· marriage,
20–21 My s· marriage was very unfortunate,
34–14 S· : It is more effectual than drugs.
40–22 my notices for a s· lecture
68– 3 s·, in the name of human concept,
70–20 The s· appearing of Jesus
88– 4 S· : Another command of the Christ,
Un. 3– 8 the s· death, of which we read
20– 8 S· : The Lord knows it.
20–13 S· : He knows it not.
30–16 The apostle refers to the s· Adam as
31–12 the s·, that matter is substance ;
41–14 the s· death has no power.
Pul. 48– 6 s· story of the house,
59–28 * at the s· dedicatory service.
74–14 'Am I the s· Christ?'
No. 19– 8 it is the sober s· thought of
Pan. 6– 3 s·, because evil and disease
'00. 6–29 as the year of the s· coming of
7–17 hath Christ a s· appearing?
7–23 we believe in the s· coming,
12– 6 In Revelation, s· chapter,
'01. 14–25 or it will control you in the s·.
My. 39– 2 * s· session was held at two o'clock
56–29 * s· and third being repetitions
126–12 s· is no longer a mystery or a
147– 1 chapter sub-title
179– 3 first and s· chapters of Genesis,
179– 5 the s· was an opposite story,
223–15 s·, which place I do not consider
246– 1 s· degree (C.S.D.) is given
303–27 a first or s· Virgin-mother
304–30 s·, she has stolen the contents
313–30 after my father's s· marriage
314– 2 Daniel Patterson, my s· husband,
323–30 * studying in the s· class
335–18 * This was the s· case of
353–12 the s· I entitled Sentinel,

secondary
Mis. 334– 5 but this place is s·.

Second Church
Man. 112– 2 as First Church, S· C·, etc.,

Second Church of Christ, Scientist
Chicago, Ill.
My. 191–26 chapter sub-title
Minneapolis, Minn.
My. 193–13 chapter sub-title
New York
My. 201–25 chapter sub-title
231–26 S· C· of C·, S·, NEW YORK

Man. 71– 3 S· C· of C·, S·, and so on,
My. 362–28 * signature

seconding
My. 8– 8 * Judge . . . Ewing in s· the motion,

Second Reader
My. 16–18 * Mrs. Ella E. Williams, S· R· ;
31–24 * S· R· Mrs. Laura Carey Conant,

Second Readers
Man. 32– 4 S· R· shall read the BIBLE texts.
99–27 appointed by the First and S· R·
My. 249–26 If both the First and S· R·

secret

Mis.	50– 7	*is there a s· back of*
	50–14	no additional s· outside of its
	133–16	thy Father which is in s· ; — *Matt.* 6 : 6.
	133–16	seeth in s· — *Matt.* 6 : 6.
	133–25	"seeth in s·," — *Matt.* 6 : 6.
	144–14	laid away as a sacred s·
	165–29	s· stores of wisdom
	177– 6	leagued together in s· conspiracy
	223– 3	into the s·" — *see Gen.* 49 : 6.
	250–23	unselfish deed done in s· ;
	277–16	falsehoods, and a s· mind-method,
	292–27	searched the s· chambers of sense
	323–14	masters their s· and open attacks
	339– 7	out of defeat comes the s· of
	350– 3	organized a s· society
	365–13	the s· of its success lies in
	389–19	sweet s· of the narrow way,
Ret.	15–27	who divulged their s· joy
	33–11	I found, . . . one pervading s· ;
	71–27	S· mental efforts to obtain help
	72– 7	portrays the result of s· faults,
Pul.	5– 9	holds in her s· chambers
	9–23	Christians rejoice in s·,
	83– 4	* In our s· heart our better self
No.	3–17	must pore over it in s·,
	18–10	the s· of its presence lies in the
	39–10	glorified God in s· prayer,
'00.	9– 8	s· of C. S. in right thinking
Po.	4–18	sweet s· of the narrow way,
My.	133–22	I have a s· to tell you
	133–24	then my sacred s· is incommunicable,
	134– 3	tell my long kept s·
	188–10	"the s· place of the— *Psal.* 91 : 1.
	211–32	induced by this s· evil influence
	244–15	The "s· place," — *Psal.* 91 : 1.
	261–23	involves an open s·,
	280– 2	God's open s· is seen through grace,

secretaries

My.	223– 8	not read by me or by my s·.
	231–16	to the waste-basket by her s·.

Secretary

My.	63– 8	* WILLIAM B. JOHNSON, S·.

secretary

Mis.	132–17	answers through my s·,
	157– 7	caused my s· to write,
My.	25–10	* from the report of the s·
	242–21	I have requested my s· not to
	358–21	Mr. Adam Dickey is my s·,

secretions

Mis.	243–29	s· of the gastric juice,

secretly

Mis.	114– 9	that these be not s· robbed,
	267–12	s· striving to injure me.
Ret.	71–18	He who s· manipulates mind

secrets

Mis.	202–29	relieve my heart of its s·,
	343–16	uncovering the s· of sin

sect

Mis.	150–26	appropriated by no s·.
	325– 5	of different s·, and of no sect ;
Un.	11–20	theologian of some bigoted s·,
Pul.	28–16	* from that of any other s·,
	47– 6	* official organ of this s·.
	64–26	* of the Founder of that s·,
	65– 6	* Boston s· of Christian Scientists,
	70–12	* founded a s· that has
No.	9–22	not the shibboleth of a s·
	14–20	more than any other religious s·,
'01.	33–28	one s· to persecute another
My.	84–23	* methods and tenets of the s·.
	89–11	* A s· that leaves such a monument
	92–17	* every other s· in the country
	94– 2	* every other s· will be left behind
	94–10	* consistent growth of the s·
	99– 3	* good things that this s· is doing.
	100– 6	* property of no poverty-stricken s·.
	100–12	* C. S. s· made its appearance
	148–27	opinions of a s· struggling to
	148–28	scourging the s· in advance of it.
	292–14	"Why did Christians of every s·
	303– 8	Catholics, or any other s·.
	316– 3	Truth divides between s· and Science
	328–20	* issued to the healers of this s·
	329– 5	* relieved the healers of this s· from

Section

2		
Mis.	272–12	* Public Statutes, Chapter 115, S· 2,
3		
My.	15– 3	* S· 3 of Article XLI
4		
Mis.	272– 4	* Act of 1874, Chapter 375, S· 4.

section

Ret.	82–12	locate permanently in one s·,
My.	84–15	* in that s· of the Back Bay.
	327–20	* s· of an act in the Legislature
	327–23	* The s· formerly read,
	328–23	* the s· of the machinery act
	328–26	* The s·, after enumerating

Section 1.

Article I.
Man.	25– 4	Names.

Article II.
Man.	29–20	Election.

Article III.
Man.	31– 4	Moral Obligations.

Article IV.
Man.	34– 4	Believe in C. S.

Article V.
Man.	35–10	Students of the College.

Article VI.
Man.	37–16	Pupils of Normal Students.

Article VII.
Man.	38–17	Members who once Withdrew.

Article VIII.
Man.	40– 4	A Rule for Motives and Acts.

Article IX.
Man.	49–19	A Legal Ceremony.

Article X.
Man.	50– 7	No Unauthorized Debating.

Article XI.
Man.	50–13	Departure from Tenets.

Article XII.
Man.	55–10	Probation.
	85– 9	provisions of Article XII, S· I,

Article XIII.
Man.	56–10	Annual Meetings.

Article XIV.
Man.	58– 4	Ordination.

Article XV.
Man.	58–20	Announcing Author's Name.

Article XVI.
Man.	59–15	The Leader's Welcome.

Article XVII.
Man.	60– 3	Continued Throughout the Year.

Article XVIII.
Man.	61– 8	No more Communion.

Article XIX.
Man.	61–18	Soloist and Organist.

Article XX.
Man.	62– 8	The Sunday School.

Article XXI.
Man.	63–14	Establishment.

Article XXII.
Man.	64–13	The Title of Mother Changed.

Article XXIII.
Man.	70–10	Local Self-government.

Article XXIV.
Man.	75– 3	Church Edifice a Testimonial.

Article XXV.
Man.	79–18	Board of Trustees.

Article XXVI.
Man.	83– 4	Motive in Teaching.

Article XXVII.
Man.	86– 3	Authorized to Teach.

Article XXVIII.
Man.	88– 4	Officers.

Article XXIX.
Man.	89–11	Normal Teachers.

Article XXX.
Man.	90– 8	Sessions.

Article XXXI.
Man.	93– 4	Election.

Article XXXII.
Man.	95– 3	From the Directors.

Article XXXIII.
Man.	97– 3	In The Mother Church.

Article XXXIV.
Man.	102– 3	Building Committee.

Article XXXV.
Man.	72– 3	See Article XXXV, S·. I.
	104– 3	For The Mother Church Only.

Sect. 2.

Article I.
Man.	25– 8	President.

Article II.
Man.	30– 1	Eligibility.

Article III.
Man.	31–15	First Readers' Duties.

Article IV.
Man.	34–17	Free from Other Denominations.

Article V.
Man.	35–17	Other Students.

Article VI.
Man.	36– 2	as provided in Article VI, S·. 2,
	37–22	Members of The Mother Church.

sections
  My. 73–27 * extra s· of trains are due
       74– 1 * western s· of this country.
       74– 4 * s· within two or three days' ride,
       82–26 * trains . . . in double s·.

sects
  Mis. 111–21 Christianity that is merely of s·,
       111–25 Catholic and Protestant s·.
       297–13 his lofty scorn of the s·,
       325– 5 believers of different s·,
  Man. 59–17 of all s· and denominations
  Pul. 21–21 our denomination and other s·,
        57–22 * several s· of mental healers,
  '00.   4– 1 has it not tainted the religious s·?
  '01.   2–17 feverish pride of s· and systems
        22–23 and the different religious s·
        23– 3 little left that the s· and faculties
        31– 3 only opposing element that s· or
  My.   40–15 * divided into warring s· ;
       148–27 power over contending s·

secular
  Mis. 38– 8 education, s· and religious,
       272–22 * for any s· purposes ;
  My. 135– 9 attended to my s· affairs,
       137–12 to my s· affairs, to my income,
       223–13 questions about s· affairs,

secure
  Ret.   5–28 * untiring in her efforts to s· the
  My.   12– 6 * to s· the large parcel of land
        63– 2 * to s· the services of Mr. Whitcomb
        80–29 * to s· seats in the main body of the
       245– 8 s· a thorough preparation of

secured
  My.   30–25 * collections s· by evangelists
        54–22 * Rooms were again s·.
        77–30 * s· by voluntary subscription.
        82–12 * s· express wagons enough to
       134–26 * "Permission has been s· from

securely
  Mis. 201–25 protect our dwellings more s·

secures
  Mis. 135–11 conquers . . . and s· success.
       252–28 s· the success of honesty.

securing
  Mis. 333–20 s· the sweet harmonies of
  Pul. 64– 5 * s· sufficient funds for the
  My.   75–15 * matter of s· accommodations.

security
  Mis. 227– 7 s· from slanderers

sedentary
  Mis. 329–20 challenging the s· shadows

sedulously
  Mis. 114–21 Scientists cannot watch too s·,

see
  Mis.   8–11 Can you s· an enemy,
        14– 5 where will you s· or feel evil,
        28– 3 Matter can neither s·, hear,
        34–16 s· them as they were before death,
        35–30 * S· the sixth edition.
        58–13 "Having eyes, s· ye not?" — Mark. 8 : 18.
        58–15 As matter, the eye cannot s· ;
        67–20 if you s· the danger menacing
        76– 5 shall never s· death." — John 8 : 51.
        81–10 Do we not s· in the commonly accepted
        81–18 or s· many of the people from
        81–20 hear this voice, or s· the dove,
        82–21 which finite mortals s·
        86–28 What mortals hear, s·, feel,

see
  Mis. 94– 5 s· himself and the hallucination of
        99–·4 "Having eyes ye s· not, — see Mark 8 : 18.
       109– 8 s· what, and how much, sin claims
       112–26 inability to s· one's own faults,
       117–15 We s· eye to eye and know as we
       129–20 s· somebody's faults to magnify
       135–28 You may be looking to s· me
       149–12 s· that nothing has been lost.
       156– 9 s· clearly the signs of Truth
       158–11 you s· we both had first to obey,
       168– 3 tell what things ye shall s·
       168–16 "Come and s·." — Rev. 6 : 1.
       170–29 as having any power to s·.
       170–29 Having eyes, ye s· not ;
       171–13 and s· what manner they are of.
       186– 5 we s· the material self-constituted
       186–19 we shall s· that man cannot
       194–17 we then s· the supremacy of Spirit
       197–13 let us s· what it is to believe.
       212–26 open his eyes to s· this error?
       218– 8 matter can neither s·, hear,
       233–32 we s· and feel disease only by
       240–25 If they s· their father with a cigarette
       241–27 you s·, it is easier to heal the physical
       244–20 the blind to s·, the deaf to hear,
       249– 3 to s· if C. S. could not obviate its
       277–32 I rebuke it wherever I s· it.
       280– 7 S· thou hurt not the holy things
       299–15 good which the material senses s· not
       299–16 evil which these senses s· not
       300–32 S· the revised edition of 1890,
       318–28 S· edition of 1909.
       321–27 I have no desire to s· or to
       324–18 tired of sin, can s· the Stranger.
       347–19 I s· the way now.
       352– 7 But it must first s· the error
       359–11 we s· through a glass, — I Cor. 13 : 12.
       367–24 He sees light, and cannot s· darkness.
       371– 5 opened his eyes to s· the need
       375–28 * to s· produced to-day that art
       378–20 cannot fail to s· that metaphysical
       379– 4 asked if I could s· his pennings
       379–32 S· S. and H., p. 47,
       385–19 Now s· thy ever-self ;
       392–23 Scenes that I would s· again.
       393–10 we s· Soon abandoned
       397– 6 I s· Christ walk,
  Man. 25–17 S· under "Deed of Trust"
        44–20 to s· that these periodicals are ably
        61– 1 (S· S. AND H., page 140.)
        64–25 S· also Article XXV, Sect. 7.
        72– 3 S· Article XXXV, Sect. I.
        78–15 (S· Article I, Sect. 6.)
        98–13 s· that it is published according to copy ;
       109–15 s· that names are legibly written,
       111–19 (s· Art. V, Sect. 4),
       112– 6 S· Article XXIII, Sect. 2.
  Ret. 14–27 s· if there be any wicked — Psal. 139 : 24.
        21– 9 came to s· me in Massachusetts.
        38–15 started for Lynn to s· me.
        40– 7 I asked permission to s· her.
        50–23 I s· clearly that students in C. S.
        64–16 shall never s· light. — Psal. 49 : 19.
        91–17 we s· Jesus ministering to the
  Un.   8– 6 What you s·, hear, feel, is a
        18– 4 Dwelling in light, I can s· only
        20–16 then s· if this Love does not
        20–21 He can s· nothing outside of
        22–10 to eat or be eaten, to s· or be seen,
        24–24 and is able to s·, taste, hear,
        34– 2 mortal mind says, "I cannot s· ;"
        34– 7 that mortal mind cannot s·
        36–11 Thus we s· that Spirit is Truth
        46– 5 We do not s· much of the real man
        49– 8 I s· it to be sinless,
  Pul. 18–15 I s· Christ walk,
        21– 7 to s· this love demonstrated.
        39–24 * I s· the hurrying throng
        39–25 * 'mid them all I only s· one face,
        44– 3 * At last you begin to s· the fruition
        85– 8 * s· and acknowledge it.
  Rud.   5–19 The body does not s·, hear,
         5–22 we could not s· materially ;
        10–14 matter cannot feel, s·, or
        16–11 I s· that some novices,
  No.   7–11 to s· every error they possess,
        12– 5 leading us to s· spirituality
        27– 6 get near enough to God to s· this,
        31–27 shall never s· death ;" — John 8 : 51.
  '00.   1– 2 s· your glad faces, aglow with
         5–14 I s· no other way under heaven
         9– 9 few, comparatively, s· it ;
        15–13 to s· through sin's disguise
        15–14 to s· that sin has no claim,
  '01.   11– 6 s· the Son of man in divine Science ;

see

'01.	12–23	we then *s·* the allness of Spirit,
	27– 5	* I look to *s·* some St. Paul arise
'02.	16–13	no man shall *s·* the— *Heb. 12 : 14.*
Hea.	6–20	whatever manifestation we *s·*.
	6–25	producing the effect we *s·*.
	11– 3	gladly waken to *s·* it was unreal.
	16– 8	*S·* to it, O Christian Scientists,
	16–20	They can neither *s·*, hear, feel,
Po.	12–15	I *s·* Christ walk,
	17– 3	rest till I *s·* My loved ones
	26–19	charter I have lived to *s·* Purged
	48–13	Now *s·* thy ever-self ;
	51– 5	Scenes that I would *s·* again.
	51–15	we *s·* Soon abandoned
	70– 8	the glory that eye cannot *s·*.
My.	26–20	trust that you will *s·*,
	33–11	*s·* if there be any wicked— *Psal.* 139 : 24.
	41–16	* So we *s·* that C. S.
	45–23	* as in retrospect we *s·* the
	71–25	* *s·* and hear the two Readers
	71–30	* each of whom could *s·* the Readers,
	79– 7	* those who seem to *s·* no good in
	93–20	* *s·* only its ridiculous phases,
	117– 3	went ye out for to *s·*?''— *Matt.* 11 : 8.
	117–16	But when may we *s·* you,
	118–12	you would not *s·* me,
	119–28	you would not *s·* me thus,
	122–31	refused to *s·* the power of Truth
	123–19	Ere long I will *s·* you in this hall,
	129– 1	*s·* if there be found anywhere a
	132–20	see God and live, *s·* good in good,
	138–15	persons whom I desire to *s·*
	146– 2	(*s·* page 177),
	149–26	could not *s·* London for its houses.
	150–16	*S·* therein the mirrored sky
	161–11	ye shall *s·* Abraham,— *Luke* 13 : 28.
	170– 4	that they might *s·* the Leader of C. S.
	180–19	refuses to *s·* this grand verity
	183–20	blind *s·* out of obscurity.
	189–18	to *s·* how soon earth's fables flee
	206–13	or believing that you *s·* an individual
	207–24	(*S·* S. and H., p. 227.)
	213–20	*s·* whether they lead you to God
	216–27	and *s·* the need of self-culture,
	216–30	I *s·* that you should begin now
	224– 1	*s·* or understand the importance of
	237–13	*S·* S. and H., page 442, line 30,
	239–14	*and s· their apparent identity*
	243–16	will *s·* that it is wise to remain
	256–22	and *s·* whence they came
	259– 1	will *s·* the sweetest sculptured face
	268–28	and you *s·* the heart of humanity
	268–29	you *s·* male and female one
	268–30	you *s·* the designation *man*
	268–31	you *s·* the whole universe included
	277– 6	I will say I can *s·* no other way
	297–22	we should *s·* him here
	300–19	shall never *s·* death.''— *John* 8 : 51.
	307–13	* ''I *s·* now what you mean,
	307–14	* and I *s·* that I am John,
	309–32	Let us *s·* what were the fruits
	310–28	* ''When do you ever *s·* Mary angry?''
	324–27	* he wanted to *s·* if there was one
	345– 1	*s·* that your mind is in such a state
	355– 2	to *s·* in her spiritualized thought
		(*see also* **God**)

seed

Mis.	26– 9	ponders the history of a *s·*,
	26–13	Whence came the first *s·*,
	83– 9	*springing from a s· of thought,*
	111–15	Leaving the *s·* of Truth
	121–12	believed to be the *s·* of the Church.
	144–26	As in the history of a *s·*,
	281–31	*s·* of the righteous shall— *Prov.* 11 : 21.
	338–29	* Shall be a fruitful *s·* ;
	356–16	*s·* of C. S., which when sown
Ret.	43– 4	From this *s·* grew the
Un.	6– 2	*s·* within itself,''— *see Gen.* 1 : 11.
'01.	33– 6	hand of love must sow the *s·*.
Po.	31– 3	celestial *s·* dropped from Love's
	79– 8	God able is To raise up *s·*
My.	177–18	* the *s·* of the Church ;''
	182–13	small sowing of the *s·* of Truth,
	222–11	a grain of mustard *s·*,— *Matt.* 17 : 20.
	273–12	nor his *s·* begging bread.''— *Psal.* 37 : 25.

seedling

Mis.	26–10	that his crops come from the *s·*
	343–24	until no *s·* be left to propagate
'00.	4– 1	This *s·* misnomer couples love and

seeds

Mis.	356–17	''the least of all *s·*,''— *Matt.* 13 : 32.
	357–13	*s·* of Truth fall by the wayside,
Rud.	9– 4	*s·* of discord and disease.
My.	182–14	seemed the least among *s·*,

seedtime

Mis.	332– 8	Its *s·* has come to enrich earth
	356–12	remember that the *s·* is passed,

seeing

Mis.	107–25	lack of *s·* one's deformed mentality,
	109–17	*s·* the need of somethingness
	225–18	* *s·*, I may be led to believe.''
	319– 8	not *s·* their own belief in sin,
	319– 8	*s·* too keenly their neighbor's.
	326–21	*S·* the wisdom of withdrawing
	336–15	*s·* clearly how to cast the mote of
Ret.	26–15	*s·* therein the operation of the
Un.	20– 2	by *s·* it in its proper light,
Pul.	79–14	* *s·* notices of C. S. meetings,
Rud.	5–21	this belief of *s·* with the eye,
Pan.	11– 3	*s·* that ye have put off— *Col.* 3 : 9.
'00.	9–10	or, *s·* it, shut their eyes
My.	105–24	*s·* her immediately restored by me
	119–20	*s·* your personal self,
	119–27	give you the opportunity of *s·*
	120–10	bliss of *s·* the risen Christ,
	123–27	*S·* that we have to attain to the
	169– 5	as simply *s·* Mother.
	171–10	I think you would enjoy *s·* it.
	206–12	*S·* a man in the moon,
	206–12	or *s·* a person in the picture of
	206–15	not *s·* the spiritual idea of God ;
	206–15	it is *s·* a human belief,
	322–28	* *S·* my great interest in the subject,

seek

Mis.	13–28	*S·* the Anglo-Saxon term for God,
	52– 1	refer to such as *s·* the material
	63–15	Jesus came to *s·* and to save
	124– 5	*s·* and cannot find God in matter,
	129–15	*s·* occasion to balloon an atom
	133–22	to *s·* the divine blessing
	138–11	Each student should *s·*
	178–11	*s·* those things which are— *Col.* 3 : 1.
	194– 5	Let us, then, *s·* this Science ;
	200–23	compels me to *s·* the remedy
	206–26	all who diligently *s·* God.
	215–10	not *s·* to climb up some other way,
	236–23	*s·* in divine Love the remedy
	270–11	To *s·* or employ other means
	270–14	''*S·* ye first the kingdom— *Matt.* 6 : 33.
	326–18	forced to *s·* the Father's house,
	342–24	*S·* Truth, and pursue it.
	344–19	would *s·* a correct conclusion.
	348– 7	It is not *mine* but *Thine* they *s·*.
	357– 5	Let them *s·* the lost sheep
	387–18	*S·* holy thoughts and heavenly
	393–20	Points the plane of power to *s·*.
	400–21	Thee I *s·*, Patient, meek,
Man.	94–11	he who goes to *s·* truth
Chr.	55–10	*s·* ye first the kingdom— *Matt* 6 : 33.
Ret.	31–12	*s·* diligently for the knowledge
	85–16	*S·* to occupy no position whereto
	90– 3	or *s·* to stand in God's stead.
Un.	5–10	to *s·* the divine Science of this
	62–23	*s·* ye the living among— *Luke* 24 : 5.
Pul.	67–14	* which *s·* to give expression
	81–16	* all those who *s·* the brightness
No.	3–22	*s·* not so much thine own as
	40– 4	mortals *s·*, and expect to receive,
'00.	14–11	*s·* thou the divine import of
'01.	1–22	you *s·* to define God to your
	30–12	to retaliate or to *s·* redress ;
'02.	11– 2	who *s·* for a better country
	17– 6	*s·* and obey what they love.
Po.	6–13	*S·* holy thoughts and heavenly
	8– 4	*s·* the loving rose,
	33– 6	*s·* for deliverance strong
	52– 4	Points the plane of power to *s·*.
	69– 9	Thee I *s·*, Patient, meek,
My.	34– 8	of them that *s·* him,— *Psal.* 24 : 6.
	34– 9	*s·* thy face, O Jacob.— *Psal.* 24 : 6.
	55–22	* obliged to *s·* other quarters,
	98–11	* critics who *s·* the light
	117–29	to *s·* the one divine Person,
	118–13	hence I *s·* to be
	149–12	*S·* these till you make
	163– 2	to *s·* the haven of hope,
	188–28	man will naturally *s·* the Science
	209– 4	those that *s·* and serve Him.
	261– 5	who *s·* wisdom of God,
	276–19	* no one should *s·* to dictate
	313–24	nor did . . . *s·* my advice.
	338–17	they *s·* a higher source
	341–15	* ''Tis peace not power I *s·*,
	345–27	They *s·* the finer essences.

seeker

Mis.	89–22	for I am a *s·* after *Truth.*
Ret.	52– 8	a home for every true *s·*
Pul.	6–23	*s·*, and servant of Truth,

seeker

'01. 19– 6 prayer brings the s· into
My. 4–22 s· and finder of C. S.
178– 2 do not mislead the s· after Truth.

seekers

Mis. 32–20 unfortunate s· after Truth
114– 2 value to all s· after Truth.
156– 3 number of earnest readers, and s·
317–17 by the most faithful s· ;
Man. 17– 2 earnest s· after Truth
Pul. 14–14 simple s· for Truth,
My. 40– 7 * s· everywhere may be satisfied.

seekest

My. 150– 4 if thou s· this guidance.

seeketh

Mis. 184–27 that s· not her own,
358–11 s· aught besides God,
'00. 14–19 that s· not only her own,
'01. 34–18 which s· not her own
My. 19–22 "s· not her own" — *I Cor.* 13 : 5.
150– 3 that which s· to save,

seeking

Mis. 171–16 s· out of the basis upon which
228–12 s· to raise those barren natures
245–26 s· to stereotype infinite Truth,
246–32 s· after practical truth
260–21 s· to dethrone Deity.
276–26 s· light from matter instead of
322–26 zealous affection for s· good,
324–27 s· peace but finding none.
335–31 s· power or good aside from God,
340– 8 s· no other pursuit
341–10 S· is not sufficient
353–32 world worship, pleasure s·,
389–20 S· and finding,
Ret. 2– 8 s· "freedom to worship
13–20 s· His guidance.
52– 3 s· to broaden its channels
Pul. 21– 8 s· and praying for it
38–28 * spirituality s· expression.
Po. 4–19 S· and finding,
My. vi– 3 * are earnestly s· Truth ;
130– 9 s· only public notoriety,
174–29 Thus s· and finding

Seeking and Finding

Mis. 373– 4 picture "S· and F·."

seeks

Mis. 53–17 s· what is below instead of
55–10 s· the proportions of good.
147–25 He s· no mask to cover him,
302– 5 s· again to "cast lots — *Matt.* 27 : 35.
324–21 s· to leave the odious company
325–13 patiently s· another dwelling,
326– 5 s· the dwelling-place of mortals
369–15 s· a wisdom that is higher
Man. 47– 2 s· to overcome evil with good.
Un. 15–24 who s· to do them mischief,
17– 2 s· to fasten all error upon
17–10 or s· so to do,
45–23 not the goal which Truth s·.
'01. 19– 7 thus he finds what he s·,
My. 153–23 s· personality for support,
349–32 s· cause in effect,

seem

Mis. 2–14 and the laborers s· few.
5–22 s· a miracle and a mystery
5–29 can s· solid substance to
9–16 friends s· to sweeten life's cup
32– 7 s· not to know in what manner they
61–30 Mortals s· very material,
112–12 s· to belong to the latter days,
121– 8 good and evil, s· to grapple,
136–12 verities of being s· to you as to me,
222–27 good should s· more natural than
234– 8 attempt to s· . . . a Christian.
273– 6 where I now s· to be most needed,
278–20 s· stronger to resist temptation
318–27 making sin s· either too large or
337–21 and thus s· to extinguish it.
396– 7 More sorrowful it scarce could s· ;
Man. 80–15 such reasons as . . . s· expedient.
Ret. 69–12 matter shall s· to have life
80– 4 yet it may s· severe.
Un. 17– 3 and so make the lie s· part of
45– 1 this lie shall s· truth]."
Rud. 11–11 s· to be disease, vice, and
No. 20– 9 it may s· distant or cold, until
20–18 Love must s· ever absent to
'00. 4–16 It should s· rational
'01. 31– 9 that now s· troublesome.
Hea. 11–11 though it may s· to the age like the
Po. 58–19 More sorrowful it scarce could s· ;
My. 15–28 * S· hungering and thirsting

seem

My. 47–24 * s· but a short time.
79– 7 * who s· to see no good in C. S.,
82–18 * It would s· that this ability
93– 7 * if their opinions s· visionary,
130–32 should s· reasonable.
159– 4 s· to me, and must s· to thee,
208– 4 s· as if the whole import of C. S.
262–24 s· a human mockery in mimicry
290– 4 and the tried and true s· few.
290–17 earthly joys s· most afar.
317–14 s· ambiguous to the reader.

seemed

Mis. 22–29 s· to fall by reason of its own
99–19 In no other one thing s·
142–22 A boat song s· more Olympian
163–16 In no one thing s· he less human
164–13 babe Jesus s· small to mortals ;
378–12 His treatment s· at first to
Ret. 23– 7 cloud of mortal mind s· to
26–13 s· to me supernatural.
Un. 59–20 to which he s· to conform :
62–19 The fleshly Jesus s· to die,
Pul. 20–14 s· type and shadow of the warfare
'00. 9–29 no one else has s· equal to
'01. 32–10 s· to shield the whole world
My. 56–15 * s· that there would be ample room
61– 7 * it s· impossible for the building to
61–23 * s· to move as by magic ;
63–19 * s· to say that all the world
182–14 s· the least among seeds,
307–11 that s· at first new to him.
311–14 s· to culminate at twelve years
320– 5 *He also s· very much pleased
320–12 * s· quite proud of his having had
321– 2 * He s· very proud to think that he
322–23 * s· inclined to banter me

seemeth

Mis. 260–20 whatever else s· to be intelligence

seeming

Mis. 30–26 s· mysticism surrounding realism
53–28 Its s· abstraction is the
57–22 or it would have no s·.
83–10 *explain this s· contradiction?*
107– 8 above the s· mists of sense,
298–22 the s· power of error,
'01. 2–11 a fair s· for right being,
'02. 20–18 thus breaking any s· connection
My. 21–15 * compensates for every s· trial

seemingly

Mis. 1–20 s· rolled up in shades,
Man. 110– 5 these s· strict conditions
Rud. 8–26 the health is s· restored,

seemliest

My. 89– 1 * one of the largest and s· in

seems

Mis. 4–18 periodical . . . . s· alone adequate to
7–19 so loaded with disease s· the very air.
15–26 goodness s· in embryo.
71–27 What s· to be of human origin
85–22 mind which s· to be matter
102–24 Whatever s· material,
102–25 s· thus only to the material senses,
108–20 wherein evil s· as real as good,
113– 6 when evil s· to predominate
145– 6 form of godliness s· as requisite
168–15 voice from heaven s· to say,
179–19 What is it that s· a stone
188–11 s· to be a war between the
198–29 whatever s· to punish man
204– 1 a mortal s· a monster,
222–15 because the false s· true.
222–26 whose power s· inexplicable,
234–26 s· to them still more inconceivable.
247–19 C. S. s· a mystery,
247–24 s·, to the common estimate, solid
260–24 evil is naught, although it s· to be.
289–11 s· to rest on this basis.
354–11 and sense s· sounder than
369–12 madness it s· to many onlookers.
372–17 * the artist s· quite familiar with
Ret. 32–17 * Whose most constant substance s·
33–13 s· to prove the Principle
81–29 s· to be requisite at every
94– 5 that whatsoever s· true,
94– 7 whatsoever s· to be good,
Un. 43– 3 s· too material for any
Pul. 45– 8 * s· impossible to mortal senses.
No. 32–23 It s· a great evil to belie
41–22 Church s· almost chagrined
Pan. 7–21 wherein theism s· meaningless,
'00. 13–26 * s· not to have been wholly
'01. 18–13 C. S. s· transcendental

seems

01.	33– 2	that to-day *s·* to be fading
'02.	1–15	*s·* calculated to displace
Hea.	10–16	when sorrow *s·* to come,
My.	13–13	Jerusalem *s·* to prefigure
	47– 3	* It *s·* meet at this time,
	69–28	* the dome *s·* to dominate
	177– 8	*s·* to be no special need of
	220–30	*s·* less divine,
	220–31	*s·* more divine to-day
	258– 6	*s·* illuminated for woman's hope
	261– 5	*s·* to have amply provided for
	281–19	* *s·* to offer an appropriate occasion
	290– 4	the near *s·* afar,

seen

Mis.	2–11	Adam legacy must first be *s·*,
	3–23	as *s·* in the truth of being,
	21–12	C. S. will be seen to
	23–25	God is *s·* only in that which
	36–10	ferocious mind *s·* in the beast
	43– 3	without even having *s·* the individual,
	57–14	*s·* when Truth, God, denounced it,
	60–30	it will be *s·* that material belief,
	62– 8	*s·* only in the true likeness
	66–20	things which are *s·*, — *II Cor.* 4 : 18.
	66–21	which are not *s·*." — *II Cor.* 4 : 18.
	82–12	what eye hath not *s·*.
	88–26	* had never *s·* water freeze."
	95– 4	* will be *s·* by what follows,
	97–25	we have not *s·* all of man ;
	97–27	I have not *s·* a perfect man
	104– 4	superior to that which was *s·*,
	107– 5	Its redemptive power is *s·*
	108–27	not be *s·* believing in,
	109–12	must be *s·* as a mistake,
	109–14	sins be *s·* and repented of,
	115–12	pitiable, and plain to be *s·*.
	125–15	whom, not having *s·*, we love.
	127– 4	I have *s·*, that in the ratio
	138–12	heard, and *s·* in me, — *Phil.* 4 : 9.
	133–13	may be *s·* of men. — *Matt.* 6 : 5.
	150–15	already *s·* the salvation of
	164– 8	*s·* more clearly until it
	165– 4	was *s·* that he had grown beyond
	166–28	*s·* as diffusing richest blessings.
	175–18	Thus it can be *s·* that the Science of
	182–21	no mortal hath *s·* the spiritual man,
	182–22	than he hath *s·* the Father.
	183– 6	the power of Truth must be *s·*
	187– 8	discord, as *s·* in disease and death,
	188–17	upon the basis of what is *s·*,
	195–17	divine logic, as *s·* in our text,
	205–19	eye hath not *s·* it,
	212– 9	had suffered, and *s·* their error.
	213–12	if *s·*, can be destroyed,
	219–13	beginning to be *s·* by thinkers,
	231– 5	had *s·* sunshine and shadow
	234–24	has *s·* far into the spiritual facts of
	278–12	and *s·* as my Father seeth them.
	280– 2	It is *s·* in C. S. that the
	286–29	Science of being is *s·*, understood,
	292–26	good, both *s·* and unseen ;
	299– 3	error that is *s·* aright as error,
	317– 1	students whom I have not *s·*
	317–25	*s·* in many instances their talents,
	325–22	and *s·* working for it !
	332– 1	Mind is *s·* kindling the stars,
	330– 9	His highest idea as *s·* to-day?
	355–29	rainbow *s·* from my window
	363–20	is *s·* the brightness of His coming.
	372–26	having *s·* the painter's masterpieces ;
	373– 9	I had never before *s·* it :
	375–25	* many times have I *s·* these
	390–19	As smiles through teardrops *s·*,
Chr.	55– 8	have *s·* a great light : — *Isa.* 9 : 2.
Ret.	37–24	*s·* in the following circumstances,
Un.	7– 9	clearly *s·* and most sensibly felt
	22–10	to see or be *s·*,
	28–11	not a spectre had ever been *s·*
	28–22	"eye hath not *s·*, — *I Cor.* 2 : 9.
	29–20	sense declares can never be *s·*
	34– 7	That matter is not *s·* ;
	34–24	Nothing would remain to be *s·*
	38–23	not *s·* in the mineral, vegetable, or
	51– 5	is neither *s·*, felt, heard, nor
	53– 9	here to be *s·* and demonstrated ;
	62– 6	"The things which are *s·* — *II Cor.* 4 : 18.
	62– 7	things which are not *s·* — *II Cor.* 4 : 18.
Pul.	13– 9	nothingness of error is *s·* ;
	30– 1	* *s·* members of their own families,
	32– 3	* so often *s·* in New England,
	33–23	* no one else had *s·* him,
	41–20	* all who wished had heard and *s·* ;
	72– 9	* was one of the first to be *s·*.
	73–18	* When *s·* yesterday she emphasized

seen

Pul.	80–12	* Mrs. Eddy we have never *s·* ;
Rud.	5–12	who has ever *s·* spiritual substance
No.	22–16	No man hath *s·* the person of good
	25–21	Mortals have not *s·* it.
	27–19	* "No man living hath yet *s·* man."
	27–24	Who living hath *s·* God
Pan.	1–16	hopeth for what he hath not *s·*,
'01.	5–26	nature of God must be *s·* in man,
	7–28	because thou hast *s·* — *John* 20 : 29.
	7–29	they that have not *s·*, — *John* 20 : 29.
	12– 9	would be *s·* in such company."
	13– 5	ought not to be *s·*, felt, or
	32–13	courage of their convictions was *s·*.
'02.	6–13	human woe is *s·* to obtain in
	19–14	repentance *s·* in a tear
Hea.	2– 8	never *s·* amid the smoke of battle.
	11– 5	*s·* wholly apart from the dream.
	19– 9	had *s·* that a vein had not been
Peo.	9–23	is *s·* to rise above physics,
Po.	55–20	smiles through teardrops *s·*,
My.	18– 1	I have *s·*, that in the ratio
	21– 7	* it will thus be *s·* that
	29–14	* have been *s·* in this country
	45–14	* have long prophetically *s·*
	69–31	* building and dome can be *s·*
	87–20	* I do not think I have ever *s·*
	103– 2	reluctantly *s·* and acknowledged.
	108– 8	in proportion as it is *s·* to act apart
	118–17	they that have not *s·*, — *John* 20 : 29.
	124–28	*s·* of men, and spiritually
	129–15	*s·* through the lens of Spirit,
	143–11	am *s·* daily by the members of my
	149–28	*s·* and forgotten in the same hour ;
	152–25	It will also be *s·* that this
	184– 5	neither hath the eye *s·*,
	270–30	C. S. will ultimately be *s·* to
	273–11	yet have I not *s·* the — *Psal.* 37 : 25.
	289– 2	God's open secret is *s·*
	309–12	I have *s·* only extracts,
	322– 3	* she had *s·* the manuscript.
	322–17	* I had *s·* you the day before
	342– 9	* often *s·* in reproductions,
	361– 0	I have not *s·* Mrs. Stetson

seer (*see also* seer's)

Mis.	1–13	The *s·* of this age should be
My.	307–20	he was quite a *s·* and understood

seer's

Pul.	4–16	is the *s·* declaration true,

seers

'01.	9– 9	so pure it made *s·* of men,

sees

Mis.	58–16	eye cannot . . . it is a belief that *s·*.
	92–10	He who *s·* most clearly
	173– 3	*s·* nothing but a law of matter.
	228–21	Whatever man *s·*, feels, or
	297– 2	one readily *s·* that this Science
	321– 7	*s·* the steady gain of Truth's idea
	325–28	*s·* robbers finding ready ingress
	361– 2	pure heart that *s·* God.
	367–24	and in the light He *s·* light,
	374–25	the other *s·* "Helen's beauty in a
Man.	96–10	where he *s·* there is special need,
Ret.	25–25	neither *s·*, hears, nor feels Spirit,
	76–26	*s·* each mortal in an impersonal
	80–24	He who *s·* the door and turns away
	84– 7	He who *s·* clearly and enlightens
Un.	18– 7	if He knows and *s·* it not ;
	25– 8	It *s·*, hears, feels, tastes, smells
	33–26	Mortal mind declares that matter *s·*
	33–27	or that mind *s·* by means of
	34– 4	Mortal mind admits that it *s·* only
	49–25	affirm it to be something which God *s·*
	60–27	material sense, which *s·* not God.
Pul.	15–12	one who *s·* the foe?
No.	31– 2	admit that God sends it or *s·* it.
'02.	2– 1	*s·* through the mist of mortal strife

seest

Hea.	8–16	* "What thou *s·*, that thou beest."

seeth

Mis.	133–16	Father which *s·* in secret — *Matt.* 6 : 6.
	133–25	Father which "*s·* in secret," — *Matt.* 6 : 6.
	213–26	he *s·* the wolf coming.
	278–13	seen as my Father *s·* them.
Pan.	1–15	what a man *s·* he hopeth not for,
My.	109–18	now mine eye . . . *s·* Thee." — *Job.* 42 : 5.

seething

Mis.	264– 5	midst of this *s·* sea of sin.
	338–11	in the midst of *s·* evil ;

seize

Mis.	319–29	*s·* them, trust the divine Providence,
	325–11	*s·* his pearls, throw them away,
My.	131–14	above the symbol *s·* the spirit,

seized
My. 11–19 * having s· upon this privilege and
277–22 if our nation's rights . . . were s·,
312–20 s· with yellow fever

seizure
My. 336–16 * s· of disease was so sudden

seldom
Mis. 75–16 this term should s· be employed
283–22 s· the case with loyal students,
283–31 s· calls on his teacher or musician to
316– 8 speak to my church . . . very s·.
Ret. 83– 7 s· benefited by the teachings of
Rud. 15– 3 s· that a student, if healed in a class,
'01. 6–21 its theory even s· named.
My. 79–13 * s· witnessed anywhere
147–26 be with you personally very s·.
160– 4 is s· alight with love.
215– 8 I s· taught without
249– 3 condemn persons s·, if ever.
264– 5 and this s·, until mankind learn more
313–19 but I s· took one.

select
Mis. 256–15 s· number of students.
Man. 30– 2 shall s· intelligible Readers
83– 9 shall carefully s· for pupils
My. 135–13 s· a Board of Trustees to
137–21 s· a Board of Trustees to
137–30 able to s· the Trustees I need
214– 1 s· one only to place on the walls

selected
Mis. 315–13 thirty-three students, carefully s·,
Man. 62– 4 any special hymn s· by the Board
84–21 assemble a s· number of them,
Ret. 90– 9 To these s· ones
Pul. 20–22 s· and observed in the East as the
55–17 * Afterward she s· the name C. S.
60–12 * s· for him from Mrs. Eddy's book.
My. 137–14 personally s· all my investments,
137–27 I s· said Trustees because I
312–27 The Free Masons s· my escort,

selecting
Man. 99–11 in s· this Committee,
My. 20–11 May I relieve you of s·,

selection
My. 137–29 to make this s·.

selections
Mis. 314–18 read all the s· from S. and H.
314–28 s· from both the Bible and the
315– 1 s· taken from the Scriptures and
Man. 31–19 Suitable S·.
31–21 s· from the SCRIPTURES, and from
Pul. 12– 1 following s· from ''S. and H.
28–24 * s· from Whittier and Lowell,
29–15 * s· from the Bible and from S. and H.
43–16 * S· from the Scriptures and from
My. 17–17 * reading of s· from ''S. and H.
80–18 * s· from ''S· and H.
214– 3 promiscuous s· would write your

Selections read on June 12, 1906
My. 39– 7 to 10 references from Bible and S. and H.

selects
Man. 81–26 Publishing Society of The . . . s·,

self (see also **self's**)
and matter
Mis. 343–12 sordid soil of s· and matter.
and sin
Ret. 79–21 victory over s· and sin.
another
Mis. 1–20 reveals another scene and another s·
better
Pul. 83– 4 * our better s· is shamed and
'01. 17– 7 departed from his better s·
My. 6– 7 To abide in our unselfed better s·
cleansed of
My. 265–25 cleansed of s· and permeated with
deification of
Rud. 17–10 rivalry, or the deification of s·.
deny
No. 2–11 taught his students to deny s·,
dissolving
Mis. 1–17 from the ashes of dissolving s·,
egotistic
Ret. 74– 7 corporeality, or egotistic s·.
evil in
Mis. 254–16 kill this evil in ''s·'' in order to
exterminate
'00. 8–21 We must exterminate s· before we
forget
Mis. 155– 7 Forget s· in laboring for mankind ;
forgetting
Mis. 107–12 forgetting s·, forgiving wrongs

self
higher
No. 36–15 Jesus had a resort to his higher s·
how to leave
Mis. 194–22 how to leave s·, the sense material,
human
Mis. 162–29 he must be oblivious of human s·.
My. 194–14 human s· lost in divine light,
ignorance of
My. 233–19 Ignorance of s· is the most stubborn
immortality's
My. 275–25 is immortality's s·.
inflate
Mis. 301–30 stop the ears of . . . and inflate s· ;
irrespective of
Mis. 357–21 love that is irrespective of s·,
is lost
My. 283–22 when s· is lost in Love
leaving
Peo. 9– 5 love leaving s· for God.
loses
'00. 3– 3 he loses s· in love,
love of
Un. 27– 9 a passionate love of s·,
mortal
Ret. 86– 9 the falsity of this mortal s· !
one's
Mis. 38– 7 support one's s· and a Cause?
108–18 namely, the knowledge of one's s·,
118–25 warfare with one's s· is grand ;
119–27 justly reserves to one's s·,
129– 6 first lesson is to learn one's s· ;
131– 5 The darkness in one's s· must
227–31 Not to avenge one's s· upon
283– 8 suit one's s· in the arrangement
287–28 makes one ruler over one's s·
Pan. 9–20 to help such a one is to help one's s·.
9–22 loves one's neighbor as one's s· ;
My. 122– 2 for one's s· and for the world
personal
My. 119–27 pastime of seeing your personal s·,
pride and
Mis. 92–32 divests himself of pride and s·,
Ret. 84–20 divests himself most of pride and s·,
real
Un. 55– 4 In his real s· he bore no infirmities.
renounced
Mis. 238–22 Have you renounced s·?
sacrifice
Mis. 155– 6 Sacrifice s· to bless one another,
'01. 35– 5 to sacrifice s· for the Cause
sceptre of
'00. 10–19 the sceptre of s· and pelf
scorn
Pul. 81–15 * scorn s· for the sake of love
selfish
Pul. 82–27 * Why should our selfish s·
sense and
Mis. 125– 9 his own sinful sense and s·.
silencing
Ret. 67–13 Silencing s·, alias rising above
sin, and
Mis. 328–17 burdened by pride, sin, and s·,
spiritual
Mis. 84–15 his spiritual s·, or Christ,
subordination of
My. 194–12 complete subordination of s·.
thine own
Mis. 226–15 * To thine own s· be true,
Ret. 81–24 * To thine own s· be true ;
this
Ret. 86– 8 be introduced to this s·.
Un. 45– 8 most of all to be rid of this s·,
victory over
Ret. 79–21 victory over s· and sin.
'01. 10–23 victory over s·, sin, disease,
was forgotten
'02. 13– 2 In this endeavor s· was forgotten,

Mis. 50–28 from s· to benevolence and love
299– 7 iens of C. S., not of ''s·,''
322–17 senses satisfied, or s· be justified.
My. 90–12 * for s· or dear ones.
160– 4 The heart that beats mostly for s·
283–19 When pride, s·, and human reason

self-abandonment
Ret. 91–30 humility, unworldliness, and s·

self-abnegation
Mis. 15–16 moments of s·, self-consecration,
100–13 meaning nor the magnitude of s·,
154–27 Strive for s·, justice, meekness,
298–21 absolute C. S., — s· and purity ;
Pul. 12–22 S·, by which we lay down all
My. 6–28 prefigures s·, hope, faith ;
81– 6 * so complete this s·,

self-adulation
    My. v–12 * mesmerism of personal pride and *s·*
self-aggrandizement
    Pul. 21–28 Popularity, *s·*, aught that can darken
    Rud. 17– 3 to convert from mere motives of *s·*
self-annihilated
    Mis. 2–25 he would be inevitably *s·*.
self-arrayed
    Ret. 67–10 finite was *s·* against the infinite,
self-asserting
    Mis. 281– 4 It is the *s·* mortal will-power
self-assertion
    Mis. 224– 4 feels hurt by another's *s·*.
    Pul. 32– 8 * to control, not by any crude *s·*,
self-assertive
    Mis. 268–30 *s·* error dies of its own elements.
self-conceit
    Mis. 78–17 *et cetera* of ignorance and *s·*
      265–32 compels the downfall of his *s·*.
      354–21 *s·*, ignorance, and pride
    Un. 27– 7 *Egotism* implies vanity and *s·*.
self-condemnation
    Mis. 112–26 loss of self-knowledge and of *s·*,
self-conscious
    Mis. 183–11 pleasures and pains of *s·* matter.
    Un. 46–23 equally identical and *s·*
      52–27 supposed modes of *s·* matter,
    Rud. 2– 2 * ''a living soul ; a· s· being ;
self-consecration
    Mis. 15–16 moments of self-abnegation, *s·*,
self-constituted
    Mis. 186– 5 material *s·* belief of the Jews
    Ret. 61–14 saith . . . you are a *s·* falsity,
self-contradictions
    '01. 25–29 Jesus likened such *s·* to
self-contradictory
    Un. 53–14 for being *s·*, it is also
    '01. 26–28 was problematic and *s·*.
    My. 113– 6 *s·*, or unprofitable to
self-control
    My. 161–14 who gains self-knowledge, *s·*,
self-created
    Mis. 76– 2 *s·* or derived capacity
      173–32 it must have been *s·*.
      217– 7 cause is the *s·* Principle,
      364–20 *s·* or evolves the universe.
    Ret. 67–23 but supposititiously *s·*.
    No. 20– 3 are neither *s·*, nor
self-creative
    Mis. 20–19 *s·*, and infinite Mind.
    Un. 45–26 is *o·* and self-sustained,
self-culture
    My. 216–27 and see the need of *s·*,
self-damnation
    My. 200–24 bottomless abyss of *s·*,
self-deceived
    Mis. 184–22 destroys his *s·* sense of power in
      319–15 they are *s·* sinners
self-deception
    Ret. 72– 8 presumptuous sins, and *s·*,
self-defence
    My. 288– 4 gives little thought to *s·* ;
self-defense
    '02. 16–22 opening not his mouth in *s·*
self-degradation
    Mis. 227–16 from their choice of *s·*
self-deification
    My. 302–20 I regard *s·* as blasphemous.
self-denial
    My. 121–24 *S·* is practical, and is not only
self-denials
    Mis. 107– 6 is seen in sore trials, *s·*,
self-destroyed
    Mis. 2–23 evil must be mortal and *s·*.
      104–20 must stand . . . until *s·*.
      209–12 demonstrates . . . when sin is *s·*.
      210– 3 evil, uncovered, is *s·*.
    No. 32– 8 must suffer, until it is *s·*.
    My. 269–30 The lie and the liar are *s·*.
self-destroying
    Un. 52–19 *s·* elements of this world,
      55–15 reveals the *s·* ways of error
    No. 10–16 matter, . . . is a *s·* error.
      26–18 would be annihilated, for evil is *s·*.
self-destruction
    My. 211–20 would induce their *s·*.

self-destructive
    Mis. 2–22 good dies not and evil is *s·*,
    Un. 53–15 self-contradictory, it is also *s·*.
    No. 18– 7 If Science . . . it would be *s·*,
self-distrust
    Rud. 17–11 could tell you of timidity, of *s·*,
self-evident
    Mis. 23–11 The answer is *s·*,
      26– 3 will be known as *s·* truth,
      46– 4 The leading *s·* proposition of
      49–31 Truth never created . . . is *s·* ;
      186–22 *s·* proof of immortality ;
      193– 7 *s·* demonstrable truth.
      269–19 These are *s·* propositions :
      346–19 *s·* proposition of C. S.,
    Ret. 31– 6 *s·* propositions of Truth
    Un. 25– 4 and dispute *s·* facts ;
    No. 4–15 *s·* proposition, in the Science
    Pan. 4–28 By admitting *s·* affirmations
    '00. 5– 7 corroborating this as *s·*.
    '01. 14–17 *s·* that error is not Truth ;
    Hea. 4–23 with such *s·* contradictions
      12– 6 *s·* it can do nothing,
    My. 111–30 valid, simple, real, and *s·*,
      143–17 It is *s·* that the discoverer of
      179–13 Testaments contain *s·* truths
      302– 8 *s·* fact is proof that mind
      349– 6 *s·* that matter, or the body,
self-examination
    Mis. 137–23 must give much time to *s·*
      154–27 spiritual observation and *s·*.
self-existence
    Pan. 8– 9 deny the *s·* of God?
self-existent
    Mis. 26–17 Was it *s·*?
      187–22 The *s·*, perfect, and eternal
      198–28 a belief in *s·* evil,
    Ret. 00– 3 as eternal, *s·* Mind ;
    Pan. 3–19 supreme, holy, *s·* God,
      4– 4 will of a *s·* divine Being,
      5– 8 or is evil *s·*,
      12–23 demonstrably the *s·* Life,
    '00. 5–12 God is *s·*, the essence
    '01. 3–13 * Supreme Being, *s·* and eternal.''
    Peo. 5–23 The ego is not *s·* matter
self-extinction
    '01. 5–18 leave all sin to God's fiat — *s·*,
self-extinguished
    Mis. 362–20 until *s·* by suffering !
self-forgetful
    Mis. 234–19 and, *s·*, should have gone on to
      250–24 the *s·* heart that overflows ;
      354– 6 *s·*, faithful Christian Scientists
    My. 247–29 *s·*, patient, unfaltering
self-forgetfulness
    Mis. 213– 4 flowed through cross-bearing, *s·*,
    Pul. 9–24 *S·*, purity, and love are treasures
self-glorification
    My. vii–13 * emotionalism which is largely *s·*
self-governed
    '01. 20– 5 Man is properly *s·*, and
    My. 247– 5 man governed by his creator is *s·*.
      254–26 man governed by his creator is *s·*.
self-government
    Mis. 240–24 Teach the children early *s·*,
      317– 7 demonstrate self-knowledge and *s·* ;
    Man. 70–10 Local *S·*.
      71–11 in its By-Laws and *s·*,
    Ret. 71–14 freedom of choice and *s·*.
    '00. 10–13 liberty, human rights, and *s·*
    '02. 3–13 *s·* under improved laws.
selfhood
    Mis. 104–20 must stand the friction of false *s·*
      183–24 Asserting a *s·* apart from God,
      333– 1 that sin — yea, *s·* — is apart from **God,**
      363– 4 ''ego'' that claims *s·* in error,
    Ret. 73–15 above physical personality, or *s·*
    Un. 6– 5 spotless *s·* of God
      6– 7 higher *s·*, derived from God,
      13– 9 God is harmony's *s·*.
      26– 2 having its own innate *s·*.
      39–14 That *s·* is false which opposes
      42–25 true sense of *s·* and Godhood ;
      46–14 taught no *s·* as existent in matter.
    No. 26–17 Man's real ego, or *s·*, is goodness.
      36–19 retreat from material to spiritual *s·*
    '01. 8–24 Christ was Jesus' spiritual *s·* ;
      9– 3 referring to his eternal spiritual *s·*
self-identification
    My. 83– 7 * buttons, for their own *s·*,

self-ignorance
Mis. 9– 3 pride, s·, self-will, self-love,
118–21 S·, self-will, self-righteousness,
self-immolated
Mis. 10–22 and their fear is s·.
self-immolation
Pul. 10– 1 It was our Master's s·,
'02. 17– 9 in blessing others, and s·
self-imposed
Mis. 122–30 his sufferings, s· ;
361– 4 through s· suffering,
self-inflicted
Mis. 209–27 suffering is s·, and good is the
Pul. 56–22 * mourn our s· pain.''
'01. 17– 1 s· sufferings of mortals
self-instruction
Man. 34–14 textbooks for s· in C. S.,
self-interest
Mis. 371–17 has s· in this mixing
self-interests
Mis. 291– 4 affinities, s·, or obligations,
selfish
Mis. 9–22 this cup of s· human enjoyment
118– 3 s· motives, and human policy.
262–28 s· in me sometimes to relieve my
288–23 The s· rôle of a martyr
Ret. 71–21 Sinister and s· motives entering
89–29 Corporeal and s· influence
Pul. 81–12 * call her "s·" because she
82–27 * Why should our s· self
'01. 29–12 s· in showing their love.
My. 121–12 never s·, stony, nor stormy,
selfishly
'02. 17– 5 S·, or otherwise, all are ready
selfishness
Mis. 211–21 Cowardice is s·.
237–20 inquiry, speculation, s· ;
240–22 appetites, pride, s·,
297–26 s·, unmercifulness, tyranny,
298–15 To build on s· is to build on sand.
343–16 cold, hard pebbles of s·,
No. 20–19 absent to ever-present s·
'00. 8–16 sensitiveness is sometimes s·,
'02. 17– 1 s·, worldliness, hatred,
Hea. 1–10 We have asked, in our s·,
Po. 33– 7 s·, sinfulness, dearth,
My. 229–14 and thus lose all s·,
self-justification
Mis. 9– 4 self-will, self-love, s·.
153–15 hatred, self-will, and s· ;
293–29 sensuality, ease, self-love, s·,
self-knowledge
Mis. 109–30 Watch and pray for s· ;
112–25 of s· and of self-condemnation,
317– 7 s· and self-government ;
355–12 First, s·.
358–14 S·, humility, and love
My. 161–14 He who gains s·, self-control,
selfless
Mis. 294– 7 With s· love, he inscribes on the
My. 41–31 * supports such s· devotion,
selflessness
Rud. 17–16 Meekness, s·, and love
self-love
Mis. 9– 4 self-will, s·, self-justification.
293–29 ease, s·, self-justification,
self-made
Pan. 5–10 Since evil is not s·,
self-mesmerism
My. 118– 6 s·, wherein the remedy is worse
self-oblivious
Mis. 172– 6 Intrepid, s· Protestants
My. 275–25 Intrepid, s· love fulfils the
self-preservation
My. 227–22 individual rights, s·,
self-proved
Un. 7–18 Certain s· propositions
self-renunciation
Mis. 185– 7 S· of all that constitutes
Ret. 28–17 Purity, s·, faith, and
30– 5 Ceaseless toil, s·, and love,
54– 5 It demands less cross-bearing, s·,
self-respect
Mis. 99– 8 temporary loss of his s·.
226– 9 losing his own s·?
self-respected
Mis. 227–21 calm, s· thoughts abide in

self-righteousness
Mis. 118–21 Self-ignorance, self-will, s·,
398– 7 Make s· be still,
Ret. 46–13 Make s· be still,
65– 6 lead to s· and bigotry,
Pul. 17–12 Make s· be still,
No. 40– 3 Because of vanity and s·,
'01. 14– 5 s· crucified Jesus.
Po. 14–11 Make s· be still,
My. 228–21 taints of s·, hypocrisy, envy,
334–23 s· crucified Jesus.''
self's
My. 133–15 free from s· sordid sequela ;
self-sacrifice
Mis. 143–28 sometimes at much s·,
358–27 Scientists who have grown to s·
No. 33–13 S· is the highway to heaven.
My. 28–11 * loving s·, of those who have
167– 2 especially for the s· it may have
298– 6 s·, etc., that has distinguished all my
self-sacrifices
My. 21– 3 * s· which have been made
self-sacrificing
Mis. 312– 5 s·, unutterably kind ;
No. v– 4 s· spirit of Love
self-same
Un. 3–27 this s· God is our helper.
Po. 10–16 ''Thou of the s· spirit,
My. 218–10 even the s· Lazarus.
314–23 letter from me to this s· husband,
337–17 ''Thou of the s· spirit,
self-satisfaction
Mis. 9–21 dreamy objects of s· ;
self-satisfied
Mis. 265–29 s·, unprincipled students.
My. 180–24 the disguised or the s· mind,
self-seeking
Mis. 288–24 nothing short of s· ;
'02. 18– 8 cowardice and s· of his disciples
My. 210–12 s· pride of the evil thinker
self-support
Ret. 20–11 had no training for s·,
My. 216–26 in the knowledge of s·,
312–17 * only one effort at s·.
self-surrender
Pan. 9–17 s·, and spiritual endeavor
self-sustained
Mis. 209–26 Joy is s· ;
316– 9 Mother Church must be s·
Un. 45–26 Mortal mind is self-creative and s·,
self-sustaining
My. 275–26 love . . . is s· and eternal.
self-testimony
Un. 33–19 s· of the physical senses is false.
self-will
Mis. 9– 4 s·, self-love, self-justification.
118– 3 false suggestions, s·, selfish motives,
118–21 Self-ignorance, s·, self-righteousness,
153–15 hatred, s·, and self-justification ;
162–25 worldliness, human pride, or s·,
224– 3 s· that makes another's deed
366–27 dishonesty, s·, envy, and lust.
'02. 16–27 pride, s·, envy, or hate.
My. 41–10 * arrogance, and s· are unmerciful,
sell
Mis. 113– 9 ''no man might buy or s·,— Rev. 13: 17.
140–11 No one could buy, s·, or mortgage
269–31 ''no man might buy or s·,— Rev. 13: 17.
299–25 s· them or loan them to you?
342–23 ''Go to them that s·,— see Matt. 25: 9.
Man. 43–22 shall neither buy, s·, nor
'02. 14– 4 can neither rent, mortgage, nor s·
15–18 I declined to s· them
sellers
Mis. 80– 1 s· of impure literature,
selleth
Mis. 252–32 he goeth and s· all that he hath
selling
Mis. 381–23 publishing, s·, giving away,
sells
Mis. 227– 1 s· himself in a traffic by which he
selves
Mis. 104–24 How shall we reach our true s·?
'01. 11– 9 saved, and that not of our s·,
semblance
Mis. 374–29 perceives a s· between the

semi-annual
  Man. 38–13 s˙ meetings held for this purpose.
  My. 121– 3 holding our s˙ church meetings,
semi-annually
  Man. 68–11 shall be paid s˙ at the rate of
  76–10 to have the books . . . audited s˙,
  80– 5 be paid over s˙ to the Treasurer
semi-circular
  My. 78–12 * s˙ sweep of mahogany pews
semi-individuality
  My. 211–30 victim is in a state of s˙,
seminaries
  My. 266–12 decrease of students in the s˙
send
  Mis. 27–18 "Doth a fountain s˙ forth— *Jas.* 3 : 11.
  41– 1 that only the cruel and evil can s˙
  69–27 I will s˙ his address to any one
  129–17 s˙ it into the atmosphere of mortal
  142–23 So I s˙ my answer in a
  149–20 to s˙ him to aid me.
  155–21 s˙ them to the editors of *The*
  156– 7 s˙ in your contributions as usual
  159– 6 then s˙ it to Rev. Mr. Norcross,
  214– 5 that I am come to s˙ peace— *Matt.* 10 : 34.
  214– 5 I came not to s˙ peace, — *Matt.* 10 : 34.
  227–20 the sweeter the odor they s˙ forth
  256–18 s˙ to each applicant a notice
  273–20 s˙ out students from these sources of
  305–27 * s˙ with the amount the name of
  306– 2 * s˙ fullest historical description.
  310–21 s˙ in their petitions to this effect
  313–21 to s˙ forth more laborers
  Man. 37–10 shall s˙ to the applicant a notice
  55– 2 nor s˙ notices to The Mother Church,
  100– 3 s˙ to the First Reader of the church
  100– 6 Or if she shall s˙ a special request
  Pul. 14–18 What if the old dragon should s˙ forth
  44– 6 * I s˙ my hearty congratulations.
  52– 2 * treasurer has to s˙ out word
  73– 3 * will s˙ to us those who have faith,
  '00. 10–30 s˙ me some of his hard-earned money
  '01. 31–10 "I came not to s˙ peace— *Matt.* 10 : 34.
  Po. 16–16 voice of the night-bird must here s˙
  24–21 S˙ us thy white-winged dove.
  31– 1 S˙ to the loyal struggler
  My. 8–26 * s˙ our greeting to you,
  20–12 S˙ her only what God gives
  20–16 S˙ no gifts to her
  23– 4 * what amount each shall s˙
  23–20 * s˙ their loyal and loving greetings
  27–15 * requested to s˙ no more money
  53– 6 * to s˙ forth her book
  59–26 * "S˙ those who say
  62–20 * s˙ you loving greetings
  72–15 * do not s˙ us any more money
  98–16 * requested to s˙ no more money
  153– 3 s˙ these floral offerings
  154– 7 to s˙ flowers to this little hall
  154– 0 S˙ flowers and all things fair
  159– 7 I s˙ to you the throbbing of
  167–23 s˙ forth a pæan of praise
  197–26 I s˙ loving congratulations,
  215–27 s˙ forth his students
  250–12 s˙ to the Editor of our periodicals
  253–23 I s˙ with this a store of wisdom
  256– 0 I beg to s˙ to you all a
  256–12 to s˙ to your Leader.
  257–26 and s˙ you my Christmas gift,
  264–10 * s˙ through the *Globe* to the people
  289–25 s˙ a few words of condolence,
  291–29 s˙ her more laborers,
  300–23 s˙ out students according to
  326–12 I s˙ for publication in our
  358–13 to read all that you s˙ to me,
  358–18 thank you for the money you s˙
  362–18 * s˙ you their loving greetings.
sending
  Mis. 135–16 S˙ forth currents of Truth,
  368–15 s˙ forth a poison more deadly
  Man. 67–19 s˙ gifts, congratulatory despatches
  98–15 s˙ a copy to the Clerk
  109–16 s˙ them to the Clerk
  My. 152–31 s˙ to you weekly flowers
  244– 2 my purpose in s˙ for you,
  269–22 s˙ forth their rays of reality
sends
  Mis. 18–31 to believe that aught that God s˙
  340–11 which s˙ forth a barrister
  Man. 82– 2 books and literature it s˙ forth.
  Ret. 56–22 The sun s˙ forth light,
  Pul. 12–21 Love s˙ forth her primal and
  Rud. 8– 5 Spirit s˙ forth its own harmless
  No. 31– 2 if you admit that God s˙ it

sends
  My. 155–29 Leader's love, which she s˙ to them
  249–12 s˙ forth a mental miasma
  274–17 * chapter sub-title
senior
  Mis. 235–25 superstitions of a s˙ period.
sensation
  and consciousness
  Mis. 228–23 perception, s˙, and consciousness
  360–23 spiritual s˙ and consciousness.
  and life
  Mis. 53– 1 false claim of s˙ and life
  belief of
  Mis. 93–19 belief of s˙ in matter :
  bodily
  My. 110–19 if waking to bodily s˙ is real
  110–20 if bodily s˙ makes us captives?
  diseased
  My. 106–19 the evidence of diseased s˙.
  false
  Mis. 73–20 subjective states of false s˙
  has no
  Mis. 44–19 for matter has no s˙.
  having no
  Mis. 28– 3 having no s˙ of its own.
  is not in matter
  Mis. 233–31 learn that s˙ is not in matter,
  life, nor
  Ret. 69–20 has no intelligence, life, nor s˙,
  material
  Mis. 198– 6 so-called laws and material s˙,
  331–29 their dream of material s˙,
  No. 4– 8 material s˙ and mental delusion.
  Mind nor
  Un. 50–17 matter has neither Mind nor s˙.
  no
  Ret. 61–22 for matter has no s˙
  No. 19–17 and feel no s˙ of divine Love,
  of mind
  My. 228– 4 so-called disease is a s˙ of mind,
  pains of
  Pan. 1–13 pleasures and pains of s˙
  physical
  Mis. 123–31 far apart from physical s˙
  205–27 material life or physical s˙,
  produced a
  Pul. 51–17 * produced a s˙ in religious circles,
  real
  Mis. 72–26 Real s˙ is not material ;

  Mis. 51–15 declaration . . . that s˙ belongs to
  Rud. 7–19 Matter, . . . has neither s˙ nor
  No. 5–10 the belief that matter has s˙
sensationless
  Rud. 5–10 Matter is inert, inanimate, and s˙,
sensations
  Mis. 44–22 or that mind is . . . reporting s˙,
  86–18 pleasant s˙ of human belief,
sense
  accepted
  No. 31–24 in the generally accepted s˙,
  all
  Mis. 78– 4 all s˙ of sin, sickness, and death,
  286–28 shut out all s˙ of other claims.
  Un. 1–19 they lose all s˙ of error.
  32–12 destroys all s˙ of matter
  No. 30– 3 destroying all s˙ of sin and death.
  Pan. 11–25 destroys all s˙ of evil,
  My. 364–11 all s˙ of the realism
  and power
  Mis. 293–12 the s˙ and power of Truth
  and self
  Mis. 125– 9 over his own sinful s˙ and self.
  and sin
  Mis. 172– 8 defeat the claims of s˙ and sin,
  and Soul
  Mis. 102–28 conflict between s˙ and Soul.
  No. 12–25 both s˙ and Soul, man and Life,
  anthropomorphic
  '01. 6–24 in the corporeal or anthropomorphic s˙.
  any
  Rud. 12–25 from any s˙ of subordination to
  arbitrary
  My. 49– 6 * and control, in no arbitrary s˙,
  awakened
  My. 155–20 awakened s˙ of the risen Christ.
  barriers of
  No. 28– 5 will burst the barriers of s˙,
  best
  My. 46– 8 * In the best s˙ it stands in prophetic
  bitter
  My. 267–23 with a bitter s˙ of lost opportunities
  bitter to
  My. 252– 5 sweet things which, if bitter to s˙,

sense

boastful
Un. 11–13   boastful *s·* of physical law
captive
My. 133–15   set the captive *s·* free
certain
Mis. 80–24   In a certain *s·*, we should
Pul. 13–13   sweet and certain *s·* that God
chambers of
Mis. 292–28   searched the secret chambers of *s·*
chastened
Ret. 31–27   spoke to my chastened *s·*
Christian Scientist's
'01. 5– 6   Christian Scientist's *s·* of Person
common
Mis. 105–13   no conflict with Life or common *s·*,
    105–16   the too common *s·* of its opposites
    285–27   common *s·*, and common honesty,
No. 2– 5   scorned by people of common *s·*.
My. 93–22   * saneness and common *s·* which underlie
complete
Mis. 75–17   can be used and make complete *s·*.
corporeal
Mis. 205–15   last scene in corporeal *s·*.
    308–29   invisible to corporeal *s·*.
darkling
Po. 79–10   darkling *s·*, arise, go hence !
deluded
Mis. 107–21   deluded *s·* must first be shown its
'01. 15–19   waken such a one from his deluded *s·* ;
    15–19   for all sin is a deluded *s·*,
delusion of
My. 5– 8   this illusion and delusion of *s·*,
discords of
Mis. 202– 3   to correct the discords of *s·*,
divine
Un. 21–21   or a divine *s·* of being.
'02. 6–17   lets in the divine *s·* of being,
diviner
Mis. 385–17   diviner *s·*, that spurns such toys,
Ret. 81–10   diviner *s·* of liberty and light.
Un. 4–12   diviner *s·* that God is all
Peo. 5–19   diviner *s·* of Life and Love,
Po. 48–11   diviner *s·*, that spurns such toys,
doubtful
My. 260–15   doubtful *s·* that falls short of
dream of
Mis. 176– 1   truth that breaks the dream of *s·*,
dyspepsia of
My. 230–9   silences the dyspepsia of *s·*.
enlarged
Mis. 193–26   this enlarged *s·* of the spirit
    282– 3   an enlarged *s·* of Deity.
enlightened
Mis. 173– 3   most enlightened *s·* herein sees
My. 283–27   enlightened *s·* of God's government.
escape from
Mis. 85–28   to escape from *s·* into the
every
Mis. 187– 5   above every *s·* of matter,
Ret. 61–24   If you rule out every *s·* of disease
Pul. 37–12   * In every *s·* she is the recognized
evil
Mis. 219–28   if he can change this evil *s·*
    332–19   an evil *s·* that blinded the eyes of
exaggerating
Mis. 112–27   an exaggerating *s·* of other people's.
ex-common
Mis. 112– 7   microbes, X-rays, and ex-common *s·*,
fallibility of
Ret. 60–30   arises from the fallibility of *s·*,
false
Mis. 9–30   false *s·* of what constitutes
    42–26   we drop our false *s·* of Life
    57–23   false *s·* and error of creation
    73– 9   separates the false *s·* from the true,
    74– 4   subdues not only the false *s·*
    76–24   an error or false *s·* of mentality
    175– 6   likened to the false *s·* of life,
    175– 9   Science changes this false *s·*,
    182– 9   lose their false *s·* of existence,
    189–17   presents a false *s·* of existence,
    190– 5   Mind as dispelling a false *s·*
    209–20   destroy the peace of a false *s·*.
    222– 2   gives him a false *s·* of both
    276–21   When a false *s·* suffers,
    351–28   punishes the joys of this false *s·*
Ret. 21–19   false *s·* of life and happiness,
    21–21   awakening from a false *s·* of life,
    69–15   transient, false *s·* of an existence
    74– 6   from the false *s·* of corporeality,
Un. 38–18   idolatrous and false *s·* of life
    42–25   Science, dispelling a false *s·*
    55–14   from the false *s·* of the flesh
    58– 1   false *s·* of life and happiness.
    60–27   false *s·* of substance must yield

sense

false
Un. 62–16   false *s·* of Life and good.
No. 28– 2   How long this false *s·* remains
    29– 5   a false *s·* of Soul and body.
    30– 4   does more than forgive the false *s·*
    37–25   buried in a false *s·* of being.
    39–13   false *s·* of Life, Love, and Truth,
'02. 18–18   It is a false *s·* of love
My. 119–23   Truth, which destroys the false *s·*
    233–26   [his false *s·* of life]
famine of
My. 263– 7   a feast of Soul and a famine of *s·*.
feeble
Mis. 172–19   presents but a finite, feeble *s·*
finite
Un. 4– 2   finite *s·* of sin, sickness, or death,
'01. 26– 7   only a finite *s·* of the infinite :
Hea. 4–11   to possess our finite *s·*,
    5– 1   our own erring finite *s·* of God,
Peo. 2– 5   As the finite *s·* of Deity, based on
fleeting
Mis. 9–26   failure . . . to relish this fleeting *s·*,
fogs of
Mis. 374–11   Above the fogs of *s·*
following
Mis. 376– 4   * *most authentic* in the following *s·* :
frightened
Un. 5–12   undisturbed by the frightened *s·* of
fuller
Mis. 320– 7   Christ's appearing in a fuller *s·*
fullest
Mis. 223–21   name of Christ in its fullest *s·*,
    303–11   brethren in the fullest *s·*
good
Mis. 219–29   good *s·*, or conscious goodness,
grateful a
Mis. 273– 9   so grateful a *s·* of my labors
gratified by
My. 117– 6   A personal motive gratified by *s·*
higher
Mis. 16–18   we must entertain a higher *s·* of
    84–29   to a new and higher *s·* thereof,
    111–12   higher *s·* of the true idea.
    113–12   not gaining a higher *s·* of Truth
    172– 7   a higher *s·* than ever before,
    195–29   higher *s·* of Christianity.
    292–12   higher *s·* I entertain of Love,
Un. 2–13   gains a higher *s·* of God,
    5–17   unfold in us a higher *s·* of Deity ;
Peo. 13–22   to a higher *s·* of Life.
    14–16   higher *s·* of omnipotence ;
highest
Un. 61–17   Our highest *s·* of infinite good
Rud. 9– 4   not a Christian, in the highest *s·*,
My. 244–21   In the highest *s·* of a disciple,
human
    (see **human**)
illuminated
Mis. 75–26   It was evidently an illuminated *s·*
immature
Mis. 87– 6   immature *s·* of spiritual things,
immortal
Mis. 74–15   immortal *s·* of the ideal world.
Un. 52–13   Christ's immortal *s·* of Truth,
imperfect
Rud. 16– 8   an imperfect *s·* of the spiritual
increasing
My. 174–26   An increasing *s·* of God's love,
inspired
Mis. 187–15   not lifted to the inspired *s·* of the
instead of soul
Un. 29–23   reading *s·* instead of *soul*,
lingering
'02. 3– 8   any lingering *s·* of the North's
literal
'01. 3–15   literal *s·* of the lexicons :
lively
Ret. 5–29   * lively *s·* of the parental obligation,
lost
Mis. 185– 1   lost *s·* of man in unity with,
    186–31   the lost *s·* of man's perfection,
    190–26   the lost *s·*, must yield to the right
No. 10–17   Truth restores that lost *s·*,
lower
Mis. 102– 9   In this limited and lower *s·*
Un. 30– 9   Hence this lower *s·* sins and suffers,
make
My. 226– 3   only where you can . . . make *s·*.
material
    (see **material**)
may say
Rud. 8–22   *s·* may say the unchristian
mental
Un. 9– 2   the mental *s·* of the disease,

sense

mistaken
My. 357– 8   only incentive of a mistaken *s·*
mists of
Mis. 107– 9   above the seeming mists of *s·*,
modern
Ret. 89– 6   modern *s·* of the term.
moral
Mis. 223–11   I respect that moral *s·* which
269– 5   commits his moral *s·* to a dungeon.
352–30   moral *s·* be aroused to reject the
No. 23–17   moral *s·* of the word *devil*,
My. 249– 2   without harming . . . your own moral *s·*,
mortal
        (*see* **mortal**)
mortal mind
Mis. 254–22   *Per contra*, it is the mortal mind *s·*
mounting
Mis. 1–16   The mounting *s·* gathers fresh forms
my
Mis. ix– 2   suits my *s·* of doing good.
24–12   healing Truth dawned upon my *s·* ;
86–14   My *s·* of the beauty of the universe is,
96–21   It brings to my *s·*,
97–25   To my *s·*, we have not seen all of
373– 5   my *s·* of Soul's expression
392–21   To my *s·* a sweet refrain ;
Ret. 27–24   first broke upon my *s·*,
No. 15– 5   such a statement is
Pan. 3– 6   My *s·* of nature's rich glooms is,
'01. 6–29   is not my *s·* of Him.
10–15   enthrall my *s·* of the Godhead,
11–17   To my *s·* the Sermon on the Mount,
Po. 51– 3   To my *s·* a sweet refrain ;
My. 262–11   my *s·* of the eternal Christ, Truth,
266– 3   To my *s·*, the most imminent dangers
natural
Mis. 72–19   *disappear only to the natural s·*
new
My. 63–22   * new *s·* of the magnitude of C. S.,
new-born
Mis. 74– 3   new-born *s·* subdues not only the
no
Mis. 76–25   and matter has no *s·*.
112–18   He had no *s·* of his crime ;
198– 9   understanding that matter has no *s·* ;
Un. 21–19   no *s·* in matter ;
23–25   has no *s·* whereby to cognize
33– 3   (matter really having no *s·*)
'01. 22–27   receive no *s·* whatever of it.
My. 96– 8   * can in no *s·*, save one, be compared
objects of
Mis. 344– 9   disengage the soul from objects of *s·*,
Peo. 7–24   objects of *s·* called sickness and
of being
Mis. 47–17   which is the truer *s·* of being.
101–14   scientific *s·* of being which establishes
175– 1   whole *s·* of being is leavened
186–27   immortal and true *s·* of being.
Un. 21–21   or a divine *s·* of being.
40–18   not by a material *s·* of being.
43– 6   mortal *s·* of being is too finite for
No. 29– 4   and a deathless *s·* of being.
37–25   buried in a false *s·* of being.
'02. 6–17   lets in the divine *s·* of being,
My. 275–22   the true *s·* of being goes on.
of Christian Science
My. 147–17   enlightens the people's *s·* of C. S.
of death
Un. 2–21   awake from a *s·* of death
40–19   A *s·* of death is not requisite
of Deity
Mis. 282– 3   enlarged *s·* of Deity.
Un. 5–17   unfold in us a higher *s·* of Deity ;
Rud. 2–14   to retain the proper *s·* of Deity
2–19   enlarges our *s·* of Deity,
Peo. 2– 5   As the finite *s·* of Deity, based on
of discomfort
Mis. 219–20   a *s·* of discomfort in sin
of disease
Ret. 61–24   If you rule out every *s·* of disease
Rud. 12– 6   Wrong . . . strengthen the *s·* of disease,
of divine Love
Pul. 74–25   in the *s·* of divine Love
of error
Mis. 352–31   aroused to reject the *s·* of error ;
Un. 1–19   they lose all *s·* of error.
of evil
Mis. 332–18   A *s·* of evil is supposed to have
Un. 20–17   all hate and the *s·* of evil.
64–13   and the haunting *s·* of evil
No. 32–22   good destroys the *s·* of evil.
Pan. 11–25   destroys all *s·* of evil,
of existence
Mis. 82–26   mythical or mortal *s·* of existence
182– 9   lose their false *s·* of existence,

sense

of existence
Mis. 186–25   material *s·* of existence is not the
189–17   presents a false *s·* of existence,
189–23   not merely a *s·* of existence,
310– 8   the material *s·* of existence
Ret. 58– 7   not merely a *s·* of existence,
Un. 42–16   not merely a *s·* of existence,
No. 4– 9   But an erring *s·* of existence,
offspring of
My. 5– 5   offspring of *s·* the murderers of
of God
Mis. 186–26   spiritual *s·* of God and His
Un. 2–13   and gains a higher *s·* of God,
No. 12–25   so enlarges our *s·* of God
Hea. 5– 1   our own erring finite *s·* of God,
Peo. 3–22   This limited *s·* of God as good
of good
Mis. 222– 2   a man's proper *s·* of good,
341–18   to win the spiritual *s·* of good.
Un. 41– 8   a loss of the true *s·* of good,
of gratitude
Mis. 131–23   that loving *s·* of gratitude
of harmony
Un. 2–18   gain that spiritual *s·* of harmony
22– 3   in a *s·* of harmony and immortality,
24– 6   the supreme *s·* of harmony.
'00. 11– 4   the true *s·* of harmony,
of imperfection
Un. 4–11   destroys our *s·* of imperfection,
of its nullity
'01. 13–11   with such a *s·* of its nullity
of justice
Mis. 121–30   borrow their *s·* of justice from
of Life
Mis. 19–31   spiritual *s·* of Life and its
20– 1   *s·* of Life illumes our pathway
42–26   false *s·* of Life in sin
67–11   strike at the eternal *s·* of Life
67–12   thine own *s·* of Life shall be
70–15   in a spiritual *s·* of Life
84–28   from our lower *s·* of Life to a
84–31   a clearer and nearer *s·* of Life
189–19   a released *s·* of Life in God
194–27   *s·* of Life that knows no death,
Un. 2–22   to a *s·* of Life in Christ,
40–20   proper or true *s·* of Life,
40–25   Holding a material *s·* of Life,
41– 5   shuts out the real *s·* of Life,
62–16   death is a false *s·* of Life
No. 30–13   our false *s·* of Life,
Peo. 5–19   diviner *s·* of Life and Love,
13–22   to a higher *s·* of Life.
My. 191–16   human *s·* of Life and Love,
of life
Mis. 82–22   material *s·* of life, is put off,
84–21   Paul's *s·* of life in matter,
175– 6   likened to the false *s·* of life,
341–17   parting with a material *s·* of life
Ret. 21–19   from a material, false *s·* of life
21–21   awakening from a false *s·* of life,
Un. 38–14   A material *s·* of life robs God,
38–18   false *s·* of life is all that dies,
58– 1   false *s·* of life and happiness.
My. 178–14   true *s·* of life is lost to
233–26   [this false *s·* of life]
274– 1   true *s·* of life and of righteousness,
274– 6   a false material *s·* of life,
of love
Mis. 17– 4   opposed to the material *s·* of love ;
351–28   punishes . . . this false *s·* of love,
'02. 18–18   It is a false *s·* of love that,
My. 287–15   true *s·* of love for God,
of man
Mis. 57–24   *s·* of man and the universe
185– 1   lost *s·* of man in unity with,
185–19   spiritualization of our *s·* of man
Un. 30–18   spiritual *s·* of man as immortal
My. 118–24   not by the spiritual *s·* of man,
of matter
Mis. 74–13   Christ Jesus' *s·* of matter
187– 5   over and above every *s·* of matter,
Un. 32–12   destroys all *s·* of matter as substance
of might
Un. 42–17   a *s·* of might and ability to subdue
of mortality
Mis. 181–25   lose their *s·* of mortality
of music
My. 267–21   awaken . . . with a *s·* of music ;
of personality
Mis. 282– 4   *s·* of personality in God
of power
Mis. 184–23   self-deceived *s·* of power in evil.
Ret. 58– 8   *s·* of power that subdued matter
of religion
Pan. 3– 2   not at all the Christian *s·* of religion.

sense

of Science
Mis. 12–29   our *s·* of Science will be measured by
    174– 8   attach our *s·* of Science to
My. 212–25   destroys the true *s·* of Science,
of sickness
Un.   2–17   the sick lose their *s·* of sickness,
of sin
Mis.   78– 4   thus it destroys all *s·* of sin,
    107–16   (1) A proper *s·* of sin ;
    319– 7   If the *s·* of sin is too little,
Un.   2–12   The sinner loses his *s·* of sin,
    4– 2   our mortal, finite *s·* of sin,
    9– 3   Destroy the *s·* of sin,
    56–20   physicality and the *s·* of sin.
    62–15   Destroy this *s·* of sin,
No.   30– 3   destroying all *s·* of sin
’01.   13–25   *s·* of sin, and not a sinful soul,
    13–27   To lose the *s·* of sin we must first
    16– 5   poignant present *s·* of sin
    17– 3   mortal *s·* of sin and mind in matter
of sinning
Mis. 219–20   change the patient's *s·* of sinning
of Spirit
Mis.   17–31   gains a truer *s·* of Spirit
    24–20   shutting out the true *s·* of Spirit.
Un.   21–19   *s·* of Spirit, and this is the only
of substance
Mis.   86–20   gain the glorified *s·* of substance
Un.   60–27   This false *s·* of substance must yield
of the body
Mis.   47–15   In sleep, a *s·* of the body
of the existence
Mis.   13–16   *s·* of the existence of good.
of the word
Un.   8–11   not real, in our *s·* of the word.
No.   23–17   moral *s·* of the word *devil,*
    32– 6   in the popular *s·* of the word,
of Truth
Mis. 113–12   not gaining a higher *s·* of Truth
    235–16   gives a keener *s·* of Truth
    268–31   we must possess the *s·* of Truth ;
Un.   52–13   Christ's immortal *s·* of Truth,
Rud.   9–12   false and temporal *s·* of Truth,
My. 122–20   our *s·* of Truth is not demoralized,
    122–27   *s·* of Truth of the real Christian
of unity
Pul.   4–10   a scientific, positive *s·* of unity
of words
Mis.   67–26   *s·* of words in one language
of worship
My. 139–19   turn your *s·* of worship from the
one's
Ret.   74– 1   increases one's *s·* of corporeality,
only as a
Un.   62–14   Sin exists only as a *s·*,
opposite
Mis. 292–19   to shut out all opposite *s·*.
or consciousness
Mis.   93–29   a sinning *s·* or consciousness
Un.   7–24   *s·* or consciousness of sin,
overwhelming
Ret.   81–16   overwhelming *s·* of error's vacuity,
pains of
Mis.   17–30   accumulating pains of *s·*,
    85–26   pleasures— more than the pains— of *s·*,
peculiar
My.   50–12   * felt a peculiar *s·* of isolation,
personal
Mis.   97–26   more than personal *s·* can cognize,
    287– 9   personal *s·*, discerning not the
    290–22   personal *s·* of things, conjectural and
    309– 1   the personal *s·* of any one,
    357– 3   ways and means of personal *s·*.
Ret.   67–15   testimony of material personal *s·*
My. 117–11   one's own dream of personal *s·*,
    227– 4   his own personal *s·* of righteousness
    273–19   material or personal *s·* of pleasure,
physical
Ret.   57–12   had known that physical *s·*, not Soul,
poured on the
Po.   31–19   Poured on the *s·* which deems
practical
Mis. 192– 1   more spiritual and practical *s·*.
present
Mis.   9–14   far beyond the present *s·*
’01.   16– 5   poignant present *s·* of sin
profoundest
My. 295–15   in its largest, profoundest *s·*
proper
Mis. 107–16   A proper *s·* of sin ;
    187– 5   proper *s·* of the possibilities of
    222– 2   a man's proper *s·* of good,
Rud.   2–14   the proper *s·* of Deity
pure
’02.   18– 4   thrust upon the pure *s·* of the

sense

purifies
’00.   8–24   fire that purifies *s·* with Soul
quickened
Un.   56– 9   Holding a quickened *s·* of
Pul.   10– 4   raised . . . to a quickened *s·* of
rapt
Mis. 387– 1   rapt *s·* the heart-strings gently sweep,
Po.   50–18   rapt *s·* the heartstrings gently sweep
right
Mis. 190–27   must yield to the right *s·*,
Ret.   78–14   right *s·* of metaphysical Science.
rises
No.   19–24   *s·* rises to the fulness of the
sacred
Mis. 196–17   sacred *s·* and permanence of
Un.   41–15   The sweet and sacred *s·* of
sad
Po.   31– 5   Sad *s·*, annoy No more
Science and
Mis. 184– 4   Science and *s·* conflict,
scientific
Mis. 101–14   The scientific *s·* of being
No.   25–24   in a spiritually scientific *s·*.
’00.   6–11   the scientific *s·* which interprets
’01.   4–18   personal in a scientific *s·*,
    6–22   in the infinite scientific *s·*
seems
Mis. 354–11   *s·* seems sounder than Soul,
sickened
Mis. 124–10   We turn, with sickened *s·*,
sight and
Un.   47– 2   destroying . . . to sight and *s·*.
sight or
My. 116–17   based upon personal sight or *s·*.
simple
Mis.   43–12   The simple *s·* one gains of this
sinful
Mis. 125– 9   over his own sinful *s·* and self.
No.   19–20   A sinful *s·* is incompetent to
My. 200–21   Pale, sinful *s·*, at work to
sinless
Po.   70–12   For sinless *s·* is here
sinning
Mis.   93–29   a sinning *s·* or consciousness
No.   7–13   the enemy of sinning *s·*,
    29– 9   they believe . . . sinning *s·* to be soul ;
slave of
Mis. 183–10   he is neither the slave of *s·*, nor
Soul and
’02.   4–11   peace between Soul and *s·*
soul as
Mis.   15–21   shall soul as *s·* be satisfied,
soul for
Mis.   76–20   exchange the term *soul* for *s·*
Un.   30– 4   uses the word *soul* for *s·*.
soul from
My. 139–28   redeem . . . your soul from *s·* ;
soul means
No.   28–26   Here *soul* means *s·* and organic life ;
Soul, not
Po.   70–21   heraldry of Soul, not *s·*,
My. 118–19   Soul, not *s·*, receives and gives
Soul over
Mis. 321–12   triumphs . . . of Soul over *s·*.
Hea.   10–20   the triumph of Soul over *s·*.
Peo.   11–11   supremacy of Soul over *s·*,
spiritual
    (see **spiritual**)
supreme
Hea.   15–10   as it rises to that supreme *s·*
sweet
Mis. 135– 9   sweet *s·* of journeying on together,
My. 163– 2   sweet *s·* of angelic song
that very
Un.   29–20   soul which that very *s·* declares
their
Mis. 121–30   borrow their *s·* of justice from
    181–25   will lose their *s·* of mortality
    191– 7   meaning of the term, to their *s·*,
Un.   2–17   sick lose their *s·* of sickness,
’01.   22–26   receive their *s·* of the Science,
this
Mis. 102–29   Mortal thought wars with this *s·*
    105–13   if this *s·* were consistently sensible.
    186–32   restored this *s·* by the spiritual
    332–22   What was this *s·* ?
Ret.   64– 1   and in this *s·* they are one.
Un.   57– 5   but as this *s·* disappears
    62–15   Destroy this *s·* of sin,
No.   32–19   When this *s·* is attained,
’00.   11– 4   this *s·* will harmonize, unify,
My. 273–15   This *s·* of rightness acquired
tired
’01.   26– 2   my tired *s·* of false philosophy

sense

to Soul
Mis. 267–22 must gravitate from *s·* to Soul,
Un. 25–15 removing its evidence from *s·* to Soul,
'02. 10–16 and rise from *s·* to Soul,
My. 117–30 footsteps from *s·* to Soul.
    142–20 their passage from *s·* to Soul.
    156–13 the passover from *s·* to Soul,
    163– 6 from *s·* to Soul, from gleam to glory,
    234–14 from light to Love, from *s·* to Soul.

trifling
Mis. 43–11 into other minds a trifling *s·* of it

true
Mis. 24–20 shutting out the true *s·* of Spirit.
    28–12 to the true *s·* of reality,
    59– 2 no true *s·* of the healing theology
    84–26 true *s·* of the falsity of material
    124–19 man's true *s·* is filled with peace,
    186–27 immortal and true *s·* of being.
    190– 6 giving the true *s·* of itself,
    234–10 true *s·* of Love as God ;
    276–21 the true *s·* comes out,
    282– 2 a true *s·* of the infinite good,
    291– 5 it dims the true *s·* of God's reflection,
    319– 1 true *s·* of the unity of good
    347–19 A true *s·* not unfamiliar
    372–31 true *s·* of meekness and might.
Ret. 54–24 impressed with the true *s·* of the
Un. 40–20 proper or true *s·* of Life,
    41– 8 a loss of the true *s·* of good,
    42–25 leading man into the true *s·* of
Pul. 3–15 gives us the true *s·* of victory,
    21–16 a true *s·* of goodness in others,
Rud. 10–18 true *s·* that God is Love,
'00. 11– 4 the true *s·* of harmony,
My. 116– 3 true *s·* of the omnipotence of Life,
    100–25 waking to a true *s·* of itself,
    178–14 true *s·* of life is lost to those who
    212–25 destroys the true *s·* of Science,
    274– 1 gives the true *s·* of life
    275–22 the true *s·* of being goes on.
    287–15 true *s·* of love for God,

truer
Mis. 17–31 gains a truer *s·* of Spirit
    47–17 is the truer *s·* of being.
No. 34– 5 truer *s·* of following Christ
'01. 9– 7 their truer *s·* of Christ baptized them

unreal
Un. 41– 6 unreal *s·* of suffering and death.
No. 5–12 this unreal *s·* substitutes for Truth an

Virgin-mother's
Un. 29–28 Virgin-mother's *s·* being uplifted to

whatever
My. 154–30 take it in whatever *s·* you may.

wings of
Mis. 230–19 floating off on the wings of *s·* :

without the Science
Mis. 302– 9 *s·* without the Science, of Christ's

wounded
Mis. 145–16 a wounded *s·* of its own error,

Mis. 75–20 substitution of *s·* for *soul*
    96–21 to the *s·* of all who entertain this
    107–22 Without a *s·* of one's
    159–24 *s·* of Thy children grown to
    179–23 old consciousness of Soul in *s·*.
    181–27 *s·* of man's spiritual preexistence
    186–31 even the *s·* of the real man
    282– 2 a *s·* that does not limit God,
    353– 1 allowed to rejoice in the *s·* that
    354– 1 pleasure seeking, and *s·* indulgence,
Un. 8– 7 than the *s·* you entertain of it.
    29–25 O my soul [*s·*] — *Psal.* 42 : 11.
Rud. 8– 4 To *s·*, the lion of to-day
No. 2–11 to deny self, *s·*, and take up the
    10–19 former position, that *s·* is organic
    34–15 one upon whom the world of *s·*
'01. 8– 9 in the *s·* that one ray of light is
    9– 8 a *s·* so pure it made seers of men,
    10–11 son of man only in the *s·* that
My. 106–22 In what *s·* is the . . . Scientist a
    106–28 In what *s·* is the . . . a charlatan?
    349– 8 disease is in a *s·* susceptible of

senseless
Mis. 355–19 Mental darkness is *s·* error,
Un. 11–22 for restoring his *s·* hand ;

senses *(see also* senses')

afford no evidence
Hea. 16–19 *s·* afford no evidence of Truth?

cannot define
Un. 29–15 that which the *s·* cannot define

claims of the
My. 222–14 admitting the claims of the *s·*

cognized by the
Mis. 22–29 simple fact cognized by the *s·*,

senses

corporeal
Ret. 54– 7 claims of the corporeal *s·*

could not prophesy
Ret. 23–11 *s·* could not prophesy sunrise

delusion that the
Un. 30– 4 delusion that the *s·* can reverse

doubleminded
Mis. 198–23 adherence to the "doubleminded" *s·*,

dull
Mis. 100– 5 was to awaken the dull *s·*,

erring
Mis. 13–22 testimony of the five erring *s·*,

error of the
Un. 42–11 is an error of the *s·* ;

evidence of the
    (see **evidence***)*

evidences of the
Mis. 58–11 *deny the evidences of the s·?*
Hea. 15– 1 repudiates the evidences of the *s·*

false
Mis. 107–19 false *s·* pass through three states

fear of the
Ret. 74– 2 begets a fear of the *s·*

feasting the
Ret. 65–10 Feasting the *s·*, gratification of

finite
Hea. 4– 8 we limit . . . to the finite *s·*.

five
Mis. 351–23 the five *s·* give to mortals pain,
Un. 25– 5 the testimony of the five *s·*.
    28–18 the five *s·* take no cognizance of
Rud. 5–26 the five *s·* as organized matter,

foul
Mis. 399– 7 Cleanse the foul *s·* within ;
Po. 75–14 Cleanse the foul *s·* within ;

habitation of the
Mis. 328–19 tarried in the habitation of the *s·*,

human
My. 189–18 When the human *s·* wake

illusion of the
Mis. 368– 5 dispel this illusion of the *s·*,

instead of the
Hea. 7– 8 language of Soul instead of the *s·* ;
Peo. 2–13 of Soul instead of the *s·*,

intoxicated
Mis. 277–30 the cloud of the intoxicated *s·*.

join issue
Mis. 105–26 *s·* join issue with error,

material
    (see **material***)*

misguided
Mis. 268–21 enlightening the misguided *s·*,

mortal
Mis. 13–20 the shifting mortal *s·* confirm
Pul. 45– 8 * seems impossible to mortal *s·*.
    45–21 * evidence of the mortal *s·* is

obtained from the
Mis. 251–18 knowledge obtained from the *s·*

personal
Mis. 28– 4 Perception by the five personal *s·*
    65– 1 from the five personal *s·*.
    96–31 evidence before the personal *s·*,
    100–12 The five personal *s·*,
    172–19 taken in by the five personal *s·*,
    172–25 Science, and the five personal *s·*,
    198–15 false belief of the personal *s·* ;
    200–25 apart from the personal *s·*.
    218–15 the five personal *s·* can take no
Un. 21–12 the evidence of your personal *s·*
'01. 18–15 evidence of the five personal *s·*,
    26– 7 The five personal *s·* can have
Hea. 16–16 A word about the five personal *s·*,
    17– 4 or the pains of the personal *s·*
    17– 6 material man and the personal *s·*
    17–10 material man and the personal *s·*,
My. 273–25 personal *s·* are perishable :
    273–29 in possession of the five personal *s·*,

physical
    (see **physical***)*

rebuke the
Mis. 203–17 baptism serves to rebuke the *s·*

satisfied
Mis. 322–17 *s·* satisfied, or self be justified.

say
Mis. 103–10 the *s·* say vaguely :

scope of the
Mis. 100–17 scope of the *s·* is inadequate

so-called
My. 275– 6 so-called *s·* do not perceive this

spiritual
Mis. 104–18 physical senses with his spiritual *s·*.
Rud. 5– 1 spiritual *s·* afford no such evidence,
No. 19–19 spiritual *s·* are drinking in the
Hea. 17–17 when the spiritual *s·* were hushed

senses

testimony of the
Mis. 103– 2   annuls the testimony of the *s·*,
    105– 9   came from the testimony of the *s·*,
    164–31   arose from the testimony of the *s·*.
No.   6– 8   validity of the testimony of the *s·*,
these
Mis. 198–15   if we deny the claims of these *s·*
    299–16   the evil which these *s·* see not
Un.   33– 5   Now these *s·*, being material,
Hea. 16–18   is furnished by these *s·* ;
those
Hea. 16–24   those *s·* through which it is impossible to
thraldom of the
Mis. 101– 5   departing from the thraldom of the *s·*
would say
Mis. 367–28   *s·* would say that whatever saves from

Mis.   98– 6   chapter sub-title
    100–19   Science speaks when the *s·* are
    101– 8   C. S. and the *s·* are at war.
    105– 7   anathema of priesthood and the *s·* ;
    161– 9   To the *s·*, Jesus was the son of man :
    166–21   more spiritual than the *s·* could
    190–17   interpretations that the *s·* give
    191– 3   which the *s·* are supposed to
    214–12   closed — to the *s·* — that wondrous life,
    310– 1   studying Truth through the *s·*,
Un.   41–26   To the *s·*, matter appears to
    52–26   The *s·*, not God, Soul, form the
Hea. 17– 2   Not by the *s·* — the lusts of the
Po.   68–11   Enchant deep the *s·*,

senses'

My. 230– 7   during the *s·* assimilation thereof,

sensibilities

Mis. 224–21   shall not wear upon our *s·* ;

sensibility

Mis. 204–19   and so quickens moral *s·*
    293–28   consigns *s·* to the charnel-house
Ret.   74– 2   perpetually egotistical *s·*.

sensible

Mis. 105–13   if this sense were consistently *s·*.
    126–15   not yet quite *s·* of what we owe
Ret.   73–16   true Mind, where *s·* evil is lost
Un.   21–18   There is no *s·* matter,
    50– 8   belief in matter as *s·* mind.
No.   6–18   is as *s·* and real as the
    14– 6   all *s·* phenomena are
    38– 4   falsity of . . . are *s·* claims,
'01.   30–29   * *s·*, and well-bred man will not
My. 349– 9   and matter is not *s·*.

sensibly

Un.   7– 9   clearly seen and most *s·* felt
'01.   33– 3   fading so *s·* from our sight.

sensitive

Mis. 108– 1   The *s·*, sorrowing saint
    360–28   to *s·* ears and dark disciples,

sensitiveness

Mis. 112–25   shows itself in extreme *s·* ;
    116– 2   destroy your own *s·* to the
'00.   8–15   remember that *s·* is sometimes

sensual

Mis. 196–11   become material, *s·*, evil.
    328–11   acquaint *s·* mortals with the
    361– 3   mortal mind, *s·* conception,
    363–22   avoid the shoals of a *s·* religion
Un.   9– 5   Material and *s·* consciousness
'00.   13–17   was devoted to a *s·* worship.
'01.   26– 8   metaphysician is *s·* that combines
Peo.   1– 8   as they pass from the *s·* side
    11–12   the sick, the *s·*, are slaves,
My.   48–23   * The scorn of the gross and *s·*,
    262–22   mortal, material, *s·* giving

sensualism

Mis. 325–27   as a testimony against *s·*
    337–31   *s·*, as heretofore, would hide
No.   21– 1   forbidden by-paths of *s·*,

sensualist

'01.   30–30   The *s·* and world-worshipper

sensuality

Mis. 234–26   so sunken in sin and *s·*,
    285–16   the whole warfare of *s·*
    289– 5   Drunkenness is *s·* let loose,
    293–28   the charnel-house of *s·*,
    298–19   all the claims of *s·*.
Hea. 10– 4   vision of envy, *s·*, and malice,
My. 139–28   redeem . . . your being from *s·* ;

sensuous

Mis. 87– 7   of the beauties of the *s·* universe :
    113– 1   result of *s·* mind in matter.
    217–17   *S·* and material realistic views

sensuous

Mis. 286–13   of spiritual power over *s·*,
    351–22   and *s·* love is material,
Ret.   25–13   physical senses, or *s·* nature,
No.   26–10   Theirs is the *s·* thought,
    26–11   brings forth its own *s·* conception.

sent

Mis.   6– 1   that sickness is *s·* as a discipline
    60– 2   *He s· His Son to save from*
    87–15   *inform us, . . . if you s·*
    87–16   *She said that you s· her there to*
    158–26   divine directions *s·* out to the
    249–18   not one has been *s·* to my house,
    275–29   floral offerings *s·* to my apartments
    299–10   following question *s·* to me ;
    304–14   * *s·* to the next World's Exhibition,
    305–11   * circular is *s·* to every member
    306–12   * Contributions should be *s·* to the
    317–30   "Whom God hath *s·* — *John 3 : 34.*
    326–27   stonest them which are *s·* — *Matt. 23 : 37.*
    339–26   *s·* along the ocean of events a wave
Man. 66–25   an order . . . that she has not *s·*,
    98–19   letter *s·* to the Pastor Emeritus
Ret.   20– 8   was *s·* away from me,
    48–21   *s·* to all parts of our country,
    52–23   June, 1889, I *s·* a letter,
    90– 7   towns whither he *s·* his disciples ;
Un.   4–25   Jesus Christ, whom He has *s·*.
Pul. 41–11   * listen to the Message *s·* them by
    41–14   * New York *s·* its hundreds,
    80–12   * *s·* us by interested friends,
'00.   10–25   *s·* to me, in the name of a
Po.   43– 1   *s· me the picture depictive of*
My.   14– 1   whereto [God, Spirit] *s·* it." — *see Isa. 55 : 11.*
    49–18   * *s·* an invitation to Mrs. Eddy,
    57–29   * Treasurer has *s·* out word
    72–19   * *s·* forth to the thirty thousand
    94–25   * *s·* greetings in which she declared
    96–21   * money was *s·* in such quantities
    144– 1   * Mrs. Eddy also *s·* the following
    150–27   when he *s·* them forth to heal
    159–10   hath *s·* forth His word to heal
    173–12   a note, *s·* at the last moment,
    215–11   *s·* me the full tuition money.
    215–23   When the great Master first *s·* forth his
    223– 9   *s·* to the C. S. practitioners
    242–19   *s·* to the C. S. Board of Directors
    253–13   that Thou hast *s·* me." — *John 17 : 25.*
    258–30   *s·* me that beautiful statuette
    272–21   * an article *s·* to us by Mrs. Eddy,
    274–18   * *s·* the following to the *Herald :*
    335–24   * *s·* for the distinguished physician

sentence

Mis.   8–28   *s·*, can only be fulfilled
    21–23   order of this *s·* has been conformed
    121–20   this *s·* passed upon innocence
    133– 4   to build a *s·* of so few words
Pul. 59– 5   * There was no special *s·* or prayer
    59–13   congregation repeating one *s·*
No.   44–13   could *s·* men to the dungeon or stake
'01.   20–28   and will pass *s·* on the
    26– 9   In one *s·* he declaims against
My. 104–18   suspend judgment and *s·*
    161– 8   never remits the *s·* necessary

sentenced

Mis. 261– 1   doomed, already *s·*, punished ;
Hea.   7–21   *s·* it as our judges would not

sentences

Mis. 125–19   meanings of these short *s·* :
My. 110–31   *s·* or paragraphs torn from
    113–10   Paul declares . . . in these brief *s·* :

sentencing

'02.   10–28   *s·* a man for communicating

sentiment

Mis. 127–29   tender *s·* felt, or a kind word
    174– 9   what touches the religious *s·*
    250–10   no *s·* less understood.
    295–21   English *s·* is not wholly
    315–18   that they prove sound in *s·*,
Man. 83–17   that they prove sound in *s·*
Un.   26–20   its *s·* is foreign to C. S.
Pul. 21–30   Only what feeds and fills the *s·*
    79–23   * requires the religious *s·*
    80– 4   * religious *s·* in women is so strong
No.   1– 1   kindle in all minds a common *s·*
    1–11   when public *s·* is aroused,
Pan.   2–21   to which the religious *s·* is directed.
'00.   7– 4   religious *s·* has increased ;
'01.   17–19   when the public *s·* would allow it,
My. 224–10   public *s·* is helpful or dangerous
    264–12   * will you please send . . . a *s·* on
    281–21   * a *s·* on some phase of the subject,

sentimental

My.	41–19	* teaches us to rise from *s·* affection
	48–29	* or paralyzed by *s·* fiction.

sentiments

Mis.	13– 3	permit me to exercise these *s·*
	143– 3	and the "square" of moral *s·*
	250– 9	should be repressed by the *s·*.
	295–14	lost these *s·* from his
Chr.	55– 1	basis of the *s·* in the verses,
No.	1–15	stir of contending *s·* cease,
	42– 4	Such *s·* are wholesome
Hea.	18–13	world would accept our *s·* ;
My.	170– 7	*s·* uttered in my annual
	175–30	very opposite of my real *s·*.
	316–19	freedom of Christian *s·*,

Sentinel

Christian Science

Man.	27–15	*The C. S. Journal, C. S. S·*,
	81–11	*The C. S. Journal, C. S. S·*,
My.	vi–28	* she established the *C. S. S·*
	10– 1	*[C. S. S·,* May 16, 1903]
	11–22	* Editorial in *C. S. S·*,
	12–15	* Mrs. Eddy in *C. S. S·*,
	14–10	* [Editorial in *C. S. S·*,
	15– 1	*[C. S. S·,* March 5, 1904]
	19– 3	*The C. S. Journal, C. S. S·*,
	24–16	* Editorial in *C. S. S·*,
	25– 5	*[C. S. S·,* March 17, 1906]
	26– 1	*[C. S. S·,* April 14, 1906]
	26– 7	*[C. S. S·,* April 28, 1906]
	27–20	* Editorial in *C. S. S·*,
	29– 1	* *C. S. S·*, June 16, 1906.
	58– 4	* notice was published in the *C. S. S·*
	63–10	* Editorial in *C. S. S·*,
	72–22	also through the *C. S. S·*
	98–14	* last issue of the *C. S. S·*
	220–27	editor-in-chief of the *C. S. S·*
	232–11	which Appeared in the *C. S. S·*,
	276 1	*[C. S.* May 16, 1908]
	279–20	*[C. S. S·,* June 17, 1905]
	280–14	*[C. S. S·,* July 1, 1905]
	280–26	*[C. S. S·,* July 22, 1905]
	316– 9	*[C. S. S·,* January 19, 1907]
	334– 9	* weekly issue of the *C. S. S·*,
	356–13	*Editor C. S. S·:*
	363–18	Reprinted in *C. S. S·*,

Man.	65–11	editors of the *C. S. Journal, S·*,
Pul.	88–22	* *S·*, Eastport, Me.
	90– 5	* *S·*, Indianapolis, Ind.
	90– 6	* *S·*, Milwaukee, Wis.
My.	27–23	* in this issue of the *S·*
	142– 6	* Editor *S·*.
	217–17	In the last *S·* [Oct. 12, 1899]
	237– 2	in the *S·* a few weeks ago,
	237–22	in the *S·* of September 10 [1910]
	241–29	* Please give the truth in the *S·*,
	317– 2	* *S·* of December 1, 1906,
	338–10	* Editor *S·*.
	351– 2	* the *S·* is privileged to publish
	353–12	the second I entitled *S·*,
	355– 4	* Editor *S·*.]
	359–17	* In the *S·* of July 31, 1909,

sentinel

Mis.	392–10	Whate'er thy mission, mountain *s·*,
Ret.	18– 8	*s·* hedgerow is guarding repose,
Po.	20–14	Whate'er thy mission, mountain *s·*,
	63–17	*s·* hedgerow is guarding repose,

sentinels

Mis.	291–28	as *s·* along the lines of thought,
	370– 9	Let the *s·* of Zion's watch-towers

separate

Mis.	8–14	*s·* you from the Love
	18–22	could never *s·* himself from
	18–26	can we in belief *s·* one man's
	18–28	to *s·* Life from God.
	36–29	in matter and *s·* from God,
	110–18	time and space, . . . do not *s·* us.
	117– 4	*s·* the tares from the wheat ;
	136–15	and be ye *s·*, — *II Cor.* 6 : 17.
	196– 8	*s·* mind from God
	370–29	*s·* the sheep from the goats;
Ret.	60– 5	mind as something *s·* from God.
	64– 2	cannot *s·* sin from the sinner,
	67– 8	and yet are *s·* from God.
	81– 5	Nothing except sin, . . . can *s·*
Un.	24–22	*Evil.* I am something *s·*
	37–12	no boundary of time can *s·* us
Pul.	29–12	* composed of three *s·* panels,
	30– 4	* enticing a *s·* congregation
	61– 1	* enclosed in *s·* swell-box,
Rud.	15–16	should have *s·* departments,
No.	9–12	regenerate and *s·* wisely

separate

	'01. 6– 3	and have no *s·* identity?
My.	121– 4	in order to *s·* these sessions
	124–30	to *s·* the tares from the wheat,
	344– 4	and each *s·* ray for
	358–10	cannot *s·* you from your Leader

separated

Mis.	70–21	inevitably *s·* through Mind.
	135– 8	not one of you can be *s·* from
	186–19	man cannot be *s·* from
	214–29	must be *s·* from the wheat
	223–11	cannot be *s·* from it.
Ret.	21–29	are *s·* from their premises,
	57–23	not our own, *s·* from Him.
	81– 8	law of God, *s·* from its spirit,
	94– 9	As dross is *s·* from gold,
Un.	7–10	this has not *s·* me from God,
	32– 9	cannot be *s·* in origin and action.
	52–11	man *s·* from his Maker.
Pul.	76– 9	* are *s·* from the apartment
Hea.	6– 1	the more are we *s·* from the
My.	111–11	chaff is *s·* from the wheat.
	315– 6	* wife, from whom he was *s·*.
	316– 1	has *s·* the tares from the wheat,

separately

Man.	55– 6	shall *s·* and independently discipline

separates

Mis.	73– 9	it *s·* the false sense from
	151– 6	He *s·* the dross from the gold,
	186– 9	*s·* its conception of man from
	205– 7	*s·* the dross from the gold,
Un.	10– 2	*s·* my system from all others.
My.	167– 5	*s·* us from the spiritual world,

separating

Mis.	172– 3	*s·* the tares from the wheat,
My.	269–17	*s·* the tares from the wheat.

separation

Ret.	20–16	poem, . . . written after this *s·* :
My.	315– 7	* cause of the *s·* being wholly

separator

Mis.	150–10	Space is no *s·* of hearts.

September

(*see* **months**)

sepulchre

Mis.	123–18	stone from the *s·* of our Lord ;
	180–14	I found the open door from this *s·*
	27b– 5	stone from the door of this *s·*
Ret.	88– 6	lifted his own body from the *s·*.
No.	36–25	rolled away the stone from the *s·*,
	45–14	"last at the cross and first at the *s·*,"
Peo.	5–15	it sitteth beside the *s·*
My.	119–13	*stooped down* and looked into the *s·*
	214–11	Jesus' three days' work in the *s·*
	258– 9	To the woman at the *s·*,

sepulchres

Mis.	292–15	turn away from the open *s·* of sin,
	'01. 25–18	denounced all such gilded *s·*
Peo.	8–23	to light our *s·* with immortality.
My.	191–19	The *s·* give up their dead.

sequel

Hea.	12–23	and the *s·* proves it ;
Po.	16– 9	*s·* of power, of glory, or gold ;

sequela

My.	133–16	free from self's sordid *s·* ;

sequence

Mis.	65–26	*s·* proves that strict adherence to
	100 24	*s·* of knowledge would be lacking,
	217– 2	in logical *s·*, nature, reason, and
	336–29	the *s·* proves.
	366–28	To destroy sin and its *s·*,
Un.	33–17	Hence the logical *s·*,
Pan.	7–24	logical *s·* of this error is idolatry
My.	275– 4	As the *s·* of divine Love
	279–14	Hence the *s·* : Had all peoples

seraphic

Po.	22– 8	New themes *s·*, Life divine,

seraph's

Po.	65–19	rise to a *s·* new song.

seraphs

Po.	16–22	call to my spirit with *s·* to dwell ;

sere

Po.	41– 8	fountain and . . . are frozen and *s·*,

serene

Mis.	206– 4	from foul to pure, from torpid to *s·*,
	323– 3	in *s·* azure and unfathomable glory :
	323–15	masters their . . . attacks with *s·*
	369–13	This method sits *s·* at the portals
	400– 9	In thy heart Dwell *s·*,
Ret.	42–14	resting on his *s·* countenance.

serene

Pul.	5–14	his athletic mind, scholarly and *s·*,
	16–21	In thy heart Dwell *s·*,
Po.	76–20	In thy heart Dwell *s·*,
My.	87–24	* such *s·*, beautiful expressions,

serenely

Mis.	162– 9	walk *s·* over their fretted, foaming

serenity

My.	88–21	* *s·* of faith, life, and love

series

Ret.	91–14	this *s·* of great lessons
No.	20–26	a continued *s·* of mortal hypotheses,
'00.	13–13	after a *s·* of wars it was taken
My.	78– 9	* beneath a *s·* of arches

serious

Mis.	239–25	made them more *s·* over it.
Man.	43–18	calls more *s·* attention to the
Un.	26–24	All is real, all is *s·*.
Pul.	33–20	* high counsel and *s·* thought.
My.	51–11	* a *s·* blow to her Cause

seriously

Un.	14– 5	Can it be *s·* held, by any thinker,

sermon

Mis.	68– 7	*The Rev. —— said in a s·:*
	126– 2	to one eternal *s·* ;
	161– 1	chapter sub-title
	168–21	chapter sub-title
	171–21	chapter sub-title
	177–26	* was announced to preach the *s·*,
	178–19	* to preach a *s·* on C. S.,
	178–25	* At the conclusion of the *s·*,
	301– 1	compiling and delivering that *s·*
	314–32	*s·* shall be preached to the children,
Man.	59–18	to listen to the Sunday *s·*
Ret.	16–12	for the sick to be healed by my *s·*.
	91– 5	well be called "the diamond *s·*."
Pul.	32–17	* *s·*, which dealt directly with the
	40–13	* S· by Rev. Mary Baker Eddy,
	43–22	* *s·* prepared for the occasion by
	43–29	* Before presenting the *s·*,
	57– 8	* *s·*, prepared by Mrs. Eddy,
	59–16	* The *s·*, prepared by Mrs. Eddy,
No.	29–11	*s·* on The Ministry of Healing,
	41–25	Baptist clergyman, said in a *s·* :
	42–28	* to support me through a *s·*."
	43– 7	stimulate and sustain a good *s·*.
'01.	6–19	consistent with Christ's hillside *s·*,
	11–22	saith there is no *s·* without personal
	11–25	a *s·* from his personal God !
My.	50–31	* her farewell *s·* to the church.
	186– 9	its song and *s·* will touch the heart,
	194– 1	may song and *s·* generate only
	197–27	join with you in song and *s·*.

Sermon on the Mount

Mis.	12–13	loyalty to Jesus' *S· on the M·*,
	21– 4	unity with Christ's *S· on the M·*,
	25– 9	Christ's *S· on the M·*, in its direct
	93–30	obey Christ's *S· on the M·*,
	114–14	Decalogue, the *S· on the M·*,
Man.	63– 3	*S· on the M·*
Ret.	75– 4	tramples upon Jesus' *S· on the M·*,
	91– 7	known as the *S· on the M·*,
Rud.	3–15	called the *S· on the M·*,
	12– 4	practises Christ's *S· on the M·*.
'01.	11–17	*S· on the M·*, read each Sunday
	32–23	Ninety-first Psalm, the *S· on the M·*,
'02.	5–22	breathed in the *S· on the M·*.
My.	180– 6	uttered Christ's *S· on the M·*,
	229–22	ascent of Christ's *S· on the M·*,

sermons

Mis.	133– 7	to read my *s·* and publications.
Ret.	89– 8	for . . . ceremonies, not for *s·*.
Pul.	5–29	palpably working in the *s·*,
	9–18	excellent *s·* from the editor
	45–28	* *s·* hereafter will consist of
No.	29–22	Such *s·*, though clad in soft
	43–11	* "Your book leavens my *s·*."
'01.	32–16	the *s·* their lives preached
My.	185–30	*s·* in stones, refuge in mountains,
	194– 2	*s·* that fell forests

serpent (*see also* serpent's)

cast out

Mis.	373– 9	*s·* cast out of his mouth,
Pul.	14– 8	*s·* cast out of his mouth — *Rev. 12 : 15.*

handle the

Mis.	336– 5	to handle the *s·* and bruise its

head of the

Mis.	210–17	puts her foot on the head of the *s·*,

kill the

Mis.	336– 7	to kill the *s·* of a material mind.

lurking

Mis.	210–21	kill this lurking *s·*, intemperance,

serpent

named

'01.	16–13	*devil* is named *s·* — *liar*

of sin

Pul.	13–15	and fail to strangle the *s·* of sin

placing the

Mis.	373– 3	placing the *s·* behind the woman

said

Mis.	196–11	bear in mind that a *s·* said that ;
Peo.	4–11	because a *s·* said it.

so-called

Ret.	69– 8	pantheistic error, or so-called *s·*,

talking

Mis.	24–28	not to believe the talking *s·*,
Pan.	6–12	in the form of a talking *s·*,

this

Mis.	191– 4	and then defines this *s·* as
Un.	45– 3	Bruise the head of this *s·*,

was the emblem

'00.	13–19	*s·* was the emblem of Æsculapius.

wisdom of a

Mis.	210–12	wisdom of a *s·* is to hide itself.

Mis.	23–17	and the *s·*, Satan,
	190–29	*s·*, liar, the god of this world,
	191– 3	in another term, *s·*,
	191– 7	*s·* became a symbol of wisdom.
	210–13	brings the *s·* out of its hole,
Ret.	68– 2	although as a *s·* it claimed to
Un.	54–26	*s·*, who pushed that claim
Pan.	6–10	chapter sub-title
	6–20	between good and evil, God and a *s·*?
Hea.	17–18	claimed audience with a *s·*.

serpent's

Mis.	123– 9	the *s·* biggest lie !
Un.	44–19	carrying out the *s·* assurance :

serpents

Mis.	24–30	his followers should handle *s·* ;
	90–17	wise as *s·*." — *Matt. 10 : 16.*
	210– 7	Do men whine over a nest of *s·*,
	210–10	"They shall take up *s·* ;" — *Mark 16 : 18.*
	210–11	wise as *s·* and harmless as — *Matt. 10 : 16.*
	211– 5	it teaches mortals to handle *s·*
	323–11	Venomous *s·* hide among the rocks,
	323–20	hushing the hissing *s·*,
'02.	17–18	and to be wiser than *s·* ;
Hea.	1– 3	*they shall take up s· ;— Mark 16 : 18.*
	7–25	"They shall take up *s·* ; — *Mark 16 : 18.*
	15–10	"take up *s·*" — *Mark 16 : 18.*
My.	47–31	* they shall take up *s·* ; — *Mark 16 : 18.*
	146– 4	"They shall take up *s·* ; — *Mark 16 : 18.*
	150–29	wise as *s·*, and harmless as — *Matt. 10 : 16.*
	205– 5	wise as *s·*, and harmless as — *Matt. 10 : 16.*

servant

Mis.	47–18	body is the *s·* of Mind,
	108–25	then we are its master, not *s·*.
	122–26	good and faithful *s·*, — *Matt. 25 : 23.*
	206– 2	the former being *s·* to the latter,
	256–12	remaining at present a public *s·* :
	266–10	unacknowledged *s·* of mankind.
	272–14	* any officer, agent, or *s·* of
	335– 3	if that evil *s·* shall say — *Matt. 24 : 48.*
	335– 7	"The lord of that *s·* shall — *Matt. 24 : 50.*
Man.	28–10	"That *s·*, which knew — *Luke 12 : 47.*
Ret.	9–11	for Thy *s·* heareth." — *I Sam. 3 : 9.*
Pul.	6–23	seeker, and *s·* of Truth,
	33– 8	* for Thy *s·* heareth." — *I Sam. 3 : 9.*
Pan.	8–27	make man the *s·* of matter,
'00.	3–11	by no means his *s·*, but his master.
My.	62– 3	* good and faithful *s·* ; — *Matt. 25 : 23.*
	145–21	makes me the *s·* of the race
	165– 4	the Master became the *s·*.
	207–21	good and faithful *s·* ; — *Matt. 25 : 21.*
	295–27	the *s·* of God and man,
	332–13	* Your friend and obedient *s·*,

servants

Mis.	19– 5	obedience demanded of His *s·*
	46– 3	*s·* to obey, — *Rom. 6 : 16.*
	46– 3	his *s·* ye are." — *Rom. 6 : 16.*
	120– 8	*s·* to obey, — *Rom. 6 : 16.*
	120– 8	his *s·* ye are — *Rom. 6 : 16.*
	158–19	God's *s·* are minute men
	275–28	The *s·* are well-mannered,
	346–18	*s·* to obey, — *Rom. 6 : 16.*
	346–18	his *s·* ye are." — *Rom. 6 : 16.*
No.	32–20	no longer be the *s·* of sin,

serve

Mis.	x–14	*s·* as mile-stones measuring
	40– 6	*s·* "other gods." — *Exod. 20 : 3.*
	52– 6	if he were to *s·* one master,
	89– 2	"No man can *s·* two — *Matt. 6 : 24.*
	221–28	might *s·* as the multiplicand.
	237– 8	Not a few individuals *s·* God
	269– 6	"No man can *s·* two — *Matt. 6 : 24.*

serve

Mis.	269– 9	cannot *s·* God and — *Matt.* 6 : 24.
	271–13	whom ye will *s·*.'' — *Josh.* 24 : 15.
	286–12	will *s·* to illustrate the
	303–13	Let us *s·* instead of rule,
	350–28	I cannot *s·* two masters ;
Man.	69– 6	has been called to *s·* our Leader
	99– 2	to *s·* in their localities.
	99–10	to *s·* in its locality.
Un.	49–15	You cannot simultaneously *s·*
	60–18	to choose whom they would *s·*.
	60–19	If God, then let them *s·* Him,
Pul.	21–17	we cannot *s·* mammon.
Rud.	14– 1	Neither can they *s·* two masters,
No.	25– 6	*s·* in newness of spirit, — *Rom.* 7 : 6.
'01.	20– 4	to *s·* God and benefit mankind.
'02.	3–28	to *s·* God and to help the race.
Peo.	9–21	cannot *s·* two masters.'' — *see Matt.* 6 : 24.
My.	5–22	to love more and to *s·* better.
	5–27	to choose whom ye will *s·*.
	5–29	indulging sin, men cannot *s·* God ;
	6– 3	We cannot *s·* two masters.
	42–14	* to *s·* you in this capacity,
	110–32	may *s·* to call attention to
	134– 7	daily lives *s·* to enhance
	138–16	''*s·* two masters.'' — *Matt.* 6 : 24.
	145–22	if in this way I can *s·* equally
	152–21	and *s·* no other gods.
	174–28	pray to *s·* Him better.
	192– 2	Ye worship Him whom ye *s·*.
	209– 4	those that seek and *s·* Him.
	224–31	* ''They also *s·* who only stand
	325–13	* in which I could *s·* you,
	356–22	*s·* two masters : — *Matt.* 6 : 24.
	356–24	cannot *s·* God and — *Matt.* 6 : 24.

served

Mis.	203–13	*s·* the imagination for centuries.
Man.	16– 0	his resurrection *s·* to uplift faith
	26– 6	who have *s·* one year or more,
	80–26	who have *s·* one year or more
Ret.	6–26	*s·* the public interests faithfully
	21–10	he had *s·* as a volunteer
Pul.	8–15	*s·* to erect this ''miracle in

serves

Mis.	203–17	baptism *s·* to rebuke the senses
	210–20	*s·* to uncover and kill this lurking
	292–23	Charity thus *s·* as admonition
	341–21	*s·* to illustrate the evil of
	373– 1	One incident *s·* to illustrate the
Ret.	76–20	*s·* to constitute the Mind-healer a.
'02.	7–24	passage which *s·* to confirm C. S.
My.	91–17	* *s·* to call attention to one of the
	342–17	* which *s·* as a library,

service

My.	184–22	*s·* acceptable in God's sight.
	250– 9	three years of acceptable *s·* as

after the

My.	38–25	* Scientists said after the *s·*

another

Pul.	42– 4	* At 10 : 30 o'clock another *s·* began,

before the

My.	54– 8	* crowded one hour before the *s·*

charity, and

'00.	15–24	charity, and *s·*, and faith, *Rev.* 2 : 19.

children's

Mis.	315– 4	The children's *s·* shall be held
My.	78–26	* chapter sub-title

Christian

My.	36–11	* holy Christian *s·* that shall be

Christ's

My.	147–24	already dedicated to Christ's *s·*,

church

Mis.	177–23	* the hour for the church *s·*

Communion

Mis.	314–28	observed at the Communion *s·* ;

communion

My.	27– 6	annual meeting and communion *s·*,
	29– 3	* chapter sub-title
	140–14	* dropping the annual communion *s·* of
	141– 3	* The general communion *s·* of

consecration

Pul.	31– 1	* its consecration *s·* on January 6

dedication

Pul.	41–29	* until the hour for the dedication *s·*

dedicatory

Pul.	59–29	* at the second dedicatory *s·*.
My.	31–30	* as the opening of the dedicatory *s·*.

each

My.	35–27	* During the progress of each *s·*,
	38–12	* church was filled for each *s·*

Easter

Mis.	180–16	I *love* the Easter *s·* :

end of the

My.	32– 4	* at the end of the *s·*,

service

evening

My.	29–31	* until the close of the evening *s·*,

faithful

Mis.	158–15	reward for your faithful *s·*,
Pan.	14–21	and their faithful *s·* thereof,

first

My.	56–30	* repetitions of the first *s·*.

God's

My.	195–16	use in God's *s·* the one talent

half past twelve

My.	78–28	* of the half past twelve *s·* ;

His

'01.	1– 6	so long as you are in His *s·*.
My.	251–26	armors, and tests in His *s·*,

its

Pul.	28–17	* save that its *s·* includes

Memorial

My.	284–13	referring to the Memorial *s·*
	284–19	the aforesaid Memorial *s·*

morning

Man.	58–12	Lesson-Sermon in the morning *s·*
Pul.	34– 9	* before proceeding to his morning *s·*,
My.	56– 6	* repetition of the morning *s·*.
	56–25	* crowded condition of the morning *s·*

much

My.	324– 9	* no one could be of much *s·*

next

My.	38–11	* admitted until the next *s·*.

of Christian Science

Mis.	91–17	employed in the *s·* of C. S.

one

Pul.	59–29	* Before one *s·* was over and the

order of

Pul.	28–14	* heading
	28–15	* order of *s·* in the C. S. Church
	60– 3	* new order of *s·* went into operation.
My.	32–12	* order of *s·* was as follows :

postal

'02.	11–13	postal *s·*, a steam engine,

reasonable

Mis.	184–11	which is our reasonable *s·* ;
My.	vii–13	* a reasonable *s·* which all

repeated

Pul.	40–12	* *S·* Repeated Four Times

rules of

My.	342–31	its present rules of *s·*

said

Mis.	302–22	destroyed . . . after said *s·*.

such

Man.	69–12	during the time of such *s·*.

such a

Mis.	80– 3	By rendering error such a *s·*,

Sunday

Mis.	302–21	reading my works for Sunday *s·* ;
	315– 4	after the manner of the Sunday *s·*.
My.	54–31	* Sunday *s·* held in Chickering Hall
	56– 3	* Attendance at the Sunday *s·*
	74– 8	* in time for the first Sunday *s·*.
	147– 1	chapter sub-title

telephone

My.	73–24	* telegraph and telephone *s·*.

ten o'clock

My.	30–30	* admission at the ten o'clock *s·*,

term of

Man.	69– 5	Incomplete Term of *S·*.

that

Mis.	314–31	such as is adapted to that *s·*.

their

My.	38–21	* their *s·* was the same as all

this

Man.	61–14	at this *s·* the Tenets
Pul.	42– 1	* Before this *s·* had closed
My.	42–18	* endeavor to perform this *s·*
	54–32	* Mrs. Eddy preached at this *s·*

was repeated

Pul.	41–19	* Hence the *s·* was repeated until
	42– 5	* at 3 p. m. the *s·* was repeated

Pul.	29– 9	* *s·* held in Copley Hall
	29–14	* pressed into *s·* for the
	66–17	* belief and *s·* are well suited to
My.	30– 2	* either coming from a *s·* or
	30–27	* for the *s·* at half past seven,
	38–16	* for the *s·* at half past twelve
	61–18	* ready for the *s·*, June 10.''
	150– 9	* the *s·* of such a mission.

serviceable

Mis.	278–22	This may be a *s·* hint,

services

afternoon

My.	147– 5	morning and afternoon *s·*

after the

My.	50–32	* committee met after the *s·*

services

all the
  My. 22– 6 * attendance at all the *s*,
      30– 3 * As all the *s* were . . . the same
any
  Pul. 87– 2 * any *s* that may be held therein.
attended
  My. 141– 6 * *s* attended last Sunday [June 14] by
Church
  Man. 63– 8 Quarterly Lessons, read in Church *s*.
church
  Man. 72– 9 church *s* conducted by reading the
  Pul. 9–17 church *s* were maintained by
communion
  My. 56–32 * Our communion *s* and annual
conduct the
  My. 71–26 Readers who conduct the *s*
continuous
  Pul. 59– 6 * continuous *s* were held
dedicatory
  My. 29– 7 * incident of the dedicatory *s*
      58–29 * attended the dedicatory *s*
      82–14 * At the dedicatory *s* of
      94–20 * dedicatory *s* were being held
     195– 5 invitation to the dedicatory *s*
desire for
  My. 54–21 * desire for *s* was so great
Easter
  Mis. 177–21 chapter sub-title
four
  Pul. 57– 7 * at the four *s* on the day of
gratuitous
  Mis. 349–27 to receive my gratuitous *s*,
identical
  My. 86–30 * At each of the identical *s*,
introductory
  My. 80–16 * introductory *s* were identical,
menial
  Pul. 8–18 never before devoted to menial *s*,
morning
  Man. 59–24 come to attend the morning *s*.
my
  Ret. 40– 3 refusing to take any pay for my *s*
  My. 244–27 No charge will be made for my *s*.
     325–12 * Years ago I offered my *s*
of Sunday
  My. 66–27 * *s* of Sunday will mark an epoch
order of the
  My. 16–21 * The order of the *s*,
other
  Man. 58–15 shall be repeated at the other *s*
public
  Mis. 299–14 * and read them for our public *s*?"
     301–21 and read them for our public *s*?"
  Man. 74– 2 C. S. society holding public *s*,
  My. 51–11 * to have the public *s* discontinued
regular
  Pul. 68–17 * It now holds regular *s*
secure the
  My. 63– 2 * secure the *s* of Mr. Whitcomb
six
  My. 66–22 * when six *s* will be held,
     78– 3 * six *s*, identical in character,
Sunday
  Mis. 176– 4 chapter sub-title
     302–15 through C. S. Sunday *s*.
     314– 3 From this date the Sunday *s*
     382–29 denominational form of Sunday *s*,
  Man. 31–17 principal part of the Sunday *s*,
     61– 5 not hold two or more Sunday *s*
  My. 54–19 * the Sunday *s* were postponed.
     55–19 * In the mean time Sunday *s*
     55–26 * in that place Sunday *s* were held
     56– 7 * inauguration of two Sunday *s*
their
  Rud. 14– 3 must give Him all their *s*,
     14– 5 suitable price for their *s*,
these
  Pul. 42– 8 * exercises at any one of these *s*.
those
  Pul. 81– 5 * than it was during those *s*,
three
  My. 56–29 * three *s* were held each Sunday,
two
  My. 56– 4 * in consequence two *s* were held,
uninterrupted
  Man. 60– 2 *s* UNINTERRUPTED.
valuable
  My. 62–26 * valuable *s* rendered to this Board
     63– 5 * and for their valuable *s*,
Wednesday evening
  Man. 31–21 of the Wednesday evening *s*,

  Man. 60– 4 *s* of The Mother Church
     72–14 *s* of such a church may be
  My. 31–25 * soloist for the *s*, Mrs. Hunt,

services
  My. 32– 2 * striking features of the *s*.
     51–30 * all who have attended the *s*,
     53–11 * The *s* were held there until
     61–10 * announcement that the *s* would
     62–29 * also the *s* of other members
     78–14 * at the beginning of the *s*
     78–21 * remarkable features of the *s*
    141–12 * announcement in regard to the *s*
serving
  Mis. 7–12 if *s* Christ, Truth,
    303–16 If ever I wear out from *s* students,
  Man. 67–24 Opportunity for *S* the Leader.
     68–10 Members thus *s* the Leader
  Ret. 90– 5 while he is *s* another fold?
  Pul. 38–29 * *s* those who find in one form
  '00. 10–29 for a soldier *s* his country
  My. 287– 8 *s* as admonition, instruction, and
servitude
  '00. 3– 9 worker's *s* is duly valued,
  My. 218–25 My private life is given to a *s*
session
  Mis. 134–11 at the annual *s* of the National
    136–22 I recommend that the June *s*
  My. 39– 2 * a second *s* was held at two o'clock
sessions
  Mis. 136–24 hold three *s* annually,
  Man. 57–10 (excepting its regular *s*)
     90– 8 *S*.
     90–11 *s* will continue not over one week.
     90–14 shall be present at the *s*,
  Pul. 4–29 used, in all its public *s*,
  My. 82–15 * at the *s* of the annual meeting,
    121– 4 in order to separate these *s* from
set
  Mis. 9–23 *s* it aside as tasteless
    71–11 *Does C. S. s* aside the law of
    72–15 teeth are *s* on edge— *Ezek.* 18 : 2.
    76–15 to *s* a human soul free from its
   133–19 to *s* you right on this question,
   187–16 as *s* forth in original Holy Writ.
   194–31 *s* forth in the text,
   214– 6 to *s* a man at variance— *Matt.* 10 : 35.
   255– 3 *s* themselves on pedestals,
   323– 2 "a city *s* upon a hill,"— *see Matt.* 5 : 14.
   337–12 *s* him in the midst of— *Matt.* 18 : 2.
   ,345– 8 * "I will *s* the beasts upon you,
   345–11 *s* fire to the fagots,
   353–14 *s* a man who applied for work,
   353–27 *s* up housekeeping alone.
   361–19 race that is *s* before us,— *Heb.* 12 : 1.
  Man. 51– 1 By-Laws or Rules herein *s* forth,
  Ret. 2– 5 *s* forth in the pages of
    22–11 joy that was *s* before him— *Heb.* 12 : 2.
    22–12 *s* down at the right hand of— *Heb.* 12 : 2.
    38–10 I *s* to work, contrary to my
    50– 1 impelled me to *s* a price on
    62– 4 find that the views here *s* forth
    79–23 jewels of Love, *s* in wisdom.
    95– 7 * And *s* apart Unto a life of
  Un. 1– 3 may be *s* down as one of the
  Pul. 16– 1 *S* to the Church Chimes
    21–30 Popularity, . . . must be *s* aside.
    49–26 * the will of the woman *s* at work,
    54–22 * they are fully *s* forth.
    58–13 * In the belfry is a *s* of
    59–28 * seats were especially *s* apart
    60–11 * Scripture parallels, as *s* down
    76– 5 * superb archway . . . *s* in the wall.
    81– 6 * *s* forth as the power of God
  Rud. 7– 6 *s* forth in my work S. and H.
  Pan. 14– 4 *S* your affections on things above ;
  '01. 6–20 which is *s* aside to some degree,
  '02. 9–13 Loving chords *s* discords in harmony.
  Peo. 13–21 *s* fire to the fagots,
  Po. 1–10 from chaos dark *s* free,
    68–20 star of our friendship arose not to *s* ;
  My. 22–18 * every purpose she has *s* in motion,
    36–28 * and *s* up this tabernacle,
    43–17 * were *s* up on the other side
    67–18 * Two million dollars was *s* aside
    71– 1 * a *s* of cathedral chimes,
    71–20 * traditions . . . have been *s* aside
    72– 2 * necessary to *s* aside the traditions
    80– 7 * when having broken bones *s* ;
    85–20 * another "landmark" *s* in the illustrious
    91– 7 * Christian Scientists *s* a good example
    96–22 * before the day *s* for the dedication
   103–18 I have *s* forth C. S.
   133–15 *s* the captive sense free
   155–14 the race *s* before it,
   161– 2 paid our debt and *s* us free
   179– 2 synoptic Scriptures, as *s* forth in
   197–20 for the hope *s* before us

set
My. 214–11   s· the seal of eternity on time.
     216– 1   plainly s· forth in the Scriptures.
     258–14   for the joy that was s· before him
     258–16   and is s· down at the right hand of
     310–24   * s· the house in an uproar,''

sets
Mis. 72– 4   Science s· aside man as a creator,
     101–17   and s· the captive free,
     329– 6   s· the earth in order ;
Pul. 62–22   * little s· of silver bells
     80–19   * speak of the system it s· forth,
Po.   3– 9   Till sleep s· drooping fancy free

setting
Ret. 27– 2   s· forth their spiritual
My. 203–12   nor by s· up to be great,
     248– 7   You are not s· up to be great ;

settings
My. 12–29   gems in the s· of manhood

settle
Mis. 265–27   constantly called to s· questions
Pul.   9–15   and helped s· the subject.
My. 181– 2   to s· all points beyond cavil,
     277–20   can s· all questions amicably
     358–15   will s· the question whether or not
     360–13   if I can s· this church difficulty

settled
Mis. 165–25   accordingly as this account is s·
     224–22   with an equanimity so s·
Ret. 87– 9   s· and systematic workers,
Pul. 51–10   * There is really nothing s·.
My. 277– 4   s· peacefully by statesmanship
     286– 9   wisely, fairly ; and fully s·.

settlement
My. 279–24   amicable s· of the war

settlers
No. 46–14   first s· of New Hampshire.

settles
Mis. 192–31   This declaration . . . s· the question ;
     204–15   This mental condition s· into strength,
'02. 12– 4   s· the whole question on the basis that
My. 277–10   never s· the question of his life.

settling
Mis. 380– 1   and s· the question,
My. 277– 7   no other way of s· difficulties
     309– 5   making out deeds, s· quarrels,

set-to
Mis. 231–22   instead of a real s· at crying,

seven
Mis. 279–17   s· times around these walls,
     279–17   the s· times corresponding to
     279–18   the s· days of creation :
     348–18   once in about s· years
Man. 62– 1   six or s· minutes for the postlude,
Pul.   6–17   * an ailment of s· years' standing.
     37–27   * was organized . . . by s· persons,
     58–14   * s· excellent class-rooms,
     67–26   * was organized by s· persons,
No. 23–11   Out of . . . Jesus cast s· devils ;
Pan. 3–28   His pipe of s· reeds denotes
     3–29   harmony of the s· planets ;
'00. 12– 3   "holdeth the s· stars — Rev. 2 : 1.
     12– 4   s· golden candlesticks" — Rev. 2 : 1.
     14– 6   He goes on to portray s· churches,
'pc. 13– 5   During the last s· years
My. 30–28   * for the service at half past s·,
     30–32   * Before half past s· the chimes
     68–28   * s· broad marble stairways,
     69–16   * auditorium contains s· galleries,
     70–28   * s· combination pedals,
     80–31   * long before s· the auditorium
     (see also **numbers, values**)

seven-eighths
Rud. 14– 9   gave fully s· of her time

seven-fold
My. 200–18   s· shield of honesty, purity,

seven-hued
Chr. 53–38   now blends In s· white !

seven-pointed
Pul. 25–17   * sunburst with a s· star,
     42–21   * a huge s· star was hung

seventeen
Ret. 50–16   as many as s· in one class.
Rud. 14–14   sometimes s·, free students
My. 311–14   at the age of s·

seventeenth
Ret. 2–19   s· and eighteenth centuries.
My. 221–32   In the s· chapter of the Gospel

seventh
Mis. 225– 9   s· modern wonder, C. S. ;
     279–19   the s· is the day of rest,
My. 336– 2   * would have died on the s· day.

seventieth
Mis. 191– 8   John, sixth chapter and s· verse,

seventy-eight
     (see **numbers**)

seventy-fifth
     (see **numbers**)

seventy-five
     (see **values**)

seventy-four
My. 148–17   membership of s· communicants,

Seventy-third Edition
Man. 104–12   S· Edition the Authority.
     104–15   keep a copy of the S· Edition

seventy-two
My. 69– 3   * each suspending s· lamps,
     70–26   * s· stops, nineteen couplers,

several
Mis. 141–29   return . . . to the s· contributors,
     144–10   on which appear your s· names
     169–28   * Taking s· Bible passages,
     191 19   s· individuals cast out of
     236– 6   after eating s· ice-creams,
     048–26   Hence I tried s· doses of
     349–18   and s· other students with him.
     378– 9   in company with s· other patients,
Man. 28–17   the functions of their s· offices
     77–15   performance of their s· offices
Pul. 23–12   * under s· different aspects
     42–10   * presence of s· hundred children
     57–22   * s· sects of mental healers,
     69– 8   * after s· doctors had pronounced
Rud. 14–13   without s·, . . . free students in it ;
No. 22–21   That Jesus cast s· persons out of
Hea. 3–17   Josephus alludes to s· individuals
My. 55– 5   * S· places were considered,
     73–14   * as they have been for s· days past
     73–15   * and will be for s· days to come,
     78– 9   * series of arches in the s· facades.
     216–23   work in your own s· localities,
     243– 3   the s· churches in New York City
     014– 6   * doctor practised in s· towns,
     320–20   * I called on Mr. Wiggin s· times
     320–31   * s· times subsequent thereto,
     320–32   * I saw Mr. Wiggin s· times
     346–12   * made s· turns about the court-house
     (see also **years**)

severe
Mis. 35– 5   s· casualty pronounced . . . incurable,
     107–20   and repentance so s· that it
     203–21   gain s· views of themselves ;
     250–11   this imposes on me the s· task of
Ret. 80– 4   gentle, yet it may seem s·.
Pul. 34– 6   * met with a s· accident,
No. 5– 6   s· realities of this error.
     41–15   is to subject them to s· scrutiny.
'00. 2–24   more sudden, s·, and lasting
My. 80– 8   * s· tax upon frail human credulity,
     149–32   no condition, be it ever so s·,
     190–15   failing to cure a s· case of lunacy,

severed
Mis. 105–21   his ideal can never be s·.
     386–13   "When, s· by death's dream,
Po. 49–19   "When, s· by death's dream,
My. 129–17   never s· from Spirit !

severely
Mis. 12– 7   punish, more s· than you could,

severest
My. 103– 3   summons the s· conflicts of the ages

severs
Mis. 285–23   s· the marriage covenant,

sex
Man. 50– 4   by one of her own s·.
Pul. 82–21   * for their people, not for their s·.
     82–24   * singing most for their own s·.
My. 239–27   a kind of man who is identified by s·
     249–27   without reference to s· I should
     268–30   s· or gender eliminated ;

sexes
No. 45–19   vindicated by the noblest of both s·.
My. 247– 9   equality of the s·, rotation in office.
     255– 2   equality of the s·, rotation in office.''

shackle
Mis. 246–17   to s· conscience, stop free speech,

shackles
My. 44– 3   * the s· of sin are being broken,

shade

Mis. 392– 9 Thy sheltering s·,
396–16 Beneath the maple's s·.
399– 3 will lift the s· of gloom,
Ret. 90– 2 s· God's window which lets in light,
Un. 27– 4 really have a s· of difference
Pul. 2–10 Material light and s· are temporal,
63–11 * s· her delightful country home
Pan. 3–16 * or in thy evening s·,
Po. 20–12 Thy sheltering s·,
29–14 Was but thy s· !
59– 8 Beneath the maple's s·.
67–15 s· o'er the dark wavy grass.
75–10 will lift the s· of gloom,
My. 107–22 or scatter the s· of one who
166–14 Days of s· and shine
342–12 * s· of which is so hard to catch,

shaded

Mis. 142–18 s· as autumn leaves

shades

Mis. 1–21 seemingly rolled up in s·,
372–30 gives scopes and s· to the
Pul. 48– 8 * in the lights and s· of spring
Rud. 16–23 Minor s· of difference in
Po. 78– 8 S· of our heroes !

shading

Po. 53– 5 And soft thy s· lay

shadow

Mis. 33– 9 s· of Truth's appearing
88–16 in the s· of darkling criticism
105–22 the s· cast by this error.
131–10 so s· forth the substance
134–15 is bigger than the s·,
144–17 s· of a great rock — Isa. 32 : 2.
157–14 under the s· of His wing.
180– 5 dark s· and portal of death,
203–16 topically as type and s·.
231– 5 had seen sunshine and s·
239– 8 my s· is not growing less ;
253–20 type and s· of this hour.
263– 9 s· of a great rock — Isa. 32 : 2.
368– 9 * Standeth God within the s·,
386– 2 Beyond the s·, infinite appear
389–18 Beneath the s· of His mighty wing ;
Chr. 55– 9 the s· of death, — Isa. 9 : 2.
Ret. 18–25 This life is a s·, and hastens
21–16 "as the s· when it — see Psal. 102 : 11.
25–14 I called error and s·
Un. 14–18 neither s· of turning." — Jas. 1 : 17.
27–14 fleeing like a s· at daybreak ;
40– 4 this dark s· of material sense,
57– 7 s· of the Almighty." — Psal. 91 : 1.
63– 9 no variableness or s· of turning,
Pul. 20–15 type and s· of the warfare
20–16 s· whose substance is the
20–19 s· of a great rock — Isa. 32 : 2.
Po. 4–17 s· of His mighty wing ;
23– 1 a s· on thy brow
42– 1 there's never a s· where
49– 4 Beyond the s·, infinite appear
64–22 This life is a s·,
My. 107–23 s· of the Almighty"? — Psal. 91 : 1.
182–21 Love that reigns above the s·,
190– 1 Did that midnight s·,
206–14 through the s· called death,
210–15 under the s· of the Almighty.
260– 7 and the s· of frivolity
268–21 flutters . . . as an unreal s·,
290–20 has passed earth's s·
294–29 through the s· of death
350–21 Stygian s· of a world of glee

shadowed

Un. 5–25 s· forth in scientific thought.

shadows

Mis. 71–28 human concepts, mortal s·
205– 5 melting away the s· called sin,
222–32 dawns the morning light and s· flee,
264– 8 s· thrown upon the mists of time,
329–21 challenging the sedentary s· to
352–11 human s· of thought lengthen
372–30 shades to the s· of divinity,
Ret. 21–17 heavenly intent of earth's s·
Un. 44– 6 are vain s·, repeating
Po. 3– 4 When noonday's length'ning s· flee,
8– 1 sitting alone where the s· fall
24–15 Come when the s· fall,
30–15 dark s· cast on Thy blest name,
My. 19–18 our s· follow us in the sunlight
184–19 a love which stays the s· of years.

shadowy

Un. 46– 2 These are the s· and false,
Po. 25– 6 s· throng Around you in memory rise !
27– 6 grow tremulous with s· night !

shaft

My. 128–28 s· aimed at you or your practice

shafts

Mis. 277– 8 becomes the mark for error's s·.

shake

Mis. 330–14 to s· out their tresses
Hea. 12–21 cannot s· the poor drug without

shaken

No. 22–11 reeds s· by the wind.
My. 21–19 * pressed down, and s· — Luke 6 : 38.
108–27 * "Mrs. Eddy not s·"
117– 6 "a reed s· with the wind," — Matt. 11 : 7.

Shakers

My. 313–22 interested in the S·,

Shakespeare (see also Shakespeare's)

Mis. 8–21 S· writes : "Sweet are the uses of
226–13 S·, the immortal lexicographer
267–15 signature
Ret. 81–22 S· puts this pious counsel into

Shakespearean

Un. 23– 9 How well the S· tale agrees with

Shakespeare's

Un. 22–23 In S· tragedy of King Lear,

shaking

Hea. 13– 6 s· the preparation thirty times

shallow

Mis. 265–15 egotistical theorist or s· moralist
296– 9 to overflow in s· sarcasm,
357–14 on stony ground and s· soil.

sham

Mis. 250–19 cast aside the word as a s· and
365–24 infidelity, bigotry, or s· has never

shambles

Mis. 269–25 C. S. may be sold in the s·.
285–24 puts virtue in the s·,

shame

Mis. 267–17 suffered temporary s· and loss
296–31 his s· would not lose its blush !
Ret. 22–12 despising the s·, — Heb. 12 : 2.
Un. 56– 8 "put him to an open s·." — Heb. 6 : 6.
My. 258–15 despising the s·, — Heb. 12 : 2.

shamed

Mis. 332–21 s· the face of mortals.
Pul. 83– 4 * our better self is s· and

shameful

Peo. 13–14 forcing from the lips of manhood s·

shameless

Mis. 121–24 s· insult to divine royalty,
210–25 s· brow of licentiousness,

shamelessness

My. 340–16 shorn of some of its s·

shames

Mis. 183–23 while it s· human pride.

shape

Pan. 11–18 in order to be in proper s·,
My. 65–20 * in the s· of a triangle,
66– 3 * in the s· of a triangle,
67– 7 * S·, triangular . . . 220x220x236 ft.

shapeless

Peo. 7–12 * carved the dream on that s· stone

share

Mis. 290–26 s· the benefit of that radiation.
290–30 all who are receptive s· this
321–24 to s· the hospitality of their
391–17 S· God's most tender mercies,
Pul. 51–27 * s· of attention it deserves,
'01. 16–12 surviving defamers s· our pity.
35–17 the working hitherto — Shall we s· it
Po. 38–16 S· God's most tender mercies,
My. 83–31 * s· of the necessary expense
120–10 s· with me the bliss of seeing the
218–26 fruit of which all mankind may s·.
220–30 s· alike liberty of conscience,
244– 4 wish to s· this opportunity
317– 6 * that Mr. Wiggin had a s· in the

shared

Mis. 55– 7 as much . . . as he s·,
278–19 have s· less of my labors
369–23 which he s· with the swine,
My. 51–30 * gratitude s· by all who

shares

Un. 56–14 s· his cup of sorrows.
My. 217–11 equal s· to each contributor.

sharing

Mis. 239–21 Her apparent pride at s·
My. 63–19 * s· in our joy.

Sharon's

Chr. 53–31 S· rose must bud and bloom

sharp

Mis.	13– 5	s· return of evil for good
	246–15	another s· cry of oppression.
	396– 5	cricket's s·, discordant scream
Pan.	12–15	the burden of s· experience
	12–27	by bold conjecture's s· point,
'00.	15–15	it yields to s· conviction
Peo.	7–13	* With many a s· incision.
	7–21	* With many a s· incision,
Po.	58–17	cricket's s·, discordant scream
My.	69– 6	* no s· angles are visible,
	244–18	a struggle or s· experience,

sharper

'02.	13– 4	incurred a s· fire from enmity.

sharply

Mis.	277–29	and s· lighten on the cloud of
Ret.	8–20	Mehitable then said s·,

shattered

Pul.	9– 7	never be s· in our hearts,

shatters

My.	206– 4	and s· whatever hinders the

sheathed

Ret.	11– 9	The sword is s·,
Po.	60– 6	The sword is s·,
My.	185– 9	nor will it be s· till Truth

sheaves

Mis.	313–20	the rich s· are ripe,
	332–10	hues of heaven, ripened s·,
Po.	47–20	are the s· and the gladness
My.	170–30	bearing your s· with you.
	202–26	bringing your s· into the
	291–25	her s· garnered, her treasury filled,

shed

Mis.	65–31	shall his blood be s·." — Gen. 9 : 6.
	385–25	faith . . . s· Majestic forms ;
Ret.	17–11	when the dewdrop is s·
	81– 3	The unavailing tear is s·
Po.	9– 9	leaves all faded, the fruitage s·,
	25–11	Sweetly to s· Fragrance fresh
	46– 6	Its leaves have s· or bowed the
	47–15	Over the tears it has s· ;
	48–22	faith . . . s· Majestic forms ;
	62–14	when the dewdrop is s·
My.	62–12	* s· its brightest beams on your
	91–12	* and s· sunshine about them
	294–31	s· "the unavailing tear."
	347– 12	* boughs, that cannot s· Your leaves,

sheddeth

Mis.	65–30	"whoso s· man's blood, — Gen. 9 : 6.

shedding

No.	33–20	though s· human blood
My.	350–14	the scalding tear man's s·,

sheep (see also sheep's)

Mis.	151– 1	folds the s· of His pasture;
	151– 3	"My s· hear my voice, — John 10 : 27.
	213–22	"My s· hear my voice, — John 10 : 27.
	244–24	"And other s· I have, — John 10 : 16.
	357– 5	Let them seek the lost s·
	370–20	separate the s· from the goats ;
	397–21	poem — John 21 : 16.
	397–25	How to feed Thy s· ;
Ret.	page 46	poem — John 21 : 16.
	46– 6	How to feed Thy s·;
	52–11	provide folds for the s·
	80–23	the older s· pass into the fold
	85–24	scatter the s· abroad ;
Pul.	14– 1	poem — John 21 : 16.
	17– 5	How to feed Thy s· ;
Po.	page 14	poem — John 21 : 16.
	14– 4	How to feed Thy s· ;

sheepcot

Ret.	80–23	carries his lambs . . . to the s·,

sheep's

Mis.	294–18	from wolves in s· clothing
	323–13	wolves in s· clothing are ready to
	325– 6	Christian Scientists in s· clothing ;
	370–20	a wolf in s· clothing?
My.	215–21	wolves in s· clothing," — see Matt. 7 : 15.

sheer

Mis.	230–17	spend no time in s· idleness.
Un.	16– 4	would they be s· nonsense,
No.	43–26	through the s· ignorance of people,

sheet

Man.	98–12	shall read the last proof s·

shelf

Mis.	250–14	not something put upon a s·,

shelter

Mis.	154– 5	reaching out their broad s·
	347– 8	people prepare s· in caves
	362–25	find s· from the storm

shelter

Ret.	52– 5	should s· its perfections
Pul.	10–24	s· of this house,
My.	147– 7	flung its foliage in kindly s·
	182–28	find s· from the storm

sheltered

Mis.	14–31	But the sinner is not s·
	152–24	s· in the strong tower
Rud.	13–27	to be fed, clothed, and s·

sheltering (see also shelt'ring)

Mis.	392– 9	pouring down Thy s· shade,
Po.	20–12	pouring down Thy s· shade,
My.	36–25	* by this s· dome ;

shelt'ring

Mis.	387– 8	Brood o'er us with Thy s· wing,
Po.	6– 1	Brood o'er us with Thy s· wing,

Shepherd

Mis.	9– 6	Well is it that the S· of Israel
	150– 3	you have the great S· of Israel
	150–31	hence God is our S·.
	275–14	May the great S· that
	322–14	S· that feedeth my flock,
	357– 7	have lost their great S·
	357–28	the true fold and the great S·,
	370–28	good S· does care for all,
	371– 6	the care of the great S·,
	397–22	S·, show me how to go
	398–20	S·, wash them clean.
Ret.	46– 3	S·, show me how to go
	46–26	S·, wash them clean.
Pul.	17– 2	S·, show me how to go
	17–25	S·, wash them clean.
Po.	14– 1	S·, show me how to go
	14–24	S·, wash them clean.
My.	31– 3	"S·, show me how to go ;"
	162–25	S· of this feeble flock
	177–19	the great S· has nurtured

shepherd (see also shepherd's)

Mis.	162–31	simple as the s· boy,
	270–19	one fold, and one s· ;" — John 10 : 16.
	303– 5	kindly s· has his own fold
	321– 2	watchful s· chants his welcome
	370–27	the good s· cares for all
Chr.	55–25	one fold, and one s·. — John 10 : 16.
Ret.	80–22	The kindly s· of the East
	90– 4	Does the faithful s· forsake
My.	257– 4	To-day the watchful s·

Shepherd of Israel

Mis.	150– 3	S· of I· watching over you.

shepherd's

Mis.	195–25	s· sling would slay this Goliath.
Pan.	3–29	his s· crook, that care and

shepherds

Mis.	168–19	s· shout, "We behold the
Ret.	59–11	sheep that were without s·,
Pan.	3–26	Pan was the god of s·

shibboleth

No.	9–22	Science is not the s· of a sect

shield

Mis.	113–25	our hope, strength, and s·.
	358–10	his s· and great reward.
Un.	11– 1	to s· them from the penalty
'01.	32–11	s· the whole world in their hearts,
'02.	14– 7	life-giving spiritual s·
	19–13	his s· and his buckler.
Po.	43–12	S· and guide and guard them ;
My.	200–18	the seven-fold s· of honesty,
	292–10	O may His love s·, support,

shielded

Pan.	14–24	s· by the power that saved
'02.	14–24	What has s· and prospered
My.	210– 9	s· from the attacks of error

shift

Mis.	233–20	a poor s· for the weak
	288–23	the s· of a dishonest mind,
My.	287–11	a poor s· for the weak

shifting

Mis.	13–19	the s· mortal senses confirm
Ret.	81–27	s· scenes of human happiness,
Un.	14–19	the s· vane on the spire,

shifts

Mis.	286–17	put ingenuity to ludicrous s· ;
'01.	29–20	waiting 'till the wind s·.
Peo.	3–25	certain unspiritual s·, such as

shimmer

Pul.	2– 7	soft s· of its starlit dome.
	76–10	* which in certain lights has a s·

shine

Mis.	54– 4	Has the sun forgotten to s·,
	303– 2	s· from their home summits

shine
Mis. 340–29 s· with the reflected light of God.
Hea. 20– 4 * Which in our Saviour s·,
Po. 70–22 S· on our 'wildered way,
     79– 3 storm or s·, pure peace is thine,
My. 166–14 Days of shade and s· may come
    183–27 "Arise, s·; for thy light is— Isa. 60: 1.
    191–11 Let your light s·.
    206–21 neither of the moon, to s·— Rev. 21: 23.
    355–22 s· with the reflection of light

shined
Chr. 55– 9 upon them hath the light s·.— Isa. 9: 2.

shines
Mis. 363–18 His manifold wisdom s· through the
Ret. 57–15 Man s· by borrowed light.
Un. 58–20 midnight sun s· over the Polar Sea.
Pul. 28– 4 * star of Bethlehem s· down
     83–25 * royalty which s· from her brow.
'02. 17–20 sun s· but to show man the
My. 110– 7 and it s· as of yore,
    301– 2 it s· with borrowed rays
    355–25 and their light s·.

shineth
Mis. 368– 3 light that s· in darkness,
Un. 63–10 light which s· in darkness,
My. 110– 8 "s· in darkness ; — John 1: 5.

shining
Mis. 171–29 all clad in the s· mail
    205– 4 s· through the mists of materiality
My. 355–20 * He hides a s· face."

Shintoism
'02.   3– 5 Buddhism and S· are said to

ship
Pul. 80– 2 * s· when under stress of storm

shipwreck
Mis. 268–16 suffers no s· in a starless night

shirk
Un. 26– 7 I s· all responsibility for myself

shoals
Mis. 268–17 on the s· of vainglory.
    363–22 avoid the s· of a sensual religion

shock
Mis. 397–11 waves can s·, Oh, nevermore !
Pul. 18–20 waves can s·, Oh, nevermore !
Rud. 15– 6 is a s· to the mind ;
Po. 12–21 waves can s·, Oh, nevermore !
     18–18 and earthquakes may s·,

shocked
Mis. 210–16 will not be s· when she
Pul. 14– 5 s· into another extreme mortal mood,
     74– 2 * chapter sub-title

shocking
Mis. 112–26 s· inability to see one's own faults,
    350– 5 * not "terrible and too s· to relate."
No. 29–18 such a statement is a s· reflection
     35–17 s· human idolatry that presupposes
My. 276–10 s· fact that she is minding her own

shockingly
Peo.   2–16 s· material in practice,

shocks
Pul. 74–15 "Even the question s· me.

shoes
Mis. 17– 8 you take off your s·
    120– 2 take off their s· at our altars ;
No. 27–25 take off thy s· and tread lightly,

shone
Chr. 53– 3 s· One lone, brave star.
Ret.   4–15 peaches, pears, and cherries s·
Peo.   7–14 * With . . . light the sculptor s·,

shoot
No.   3– 2 envy will bend its bow and s·

shore
Mis. 81–21 has not Truth yet reached the s·?
     82–11 stand upon the s· of eternity,
    111–10 will not pull for the s· ;
    206– 6 dashing against the receding s·,
    212– 7 On the s· of Gennesaret
    251– 5 from the Pacific to the Atlantic s·,
    385–14 Spirit emancipate for this far s·
    397–10 Life's s·, 'Gainst which the winds
    398– 9 Strangers on a barren s·,
Ret. 46–15 Strangers on a barren s·,
Pul. 17–14 Strangers on a barren s·,
     18–19 Life's s· ; 'Gainst which the winds
'02. 11– 1 to leave on a foreign s·.
Po. 12–19 Life's s·, 'Gainst which the winds
     14–13 Strangers on a barren s·,
     48– 7 Spirit emancipate for this far s·
     73– 5 hoarse wave revisits thy s· !
My. 126– 5 swimmer struggling for the s·,

shoreless
Mis. 82– 6 floweth . . . into a s· eternity.

shores
Mis. 176–16 sought the New England s·,
    205–31 Mortals who on the s· of time
    295–24 resound from Albion's s·.
    393–16 From the s· afar, complete.
Ret. 91–15 s· of the Lake of Galilee,
Pul. 10–10 On s· of solitude, at Plymouth Rock,
No.   2–21 along the s· of erudition ;
'02. 11– 3 to wander on the s· of time
Po. 51–21 From the s· afar, complete.
My. 232– 5 looms of love that line the sacred s·.

shorn
Mis. 275–14 * "tempers the wind to the s· lamb,"
Hea. 18–25 no blind Samson s· of his locks.
My. 205–23 C. S., s· of all personality,
    340–16 s· of some of its shamelessness by

short
Mis. 24–15 That s· experience included a
    125–19 meanings of these s· sentences :
    224–28 Nothing s· of our own errors
    233–27 if some fall s·, others will
    285–10 Human life is too s· for foibles
    288–24 nothing s· of self-seeking ;
    297– 1 Taking into account the s· time
    380– 4 in s·, how can sinful mortals
    389– 3 In s·, the right to work
Ret.   7– 3 after a s· illness,
      7–10 * throughout his s· life.
     79–19 s· of the wisdom requisite for
     82–23 or fall s· of other religionists ;
Pul. 12–15 he hath but a s· time.— Rev. 12: 12.
     13–22 devil knoweth his time is s·.
'01.   2–15 if some fall s· of Truth,
     15–17 s· of the old orthodox hell
Po. 21–17 In s·, the right to work
My. 26–16 too s· to be printed in book form,
     39–11 * Then followed a s· silent prayer
     47–24 * the years . . . seem but a s· time.
     88– 6 * the development of a s· lifetime.
    114– 5 in s·, Do unto others
    173–23 Scientists' s· stay so pleasant.
    260–15 sense that falls s· of substance,
    262–10 falls far s· of my sense of the
    314– 3 * "lived for a s· time at Tilton,

shortcomings
Un. 14–11 s· of the Puritan's model?
My. 195–19 discontent with our s·.

shorten
Mis. 213– 7 point the way, s· the process,

shortened
Mis. 171– 1 "His hand is not s·— see Isa. 59: 1.
My. 292– 6 way pointed out, the process s·,

shortens
'02. 10–21 reformer . . . s· the distance,

shorthand
Mis. 95– 8 * s· reporter who was present,

short-lived
Ret. 32–16 * S· joy, that ends in sadness,
No. 37– 7 license of a s· sinner,

shortly
My. 57–27 * S· before the dedication of
    311– 7 S· after, . . . my good housekeeper

short-sighted
Mis. 209–12 S· physics admits the

shot
Mis. 223–30 arrow s· from another's bow

shoulder
Mis. 161– 6 shall be upon his s·:— Isa. 9: 6.
    166–21 shall be upon his s·."— Isa. 9: 6.
    167–21 shall be upon his s· !"— Isa. 9: 6.

shoulders
Ret. 16–14 carrying them on their s·.

shout
Mis. 168–19 shepherds s·, "We behold the appearing
    274–24 s· for class legislation,
    279–25 they had all to s· together
    342–17 they heard the s·,
    370– 9 sentinels of Zion's watch-towers s·
Po. 73– 6 waters s·, And the stars peep out,
My. 289–18 s· of love lives on in the heart

shouted
Mis. 259–21 sons of God s· for joy."— Job 38: 7.
Un. 42–15 sons of God s· for joy."— Job 38: 7.

shoutings
Mis. 400– 7 Dirge and song and s· low
Pul. 16–19 Dirge and song and s· low,
Po. 76–18 Dirge and song and s· low

shouts

Mis.	328– 1	Stranger s·, "Let them alone ;
	369– 2	look up with s· and thanksgiving,
My.	257– 4	watchful shepherd s· his welcome

shoveled

Pul.	8–18	Little hands, . . . s· snow,

show

Mis.	ix– 4	* the best alms are to s· and
	64– 4	to s· his power over death ;
	100– 8	s· the word and might of Truth
	100–15	finally s· the fruits of Love.
	114–28	s· us the powerlessness of evil,
	205–11	s· it unto you." — *John* 16 : 15.
	212–28	and tries to s· his errors to him
	221– 7	s· the fundamental Principle of
	348–13	and s· the plan of battle.
	363–32	s· their marked consonance with
	397– 1	s· Life's burdens light.
	397–22	Shepherd, s· me how to go
Man.	41– 6	s· the great gulf between C. S. and
	44– 2	writings must s· strict adherence to
	85–14	unless he has a certificate to s·
Ret.	11–15	Hero and sage arise to s·
	25– 1	take the things of God and s· them
	27– 7	s· that after my discovery of
	40–24	simply to s· the opposition
	46– 3	Shepherd, s· me how to go
	90– 6	There is no evidence to s·
Un.	18–17	s· My pity through divine law,
	45–15	to s· its all-pervading presence
Pul.	17– 2	Shepherd, s· me how to go
	18 10	his unveiled, sweet mercies s·
	50–27	* to s· even some one side of it
	55– 3	* Not for s· of power,
	67–10	* probably s· a greater number
		and s· the power of Love.
No.	9–21	his purpose was to s· them
	33–26	to s· the allness of Love
	35–11	to s· mortals the awful price
	35–14	s· the annual death-rate
'*00.*	7– 3	s· man the beauty of holiness
'*02.*	17–21	to s· its helplessness.
Hea.	3– 3	to s· itself infinite again.
	4–17	"I will s· thee my faith — *Jas.* 2 : 18.
Po.	5–24	s· Life's burdens light.
	12–10	Shepherd, s· me how to go
	14– 1	Hero and sage arise to s·
	60–12	"S· me thy faith — *Jas.* 2 : 18.
My.	3–12	* will s· the dollars and cents
	28– 8	"Shepherd, s· me how to go ;"
	31– 3	* reputation, time will s·.
	52–23	* s· a membership of 41,944.
	57–24	* all of which goes to s·
	76–15	* might s· that the Scientists
	97–12	s· conclusively that C. S.
	103– 8	to s· the folly of believing that
	106– 8	should s· us that even mortals
	110–23	to s· others the footsteps
	117–30	s· you a large upper room — *Luke* 22 : 12.
	156–16	cannot s· my love for them
	163–13	s· in livid lines that the
	177–18	s· that thirty years ago
	181–25	s· explicitly the attitude of
	199–14	s· forth the praises — *I Pet.* 2 : 9.
	206 14	Statistics s· that C. S.
	227–30	* which records s· really existed
	334–13	

showed

Mis.	44– 2	pattern s· to thee— *Heb.* 8 : 5.
	169–28	* Mrs. Eddy s· how beautiful
	201 12	he also s· forth the error
	248– 9	Greeks s· a just estimate
Ret.	40–12	they s· me the clothes
Un.	11– 9	He s· the need of changing this mind
No.	21–11	s· man as reflecting God
'*02.*	15–26	I s· it to my literary friends,
My.	16– 4	* report . . . s· that a total of
	38 11	* the visitors s· a tendency to
	47–19	* s· a forward effort
	50–25	* s· that still further provision
	145– 6	He drew the plan, s· it to me,
	288–23	s· that every effect or amplification

shower

Mis.	390–18	When sunshine beautifies the s·,
Po.	55–19	When sunshine beautifies the s·,
	70– 3	A bright and golden s·
My.	134–18	like a soft summer s·,
	343–18	a s· of abuse upon my head,

showers

Mis.	355–27	fall in mist and s· from
Po.	46– 5	Nor April's changeful s·,

showeth

Mis.	175– 3	s· them unto the creature,
	261–17	s· mercy by punishing sin.

showeth

Pan.	12–14	s· to all peoples the way of escape
'*01.*	9–23	s· them unto the creature ;

showing

Mis.	53–19	s· his ignorance of the meaning of
	105–10	after s· us the way to escape
	162–20	s· mortals how to escape from
	245– 1	no record s· that our Master ever
	285–21	s· its relation to C. S.
	327–23	s· them their folly,
	367– 8	s· that error is not Mind,
Ret.	31– 4	s· this solemn certainty in
Un.	11– 8	s· them to be laws of mortal mind,
	25–17	by s· God as its source.
Pul.	64–27	* s· that belief in that curious
'*01.*	29–13	inapt or selfish in s· their love.
'*02.*	6–12	a lie fathers itself, thereby s·
	18–26	s· their unfitness to follow him,
Hea.	12– 9	s· he was right.
Peo.	9–20	s· our greater faith in matter,
My.	24–13	* s· that The Mother Church
	269– 3	s· forth the infinite divine
	288–21	s· that all suffering

shown

Mis.	11–12	s· them the sure way of salvation,
	28–17	this great truth was s· by
	70– 5	Thus it was s· that the healing
	84– 1	Jesus' wisdom ofttimes was s· by
	107–21	sense must first be s· its falsity
	158–13	meaning of it all, as now s·,
	312–15	* s· in the raising up of the
	321–10	as s· by the triumphs of Truth
	322–23	hath s· you the amplitude of His mercy,
Man.	112– 4	as s· on page 118.
Ret.	47– 9	Example had s· the dangers
	50–10	God has since s· me,
Un.	7– 4	s· by the changes at Andover Seminary
	31–21	It can be s·, in detail,
Pul.	44–20	* has s· its power over its students,
	58–12	* Its appearance is s· in the
	66–19	* has s· an uncommon development
	74– 8	* was s· to Mrs. Mary Baker Eddy,
	79–17	* has s· a vitality so unexpected.
Rud.	15– 1	experience has s· that this defrauds
No.	6–23	Copernicus has s· that what
My.	22–13	* s· the absolute necessity of giving.
	22–20	* she has s· wisdom, faith, and
	25– 8	* s· by their contributions to the
	97– 7	* It has yet to be s· that of the
	152–20	even as the ages have s·.
	294–21	in what is s· him by God's works
	325– 1	* kindnesses and s· them,
	328–24	* machinery act . . . was s·,
	329 24	* s· by the fair attitude of the press
	333– 5	* s· that on the twenty eighth day of

shows

Mis.	6–14	rapid growth of the work s·.
	22–14	It s· the impossibility of
	26–20	Natural history s· that
	29–20	s· that longevity has *increased*.
	72–24	s· that nothing which is material
	112–24	s· itself in extreme sensitiveness ;
	113–17	s· that there is a way of escape
	148– 1	never s· us a smiling countenance
	258–31	s· that nature and man are as
	354–23	s· that humility is the first step
	365–22	s· the real value of C. S.
Pul.	23–19	* History s· the curious fact that
	54–19	* s· that he observed, in his practice
Rud.	8–23	s· that he makes morally worse the
No.	11–25	Revelation s· this Principle,
	15 21	s· that matter and mortal mind
	16– 9	C. S. s· that matter, evil,
	19– 4	s· its real value to the race.
	22–18	s· that the term devil is generic,
	39–22	s· us more clearly than we saw
	39–23	it s· us what God is.
Pan.	5–18	It s· that evil is both liar and
	7– 3	Science s· that a plurality of
'*00.*	10 17	History s· that error repe
'*01.*	9– 4	C. S. s· clearly that C·· is one of
	28–15	Sacred history s· C. S.
'*02.*	8– 9	s· what true call parts,
My.	41–24	* s· man mental and physical
	58–12	* s· the unpunished sin
	79–13	* s· er not only equalling but
	88– 6	frequency of divorce s· that
	11	ment that the clerk's book s·

shrank
Ret. 50– 8 I s· from asking it,

shrewd
My. 81–32 * hard-headed s· business men.

shriek
Mis. 326– 7 sufferers s· for help :

shrieked
Pan. 1– 7 winds of March have s·

shrill
Mis. 390– 6 The lark's s· song doth wake
Po. 55– 7 The lark's s· song doth wake
My. 38–20 * their s· trebles rising with
78–31 * joining with their s· voices

shrine
Mis. 159–21 offer at the s· of C. S.,
Ret. 18–14 as the s· Or fount of real joy
Po. 34–14 Divinely desolate the s· to paint?
43–13 when At some siren s·
64– 5 as the s· Or fount of real joy
71– 5 Knelt worshiping at mammon's s·.

shrines
My. 96– 9 * Mecca and the Hindu s·,

shrink
My. 297– 3 s· from such salient praise.

shrubs
Pul. 48– 3 * dotted with beds of flowering s·,

shrunk
Mis. 236– 6 until thought has s· from
My. 52–28 * authors would have s·,

shuddered
Mis. 180–13 s· at her material approach ;

shudders
Mis. 141–13 s· at the freedom, might, and

shuffling
Ret. 79–10 in s· off scholastic rhetoric,

shun
Mis. 395–22 For joy, to s· my weary way,
Un. 49–27 commands mortals to s· or
Pul. 21–16 s· whatever would isolate us from
'00. 3–17 to s· him as their tormentor.
Po. 58– 7 to s· my weary way,

shuns
Ret. 47–10 C. S. s· whatever involves material

shut
Mis. 133–15 when thou hast s· thy door, — Matt. 6 : 6.
209– 5 wouldst s· the mouth of His prophets,
276–29 learned when the door is s·.
286–28 s· out all sense of other claims.
292–18 to s· out all opposite sense.
317–11 door to my teaching was s·
324– 5 The door is s·.
342–22 The door is s·.
Pan. 12–14 a door that no man can s· ;
'00. 9–10 s· their eyes and wait for a more
My. 188–19 s· me out from your presence,

shuts
Un. 41– 5 sin s· out the real sense of Life,
Rud. 8–20 This falsity s· against him the Truth

shutteth
'00. 14–22 openeth and no man s·, — Rev. 3 : 7.
14–22 s· and no man openeth ;" — Rev. 3 : 7.

shutting
Mis. 24–19 s· out the true sense of Spirit.
276–28 thus s· out spiritual light.

shuttlecock
Mis. xi–18 s· of religious intolerance

sick (noun)
and sinful
Mis. 364– 8 to have healed, . . . the s· and sinful,
and sinner
No. 15– 1 falling on the s· and sinner,
and sorrowing
My. 139–23 divine blessing on the s· and sorrowing,
and ṭhṛing
Mis. 74– 3 in my name to the s· and suffering.
259–2... ...er to heal the s· and the sinner,
Man. 92– 4 ...ed the s· and the sinner ;
'00. 15–21 ...effe...
8–10 ...that is the s· and the sinner,
'02. 5–30 heals ... and the sinner with Truth
My. 158–20 healing ... the sinner !
180– 2 ...red the sinner.
are aided
Rud. 12–13 If the s· ...e... the sinner.
are being healed
My. 44– 2 * the s· are be...er.

sick (noun)
are healed
Mis. 171–19 By these signs . . . the s· are healed ;
364– 4 whereby the s· are healed,
Ret. 60–20 and the s· are healed.
Pul. vii–18 s· are healed and sinners saved,
My. 178– 6 s· are healed and sinners saved,
258– 2 is reformed and the s· are healed.
belief of the
Ret. 63–10 belief of the s· in the reality of
benefit the
Mis. 378–16 ask him how . . . could benefit the s·.
care of the
Man. 49–13 can take proper care of the s·.
cure of the
No. 6–11 consequent cure of the s·,
30–26 cure of the s· demonstrates this
extended to the
Hea. 18–20 Jesus' mission extended to the s·
fear of the
Rud. 12– 8 or else quiet the fear of the s·
giving to the
Mis. 262–16 giving to the s· relief from pain ;
hands on the
Mis. 29– 1 lay hands on the s·, — Mark 16 : 18.
192–30 lay hands on the s·, — Mark 16 : 18.
248– 2 "lay hands on the s·, — Mark 16 : 18.
248– 4 "lay hands on the s·" — Mark 16 : 18.
Ret. 35–17 lay hands on the s·, — Mark 16 : 18.
Hea. 1– 4 lay hands on the s·, — Mark 16 : 18.
8–10 lay hands on the s·, — Mark 16 : 18.
19–27 lay hands on the s·, — Mark 16 : 18.
Peo. 12– 5 lay hands on the s·, — Mark 16 : 18.
My. 48– 2 * lay hands on the s·, — Mark 16 : 18.
healed the
Mis. 28–28 healed the s· and raised the dead.
74–18 healed the s· and the sinner ;
Un. 11– 6 he healed the s·,
Pul. 66– 3 * as it did when Christ healed the s·.
No. 1–20 Truth, and Love, which healed the s·
Pan. 5–24 healed the s·, and saved sinners.
'01. 19–17 great Metaphysician healed the s·,
My. 37–13 * Christ which has ever healed the s·.
107– 1 healed the s· as a token of their
288–23 cast out devils and healed the s·.
345–18 and healed the s·,
348–26 healed the s· and reformed the sinner
healeth the
Mis. 322–21 healeth the s· and cleanseth the
healing of the
Man. 47–14 in regard to the healing of the s·
My. 104–32 healing of the s·, the saving of
182–16 healing of the s·, the reforming of
healing the
Mis. 19– 8 healing the s· is far lighter than
25–18 healing the s·, casting out evil,
25–30 drugs for healing the s·,
30– 4 Jesus' example in healing the s·
39–29 work with God in healing the s·,
55– 3 simplest problem . . . is healing the s·,
60– 5 Jesus came healing the s·
71– 9 healing the s· is a very right thing
77–31 healing the s·, casting out evils,
99–30 casting out evils and healing the s· ;
100– 9 healing the s· and reclaiming the
124–17 healing the s·, cleansing the leper,
175– 2 casting out error and healing the s·.
187– 2 casting out evils, healing the s·,
195–27 relative to healing the s·,
247–16 demonstrate . . . by healing the s· ;
252–25 lost element, namely, healing the s·.
268–12 healing the s· and casting out error.
270–17 requisite for healing the s·.
308–15 only by healing the s·
Man. 16– 3 healing the s· and overcoming sin
43– 8 or for healing the s·.
92– 4 Healing the s· and the sinner
Ret. 65–23 casting out evils and healing the s· ;
66– 1 to be utilized in healing the s·,
Pul. 72–27 * doing good and healing the s·.
Rud. 2–22 Is healing the s· the whole of Science?
8– 8 demonstrate C. S. in healing the s·?
14– 7 practising . . . healing the s·.
No. 12–19 casting out evil, healing the s·,
43–14 * S. and H. is healing the s·,
'00. 5–29 casting out . . . and in healing the s·.
'01. 4–10 Love . . . healing the s· ;
'02. 6–11 saving the sinner and healing the s·.
Peo. 5–21 demonstration . . . in healing the s·.
12–21 healing the s· and raising the dead
13– 8 casting out error and healing the s·.
My. v–16 * healing the s· and reforming the
4–28 healing the s· and saving the sinner.
58–23 * healing the s· and reforming the sinful,
110– 3 casting out evils, healing the s·,
113–27 healing the s·, and uplifting

sick (noun)
healing the
My. 122–29	healing the s· and saving sinners.
126–13	casting out evil and healing the s·.
128–22	preaching the gospel and healing the s·.
150–21	healing the s·, bringing the
153–26	casting out evil and healing the s·.
155– 1	healing the s· and reforming
180– 2	healing the s· and the sinner.
231–12	qualified students for healing the s·,
253– 2	healing the s·, soothing sorrow,
270–27	anoints with Truth, . . . healing the s·.
271– 6	healing the s· and reforming the
301–17	but healing the s· is *not* sin.
343–16	as I learned while healing the s·.

heals the
Mis. 193–13	heals the s·, casts out error,
259–28	power of God which heals the s·
379–26	Mind, that heals the s·
380– 5	divine Principle heals the s·,
Man. 17–18	casts out error, heals the s·,
92– 9	C. S. heals the s· quickly
Pul. 14–26	When God heals the s·
Rud. 15– 2	though it heals the s·.
No. 12– 3	heals the s· and exalts the race.
15–12	Christianity that heals the s·
'02. 8–20	saves sinners and heals the s·
Hea. 12– 3	Mind instead of matter heals the s·.
13–24	casts out error and thus heals the s·.
18–22	Christ, Truth, heals the s·.
My. 5–30	divine Mind that heals the s·
28–22	* a religion which heals the s·
106–29	he heals the s· without drugs
107–17	that with these . . . he heals the s·.
113– 2	heals the s· and reclaims sinners
147–16	heals the s· and enlightens the
158–20	it is the Spirit that heals the s·
185–20	Christ, as aforetime, heals the s·,
200–25	casts out evils, heals the s·,
292–27	prayer of the righteous heals the s·,
348–19	divine Mind heals the s·

heal the
Mis. 2– 2	power of . . . Love to heal the s·.
3– 7	power to heal the s·
4–30	mission of C. S. to heal the s·,
5– 9	and ministers, to heal the s·
17–21	divine power to heal the s·.
35–16	*teach its readers to heal the s·,*
37–15	heal the s·.'' — *Matt.* 10 : 8.
38–19	to benefit the race, heal the s·,
62–15	*essential to heal the s·,*
194– 2	power of a drug to heal the s· !
214–26	cannot heal the s·, and take
225–12	power of Christ, . . . to heal **the s·.**
247– 1	cast out error and heal the s·,
326– 1	heal the s·, — *Matt.* 10 : 8.
352–22	to heal the s· or the sinful.
Chr. 55–22	Heal the s·, — *Matt.* 10 : 8.
Ret. 36– 1	''Heal the s·,'' — *Matt.* 10 : 8.
87–15	''heal the s·'' — *Matt.* 10 : 8.
Pul. 22–13	to heal the s· in his name.
20 18	* ''heal the s·, *Matt.* 10 : 8.
66–12	* ''heal the s·'' — *Matt.* 10 : 8.
69–21	* power to heal the s·
73–13	* to do good and heal the s·.
No. 6– 4	in order to heal the s·.
14–10	''Heal the s·, — *Matt.* 10 : 8.
21–27	A philosophy which cannot heal the s·
40–23	cast out fear and heal the s·,
41–21	''Heal the s·, — *Matt.* 10 : 8.
42–15	and so heal the s·.
'00. 15–21	heal the s· and the sinner !
'01. 9–26	they cast out evils and heal the s·.
25–13	which because of . . . heal the s· !
Hea. 2–25	to cast out error and heal the s·.
3– 5	to cast out error, and heal the s·.
7–28	and ability of Christians to heal the s· ;
8– 4	pray to heal the s·.
11–26	imbued with Truth to heal the s· ;
Peo. 4–27	false ideals . . . cannot heal the s·
8– 3	cast out error and heal the s·.
8– 6	incompetency that cannot heal the s·,
9–18	divine aid of Spirit to heal the s·,
My. 5–17	heal the s·, reform the sinner,
46–16	* preach the gospel and heal the s·
51–15	* to heal the s· and reform the sinner.
51–32	* to heal the s·, and reform the sinner,
52–14	* Life, and Love, . . . does heal the s·,
52–18	* heal the s·, and preach the gospel,
109–11	taught his followers to heal the s·,
114– 5	cast out evil and heal the s· ;
150–27	sent them forth to heal the s·
152– 5	were supposed to heal the s·,
172–16	'heal the s·,' — *Matt.* 10 : 8.
192– 4	Heal the s·, make spotless the
230–13	his capacity to heal the s·,

sick (noun)
heal the
My. 270–21	My writings heal the s·,
294– 4	they heal the s· on the basis that
300–26	''Heal the s·, — *Matt.* 10 : 8.
364–14	and to heal the s·, by

health to the
Mis. 168– 1	health to the s·, salvation from

helpless
Un. 61–28	helpless s· are soonest healed

letters from the
My. 223– 8	Letters from the s· are not read

lose
Un. 2–17	s· lose their sense of sickness,

may look
Mis. 307–26	at which the s· may look

preparations for the
Mis. 268–22	God's preparations for the s·
268–25	His preparations for the s·

recovery of the
Mis. 59–11	*to pray for the recovery of the s·?*
308–27	prevents the recovery of the s·.
380–19	the immediate recovery of the s·,

restored the
No. 4– 1	has restored the s· to health ;

said to the
No. 42– 8	Jesus said to the s·,

satisfy the
Mis. 380–21	wherewith to satisfy the s· that

save the
No. 41–26	* prayer of faith shall save the s·,
My. 221–32	shall save the s·'' ? — *Jas.* 5 : 15.

saying to the
Mis. 369–28	privilege of saying to the s·,

sinner and the
Mis. 382– 9	the sinner and the s· are helped

the dear
My. 154–10	comforting to the dear s·,

tonic for the
Mis. 252– 1	Truth is the tonic for the s·,

treatment of the
Mis. 66–23	scientific treatment of the s·.

who are dis-eased
Mis. 241–30	the s· who are dis-eased,

who are healed
Mis. 133–32	behold the s· who are healed,

Mis. 22–24	with the s·, the lame, the deaf,
25–25	s· are more deplorably situated
25–26	if the s· cannot trust God for help
43–15	far more advantageous to the s·
54–15	the s·, . . . are testifying thereto.
85–30	s· often are thereby led to Christ,
357– 4	Scientists minister to the s· ;
Ret. 16–12	for the s· to be healed by my
73–23	is like the s· talking sickness.
'01. 12– 4	heals the sinning and the s·.
27–18	an equal number of s· healed,
Peo. 11–12	The lame, the blind, the s·,
My. 3–15	nor a . . . that heals only the s·.
90–17	* readily grasped by s· or well.
97– 7	* of the s· who abjure medicine
132–26	s·, dreaming of suffering matter ;
147–29	the s· and the heavenly homesick
204–24	the s· whom you have not healed
219– 4	anticipation on the part of the s·

sick (adj.)
Mis. 36– 1	is erring, sinful, s·, and dying,
70– 4	cast out the s· man's illusion,
71– 9	he healed others who were s·.
79–19	A mortal who is sinning, s·, and
85– 4	*Is a Christian Scientist ever s·,*
85– 5	*has he who is s· been regenerated?*
184–18	to sin and be s·,''
184–18	believing that he is s· and a
186–11	in a s· and sinning mortal
187–25	create a s·, sinning, dying man?
187–29	s· and a sinner in order to be
197–32	he can neither be s· nor forever a
219–15	one person feels s·, another feels
219–23	mortal mind makes s·,
220– 4	suppose that there is a s· person
220– 9	aim to refute the s· man's thoughts,
220–25	people believe that a man is s·
220–26	speak of him as being s·,
220–27	minds of others that he is s·,
220–29	he will believe that he is s·,
229– 8	than he does the s· man's.
235– 3	no longer obliged to sin, be s·,
238–24	chapter sub-title
238–25	* public allegement that I am ''s·,
241– 5	man will no more enter heaven s· than
241–19	''God never made you s· :
252–13	s· thoughts are unreality
355–24	mind that makes his body s·,

sick (adj.)

Man.	49–12	wisdom necessary in a s· room,
Ret.	40–10	s· woman rose from her bed,
Un.	62– 2	that they never were s·.
Pul.	14–29	it makes them s· or sinful.
	73– 3	* If we become s·, God will
Rud.	3– 2	they do not love to be s·.
	7–13	fallen, s·, depraved, mortal.
	12–10	that they are first made s· by
No.	29–12	* ''The forgiven soul in a s· body
	29–20	A mortal pardoned by God is not s·,
	31– 5	and they are yet s· and sinful.
Hea.	6–19	Man thinks . . . that when he is s·,
Peo.	4–21	sinning, s·, and dying mortals.
	6– 2	* ''I am s· of learned quackery.''
	10–18	have made men sinning and s·,
My.	97– 3	* faith on the part of a s· person,
	117–15	when saw we thee s·, — *Matt.* 25 : 39.
	132–30	whose whole head is s·
	144– 5	to lies afloat that I am s·,
	275–13	the report that I am s·
	276– 4	a criminal or a s· person,
		(*see also* **man**)

sick-bed

Hea.	18–24	religion at the s· will be

sick-bound

No.	46–20	has dawned on the s· and

sickened

Mis.	124–10	We turn, with s· sense,

sickle

Un.	12– 5	s· of Mind's eternal circle,
My.	269–17	God hath thrust in the s·,

sickly

Mis.	211– 7	s· charity that supplies criminals
	219–14	think also after a s· fashion.
My.	116– 8	This state of mind is s· ;
	345–13	I was a s· child.

sickness

action of
Mis.	353– 4	they are like the action of s·,

all
Ret.	34–12	the antidote for all s·,
	61–13	''You are the cause of all s· ;

all our
Mis.	173– 6	healeth all our s· and sins

and death
Mis.	96– 2	salvation from s· and death,
Hea.	17–22	s· and death are supposed physical
	17–25	s· and death were produced by sin.
	17–27	If s· and death came through
Peo.	12–19	salvation from s· and death.

and disease
Pul.	73– 2	* worry . . . about s· and disease?
Peo.	7–24	objects . . . called s· and disease,
My.	364–16	all manner of s· and disease,

and of sin
Hea.	9– 9	think most of s· and of sin ;

and sin
Mis.	37–23	as do s· and sin.
	85–31	way out of both s· and sin.
	98– 4	from inharmony, s·, and sin,
	179–17	the consciousness of s· and sin
	262–20	looseth the chains of s· and sin,
	399–10	sorrow and s· and sin.''
Ret.	63– 3	need of healing s· and sin
No.	30– 7	s· and sin have no relapse.
Pan.	5–28	and thus healed s· and sin.
	8–26	s· and sin, life and death.
Po.	75–17	sorrow and s· and sin.''
My.	50–12	* dogma, creed, s·, and sin,
	122–18	saves from s· and sin
	257–16	all sorrow, s·, and sin.

and sorrow
Mis.	250–28	want and woe, s· and sorrow

and suffering
Rud.	10–17	which causes s· and suffering.

antidote for
Mis.	33–27	antidote for s·, as well as for sin,
	255–23	antidote for s·, as well as for sin,

beds of
My.	36–14	* delivered from beds of s·

believes in
My.	300– 8	Does he who believes in s·

believe that
Hea.	15–20	and believe that s· is something

called
Un.	54– 3	a false claim, called s·,

calls
Un.	59–22	illusion which calls s· real,

can master
Hea.	8– 6	Mind can master s· as well as

casts out
Mis.	241– 6	Christianity casts out s·

sickness

culminate in
Mis.	366–25	culminate in s·, sin,

destroying
Mis.	40– 7	effectual in destroying s·

disease, and death
Mis.	14–30	sin, s·, disease, and death.
	187– 3	sin, s·, disease, and death.
	194– 4	sin, s·, disease, and death
No.	6– 9	phenomena, — s·, disease, and death.
My.	180–15	sin, s·, disease, and death.

disease, or death
Mis.	65– 4	sin, s·, disease, or death,

dream of
Rud.	11–17	awake from the dream of s· ;

error and
Mis.	221– 9	that error and s· are one,

healing
Ret.	63– 3	need of healing s· and sin?
My.	194– 9	healing s· and destroying sin,

healing of
Mis.	352–29	and the healing of s·

heals
Ret.	63– 4	heals sin as it heals s·,

health and
Ret.	57–27	health and s·, life and death ;
'00.	4– 2	good and evil, health and s·,

health, not of
Un.	3–18	of health, not of s· ;

health over
Mis.	321–11	triumphs . . . of health over s·,

is a belief
Ret.	61– 3	declares that s· is a belief,

is healed
Mis.	352–14	In Science, s· is healed
Un.	8–18	same basis whereby s· is healed,

is the schoolmaster
Rud.	11– 3	S· is the schoolmaster,

last
My.	331–24	* during his last s·,

less
Peo.	6–10	* there would be less s· and

moral
Mis.	352–19	in healing the moral s· ;

more dangerous than
Ret.	63–20	is more dangerous than s·,

must be covered
Mis.	352–31	s· must be covered with the

never made
Mis.	247–30	He never made s·.
No.	4–10	never made s· a stubborn reality.

no
Mis.	293–25	and there is no s·
Rud.	11–10	no s·, sin, and death in the divine
My.	300– 9	there is no s· or disease,

no more
No.	35– 9	there will be no more s·,

no reality in
Mis.	63–12	If there is no reality in s·,

nor sin
Ret.	63– 6	no evil neither s· nor sin.

or death
Peo.	12– 5	s· or death is a law of mortal belief,

or disease
My.	300– 9	declare that there is no s· or disease,

pain and
Mis.	68–12	to believe that pain and s· are

physical
Rud.	2–23	Healing physical s· is the smallest

recovered from
Un.	62– 1	''I have recovered from s· ;''

redemption from
Mis.	96–19	man's redemption from s·

sense of
Un.	2–17	the sick lose their sense of s·,

sin and
	(*see* **sin**)

sin, and death
Mis.	6–21	we conquer s·, sin, and death.
	37–10	belief . . . in s·, sin, and death.
	61–27	of error, . . . of s·, sin, and death.
	62–18	error of s·, sin, and death,
	63– 9	opposite triad, s·, sin, and death.
	64– 6	nothingness of s·, sin, and death,
	86– 6	to strive with s·, sin, and death
	181–26	disease, s·, sin, and death
	182–31	s·, sin, and death will yield to it,
	234–30	our Saviour from s·, sin, and death.
	340–32	Human wrong, s·, sin, and death
	351–24	pain, s·, sin, and death,
Un.	39– 1	s·, sin, and death yield to holiness,
	60–11	descant upon s·, sin, and death as
	64– 7	conscious of s·, sin, and death,
Rud.	11–10	no s·, sin, and death in the divine
No.	17–27	s·, sin, and death would be as

sickness

sin, and death
No. 33–24 in overcoming s·, sin, and death.
Po. 70–24 s·, sin, and death are banished hence.

sin, . . . and death
(see **sin**)

sin, . . . and disease
Mis. 251–29 Sin, s·, and disease flee before the

sin or
Hea. 9–24 He never made sin or s·,

sin, or death
Un. 62–15 S·, sin, or death is a false sense

sin, . . . or death
Mis. 17– 6 opposed to . . . sin, s·, or death.
Un. 4– 3 finite sense of sin, s·, or death,
Hea. 9– 7 less said . . . of sin, s·, or death,
16–18 only evidence . . . of sin, s·, or death

sorrow and
Mis. 399–10 thy sorrow and s· and sin."
No. 30–24 Sympathy with sin, sorrow, and s·
Po. 75–17 thy sorrow and s· and sin.

talking
Ret. 73–23 is like the sick talking s·.

the most
Mis. 6–28 there is the most s·.

there is no
Mis. 60– 4 *believe there is no s·,*

to health
Mis. 220–17 consciousness from s· to health.

to regard
Un. 54– 7 To regard s· as a false claim,

unusual
My. 333–32 * reports of unusual s·

worse than
Ret. 63–23 Sin is worse than s· ;

Mis. 6– 1 We hear from the pulpits that s· is
6– 3 s· often leaves mortals but little
6–32 s· is by no means the exception.
63– 1 and the s· of matter.
83– 8 "S· is a growth of illusion,
89– 5 *to care for . . . a friend in s·,*
105–28 Destroy the thought of sin, s·,
192– 8 s·, sin, disease, and death,
241–30 much more should these heal, of s·,
259– 6 of health, not of s· ;
Ret. 60–22 S· is something besides
63–10 belief . . . in the reality of s·,
Un. 54– 4 is to admit all there is of s· ;
54–11 As with s·, so is it with sin.
Pul. 13–15 serpent of sin as well as of s· !
No. 4– 4 be undertaken in health than s·.
17–26 Then . . . s· as real as health,
40–19 Only when s·, sin, and fear
Pan. 10–29 Sin, s·, appetites, and passions,
Hea. 18–18 never did anything for s·
Peo. 10–23 The emancipation . . . from s·
My. 161–24 S· is possible because one's

sick-producing
Pul. 69–11 * evil and s· thoughts,

sick-room
Mis. 296–12 who minister in the s·,
Ret. 41– 2 welcome into the s·.

side (noun)

bad
Hea. 10–14 a good and a bad s· to existence.

better
'01. 1–21 It is the better s· of man's nature

bright
Hea. 10–17 if you will look on the bright s· ;

either
Hea. 13– 3 and accomplish less on either s·.
My. 69–17 * galleries, two on either s·
259– 4 on either s· lace and flowers.

evil
Hea. 10–11 it has no evil s· ;

father's
Ret. 1– 3 great-grandfather, on my father's s·,
Pul. 32–23 * On her father's s· Mrs. Eddy came

God's
Mis. 102–31 "one on God's s· is a majority."
Pul. 4–16 "one on God's s· is a majority."
No. 46– 1 "One on God's s· is a majority ;"

good
Hea. 10–12 and that is the good s·.

her
Ret. 8–14 I sat in a little chair by her s·,
40–10 I had stood by her s·
Po. 66– 8 whisper of one who sat by her s·

his
Ret. 20–13 * I knelt by his s· throughout
82–20 accumulation of power on his s·
Pul. 33–19 * suddenly appeared at his s·,

material
Mis. 140–18 material s· of this question.

side (noun)

mortal
My. 50–16 * steadfastly from the mortal s·,

of Adam
Mis. 244– 1 from the s· of Adam, — see Gen. 2 : 21.

of error
My. 146–28 Others who take the s· of error

of existence
Mis. 65–14 not consider the false s· of existence
Peo. 1– 9 the sensual s· of existence

of God
Mis. 226– 5 carried the case on the s· of God ;
321–10 adjusted more on the s· of God,

of good
Mis. 104–30 gain a balance on the s· of good,

of happiness
Hea. 10–21 on the s· of happiness ;

of right
Mis. 255– 8 action on the s· of right,

of sin
My. 146–27 audibly takes the s· of sin,

of Spirit
Mis. 180– 2 so far as to take the s· of Spirit,

of Truth
Mis. 46–18 acts on the s· of Truth,
'02. 6–25 victory on the s· of Truth.

one
Mis. 280–16 working on one s· and in Science.
288– 9 regards only one s· of a question,
Pul. 50–27 * to show even some one s· of it
Hea. 10–10 There is but one s· to good,
10–11 there is but one s· to reality,
My. 234–17 when regarded on one s· only,

other
My. 43–17 * set up on the other s· for a

physical
Ret. 33– 1 physical s· of this research was aided by
Pul. 47–11 * knowledge concerning the physical s·

right
Mis. 111–12 cast their nets on the right s·,
212–11 cast their nets on the right s·.
263–21 wavering balance on the right s·,
My. 277–19 tips the beam on the right s·,

safe
Mis. 117– 9 place him on the safe s· of practice.

side by
Mis. 231– 4 exuberant with joy, — ranged side by s·.
Ret. 71–24 growing side by s· with the wheat,
Pul. 84– 6 * side by s·, equal partners in
My. 227–26 side by s· with Christ's command,

south
Pul. 48– 6 * broad piazza on the south s·

under
Pul. 86– 8 * On the under s· of the cover

wrong
Hea. 9– 6 talking on the wrong s· of the question.

Mis. 172–26 on the s· of immutable right,
270– 2 let us take the s· of him who
Ret. 7–18 * of the s· he deemed right.
Hea. 10–21 take the s· you wish to carry,

side (adj.)
Mis. 250–26 out of a s· door ;
My. 69– 5 * ceiling or roof and s· walls

sides
Mis. 146–10 regarding both s· of the subject,
266– 4 these s· are moral opposites,
287–20 preserve affection on both s·.
Rud. 15–17 should be fortified on all s·
Hea. 10–22 be careful not to talk on both s·,
My. 69–11 * placed on the two s· of the organ.
234–18 both s· of the great question of

sidewalk
Mis. 239–11 upon the s· one winter morning,
250–26 little feet tripping along the s· ;

sidewalks
Pul. 42– 2 * the s· around the church

siege
Mis. 99–17 to stand a long s·,
My. 127–22 A s· of the combined centuries,

sieges
My. 124–12 bloodless s· and tearless triumphs,

sift
Mis. 79– 6 will s· the chaff from the wheat,

sifted
'00. 7– 5 creeds and dogmas have been s·,

sifting
Mis. 215– 2 the s· and the fire.

sigh
Mis. ix–13 s·, and smile commingled,
106–26 s· of angels answering,
206–32 and betimes s· for rest

sigh

Mis.	386–10	gathered from her parting *s·* :
Ret.	4–18	winds *s·* low requiems
Pan.	14– 1	weigh a *s·*, and rise into
'00.	11–11	The human *s·* for peace
Po.	30– 7	dayspring ! 'reft of mortal *s·*
	49–15	gathered from her parting *s·*.
	65–15	We waken to life's dreary *s·*.
	73–19	Or hypocrite *s·*,
My.	189–22	last-drawn *s·* of a glory gone,

sighing

Po.	15– 1	soft *s·* zephyrs through foliage
My.	171– 6	*s·* shall flee away."— *Isa.* 35 : 10.

sighs

Mis.	386– 4	yearnings come not, *s·* are stilled,
	395–24	languid brooklets yield their *s·*,
Po.	49– 6	yearnings come not, *s·* are stilled,
	58– 9	languid brooklets yield their *s·*,

sight

and sense

Un.	47– 2	by destroying . . . to *s·* and sense.

deplorable

'01.	15–14	The most deplorable *s·* is

faith in

My.	149–24	cause in effect, and faith in *s·*,

faith, not

Mis.	158–12	through faith, not *s·*.

first

My.	31–20	* first *s·* which the visitors caught

give

Mis.	242– 9	give *s·* to one born blind.

gives

Mis.	362– 9	gives *s·* to these blind,

God's

Mis.	144–22	precious in God's *s·*
My.	184–22	service acceptable in God's *s·*.

His

'01.	15–26	* to have you in His *s·*.
My.	167–17	acceptable in His *s·*,

human

Mis.	194–17	the divine power to human *s·* ;
'01.	12–23	magnifies the divine power to human *s·*;

lose

Mis.	100–13	may lose *s·* thereof ;
	319–15	they must not lose *s·* of sin ;
	327–28	and lose *s·* of their guide ;
Un.	54– 5	one must lose *s·* of a false claim.

lost

Mis.	179– 5	believing we have lost *s·* of Truth,
	212–32	His disciples, . . . lost *s·* of him ;
My.	243– 7	You cannot have lost *s·* of the rules
	339– 5	C. S. cannot be lost *s·* of,

material

Un.	34– 9	material *s·* is an illusion, a lie.
My.	265– 6	less subordinate to material *s·*

of thee

Mis.	326–32	"The *s·* of thee unveiled my sins,

or sense

My.	116–17	based upon personal *s·* or sense.

our

'01.	33– 3	fading so sensibly from our *s·*.
Hea.	5–20	constantly covered, . . . from our *s·*.

out of

Mis.	292–17	to bury the dead out of *s·* ;
My.	160– 1	and keeps Mind much out of *s·*.
	191–13	Keep personality out of *s·*,

receive

Mis.	168– 4	how the blind, . . . receive *s·* ;

restored

Mis.	258– 7	he restored *s·* to the blind,
My.	105–17	physically restored *s·* to the blind,

their

Mis.	212–31	buried it out of their *s·*.
	324–16	passions have so dimmed their *s·*

your

Po.	67–15	pass From your *s·* as the shade

Un.	33–26	*S·*. Mortal mind declares that
Rud.	5–13	who has found *s·* in matter,
My.	23–24	* not only to faith but also to *s·* ;
	29–12	* *s·* which no one who saw
	184–25	precious in the *s·* of divine Love,

sign

Mis.	145–20	modest *s·* be nothingness.
	320–18	shall be the *s·* of his appearing
	380– 2	outward *s·* of such a practice :
	380–18	without a *s·* save the . . . recovery of
	380–20	and people generally, called for a *s·*
Man.	110–14	Women must *s·* "Miss" or "Mrs."
	111– 6	must *s·* her own Christian name,
	111– 8	unmarried women must *s·* "Miss."
	111–19	whose teachers refuse, . . . to *s·*
Ret.	1–13	no *s·* that she inherited a spark from
	42– 6	symbolic words on his office *s·*.

sign

Un.	10–23	like commencing with the minus *s·*,
	61–18	is but the *s·* and symbol,
Pul.	30–11	* *s·* a brief "confession of faith,"
	35–30	* on the *s·* at his door.
Po.	24– 7	A *s·* that never can depart.
My.	36–29	* a *s·* of your understanding
	354–18	Sweet *s·* and substance

signal

Pul.	39– 2	* *s·* proof of the divine origin
My.	187– 8	and *s·* the perfect path

signalize

Chr.	53–25	wherefore *s·* the birth
My.	234– 1	*s·* the thinking of person.

signalled

Pul.	6–24	William R. Alger of Boston, *s·* me

signally

Mis.	378–13	*s·* failed in healing her case.
'00.	9–23	attempts to . . . will *s·* fail ;
My.	228– 5	Evil minds *s·* blunder
	326–16	*s·* honored his memory,

signature

Mis.	x–17	My *s·* has been slightly changed
	x–26	adopted that form of *s·*,
Man.	36–11	approval and *s·* of their teachers,
	89– 2	resign over her own *s·*
	91– 4	The *s·* of the teacher
	111– 7	prefix her *s·* with "Mrs ;"
My.	175–28	purporting to have my *s·*,
	299– 3	*s·* "A Priest of the Church,"

signatures

Armstrong

Pul.	87– 7	* Joseph A·,
My.	21–29	* Joseph A·,

Baker

My.	332–14	* George S. B·.

Bancroft

My.	60–21	* S. P. B·.

Bates

Pul.	77–19	* Edward P. B·,
	77–20	* Caroline S. B·.
	78–17	* Edward P. B·,
	78–18	* Caroline S. B·.
My.	322– 7	* Edward P. B·.

Board of Directors

Pul.	87– 9	* The C. S. B· of D·.
My.	21–32	* The C. S. B· of D·.
	63– 7	* The C. S. B· of D·,

Chase

Pul.	87– 8	* Stephen A. C·,
My.	21–30	* Stephen A. C·,
	27–17	* Stephen A. C·,

Churches and Societies in New York

My.	361–24	* First Church of Christ, Scientist,
	362–27	* First Church of Christ, Scientist,
	362–28	* Second Church of Christ, Scientist,
	363– 1	* Third Church of Christ, Scientist,
	363– 2	* Fourth Church of Christ, Scientist,
	363– 3	* Fifth Church of Christ, Scientist,
	363– 4	* Sixth Church of Christ, Scientist,
	363– 5	* First Church of Christ, Scientist, Brooklyn,
	363– 6	* Fourth Church of Christ, Scientist, Brooklyn,
	363– 7	* First Church of Christ, Scientist, Staten Island,
	363– 8	* C. S. Society, Bronx,
	363– 9	* C. S. Society, Flushing, L. I.,

Churches . . . in Missouri

My.	207–16	* Churches and Societies of C. S. in Missouri.

Dean

My.	361–26	* Charles D·, *Chairman,*

Desha

Mis.	306–10	* Mary D·,

Dickey

Po.	vii–16	* Adam H. D·.

Eddy

(see **Eddy-signatures**)

Frye

Ret.	49–31	C. A. F·, *Clerk.*

Harrison

My.	334–24	* Mary Hatch H·.

Hollis

My.	138–30	* Allen H·, *Justice of the Peace.*

Johnson

Pul.	87– 8	* William B. J·,
My.	21–30	* William B. J·,
	38– 7	* William B. J·, *Clerk.*
	46–31	* William B. J·, *Clerk.*
	63– 8	* William B. J·, *Secretary.*
	280–12	* William B. J·, *Clerk.*

signatures
  Knapp
    Pul. 87– 7   * IRA O. *K·*,
    My. 21–29   * IRA O. *K·*,
  McLellan
    My. 21–31   * ARCHIBALD *M·*,
  Morse
    My. 315–19   * H. M. *M·*, *Justice of the Peace.*
  Norcross
    Pul. 44–14   * "LANSON P. *N·.*"
  Probst
    My. 361–27   * ARTHUR O. *P·*, *Clerk.*
  Rome
    My. 62–15   * JAMES J. *R·*.
  Rounsevel
    My. 315–15   * R. D. *R·*.
  Snider
    My. 325–18   * CARRIE HARVEY *S·*.
  White
    Mis. 394–22   * JAMES T. *W·*.
    Po. 57– 8   * *James T. W·*.
  Whiteside
    My. 323–14   * FLORENCE *W·*.
  Whiting
    Pul. 40– 5   * LILIAN *W·*.

  Man. 91– 4   *S·*.
  Pul. 86– 8   * facsimile *s·* of the Directors,

signed
  Mis. 281–25   have *s·* your names.
    381–17   drawn up and *s·* by counsel.
  Man. 15– 1   *To be s· by those uniting with*
    35–14   *s·* by the C. S. Board of Directors
    36–20   a recommendation *s·* by three members
    65–16   order, *s·* by Mary Baker Eddy,
    69– 2   *s·* agreement to remain with Mrs. Eddy
  My. 315–15   * (*S·*) R. D. ROUNSEVEL.
    315–18   * statement by him *s·* is true.
    315 10   * (*S·*) H. M. MORSE,
    319– 7   little pamphlet, *s·* "Phare Pleigh."
    332–14   * (*S·*) GEORGE S. BAKER.

signet
  Mis. 35– 7   with the *s·* of C. S.
    121–21   thereby giving the *s·* of God to
  Hea. 19–16   Heaven's *s·* is Love.
  My. 131–12   The *s·* of the great heart,

significance
  Mis. 46–21   *s·* of what the apostle meant
    250–11   divine *s·* of Love
    250–22   glorious *s·* of affection
  Ret. 38–29   must also gain its spiritual *s·*,
    88–10   spiritual *s·* of this command,
  Pul. 27–28   * and others of pictorial *s·*.
    44–12   * comprehends its full *s·*.
    57– 9   * rehearsed the *s·* of the building,
    84–17   * Of the *s·* of this achievement
  No. 34–25   deep *s·* of the blood of Christ.
    46–19   full-orbed *s·* of this destiny
  '02. 9– 8   When the full *s·* of this saying is
  My. 6–25   giving to the material spiritual *s·*
    28–17   * The *s·* of this building is
    42–22   * *s·* of this momentous occasion.
    40– 6   * without this spiritual *s·* it were
    60–16   * spiritual *s·* of the first chapter of
    64– 1   * As one thought upon the *s·* of
    85– 3   * in the *s·* of the occasion.
    88–12   * more than usual ecclesiastic *s·*.
    90–26   * event of . . . momentous *s·*.
    94–29   giving . . . a spiritual *s·*
    259–22   chapter sub-title

significant
  Mis. 91– 2   *s·* as a type of the true worship,
  Un. 56–10   *s·* of that state of mind which
  Pul. 32–16   * experiences which alone are *s·*.
    79–12   * it is a *s·* fact that one
  My. 28– 3   * announcement will be deeply *s·*.
    45– 6   * *s·* events associated with this,
    228–11   chapter sub-title

signification
  Mis. 190–16   spiritual *s·* of its terms
  Man. 66– 9   *s·* of the communications
  Ret. 10–16   man's origin and *s·*.
    25– 5   Their spiritual *s·* appeared ;
    59–14   has the *s·* of Life.
  Rud. 16– 8   spiritual *s·* of the Bible,
  No. 12–24   spiritual *s·* of the Word
  Hea. 7–10   spiritual instead of the material *s·*.
  My. 220–13   the moral *s·* of law.
    245–26   *s·* of the letters of

significations
  Ret. 59– 4   terms have no contradictory *s·*.
  My. 266–28   modes and *s·* are adopted.

signified
  Mis. 74– 2   correspondence of . . . are here *s·*.
  Hea. 3–19   *s·* a "good man," — *John* 7 : 12.
  My. 339–15   and all that it formerly *s·*,

signifies
  Mis. 27–21   evil *s·* the absence of good,
  Pan. 7– 4   *s·* more than one God,
  '00. 14– 7   which *s·* a complete time
    14–14   the name whereof *s·*
  '02. 7–11   Latin *omni*, which *s· all*,
    7–12   *s·* all-power, all-presence,
  Hea. 7– 1   in Hebrew it is *belial*, and *s·*
    7– 5   *s·* those who understand
  My. 264–16   *s·* to the minds of men
    265– 3   It *s·* that love, unselfed,
    265–14   It *s·* that the Science of

signify
  Mis. 18–12   commands of infinite wisdom, . . . *s·* :
    28–23   does not *s·* a graven idol,
    75–19   warped to *s·* human quality,
    171– 2   to *s·* human hands.
  Man. 42–16   nor *s·* a belief in more than one
  Ret. 88–21   should not be so warped as to *s·*
  No. 20– 8   Principle is used to *s·* Deity
  Pan. 9– 7   *s·* a good Spirit and an evil spirit.
  '00. 5–11   they *s·* one God.
  My. 264–13   * should *s·* to all mankind?

signifying
  Un. 27– 8   *s·* a passionate love of self,

signs
  and symbols
    My. 185–30   are rich in *s·* and symbols,
  following
    Mis. 25–16   with "*s·* following," — *Mark* 16 : 20.
      29–28   the *s·* following Christianity,
      65–24   and with *s·* following.
      133–31   with "*s·* following." — *Mark* 16 : 20.
      154–24   "*s·* following" — *Mark* 16 : 20.
    No. 37–20   "*s·* following." — *Mark* 16 : 20.
    My. 147–11   with "*s·* following," — *Mark* 16 : 20.
      190–27   with "*s·* following." — *Mark* 16 : 20.
      258– 2   "*s·* following." — *Mark* 16 : 20.
  foreshadowed by
    Mis. 1– 5   foreshadowed by *s·* in the
  for the wayfarer
    Ret. 79– 9   *s·* for the wayfarer in divine Science
  no
    Mis. 242–16   "where there shall no *s·* — see *Matt.* 12 : 39.
  of the heart
    Po. page 24   poem
  of these times
    Mis. 2– 6   The *s·* of these times portend
      278– 3   and are the *s·* of these times ;
      347–10   the mental *s·* of these times,
    My. 270– 5   repeat the *s·* of these times.
  of the times
    Mis. 1– 8   discern the *s·* of the times?" — *Matt.* 16 : 3.
      317– 6   to appreciate the *s·* of the times ;
    '00. 4–14   are progressive *s·* of the times
    My. 113–29   The *s·* of the times emphasize
      114– 1   discern the *s·* of the times?" — *Matt.* 16 : 3.
      200– 4   praised for the *s·* of the times.
      235–14   chapter sub-title
      265–31   For these *s·* of the times we thank
      266–14   to the "*s·* of the times" — *Matt.* 16 : 3.
      266–22   special "*s·* of the times" — *Matt.* 16 : 3.
  of Truth
    Mis. 156–10   will see clearly the *s·* of Truth
  pioneer
    Mis. xii– 1   pioneer *s·* and ensigns of war,
  referred to
    Hea. 7– 2   *s·* referred to are the manifestations
  spiritual
    Mis. 18– 6   these spiritual *s·* of the new birth
  these
    Mis. 28–31   "These *s·* shall follow — *Mark* 16 : 17.
      171–18   By these *s·* are the true disciples
      192–28   these *s·* shall follow — *Mark* 16 : 17.
    Ret. 16–14   these *s·* shall follow — *Mark* 16 : 17.
    Hea. 1– 1   *these s· shall follow* — *Mark* 16 : 17.
      6–26   these *s·* shall follow — *Mark* 16 : 17.
      19–26   "these *s·* shall follow — *Mark* 16 : 17.
    My. 47–29   * these *s·* shall follow — *Mark* 16 : 17.
      265–31   For these *s·* of the times we thank
  truest
    '00. 10– 6   Conflict and . . . are the truest *s·* that

  Mis. 133–32   as to "*s·*," behold the — *Mark* 16 : 20.

silence
  Mis. 114–24   Scientists will *s·* evil suggestions,
    124–21   *s·* wherein to muse His praise,
    129–13   let *s·* prevail over his remains.

silence

Mis. 134–26   neither s· nor disarm God's voice.
152–28   to s· the right intuition which
193–18   a modification of s· on this subject,
212–14   The ultimatum . . . ought to s· ours.
277–17   s· Truth? Never.
299–30   does this s· your conscience?
339– 5   s· for the space of half an hour.
No.   8– 5   s· whenever it can substitute censure.
'02.   14–27   s· all private criticisms,
15–23   came to me in the s· of night,
Po.   2–19   thy deep s· is unbroken still.
15– 5   Break not on the s·,
27–16   Hearts bleeding ere they break in s·
My.   104–21   sufficient reason for his s·
124–22   s·, or with finger pointing upward,
170–28   sacred s· in blest communion
195–18   best way to s· a deep discontent
246–13   and sought in solitude and s·
249–15   patience, s·, and lives of saints.
262–29   eloquent s·, prayer and praise
339–27   S· . . . all that wars against Spirit

silenced

Mis. 277–13   stake and scaffold have never s· the
360–25   When mortal mind is s· by
Ret.   22– 5   spiritual numenon s· portraiture.
My.   243– 6   should be s· at its inception.

silences

Mis. 198– 9   s· the mortal claim to life,
259– 8   s· the supposition that evil is a
'02.   5–30   s· all questions on this subject,
My.   230– 8   Soul s· the dyspepsia of sense.

silencing

Ret.   67–13   S· self, alias rising above

silent

Mis.   12–22   human mind in its s· arguments,
70–28   working out, even in the s· tomb,
100–19   speaks when the senses are s·,
114–32   against evil and its s· modes,
126–20   s· lesson of a good example.
143– 8   with this s· benediction :
152– 8   breathe a s· benediction
220– 7   supports this s· mental force
238– 9   s· endurance of his love.
250–23   the s·, ceaseless prayer ;
260–31   s· mental methods whereby
269–29   opening of this s· mental seal,
275–10   wife or husband, s· and alone,
351– 7   weapons of the s· mental malpractice.
368–19   The s· address of a mental
400– 6   Grave, s·, steadfast stone,
Chr.   53–43   s· healing, heaven heard,
Ret.   38–24   disgusted . . . and become s·.
61– 6   unconsciously in the s· thought,
76–27   I have long remained s·
Pul.   10– 8   fallen fanes and s· Aventine
16–18   Cold, s·, stately stone,
No.   1– 5   changed by its s· influence.
1–13   for the s· cultivation of the
39– 2   s· intercession and unvoiced
Pan.   3–10   s· as the storm's sudden hush ;
'02.   5– 1   As s· night foretells the dawn
Po.   66–10   that heart is s· and sad,
76–17   Grave, s·, steadfast stone,
My.   29– 4   * kneeling in s· communion ;
32– 3   * five minutes of s· communion
32–29   * s· communion, which concluded with
38–24   * than the s· communion.
70–14   * stood in s· admiration
78–19   * knelt in s· communion,
79– 2   * kneeling for s· communion
106– 3   speak charitably . . . or to keep s·,
171–21   * s· greetings of the people
189– 9   s· prayers of our churches,
194– 8   a s·, grand man or woman,
211–13   by unseen, s· arguments.
211–14   in their s· allurements to
268–18   as s· as the dumb centuries
332– 4   * The s· gush of grateful tears alone
(see also **prayer**)

silently

Mis.   78–12   I know not how to teach . . . s· ;
159–15   sit s·, and ponder.
225–24   s·, through the divine power,
231–32   gazing s· on the vacant seat
315–24   Teachers shall not s· mentally
My.   46– 4   * s· but eloquently beckoning
247–15   I stood s· beside it,

silk

Pul.   77– 6   * casket with white s· linings.

silly

Mis.   183–11   nor a s· ambler to the
254–24   resting in s· peace upon the
My.   313– 1   a paraphrase of a s· song

silver

Mis. 159–28   embroidery, s·, gold, and jewels,
305–21   * gold, s·, bronze, copper, and
346–24   in pictures of s·." — Prov. 25 : 11.
Ret.   12– 3   Minerva's s· sandals still
23– 8   seemed to have a s· lining;
Pul.   25–26   * s· lamps of Roman design,
26–11   * s· lamps eight feet in height.
62–23   * down to little sets of s· bells
76–11   * in certain lights has a shimmer of s·.
Po.   61– 1   Minerva's s· sandals still
My.   30–22   * with bills, with s·, and with gold.

silver-throated

Pul.   11– 2   sweet song of s· singers,

silvery (see also silv'ry)

Po.   53–11   Till heard at s· eve

silv'ry

Po.   8–12   O'er the s· moon and ocean
73–11   Laving with surges thy s· beach !

similar

Mis. 272– 8   * were granted for s· colleges,
296–17   by no means identical — nor even s·.
Man.   54–23   a second s· offense shall remove
Ret.   43– 6   granted for s· purposes after
Un.   6–24   discussion and horror, s· to
Rud.   9–19   s· effects come from pride,
Po.   v–22   * S· requests continued to reach
My.   73– 3   * necessary to issue a s· notice
76–13   * A s· decision was reached

similarly

Pul.   65–27   * s· expresses the faith of

similes

Mis. 263– 6   sweetest s· to be found

similitude

Mis. 162–23   after the s· of the Father,
Un.   60–14   after the s· . . . of God. — Jas. 3 : 9.
No.   27– 8   s· of the Apocalyptic pictures.

simple

Mis.   22–29   s· fact cognized by the senses,
30– 4   adopt the "s· addition" in C. S.
43–12   s· sense one gains of this Science
53–22   why is it not more s·,
53–23   The teachings of Jesus were s· ;
53–26   C. S. is s·, and readily understood
53–29   godliness is s· to the godly ;
54–29   the pupil in s· equations
112–18   regarded his act as . . . s· justice,
148–18   hence their s·, scientific basis,
162–30   s· as the shepherd boy,
196–30   require more than a s· admission
248–11   s· falsehoods uttered about me
262–10   however s· the words,
265–16   innovations upon s· proof ;
373– 1   the s· nature of art.
Man.   3–14   hence their s·, scientific basis,
Ret.   82– 3   dealing with a s· Latour exercise
92– 2   not too s· to be sublime,
Un.   9–17   s· teaching and life of Jesus
49– 5   s· appeal to human consciousness.
Pul.   14–14   s· seekers for Truth,
40–16   * s· ceremonies, four times repeated,
50–22   * s· and direct as they are,
Rud.   6– 1   s· solution of the problem of being,
'00.   6–13   through his s· faith and purity,
'01.   22–30   s· statement as to Spirit and
My.   50–21   * s· but suggestive words,
67–26   * will in its s· grandeur surpass
111–30   C. S. is valid, s·, real,
172–28   as a s· token of love."
340–13   a s· board of health,
356–27   This s· statement of oneness

simpler

Man.   62–22   to grasp the s· meanings
My.   vi– 4   * to state truth absolutely in a s·

simplest

Mis.   55– 2   The s· problem in C. S.
Rud.   6–24   in the s· . . . form of healing,
7– 2   s· case, healed in Science,

simplicity

Ret.   91–17   In this s·, and with such fidelity,
Pul.   43–13   * utmost s· marked the exercises.
My.   29–17   * impressiveness . . . in its very s· ;
79–26   * a s· which sprang from the
342–22   s· of the oneness of God ;

simplified

My.   361– 1   directions of God as s· in C. S.,

simply

Mis.   8–17   S· count your enemy to be that
9–11   S·, in that those unfortunate
34– 8   physique is s· thought made manifest.
43– 4   or s· after having been

simply

Mis. 137– 7 it was s· to give you the privilege,
272–20 * have s· an incorporated grant,
299– 9 s· answer the following question
363– 6 s· the supposition that the absence
Ret. 39– 2 were healed s· by reading it,
40–24 s· to show the opposition
64–13 are alike s· nothingness ;
Pul. 4–10 s· to preserve a scientific,
35– 7 * was s· a natural fulfilment of
80–17 * but s· state the fact.
81–10 * s· the woman of the past
No. 25– 1 S· uttering this great thought
Peo. 10– 3 s· because it is more ethereal.
My. 31–28 * announced s· that they would sing
81–19 * spoke s· and gratefully,
106– 8 s· to show the folly of believing
114–10 S· because the treasures of this
169– 5 as s· seeing Mother.
170– 3 s· my acquiescence in the request
273– 2 * This manuscript is presented s· as
280–29 s· to pause in special prayer
305–24 s· how to do his works.
343–15 I have s· taught as I learned

simulates

Mis. 334– 8 Whatever s· power and Truth

simultaneously

Un. 49–15 You cannot s· serve the
Pul. 7– 8 s· praised and persecuted

sin (see also sin's)

abandonment of
Mis. 205–26 absolute abandonment of s·
all
Mis. 3–21 holds in itself all s·,
184–26 all s·, sickness, and death ;
204–13 Truth cleansing from all s· ;
208– 4 it covers all s· and its effects.
317– 8 over all s·, disease, and death.
Man. 41–23 and rule out of me all s· ;
Pul. 12–18 mighty conquest over all s·
13–26 to remove all s·, must depend upon
'01. 5–17 leave all s· to God's fiat
15–19 all s· is a deluded sense,
My. 120–11 takes away all s·, disease, and death,
301–17 All s· is insanity.
and death
Mis. 3–24 elements of s· and death.
30–21 law of v· and death ” — Rom. 8 : 2.
36–23 and the law of s· and death.
49–26 non-intelligence, s·, and death.
90– 5 s· and death to be powerless.
201–19 law of s· and death ;” — Rom. 8 : 2.
321–16 law of s· and death.” — Rom. 8 : 2.
326– 3 law of s· and death.” — Rom. 8 : 2.
Man. 16– 4 overcoming s· and death.
19– 5 saving the world from s· and death ;
Un. 42– 3 s·, and death are not the outcome of
42– 5 What then are matter, s·, and death?
56–17 from the law of s· and death.
62–21 human error, s·, and death
No. 30– 3 all sense of s· and death.
34–28 freedom . . . from s· and death.
35– 9 sickness, sorrow, s·, and death.
35–12 nothingness of hate, s·, and death,
'02. 9–13 law of s· and death.” — Rom. 8 : 2.
My. 5–11 creation of matter, s·, and death,
113–14 law of s· and death.” — Rom. 8 : 2.
239–11 by overcoming s· and death.
272– 7 law of s· and death.” — Rom. 8 : 2.
293–29 law of s· and death.” — Rom. 8 : 2.
and Deity
Un. 6–24 declarations about s· and Deity
and disease
Mis. 101–25 including s· and disease.
No. 4–18 S· and disease are not scientific,
My. 147–20 to heal both s· and disease.
221–20 with which to heal s· and disease.
and fear
No. 40–19 when sickness, s·, and fear
and flesh
'00. 7–30 if s· and flesh are put off,
and mortality
Pan. 8– 5 lunacy, s·, and mortality.
My. 192–11 conquest over s· and mortality,
and self
Mis. 328–17 burdened by pride, s·, and self,
and sensuality
Mis. 234–26 sunken in s· and sensuality,
and sickness
Mis. 189–29 healing s· and sickness,
241–22 bondage to s· and sickness.
No. 18– 2 never diminished s· and sickness,
My. 113–16 healing s· and sickness,
207–13 * s· and sickness are destroyed

and sinners
Un. 60– 7 talk of s· and sinners as real.
My. 180–22 struggles with s· and sinners,
and sorrow
Pul. 82– 4 * cold haunts of s· and sorrow,
and suffering
Mis. 261– 4 s· and suffering it occasions
261– 6 s· and suffering are not cancelled by
My. 248–24 exterminating s· and suffering
annihilated
Un. 31–10 overruled . . . as they annihilated s·.
as a claim
Ret. 63–19 S·, as a claim, is more dangerous
as well as
Ret. 34–12 all sickness, as well as s·,
Hea. 8– 7 can master sickness as well as s·,
Peo. 11– 7 from disease as well as s· ;
at ease in
Mis. 241–29 the sinner who is at ease in s·,
atones for
My. 288–27 Love atones for s·
attaches to
Mis. 209– 1 attaches to s· due penalties
authority of
Ret. 63–12 When we deny the authority of s·,
author of
Mis. 83–17 sin is the author of s·.
away from
Chr. 53–53 away from s· Christ summons thee !
because of
Chr. 55–16 body is dead because of s· ; — Rom. 8 : 10.
belief in
(see belief)
believe in
My. 299–17 Do Christians, who believe in s·,
blotted-out
'01. 35–15 the bliss of blotted-out s·
brought death
Mis. 201– 6 S· brought death ; and death is an
called
Mis. 205– 5 melting away the shadows called s·,
Ret. 67–16 the false claim called s·
No. 31–23 If the evils called s·, sickness, and
'01. 13– 2 The outcome of evil, called s·,
calls
Un. 59–21 illusion which calls s· real,
cancels not
Mis. 338–13 cancels not s· until it be destroyed,
can do nothing
Mis. 93–17 S· can do nothing :
claim of
Un. 31–12 first idolatrous claim of s· is,
'00. 15–14 to see . . . the claim of s·,
'01. 13–28 first detect the claim of s· ;
claims
Mis. 109– 8 and see what, . . . s· claims of you ;
claims of
Mis. 109–26 to escape from the false claims of s·.
cleaves
No. 32–13 cleaves s· with a broad battle-axe.
clouds of
Mis. 355–26 Let no clouds of s· gather
cognizant of
Un. 15– 7 declare Him absolutely cognizant of s· ?
commensurate with
My. 288–22 suffering is commensurate with s· ;
conception of
'01. 13–18 destroy the conception of s·
condition of
Mis. 109–18 Ignorance was the first condition of s·
conquer
Mis. 235– 4 empowered to conquer s·,
My. 125– 2 Have you learned to conquer s·,
conquer this
Mis. 40–30 requires more . . . to conquer this s·
consciousness of
Un. 7–24 the sense or consciousness of s·,
conscious of
Un. 13–13 If God could be conscious of s·,
constitutes
Ret. 67– 4 s· constitutes the human or physical
correct
My. 249– 4 opportunity to correct s·
defense from
Mis. 115–16 protection and defense from s·
definition of
Mis. 108–26 Jesus' definition of s· as a lie.
departure of
My. 197– 1 comes with the departure of s·.
destroy
Mis. 4–30 to destroy s· in mortal thought.
366–28 To destroy s· and its sequence,
My. 221– 9 which was to destroy s·,

sin

destroying
Un. 47– 1   burden of disproof by destroying s·,
Peo. 6–22   are found destroying s·, sickness, and
My. 194– 9   healing sickness and destroying s·,
265–18   destroying s·, disease, and death ;

destroys
Mis. 189–25   subordinates matter and destroys s·,
Ret. 67–14   reforms the sinner and destroys s·.
Un. 54–14   then s· destroys the at-one-ment,
No. 13– 2   and thus destroys s· quickly
My. 288–27   through love that destroys s·.

destruction of
Mis. 40– 8   as in the destruction of s·.
Man. 15–11   in the destruction of s·
No. 31–12   which is the sure destruction of s· ;
31–13   I insist on the destruction of s·

diminishes
Ret. 67–15   personal sense ceases, s· diminishes,

diminishing
Mis. 8– 2   abating suffering and diminishing s·,

disappears
Un. 62–15   Destroy this . . . and s· disappears.
'01. 13–20   destroy . . . and s· disappears.
13–29   we get the victory, s· disappears,

discomfort from
My. 233–12   Is not discomfort from s· better

discomfort in
Mis. 219–21   a sense of discomfort in s·

disease and
(see disease)

disease, and death
Mis. 17–17   materialism, — s·, disease, and death.
60– 6   To regard s·, disease, and death
103– 8   such as s·, disease, and death,
177–19   error, s·, disease, and death?
189–25   destroys s·, disease, and death.
192– 8   sickness, s·, disease, and death,
200– 5   than s·, disease, and death.
205– 5   called s·, disease, and death.
270– 9   power over s·, disease, and death,
317– 8   over all s·, disease, and death.
366–25   in sickness, s·, disease, and death.
No. 4–24   unreality of s·, disease, and death,
29–20   He in whom s·, disease, and death
36–12   of matter, of s·, disease, and death,
Pan. 7–28   makes s·, disease, and death inevitable,
12–15   escape from s·, disease, and death ;
'01. 10–21   dark passage of s·, disease, and death
10–23   over self, s·, disease, and death,
11– 4   over s·, disease, and death,
15– 7   to lessen s·, disease, and death,
17– 1   from s·, disease, and death
23–21   matter, s·, disease, and death,
'02. 7– 5   s·, disease, and death enter not
11– 5   subject to s·, disease, and death.
11–17   from s·, disease, and death.
My. 120–11   takes away all s·, disease, and death,
154– 1   from s·, disease, and death.
156–23   victory over s·, disease, and death.
210– 3   s·, disease, and death cannot enter
221– 9   to destroy s·, disease, and death,
265–18   destroying s·, disease, and death ;
350– 6   its effects, s·, disease, and death.

disease, . . . and death
Un. 10– 1   unreality of disease, s·, and death,
My. 106–19   expressed in disease, s·, and death,

dis-ease in
'01. 15–20   dis-ease in s· is better than ease.
My. 233–11   prefer, ease or dis-ease in s· ?

disease, or death
My. 146–27   takes the side of s·, disease, or death.

divine
Un. 16– 2   In Truth, such terms as divine s·

does not commit
Mis. 61–13   image of God, does not commit s·.'

does not constitute
Ret. 67– 4   human thought does not constitute s·,

does not test
Mis. 93–25   does not test s· and the fact of

ease in
Mis. 343– 2   the temptation of ease in s· ;
My. 233–13   better . . . than ease in s· ?

easily-besetting
Mis. 307–22   Idolatry is an easily-besetting s·

effect of
Mis. 221–11   the effect of s· on himself,

effects of
Mis. 115–29   effects of s· on yourself,

encourages
Ret. 63–24   it encourages s· to say,

error and
No. 37–27   if error and s· existed in
My. 323–23   * triumph over error and s·,

sin

every
Mis. 83– 6   "Every s· is the author of itself,
No. 8–16   every s· will so punish itself

evil or
'01. 12–25   chapter sub-title

except
Ret. 81– 4   Nothing except s·, in the students

expiate their
Pul. 13–20   expiate their s· through suffering.

fear nor
Mis. 93–21   neither fear nor s· can bring on

fear not
Mis. 109–29   fear not s·, lest thereby it

fear or
Mis. 93– 6   Can fear or s· bring back old

fear to
Mis. 109–30   but only fear to s·.

fondness for
Un. 2– 9   takes away man's fondness for s·

forgiven
No. 30– 1   chapter sub-title

forgiveness of
Man. 15–10   acknowledge God's forgiveness of s·
Pul. 80–20   * the forgiveness of s· by God,

forms of
No. 41–16   sublest forms of s· are trying to

forsake
Mis. 123–25   repent, forsake s·, love God,

freed from
Mis. 90–15   Do you desire to be freed from s· ?

freedom from
Peo. 10–24   the mind's freedom from s· ;

from the sinner
Ret. 64– 2   cannot separate s· from the sinner,

giant
Mis. 55–13   This giant s· is the sin against

gloom is
My. 90–16   * teaches . . . that gloom is s·,

God and
Un. 6–16   questions about God and s·,

god of
Mis. 123–14   Merodach, or the god of s·,

great
My. 309–16   slavery he regarded as a great s·.

greatest
Mis. 130–24   greatest s· that one can commit

growing
Mis. 284–19   This growing s· must now be dealt with

grow out of
Peo. 3–28   whereby we grow out of s·

hallucination of
Mis. 94– 5   see . . . the hallucination of s· ;

has no claim
'00. 15–14   thence to see that s· has no claim,

has no power
Mis. 93–15   This being true, s· has no power ;

has produced
Mis. 221–12   believes that s· has produced the

healed
No. 31–19   healed disease as he healed s· ;

healing of
Mis. 352–28   healing of s· and the healing of
Rud. 2–27   purpose of . . . is the healing of s· ;

heal, of
Mis. 241–29   Truth and Love heal, of s·,

heals
Ret. 63– 4   C. S. heals s· as it heals sickness,
My. 180–15   this Principle heals s·,

hiding
My. 211– 6   This mistaken way, of hiding s·

his own
No. 29– 2   put to death for his own s·,

human
Un. 15–19   human s· become only an echo of

human concept of
Ret. 67– 2   before the human concept of s·

ignorance of
Un. 6–19   blindness . . . and ignorance of s·.

ignorant of
Un. 49– 9   as ignorant of s· as is the perfect

indulge in
Mis. 115–29   if you in any way indulge in s· ;

indulging
My. 5–28   indulging s·, men cannot serve God ;

in its citadels
Mis. 211–27   Jesus stormed s· in its citadels

in itself
'01. 14–19   to conceive of . . . is s· in itself.

is a lie
'01. 13– 7   s· is a lie from the beginning,
13–14   evil, alias devil, s·, is a lie

is destroyed
'01. 16– 6   till the s· is destroyed.

is healed
Mis. 352–15   by the same rule that s· is healed.

sin

is impotent
Mis. 90– 2   hence, that *s·* is impotent.

is inadmissible
Mis. 147–11   learned that *s·* is inadmissible,

is losing
No. 41–23   *s·* is losing prestige and power.

is mortal
'01. 13–27   Soul is immortal, but *s·* is mortal.

is not Mind
No. 27– 1   *S·* is not Mind ;

is obsolete
Mis. 173–21   matter is nowhere and *s·* is obsolete.

is removed
'01. 13–23   only as the *s·* is removed

is self-destroyed
Mis. 209–12   when *s·* is self-destroyed.

is sin
'01. 13– 9   the position that *s·* is sin

is the sinner
Ret. 64– 3   *s·* is the sinner, and *vice versa*,

is worse
Ret. 63–23   *S·* is worse than sickness ;

itself
Un. 9– 3   and *s·* itself disappears.
'01. 14– 3   *s·* itself, that clings fast to iniquity.
My. 334–21   *s·* itself, that clings fast to iniquity.

knowing
No. 30–15   becoming human, and knowing *s·*,

knowledge of
   (*see* **knowledge**)

knows
Un. 54–17   If God knows *s·*,

law of
   (*see* **law**)

leaving
No. 19–24   leaving *s·*, sense rises to the

leprosy of
Pul. 29–23   * to cleanse the leprosy of *s·*,

lose sight of
Mis. 319–15   or they must not lose sight of *s·* ;

makes something of
'01. 13–17   When man makes something of *s·*

manifestation of
Ret. 67– 9   first iniquitous manifestation of *s·*

materialism or
Mis. 19–27   out of materialism or *s·*,

matter and
My. 4– 1   losing his faith in matter and *s·*,

most fearful
Mis. 19–19   most fearful *s·* that mortals can

motives for
Peo. 9– 5   washing away the motives for *s·* ;

must be obsolete
No. 26–28   *S·* must be obsolete,

must be *uncovered*
Mis. 352–29   *s·* must be *uncovered* before it

named
No. 30– 4   the false sense named *s·*,

nature of
Un. 5–24   as to the nature of *s·*

never pardons the
Peo. 9–15   never pardons the *s·* that deserves to

no
Mis. 63–11   *If there is no s·, why did Jesus*
   125– 5   rise to know that there is no *s·*,
   293–25   there is no sickness and no *s·*,
Ret. 63–24   to say, "There is no *s·*,"
Un. 56– 6   no *s·* or suffering in the Mind which
No. 35–26   Hence there is no *s·*,

no intelligent
No. 38– 5   no intelligent *s·*, evil *mind* or

no knowledge of
Un. 2–16   God, has no knowledge of *s·*.
No. 17–22   God who has no knowledge of *s·*

no reality in
Un. 64– 3   there is no reality in *s·*,
'01. 14– 2   To assume there is no reality in *s·*,
My. 334–20   "To assume there is no reality in *s·*,

no refuge from
Un. 2– 6   The sinner has no refuge from *s·*,

not
My. 301–17   but healing the sick is *not s·*.

nothing but
Rud. 10–19   Love punishes nothing but *s·*,

obdurate
My. 36–15   * redeemed from obdurate *s·*.

of any sort
Mis. 108– 4   To allow *s·* of any sort
   337–31   *S·* of any sort tends to hide from

of every sort
Mis. 37–21   *s·* of every sort, is destroyed in
   67–19   Justice uncovers *s·* of every sort ;
   241– 6   sickness as well as *s·* of every sort.

of sins
'01. 20–19   This unseen evil is the *s·* of sins ;

sin

of the world
'01. 9–18   the *s·* of the world ;" — *John* 1 : 29.

operation of
Un. 20–20   knowledge and the operation of *s·*,

or death
Mis. 30–11   without pain, *s·*, or death.
Un. 62–16   *s·*, or death is a false sense of

or disease
Mis. 191–30   *s·* or disease made manifest.

original
Mis. 114–19   original *s·*, appearing in its myriad
   201– 4   its original *s·*, or human will

or sense
Mis. 42–27   sense of Life in *s·* or sense material,

or sickness
Hea. 9–24   He never made *s·* or sickness,

or suffering
Un. 56– 6   no *s·* or suffering in the Mind which

or suicide
Mis. 53– 7   Not through *s·* or suicide,

overcome
Mis. 55– 8   utilizes its power to overcome *s·*.
My. 6–10   When we have overcome *s·*
   300– 4   enabling the sinner to overcome *s·*

overcoming
Mis. 319–16   overcoming *s·* in themselves,
Man. 16– 4   healing the sick and overcoming *s·*
My. 239–11   by overcoming *s·* and death.

paid by
No. 35–14   the awful price paid by *s·*,

pain and
Po. 22–18   dark domain of pain and *s·*

pardon
My. 299–18   those who claim to pardon *s·*,

penalty for
Mis. 237– 6   accepted as the penalty for *s·*.

percentage of
No. 32–25   diminishing the percentage of *s·*.

pleasure in
Mis. 90– 3   power of sin is the pleasure in *s·*.
   241–11   "You have no pleasure in *s·*,"
My. 132–26   sinner, dreaming of pleasure in *s·* ;

pleasure of
Ret. 63– 8   belief in the pleasure of *s·*,

power over
Mis. 40–24   must gain the power over *s·*
   270– 9   demonstrated his power over *s·*,

prevent
Mis. 302–29   when it is necessary to prevent *s·*

price of
Mis. 165–24   they never paid the price of *s·*.

produced by
Hea. 17–26   sickness and . . . produced by *s·*.

proof that
No. 37–15   or as a proof that *s·* is known to

punish
Mis. 209– 5   wouldst teach God not to punish *s·* ?

punishes itself
Mis. 93–27   *S·* punishes itself, because it cannot
My. 288–25   that *s·* punishes itself ;

punishing
Mis. 261–18   showeth mercy by punishing *s·*.

punishing of
Mis. 290– 7   This uncovering and punishing of *s·*

punishment for
Mis. 279– 4   Individual punishment for *s·*
'01. 13–23   removes the punishment for *s·*

punishment of
'01. 16– 3   chapter sub-title

quenching
'02. 9– 3   the All-presence — quenching *s·* ;

reality of
Ret. 63– 8   *alias* the reality of *s·*, which makes

rebukes
No. 13– 1   This Science rebukes *s·*

rebuking
Man. 40–10   amenities of Love, in rebuking *s·*,

recognizes
Un. 54–15   unity which *s·* recognizes as its

recovery from
Mis. 100–31   of man's recovery from *s·*

redemption from
Mis. 165–23   of mortals' redemption from *s·* ;

result of
Mis. 115– 8   only as the result of *s·* ;

rolling
Mis. 130–11   "rolling *s·* as a sweet morsel

root of
'01. 13–16   lays the axe at the root of *s·*,

salvation from
   (*see* **salvation**)

saved from
Mis. 197– 8   man saved from *s·*, sickness,
Un. 2– 8   in order to be saved from *s·*.

sin

save from
  Mis. 60– 3 *sent His Son to save from s·,*
      197–16 no more help to save from s·, than
save him from
  Ret. 63– 9 and save him from s· ;
save man from
  Un. 18– 6 can never save man from s·, if
saves from
  Mis. 90– 6 practical Truth saves from s·,
      367–28 that whatever saves from s·,
save them from
  Rud. 3– 5 all efforts to save them from s·
sea of
  Mis. 264– 5 midst of this seething sea of s·.
secrets of
  Mis. 343–16 uncovering the secrets of s·
self and
  Ret. 79–21 the victory over self and s·.
sense and
  Mis. 172– 8 defeat the claims of sense and s·,
sense of
    (*see* **sense**)
sepulchres of
  Mis. 292–15 from the open sepulchres of s·,
serpent of
  Pul. 13–15 fail to strangle the serpent of s·
servants of
  No. 32–20 no longer be the servants of s·,
shackles of
  My. 44– 3 * shackles of s· are being broken,
shuts out
  Un. 41– 5 s· shuts out the real sense of Life,
sickness and
    (*see* **sickness**)
sickness, and death
  Mis. 2–18 remedy for s·, sickness, and death ;
      3–21 all s·, sickness, and death,
     16–14 over s·, sickness, and death.
     78– 4 sense of s·, sickness, and death,
    105– 5 over s·, sickness, and death,
    106– 1 where are s·, sickness, and death?
    179–11 is in s·, sickness, and death.
    184–26 all s·, sickness, and death ;
    196–20 from s·, sickness, and death.
    197– 8 saved from s·, sickness, and death ;
    235– 4 to conquer s·, sickness, and death ;
    260–15 s·, sickness, and death are its
    320–15 from s·, sickness, and death.
  Ret. 56–16 disclaims s·, sickness, and death,
     62– 5 illusion of s·, sickness, and death ;
     64–21 classify s·, sickness, and death as
     69–18 that s·, sickness, and death are
  Un. 1–11 *behold s·, sickness, and death ?*
     3–15 fruit of s·, sickness, and death,
     6– 8 from s·, sickness, and death
    13–15 knowledge of s·, sickness, and death,
    32–18 material, in s·, sickness, and death,
    46–21 S·, sickness, and death were evil's
    47– 1 destroying s·, sickness, and death,
    50–20 evade s·, sickness, and death,
    58–18 unreality of s·, sickness, and death
  Pul. 70–23 * all error, s·, sickness, and death.
  No. 8–22 of s·, sickness, and death.
    16– 9 evil, s·, sickness, and death
    16–23 of matter — s·, sickness, and death
    29–24 waves of s·, sickness, and death.
    31–23 called s·, sickness, and death
    36–20 over s·, sickness, and death.
    38– 4 that s·, sickness, and death are
  Pan. 5–26 brought s·, sickness, and death
  '01. 18–28 triad — s·, sickness, and death,
  Hea. 9–25 s·, sickness, and death are this
    17–10 evidences of s·, sickness, and death,
    17–18 S·, sickness, and death never
    17–19 S·, sickness, and death are error ;
  Peo. 3–10 produced s·, sickness, and death ;
    4– 5 s·, sickness, and death originated in
    6–22 destroying s·, sickness, and death ;
sickness, . . . and death
    (*see* **sickness**)
sickness, and disease
  Mis. 251–29 S·, sickness, and disease flee
sickness and of
  Hea. 9– 9 think most of sickness and of s· ;
sickness nor
  Ret. 63– 7 no evil, neither sickness nor s·.
sickness, or death
  Mis. 17– 6 law of s·, sickness, or death.
  Un. 4– 3 finite sense of s·, sickness, or death,
  Hea. 9– 7 thought of s·, sickness, or death,
    16–18 evidence we have of s·, sickness, or death
single
  Pul. 12–16 For victory over a single s·,
  My. 152–27 nor pardon a single s· ;

sin

sinner and
  Ret. 64– 4 sinner and s· will be destroyed by
sinner and the
  Mis. 94– 7 sinner and the s· are the twain
  Ret. 64–13 the sinner and the s· are alike
sinner from his
  Ret. 64– 3 nor the sinner from his s·.
spectacle of
  '02. 18– 4 The constant spectacle of s·
storming
  '01. 2–19 storming s· in its citadels,
struggle with
  Mis. 41–17 struggle with s· is forever done.
subdues
  My. 131– 2 removes fear, subdues s·,
subject of
  Mis. 115– 4 subject of s· and mental malpractice,
subtleties of
  Mis. 112– 2 with the subtleties of s· !
success in
  Mis. 354– 4 sanguine of success in s·,
  '00. 10– 1 Success in s· is downright defeat.
suffering due to
  Mis. 122–23 for the suffering due to s·.
suffering for
  Mis. 15–27 By suffering for s·, and the
suffering from
  Mis. 14–32 not sheltered from suffering from s· :
sum total of
  My. 212–13 to complete the sum total of s·.
superinduced by
  Mis. 66–24 Disease that is superinduced by s·
sympathy with
  No. 30–24 Sympathy with s·, sorrow, and sickness
take possession of
  '01. 13–11 take possession of s· with such a sense
temptation and
  Mis. 53– 8 by *overcoming* temptation and s·,
termed
  Ret. 64–20 in belief an illusion termed s·,
that
  Mis. 246–10 purged of that s· by human gore,
there is no
  Mis. 60– 1 *you believe there is no s·;*
  Un. 2–13 of God, in whom there is no s·.
  '00. 15–13 that saith "there is no s·,"
this
  Mis. 40–30 requires more . . . to conquer this s·
    222–19 This s· against divine Science
  '00. 14–27 lay not this s· to their — *Acts* 7 : 60.
thought of
  Mis. 105–28 Destroy the thought of s·,
  Un. 15–17 if the thought of s· could be
  Hea. 9– 7 The less said or thought of s·,
thrall of
  '00. 6–22 from the stubborn thrall of s· to a
tired of
  Mis. 324–18 his own heart tired of s·,
to efface
  Ret. 64– 6 to efface s·, *alias* the sinner,
to holiness
  Un. 37–10 a change . . . from s· to holiness,
  '02. 10–23 yea, from s· to holiness
to meet
  Mis. 3–31 to meet s·, and uncover it ;
treated for
  Mis. 90– 9 *to have a husband treated for s·,*
turn from
  Mis. 197– 5 exhort people to turn from s·
types of
  '01. 16– 7 St. John's types of s·
ultimates
  Ret. 64– 1 S· ultimates in sinner,
unless it be a
  Un. 37–15 Not unless it be a s· to believe that
unpunished
  My. 160–24 unpunished s· is this internal fire,
unreality of
  Un. 58–18 the absolute unreality of s·,
  No. 4–24 unreality of s·, disease, and death,
unseen
  Mis. 318–25 chapter sub-title
  Ret. 31–17 the unseen s·, the unknown foe,
unto death
  Mis. 120– 9 whether of s· unto death, or of
visible
  '01. 13– 5 The visible s· should be invisible :
vision of
  Un. 4–26 the vision of s· is wholly excluded.
wages of
  Mis. 76–27 wages of s· is death." — *Rom.* 6 : 23.
  '00. 2–20 his stock in trade, the wages of s· ;
was first
  Hea. 17–24 S· was first in the allegory,

sin

whatsoever is of
Ret. 94–11 consumes whatsoever is of *s*.

without
Un. 58–17 yet without *s*." — *Heb.* 4 : 15.
Mis. 14–30 destroys all error, *s*, sickness,
27–12 *s*, disease, death) are *unreal*.
33–28 for sickness, as well as for *s*,
45–17 *S* is not the master of
55–14 is the *s* against the Holy Ghost
61–19 * held responsible for the '*s*.' "
65– 3 *s*, sickness, disease, or death,
66–15 *s* is identical with suffering,
70–18 *s* was destroying itself,
83–17 *s* is the author of sin.
90– 3 power of *s* is the pleasure in sin.
93–26 believing that *s* is pardoned
96–20 from sickness as well as from *s*.
103– 2 say that *s* is an evil power,
104–11 Herein *s* is miraculous and
107–32 too much or too little of *s*.
108– 3 thinks too little of *s*.
108–14 *S* should be conceived of only as
108–23 *S* needs only to be known
187– 3 Jesus demonstrated over *s*,
194– 4 *s*, sickness, disease, and death are
198–21 product of mortal thought as *s* is.
237–21 *s* can only work out its own
255–24 for sickness, as well as for *s*,
268–21 curing alike the *s* and the
278–16 a curse on *s* is always
318–27 making *s* seem either too large or
319–12 protest against the reality of *s*,
319–12 tends to make *s* less or more
333– 1 *s* . . . is apart from God,
354– 3 *S* in its very nature is
361–18 *s* which doth so easily — *Heb.* 12 : 1.
367–29 would say that . . . must know *s*.
Ret. 67– 1 *S* existed as a false claim before
67– 6 *S* is both concrete and abstract.
67– 6 *S* was, and *is*, the lying supposition
67–18 created neither himself nor *s*,
67–18 but *s* created the sinner ;
94–20 not of faith is *s*." — *Rom.* 14 : 23.
Un. 1– 3 God knows no such thing as *s*.
19–13 there would be *s* in Deity,
23–19 But mortal mind and *s*
24– 2 *s* the opposite of goodness.
36–22 and yet admit the reality of . . . *s*,
51– 4 and hence that *s* is eternal,
54–11 As with sickness, so is it with *s*.
54–11 To admit that *s* has any claim
56–22 he suffers least from *s* who is
58– 1 *s*, pain, death, — a false sense of
62–14 *S* exists only as a sense,
64– 1 If *s* has any pretense of
Pul. 13–20 The *s*, which one has made his
No. 30– 5 will not let *s* go until it is
32–10 chapter sub-title
32–14 It gives the lie to *s*,
32–15 other theories make *s* true.
Pan. 10–26 in loathsome habits or in *s*,
10 29 *S*, sickness, appetites, and
'01. 13–12 *S* can have neither entity, verity,
14– 1 or believe in the power of *s*,
14– 3 To assume . . . and yet commit *s*,
Hea. 17–21 *S* is a supposed mental condition ;
17–26 Then was not *s* of mental origin,
Po. 31–21 sting of death — *s*, pain.
My. 4– 5 Lust, dishonesty, *s*, disable the
41–17 * makes no compromise with evil, *s*,
116–14 Hence the *s*, the danger and
122– 7 *S* is like a dock root.
161–32 *s*, suffering, and death
219–12 To say that it is *s* to ride to
233–21 apathy, dishonesty, *s*.
283–15 *S* is its own enemy.
334–21 "To assume . . . and yet commit *s*,

sin (verb)

Mis. 12–16 temptations to *s* are increased
61–13 What then does *s*?
61–22 Does God's essential likeness *s*,
76– 3 derived capacity to *s*.
184–17 saying, "I have the power to *s*"
198– 3 will have no desire to *s*.
198–13 When tempted to *s*, we should
235– 2 no longer obliged to *s*,
237–13 impossible . . . to *s* and not suffer.
Pul. 3–10 what can cause you to *s*
Rud. 3– 1 while mortals love to *s*,
My. 288–25 "*S* no more, — *John* 5 : 14.

Sinai

Mis. 17– 1 awful detonations of *S*.
151–10 speaketh . . . in tones of *S* :
'02. 5–21 voiced in the thunder of *S*,

since

Mis. x– 7 published . . . *s* April, 1883,
8– 5 cannot, produce health . . . *s*
11–27 *s* they permit me no other way,
23–30 *s*, according to natural science,
24–16 I have *s* tried to make plain
25– 8 *s* God is Truth, and All-in-all.
27–15 *s* the Scriptures maintain
29–16 *S* that date I have known
29–18 The census *s* 1875
34– 8 *s* the physique is simply
65–28 *s* both constitute the divine law
66– 2 *s* false testimony or mistaken
75– 3 *s* Life and Truth were the way
93–22 *s* there is in reality no disease.
96–18 atonement becomes more to me *s* it
108– 8 *s* a lie, being without foundation
108–20 *s* that which is truly conceived of,
109–31 *s* then, . . . cometh repentance,
110–16 months into years, *s* last we met ;
115–20 *s* God, good, is All-in-all.
125– 6 *s* all that is *real* is *right*.
131–14 *s* the erection of the edifice of
136–19 well afford to give me up, *s* you
137–11 *S* then you have doubtless
139–25 wisdom whereof a few persons have *s*
142–13 Each day *s* they arrived
163–12 has *s* ripened into interpretation
182–20 *s* he is and ever was the image
229–10 *s* God is omnipresence,
236– 3 *s* undertaking the labor of
238– 8 *s* no sacrifice is too great for the
243–19 *s* my system of medicine is
247–13 *s* those bringing them do not
248–27 *s* which time I have not
249–17 *s* my residence in Boston ;
278–23 *s* necessities and God's providence
290– 9 *s* whatever is false should disappear.
294–25 *S* my residence in Concord,
297– 2 *s* the discovery of C. S.,
301–17 *s* my private counsel they disregard.
311–20 *s* by breaking Christ's command,
330–11 *s* man's possibilities are infinite,
334–14 *s* there is no disease
345–16 * *s* the reign of Christianity began
350–18 and we have not met *s*.
369–11 *s* madness it seems to many
370–22 *s* the good shepherd cares for all
380–17 *s* God is good, and loss is gain.
Man. 18–21 others that have *s* been elected
85–19 *s* receiving instruction as above,
86–21 revised editions *s* 1902,
Ret. 16– 7 she left the choir
26–24 *s* none but the pure in heart
28–25 but I have *s* understood it.
43– 2 of healing *s* the apostolic days.
50–10 God has *s* shown me,
64–20 *S* there is in belief an illusion
87–24 *s* it is only through the lens of
94–23 *s* Science is eternally one,
Un. 9–25 *s* the days of Christ.
13–16 *s* He is, in the very fibre of His
28–17 *s* we learn Soul only as we learn
38–12 *s* matter has no life,
56– 4 *s* all suffering comes from mind,
Pul. 5– 1 used, . . . my form of prayer *s* 1866 ;
9 16 * for which I had hungered *s* girlhood,
15– 5 *s* exposure is necessary to
35–10 "*s* only the 'pure in — *Matt.* 5 : 8.
36–18 * met Mrs. Eddy many times *s*
55–14 * *S* then she has revised it
66– 6 * *s* then the number of believers
67–16 * unknown a decade *s*,
Rud. 5– 5 *s* God is Mind.
No. 20–23 over *s* the flood,
24–13 *s* evil subordinates good
Pan. 1– 5 *s* last you gathered at the
5– 9 *S* evil is not self-made,
'00. 10–24 *s* publishing this page I have
'01. 2–14 *s* it has a divine . . . Principle
2–30 added *s* last November
8–15 Can he be too spiritual, *s* Jesus said,
15–27 * *s* you have sat here in the house
22– 6 not try to mix matter and Spirit, *s*
25–26 which has *s* been avowed to be
27–10 nothing has *s* appeared that
28– 8 writers *s* the first century
30– 2 *s* ever the primitive Christians,
'02. 5–25 *S* God is Love, and infinite,
6– 1 *s* it is impossible to have aught
6– 6 *s* knowledge of evil, . . . brought
Hea. 6–10 abused me . . . and have ever *s* ;
Peo. 13–25 * "*S* ever the history of Christianity
Po. vi–13 *Boston has s been the pioneer of*
3–11 *S* first we met, in weal or woe

since

Po.	4–16	*s·* God is good
	39–17	*S·* temperance makes your laws.
	54– 2	*S·* joyous spring was there.
	70–17	Immortal Truth, — *s·* heaven rang,
My.	8–29	* "*S·* the last report, in 1900,
	22–14	* *S·* 1866, almost forty years ago,
	47–17	* *s·* the inception of this great
	47–23	* the years that have passed *s·*
	61– 2	* every night *s·* that time.
	61– 6	* *s·* it seemed impossible
	66–28	* *S·* the discovery by Mrs. Eddy,
	73– 5	* in other countries *s·* that time,
	86–16	* *s·* he had enough.
	91–19	* *s·* C. S. was announced
	92–15	* *s·* 1890 its following had
	95–28	* It is doubtful if, *s·* the days of
	100–11	* *s·* the C. S. sect
	114–26	meaning of this book *s·* writing it.
	116–22	Every loss . . . *s·* time began,
	127–11	religions *s·* the first century.
	146– 7	*s·* the third century.
	147–24	*s·* Christian Scientists never
	181–26	*S·* that time it has steadily
	184– 4	*S·* the world was, men have
	187–24	*S·* the day in which you were
	215–31	*s·* we have no hint of his changing
	219–19	*s·* Christianity must be
	219–22	*s·* Christ, the great demonstrator
	220–13	*s·* justice is the moral signification
	221–26	*s·* matter is not conscious ;
	224–25	*s·* the Scripture declares,
	233– 4	in your daily life, *s·*
	235–26	*s·* there are none
	237– 3	I have *s·* decided not to publish.
	239–29	going on *s·* ever time was.
	266–19	*s·* God is Spirit
	266–20	*s·* this great fact is to be
	266–22	*S·* 1877, these special "signs — *Matt.* 16 : 3.
	267– 2	why not, *s·* Christianity is
	275–18	twice *s·* I came to Massachusetts.
	276– 3	*S·* Mrs. Eddy is watched,
	284–18	*S·* my residence in Concord,
	321–21	* twenty years *s·* I first saw you
	322– 1	* It is not long *s·* I met a
	330– 4	* *s·* the great Master himself
	330– 9	* *s·* Mrs. Eddy was not then a
	334–12	* *s·* this critic places certain
	348–17	*s·* Science demanded a rational
	349– 8	cannot cause disease, *s·* disease
	361–10	not written to her *s·* August 30,

sincere

Mis.	x– 3	sacred and *s·* in trial
	288– 1	your *s·* and courageous convictions
	301–15	too *s·* and morally statuesque
No.	3– 4	modest, generous, and *s·* !
My.	17– 6	the *s·* milk of the word, — *I Pet.* 2 : 2.
	44–26	* convey to you their *s·* greetings
	46–23	* a more *s·* and Christly love
	62–14	* Your *s·* follower,
	86– 3	* will be constant and *s·*.
	292–22	though both are equally *s·*.
	358– 3	if you are *s·* in your protestations

sincerely

Mis.	229– 5	If he believed as *s·* that health
Ret.	19–14	*s·* lamented by a large circle
My.	51– 6	* most *s·* regret that our pastor,
	52– 8	* *s·* acknowledge our indebtedness
	272–15	*S·* yours,
	285–29	Most *s·* yours,
	330–25	*s·* lamented by a large circle
	361–11	*S·* yours,

sincerity

Mis.	106–27	"So live, that your lives attest your *s·*
	175–16	unleavened bread of *s·* — *I Cor.* 5 : 8.
	200–21	sweet *s·* of the apostle,
Man.	39–11	thoroughly to test his *s·*,
'00.	9–18	*S·* is more successful than genius
'01.	1–19	Truth comes from a deep *s·*
My.	74–18	* monument to the *s·* of their faith ;
	81–22	* was the depth of *s·*,
	203–19	A deep *s·* is sure of success,

sin-enslaved

No.	46–20	the sick-bound and *s·*.

sinful

Mis.	19–28	*s·*, material, and perishable,
	25–26	more deplorably situated than the *s·*,
	25–27	and the *s·* can.
	36– 1	erring, *s·*, sick, and dying,
	49–17	*can it be wrong, s·, or*
	125– 8	dominion over his own *s·*
	134– 1	the *s·* and ignorant who
	198– 2	man has no *s·* thoughts
	352–22	to heal the sick or the *s·*.

sinful

Mis.	364– 8	healed, through Truth, the . . . *s·*,
	380– 4	how can *s·* mortals prove that
Un.	14–16	created children proved *s·* ;
	15–16	called . . . man the *s·*;
	51– 4	that immortal Soul is *s·*,
	52– 2	that there can be *s·* souls
Pul.	14–29	when it makes them sick or *s·*.
No.	1–20	and cleansed the *s·*.
	7–10	eyes of *s·* mortals must be opened
	19–20	A *s·* sense is incompetent to
	25–25	*s·* mortal is but the counterfeit of
	27–20	This material *s·* personality,
	31– 5	they are yet sick and *s·*.
'01.	13–26	sense of sin, and not a *s·* soul,
	15–28	* your *s·*, wicked manner of
My.	28–23	* heals the sick and reforms the *s·*
	58–23	* healing the sick and reforming the *s·*,
	200–21	Pale, *s·* sense, at work to

sinfulness

Po.	33– 7	From selfishness, *s·*, dearth,

sing

Mis.	387–10	brother birds, that soar and *s·*,
	389–20	with the angels *s·* :
Man.	62– 4	not neglect to *s·* any special hymn
Ret.	16– 6	"Did you hear my daughter *s·*?
Pul.	82–23	* who *s·* best by singing most
Po.	4–19	with the angels *s·* :
	6– 5	brother birds, that soar and *s·*,
	28–10	Aid our poor soul to *s·*
	34–11	Or *s·* thy love-lorn note
	page 65	poem
	65– 1	O *S·* me that song !
	65–10	O *s·* me "Sweet hour of prayer" !
My.	15–31	* I *s·* the NEW, NEW SONG,
	31–28	* would *s·* Hymn 161,
	155–24	*s·* as the angels heaven's symphonies
	166–22	*s·* the old-new song of salvation,
	174–25	my soul can only *s·* and soar.
	192–26	Of this, however, I can *s·* :
	203– 5	*s·* in faith.

singer

Man.	62– 3	solo *s·* shall not neglect to sing
Pul.	59–20	* solo *s·*, however, was a Scientist,
Pan.	4–21	in the words of the Hebrew *s·*,

singers

Pul.	11– 2	song of silver-throated *s·*,
	43– 3	* thirty-five *s·* in all

singing

Mis.	392–20	Isle of beauty, thou art *s·*
Ret.	4–19	*s·* brooklets, beautiful wild flowers,
Pul.	28–20	* *s·* is from a compilation called
	43– 3	* led the *s·*,
	59–10	* *s·* by a choir and
	82–23	* *s·* most for their own sex.
Po.	47– 3	*S·* the olden and dainty refrain,
	51– 2	Isle of beauty, thou art *s·*
My.	31–30	* And what *s·* it was !
	33– 1	* *S·* the Communion Doxology.
	38–19	* when it came to the *s·*,
	59–23	* attempts to lead the *s·*.
	78–22	* *s·* in perfect unison.
	79– 1	* in the *s·* and responsive reading,
	148–21	*s·* of this dear little flock,
	341–11	The bird of hope is *s·*

single

Mis.	45–19	Science in a *s·* instance decides
	80– 4	on the *s·* issue of opposition to
	110– 3	had not the value of a *s· tear.*
	130–20	without one *s·* mistake,
	145– 8	Does a *s·* bosom burn for fame
	234–17	it never has advanced man a *s·* step
	242–20	if he will heal one *s·* case of
	247–10	to furnish a *s·* instance of
	263–29	a *s·* original conception,
	264–29	A *s·* mistake in metaphysics,
	265–12	Whosoever understands a *s·* rule
	266– 6	to abridge a *s·* human right
	278–11	occasion for a *s·* censure,
	333–27	in a *s·* quality or quantity !
Man.	84–23	A *S·* Field of Labor.
Un.	4– 2	without a *s·* taint of our mortal,
Pul.	4–18	A *s·* drop of water may help to
	12–16	For victory over a *s·* sin,
	26–15	* the gift of a *s·* individual
	28– 3	* by the light of a *s·* candle,
	67–21	* *s·* believers or little knots of them
Pan.	5– 2	Can a *s·* quality of God,
Hea.	13–12	a *s·* drop of this harmless
Peo.	6– 8	* if there was not a *s·* physician,
	10–27	but in a *s·* instance when
My.	69–17	* not a *s·* pillar or post
	112–13	not inconsistent in a *s·* instance
	152–27	nor pardon a *s·* sin ;

single

My. 294–13 mightily rebuke a *s·* doubt
342–30 * directed by a *s·* earthly ruler?"

single-handed

Pul. 2–18 *s·* to combat the foe?

singleness

Mis. 317–26 *s·* of purpose to uplift the race.

sin god

Pan. 8– 4 sun god, moon god, and *s· g·*

sings

Mis. 204–10 while white-winged peace *s·*
329–30 brooklet *s* melting murmurs
Un. 26–22 as *s·* another line of this hymn,
Pul. 81–18 * the lark who soars and *s·*
Hea. 20– 6 * vie with Gabriel, while he *s·*,
Po. 66–14 cheer it, perchance, when she *s·*.
My. 192–17 and *s·* of our Redeemer.

singularly

Pul. 31–26 * *s·* graceful and winning

sin-healing

Mis. 66–25 beginner in *s·* must know this,

sinister

Mis. 43–21 such *s·* rivalry does a vast amount of
263– 1 but if my motives are *s·*,
Man. 53–19 a complaint . . . for a *s·* purpose.
Ret. 71–21 *S·* and selfish motives
78– 8 carnal and *s·* motives,

sink

Pul. 14–20 nor again *s·* the world into the

sinking

Rud. 5–26 and *s·* into oblivion.
My. 117–24 except by *s·* its divine

sinks

Ret. 81–20 and so *s·* into deeper darkness.

sinless

Mis. 17–27 primitive, *s·*, spiritual existence
76– 2 hence it must be *s·*,
104–15 *s·*, deathless, harmonious, eternal.
Un. 15–16 God is commonly called the *s·*,
15–18 would Deity then be *s·*?
29– 7 Soul is *s·*, and is God.
49– 9 the more I see it to be *s·*,
52– 1 Soul is *s·* and immortal,
Po. 70–12 For *s·* sense is here
My. 181– 9 scientific, *s·* life of man

sinned

Mis. 76–26 if Soul *s·*, it would die ;
278–14 Job *s·* not in all he said,

sinner (*see also* sinner's)

and sin
Ret. 64– 4 both *s·* and sin will be destroyed
and the sick
Mis. 382– 9 *s·* and the sick are helped thereby,
and the sin
Mis. 94– 7 *s·* and the sin are the twain that are
Ret. 64–13 obvious that the *s·* and the sin are
awaken the
My. 230–14 and to awaken the *s·*.
cleanseth the
Mis. 322–21 healeth . . . and cleanseth the *s·*.
condemned the
Un. 29– 4 Jewish law condemned the *s·*
converting the
Mis. 39–30 than in converting the *s·*.
created the
Ret. 67–19 sin created the *s·* ;
from his sin
Ret. 64– 2 nor the *s·* from his sin.
greatest
Hea. 9– 8 The greatest *s·* and the most hopeless
hardened
Un. 56–22 suffers least . . . who is a hardened *s·*.
has no refuge
Un. 2– 6 The *s·* has no refuge from sin,
infinite
Un. 15–19 precedence as the infinite *s·*,
16– 3 such terms as . . . and *infinite s·*
is consumed
My. 160–26 *s·* is consumed, — his sins destroyed.
is not sheltered
Mis. 14–31 But the *s·* is not sheltered from
is reformed
My. 258– 1 *s·* is reformed and the sick are
loses
Un. 2–12 The *s·* loses his sense of sin,
makes him a
Ret. 63– 8 which makes him a *s·*,
mortal
Mis. 268–22 curing . . . sin and the mortal *s·*.
must endure
Mis. 15– 2 *s·* must endure the effects of his

sinner

none but the
Mis. 165–25 This cost, none but the *s·* can pay ;
obstinate
My. 180–19 The obstinate *s·*, however,
poor
Mis. 344–14 poor *s·* struggling with temptation,
reclaiming the
Mis. 100– 9 healing . . . and reclaiming the *s·*
reclaim the
My. 161– 8 necessary to reclaim the *s·*.
reformed the
Mis. 219–30 and he has reformed the *s·*.
My. 348–26 healed the sick and reformed the *s·*
reforming of the
My. 182–17 the reforming of the *s·*,
reforming the
My. v–16 * reforming the *s·* quickly
155– 2 healing the sick and reforming the *s·*
271– 7 healing the sick and reforming the *s·*,
reforms the
Ret. 67–14 reforms the *s·* and destroys sin.
reform the
Mis. 38–20 enlighten and reform the *s·*,
362–30 to prevent sin or reform the *s·*.
My. 5–17 heal the sick, reform the *s·*,
51–16 * heal the sick and reform the *s·*.
52– 1 * heal the sick, and reform the *s·*,
sad
'01. 17– 8 meet the sad *s·* on his way
saint and
My. 4–11 blessing saint and *s·* with the leaven of
saved the
No. 37–23 saved the *s·* and raised the dead,
saves the
My. 348–19 heals the sick and saves the *s·*.
save the
Mis. 129–23 Were they to save the *s·*,
saving the
'02. 6–11 saving the *s·* and healing the sick.
My. 4–29 healing the sick and saving the *s·*.
short-lived
No. 37– 7 the license of a short-lived *s·*,
sick and
No. 15– 1 falling on the sick and *s·*,
sick and the
(*see* sick)
sin from the
Ret. 64– 2 cannot separate sin from the *s·*,
sin is the
Ret. 64– 3 sin is the *s·*, and *vice versa*.
sordid
Mis. 108– 2 sordid *s·*, . . . thinks too little of sin.
ultimates in
Ret. 64– 1 Sin ultimates in *s·*,
veriest
Mis. 172–11 shall cover . . . the veriest *s·*.
was the antipode
Ret. 67–11 a *s·* was the antipode of God.
willing
Mis. 22–27 he who is a willing *s·*,

Mis. 61–23 a *s·*, — anything but a man !
61–24 Then, what is a *s·*?
62– 4 opposite image of man, a *s·*,
130–13 same power to make you a *s·*
165–26 is the *s·* ready to avail himself of
168– 2 salvation from sin to the *s·*
184–19 believing that he is sick and a *s·*.
187–30 sick and a *s·* in order to be
198– 1 neither be sick nor forever a *s·*.
221–13 and knows he is a *s·* ;
221–14 or, knowing that he is a *s·*,
241– 5 man will no more enter . . . as a *s·*,
241–29 the *s·* who is at ease in sin,
277–29 I thunder His law to the *s·*,
399– 6 *S·*, it calls you,
Ret. 64– 7 to efface sin, *alias* the *s·*,
67–18 *s·* created neither himself nor sin,
Un. 29– 3 If Soul sins, it is a *s·*,
49– 7 the *s·*, wrongly named *man*.
53–21 is not a mortal mind or *s·* ;
53–23 not a mortal mind and a *s·* ;
59–21 calls sin real, and man a *s·*,
No. 19–22 A *s·* can take no cognizance
29–14 the immortal part of man a *s·*?
'01. 15–13 A *s·* ought not to be at ease,
Hea. 18–20 the sick as much as to the *s·* :
Po. 75–13 *S·*, it calls you,
My. 132–26 the *s·*, dreaming of pleasure in sin ;
150–21 bringing the *s·* to repentance,
227–29 The *s·* may sneer at this beatitude,
300– 3 enabling the *s·* to overcome sin

sinner's

Ret. 63– 7 We attack the *s·* belief in

sinners

addressed to
Mis. 60– 3 Bible is addressed to s·
also love
Mis. 13–12 s· also love those that— Luke 6 : 32.
apprehension of
Mis. 201–22 beyond the common apprehension of s· ;
contradiction of
Ret. 22–10 such contradiction of s·— Heb. 12 : 3.
My. 196–21 such contradiction of s·— Heb. 12 : 3.
conversion of
Mis. 229–12 clergyman's conversion of s·.
death of
Un. 50–27 growth, maturity, and death of s·,
hated by
Mis. 1–10 Christianity, hated by s·.
in all societies
No. 41–12 There are s· in all societies,
makes
Mis. 219–24 that mortal mind makes s·,
pray for
'01. 18–30 clergymen pray for s· ;
reclaims
My. 113– 2 reclaims s· in court and in
reformed
·01. 27–19 sick healed, also s· reformed
saints or
Mis. 293–26 makes mortals either saints or s·.
save
Mis. 63–11 why did Jesus come to save s·?
'01. 19– 4 He worketh with them to save s·.
My. 200–27 lessen its depths, save s·
saved
Pul. vii–18 sick are healed and s· saved,
Pan. 5–24 healed the sick, and saved s·.
My. 178– 6 sick are healed and s· saved.
saves
'01. 34– 2 whereby Christendom saves s·,
'02. 8–20 The energy that saves s·
My. 185–21 heals the sick, saves s·,
saving
Mis. 124–18 raising the dead, saving s·.
My. 122–29 healing the sick and saving s·.
saving of
My. 104–32 healing of . . . the saving of s·,
sin and
Un. 60– 7 then talk of sin and s· as real.
My. 180–22 In our struggles with sin and s·,
suffer
Mis. 123–24 s· suffer for their own sins,
world of
Mis. 122– 7 salvation of a world of s·,

Mis. 248–15 malice aforethought of s·."
319–15 self-deceived s· of the worst sort.
Un. 52– 3 sinful souls or immortal s·.

sinneth

Mis. 75–27 "The soul that s·,— Ezek. 18 : 20.
75–29 material sense) that s·, shall die ;
76–23 sense, which s· and shall die ;
Un. 28– 2 "The soul that s·,— Ezek. 18 : 20.
No. 28–25 "the soul that s·,— Ezek. 18 : 20.

sinning

Mis. 12–14 s· unseen and unpunished
36–14 animal qualities of s· mortals ;
79–19 A mortal who is s·, sick, and
90– 9 when she knows he is s·,
93–29 to indulge a s· sense
186–11 in a sick and s· mortal.
187–25 to create a sick, s·, dying man?
219–20 change the . . . sense of s· at ease
Pul. 14–26 When God heals the sick or the s·,
No. 7–13 away from the enemy of s· sense,
29– 9 believe . . . s· sense to be soul ;
'01. 12– 3 heals the s· and the sick.
15–14 or he would never quit s·.
Peo. 4–21 s·, sick, and dying mortals.
10–18 beliefs, . . . made men s· and sick,

sin's

Ret. 80–13 pulling down of s· strongholds,
Un. 54–13 if s· claim be allowed
Pul. 13–26 must depend upon s· obduracy.
'00. 15–13 to see through s· disguise

sins

her
My. 126–16 her s· have reached unto— Rev. 18 : 5.
his
Mis. 107–29 Without a knowledge of his s·,
213– 9 "He that covereth his s·— Prov. 28 : 13.
Un. 55– 6 he bore not his s·, but ours,
My. 160–27 sinner is consumed,— his s· destroyed.
his own
Un. 56– 7 Not his own s·, but the sins of

sins

indulgence of the
My. 64–21 * against the indulgence of the s·
mistakes or
Mis. 72– 3 because of his parent's mistakes or s·,
my
Mis. 326–32 "The sight of thee unveiled my s·,
of a few
Peo. 8– 7 for the s· of a few tired years
of the flesh
Mis. 162–21 to escape from the s· of the flesh.
My. 6– 7 done forever with the s· of the flesh,
of the world
Mis. 246– 2 covers the s· of the world,
Un. 56– 7 but the s· of the world,
one's
Mis. 109–14 should one's s· be seen
open
My. 212– 7 older and more open s·,
other people's
My. 233–14 the effects of other people's s·
others'
Mis. 115–31 of your own as well as of others' s·.
presumptuous
Ret. 72– 8 presumptuous s·, and self-deception,
saved from the
'01. 11–10 saved from the s· and sufferings
sickness and
Mis. 173– 7 healeth all our sickness and s·?
sin of
'01. 20–19 This unseen evil is the sin of s· ;
their
My. 28–27 * of their diseases and their s·,
their own
Mis. 123–24 sinners suffer for their own s·,
thy
No. 42– 9 "Thy s· are forgiven— see Luke 5 : 23.
trespasses and
My. 133–15 "dead in trespasses and s·,"— Eph. 2 : 1.
150–22 dead in trespasses and s·
your
Un. 60–25 are yet in your s·."— I Cor. 15 : 17.

Mis. 61–20 What s·?
Ret. 25–12 That which s·, suffers, and dies,
Un. 29– 3 If Soul s·, it is a sinner,
29– 6 Spirit never s·,
30– 7 Soul is Life, and . . . never s·.
30– 9 Hence this lower sense s·
No. 29– 3 Not Soul, but mortal sense, s·

sinuous

Un. 54–28 diabolical and s· logic?

Sion

My. 17–15 Behold, I lay in S· a— I Pet. 2 : 6.

sir

Mis. 132–12 Dear S· :— In your communication
134– 3 dear s·, as you have expressed
My. 118– 9 My Dear S· :— I beg to thank you
137–11 Respected S· :— It is over forty years

sire

Po. 1– 1 s·, unfallen still thy crest !

siren

Po. 43–13 and, when At some s· shrine

sirens

Mis. 280–29 rocks and s· in their course,

Sisera

Un. 17– 7 fought against S·.— Judges 5 : 20.

sister

Mis. 151–18 Brother, s·, beloved in the Lord,
Man. 64–21 such as s· or brother.
Chr. 55–24 my brother, and s·,— Matt. 12 : 50.
Ret. 20– 6 s· of Lieutenant-Governor
'02. 3–18 rejoices with our s· nation
Peo. 10–10 It were well if the s· States
Po. 65–11 Ah, sleep, twin s· of death
My. 313–27 My oldest s· dearly loved me,
(see also Eddy)

sisterhood

'02. 3–10 joy in the s· of States.

sisters

Mis. 167–16 his parents, brothers, and s·?
Ret. 6–10 parents, brothers, and s·,
13– 7 if my brothers and s· were to be
14–16 safety with my brothers and s·,
Po. 25– 5 S· of song,
My. 62– 9 * give it to my brothers and s·?"
217– 3 your parents, brothers, or s·.

sit

Mis. 17–12 to s· at the feet of Jesus.
73–24 shall s· in the throne— Matt. 19 : 28.
73–25 s· upon twelve thrones,— Matt. 19 : 28.
125–11 s· down at the Father's right hand :

sit

Mis.	125–12	s· *down;* not stand waiting
	154–13	s· beneath your own vine
	159–15	s· silently, and ponder.
	171– 8	that Christian Scientists s· in
	361–16	s· at the feet of Jesus.
	373–28	s· down at the right hand of the
	388–25	The right to s· at Jesus' feet ;
	400– 5	be in thy place : Stand, not s·.
Pul.	16–17	be in thy place : Stand, not s·.
	48– 7	* can s· in her swinging chair,
'00.	15– 5	To s· at this table of their
'02.	3–21	will s· easier on the brow of
Po.	21–14	The right to s· at Jesus' feet ;
	76–16	be in thy place : Stand, not s·.
My.	192– 1	Ye s· not in the idol's temple.
	228–18	who s· at the feet of Truth,
	324–27	* to s· through your class.

site

Mis.	139–23	had this desirable s· transferred
Man.	103– 6	nor removed from the s·
Pul.	57–25	* s· of the new Music Hall,
My.	9–23	purchase of more land for its s·,
	15– 8	nor removed from the s·
	16– 8	the s· of the new building.
	67– 9	* Area of s· . . . 40,000 sq. ft.
	215–19	to purchase the s· for a church

sits

Mis.	ix–13	now hope s· dove-like.
	369–12	This method s· serene at the portals
'00.	15–15	it s· in sackcloth
My.	192–16	s· smilingly on these branches
	349–13	s· at the feet of Jesus

sitteth

Mis.	126–28	she s· in high places ;
	126–30	"He that s· in the heavens — *Psal.* 2 : 4.
	178–12	s· on the right hand of God'' — *Col.* 3 : 1.
Peo.	5–15	it s· beside the sepulchre

sitting

Po.	page 8	poem
	8– 1	s· alone where the shadows fall
My.	159– 7	S· at his feet,

sitting-at-table

Mis.	231–26	his first s· on Thanksgiving

situated

Mis.	25–25	The sick are more deplorably s·
	139–19	s· near the beautiful Back Bay Park,
	144– 3	s· in the second story of the
Man.	99–19	in which London, England, is s·
Ret.	4–10	s· on the summit of a hill,
	5– 1	small town s· near Concord.
My.	66–15	* so well s· for church purposes
	271–13	* modest, pleasantly s· home
	309–18	an extensive farm s· in Bow

situation

Mis.	236– 1	has not suffered from the s·
	265–14	is master of the s·.
	298– 3	St. Paul's words take in the s· :
Man.	75–12	now understands the financial s·
	75–15	Financial S·.
Ret.	44–17	Examining the s· prayerfully
My	10–10	* best of design, material, and s·.
	217–06	understanding the s· in C. S.''
	302–26	and the s· was satisfactory.

six

Mis.	243– 9	bandages to remain s· weeks,
	279–18	the s· days are to find out the
Man.	62– 1	s· or seven minutes for the postlude,
Ret.	5– 7	youngest of my parents' s· children
	43–22	by myself and s· of my students
Pul.	6–13	*''S· months ago your book, S. and H.,
	26–11	* bearing s· . . . silver lamps,
	27–14	* with s· small windows beneath,
	27–15	* the s· water-pots referred to
	86– 2	* s· inches in each dimension,
'02.	15–21	S· weeks I waited on God to
	16– 1	S· months there after Miss Dorcas
My.	29–11	* repeated s· times during the day.
	30–19	* The s· collections were large,
	31– 9	* Promptly at half past s·
	66–22	* when s· services will be held,
	70–25	* it is a combination of s· organs,
	77–22	* at s· o'clock this morning.
	78– 3	* s· services, identical in character,
	164–16	s· dear churches are there,
	312– 7	* s· months after his marriage,
	333–28	* brief space of s· months,
	(see also **numbers***)*	

sixteen

Man.	73– 1	organized with less than s·
My.	304– 9	At s· years of age,
	(see also **numbers;**	

sixteenth

Mis.	83–28	* Quoted from the s· edition.
My.	138–26	* On this s· day of May,

sixth

Mis.	35–30	* See the s· edition.
	57–25	*of the s· and last day,*
	191– 8	in John. s· chapter

Sixth Church of Christ, Scientist

My.	363– 4	* signature

sixty

Pul.	32–20	* must have been some s· years of age,
Po.	35–15	Written more than s· years ago
	(see also **numbers***)*	

sixty-five

Mis.	279–12	AN ATTENDANCE OF S· STUDENTS.

sixty-four

	(see **numbers***)*	

sixty-two

Ret.	37–10	it had reached s· editions.
	(see also **numbers***)*	

size

My.	11–26	* The s· of the building was decided
	67–27	* Notwithstanding its enormous s·,
	68– 8	* twice the s· of the dome on the
	69–26	* chapter sub-title
	69–27	* an idea of the s· of this building
	77– 2	* its great s·, beautiful architecture,
	86–28	* the great s· of the auditorium
	89– 2	* in its s·, if not in its aspect,

sizes

Pul.	62–22	* as they range in all s·,

skeleton

Mis.	302– 7	the s· without the heart,

skeptic

No.	42–28	Here a s· might well ask if the
My.	94–14	* much to convince the s·.
	98– 1	* impress the most determined s·.

skepticism

Mis.	7–11	s· and incredulity prevail in
My.	179–15	Some dangerous s· exists

sketch

Mis.	373–19	master's thought presents a s· of
	376–10	* small s· handed down from
Pul.	46–11	* touched upon in this brief s·.
	61–18	* which stands at the head of this s·.
	67– 4	* S· OF ITS ORIGIN AND GROWTH

sketches

Ret.	2– 6	in John Wilson's s·.

sketching

Po.	8–13	s· in light the heaven of my youth

skies

Mis.	262–24	With all the homage beneath the s·,
	329–30	of fair earth and sunny s·.
	347– 9	discern the face of the s·
	387– 4	mount upward unto purer s· ;
	392– 3	s· clasp thy hand,
	395–26	Of sunny days and cloudless s·,
Po.	20– 3	s· clasp thy hand,
	25– 4	Soft tints of the rainbow and s·
	50–22	mount upward unto purer s· ;
	58–11	Of sunny days and cloudless s·,
My	129–11	The oracular s·, the verdant earth
	193– 7	gorgeous s· of the Orient
	265–27	clearer s·, less thunderbolts,

skilful

Mis.	81– 2	s· and scholarly physicians
	231–11	s· carving of the generous host,
	349– 6	who are s· obstetricians.
Hea.	14–11	be sure he is a learned man and s· ;
My.	152–32	flowers that my s· florist has
	294–16	s· surgeon or the faithful M.D.
	311–10	considered a rarely s· dentist.

skill

Mis.	29–23	diseases that had defied medical s·.
	49– 8	had the s· and honor to state,
	232–13	Human s· but foreshadows
	270– 5	What artist would question the s· of
	351– 7	I have no s· in occultism ;
Ret.	26– 1	and his marvellous s· in
	95– 4	* Ask God to give thee s·
Pul.	55– 2	Not in cunning sleight of s·,
Peo.	8–28	s· proved a million times unskilful.
My.	190–18	as to the relative value, s·, and
	273– 8	* s·, determination, and energy

skin

Pan.	3–30	his spotted s·, the stars ;

skins

Pul.	76–15	* of s· of the eider-down duck,

skirmishing

Pul.	50–25	* after a little s·, finally subsides.

skirt
Pul. 48–12   * woods that s· the valley
skulking
My. 228– 7   The evil mind calls it "s·,"
skull
Mis. 55–29   If Mind is . . . beneath a s· bone,
Un. 33–15   is only matter within the s·,
sky
Mis. 1– 7   discern the face of the s· ; — *Matt.* 16 : 3.
  87– 2   clear ether of the blue temporal s·.
  376–18   splendor of a November s·
Ret. 17–13   has stolen the rainbow and s·,
Pul. 4– 6   I'll tarry in the s·.' "
  39–19   * The splendor of the s·
Rud. 6– 3   *glories of earth and s·,*
No. 14–14   coruscations of the northern s·
Po. 8–16   dreaming alone of its changeful s·
  19– 2   breezes that waft o'er its s· !
  30– 4   new-born beauty in the emerald s·,
  32– 9   sunbeams enkindling the s·
  35–14   Bird, bear me through the s· !
  62–16   has stolen the rainbow and s·,
My. 149–27   Clouds . . . that swing in the s·
  150–16   See therein the mirrored s·
  151–19   * 'neath the temple of uplifted s·
  234– 5   they only cloud the clear s·,
sky-lines
My. 85–31   * one of the few perfect s·
slain
Mis. xi–26   sadly to survey the fields of the s·
My. 185–17   Life is the "Lamb s·— *Rev.* 13 : 8.
slander
Mis. 32–28   should never envy, elbow, s·,
  226– 8   chapter sub-title
  226–29   *S·* is a midnight robber ;
  246–17   stop free speech, s·, vilify ;
  347–32   targets for envy, rivalry, s· ;
Man. 81–23   No idle gossip, no s·,
No. 32–26   s· loses its power to harm ;
slanderer
Mis. 248–10   estimate of the person they called s·,
slanderers
Mis. 227– 7   s· —those pests of society
  345–22   pagan s· affirmed that Christians
slanderous
Mis. 277–15   namely, by s· falsehoods
slanderously
Mis. 298– 4   as we be s· reported, — *Rom.* 3 : 8.
slang
My. 108–20   Ignorance, s·, and malice
  308–28   no profanity and no s· phrases.
slaughtering
My. 286– 4   no more barbarous s· of
slaughters
Mis. 123– 2   same spirit that . . . s· innocents.
slave
Mis. 183–10   he is neither the s· of sense, nor
  246–13   The cry of the colored s·
Peo. 10– 8   succored a fugitive s· in 1853,
Po. 25–15   Be he monarch or s·,
  78–10   Tears of the bleeding s·
slavery
Mis. 237–28   fetters of one form of human s·.
Peo. 10–27   when African s· was abolished
Po. vi–20   *prohibiting s· in the United States."*
My. 266– 6   industrial s·, and insufficient freedom
  309–15   s· he regarded as a great sin.
slaves
'02. 15–18   much of his property was in s·,
Peo. 11–13   the sick, the sensual, are s·,
My. 197– 2   becoming s· to pleasure
slay
Mis. 195–25   sling would s· this Goliath
  250– 8   fattening the lamb to s· it.
slays
Mis. 254–11   when brother s· brother,
sleep
Mis. 23– 5   * Does mind "s· in the mineral,
  36–28   as in the dreams of s·.
  47–15   In s·, a sense of the body
  215–18   as when a child in s· walks on the
  298–26   relief from pain in . . . s·."
  335–23   zealots, who, like Peter, s· when
  400–16   Guard me when I s· ;
Ret. 61– 6   s· when you awaken from s·
  69– 6   deep s·, in which originated the
'02. 17–12   Many s· who should keep themselves
Hea. 17–16   the "deep s·" — *Gen.* 2 : 21.
Po. 3– 9   s· sets drooping fancy free

sleep
Po. 65–11   s·, twin sister of death
  69– 4   Guard me when I s· ;
My. 83–16   * will have time to rest and s·,
  132–28   satisfied to s· and dream.
  296–12   neither does he s· nor rest from
sleeper
My. 133–14   should waken the s·,
sleepers
Mis. 60–17   s·, in different phases of thought,
  325–29   ingress to that dwelling of s·
  342–15   brooded over earth's lazy s·.
sleeping
My. 150–15   s· amid willowy banks
sleeps
Mis. 60–19   or for one who s· to communicate
  209–17   God neither slumbers nor s·.
  257– 4   presupposes that God s·
Pan. 9– 1   * "s· in the mineral,
sleeve
Pul. 49–14   * touching my s· and pointing,
sleight
Pul. 55– 2   * Not in cunning s· of skill,
sleight-of-hand
Hea. 5–16   except s· and hallucination
slender
Mis. 330–32   to put forth its s· blade,
Pul. 31–28   * Her figure was tall, s·, and
slept
Mis. 225–27   deep flush faded . . . and he s·.
  245– 6   Asa s· with his fathers." — *II Chron.* 16 : 13.
slight
Mis. 240–23   s· sway over the fresh, unbiased
  300–31   he who withholds a s· equivalent
Rud. 17– 1   A s· divergence is fatal
No. 29– 8   mind-quacks have so s· a knowledge
  34–14   Physical torture affords but a s·
My. 88–19   * a s· and material development
slightest
Mis. 221– 1   does not, produce the s· effect,
  289– 3   its s· use is abuse ;
  349–24   before I would accept the s·
My. 75–14   * has not been the s· hitch
  75–20   * not the s· evidence of temper,
  96– 7   * none . . . with the s· trace of
slightly
Mis. x–17   My signature has been s· changed
  209– 7   healest the wounds of my people s·
  380–17   practised in s· differing forms.
My. 233–17   healed . . . my people s·, — *Jer.* 6 : 14.
sling
Mis. 195–25   s· would slay this Goliath.
My. 125– 9   the s· of Israel's chosen one
slipping
Mis. 341– 7   after much s· and clambering,
slips
Mis. 9–18   but it s· from our grasp,
slopes
Pul. 48– 1   * well placed upon a terrace that s·
Po. 41–13   green sunny s· of the woodland
sloping
Ret. 91–15   near the s· shores of the Lake of
My. 309–24   My father's house had a s· roof,
sloth
Mis. 342– 5   They heeded not their s·,
slothful
My. 132–27   s·, satisfied to sleep and dream.
slow
Mis. 117–24   inclined to be too fast or too s· :
  223–26   "He that is s· to anger — *Prov.* 16 : 32.
  340–23   however s·, thy success is sure :
  400–24   Be it s· or fast,
Ret. 78– 2   being too fast or too s·.
Hea. 8–12   The world is s· to perceive
Peo. 1–10   footsteps of thought, . . . are s·,
Po. 65– 3   Life's pulses move fitful and s· ;
  69–12   Be it s· or fast,
My. 44– 7   * may be fast or it may be s·,
  196– 9   s· to speak, s· to wrath." — *Jas.* 1 : 19.
  196–10   "He that is s· to anger — *Prov.* 16 : 32.
slowly
Mis. 216–20   * "vanished quite s·,
  316–18   turn them s· toward the haven.
Ret. 80– 8   * mills of God grind s·
Hea. 11– 7   yielding s· to metaphysics ;
  11–10   her modest tower rises s·,
My. 342– 3   * s· descending the stairs.

slumber

'02. 15–24 when s· had fled,
My. 189–18 senses wake from their long s·

slumbered

No. 41–19 Through long ages people have s·

slumberers

Mis. 326–10 thence they spread to the house of s·

slumbering

Mis. 283–11 rouse the s· inmates,
'00. 3–13 the s· capability of man.

slumbers

Mis. 209–17 God neither s· nor sleeps.
400– 2 S· not in God's embrace ;
Pul. 16–14 S· not in God's embrace ;
Po. 76–13 S· not in God's embrace ;
My. 252–30 that neither s· nor is stilled by

small

Mis. 6–31 s· families of one or two children,
27–29 it is a s· manifestation of Mind,
134–26 "still, s· voice" — I Kings 19 : 12.
138–27 "still, s· voice" — I Kings 19 : 12.
147–11 and indicates a s· mind?
164–13 babe Jesus seemed s· to mortals ;
175– 1 "still, s· voice" — I Kings 19 : 12.
294–13 but he is a s· animal :
305–16 * s· contributions from many persons
325– 7 s· conceptions of spiritual riches,
360–25 "still, s· voice" — I Kings 19 : 12.
376–10 * s· sketch handed down from
Man. 72–17 not more than two s· churches
112– 5 capitalized (The), or s· (the),
Ret. 5– 1 s· town situated near Concord,
40– 3 and living on a s· annuity.
52– 6 have a s· portion of its letter
80– 9 * Yet they grind exceeding s· ;
Un. 5– 3 rejoice in the s· understanding
Pul. 3–27 so s· that I am afraid.
4– 4 'So s· a drop as I
27–14 * with six s· windows beneath,
27–17 * Beneath are two s· windows
62–23 * placed on a s· centre table.
65– 7 * which is rather s· and new,
69–16 * It would take a s· book to explain
Rud. 7– 3 scientific, in a s· degree,
No. 1– 4 still, s· voice," — I Kings 19 : 12.
1– 7 S· streams are noisy
8– 4 To this s· effort let us add
32–19 evil, must be s· and unreal.
38– 2 is to-day proving in a s· degree,
'00. 7–15 learned, in a s· degree, the Science
'02. 15–30 "still, s· voice" — I Kings 19 : 12.
My. 42–25 * to comprehend, even in s· degree,
45–11 * represent only a s· part of the
78–16 * and none proffering s· change.
83–10 * Scientists frequently wear a s· pin,
123–25 s· beginnings have large endings.
123–28 we must not overlook s· things
145– 3 acquainted with the s· item
162– 7 A s· group of wise thinkers
169– 4 so long a trip for so s· a purpose
182–13 s· sowing of the seed of Truth,
249– 5 "still s· voice" — I Kings 19 : 12.
309–22 * a s·, square box building

smaller

My. 82–10 * and s· articles of baggage
342–16 * in the other and s· parlor

smallest

Mis. 224–17 into life with the s· expectations,
Rud. 2–23 Healing . . . sickness is the s· part
13– 7 even in the s· degree.
My. 88–17 * constitute the s· feature of the

smallpox

Mis. 257–32 may infect you with s·,
344–15 or to a man with the s·
My. 344–28 the fear of catching s· is

smart

Mis. 297–10 S· journalism is allowable,

smartly

Mis. 230–12 Rushing around s· is no proof of

smell

Mis. 28– 3 Matter can neither see, . . . nor s· ;
86–28 What mortals hear, see, . . . s·,
Un. 24–15 to see, taste, hear, feel, s·.
Rud. 5–20 The body does not see, hear, s·,
Hea. 16–21 can neither see, . . . nor s· God ;

smells

Un. 25– 9 s· as Mind, and not as matter.

smile

Mis. ix–13 hope, disappointment, sigh, and s·
203– 6 as I look on this s· of C. S.,
388–15 won from vice, by virtue's s·,

smile

Ret. 20–17 Thy s· through tears,
42–13 with a s· of peace and love
Pan. 1– 8 frown and s· of April,
Peo. 7–10 * his face lit up with a s· of joy
Po. 21– 3 won from vice, by virtue's s·,
74– 4 S· on me yet, O blue eyes and jet,
My. 6– 9 s· and deceit of damnation.
129–11 there is no day but in His s·.
271–16 * This lady with sweet s·
342– 4 * She entered with a gracious s·,
345– 9 * "Not," with a s·, "if it is really

smiled

Mis. 126–27 hath indeed s· on my church,
127– 2 s· on His "little ones," — Matt. 18 : 6.
Hea. 6– 5 pardon me if I s·.
My. 17–30 s· on His 'little ones,' — Matt. 18 : 6.
29–25 * Even the sun s· kindly upon the

smiles

Mis. 179–27 to give us these s· of God !
231– 2 middle age, in s· and the
390–19 As s· through teardrops seen,
Pul. 82– 4 * her words are s·
82– 4 * her s· are the sunlight
Po. 55–20 As s· through teardrops seen,

smileth

Po. 15–16 Here s· the blossom

smiling

Mis. 148– 1 never shows us a s· countenance
339–17 s· saith, "Thou hast — Matt. 25 : 23.
Peo. 14– 5 cool grottos, s· fountains,
Po. 26–16 And s·, say'st, " 'Tis done !
My. 49– 2 * when these s· people say,
155–31 flowers . . . s· upon them.

smilingly

'00. 2–19 is supposed to answer s· :
My. 192–16 dove of peace sits s·

smite

Mis. 335– 5 shall begin to s· — Matt. 24 : 49.
Ret. 30– 2 endeavoring to s· error with the
45–20 "Whosoever shall s· — Matt. 5 : 39.
81– 1 which s· the heart and threaten
'02. 10–20 s· the reformer who finds the
My. 227–27 "Whosoever shall s· — Matt. 5 : 39.

smites

Mis. 257–28 pitiless power s· with disease

Smith (see also Smith's)

Hon. Hoke

Pul. 48–19 * photograph of Hon. Hoke S·,

'00. 13–25 S· writes : "In this city

Smith, LL.B., C. S. B.,

Judge Clifford P.

My. 142– 8 JUDGE CLIFFORD P. S·, LL.B., C.S.B.,

Smith's

Mr.

Mis. 299–18 If I enter Mr. S· store
299–21 These garments are Mr. S· ;

Smith's grammar

My. 311–30 * finished S· grammar and

smitten

Mis. 11–29 When s· on one cheek,

smoke

Mis. xii– 7 above the s· of conflict,
Hea. 2– 9 amid the s· of battle.

smoked

Mis. 69–26 was — eating s· herring.

smoking

Mis. 90–10 or for drinking and s·?
240–27 habit of s· is not nice,
'02. 18–11 quenched not the s· flax,

smooth

Mis. 347–21 It may be s·, or it may be rugged ;
Un. 64–15 Mortals may climb the s· glaciers,
My. 166–18 in the s· seasons and calms

smoothing

Mis. 257–31 S· the pillow of pain

smoothly

Mis. 118–13 and pass a friend over it s·,

smooth-tongued

Mis. 19–23 or would have in a s· hypocrite

smoulder

My. 211– 8 allowing it first to s·,

Smyrna

'00. 13–12 founded the city of S·,
13–14 writes of this church of S· :

snake

Un. 44–11 a false personality, — a talking s·,

snare
 Mis. 389–11 Can I behold the *s*,
   389–22 No *s*, no fowler, pestilence or
 Po. 4–10 Can I behold the *s*,
   5– 1 No *s*, no fowler, pestilence or

snares
 Mis. 307–27 should beware of unseen *s*,

snatch
 Rud. 16–26 *s* at whatever is progressive,

snatched
 My. 178–23 *s* this book from the flames.
   315–28 *s* me from the *cradle* and

sneer
 Mis. 69– 3 A *s* at metaphysics is a scoff at
   86–23 is something that defies a *s*.
 My. 92–22 * cannot *s* away the two-million-dollar
   94– 6 * cannot *s* away the two-million-dollar
   96–25 * It is the custom to *s* at C. S.,
   227–29 sinner may *s* at this beatitude,

sneered
 Ret. 37–11 Those who formerly *s* at it,

sneering
 My. 96–26 * will soon be beyond the *s* point.

sneers
 '01. 18– 6 the *s* forty years ago

Snider
 Carrie Harvey
 My. 325–18 * signature
 Mr.
 My. 323–28 * Mr. *S* and myself boarded in the

snow
 Mis. 329–29 stricken . . . with winter's *s*,
 Pul. 8–18 Little hands, . . . shoveled *s*,
 Po. 65– 6 robes were as spotless as *s* :

snow-bird
 Mis. 329–25 The *s* that tarried

snows
 My. 153– 1 despite our winter *s*.

snowstorm
 Pul. 60– 1 * (despite the *s*) were crowded

snowy
 Pul. 33–18 * an old man with a *s* beard
 My. 271–16 * with sweet smile and *s* hair

snuff-taker
 No. 22– 8 an inveterate *s*.

snuggled
 '00. 10–28 gold pieces *s* in Pears' soap.

snugly
 My. 342–16 * When we were *s* seated

soap
 '00. 10–28 gold pieces snuggled in Pears' *s*.
   10–30 to part with his *s*,

soar
 Mis. 87– 1 *s* above, as the bird in the
   267–19 whose right wing flutters to *s*,
   277– 4 but Truth will *s* above it.
   361–21 mortals *s* to final freedom,
   387–10 brother birds, that *s* and sing,
 Ret. 18–17 May *s* above matter,
 Hea. 20– 5 * *s* and touch the heavenly strings,
 Po. 6– 4 brother birds, that *s* and sing,
   28–13 The dove's to *s* to Thee !
   34–20 in azure bright *s* far above ;
   64– 8 May *s* above matter,
 My. 131–15 and may thought *s*
   174–25 my soul can only sing and *s*.
   202– 2 *s* above it, pointing the path
   248–20 You *s* only as uplifted by

soared
 Mis. 385–22 "When hope *s* high,
 Po. 48–16 "When hope *s* high,

soareth
 Mis. 354–32 he *s* to fashion his nest,
 Po. 18–10 he *s* to compass his rest,

soaring
 Ret. 9–24 * My *s* soul Now hath redeemed her
 Po. 18– 3 His *s* majestic, and feathersome fling
 My. 281– 7 *s* to the Horeb height,
   290–22 where no arrow wounds the eagle *s*,

soars
 Mis. 68–30 * which *s* beyond the bounds of
 Pul. 81–18 * the lark who *s* and sings

sobbing
 Po. 47–14 Weary of *s*, like some tired child

sober
 Mis. 384– 8 To thought and deed Give *s* speed,
 Pul. 83– 5 * from Philip drunk to Philip *s*,
 No. 19– 8 it is the *s* second thought of
 Po. 36– 7 To thought and deed Give *s* speed,

soberly
 Mis. 240–28 *s* inform them that "Battle-Axe Plug"
   309–29 Let them *s* adhere to the Bible

sober-suited
 Mis. 231– 4 The *s* grandmother,
   332– 9 may its *s* autumn follow

so-called
 Mis. 12–22 effects of this *s* human mind ;
   23– 8 subordinates *s* material laws ;
   28–10 this *s* life is a dream soon told.
   36–16 qualities of the *s* animal man ;
   36–22 relative to the *s* material laws,
   48– 6 its *s* power is despotic,
   55–20 antipodes of the *s* facts of
   73– 2 *s* material body is said to suffer,
   73–19 *s* pleasures and pains of matter
   73–30 the *s* material senses.
   76–21 the *s* soul in the body,
   95–16 between the *s* dead and living.
   107–22 knowledge of evil as evil, *s*.
   108– 2 or the *s* Christian asleep,
   123–13 to appease the anger of a *s* god
   128– 3 The lessons of this *s* life
   173–14 an opposite *s* science,
   183–11 *s* pleasures and pains of
   185– 8 constitutes a *s* material man,
   185–20 that the *s* material senses would
   193–16 "the *s* Christian Scientists."
   198–25 based on physical material law *s*
   199–27 *s* miracles contained in Holy Writ
   200–16 *s* miracles of our Master,
   200–28 the *s* pains and pleasures of matter
   203–15 hydrology handles it with *s* science,
   209–13 physics admits the *s* pains of matter
   250– 6 *s* affection pursuing its victim
   254–23 hurling its *s* healing at random,
   257–10 The *s* law of matter is an
   257–12 This *s* force, or law,
   257–22 governed by this *s* law,
   271– 7 compounded metaphysics (*s*)
   272–22 * these *s* charters bestow no rights to
   294– 2 last infirmity of evil is *s* man,
   325– 6 some, *s* Christian Scientists
   325–25 charnel-house of the *s* living,
   341–30 the *s* pleasures or pains
 Ret. 23– 2 illusion that this *s* life
   60–26 matter and its *s* organizations
   69– 8 pantheistic error, or *s* *serpent*,
   78–11 not to read *s* scientific works,
   88– 8 the *s* dead forthwith emerged
 Un. 10– 3 these *s* existences I deny,
   11– 7 and *s* natural science.
   30– 8 is the *s* material life.
   34– 1 the *s* material structure,
   34–22 its own *s* substance,
   35– 8 *s* material senses are found,
   35–19 *are* the *s* forces of matter?
   37–21 The *s* material senses,
   52–16 God is not the *s* ego of evil ;
   54– 9 the *s* fact of the *claim*.
   55–18 the *s* sufferings of the flesh
   58– 2 if at ease in *s* existence,
   63– 7 *s* appearing, disappearing,
 Pul. 50–24 * *s* orthodox religious bodies
 Rud. 7–12 *s* physical senses,
   7–25 than natural science, *s*,
   10–11 mortal material universe, — *s*,
   12–18 a *s* material organism
   17– 4 these *s* schools are clogging
 No. 10–15 relates to its *s* attributes,
   10–16 When a *s* material sense is lost,
   18–24 the *s* mortal mind asks for
   18–26 militates against the *s* demands of
   31– 3 mortal mind-healing (*s*) has
 Pan. 4–15 that there are many *s* minds ;
 '00. 6–17 fact proves that the *s* fog of
   13– 9 *s* prophetic illumination.
 '01. 12–26 embodies itself in the *s* corporeal,
   25– 1 Hence the mysticism, *s*,
   25– 9 metaphysics (*s*) which mix
 '02. 9–16 tones of *s* material life
 Hea. 6–12 intercommunion between the *s* dead
   13– 9 *s* drug loses its power.
   15–13 the *s* miracles recorded in
   17– 8 makes the material *s* man,
   17– 9 therefore the *s* material man
 My. 91– 6 * in this *s* commercial age.
   181– 3 and *s* natural science,
   219–27 spread of *s* infectious
   228– 4 *s* disease is a sensation of mind,

so-called
My. 232–27 If *s·* watching produces fear
239–25 is the material, *s·* man
274– 3 apart from the *s·* life of matter
275– 6 human, material, *s·* senses
293– 3 and the *s·* power of matter,
302– 9 manifest through *s·* matter.
315–21 what is the *McClure* "history," *s·*,
348– 1 absolutely healed of *s·* disease
349–21 beyond the *s·* natural sciences
(*see also* **laws, mind**)

Social
Po. 39–19 "*S·*," or grand, or great,

social
Mis. 32–25 denominational and *s·* organizations
Pul. 23–17 * potent factors in the *s·* evolution
Pan. 6–13 thereby obtaining *s·* prestige,
'*00.* 10–12 civic, *s·*, and religious rights
My. 93–25 * economy of our *s·* and religious life.
96– 6 * figures in the *s·* and business world,
163–13 show my love for them in *s·* ways
184–23 rural chapel is a *s·* success
309–30 * supplied the only *s·* diversions,

socially
Mis. 136– 2 it was a departure, *s·*, publicly,
Pul. 80– 9 * women's paradise, — numerically, *s·*,
My. 130– 6 *s·*, physically, and morally

Societies
Man. 95–14 From *S·*.
My. 207–16 * signature

societies
Mis. 32–26 social organizations and *s·*
136– 4 as society and our *s·* demand.
297–13 lofty scorn of the sects, or *s·*,
305– 3 * representative from the patriotic *s·*,
Man. 45– 9 members of other *s·*
74–11 churches and *s·* are required to
74–19 *s·* advertised in said *Journal,*
Pul. 1– 4 * One or more organized *s·*
66– 7 * until now there are *s·* in every
No. 41–12 There are sinners in all *s·*,
My. 57–25 * The number of *s·* advertised
207– 8 * representatives of churches and *s·*
362–14 * churches and *s·* of Greater New York,
362–23 * churches and *s·* in this field

Society
Mis. 350– 7 P. M. (Private Meeting) *S·*
Man. 82– 3 the *S·* will not publish them.
82– 8 nor republished by this *S·*
95–15 may lecture for a *S·*.
Pul. 48–22 * *S·* of the Daughters of the Revolution.

society
above
My. 66– 3 * gives to the above *s·* the ownership
66– 9 * purchase of . . . by the above *s·*,
American
Mis. 296– 6 Was it ignorance of American *s·*
benefits
'*00.* 2–12 benefits *s·* by his example
cement of
Mis. 145– 1 at present is the cement of *s·*,
Pul. 2– 6 the cement of *s·*, the hope of
Christian endeavor
Pul. 21–12 Let this be our Christian endeavor *s·*,
Christian Science
Man. 74– 2 C. S. *s·* holding public services,
church and
Pul. 20– 3 purchased by the church and *s·*.
church or
Mis. 314– 5 Each church, or *s·* formed for
conforming to
Mis. 138– 6 The detail of conforming to *s·*,
dissolved the
Mis. 350–17 I dissolved the *s·*,
each
Mis. 81– 6 let each *s·* of practitioners,
effect on
Ret. 62– 3 Test C. S. by its effect on *s·*,
fashionable
Mis. 111–22 the pulpit, and fashionable *s·*,
individuals and
'*00.* 8–10 or a bane upon individuals and *s·*.
My. 211– 4 unseen wrong to individuals and *s·*
member of the
Mis. 305– 1 * sent to every member of the *s·*,
305–24 * Each member of the *s·* is asked to
mutual aid
My. 155– 2 mutual aid *s·*, which is effective
our
Mis. 304–10 * under the care of our *s·*.
pests of
Mis. 227– 7 slanderers — those pests of *s·*

society
secret
Mis. 350– 3 I temporarily organized a secret *s·*
sweet
Pul. 8–24 Sweet *s·*, precious children,
thanks of the
My. 49–28 * merited the thanks of the *s·*
this
Mis. 350– 6 brings up the question of this *s·*,
wish for
Mis. 126– 4 Truly, I half wish for *s·* again ;
withdrawal from
My. 118–20 One's voluntary withdrawal from *s·*,
withdrew from
Ret. 24–22 I then withdrew from *s·*

Mis. 126–10 and in *s·* his tongue?
136– 3 as *s·* and our societies demand.
Man. 45– 4 Joining Another *S·*.
74– 4 a branch church and a *s·* ;
'*00.* 2–11 he gives little time to *s·* manners
My. 53–17 * if she would preach for the *s·*
66–11 * use the *s·* will make of the
93– 4 * in no wise at war with *s·* ;
216–22 request that . . . you disband as a *s·*,

Society of German Patriots
Mis. 305– 5 * the *S· of G· P·*,

Socrates
Mis. 345– 2 St. Paul stood where *S·* had stood
361–14 *S·*, Plato, Kant, Locke,
'*01.* 24–18 It dates beyond *S·*,

sod
Mis. 385– 2 * triune, Above the *s·*
396– 9 Yet here, upon this faded *s·*,
Ret. 18–16 the eaglet that spurneth the *s·*,
Peo. 5–17 has risen above the *s·* to declare
Po. 37– 2 * triune, Above the *s·*
46–11 Fresh as the fragrant *s·*,
59– 1 Yet here, upon this faded *s·*,
64– 7 eaglet that spurneth the *s·*,
My. 160–15 cuts its way through iron and *s·*,

Sodom
No. 7–14 imperfection in the land of *S·*,

soever
My. 293 31 "What things *s·* ye — *Mark* 11 : 24.

sofa
Mis. 225–21 sat down beside the *s·*.
My. 342– 6 * took a seat on a *s·*.

soft
Mis. 106–26 the *s·*, sweet sigh of angels
126– 5 to hear the *s·* music of our Sabbath
231–21 *s·* as thistle-down, on the floor ;
231–23 *s·* little palms patting together,
329–16 stirring the *s·* breeze ;
329–23 and sweep in *s·* strains her
343–26 Among the manifold *s·* chimes
373–17 as clad not in *o·* raiment
385–13 *S·* gales celestial, in sweet music
390–14 And *s·* thy footstep falls upon
394– 8 tears, as the *s·* summer rain,
Man. 41– 9 "A *s·* answer turneth — *Prov.* 15 : 1.
Ret. 13–21 *s·* glow of ineffable joy
17– 6 Muses' *s·* echoes to kindle the grot.
31–25 *s·* as the heart of a moonbeam,
Pul. 2– 7 *s·* shimmer of its starlit dome.
82– 7 * she is *s·* and gentle,
No. 29–22 though clad in *s·* raiment,
Pan. 3– 9 in stillness, *s·*, silent as the
'*02.* 4–15 ringing like *s·* vesper chimes
17–28 world's *s·* flattery or its frown.
Po. 15– 1 *s·* sighing zephyrs through foliage
15–12 Their wooings are *s·*
25– 3 *S·* tints of the rainbow
41– 3 Was that fold . . . *s·* virtue's repose,
45–10 as the *s·* summer rain,
48– 6 *S·* gales celestial, in sweet music
53– 5 And *s·* thy shading lay
55–15 And *s·* thy footstep falls upon
62– 6 Muses' *s·* echoes to kindle the grot.
66– 6 spirit of love, at *s·* eventide
74– 6 *S·* as when parting
My. 78–10 * an interior done in *s·* gray
134–18 tears like a *s·* summer shower,
174– 4 *s·* greensward proved an ideal

softened
Mis. 354–16 a heart *s·*, a character subdued,
376–23 *s·*, grew gray, then gay,

softening
Hea. 4– 9 a person with *s·* of the brain

softly
Ret.	18– 5	colored *s·* by blossom and leaves ;
Po.	53– 9	More *s·* warm and weave
	63–13	colored *s·* by blossom and leaves ;

soil
Mis.	26–14	and what made the *s·*?
	211–12	are not indigenous to her *s·*.
	251–28	to enrich the *s·* for fruitage.
	265–26	is not in the culture but the *s·*.
	343–12	away from the sordid *s·* of self
	343–24	tear them away from their native *s·*,
	357–14	stony ground and shallow *s·*.
	392–16	deeply rooted in a *s·* of love ;
Po.	20–20	deeply rooted in a *s·* of love ;
My.	160–13	a sapling within rich *s·*

soiled
Mis.	391–16	With bare feet *s·* or sore,
Ret.	86–12	this wanderer's *s·* garments,
Pan.	1–12	wornout, or *s·* garments
Po.	38–15	With bare feet *s·* or sore,

soils
Mis.	340–14	dug into *s·* instead of delving into

sojourn
My.	43– 9	* During their *s·* in the wilderness

sojourning
Mis.	178– 1	the place of my own *s·*

Sol
My.	133–16	and one more round of old *S·*

solace
'01.	34–17	*s·* us with the song of angels
My.	135– 7	applied to old age, is a *s·*.
	268–21	*s·* the sore ills of mankind

solar
Mis.	174–13	broader than the *s·* system
No.	14–14	to *s·* heat and light.
	39–26	as photography grasps the *s·* light
My.	114–18	light of revelation and *s·* light.

sold
Mis.	269–25	C. S. may be *s·* in the shambles.
	270– 3	of them that *s·* doves,'' — *Matt.* 21 : 12.
	285– 8	were mistaken for . . . and *s·*.
Man.	64– 4	The literature *s·* or exhibited
	64– 9	literature published or *s·* by
	81–22	C. S. textbook is published or *s·*.
'00.	7– 8	more Bibles *s·* than in all the
'01.	29–28	every book of mine that they *s·*.
My.	v–23	* four hundred thousand copies . . . *s·*
	354– 6	nothing but what is published or *s·* by

soldier
Pul.	65–22	* a Roman *s·* parted his mantle
'00.	10–25	a private *s·* who sent to me,
	10–29	Surely it is enough for a *s·*
My.	277–22	every citizen would be a *s·*
	297– 2	*s·*, patriot, philanthropist,

soldiers
Mis.	138–26	God will give to all His *s·*
Un.	39–20	As *s·* of the cross we must be brave,
Pan.	14–19	remember our brave *s·*,

soldier-shroud
Po.	71–20	O war-rent flag ! O *s·* !

sole
Mis.	24–17	this Life being the *s·* reality
	200–17	*s·* reason that it is their basis.
	308– 1	divine Mind as its *s·* centre
Un.	10– 5	built on Him as the *s·* cause.
	30– 1	Spirit as the *s·* origin of man,
Pul.	42–13	* for the *s·* use of Mrs. Eddy.
	55–28	* Truth is the *s·* recognized authority.
'02.	14–13	*s·* proof that Christ, . . . is the way.
My.	271–10	the *s·* proof of rightness.
	304–17	*s·* editor of that periodical.

solely
Mis.	48–30	*s·* to injure her or her school.
	187–14	*s·* because their transcribing thoughts
	276– 6	*s·* because so many people
	351–11	*s·* from mental malicious practice,
Man.	75–22	and not *s·* to the Directors.
Pul.	82–15	* created *s·* for man.
My.	138–16	but decline to receive *s·* because
	152–12	rests *s·* on spiritual understanding,

solemn
Mis.	13–10	the *s·* consideration of all
	148–10	originated not in *s·* conclave
	177– 1	Never was there a more *s·*
	286– 3	the *s·* vow of fidelity,
	341–24	takes the most *s·* vow of celibacy
Man.	3– 5	originated not in *s·* conclave
Ret.	31– 4	in showing this *s·* certainty
'01.	15–29	* of attending His *s·* worship.
Po.	31–17	*s·* splendor of immortal power,

solemn
My.	46–21	* On this *s·* occasion,
	79– 3	* *s·* little faces turned upward.
	289–11	should upon this *s·* occasion

solemnized
Ret.	42– 2	*s·* at Lynn, Massachusetts,

solemnly
Mis.	176– 6	deeply and *s·* expounded
Man.	16– 9	*s·* promise to watch, and pray

solicit
Man.	87–10	shall not *s·*, or cause or permit
	87–11	or permit others to *s·*,
My.	149–30	*s·* every root and every leaf

solicitations
Mis.	236–15	*s·* of husband or wife
My.	231– 4	in compliance with *s·*

solicited
Pul.	8–11	nor a loan *s·*,
My.	60– 1	* I have been *s·* by many
	89–16	* and subscriptions are not *s·*.

solicitude
Ret.	5– 8	object of their tender *s·*.
	90–20	What other heart yearns with her *s·*,
My.	280– 6	* loving *s·* for the welfare of
	331- 4	* Such watchful *s·* as Mrs. Eddy

solid
Mis.	5–29	seem *s·* substance to this thought.
	66–11	This sacred, *s·* precept
	103– 4	more impregnable and *s·* than matter ;
	156–26	students in acquiring *s·* C. S.
	247–24	seems, . . . *s·* and substantial.
Pul.	77– 4	* a scroll of *s·* gold,
	86– 2	* contains a *s·* gold box,
'02.	14–13	accomplished on this *s·* basis.
My.	45–32	* In *s·* foundation, in symmetrical
	301– 8	leaving a *s·* Christianity at the

solidity
Pan.	3–31	the *s·* of the earth ;
My.	89– 8	* joined lightness and grace to *s·*,

solitary
Mis.	246–18	refuse the victim a *s·* vindication
	282–18	There are *s·* exceptions to

solitude
Mis.	331–25	In sacred *s·* divine Science evolved
Ret.	91–24	*s·* was peopled with holy messages
Pul.	10–10	On shores of *s·*, at Plymouth Rock,
	28– 2	* panel represents her in *s·*
Pan.	3– 3	to preside over sylvan *s·*,
	3– 8	to whisper, "*S·* is sweet."
	3–14	* "O sacred *s·* ! divine retreat !
Po.	31– 7	peace of Soul's sweet *s·* !
	34–12	In deeper *s·*, where nymph or saint
My.	3–13	not a dweller apart in royal *s·* ;
	230–22	give my *s·* sweet surcease.
	246–13	sought in *s·* and silence

solo
Man.	62– 3	*s·* singer shall not neglect to
Pul.	59–20	* *s·* singer, however, was a Scientist,
My.	32–24	* *S·*, "Communion Hymn," words by
	71– 4	* There is also a *s·* organ attached.

soloist
Man.	61–18	*S·* and Organist.
My.	31–25	* *s·* for the services, Mrs. Hunt,

Solomon (see also Solomon's)
Mis.	203– 9	*S·* saith, "As in water — *Prov.* 27 : 19.
	281–29	remember the words of *S·*,
	347– 1	this first command of *S·*,
Pul.	2– 2	saw the house *S·* had erected.
My.	133–17	give birth to the sowing of *S·*.

Solomon's
Mis.	348–14	Hence, *S·* transverse command :

solution
Mis.	65–15	to gain the true *s·* of Life
	291–29	would aid the *s·* of this problem,
	379–24	assiduously pondering the *s·* of
Un.	9–18	true *s·* of the perplexing problem
Rud.	6– 1	simple *s·* of the problem of being,
Hea.	13–12	single drop of this harmless *s·*,
My.	348–31	nothing . . . ill can enter into the *s·* of

solve
Mis.	54–30	to *s·* a problem involving logarithms ;
	62–24	attempts to *s·* its divine Principle by
Ret.	34– 4	could *s·* the mental problem.
Un.	5–13	attempting to *s·* every Life-problem
My.	110–22	*s·* the blind problem of matter.

solved
Un.	36–10	met and *s·* by C. S.
My.	181–15	would have *s·* ere this the problem of
	348– 9	*s·* sufficiently to give a reason for

solves

My. 180–31	the latter *s·* the whence and why
306–18	Divinity alone *s·* the problem of
348–30	it *s·* the problem of being ;

solving

Mis. 52–28	before *s·* the advanced problem.

somber

Po. 8– 3	In *s·* groups at the vesper-call,

some

Mis. x–13	To *s·* articles are affixed data,
7–20	to be depicted in *s·* future time
7–22	will counteract to *s·* extent
30– 2	*s·* feeble demonstration thereof,
32– 6	I infer that *s·* of my students
32–31	query in regard to *s·* clergyman's
38–23	*s·* speculative view too vapory
39– 8	*s·* grossly incorrect and false
40–13	In *s·* instances the students
48–21	hidden nature of *s·* tragic events
49– 5	manifested *s·* mental unsoundness,
50– 8	*is there a secret . . . as s· say ?*
51–28	* transparent like *s·* holy thing."
60–28	its counterfeit in *s·* matter belief.
81– 2	as *s·* of the most skilful
81–23	Every individual . . . at *s·* date
89–17	to refuse help to *s·* who sought
96–26	I can name *s·* means by which
112–14	*s·* of the many features and forms
115– 4	apathy of *s·* students on the subject
155–28	to furnish *s·* reading-matter
159–30	and *s·* from abroad,
171– 8	according to the report of *s·*,
198–23	of adherence . . . to *s·* belief,
215–10	not seek to climb up *s·* other way,
216– 9	review of, and *s·* extracts from,
225–30	* you shall have *s·* gruel."
227–12	*S·* uncharitable one may give
230–11	planning for *s·* amusement,
233–27	if *s·* fall short, others will
234–24	she has made *s·* progress,
236–26	at *s·* step in one's efforts
243–26	*s·* of the medical faculty
249– 2	*s·* large doses of morphine,
249–21	*s·* malignant students,
264–19	*S·* students leave my instructions
278–21	than *s·* of those who have had
278 32	led to *s·* startling departures
280–27	to answer *s·* questions
285– 7	*s·* of these pamphlets were
285–22	*s·* extra throe of error
293– 7	will come, at *s·* date,
295–10	* for *s·* manner of notoriety."
298– 4	as *s·* affirm that we say, *Rom. 3 : 8.*
311–11	*s·* of the older members are not
318– 7	*s·* of those devoted students
318– 8	better than *s·* of mine who are
325– 6	*s·*, so-called Christian Scientists
338– 3	brings to humanity *s·* great good,
349–20	*s·* of these students have
368–23	*S·* of the mere puppets of the hour
390– 8	Gives back *s·* maiden melody,
391–20	*S·* good ne'er told before,
397–17	My prayer, *s·* daily good to do
Man. 59– 5	lose *s·* weight in the scale of
Ret. 2 21	*s·* newspapers, yellow with age.
2–22	*S·* of these, however, were not very
8– 3	For *s·* twelve months,
13– 4	*s·* circumstances are noteworthy.
48–13	following are *s·* of the resolutions
54– 2	*s·* of the cures wrought through
87–14	Let *s·* of these rules be here stated.
94– 4	At *s·* period and in some way
Un. 11–19	a theologian of *s·* bigoted sect,
28– 9	declare *s·* old castle to be peopled with
44 2	*s·* of which are as unkind and unjust
57–28	existence in the flesh is error of *s·* sort,
Pul. 3–26	Perchance *s·* one of you may say,
5– 8	glow of *s·* deathless reality.
8–19	*S·* of these lambs my prayers had
13– 3	Every mortal at *s·* period,
14– 3	with fetters of *s·* sort,
19– 1	My prayer, *s·* daily good to do
28–13	* valued at *s·* forty thousand dollars.
31–14	* during *s·* year in the early '80's
32–20	* *s·* sixty years of age,
36–28	* *s·* of the data of this paper.
45– 1	* *s·* giving a mite
45– 2	* and *s·* substantial sums.
49– 5	* reproductions of *s·* of Europe's
50–20	* will awaken *s·* sort of interest.
50–27	* to show even *s·* one side of it
51–25	* *s·* may be satisfied and *s·* will not.
52– 5	* What a pity *s·* of our practical
56– 7	* In *s·* churches a majority of

Pul. 59– 9	* program was for *s·* reason not
64– 9	* *s·* giving a pittance,
66–25	* *s·* of the pre-Christian ideas
69– 8	* *s·* twelve years ago, after several
81–11	* *S·* of her dearest ones
84–19	* *s·* measure of understanding
Rud. 16–12	I see that *s·* novices,
16–12	*s·* impostors are committing
No. 2–22	*s·* marked success in healing
3– 1	in *s·* vital points lack Science.
3– 9	in 1878, *s·* irresponsible people
9–15	towards *s·* of my students
16–18	inference of *s·* other existence
44– 9	To climb up by *s·* other way
'00. 6–28	*S·* modern exegesis on the
9–26	to have *s·* one take my place
10– 3	is *s·* manifestation of God
10–30	*s·* of his hard-earned money
'01. 2–15	if *s·* fall short of Truth,
15–20	*S·* mortals may even need
17–28	this attenuation in *s·* cases
22– 3	to *s·* extent a Christian Scientist.
25–15	ends in *s·* specious folly.
27– 5	* I look to see *s·* St. Paul arise
27–11	cannot be traced to *s·* of those
28–11	*S·* of his writings have been
31–28	taught by *s·* grand old divines,
'02. 9–29	*s·* new-old truth that counteracts
12–21	*s·* matters of business that
Peo. 3– 9	*s·* of the false beliefs that
8– 4	partiality that elects *s·* to
10– 4	that lose *s·* materiality ;
Po. v– 7	* *s· experience that claimed*
v–17	* *S· tourists who were passing,*
13– 5	My prayer, *s·* daily good to do
34– 5	*S·* dear remembrance in a
34–13	Has wooed *s·* mystic spot,
38–19	*S·* good ne'er told before,
43–13	At *s·* siren shrine
47–14	sobbing, like *s·* tired child
55– 9	Gives back *s·* maiden melody,
77–17	*s·* dear lost guest
My. 7– 4	*s·* matters of business that
10–11	* *S·* money has been paid in
10–12	* *s·* of the churches and other
10–22	* on the part of *s·* one else.
26–23	should date *s·* special reform,
30–22	* *S·* of these contributions were
30–24	* gave a sum surpassing *s·* of
40– 9	* It may even imply that *s·* who
49–24	* giving *s·* useful hints as to
53–27	* *s·* very interesting statements,
54–20	* that *s·* place would be obtained,
55– 4	* purchase *s·* building, or church,
57–32	* What a pity *s·* of our practical
59– 6	* in *s·* far distant day beyond our
59–25	* *S·* say she did not."
69–30	* Cambridge, *s·* four miles away.
71– 2	* and *s·* of the most intricate
84– 7	* a rule in *s·* denominations
86–24	* *s·* of its aspects the most notable
89–28	* It is, in *s·* respects, the greatest
90–31	* the efficacy of which to *s·* extent
92 20	* *s·* such comfort as it promises.
94– 5	* *s·* of the evidence appears in
100– 2	* *s·* of the facts and figures
111–18	to get *s·* good out of your
134–12	eclipsed by *s·* lost opportunity,
134–12	*s·* imperative demand not yet met.
138–12	* of my students and trusted
152–15	or do I climb up *s·* other way?
155–28	may they find *s·* sweet scents
158–22	*s·* practise what they say.
170–27	Beloved, *s·* of you have come
179–15	*S·* dangerous skepticism exists
187– 4	I may at *s·* near future
210– 3	through *s·* favored student.
224–15	not caught in *s·* author's net,
237– 5	wrote . . . *s·* twenty-five years **ago**
251–16	evidently *s·* misapprehension
256– 3	to improvise *s·* new notes,
268– 6	*s·* fundamental error is engrafted
281–22	* on *s·* phase of the subject,
284–19	in *s·* church in Concord, N. H.
306–31	*S·* words in these quotations
307–20	in *s·* respects he was quite
307–21	better than *s·* others did.
313–18	by *s·* responsible individual
318– 8	because at that date *s·* critics
319–16	* conversant with *s·* facts
319–30	* had done *s·* literary work
320–13	* something to do with *s·* editions.
323– 6	* *s·* minister in the far West.
323–32	* We were at that time *s·* eight days
329–26	* *s·* interesting facts concerning

some

My.	329–27	* s· incidents of her life
	334– 3	* s· insidious disease was raging
	334–14	* May it not be, . . . s· other one?
	340–16	shorn of s· of its shamelessness
	345–31	* many subjects, s· only of which
	363–23	misunderstood by s· students.

(*see also* **degree, people, time, way**)

somebody (*see also* somebody's)

Mis.	111–30	belief . . . that s· in the flesh is
	123– 5	idolizing something and s·, or
	129–19	he will always find s· in his way,
	130–10	for a fault in s· else,
	223–28	* I should make him hate s·."
	238–13	utilized in the interest of s·.
	239–15	"Ah!" thought I, "s· has to take it ;
	265– 4	original, or wiser than s· else,
Ret.	8– 9	I heard s· call *Mary,*
My.	61–11	* I saw at once that s· had to
	299– 4	s·, kindly referring to my address

somebody's

Mis.	129–20	will see s· faults to magnify
	335–24	would cut off s· ears.

Some Objections Answered

Pul.	38–12	"S· O· A·,"

something

and somebody
Mis.	123– 5	idolizing s· and somebody, or

apart
Ret.	60– 1	sense defines life as s· apart from

below
No.	26–16	into s· below infinitude.

beside God
Un.	25–12	claiming to be s· beside God,

besides God
Mis.	27–22	claims s· besides God,
	333–25	They believed that s· besides God
Ret.	60– 8	says that . . . is s· besides God.
'02.	6– 7	knowledge of evil, of s· besides God,

besides Him
Mis.	173–25	whence, then, is s· besides Him
	332–30	that there is s· besides Him ;
Ret.	60–22	saith, . . . is s· besides Him,

cast
Mis.	280–14	cast s· into the scale of Mind,

create
Mis.	362–17	out of nothing would create s·,

desirable
Un.	54–21	held it up before man as s· desirable

else
Mis.	178–20	* 'Much learning' — or s· else
Un.	38–15	that s· else also is life,

evil is not
Mis.	284–24	Evil is not s· to fear

for the toilers
Pul.	50– 6	* do s· for the toilers,

good
Pul.	51–29	* have done s· good for the sake of

goodness is
Ret.	63–14	God is good, hence goodness is s·,

higher
Ret.	31–10	s· higher and better
	48–24	s· higher than physic or
My.	221– 6	looked for s· higher
	308– 8	S· higher, nobler, more imperative

impossible
My.	118–22	s· impossible in the Science of

in a name
My.	353– 8	chapter sub-title

inmost
My.	133–26	inmost s· becomes articulate,

in the constitution
Pul.	79–22	* s· in the constitution of

knows
Un.	13–19	that He knows s· which

less
Pan.	11–20	s· less than perfection

makes
'01.	13–17	When man makes s· of sin

matter claims
Mis.	27–22	matter claims s· besides God,

mighty
My.	164–18	A great sanity, a mighty s·

more
Mis.	4–27	s· more than faith is necessary,
My.	79–20	* must be s· more than a fad

new
Hea.	6– 5	pioneer of s· new under the sun

nothing and
Mis.	86–11	*Nothing* and s· are words which

of a novelty
Pul.	62– 1	s· of a novelty in this country,

opposite of
No.	32–17	nothing, or the opposite of s·.

something

real
Mis.	108–23	conception of it at all as s· real,

sanity and
My.	14– 8	a sanity and s· from the

separate
Ret.	60– 5	as s· separate from God.
Un.	24–22	*Evil.* I am s· separate from

suggestive
My.	131–21	There is s· suggestive to me in

superb
Pul.	62–15	* quality of tone is s· superb,

sweet
Mis.	240–31	takes from their bodies a sweet s·

tangible
'01.	7–21	not believe there must be s· tangible

that defies
Mis.	86–23	s· that defies a sneer.

that enjoys
'01.	14– 9	and No, as s· that enjoys,

this
Mis.	333– 1	that this s· is intelligent
Un.	22–14	that a knowledge of this s· is
My.	164–21	this s·, this phœnix fire,
	233– 7	if this s·, . . . frightens you,

to be denied
Un.	50– 5	it is s· to be denied

to be desired
Mis.	86–15	and is s· to be desired.

to be proud of
My.	84–13	* temple is s· to be proud of.

to do
My.	320–13	* having had s· to do with

to forget
Mis.	353– 2	but s· to forget.

to know
Un.	22– 9	not admit that error is s· to know

to watch
My.	233– 3	Is there not s· to watch in

understand
Mis.	54– 7	understand s· of what cannot be lost.
Peo.	6–26	we should understand s· of

unlike Him
Mis.	55–30	it is in s· unlike Him ;
No.	16–19	of s· unlike Him

unreal
No.	17– 1	s· unreal, material, and

Mis.	5–27	is s· not easily accepted,
	38– 6	s· to support one's self and
	235–20	and know s· of the ideal man,
	239–27	s· that she ought not to have,
	249–18	unless it was s· to remove stains or
	250–14	Love is not s· put upon a shelf,
	281– 8	could neither deprive me of s· nor
	327– 2	to take s· out of it,
	342–25	It should cost you s· :
	380–21	that s· was being done for them ;
Un.	22–13	*Evil.* But there is s· besides
	28– 8	define Soul as s· within man?
	49–25	s· which God sees and knows,
Pul.	49–19	* s· of her domestic arrangements,
Pan.	5–22	not believe that . . . can be s·,
	10– 3	think himself to be s·, — *Gal.* 6: 3.
'01.	13– 8	assumption that nothing is s·.
	13–18	conception of sin as s·,
'02.	6–15	false claim, . . . s· that is not of
Hea.	15–20	believe that sickness is s·
My.	8–14	* that there should be s· done,
	24– 6	* s· of the vastness of the truth it
	29–18	* There was s· emanating from
	60– 2	* s· about the early history of
	82–17	* in s· like ten minutes.
	91– 3	* they did not find in other

somethingness

Mis.	109–17	seeing the need of s· in its stead,
	201–14	great s· of the good we possess,
Ret.	55– 7	brings out . . . the eternal s·,

sometimes

Mis.	xi–24	thought s· walks in memory,
	52–12	often convenient, s· pleasant,
	52–14	It s· presents the most wretched
	53–11	*Do you* s· *find it advisable to*
	75–18	may s· be used metaphorically ;
	88– 2	s· feel the need of physical help,
	90–11	s·, under circumstances exceptional,
	117–25	and, s· out of season,
	128– 1	needs often to be *stirred,* s· roughly,
	138–10	but s· to coelbow !
	143–28	s· at much self-sacrifice,
	204– 6	This mental period is s· chronic,
	238– 2	are s· made to believe a lie,
	255– 2	It is s· said, cynically,
	255–18	s· asked, What are the advantages of
	262–28	s· to relieve my heart of its

sometimes

Mis.	280–31	s· just at the moment when you
	282–23	it is s· wise to do so,
	294–12	*vice versa* of this man is s· called
	309–28	s· take things too intensely.
	350–21	An individual state of mind s·
	351– 1	I have s· called on students to
Man.	43–11	S· she may strengthen the faith by
Ret.	8– 6	s· went to her, beseeching her
	54– 1	Why are faith-cures s· more speedy
Un.	9–20	S· it is said, by those who fail to
	52–25	is s· the home of vice.
Pul.	49– 2	* or s· "Mother's room,"
Rud.	2–27	this task, s·, may be harder than
	14–13	s· seventeen, free students
No.	1–10	thrilled by a new idea, are s·
	40– 8	s· wise to hide . . . pure pearls of
Pan.	9–27	s· object to the philosophy of C. S.,
'00.	8–16	sensitiveness is s· selfishness,
	8–29	I s· advise students not to
	9– 3	I s· withdraw that advice and say :
'01.	3–20	It is s· said : "God is Love,
	29–12	well-meaning people s· are inapt or
My.	109–17	yet we may s· say with Job,
	160–22	Physical science has s· argued
	206–30	"Ye were s· darkness,— *Eph.* 5 : 8.
	215– 9	s· a dozen or upward in one class.
	317–18	s· saying, "I wouldn't express it

somewhat

Mis.	77–23	learn, in divine Science, s· of
	117–25	he works s· in the dark ;
	199–18	We learn s· of the qualities of
	237– 3	has yielded s· to the
	264–17	abstract Science is s· untested.
	325–13	S· disheartened, he patiently
Pul.	59– 3	* in a s· novel way.
'00.	12–18	have s· against thee,— *Rev.* 2 : 4.
My.	121–14	is s· out of fashion.
	149– 1	must know s· of the divine Principle
	320–25	* were at times s· long
	324– 3	* Mr. Wiggin had s· of a

somewhere

Pul.	32–18	* s· in the early decade of

somnambulist

Mis.	215–19	because he is a s·,

Son

and Holy Ghost

Un.	51–22	revealed as Father, S· and Holy Ghost ;
'00.	5–11	Father, S·, and Holy Ghost mean

beloved

Mis.	121–22	crucifixion of His beloved S·,
	206– 8	"This is my beloved S·."— *Matt.* 17 : 5.

dear

My.	206–30	kingdom of His dear S·."— *Col.* 1 : 13.

His

Mis.	60– 2	*when He sent His S· to save*
Man.	15– 7	We acknowledge His S·, one Christ ;
Pul.	30–17	* His S·, and the Holy Ghost,
Po.	32–19	pardon and grace, through His S·,

His favorite

Peo.	3– 9	torture of His favorite S·,

of God

Mis.	63–27	Christ as the S· of God was divine.
	77– 2	*Jesus Christ was the S· of God*
	84–15	Christ, was the S· of God ;
	84–17	manifestation of the S· of God
	161–11	the Christ, or S· of God :
	164– 2	incorporeal idea, or S· of God ;
	164–25	as the only S· of God,
	180–30	S· of God and the Son of man ;
	197–14	as a man, as the S· of God,
	309–16	we reach the Christ, or S· of God,
Chr.	55– 7	voice of the S· of God :— *John* 5 ; 25.
	55–21	unto the S· of God.— *Heb.* 7 : 3.
Un.	61–21	faith of the S· of God." *Gal.* 2 : 20.
No.	31–14	S· of God was manifested,— *I John* 3 : 8.
	36–28	ideal Christ was the S· of God,
'01.	9– 2	S· of God and the Son of man
	10– 8	Christ being the S· of God,
	10–16	and of Jesus as the S· of God
	11– 2	Christ, the eternal S· of God,
'02.	12–13	but is the S· of God.

of man

Mis.	73–24	*the S· of man shall*— *Matt.* 19 : 28.
	74– 8	which enthrone the S· of man
	83–20	"*the S· of man*"— *Matt.* 16 : 13.
	84–17	was called the S· of man,
	180–30	Son of God and the S· of man ;
	195–11	S· of man is come— *Matt.* 18 : 11.
Ret.	85–14	the S· of man will be glorified,
Un.	59– 9	S· of man *which is in*— *John* 3 : 13.
No.	36– 9	S· of man which is in— *John* 3 : 13.
'01.	9– 2	Son of God and the S· of man
	11– 1	his mission . . . as the S· of man,

Son

of man

'01.	11– 6	S· of man in divine Science ;
	12–11	the S· of man cometh,— *Luke* 18 : 8.

of the Blessed

Mis.	337– 9	immaculate S· of the Blessed

represented by the

Pul.	13– 2	Truth, represented by the S· ;

Thy

Mis.	83–25	glorify Thy S·,— *John* 17 : 1.
	83–25	that Thy S· also may — *John* 17 : 1.

son

adopted

Ret.	43–10	adopted s·, Ebenezer J. Foster-Eddy,

and daughter

Mis.	167– 8	Both s· and daughter :
My.	282–24	s· and daughter of all nations

bastard

Un.	23– 2	from his bastard s· Edmund

clergyman's

Mis.	225–13	clergyman's s· was taken violently ill.
	226– 6	clergyman's s· returned home— *well.*

every

Mis.	18– 4	and scourgeth every s·— *Heb.* 12 : 6.
Ret.	80– 6	And scourgeth every s·— *Heb.* 12 : 6.
My.	282–24	importance to every s· and daughter

Father and

'02.	12–18	Father and s·, are one in being.

is given

Mis.	161– 5	*unto us a s· is given* :— *Isa.* 9 : 6.
	166–11	unto us a s· *is given* :— *Isa.* 9 : 6.
	168–18	"Unto us a s· is given."— *Isa.* 9 : 6.
	370–10	unto us a s· is given."— *Isa.* 9 : 6.

lawful

Un.	23– 5	His lawful s·, Edgar,

Mary's

Mis.	84–18	Son of man, or Mary's s·.

my

Mis.	225–18	* "If you heal my s·,
Ret.	21– 4	informed that my s· was lost.
My.	313–30	obliged to be parted from my s·,

my little

Ret.	20– 8	my little s·, about four years of age,
	21– 1	letter was read to my little s·,

of a year

Mis.	180–27	month is called the s· of a year.

of God

Mis.	111–31	that somebody . . . is the s· of God.
	161–10	in Science, man is the s· of God.
	164–28	reveal man . . . to be the s· of God.
	180–26	power to become the s· of God
	182–12	power to become the s· of God,

of man

Mis.	63–26	Jesus as the s· of man was human :
	161– 9	Jesus was the s· of man ;
	309–14	personality of Jesus, the s· of man,
'01.	10–10	s· of man only in the sense that
	10–16	Son of God and the s· of man.

of Mary

Un.	59–11	divine idea . . . in the s· of Mary.
'01.	10–10	Jesus was the s· of Mary,

or daughter

Mis.	167– 7	Is the babe a s·, or daughter?

prodigal

Mis.	369–23	as tired as was the prodigal s· of the
Ret.	91– 3	The parable of "the prodigal s·"

the word

Mis.	180–27	In the Hebrew text, the word "s·"

Un.	23–11	what s· is he whom— *Heb.* 12 : 7.

sonare

Rud.	1–15	*per* (through) and s· (to sound).

song

Mis.	142–22	A boat s· seemed more Olympian
	145–28	and echo the s· of angels :
	204–10	sings to the heart a s· of angels.
	372– 8	through s· and object-lesson.
	390– 6	lark's shrill s· doth wake the dawn :
	396–24	and breathed in raptured s·,
	400– 7	Dirge and s· and shoutings low
Ret.	10–17	Prosody, the s· of angels,
	17– 3	spirit of s·,— midst the zephyrs
Pul.	11– 2	sweet s· of silver-throated singers,
	12–18	A louder s·, sweeter than has
	16–19	Dirge and s· and shoutings low,
	18– 8	and breathed in raptured s·,
'00.	2– 7	The s· of C. S. is, "Work— work
'01.	34–17	solace us with the s· of angels
Po.	12– 8	and breathed in raptured s·,
	24–18	With s· of morning lark,
	25– 5	Sisters of s·, What a shadowy throng
	29– 8	No cradle s·, No natal hour
	30–19	sacred s· and loudest breath of
	39– 3	Temperance and truth in s· sublime

song

Po.	54– 4	With light and *s·* and prayer !
	55– 7	lark's shrill *s·* doth wake the dawn :
	62– 1	spirit of *s·*, — midst the zephyrs
	page 65	poem
	65– 1	O sing me that *s·* !
	65–19	To rise to a seraph's new *s·*.
	71–17	holy meaning of their *s·*.
	76–18	Dirge and *s·* and shoutings low
My.	14– 4	above the *s·* of angels,
	15–31	* I sing the NEW, NEW *S·*,
	31–32	* joined in the *s·* of praise.
	81–22	* holy *s·* rose tingling
	163– 1	bursting into the rapture of *s·*
	163– 3	sweet sense of angelic *s·*
	166–22	the old-new *s·* of salvation,
	175–25	The *s·* of my soul must remain
	186– 9	its *s·* and sermon will touch
	189–27	the *s·* and the dirge, surging
	194– 1	*s·* and sermon generate only
	197–27	join with you in *s·* and sermon.
	201–10	Your Soul-full words and *s·*
	269–19	Its harvest *s·* is world-wide,
	313– 2	paraphrase of a silly *s·*
	316– 5	harvest *s·* of the Redeemer
	347–15	bird, and *s·*, to salute me.
	354–24	And the *s·* of songs.

songlet

Ret.	18– 9	grotto and *s·* and streamlet
Po.	63–18	grotto and *s·* and streamlet

songs

Mis.	332–11	sheaves, and harvest *s·*.
	356–13	*s·* should ascend from the mount
Pul.	28–21	* its *s·* are for the most part
Po.	53–20	The vernal *s·* and flowers.
	66– 5	*s·* float in memory's dream.
My.	171– 5	with *s·* and everlasting joy
	176–10	palms of victory and *s·* of glory.
	194– 3	*s·* of joy and gladness.
	354–21	Give us not only angels' *s·*,
	354–24	And the song of *s·*.

songsters'

Mis.	396–11	*s·* matin hymns to God
Po.	59– 3	*s·* matin hymns to God

sonnet

Mis.	379–19	one could write a *s·*.
Ret.	1–12	wrote a stray *s·* and an

sonnets

Ret.	1– 9	containing Scriptural *s·*,

Son of God

(see **Son**)

Son of man

(see **Son**)

sonorous

My.	59–19	* as I heard the *s·* tones

Sons

Po.	40– 2	Good "*S·*," and daughters, too,

sons

Mis.	174–12	Above Arcturus and his *s·*,
	176–13	liberty of the *s·* of God.
	180–22	*to become the s· of God,* — *John* 1 : 12.
	181–25	to become the *s·* of God." — *John* 1 : 12.
	182–25	His *s·* and daughters.
	185–18	to become the *s·* of God." — *John* 1 : 12.
	185–26	to become the *s·* of God." — *John* 1 : 12.
	251–14	the liberty of the *s·* of God,
	259–21	all the *s·* of God — *Job* 38 : 7.
	321–21	Press on, press on ! ye *s·* of light,
Un.	5–20	the liberty of the *s·* of God,
	23–11	with you as with *s·* ; — *Heb.* 12 : 7.
	23–14	bastards, and not *s·*" — *Heb.* 12 : 8.
	42–14	all the *s·* of God — *Job* 38 : 7.
Peo.	11– 1	full liberty of the *s·* of God
Po.	39–14	*S·* of the old Bay State,
My.	185–29	*s·* and daughters of the Granite State

sonship

Mis.	83–22	he declared his *s·* with God :
	83–27	his eternal Life and *s·*.
	181– 3	Is man's spiritual *s·* a personal
	181– 7	in order to understand his *s·*,
	181–20	His *s·*, referred to in the text,
	183–25	denial of man's spiritual *s·* ;
	360–11	scientific *s·* with God.
Un.	39–16	and denies spiritual *s·* ;

soon

Mis.	10–32	*S·* or late, your enemy will
	28–11	so-called life is a dream *s·* told.
	70–27	our Lord would *s·* be rising
	145–17	let not . . . resuscitate too *s·*.
	150– 2	May He *s·* give you a pastor ;
	158– 8	I little knew that so *s·*

soon

Mis.	225–13	*S·* after this conversation,
	253–18	as *s·* as it was born,
	311–20	as *s·* harm myself as another ;
	343– 5	Too *s·* we cannot turn from
	393–11	*S·* abandoned when the Master
Ret.	6–25	was *s·* elected to the Legislature
	7–21	* sad event will not be *s·* forgotten.
	20–28	The family . . . very *s·* removed
Pul.	34–14	* *S·*, to their bewilderment and fright,
No.	28–13	none too *s·* for entering this path.
	28–17	is never understood too *s·*.
'02.	18–19	summer brook, *s·* gets dry.
	19– 2	So *s·* as he burst the bonds of
Hea.	10– 3	as *s·* as it was born," — *Rev.* 12 : 4.
Po.	51–16	*S·* abandoned when the Master
	71–21	nor too *s·* Is heard your
	72– 1	O not too *s·* is rent the chain
My.	12– 3	* as *s·* as the money in hand
	56– 7	* It was *s·* evident that
	61–22	* as *s·* as the workmen began to admit
	92–18	* country would *s·* be left behind.
	95– 1	* C. S. would *s·* be included among
	96–26	* cult will *s·* be beyond the
	130–18	left to itself is not so *s·* destroyed
	140–22	abandoned so *s·* as God's Way-shower,
	169– 8	which I hope *s·* to name to them.
	189–19	how *s·* earth's fables flee
	291– 6	a uniting of breaches *s·* to widen,
	321–21	* will *s·* be twenty years since I
	335– 5	* He was *s·* exalted to the
	346– 9	* *S·* after I reached Concord

sooner

Mis.	11–17	would one *s·* give up his own?
	43–18	letter is gained *s·* than the spirit
	115–30	if . . . *s·* or later, you will fall
	278–27	*s·* this lesson is gained the better.
Ret.	44–24	No *s·* were my views made known,
Un.	6– 4	*S·* or later the whole human race
	41–12	must come to all *s·* or later ;
No.	7–10	*S·* or later the eyes of . . . mortals
	28– 4	mists of error, *s·* or later, will melt
Pan.	13–18	*S·* or later all shall know Him,
'01.	20–20	agony . . . it must *s·* or later cause

soonest

Un.	61–27	contrite heart *s·* discerns this truth,
	61–28	helpless sick are *s·* healed
Pul.	5–10	firmest to suffer, *s·* to renounce.
'01.	29–25	who *s·* will walk in his footsteps.
Hea.	13– 8	higher natures are reached *s·* by

soothing

My.	253– 2	healing the sick, *s·* sorrow,

sophist

Mis.	363–27	exposes the subtle *s·*,

sophistry

Mis.	366–32	false theories . . . gilded with *s·*
	370–26	*s·* that such is the true fold for
No.	11–27	Revelation must subdue the *s·* of

soprano

Ret.	16– 1	a *s·*, — clear, strong, sympathetic,
Pul.	37–19	* Miss Elsie Lincoln, the *s·* for the choir

sordid

Mis.	108– 2	*s·* sinner, . . . thinks too little of sin.
	343–12	*s·* soil of self and matter.
My.	133–16	from self's *s·* sequela ;

sore

Mis.	15–20	*s·* travail of mortal mind
	71– 7	that he had *s·* eyes ;
	72– 4	were *s·* injustice.
	107– 5	in *s·* trials, self-denials, and
	253–28	the spiritual Mother's *s·* travail,
	391–16	With bare feet soiled or *s·*,
'01.	29– 3	known of his *s·* necessities?
Po.	22–15	To heal humanity's *s·* heart ;
	38–15	With bare feet soiled or *s·*,
My.	268–21	solace the *s·* ills of mankind

sore-footed

Mis.	327–27	*s·*, they fall behind

sorely

My.	215– 2	Though *s·* oppressed,

sorrow

all

My.	257–16	all *s·*, sickness, and sin.

and loss

Ret.	7–23	* too much of *s·* and loss.

and mortality

Mis.	103–11	say . . . life is *s·* and mortality ;

and sickness

Mis.	399–10	thy *s·* and sickness and sin."
No.	30–24	Sympathy with sin, *s·*, and sickness
Po.	75–17	thy *s·* and sickness and sin."

sorrow

and sighing
My. 171– 6   s· and sighing shall — Isa. 35: 10.
becomes
Mis. 351–25   joy that becomes s·.
dismissal of
Mis. 101– 7   and the dismissal of s·.
endureth
Hea. 10–17   s· endureth but for the night,
is the harbinger
Un. 57–25   S· is the harbinger of joy.
multiply thy
Mis. 57–16   multiply thy s·." — Gen. 3: 16.
nation's
My. 292– 8   sanctify our nation's s·
no
'02. 20– 7   no s·, no pain ;
pain and
Un. 18–11   If pain and s· were not in
seems to come
Hea. 10–16   when s· seems to come, if you will
sickness and
Mis. 250–28   want and woe, sickness and s·
sin and
Pul. 82– 4   * cold haunts of sin and s·,
soothing
My. 253– 2   healing the sick, soothing s·,
subdued
My. 290–26   him who suffered and subdued s·.
tears of
My. 36–16   * exchanged the tears of s· for
your
Hea. 10–18   Then will your s· be a dream,

Mis. ix–12   joy, s·, hope, disappointment,
204– 7   hope, s·, joy, defeat, and
327– 1   turned my misnamed joys to s·.
400– 9   and s·?   No, It has none,
Pul. 16–21   and s·?   No, It has none,
No. 35– 9   no more sickness, s·, sin, and
Hea. 10–23   or to argue stronger for s· than
Po. 76–20   and s·?   No, It has none,
My. 273–20   joy, s·, life, and death.

sorrowful

Mis. 133–32   the s· who are made hopeful,
396– 7   More s· it scarce could seem ;
Po. 58–19   More s· it scarce could seem ;
My. 50–15   * this meeting . . . was rather s· ;"

sorrowing

Mis. 108– 1   s· saint thinks too much of it :
133–23   blessing on the sick and s·,

sorrows

Mis. 10– 2   and enhance its s·.
84–14   "man of s·" — Isa. 53: 3.
84–26   falsity of material joys and s·,
Un. 55– 5   "a man of s·, — Isa. 53: 3.
56–14   shares his cup of s·.
'02. 18– 5   made him a man of s·.
Po. 33–14   Whose mercies my s· beguile,

sorrow-worn

My. 40–18   * pain-racked and s· humanity.

sorry

Mis. 132–28   * "If we have . . . we are s·."
311–32   I have been s· that I spoke at all,
'01. 21–14   I am s· for my critic,
My. 313–29   that was a s· offence.

sort

Mis. 37–22   impurity, sin of every s·,
40–18   error, discord of whatever s·.
67–19   Justice uncovers sin of every s· ;
108– 4   To allow sin of any s·
131– 8   let the leaner s· console this
178–16   * wondered what s· of people you were,
241– 6   as well as sin of every s·.
307–10   to suffering of every s·.
313–22   laborers of the excellent s·,
319–16   sinners of the worst s·.
337–32   Sin of any s· tends to hide from
353–11   of the misguided, fallible s·,
371–16   not productive of the better s·,
Man. 97–20   or circulated literature of any s·.
Ret. 61–12   fear or suffering of any s·.
Un. 11–21   the ruder s· then prevalent,
58– 1   error of some s·, — sin, pain,
Pul. 5–10   those characters of holiest s·,
14– 3   will chain, with fetters of some s·,
43–27   * that s· of personal worship
50–20   * will awaken some s· of interest.
60– 4   * There was no address of any s·,
'01. 1–18   All that is true is a s· of necessity,
32– 7   I loved Christians of the old s·
My. 147–10   a s· of C. S. kindergarten
210– 9   attacks of error of every s·.
229– 5   cannot be found . . . one of this s·.

sorts

Mis. 370–25   would gather all s· into a
My. 104– 5   all s· of institutions flourish

sought

Mis. 89–18   to some who s· his aid ;
140–17   till mortal man s· to know
163– 1   he s· to conquer the
176–16   s· the New England shores,
199–16   rulers s· the life of Jesus ;
232–26   s· from the love of good,
245– 5   s· not to the Lord, — II Chron. 16: 12.
303– 3   s· and found as healers
357–27   have s· the true fold
372–13   I s· the judgment of sound
Chr. 53–15   Through understanding, dearly s·,
Ret. 23–18   my affections had diligently s·
33– 7   I s· knowledge from the different
34– 5   If I s· an answer from the
88– 1   and different aid is s·.
89–28   not . . . known to them or s· by them.
Pul. 47–10   * she states that she s· knowledge
80– 8   * s· the line of least resistance.
Rud. 14– 8   never s· charitable support,
'02. 15– 4   nor s· the protection of the laws
My. 111– 2   the reader would not have s·.
142–12   I s· God's guidance in doing
189–21   that which defies decay . . . is s·
246–13   s· in solitude and silence
247–17   s· their food of me.
343–14   s· no such distinction.
348– 5   I s· this cause,

Soul (see also Soul's)

allness of
Man. 16– 7   even the allness of S·, Spirit,
alone
Ret. 25–14   S· alone is truly substantial.
and body
No. 29– 5   a false sense of S· and body.
and intelligence
No. 35–18   presupposes . . . S·, and intelligence
and sense
'02. 4–11   peace between S· and sense
and substance
Mis. 145– 7   to express S· and substance.
bands of
Un. 12– 6   bind it with bands of S·.
cannot be formed
Mis. 75–31   S· cannot be formed . . . by
consciousness of
Mis. 170–23   old consciousness of S· in sense.
define
Un. 28– 8   define S· as something within man?
described
Un. 28– 5   has not descried nor described S·.
dignity of
Mis. 126–12   lift us to that dignity of S·
emanates from
Mis. 16–25   emanates from S· instead of body,
essence of
My. 204–11   sacred ave and essence of S·
evergreen of
Mis. ix–22   is not the evergreen of S· ;
evidence of
My. 119–24   with the evidence of S·,
feast of
My. 263– 6   feast of S· and a famine of sense.
flow of
Mis. 149– 5   this feast and flow of S·.
from clay to
Pan. 11–12   turn from clay to S· for the model
furnace of
My. 269–19   is molten in the furnace of S·.
harmony of
Mis. 85–28   immortality and harmony of S·.
has man a
No. 28–24   chapter sub-title
hath part
Mis. 390–23   In which the S· hath part,
Po. 56– 2   In which the S· hath part,
haven of
Mis. 152–27   Into His haven of S·
heaven of
Mis. 394– 5   the home, and the heaven of S·.
Po. 45– 7   the home, and the heaven of S·.
My. 163– 2   the haven of hope, the heaven of S·,
heavens of
Mis. 360–14   stars in the heavens of S·.
heraldry of
Po. 70–21   A painless heraldry of S·,
immortal
Un. 51– 4   that immortal S· is sinful,
No. 11– 4   Man has an immortal S·,
29– 4   Immortal man has immortal S·
impulse of
My. 308– 9   impels the impulse of S·.

Soul

infinite
Un. 48–18 The Ego is God . . . infinite *S·*.
Pul. 2–24 eternal harmony of infinite *S·*.
informing
My. 259–30 represents the eternal informing *S·*
instead of
Peo. 2–13 of *S·* instead of the senses,
is a synonym
Mis. 75–11 *S·* is a synonym of Spirit,
is immortal
'01. 13–26 *S·* is immortal, but sin is mortal.
My. 273–25 body is mortal, but *S·* is immortal ;
is Life
Un. 30– 7 *S·* is Life, and . . . never sins.
is not in body
Un. 51–27 *S·* is not in body, but is God,
is one
Mis. 75–13 hence *S·* is one, and is God ;
is right
Ret. 57– 9 *S·* is right ;
is sinless
Un. 29– 7 *S·* is sinless, and is God.
52– 1 *S·* is sinless and immortal,
is substance
Mis. 103– 3 Spirit, *S·*, is substance,
is the divine Mind
Mis. 75–30 *S·* is the divine Mind,
is the Life
Mis. 76–25 *S·* is the Life of man.
is the synonym
Ret. 57–10 *S·* is the synonym of Spirit,
knowledge of
No. 29– 8 so slight a knowledge of *S·*
language of
Hea. 7– 8 language of *S·* instead of the senses ;
legitimate affection of
Mis. 287– 9 not the legitimate affection of *S·*,
Life that is
My. 274– 3 even the Life that is *S·* apart from
living
Un. 30–25 living *S·* shall be found a
music of
Mis. 106–28 music of *S·* affords the only
'00. 11– 8 spiritual music, the music of *S·*.
must be God
Un. 28–17 *S·* must be God ;
my
Un. 29–27 [my *S·*, immortality].
never saw
Un. 59–17 *S·* never saw the Saviour come
no cognizance of
Un. 28–19 senses take no cognizance of *S·*,
not sense
Po. 70–21 heraldry of *S·*, not sense,
My. 118–19 *S·*, not sense, receives and gives it.
of all being
Un. 29–10 declares God to be the *S·* of all being,
of man
Rud. 1– 7 the *S·* of man and the universe.
one
Mis. 75– 6 *there is but one S·*,
Ret. 57–11 hence there is but one *S·*,
Un. 29–12 There is but one God, one *S·*,
or Mind
Mis. 189–15 supposition that *S·*, or Mind,
Un. 29–12 There is but one God, one *S·*, or Mind,
or Spirit
No. 26– 4 and that *S·*, or Spirit, is subdivided
over sense
Mis. 321–12 of Life over death, and of *S·* over sense.
Hea. 10–20 even the triumph of *S·* over sense.
Peo. 11–10 supremacy of *S·* over sense,
penetration of
Mis. 292–27 with the penetration of *S·*,
purifies sense with
'00. 8–24 fire that purifies sense with *S·*
reality and
Peo. 1– 9 reality and *S·* of all things,
restores
Un. 30–11 restores *S·*, or spiritual Life.
Science of
    (*see* Science)
Science reveals
Un. 29–15 Science reveals *S·* as that which
sense and
Mis. 102–28 conflict between sense and *S·*.
No. 12–25 it makes both sense and *S·*,
sense to
    (*see* sense)
silences
My. 230– 8 digested only when *S·* silences
soul to
My. 129–23 divine law . . . gives a soul to *S·*,
Spirit, or
No. 29– 6 He believes that Spirit, or *S·*,

Soul

springtide of
Pan. 1–14 waiting — for the springtide of *S·*.
stands
Un. 28–22 *S·* stands in this relation to
sublime
Mis. 393– 5 *S·*, sublime 'mid human *débris*,
Po. 51–10 *S·*, sublime 'mid human *débris*,
substance of
Mis. 104– 7 safe in the substance of *S·*,
sunlight of
Mis. 202– 4 into the sunlight of *S·*.
supremacy of
Peo. 11–10 even the supremacy of *S·*
the word
Mis. 75–18 The word *S·* may sometimes
we learn
Un. 28–17 we learn *S·* only as we learn God,
what is
Un. 28– 3 What is *S·*?
would place
Mis. 344–17 They would place *S·* wholly inside

———

Mis. 75– 7 *S· is not in the body*
75–15 *S·* is a term for Deity,
76–26 if *S·* sinned, it would die ;
186– 4 in which *S·* is supposed to
287–12 *S·* is the infinite source of bliss :
354–12 and sense seems sounder than *S·*,
Ret. 25–14 *S·* I denominated *substance*,
56– 6 or divides . . . *S·* into souls,
57–13 sense, not *S·*, causes . . . ailments,
60–29 but one Spirit, Mind, *S·*.
Un. 29– 3 If *S·* sins, it is a sinner,
29–25 Hope thou in God [*S·*] :—*Psal.* 42 : 11.
42– 3 *S·*, Spirit, is deathless.
45–25 substance of Spirit, . . . *S·*.
52–26 The senses, not God, *S·*,
62–14 only as a sense, and not as *S·*.
Rud. 5–11 who has ever found *S·* in the body
5–18 *S·* is the only real consciousness
No. 29– 3 Not *S·*, but mortal sense, sins
29–14 statement . . . that *S·* is in matter,
35–21 the only Mind, Life, substance, *S·*
My. 119–31 Truth that leadeth . . . from body to *S·*,
131–16 may thought soar and *S·* be.
225–29 Truth, Life, Spirit, Mind, *S·*,
252– 6 will be salutary as *S·* ;
269–13 * and God the *S·*.
351–16 meet in that hour of *S·* where are no

soul (*see also* **soul's**)

alone in
My. 189–32 Am I not alone in *s·*?
and life
Ret. 59– 3 a mortal mind and *s·* and life,
another's
Mis. 338–23 * Another's *s·* wouldst reach ;
as sense
Mis. 15–21 shall *s·* as sense be satisfied,
belief that
Mis. 76– 9 mortal belief that *s·* is in body,
body and
Mis. 354–19 body and *s·* in accord with God.
dear to the
Pul. 82–11 * many things dear to the *s·*
disengage the
Mis. 344– 8 disengage the *s·* from objects of
feast of
My. 191–29 invitation to this feast of *s·*
forgiven
No. 29–12 * "The forgiven *s·* in a sick body
for sense
Mis. 76–20 exchange the term *s·* for *sense*
Un. 30– 3 uses the word *s·* for *sense*.
from sense
My. 139–28 redeem . . . your *s·* from sense ;
gives to
My. 120–12 gives to *s·* its native freedom.
her
Pul. 84– 1 * not in her hand, but in her *s·*.
her own
Pul. 81–22 * her own *s·* plays upon magic strings
his
Pul. 79–24 * breath of his *s·* is a belief in
My. 34– 4 not lifted up his *s·* unto— *Psal.* 24 : 4.
human
Mis. 76–15 to set a human *s·* free from its
76–23 misnamed human *s·* is material sense,
Un. 51–26 man is reflected not as human *s·*,
Pul. 53–22 * the power of the human *s·*.
image of the
Po. 23– 8 An image of the *s·*,
is deathless
Mis. 75–30 that *s·* is deathless.

soul

is emancipate
My. 267–27   whereby *s·* is emancipate
living
Mis. 185–27   *was made a living s· ; — I Cor.* 15 : 45.
Un.   30–14   was made a living *s· ; — I Cor.* 15 : 45.
Rud.   2– 2   * *person*, . . . "a living *s· ;*
man's
My. 200–15   man's *s·* is safe ;
means sense
No.   28–26   Here *s·* means sense
miscall
Un.   29–17   the physical senses miscall *s·*,
must overflow
Mis. 338–22   * Thy *s·* must overflow,
my
Mis.   75–22   "My *s·* doth magnify — *Luke* 1 : 46.
    317–29   My *s·* abhors injustice,
Ret.   20–20   earthly hope, babe of my *s·*.
Un.   29–24   cast down, O my *s· — Psal.* 42 : 11.
    30– 1   "My *s·* . . . doth magnify — *Luke* 1 : 46.
    30–11   "He restoreth my *s·*," — *Psal.* 23 : 3.
Pan.   4–22   cast down, O my *s·* ? — *Psal.* 42 : 11
Po.   32–20   comfort my *s·* all the wearisome day,
    65– 9   My *s·* is enchained to life's
My. 118– 1   My *s·* thanks the loyal,
    174–25   my *s·* can only sing and soar.
    175–25   The song of my *s·* must remain
    262–12   celebrate Christmas with my *s·*,
    290–12   My *s·* reaches out to God
    360–17   I advise you with all my *s·*
no
Po.   2– 1   no *s·* those looks betray ;
of divine philosophy
Mis. 364–11   It is the *s·* of divine philosophy,
of man
My. 344– 9   * "And the *s·* of man?"
of melody
Po.   34– 2   *s·* of melody by being blest
palace of the
Pul. 82– 1   * the body . . . the palace of the *s·*,
poor
Po.   28–10   Aid our poor *s·* to sing
redemption of
Un.   52–12   precious redemption of *s·*,
save the
Mis. 244– 8   states that God cannot save the *s·*
sense instead of
Un.   20–23   by reading *sense* instead of *s·*,
sense of a
Un.   29–19   that material sense of a *s·* which
sinful
'01.   13–26   a sense of sin, and not a sinful *s·*,
soaring
Ret.   9–24   * My soaring *s·* Now hath
so-called
Mis.   76–21   the so-called *s·* in the body,
stricken
Pul. 82– 5   * which heals the stricken *s·*.
that sinneth
Mis.   75–27   "The *s·* that sinneth, — *Ezek.* 18 : 4.
Un.   28– 1   "The *s·* that sinneth, — *Ezek.* 18 : 4.
No.   28–25   "the *s·* that sinneth, — *Ezek.* 18 : 4.
the word
Un.   30– 3   the word *s·* for *sense.*
this
No.   29–10   and then they doctor this *s·*
thrills the
My. 125–18   which always thrills the *s·*.
thy
My. 183– 2   and with all thy *s·*, — *Luke.* 10 : 27.
to Soul
My. 129–23   gives a *s·* to Soul,
truth of the
Po.   72–20   mock the bright truth of the *s·*.
upborne
Po.   23–15   *s·*, upborne on wisdom's wings,
with soul
My. 154–28   mind with mind, *s·* with soul,

Mis.   75–20   a substitution of *sense* for *s·*
Ret.   57– 6   Plato believed he had a *s·*,
Pul. 10–28   Speak out, O *s·* !
No.   29– 9   believe material . . . sense to be *s·* ;
My. 179– 9   In other words, *s·* enters
    363–15   This proof that . . . is *s·* inspiring.

Soul-full
My. 201–10   Your *S·* words and song

soulfully
My. 139– 5   *s·* founded upon the rock,

Soul-less
Mis. 311–14   impractical, unfruitful, *S·*.

soulless
Ret.   23–20   *S·* famine had fled.
    74– 5   *corpus sine pectore* (*s·* body),

Soul's

Mis. 373– 5   *S·* expression through the brush ;
    385–17   To *S·* diviner sense,
Hea.   10–27   the true fount and *S·* baptism.
Po.   31– 7   peace of *S·* sweet solitude !
    48–11   To *S·* diviner sense,
My. 344–15   approaches to *S·* perfection."

soul's
Po.   70– 5   the *s·* glad immortality,

souls
Mis.   76–13   belief the . . . contain immortal *s·* !
    76–13   for these *s·* to escape
    153–27   * *S·* that are gentle and still
Ret.   56– 7   Soul into *s·*, . . . is a misstatement
Un.   28–13   common hypotheses about *s·*
    52– 2   sinful *s·* or immortal sinners.
Pul.   56–15   * comfort to many weary *s·*.
    63– 9   nourish trees as well as *s·*,"
No.   26– 5   spirits, or *s·*, — *alias* gods.
'01.   32–28   sanctified *s·* would take in the

soul-visit
My. 297– 6   description of her *s·*,

sound
Mis.   46–27   even as the idea of *s·*, in tones,
    120–18   *s·* of vintage bells to villagers
    140–27   Our title . . . will be safe and *s·*
    315–18   prove *s·* in sentiment, health, and
    356–14   sweeter than the *s·* of vintage bells.
    372–14   sought the judgment of *s·* critics
    398–22   Heard ye the glad *s·* ?
Man.   83–17   *s·* in sentiment and practical
Pul.   11– 3   organ's voice, as the *s·* of many waters,
Rud.   1–15   *per* (through) and *sonare* (to *s·*)
No.   13–25   A theory may be *s·* in spots,
    14– 1   C. S. is *s·* in every part.
    29–13   Is this . . . statement *s·* theology,
'00.   11–13   Music is more than *s·* in unison.
'01.   26–20   *s·* faith and charity,
'02.   9–21   When first I heard the life-giving *s·*
Hea.   20– 3   * Oh, could we *s·* the glories forth,
Po.   71–15   Joy for the captive ! *S·* it long !
    75– 2   Heard ye the glad *s·* ?
My.   v–15   * established the Cause on a *s·* basis
    vii–10   * Deeds, . . . are the *s·* test of love ;
    164–17   not only possess a *s·* faith, but
    189–11   go forth in waves of *s·*,
    265– 6   subordinate to material sight and *s·*
    277– 9   and *s·*, well-kept treaties.
    304–22   * a woman of *s·* education
    316–23   *s·* appreciation of the rights of

sounded
My. 199–19   *s·* the tocsin of a higher hope,
    258–23   memories of him who *s·* all depths of

sounder
Mis. 354–11   sense seems *s·* than Soul,

sounding
Mis. 292–11   such as eternity is ever *s·*.
    316–23   pounding . . . love into *s·* brass ;
No.   45– 3   "as *s·* brass, — *I Cor.* 13 : 1.
'01.   26–23   as *s·* brass, — *I Cor.* 13 : 1.

soundness
Mis. 350–23   *s·* of the argument used

sounds
Mis. 324– 6   *s·* of festivity and mirth ;
    329–20   *s·* her invisible lute,
Rud.   6– 3   *sweet s· and glories of earth*

sour
Mis.   72–14   have eaten *s·* grapes, — *Ezek.* 18 : 2.
Un.   35– 2   this is sweet, this is *s·*."
    35– 2   and say that *s·* is sweet,
    35– 4   believed sweet to be *s·*,

source

any other
Pul. 21–28   cannot come from any other *s·*.
correct
Hea.   16–27   evidences . . . from the correct *s·*.
divine
Mis.   19–17   God, its divine *s·*.
    22– 7   if not from the divine *s·*,
    333–18   from the divine *s·* of being,
Pul.   4–11   unity with your divine *s·*,
essence and
'00.   5–13   essence and *s·* of the two latter,
evil
Mis. 113–17   suggestions from an evil *s·*.
exhaustless
Mis.   39–19   this saving, exhaustless *s·*
higher
My. 338–18   they seek a higher *s·*
infinite
Mis. 287–12   Soul is the infinite *s·* of bliss :
My. 165–31   found and felt the infinite *s·*

source

is infinite Mind
Un. 24–15 man, whose s· is infinite Mind.
is Spirit
Un. 25–23 whose only s· is Spirit.
its
Un. 25–17 by showing God as its s·.
mighty
Ret. 11–16 Science the mighty s·,
Po. 60–13 Science the mighty s·,
of appeal
My. 90–14 * not the only s· of appeal.
of being
Mis. 333–18 from the divine s· of being,
Ret. 69–3 and ultimate s· of being;
Un. 46–12 spiritual sense and s· of being.
of death
Ret. 59–7 that which is the s· of death,
one
My. 153–32 up to the one s·, divine Life
prolific
Ret. 69–21 prolific s· of all suffering?
same
Mis. 92–15 from the same s·.
spiritual
Mis. 225–24 spiritual s· and ever-present help,
their
Mis. 354–15 prove the nature of their s·.
Pul. 3–22 have their s· in God,
this
Mis. 347–5 To avoid danger from this s·
unerring
Ret. 34–2 unmixed, unerring s·,

Ret. 34–13 mortal mind as the s· of all the ills
Un. 9–14 conclusions as to the s· and

sources

Mis. 113–31 prolific s· of spiritual power
223–7 flow from corrupt s·.
273–21 from these s· of education, to
'02. 15–14 my income from literary s·
My. 90–28 * s· of her power and following

South

Ret. 19–6 I went with him to the S· ;
'02. 3–9 half-hostility to the S·,
My. 176–6 you of the dear S·
189–26 erected in the sunny S·
304–12 magazines in the S· and North.
322–20 * journeying from the far S·,
331–28 * characterized the people of the S·,

south

Pul. 48–6 * broad piazza on the s· side
76–14 * gold decoration adorns the s· wall,
82–3 * When she comes like the s· wind
My. 63–29 * and from the s·,"— Psal. 107 : 3.

South Africa

'02. 3–19 close of the conflict in S· A· ;
My. 30–16 * from Switzerland, from S· A·,

South Carolina and S. C.

My. 312–6 * took his bride to Wilmington, S· C·,
329–28 * her life in North and S· C·
(see also **Charleston**)

South Congregational church

My. 289–24 meeting in the S· C· c·

Southern

Mis. 246–6 It was the S· pulpit and press
My. 326–9 * in the S· and Northern States
331–13 * whose S· chivalry would have

Southern States

Pul. 89–16 * heading

Southron

My. 188–21 heart of a S· has welcomed

Southrons

My. 327–1 turning the hearts of the noble S·

southward

'00. 12–13 its gates, . . . led northward and s·.

souvenir

Pul. 76–22 * chapter sub-title
86–11 * beautiful s· is encased in

souvenirs

Pul. 46–17 * Among the many s·

sovereign

Mis. 121–14 would make this . . . just and s·,
249–29 it hath range and is s· !
355–18 to lift . . . is a s· panacea.
Pul. 3–7 s· power to think and act rightly,
Pan. 6–23 If Spirit is s·, how can matter be
My. 108–17 divine Mind is the s· appeal,
283–24 s· remedies for all earth's woe.

sovereigns

My. 290–8 Few s· have been as venerable,

sovereignty

Mis. 234–32 makes His s· glorious.
Un. 51–12 usurpation, . . . of the heavenly s·.
Pan. 7–11 lose the character and s· of

sow

Mis. 397–24 How to gather, how to s·,
Ret. 46–5 How to gather, how to s·,
Pul. 17–4 How to gather, how to s·,
No. 3–23 to s· by the wayside for the way-weary,
'01. 33–6 hand of love must s· the seed.
Po. 14–3 How to gather, how to s·,
47–22 Or to the patient who s·

soweth

Mis. 66–7 "Whatsoever a man s·,— Gal. 6 : 7.
105–29 "Whatsoever a man s·,— Gal. 6 : 7.
348–4 whatsoever a man s·, that shall he
No. 32–9 "Whatsoever a man s·,— Gal. 6 : 7.
Hea. 5–27 "whatsoever a man s·,— Gal. 6 : 7.
My. 6–6 whatsoever a man s·,— Gal. 6 : 7.
185–1 he that s· shall reap.

sowing

Mis. 144–27 may our earthly s· bear fruit that
Rud. 9–4 s· the seeds of discord and disease.
Po. 47–16 Weary of s· the wayside
My. 133–17 give birth to the s· of Solomon.
182–13 small s· of the seed of Truth,

sown

Mis. 38–10 "If we have s· unto you— I Cor. 9 : 11.
80–26 have planted and s· and reaped
356–16 seed of C. S., which when s· was
357–16 Much of what has been s·
Po. 31–2 nor yet by nature s·,
My. 40–21 * fruit of righteousness is s·— Jas. 3 : 18.
129–6 and Christianity s· broadcast
182–14 seed of Truth, which, when s·,

sows

Mis. 15–2 will reap what he s· ;

space

airy
My. 110–16 dreams of flying in airy s·,
all
Mis. 14–1 it fills all s·, being omnipresent ;
173–20 If God is Mind and fills all s·,
331–24 Mind-force, filling all s·
332–2 reflecting all s· and Life,
Un. 51–21 radiating throughout all s·
Pul. 4–21 lives in all Life, through all s·.
Rud. 3–27 ever-present I am, filling all s·,
'00. 1–6 ever-present Love filling all s·,
brief
My. 333–28 * brief s· of six months,
celestial
Mis. 376–29 spangled the gloom in celestial s·
dashing through
Mis. 266–13 comet's course, dashing through s·
economy of
Pul. 62–7 * advantage of great economy of s·,
intermediate
Mis. 215–4 Truth comes into the intermediate s·,
miles of
Pul. 44–5 * Across two thousand miles of s·,
more
Ret. 6–14 would require more s· than
no
My. 210–6 and no s· for evil to fill
occupying a
Pul. 62–8 * occupying a s· not more than
of time
Mis. 147–4 another s· of time has been given us,
open
Mis. 347–6 from their houses to the open s·.
My. 89–9 * needs only an open s· about it,
seating
My. 38–10 * when all seating s· had been filled
time and
Mis. 110–17 time and s·, when encompassed by
No. 16–13 destitute of time and s· ;
My. 110–13 forces annihilating time and s·,
vast
My. 69–18 * anywhere in the vast s·
without
Mis. 173–18 Does an evil mind exist without s·

Mis. 22–12 defining the line, plane, s·, and
150–10 S· is no separator of hearts.
339–5 silence for the s· of half an hour.
364–14 all time, s·, immortality,
380–6 governs the universe, time, s·,
Un. 60–23 s·, substance, and immortality
Pul. 56–10 * S· does not admit of an elaborate
No. 21–9 all time, s·, immortality,
'02. 10–5 power over matter, molecule, s·,
My. 343–3 * looking large-eyed into s·,

spacious
Mis. 276– 3 s· rooms of the Palmer House,
Pul. 26– 6 * organ and choir gallery is s·
 29– 9 * s· apartment was thronged
 31–23 * I rang the bell at a s· house
 42– 1 * the s· lobbies and the sidewalks
 60–19 * recess behind the s· platform,
My. 66–21 * s· and elegant edifice
 174– 7 opening their s· club-house

Spain
Pan. 14–28 war between United States and S·
My. 277– 4 between the United States and S·

spake
Mis. 23–10 Was it Mind or matter that s·
 68–15 cast out a devil, and the dumb s· ;
 76–16, 17 who s· as never man s·,
 83–23 "These words s· Jesus,—John 17 : 1.
 100– 1 He s· of Truth and Love
 126–30 s· after this manner :
 159– 1 He s· in their synagogues,
 185–30 first s· from their standpoint
 190–12 the dumb s·.—Luke 11 : 14.
 192–13 words of him who s· divinely,
 269–11, 12 "s· as never man s·,"— see John 7 : 46.
 280– 1 Mind s· and form appeared.
Mis. 312–24 He s· inspired ;
 359– 8 I s· as a child,— I Cor. 13 : 11.
Ret. 91–16 Lake of Galilee, where he s·
Un. 17–16 "s· as never man s·,"— see John 7 : 46.
'00. 14–20 angel that s· unto the churches
'02. 8–27 He s· of man not as the
My. 135– 3 I s· as a child,— I Cor. 13 : 11.
 162–19 which s· thus in olden time
 227– 3 he s· as God's representative
 261–16 I s· as a child,— I Cor. 13 : 11.
 351–13 his garment who s· divinely.

span
Mis. 355–30 will s· thy heavens of thought
My. 155–21 s· the horizon of their hope

spangled
Mis. 376–28 s· the gloom in celestial space

Spanish
Ret. 32–11 Calderon, the famous S· poet,
Rud. 1–13 In S·, Italian, and Latin,
Pan. 14–26 blotted out the S· squadron.

spanned
Mis. 163– 8 dated time, . . . and s· eternity,
Ret. 23– 9 Matter was no longer s· with

spans
'01. 10–21 Love s· the dark passage of sin,
Peo. 3–15 s· the moral heavens with light,
Po. 71– 9 S· our broad heaven of light.

spare
Mis. 114– 4 and should s· no research
 129–23 to save the sinner and to s· his
 155–24 If my own students cannot s· time
 287–26 it will s· you much bitterness.
 300–14 does it s· our Master's
 342–22 The wise virgins had no oil to s·,
My. 144– 5 s· not a moment's thought to lies
 200–27 God s· this plunge,
 285– 6 I cannot s· the time requisite

spared
Mis. 89–25 false concept that is not s·
Man. 76– 1 funds, which can be s·
Ret. 7–13 * Had life and health been s·
 19– 6 s· to me for only one brief year.
'01. 32–15 and s· no denunciation.
'02. 18–12 nor s· through false pity

spares
Mis. 300–13 and s· you the printer's bill,
My. 249–12 burns the wheat, s· the tares,

sparing
Mis. 302–12 thus s· their teacher a task

spark
Mis. 132–29 desire to be just is a vital s· of
Ret. 1–13 no sign that she inherited a s· from

sparkle
No. 13–25 and s· like a diamond,

sparkles
Mis. 257–22 Electricity, . . . s· on the cloud,

sparkling
Mis. 240– 4 s· eyes, and ruby cheeks

sparrow (see also **sparrow's**)
Mis. 174–11 from the falling of a s· to
 184– 5 from . . . to the death of a s·.
Un. 40– 1 from . . . to the fall of a s·.

sparrow's
Mis. 157– 5 He that marketh the s· fall
My. 226–13 that marks the s· fall,

sparse
Mis. 119–26 s· individual rights which one

spasmodic
Ret. 87–10 unsettled and s· efforts.

spat
Mis. 170–25 he is said to have s· upon the dust.
 258– 8 literally s· upon matter ;

speak
Mis. 44– 1 Honest students s· the truth
 84– 1 shown by his forbearing to s·,
 99–25 s· louder than to-day.
 141– 3 It will s· to you of the
 168–26 * would s· before the Scientist
 180–29 The Scriptures s· of Jesus as the
 192– 1 When we s· of a good man,
 220–26 and s· of him as being sick,
 238–26 * unable to s· a loud word,"
 256–22 to s· of gravitation as a law
 266–20 I s· of them as I feel,
 283– 3 s· the truth audibly ;
 316– 7 s· to your church in Boston?
 316– 8 I shall s· to my dear church
 322– 6 expecting to hear me s·
 338–28 * S· truly, and each word
Ret. 5–15 I cannot s· as I would,
 6–12 To s· of his beautiful character
 9–10 "S·, Lord ; for Thy servant—I Sam. 3 : 9.
 16– 9 she could not s· a loud word,
 40– 4 I was called to s· before the
 50–17 students s· with delight of
 75–15 lightly s· evil of me."—Mark 9 : 39.
Un. 7– 6 Nevertheless, though I thus s·,
 23–18 incompetent to s·.
 43–12 of myself I cannot s·
 46– 2 which neither think nor s·.
Pul. 10–28 S· out, O soul !
 29– 7 * I shall venture to s·,
 33– 8 * "S·, Lord, for Thy servant—I Sam. 3 : 9.
 46– 6 * the words of the judge s·
 75– 7 But to think or s· of me
 80–19 * s· of the system it sets forth,
 84–18 * we shall not undertake to s·
 87–18 s· to you each Sunday.
No. 7–23 s·, teach, and write the truth
 39– 2 than we can write or s·.
Pan. 2– 4 who know whereof they s·
'01. 26–21 "Though I s· with—I Cor. 13 : 1.
Hea. 1– 2 s· with new tongues ;—Mark 16 : 17.
 20– 2 * s· the matchless worth,
Po. 8–18 love, that no words could s·
My. 42–22 * I shall not attempt to s· of
 47–31 * s· with new tongues ;—Mark 16 : 17.
 84– 1 * the facts s· more plainly than
 104–20 of whom these pioneers s·.
 106– 3 either to s· charitably of all
 107– 9 Here I s· from experience.
 131–15 s· the "new tongue"— see Mark 16 : 17.
 147–19 s· the truth that to-day,
 175–16 s· for themselves.
 196– 9 slow to s·,— Jas. 1 : 19.
 214–23 a hall in which to s·,
 224–27 also s· in loving terms of
 264– 4 kind enough to s· well of
 264– 6 can s· justly of my living,
 308–14 compels me . . . to s·.

speaker
Mis. 168–29 * distinguished s· began by saying :
Man. 95–12 may apply . . . for a s·,
Pul. 72–25 * added the s·
 73– 1 * inquired the s·.

speakers
Mis. 253– 8 s· that will now address you
'00. 9–21 challenge the thinkers, s·, and
My. 124–16 hearts of these hearers and s·,

speaketh
Mis. 24–26 "When he s· a lie,—John 8 : 44.
 24–26 he s· of his own :—John 8 : 44.
 151–10 He s· to the unfruitful in tones of
 198–11 "When he s· a lie,—John 8 : 44.
 198–11 of his own."—John 8 : 44.
 317–30 s· the words of God :—John 3 : 34.
No. 34–18 blood of Christ s· better things
Pan. 5–15 When he s· a lie,—John 8 : 44.
 5–16 he s· of his own :—John 8 : 44.
'01. 9–28 he s· wisely, for the spirit of
 9–29 his Father s· through him ;
My. 33–18 s· the truth in his heart.—Psal. 15 : 2.
 228–24 s· the truth in his heart."—Psal. 15 : 2.

speaking
Mis. 19– 2 Envy, evil thinking, evil s·,
 24–24 S· of the origin of evil,
 59–23 benefit in s· often one to another,
 84– 2 by s·, the whole truth.

speaking

Mis.	137– 8	s· a few words aside to your teacher.
	158– 7	I insisted on your s· without notes,
	178–27	I wished to be excused from s·
	184–10	Paul refers to this when s· of
	204–32	evil thinking, evil s· and acting ;
	227–22	s· the truth in the heart ;
	253– 7	not enough . . . for outdoor s·,
	277– 4	Truth is s· louder, clearer,
Man.	81–24	no evil s· shall be allowed.
Ret.	35–16	When s· of his true followers
Un.	35–11	strictly s·, there is no mortal mind,
Pul.	7– 1	s· of my work, said :
	49– 2	* s· of her many followers
No.	16–27	strictly s·, no mortal mind.
	39– 7	s· loud enough to be heard ;
Pan.	8–20	S· of himself, Jesus said,
My.	12–22	lost in s· or in acting,
	156–12	spiritually s· is the passover from
	186–22	while they are yet s·, — Isa. 65 : 24.
	225–25	either in s· or in writing,
	257–12	The Christ is s· for himself
	280–19	only because of oft s·,

speakings

My.	17– 5	and all evil s·, — I Pet. 2 : 1.

speaks

Mis.	15– 5	St. Paul s· of the new birth
	88–14	critic who knows whereof he s·.
	100–19	s· when the senses are silent,
	130–22	know well whereof he s·.
	180–16	it s· to me of Life,
	212–27	s· plainly to the offender
	262–10	When the heart s·,
	296–31	but knew whereof he s·,
	388–12	S· kindly when we meet and part.
	394–12	mandate that s· from above,
Rud.	9– 5	Even the truth he s·
'00.	8–27	When God s· to you
	13–29	Revelator s· of the angel
Po.	7–12	S· kindly when we meet and part.
	45–15	mandate that s· from above,
My.	28–28	* It s· for the successful labors
	58–16	* s· more than words can picture
	97–16	* s· of "the audacious,
	137– 6	* Boston Globe, . . . s· of it as,

special

Mis.	11–23	If s· opportunity for doing good
	11–27	I do it with earnest, s· care
	13– 4	taking s· care to mind my
	160–10	There is a s· joy in knowing
	162– 1	at times of s· enlightenment,
	210–15	woman's s· adaptability to lead
	293– 5	to the s· care of the unerring
	296– 1	by s· invitation, have allowed
	298–13	s· application to Christian Scientists ;
	300–28	but this was a s· privilege,
	306–19	* s· request of the late Mrs. Harrison,
	357–27	and need s· help.
Man.	27– 5	shall order no s· action
	54–19	S· Offense.
	56– 9	REGULAR AND S· MEETINGS.
	57– 5	S· meetings may be held
	60–13	shall be no s· observances.
	61– 1	No s· trowel should be used.
	62– 4	shall not neglect to sing any s·
	90–17	S· Instruction.
	96–11	where he sees there is s· need,
	100– 6	if she shall send a s· request
	109– 1	heading.
	111–20	will be furnished s· forms
Ret.	6– 8	accorded s· household privileges.
	42– 9	also taught a s· Bible-class ;
	45–16	in accord with my s· request,
	48–12	At a s· meeting of the Board
Pul.	23–21	* scholars of s· research,
	29–22	* s· lesson was to be taken
	34– 4	* no s· record is to be made.
	44–26	* without any s· appeal,
	59– 5	* There was no s· sentence
	76–12	* mahogany in s· designs,
Rud.	13–20	then give s· attention to
'01.	3– 2	The s· benediction of our
'02.	1– 3	With no s· effort to achieve
	7–27	called his disciples' s· attention
My.	11–18	* it needs no s· insight
	25– 3	* in making a s· effort
	26–23	should date some s· reform,
	33– 8	* the s· Lesson-Sermon was
	68–22	* above the Readers' s· rooms.
	73–26	* chapter sub-title
	73–27	* S· trains and extra sections
	87–27	* whatever one's s· creed
	132– 2	is . . . the s· demand.
	173–25	S· thanks are due
	177– 8	no s· need of my personal

special

My.	266–22	Since 1877, these s·
	280–17	cease s· prayer for the peace
	280–30	in s· prayer for peace.
	289–11	s· meeting of its First Members
	305–21	I claim no s· merit
	333– 6	* a s· meeting was convened
	340– 5	s· days and seasons for
	341–24	* it was a s· favor
	347–22	S· contribution to "Bohemia."
	353–24	nothing . . . of any s· interest.

Special Correspondence

Pul.	23– 8	* S· C·.

specially

Mis.	111–27	s· call the attention of
	114–30	who does not s· instruct
	148–25	s· desire that you collect no
	161–23	he was s· endowed
	315–10	s· spiritually fitted for
Man.	71–19	s· allowed and named
Ret.	85– 1	s· responsible for
No.	3–20	which Mind-healers s· need ;
My.	32–28	* s· prepared Lesson-Sermon.
	38–17	* s· reserved for them.
	227–20	not s· protected by law.
	256– 3	notes, not s· musical
	339– 7	s· requested to be wise

specialty

Mis.	4–22	so that its religious s·

species

Mis.	23–31	could not change its s·
	26–21	neither a genus nor a s·
	27–13	no s· ever produces its opposite.
	346–13	This belief is a s· of idolatry,
Un.	51–15	Woman is the highest s· of
Rud.	7–24	Spirit no more changes its s·,
	7–26	bring about alteration of s·
My.	12–22	is a s· of intoxication,
	301–24	is in itself a s· of insanity.

specific

Mis.	217–14	the s· nature of all things
	244–16	* visible agencies for s· ends?"
'01.	6–15	Is this pure, s· Christianity?
	31– 5	all error, s· or universal.
My.	181– 1	The s· quest of C. S.
	302–10	s· insanity is that brain, matter,

specifically

My.	10–14	* donation to be s· subscribed

specifications

My.	335–14	* s· of which were kept by

specified

Man.	45–10	s· in The Mother Church Manual,
	69– 3	during the time s· in the
	78– 8	such debts as are s· in
	99– 7	except as hereinafter s·,
Ret.	15–24	Among . . . they s· cancers.

specimen

No.	43–12	a s· of those received daily :

specimens

Mis.	294–19	Love such s· of mortality
No.	20–24	s· of every kind emerged

specious

'01.	25–16	ends in some s· folly.

specks

My.	109–21	but s· in His universe,

spectacle

'02.	18– 4	The constant s· of sin
My.	79–11	* s· of thirty thousand people

spectators

Mis.	299–24	The s· may ask,

spectre

Un.	28–11	not a s· had ever been seen

speculate

Mis.	327–10	to s· in worldly policy,
'02.	5–27	or s· on the existence of
Peo.	8–15	and s· concerning material forces.
My.	13– 1	They s· neither on the past,

speculation

Mis.	237–20	period of doubt, inquiry, s·,
	286–31	human s· will go on,

speculative

Mis.	29–13	between it and any s· theory.
	34–14	s· opinion and human belief.
	38–23	s· view too vapory and hypothetical
	64–20	resist s· opinions and fables.
	68–30	* "A s· science, which
	234– 4	by s· views of Truth.
	361–22	subtlety of s· wisdom
Ret.	70–12	s· theories as to the recurrence of
Peo.	3– 3	crudest ideals of s· theology

sped

Mis.	385–26	radiant glory *s·* The dawning day.
Chr.	53– 5	Spirit *s·* A loyal ray
Po.	49– 1	radiant glory *s·* The dawning day.

speech

Mis.	190–25	*s·* belongs to Mind instead of
	246– 2	the prohibiting of free *s·*,
	246–17	to shackle conscience, stop free *s·*,
	338–25	* To give the lips full *s·*.
Ret.	61–18	no *s·* nor language, — *Psal.* 19 : 3.
Po.	73–14	Witness my presence and utter my *s·*.
My.	105–17	hearing to the deaf, *s·* to the dumb,
	226– 6	termed in common *s·* the principle
	345–29	make them our figures of *s·*.

speechless

Mis.	191–28	would be impossible if he were *s·*.
	275–25	They moved me to *s·* thanks.
	312– 6	*s·* and alone, bears all burdens,
My.	150–17	in *s·* prayer, ask God to enable you to

speed

Mis.	384– 8	To thought and deed Give sober *s·*,
'02.	2–14	God *s·* the right!
	10–22	increases the *s·* of mortals' transit
Po.	36– 7	To thought and deed Give sober *s·*,
My.	6–26	*s·*, beauty, and achievements of
	94–30	*s·*, beauty, and achievements of
	124–26	rate of *s·*, the means of travel,
	127– 7	*s·* of the chariot-wheels of Truth

speedily

Mis.	141–19	Let this be *s·* done.
	144–30	*s·* wake the long night of
My.	181–17	that all nations shall *s·* learn

speedy

Mis.	212–15	*s·* return under the reign of
Ret.	54– 2	sometimes more *s·* than some of the
My.	12– 8	* *s·* accumulation of a sum sufficient

spell

Mis.	390–11	Enraptured by thy *s·*,
	392–11	thou art a power and *s·*;
Ret.	18–21	communion with home's magic *s·*!
Po.	20–15	thou art a power and *s·*;
	55–12	Enraptured by thy *s·*,
	64–15	communion with home's magic *s·*!
	08–13	stronger than these is the *s·* that hath

Spencer

Mis.	361–15	Tyndall, Darwin, and *S·*
My.	349–10	Berkeley, Tyndall, and *S·*

spend

Mis.	230–17	*s·* no time in sheer idleness,
My.	231–10	*s·* no more time or money in

spends

Pul.	81–13	* *s·* her whole time helping

spent

Mis.	213–28	the night is far *s·*,
	075 14	* I *s·* two years in Paris,
Ret.	6–20	but later Albert *s·* a year
Pan.	1–17	The night is far *s·*,
My.	67–23	* sums of money were *s·* in
	202 7	tho night is far *s·*

sphere

Mis.	284– 9	*s·* of his present usefulness.
	386– 1	glorious life's *s·*,
Ret.	60– 3	Life as a complete *s·*,
	60– 5	life as a broken *s·*,
	89–25	enlarge their *s·* of action.
Un.	3– 4	another *s·* of experience,
	45–20	into an imaginary *s·*
	61–17	good in this mortal *s·*
No.	37– 9	and when, as a *s·* of Mind,
Po.	28– 2	Of every rolling *s·*,
	49– 3	glorious life's *s·*,
My.	253– 2	brightening this lower *s·*

spheres

Po.	30–21	the hymning *s·* of light,
My.	13–27	cycles of systems and *s·*.

spider

My.	252– 6	will not be like the *s·*,

spilled

Hea.	18– 7	break and the wine be *s·*.

spilling

No.	33–17	*s·* of human blood

Spinoza (see also Spinoza's)

No.	22– 4	Fichte, Hegel, *S·*,
	24– 6	according to *S·*.

Spinoza's

No.	24– 3	According to *S·* philosophy

spire

Mis.	144–32	the *s·* of this temple.
Un.	14–19	shifting vane on the *s·*,
Po.	30–18	with its triumphal *s·*.
My.	13–24	the spiritual *s·* of which

Spirit (see also Spirit's)

abode of

Mis.	174–16	abode of *S·*, the realm of the real.

absence of

No.	17– 4	evil, is the absence of *S·*

according to

Mis.	360–21	"the Israel according to *S·*"

after the

Mis.	188–15	but after the *S·*." — *Rom.* 8 : 1.
My.	113–13	but after the *S·*. — *Rom.* 8 : 1.
	205– 3	but after the *S·*." — *Rom.* 8 : 1.

aid of

Peo.	9–18	invoke the divine aid of *S·*

All-in-all of

Ret.	34– 3	Science of Mind, the All-in-all of *S·*,

all is

My.	178–13	Then all is *S·* and spiritual.

All must be

Un.	31– 6	for the divine All must be *S·*.

allness of

Ret.	26–28	and the allness of *S·*,
'01.	12–23	and we then see the allness of *S·*,

alone

Mis.	359– 7	instantaneously, and through *S·* alone.
Un.	31–23	God, or good, is *S·* alone;

and flesh

Mis.	85–21	*S·* and flesh antagonize.

and good

Ret.	60–10	as real as *S·* and good.

and immortal

Mis.	201–14	which is of *S·*, and immortal.

and infinite

'01.	25–27	if indeed *S·* and infinite,

and law

Mis.	256–21	chapter sub-title

and matter

Mis.	55–16	*the facts of both S· and matter?*
	121– 7	*S·* and matter, good and evil,
'01.	22 10	Truth and error, *S·* and matter,
	22–30	statement as to *S·* and matter,
Hea.	18– 8	no connection between *S·* and matter.

and Spirit

'01.	22– 9	*S·* and Spirit is not:

and the bride

My.	153–27	"the *S·* and the bride," — *Rev.* 22 : 17.

and Truth

Mis.	363–25	Word that *is* God, *S·*, and Truth.

and Word

Ret.	76– 9	touched with the *S·* and Word

antipode of

Mis.	217–12	antipode of *S·*, namely, matter.
	267–24	antipode of *S·*, which we name *matter*,
Un.	31–19	matter, the antipode of *S·*,

approach

No.	16–24	in proportion as mortals approach *S·*,

as well as

Mis.	333–12	in matter as well as *S·*?

at war with

Un.	36–14	flesh at war with *S·*;

baptism of

Mis.	30–31	bathe in the baptism of *S·*,
	82– 8	out of the baptism of *S·*,
	205 13	The baptism of *S·*,
Peo.	9– 9	It is the baptism of *S·* that

baptism of the

'01.	1–15	The baptism of the *S·*,

baptized in

Pan.	14– 9	and be baptized in *S·*.

baptized of

Mis.	206 7	to the baptized of *S·*:

baptized them in

'01.	9– 8	Christ baptized them in *S·*

becomes

Mis.	218– 1	in which nature becomes *S·*;

behold

Un.	30– 1	uplifted to behold *S·* as the

belief that

Peo.	4– 6	belief that *S·* materialized into

bestows

Mis.	345– 1	*S·* bestows spiritual gifts,

blind us to

Mis.	234– 2	no longer to blind us to *S·*,

born of

Mis.	184– 9	man born of *S·* is spiritual,
My.	261–26	born of *S·* and not of matter.

born of the

'01.	27–26	born of the *S·* and not matter.

Spirit

can never
Un. 41–22 S· can never dwell in its
claims of
Mis. 140–10 the claims of S· over matter
conceived of
My. 262–14 conceived of S·, of God
conception of
My. 152–11 conception of S· and its all-power.
concerning
Un. 23–17 they testify concerning S·,
constitutes
Mis. 56–13 to conclude that S· constitutes
controls body
Mis. 247–20 that S· controls body.
could not change
Mis. 23–31 God, S·, could not change
creates
Mis. 27– 5 or that S· creates its opposite,
defies
Un. 31–19 all that denies and defies S·,
demonstrate
Mis. 258–21 neither name nor demonstrate S·.
demonstration of
Mis. 74–20 His demonstration of S· virtually
departure from
My. 151–28 This departure from S·,
derived from
Mis. 162–15 his power, derived from S·,
disagreement with
Un. 41–28 perpetual disagreement with S·.
divine
(see **divine**)
dominion of
Mis. 16–14 reflect the full dominion of S·
dream of
Mis. 180– 1 the dream of S· in the flesh
eternal
Un. 22–19 cometh not from the eternal S·,
evidences of
Ret. 56–12 between the evidences of S· and
existence in
Un. 45–27 no origin or existence in S·,
facts of
Mis. 55–18 C. S. is based on the facts of S·
faith in
Peo. 9–24 and rest all faith in S·,
false conceptions of
Peo. 2–14 false conceptions of S·, based on
finds
No. 15–20 finds S· neither in matter nor in
flesh and
(see **flesh**)
flesh not
'02. 6– 6 fruits of the flesh not S·.
flesh to
Un. 56–25 ere he can change from flesh to S·,
fourth dimension of
Mis. 22–12 and fourth dimension of S·.
from matter to
Mis. 194–22 turn from matter to S· for healing ;
fruit of the
My. 167– 4 "the fruit of the S·." — Gal. 5 : 22.
fruits of
(see **fruits**)
functions of
My. 288–19 to perform the functions of S·,
giveth Life
Ret. 65– 8 Pharisaism killeth ; S· giveth Life.
God is
(see **God**)
God is a
Mis. 219– 8 "God is a S· : — John 4 : 24.
Un. 31– 1 "God is a S·" — John 4 : 24.
God, or
Un. 10–11 Life is God, or S·,
No. 16–14 there is none beside God or S·
good
Pan. 9– 7 a good S· and an evil spirit.
good is
No. 38– 7 He is good, and good is S· ;
governed by
Mis. 267–23 should be governed by S·,
graces of the
Mis. 149–22 all the rich graces of the S·.
grandeur of
Mis. 86–25 divine beauty and the grandeur of S·.
harmonies of
Mis. 333–20 securing the sweet harmonies of S·
heaven of
My. 195–28 eternal in the heaven of S·.
He is
No. 15–25 He is S· ;
Holy
Mis. 161–23 endowed with the Holy S· ;
'01. 9–22 Holy S· takes of the things of God

Spirit

holy
Mis. 70–24 body of the holy S· of Jesus
idea of
Mis. 60–27 every creation or idea of S·
No. 16–14 God or Spirit and the idea of S·.
image of
Rud. 5– 8 in the image of S·, or God.
'01. 8–20 The reflex image of S· is not
individual
Rud. 2–17 but one infinite individual S·,
infinite
Mis. 16–31 with the laws of infinite S·;
56– 4 Life is inorganic, infinite S· ;
72–29 Being is God, infinite S· ;
181–12 Infinite Principle and infinite S·
190– 3 it is infinite S·, Truth, Life,
219– 5 the personality of infinite S·
Rud. 2–11 if by person is meant infinite S·.
Pan. 9– 3 "Infinite S·" means one God
'01. 5–20 God is infinite S· or Person,
7– 2 infinite Love, infinite S·,
Hea. 4–16 and, after infinite S· is forced in
My. 235–17 Did infinite S· make that
infinity or
Ret. 58– 4 the problem of infinity or S·,
instead of
Mis. 276–27 from matter instead of S·,
Peo. 12–25 power to matter instead of S·.
intelligent
Mis. 103– 3 Intelligent S·, Soul, is substance,
is All and is all
Un. 36– 5 against the fact that S· is All,
My. 357–22 Spirit is infinite ; therefore S· is all.
is causation
Hea. 19–12 S· is causation,
is deathless
Un. 42– 3 Soul, S·, is deathless.
is God
Mis. 21–20 S· is God, and man is His image
218– 2 S· is God, and God is good.
Un. 25– 6 S· is God, and God is good ;
29– 6 Spirit never sins, because S· is God.
My. 235–21 Because S· is God and infinite ;
356–25 S· is God, and this God is infinite
is immortal Truth
Mis. 21–18 S· is immortal Truth ;
is infinite
Pan. 13–19 great truth that S· is infinite,
My. 271– 1 God, S·, is infinite,
357–22 S· is infinite ; therefore Spirit is all.
is omnipotent
Mis. 232–18 S· is omnipotent ;
is sovereign
Pan. 6–23 If S· is sovereign, how can matter
is substance
Ret. 57–17 S· is substance in Truth.
is the lawgiver
Mis. 364–25 If S· is the lawgiver to matter,
is the only creator
Un. 32– 6 S· is the only creator,
35–26 S· is the only creator.
is the only substance
Mis. 47–20 God, S·, is the only substance ;
Un. 25– 6 Good. S· is the only substance.
is the real
Mis. 21–19 S· is the real and eternal ;
is true
'01. 22–12 S· is true and infinite,
is Truth
Un. 36–11 Thus we see that S· is Truth
itself
Mis. 46–22 S· itself beareth witness — Rom. 8 : 16.
255–14 S· itself beareth witness — Rom. 8 : 16.
jubilee of
Mis. 135–15 to the jubilee of S·
kingdom of
'02. 20– 5 desired haven, the kingdom of S· ;
language of
My. 180–10 in the language of S·,
law of
(see **law**)
law of the
(see **law**)
laws of
Mis. 260–12 laws of S·, not of matter ;
leavened with
Mis. 175– 5 sense of being is leavened with S·.
lens of
My. 129–15 seen through the lens of S·,
less than
Mis. 217– 6 cannot become less than S· ;
Life is
Un. 41–22 All Life is S·,
Hea. 9–26 Life is S· ; and when we

Spirit

Life of
  No. 34–22 The real blood or Life of *S·*
Life, or
  Mis. 56– 4 if Life, or *S·*, were organic,
Life was
  Un. 42–23 To him, Life was *S·*.
likeness of
  Mis. 62– 1 man in the likeness of *S·* is spiritual.
  Rud. 13–10 body is not the likeness of *S·* ;
love
  Mis. 18–13 Thou shalt love *S·* only,
made all
  Pan. 6–16 if *S·* made all that was made,
majesty of
  Mis. 141–13 might, and majesty of *S·*,
matter and
  (*see* **matter**)
matter to
  '02. 10–23 transit from matter to *S·*
  My. 163– 7 from matter to *S·*.
  181–11 departure from matter to *S·*,
matter with
  '01. 26– 9 that combines matter with *S·*.
meaning of
  Hea. 11– 9 would catch the meaning of *S·*.
might be found
  Mis. 64– 1 *S·* might be found "All-in-all."
Mind of
  Un. 32–11 It is not the Mind of *S·* ;
my
  My. 154–12 "my *S·*, saith the Lord ;"—*Zech.* 4: 6.
name without the
  Mis. 302– 7 teaching the name without the *S·*,
nativity in
  Mis. 162–17 therefrom rise to his nativity in *S·*.
nature of
  Mis. 218–25 not express the nature of *S·*,
negations of
  No. 16–10 are but negations of *S·*, Truth,
never entered
  Hea. 18– 9 *S·* never entered . . . matter ;
never sins
  Un. 29– 6 *S·* never sins, because
new-born of
  Pul. 10–29 This is the new-born of *S·*,
no cognizance of
  Mis. 218–14 take no cognizance of *S·*
nod of
  My. 129–14 The nod of *S·* is nature's natal.
not formed by
  Un. 35–23 molecule, . . . is not formed by *S·* ;
nothing but
  Un. 34–12 therefore there is nothing but *S·* ;
notion of
  Mis. 218–21 notion of *S·* as cause and end, with
not matter
  Mis. 5–18 power of *S·*, not matter,
  '01. 5–22 man reflects *S·*, not matter.
  Peo. 9– 2 this faith builds on *S·*, not matter ;
obscuration of
  Mis. 2– 8 causing great obscuration of *S·*.
offspring of
  Mis. 181–18 offspring of *S·*, and not of the flesh ;
  Ret. 68–28 "Man is the offspring of *S·*.
  My. 257– 5 Christ, . . . the offspring of *S·*,
of life
  Mis. 201–18 *S·* of life in Christ Jesus—*Rom.* 8: 2.
  321–15 *S·* of life in Christ Jesus—*Rom.* 8: 2.
  326– 2 *S·* of life in Christ Jesus—*Rom.* 8: 2.
  '01. 9–10 "*S·* of life in Christ Jesus,"—*Rom.* 8: 2.
  '02. 9–12 *S·* of life in Christ Jesus—*Rom.* 8: 2.
  My. 41–23 * *S·* of life in Christ Jesus,"—*Rom.* 8: 2.
  113–13 *S·* of life in Christ Jesus—*Rom.* 8: 2.
  272– 6 *S·* of life in Christ Jesus—*Rom.* 8: 2.
  293 28 *S·* of life in Christ Jesus—*Rom.* 8: 2.
of the Lord
  My. 128–11 "Where the *S·* of the Lord—*II Cor.* 3: 17.
omnipotence of
  Ret. 31–24 before the omnipotence of *S·*,
omnipresence of
  Ret. 56–10 omniscience, and omnipresence of *S·*,
omnipresent
  Un. 43–27 omnipresent *S·* which knows no matter.
one
  Ret. 22–20 his father and mother are the one *S·*,
  60–29 but one *S·*, Mind, Soul.
  Pan. 9– 5 "spirits" means more than one *S·* ;
only
  Mis. 18–13 Thou shalt love *S·* only,
  Rud. 4–18 not in matter, but in *S·* only.
  My. 152–15 worship only *S·* and spiritually,
opposed to
  Mis. 199–21 the qualities opposed to *S·*

Spirit

opposite of
  Mis. 26–18 it is the very opposite of *S·*,
  Un. 32–19 saying, "I am the opposite of *S·*,
  36–13 that matter is the opposite of *S·*,
or God
  Rud. 5– 8 in the image of *S·*, or God.
or good
  No. 17– 4 evil, is the absence of *S·* or good.
or matter
  Mis. 28–22 What meaneth this Me,—*S·*, or matter?
or Soul
  No. 29– 6 He believes that *S·*, or Soul,
or Truth
  No. 5–15 sense also avers that *S·*, or Truth,
outcome of
  Un. 42– 4 not the outcome of *S·*, holiness,
over matter
  Ret. 26–11 superiority of *S·* over matter.
paradise in
  My. 118–28 finds its paradise in *S·*,
paradise of
  Mis. 70–14 paradise of *S·* would come to
permanence of
  Mis. 47– 7 glory and permanence of *S·* :
  74–28 and the power and permanence of *S·*.
personal
  Peo. 13– 3 believe that God is a personal *S·*.
phenomena of
  Mis. 73–31 phenomena of *S·* in C. S.,
  No. 19–23 noumenon or the phenomena of *S·* ;
phenomenon of
  Mis. 217–12 or, that the phenomenon of *S·*
pleads for
  Mis. 174–21 Shall that . . . which pleads for *S·*
possibilities of
  Mis. 187– 6 sense of the possibilities of *S·*.
power of
  (*see* **power**)
prerogative of
  My. 179– 8 the power and prerogative of *S·*
Principle and
  Un. 61–14 but the divine Principle and *S·*
proved
  Mis. 63–29 in which *S·* proved its supremacy
qualities of
  Mis. 201– 6 bringing the qualities of *S·*
quickening
  Un. 30–24 last Adam as a quickening *S·*,
  30–26 shall be found a quickening *S·* ;
reflection of
  Ret. 73– 8 is found in the reflection of *S·*.
reflects only
  Mis. 205–17 consciousness reflects only *S·*,
retained by
  Mis. 218–26 neither eliminated nor retained by *S·*.
reveals
  Ret. 60– 6 Science reveals *S·* as All,
revelation of
  Mis. 56–20 at the full revelation of *S·*,
rights of
  Mis. 56–13 and infringes the rights of *S·*.
saith
  '00. 11–26 *S·* saith unto the—*Rev.* 2: 7.
  14–10 hear what the *S·* saith unto the
sends forth
  Rud. 8– 5 *S·* sends forth its own
sense of
  Mis. 17–32 gains a truer sense of *S·*
  24–20 shutting out the true sense of *S·*.
  Un. 21–20 spiritual sense, a sense of *S·*,
side of
  Mis. 180– 2 so far as to take the side of *S·*,
Soul, or
  No. 26– 4 and that Soul, or *S·*, is subdivided
source is
  Un. 25–24 whose only source is *S·*.
sprung from
  Mis. vii–17 My world has sprung from *S·*,
strives against
  Mis. 119–15 flesh strives against *S·*,
subjection to
  Mis. 201– 6 bringing . . . into subjection to *S·*.
substance of
  Mis. 56– 8 substance of *S·* is divine Mind.
  104– 7 was safe in . . . the substance of *S·*,
  Un. 45–25 It lacks the substance of *S·*,
supremacy of
  (*see* **supremacy**)
sword of
  Mis. 215–26 at this stage use the sword of *S·*.
  My. 189– 2 grasping the sword of *S·*,
sword of the
  My. 185– 9 sword of the *S·* is drawn ;

Spirit

synonym of
Mis. 75–11 Soul is a synonym of *S*·,
Ret. 57–10 Soul is the synonym of *S*·,
tabernacle of
Mis. 362–26 in the tabernacle of *S*·.
teaches
My. 167– 7 *S*· teaches us to resign what we
temple of
My. 64–26 * in the universal temple of *S*·,
that heals
My. 158–20 it is the *S*· that heals the sick
"the way" in
Un. 55–13 "The way," in *S*·, is — *John* 14 : 6.
things of
Mis. 342–32 faithful over the few things of *S*·,
'01. 9–28 liveth most the things of *S*·,
My. 260–10 the things of *S*·, not of matter.
this force is
Rud. 4–11 This force is *S*·,
this one is
My. 356–25 and this one is *S*· ;
to apprehend
Ret. 28–10 in order to apprehend *S*·.
Pul. 35–14 in order to apprehend *S*·.
torches of
Ret. 23–17 the midnight torches of *S*·.
triumph of
Ret. 56–15 triumph of *S*· in immutable harmony.
triumphs of
Un. 3–12 through . . . the triumphs of *S*·.
understanding of
Un. 50–10 by a dominant understanding of *S*·.
unity of
Mis. 198– 4 arrive at this point of unity of *S*·,
My. 167– 8 what we are in the unity of *S*·
unlike
Mis. 55–23 destruction of all that is unlike *S*·.
'01. 8–21 image of Spirit is not unlike *S*·.
verities of
Mis. 55–21 verities of *S*· assert themselves over
war against
Mis. 2–30 beliefs that war against *S*·,
warreth against
Mis. 124– 8 which warreth against *S*·,
wars against
My. 339–28 and all that wars against *S*·
with matter
My. 206– 2 would unite . . . *S*· with matter
works of the
Ret. 65– 5 or the works of the *S*·.
worship of
My. 23–25 * represents the worship of *S*·,
would destroy
Mis. 56– 5 would destroy *S*· and annihilate man.

Mis. 18– 1 baptismals that come from *S*·,
23–22 God, *S*·, Mind, are terms synonymous
24–17 Life in and of *S*· ;
26–23 *S*·, God, has no antecedent ;
27– 3 terms God and good, as *S*·, are
27–24 being in and of *S*·, Mind,
28–23 and must mean *S*·.
56–29 Your question implies that *S*·,
57– 7 not from dust, . . . but from *S*·,
72–21 *imply that S· takes note of matter ?*
76–29 The Science of Soul, *S*·,
96–32 not of the flesh, but of the *S*·.
113– 4 *S*· is our Father and Mother,
123–29 God is Love, is *S*· ;
169–27 which is enmity toward God, *S*·.
181–13 over what is the person of *S*·,
187–24 Did the substance of God, *S*·,
198–16 man as governed by God, *S*·,
200– 7 because *S*· was to him All-in-all,
201– 8 element of matter, . . . never of *S*·.
217– 5 *S*· cannot become less than
217–16 nature is consituted of and by *S*·.
217–30 matter must . . . for *S*· to appear.
218– 3 Deity was forever Mind, *S*· ;
286–26 *S*·, God, is the only creator :
317–31 God giveth not the *S*· by — *John* 3 : 34.
363–14 "Let us [*S*·] make man perfect ;"
364–22 hypotheses predicate matter of *S*·
399– 8 'T is the *S*· that makes pure,
Man. 16– 7 even the allness of Soul, *S*·,
Chr. 53– 5 *S*· sped A loyal ray
55–16 *S*· [God-likeness] is life — *Rom.* 8 : 10.
Ret. 25–18 *S*· I called the *reality* ;
25–25 neither sees, hears, nor feels *S*·,
28–15 For *S*· to be supreme
56– 6 or divides . . . *S*· into spirits,
58–14 not the result of . . . it was *S*·.
69– 2 *S*· is his primitive . . . source
69–12 God, *S*·, who *is* the only Life.'
Un. 24–17 *S*· is all that endureth,

Spirit

Un. 29– 7 as *S*·, Soul is sinless, and is God.
31–18 usurps the authority of God, *S*· ;
31–22 evil does not obtain in *S*·,
34–26 *S*·, Life, Truth, and Love.
35–12 is not matter, but *S*·.
35–24 *S*· is *spiritual* consciousness
35–25 can form nothing unlike itself, *S*·,
46– 4 from *S*·, not from flesh.
Pul. 2–24 *S*·, God, the eternal harmony
35–19 For *S*· to be supreme
Rud. 1– 8 It is substance, *S*·, Life, Truth,
4–17 *S*· is not in matter,
7–21 *S*· cannot originate its opposite,
7–23 According to divine Science, *S*·
7–24 by evolving matter from *S*·,
No. 3–13 not having lost the *S*· which
27–10 *S*· will be the light of the city,
Pan. 4–20 *S*·, is indeed the preserver of man.
5– 3 *S*·, be discovered in matter?
7– 1 *S*·, God, is infinite,
7– 8 belief, that after God, *S*·, had
7–17 infinity of God, *S*·
7–24 which implies Mind, *S*·, God ;
12– 5 * *S*·, is ever in universal nature."
12– 6 we naturally ask, how can *S*· be
12–24 Life, Truth, Love, substance, *S*·,
'01. 3–19 called in Scripture, *S*·, Love.
3–25 loses the nature of God, *S*·,
8–17 Is God *S*· ? He is.
'02. 7– 3 It accords all to God, *S*·,
8– 5 likeness of God, *S*·, is spiritual,
Po. 75–15 'Tis the *S*· that makes pure,
My. 14– 1 whereto [God, *S*·] sent it." — see *Isa.* 55 : 11.
129–18 never severed from *S*· !
151–22 Subject: "Not Matter, but *S*'"
191–19 *S*· is saying unto matter :
225–29 Truth, Life, *S*·, Mind, Soul,
232–25 man created by and of *S*·,
235–17 Is God *S*· ? He is.
238–10 God being *S*·, His language and
239–27 spiritual man, created by God, *S*·,
288–18 matter was not the auxiliary of *S*·.
349–29 and deduced from God, *S*· ;
357– 4 spiritual fulness of God, *S*·,

spirit (see also spirit's)

and in truth
Mis. 150–20 "in *s*· and in truth," — *John* 4 : 23.
219– 9 in *s*· and in truth." — *John* 4 : 24.
321–14 in *s*· and in truth." — *John* 4 : 23.
Ret. 65–13 "in *s*· and in truth." — *John* 4 : 23.
Un. 31– 4 in *s*· and in truth." — *John* 4 : 24.
Pul. 21– 7 Scientists in *s*· and in truth.
No. 34–11 in *s*· and in truth." — *John* 4 : 23.
Pan. 14– 6 worship in *s*· and in truth ;
My. 5–25 "in *s*· and in truth," — *John* 4 : 23.
25–22 "in *s*· and in truth." — *John* 4 : 23.
270–32 in *s*· and in truth." — *John* 4 : 24.
and mission
Mis. 372–22 concerning the *s*· and mission of
and power
Mis. 193–26 *s*· and power of Christianity.
Ret. 86– 3 *s*· and power of C. S.,
and the flesh
My. 293–19 yea, the *s*· and the flesh
and the letter
Mis. 146–17 *s*· and the letter of this Scripture :
195– 9 *s*· and the letter are requisite ;
My. 129–30 they include the *s*· and the letter
and the Word
My. 246–21 *s*· and the Word appeared,
and understanding
'01. 32–23 *s*· and understanding of C. S.
animus and
My. 45–12 * animus and *s*· of our movement.
Christian
Man. 77–26 in a Christian *s*· and manner,
Christly
Ret. 48–29 whose Christly *s*· has led to higher ways,
divine
Pul. 65–25 * was called the divine *s*· of giving,
evil
Pan. 9– 7 a good Spirit and an evil *s*·.
'01. 16–20 refer to an evil *s*· as *dumb*,
fevered
'00. 11–24 * it lay on my fevered *s*·
following Christ in
No. 34– 5 following Christ in *s*·,
foul
My. 126–26 hold of every foul *s*·, — *Rev.* 18 : 2.
full
Mis. 311–12 the full *s*· of that charity
His
Ret. 18–18 adore all His *s*· hath made,
Rud. 4–23 love Him through His *s*·,
Po. 64– 9 adore all His *s*· hath made,

spirit

his
Mis. 387–16 Pray that his s· you partake,
Po.   6–11 Pray that his s· you partake,
My. 196–11 and he that ruleth his s· — Prov. 16 : 32.
hopeful
Pul. 80–25 * it has brought a hopeful s·
imbibe the
Mis. 303–18 imbibe the s· of Christ's Beatitudes.
My. 239– 8 imbibe the s· and prove the
its
Mis. 145– 6 as requisite to manifest its s·,
195– 6 but possesses not its s·,
292– 3 and its s· is baptismal ;
Ret. 52– 7 and less of its s·.
81– 8 The letter . . . separated from its s·,
letter without the
My. 158–19 The letter without the s· is dead :
matter or
My. 235–20 Is mortal man . . . matter or s·?
meek in
Mis. 152–20 pure in affection, the meek in s·,
more of the
Ret. 49– 9 more of the s· instead of the letter,
my
Po. 16–22 call to my s· with seraphs to dwell ;
65– 1 Sing me that song ! My s· is sad,
My. 303– 1 mysteriously upon my s·.
need the
Mis. 345– 7 need the s· of the pious Polycarp,
newness of
No. 25– 6 serve in newness of s·, — Rom. 7 : 6.
of beauty
Pul. 2– 6 s· of beauty dominates The
of bigotry
My. 93– 4 * have little of the s· of bigotry.
of Christ
Mis. 25–21 manifests the s· of Christ.
141–17 s· of Christ actuating all the parties
370– 7 greater s· of Christ is also abroad,
374– 4 Pharisees scorned the s· of Christ
Ret. 47–16 richly imbued with the s· of Christ,
Pul. 21–27 rest on the s· of Christ
75– 3 has most of the s· of Christ,
of Christianity
My. 246–16 s· of Christianity, dwelling forever
of Christian Science
Mis. 43–18 gained sooner than the s· of C. S. :
Pul. 80–20 * the s· of C. S. ideas has caused
of Christmas
My. 260–24 true s· of Christmas elevates
of divine Love
'01. 9–14 the s· of divine Love,
of evil
Mis. 370– 6 antagonistic s· of evil is still abroad ;
My. 212– 5 essence, or s·, of evil,
of faith
My. 85–26 * s· of faith and brotherhood
of God
'01. 9–16 s· of God is made manifest
My. 344–10 "It is not the s· of God,
of his Father
'01. 9–29 s· of his Father speaketh
of his mission
My. 246–26 and the s· of his mission,
of his prayer
Mis. 211–30 lived the s· of his prayer,
of humanity
My. 129– 5 the s· of humanity, ethics, and
of idolatry
Mis. 123– 6 the s· of idolatry, envy,
of levity
My. 93–18 * to approach it in a s· of levity,
of lies
Mis. 200–28 The s· of lies is abroad.
of Love
Mis. 288–29 s· of Love that nerves the struggle.
No. v– 4 self-sacrificing s· of Love
of love
Po. 66– 6 s· of love, at soft eventide
of our Master
Mis. 370– 2 say, in the s· of our Master,
of sacrifice
Mis. 261–23 This s· of sacrifice always has
of song
Ret. 17– 3 s· of song, — midst the zephyrs
Po. 62– 1 s· of song, — midst the zephyrs
of St. Paul
Mis. 344–29 We need the s· of St. Paul,
of the prayer
My. 292–26 s· of the prayer of the righteous
of these rights
Mis. 289–29 are the s· of these rights,
of this orison
My. 281– 8 s· of this orison is the fruit of

spirit

of true watching
My. 233– 1 the s· of true watching,
of Truth
Mis. 40–23 must possess the s· of Truth
49–19 s· of Truth leads into all truth,
204–12 s· of Truth cleansing from
205–10 s· of Truth and Love on
Ret. 81–10 s· of Truth extinguishes
Pul. 75– 2 the s· of Truth and Love,
No. 32–14 in the s· of Truth ;
My. 4– 2 one finds the s· of Truth,
119–30 s· of Truth that leadeth away
130–12 s· of Truth is the lever
225– 3 worker in the s· of Truth
238–18 the s· of Truth, whereby the
of unselfishness
My. 87–26 * imbued with the s· of unselfishness
omitting the
No. 28–22 omitting the s· of this Science
one
Pan. 6–27 belief in more than one s·,
14– 6 at the table of our Lord in one s· ;
oneness in
Mis. 289–18 Oneness in s· is Science,
or letter
Man. 44– 5 s· or letter of this By-Law
our
Mis. 46–23 witness with our s·, — Rom. 8 : 16.
255–14 witness with our s·, — Rom. 8 : 16.
placid
Ret. 5–23 * sympathizing heart, and a placid s·.
poor in
Mis. 325– 3 the poor in s· : — Matt. 5 : 3.
Ret. 26–26 none but the "poor in s·" — Matt. 5 : 3.
'01. 2–19 blessing the poor in s·
pure in
Mis. 168–13 only such as are pure in s·,
'01. 26–18 the pure in s·, and the meek
quickening
Mis. 185–28 made a quickening s·. — I Cor. 15 : 45.
188–32 "a quickening s· ;" — I Cor. 15 : 45.
189–17 quickening s· takes it away :
Un. 30–15 made a quickening s·." — I Cor. 15 : 45.
requires the
Pul. 15– 8 requires the s· of our blessed Master
sainted
Ret. 6– 2 * impressions of that sainted s·,
same
Mis. 123– 1 same s· that in our time massacres
347–13 operation by the same s·.
self-same
Po. 10–16 "Thou of the self-same s·,
My. 337–17 "Thou of the self-same s·,
thereof
Mis. 291–19 if the s· thereof be lacking.
this
Pul. 75– 6 a greater degree of this s·
'01. 9–16 This s· of God is made manifest
My. 165– 9 and by this s· man lives
292–27 but this s· is of God,
underlying
My. 71– 8 * fussing about the underlying s·
unity of
Mis. 145–21 the visible unity of s· remains,
Pul. 22–18 there will be unity of s·,
uplifting of
Mis. 169–12 The uplifting of s· was the
with thee in
Po. 73– 8 I am with thee in s· once more.
with you in
Pul. 1–18 being with you in s·,
My. 148–19 am with you in s·,
wounded
Mis. 258– 9 anointing the wounded s·
your
Man. 47–12 and in your s·, — I Cor. 6 : 20.

Mis. 124– 4 must worship Him in s·.
195– 7 hath the s· without the letter,
207– 4 s· of my life-purpose,
260–27 The s·, and not the letter,
355– 5 not of the letter, but the s·.
385–14 S· emancipate for this far shore
Man. 43–26 s· in which the writer has written
Ret. 69–11 saying, . . . 'I will put s· into
88–25 s· of the Saviour's ministry,
Pul. 2– 3 no more s· in her ;" — I Kings 10 : 5.
'01. 9–30 s· giveth him liberty :
24–30 to attain the s· or mystery of
'02. 9–19 s· of the healing Christ,
Po. 48– 7 S· emancipate for this far shore
My. 125–17 s· of the Mars' Hill orator,
131–15 above the symbol seize the s·,
180–28 in the s· of our great Exemplar
188–17 In s· I enter your inner sanctuary,

spirit
My.	194– 6	but the s· of it is immortal.
	194–23	gratefully accept the s· of it ;
	233– 2	s· of our Master's command
	343– 2	* in Mrs. Eddy's own s·.

spirited
Pul.	29–14	* The music was s·,

spiritless
No.	29–22	Such sermons, . . . are s· waifs,
Peo.	5–12	barbarisms of s· codes.
Po.	67– 3	Grow cold in this spot as the s· clay,

spirit-rappings
Mis.	231– 9	though I take no stock in s·

Spirit-revelator
Mis.	3–14	through Christ, the S·,

Spirit's
Un.	58–10	by the law of S· supremacy ;

spirit's
Ret.	9–19	* naught my s· breathings to control,

spirits (*see also* **spirits'**)
Mis.	34–23	are called "communications from s·,"
	171–13	"try the s·" — *I John* 4 : 1.
	171–15	s· supposed to have departed
	278– 2	the distilled s· of evil,
	387– 9	'Neath which our s· blend
Ret.	56– 6	Spirit into s·, . . . is a misstatement
No.	26– 4	s·, or souls, — *alias* gods.
Pan.	9– 4	term "s·" means more than one
Hea.	6–15	ignorantly imputed to s·.
Po.	3–13	Till bursting bonds our s· part
	6– 3	'Neath which our s· blend
My.	211–10	the unclean s· cried out,
	313–21	I was not a medium for s·.

spirits'
Mis.	387– 6	in what glad surprise, Our s· own !"
Po.	50–24	in what glad surprise, Our s· own !"

Spirit-substance
Mis.	205–20	disembodied individual S·

spiritual
abstractions
Mis.	195–27	s· abstractions, impractical and

achievement
My.	37–16	* By reason of your s· achievement

advent
Ret.	70–21	s· advent of the advancing idea

Æsculapius
My.	205–16	s· Æsculapius and Hygeia,

afflatus
Ret.	31–30	potency of a present s· *afflatus.*

altitude
Mis.	16–28	this new-born s· altitude
	289–31	allowed to rise to the s· altitude

and eternal
(*see* **eternal**)

animus
Mis.	113–32	moral, and s· animus is felt
Man.	31–13	s· *animus* so universally needed.
Pul.	3–30	unfitness for such a s· animus
	32– 9	* but a s· animus.

application
Mis.	170–21	s· application bears upon our

apprehension
Mis.	363–31	s· apprehension of the Scriptures,
My.	183–12	S· apprehension unfolds,

armament
Un.	6–27	manual of their s· armament.
My.	355–14	the untiring s· armament.

ascendency
'01.	19–19	through s· ascendency alone.

aspirations
My.	91–10	* no person's s· aspirations were

attainments
Mis.	345–32	directed them to s· attainments.
'00.	1–14	rich s· attainments,
My.	64– 5	* through her s· attainments,
	244–11	impulse to our s· attainments,

attitude
Ret.	88–26	abide in such a s· attitude

attraction
My.	159–18	tend to check s· attraction

axis
Ret.	88–30	Mind revolves on a s· axis,

bankruptcy
Mis.	122–24	Neither s· bankruptcy nor

basis
Un.	25–19	a material, not a s· basis.
Hea.	1–21	more s· basis and tendency

beauty
My.	141–28	blossomed into s· beauty,

behest
'02.	19–24	a s· behest, in reversion,

spiritual
being
Mis.	105–10	his individual s· being,
	113–13	scale of moral and s· being,
	352– 1	the bliss of s· being ;
Peo.	2– 6	material conceptions of s· being,

beings
Peo.	1–18	understanding that we are s· beings

birth
Mis.	17–18	This s· birth opens to the
	17–27	With the s· birth, man's

body
My.	218–11	The s· body, the incorporeal

call
My.	172–13	symbol of my s· call

chemicalization
Pul.	5–30	This s· chemicalization is the

child
Mis.	18–15	as God's s· child only,

Christ
Mis.	84–12	s· Christ was infallible ;

Christianity
Mis.	2–15	view of a more s· Christianity,
	232–18	a more s· Christianity will be
	246–28	Shall we have a s· Christianity
No.	46– 4	a practical, s· Christianity,
'01.	2– 3	The highest s· Christianity
Peo.	5– 2	recommends the more s· Christianity,

coexistence
Mis.	47–24	s· coexistence with his Maker.

communion
Mis.	90–30	is the s· communion which
My.	139–24	the material to the s· communion ;

compact
Ret.	47– 3	wars with Love's s· compact,

concept
Un.	32– 7	man . . . is His s· concept.

conception
Mis.	286–11	more s· conception and education of

concepts
Mis.	361–10	s· concepts testifying to one

conclusions
Ret.	21–28	if s· conclusions are separated from

condition
Un.	7–13	In the same s· condition

consciousness
Un.	23–25	a purely good and s· consciousness
	35–24	Spirit is s· consciousness alone.
	35–24	Hence this s· consciousness

cooperation
My.	162– 9	Unity is s· cooperation,

cosmos
Mis.	26–25	God's consequent is the s· cosmos.
	362–24	s· cosmos and Science of Soul.

creation
My.	179– 5	gave an account of the s· creation,

danger
No.	23– 4	is fraught with s· danger.

dawn
Mis.	78– 1	s· dawn of the Messiah,
'02.	5– 4	s· dawn of the twentieth century

death
Un.	29– 8	there can be, no s· death.

demand
Pul.	23–14	* common identity of s· demand.
Hea.	19–20	Science makes a more s· demand,

development
My.	48–20	* a means of s· development

dictionary
Mis.	252–30	the wise man's s· dictionary ;

discernment
Mis.	112–29	intellectual, and s· discernment,
	215–32	a wise s· discernment must be used
	312–21	his own s· discernment,
My.	22–21	* a s· discernment of the needs of

effect
My.	318–13	declare the moral and s· effect

element
Ret.	65– 7	freeze out the s· element.

elements
Mis.	2–30	putting on the s· elements

elevator
Mis.	259–23	s· elevator of the human race,

endeavor
Pan.	9–17	s· endeavor to bless others,

ends
Ret.	47–11	means for the promotion of s· ends.

existence
Mis.	17–28	primitive, sinless, s· existence
	182–15	man's primal, s· existence,
Ret.	23–14	heart's bridal to more s· existence.

eye
Po.	32–11	illumines my s· eye,

fact
Mis.	42–22	the s· fact of Life is,
My.	109– 6	not the s· fact of being.

spiritual

facts
Mis. 8– 1 More . . . than to s· facts.
37– 6 the s· facts of being.
174–28 that reveals the s· facts
234–24 has seen far into the s· facts
Ret. 60–26 the s· facts of the universe,
Un. 30– 5 can reverse the s· facts

faith
My. 132– 8 s· faith and understanding

famine
Mis. 246–23 the s· famine of 1866,

force
Mis. 257– 9 a moral and s· force
Rud. 4–10 represents a moral and s· force,

forces
'02. 10– 3 unfolds s· forces,

foresight
My. 281– 1 Because a s· foresight of

form
Pul. 33–24 * his visitor was a s· form from

formation
Ret. 49–12 s· formation first, last, and always,

forms
Mis. 91–18 most s· forms of thought

foundation
Mis. 74– 7 s· foundation for the affections
341– 4 s· foundation and superstructure
Pul. 6– 6 s· foundation of Christ's healing.
My. 357–16 on a wholly s· foundation,
357–19 Christ, the s· foundation.

freedom
Ret. 45–13 in order to gain s· freedom

fulness
My. 357– 3 until we arrive at the s· fulness

gates
Ret. 79–28 its s· gates not captured,

Genesis
Mis. 258–12 the s· Genesis of creation,

gifts
Mis. 345– 1 Spirit bestows s· gifts,

glow
Mis. x– 1 s· glow and grandeur of
356– 3 s· glow and understanding.

goal
No. 44– 8 swerves not . . . from the s· goal.

good
Mis. 140– 7 all s· good comes to
Un. 38–23 s· good, is not seen in

grace
Un. 57–21 s· grace was sufficient

gravitations
Mis. 19–26 material and s· gravitations,

groan
Mis. 231–10 table give a s· groan

growth
Mis. 41–14 it promotes s· growth,
308–25 impedes s· growth ;
317–13 by s· growth and by the study
330–20 reported more s· growth.
350–30 promote health and s· growth.
380– 8 as if centuries of s· growth
Ret. 44–11 and its s· growth kept pace with
45–10 retards s· growth,
75–20 dishonesty retards s· growth
Un. 43–11 time and immense s· growth.
My. 116–22 loss in grace and growth s·,
211–31 intellectual culture or s· growth.
213– 2 brotherly love, s· growth

harvests
Ret. 79– 5 We glean s· harvests from our

healing
Mis. 163–28 s· healing of body and mind.
246–29 a s· healing, or a materialistic
346– 4 demonstration of moral and s· healing

heaven is
My. 267–16 Heaven is s·.

heavens
Mis. 254–20 stars from the s· heavens,

help
My. 153–18 s· help of divine Love.

hero
My. 203–13 A s· hero is a mark for gamesters,

heroes
My. 248– 9 S· heroes and prophets

homœopathist
'01. 22– 7 I am a s· homœopathist

house
My. 17–11 built up a s· house, — I Pet. 2 : 5.

idea
Mis. 2–20 Christ, the s· idea of God,
17–13 before the Christ, the s· idea
77–12 divine Principle and s· idea ;
140–31 the s· idea would live,
151–26 wedded to the s· idea, Christ ;
163–27 s· idea which leadeth into

spiritual

idea
Mis. 164– 3 the former is the s· idea
164–11 s· idea of the Principle of man
164–21 understanding of Christ, the s· idea,
164–32 This s· idea that the personal
165– 7 s· idea of God and of man,
166– 2 Principle and s· idea of being.
166–13 This child, or s· idea,
166–23 s· idea, named in this century
166–29 This s· idea, or Christ,
167– 4 pertain to the s· idea,
175– 3 woman, the s· idea,
306–28 it is a s· idea that lights
328– 8 Christ, the s· idea which
Ret. 68– 7 the s· idea, or ideal man,
93– 3 the s· idea, appeared to
Un. 52–14 s· idea, *man* and *woman*.
Pul. 10–17 Christ, the true, the s· idea,
14–22 s· idea will be understood.
No. 1– 2 s· idea emanating from
19–17 senses receive no s· idea,
26–12 s· idea which transfigures
'01. 8– 3 Holy Ghost, or s· idea of
'02. 12– 5 Messiah, the true s· idea,
16–19 a glorified s· idea
Peo. 3–16 s· idea of good and Truth
My. 120–11 s· idea that takes away all sin,
122–22 to grasp the s· idea
139– 6 even the s· idea of Life,
181–29 return of the s· idea to
206–15 not seeing the s· idea
219–15 the ever-present s· idea,
262–21 His s· idea, man
263– 1 to obliterate the s· idea
303–19 to understand the s· idea.

ideal
Mis. 124–12 find rest in the s· ideal,
Ret. 75–16 If one's s· ideal is comprehended
93–15 s· ideal is made our own,
Peo. 5– 8 for their more s· ideal,
My. 319– 3 s· ideal is the only real man

idealism
My. 5–15 s· idealism and realism

ideas
Mis. 82– 1 peoples the mind with s· ideas,
307– 1 gives you His s· ideas,
'00. 3–17 the pioneer of s· ideas,

identity
Mis. 185–10 s· identity as the child of God,

ignorance
Mis. 298–10 in the same s· ignorance

illumination
Mis. 342–16 With no . . . s· illumination

image
Rud. 13– 9 divine and s· image of God.

import
Mis. 162– 4 s· import to mankind !
'00. 12– 3 the s· import whereof
'01. 25–12 because of their more s· import
My. 46–27 * Manual in its s· import,
270– 4 magnitude of their s· import,

individuality
Mis. 103–27 s· individuality that reflected the
Ret. 73–15 man's s· individuality in God,
Un. 37–19 s· individuality is immortal.
38– 1 no cognizance of s· individuality,

influx
My. 212–20 s· influx impossible under other

insight
Mis. 169– 5 her s· insight had been darkened
189–10 S· insight of Truth and Love
Ret. 32– 4 s· insight, knowledge, and being.

instruction
Mis. 169–21 left for our s· instruction.

interpretation
Mis. 248– 3 s· interpretation they refuse to
314–17 s· interpretation of the
Ret. 27– 2 setting forth their s· interpretation,
Pul. 43–20 * with its s· interpretation
No. 37–11 s· interpretation of the vicarious
My. 17–26 * its s· interpretation, as given in
32–18 * its s· interpretation as given in

interpretations
Ret. 35–12 but the s· interpretations thereof.

issues
Mis. 235–15 touches mind to more s· issues,
My. 287–23 touches thought to s· issues,

joy
Ret. 21–20 s· joy and true estimate of being.

knowledge
My. 294–12 s· knowledge of God.

lack
No. 45–11 such efforts arise from a s· lack,

spiritual

latitudes
Ret. 73–11 floated into more s· latitudes
No. 45–23 anchor . . . in more s· latitudes,
Peo. 1–13 drift into more s· latitudes.

law
Mis. 17– 2 thunderings of the s· law of Life,
17– 3 s· law of Love, as opposed to
95–21 reveals itself . . . through s· law.
116–19 final obedience to s· law.
199– 7 amenable only to moral and s· law,
200–19 the supremacy of s· law
Rud. 10–22 disobedience to His s· law.
No. 21– 8 it grasped in s· law the universe,

laws
Mis. 198–26 divine Principle, and its s· laws.
My. 159–23 s· laws enforcing obedience

Leader
Pul. 49– 3 * consider her their s· Leader

leaven
Mis. 175– 8 s· leaven of divine Science

Life
Mis. 16– 1 new and more s· Life and Love.
361– 7 s· Life, whose myriad forms
Un. 30– 7 Soul is Life, and being s· Life,
30–11 restores Soul, or s· Life.

life
Mis. 351–30 the antipode of s· life ;
My. 113–28 more s· life and love?

light
Mis. 113– 2 God's presence gives s· light,
276–28 thus shutting out s· light.
341–31 for the neglect of s· light,
342– 6 decline of s· light, until,

lines
Mis. 81– 5 into more s· lines of life

Love
Mis. 288– 7 and weighed by s· Love,

love
Mis. 15–17 heaven-born hope, and s· love.
Ret. 76–15 which lead up to s· love.
'01. 26–21 charity— s· love.
'02. 8–22 the rule of s· love ;
8–29 S· love makes man conscious that

man
Mis. 17–32 truer sense of Spirit and s· man.
79–22 s· man is that perfect and unfallen
162–23 The s· man, or Christ,
182–21 no mortal hath seen the s· man,
186– 1 history of the s· man
186– 8 s· man made in the image
186–17 spiritual Principle of s· man.
187–16 inspired sense of the s· man,
Un. 61–15 Spirit and s· man are
No. 19–18 s· man and his spiritual senses
'01. 5–19 real s· man and universe.
'02. 7–17 s· man and the universe
Hea. 17– 7 Love makes the s· man,
My. 239–26 and is not the s· man,
296–14 to destroy the real s· man.

manifestation
'02. 2–21 to a more s· manifestation,

meaning
Mis. 18–12 new tongue, their s· meaning,
73– 9 discern their s· meaning,
300–27 s· meaning of Bible texts ;
Ret. 25– 7 in their s· meaning,
Pul. 35– 2 I apprehended the s· meaning
'00. 6–10 dawns the s· meaning thereof ;
Hea. 7– 7 s· meaning as opposed to
My. 178– 3 s· meaning of Holy Writ

means
Mis. 152–30 His s· means and methods,
'01. 19–12 mixing material and s· means,
26–12 from Christ's purely s· means
My. 357– 7 s· means, manifestation,

mentality
Pul. vii–13 lenses of more s· mentality,

mind
Peo. 4–22 No . . . can make a s· mind out of

mode
Ret. 89– 2 potency of this s· mode of Mind,

modes
My. 266–27 more s· modes and significations

modesty
My. 357–12 s· modesty of C. S.,

molecule
Mis. 313– 6 points to the scientific s· molecule,

monitor
Mis. 100–20 s· monitor understood is coincidence

music
'00. 11– 8 s· music, the music of Soul.

nature
Mis. 119–14 strives . . . against the s· nature ;
My. 188–29 seek the Science of his s· nature,

spiritual

need
Mis. 245–16 s· need that C. S. should remove

needs
Ret. 91–18 ministering to the s· needs of all
My. 147–18 moral, and s· needs of humanity,

noumenon
Ret. 22– 4 His s· noumenon and phenomenon

nutriment
My. 230– 5 digestion of s· nutriment

obedience
'01. 34– 6 in s· obedience to Christ's mode

observation
Mis. 154–26 post of s· observation and self-examination.

order
Ret. 10–16 Syntax was s· order and unity.

organization
Mis. 138–29 march on in s· organization.

origin
Mis. 18–17 of s· origin, God's reflection,
75–27 discovered the s· origin of man.
166–17 how to declare its s· origin,

peace
My. 93–14 * physical health and s· peace.

perception
Mis. 139–25 but to my s· perception,
My. 37–22 * known through your s· perception

perfectibility
Pan. 11–27 man's unfallen s· perfectibility.

perfection
Mis. 42–26 exists only in s· perfection,
My. 345–23 as we near a state of s· perfection.

perfectly
Pul. 54– 8 * The . . . is the perfectly s·.

personality
Mis. 218–31 * purely s· personality in God.''

phenomena
Un. 10–12 s· phenomena of this one infinite
10–13 S· phenomena never converge toward

plane
My. 46– 5 * more s· plane of living,

points
Mis. 143– 5 our s· points, above the plane of

power
Mis. 3–17 never are needed to aid s· power.
113–31 prolific sources of s· power
170–32 in Bible usage, often means s· power.
189–24 s· power that subordinates matter
189–29 s· power, healing sin and sickness,
193–31 man's capabilities and s· power.
248– 6 its moral meaning, . . . is s· power,
268–29 human pride forfeits s· power,
286–12 superiority of s· power over sensuous,
352–21 not sufficient s· power in the
Ret. 43– 7 teaching the pathology of s· power,
44–28 love, prosperity, and s· power.
Rud. 9–21 s· power of a scientific, right thought,
Hea. 15– 7 in s· power divinely directed.
My. 3– 7 not . . . but with s· power.
152–13 spiritual worship, s· power.
226–11 by evolved s· power,
339–29 wars against Spirit and s· power.

preexistence
Mis. 181–27 man's s· preexistence as God's child ;

presence
Mis. 328–22 s· presence and idea of God.

Principle
Mis. 186–17 s· Principle of spiritual man.
Ret. 37–17 demonstrating the s· Principle

progress
Mis. 124–23 proportion to a man's s· progress,
192– 6 importance to man's s· progress,
My. 114–30 each step of mental and s· progress,

qualifications
Man. 87–15 moral and s· qualifications
My. 241– 1 * moral and s· qualifications

realities
Mis. 53– 2 up to the s· realities of existence,

reality
Mis. 60–29 hints the existence of s· reality ;
87– 9 s· reality and substance of form,

recognition
Mis. 196–26 arise to s· recognition of being,

refreshment
Mis. 170– 8 symbolize the s· refreshment of

regeneration
Mis. 187– 1 s· regeneration of both mind and

relation
Mis. 181–21 his s· relation to Deity :

religion
Mis. 365–16 Good health and a more s· religion
No. 18–22 Good health and a more s· religion
Hea. 1–11 more practical and s· religion

resurrection
Mis. 179–22 come into the s· resurrection by

spiritual
understanding
My. 140– 1 abiding s· understanding
152–13 rests solely on s· understanding,
161–24 becloud s· understanding,
180– 8 s· understanding of the Scriptures
205–19 with s· understanding,
206– 5 tender grace of s· understanding,
234–12 from . . . to s· understanding,
260–18 s· understanding of joy
267–25 obscure s· understanding,
267–29 within man's s· understanding
273–22 s· understanding of Life
292–16 faith or s· understanding,
union
Ret. 42– 2 a blessed and s· union,
unity
Mis. 358–32 a higher s· unity is won,
My. 243–22 s· unity with your Leader.
universe
Mis. 21– 7 the s· universe, whereof
361–25 s· universe, including man
Un. 14–14 rectify His s· universe?
No. 26–24 in the s· universe he is
values
My. 48–24 * subordination . . . to s· values,
verity
Pul. 3–27 evidence of s· verity
version
Hea. 16– 2 and given its s· version,
vision
Mis. 373–13 s· vision that should, does, guide
Un. 61– 6 to immortal and s· vision he was
My. 126–23 which the Revelator saw in s· vision
voice
My. 265– 5 revelation, s· voice and vision,
warfare
Ret. 86– 1 energize wholesome s· warfare,
way
'02. 10–20 reformer who finds the more s· way,
wholly
Mis. 16–24 awakened consciousness is wholly s·;
91–11 This bond is wholly s· and inviolate.
My. 238–10 His language and . . . are wholly s·.
wickedness
Mis. 116– 4 "s· wickedness in high — Eph. 6 : 12.
134–27 S· wickedness is standing in
world
'01. 21–10 * ideas about the s· world
My. 167– 5 s· world, which is apart from matter,
worship
My. 152–13 s· worship, spiritual power.

Mis. 5– 4 Science reveals man as s·,
19–29 s·, joy-giving, and eternal
21–22 man is not material; he is s·."
25–13 s· and original meaning of the
26– 5 period more humane and s·.
27–25 must be s· and mental.
27–27 But, say you, is a stone s·?
30–10 They were s·, not material;
37–12 s· and immortal Mind,
37–13 leave the animal for the s·,
40– 4 material methods with the s·,
47–22 man, . . . is s·, not material.
52– 2 to such as seek . . . to aid the s·,
62– 1 man in the likeness of Spirit is s·.
64–22 It is s·, and not material.
73–10 reality of what is s·,
74–14 his nativity was a s· and immortal
85–17 s·, individual existence.
86– 2 The individual and s· are perfect;
142–19 with bright hues of the s·,
155– 5 All power and happiness are s·,
166–21 whose origin was more s·
179–15 more true, more s·"
181–19 s·, and not material laws;
181–20 as s·, and not material.
184– 9 man . . . is s·, not material.
187–20 might have been as s· as the New.
187–29 material, before s·;
190– 8 nor does . . . ultimate in the s·;
191–32 more s· and practical sense.
217– 6 the universe of God is s·,
232–26 most s· and unselfish motives.
253–27 the s· Mother's sore travail,
287–15 the s· over the animal,
351–21 Love is s·,
352– 5 as material and not s·,
352– 5 or as both material and s·,
363–12 the immortal modes of Mind are s·,
365–20 moral and s·, as well as physical,
375– 4 the counterfeit of the s·
Ret. 25–11 compassionate, helpful, and s·.
35– 1 s·, scientific Mind-healing,
48–28 s· and scientific impartation of
59–20 harmonious, immortal, and s·:
65–15 Jewish religion was not s·;

spiritual
Ret. 67– 8 both material and s·,
73– 1 immortal man being s·,
78–16 wholly Christlike and s·.
91–21 His power over others was s·,
Un. 10–14 Their gradations are s· and divine;
24–21 Man, as God's offspring, must be s·,
25–22 Evil is not s·,
35–17 forces of Truth are moral and s·,
40–18 by a s· and not by a material sense
42–11 material before he can be s·,
42–27 nor the material the s·,
46–16 were real to him only as s·
Pul. 69–19 * s· or metaphysical standpoint.
Rud. 3–11 more because of his s· than
3–17 Jesus' healing was s· in its nature,
4– 3 universe is s·, peopled with
7– 8 Is man material or s·?
No. 6– 5 God's formations are s·,
12– 5 leading us . . . to be s·,
17– 9 a s· and individual being,
19– 2 moral and s·, as well as physical,
25–22 S· . . . man alone is God's likeness,
34– 6 s· and infinite meaning
40– 6 s· and immortal Truth.
'01. 8–14 Can he be too s·, since Jesus said,
8–19 can man be . . . less than s·
8–20 is he not wholly s·?
8–28 s· and material Christ Jesus,
9–24 and these things being s·,
10– 8 a s·, divine emanation,
10– 9 Christ must be s·, not material.
11–20 not too s· to be practical,
27–25 left C. S. as it is, purely s·,
'02. 8– 6 likeness of God, Spirit, is s·,
9–15 was loving and s·,
10–18 man becomes finally s·.
10–19 correct, and inevitably s·.
Hea. 5–28 The more s· we become here,
7–10 s· instead of the material
Peo. 1– 2 is a step more s·.
6–18 more s· and true ideal of Deity
7–30 his mind-models are more or less s·.
7–32 and our methods grow more s·
14– 1 As our ideas of Deity become more s·,
14– 8 ideas of Life have grown more s·;
My. 50–16 * and looked towards the s·,
91– 5 * s· and mystic mediation
121–11 This peace is s·; never selfish,
133–29 s· bespeaks our temporal history.
139–20 from the material to the s·,
160– 2 Christian, . . . strives for the s·;
160– 6 relation with the divine, the s·,
166–23 measure of time and joy be s·,
178–13 Then all is Spirit and s·.
181– 8 Progress is s·.
193–15 The s· dominates the temporal.
221–17 other than the s· and divine,
221–20 no other . . . means than the s·
235–18 that which is not s·?
252–29 it is moral, s·, divine.
267–15 Is heaven s·?
303–22 the material to the s·,
349–22 because they are s·,
349–28 is correct only as it is s·,
353–25 s· have all place and power.

Spiritual Interpretation
Man. 63– 2 S· I· by Mary Baker Eddy,

spiritualism
Mis. 29–13 between C. S. and s·,
34–10 Is s· or mesmerism included
34–13 s·, so far as I understand it,
296–16 with theosophy and s·;
Man. 41– 7 theosophy, hypnotism, or s·,
47–26 theosophy, hypnotism, or s·,
Ret. 28–28 Am I a believer in s·?
29– 2 s· is the antipode of C. S.
Pul. 38–18 * not accept the belief we call s·.
No. 13–16 chapter sub-title
13–21 C. S., s·, and theosophy.
Pan. 9– 6 in s· they imply men and
Hea. 5–12 * "between Christianity and s·,
5–25 s· would lead our lives to

spiritualist
Mis. 95–14 Am I a s·?
249–12 well known that I am not a s·,
No. 14– 2 If a s· medium understood

spiritualists
Mis. 95–18 which s· have miscalled
Ret. 24– 3 s· would associate therewith,
Hea. 6– 9 s· abused me for it then,

spirituality
accession of
Mis. 204–28 Through the accession of s·,

spirituality
advance in
  Mis. 21–12 As the ages advance in *s·*,
begotten of
  Ret. 26–24 It must be begotten of *s·*,
  Pul. 35–10 "Divine Science is begotten of *s·*,"
demonstrate
  My. 242– 3 You can never demonstrate *s·* until
God of
  Un. 49–16 and the God of *s·*.
growth of
  Mis. 154–14 as the growth of *s·*
higher
  Pul. 38–28 * a higher *s·* seeking expression.
      67–15 * to give expression to a higher *s·*.
his
  Hea. 2–22 his *s·* rebuked their carnality,
increase of
  Mis. 21–14 in no wise except by increase of *s·*.
increase the
  My. 230–12 increase the *s·* of him who obeys it,
individual
  Mis. 165–15 individual *s·*, perfect and eternal,
is the basis
  Mis. 156–23 *S·* is the basis of all true thought
lack of
  Mis. 53–25 because of their great lack of *s·*.
life of
  My. 352– 9 * for your life of *s·*,
man's
  Mis. 105– 2 facts of man's *s·*, individuality,
morals, and
  Mis. 245–13 morals, and *s·* of mankind.
of Truth
  No. v–13 apprehend the pure *s·* of Truth.
our
  Pul. 21–29 aught that can darken . . . our *s·*,
price of
  My. 221– 1 earthly price of *s·* in religion
purest
  No. 38–26 loses a part of its purest *s·*
refuge is in
  Un. 57– 7 Man's refuge is in *s·*,
to see
  No. 12– 5 leading us to see *s·*
true
  '02. 8– 9 shows what true *s·* is,
we approach
  Mis. 30–29 will vanish as we approach *s·*,
  Pul. 39– 4 * the peace of the Lord in *s·*.

spiritualization
  Mis. 10–27 this is the advent of *s·*.
      15– 9 Nothing aside from the *s·*
      42–11 states that *s·* of thought is
      73–29 the *s·* that comes from
    185–19 The *s·* of our sense of man
  Un. 28–18 we learn Soul only . . . by *s·*.
      32–12 *s·* of thought destroys
  No. 12–20 impels a *s·* of thought
      32– 2 and the *s·* of the race.
  My. 266–17 final *s·* of all things,
    266–21 verified by the *s·* of all?

spiritualize
  Mis. 92– 5 and to *o·* human life,
    217–31 but *s·* human thought,
  Ret. 89–30 better adapted to *o·* thought
      84– 5 to *s·* his own thoughts
  Un. 31– 7 to *s·* thought and action.
  No. 11–27 and *s·* consciousness with the
  Hea. 19–17 to *s·* thought, motive, and
  Peo. 7–31 our thoughts must *s·* to

spiritualized
  Mis. 86–19 sensations . . . must be *s·*, until we
  Ret. 28– 9 learned that thought must be *s·*,
  Pul. 35–13 learned that thought must be *s·*
  Peo. 11– 6 feeblest mind, enlightened and *s·*,
  My. 122–28 *s·* to behold this Christ,
    127– 1 Science, whereby thought is *s·*,
    355– 2 to see in her *s·* thought

spiritualizes
  Mis. 92–20 this *s·* their thoughts.
     92–32 *s·* his own thought,
    252–24 It *s·* religion
    267–28 *s·* man's motives and methods,
  My. 4– 3 obedience to this rule *s·* man,
    249–30 which *s·* the congregation.

spiritualizing
  No. 10–24 dematerializing and *s·* mortals
spiritually
  Mis. ix–10 morally, physically, *s·*.
     3– 1 physically, morally, and *s·*,
    24– 2 makes man *s·* minded.
    24– 4 but to be *s·* minded — *Rom.* 8 : 6.
    25–18 and raising the *s·* dead.
    30– 8 St. John *s·* discerned

spiritually
  Mis. 31– 6 morally, physically, or *s·*
    43–16 those who are *s·* unqualified.
    51– 2 its effect physically as well as *s·*,
    56–29 first *s·* created the universe,
    57– 7 but from Spirit, *s·*.
    57–23 universe with man created *s·*.
    58–17 but I must *s·* understand them
    64–17 ethics which guide thought *s·*
    85– 6 learns *s·* all that he knows
    86–16 Earth is more *s·* beautiful
    88–21 * Science is natural, *s·* natural;
    90–28 *s·* prepared breakfast,
   108– 9 *s·*, literally, it *is nothing*.
   111–31 or is a *s·* adopted child,
   123–31 must worship Him *s·*,
   138–14 ethically, physically, and *s·*.
   140– 6 morally and *s·* inalienable.
   150–11 *S·*, I am with all who
   168– 4 the blind, and physically,
   169–16 must be *s·* discerned.
   170–15 Jesus interpreted all *s·*:
   172–21 affections, *s·* understood,
   172–24 *s·* discerned, understood,
   182– 1 *s·* instead of materially
   252–20 physically, as well as *s·*,
   315–10 *s·* fitted for teachers,
   317–16 is yet assimilated *s·*
   362–10 physically, morally, *s·*.
  Man. 46– 2 a *s·* adopted child
     46– 3 a *s·* adopted husband
  Ret. 34–19 advanced morally and *s·*.
    44–30 this *s·* organized Church
    68–10 idea is *s·* real.
    76–14 The *s·* minded meet on the
  Un. 36–20 mentally, morally, *s·*.
    37–17 physically mortal, but *s·* immortal.
  Pul. 29–22 * lesson was to be taken *s·*
  No. 13–20 physically, morally, and *s·*,
    22–10 morally, *s·*, or physically.
    25–24 in a *s·* scientific sense.
  Pan. 7– 9 had created all things *s·*,
    11–16 If man is *s·* fallen,
  '00. 6–28 physically, morally, and *s·*.
    14– 9 let him . . . (that discerneth *s·*)
    14–23 toiled for the *s·* indispensable.
    15– 8 Passover, *s·* discerned,
  '01. 5–15 their personality is defined *s·*,
    20–16 physically, morally, or *s·*,
  '02. 6–28 that man becomes *s·* minded
    6–29 to be *s·* minded — *Rom.* 8 : 6.
    8–15 *s·* minded are inspired with
  Hea. 17–14 when *s·* understood,
  Peo. 6–19 improves the race physically and *s·*.
  My. 4–11 meekly, patiently, *s·*,
   119–19 could not identify Christ *s·*,
   124–29 seen of men, and *s·* understood;
   135–29 *s·* and scientifically understand
   140–20 Relinquishing . . . advances it *s·*.
   150–22 *s·* dead in trespasses
   152–15 worship only Spirit and *s·*,
   156–12 *s·* speaking is the passover
   180–32 defines noumenon . . . *s·*,
   187– 2 *s·* as well as literally,
   196–26 even the *s·* indispensable,
   275–27 *s·* understood and demonstrated,
   350– 9 she *s·* discerned the divine idea

spiritually-minded
  Po. vii–13 * *gems . . . from this s· author*
  My. 249–28 student who is most *s·*.
Spiritward
  Mis. 360–19 lift every thought-leaflet *S·*;
spite
  My. 38–13 * in *s·* of the fact that many
    78–29 * in *s·* of its vast interior,
   294–19 in *s·* of the constant stress
spitting
  Mis. 170–26 *S·* was the Hebrew method of
spittle
  Mis. 171– 7 anoint the . . . eyes with his *s·*,
splendid
  My. 48–15 * *s·* appreciation of her efforts
    99–14 * recently built a *s·* cathedral
splendor
  Mis. 330–29 unveils its regal *s·* to the sun;
    376–17 brave *s·* of a November sky
  Pul. 39–19 * *s·* of the sky Repeats its glory
  Po. 31–17 solemn *s·* of immortal power,
  My. 262–31 The *s·* of this nativity of Christ
splints
  Mis. 243– 8 regular doctor had put on *s·*
spoil
  My. 123–30 *s·* the vines." — *Song* 2 : 15.

spoiled

Mis. 344–16 are s· by lack of Science.

spoiling

My. 211–25 s· that individual's disposition,

spoils

My. 236–11 Too much of one thing s· the whole.

spoke

Mis. 170–12 she s· of the hades, or hell of
312– 1 sorry that I s· at all,
344–21 which Paul understood when he s· of
Ret. 13–16 of these things he now s·,
31–27 s· to my chastened sense as by
Un. 59– 8 Jesus, who s· of the Christ as
No. 36– 8 He once s· of himself . . . as
My. 30–10 * It s· much for the devotion of
81–19 * s· simply and gratefully,
146– 3 Jesus s· the truth.
172– 9 * Mrs. Eddy s· as follows
185–22 s· to an attentive audience
185–24 I foresaw this hour, and s· of
266–15 of which Jesus s·.
315– 6 * He s· of her being a
320–11 * Mr. Wiggin s· of "S· and H·
320–14 * always s· of you as the author
320–23 * and s· of your ability
320–32 * s· in a very animated manner
322–20 * s· of my journeying from
322–29 * s· earnestly and beautifully of you
324– 1 * often s· his thoughts freely
325– 1 * and s· of one especial day

spoken

Mis. 23–14 It is plain that the Me s· of
25–16 s· of by St. Mark.
55–14 s· of in Matt. xii. 31, 32.
89–16 "be evil s· of."— *Rom.* 14 : 16.
122– 6 Would Jesus thus have s·
127–29 word s·, at the right moment,
151–22 Glorious things are s· of
154–19 word that is s· unto you,
166– 6 Truth he has taught and s·
266–28 Because Truth has s· aloud,
316–16 the word s· at this date.
332–18 evil is supposed to have s·,
337–10 s· of them as the Golden Rule
346–23 "A word fitly s·"— *Prov.* 25 : 11,
Un. 9– 8 words would not have been s·.
43–12 I have by no means s· of myself,
Pul. 8– 2 press has s· out historically,
11– 4 Word s· in this sacred temple
27–23 * woman s· of in the Apocalypse,
81– 4 * nowhere s· with more reverence
No. 2–15 by the s· than the unspoken word.
'00. 14– 8 s· of in the Scriptures.
'01. 9–10 s· of by St. Paul.
My. 20– 2 s· of for a memorial — *Mark* 14 : 9.
104–29 anathema s· of in Scripture :
162–17 This was s· derisively.
185–11 wherever thought, felt, s·,
225– 5 s· by our Master.
344– 1 even been s· of as a Christ,

sponsors

My. 248–14 the inevitable s· for the

spontaneity

My. 185–16 Life is the s· of Love,

spontaneous

Mis. 101– 2 healing becomes s·,
Ret. 31–13 first s· motion of Truth
Po. v– 5 * *the s· outpouring of a*
My. 11–16 * response was instant, s·,
12– 5 * s· and liberal donations
32– 1 * S· unanimity and repetition

spontaneously

Mis. 20– 2 heals man s·, morally and
'01. 3– 1 spring s· the higher hope,
My. 4– 3 practises the Golden Rule s· ;
128–10 Truth crushed . . . springs s· upward,

sport

Po. 2– 2 to s· at mortal clay
My. 166–21 s· would be more irksome than work.
303–23 His metaphysics is not the s· of

spot

Mis. 150–25 God is universal ; confined to no s·,
Ret. 17– 5 while I worship in deep sylvan s·,
18–20 s· where affection may dwell
94–14 s· and blemish on the disk of
Pul. 1–16 This s· whereon thou troddest
65–21 * Frankish church was reared upon the s·
Po. 34–13 Has wooed some mystic s·,
42– 3 sunshine without a dark s· ;
62– 5 while I worship in deep sylvan s·,
64–12 s· where affection may dwell
67– 3 Grow cold in this s· as the

spot

My. 145–14 I healed him on the s·.
197– 6 without s· or blemish.
356– 2 praise and love the s· where God

spotless

Un. 6– 5 the s· selfhood of God
Po. 65– 6 robes were as s· as snow :
My. 192– 5 make s· the blemished,
262– 4 s· purity and original perfection.

spots

No. 13–25 A theory may be sound in s·,

spotted

Pan. 3–30 his s· skin, the stars ;

sprain

Mis. 243– 7 In the case of s· of the wrist-joint,

sprains

Mis. 243– 6 although students treat s·,

sprang

Mis. 148–14 They s· from necessity,
163– 7 from which s· a sublime and
179–26 before it s· from the earth :
235– 7 Mind whence s· the universe.
Man. 3–11 They s· from necessity,
No. 14– 9 s· from the Oriental philosophy of
Peo. 4– 4 Idolatry s· from the belief that
Po. 71–12 Injustice to the combat s· ;
My. 29–17 * its grandeur s· from the
79–26 * which s· from the conviction that
182–14 From this . . . s· immortal fruits
195–26 s· from the temples erected first in
348–11 s· from the belief that the man Jesus,

spray

Mis. 329–16 nursing the timid s·,

sprays

Pul. 26–24 * s· of fig leaves bearing fruit.

spread

Mis. 137–16 to s· your own so bravely.
225–27 a cool perspiration s· over it,
234– 3 We s· our wings in vain when
326– 9 thence they s· to the house of
No. 2–28 We should not s· abroad
Pan. 15– 6 hath s· for us a table
Po. 78– 3 will s· over their tomb ;
My. 118– 4 Only . . . s· personal contagion,
219–27 the s· of so-called infectious
256–24 the festive boards are s·,
302–17 the word s· like wildfire.
336– 3 * The disease s· so rapidly
353–16 to s· undivided the Science

spreading

Mis. 135–17 and so s· the gospel
154– 3 The s· branches of The Church
Ret. 85–26 rapidly s· over the globe ;
My. 52–12 * s· world wide of this great truth,
55–10 * the Cause itself was s·
191– 6 C. S. is s· steadily
313– 9 s· the road in front of

spreads

Mis. 12– 2 s· its virus and kills
Po. 33–16 s· her pinions abroad,

spreadst

Po. 77– 8 impartial, blessings s· abroad,

Spring *and* spring

Mis. 51–27 * sunshine of the world's new s·,
251–22 burdened for an hour, s· into liberty,
262– 8 new and costly s· dress.
329– 1 chapter sub-title
329– 6 In s·, nature like a thrifty
329–10 S· is my sweetheart,
329–14 S· passes over mountain and
329–18 Whatever else droops, s· is gay :
332– 6 S· is here !
343–12 fruits of C. S. s· upward,
Man. 17– 1 In the s· of 1879,
Ret. 75– 2 s· from this ill-concealed
80–19 will be within him a s·,
Un. 5–22 Let no enmity, . . . s· up
Pul. 43–16 * corner-stone laying last s·,
46–27 * Her last marriage was in the s· of
48– 8 * lights and shades of s·
82– 9 * stop the coming of s·.
Rud. 9– 6 and this error will s· up
No. 7– 5 root of bitterness to s· up
'00. 14–18 Let no root of bitterness s· up
'01. 3– 1 s· spontaneously the higher hope,
Po. page 53 poem
53– 1 Come to thy bowers, sweet s·,
54– 2 Since joyous s· was there.
My. 56–24 * In the s· of 1905
341– 8 chapter sub-title
341–10 accept your Leader's S· greeting,
347–13 * nor ever bid the S· adieu !

Springfield, Mass.
Pul. 88–21   * *Republican, S·, M·.*
Springfield (Mass.) Republican
My. 92– 8   * [S· (M·.) R·]
Springfield Republican
My. 94– 9   * says the S· R·.
springing
Mis. 83– 8   *s· from a seed of thought,*
   285–25   S· up from the ashes of
Rud. 16–24   s· up among unchristian students,
'00.   2– 3   s· up in the above-named cities,
My. 68– 5   * s· from the tops of great stone piers,
   243– 3   belief is s· up among you
springs
'01. 31– 5   s· from the very nature of Truth,
My. 74–24   * the satisfaction that s· from
   128– 9   s· spontaneously upward,
   201–29   Hope s· exultant on this blest morn.
   256–21   s· aside at the touch of Love.
   287–18   Mind whence s· the universe.
springtide
Mis. 330– 6   pray for the perpetual s·
   330–10   s· of Christ's dear love.
   331–10   s· of freedom and greatness.
No. 14–13   to the sweet breath of s·,
   27– 6   s· of Truth in C. S.
Pan. 1–14   for the s· of Soul.
springtime
Po. 16–24   breath from the verdant s·,
sprinkle
Ret. 17–14   s· the flowers with exquisite dye.
Po. 62–17   s· the flowers with exquisite dye.
sprinkled
Hea. 2–27   s· the altar of Love
sprung
Mis. vii–17   My world has s· from Spirit,
   159–26   many weary wings s· upward !
   196–16   gods'' which s· from it.— *Exod.* 20 : 3.
   356–17   has s· up, borne fruit,
Pul. 56– 1   * organized societies have s· up
No. 9– 3   the factions which have s· up
My. 199– 5   light hath s· up.
spurious
Mis. 43–15   s· teaching of those who are
   80– 2   s· works on mental healing.
   271–14   cobwebs which s· "compounds"
Un. 23–15   s· evidence of the senses
No. 2– 3   s· and hydra-headed mind-healing
Peo. 12– 8   s·, imaginary laws of matter
spurned
Mis. 122–21   Love divine s·, lessens not the
spurneth
Ret. 18–16   eaglet that s· the sod,
Po. 64– 7   eaglet that s· the sod,
spurns
Mis. 385–17   diviner sense, that s· such toys,
Po. 48–11   diviner sense, that s· such toys,
squadron
Pan. 14–26   blotted out the Spanish s·.
square
Mis. 143– 3   "s·" of moral sentiments.
Pul. 24–26   * twenty-one and one half feet s·
'02. 17–19   s· accounts with each passing hour.
My. 309–22   * a small, s· box building
squarely
Mis. 378–17   He answered kindly and s·,
   399–24   (Heaven chiselled s· good)
Pul. 16– 9   (Heaven chiselled s· good)
Po. 76– 8   (Heaven chiseled s· good)
My. 112–10   founded s· and only on the
squills
Mis. 240– 2   doctor's s· and bills
staff
Mis. 118–20   His rod and His s· comfort you.
   158–20   with sandals on and s· in hand,
   358–28   awaiting, with s· in hand,
Man. 43– 1   or treats our Leader or her s·
My. 174– 9   city marshal and his s·
   292– 9   His rod and His s· comfort the
   310–14   s· of the Governor of New Hampshire.
   312–25   Governor of the State and his s·,
stage
Mis. 108–17   second s· of human consciousness,
   109–11   most hopeful s· of mortal mentality.
   109–23   through the second to the third s·,
   200–13   applicable to every s· and state of
   215–25   at this s· use the sword of Spirit.
   288–22   in every state and s· of being.
   355– 2   present s· of progress in C. S.

stage
Mis. 356–22   second s· of mental development
   357–19   third s· of mental growth
Ret. 81–30   at every s· of advancement.
No. 38–23   of any other state or s· of being.
'01. 17–20   had overcome a difficult s·
   17–22   next more difficult s· of action
   28– 2   last s· of the great naturalist's
Hea. 13–14   cured the incipient s· of fever.
My. 75– 4   * holding the centre of the s·
   236–28   of great importance at this s· of
   239–28   state and s· of mental
stages
Mis. 56–27   *successive s· of existence*
   100–31   indicates the different s· of
   107–20   three states and s· of human
   112–12   The mental s· of crime,
   206–11   advancing s· of C. S.
   208–17   states and s· of human error
   355–11   pass through three s· of growth.
   357–20   all s· and states of being ;
Ret. 45–12   first s· of mortal existence
Un. 50–16   no material states or s· of
'01. 17–16   the last s· of consumption,
   27–28   * goes through three s·.
   28– 1   passed through the first two s·,
   29– 6   advancing s· of their careers
'01. 33– 8   * decaying s· of religion,
My. 47– 8   * a few of the s· of its progress,
   47–14   * epoch-marking s· of its growth,
   80– 5   * of consumption in its advanced s·,
   105– 8   healed consumption in its last s·,
   107–30   s· of organic and inflammatory
   304–26   * goes through three s·.
stagger
My. 79– 8   * must s· their faith not a little
staging
Peo. 11–10   another s· for diviner claims,
stagnant
My. 149–30   waken the s· waters
staid
My. 79–15   * this occurred in s· old Boston,
stain
Mis. 141–20   s· the early history of C. S.
Ret. 86–11   Cleanse every s· from this wanderer's
stained
Pul. 24–28   * The windows of s· glass
   58–30   * portrait of her in s· glass ;
'02. 10– 9   footprints . . . are s· with blood,
   14– 9   * not like Cæsar, s· with blood,
My. 248– 5   * not like Caesar, s· with blood,
stains
Mis. 249–19   to remove s· or vermin.
   327–32   wipes away the blood s·,
staircases
Pul. 25–14   * the s· are of iron,
stairs
Ret. 76–14   meet on the s· which lead
Pul. 25–15   marble s· of rose pink,
My. 342– 3   * lady slowly descending the s·.
stairways
My. 46– 2   * commodious foyer and broad s·,
   68–28   * seven broad marble s·,
stake
Mis. 277–13   The s· and scaffold have never
   345–11   bound him to the s·,
   368–24   and at a fearful s·.
No. 44–14   sentence men to the dungeon or s·
Peo. 13–20   they bound him to the s·,
stale
Mis. 30–22   The s· saying that C. S.
stalk
Mis. 331– 1   construct the o·, instruct the ear,
   396– 4   Where ghosts and goblins s·.
Po. 58–16   Where ghosts and goblins s·.
stalled
Mis. 121–13   S· theocracy would make this
stall-fed
No. 43– 6   whether s· or famishing,
stamp
Hea. 19–16   We need it to s· our religions
stamped
Pul. 42–16   * golden beehive s· upon it,
stand
Mis. 16–30   Here you s· face to face with
   16–32   You s· before the awful detonations
   82–10   s· upon the shore of eternity,
   99–16   to s· a long siege,
   104–20   s· the friction of false self-hood

stand

Mis.	125–12	not s· waiting and weary ;
	140–29	church will s· the storms of ages :
	158–20	I s· with sandals on
	178–18	* s· before you to preach a sermon
	197–27	and therefore cannot s·.
	227– 3	may s· in the place of a virtue ;
	276–31	Scientists s· firmer than ever
	307–20	I must s· on this absolute basis
	347–17	Between the two I s· still ;
	369– 7	to s· erect on sublime heights,
	392– 2	monarch, at whose feet I s·,
	400– 5	be in thy place : S·, not sit.
Man.	75–17	with the land whereon they s·,
Chr.	55–26	Behold, I s· at the door, — *Rev.* 3 : 20.
Ret.	90– 3	or seek to s· in God's stead.
Un.	64–16	s· on the summit of Mont Blanc ;
Pul.	16–17	be in thy place ; S·, not sit.
	26–10	* lamp s· of the Renaissance period
	84– 7	* shall s· the new man with
Pan.	2–23	s·, in the term pantheism, for the
	9– 5	in paganism they s· for gods ;
'01.	25–30	a kingdom . . . that cannot s·.
Peo.	7–16	* "Sculptors of life are we as we s·
Po.	20– 2	monarch, at whose feet I s·,
	76–16	be in thy place : S·, not sit.
My.	34– 2	s· in his holy place? — *Psal.* 24 : 3.
	36–29	* to s· as an enduring monument,
	106–16	would weary, and the world s· still.
	150–15	S· by the limpid lake,
	158–28	s· through all time for
	205– 3	"S· fast therefore in the — *Gal.* 5 : 1.
	216– 5	All systems of religion s· on this
	224–31	* "They also serve who only s· and
	230– 4	s· when those have passed to rest.
	302–18	I s· in relation to this century as
	305–11	manuscripts . . . s· in evidence.
	322– 5	* facts . . . and they must s·.
	344– 4	rays collectively s· for Christ,
	344–24	* How does C. S. s· as to

standard

Mis.	50–21	a change . . . to the divine s·,
	53–18	the s· of metaphysics ;
	186– 8	far below man's original s·,
	232–12	s· of right that regulates human
	233–12	s· of metaphysical healing
	233–21	think the s· of C. S. too high
	233–27	having a true s·,
	233–29	they only who adhere to that s·.
Man.	61–21	s· of musical excellence ;
Ret.	53– 5	s· of genuine C. S.
Un.	38–27	not up to the Christian s· of Life,
Pul.	10–16	planted your s· on the rock
No.	2– 1	on its s· have emblazoned
	10–11	but one s· statement, one rule,
	46–15	Puritan s· of undefiled religion.
	46–17	let us lift their s· higher,
Pan.	11–21	the original s· of man
'01.	2– 6	the healing s· of C. S.
	2–12	the s· of Christ's healing
	34–10	look for the s· of Christianity
Peo.	10–15	alone grasps the s· of liberty,
My.	41–18	* maintains the perfect s· of truth
	180–11	primordial s· of Truth.
	283–24	is the s· of C. S.

standard-bearers

Mis.	177–11	against the lives of our s·.

Standard Dictionary

Pan.	2–19	S· D· has it that pantheism

Standard dictionary's

'01.	3–11	S· d· definition of God,

standards

Mis.	353– 6	are neither s· nor models.
My.	91–11	* or his moral s· debased
	224–24	to accept the latter as s·.

standest

Mis.	341–16	place whereon thou s·

standeth

Mis.	368– 9	* S· God within the shadow,

standing

Mis.	133–12	they love to pray s· in — *Matt.* 6 : 5.
	134–27	wickedness is s· in high places ;
	140– 4	and the church s· on it,
	178–22	* I should not be s· before you :
	301–25	injustice s· in a holy place.
Man.	36–21	members thereof in good s·,
	50–17	another member in good s·
	51–11	are in good and regular s·
	73– 8	Members in good s· with The
	73–13	Also members in good s·
	76–17	members of this Church in good s·.
Un.	49–19	S· in no basic Truth,
Pul.	6–17	* ailment of seven years' s·.

standing

'02.	16–18	angel, s· in the sun,
My.	9–14	* you, who are s· in the forefront
	64–18	* high s· of C. S. before the world.
	80– 3	* people of substance and of s·,
	81–31	* people of s· and of substance,
	126– 7	the recording angel, s· with
	199–18	This year, s· on the verge of the
	246– 4	in good and regular s·.
	296–28	s· and seating capacity,
	305–18	* "s· eighth in a list of twenty-two
	330–12	* by a Mason of good s·
	331– 9	* indicates her irreproachable s·

standing-room

My.	54–12	* ' No more s·.' "
	56–28	* there was not even s·.

standpoint

Mis.	14–21	appears to mortals from their s·
	52–30	up, to its spiritual s·.
	185–30	first spake from their s·
	228– 6	is to take a new s·
	289– 8	From a human s· of good,
	373–12	Neither material finesse, s·, nor
	379–22	a mental s· not understood,
Un.	29–16	from any s· of their own.
Pul.	69–19	* spiritual or metaphysical s·.
No.	9–10	their own s· of experience,
	12– 2	from a purely Christian s·.
Pan.	9–27	From a material s·,
My.	346– 1	* from the s· of C. S.,

standpoints

Peo.	1–16	from material to spiritual s·.

stands

Mis.	206–29	s· upon the mount of holiness,
	323–16	eventually s· in the valley
	364–17	s· on this Scriptural platform :
	399–25	on this rock . . . S· His church,
Man.	71–12	The Mother Church s· alone ;
	104– 7	It s· alone, uniquely
Ret.	70–27	he virtually s· at the head of
	80–10	* with patience He s· waiting,
Un.	29– 1	Soul s· in this relation to
Pul.	16–10	on this rock . . . S· His church,
	20– 1	The land whereon s· The
	61–17	* s· at the head of this sketch.
Rud.	2– 5	s· for one of the three subjects,
No.	3– 5	foe who s· in its way.
	33–22	Jesus' sacrifice s· preeminently
'01.	4– 2	then Love . . . s· for God
'02.	14– 5	the land whereon it s·.
Hea.	11–10	it s· and is the miracle of
Po.	46– 7	But gracefully it s·
	76– 9	on this rock . . . S· His church,
My.	28–21	s· as the visible symbol
	45–15	* edifice s· a fitting monument
	45–31	* s· a material type of
	46– 4	* the great structure s·, silently
	46– 8	* In the best sense it s·
	49– 7	* s· a great chance of sweeping
	55–12	* The Mother Church now s·.
	143–15	s· the eternal fact of C. S.
	143–21	s· forever as an eternal
	159–13	s· at the vestibule of C. S.,
	194–14	s· for human self lost in
	194–15	s· for meekness and might,
	227–21	above quotation . . . s· for this :
	227–26	it s· side by side with
	247– 1	It s· for the inalienable,
	254–23	It s· for the inalienable,
	260– 9	Christmas s· for the real,
	295–18	It s· the storm.
	338–24	s· alone in word and deed,
	344– 3	If we say that the sun s· for God,

standstill

Ret.	38–18	He had come to a s·
My.	171–23	* Her carriage came to a s·

stanza

Un.	26–20	protest against this s· of Bowring's,

Star

Pul.	90– 7	* S·, Kansas City, Mo.

star

Mis.	1– 4	watched the appearing of a s· ;
	164–12	spiritual idea . . . appeared as a s·.
	168–20	behold the appearing of the s· !"
	276– 2	and the crescent with a s·.
	320– 9	s· that looked lovingly down
	320–17	polar s·, fixed in the heavens
	320–23	The s· of Bethlehem
	320–23	is the s· of Boston,
	320–27	s· of Bethlehem is the light of
	321– 1	wise men follow this guiding s· ;
Chr.	53– 4	One lone, brave s·.

star
Chr.	53–37	faith's pale s· now blends
	55– 4	bright and morning s·. — *Rev.* 22 : 16.
	57– 4	give him the MORNING S·. — *Rev.* 2 : 28.
Ret.	20–20	S· of my earthly hope,
Un.	17– 4	* "Hitch your wagon to a s·."
Pul.	25–18	* sunburst with a seven-pointed s·,
	26– 2	* electric lights in the form of a s·,
	28– 4	* s· of Bethlehem shines down from
	28– 9	* the crown and the s· are presented
	42–21	* a huge seven-pointed s·
	42–21	* a s· of lilies resting on palms,
Po.	9– 2	Turned to his s· of idolatry.
	46–15	Bright as her evening s·,
	68–19	s· of our friendship arose
	68–21	and bright as the s·,
	78– 9	s· whose destiny none may outrun ;
My.	110– 5	this Bethlehem s· looks down

stark
Po.	53– 2	paint the gray, s· trees,

starless
Mis.	268–16	no shipwreck in a s· night

starlight
Ret.	23–12	could not prophesy sunrise or s·.
Po.	3– 1	s· blends with morning's hue,

star-lit and **starlit**
Mis.	400– 1	*Laus Deo*, night s·
Pul.	2– 8	soft shimmer of its s· dome.
	16–13	*Laus Deo*, night s·
Po.	8–11	watching alone o'er the s· glow,
	76–12	*Laus Deo*, night s·

starry
Po.	8–15	Its s· hopes and its waves

stars
Mis.	188– 4	when the s· first sang together,
	254–19	s· from the spiritual heavens,
	259–20	morning s· sang together, — *Job* 38 : 7.
	319–27	feel themselves alone among the s·.
	332– 1	Mind is seen kindling the s·,
	340–28	like the s·, comes out in
	360–13	s· of the first magnitude
	360–13	fixed s· in the heavens of Soul.
	395– 6	The s· reject his pains,
Ret.	28–27	higher than the s· of heaven.
	65–28	magnitude and distance of the s·,
Un.	14– 7	"the s· also," — *Gen.* 1 : 16.
	17– 6	s· in their courses — *Judg.* 5 : 20.
	42–14	morning s· sang together, *Job* 38 : 7.
Pul.	4–18	water may help to hide the s·,
	83–29	* a crown of twelve s·." — *Rev.* 12 : 1.
Pan.	3–31	his spotted skin, the s· ;
'00.	12– 3	"holdeth the seven s· — *Rev.* 2 : 1.
'02.	15–23	steadfast s· watched over the world,
Po.	2–15	s·, so cold, so glitteringly bright,
	57–13	The s· reject his pains,
	70–18	The while the glad s· sang
	73– 7	And the s· peep out,
My.	13–25	reach the s· with divine overtures,
	125–22	are s· in my crown of rejoicing.

start
Mis.	53–12	to s· the patient's recovery ?
	215–11	or s· from wrong motives.
	235–22	s· the wheels of reason aright,
	366–24	s· from this false premise,
'00.	15– 7	s· forward with true ambition.
'01.	27–16	s· thirty years ago without a
Hea.	4– 1	unlimited Mind cannot s· from
My.	5– 3	man is supposed to s· from dust
	201–18	not to a s·, but to a tenure of
	215–16	I earned the means with which to s· a
	308–23	as they were about to s· for church.

started
Mis.	107–18	it never s· with time,
	139–15	I s· the *Journal* of C. S.,
Ret.	38–15	s· for Lynn to see me.
	38–16	s· for Boston with my finished
	52–20	I s· it, April, 1883, as editor and
Un.	34–11	wherewith we s· :
'01.	17–13	and s· the Great Cause
	17–18	that s· the inquiry, What is it ?
My.	189– 2	s· in this sublime ascent,
	304–16	I s· *The C. S. Journal*,

starting
Mis.	51–26	* s· fresh, as from a second birth,
Pul.	79–10	* which, s· fifteen years ago,
No.	20–16	of an infinite Mind s· from
'01.	29–26	To aid my students in s·
My.	50–11	* s· out on their labors
	204–21	when s· this great Cause,
	312–31	s· that educational system

startle
Mis.	70–13	should s· him from the dream

startled
Mis.	324–19	S· beyond measure at beholding
Pul.	71–14	* s· and greatly discomfited
Peo.	13–12	On the s· ear of humanity
My.	294– 9	the s· or the unrighteous
	307–12	s· me by saying what I cannot forget

startles
Hea.	5–11	clergymen s· us by saying

startling
Mis.	84– 3	to receive s· announcements.
	193– 1	entertaining the s· inquiries,
	278–32	led to some s· departures
	301–10	There are s· instances of
	361–13	understood in s· contradiction of
Ret.	50– 6	a s· sum for tuition
'01.	21–17	s· ignorance of C. S.
My.	9–21	pledged yourselves with s· grace
	99–25	* with a rapidity that is s·,

starts
Mis.	325–19	s· up in blank amazement
	339– 8	to-morrow s· from to-day
My.	213– 5	It s· factions and engenders
	288– 1	it s· the wheels of right reason,

starve
Ret.	90– 9	left them to s· or to stray.

starving
Pan.	15– 1	fed her s· foe,

State
Mis.	11– 5	abide by our S· statutes ;
	144– 2	New Hampshire, my native S·,
	251–10	of this city and of my native S·
	263–24	aid and protection of S· laws.
	305– 1	* women representing each S·
Man.	45–26	under the *laws* of the S·.
	70–17	located in the same S·,
	70–18	on a statute of said S·,
	70–20	of the churches in said S·.
	98–21	S· Committees on Publication
	98–25	in each S· of the United States
	99– 3	the S· of California shall be
Ret.	4– 6	in the S· of New Hampshire.
	6–25	Legislature of his native S·,
	7– 2	the largest vote of the S· ;
	49–19	thank the S· for its charter,
Pul.	7– 4	especially the laws of the S·
	20– 9	by means of a statute of the S·,
	24–24	* Mrs. Eddy's native S·.
	41– 5	* From every S· in the Union,
	57– 5	* from every S· in the Union,
	68–11	* residence in her native S·.
No.	44–21	will again unite Church and S·,
'02.	20–25	metropolis of my native S·,
Peo.	12–11	as with an inhuman S· law ;
My.	94–22	* from every S· in the Union
	138–25	* S· OF NEW HAMPSHIRE,
	157– 8	* capital city of your native S·.
	167–26	the laws of my native S·.
	184– 9	Scientists of my native S·
	186– 2	forests of our native S·
	196– 5	a S· whose metropolis is called the
	196– 8	engrafted in church and S· :
	204–16	IN COMPLIANCE WITH THE S· LAWS
	204–19	practice of C. S. in your S·,
	227– 9	under the protection of S·
	270– 9	newspapers of my native S·
	269–28	the capital of my native S·
	312–25	The Governor of the S·
	326–14	the S· where my husband,
	320–15	the S· that so signally honored
	327– 2	practice of C. S. in that S·.
	327– 4	New Hampshire, my native S·,
	327–16	* practice of C. S. in our S·.
	327–22	* representative men of our dear S·
	327–29	* when the laws of every S·
	328–21	* healers of this sect in the S·.
	328–28	* to carry them on in this S·,
	331– 7	* the Governor of the S·,
	340–15	of making laws for the S·
	340–21	leaders of our rock-ribbed S·.
	341– 5	on the escutcheon of this S·,

state (noun)
affairs of
My.	340–26	to rule . . . the affairs of s·.

and stage
Mis.	288–22	in every s· and stage of being.
My.	239–28	The millennium is a s· and stage of

any other
No.	38–23	any other s· or stage of being.

Christian
Mis.	229–25	A calm, Christian s· of mind

Christianity's
Mis.	373–20	a sketch of Christianity's s·,

first
Mis.	108–18	The first s·, namely, the knowledge of

state (noun)

harmonious
Un. 51–18 none . . . lost their harmonious s`,

healthy
My. 14–25 * but it is in such a healthy s`

induced
My. 211–32 s` induced by this secret evil

last
Mis. 59– 9 in which the last s` of patients
Rud. 9– 1 last s` of that man — Matt. 12 : 45.
No. 5–28 makes the last s` of one's patients

material
Mis. 64–30 or of a material s` and universe,

mental
Mis. 107–25 this deplorable mental s` is
109–20 Their mental s` is not desirable,
112–17 the mental s` called moral idiocy.
174–24 kingdom of heaven . . . is a mental s`.
220–18 The patient's mental s` is now the
229– 2 This mental s` prepares one to
355–13 the mental s` of his patient.
Ret. 54–17 this mental s` called belief ;
Rud. 9–18 his mental s` weighs against his
10–23 erroneous physical and mental s`.
My. 349– 6 disease is a mental s` or error

normal
Mis. 200– 3 regarded good as the normal s`

objective
Ret. 34–19 objective s` of the mortal mind,

of agitation
Pul. 51–11 * more or less in a s` of agitation.

of being
Mis. 161–12 approximation to this s` of being
No. 5–18 and is itself a s` of being,
17–17 there is no fallen s` of being ;

of combat
Mis. 216– 2 your own s` of combat with error.

of consciousness
Mis. 219–25 s` of consciousness made manifest
367–21 evil is a different s` of consciousness.
'02. 9–16 urging a s` of consciousness

of evil thoughts
Mis. 18–25 entering into a s` of evil thoughts,

of exhilaration
Pul. 36–16 * a s` of exhilaration and energy

of existence
Mis. 34–18 in our present s` of existence,
34–20 pass on to their s` of existence,
42– 7 still in a conscious s` of existence ;
42–27 recognize a better s` of existence.

of false consciousness
Mis. 222– 6 This s` of false consciousness

of feeling
Mis. 222– 8 conviction of his wrong s` of feeling
229– 6 would catch their s` of feeling

of health
Mis. 219–25 a s` of health is but a
My. 349– 3 A scientific s` of health

of human existence
Mis. 200–14 stage and s` of human existence.

of mind
Mis. 112–31 This s` of mind is the
115– 7 this s` of mind in the teacher
203–21 a s` of mind which rends the veil
204–23 this s` of mind permeates with
229–25 calm, Christian s` of mind
348–28 in a proper s` of mind.
350–21 An individual s` of mind
Un. 56–11 are significant of that s` of mind
My. 116– 8 This s` of mind is sickly ;

of misled consciousness
Mis. 222–12 In this s` of misled consciousness,

of mortality
Mis. 64–28 that he is in a s` of mortality.

of mortal mind
No. 8–24 this s` of mortal mind,
My. 109– 1 subjective s` of mortal mind.

of mortal thought
Mis. 44–19 s` of mortal thought made manifest

of perfection
Mis. 14– 8 his original s` of perfection,
78–25 fallen from a s` of perfection ?

of spiritual perfection
My. 345–23 a s` of spiritual perfection.

of thought
Mis. 105–25 their own subjective s` of thought,
My. 221–25 correct or incorrect s` of thought,

probationary
Un. 3– 6 pass through another probationary s`

ring of
'02. 3–25 hallow the ring of s`.

spiritual
My. 244–16 man's spiritual s` in God's own

stricken
Mis. 203–20 stricken s` of human consciousness,

state (noun)

subjective
Mis. 24–19 subjective s` which it names matter,
86–26 subjective s` of high thoughts.
102–26 subjective s` of mortal and material
105–25 their own subjective s` of thought.
266– 8 subjective s` of his own mind
My. 109– 1 subjective s` of mortal mind.
265–26 reflect this purified subjective s`

such a
My. 345– 1 see that your mind is in such a s`

Mis. 138–20 to the s` of general growth
358– 6 S` honors perish,
My. 211–30 in a s` of semi-individuality,

state (verb)
Mis. 49– 8 had the skill and honor to s`,
131–27 let her s` the value thereof,
132–14 you s` that you would "like to
297–16 s`, in unmistakable language,
349–23 will s` that I preached four years,
Man. 57–13 to s` definitely the purpose
Ret. 26–26 could first s` this Principle,
Pul. 80–17 * but simply s` the fact.
My. vi– 4 * to s` truth absolutely in a simpler
24–17 * We are prompted to s`,
50–13 * for their records s`,
51–21 * but, as the records s`,
99–19 * s` that the contribution baskets
224–21 My books s` C. S. correctly.
242–13 you must s` its Principle correctly,
314–14 the court record may s` that
334–15 * We can s` Mrs. Eddy's teaching
354– 5 it is due the field to s` that I
356–14 will you please s` that within

State Commissioner
Pul. 20– 8 not, however, through the S· C·,

State Committee
Man. 99–26 S· C· shall be appointed by

stated
Mis. 57–27 s` in mathematical order,
289–28 fairly s` by a magistrate
318– 4 brotherhood of man is s`
Ret. 37–15 Mind-healing as therein s`.
61–27 demand that C. S. be s`
78–20 other than is s` in S. and H.
87–14 Let some of these rules be here s`.
88–24 s` occupant of that pulpit.
Pul. 43–26 * heretofore s` in The Herald,
73–22 * She s` that man of himself
No. 22–22 is not s`, and is impossible.
My. 54–23 * "It should be here s`
66–12 * what use . . . has not been s`,
225–27 In their textbook it is clearly s`
313–17 as s` by McClure's Magazine.
314–28 just as I have s` them.
322–26 * so clearly s` that I was surprised
342–24 perfecting of man s` scientifically."
346–21 * s` that her successor would be
361– 5 All I say is s` in C. S.

State House
Pul. 47–22 * one mile from the S· H·
My. 68– 8 * size of the dome on the S· H·,
68–12 * higher than that of the S· H·.
86– 4 * loved its golden S· H· dome,
(see also **Massachusetts State House**)

stateliness
My. 63–25 * its purity, s`, and vastness ;

stately
Mis. 239–12 draw up before a s` mansion ;
245–10 s` goings of C. S.,
332–15 midst the s` palms,
Un. 5–26 s` goings of this wonderful part
Pul. 16–18 Cold, silent, s` stone,
44–17 * chapter sub-title
My. 23–28 * As the s` structure grows
36–25 * By these s` walls ;
84–14 * s` cupola is a fitting crown

statement

abstract
Mis. 200–32 abstract s` that all is Mind,

admits in
Hea. 15–17 admits in s` what he denies in proof?

basal
Mis. 27–10 the pith of the basal s`,

by Mrs. Eddy
My. 356–12 chapter sub-title

complete
Ret. 37– 2 the complete s` of C. S.,

correct
Mis. 14–13 begin with the correct s`,

corrections of the
Mis. 133– 1 not delay corrections of the s`

statement

definite
My. 343–11 * Here, then, was the definite s·
distinct
Ret. 34– 8 or give me one distinct s·
Pul. 47–14 * any distinct s· of the Science
64–19 * gave her no distinct s· of
error of
Mis. 56–21 Organic life is an error of s·
following
Mis. 133–21 in making the following s· :
Un. 7– 8 to make also the following s· :
My. 141–20 * According to the following s·,
157–21 * Mrs. Eddy made the following s· :
317– 1 * following s·, which was published
her
My. 319–13 * confirm her s· regarding the
his
My. 320– 7 * his s· of what he had done
his own
My. 330 8 * contradicting his own s·,
in Christian Science
Un. 1– 9 whose s· in C. S.
in my letter
My. 146– 8 The s· in my letter
its
Man. 43–24 not correct in its s·
Mrs. Eddy's
My. 317– 8 chapter sub-title
my
Mis. 247–13 understand my s· of the Science
My. 241–22 * said that my s· was wrong,
303–16 my s· of C. S. would be
317–12 criticisms of my s· of C. S.,
of being
Ret. 94– 1 this scientific s· of being.
My. 19– 7 * "the scientific s· of being,"
33– 4 * "the scientific s· of being"
111–26 "The scientific s· of being"
of Deity
Hea. 4–28 our inconsistent s· of Deity,
of existence
Mis. 182–26 metaphysical s· of existence
of Hudson
Pul. 54–12 * We accept the s· of Hudson :
of the Christ
Pul. 74–24 one conclusion and s· of the Christ
of the Science
Mis. 247–13 my s· of the Science
Ret. 78–17 s· of the Science of Mind-healing,
Pul. 47–14 * s· of the Science of Mind-healing.
64–19 * s· of the Science of Mind-healing.
pantheistic
No. 29–13 Is this pantheistic s· sound
regarding a
Pul. 74– 5 * regarding a s· made by
remarkable
Pul. 63–14 * This is a remarkable s·,
scientific
Ret. 94– 1 this scientific s· of being.
'00. 5– 2 This scientific s· of the origin,
'01. 8– 4 Is this scientific s· more
23–11 scientific s·, tho divine Principle,
Hea. 9–22 scientific s· that evil is unreal ;
My. 19– 7 * "the scientific s· of being,"
33– 4 * "the scientific s· of being"
111–26 "The scientific s· of being"
simple
'01. 22–30 its absolute simple s· as to
My. 350–27 This simple s· of oneness
such a
Pul. 75– 8 Such a s· would not only be false,
No. 29–18 such a s· is a shocking reflection
that
No. 4–18 vouches for the validity of that s·.
thereof
Man. 55–23 contrary to the s· thereof
the within
My. 315–17 * made oath that the within s·
this
Mis. 16–29 this s· demands demonstration.
76– 5 This s· of our Master
201– 1 this s· receives the
Ret. 58– 2 then departing from this s·
93–18 This s· is in substance identical
Hea. 16– 6 demonstrating of this s·?
My. 52–29 * This s· "Phare Pleigh"
220– 5 This s· should be so interpreted
270–23 to the truth of this s·.
276–22 * she has given out this s· :
299–20 subscribe to this s· ;
338– 9 * fully corroborate this s·.
unqualified
Hea. 7–27 unqualified s· of the duty
unscientific
Mis. 217–10 fallacy of an unscientific s·

statement

was made
My. 346–24 * when the s· was made,
your
Mis. 133– 6 In refutation of your s·
My. 242– 2 scientifically correct in your s·
322– 9 * I have just read your s·

Mis. 92– 4 s· of the inexhaustible topics
Ret. 84– 1 s· of the inexhaustible topics
No. 10–12 there is but one standard s·,
My. 14–14 * good authority for the s·
311–12 My reply to the s· that

statements

Mis. 19–21 one who abides by his s·
56–23 the correctness of my s·,
78–19 false s· and claims.
295–18 flaunting and floundering s·
Un. 20– 4 We undo the s· of error by
20– 5 Through these three s·,
No. 43–23 Stealing or garbling my s·
Hea. 3–26 three s· of one Principle.
16–10 abide by your s·, and
My. 53–27 * some very interesting s·,
58– 9 * s· that have been made
79–26 * making their remarkable s·
112–18 demonstrates . . . its s·,
138–20 s· herein made by me
138–27 * s· contained in the annexed
143– 8 chapter sub-title
235–25 adopt as truth the above s·?
320–18 * did not endorse all the s·
321–18 * the manner in which the s·
330–11 * s·, relating to her husband

State Militia
My. 309–13 New Hampshire S· M·,

Staten Island
My. 363– 7 First Church . . . S· I·,

state prison
My. 175–15 well-conducted jail and s· p·,

States (see also States')
Man. 99– 4 as though it were two S·,
99–15 This By-Law applies to all S·
Ret. 6–22 admitted to the bar in two S·,
52–16 branch associations in other S·,
Pul. 41–15 * and even from the distant S·
'02. 3–10 and joy in the sisterhood of S·.
Peo. 10–11 It were well if the sister S·
My. 30–17 * from Hawaii, from the coast S·
326– 9 * in the Southern and Northern S·
327– 6 to practise C. S. in these S·
340–11 in excess of other S·,
340–12 In many of the S· in our Union
344–22 * the health laws of the S·

states

all
Mis. 208–17 All s· and stages of human error
conflicting
My. 293–13 conflicting s· of the human mind,
material
Un. 50–16 In reality there are no material s·
of being
Mis. 357–20 all stages and s· of being ;
of existence
Un. 49–17 not . . . two opposite s· of existence.
of false belief
Un. 50–21 but s· of false belief,
of mind
Mis. 221–15 these s· of mind will stultify the
Pul. 87–22 More effectual . . . are our s· of mind,
subjective
Mis. 73–20 subjective s· of false sensation
260–16 are its subjective s· ;
286–20 subjective s· of the human erring
367– 5 subjective s· of error or
Rud. 10–10 the subjective s· of thought,
No. 14– 7 subjective s· of mortal mind.
16–12 subjective s· of evil, called
these
Mis. 3–22 imparts these s· to the body ;
221–15 these s· of mind will stultify the
three
Mis. 107–19 three s· and stages of human

Mis. 42–10 s· that spiritualization of thought
244– 8 He further s· that God cannot
371–.3 the gentleman aforesaid s·,
Pul. 47–10 * s· that she sought knowledge
My. 50–30 * The record of May 23, . . . s· :
309–26 McClure's Magazine s· :
330–16 * who she s· was of Charleston,
333–22 * The Chronicle s· :
336–11 * In this book (p. 20) she also s·,

States'
  My. 309–15 strong believer in *S·* rights,
statesmanship
  My. 277– 5 settled peacefully by *s·*
stateswoman
  My. 297– 2 philanthropist, moralist, and *s·*,
stating
  Ret. 58– 1 *S·* the divine Principle,
station
  Mis. 291–28 *s·* justice and gratitude as
stationary
  Mis. 266–10 *S·* in the background,
  Ret. 93–14 *s·* power, stillness, and strength ;
stationed
  My. 71– 1 * chimes, *s·* in one of the towers,
stations
  My. 82–24 * *s·* were taxed to the utmost
  260–12 it hath . . . no half-way *s·*.
statistics
  Mis. 185–22 having no need of *s·* by which to
  271–28 * following history and *s·*
  '00. 7– 3 *s·* show the annual death-rate
  My. 92–18 * mere *s·* give a feeble impression
  92–21 * The *s·* have been ridiculed by
  93–27 * certain *s·* brought to light
  181–25 The *s·* of mortality show that
  227–30 *S·* show that C. S. cures
statuary
  Pul. 65–19 * arrangement of *s·* and paintings
statue
  Mis. 224– 8 mob had broken the head of his *s·*
statuesque
  Mis. 301–15 sincere and morally *s·*
  Pan. 10–28 Whatever promotes *s·* being,
statuette
  My. 258–30 beautiful *s·* in alabaster
stature
  Mis. 15–25 fulness of the *s·* of man in Christ
  102– 1 nature and *s·* of Christ,
  172–14 and he arrives at fulness of *s·* ;
  227–28 grows into the full *s·* of wisdom,
  Un. 2–24 *s·* of manhood in Christ Jesus,
  No. 19–24 fulness of the *s·* of man in Christ.
  Pan. 11– 9 his *s·* in Christ, Truth,
  11–18 regain his native spiritual *s·*
  '01. 11– 1 fulness of his *s·* in Christ,
  My. 103–13 the *s·* of man in Christ
status
  Mis. 45–14 The moral *s·* of the man
  183–31 arrive at the true *s·* of man
  264–25 moral and spiritual *s·* of thought
  357– 9 above the present *s·* of religion
  Ret. 57–28 making mortality the *s·* and rule of
  Un. 39–21 the immortal *s·* of man,
  No. 45–26 spiritual *s·* is urging its highest
  My. 29–24 * different *s·* before the world !
  111–13 spiritual *s·* of a perfect life
statute
  Mis. 119–25 prominent *s·* in the divine law,
  297–15 chapter sub-title
  297–17 *s·* in the *morale* of C. S. :
  Man. 70–18 confer on a *s·* of said State,
  Pul. 20– 9 but by means of a *s·* of the State,
  '02. 4–21 a divine *s·* for yesterday, and
statutes
  Mis. 11– 5 to abide by our State *s·* ;
  79–28 *for violation of medical s·*
  Peo. 12– 2 these divine *s·* of God :
  My. 220–29 human nature and human *s·*.
Statutes of 1883
  Chapter 268
  Mis. 272–13 * *S·* of 1883, Chapter 268,
St. Augustine
  Ret. 63–22 *St. A·* once said,
  '01. 28–10 none lived a more . . . than *St. A·*.
staunch
  My. 127–26 it is rich beyond price, *s·* and
  307–16 At that date I was a *s·* orthodox,
stay
  Mis. 302–32 *s·* within their own fields
  334– 3 none can *s·* His hand, — *Dan.* 4 : 35.
  335–26 get out of a burning house, or *s·*
  384–10 *S·* ! till the storms are o'er
  '00. 12–24 During St. Paul's *s·* in that city
  Po. 29–22 our saint, Our *s·*, alway.
  36– 9 *S·* ! till the storms are o'er
  My. 134– 8 to enhance or to *s·* its glory.
  173–23 short *s·* so pleasant.
  200– 7 none can *s·* His hand — *Dan.* 4 : 35.

stay
  My. 276– 6 or a dignified *s·* at home,
  280–20 none can *s·* His hand nor say
  315– 4 * During his *s·*, at different times,
stayed
  My. 290–15 mind is *s·* on Thee : — *Isa.* 26 : 3.
  327–18 * Scientists who *s·* on the field
stays
  My. 184–19 *s·* the shadows of years.
  311– 8 * "If this blind girl *s·*
St. Catherine
  (*see* **Eddy**)
stead
  Mis. 109–17 need of somethingness in its *s·*,
  Ret. 90– 3 or seek to stand in God's *s·*.
steadfast
  Mis. 12–15 watchful and *s·* in Love,
  172– 2 their claims and lives *s·* in Truth.
  176–17 *s·* in faith and love,
  189– 8 Nazarene's *s·* and true knowledge of
  267– 3 *s·* in their consciousness of
  400– 6 Grave, silent, *s·* stone,
  Ret. 26– 8 *s·* to the end in his obedience to
  50–20 *s·* justice, and strict adherence to
  '01. 34–22 be *s·*, abide and abound in faith,
  '02. 15–23 *s·* stars watched over the world,
  Hea. 2– 2 a calm and *s·* communion with God ;
  Po. 76–17 Grave, silent, *s·* stone,
  My. 108–28 I remain *s·* in St. Paul's faith,
  127– 7 *s·*, calm coherence in the ranks of
  155– 5 *s·* in Christ, always abounding in
  191– 9 *s·* in Love and good works.
  275–16 Love that is Life — is sure and *s·*.
steadfastly
  Mis. 19–16 *s·* flowing on to God,
  107– 8 plant the feet *s·* in Christ.
  110–19 wrought *s·* at the same
  149–30 abide *s·* in the faith of Jesus' words :
  241– 2 should centre as *s·* in God
  338–11 hope holding *s·* to good
  Ret. 90–24 walk *s·* in wisdom's ways.
  No. 9–19 point *s·* to the power of grace
  Pan. 13– 1 witness more *s·* to its practical
  My. 50–15 * turned *s·* from the mortal side,
  153–16 it keeps *s·* the great and first
  251–28 Cherish *s·* this fact.
  272– 1 *s·* and actively strives for
steadfastness
  '02. 1– 5 increase in number, unity, *s·*.
steadily
  Mis. 160– 6 lives *s·* on, through time and
  315–27 shall *s·* and patiently strive to
  Man. 18– 8 little Church went *s·* on,
  My. 53–20 * number of attendants *s·* increased.
  53–28 * *s·* increasing interest in C. S.
  56–21 * attendance . . . *s·* grew,
  118– 3 *s·* go on promoting the true Principle
  181–27 Since that time it has *s·* decreased.
  191– 6 C. S. is spreading *s·*
steadiness
  Mis. 204–26 gives *s·* to resolve,
steady
  Mis. 87–30 imagine they can . . . *s·* God's altar
  92–27 attempting to *s·* the ark of Truth,
  287–31 attempts to *s·* other people's altars,
  321– 8 sees the *s·* gain of Truth's idea
  342– 6 *s·* decline of spiritual light,
  386–16 a love that *s·* turns To God ;
  Ret. 84–16 attempting to *s·* the ark of Truth,
  No. 32–13 Mind-healing lifts with a *s·* arm,
  Po. 49–24 a love that *s·* turns
  My. 55–29 * *s·* increase in attendance.
  83–29 * made *s·* gains in recent years.
  94–10 * *s·*, consistent growth of the sect
  113–30 rapid and *s·* advancement of
  329–22 * recognizing the *s·* progress
steadying
  My. 278–19 *s·*, elevating power of
steal
  Mis. 2– 4 they *s·* from their neighbor,
  67– 7 "Thou shalt not *s·* ;" — *Ex.* 20 : 15.
  119–30 that others . . . *s·* your possessions,
  234–14 his effort to *s·* from others
  335–17 to murder, *s·*, commit adultery,
  354– 4 can *s·*, and lie and lie,
  No. 41–18 never admit such as come to *s·*
  '00. 8–11 may *s·* other people's good thoughts,
stealing
  Mis. 250–25 *s·* on an errand of mercy,
  324–22 *S·* cautiously away from
  Ret. 71–29 same as other forms of *s·*,
  No. 43–23 *S·* or garbling my statements

steam
  Peo. 10– 2 steam is more powerful

steam engine
  '02. 9–27 with the inventor of a *s· e·*?
      11–13 a *s· e·*, a submarine cable,
  My. 345–10 * the telephone, the *s· e·*

Stebbin's, Mrs.
  Mis. 157–20 relative to Mrs. *S·* case.

steel
  Pul. 82– 6 * *s·* tempered with holy resolve,

steep
  Mis. 206–28 the *s·* ascent of C. S.,
     397–23 O'er the hillside *s·*,
  Ret. 46– 4 O'er the hillside *s·*,
  Pul. 17– 3 O'er the hillside *s·*,
  Hea. 19–24 up the *s·* ascent, on to heaven,
  Po. 14– 2 O'er the hillside *s·*,
     53– 8 Light o'er the rugged *s·*.
  My. 229–21 scaling the *s·* ascent of

steepeth
  Po. 16–14 *s·* the trees when the day-god

steer
  Mis. 353–19 *s·* the regulator of mankind.

steering
  My. 232– 3 *S·* thus, the waiting waves

stellar
  Mis. 65– 6 *ipse dixit* as to the *s·* system
  No. 6–23 Science of the *s·* universe.

stem
  Mis. 162– 9 *s·* these rising angry elements,
    162–14 *s·* the tide of Judaism,
  Po. 46– 6 leaves have shed or bowed the *s·* ;

stenchpots
  Un. 57– 1 More obnoxious than Chinese *s·*

step
  advanced
    Mis. 311–12 to take this advanced *s·*
    My. 140–23 points the advanced *s·*.
  advancing
    My. 45–26 * for each advancing *s·*
  backward
    Mis. 340– 1 One backward *s·*, . . . has torn the
  each
    Mis. 117–21 watch that each *s·* be taken,
    My. 11 11 * grow into readiness for each *s·*,
    114–30 trace its teachings in each *s·*
  every
    Mis. 117–20 To point out every *s·* to a student
    '02. 10–30 walking every *s·* over the land route,
    Peo. 1– 2 Every *s·* of progress is a step more
    My. 215– 6 it prospered at every *s·*,
    234–12 guide them every *s·* of the way
  first
    Mis. 354–23 humility is the first *s·* in C. S.,
  forward
    Mis. 212–25 who will *s·* forward and
    '02. 3–11 Our nation's forward *s·* was
    14–18 every forward *s·* has been
  higher
    My. 142–19 a *s·* higher in their passage from
    151–30 it took a *s·* higher ;
  in advance
    My. 252–25 was a *s·* in advance.
  last
    My. 217–30 does not require the last *s·* to be
  light
    My. 342– 5 * walking . . . with light *s·*,
  next
    Mis. 193–22 next *s·* for ecclesiasticism to take,
    270–29 The next *s·* is Mind-medicine.
    My. 217–26 aids in taking the next *s·*
  one
    Mis. 212–14 one *s·* away from the direct line
    My. 217–25 "An improved belief is one *s·* out
  onward
    My. 10–29 * necessitates this onward *s·*.
  Scriptural
    Mis. 129–12 then take the next Scriptural *s·* :
  single
    Mis. 234–17 never has advanced man a single *s·*
  some
    Mis. 236–26 in some way or at some *s·*
  step by
    Mis. 18– 2 develop, step by *s·*, the original
  take
    Mis. 138–28 we all shall take *s·*
    My. 155–10 take *s·* with the twentieth century,
  this
    Ret. 13– 5 Before this *s·* was taken,
    My. 241– 7 * Students who are ready for this *s·*

  Mis. 359–17 to *s·* upon the Atlantic

step
  '00. 9–26 I have desired to *s·* aside
  Peo. 1– 2 is a *s·* more spiritual.
  My. 11–12 * never urged upon us a *s·* that

stepfather
  Ret. 20–25 his *s·* was not willing

stepped
  Mis. 162– 7 *s·* suddenly before the people

stepping
  My. 31–26 *S·* to the front of the platform,

stepping-stone
  Mis. 1–15 Humility is the *s·* to
  Un. 37– 8 *s·* to Life and happiness.
    56– 1 *s·* to the cosmos of
    61–25 *s·* to the understanding

steps
  Mis. 10–15 retrace their *s·*, and reinstate His
    231–19 one, two, three *s·*,
    347–18 take a few *s·*, then halt.
  Pul. 42–25 * the *s·* of the platform were
    58–18 * the *s·* marble,
  No. 34–24 *s·* of uplifted humanity,
  '00. 4–12 forward *s·* in religion,
  '02. 10–14 taking *s·* outward and upwards.
  My. 10–13 * taken *s·* in this direction,
    47– 6 * the *s·* by which this church
    65–18 * chapter sub-title
    110–11 guiding the *s·* of progress
    114–32 find these progressive *s·*
    129–19 plant thy *s·* in Christ,
    129–29 Trust God to direct your *s·*.
    141–16 * has taken *s·* to abolish
    196–17 should follow his *s·* : — *I Pet.* 2 : 21.
    211–12 its ascending *s·* of evil,
    302–30 upon the *s·* of its altar.

stereotype
  Mis. 245–26 seeking to *s·* infinite Truth,

stereotyped
  Mis. 232– 9 should religion be *s·*,
  No. 45–28 Truth cannot be *s·* ;

stern
  Mis. 74– 9 through the *s·* mandate of Science,
    254– 4 gentle entreaty, the *s·* rebuke
  Pan. 13–11 its *s·* condemnation of all error,
  '02. 2–13 has passed from *s·* Protestantism
  Po. 2– 1 *S·*, passionless, no soul
    23–14 A *s·* rebuke to wrong !
    30–15 *s·*, dark shadows cast on Thy
  My. 18–19 its *s·* condemnation of all error,
    247–20 not a *s·* but a loving look

sterner
  Ret. 23– 7 became clearer, they grew *s·*.

sternly
  Mis. 77–25 *s·* to rebuke the mortal belief

sternness
  Ret. 80–16 mingled *s·* and gentleness

stethoscope
  My. 105– 9 by verdict of the *s·*

Stetson
  Mrs.
    My. 350–24 * letter was forwarded . . . by Mrs. *S·*
    359–26 * Mrs. Eddy wrote to Mrs. *S·*
    361– 9 not seen Mrs. *S·* for over a year,
  Mrs. Augusta E.
    My. 357–27 Mrs. AUGUSTA E. *S·*, NEW YORK
    359–20 * written to Mrs. Augusta E. *S·*

stewards
  Pul. 15–14 designate those as unfaithful *s·*

Stewart
  Mr. and Mrs.
    Mis. 157– 8 to write, to Mr. and Mrs. *S·*,
  Rev. Samuel Barrett
    Ret. 42– 3 by the Rev. Samuel Barrett *S·*,

stick
  Mis. 370–21 braying donkey whose ears *s·* out
  My. 225–23 expected to *s·* to their text,
    308–24 declined to accept the *s·*,

sticklers
  My. 211– 1 *s·* for a false, convenient peace,

sticks
  Mis. 27– 8 C. S. *s·* to its text,
  '01. 14– 1 So long as we indulge . . . it *s·* to us

stifled
  Mis. 356– 8 they should be *s·* from lack of air

still
  Mis. ix–15 course of years *s·* and uniform,
    xi– 6 *s·* in advance of their time ;
    42– 7 is *s·* in a conscious state of
    99–24 *s·* live, and to-morrow speak

still

Mis.	124–27	and *s·* crowns Christianity :
	134–26	"*s·*, small voice" — *I Kings* 19 : 12.
	136– 5	I am *s·* with you on the field of
	138–27	"*s·*, small voice" — *I Kings* 19 : 12.
	146–13	and *s·* maintain this position.
	153–27	* Souls that are gentle and *s·*
	163–20	they *s·* live ; and are the basis
	166– 9	ideal Christ . . . is *s·* with us.
	170– 4	may *s·* believe in death
	174–32	"*s·*, small voice" — *I Kings* 19 : 12.
	209–25	happiness should *s·* attend it.
	230–24	* *S·* achieving, *s·* pursuing,
	233–17	*s·* worse in the eyes of Truth
	234–11	and rise — and *s·* rise
	234–27	to them *s·* more inconceivable.
	261–23	and *s·* saves mankind ;
	285–18	*s·* at work, deep down in
	307– 9	"Peace, be *s·*" — *Mark* 4 : 39.
	321–21	*S·* treading each temptation down,
	340–32	sin, and death *s·* appear
	347–17	Between the two I stand *s·* ;
	360–25	"*s·*, small voice" — *I Kings* 19 : 12.
	370– 6	spirit of evil is *s·* abroad ;
	398– 7	Make self-righteousness be *s·*,
Ret.	4– 7	*s·* cultivated and owned by
	12– 3	Minerva's silver sandals *s·*
	12– 5	echoes *s·* my day-dreams thrill,
	21– 8	learned that his mother *s·* lived,
	22–14	mortal life-battle *s·* wages,
	45– 1	Church of Christ, . . . *s·* goes on.
	46–13	Make self-righteousness be *s·*,
	60–15	"Be *s·*," — *Mark* 4 : 39.
	69– 9	insists *s·* upon the opposite
	69–26	voice of Truth *s·* calls :
	86– 7	Art thou *s·* unacquainted with thyself?
Un.	3– 2	and *s·* believe in matter's reality,
	4–14	as we get *s·* nearer Him,
	46–19	is *s·* claimed by the worldly-wise.
Pul.	13–16	They are dwellers *s·* in the
	17–12	Make self-righteousness be *s·*,
	27–29	* the windows are of *s·* more unique
	42– 4	* and at noon *s·* another.
	56–19	* "And *s·* we love the evil cause,
	67–16	* it was *s·* practically unknown
	82–15	* Too many *s·* are Jews who
Rud.	14– 2	and *s·* be Christian Scientists.
	14–22	If . . . are *s·* impecunious,
No.	1– 4	*s·*, small voice," — *I Kings* 19 : 12.
	11–13	and (worse *s·*) by those who
	12–26	immaterial, though *s·* individual.
	13–11	though the hiatus be longer *s·*
Pan.	10–20	better *s·*, they reform desperate
	14–14	*s·* guide and bless our
'01.	1–11	rise higher and *s·* higher
'02.	15–30	"*s·*, small voice" — *I Kings* 19 : 12.
Hea.	2–14	*s·* another Christian hero,
Peo.	11–17	hold . . . *s·* in bondage.
Po.	1– 1	unfallen *s·* thy crest !
	2–12	*s·* art thou drear and lone !
	2–19	thy deep silence is unbroken *s·*.
	14–11	Make self-righteousness be *s·*,
	16–19	when the winds are all *s·*.
	17– 4	in glory *s·* waiting for me.
	19– 1	oh, *s·* be it high,
	25–16	heart bore its grief and is *s·* !
	30– 9	thy *s·* fathomless Christ-majesty.
	53–19	*s·* and dead are all The vernal songs
	61– 1	Minerva's silver sandals *s·*
	61– 3	echoes *s·* my day-dreams thrill,
	65–12	'neath thy drap'ry *s·* lie.
	79–20	His likeness *s·* — Is satisfied.
My.	11–27	* *s·* remained for definite decision
	23– 7	* is *s·* with us, and will bless us
	31– 7	* "*S·*, *s·* with Thee ;"
	37–25	* will *s·* be the pretext for our
	56–26	* *s·* further provision must be made,
	106–16	and the world stand *s·*.
	117–13	the old question *s·* rampant?
	122–18	Are we *s·* searching diligently
	145–19	and *s·* be at home attending to
	161– 3	for which we are *s·* his debtors,
	185– 6	* *S·* achieving, *s·* pursuing,
	223–29	"Be *s·*, and know that I — *Psal.* 46 : 10.
	241–22	* I *s·* lived in my flesh.
	245–24	these credentials are *s·* required
	249– 5	"*s·* small voice" — *I Kings* 19 : 12.
	267–22	* another with a bitter sense of
	275– 8	"Be *s·*, and know that I — *Psal.* 46 : 10.
	279–13	is sufficient to *s·* all strife.
	282– 6	my hope must *s·* rest in God,
	287–16	so rise and *s·* rise to His image
	295–28	he *s·* lives, loves, labors.
	302–17	I *s·* must think the name is not
	305–22	I *s·* wait at the cross to
	307–23	*s·* think that it was profane.

still

My.	316– 4	I *s·* hear the harvest song
	319– 2	I should *s·* know that God's
	319–28	* and do so *s·*.
	331–24	* who *s·* extended their care and
	334–10	* *s·* contain the original account
		(*see also* **waters**)

stilled

Mis.	386– 4	yearnings come not, sighs are *s·*,
'02.	20– 3	voice of him who *s·* the tempest
Po.	49– 7	yearnings come not, sighs are *s·*,
My.	252–30	neither slumbers nor is *s·*
	278–16	chapter sub-title

stillness

Ret.	89– 1	eternal *s·* and immovable Love.
	93–15	stationary power, *s·*, and strength ;
Pul.	12– 3	impressive *s·* of the audience
Pan.	3– 9	find an indefinable pleasure in *s·*,
	3–10	nature's *s·* is voiced with
My.	29– 5	* a *s·* profound ;
	61–26	* in the dark *s·* of the night,
	79– 3	* in absolute *s·*, their eyes closed

stills

Chr.	53–12	That *s·* all strife.
'02.	5– 6	C. S. *s·* all distress over
	19–18	The thought of it *s·* complaint ;
Hea.	2– 6	*s·* the tempest of error ;

stimulate

Mis.	238–18	*s·* philanthropy and
No.	43– 7	to *s·* and sustain a good sermon.

stimulated

Mis.	214–11	This action of Jesus was *s·* by
No.	12–13	*s·* true Christianity in all ages,
My.	28–13	* has *s·* those gentle qualities

stimulates

Mis.	355–15	for the remainder only *s·*

sting

Mis.	96– 3	robbed . . . death of its *s·*.
	210–14	handles it, and takes away its *s·*,
	294–13	with *s·* ready for each kind touch,
Un.	48–10	deprives death of its *s·*,
Pul.	84– 4	* ingratitude of her *s·*,
Po.	31–21	wipes away the *s·* of death
My.	191–23	Death has lost its *s·*,

stings

Mis.	210– 9	because they have *s·*
	294–21	their *s·*, and jaws, and claws ;
Un.	45– 4	and it *s·* your heel,

stingy

'00.	2–16	idler earns little and is *s·* ;

stipulating

My.	250–16	*s·* three years as the term for its

stipulation

Mis.	381–16	*s·* for a judgment and a decree

stir

Mis.	210– 8	not to *s·* up these reptiles
	283– 5	*s·*, upset, and adjust his thoughts
	351–13	falsehood designed to *s·* up strife
	372–13	this book would produce a *s·*,
Ret.	80–13	it may *s·* the human heart
No.	1–15	*s·* of contending sentiments cease,
My.	150–17	This will *s·* your heart.
	244– 3	in order to avoid the *s·*

stirred

Mis.	127–32	needs often to be *s·*,
	390–16	To melting murmurs ye have *s·*
Ret.	40–21	demonstration so *s·* the doctors
Pul.	51–21	* belief has *s·* up feeling,
Po.	34– 4	Like thee, my voice had *s·*
	55–17	To melting murmurs ye have *s·*
My.	105– 2	had of a verity *s·* the people

stirreth

My.	104– 8	*s·* up the people." — *Luke* 23 : 5.
	104–15	"*s·* up the people" — *Luke* 23 : 5.
	222–18	*s·* up the people." — *Luke* 23 : 5.

stirring

Mis.	329–16	*s·* the soft breeze ;
My.	v– 4	* In these *s·* times

stirs

Mis.	391–12	It *s·* no thought of strife ;
Po.	38–11	It *s·* no thought of strife ;

St. James (*see also* **James**)

Ret.	31–19	As says *St. J·* : "Whosoever — *Jas.* 2 : 10.

St. John (*see also* **John, Revelator, St. John's**)

Mis.	21– 5	in the Revelation of *St. J·*,
	30– 8	*St. J·* spiritually discerned and
	205–11	in the words of *St. J·*,
	317–30	*St. J·* writes : "Whom God — *John* 3 : 34.
	339– 3	that which *St. J·* informs us
Ret.	90–10	to whom *St. J·* addressed one of

St. John

'00.	11–26 In Revelation *St. J·* refers to
	12–27 The Revelation of *St. J·*
	15–22 In the words of *St. J·*,
'01.	12– 4 If *St. J·* should tell that man
'02.	5–17 Divine metaphysics and *St. J·* have
Hea.	9–28 *St. J·* saw the vision of life in
My.	3– 7 *St. J·* writes: "Blessed are— *Rev.* 22 : 14.
	119–32 *St. J·* found Christ, Truth, in the
	187–13 *St. J·* says : "For this is— *I John* 3 : 11.
	285–17 In Revelation 2 : 26, *St. J·* says :
	339–17 disciples of *St. J·* the Baptist said

St. John's

Mis.	292– 2 divinity of *St. J·* Gospel
'01.	16– 6 *St. J·* types of sin
	32–24 Sermon on . . . and *St. J·* Revelation,

St. John's Lodge

My.	333– 4 * records of *St. J· L·*, Wilmington,

St. Joseph, Missouri and Mo.

Pul.	89–32 * *Herald, St. J·, M·*.
	89–37 * *News, St. J·, M·*.
My.	207–18 * *St. J·, M·*, January 5, 1909.

St. Louis

Mo.

My.	196–24 chapter sub-title
	351– 4 * Mr. John C. Higdon of *St. L·*, Mo.

'00.	1–21 *St. L·*, Denver, Salt Lake City,

St. Louis Democrat

Mis.	248–20 The *St. L· D·* is alleged to have

St. Mark (see also Mark)

Mis.	25–17 spoken of by *St. M·*.
	373–22 and, as *St. M·* writes,
My.	147–12 of which *St. M·* prophesies.
	238–15 of which *St. M·* prophesied

St. Matthew (see also Matthew)

Mis.	189–26 insomuch that *St. M·* wrote,
	298–12 These words of *St. M·*
My.	222– 1 Gospel according to *St. M·*,

stock

Mis.	231– 8 though I take no *s·* in spirit-rappings
	239–24 familiarity with what the *s·* paid,
	272–12 * such as any *s·* company may
'00.	2–20 his *s·* in trade, the wages of sin ;

stockholders

Mis.	239–23 with that of the household *s·*,

Stoic

Mis.	162– 8 Gnostic, Epicurean, and *S·*.

stole

Hea.	3–11 material element *s·* into religion,

stolen

Mis.	201–26 our jewels have been *s·* ;
Ret.	17–13 Flora has *s·* the rainbow and sky,
	76– 7 The Bible is not *s·*,
Po.	62–16 Flora has *s·* the rainbow and sky,
My.	304–30 second, she has *s·* the contents of

stomach (see also stomach's)

Mis.	69–31 dominion over the fish in his *s·* ?
	210–20 membranes, *s·*, and nerves ;
	243–27 cause the coats of the *s·* to thicken

stomach's

Mis.	243–25 for thy *s·* sake"— *I Tim.* 5, 20.

Stone

(see **Corner Stone**)

stone (noun)

art and

Pul.	65–25 * memorialized in art and *s·*

as substance

Mis.	27–31 Mortals can know a *s·* as substance,

Bedford

My.	45–29 * New Hampshire granite and Bedford *s·*,
	68–19 * harmonize with the Bedford *s·*
	68–25 * Bedford *s·* and marble form the
	68–30 * bronze, marble, and Bedford *s·*.

corner

My.	16–26 precious corner *s·*,— *Isa.* 28 : 16.
	17–15 a chief corner *s·*,— *I Pet.* 2 : 6.

cut in a

Mis.	376–12 * engraving cut in a *s·*.

every

Pul.	41– 2 * with every *s·* paid for

first

Mis.	285–18 book that cast the first *s·*,

foundation

Hea.	2–27 eternity's foundation *s·*,
	11–18 foundation *s·* of mental healing ;

gray

Mis.	340–14 forsook Blackstone for gray *s·*,
My.	78– 6 * imposing structure of gray *s·*

stone (noun)

head

Mis.	196–24 head *s·* of the corner,"— *Psal.* 118 : 22.

is rolled away

My.	191–22 The *s·* is rolled away.

light

My.	89– 5 * The building is of light *s·*,

living

My.	17– 9 as unto a living *s·*,— *I Pet.* 2 : 4.

miracle in

Pul.	8–15 erect this "miracle in *s·*."
Hea.	11–12 pyramid . . . a miracle in *s·*.

pillows of

Mis.	144–25 from earth's pillows of *s·*,

prayer in

(see **prayer**)

roll away the

Mis.	179– 2 roll away the *s·* ?"— see *Mark* 16 : 3.
	275– 5 Who can roll away the *s·*

rolled away the

Mis.	74–19 rolled away the *s·* from the
	123–18 rolled away the *s·* from the
No.	36–24 rolled away the *s·* from the

shapeless

Peo.	7–12 * the dream on that shapeless *s·*

stately

Pul.	16–18 Cold, silent, stately *s·*,

steadfast

Mis.	400– 6 Grave, silent, steadfast *s·*,
Po.	76–17 Grave, silent, steadfast *s·*,

testimonial in

My.	58–16 * this fitting testimonial in *s·*,

this

Mis.	400– 4 Like this *s·*, be in thy place :
Pul.	16–16 Like this *s·*, be in thy place ;
Po.	76–15 Like this *s·*, be in thy place :

tried

My.	16–25 a tried *s·*,— *Isa.* 28 : 16.

white

Mis.	320–29 white *s·* in token of purity

wood and

Peo.	13– 1 worshippers of wood and *s·*

wood or

Mis.	346–15 an image graven on wood or *s·*
Peo.	2–18 form its Deity . . . of wood or *s·*.

yielding

Peo.	7–20 * carve it then on the yielding *s·*

Mis.	5–20 *s·* that the builders have rejected,
	27–27 But, say you, is a *s·* spiritual?
	28– 1 tho *s·* itself would disappear,
	127–12 it is not given a *s·*,
	179– 3 The *s·* has been rolled away
	179–19 What is it that seems a *s·*
	196–23 *s·* which the builders— *Psal.* 118 : 22.
	293–28 rolls on the human heart a *s·* ;
	399–20 Rolled away from loving heart Is a *s·*.
Man.	18– 1 *s·* which the builders— *Matt.* 21 : 42.
Un.	57–18 This is earth's Bethel in *s·*,
Pul.	10–19 *s·* which the builders *Matt* 21 : 42.
	16– 5 Rolled away from loving heart is a *s·*.
'01.	25– 5 The *s·* which the builders reject
'02.	2–15 *s·* at the head of the corner ;
Hea.	3– 8 The *s·* which the builders rejected
Po.	76– 4 Rolled away from loving heart Is a *s·*.
My.	16–25 for a foundation a *s·*,— *Isa.* 28 : 16.
	18– 9 it is not given a *s·*,
	23–29 * and *s·* is laid upon *s·*,
	48– 6 * the *s·* that had been rejected,
	60–12 * *s·* which the builders— *Matt.* 21 : 42.
	129–20 *s·* which the builders— *Matt.* 21 : 42.
	188– 1 the *s·* which the builders rejected

stone (adj.)

Mis.	325– 1 enters a massive carved *s·* mansion,
Ret.	5–12 inscribed on the *s·* memorials in
Pul.	24–11 * *s·* porticos and turreted corners.
	41–23 * chimes in the great *s·* tower,
	58–19 * the steps marble, and the walls *s·*,
	86–13 * Accompanying the *s·* testimonial
My.	68– 6 * from the tops of great *s·* piers,
	68–23 * It has an architectural *s·* screen
	92–23 * two-million-dollar *s·* edifice
	94– 7 * two-million-dollar *s·* edifice

stone (verb)

No.	41– 6 do ye *s·* me?"— *John* 10 : 32.
My.	108–24 do ye *s·* me,"— *John* 10 : 32.
	227– 2 do ye *s·* me?"— *John* 10 : 32.

stoned

'00.	14–25 if you are *s·* from the pulpit,
My.	108–22 To be *s·* for that which our Master

stones

Mis.	224– 8 broken the head of his statue with *s·*
	336– 6 cannot, . . . resort to *s·* and clubs,
Peo.	14– 6 dismal gray *s·* of churchyards

stones
Peo.	14– 9	* "bat and owl on the bending *s*,
Po.	79– 6	of these *s*, or tyrants' thrones,
My.	17–11	"Ye also, as lively *s*, — *I Pet.* 2 : 5.
	43–16	* twelve *s* taken from the midst of
	43–19	* "What mean ye by these *s* ?" — *Josh.* 4 : 6.
	43–32	* "What mean ye by these *s* ?" — *Josh.* 4 : 6.
	61–14	* climbing over *s* and planks
	64–25	* "living *s*" — see *I Pet.* 2 : 5.
	185–30	signs and symbols, sermons in *s*,

stonest
Mis.	326–26	*s* them which are sent — *Matt.* 23 : 37.

stony
Mis.	357–14	on *s* ground and shallow soil.
My.	121–12	never selfish, *s*, nor stormy,

stood
Mis.	178–23	* could not have *s* up again *to* preach,
	253–17	*s* ready to devour the child
	344–29	*s* on Mars' hill at Athens,
	345– 2	St. Paul *s* where Socrates
	345– 3	*s* four hundred years before,
Ret.	30– 1	I *s* alone in this conflict,
	31–22	I gazed, and *s* abashed.
	40–10	*s* by her side about fifteen minutes
Pan.	3–23	Pan *s* for "universal nature
Hea.	10– 2	dragon that . . . *s* ready
Peo.	7– 8	* "Chisel in hand *s* a sculptor-boy,
My.	56– 4	* many *s* in the aisles,
	61–26	* *s* under the great dome,
	62– 1	* *s* at the breast-works
	70–14	* and *s* in silent admiration
	92– 3	* *s* the test of time.
	105–16	so that it *s* out like a cord.
	105–23	physician, who *s* by her bedside,
	194–29	* *s* the storm when seas were rough,
	247–15	I *s* silently beside it,
	247–16	to the rim where I *s*.

stool
Mis.	131– 8	kneels on a *s* in church,

stoop
Mis.	226–26	dignified natures cannot *s* to
My.	165– 5	The grand must *s* to the menial.

stooped
Un.	11–14	Jesus *s* not to human
My.	119–13	*s* down and looked into the sepulchre

stoops
Mis.	330–30	*s* meekly before the blast ;

stop
Mis.	114–25	and *s* their hidden influence
	157–27	it cannot *s* the eternal currents
	246–17	to shackle conscience, *s* free speech,
	265–31	student must *s* at the foot of the
	274– 6	I must *s* teaching at present.
	286–32	*s* at length at the spiritual
	288–25	real suffering would *s* the farce.
	301–29	blind the eyes, *s* the ears
	307–14	thought best to *s* its publication.
	327–20	Despairing . . . they conclude to *s*
	358–21	to *s* teaching, to dissolve their
Pul.	64–12	* in order to *s* the continued inflow of
	82– 9	* no more . . . than winter could *s* the
Peo.	8–26	* trusting where there is no trust,
My.	116– 5	C. S. realized will *s* a contagion.
	147–25	never *s* ceremoniously to dedicate
	165–26	and never *s* from exhaustion.
	203– 9	and never *s* working.
	327–16	* or *s* the practice of C. S.

stoppage
Mis.	69–19	I removed the *s*, healed him
	69–26	cause of the inflammation and *s*

stopped
Mis.	275–27	Palmer House, where we *s*,
Ret.	38– 4	and yet he *s* my work.
Hea.	19– 6	could not have been *s* by mind
My.	70–13	* workingmen *s* in the street
	318–29	would have continued . . . but I *s* him.

stopping
Mis.	107–28	*s*, the growth of Christian Scientists.

stopping-place
My.	348–17	Here, however, was no *s*,

stops
Mis.	44–13	*and nothing s* it until I
	44–27	belief in pain ceases, the pain *s* ;
	308– 7	greatly errs, *s* his own progress,
Pul.	87–23	This wish *s* not with my pen
'00.	8–21	he *s* quarrelling with others.
'01.	20–22	till he . . . . *s* practising it.
My.	107–31	*s* decomposition, removes enteritis,
	291–27	She *s* to think, to mourn,
	(see also **organ**)	

store
Mis.	149– 7	and replenish your scanty *s*.
	299–18	If I enter Mr. Smith's *s*
	391– 6	An item rich in *s* ;
Pul.	78–26	* window of J. C. Derby's jewelry *s*.
Po.	38– 5	An item rich in *s* ;
My.	253–23	I send with this a *s* of wisdom

storehouse
Mis.	139– 4	bring your tithes into the *s*,
	159–18	This is my Christmas *s*.
	313–20	the *s* is ready :
My.	14– 2	brought their tithes into His *s*.
	20–13	your tithes into His *s*,
	131–25	tithes into the *s*, — *Mal.* 3 : 10.
	202–26	sheaves into the *s*.

stores
Mis.	165–29	secret *s* of wisdom must be
My.	149–11	its radiant *s* of knowledge

storied
'00.	1– 4	chinked within the *s* walls

storics
Mis.	48–29	like a hundred other *s*,
Ret.	2–28	*s* about General Knox,
My.	82– 1	* all have the same *s*
	313– 8	*s* told by *McClure's Magazine*

storm (*see also* storm's)
Mis.	ix–16	darkness of *s* and cloud
	152–22	when *s* and tempest beat
	152–26	till *s* has passed.
	329–26	that tarried through the *s*,
	362–26	shelter from the *s* and tempest
Ret.	17–16	to the lightning and *s*,
	60–15	saith to the wave and *s*,
Pul.	80– 2	* ship when under stress of *s*
Hea.	2– 5	while it reasons with the *s*,
Po.	29– 4	born where *s* enshrouds
	46– 4	Nor blasts of winter's angry *s*,
	53–15	Where wind nor *s* can numb
	62–21	to the lightning and *s*,
	79– 3	*s* or shine, pure peace is thine,
My.	182–28	find shelter from the *s*
	194–29	* stood the *s* when seas were rough,
	205–12	* And rides upon the *s*."
	252–13	and run away in the *s*,
	295–19	It stands the *s*.
	356– 8	* And rides upon the *s*."

stormed
Mis.	211–27	Jesus *s* sin in its citadels

storming
'01.	2–19	ever *s* sin in its citadels,

storm's
Pan.	3–10	silent as the *s* sudden hush ;

storms
Mis.	140–29	will stand the *s* of ages :
	374–11	Above the . . . *s* of passion,
	384–10	Stay ! till the *s* are o'er
	392–15	wrestle with the *s* of time ;
'00.	15–27	Watch ! till the *s* are o'er
'01.	24–13	when the *s* of disease beat
Po.	20–19	to wrestle with the *s* of time ;
	36– 9	Stay ! till the *s* are o'er
My.	11– 6	* *s* that have surged against her
	204– 5	which *s* awaken to vigor

stormy
My.	121–12	never selfish, stony, nor *s*,

story
Mis.	144– 4	situated in the second *s*
	216–19	*s* of the Cheshire Cat,
	238– 1	I had heard the awful *s*
	239–19	tired look, told the *s* ;
Un.	44– 8	The old, old *s*,
Pul.	vii– 2	*s* of the birth of C. S.,
	27–20	* window tells its pictorial *s*
	32–14	* She told me the *s* of her life,
	33– 7	* related to her the *s* of Samuel,
	46– 1	* A *s* has been abroad that
	48– 7	* the second *s* of the house,
	65–18	* *s* of the cathedral of Amiens,
	84–21	* the *s* of its mighty meaning
My.	14–19	* pronounced the *s* a fabrication
	15–18	* I love to tell the *s*,
	15–22	* I love to tell the *s*,
	15–26	* I love to tell the *s* ;
	15–32	* 'Twill be the OLD, OLD *S*
	38– 5	* the *s* of our love for you
	68–27	* floors of the first *s* are of marble.
	84–19	* It is a remarkable *s*
	179– 5	the second was an opposite *s*,
	321–27	* told the same *s* to every one

stout
Mis.	222–23	will make *s* hearts quail.

stoutest
My. 88–27 * *s·* enemies of C. S.
stoutly
Mis. 327–16 They *s·* belay those who,
Ret. 14–14 I *s·* maintained that I was willing
St. Paul (*see also* **Paul, St. Paul's**)
admonishes
Peo. 10–24 as *St. P·* admonishes, we should
avers
Mis. 253– 3 not merely a gift, as *St. P·* avers,
complains
'01. 11–28 *St. P·* complains of him whose
declared
Ret. 30–17 *St. P·* declared that the law
declares
Mis. 30–20 law of Life, which *St. P·* declares
71–23 *St. P·* declares astutely,
defines
'01. 16–14 *St. P·* defines this world's god as
handkerchief of
My. 152– 4 and the handkerchief of *St. P·*
learned
My. 104– 3 thought that the learned *St. P·*,
modern
'01. 27–16 Or if a modern *St. P·* could start
rule of
My. 12–17 This was an emphatic rule of *St. P·* :
said
Ret. 93–17 *St. P·* said to the Athenians,
No. 25 4 *St. P·* said, "But now — *Rom.* 7 : 6.
45– 3 *St. P·* said that without charity
'01. 26–21 *St. P·* said: "Though I — *I Cor.* 13 : 1.
says
Mis. 359– 8 *St. P·* says: "When I was — *I Cor.* 13 : 11.
Un. 60–24 *St. P·* says, "And if Christ — *I Cor.* 15 : 17.
speaks
Mis. 15– 5 *St. P·* speaks of the new birth
spirit of
Mis. 344–29 We need the spirit of *St. P·*,
stood
Mis. 345– 2 *St. P·* stood where Socrates
summarized
Ret. 22– 8 *St. P·* summarized the character of
terms
No. 27–21 *St. P·* terms "the old man — *Col.* 3 : 9.
words of
(*see* **words**)
writes
Mis. 24– 2 *St. P·* writes: "For to be — *Rom.* 8 : 6.
'02. 6–26 *St. P·* writes: "For to be — *Rom.* 8 : 6.
16–12 *St. P·* writes: "Follow peace — *Heb.* 12 : 14.
My. 293–28 *St. P·* writes: "For the law — *Rom.* 8 : 2.
wrote
Mis. 330–10 *St. P·* wrote, "Rejoice in — *Phil.* 4 : 4.
My. 261–15 *St. P·* wrote, "When I was — *I Cor.* 13 : 11.

Mis. 186– 6 as referred to by *St. P·*.
188–16 *St. P·* first reasons upon the basis
Man. 47–13 which are God's" (*St. P·*). — *I Cor.* 6 : 20.
Rud. 17– 2 Jews whom *St. P·* had hoped to convert
Pan. 11– 3 It caused *St. P·* to write,
'00. 4–29 *St. P·* beautifully enunciates this
12–13 travelled to meet *St. P·*
12–23 It were well if we had a *St. P·*
'01. 9 10 spoken of by *St. P·*.
27– 5 * I look to see some *St. P·* arise
My. 104–11 call *St. P·* a "pest," — *see Acts* 24 : 5.
113– 8 *St. P·* was a follower but not
113–15 Was it profane for *St. P·* to
123–32 let us say with *St. P·* :
228–30 against that day" (*St. P·*). — *II Tim.* 1 : 12.
St. Paul, Minn.
Pul. 90– 2 * *Pioneer-Press*, *St. P·*, *M·*.
St. Paul's
Mis. 191–31 Let us obey *St. P·* injunction
208 3 *St. P·* words take in the situation :
Ret. 93–23 If C. S. reiterates *St. P·* teaching,
94– 6 divine Science and *St. P·* text,
'00. 12–10 *St. P·* life furnished items
12–21 influence of *St. P·* preaching
12–24 During *St. P·* stay in that city
My. 108–28 I remain steadfast in *St. P·* faith,
340– 3 *St. P·* days for prayer were
St. Paul's School
Pul. 49–25 * "Eton of America," *St. P· S·*.
St. Paul Street
My. 66– 9 * the last parcel on *St. P· S·*
straggling
Pul. 29–11 * no *s·* of late-comers.
straight
Mis. 32–21 from the *s·* and narrow path.
99–27 "Make *s·* God's paths ;
245–28 the *s·* and narrow way ;

straight
Mis. 246–25 make His paths *s·*." — *Matt.* 3 : 3.
268–14 Scientist keeps *s·* to the course.
323–23 up the hill it is *s·* and narrow,
347–22 but it is always *s·* and narrow ;
Ret. 71– 8 *s·* and narrow path of C. S.
Pul. 48– 5 * Mrs. Eddy took the writer *s·* to
48–14 * *S·* as the crow flies,
My. 75–10 * headed *s·* for Horticultural Hall,
140– 5 and crooked things *s·* — *Isa.* 42 : 16.
straightforward
Mis. 233–19 fair-seeming for *s·* character,
340– 6 unremitting, *s·* toil ;
straightway
Mis. 81–14 *coming up s· out of the*
Un. 13–14 would *s·* reduce the universe to
49–26 He *s·* commands mortals
strain
Mis. 184–12 brings to remembrance the Hebrew *s·*,
339–13 the *s·* of intellectual wrestlings,
365– 1 will bear the *s·* of time and
387–18 Seek holy thoughts and heavenly *s·*,
396–19 There sweeps a *s·*,
Pul. 12–22 her primal and everlasting *s·*.
18– 3 There sweeps a *s·*,
No. 21–22 bears the *s·* of time,
Po. 6–13 holy thoughts and heavenly *s·*,
12– 2 There sweeps a *s·*,
31– 5 Prolong the *s·* "Christ risen !"
35– 3 *s·* which hath strange power
41–21 *s·* of enchantment that flowed
My. 130–27 enormous *s·* put upon it,
276– 9 do not *s·* at gnats
strained
My. 87– 3 * have been *s·* to their utmost
straining
My. 211– 2 sticklers . . . *s·* at gnats
218–19 namely, *s·* at gnats
235– 5 *S·* at gnats, one may swallow camels.
strains
Mis. 106–29 affords the only *s·* that thrill
116–14 emphasizing its grand *s·*,
116–16 varied *s·* of human chords
142–23 the psalm in spiritual *s·*
329–24 sweep in soft *s·* her Orphean
345– 5 in immortal *s·* of eloquence.
396–12 Are poured in *s·* so sweet,
Ret. 12– 1 *S·* nobler far than clarion call
Po. 59 4 Are poured in *s·* so sweet,
60–21 *S·* nobler far than clarion call
strait
Ret. 55– 1 this *s·* and narrow path,
'01. 28– 6 the *s·* and narrow way,
My. 104– 1 the *s·* and narrow way
stranded
Ret. 79–18 *s·* on the quicksands of
strange
Mis. 1–17 *s·* fire from the ashes of
250– 3 By what *s·* perversity is the
275–13 words of *s·* import.
Ret. 21– 8 by a *s·* providence had learned
50– 9 led, by a *s·* providence,
Po. 35– 3 strain which hath *s·* power
My. 114–17 *s·* coincidence or relationship
strangeness
My. 50– 7 * Pilgrims felt the *s·* of their
Stranger
Mis. 323– 7 *S·* wending his way downward,
323–13 but the *S·* meets and
323–16 *S·* eventually stands in the
324–18 he alone . . . can see the *S·*.
324–22 he seeks . . . to find the *S·*.
324–24 to go on and to meet the *S·*.
324–31 the reappearance of the *S·*,
325– 1 The *S·* enters a massive
325–10 fear not to fall upon the *S·*,
325–20 and looks at the *S·*,
325–25 the *S·* turns quickly,
326–22 the *S·* returned to the valley ;
326–30 the *S·* saith unto him,
327– 5 the *S·* saith unto him,
327– 8 saith the *S·*, "thou hast chosen
327–23 the *S·* is pointing the way,
328– 1 suddenly the *S·* shouts,
328– 8 the *S·* the ever-present Christ,
stranger
Mis. 155– 9 win the pilgrim and *s·* to your
178–16 * I strayed into this hall, a *s·*,
Ret. 86–11 "*s·* that is within — *Deut.* 5 : 14.
89–14 hortatory compliment to a *s·*,
90–18 to the care of nurse or *s·*.
Pul. 33–21 * as to whence the *s·* came

stranger

Po. 65–20 the s· who roams
My. 91–26 * even s· is its increase in wealth.
117–14 "When saw we thee a s·, — *Matt.* 25 : 38.

strangers

Mis. 308–18 Friends, s·, and Christian Scientists,
398– 9 S· on a barren shore,
Man. 59–14 WELCOMING S·.
59–23 s· who may come to attend
Ret. 46–15 S· on a barren shore,
Pul. 17–14 S· on a barren shore,
Po. 14–13 S· on a barren shore,
My. 85–24 * but for a multitude of s·
231– 4 solicitations or petitions from s·,

strangle

Pul. 13–15 to s· the serpent of sin

strangled

Mis. 233–11 and so s· in its attempts.

straw

My. 313–10 with tan-bark and s·,

stray

Mis. 281–13 a s· copy of the Scriptures
398– 2 Lest my footsteps s· ;
Ret. 1–12 wrote a s· sonnet
46– 8 Lest my footsteps s· ;
90– 9 left them to starve or to s·.
Pul. 17– 7 Lest my footsteps s· ;
Po. 14– 6 Lest my footsteps s· ;
41–12 and left them to s·
My. 41–13 * howsoever far he may s·,
201–22 Lest my footsteps s· ;

strayed

Mis. 32– 8 or such as have s· from
178–15 * I s· into this hall, a stranger,
357– 6 having s· from the true fold,
357–28 lambs that have . . . s· innocently ;
Man. 55–12 decided that a teacher has so s·
85– 4 Caring for Pupils of S· Members.
85– 8 member of this Church who has so s·

strayest

Mis. 328– 3 and if thou s·, listen for the

strayeth

Ret. 80–25 while innocence s· yearningly.

straying

Mis. 32–20 s· from the straight and narrow path.
No. 20–28 s· into forbidden by-paths

stream

Pan. 3–16 * By thy pure s·,
Hea. 7–14 in order to purify the s·.
Po. 66– 3 walk by that murmuring s· ;

streaming

My. 72–10 * there are s· into town

streamlet

Ret. 18– 9 songlet and s· that flows
Po. 63–18 songlet and s· that flows

streamlets

Ret. 11–13 from this fount the s· flow,
Po. 60–10 from this fount the s· flow,

streams

Mis. 223– 6 S· which purify, necessarily have
223– 7 impure s· flow from corrupt
323–21 and bathe in its s·,
329–21 the s· to race for the sea.
330–14 The alders bend over the s·
332–16 crystal s· of the Orient,
No. 1– 7 Small s· are noisy
Hea. 10–28 Earth's fading dreams are empty s·,
12– 7 goes to the fount to govern the s· ;
Po. 35– 8 s· will never dry or cease to flow;

street

Mis. 274–16 *Truth is fallen in the s·,* — *Isa.* 59 : 14.
Pul. 59–30 * the front vestibule and s·
My. 68–11 * the dome . . . above the s·,
70–14 * workingmen stopped in the s·

street-car

My. 83–13 * s· men and policemen,

Streeter, Lawyer

My. 137–26 * I had consulted Lawyer S·

Street Fund

My. 176– 4 THE CONCORD (N. H.) S· F·

Streets

'02. 13–17 Falmouth and Caledonia . . . S· ;

streets

Mis. 133–13 in the corners of the s·, — *Matt.* 6 : 5.
237–25 s· through which Garrison
274–29 s· besmeared with blood.
324– 2 s· of a city made with hands.
324–27 rushes again into the lonely s·,
Ret. 79–28 nor its golden s· invaded,

streets

My. 66– 6 * property on these s·,
77–19 * filled the s· leading to the
80–28 * waiting vainly in the s·.
82–30 * living in the s· leading directly to
175–18 greatly needs improved s·.

strength

and beauty
My. 39–29 * s· and beauty of her character.
and growth
My. 83–28 * s· and growth of their
and permanence
Mis. 287–20 giving them s· and permanence.
and shield
Mis. 113–24 Love is our hope, s·, and shield.
beauty and
My. 68– 3 * beauty and s· of the design.
calm
Mis. 338–17 calm s· will enrage evil.
divine
Mis. 170–18 refreshment of divine s·,
358–15 humility, and love are divine s·.
Un. 39–12 removes . . . weakness by divine s·,
from on high
Po. 32–13 resolutions, with s· from on high,
gathering
Mis. 354–27 gathering s· for a flight well begun,
health and
Mis. 7–29 think that health and s· would have
Pul. 52–16 * receive light, health, and s·,
hidden
My. 166–16 they develop hidden s·.
His
Mis. 263–10 safe in His s·, building on His
his
Mis. 130–28 renews his s·, and is exalted
holy
Po. 23–13 Yielding a holy s· to right,
human
Mis. 138–17 I once thought . . . was human s· ;
138–18 know that human s· is weakness,
My. 132–14 no longer to appeal to human s·,
in union
Mis. 98–18 and to find s· in union,
is in man
My. 162– 6 S· is in man, not in muscles ;
its
Mis. 341–10 its s· in exalted purpose.
little
'00. 14– 2 "Thou hast a little s·, — *Rev.* 3 : 8.
moral
Mis. 268–27 From lack of moral s·
Pul. 83– 6 * has not yet the moral s·
of human belief
Rud. 11–19 on the s· of human belief.
of peace
My. 121– 7 we learn that the s· of peace
of the hills
My. 185–27 * For the s· of the hills, we bless
of the Lord God
Ret. 15– 8 s· of the Lord God : — *Psal.* 71 : 16.
of union
Mis. 254–12 the s· of union grows weak with
of weakness
Po. 2–10 With all the s· of weakness
physical
Mis. 240–12 physical s· and freedom.
reality and
Mis. 252–14 healthy thoughts are reality and s·.
requires
Mis. ix–17 requires s· from above,
salvation and
Pul. 12– 6 salvation, and s·, — *Rev.* 12 : 10.
settles into
Mis. 204–15 settles into s·, freedom,
shows
My. 88– 7 * It shows s· in all parts,
stillness, and
Ret. 93–15 power, stillness, and s· ;
their
Mis. 10–20 tried their s· and proven it ;
10–21 their s· made perfect in weakness,
Pul. 30– 5 * offering their s· to unite with
this
My. 121–10 This s· is like the ocean,
thy
My. 183– 3 and with all thy s·, — *Luke* 10 : 27.
252–17 so shall thy s· be." — *Deut.* 33 : 25.
270–17 so shall thy s· be." — *Deut.* 33 : 25.
time and
Mis. 296–12 give their time and s· to
to bear
Un. 6–12 as the age has s· to bear.
to build
Mis. 98–18 s· to build up,

strength

to nourish
Pul. 63– 8 * has the s· to nourish trees
wisdom and
My. 164–27 is reserved wisdom and s·.
your
Mis. 364– 6 renew your s·." — see Isa. 40 : 31.

Mis. 126–16 s·, meekness, honesty, and
162–32 in the s· of an exalted hope,
Pul. 4– 1 may say, . . . my s· is naught
My. 287– 8 giving to human weakness s·,

strengthen

Mis. 98–17 s· and perpetuate our organizations
328–26 lift the fallen and s· the weak.
Man. 43–11 s· the faith by a written text
Pul. 2–19 s· your citadel by every means
Rud. 12– 6 Wrong thoughts . . . s· the sense of
My. 213–22 s· your own citadel

strengthened

Mis. 298–11 would I be s· by having my
Ret. 27–20 * are lifted up and s·.
Pul. 50–19 * comforted and s· by them.
My. 95– 5 * constantly s· by members
132–16 Divine Love has s· the hand
152– 8 said, . . . tonic has s· you."
199–19 a higher hope, of s· hands,

strengthening

Mis. 262–17 lifting the fallen and s· the

strengthens

Mis. 362–31 no crime except when it s·
My. 129–27 expatiates, s·, and exults.
131– 1 s· them, removes fear,

stress

Pul. 80– 2 * a ship when under s· of storm
'01. 30–22 or by the s· of the appetites
My. 294–19 in spite of the constant s·

stretch

Mis. 124–22 s· out our arms to God.
370– 2 "S· forth thy hand, — see Matt. 12 : 13.

stretched

Mis. 325–17 lie s· on the floor,
Ret. 4–13 Where once s· broad fields
My. 215– 4 God s· forth His hand.

stretches

Pul. 48– 3 * green s· of lawns, dotted with
48–11 * S· on through an intervale
My. 200–12 unbroken, s· across the sea

stricken

Mis. 203 10 s· state of human consciousness,
275– 8 the faithful, s· mother,
329–28 robin, though s· to the heart
Ret. 13–11 pronounced me s· with fever.
Pul. 82– 5 * which heals the s· soul.
Po. 41– 1 * rest in this bosom, my own s· deer.
My. 291–26 suddenly s·, — called to mourn

strict

Mis. 65–26 proves that s· adherence to one is
119–23 s· obedience thereto, tests and
248–18 s· obedience to the Mosiac Decalogue,
Man. 44– 2 s· adherence to the Golden Rule,
110– 5 these seemingly s· conditions
Ret. 50–21 s· adherence to divine Truth
Pul. 38–24 * s· fidelity to what they believe
66–13 * s· fidelity to what they
No. 7–19 will not release them from the s·
My. 45– 1 * s· and intelligent recognition of
212–16 s· accordance with the teaching of
256– 5 phrasing s· observance

strictest

Ret. 14– 5 the s· Presbyterian doctrines.
76–28 s· observance of moral law

strictly

Mis. 6–26 where laws of health are s·
22– 1 I am s· a theist
92–16 the teacher should s· adhere to
112–13 s· classified in metaphysics as
114–11 Teachers must conform s· to the
284–10 Students who s· adhere to the right,
Man. 51–17 requirements . . . s· obeyed,
67– 6 A s· private communication
70– 6 adhering s· to her advice
80– 2 on a s· Christian basis,
Ret. 84– 9 s· adheres to the teachings in
Un. 35–11 s· speaking, there is no mortal mind,
40–27 s· belonging to the nature and
Pul. 73– 5 * s· an ardent follower after God.
Rud. 14– 6 s· practising Divine Science,
No. 16–27 s· speaking, no mortal mind.
Pan. 12–21 The Science of Christianity is s·

strictly

'01. 5– 2 defined s· by the word Person,
34–24 obey s· the laws for he be,
My. 13–12 * s· a mother and a ruling church."
226– 3 This rule s· observed will
282– 3 I believe s· in the Monroe doctrine,
345–32 * her views, s· and always
364– 4 s· to handle no other mentality

strife

Mis. 41–12 victory in the ennobling s·.
222– 4 passion, evil-speaking, and s·.
333– 4 commingle, and are forever at s· ;
341–12 glory of the s· comes of honesty
343–15 malice, envy, and s·
351–13 to stir up s· between brethren,
386–14 and could not know the s·
388– 8 Free us from human s·.
391–12 It stirs no thought of s· ;
Chr. 53–12 That stills all s·.
'01. 32–14 They were heroes in the s· ;
'02. 2– 2 through the mist of mortal s·
Po. 7– 8 Free us from human s·.
29–18 far above All mortal s·,
38–11 It stirs no thought of s·
49–22 and could not know the s·
My. 278–16 chapter sub-title
279–13 is sufficient to still all s·.

strike

Mis. 67–10 thou shalt not s· at the
355–16 To s· out right and left
Un. 18–22 in order to s· at its root ;
Pul. 51– 1 * C. S. does not s· all as a

strikes

Mis. 237–11 that conscience s· home ;
257–23 s· down the hoary saint.
Ret. 75–21 s· at the heart of Truth.
Pul. 24– 2 * s· a keynote of definite

striking

Mis. 232–29 from s· out promiscuously,
312–13 * "No more s· manifestation
Pul. 45–20 * proved, in most s· manner,
76– 2 * A s· feature of the church
'00. 10–13 s· at liberty, human rights,
My. 32– 2 * two of the most s· features
88–19 * s· as are its beauties,

strikingly

Pul. 49–27 * a s· well-kept estate

strings

Pul. 81–23 * her own soul plays upon magic s·
Hea. 20– 5 * soar and touch the heavenly s·,
Po. 66–11 No melody sweeps o'er its s· !

stripes

Mis. 3–12 "through his s·" — see Isa. 53 : 5.
162–19 through his s· we are healed.
260– 2 "s· we are healed." — Isa. 53 : 5.
Man. 28–13 beaten with many s·." — Luke 12 : 47.
Un. 55– 8 s· we are healed." — Isa. 53 : 5.

strips

Mis. 185– 6 s· matter of all claims,
210– 1 s· off its disguises,
Pan. 11–22 whatever s· off evil's disguise

strive

Mis. 7– 9 we must s· to emulate.
86– 6 Scientist must continue to s·
154–27 S· for self-abnegation, justice,
176–12 s· valiantly for the liberty of the
180– 2 and s· to cease my warfare.
197– 6 and to s· after holiness ;
315–27 s· to educate their students
341–12 Seeking is not . . . you must s· ;
Man. 45–11 s· to promote the welfare of all
55– 4 shall s· to overcome these errors.
92– 8 shall s· to demonstrate by
My. vii– 3 * S· it ever so hard, The Church
132–14 to s· with agony ;
150– 8 S· thou for the joy and crown
207–10 * pledge themselves to s· more

striven

Mis. 11–28 though with tears have I s· for it.
12– 8 him who has s· to injure you.
My. 130–10 and s· to uplift morally

strives

Mis. 119–14 s· to tip the beam against the
119–15 the flesh s· against Spirit,
371–23 but error always s· to
My. 160– 1 s· for the spiritual ;
228–26 He who s·, and attains ;
249– 4 error s· to be heard above Truth,
272– 2 actively s· for perfection,
334– 1 * s· to give the impression that

striving
Mis. 267–12 secretly s' to injure me.
328–24 mortals who are s' to enter the
My. 200–14 S' to be good, to do good,
300–17 s' to reach the summit of

strivings
Mis. 61– 6 vain s' of mortal mind,

stroke
Mis. 195–22 s' of unskilled swordsmen.
Ret. 35–21 beneath the s' of artless workmen.

strokes
My. 291– 7 His work began with heavy s',

stroll
Man. 48–13 continually s' by her house,

strong
Mis. xii– 7 with s' wing to lift my readers
2– 6 s' determination of mankind to
4–24 a very s' will-power
126–24 Scientists have a s' race to run
139–11 *pulling down of s' holds ; — II Cor.* 10: 4.
152–24 s' tower of hope, faith, and
223–12 is sufficiently s' to discern
238– 6 honest . . . and s' of purpose.
240–10 s' promotors of health and
250–16 I make s' demands on love,
252–30 children's toy and s' tower ;
277–10 heart loyal to God is patient and s'.
288–26 a s' impulse from the cause of
289– 2 S' drink is unquestionably an evil,
313–19 the reapers are s',
345–12 his pure and s' faith rose higher
369–10 s' in the unity of God and man.
392–15 s' to wrestle with the storms of
393–18 In a beauty s' and meek
Ret. 5–14 a s' intellect and an iron will.
5–22 * She possessed a s' intellect,
16– 2 a soprano, — clear, s', sympathetic,
Un. 43– 3 too material for any s' demonstration
Pul. 62–10 * required a s' man to ring them,
67–20 * Toronto and . . . have s' churches,
80– 4 * religious sentiment in women is so s'
Rud. 8–12 thou wilt be s' in God,
No. 42–27 * He said : . . . drink s' coffee to
Pan. 12–10 will make s' claims on religion,
'00. 9–13 S' desires bias human judgment
Hea. 2–12 * "Old Adam is too s' for
6–18 if the belief is s' enough
Po. 20–19 s' to wrestle with the storms
22–17 life perfected, s' and calm.
23–12 With utterance deep and s',
33– 6 hourly seek for deliverance s'
52– 2 In a beauty s' and meek
My. 126– 5 to drown the s' swimmer
126–21 s' is the Lord God — *Rev.* 18: 8.
129– 7 is taking s' hold of the public
229–30 Truth is s' with destiny ;
252–15 wait on God, the s' deliverer,
258– 9 bowed in s' affection's anguish,
290– 1 felt by the s' hearts of New England
291–24 while her reapers are s',
309–15 s' believer in States' rights,
355–11 a s' supporting arm to religion
355–13 the s', the faithful, the untiring

stronger
Mis. 10–12 rise again, s' than before
160–14 trial of our faith in God makes us s'
235–17 and a s' desire for it.
278–20 seem s' to resist temptation
339–15 if it yields not, grows s'.
Rud. 12– 9 until they hold s' than before
Pan. 10–14 s' and better than before it.
Hea. 10–23 or to argue s' for sorrow
Peo. 10– 2 and the s' element of action ;
Po. 68–13 s' than these is the spell
My. 162– 8 s' than the might cf empires.
283–18 his grasp of goodness grows s'.

strongest
Mis. 399–11 S' deliverer, friend of the
Ret. 82– 9 widest power and s' growth
Po. 75–18 S' deliverer, friend of the
My. 211–22 where courage should be s',

strongholds
Mis. 303– 9 garrisons these s' of C. S.,
Ret. 80–13 pulling down of sin's s',
My. 40–13 * abandon their s' of rivalry.
127–23 cannot demolish our s'.

strongly
Mis. 271–26 * more s' mark the difference
295–20 for whose ability . . . Mr. Wakeman s'
Pul. 27–11 * members s' insist upon.
37–16 * Mrs. Eddy feels very s',"
37–21 * "Mother feels very s',"

strongly
No. 9–17 opposed occasionally and s'
My. 213–22 strengthen your own citadel more s'.

strove
'00. 9–28 s' earnestly to fit others for this

struck
Mis. 249– 5 The hour has s',
317– 5 The hour has s' for . . . Scientists
Peo. 11– 4 s' the keynote of higher claims,
My. 81– 2 * s' with the air of well-being

structure
Un. 34– 1 the so-called material s',
44– 5 like the s' raised thereupon,
Pul. 23– 5 * MOST UNIQUE S' IN ANY CITY
24– 5 * most unique s' in any city.
41– 1 * s' came forth from the hands of
41– 7 * to help erect this beautiful s',
65–16 * beautiful s' of gray granite,
75–26 * most nearly fire-proof church s'
77– 7 * golden key of the church s'.
Rud. 12– 1 * of the material body.
My. 23–28 * As the stately s' grows,
24–26 * the s' is worthy of our Cause
28–18 * not . . . in the material s',
31–11 * first glimpse of the great s',
32– 7 * acoustic properties of the new s'
46– 3 * the great s' stands,
58–15 * This magnificent s', this fitting
62– 5 * But what of this magnificent s'?
62–12 * crowns the completion of this s'
66–26 * giving her blessing to the s'.
76–31 * s', which is now completed,
78– 5 * imposing s' of gray stone
84–27 * dedication of the beautiful s'
85–16 * in the building of a church s'
85–27 * rested on this s',
94–19 * the s' was free from debt.
98–18 * s' cost about two million dollars,
171–13 view this beautiful s',
342–11 * depend upon the osseous s' ;

struggle
Mis. 41–17 s' with sin is forever done.
64– 2 human cry which voiced that s';
87–31 this interference prolongs the s'
101– 9 It is a revolutionary s'.
101–12 Now cometh a third s' ;
163–25 After his brief brave s',
221–25 s' against both evil and disease,
266– 1 that student must s' up,
288–29 spirit of Love that nerves the s'.
378– 8 and a s' with pride,
Ret. 94– 3 a s' for its demonstration.
Pul. 21–11 faithfully s' till it be accomplished
No. 8–16 s' into freedom and greatness,
33– 8 It requires sacrifice, s', prayer,
'00. 8–15 In this s' remember that
10– 8 and a world-imposed s'.
'02. 6–24 heaven here, — the s' over,
14–24 nor protection in the great s'.
Peo. 10– 5 as we s' through the cold night
My. 158–13 heaven here, the s' over ;
244–18 mortals do not enter without a s'
307–28 mental s' might have caused

struggled
'02. 15– 8 I s' on through many years ;
My. 293–20 spirit and the flesh — s',

struggler
Po. 31– 1 the loyal s' for the right,
My. 350–13 Lift from despair the s'

struggles
Mis. 116–23 watchfulness, prayer, s', tears,
121– 9 human s' against the divine,
131–20 to consider the great s'
204– 1 agony s', pride rebels,
241–16 constant combat and direful s',
324–28 this time he s' on,
Un. 5– 7 mental s' and pride of opinion
No. 35– 7 When human s' cease,
'01. 30– 9 s' to articulate itself.
My. 60– 1 * one who knew of your early s'.
180–22 In our s' with sin and sinners,

struggling
Mis. 63–24 Even as the s' heart,
126– 9 when s' with mankind
344–14 poor sinner s' with temptation,
Pul. 13–17 not s' to lift their heads
No. 40–22 thought s' for freedom.
'01. 17– 7 repentant prodigal . . . s' to return
My. 126– 5 swimmer s' for the shore,
148–27 a sect s' to gain power
150–13 and never weary of s'
159–13 s' to enter into the perfect love

St. Stephen
'00. 14–26   as the devout *St. S·* said :

stubbly
Pul. 49–24   * She chose the *s·* old farm

stubborn
Mis. 119–11   more *s·* than the circumstance,
    398– 5   Thou wilt bind the *s·* will,
Ret. 46–11   Thou wilt bind the *s·* will,
Un. 5–15   No *s·* purpose to force
Pul. 17–10   Thou wilt bind the *s·* will,
Rud. 12–14   will return, and be more *s·*
No. 2– 6   To aver that disease is . . . *s·* reality,
    4–10   never made sickness a *s·* reality.
    5–21   becomes indeed a *s·* reality,
    7–13   sinning sense, *s·* will,
'00. 6–22   from the *s·* thrall of sin
Po. 14– 9   Thou wilt bind the *s·* will,
My. 99–27   * Facts and figures are *s·* things,
    233–20   most *s·* belief to overcome,

student (*see also* student's)
affectionate
My. 322– 6   * Your affectionate *s·*,
another
Mis. 283–15   to treat another *s·* without his
Ret. 89–23   employing another *s·* to take charge
any
Mis. 318–14   Any *s·*, having received instructions
at Harvard College
Ret. 75–21   If a *s·* at Harvard College
become a
Mis. 35–17   *is one obliged to become a s·*
beloved
Mis. 158– 2   *My Beloved S· :*— In reply
My. 135– 2   *Beloved S· :*— The wise man has
    234–16   *Beloved S· :*— The report of the
    247–11   *Beloved S· :*— Christ is meekness
    289– 8   *Beloved S· :*— I deem it proper that
    351– 7   *Beloved S· :*— Your interesting
    357–28   *Beloved S· :*— I have just finished
calls a
Man. 68–24   calls a *s·* in accordance with
can enter
Ret. 47–21   *s·* can enter upon the gospel work
can write
Ret. 76– 4   A *s·* can write voluminous works
class
Ret. 47–16   A Primary class *s·*,
    47–18   a Normal class *s·*
dear
Mis. 157– 2   *My Dear S· :*— It is a great thing
My. 285– 2   *Dear S· :*— Please accept
    295–12   *Dear S· :*— I am in grateful receipt
    359–27   *My Dear S· :*— Awake and arise
    360–29   *My Dear S· :*— Your favor of the
derived
Mis. 302–26   benefit which the *s·* derived
desiring growth
Ret. 86–17   A *s·* desiring growth in the
disable the
My. 4– 5   dishonesty, sin, disable the *s·* ;
each
Mis. 138–10   Each *s·* should seek alone the
    283–24   Each *s·* should, must, work out his
Man. 85– 1   Outside of this Board each *s·*
earnest
My. 110–16   The earnest *s·* of this book,
    240– 6   An earnest *s·* writes to me !
faithful
Mis. 88– 2   A faithful *s·* may even
favored
My. 219– 3   through some favored *s·*.
first
Mis. 29–15   taught the first *s·* in C. S.
    380–12   teach the first *s·* in C. S.
    382–15   first *s·* in C. S. Mind-healing ;
Ret. 42– 1   first *s·* publicly to announce
her
My. 240–23   * replies, through her *s·*,
impart to the
Mis. 292–11   Could I impart to the *s·* the
is not willing
'00. 9– 6   because the *s·* is not willing
letter from a
My. 355– 6   letter from a *s·* in the field
literary
My. 320– 1   * that he was a fine literary *s·*
lover and
'01. 32– 6   lover and *s·* of vital Christianity.
loyal
Mis. 91–25   never dreamed, . . . that a loyal *s·*
    318–15   from a loyal *s·* of C. S.,
Man. 38– 5   If the approver is not a loyal *s·* of
Ret. 47–20   from me, or a loyal *s·*,
may mistake
Ret. 83–13   *s·* may mistake in his conception of

student
must have studied
Mis. 318–20   *s·* must have studied faithfully
must stop
Mis. 265–30   If impatient . . . the *s·* must stop
my
Mis. 157–15   Yes, my *s·*, my Father is your
    242–28   he was my *s·* in December, 1884 ;
Ret. 51– 2   my *s·*, Mr. Ira O. Knapp
no
Ret. 44–14   no *s·*, at that time, was found able
Normal
Man. 37–17   One Normal *s·* cannot recommend
    37–18   pupil of another Normal *s·*,
of Christian Science
Mis. 41–10   The honest *s·* of C. S.
    117– 4   The *s·* of C. S. must first
    280–28   import to the *s·* of C. S.,
    318–15   a loyal *s·* of C. S.,
    380–30   issued by a *s·* of C. S.
No. 2–17   honest *s·* of C. S. is modest
of Christ Jesus
'01. 28–28   is not a *s·* of Christ Jesus.
of Mind-healing
Mis. 221–22   baffles the *s·* of Mind-healing,
of mine
Mis. 243– 9   a *s·* of mine removed these
    283–14   For a *s·* of mine to treat
My. 251–18   Primary *s·* of mine can teach
of science
Mis. 52–22   What progress would a *s·* of science
of the Bible
Mis. 64–23   aids to a *s·* of the Bible
of this book
My. 112–24   *s·* of this book will tell you
of this Science
Mis. 43– 9   *s·* of this Science who understands
My. 237– 7   a present *s·* of this Science.
one
Mis. 43–21   If one *s·* tries to undermine
Man. 90–21   One *s·* in the class shall
Ret. 43– 3   I began by teaching one *s·*
possesses
Mis. 55– 6   will come when the *s·* possesses
preparation of the
My. 245– 8   thorough preparation of the *s·*
Primary
My. 251–18   A Primary *s·* of mine can teach
    251–20   Primary *s·* can himself be examined
said
Man. 69– 1   said *s·* shall come under a
should explain
Ret. 83–18   the *s·* should explain only
success of a
Mis. v– 6   CONSTITUTE THE SUCCESS OF A *S·*
such
Man. 69– 9   such *s·* shall pay to Mrs. Eddy
such a
Ret. 90–29   gladdening to find, in such a *s·*,
taught the
'02. 2–30   taught the *s·* to overcome evil
teacher and
Man. 87–21   better . . . for both teacher and *s·*.''
Ret. 84–26   better . . . for both teacher and *s·*.
that
Mis. 88– 5   the better it is for that *s·*.
    266– 1   Then that *s·* must struggle up,
My. 249–28   I should prefer that *s·* who
the very
Mis. 350– 6   with advice of the very *s·* who
this
Mis. 265–23   misconduct of this *s·*.
    340–11   This *s·* had taken the above-named
white
My. 259– 4   I have named it my *white s·*.
who heals
Mis. 358– 4   *s·* who heals by teaching
who pays
Rud. 14–16   *s·* who pays must of necessity
worthy
My. 215–17   home for the poor worthy *s·*,
your
My. 325–17   * ever faithfully your *s·*,

Mis. 38–27   to make each patient a *s·*
    40–19   the *s·* does not in every case
    40–26   *s·* or practitioner has to master
    50–15   essential that the *s·* gain the
    117–20   To point out every step to a *s·*
    157– 1   chapter sub-title
    158– 1   chapter sub-title
    264–28   mental development of the *s·* ;
    265–22   Truth and its ethics to a *s·*,
    292–28   I never knew a *s·* who fully
    293–14   If . . . is not dominant in a *s·*,
    316–12   hour best for the *s·*,

student

Mis.	348–32	A s· who consulted me
Man.	35– 5	by a s· of the Board of Education,
	38– 6	or a s· of the Board of Education
	69– 6	s· who has been called to serve our
Ret.	78– 4	In healing . . . the s· has not yet
	90– 1	s· should be most careful not to
Rud.	15– 3	a s·, if healed in a class,
Hea.	14–23	I waited many years for a s· to
My.	239– 6	acquaint the s· with God.
	285– 1	chapter sub-title
		(see also **Eddy**)

student's

Mis.	156–15	one s· opinions or *modus*
	349– 8	materialization of a s· thought,
Man.	84–13	s· price for teaching C. S.
	86– 4	After a s· pupil has been duly

students (see also **students'**)

advise
No.	8–10	Advise s· to rebuke each other
'00.	8–30	I sometimes advise s·

affectionate
Pul.	86– 6	* from her affectionate S·,

all
Mis.	32–18	to talk with all s· of C. S.,
	272–29	to act toward all s· of C. S.

and patients
Ret.	83– 4	will commend s· and patients

any
Mis.	349–17	no jurisdiction over any s·.

are examined
Man.	90– 3	S· are examined and given

association of
Man.	86–13	in charge of an association of s·
Pul.	58– 5	* gathered an association of s·,

beloved
Mis.	93– 3	Beloved s·, *so teach that*
	110–15	*Beloved S· :— Weeks have passed*
	116–11	*Beloved S· :— This question,*
	120–11	Beloved s·, loyal laborers
	134–10	*Beloved S· :— Meet together*
	135–28	*Beloved S· :— You may be looking*
	142–11	*Beloved S· and Friends :*
	143–14	*Beloved S· :— On the 21st day*
	146– 6	*Beloved S· :— I cannot conscientiously*
	147– 3	*Beloved S· :— Another year*
	155–16	*Beloved S· :— Because Mother*
	159–11	*Beloved S· :— My heart has*
	203– 1	*Beloved S· :— In thanking you*
	206–24	Beloved s·, you have entered
	278–18	beloved s·, who are absent
My.	20– 8	*Beloved S· :— The holidays are*
	26– 9	*Beloved S· :— Your generous*
	139– 2	*Beloved S· :— Rest assured*
	142–26	*Beloved S· :— I thank you*
	167–15	*Beloved S· :— May this, your first*
	171– 9	*Beloved S· :— The new Concord church*
	183–24	*Beloved S· and Church :— Thanks for*
	192–20	*Beloved S· :— Your kind letter,*
	194–19	*Beloved S· :—Your telegram,*
	197–10	*Beloved S· :— Words are inadequate*
	198– 3	*Beloved S· and Brethren :* —Your letters
	199– 3	BELOVED S· AND BRETHREN : — I rejoice
	201– 1	God is blessing you, my beloved s·
	203–24	*Beloved S· :— You have laid the*
	224–30	Beloved s·, just now let
	226–21	Beloved s·, in this you learn
	229–20	Will those beloved s·, whose growth
	230–18	*Beloved S· :— I read with pleasure*
	236– 2	Will the beloved s· accept
	243– 2	BELOVED S· :— According to reports,
	248– 2	*Beloved S· :— I am more than*
	250–15	*Beloved S· :— The By-law of*
	251–24	*Beloved S· :— I call you mine,*
	252–19	*Beloved S· :—Your letter and*
	253–21	*Beloved S· :— You will accept*
	254–10	*Beloved S· :— Responding to*
	257–24	*Beloved S· :— For your manifold*

best
Pan.	10–13	best s· in the class averred

called on
Mis.	351– 1	called on s· to test their ability

came
Pul.	68– 6	* S· came to it in hundreds

can confer
Man.	88–20	s· can confer with their teachers

certain
Mis.	353–28	Certain s·, being too much

charity
Mis.	267– 6	Charity s·, for whom I have

Christian
Mis.	132–25	and to my Christian s·.
	243–18	My Christian s· are . . . modest :
	301–13	My Christian s· who have read copies
	303– 6	Christian s· should have their own

students

Christian
Ret.	54–24	My Christian s·, impressed with the
No.	9– 1	as my Christian s· can testify ;

Christian Science
Un.	5–22	C. S. s· and Christians who

class of
Mis.	32–16	to the above-named class of s·

crowded with
Mis.	5– 6	crowded with s· who are willing to

dear
Mis.	137– 2	*My Dear S· and Friends :*
	143– 4	My dear s· may have explained
	159–21	gifts that my dear s· offer
	262–13	I thank you, my dear s·,
My.	234– 7	Did the dear s· know how much I
	358–23	love to your dear s· and church.

decrease of
My.	266–12	decrease of s· in the seminaries

devoted
Mis.	318– 7	love some of those devoted s·

disloyal
Mis.	32– 4	*students of disloyal s·*
My.	130– 8	effort of disloyal s· to blacken me

early
My.	321–27	* that I was among your early s·

employed
Man.	69–21	S· employed by Mrs. Eddy

faithful
Mis.	356–20	Now let my faithful s·

five thousand
Mis.	29–17	about five thousand s·.

free
Rud.	14–14	sometimes seventeen, free s· in it ;

good
My.	219– 6	My good s· have all the honor of

her
Mis.	37–27	leaving to her s· the work of
	40–22	Founder of C. S. teaches her s·
	54–10	Thousands . . . are her s·,
Man.	18–14	twelve of her s·
My.	48–11	* insisted that her s· make,
	53–22	* pulpit was supplied . . . by her s·
	359–21	* by twenty-four of her s·

his
Mis.	92–14	and his s· will answer them
	92–31	teacher does most for his s·
	97– 8	Master said of one of his s·,
	212– 8	tersely reminded his s·
	265– 7	also predisposes his s· to
	265–17	visited upon himself and his s·,
	293– 9	should impart to his s· the
	315–16	look after the welfare of his s·,
Ret.	68–13	Our Master instructed his s·
	84–19	teacher does most for his s· who
No.	2–11	Our Master taught his s·
'01.	33–23	which he enjoined his s· to teach
My.	215–23	Master first sent forth his s·,
	215–28	Why did he send forth his s·
	364–13	should teach his s· to defend

his own
Ret.	89–19	method was to instruct his own s· ;

honest
Mis.	44– 1	Honest s· speak the truth

hundreds of
Pul.	36– 8	* hundreds and hundreds of s·,

imposed by
Mis.	351– 3	to lift the burdens imposed by s·.

in Christian Science
Ret.	50–23	I see clearly that s· in C. S.

indigent
Mis.	11– 8	taught indigent s· gratuitously,
'02.	15– 7	rooming and boarding indigent s·
My.	214–24	C. S. home for indigent s·,

in mathematics
Mis.	29–30	Christians, like s· in mathematics,

in New York
My.	243–15	s· in New York and elsewhere

its
Mis.	40–11	why do not its s· perform as
Pul.	44–20	* has shown its power over its s,

I warn
Mis.	309–18	I warn s· against falling into

Jesus'
No.	14–22	are not confined to Jesus' s·
My.	190–14	Jesus' s·, failing to cure a severe

letters from
My.	319–11	* heading
	319–12	* following letters from s·

loving
Pul.	86–20	* In behalf of your loving s·

loyal
Mis.	266–19	my loyal s· in Chicago,
	283–12	is seldom the case with loyal s·,
Man.	35– 4	by one of Mrs. Eddy's loyal s·,
	36– 6	coming from pupils of loyal s·

students

loyal
Man. 38– 3 loyal s· of the textbook,
89–11 Loyal s· who have been taught
109– 7 except loyal s· of Mrs. Eddy,
Ret. 50–12 ask my loyal s· if they
50–17 Loyal s· speak with delight
82–10 attained by those loyal s·
Rud. v– 5 LOYAL S·, WORKING and WAITING
'00. 9–25 loyal s· will tell you that
My. 182–16 faithful labor of loyal s·,
244–21 all loyal s· of my books

loyalty in
Ret. 50–19 By loyalty in s· I mean this,

malignant
Mis. 249–21 efforts of some malignant s·,

many
Mis. 264–13 Many s· enter the Normal class
299–12 to the minds of many s·.
Rud. 14–26 Many s·, who have passed through
My. 360–14 as many s· think I can,

Mrs. Eddy's
Man. 18–19 Mrs. Eddy's s· and members of

my
Mis. 32– 6 some of my s· seem not
87–22 My s· are taught the divine
88– 1 to blight the fruits of my s·.
115–13 May God enable my s·
137–14 rejoice over the growth of my s·
137–29 My s· can now organize
159–12 to the memory of my s·.
203– 4 my s· and your students ;
203– 7 this gift from my s·
214–19 My s· need to search the
215–23 My s· are at the beginning
242– 6 offered me, . . . or one of my s·,
264–15 taught their first lessons by my s· ;
273– 8 My s· have never expressed
273–13 gather all my s·, in the
276–10 My s·, our delegates,
276–24 I pray that all my s·
278–25 perpetual instruction of my s·
279–13 My s·, three picture-stories
281–23 Among the gifts of my s·,
302– 9 My s· are expected to know
316–25 had my s· achieved the point
318– 1 chapter sub-title
318– 5 not alone for my s·,
356–10 My s·, with cultured intellects,
380–17 My s· at first practised
Ret. 43–22 six of my s· in 1876,
52–12 I suggested to my s·,
82– 5 my s· should not allow
82–14 my s· should locate in
90–20 One of my s· wrote to me :
Un. 1–14 I counsel my s· to defer
No. 8–19 my s· to hold no controversy
9–16 my s· who fall into error,
40–14 I instruct my s· to pursue
'01. 17–21 into the hands of my s·
29–26 To aid my s· in starting
My. 121–17 presented to me by my s·
130–17 my s· reprove, rebuke,
138–12 my s· and trusted personal friends
153– 7 gospel ministry of my s·
244–22 are indeed my s·,
249–27 If both . . . Readers are my s·,

my own
Mis. 155–24 If my own s· cannot spare time

no aid to
Mis. 150–26 no aid to s· in acquiring

noble
Mis. 264– 3 My noble s·, who are loyal to

Normal
Man. 37–16 Pupils of Normal S·.

not
Mis. 271– 6 (and many who are not s·)

number of
Mis. 256–15 but a select number of s·.
Rud. 15–19 very limited number of s·

of Christian Science
Mis. 32–18 to talk with all s· of C. S.,
40–13 In some instances the s· of C. S.
271– 5 S· of C. S. (and many who
272–29 to act toward all s· of C. S.
357–22 those s· of C. S. whose
Man. 45–23 S· of C. S. must drop the titles of
91–19 S· of C. S., duly instructed

of mine
Mis. 87–19 to teach s· of mine.
Ret. 43–19 These s· of mine were the only

of Mrs. Eddy
Man. 35–20 s· of Mrs. Eddy, loyal to the
109– 7 except loyal s· of Mrs. Eddy,
My. 319–12 * letters from s· of Mrs. Eddy

students

of students
Mis. 317–24 enlisted for the s· of students ;

of the Christ
My. 190–25 become s· of the Christ,

of the College
Mis. 64– 9 prospective s· of the College
Man. 35–10 S· of the College.

older
My. 323–26 * should mean to your older s·

other
Mis. 349–19 several other s· with him.
Man. 35–17 Other S·.
Ret. 82– 6 to be controlled by other s·,
83– 8 by the teachings of other s·,
My. 138–14 Mr. Calvin A. Frye and other s·
361– 5 your relations with other s·.

Oxford
Hea. 18–27 Oxford s· proved this :

practising
Mis. 4–15 and to the practising s·,

Primary
Man. 91–19 Primary S·.
Rud. 14–22 If the Primary s· are

progress of
Mis. 156–20 clogs the progress of s·,

prospective
Mis. 64– 9 What can prospective s· of the College

qualified
My. 231–11 She has qualified s· for healing

scientific
Mis. 308–12 scientific s· are ready for

send out
Mis. 273–20 to send out s· from these sources
My. 300–24 send out s· according to Christ's

serving
Mis. 303–17 If ever I wear out from serving s·,

sixty-five
Mis. 279–12 ATTENDANCE OF SIXTY-FIVE S·.

some
Mis. 115– 4 the apathy of some s·
264–19 Some s· leave my instructions
My. 363–23 misunderstood by some s·.

students'
Mis. 155–20 First, that you, her students' s·,
316– 5 chapter sub-title

such
Mis. 264–22 Such s· are more or less subject
317–27 Such s· should not pay the
No. 42 22 Such s· come to my College
My. 197–15 Comparing such s· with those

taught
My. 215– 7 taught s· for a tuition of

their
Mis. 137–29 organize their s· into associations,
138– 1 their s· will sustain themselves
203– 8 from my students and their s·,
303– 8 teaching and guiding their s·.
315–25 nor allow their s· to do thus,
315–28 strive to educate their s·
315–32 They shall teach their s·
Ret. 85– 4 band together their s· into
89–24 to take charge of their s·,
No. 3–16 and recommend it to their s·,

their own
Ret. 80 21 or for neglecting their own s·.

these
Mis. 349–21 some of these s· have openly
Ret. 43–19 These s· of mine were the only

thirty-three
Mis. 315–13 consist of not over thirty-three s·,

those
Mis. 357–22 those s· of C. S.
Pan. 10–15 present and future of those s·

those very
My. 215–11 those very s· sent me the

thy
Mis. 318– 1 chapter sub-title
318– 6 not alone for . . . but for thy s·,

to fit
Rud. 16– 5 will never undertake to fit s· for

to qualify
Mis. 43–19 to qualify s· for the great ordeal

treat
Mis. 243– 6 although s· treat sprains,

true-hearted
Mis. 301–19 question of my true-hearted s·,

two
My. 243–14 two s· who are adequate to

unchristian
Rud. 16–25 among unchristian s·,

unprincipled
Mis. 265–30 self-satisfied, unprincipled s·.

Western
My. 197–13 of our far Western s·,

students

wise
Mis. 393–13 S· wise, he maketh now
Po. 51–18 S· wise, he maketh now
with Mrs. Eddy
Man. 69–21 S· with Mrs. Eddy.
with the degree
Mis. 349– 6 s· with the degree of M. D.,
your
Mis. 54–19 treatment by one of your s·.
54–25 Because none of your s· have
119–29 manipulate your s·, . . . No !
203– 4 between my students and your s· ;
My. 63– 6 * gratefully your s·,
319–18 * observation of many of your s·,
358–19 was given you by your s·.
359–29 allowing your s· to deify you
359–30 get your s· to help you

Mis. ix– 7 among my thousands of s·
11–13 my whole duty to s·.
32– 3 s· of disloyal students
32– 8 the s· of false teachers,
87–17 to look after the s·;
91–28 I supposed that s· had
92–19 require the s· . . . to study it
138– 9 For s· to work together
156– 6 chapter sub-title
263–16 The need of . . . felt by s·,
280–18 s· of this Primary class,
284–10 S· who strictly adhere to the right,
298–24 chapter sub-title
302–19 s· working faithfully for Christ's
302–32 I recommend that s· stay
311– 7 to Christian Scientists' s·,
317– 1 To the s· whom I have not seen
318– 6 for s· of the second generation.
348–29 have by no means encouraged s· of
358–30 When s· have fulfilled all the
Man. 17– 5 s· of Mrs. Mary Baker Eddy
35–12 s· of the Massachusetts Metaphysical
73– 9 or s· in any university
88–17 is not to be consulted by s·
109– 8 s· of the Board of Education
Ret. 36– 7 writing out my manuscripts for s·
47– 4 S· from all over our continent,
48–22 s· instructed in C. S. Mind-healing,
50–29 S· are not environed with such
78–11 I recommend s· not to
81– 4 Nothing except sin, in the s·
83– 7 S· whom I have taught
91–22 s· whom he had chosen,
Pul. 79– 9 * as s· of public questions
Rud. 14–19 furnished s· with the means of
15–14 besides invalids for s·,
No. 7–20 s· must now fight their own battles.
Pan. 10–11 s· at the Massachusetts Metaphysical
'01. 21– 4 s· of a demonstrable Science
29–29 this percentage,'' s· wrote me,
My. 26–21 the lie that s· worship me
125–21 in my last class in 1898
130– 9 s· seeking only public notoriety,
190–22 gave his disciples (s·) power over
236–29 it will greatly aid the s·
241– 6 * S· who are ready for this step
244– 6 if . . . were advantageous to the s·.
245–22 S· . . . have received certificates,
245–32 to s· of the Primary class ;
246– 5 * S· who enter the . . . College,
251– 7 * s·, whom I have taught,
253–19 chapter sub-title
302–14 I begged the s· who first

students'

Mis. 93– 1 able to empty his s· minds,
138–23 members of s· organizations.
155–20 her s· students, who write such
266–26 in accordance with my s· desires,
316– 5 chapter sub-title
380–19 my s· patients, and people generally,
Man. 36– 4 S· Pupils.
Ret. 84–21 to empty his s· minds of error,

studied

Mis. 58–10 that she has read and s· correctly,
147–26 for he acts no s· part ;
318–16 s· thoroughly ''S. and H.
318–20 student must have s· faithfully
344– 5 have you s· music, astronomy, and
344–11 had not s· those branches,
375–12 * s· the old masters and their great
Man. 35–13 s· with Rev. Mary Baker Eddy,
35–18 who have not s· C. S. with
111–10 s· C. S. with an authorized teacher ;
111–12 not s· C. S. with a teacher.
Ret. 10–10 My brother s· Hebrew
47–20 s· thoroughly S. and H.,

studied

Ret. 47–24 s· the latest editions of my works,
75–22 s· a textbook written by
Pul. 64–15 * She s· the Scriptures and
73– 9 * s· and meditated over His
My. 60– 8 * told that I had s· with you.
239– 7 In the ratio that C. S. is s·

studies

Mis. 64–10 take for preliminary s·?
Ret. 10– 7 My favorite s· were
Pul. 46–23 * applied herself, . . . to her s·,
Pan. 3–23 (one of my girlhood s·),
My. 113– 5 s· it and thereby is healed
237– 9 his earliest s· or discoveries.
304– 5 finished my course of s·
304– 7 Among my early s· were

studio

My. 259– 1 take a peep into my s· ;

study (noun)

and foundation
Pul. 71–20 * the s· and foundation of the faith
careful
Pul. 64–20 * After careful s· she became
My. 237–23 I recommend its careful s·
close
Pan. 7–18 close s· of the Old and New
continue the
Mis. 92–23 continue the s· of this textbook.
incessant
Ret. 7– 9 * intense and almost incessant s·
more
Mis. 366– 4 requires more s· to understand
No. 11–19 requires more s· to understand
observation or
Mis. 308–33 from their observation or s·
of literature
Mis. 64–10 s· of literature and languages
of music
Mis. 375–15 * s· of music and art.
of Science and Health
My. 112–26 conscientious s· of S. and H.
pastor's
Pul. 27– 7 * class-rooms and the pastor's s·.
58–23 * Adjoining . . . is a pastor's s· ;
prayerful
My. 48–11 * prayerful s· of the Bible,
proper
Mis. 48–26 proper s· of Mind-healing would
searching
Pul. 73–20 * a careful and searching s·
unbiased
My. 96–15 * intelligent and unbiased s·
weary with
Mis. 236– 8 and become weary with s·
without
Mis. 279–15 from which we learn without s·.

Mis. 156–18 through the s· of my works
284–11 make the Bible and S. and H. a s·,
317–14 by the s· of what is written.

study (verb)

Mis. 5–11 Many say, ''I should like to s·,
35–18 if one is obliged to s·
35–22 and then s· it at college
38–25 Is it necessary to s· your Science
54–17 Must I s· your Science in order to
87–24 s· thoroughly the Scriptures
91–31 to require their pupils to s· the
92– 7 needs continually to s· this textbook.
92–20 to s· it before the recitations ;
315–29 to s· His revealed Word,
375–20 * s· each illustration thoroughly,
Man. 83–21 to s· the Scriptures and S. AND H.
Ret. 83–26 s· each lesson before the recitation.
84– 4 should continue to s· this textbook,
84–12 continue to s· and assimilate this
No. 28–19 S· C. S. and practise it,
'01. 34–23 s· the Bible and the textbook

studying

Mis. 5– 9 by s· this scientific method
48–23 made insane by s· metaphysics ?
310– 1 s· Truth through the senses,
Hea. 12–14 When s· the . . . remedies of the Jahr,
My. 323–30 * s· in the second class with you

stuff

Mis. 227–11 to get their weighty s· into the
354– 7 to overbalance this foul s·.
My. 313–11 Nor do I remember any such s·

stuffed

My. 99–20 * s· and jammed with money.

stultifies
Mis. 288–32 s· and causes him to degenerate
Un. 36–24 This error s· the logic of
No. 3–19 Dishonesty necessarily s· the

stultify
Mis. 221–15 will s· the power to heal mentally.
Un. 25– 3 s· my intellect, insult my

stultifying
Mis. 265– 9 Diverse opinions in Science are s·.

stumble
Mis. 10–12 stronger than before the s·.
264– 6 others s· over misdeeds,
328–24 causing to s·, fall, or faint,
Pul. 7–21 s· onward to their doom ;
My. 11– 3 * although we may falter or s·
152–19 s· into doubt and darkness,

stumbled
Mis. 328–17 hast thou turned back, s·,

stumbling
Mis. 327–29 s· and grumbling, and fighting

stung
Pul. 13–24 dragon is at last s· to death
'01. 31– 1 world-worshipper are always s· by

stunning
My. 71–10 * a s· piece of architecture

stupefied
Mis. 328–19 pleased and s·, until wakened

stupendous
Mis. 99– 7 The risk is s·.
213–10 No risk is so s· as
380–11 impelled me to begin this s· work
My. 14– 8 s·, Godlike agency of man.
97–16 * s·, inexplicable faith
97–29 * produced by that s· gathering.
165–17 portion of one s· whole,
269–12 * parts of one s· whole,

stupid
Mis. 343–22 O s· gardener !
398– 8 Break earth's s· rest.
Ret. 46–14 Break earth's s· rest.
Pul. 17–13 Break earth's s· rest.
Po. 14–12 Break earth's s· rest.

sturdy
Mis. 240–17 while the s· oak, with form
Ret. 2– 2 s· Calvinistic devotion to
17–19 s· horse-chestnut for centuries
Po. 63– 5 s· horse-chestnut for centuries

Stygian
No. 22–14 as S· night to the kindling dawn.
My. 350–21 S· shadow of a world of glee) ;

style
Mis. 294–27 terse, graphic, and poetic s·
366–17 new s· of imposition in the field
Pul. 59–20 * in a clear emphatic s·.
No. 10– 9 The former is the highest s· of man ;
My. 68– 1 * Italian Renaissance s·,
309–24 prevailing s· of architecture
318– 2 constituted a new s· of language.

styled
'01. 01– 6 s· the laws of nature,

subdivide
Ret. 56–23 does not s· Mind, or good,
Un. 44–16 would multiply and s· personality

subdivided
No. 26– 4 s· into spirits, or souls,

subdivides
Ret. 28–19 which divides, s·, increases,

subdivision
Ret. 56–20 by the reflection, not the s·,

subdue
Un. 42–17 ability to s· material conditions.
Pul. 84– 2 * shall s· the whole earth with the
No. 11–26 Revelation must s· the sophistry of

subdued
Mis. 2–12 s· and recompensed by justice,
200–30 s· it with this understanding.
354–17 a character s·, a life consecrated,
Ret. 58– 8 sense of power that s· matter
My. 200–26 him who suffered and s· sorrow.

subdues
Mis. 74– 3 new-born sense s· not only the
My. 131– 2 removes fear, s· sin, and

subduing
'02. 10–13 subjugating the body, s· matter,
Po. 68–11 Enchant deep the senses, — s·,

subject (noun)
abstract
Mis. 38–15 *such a dry and abstract s·?*
considering a
Mis. 271–15 considering a s· that is unworthy
following
Mis. 349–22 a question on the following s·,
for lessons
Man. 62–24 S· for Lessons.
My. 231–29 By-law, "S· for Lessons"
general
My. 107– 6 general s· under discussion,
given out
Mis. 350– 8 s· given out for consideration
350–15 s· given out at that meeting was,
gives the
My. 234–20 gives the s· quite another aspect.
great
Mis. 7–32 enlightened on this great s·.
Hea. 1–12 great s· of Christian healing ;
My. 339– 8 great s· of C. S.
greater
Mis. 65– 9 greater s· of human weal and woe
her
My. 346– 3 * as one who has lived with her s·
important
Un. 1– 8 reason together on this important s·,
inexhaustible
Ret. 84–13 assimilate this inexhaustible s·
interest in the
My. 322–28 * Seeing my great interest in the s·,
leaves the
Mis. 188–19 and right there he leaves the s·.
leave the
Ret. 63–25 and leave the s· there.
Un. 1–16 better leave the s· untouched,
my
Pan. 13–27 only traversed my s· that you may
'02. 4–13 My s· to-day embraces the
new
Un. 7– 2 apprehension of this new s·,
of Christian Science
Mis. 382– 3 No works on the s· of C. S.
My. 125–24 looking into the s· of C. S.,
339– 8 the great s· of C. S.
of mental practice
Man. 90–20 s· of mental practice and *malpractice.*
of sin
Mis. 115– 4 s· of sin and mental malpractice,
of the Trinity
My. 338– 7 * upon the s· of the Trinity,
our
Mis. 188–16 On our s·, St. Paul first reasons
said
Man. 67–16 conferred with her on said s·.
70– 6 first consulting her on said s·
90–22 shall prepare a paper on said s·
same
My. 322–13 * letter to you on the same s· ;
scarcely awakes
Mis. 222–18 the s· scarcely awakes in time,
settle the
Pul. 9–15 and helped settle the s·
silence on the
My. 104–21 reason for his silence on the s·,
takes up the
My. 217–29 Jesus . . . first takes up the s·.
that
Mis. 306– 6 * any ideas on that s·
Man. 94–13 depart in quiet *thought* on that s·
this
Mis. 32–14 will find my views on this s· ;
44– 4 are ready to investigate this s·,
76–18 his authority on this s·
115–11 ignorance of the community on this s·
130– 9 What do we find . . . on this s·?
130–15 Note the Scripture on this s·.
156–17 read "Retrospection" on this s·.
185–29 When reasoning on this s· of man
192–25 Mark is emphatic on this s· ;
193–18 modification of silence on this s·,
269– 6 Hear the Master on this s· :
310–24 action of the church on this s·.
348–32 consulted me on this s·,
382–16 the first books on this s· ;
Man. 59– 4 at random on this s·,
87– 7 not to be consulted on this s·.
Ret. 35– 9 before a work on this s· could
Un. 5–16 force conclusions on this s·
7–17 views here promulgated on this s·
31–21 This s· can be enlarged.
Pul. 80–16 * On this s· we have no opinion
Rud. 15–20 grapple with this s·,
No. 32–11 Frequently when I touch this s·
'01. 14–11 Our only departure . . . on this s· is,
21–25 knows more than any man on this s·,

subject (noun)

this

'01.   26–25   this s· of the old metaphysicians,
     27–11   correct on this s·
'02.   5–30   silences all questions on this s·,
My.   250–24   favored moment to act on this s·.
     256–13   close the door of mind on this s·,
     303– 6   Scriptures relative to this s·.

this very

Mis.   32–12   and in my books, on this very s·.

whole

Un.   36–10   This whole s· is met
My.   363–23   gist of the whole s· was not to

works on the

Mis.   382– 3   No works on the s· of C. S.

Mis.   4–20   on the s· of metaphysical healing,
     116–10   S· : Obedience.
     132– 2   on a s· the substance whereof you
     146–11   regarding both sides of the s·,
     161– 4   S· : The Corporeal and Incorporeal
     299–26   this question on the s·,
Man.   58–11   The s· of the Lesson-Sermon
Ret.   35– 7   so unfamiliar with the s·
Pul.   72– 7   * conversations upon the s·.
Rud.   11–26   the s· of human anatomy ;
     15–25   a s· laid bare for anatomical
No.   13–23   on the s· of mediumship,
Pan.   1– 4   S· : Not Pantheism, but C. S.
'01.   26–29   on the s· of metaphysical healing
My.   33– 8   * s· of the special Lesson-Sermon
     53–31   * address them on the s·.
     60– 4   * to instruct them on the s·
     97–10   * kept no books on the s·,
     151–22   S· : "Not Matter, but Spirit"
     281–22   * on some phase of the s·,
     294– 2   on the s· of divine metaphysics ;
     305– 8   the s· of "vulgar metaphysics,"
     338–12   s· "The Unknown God Made Known,"

subject (adj. and verb)

Mis.   36–25   not s· to the law of God, — Rom. 8 : 7.
     39– 4   To avoid being s· to disease,
     54–22   But not to be s· again to
     82–31   not s· to growth, change, or
     104– 4   not s· to the temptations of
     264–22   Such students are more or less s· to
     284– 5   C. S., . . . is s· to abuses.
     338–15   will s· one to deception ;
     341–15   is s· to terrible torture if the
Man.   25– 9   s· to the approval of
     28– 1   s· to the approval of
     46–17   failure to do this shall s· the
     63–22   s· to the approval of
     65–23   shall be s· to the approval of
     78–14   and be s· to the approval of
     80– 7   hold this money s· to the order of
     80–21   s· to her approval.
     88–14   shall be s· to the approval of
     93– 7   s· to the approval of
Ret.   48– 8   s· to the one builder and maker,
No.   41–15   to s· them to severe scrutiny,
'01.   19–24   to s· mankind unwarned and
'02.   11– 5   s· to sin, disease, and death.
Peo.   11–11   is made s· to his Maker.

subjected

Ret.   71–15   Who is willing to be s· to such

subjection

Mis.   67–28   without his s· to death,
     201– 6   into s· to Spirit.

subjective

Mis.   24–18   s· state which it names matter,
     73–20   s· states of false sensation
     86–26   s· state of high thoughts.
     102–26   s· state of mortal . . . thought.
     105–25   their own s· state of thought.
     260–16   sickness, and death are its s· states ;
     266– 8   s· state of his own mind
     286–22   s· states of the human . . . mind ;
     367– 5   Matter and evil are s· states of
Rud.   10–10   from the s· states of thought,
No.   14– 7   s· states of mortal mind.
     16–11   The s· states of evil,
My.   109– 1   s· state of mortal mind.
     265–26   reflect this purified s· state

subject-matter

Ret.   82–29   makes the s· clearer than any

subjects

Mis.   146–13   declined to be consulted on these s·,
     317–21   s· of such earnest import.
     339– 2   confine their talk to s· that are
     350–20   misconception of those s·
Man.   53–13   trouble her on s· unnecessarily
     88–20   s· essential to their progress.
Rud.   2– 6   s·, or agents, constituting the

subjects

Hea.   9–12   s· they would gladly discontinue to
     16–17   leave our abstract s· for this time.
     16–26   that we look into these s·,
Peo.   7–25   appeal to mind to improve its s·
My.   242–22   not to make inquiries on these s·,
     338–16   their s· or the handling thereof,
     345–31   * We talked on many s·,

subjugate

Un.   50– 9   s· it as Jesus did,

subjugated

Mis.   118– 1   Human will must be s·.

subjugates

Mis.   260–17   s· and destroys any suppositional
'02.   10– 1   Whatever . . . s· matter, has a fight

subjugating

'02.   10–13   it is s· the body,

subjugation

Mis.   361– 1   rather was it their s·,

sublime

Mis.   131–10   substance of our s· faith,
     137–22   the s· ends of human life.
     163– 7   a s· and everlasting victory !
     227–25   s· summary of an honest life
     369– 8   to stand erect on s· heights,
     393– 5   Soul, s· 'mid human débris,
Ret.   92– 2   not too simple to be s·,
Un.   58–14   Master's s· triumph over all
Pul.   2–25   would overthrow this s· fortress,
'02.   16–21   The meek might, s· patience,
Po.   39– 4   Temperance and truth in song s·
     51–10   Soul, s· 'mid human débris,
     68–11   rock and the sea . . . subduing, s· ;
My.   121– 8   strength of peace . . . is s·,
     189– 3   started in this s· ascent,
     277–12   answer to the s· question

sublimity

Mis.   88–24   * those who do not enter into its s·
My.   25–25   s· of this superb superstructure,

sublunary

Pul.   2–11   Turning the attention from s·
Hea.   11– 2   survey the cost of s· joy,

submarine

'02.   11–13   a steam engine, a s· cable,

submerge

My.   259–28   too much to s· itself

submerged

Mis.   184–32   s· in the humane and divine,
'01.   9– 8   s· them in a sense so pure
My.   179– 8   power and . . . are s· in matter.

submit

Mis.   65– 8   s· to the affirmations of Science
     208–11   Mortals have only to s· to the
Man.   77– 6   Treasurer of this Church shall s· them
My.   26–19   enclosed notice I s· to you,
     219–30   that an individual s· to this process,
     220– 3   s· to the providence of God,
     299–10   I s· that C. S. has been widely

submitted

Mis.   271–29   * statistics are officially s· :
My.   195–10   so have s· to necessity,
     213–29   three quotations . . . are s·
     314–19   After the evidence had been s·

subordinate

Mis.   29–30   matter is proven powerless and s· to
Un.   46–11   would s· the fleshly perceptions
Rud.   16– 6   s· to thorough class instruction
My.   265– 6   less s· to material sight

subordinated

'02.   5–12   s· to this commandment,
My.   303–21   His life-work s· the material

subordinates

Mis.   23– 8   s· so-called material laws ;
     189–24   spiritual power that s· matter
Un.   40– 9   s· the belief in death,
No.   24–13   evil s· good in personality.

subordination

Ret.   50–20   s· of the human to the divine,
Rud.   12–25   from any sense of s· to their
My.   48–23   * the s· of merely material
     194–12   in a complete s· of self.

subscribe

Man.   44–18   to s· for the periodicals
My.   299–20   firmly s· to this statement ;
     353– 1   s· for and read our daily newspaper.
     360–15   cheerfully s· these words of love :

subscribed
Pul. 52– 3 * no sums except those already s·
My. 10–14 * donation to be specifically s·
57–30 * no sums except those already s·
72–25 * two million dollars has been s·

subscribing
Mis. 281–27 responsibility you assume when s· to

subscription
Mis. 144– 9 s· list on which appear your
My. 77–30 * secured by voluntary s·.

subscriptions
Pul. 50–15 * no . . . sums outside of the s·
My. 14–16 * further payments or s· were not
89–16 * s· are not solicited.

subsequent
Mis. xi– 4 the initial "G" on my s· books.
Man. 104–16 s· editions of the Church Manual ;
Pul. 31–10 * s· development of some degree of
My. 86–12 * s· ceremonies and exercises.
303–28 her duplicate, antecedent, or s·.
304–20 for ten s· years he
320–22 * several times s· thereto,

subsequently
Mis. 35– 4 and s· her recovery,
191– 5 S·, the ancients changed the meaning
Po. v–21 * which was s· mailed to them.

subserve
Mis. 246– 8 to s· the interests of wealth,
My. 147–14 May this little sanctum . . . s· it.
339– 1 s· the interest of mankind,

subserved
My. 278– 3 s· by the battle's plan

subserves
My. 4–17 such an individual s· the

subsidence
My. 40– 8 * imply the s· of criticism

subsides
Pul. 50–25 * after a little skirmishing, finally s·.
Rud. 15–11 until this impulse s·.

subsist
My. 216– 8 s· on demand and supply,

substance
actual
Hea. 16– 7 which to you hath the most actual s·,
all
Mis. 199–26 all s·, Life, and intelligence
and immortality
Un. 60–23 s·, and immortality be lost.
and intelligence
Mis. 309–12 spiritual s· and intelligence.
Hea. 16– 5 Life, s·, and intelligence
and life
Mis. 187–21 s·, and life of man are one,
and mind
Ret. 21–21 false sense of life, s·, and mind
and penmanship
My. 137– 9 * in both s· and penmanship :
and practicality
Mis. 193– 8 s· and practicality of all
and reality
My. 109– 2 no more s· and reality in our
becomes the
Mis. 301–13 And Love becomes the s·,
Po. 38–12 Love becomes the s·,
called matter
Un. 33– 5 existence of a s· called matter.
constant
Ret. 32–17 * Whose most constant s· seems
divine
Mis. 68– 1 fact of divine s·, intelligence,
falls short of
My. 260–15 sense that falls short of s·,
her
My. 19–21 her s·, the immortal fruition of
his
Mis. 167–11 His s· outweighs the material
intelligence, nor
Mis. 21–17 intelligence, nor s· in matter.
its
Ret. 23–22 its s·, cause, and currents
My. 295– 5 holds its s· safe in the
Life, and
Mis. 55–25 the only Mind, Life, and s·.
life, . . . and intelligence
Mis. 175– 6 sense of life, s·, and intelligence,
218– 9 of life, s·, and intelligence,
Ret. 67– 7 that life, s·, and intelligence are
Life's
My. 290–20 passed earth's shadow into Life's s·.
make room for
My. 260– 7 to make room for s·,

substance
material
Un. 24–16 There is no material s·,
means more
Mis. 47– 6 s· means more than matter :
mortal sense of
Mis. 28– 1 Take away the mortal sense of s·,
nor intelligence
Ret. 93–20 s·, nor intelligence in matter."
of Christian Science
Mis. 357–31 Divine Love is the s· of C. S.,
My. 37–22 * the s· of C. S.,
of form
Mis. 87– 9 spiritual reality and s· of form,
of God
Mis. 104– 7 yea, the s· of God,
187–24 Did the s· of God, Spirit,
of good
Mis. 103–12 who knoweth the s· of good?"
Ret. 57–16 is . . . the s· of good.
Un. 61–18 is . . . not the s· of good.
of life
Mis. 103–11 say . . . "The s· of life is sorrow
of my Address
Mis. 98– 7 S· of my Address at the National
of my reply
Mis. 287–23 the s· of my reply is :
of Soul
Mis. 104– 6 safe in the s· of Soul,
of Spirit
Mis. 56– 8 s· of Spirit is divine Mind.
104– 7 the s· of Spirit, . . .of God,
Un. 45–25 It lacks the s· of Spirit,
of the truth
My. 130–30 s· of the truth that is taught ;
of things
Mis. 27–30 s· of things hoped for." — Heb. 11 : 1.
103– 9 s· of things not hoped for.
175–11 s· of things hoped for." — Heb. 11 : 1.
Pan. 15– 8 "s· of things hoped for" Heb. 11 : 1.
My. 226–18 "s· of things hoped for ;" — Heb. 11 : 1.
of this textbook
Ret. 75–24 the s· of this textbook
of Truth
'01. 18–14 s· of Truth transcends the
or intelligence
My. 235–19 Matter as s· or intelligence never was
or law
'02. 6– 3 knowledge of life, s·, or law,
or Life
Mis. 367– 8 error is not Mind, s·, or Life.
or mind
Mis. 198–10 claim to . . . s·, or mind in matter,
My. 296–16 dream of life, s·, or mind in matter,
people of
My. 80– 3 * people of s· and of standing,
physical
'01. 23–27 declared physical s· to be "only
real
Un. 34–26 Immortal Mind is the real s·,
reality and
Un. 49–10 reality and s· of being are good,
reflection is
Ret. 57–16 and this reflection is s·,
sense of
Mis. 86–20 gain the glorified sense of s·
Un. 60 27 This false sense of s· must yield to
sign and
My. 354–18 Sweet sign and s·
so-called
Un. 34–22 its own so-called s·,
solid
Mis. 5–30 can seem solid s· to this thought.
Soul and
Mis. 145– 7 to express Soul and s·.
Soul, is
Mis. 100– 4 Spirit, Soul, is s·,
Spirit is
Ret. 57–17 Spirit is s· in Truth.
spiritual
Mis. 27–30 a type of spiritual s·,
309–12 spiritual s· and intelligence.
Rud. 5–12 who has ever seen spiritual s·
My. 226–18 spiritual "s· of things — Heb. 11 : 1.
the only
Mis. 47–21 Spirit, is the only s· ;
200– 9 while God was the only s·,
361–26 the only s· and divine Principle
Un. 24–17 and hence is the only s·.
25– 6 Spirit is the only s·.
25–17 good is the only s·,
to translate
Mis. 74–16 mission was to translate s·
true
Mis. 103–15 dwell . . . as tangible, true s·,

substance

visionary
Un. 45–24 the visionary *s·* of matter.

Mis. 18–14 in every God-quality, even in *s·* ;
27–31 know a stone as *s·*, only by
47– 5 adipose belief of yourself as *s·* ;
56– 7 If Mind is not *s·*, form, and
74–23 theory that matter is *s·* ;
74–31 matter is neither *s·*, intelligence,
103– 3 which say that . . . *s·* is perishable.
103– 8 as . . . mortals virtually name *s·*;
103–10 lack of knowing what *s·* is,
131–10 *s·* of our sublime faith,
132– 2 subject the *s·* whereof you had
239– 8 *s·* is taking larger proportions.
272–11 * "The *s·* of this Act is at present
301– 8 periodicals whose *s·* is made up of
349–20 My counsel to all of them was in *s·*
350–15 The subject . . . was, in *s·*,
378–17 He answered . . . in *s·*,
381–14 and he replied, in *s·*,
Ret. 25–14 Soul I denominated *s·*,
57–17 Matter is *s·* in error,
93–18 This statement is in *s·* identical
Un. 24–23 *Evil*. . . . I am *s·*.
31–13 claim . . . that matter is *s·* ;
32–13 destroys all sense of matter as *s·*,
34–20 could not feel what it calls *s·*.
34–25 What is *s·*?
Pul. 20–16 whose *s·* is the divine Spirit,
Rud. 1– 8 It is *s·*, Spirit, Life, Truth,
No. 20–10 This Principle is Mind, *s·*, Life,
35–18 Life, *s·*, Soul, and intelligence
35–21 God is the only Mind, Life, *s·*,
Pan. 12–24 Life, Truth, Love, *s·*, Spirit,
My. 81–32 * people of standing and of *s·*,
146– 9 The statement in my letter . . . in *s·*
339–20 he answered them in *s·* :

substanceless
Mis. 56– 8 If . . . God is *s·* ;
361– 5 its substances are found *s·*,

substances
Mis. 361– 5 its *s·* are found substanceless,

substantial
Mis. 27–32 first admitting that it is *s·*.
247–24 seems, . . . solid and *s·*.
Ret. 25–14 Soul alone is truly *s·*.
Un. 34–19 What evidence . . . that matter is *s·*,
Pul. 45– 2 * and some *s·* sums.
49–22 * there to build a *s·* home
My. 24–23 * *s·* and enduring character of its

substantially
Ret. 89– 5 preaching and teaching were *s·*

substantiated
Ret. 35–20 and its claim is *s·*,

substantiates
Mis. 47–23 *s·* man's identity,
No. 38– 5 God *s·* their evidence
44– 1 *s·* his ignorance of its Principle

substitute
Mis. 278–25 *s·* my own for their growth,
Man. 65– 1 and to *s·* Leader,
92– 6 nothing can *s·* this demonstration.
Ret. 58– 6 false, and finite *s·*.
No. 8– 5 whenever it can *s·* censure.
21–13 and *s·* matter and evil
'01. 2–10 to *s·* good words for good deeds,
My. 226– 2 use it only where you can *s·*

substituted
Mis. 92–25 cannot be *s·* for God's revelation.
Ret. 84–14 cannot be *s·* for God's revelation.

substitutes
Mis. 122–22 nor *s·* the suffering of the
No. 5–12 *s·* for Truth an unreal belief,
My. 197–16 those whose words are but the *s·*

substituting
Mis. 233–18 *S·* good words for a good life,
310– 4 misused by *s·* personality

substitution
Mis. 75–19 a *s·* of *sense* for *soul*
121–32 *s·* of a good man to suffer
334–26 *s·* of Truth demonstrated,
Pul. 62– 5 * They are a *s·* of tubes

substratum
No. 16–26 matter is the *s·* of evil,

subterfuge
Ret. 78–17 a resort to *s·* in the statement

subtle
Mis. 24–30 put down all *s·* falsities
26– 7 in the most *s·* ether,
108–19 evil and its *s·* workings
191– 5 "more *s·* than — *Gen.* 3 : 1.
335–12 for opposing the *s·* lie,
363–27 exposes the *s·* sophist,
Ret. 63–20 more *s·*, more difficult to heal.
My. 14–22 * *s·* lie with which to ensnare
128–25 as does a *s·* conspirator ;
150–31 to call this "a *s·* fraud,"

subtler
Mis. 115–23 against the *s·* forms of evil,
Rud. 7– 5 *s·* conceptions and consistencies
No. 31– 6 appear to-day in *s·* forms

subtlest
No. 41–16 *s·* forms of sin are trying

subtleties
Mis. 112– 2 with the *s·* of sin !
196– 6 in all manner of *s·*

subtlety
Mis. 36–13 passions, anger, revenge, *s·*,
361–22 *s·* of speculative wisdom
Ret. 64–27 forms, methods, and *s·* of error,
Rud. 6–15 * this is not "any metaphysical *s·*,"
No. 35–10 also the drear *s·* of death.

subtly
Ret. 85–13 the *s·* hidden suggestion
My. 213–16 working so *s·* that we mistake

subtracted
'00. 10–19 not added but *s·* from

subtraction
Mis. 60–16 to say that addition is not *s·*
Ret. 59– 9 saying that addition means *s·*
Un. 53–18 assertion that . . . is the rule of *s·*,

suburbs
Ret. 17– 2 in the beautiful *s·* of Boston.
Po. vii– 2 * *in the beautiful s· of Boston*);
My. 56–10 * churches in such *s·* of Boston
56–23 * established in other *s·*,

subversion
Mis. 31–10 *s·* of right is not scientific.

subvert
Mis. 302–30 to *s·* or to liquidate.

subverts
Mis. 31– 7 *s·* the scientific laws

succeed
Mis. 6–16 Truth must ultimately *s·*
31–22 *s·* with his wrong argument,
216–28 * the attempt . . . may *s·*,
Pul. 83–19 * She must and will *s·*,
My. 166– 4 fail to *s·* and fall to the earth.

succeeded
Mis. 110–27 defense of Truth, and have *s·*.
Ret. 6–23 In 1837 he *s·* to the law-office
Pul. 45–25 * *s·* by the grandest of ministers
My. 31– 1 * *s·* by the following hymns
340–29 *s·* by our time of abundance,

succeeding
Pul. 38– 6 * During these *s·* twenty years
My. 177–18 *s·* years show in livid lines that

succeeds
My. 108– 2 *s·* as well . . . without drugs
193–23 * if it *s·*, it is a right thing."

success

achieving
Mis. 266–23 toiling and achieving *s·*
Christian
Mis. 120–14 Christian *s·* is under arms,
conspicuous
My. 272–26 * leads with such conspicuous *s·*
desires
Mis. 32– 1 if indeed he desires *s·* in this
doctor's
Mis. 229–11 doctor's *s·*, and the clergyman's
each
'02. 13– 3 each *s·* incurred a sharper fire from
element of
Pul. 53–20 * essential element of *s·* in
essential to
Pul. 54–21 * conditions . . . that are essential to *s·*.
fail of
Mis. 147–30 rather fail of *s·* than attain it by
genuine
'02. 14–11 The only genuine *s·* possible
good
My. 246– 9 practised C. S. . . . with good *s·*.
her
My. 64–18 * her *s·* in so doing is what

success

his
My. 165– 1 promote and pervade all his *s·*
honor and
'01. 29–22 All honor and *s·* to those who
in healing
No. 2–22 and some marked *s·* in healing
in life
Mis. 230– 2 *S·* in life depends upon
in sin
Mis. 354– 4 sanguine of *s·* in sin,
'00. 10– 1 *S·* in sin is downright defeat.
insures
My. 287–23 systematizes action, and insures *s·* ;
is dangerous
My. 283–29 Lured by fame, . . . *s·* is dangerous,
its
Mis. 365–14 secret of its *s·* lies in supplying
labor and
My. 197–11 labor and *s·* in completing
motive and
My. 236–19 a far-reaching motive and *s·*,
never-ending
My. 357–20 to their never-ending *s·*,
no
Ret. 79–17 cometh no *s·* in Truth.
of a student
Mis. v– 6 CONSTITUTE THE *S·* OF A STUDENT
of Christian Science
My. 234–16 *s·* of C. S. in benighted
of honesty
Mis. 252–29 secures the *s·* of honesty.
of others
My. 212–28 hindering . . . the *s·* of others.
of this church
My. 195–24 praiseworthy *s·* of this church,
secures
Mis. 135–11 conquers all . . . and secures *s·*.
social
My. 184–23 rural chapel is a social *s·*
sure of
My. 203–19 sincerity is sure of *s·*,
temporary
Mis. 43–26 occasional temporary *s·* of such
tend to
My. 274–12 tend to *s·*, intellectuality,
their
My. 219– 6 honor of their *s·* in teaching
357–17 estimate their *s·* and glory
the only
'02. 14–12 the only *s·* I have ever achieved
thy
Mis. 340–23 however slow, thy *s·* is sure :
without
Ret. 21– 6 employed . . . but without *s·*.
your own
Ret. 78–24 against your own *s·*
zenith of
My. 225– 4 rising to the zenith of *s·*,

Mis. 59–23 *s·* that one individual has with
204–27 gives . . . *s·* to endeavor.
228–14 momentary *s·* of all villainies,
267–29 crowns them with *s·* ;
My. 244–31 *s·* of this Christian system of
269–22 interest you manifest in the *s·* of

successful

Mis. 5–20 metaphysics comes in, . . . and is *s·*.
43–12 make safe and *s·* practitioners.
171– 4 first effort . . . was not wholly *s·* ;
230– 6 If one would be *s·* in the future,
230–14 *s·* individuals have become such
305–13 * in making the undertaking *s·*.
340–20 The conscientious are *s·*.
Ret. 7–16 * *s·* practice of a very large
42–12 remarkably *s·* in Mind-healing,
53– 3 had been made *s·* and prosperous
Un. 17– 1 one chance of *s·* deception.
No. 6–15 mistaken healer is not *s·*,
'00. 2–29 he answers : "I am not so *s·*
9–18 Sincerity is more *s·* than
'01. 28–29 After a hard and *s·* career
'02. 14–15 *s·* end could never have been
My. 28–28 * It speaks for the *s·* labors
42–28 * and how *s·* she is in the
51–32 * *s·* instructions to heal the sick,
111–19 become *s·* healers and models of
213–13 they will be proportionately *s·*
227–20 whether *s·* or not,
352–28 thanks for your *s·* plans

successfully

Mis. 243– 7 students treat sprains, . . . *s·*.
Man. 89–21 practised C. S. healing *s·*
'00. 8–22 before we can *s·* war with

succession
My. 360–23 for forty years in *s·*.

successive
Mis. 26– 4 Each *s·* period of progress
56–27 and have had *s·* stages of
80–25 doctors, who, in *s·* generations
Ret. 40– 1 four *s·* years I healed,
52– 1 For many *s·* years I have
'01. 30– 6 *s·* utterances of reformers

successor
My. 343– 7 ask, perhaps, whether my *s·*
343–12 * that Mrs. Eddy's immediate *s·* would,
346–18 * chapter sub-title
346–22 * stated that her *s·* would,
346–27 a man would be my future *s·*.
347– 3 and reveal my *s·*,

successors
Pan. 12–10 closing century, and its *s·*,
My. 172–22 * myself and my *s·* in office."

succor
Pan. 14–22 May the divine Love *s·* and

succored
Peo. 10– 8 *s·* a fugitive slave in 1853,

such
Mis. 6–24 uselessness of *s·* material methods,
11–26 to *s·* as hate me,
31–10 *s·* a subversion of right is
31–12 *S·* false faith finds no place in,
32– 8 *s·* as have strayed from the
38–15 *s·* a dry and abstract subject ?
39– 9 of *s·* beware.
40– 2 demands *s·* cooperation ;
43–21 *s·* sinister rivalry does a vast
43–26 success of *s·* an one is
43–28 to recognize, as *s·*, the . . . errors
46–12 There are no *s·* indications
46–13 *s·* a misconception of Truth
47– 1 there is no *s·* thing as matter,
48– 8 If *s·* be its power, I am opposed
48–25 *S·* an occurrence would
49–31 never created error, or *s·* a
52– 1 to *s·* as seek the material
63–15 to save *s·* as believe in the
76– 9 *s·* as the mortal belief that
80– 3 By rendering error *s·* a service,
82– 9 *S·* Christians as John
95–22 to *s·* as are "waiting — *Rom.* 8 : 23.
97–11 *S·* suppositional healing
97–28 *s·* must be the personality of
103– 7 destructive forces, *s·* as sin,
122– 9 *s·* a monstrous work?
122–16 *S·* an inference were impious.
123–32 sensation *s·* as attends eating
124–15 comforting *s·* as mourn,
130–20 *s·* Herculean tasks as they
134– 5 reiterate *s·* words of apology
134–13 blessing *s·* as you never before
136– 3 routine of *s·* material modes
137–12 *s·* opportunity might have been
139– 5 blessing *s·* as you even yet
140– 1 *s·* as error could not control.
142–17 *s·* varying types of true affection,
145 22 *s·* as Isaiah prophesied :
148–11 nor dictatorial demands, *s·* as
155–20 write *s·* excellent letters to her
162– 4 of *s·* wonderful spiritual import
168–12 only *s·* as are pure in spirit,
187–32 *s·* as crucified our Master,
192–13 *S·* are the words of him who
195 15 authority for *s·* a conclusion,
197–15 *s·* an action of mind would
221–21 *S·* denial dethrones demonstration,
221–23 *S·* denial also contradicts the
226–25 *s·* as manages to evade the law,
230–14 have become *s·* by hard work ;
231–28 *s·* tones of heartfelt joy
233– 6 are *s·* in name only,
234–18 on *s·* unfamiliar ground,
234–21 against *s·* odds,
237–11 gives them *s·* a cup of gall
242–25 I cured precisely *s·* a case
262–21 opening the prison doors to *s·*
264–22 *S·* students are more or less
270– 4 of *s·* as barter integrity
272–21 * *s·* as any stock company may
272–24 * institutions, under *s·* charters,
276–28 *S·* an error and loss will
292–10 *s·* as eternity is ever sounding.
294–19 Love *s·* specimens of mortality
294–23 to help even *s·* as these.
295–25 *s·* an organization as the
295–29 with *s·* dignity, clemency, and
296–23 Why fall into *s·* patronage,
297–22 unless *s·* claims are relinquished

such

Mis.	306–19	* having been made *s·* by the
	314–31	this Lesson shall be *s·*
	315–14	*s·* as have promising proclivities
	317–21	subjects of *s·* earnest import.
	317–27	*S·* students should not pay the
	335–24	*S·* people say,
	337–24	*s·* as lived according to
	344–13	*s·* a material science
	344–19	*S·* philosophy can never
	344–22	*S·* philosophy is far from the
	349– 7	*S·* a course with *s·* a teacher
	350–29	teach the use of *s·* arguments
	351–18	nor benefit mankind by *s·* endeavors.
	370– 4	*s·* deeds of mercy,
	370–26	sophistry that *s·* is the true fold
	372–15	*s·* replies as the following :
	375–27	* gave me *s·* a thrill of joy
	376– 1	* attention to *s·* matters,
	377– 1	fashions forever *s·* forms,
	378–22	removed from *s·* thoughts
	380– 2	outward sign of *s·* a practice :
	385–17	diviner sense, that spurns *s·* toys,
	393–12	Crowns life's Cliff for *s·* as we.
	394–18	* *S·* old-time harmonies *retune*,
Man.	3– 8	dictatorial demands, *s·* as
	32–15	*S·* announcement shall be made
	37–11	notice of *s·* rejection ;
	46–15	also *s·* information as may
	48– 2	who do believe in *s·* doctrines,
	48–15	for *s·* a purpose.
	49–14	The cards of *s·* persons
	51– 4	to accept *s·* admonition,
	57– 2	transaction of *s·* other business
	63– 5	*s·* questions and answers
	64–21	*s·* as sister or brother.
	69– 9	*s·* student shall pay to Mrs. Eddy
	69–12	during the time of *s·* service.
	71– 8	in naming *s·* churches.
	71–14	to assume *s·* position would
	72–15	services of *s·* a church
	73–11	at *s·* university or college,
	74–18	required to acknowledge as *s·*
	78– 8	except *s·* debts as are specified
	78–23	for the payment of *s·* bills.
	78–23	*S·* payments shall be reported,
	79– 6	shall transact . . . *s·* business
	80–15	for *s·* reasons as to the Board may
	83–10	shall carefully select for pupils *s·*
	85–18	*S·* members who have not been
	89–15	*s·* credentials as are required
	95– 7	at *s·* places and at *s·* times
	98–12	read the *last proof sheet* of *s·*
	98–15	papers containing *s·* an article,
	102–18	incorporated in all *s·* deeds
Chr.	55–18	*s·* as I have give I thee :— *Acts* 3 : 6.
Ret.	21–27	*s·* narrations may be admissible
	22–10	endured *s·* contradiction— *Heb.* 12 : 3.
	38–13	not thought of *s·* a result,
	44– 4	first *s·* church ever organized.
	50–29	*s·* obstacles as were encountered
	57–27	*s·* opposite effects as good and evil,
	57–29	*s·* methods can never reach the
	59– 7	*S·* an inference is unscientific.
	64– 4	*s·* is the unity of evil ;
	65–17	constituted of *s·* elements as
	70–13	the recurrence of *s·* events.
	70–29	*S·* a post of duty, *s·* exalts
	71–15	subjected to *s·* an influence?
	73–23	*S·* errancy betrays a
	78–13	*s·* works and words becloud the
	81–28	*s·* as first led me to the feet of
	87–26	Truth beams with *s·* efficacy
	88–11	It implies *s·* an elevation
	88–26	in *s·* spiritual attitude
	90–28	to find, in *s·* a student,
	91–17	with *s·* fidelity, we see Jesus
Un.	1– 3	knows no *s·* thing as sin.
	1– 4	*s·* as the apostle Peter
	4–25	Surely from *s·* an understanding
	4–26	Surely from . . . *s·* knowing,
	6–17	far from ready to assimilate *s·*
	7–20	here is one *s·* conviction :
	13–21	*S·* a view would bring us upon
	14– 1	which contains *s·* planks as
	15–21	*S·* vagaries are to be found
	16– 2	*s·* terms as *divine sin*
	18–27	If *s·* knowledge of evil were
	23– 8	and Truth knows only *s·*.
	26–11	which leads to *s·* teaching
	38–12	*s·* misbelief must enthrone
	41–27	*s·* a theory implies
	50–13	really there is no *s·* thing as
	53–16	not built on *s·* false foundations,
	56–26	*S·* mental conditions as
	60– 1	*s·* thoughts — mortal inventions,

such

Un.	64–10	nearer we approximate to *s·* a Mind,
Pul.	3– 1	*S·* being its nature, how can
	3–13	*S·* . . . assurance ends all warfare,
	3–30	unfitness for *s·* a spiritual animus
	5–11	*S·* was the founder of the
	9– 6	the full chords of *s·* a rest.
	32– 9	* Of course *s·* a personality,
	36–10	* and *s·* earnestness of attention
	41–28	* others *s·* — were chimed until
	46– 7	* no *s·* inference is to be drawn
	57–15	* organization of *s·* a church,
	57–20	* *S·* is the excellent name given to
	64– 6	* *s·* was not the experience of
	66–21	* *S·* a rapid departure from
	75– 8	*S·* a statement would not only be
Rud.	5– 1	spiritual senses afford no *s·*
	5–15	If there is any *s·* thing as matter,
	8–26	If by *s·* lower means the health
	15–26	lectures cannot be *s·* lessons
	16– 5	to fit students for practice by *s·* means,
No.	2–14	through *s·* an admission,
	2–20	Institutes furnished with *s·* teachers
	3–26	*s·* compilations, instead of
	22– 1	*S·* philosophy has certainly not
	22–10	*S·* miscalled metaphysical systems
	23–22	can have no *s·* warfare
	26– 9	*s·* material and mortal views
	27–25	In presence of *s·* thoughts
	29–16	impute *s·* doctrines to mortal opinion
	29–18	*s·* a statement is a shocking
	29–22	*S·* sermons, though clad in soft
	32– 1	misinterpretation of *s·* passages
	32–10	chapter sub-title
	35– 4	demonstrate the Principle of *s·* Life ;
	39–14	*S·* prayer humiliates, purifies,
	41–18	will never admit *s·* as come to steal
	42– 2	* *s·* manifestations of God's power
	42– 3	*S·* sentiments are wholesome
	43–22	*S·* students come to my College
	45– 9	*S·* an attempt indicates weakness,
	45–10	*s·* efforts arise from a
Pan.	9–19	kiss the feet of *s·* a messenger,
	9–20	to help *s·* a one is to help
'00.	1–19	cities, *s·* as Boston, New York,
	2–23	doom of *s·* workers will come,
	10– 8	*S·* conflict never ends till
	13–16	A glad promise to *s·* as wait
'01.	12– 1	to *s·* a one our mode of worship
	12– 9	would be seen in *s·* company.''
	13–11	with *s·* a sense of its nullity
	15–18	to waken *s·* a one from his deluded
	19–23	*s·* as mesmerism, hypnotism,
	19–26	flow through no *s·* channels.
	21–16	*s·* foreseeing is not foreknowing,
	22– 8	I do not believe in *s·* a compound.
	25–14	or required in *s·* metaphysics,
	25–18	all *s·* gilded sepulchres
	25–28	Jesus likened *s·* self-contradictions to
	26–18	Let it be left to *s·* as see God
	27–14	healed hopeless cases, *s·* as
	32–21	*S·* churchmen and the Bible,
	33–10	* influence in *s·* things ;
'02.	10–18	If *s·* is man's ultimate,
Hea.	3– 1	*S·* Christianity requires neither
	4–23	*s·* self-evident contradictions
	5–18	*S·* hypotheses ignore Biblical
Peo.	2–19	*S·* a theory has overturned empires
	3–25	*s·* as dependence on personal
	4–26	grown out of *s·* false ideals
Po.	vi–16	*assailed* . . . *Garrison with s· fury*
	32–15	*S·* physical laws to obey,
	48–11	diviner sense, that spurns *s·* toys,
	51–17	Crowns life's Cliff for *s·* as we.
	57– 4	* *S·* old-time harmonies *retune*,
My.	4–17	*s·* an individual subserves the
	14–25	* but it is in *s·* a healthy state
	21– 2	* expended in *s·* an event.
	22– 8	* to erect *s·* a building
	29– 6	* *S·* was the closing incident of
	29–10	* *s·* was the scene repeated six times
	41–18	* supports *s·* selfless devotion,
	45–21	* results of *s·* following have been
	48–21	* build *s·* truth as they do gain
	51–12	* *s·* an interest manifested
	56–10	* in *s·* suburbs of Boston as would
	59–30	* has accomplished *s·* a work
	61–30	* in *s·* an immense undertaking,
	62–10	* thank God . . . for *s·* an one,
	66–30	* never before has *s·* a grand church
	69– 6	* *s·* meetings presenting an oval
	71–30	* with *s·* . . . acoustic properties
	74–25	a belief in *s·* emancipation,
	74–26	* as *s·* they are welcome.
	82–27	* came to Boston in *s·* numbers
	82–28	* with *s·* remarkable expedition,

such

My.	86–24	* most notable of s· occasions.
	87–23	* s· serene, beautiful expressions,
	89– 9	* an open space about it, s· as
	89–11	* A sect that leaves s· a monument
	92–29	* some s· comfort as it promises.
	95–29	* s· a wonderful demonstration
	96–21	* money was sent in s· quantities
	98– 9	* s· as religious annals hardly parallel
	99–24	* hundreds of s· churches.
	113– 5	Can s· a book be ambiguous,
	118–14	s· circumstances embarrass the
	119– 3	on s· a basis to demonstrate the
	119–12	C. S. destroys s· tendency.
	122–13	was s· as to command respect
	126– 6	s· as drink of the living water.
	132–31	comforts s· as mourn,
	150– 9	joy and crown of s· a pilgrimage
	150–10	the service of s· a mission.
	154–30	S· communing uplifts man's being;
	162–10	the bond of blessedness s· as
	164– 1	knowing that s· an effort
	175–16	if, indeed, s· must remain
	176– 8	grant that s· great goodness,
	179–30	They afford s· expositions of
	185– 2	To s· as have waited patiently
	196–20	endured s· contradiction — Heb. 12 : 3.
	197–15	Comparing s· students with
	197–21	of s· is the kingdom — Matt. 19 : 14.
	201–11	S· elements of friendship, faith,
	204– 8	that mutual friendships s· as ours
	208–15	expectation of just s· blessedness,
	218–26	S· labor is impartial,
	219– 3	S· practice would be erroneous,
	219– 4	s· an anticipation on the part of
	223–17	All s· questions are superinduced
	228–31	s· a one was never called to
	229– 4	I have no use for s·,
	230–13	to comfort s· as mourn,
	230–21	fitness and fidelity s· as thine
	230–23	s· as the Christian education of
	231– 2	s· purposes only as God indicates.
	231–10	s· uncertain, unfortunate investments.
	233–23	watch against s· a result?
	249–17	should countenance s· evil tendencies.
	260– 6	would flee before s· reality,
	272–26	* leads with s· conspicuous success
	276–19	* in s· matters no one should
	278–20	civilization destroys s· illusions
	284–16	* that s· an event has occurred."
	295– 2	our dear God comforts s·
	297– 3	shrink from s· salient phase.
	306– 7	s· was Ralph Waldo Emerson ;
	311– 7	tenderness and sympathy were s· that
	312–23	would need on s· an excursion.
	313–11	Nor do I remember any s· stuff
	316–16	S· a dignified, eloquent appeal
	316–23	s· sound appreciation of the rights
	317–11	It was for no s· purpose.
	318–25	* that there ever was s· a man
	319– 1	s· a person as the Galilean
	322–24	* to banter me on s· enthusiasm,
	323–21	* giving this age s· a Leader
	331– 1	* S· watchful solicitude
	331–14	* extend s· unrestrained hospitality
	340–17	immediately annulling s· bills
	343–15	I have sought no s· distinction.
	345– 1	see that your mind is in s· a state
	348–14	writer's departure from s· a religion
	362–22	* our intention to take s· action
	(see also cases)	

suckling

My.	113–19	a s· in the arms of divine Love,

sucklings

Pul.	8–22	mouths of babes and s· — Matt. 21 : 16.

sudden

Mis.	48–21	tragic events and s· deaths
Man.	49–23	S· Decease.
Pan.	3–10	silent as the storm's s· hush ;
'00.	2–23	more s·, severe, and lasting
My.	201–17	that its s· sallies may help us,
	280–14	world's loss, in the s· departure of
	290– 3	s· international bereavement,
	294–23	sad, s· announcement of the decease of
	336–17	* seizure of disease was so s·

suddenly

Mis.	162– 7	stepped s· before the people
	328– 1	but s· the Stranger shouts,
Man.	49–24	If a member . . . shall decease s·,
Ret.	19– 9	s· attacked by this insidious
Pul.	33–19	* s· appeared at his side,
	34–11	* she s· became aware of a divine
	35– 1	s· I apprehended the spiritual
	53–11	* Can drugs s· cure leprosy?

suddenly

Rud.	15– 6	glad surprise of s· regained health
My.	291–25	she is s· stricken,
	312–20	s· seized with yellow fever

sue

Man.	46–20	shall not, . . . s· his patient

suffer

Mis.	8–20	however much we s· in the process.
	11– 1	to s· for his evil intent ;
	66– 3	innocent to s· for the guilty.
	73– 2	material body is said to s·,
	91–10	"S· it to be so now." — Matt. 3 : 15.
	93–31	even if you s· for it
	99–16	ready to s· for a righteous cause,
	118–18	willing to s· patiently for error
	121–15	innocent shall s· for the guilty,
	122– 1	good man to s· for evil-doers
	123–24	sinners s· for their own sins,
	141– 7	no one can s· from it,
	157– 3	worthy to s· for Christ, Truth.
	157– 4	"If we s·, we shall also — II Tim. 2 : 12.
	184–21	must s· for this error until he
	198–32	therefore he must s· for it.
	209–21	s· for having "other gods — Exod. 20 : 3.
	210–27	it may s· long, but has neither
	210–31	lest it should s· from an encounter.
	211–16	break his peace and cause him to s·
	211–19	you afraid to do this lest he s·,
	222–18	s· its full penalty after death.
	237–13	impossible . . . to sin and not s·.
	261– 9	mortals s· from the wrong they
	278–27	learn by the things they s·,
	291–25	worthy to s· for righteousness,
	328– 3	learn from the things they s·.
	380–22	"S· it to be so now," — Matt. 3 : 15.
Ret.	48–27	"S· it to be so now," — Matt. 3 : 15.
	61–23	has no sensation and cannot s·.
Un.	57–23	was found worthy to s· for Christ ;
	57–24	to s· with him is to reign
	59–14	to s· before Pilate and on Calvary,
Pul.	3–11	what can cause you to sin or s· ?
	5–10	bravest to endure, firmest to s·,
No.	30– 6	to s·, or to be punished.
	32– 8	must s·, until it is self-destroyed.
Po.	41–16	And this life but one given to s·
My.	41–15	* hatred he may practise and s· from.
	140–21	"S· it to be so now," — Matt. 3 : 15.
	162– 3	"S· it to be so now : — Matt. 3 : 15.
	165– 8	righteous s· for the unrighteous ;
	218– 3	"S· it to be so now ' — Matt. 3 : 15.
	220–29	That the innocent should s· for
	222– 6	how long shall I s· you? — Matt. 17 : 17.
	357– 2	"S· it to be so now" — Matt. 3 : 15.

suffered

Mis.	71– 3	John B. Gough is said to have s· from
	84–16	mind, not the immortal Mind, s·.
	162–20	s· in the flesh,
	198–30	s· from inclement weather,
	212– 9	had s·, and seen their error.
	235–29	Who . . . has not s· from the
	267–17	s· temporary shame and loss
Ret.	40–19	"I never before s· so little
Un.	56– 3	If Jesus s·, as the Scriptures
	56–18	Prophets and apostles s·
No.	33–24	Jesus s· for all mortals
	35–13	to show the allness of Love . . . , Jesus s·.
	35–14	He s·, to show mortals the
	35–17	s· because of the shocking
'00.	7–14	my great reward for having s·,
'01.	11– 2	never s· and never died.
Hea.	11–14	he who has s· from intolerance
My.	43– 9	in the wilderness they s· defeats
	166–16	Had I never s· for The Mother Church,
	196–16	"Christ also s· for us, — I Pet. 2 : 21.
	196–18	when he s·, — I Pet. 2 : 23.
	231– 6	she has s· most from
	232–16	not have s· his house — Luke 12 : 39.
	290–26	the words of him who s·

sufferer

Mis.	72– 3	to be born a lifelong s·
	241–18	to the bedridden s·
	332–25	supposer, false believer, s·
'01.	17– 2	to awaken the s· from the

sufferers

Mis.	326– 6	and s· shriek for help :

suffereth

Mis.	338–12	charity that s· long and is kind,
Ret.	79–26	kingdom . . . s· violence, — Matt. 11 : 12.
Un.	56–14	He also s· in the flesh,
No.	45– 5	"Charity s· long — I Cor. 13 : 4.
My.	231–17	"Charity s· long — I Cor. 13 : 4.
	260–23	love that "s· long, — I Cor. 13 : 4.

suffering (noun)

abating
Mis. 8– 2 If we can aid in abating *s·*
above the
My. 99– 4 * above the *s·* of petty ills ;
all
Mis. 185–13 destroying all *s·*,
198–21 All *s·* is the fruit of
200–23 pain, and all *s·* of the flesh,
Ret. 69–21 prolific source of all *s·*
Un. 56– 4 all *s·* comes from mind,
My. 288–22 all *s·* is commensurate with sin ;
and death
Un. 41– 6 unreal sense of *s·* and death.
My. 161–32 their ultimatum, sin, *s·*, and death.
and sacrifice
Mis. 350–31 through nameless *s·* and sacrifice,
baptism of
No. 34– 2 through the baptism of *s·*,
brings
Mis. 12– 4 brings *s·* upon suffering to its
casts out the
Mis. 73– 4 when Mind casts out the *s·*.
disease and
Ret. 61–24 every sense of disease and *s·*
dis-ease and
Mis. 219–18 consciousness of dis-ease and *s·*
dream of
Mis. 70–14 startle him from the dream of *s·*.
driven by
Mis. 328–15 Hast thou been driven by *s·*
fear or
Ret. 61–11 you cannot awake in fear or *s·*
My. 267–22 relief from fear or *s·*,
fervent heat of
No. 28– 5 melt in the fervent heat of *s·*,
fires of
Mis. 125– 2 the fires of *s·* ;
for others
No. 34–13 unseen glory of *s·* for others.
for sin
Mis. 15–27 By *s·* for sin, . . . thought is
from sin
Mis. 14–32 not sheltered from *s·* from sin :
gospel of
Ret. 30–20 through the gospel of *s·*,
Un. 57–17 gospel of *s·* brought life and bliss.
his
My. 161– 6 were it not that his *s·* reforms
human
Mis. 179– 3 rolled away by human *s·*.
Ret. 62– 2 and human *s·* will increase.
identical with
Mis. 66–15 sin is identical with *s·*,
its
'01. 16– 5 sense of sin and its *s·*,
loss of
Mis. 219–19 ease and loss of *s·* ;
no
Mis. 125– 6 to know . . . that there is no *s·* ;
Po. 31–19 which deems no *s·* vain
physical
Mis. 222– 7 causes the victim great physical *s·* ;
No. 33–23 physical *s·* and human woe.
real
Mis. 288–24 and real *s·* would stop the farce.
sacrifice and
Mis. 257–15 repays . . . with sacrifice and *s·*.
Science or
Mis. 362–27 won through Science or *s·* :
self-extinguished by
Mis. 362–21 until self-extinguished by *s·* !
self-imposed
Mis. 361– 4 dissolves through self-imposed *s·*,
sick and
My. 153– 4 send these . . . to the sick and *s·*.
sickness and
Rud. 10–17 which causes sickness and *s·*.
sin and
Mis. 261– 4 and the sin and *s·* it occasions
261– 6 sin and *s·* are not cancelled by
My. 248–24 of exterminating sin and *s·*
sin or
Un. 56– 6 no sin or *s·* in the Mind which
summary of
My. 203–15 the summary of *s·* here
through
Mis. 356– 8 that they be destroyed through *s·* ;
Ret. 94–10 his purification through *s·*,
Pul. 13–20 expiate their sin through *s·*.
Peo. 9–16 destroyed only through *s·*.
vicarious
Mis. 123–22 not through vicarious *s·*,
which leads
Un. 55–12 *s·* which leads out of the flesh.

———

Mis. 12– 4 **brings suffering upon *s·* to its**

suffering (noun)

Mis. 66–16 *s·* is the lighter affliction.
102–23 Science supports harmony, denies *s·*,
122–23 the *s·* of the Godlike
122–23 the *s·* due to sin.
124–28 it gives to *s·*, inspiration ;
165–28 example, and *s·* of our Master.
198–27 *S·* is the supposition of another
209–27 *s·* is self-inflicted,
211–15 is unconscious of *s·*.
213– 5 *S·* or Science, or both,
237– 3 *s·* is a thing of mortal mind
261– 2 *s·* is commensurate with evil,
262–16 giving joy to the *s·* and hope to
265–32 until *s·* compels the downfall of
299– 1 *s·* and mistakes recur until one is
307– 9 to *s·* of every sort.
323–11 privation, temptation, toil, *s·*.
332–23 second, a false belief ; third, *s·* ;
350–27 which consign people to *s·*.
362–28 And *s·* has no reward, except
Man. 47–18 description of symptoms or of *s·*,
Ret. 61–21 the fact that, if *s·* exists,
Un. 57–20 *S·* was the confirmation of Paul's
Po. 47–12 Will the hereafter from *s·* free
My. 121–27 strength of peace and of *s·* is

suffering (adj.)
Mis. 156– 1 in behalf of a *s·* race,
Ret. 92– 3 for the needs of *s·* mortals,
My. 132–27 dreaming of *s·* matter ;
190– 4 larger sympathy for *s·* humanity

suffering (verb)
Mis. 332–27 Supposing, false believing, *s·* are
Un. 56–10 *s·* from mentality in opposition to
No. 42–26 * "I am *s·* from nervous prostration,
Pan. 8–27 *s·* because of it,
My. 29–30 * without *s·* the inconveniences of

sufferings
Mis. 83– 7 *cause of his own s·."*
89–12 or alleviate his *s·*,
105– 8 His physical *s·*, which
122–29 his *s·*, self-imposed ;
221– 7 Error produces physical *s·*,
221– 7 these *s·* show the fundamental
Ret. 30– 8 relieve the *s·* of humanity
60–21 when will my *s·* cease?
Un. 3–14 through the *s·* of the flesh
55–18 *s·* of the flesh are unreal.
'01. 11–10 sins and *s·* of the flesh,
17– 1 self-inflicted *s·* of mortals

suffers
Mis. 66– 9 for the offender alone *s·*,
268–16 hence he *s·* no shipwreck
276–21 When a false sense *s·*,
312– 7 alone, . . . *s·* all inflictions,
Ret. 25–12 That which sins, *s·*, and dies,
Un. 30– 9 this lower sense sins and *s·*,
56–21 he *s·* least from sin who
No. 43–26 Science often *s·* blame through
'01. 14–10 something that enjoys, *s·*,
20–22 till he *s·* up to its extinction

suffice
'01. 17– 2 *s·* so to awaken the sufferer
My. 20–16 let this *s·* for her rich portion
28–12 * *S·* it to say, however,

suffices
My. 303– 5 It *s·* me to learn the Science of
340–27 *s·* for the Christian era.

sufficiency
My. 156– 8 all *s·* in all things, — *II Cor.* 9 : 8.

sufficient
Mis. 5–11 have not *s·* faith
41–28 is *s·* for all emergencies.
100–28 Who is *s·* for these things?
111– 2 is scarcely *s·* to demonstrate
341–11 Seeking is not *s·* whereby to
349–25 When the church may *s·* members
352–21 not *s·* spiritual power in the human
Man. 15– 4 our *s·* guide to eternal Life.
39–10 when *s·* time has elapsed
45– 2 dutiful and *s·* occupation for all
52–15 deemed *s·* . . . for forgiveness
53–22 shall be considered a *s·* evidence
55–10 For *s·* reasons it may be decided
60– 7 One meeting on Sunday . . . is *s·*.
65–18 *s·* cause for the removal of
111–19 refuse, without *s·* cause, to sign
Ret. 15–15 not *s·* to seat the audience
40–17 *s·* to add her babe was safely born,
55– 4 gain *s·* knowledge of error to
57–19 infinite Mind is *s·* to supply all
Un. 43–13 "*s·* for these things." — *II Cor.* 2 : 16.
57–22 learned that spiritual grace was *s·*
Pul. 64– 5 * in securing *s·* funds

sufficient
No.   23–23   not s· to inform us as to the
My.   12– 8   * accumulation of a sum s· to
      27–14   * s· funds have been received
      27–23   * s· funds have been received
      58– 8   * s· refutation of the statements
     104–21   a s· reason for his silence
     123–22   My little hall, . . . is less s· to
     130–23   Quotation-marks are not s·.
     161–22   s· unto each day is the duty
     161–26   do not afford a s· defence against
     179–20   s· to authenticate Christ's
     223–14   First, because I have not s· time
     231–21   more . . . than one woman is s· to
     263– 5   A word to the wise is s·.
     279–13   is s· to still all strife.
     297–27   not had s· interest in the matter
     339–26   not s· to meet his demand.

sufficiently
Mis.   7–31   is not s· enlightened
      11– 4   I used to think it s· just
      40–20   possess s· the Christ-spirit
      43– 8   C. S. is not s· understood
      44–11   one who understands this Science s·
      91–30   s· to do this, and also to
      92– 5   become s· understood to
     194–32   s· to exclude all faith in
     223–12   s· strong to discern
     302–11   s· to discriminate between
     334–31   s· to understand this Golden Rule
     340–31   not s· enlightened mankind.
Ret.   28– 6   s· to demonstrate, even in part,
      84– 2   s· understood to be fully
Pul.   22–13   s· to heal the sick in his name.
Rud.   15– 4   understanding s· the Science
'02.   7–10   s· to fulfil the First Commandment.
My.   161–17   drink s· of the cup of
     310– 2   education, s· advanced
     348– 9   solved s· to give a reason for

suffocate
Hea.   8–18   s· reason by materialism.

suffocated
Mis. 274–27   the *vox populi* is s·,

suffrage
Mis. 295– 7   * from female s·, past a
     296–27   a wish to promote female s·?

suffused
Mis. 239–18   red nose, s· eyes, cough,

sugar
Hea. 12–27   giving the unmedicated s·
      13–16   using only the s· of milk ;

sugar-tongs
Mis. 250–15   to be taken down . . . with s·

suggest
Mis. 54–27   *does it not s· the possibility*
     240–26   s· to them that the habit
     200– 5   * the sweetest similes
Pul.   76–17   * s· the tribute of loving friends.
'02.   14– 6   I s· as a motto for
      15–21   to s· a name for the book
My.   236–14   for the one which I s·,
     347–14   s· that nature had reproduced

suggested
Mis. 22–28   falling apple s· to Newton
Ret.   52–11   I s· to my students,
My.   21– 7   * course s· will not only hasten
      25– 1   * and it is s· to our readers
      57– 7   * she s· the need of a larger
     121– 2   I have s· a change
     145– 8   s· the details outside and
     236– 5   Because I s· the name for
     319–23   * you s· that I call on the
     340–22   has s· to his constituents

suggestion
Man. 42– 6   against aggressive mental s·,
Ret.   85–13   the subtly hidden s·
'01.   20–13   s· of the inaudible falsehood,
'02.   15–25   recorded the hallowed s·.
My.   243– 5   This is a s· of error,
     324– 4   * and he scorned the s·

suggestions
Mis. 113–16   and rises superior to s·
     114–24   Scientists will silence evil s·,
     118– 3   false s·, self-will,
     119– 1   If malicious s· whisper
     306– 7   * welcome s· of events
Pul.   61–15   * Beautiful s· greet you in
My.   128–31   evil s·, in whatever guise,
     130– 3   guard . . . against evil s·
     213–16   we mistake its s· for the
     223–18   wrong motives or by "evil s·,"

suggestive
Pul.   29–24   * helpful in its s· interpretation.
Pan.   2–13   Webster's *derivation* . . . is most s·.
My.   50–22   * simple but s· words,
     131–21   There is something s· to me

suggests
Mis. 28–21   First Commandment, . . . s· the inquiry,
      85–23   s· pleasure and pain in matter ;
Pul.   65–17   * s· to recollection the story of
'01.   5–13   This s· another query :

suicidal
Mis. 129– 9   To avenge . . . wrong, is s·.

suicide
Mis. 52–20   *why not commit s·?*
      53– 4   Committing s· to dodge the
      53– 7   Not through sin or s·,
     122–31   and he ends — with s·.
     212– 3   betrays you, and commits s·.
'01.   16–11   outdoes itself and commits s·.
My.   128–17   Men cannot punish a man for s· ;

suing
My. 204–25   the s· for payment, hypnotism,

suit
Mis.   xi–18   to s· and savor all literature.
     283– 7   s· one's self in the arrangement
     381–19   her cost of s·, taxed at
Ret.   39– 3   I entered a s· at law,
'01.   2–11   may s· the weak or the worldly
My.   136–15   Henry M. Baker, who won a s·
     138– 6   This s· was brought without my
     250–18   branch churches to follow s· ;
     309–10   and my father won the s·.

suitable
Mis. 228–17   as the only s· fabric
     258–28   only s· or true idea of Him ;
     302–23   so elect and give s· notice,
Man. 27–13   to provide a s· building
      27–20   to provide s· rooms,
      29–14   five s· members of this Church
      31– 6   s· portion of their time
      31–19   S· Selections.
      61–22   in a dignified and s· manner.
      81– 5   S· Employees.
      81– 8   is not accepted . . . as s·,
     100–25   If a s· man is not obtainable
     100–27   a s· woman shall be elected.
Rud.   14– 5   s· price for their services,
      15–17   s· and thorough guardianship
My.   54–18   * no place s· could be found
      55– 5   * church, in a s· location.
      57–11   * building a s· edifice.

suitably
Man. 30–19   s· furnish the house,
Pul.   77– 5   * s· engraved, and encased

suited
Ret.   11– 1   Poetry s· my emotions
Pul.   66–17   * well s· to satisfy a taste

suits
Mis.   ix– 2   s· my sense of doing good.
     340–15   instead of delving into s·,
Pan.   3– 2   while pantheism s· not at all

sulphate
My. 109– 1   carbonate and s· of lime ;

sum
Mis. 30– 8   s· total of transcendentalism.
      52–29   Mortals have the s· of being
     105–32   God is the s· total of the
     143–23   s· of forty-two thousand dollars
     242– 6   s· of one thousand dollars
     293–21   s· total of Love reflected
     378–18   the s· of what he taught her
     386–30   to reap, . . . Of bliss the s·.
Man. 78–21   deposit the s· of $500
Ret.   50– 6   a startling s· for tuition
'02.   13–18   paying for it the s· of $4,963.50
Po.   50–17   to reap, . . . Of bliss the s·.
My.   12– 8   * accumulation of a s· sufficient
      13–29   pledged this munificent s·
      16– 7   * the s· of $199,607.93,
      22– 8   * s· of money adequate to erect
      23–14   * the s· of $2,000,000
      26–12   gift is the largest s· of money
      30–24   * Scientists gave a s· surpassing
     146–10   lengthens my s· of years
     157–23   conveyed to them the s· of
     164–25   s· of all reality and good.
     165–13   s· of ten thousand dollars
     177–10   lengthens my s· of years
     212–13   complete the s· total of sin.
     217– 7   s· of four thousand dollars
     217–10   This s· is to remain on interest

summarily

Mis. 12–23 s· dealt with by divine justice.
211– 9 dealt with s· by the good judgment of
Pan. 5–27 Jesus treated the lie s·.

summarized

Ret. 22– 8 St. Paul s· the character of Jesus

summary

Mis. 35–11 complete, s· of the matter :
227–25 sublime s· of an honest life
Un. 34–10 s· of the whole matter,
My. 203–14 s· of suffering here and of heaven

summed

Mis. 214–13 s· up its demonstration in

summer

Mis. 136–23 close your meetings for the s· ;
144–24 fresh as a s· morn,
329–28 back to their s· homes.
394– 8 our tears, as the soft s· rain,
Man. 48–14 or make a s· resort near
Pul. 48– 8 * lights and shades of spring and s·
'02. 18–19 like the s· brook, soon gets dry.
Po. 24– 2 Breathe through the s· air
45–11 our tears, as the soft s· rain,
46– 3 Within life's s· bowers !
53–18 To empty s· bowers,
My. 54–17 * During the s· vacation,
61– 8 * before the end of s·,
133–11 Message from me this s·,
134–18 tears like a soft s· shower,
158– 8 upon the glories of s· ;
196–29 Over the glaciers . . . the s· glows.
314–11 fancied, for a s· home.

summer-house

Pul. 48– 4 * with . . . a fountain or s·.

summing

Mis. 62–10 s· up positive and negative

summit

Mis. 41–16 gains the s· in Science
66–16 To reach the s· of Science,
162– 6 dazzling, God-crowned s·,
215–19 walks on the s· of the roof
266– 2 s· of unselfish and pure aims
323– 7 Then from this sacred s·
327–19 Despairing of gaining the s·,
328– 9 from the s· of bliss surveys
347–23 the s· can be gained.
358–18 reach the heaven-crowned s·
392– 1 poem
392– 8 And from thy lofty s·,
Ret. 4–10 situated on the s· of a hill,
76–23 gains the God-crowned s·
Un. 64–16 on the s· of Mont Blanc ;
Po. page 20 poem
20–11 And from thy lofty s·,
My. 133– 6 God-crowned s· of divine Science ;
300–18 striving to reach the s·

summits

Mis. 303– 2 shine from their home s·

summoned

Ret. 8–22 asked her if she had s· me?
13–11 family doctor was s·,

summons

Chr. 53–54 away from sin Christ s· thee!
My. 103– 3 s· the severest conflicts
148–29 Christianity is the s· of divine Love

sumptuous

'00. 15– 3 you have come to a s· feast,

sums

Un. 53–19 s· done under both rules
Pul. 45– 2 * some giving . . . substantial s·.
50–14 * no additional s· outside of the
52– 2 * no s· except those already subscribed
64–10 * others donating large s·.
My. 57–30 * no s· except those already subscribed
67–23 * vaster s· of money were spent
231– 8 to whom she has given large s·

Sun

Pul. 88–23 * S·, Attleboro, Mass.
89–12 * S·, New York City.

sun (*see also* sun's)

before the
Mis. 251–30 mountain mists before the s·.
bright as the
Pul. 83–13 * as bright as the s·, — *see Song* 6 : 10.
clothed with the
Pul. 83–28 * clothed with the s·, — *Rev.* 12 : 1.
detains the
Pul. 87–24 church's tall tower detains the s·,
full-orbed
'01. 8–10 but it is not the full-orbed s·.

sun

great
Pul. 81–18 * soars and sings to the great s·.
his eye on the
Mis. 354–26 his eye on the s·,
in the centre
My. 13–10 * like a s· in the centre of its system,
like the
'02. 17–29 like the s· beneath the horizon,
midnight
Mis. 88–17 glows . . . like a midnight s·.
Un. 58–20 midnight s· shines over the
moonbeams to the
No. 22–13 they are as moonbeams to the s·,
no need of the
No. 27–10 There will be no need of the s·,
My. 206–20 city had no need of the s·, — *Rev.* 21 : 23.
nor need of the
Mis. 323– 5 nor need of the s·,
one with the
'02. 12–18 a ray of light one with the s·,
outlives the
'02. 17–20 Then thy gain outlives the s·,
reflects the
Pul. 4–14 A dewdrop reflects the s·.
rising of the
My. 114–20 until the rising of the s·.
sends forth
Ret. 56–22 The s· sends forth light,
shines
'02. 17–20 the s· shines but to show man
smiled
My. 29–25 * the s· smiled kindly upon the
standing in the
'02. 16–18 the angel, standing in the s·,
under the
Mis. 267–27 cause of all . . . under the s·,
Pul. 53– 6 * no new thing under the s·." — *Eccl.* 1 : 9.
Pan. 9– 8 a religion under the s· that hath
Hea. 6– 5 something new under the s·
My. 324–28 * one woman under the s· who could
worshipped the
Mis. 333–24 worshippers of Baal worshipped the s·.

Mis. 54– 4 Has the s· forgotten to shine,
192–16 as long as the s·." — *Psal.* 72 : 17.
330–29 unveils its regal splendor to the s· ;
Un. 14– 7 plants, the s·, the moon, and
64– 4 than the s· can coexist with
No. 6–17 evidence that . . . the s· revolves
6–21 error of the revolution of the s·
Pan. 8– 4 find expression in s· worship,
My. 344– 3 If we say that the s· stands for

sunbeams

Hea. 11– 1 fountains play in borrowed s·,
Po. 32– 8 s· enkindling the sky

sunburst

Pul. 25–17 * In the ceiling is a s·
25–29 * s· in the centre of the ceiling
58–22 * In the ceiling is a beautiful s·

Sunday

service
  (*see* **service**)
services
  (*see* **services**)

Mis. 120–23 love to be with you on S·,
161– 3 S· BEFORE CHRISTMAS, 1888.
314– 5 formed for S· worship,
314–31 On the first S· of each month,
314–32 except Communion S·,
315– 5 S· following Communion Day.
349–28 each S· when I preached.
Man. 31– 7 reading of the S· lesson,
40–19 the first S· of each month.
56–12 Monday following the first S·
57– 4 preceding the first S· in June,
58–15 repeated at the other services on S·.
59–18 listen to the S· sermon
60– 6 One meeting on the S· during
61–13 on the second S· in January
Ret. 10– 7 I had to repeat every S·.
16– 1 One memorable S· afternoon,
44–10 in the pulpit every S·,
Pul. 29– 8 * Last S· I gave myself the
34– 8 * a S· morning when her pastor
56–26 * dedicated in Boston on S·,
59– 3 * dedicated on New Year's S·
60– 3 * next S· the new order of service
68–19 * The dedication in Boston last S·
74– 7 * meets every S· in Hodgson Hall,
75–19 * ceremonies at Boston last S·
87–18 I already speak to you each S·.
'01. 11–17 Sermon on the Mount, read each S·
'02. 12–28 their presence on Communion S·.

Sunday

Po.	11– 5	*Boston Herald, S·,* May 15, 1898.
My.	7–11	their presence on Communion *S·.*
	26– 6	* communion, *S·,* June 10, 1906.
	50–20	* Communion *S·,* however,
	50–22	* "*S·,* January 4, 1880.
	53–17	* preach . . . for ten dollars a *S·,*
	54–25	* Hawthorne Rooms, *S·* after *S·."*
	56–29	* services were held each *S·,*
	58–30	* services at the C. S. church last *S·*
	66–22	* elaborate observances of *S·,*
	66–27	* services of *S·* will mark an epoch
	82–15	* dedicatory services . . . on *S·,*
	84–28	* to take place on *S·,*
	85–26	* Last *S·* it was entirely credible
	88–10	* The dedication, *S·,* in Boston,
	92–24	* entered its portals *S·.*
	94– 8	* entered its portals *S·,"*
	96– 1	* zeal . . . exhibited at Boston, *S·,*
	100– 7	* On the *S·* of the dedication,
	141– 7	* services . . . *S·* [June 14]
	147– 8	my childhood's *S·* noons.
	170– 8	my annual Message to the church last *S·*
	289–24	on *S·* evening, February 3,
	337– 1	[*Boston Herald, S·,* May 15, 1898]

Sunday Lesson

Mis.	106–17	Your *S· L·,* composed of

Sunday Lessons

Mis.	114– 1	our *S· L·,* are of inestimable value
	314–19	referred to in the *S· L·.*

Sundays

My.	51–17	* remain with us for a few *S·*
	90– 2	* *S·* or on week-days

Sunday School

Order of Exercises

Man.	127– 1	heading

Mis.	382–29	form of Sunday services, *S· S·,*
Man.	62– 7	*S· S·.*
	62– 8	The *S· S·.*
	62– 9	received in the *S· S·* classes
	62–13	*S· S·* of any Church of Christ,
	62–16	attend the *S· S·* exercises.
Ret.	42– 8	C. S. *S· S·,* which he superintended.
Pul.	9–20	together with the *S· S·*
	46–29	* organizer of a C. S. *S· S·,*
Po.	page 43	poem
My.	25– 8	* *S· S·* of The Mother Church
	25–11	* report of the secretary of the *S· S·*
	55– 2	* date . . . the *S· S·* was formed.
	69–22	* *S· S·* and the . . . offices,
	155–26	May the dear *S· S·* children
	162–11	dear *S· S·* children,
	230–15	chapter sub-title
	230–17	TEACHERS OF THE MOTHER CHURCH *S· S·*
	231–25	chapter sub-title
	231–26	*S· S·* OF SECOND CHURCH . . . NEW YORK

Sunday School Lesson

Mis.	314–12	*S· S· L·* of the *C. S. Quarterly,*

Sunday School Lessons

Mis.	114– 3	Committee on *S· S· L·*

Sunday Schools

Pul.	5–29	sermons, *S· S·,* and literature of

Sunday Services

Man.	120– 4	heading

sunder

My.	185–16	the trinity no man can *s·.*
	268–10	God hath joined . . . man cannot *s·.*

sunders

Ret.	31– 1	*s·* the dominant ties of earth

sundries

My.	133–12	in *s·* already given out.

sung

Ret.	16– 7	she has not *s·* before since she
Un.	26–12	hymn-verse so often *s·* in church :
Pul.	16– 1	and *S·* on This Occasion
	43–16	* *s·* by the congregation.
Hea.	20– 1	The following hymn was *s·*
Po.	vi– 7	* *was s· by the audience*

sun god

Pan.	8– 3	*s· g·,* moon god, and sin god

sunk

Peo.	5–28	* *s·* to the bottom of the sea,
My.	53– 3	* were *s·* into the bottomless sea of
	350–23	*S·* from beneath man,

sunken

Mis.	234–26	an age so *s·* in sin and sensuality,

sunlight

Mis.	202– 4	into the *s·* of Soul.
	331– 9	*s·* of prayer and praise

sunlight

Mis.	376–23	deeply dazzling *s·,* softened,
Ret.	4–14	waving gracefully in the *s·,*
Pul.	82– 5	* and her smiles are the *s·*
	83– 7	* and the *s·* cannot long be delayed.
Hea.	19–26	in the *s·* of our deeds ;
My.	19–19	our shadows follow us in the *s·*
	114–22	as gloriously as the *s·*
	202–22	The taper unseen in *s·*
	282–25	the *s·* of the law and gospel.

sunlit

Po.	77–19	Bears hence its *s·* glow

sunny

Mis.	329–29	fair earth and *s·* skies.
	395–26	Of *s·* days and cloudless skies,
Pul.	49– 1	* This big, *s·* room
Po.	41–13	From the green *s·* slopes
	58–11	Of *s·* days and cloudless skies,
My.	189–25	erected in the *s·* South
	194–30	* Ne'er in a *s·* hour fall off."

sunrise

Mis.	304–23	* It shall ring at *s·* and sunset ;
	376–16	chapter sub-title
Ret.	23–12	could not prophesy *s·* or starlight.

sun's

Po.	2–17	the *s·* more genial, mighty ray ;

suns

Ret.	56–22	sun sends forth light, but not *s·* ;

sunset (*see also* sunset's)

Mis.	304–23	* It shall ring at sunrise and *s·* ;
	356– 1	radiant *s·,* beautiful as blessings
Pul.	39–15	* The *s·,* burning low,
My.	114–19	I could not write these notes after *s·.*

sunset's

Po.	70– 4	At *s·* radiant hour,

sunshine (*see also* sunshine's)

Mis.	51–27	* *s·* of the world's new spring,
	231– 5	had seen *s·* and shadow fall
	231–27	brought *s·* to every heart.
	279– 8	*s·* and joy unspeakable.
	343–10	Warmed by the *s·* of Truth,
	343–19	freshness and *s·* of enlightened faith
	390–18	When *s·* beautifies the shower,
Ret.	20–17	as *s·* o'er the sea,
	87–26	*s·* of Truth beams with such efficacy
Pul.	9–12	as *s·* from the clouds ;
'00.	9–15	his lightning, thunder, and *s·*
Po.	15–16	Here smileth the blossom and *s·*
	42– 1	never a shadow where *s·* is not,
	42– 3	never the *s·* without a dark spot ;
	55–19	When *s·* beautifies the shower,
My.	87–22	* make *s·* on the grayest day.
	91–13	* cheerful and shed *s·* about them
	252–13	not work in the *s·* and run away in
	252–21	rays from the eternal *s·* of Love,

sunshine's

Po.	53– 7	With *s·* lovely ray

sun-worshippers

My.	151–24	Baalites or *s·* failed to

sup

Chr.	55–27	will *s·* with him, — *Rev. 3 : 20.*

superb

Mis.	276– 1	The floral offerings , , , were *s·,*
Pul.	42–13	* a *s·* apartment intended for
	62–15	* quality of tone is something *s·,*
	76– 4	* archway of Italian marble
	76–13	* *s·* mantel of Mexican onyx
My.	25–25	sublimity of this *s·* superstructure,

superbly

Pul.	39–10	poem that I consider *s·* sweet

supercilious

'00.	15–12	*s·* consciousness that saith

superficial

No.	46– 5	material medicine and *s·* religion

superfine

Mis.	285–28	in the *rôle* of a *s·* conjugality ;

superfluous

Mis.	107– 5	Christianity is not *s·.*
My.	276– 6	to be criticized . . . is *s·.*

superinduced

Mis.	66–23	Disease that is *s·* by sin
	117– 6	act *s·* by the wrong motive
My.	223–17	All such questions are *s·* by

superintended

Ret.	42– 8	C. S. Sunday School, which he *s·.*

superintendent

Pul.	46–30	* of which he was the *s·,*
My.	230–16	TO THE *S·* AND TEACHERS

superintends
Pul. 37–10 * s· the church in Boston,
superior
Mis. 104– 3 His unseen individuality, so s· to
113–16 rises s· to suggestions
Pan. 11–14 will demonstrate man to be s·
'01. 25–24 good and evil, and the latter s·,
Hea. 15–21 as if drugs were s· to Deity.
Superior Court
My. 137– 3 * Robert N. Chamberlin of the S· C·,
superiority
Mis. 28–30 s· of the higher law ;
30–18 proved the s· of Mind
109–32 your s· to a delusion is won.
140– 9 s· of the claims of Spirit
286–12 the s· of spiritual power
379–29 Mind and its s· over matter,
Ret. 26–10 s· of Spirit over matter.
34–16 s· of metaphysics over physics.
superlative
Mis. 223–29 To punish ourselves . . . is s· folly.
super-modest
My. 115– 8 I cannot be s· in
supernal
Mis. 160– 9 meet and mingle in bliss s·.
387–23 Whence joys s· flow,
Ret. 85–15 the order prescribed by s· grace.
Un. 5–27 left to the s· guidance.
Po. 6–18 Whence joys s· flow,
supernatural
Mis. 3– 4 we shall claim . . . no s· power.
88–22 * that Christian healing is s·, or
104–11 sin is miraculous and s· ;
199–28 neither s· or preternatural ;
Ret. 26–13 had before seemed to me s·,
Pul. 72– 1 * as though inspired . . . by s· power.
My. 95–24 * can banish faith in the s·,
supernaturally
Pan. 3–20 who reveals Himself s· to
superscription
My. 170–17 it has His image and s·.
supersede
My. v–10 * threatens to s· persecution,
supersedes
Un. 40– 8 As Truth s· error,
supersensible
Mis. 86–31 to reach the glory of s· Life ;
Ret. 73–17 evil is lost in s· good.
Un. 10–11 God, or Spirit, the s· eternal.
supersensual
Mis. 77–19 s·, impartial, and unquenchable Love.
superstition
Mis. 30–24 wisdomless wit, weakness, and s·.
123– 7 s·, lust, hypocrisy, witchcraft.
199–18 denied and defied their s·.
'02. 9–30 counteracts ignorance and s· ?
My. 245–13 devouring beasts, s· and jealousy.
superstitions
Mis. 235–24 Christianity unbiased by the s· of
superstitious
My. 313–23 * nor did "the s· country folk
superstructure
Mis. 140– 2 God's gift, foundation and s·,
140–29 though the material s· should crumble
341– 5 s· that is real, right, and eternal
357–32 yea, its foundation and s·.
Pul. 2–29 s· of Truth, reared on the
'01. 25– 4 s· eternal in the heavens,
Hea. 11– 9 immortal s· is built on Truth ;
My. 6–23 a s· high above the work of
25–25 sublimity of this superb s·,
94–27 a s· high above the work of
supervision
Man. 74– 4 neither shall he exercise s· or
supine
Mis. 312–23 reason too s· or misemployed
supper
Mis. 90–26 the Passover, or last s·,
170– 8 drinking of wine at the Lord's s·,
supplant
Pul. 66–26 * are eventually to s· those
supplemented
Pul. 60–10 * Each paragraph he s· first with
supplied
Mis. 148–16 must be s· to maintain the dignity
Man. 3–13 must be s· to maintain the dignity
30–10 and the vacancy s·.

supplied
Man. 65–21 vacancy shall be s· by a
78– 4 vacancy s· by the Board.
Un. 51–11 s· by the pretentious usurpation,
My. 23– 5 * s· the means to consummate the
53–20 * The pulpit was s· by Mrs. Eddy,
309–30 * s· the only social diversions,
supplies
Mis. 211– 8 s· criminals with bouquets
307– 2 they give you daily s·.
313–22 garner the s· for a world.
Man. 45– 1 s· within the wide channels of
No. 42– 8 divine Spirit s· all human needs.
My. 12–26 Love s· the ever-present help
91– 2 * proof positive that it s· these
260–26 s· every need of man.
supply
Mis. 45–16 s· invariably meets demand,
365–19 what immortal Mind alone can s·.
Man. 96–12 he is at liberty to s· that need
102– 8 elect, dismiss, or s· a vacancy
Ret. 57–20 infinite Mind is sufficient to s· all
82–17 ample to s· many practitioners,
Pul. 10– 5 power and purpose to s· them.
15–17 God will s· the wisdom
No. 18–25 for what Mind alone can s·.
'01. 7–16 and s· the differing needs of
16– 9 s· sacrilegious gossip with the
My. 118–21 to s· the blessings of the infinite,
186–14 will s· all your needs
216– 8 subsist on demand and s·,
231–21 more . . . than . . . is sufficient to s·.
261– 7 the full s· of juvenile joy.
312– 2 to s· the place of his leading
supplying
Mis. 193–19 s· the word Science to Christianity,
263–20 responsible for s· this want,
365–14 s· the universal need of
Ret. 56–20 s· all Mind by the reflection,
Un. 29–12 s· all that is absolutely immutable
My. 349–30 s· all the needs of man.
support
Mis. 38– 6 to s· one's self and a Cause
39–22 Scientist . . . needs s· at times ;
52– 2 s· God's power to heal
66–32 to s· the liberated thought
77–14 to s· their ideal man.
80– 7 in s· and defense of
193–11 s· unequivocally the proof
381–11 evidence to s· his claim
383– 5 approval and s· of . . . Scientists.
Ret. 19–15 sympathy helped to s· me
26– 3 s· the divine power which heals.
Un. 43–15 words of the Master in s· of
Rud. 14– 8 The author never sought charitable s·,
No. 15–11 s· the Christianity that heals
38–15 basis and s· of creation,
42–27 * drink strong coffee to s· me
My. 8– 3 * In s· of the motion,
51– 9 * has not met with the s· that she
76–16 * in the s· of their church work,
153–23 seeks personality for s·,
227–13 turn to divine justice for s·
276–24 to help s· a righteous government ;
290–13 your s·, consolation, and victory.
292–10 O may His love shield, s·, and
312–16 * entirely without means of s·.
312–29 writing gave me ample s·.
330–27 sympathy helped to s· me
360–18 s· the Directors of The
supported
Mis. xii– 5 S·, cheered, I take my pen
66–12 is s· in the Scripture by
93–17 s· by the unerring Principle
93–20 nor s· by facts,
96–30 is not s· by the evidence
Ret. 64–14 this view is s· by the Scripture,
'00. 13– 8 were part of a system s· by
'01. 26– 5 s· it by his words and deeds.
My. 68– 4 * ceiling, s· on four arches
supporting
Un. 57–18 s· the ladder which reaches
Peo. 2–13 by revelation s· reason.
My. 355–11 a strong s· arm to religion
360–19 s· The Mother Church Directors.
supports
Mis. 71–14 never averts law, but s· it.
102–23 Science s· harmony,
200–32 s· the entire wisdom of the
220– 7 he s· this silent mental force
My. 41–31 * s· such selfless devotion,

suppose
Mis.	171– 5	To *s·* that Jesus did actually
	220– 4	*s·* that there is a sick person
	290–10	To *s·* that human love,
My.	345– 4	I do not *s·* their mental

supposed
Mis.	3–27	their only *s·* efficacy is in
	24–31	and thus destroy any *s·* effect
	53– 5	error of *s·* life and intelligence
	72– 9	God is *s·* to impart to man
	74–21	matter and its supposed laws.
	91–28	I supposed that students had followed
	140–12	I *s·* the trustee-deed was legal ;
	171–15	spirits *s·* to have departed
	186– 4	Soul is *s·* to enter the
	191– 3	which the senses are *s·* to take in,
	191–24	was *s·* to have outtalked even Truth,
	200–19	every *s·* material law.
	201–13	nothingness of *s·* life in matter,
	202– 1	basis of all *s·* miracles ;
	205–26	dissolves all *s·* material life
	332–18	sense of evil is *s·* to have spoken,
	339–11	the *s·* activity of evil.
	352–16	To know the *s·* bodily belief
Man.	66–21	authority *s·* to come from her
Un.	52–27	*s·* modes of self-conscious matter,
Rud.	8–24	invalid whom he is *s·* to cure.
	12– 2	parts of the body *s·* to be ailing.
No.	35–16	*s·* existence apart from God.
Pan.	3– 3	Pan, as a deity, is *s·* to preside
'00.	2–18	satanic majesty is *s·* to answer
'01.	16–21	was *s·* to outtalk Truth
Hea.	10– 6	*s·* to have fought the manhood of
	11–25	*s·* to be both mind and matter.
	13–27	while it is *s·* to cure
	17–21	Sin is a *s·* mental condition ;
	17–22	sickness and death are *s·* physical
My.	5– 3	man is *s·* to start from dust
	79–10	* *s·* fountain of knowledge
	152– 5	were *s·* to heal the sick,
	173–12	I scarcely *s·* that a note,
	292–25	those drugs are *s·* to possess
	293– 5	properties of drugs are *s·* to act
		(*see also* **power**)

supposedly
My.	119–16	away from the *s·* crucified

supposer
Mis.	332–25	Is man the *s·*, false believer,

supposing
Mis.	332–27	*S·*, false believing, suffering

supposition
Mis.	73– 3	this *s·* is proven erroneous
	74–23	any *s·* that matter is intelligent,
	175–22	*s·* is, that there are other minds
	189–15	*s·* that Soul, or Mind,
	191–21	destroys all consistent *s·* of
	196– 4	Idolatry, the *s·* of the existence of
	198–27	Suffering is the *s·* of another
	259– 8	*s·* that evil is a claimant
	260–15	holds only in itself the *s·* of evil,
	332–23	first, a *s·* ; second, a false belief ;
	332–29	*s·* is, that God and His idea
	363– 6	*s·* that the absence o· good is mind
Ret.	67– 7	Sin was, and *is*, the lying *s·* that
Un.	18–20	destroy, every *s·* of discord.
	52– 2	in contradistinction to the *s·* that,
	52–16	evil, as a *s·*, is the father of itself,
No.	27– 1	Sin is not Mind ; it is but the *s·*
Hea.	17–23	*s·* of life and intelligence in
My.	301–23	*s·* that we can correct insanity

suppositional
Mis.	14–27	Thus evil is . . . *s·* ;
	19–15	endeavors of *s·* demons
	71–19	they are *s·* modes,
	97–11	Such *s·* healing I deprecate.
	217–19	*s·* unity and personality,
	260–17	*s·* or elementary opposite
	289– 7	It is *s·* absence of good.
	334–18	diabolism of *s·* evil
	363–11	material mode of a *s·* mind ;
	367– 7	exposes the lie of *s·* evil,
Un.	32–15	a false claim, a *s·* mind,
My.	167– 4	The *s·* world within us
	235– 3	the *s·* opposite of life,
	297–12	A *s·* gust of evil in this

supposititious
Mis.	17– 5	opposed to any *s·* law of sin
	355–20	responsible for its *s·* presence.
Ret.	64–22	They are *s·* claims of error ;
My.	161–30	the falsity of *s·* life

supposititiously
Ret.	67–23	but *s·* self-created.

suppression
Pul.	54– 7	* not in . . . *s·*, or violation of it,

supremacy
and allness
My.	364–15	the *s·* and allness of good.

freedom and
Ret.	45–13	spiritual freedom and *s·*.

God's
No.	18– 8	God's *s·* and omnipotence.
Hea.	7– 5	those who understand God's *s·*,

numerical
My.	94– 3	* in the race for numerical *s·*.

of God
Hea.	15– 2	rests upon the *s·* of God.

of good
Ret.	26–10	the *s·* of good over evil,
	64– 5	destroyed by the *s·* of good.

of Mind
Mis.	35– 4	*s·* of Mind over matter,

of right
Mis.	267– 4	consciousness of . . . the *s·* of right.

of Soul
Peo.	11–10	the *s·* of Soul over sense,

of Spirit
Mis.	17–19	*s·* of Spirit, and of man
	70–27	rising to the *s·* of Spirit,
	176–19	*s·* of Spirit and the nothingness of
	194–17	*s·* of Spirit and the nothingness of
	321–10	witnesses . . . the *s·* of Spirit ;

of spiritual law
Mis.	200–18	from the *s·* of spiritual law

of the law
Mis.	258–10	*s·* of the law of Life

of Truth
Pul.	13– 8	conscious of the *s·* of Truth,

over matter
Mis.	63–30	Spirit proved its *s·* over matter.

over sin
Mis.	16–14	its *s·* over sin, sickness, and

Spirit's
Un.	58–10	by the law of Spirit's *s·* ;

supreme
Mis.	3–22	*s·* and perfect Mind,
	3–25	God is *s·* and omnipotent,
	45– 1	prove the fact that Mind is *s·*.
	47–19	Mind is *s·*.
	80–23	until right is found *s·*.
	156–12	reign of peace and harmony be *s·*
	102–10	prove his power, . . . to be *s·* ;
	176 9	*s·* devotion to Principle
	234–29	God is regarded more as absolute, *s·* ;
	259–17	Science, in which God is *s·*,
	260–19	Truth is *s·* and omnipotent.
	277–24	proof that God, good, is *s·*.
	331–26	This *s·* potential Principle reigns
	333–14	denying that God, good, is *s·*,
	336– 1	Mind is *s·* : Love is the master of
	368–29	rejoice in His *s·* rule,
Man.	15– 6	adore one *s·* and infinite God.
Ret.	28–15	For Spirit to be *s·* in demonstration,
	28–15	it must be *s·* in our affections,
	81–15	*s·* advent of Truth in the heart,
Un.	19–11	if the *s·* good could
	24– 6	*s·* sense of harmony.
	56–16	but the divine law is *s·*,
Pul.	35–19	For Spirit to be *s·* in demonstration,
	35–19	it must be *s·* in our affections,
Rud.	2–18	*s·* good, Life, Truth, Love.
No.	24–27	glorious truth, that good is *s·*.
	26–19	reflect the *s·* individual Being,
	35–27	God's kingdom is everywhere and *s·*,
Pan.	3–19	*s·*, holy, self-existent God,
	6– 6	illusive claim that God is not *s·*,
	11–24	good *s·* destroys all sense of evil,
'01.	2– 1	*s·* certainty that Christianity is
Hea.	15–10	as it rises to that *s·* sense that
Peo.	8–16	Mind is *s·*; and yet we
Po.	23–19	*S·* and omnipresent God,
My.	37–20	* grand truth that God is the *s·* cause
	126–28	it reigns *s·* to-day, to-morrow,
	205–20	makes God more *s·* in consciousness,
	267–10	He is *s·*, infinite,
	278– 7	government of divine Love is *s·*.
	294– 6	omniscient, omnipresent, *s·* over *all*.
	339– 6	one God, *s·*, infinite,

Supreme Being
Mis.	82–15	offspring and idea of the *S· B·*,
	96– 8	I believe in God as the *S· B·*,
Ret.	59–13	every other name for the *S· B·*,
Un.	48–12	He is best understood as *S· B·*,
Pul.	30–17	* a *S· B·*, and His Son,
Rud.	1– 6	*S· B·*, infinite and immortal Mind,
No.	19–15	the fatherliness of this *S· B·*.
'01.	3–11	* definition of God, "A *S· B·*,"

Supreme Being
'01. 3–12 * S· B·, self-existent and eternal."
Hea. 15– 4 the omnipotence of the S· B·
Peo. 2– 5 improved views of the S· B·.
    4–27 false ideals of the S· B·
    (see also **Being**)

Supreme God
My. 36–30 * our S· G·, through His power

supremely
Mis. 50–30 one God and loving Him s·,
   206–27 if you love good s·,
   328–30 loving God s· and thy neighbor
   360– 9 s· natural transforming power
   367– 4 and to love God s·.
My. 6– 4 Do we love God s·?
   276–25 love God s·, and my neighbor
   286– 7 love God s·, and love their neighbor

surcease
My. 230–22 give my solitude sweet s·.

sure
Mis. 11–12 the s· way of salvation,
   81– 1 broad and s· foundation of Science ;
   82–10 reach the s· foundations of time,
   90–18 be s· that your means for doing good
   109– 6 a s· pretext of moral defilement.
   117–31 Be s· that God directs your way ;
   143– 2 broad basis and s· foundation
   146–23 I feel s· that as Christian Scientists
   152– 7 Of this we may be s· :
   152–23 against this s· foundation,
   229–28 is a s· defense.
   237–25 but it is s· to follow.
   252–27 with safe and s· medicine ;
   288– 5 s· of being a fit counsellor.
   337–20 Where these exist, C. S. has no s·
   340–23 however slow, thy success is s· :
Man. 28–15 Directors to watch and make s·
Ret. 60–24 the only s· basis of harmony.
   73–21 s· victim of his own corporeality.
   83–14 is s· to be corrected.
   91– 1 God is their s· defense
Pul. 65– 7 * small and new, to be s·,
No. 28– 3 but this is s·, that the mists
   31–12 the s· destruction of sin ;
Pan. 10– 7 we are s· the honest verdict
'01. 2–26 fearless wing and a s· reward.
   33–11 * the s· precursor that they
'02. 15–28 feeling s· that God had led
Hea. 14–10 be s· he is a learned man
My. 8–13 * "Now I am s· that I have
   16–26 a s· foundation :— Isa. 28 : 16.
   21–10 * We therefore feel s· that all
   40– 5 * we are s· that now
   44– 8 * our progress . . . will be s·,
   143– 3 s· that they are blessed in
   146–20 s· that what I wrote is true,
   175–27 I am s· that the . . . letters
   203–18 s· precursor that its possessor is
   203–19 sincerity is s· of success,
   203–20 I am s· that He will
   224–14 Also be s· that you are not
   230–11 Of this I am s·,
   247–26 be s· that after many . . . days
   254–11 s· reward of right thinking
   256– 4 not specially musical to be s·,
   275–16 Life — is s· and steadfast.
   324–15 * s· that neither Mr. Wiggin nor
   325– 7 * s· Back Bay property would never
   363–25 to be s· that one is not

surely
Mis. 6–13 it s· does, to many thinkers,
   29–24 S· the people of the Occident
   37–23 yields to Science as directly and s·
   57–17 thou shalt s· die."— Gen. 3 : 17.
   81– 8 wait on God to decide, as s· He will,
   173–27 S· not from God,
   208– 2 "Thou shalt s· die."— Gen. 2 : 17.
   229– 7 quite as s· and with better effect
   261–13 S· "the way of — Prov. 13 : 15.
   367–17 thou shalt s· die."— Gen. 2 : 17.
Ret. 81– 7 our friendship will s· continue.
Un. 4–25 S· from such an understanding
   15–28 S· this is no Christian worship !
   17–23 declares . . . they must s· die.
   31– 5 s· there can be no matter ;
Pul. 44– 9 * S· it marks an era in the
   80– 1 * as s· as of a ship
   80– 3 * will s· find the other.
   85–14 * s· she, as the one chosen of God
No. 27–26 S· the probation of mortals
'00. 10–18 S· the wisdom of our forefathers
   10–28 S· it is enough for a soldier
My. 111– 2 S· "the wrath of man — Psal. 76 : 10.

surely
My. 184–28 S·, the Word that is God must
   187– 1 S·, your fidelity, faith, and
   188–19 He s· will not shut me out
   233– 9 I s· should.
   300–30 as s· it is not,
   343–14 s· I have sought no such

surety
Pul. 3–11 Our s· is in our confidence

surf
'02. 19–19 heaving s· of life's troubled sea

surface
Mis. 65– 5 that the earth's s· is flat,
My. 69– 8 * gently curved and panelled s·,
   225– 2 come to the s· to pass off,

surge (see also surge's)
Mis. 339–27 s· dolefully at the door of

surged
My. 11– 6 * storms that have s· against her

surgeon (see also surgeon's)
Mis. 311–25 as a s· who wounds to heal.
Peo. 6– 8 * not a single physician, s·,
My. 106–14 impossible for the s· or
   294–16 If the skilful s· or the
   345–21 "The work done by the s·

Surgeon Extraordinary to the King
Peo. 6– 5 Dr. James Johnson, S· E· to the K·,

surgeon's
My. 105–12 s· instruments were lying on

surgery
Mis. 243– 5 not yet made s· one of the
Ret. 24–14 neither medicine nor s· could
My. 345–20 * "But s·?"
   348– 2 s·, hygiene, electricity,

surge's
Ret. 20–18 new beauty in the s· roll !

surges
Po. 73–11 Laving with s· thy silv'ry beach !

surgical
Mis. 244– 4 even a "s· operation"
   244– 6 before s· instruments were
   349– 5 the s· part of midwifery.
Ret. 40–15 received from a s· operation
My. 345–24 about advice on s· cases."

surging
Pul. 13–17 in the s· sea of error,
My. 189–27 song and the dirge, s· my being,

surly
Mis. 297–12 a s· censor ventilating his

surmounting
My. 68– 7 * dome s· the building

surmounts
Mis. 135–11 s· all obstacles,

surpass
Mis. xi–17 found to s· imagination,
My. 67–26 * s· any church edifice

surpassing
My. 30–24 * Scientists gave a sum s·

surplus
Man. 91–15 S· Funds.
   91–15 Any s· funds left

surprise
Mis. 387– 5 waiting, in what glad s·,
Rud. 15– 6 glad s· of suddenly regained health
'00. 4–14 ought not this to be an agreeable s·,
Po. 50–23 waiting, in what glad s·,
My. 31–15 * expressions of s· and of admiration
   122–14 created s· in our good city
   310–31 * It does not s· me,

surprised
Ret. 8–17 Greatly s·, my cousin turned to
   38–18 We met . . . and were both s·,
Pul. 71–11 * SCIENTISTS OF SYRACUSE S·
'00. 4–11 * at the new . . . steps in religion,
Hea. 13–19 you cannot be s· that we
My. 322–26 * so clearly stated that I was s·
   330– 3 * I presume we should not be s·

surprises
'00. 3–21 To-day it s· us that
My. 248– 3 its grandeur almost s· me.

surprising
Mis. 66– 5 s· wisdom of these words
   224– 9 * s·, but I don't feel hurt
My. 276–12 recommends this s· privilege
   346– 2 * her views, . . . were continually s·.

surrender
Mis.	15–14	moments of *s·* to God,
	231–15	caused unconditional *s·*.
Ret.	29– 1	cause a *s·* of this effort.
My.	127–24	forts of C. S. . . . . can never *s·*.

surrendered
My.	127–28	not . . . *s·* in conquest,

surrenders
Mis.	257–30	where the good man *s·* to death
	289–13	*s·* independent action
Po.	22–19	dark domain of pain and sin *S·*

surrounded
My.	312–23	I was *s·* by friends,

surrounding
Mis.	30–27	any seeming mysticism *s·* realism
Pul.	vii–17	*s·* the cradle of this grand verity
	47–27	* Concord and its *s·* villages.
My.	173–27	green *s·* the high school ;
	174– 1	beautiful lawn *s·* their church

survey
Mis.	xi–26	*s·* the fields of the slain
Hea.	11– 2	*s·* the cost of sublunary joy,
My.	316–14	*S·* of the C. S. Movement,''

surveying
Mis.	324–11	*s·* him who waiteth at the door.
	369– 8	*s·* the immeasurable universe

surveys
Mis.	328– 9	*s·* the vale of the flesh,

survival
No.	25–13	* "the *s·* of the fittest."

survive
Mis.	26– 1	can *s·* the wreck of time ;
	140–30	the fittest would *s·*,

survived
My.	191– 1	if there *s·* more of the wisdom

survives
My.	166– 6	but the fittest *s·* ;

surviving
'01.	16–12	*s·* defamers share our pity.

susceptibility
'01.	4–10	*s·* of scientific proof.

susceptible
Mis.	27–26	and is *s·* of proof.
	52–13	Marriage is *s·* of many definitions.
	200–12	rule that is *s·* of proof,
No.	13–17	Science is not *s·* of
'01.	19–23	*s·* misuse of the human mind,
'02.	17–30	cheer the heart *s·* of light
My.	349– 8	*s·* of both ease and dis-ease,

suspect
Mis.	328– 6	Dear reader, dost thou *s·*

suspects
Hea.	1–16	* man *s·* himself a fool ;

suspend
My.	104–18	that men *s·* judgment

suspended
Man.	54– 3	the offender shall be *s·*

suspending
My.	69– 3	* *s·* seventy-two lamps,

suspicion
Mis.	257–17	*s·* where confidence is due,

suspicious
My.	211–21	fosters *s·* distrust where

sustain
Mis.	138– 1	students will *s·* themselves
Ret.	48– 3	Who else could *s·* this institute,
Rud.	17–13	miraculous vision of light,
No.	43– 7	Truth to stimulate and *s·*
My.	52–10	* to *s·* her in her work.
	216–11	without a cent to *s·* it?
	359– 1	maintain them and *s·* them.

sustained
Mis.	175– 7	says, I am *s·* by bread,
'02.	1–20	should be welcomed and *s·*.
Peo.	10–11	followed her example and *s·*
My.	226–20	the cosmos is *s·* by the
	330–19	* *s·* by Masonic records

sustaining
Ret.	33– 2	*s·* my final conclusion

sustains
Mis.	50–23	belief that . . . *s·* life,
	126–12	dignity of Soul which *s·* us,
Ret.	28–20	*s·*, according to the law of God.
Un.	48– 7	He *s·* my individuality.
	52– 5	reveals and *s·* the unbroken
No.	3–13	*s·* the genuine practice,
	33–19	*s·* man's at-one-ment with God ;
Po.	1– 6	What power *s·* thee in thy

swaddling-clothes
No.	45–25	clamor to leave cradle and *s·*.
My.	257– 8	his *s·* (material environments)

swallow
Mis.	257–24	Floods *s·* up homes and households ;
	297–11	the public cannot *s·* reports of
My.	235– 5	Straining at gnats, one may *s·* camels.
	276– 9	strain at gnats or *s·* camels

swallowed
Mis.	61– 8	*s·* up by the reality and
	361– 6	death itself is *s·* up in Life,
Pul.	14–12	*s·* up the flood — *Rev.* 12 : 16.
No.	13– 7	death must be *s·* up in Life,
'01.	15–24	* *s·* up in everlasting destruction.
My.	107–13	pellets can be *s·* without harm
	127–15	Aaron's rod *s·* up the rods of
	133–11	Message is *s·* up in sundries

swallowing
My.	211– 3	straining at gnats and *s·* camels.
	218–20	straining at gnats and *s·* camels.

swallows
Po.	53–13	Bid faithful *s·* come

Swampscott, Mass.
Po.	28–18	*S·, M·, January* 1, 1868.

sway
Mis.	204–21	holding *s·* over human consciousness.
	240–23	slight *s·* over the fresh, unbiased
Ret.	91–20	*s·* of his own perfect understanding.
Hea.	18–23	will cease to assert their Cæsar *s·*
Po.	70–23	Give God's idea *s·*,
My.	89–31	* movement of international *s·* ;

swayed
Mis.	294– 2	*s·* by the maëlstrom of human

sways
Mis.	368– 8	* Yet that scaffold *s·* the future,
'00.	10–19	whatever *s·* the sceptre of self

swearer
My.	106–25	tobacco user, a profane *s·*,

sweareth
My.	33–23	*s·* to his own hurt, — *Psal.* 15 : 4.

sweep
Mis.	99–23	winds of time *s·* clean the centuries,
	329–23	*s·* in soft strains her Orphean lyre.
	387– 1	the heart-strings gently *s·*,
Pul.	26– 9	* following the *s·* of its curve,
Po.	50–19	the heartstrings gently *s·*
	68–15	To *s·* o'er the heartstrings
My.	16–29	hail shall *s·* away — *Isa.* 28 : 17.
	78–13	* semi-circular *s·* of mahogany pews
	149–10	tides of truth that *s·* the

sweeping
My.	49– 7	* stands a great chance of *s·* the

sweeps
Mis.	396–19	There *s·* a strain,
Pul.	18– 3	There *s·* a strain,
Po.	12– 2	There *s·* a strain,
	66–11	No melody *s·* o'er its strings !

sweet
Mis.	8–21	* "*S·* are the uses of adversity."
	9– 4	*S·*, indeed, are these uses of
	15–30	it drinks in the *s·* revealings
	37–18	*s·* water and bitter?" — *Jas.* 3 : 11.
	106–26	*s·* sigh of angels answering,
	116–18	gain of its *s·* concord,
	130–12	"rolling sin as a *s·* morsel
	135– 0	*s·* sense of journeying on
	144–23	*s·* as the rest that remaineth
	145–21	*s·* memorial such as Isaiah
	146– 1	'T is *s·* to remember thee,
	148–28	invitation to this *s·* converse
	160– 8	flow on in the same *s·* rhythm
	196–17	*s·*, sacred sense and permanence
	200–21	*s·* sincerity of the apostle,
	202– 2	the *s·* harmonies of C. S.
	224–25	*s·* enough to neutralize
	227–25	isles of *s·* refreshment,
	239–17	a tiny, *s·* face appeared
	239–26	What if that *s·* child,
	240– 6	must not take the *s·* freshness
	240–30	a *s·* something which belongs
	307– 8	This *s·* assurance is the
	316–19	accumulative, *s·* demands
	320–15	*s·* immunity these bring
	329–11	restoring in memory the *s·* rhythm
	333–20	the *s·* harmonies of Spirit
	385–13	gales celestial, in *s·* music
	388–11	life most *s·*, as heart to heart
	388–24	To nurse the Bethlehem babe so *s·*,
	389–19	*s·* secret of the narrow way,
	392–21	To my sense a *s·* refrain ;
	394–20	* So full of *s·* enchantment

sweet
Mis.	395– 9	When s· *rondeau* Doth play a part,
	396–12	Are poured in strains so s·,
	396–20	sweeps a strain, Low, sad, and s·,
	397– 1	His unveiled, s· mercies show
Man.	40– 9	reflects the s· amenities of Love,
Ret.	27–21	As s· music ripples in one's
Un.	35– 1	this is s·, this is sour."
	35– 3	and say that sour is s·,
	35– 4	believed s· to be sour,
	41–15	s· and sacred sense of the
Pul.	8–24	S· society, precious children,
	11– 2	s· song of silver-throated singers,
	13–13	s· and certain sense that God is
	18– 4	sweeps a strain, Low, sad, and s·,
	18–10	His unveiled, s· mercies show
	39–10	that I consider superbly s·
	61–25	* s·, musical tones attracted
Rud.	4–12	"bind the s· influences— *Job* 38 : 31.
	6– 3	s· sounds and glories of earth
No.	14–13	the s· breath of springtide,
	45–20	with all its s· amenities
Pan.	3– 8	to whisper, "Solitude is s·."
'01.	34–18	s· charity which seeketh not
Po.	4–18	s· secret of the narrow way,
	7–11	life most s·, as heart to heart
	12– 3	sweeps a strain, Low, sad, and s·,
	12–10	His unveiled, s· mercies show
	21–13	To nurse the Bethlehem babe so s·,
	31– 7	peace of Soul's s· solitude !
	33–17	s· when I ponder the days
page 34		poem
	34– 1	O for thy wings, s· bird !
	46–14	S· as the poetry of heaven,
	48– 6	gales celestial in s· music
	51– 3	To my sense a s· refrain ;
	53– 1	Come to thy bowers, s· spring,
	57– 6	* So full of s· enchantment
	57–10	When s· *rondeau* Doth play a part,
	59– 4	poured in strains so s·,
	65–10	O sing me "S· hour of prayer" !
	65–16	moments most s· are fleetest alway,
	66– 6	S· spirit of love, at soft eventide
	68– 5	s· pledge to my lone heart
My.	37–28	* deeply touched by its s· entreaty,
	152–31	I have the s· satisfaction of
	153–30	s· flowers should be to us His
	155–28	s· scents and beautiful blossoms
	159– 3	Never more s· than to-day,
	163– 2	s· sense of angelic song
	173–21	s· to observe with what unanimity
	216–16	your s· industry and love
	230– 6	as both s· and bitter,
	230– 6	s· in expectancy and bitter in
	230–22	give my solitude s· surcease.
	236–15	s· alacrity and uniformity
	247–17	Then I fed these s· little
	252– 5	bee, always distributing s· things
	271–15	* with s· smile and snowy hair
	284– 4	'tis s· to be remembered.
	347–20	with all its s· associations.
	354–18	S· sign and substance

sweeten
Mis.	9–16	seem to s· life's cup

sweeter
Mis.	227–20	the s· the odor they send forth
	356–14	s· than the sound of vintage bells.
Pul.	12–18	A louder song, s· than has
My.	175–22	S· than the balm of Gilead,
	201– 6	s· than a sceptre,

sweetest
Mis.	263– 5	suggest the s· similes
	343–27	Among the manifold . . . this is the s· :
My.	259– 2	will see the s· sculptured face

sweetheart
Mis.	329–10	Spring is my s·,

sweetly
Mis.	120–18	come more s· to our ear
Pul.	61–20	* chapter sub-title
Po.	25–11	S· to shed Fragrance fresh
	47– 2	As s· they came of yore,

sweetness
Mis.	107– 1	but even the s· and beauty
Pul.	62–14	* purity and s· of their tones.
	81–14	* beauty, s·, and nobility

sweet-smelling
Ret.	65– 9	not the s· savor of Truth

swell
Mis.	107–13	should s· the lyre of human love.
Po.	16–21	hear the glad voices that s·,
My.	19–27	s· the hearts of the members

swell-box
(see **organ**)

swelled
Mis.	388– 2	Which s· creation's lay :
'02.	20–11	Which s· creation's lay,
Po.	7– 2	Which s· creation's lay :

swelling
Mis.	116–14	s· the harmony of being
My.	81–23	* rose . . . s· as one voice.
	186–12	s· the loud anthem
	332– 4	* feelings of a s· bosom.

swell organ
(see **organ**)

swells
Chr.	53–59	s· Christ's music-tone,
(see also **organ**)

swept
Mis.	79– 4	s· clean by the winds
Pul.	23–11	* that has s· over the country,
	52–21	* bigotry that s· over the world
'02.	20–13	That s· the clouds away ;
Peo.	8–21	s· by the divine *Talitha cumi*,
My.	111–10	he s· away their illogical

swerved
Pul.	6–30	whose mind never s· from

swerves
No.	44– 8	s· not from the highest ethics

swift
Mis.	156– 2	pages of this s· vehicle
My.	92–13	* s· growth of the new faith
	115– 1	on the s· and mighty chariot
	124–14	waiting only your s· hands,
	196– 9	be s· to hear,— *Jas.* 1 : 19.
	229–23	thanks for their s· messages
	238–16	s· pinions of spiritual thought

swimmer
My.	126– 5	s· struggling for the shore,

swimming
'02.	10–30	s· the ocean with a letter

swindler
Mis.	226–30	s·, who sells himself in a

swine
Mis.	7–14	Cast not your pearls before s· ;
	89–17	"pearls before s·"— *Matt.* 7 : 6.
	369–23	which he shared with the s·,
My.	227–24	pearls before s·,— *Matt.* 7 : 6.

swing
My.	149–27	Clouds . . . that s· in the sky

swinging
Pul.	48– 7	* she can sit in her s· chair,

Switzerland
My.	30–16	* from Germany, from S·,

sword
Mis.	214– 1	chapter sub-title— *John* 18 : 11.
	214– 6	not . . . but a s·.— *Matt.* 10 : 34.
	214–14	"Put up thy s·."— *John* 18 : 11.
	214–16	"Put up thy s· ;"— *John* 18 : 11.
	214–16	s· must have been drawn
	215–26	use the s· of Spirit.
Ret.	2–11	a heavy s·, encased in
	11– 9	The s· is sheathed,
Pul.	46–19	* a heavy s·, encased in
	46–20	* the s· had been bestowed
	65–23	* parted his mantle with his s·
	83–15	* the ruthless s· of injustice.
'01.	31–10	not . . . but a s·."— *Matt.* 10 : 34.
Po.	26– 8	While Justice grasped the s·
	60– 6	The s· is sheathed,
My.	185– 8	s· of the Spirit is drawn ;
	189– 2	grasping the s· of Spirit,
	278–28	pierced by its own s·.

swords
Mis.	10–18	crossing s· with temptation,
	285–15	crossed s· with free-love,

swordsmen
Mis.	195–22	stroke of unskilled s·.

sworn
Mis.	177–11	s· enmity against the lives of
My.	34– 4	nor s· deceitfully.— *Psal.* 24 : 4.

swung
Pul.	80– 3	* pendulum that has s· to one extreme

Sydney
My.	208– 2	chapter sub-title

syllogism
Mis.	195–20	That perfect s· of Jesus
Un.	34– 6	What then is the line of the s·

syllogisms
My.	111–11	swept away their illogical s·

sylvan

Ret.	17– 5	I worship in deep s· spot,
Pan.	3– 3	preside over s· solitude,
Po.	62– 5	I worship in deep s· spot,

symbol

Mis.	170–11	This is the reality behind the s·.
	191– 7	serpent became a s· of wisdom.
Un.	61–18	sign and s·, not the substance
My.	8–11	* let us have the best material s·
	28–22	* s· of a religion which heals
	86– 5	* find pleasure in this new s·,
	131–12	given to me in a little s·,
	131–14	above the s· seize the spirit,
	151–27	to look no higher than the s·.
	172–13	material s· of my spiritual call
	248–19	No fetishism with a s·
	355– 3	* a s· of the glad New Year

symbolic

Mis.	61– 5	material s· counterfeit sciences.
Ret.	42– 6	s· words on his office sign.
Pul.	58–21	* pictures s· of the tenets of
'00.	11–28	His s· ethics bravely rebuke
	12–27	s·, rather than personal

symbolisms

My.	88–13	* architectural s· of aspiration

symbolize

Mis.	170– 8	s· the spiritual refreshment
My.	24– 7	* to s· your unmeasured love for
	63–24	* s· this revelation,
	89– 3	* may be held to s· that faith

symbolized

Mis.	82– 5	brings the peace s· by a dove ;

symbols

Mis.	82–10	cognize the s· of God,
	142–10	a number of masonic s·.
	142–26	s· of freemasonry depicted on
Pul.	30–13	* outward s· of bread and wine,
My.	185–30	are rich in signs and s·,

symmetrical

Mis.	167– 6	He is wholly s· ;
My.	45–32	* In solid foundation, in s· arches,
	85–28	* its s· and appropriate design.

sympathetic

Mis.	312– 5	Love is consistent, uniform, s·,
Ret.	16– 2	clear, strong, s·,
My.	291–17	uniform, consistent, s·,

sympathies

Mis.	32–15	My s· extend to the
	317–24	My s· are deeply enlisted for

sympathize

Mis.	371–21	To s· in any degree with error,
My.	151– 4	I s· with their ignorance
	295– 1	I s· with those who mourn,

sympathizing

Ret.	5–23	* a s· heart, and a placid spirit.

sympathy

Mis.	109–10	s· of His eternal Mind
	118–14	one's s· can neither atone for error,
	208–12	come into s· with it,
	253–23	should it not appeal to human s·
	379–18	his rare humanity and s·
Ret.	19–15	s· helped to support me
	95– 8	* set apart Unto a life of s·.
Un.	18–18	My s· with and My knowledge of
Pul.	35–29	s· with her own views,
No.	30–17	His s· is divine, not human
	30–24	s· with sin, sorrow, and
	30–25	Truth has no s· for error,
Hea.	14–27	in s· with all that is right
Po.	74– 6	when parting thy s· glowed !
My.	30– 9	* from curiosity, and from s·, too.
	190– 4	s· for suffering humanity
	287– 5	enlists my hearty s·.
	289–13	s· with the bereaved nation,
	311– 6	my tenderness and s· were such
	320–17	* in s· with the movement,
	330–27	whose kindness and s· helped to
	331–24	* extended their care and s·
	331–30	* s· extended to her after his

symphonies

My.	155–24	heaven's s· that come to earth.

Symphony Hall

My.	57– 3	* in S· H·, and in the Mechanics Building,

symposium

My.	347–22	contribution to "Bohemia." A s·

symptom

My.	116–19	not a s· of this contagious malady,

symptoms

Mis.	100–30	s· by which our Father indicates
Man.	47–19	description of s· or of suffering,
Ret.	26– 1	as to their disease or its s·,
Hea.	12–16	the general and moral s·
My.	116–17	Its s· are based upon personal

synagogue

Mis.	326–13	crept unseen into the s·,
Ret.	89–17	once again entered the s·
'00.	12–25	he labored in the s·,
	14– 3	s· of Satan — *Rev. 3: 9.*

synagogues

Mis.	133–12	love to pray standing in the s·
	159– 1	He spake in their s·,
	373–22	Christianity entered into s·,
Ret.	65–17	ruled Christ out of the s·,
	89– 9	s·, scattered about in cities
'01.	28–17	have been scourged in the s·
Hea.	2– 4	s· as of old closed upon it,
My.	285–23	neither in the s·, — *Acts 24: 12.*

Syndicates

Man.	27–25	Trusteeships and S·.
	27–26	Boards of Trustees and S·

synonym

Mis.	75–11	Soul is a s· of Spirit,
Ret.	57–10	Soul is the s· of Spirit,

synonymous

Mis.	23–22	terms s· for the one God,
	27– 4	terms God and good, . . . are s·.
	248–10	made the word s· with devil.
'00.	5–10	Father and Mother are s· terms ;
My.	5– 4	marriage s· with legalized

synonyms

Un.	27– 4	used as if they were s·,
My.	225–28	His s· are Love, Truth, Life,

synopsis

Mis.	95–12	insufficient for even a s· of C. S.,

synoptic

My.	179– 2	s· Scriptures, as set forth in the

syntax

Ret.	10–16	S· was spiritual order and unity.

Syracuse
New York

Pul.	71– 9	* *The Post*, S·, New York,

N. Y.

Pul.	69– 3	* Miss Cross came from S·, N. Y.,
Pul.	71–11	* CHRISTIAN SCIENTISTS OF S·

system
barmaid

Mis.	295– 5	* "cursed barmaid S·"

best

Mis.	233– 4	a malpractice of the best s·

complete

My.	113–10	truth of the complete s· of C. S.

educational

Mis.	263–23	educational s· of C. S.
My.	245– 6	This Christian educational s·
	312–31	educational s· in New Hampshire.

entire

Mis.	382–30	entire s· of teaching and

gospel-opposing

Mis.	301–11	gospel-opposing s· of authorship,

homœopathic

My.	107– 8	namely, the homœopathic s·,
	107–19	efficiency of the homœopathic s·.

human

Mis.	48–16	effect of alcohol, . . . on the human s·,
	244– 6	Mind alone constructing the human s·,

hygienic

No.	10–14	My hygienic s· rests on Mind,

its

My.	13–10	* like a sun in the centre of its s·,

learn a

No.	43–22	come to my College to learn a s·

medical

Mis.	80–31	to understand the medical s· of

mental

Mis.	35– 9	this mental s· of treating disease.
Hea.	13–25	this mental s· of healing

metaphysical

Ret.	43– 1	the first purely metaphysical s·
Un.	9–28	difference in my metaphysical s·

mighty

Mis.	234–20	mighty s· of metaphysical healing,

my

Mis.	243–19	since my s· of medicine is not
Un.	10– 2	separates my s· from all others.
No.	4–17	and the efficacy of my s·,
	11– 8	my s· of Christian metaphysics
	24– 8	at variance with my s· of metaphysics,

system

my
No. 44– 7 My s· of Mind-healing
My. 105–26 a work describing my s· of healing.
nebulous
Mis. 378–22 than the nebulous s· is from the earth.
of Christianity
'01. 34–13 new s· of Christianity,
of faith
My. 59– 8 * a new s· of faith and worship,
of healing
Mis. 33–21 *advantages of your s· of healing,*
255–19 advantages of your s· of healing?
Ret. 43– 1 purely metaphysical s· of healing
Pul. 85–13 * the s· of healing of Jesus
Hea. 13–25 this mental s· of healing
My. 105–26 describing my s· of healing.
244–31 Christian s· of healing all manner of
of medicine
Mis. 81– 9 which is the true s· of medicine.
243–13 every s· of medicine claims more than
243–19 since my s· of medicine is not
My. 105–31 misrepresenting a s· of medicine
of metaphysics
No. 24– 8 at variance with my s· of metaphysics,
'01. 26– 4 founded his s· of metaphysics
My. 105–28 curative s· of metaphysics.
of ministry
Pul. 20–11 s· of ministry and church
of religion
Mis. 284– 4 any other s· of religion,
296– 1 s· of religion,— widely known ;
My. 129– 4 and a lax s· of religion.
258– 3 that lifts a s· of religion to
of truth
Pul. 51– 1 * not strike all as a s· of truth.
part of a
'00. 13– 8 part of a s· supported by
proper
Man. 28– 7 Without a proper s· of government
public school
'02. 3–16 improved her public school s·
sanitary
Ret. 30– 9 a sanitary s· that should include
scientific
My. 127–12 Comparing our scientific s· of
solar
Mis. 174–13 broader than the solar s·
speak of the
Pul. 80–19 * speak of the s· it sets forth,
stellar
Mis. 65– 6 man's *ipse dixit* as to the stellar s·
this
Mis. 235– 1 By this s·, too, man has
296– 1 Founder of this s· of religion,
369–11 "method" in the "madness" of this s·,
Un. 10– 4 this s· is built on Him
No. 11–11 As a Science, this s· is held back by
My. 107–20 identifies this s· with mind,
type, and
'00. 11–28 human action, type, and s·.
whole
Mis. 38– 7 our whole s· of education,

system

your
Mis. 33–21 *advantages of your s· of healing,*
255–19 advantages of your s· of healing
Mis. 34– 2 "after effects" of these in the s· ;
243–14 If the s· is Science, it includes
'02. 1–19 a s· that honors God
Hea. 19– 4 proved that every organ of the s·,
systematic
Ret. 87– 9 settled and s· workers,
87–11 s· and law-abiding people on earth,
Rud. 15–10 deep s· thinking is
systematically
My. 245– 5 cautiously, s·, scientifically.
systematized
Mis. 113–28 s· centres of C. S.
systematizes
Mis. 235–15 s· action, gives a keener sense of
My. 287–23 s· action, and insures success ;
systems
and practices
My. 221– 6 s· and practices of their times.
and spheres
My. 13–26 all cycles of s· and spheres.
erudite
Ret. 31–28 Erudite s· of philosophy
four
Pul. 25– 5 * four s· with motor electric power.
human
Mis. 74–10 all human s· of etiology
Ret. 57–24 Human s· of philosophy
material
Mis. 232–14 part with material s· and theories,
Peo. 8–25 fossils of material s·,
materialistic
Ret. 78–13 which advocate materialistic s· ;
medical
Mis. 252– 3 medical s· of allopathy
metaphysical
No. 22–11 Such miscalled metaphysical s·
modern
My. 103–22 nothing in ancient or in modern s·
of crime
Mis. 246– 3 all unmitigated s· of crime ;
of *materia medica*
Peo. 4– 2 to all s· of *materia medica*
of religion
Mis. 27– 8 and other s· of religion
'00. 5–25 foundation of all s· of religion.
Peo. 4–25 S· of religion and of medicine
My. 216– 4 All s· of religion stand on this basis.
ordinary
'02. 1–16 ordinary s· of religious beliefs
other
Mis. 27– 8 other s· of religion abandon
No. 4–17 beyond other s· of medicine,
Hea. 11–28 excellence above other s·.
pathological
Mis. 297– 4 pathological s· for physical and
sects and
'01. 2–17 feverish pride of sects and s·

Pan. 11– 8 s·, doctrines, and dogmas of men

T

T——, Professor
Mis. 242– 2 The article of Professor T·,
tabernacle
Mis. 152–11 those who worship in this t· :
362–26 in the t· of Spirit.
My. 33–15 abide in thy t·?— *Psal.* 15 : 1.
36–28 * and set up this t·,
188–12 your t· of the congregation
tabernacles
Mis. 227–22 abide in t· of their own,
Pul. 7–21 their t· crumble with dry rot.
table
Mis. 106–20 crumbs fallen from this t· of Truth,
231– 9 would I have had the t· give a
311– 7 ready for the t· of our Lord :
369–20 crumb that falleth from his t·.
Pul. 62–23 * might be placed on a small centre t·.
No. 9–20 a t· in the wilderness"— *Psal.* 78 : 19.
Pan. 14– 5 commune at the t· of our Lord
15– 6 spread for us a t· in the wilderness
'00. 15– 5 To sit at this t· of their Lord
'01. 22–16 with the numeration t· of C. S.
22–21 numeration t· of C. S.,

table
'01. 22–25 they have learned its numeration t·,
22–28 Even the numeration t· of C. S.
23– 2 losing the numeration t·
My. 105–13 instruments were lying on the t·
178–22 on a t· in a burning building.
178–24 t· sank a charred mass.
tables
Mis. 270– 2 "overthrew the t· of — *Matt.* 21 : 12.
tablet
Pul. 24–12 * On the front is a marble t·,
26–22 * golden letters on a marble t·,
63–25 * a t· imbedded in its wall
'02. 2– 6 t· of one's own heart,
tablets
Mis. 121– 3 are engraved upon eternity's t·.
295–25 ideas are inscribed on t· of
No. 1–17 read more clearly the t· of Truth.
tabret
Chr. 55–12 The t·, and pipe, and wine,— *Isa.* 5 : 12.
tacit
Mis. 291–10 t· acquiescence with others' views

tacitly
Mis. 109– 3 *t·* assent where they should dissent ;

tail
Mis. 216–21 * beginning with the end of the *t·*,

taint
Mis. 223–23 or *t·* their examples.
Un. 4– 2 without a single *t·* of our mortal,
Po. 29–19 cruel creed, or earth-born *t·* :

tainted
'00. 3–30 has it not *t·* the religious sects

taints
My. 228–20 washing it clean from the *t·* of

take
Mis. vii– 1 * *t·* care, that tak'st my book in hand,
xii– 5 I *t·* my pen and pruning-hook,
6–29 *T·* a large family of children
14– 4 *t·* in only the immortal facts
17– 8 you *t·* off your shoes
27–32 *T·* away the mortal sense
30–26 *T·* courage, dear reader,
37–25 *Does Mrs. Eddy t· patients ?*
39– 2 to *t·* a course of instruction
39–13 *Can you t· care of yourself ?*
39–17 not afraid to *t·* their own medicine,
47– 9 material senses cannot *t·* in.
52– 2 may refer to such as . . . *t·* drugs
58–25 *T·* away the theology of
58–26 and you *t·* away its science,
64– 9 *t·* for preliminary studies ?
79–26 *What course should . . . Scientists t·*
87– 3 To *t·* all earth's beauty into one
90– 3 *T·* away this pleasure,
91–25 did not *t·* his textbook with him
92–12 He will *t·* the textbook of C. S.
97– 3 *t·* hold of the eternal energies
99–15 *t·* not back the words of Truth.
99–17 in the front rank, face the foe,
109– 4 *t·* me as authority for what I
115–13 to *t·* up the cross as I have done,
120– 2 *t·* off their shoes at our altars ;
129–11 *t·* the next Scriptural step :
132– 3 *t·* this as a favorable omen,
135–15 *t·* this cross, and the crown
137–17 dear ones, if you *t·* my advice
138 28 all shall *t·* step and march on
180– 2 to *t·* the side of Spirit,
191– 4 senses are supposed to *t·* in,
193–22 next step for ecclesiasticism to *t·*,
199–11 *t· pleasure in infirmities,*— II Cor. 12 : 10.
200–21 *t· pleasure in infirmities,"*— II Cor. 12 : 10.
205–11 *"shall t· of mine*— John 16 : 15.
205–32 *t·* rapid transit to heaven,
210–10 shall *t·* up serpents ;"— Mark 16 : 18.
214–26 cannot . . . *t·* error along with Truth,
215–11 if we *t·* the end for the beginning
215–27 cannot . . . *t·* the attitude, nor
218–13 can *t·* no cognizance of Spirit
227–32 *t·* this to be a safer guide
228– 5 is to *t·* a new standpoint
231– 8 I *t·* no stock in spirit-rappings
236–20 "*T·* no counsel of a mortal,
239–13 alight, and *t·* from his carriage the
239–15 "somebody has to *t·* it ;
240– 6 doctors must not *t·* the sweet
240–14 nature would *t·* it out as gently,
243–24 "*T·* a little wine for*— see I Tim. 5 : 23.
245– 3 *T·* no thought,— Matt. 6 : 31.
248–16 That I *t·* opium ; . . . is not more true
254–19 *t·* away a third part of the stars
262–29 because I *t·* so much pleasure
264–29 *t·* its hue from the divine Mind.
270– 1 let us *t·* the side of him who
271–10 should *t·* our magazine,
271–16 *t·* in this axiomatic truism :
275– 3 would you *t·* away even
294–22 thank God and *t·* courage,
298– 3 St. Paul's words *t·* in the
299–18 *t·* from it his garments
308–10 *t·* their proper place in history,
309–28 *t·* things too intensely.
311–11 to *t·* this advanced step
311–28 *t·* the cup, drink all of it,
316– 6 When will you *t·* a class
319–22 *T·* thither thy saintly offerings,
326–24 *t·* them up the mountain.
327– 2 to *t·* something out of it,
327– 6 *t·* nothing of thine own
327–21 only to *t·* them up again,
336–28 only to *t·* away its frailty.
347–16 *T·* the opposite direction !
347–18 *t·* a few steps, then halt.
347–26 Those who . . . *t·* His hand,
349– 2 to *t·* lessons outside of my College,
356– 1 when they *t·* their flight,

take
Mis. 368–11 chapter sub-title
398–16 *T·* them in Thine arms ;
Man. 15– 3 we *t·* the inspired Word
49–13 *t·* proper care of the sick.
62– 3 required to *t·* the collection.
63–20 *t·* charge of the Reading Rooms
67–12 nor *t·* legal action on a case
69–23 not *t·* care of their churches or
71– 2 *t·* the title of First Church
Chr. 53–55 Just *t·* Me in !
Ret. 14–15 to trust God, and *t·* my chance
24–24 should *t·* the things of God
40– 2 refusing to *t·* any pay for my
46–22 *T·* them in Thine arms ;
60–26 *t·* no cognizance of the
65–12 Mortals must *t·* up the cross
70–14 No person can *t·* the . . . place of
70–16 No person can *t·* the place of
79–27 violent by force !"— Matt. 11 : 12.
83–21 Scientists should *t·* their textbook
84–27 teacher should *t·* charge only of
89–23 to *t·* charge of their students,
Un. 15–18 *t·* precedence as the infinite sinner,
25–25 evil can never *t·* away.
28–18 five senses *t·* no cognizance of Soul,
28–19 they *t·* no cognizance of God.
34–14 *T·* another train of reasoning.
34–19 *T·* away mortal mind,
34–21 *T·* away matter,
38– 1 *t·* no cognizance of spiritual
Pul. 13–25 how many periods of torture it may *t·*
17–21 *T·* them in Thine arms ;
31– 8 * and *t·*, as the point of departure,
51–28 * can only aspire to *t·* its place
69–16 * It would *t·* a small book
72–26 * we *t·* Christ as an example.
79–12 * one cannot *t·* up a daily paper
81–19 * they want no time to *t·*,
87– 1 * and *t·* charge of any services
Rud. 12–23 "*T·* no thought— Matt. 6 : 25.
14–14 to *t·* the full price of tuition
16– 2 then public lectures can *t·* the place of
No. v–11 *t·* the unadulterated milk of
2–11 and *t·* up the cross.
6– 8 *t·* cognizance of their own phenomena,
16–21 can *t·* in no more than all.
19–22 sinner can *t·* no cognizance of
27–25 *t·* off thy shoes and tread lightly,
33–18 they *t·* hold of harmony,
40–17 never to *t·* away the rights,
43–18 who *t·* it up from mercenary motives,
'00. 2–26 to *t·* some time for myself ;
9–26 to have some one *t·* my place
14– 5 that no man *t·* thy crown."— Rev. 3 : 11.
'01. 13–10 *t·* possession of us and
13–11 *t·* possession of sin with such a
16– 4 *t·* in a poignant present sense of
32 28 *t·* in the spirit and understanding
'02. 13–25 nor to *t·* the property off my hands,
17–26 *t·* its answer as to thy aims,
Hea. 1– 3 shall *t·* up serpents ;— Mark 16 : 18.
1–14 "Then there were no cross to *t·* up,
6–10 they *t·* pleasure in calling me a medium.
7–25 shall *t·* up serpents ;— Mark 16 : 18.
10–21 *t·* the side you wish to carry,
15–10 shall "*t·* up serpents"— Mark 16 : 18.
Pev. 12–18 we shall *t·* in the remaining
Po. v–15 * began to *t·* form in her thought,
14–20 *T·* them in Thine arms ;
27–21 and may *t·* thy rest,
35– 1 O *t·* me to thy bower !
My. 31–19 * can *t·* a place in the front rank
47–31 * shall *t·* up serpents ;— Mark 16 : 18.
51– 2 * no one . . . who could *t·* her place
62– 8 * *t·* this precious truth and give
75–17 * *t·* it all very good-naturedly.
84–28 * to *t·* place on Sunday,
86–12 * to *t·* part in the . . . ceremonies
96–12 * *t·* joy in attesting their faith
128–31 that evil suggestions, . . . *t·* no root
135–14 *t·* the charge of my property ;
137–21 to *t·* charge of my property ;
138– 2 gave them my property to *t·* care of
138– 4 to *t·* care of my property
140–18 *T·* courage. God is leading you
146– 4 shall *t·* up serpents ;— Mark 16 : 18.
146–27 Others who *t·* the side of error
154–30 *t·* it in whatever sense you may.
155–10 * step with the twentieth century,
160–27 This may *t·* millions of cycles,
173–17 to *t·* a peep at this church edifice
177– 9 I am quite able to *t·* the trip
180–27 *T·* it up,— it wins the crown ;
193–16 Love gives nothing to *t·* away.
215–24 bade them *t·* no scrip

take

My.	215–26	Next, . . . he bade them *t·* scrip.
	217–12	disbursal will *t·* place when the
	236–23	chapter sub-title
	237– 4	chapter sub-title
	237–12	chapter sub-title
	237–20	chapter sub-title
	242–15	chapter sub-title
	243–14	who are adequate to *t·* charge
	251– 8	* to *t·* both Primary and Normal
	258–32	*t·* a peep into my studio ;
	335–22	* to *t·* the remains to Charleston.
	336– 5	* to *t·* her back to the North.
	351–22	chapter sub-title
	358–29	chapter sub-title
	362–22	* to *t·* such action as will unite the

taken

Mis.	67–31	footsteps requisite have been *t·*
	95– 7	* which reply was *t·* in full
	117–21	then watch that each step be *t·*,
	124–20	C. S. has *t·* expressive silence
	144– 1	granite for this church was *t·* from
	172–18	evidences whereof are *t·* in by the
	225–14	clergyman's son was *t·* . . . ill.
	231–21	grandpa was *t·* napping.
	242–23	having *t·* it twenty years ;
	248–28	I have not *t·* drugs,
	250–14	*t·* down . . . with sugar-tongs
	285–20	We have *t·* the precaution to
	311–13	and if it be not *t·* thus,
	314–29	shall be *t·* from the *Quarterly*,
	315– 1	selections *t·* from the Scriptures
	349–11	*t·* the above-named course
	376– 8	* having been *t·* by Fra Angelico
	381– 5	Testimony was *t·* on the part of
Man.	27– 6	no special action to be *t·*
	36– 6	loyal students who have *t·*
	66–10	before action is *t·* it shall be
	85–15	or has *t·* a Normal Course
Ret.	13– 5	Before this step was *t·*,
	20–12	night before my child was *t·*
	20–15	are *t·* from my poem,
Un.	14–23	model would be *t·* away.
	28–20	Whatever cannot be *t·* in by
Pul.	29–22	* lesson was to be *t·* spiritually
	72–17	* "I have not *t·* any medicine
	79– 6	* no debt had to be *t·* care of
	79–19	* had *t·* possession of men's minds,
Rud.	14–10	The only pay *t·* for her labors
	15–13	Few were *t·* besides invalids
'00.	13–13	it was *t·* and sacked.
'01.	7–19	have not *t·* away their Lord,
	24–10	* having *t·* this medicine
	27–23	*t·* out of its metaphysics all matter
'02.	19–21	its treasures, *t·* away from you?
Hea.	5– 8	if a man has *t·* cold by
	13– 9	they have *t·* no medicine,
Peo.	5– 5	have not *t·* away our Lord,
My.	10–12	* *t·* steps in this direction,
	22–25	* position *t·* by our Pastor Emeritus
	25–10	* figures are *t·* from the report
	31–27	* congregation had *t·* their seats,
	43–16	* stones *t·* from the midst of the
	65–22	* deed being *t·* by Ira O. Knapp
	78–14	* offertory *t·* at the beginning
	137–19	affairs carefully *t·* care of
	141–16	* *t·* steps to abolish its
	172– 2	* *t·* from the old Yale College
	217–30	last step to be *t·* first.
	311–22	*t·* in connection with her own
	312–13	* *t·* to her father's home
	317–23	The liberty that I have *t·*
	329– 2	* was accordingly *t·* out.
	329–15	* *t·* from the . . . *Chronicle*

takes

Mis.	5–19	*t·* up the case hopefully
	28– 8	Matter *t·* no cognizance of matter.
	42– 1	*After the change called death t· place*,
	72–21	*imply that Spirit t· note of*
	84–27	*t·* them away, and teaches Life's
	138– 3	time it *t·* yearly to prepare for
	175– 3	*t·* of the things of God
	175–23	one belief *t·* the place of another.
	189–17	quickening spirit *t·* it away:
	210–14	handles it, and *t·* away its sting.
	218– 1	spiritual sense *t·* in new views,
	222– 1	It *t·* away a man's proper sense of
	228–21	or in any way *t·* cognizance of,
	240–15	*t·* the frost out of the ground
	240–29	"Battle-Axe Plug" *t·* off men's heads ;
	240–30	*t·* from their bodies a sweet something
	304–15	* *t·* place at Paris, France.
	341–24	*t·* the most solemn vow of celibacy
Man.	68–21	This By-Law *t·* effect on Dec. 15, 1908.
Un.	2– 9	*t·* away man's fondness for sin

takes

Un.	30–10	understanding *t·* away this belief
	53– 1	lie *t·* its pattern from Truth,
	61– 2	*t·* hold of eternal Truth.
Pul.	25–29	* *t·* the place of chandeliers.
	37– 9	* she *t·* a daily walk
	46–12	* Mrs. Eddy *t·* delight in going back to
	50– 2	* in whom she *t·* a vital interest.
Rud.	2–20	*t·* away the trammels assigned to
	6–10	to the material senses, evil *t·* the
	11–21	*t·* away every human belief,
No.	13–18	It *t·* hold of eternity,
Pan.	10– 1	it *t·* away man's personality
'00.	2–13	He *t·* no time for amusement,
	6–14	he *t·* in its spiritual sense
	8–13	till God's discipline *t·* it off
'01.	9–22	Holy Spirit *t·* of the things of God
	14–11	our faith *t·* hold of the fact
My.	26– 3	* Board of Directors *t·* pleasure in
	83–22	* *t·* on a tone of deserved satisfaction,
	120–11	*t·* away all sin, disease, and death,
	129–24	good man's heart *t·* hold on heaven,
	146–26	*t·* the side of sin, disease, or
	166– 8	God *t·* care of our life.
	203–19	for God *t·* care of it.
	217–29	Jesus of Nazareth, first *t·* up the
	229–31	it *t·* life profoundly ;
	247–22	*persuasion that t· away their fear,*

taketh

'01.	9–17	*t·* away the sin of — *John* 1 : 29.
My.	4– 8	*t·* not his cross, — *Matt.* 10 : 38.
	33–20	nor *t·* up a reproach — *Psal.* 15 : 3.
	33–26	nor *t·* reward against — *Psal.* 15 : 5.
	196–11	he that *t·* a city." — *Prov.* 16 : 32.
	233–24	*t·* not his cross, — *Matt.* 10 : 38.

taking

Mis.	11–16	save it only . . . by *t·* another's,
	11–31	*t·* by the hand all who love me not,
	13– 4	*t·* special care to mind my
	19–18	*t·* the livery of heaven wherewith to
	78–20	*t·* its money in exchange for this
	136– 5	*t·* forward marches,
	169–28	* *T·* several Bible passages,
	223–24	chapter sub-title
	239– 8	substance is *t·* larger proportions.
	241–13	*t·* a dose of error big enough
	242–21	*t·* morphine . . . at the rate of
	249– 2	experimented by *t·* some large doses
	292–21	enjoins *t·* them by the hand
	297– 1	*T·* into account the short time
	300– 4	* this copy into the pulpit,
	327–13	insisted upon *t·* all of it with them,
	329– 7	*t·* up the white carpets
	371– 5	*t·* them out of the care of
	381– 7	The time for *t·* testimony
Ret.	19– 3	*t·* place under the paternal roof
	36– 5	after *t·* out my first copyright,
	58– 2	*t·* the rule of finite matter,
	86–18	*t·* up his cross and following Truth.
Un.	11–18	*t·* away the material evidence.
Pul.	56–12	* *t·* place on the 6th of January,
	70–19	* *T·* her text from the Bible,
	72–30	* ever hear of Jesus' *t·* medicine
Rud.	17–13	*t·* the first footsteps in this
No.	2–25	*T·* advantage of the present ignorance
'02.	10–14	*t·* steps outward and upwards.
Hea.	13– 2	*t·* hold of both horns of the
My.	13– 2	*t·* no thought for the morrow,
	129– 7	*t·* strong hold of the public thought
	193–24	*t·* the first by the forelock
	212– 6	*t·* the place of older . . . sins,
	214–17	*t·* pay for their labors,
	214–20	*t·* no remuneration for my labors,
	217–25	aids in *t·* the next step
	224–22	not be as *t·* to those ignorant of
	227–15	*t·* a case of malignant disease.
	229–20	*t·* in the Ten Commandments
	233–19	*t·* the name of God in vain.

tak'st

Mis.	vii– 1	* that *t·* my book in hand,

tale

Ret.	21–16	"as a *t·* that is told," — *Psal.* 90 : 9.
Un.	23– 9	How well the Shakespearean *t·* agrees
	48– 2	to repeat my twice-told *t·*,
	48– 3	*t·* already told a hundred times,
My.	186– 8	tells the *t·* of your little church,

talent

Un.	9–12	*t·* and genius of the centuries
'00.	9–19	more successful than genius or *t·*.
My.	195–17	the one *t·* that we all have,
	195–18	only means of adding to that *t·*

talented
Ret. 6–16 reputed one of the most *t*·,
Pul. 39–11 Miss Whiting, the *t*· author
My. 338–18 The *t*· author of this lecture

talents
Mis. 317–26 having already seen . . . their *t*·,
Ret. 7–21 * from his *t*· and acquirements.
11–17 laud the land whose *t*·
Po. 60–14 laud the land whose *t*·
My. 104–26 of the highest *t*·, scholarship,
117–26 their *t*· and loving hearts

tales
Pul. 8– 3 Like the winds telling *t*·
My. 81–31 * *t*· of people of standing

talisman
Po. 68–17 Of the past 'tis the *t*·,

Talitha cumi
Peo. 8–21 swept by the divine *T*· *c*·,

talk
Mis. 23–17 Matter cannot even *t*· ;
32–17 If I had the time to *t*· with
127–27 Wise sayings and garrulous *t*·
159–22 Here I *t*· once a year,
174– 3 it is a lie, claiming to *t*·
239– 3 I can *t*· — and laugh too !
330–19 *t*· with our past hours,
339– 2 confine their *t*· to subjects that
397– 8 and tenderly, Divinely *t*·.
Un. 6–21 will *t*· to her babe about the
21– 7 good and evil *t*· to one another ;
25–10 Matter cannot *t*· ;
33–11 it cannot *t*· or testify ;
60– 7 *t*· of sin and sinners as real.
Pul. 18–17 and tenderly, Divinely *t*·.
74–22 as I have heard her *t*·.
No. 26– 5 infantile *t*· about Mind-healing
Hea. 9–11 moral advisers *t*· for them
10–22 careful not to *t*· on both sides,
Po. 12–17 and tenderly, Divinely *t*·.
My. 59–27 * I heard her *t*· it before
158–22 Most men and women *t*· well,
189– 8 nor *t*· of unknown love.
321–12 * with whom he had occasion to *t*·,

talked
Mis. 293–27 Truth *t*· and not lived,
312– 2 may the love that is *t*·,
345–27 *t*· of the crucified Saviour ;
Pul. 49–18 * Mrs. Eddy *t*· earnestly
My. 65–12 * It was not even *t*· over,
287–11 Love *t*· and not lived
291–15 not *t*· but felt and lived.
321–15 * differing from what he *t*·
345–31 * We *t*· on many subjects,

talker
Mis. 23–17 Satan, the first *t*· in its behalf,
191–24 original devil was a great *t*·,
295– 9 anonymous *t*· further declares,
My. 210–14 evil thinker is the proud *t*·

talking
Mis. 24–28 not to believe the *t*· serpent,
88–18 task of *t*· to deaf ears
130–10 *t*· about it, thinking it over,
230– 4 time is consumed in *t*· nothing,
230–18 *t*· when they have nothing to say,
Ret. 73–23 is like the sick *t*· sickness.
Un. 44–11 a false, personality, — a *t*· snake,
Pan. 6–12 in the form of a *t*· serpent,
Hea. 9– 5 *t*· on the wrong side
My. 343– 2 * She has a rapt way of *t*·,

talks
Un. 27– 6 one who *t*· much of himself,
Pul. 36–11 * was given to her morning *t*·
Rud. 11–28 He never *t*· about the structure of
My. 341–19 * chapter sub-title
346– 2 * She *t*· as one who has lived with

tall
Pul. 31–28 * Her figure was *t*·, slender,
87–24 church's *t*· tower detains the sun,
Po. 67–11 winds bow the *t*· willow's head !
68– 9 the sea and the *t*· waving pine
My. 308–15 * my father's "*t*·, gaunt frame"

Talmage, Rev. Dr.
Mis. 117–11 I agree with Rev. Dr. *T*·,

Talmudical
Mis. ix– 1 apothegm of a *T*· philosopher

taming
Mis. 323–20 *t*· the beasts of prey,

tampered
Mis. 282–13 would we have our minds *t*· with.
Ret. 83– 9 ought not to be *t*· with.

tampering
No. 5–24 *t*· with the realities of God

tan-bark
My. 313–10 his house with *t*· and straw,

tangibility
Mis. 56– 7 substance, form, and *t*·,

tangible
Mis. 103–15 as *t*·, true substance,
Un. 54– 7 as *t*· as any reality.
Pul. 63–20 * *t*· and material manner
Rud. 6– 4 *are they not t*· *and material ?*
'01. 7–21 there must be something *t*·
Hea. 6–16 were evolved and made *t*· ;
My. 98–10 * church, . . . is a *t*· reality,

tape
Un. 11–23 neither red *t*· nor indignity hindered

taper
My. 202–22 The *t*· unseen in sunlight

tapestried
Mis. 324– 7 the gorgeously *t*· parlors,

tapestry
Pul. 76–13 * upholstery is in white and gold *t*·.

tap-rooms
Mis. 296–19 Do manly Britons patronize *t*·

tardy
Mis. 275– 2 Oh, *t*· human justice !
358– 9 naught but *t*· justice,

tares
Mis. 111–16 the *t*· cannot hinder it.
117– 5 separate the *t*· from the wheat ;
172– 4 separating the *t*· from the wheat,
214–29 possibility of destroying the *t*· :
Ret. 71–23 *t*· growing side by side with the wheat,
'02. 18–12 nor spared . . . the consuming *t*·.
My. 124–30 separate the *t*· from the wheat,
249–12 burns the wheat, spares the *t*·,
269–18 separating the *t*· from the wheat.
316– 2 separated the *t*· from the wheat,

targets
Mis. 347–31 Loyal Scientists are *t*· for envy,

tariff
My. 216– 7 manufacture, agriculture, *t*·,

tarried
Mis. 328–18 *t*· in the habitation of the senses,
329–25 snow-bird that *t*· through the storm,

tarry
Pul. 4– 6 I'll *t*· in the sky.' "
My. 38–14 * visitors showed a tendency to *t*·

tarrying
Mis. 340– 2 faithless *t*·, has torn the laurel from

tar-water
No. 22– 7 on the healing properties of *t*·,
'01. 24– 9 descanting on the virtues of *t*·,
24–16 from divine metaphysics to *t*· !

task
Mis. 19– 8 The *t*· of healing the sick
88–18 closes the *t*· of talking to
114– 4 time and attention to their *t*·,
256–11 severe *t*· of remaining at present
302–12 thus sparing their teacher a *t*·
Ret. 38–11 to fulfil this painful *t*·,
Pul. 72– 1 * inspired in her great *t*· by
Rud. 2–27 this *t*·, sometimes, may be harder
No. 4– 2 the *t*· of learning thoroughly
Hea. 14–18 most arduous *t*· I ever performed.
My. 39–14 * my modest *t*· will be ended.
64–24 * holy *t*· of overcoming
334–10 and not *t*· themselves with
258–12 resurrection and *t*· of glory,

tasks
Mis. 130–20 such Herculean *t*· as they have
242–14 I performed more difficult *t*·
273–10 so capable of relieving my *t*·
Ret. 90–24 those first sacred *t*·,
Pul. 9– 5 when your tireless *t*· are done
No. 7–18 God has appointed . . . high *t*·,
My. 42–29 * performance of her daily *t*·.
231–22 for her to undertake new *t*·,

taste
Mis. 28– 3 neither see, hear, feel, *t*·,
86–28 hear, see, feel, *t*·, smell,
Un. 22– 8 would *t*· and know error
24–25 to see, *t*·, hear, feel, smell.
35– 1 *T*·. Mortal mind says, "I *t*· ;
Pul. 36–24 * one of the utmost *t*· and luxury,
66–18 * satisfy a *t*· for the mystical
Rud. 5–20 does not see, hear, smell, or *t*·.
'01. 26–27 a native or an acquired *t*· for
Hea. 16–21 feel, *t*·, nor smell God ;

tasted

Mis.	9–19	having *t·* its tempting wine,
My.	17– 8	"If so be ye have *t·* — *I Pet.* 2 : 3.

tasteless

Mis.	9–23	set it aside as *t·*

tastes

Mis.	119–13	its habits, *t·*, and indulgences.
	224–13	ambitions, *t·*, and loves ;
Un.	25– 9	feels, *t·*, smells as Mind,

tasting

Ret.	30–24	without *t·* this cup.

tatters

Po.	79–12	fears are foes — truth *t·* those,

taught

Mis.	3–11	his demonstration hath *t·* us
	11– 8	if I *t·* indigent students
	29–15	In 1867, I *t·* the first student in
	35–25	*t·* its Science by the author of
	38–16	Metaphysics, as *t·* by me at the
	43–29	the barefaced errors that are *t·*
	48– 4	should neither be *t·* nor practised,
	65–23	and I have *t·* them both
	78– 7	*t· to those who are absent?*
	78– 9	can no more be *t·* thus, than
	87–22	*t·* the divine Principle and rules
	87–28	the truth they have been *t·*.
	91–28	as authority for what he *t·*.
	111– 3	to demonstrate what you have . . . *t·* ;
	150–20	as *t·* by our great Master.
	163–10	He healed and *t·* by the wayside,
	166– 6	Truth he has *t·* and spoken lives,
	174–25	and *t·* us to pray,
	189–27	*t·* them as one having — *Matt.* 7 : 29.
	213– 3	All that I have written, *t·*, or
	229–16	would teach man as David *t·* :
	239–28	had been *t·* the value of
	243– 6	mental branches *t·* in my college ;
	247–15	are unwilling to be *t·* it,
	264–15	*t·* their first lessons by my
	273–27	When these were *t·*,
	291–25	*t·* the truth which is energizing,
	308–22	*t·* me more than it has others),
	308–28	C. S. is *t·* through its divine
	317–13	to be *t·* in a class,
	331–16	*t·* them the Lord's Prayer
	337–26	him who *t·* — by the wayside,
	340–19	by practising what he was *t·*.
	349–10	obstetrics *t·* in my College.
	357–25	no matter who has *t·* them.
	357–25	If they have been *t·* wrongly,
	371– 1	*t·* by our great Master.
	378–18	sum of what he *t·* her
	380–24	*t·* me the impossibility of
	382–14	I *t·* the first student in C. S.
Man.	17–17	*t·* and demonstrated by our Master,
	62–19	children shall be *t·* the Scriptures,
	62–23	divine Principle that they are *t·*.
	69–11	charge for what she has *t·* him
	85–14	that he has been *t·* by Mrs. Eddy
	88– 9	Obstetrics will not be *t·*.
	89–12	*t·* in a Primary class by Mrs. Eddy
	90–15	no . . . *t·* under the auspices of
Chr.	53–13	What the Beloved knew and *t·*,
Ret.	10– 1	*t·* to believe that my brain was
	15–10	*t·* me from my youth :— *Psal.* 71 : 17.
	36– 5	I *t·* the Science of Mind-healing,
	40– 2	and *t·* in a general way,
	42– 9	He also *t·* a special Bible-class ;
	43– 9	Asa G. Eddy, *t·* two terms in my
	43–16	*t·* the Primary, Normal,
	43–18	*t·* one Primary class, in 1889,
	58–10	*t·* them as one having — *Matt.* 7 : 29.
	61–28	however little be *t·* or learned,
	65–22	as *t·* in the four Gospels.
	75–12	understood or *t·* by those who
	83– 7	Students whom I have *t·*
	87– 7	Experience has *t·* me that the
	90– 8	*t·* a few hungry ones,
Un.	1– 5	*t·* by his fellow-apostle Paul,
	10– 7	apostles, who have thus *t·*
	17–13	Jesus distinctly *t·* the arrogant
	42–19	*t·* them as one having — *Matt.* 7 : 29.
	44–12	pretender *t·* the opposite of Truth.
	46–13	He *t·* no selfhood as existent in
	58–10	after the manner that he had *t·*,
Pul.	36– 2	* College in Boston, in which he *t·*.
	46– 4	* in search of the truth as *t·*.
	52–19	* *t·* and practised by Jesus
	52–25	* revived belief in what he *t·*
	68– 5	* and here she *t·* the principles
	74–22	it is not what I have *t·* her,
Rud.	14–13	She has never *t·* . . . without
	15–21	assimilate what has been *t·*
No.	2–10	*t·* his students to deny self,

taught

No.	2–19	what he has been *t·*.
Pan.	8–14	Christianity, as *t·* and demonstrated
	8–21	as he *t·* and demonstrated it,
	10–17	utility of what they had been *t·*.
'00.	4–17	as *t·* by our great Master ;
'01.	2– 2	Christ Jesus *t·* and demonstrated
	9–15	*t·* his followers to do likewise.
	18–12	*t·* his disciples none other.
	21–10	* which are now *t·* in C. S."
	22–29	C. S. is not *t·* correctly by those who
	23–19	*t·* his disciples and followers
	25–21	He demonstrated what he *t·*.
	25–22	he *t·* the power of Spirit,
	31–27	*t·* by some grand old divines,
	33–22	after the manner *t·* by Jesus,
'02.	2–30	*t·* the student to overcome evil
	15– 8	indigent students that I *t·*
Peo.	7–28	*t·* me that the health and character
My.	52–13	* *t·* and expressed by our pastor,
	54– 5	* the eternal truth she *t·* them."
	61–24	* *t·* me that I should be willing to
	109–10	Christ *t·* his followers to heal
	112– 9	doctrines *t·* by divine Science
	130–30	substance of the truth that is *t·*;
	163– 4	won the way and *t·* mankind
	180– 7	*t·* his disciples the healing
	182–11	I *t·* a class in C. S.
	215– 7	*t·* students for a tuition of
	215– 9	I seldom *t·* without having
	219–21	what Christ Jesus *t·* and did;
	230–27	all *t·* of God." — *John* 6 : 45.
	239–14	*and all are t· of God*
	251– 7	* students, whom I have *t·*,
	251–14	is *t·* in the Board of Education
	261– 8	children should not be *t·* to
	292– 4	All good that ever was written, *t·*,
	310– 3	they all *t·* school acceptably
	312–17	* For a brief season she *t·* school."
	327–30	* *t·* and practised in C. S.,
	343–15	I have simply *t·* as I learned
		(*see also* **Jesus**)

taunt

Un.	11–16	He heeded not the *t·*,

tax

Ret.	71– 2	with the *t·* it raises on calamity
My.	80– 8	* *t·* upon frail human credulity,
	309–20	paid the largest *t·* in the colony.

taxed

Mis.	381–19	her cost of suit, *t·* at ($113.09)
My.	82–24	* were *t·* to the utmost

taxes

Man.	30–17	*t·* and rent on this property ;
My.	327–21	* act in the Legislature regulating *t·*,

taxing

Mis.	140– 8	to the end of *t·* their faith

tea

Mis.	348–19	not even coffea (coffee), thea (*t·*),

teach

Mis.	35–16	*t· its readers to heal the sick,*
	43– 7	*Do all . . . t· it correctly?*
	43–25	to practise or *t·* C. S.
	44– 4	*t·* people, who are ready
	46–10	*Do you t· that you are equal with God?*
	51–13	*t· him life in matter?*
	66–14	Truth and Love *t·*, through divine
	78–11	to *t·* either Euclid or the
	87–19	to *t·* students of mine.
	91–23	*in his schoolroom and t· from it?*
	93– 3	Beloved students, *so t·* that
	98–27	* if thou the truth would'st *t·* ;
	100–18	and *t·* the eternal.
	114–14	and *t·* others to employ
	115–15	to practise, *t·*, and live C. S. !
	128– 4	too vast . . . to *t·* briefly ;
	132–23	as to what I believe and *t·*,
	137–28	*t·* with increased confidence.
	151–27	heal, and *t·*, and preach,
	161–21	that none should *t·* or preach
	163– 4	preparing to heal and *t·*
	169–15	truths they *t·* must be spiritually
	174–26	did not *t·* us to pray for death
	209– 4	wouldst *t·* God not to punish sin?
	229–15	would *t·* man as David taught :
	240–24	*T·* the children early
	240–24	*t·* them nothing that is wrong.
	244–23	not to *t·* himself, but others,
	247– 8	I found health in just what I *t·*.
	273–29	if I should *t·* that Primary class,
	293– 1	safe not to *t·* prematurely the
	315–11	*t·* annually three classes
	315–11	*t·* from the C. S. textbook.

teach

Mis.	315–32	*t·* their students how to defend
	330–24	*t·* man to be kind,
	338–21	* If thou the truth wouldst *t·* ;
	350–29	*t·* the use of such arguments
	366– 5	demonstrate what they *t·*
	380–12	and *t·* the first student in C. S.
Man.	55–22	or to *t·* C. S. contrary to the
	84– 8	shall *t·* but one class yearly,
	84–24	not *t·* another loyal teacher's pupil,
	85– 6	*t·* and receive into his association
	85–12	not *t·* pupils C. S. unless he
	85–20	not *t·* C. S. without the approval of
	86– 3	Authorized to *T·*.
	86–17	shall *t·* from the chapter "Recapitulation"
	86–22	*t·* nothing contrary thereto.
	87– 3	Neither . . . shall *t·* Roman Catholics
	87–10	authorized by its By-Laws to *t·*
	92–13	duly qualified to *t· C. S.,*
	92–14	should *t·* yearly one class.
Ret.	83–25	to corroborate what they *t·*.
Un.	9–25	healing, as I *t·* it, has not been
	59–16	*t·* mankind only through this
Pul.	39– 5	* *t·* that one great truth,
Rud.	12–26	*t·* them that the divine Mind,
	15–22	to *t·* thorough C. S.
No.	7–23	speak, *t·*, and write the truth of
	10–11	postulate of all that I *t·*,
	11–20	demonstrate what these works *t·*,
	11–21	because they *t·* divine Science,
	33– 9	demonstrate what these volumes *t·*,
	36– 2	He did not *t·* that there are two
	37–21	Scriptures *t·* an infinite God,
'01.	33–23	enjoined his students to *t·* and
Hea.	5–27	*t·* him that "whatsoever a man — *Gal.* 6 : 7.
	14–21	you must *t·* them how to learn,
	14–24	to reach the ability to *t·* ;
My.	51–24	* to go into new fields to *t·*
	218–23	can either *t·* or heal by
	220–13	I practise and *t·* this obedience,
	234–27	to *t·* and to demonstrate C. S.
	235– 2	To *t·* the truth of life
	235– 8	Can I *t·* my child the correct
	235–12	and *t·* truth scientifically.
	245–24	all who claim to *t·* C. S.
	251–18	can *t·* pupils the practice of C. S.,
	300–23	*t·* the Christianity which heals,
	301–10	*t·* us the life of Love.
	303– 2	I believe in one Christ, *t·* one Christ,
	364–13	And he should *t·* his students to

Teacher

Mis.	121–32	*T·* of both law and gospel
'02.	18–23	prophecy of the great *T·* is fulfilled
My.	190–15	asked their great *T·*,
	267–28	Our great *T·* hath said :
	338–26	great *T·* of Christianity,

(see also **Eddy**)

teacher *(see also* **teacher's***)*

and guide
Pul. 30–19 * *t·* and guide to salvation ;
and members
Man. 90–13 None but the *t·* and members
and preacher
Mis. 252–26 inspires the *t·* and preacher ;
and student
Man. 87–21 for both *t·* and student."
Ret. 84–26 for both *t·* and student.
authorized
Man. 111–11 with an authorized *t·* ;
error in the
Mis. 265– 7 error in the *t·* also predisposes
every
No. 3–10 Every *t·* must pore over it
faithful
My. 254–14 the faithful *t·* of this class
former
Mis. 264–23 influence of their former *t·*.
Man. 86– 8 jurisdiction of his former *t·*.
given to the
Man. 91– 1 this paper shall be given to the *t·*,
great
'01. 26– 3 The great *t·*, preacher, and
healer and
Ret. 47–17 is a better healer and *t·*
his
Mis. 283–31 seldom calls on his *t·* or
     340–18 Is a musician made by his *t·*?
Ret. 75–22 a textbook written by his *t·*,
in Christian Science
Mis. 114–30 *t·* in C. S. who does not
leading
My. 312– 2 supply the place of his leading *t·*
new
Mis. 171–17 works by which the new *t·* would

teacher

of Christian Science
Mis.	91–21	*Should not the t· of C. S.*
	92– 6	*t·* of C. S. needs continually
	264–32	If a *t·* of C. S. unwittingly
Man.	55–13	or a *t·* of C. S.
	84–24	loyal *t·* of C. S. shall not
	85– 5	loyal *t·* of C. S. may
	86– 5	authorized to be a *t·* of C. S.,
	88– 8	vice-president, and *t·* of C. S.
Ret.	30–22	Discoverer and *t·* of C. S. ;
	70–26	right *t·* of C. S.

of divine metaphysics
Mis. 293– 8 *t·* of divine metaphysics should
of Mind-healing
Rud. 9– 3 *t·* of Mind-healing who is not a
one
Man. 73–25 the pupils of one *t·*.
or healer
Rud. 11–25 lecturer, *t·*, or healer who is
replied
Mis. 344– 4 "Very well," the *t·* replied ;
seaside
Ret. 91–28 this hillside priest, this seaside *t·*,
shall be elected
Man. 88–13 *t·* shall be elected every third year
should require
Mis. 92–22 *t·* should require each member to
signature of the
Man. 91– 5 signature of the *t·* and of the
such a
Mis. 349– 7 Such a course with such a *t·*
that
Mis. 92–31 That *t·* does most for his students
Ret. 84–19 That *t·* does most for his students
well qualified
Man. 90–18 lessons by a well qualified *t·*
your
Mis. 136–20 your *t·* and guide.
My. 300–30 God is above your *t·*,

Mis.	32–20	seekers after Truth whose *t·* is
	92–15	*t·* should strictly adhere to the
	115– 8	this state of mind in the *t·*
	315–15	*t·* shall hold himself . . . obligated to
Man.	55–11	it may be decided that a *t·* has
	83–12	*t·* shall not assume personal control
	86–10	whose *t·* has left them,
	87–18	"The less the *t·* personally controls
	91–13	presentation of the card to the *t·*.
	111–13	have not studied C. S. with a *t·*.
Ret.	84– 4	The *t·* himself should continue to
	84–24	The less the *t·* personally controls
	84–27	A *t·* should take charge only of
No.	18–20	but the *t·* is morally responsible.
My.	130–29	your public ministrations, as *t·*

(see also **Eddy**)

teacher's

Mis.	115– 6	even the *t·* own deficiency
	263–16	The need of their *t·* counsel,
	264–26	The tone of the *t·* mind
Man.	84–25	not teach another loyal *t·* pupil,

teachers *(see also* **teachers'***)*

and healers
My. 218–25 My published works are *t·* and healers.
and practitioners
Man. 74–11 *T·* and practitioners of C. S,
Ret. 82– 7 even if they are *t·* and practitioners
and preachers
Ret. 82–17 practitioners, *t·*, and preachers
and pupils
Man. 62–16 except the officers, *t·*, and pupils
are deceased
Man. 36–15 Scientists whose *t·* are deceased,
     111–17 Those whose *t·* are deceased,
assistant
Ret. 43–20 assistant *t·* in the College.
association of
My. 251–23 chapter sub-title
     253–10 chapter sub-title
become
Mis. 318–24 all those who become *t·*.
My. 251– 9 * in order to become *t·* of
Canadian
My. 253–14 chapter sub-title
children's
Man. 63– 9 children's *t·* must not deviate from
faithful
My. 244–23 your wise, faithful *t·*
false
Mis. 32– 8 the students of false *t·*,
     39– 9 false *t·* of what they term C. S. ;
     271–27 * false *t·* of mental healing,
fitted for
Mis. 315–10 spiritually fitted for *t·*,

teachers

her
Pul. 82–11   * far better than her *t·*.
loyal
Man. 84–17   the pupils of loyal *t·*
    92–25   loyal *t·* of C. S.
must conform
Mis. 114–10   *T·* must conform strictly to
Normal
Man. 89–11   Normal *T·*.
of Christian Science
Mis. 114– 7   *t·* of C. S. need to watch
Man. 84– 1   *t·* of C. S. shall teach
    87–14   *T·* of C. S. must have the
    92–25   loyal *t·* of C. S.
Ret. 85– 3   *T·* of C. S. will find
My. 251– 4   chapter sub-title
other
Mis. 91–29   my example, and that of other *t·*,
Ret. 83–22   the same as other *t·* ;
    85– 1   other *t·* who should be specially
our
'02. 2–11   making the children our *t·*.
previous
Un. 10– 6   to name any previous *t·*,
refuse
Man. 111–18   *t·* refuse, without sufficient cause,
religious
Pul. 43–28   * which religious *t·* so often receive.
Pan. 10–22   other religious *t·* are unable to
shall instruct
Man. 84– 2   *T·* shall instruct their pupils
such
No. 2–20   Institutes furnished with such *t·*
superintendent and
My. 230–16   To the Superintendent and *T·*
their
Man. 36–12   signature of their *t·*,
    88–20   can confer with their *t·*
without
Man. 86– 9   Without *T·*.

        ———

Mis. 143–20   physicians, *t·*, editors, and
    315–21   *T·* shall form associations
    315–24   *T·* shall not silently mentally
Man. 36–16   whose *t·*, for insufficient cause,
    55– 9   *T·*.
    83– 3   *T·*.
    83– 9   Christian Scientists who are *t·*
    84–20   *T·* shall not call their pupils
    85–11   *T·* must have Certificates.
    86–16   *t·* of the Normal class shall
    86–22   *t·* of the Primary class
No. 2–21   and many who are not *t·* have

teachers'

Man. 74–10   *T·* and Practitioners' Offices.
    84–19   not by their *t·* personal views.
My. 252–18   chapter sub-title

teaches

Mis. 19– 6   carrying out what He *t·*
    40–22   *t·* her students that they
    54– 6   demonstrated, and *t·* C. S.
    84–27   *t·* Life's lessons aright.
    211– 4   *t·* mortals to handle serpents
    219– 4   nor *t·* that nature and her laws
    358– 4   student who . . . *t·* by healing,
Man. 68–13   members whom she *t·* the course
Ret. 64–10   which *t·* that good is equally
    70–27   lives the truth he *t·*.
'01. 18–20   *t·* that a human hypothesis
Hea. 16– 4   *t·* us there is no other Life,
My. 41–19   * It *t·* us to rise from
    90–15   * *t·* that hate is atheism,
    114– 3   C. S. *t·* : Owe no man ;
    167– 7   Spirit *t·* us to resign what
    188–26   C. S. *t·* the majesty of man.
    212–30   saying . . . that Mrs. Eddy *t·*

teacheth

Mis. 392–12   A lesson grave, of life, that *t·* me
Po. 20–16   A lesson grave, of life, that *t·* me

teaching (noun)

and demonstrating
Ret. 79–20   requisite for *t·* and demonstrating
and demonstration
Ret. 25– 7   Jesus' *t·* and demonstration
and healing
Mis. 162–13   good will, love, *t·*, and healing.
Rud. 15–16   *T·* and healing should have
and life
Un. 9–17   simple *t·* and life of Jesus
and practice
Ret. 65– 4   the *t·* and practice of Jesus,
My. 190–27   declared that his *t·* and practice

teaching (noun)

and preaching
Mis. 359– 4   Christly method of *t·* and preaching
and proof
'01. 23–16   the Master's *t·* and proof.
basis for
Man. 86–16   Basis for *T·*.
better than
Man. 92– 3   Healing Better than *T·*.
books and
Ret. 85– 9   books and *t·* are but a ladder
Christ's
Ret. 65–21   Christ's *t·* and example,
'01. 28–16   followed exclusively Christ's *t·*,
class
Mis. 87–20   After class *t·*, he does best
Man. 87– 8   Class *T·*.
My. 240–22   * chapter sub-title
    240–25   * Does Mrs. Eddy approve of class *t·* :
    241– 2   * Class *t·* will not be abolished until
correct
My. 241–15   * absolute and correct *t·*.
    297–19   clear, correct *t·* of C. S.
exclusive
Mis. 273–32   call is for my exclusive *t·*.
false
Mis. 368–17   false *t·* and false practice
gave up
Ret. 43–10   After I gave up *t·*,
healing and
Ret. 78– 4   In healing and *t·* the student has
    83– 1   scientific healing and *t·*.
immortal
Ret. 91–22   his immortal *t·* was the bread of
incorrect
Mis. 263–26   hampered by incorrect *t·* ;
its
'01. 21–13   in its *t·* and authorship
less
Mis. 355– 6   Less *t·* and good healing
motive in
Man. 83– 4   Motive in *T·*.
motives for
Rud. 16– 2   If . . . are the motives for *t·*,
Mrs. Eddy's
My. 334–15   * Mrs. Eddy's *t·* on the unreality of
my
Mis. 274– 9   my *t·* would advance it :
    317–10   door to my *t·* was shut
Un. 10– 8   If there be any *monopoly* in my *t·*,
of Christian Science
Mis. 302–10   to know the *t·* of C. S.
My. 4– 6   practice or efficient *t·* of C. S.,
    212–17   the *t·* of C. S. Mind-healing.
    297–19   correct *t·* of C. S.
of Jesus
Pul. 35– 2   spiritual meaning of the *t·* of Jesus
or lecturing
Mis. 266–24   in *t·* or lecturing on C. S.,
platform and
Man. 34– 9   according to the platform and *t·*
scientific
Ret. 94–17   scientific *t·*, preaching, and
spurious
Mis. 43–16   spurious *t·* of those who are
stop
Mis. 274– 6   I must stop *t·* at present.
    358–21   not require . . . Scientists to stop *t·*,
St. Paul's
Ret. 93–23   If C. S. reiterates St. Paul's *t·*,
success in
My. 219– 7   their success in *t·* or in healing.
such
Un. 26–11   leads to such *t·* as we find in
that matter
Un. 45–13   falsity is the *t·* that matter can
this
Mis. 38– 5   as this *t·* certainly does,
    292– 4   he chronicles this *t·*,

        ———

Mis. 38– 3   When *t·* imparts the ability to
    165–27   *t·*, example, and suffering of our
    179–13   In the new religion the *t·* is,
Ret. 48–27   the *t·* was a purely spiritual and
    89– 5   In those days preaching and *t·* were
'00. 4– 7   *t·* of the righteous Galilean,
My. 230–15   chapter sub-title
    240–26   * when the *t·* is done by those who
    246–15   *t·* and letter of Christianity

teaching (verb)

Mis. 11– 9   did not cease *t·* the wayward ones
    19– 9   *t·* the divine Principle and rules
    38– 1   *Why do you charge for t· C. S.,*
    38–21   *T·* metaphysics at other colleges
    43– 6   *Do all who . . . claim to be t· C. S.,*

teaching (verb)

Mis.	64– 5	relinquished his earth-task of *t·* and
	132–20	editing a magazine, *t·* C. S.,
	232–20	*t·* and practising in the *name* of
	239– 7	Lecturing, writing, preaching, *t·*,
	302– 7	*t·* the name without the Spirit,
	303– 8	in *t·* and guiding their students.
	315–20	T· C. S. shall be no question of
	318–18	the gospel work of *t·* C. S.,
	358– 4	The student who heals by *t·*
	358–24	College for *t·* C. S. Mind-healing,
	380–16	I . . . commenced *t·*.
	382–30	system of *t·* and practising C. S.
	393–21	Isle of beauty, thou art *t·*
Man.	34–15	for *t·* . . . metaphysical healing.
	43– 7	as auxiliaries to *t·* C. S.
	62–18	T· the Children.
	83– 1	heading
	83– 4	T· C. S. shall not be a question of
	84–14	A student's price for *t·* C. S.
Ret.	43– 3	I began by *t·* one student C. S.
	43– 7	*t·* the pathology of spiritual power,
	47–22	the gospel work of *t·* C. S.,
	49–20	*t·* the Science of Mind-healing ;
Pul.	58– 4	* about 1880, she began *t·*,
'01.	15– 9	through Christ, Truth, *t·* him
Po.	52– 5	Isle of beauty, thou art *t·*
	77–13	T· us thus of Thee,
My.	51– 3	* in *t·* us the Science of Life."
	64–16	* she has been *t·* her followers
	109–11	*t·* them the same heavenly
	147–10	C. S. kindergarten for *t·* the
	234–23	*t·* C. S. in her country.
	343–19	*t·* and organizing,

Teaching Christian Science

Man.	83– 1	heading
Pul.	38–14	"C. S. Practice," "T· C· S·,"

teachings

accepted
Mis. 81–10 *in the commonly accepted t·*
and demonstration
Mis. 244–26 *t·* and demonstration of Jesus
and demonstrations
Mis. 187–18 later *t·* and demonstrations of
My. 103–23 except the *t·* and demonstrations of
and example
Pul. 75– 5 my writings, *t·*, and example
My. 127–10 more of Christ's *t·* and example
120–31 *t·* and example of Christ Jesus.
and life
Mis. 25–15 *t·* and life of our Lord.
books and
Pul. 74–23 "My books and *t·* maintain but
Christ's
Mis. 141–25 ambassador of Christ's *t·*,
193– 8 practicality of all Christ's *t·*
311– 8 so, should we follow Christ's *t·* ;
Pul. 9–30 enlightened faith is Christ's *t·*
'01. 25– 3 on the rock of Christ's *t·*,
My. 127–10 possesses more of Christ's *t·*
228–10 and yet depart from Christ's *t·*.
232–18 Are Christ's *t·* the true authority
counsel and
My. 129–29 Accept my counsel and *t·* only as
divine
Mis. 302–29 divine *t·* contained in "S. and H.
exalted
Ret. 91– 6 No purer and more exalted *t·*
false
Peo. 11–14 are clasped by the false *t·*,
her
My. 40–32 * as well as by her *t·*,
273– 4 * the value of her *t·*.
His
Pul. 72–23 * faith in Him and His *t·*.
his
Un. 11– 4 His *t·* beard the lions
43–21 with the power of his *t·*,
Pul. 52–24 * all vital belief in his *t·*.
My. 111– 8 They disputed his *t·*
its
Mis. 50–14 no . . . secret outside of its *t·*,
My. 50–27 * and few knew of its *t·*,
112– 7 those who abide in its *t·*
114–30 You can trace its *t·* in
Jesus'
Ret. 94–29 Jesus' *t·* bore much fruit,
'01. 24–25 necessary to follow Jesus' *t·*,
life and
Mis. 244–18 life and *t·* of Jesus?
No. 21– 1 contrary to the life and *t·* of
literal
Pul. 66–14 * the literal *t·* of the Bible
metaphysical
Pul. 6–27 * in Mrs. Eddy's metaphysical *t·*

teachings

Mrs. Eddy's
Mis. 48–29 * by Mrs. Eddy's *t·*,"
49– 9 "Mrs. Eddy's *t·* had not produced
Man. 42–15 in accord with all of Mrs. Eddy's *t·*,
my
Mis. 249–11 and especially through my *t·*,
265–23 My *t·* are uniform.
No. 15– 6 comprehension of my *t·* would
My. 237–10 accept only my *t·* that
obedience to the
My. 43–25 * Obedience to the *t·* of this book
of Christ
Pul. 38–25 * the literal *t·* of Christ.
of Christian Science
Man. 49– 4 understand the *t·* of C. S.
Ret. 43–15 embraced the *t·* of C. S.,
My. 130– 4 disloyal to the *t·* of C. S.
272–32 * indorsement to the *t·* of C. S.,
352–13 * so reflect . . . the *t·* of C. S.
of Jesus
Mis. 53–23 The *t·* of Jesus were simple ;
195–26 the practice and *t·* of Jesus
244–18 from the life and *t·* of Jesus?
310– 4 Even the *t·* of Jesus would
No. 21–21 reproduces the *t·* of Jesus,
of John
Mis. 81–11 *mingled with the t· of John*
of the Bible
'01. 8–22 if we follow the *t·* of the Bible.
My. 251–29 Adhere to the *t·* of the Bible,
of the textbook
Man. 35–21 loyal to the *t·* of the textbook,
of this book
Ret. 83– 5 to the *t·* of this book,
My. 113– 4 practises the *t·* of this book
pastor's
My. 52–18 * our pastor's *t·*, namely,
practical
Mis. v– 4 DEDICATE THESE PRACTICAL *t·*
practice and
Mis. 195–26 practice and *t·* of Jesus relative to
prayer and
Pul. 85–18 * prayer and *t·* of Jesus Christ.
sacred
My. 46–25 * obedience to the sacred *t·*
these
My. 114– 8 the maximum of these *t·*?
your
My. 44–29 * continued loyalty to your *t·*,
215–14 * "Your *t·* are worth much

Mis. 188– 1 whose *t·* opposed the doctrines of
Ret. 83– 8 benefited by the *t·* of other students,
84–10 *t·* in the chapter on Recapitulation.

tear

Mis.	110– 3	had not the value of a single *t·*.
	119–28	should *t·* up your landmarks,
	339–28	pour forth the unavailing *t·*.
	343–23	*t·* them away from their native soil,
	354–30	No *t·* dims his eye,
	389–14	glad for every scalding *t·*,
	398–14	T· or triumph harms,
Ret.	18–12	earth yields you her *t·*,
	46–20	T· or triumph harms,
	81– 2	The unavailing *t·* is shed
Pul.	17–19	T· or triumph harms,
'00.	11– 1	cost me a *t·* !
'02.	19–15	repentance seen in a *t·*
Po.	4–13	glad for every scalding *t·*,
	14–18	T· or triumph harms,
	18– 7	glad a *t·* dim his eye,
	27–15	Though thou must leave the *t·*,
	29– 9	No natal hour and mother's *t·*,
	64– 2	earth yields you her *t·*
	65–23	*man* is the cause of its *t·*.
My.	132–32	the unavailing, tired *t·*,
	294–31	shed "the unavailing *t·*."
	350–14	heed'st Thou not the scalding *t·*

tear-dews
Po. 8– 4 Where *t·* of night seek the

teardrops
Mis. 390–19 As smiles through *t·* seen,
Po. 55–20 As smiles through *t·* seen,

tear-drops
Mis. 389–24 aftersmile earth's *t·* gain,
Po. 5– 4 aftersmile earth's *t·* gain,

tear-filled
Mis. 231–30 *t·* eyes looking longingly
'00. 15– 9 *t·* sea of repentance
Po. 31– 8 *t·* tones of distant joy,

tearful
Mis. 249– 4 I say with t· thanks,
    329–13 touching tenderly its t· tones.
Ret. 31–27 the t· lips of a babe.

tearfully
Ret. 14–20 but t· I had to respond

tearless
My. 124–12 bloodless sieges and t· triumphs,

tears
Mis. 11–28 though with t· have I striven
    116–23 struggles, t·, and triumph.
    120– 6 or repeat their work in t·.
    203–22 T· flood the eyes,
    210–24 t· the black mask from the
    385– 1 * "Faith, hope, and t·, triune,
    394– 8 It comes through our t·,
    399– 2 Love wipes your t· all away,
Ret. 16– 5 t· of joy flooding her eyes
    20–17 Thy smile through t·,
    86–13 wipe . . . the t· from his eyes,
Un. 18–12 wipe the t· from the eyes of
    57–27 divine Science wipes away all t·.
Pul. 7–12 O ye t· ! Not in vain did ye flow.
    33–10 * This caused her t· of remorse
Peo. 9– 4 but t· of repentance,
Po. 16– 1 gentle cypress, in evergreen t·,
    22– 9 bliss that wipes the t· of time
    37– 1 * "Faith, hope, and t·, triune,
    45–10 It comes through our t·,
    47– 6 Ever to gladness and never to t·,
    47–15 Over the t· it has shed ;
    54– 3 O come to clouds and t·
    67– 7 t· be bedewing them fresh-smiling
    67–18 mourn with her evergreen t·,
    75– 9 Love wipes your t· all away,
    77–12 joy and t·, conflict and rest,
    78–10 T· of the bleeding slave
My. 36–16 * exchanged the t· of sorrow
    44– 4 * t· are being wiped away,
    134–18 Love comes to our t·
    161– 4 washing the . . . feet with t· of joy.
    191–17 Love, which wipes away all t·.
    228–20 with t· of repentance
    291–27 T· blend with her triumphs.
    314–27 told me that with t· of gratitude
    332– 4 * silent gush of grateful t·

teaspoonful
Ret. 33–16 one t· of the water mixed with
Hea. 13–13 administering one t· of this water

technical
My. 149–23 Losing the comprehensive in the t·,

Te Deum
My. 275–28 unite in one T· D· of praise.

tedious
My. 122–10 Now I am done with . . . t· prosaics.

teeth
Mis. 72–15 t· are set on edge — Ezek. 18 : 2.
Pul. 80–14 * fairly broken our mental t·
My. 161–11 weeping and gnashing of t·,— Luke 13 : 28.

Telegram
Pul. 89–13 * T·, Philadelphia, Pa.
    89–14 * T·, Troy, N. Y.
    89–20 * T·, New Orleans, La.
    90– 8 * T·, Portland, Ore.

telegram
My. 36– 3 * The t· from the church
    44–14 * heading
    194–19 Your t·, in which you present
    207– 6 * chapter sub-title
    253–22 thanks for your letter and t·.
    281–17 * [T·]
    361–15 chapter sub-title
    361–16 [T·]

telegrams
My. 234– 1 fifty t· per holiday
    234– 4 cannot . . . while reading t· ;
    259–13 t· to me are refreshing

telegraph
Pul. 74– 3 * [By T· to the Herald]
'02. 11–14 a submarine cable, a wireless t·,
My. 73–24 * t· and telephone service.

telegraphs
Un. 45–19 it t· and telephones

telegraphy
'02. 9–26 Morse's discovery of t· ?
My. 110–14 t·, navigation of the air;

teleology
Mis. 74–10 systems of etiology and t·.
    218–30 * "The recognition of t·
    219– 1 t· is the science of the final cause

telephone
My. 73–24 * telegraph and t· service.
    345–10 * the t·, the steam engine

telephones
Un. 45–19 it telegraphs and t·

telescope
Ret. 65–27 to determine, without a t·,
Pul. vii–11 to turn backward the t·

tell
Mis. 121–26 "If I t· you, ye will — Luke 22 : 67.
    125–28 to t· the towers thereof
    129–10 to t· thy brother his fault
    168– 3 t· what things ye shall see
    181–14 who can t· what is the form
    221–30 Who would t· another of a crime
    226–20 * when he shall t· the truth."
    242–28 t· you that he was my student
    243–27 the medical faculty will t· you
    253–23 Can a mother t· her child
    311–24 and my necessity was to t· it ;
    316–17 My juniors can t· others
Ret. 8– 7 to t· me what she wanted.
    14–19 minister then wished me to t· him
    38–19 come to t· me he wanted more,
Pul. 15– 7 when you t· them their virtues
    15– 8 when you t· them their vices.
    15– 9 to t· a man his faults,
    34–22 "How, I could not t·,
    84–21 * the future will t· the story
Rud. 17–10 could t· you of timidity,
'00. 7–11 will t· you they never loved the Bible
    9–25 My loyal students will t· you
'01. 12– 4 If St. John should t· that man
Hea. 3–26 We cannot t· what is the person of
Po. 1– 5 Beyond the ken of mortal e'er to t·
    17– 2 O t· of their radiant home
    66–10 And t· how that heart is silent
    71–16 can t· The holy meaning
My. 15–18 * I love to t· the story,
    15–22 * I love to t· the story,
    15–26 * I love to t· the story ;
    60–27 * to t· you of the interesting
    63–29 * to t· by their presence that
    111–12 will t· you that he has found the
    112–16 its readers . . . will t· you this.
    112–25 student of this book will t· you
    123–12 "T· it not in Gath" !— II Sam. 1 : 20.
    124–17 What more . . . pen may not t·.
    133–22 I have a secret to t· you
    134– 2 t· my long-kept secret
    313– 5 * T· her I love her ;
    317–16 he will t· you that Mr. Wiggin
    323–17 * My heart has been too full to t· you
    332– 5 * grateful tears alone can t· the

telling
Pul. 8– 3 Like the winds t· tales
    15–11 Who is t· mankind of the foe
My. 95–20 * t· of miracles performed
    324–12 * I remember t· you of this,

tells
Mis. 62–26 especially when she t· them that
Un. 14–17 but the New Testament t· us of
Pul. 27–20 * window t· its pictorial story
My. 81–30 * t· his or her experience.
    84–20 * story which the gathering here t·.
    107–16 he t· you, and you believe him,
    186– 8 neither dome nor turret t· the tale
    345– 5 But every thought t·,

temerity
Pul. 3–29 to reach out for . . . savors of t·.

temper
Mis. 126–10 when struggling . . . his t·,
    224–20 with a t· so genial
Po. 43–18 T· every trembling footfall,
My. 29–27 * cooling breeze to t· the heat,
    75–21 * not the slightest evidence of t·,
    215–32 should t· human affairs,
    310–26 * "hysteria mingled with bad t·."

temperament
Pul. 32– 7 * the t· to dominate, to lead,

temperance
Mis. 201–27 t·, virtue, and truth,
    288–26 cause of t· receives a strong impulse
    288–27 t· and truth are allies,
    288–31 to promote the ends of t· ;
    289– 4 only t· is total abstinence.
    297– 5 In the direction of t·
Ret. 45–22 long-suffering and t·,
    79–23 Meekness and t· are the jewels
Po. vi– 5 * poem
    page 39 poem
    39– 3 T· and truth in song sublime

temperance
Po. 39–17 Since *t·* makes your laws.
39–20 blazoned, brilliant *t·* hall
40– 3 We dedicate this *t·* hall

temperate
Ret. 79–22 Be *t·* in thought, word, and deed.
My. 114– 3 Owe no man ; be *t·* ;

temperately
Mis. 289– 3 evil cannot be used *t·* :

temperature
Hea. 5– 5 by changes of *t·*,

tempered
Pul. 82– 6 * steel *t·* with holy resolve,

tempers
Mis. 275–14 * "*t·* the wind to the shorn lamb,"

tempest (*see also* tempest's)
Mis. ix–17 darkness of storm and cloud and *t·*,
144–17 a covert from the *t·* ; — *Isa.* 32 : 2.
152–23 when storm and *t·* beat against
362–26 shelter from the storm and *t·*
Un. 46–25 earthquake, thunderbolt, and *t·*.
'02. 20– 3 voice of him who stilled the *t·*
Hea. 2– 6 stills the *t·* of error ;
My. 106–20 expressed . . . in *t·* and in flood,
182–29 a covert from the *t·*.

tempest's
Po. 28–11 Above the *t·* glee ;

tempests
Un. 52–20 its unkind forces, its *t·*,

temple
ample
My. 13–19 an ample *t·* dedicate to God,
beautiful
Pul. 23– 5 * BEAUTIFUL *T·* AND ITS FURNISHINGS
My. 88–19 * this beautiful *t·*, striking as
187–23 to consecrate your beautiful *t·*
202–14 builders of this beautiful *t·*,
build a
My. 13–24 to build a *t·* the spiritual spire
cathedral or
My. 71–14 * this new cathedral or *t·*
Christian Science
Pul. 79– 4 * a C. S. *t·* costing over
81– 1 * The chimes on the C. S. *t·*
My. 70–11 * The chimes for the new C. S. *t·*
72–19 * fund of the new C. S. *t·*,
91–16 * The dedication of a C. S. *t·*
100 1 * dedication of a C. S. *t·*
church
Mis. 141– 8 and against this church *t·*
earlier
'00. 12–15 The earlier *t·* was burned
erection of the
Pul. 56–11 * erection of the *t·*, in Boston,
giant
My. 76–24 * chapter sub-title
God is the
Mis. 323– 5 for God is the *t·* thereof ;
godly
Pul. 3– 1 how can our godly *t·* possibly be
God's
Mis. 140–17 to know who owned God's *t·*,
goodly
My. 162–31 towering top of its goodly *t·*
great
My. 45–13 * The great *t·* is finished !
45–28 * The great *t·* is finished !
86–15 * building fund of the great *t·*
her
Pul. 59– 2 * has not yet visited her *t·*,
holy
My. 24–14 * unto an holy *t·* — *Eph.* 2 : 21.
idol's
My. 192– 1 Ye sit not in the idol's *t·*.
its
My. 88–21 * finds its *t·* in the heart of
lofty
My. 193–25 lofty *t·*, dedicated to God
magnificent
Pul. 25–17 * entrance to this magnificent *t·*.
My. 6–14 magnificent *t·* wherein to enter
43–31 * dedication of our magnificent *t·*,
59–13 * gallery of that magnificent *t·*,
77–20 * magnificent *t·* of the C. S. church,
massive
Pul. 52–11 * erection of a massive *t·* in Boston
'neath the
My. 151–19 * 'neath the *t·* of uplifted sky
new
My. 67–25 * new *t·*, begun nearly two years ago,
73–17 * dedication of the new *t·*.
83–25 * construction of the new *t·*

temple
new
My. 84–13 * new *t·* is something to be proud of.
88– 5 * opening of their great new *t·*.
92–11 * a new *t·* to Isis and Osiris
94–18 * magnificent new *t·* of the cult.
97–27 * to dedicate the new *t·*, just built
new-built
Pul. 41–11 * to view the new-built *t·*
no
Mis. 323– 4 having no *t·* therein,
of Diana
'00. 12–14 *t·* of Diana, the tutelary divinity
of Spirit
My. 64–26 * in the universal *t·* of Spirit,
of thought
Mis. 369–13 at the portals of the *t·* of thought,
one
Ret. 89– 7 Men assembled in the one *t·*
our
Mis. 145–11 in this corner-stone of our *t·* :
Pul. 84–24 * our *t·* is completed as God intended
My. 13–32 a foundation for our *t·*,
63–24 * Grandly does our *t·* symbolize this
sacred
Pul. 11– 4 Word spoken in this sacred *t·*
this
Mis. 107– 2 beauty in and of this *t·*
144–11 His people in this *t·*,
144–32 the spire of this *t·*.
Pul. 3– 4 Referring to this *t·*,
3– 5 "Destroy this *t·*, — *John* 2 : 19.
27– 8 * remarkable feature of this *t·*.
51–23 * erection of this *t·* will doubtless
85– 2 * to lay the foundation of this *t·*,
My. 23–24 * that this *t·*, . . . is being built
71–20 * have been set aside in this *t·*,
77– 3 * This *t·* is one of the largest
true
Pul. 2–29 true *t·* is no human fabrication,
vast
My. 79– 9 * dedication of the vast *t·*
92–21 * dedication of this vast *t·*.
veil of the
Mis. 364–31 C. S. rends this veil of the *t·*
white
My. 202– 2 white wings overshadow this white *t·*
wonderful
My. 60–13 * corner-stone of this wonderful *t·*
your
My. 158–27 may your *t·* and all who worship
103– 1 dedicate your *t·* in faith unfeigned,

Mis. 149–29 first *t·* for C. S. worship
166–19 to go to the *t·* and be purified,
Ret. 51– 6 *t·* for C. S. worship.
Pul. 40– 9 * chapter sub-title
75–25 * The *t·* is believed to be the most
'02. 18– 1 Be faithful at the *t·* gate of
Po. 39– 6 A *t·*, whose high dome
My. 77–27 * *t·* . . . absolutely free of debt,
78– 1 * seating capacity of the *t·* is
78 23 * acoustic properties of the *t·*,
79–13 * to gain admission to the *t·*
91–26 * *t·* which has just been dedicated
100– 4 * *t·* recently dedicated at Boston
158–25 chief corner-stone of the *t·*
194– 6 a *t·* but foreshadows the idea of
285–21 neither found me in the *t·* — *Acts* 24 : 12.

temples
Ret. 13–18 she bathed my burning *t·*,
My. 195–26 *t·* erected first in the hearts of
195–30 fill these spiritual *t·* with grace,

Temples of Honor
Po. 39–18 "*T·* of *H·*," all,

temporal
Mis. 21–20 matter is the unreal and *t·*.
87– 1 clear ether of the blue *t·* sky.
93–13 Evil is *t·* : it is the illusion of
103– 5 one is *t·*, while the other is
103–18 and knows not the *t·*.
103–19 Neither does the *t·* know the eternal.
Ret. 25–17 its antipodes, or the *t·*,
59– 5 Life is not *t·*, but eternal,
68–12 One is *t·*, but the other is eternal.
73– 3 material, corporeal, and *t·*.
Un. 40–27 regard all things as *t·*.
62– 7 which are seen are *t·* ; — *II Cor.* 4 : 18.
Pul. 2–10 Material light and shade are *t·*,
13–23 Scriptures declare that evil is *t·*,
Rud. 9–12 false and *t·* sense of Truth,
No. 37– 8 evil is *t·* and God is eternal,
'01. 9– 3 referring to . . . his *t·* manhood.
24–11 * greatest of all *t·* blessings,

temporal

Peo.	4– 8	belief that . . . the eternal entered the *t·*.
My.	134– 1	spiritual bespeaks our *t·* history.
	143–18	cannot be a *t·* fraud.
	193–15	The spiritual dominates the *t·*.

temporarily

Mis.	85–10	though his power is *t·* limited.
	350– 3	I *t·* organized a secret society
No.	1–12	turn *t·* from the tumult,

temporary

Mis.	43–25	*t·* success of such an one
	84– 9	the world's *t·* esteem ;
	99– 8	*t·* loss of his self-respect.
	247–23	That which is *t·* seems,
	267–17	*t·* shame and loss
	356– 7	need no *t·* indulgence
Ret.	89–29	is human, fallible, and *t·* ;
Un.	4– 7	To gain a *t·* consciousness of
	41– 9	involves a *t·* loss of God,
Hea.	4–18	after a *t·* lapse,
My.	87– 5	* *t·* increase of the population
	159–20	towards the *t·* and finite.
	188–13	will not be *t·*,
	259–29	merely *t·* means and ends.
	312– 2	during her *t·* absence.

temptation

Mis.	10–18	crossing swords with *t·*,
	12–20	danger of yielding to *t·*
	53– 7	*overcoming* *t·* and sin,
	85–21	*T·*, . . . suggests pleasure
	85–24	so long as this *t·* lasts,
	114–28	He will deliver us from *t·*
	115–17	that you enter not into *t·*
	198–17	the *t·* will disappear.
	278–20	seem stronger to resist *t·*
	301–16	to be long led into *t·* ;
	302–13	the *t·* to be misled.
	312– 2	to guard against that *t·*.
	321–21	treading each *t·* down,
	323–11	beset with peril, privation, *t·*,
	343– 2	that we enter not into the *t·*
	344–15	sinner struggling with *t·*,
Ret.	45–24	the *t·* of popularity
Un.	50– 7	that we enter not into the *t·*
	57–10	Without it there is neither *t·* nor
'01.	14–22	that he enter not into *t·*
My.	6– 9	the tempter and *t·*,
	358– 6	enter not into *t·*." — *Matt.* 26 : 41.
	359–27	arise from this *t·*

temptations

Mis.	12–16	*t·* to sin are increased
	104– 4	was not subject to the *t·* of
Ret.	71– 7	Great *t·* beset an ignorant

tempted

Mis.	198–13	When *t·* to sin, we should
Un.	58–16	"in all points *t·* — *Heb.* 4 : 15.
Pul.	31– 7	* *t·* to "begin at the beginning"
	50–18	* *t·* to examine its principles,
My.	122–11	my church *t·* me tenderly

tempter

Ret.	85–22	The *t·* is vigilant,
My.	6– 8	*t·* and temptation, the smile and

tempting

Mis.	9–20	having tested its *t·* wine,
No.	3–28	are *t·* and misleading.

tempts

My.	211–16	*t·* into the committal of acts

ten

Mis.	95– 6	* allowed *t·* minutes in which to reply
	221–26	five times *t·* are fifty
	221–26	while *t·* times five are not
	341–21	*t·* virgins" — *Matt.* 25 : 1.
	353–16	bucket of water every *t·* minutes
Man.	52– 8	within *t·* days thereafter,
	68– 3	to go in *t·* days to her,
Ret.	10– 4	At *t·* years of age I was as
Pul.	53–11	* When the *t·* lepers were cleansed
'00.	10–27	*t·* five-dollar gold pieces
My.	10– 6	* externalized itself, *t·* years ago,
	30–30	* admission at the *t·* o'clock service,
	38–30	* Tuesday, June 12, at *t·* o'clock
	66– 7	* *t·* estates having been conveyed
	76– 3	* Up to within *t·* days
	80–24	* it took *t·* meetings to accommodate
	82–18	* in something like *t·* minutes.
	127–18	the *t·* of *materia medica*.
	304–10	and for *t·* subsequent years
	310–23	* Mary, a child *t·* years old,
		(*see also* **numbers, values**)

tenants

My.	231–24	to receive more *t·*.

Ten Commandments

Mis.	303–18	help them to obey the *T· C·*
Man.	62–25	should be the *T· C·*
Rud.	12– 3	keeps unbroken the *T· C·*,
My.	129–30	the letter of the *T· C·*,
	229–21	taking in the *T· C·*

tend

Mis.	47–13	*t·* to elucidate your day-dream,
	124– 2	*t·* to disturb the divine order,
	181– 9	*t·* to obscure the order of Science,
	209–19	*t·* to rebuke appetite
	353–18	Some people try to *t·* folks,
Ret.	21–23	lessons of Love which *t·* to this
My.	159–18	Material theories *t·* to check spiritual
	256–22	whence they came and whither they *t·*.
	259–24	*t·* to give the activity of man
	263– 1	*t·* to obliterate the spiritual idea
	274–11	in youth *t·* to success,
	340–24	should *t·* to enhance their confidence
	345–20	They all *t·* to newer, finer,

tended

Mis.	341–32	must be *t·* to keep aglow the flame
'02.	9–22	not whence it came nor whither it *t·*,

tendencies

Mis.	10–25	material *t·* of human affections
	245–19	in all the good *t·*, charities,
My.	151–30	discerned its idolatrous *t·*,
	249–18	should countenance such evil *t·*.

tendency

Mis.	3–29	*t·* of mental healing is to uplift
	4– 4	marked *t·* of mortal mind
	49– 2	had a *t·* to monomania,
	214–23	their motives, aims, and *t·*.
	215– 2	The *t·* of mortal mind is to
Un.	31– 7	*t·* of Christianity is to spiritualize
Pul.	14– 4	present apathy as to the *t·* of
No.	46–21	unfolding of this upward *t·*
'02.	10–14	This upward *t·* of humanity will finally
Hea.	1–21	more spiritual basis and *t·*
My.	38–14	* visitors showed a *t·* to tarry
	119–12	C. S. destroys such *t·*.
	159–19	the *t·* towards God,
	320–19	* but his *t·* was friendly.

tender

Mis.	xi–24	With *t·* tread, thought sometimes
	127–28	*t·* sentiment felt, or a kind word
	142–27	touched *t·* fibres of thought,
	230–28	to render it pathetic, *t·*, gorgeous.
	250–23	*t·*, unselfish deed done in secret ;
	254– 5	brooded tireless over their *t·* years
	311– 6	I would extend a *t·* invitation to
	319–18	Scientists accept my *t·* greetings
	391–17	Share God's most *t·* mercies,
Man.	64–21	*t·* term such as sister or brother.
Chr.	53– 5	In *t·* mercy, Spirit sped
Ret.	5– 8	object of their *t·* solicitude.
	19–19	*t·* devotion to his young bride
Pul.	82– 6	* Her hand is *t·*
'00.	7–26	*t·*, loving Christ is found near,
'01.	29– 7	*t·* care of those who want to help
Po.	38–16	Share God's most *t·* mercies,
	44– 1	Then, O *t·* Love and wisdom,
My.	13–22	lovingkindness and *t·* — *Psal.* 103 : 4.
	36–27	* in *t·* affection for the cause of
	51– 7	* her duty to *t·* her resignation,
	51–28	* *t·* . . . the heartfelt thanks
	64– 7	* were thrilled with *t·* gratitude,
	150– 1	where its *t·* lesson is not awaiting
	158–21	makes the heart *t·*, faithful, true.
	186– 5	like *t·* nestlings in the crannies
	194–13	*t·* memorial engraven on your grand
	196– 7	accept my *t·* counsel in these words
	206– 5	*t·* grace of spiritual understanding,
	235– 6	*t·* mother, guided by love,
	247–21	*t· persuasion* that takes away their
	289–26	may be read on that *t·* occasion.
	290–19	Thy *t·* husband, our nation's chief
	292–17	in which one earnest, *t·* desire
	312–25	provisions in my behalf were most *t·*.
	326–18	in long procession with *t·* dirge
	330–30	*t·* devotion to his young bride
	351–14	It was truly Masonic, *t·*, grand
	352– 9	* with its years of *t·* ministry,
	352–20	I thank you . . . for your *t·* letter

tendered

My.	173–25	thanks are due and are hereby *t·*

tenderest

My.	37– 8	* from the depths of *t·* gratitude,
	258– 8	the *t·* tendril of the heart

tenderly

Mis.	249–25	more *t·* to save and bless.
	329–12	touching *t·* its tearful tones.
	354–16	a few truths *t·* told,

tenderly
Mis. 397– 7   and t·, Divinely talk.
Pul.   v– 7   BOOK IS t· DEDICATED
    18–16   and t·, Divinely talk.
Rud.   v– 3   t· AND RESPECTFULLY DEDICATED
No.   v–10   saith t·,"Come and drink ;"
Po.   12–16   and t·, Divinely talk.
    27–12   heal her wounds too t·
My. 122–11   tempted me t· to be proud !
    204–17   I congratulate you t· on the
    216–15   T· thanking you for your

tenderness
Mis. 251– 7   my heart will with t·
    331–14   in tones tremulous with t·,
'02.   8–15   inspired with t·, Truth, and Love.
Po.   35– 7   Or pining t·
My. 215–11   Afterwards, with touching t·,
    247–30   patient, unfaltering t·.
    257–11   with ineffable t·.
    291–15   t· not talked but felt
    311– 6   my t· and sympathy were
    343–28   I wrote to each church in t·,

tendeth
Mis. 254– 8   mother-bird t· her young

tending
Mis. 353–20   t· the action that He adjusts.
    353–23   folly of t· it is no mere jest.
    354–12   the children are t· the regulator ;
    393–19   As the rock, whose upward t·
Ret.   90– 5   salary for t· the home flock
'02.   10–18   his predicate t· thereto is correct,
Po.   52– 3   As the rock, whose upward t·
My. 129– 9   t· to counteract the trend of

tendril
My. 258– 8   tenderest t· of the heart

tendrils
My. 125– 7   to bend upward the t·

tends
Mis. 52–16   t· to lift mortals higher.
    85–29   t· to destroy error :
    88– 1   t· to blight the fruits of my
    115–27   whatever t· to impede progress.
    301–28   error t· to harden the heart,
    303– 5   t· his own flock.
    310–12   t· to make sin less or more
    337–32   t· to hide from an individual
    341–26   if the lamp she t· is not replenished
    369–27   vine which our Father t·.
Man. 43–19   t· to prevent C. S. from
Ret. 81– 9   t· to demoralize mortals,
My. 119–10   Think not that C. S. t· towards
    218–18   t· to confuse the mind of the reader,
    266–16   t· in one ultimate
    267–24   Material thought t· to obscure
    316–19   t· to turn back the foaming torrents

Tenet
Man. 105– 2   No new T· or By-Law shall be
    105– 3   T· or By-Law amended or annulled,

tenet
Ret. 14– 9   as John Calvin . . . called his own t·

Tenets
Man.   page 15 heading
    17–15   to draft the T· of The Mother Church
    28– 6   ultimate in annulling its T·
    33– 7   shall maintain the T·, Rules, and
    50–13   Departure from T·.
    50–15   If a member . . . depart from the T·
    54– 8   The Mother Church of Christ, . . . T·.
    54–11   T· as to unjust and unmerciful
    61–14   T· of The Mother Church are to be
    71–20   T· Copyrighted.
    71–21   not write the T· of The Mother Church
    71–24   as T· of The Mother Church,
My.   vi–14   * wrote its Church Manual and T·,
    32–22   * Reading of T· of The Mother Church.

tenets
Mis. 285–12   impersonal in its tenor and t·.
Pul. 38–23   * which are the t· of theosophy.
    57–13   * t· of the Christian Scientists,
    58–21   * pictures symbolic of the t· of
My. 49–14   * also the t· and church covenant
    59–10   * t· be accepted wholly or in part
    84–23   * methods and t· of the sect.
    94–13   * in the interpretation of its t·,
    95– 4   * t· first presented by Mrs. Eddy
    178– 2   Your . . . pastor and ethical t·,
    182–30   beloved church adhere to its t·,

tenfold
Mis. 11– 2   its punishment is t·.

Tennessee and **Tenn.**
Pul. 25–25   * base and cap are of pink T· marble.
    (see also **Chattanooga**)

Tennyson's
Mis. 106– 5   poor parody on T· grand verse,

tenor
Mis. 285–12   impersonal in its t· and tenets.
Ret. 65–21   t· of Christ's teaching and example,

tension
Mis. 339–14   moral t· is tested,

tenth
My. 319–20   * On the t· day of January, 1887,

tents
Pul. 84– 6   * shall dwell in the t· of hate ;

tenure
'02. 17–24   what we give . . . through His t·,
My. 201–18   to a t· of unprecarious joy.

term (noun)
    class
Mis. 11–10   at close of the class t·,
    315–17   not only through class t·,
Man. 83–16   not only during the class t·
    "devil"
Mis. 190–13   meaning of the t· "devil" — Luke 11 : 14.
    191– 2   Hebrew embodies the t· "devil"— Luke 11 : 14.
No. 22–18   the t· devil is generic,
    divine Principle
No. 20– 8   When the t· divine Principle is used
    employed
Ret. 37– 3   t· employed by me to express
    for Deity
Mis. 75–15   Because Soul is a t· for Deity,
    192– 2   Hebrew t· for Deity was "good,"
    for God
Mis. 13–28   Anglo-Saxon t· for God,
    26–29   Saxon t· for God is also good.
Pul. 6– 7   Good, the Anglo-Saxon t· for God,
My. 185–14   Love is the generic t· for God.
    generic
Un. 51–14   generic t· for all humanity.
    51–16   generic t· for all women ;
'01. 10–11   generic t· for both male and female.
My. 185–14   Love is the generic t· for God.
    239–19   generic t· for men and women.
    347– 5   man the generic t· for mankind."
    God
Hea. 3–14   t· God was derived from the
    Hebrew
Mis. 192– 2   Hebrew t· for Deity was "good,"
Peo. 2– 8   Hebrew t· that gives another letter
    implies
Pan. 12–25   includes all that the t· implies,
    Life is a
Ret. 59–12   Life is a t· used to indicate Deity ;
    meaning of the
Mis. 53–19   meaning of the t· and of C. S.
    190–13   meaning of the t· "devil" — Luke 11 : 14.
    191– 6   changed the meaning of the t·,
    of Mother
Man. 64–17   endearing t· of Mother.
    of office
Man. 25–15   t· of office for the Clerk
    80–22   t· of office for the editors
    94–16   His t· of office, if approved,
    of Readership
Man. 90–14   during his t· of Readership,
    95–21   during his t· of Readership.
    of service
Man. 60– 5   Incomplete T· of Service.
    one
Ret. 43–17   taught the Primary, . . . class one t·.
    opening
Mis. 256–19   previous to the opening t·.
    pantheism
Pan. 2–23   stand, in the t· pantheism, for the
    pope
My. 343–21   t· pope is used figuratively.
    serpent
Mis. 191– 3   in another t·, serpent,
    soul
Mis. 76–20   exchange the t· soul for sense
    "spirits"
Pan. 9– 4   t· "spirits" means more than
    tender
Man. 64–21   tender t· such as sister or
    that
Rud. 4–14   if by that t· you mean material
    the only
No. 20–11   found to be the only t· that fully
    this
Mis. 75–16   this t· should seldom be employed
    75–19   if this t· is warped to signify
    180–28   This t·, as applied to man,
Man. 65– 7   when this t· is used in connection
Rud. 2–19   This t· enlarges our sense of Deity,

term (noun)
  three years'
    My. 250– 3   three years' *t·* for church Readers,
  winter's
    My. 327–14   * winter's *t·* of our Legislature,

    Mis. 191–20   *t·*, being here employed in its
    Man. 90– 8   *t·* of the . . . Metaphysical College
    Ret. 89– 7   in the modern sense of the *t·*.
    My. 250–17   as the *t·* for its Readers,
term (verb)
    Mis. 39– 9   false teachers of what they *t·* C. S. ;
    Pul. 31– 4   * C. S., as they *t·* her work
    66– 1   * they *t·* the divine art of healing,
termed
    Mis. 36– 1   *t·* material or mortal man,
    45–26   intelligence or mind *t·* evil.
    172–17   That which is *t·* "natural science,"
    205–20   *t·* in Christian metaphysics the
    233–15   force of mortal mind, *t·* hypnotism,
    Ret. 32–10   *t·* mortal and material existence
    64–20   in belief an illusion *t·* sin,
    Pul. 24– 7   * is *t·* by its Founder,
    70–25   * Mind-healing, which she *t·* C. S.
    No. 10–15   What is *t·* matter,
    Hea. 18–26   what is *t·* death has been produced
    My. 41–23   * hourly application what Paul *t·*
    226– 6   What are *t·* in common speech
terming
    Mis. 233–17   *t·* it metaphysics !
terms
  and nature
    Mis. 192– 9   *t·* and nature of Deity and devil
  belief and understanding
    Pul. 47–18   * upon the *t·* belief and understanding,
  better
    My. 334–16   * in no better *t·* than to quote
  class
    Mis. 256–17   intervals between my class *t·*,
  finite
    Ret. 59–11   even as mortals apply finite *t·*
  its
    Mis. 190–16   spiritual signification of its *t·*
  loving
    My. 224–27   speak in loving *t·* of their efforts,
  lowest
    No. 32–26   reduce this evil to its lowest *t·*,
  material
    No. 11– 9   is hampered by material *t·*,
  obsolete
    Mis. 318– 2   Mine and thine are obsolete *t·*
  opprobrious
    My. 104–10   vented their . . . in opprobrious *t·*.
  other
    My. 307–11   that word, as well as other *t·*
  physical
    Mis. 50–13   the metaphysical in physical *t·*.
    171–12   expressed in literal or physical *t·*,
  proper
    Mis. 365–27   hampered by lack of proper *t·*
  scientific
    Ret. 59– 4   Scientific *t·* have no contradictory
  such
    Un. 16– 2   such *t·* as *divine sin* and
  synonymous
    Mis. 23–22   Spirit, Mind, are *t·* synonymous
    '00. 5–11   Father and Mother are synonymous *t·* ;
  these
    Mis. 190–18   these *t·* will be found to include
  those very
    My. 324–13   * those very *t·* revealed to you.
  three
    Peo. 4–19   three *t·* for one divine Principle
  two
    Ret. 43– 9   taught two *t·* in my College.

    Mis. 27– 3   the *t·* God and good, as Spirit, are
    No. 27–21   what St. Paul *t·* "the old man— *Col.* 3 : 9.
terrace
    Pul. 48– 1   * well placed upon a *t·*
    49– 9   * tree-tops on the lower *t·*,
terra cotta
    Pul. 25–12   * roof is of *t· c·* tiles,
Terre Haute (Ind.) ***Star***
    My. 90–21   * [*T· H· (I·.) S·*]
terrestrial
    Mis. 100–24   They unite *t·* and celestial joys,
    376–19   According to *t·* calculations,
terrible
    Mis. 69–17   barely alive. and in *t·* agony.
    246–20   conflict more *t·* than the battle of
    341–25   subject to *t·* torture if the lamp

terrible
    Mis. 350– 4   * not "*t·* and too shocking to relate."
    356– 5   need no *t·* detonation to free them.
    Ret. 19–16   in this *t·* bereavement.
    Pul. 83–13   * *t·* as an army with banners"— *Song* 6 : 10.
    No. 28– 7   purifying processes and *t·* revolutions
    35–15   He atoned for the *t·* unreality of
    My. 330–28   in this *t·* bereavement.
    335–25   * attended cases of this *t·* disease
terrifies
    Ret. 73–20   wrongs it, or *t·* people over it,
Territory
    Mis. 305– 1   * representing each State and *T·*,
territory
    Pul. 41–10   * *t·* that lies between,
Territory of Dakota
    Ret. 21–12   Marshal of the *T· of D·*.
terrors
    Ret. 72–10   consumed with *t·*."— *Psal.* 73 : 19.
terse
    Mis. 294–27   *t·*, graphic, and poetic style
tersely
    Mis. 212– 7   he *t·* reminded his students
test
    Mis. 93–25   does not *t·* sin and the fact of
    114–27   will *t·* all mankind on all questions ;
    158–17   to *t·* your humility and obedience in
    241– 7   *T·*, if you will, metaphysical healing
    249– 1   to *t·* that malpractice
    351– 1   called on students to *t·* their ability
    Man. 39–11   thoroughly to *t·* his sincerity,
    Ret. 62– 3   *T·* C. S. by its effect
    Un. 58–15   to *t·* the full compass of human woe,
    No. 2–13   to *t·* the feasibility of
    '02. 17– 4   obedience is the *t·* of love ;
    Hea. 19– 1   to *t·* the power of mind over body ;
    19– 2   and they did *t·* it,
    My. vii–10   * Deeds, . . . are the sound *t·* of love ;
    92– 3   * until it has stood the *t·* of time.
    138–10   present proceedings *t·* my trust
    215–29   Doubtless to *t·* the effect of both
Testament
    (see **Greek, Old,** *and* **New Testament**)
Testaments
  Old and New
    Pan. 7–18   study of the Old and New *T·*
  Old and the New
    My. 179–13   The Old and the New *T·* contain
tested
    Mis. 22–26   He who has not *t·* it,
    46– 6   needs only to be *t·* scientifically
    76– 8   can never be *t·* or proven true upon
    201–23   *t·* and developed latent power.
    339–14   moral tension is *t·*,
    My. 70–15   * were being *t·* the other day.
testified
    Ret. 15–22   persons who feelingly *t·*
    My. vii– 8   * *t·* to by Jesus and the prophets.
testifies
    Un. 33–10   matter *t·* of itself,
    My. 331–11   * *t·* to the love and respect
testify
    Ret. 15–30   were too timid to *t·* in public.
    25–24   material senses *t·* falsely,
    Un. 1–17   able to *t·*, by their lives,
    2–14   is ready to *t·* of God
    23–16   when they *t·* concerning Spirit,
    33– 6   *t·* from their own evidence,
    33–11   it cannot talk or *t·* ;
    33–14   Brain, thus assuming to *t·*,
    37–16   Evil and disease do not *t·* of Life
    39–22   senses, which *t·* that man dies.
    39–24   The material senses *t·* falsely.
    Rud. 4–26   senses *t·* to the existence of matter.
    No. 9– 1   as my Christian students can *t·* ;
    My. 81– 7   * bursting with a desire to *t·*
    84– 5   * Many a clergyman can *t·* from
testifying
    Mis. 54–16   the sick, unasked, are *t·* thereto.
    361–11   spiritual concepts *t·* to one creator,
    No. 17–14   witness, *t·* of Himself.
testimonial
    Man. 75– 3   Church Edifice a *T·*.
    75– 8   church edifice as a *T·*
    Pul. 24–15   * A *t·* to our beloved teacher,
    27–10   * the entire church is a *t·*,
    40–21   * *t·* to the Discoverer
    56–27   * intended to be a *t·*
    63–26   * *t·* to our beloved teacher,
    70–14   * as a *t·* to her labors,

testimonial
Pul. 75–23 * a *t·* to the Discoverer
77–13 * built as a *t·* to Truth,
77–16 * formally accept this *t·*
77–24 * chapter sub-title
78– 1 * a *t·* which is probably
78–11 * built as a *t·* to Truth,
78–14 * formally accept this *t·*
78–23 * *t·* is encased in a white
85–21 * chapter sub-title
85–26 * a beautiful and unique *t·*
86–13 * Accompanying the stone *t·*
86–22 * *t·* of love and gratitude
My. 58–15 * fitting *t·* in stone,

testimonials
Mis. 54– 9 lives are worthy *t·*,
Man. 47–11 *T·*.
47–21 This By-Law applies to *t·*

testimony
against sensualism
Mis. 325–27 a *t·* against sensualism
bear
Man. 48– 3 to bear *t·* to Truth
93–13 to bear *t·* to the facts
'02. 3– 2 bear *t·* to this fact.
beareth
Man. 42–18 the Scripture beareth *t·*.
bears
Mis. 21– 8 C. S. now bears *t·*.
bore
Mis. 225–11 bore *t·* to the power of Christ,
brief
Ret. 22– 3 Gospel narratives bear brief *t·*
death-bed
Mis. 24– 6 I give it to you as death-bed *t·*
deny the
Rud. 5– 2 deny the *t·* of the material
entire
My. 301–19 entire *t·* of the material
false
Mis. 66– 2 false *t·* or mistaken evidence
Ret. 30–12 false *t·* of the physical senses.
Un. 36– 8 reverses false *t·* and gains a
fitting
My. 352–14 * daily living may be a fitting *t·*
give
My. 80–26 * throngs who wanted to give *t·*
His
Rud. 17–16 are the paths of His *t·*
his
Hea. 2–15 Christian hero, . . . added his *t·* :
loving
'01. 31–18 church would bear loving *t·*.
mingle the
Mis. 73– 7 mingle the *t·* of immortal Science
my
My. 59–29 * Now my *t·* is not needed.
of material sense
Mis. 218– 6 The *t·* of material sense
of spiritual sense
Mis. 188–18 the *t·* of spiritual sense ;
of the five senses
Un. 25– 5 the *t·* of the five senses.
of the physical senses
No. 6–26 the *t·* of the physical senses.
of the senses
Mis. 103– 1 annuls the *t·* of the senses,
105– 9 from the *t·* of the senses,
164–30 from the *t·* of the senses.
No. 6– 7 refutes . . . the *t·* of the senses,
overturns the
Mis. 13–22 overturns the *t·* of the five erring
pretended
Un. 33– 1 give the only pretended *t·*
put in
Mis. 381– 9 he should not put in *t·*.
receive
My. 81–12 * were ready to receive *t·*,
reverses the
Un. 30– 6 Science reverses the *t·*
taking
Mis. 381– 7 taking *t·* on the part of the
their
Un. 33–22 the foundations of their *t·*,
Pul. 12–10 by the word of their *t·* ; — *Rev.* 12 : 11.
Hea. 16–19 how can we rely on their *t·*
this
Man. 47–18 This *t·*, however, shall not
was taken
Mis. 381– 5 *T·* was taken on the part of
which
Rud. 5– 3 Which *t·* is correct?

Mis. 73–30 *t·* of the so-called material senses.
Man. 47–13 *T·* in regard to the healing

testimony
Ret. 67–15 *t·* of material personal sense
My. 79–29 * at the *t·* meetings that marked
315–26 *t·* they have thereby given

tests
Mis. 119–23 *t·* and discriminates between
156–27 the aids and *t·* of growth
My. 90– 8 * and is given very real *t·*.
251–25 armors, and *t·* in His service,

Tex. (State)
(*see* **Dallas**)

text
Hebrew
Mis. 180–26 In the Hebrew *t·*, the word "son"
her
Pul. 70–19 * Taking her *t·* from the Bible,
My. 324–29 * who could keep to her *t·*.
meaning of the
Mis. 197–12 comprehend the meaning of the *t·*,
misinterprets the
Ret. 83–15 misinterprets the *t·* to his pupils,
my
'01. 22–19 my *t·*, that one and one are two
original
Mis. 192– 5 the original *t·* defines devil as a
Pan. 7–19 the original *t·* indicates,
'01. 16–16 original *t·* defines *devil*
Hea. 3–14 In the original *t·* the term *God*
our
Mis. 161–15 we have chosen for our *t·*,
164–17 In our *t·* Isaiah foretold,
191–23 our *t·* refers to the devil as
195–17 divine logic, as seen in our *t·*,
Scriptural
Mis. 194–19 the foregoing Scriptural *t·*
St. Paul's
Ret. 94– 6 contradicts . . . St. Paul's *t·*,
their
My. 225–24 expected to stick to their *t·*,
this
Mis. 52– 1 This *t·* may refer to such as
197– 7 the full import of this *t·* is not
wisdom of the
Mis. 201– 1 the entire wisdom of the *t·* ;
written
Man. 43–12 strengthen the faith by a written *t·*

Mis. 21–23 has been conformed to the *t·* of
27– 8 C. S. sticks to its *t·*,
84–19 the *t·*, "For to me to live — *Phil.* 1 : 21.
161– 5 *T·* : "For unto us a child is — *Isa.* 9 : 6.
168–22 *T·* : Ye do err, — *Matt.* 22 : 29.
171–23 *T·* : *The kingdom of heaven* — *Matt.* 13 : 33.
178–11 * *t·*, "If ye then be risen — *Col.* 3 : 1.
181–21 His sonship, referred to in the *t·*,
182–26 The *t·* is a metaphysical statement
194–31 first condition set forth in the *t·*,
197– 4 *t·* is one more frequently used
200–12 that we have chosen for a *t·* ;
Pul. 1– 1 *T·* : *They shall be — Psal.* 36 : 8.
Hea. 1– 1 *T·* : *And these signs shall — Mark* 10 : 17.
Peo. 1– 1 *T·* : *One Lord, one faith,* — *Eph.* 4 : 5.

textbook
author of its
Pul. 64– 2 * author of its *t·*, 'S. and H.
70– 7 * author of its *t·*, 'S. and H.
86–24 * author of its *t·*, "S. and H.
My. 23–24 * Founder of . . . and author of its *t·*.
author of the
Pul. 52–14 * Mary Baker Eddy, . . . author of the *t·*
Christian Science
Mis. 92–20 C. S. *t·* is the Key.
130– 8 and in the C. S. *t·*,
314–20 and add to this . . . "the C. S. *t·*."
314–29 Bible and the C. S. *t·*
315–12 teach from the C. S. *t·*.
317–16 the Scriptures and the C. S. *t·*,
383– 2 Bible, and . . . the C. S. *t·*,
Man. 34–10 contained in the C. S. *t·*,
37–20 loyal . . . to the C. S. *t·*,
60– 9 Scriptures or the C. S. *t·*.
69–14 author of the C. S. *t·*
72–10 SCRIPTURES and the C. S. *t·*.
81–22 where the C. S. *t·* is published
Pul. 7–25 Bible and the C. S. *t·*,
43–21 * given in the C. S. *t·*,
'00. 6–30 In that year the C. S. *t·*,
'01. 24–23 S. and H., the C. S. *t·*.
My. v–21 * C. S. *t·*, "S. and H.
17–27 * given in the C. S. *t·*,
32–19 * given in the C. S. *t·*.
115– 9 my estimate of the C. S. *t·*.
147–15 Bible and the C. S. *t·*

textbook

Christian Science
My. 178–21 C. S. *t·* lay on a table
 305–15 author of the C. S. *t·*,
her
My. 48– 9 * With the reading of her *t·*,
his
Mis. 91–25 did not take his *t·* with him
My. 111–14 he has found . . . through his *t·*.
my
Ret. 25– 3 The Bible was my *t·*.
my only
Pul. 34–27 "the Bible was my only *t·*.
of Christian Science
Mis. 50–10 complete *t·* of C. S. ;
 92–12 take the *t·* of C. S.
 364– 1 consonance with the *t·* of C. S.
 372– 5 *t·* of C. S. is transforming
Ret. 38–27 S. and H. is the *t·* of C. S.
 68–16 S. and H., the *t·* of C. S.,
My. 111–15 The *t·* of C. S. maintains
 232–19 *t·* of C. S., "S. and H.
our
Mis. 91–22 *Should not the teacher . . . have our t·*,
 356–27 must be had to understand our *t·* ;
Man. 53– 9 the author of our *t·*
 105– 5 author of our *t·*, S. AND H.
My. 43–23 * later she gave us our *t·*,
 46–25 * the Bible and our *t·*,
 163–21 to revise our *t·*, "S. and H.
Science and Health
Mis. 91–22 *t·*, "*S. and H. with Key to the*
 114–12 Bible and their *t·*, "S. and H.
 144–10 your *t·*, "S. and H. with Key to the
Man. 34–10 *t·*, S. AND H. WITH KEY TO THE
 35–21 teachings of the *t·*, S. AND H.
 38– 3 students of the *t·*, S. AND H.
 55–24 in its *t·*, S. AND H.
 105– 5 author of our *t·*, S. AND H.
Pul. 7–25 C. S. *t·*, "S. and H.
 64– 2 * author of its *t·*, 'S. and H.
 70– 7 * author of its *t·*, "S. and H.
 86–24 * author of its *t·*, "S. and H.
'00. 6–30 C. S. *t·*, "S. and H.
My. v–21 * C. S. *t·*, "S. and H.
 43–23 * gave us our *t·*, "S. and H.
 48– 9 * reading of her *t·*, "S. and H.
 163–21 to revise our *t·*, "S. and H.
 305–15 author of the C. S. *t·*, " S. and H.
their
Mis. 114–12 Bible and their *t·*, "S. and H.
 115– 3 With S. and H. for their *t·*,
Man. 63–11 C. S. contained in their *t·*.
 64–16 given to the author of their *t·*,
Ret. 83–21 should take their *t·* into the
Pul. 60– 5 * no explanation of . . . their *t·*.
My. 225–27 In their *t·* it is clearly stated
this
Mis. 92– 7 continually to study this *t·*.
 92–24 continue the study of this *t·*.
Ret. 75–24 the substance of this *t·* ?
 84– 4 should continue to study this *t·*,
My. 114–11 the treasures of this *t·* are
your
Mis. 144–10 your *t·*, "S. and H. with Key
Pul. 87–17 Through my book, your *t·*,
My. 178– 1 Your Bible and your *t·*,
 214– 3 would write your *t·* on the walls
 320–18 * the statements in your *t·* ;

Mis. 309–27 My Christmas poem . . . not a *t·*.
Ret. 75–22 a *t·* written by his teacher,
'01. 34–24 study the Bible and the *t·*
My. 112–23 better . . . than the *t·* itself, is not

textbooks

Man. 34–14 his only *t·* for self-instruction
 42–12 the C. S. *t·*,
Pul. 45–21 * declarations of our *t·*,
My. 103– 5 demanded of man in our *t·*,
 203– 4 all is in your *t·*.

texts

Mis. 191–26 the original *t·* define him as
 300–27 spiritual meaning of BIBLE *t·* ;
Man. 32– 3 correlative *t·* in S. AND H.
 32– 5 Second Readers shall read the BIBLE *t·*.
 58–16 correlative Biblical *t·* in the
Chr. 55– 1 These Scriptural *t·* are the basis
Pul. 25–27 * illuminated *t·* from the Bible
My. 317–20 quoting corroborative *t·* of Scripture.

textual

Ret. 78– 5 *t·* explanation of this practice

thank

Mis. 13–11 what *t·* have ye? — *Luke* 6 : 32.
 167–23 "I *t·* Thee, O Father, — *Luke* 10 : 21.
 218–29 "Pretty well, I *t·* you !"

thank

Mis. 262–13 I just want to say, I *t·* you,
 275–17 we *t·* Thee that Thy light
 308–18 I *t·* you, each and all,
 313–12 I *t·* the contributors to *The*
Ret. 49–19 *Resolved,* That we *t·* the State
 49–21 that we *t·* the public for its
No. 44–28 "I *t·* Thee, O Father, — *Luke* 10 : 21.
Peo. 8–24 We *t·* our Father that to-day
My. 6–16 deeply do I *t·* you for this proof
 38– 4 * we *t·* you and renew the story of
 62–10 * ever *t·* you enough
 118– 9 I beg to *t·* you for your
 127– 6 We *t·* the Giver of all good
 142–26 I *t·* you for your kind
 157–12 * We *t·* you for this renewed
 163–27 and *t·* their ancestors for helping
 165–12 I beg to *t·* the dear brethren
 173– 6 *t·* the citizens of Concord
 174–10 I *t·* the distinguished editors
 194–23 profoundly *t·* you for it,
 197–20 I *t·* divine Love for the hope
 201–12 I *t·* you out of a full heart.
 202–21 I *t·* you for the words of cheer
 253–11 *Beloved Brethren:* — I *t·* you.
 254–14 I *t·* the faithful teacher
 265–31 we *t·* our Father-Mother God.
 282–21 Deeply do I *t·* you for the
 295–16 I *t·* you for it.
 298– 8 I *t·* Miss Wilbur and the Concord
 315–25 allow me to *t·* the enterprising
 327–27 * We *t·* our heavenly Father
 352–20 I *t·* you not only for
 357–29 I *t·* you for acknowledging
 358–18 I *t·* you for the money
 (*see also* **God**)

thanked

Mis. 112–21 The jailer *t·* me, and said,
Un. 11–22 he never *t·* Jesus for restoring
My. 308–23 My father *t·* the Governor,

thankful

Mis. 193–17 I am *t·* even for his allusion to
 245–27 it is a thing to be *t·* for
 273– 2 I am *t·* that the neophyte
My. 62–23 * *t·* appreciation of your wise
 332– 5 * emotions of the *t·* heart,

thankfulness

My. 9– 8 * to turn in loving *t·* to

thanking

Mis. 203– 1 In *t·* you for your gift
My. 5–25 lovingly *t·* your generosity
 15–15 *t·* you for your gracious reception
 174–17 I have the pleasure of *t·* you
 216–15 Tenderly *t·* you for your

thanks (noun)

bankrupt in
My. 9–20 I am bankrupt in *t·* to you,
breath of
My. 256–10 heartfelt breath of *t·* for
card of
My. 173– 1 chapter sub-title
Christian Science
My. 264– 8 * chapter sub-title
cordial
My. 184–14 and to return my cordial *t·*
deep
My. 167– 1 Accept my deep *t·* therefor,
 208– 3 Accept my deep *t·* for your
give
Mis. 311–29 drink all of it, and give *t·* ?
Pul. 12–16 we give *t·* and magnify the Lord
 14–23 Those ready for . . . will give *t·*.
 53–12 * one returned to give *t·*
My. 131–11 for the cup . . . we give *t·*.
giving
Mis. 211–28 He drank this cup giving *t·*,
'02. 11–19 which he drank, giving *t·*,
My. 131– 7 we unite in giving *t·*.
 206–26 "Giving *t·* unto the Father, — *Col.* 1 : 12.
heartfelt
My. 51–29 * the heartfelt *t·* and gratitude
knelt in
My. 302–29 knelt in *t·* upon the steps
Leader's
My. 9–18 chapter sub-title
letter of
My. 295– 9 LETTER OF *T·* FOR THE GIFT OF A
 331–10 * The following letter of *t·*,
love and
My. 257–27 two words enwrapped, — *love* and *t·*.
many
My. 62–26 * We acknowledge with many *t·*
 198– 6 received with many *t·* to you
 332– 9 * Many *t·* are due Mr. Cooke,

thanks (noun)
  merited the
    My. 49–27   * merited the *t·* of the society
  Mrs. Eddy's
    My. 352–26   chapter sub-title
  my
    Mis. 137– 2   Accept my *t·* for your card
    142–11   my *t·* for the beautiful boat
    242–10   Will the gentleman accept my *t·*
    Pul. 8– 5   repeat my *t·* to the press.
    My. 42–15   * opportunity to express my *t·*
    142–10   Accept my *t·* for your approval
    164– 9   yearned to express my *t·*
    172–18   You will please accept my *t·*
    186–25   Accept my *t·* for your cordial
    191–30   Accept my *t·*.
    231–28   You will accept my *t·* for your
    274–20   my *t·* for their magnificent gifts,
    285– 2   my *t·* for your kind invitation,
    352–27   my *t·* for your successful plans
  our
    My. 331–21   * to return our *t·* and express
  poor in
    My. 9–25   never before felt poor in *t·*,
  profound
    Pul. 87–14   accept my profound *t·*.
    My. 229–22   accept profound *t·* for their
    253–22   accept my profound *t·*
  sends
    My. 274–17   * chapter sub-title
  special
    My. 173–25   Special *t·* are due
  speechless
    Mis. 275–25   moved me to speechless *t·*.
  tearful
    Mis. 249– 4   I say with tearful *t·*,
  the word
    Mis. 100– 4   uttering the word *t·*,
  to God
    '00. 2– 4   and, *t·* to God,
  your
    My. 252–26   It expressed your *t·*,

    Mis. 280–25   fellow-students' *t·* to their teacher.
    My. 183–24   *T·* for invitation to your

thanks (verb)
    My. 118– 1   My soul *t·* the loyal,

Thanksgiving
    Mis. 230–26   chapter sub-title
    Man. 67–21   letters to the Pastor Emeritus on *T·*,
    Po. page 77   poem
    My. 25– 1   * the present *T·* season ;

thanksgiving
    Mis. 110–21   We may well unite in *t·*
    369– 3   look up with shouts and *t·*,
    My. 27–22   * will read with much joy and *t·*
    77–21   * a first hymn of *t·*

Thanksgiving Day
    Mis. 231–26   his first sitting-at-table on *T· D·*
    231–29   heartfelt joy on *T· D·*
    Man. 123– 1   heading
    My. 167–14   chapter sub-title
    167–15   first *T· D·* . . . in our new church
    252–24   "*T· D·*," instituted in England on
    264–11   * the birthplace of *T· D·*,
    264– 9   * last *T· D·* of the nineteenth
    264–15   last *T· D·* of this century
    322–14   * *T· D·* twenty years ago,

The
    Man. 71– 6   "*T·*" must not be used before
    112– 5   capitalized (*T·*), or small (the),

the
    Man. 112– 4   The article "*t·*" . . . must not be used
    112– 5   capitalized (The), or small (*t·*),

thea
    Mis. 348–19   not even coffea (coffee), *t·* (tea),

The Arena
    My. 316–11   January number of *T· A·*

theatres
    Pul. 62–21   * *t·*, concert halls, and

The Board of Education
    (*see* **Board of Education**)

The Christian Science Board of Directors
    (*see* **Board of Directors**)

The Christian Science Board of Lectureship
    (*see* **Board of Lectureship**)

The Christian Science Publishing Society
    (*see* **Publishing Society**)

The Church of Christ, Scientist
    Mis. 139–21   to be called *T· C· of C·, S·*.
    145–31   *T· C· of C·, S·*, in Boston,
    154– 3   branches of *T· C· of C·, S·*.
    193–14   Referring to *T· C· of C·, S·*,
    300–23   *T· C· of C·, S·*, in Boston,
    314– 1   pastor of *T· C· of C·, S·*,
    My. vii– 3   * *T. C· of C·, S·*, can never
    48– 7   * of *T· C· of C·, S·*,
    51–28   * members of *T· C· of C·, S·*,
    54– 6   * "*T· C· of C·, S·*, had their
    243–10   Readers of *T· C· of C·, S·*,
    249–23   First Reader in *T· C· of C·, S·*,
    342–19   continuity of *T· C· of C·, S·*,"
    (*see also* **Church of Christ, Scientist**)

Thee and thee
    Mis. 83–25   Son also may glorify *T·*." — *John* 17 : 1.
    151–16   in heaven but *t·*? — *Psal.* 73 : 25.
    151–17   desire beside *t·*." — *Psal.* 73 : 25.
    159–25   grown to behold *T·* !
    167–23   "I thank *T·*, O Father, — *Luke* 10 : 21.
    275–17   we thank *T·* that Thy light
    397–14   From . . . grief afar, And nearer *T·*,
    397–18   To Thine, for *T·* ;
    400–18   Guide my little feet Up to *T·*.
    400–21   lovingly *T·* I seek,
    400–25   Be it slow or fast, Up to *T·*.
    Pul. 18–23   From . . . grief afar, And nearer *T·*,
    19– 2   To Thine, for *T·* ;
    No. 44–28   "I thank *T·*, O Father, — *Luke* 10 : 21.
    '02. 1–13   shall praise *T·* :— *Psal.* 76 : 10.
    Po. 13– 2   From . . . grief afar, And nearer *T·*,
    13– 6   To Thine, for *T·* ;
    24–11   The Life that lives in *T·* !
    28–13   The dove's to soar to *T·* !
    39– 5   An offering bring to *T·* !
    39–21   temperance hall To *T·* we dedicate.
    69– 6   Guide my little feet Up to *T·*.
    69– 9   lovingly *T·* I seek,
    69–13   Be it slow or fast, Up to *T·*.
    77– 1   to *T·* we raise A nation's holiest
    77–13   of *T·*, who knowest best !
    77–14   to *T·* we'll meekly bow,
    My. 4–30   Glory be to *T·*, Thou God
    31– 5   * "I need *T·* every hour ;"
    31– 7   * "Still, still with *T·* ;"
    109–18   [spiritual sense] seeth *T·*." — *Job* 42 : 5.
    111– 3   shall praise *T·*." — *Psal.* 76 : 10.
    151–11   shall praise *T·* :— *Psal.* 76 : 10.
    185–27   * we bless *T·*, Our God,
    253–12   world hath not known *T·*.— *John* 17 : 25.
    253–13   but I have known *T·*, — *John* 17 : 25.
    290–15   whose mind is stayed on *T·* :— *Isa.* 26 : 3.
    290–16   because he trusteth in *T·*." — *Isa.* 26 : 3.
    290–16   I cried unto *T·*." — *Psal.* 130 : 1.

The Evening Press
    My. 271–11   * *T· E· P·*, Grand Rapids, Mich.,
    271–20   * editor of *T· E· P·*
    271–28   *Editor of T· E· P·*

The First Church of Christ, Scientist
    Mis. 131–15   of the edifice of *T· F· C· of C·, S·*,
    139– 8   chapter sub-title
    141– 1   *T· F· C· of C·, S·* our prayer
    143 16   "*T· F· C· of C·, S·*," in Boston.
    146– 4   chapter sub-title
    147– 1   chapter sub-title
    148– 8   Manual of *T· F· C· of C·, S·*,
    310–12   gone out of *T· F· C· of C·, S·*,
    Man. 3– 4   Manual of *T· F· C· of C·, S·*,
    15– 1   *uniting with T· F· C· of C·, S·*,
    18–16   named it, *T· F· C· of C·, S·*.
    19– 1   *T· F· C· of C·, S·*, IN BOSTON,
    34– 6   *T· F· C· of C·, S·*, in Boston,
    37– 8   membership with *T· F· C· of C·, S·*,
    45–15   member of *T· F· C· of C·, S·*,
    58– 7   *T· F· C· of C·, S·*, in Boston,
    65– 4   member of *T· F· C· of C·, S·*,
    70–21   "*T· F· C· of C·, S·*" is the legal
    72–26   branch church of *T· F· C· of C·, S·*,
    75– 5   in behalf of *T· F· C· of C·, S·*,
    77–21   Mother Church, *T· F· C· of C·, S·*,
    92–19   not a member of *T· F· C· of C·, S·*,
    102–11   land for *T· F· C· of C·, S·*,
    103– 1   *T· F· C· of C·, S·*, in Boston,
    103– 4   *T· F· C· of C·, S·*, in Boston,
    104– 4   Manual of *T· F· C· of C·, S·*,
    Pul. v– 5   ROOM IN *T· F· C· of C·, S·*,
    1—   chapter heading
    7–26   pastor of *T· F· C· of C·, S·*,
    8–27   Room in *T· F· C· of C·, S·*,
    20– 1   whereon stands *T· F· C· of C·, S·*,
    23– 3   * COMPLETION OF *T· F· C· of C·, S·*.
    24– 6   * *T· F· C· of C·, S·*,
    24–14   * "*T· F· C· of C·, S·*, erected
    40–20   * home for *T· F· C· of C·, S·*,

theology

would teach
Mis. 229-15 *t·* would teach man as David taught :

Mis. 58-21 Without its *t·* there is no
62-14 *that their t· is essential to heal*
203-13 T· religiously bathes in water,
Un. 13- 1 evidence of the senses in *t·*,
Pul. 55-21 * *t·* . . . of C. S. is contained in
Pan. 2-25 belief concerning Deity in *t·*.
'01. 6- 6 Person is defined differently by *t·*,

theology's
'01. 6- 2 *t·* three divine persons,

theorems
Mis. 173- 2 man's *t·*, misstate mental Science
312-22 human *t·* or hypotheses,
My. 248-16 rising above *t·* into the

theoretic
Mis. 369-22 we are tired of *t·* husks,

theoretically
Mis. 48- 1 no . . . mesmerism, practically or *t·*,
264-24 Their knowledge . . . may be right *t·*,
'01. 10-19 T· and practically man's salvation
My. 136- 4 cannot be fully understood, *t·* ;

theories

and practice
No. 2-28 with conflicting *t·* and practice.
crude
My. 111- 5 crude *t·* or modes of metaphysics.
difference in the
Pul. 47-17 * difference in the *t·* between
false
Mis. 366-31 false *t·* whose names are legion,
Peo. 11-15 false *t·*, false fears,
finite
Ret. 56- 2 antagonized by finite *t·*,
human
Mis. 365- 5 Human *t·* weighed in the
Un. 44-15 Human *t·* call, or miscall,
No. 18-13 Human *t·*, when weighed in the
man-made
Mis. 64-15 Man-made *t·* are narrow,
material
Un. 28-15 material *t·* are built on the
My. 159-18 Material *t·* tend to check
of agnosticism
Mis. 55-31 *t·* of agnosticism and pantheism,
other
Mis. 25-13 rejects all other *t·* of causation,
No. 32-15 but other *t·* make sin true.
speculative
Ret. 70-12 speculative *t·* as to the recurrence
systems and
Mis. 232-15 part with material systems and *t·*,

theorist
Mis. 265-15 egotistical *t·* or shallow moralist

theorizing
'02. 18-24 effective healers and less *t·* ;

theory

abjure a
Mis. 197-29 Let man abjure a *t·* that is in
and practice
Ret. 79- 2 *honest* metaphysical *t·* and practice.
No. 5-27 in both *t·* and practice.
'01. 26- 1 consistency of Jesus' *t·* and practice
Peo. 2- 3 *t·* and practice of religion
5- 1 *t·* and practice of medicine
bacteria
My. 344-16 * reject utterly the bacteria *t·*
embraced in the
Un. 6-19 is embraced in the *t·* of God's
fallacy of the
Mis. 74-22 he proved the fallacy of the *t·*
its
'01. 6-21 its *t·* even seldom named.
man-made
Mis. 38-22 elaborating a man-made *t·*,
may be sound
No. 13-25 A *t·* may be sound in spots,
mere
No. 13-17 being held as a mere *t·*.
metaphysical
Ret. 79- 2 as against *honest* metaphysical *t·*
No. 22- 6 Berkeley ended his metaphysical *t·*
opposite
Ret. 64- 9 any opposite *t·* is heterodox
practice more than
Mis. 195-29 practice more than *t·*,
281-32 need, . . . *practice* more than *t·*.
same
Pul. 73-19 * same *t·* as Mrs. Copeland.
speculative
Mis. 29-14 between it and any speculative *t·*.

theory

such a
Un. 41-28 such a *t·* implies perpetual
Peo. 2-19 Such a *t·* has overturned
their
Ret. 54-21 far in advance of their *t·*.

Mis. 76-14 The *t·* that death must occur,
102- 5 a *t·* to me inconceivable,
198-24 belief, fear, *t·*, or bad deed,
No. 6- 5 that God's formations are
Peo. 2-16 that make a Christian only in *t·*,

theosophy
Mis. 296-15 with *t·* and spiritualism ;
Man. 41- 7 gulf between C. S. and *t·*,
47-26 *t·*, hypnotism, or spiritualism,
Ret. 23-21 pantheism, and *t·* were void.
Pul. 38-24 * which are the tenets of *t·*.
Rud. 13- 3 pantheism and *t·* are not Science.
No. 13-16 chapter sub-title
13-21 C. S., spiritualism, and *t·*.
14- 8 T· is a corruption of Judaism.
14-11 T· is no more allied to C. S. than

therapeutics
Mis. 5-22 *t·* can seem a miracle
80-27 pathology, hygiene, and *t·*,
268-23 His *t·* are antidotes for
378-21 *t·*, as in C. S.,
Pul. 54-20 * in his practice of mental *t·*,
Pan. 4-27 hygiene, and medical *t·*,
'01. 30-16 Even religion and *t·* need
My. 127-12 system of metaphysical *t·*
179-31 They afford such expositions of the *t·*,
204-29 *t·*, based as aforetime on
265-16 religion and scientific *t·*
267- 1 the only religion and *t·*
306-31 on my views of mental *t·*.
349-11 divine metaphysics or its *t·*.

thereabout
My. 100-11 * twenty-five years, or *t·*,

thereabouts
Mis. 381-28 thirty-eight hundred or *t·*,

thereafter
Mis. x-26 *t·* adopted that form of
24-10 On the third day *t·*,
87-24 What they need *t·* is to
120-13 *t·* "let the dead — *Matt.* 8 : 22.
Man. 52- 8 within ten days *t·*, the Clerk
Ret. 83-16 *t·* he will find it more difficult
'02. 16- 1 Six months *t·* Miss Dorcas Rawson
My. 158-26 *t·* dedicate to Truth and Love,
296-29 *t·* gave her discovery to

thereby
Mis. 9- 7 *t·* numbering them, and giving them
10-19 they *t·* have tried their strength
14-30 and *t·* destroys all error,
24-19 *t·* shutting out the true sense
33- 4 *t·* they lost, and he won, heaven.
45- 8 *t·* avoiding the fatal results
50-25 live *t·*, and have being.
84- 5 and *t·* hasten or permit it.
85-30 sick often are *t·* led to Christ,
109-29 lest *t·* it master you ;
121-20 *t·* giving the signet of God
129-10 tell thy brother his fault and *t·* help
130- 1 hope remained of *t·* benefiting
155-23 *t·* give to us all the pleasure
169- 5 insight had been darkened *t·*,
221- 6 *t·* learns more of its divine
287-10 on a false basis and *t·* lose it.
382-10 sinner and the sick are helped *t·*,
Ret. 33-19 matter is *t·* rarefied to
51- 5 the premises *t·* conveyed,
Pul. vii-16 impetus *t·* given to Christianity ;
81-17 * the moth to be destroyed *t·*,
Pan. 6-12 and *t·* obtaining social prestige,
'00. 3-10 he is not *t·* worshipped.
'01. 7-27 nor can they gain any . . . *t·*.
'02. 6-12 *t·* showing that God made
My. 6-16 impressed and encouraged *t·*,
17- 7 that ye may grow *t·* :— *I Pet.* 2 : 2.
21-12 * *t·* aid the progress of our Cause
52- 5 * *t·* giving in her Christian example,
113- 5 and *t·* is healed of disease.
164- 4 I consented, hoping *t·* to
210-11 but all . . . are *t·* benefited.
229-15 *t·* help themselves and
315-26 testimony they have *t·* given

The Recent Reckless and Irresponsible Attacks on Christian Science etc.

My. 316-12 T· R· R· and I· A· on C· S·

therefor

Mis.	107–26	and of *repentance t·*,
	119–31	and escape the penalty *t·*?
	301– 3	and receive pay *t·*,
Man.	67–23	and are amenable *t·*.
	69–17	appoint a proper member . . . *t·*,
	89–23	evidence of their eligibility *t·*,
Un.	64– 2	If . . . God is responsible *t·* ;
My.	167– 1	Accept my deep thanks *t·*,

therefore

Mis.	2–23	*t·* evil must be mortal
	14–17	*t·* to him evil is as real and
	14–28	*t·*, wholly problematical.
	16–18	*t·*, we must entertain a higher sense
	18– 5	*t·* rejoice in tribulation,
	21–21	*T·* man is not material ;
	22–18	*t·* these are null and void.
	24–22	*t·* it cannot be true.
	27– 2	*T·* the Science of good calls evil *nothing.*
	31– 8	*t·*, is not the use but the abuse of
	45–15	*t·*, under the deific law that
	50– 2	*t·* your answer is, that error is
	50–21	"Be ye *t·* perfect ;"— *Matt. 5 : 48.*
	72–29	*t·* it cannot cognize aught material,
	73–14	Human wisdom *t·* can get no
	85–14	"Be ye *t·* perfect,— *Matt. 5 : 48.*
	96–10	*t·*, I worship that of which I can
	103–31	*t·* is forever with the Father.
	119–31	"*T·* all things whatsoever — *Matt. 7 : 12.*
	128– 5	*T·* I close here,
	155– 1	*t·*, . . . there is but one cause and
	182– 8	*t·*, . . . they lose their false sense
	184–19	If he says, "I am of God, *t·* good,"
	186–15	*t·* divine Love is the
	188–13	*t·* now no condemnation — *Rom. 8 : 1.*
	190–21	*t·* the devil herein referred to
	196–12	*t·* that saying came not from Mind,
	197–26	*t·* cannot stand.
	198–31	*t·* he must suffer for it.
	199–11	*T· I take pleasure in* — *II Cor. 12 : 10.*
	210–10	"Be ye *t·* wise— *Matt. 10 : 16.*
	254–25	"What shall, *t·*, the Lord— *Mark 12 : 9.*
	273–19	*t·* they should continue,
	274–10	*t·* I leave all for Christ.
	292–20	who know not . . . and *t·* curse him ;
	293– 3	*t·* it is best to leave the
	303–11	*t·* no queries should arise as to
	311–25	*t·* I did this even as a surgeon
	313–21	pray ye *t·* the God of harvest
	322–18	*T·*, beloved, my often-coming is
	328–26	*T·*, give up thy earth-weights ;
	350–28	*t·* I teach the use of
	384–17	You *t·* cannot part.
Man.	59– 6	*T·* it is the duty of every member
	71–15	*T·*, no Church of Christ, Scientist,
Ret.	25–25	is *t·* inadequate to form any
	45–15	*T·*, in accord with my special request,
	49–18	*t· Resolved*, That we thank the State
	60–13	*t·* evil is unreal
	67–21	*T·* the lie was, and *is*, collective
	72– 4	*t·* it deteriorates one's ability
	75–18	and is *t·* honest.
	76–10	*T·* the mind to which this
	78–16	*T·* the adoption of a worldly policy
	79–27	*T·* are its spiritual gates
	81– 5	*T·* we should guard thought
	82–23	*t·* their examples either excel or
	82–30	it is *t·* better adapted to
	87–24	can *t·* bear the weight of
	94–11	*T·* this purgation of
Un.	8–10	not absolute, and *t·* not real,
	15–24	whom *t·* they wish to bribe
	18– 3	*t·* I know not evil.
	19–14	"If *t·* the light — *Matt. 6 : 23.*
	20–14	We *t·* need not fear it.
	25–23	*t·* has no groundwork in Life,
	27–10	An *egoist, t·*, is one
	29– 7	*T·* there is, . . . no spiritual death.
	34– 8	*t·* that the whole function
	34–11	*t·* there is nothing but Spirit ;
	38– 4	*t·* it is not in accordance with
	40–13	*t·* mortals can no more receive
	41–23	Life, *t·*, is deathless, because
	60–11	its opposite, and *t·* unreal ;
Pul.	4– 8	and *t·* whole number,
	4–15	*t·* is the seer's declaration true,
	12–11	*t·* rejoice, ye heavens,— *Rev. 12 : 12.*
	20– 4	*t·* I paid it,
	25– 7	* *t·* as literally fire-proof as
	55–12	* We do not, *t·*, regard it as a
	80–19	* We do not, *t·*, speak of
	86–26	* We *t·* respectfully extend
Rud.	2–14	*t·* I prefer to retain the
	5– 6	*T·* in divine Science there is
	11– 8	*t·* good is one and All.
No.	5–10	*T·* this material sense,

therefore

No.	5–22	*t·* the mind that attacks a
	23– 9	and *t·* was not a *devil*,
	24– 4	He is in all things, and *t·*
	36– 4	and *t·* as the All-in-all ;
Pan.	2– 5	*t·* is neither hypothetical nor
	5–19	*T·* we should neither believe
	9–11	"Be ye *t·* perfect,— *Matt. 5 : 48.*
	10–25	*t·* no pleasure in loathsome
	10–30	*T·* it required the divinity of
	11–30	"Be ye *t·* perfect,"— *Matt. 5 : 48.*
'00.	9– 6	*t·*, not ready — to obey.
'01.	3–26	*t·* it is illogical
	5–11	*t·* divine metaphysics
	5–21	*t·* man reflects Spirit,
	8–10	*T·* we have the authority of
	8–15	"Be ye *t·* perfect,— *Matt. 5 : 48.*
	8–24	*t·* Christ existed prior to Jesus,
	10– 6	Fear them not *t·* :— *Matt. 10 : 26.*
	10–10	*t·* the son of man only in
	12–23	*t·* the nothingness of matter.
	13–14	*t·* is nothing and the father of
	14–15	*t·* as unreal as a mirage
	14–27	*t·* man is its master.
	15– 6	to prove it false, *t·* unreal.
	16–17	*t·*, according to Holy Writ
	22– 6	*T·* I do not try to mix
	22–13	*t·* matter cannot be a reality.
	23–20	*t·* he demonstrated his power
	26– 8	*t·* the metaphysician . . . that combines
'02.	11–20	*T·* it is thine, advancing Christian,
	14–24	*T·*, I ask : What has shielded
Hea.	3–18	*T·* Christ Jesus was an honorary title ;
	10– 9	*t·* evil is impotent.
	17– 9	*t·* the so-called material man
	17–21	and *t·* are not TRUE.
Peo.	5–24	*t·* a Truth-filled mind makes a
Po.	vii–10	* *With grateful acknowledgment, t·*,
	36–16	You *t·* cannot part.
My.	11–25	* The location is, *t·*, determined.
	16–24	"*T·* thus saith the— *Isa. 28 : 16.*
	21–10	* We *t·* feel sure that all
	22–26	* Is it not *t·* the duty of all
	24–30	* It *t·* occurs to us that
	56–11	* *t·* three branch churches
	56–28	* *T·*, beginning October 1, 1905,
	83–13	* *T·*, with the exception of
	100– 6	* is *t·* the property of
	109–19	*T·* there can be but one God,
	113–11	"There is *t·* now no— *Rom. 8 : 1.*
	126–20	*T·* shall her plagues— *Rev. 18 : 8.*
	128– 3	"*T·* . . . let us go on — *Heb. 6 : 1.*
	128–22	*T·* be wise and harmless,
	130–15	*T·* I ask the help of others
	136– 4	*t·* it is best explained by
	146–25	*T·* a Christian Scientist never
	150– 2	*T·* despair not nor murmur,
	150–28	"Be ye *t·* wise— *Matt. 10 : 16.*
	153–21	"whom *t·* ye ignorantly— *Acts 17 : 23.*
	161–19	*T·*, said Jesus, " Ye shall drink— *Matt. 20 : 23.*
	171–11	*T·* I hereby invite all my
	178–16	*t·* if evil exists, it exists without
	202– 8	"Render *t·* to all— *Rom. 13 : 7.*
	205– 1	"There is *t·* now no— *Rom. 8 : 1.*
	205– 4	"Stand fast *t·*— *Gal. 5 : 1.*
	205– 5	"Be ye *t·* wise as— *Matt. 10 : 16.*
	214–25	I *t·* halted from necessity.
	218–28	*T·* an individual should not
	224–23	less correct and *t·* less profound.
	231– 9	She has, *t·*, finally resolved
	231–21	It would *t·* be as unwise
	269–11	This, *t·*, is Christ's plan
	273–23	ever-present good, and *t·*
	276– 5	*t·* to be criticized or judged
	288–22	*t·*, he cast out devils
	299–17	*T·* I query :
	351–24	*T·* I have not endorsed it,
	357–22	*t· Spirit is all.*
	358– 2	*t·*, if you are sincere

therefrom

Mis.	vii–15	Nothing have we gained *t·*,
	33–20	recognize the help they derive *t·*.
	115– 1	to protect themselves *t·*,
	162–17	*t·* rise to his nativity in Spirit.
	288–12	any conclusion drawn *t·*
Man.	110– 4	confusion that might result *t·*.
Ret.	50–28	the blessings which arose *t·*.
Pul.	46– 7	* no such inference is to be drawn *t·*
'02.	13–11	I receive no personal benefit *t·*
My.	133–14	fragments gathered *t·* should
	242– 7	and must be practised *t·*.

therein

Mis.	28–26	find neither pleasure nor pain *t·*.
	146–17	be governed *t·* by the spirit
	158–27	order *t·* given corresponds to

therein

Mis.	169– 3	way of her researches *t·*,
	189– 5	interpretation *t·* will be found to be the
	323– 4	having no temple *t·*,
	323–18	saith unto the patient toilers *t·* :
	325– 2	saith unto the dwellers *t·*,
	344–26	shall in no wise enter *t·*.''— *Luke* 18 : 17.
Man.	68–19	or allows to visit or to locate *t·*
	69– 9	expiration of the time *t·* mentioned
	79–23	manage the property *t·* conveyed,
	91–20	Students of C. S., duly instructed *t·*
Ret.	26–16	seeing *t·* the operation of the divine
	37–15	Science of Mind-healing as *t·* stated.
	82–16	in large cities, . . . and *t·* abide.
	94–30	the Father was glorified *t·*.
Un.	14–22	if . . . all cannot be good *t·*.
	28–11	never a light . . . was discerned *t·*,
	33–17	and you find no mind *t·*.
	36–19	(instead of acquiescence *t·*)
Pul.	58–29	* *T·* is a portrait of her
	87– 2	* any services that may be held *t·*.
No.	17–17	*t·* is no inverted image of God,
My.	33–29	they that dwell *t·*.— *Psal.* 24 : 1.
	150–16	See *t·* the mirrored sky
	158–28	your temple and all who worship *t·*
	199–14	joint resolutions contained *t·*
	298– 6	the good acomplished *t·*,

thereof

Mis.	28– 2	reappear in the spiritual sense *t·*.
	30– 3	some feeble demonstration *t·*,
	30–12	The gates *t·* he declared were
	55– 4	understanding and demonstration *t·*
	57–16	day that thou eatest *t·*— *Gen.* 2 : 17.
	67–21	you shall, . . . inform them *t·*.
	84–29	a new and higher sense *t·*,
	91–24	I never dreamed, until informed *t·*,
	93– 1	and by reason *t·* is able to
	100 13	may lose sight *t·* ;
	121–31	from the divine Principle *t·*,
	125–28	to tell the towers *t·*
	131–27	let her state the value *t·*,
	144– 5	and the name *t·*,
	156–19	daily Christian demonstration *t·*.
	158–10	comes the interpretation *t·*.
	189–18	revealing, in place *t·*, the power
	244– 1	closed up the wound *t·*,— *see Gen.* 2 : 21.
	291–16	If any are not partakers *t·*,
	291–19	if the spirit *t·* be lacking.
	302–27	received from his reading *t·* :
	306–21	* was at that time the President *t·*.
	323– 5	for God is the temple *t·* ;
	330–13	consciousness *t·* is here and now
	358–32	leaving the material forms *t·*
	365– 9	gets things wrong, and is ignorant *t·*.
	367–17	day that thou eatest *t·*,— *Gen.* 2 : 17.
Man.	29–10	shall complain *t·* to the Clerk
	36–21	signed by three members *t·*
	50– 1	and the cause *t·* be unknown,
	53–22	considered a sufficient evidence *t·*.
	55–24	contrary to the statement *t·*
	66–13	to await her explanation *t·*.
	68– 8	upon Mrs. Eddy's complaint *t·*
	75–10	with grateful acknowledgments *t·*,
	78– 1	demand that each member *t·*
	110– 9	and become a part *t·*.
Ret.	35–12	spiritual interpretations *t·*
	83– 5	and the healing efficacy *t·*,
	84–20	and by reason *t·* is able to
	87–14	in the orderly demonstration *t·*.
Un.	19– 8	must have had foreknowledge *t·* ;
	44–20	"In the day ye eat *t·*— *Gen.* 3 : 5.
Pul.	1–13	great is the value *t·*.
	5– 7	we kindle in place *t·*
No.	7–26	discriminations and guidance *t·*
	8–14	the remainder *t·* He will restrain.
Pan.	1–17	waiteth patiently the appearing *t·*.
	14–21	and their faithful service *t·*,
'00.	6–10	dawns the spiritual meaning *t·* ;
'01.	27–16	rejoice in being informed *t·*.
'02.	5–28	Love and the manifestation *t·*
	8–21	Love is the Principle *t·*.
	9–21	heard the life-giving sound *t·*,
Hea.	3– 5	more than a profession *t·* ;
Peo.	5–21	the demonstration *t·* in healing
My.	8– 5	* outgrowing the institutional end *t·*.
	33–28	and the fulness *t·* ;— *Psal.* 24 : 1.
	161–23	unto each day is the duty *t·*.
	184–13	to wire an acknowledgment *t·*
	186–20	eat the fruit *t·*.
	197–21	in the Word and in the doers *t·*,
	206–22	Lamb is the light *t·*.''— *Rev.* 21 : 23.
	207– 5	remainder *t·* He will restrain.
	225– 1	the present persecution *t·*.
	230– 8	senses' assimilation *t·*,
	237– 9	understanding of the principle *t·*,
	275–14	(and I trust the desire *t·*)

thereof

My.	338–17	subjects or the handling *t·*,
	348–20	demonstration *t·* was made,

thereon

Mis.	124–19	As we think *t·*, man's true sense
	139–21	erected *t·* a church edifice
Man.	70– 6	adhering strictly to her advice *t·*.
My.	217–14	with interest *t·* up to date,

thereto

Mis.	54–16	the sick, unasked, are testifying *t·*.
	66– 1	obedience *t·* may be found faulty,
	85–12	regeneration leading *t·* is gradual,
	119–23	or strict obedience *t·*,
	124– 9	will not be reconciled *t·*.
	296–27	or are they incited *t·* by their
Man.	83–23	habitually to study . . . as a help *t·*.
	86–22	shall teach nothing contrary *t·*.
Ret.	14–13	if assent . . . was essential *t·*.
	53– 3	and the funds belonging *t·*.
Un.	38– 5	but antagonistic *t·*.
Pul.	84–19	* All who are awake *t·*
Pan.	9– 9	four first rules pertaining *t·*,
'01.	35–18	walk in Patient faith the way *t·*
'02.	10–19	his predicate tending *t·* is correct,
My.	233–15	can you . . . by indifference *t·* ?
	237–14	and give daily attention *t·*.
	241–13	* and Mrs. Eddy's reply *t·*.
	284–22	I consented *t·* only as other
	320–22	* several times subsequent *t·*,

thereunto

Mis.	272– 3	* privileges pertaining *t·*

thereupon

Man.	77– 8	decide *t·* by a unanimous vote,
Un.	44– 6	like the structure raised *t·*,
Pul.	58– 2	* and *t·* devoted herself to

therewith

Mis.	296–19	is by no means associated *t·*.
	309–20	whatever is connected *t·*,
Man.	27–24	other literature connected *t·*.
	37– 3	application for membership *t·*
	66– 5	then act in accordance *t·*.
	74–14	nor in rooms connected *t·*.
Ret.	24– 3	would associate *t·*,
Un.	60–14	and *t·* curse we men,— *Jas.* 3 : 9.
'02.	13–20	the note *t·* became due,
My.	175– 4	organizations connected *t·*,
	210– 8	clad *t·* you are completely shielded
	253–25	and my joy *t·*.

The Science of Man

Ret.	35– 2	entitled "*T· S· of M·*."

"The Temptation"

Mis.	313–17	"*T· T·*," a poem by J. J. Rome,

The Unknown God Made Known

My.	338–12	subject "*T· U· G· M· K·*,"

The World Beautiful

Pul.	39–11	* author of "*T· W· B·*."

thick

Pul.	78– 5	* an eighth of an inch *t·*.
My.	191–22	Mortality's *t·* gloom is pierced.

thicken

Mis.	243–28	cause the coats of the stomach to *t·*

thief (*see also* **thief's**)

Mis.	70–10	*when he said to the dying t·*,
	70–17	*t·* was not equal to the demands
	70–25	*t·* would be with Jesus only in a
'02.	18– 2	wilt know when the *t·* cometh.
My.	232 15	hour the *t·* would come,— *Luke* 12 : 39.

thief's

Mis.	70–20	the poor *t·* prayer for help
	70–22	The *t·* body, as matter,

thieves

'01.	14–23	against the approach of *t·*.

thin

Mis.	291–23	will at length dissolve into *t·* air.

Thine

Mis.	212–21	"Not my will, but *T·*,— *Luke* 22 : 42.
	348– 7	It is not *mine* but *T·* they seek.
	397–15	where *T·* own children are,
	397–18	To *T·*, for Thee ;
	398–12	And Thou know'st *T·* own ;
	398–16	Take them in *T·* arms ;
Ret.	15– 9	even of *T·* only.— *Psal.* 71 : 16.
	46–18	And Thou know'st *T·* own.
	46–22	Take them in *T·* arms ;
Pul.	17–17	And Thou know'st *T·* own.
	17–21	Take them in *T·* arms ;
	18–24	where *T·* own children are,
	19– 2	To *T·*, for Thee ;
Po.	13– 3	where *T·* own children are,
	13– 6	To *T·*, for Thee ;
	14–16	And Thou know'st *T·* own ;

Thine

Po.	14–20	Take them in *T·* arms ;
	24–13	This heart of *T·*
	43–11	Ever thus as *T·* !
My.	253–16	through *T·* own name— *John* 17 : 11.

thing

any

Mis.	259– 2	was not any *t·* made."— *John* 1 : 3.
My.	202–10	Owe no man any *t·*,— *Rom.* 13 : 8.
	267– 8	was not any *t·* made— *John* 1 : 3.

any other

Un.	48– 7	no faith in any other *t·* or being.

any such

Rud.	5–15	If there is any such *t·* as matter,

bad

My.	87–24	* it would not be a bad *t·* if

best

'00.	9– 5	not because it is the best *t·* to do,

deadly

Mis.	28–32	drink any deadly *t·*,— *Mark* 16 : 18.
	249– 6	drink any deadly *t·*,— *Mark* 16 : 18.
Hea.	1– 3	*drink any deadly t·,— Mark 16 : 18.*
	7–26	drink any deadly *t·*,— *Mark* 16 : 18.
	15–11	drink any deadly *t·*,— *Mark* 16 : 18.
Peo.	12– 4	drink any deadly *t·*,— *Mark* 16 : 18.
My.	48– 1	* drink any deadly *t·*,— *Mark* 16 : 18.
	146– 5	drink any deadly *t·*,— *Mark* 16 : 18.

every high

Mis.	139–12	*every high t· that exalteth— II Cor.* 10 : 5.

first

Mis.	375–17	* "The first *t·* that impressed me

great

Mis.	38–11	is it a great *t·* if we— *I Cor.* 9 : 11.
	157– 2	great *t·* to be found worthy

holy

Mis.	51–28	* walk transparent like some holy *t·*."

instead of a

Mis.	271– 4	a thought, instead of a *t·*.

made

My.	205–18	* as the *t·* made is good or bad,

most important

My.	289– 1	The *t·* most important is

no new

Pul.	53– 6	* no new *t·* under the sun."— *Eccl.* 1 : 9.

no such

Mis.	47– 1	*there is no such t· as matter*
Un.	1– 3	God knows no such *t·* as sin.
	50–13	there is no such *t·* as *mortal mind,*

of mortal mind

Mis.	237– 4	suffering is a *t·* of mortal mind

of the past

Mis.	375–30	* a *t·* of the past,

of thought

Rud.	10–15	Disease is a *t·* of thought

one

Mis.	48– 5	One *t·* is quite apparent ;
	99–19	In no other one *t·* seemed Jesus
	127– 7	One *t·* I have greatly desired,
	163–16	In no one *t·* seemed he less human
	230– 4	more than upon any other one *t·*.
No.	9– 8	but this one *t·* can be done,
'00.	6– 5	this one *t·* I do,—*Phil.* 3 : 13.
Hea.	4–25	model is one *t·* at one time,
My.	18– 4	"One *t·* I have greatly desired,
	44– 8	* one *t·* is certain, it will be sure,
	70– 3	* One *t·* is certain:
	87–26	* There is one *t·* about it:
	126–28	One *t·* is eternally here;
	126–32	This is that needful one *t·*
	236–11	Too much of one *t·* spoils the
	271–10	the one *t·* needful and the sole proof
	325– 4	* One *t·* more, that I think will

person and

Un.	45– 6	mind and matter, person and *t·*?"

place or a

'01.	13– 1	a man or a woman, a place or a *t·*,

proper

Ret.	90–27	* "I believe the proper *t·* for us to do

remarkable

My.	89–13	* remarkable *t·* in this building

right

Mis.	71–10	is a very right *t·* to do.
My.	193–23	* if it succeeds, it is a right *t·*."

same

Mis.	381–32	* discoverer of the same *t·*."

such

No.	32–10	chapter sub-title

that

Ret.	94–18	that *t·* which he alloweth.— *Rom.* 14 : 22.

the very

Un.	58– 8	This was the very *t·* he *was* doing,

vain

My.	103–17	imagine a vain *t·*?"— *Psal.* 2 : 1.
	200– 5	imagine a vain *t·* ;"— *Psal.* 2 : 1.
	270–14	Let error rage and imagine a vain *t·*.

thing

worse

My.	288–26	lest a worse *t·* come— *John 5 :* 14.

Mis.	8–10	*t·* outside thine own creation?
	245–27	it is a *t·* to be thankful for
Pul.	53– 4	* "The *t·* that hath been,— *Eccl.* 1 : 9.
No.	3–22	How good and pleasant a *t·* it is
My.	14– 1	in the *t·* whereto— *Isa.* 55 : 11.
	164–11	a *t·* focusing light where love,
	193–22	* Carlyle writes, "Give a *t·* time ;

things

above

Mis.	391– 4	For *t·* above the floor,
Pan.	14– 4	Set your affections on *t·* above ;
Po.	38– 3	For *t·* above the floor,
My.	15–19	* tell the story, Of unseen *t·* above,

all

Mis.	10–24	and all *t·* become new.
	45–28	"All *t·* were made— *John* 1 : 3.
	59–13	God *has* given all *t·* to those who
	68–27	* causes of all *t·* existing,"
	71–25	to Him, are all *t·*,"— *Rom.* 11 : 36.
	119–31	all *t·* whatsoever— *Matt.* 7 : 12.
	159–13	where all *t·* are pure
	217–14	specific nature of all *t·* is unchanged,
	222– 4	It reverses C. S. in all *t·*.
	232–17	maximum of perfection in all *t·*.
	235–28	"All *t·* whatsoever— *Matt.* 7 : 12.
	258–17	infinite Mind governs all *t·*.
	259– 1	"all *t·* were made— *John* 1 : 3.
	310–16	"Let all *t·* be done— *I Cor.* 14 : 40.
	367–13	Error says that knowing all *t·*
	373–25	gave man dominion over all *t·* ;
Man.	42–22	"All *t·* whatsoever— *Matt.* 7 : 12.
Ret.	23– 3	All *t·* earthly must ultimately
	26–25	Principle of all *t·* pure ;
	28–18	reduce all *t·* real to their own
Un.	10–10	the one God, to whom belong all *t·*.
	15– 8	God created all *t·*,
	17–11	because He knows all *t·* ;
	40–26	and regard all *t·* as temporal.
	56–26	and endureth all *t·*.
Pul.	85–12	* divine Principle of all *t·*
No.	24– 4	He is in all *t·*,
	42– 2	* to believe all *t·* written in the
	43– 8	* "Only He who knows all *t·*
Pan.	5– 4	"all *t·* were made— *John* 1 : 3.
	7– 9	had created all *t·* spiritually,
'00.	5– 3	nature, and government of all *t·*
	11–10	"all *t·* work together— *Rom.* 8 : 28.
'01.	21–26	for did He not know all *t·*
Peo.	1– 9	reality and Soul of all *t·*,
My.	52–15	* bring out the perfection of all *t·*,
	123–28	ministry of righteousness in all *t·*,
	143–21	all *t·* work together— *Rom.* 8 : 28.
	152–23	an ever-present help in all *t·*,
	154– 9	Send flowers with all *t·* fair
	156– 8	sufficiency in all *t·*,— *II Cor.* 9 : 8.
	158–12	it endureth all *t·* ;
	180–15	to whom all *t·* are possible ;
	181–19	and thus exemplify in all *t·*
	194– 5	dies, as do all *t·* material,
	266–17	final spiritualization of all *t·*,
	267– 7	"All *t·* were made— *John* 1 : 3.
	285–27	believing all *t·*— *Acts* 24 : 14.
	293– 1	knowledge that all *t·* are possible
	349– 3	to whom all *t·* are possible.

all the

My.	280– 8	* all the *t·* which make for

better

No.	34–18	blood of Christ speaketh better *t·*

carnal

Mis.	38–12	reap your carnal *t·*?"— *I Cor.* 9 : 11.

cause of

Mis.	219– 2	the final cause of *t·* ;

certain

'00.	8–30	advise students not to do certain *t·*

childish

Mis.	359–10	I put away childish *t·*.— *I Cor.* 13 : 11.
My.	135– 5	I put away childish *t·*."— *I Cor.* 13 : 11.
	261–18	I put away childish *t·*."— *I Cor.* 13 : 11.

crooked

My.	140– 5	crooked *t·* straight.— *Isa.* 42 : 16.

divine

Ret.	31–10	and thirst after divine *t·*,

few

Mis.	116–29	"faithful over a few *t·*."— *Matt.* 25 : 23.
	339–18	faithful over a few *t·*."— *Matt.* 25 : 23.
	340–17	not been faithful over a few *t·*.
	340–25	been faithful over a few *t·*.
	342–32	faithful over the few *t·* of Spirit,
Pul.	13– 7	faithful over a few *t·*,— *Matt.* 25 : 23.

fitness of

Mis.	316–11	depend on the fitness of *t·*,

things

glorious
Mis. 151–22 Glorious *t·* are spoken of you
good
Un. 15– 9 Was evil among these good *t·?*
My. 13–23 thy mouth with good *t·* ;— *Psal.* 103 : 5.
99– 2 * good *t·* that this sect is doing.
197– 1 Enjoying good *t·* is not evil,
hard
Mis. 266–18 assertion that I have said hard *t·*
Un. 1– 4 "*t·* hard to be understood," — *II Pet.* 3 : 16.
hidden
My. 124– 1 hidden *t·* of dishonesty, — *II Cor.* 4 : 2.
holy
Mis. 280– 7 not the holy *t·* of Truth.
hoped for
My. 260–16 *t·* hoped for and the evidence
many
Mis. 117– 1 over many *t·*." — *Matt.* 25 : 23.
341– 9 made ruler over many *t·*.
375–22 * resemblance in many *t·*,
Pul. 82–11 * many *t·* dear to the soul
material
(*see* **material**)
material basis of
Mis. 341– 4 unreal material basis of *t·*,
material sense of
Mis. 120– 3 unclasp the material sense of *t·*
mortal
Hea. 19–12 the origin of all mortal *t·*.
mortal sense of
Mis. 188–26 unreal or mortal sense of *t·* ;
Un. 30–23 change in the mortal sense of *t·*,
most essential
Mis. 232–11 in *t·* most essential,
234–12 *t·* most essential and divine.
new
'00. 8–14 *t·* new and old." — *Matt.* 13 : 52.
of earth
Mis. 390–24 like *t·* of earth,
Po. 56– 3 like *t·* of earth,
of God
Mis. 175– 3 takes of the *t·* of God
Ret. 24–24 should take the *t·* of God
'01. 9–23 takes of the *t·* of God
of man
Mis. 332–17 pondered the *t·* of man and God.
of Spirit
Mis. 342–32 faithful over the few *t·* of Spirit,
'01. 9–28 liveth most the *t·* of Spirit,
My. 260–10 *t·* of Spirit, not of matter.
old
Mis. 10–24 wherein old *t·* pass away
personal sense of
Mis. 290–22 from a personal sense of *t·*.
Principle of
Mis. 232– 7 the perfect Principle of *t·* ;
prove the
My. 285–24 prove the *t·* whereof they — *Acts* 24 : 13.
reality of
'01. 1–19 portion of the primal reality of *t·*.
20– 9 alone . . . with the reality of *t·*.
small
My. 123–28 not overlook small *t·* in goodness
spiritual
(*see* **spiritual**)
stubborn
My. 99–27 * Facts and figures are stubborn *t·*,
substance of
(*see* **substance**)
such
'01. 33–10 * originating influence in such *t·* ;
sweet
My. 252– 5 always distributing sweet *t·*
that are Cæsar's
Mis. 374–25 "the *t·* that are Cæsar's ;" — *Mark* 12 : 17.
Ret. 71– 5 the *t·* that are Cæsar's, — *Mark* 12 : 17.
My. 220–10 the *t·* that are Cæsar's,' — *Mark* 12 : 17.
344–25 the *t·* that are Cæsar's.' — *Mark* 12 : 17.
that are God's
Ret. 71– 6 the *t·* that are God's." — *Mark* 12 : 17.
My. 220–11 the *t·* that are God's.' " — *Mark* 12 : 17.
these
Mis. 72–21 *need of all these t·*," — *Matt.* 6 : 32.
73–18 We have need of *these t·* ;
100–28 Who is sufficient for these *t·?*
128–11 think on these *t·*. — *Phil.* 4 : 8.
167–24 hid these *t·* from the wise — *Luke* 10 : 21.
270–15 these *t·* shall be added — *Matt.* 6 : 33.
Chr. 55–10 these *t·* shall be added — *Matt.* 6 : 33.
Ret. 13–16 of these *t·* he now spoke,
Un. 43–13 "sufficient for these *t·*." — *II Cor.* 2 : 16.
60–17 these *t·* ought not so to be." — *Jas.* 3 : 10.
No. 45– 1 hid these *t·* from the wise — *Luke* 10 : 21.
'01. 9–24 and these *t·* being spiritual,
10– 3 "For all these *t·* — *see Matt.* 10 : 17.

things

these
'02. 19–23 need of all these *t·*." — *Matt.* 6 : 32.
My. 33–27 He that doeth these *t·* — *Psal.* 15 : 5.
90– 5 * all these *t·* are new,
140– 6 These *t·* will I do — *Isa.* 42 : 16.
143–23 when these *t·* cease to bless
143–28 say to these *t·?* — *Rom.* 8 : 31.
153– 9 "these *t·* saith He — *Rev.* 3 : 7.
229– 5 "For all that do these *t·* — *Deut.* 18 : 12.
300–20 these *t·*, inseparable from C. S.,
they suffer
Mis. 278–27 must learn by the *t·* they suffer,
328– 2 learn from the *t·* they suffer.
those
Mis. 128–11 Those *t·*, which — *Phil.* 4 : 9.
178–12 those *t·* which are above, — *Col.* 3 : 1.
328–28 "Forgetting those *t·* — *Phil.* 3 : 13.
'00. 6– 6 forgetting those *t·* — *Phil.* 3 : 13.
6– 7 those *t·* which are before, — *Phil.* 3 : 13.
My. 155–11 those *t·* that are behind,
256–10 thanks for those *t·* of beauty
thought as
Mis. 331–26 nature as thought, and thought as *t·*.
thoughts are
Pul. 80–26 * belief that "thoughts are *t·*,"
two
My. 92–26 * two *t·* to be said in favor of
165– 2 Of two *t·* fate cannot rob us ;
unseen
My. 15–19 Of unseen *t·* above,
95–25 * without faith in the *t·* unseen.
what
Mis. 168– 3 tell what *t·* ye shall see
My. 293–30 "What *t·* soever ye desire, — *Mark* 11 : 24.
whatsoever
Mis. 128– 7 whatsoever *t·* are true, — *Phil.* 4 : 8.
128– 7 whatsoever *t·* are honest, — *Phil.* 4 : 8.
128– 8 whatsoever *t·* are just, — *Phil.* 4 : 8.
128– 8 whatsoever *t·* are pure, — *Phil.* 4 : 8.
128– 9 whatsoever *t·* are lovely, — *Phil.* 4 : 8.
128– 9 whatsoever *t·* are of — *Phil.* 4 : 8.
which are not seen
Mis. 66–21 *t·* which are not seen." — *II Cor.* 4 : 18.
Un. 62– 7 *t·* which are not seen are — *II Cor.* 4 : 18.
which are seen
Mis. 66–20 at the *t·* which are seen, — *II Cor.* 4 : 18.
Un. 62– 6 *t·* which are seen are — *II Cor.* 4 : 18.
wrong
Mis. 365– 8 gets *t·* wrong, and is ignorant
No. 18–20 gets *t·* wrong, and knows it not ;

Mis. 28– 8 In dreams, *t·* are only what
263–15 chapter sub-title
309–28 sometimes take *t·* too intensely.

think

Mis. 7–28 they *t·* that health and strength
11– 4 I used to *t·* it sufficiently just
52–11 *What do you t· of marriage?*
124–18 As we *t·* thereon, man's true sense
128–11 *t·* on these things. — *Phil.* 4 : 8.
158–25 forthcoming completion (as I now *t·*)
171– 7 is as absurd as to *t·*, . . . that
178–15 * "I *t·* it was about a year ago
214– 4 "*T·* not that I am come to — *Matt.* 10 : 34
219–12 admitted that mortals *t·* wickedly
219–14 mortals *t·* also after a sickly
233–21 weak and worldly who *t·* the
233–23 What *t·* you of a scientist
251–20 *T·* of this inheritance !
256–22 accustomed to *t·* and to speak
263– 9 blessed it is to *t·* of you as
280–13 As we commonly *t·*, we imagine
281–20 *t·* instead, of our poverty
338–26 * "*T·* truly, and thy thoughts
344– 6 do you *t·* it possible for you
353–28 *t·* of helping others, go their way.
Man. 59– 4 *t·* at random on this subject,
Ret. 50– 2 I could *t·* of no financial equivalent
74– 9 I desire never to *t·* of it,
74– 9 it cannot *t·* of me.
Un. 18– 2 let us *t·* of God as saying,
40– 2 which neither *t·* nor speak.
Pul. 2–12 *t·* for a moment with me
3– 8 power to *t·* and act rightly,
74–20 "I *t·* Mrs. Lathrop was not understood.
75– 7 But to *t·* or speak of me in
Rud. 2–12 if we *t·* of Him as less
No. 7–22 *t·*, speak, teach, and write
39– 1 the way we can *t·* more lucidly
43–19 *t·* to build a baseless fabric
Pan. 10– 3 "If a man *t·* himself — *Gal.* 6 : 3.
'02. 5–23 "*T·* not that I am — *Matt.* 5 : 17.
Hea. 5–14 Does any one *t·* the departed
9– 9 *t·* most of sickness and of sin ;

think
Peo.	12– 1	should *t·* for one moment
Po.	3– 6	I *t·* of thee, I *t·* of thee !
	17– 3	Then I'll *t·* of its glory,
	74– 2	*T·* kindly of me,
My.	3–21	compels him to *t·* genuine,
	41– 2	* so that they *t·* rightly
	87– 7	* And so, we *t·*, must be
	87–20	* I do not *t·* I have ever seen
	95–23	* may *t·* they can banish
	100–16	* who *t·* for themselves.
	119–10	*T·* not that C. S. tends
	133– 3	Ofttimes I *t·* of this in the
	156– 6	that we ask or *t·*,"— *Eph.* 3 : 20.
	163–15	which I *t·* do them more good.
	171–10	I *t·* you would enjoy seeing it.
	187– 5	to *t·* of doing so at present.
	212– 2	*t·* or do voluntarily.
	219–23	"*T·* not that I am— *Matt.* 5 : 17.
	259–16	to *t·* and work for others.
	291–28	She stops to *t·*, to mourn,
	302–17	I still must *t·* the name
	307–23	still *t·* that it was profane.
	313–14	everything they could *t·* of
	321– 2	* He seemed very proud to *t·*
	325– 5	* I *t·* will amuse you :
	335–26	* (Dr. McRee we *t·* it was),
	344–19	I should *t·* myself in danger of
	360–14	as many students *t·* I can,

thinker
Mis.	374–29	between the *t·* and his thought
Un.	14– 5	Can it be seriously held, by any *t·*,
'00.	2– 9	the right *t·* and worker,
	2–11	The right *t·* works ;
	3– 4	The right *t·* and worker
	3– 9	If the right *t·* and worker's
	3–14	what the best *t·* and worker has
	3–18	Only the good man loves the right *t·*
My.	210–12	self-seeking pride of the evil *t·*
	210–14	The evil *t·* is the proud talker
	210–15	right *t·* abides under the shadow of

thinkers
Mis.	6–13	it surely does, to many *t·*,
	112– 3	Even honest *t·*, not knowing
	219–13	beginning to be seen by *t·*,
	234–23	grave wonderment to profound *t·*.
	383–15	rise higher in the estimation of *t·*
Un.	6–14	even the *t·* are not prepared to
	8– 2	much trouble to many earnest *t·*
	9–22	spiritual *t·* in all ages.
No.	9– 5	errors of one class of *t·*
	13–23	revolution in the minds of *t·*
'00.	9–21	will challenge the *t·*,
'01.	17–15	the respect of our best *t·*.
'02.	9–25	Did the age's *t·* laugh long
My.	113–31	the deep *t·*, the truly great
	162– 7	A small group of wise *t·*
	347–24	Most *t·* concede that Science

thinketh
Mis.	70– 7	"*t·* in his heart,— *Prov.* 23 : 7.
	311–13	charity which *t·* no evil ;
No.	45– 6	*t·* no evil,— *I Cor.* 13 : 5.
Peo.	3– 2	"*t·* in his heart,— *Prov.* 23 : 7.

thinking
Mis.	x–22	*t·* that otherwise the name
	19– 1	Envy, evil *t·*, evil speaking,
	117–14	basis of all right *t·* and acting ;
	130–11	*t·* it over, and how to meet it,
	204–32	evil *t·*, evil speaking and acting ;
	230–10	*t·* of nothing or planning for some
	233–13	*t·* to put into the old garment of
	245–23	*t·* that it was following Christ ;
	365–12	Its genius is right *t·*
Man.	59– 5	weight in the scale of right *t·*.
Ret.	81–11	false *t·*, feeling, and acting ;
Pul.	6–12	mistake of *t·* she caught her notions
Rud.	15–10	systematic *t·* is impracticable until
No.	12– 4	essence of this Science is right *t·*
	15–23	*T·* otherwise is what estranges
	18– 9	Right *t·* and right acting,
'00.	3– 5	does the *t·* for the ages.
	9– 8	secret of C. S. in right *t·*
'01.	30– 4	in *t·* the object of vital Christianity
Hea.	3– 7	foundation of right *t·*
	9– 5	*t·* and talking on the wrong side
Po.	8–20	I'm *t·* alone of a fair young bride,
My.	vii–11	* consistent and constant right *t·*
	vii–12	* intelligent *t·* untainted by the
	41– 5	* the law of right *t·*,
	209– 5	right *t·* and right acting,
	233–31	*T·* of person implies that
	234– 1	is not *t·* of Principle,
	234– 2	signalize the *t·* of person.
	254–11	of right *t·* and acting,

thinking
My.	273–14	spiritual sense of *t·*, feeling,
	274–10	right *t·*, right feeling,
	346–14	* looking forward, *t·*, *t·*,

thinks
Mis.	71– 6	one writer *t·* that he was
	88– 8	* "*What Quibus T·.*"
	107–32	Mankind *t·* either too much or
	108– 1	saint *t·* too much of it :
	108– 2	sinner, . . . *t·* too little of sin.
	145–11	And if he *t·* that he is,
	215–20	*t·* he is where he is not,
	298–29	one *t·* he is not mistaken,
Ret.	76–25	He *t·* of every one in his real
Pul.	81–12	* she *t·* so much of herself
Hea.	6–18	*t·* he is a medium of disease ;
My.	271– 9	what a man *t·* or believes

third
Mis.	24–10	On the *t·* day thereafter,
	34– 4	*T·* : One who has been healed
	76– 4	*T·* : Jesus said,
	101–12	Now cometh a *t·* struggle ;
	109–23	through the second to the *t·* stage,
	142–16	my second, a psalm ; my *t·*, a letter.
	162– 3	*t·* event of this eventful period,
	205–13	*T·* : The baptism of Spirit,
	210– 6	the remaining *t·* kills itself.
	217–21	a *t·* quality unlike God.
	219–16	A *t·* person knows that if
	242– 3	in *Zion's Herald*, December *t·*,
	254–19	take away a *t·* part of the
	256– 1	*T·* : Persons who have been healed
	276–12	*t·* convention of our National
	280– 3	The *t·* picture-lesson is from
	290– 1	A *t·* person is not a party to
	301–28	*T·* : All error tends to harden
	309–25	*t·* and fourth paragraphs,
	318–10	must go on *ad libitum* unto the *t·*
	332–13	*t·* chapter and ninth verse,
	332–23	*t·*, suffering ; fourth, death.
	355–14	the last *t·* pierces itself,
	357–19	*t·* stage of mental growth
Man.	26–12	Every *t·* year Readers shall be
	88–13	shall be elected every *t·* year
Ret.	34–17	*T·* : A person healed by C. S.
	88–17	*T·* : This leads inevitably to
Un.	20– 9	*T·* : I am afraid of it.
	20–14	*T·* : We therefore need not fear it.
	31–13	*t·*, that matter has intelligence ;
	43–24	*t·* chapter of Philippians,
Pan.	7–19	in the *t·* chapter of Genesis,
'01.	8– 6	*t·* person in the Godhead?
Peo.	4–14	would form a *t·* person,
My.	56–30	* second and *t·* being repetitions
	146– 7	since the *t·* century.
	305– 7	S. and H., page 68, *t·* paragraph,
	335–23	* the *t·* day of her husband's illness,
	353–13	*t·*, *Der Herold der C. S.*,

Third Church of Christ, Scientist
London, England
My.	205–13	chapter sub-title
My.	363– 1	* signature

thirst
Mis.	369–26	*t·* for inspiring wine from
Ret.	31–10	and *t·* after divine things,
My.	40– 4	* to those who hunger and *t·*

thirsteth
Mis.	148–29	"Ho, every one that *t·*,— *Isa.* 55 : 1.

thirsting
Mis.	235–18	*t·* after a better life,
My.	15–28	* Seem hungering and *t·*

thirteen
Ret.	4– 1	grandmother had *t·* children,
		(*see also* **values**)

thirtieth
Ret.	33–14	One drop of the *t·* attenuation

thirty
Mis.	161–19	when he was *t·* years of age ;
	163– 4	He had for *t·* years been preparing
	341–24	vow of celibacy for *t·* years,
	382– 7	has cost more than *t·* years of
Man.	84– 9	consist of not more than *t·* pupils.
	84–12	Normal class not exceeding *t·* pupils.
Pul.	vii– 4	during the ensuing *t·* years.
	32–21	* elastic bearing of a woman of *t·*,
	75–19	* to the number of *t·*,
	85– 1	* nearly *t·* years ago began to
'01.	27–16	could start *t·* years ago
Hea.	1–16	* "At *t·*, man suspects himself a fool ;
	13– 6	shaking the preparation *t·* times
My.	70– 4	* organized only *t·* years,
	85– 4	* *T·* years ago it was comparatively

thirty
My. 104–28 learn of her who, t· years ago,
181–21 T· years ago (1866) C. S.
181–25 t· years ago the death-rate was
182– 1 T· years ago Chicago had
182– 3 T· years ago at my request
182– 7 and a membership of t· years
 (*see also* **numbers**)

thirty-eight
 (*see* **numbers**)

thirty-eighth
Mis. 191–12 ninth chapter and t· verse,

thirty-five
Pul. 43– 3 * numbering t· singers in all

thirty-four
Ret. 21– 7 had reached the age of t·,

thirty-one
Ret. 7– 3 passed away at the age of t·,
 (*see also* **numbers**)

thirty-six
 (*see* **numbers**)

thirty-third
Mis. 32–13 commencing at the t· verse,

thirty-three
Mis. 315–13 shall consist of not over t·

thirty-two
My. 69– 3 * lamp of t· candle-power.
70–30 * which is t· feet long.

thistle-down
Mis. 231–21 baby has tumbled, soft as t·

thistles
Mis. 27–17 or figs of t·?'' — *Matt.* 7 : 16.
336–18 grapes of thorns, nor figs of t·.

thither
Mis. 319–22 Take t· thy saintly offerings,
My. 124–23 pointing upward, — T· !
229–13 incentive for going t·.

thitherward
My. 124–25 facts relating to the t·,

Thomas
Mis. 28–15 his doubting disciple, T·.
'01. 7–27 "T·, because thou hast — *John* 20 : 29.

thorn
Mis. 71– 6 Paul had a t· in the flesh :
Un. 57–21 "a t· in the flesh" — *II Cor.* 12 : 7.

Thorne, John C.
My. 174–15 Edward A. Moulton, John C. T·,

thorns
Mis. 27–17 gather grapes of t·, — *Matt.* 7 : 16.
336–18 we gather not grapes of t·,
'02. 18– 9 helped crown with t· the life of
My. 201–13 Even the crown of t·, which

thorny
Un. 58– 5 walked with bleeding feet the t·

thorough
Man. 90– 2 must be t· English scholars.
90–18 Not less than two t· lessons
Ret. 6–17 one of the most , . . t· scholars
48–19 t· understanding of metaphysics,
Rud. 15–18 t· guardianship and grace.
15–22 impossible to teach t· C. S. to
16– 3 a t· knowledge of C. S.,
16– 7 subordinate to t· class instruction
My. 245– 8 t· preparation of the student

thoroughly
Mis. 43–19 time is required t· to qualify
87 24 to study t· the Scriptures
92–19 require the students t· to study it
114–18 They cannot arm too t·
242–29 t· addicted to the use of opium
265–21 After t· explaining spiritual Truth
318–16 afterwards studied t· "S. and H.
375–13 * studied the old masters . . . t·,
375–20 * study each illustration t·,
Man. 39–10 t· to test his sincerity,
49–11 t· understands the practical wisdom
76–22 and keep themselves t· informed
90–23 t· discussed, and understood ;
Ret. 47–20 afterwards studied t· S. and H.,
83–28 necessity of t· understanding
87– 8 more t· and readily acquired
Un. 6–26 are not yet t· drilled in
Pul. 50–21 * t· carried away with the
No. 4– 2 task of learning t· the Science
'02. 5–12 For man to be t· subordinated
My. 59–31 * so t· endorsed or so completely
96–11 * Scientists are t· in earnest
204–19 t· recommend it

Thou
Mis. 63–23 hast T· forsaken me ?'' — *Mark* 15 : 34.
167–24 T· hast hid these things — *Luke* 10 : 21.
331–20 T· Love that guards the nestling's
331–21 Keep T· my child on upward wing
334– 4 What doest T·?'' — *Dan.* 4 : 35.
347–28 None can say . . . What doest T·?
384– 1 poem
384– 6 Come T· ! and now, anew,
385– 5 T· hast heard my prayer ;
385– 8 T·, here and *everywhere.*
388– 7 T· to whose power our hope we give,
389– 8 T· Love that guards the nestling's
389– 9 Keep T· my child on upward wing
398– 5 T· wilt bind the stubborn will,
398–12 And T· know'st Thine own ;
399–13 T· the Christ, and not the creed ;
399–14 T· the Truth in thought and deed ;
399–15 T· the water, the bread, and the
400–23 In the way T· hast,
Ret. 15–10 T· hast taught me — *Psal.* 71 : 17.
46–11 T· wilt bind the stubborn will,
46–18 And T· know'st Thine own.
Pul. 1– 2 T· shalt make them drink — *Psal.* 36 : 8.
3–17 T· shalt make them drink — *Psal.* 36 : 8.
7–30 T· shalt make them drink — *Psal.* 36 : 8.
8–22 T· hast perfected — *Matt.* 21 : 16.
10–27 breathe T· Thy blessing
17–10 T· wilt bind the stubborn will,
17–17 T· know'st Thine own.
No. 45– 1 T· hast hid these things — *Luke* 10 : 21.
'02. 1–13 wrath shalt T· restrain.'' — *Psal.* 76 : 10.
Po. 4– 5 T· Love that guards the nestling's
4– 7 Keep T· my child on upward wing
7– 7 T· to whose power our hope we give,
14– 9 T· wilt bind the stubborn will,
14–16 And T· know'st Thine own ;
22–14 how great, how good T· art
28– 9 Knowing T· knowest best.
28 17 In knowing what T· art !
30–10 T· gildest gladdened joy,
30–12 fan T· the flame
30–17 Lift T· a patient love above
33– 3 Increase T· my faith
page 36 poem
36– 5 Come T· ! and now, anew,
37– 5 T· hast heard my prayer ;
37– 8 T·, here and *everywhere.*
43–21 Just the way T· hast :
69–11 In the way T· hast,
75–20 T· the Christ, and not the creed ;
75–21 T· the Truth in thought and deed ;
75–22 T· the water, the bread, and
77– 8 T· who, impartial, blessings
77–10 T· wisdom, Love, and Truth,
77–15 learned of Truth what T· doest
77–19 T· knowest best !
78– 6 T· knowest best !
78–12 T· knowest best !
My. 4–30 T· God most high and nigh.
151–11 wrath shalt T· restrain.'' — *Psal.* 76 : 10.
220–27 T· knowest best what we need
253–13 T· hast sent me.'' — *John* 17 : 25.
253–17 T· hast given me, — *John* 17 : 11.
280–21 nor say unto Him, What doest T·?
290–14 "T· wilt keep him — *Isa.* 26 : 3.
290–25 T· hearest me always,'' — *John* 11 : 42.
350–12 T· the dark wave treading
350–14 heed'st T· not the scalding tear
350–15 know'st T· not the pathway
350–19 T· all, T· infinite — dost doom above.

thought (noun)
accompanies
Mis. 47–16 sense of the body accompanies t·
according to
Mis. 247 28 reflects , . . according to t·.
Adam's
Ret. 67–23 in no way contingent on Adam's t·,
address the
Mis. 315–24 not silently mentally address the t·,
advancing
Mis. 2– 1 evolutions of advancing t·,
and action
Mis. 255– 8 t· and action on the side of right,
264–12 demands oneness of t· and action.
Ret. 28– 5 guiding our every t· and action ;
81– 6 we should guard t· and action,
Un. 31– 7 to spiritualize t· and action.
Rud. 2–24 bugle-call to t· and action,
8–16 higher condition of t· and action,
Peo. 3–23 limits human t· and action
My. 153–29 to all human t· and action,
and conduct
My. 161–25 because one's t· and conduct

thought (noun)

and deed
Mis. 384– 7   To t· and deed Give sober speed,
    399–14   Thou the Truth in t· and deed ;
Po.   36– 6   To t· and deed Give sober speed,
    75–21   Thou the Truth in t· and deed ;
    79– 8   raise up seed — in t· and deed
and desire
Mis. 15–10   Christianization— of t· and desire,
and knowledge
Mis. 68–23   * necessary to t· and knowledge ;
and method
No.   12–21   spiritualization of t· and method,
another's
Mis. 97– 6   transmitted to another's t· from the
any other
My. 324–16   * any other t· but that you were
ascends
Mis. 96–12   as t· ascends the scale of being
atmosphere of
Mis. 12–32   radius of our atmosphere of t·.
awakened
Mis. 123–20   there has risen to the awakened t·
begins
Peo.   3–20   t· begins wrongly to apprehend the
budding
Mis. 330–18   arranging . . . each budding t·.
Man. 104– 8   adapted to form the budding t·
causes
Mis. 138– 4   if it causes t· to wander
chambers of
My. 156–19   upper chambers of t· prepared for
child's
Mis. 51–17   make clear to the child's t·
classifies
Mis. 252– 8   C. S. classifies t· thus :
collisions of
Un.   6–12   forcible collisions of t·
continue in
Mis. 42– 2   or does life continue in t· only
continuity of
My. 53–30   * even though the continuity of t·
deed and
My.   9–10   * glory in every good deed and t·
desire and
Pul. 55–20   * has its origin in desire and t·.
destroy the
Mis. 37–20   can and does destroy the t· that
    105–28   Destroy the t· of sin, sickness, death,
divine
Un.   5– 5   toward the perfect t· divine.
dominant
Ret. 20–24   My dominant t· in marrying again
dwell in
Mis. 309– 1   and not to dwell in t· upon their
dwells in God
Mis. 290–23   When t· dwells in God,
early
Mis. 240–19   easier to incline the early t·
encompass
Ret. 68–21   Darkness and doubt encompass t·,
enlightened
My. 187– 7   lighteth every enlightened t·
error in
Hea.   7– 3   and, correcting error in t·,
error of
No.   4–13   error of t· becomes fable
My. 211–16   impels . . . into error of t·,
errors of
Rud. 10–13   ills are but errors of t·,
every
Mis. 85– 9   every t· and act leading to good.
    139–13   into captivity every t· — II Cor. 10 : 5.
Ret. 28– 5   guiding our every t·
My. 345– 5   But every t· tells,
evil
Pul. 29–23   * cast out the demons of evil t·.
exist in
'01. 14– 9   evil, . . . does exist in t· ;
expressed the
My. 60–10   * He only expressed the t· of
faith-lighted
Mis. 15–22   What a faith-lighted t· is this !
fibres of
Mis. 142–27   touched tender fibres of t·,
finite
Rud. 2–21   assigned to God by finite t·,
flow of
'00.   9–20   in the ebb and flow of t·
footsteps of
Peo. 1– 8   footsteps of t·, as they pass
forbids the
'02.   6– 1   forbids the t· of any other
forms of
Mis. 91–19   forms of t· and worship

thought (noun)

freer breath to
Hea.   4– 4   give freer breath to t·
gardens of
Mis. 343–13   clearing the gardens of t·
general
Mis.   8– 4   bring to the general t·
My. 159–28   general t· chiefly regards
great
No.   25– 1   Simply uttering this great t·
guide
Mis. 64–17   ethics which guide t· spiritually
harmonious
Mis. 220–13   the harmonious t· has the full
has shrunk
Mis. 236– 6   until t· has shrunk from
heavens of
Mis. 355–31   will span thy heavens of t·.
helm of
Mis. 113–26   when Love is at the helm of t·,
her
Po.   v–15   * began to take form in her t·,
higher
Pul. 2– 9   there is a t· higher and deeper
his
Mis. 374–29   between the thinker and his t·
his own
Mis. 93– 1   spiritualizes his own t·,
    265– 1   intentionally offers his own t·,
holding in
Mis. 62– 5   holding in t· the form of a
human
    (see **human**)
imagery of
Mis. 142–20   imagery of t· gave place to
images of
Mis. 96–29   transference of human images of t·
improve the
My. 10– 3   * C. S. should improve the t·,
inclining
My. 261–12   and inclining t· of childhood.
individual
Un.   5–18   or enlighten the individual t·.
No.   1–21   correcting the individual t·,
infant
Mis. 293– 2   the infant t· in C. S.
infantile
Mis. 167– 2   the infantile t· of God's man,
involuntary
Hea. 12–22   without the involuntary t·,
is developed
Mis. 15–28   By suffering . . . t· is developed
is spiritualized
My. 126–32   whereby t· is spiritualized,
is the essence
Peo. 10– 1   T· is the essence of an act,
jewels of
Mis. 313–13   jewels of t·, so adapted to
labors, and
My. 137–18   my time, labors, and t·,
let loose
My. 110–17   luxury of t· let loose,
liberated
Mis. 41– 3   power of liberated t· to do good,
    67– 1   to support the liberated t·
line of
Mis. 3–16   this line of t· or action.
    186–28   proceeds in this line of t·,
    188–20   in the intermediate line of t·,
lines of
Mis. 291–29   sentinels along the lines of t·,
My. 124–20   between these lines of t· is written
little
My. 288– 4   gives little t· to self-defence ;
lofty trend of
Po. vii– 3   * by the same lofty trend of t·
loving
Mis. xii– 4   interluding with loving t·
made manifest
Mis. 34– 8   physique is simply t· made manifest.
master's
Mis. 373–19   This master's t· presents a sketch
material
Mis. 102–26   state of mortal and material t·.
Peo. 3–17   Truth meets the old material t·
My. 267–24   Material t· tends to obscure
moment's
My. 144– 5   spare not a moment's t· to
more
Mis. 7–32   More t· is given to material
mortal
    (see **mortal**)
mounted
My. 115– 1   mounted t· on the swift and
movement of
Mis. 235–21   This movement of t· must push on

thought (noun)

must be spiritualized
Ret. 28– 9 t must be spiritualized,
Pul. 35–13 t must be spiritualized

my
Mis. vii– 4 * my t looks Upon thy
279–14 present themselves to my t ;
357–22 clear to my t that those students
'00. 11–21 Adelaide A. Proctor breathes my t :
'01. 32–24 educated my t many years,
My. 268–20 flutters in my t as an unreal shadow,

nature as
Mis. 331–25 Science evolved nature as t,

night
My. 110–20 night t, methinks, should unfold
110–23 night t should show us

no
Mis. 391–12 It stirs no t of strife ;
Po. 38–11 It stirs no t of strife ;
My. 13– 2 taking no t for the morrow,

objects of
Peo. 7–26 its subjects and objects of t,

ocean of
No. 29–23 driftwood on the ocean of t ;

of contempt
My. 324– 3 * a t of contempt for the unlearned,

of fleshly sacrifice
Mis. 345–31 away from the t of fleshly sacrifice,

of sin
Mis. 105–28 Destroy the t of sin,
Un. 15–17 if the t of sin could be possible

or action
Mis. 3–16 this line of t or action.
260– 7 the line of Jesus' t or action.
My. 278–30 brings into human t or action
308– 7 aroused to t or action

or word
Mis. 387–15 By t or word unkind,
Po. 6–10 By t or word unkind,

our
Un. 49–21 masquerades as the real, in our t.

our own
Mis. 224– 1 unless our own t barbs it.
My. 213–17 impulses of our own t,

pearls of
Mis. 211–20 trample on your pearls of t,

phases of
Mis. 60–18 in different phases of t,

pleasant
No. 39–27 to portray the face of pleasant t.

power of
Hea. 12–18 power of t brought to bear on the

power was the
Hea. 12– 24 prove that the power was the t,

preoccupied in
Mis. 47–10 preoccupied in t when moving your

present to the
Un. 54– 6 If the claim be present to the t,

procurator of the
Rud. 10–16 fear is the procurator of the t

public
Mis. 78–23 public t concerning it.
Peo. 11–23 leaders of public t who are mistaken
My. 129– 7 taking strong hold of the public t
224– 9 Hurried conclusions as to the public t
226–28 until the public t becomes

purest
Po. vii–12 * these gems of purest t

purify
Mis. 341– 6 purify t, then put thought into

purifying
Mis. 7–24 with healing, purifying t.

quality of
My. 249–29 devout, unselfed quality of t

quiet
Man. 94–12 in quiet t on that subject.

random
Mis. 264– 2 every random t in line with mine.

reaches the
Hea. 8–13 reaches the t that has produced this,

reach, in
Un. 49–12 I reach, in t, a glorified

realms of
Ret. 73–11 and purer realms of t.

reciprocal
Mis. 265–19 whole line of reciprocal t.

reflects
Peo. 10–22 the images that t reflects

replenish
Mis. 92– 8 His work is to replenish t,

ridding the
Ret. 79–11 ridding the t of effete doctrines,

right
Rud. 9–21 power of a scientific, right t,

satisfies the
Rud. 15– 7 this holds and satisfies the t

---

thought (noun)

scale of
My. 152– 7 far lower in the scale of t,

scientific
Mis. 156– 2 swift vehicle of scientific t ;
Un. 5–25 shadowed forth in scientific t.

second
No. 19– 8 sober second t of advancing

seed of
Mis. 83– 9 *springing from a seed of t,*

sensuous
No. 26–10 Theirs is the sensuous t,

serious
Pul. 33–20 * high counsel and serious t.

shadows of
Mis. 352–12 human shadows of t lengthen

silent
Ret. 61– 6 unconsciously in the silent t,

spiritual
My. 136–28 peace, and time for spiritual t
238–16 swift pinions of spiritual t

spiritualization of
Mis. 42–11 spiritualization of t is not attained by
Un. 32–12 spiritualization of t destroys
No. 12–21 impels a spiritualization of t

spiritualize
Ret. 82–30 better adapted to spiritualize t
Un. 31– 7 to spiritualize t and action.
Hea. 19–17 We need it . . . to spiritualize t,

spiritualized
My. 355– 3 * to see in her spiritualized t

standpoint of
Mis. 185–31 spake from their standpoint of t ;

state of
Mis. 105–25 their own subjective state of t.
My. 221–26 correct or incorrect state of t,

states of
Rud. 10–10 the subjective states of t,

status of
Mis. 264–25 moral and spiritual status of t

struggling
No. 40–22 the t struggling for freedom.

student's
Mis. 349– 9 materialization of a student's t,

take no
Mis. 245– 3 "Take no t,— Matt. 6 : 31.
Rud. 12–23 "Take no t — Matt. 6 : 25.

temperate in
Ret. 79–22 Be temperate in t, word, and

temple of
Mis. 369–13 portals of the temple of t,

thing of
Rud. 10–15 Disease is a thing of t

this
Mis. 5–30 seem solid substance to this t.
346– 2 carries this t even higher,

throes of
Peo. 1–15 throes of t are unheard,

thy
Pul. 55– 4 * Nature's marvel in thy t."

time and
Mis. 119– 7 occupy time and t ;
Hea. 12–20 To prepare . . . requires time and t ;

time nor
Un. 11–24 neither cycles of time nor t

to lift
Ret. 73–14 I endeavored to lift t above

touches
My. 287–22 touches t to spiritual issues,

transference of
Ret. 68–18 and the transference of t,

transfigures
No. 26–12 idea which transfigures t.

treasures of
'01. 1–13 to add to your treasures of t

trend of
My. 305–31 was not the trend of t,

true
Mis. 156–23 the basis of all true t
My. 159–15 true t escapes from the inward

unanimity of
My. 29–18 * unanimity of t and of purpose.

unbiased
Mis. 240–23 over the fresh, unbiased t.

unconscious
Hea. 6–24 back in the unconscious t,

underlying
Un. 50–15 express the underlying t.

unfolds the
My. 164–24 unity, which unfolds the t

unity of
My. 24–12 * unity of t and purpose

unprepared
Mis. 307–22 before the unprepared t.

unspoken
Mis. 55–11 power of the unspoken t,

thought (noun)

unworthy of
Mis. 271–16 subject that is unworthy of *t*·,

vein of
Mis. 379–11 usually ran in the vein of *t*·

vocabulary of
No. 10– 6 words in the vocabulary of *t*·

waiting
Un. 7–19 pour into my waiting *t*·

weight of
My. 146–30 lays his whole weight of *t*·,

white-robed
Peo. 5–18 white-robed *t*· points away from

will enable
Ret. 88–12 as will enable *t*· to apprehend

woman's
Un. 57–12 influence of the woman's *t*· ;

world's
Pul. 51–27 * cannot absorb the world's *t*·.

your
Mis. 14– 2 Divest your *t*·, then, of
  290–16 * I felt the influence of your *t*·
  322–16 your *t*· must not be diverted
My. 8– 7 * beyond resistance in your *t*·."
  128–32 take no root in your *t*·
  216–20 which I present to your *t*·.

your own
Mis. 83– 9 your own *t*· or another's."
  83–14 at the door of your own *t*·

Mis. xi–24 *t*· sometimes walks in memory,
  4– 1 *T*· imbued with purity, Truth, and
  46–27 *t*· has not yet wholly attained unto
  53–27 *t*· educated away from it
  88–11 whose *t*· is appreciated by many
  117– 5 discern between the *t*·, motive, and
  271– 4 a *t*·, instead of a thing.
  331–26 evolved . . . *t*· as things.
  341– 6 then put *t*· into words,
  343– 7 *T*· must be made better,
  364–15 *t*·, extension, cause, and effect ;
Pul. 79–26 * the *t*· of the world's scientific
No. 21– 9 all time, space, immortality, *t*·,
'01. 28–30 Has the *t*· come to . . . Scientists,
'02. 19–18 The *t*· of it stills complaint ;
Po. 23– 4 a *t*· of vanished hours
  67– 5 And *t*· be at work with
My. 55– 7 * the *t*· of obtaining a church
  131–15 may *t*· soar and Soul be.
  154– 9 to infringe . . . even in *t*·.
  205–17 * "As the *t*· is, so is the deed ;
  271–14 * followers of the *t*· that has
  272–30 * in this presentation of the *t*· of
  324–18 * too honorable to allow the *t*·

thought (verb)
Mis. 11– 7 I *t*·, also, that if I
  44–17 What you *t*· was pain in the bone
  58– 6 proves to him who *t*· he died
  67–15 nor cause it to be *t*·.
  108–29 What would be *t*· of a
  108–32 What should be *t*· of an individual
  109– 5 or mayhap never have *t*· of,
  138–17 I once *t*· that in unity
  158– 6 I little *t*· of the changes
  239–15 *t*· I, "somebody has to take it ;
  239–28 and which mamma *t*· must be
  263–15 chapter sub-title
  265– 4 in order to be *t*· original,
  290–18 I had not *t*· of the writer
  307–14 *t*· best to stop its publication.
  359– 9 I *t*· as a child :— I Cor. 13 : 11.
  376–30 Then *t*· I, What are we,
Ret. 8– 5 I *t*· this was my mother's voice,
  38–13 I had not *t*· of such a result,
Pul. 34–15 "and they *t*· I had died,
  44– 7 * I *t*· you would willingly pause
  57–13 * Whatever may be *t*· of the peculiar
'01. 14–24 Wrong is *t*· before it is acted ;
Hea. 9– 6 The less said or *t*· of sin,
My. 26–16 I *t*· it better to be brief
  56– 1 * it was *t*· the seating capacity
  59– 6 * we *t*· this might be true
  59–21 * I *t*· of the little melodeon
  60– 4 * if Mrs. Eddy *t*· it wise to
  61– 6 * At first I *t*· that, since
  61–27 * I have often stood . . . and *t*·,
  64– 1 * As one *t*· upon the significance
  104– 3 *t*· that the learned St. Paul,
  104–11 what would be *t*· to-day of
  104–12 what will be *t*· to-morrow of
  135– 4 I *t*· as a child :— I Cor. 13 : 11.
  185–11 wherever *t*·, felt, spoken,
  306–11 than to be *t*· great.
  319–15 * what he himself *t*·
  324–10 * he often hinted that he *t*·

thought (verb)
My. 324–20 * the impression that he *t*·
  324–21 * always *t*· that Mr. Wiggin
  345– 4 not . . . *t*· to matter much.

thoughtful
Pul. 80–24 * more *t*· and devout ;

thought-leaflet
Mis. 360–19 shall lift every *t*· Spiritward ;

thoughts

adverse
My. 41– 9 * *t*· adverse to the law of love.

all
Mis. 37– 5 all *t*· and desires that draw
My. 114–19 All *t*· in the line of Scriptural

and actions
Mis. 280– 5 to weigh the *t*· and actions
  291–10 other people's *t*· and actions.

and acts
Mis. 46–18 weight of his *t*· and acts
  119– 3 responsible for our *t*· and acts ;
Hea. 5–22 of our own *t*· and acts ;
My. 352–13 * so reflect in our *t*· and acts

and being
Mis. 42– 9 with *t*·, and being, as material as

angelic
Ret. 85–11 angelic *t*· ascend and descend,

are outlined
Mis. 103–13 *t*· are outlined, individualized

are things
Pul. 80–26 * belief that "*t*· are things,"

aroused
Ret. 13–10 perturbed was I by the *t*· aroused

borrows the
My. 224–17 when he borrows the *t*·,

crowding
My. 323–20 * crowding *t*· of gratitude

evil
Mis. 18–26 into a state of evil *t*·,
  252–11 evil *t*· are impotent,

first
Ret. 27–21 ripples in one's first *t*·

good
Mis. 252–10 Good *t*· are potent ;
Pul. 69–12 * so fill the mind with good *t*·
'00. 8–11 he may steal other people's good *t*·,
My. 210– 7 Good *t*· are an impervious armor ;

healthy
Mis. 252–14 healthy *t*· are reality and

her
Mis. 169– 3 whenever her *t*· had wandered

high
Mis. 86–26 subjective state of high *t*·.

his
Mis. 46–18 to throw the weight of his *t*·
  59–24 leading his *t*· away from the
  283– 5 upset, and adjust his *t*·
'00. 3– 2 his *t*· are right, active, and
My. 210–16 His *t*· can only reflect peace,
  324– 1 * He often spoke his *t*· freely

his own
Mis. 126– 9 has his own *t*· to guard,
Ret. 84– 5 to spiritualize his own *t*·

holy
Mis. 280– 7 messengers of pure and holy *t*·
  387–18 holy *t*· and heavenly strain,
Po. 6–13 holy *t*· and heavenly strain,

human
Mis. 393–10 the misty Mine of human *t*·,
Un. 21– 2 wherein human *t*· are
Po. 51–15 the misty Mine of human *t*·,

illumed
Mis. 396–23 throng Of *t*·, illumed By faith,
Pul. 18– 7 throng Of *t*·, illumed By faith,
Po. 12– 7 throng Of *t*·, illumed By faith,

imperative
Mis. 288– 6 Positive and imperative *t*·

indicate
No. 11–10 which must be used to indicate *t*·

kind
My. 236– 3 love for them and their kind *t*·.

little
My. 247–17 Then I fed these sweet little *t*·

my
Mis. 291–15 to be benefited by my *t*·
Ret. 14–26 and know my *t*· :— Psal. 139 : 23.
  48– 7 recent experience . . . fresh in my *t*·,
Po. 65–12 My *t*· 'neath thy drap'ry
My. 33–11 and know my *t*· :— Psal. 139 : 23.
  39–21 * My *t*· revert to a former

no sinful
Mis. 198– 2 When . . . man has no sinful *t*·

of men
Peo. 3–18 while it inscribes on the *t*· of men

thoughts

  of others
    Un. 56–18 suffered from the *t·* of others.
    '01. 20– 3 influencing the *t·* of others,
  of the practitioner
    Rud. 9–24 *t·* of the practitioner should be
  of you
    Pul. 40– 2 * *t·* of you forever cling to me :
  our
    Mis. 119– 3 responsible for our *t·* and acts ;
    136–17 All our *t·* should be given to
    '02. 4–28 Our *t·* of the Bible utter our lives.
    Hea. 9– 4 employed our *t·* more in
    Peo. 7–30 our *t·* must spiritualize
    7–32 to accord with our *t·*.
    14– 3 clothe our *t·* of death with
    My. 203–15 Our *t·* beget our actions ;
    352–13 * so reflect in our *t·* and acts
  overflowing
    Mis. 310–25 chapter sub-title
  people's
    Ret. 89–27 upon other people's *t·*,
  right
    Mis. 252– 8 Right *t·* are reality and power ;
    My. 283–14 Right *t·* and deeds are the
  scientific
    Ret. 68–26 scientific *t·* are true thoughts,
  self-respected
    Mis. 227–21 wherein calm, self-respected *t·* abide
  sick
    Mis. 252–13 learn that sick *t·* are unreality
  sick man's
    Mis. 220–10 to refute the sick man's *t·*,
  sick-producing
    Pul. 69–11 * from evil and sick-producing *t·*,
  spiritual
    My. 261–28 Virgin Mary's spiritual *t·* of Life
  such
    Mis. 378–22 are farther removed from such *t·*
    Un. 60– 1 From such *t·* — mortal inventions,
    No. 27–25 In presence of such *t·*
  that express
    '01. 7–13 the *t·* that express the different
  their
    Mis. 92–21 for this spiritualizes their *t·*.
    My. 186– 6 preen their *t·* for upward flight.
    355–24 their *t·* are upward ;
  their own
    Mis. 114– 8 the trend of their own *t·* ;
    Un. 43–21 unite the influence of their own *t·*
    Pul. vii– 8 inclination given their own *t·*
    My. vii– 6 * can so protect their own *t·*
  thy
    Mis. 338–26 * "Think truly, and thy *t·*
  transcribing
    Mis. 187–15 their transcribing *t·* were not
  true
    Mis. 22–16 true *t·* revolve in God's orbits :
    Ret. 68–26 scientific thoughts are true *t·*,
  woman's
    '02. 8–24 woman's *t·* . . . hallow the
  works and
    Ret. 64–18 God's ways and works and *t·*
  wrong
    Mis. 252– 9 wrong *t·* are unreality and powerless,
    Rud. 12– 6 Wrong *t·* and methods
  your
    My. 210–10 all whom your *t·* rest upon
    213–20 Watch your *t·*, and see whether
    256–11 forming themselves in your *t·*
  your own
    My. 130– 2 guard your own *t·*

    Mis. 152– 7 *t·* winged with peace and love
    169–29 * *t·* when rightly understood.
    Ret. 76– 9 *T·* touched with the Spirit
    No. 40–11 *t·* are our honest conviction.

Thoughts on the Apocalypse
  My. 13– 4 * book title

thought-tired
  Mis. 125–27 *t·*, turns to-day to you ;

thousand
  My. 91–21 * The few *t·* persons who followed
  332– 2 * more than a *t·* miles,
  (*see also* **numbers, values**)

thousandfold
  My. 164–23 *t·* expansion that will engirdle the

thousands
  Mis. ix– 7 among my *t·* of students
  54– 8 *T·* in the field of metaphysical
  Pul. 58– 8 * *t·* of believers throughout this
  60–14 * among the *t·* of adherents
  71–21 * *t·* throughout the United States
  No. 32–25 Cause which is healing its *t·*

thousands
  My. 24–10 * prayers and offerings of the *t·*
  28–15 * influence upon the lives of *t·*
  29–19 * emanating from the *t·* who
  29–27 * *t·* who began to congregate
  31–15 * *t·* had been seated,
  47– 4 * *t·* of Christian Scientists
  58–28 * Of the many *t·* who attended
  59–10 * by the hundreds of *t·*
  63–27 * the *t·* who had come,
  76–11 * by the *t·* of church members
  80– 4 * assure *t·* of auditors
  85–23 * its *t·* of worshippers,
  86– 9 * *T·* of Christian Scientists
  90– 1 * should number many *t·*
  90–8, 9 * *T·* upon *t·* believe that it
  92–17 * from . . . to hundreds of *t·*,
  93–31 * number hundreds of *t·*,
  100–14 * members are numbered by *t·*
  111–30, 31 *t·* upon *t·* attest with their
  113– 1 and in *t·* of homes,
  173–13 *t·* here yesterday ;
  228– 3 *t·* are healed by learning that
  271–17 * beloved of *t·* of believers
  293– 9 *t·* of others believed the same,
  293–10 Hundreds of *t·* who prayed for him

thousandth
  (*see* **numbers**)

thraldom
  Mis. 86–30 even this pleasing *t·*,
  101– 4 departing from the *t·* of the senses

thraldoms
  Pul. 55–11 * *t·*, prejudices, and oppressions

thrall
  No. 11–26 rescue reason from the *t·* of error.
  '00. 6–22 lifts him from the stubborn *t·* of sin
  Po. 79–15 lifteth me, Ayont hate's *t·* :

thread
  Mis. 99– 5 To weave one *t·* of Science

threaten
  Ret. 81– 2 *t·* to paralyze its beneficence.

threatened
  Peo. 13–18 *t·* to let loose the wild beasts
  My. 196–18 he *t·* not ; — *I Pet.* 2 : 23.

threatening
  My. 129– 3 danger *t·* our nation,

threatens
  My. v–10 * popularity *t·* to supersede

threats
  '02. 15– 2 contained *t·* to blow up the hall

three
  Mis. 51– 7 All mesmerism is of one of *t·* kinds;
  69–15 *t·* doses of Croton oil,
  107–14 *T·* cardinal points must be gained
  107–19 false senses pass through *t·* states
  133–22 *T·* times a day, I retire to
  136–24 hold *t·* sessions annually,
  143–22 within about *t·* months,
  166–22 hid in *t·* measures of meal,
  171–24 *in t· measures of meal,* *Matt.* 13 · 33.
  172–13 until the *t·* measures be
  174–30 hid in *t·* measures of meal,
  175– 5 The *t·* measures of meal may well be
  177–23 * *t·* o'clock, the hour for the
  230– 0 *T·* ways of wasting time,
  231–19 walking one, two, *t·* steps,
  242–24 to cure that habit in *t·* days,
  273–29 *t·* classes . . . would be delayed.
  279–13 *t·* picture-stories from the Bible
  279–14 *t·* of those pictures from which we
  315–11 teach annually *t·* classes only.
  315–23 as often as once in *t·* months.
  349– 5 twelve lessons, *t·* weeks' time,
  355–11 through *t·* stages of growth.
  Man. 36–20 recommendation signed by *t·* members
  68–14 remain with her *t·* consecutive years,
  76–17 shall consist of *t·* members
  79– 4 not less than *t·* loyal members
  88– 7 consisting of *t·* members,
  91–24 once in *t·* years
  91–25 for *t· consecutive* years under
  98–25 the *t·* largest branch churches
  99– 8 its *t·* largest branch churches,
  102– 5 consisting of not less than *t·* members,
  Ret. 4–12 undulating lands of *t·* townships.
  8– 5 *t·* times, in an ascending scale.
  8–10 call *Mary*, *t·* times !"
  50– 7 tuition lasting barely *t·* weeks.
  Un. 20– 5 Through these *t·* statements,
  33–24 two or *t·* witnesses — *Matt.* 18 : 16.
  Pul. vii– 4 *T·* quarters of a century hence,
  3– 5 and in *t·* days — *John* 2 : 19.
  6–14 * I had not read *t·* pages before I

three

Pul.	27– 7	* *t·* large class-rooms and the pastor's
	27–30	* composed of *t·* separate panels,
	61–11	* *t·* affecting great and pedal
	61–11	* *t·* affecting swell and pedal
Rud.	2– 6	one of the *t·* subjects,
	8– 1	the *t·* great kingdoms.
No.	30–11	God's law is in *t·* words,
Pan.	7–14	We know of but *t·* theistic religions,
'00.	2– 9	*t·* types of human nature
'01.	4– 5	four times *t·* is twelve,
	4– 5	*t·* times four is twelve.
	4–23	One instead of *t·*,
	4–26	these *t·* are one in essence
	6– 2	theology's *t·* divine persons
	6– 6	which reckons *t·* as one
	6–12	Who can conceive . . . of *t·* infinites?
	6–15	must be One although He is *t·*.
	17–17	in from one to *t·* interviews,
	22–17	do not say that one added to one is *t·*,
	23– 1	neither more nor less than *t·* ;
	27–14	in one to *t·* interviews
	27–28	* truth goes through *t·* stages.
'02.	2–16	hid in *t·* measures of meal,
Hea.	3–26	*t·* statements of one Principle.
Peo.	4–19	*t·* terms for one divine Principle
	4–19	are the *t·* in one
Po.	68–17	when *we* *t·* met,
My.	56–12	* *t·* branch churches were organized,
	56–19	* *t·* foregoing named churches
	56–29	* *t·* services were held each Sunday,
	69–17	* and *t·* at the back,
	70–27	* *t·* balanced swells,
	74– 4	* within two or *t·* days' ride,
	80–29	* *t·* o'clock in the afternoon
	157–22	deed of trust to *t·* individuals
	213–28	*t·* quotations from "S. and H.
	214–11	Jesus' *t·* days' work in the sepulchre
	227–11	one out of *t·* of their patients,
	243–15	to take charge of *t·* or more churches.
	244–26	not exceed *t·* in number.
	250– 3	*t·* years' term for church Readers,
	253–23	a store of wisdom in *t·* words :
	304–25	* truth goes through *t·* stages.

(*see also* **dates, numbers, persons, values, years**)

threefold
Un.	55–15	This *t·* Messiah reveals the

three-in-one
Mis.	163– 1	sought to conquer the *t·* of error :

three-manual
Pul.	60–22	* It is of *t·* compass,

three-years
Mis.	163– 5	his *t·* mission was a marvel of

threshold
Mis.	120– 3	at the very *t·* of C. S. :
	324– 4	Pausing at the *t·* of a palatial
My.	264– 9	* *t·* of the twentieth century,

thrice
Ret.	8–19	same call was *t·* repeated.

thrifty
Mis.	329– 6	nature like a *t·* housewife

thrill
Mis.	106–29	strains that *t·* the chords of feeling
	132–26	with a *t·* of pleasure that I read
	375–27	* "It gave me such a *t·* of joy
Ret.	12– 5	echoes still my day-dreams *t·*,
Po.	16–17	send a *t·* To the heart of the leaves
	61– 3	echoes still my day-dreams *t·*,
	66– 4	like the *t·* of that mountain rill,

thrilled
Pul.	31–17	* largely *t·* and pervaded by a
No.	1–10	So men, when *t·* by a new idea,
My.	39–25	* hearts were *t·* by her compassion,
	64– 6	* *t·* with tender gratitude

thrills
My.	125–18	which always *t·* the soul.

thrive
Mis.	80–21	Tyranny can *t·* but feebly under our
My.	4–19	they *t·* together,

thrives
My.	139–10	Scientist *t·* in adversity ;
	165– 9	by this spirit man lives and *t·*,

throb
Mis.	152–13	pulsates with every *t·* of theirs

throbbing
My.	159– 8	the *t·* of every pulse

throbbings
Peo.	1–15	ceaseless *t·* and throes of thought

throe
Mis.	285–22	some extra *t·* of error

throes
Un.	57–25	Mortal *t·* of anguish
Peo.	1–15	throbbings and *t·* of thought

throne
Mis.	67–31	taken up to the very *t·*,
	73–24	*t·* of his glory, — *Matt.* 19 : 28.
	328–31	up to the *t·* of everlasting glory.
	368– 7	* Wrong forever on the *t·*.
	388–16	Her dazzling crown, her sceptred *t·*,
Ret.	22–13	the *t·* of God." — *Heb.* 12 : 2.
Pul.	82– 2	* brain for its great white *t·*.
Rud.	10– 1	unjust usurper of the *t·*
No.	34–24	mounting to the *t·* of glory
'00.	10–22	habitation of His *t·* forever.
Po.	21– 5	Her dazzling crown, her sceptered *t·*,
	26– 9	grasped the sword to hold her *t·*,
	31– 4	seed dropped from Love's *t·*.
	39– 8	from its altar to Thy *t·*
My.	258–16	the *t·* of God." — *Heb.* 12 : 2.

thrones
Mis.	73–25	*shall sit upon twelve t·*, — *Matt.* 19 : 28.
Po.	79– 6	of these stones, or tyrants' *t·*,
My.	200–22	on crumbling *t·* of justice

throng
Mis.	396–22	wake a white-winged angel *t·*
Ret.	8– 2	*t·* the chambers of memory.
Pul.	18– 6	wake a white-winged angel *t·*
	29–14	* for the overflowing *t·*.
	39–24	* I see the hurrying *t·*
	41–18	* incapable of receiving this vast *t·*,
	54– 4	* We touch him in life's *t·*
	61–25	* attracted quite a *t·* of people,
Po.	12– 6	wake a white-winged angel *t·*
	25– 6	What a shadowy *t·*
My.	79–18	* not a gathering of "the vulgar *t·* ;"
	86–29	* could accommodate the *t·*
	189–29	why *t·* in pity round me?

thronged
Pul.	29–10	* was *t·* with a congregation
	57– 7	* was *t·* at the four services

throngs
My.	80–25	* to accommodate the great *t·*

throttle
My.	26–21	Now is the time to *t·* *the lie*

throttled
Mis.	286– 5	can neither be obscured nor *t·*.

throughout
Mis.	12– 4	*t·* time and beyond the grave.
	92–15	*T·* his entire explanations,
	113–32	spiritual animus is felt *t·* the land.
	127– 3	*T·* my entire connection with The
	192–27	extends . . . *t·* all Christendom.
	204– 7	attended *t·* with doubt, hope,
	217–13	Nature declares, *t·* the mineral,
	236– 3	*T·* our experience since
	278– 8	*t·* my labors, and in my history
	312–26	emphasis *t·* the entire centuries,
	314– 1	*t·* our land and in other lands.
	364–24	*t·* time and eternity.
Man.	60– 3	Continued *T·* the Year.
	97– 8	*t·* the United States, Canada,
Ret.	7–10	* incessant study *t·* his short life.
	20–13	I knelt by his side *t·* the dark
	21–10	*t·* the war for the Union,
	84– 9	*T·* his entire explanations
Un.	46–22	extend *t·* the universe,
	51–21	eternally radiating *t·* all space
Pul.	8– 2	*t·* our land the press has spoken
	24–25	* The architecture is Romanesque *t·*.
	58– 8	* believers *t·* this country
	60–21	* pneumatic wind-chests *t·*,
	63– 5	* An Immense Following *T·* the
	71–21	* thousands *t·* the United States
'01.	11–18	and obeyed *t·* the week,
My.	17–31	*T·* my entire connection with The
	20– 1	*t·* the whole world, — *Mark* 14 : 9.
	31– 2	* following hymns *t·* the day :
	111–16	*t·* is logical in premise and in
	129– 7	*t·* our beloved country
	174– 9	courtesy . . . extended to me *t·*.
	175–21	to macadamize North State Street *t·*
	185– 1	acceptance *t·* the earth,
	240– 3	acknowledged *t·* the earth.
	301–19	*t·* the entire testimony of the

(*see also* **world**)

throw
Mis.	46–17	*t·* the weight of his thoughts
	255– 7	to *t·* the weight of thought
	275–19	*t·* wide the gates of heaven.
	313– 9	*t·* the light of penetration on
	325–11	*t·* them away, and afterwards try to
Un.	15– 5	which God never can *t·* off?
'02.	16–16	and they *t·* a light upon the

throwing
My. 174– 2   *t·* open their doors for the
   221–28   thus *t·* the door wide open

thrown
Mis. 23–28   likeness *t·* upon the mirror
   264– 8   *t·* upon the mists of time,
My. 31–10   * doors of the church were *t·* open
   73–18   * headquarters was *t·* open

throws
Pul. 39–16   * *T·* o'er the Charles its flood of

thrust
Mis. 84– 7   prophets *t·* disputed points
Ret. 90– 1   not to *t·* aside Science,
'02. 18– 4   spectacle of sin *t·* upon the
My. 161–13   yourselves *t·* out."— Luke 13 : 28.
   269–17   God hath *t·* in the sickle,

Thummim
Mis. 194– 7   *T·* of priestly office,
Ret. 35–23   *T·* of priestly office,
'01. 12–13   *T·* of priestly office,

thunder
Mis. 277–29   I *t·* His law to the sinner,
   374–13   hatred — earth's harmless *t·*
'00. 9–15   his lightning, *t·*, and sunshine
'02. 5–21   voiced in the *t·* of Sinai,

thunderbolt
Un. 46–24   earthquake, *t·*, and tempest.
'01. 15–21   *t·* of Jonathan Edwards :
Hea. 2– 6   hurls the *t·* of truth,

thunderbolts
My. 149–28   in the sky with dumb *t·*,
   265–27   clearer skies, less *t·*, tornadoes,

thundered
Mis. 106–10   Volleyed and *t·* !

thunderings
Mis. 17– 2   You hear and record the *t·* of

thunders
Ret. 9–21   * where dying *t·* roll

Thursday
My. 333–21   * died on *T·* night,

thwarted
Mis. 11– 2   *t·*, its punishment is tenfold.

Thy and thy
Mis. 83–25   glorify *T·* Son,— John 17 : 1.
   80–25   *T·* Son also may glorify — John 17 : 1.
   159–25   *T·* children grown to behold Thee !
   174–25   " *T·* kingdom come ; " — Matt. 6 : 10.
   208– 1   chapter sub-title — Matt. 6 : 10.
   208–23   kept *T·* word," — Psal. 119 : 67.
   211–30   " *T·* kingdom come." — Matt. 6 : 10.
   248– 7   works of *T·* hands." — Psal. 92 : 4.
   275–17   *T·* light and *T·* love reach earth,
   384– 9   *T·* will to know, and do.
   385– 7   This is *T·* high behest :
   387– 8   Brood o'er us with *T·* shelt'ring
   388– 9   Fed by *T·* love divine we live,
   397–25   How to feed *T·* sheep ;
   398– 1   I will listen for *T·* voice,
   398–15   Lead *T·* lambkins to the fold,
Man. 41–21   " *T·* kingdom come ; " — Matt. 6 : 10.
   41–23   may *T·* Word enrich the affections
Ret. 9–11   *T·* servant heareth." — I Sam. 3 : 9.
   15– 9   mention of *T·* righteousness, — Psal. 71 : 16.
   15–11   *T·* wondrous works." — Psal. 71 : 17.
   46– 6   How to feed *T·* sheep ;
   46– 7   I will listen for *T·* voice,
   46–21   Lead *T·* lambkins to the fold,
Un. 5–28   parts of *T·* ways," — see Job 26 : 14.
Pul. 1– 1   fatness of *T·* house; — Psal. 36 : 8.
   1– 2   river of *T·* pleasures. — Psal. 36 : 8.
   3–16   fatness of *T·* house ; — Psal. 36 : 8.
   3–17   river of *T·* pleasures. — Psal. 36 : 8.
   4–26   fatness of *T·* house." — Psal. 36 : 8.
   7–29   fatness of *T·* house ; — Psal. 36 : 8.
   7–30   river of *T·* pleasures." — Psal. 36 : 8.
   10–27   breathe Thou *T·* blessing
   17– 5   How to feed *T·* sheep ;
   17– 6   I will listen for *T·* voice,
   17–20   Lead *T·* lambkins to the fold,
   22– 7   " *T·* kingdom come. — Matt. 6 : 10.
   22– 7   *T·* will be done — Matt. 6 : 10.
   33– 8   * *T·* servant heareth." — I Sam. 3 : 9.
Po. 6– 1   Brood o'er us with *T·* shelt'ring
   7– 9   Fed by *T·* love divine we live,
   14– 4   How to feed *T·* sheep ;
   14– 5   I will listen for *T·* voice,
   14–19   Lead *T·* lambkins to the fold,
   24–21   Send us *t·* white-winged dove.
   28– 7   To *T·* all-wise behest
   30–15   cast on *T·* blest name,
   36– 8   *T·* will to know, and do.

Thy and thy
Po. 37– 7   This is *T·* high behest :
   39– 8   And from its altar to *T·* throne
   43–10   in *T·* great heart hold them
   44– 3   With the guerdon of *T·* bosom,
   77– 5   peace abound at *T·* behest,
   77– 6   wherefore this *T·* love?
My. 33–15   abide in *t·* tabernacle? — Psal. 15 : 1.
   33–16   dwell in *t·* holy hill? — Psal. 15 : 1.
   201–21   I will listen for *T·* voice,
   220–22   make them *T·* friends ;
   225–26   "Hallowed be *T·* name." — Matt. 6 : 9.
   228–23   dwell in *T·* holy hill? — Psal. 15 : 1.
   229–27   *T·* ways are not as ours.
   281– 4   "*T·* kingdom come. — Matt. 6 : 10.
   281– 4   *T·* will be done — Matt. 6 : 10.

Thyatira
'00. 13–24   deity in the city of *T·*

tide
Mis. 162–14   to stem the *t·* of Judaism,
   316–11   *t·* which flows heavenward,
Pul. 41– 3   * *t·* of contributions which
Po. 16–10   and roll on with its *t·*,
My. 54–10   * the *t·* of men and women

tides
Mis. 292– 3   overwhelming *t·* of revelation,
   360–23   *t·* of spiritual sensation
My. 149–10   the ever-flowing *t·* of truth

tidings
Mis. 369– 4   the gospel of glad *t·*
   386– 7   "Bearest thou no *t·* from our
Ret. 45– 3   "bringeth good *t·*, — Isa. 52 : 7.
Po. 49–11   "Bearest thou no *t·* from our
My. 184–27   bringeth good *t·*, — Isa. 52 : 7.

ties
Ret. 31– 2   sunders the dominant *t·* of earth
Un. 17– 9   evil *t·* its wagon-load of offal to
'02. 19–21   Are earth's pleasures, its *t·* and

tiles
Pul. 25–12   * the roof is of terra cotta *t·*,

till
Mis. vii–11   *T·* time shall end more timely,
   115–18   *t·* you intelligently know and
   140–17   *t·* mortal man sought to know
   145– 5   *T·* then, this form of godliness
   152–26   *t·* the storm has passed.
   160– 9   *t·* they meet and mingle in bliss
   169– 5   *t·* she was God-driven back
   171–24   *t· the whole was leavened. — Matt.* 13 : 33.
   227–27   *t·* it grows into the full stature
   264– 7   *t·*, like camera shadows
   272– 9   * *t·* the repealing of said Act
   302–18   *t·* this permission was *withdrawn,*
   384–10   Stay ! *t·* the storms are o'er
   398–18   *T·* the morning's beam ;
Man. 55–16   shall not be counted loyal *t·*
Ret. 8–19   but I answered not, *t·*
   15– 4   *t·* I founded a church
   15–27   *t·* the persons who divulged their
   22–15   *t·* its involved errors are vanquished
   33– 6   *t·* I was weary of "scientific guessing,"
   46–24   *T·* the morning's beam ;
   90–24   *t·* her children can walk steadfastly
   94–16   not *t·* then, will immortal Truth
Un. 30– 9   *t·* divine understanding takes
   43–16   *t·* all be fulfilled." — Matt. 5 : 18.
Pul. 6– 3   And it will continue *t·* the
   17–23   *T·* the morning's beam ;
   21–11   struggle *t·* it be accomplished?
No. 1– 8   *t·* they rise in floods
Pan. 13–16   *t·* God's will be witnessed
'00. 7–29   *t·* the long night is past
   8– 3   *t·* we awake in his likeness.
   8–12   *t·* God's discipline takes it off
   9–15   *t·* the mental atmosphere is clear.
   10– 9   Such conflict never ends *t·*
   15–27   Watch ! *t·* the storms are o'er
'01. 16– 6   *t·* the sin is destroyed.
   20–22   *t·* he suffers up to its extinction
   29–20   no excuse for waiting *t·* the wind
Po. 3– 9   *T·* sleep sets drooping fancy free
   3–13   *T·* bursting bonds our spirits part
   8– 9   *T·* vestal pearls that on leaflets
   14–22   *T·* the morning's beam ;
   17– 3   rest *t·* I see My loved ones
   36– 9   Stay ! *t·* the storms are o'er
   43–19   *T·* they gain at last
   53–11   *T·* heard at silvery eve
   65–18   *T·* darkness and death like mist
   72– 3   *T·* God is God no longer
   78– 6   *T·* molds the hero form
My. 9–26   *t·* I am satisfied with what my
   18–24   *t·* God's will be witnessed

till

My. 104–19 t· they know of what and of whom
148–13 unthought of t· the day had passed !
149–13 t· you make their treasures yours.
155–14 t·, home at last, it finds the
183– 7 * "When Christ reigns, and not t· then,
185– 9 t· Truth shall reign triumphant
189–12 t· truth and love, commingling in
216– 1 T· Christian Scientists give all
217–10 t· it is disbursed in equal shares
240– 1 t· all men shall know Him
307– 5 t· one day I declared to him
335– 7 * membership in both t· his decease.
338–13 unknown to me t· after the lecture

Tilton

N. H.

My. 174–24 Congregational Church in T·, N. H.
310–12 establishment in T·, N. H.
312–28 to my father's home in T·, N. H.

Ret. 5– 9 my parents removed to T·,
5–19 for many years had resided in T·
19– 4 under the paternal roof in T·.
My. 310–10 * workman in a T· woolen mill."
314– 3 * "lived for a short time at T·,
314– 6 * from T· to North Groton

Tilton, Alexander

My. 310–11 joint partner with Alexander T·,
310–30 Dr. Ladd said to Alexander T· :

Tilton Congregational Church

My. 311–13 I joined the T· C· C·

Time

Mis. 390– 5 Old T· gives thee her palm.
Po. 55– 6 Old T· gives thee her palm.

time (see also time's)

six o'clock
My. 77–22 * at s· o· this morning.
7 : 30 a. m.
Pul. 41–23 * At 7 : 30 a. m. the chimes in the
eight o'clock
My. 16–13 * at e· o· in the forenoon.
9. a. m.
Pul. 41–30 * At 9 a. m. the first congregation gathered.
nine o'clock
Mis. 304–23 * n· o· in the morning
304–28 * It will always ring at n· o·
nine to four o'clock
Pul. 59– 6 * were held from n· to f· o·,
ten o'clock
My. 30–30 * admission at the t· o· service,
38–30 * Tuesday, June 12, at t· o·
10 : 30 a. m.
Pul. 42– 8 * at 10 : 30 a. m., however,
10 : 30 o'clock
Pul. 42– 3 * At 10 : 30 o· another service began,
twelve o'clock
Mis. 304–26 * at t· o· on the birthdays of
12 . 30 P. M.
My. 169– 4 on July 5, at 12 . 30 P. M.,
two o'clock
My. 39–3 * at t· o· in the afternoon.
171–13 at t· o· in the afternoon,
3 p. m.
Pul. 42– 5 * at 3 p. m. the service was repeated
three o'clock
Mis. 177–23 * said that at t· o·,
My. 80–29 * t· o· in the afternoon
four o'clock
Mis. 304–27 * at f· o· it will toll
about the
My. 27– 5 about the t· of our annual meeting
acceptable
No. 28–11 now is the most acceptable t·
accepted
My. 12–18 now is the accepted t·." — II Cor. 6 : 2.
advance of the
'02. 10– 8 or in advance of the t·,
all
Mis. 189–30 it extends to all t·,
244–27 for all peoples and for all t· ;
364–14 all t·, space, immortality,
Ret. 26– 9 demonstrated for all t· and peoples
36– 1 or its application in all t·
No. 21– 9 all t·, space, immortality,
Pan. 5–11 the proper answer for all t·
'01. 25–18 of his time and of all t·.
Po. 30– 8 To glorify all t· — eternity
My. 28–24 * Jesus' gospel was for all t·
158–28 stand through all t· for God and
all the
Mis. 32–23 all the t· and attention that they
223– 3 I was saying all the time,
almost perfect
My. 38–21 * in almost perfect t·.

time

ample
Man. 82–20 devote ample t· for faithful practice.
and attention
Mis. 32–23 all the t· and attention that they
112–11 demands our t· and attention.
114– 4 cannot give too much t· and attention
138– 7 to give t· and attention to hygiene
Ret. 44–20 t· and attention must be given to
My. 163–14 demands on my t· and attention
192–25 demands upon my t· and attention
231–20 demands on her t· and attention
243–17 give all possible t· and attention
and circumstance
Mis. 160– 6 through t· and circumstance,
and eternity
Mis. 68– 3 it requires both t· and eternity.
147– 6 victory won for t· and eternity?
264– 5 They build for t· and eternity.
364–24 or quarrel throughout t· and eternity,
382–10 t· and eternity bear witness to
Ret. 70–19 fill his own niche in t· and eternity.
'01. 25– 5 encompassing t· and eternity.
My. 19–26 vibrant through t· and eternity
and for eternity
'02. 5–19 the theme for t· and for eternity ;
and goodness
My. 306–12 T· and goodness determine greatness.
and immortality
'00. 1– 6 all space, t·, and immortality
and joy
My. 166–23 let our measure of t· and joy
and labor
My. 193–24 you have grasped t· and labor,
and place
My. 169–20 beauty of t· and place
and retirement
My. 117– 8 t· and retirement to pursue the
and space
Mis. 110–17 t· and space, when encompassed by
No. 16–13 destitute of t· and space ;
My. 110–13 forces annihilating t· and space,
and thought
Mis. 112– 7 occupy t· and thought ;
Hea. 12–20 requires t· and thought ;
another
Mis. 29– 7 At another t· he prayed,
any
Mis. 321–25 at any t· during the great wonder
Man. 30– 6 be found at any t· inadequate
32–21 no remarks . . . at any t·,
57– 6 meetings may be held at any t·
81–15 shall at any t· be published
101– 1 any t· the C. S. Board of Directors
My. 325–14 * Command me at any t·,
approaches
Mis. 2–17 t· approaches when divine Life,
appropriate
My. 24–31 * no more appropriate t· for
at one
Ret. 3– 2 at one t· held the position of
40– 4 At one t· I was called to speak
attention and
My. 175– 5 my constant attention and t·,
awakes in
Mis. 222–18 subject scarcely awakes in t·,
babe of
Pul. 1– 4 a nursling, a babe of t·,
before the
'00. 9–12 before the t·?" — Matt. 8 : 29.
'02. 10– 6 before the t·?" — Matt. 8 : 29.
began
My. 116–22 growth spiritual, since t· began,
bells of
My. 31– 7 * clanging bells of t· ;"
best
Mis. 80–20 at the best t·, will redress
boundary of
Un. 37–11 no boundary of t· can separate
cannot quench
Po. 15–22 t· cannot quench in oblivion's wave.
cannot spare
Mis. 155–24 cannot spare t· to write to God,
change in the
My. 121– 3 change in the t· for holding
cometh
Mis. 145– 3 But the t· cometh when the
286–19 The t. cometh, and now is,
complete
'00. 14– 8 signifies a complete t· or number
consumed
My. 25–17 Owing to the t· consumed
consumes
Mis. 117–21 To point out . . . consumes t·,

time

corridors of
'02. 4–16 adown the corridors of t·,
My. 189–10 through the dim corridors of t·,
cycles of
Un. 11–24 required neither cycles of t· nor
dated
Mis. 163– 8 He who dated t·, the Christian era,
My. 180– 8 by him who . . . dated t·:
dial of
Mis. 71–29 flitting across the dial of t·.
due
Mis. 373–21 in due t· Christianity entered into
Ret. 1–17 in due t· was married
during the
My. 323–30 * during the t· of our studying
easel of
Mis. ix–10 easel of t· presents pictures
expiration of the
Man. 69– 9 before the expiration of the t·
first
Mis. 16–31 behold for the first t· the
17–16 behold for the first t· the divine
344–30 Christianity for the first t·
352– 6 able for the first t· to discern the
Ret. 25– 6 I apprehended for the first t·,
My. 166–27 I am for the first t· informed of
284–15 * first t· in the history of
362–14 * first t· gathered in one place
flourishes for a
My. 112– 4 false philosophy flourishes for a t·
flourish for a
My. 95– 2 * cults which flourish for a t·
footsteps of
Po. 15– 4 moans from the footsteps of t· !
foundations of
Mis. 82–10 reach the sure foundations of t·,
fulness of
Pul. 85– 7 * will, in the fulness of t·, see
future
Mis. 7–20 to be depicted in some future t·
give a thing
My. 193–22 * Carlyle writes, "Give a thing t· ;
God's
Mis. 117–23 God's t· and mortals' differ.
My. 13– 3 act in God's t·.
God's own
My. 306–19 and that in God's own t·,
have kept
Mis. 110–18 Our hearts have kept t· together,
have not had
My. 195– 9 privileges I have not had t· to
her
Mis. 37–26 Her t· is wholly devoted to
Rud. 14– 9 gave fully seven-eighths of her t·
My. 231–20 demands on her t· and attention
his
Mis. 214– 4 mortal thought, of his t·.
Pul. 13–22 devil knoweth his t· is short.
'01. 25–18 of his t· and of all time.
hoary with
No. 13–18 It is hoary with t·.
illusion of
Mis. 93–13 it is the illusion of t· and mortality.
improved
Pul. 1 10 t· improved is eloquent
indefinite
Pul. 58–24 * but for an indefinite t·
is at hand
My. 10–13 * but the t· is at hand, now,
is consumed
Mis. 230– 4 great amount of t· is consumed
is money
'00. 3– 7 to him t· is money,
is required
Mis. 43–18 t· is required thoroughly to
Jesus'
My. 211–10 even as in Jesus' t·
lack of
Mis. 256–16 the old impediment, lack of t·,
last
Pul. 42– 6 * service was repeated for the last t·.
less
Man. 68– 6 member who leaves her in less t·
little
Mis. 4–15 but little t· has been devoted to
6– 3 but little t· free from complaints
'00. 2–11 he gives little t· to society
looms of
Mis. 99– 6 through the looms of t·,
many a
Pul. 80–12 * has many a t· been sent us
matures
Mis. 286– 6 Until t· matures human growth,

time

may commence
Mis. 15–18 T· may commence, but it
mean
My. 55– 8 * In the mean t·, not only was the
55–19 * In the mean t· Sunday services
mists of
Mis. 264– 8 shadows thrown upon the mists of t·,
more
My. 259–16 and give me more t· to think
most
Mis. 267– 7 I have sacrificed the most t·,
moth of
My. 230– 1 the sacrilegious moth of t·,
much
Mis. 137–23 give much t· to self-examination
Ret. 44–20 much t· and attention must be given
my
Mis. x–10 manifold demands on my t·
132–16 great demand upon my t·,
My. 135–11 increasing demands upon my t·
137–17 increasing demands upon my t·,
163–14 demands on my t· and attention
192–25 demands upon my t· and attention
275–19 demands upon my t· at home,
next
Ret. 9–14 resolving to do, next t·, as my mother
no
Mis. 230–17 spend no t· in sheer idleness,
238– 7 reformer has no t· to give in
282–27 when there is no t· for ceremony
290– 8 no t· for detailed report
357– 1 no t· for idle words,
Pul. 81–19 * they want no t· to take,
'00. 2–13 He takes no t· for amusement,
'01. 32–10 no t· or desire to defame
no better
My. 329–21 * At no better t· than now,
of contagious disease
My. 116– 2 At a t· of contagious disease,
of election
Man. 26– 5 from the t· of election to office.
80–25 dating from the t· of election
of such service
Man. 69–12 during the t· of such service.
of the dedication
My. 76–14 * at the t· of the dedication
320–30 * at the t· of the dedication
of the divorce
My. 314–30 up to the t· of the divorce.
of the occurrence
Mis. 290–15 naming the t· of the occurrence,
of times
Pul. 84– 1 * "The t· of times" is near
olden
My. 147–20 to-day, as in olden t·,
162–19 which spake thus in olden t·
one
Hea. 4–25 is one thing at one t·,
My. 308–20 One t· when my father was visiting
309–14 justice of the peace at one t·.
343–26 I found at one t· that they had
one's
My. 234– 3 absorbing one's t· writing or
one week's
Mis. 135–14 give one week's t· and expense
or attention
Mis. 366– 2 the t· or attention that
or money
My. 231–10 spend no more t· or money in
our
Mis. 112–11 demands our t· and attention.
123– 1 same spirit that in our t· massacres
Ret. 70–10 in our t· no Christian Scientist
My. 111– 8 same class of . . . as we have in our t·.
340–29 succeeded by our t· of abundance,
outweighs
'02. 17–15 that which outweighs t· ;
past
Pul. 1– 9 T· past and time present,
posterns of
Mis. 383–13 go down the dim posterns of t·
precise
Ret. 14–21 could not designate any precise t·.
present
Mis. 56–28 stages of existence to the present t· ?
Pul. 1– 9 Time past and t· present,
My. 24–21 * and at the present t· there are
110– 5 At the present t· this Bethlehem star
Queen Elizabeth's
No. 44–13 In Queen Elizabeth's t· Protestantism
question of
Mis. 348–12 It is only a question of t·
required
Man. 62– 2 t· required to take the collection.

time

requires
Mis.	6–22	it requires *t·* to óvercome
Un.	43–10	requires *t·* and immense . . . growth.
Hea.	12–20	To prepare the medicine requires *t·*

requisite
My.	285– 6	I cannot spare the *t·* requisite

right
Mis.	359–23	and is available at the right *t·*.

ripeness of
Mis.	164– 6	appeared in the ripeness of *t·*,

sacred
My.	36– 9	* have assembled at this sacred *t·*

same
Mis.	109– 1	at the same *t·* declaring the unity
	256– 3	at the same *t·* improved morally.
Ret.	38–14	at the same *t·*, finished printing
	52– 7	At the same *t·* I have worked to
Pul.	37–14	* At the same *t·* it is her most earnest aim
Hea.	15–16	when at the same *t·* he calls God
My.	vi–23	* at the same *t·* she presented to
	70– 6	* edifices to its credit in the same *t·*
	82– 9	* to get away at the same *t·*.
	131– 4	refines character at the same *t·*
	224–19	at the same *t·* giving full credit

shores of
Mis.	205–31	Mortals who on the shores of *t·*
'02.	11– 3	to wander on the shores of *t·*,

short
Mis.	297– 1	Taking into account the short *t·*
Pul.	12–15	he hath but a short *t·*.— *Rev.* 12 : 12.
My.	47–25	* the years . . . seem but a short *t·*.
	314– 3	* "lived for a short *t·* at Tilton,

some
Mis.	78–22	will some *t·* appear all the clearer
	87– 9	shall know, some *t·*, the spiritual
	136–13	as they must some *t·*,
	147–17	by affections which may some *t·*
	216–22	* some *t·* after the rest of it had
	273– 1	some *t·*, as . . . Scientists,
	278–24	I have felt for some *t·* that
	339–27	will some *t·* flood thy memory,
	357–21	For some *t·* it has been clear
	368–28	this earth shall some *t·* rejoice
Ret.	89–16	when he had been some *t·* absent
Un.	9– 6	some *t·* and in some way,
Pul.	62– 2	* for some *t·* well . . . known in
No.	28–10	must be learned some *t·*,
'00.	2–26	to take some *t·* for myself ;
My.	142–18	some *t·* learn this and rejoice with me,
	184–29	must at some *t·* find utterance

space of
Mis.	147– 5	another space of *t·* has been given

specified
Man.	69– 3	*t·* specified in the Church Manual.

storms of
Mis.	392–15	to wrestle with the storms of *t·* ;
Po.	20–19	to wrestle with the storms of *t·* ;

strain of
Mis.	365– 1	will bear the strain of *t·*
No.	21–22	bears the strain of *t·*,

sufficient
Man.	39–10	when sufficient *t·* has elapsed
My.	223–14	because I have not sufficient *t·*

tears of
Po.	22– 9	bliss that wipes the tears of *t·*

test of
My.	92– 4	* until it has stood the test of *t·*.

that
Mis.	137–13	but that *t·* has passed.
	193– 5	deemed it safe to say at that *t·*.
	290–19	not thought of the writer at that *t·*.
	306–20	* was at that *t·* the President
Ret.	27–13	Up to that *t·* I had not fully
	44–14	no student, at that *t·*, was found able
Un.	9– 7	That *t·* has partially come,
Pul.	34– 4	* and from that *t·* until 1866
My.	29–31	* From that *t·*, until the close of
	56– 1	* at that *t·* it was thought
	60–11	* Christian (?) people at that *t·*.
	61– 3	* every night since that *t·*.
	61– 9	* postponed until that *t·*.
	73– 5	* in other countries since that *t·*,
	145– 7	From that *t·*, October 29, 1897,
	181–26	Since that *t·* it has steadily decreased.
	314–11	At that *t·*, he owned a house in
	315–11	* At that *t·* I had no knowledge of
	321–22	* During that *t·*, from my
	323–32	* were at that *t·* some eight days in
	331– 9	* in your city at that *t·*.
	334– 4	* disease was raging at that *t·*.

their
Mis.	xi– 6	in advance of their *t·* ;
	296–12	give their *t·* and strength
Man.	31– 7	suitable portion of their *t·*
Rud.	13–26	give all their *t·* to C. S. work,

time

their
Rud.	14– 2	giving only a portion of their *t·*
My.	62–30	* gave freely of their *t·* and efforts
	216– 2	all their *t·* to spiritual things,

this
Mis.	324–28	this *t·* he struggles on,
	327–23	All this *t·* the Stranger is
Ret.	47– 6	At this *t·* there were over three
Pul.	34–11	* During this *t·* she suddenly
	34–26	"During this *t·*," she said,
'00.	15–17	all this *t·* divine Love
Hea.	16–17	will leave our . . . for this *t·*.
My.	11–11	* in all this *t·* she has never
	21–11	* a visit to Boston at this *t·*,
	47– 3	* It seems meet at this *t·*,
	54–15	* At this *t·* the Hawthorne Rooms,
	55–24	* At this *t·* the church removed
	89–25	* not to this *t·* alone,
	132–12	at this *t·* and in every heart
	145– 2	by this *t·* acquainted with
	244– 5	gladly give it at this *t·*

this very
Mis.	54–15	curing hundreds at this very *t·* ;

three weeks'
Mis.	349– 5	twelve lessons, three weeks' *t*,

throughout
Mis.	12– 5	throughout *t·* and beyond the grave.

to follow
Mis.	359– 1	*t·* to follow the example of the

to preach
My.	53–21	* when she could give the *t·* to preach,

to receive
My.	163– 9	Not having the *t·* to receive all

to rest
My.	83–16	* will have *t·* to rest and sleep,

to talk
Mis.	32–17	If I had the *t·* to talk with all

to throttle
My.	26–20	Now is the *t·* to *throttle the lie*

touches
Mis.	336–28	touches *t·* only to take away its

to work
Mis.	340– 5	the *t·* to work, is *now*.

treasure of
Mis.	394–10	the treasure of *t·* ;
Po.	45–13	the treasure of *t·* ;

veil of
My.	256–20	veil of *t·* springs aside

want of
Mis.	351– 4	for want of *t·*, . . . I neglect myself.

wasting
Mis.	230– 8	Three ways of wasting *t·*,

whole
Pul.	81–13	* spends her whole *t·* helping others.

will remove
My.	223–28	burdens that *t·* will remove.

will show
My.	52–22	* "Whatever is . . . *t·* will show.

winds of
Mis.	99–23	winds of *t·* sweep clean the

wreck of
Mis.	26– 1	can survive the wreck of *t·* ;

your
Mis.	230– 1	chapter sub-title
My.	60–27	* I ask a little of your *t·* to tell you

Mis.	vii–11	Till *t·* shall end more timely,
	95–11	*t·* so kindly allotted me is
	107–18	it never started with *t·*,
	111–26	in *t·*, that church will love C. S.
	138– 3	The *t·* it takes yearly to
	155–16	Because Mother has not the *t·*
	182– 9	in *t·* they lose their false sense
	248–27	since which *t·* I have not
	267–10	there never was a *t·* when I
	281–12	in the *t·* of the French Huguenots,
	349–27	I accepted, for a *t·*, fifteen dollars
	380– 5	governs the universe, *t·*, space,
	381– 7	The *t·* for taking testimony
Man.	44– 7	possible loss, for a *t·*, of C. S.
Pul.	23– 9	* of the *t·* of Jonathan Edwards
	32–19	* At the *t·* I met her
	45– 7	* get their buildings finished on *t·*,
	51–21	* but as *t·* has gone on,
Pan.	13– 1	every hour in *t·* and in eternity
'00.	12–10	in the *t·* of . . . Emperor Augustus.
'02.	10– 5	molecule, space, *t·*, mortality ;
Po.	31– 2	not of *t·*, nor yet by nature sown,
My.	22–17	* *t·* has put its seal of affirmation
	51–12	* at a *t·* when there is such an
	55– 8	* although given up for a *t·*,
	56–19	* From the *t·* that the three foregoing
	61–13	* I fought hard . . . for a *t·* ;
	74– 8	* in *t·* for the first Sunday service.
	116– 6	In *t·* of religious . . . prosperity,

time

My. 130–14 I have neither the *t·* nor the
136–27 and *t·* for spiritual thought
142–16 might in *t·* lose its sacredness
160–28 but of the *t·* no man knoweth.
214–12 set the seal of eternity on *t·*.
235–28 Had I known . . . in *t·* to have
239–29 going on since ever *t·* was.
250–22 But if now is not the *t·*,
319–27 * considered the *t·* an important one
320–21 * at the *t·* above referred to
342–31 "In *t·* its present rules
355– 1 * were with her at the *t·*,
358–14 I have not the *t·* to do so.

time-honored

My. 174–19 our *t·* First Congregational Church

timely

Mis. vii–11 Till time shall end more *t·*,
4–11 chapter sub-title
17–24 according to the *t·* or untimely
Ret. 80–17 he will not scorn the *t·* reproof,
Pul. 10–24 the *t·* shelter of this house,
My. 62–23 * wise counsel, *t·* instruction, and

time's

Mis. xi–16 and thus may *t·* pastimes become
Pul. 1– 8 An old year is *t·* adult,
Po. 27–23 Pillow thy head on *t·* untired

Times

Pul. 89–15 * *T·*, Trenton, N. J.
89–21 * *T·*, New Orleans, La.
90– 9 * *T·*, Chicago, Ill.
90–10 * *T·*, Minneapolis, Minn.

times

abreast of the
Man. 44–22 and kept abreast of the *t·*.
all
Mis. 96– 4 help in all *t·* of trouble,
My. 127–32 all *t·*, climes, and races.
apostolic
Pul. 54–11 * as were necessary in apostolic *t·*.
at all
Mis. 44–23 is but a dream at all *t·*.
91–13 It is imperative, at all *t·*
147–22 at all *t·* the trusty friend,
Pul. 15–16 At all *t·* and under all circumstances,
'00. 14–24 At all *t·* respect the character and
behind the
Mis. 232–11 will never do to be behind the *t·*
demand of the
Mis. 232–22 C. S., is a demand of the *t·*.
different
My. 315– 5 * at different *t·*, I had conversation
five
Mis. 221–26 five *t·* ten are fifty
four
Pul. 40–13 * SERVICE REPEATED FOUR *T·*
40–16 * simple ceremonies, four *t·* repeated,
59– 8 * these exercises four *t·* repeated.
'01. 4– 5 four *t·* three is twelve,
hundred
Un. 18– 3 tale already told a hundred *t·*,
like these
Mis. 278– 7 In *t·* like these it were well to lift the
many
Mis. 375–24 * how many *t·* have I seen these hands
Pul. 36–18 * met Mrs. Eddy many *t·* since then,
55–15 * she has revised it many *t·*,
My. 130–11 has been made too many *t·*
million
No. 33–15 million *t·* greater than the brief agony
Pev. 8–28 proved a million *t·* unskilful.
modern
My. 98–10 * annals hardly parallel in modern *t·*,
ninety-nine
Mis. 118– 9 ninety-nine *t·* in one hundred
of hate
Mis. 277–27 especially near in *t·* of hate,
of need
'01. 26–13 for help in *t·* of need.
of persecution
'02. 1– 2 His people in *t·* of persecution
of trouble
Mis. 10–13 God, their help in *t·* of trouble.
96– 4 help in all *t·* of trouble,
'01. 19– 3 is given to them in *t·* of trouble,
olden
Pul. 82–12 * In olden *t·* the Jews claimed to be
83–16 * In olden *t·* it was the Amazons
our
Mis. 176–25 what of ourselves, and our *t·*
pagan
Pul. 65–22 * the spot where, in pagan *t·*,

times

past
Mis. 92–26 not be forgotten that in *t·* past,
Ret. 84–15 In *t·* past, arrogant pride,
No. 9– 2 if it had been heeded in *t·* past
Pan. 15– 5 God, who in *t·* past hath
My. 323–27 * not . . . able to appreciate in *t·* past.
Phariseeism of the
Mis. 234–13 the Phariseeism of the *t·*,
seven
Mis. 279–17 seven *t·* around these walls,
279–17 seven *t·* corresponding to the
several
My. 320–20 * I called on Mr. Wiggin several *t·*
320–22 * and several *t·* subsequent thereto,
320–28 * I saw Mr. Wiggin several *t·*
signs of the
(*see* signs)
signs of these
Mis. 2– 6 signs of these *t·* portend a
278– 3 and are the signs of these *t·* ;
347–10 discern the mental signs of these *t·*,
My. 270– 5 repeat the signs of these *t·*.
six
My. 29–11 * repeated six *t·* during the day.
stirring
My. v– 4 * stirring *t·* of church building,
such
Man. 95– 7 such *t·* as the cause of C. S. demands.
support at
Mis. 39–23 needs support at *t·* ;
ten
Mis. 221–26 ten *t·* five are not
their
My. 221– 7 systems and practices of their *t·*.
thirty
Hea. 13– 6 shaking the preparation thirty *t·*
three
Mis. 133–22 Three *t·* a day, I retire to
Ret. 8– 5 three *t·*, in an ascending scale.
8–10 heard somebody call . . . three *t·* !"
'01. 4– 6 three *t·* four is twelve.
time of
Pul. 84– 1 * "The time of *t·*" is near
two thousand
Hea. 13– 5 reducing . . . two thousand *t·*,
various
My. 310– 3 at various *t·* and places.

Mis. 111– 5 At *t·*, your net has been so full
162– 1 at *t·* of special enlightenment,
'00. 2–25 intermediate worker works at *t·*,
My. 266–11 chapter sub-title
320–25 * Our conversations were at *t·*

Times-Herald

Pul. 89–22 * *T·*, Dallas, Tex.

time-table

My. 124–24 produce thy records, *t·*, log,

time-tables

My. 167–16 Thanksgiving Day, according to *t·*,

time-world

My. 268–20 This *t·* flutters in my thought

time-worn

My. 295–12 your *t·* Bible in German.

timid

Mis. 329–15 nursing the *t·* spray,
390–17 The *t·*, trembling leaves.
Ret. 15–30 were too *t·* to testify in public.
Po. 53–10 The patient, *t·* grass,
55–18 The *t·*, trembling leaves.
My. 340–19 paltering, *t·*, or dastardly policy,

timidity

Mis. x–18 *T·* in early years
Rud. 17–11 could tell you of *t·*,

Timothy

Mis. 243–23 alludes to Paul's advice to *T·*.

tincture

Mis. 369–16 higher than a rhubarb *t·*
Pul. 48–24 * a *t·* of blue and brave blood,
'01. 18– 1 "mother *t·*" of one grain

tinged

Ret. 32– 8 hope, if *t·* with earthliness,

tingling

My. 81–23 * rose *t·* to the great dome,

tinkling

No. 45– 4 or a *t·* cymbal ;" — *I Cor.* 13 : 1.
'01. 26–23 or a *t·* cymbal." — *I Cor.* 13 : 1.

tinsel

Po. 27– 2 pomp and *t·* of unrighteous

tint
Mis. 264–28   *t·* of the instructor's mind
Ret. 31–24   and a *t·* of humility,
Pul. 32– 3   * transparency and rose-flush of *t·*
My. 85–30   * noble dome of pure gray *t·*,

tints
Pul. 25–24   * wainscoting repeats the same *t·*.
26– 5   * prisms which reflect the rainbow *t·*.
Po. 25– 3   Soft *t·* of the rainbow and skies

tiny
Mis. 239–17   Just then a *t·*, sweet face appeared
My. 83– 6   * wore *t·* white, unmarked buttons,

tip
Mis. 119–14   material nature strives to *t·* the beam
My. 146–24   beliefs of mortals *t·* the scale

tipping
'02. 20– 5   hues of heaven, *t·* the dawn

tips
My. 277–19   mercy *t·* the beam on the right side,

tire
My. 165–25   Goodness and benevolence never *t·*.

tired
Mis. 52–19   *if one gets t· of it, why not*
52–23   if, when *t·* of mathematics
239–18   suffused eyes, cough, and *t·* look,
316–20   *t·* aphorisms and disappointed ethics ;
324–18   his own heart *t·* of sin,
368–29   *t·* watchmen on the walls of Zion,
369–22   we are *t·* of theoretic husks,
369–22   as *t·* as was the prodigal son of the
397–13   From *t·* joy and grief afar,
Ret. 84–23   *t·* tongue of history be enriched.
Pul. 18–22   From *t·* joy and grief afar,
'01. 26– 2   my *t·* sense of false philosophy
Peo. 8– 7   for the sins of a few *t·* years
Po. 13– 1   From *t·* joy and grief afar,
16–12   *t·* wings flitting through
47–14   sobbing, like some *t·* child
My. 132–32   wipes away the unavailing, *t·* tear,
165–23   Human reason becomes *t·*

tireless
Mis. 254– 5   love which brooded *t·* over their
386– 8   The toiler *t·* for Truth's new birth
Pul. 9– 5   when your *t·* tasks are done
Hea. 19–18   T· Being, patient of man's
Po. 49–13   toiler *t·* for Truth's new birth
My. 51–26   * of Mrs. Eddy's *t·* labors,

tithe
Mis. 253–24   one *t·* of the agonies that
'01. 29–26   under a *t·* of my own difficulties,
My. 191– 5   Injustice has not a *t·* of the power

tithes
Mis. 139– 4   bring your *t·* into the storehouse,
My. 14– 2   brought their *t·* into His storehouse.
20–13   all your *t·* into His storehouse,
131–24   "Bring ye all the *t· — Mal. 3 : 10.*

title
Mis. 140– 3   hold a wholly material *t·*.
140–26   Our *t·* to God's acres will be
140–27   * when we can "read our *t·* clear"
314–24   announcing the full *t·* of this book,
314–27   unnecessary to repeat the *t·*
Man. 18–25   changed the *t·* of "First Members"
32–14   announce the full *t·* of the book
64–13   The T· of Mother Changed.
70–22   legal *t·* of The Mother Church.
71– 2   *t·* of First Church of Christ,
Ret. 91–10   this *t·* really indicates more the
Pul. 46– 9   * under the *t·* of "Retrospection and
53–24   * earned the *t·* of Saviour of
'00. 15– 4   are distinguished above human *t·*
'02. 15–22   Its *t·*, S. and H., came to me
15–27   to drop both the book and the *t·*.
Hea. 3–19   Christ Jesus was an honorary *t·* ;
My. 87–11   * visitors of *t·* and distinction,
310–13   His military *t·* of Colonel
351–10   the *t·* of your gem quoted,

titled
My. 72– 8   * members of the *t·* aristocracy
113–31   among the scholarly and *t·*,

titles
Mis. 140–10   or merely legal *t·*.
Man. 45–23   Legal T·.
45–24   must drop the *t·* of Reverend
45–26   *t·* under the *laws* of the *State*.
70–21   T·.
71– 6   must not be used before *t·*
112– 6   before *t·* of branch churches.
Pul. 38– 9   * whose *t·* are as follows :

to and fro
Mis. 266–29   running *t· and f·* in the earth,
277– 5   walking *t· and f·* in the earth,
'02. 11– 4   tossed *t· and f·* by adverse

tobacco
Mis. 240–28   nothing but a . . . worm *naturally* chews *t·*.
Ret. 65– 9   persecution, *t·*, and alcohol
Pan. 10–21   cases of intemperance, *t·* using,
'00. 6–19   to a man who uses *t·*,
My. 106–25   an alcohol drinker, a *t·* user,
114– 4   abstain from alcohol and *t·* ;

tocsin
My. 199–19   sounded the *t·* of a higher hope,

to-day (noun)
Mis. 175–24   But this ism of *t·* has
245–20   charities, and reforms of *t·*.
310– 9   is the lesson of *t·*.
339– 8   to-morrow starts from *t·*
Ret. 65–16   If the religion of *t·* is
85–27   will crown the effort of *t·*
Pul. vii– 5   when the children of *t·* are the
Rud. 8– 4   the lion of *t·* is the lion of
No. 28–13   *t·* is none too soon for entering
'01. 2–22   his followers of *t·* will prove,
'02. 4–21   yesterday, and *t·*, and forever.
5– 2   as the dulness of *t·* prophesies
Hea. 1– 6   to-morrow grows out of *t·*.
11–13   burn upon the altars of *t·* ;
Po. 27–13   let *t·* grow difficult and vast
My. 119–15   the Mary of *t·* looks up
158–11   for all mankind *t·* hath its
158–14   *t·* lends a new-born beauty

to-day (adv.)
Mis. 2–14   T· we behold but the first
12–12   should be *t·* a law to himself, herself,
30–23   is *t·* the fossil of wisdomless wit,
70–11   "T· shalt thou be with me — *Luke* 23 : 43.
99–25   speak louder than *t·*.
99–25   They are *t·* as the voice of one
111–24   no greater difference . . . than *t·* exists
116–12   This question, . . . is *t·* uppermost :
120–28   whose character we *t·* commemorate,
125–27   thought-tired, turns *t·* to you ;
144–21   T·, be this hope in each of
144–29   T· I pray that divine Love,
150–12   *t·* are repeating their joy
178–18   * had said to me that *t·*
178–28   to be excused from speaking *t·*,
178–32   has been given to the world *t·*.
179–10   He is saying to us *t·*,
179–16   Can we say this *t·* ?
194– 1   How many *t·* believe that the
200–20   Christians *t·* should be able to say,
251– 7   my hand may not touch yours *t·*,
251–12   T· we commemorate not only our
258–32   nature and man are as harmonious *t·*
279–27   We, *t·*, in this class-room,
286–18   although it is *t·* problematic.
316–27   *t·* there would be on earth
320–28   *t·* christening religion undefiled,
336– 9   His highest idea as seen *t·*
355– 6   good healing is *t·* the acme of
375–28   * to see produced *t·* that art
Chr. 53–53   T·, as oft, away from sin
Ret. 94–23   *t·*, and forever," — *Heb.* 13 : 8.
Un. 61– 4   *t·*, and forever." — *Heb.* 13 : 8.
Pul. 1–18   T·, being with you in spirit,
7– 5   T·, as of yore, her laws
10–21   If you are less appreciated *t·*
34–19   * it is as true *t·* as it was
35– 8   * as operative in the world *t·*
44–23   * church which will be dedicated *t·*
49–27   * *t·* a strikingly well-kept estate
54–11   * conditions . . . *t·* are the same
66– 2   * exists as much *t·* as it did
67–10   * which are to be found there *t·*
67–16   * but *t·* it numbers over a
74– 9   * shown to Mrs. Mary Baker Eddy, . . . *t·*.
82–10   * and *t·* she knows many things
82–22   * T· there are ten thousand Esthers,
No. 31– 6   appear *t·* in subtler forms
38– 2   what C. S. is *t·* proving
41–26   * and it is doing it *t·* ;
44–25   * "Heretics of . . . are martyrs *t·*."
Pan. 9–14   What mortal *t·* is wise enough
'00. 3–21   T· it surprises us that during the
4–11   T· people are surprised at
15– 2   T· you have come to a
15–18   T· you have come to Love's feast,
'01. 1– 1   brethren, *t·* I extend my
1–10   T· you meet to commemorate
9–13   Truth that is persecuted *t·*,
17–14   that *t·* commands the respect
18– 8   more honored and respected *t·*

to-day (adv.)
'01. 32–27 if those . . . Christians were here t·,
33– 2 holiness that t· seems to be
'02. 4–13 My subject t· embraces the
11–29 while t· Jew and Christian can
16– 7 T· I am the happy possessor
Hea. 7–21 would not have done t·.
Peo. 8–24 We thank our Father that t·
14– 2 T· we clothe our thoughts
Po. vi–18 T·, by order of Governor Andrew,
29–20 Fill us t· With all thou art
My. vi– 6 * That no one on earth t·,
24– 3 * truth . . . is t· being proven
28–25 * as effective t· as it was
39–27 * realize her presence with us t·.
43–26 * t· we rejoice that we have
47–16 * T· we look back over the
57–17 * membership of this church t·
64– 8 * If t· we feel a pardonable pride
73–14 * flocking . . . to Boston t·,
82–21 * at noon t· [June 14]
85– 7 * T· its adherents number
93–30 * T· its adherents number
98– 4 * C. S. army in this country t·,
99–23 * T· there are hundreds of such
100–14 * numbered by thousands t·,
104– 5 t· all sorts of institutions
104–11 what would be thought t·
109–11 he is t· teaching them the
109–13 t·, and forever." — Heb. 13 : 8.
112– 6 C. S. makes practical t·
115– 2 t· is circling the whole world.
122–23 Can we say with the angels t· :
123–10 T· in Concord, N. H., we have
124– 9 who would say t·,
126–28 it reigns supreme t·,
146–18 as true t· as they will be
147–20 speak the truth that t·,
148–17 T·, with the large membership
152–20 T·, if ye would hear His voice,
153–11 T· our great Master would say
155–23 May those who discourse music t·,
155–28 T· may they find some sweet
158–26 temple which t· you commemorate,
159– 3 Never more sweet than t·,
170–15 present a gift to you t·,
171– 3 T· is fulfilled the prophecy of Isaiah :
174–25 T· my soul can only sing and soar.
177–20 T· the glory of His presence
182– 2 T· it is said to have a majority
183–11 T· a nation is born.
184– 8 T· I am privileged to congratulate
190–30 wherefore vilify His prophets t·
199– 6 reward . . . is given thee t·.
220–31 seems more divine t· than
246–28 the same t· as yesterday
257– 4 T· the watchful shepherd shouts his
257–13 T· the Christ is, more than
257–28 T· Christian Scientists have their
271–22 * dearest to your heart t·?''
292–12 same yesterday, t·, and forever ;
294–11 If he were personally with us t·,
296–15 He is wiser t·, healthier and
314–16 Individuals are here t· who were
324–17 * were he here t· he would
346–28 did not mean any man t· on earth.

together
Mis. xi–22 grant us peace, t· with pardon
10– 6 "work t· for good — Rom. 8 : 28.
22–24 t· with the sick, the lame,
28–27 t· with his divine Love,
47–23 t· with his immortality and
59–20 let us reason t·." — Isa. 1 : 18.
94– 8 which God hath not joined t·.
98–10 brought us t· to minister and to be
110–18 Our hearts have kept time t·,
134–10 Meet t· and meet en masse,
135– 9 sweet sense of journeying on t·,
138– 9 For students to work t·
145–25 lion and the fatling t· ; — Isa. 11 : 6.
145–26 hearts of . . . Scientists are woven t·
156–24 Assembling themselves t·,
177– 6 leagued t· in secret conspiracy
188– 4 when the stars first sang t·,
231–24 little palms patting t·,
259–21 morning stars sang t·, — Job 38 : 7.
275–12 little ones, wondering, huddle t·,
279–22 met t· in an upper chamber ;
279–25 they had all to shout t·
296– 7 t· with unfamiliarity with the
310–28 t· with those who never have
Man. 34–12 The Bible, t· with S. and H.
84–21 shall not call their pupils t·,
Ret. 64– 4 and t· both sinner and sin
82–25 found dwelling t· in harmony,
85– 4 advisable to band t· their students

together
Un. 1– 8 Let us then reason t·
42–14 morning stars sang t·, — Job 38 : 7.
Pul. 9–19 t· with the Sunday School
21–27 spirit of Christ calling us t·.
64–26 * drawing t· six thousand people
'00. 11–10 work t· for good — Rom. 8 : 28.
Hea. 14–22 t· with what they learn.
18–10 good and evil never dwelt t·.
Po. vi– 2 * t· with "The Valley Cemetery,"
My. vii– 1 * t· with The C. S. Journal,
4–19 and they thrive t·,
21–20 * and shaken t·, — Luke 6 : 38.
24–14 * "fitly framed t· — Eph. 2 : 21.
32– 5 * began all t·, and their voices
48–24 * t· with the discouragement of
69– 5 * roof and side walls come t·
81–28 * two or more of them are met t·,
104–27 that brought t· this class
143–25 work t· for good — Rom. 8 : 28.
163–23 t· with the retirement
166–22 let us t· sing the old-new song
174–30 may we not t· rejoice in the
175– 3 t· with the organizations connected
243– 4 come t· and form one church.
268–10 What God hath joined t·,
310–11 t· they owned a large manufacturing

toil
Mis. 212–17 darkness, and unrequited t·.
323–11 peril, privation, temptation, t·,
340– 7 unremitting, straightforward t· ;
340–24 t· is triumph ;
382– 8 years of unremitting t·
Ret. 30– 5 Ceaseless t·, self-renunciation, and
86– 3 to crown patient t·, and
Rud. 17–11 of friendlessness, t·, agonies,
'01. 2–24 doubt, and unrequited t·
Po. 16–11 And bustle and t· for its pomp
My. 64– 6 * and her years of t·,
136–25 the fruits of honest t·,
154–20 * "If the poor . . . t· that we have food,
154–21 * t· for him in return,
196–27 The poor t· for our bread,
217– 5 reward your hitherto unselfish t ,

toiled
Mis. 111– 4 you have t· all night ;
Pul. 44– 4 * worked, t·, prayed for.
'00. 14–23 in other words, he that t· for
'01. 29–14 nurtured them, t· for them,

toiler
(see Eddy)

toilers
Mis. 323–17 He saith unto the patient t·
Pul. 50– 7 * do something for the t·,
My. 252– 4 you will be t· like the bee,

toilet
Pul. 27– 1 * are t· apartments, with

toiling
Mis. 266–22 who are t· and achieving
Po. 47– 8 Never to t· and never to fears,

token
Mis. 132– 4 t· that heavy lids are opening,
160– 6 may give no material t·,
320–30 white stone in t· of purity
No. 24–12 By the same t·, evil is not
'00. 10–22 I received a touching t·
My. 107– 1 as a t· of their Christianity.
172–28 as a simple t· of love."
194–21 t· of your gratitude and love.

told
Mis. 28–11 so-called life is a dream soon t·.
57–21 t· in the name of Truth,
170–30 he had just t· them.
224– 7 A courtier t· Constantine
239–18 tired look, t· the story ;
284–17 t· him his fault,
354–16 a few truths tenderly t·,
391–20 Some good ne'er t· before,
Ret. 9– 4 Mother t· Mehitable all about
21–16 It is "as a tale that is t·," — Psal. 90 : 9.
40– 6 t· me that her next-door neighbor
40–13 t· me that her physicians had
Un. 17–21 t· our first parents that
48– 3 already t· a hundred times,
Pul. 2– 4 the half was not t· me :— I Kings 10 : 7.
8–11 t· their privileged joy
29–27 * Later I was t· that almost the entire
30– 2 * I was further t· that once
30– 6 * I was t· he replied that the C. S.
32–14 * She t· me the story of her life,
32–22 * this, she t· me, was due to the
33–24 * so a friend has t· me,
46–10 * much is t· of herself in detail

told

Pul.	49–19	* She *t·* something of her domestic
	72–28	* Christ has *t·* us to do his work,
'00.	14–29	being *t·* they are distinguished
'01.	16–27	commence with one truth *t·*
	16–28	one hundred falsehoods *t·* about it
Hea.	6– 3	When I was *t·* the other day,
Po.	38–19	Some good ne'er *t·* before,
My.	43–19	* it was *t·* them :
	59– 4	* When you *t·* us that the truth
	60– 8	* when *t·* that I had studied with you.
	79–28	* *t·* of cures from diseases,
	81–13	* They had been *t·* to name,
	226–26	*t·* by the alert editor-in-chief
	313– 3	so I have been *t·* :
	313– 8	*t·* by *McClure's Magazine*
	314–26	A Christian Scientist has *t·* me
	319–30	* You *t·* me that he had done
	320– 8	* agreed with what you had *t·* me
	321–11	* *t·* the same story to every one
	321–32	* *t·* me of their knowledge of your
	322– 2	* she *t·* me she knew you
	322–26	* I was surprised when he *t·* me
	322–28	* *t·* me of his acquaintance with you
	324–26	* *t·* us laughingly why he accepted
	328–16	* is *t·* in the *Kinston Free Press*
	335–26	* was *t·* by him that he could not
	335–31	* was *t·* by the expert physician

Toledo

Pul.	56– 3	* Detroit, *T·*, Milwaukee, Madison,

tolerant

Mis.	247– 6	familiar with my history are more *t·* ;

toll

Mis.	304–27	* it will *t·* on the anniversaries of
My.	189–30	Wherefore, pray, the bell did *t·*?

tolling

'02.	17– 2	knells *t·* the burial of Christ.

tomb

Mis.	70–28	even in the silent *t·*,
	74–20	the door of his own *t·*.
	388–21	First at the *t·* to hear his word :
	395–25	A requiem o'er the *t·*
Ret.	88– 7	called the physical man from the *t·*
Pul.	10– 8	silent Aventine is glory's *t·* ;
'02.	19– 3	burst the doors of the *t·*
Po.	21–10	at the *t·* to hear his word :
	39–11	First at the *t·*,
	58–10	A requiem o'er the *t·*
	78– 4	will spread over their *t·* ;
My.	191–18	from the *t·* of the past,
	290– 6	lose their lustre in the *t·*,

to-morrow

Mis.	99–25	*t·* speak louder than to-**day.**
	307– 2	Never ask for *t·* :
	339– 7	*t·* starts from to-day
Pul.	50–13	* will be dedicated *t·*.
'02.	5– 2	renewed energy for *t·*,
Hea.	1– 6	*t·* grows out of to-day.
My.	75–27	* dedicated *t·* free from debt.
	76–25	* dedicated in Boston *t·*
	104–12	what will be thought *t·*
	126–29	it reigns supreme to-day, *t·*,
	146–18	true to-day as they will be *t·*.
	158–26	*t·* complete, and thereafter dedicate
	161–22	cannot boast ourselves of *t·* ;

tone

Mis.	264–26	The *t·* of the teacher's mind
	282–15	metaphysical *t·* of his command,
	292–10	new *t·* on the scale ascending,
	312–25	he touched a *t·* of Truth
	366–11	this is the prolonged *t·* :
Ret.	5–25	* the *t·* of conversation in the
Pul.	26–18	* fine range and perfect *t·*.
	62–14	* quality of *t·* is something superb,
'00.	1– 2	*t·* of your happy hearts,
	11–18	quantity, and variation in *t·*,
	11–19	if the divine *t·* be lacking,
	11–20	human *t·* has no melody for me.
My.	32–10	* above the usual platform *t·*,
	50–13	* *t·* of this meeting for deliberation
	83–22	* naturally takes on a *t·* of
	202–25	From the dear *t·* of your letter,
	291–19	May his history waken a *t·*

toned

Pul.	26–25	* room is *t·* in pale green

tones

Mis.	46–27	idea of sound, in *t·*, represents
	106–31	organ, in imitative *t·*
	116–14	with *t·* whence come glad echoes
	126– 6	in *t·* that leap for joy,
	151–10	to the unfruitful in *t·* of Sinai :
	213–21	These are its inspiring *t·*

tones

Mis.	231–28	How many homes echo such *t·*
	295–24	high and pure ethical *t·*
	329–13	touching tenderly its tearful *t·*.
	331–13	in *t·* tremulous with tenderness,
Ret.	9– 6	name pronounced in audible *t·*.
Pul.	60– 8	* clear, manly, and intelligent *t·*,
	61–25	* The sweet, musical *t·*
	62–14	* purity and sweetness of their *t·*.
'00.	11–14	besieges you with *t·* intricate,
'02.	9–16	consciousness that leaves the minor *t·*
Po.	31– 8	tear-filled *t·* of distant joy,
	65–22	life hath its music in low minor *t·*,
My.	39–25	* harmonious *t·* of her gentle voice.
	59–20	* sonorous *t·* of the powerful organ

tongue

and pen

My.	146–31	weight of thought, *t·*, and pen

Anglo-Saxon

Mis.	216–13	given to the Anglo-Saxon *t·*,

Christian

'01.	28–12	into almost every Christian *t·*,

examines the

Hea.	12– 5	feels the pulse, examines the *t·*,

her

My.	42– 3	* in her *t·* is the law of — *Prov.* 31 : 26.

his

Mis.	126–10	guard, . . . in society his *t·*?

new

Mis.	18–12	translated into the new *t·*,
	25–16	religion's "new *t·*," — see *Mark* 16 : 17.
	248– 1	This is the "new *t·*," — see *Mark* 16 : 17.
	248– 6	found in the "new *t·*," — see *Mark* 16 : 17.
	364– 3	in the "new *t·*," — see *Mark* 16 : 17.
Ret.	25– 5	a new meaning, a new *t·*.
Rud.	16–11	into the "new *t·* ;" — see *Mark* 16 : 17.
No.	44– 6	It is the "new *t·*" — see *Mark* 16 : 17.
Hea.	7– 7	"The new *t·*" is the — see *Mark* 16 : 17.
My.	131–15	speak the "new *t·*" — see *Mark* 16 : 17.
	147–11	teaching the "new *t·*" — see *Mark* 16 : 17.
	225– 8	the old "new *t·*," — see *Mark* 16 : 17.
	238–14	C. S. . . . or "new *t·*" — see *Mark* 16 : 17.
	306–15	in the "new *t·*," — see *Mark* 16 : 17.
	318– 1	express the "new *t·*," — see *Mark* 16 : 17.

of angels

My.	354–23	The *t·* of angels

original

My.	180–10	restores their original *t·*

their

Mis.	368–22	under their *t·*." — see *Rom.* 3 : 13.

tired

Ret.	84–23	tired *t·* of history be enriched.

your

Mis.	130–12	sweet morsel under your *t·*,"
Un.	60–13	With the *t·* "bless we God, — *Jas.* 3 : 9.
My.	33–19	backbiteth not with his *t·*, — *Psal.* 15 : 3.
	93–20	* with the *t·* of facetiousness.

tongues

Ret.	10– 9	lessons in the ancient *t·*,
Pan.	13–22	all nations, peoples, and *t·*,
'01.	26–22	speak with the *t·* of men — *I Cor.* 13 : 1.
Hea.	1– 2	*speak with new t· ;— Mark* 16 : 17.
My.	47–22	* many of different races and *t·*
	47–31	* speak with new *t·* ;— *Mark* 16 : 17.

tonic

Mis.	252– 1	Truth is the *t·* for the sick,
My.	152– 8	said, "My material *t·* has

to-night

Mis.	331–21	on upward wing *t·*.
	389– 9	on upward wing *t·*.
	393–22	Lessons long and grand, *t·*,
Chr.	53–55	Truth pleads *t·* : Just take Me in !
Po.	4– 8	on upward wing *t·*.
	52– 6	Lessons long and grand, *t·*,
My.	73–28	* due to arrive in Boston *t·*,
	82–23	* more visitors by midnight *t·*.

took

Mis.	77– 5	*believe t·* its original meaning,
	139–30	I *t·* care that the provisions for
	171–24	*leaven, which a woman t·*,— *Matt.* 13 : 33.
	174–30	leaven which a woman *t·* and hid
	201–16	Paul *t·* pleasure in infirmities,
	201–19	he *t·* pleasure in
	201–23	he *t·* pleasure in
	212–30	*t·* down from the cross
	223– 4	*t·* up the research
	242–29	he *t·* a patient
	243–32	"He *t·* a bone — see *Gen.* 2 : 21.
	248–25	prescribed morphine, which I *t·*,
	339– 3	*t·* place once in heaven,
	345–23	*t·* their infants to a place of
	370– 5	they went away and *t·* counsel
	383– 4	*t·* effect the same year,

took
Ret. 37– 6 critics *t·* pleasure in saying,
Pul. 38– 4 * ceremony *t·* place in 1881.
48– 5 * *t·* the writer straight to her beloved
75–19 * *t·* part in the ceremonies
Pan. 7– 9 that . . . material creation *t·* place,
'01. 31–27 what He *t·* away.
My. 45–24 * ''He *t·* not away the— *Exod.* 13 : 22.
64– 3 * *t·* on a larger and truer meaning.
80–24 * it *t·* ten meetings
117–14 a stranger, and *t·* thee in?— *Matt.* 25 : 38.
151–30 it *t·* a step higher ;
312– 6 * *t·* his bride to Wilmington,
312–22 He *t·* with him the usual amount
312–28 *t·* me to my father's home
313–19 when I *t·* an evening walk,
313–19 but I seldom *t·* one.
342– 5 * *t·* a seat on a sofa.

tools
My. 211–18 lend themselves as willing *t·*

tooth
Mis. 44–14 *until I have the t· extracted,*
44–24 if the *t·* were extracted,

toothache
Mis. 44–13 *If I have the t·,*
45– 6 more than to heal a *t·* ;

top
Mis. 165–12 rends . . . from *t·* to bottom.
Pul. 9–14 to the *t·* of the tower,
My. 68–10 * The *t·* of the dome is
69–29 * view is on *t·* of the tower
122– 7 To cut off the *t·* of a plant
162–31 towering *t·* of its goodly temple

topaz
Mis. 376–27 *t·*, opal, garnet, turquoise,

Topeka (Kan.) *Daily Capital*
My. 93–16 * [*T· (K·.) D· C·*]

Topeka, Kans.
Pul. 89–34 * *Journal, T·, K·.*

topic
Mis. 280–28 allude briefly to a *t·*
309–26 elucidates this *t·.*

topically
Mis. 203–16 metaphysics appropriates it *t·.*

topics
Mis. 76–18 other *t·* less important.
92– 5 inexhaustible *t·* of that book
236– 9 giving advice on personal *t·.*
350–19 consideration of these two *t·.*
Man. 93–12 *t·* condemning C. S.,
Ret. 42–10 lectured so ably on Scriptural *t·*
84– 2 inexhaustible *t·* of S. and H.
Pul. 47– 2 * lectures upon Scriptural *t·.*
My. 319–25 * analyzing and arranging the *t·*,

topmost
Mis. 376–22 *t·* pall, drooping over a deeply

tops
My. 68– 5 * *t·* of great stone piers,

torches
Ret. 23–17 the midnight *t·* of Spirit.

torment
Mis. 293–18 brings greater *t·* than ignorance.
'00. 9–12 come hither to *t·* me— *see Matt.* 8 : 29.
'02. 10– 6 come hither to *t·* us— *Matt.* 8 : 29.

tormentor
Mis. 278– 6 the presence of its *t·.*
'00. 3–18 to shun him as their *t·.*

torments
Mis. 210–25 belief in . . . *t·* its victim,

torn
Mis. 186–21 idea cannot be *t·* apart from
340– 2 had *t·* the laurel from many a brow
My. 110–31 *t·* from their necessary contexts,

tornado
Mis. 240–18 the sturdy oak, . . . breasts the *t·*

tornadoes
My. 265–27 less thunderbolts, *t·*, and

Toronto
Canada
Mis. 142– 6 chapter sub-title
157– 8 Mrs. Stewart, of *T·*, Canada
Pul. 75–13 * *The Globe, T·,* Canada,
My. 184– 2 chapter sub-title
— —
Mis. 142– 8 presented by Christian Scientists in *T·*,
Pul. 56– 4 * Scranton, Peoria, Atlanta, *T·*,
67–20 * *T·* and Montreal have strong churches,
75–17 * MANY *T·* SCIENTISTS PRESENT
75–18 * Christian Scientists of *T·*,

torpid
Mis. 206– 4 from foul to pure, from *t·* to serene,

torrents
My. 316–20 foaming *t·* of ignorance, envy,

torrid
'00. 10–29 serving his country in that *t·* zone

torture
Mis. 244–13 are they bodily penance and *t·*,
341–25 and is subject to terrible *t·*
Pul. 13–25 how many periods of *t·* it may take
No. 34–14 Physical *t·* affords but a slight
Peo. 3– 9 sacrifice and *t·* of His favorite Son,
My. 160–26 burning in *t·* until the sinner

tortured
Mis. 123–12 or *t·* to appease the anger of

tortures
Ret. 26– 7 to allay the *t·* of crucifixion.

tossed
'02. 11– 4 *t·* to and fro by adverse

tosses
Mis. 331– 3 *t·* earth's mass of wonders into

total
Mis. 2–10 admit the *t·* depravity of mortals,
30– 9 sum *t·* of transcendentalism.
105–32 God is the sum *t·* of the universe.
112–29 ends in a *t·* loss of moral,
112–32 exemplification of *t·* depravity,
289– 4 temperance is *t·* abstinence.
293–21 sum *t·* of Love reflected
'02. 1– 8 members have been added . . . making *t·*
My. 16– 4 * *t·* of $425,893.66 had been received
23– 3 * *t·* membership of The Mother Church
23–12 * *t·* receipts . . . $891,460.49.
25–14 * *t·*, $2,579.19.
57–21 * *t·* number admitted during the
57–22 * *t·* number of branch churches
212–13 to complete the sum *t·* of sin.
256– 8 *t·* exemption from Christmas gifts.

totally
No. 30–16 could not destroy our woes *t·* if
My. 311– 4 a girl, *t·* blind, knocked

touch
Mis. ix–11 the *t·* of God's right hand.
97–17 *t·* the hem of His garment ;
143– 1 *t·* of heart to heart
175–13 increase by every spiritual *t·*,
180–12 "*T·* me not."— *John* 20 : 17.
200–29 the *t·* of weakness, pain,
230–28 canvas and the *t·* of an artist
251– 6 my hand may not *t·* yours
294–14 with sting ready for each kind *t·*,
306–24 *t·* of the breast of a dove ;
306–26 Oh, may you feel *this t·*,
372–24 to reproduce, with reverent *t·*,
Ret. 27–19 * *T·* God's right hand
95–12 * Of Christlike *t·.*
Un. 22– 7 ye shall not *t·* it, lest ye die.
34–14 *T·.* Take another train of
Pul. 54– 4 * We *t·* him in life's throng
No. 32–11 when I *t·* this subject
40–15 never to *t·* the human thought save to
'00. 11–25 * With a *t·* of infinite calm,
15–20 *t·* of the hem of this garment
'01. 9–19 foams at the *t·* of good ;
21–27 felt the incipient *t·* of divine Love.
Hea. 16–14 *t·* but the hem of Truth's garment.
20– 5 * We'd soar and *t·* the heavenly
Peo. 11–26 that they themselves will not *t·*
My. 26–11 emotion at the *t·* of memory.
93–19 * too often disposed to *t·* upon it
108–20 slang, and malice *t·* not the hem
108–21 for if they did once *t·* it,
121–11 yielding to the *t·* of a finger
125–16 I have felt the *t·* of the spirit
147– 3 moments when at the *t·* of memory
152– 4 the *t·* of Jesus' robe
186– 9 song and sermon will *t·* the heart,
256–21 springs aside at the *t·* of Love.

touched
Mis. 75– 1 you will have the hem of
112–19 My few words *t·* him ;
142–27 *t·* tender fibres of thought,
312–24 he *t·* a tone of Truth
395–20 *T·* by the finger of decay
Ret. 23–23 I had *t·* the hem of C. S.
76– 9 Thoughts *t·* with the Spirit and
Un. 28– 5 was never *t·* by the scalpel
29–21 weighed or *t·* by physicality.
57–11 "Who hath *t·* me ?"— *see Mark* 5 : 31.
Pul. 46–10 * detail that can only be *t·* upon
No. 22– 2 certainly not *t·* the hem of the
'00. 1– 1 methinks even I am *t·* with

touched

Po. 58– 5 T· by the finger of decay
My. 22–27 * t· the healing hem of C. S.,
37–28 * deeply t· by its sweet entreaty,
47–11 * t· by its influence for good,
47–18 * t· by each landmark of progress
150–11 A heart t· and hallowed by
192– 7 Thou hast t· its hem,
319– 5 My saying t· him,
345–32 * which are here t· upon,

touches

Mis. 29– 6 t· universal humanity.
174– 9 t· the religious sentiment
235–15 t· mind to more spiritual issues,
253–22 mother's love t· the heart of God,
289–26 Science t· the conjugal question
336–28 t· time only to take away its
Pul. 13–11 t· the hem of Christ's robe
My. 66–18 * chapter sub-title
205–22 t· but the hem of C. S.,
287–22 it t· thought to spiritual issues,
294–24 t· the heart and will move the pen
351–12 t· the hem of his garment

touching

Mis. 60–18 even if t· each other corporeally ;
143–29 t· letter breathing the donor's
275–24 love and loyalty were very t·.
329–12 t· tenderly its tearful tones.
Pul. 49–14 * t· my sleeve and pointing,
'00. 10–23 t· token of unselfed manhood
My. 215–10 Afterwards, with t· tenderness,
347–11 illustrated by Keats' t· couplet,

touchingly

Pul. 8–11 t· told their privileged joy

tourists

Po. v–17 * Some t· who were passing,

toward

Mis. 13– 2 mercy and charity t· every one,
13– 3 exercise these sentiments t· them,
37– 6 desires that draw mankind t· purity,
63–24 reaching t· a higher goal,
74– 5 enmity of mortal man t· God.
133–23 with my face t· the Jerusalem of
143–24 t· building The Mother Church.
169–26 carnal mind, which is enmity t· God,
250–27 door that turns t· want and woe,
265–28 disaffections t· C. S. growing out of
272–29 I have endeavored to act t· all
304–25 * the world's progress t· liberty ;
315–14 promising proclivities t· C. S.
316–18 turn them slowly t· the haven.
338– 4 to be able to lift others t· it.
Man. 48– 1 cherish no enmity t· those who
74–20 maintain t· them an attitude of
83–11 promising proclivities t· C. S.
Ret. 76–10 gravitate naturally t· Truth.
Un. 2–24 their lives have grown so far t· the
5– 5 t· the perfect thought divine.
10–13 Spiritual phenomena never converge t·
61–12 Human perception, advancing t·
Pul. 8–19 earn a few pence t· this
37– 3 * attitude t· all questions."
50– 7 * t· the advancement of
65– 9 * attitude Rome may assume t· it.
72– 4 * t· the reported deification of
'00. 6– 7 press t· the mark — Phil. 3 : 14.
My. 156– 7 grace abound t· you ; — II Cor. 9 : 8.
(see also men)

towards

Mis. 32– 3 How shall we demean ourselves t·
32– 7 in what manner they should act t·
32–15 admissible t· friend and foe.
32–19 do my best t· helping
232– 6 reaching out t· the perfect
232– 7 pushing t· perfection in art,
290–20 involuntarily flow out t· all.
336–11 right obligations t· him.
348– 2 press forward t· the mark
Man. 48– 9 impertinent t· religion,
Chr. 53–35 grace t· you and me,
Ret. 3–12 t· the close of the War
13–15 merciless t· unbelievers ;
No. 9–15 * some of my students
'02. 10–12 advancing above itself t· the
18–26 ignoble conduct of his disciples t·
My. 9–22 t· the purchase of more land
10–11 * paid in t· the fund,
19–29 t· its church building fund.
46– 4 * beckoning us on t· a
50–16 * looked t· the spiritual,
86–20 * maintain t· their church.
96–17 * generosity of its adherents t·
97– 4 * t· making the patient well.
119–11 Think not that C. S. tends t·

towards

My. 125– 7 incline the vine t· the
159–19 the tendency t· God,
159–20 t· the temporary and finite.
176– 3 FIFTY DOLLARS IN GOLD t·
189–23 we are drawn t· God.
191– 4 Be patient t· persecution.
199–15 t· me and t· the Cause
201– 2 Press on t· the high calling
242– 6 nor advancing t· it ;
244–14 contribute my part t· this result.
245–13 T· the animal elements
261–11 t· guarding and guiding
262–28 letting good will t· man,
282–11 helped onward t· justice,
322–11 * work for and attitude t·
331–22 * gratitude we owe and cherish t·
338–19 love t· God and man.
338–29 instructed to be, charitable t·
(see also men)

tower

Mis. 144– 4 in the second story of the t·
152–24 safely sheltered in the strong t·
203– 6 From my t· window,
252–30 dear children's toy and strong t· ;
Pul. 9–14 climbed . . . to the top of the t·,
24–10 * Romanesque t· with a circular front
24–25 * t· is one hundred and twenty feet
39–21 * angels, on the gray church t·,
41–23 * chimes in the great stone t·,
58–27 * In the t· is a room devoted to
61–22 * first peal of the chimes in the t·
87–24 church's tall t· detains the sun,
Hea. 11–10 her modest t· rises slowly,
My. 69–29 * t· in Mt. Auburn cemetery
145–10 from the foundations to the t·,

towering

My. 46– 3 * in t·, overshadowing dome,
162–31 t· top of its goodly temple

towers

Mis. 125–28 to tell the t· thereof the
My. 71– 1 * stationed in one of the t·,

town

Ret. 5– 1 small t· situated near Concord,
Pul. 79–13 * daily paper in t· or village
My. 72–10 * streaming into t· lords and
87– 3 * transportation facilities of the t·
87–10 * multitude that has invaded the t·.
92– 1 * every important t· and city
134–16 happifies life in the hamlet or t· ;
309– 4 to do much business for his t·,
346–11 * Mrs. Eddy's carriage drove into t·

towns

Mis. 81–18 cities and t· of Judea,
Ret. 4– 5 adjoining t· of Concord and Bow,
90– 7 t· whither he sent his disciples ;
Pul. 67–21 * in many t· and villages
My. 309– 6 between the t· of Loudon and Bow,
314– 6 * doctor practised in several t·,

townships

Ret. 4–12 undulating lands of three t·.

toy

Mis. 231–23 a look of cheer and a t· from mamma
252–29 children's t· and strong tower ;

toys

Mis. 385–17 diviner sense, that spurns such t·,
Po. 48–11 diviner sense, that spurns such t·,

trace

Ret. 24– 8 trying to t· all physical effects to
My. 79–25 * without a t· of fanaticism,
96– 7 * none . . . with the slightest t· of
114–29 You can t· its teachings

traceable

My. 349–25 lawless and t· to mortal mind

traced

Mis. 388– 5 Love whose finger t· aloud
'01. 21– 9 * may be t· many of the ideas
27–11 the basis whereof cannot be t· to
'02. 20–14 Love whose finger t· aloud
Po. 7– 5 Love whose finger t· aloud
My. 296–26 t· its emotions, motives, and object.

tracing

Pul. 46–13 * t· those branches which are

track

Po. 26– 2 t· behind thee is with glory crowned ;

tractable

Rud. 15– 9 inquisitive, plastic, and t· ;

trade

'00. 2–20 his stock in t·, the wages of sin ;

trades
   My. 24–22 * fifteen different *t·* represented.
tradition
   Mis. 370– 8 risen from the grave-clothes of *t·*
   My. 260–19 not because of *t·*, usage, or
   340–19 Not the *t·* of the elders,
traditional
   Ret. 22– 7 legendary and *t·* history
traditions
   No. 8–20 enmity over doctrines and *t·*,
   My. 71–19 * nearly all the *t·* of church
   72– 3 * *t·* of interior church architecture.
   340– 7 *t·*, old-wives' fables, and
traduced
   Mis. 233–12 metaphysical healing is *t·* by
   '01. 2– 7 standard of C. S. was and is *t·* by
traffic
   Mis. 227– 1 *t·* by which he can gain nothing.
trafficking
   Mis. 356–32 it has no moments for *t·*
tragedy
   Mis. 124–24 last act of the *t·* on Calvary
   Un. 22–23 In Shakespeare's *t·* of King Lear,
tragic
   Mis. 48–21 hidden nature of some *t·* events
   My. 312– 4 the *t·* death of my husband,
train
   Un. 34–14 Take another *t·* of reasoning.
   Pan. 14– 3 righteousness with its triumphant *t·*.
   My. 233–21 dishonesty, sin, follow in its *t·*.
   331– 8 * accompanied her to the *t·*
trained
   Mis. 9–28 *t·* in treacherous peace
   Ret. 7– 8 * he *t·* and schooled them
   Pul. 80–27 * *t·* into harmony with the laws of God,
   Po. 2– 8 *t·* falcon in the Gallic van,
   My. 31–30 * As though *t·* carefully under
   38– 8 * carefully *t·* corps of ushers,
training
   Mis. 169– 7 Early *t·*, . . . had been the underlying
   Ret. 20–11 had no *t·* for self-support
   My. 310– 5 In addition to my academic *t·*,
trainloads
   My. 77–13 * daily *t·* of pilgrims
trains
   My. 73–26 * chapter sub-title
   73–27 * Special *t·* and extra sections of *t·*
   74– 5 * night *t·* of Saturday will bring
   82–25 * *t·* pulled out of the city
traitorous
   Un. 23– 1 *t·* and cruel treatment
traitors
   Mis. 106– 7 *T·* to right of them,
   Po. 27–14 With *t·* unvoiced yet?
traits
   Mis. 72– 8 bad *t·* of the parents
   191–17 evils, apparent wrong *t·*,
trammels
   Rud. 2–20 takes away the *t·*
tramping
   My. 308–10 * old man *t·* doggedly along
trample
   Mis. 211–19 *t·* on your pearls
   My. 227–24 lest they *t·* them under — *Matt.* 7 : 6.
trampled
   Mis. 227–19 the more *t·* upon,
   247– 5 treated not as pearls *t·* upon.
   No. 40–10 lest your pearls be *t·* upon.
   Peo. 12–10 *t·* under the feet of Truth.
   My. 199 10 flourish when *t·* upon,
tramples
   Ret. 75– 4 *t·* upon Jesus' Sermon on the
trampling
   Po. 72– 2 *t·* right in dust !
trance
   My. 313–25 I never went into a *t·*
tranquillity
   My. 280– 7 * peaceful *t·* of the race.
transact
   Man. 79– 5 shall *t·* . . . such business as
transacted
   Man. 27– 2 The business . . . shall be *t·* by
   My. 358–22 through whom all my business is *t·*.
transaction
   Mis. 139–26 this *t·* will in future be
   141–23 divine will . . . rule this business *t·*,
   Man. 57– 1 *t·* of such other business

transaction
   Man. 70– 3 nor enter into a business *t·* with
   78–20 not exceeding $200 for any one *t·*,
   79–10 *t·* of the business assigned to them
   Pul. 54–14 * *t·* was in perfect obedience to
   My. 135–19 of this, the aforesaid *t·*.
transactions
   Mis. 350–11 no *t·* at those meetings which I
   '02. 12–23 financial *t·* of this church,
   My. 7– 7 financial *t·* of this church,
transcended
   Pul. 45–13 * *t·* human possibility.
   54–13 * no law of nature violated or *t·*.
transcendent
   Mis. 199–20 his *t·* goodness is manifest
transcendental
   '01. 6– 1 more *t·* than theology's three divine
   8– 5 scientific statement more *t·* than
   8–14 more *t·* than God made him?
   8–22 makes man none too *t·*,
   11–21 nor too *t·* to be heard
   12– 7 reply, "That is too *t·* for me
   18–13 C. S. seems *t·* because the
   My. 248–16 above theorems into the *t·*,
transcendentalism
   Mis. 30– 9 revealed the sum total of *t·*.
   '01. 18– 9 who laugh at or pray against *t·*
   My. 3–14 nor a *t·* that heals only the sick.
transcendentalists
   '01. 5–23 We are not *t·* to the extent of
transcending
   Un. 29– 9 *T·* the evidence of the material
   My. 154– 5 *t·* the law of death.
transcends
   '01. 18–14 Truth *t·* the evidence of the
   My. 262–22 a gift which so *t·* mortal, . . . giving
transcribed
   Mis. 95– 8 * and is *t·* below.
   187–31 *t·* by pagan religionists,
   '00. 3–23 afterwards *t·* Jehovah ;
transcribes
   Mis. 294– 8 *t·* on the page of reality
transcribing
   Mis. 187–15 because their *t·* thoughts were
   311–27 who can refrain from *t·*
transept
   My. 71–21 * neither nave, aisles, nor *t·*
transfer
   Man. 62–11 by *t·* from another Church
   94–20 nor *t·* this sacred office.
   '02. 13– 9 (which was a part of this *t·*)
transference
   Mis. 96–29 it is not the *t·* of
   Ret. 68–17 the *t·* of thought,
   68–24 no *t·* of mortal thought
transferred
   Mis. 139–23 this desirable site *t·*
   Ret. 28–13 *t·* to a perception of
   Pul. 35–17 *t·* to a perception of
   '02. 13– 5 *t·* to The Mother Church,
   My. 332–27 * Masonic records were *t·* to
transferring
   My. 21– 4 * *t·* to this fund the money
transfiguration
   Mis. 360– 5 hammering, chiselling, and *t·*
   Un. 2–26 ready for a spiritual *t·*,
transfigures
   No. 26–12 spiritual idea which *t·* thought.
   My. 183–12 unfolds, *t·*, heals.
transform
   Mis. 220–19 practitioner undertook to *t·* it,
   294–20 to reform and *t·* them,
   Un. 17–17 *t·* the universe into a home
   My. 15–13 *t·* you into His own image
transformation
   My. 61– 3 * To watch the *t·* has been
transformed
   My. 37–19 * the philosophy of the ages *t·*.
transforming
   Mis. 360–10 *t·* power of Truth ;
   372– 5 textbook . . . is *t·* the universe.
   Rud. 7–26 *t·* minerals into vegetables
   My. 10– 2 * *t·* influence of C. S.
transfused
   My. 306–14 wait to be *t·* into the practical
transgress
   My. 160– 3 which it were impious to *t·*,

transgressing
  Ret. 71–17 knowingly *t·* Christ's command.
transgression
  Mis. 293–18 wilful *t·* brings greater torment
transgressor
  Mis. 261–15 way of the *t·* — *see Prov.* 13 : 15.
transient
  Mis. 291– 1 *t·* views are human :
  Ret. 69–14 *t·*, false sense of an existence
transit
  Mis. 125–30 rapid *t·* from halls to churches,
    205–32 take rapid *t·* to heaven,
  '02. 10–22 *t·* from matter to Spirit
transition
  Mis. 84–28 *t·* from our lower sense of
  Un. 2–28 reach this *t·*, called *death,*
    38–11 *t·* called *material death,*
  No. 14– 5 have not passed the *t·* called death,
    28– 2 after the *t·* called death.
transitory
  Un. 36–14 matter is erroneous, *t·*,
translate
  Mis. 74–16 *t·* substance into its original
  Pul. 32–15 * may *t·* those inner experiences
  My. 306–13 almost unutterable truths to *t·*,
translated
  Mis. 18–11 *t·* into the new tongue,
  Un. 31– 1 or, more accurately *t·*,
  '01. 28–11 *t·* into almost every
  My. 206–29 hath *t·* us into the— *Col.* 1 : 13.
translates
  Mis. 22–10 C. S. *t·* Mind, God,
    25–12 *t·* matter into Mind,
    124–28 it *t·* love ;
  Hea. 7– 8 *t·* matter into its original language,
translation
  Mis. 67–24 *Do you believe in t·?*
    68– 2 This *t·* is not the work of
    97–23 I commend the Icelandic *t·* :
    373– 8 *t·* of the New Testament
  Rud. 16–10 in their *t·* of the Scriptures
  '02. 16– 3 Wyclif's *t·* of the New Testament,
  Peo. 1– 6 *t·* of law back to its original
  My. 295–10 MARTIN LUTHER'S *T·* INTO GERMAN
translations
  Mis. 171–11 spiritual *t·* of God's messages,
  No. 15– 8 Bible *t·* and voluminous commentaries
  My. 178–31 reported as his sayings are *t·*.
    179–14 being *t·*, the Scriptures are
    179–24 renderings or *t·* of Scripture
    238–11 Uninspired knowledge of the *t·* of
    299–15 undiscovered in the *t·* of the Bible
translator
  Mis. 188– 5 It is the *t·*, not the original Word,
translators
  Mis. 187–13 *t·* of the older Scriptures
    187–17 both writers and *t·* in that age
  Ret. 91– 9 compilers and *t·* of the Bible,
translucent
  My. 197–17 *t·* atmosphere of the former
transmigration
  Mis. 22–13 refutes the amalgamation, *t·*,
transmission
  Mis. 71–11 *law of t·, prenatal desires, and*
transmit
  Mis. 72– 1 can *t·* to man . . . nothing evil,
  Ret. 68–19 can matter originate or *t·* mind?
transmitted
  Mis. 72– 8 *t·* to their helpless offspring,
    97– 6 not one mortal thought *t·* to
  My. 258–26 A *t·* charm rests on them.
transmitting
  Mis. 22–15 impossibility of *t·* human ills,
transparency
  Mis. 59–27 becomes a *t·* for the divine Mind,
    183–14 Through the *t·* of Science we learn
    330–16 looking through Love's *t·*,
  Pul. 32– 2 * had the *t·* and rose-flush
transparent
  Mis. 51–28 * walk *t·* like some holy thing."
  No. v– 7 *t·* to the hearts of all
transpired
  My. 321–28 * *t·* during the past twenty years.
transportation
  My. 82–24 * *T·* facilities at the two stations
    87– 2 * *t·* facilities of the town
transported
  '02. 4–25 Alternately *t·* and alarmed by

transverse
  Mis. 348–14 Hence, Solomon's *t·* command :
trash
  Mis. 67– 9 money, which is but *t·*,
travail
  Mis. 15–20 sore *t·* of mortal mind
    17–29 through the *t·* of mortal mind,
    253–16 of the woman in *t·*,
    253–28 spiritual Mother's sore *t·*,
travel
  Mis. 88–13 reading, writing, extensive *t·*,
    230–11 *t·* of limb more than mind.
  My. 25–18 time consumed in *t·*,
    124–26 rate of speed, the means of *t·*,
traveling
  Man. 96– 6 The lecturer's *t·* expenses
travelled and **traveled**
  Mis. 385–16 "You've *t·* long, and far
  '00. 12–12 elders *t·* to meet St. Paul,
  Po. 48– 9 "You've *t·* long, and far
  My. 75–21 * no matter how far they had *t·*
Traveller
  Pul. 39–14 * [Written for the *T·*]
traveller (*see also* **traveller's**)
  Mis. 84–24 turn one, like a weary *t·*,
    177–28 *t·* in foreign lands
  '01. 14–15 misleads the *t·* on his way home.
  Peo. 1–10 a long night to the *t·* ;
traveller's
  My. 124–24 time-table, log, *t·* companion,
    257–29 the Christian *t·* resting-place.
travellers
  Mis. 327–15 The encumbered *t·* halt
  '02. 11– 4 *t·*, tossed to and fro
travels
  My. 75–22 * might have endured in their *t·*.
traversed
  Mis. 320–19 it hath *t·* night,
  Pan. 13–26 I have only *t·* my subject
  My. 257– 5 This truth has *t·* night,
travesties
  Mis. 260– 9 the *t·* of mortal mind.
  My. 288–13 partook not of the *t·* of
treacherous
  Mis. 9–28 trained in *t·* peace?
    82–27 *t·* glare of its own flame
  Un. 64–16 scale the *t·* ice, and stand on
  Po. 43–17 Rough or *t·* way.
treachery
  '02. 19– 1 injustice, ingratitude, *t·*,
tread
  Mis. xi–24 With tender *t·*, thought sometimes
    324– 7 gayly *t·* the gorgeously tapestried
    395–17 The turf, whereon I *t·*,
  Pul. 56–21 * We *t·* upon life's broken laws,
  No. 27–26 take off thy shoes and *t·* lightly,
  Peo. 13–12 iron *t·* of merciless invaders,
  Po. 58– 2 The turf, whereon I *t·*,
  My. 306– 4 to *t·* on the ashes of the dead
    308–11 *t·* not ruthlessly on their ashes.
treading
  Mis. 321–21 Still *t·* each temptation down,
  Un. 58– 6 *t·* "the winepress — *Isa.* 63 : 3.
  '00. 10– 2 that is *t·* on its head
  My. 350–12 did'st not Thou the dark wave *t·*
treason
  Mis. 341–20 implicit *t·* to divine decree.
  Peo. 6–23 no longer be deemed *t·* to understand
treasure
  Mis. 394–10 harp of the minstrel, the *t·* of time ;
  Po. 45–13 harp of the minstrel, the *t·* of time ;
  My. 184–17 I *t·* it next to your compliments.
    347–20 I shall *t·* my loving-cup
treasured
  Ret. 6– 9 Among the *t·* reminiscences of
Treasurer and **treasurer** (*see also* **Church Treas-urer, Treasurer's** and **treasurer's**)
  Man. 25– 6 a President, a Clerk, a *T·*,
    25–15 Clerk and *T·*,
    25–16 Clerk and the *T·* of this Church
    56–15 reports of *T·*, Clerk, and
    76–24 *T·* of The Mother Church,
    77– 6 *T·* of this Church shall
    77–13 Board of Directors and the *T·*
    78–16 The *T·*, personally, or
    80– 6 *T·* of The Mother Church.
    91–17 paid over annually to the *T·*
  Pul. 52– 2 * Here is a church whose *t·* has
  My. 16– 2 * *t·* of the building fund

Treasurer and treasurer

My. 23– 4 * amount each shall send the T·.
27–18 * T· of the Building Fund.
27–24 * t· of the building fund,
39–15 * T·, Stephen A. Chase, C.S.D. ;
57–29 * Here is a church whose T· has
72–18 * t· of the building fund
86–15 * t· of the building fund

Treasurer's and treasurer's

My. 16– 1 * chapter sub-title
23– 9 * Extract from the T· Report
28– 8 * t· books will show the

treasures

Mis. 165–20 nor appropriate his t·
165–30 their t· reproduced
Ret. 2–21 Among grandmother's t·
Pul. 9–25 purity, and love are t· untold
'01. 1–13 to add to your t· of thought
'02. 19–21 its t·, taken away from you?
My. 114–11 the t· of this textbook are
149–13 till you make their t· yours.
149–31 with the t· of rain,

treasure-troves

Mis. 22–32 concealed in the t· of Science.

treasury

Mis. 140–16 generously poured into the t·.
Hea. 7–18 dropped her mite into the t·,
My. 214–27 cast my all into the t· of Truth,
291–25 sheaves garnered, her t· filled,

treat

Mis. 71– 1 Is it right for me to t· others,
88–27 a Scientist to t· with a doctor ?
89– 6 would it be right to t· this
89–10 that Scientists do not t· them,
243– 6 although students t· sprains,
282–21 to t· him without his knowing it,
283–15 For a student of mine to t·
284–13 How shall I t· malicious
334–13 Why do . . . t· disease as disease,
334–22 How shall we t· a negation,
Man. 53– 8 to t· the author of our textbook
Rud. 13–18 not Science to t· every organ
My. 359–29 T· yourself for it and get your
364– 5 t· this mind to be Christly.

treated

Mis. 42–29 Can I be t· without being present
90– 8 to have a husband t· for sin,
198–18 disease also is t· and healed.
247– 4 t· not as pearls trampled upon.
282– 7 t· . . . without their knowledge
284–15 for this evil to be t· personally,
Ret. 15–25 t· and given over by physicians
71–11 knowledge of the individual t·,
Pul. 82–13 * they t· woman as a chattel,
Rud. 7– 4 the most difficult case so t·.
No. 31–19 but he t· them both,
Pan. 5–26 Jesus t· the lie summarily.
Hea. 14– 4 until disease is t· mentally
My. 97– 9 * those who were medically t·.
330– 6 * his followers would be so t·.

treaties

My. 277– 9 and sound, well-kept t·.

treating

Mis. 35– 9 mental system of t· disease.
45–17 effectual in t· moral ailments.
65–18 right way of t· disease
97–14 other methods of t· disease
368–18 Science of t· disease through Mind.
379– 1 After t· his patients, Mr. Quimby
Rud. 13–18 When t· a patient, it is not
Hea. 14– 4 the science of t· disease
My. 363–27 patient whom he is t·,

treatise

No. 22– 6 t· on the healing properties of

Treatise Concerning the Principle of Human Knowledge

'01. 23–24 book title

treatment

Mis. 31– 8 the abuse of mental t·,
33–16 when they began t·, had no faith
42–29 without being present during t·?
49– 7 restored by C. S. t·.
54–19 after one month's t· by one of your
66–23 as to the scientific t· of the sick.
89– 9 under material medical t·,
315–26 needing it asks for mental t·.
378–12 His t· seemed at first to relieve her,
Ret. 71– 9 mental t·, without the consent or
71–12 indications of mental t·,
Un. 23– 1 cruel t· received by old Gloster
Pul. 30– 2 * healed by C. S. t· ;

treatment

Pan. 5–28 His t· of evil and disease,
Hea. 14–21 metaphysical t· of disease ;
My. 103–19 application to the t· of disease
204–23 The too long t· of a disease,
204–24 a full fee for t·,
237–17 charges for t· equal to those of
307– 6 his magnetic t· and manipulation of
307–26 improved . . . under his t·,
363–26 avoid naming, in his mental t·,

treats

Mis. 69– 1 t· of the existence of God,
Man. 42–26 malpractises upon or t· our Leader
Ret. 68–17 t· of the human concept,

treaty

My. 281–23 * parties to the t· of Portsmouth,
281–29 t· of Portsmouth is not an executive

trebles

My. 38 20 * their shrill t· rising with the

tree (see also tree's)

Mis. 37–17 axe at the root of the t·.
198–22 the fruit of the t· of
223– 9 t· is known by its fruit ;
235–12 axe at the root of the t·
356–20 carry the fruit of this t· into
367–16 this fruit of the t·
392–13 the Hebrew figure of a t·.
Ret. 95– 1 this "t· of life" — Rev. 22 : 2.
Un. 3–16 the "t· of life." — Gen. 2 : 9.
21–10 every t· of the garden." — Gen. 3 : 1.
55– 7 own body on the t·." — I Pet. 2 : 24.
Pul. 4–19 or crown the t· with blossoms.
46–13 * going back to the ancestral t·
'00. 8– 8 characteristics of t· and flower,
Po. 20–17 the Hebrew figure of a t·.
My. 3– 9 have right to the t· of life, — Rev. 22 : 14.
111–21 Is not the t· known by its fruit?
112–24 The t· is known by its fruit.
287–21 axe at the root of the t·
300–28 The t· is known by its fruit.

tree's

Mis. 264–18 * twig is bent, the t· inclined."

trees

Pul. 63– 8 the strength to nourish t·
Po. 16–14 Which steepeth the t· when the
53– 2 paint the gray, stark t·,
My. 296– 4 the root of the t·," — Matt. 3 : 10.

tree-tops

Pul. 49– 8 * t· on the lower terrace,

tremble

Ret. 17– 8 t· with accents of bliss.
Po. 62– 8 t· with accents of bliss.
My. 344–27 I should t· for mankind ;

trembled

My. 62– 6 * that t· in one human heart

trembler

Mis. 341–14 is joy a t·?

trembling

Mis. 275– 3 woman's t·, clinging faith
390–17 The timid, t· leaves.
Peo. 8–20 t· chords of human hope
Po. 43–18 Temper every t· footfall,
55–18 The timid, t· leaves.
My. 153–22 This t· and blind faith,
293–13 of t· faith, hope, and of fear,
300– 5 with fear and t·. — Phil. 2 : 12.

tremendous

My. 90–24 * its t· outpouring of eager
93–24 * missed entirely its t· growth

Tremont Street

My. 54–28 * Chickering Hall on T· S·,

Tremont Temple

Mis. 95– 1 chapter sub-title
95– 3 * Monday lectureship in T· T·,
My. 57– 2 * were overcrowded in T· T·,

tremor

Ret. 14–12 which I answered without a t·,

tremulous

Mis. 331–13 tones t· with tenderness,
Po. 27– 6 t· with shadowy night !
My. 121– 9 neither t· nor relapsing.

trenchant

My. 160–14 t· truth that cuts its way

trend

Mis. 21–13 to depart from the t· of other
114– 8 the t· of their own thoughts ;
Ret. 23– 1 t· of human life was too eventful
65–20 t· and tenor of Christ's teaching
Po. vii– 3 * same lofty t· of thought

trend
  My. 100– 4 * unmistakable in their *t·.*
  129– 9 counteract the *t·* of mad ambition.
  305–30 was not the *t·* of thought,
Trenton, N. J.
  Pul. 89–15 * *Times, T·, N. J.*
trespass
  Mis. 184–15 would *t·* upon divine Science,
  283–18 conscious *t·* on the rights of
  Ret. 87–18 to *t·* upon the rights of
  89–26 *t·* not intentionally upon
  Pul. 3– 9 nothing can . . . *t·* on Love.
  No. 40–16 never to *t·* mentally on
trespassers
  Mis. 119–26 *t·* upon the sparse individual rights
trespasses
  My. 133–14 "dead in *t·* and sins," — *Eph.* 2 : 1.
  150–22 spiritually dead in *t·* and sins
trespassing
  Ret. 76– 5 student can write . . . without *t·,* if
  No. 3– 4 *t·* error murders either friend or
tresses
  Mis. 330–15 to shake out their *t·*
triad
  Mis. 63– 9 infinite remedy for the opposite *t·,*
  '01. 18–28 popular *t·* — sin, sickness, and death
trial
  Mis. x– 3 sincere in *t·* or in triumph.
  121–21 arrest, *t·,* and crucifixion of
  160–14 every *t·* of our faith in God
  335–24 when the hour of *t·* comes
  Man. 67– 4 cases of those on *t·*
  Ret. 20–14 vision of relief from this *t·.*
  My. 21–16 * every seeming *t·* and deprivation
  143–23 I do not regard this . . . as a *t·,*
  270–17 proven under *t·,* and evidences
trials
  Mis. 107– 5 redemptive power is seen in sore *t·,*
  126–11 have learned that *t·* lift us
  298–18 *T·* purify mortals
  No. 36–16 could find rest from unreal *t·*
  My. 47–15 * memories of *t·,* progress, and
  50– 9 * knew not the *t·* before them,
triangle
  My. 65–20 * in the shape of a *t·,*
  66– 3 * also in the shape of a *t·,*
triangular
  Pul. 24– 9 * on a *t·* plot of ground,
  My. 67– 7 * Shape, *t·* . . . 220x220x236 ft.
tribal
  Mis. 123–16 Jehovah, was the Jewish *t·* deity.
  '02. 5– 3 pagan philosophies and *t·* religions
  My. 288–14 pagan mysticisms, *t·* religion,
tribe
  Mis. 329–27 calling the feathered *t·* back to
tribes
  Mis. 73–26 *twelve t· of Israel." — Matt.* 19 : 28.
tribulation
  Mis. 18– 5 therefore rejoice in *t·,*
  No. 25– 3 Having won through great *t·*
  Peo. 14–14 be patient in *t·,*
  My. 132– 6 ye shall have *t· ; — John* 16 : 33.
tribunals
  Mis. 121–29 Human *t·,* if just,
  My. 277– 8 by means of their wholesome *t·,*
Tribune
  Pul. 90–11 * *T·,* Minneapolis, Minn.
  90–12 * *T·,* Salt Lake City, Utah.
tributary
  Mis. 127–17 the *t·* of divine Love,
  Un. 13– 3 makes God *t·* to man,
  Pul. 3–21 a *t·* of divine Love,
  My. 18–14 the *t·* of divine Love,
tribute
  Pul. 76–17 * the *t·* of loving friends.
  My. 202– 8, 9 *t·* to whom *t·* is due ; — *Rom.* 13 : 7.
  291– 1 chapter sub-title
  295– 8 chapter sub-title
  332– 8 * meagre *t·* for so noble an effort
  332– 8 * as a *t·* of grateful hearts?
  333– 8 * the last *t·* of respect
  351– 5 * beautiful *t·* to Free Masonry.
tributes
  My. 289– 6 chapter sub-title
tried
  Mis. xl–27 I have *t·* to remove the
  10–19 I *t·* their strength and proven it ;
  24–16 *t·* to make plain to others,
  235–27 *t·* to follow the divine precept,

tried
  Mis. 278–17 who are *t·* in the furnace
  348–26 I *t·* several doses of medicine,
  Man. 50–20 offender's case shall be *t·*
  My. 11– 9 * not *t·* to guide us by means of
  16–25 a stone, a *t·* stone, — *Isa.* 28 : 16.
  121– 8 a true, *t·* mental conviction
  290– 4 the *t·* and true seem few.
  306–26 *t·* to get them published
triennial
  My. 141–10 * except on the *t·* gatherings,
triennially
  Mis. 120–20 Association hereafter meet *t· :*
  Man. 84–11 shall have one class *t·,*
tries
  Mis. 43–21 If one student *t·* to undermine
  212–28 *t·* to show his errors to him
  My. 212–26 He *t·* to compensate himself for
trifle
  Mis. 257–16 code whose modes *t·* with joy,
  My. 123–21 a *t·* over two hundred people,
trifles
  My. 75–18 * do not get excited over *t·.*
  123–29 * "*t·* make perfection,"
trifling
  Mis. 43–11 a *t·* sense of it as being
trimmed
  Mis. 92–11 keeps his own lamp *t·*
  276–25 shall have their lamps *t·*
  Ret. 84– 8 his own lamp *t·* and burning.
  My. 125–27 Are our lamps *t·* and burning?
trimmings
  Pul. 24–23 * with *t·* of the pink granite
Trinitarian
  Ret. 13– 2 Congregational (*T·*) Church,
  Rud. 2– 5 He adds, that among *T·* Christians
Trinity
  My. 338– 7 * upon the subject of the *T·,*
trinity
  Mis. 63– 9 divine *t·* is one infinite remedy
  Un. 62–17 Destroy this *t·* of error,
  63– 4 *t·* of Love lives and reigns
  Rud. 3– 8 Life, Truth, and Love — this *t·* of good
  4– 2 Life, Truth, and Love are this *t·*
  No. 1–19 divine oneness of the *t·,*
  1–20 *t·* in unity, correcting the
  '01. 7– 4 *t·* of the Godhead in C. S.
  Hea. 3–25 "God is . . . a *t·* in unity ;
  My. 185–15 Love formed this *t·,*
  185–15 the *t·* no man can sunder.
trip
  Mis. 329–18 her little feet *t·* lightly on,
  My. 169– 4 so long a *t·* for so small a
  177–10 I am quite able to take the *t·*
  312–19 While on a business *t·*
  312–21 I was with him on this *t·.*
triple
  My. 78–13 * and in *t·* galleries.
tripping
  Mis. 250–26 little feet *t·* along the sidewalk ;
triturations
  My. 107–11 same *t·* of medicine have not
triumph
  and rest
  Po. 78– 5 their reward, *t·* and rest,
  crowning
  My. 323–22 * Your crowning *t·* over error
  defeat, and
  Mis. 204– 8 sorrow, joy, defeat, and *t·.*
  of art
  '00. 11–16 his composition is the *t·* of art,
  of good
  Mis. 201–31 *t·* of good that has pleasure in
  of mind
  Peo. 13–17 *t·* of mind over the body,
  My. 74–13 * *t·* of mind over matter.
  of Soul
  Hea. 10–19 *t·* of Soul over sense.
  of Spirit
  Ret. 56–14 *t·* of Spirit in immutable harmony.
  over death
  Un. 43–10 complete *t·* over death,
  over sin
  No. 36–20 *t·* over sin, sickness, and death.
  over the grave
  Mis. 74–25 His *t·* over the grave
  sublime
  Un. 58–14 The Master's sublime *t·*

triumph

tear or
  Mis. 398–14   Tear or *t·* harms,
  Ret. 46–20   Tear or *t·* harms,
  Pul. 17–19   Tear or *t·* harms,
  Po. 14–18   Tear or *t·* harms,

tears and
  Mis. 116–24   prayer, struggles, tears, and *t·*.

this
  Ret. 22–16   but this *t·* will come !

toil is
  Mis. 340–24   Be active, . . . toil is *t·* ;

to the truth
  Po. 23–21   Give peaceful *t·* to the truth,

———

  Mis. x– 3   sincere in trial or in *t·*.
     200–26   *t·* of a reasonable faith
     201–17   enabled him to *t·* over them,
     248– 7   "I will *t·* in the works of — *Psal.* 92 : 4.
  '02. 3–23   *t·* canker not his coronation,
  My. 134– 8   To *t·* in truth, to keep the faith
     161–31   can *t·* over their ultimatum,
     227–28   I abide by this rule and *t·* by it.

triumphal
  Mis. 130–30   *t·* march out of the wilderness,
  Po. 30–18   Piercing the clouds with its *t·*

triumphant
  Man. 19– 6   Church Universal and *T·*
  Mis. 100–20   the evermore of Truth is *t·*.
     124–30   to understanding, Love *t·* !
     138–25   equal to the march *t·*,
     153– 5   Truth is restful, and Love is *t·*.
     374–12   and its art will rise *t·* ;
     385–25   faith *t·* round thy death-couch
  Pul. 3–19   of the church *t·* ;
  Pan. 14– 2   righteousness with its *t·* train.
  Po. 48–21   faith *t·* round thy death-couch
  My. 133– 8   rise to the church *t·*,
     154–27   foreshadowing of the church *t·*.
     174–30   rejoice in the church *t·*
     185–10   till Truth shall reign *t·*
     259–18   a lowly, *t·* trust,

triumphantly
  No. 29–24   walks *t·* over the waves of sin,
  My. 273– 7   * emerging *t·* from all attacks

triumphed
  '02. 19–26   great Master *t·* in furnace fires.

triumphs
  Mis. 260– 3   By conflicts, defeats, and *t·*,
     281– 2   chant hymns of victory for *t·*.
     298–23   faith vested in righteousness *t·* !
     321–11   *t·* of Truth over error,
     356–23   This virtue *t·* over the flesh ;
  Un. 3–12   and the *t·* of Spirit.
  Po. 25–19   Wreaths for the *t·* o'er ill !
  My. 124–13   bloodless sieges and tearless *t·*,
     291–27   Tears blend with her *t·*.

triune
  Mis. 63– 8   *t·* Principle of all pure theology ;
     385– 1   * "Faith, hope, and tears, *t·*,
  '01. 4–25   *t·*, because He is Life, Truth, Love,
     5– 7   one divine infinite *t·* Principle,
  Po. 37– 1   "Faith, hope, and tears, *t·*,

trod
  Po. 26– 4   The turf where thou hast *t·*
  My. 151–18   * aisles by flaunting folly *t·*,

trodden
  Mis. 274–28   individual rights are *t·* under
     301–31   *t·* the winepress alone ;— *Isa.* 63 : 3.
  My. 190–13   belied, and *t·* upon.

troddest
  Pul. 1–16   This spot whereon thou *t·*

tropic
  Mis. 394– 4   An infinite essence from *t·* to pole,
  Po. 45– 5   An infinite essence from *t·* to pole,

troth
  Mis. 298–12   my best friend break *t·* with me?

trouble
  Mis. 10–13   their help in times of *t·*.
     54–18   *I was healed of a chronic t·*
     80–18   and full of *t·*." — *Job.* 14 : 1.
     96– 4   help in all times of *t·*,
  Man. 53–12   If a member, . . . shall *t·* her
  Chr. 55–14   and full of *t·*. — *Job.* 14 : 1.
  Un. 2– 5   present help in *t·*." — *Psal.* 46 : 1.
     8– 2   much *t·* to many earnest thinkers
  '01. 19– 4   given to them in times of *t·*,
  My. 162– 3   present help in *t·*'" — *Psal.* 46 : 1.
     167– 9   ever-present help in *t·*,
     359– 3   neither do they *t·* me with their

troubled
  Mis. 71– 7   thinks that he was *t·* with
     277– 2   their hearts are not *t·*.
     324–20   growing more and more *t·*,
     389–23   drops down upon the *t·* breast,
     397– 5   o'er earth's *t·*, angry sea
  Ret. 13– 6   predestination, greatly *t·* me ;
     50– 7   This amount greatly *t·* me.
  Un. 50–22   awake from the *t·* dream,
  Pul. 18–14   o'er earth's *t·*, angry sea
  '00. 7–22   walking the wave of earth's *t·* sea,
  '02. 19–19   heaving surf of life's *t·* sea
  Po. 5– 2   drops down upon the *t·* breast,
     12–14   o'er earth's *t·*, angry sea
  My. 152– 3   anchored its faith in *t·* waters.
     325– 6   * Mr. Wiggin was very much *t·*

troubles
  Mis. 236– 5   little else than the *t·*,
  Ret. 3– 6   Indian *t·* of 1722–1725,
  Un. 18–15   console others in *t·* that you
  My. 212–29   animal magnetism never *t·* him,
     311– 9   * "she *t·* me so much."

troublesome
  Mis. 370–22   braying donkey . . . is less *t·*.
  '01. 31– 9   truths . . . that now seem *t·*.

trow
  Mis. 395– 8   And yet I *t·*,
  Po. 57–15   And yet I *t·*,
  My. 20– 9   I *t·* you are awaiting

trowel
  Man. 61– 1   No special *t·* should be used.

Troy, N. Y.
  Pul. 89–14   * *Telegram, T·, N. Y.*

truant
  Pul. 48–13   * little *t·* river, as it wanders

true
  Mis. 15–10   can give the *t·* perception of God
    18–15, 16   the *t·* man and *t·* woman,
     22–16   all *t·* thoughts revolve in
     22–32   *T·*, Newton named it gravitation,
     23– 4   Is pantheism *t·*?
     24–23   therefore it cannot be *t·*.
     40–14   All *t·* healing is governed by,
     41–31   Principle that he knows to be *t·*.
     46– 7   tested scientifically to be found *t·*,
     47–30   accepts as either useful or *t·*.
     57– 3   If the first record is *t·*,
     57– 8   the *t·* creation was finished,
     57–17   opposite error said, "I am *t·*,"
     62–12   aggregate positive, or *t·* quantity,
     65– 7   this is because Science is *t·*,
     65–15   to gain the *t·* solution of Life
     69– 5   the unfolding of *t·* metaphysics ;
     70– 2   That the Bible is *t·*
     72– 6   the only living and *t·* origin, God.
     73–10   separates the false sense from the *t·*,
     74– 6   the *t·* basis of being,
     76– 6   statement of our Master is *t·*,
     76– 8   never be tested or proven *t·* upon a
     79–21   *t·* ideal of immortal man's divine
     80–19   promotes and impels all *t·* reform ;
     81– 9   which is the *t·* system of medicine.
     91– 2   as a type of the *t·* worship,
     93–15   This being *t·*, sin has no power ;
     98–27   * "Thou must be *t·* thyself,
     103–15   as tangible, *t·* substance,
     104–24   How shall we reach our *t·* selves?
     104–28   would not gain the *t·* ideal
     104–31   on the side of good, my *t·* being.
     108–15   This *t·* conception would remove
     113– 4   If, as is indisputably *t·*,
     113–23   resisted by *t·* Christianity.
     117– 7   the wrong motive or the *t·*
     128– 7   whatsoever things are *t·*, — *Phil.* 4 : 8.
     135– 1   Christians, and all *t·* Scientists,
     139–26   like all *t·* wisdom,
     140– 5   the *t·* nature of the gift ;
     142–18   varying types of *t·* affection,
     143– 2   *t·* friendship's "level"
     156–23   the basis of all *t·* thought
     157–12   Every *t·* Christian Scientist
     171– 2   never be wrested from its *t·* meaning
     171–18   By these signs are the *t·* disciples
     176–23   establish a nation in *t·* freedom,
     179–15   more *t·*, more spiritual."
     181–15   understand man's *t·* birthright,
     183–30   will arrive at the *t·* status
     185–14   the *t·* image and likeness.
     187–12   must be accepted as *t·*
     189–12   brings to light the *t·* reflection :
     193– 2   Are they *t·*?
     193– 4   that the Scripture is *t·* ;
     206–16   of what constitutes *t·* manhood.

true

Mis.	216– 3	There *remaineth*, it is *t*·,
	217– 1	*T*· idealism is a divine Science,
	222–15	because the false seems *t*·.
	226–15	* To thine own self be *t*·,
	228–16	a kind, *t*·, and just person,
	233–20	the practice of *t*· medicine,
	233–27	having a *t*· standard,
	238– 5	for all who dare to be *t*·,
	248–19	is not more *t*· than
	250–20	having no ring of the *t*· metal.
	264–27	must be pure, grand, *t*·,
	266– 9	The *t*· leader of a *t*· cause
	271–27	* between *t*· and false teachers
	278–31	on the part of *t*· followers,
	291–22	the *t*· and unswerving course
	294–28	the *t*· ideas of humanity
	298–25	*t*· consciousness is the *t*· health.
	299–27	*t*·, it saves your purchasing these
	309–10	*t*· contemplation of his character.
	309–13	Experience proves this *t*·.
	311– 3	*t*· . . . Scientists will be welcomed,
	321–13	*t*· worshippers shall — *see John* 4 : 23.
	336– 4	a lie is never *t*·
	336–22	cognomen of all *t*· religion,
	338–20	* "Thou must be *t*· thyself,
	344– 1	chapter sub-title
	346–14	is not more *t*· or real than
	352–10	*t*· consciousness of God,
	357– 6	having strayed from the *t*· fold,
	357–28	lambs that have sought the *t*· fold
	363– 3	divine Mind and *t*· happiness.
	366– 4	*T*·, it requires more study to
	369– 1	*t*· . . . Scientist at the foot of
	370–26	*t*· fold for Christian healers,
	372–28	*t*· hue and character of the
	375–14	* idea of what constitutes *t*· art.
	375–19	* is the foundation of *t*· art.
	375–28	* the only *t*· art
	376– 2	* *t*· art of the oldest, most revered,
	384– 4	And *t*· hearts greet,
Man.	40–10	in *t*· brotherliness, charitableness,
	93–12	a *t*· and just reply to public
Ret.	21–20	*t*· estimate of being.
	25–28	witness is not *t*·." — *John* 5 : 31.
	35–16	speaking of his *t*· followers
	44–29	that hour holds this *t*· record.
	52– 8	a home for every *t*· seeker
	68–11	while the other is *t*·.
	68–26	scientific thoughts are *t*·
	73–16	in the *t*· Mind,
	81–24	* To thine own self be *t*· ;
	86– 4	we must ourselves be *t*·.
	87– 4	so eternally *t*·, so axiomatic,
	90–16	The *t*· mother never willingly neglects
	93–22	but it is nevertheless *t*·.
	94– 5	seems *t*·, and yet contradicts
	94– 8	acknowledging the *t*· way,
	94–16	immortal Truth be found *t*·,
Un.	1–18	closer to the *t*· understanding of God
	2–14	The *t*· man, really *saved*,
	4–13	God is all *t*· consciousness ;
	9–18	*t*· solution of the perplexing problem
	13– 4	the reverse is *t*· in Science,
	13–12	*t*· understanding of Deity.
	17– 2	to be accounted *t*·.
	21–20	belonging to *t*· individuality,
	23– 2	which makes *t*· the lines :
	26–17	Now if it be *t*· that God's power
	26–18	can it be also *t*· that *chance*
	32–16	*T*· Mind is immortal.
	33– 9	witness is not *t*·." — *John* 5 : 31.
	42–28	*t*· manhood and womanhood go forth
	49– 8	The more I understand *t*· humanhood,
	53–22	he has lost his *t*· individuality
	61– 1	the *t*· evidence of Life,
	62–12	the *t*· ideal of omnipotent and
Pul.	2–28	*t*· temple is no human fabrication.
	4–16	seer's declaration *t*·,
	9–11	Woman, *t*· to her instinct,
	10–17	Christ, the *t*·, the spiritual idea,
	33–25	* It is certainly *t*· that many
	34–19	* and that it is as *t*· to-day
	80–20	* but this much is *t*· :
	81–24	* She is the apostle of the *t*·,
	82–19	* *T*·, there were Miriam and Esther,
Rud.	3–19	Mind, which gives all *t*· volition,
	5– 4	"Let God be *t*·, — *Rom.* 3 : 4.
	6–19	*t*· evidence of spiritual sense
	7–15	*t*· evidence of the being of God
	8–11	be *t*· to thyself, and *t*· to others ;
	11–20	based on a *t*· understanding of God
	17– 5	*t*· character of C. S.,
	17– 8	*t*· understanding of C. S.
No.	v– 9	life-giving waters of a *t*· divinity,
	4–22	*t*· constituency of being.

true

No.	5– 1	All *t*· Christian Scientists are
	7– 2	to be wise and *t*· rejoices every
	9– 4	It is *t*· that the mistakes,
	10– 3	C. S. is demonstrably as *t*·,
	11–18	It is *t*· that it requires more study
	12–14	*t*· Christianity in all ages,
	12–18	Living a *t*· life, casting out evil,
	13– 7	If this be *t*·, then death must be
	13–13	declaration is nevertheless *t*·,
	17– 8	it is impossible for the *t*· man
	28–21	demonstrably *t*· cannot be gainsaid ;
	32–15	other theories make sin *t*·.
	34–10	the *t*· worshippers shall — *John* 4 : 23.
	34–13	who discern his *t*· merit,
	36– 6	Jesus' *t*· and conscious being
	38– 6	established the only *t*· idealism
	38– 9	*t*· philosophy and realism.
	39–17	*T*· prayer is not asking God for love ;
	42–20	declaring itself both *t*· and good.
Pan.	9–26	chapter sub-title
	11–28	man is the *t*· image of God,
	12–28	It is divinely *t*·,
'00.	15– 7	start forward with *t*· ambition.
'01.	1–18	All that is *t*· is a sort of necessity,
	5–24	anything that is real, good, or *t*· ;
	11–13	*T*·, I have made . . . the pastor
	22– 1	That God is good, that Truth is *t*·,
	22–11	so if one is *t*·, the other is false.
	22–12	If Truth is *t*·, its opposite,
	22–13	if Spirit is *t*· and infinite,
'02.	3–28	the only *t*· ambition is to
	7– 1	the *t*· nature of Love intact
	8– 9	shows what *t*· spirituality is,
	12– 5	Messiah, the *t*· spiritual idea,
	17–17	Who . . . ever found her *t*· ?
	18–13	Jesus was compassionate, *t*·,
	19– 4	*T*· to his divine nature,
Hea.	10–27	*t*· fount and Soul's baptism.
	17–21	and therefore are not *T*·
Peo.	2– 2	*t*· glory of immortality.
	6–18	spiritual and *t*· ideal of Deity
Po.	36– 3	And *t*· hearts greet,
My.	4–20	Thus unfolding the *t*· metal
	4–32	natural and demonstrably *t*·,
	6– 4	Are we *t*· to ourselves?
	15–23	* Because I know 'tis *t*· ;
	26–24	the *t*· animus of our church
	28– 6	* this has been proved *t*·
	42– 2	* We have found it *t*· that
	46–14	* work of *t*· Christian Scientists.
	59– 6	* we thought this might be *t*·
	91–13	* element in *t*· Christianity.
	118– 3	go on promoting the *t*· Principle
	119–31	*t*· image and likeness of God.
	121– 8	a *t*·, tried mental conviction
	121–18	found in a *t*· character,
	123–24	the *t*· Christian Scientist is not
	130– 1	correct the false with the *t*·
	138–29	that the statements . . . are *t*·.
	146–17	if they are *t*· at all,
	146–18	as *t*· to-day as they will be
	146–21	what I wrote is *t*·,
	150– 6	the character of *t*· greatness :
	158–21	the heart tender, faithful, *t*·.
	159–15	the *t*· thought escapes from the
	179–23	a *t*· divinity and humanity.
	181–13	the motive of *t*· religion,
	204– 9	C. S. unites its *t*· followers
	213–21	harmony with His *t*· followers.
	229– 9	*t*· that loyal Christian Scientists,
	232–18	the *t*· authority for C. S.?
	233– 1	the spirit of *t*· watching,
	235–30	commemorated . . . what is not *t*·,
	252–11	purpose of *t*· education
	259–19	a *t*· heart, and a helping hand
	260–24	The *t*· spirit of Christmas
	266–29	undoubtedly *t*· that C. S.
	267–25	to darken the *t*· conception
	290– 4	the tried and *t*· seem few.
	306–10	making the *t*· apparent.
	315–18	* statement by him signed is *t*·.
	334– 2	* that the rumor is not *t*·.
	357–23	the axiom of *t*· C. S.,
	357–30	I know that every *t*· follower
	358– 2	the *t*· following of their Leader ;

(*see also* **Christian, God, idea, knowledge, likeness, Science, sense**)

true-hearted

Mis.	301–19	question of my *t*· students,

truer

Mis.	17–31	gains a *t*· sense of Spirit
	47–17	which is the *t*· sense of being.
No.	34– 5	when we gain the *t*· sense of
'01.	9– 7	*t*· sense of Christ baptized them

truer

Peo. 12–17 advance to t· conceptions,
My. 64– 3 * a larger and t· meaning.

truest

Mis. 375– 5 t· art of C.· S. is to be a
'00. 10– 6 the t· signs that can be given
My. 213–10 the t· friends of mankind,

truism

Mis. 46– 6 t· needs only to be tested
259–24 t· that Truth demonstrates good,
271–16 take in this axiomatic t· :
382– 1 either a t· or a rule,
Ret. 87– 4 that it has become a t· ;
No. 39– 1 It is a t· that we can think

truisms

My. 160–11 willingly accept dead t·

truly

Mis. ix–18 T· may it be said :
98–25 T· is it written :
108–21 that which is t· conceived of,
126– 4 T·, I half wish for society again ;
134– 7 Very t·,
170– 2 for by following Christ t·,
338–26 * "Think t·, and thy thoughts
338–28 * Speak t·, and each word of thine
338–30 * Live t·, and thy life shall be
372–17 * are t· a work of art,
Ret. 14–22 that I had been t· regenerated,
25–15 Soul alone is t· substantial.
Un. 3– 6 before it can be t· said of them :
45–28 Matter is not t· conscious ;
No. 3– 6 T· it is better to fall into the hands
16– 2 must t· and eternally exist.
Pan. 13–26 T· there is no rest in them,
'02. 10–10 Rev. Hugh Black writes t· :
My. 4–10 follow t·, meekly, patiently,
42– 1 * to be t· grateful to her who
98– 2 * t· make up a mighty host,
113–32 the t· great men and women
142–21 Most t· yours,
158– 4 Very t·,
282–27 Most t· yours,
351–14 t· Masonic, tender, grand in you
361–21 * t· democratic and liberal

trumpet-call

My. 155–10 May it catch the early t·,

trunk

My. 125– 8 incline . . . towards the parent t·.

trunks

Mis. 274–25 headless t·, and quivering hearts
My. 82–10 * t· and smaller articles of baggage

Trust

Deed of
(see **Deed of Trust**)

trust

childlike
Mis. 15–15 childlike t· and joyful adoption of
deed of
My. 157–18 * in her original deed of t·,
157 22 a deed of t· to three individuals
executive
Pan. 14–16 associated with his executive t· .
feeling of
My. 50–17 * a feeling of t· in the
fond
My. 158– 9 in attune with faith's fond t·.
his
Mis. 107–31 placing his t· in this grand Truth,
my
My. 138 10 test my t· in divine Love.
no
Peo. 8–27 trusting where there is no t·,
our
My. 200– 6 our t· is in the Almighty God,
proclaims the
My. 58–13 * proclaims the t·, the willingness of
that
Mis. 284–31 to fulfil that t·
this
Ret. 31–17 for this t· is the unseen sin,
triumphant
My. 259–19 a lowly, triumphant t·, a true heart,

Mis. vii–12 There's nothing here to t·.
25–26 if the sick cannot t· God for help
48–19 has, we t·, been made in season to
157–20 t· also in Him ;— Psal. 37 : 5.
269– 1 t· also in Him ;— Psal. 37 : 5.
269–27 Error is vending itself on t·,
271–16 * "T· her not, she's fooling thee ;"
297–28 T· Truth, not error ;
298– 1 "T· in the Lord with— Prov. 3 : 5.
320– 1 t· the divine Providence,

trust

Mis. 369–17 t· Christ more than it does drugs.
Man. 96–13 t· to contributions for his fee.
Ret. 14–15 I was willing to t· God,
No. v– 7 import of this edition is, we t·,
3–24 t· Love's recompense of love.
'01. 34–29 "T· in the Lord— Prov. 3 : 5.
'02. 19–27 Then, Christian Scientists, t·,
Hea. 14–11 never t· yourself in the hands of
My. 26–19 t· that you will see, as I foresee,
120– 4 t· that you and I may meet in truth
129–28 T· God to direct your steps.
161–26 T· in God, and "He shall— Prov. 3 : 6.
167–27 will, I t·, never be marred by
170–20 "T· in the Lord,— Psal. 37 : 3.
170–23 t· also in Him ;— Psal. 37 : 5.
171– 1 T· in Truth, and have no other
217– 6 deeded in t· to The Mother Church
275 14 (and I t· the desire thereof)
290–13 T· in Him whose love enfolds thee.
343–20 and t· in me grew.

trusted

My. 138–12 students and t· personal friends

trustee-deed

Mis. 140–13 and I supposed the t· was legal ;

Trustees and trustees (see also **Board of Trustees**)

Man. 27–26 Boards of T· and Syndicates
65–13 T· of The C. S. Publishing Society,
80–20 remaining t· shall fill the vacancy,
Pul. 20– 4 and through t· gave back the land
20– 6 to recover the land from the t·,
'02. 13–29 gave to my church through t·,
My. vi–22 * she made over to t· under agreement
66– 1 * taken by Ira O. Knapp et al., t·.
136–24 To my aforesaid T· I have
137–27 I selected said T· because I had
137–30 able to select the T· I need
199–11 Directors and T· of this church
362–12 * The T· and Readers of all the

Trusteeship and trusteeship

Man. 80–12 Vacancies in T·.
80–14 to declare vacancies in said t·,

Trusteeships

Man. 27–25 T· and Syndicates.

trusteth

My. 290–15 because he t· in Thee."— Isa. 26 : 3.

trustful

Mis. 127–14 If this heart, humble and t·,
Pul. 45–17 * heaped upon the hopeful, t· ones,
My. 18–10 If this heart, humble and t·,

trusting

'02. 19–27 and t·, you will find divine Science
Peo. 8–27 t· where there is no trust,
My. 138–19 T· that I have not exceeded the

trustingly

My. 182–19 gratefully, t·, I dedicate

trusts

Man. 87–19 t· them to the divine Truth
102–13 shall have named in them all the t·
Ret. 84 25 t· them to the divine Truth
'02. 4– 2 dishonesty in t·, begin with
My. 171– 2 and have no other t·.
230–23 faithful over foundational t·,
265– 8 invests less in t·, loses capital,
266– 8 ritual, creed, and t· in place of

trustworthiness

Mis. 118–17 meritorious faith or t·
153–20 positive proof of t·.
Hea. 5–13 * t· of the communications,

trustworthy

Rud. 13–23 methods of t· Christian Scientists

trusty

Mis. 147–22 at all times the t· friend,

Truth (see also **Truth's**)

abiding in
Mis. 331– 8 abiding in T·, the warmth and
above
Mis. 277– 6 trying to be heard above T·,
My. 249– 5 error strives to be heard above T·,
absolute
Mis. 311–24 The works . . . contain absolute T·,
My. 293–16 prevented the power of absolute T·
according as
Mis. 147–15 according as T· and the voice of
adherents
Mis. 213–19 the faithful adherents of T·
Man. 15– 3 As adherents of T·, we take
admits
Ret. 54–14 admits T· without understanding it.
advent of
Ret. 81–15 After the supreme advent of T·

Truth

against
Mis. 328–14 and closed it against *T·*,
aiming for
My. 126– 6 human mind . . . aiming for *T·*,
all
Mis. 163–27 which leadeth into all *T·*
    174–32 that leadeth into all *T·* ;
Un. 46– 3 All *T·* is from inspiration
No. 9–24 it . . . includes all *T·*.
alone
No. 5– 7 As *T·* alone is real,
alterative
Mis. 241–10 the great alterative, *T·* :
    241–19 administer this alterative *T·* :
and error
Mis. 65–10 question between *T·* and error,
    188–12 contest between *T·* and error ;
'01. 22–10 *T·* and error, Spirit and matter,
and Life
Mis. 320–22 words of *T·* and Life.
Chr. 53–10 God anoints Of *T·* and Life ;
Un. 32– 2 false to *T·* and Life.
No. 16–10 negations of Spirit, *T·*, and Life,
Hea. 3–24 "God is Love, *T·*, and Life,"
My. 221–30 divine Mind, *T·* and Life,
    257–21 and the reign of *T·* and Life
    261–26 *T·* and Life born of God
and Love
Mis. 2– 2 *T·* and Love to heal the sick.
    3– 8 the power of *T·* and Love.
    4– 1 imbued with purity, *T·*, and Love,
    5–13 healing power is *T·* and Love,
    19–13 divine claims of *T·* and Love
    36–29 that intelligence, *T·*, and Love,
    40–23 possess the spirit of *T·* and Love,
    66–14 law and gospel of *T·* and Love
    92– 9 open fount of *T·* and Love.
    100– 1 spake of *T·* and Love
    103–30 Life, infinite *T·* and Love.
    135– 5 watchwords are *T·* and Love ;
    157–13 as free in *T·* and Love,
    164–16 manifestation of *T·* and Love,
    165–21 his treasures of *T·* and Love,
    166– 8 *T·* and Love — is still with us.
    166–15 understanding of *T·* and Love.
    189–11 Spiritual insight of *T·* and Love
    205– 4 *T·* and Love, shining through the
    205–10 of the spirit of *T·* and Love
    241–28 divine *T·* and Love heal,
    260–28 vital functions of *T·* and Love.
    284–18 vindicated divine *T·* and Love
    285–11 hold high the banner of *T·* and Love,
    317– 3 When born of *T·* and Love,
    320–14 beckons him on to *T·* and Love
    333–29 exemplify the power of *T·* and Love.
    336–24 Part and parcel of *T·* and Love,
    354–25 by wisdom, *T·*, and Love.
    356–31 the way of *T·* and Love.
    371–15 more and more of *T·* and Love ;
    373–32 demonstration of *T·* and Love.
Man. 60–10 *T·* and Love rest the weary
    87–20 to the divine *T·* and Love,
Ret. 30–14 infinite energies of *T·* and Love,
    31–14 spontaneous motion of *T·* and Love,
    49– 2 advancement . . . in *T·* and Love ;
    50–21 adherence to divine *T·* and Love.
    64–25 deathless *T·* and Love.
    65– 2 their opinions of *T·* and Love
    65–10 savor of *T·* and Love.
    66– 1 ever-present *T·* and Love.
    84– 6 open fount of *T·* and Love.
    84–25 to the divine *T·* and Love,
    85–10 from the heaven of *T·* and Love,
    92– 4 he healed by *T·* and Love.
Un. 2–23 a knowledge of *T·* and Love
    48–20 able to demonstrate *T·* and Love.
Pul. 3–12 dwellers in *T·* and Love,
    75– 2 spirit of *T·* and Love,
Rud. 3– 5 spiritual *T·* and Love,
    8–13 Heal through *T·* and Love ;
No. 7–15 rescue and refuge in *T·* and Love.
    8–18 commandments of Christ, — *T·* and Love.
    11–28 demonstration of *T·* and Love.
    34– 7 efficacy of *T·* and Love,
    40–23 It is *T·* and Love that cast out fear
    44–19 healing balm of *T·* and Love
'02. 8–16 with tenderness, *T·* and Love,
Hea. 16– 7 wealth and fame, or *T·* and Love?
Po. 31–15 *T·* and Love attest The solemn
My. 60–14 * temple of "wisdom, *T·*, and Love."
    114–24 divine power of *T·* and Love,
    129– 1 a deterrent of *T·* and Love,
    153– 5 power of *T·* and Love will fulfil
    158–27 thereafter dedicate to *T·* and Love.
    210– 3 minds so filled with *T·* and Love,

Truth

and Love
My. 232– 7 even the way of *T·* and Love
    245–17 voice of *T·* and Love be heard
    264–17 *T·* and Love made more practical ;
    323–12 * living witness to *T·* and Love,
and the Life
Ret. 36– 2 Christ as the *T·* and the Life,
Un. 63– 3 The Way, the *T·*, and the Life
'00. 7–16 Christ, the Way, the *T·*, and the Life.
My. 139–12 nearing the Way, the *T·*, and the Life,
    260–29 the Way, the *T·*, and the Life.
and Truth
'01. 22– 9 *T·* and Truth is not a compound ;
and wisdom
Mis. 391– 9 And learn that *T·* and wisdom
Po. 38– 8 And learn that *T·* and wisdom
animus of
Mis. 38–18 Science that has the animus of *T·*.
announcing
No. 35–24 Jesus came announcing *T·*,
anoints with
My. 270–27 C. S., which anoints with *T·*,
appearing of
My. 185– 3 for the appearing of *T·*,
ark of
Mis. 92–28 attempting to steady the ark of *T·*,
Ret. 84–16 attempting to steady the ark of *T·*,
armor of
Peo. 14–14 put on the whole armor of *T·* ;
as attested
My. 194–16 *T·* as attested by the Founder of
as demonstrated
No. 28–18 *T·*, as demonstrated by Jesus,
attribute of
Mis. 2–13 justice, the eternal attribute of *T·*,
auxiliaries of
Mis. 260–26 not always the auxiliaries of *T·*.
availability of
My. 353–15 activity and availability of *T·* ;
being the cure
Mis. 221–18 If error . . . *T·* being the cure,
believe in
My. 193–18 unite with all who believe in *T·*.
bestows
Rud. 10– 3 the power that *T·* bestows,
betrays
My. 128–24 A lack of wisdom betrays *T·*
birth of
My. 262–15 the birth of *T·*, the dawn of
bright gold of
Un. 54– 1 bright gold of *T·* is dimmed by
built on
Hea. 2–26 his name who built, on *T·*,
    11–10 superstructure is built on *T·* ;
can know
Un. 19–17 actuality which *T·* can know.
canonized
My. 268–24 *T·*, canonized by life and love,
casting out evils
Ret. 65–23 *T·*, casting out evils and healing
casts out
Mis. 68–17 error which *T·* casts out.
    191–17 that Christ, *T·*, casts out.
Cause of
Un. 5–17 promote the Cause of *T·*
No. 9– 4 hindrance of the Cause of *T·*.
cause of
My. 49–28 * labors in the cause of *T·*,"
challenged by
My. 233– 7 when challenged by *T·*,
channels of
Mis. 220–11 turn them into channels of *T·*.
chariot-wheels of
My. 127– 7 speed of the chariot-wheels of *T·*
Christ is
Mis. 180– 9 I replied ; "Christ is *T·*,
comes
Mis. 215– 3 *T·* comes into the intermediate space,
    218–16 *T·* comes to the rescue
'01. 1–19 *T·* comes from a deep sincerity
coming anew of
My. 307–19 referred to the *coming* anew of *T·*,
conception of
Ret. 83–13 mistake in his conception of *T·*,
confirms
Un. 36– 7 it unwittingly confirms *T·*,
conflict against
My. 358– 9 conflict against *T·* is engendered
consciousness of
My. 63–14 * expanding consciousness of *T·*,
controvert
Mis. 109– 6 invert, or controvert, *T·* ;
crucible of
Mis. 79– 3 dissolved in the crucible of *T·*,

Truth

crushed to earth
  My. 128– 9 *T·* crushed to earth springs
currents of
  Mis. 135–16 Sending forth currents of *T·*,
  157–28 the eternal currents of *T·*.
dawned
  Mis. 24–12 *T·* dawned upon my sense ;
  169– 9 before *T·* dawned upon her
defeat in
  My. 278–26 Victory in error is defeat in *T·*.
defense of
  Mis. 110–27 dared the perilous defense of *T·*,
delightful
  My. 350–26 *T·* delightful, crowned with endless
delivers
  Mis. 298–21 then *T·* delivers you from
demands
  Chr. 53–19 To celebrate As *T·* demands,
demands of
  Mis. 201– 3 immortal demands of *T·*.
demonstrated
  Mis. 251–27 will fall before *T·* demonstrated,
  334–26 substitution of *T·* demonstrated,
  ’02. 6– 9 Christ, *T·*, demonstrated
demonstrates
  Mis. 116–26 Obeying . . . demonstrates *T·*.
  259–24 truism that *T·* demonstrates good,
  Man. 92– 4 *T·* demonstrates what we affirm
  My. 288– 9 it demonstrates *T·* and reflects
demonstrating
  Mis. 116–22 the Word — demonstrating *T·*
demonstration of
  Mis. 192– 7 to his demonstration of *T·*
  373–32 demonstration of *T·* and Love,
  Ret. 75–11 and demonstration of *T·*,
  No. 11–28 demonstration of *T·* and Love.
denial by
  Mis. 247–32 met, . . . with a denial by *T·*.
denial of
  Mis. 31– 2 malpractice is a bland denial of *T·*,
denying
  Un. 25–12 denying *T·* and its demonstration
destroyed by
  Mis. 37–22 sin . . . is destroyed by *T·*.
destroy it with
  Ret. 55– 5 to destroy it with *T·*.
destroys
  Mis. 56–21 an error . . . that *T·* destroys.
  62–19 error . . . that *T·* destroys.
  65–13 which the positive *T·* destroys ;
  105–24 *T·* destroys error.
  241–20 *T·* destroys the error that insists
  My. 349– 6 state or error that *T·* destroys.
disclaim against
  Mis. 174– 4 to talk and disclaim against *T·* ;
discoveries of
  No. 41–23 by new discoveries of *T·*
dispensation of
  My. 221– 7 the new dispensation of *T·*
divides
  My. 316– 3 *T·* divides between sect and Science
divine
  (see **divine**)
divinity of
  Mis. 102–24 destroys it with the divinity of *T·*.
effects of
  Mis. 188–17 effects of *T·* on the material senses ;
  My. 103–21 effects of *T·* on the health,
efficacy of
  Mis. 89–30 avail himself of the efficacy of *T·*,
  No. 34– 7 meaning and efficacy of *T·*
embodiment of
  ’00. 7–25 far from the embodiment of *T·*
energies of
  Mis. 97– 4 eternal energies of *T·*,
  Ret. 30–14 infinite energies of *T·* and Love,
engrounds me
  Mis. 397– 9 *T·* engrounds me on the rock,
  Pul. 18–18 *T·* engrounds me on the rock,
  Po. 12–18 *T·* engrounds me on the rock,
epoch of
  Mis. 363–31 every advancing epoch of *T·*
equipped with
  Hea. 14–13 In proportion as . . . equipped with *T·*,
error and
  Mis. 302–11 to discriminate between error and *T·*,
error is not
  ’01. 14–17 self-evident that error is not *T·* ;
error versus
  Mis. 332–22 Error versus *T·* : first, a supposition ;
eternal
  Mis. 182–30 eternal *T·* will be understood ;
  Un. 17– 3 make the lie seem part of eternal *T·*.
  61– 2 takes hold of eternal *T·*.
  No. 10–14 rests on Mind, the eternal *T·*.

Truth

eternal as
  Mis. 163–23 are as eternal as *T·*,
  Ret. 69–11 as real and eternal as *T·*.
ethics of
  Ret. 21–27 they illustrate the ethics of *T·*.
evangel of
  Mis. 251–30 flee before the evangel of *T·*
evermore of
  Mis. 100–20 evermore of *T·* is triumphant.
expression of
  My. 248–30 nearest the scientific expression of *T·*.
eyes of
  Mis. 233–17 is still worse in the eyes of *T·*
facts of
  Mis. 352– 8 able to behold the facts of *T·*
faith in
  Mis. 111–18 Jesus’ faith in *T·* must not exceed
falchion of
  Ret. 30– 3 smite error with the falchion of *T·*.
fall short of
  ’01. 2–16 if some fall short of *T·*,
false to
  Un. 32– 2 false to *T·* and Life.
feast of
  Mis. 233– 8 the death’s-head at the feast of *T·* ;
fed them with
  Mis. 254– 6 love that hath fed them with *T·*,
feet of
  Peo. 12–10 trampled under the feet of *T·*.
  My. 228–19 The meek, who sit at the feet of *T·*,
fidelity to
  Pul. 22–10 attest their fidelity to *T·*,
filled with
  Mis. 93– 2 that they may be filled with *T·*.
  Ret. 84–22 that they may be filled with *T·*.
  My. 210– 3 keep your minds so filled with *T·*
follow
  My. 4–10 We follow *T·* only as we follow truly,
following
  Ret. 86–19 taking up his cross and following *T·*.
follows
  My. 160– 3 and follows *T·* fearlessly.
footsteps of
  Mis. 81–13 *footsteps of T· being baptized of*
  Hea. 17– 1 through the footsteps of *T·*.
forces of
  Un. 35–17 forces of *T·* are moral and spiritual,
foretelling
  Mis. 82– 7 He who knew the foretelling *T·*,
form of
  Mis. 310– 6 impersonal form of *T·*,
forthcoming
  Mis. 82 7 beheld the forthcoming *T·*,
foundation in
  ’01. 2–25 Only a firm foundation in *T·* can
friends to
  Mis. 319–29 faith and resolve are friends to *T·* ;
full
  Un. 51–23 full *T·* is found only in divine
fusion of
  No. 5–26 Any contradictory fusion of *T·* with
genuine as
  Un. 29–15 *Evil.* . . . A lie is as genuine as *T·*,
give utterance to
  Mis. 183–19 to give utterance to *T·*.
glorious
  Mis. 159–24 “O glorious *T·* ! O Mother Love !
God as
  No. 30–25 would dethrone God as *T·*,
God is
  Mis. 25– 9 God is *T·*, and All-in-all.
  49–30 God is *T·*, the Scriptures aver ;
  Un. 35–16 But God is *T·*,
good and
  Mis. 36– 4 in contradistinction to good and *T·*,
  Peo. 3–10 spiritual idea of good and *T·*
good, or
  Mis. 196–13 came not from Mind, good, or *T·* .
gospel of
  Mis. 66–14 law and gospel of *T·* and Love
  No. 12–19 preaching the gospel of *T·*,
grace and
  Mis. 164–26 full of grace and *T·*,
grand
  Mis. 197–31 placing his trust in this grand *T·*,
great
  Mis. 47–22 This great *T·* does not destroy but
guest-chamber of
  Mis. 342– 9 entering the guest-chamber of *T·*,
happifies life
  My. 134–16 *T·* happifies life in the hamlet or
has become
  Mis. 179–14 *T·* has become more to us,
has reappeared
  No. 28–20 will know that *T·* has reappeared.

Truth

has spoken
  Mis. 266–28   Because *T·* has spoken aloud,
healing
  Mis.   24–12   healing *T·* dawned upon my sense ;
heals
  Mis. 241–16   *T·* heals him of the moral malady.
  Hea.   18–21   Christ, *T·* heals the sick.
heart of
  Ret.   75–21   strikes at the heart of *T·*.
higher sense of
  Mis. 113–12   gaining a higher sense of *T·*
his
  Mis. 214–14   The very conflict his *T·* brought,
horizon of
  Pan.   1–18   not distant in the horizon of *T·*
idea of
     (*see* **idea**)
identical with
  Un.   33–13   Mind that is identical with *T·*.
imbued with
  Hea.   11–26   requires mind imbued with *T·*
immortal
  Mis.   21–19   Spirit is immortal *T·* ;
  Ret.   94–16   then, will immortal *T·* be found true,
  No.   40– 7   spiritual and immortal *T·*.
  Po.   70–17   Immortal *T·*, — since heaven rang,
immortality of
  Mis. 163–17   faith in the immortality of *T·*.
impartation of
  Ret.   48–28   scientific impartation of *T·*,
in divine Science
  Un.   61–25   *T·*, in divine Science, is the
infinite
  Mis.   1–12   welling up from infinite *T·*
     103–30   eternal Life, infinite *T·* and Love.
     245–27   seeking to stereotype infinite *T·*,
  Hea.   4– 7   the power of infinite *T·*.
      4–14   expect infinite *T·* to mix with
  Po.   29–17   *T·* infinite, — so far above
inspiration of
  Peo.   7–28   discovery and the inspiration of *T·*
in thought
  Mis. 399–14   Thou the *T·* in thought and deed ;
  Po.   75–21   Thou the *T·* in thought and deed ;
is admitted
  Ret.   54–17   if *T·* is admitted, but not understood,
is All
  Un.   4– 6   This law declares that *T·* is All,
is always here
  Mis. 180–10   and *T·* is always here,
is God
  Un.   4– 5   *T·* is God, and in God's law.
is immortal
  My. 269–30   *T·* is immortal.
is moulding
  No.   20– 6   *T·* is moulding a Godlike man.
is neutralizing
  Pul.   6– 1   when *T·* is neutralizing error
is not in matter
  Mis. 179–14   *T·* is not in matter ;
is not lost
  Peo.   5–11   *T·* is not lost in the mists of
is restful
  Mis. 153– 4   *T·* is restful, and Love is triumphant.
is speaking
  Mis. 277– 4   *T·* is speaking louder, clearer,
is strong
  My. 229–30   *T·* is strong with destiny ;
issues of
  No.   40–16   never . . . save to issues of *T·* ;
is supreme
  Mis. 260–19   *T·* is supreme and omnipotent.
is the power
  Mis. 259–27   *T·* is the power of God
is the real
  Hea. 10–14   *T·* is the real ; error is the unreal.
      18–11   *T·* is the real ; error, the unreal.
is the tonic
  Mis. 251–30   *T·* is the tonic for the sick,
is the way
  '02.   10–24   Christ, *T·*, is the way.
is true
  '01.   22– 1   *T·* is true, and Science is
      22–12   If *T·* is true, its opposite,
is won
  Mis. 362–27   *T·* is won through Science or
knowledge of
  Mis. 160–11   knowledge of *T·* and divine Love.
  Ret.   86–17   growth in the knowledge of *T·*,
  Un.   2–23   knowledge of *T·* and Love
knows
  Un.   23– 7   and *T·* knows only such.
last appearing of
  Mis. 165– 7   The last appearing of *T·* will be

Truth

law of
  Mis. 208– 2   This is the law of *T·* to error,
  Un.   4– 6   This law of *T·* destroys every
  Rud. 10–22   His law of *T·*, when obeyed,
learned of
  Po.   77–15   When we have learned of *T·*
leaven of
  Mis.   39–20   with enough of the leaven of *T·* to
Life and
     (*see* **Life**)
Life, and Love
  Mis.   5–27   perfect in God, in *T·*, Life, and Love,
      12–31   imparting, . . . *T·*, Life, and Love
  Man. 16– 2   through *T·*, Life, and Love,
      19– 4   divine *T·*, Life, and Love,
      41–22   reign of divine *T·*, Life, and Love
  Rud.   9–12   sense of *T·*, Life, and Love.
  Hea. 15– 5   *T·*, Life, and Love, understood,
      16–23   understanding of *T·*, Life, and Love
      17–19   never . . . from *T·*, Life, and Love.
  My. 134–14   *T·*, Life, and Love will never lose
     185–10   *T·*, Life, and Love are formidable,
     195–31   with grace, *T·*, Life, and Love.
     353–13   to hold guard over *T·*, Life, and Love ;
Life, . . . and Love
     (*see* **Life**)
life of
  Peo.   9–11   bathes us in the life of *T·*
Life, . . . or Love
  Mis.   67– 6   not adulterate Life, *T·*, or Love,
Life that is
  My. 214– 9   demonstrating the Life that is *T·*,
light of
  Mis. 320–11   light of *T·*, to cheer, guide, and
  My. 241–26   * after coming to the light of *T·*,
line of
  Mis. 268–16   lie in the line of *T·* ;
lips of
  Mis.   51–22   * "When from the lips of *T·*
living
  Mis. 115– 1   through Christ, the living *T·*,
logic of
  '01.   5–25   or the logic of *T·*,
lost sight of
  Mis. 179– 5   believing we have lost sight of *T·*,
love
  My. 316– 3   uniting . . . those who love *T·* ;
Love and
     (*see* **Love**)
love of
  Mis. 235–11   the light and love of *T·*.
loyalty to
  My.   21–16   * deprivation in our loyalty to *T·*,
makes haste
  '02.   2– 9   *T·* makes haste to meet and to
mandate of
  Mis. 283–29   Science is the mandate of *T·*
manifest as
  Mis. 185– 5   is made manifest as *T·*,
manifestation of
  Mis. 164–15   manifestation of *T·* and Love.
  Rud.   3–22   manifestation of *T·* upon the body
march of
  My. 155–13   in the onward march of *T·*,
meekness and
  My. 247–11   meekness and *T·* enthroned.
meets error with
  My. 180–17   C. S. meets error with *T·*,
methods of
  Mis. 141–12   the bonds and methods of *T·*,
might of
  Mis.   52– 8   even the might of *T·*,
     100– 9   the word and might of *T·*
  My.   3– 5   The divine might of *T·*
mighty
  Mis.   43–27   unacquainted with the mighty *T·*
Mind is
  Mis. 332– 3   this Mind is *T·*,
misconception of
  Mis.   46–14   a misconception of *T·* is not
  Ret.   83–16   his misconception of *T·*,
must be
  No.   16– 6   made manifest, and must be *T·*.
name of
  Mis.   57–21   must be told in the name of *T·*,
      59– 4   will practise . . . in the name of *T·*.
naturalness of
  Mis. 200– 1   naturalness of *T·* in the mind of
nature of
  '01.   31– 6   from the very nature of *T·*,
needs
  No.   43– 7   theology needs *T·* to stimulate
never created error
  Mis.   49–30   that *T·* never created error,

Truth

never dies
 Un. 45–22 But *T·* never dies,
never engraft
 No. 43–21 can never engraft *T·* into error.
never falters
 My. 130–19 *T·* never falters nor fails ;
"new tongue" of
 No. 44– 6 "new tongue" of *T·*, — see Mark 16 : 17.
no
 Mis. 285–29 having no *T·*, it will have no past,
no basic
 Un. 49–19 Standing in no basic *T·*,
not error
 Mis. 71–16 Law brings out *T·*, not error ;
 297–28 Trust *T·*, not error ;
 My. 239– 1 *T·*, not error ; Love, not hate.
of divine Science
 Un. 10–18 in the *T·* of divine Science,
of existence
 Mis. 182– 7 receive the *T·* of existence ;
of healing
 Rud. 9–17 Science . . . is the *T·* of healing.
of Life
 Un. 39– 2 *T·* of Life is rendered practical
omnipotence of
 Mis. 61– 9 omnipotence of *T·* over error,
 192–14 well knowing the omnipotence of *T·*.
omnipresent
 Mis. 105–18 unknown to the omnipresent *T·*.
one
 Ret. 60–28 one *T·*, Life, Love,
opposed to
 Un. 22– 6 ungodliness, which is opposed to *T·*,
 28– 6 Death, then, is error, opposed to *T·*,
opposite of
 Mis. 24–22 error, the opposite of *T·* ;
 Ret. 69– 9 the opposite of *T·*, saying,
 Un. 44–12 pretender taught the opposite of *T·*.
opposition to
 Un. 56–10 mentality in opposition to *T·*,
or Christ
 Pul. 12–23 we lay down all for *T·*, or Christ,
 My. 118–27 in which *T·*, or Christ, finds its
or Life
 Un. 62–20 *T* or Life in divine Science
outcomes of
 Mis. 267–17 the vital outcomes of *T·*
outtalk
 '01. 16–21 was supposed to outtalk *T·*
outtalked even
 Mis. 191–25 supposed to have outtalked even *T·*,
over error
 Mis. 61– 9 omnipotence of *T·* over error,
 97– 1 it is *T·* over error ;
 321–11 triumphs of *T·* over error,
 Pul. 30–21 * power of *T·* over error,
 My. 154– 3 power of *T·* over error.
 302– 5 right over wrong, of *T·* over error.
part of
 Un. 5–26 of this wonderful part of *T·*
 No. 21– 4 one-hundredth part of *T·*,
pattern from
 Un. 53– 2 a lie takes its pattern from *T·*,
penetration of
 Un. 2–15 in the infinite penetration of *T·*,
perceive
 Mis. 179–29 perceive *T·*, and say with Mary,
person of
 Hea. 3–27 person of *T·*, the body of the
perverted
 Mis. 203–22 *T·* perverted, in belief, becomes the
pleads
 Chr. 53–55 *T·* pleads to-night :
postulate of
 '01. 21–21 predicate nor postulate of *T·*,
potency of
 Mis. 222–31 ways, means, and potency of *T·*
power and
 Mis. 334– 8 Whatever simulates power and *T·*
power of
 (*see* **power**)
practical
 Mis. 90– 6 practical *T·* saves from sin,
premises of
 Mis. 93– 9 to be the premises of *T·*,
prerogative of
 My. 218– 9 power and prerogative of *T·*
price of
 Mis. 342–27 if you pay the price of *T·*,
prism of
 Ret. 35–13 Science is the prism of *T·*,
proclaim
 My. 248–11 to proclaim *T·* so winningly

Truth

proclaims
 Mis. 277– 8 Whosoever proclaims *T·* loudest,
propositions of
 Ret. 31– 6 self-evident propositions of *T·*
question of
 Un. 5–11 to seek . . . this question of *T·*
ray of
 Mis. 333– 4 every ray of *T·*, of infinity,
rays of
 Mis. 194–14 to divide the rays of *T·*,
 '01. 12–21 to divide the rays of *T·*,
real fruits of
 Mis. 265–20 bring forth the real fruits of *T·*.
reality of
 No. 4–14 demonstrates the reality of *T·*
 5– 4 In . . . thought the reality of *T·* has
realize
 Mis. 171– 3 Jesus' first effort to realize *T·*
reappearing of
 No. 13–11 before this reappearing of *T·*,
rebukes error
 No. 43– 5 *T·* rebukes error ;
receive
 Mis. 168–14 only such . . . receive *T·*.
reception of
 My. 156–20 prepared for the reception of *T·*
reflecting
 Mis. 77–27 that man, . . . reflecting *T·*,
remedy of
 Mis. 45–15 demands the remedy of *T·*
replies
 Mis. 367–29 *T·* replies that God is too pure to
resist
 Ret. 80–14 to stir the human heart to resist *T·*,
restores
 No. 10–17 *T·* restores that lost sense,
revealed
 Mis. 302–16 in interpreting revealed *T·*,
reversing
 Un. 53– 2 lie takes its . . . by reversing *T·*.
rock of
 No. 38–10 godliness was the rock of *T·*,
said
 Mis. 363–13 *T·* said, and said from the beginning,
saith
 Mis. 109–28 Christ, *T·*, saith unto you,
sanctuary of
 Mis. 77–23 the spiritual sanctuary of *T·*,
Saviour, which is
 Mis. 164– 9 Saviour, which is *T·*, be comprehended.
Science of
 Mis. 14–29 Science of *T·* annihilates error,
 My. 353–12 the divine Science of *T·* ;
seed of
 Mis. 111–15 Leaving the seed of *T·* to its own
 My. 182–13 small sowing of the seed of *T·*,
seeds of
 Mis. 357–13 seeds of *T·* fall by the wayside,
seek
 Mis. 342–24 Seek *T·*, and pursue it.
seeker after
 Mis. 80–22 for I am a seeker after *T·*.
 My. 178– 2 not mislead the seeker after *T·*.
seekers after
 Mis. 32–20 seekers after *T·* whose teacher is
 114– 2 value to all seekers after *T·*.
 156– 4 readers, and seekers after *T·*.
 Man. 17– 2 band of earnest seekers after *T·*
seekers for
 Pul. 14–15 simple seekers for *T·*,
seeking
 My. vi– 3 * who are earnestly seeking *T·* ;
seeks
 Un. 45–23 not the goal which *T·* seeks.
sense of
 (*see* **sense**)
servant of
 Pul. 6–24 seeker, and servant of *T·*,
shall reign
 My. 185– 9 till *T·* shall reign triumphant
side of
 Mis. 46–18 and acts on the side of *T·*,
 '02. 6–25 victory on the side of *T·*.
signs of
 Mis. 156–10 you will see clearly the signs of *T·*
silence
 Mis. 277–17 can the present mode . . . silence *T·*?
Spirit, and
 Mis. 363–25 Word that *is* God, Spirit, and *T·*.
Spirit is
 Un. 36–12 Thus we see that Spirit is *T·*
spirit of
 (*see* **spirit**)

Truth

Spirit, or
No. 5–15 avers that Spirit, or *T·*, cannot

spiritual
Mis. 265–21 thoroughly explaining spiritual *T·*
Ret. 54– 5 than to understand spiritual *T·*.
Rud. 3– 5 through Christ, spiritual *T·*

spirituality of
No. v–13 the pure spirituality of *T·*.

springtide of
No. 27– 7 the springtide of *T·* in C. S.

standard of
My. 180–11 that primordial standard of *T·*.

steadfast in
Mis. 172– 2 lives steadfast in *T·*.

studying
Mis. 310– 1 of studying *T·* through the senses,

substance in
Ret. 57–18 Spirit is substance in *T·*.

substance of
'01. 18–14 substance of *T·* transcends the

substitutes for
No. 5–12 substitutes for *T·* an unreal belief,

success in
Ret. 79–17 cometh no success in *T·*.

sunshine of
Mis. 343–10 Warmed by the sunshine of *T·*,
Ret. 87–26 the sunshine of *T·* beams with

supersedes error
Un. 40– 8 As *T·* supersedes error,

superstructure of
Pul. 2–30 superstructure of *T·*, reared on

supremacy of
Pul. 13– 8 conscious of the supremacy of *T·*,

table of
Mis. 106–21 fallen from this table of *T·*,

tablets of
No. 1–17 read more clearly the tablets of *T·*.

talked
Mis. 293–27 *T·* talked and not lived,

testimonial to
Pul. 77–13 * built as a testimonial to *T·*,
78–12 * built as a testimonial to *T·*,

testimony to
Man. 48– 4 to bear testimony to *T·*

that destroys
Mis. 194–26 *T·* that destroys all error,
Ret. 61–19 *T·* that destroys error

that is Life
My. 214– 9 and the *T·* that is Life.

the rock
Pan. 15– 5 on *T·*, the rock of Christ,

the victor
Mis. 336– 1 *T·*, the victor over a lie.

things of
Mis. 280– 8 hurt not the holy things of *T·*.

this
No. 38–13 This *T·* is the rock which

through
Mis. 364– 8 to have healed, through *T·*, the sick
Man. 16– 2 through Christ, through *T·*,
Un. 41–21 not through error, but through *T·*.

to bring out
Mis. 346–25 requisite to bring out *T·*.

to error
Mis. 208– 2 This is the law of *T·* to error,
268–11 from *T·* to error, in pursuit of

tone of
Mis. 312–25 he touched a tone of *T·*

toward
Ret. 76–10 gravitate naturally toward *T·*.

treasury of
My. 214–27 into the treasury of *T·*,

trust in
My. 171– 2 *Trust in T·, and have no*

understanding of
Mis. 166–15 the scientific understanding of *T·*
Un. 40– 9 understanding of *T·* subordinates
Hea. 16–23 can gain no understanding of *T·*,
My. 232–23 understanding of *T·* which destroys

unfit for
Mis. 268–10 He is unfit for *T·*,

unfolding of
Ret. 50–25 furtherance and unfolding of *T·*,

unity of
Mis. 109– 2 declaring the unity of *T·*,

unknown to
No. 31– 9 are unreal, *unknown* to *T·*,

utilize
Ret. 26–28 utilize *T·*, and absolutely reduce

versus error
Mis. 346–22 chapter sub-title

views of
Mis. 234– 5 speculative views of *T·*.
No. 21– 6 Jesus . . . whose views of *T·*

Truth

vineyard of
Ret. 52– 9 worker in this vineyard of *T·*.

vision of
No. 27–12 vision of *T·* is fully interpreted

voice of
(*see* voice)

walks triumphantly
No. 29–24 *T·* walks triumphantly over the

way of
Mis. 356–31 or you will miss the way of *T·*
Un. 55–16 and the life-giving way of *T·*.
My. 104– 2 the strait and narrow way of *T·*.
232– 7 even the way of *T·* and Love

will arise
'02. 9– 9 *T·* will arise in human thought

will destroy
Rud. 10–25 is an error which *T·* will destroy.

will give
Mis. 297–28 *T·* will give you all that belongs to

will soar
Mis. 277– 3 but *T·* will soar above it.

with us
My. 109–24 it is *T·* with us,

Word of
No. 22–13 meaning of the Word of *T·*,

word of
Mis. 100–17 to grasp the word of *T·*,
334–16 without one word of *T·* in it.

words of
Mis. 99–15 take not back the words of *T·*.
320–22 words of *T·* and Life.

you find
Un. 62–17 Destroy . . . and you find *T·*.

your
Mis. 241–14 apparently to neutralize your *T·*,

———

Mis. 6–16 *T·* must ultimately succeed
7–13 for if serving Christ, *T·*,
18– 7 law and gospel of Christ, *T·*.
23–26 reflects good, Life, *T·*, Love
33– 6 ministries of Christ, *T·*.
40– 6 *T·* is as effectual in
41–11 is purged through Christ, *T·*,
53– 6 only as we master error with *T·*.
57–14 *T·*, God, denounced it,
59–26 guiding them with *T·*.
61–27 of error, not of *T·* ;
62–17 The theology of C. S. is *T·* ;
63– 7 Life, *T·*, Love are the triune
66–19 and *T·* be enthroned,
77–18 *T·* that knows no error,
81–21 *has not T· yet reached the shore?*
84–25 is to live in Christ, *T·*,
85–30 are thereby led to Christ, *T·*,
100–10 for *T·* to deny or to destroy.
124–14 ever-living Life, *T·*, Love :
150–11 I am with all who are with *T·*,
157– 3 worthy to suffer for Christ, *T·*,
166– 5 The *T·* he has taught and spoken
187–22 one is God, — Life, *T·*, Love.
188– 2 demonstrated the opposite, *T·*.
190– 3 infinite Spirit, *T·*, Life,
193–24 of our Lord and His Christ, *T·* ;
195– 1 *T·* that antidotes all error.
204– 4 *T·*, searching the heart,
214–27 cannot . . . take error along with *T·*,
218– 6 by reversion, as error declares *T·*.
221– 9 and *T·* is their remedy.
222–25 Error is more abstract than *T·*.
225–11 power of Christ, *T·*, to heal
264– 3 who are loyal to Christ, *T·*,
268–32 and *T·* is used to waiting.
274–16 *T· is fallen in the street, — Isa.* 59: 14.
281–22 always as debtors to Christ, *T·*.
322–13 the *T·* they illustrate,
334–23 Is matter *T·* ? No !
351–20 it says, "I am *T·*,"
352– 4 error of regarding Life, *T·*, Love as
354–11 error to *T·*, and evil to good,
365– 4 which is Christ, *T·*.
366–28 is the office of Christ, *T·*,
368– 7 * "*T·*" forever on the scaffold,
371–23 with *T·*, to give it buoyancy.
398–24 'T was the *T·* that made us free,
Chr. 53–41 The Way, the *T·*, the Life
Ret. 88– 6 In him, *T·* called the physical man
93–11 *T·* is not fragmentary,
Un. 16– 2 In *T·*, such terms . . . are unheard-of
17–15 the would-be murderer of *T·*.
18–14 *T·*, God, says you oftenest console
25–25 the eternal All, — Life, *T·*, Love,
29–13 eternal, — *T·*, Life, Love.
42–24 *T·*, defiant of error or matter,
45– 3 as *T·* and "the woman" — *Gen.* 3: 15.
Pul. 3– 3 Can *T·* be uncertain ?

Truth

Pul. 13– 2   *T*·, represented by the Son ;
    55–28   * *T*· is the sole recognized authority.
Rud. 2–19   supreme good, Life, *T*·, Love.
    8–16   In . . . *T*· is in the minority
    8–21   This falsity shuts against him the *T*·
No. 1– 4   must be done gradually, for *T*· is as
    5– 7   To *T*· there is no error.
    5– 9   would be to make it *T*·.
    20–10   Mind, substance, Life, *T*·,
    28–16   *T*· is never understood too soon.
    30–25   *T*· has no sympathy for error.
    42–24   would make a lie the author of *T*·,
    42–24   and so make *T*· itself a
    44– 9   by some other way than *T*·
    45–27   *T*· cannot be stereotyped ;
Pan. 7– 5   demonstration that . . . *T*·, gave
    11–10   his stature in Christ, *T*·,
    12–24   Life, *T*·, Love, substance, Spirit,
    14– 7   living the divine Life, *T*·, Love,
'01. 4–26   because He is Life, *T*·, Love,
    5– 8   named in the Bible Life, *T*·, Love
    7– 5   in C. S. being Life, *T*·, Love,
    11– 8   Through this redemptive Christ, *T*·,
    15– 9   overcomes them through Christ, *T*·,
    18–26   The divine Life, *T*·, Love
    20– 6   guided by no other mind than *T*·,
    22– 5   Is *T*· material? No !
    26– 5   founded his system . . . on Christ, *T*·,
    28–22   beyond a doubt that Christ, *T*·,
    31– 4   *T*· opposed to all error,
'02. 6–23   Through Christ, *T*·,
Hea. 16–20   senses afford no evidence of *T*·
    17–20   not *T*·, and therefore are not TRUE.
Peo. 2–11   divine Principle,— Life, *T*·, Love ;
    2–24   *T*· without a lapse or error, and
Po. 40– 4   To God, to *T*·, and you !
    47– 9   Ever to *T*· and to Love
    page 70   poem
    70–10   *T*· is eternal light,
    70–13   In *T*·, the Life, the Principle of
    75– 4   'Twas the *T*· that made us free,
My. 52–13   * Mind, *T*·, Life, and Love,
    52–23   * if only . . . *T*· may be glorified.
    63–30   * had been healed by Christ, *T*·,
    104–15   healer of men, the Christ, the *T*·,
    105– 1   the words of Christ, *T*·,
    119–17   to the ascended Christ, to the *T*·
    119–23   *T*·, which destroys the false sense
    119–32   St. John found Christ, *T*· in the
    122–26   but is *T*·, even as Jesus declared ;
    122–28   Christ, *T*·, again healing the sick
    126– 1   the body of Christ, *T*· ;
    129–19   plant thy steps in Christ, *T*·,
    161–16   is saved through Christ, *T*·.
    165– 7   for the cause of Christ, *T*·,
    182– 9   Christ, *T*·, as the chief corner-stone.
    185–15   this trinity, *T*·, Life, Love,
    190–25   become students of the Christ, *T*·,
    191–17   Christ, *T*·, has come forth from
    206–17   fact that portrays Life, *T*·, Love.
    219–15   Christ, *T*·, the ever-present spiritual
    225–28   Love, *T*·, Life, Spirit, Mind,
    262–11   Christ, *T*·, never born and never
    339–22   have not the Christ, *T*·, within
    348–29   Divine Life, *T*·, Love is the
    349– 5   gained through Christ, *T*· ;

truth

abode not
Un. 32–22   The *t*· abode not in you.
Rud. 7–17   "the *t*· abode not— *see John* 8 : 44.
No. 24–23   the *t*· abode not— *see John* 8 : 44.
abode not in the
Pan. 5–14   abode not in the *t*·— *John* 8 : 44.
absolute
My. 146–19   absolute *t*· of his sayings
adopt as
My. 235–25   adopt as *t*· the above statements?
advancing
Mis. 247– 3   *proofs* of advancing *t*·
all
Mis. 49–19   spirit of Truth leads into all *t*·,
    189– 7   that leadeth into all *t*·.
allusion to
Mis. 193–17   even for his allusion to *t*· ;
and error
Un. 60– 5   he articulates *t*· and error.
Pan. 8–25   matter and Spirit, *t*· and error,
and love
My. 148– 7   God of all grace, *t*·, and love
    189–13   *t*· and love, commingling
    272– 3   justice, mercy, *t*·, and love.
    280–22   with His own *t*· and love.
    289– 3   through grace, *t*·, and love.

truth

and the life
Mis. 74–12   *the t*·, *and the life*," — *John* 14 : 6.
No. 12–17   the *t*·, and the life." — *John* 14 : 6.
Hea. 16–28   the *t*·, and the life. — *John* 14 : 6.
My. 257–14   the *t*·, and the life," — *John* 14 : 6.
    349–19   the *t*·, and the life." — *John* 14 : 6.
any
My. 299– 6   * have any *t*· to reveal
basic
Mis. 6–20   with that basic *t*· we conquer
beginnings of
My. 303– 1   beginnings of *t*· fell mysteriously
brightness of
Pul. 81–17   * those who seek the brightness of *t*·
clothed in
My. 349–14   at the feet of Jesus clothed in *t*·,
contemplating
Man. 94–11   should go away contemplating *t*· ;
declares the
My. 113– 9   Paul declares the *t*· of the complete
declaring the
My. 116–18   Declaring the *t*· regarding an
define
My. 235– 4   impossible as to define *t*· and not
demonstrable
Mis. 193– 7   self-evident demonstrable *t*·.
My. 260–21   fundamental and demonstrable *t*·,
demonstrate
My. 3– 6   in order to demonstrate *t*·,
demonstrated its
Mis. 70– 3   *demonstrated* its *t*· when I
demonstrates the
'01. 22– 3   whosoever demonstrates the *t*·
demonstration of the
Mis. 87–27   demonstration of the *t*·
deride
Man. 94–10   goes to hear and deride *t*·,
discovers the
Mis. 352–10   when it discovers the *t*·,
dogma and
Pul. 56–17   * dogma and *t*· could not unite,
elucidation of
'01. 31– 1   stung by a clear elucidation of *t*·,
establishing the
Mis. 177–17   great work of establishing the *t*·,
eternal
My. 54– 4   * for the sake of the eternal *t*·
    143–18   the discoverer of an eternal *t*·
evangelic
Ret. 65–20   C. S. is the pure evangelic *t*·.
every
Pul. 51–11   * Every *t*· is more or less in a state of
exclusive
No. 4–25   rests on the exclusive *t*· that
faith in
My. 292–30   faith in *t*· and faith in error.
find the
Mis. 176– 1   find the *t*· that breaks the dream of
found it
Mis. 178–23   * if I had not found it *t*·,
fountains of
Mis. 113–29   are life-giving fountains of *t*·.
full of
Mis. 147–27   full of *t*·, candor, and humanity.
give the
My. 241–29   * give the *t*· in the *Sentinel*,
glorious
No. 24–27   another and more glorious *t*·,
    35–20   The glorious *t*· of being
grace and
Mis. 292–25   C. S., full of grace and *t*·,
grand
Hea. 5–19   obscure the one grand *t*·
    9–28   shall learn this grand *t*· of being.
My. 87–20   * grand *t*· that God is the supreme
great
Mis. 28–17   and this great *t*· was shown by
    83–26   the avowal of this great *t*·,
    258– 9   the great *t*· that God is All
    321– 3   over the cradle of a great *t*·,
Pul. 39– 5   * all teach that one great *t*·,
Pan. 13–19   great *t*· that Spirit is infinite,
Peo. 12–21   Master demonstrated this great *t*·
My. 52–13   * spreading world wide of this great *t*·,
    117–20   great *t*· of God's impersonality
    279–16   this great *t*·, when understood
he speaks
Rud. 9– 5   Even the *t*· he speaks
his
My. 216–12   or his *t*· not worth a cent.
impart
My. 165–20   able to impart *t*·, health, and
in Christian Science
Mis. 195–23   to try the edge of *t*· in C. S.,
Rud. 6–12   *t*· in C. S. met a response

truth

in the Scriptures
My. 179–20 the *t·* in the Scriptures,
is leading
Pul. 6–21 * I feel the *t·* is leading us
it represents
My. 24– 6 * vastness of the *t·* it represents,
justice and
Peo. 10–14 Justice and *t·* make man free,
My. 316–17 in behalf of common justice and *t·*
know the
Mis. 241–22 'Ye shall know the *t·*,— *John* 8 : 32.
316– 3 to know the *t·* that makes free,
Man. 84– 5 to know the *t·* that makes free,
'01. 10– 1 "Ye shall know the *t·*,— *John* 8 : 32.
My. 252–11 to make one not only know the *t·*
learned the
My. 271– 7 learned the *t·* of what I had written.
legacy of
My. 303–22 he left his legacy of *t·*
life in
My. 273–21 life in *t·*, is a scientific knowledge
light and
My. 154–24 light and *t·*, emanating from the
live
My. 160–12 a live *t·*, . . . frightens people.
lives the
Ret. 70–26 lives the *t·* he teaches.
manifestation of the
My. 124– 3 but by manifestation of the *t·*
207–12 * perfect manifestation of the *t·*
meet in
My. 120– 5 trust that you and I may meet in *t·*
mercy and
Mis. 151–24 May mercy and *t·* go before you :
metaphysical
My. 52– 1 * by metaphysical *t·* or C. S.,
mirrored in
Po. 23– 9 Mirrored in *t·*, in light and joy,
new-old
'02. 9–29 new-old *t·* that counteracts ignorance
no
Mis. 371–20 has no *t·* to defend.
Pan. 5–15 no *t·* [reality] in him— *John* 8 : 44.
of being
Mis. 3–23 as seen in the *t·* of being,
182–18 beholding the *t·* of being ;
185–17 accept the *t·* of being,
190–24 cast out by the spiritual *t·* of being ;
260–17 pure Mind is the *t·* of being
Un. 55–20 and behold the *t·* of being,
Rud. 13–11 it is not the *t·* of being,
No. 4–11 harmony is the *t·* of being,
35–20 The glorious *t·* of being
Hea. 9–28 learn this grand *t·* of being
13–23 *t·* of being that casts out error
My. 275–16 keenly alive to the *t·* of being
of Christian Science
Ret. 61– 9 conscious of the *t·* of C. S.,
No. 7–23 write the *t·* of C. S.
My. 111– 4 nature and *t·* of C. S.
297–23 fundamental *t·* of C. S.
of God
No. 8– 6 utter the *t·* of God
'00. 4–19 *t·* of God, and of man and the
of its statements
My. 112–17 the *t·* of its statements,
of Jesus' words
Mis. 133–29 attest to the *t·* of Jesus' words.
of Life
Peo. 9–11 life of Truth and the *t·* of Life.
of life
My. 235– 2 To teach the *t·* of life
273–20 The *t·* of life, or life in truth,
of Love
Mis. 287–11 corrects . . . with the *t·* of Love,
337– 2 reveals the *t·* of Love,
of man
Mis. 57–12 *t·* of man had been demonstrated,
of man's being
My. 4– 7 the *t·* of man's being.
of Mind-healing
Mis. 260–22 *t·* of Mind-healing uplifts
of prophecy
Mis. 192–21 to prove the *t·* of prophecy.
of Science
Rud. 16–12 novices, in the *t·* of Science,
of the axiom
My. 58– 6 * proves the *t·* of the axiom,
of the Scripture
No. 17–20 and the *t·* of the Scripture,
of the Scriptures
My. 299–12 entire *t·* of the Scriptures,
of the soul
Po. 73–20 the bright *t·* of the soul.

truth

of this statement
My. 270–23 to the *t·* of this statement.
old
My. 257– 5 new cradle of an old *t·*.
one
'01. 16–27 commence with one *t·* told
order and
Mis. 215–13 C. S. demands order and *t·*.
or science
My. 107–25 classification as *t·* or science
page of
Po. 28– 5 to write a deathless page Of *t·*,
portions of
My. 299–12 whatever portions of *t·* may be found
practical
Mis. 246–32 earnest seeking after practical *t·*
Pan. 13– 2 steadfastly to its practical *t·*.
precious
My. 62– 8 * may I not take this precious *t·*
realizes the
Rud. 13–22 if the *healer realizes* the *t·*,
rejoiceth in the
No. 45– 7 rejoiceth in the *t·*."— *I Cor.* 13 : 6 .
religious
Pul. 51–10 * searching after religious *t·*.
saw the
Pul. 53–26 * Whittier, . . . saw the *t·* :
scientific
Mis. 113–19 escape . . . through scientific *t·* ;
No. 10–13 for all scientific *t·*.
'01. 27–27 * "Every great scientific *t·*
My. 304–25 * "Every great scientific *t·*
search of
Pul. 51–25 * will go there in search of *t·*,
search of the
Pul. 46– 4 * in search of the *t·* as taught.
self-evident
Mis. 26– 3 will be known as self-evident *t·*,
shall seem
Un. 45– 2 this lie shall seem *t·*
sincerity and
Mis. 175–17 bread of sincerity and *t·*."— *I Cor.* 5 : 8.
speaketh the
My. 33–18 speaketh the *t·* in his heart.— *Psal.* 15 : 2.
228–25 speaketh the *t·* in his heart."— *Psal.* 15 : 2.
speaking the
Mis. 227–23 speaking the *t·* in the heart ;
speak the
Mis. 44– 1 Honest students speak the *t·*
283– 3 can to advantage speak the *t·*
My. 147–19 speak the *t·* that . . . is found **able**
spirit and in
(see **spirit**)
spiritual
Mis. 101– 5 and accepting spiritual *t·*,
190–24 by the spiritual *t·* of being ;
Ret. 79– 3 spiritual *t·* learned and loved ;
Peo. 12–15 when imbued with the spiritual *t·*
spoke the
My. 146– 3 that Jesus spoke the *t·*.
standard of
My. 41–18 * maintains the perfect standard of *t·*
state
My. vi– 4 * to state *t·* absolutely in a
substance of the
My. 130–30 substance of the *t·* that is taught ;
such
My. 48–21 * such *t·* as they do gain
system of
Pul. 51– 1 * does not strike all as a system of *t·*.
tatters
Po. 79–12 fears are foes— *t·* tatters those,
taught the
Mis. 291–26 taught the *t·* which is energizing,
teach
My. 235–12 and teach *t·* scientifically.
tell the
Mis. 226–20 * when he shall tell the *t·*."
temperance and
Mis. 288–28 temperance and *t·* are allies,
Po. 39– 3 Temperance and *t·* in song sublime
that is Life
My. 260– 2 in the *t·* that is Life,
this
Un. 61–27 contrite heart soonest discerns this *t·*,
No. 36– 5 shall know this *t·* when we awake
Hea. 5–20 This *t·* is, that we are to work out
Peo. 9–27 This *t·* of Deity, understood,
My. 257– 5 This *t·* has traversed night,
thunderbolt of
Hea. 2– 6 hurls the thunderbolt of *t·*,
tides of
My. 149–10 the ever-flowing tides of *t·*
tone of
My. 291–20 waken a tone of *t·* that shall

tumble
Mis. 134–28 blind to its own fate, it will t· into
My. 200–23 will t· from this scheme into

tumbled
Mis. 231–21 baby has t·, soft as thistle-down,

tumbler-full and **tumblerful**
Ret. 33–15 in a t· of water,
Hea. 13–12 dropped into a t· of water a single

tumor
Mis. 313–14 without ill-humor or hyperbolic t·.

tumult
Pul. 3–13 ends all warfare, and bids t· cease,
32–10 * wonderful t· in the air
No. 1–13 turn temporarily from the t·,
Hea. 2– 3 a t· on earth,

tune
Mis. 395– 3 out of t· With love and God ;
Po. 57–10 out of t· With love and God ;

tuned
Pul. 62–16 * The tubes are carefully t·,

turf
Mis. 395–17 The t·, whereon I tread,
Po. 26– 4 The t· where thou hast trod
58– 2 The t·, whereon I tread,

turkey
Mis. 231–12 mammoth t· grew beautifully less.

turmoil
Po. 73–17 afar from life's t· its goal.

turn
Mis. 28–11 In proportion as mortals t· from
52–27 to t· back and work out the previous
80–22 "t· and overturn" — see Ezek. 21 : 27.
84–24 t· one, like a weary traveller,
98– 4 should t· away from inharmony,
119–10 Evil is impotent to t· the righteous
124–10 We t·, with sickened sense, from
133–27 I t· constantly to divine Love for
138– 1 until, in t·, their students will
156–22 preys, and in t· becomes a prey.
181– 6 Principle, which in t· is requisite
194–21 t· from matter to Spirit for healing ;
197– 5 to exhort people to t· from sin
211–20 t· on you and rend you?
220–11 t· them into channels of Truth.
244–20 t· the water into wine,
246–18 to invite its prey, then t· and
292–14 causes mortals to t· away from
307– 2 in t·, they give you daily supplies.
307–30 human thought must t·
316–17 t· them slowly toward the haven.
335– 1 shall you t· away from this
343– 5 Too soon we cannot t· from disease
345–21 To t· the popular indignation
353–25 t· from the metaphor of the mill
Man. 48–20 t· away from personality
67–18 t· their attention from the divine
Ret. 21–19 t· it gladly from a material,
45–21 t· to him the other — Matt. 5 : 39.
Un. 23– 6 God has no bastards to t· again
64–17 can never t· back what Deity knoweth,
Pul. vii–11 t· backward the telescope of
82– 8 * but you could no more t· her
85– 5 * t· their hearts in gratitude to her
No. 1–12 They should then t· temporarily
8–24 lest it t· and rend you ;
Pan. 11–12 to t· from clay to Soul
'02. 4–26 we are liable to t· from them
11–14 each in t· has helped mankind,
Peo. 7– 6 t· often from marble to model,
My. 9– 8 * to t· in loving thankfulness
63–17 * as friend met friend at every t·
88–25 * t· with respect and affection.
139–19 It was to t· your sense of worship
182–26 t· hither with satisfied hope.
227–13 we naturally t· to divine justice
227–25 t· again and rend you." — Matt. 7 : 6.
227–27 t· to him the other — Matt. 5 : 39.
311–10 to t· the blind girl out,
316–19 tends to t· back the foaming

turned
Mis. 11–29 I have t· the other :
74–17 he t· the water into wine ;
206– 1 on which have t· all revolutions,
309–10 it has t· many from the true
327– 1 t· my misnamed joys to sorrow.
328–17 hast thou t· back, stumbled,
345–31 Christianity t· men away from the
380–15 in faith, t· to divine help,
Ret. 8–17 my cousin t· to me
Un. 11– 5 He t· the water into wine,
57–11 When Jesus t· and said,
Pul. 6–18 * t· to the 'great Physician.'

turned
Po. 9– 2 T· to his star of idolatry.
My. 6– 2 knows will be t· against himself.
30–28 * hundreds had to be t· away,
50–15 * t· steadfastly from the mortal
54–11 * was t· from the door with the
79– 4 * solemn little faces t· upward.
87–25 * if all the world t· to the new
119–20 He t· to the person,
152– 1 t· to another form of idolatry,

turnest
Mis. 333–17 t· away from the divine source of

turneth
Man. 41– 9 t· away wrath." — Prov. 15 : 1.

turning
Mis. 136–10 in t· aside for one hour
198– 5 t· away from material gods ;
232– 2 t· from it, in a bumper of
329–19 t· up the daisies,
333–14 are t· away from the
340– 7 t· neither to the right nor
Un. 14–18 neither shadow of t·." — Jas. 1 : 17.
20– 3 then t· it or t· from it.
63– 9 variableness or shadow of t·,
Pul. 2–11 T· the attention from sublunary
My. 326–20 in t· the hearts of the noble

turns
Mis. 101–19 t· to the body for evidence,
115–23 t· us more unreservedly to Him
125–27 Mother, . . . t· to-day to you ;
125–27 t· to her dear church,
128– 1 and given a variety of t·,
129–21 lens that he never t· on himself.
250–27 t· toward want and woe,
324–23 he departs ; then t· back,
325–26 the Stranger t· quickly,
351–29 t· it into the opposite channels.
386–16 waking with a love that steady t·
Ret. 80–24 sees the door and t· away
No. 10–24 t· like the needle to the pole
'00. 11– 9 t· mortals away from earth
'01. 26–11 t· away from Christ's
Po. 1–16 the bitter draft which t·
49–24 waking with a love that steady t·
My. 346–12 * and made several t· about the

turquoise
Mis. 376–28 garnet, t·, and sapphire

turret
My. 186– 8 neither dome nor t· tells

turreted
Pul. 24–11 * porticos and t· corners.

turtle
Mis. 329–24 "The voice of the t· — Song 2 : 12.

tutelary
'00. 12–14 t· divinity of Ephesus.

tutored
My. 310– 6 I was privately t· by him.

Twain, Mark
My. 302–13 chapter sub-title

twain
Mis. 94– 7 the t· that are one flesh,
289–17 t· shall be one flesh." — Matt. 19 : 5.

Twain's, Mark
My. 303–13 Mark T· wit was not wasted

twelve
Mis. 29– 7 prayed, not for the t· only,
73–25 upon t· thrones, — Matt. 19 : 28.
73–26 t· tribes of Israel." — Matt. 19 : 28.
191–10 chosen you t·, — John 6 : 70.
304–26 * t· o'clock on the birthdays of
349– 4 included about t· lessons,
Man. 18–13 t· of her students and
35– 1 Children when T· Years Old.
35– 2 arrived at the age of t· years,
54–18 branch church for t· years.
60– 5 continued t· months each year.
Ret. 8– 3 For some t· months,
13– 1 At the age of t· I was
40–18 and weighed t· pounds.
50–14 my instruction during t· half-days,
90–14 one of the t· whom he kept near
Pul. 69– 8 * cured . . . some t· years ago,
81–25 * all that the t· have left undone.
83–29 * crown of t· stars." — Rev. 12 : 1.
No. 22–25 chosen you t·, — John 6 : 70.
Pan. 10–15 With t· lessons or less,
'01. 4– 5 four times three is t·,
4– 6 three times four is t·,
My. 38–13 * and was emptied in t·,
38–17 * the service at half past t·

twelve

My.	43–16	* *t·* stones taken from the midst of
	55–13	* *t·* of the members of the church
	55–31	* *T·* years ago . . . the corner-stone
	68–15	* built *t·* years ago,
	68–28	* There are *t·* exits and
	70– 5	* its first church only *t·* years ago,
	72–29	* first church in Boston *t·* years ago
	78– 9	* passed through the *t·* entrances
	78–28	* the half past *t·* service ;
	169– 6	Busy Bees, under *t·* years of age,
	311- 15	seemed to culminate at *t·* years
	347–16	*t·* beautiful pearls that crown this

(*see also* **numbers**)

twentieth

Pul.	vii– 6	the elders of the *t·* century,
	8–30	They belong to the *t·* century.
	22–10	I predict that in the *t·* century
	77–16	* on the *t·* day of February,
'00.	9–20	*t·* century in the ebb and flow
'02.	5– 4	spiritual dawn of the *t·* century
My.	95–20	* performed in this *t·* century
	98– 3	* a *t·* of the C. S. army
	155–10	take step with the *t·* century,
	199–18	on the verge of the *t·* century,
	229–23	the *t·* century Church Manual
	248–15	sponsors for the *t·* century,
	264– 9	* the threshold of the *t·* century,
	319–25	* the *t·* of the above-named month.·

twentieth-century

My.	316–21	* "*t·* review of opinion"

twenty

Mis.	88–13	*t·* years in the pulpit,
	242–23	having taken it *t·* years ;
Man.	18–18	*t·* others of Mrs. Eddy's students
	62–11	up to the age of *t·* years,
	62–15	after reaching the age of *t·*.
Ret.	24– 7	During *t·* years prior to my
Pul.	38– 7	* these succeeding *t·* years
My.	38–12	* in about *t·* minutes,
	321–21	* It will soon be *t·* years
	321–29	* during the past *t·* years.
	322–14	* Thanksgiving Day *t·* years ago,
	342– 9	* portraits of *t·* years ago,

(*see also* **numbers, values**)

twenty-eighth

My.	333– 6	* *t·* day of June, 1844,

twenty-fifth

Man.	79–21	on January *t·*, 1898,
My.	60–29	* On the *t·* of last March

twenty-first

My.	55–31	* the *t·* of last month,

twenty-five

Pul.	67–15	* Founded *t·* years ago,
My.	100–11	* It is only *t·* years,
	237– 5	What I wrote . . . *t·* years ago

(*see also* **numbers, values**)

twenty-four

Mis.	243– 1	if she went without it *t·* hours
My.	359–20	* by *t·* of her students

(*see also* **numbers**)

twenty-fourth

Pul.	87– 3	* on the *t·* day of March,

twenty-nine

My.	68–11	* altitude *t·* feet higher

twenty-one

Pul.	26– 2	* *t·* inches from point to point,

(*see also* **numbers, values**)

twenty-seven

My.	76–28	* *t·* years ago was founded

twenty-seventh

My.	333– 9	* died on the night of the *t·*.
	333–21	* Thursday night, the *t·* of June.

twenty-six

Man.	18– 4	members, *t·* in number,
Ret.	16–18	members, *t·* in number,
	44– 6	members, *t·* in number,
Pul.	30–27	* It opened with *t·* members,
	37–28	* was founded with *t·* members,
	66– 5	* with a membership of only *t·*,
	67–27	* founded . . . with *t·* members,
	78– 4	* gold scroll, *t·* inches long,
My.	48–14	* and *t·* years later the
	50–29	* more than *t·* years ago,
	76–30	* membership of *t·* persons.

(*see also* **numbers**)

twenty-third

Man.	18–12	On the *t·* day of September, 1892,
My.	55–13	* *t·* day of September, 1892,

twenty-two

My.	305–19	* eighth in a list of *t·*

twice

Mis.	350– 8	The P. M. . . . Society met only *t·*.
Man.	39–17	*t·* notified of his excommunication,
My.	68– 7	* more than *t·* the size of the
	275–18	*t·* since I came to Massachusetts.

twice-told

Un.	48– 2	to repeat my *t·* tale,

twig

Mis.	264–18	* "As the *t·* is bent, the tree's

twilight

Un.	61–10	*t·* and dawn of earthly vision,
'00.	11–22	* It flooded the crimson *t·*
My.	155–22	a dawn that knows no *t·*
	189–21	*t·* of the world's pageantry,

twin

Po.	65–11	*t·* sister of death and of night !

twined

Ret.	11–19	wreaths are *t·* round Plymouth Rock,
Po.	60–16	wreaths are *t·* round Plymouth Rock,

twines

Mis.	370–16	babe that *t·* its loving arms

twist

Mis.	233–14	or by trying to *t·* the
'01.	2– 8	to *t·* the fatal magnetic element of

two

Mis.	6–32	families of one or *t·* children,
	11–30	I have but *t·* to present.
	60–17	of *t·* individual sleepers,
	89– 2	serve *t·* masters ;"— *Matt.* 6 : 24.
	101– 9	We already have had *t·*
	168– 5	halting between *t·* opinions
	191–28	These *t·* opposite characters
	221–27	multiplication of the same *t·*
	231–16	*t·* incisors, in a big pippin,
	231–19	one, *t·*, three steps,
	241– 7	metaphysical healing on *t·* patients :
	242–23	one ounce in *t·* weeks,
	256–19	notice from one to *t·* weeks
	263– 5	These *t·* words in Scripture
	268– 3	*T·* personal queries give point
	269– 6	serve *t·* masters : — *Matt.* 6 : 24.
	273–30	one Primary and *t·* Normal
	278–29	For *t·* years I have been gradually
	280–12	There are not *t·*,
	289– 9	of *t·* evils choose the less ;
	289–16	by the marriage contract *t·* are made one,
	289–20	has *divorced* *t·* minds in one.
	290– 1	the compact of *t·* hearts.
	290– 2	*t·* persons only, should be
	302–16	of *t·* evils the less would be
	305–18	* They are to be of *t·* kinds :
	307–12	rapid sale already of *t·* editions
	314– 6	shall elect *t·* Readers :
	318–20	*T·* points of danger beset mankind ;
	332–14	*t·* mortals, walking in the cool of the
	347–14	*T·* individuals, with all the
	347–16	Between the *t·* I stand still ;
	350–19	consideration of these *t·* topics,
	350–28	I cannot serve *t·* masters ;
	355– 3	presents *t·* opposite aspects,
	372– 8	In *t·* weeks from the date
	375–14	* I spent *t·* years in Paris,
	384– 3	When *t·* hearts meet.
Man.	25– 6	a Treasurer, and *t·* Readers.
	61– 4	*t·* or more Sunday services
	63–16	*t·* or more churches may unite
	72–17	not more than *t·* small churches
	90–18	Not less than *t·* thorough lessons
	99– 4	as though it were *t·* States,
	111– 9	There are *t·* regular forms
Ret.	6–18	*t·* or three years he read law
	6–22	admitted to the bar in *t·* States,
	6–26	for *t·* consecutive years.
	16– 3	*t·* ladies pushing their way
	21– 7	had a wife and *t·* children,
	43– 9	taught *t·* terms in my College.
Un.	21– 6	mortal is not *t·* personalities,
	21– 8	yet they are not *t·* but one,
	27– 3	There are *t·* English words,
	33–24	"In the mouth of *t·* or three— *Matt.* 18 : 16.
	49–17	There are not *t·* realities of being,
	49–17	*t·* opposite states of existence.
Pul.	25– 3	* generated by *t·* large boilers
	27–12	* In the auditorium are *t·* rose windows
	27–17	* Beneath are *t·* small windows
	28–20	* reading is from the *t·* alternately ;
	28–26	* For the past year or *t·*
	37–19	* and one or *t·* other friends
	43– 1	*T·* combined choirs— that of First
	45–29	* read from the *t·* books by Readers.

two

Pul.	47–20	* definitions of these *t·* healing arts.
	49–13, 14	"*t·* and a half, only *t·* and a half
	67–28	* charter was obtained *t·* months later.
	75–20	* and for the day or *t·* following,
	76– 8	* *t·* alcoves are separated
	76–18	* One of the *t·* alcoves is a
	79–16	* We believe there are *t·* reasons
Rud.	14– 1	Neither can they serve *t·* masters,
No.	10– 6	*t·* largest words in the vocabulary
	17–21	If mortals could grasp these *t·* words
	23–16	Which of the *t·* is the more important
	27–18	the *t·* should not be confounded.
	36– 1	infinite as one, and not as *t·*.
	36– 2	not teach that there are *t·* deities,
Pan.	2–11	is derived from *t·* Greek words
	4–17	making *t·* creators ;
	6–19	Did one Mind, or *t·* minds,
	6–21	if *t·* minds, what becomes of
	6–23	Christian religion has at least *t·* Gods.
	8– 7	Does not the belief . . . imply *t·* Gods,
'00.	5–13	essence and source of the *t·* latter,
	12–24	St. Paul's stay in that city — over *t·* years
'01.	22–19	my text, that one and one are *t·*
	23– 1	one and *t·* are neither more nor less
	28– 1	passed through the first *t·* stages,
'02.	4–22	consider these *t·* commandments
	16– 8	gift of *t·* Christian Scientists,
Hea.	7–24	his understanding of these *t·* facts,
Peo.	9–21	serve *t·* masters." — *Matt.* 6 : 24.
Po.	36– 2	When *t·* hearts meet,
My.	6– 3	We cannot serve *t·* masters.
	32– 2	* *t·* of the most striking features
	39– 3	* at *t·* o'clock in the afternoon.
	50–24	* *t·* new members were added
	56– 4	* *t·* services were held,
	56– 7	* *t·* Sunday services
	65–12	* beyond *t·* brief explanations
	66– 5	* During the past *t·* weeks
	67–25	* begun nearly *t·* years ago,
	69–10	* *T·* large marble plates
	69–11	* on the *t·* sides of the organ.
	69–16	* *t·* on either side
	71–26	* *t·* Readers who conduct the services
	74– 4	* within *t·* or three days' ride,
	74–28	* Within *t·* weeks we have had here
	74–29	* the *t·* poles of healing,
	81–28	* wherever *t·* or more of them are met
	82–24	* facilities at the *t·* stations
	92–26	* *t·* things to be said in favor of
	123–23	"five loaves and *t·* fishes" — *Matt.* 14 : 17.
	137–15	except in one or *t·* instances,
	138–16	"serve *t·* masters." — *Matt.* 6 : 24.
	145–17	past year and *t·* months,
	165– 2	Of *t·* things fate cannot rob us ;
	171–13	at *t·* o'clock in the afternoon,
	179– 3	in *t·* distinct manuscripts.
	181–31	first *t·* years of my discovery of
	243–11	and *t·* individuals would
	243–14	*t·* students who are adequate to
	257–26	*t·* words enwrapped,
	268–14	*T·* commandments of the
	281–23	* *t·* parties to the treaty of
	318– 6	and for only *t·* of my books.
	328–18	* *t·* C. S. healers in this city.
	347– 2	His *t·* witnesses.
	356–22	serve *t·* masters : — *Matt.* 6 : 24.

(*see also* **numbers, values**)

two-sided

Mis.	266– 4	To be *t·*, when these sides are
My.	210–20	notion that . . . should be *t·*,

two-thirds and two thirds

Mis.	210– 6	found out, is *t·* destroyed,
	355–14	found out is *t·* destroyed,
Peo.	12–18	we shall take in the remaining *t· t·*

tympanum

Mis.	119– 2	through the mind's *t·*,
	168– 8	"*t·* on the brain"

Tyndall

Mis.	361–15	Locke, Berkeley, *T·*, Darwin,
My.	349–10	Berkeley, *T·*, and Spencer

type

Mis.	27–29	a *t·* of spiritual substance,
	33– 9	present the *t·* and shadow of
	61– 2	*t·* and representative of verities
	88–21	* Jesus was the highest *t·* of
	91– 2	as a *t·* of the true worship,
	140– 4	must be conveyed through a *t·*
	140– 5	a *t·* morally and spiritually
	140–31	*t·* of the divine Principle it reflects.
	141–11	proposed *t·* of universal Love ;
	184–29	a *t·* of physical cleanliness
	203–16	topically as *t·* and shadow,
	253–20	*t·* and shadow of this hour.
	261–21	No greater *t·* of divine Love
Ret.	2–18	printed in olden *t·* and replete with
	93–13	best spiritual *t·* of Christly method
Pul.	20–14	*t·* and shadow of the warfare between
'00.	11–28	human action, *t·*, and system.
My.	45–31	* *t·* of Truth's permanence.
	52– 7	* highest *t·* of womanhood,
	335–17	* yellow fever of the worst *t·*.

types

Mis.	91–15	*t·* of these mental conditions,
	91–17	all *t·* employed in the service of
	142–18	varying *t·* of true affection,
'00.	2– 9	three *t·* of human nature
	11–29	His *t·* of purity pierce corruption
'01.	16– 7	St. John's *t·* of sin scarcely equal

typical

Pul.	27–18	* lamps, *t·* of S. and H.
	28– 1	* *t·* of the work of Mrs. Eddy.

typified

Mis.	261–19	*t·* in the law of Moses,

typifies

Mis.	86–15	that beauty *t·* holiness,

typify

Mis.	144–15	there to *t·* the prophecy

tyrannical

Pul.	6– 4	a national or *t·* religion,
Peo.	10– 9	a *t·* prohibitory law
My.	265–20	no longer *t·* and proscriptive ;

Tyrannus

'00.	12–25	in the school of *T·*,

tyranny

Mis.	80–21	*T·* can thrive but feebly under our
	297–27	unmercifulness, *t·*, or lust.
No.	44–16	Ecclesiastical *t·* muzzled the

tyrant (*see also* **tyrant's**)

Peo.	2–22	no longer a personal *t·*

tyrant's

Po.	71–11	Feared for an hour the *t·* heel !

tyrants (*see also* **tyrants'**)

Mis.	99–11	weapon in the hands of *t·*.
My.	191– 7	Persecution is the weakness of *t·*

tyrants'

Po.	79– 6	these stones, or *t·* thrones,

U

ulceration

Mis.	243–29	*u·*, bleeding, vomiting,

ultimate

Mis.	14– 7	the origin or *u·* of good?
	68–28	* the *u·* grounds of being,
	103– 5	*u·* and predicate of being.
	116–20	*u·* of scientific research
	190– 8	nor does the material *u·* in
	257–16	immediate or *u·* death.
	286–32	at the spiritual *u·* :
	364–28	This error, carried to its *u·*,
Man.	28– 5	*u·* in annulling its Tenets
Ret.	27–15	express in feeble diction Truth's *u·*.
	69– 3	*u·* source of being ;
	70–23	scientific *u·* of this God-idea
'02.	10–18	If such is man's *u·*,
My.	6–22	Its crowning *u·* rises to
	45– 4	* in the *u·* regeneration of its

ultimate

My.	94–26	"crowning *u·*" of the church
	123– 9	as the *u·* of C. S.
	181– 6	*u·* in unsolved problems
	239–12	the *u·* of the *millennium*
	266–16	flux and flow . . . tends in one *u·*
	272– 8	This predicate and *u·* of
	273–13	his *u·* or spiritual sense

ultimately

Mis.	6–16	Truth must *u·* succeed
	9–13	Primarily and *u·*, they are
	26– 2	*u·* will be known as
	30– 6	despair of *u·* reaching them,
	290– 6	must *u·* break all bonds
Ret.	23– 4	must *u·* yield to the
Peo.	3– 1	lift man *u·* to the understanding
My.	270–30	will *u·* be seen to control

ultimates
Mis. 123– 9 *u·* in a religion of pagan priests
   186–10 and *u·* in the opposite of
Ret. 64– 1 Sin *u·* in sinner,
My. 218–19 *u·* in what Jesus denounced,

ultimating
Mis. 122–16 nor good *u·* in evil.

ultimatum
Mis. 76– 7 the *u·* of C. S. ;
  79–10 man is the *u·* of perfection,
 113–18 the latter-day *u·* of evil,
 212–13 *u·* of their human sense
Un. 43– 9 achievement of this *u·* of Science,
My. 161–31 can triumph over their *u·*,
 273–18 *u·* of life here and hereafter

ultra
'01. 23–16 He was *u·* ; he was a reformer ;

umpire
Mis. 14–18 evil's *u·* and empire,
 348– 1 is well paid by the *u·*.

unable
Mis. 168–29 * had to go away *u·* to obtain seats.
 195– 6 is *u·* to demonstrate this Science ;
 238–25 * *u·* to speak a loud word,"
Man. 96–11 *u·* to meet the expense,
Pul. 20– 3 they were *u·* to pay the mortgage ;
No. 42– 5 God is not *u·* or unwilling to heal,
Pan. 10–22 religious teachers are *u·* to effect.
My. 41–21 * *u·* to cherish any enmity.
 74–13 * are *u·* to accompany them
 74–22 * if those outside are *u·* to believe
 336–17 * he was *u·* to make a will.

unaccountable
My. 90– 7 * *U·* ? Hardly so.

unaccustomed
My. 86– 2 * *u·* to fine architectural effects,

unacknowledged
Mis. 266– 9 is the *u·* servant of mankind.
No. 45–11 spiritual lack, felt, though *u·*.

unacquainted
Mis. 43–27 *u·* with the mighty Truth
Ret. 86– 7 Art thou still *u·* with thyself?

unadored
Mis. 106–24 most adorable, but most *u·*,

unadorned
My. 83–12 * and the men go entirely *u·*.

unadulterated
No. v–12 *u·* milk of the Word,

unambitious
Pul. 21– 4 *u·*, impartial, universal,

unanimity
My. 29–18 * *u·* of thought and of purpose.
 32 1 * *u·* and repetition in unison
 65–11 * passed with both *u·* and assurance.
 173–22 with what *u·* my fellow-citizens

unanimous
Man. 20– 8 *u·* vote of the C. S. Board
 36–22 *u·* vote of the Board of Directors
 39–14 *u·* vote of the C. S. Board
 73–16 *u·* vote of, the active members
 77– 8 decide thereupon by a *u·* vote,
 81– 2 *u·* vote of the C. S. Board
 97–10 *u·* vote of the C. S. Board
My. 49–11 * *u·* invitation to Mrs. Eddy

unanimously
Ret. 47–14 *u·* voted that the school be
 48–15 presented and passed *u·* :
 49–27 it was *u·* voted :
My. 8–22 * motion was carried *u·*.
 44–18 * The motion was carried *u·*
 49–26 * it was *u·* voted that

unannounced
Mis. 283– 1 *u·* mental practice where

unapproachable
Mis. 377– 4 so *u·*, and yet so near

unasked
Mis. 54–15 the sick, *u·*, are testifying thereto.
Ret. 88–23 to enter *u·* another's pulpit,

unattractive
Mis. 369–24 wholesome but *u·* food.

unauthorized
Man. 60– 7 No *U·* Debating.
 66–23 *U·* Reports.
 67–10 *U·* Legal Action

unavailable
Ret. 92– 3 nor was his power . . . *u·*

unavailing
Mis. 59–17 that is *u·* in divine Science.
 339–28 pour forth the *u·* tear.
Ret. 81– 2 The *u·* tear is shed
My. 132–32 wipes away the *u·*, tired tear,
 294–31 relatives shed "the *u·* tear."

unaware
Ret. 71–11 People *u·* of the indications
 71–28 one who is *u·* of this attempt,

unawares
Peo. 5–22 not entertain the angel *u·*.

unbar
Mis. 394–16 * The gates of memory *u·* :
Po. 57– 2 * The gates of memory *u·* :

unbarred
Mis. 325–30 without watchers and the doors *u·* !

unbecoming
Mis. 243–17 Boasting is *u·* a mortal's

unbelief
Mis. 169–23 often is the foundation of *u·*
My. 222– 9 "Because of your *u·*" — Matt. 17 : 20.
 294– 8 because of their *u·*," — Matt. 13 : 58.

unbelievers
Ret. 13–15 a Jehovah merciless towards *u·* ;
 14– 7 to have *u·* in these dogmas
Pul. 54–23 * He kept the *u·* away,

unbelieving
Pul. 65–25 * whose *u·* exemplar afterward

unbiased
Mis. 43–13 *u·*, contemplative reading of
 226– 4 *u·* youth and the aged Christian
 235–24 *u·* by the superstitions of a
 240–23 over the fresh, *u·* thought.
My. 96–14 * intelligent and *u·* study
 316–23 manifesting its *u·* judgment by

unbidden
Mis. 396–13 My heart *u·* joins rehearse ;
Po. 59– 5 My heart *u·* joins rehearse,

unborn
Mis. 71–12 *influences on the u· child*

unbridled
Ret. 71–15 Ask the *u·* mind-manipulator if he
'01. 19–25 *u·* individual human will.

unbroken
Mis. 208–13 *u·* motion of the law of divine
Ret. 80–27 and an *u·* friendship.
Un. 52– 5 the *u·* and eternal harmony
Rud. 12– 3 keeps *u·* the Ten Commandments,
Po. 2–19 thy deep silence is *u·* still.
My. 37–24 * *u·* activity of your labors,
 200–12 chain of Christian unity, *u·*,

unburdened
My. 192– 4 unto the possession of *u·* bliss.

uncalled
Mis. 87–28 obsequious helpers, who, *u·* for,

uncapitalized
Pan. 2–13 His *u·* word "god"

uncarved
Mis. 360– 2 Human lives are yet *u·*,
Peo. 7–17 * With our lives *u·* before us,

unceasing
Ret. 80–19 welling up into *u·* spiritual rise

unceasingly
My. 47–13 * labored *u·* for the work

uncertain
Mis. 372–21 gives no *u·* declaration
Un. 27–10 An egoist, therefore, is one *u·* of
Pul. 3– 3 Can Truth be *u·* ?
My. 231–10 in such *u·*, unfortunate investments.
 282– 9 is no *u·* ray of dawn.

unchained
My. 201– 5 Satan is *u·* only for a season,

unchangeable
Mis. 124–13 *u·*, all-wise, all-just,
Un. 43– 2 perfections, unchanged and *u·*.
 61–15 Spirit and spiritual man are *u·*,

unchangeableness
Un. 13– 9 His universal laws, His *u·*,

unchanged
Mis. 217–15 nature of all things is *u·*,
Ret. 82– 3 law of the chord remains *u·*,
Un. 43– 1 perfections, *u·* and unchangeable.

unchanging
Mis. 328–12 *u·*, unquenchable Love
Ret. 94–24 Science is eternally one, and *u·*,

uncharitable
Mis. 129– 3 is inclined to be *u·*,
211– 4 His mode is not cowardly, *u·*,
227–12 Some *u·* one may give it a
Man. 48– 6 *U·* Publications.
48– 8 article that is *u·* or impertinent

unchristian
Mis. 68–12 It is *u·* to believe that pain
81– 4 all unpleasant and *u·* action
89–14 it is humane, and not *u·*,
266–17 chapter sub-title
372– 2 contradictory, unscientific, *u·* ;
Man. 53– 7 No *U·* Conduct.
Un. 37–14 Is it *u·* to believe there is no
38–11 It is *u·* to believe in the
Rud. 8–22 may say the *u·* practitioner
12–15 because the relief is *u·*
16–25 springing up among *u·* students,

unchristly
Pul. 21–23 Go not into the way of the *u·*,

uncivil
Mis. 295–21 as both untrue and *u·*.
My. 278–25 burlesque of *u·* economics.

unclasp
Mis. 120– 2 *u·* the material sense of things

uncle
My. 60– 6 * remember the words of my *u·*,

unclean
My. 126–27 cage of every *u·* — *Rev.* 18 : 2.
211–10 the *u·* spirits cried out,

uncleanness
Mis. 185–13 cleansing mortals of all *u·*,

uncomfortable
Mis. 128– 2 *u·* whereon to repose.

uncomforted
My. 41– 8 * proud are lonely and *u·*,

uncommon
Mis. 95–18 phenomena of an *u·* order,
Ret. 7– 7 * young man of *u·* promise.
16–11 not an *u·* occurrence
Pul. 66–19 * shown an *u·* development

uncomplaining
'02. 16–16 *u·* agony in the life of

uncomprehended
No. 16–15 *u·*, yet forever giving forth

unconceived
'02. 5– 9 this almost *u·* light

uncondemned
'01. 15– 4 Error *u·* is not nullified.

unconditional
Mis. 231–14 caused *u·* surrender.
Ret. 13– 5 doctrine of *u·* election,

unconfined
Mis. 30–16 illustrated Life *u·*,

unconquerable
'00. 10– 9 till *u·* right is begun anew,

unconquered
'01. 13–20 man's fear, *u·*, conquers him,

unconscious
Mis. 209–32 Love, as *u·* as incapable of
211–15 is *u·* of suffering.
298–26 relief from pain in *u·* sleep.''
298–29 When *u·* of a mistake,
Un. 25– 2 If you say that matter is *u·*,
No. 36–12 Christ was *u·* of matter,
Hea. 6–24 back in the *u·* thought,

unconsciously
Mis. 78–18 that some people employ the . . . *u·*,
152– 9 brood *u·* o'er the work of
208– 9 enters *u·* the human heart
212–24 If, consciously or *u·*, one is
Ret. 61– 5 This fear is formed *u·*
'00. 8– 6 exhales consciously and *u·*
My. 22–10 * let us not be *u·* blind
292–17 desire works *u·* against the

unconsciousness
Mis. 298–27 through *u·* one no more gains

unconstitutional
Mis. 80–16 *U·* and unjust coercive

uncontaminated
Mis. 30–16 *u·*, untrammelled, by matter.
110– 6 faithful affection, *u·* lives.
Man. 31–11 unspotted . . . *u·* with evil,

uncover
Mis. 3–32 to meet sin, and *u·* it ;
114–24 *u·* their methods, and stop their
210–21 to *u·* and kill this lurking serpent,

uncover
Mis. 348– 8 When God bids one *u·* iniquity,
My. 211– 5 too ignorant, or too wicked to *u·*,
235–12 name the error, *u·* it,

uncovered
Mis. 12–23 *u·* and summarily dealt with
210– 2 evil, *u·*, is self-destroyed.
334–28 Because I have *u·* evil,
352–29 *u·* before it can be destroyed,
No. 24–18 evil . . . is *u·* by Science ;
24–19 evil, being thus *u·*, is found out,
My. 114–11 treasures of . . . are not yet *u·*

uncovering
Mis. 293– 6 This *u·* and punishing of sin
343–16 *u·* the secrets of sin
Ret. 30–11 as one intelligence, analyzing, *u·*,

uncovers
Mis. 67–19 Justice *u·* sin of every sort ;
352–10 this *u·* the error and quickens the
Un. 32–27 a claim which C. S. *u·*,
'02. 10– 3 new ideas, unfolds spiritual
My. 126– 9 *u·* and kills this mystery of iniquity
133–28 *u·* my life, even as your heart has
288– 3 Love . . . *u·* hidden evil.

uncremated
Peo. 8–24 *u·* fossils of material systems,

unction
'00. 11–18 but the *u·* of Love.

unctuous
Pan. 1–11 In *u·* unison with nature,

uncultivated
My. 168– 1 *u·* understanding has passed.

undefended
'01. 19–25 to subject mankind unwarned and *u·*

undefiled
Mis. 98–20 that pure and *u·* religion
320–28 to-day christening religion *u·*,
Ret. 71–20 according to pure and *u·* religion.
No. 46–16 Puritan standard of *u·* religion.
My. 41–26 * ''incorruptible and *u·*''— *I Pet.* 1 : 4.

undemonstrable
Un. 49–23 it is *u·*, without proof.

undeniable
No. 33–14 The sacrifice . . . is *u·*,
'00. 4–21 being demonstrable, they are *u·* ;

under
Mis. 9– 6 passes all His flock *u·*
17–16 redeems man from *u·* the curse
18– 6 *u·* the law and gospel of Christ,
33–17 place themselves *u·* my care,
35–17 *u·* your personal instruction?
35–18 *if one is obliged to study u· you,*
37–11 *u·* the control of God,
45–15 therefore, *u·* the deific law
50–12 *u·* the necessity to express
53–16 *u·* difficulties the former is not
59–16 to admit that it has been lost *u·*
79–31 they chance to be *u·* arrest
80–21 thrive but feebly *u·* our Government.
89– 9 *u·* material medical treatment,
90–11 *u·* circumstances exceptional,
91– 3 *u·* every circumstance,
117–32 follow *u·* every circumstance.
118– 7 Honesty . . . *u·* every circumstance,
120–15 Christian success is *u·* arms,
127–22 know yourself, *u·* God's direction,
129–20 to magnify *u·* the lens
130–12 sweet morsel *u·* your tongue,''
131–18 did not act *u·* that By-law ;
132–13 March 18, *u·* the heading,
135– 1 marching *u·* whatsoever ensign,
138–27 *u·* the banner of His love,
140–20 I redeemed from *u·* mortgage.
157–14 *u·* the shadow of His wing.
160– 2 *u·* the *régime* of C. S. !
161–21 preach in public *u·* that age.
185–15 no other way *u·* heaven
210–20 hides itself *u·* the false pretense
212–16 *u·* the reign of difficulties,
222–22 *u·* this new *régime* of mind-power,
229– 1 *u·* certain predisposing or
231–11 *U·* the skilful carving of the
272– 4 * *u·* Act of 1874,
272–24 * *u·* such charters, *colleges,*
274–28 rights are trodden *u·* foot,
288–14 nearest right *u·* the circumstances,
298– 9 *U·* the same circumstances,
304–10 * *u·* the care of our society.
304–18 * *u·* the care of the Daughters of
311–26 I was a scribe *u·* orders ;
326–16 *u·* every hue of circumstances,
331–13 nestles them *u·* her wings.

under

Mis.	348–23	*u·* this new *régime* of medicine,
	358– 5	will graduate *u·* divine honors,
	368–21	poison of asps is *u·* their — *Rom.* 3 : 13.
	371–24	What is *u·* the mask,
	381–21	*u·* the seal of the said Court,
	381–28	*u·* the edge of the knife,
Man.	18–15	reorganized, *u·* her jurisdiction,
	25–17	See *u·* "Deed of Trust"
	45–26	*u·* the *laws* of the *State.*
	46–20	shall not, *u·* pardonable circumstances,
	49–15	*u·* rules established by the
	69– 1	shall come *u·* a signed agreement
	72–18	*u·* one church government
	85– 8	*u·* the provisions of Article XII,
	86– 5	*u·* the personal instruction of
	86– 7	no longer *u·* the jurisdiction of
	88– 5	*u·* the auspices of Mary Baker Eddy,
	90–15	*u·* the auspices of this Board.
	91–26	*u·* Mrs. Eddy's daily conversation
	98–22	*u·* the direction of this Committee
Ret.	15–29	had been healed *u·* my preaching,
	19– 3	*u·* the paternal roof in Tilton.
	20– 9	*u·* the care of our family nurse,
	27–28	*u·* the guidance of the great Master.
	48– 3	*u·* all that was aimed at its
	53– 4	prosperous *u·* difficult circumstances,
	80–24	*u·* his compelling rod.
	84–29	place themselves *u·* his direction ;
	87–29	*u·* the care of a regular physician,
	91–19	placed themselves *u·* his care,
	91–20	*u·* the sway of his own perfect
Un.	10–28	hide from His presence *u·* their
	30– 4	This it does *u·* the delusion that
	53–19	sums done *u·* both rules
	57– 7	"*u·* the shadow of the— *Psal.* 91 : 1.
Pul.	6–20	* He went out *u·* the auspices of
	15–16	At all times and *u·* all circumstances,
	23–12	* *u·* several different aspects
	23–12	* and *u·* various names,
	23–14	* *u·* the guise of C. S.,
	26– 4	* each ray *u·* prisms which reflect
	29–20	* could, *u·* certain conditions,
	39–26	* *U·* the meadow grass.
	43– 4	* led the singing, *u·* the direction,
	46– 9	* published *u·* the title of
	66–11	* *u·* the injunction to
	69– 4	* were *u·* the instruction of
	80– 2	* ship when *u·* stress of storm
	83–14	* *u·* the black flag of oppression
	83–28	* the moon *u·* her feet,— *Rev.* 12 : 1.
	86– 8	* On the *u·* side of the cover
Rud.	17–12	agonies, and victories, *u·* which she
Pan.	14–12	for her victory *u·* arms ;
'00.	5–15	I see no other way *u·* heaven
	12–21	*U·* the influence of St. Paul's
'01.	2–23	costs a return *u·* difficulties ;
	16–23	*u·* sanction of the gown,
	20–23	The crimes committed *u·* this
	24–12	* *u·* Providence I owe my life to it."
	29–26	*u·* a *litho* of my own difficulties,
	00 27	*u·* all circumstances to obey the
'02.	3–13	self-government *u·* improved laws.
Peo.	10– 6	*u·* the microscope of Mind,
	12–10	trampled *u·* the feet of Truth.
Po.	vi– 9	* *u· the date of February* 3, 1865.
	10–20	Is marching *u·* orders ;
My.	vi–22	* made over to trustees *u·* agreement
	28–18	* *u·* the consecrated leadership of
	29–20	* *u·* the dome of the great edifice
	31–31	* trained carefully *u·* one leader,
	01–26	* stood *u·* the great dome,
	104– 5	*u·* the name of this
	107– 6	general subject *u·* discussion,
	107–23	*u·* the shadow of the— *Psal.* 91 : 1.
	125–19	*u·* the auspices of the
	169– 6	*u·* twelve years of age,
	188–14	*u·* the wings of the cherubim,
	195–11	hidden *u·* an appearance of
	200– 1	*u·* the Constitution of our nation
	204–20	recommend it *u·* the circumstances.
	210–15	*u·* the shadow of the Almighty.
	212–20	impossible *u·* other conditions,
	224–32	*u·* the present persecution
	227– 9	*u·* the protection of State
	227–24	*u·* their feet,— *Matt.* 7 : 6.
	246– 6	examined *u·* its auspices
	266– 5	*u·* the warrant of the Scriptures ;
	270–16	Her life is proven *u·* trial,
	282–24	*u·* the sunlight of the law
	304– 5	*u·* Professor Dyer H. Sanborn,
	307–25	*u·* his treatment,
	316–22	*u·* Mr. Flower's able guardianship
	319–17	* have not come *u·* the observation of
	337–21	Is marching *u·* orders ;
	343–26	five churches *u·* discipline.

under

My.	354– 7	Scientists are *u·* no obligation to
	359–17	* *u·* the heading "None good but
		(*see also* **sun**)

underived

Mis.	46–16	no power *u·* from its creator.
	249–29	the *u·*, the incomparable,
	255– 6	and has no *u·* power.
Un.	39–14	Man has no *u·* power.
Hea.	9–19	not a faculty or power *u·* from
My.	202–24	*u·* glory, the divine *Esse.*

underlie

My.	93–22	* *u·* many of the practices

underlying

Mis.	169– 8	had been the *u·* cause of
Un.	50–14	to express the *u·* thought.
My.	71– 8	* *u·* spirit that built the

undermine

Mis.	43–21	If one student tries to *u·*
'00.	10–11	would *u·* the civic, social, and

undermines

Mis.	101–16	It *u·* the foundations

undermining

My.	211–26	*u·* his health, and sealing his

underneath

'02.	19–20	*u·* is a deep-settled calm.

understand

Mis.	vii– 2	* To read it well ; that is, to *u·*.
	5–23	to those only who do not *u·*
	7–27	because people do not *u·*
	30– 1	Do we really *u·* the
	33– 7	may not *u·* the illustrations
	34–14	so far as I *u·* it,
	50–19	We do believe, and *u·*
	53–22	*so that all can readily u· it?*
	53–24	difficult to make the rulers *u·*,
	54– 7	does *u·* something of what
	58–17	I must spiritually *u·* them
	59– 3	can neither *u·* nor demonstrate
	63–18	*u·* the final fact, — that God is
	65–20	those who *u·* my instructions
	75–21	assists one to *u·* C. S.
	77– 6	to *u·* those great truths
	80–30	not until it shall come to *u·*
	88–24	* who do not . . . *u·* its modes
	90– 7	will save all who *u·* it.
	94– 4	to *u·* me, or himself.
	95–15	I *u·* the impossibility of
	95–19	I clearly *u·* that no human
	96– 3	I *u·* that God is an ever-present
	99– 5	neither can you *u·*," — see *Mark* 8 : 17.
	109–26	To *u·* good, one must discern
	116–25	you profess to *u·* and love,
	130– 6	Do we yet *u·* how much better
	136–13	*u·* the necessity for my seclusion,
	141–16	I believe, — yea, I *u·*,
	159– 6	and he will *u·*.
	181– 7	in order to *u·* his sonship,
	181–15	*u·* man's true birthright,
	181–17	*u·* that man is the offspring of
	197–17	to *u·* the beauty of holiness,
	197–23	does not *u·* life in Christ.
	200–27	*u·* and obey the Way-shower,
	214–20	to *u·* the personal Jesus' labor
	214–22	need to do this even to *u·* my works,
	215–13	first *u·* the Principle
	217– 5	*u·* that Spirit cannot become less
	220–23	should *u·* with equal clearness,
	247–13	do not *u·* my statement of the
	247–15	If they did *u·* it, they could
	247–10	*u·* that Spirit controls body.
	271– 6	*u·* enough of this to keep out of
	293–15	not *u·* all your instructions ;
	311–19	As I now *u·* C. S.
	325– 4	But they *u·* not his saying.
	334–31	to *u·* this Golden Rule
	344– 6	to *u·* aught of that which leads to
	355–13	*u·* the mental state of his patient.
	356–27	to *u·* our textbook ;
	366– 4	to *u·* and demonstrate what they
Man.	16– 6	uplift faith to *u·* eternal Life,
	49– 4	all who *u·* the teachings of C. S.
	66– 2	which he does not fully *u·*,
Ret.	28– 5	*u·* the omnipresence of good
	29– 1	As I *u·* it, spiritualism is the
	36– 2	*u·* Christ as the Truth
	54– 4	to *u·* spiritual Truth.
Un.	3– 3	not ready to *u·* immortality.
	4– 1	To *u·* Him, . . . is to approach Him
	9–20	by those who fail to *u·* me,
	49– 2	I *u·* that man is as
	49– 8	The more I *u·* true humanhood,
	59–10	*u·* Christ to be the divine idea

understand

Un.	62–10	Mortals can *u·* this only as they
Pul.	30– 9	* this estimate, as I *u·*,
	69–23	* must *u·* these laws aright.
	80–15	* That we could not *u·* it might be
	85– 5	* who now, in part, *u·* her mission,
	85– 7	* those who do not *u·* it
Rud.	6–21	so far as you perceive and *u·* this
	6–26	question of how much you *u·* of
No.	6–11	as all *u·* who practise the
	11–19	more study to *u·* and demonstrate
	12– 5	to *u·* and to demonstrate God.
	16–17	Mortals do not *u·* the All ;
	19–20	A sinful sense is incompetent to *u·*
	33– 9	to *u·* and demonstrate what
'00.	6–13	can measurably *u·* C. S.,
	6–26	accept it, *u·* and practise it,
'01.	4–17	*u·* that God is personal in it.
	4–18	We *u·* that God is not finite ;
	4–22	misjudge us because we *u·*
	15– 3	in order to *u·* and demonstrate
Hea.	3–22	we must *u·* in part this
	7– 5	signifies those who *u·*
	8–19	When we *u·* that God is
	16– 3	having ears, hear and *u·*.
Peo.	6–25	we should *u·* something of that
My.	13–16	I *u·* that the members of
	41–30	* *u·* how illimitable is the Love
	111–28	professionals who fail to *u·*
	135–27	you *u·* the Scripture,
	135–29	scientifically *u·* that God is
	146– 6	believe this saying because I *u·*
	151– 7	can or does *u·* this Science
	167– 8	and to *u·* what we are
	195–15	nor *u·* what is not ripening in us.
	224– 1	*u·* the importance of that demand
	242– 4	*u·* that you are so.
	253–26	We *u·* best that which begins in
	299–21	*u·* it and the law governing it,
	300–14	*u·* or aver that there is no death,
	303–19	it is essential to *u·*
	313– 1	but is, I *u·*, a paraphrase
		(*see also* **God**)

understandable

My.	238–21	God is *u·*, knowable,

understandeth

Ret.	64–16	Man that . . . *u·* not,— *Psal.* 49 : 20.

understanding (noun)

absolute

My.	293–15	absolute *u·* of God's omnipotence,

affections and

Un.	2–26	their affections and *u·*.

all

Mis.	125–14	that passeth all *u·* ;
No.	8– 8	passeth all *u·*," — *Phil.* 4 : 7.

all-important

Peo.	13– 8	This all-important *u·*

and demonstration

Mis.	55– 4	*u·* and demonstration thereof
Man.	19– 3	*u·* and demonstration of divine Truth,

and obedience

Mis.	160–15	firmer in *u·* and obedience.

and works

'01.	21– 2	Science, *u·*, and works

belief and

Pul.	47–19	* the terms belief and *u·*,

better

Pul.	69–24	* patient may gain a better *u·*

brought to the

Mis.	3–13	divine Science, brought to the *u·*

clear

Man.	66– 4	obtain a clear *u·* of the matter,

clearer

My.	207–11	* clearer *u·* and more perfect

darkens the

Mis.	291– 6	and darkens the *u·*

divine

Mis.	40–30	requires more divine *u·* to conquer
Un.	30–10	divine *u·* takes away this belief

ears of

Mis.	301–29	stop the ears of *u·*,

elevation of the

Ret.	88–12	implies such an elevation of the *u·*

enlightened

No.	45–17	highest measure of enlightened *u·*
My.	128–17	conscience and enlightened *u·*.

enraptured

Mis.	17–18	opens to the enraptured *u·*

faith and

    (*see* **faith**)

faith with

Mis.	97–16	combines faith with *u·*,

feeble

Un.	61–19	faith and a feeble *u·* make

understanding (noun)

full

Mis.	45– 3	full *u·* that God is Mind,
My.	237– 8	has not attained the full *u·*

get

My.	60–19	* get *u·*." — *Prov.* 4 : 7.

glow and

Mis.	356– 4	with spiritual glow and *u·*.

growth and

Mis.	156–28	tests of growth and *u·*

guides the

Mis.	81–30	It . . . guides the *u·*,

her

Mis.	169–10	Truth dawned upon her *u·*,

higher

Mis.	342–11	wedded to a higher *u·* of God.
My.	51–14	* to lead us to the higher *u·* of
	246–14	higher *u·* of the absolute

highest

Mis.	146–25	highest *u·* of justice and mercy.
'01.	28–10	life up to his highest *u·*

his

Mis.	31–21	parts with his *u·* of good,
Hea.	7–23	his *u·* of these two facts,

human

    (*see* **human**)

implies

Mis.	193–32	the Hebrew of which implies *u·*.

is required

Mis.	334–25	No : *u·* is required to do this.

lack of

Mis.	195– 8	by reason of the lack of *u·*.
Rud.	10–27	It is only a lack of *u·* of the

life and

Pan.	15– 9	life and *u·* of God,

life-giving

No.	46– 8	life-giving *u·* C. S. imparts,

means, and

Ret.	48–29	to higher ways, means, and *u·*,

measure of

Pul.	84–20	* have some measure of *u·* of

misguides the

My.	153–19	Faith in . . . misguides the *u·*;

my

Mis.	25– 5	to my *u·* it is the heart of
My.	344– 2	to my *u·* of Christ

not

Ret.	54– 3	faith is belief, and not *u·* ;

of Christ

Mis.	164–20	Wisemen grew in the *u·* of Christ,
My.	344– 2	to my *u·* of Christ

of Christian Science

Un.	56–11	actual *u·* of C. S.
Pul.	22–12	approximate the *u·* of C. S.
Rud.	17– 8	true *u·* of C. S. Mind-healing
No.	38–17	approximate the *u·* of C. S.,
'01.	32–28	spirit and *u·* of C. S.

of divine Love

Mis.	125–13	rest, in the *u·* of divine Love
My.	162–28	their *u·* of divine Love.

of divine Principle

Man.	83–15	in the *u·* of divine Principle,

of God

    (*see* **God**)

of good

Mis.	31–21	parts with his *u·* of good,
	107–17	(3) the *u·* of good.

of His presence

Un.	4–10	the *u·* of His presence,

of Life

My.	273–22	spiritual *u·* of Life

of Love

My.	278–11	faith armed with the *u·* of Love,

of Mind-healing

Mis.	356–26	to the *u·* of Mind-healing ;

of mortals

Mis.	260– 4	reduced to the *u·* of mortals,

of omnipotence

My.	294–18	his conscious *u·* of omnipotence,

of Science

Un.	4–25	such an *u·* of Science,

of Spirit

Un.	50– 9	by a dominant *u·* of Spirit.

of the Science

Mis.	54–23	require an *u·* of the Science
	96–22	this *u·* of the Science of God,
	221–20	saps one's *u·* of the Science

of Truth

Mis.	166–14	*u·* of Truth and Love.
Un.	40– 9	*u·* of Truth subordinates
Hea.	16–22	gain no *u·* of Truth, Life,
My.	232–22	precede that *u·* of Truth

passeth

Mis.	133–30	peace that passeth *u·*,

patience, and

No.	8–27	power, patience, and *u·*

understanding (noun)

peace, and
Mis. 290–18 * illumination, peace, and u˙ ; "
perfect
Ret. 91–20 his own perfect u˙.
praise and
Mis. 331– 9 prayer and praise and u˙
present
Un. 6– 1 Our present u˙ is but
presents to the
Pul. 6– 8 presents to the u˙, not matter,
priceless
Mis. 30–13 priceless u˙ of man's real
proper
Un. 8–14 proper u˙ of the unreality of
reach the
No. 35– 6 to reach the u˙ of this
resurrect the
Mis. 154–16 Love to resurrect the u˙,
scientific
Mis. 118– 5 scientific u˙ guides man.
166–14 scientific u˙ of Truth and Love.
small
Un. 5– 3 rejoice in the small u˙ they have
spiritual
(see **spiritual**)
that matter
Mis. 198– 8 u˙ that matter has no sense ;
their
Mis. 170–10 whose entrance into their u˙
Man. 62–21 according to their u˙
My. 162–28 their u˙ of divine Love.
thine own
Mis. 298– 2 unto thine own u˙." – Prov. 3 : 5.
'01. 34–30 unto thine own u˙.— Prov. 3 : 5.
this
Mis. 96–22 this u˙ of the Science of God,
200–31 subdued it with this u˙.
281–21 helplessness without this u˙,
Un. 40– 9 this u˙ of Truth subordinates
thorough
Ret. 18–19 to impart a thorough u˙
true
Un. 1–18 closer to the true u˙ of God
13–12 the true u˙ of Deity.
Rud. 11–20 based on a true u˙ of God
17– 8 Tho true u˙ of C. S.
uncultivated
My. 168– 1 or of an uncultivated u˙
upright
Mis. 265– 6 cannot regain, . . . upright u˙.
your
My. 36–30 * a sign of your u˙

Mis. 39– 5 the u˙ of how you are healed.
50–21 the u˙ that God is our Life,
59–12 pray . . . with the u˙ that God has
114–15 the u˙ . . . according to Christ.
124–30 to hope, faith ; to faith, u˙ ;
124–30 to u˙, Love triumphant !
169–11 With the u˙ of Scripture-meanings,
182–19 the u˙ that man was never lost
193–30 the u˙ of man's capabilities
307– 6 through the u˙ of omnipresent Love !
360–22 the divine energies, u˙, and
Chr. 53–15 Through u˙, dearly sought,
Un. 48–20 I believe . . . through the u˙,
'01. 34–23 abound in faith, u˙, and good works ;
Peo. 1–17 the u˙ that we are spiritual beings
3– 1 the u˙ that our ideals form our
My. 3–18 highway of hope, faith, u˙.
170–29 faith, u˙, prayer, and praise
240–14 highway of hope, faith, u˙."

understanding (ppr.)

Mis. 82– 4 U˙ this fact in C. S.,
92– 2 necessity for u˙ Science,
201–16 U˙ this, Paul took pleasure in
333–19 to aid in u˙ and securing
Man. 65–25 U˙ Communications.
Ret. 54–15 admits Truth without u˙ it.
83–28 the necessity of thoroughly u˙
Pul. 69–27 * u˙ and demonstrating the
Rud. 15– 4 u˙ sufficiently the Science of
Hea. 8– 5 U˙ the truth regarding mind and
15– 8 By rightly u˙ the power
My. 5–21 Him whom, u˙ even in part,
78–31 * apparently u˙ all they heard,
112–16 student of this book, u˙ it,
217–26 u˙ the situation in C. S."
248–23 The Christ mode of u˙ Life
349–10 afford little aid in u˙

understandingly

Mis. 352–11 act more u˙ in destroying this
Man. 32–19 They shall read u˙
No. 4– 3 and demonstrating it u˙

understands

Mis. 19–22 as high a basis as he u˙,
43– 9 student of this Science who u˙ it
44–10 conducted by one who u˙ this Science
52– 7 Whosoever u˙ the power of Spirit,
85– 7 demonstrates what he u˙.
100–27 He u˙ this Principle,— Love.
183–20 Who u˙ these sayings?
243–16 in proportion as he u˙ it.
265–12 u˙ a single rule in Science,
269–14 Who is it that u˙, unmistakably,
Man. 49–11 thoroughly u˙ the practical wisdom
52–25 what she u˙ is advantageous to this Church
75–11 she now u˙ the financial situation
Un. 39– 9 Who u˙ these sayings?
40–21 to him who fully u˙ Life.
No. 16–20 He who is All, u˙ all.
Pan. 11–15 who u˙ not this Science.
'01. 15–11 in proportion as one u˙ it
Peo. 13– 5 u˙ that the Divine Being is more than
My. 180– 3 Whosoever u˙ C. S. knows

understood

Mis. 1–13 infinite Truth needs to be u˙.
4–23 specialty and . . . are not u˙.
5– 5 This should be u˙.
9– 2 through affliction rightly u˙,
12–19 in a manner least u˙ ;
14–19 that good, God, u˙, . . . destroys.
25–12 Science, u˙, translates matter into
36– 3 to be u˙, we shall classify evil
43– 8 C. S. is not sufficiently u˙
53–26 readily u˙ by the children ;
56–22 Science of Life needs only to be u˙ ;
59– 7 divine power u˙, as in C. S. ;
63– 7 Our Master u˙ that Life, Truth, Love
74– 2 noumenon and phenomenon u˙,
75–10 includes a rule that must be u˙,
92– 5 become sufficiently u˙
97– 2 Truth . . . that u˙, gives man ability
100–21 The spiritual monitor u˙ is
101– 3 how the divine Mind is u˙
154–21 healing Christ . . . u˙ and glorified.
156–17 best u˙ through the study of my
164– 8 until it be acknowledged, u˙,
164–22 continue, as it shall become u˙,
166–18 the idea of man was not u˙.
169–30 * thoughts when rightly u˙.
172–21 spiritually u˙, and demonstrated
172–24 spiritually discerned, u˙, and
172–29 rule of Science must be u˙
175–19 mental healing must be u˙.
182–30 this eternal Truth will be u˙ ;
190–15 When the Scripture is u˙,
190–16 signification of its terms will be u˙,
192– 9 nature of Deity and devil be u˙.
196–27 not through death, but Life, God u˙.
200– 6 u˙ omnipotence to be All-power :
232–27 u˙ to be of God,
233–10 if not u˙ and withstood,
233–30 Matter must be u˙ as a
243–20 is not generally u˙.
250–10 no sentiment less u˙.
278–12 when my motives and acts are u˙
286–20 recognized and u˙ in Science.
286–26 It should be u˙ that Spirit,
286–29 is seen, u˙, and demonstrated
287– 1 u˙ as the most exalted
288–19 before it is u˙ is impossible,
292–29 u˙ my instructions on this point
331–31 hieroglyphics of Love, are u˙ ;
333–32 the prophet better u˙ Him
337–17 harmony is not u˙ unless
337–25 u˙ the concrete character
344–21 the Science which Paul u˙
346– 4 God is u˙ and illustrated.
352–20 must be u˙ in order to
358–20 Be it u˙ that I do not require
359– 9 I u˙ as a child,— I Cor. 13 : 11.
360–30 and this idea is u˙,
361–13 u˙ in startling contradiction of
365–31 must be conscientiously u˙
367–10 in the proportion that Science is u˙,
369– 4 shall be finally u˙ ;
379–22 a mental standpoint not u˙,
399–26 God is Love, and u˙
Man. 90–23 thoroughly discussed, and u˙ ;
Ret. 28–25 but I have since u˙ it.
33–24 methods of medicine, when u˙,
54–18 admitted, but not u˙,
69–19 When will it be u˙ that
75–12 cannot be, u˙ or taught by
81–14 so apparent as to be well u˙.
84– 2 sufficiently u˙ to be fully
87–28 u˙ that Christian Scientists
Un. 1– 4 "things hard to be u˙,"— II Pet. 3 : 16.

understood
Un.	6– 5	selfhood of God is *u·*,
	30–24	*u·* the meaning of the declaration
	39– 3	Eternal Life is partially *u·* ;
	48–12	best *u·* as Supreme Being,
	51– 5	neither seen, felt, heard, nor *u·*.
Pul.	14–22	the spiritual idea will be *u·*.
	16–11	God is Love, and *u·*
	54–15	* He *u·* the law perfectly,
	54–16	* as no one before him *u·* it ;
	74–20	"I think Mrs. Lathrop was not *u·*.
	74–21	intention to be thus *u·*,
Rud.	6–23	*u·* in practical demonstration.
	13–16	propositions *u·* in their Science,
No.	11–10	are to be *u·* metaphysically.
	11–14	*u·* and conscientiously introduced.
	14– 3	*u·* the Science of Mind-healing,
	20–11	When *u·*, Principle is found to be
	28–17	Truth is never *u·* too soon.
	31– 8	*u·* that disease and sin are unreal,
	34–22	atonement . . . needs to be *u·*.
Pan.	10–24	the effect of God *u·*.
	11–13	Science of being, *u·* and obeyed,
'00.	5–27	spiritual sense of the Scriptures *u·*
'01.	11–21	to be heard and *u·*.
	22–24	as if they *u·* its Principle
'02.	5–14	intelligently considered and *u·*.
	9– 8	significance of this saying is *u·*,
	12–14	This declaration of Christ, *u·*,
Hea.	9– 3	if we *u·* the Principle better
	14–24	included more than they *u·*.
	15– 5	Truth, Life, and Love, *u·*,
	16– 1	Prayer, *u·* in its spiritual sense,
	17–14	allegory of Adam, when spiritually *u·*,
	18–24	when metaphysics is *u·* ;
Peo.	4–20	three in one that can be *u·*,
	6–21	divine Principle, *u·* in part,
	9–27	This truth of Deity, *u·*,
	12– 8	When this great fact is *u·*,
Po.	76–10	God is Love, and *u·*
	79–13	truth tatters those, When *u·*.
My.	52–15	* *u·*, does bring out the perfection
	103–11	Science, until *u·*, has been persecuted
	109– 7	scientific classification is *u·*,
	112–19	is demonstrable when *u·*,
	112–20	is fully *u·* when demonstrated.
	113–26	as this Principle and rule are *u·*,
	124–29	seen of men, and spiritually *u·* ;
	135– 3	I *u·* as a child, — *I Cor.* 13 : 11.
	136– 4	cannot be fully *u·*, theoretically ;
	146– 2	It is *u·* by all Christians
	152–24	and C. S. will be *u·*.
	152–28	God, . . . when *u·* and demonstrated,
	153–24	Love, which can be *u·*,
	154– 5	Life *u·* by the practitioner
	170– 1	desirous that it should be *u·*
	178– 7	Christianity is not generally *u·*,
	225– 9	C. S. is not *u·* by the
	232–25	*u·* and recognized as the true
	238– 9	discerned, *u·*, and demonstrated.
	239– 7	ratio that C. S. is studied and *u·*,
	261–16	I *u·* as a child, — *I Cor.* 13 : 10.
	261–23	secret, *u·* by few — or by none
	264–16	the Bible better *u·*
	265–21	as *u·* in divine Science,
	271– 5	little *u·* all that I indited ;
	275–27	spiritually *u·* and demonstrated,
	279–17	*u·* in its divine metaphysics,
	298– 4	if correctly narrated and *u·*,
	302–14	It is a fact well *u·* that I
	303– 9	*u·* as following the divine Principle
	306–15	*u·* in the "new tongue." — *see Mark* 16 : 17.
	307–21	*u·* what I said better than some
	342–15	* not be *u·* that I mean weak,
	348– 7	*u·* through divine Science.
	349–12	*u·* by and divinely natural to him
	349–17	Thus the great Way-shower, . . . is *u·*,
	357–10	and this must be *u·*.

undertake
Pul.	84–18	* we shall not *u·* to speak
Rud.	8– 7	*How should I u· to demonstrate*
	16– 5	*u·* to fit students for practice
My.	231–22	unwise for her to *u·* new tasks,

undertaken
Mis.	249– 1	first *u·* by a mesmerist,
No.	4– 4	had better be *u·* in health

undertakes
Ret.	86–19	*u·* to carry his burden

undertaking
Mis.	236– 3	since *u·* the labor of
	305–13	* making the *u·* successful.
My.	61–30	* in such an immense *u·*,

undertook
Mis.	220–19	when the mental practitioner *u·* to

undeserving
My.	231– 7	also from the *u·* poor

undeveloped
No.	21–15	philosophy has an *u·* God,

undisciplined
Mis.	320–21	to dull ears and *u·* beliefs

undiscovered
My.	299–15	hitherto *u·* in the translations of

undisturbed
Ret.	23– 2	too eventful to leave me *u·*
Un.	5–12	*u·* by the frightened sense of
	62–20	*u·* by human error,
My.	68–16	* Mrs. Eddy's famous room will be *u·*.
	266–26	at that date *u·*, are now agitated,

undivided
Mis.	341– 3	an *u·* affection that leaves the
My.	353–16	to spread *u·* the Science

undo
Un.	20– 4	*u·* the statements of error by

undone
Mis.	274– 8	left *u·* might hinder the progress
Pul.	81–25	* all that the twelve have left *u·*.
My.	124–14	the *u·* waiting only your

undoubtedly
Mis.	121– 4	*U·* our Master partook of
	186–29	*u·* refers to the last Adam
Pul.	65– 7	* but is *u·* an interesting faith
My.	179– 1	*u·* the beginning of the gospel
	266–29	It is *u·* true that C. S.

undulating
Ret.	4–12	*u·* lands of three townships.

unduly
Ret.	73–23	or accuse people of being *u·* personal,

unearthed
My.	130– 6	will ere long be *u·* and punished

uneducated
My.	305– 1	(an obscure, *u·* man),

unemployed
Pul.	8– 8	*u·* in our money centres,

unenvironed
My.	122–22	spiritual idea *u·* by materiality

unequal
Mis.	195–24	is *u·* to the conflict,
No.	18–14	found *u·* to the demonstration

unequivocally
Mis.	193–11	support *u·* the proof

unerring
Mis.	3–19	God, *u·* and immortal Mind.
	22– 4	the *u·* manifesto of Mind,
	27–28	but to *u·* spiritual sense,
	93–17	supported by the *u·* Principle
	172–12	*u·* Mind measures man,
	232–24	The *u·* and fixed Principle
	293– 6	*u·* modes of divine wisdom,
	315–28	*u·* wisdom and law of God,
Man.	83–20	in conformity with the *u·* laws
Ret.	34– 2	the unmixed, *u·* source,
	56– 8	*u·* divine Principle of Science,
Un.	53–24	the immortal and *u·* Mind, God,
No.	8– 1	the Father, whose wisdom is *u·*
	39–16	in the direction that is *u·*.
My.	vi–16	* wise and *u·* counsellor.
	3–16	a persuasive animus, an *u·* impetus,
	44–29	* *u·* wisdom of your leadership,
	205–28	demonstrated by perfect rules ; it is *u·*.

unexpected
Pul.	79–17	* has shown a vitality so *u·*.
My.	26–14	quite *u·* at this juncture,
	194–21	*u·* token of your gratitude
	228– 6	I am always saying the *u·*

unexpectedly
My.	42–13	* Most *u·* to me came the call
	343– 5	* reaching an answer often *u·*

unexplained
My.	218–18	divine Principle of C. S. *u·*,
	243–21	in Concord at my *u·* call

unexplored
Mis.	xi–13	hitherto *u·* fields of Science.

unfailing
My.	62– 1	* unflinching faith and *u·* fidelity
	348–22	an actual, *u·* causation,

unfair
My.	323– 5	* answer to an *u·* criticism

unfaithful
Pul.	15–13	designate those as *u·* stewards
'02.	19– 3	console his *u·* followers

unfallen
Mis.	79–23	that perfect and *u·* likeness,
Pul.	8– 4	leaves of an ancient oak, *u·*,
Pan.	11–26	man's *u·* spiritual perfectibility.
Po.	1– 1	*u·* still thy crest !

unfaltering
Mis.	163–17	*u·* faith in the immortality of
'02.	20– 8	glorifying thy *u·* faith
My.	155– 6	*u·* faith in the prophecies,
	247–29	patient, *u·* tenderness.

unfamiliar
Mis.	234–18	ventured on such *u·* ground,
	347–19	A true sense not *u·*
Ret.	35– 6	men were so *u·* with the subject
My.	338–21	*u·* with his broad views

unfamiliarity
Mis.	296– 7	*u·* with the work and career

unfathomable
Mis.	323– 4	in serene azure and *u·* glory :
Ret.	57– 2	the *u·* sea of possibilities.
Un.	28–21	must be the *u·* Mind,

unfeasted
Mis.	231–10	groan for the *u·* ones.

unfeigned
Mis.	136–11	and of the faith *u·*.
My.	187–13	and of faith *u·* ;" — *I Tim.* 1 : 5.
	193– 1	dedicate your temple in faith *u·*,

unfettered
Ret.	9–26	* And won, . . . her own *u·* way !

unfinited
Peo.	2–21	has been dematerialized and *u·*

unfit
Mis.	25–29	then they are bad and *u·* for man ;
	195–24	and *u·* to judge in the case ;
	268–10	He is *u·* for Truth,
Hea.	4–12	to bless what is *u·* to be blessed.

unfitness
Mis.	309– 8	this declares its *u·* for
Pul.	3–30	*u·* for such a spiritual animus
'01.	21–18	a manifest *u·* to criticise it
'02.	18–26	showing their *u·* to follow

unflinching
My.	61–32	* *u·* faith and unfailing fidelity

unfold
Un.	5–16	*u·* in us a higher sense of Deity ;
Pul.	84–21	* *u·* it to the comprehension of
Po.	16– 8	These vaults will *u·*
My.	110–21	*u·* in part the facts of day,

unfolded
Mis.	189– 5	as *u·* in divine Science,
Pul.	85– 9	* *u·* and demonstrated divine Love,
My.	103–13	Infinite perfection is *u·*
	207–12	* truth which you have *u·*
	248–19	God *u·* the way,

unfoldeth
No.	45–28	Truth . . . *u·* forever.

unfolding
Mis.	69– 5	C. S. is the *u·* of true
	82–17	*u·* the endless beatitudes
	83– 2	rhythmic round of *u·* bliss,
	293– 4	the righteous *u·* of error
Man.	15–15	*u·* man's unity with God
Ret.	50–25	furtherance and *u·* of Truth,
Pul.	4–23	*u·* its eternal Principle.
No.	45– 8	To hinder the *u·* truth,
	46–21	*u·* of this upward tendency
Po.	18– 6	*u·* a quenchless desire.
My.	3–18	*u·* the highway of hope,
	4–20	Thus *u·* the true metal
	216–21	your present *u·* capacity.
	240–13	*u·* the highway of hope,
	261–14	and in *u·* the immortal model,

unfolds
Mis.	71–16	*u·* divine Principle,
	72– 5	*u·* the eternal harmonies
	100–14	Science . . . *u·* infinite good,
	117– 2	that *u·* its immortal Principle.
	183–22	divine Science *u·* omnipotence,
	218– 2	Science *u·* the fact that
	218–17	*u·* the real nature of God
Chr.	53–51	same hand *u·* His power,
No.	10– 9	aggregates, amplifies, *u·*,
	21–15	*u·* Himself through material modes,
	37–12	*u·* the full-orbed glory
'02.	10– 3	*u·* spiritual forces,
My.	42–24	* only as infinite good *u·*
	164–24	*u·* the thought most within us
	183–12	*u·*, transfigures, heals.
	288– 3	Love *u·* marvellous good

unforgotten
Mis.	329–12	sweet rhythm of *u·* harmonies,
Po.	34–22	O'er joys departed, *u·* love.

unfortunate
Mis.	9–12	those *u·* individuals are virtually
	32–19	*u·* seekers after Truth
Ret.	20–21	My second marriage was very *u·*,
My.	231–10	uncertain, *u·* investments.
	301–20	*u·* people who are committed to
	332– 7	* an effort in behalf of the *u·*,

unfruitful
Mis.	151–10	He speaketh to the *u·*
	311–14	impractical, *u·*, Soul-less.

unfurling
My.	232– 2	*u·* your banner to the breeze

ungodliness
Un.	22– 6	but as to the fruit of *u·*,

ungodly
Mis.	53–30	to the unspiritual, the *u·*, it is dark

ungrammatical
My.	318– 9	as *u·* as it was misleading.

unharmed
Mis.	383–13	down the dim posterns of time *u·*,
Hea.	15–10	"take up serpents" *u·*, — *Mark* 16 : 18.

unhealing
Ret.	65–30	unspiritual and *u·* religion.

unheard
Peo.	1–15	throes of thought are *u·*,

unheard-of
Un.	16– 3	*u·* contradictions, — absurdities ;

unholiness
Un.	11– 1	mountains of *u·* to shield them

uniform
Mis.	ix–15	long course of years still and *u·*,
	ix–16	amid the *u·* darkness of storm
	265–24	My teachings are *u·*.
	312– 4	Love is consistent, *u·*,
	365–19	If the *u·* moral and spiritual,
Man.	55–19	proved by *u·* maintenance of
No.	19– 1	If the *u·* moral and spiritual,
My.	291–17	His public intent was *u·*,

uniformity
My.	236–15	with the sweet alacrity and *u·*

uniformly
Mis.	309– 9	The face of Jesus has *u·* been
Pul.	88– 5	*u·* kind and interesting articles
My.	112–21	because of their *u·* pure morals
	309– 2	was *u·* dignified
	338– 8	* *u·* held and expressed by her.

unify
'00.	11– 5	harmonize, *u·*, and unself you.

unimpeachable
My.	103– 2	because Science is *u·*,

uninspired
Ret.	26–14	though *u·* interpreters ignorantly
My.	238–11	*U·* knowledge of the translations of

unintentionally
Mis.	40–31	*u·* harms himself or another.
Ret.	83–16	and communicates, even *u·*,

uninterrupted
Man.	60– 2	services *u·*.

uninvited
Ret.	88–21	to signify that we . . . may go, *u·*, to

Union
Ret.	21–11	throughout the war for the *U·*,
Pul.	41– 5	* From every State in the *U·*,
	57– 5	* from every State in the *U·*,
Po.	78– 8	the *U·* now is one,
My.	94–22	* from every State in the *U·*
	340–13	In many of the States in our *U·*

union
Mis.	42–12	by a conscious *u·* with God.
	52–16	a *u·* of the affections
	77–13	indissoluble bond of *u·*,
	98–18	and to find strength in *u·*,
	254–12	strength of *u·* grows weak
Ret.	42– 2	a blessed and spiritual *u·*,
Un.	17– 9	*u·* predestined from all eternity ;
My.	343–30	brought all back to *u·* and love

Union Chapter, Number 3
Ret.	19–12	*U· C·, N·* 3, of Royal Arch masons.
My.	330–24	*U· C·, N·* 3, of Royal Arch Masons.
	335– 6	* Royal Arch Mason in "*U· C·, N·* 3,"

Union Signal, The
Pul.	79– 1	*[The *U· S·*, Chicago]

unique

Man.	71— 9	Mother Church *U·*.
Pul.	v— 6	THIS *u·* BOOK IS TENDERLY DEDICATED
	5— 5	read by . . . in that *u·* assembly.
	23— 5	* MOST *u·* STRUCTURE IN ANY CITY
	24— 5	* most *u·* structure in any city.
	27—29	* windows are of still more *u·* interest.
	40—18	* the *u·* and costly edifice
	61—16	* in every part of this *u·* church,
	85—26	* a beautiful and *u·* testimonial
My.	71—13	* chapter sub-title
	85—28	* absolutely *u·* in its symmetrical
	320—12	* as being a very *u·* book,
	324—25	* as entirely *u·* and original.

uniquely

Man.	104— 8	*u·* adapted to form the budding

unison

Mis.	40— 3	but this *u·* and its power
	266—23	toiling and achieving success in *u·*
Pan.	1—11	In unctuous *u·* with nature,
'00.	11—13	Music is more than sound in *u·*.
My.	29— 5	* rising in *u·* from the vast congregation,
	32— 1	* unanimity and repetition in *u·*
	78—22	* congregation singing in perfect *u·*.

unit

Mis.	65—24	They are a *u·* in restoring the
Pul.	4— 8	mathematically number one, a *u·*,

Unitarian

Pul.	28—25	* hymn-books of the *U·* churches.
My.	171—22	* on the lawn of the *U·* church
	173—29	committee of the *U·* church,

unite

Mis.	100—24	They *u·* terrestrial and celestial joys,
	110—21	We may well *u·* in thanksgiving
	142—29	I may not *u·* with you in freemasonry,
	152— 6	*u·* in the purposes of goodness.
	160— 3	Never did . . . *u·* more honestly
	311— 2	to come and *u·* with The Mother Church
	371—23	but error always strives to *u·*,
Man.	35—19	can *u·* with this Church only by
	44—24	shall not *u·* with organizations which
	63—17	may *u·* in having Reading Rooms,
	94— 3	to *u·* in their attendance
	109— 4	approve candidates to *u·* with this Church.
Ret.	14—12	never could I *u·* with the church, if
Un.	43—20	*u·* the influence of their own thoughts
Pul.	15—20	*u·* all interests in the one divinity.
	21—10	Who will *u·* with me in this
	22— 5	rejoicing that we *u·* in love,
	30— 5	* to *u·* with churches already established
	30—12	* and to *u·* in communion
	56—18	* dogma and truth could not *u·*,
No.	44—21	will again *u·* Church and State,
'02.	11—29	Jew and Christian can *u·* in doctrine
Po.	11— 2	*U·* your battle-plan ;
My.	131— 7	we *u·* in giving thanks.
	193—18	*u·* with all who believe in Truth.
	206— 1	would *u·* dead matter with
	207— 9	* *u·* in loving greetings to you,
	275—28	*u·* in one *Te Deum* of praise.
	283—21	*u·* harmoniously on the basis of
	285—14	*u·* with us in the grand object
	301—10	*u·* as brethren in one prayer :
	338— 2	*U·* your battle-plan ;
	360—18	*u·* with those in your church
	362—22	* will *u·* the churches and societies

united

Ret.	19— 1	I was *u·* to my first husband,
	90—13	on their *u·* pilgrimages.
Pul.	21—18	*u·* to only that which
Pan.	13—14	churches are *u·* in purpose,
'02.	12—25	before making another *u·* effort
My.	7— 8	before making another *u·* effort
	18—22	churches are *u·* in purpose,
	50— 6	*u·* themselves into a little band
	195—25	*u·* efforts to build an edifice
	333—27	* to whom he had been *u·*

unitedly

My.	362—16	* confer harmoniously and *u·*

United States

Mis.	305—31	* the first President of the *U· S·*,
Man.	27— 5	The manager . . . in the *U· S·*
	60—12	In the *U· S·* there shall be
	94—18	shall lecture in the *U· S·*,
	97— 8	*U· S·*, Canada, Great Britain
	98—26	each State of the *U· S·*
Ret.	6—20	afterwards President of the *U· S·* ;
Pul.	44—25	* from all parts of the *U· S·*
	63— 5	* THROUGHOUT THE *U· S·*,
	64— 8	* from all parts of the *U· S·*.
	67—18	* majority of whom are in the *U· S·*,

United States

Pul.	68—22	* church edifices in the *U· S·*
	71—21	* thousands throughout the *U· S·*
Pan.	14—28	war between *U· S·* and Spain
'00.	7— 2	From that year the *U· S·*
	10—26	first lieutenant of the *U· S·* infantry
'02.	2—12	religion in the *U· S·* has
	3— 7	the President of the *U· S·*
Po.	vi—21	*slavery in the U· S·*.''
	page 10	poem
My.	65— 5	* largest ever held in the *U· S·*
	92— 1	* town and city of the *U· S·*.
	96—29	* from all parts of the *U· S·*.
	112—30	the President of the *U· S·*,
	128— 7	Constitution of the *U· S·*,
	182— 3	over any other city in the *U· S·*.
	222—22	Constitution of the *U· S·*
	227— 9	protection of State or *U· S·*
	250—19	churches in the *U· S·* and Canada.
	277— 4	between the *U· S·* and Spain
	278— 4	by the intervention of the *U· S·*,
	290— 2	of New England and the *U· S·*.
	292—14	of every sect in the *U· S·*
	309— 8	afterwards President of the *U· S·*,
	337— 2	poem

United States Circuit Court

Mis.	300—22	record of theft in the *U· S· C· C·*.
	380—27	was filed in the *U· S· C· C·*

United States Marshal

Ret.	21—12	was appointed *U· S· M·*

United States Tubular Bell Company

Pul.	61—27	* *U· S· T· B· C·*, of Methuen, Mass.,

unites

Mis.	205—24	*u·* all periods in the divine design.
Pul.	6— 7	*u·* Science to Christianity.
'02.	12— 9	Jew *u·* with the Christian idea
	12—12	*u·* with the Jew's belief in one God,
Peo.	2— 9	*u·* Science and Christianity,
My.	167— 6	and *u·* us to one another.
	204— 9	C. S. *u·* its true followers

uniting

Man.	15— 1	*To be signed by those u· with The*
Ret.	49—25	*u·* them in one common brotherhood.
Pul.	30—11	* ceremonial of *u·* is to sign a
	30—14	* by *u·* in silent prayer.
My.	279—10	*u·* all periods in the design of
	291— 6	a *u·* of breaches soon to widen,
	291—11	*u·* the interests of all people ;
	316— 2	*u·* . . . those who love Truth

unity

among brethren

My.	274—24	*u·* among brethren, and love to God

and consistency

'01.	26— 1	*u·* and consistency of Jesus' theory

and harmony

My.	270—31	religion and art in *u·* and harmony.

and love

My.	6—17	your progress, *u·*, and love.

and power

My.	162— 6	*u·* and power are not in atom

and progress

My.	123— 1	Our *u·* and progress are proverbial,

and the purity

'00.	13— 1	*u·* and the purity of the church.

any

My.	306— 5	any *u·* that may exist between

bond of

Pul.	22— 3	one bond of *u·*, one nucleus

Christian

My.	200—11	The chain of Christian *u·*, unbroken,

commemorate in

'01.	1—10	you meet to commemorate in *u·*

communicants in

'00.	1—13	sixteen thousand communicants in *u·*,

eternal

Mis.	77—11	eternal *u·* of man and God,

final

Peo.	1— 7	final *u·* between man and God.

fourfold

My.	199—20	of fourfold *u·* between the churches of

in Christian Science

My.	251—28	namely, the *u·* in C. S.

individual

Man.	70—19	on individual *u·* and action

inherent

My.	262— 3	inherent *u·* with divine Love,

is divine might

Mis.	138—19	*u·* is divine might,

its

Mis.	307—16	as to Christianity and its *u·*

love and

My.	39—28	* our own growth in love and *u·*
	205—15	Love and *u·* are hieroglyphs

unity

man's
Mis. 196–18 man's *u·* with his Maker,
Man. 15–16 unfolding man's *u·* with God
Un. 41–16 man's *u·* with his Maker
meet in
Mis. 147– 7 Do you meet in *u·*,
mere
Mis. 80– 4 more than can be gained by mere *u·*
moral
Un. 19–14 would be the end of infinite moral *u·*.
of action
My. 212–18 there would be *u·* of action.
of doctrine
Ret. 15–20 if not in full *u·* of doctrine.
of eternal Love
Mis. 286–10 the *u·* of eternal Love.
of faith
My. 170–28 *u·* of faith, understanding,
of God
Mis. 266–16 inseparable from the *u·* of God.
369–10 strong in the *u·* of God and man.
'02. 9–18 *u·* of God and man is not the dream
of good
Mis. 135–19 noble offering to the *u·* of good,
319– 2 true sense of the *u·* of good
366–21 evil insists on the *u·* of good and evil
Ret. 76–19 *u·* of good and bond of perfectness.
No. 38–16 the infinity and *u·* of good.
of man
Un. 5–24 marvellous *u·* of man with God
of Mind
Peo. 13– 11 *u·* of Mind and oneness of Principle.
of Spirit
Mis. 198– 4 at this point of *u·* of Spirit,
My. 167– 8 what we are in the *u·* of Spirit
of spirit
Mis. 145–21 visible *u·* of spirit remains,
Pul. 22–18 there will be *u·* of spirit,
of thought
My. 24–12 * rejoice in the *u·* of thought
of Truth
Mis 109– 1 declaring the *u·* of Truth,
order and
Ret. 10–17 was spiritual order and *u·*.
perfect
Mis. 21– 4 It goes on in perfect *u·*
preserve
Mis. 131–10 Christian Scientists preserve *u·*,
prevailed
Mis. 140–16 *U·* prevailed, till mortal man
Principle of
Mis. 117–14 Love is the Principle of *u·*,
question of
My. 236–17 seals the question of *u·*,
rests on
Ret. 75–19 excludes opposites, and rests on *u·*.
scientific
My. 246–14 absolute scientific *u·* which
sense of
Pul. 4 10 positive sense of *u·* with
spiritual
Mis. 358–32 higher spiritual *u·* is won,
My. 243–22 your spiritual *u·* with
suppositional
Mis. 217–20 suppositional *u·* and personality,
this
My. 164–27 This *u·* is reserved wisdom
195–29 grant that this *u·* remain,
trinity in
Rud. 4– 2 are this trinity in *u·*,
No. 1–21 This trinity in *u·*,
Hea. 3–25 a trinity in *u·* ;
with churches
Pul. 21–26 Our *u·* with churches of other
with God
Mis. 181– 7 his sonship, or *u·* with God,
Man. 15–16 unfolding man's *u·* with God
with Rome
Pul. 65– 5 * In inviting . . . to *u·* with Rome,

Mis. 138–17 I once thought that in *u·* was
185– 1 man in *u·* with . . . his Maker.
264–10 *U·* is the essential nature of C. S.
Ret. 64– 4 for such is the *u·* of evil ;
Un. 54–15 a *u·* which sin recognizes as
'02. 1– 5 increase in number, *u·*, steadfastness.
My. 162– 9 *U·* is spiritual cooperation,
164–22 *u·*, the bond of perfectness,
164–24 *u·*, which unfolds the thought

universal

Man. 19– 6 Church *U·* and Triumphant
Mis. 29– 6 touches *u·* humanity.
55– 9 *u·* claim of evil that seeks the
99–28 health, holiness, *u·* harmony,
102–12 He is *u·* and primitive.

universal

Mis. 134–19 the reign of *u·* harmony,
141–11 proposed type of *u·* Love ;
144–31 *u·* dawn shall break upon
150–25 God is *u·* ; confined to no spot,
150–29 Principle, with its *u·* manifestation,
155–30 to contemplate the *u·* charge
186–14 He is the *u·* Father and Mother
208– 8 the *u·* law of God has no
213–28 God's *u·* kingdom will appear,
252–18 C. S. . . . is *u·*.
259–29 the *u·*, intelligent Christ-idea
288–21 To reckon the *u·* cost and gain,
290–28 from individual as from *u·* love :
318– 3 *u·* brotherhood of man
365–14 *u·* need of better health
383– 4 *u·* approval and support of
Un. 6–23 the assertion of *u·* salvation
13– 9 His *u·* laws, His unchangeableness,
26–18 can it be . . . *chance* and *change* are *u·*
Pul. 21– 4 unambitious, impartial, *u·*,
Rud. 1– 4 Principle and rule of *u·* harmony.
No. 8– 2 and whose love is *u·*.
18–11 *u·* need of better health and
Pan. 3–24 * Pan stood for "*u·*" nature
12– 5 * Spirit, is ever in *u·* nature."
'01. 13–25 hence the hope of *u·* salvation.
23–30 * by the operations of the *u·* mind,
31– 5 all error, specific or *u·*.
Peo. 2–10 we learn that God, good, is *u·*,
2–25 Love *u·*, infinite, eternal.
Po. 1– 9 far the *u·* fiat ran,
My. 8–13 * expressed the *u·* voice of
37–15 * before the gaze of *u·* humanity.
64– 25 * in the *u·* temple of Spirit,
141–29 communion *u·* and divine.
165–18 identifies man with *u·* good.
181–19 the *u·* equity of Christianity.
186– 1 refuge in mountains, and good *u·*.
226– 9 an effect of one *u·* cause,
245– 3 demand for this *u·* benefice
247– 2 inalienable, *u·* rights of men.
248–15 reaching deep down into the *u·*
248–28 to challenge *u·* indifference,
254–23 inalienable, *u·* rights of men.
265–21 divine Love, impartial and *u·*,
275– 2 chapter sub-title
275– 3 and does produce *u·* fellowship.
280– 9 * the establishment of a *u·*, loving
291–12 it ended with a *u·* good
301–18 There is a *u·* insanity which
348– 5 the offspring of a *u·* cause.
353–14 *u·* activity and availability of Truth ;

Universalist

Pul. 60–18 * gift of a wealthy *U·* gentleman,

universality

Mis. 102–32 defines *omnipresence* as *u·*,

universally

Man. 31–13 spiritual *animus* so *u·* needed.
Rud. 6–16 * fact "almost *u·* accepted,
My. 225–20 Mankind almost *u·* gives to
236–24 I request the Christian Scientists *u·*

universe

and man
Mis. 65–13 God's *u·* and man are immortal,
Un. 10–12 *u·* and man are the spiritual
beauty of the
Mis. 86–15 My sense of the beauty of the *u·*
coexistent
'02. 7–18 the *u·* coexistent with God.
conceive the
Mis. 216–27 * to conceive the *u·* as a *phenomenon*
created the
Mis. 56–30 first spiritually created the *u·*,
doctrine that the
Pan. 2–15 * doctrine that the *u·*, . . . is God ;
4– 2 doctrine that the *u·* owes its origin
evolves the
Mis. 364–21 self-created or evolves the *u·*.
existing
Pan. 2–18 * manifested in the existing *u·*."
facts of the
Ret. 60–27 the spiritual facts of the *u·*,
Father of the
My. 148–15 Father of the *u·* and the father of
fresh
Ret. 27–30 a fresh *u·* — old to God, but
from the
Un. 60–22 from Himself nor from the *u·*.
God, and the
(see **God**)
God's
Mis. 65–13 God's *u·* and man are immortal.

universe

governs the
　Mis. 41–27　Principle which governs the *u·*,
　　258–15　He governs the *u·*.
　　380– 5　as well as governs the *u·*,
　No. 13–19　voices the infinite, and governs the *u·*.
　Pan. 3–30　by which he governs the *u·* ;
　Peo. 8–18　Mind, that governs the *u·*,
　My. 182–22　created and governs the *u·*

grasping the
　Mis. 364–14　right hand grasping the *u·*,

harmonies of the
　Pul. 81–22　* all the harmonies of the *u·*

His
　Mis. 186–26　sense of God and His *u·*
　'00. 5–24　Science of God and His *u·*,
　My. 109–21　individually but specks in His *u·*,

includes
　Pan. 12– 7　for the *u·* includes man

including man
　Mis. 23–20　The *u·*, including man, is not a
　　333–21　relate to the *u·*, including man

including the
　Un. 32– 6　man, including the *u·*, is His

indestructibility of the
　Mis. 206–10　scientific indestructibility of the *u·*

informing the
　Mis. 332– 3　Wisely governing, informing the *u·*,

is spiritual
　Rud. 4– 2　and their *u·* is spiritual,

laws of the
　My. 340–30　beneficence of the laws of the *u·*

logical
　Pul. 67– 8　* the hub of the logical *u·*,

made the
　Un. 14– 6　long after God made the *u·*,

man and
　'01. 5–19　real spiritual man and *u·*.
　My. 253– 4　perfect original man and *u·*.

man and the
　Mis. 57–24　sense of man and the *u·*
　　72– 1　can transmit to man and the *u·*
　Rud. 1– 7　the Soul of man and the *u·*.
　　5–25　believe man and the *u·* to be the
　'00. 4–19　truth of God, and of man and the *u·*.
　　4–26　Man and the *u·* coexist with God
　'02. 2– 8　Science of man and the *u·*,
　　7– 4　manifestations of love— man and the *u·*.
　　7–18　man and the *u·* coexistent with God.
　My. 106–15　Without Mind, man and the *u·*
　　226–15　Withdraw God, . . . from man and the *u·*,
　　226–16　man and the *u·* would no longer exist.
　　226–17　man and the *u·* would remain
　　262–21　His spiritual idea, man and the *u·*,
　　266–18　spiritualization . . . of man and the *u·*.
　　267–10　Alpha and Omega of man and the *u·* ;
　　294–15　conditions of man and the *u·*.
　　348–23　the laws of man and the *u·*,

man or the
　Mis. 37– 3　creating or governing man or the *u·*.
　　164–12　Principle of man or the *u·*,

material
　　　　(*see* material)

mingling with the
　Mis. 396–15　When mingling with the *u·*,
　Po. 59– 7　When mingling with the *u·*,

miracle in the
　Mis. 294– 7　miracle in the *u·* of mortal mind.

of God
　Mis. 217– 6　the *u·* of God is spiritual,

of Mind
　Mis. 369– 8　immeasurable *u·* of Mind,

reduce the
　Un. 13–14　would . . . reduce the *u·* to chaos.

rhythm of the
　Ret. 61–11　than the rhythm of the *u·*,

rules the
　My. 278– 8　Love rules the *u·*,

sensuous
　Mis. 87– 8　beauties of the sensuous *u·* :

spiritual
　Mis. 21– 8　spiritual *u·*, whereof C. S.
　　361–25　spiritual *u·*, including man
　Un. 14–14　rectify His spiritual *u·*?
　No. 26–24　in the spiritual *u·* he is

stellar
　No. 6–23　true Science of the stellar *u·*.

throughout the
　Un. 46–22　must extend throughout the *u·*,

transforming the
　Mis. 372– 6　C. S. is transforming the *u·*.

transform the
　Un. 17–18　transform the *u·* into a home of

visible
　Mis. 218– 5　visible *u·* declares the invisible

universe

whole
　My. 269– 1　whole *u·* included in one infinite Mind

would disappear
　Un. 60–22　Without Him, the *u·* would disappear,

　Mis. 4– 8　and of the *u·* as His idea,
　　57–22　the *u·* with man created spiritually.
　　64–30　or of a material state and *u·*,
　　106– 1　God is the sum total of the *u·*.
　　235– 7　Mind whence sprang the *u·*.
　　257– 2　excludes God from the *u·*, or
　　368– 1　a *u·* in His own image and likeness.
　Un. 29–11　only Mind and intelligence in the *u·*.
　No. 21– 8　it grasped in spiritual law the *u·*,
　My. 149–10　tides of truth that sweep the *u·*,
　　248–18　reality of God, man, nature, the *u·*.
　　287–18　Mind whence springs the *u·*.

universities
　Pul. 5–23　colleges, and *u·* of America ;

University
　Ret. 75–23　when he leaves the *U·*,

university
　Man. 73–10　students in any *u·* or college,
　　73–12　at such *u·* or college,
　　73–14　graduates of said *u·* or college,
　　73–18　rules of the *u·* or college
　　73–20　said *u·* or college organization.
　Ret. 91–27　nature's haunts were the Messiah's *u·*.

University Avenue
　Pul. 72– 8　* Mrs. D. W. Copeland of *U· A·*

University Press
　My. 318–11　proofreader for the *U· P·*,

unjust
　Mis. 18–31　that aught that God sends is *u·*,
　　19– 1　bring to . . . that which is *u·*,
　　80– 4　opposition to *u·* medical laws.
　　80–16　*u·* coercive legislation and
　　87– 5　which is *u·* to human sense
　　123–23　the just obtain a pardon for the *u·*,
　　290–12　partial, unmerciful, or *u·*,
　Man. 53–23　Publications *U·*.
　　53–25　an article that is false or *u·*,
　　54–11　as to *u·* and unmerciful conduct
　Un. 44– 2　which are as unkind and *u·* as
　　54–12　any claim whatever, just or *u·*,
　Pul. 7–19　*u·*, unmerciful, and oppressive
　Rud. 10– 1　an *u·* usurper of the throne
　'02 14–28　all *u·* public aspersions.

unjustly
　Man. 51– 8　member who shall *u·* aggrieve
　My. 138–13　*u·*, and wrongfully accused.

unkind
　Mis. 387–15　By thought or word *u·*,
　Un. 44– 2　which are as *u·* and unjust as
　　52–19　its *u·* forces, its tempests,
　Po. 6–10　By thought or word *u·*,
　My. 180–26　and calls them *u·*.
　　231–18　else . . . giving is *u·*.

unknow
　Un. 13–20　which He must learn to *u·*,

unknowingly
　'00. 8– 4　imparts knowingly and *u·* goodness ;

unknown
　Mis. xi–10　not *u·* to nor unrewarded by Him.
　　105–18　*u·* to the omnipresent Truth.
　　295–19　statements of the great *u·*
　　296– 8　*u·* author cited by Mr. Wakeman
　　296–21　in this *u·* gentleman's language,
　　296–29　What manner of man *is* this *u·*
　　368– 8　* and, behind the dim *u·*,
　　385–21　never of the dead : The dark *u·*.
　Man. 50– 1　and the cause thereof be *u·*,
　Ret. 31–17　the unseen sin, the *u·* foe,
　　38–25　motives and circumstances *u·* to me.
　Un. 5–15　*mystery* involves the *u·*.
　　50– 6　and is *u·* to the Divine.
　Pul. 67–16　* practically *u·* a decade since,
　No. 31– 9　unreal, *u·* to Truth,
　Hea. 6–23　wholly *u·* to the individual,
　Po. 48–15　never of the dead : The dark *u·*.
　My. 5–20　to worship, not an *u·* God,
　　43– 2　* An *u·* wilderness
　　85– 5　* years ago it was comparatively *u·* ;
　　153–20　appeals to an *u·* power
　　167– 3　mysticism of good is *u·* to the
　　189– 8　nor talk of *u·* love.
　　192– 2　Ye build not to an *u·* God.
　　193– 2　not to the *u·* God, but unto
　　251– 5　question from *u·* questioners :
　　338–12　"The *U·* God Made Known,"
　　338–13　*u·* to me till after the lecture

unlawful
Mis. 380–29 the u· publishing and use of an
381–29 their u· existence destroyed,

unlearned
Un. 1– 6 u· and unstable— II Pet. 3 : 16.
My. 307–22 For one so u·, he was a remarkable
324– 4 * a thought of contempt for the u·,

unleavened
Mis. 175–16 u· bread of sincerity— I Cor. 5 : 8.

unless
Mis. 12–15 u· one be watchful and steadfast
112–10 u· he knows how to be just ;
112–28 U· this mental condition be
181–10 u· that requirement should express
197– 9 u· this be so, no man can be
221–12 u· he believes that sin has
224– 1 u· our own thought barbs it.
224–27 u· the offense be against God.
249–18 u· it was something to remove stains
250–18 U· these appear, I cast aside the
296–23 u· from their affinity for the
297–21 u· such claims are relinquished
337–17 u· it produces a growing affection
345– 9 * u· you yield your religion,"
346–25 never to repeat error u·
Man. 30–11 U· Mrs. Eddy requests otherwise,
51–17 u· a By-Law governing the
70–16 u· it be when our churches,
85–13 u· he has a certificate
Ret. 21–26 u· they illustrate the ethics of
61–30 U· this method be pursued,
Un. 10–27 u·, pursued by their fears,
23–20 u· God has created them?
33–11 u· matter is mind, it cannot
37–15 Not u· it be a sin to believe
'00. 3– 3 u· he loses the chord.
'02. 8–11 u· he is actuated by love
Hea. 16–11 u· you do this you are not
Peo. 9–26 u· omnipotence is the All-power.
Po. 15– 5 Break not on the silence, u·
My. 87–11 * u· they are pointed out.
152–18 U· this be so, the blind is
211–27 u· the cause of the mischief is
213–15 U· one's eyes are opened to
219– 1 u· I am personally present.
229– 2 u· I mistake their calling.
242– 8 U· you fully perceive that
249–11 U· withstood, the heat of hate
347–27 u· it be the manifestation of

unlike
Mis. 39–16 U· the M. D.'s, Christian Scientists
55–23 all that is u· Spirit.
55–30 in something u· Him ;
72– 2 nothing evil, or u· Himself.
103–16 U· mortal mind, which must
217–21 a third quality u· God.
259–12 good as being u· itself,
292–18 u· the risen, immortal Love ;
355–22 what in thine own mentality is u·
300–13 He is in nothing u· Himself ;
Ret. 49–17 conquering all that is u·
Un. 3–25 of anything u· Himself ;
18– 8 everything that is u· Myself.
23–21 anything so wholly u· Himself
35–25 can form nothing u· itself,
38–22 in aught which is u· God,
No. 15–25 in nothing is He u· Himself.
16–19 of something u· Him.
37–16 what is u· God demands His
37–26 null and void whatever is u· God ;
Pan. 14– 1 of whatever is u· good,
'01. 8–20 Image of Spirit is not u· Spirit.
'02. 6– 2 to have aught u· the infinite.
6–30 producing nothing u· Himself,
My. 64–24 * overcoming all that is u· God,
127–25 U· Russia's armament, ours is
240–17 all that is u· God, good

unlimited
Mis. 102– 5 infinite finite being, an u· man,
102– 6 the u· and immortal Mind
103–17 the eternal Mind is free, u·,
Pul. 73– 4 * His u· and divine power.
Hea. 4– 1 u· Mind cannot start from a

unlock
Mis. 283– 7 u· the desk, displace the furniture,
Ret. 37–19 to u· this "mystery— I Tim. 3 : 16.

unlooked-for
Mis. 380–10 u·, imperative call for help
Pul. 65– 3 * has penetrated . . . to an u· extent.

unloose
Mis. 341–15 u· the latchet of thy sandals ;
Ret. 92– 6 May we u· the latchets of

unloose
My. 222–20 u· the sandals of thy Master's feet.
338–27 whose sandals none may u·.

unlovely
'02. 6–30 Love, including nothing u·,

unloving
'02. 8– 8 mortals hating, or u·,

unmanageable
Mis. 326–11 until they became u· ;

unmarked
My. 83– 7 * wore tiny white, u· buttons,

unmarried
Man. 111– 8 u· women must sign "Miss."

unmasked
Ret. 69–19 "When will the error . . . be u·?

unmeasured
My. 24– 7 * your u· love for humanity,

unmedicated
Hea. 12–27 giving the u· sugar

unmentioned
Mis. 238–12 reformer works on u·,

unmerciful
Mis. 19– 7 never u·, never unwise.
121–29 Love,— that cannot be u·.
290–12 partial, u·, or unjust,
Man. 54–11 unjust and u· conduct
Pul. 7–19 u·, and oppressive priesthood
My. 41–10 * arrogance, and self-will are u·,

unmercifulness
Mis. 297–26 u·, tyranny, or lust.
Peo. 8– 7 u·, that for the sins of a few

unmindful
Mis. 310–15 not u· that the Scriptures enjoin,
My. 153–23 u· of the divine law of Love,

unmistakable
Mis. 193– 6 His words are u·, for they
193–28 u· declaration of the right
297–16 I hereby state, in u· language,
366– 8 given rule, and u· proof.
No. 11–22 given rule, and u· proof.
33–11 given rule, and u· proof.
My. 100– 4 * they are u· in their trend.
342–10 * The likeness . . . was u·.

unmistakably
Mis. 269–14 Who is it that understands, u·,
My. 266–14 points u· to the
305– 8 express myself u· on the subject of
348–21 I had found u· an actual,

unmitigated
Mis. 246– 3 all u· systems of crime ;

unmixed
Ret. 34– 2 more of the u·, unerring source,

unmolested
Mis. 303– 7 u·, be governed by divine Love

unnatural
Mis. 74– 4 u· enmity of mortal man toward God.
My. 288–10 Evil is u· ; it has no origin

unnaturally
Mis. 300– 9 has uniformly been so u· delineated

unnecessarily
Man. 53–13 trouble her on subjects u·

unnecessary
Mis. 314–26 u· to repeat the title or page.
322–18 my often-coming is u· ;
My. 42–11 * further words of mine are u·.

unnoticed
My. 67–28 * its massiveness is u·

unnumbered
Pul. 80–25 * homes of u· invalids.

unparalleled
My. v–23 * an u· record for a work of

unpierced
Ret. 70–29 post of duty, u· by vanity,
Pan. 12–26 u· by bold conjecture's sharp

unpleasant
Mis. 81– 4 u· and unchristian action

unplucked
Po. 46– 9 U· by ruthless hands.

unprecarious
My. 201–19 a tenure of u· joy.

unprecedented
Mis. 110–22 u· prosperity of our Cause.
246–19 in this most u· warfare.
Ret. 45–16 followed that noble, u· action
47– 4 u· popularity of my College.

unprecedented
'00. 1–11 crowned with u· prosperity ;
My. 86–27 * u·, as regards numbers.
134– 5 u· progress of C. S.
246–12 in the midst of u· prosperity,

unprejudiced
Pul. 14–14 Millions of u· minds

unprepared
Mis. 84– 8 on minds u· for them.
307–21 pearls before the u· thought.
Rud. 14–23 u· to enter higher classes.

unpretentious
Mis. 360– 7 u· yet colossal characters,
My. 178– 3 These u· preachers cloud not

unprincipled
Mis. 263–26 especially by u· claimants,
265–29 self-satisfied, u· students.
274–21 inordinate, u· clans.
Ret. 71– 7 an ignorant or an u· mind-practice

unprofitable
My. 113– 6 self-contradictory, or u· to mankind

unprohibited
Mis. 286– 7 will continue u· in C. S.

unpromising
Pul. 49–11 * barren waste of most u· ground

unprotected
Man. 28– 8 individuals, and religion are u· ;

unprovided
My. 75–29 * with any part of the . . . u· for,

unpublished
Ret. 36– 9 and u· manuscripts extant,

unpunished
Mis. 12–14 sinning unseen and u·
93–27 because it cannot go u·
281–30 shall not go u· : — see Prov. 11 : 21.
My. 160–24 u· sin is this internal fire,

unqualified
Mis. 43–16 those who are spiritually u·.
Hea. 7–26 This is an u· statement of
My. 359–25 * with the latter's u· approval.

unquenchable
Mis. 77–19 impartial, and u· Love.
328–12 unchanging, u· Love

unquestionable
Mis. 249–15 whose morals are not u·.
My. 286–10 u·, however, that at this hour

unquestionably
Mis. 71– 9 u· right to do right ;
289– 2 Strong drink is u· an evil,
295–28 u· the best queen on earth ;
Ret. 70–20 second appearing of Jesus is, u·,
Pul. 71–23 * u· looked upon as having
My. 244–15 u· man's spiritual state
287– 5 They were u· used in a

unready
Mis. 116–28 never u· to work for God,

unreal
absolutely
No. 6–25 appears real, . . . is absolutely u·.
and temporal
Mis. 21–20 matter is the u· and temporal.
and the real
Mis. 86–14 of the u· and the real.
belief
No. 5–13 substitutes . . . an u· belief,
called
My. 334–18 * while being called u·.
cast out the
Pan. 11– 2 cast out the u· or counterfeit.
concept
'01. 24– 2 * an impossible and u· concept."
discord is the
Rud. 13–20 and discord is the u·,
disease
No. 4– 5 chapter sub-title
13– 3 It makes disease u·,
disease is
Rud. 13– 1 in Science, disease is u· ;
No. 4–16 that disease is u· ;
error is the
Hea. 10–15 error is the u·.
error, the
Hea. 18–11 Truth is the real ; error, the u·.
evil as
Man. 15–12 that casts out evil as u·.
evil is
Ret. 60–14 therefore evil is u·
'01. 15– 1 declaration that evil is u·,
Hea. 9–23 statement that evil is u· ;
My. 178–19 that evil is u· ;

unreal
matter is
My. 217–18 * "If all matter is u·, why do we
mortal as
No. 36–18 holding the mortal as u·,
necessarily
Mis. 346–21 opposite is necessarily u·,
real and the
Mis. 49–20 between the real and the u·.
119–24 the real and the u· Scientist.
sense
Un. 41– 6 u· sense of suffering and death.
No. 5–12 this u· sense substitutes for Truth
shadow
My. 268–20 in my thought as an u· shadow,
small and
No. 32–19 must be small and u·.
something
No. 17– 2 something u·, material, and mortal.
to Jesus
Mis. 200–29 were alike u· to Jesus ;
trials
No. 36–16 find rest from u· trials

Mis. 27–12 sin, disease, death) are u·.
42–23 the former is a dream and u·,
46– 5 evil, good's opposite, is u·.
63–16 such as believe in the . . . u· ;
73–21 states of false sensation — are u·.
89–20 If mortal man is u·, how can he
122–29 The hater's pleasures are u· ;
188–25 the u· or mortal sense of things ;
218–15 they make Deity u· and
341– 3 u· material basis of things,
Ret. 25–18 the temporal, I described as u·.
68–10 human material concept is u·,
Un. 9– 6 they must, . . . be reckoned u·.
36–15 matter is erroneous, transitory, u·.
49–18 and the other u·,
49–20 the u· masquerades as the real,
55–18 sufferings of the flesh are u·.
60–11 its opposite, and therefore u· ;
Rud. 11–13 These illusions are not real, but u·.
No. 5–12 is of necessity u·.
6–20 in both cases to be u·.
31– 9 disease and sin are u·,
35–28 is nowhere, and must be u·.
'01. 14–15 u· as a mirage that misleads the
14–18 and if untrue, u· ; and if u·, to
14–20 from believing in what is u·,
14–26 it must become u· to us :
15– 6 prove it false, therefore u·.
Hea. 11– 3 gladly waken to see it was u·.

unrealities
Mis. 60– 7 as the woeful u· of being,

unreality
Mis. 58– 4 one learns its u· ;
60–10 make the u· of both apparent
63–14 on the basis of its u·
73–11 and the u· of materiality.
187– 9 opposite of man, hence the u· ;
187–11 and discord the u·.
252– 9 wrong thoughts are u·
252–13 sick thoughts are u· and weakness ;
319– 2 true sense of . . . the u· of evil
363– 2 more conscious . . . of its own u·,
Ret. 25–19 and matter, the u·.
62– 7 demonstration of the u· of evil
Un. 8–14 u· of matter and evil
9–28 by knowing the u· of disease,
38– 7 even the u· of mortal mind,
58–18 u· of sin, sickness, and death
Rud. 11–14 consciousness of the u· of pain
No. 4–15 demonstrates . . . the u· of the error.
4–24 u· of sin, disease, and death,
17–19 Hence the u· of error,
35–15 He atoned for the terrible u· of
'01. 13–29 disappears, and its u· is proven.
15– 2 his belief in this awful u·,
15– 4 understand and demonstrate its u·.
My. 334–15 * on the u· of evil

unreasonable
Mis. 38– 5 is it u· to expect

unrelenting
Mis. 258– 5 u· false claim of matter

unreliable
Pul. 45–22 * the evidence . . . is u·."

unremitting
Mis. 340– 6 u·, straightforward toil ;
382– 8 years of u· toil and unrest ;

unrent
'01. 26–15 to preserve Christ's vesture u· ;

unrequited
   Mis. 212–16 difficulties, darkness, and *u·* toil.
   '01. 2–24 darkness, doubt, and *u·* toil
unreservedly
   Mis. 115–24 turns us more *u·* to Him for help,
unrest
   Mis. 382– 8 of unremitting toil and *u·* ;
   Pul. 23–20 * manifested in *u·* or in
unrestrained
   My. 331–14 * to extend such *u·* hospitality
unrewarded
   Mis. xi–10 not unknown to nor *u·* by Him.
unrighteous
   Po. 27– 2 pomp and tinsel of *u·* power ;
   My. 165– 8 righteous suffer for the *u·* ;
   294– 9 *u·* contradicting minds of
unrolled
   Po. 26–15 dark record of our guilt *u·*,
unsafe
   No. 21– 4 *u·* decoction for the race.
unsatisfying
   Ret. 57–21 as *u·* as it is unscientific.
unscientific
   Mis. 217–10 fallacy of an *u·* statement
   372– 2 incorrect, contradictory, *u·*,
   Ret. 57–22 as unsatisfying as it is *u·*.
   59– 8 Such an inference is *u·*.
   Rud. 12–15 the relief is unchristian and *u·*.
   My. 111–20 book itself be absurd and *u·*?
   111–23 Were the apostles absurd and *u·*
   111–29 absurd, ambiguous, *u·*.
   113–23 is that *u·* which all around us is
   303–10 *u·* worshippers of a human being.
unscriptural
   My. 113–18 Neither is it presumptuous or *u·*
unscrupulous
   My. 212–32 in furtherance of *u·* designs.
unsealed
   Ret. 31–28 Frozen fountains were *u·*.
   Pul. 7–14 God has now *u·* their receptacle
   Po. 9– 5 *u·* fountains of grief and joy
unseemly
   No. 45– 6 not behave itself *u·*, — *I Cor.* 13 : 5.
   My. 308–27 attributes to my father language *u·*,
Unseen
   Un. 7–21 perfection of the infinite *U·*
unseen
   Mis. xi–12 pointing the path, dating the *u·*,
   12–14 The means for sinning *u·*
   47– 8 that which is hoped for but *u·*,
   104 3 His *u·* individuality, so superior
   188–18 thence, up to the *u·*,
   260–30 lawless mind, with *u·* motives,
   292–26 great good, both seen and *u·* ;
   301–24 an *u·* form of injustice
   307–27 should beware of *u·* snares,
   318–25 chapter sub-title
   326–13 crept *u·* into the synagogue,
   Ret. 31–17 for this trust is the *u·* sin,
   Un. 37–21 this *u·* individuality is real
   Pul. 14– 4 active yet *u·* mental agencies
   No. 10– 4 the *u·* verities of being,
   34–13 *u·* glory of suffering for others.
   '01. 20–19 This *u·* evil is the sin of sins ;
   My. 15–19 * Of *u·* things above,
   95–26 * without faith in the things *u·*,
   164–19 buried in the depths of the *u·*,
   202–22 The taper *u·* in sunlight
   211– 3 The *u·* wrong to individuals
   211–13 by *u·*, silent arguments.
   260–16 and the evidence *u·*.
unself
   '00. 11– 5 harmonize, unify, and *u·* you.
   My. 161–18 *u·* mortality and to destroy its
unselfed
   Mis. 238– 9 What has not *u·* love achieved
   '00. 10–23 touching token of *u·* manhood
   '01. 30–26 heart of the *u·* Christian hero.
   '02. 16–16 watch fires of *u·* love,
   My. 6– 7 To abide in our *u·* better self
   19–21 fruition of her *u·* love,
   62–10 * for your *u·* love.
   165–28 The best man . . . is the most *u·*.
   195–27 *u·* love that builds without hands,
   200–19 honesty, purity, and *u·* love.
   249–29 devout, *u·* quality of thought
   265– 3 It signifies that love, *u·*,
   291–19 was wise, brave, *u·*.
   298– 9 for their *u·* labors in
   306–16 patience and *u·* love,

unselfish
   Mis. 35–14 * so *u·* an individual.''
   100–14 Science voices *u·* love,
   232–27 spiritual and *u·* motives.
   250–23 *u·* deed done in secret ;
   263– 2 I shall have the *u·* joy of
   266– 2 *u·* and pure aims
   Ret. 28–10 It must become honest, *u·*,
   79–10 in *u·* motives and acts,
   80– 1 *u·* affection or love,
   Pul. 21– 3 a love *u·*, unambitious,
   35–14 It must become honest, *u·*,
   84–27 * *u·*, and zealous effort
   My. 19–12 * chapter sub-title
   28–10 * a hint of the *u·* efforts,
   52–16 * *u·* labor to establish these
   157–13 * evidence of your *u·* love.''
   217– 5 your hitherto *u·* toil,
unselfishly
   Ret. 49–16 the bliss of loving *u·*,
unselfishness
   Mis. 110– 6 innocence, *u·*, faithful affection,
   Ret. 87–25 through the lens of their *u·*
   My. 87–27 * spirit of *u·* and helpfulness,
   274–11 honesty, purity, *u·*
unselfs
   Mis. 204–26 it *u·* the mortal purpose,
   My. 288– 2 *u·* men and pushes on the ages.
unsettled
   Mis. 125–30 from *u·* questions to permanence,
   Ret. 87– 9 *u·* and spasmodic efforts.
unshaken
   My. 44–29 * their *u·* confidence in the
unsheathed
   Mis. 105–22 He who never *u·* his blade
unshod
   Mis. 77–29 to enter *u·* the Holy of Holies,
unsipped
   Mis. 324– 9 music is dull, the wine is *u·*,
unskilful
   Peo. 8–28 skill proved a million times *u·*.
unskilled
   Mis. 195–22 beneath the stroke of *u·* swordsmen.
unsolved
   Ret. 79–15 inscrutable problem of being *u·*.
   My. 181– 6 and ultimate in *u·* problems
unsought
   Mis. 282–26 which may call for aid *u·*,
unsoundness
   Mis. 49– 5 had manifested some mental *u·*,
unsparingly
   Ret. 36– 8 and distributing them *u·*.
unspeakable
   Mis. 279– 8 eternal sunshine and joy *u·*.
unspent
   My. 353–16 the Science that operates *u·*.
unspiritual
   Mis. 53–30 to the *u·*, the ungodly,
   124– 1 It is plain that aught *u·*,
   Ret. 65–29 *u·* and unhealing religion
   Peo. 3–25 has implanted . . . certain *u·* shifts,
   4–15 *u·* and mysterious ideas of God
unspoken
   Mis. 55–11 power of the *u·* thought,
   302–17 *not* to leave the Word *u·*
   No. 2–15 by the spoken than the *u·* word.
unspotted
   Man. 31–10 They must keep themselves *u·*
   Ret. 65–24 keeping man *u·* from the world,
unstable
   Mis. 147–18 a loose and *u·* character.
   Un. 1– 6 are unlearned and *u·* — *II Pet.* 3 : 16.
unstained
   Mis. 108– 1 preserve these virtues *u·*,
unstimulating
   My. 309–29 * lonely and *u·* existence.
   310– 1 * ''lonely and *u·* existence.''
unsubstantial
   Pan. 13–27 prove for yourselves the *u·* nature of
unsubstantiality
   Mis. 264– 7 stumble over . . . their own *u·*,
unsurpassed
   Pul. 20–13 prosperity of this church is *u·*.
unswerving
   Mis. 291–22 *u·* course of a Christian Scientist,

unswervingly
My. 45–18 * followed u· the guidance

unsystematic
Ret. 93–11 fragmentary, disconnected, u·,

untainted
My. vii–12 * u· by the emotionalism

untalkable
Mis. 251– 7 my heart will with tenderness u·.

untamed
Ret. 31–18 the heart's u· desire

untaught
Mis. 302–18 *not* to leave the Word . . . u·.

untempered
Ret. 79–24 Restrain u· zeal.
Un. 5–21 Let no enmity, no u· controversy,

untested
Mis. 264–17 abstract Science is somewhat u·.

unthought
My. 148–13 Memorable date, all u· of till

until
Mis. 7– 4 u· their bodies become dry,
15– 3 u· he awakes from it.
15–23 u· man is found to be the image
44–13 u· *I have the tooth extracted,*
67– 1 u· its altitude reaches beyond the
71– 4 suffered from . . . u· his death ;
79– 6 u· it is clear to human comprehension
80–22 u· right is found supreme.
80–30 u· it shall come to understand
86– 5 U· this be attained,
86–19 u· we gain the glorified sense
91–24 I never dreamed u· informed thereof,
104–20 false selfhood u· self-destroyed.
118–19 u· all error is destroyed
138– 1 u·, in turn, their students will sustain
148–23 U· recently, I was not aware
164– 8 u· it be acknowledged, understood,
164–22 u· man be found in the actual
165–21 u· lifted to these by their own
166–25 u· the whole shall be leavened
172–12 u· the three measures be
175– 4 u· the whole sense of being
184–21 u· he learns that all power is good
220–12 u· the patient's mind yields,
225–30 * "Wait u· we get home,
229–23 u· the whole human race would
231–14 u· delicious pie, pudding, and
236– 6 u· thought has shrunk from contact
237–10 u· earth gives them such a cup
242– 4 came not to my notice u· January
253–25 u· she herself is become a mother?
261–12 u· he pays his full debt
265–32 u· suffering compels the downfall
276–16 u· "no night is there."— *see Rev.* 21 : 25.
286– 4 * "u· death do us part ;"
286– 6 U· time matures human growth,
286–28 U· this absolute Science of being
287–15 u· progress lifts mortals to discern
299– 1 u· one is awake to their cause
299– 5 but never u· then.
304–14 * u· 1900, when it will be sent to
304–16 * u· that Exhibition closes.
308– 1 U· this be done, man will never
316–12 U· minds become less worldly-minded,
326–10 u· they became unmanageable ;
328–19 u· wakened through the baptism of fire
338–13 cancels not sin u· it be destroyed,
342– 7 u·, the midnight gloom upon them,
343–24 u· no seedling be left to propagate
352–12 u· they are lost in light
353–10 gained the right one— and never u·
356–24 u· one has gone down
358–13 and they never should be u· then.
359– 6 u· you can cure without it
359–17 u· we can walk on the water.
362–20 u· self-extinguished by suffering !
364–24 u· this impossible partnership
Man. 34–20 u· that membership is dissolved.
37– 4 u· after the blank has been
51–15 u· the requirements according to
102– 6 shall not be dissolved u·
Ret. 5–11 there the family remained u·
7–12 * u· he had explored their
8–10 u· I grew discouraged,
20– 3 remained with my parents u·
21– 6 We never met again u· he
27– 9 u· S. and H. was written.
35– 8 I did not venture . . . u· later,
37–18 u· our heavenly Father saw fit,
56–14 must go on u· peace be declared
67–16 u· the false claim called sin
87–30 u· he has done with the case

until
Ret. 90–12 u· they were able to fulfil
Un. 1–16 u· they draw nearer to the
6–13 U· the heavenly law of health,
45–21 u· it finally dies in order to
45–26 u· it becomes non-existent.
56–21 U· he awakes from his delusion,
64–12 u· the hope of ever eluding
Pul. 34– 4 * from that time u· 1866
39– 4 * u· it finds the peace of the Lord
41–20 * u· all who wished had heard
41–28 * u· the hour for the dedication
44–27 * kept coming u· the custodian
66– 7 * u· now there are societies in
Rud. 12– 9 u· they hold stronger than before
15–10 u· this impulse subsides.
15–14 u· there were enough practitioners
No. v–12 u· you grow to apprehend
20– 9 u· better apprehended.
25– 2 u· God becomes the All
27–11 U· centuries pass,
30– 5 will not let sin go u· it is
30– 5 u· nothing is left to be forgiven,
31– 8 u· it is understood that disease
31–18 u· a perfect consciousness is
32– 8 suffer, u· it is self-destroyed.
Pan. 6– 7 fight it u· it disappears,
'00. 10–17 u· it is exterminated.
'01. 10–26 u· there shall be nothing left
13– 3 u· it annihilates its own
'02. 15–15 u·, declining dictation as to what
Hea. 1–10 wait u· the age advanced
11–20 "u· you arrive at no medicine."
13– 8 u· the fact is found out
13–11 u· it was no longer aconite,
14– 4 u· disease is treated mentally
18–17 u· it became popular.
Po. v–23 * u· *the poem finally found its*
My. 14–27 * u· the church is finished.
29–31 * From that time, u· the close
38–11 * no more were admitted u·
48– 4 * Not u· nineteen centuries had
53– 4 * not u· the authoress was satisfied
53–12 * held there u· November, 1883,
55–20 * continued there u· March, 1894,
55–27 * u· The Mother Church edifice was ready
56– 3 * u· every seat was filled
61– 9 * be postponed u· that time.
74– 3 * From now u· Saturday night
84– 8 * u· it be wholly free from debt.
87– 1 * early morning u· the evening,
92– 3 * u· it has stood the test of time.
103–11 Science, u· understood, has
114–20 leave me u· the rising of the sun.
145– 7 u· the remodelling of the house
160–15 u· compelled to glance at it.
160–26 u· the sinner is consumed,
174–22 u· I had a church of my own,
220–10 u· He whose right it is shall reign.
226–28 u· the public thought becomes better
232–23 destroys error, u· the entire
239–13 u· *every man and woman comes into*
241– 3 * not be abolished u· it has
242– 3 u· you declare yourself to be
264– 5 u· mankind learn more of
273–26 u· at length they are consigned to
275– 6 u· they are controlled by divine
283–17 u· his grasp of goodness grows
318–21 u· I began my attack on
318–23 u· he could control himself no longer
327–18 * stayed on the field u· the last.
332–11 * or remit his kind attention u· he
336–14 u· after my mother's decease."
345–13 u· they had no effect on me.
357– 3 u· we arrive at the spiritual

untimely
Mis. 17–24 timely or u· circumstances,

untired
Po. 27–23 thy head on time's u· breast.

untiring
Mis. 321–20 * U· in your holy fight,
Ret. 5–28 * she was u· in her efforts to
42–12 u· in his chosen work.
Pul. 84–26 * u·, unselfish, and zealous effort
My. 42–27 * how u· are her efforts,
355–13 the u· spiritual armament.

unto
Mis. 20– 4 "Come u· me,— *Matt.* 11 : 28.
38–10 have sown u· you— *I Cor.* 9 : 11.
46–28 attained u· the Science of being,
73–22 *Jesus said u· them,— Matt.* 19 : 28.
73–22 *Verily I say u· you,— Matt.* 19 : 28.
98–11 and to be ministered u· ;
109–28 Christ, Truth, saith u· you,

unto

Mis.	120– 9	whether of sin *u·* death,— *Rom.* 6 : 16.
	120– 9	*obedience u·* righteousness— *Rom.* 6 : 16.
	122– 2	"Woe *u·* the world— *Matt.* 18 : 7.
	131–22	May God give *u·* us all that loving
	134– 2	"wise *u·* salvation" — *II Tim.* 3 : 15.
	135– 9	doing *u·* others as ye
	135–10	would they should do *u·* you,
	146–19	should do *u·* you,— *see Matt.* 7 : 12.
	154–19	word that is spoken *u·* you,
	157–22	thy way *u·* the Lord ;— *Psal.* 37 : 5.
	161– 5	*u·* us a child is born,— *Isa.* 9 : 6.
	161– 5	*u·* us a son is given.— *Isa.* 9 : 6.
	166–10	*u·* us a child *is* born,— *Isa.* 9 : 6.
	166–11	*u·* us a son is given.— *Isa.* 9 : 6.
	167–25	revealed them *u·* babes !"— *Luke* 10 : 21.
	168–17	"*U·* us a son is given."— *Isa.* 9 : 6.
	171–23	is like *u·* leaven,— *Matt.* 13 : 33.
	175– 4	showeth them *u·* the creature,
	192–11	I go *u·* my Father.— *John* 14 : 12.
	194–20	I go *u·* my Father."— *John* 14 : 12.
	196–25	does go *u·* the Father,
	205–12	show it *u·* you."— *John* 16 : 15.
	213–23	give *u·* them eternal life ;— *John* 10 : 28.
	215– 6	not as the . . . give I *u·* thee.— *John* 14 : 27.
	223–18	doing *u·* others what we would resist
	223–18	if done *u·* ourselves.
	235–28	should do *u·* you,— *see Matt.* 7 : 12.
	254–27	vineyard *u·* others."— *Mark* 12 : 9.
	260–29	Mind, . . . is a law *u·* itself,
	268–32	thy way *u·* the Lord ;— *Psal.* 37 : 5.
	270–15	be added *u·* you."— *Matt.* 6 : 33.
	278– 4	my peace returns *u·* me.
	279– 1	woe *u·* him,— *Luke* 17 : 1.
	292– 5	I give *u·* you, — *John* 13 : 34.
	298– 2	lean not *u·* thine own— *Prov.* 3 : 5.
	301– 6	would have others do *u·* you
	316– 4	a law not *u·* others, but themselves.
	317–32	by measure *u·* him."— *John* 3 : 34.
	318– 9	*u·* the third and fourth and final
	321– 3	"*U·* us a child is born,"— *Isa.* 9 : 6.
	323–17	He saith *u·* the patient toilers
	325– 2	saith *u·* the dwellers therein,
	325–31	saith *u·* them, "Go ye into— *Mark* 16 : 15.
	326–27	which are sent *u·* thee,— *Matt.* 23 : 37.
	326–27	left *u·* you desolate."— *Matt.* 23 : 38.
	326–31	the Stranger saith *u·* him,
	327– 5	the Stranger saith *u·* him,
	328–29	reaching forth *u·* those— *Phil.* 3 : 13.
	331– 3	committing their way *u·* Him
	334– 3	or say *u·* Him,— *Dan.* 4 : 35.
	337–12	little child *u·* him,— *Matt.* 18 : 2.
	343– 1	make us wise *u·* salvation !
	347– 2	be like *u·* him."— *Prov.* 26 : 4.
	347–28	None can say *u·* Him,
	351–25	life that leads *u·* death,
	361–30	looking *u·* Jesus— *Heb.* 12 : 2.
	370–10	"*U·* us a child is born,— *Isa.* 9 : 6.
	370–10	*u·* us a son is given."— *Isa.* 9 : 6.
	373–26	power is given *u·* me— *Matt.* 28 : 18.
	374–24	one renders not *u·* Cæsar
	387– 4	mount upward *u·* purer skies ;
	390–12	*u·* the laughing hours,
Man.	16–11	to do *u·* others as we would
	16–12	would have them do *u·* us ;
	41–12	do good *u·* your enemies
	84– 6	a law, not *u·* others, but to
Chr.	55– 6	verily, I say *u·* you,— *John* 5 : 25.
	55–11	be added *u·* you.— *Matt.* 6 : 33.
	55–21	made like *u·* the— *Heb.* 7 : 3.
	57– 2	keepeth my works *u·* — *Rev.* 2 : 26.
Ret.	25–21	personal being, like *u·* man ;
	87–23	become a law *u·* themselves.
	88–27	as will draw men *u·* us.
	89–20	guarded them *u·* the end,
	92–10	shall be done *u·* you."— *John* 15 : 7.
	93– 9	draw all men *u·* me."— *John* 12 : 32.
	95– 8	*U·* a life of sympathy.
Un.	1– 7	*u·* their own destruction."— *II Pet.* 3 : 16.
	24– 8	but verily I say *u·* you,
	60–19	and He will be *u·* them All-in-all.
Pul.	12–11	their lives *u·* the death.— *Rev.* 12 : 11.
	12–13	devil is come down *u·* you,— *Rev.* 12 : 12.
	13–28	cast *u·* the earth,— *Rev.* 12 : 13.
No.	7– 8	continue to do so *u·* the end.
	43– 4	"Come *u·* me,— *Matt.* 11 : 28.
	45– 2	revealed them *u·* babes."— *Luke* 10 : 21.
Pan.	14–21	be *u·* them life-preservers !
'00.	11–27	saith *u·* the churches."— *Rev.* 2 : 7.
	13–15	"Be thou faithful *u·* death,— *Rev.* 2 : 10.
	14–10	what the Spirit saith *u·* the churches ;
	14–20	The angel that spake *u·* the churches
'01.	9–23	showeth them *u·* the creature ;
	11–27	thou also be like *u·* him."— *Prov.* 26 : 4.
	19–10	it shall be given *u·* you ;
	34–30	lean not *u·* thine own— *Prov.* 3 : 5.

unto

'02.	7–25	I give *u·* you,— *John* 13 : 34.
	18–14	*u·* one of the least— *Matt.* 25 : 40.
	18–15	have done it *u·* me."— *Matt.* 25 : 40.
	19–16	"Come *u·* me."— *Matt.* 11 : 28.
Hea.	2–17	"Come *u·* me,— *Matt.* 11 : 28.
	16–28	cometh *u·* the Father,— *John* 14 : 6.
Peo.	5–16	angel form, saying *u·* us,
	8–22	I say *u·* thee, arise."— *Mark* 5 : 41.
Po.	v–14	* *through nature, u· nature's God,*"
	34–17	*U·* thy greenwood home
	50–22	mount upward *u·* purer skies ;
	55–13	Looks love *u·* the laughing hours,
My.	13–30	returns it *u·* them
	17– 9	as *u·* a living stone,— *I Pet.* 2 : 4.
	19–31	"Verily I say *u·* you,— *Mark* 14 : 9.
	24–14	* *u·* an holy temple— *Eph.* 2 : 21.
	34– 4	his soul *u·* vanity,— *Psal.* 24 : 4.
	36–12	* that shall be acceptable *u·* God.
	44–12	* even *u·* the end— *Matt.* 28 : 20.
	46–28	* "*u·* the city of the— *Heb.* 12 : 22.
	80– 7	* when wasted *u·* death
	114– 5	Do *u·* others as ye would have
	117–16	and came *u·* thee?"— *Matt.* 25 : 39.
	126–16	reached *u·* heaven,— *Rev.* 18 : 5.
	126–17	double *u·* her double— *Rev.* 18 : 6.
	128– 3	go on *u·* perfection— *Heb.* 6 : 1.
	140– 6	will I do *u·* them,— *Isa.* 42 : 16.
	150–25	shall be done *u·* you."— *John* 15 : 7.
	150–26	what our Master said *u·* his disciples,
	150–28	I say *u·* you :
	153– 8	*U·* "the angel of— *Rev.* 3 : 7.
	156–10	have committed *u·* Him— *II Tim.* 1 : 12.
	156–14	Master saith *u·* thee,— *Luke* 22 : 11.
	159– 5	even *u·* the end."— *Matt.* 28 : 20.
	161–22	sufficient *u·* each day is the duty
	170–23	thy way *u·* the Lord ;— *Psal.* 37 : 5.
	184–28	that saith *u·* Zion,— *Isa.* 52 : 7.
	187–20	to build a house *u·* Him
	188– 6	attent *u·* the prayor— *II Chron.* 7 : 15.
	191–19	Spirit is saying *u·* matter :
	192– 4	press on *u·* the possession of
	193– 2	*u·* Him whom to know aright
	206–19	shall be *u·* thee— *Isa.* 60 : 19.
	206–26	"Giving thanks *u·* the— *Col.* 1 : 12.
	222–11	say *u·* this mountain,— *Matt.* 17 : 20.
	225–13	giving *u·* His holy name
	228–29	have committed *u·* him— *II Tim.* 1 : 12.
	229– 6	abomination *u·* the Lord :— *Deut.* 18 : 12.
	232–13, 14	say *u·* you I say *u·* all,— *Mark* 13 : 37.
	247–13	will draw all men *u·* you.
	252– 8	the good you do *u·* others
	258–13	"Looking *u·* Jesus— *Heb.* 12 : 2.
	269– 9	equal *u·* the angels ;— *Luke* 20 : 36.
	275–24	Doing *u·* others as we would
	279– 4	peace I give *u·* you :— *John* 14 : 27.
	279– 5	give I *u·* you."— *John* 14 : 27.
	280–20	nor say *u·* Him, What doest Thou?
	282– 7	"Look *u·* me,— *Isa.* 45 : 22.
	285–18	keepeth my works *u·* — *Rev.* 2 : 26.
	285–25	I confess *u·* thee,— *Acts* 24 : 14.
	288–26	worse thing come *u·* — *John* 5 : 14.
	290–10	I cried *u·* Thee."— *Psal.* 130 : 1.
	296– 3	"*u·* the root of the trees,"— *Matt.* 3 : 10.
	349–16	"looking *u·* Jesus— *Heb.* 12 : 2.
	350–20	Oft mortal sense is darkened *u·* death

untold

Pul.	9–25	purity, and love are treasures *u·*
'02.	9– 1	gives man power with *u·* furtherance.

untouched

Mis.	125–25	hitherto *u·* problems of being,
	153– 8	*u·* by the billows.
Un.	1–16	leave the subject *u·*, until they

untrammelled

Mis.	30–17	uncontaminated, *u·*, by matter.
'02.	2–18	with the glory of *u·* truth.

untranslated

My.	179–29	the *u·* revelations of C. S.

untrodden

Mis.	xi–13	enabling him to walk the *u·*

untrue

Mis.	57–14	That this addendum was *u·*, is seen
	108–28	that which we know to be *u·*.
	109– 1	believing in that which is *u·*,
	295–21	as both *u·* and uncivil.
Ret.	56–22	Whatever else claims to be . . . is *u·*.
	81–19	or else that heart is consciously *u·*
Un.	44– 3	as unkind and unjust as they are *u·* :
No.	5–11	this material sense, which is *u·*,
'01.	14–18	then it follows that it is *u·* ;
	14–18	and if *u·*, unreal ;
'02.	6–14	false claim, an *u·* consciousness,

untruthful
Rud. 9–18 If one is *u*,
untruths
Mis. 22–18 *u* belong not to His creation,
unusual
Pul. 46–24 * though perhaps with an *u* zest,
My. 69–20 * Another *u* feature is the foyer,
   333–31 * reports of *u* sickness in
   341–21 * *u* public interest centres in the
unusually
My. 69– 1 * church is *u* well lighted,
unutterable
Mis. 133–31 As to the peace, it is *u* ;
My. 134– 4 and *u* in love.
   261–24 and *u* except in C. S.
   306–13 with almost *u* truths to translate,
unutterably
Mis. 312– 5 self-sacrificing, *u* kind ;
My. 203–14 but he is *u* valiant,
unveil
Un. 39–12 *u* the Messiah, whose name is
  45–15 This pantheism I *u*.
No. 10–22 *u* the true idea, — namely, that
unveiled
Mis. 124–25 *u* Love's great legacy
  159–27 *u* to us, and to the age !"
  326–32 sight of thee *u* my sins,
  397– 1 His *u*, sweet mercies show
Ret. 31–29 Love *u* the healing promise
Pul. 18–10 His *u*, sweet mercies show
No. 12–24 *u* spiritual signification of
Po. 12–10 His *u*, sweet mercies show
My. 199–20 of *u* hearts, of fourfold unity
unveils
Mis. 330–29 *u* its regal splendor
unvoiced
No. 39– 3 intercession and *u* imploring
Po. 27–14 With traitors *u* yet?
unwarned
'01. 19–25 mankind *u* and undefended
unwary
Mis. 119– 6 If a criminal coax the *u*
unwearied
My. 184–25 Love, holding *u* watch
unweary
Mis. 393– 7 Art and Science, all *u*,
Po. 51–12 Art and Science, all *u*,
unwilling
Mis. 233–24 *u* to work hard enough
  247–14 and are *u* to be taught it,
Ret. 13– 7 was *u* to be saved, if
No. 42– 5 God is not unable or *u* to heal,
unwinged
Mis. 124–16 marking the *u* bird,
unwise
Mis. 19– 7 are never unmerciful, never *u*.
  211– 4 not cowardly, uncharitable, nor *u*,
Ret. 86–24 To the *u* helper our Master said,
No. 8–26 let the *u* pass by,
My. 231–22 *u* for her to undertake new tasks,
  306– 7 I deem it *u* to enter into a
unwisely
Mis. 281–10 if one cherishes ambition *u*,
unwittingly
Mis. 264–32 If a teacher of C. S. *u*
Un. 36– 6 it *u* confirms Truth,
'00. 4– 4 *u* consents to many minds
Peo. 11–27 conspires *u* against the liberty
My. vii– 6 * *u* made to deprive their Leader
  111–22 and *u* misguide his followers
  292–21 *u* neutralizing another,
  363–24 was not to malpractise *u*.
unworldliness
Ret. 91–30 His holy humility, *u*, and
Pul. 22– 1 fills the sentiment with *u*,
unworthy
Mis. 9–24 tasteless and *u* of human aims.
  147–21 abhor whatever is base or *u* ;
  271–15 subject that is *u* of thought,
  291– 7 above personal motives, *u* aims and
Man. 30– 7 If . . . at any time inadequate or *u*,
My. 331–14 * unrestrained hospitality to an *u*
unwritten
Pul. 81–23 * the *u* anthems of love.
upas-tree
Mis. 368–16 more deadly than the *u*
No. 14–12 than the odor of the *u* is to the

upborne
Po. 23–15 Thy soul, *u* on wisdom's wings,
upbuilding
Mis. 140–25 means for *u* the Church of Christ
  169–12 the *u* of the body.
upheaval
Pul. 6– 1 *u* produced when Truth is
upheaves
Mis. 331–24 having all power, *u* the earth.
up-hill
Mis. 347–22 and if it be *u* all the way,
uphold
Pan. 14–17 *u* our nation with the right arm of
upholds
Mis. 105–15 It *u* being, and destroys the
upholstered
Pul. 25–21 * *u* in old rose plush.
upholstery
Pul. 76–12 * the *u* is in white and gold tapestry.
uplift
Mis. 3–29 mental healing is to *u* mankind ;
  317–26 singleness of purpose to *u* the
  328–25 *u* the fallen and strengthen the
Man. 16– 6 his resurrection served to *u* faith
'00. 9–14 else they *u* them.
My. 130–11 and striven to *u* morally
uplifted
Mis. 356–18 the *u* desires of the human heart,
Un. 29–28 Virgin-mother's sense being *u* to
No. 34–25 over the steps of *u* humanity,
My. 151–19 * 'neath the temple of *u* sky
  180–25 mind, not ready to be *u*, rebels,
  248–20 only as *u* by God's power,
uplifting
Mis. 169–12 The *u* of spirit was the
  236– 4 labor of *u* the race,
  245–12 *u* influence upon the health,
  315–21 of morals and of *u* the race.
Man. 83– 7 healing and *u* the race.
Ret. 93–13 method for *u* human thought
No. 37–24 *u* the human understanding,
  39–14 Truth, *u* us to Him.
Pan. 10– 8 will attest its *u* power,
My. 113–27 *u* human consciousness to a
  268–14 *u* the motives of men.
  350– 7 revelation, *u* human reason,
uplifts
Mis. 260–22 truth of Mind-healing *u* mankind,
Ret. 76–24 never abuses the . . . but *u* it.
No. 45– 9 to ostracize whatever *u* mankind,
My. 155– 1 Such communing *u* man's being ;
upper
Mis. 159–13 *u* chamber, where all things are pure
  279–23 met together in an *u* chamber ;
My. 156–16 show you a large *u* room— *Luke 22 : 12.*
  156–19 the *u* chambers of thought prepared
uppermost
Mis. 116–12 This question . . . is to-day *u* :
upreared
Mis. 141– 2 will be . . . the monument *u*,
upright
Mis. 79–15 If God is *u* and eternal,
  99– 2 it upsets all that is not *u*.
  147–19 *u* man is guided by a
  185–21 man infinitely blessed, *u*, pure,
  258–16 which saveth the *u* — *Psal. 7 : 10.*
  265– 6 an *u* understanding.
Ret. 42–15 and behold the *u* :— *Psal. 37 : 37.*
Pan. 11–17 he is not *u*, and must regain his
uprightly
My. 33–17 He that walketh *u*, — *Psal. 15 : 2.*
  228–24 He that walketh *u*, — *Psal. 15 : 2.*
  342– 4 * walking *u* and with light step,
uprightness
Mis. 119–11 impotent to turn . . . man from his *u*.
uproar
My. 310–24 * set the house in an *u*,"
uproot
Mis. 118–24 they will *u* all happiness.
Ret. 79–14 which *u* the germs of growth
uprooted
Ret. 71–25 that must be recognized, and *u*,
Un. 8–17 All forms of error are *u*
uprooting
Mis. 343–13 *u* the noxious weeds of passion,
  343–21 not always destroyed by the first *u* ;
upset
Mis. 283– 5 *u*, and adjust his thoughts

upsets
Mis. 99– 2 *u·* all that is not upright.

upspringing
My. 192–10 Thine is the *u·* hope,

up-to-date
My. 175–14 *u·* academies, humane institutions,

upturned
Po. 9– 4 *U·* to his mother's in playful grace ;

upward
Mis. 9–30 path that winds *u·*.
159–26 weary wings sprung *u·* !
166– 3 monument whose finger points *u·*,
204–14 new affections, all pointing *u·*.
228– 6 standpoint whence to look *u·* ;
267–21 plumed for . . . *u·* flight.
320– 1 push *u·* our prayer in stone,
328– 5 the path that goeth *u·*."
330– 5 looking *u·*, does it patiently pray
331–21 on *u·* wing to-night.
343– 9 to move it onward and *u·*.
343–12 spring *u·*, and away from
386–17 a hope that ever *u·* yearns,
387– 4 mount *u·* unto purer skies ;
389– 9 on *u·* wing to-night.
393–19 rock, whose *u·* tending
Un. 5–11 following *u·* individual convictions,
Pul. 11– 1 bear you outward, *u·*,
No. 46–21 unfolding of this *u·* tendency
'02. 10–14 *u·* tendency of humanity
Peo. 14–10 * white fingers pointing *u·*."
Po. vi–27 * poem
4– 7 on *u·* wing tonight.
page 18 poem
19– 4 *u·* and heavenward borne.
50– 1 hope that ever *u·* yearns,
50–22 mount *u·* unto purer skies ;
52– 3 rock, whose *u·* tending
My. 79– 4 * little faces turned *u·*.
110–12 *u·* in the scale of being.
124–23 with finger pointing *u·*,
125– 7 to bend *u·* the tendrils
127– 1 reaching outward and *u·*
128–10 springs spontaneously *u·*,
120–27 where faith mounts *u·*,
140–19 leading you onward and *u·*.
186– 7 preen their thoughts for *u·* flight.
200–12 rises *u·* to the realms of
202–18 onward and *u·* chain of being.
215–10 a dozen or *u·* in one class.
258–29 may you move onward and *u·*,
339– 3 whose every link leads *u·*
355–24 their thoughts are *u·* ;

upwards
'02. 10–14 taking steps outward and *u·*.
My. 45– 9 * *u·* of thirty thousand

urchin
Mis. 391 15 *u·*, With bare feet soiled or sore,
Po. 38–14 *u·*, With bare feet soiled or sore,

urge
Mis. 18– 9 *u·* upon the solemn consideration of
75– 8 *First :* I *u·* this fundamental fact
Un. 43–18 I *u·* Christians to have more faith
Pul. 82–19 * and no one to *u·* them.
My. 123– 8 continue to *u·* the perfect model

urged
Mis. 14– 8 It is *u·* that, . . . man has fallen
140–18 and *u·* only the material side
281–15 He replied to his wife, who *u·* him
Po. vii– 8 * they *u·* her to allow a
My. 11–12 * she has never *u·* upon us a
22–12 * nor wait to be *u·* or to be shown
105–27 he *u·* me immediately to write a

urgent
My. 62–31 * there was *u·* need of both.

urges
Mis. 181–23 apostle *u·* upon our acceptance
My. 277–11 mental animus goes on, and *u·* that

urging
Pul. 8–13 no *u·*, begging, or borrowing ;
No. 45–26 *u·* its highest demands on mortals,
'02. 9–15 *u·* a state of consciousness that

Urim
Mis. 194– 7 *U·* and Thummim of priestly office,
Ret. 35–23 *U·* and Thummim of priestly office,
'01. 12–13 *U·* and Thummim of priestly office,

Us
Mis. 18–20 divine idea, even the divine " *U·*"
57– 5 The creative " *U·*" made all,

usage
Mis. 170–32 "Hand," in Bible *u·*, — *Isa.* 59 : 1.
My. 226– 4 an intelligent *u·* of the word

usage
My. 260–19 not because of tradition, *u·*, or
340– 5 *u·* of special days and seasons

usages
My. 220– 5 and to governmental *u·*.

use (noun)
beauty and
My. 256–11 those things of beauty and *u·*
correct
My. 225– 7 A correct *u·* of capital letters in
dexterous
Mis. 231–13 dexterous *u·* of knife and fork,
exclusive
Pul. 25–10 * for the exclusive *u·* of Mrs. Eddy ;
future
Pul. 7–13 enshrined for future *u·*,
human
'01. 6–21 as impracticable for human *u·*,
its
Mis. 304–32 * and the direction of its *u·*,
Pul. 28–19 * its *u·* of the Bible.
My. 219– 9 preventing the occasion for its *u·* ;
219– 9 otherwise its *u·* is abuse.
lack of
My. 213–25 will not rust for lack of *u·*
medical
'01. 18–17 If God created drugs for medical *u·*,
no
My. 229– 4 I have no *u·* for such,
of drugs
Mis. 108–30 believed in the *u·* of drugs,
My. 301–24 supposition that . . . by the *u·* of drugs
of hands
Mis. 242– 8 without the *u·* of hands,
of medicine
My. 97– 6 * getting well without the *u·* of medicine.
of notes
Mis. 158–16 command, to drop the *u·* of notes,
of opium
Mis. 242–30 addicted to the *u·* of opium
of such arguments
Mis. 350–29 teach the *u·* of such arguments only
of the knife
My. 294–17 by a fruitless *u·* of the knife
of the rod
Mis. 51–13 *Doesn't the u· of the rod teach him*
51–14 The *u·* of the rod is virtually a
of the word
My. 302–16 the *u·* of the word spread like
press
Pul. 31–21 * favor of an interview for press *u·*,
proposed
Mis. 304–22 * the proposed *u·* of the bell :
slightest
Mis. 289– 3 its slightest *u·* is abuse ;
sole
Pul. 42–13 * intended for the sole *u·* of Mrs. Eddy.
Wyclif's
'02. 16– 6 Wyclif's *u·* of that combination of words,
your
My. 147–23 prepared for your *u·* work rooms

———

Mis. 31– 8 not the *u·* but the abuse of mental
45– 9 follow the *u·* of that drug
304–17 * when not in *u·* in other places,
380–29 unlawful publishing and *u·* of an
Man. 46– 7 *U·* of Initials "C. S."
Un. 36– 6 *u·* of a lie is that it unwittingly
Pul. 28–17 * the *u·* of Mrs. Eddy's book,
58–15 * by the *u·* of movable partitions.
Pan. 4–13 * is capable of *u·* and of abuse,
'01. 19–22 from the *u·* of inanimate drugs to
My. 66–11 * *u·* the society will make of the
171–29 * contained a gavel for the *u·* of
212–11 The alcoholic habit is the *u·* of

use (verb)
Mis. 11–22 those who . . . despitefully *u·* one,
53–11 *Do you sometimes . . . u· medicine*
55–12 *u·* it to harm rather than to heal,
58–12 She had to *u·* her eyes to read.
72–13 that ye *u·* this proverb — *Ezek.* 18 : 2.
72–16 to *u·* this proverb in — *Ezek.* 18 : 3.
147–13 and despitefully *u·* you
215–25 *u·* the sword of Spirit.
241– 9 *U·* as your medicine the . . . Truth :
245– 2 or recommended others to *u·*,
348–18 I *u·* no drugs whatever,
376– 3 * I *u·* the words *most authentic* in
Man. 43– 6 No member shall *u·* written formulas,
43– 7 * pupils to *u·* them,
Ret. 29– 4 "despitefully *u·* you — *Matt.* 5 : 44.
Un. 50–14 *u·* the phrase in the endeavor to
Pul. 5– 3 in the words I *u·*,
53–28 * Who *u·* it in his name ;

use (verb)

Pul.	55–21	* theology — if we may *u·* the word — of
	69– 9	* He says they *u·* no medicines,
No.	9– 9	*u·* no influence to prevent their
'01.	3–17	we *u·* this phrase for God
	31–14	can *u·* the power that God gives
'02.	7–13	*U·* these words to define God,
My.	6–11	revile us and despitefully *u·* us,
	52– 5	* loving them that despitefully *u·* her,
	52–16	* we must *u·* more energy and
	174– 1	to *u·* the beautiful lawn
	195–16	*u·* in God's service the one talent
	204– 3	to *u·* their hidden virtues,
	226– 2	*u·* it only where you can substitute
	308–24	* saying, "I never *u·* a cane."
	345–29	We *u·* them, we make them our

used

Mis.	11– 4	I *u·* to think it sufficiently just
	40–10	that Jesus and the apostles *u·*,
	69–23	with the means *u·*
	75–17	where the word *God* can be *u·*
	75–18	*Soul* may sometimes be *u·*
	75–24	name of Deity *u·* in that place
	158–30	no record that he *u·* notes
	180–28	term, as applied to man, is *u·*
	197– 4	one more frequently *u·*
	215–28	the words, that Jesus *u·*
	216– 1	*u·* in your application
	245– 1	that our Master ever *u·*,
	268–32	Truth is *u·* to waiting.
	270–12	those the Master *u·*
	277–11	and is *u·* to waiting ;
	289– 3	evil cannot be *u·* temperately :
	350–23	soundness of the argument *u·*.
	350–26	and cause none to be *u·*
Man.	41–10	However despitefully *u·*
	61– 1	No special trowel should be *u·*.
	65– 2	already *u·* in our periodicals.
	65– 7	when this term is *u·*
	71– 6	"The" must not be *u·*
	76– 3	to be hereafter *u·* for
	78–22	*u·* by him for the payment
	112– 6	must not be *u·* before
Ret.	15–18	and benches were *u·*
	51– 6	to be *u·* as a temple
	59–12	term *u·* to indicate Deity ;
Un.	27– 3	two English words, often *u·*
Pul.	4–29	*u·*, in all its public sessions,
	6–18	* false remedy I had vainly *u·*,
	47–20	* *u·* in the definitions of
	76– 1	* material *u·* in its construction
	76– 1	* being that *u·* in the doors
Rud.	2– 8	*u·* by the best authorities,
No.	11–10	which must be *u·*
	20– 8	term divine Principle is *u·*
	22–19	*u·* in the plural number.
'01.	10–15	mysticism that *u·* to enthrall
	18–18	disciples would have *u·* them
	23–18	He *u·* no material medicine,
	25–19	he never *u·* them.
	31–25	*u·* faithfully God's Word,
'02.	2–30	*u·* no other means
	7–11	*u·* as an English prefix
My.	67–20	* *u·* in giving Boston an edifice
	68–31	* *u·* in the lighting fixtures,
	69–13	* white marble was *u·*,
	121–20	may be *u·* to disguise
	130–28	*u·* as a companion to the Bible
	157– 6	to be *u·* at once to build a
	219– 8	*u·* in preventing the occasion
	225–10	capital letters should be *u·*
	225–31	should not be written or *u·*
	287– 5	*u·* in a remarkable degree
	307– 5	the word science was not *u·*
	307–10	I noticed he *u·* that word,
	308–19	He never *u·* a walking-stick.
	317–22	diction, as *u·* in explaining C. S.,
	343–21	the term pope is *u·* figuratively.
	361– 6	to be *u·* as a model.

useful

Mis.	47–30	accepts as either *u·* or true.
	299–29	new patterns which are *u·*
Ret.	85– 7	commend itself as *u·* to the Cause
'01.	25–26	avowed to be as . . . *u·*, as
My.	49–24	* giving some *u·* hints

usefulness

Mis.	284– 9	sphere of his present *u·*.
'00.	2–13	by his example and *u·*.
	8–17	*U·* is doing rightly by yourself and
'01.	1–13	essential to your growth and *u·* ;
My.	250–10	higher *u·* in this vast vineyard

useless

Mis.	17–12	hygiene as worse than *u·*
	234–16	Empirical knowledge is worse than *u·* :

uselessness

Mis.	6–23	*u·* of such material methods,

user

My.	106–25	tobacco *u·*, a profane swearer,

uses

Mis.	8–21	* "Sweet are the *u·* of adversity."
	9– 5	Sweet, . . . are these *u·* of His rod !
	41– 4	*u·* it to accomplish an evil purpose.
	284– 6	Its infinite nature and *u·*
	338–16	the *u·* of good, to abuses from
Ret.	45–15	*u·* and abuses of organization.
Un.	30– 3	Human language constantly *u·* the word
Pul.	62–19	* practically no limit to the *u·*
'00.	2–17	but he *u·* them evilly.
	6–19	to a man who *u·* tobacco,
'01.	20–12	every opportunity . . . and he *u·* it.
My.	183– 1	infinite *u·* of Christ's creed,
	216–29	money for your own *u·*.

usher

Mis.	174–28	Death can never *u·* in the dawn of
	286–13	*u·* in the dawn of God's creation,

ushering

My.	352–21	*u·* into our church the hearers and

ushers

My.	38– 8	* carefully trained corps of *u·*,
	352– 4	* we, the *u·* of your church,

Ushers of The Mother Church

My.	352–16	* signature
	352–19	*Beloved U· of T· M· C·*

using

Mis.	55–12	and who are *u·* that power against
	59– 6	It is *u·* the power of human will,
	115–31	*U·* mental power in the right direction
	269– 3	By *u·* falsehood to regain his
Ret.	34– 1	utility of *u·* a material curative.
Pul.	50– 1	* *u·* her money to promote the
Rud.	2–15	*u·* the phrase *an individual* God,
Pan.	10–21	intemperance, tobacco *u·*, and
Hea.	13–16	*u·* only the sugar of milk ;
My.	226– 1	To avoid *u·* this word incorrectly,
	235– 2	without *u·* the word death,

usual

Mis.	156– 8	send in your contributions as *u·*
	350–13	deliberations were, as *u·*, Christian,
	373– 6	but, as *u·*, he finally yielded.
My.	20–29	omit this year the *u·* large gathering
	32–10	* above the *u·* platform tone.
	88–12	* ceremonial of far more than *u·*
	134–29	* her *u·* mental and physical vigor."
	145–18	I have worked even harder than *u·*,
	148–18	I, as *u·*, at home and alone,
	312–22	took with him the *u·* amount of money
	333–14	* interred with the *u·* ceremonies.
	341–23	* granting of interviews is not *u·*,

usually

Mis.	379–11	his writings *u·* ran in the vein of
Ret.	10– 4	less labor than is *u·* requisite.
Pul.	64– 5	* There is *u·* considerable difficulty
'01.	28–29	reformers *u·* are handsomely provided for.
My.	83–10	* *u·* hidden away in the laces of

usurpation

Un.	51–11	ill supplied by the pretentious *u·*,

usurper

Rud.	10– 1	an unjust *u·* of the throne

usurpest

Mis.	209– 3	*u·* the prerogative of divine wisdom,

usurps

Ret.	70– 6	*u·* the deific prerogatives
Un.	31–17	matter *u·* the authority of God,
	32– 3	matter *u·* the prerogative of God,

usury

My.	33–25	his money to *u·*, — *Psal.* 15 : 5.

Utah

(see **Salt Lake City**)

utility

Mis.	60–27	power, wisdom, and *u·* of good ;
	86–23	beauty, grandeur, and *u·*
	108–12	hence the *u·* of knowing evil aright,
	233–26	is what constitutes its *u·* :
	365–11	proof of its goodness and *u·*,
Ret.	34– 1	*u·* of using a material curative.
Pan.	10–17	thus proving the *u·* of what they
'01.	2–14	Absolute certainty . . . constitutes its *u·*,

utilization

No.	39–19	Prayer is the *u·* of the love

utilize

Mis.	69– 8	man shall *u·* the divine power.
Ret.	26–28	*u·* Truth, and absolutely reduce the
'00.	5–28	*u·* the power of divine Love

utilized
Mis. 84–31 to those who have u· the present,
238–13 u· in the interest of somebody.
Ret. 66– 1 to be u· in healing the sick,
My. 222–27 the Golden Rule u·,
340–31 which man's diligence has u·.

utilizes
Mis. 55– 7 u· its power to overcome sin.

utilizing
'02. 10– 2 U· the capacities of the human mind

utmost
Mis. 170–26 expressing the u· contempt.
Pul. 36–24 * of the u· taste and luxury,
43–13 * u· simplicity marked the exercises.
Hea. 16–25 Friends, it is of the u· importance
My. 24–21 * pushed with the u· energy,
82–25 * stations were taxed to the u·
87– 3 * have been strained to their u·
104–17 u· concern to the world
147–28 to the u· parts of the earth,

utter
Mis. 67–14 not u· a lie, either mentally or
114–29 even its u· nothingness.
375–10 * I did not u· all I felt
Un. 10– 9 u· reliance upon the one God,
No. 8– 6 u· the truth of God
'01. 14– 8 false entity, and u· falsity,
'02. 4–28 Our thoughts of the Bible u· our
Po. 73–14 Witness my presence and u· my
My. 9–11 * move us to u· our gratitude

utterance
Mis. 183–19 to give u· to Truth.
312–20 In honest u· of veritable history,

utterance
Ret. 91– 4 our Master's greatest u·
Po. 23–12 With u· deep and strong,
My. 184–29 must at some time find u·

utterances
Un. 17–16 wonderful u· of him who
Pul. vii– 2 u· which epitomize the story of
'01. 30– 6 successive u· of reformers
My. 97–19 * their teacher and her u·.''

uttered
Mis. 165–17 truth u· and lived by Jesus,
248–11 falsehoods u· about me
No. 13–10 after those words were originally u·,
My. 170– 7 sentiments in my annual
180– 6 u· Christ's Sermon on the Mount,

uttering
Mis. 160– 3 in u· the word thanks,
226–19 by u· a falsehood,
Rud. 8–19 u· falsehood about good.
No. 25– 1 u· this great thought

utterly
Mis. 266–20 u· false and groundless.
Ret. 72–10 They are u· consumed — Psal. 73 : 19.
No. 13– 3 destroys sin quickly and u·.
'01. 17–26 the drug is u· expelled,
My. 90– 5 * these things are new, u· new,
144– 7 either . . . is u· false.
273–18 u· apart from a material
344–16 * ''Do you reject u· the

utters
Mis. 81–27 Truth u· the divine verities
296–29 unknown individual who u·

V

vacancies
Man. 80–12 V· in Trusteeship.
80–14 to declare v· in said trusteeship,
My. 266–13 consequent v· occuring in the

vacancy
Man. 26–21 shall fill a v· occurring on that
29–15 shall appoint . . . to fill the v .
30–10 and the v· supplied.
65–21 The v· shall be supplied by a
78– 4 the v· supplied by the Board.
80–17 Whenever a v· shall occur,
80–21 trustees shall fill the v·,
89– 8 shall be elected to fill the v·.
100–19 another Committee to fill the v· ;
102– 8 elect, dismiss, or supply a v·

vacant
Mis. 231–32 v· seat at fireside and board
275–11 looks in dull despair at the v· seat,

vacate
Man. 89– 2 or v· her office of President

vacation
Mis. 239– 5 I have had but four days' v·
My. 54–17 * During the summer v·,

vacations
Ret. 10–11 during his college v·.

vaccinated
My. 345– 1 let your children be v·,

vaccination
My. 219–29 ''Rather than quarrel over v·,
344–26 Were v· of any avail,
344–30 Where v· is compulsory,
345– 2 v· will do the children no harm.

vacillating
Mis. 268–29 v· good or self–assertive error

vacuity
Mis. 87– 3 into one gulf of v·
Ret. 81–16 overwhelming sense of error's v·,

vagaries
Mis. 78–30 human v·, formulated views
Un. 15–21 Such v· are to be found in
No. 24– 8 All these v· are at variance with

vagary
Mis. 200–30 as only a v· of mortal belief,

vague
Mis. 14–11 admit this v· proposition,
86–13 and v· human opinions,
Un. 28–14 are even more v· than
Pan. 7–21 v· apology for contradictions.
'01. 31–14 no v·, fruitless, inquiring wonder.
Peo. 10– 6 matter will become v·,
My. 262–18 v· human philosophy

vaguely
Mis. 103–10 the senses say v· :

vain
Mis. 61– 6 knowledge and v· strivings
78–14 * These ''ways that are v·''
145–14 forbids man to be v· ;
153–22 cleansed my heart in v·.'' — Psal. 73 : 13.
168–13 vainglory and v· knowledge,
209– 3 Who art thou, v· mortal,
234– 3 We spread our wings in v·
234–13 What hinders . . . is his v· conceit,
268– 5 Earthly glory is v· ;
268– 5 not v· enough to attempt
357– 2 v· amusements, and all the
362–27 O v· mortals ! which shall it be?
383–11 elements of earth beat in v·
Ret. 38– 6 All efforts . . . were in v·.
Un. 11– 1 call in v· for the mountains
11–17 he cut off this v· boasting
44– 6 are v· shadows, repeating
60–25 your faith is v· ; — I Cor. 15 : 17.
Pul. 7–12 Not in v· did ye flow.
70–20 * she endeavored in v· to find
No. 41–12 v· to look for perfection
42–11 the v· power of dogma
Peo. 5– 8 we look in v· for their
Po. 15–13 soft as the vision mine v·
31–20 which deems no suffering v·
34–21 Nor pinest thou in v·
My. 89–12 * has not lived in v·
103–17 imagine a v· thing?'' — Psal. 2 : 1.
113–18 Neither is it . . . v· for another,
128– 1 words are not v· when the
162–31 waves and winds beat in v·.
164–29 enmity, or malice beat in v·.
200– 5 imagine a v· thing ;'' — Psal. 2 : 1.
210–18 chapter sub–title
233–19 taking the name of God in v·.
270–14 and imagine a v· thing.

vainglorious
My. 37– 2 * No v· boast, no pride of

vainglory
Mis. 168–13 emptied of v· and vain knowledge,
267–14 chapter sub–title
268–17 on the shoals of v·.
326–12 fed by the fat of hypocrisy and v·,
Ret. 86– 2 to rebuke v·, to offset boastful
My. 155–12 lay down the low laurels of v·,

vainly
Pul. 6–18 * false remedy I had v· used,
My. 80–28 * hundreds waiting v· in the streets.
149–14 When a young man v· boasted,
265–12 and justice plead not v·

vale

Mis.	328– 9	surveys the *v·* of the flesh,
Po.	32– 4	home where I dwell in the *v·*,
	53– 6	On *v·* and woodland deep ;

valiant

Mis.	155–11	be *v·* in the Christian's warfare,
My.	203–14	but he is unutterably *v·*,

valiantly

Mis.	120–12	ye that have wrought *v·*,
	176–12	strive *v·* for the liberty of the

valid

Mis.	109–10	this claim you admit as *v·*,
	261–30	or else make the claim *v·*.
Man.	29–11	the complaint be found *v·*,
	54–13	complaint being found *v·*,
Pan.	12– 1	Christ's dear demand, . . . is *v·*,
My.	108–27	the words of . . . are *v·*.
	111–30	C. S. is *v·*, simple, real,

validity

Mis.	194– 8	yet should deny the *v·*
	195–10	the *v·* of those words
Man.	52–10	as to the *v·* of the charge.
Ret.	93–24	convincing proof of the *v·*
No.	4–18	the *v·* of that statement.
	6– 7	refutes the *v·* of the testimony
	6–14	cannot be healed by denying its *v·* ;
'01.	12–15	the *v·* and permanence of
My.	239– 9	prove the practicality, *v·*, and

valley

Mis.	323– 8	a few laborers in a *v·*
	323–16	*v·* at the foot of the mountain.
	323–22	winds and widens in the *v·* ;
	324– 2	watchers and workers in the *v·*
	324–29	pleasant path of the *v·*
	326–19	would be led to the *v·*
	326–23	Stranger returned to the *v·* ;
	327–10	had entered the *v·* to speculate
	328– 6	the *v·* is humility,
Pul.	48–12	* the woods that skirt the *v·*
Po.	vi– 2	* poem
	page 15	poem
My.	186–10	point the path above the *v·*,

Valley Cemetery, The

Po.	vi– 2	* poem
	page 15	poem

Valley of Decision

Mis.	270– 1	We are in the *V· of D·*.

valleys

Mis.	203–11	waters that run among the *v·*,

valor

Mis.	287–32	venturing on *v·* without discretion,
My.	270–10	records . . . attest honesty and *v·*.

valuable

Mis.	109–24	*v·* sequence of knowledge
	169–23	makes them nothing *v·*,
Ret.	27–10	These early comments are *v·*
My.	62–26	* *v·* services rendered to this Board
	63– 5	* and for their *v·* services,

value

Mis.	39– 1	would be of less practical *v·*.
	110– 2	had not the *v·* of a single *tear*.
	114– 2	of inestimable *v·* to all seekers
	131–27	let her state the *v·* thereof,
	139–20	at $20,000 and rising in *v·*
	232–24	its infinite *v·* and firm basis.
	239–29	taught the *v·* of saying
	253– 5	its *v·*, and the price that he paid
	269–28	to buy error at par *v·*.
	273– 2	know the *v·* of these rebukes.
	365–22	shows the real *v·* of C. S.
Ret.	45– 6	organization has its *v·* and peril,
	51– 3	and rising in *v·*,
Pul.	1–13	great is the *v·* thereof.
No.	19– 5	shows its real *v·* to the race.
'02.	13– 7	property and funds, to the *v·* of
My.	28–15	* has been of immense *v·* to them.
	75– 1	* of the *v·* of the latter,
	99–30	* at their face *v·*.
	172–12	gift that has no intrinsic *v·*
	190–18	relative *v·*, skill, and certainty of
	226–22	even as you *v·* His all-power,
	265– 8	and is bought at par *v·* ;
	273– 4	* *v·* of her teachings.
	348–21	*v·* to the race firmly established.

valued

Mis.	139–20	now *v·* at $20,000 and rising
Ret.	51– 2	*v·* in 1892 at about
Pul.	28–12	* *v·* at some forty thousand dollars
'00.	3– 9	worker's servitude is duly *v·*,
'02.	13–27	now *v·* at twenty thousand dollars,
My.	vi–21	* *v·* at forty-five thousand dollars,
	vi–26	* *v·* at twenty-five thousand dollars,

values

one cent

Mis.	305–25	* contribute *o· c·* to be fused into

twenty-five cents

Mis.	305–25	* *t· c·* to pay for it.

fifty cents

'01.	29–27	*f· c·* on every book

one dollar

Man.	44–14	tax of not less than *o· d·*,
'02.	15–11	paid me not *o· d·* of royalty

two dollars

Mis.	305–26	* asked to collect *t· d·*

three dollars

Mis.	35–16	*you offer for sale at t· d·*,

five-dollar

'00.	10–27	ten *f·* gold pieces

five dollars

My.	328–14	* license of *f· d·* annually,
	328–30	* a license fee of *f· d·*.''

ten dollars

My.	53–17	* preach for the society for *t· d·*

fifteen dollars

Mis.	349–27	accepted, for a time, *f· d·*

fifty dollars

Mis.	280–20	elegant album costing *f· d·*,
My.	176– 3	A GIFT OF *F· D·* IN GOLD

$100.00

Man.	84–15	shall not exceed $100.00 per pupil.
	91– 9	Tuition . . . shall be $100.00.

one-hundred-dollar bills

My.	30–23	* contributions were *o· b·*.

($113.09)

Mis.	381–20	cost of suit, taxed at ($113.09)

one hundred thirteen and 9/100 dollars

Mis.	381–20	taxed at . . . *o· h· t· and* $\frac{9}{100}$ *d·*.

one hundred and seventy-five dollars

My.	166–28	cabinet, costing *o· h· and s· d·*,

$200

Man.	78–19	not exceeding $200 for any one

three hundred dollars

Ret.	50– 4	I was led to name *t· h· d·*
	50–12	if they consider *t· h· d·*
My.	215– 8	tuition of *t· h· d·* each,

$500

Man.	78–21	keep on deposit the sum of $500

five hundred dollars

Mis.	272–17	* fine not less than *f· h· d·*
My.	175– 6	enclosed check for *f· h· d·*,
	289– 4	enclose a check for *f· h· d·*

$621.10

My.	25–12	* contributions . . . $621.10 ;

seven hundred dollars

Ret.	38– 4	already paid him *s· h· d·*,

$845.96

My.	25–13	* contributions . . . $845.96 ;

one thousand dollars

Mis.	143–21	contributions of *o· t· d·* each,
	242– 6	liberal sum of *o· t· d·*
	272–18	not more than *o· t· d·*.
Man.	68–11	at the rate of *o· t· d·*

$1,112.13

My.	25–14	* to February 28, 1906, $1,112.13 ;

$1,489.50

Mis.	350– 1	I hold receipts for $1,489.50

two thousand dollars

Mis.	242– 8	*t· t· d·* if either
	349–32	church-fund about *t· t· d·*

two thousand five hundred dollars

Man.	29–16	at present *t· t· f· h· d·*

$2,579.19

My.	25–14	* total $2,579.19.

three thousand dollars

Mis.	242–19	I offer him *t· t· d·*

four thousand dollars

Man.	97–14	not less than *f· t· d·*.
My.	217– 7	the sum of *f· t· d·*

$4,460

Pul.	v– 4	CONTRIBUTIONS OF $4,460 WERE
	9– 1	have come $4,460.

$4,963.50

'02.	13–18	paying for it the sum of $4,963.50

five thousand dollars

'02.	14– 1	About *f· t· d·* had been paid
My.	26– 9	check of *f· t· d·*,

ten thousand dollars

Mis.	381–25	on penalty of *t· t· d·*.
My.	73– 3	* to return more than *t· t· d·*
	164–10	munificent gift . . . of *t· t· d·*.
	165–13	for the sum of *t· t· d·*
	166–10	Your munificent gift of *t· t· d·*,

eleven thousand dollars

Pul.	26–14	* and cost *e· t· d·*.
	60–17	* at a cost of *e· t· d·*,

fourteen thousand dollars

My.	123–16	cost of the estate was *f· t· d·*.

values

$20,000
Mis. 139–20 now valued at $20,000
twenty thousand dollars
Ret. 51– 3 at about *t· t· d·,*
'02. 13–28 now valued at *t· t· d·,*
My. 123–18 amount is now about *t· t· d·.*
twenty-five thousand dollars
My. vi–26 * valued at *t· t· d·,*
forty thousand dollars
Pul. 28–13 * valued at some *f· t· d·.*
forty-two thousand dollars
Mis. 143–23 munificent sum of *f· t· d·*
forty-five thousand dollars
My. vi–21 * valued at *f· t· d·,*
eighty thousand dollars
My. 162–13 gifts to me of about *e· t· d·,*
one hundred thousand dollars
My. 157– 5 your generous gift of *o· h· t· d·*
157–23 the sum of *o· h· t· d·*
one hundred and twenty thousand dollars
'02. 13– 7 value of about *o· h· and t· t· d·;*
$191,012.
Pul. 8–10 responded . . . with $191,012.
$199,607.93
My. 16– 7 * paying out the sum of $199,607.93,
two hundred thousand dollars
Pul. 30–29 * costing over *t· h· t· d·,*
50–13 * It has cost *t· h· t· d·,*
52–12 * at a cost of over *t· h· t· d·,*
57– 3 * cost over *t· h· t· d·.*
58–10 * at a cost of over *t· h· t· d·,*
68–20 * cost over *t· h· t· d·,*
79– 5 * costing over *t· h· t· d·,*
two hundred and twenty-one thousand dollars
Pul. 28–11 * The cost . . . is *t· h· and t· t· d·,*
$226,285.73
My. 16– 6 * balance of $226,285.73 on hand
$250,000
Pul. 63– 6 * A CHURCH COSTING $250,000
two hundred and fifty thousand dollars
Pul. 63–22 * a cost of *t· h· and f· t· d·,*
70–15 * cost *t· h· and f· t· d·*
quarter of a million dollars
Pul. 44–23 * with a *q· of a m· d·* expended
71– 6 * contribution of a *q· of a m· d·*
$303,189.41
My. 23–11 * Amount on hand . . . $303,189.41 ;
$388,663.15
My. 23–12 * expenditures . . . $388,663.15 ;
$425,893.66
My. 16– 4 * $425,893.66 had been received
$891,460.49
My. 23–13 * total receipts . . . $891,460.49.
$1,108,539.51
My. 23–15 * pledged . . . $1,108,539.51.
$2,000,000
My. 23–14 * to complete the sum of $2,000,000
67– 6 * Cost . . . $2,000,000
two-million-dollar
My. 76– 2 * this new *t·* edifice,
76–26 * the new *t·* cathedral,
86–11 * their new *t·* church,
92–22 * the *t·* stone edifice
94– 7 * the *t·* stone edifice
98–28 * erection . . . of the *t·* church
two million dollars
My. 7–13 chapter sub-title
8– 1 * any portion of *t· m· d·*
9– 5 * any portion of *t· m· d·*
11–30 * "any portion of *t· m· d·*
65– 8 * any part of *t· m· d·*
67–18 * *T· m· d·* was set aside for
72–24 * *t· m· d·* has been subscribed
77–28 * *t· m· d·* required to build
83–24 * *t· m· d·* needed for the
89–14 * although it cost *t· m· d·,*
90–23 * its paid-up cost of *t· m· d·*
91–27 * temple . . . cost *t· m· d·,*
95–13 * cost them about *t· m· d·,*
96–19 * approximately *t· m· d·.*
97–27 * at a cost of *t· m· d·,*
98–18 * cost about *t· m· d·,*
99–15 * at a cost of *t· m· d·,*
100– 5 * cost about *t· m· d·*
two millions of dollars
My. 9–22 any part of *t· m· of d·*
31–12 * approximates *t· m· of d·,*
57–10 * any part of *t· m· of d·*
two millions of money
My. 13–18 any part of *t· m· of m·*
millions of dollars
Pul. 8– 7 *m· of d·* unemployed

My. 48–24 * material to spiritual *v·,*

van
Po. 2– 8 trained falcon in the Gallic *v·,*

Vanderbilt Hall
My. 172– 4 * to make room for *V· H·.*

vane
Un. 14–19 not the shifting *v·* on the spire,

vanguard
My. 31–14 * *v·* of the thousands had been seated,

vanish
Mis. 30–29 mist of materialism will *v·*
205–29 mortal molecules, . . . *v·* as a dream ;

vanished
Mis. 216–20 * "*v·* quite slowly,
Ret. 10–13 *v·* like a dream.
Po. 23– 4 a thought of *v·* hours

vanisheth
'00. 10– 4 *v·* with the new birth of the

vanity
Mis. 145–14 *v·* forbids man to be vain ;
173–18 *v·* to pretend that it is man?
265– 3 makes the venture from *v·,*
363– 8 by Him who compensateth *v·*
Ret. 70–29 post of duty, unpierced by *v·,*
Un. 27– 7 *Egotism* implies *v·* and self-conceit.
No. 39– 8 no dishonesty or *v·* influences the
40– 3 Because of *v·* and self-righteousness,
Hea. 11– 2 plucked from the wings of *v·.*
Po. 2–10 all the strength of weakness — *v·* !
33– 8 *v·,* folly, and all that is wrong
My. 25–26 * of victory disappears
34– 4 his soul unto *v·,* — *Psal.* 24 : 4.

vanquished
Mis. 74–20 virtually *v·* matter
339– 6 Experience is victor, never the *v·* ;
Ret. 22–15 till its involved errors are *v·*
My. 185–14 victors never to be *v·.*

vanquishment
Mis. 105–17 *v·* is unknown to the

vapors
Peo. 3– 6 roasting amidst noxious *v·* ;

vapory
Mis. 38–23 too *v·* and hypothetical for

variableness
Un. 14–18 with whom is no *v·,* — *Jas.* 1 : 17.
63– 9 no *v·* or shadow of turning,

variance
Mis. 148– 3 one part of his character at *v·*
214– 7 at *v·* against his father, — *Matt.* 10 : 35.
324–14 drunkenness, witchcraft, *v·,*
No. 24– 8 All these vagaries are at *v·* with

variation
Pul. 42– 7 * scarcely even a minor *v·*
'00. 11–17 quality, quantity, and *v·* in tone,

varied
Mis. 116–16 *v·* strains of human chords
128– 4 are too vast and *v·* to
198– 7 *v·* forms of pleasure and pain.
374– 5 in most of its *v·* manifestations.

varies
No. 31–11 Our phraseology *v·.*

variety
Mis. 128– 1 and given a *v·* of turns,
Pul. 52– 4 * faith of the mustard-seed *v·.*
My. 57–32 * faith of the mustard-seed *v·.*

various
Mis. x–19 to assume *v·* noms de plume.
132–24 refer you . . . to my *v·* publications,
140 8 presenting the *v·* offerings,
329– 8 her *v·* apartments are
Ret. 33– 9 and from *v·* humbugs,
75– 1 *v·* forms of book-borrowing
Un. 27– 1 From *v·* friends comes inquiry
Pul. 23–13 * and under *v·* names,
53– 7 * on *v·* occasions during the
71–17 * *v·* dignitaries of the faith.
Po. vi–25 * in *v·* publications of that day.
My. 310– 3 at *v·* times and places.
313– 8 *v·* stories told by *McClure's Magazine*
346–22 * *V·* conjectures having arisen

variously
Mis. 180–27 the word "son" is defined *v·* ;

varying
Mis. 142–18 *v·* types of true affection,
Un. 26– 8 for my *v·* manifestations.
My. 170–14 but not to *v·* views.

vascular
Rud. 11–27 *v·,* or nervous operations of the

vase
  Pul. 42–29 * a *v·* filled with . . . pink roses.

vassal
  Po. 31–14 *v·* of the changeful hour,

vast
  Mis. 43–22 does a *v·* amount of injury
     77–20 *v·* idea of Christ Jesus,
    128– 3 too *v·* . . . to teach briefly ;
    156– 3 reaches a *v·* number of earnest
    312–26 into the *v·* forever.
  Ret. 9–20 * *v·* and dim And whispering woods,
    82– 4 with the *v·* Wagner Trilogy.
  Pul. vii–19 *v·* problem of eternal life,
    26–13 * It is one of *v·* compass,
    37–10 * attends to a *v·* correspondence ;
    41–18 * receiving this *v·* throng,
    41–21 * each of the four *v·* congregations
  Po. 1– 8 when first creation *v·* began,
    27–13 let today grow difficult and *v·*
  My. 29– 6 * from the *v·* congregation,
    50– 8 * *v·* gloom of the mysterious forests,
    69–18 * anywhere in the *v·* space
    71–21 * just one *v·* auditorium
    78–23 * in spite of its *v·* interior,
    79– 9 * dedication of the *v·* temple
    92–20 * dedication of this *v·* temple.
    100– 9 * representing a *v·* number
    141–19 * *v·* multitudes of . . . Scientists
    250–10 this *v·* vineyard of our Lord.
    291–21 bear its banner into the *v·*
    354–22 Science *v·*, to which belongs

vaster
  My. 67–22 * *v·* sums of money were spent

vastly
  Mis. 52– 6 he could do *v·* more.
  Un. 14– 9 could *v·* improve upon
  My. 190–12 *v·* excelling the former.

vastness
  Mis. 4–22 *v·* of its worth
  My. 24– 6 * *v·* of the truth it represents,
    31–13 * first impression was of *v·*,
    63–25 * purity, stateliness, and *v·* ;

Vatican
  Pul. 5–27 and the *V·* at Rome.
  My. 294–30 The court of the *V·* mourns him ;

vault
  Pul. 27– 4 * *v·* for the safe preservation of

vaulted
  My. 151–18 * *v·* aisles by flaunting folly trod,

vaults
  Po. 16– 7 These *v·* will unfold

vegetable
  Mis. 217–13 *v·*, and animal kingdoms,
  Un. 38–24 *v·*, or animal kingdoms.
  No. 24– 6 animal *v·*, developed through the

vegetables
  Rud. 7–26 transforming minerals into *v·*

vehicle
  Mis. 156– 2 swift *v·* of scientific thought ;
  My. 302– 1 *v·* of all modes of healing

veil
  Mis. 124–24 rent the *v·* of matter,
    165–12 rends the *v·* of the flesh
    203–22 *v·* that hides mental deformity.
    275– 7 it were well to lift the *v·*
    352–32 covered with the *v·* of harmony,
    364–31 C. S. rends this *v·*
    374–28 Looking behind the *v·*,
  No. 21–20 rends this *v·* in the pantheon
  My. 256–20 *v·* of time springs aside at the

veiled
  Mis. 250–25 *v·* form stealing on an errand of
    395–12 *V·* is the modest moon
  Po. 57–19 *V·* is the modest moon

veils
  Mis. 62– 9 Believing a lie *v·* the truth
  Po. 31–11 *v·* the leaflet's wondrous

vein
  Mis. 379–11 *v·* of thought presented by these.
  Un. 7–12 eaten its way to the jugular *v·*.
  Hea. 19– 9 a *v·* had not been opened,
  My. 105–15 and exposed the jugular *v·*

veins
  Pul. 7– 2 * "Had I young blood in my *v·*,
  No. 20–25 have run through the *v·* of all

velvet
  Pul. 78–24 * satin-lined box of rich green *v·*.

venal
  Un. 15–26 criminal appeases, . . . the *v·* officer.

vending
  Mis. 269–27 Error is *v·* itself on trust,

vendors
  Mis. 79–31 *v·* of patent pills, mesmerists,

venerable
  Mis. 225–16 he said to this *v·* Christian :
  Ret. 4– 1 This *v·* grandmother had thirteen
  '01. 32–27 I believe, if those *v·* Christians
  My. 290– 8 Few sovereigns have been as *v·*,
    297– 1 if Miss Barton were not a *v·* soldier,

venereal
  Mis. 210–24 belief in *v·* diseases

vengeance
  Mis. 130–15 "*V·* is mine ;— *Rom.* 12 : 19.

venomous
  Mis. 323–11 *V·* serpents hide among the rocks,

vent
  Mis. 41– 2 given *v·* in the diabolical practice of

vented
  My. 104– 9 *v·* their hatred of Jesus

ventilating
  Mis. 297–12 censor *v·* his lofty scorn

ventilation
  Mis. 78–18 witless *v·* of false statements

venture
  Mis. 265– 3 makes the *v·* from vanity,
  Ret. 35– 7 I did not *v·* upon its publication
  Pul. 29– 6 * of whose work I shall *v·* to speak,
  No. 34– 6 we shall no longer *v·* to
  My. 51– 9 * we *v·* to hope she will remain
    154– 7 I shall scarcely *v·* to send

ventured
  Mis. 234–18 That one should have *v·*

venturing
  Mis. 287–32 *v·* on valor without discretion,
    339–21 *v·* its all of happiness

veracity
  My. 311–23 I never doubted the *v·* of

verb
  Mis. 77– 4 Here the *v· believe* took its
  Rud. 1–14 *v· personare* is compounded of

verbally
  Mis. 127– 9 not *v·*, nor on bended knee,
  My. 18– 6 not *v·*, nor on bended knee,

verbatim
  Mis. 300– 3 Copying my published works *v·*,

verbiage
  '01. 16–10 with the *v·* of hades.

verdant
  Mis. 390–15 The *v·* grass it weaves ;
  Po. 16–23 breath from the *v·* springtime,
    55–16 The *v·* grass it weaves ;
  My. 129–11 The oracular skies, the *v·* earth
    252–20 They point to *v·* pastures,

verdict
  Mis. 73–18 Hence the *v·* of experience ;
  Un. 57–15 rendered this infallible *v·* ;
  Rud. 5–24 *v·* of these material senses,
  Pan. 10– 7 the honest *v·* of humanity
  My. 105– 9 by *v·* of the stethoscope

verdure
  Po. 16– 4 My heart hath thy *v·*,
    31–11 Love's *v·* veils the leaflet's
  My. 139– 9 Like the *v·* and evergreen

verge
  Mis. 202– 7 * Quite on the *v·* of heaven."
    357–10 quite on the *v·* of heaven.
  My. 199–18 This year, standing on the *v·* of

veriest
  Mis. 172–11 cover with her feathers the *v·* sinner.

verification
  My. 179–16 *v·* of our Master's sayings.

verified
  Mis. 66–11 precept is *v·* in all directions
  Man. 46– 5 *v·* according to the laws of our land.
  My. 95– 3 * predictions have not been *v·*.
    186–21 Here let His promise be *v·*
    266–20 since this great fact is to be *v·*
    329–17 * photographs are *v·* by the

verifies
  My. 3–22 Christian Scientist *v·* his calling.

verify
  Man. 89–15 are required to *v·* this fact,
  '01. 13–13 and we *v·* Jesus' words,
  My. 183– 5 *v·* what John Robinson wrote

verifying
My. 58–23 * v· Jesus' words,
190–31 v· his last promise,

verily
Mis. 73–22 V· I say unto you, — Matt. 19 : 28.
Chr. 55– 6 V·, v·, I say unto you, — John 5 : 25.
Un. 24– 8 v· I say unto you, God is All-in-all ;
My. 19–30 "V· I say unto you, — Mark 14 : 9.
113–17 Was it profane . . . Nay, v·.
170–21 v· thou shalt be fed. — Psal. 37 : 3.

veritable
Mis. 243–32 of material methods, and as v· :
312–20 honest utterance of v· history,
No. 27–13 but it is just as v· now
My. 119–22 proof of his Saviour, the v· Christ,
315–22 Is it myself, the v· Mrs. Eddy,

veritably
My. 297–20 is here now as v· as when he

Veritas Odium Parit
Mis. 245– 7 chapter sub-title

verities
 of being
Mis. 81–27 utters the divine v· of being
97– 5 the grand v· of being.
136–12 When the v· of being seem to
183– 4 the v· of being exist,
No. 10– 4 relative to the unseen v· of being,

Mis. 55–21 v· of Spirit assert themselves
61– 2 representative of v· priceless,
79– 5 The grand v· of Science
112– 4 may deem these delusions v·,
192–22 grand v· of Christian healing
312–19 * v· of the sacred Scriptures."
363–19 in glimpses of the eternal v·.
No. 27–15 eternal v· of God and man

verity
Mis. 28–27 knowledge of this grand v·,
31–15 grand v· of this Science,
75– 8 grand v· of C. S.,
103– 1 This v· annuls the testimony
181– 5 Man's knowledge of this grand v·
252–16 satisfy himself of their v·.
261– 8 demonstrates this v· of being ;
286– 4 this v· in human economy
286–27 recognize this v· of being,
338– 1 this grand v· in Science,
Ret. 59– 1 C. S. reveals the grand v·,
93–21 as yet this grandest v· has not
Un. 6–17 grand and all-absorbing v·
43–16 in support of this v·,
Pul. vii–17 the cradle of this grand v·
3–27 "The evidence of spiritual v·
No. 5– 3 Principle of this grand v·
17–16 divine consciousness and God's v·.
24–20 appears the grand v· of C. S. :
31– 1 this grand v· of C. S.,
'01. 13–12 neither entity, v·, nor power
14–29 apprehension of this grand v·.
31–17 To this v· every member of my
'02. 6–10 demonstrate this grand v·,
Peo. 10–17 It assures us, of a v·,
My. 37–12 * revealed the v· and rule of
46– 8 * it stands in prophetic v·
105– 2 which had of a v· stirred
146– 6 v· has not been acknowledged
180–20 refuses to see this grand v·
232–24 eternal v·, . . . is understood
251–27 convince yourselves of this grand v· :

vermin
Mis. 249–19 to remove stains or v·.

Vermont
(see Londonderry)

vernal
Mis. 343–18 v· freshness and sunshine
Po. 53–20 The v· songs and flowers.

verse
Mis. 32–14 commencing at the thirty-third v·,
106– 5 parody on Tennyson's grand v·,
191– 9 sixth chapter and seventieth v·,
191–13 ninth chapter and thirty-eighth v·,
332–14 third chapter and ninth v·,
400–12 poem
Po. page 69 poem
My. 189–28 from which I copy this v· :

versed
Pul. 73–21 * perfectly v· in all their beliefs

verse-maker
Ret. 11– 1 From childhood I was a v·.

verses
Mis. 314–22 the book, chapter, and v·.
Chr. 55– 1 the sentiments in the v·,
Ret. 1– 9 other v· and enigmas

version
Mis. 26–26 common v· of Hebrews
Hea. 16– 2 given its spiritual v·,
My. 356–28 the only possible correct v·

versus
Mis. 332–22 What was this sense? Error v· Truth :
346–22 chapter sub-title
My. 232– 9 chapter sub-title

vertebræ
Mis. 171–10 to filter from v· to v·.

vertebrata
My. 271– 3 no v·, mollusca, or radiata.

very
Mis. 3–11 taught them for this v· purpose ;
4–24 "You must have a v· strong
7–19 so loaded . . . seems the v· air.
16– 7 so v· much requisite to
26–18 it is the v· opposite of Spirit,
32–12 in my books, on this v· subject.
54–15 curing hundreds at this v· time ;
56– 1 the v· antipodes of C. S.
61–30 Mortals seem v· material ;
67–31 taken up to the v· throne,
68–14 the penalty . . . is the v· pain and
71–10 is a v· right thing to do.
78–16 deceive, if possible, the v· elect.
99– 2 revolutionary in its v· nature ;
120– 3 at the v· threshold of C. S. :
134– 7 V· truly,
175–20 the v· elect," — Matt. 24 : 24.
184– 1 v· opposite of that Maker,
185–11 opens the v· flood-gates of heaven ;
214–14 The v· conflict his Truth brought,
215– 1 through this v· process,
224– 9 * "It is v· surprising,
237–25 v· streets through which Garrison
242–21 where the patient is v· low
275–24 love and loyalty were v· touching.
306– 9 * V· cordially yours,
316– 8 I shall speak . . . v· seldom.
338–17 But the v· heavens shall laugh
339– 4 would happen v· frequently
344– 4 "V· well," the teacher replied ;
346– 1 v· centre of its faith.
350– 5 with advice of the v· student who
354– 3 Sin in its v· nature is marvellous !
376– 5 * v· closely resemble in detail the
Ret. 2–22 were not v· ancient,
5– 3 was a v· religious man,
6–12 the v· dearest of my kindred.
7–16 practice of a v· large business.
20–12 my home I regarded as v· precious.
20–21 My second marriage was v· unfortunate,
20–28 v· soon removed to . . . the Far West.
31– 9 From my v· childhood I was
50–15 my list of . . . is v· large,
60– 2 v· far from the divine likeness.
82– 8 exception . . . should be v· rare.
Un. 2– 4 "a v· present help — Psal. 46 : 1.
11–16 withered hand looks v· real
11–17 and feels v· real ;"
13–16 in the v· fibre of His being,
15–13 comes through the v· knowledge
29–20 a soul which that v· sense declares
42–11 for the v· opposite of this error
45– 9 v· far from God's likeness."
54–20 God forbade . . . at the v· beginning,
58– 8 This was the v· thing he was doing,
59–19 rescue men from these v· illusions
Pul. 5– 1 and one of the v· clergymen
9–19 with his better half, is a v· whole man
24–16 * windows of stained glass are v· rich
27– 3 * directors' room is v· beautiful
31– 2 * a v· remarkable retrospect.
36– 4 * in the v· zenith of its prosperity
37–16 * Mrs. Eddy feels v· strongly,"
37–21 * "Mother feels v· strongly,"
47–25 * she lives v· much retired,
51–18 * is v· well known.
63–20 * v· tangible and material manner
70–13 * v· recently saw completed in Boston,
72– 6 * number of v· interesting conversations
72– 9 * Mrs. Copeland is a v· pleasant
72–10 * v· much absorbed in the work
73–17 * is also a v· prominent member
Rud. Only a v· limited number of students
No. 40–15 to pursue . . . v· sacredly,
13–16 on the v· basis of nothingness.
'01. 31– 6 from the v· nature of Truth,
'02. 11–30 on the v· basis of his words

very

Hea.	9–12	the v· subjects they would gladly
My.	14–18	* Our friend v· promptly and
	21–23	* meeting v· many of them this year,
	29–16	* lay in its v· simplicity ;
	50–24	* it was a v· inspiring season
	51–25	* relative to this v· early work
	53–27	* some v· interesting statements,
	53–30	* must have been v· much broken
	61– 3	* has been v· interesting indeed,
	61– 6	* lessons . . . have been v· precious.
	73– 6	* v· few of them owe a cent.
	74–12	* v· interesting and agreeabie visitors,
	75–17	* take it all v· good-naturedly.
	75–18	* v· patient and good-natured.
	81– 6	* at the v· height of fervor,
	84–20	* Its v· magnitude and
	90– 8	* and is given v· real tests.
	91–19	* It has not been v· many years
	100–15	* are v· generally of a class who
	106–27	the v· antipode of all these?
	122–30	the v· hearts that rejected it
	131–20	this meeting is v· joyous to me.
	147–26	with you personally v· seldom.
	158– 4	V· truly,
	162– 3	''v· present help — Psal. 46 : 1.
	175–29	the v· opposite of my real sentiments.
	184–24	prosperity of Zion is v· precious
	208–26	reaching the v· acme of C. S.
	215–11	those v· students sent me the
	272–26	* her v· great following.
	272–28	* Mrs. Eddy writes v· rarely for
	273– 8	* a v· great organization
	319–26	* These dates are v· well fixed
	319–28	* I also recall v· plainly the
	320– 5	* He also seemed v· much pleased
	320–12	* as being a v· unique book,
	320–32	* spoke in a v· animated manner
	321– 2	* He seemed v· proud to
	321–26	* v· glad that I was among your
	324– 9	* so original and so v· decided
	324–13	* to have those v· terms revealed
	324–15	* I am v· sure that neither
	325– 6	* Mr. Wiggin was v· much troubled
	325– 7	* v· sure Back Bay property would
	355– 9	men are v· important factors

vesper

Ret.	17–11	And v· reclines
'02.	4–15	ringing like soft v· chimes
Po.	62–13	And v· reclines

vesper-call

Po.	8– 3	In somber groups at the v·,

vespers

Pan.	3–12	the evening's closing v·,
Po.	34– 9	Wouldst chant thy v·

vessel

My.	149–17	A v· full must be emptied

Vesta

Mis.	341–23	the sad history of V·,

vestal

Po.	8– 9	v· pearls that on leaflets lay,

vested

Mis.	258–12	law was v· in the Lawgiver,
	298–22	faith v· in righteousness

vestibule

Mis.	239–17	sweet face appeared in the v·,
Pul.	25–16	* The v· is a fitting entrance
	59–30	* the front v· and street
My.	159–13	stands at the v· of C. S.,
	320–31	* I met him in the v· of the

vestry

Ret.	15–21	Our last v· meeting was
Pul.	25–11	* ''directors' room,'' and the v·.
	27– 6	* The v· seats eight hundred people,
	42– 1	* had closed the large v· room
My.	80–11	* in the extension v·,
	80–12	* in The Mother Church v·,

vesture

Mis.	302– 5	''cast lots for his v·,'' — see Psal. 22 : 18.
'01.	26–15	to preserve Christ's v· unrent ;
My.	154–17	weaving the new-old v·

vestures

Mis.	358–15	Christ's v· are put on

Veterans

My.	284–21	When the V· indicated their desire to

vexed

Man.	66–12	to report to her the v· question

vial

My.	107–13	a v· full of the pellets can be

viands

Mis.	231– 7	rich v· made busy many appetites ;

vibrant

My.	19–25	v· through time and eternity

vibrate

Ret.	17– 8	v· and tremble with accents of
Po.	62– 8	v· and tremble with accents of

vibrating

My.	189–11	v· from one pulpit to another

vibration

My.	226– 7	principle of harmonious v·,

vicarious

Mis.	123–22	not through v· suffering,
No.	37–11	interpretation of the v· atonement

vice

Mis.	81–29	depths of ignorance and v·.
	296–24	affinity for the worst forms of v·
	388–15	won from v·, by virtue's smile,
Un.	52–26	is sometimes the home of v·.
Rud.	11–11	seem to be disease, v·, and
Po.	21– 2	won from v·, by virtue's smile,
	22–20	peace is won, and lost is v· :
My.	36–15	* reclaimed from v· or redeemed from

Vice-President

My.	245–30	conferred by the President or V·

vice-president

Man.	88– 8	a president, v·, and
	88–10	v· shall be elected annually
	89– 6	v· of the Board of Education

vices

Mis.	226–28	more than do most v·.
Un.	23– 3	* and of our pleasant v·
Pul.	15– 8	when you tell them their v·.
Rud.	9–20	lust, and all fleshly v·.
No.	42–22	cleaving to their own v·.

vice versa

Mis.	45–18	not the master . . . but v· v·;
	192– 3	term for Deity was ''good,'' and v· v·;
	218– 4	never produced Mind, and v· v·.
	219–26	manifest on the body, and v· v·;
	294–12	v· v· of this man is sometimes
	340– 4	never the reward of evil, and v· v·.
	352– 9	v· v· . . . this uncovers the error
Ret.	64– 3	sin is the sinner, and v· v·,
	67– 4	does not constitute sin, but v· v·,

vicious

Un.	42– 9	That man must be v·

vicissitudes

Pul.	10–24	chill v· have not withheld the
	58– 1	* after many v·,

victim

Mis.	112–19	regarded . . . himself as the v·.
	115–30	you will fall the v· of
	210–25	torments its v·, and thus
	222– 5	causes the v· to believe that
	222– 7	in many cases causes the v·
	246–18	then turn and refuse the v· a
	250– 7	so-called affection pursuing its v·
	254–13	The v· of mad ambition
	355–20	its v· is responsible for
Ret.	73–21	v· of his own corporeality.
Peo.	6–14	Believing that man is the v·
My.	211–13	entices its v· by unseen,
	211–29	the v· is in a state of
	212– 1	the v· is led to believe
	213–17	the v· will allow himself to
	220–27	and fell a v· to those laws.

victims

Mis.	123–11	demands human v· to be
	254–24	filling with hate its . . . v·,
Ret.	64–29	will become the v· of error.
My.	211–17	The v· lose their individuality,

victor

Mis.	105–17	C. S. is an everlasting v·,
	336– 2	Truth, the v· over a lie.
	339– 6	Experience is v·,
Po.	42– 4	Yet there's one will be v·,

Victoria (see also Queen Victoria)

My.	289–15	the late lamented V·,
	289–29	the late lamented V·,

Victoria Institute

Mis.	295–26	V· I·, or Philosophical Society
	296– 3	life-member of the V· I·,
Pul.	5–26	and the V· I·, England ;

victories

Mis.	131–32	with perils past and v· won.
	268– 7	The imaginary v· of rivalry
Rud.	17–12	toil, agonies, and v·,
No.	34–26	Nameless woe, everlasting v·,
My.	47–15	* trials, progress, and v·
	202–17	endless hopes, and glad v·

victorious
Un. 30–19 made humanity v· over death
Po. 11– 3 V·, all who live it,
My. 186–13 God, o'er all v· !
338– 3 V·, all who live it,
victoriously
Pan. 14–25 sailed v· through the jaws of death
victors
My. 185–13 v· never to be vanquished.
victory
another
Mis. 147– 6 another v· won for time and
consolation and
My. 290–13 support, consolation, and v·.
defeat and
Mis. 267–26 cause of all defeat and v·
everlasting
Mis. 74–26 an everlasting v· for Life ;
118–28 crowns . . . with everlasting v·.
163– 7 sublime and everlasting v· !
277–12 right wins the everlasting v·.
final
'00. 10–10 fresh energy and final v·.
get the
Mis. 241–16 you get the v· and Truth heals
'01. 13–29 get the v·, sin disappears,
hymns of
Mis. 281– 2 chant hymns of v· for triumphs.
in error
My. 278–26 V· in error is defeat in Truth.
its
Un. 48–11 robs the grave of its v·.
My.   5–18 rob the grave of its v·.
191–23 and the grave its v·.
Love's
My. 62–13 * with the joy of Love's v·.
mighty
Mis. 120–13 mighty v· is yet to be won,
of right
My. 362– 4 v· of right over wrong,
over evil
Pul. 15–18 occasion for a v· over evil.
over himself
My. 268–23 gives man the v· over himself.
over self
Ret. 79 21 demonstrating the v· over self
'01. 10–23 v· over self, sin, disease,
over sin
My. 156–21 v· over sin, disease, and death.
over the flesh
Pul.   3–28 so far from v· over the flesh
palms of
Pul. 27–18 * bearing palms of v·,
My. 176–10 palms of v· and songs of glory.
ready for
Mis. 41–11 ready for v· in the ennobling strife.
secret of
Mis. 339– 7 of defeat comes the secret of v·.
sense of
Pul.   3–15 Love gives us the true sense of v·.
this
Peo. 11– 7 and this v· is achieved,
under arms
Pan. 14–11 for her v· under arms,
vanity of
My. 25–26 wherein all vanity of v· disappears

Mis. 96– 3 robbed the grave of v·
Pul. 12–16 For v· over a single sin,
'00. 15–11 after this Passover cometh v·,
'02.   6–25 v· on the side of Truth.
My. 134–10 Defeat need not follow v·.
204– 0 awaken to vigor and to v·.
victory-bringing
Ret. 22–16 vanquished by v· Science ;
vie
Mis. 231–13 to v· with guests in the dexterous
Hea. 20– 6 * v· with Gabriel, while he sings,
vied
Pul.   8–16 children v· with their parents
My. 173–22 my fellow-citizens v· with each other
view
accepted
Mis. 75–29 accepted v· is that soul is deathless.
another
My. 346– 5 * another v· of her religion.
brings to
Mis. 208–20 His rod brings to v· His love,
292– 2 brings to v· overwhelming tides of
Chr. 53–45 For C. S. brings to v·
correct
Mis. 81–19 if all this be a fair or correct v·

view
drink in the
Po. 32– 2 and drink in the v·
end in
My. 68– 2 * with the end in v· of impressing
faint
Mis.   2–15 we behold but the first faint v·
human
Mis. 282– 3 to human v· an enlarged sense of
interrupts the
My. 69–18 * not a single . . . interrupts the v·
limited
Mis. 164–30 The limited v· of God's ideas
material
Mis. 14– 3 material v· which contradicts the
my
Un.   8–22 it proves my v· conclusively,
picturesque
Ret.   4–11 picturesque v· of the Merrimac
point of
Mis. 241– 1 From a religious point of v·,
Pul. 81– 9 * chapter sub-title
My. 69–29 * best point of v· is on top of the
304–22 * From every point of v· a woman of
popular
No. 36–10 popular v· of Jesus' nature.
speculative
Mis. 38–23 some speculative v· too vapory and
such a
Un. 13–21 Such a v· would bring us upon an
this
Ret. 64–14 this v· is supported by the
Pul. 69–20 * We find in this v· of the Bible

Mis. 374– 8 In v· of this, Jesus said,
Ret. 47–12 In v· of all this, a meeting was
Pul. 41–10 * to v· the new-built temple
Po. v– 5 * with a v· of making a book,
My. 20 23 * In v· of the fact that a general
83–22 * in v· of the announcement,
171–13 and v· this beautiful structure,
354– 2 In v· of complaints from the field,

views
advanced
Mis. 379–16 had advanced v· of his own,
better
Mis. 175– 9 giving better v· of Life ;
218–27 What can illustrate Dr.——'s v· better
broad
My. 338–22 * unfamiliar with his broad v·
decided
Mis.   2–32 While we entertain decided v· as to
dissolving
Mis. 290– 9 ought to be dissolving v·,
false
Mis. 291–21 False v·, however engendered,
following
My. 338– 6 * The following v· of the Rev. . . . . Eddy
formulated
Mis. 78 30 human vagaries, formulated v·
her
My. 345–32 * her v·, strictly and always
her own
Pul. 35–29 * into sympathy with her own v·,
higher
Mis. 130– 6 broader and higher v·,
his
Ret. 14–10 depended, according to his v·, upon
'01. 24–24 In contradistinction to his v·
human
My. 221– 5 with certain purely human v·.
illiberal
My. 167–30 day of heathenism, illiberal v·,
improved
Peo.   2– 4 improved v· of the Supreme Being.
mistaken
Mis. 248–13 mistaken v· of Mrs. Eddy's book,
290– 9 Mistaken v· ought to
Hea.   8–17 mistaken v· entertained of Deity
mortal
No. 26– 9 such material and mortal v·
my
Mis. 32–14 find my v· on this subject ;
247–12 charges against my v· are false,
Ret. 44–24 No sooner were my v· made known,
'01. 16– 4 My v· of a future and eternal
My. 306–31 my v· of mental therapeutics.
new
Mis. 218– 1 spiritual sense takes in new v·,
of Truth
Mis. 234– 4 by speculative v· of Truth.
No. 21– 5 whose v· of Truth Confucius and
others'
Mis. 291–11 acquiescence with others' v·

views

personal
Man. 84–20 not by their teachers' personal *v*·.
political
My. 276–22 * an expression of her political *v*·,
popular
Un. 38–26 the popular *v*· to this effect
realistic
Mis. 217–17 material realistic *v*· presuppose that
218–14 False realistic *v*· sap the Science
religious
No. 40–25 If a change in the religious *v*·
respected
Pul. 66–21 * departure from long respected *v*·
severe
Mis. 203–21 gain severe *v*· of themselves ;
sublunary
Pul. 2–11 Turning from sublunary *v*·,
these
Mis. 3– 2 and shall express these *v*·
transient
Mis. 291– 1 transient *v*· are human :
varying
My. 170–14 but not to varying *v*·.

Ret. 62– 4 find that the *v*· here set forth
Un. 7–17 *v*· here promulgated on this subject
My. 281–20 * *v*· by representative persons.

vigilant
Ret. 85–22 The tempter is *v*·,
My. 213–13 more watchful and *v*·.

vigor
My. 84–19 * numbers, wealth, *v*·,
134–30 * mental and physical *v*·."
204– 6 awaken to *v*· and to victory.
355– 3 * mental *v*· a symbol of the

vile
My. 33–22 *v*· person is contemned ;— Psal. 15 : 4.

vileness
Ret. 86–10 Behold its *v*·, and remember
Un. 17–11 *v*· may be christened purity,

vilify
Mis. 246–17 stop free speech, slander, *v*· ;
Man. 51– 9 aggrieve or *v*· the Pastor
My. 190–30 wherefore *v*· His prophets to-day

village
Ret. 5–13 Park Cemetery of that beautiful *v*·.
Pul. 79–13 * a daily paper in town or *v*·
My. 262– 9 herds of a Jewish *v*·.

villagers
Mis. 120–18 to *v*· on the Rhine.

villages
Ret. 89– 9 scattered about in cities and *v*·,
Pul. 47–27 * Concord and its surrounding *v*·.
67–21 * while in many towns and *v*·

villainy
My. 121–20 internal vulgarity and *v*·.

villainies
Mis. 228–14 momentary success of all *v*·,

vindicate
Mis. 141–15 I *v*· both the law of God and
No. 2– 1 only Mind-healing I *v*· ;
My. 125–14 divine Principle they so ably *v*·,
273– 4 * *v*· in her own person the value of

vindicated
Mis. 284–18 *v*· divine Truth and Love
No. 45–18 *v*· by the noblest of both sexes.
Peo. 10–27 *v*· but in a single instance
My. 59–31 * or so completely *v*·.

vindicates
Ret. 55– 7 *v*· the divine Principle,
Hea. 15– 3 *v*· the omnipotence of the Supreme

vindicating
Ret. 31– 5 *v*· "the ways of God" to man.— Job 40 : 19.
No. 5– 1 All true Christian Scientists are *v*·,

vindication
Mis. 246–19 *v*· in this most unprecedented

Vine
Chr. 53–19 this living V· Ye demonstrate.

vine
Mis. 154–13 beneath your own *v*· and fig-tree
154–14 *v*· whereof our Father is husbandman.
369–27 from the *v*· which our Father tends.
Po. 15– 2 zephyrs through foliage and *v*· !
My. 125– 7 to incline the *v*· towards the
159– 9 fruit of this branch of his *v*·,
182–28 this *v*· of His husbanding,
202–29 God bless this *v*· of His planting.
269–20 The *v*· is bringing forth its fruit ;

vinegar
Ret. 26– 5 "*v*· and gall,"— see Matt. 27 : 34.

vines
My. 123–30 spoil the *v*·."— Song 2 : 15.

vineyard
Mis. 7–16 faithful laborers in His *v*·.
120–12 in the *v*· of our Lord ;
254–26 Lord of the *v*·— Mark 12 : 9.
254–27 *v*· unto others."— Mark 12 : 9.
Ret. 52– 9 worker in this *v*· of Truth.
Un. 12– 3 in this *v*· of Mind-sowing
'01. 33– 5 not be admitted to the *v*· of our
Hea. 19–22 work more earnestly in His *v*·,
My. 186–20 may those that plant the *v*·
250–10 vast *v*· of our Lord.

vineyards
Ret. 88–22 to work in other *v*· than our own.

vintage
Mis. 120–18 sound of *v*· bells to villagers
356–15 sweeter than the sound of *v*· bells.

vintage-time
Mis. 311–10 go forth to the full *v*·,

violated
Mis. 198–31 or *v*· a law of matter
Pul. 54–13 * "There was no law of nature *v*·

violates
Man. 37– 5 A member who *v*· this By-Law
Ret. 75– 3 This error *v*· the law

violating
Man. 50–23 *v*· any of the By-Laws

violation
Mis. 79–27 for *v*· of medical statutes
226–23 that from the *v*· of truth
Man. 50–22 V· of By-Laws.
51– 7 V· of Christian Fellowship.
Pul. 54– 7 * not in defiance, suppression, or *v*·

violations
Mis. 107–23 oft-repeated *v*· of divine law,

violence
Mis. 153–16 wherein *v*· covereth men
274–20 gives impulse to *v*·, envy, and hate,
Ret. 75– 5 it does *v*· to the thirsty
79–26 heaven suffereth *v*·,— Matt. 11 : 12.

violent
Mis. 182– 4 *v*· means or material methods.
Man. 41–12 in return employ no *v*· invective,
Ret. 73–24 a *v*· and egotistical personality,
79–27 *v*· take it by force !"— Matt. 11 : 12.
'02. 18–28 *v*· death of all his disciples
My. 107–30 most *v*· stages of organic and
222– 3 a *v*· case of lunacy.
336–17 * so *v*· that he was unable to

violently
Mis. 225–14 was taken *v*· ill.

violet
Mis. 330–28 *v*· lifts its blue eye to heaven,
376–27 orange, pink, crimson, *v*· ;

virgin
Mis. 165–32 mode, and *v*· origin of man
'01. 8–27 was born of a *v*· mother,

Virgin Mary
Ret. 70–14 individual place of the V· M·.

Virgin Mary's
My. 261–28 V· M· spiritual thoughts of Life

Virgin-mother (see also Virgin-mother's)
Mis. 166–19 required the V· to go to the
Ret. 70– 9 Scriptural narrative of the V·
My. 303–27 to be a first or second V·

Virgin-mother's
Un. 29–28 V· sense being uplifted to

virgins
Mis. 341–21 "the ten *v*·"— see Matt. 25 : 1.
342– 3 The foolish *v*· had no oil
342–22 wise *v*· had no oil to spare,

virtually
Mis. 9–12 are *v*· thy best friends.
19–12 *v*· accepted the divine claims
51–14 The use of the rod is *v*·
53–15 which is *v*· acknowledging that
74–20 *v*· vanquished matter and its
101–24 *v*· destroys matter and evil,
103– 8 mortals *v*· name substance;
269– 3 Galileo *v*· lost it.
288– 1 which is *v*· meddlesomeness.
Ret. 54–14 Belief is *v*· blindness, when it
70–27 *v*· stands at the head
Un. 19– 8 must *v*· have intended it,
32–18 *v*· saying, "I am the opposite of
38– 8 is *v*· without existence.

virtually

Pan.	8–15	*v·* annulled the so-called laws
'02.	6–21	all devout desire, *v·* petition,
	12–11	*v·* unites with the Jew's belief
My.	5–26	*v·* what the prophet said :
	13–28	Christian Scientists *v·* pledged
	340–24	which *v·* belongs to the past,

virtue (*see also* virtue's)

activities of
Mis. 362–32 or lessens the activities of *v·*.
and heaven
Mis. 238–15 health, *v·*, and heaven ;
and truth
Mis. 201–27 temperance, *v·*, and truth,
any
Mis. 128–10 if there be any *v·*, — *Phil.* 4 : 8.
clemency, and
Mis. 295–30 dignity, clemency, and *v·*
color of
Mis. 147–18 give the color of *v·* to a
goodness and
No. 13–24 impulse to . . . goodness and *v·*.
had gone out
Un. 57–13 "*v·* had gone out of him." — *Mark* 5 : 30.
increasing
'01. 3– 2 increasing *v·*, fervor, and fidelity.
in the shambles
Mis. 285–24 puts *v·* in the shambles,
of this nature
Mis. 208– 5 by *v·* of this nature and allness
place of a
Mis. 227– 3 may stand in the place of a *v·* ;
this
Mis. 356–23 This *v·* triumphs over the flesh ;

Mis. 329– 5 a weakness, or a — *v·* ?
367–30 by *v·* of His ignorance of
No. 30– 8 by *v·* of the allness of God.

virtue's

Mis. 388–15 won from vice, by *v·* smile,
Po. 21– 2 won from vice, by *v·* smile,
41– 4 for the lambkin soft *v·* repose,

virtues

Mis.	110– 8	preserve these *v·* unstained,
	271– 1	foremost *v·* of homœopathy
Ret.	33 23	mental *v·* of the material methods
Pul.	15– 7	when you tell them their *v·*
No.	1–14	quiet practice of its *v·*.
	42–21	false claimants, aping its *v·*,
'01.	24– 9	descanting on the *v·* of tar-water,
My.	166–18	*v·* that lie concealed in the
	204– 4	to use their hidden *v·*,
	290– 6	her personal *v·* can never be lost.

virtuous

Un. 42– 9 before he can be *v·*,
My. 93– 2 * happy, gentle, and *v·*.

virus

Mis. 12– 3 spreads its *v·* and kills at last.

visible

Mis.	68– 6	*v·* to those beholding him here.
	90–27	conferred by a *v·* organization
	91–20	worship that can be made *v·*,
	144–25	our *v·* lives are rising to God.
	145–20	*v·* unity of spirit remains,
	205–18	*v·* being is invisible to the physical
	218– 5	*v·* universe declares the invisible
	244–16	* *v·* agencies for specific ends
	363–18	shines through the *v·* world
Pul.	50–12	* erection of a *v·* house of worship
'01.	13– 4	The *v·* sin should be invisible :
My.	28 –21	* *v·* symbol of a religion
	69– 6	* no sharp angles are *v·*,
	78– 7	* *v·* from every quarter of the city.
	154–26	embodied in a *v·* communion,
	338–25	the *v·* discoverer, founder,

vision

earthly
Un. 61–11 twilight and dawn of earthly *v·*,
far-seeing
'01. 30–25 far-seeing *v·*, the calm courage,
illusive
Mis. 206–14 no emasculation, no illusive *v·*,
is fled
Po. 9– 8 weeping alone that the *v·* is fled,
Jacob's
'02. 10–16 gain the scope of Jacob's *v·*,
miraculous
Rud. 17–12 she needed miraculous *v·* to
mortal
My. 59– 7 * distant day beyond our mortal *v·*.
must be clear
Mis. 211– 5 Our own *v·* must be clear

vision

my
Mis. 136– 9 so grow upon my *v·*
347–11 Where my *v·* begins and is clear,
Po. 33– 3 my faith and my *v·* enlarge,
never clears the
Mis. 355–17 To strike out . . . never clears the *v·* ;
no
Mis. 354–33 No *v·* more bright than the
of envy
Hea. 10– 3 the *v·* of envy, sensuality,
of heaven
My. 155–19 a clear *v·* of heaven here,
of life
Hea. 9–28 St. John saw the *v·* of life
of relief
Ret. 20–14 hoping for a *v·* of relief
of sin
Un. 4–26 *v·* of sin is wholly excluded.
of the Apocalypse
No. 21– 2 and the *v·* of the Apocalypse.
of the Revelator
Mis. 277–32 The *v·* of the Revelator
of the Wisemen
Mis. 164–11 To the *v·* of the Wisemen,
of Truth
No. 27–12 this *v·* of Truth is fully interpreted
our
Mis. 62– 9 veils the truth from our *v·* ;
renewed
My. 202–16 burst . . . with renewed *v·*,
Revelator's
Mis. 113– 8 and the Revelator's *v·*,
'00. 14–11 import of the Revelator's *v·*
so bright
Po. 18–11 What *v·* so bright as the dream
soft as the
Po. 15–12 Their wooings are soft as the *v·*
spiritual
Mis. 373–13 spiritual *v·* that should, does, guide
Un. 61– 6 to immortal and spiritual *v·*
My. 126–23 the Revelator saw in spiritual *v·*
voice and
My. 265– 5 spiritual voice and *v·*,

Mis. 149–23 a *v·* of the new church,

visionary

Un. 45–24 *v·* substance of matter.
My. 93– 7 * if their opinions seem *v·*,

visions

Ret. 18–15 real joy and of *v·* divine.
Pul. 33– 2 * saw *v·* and dreamed dreams.
33–27 * *v·* in their early youth.
Po. 64– 6 real joy and of *v·* divine ;

visit

Mis.	69–14	called to *v·* a sick man
	306–23	When angels *v·* us, we do not
Man.	68–18	to *v·* or to locate therein
	77–25	shall *v·* the Board of Directors,
	85– 2	may *v·* each other's churches,
Pul.	54–29	healed Mr. Whittier with one *v·*,
	77–15	* to *v·* and formally accept
	78–13	* most lovingly invited to *v·*
My.	21 11	* gladly forego a *v·* to Boston
	21–18	* forego their anticipated *v·*
	80– 1	* close of their *v·* to Boston ;
	105–14	healed at one *v·* a cancer,
	169– 7	are requested to *v·* me at a
	169–14	chapter sub-title
	171– 8	chapter sub-title
	173– 3	* *v·* of the Christian Scientists
	187– 4	at some near future *v·* your city,
	192–22	give me pleasure to *v·* you,
	302–25	first *v·* to The Mother Church
	318–16	I invited Mr. Wiggin to *v·*

visitant

Peo. 5–22 then heed this heavenly *v·*,

visited

Mis.	112–15	I *v·* in his cell the assassin
	237–29	and he *v·* my father,
	265–17	*v·* upon himself and his students,
	297–14	that perhaps he has never *v·*.
Pul.	59– 2	* has not yet *v·* her temple,
'01.	29– 2	housed, fed, clothed, or *v·*
My.	153–12	flowers *v·* his bedside :
	185–22	I *v·* these mountains
	297–21	he *v·* me a year ago.
	306–22	when I first *v·* Dr. Quimby

visiting

Ret. 8–14 Mehitable Huntoon, was *v·* us,
17– 1 while *v·* a family friend
Po. vii– 1 * while *v·* a family friend
page 67 poem
My. 308–20 was *v·* Governor Pierce,

visitor

Pul. 33–24 * that his *v·* was a spiritual form
49–28 * first impression given to the *v·*

visitors

Mis. 112–22 * "Other *v·* have brought
Man. 69–27 shall hereafter be closed to *v·*.
My. 24–25 * *v·* who have recently inspected the
30–14 * *v·* from Australia,
31–21 * first sight which the *v·* caught of
38–14 * *v·* showed a tendency to tarry
73–18 * was thrown open to *v·*
73–21 * *v·* will receive all information
74–10 * chapter sub-title
74–12 * interesting and agreeable *v·*,
75–14 * a great number of *v·*
77–15 * twenty-five thousand *v·*
82–22 * twenty thousand and more *v·*
83–27 * The thirty thousand *v·*
87– 7 * characteristics of this crowd of *v·*.
87–10 * *v·* of title and distinction,
173–19 The number of *v·*,
173–27 allowing the *v·* to assemble
353–23 shall hereafter be closed to *v·*.

vital

Mis. 132–29 *v·* spark of Christianity.
260–27 *v·* functions of Truth and Love.
267–16 the *v·* outcomes of Truth
Ret. 48– 4 was aimed at its *v·* purpose,
Pul. 50– 2 * in whom she takes a *v·* interest.
52–23 * all *v·* belief in his teachings.
No. 3– 1 in some *v·* points lack Science.
34–27 *v·* currents of Christ Jesus' life,
'01. 16–22 to carry a most *v·* point.
30– 4 We err in thinking the object of *v·*
32– 6 student of *v·* Christianity.
My. 128–13 *v·* heritage of freedom
146–23 Scientists hold as a *v·* point

vitality

Mis. 111–15 seed of Truth to its own *v·*,
Ret. 66– 3 C. S. gives *v·* to religion,
Pul. 79–17 * has shown a *v·* so unexpected.
My. 95–25 * religion of growth and *v·*
139–14 their *v·* involves Life,

vitals

Mis. 131– 4 gnawing at the *v·* of humanity.

vivacity

Mis. 117–12 * enduring *v·* among God's people."

vividly

Ret. 72– 7 The Psalmist *v·* portrays

vivify

My. 125– 6 and to *v·* the buds,

vocabulary

No. 10– 6 two largest words in the *v·*

vocal

Mis. 146– 2 May her walls be *v·* with

vocations

Man. 82–17 or pursue other *v·*,

vogue

My. 85– 6 * measured its *v·*.

voice

called
Ret. 9–10 when the *v·* called again,
came
Ret. 9–11 The *v·* came; but I was afraid,
clear
My. 342–20 * she said, in her clear *v·*,
dissenting
Ret. 44–26 without a dissenting *v·*.
from heaven
Mis. 168–15 *v·* from heaven seems to say,
gentle
My. 39–25 * harmonious tones of her gentle *v·*.
God's
Mis. 134–27 neither silence nor disarm God's *v·*.
heard a
Ret. 8– 4 I repeatedly heard a *v·*,
heard the
Ret. 8–24 my cousin had heard the *v·*,
Pul. 33– 7 * if she heard the *v·* again
hear the
Chr. 55– 7 dead shall hear the *v·* — *John* 5 : 25.
His
Ret. 9–23 * learned at last to know His *v·*
Un. 2– 4 no place where His *v·* is not heard ;
My. 152–21 To-day, if ye would hear His *v·*,
his
Mis. 81–24 his *v·* be heard divinely
its
Mis. 277– 7 its *v·* dies out in the distance.
loud
Pul. 12– 5 I heard a loud *v·* saying — *Rev.* 12 : 10.

voice

mother's
Ret. 8– 6 I thought this was my mother's *v·*,
my
Mis. 151– 3 "My sheep hear my *v·*, — *John* 10 : 27.
213–22 "My sheep hear my *v·*, — *John* 10 : 27.
Chr. 55–26 if any man hear my *v·*, — *Rev.* 3 : 20.
Po. 34– 4 Like thee, my *v·* had stirred
mysterious
Ret. 9– 5 this mysterious *v·*,
of his conscience
Mis. 147–16 Truth and the *v·* of his conscience
of their leader
My. 43–11 * obedient to the *v·* of their leader.
of the night-bird
Po. 16–16 The *v·* of the night-bird
of the turtle
Mis. 329–24 *v·* of the turtle — *Song* 2 : 12.
of Truth
Mis. 81–27 *v·* of Truth utters the divine
134–26 "still, small *v·*" of Truth ; — *I Kings* 19 : 12.
360–26 "still, small *v·*" of Truth — *I Kings* 19 : 12.
Ret. 69–26 *v·* of Truth still calls :
My. 245–17 Let the *v·* of Truth and Love
one
My. 81–23 * swelling as one *v·*.
organ's
Pul. 11– 3 organ's *v·*, as the sound of many waters,
spiritual
My. 265– 5 revelation, spiritual *v·* and vision,
still, small
Mis. 134–26 "still, small *v·*" — *I Kings* 19 : 12.
138–28 "still, small *v·*" — *I Kings* 19 : 12.
175– 1 "still, small *v·*" — *I Kings* 19 : 12.
360–25 "still, small *v·*" — *I Kings* 19 : 12.
No. 1– 4 still, small *v·*," — *I Kings* 19 : 12.
'02. 15–30 "still, small *v·*" — *I Kings* 19 : 12.
My. 249– 5 "still small *v·*" — *I Kings* 19 : 12.
their
Ret. 61–19 where their *v·* is not — *Psal.* 19 : 3.
this
Mis. 81–20 *why does not John hear this v·*,
Ret. 61–19 this *v·* is Truth that destroys error
Thy
Mis. 398– 1 I will listen for Thy *v·*,
Ret. 46– 7 I will listen for Thy *v·*,
Pul. 17– 6 I will listen for Thy *v·*,
Po. 14– 5 I will listen for Thy *v·*,
My. 201–21 I will listen for Thy *v·*,
Truth's
Mis. 267– 1 make itself heard above Truth's *v·*.
universal
My. 8–14 * universal *v·* of Christian Scientists,
was heard
Mis. 246–22 *v·* was heard crying in the wilderness,
My. 126–13 And a *v·* was heard, saying,
your
Pul. 14–20 He can neither drown your *v·*

Mis. 99–13 *v·* a higher order of Science
99–26 *v·* of one crying in the wilderness,
'02. 20– 2 *v·* of him who stilled the tempest

voiced

Mis. 64– 2 cry which *v·* that struggle ;
336– 2 Hath not Science *v·* this
Ret. 27–13 not fully *v·* my discovery.
Pan. 3–11 *v·* with a hum of harmony,
'02. 5–21 *v·* in the thunder of Sinai,

voiceless

Po. 35–10 An aching, *v·* void,

voices

Mis. 100–14 Science *v·* unselfish love,
133– 9 *v·* my impressions of prayer :
329– 1 chapter sub-title
329–10 whose *v·* are sad or glad,
333–10 C. S. *v·* this question :
372– 7 *v·* C. S. through song and
396– 8 It *v·* beauty fled.
Pul. 33– 4 * like Jeanne d'Arc, to hear "*v·*,"
33–27 * experiences of *v·* or visions
No. 13–18 *v·* the infinite, and governs
Po. 15–11 whispering *v·* are calling away
16–20 the glad *v·* that swell,
58–20 It *v·* beauty fled.
My. 32– 5 * their *v·* rose as one
32–10 * did not have to lift their *v·*
59–21 * chorus of five thousand *v·*,
79– 1 * joining with their shrill *v·*
81–20 * occasionally the *v·* would
146–29 Scientist *v·* the harmonious

voicing

Mis. 251– 9 *v·* the friendship of this city
Ret. 10–15 *v·* the idea of God
No. 8– 6 Avoid *v·* error ;

void

Mis.	22–19	therefore these are null and v.
	76–16	is rendered v by Jesus'
Man.	39– 6	their applications shall be v.
Ret.	23–21	pantheism, and theosophy were v.
No.	37–25	Jesus rendered null and v whatever
Po.	35–10	An aching, voiceless v,
My.	219–22	annul nor make v the laws

Vol. 1

My.	353– 6	V· 1, No. 1, of The C· S Monitor,
		(see also Science and Health)

volcanoes

Mis.	316–24	warming marble and quenching v·!
My.	291–10	the v· of partizanship.

volition

Mis.	28– 7	Destroy the belief . . . v· ceases;
	117– 7	God-given intent and v·
	156–24	all true thought and v·
Rud.	3–20	v·, impulse, and action;

volleyed

Mis.	106–10	V· and thundered!

Voltaire

Peo.	6–11	V· says: "The art of medicine

volume

Mis.	xi–11	May this v· be to the reader
	29–21	perusal of my v· is healing
	262– 7	now entering upon its fifth v·,
Ret.	37–	chapter sub-title
	83– 2	proven that this v· is accomplishing
Pul.	vii– 1	v· contains scintillations from
	55–22	* is contained in the v· entitled
	73–26	* large v· which Mrs. Eddy had herself
Po.	v– 1	* garnered up in this little v·
	vii–11	* little v· is presented to the public,
My.	81–22	* the v· of holy song rose
	256–13	open the v· of Life

volumes

No.	33– 9	demonstrate what these v· teach,
Po.	vii– 6	* to prepare a few bound v·

voluminous

Ret.	76– 4	student can write v· works
Pul.	88– 7	too v· for these pages.
No.	15– 8	translations and v· commentaries

voluntarily

Mis.	9–23	we v· set it aside
	289–13	each party v· surrenders
	297–18	having v· entered into wedlock,
Man.	38–21	but who have v· withdrawn,
Ret.	84–28	those who v· place themselves
My.	30–24	* Without ostentation and quite v·
	212– 3	never, otherwise, think or do v·.

voluntary

Man.	62– 1	eight or nine minutes for the v·
Pul.	43–14	* After an organ v·,
	44–21	* building a church by v· contributions,
	63–24	* v· contributions of Christian Scientists
	71– 5	* not borne out by the v· contribution
No.	v– 5	involuntary as well as v· error.
My.	32–11	* Following the organ v·
	76–22	* all contributions have been v·.
	77–30	* secured by v· subscription.
	98–23	* Contributions were entirely v·.
	118–19	One's v· withdrawal from society,

Volunteer

Un.	14–10	boatbuilder, remedies in the V· the

volunteer

Ret.	21–10	he had served as a v·

volunteered

My.	331–31	* v· to restore her to her friends

vomit

Mis.	353–32	"return to their v·," — see Prov. 26 : 11.

vomiting

Mis.	243–30	induce ulceration, bleeding, v·,

votaries

Mis.	196–15	v· to "other gods" — Exod. 20 : 3.
My.	75– 3	* Its v· are certainly holding the
	93–11	* which it holds out to its v· ;

vote

Mis.	132– 1	motion was made, and a v· passed,
Man.	26– 9	by a unanimous v· of the
	26–23	A majority v· . . . shall dismiss a
	30– 8	majority v· of the Board of Directors
	36–22	unanimous v· of the Board
	38–12	elected by majority v· of the
	39–14	unanimous v· of the C. S. Board of
	52– 1	v· on cases involving The
	65–22	supplied by a majority v·
	73–17	by the unanimous v· of,
	77– 9	by a unanimous v·,
	81– 2	officers elected, by a unanimous v·
	82–12	except by a majority v·
	97–10	by a unanimous v· of the
	102– 9	by a majority v·.
Ret.	7– 1	majority v· of seven thousand,
	7– 2	the largest v· of the State ;
My.	44–19	* carried unanimously by a rising v·.
	276–18	* those who are entitled to v·

voted

Man.	17–10	on motion of Mrs. Eddy, it was v·,
Ret.	44– 1	it was v· to organize a church
	47–14	v· that the school be discontinued.
	49–28	it was unanimously v· :
My.	49–27	* it was unanimously v· that
	49–30	* v· to instruct the Clerk to
	53– 9	* it was v· that the church
	53–15	* church v· to wait upon Mrs. Eddy,
	57– 9	* church v· to raise any part of
	65– 7	* v· yesterday afternoon to

votes

Ret.	44–26	v· passing without a dissenting

votive

Pul.	26–15	* a v· offering of gratitude

vouches

Mis.	295–20	Mr. Wakeman strongly v·,
No.	4–18	v· for the validity of that

vouchsafed

My.	345–22	last healing that will be v·

vow

Mis.	286– 4	solemn v· of fidelity,
	290– 4	nuptial v· is never annulled so long as
	341–24	takes the most solemn v· of celibacy
My.	268– 3	The nuptial v· should never

vows

Mis.	285–25	notifies the public of broken v·.

vox populi

Mis.	xi–21	v· p· is inclined to grant us peace,
	80–18	v· p·, through the providence of God,
	245–11	calling forth the v· p·
	274–27	the v· p· is suffocated,

vulgar

My.	79–18	* not a gathering of "the v· throng ;"
	104–22	atone for the v· denunciation
	305– 9	* subject of "v· metaphysics,"
	305–10	which "v·" defamers have

vulgarity

My.	121–20	used to disguise internal v·
	121–21	no v· in kindness.

W

wading

Mis.	320–19	w· through darkness and gloom,

waft

Po.	19– 2	breezes that w· o'er its sky !
	33–19	w· me away to my God.

waged

Ret.	56–12	War is w· between the evidences of
Pul.	3–14	good fight we have w· is over,

wages

Mis.	76–27	w· of sin is death." — Rom. 6 : 23.
	104–16	w· feeble fight with his individuality,
Ret.	22–14	mortal life-battle still w·,
Rud.	13–27	receiving no w· in return,
	14– 6	conscientiously earn their w·,
'00.	2–20	his stock in trade, the w· of sin ;

Wagner Trilogy

Ret.	82– 4	or with the vast W· T·.

wagon

Un.	17– 4	* "Hitch your w· to a star."
My.	313–13	cradle for me in his w·.

wagon-load

Un.	17– 9	evil ties its w· of offal to

wagons

My.	82–12	* secured express w· enough to

waif

Ret.	93–10	no longer impersonated as a w·

waifs

No.	29–23	spiritless w·, literary driftwood

wail

Mis.	267– 2	w· of evil never harms Scientists,
'01.	14– 4	Pubican's w· won his humble desire,
My.	334–22	Publican's w· won his humble desire,

wainscoting

Pul. 25–23 * w· repeats the same tints.

wait

Mis. 81– 8 patiently w· on God to decide,
225–30 * "W· until we get home,
230–25 * Learn to labor and to w·."
307– 4 if you w·, never doubting,
331– 6 cause them to w· patiently
364– 5 "W· patiently on the— see Isa. 40 : 31.
389–16 W·, and love more for every hate,
Ret. 79–24 * "Learn to labor and to w·."
85–18 w· for God's finger to point
Un. 6–27 "W· patiently on the— see Psal. 37 : 7.
Pul. 4–23 W· patiently on illimitable Love,
10–21 If you are less appreciated . . . w·
No. 46–23 continue to labor and w·.
Pan. 12–18 not w· by the roadside,
'00. 7–28 w· for the full appearing of
9–10 shut their eyes and w· for a
13–16 promise to such as w· and weep.
'01. 34–20 brethren, w· patiently on God ;
'02. 2– 5 to w· on divine Love ;
17–17 to be willing to w· on God,
Hea. 1–10 to w· until the age advanced
5– 9 must w· for the reward
Po. 4–15 W·, and love more for every hate,
My. 22–12 * nor w· to be urged or to be shown
29–29 * were able to w· patiently for the
53–16 * voted to w· upon Mrs. Eddy,
119–29 look and w· and watch and pray
184– 6 for them that w· upon Him
185– 7 * Learn to labor and to w·."
224– 4 w· on the logic of events?
224–31 * who only stand and w·."
227–13 we naturally . . . w· on God.
227–18 lying in w· to catch them
239–12 Must mankind w· for the ultimate
250–23 the branch churches can w· for
252–15 w· on God, the strong deliverer,
305–22 I still w· at the cross to
306–14 must w· to be transfused

waited

Mis. 84– 2 he w· for a preparation of
'02. 15–21 Six weeks I w· on God
Hea. 14–23 w· many years for a student to
Po. 41–23 w· to welcome the murmur
78– 5 Why w· their reward,
My. 11–10 * but has w· for us to grow
185– 2 To such as have w· patiently
324–13 * w· on the Lord to have those

waiteth

Mis. 324–11 him who w· at the door.
Pan. 1–16 w· patiently the appearing

waiting

Mis. 15– 5 "w· for the adoption,— Rom. 8 : 23.
22–25 have proven to a w· world.
95–22 "w· for the adoption,— Rom. 8 : 23.
125–12 not stand w· and weary ;
158–20 w· for the watchword
268–32 Truth is used to w·.
273–28 w· for the same class instruction ;
276–13 assemblage found w· and watching
277–11 Justice waits, and is used to w· ;
331– 2 looking up, w· on God,
331–19 Life divine, that owns each w· hour ;
384–14 Be patient, w· heart :
387– 5 w·, in what glad surprise,
389– 7 Life divine, that owns each w· hour,
396–18 O'er w· harpstrings of the mind
Ret. 23–15 I was w· and watching ;
79–25 were saved by patient w·.
80–10 * with patience He stands w·,
Un. 7–18 pour into my w· thought
12– 4 let them apply to the w· grain
Pul. 14–15 w· and watching for rest
18– 2 O'er w· harpstrings of the mind
42– 3 * filled with a w· multitude.
60– 1 * with others, w· for admission.
Rud. v– 5 LOYAL STUDENTS, WORKING AND w·
No. 2–18 w· and working to mature
Pan. 1–14 and the sackcloth of w·
'01. 29–20 w· till the wind shifts.
'02. 15–29 to my w· hope and prayer.
Peo. 7–18 * W· the hour when at God's command
10–25 "w· for the adoption,— Rom. 8 : 23.
Po. 4– 4 Life divine, that owns each w· hour,
8– 7 I'm w· alone for the bridal hour
12– 1 O'er w· harpstrings of the mind
17– 4 still w· for me.
36–13 Be patient, w· heart :
39–16 And be your w· hearts elate,
50–23 * w·, in what glad surprise,
My. 31– 8 * "O'er w· harpstrings of the mind ;"

waiting

My. 80–28 * w· vainly in the streets.
124–14 w· only your swift hands,
208–14 my w· heart, — w· in due expectation
232– 4 w· waves will weave for you
270–12 I am rewarding your w·,
322–21 * w· months in Boston

waits

Mis. 130–28 w· on God, renews his strength,
154–10 God only w· for man's worthiness
277–10 Justice w·, and is used to waiting ;
324– 5 he knocks and w·.
330–31 patient corn w· on the elements
Ret. 90–21 w· with her hope,
Pul. 83–12 * with the patience of genius she w·.
'00. 15–15 it w· in the desert
'02. 11– 6 Divine Love w· and pleads to save
Po. 39–11 First at the tomb, who w·
My. 103– 4 and w· on God.
306–16 Age, . . . w· on God.

waive

Mis. 131–16 I recommend that you w· the

wake

Mis. 11– 1 will w· from his delusion
23– 6 * dream in the animal, and w· in man"?
144–30 w· the long night of materialism,
390– 6 shrill song doth w· the dawn :
396–22 w· a white-winged angel throng
397– 3 w· to know A world more bright.
Chr. 53– 7 rouse the living, w· the dead,
Ret. 12– 2 W· freedom's welcome,
17– 7 W· chords of my lyre,
Pul. 18– 6 w· a white-winged angel throng
18–12 w· to know A world more bright.
Po. 12– 6 w· a white-winged angel throng
12–12 w· to know A world more bright.
55– 7 shrill song doth w· the dawn :
60–22 W· freedom's welcome,
62– 7 W· chords of my lyre,
66– 7 W· gently the chords of her lyre,
79–18 centuries break, the earth-bound w·,
My. 61–12 * somebody had to w· up.
189–18 human senses w· from their long

wakefully

'02. 18– 2 gate of conscience, w· guard it ;

Wakeman, Mr.

Mis. 295– 3 Mr. W· writes from London,
295–12 Is Mr. W· awake,
295–19 Mr. W· strongly vouches,
296– 9 author cited by Mr. W·

Wakeman's, Edgar L.

Mis. 294–27 become an admirer of Edgar L. W·

waken

'01. 15–18 to w· such a one from his deluded
'02. 17–13 awake and w· the world.
Hea. 9–27 w· from the dream of life in matter,
11– 3 gladly w· to see it was unreal.
Po. 16–25 w· my joy, as in earliest prime.
65–15 We w· to life's dreary sigh.
My. 132–25 w· the dreamer — the sinner,
133–14 should w· the sleeper,
149–29 which w· the stagnant waters
258–19 w· prophecy, gleams of glory,
291–19 w· a tone of truth
356– 4 w· to the privilege of knowing God,

wakened

Mis. 142–27 The symbols . . . w· memory,
328–19 w· through the baptism of fire?

wakening

Po. 30– 5 w· murmurs from the drowsy rills

wakens

My. 287–20 w· lofty desires, new possibilities,

wakes

Mis. 257– 5 and w· in a wicked man.
Pan. 9– 2 * dreams in . . . and w· in man."
Po. 10– 9 That w· thy laureate's lay.
My. 337–10 That w· thy laureate's lay.

waking

Mis. 36–27 as much in our w· moments
47–11 If never in your w· hours,
58– 4 W· from a dream, one learns
58– 5 W· from the dream of death,
329–14 Spring . . . w· up the world ;
386–16 w· with a love that steady turns
Hea. 10–19 and your w· the reality,
Po. 49–24 w· with a love that steady turns
My. 110–19 if w· to bodily sensation
160–25 w· to a true sense of itself,
296–18 w· out of his Adam-dream of evil

Waldron, Mr. George D.

My. 173–28 Mr. George D. W·, chairman of

walk

Mis. xi–13 enabling him to w· the untrodden
28– 6 Destroy the belief that you can w·,
51–28 * w· transparent like some holy
146–22 counsel and help him to w·
162– 9 w· serenely over their fretted,
168– 6 how the lame, . . . w· ;
188–14 w· not after the flesh, — *Rom.* 8 : 1.
231–20 papa knew that he could w·,
244–19 causing him to w· the wave,
244–21 deaf to hear, the lame to w·,
245–27 that one can w· alone
311– 4 to w· with us hand in hand,
358–17 we must w· in the way which
359–15 For Jesus to w· the water
359–18 until we can w· on the water.
359–24 *way* is absolute . . . w· ye in it ;
370– 1 "Rise and w·." — *see John* 5 : 8.
396– 2 To scare my woodland w·,
397– 6 I see Christ w·,
Chr. 55–19 rise up and w·. — *Acts* 3 : 6.
Ret. 90–24 till her children can w· steadfastly
Un. 9– 9 all are without excuse who w· not
11– 3 Jesus taught us to w· *over*, not *into*
Pul. 18–15 I see Christ w·,
37– 9 * she takes a daily w·
No. 8–26 while you w· on in equanimity,
42– 9 rise up and w· !" — *see Luke* 5 : 23.
Pan. 12–18 and w·, not wait by the roadside,
'00. 7–23 w· more closely with Christ ;
7–28 Thus it is we w· here below,
'01. 29–25 will w· in his footsteps.
35–17 w· in Patient faith the way thereto
Po. 12–15 I see Christ w·, And come to me,
58–14 To scare my woodland w·,
66– 3 we w· by that murmuring stream ;
67–13 Beside you they w· while you weep,
My. 105–18 have made the lame w·.
113–12 w· not after the flesh, — *Rom.* 8 : 1.
187– 9 perfect path wherein to w·,
202–28 expands as we w· in it.
205– 2 w· not after the flesh, — *Rom.* 8 : 1.
206–31 w· as children of light." — *Eph.* 5 : 8.
254– 8 not be weary, w· and not faint.
283–24 to w· humbly" — *Mic.* 6 : 8.
313–19 when I took an evening w·,

walked

Mis. 74–17 He w· upon the waves ;
Chr. 55– 8 people that w· in darkness — *Isa.* 9 : 2.
Un. 58– 5 Jesus w· with bleeding feet
Pul. 33–19 * w· with him as he worked,
34–14 * she w· into the adjoining room,
34–20 * Jesus of Nazareth w· the earth.
36–17 * w· any conceivable distance.

walketh

'00. 12– 4 w· in the midst of the — *Rev.* 2 : 1.
'02. 20– 1 Christ w· over the wave ;
My. 33–17 He that w· uprightly, — *Psal.* 15 : 2.
228–23 He that w· uprightly, — *Psal.* 15 : 2.

walking

Mis. 74–21 W· the wave, he proved the
231–19 Then he was caught w· !
277– 5 Error is w· to and fro in the earth,
332–14 w· in the cool of the day
Man. 18– 7 Although w· through deep waters,
'00. 7–22 w· the wave of earth's troubled sea,
'02. 10–30 w· every step over the land route,
My. 124– 1 not w· in craftiness,
342– 4 * w· uprightly and with light step,

walking-stick

My. 308–18 * with a huge w·."
308–19 He never used a w·.
308–22 handed him a gold-headed w·

walks

Mis. xi–24 thought sometimes w· in memory,
125–24 common w· of mankind,
202– 6 * beyond the w· of common life,
215–18 as when a child in sleep w·
357–10 beyond the w· of common life,
Ret. 5–20 in all the w· of life.
No. 29–24 Truth w· triumphantly over the
'00. 7–11 in all the w· of life,
My. 189– 6 in the common w· of life,

wall

Mis. 178–29 w· between the old and the new ;
Pul. 42–19 * On the w· of the choir gallery
63–26 * tablet imbedded in its w·
76– 5 * Italian marble set in the w·.
76–14 * superb mantel . . . adorns the south w·,

Wallace

Sir William

Ret. 2–14 bestowed by Sir William W·,
Pul. 46–21 * bestowed by Sir William W·

Ret. 2–16 "Scots wha hae wi' W· bled."

wallow

'00. 8–25 not Science for the wicked to w·

walls

Mis. 146– 2 May her w· be vocal
279–16 before the w· of Jericho.
279–17 seven times around these w·,
279–25 in order that the w· might fall ;
324–21 the odious company and the cruel w·,
369– 1 watchmen on the w· of Zion,
Pul. 2–21 and remain within the w·
25–25 * On the w· are bracketed oxidized
49– 5 * Mrs. Eddy has hung its w· with
58–19 * steps marble, and the w· stone.
76– 8 * green and gold decoration of the w·.
'00. 1– 4 storied w· of The Mother Church.
Po. vi–18 *nowhere but in the w· of a jail.*
My. 23–23 w· of our new edifice are rising,
24– 9 * As the w· are builded by the
36–25 * By these stately w· ;
58–14 * the erection of these mighty w·.
69– 5 * roof and side w· come together
188–20 w· of your grand cathedral
193–28 Within its sacred w·
214– 1 to place on the w· of their church.
214– 3 textbook on the w· of your churches.

wander

Mis. 138– 5 if it causes thought to w·
'02. 11– 3 to w· on the shores of time

wandered

Mis. 169– 3 whenever her thoughts had w·
328–18 stumbled, and w· away?
Ret. 33– 5 I w· through the dim mazes
93– 2 evangelists of those days w· about.

wanderer (see also wanderer's)

Mis. 155– 8 woo the weary w· to your door,
Ret. 93–11 impersonated as a waif or w· ;
My. 132–32 brings back the w· to the Father's
182–25 May the w· in the wilderness

wanderer's

Ret. 86–12 this w· soiled garments,

wanderers

Mis. 298– 7 we also are w·.
326–17 w· in a beleaguered city,
Pul. 14–15 weary w·, athirst in the desert

wandering

Mis. 371– 4 w· about without a leader,
Ret. 4–17 w· winds sigh low

Wanderings

Mis. 294–28 poetic style in his "W·,"

wanderings

My. 313–16 * long and lonely w·,

wanders

Pul. 48–13 * truant river, as it w· eastward.

waneth

Un. 26–15 * But His mercy w· never,
26–17 God's power *never* w·,

waning

Mis. 312–18 * to restore the w· faith of many

want

Mis. 69–32 His w· of control over
250–27 door that turns toward w· and woe,
262–13 I w· to say, I thank you,
263–20 responsible for supplying this w·,
307– 7 more we do not w· :
351– 4 The fact is, that for w· of time,
355– 4 a full-orbed promise, and a gaunt w·.
365–17 form the common w·,
365–17 this w· has worked out a moral
Pul. 8– 7 Notwithstanding . . . the w· and woe
81–19 * have so much to give they w· no
No. 42– 7 to meet a mental w·.
'00. 11–17 I w· not only quality, quantity, and
'01. 29– 7 those who w· to help them.
My. 145–11 * said to me : "I w· to be let off
162– 2 question our w· of more faith
216–29 w· money for your own uses.
217– 1 You will w· it for academics,
281– 2 and awakened a wiser w·,
307–30 w· of divinity in scholastic

wanted

Mis. 178– 6 w· to become a God-like man.
348–24 I w· to satisfy my curiosity
Ret. 8– 7 to tell me what she w·.
9– 1 said that mother w· me.
38–20 to tell me he w· more,

wanted

Pul.	33– 6	* questioning if she were w·.
My.	80–25	* w· to give testimony
	80–26	* w· to hear it.
	138– 2	because I w· it protected
	215– 1	but nobody then w· C. S.,
	302–27	w· to greet me with escort
	324–27	* He said he w· to see if there was

wanting

Mis.	288– 8	and not be found w·,
	312– 4	we be not found w·.
	365– 6	Human theories . . . are found w· ;
My.	291–16	was not found w·.

wantonly

'01.	34–15	w· bereft of the Word of God.

wants

Mis.	67– 2	Above physical w·, lie the higher
	104–28	Who w· to be mortal, or
	365–25	met the growing w· of humanity.
Ret.	52–10	the broader w· of humanity,
No.	18–23	Good health and . . . are the common w· ;
	18–23	and these w· have wrought this
	19– 7	have never met the growing w· of
Peo.	12–23	application of its Principle to human w·.
My.	216–30	Contemplating these important w·,

War

Lovewell's

Ret.	3– 8	known historically as Lovewell's W·.

of 1812

Ret.	3–12	towards the close of the W· of 1812.

war

and oppression

My.	285–10	Bloodshed, w·, and oppression

beginning of

'02.	3–21	than the beginning of w·.

close the

Pan.	13–15	to close the w· between flesh and Spirit,
My.	18–23	to close the w· between flesh and Spirit,

divorce and

My.	268–11	Divorce and w· should be exterminated
	268–17	will eliminate divorce and w·.

ending of the

My.	281–22	* on the ending of the w·,

formidable in

Pan.	15– 3	will be as formidable in w· as

for the Union

Ret.	21–11	throughout the w· for the Union,

is waged

Ret.	56–12	W· is waged between the evidences of

learn

Mis.	xii– 6	"learn w· no more," — see Isa. 2 : 4.

make

My.	278– 5	may learn to make w· no more,

no more

My.	286– 4	that there be no more w·,

on religion

My.	234–24	a w· on religion in China

opposed to

My.	284–24	and religiously opposed to w·,

preventing

My.	286–12	for the purpose of preventing w·

refers to the

Pan.	14–28	refers to the w· between United States and

will end

My.	281–28	W· will end when nations are ripe for

with Spirit

Un.	36–14	as the flesh at w· with Spirit ;

Mis.	xii– 1	pioneer signs and ensigns of w·,
	2–29	beliefs that w· against Spirit,
	101– 8	C. S. and the senses are at w·.
	134–22	at w· with the omnipotent !
	172–26	Science, and the . . . senses, are at w· ;
	188–11	w· between the flesh and Spirit,
	217–23	that death is at w· with Life,
Pul.	2–16	w· between China and Japan
No.	6–26	at w· with the testimony of the
'00.	8–22	before we can successfully w· with
Hea.	15–15	at w· with this Mind,
Po.	27– 1	"Convulsion, carnage, w· ;
My.	93– 3	* in no wise at w· with society ;
	277– 2	chapter sub-title
	278–25	W· is in itself an evil,
	278–27	W· is not in the domain of good ;
	278–27	w· weakens power and must finally
	279–24	w· between Russia and Japan ;
	286– 2	chapter sub-title

wardrobe

Mis.	159–16	In this chamber is memory's w·,

wares

My.	151– 1	I am patient with the newspaper w·

warfare

all

Pul.	3–13	heavenly assurance ends all w·,

Christian

Mis.	40–26	In this Christian w· the student
	281–19	whatever . . . in the Christian w·
Ret.	44–23	which must always lie in Christian w·.

Christian's

Mis.	155–11	be valiant in the Christian's w·,

ends the

Mis.	102–30	outmasters it, and ends the w·.

inhuman

Peo.	11– 8	not by inhuman w·, but in

is not ended

Mis.	85–24	so long as . . . the w· is not ended

long

Mis.	215–24	they have a long w· with error

my

Mis.	180– 3	and strive to cease my w·.

no such

No.	23–22	no such w against Himself.

our

Mis.	139–10	weapons of our w· — II Cor. 10 : 4.
Pul.	12–23	in our w· against error,

perpetual

Mis.	56–17	mingling in perpetual w·

shadow of the

Pul.	20–15	type and shadow of the w· between

spiritual

Ret.	86– 1	energize wholesome spiritual w·,

theological

Pul.	51–18	* implements of theological w·,

this

'00.	10– 7	provided this w· is honest

unprecedented

Mis.	246–19	in this most unprecedented w·.

whole

Mis.	285–16	the whole w· of sensuality

Mis.	118–25	the w· with one's self is grand ;
My.	180–30	No w· exists between divine

warm

Pul.	9– 9	appliances w· this house,
	49–16	brought here in w· weather,
	63–13	brought here in w· weather,
Po.	10– 3	We proffer thee w· welcome
	46– 2	thy rosebud heart rests w·
	53– 9	More softly w· and weave
My.	68–18	* auditorium is of a w· gray,
	75–20	* and w· as the day was,
	124– 9	willing hands, and w· hearts,
	337– 5	We proffer thee w· welcome

warmed

Mis.	343–10	W· by the sunshine of Truth,
Pul.	9–10	w· also our perishless hope,

warmest

My.	189– 1	w· wish of men and angels.

warming

Mis.	316–23	w· marble and quenching volcanoes !
My.	268–28	heart of humanity w· and winning.
	291– 9	w· the marble of politics

warmth

Mis.	331– 8	w· and sunlight of prayer
	342– 5	their fading w· of action ;
My.	342– 1	* to the pleasant w· within

warn

Mis.	309–18	w· students against falling into the
Un.	57– 4	w· mortals of the approach of danger
My.	64–20	* Fearlessly does she w· all her

warned

Mis.	24–27	God w· man not to believe
No.	41– 3	w· the people to beware of

warning

Mis.	210– 8	placards w· people not to
	212–10	remember the reiterated w·
	254– 3	Should not the loving w·,
	301–17	without this word of w·
Man.	28–10	and the w· of Holy Writ :
Ret.	80–18	this w· will be within him
Pul.	15–15	and yet have given no w·.

warnings

'01.	18– 4	woeful w· concerning C. S.

warns

Ret.	73–19	w· you of "personality,"

warped

Mis.	75–19	if this term is w· to signify
Ret.	88–20	should not be so w· as to
No.	14– 1	neither w· nor misconceived,

warrant

Ret.	65–11	have no *w·* in the gospel
	75–24	There is no *w·* in common law
'02.	11– 7	awaits with *w·* and welcome,
My.	266– 5	under the *w·* of the Scriptures ;

Warren Street
My.	175–20	macadamize a portion of *W· S·*

war-rent
Po.	71–20	O *w·* flag ! O soldier-shroud !

warreth
Mis.	124– 8	which *w·* against Spirit,

warring
Pul.	83–29	* to *w·* men the Prince of Peace,
My.	40–15	* became divided into *w·* sects ;

warriors
Mis.	177–15	real and consecrated *w·* ?

wars
Mis.	102–28	Mortal thought *w·* with this
Ret.	47– 2	*w·* with Love's spiritual compact,
'00.	13–13	after a series of *w·* it was taken
My.	279–18	will . . . end *w·*, and demonstrate
	339–28	all that *w·* against Spirit

Wash. (State)
(see **Seattle**)

wash
Mis.	326–23	to *w·* their feet,
	398–20	Shepherd, *w·* them clean.
Ret.	46–26	Shepherd, *w·* them clean.
Pul.	7–16	and with power to *w·* away,
	17–25	Shepherd, *w·* them clean.
Po.	14–24	Shepherd, *w·* them clean.

washed
Mis.	153–13	*w·* in the waters of Meribah,
	246–11	would have *w·* it divinely away
	358–16	"*w·* in the blood of — see *Rev.* 7 : 14.
Un.	3–11	and have *w·* their robes white

washes
Peo.	9– 9	baptism of Spirit that *w·* our robes

washing
Pul.	27–22	* Mary *w·* the feet of Jesus,
Peo.	9– 4	*w·* away the motives for sin ;
My.	161– 3	*w·* the Way-shower's feet
	228–20	*w·* it clean from the taints of

Washington
D. C.
Mis.	304– 2	* 1505 PENNA. AVE., *W·*, D. C.
	306–15	* 1505 Penna. Ave., *W·*, D. C.,
Ret.	4– 9	Henry Moore Baker of *W·*, D. C.
Pul.	63– 1	* *The Republic, W·*, D. C.,
	89–19	* *Post, W·*, D. C.
My.	136–16	suit at law in *W·*, D. C.,
	199– 9	chapter sub-title
	203– 2	chapter sub-title
	311–25	When I was last in *W·*, D. C.,

Mis.	304–17	* It will return to *W·*
	304–19	* *W·* will be its home,
'00.	1–20	Philadelphia, *W·*, Baltimore,
My.	157–15	* National Library Building in *W·*

Washington (see also Washington's)
George
Mis.	305–30	* the inauguration of George *W·*
Ret.	2–25	death and burial of George *W·*.

Washington's
My.	148–12	February 22 — *W·* birthday.

waste
Mis.	127– 6	watering her *w·* places,
	200–21	and worse than *w·* its years.
Pul.	22–20	her *w·* places budded
	49–10	* and yet from a barren *w·*
My.	3–11	abroad in Zion's *w·* places,
	18– 3	watering her *w·* places,
	166– 6	Religions may *w·* away,
	223–15	not sufficient time to *w·* on them ;

waste-basket
My.	231–16	committed to the *w·* by

wasted
Mis.	127–30	kind word . . . is never *w·*.
	138– 4	The time . . . is worse than *w·*,
	324–25	only to find the lights all *w·*
My.	80– 7	* when *w·* unto death
	231– 9	sums of money, worse than *w·*.
	303–13	not *w·* in certain directions.

wasting
Mis.	230– 8	Three ways of *w·* time,

watch
Mis.	87–26	To *w·* and pray,
	98–14	to *w·* with eager joy the
	109–30	*W·* and pray for self-knowledge ;

watch
Mis.	110– 7	You need also to *w·*, and pray
	114– 7	teachers of C. S. need to *w·*
	114– 8	*w·* that these be not
	114–21	Scientists cannot *w·* too sedulously,
	117–21	*w·* that each step be taken,
	154–26	*W·* diligently ; never desert the post
	291–31	keeps not *w·* over his emotions
	315–17	*w·* well that they prove sound in
	335–23	when the Watcher bids them *w·*,
	342–29	they *w·* the market,
	343– 1	Let us *w·* and pray
	343– 3	*w·* their reappearing,
	356–30	Cherish humility, "*w·*," — *Matt.* 26 : 41.
	368– 9	* keeping *w·* above His own."
	387–13	not from those who *w·* and love.
	389–21	*w·* and pray.
Man.	16– 9	we solemnly promise to *w·*, and pray
	28–15	to *w·* and make sure that the
	40–12	should daily *w·* and pray
	83–17	*w·* well that they prove sound in
Un.	50– 6	We should *w·* and pray
Pul.	39–17	* I *w·* the flow Of waves of light.
No.	8–21	*w·*, and pray for the amelioration of
'00.	2– 8	"Work — work — work — *w·* and pray."
	15–27	*W·* ! till the storms are o'er
'01.	14–21	one must *w·* and pray
Po.	3– 8	*w·* thy chair, and wish thee here ;
	4–20	*w·* and pray.
	6– 8	not from those who *w·* and love.
	39–12	will *w·* to cleanse from dross
My.	61– 3	* To *w·* the transformation
	119–29	*w·* and pray for the spirit of Truth
	128–30	*W·*, and pray daily that
	130– 2	*W·* and guard your own thoughts
	143– 1	*W·* and pray that God directs your
	184–25	Love, holding unwearied *w·* over a
	193– 5	privilege remains mine to *w·*
	195– 8	to work more, to *w·* and pray ;
	213–20	*W·* your thoughts, and see whether
	232–14	I say unto all, *W·*." — *Mark* 13 : 37.
	232–28	does that *w·* accord with
	232–31	watching against a negative *w·*,
	233– 1	*alias,* no *w·*,
	233– 3	something to *w·* in yourself,
	233– 5	prevents an effective *w·* ?
	233– 9	instead of *putting out your w·* ?
	233–21	*w·* to know what his errors are ;
	233–23	*w·* against such a result?
	234– 4	I cannot *w·* and pray while
	254– 6	*W·*, pray, demonstrate,
	358– 5	"*w·* and pray, — *Matt.* 26 : 41.
	358–10	you need to *w·* and pray

watch-care
Ret.	6– 3	* especially entrusted to her *w·*,

watched
Mis.	1– 3	*w·* the appearing of a star ;
Ret.	89–20	he *w·* and guarded them
'02.	15–23	when the steadfast stars *w·*
Po.	18– 1	*w·* in the azure the eagle's
My.	232–10	he would have *w·*, — *Luke* 12 : 39.
	276– 3	Since Mrs. Eddy is *w·*,

Watcher
Mis.	335–23	when the *W·* bids them watch,

watcher
Mis.	117–27	of the more provident *w·*

watchers
Mis.	324– 1	His converse with the *w·*
	325–30	without *w·* and the doors unbarred !

watches
My.	276– 3	as one *w·* a criminal

watch-fires
'02.	16–15	Kindle the *w·* of unselfed love,

watchful
Mis.	12–15	unless one be *w·* and steadfast
	319–11	Scientists must be most *w·*.
	321– 1	*w·* shepherd chants his welcome
'01.	29– 6	*w·* and tender care
Po.	9– 1	glance of her husband's *w·* eye
My.	213–12	more *w·* and vigilant.
	257– 4	To-day the *w·* shepherd shouts
	280– 5	* your *w·* care and guidance
	331– 4	* Such *w·* solicitude as Mrs. Eddy

watchfulness
Mis.	115–16	constant *w·* and prayer
	116–23	*w·*, prayer, struggles, tears,
No.	33– 8	struggle, prayer, and *w·*

watching
Mis.	12–19	hence the need of *w·*,
	150– 3	Shepherd of Israel *w·* over you.
	276–13	assemblage found waiting and *w·*
	323– 9	working and *w·* for his coming.

watching
Ret. 23–15 I was waiting and *w·*;
Pul. 14–16 and *w·* for rest and drink.
'00. 9– 2 but, *w·* them, I discern
'01. 28– 4 praying, *w·*, and working
Po. 8–11 *w·* alone o'er the starlit glow,
47–17 *W·* the husbandman fled ;
My. 60–30 * if I would care to do a little *w·*
232– 9 chapter sub-title
232–27 If so-called *w·* produces fear
232–29 Can *w·* as Christ demands
232–30 should not "*w·* out" mean,
232–31 *w·* against a negative watch,
233– 1 gaining the spirit of true *w·*,
233–10 are you not made better by *w·*?
233–22 if this *w·* destroys his peace
254–12 reward . . . of *w·* and praying,

watchman
My. 221–27 like a *w·* forsaking his post,

watchmen
Mis. 368–29 tired *w·* on the walls of Zion,

watch-towers
Mis. 370– 9 sentinels of Zion's *w·*

watchword
Mis. 158–21 waiting for the *w·*
No. 44–27 must be the *w·* of Christianity.
My. 248– 3 Let your *w·* always be :

watchwords
Mis. 135– 5 Our *w·* are Truth and Love ;

water
as a flood
Pul. 14– 9 *w·* as a flood, — Rev. 12 : 15.
as a river
Mis. 373–10 *w·* as a river, that he might cause
baptizing with
Mis. 184–29 John came baptizing with *w·*.
bathes in
Mis. 203–14 Theology religiously bathes in *w·*,
bucket of
Mis. 353–16 to pour a bucket of *w·*
cold
Pul. 14–17 Give them a cup of cold *w·*
drop of
Pul. 4–18 A single drop of *w·* may help to
'02. 12–17 drop of *w·* is one with the ocean,
drunk on
Mis. 48–14 made a man drunk on *w·*,
first
My. 121–19 a diamond of the first *w·* ;
into wine
Mis. 74–17 he turned the *w·* into wine ;
Un. 11– 5 He turned the *w·* into wine,
living
My. 126– 7 such as drink of the living *w·*.
sweet
Mis. 27–18 sweet *w·* and bitter?" — Jas. 3 : 11.
this
Hea. 13–13 one teaspoonful of this *w·*
tumbler-full of
Ret. 33–16 in a tumbler-full of *w·*,
tumblerful of
Hea. 13–12 into a tumblerful of *w·*
walk on the
Mis. 359–18 until we can walk on the *w·*.
walk the
Mis. 359–15 to walk the *w·* was scientific,

Mis. 88–26 * had never seen *w·* freeze."
152– 3 in *w·* face answereth to — Prov. 27 : 19.
154– 8 *w·* it with the dews of heaven,
203– 9 in *w·* face answereth to — Prov. 27 : 19.
244–20 turn the *w·* into wine,
298–16 material rite of *w·* baptism,
345–25 baptism not of *w·* but of blood,
399–15 *w·*, the bread, and the wine.
Ret. 33–16 one teaspoonful of the *w·*
Hea. 10–26 hart panteth for the *w·* brooks,
Peo. 10– 3 steam is more powerful than *w·*,
Po. 75–22 *w·*, the bread, and the wine.

watercresses
Mis. 329–19 paddling the *w·*,

water-cup
Po. 39– 7 Rose from a *w·* ;

water-cure
Mis. 378–10 left the *w·*, en route for

watered
Mis. 343–10 *w·* by the heavenly dews of Love,
Ret. 95– 1 *w·* by dews of divine Science,

Waterhouse, Dr. Benjamin
Peo. 6– 2 Dr. Benjamin *W·* writes :

watering
Mis. 127– 5 *w·* her waste places,
My. 18– 2 *w·* her waste places,

water-mirrors
Mis. 330–15 shake out their tresses in the *w·* ;

water-pots
Pul. 27–15 * emblematic of the six *w·*

waters
bitter
My. 132–10 waters of Meribah here — bitter *w·* ;
come ye to the
Mis. 149– 1 come ye to the *w·*, — Isa. 55 : 1.
cool
Mis. 227–27 bathes it in the cool *w·*
Ret. 18– 3 Cool *w·* at play with the
Po. 63–10 Cool *w·* at play with the
deep
Mis. 393–14 Those who fish in *w·* deep,
Man. 18– 8 Although walking through deep *w·*,
Pul. 14–21 deep *w·* of chaos and old night.
'01. 26–14 I have passed through deep *w·*
Po. 51–19 Those who fish in *w·* deep,
life-giving
No. v– 9 are athirst for the life-giving *w·*
living
Mis. 207– 3 drink with me the living *w·*
Pul. 3–22 living *w·* have their source in God,
many
Pul. 11– 4 as the sound of many *w·*,
music of
Po. 41–15 music of *w·* had fled to the sea,
of Meribah
Mis. 153–13 washed in the *w·* of Meribah,
My. 132– 9 pass through the *w·* of Meribah
ritualistic
Mis. 81–15 the ceremonial (or ritualistic) *w·*
shall overflow
My. 17– 1 *w·* shall overflow the — Isa. 28 : 17.
shout
Po. 73– 6 When *w·* shout,
stagnant
My. 149–30 which waken the stagnant *w·*
still
Mis. 207– 1 "beside the still *w·*," — Psal. 23 : 2.
227–24 green pastures, beside the still *w·*,
322–15 "beside the still *w·*." — Psal. 23 : 2.
357– 8 rest beside still *w·*.
My. 129–26 green pastures beside still *w·*,
162–26 beside the still *w·*." — Psal. 23 : 2.
troubled
My. 152– 3 anchored its faith in troubled *w·*.
upon the
My. 247–25 cast your bread upon the *w·*
will be pacified
Pul. 14–24 The *w·* will be pacified,

Mis. 203–11 *w·* that run among the valleys,
Po. 70– 7 Making its *w·* wine,
My. 126– 4 pour wormwood into the *w·*

Waterville College
My. 304–14 Boston, Portland, and at *W· C·*,

Watt's "On the Mind and Moral Science."
My. 304– 8 *W·* "*O·* the *M·* and *M· S·*."

wave
Mis. 74–22 Walking the *w·*, he proved
211–14 rescued from the merciless *w·*
244–20 causing him to walk the *w·*,
257–25 in the death-dealing *w·*.
339–26 a *w·* that will some time flood
Ret. 60–15 C. S. saith to the *w·*
Pul. 13–18 above the drowning *w·*.
14–25 Christ will command the *w·*.
23–11 * *w·* of idealism that has swept
52–21 * *w·* of materialism and bigotry
'00. 7–22 the *w·* of earth's troubled sea,
'02. 20– 1 Christ walketh over the *w·* ;
Po. 15–22 cannot quench in oblivion's *w·*.
24–10 A *w·* of welcome birth,
41–22 that flowed as the *w·*,
73– 4 hoarse *w·* revisits thy shore !
73–16 By the "Rock" or *w·*,
My. 350–12 Thou the dark *w·* treading

waver
No. 7– 3 evil influences *w·* the scales

wavering
Mis. 263–21 poise the *w·* balance

waves
Mis. 23– 9 winds, and *w·*, obey this
74–17 He walked upon the *w·* ;
206– 5 Above the *w·* of Jordan,
313–19 field *w·* its white ensign,
397–11 'Gainst which the winds and *w·*
Pul. 18–20 'Gainst which the winds and *w·*

waves
Pul. 39–18   * I watch the flow Of w· of light.
No. 29–24   w· of sin, sickness, and death.
'01. 19–18   even the winds and w·,
Po. 2–18   w· kiss the murmuring rill
     8–15   starry hopes and its w· of truth.
   12–20   'Gainst which the winds and w·
My. 162–30   w· and winds beat in vain.
  189–10   go forth in w· of sound,
  226–12   commands the w· and the winds,
  232– 4   the waiting w· will weave
  291–24   w· over land and sea,

waving
Ret. 4–14   bending grain w· gracefully
Po. 68– 9   the sea and the tall w· pine

wavy
Mis. 329–15   weaving the w· grass,
Po. 67- 16   shade o'er the dark w· grass.

Way
Mis. 355– 1   chapter sub-title
Chr. 53– 8   And point the W·
  53–11   The W· in Science He appoints,
  53–41   The W·, the Truth, the Life
Un. 63– 3   The W·, the Truth, and the Life
'00. 7–16   Christ, the W·, the Truth, and the
My. 139–12   nearing the W·, the Truth, and the Life,
  260–28   the W·, in word and in deed,
  260–29   the W·, the Truth, and the Life.

way
after the
My. 285–25   after the w· which they— Acts 24 : 14.
all the
Mis. 39–16   alway"— all the w·.— Matt. 28 : 20.
  214–16   meant, all the w· through,
  251– 4   all the w· from the Pacific
  347–23   if it be uphill all the w·,
'01. 22–19   that one and one are two all the w·
  32–25   all the w· up to its preparation for
My. 109– 3   All the w· mortals are experiencing
along the
Mis. 109– 2   all along the w· of her researches
another's
Mis. 213–16   chastened and illumined another's w·
any
Mis. 79–30   which in any w· obligates you to
  115–29   if you in any w· indulge in sin ;
  132–27   * "If we have in any w· misrepresented
  138– 6   conforming to society, in any w·,
  228–21   or in any w· takes cognizance of,
  381–24   or in any w· or manner disposing of,
Ret. 87–18   never, in any w·, to trespass upon
My. 138– 8   not for my benefit in any w·,
  325–14   * Command me at any time, in any w·,
best
Mis. 236–17   best w· to overcome them,
My. 195–18   best w· to silence a deep discontent
better
'01. 21–23   Does this critic know of a better w·
demonstrate "the
Un. 55–10   demonstrate "the w·"— John 14 : 6.
divine
Ret. 54– 9   and learn the divine w·,
No. 12–20   This divine w· impels a
effectual
Mis. 263–19   met in the most effectual w·.
everlasting
My. 33–12   in the w· everlasting."— Psal. 139 : 24.
every
Pul. 80–10   * socially, indeed every w·,
My. 62–28   * to assist us in every w· possible ;
  212–27   by hindering in every w·
every step of the
My. 234–12   and guide them every step of the w·
general
Ret. 40– 2   and taught in a general w·,
My. 92–14   * has in a general w· been familiar ;
God's
My. 293– 8   believed that . . . was God's w·.
her own
My. 343– 4   * works around a question in her own w·,
His
My. 323–22   * to reveal to us His w·.
his
Mis. 113–16   commits his w· to God,
  129–19   will always find somebody in his w·,
  323– 7   Stranger wending his w· downward,
  324– 2   and he makes his w· into the streets
  326–30   groped his w· from the dwelling of
'01. 14–16   misleads the traveller on his w·
  17– 8   to meet the sad sinner on his w·
honorable
My. 277– 5   in a w· honorable and satisfactory
in Christian Science
My. 200–20   for you know the w· in C. S.

way
in divine Science
Mis. 358– 2   to mark the w· in divine Science.
in no
Mis. 97–12   It is in no w· allied to divine power.
Ret. 67–22   It was in no w· contingent on
in Spirit
Un. 55–13   "The w·," in Spirit, is— John 14 : 6.
interesting
My. 332–21   * in a most interesting w·.
in the
Mis. 197–10   in the w· which Jesus marked out
  208–18   in the w· of God's appointing.
  215–16   in the w· of His appointment,
  358–17   in the w· which Jesus marked out,
  400–23   In the w· Thou hast,
Ret. 14–28   in the w· everlasting."— Psal. 139 : 24.
Pul. 59–12   * in the w· peculiar to
Peo. 3–28   in the w· that our Lord has appointed ;
Po. 69–11   In the w· Thou hast,
My. 45–20   * to lead you in the w·,
  91–24   * despite the obstacles put in the w·
  93–12   * in the w· of gratifying the passions
in the flesh
Un. 55–11   "The w·," in the flesh, is— John 14 : 6.
I see the
Mis. 347–19   I see the w· now.
is narrow
My. 202–27   The w· is narrow at first,
its
Mis. 267–20   while the left beats its w· downward,
Un. 7–12   which had eaten its w· to the
No. 3– 6   foe who stands in its w·.
Po. vi– 1   * found its w· into print,
My. 112–29   has won its w· into the
  160–15   cuts its w· through iron
lead the
Mis. 389– 4   * point to heaven and lead the w·."
Po. 21–18   * point to heaven and lead the w·."
light the
My. 345–28   light the w· to the Church of Christ.
literal
Mis. 169–15   interpreted in a literal w·.
living
My. 191–25   lights the living w· of Life.
  192–12   lights the living w· to Life,
loiter by the
My. 11– 4   * stumble or loiter by the w·,
Love is the
'01. 35–10   Love is the w· alway.
make
Mis. 99–27   make w· for health, holiness,
mistaken
My. 211– 6   This mistaken w·, of hiding sin
mysterious
My. 205– 9   * "God moves in a mysterious w·
narrow
Mis. 245–28   the straight and narrow w· ;
  389–19   sweet secret of the narrow w·,
'01. 28– 6   enter the strait and narrow w·,
Po. 4–18   sweet secret of the narrow w·,
My. 104– 2   strait and narrow w· of Truth,
no
Ret. 82–18   This fact interferes in no w·
'01. 31–15   in no w· except in the interest of
My. 280–28   In no w· nor manner did I request
no other
Mis. 11–28   since they permit mo no other w·,
  185–15   no other w· under heaven
  234–10   in no other w· can we reach
Ret. 86–23   this manner and in no other w·
'00. 5–15   I see no other w·
My. 277– 7   no other w· of settling difficulties
novel
Mis. 139–24   in a circuitous, novel w·,
Pul. 59– 4   * in a somewhat novel w·.
obstructs the
Mis. 39–27   what most obstructs the w·?
  328–23   Whatever obstructs the w·,
of escape
Mis. 113–18   there is a w· of escape from
Pan. 12–14   the w· of escape from sin,
of healing
Mis. 244–23   w· of healing and salvation.
of Life
Un. 55–13   "the w·" of Life, Truth, — John 14 : 6.
No. 35–10   He who pointed the w· of Life
My. 191–25   lights the living w· of Life.
of salvation
Mis. 11–12   the sure w· of salvation,
  211– 3   Christ points the w· of salvation.
Pul. 70–22   * w· of salvation demonstrated by Jesus
No. 28–14   C. S. is the w· of salvation
'01. 28–22   is indeed the w· of salvation from all
My. 9–16   * w· of salvation through Christ."

way

of salvation
My. 37– 1   * w· of salvation of all men
    58–20   * demonstrable w· of salvation.

of talking
My. 343– 2   * She has a rapt w· of talking,

of the Lord
Mis. 246–24   the w· of the Lord,— *Matt.* 3 : 3.

of the transgressor
Mis. 261–14   w· of the transgressor— *see Prov.* 13 : 15.

of the unchristly
Pul. 21–23   Go not into the w· of the unchristly,

of Truth
Mis. 356–31   miss the w· of Truth and Love.
Un. 55–16   the life-giving w· of Truth.
My. 104– 2   strait and narrow w· of Truth.
    232– 6   even the w· of Truth and Love

of wisdom
My. 356–21   chapter sub-title

one
Mis. 220– 3   a good rule works one w·,
Ret. 86– 4   but one w· of *doing* good,
    86– 5   but one w· of *being* good,
Hea. 5–19   in one w· or another,

one's
Mis. 117–28   He illumines one's w·

opens a
Rud. 8–21   but opens a w· whereby,

open the
Mis. 317–29   divine Love will open the w·
My. 357–19   open the w·, widely and impartially,

opposite
Mis. 220– 3   a false rule the opposite w·.

other
Mis. 215–10   not seek to climb up some other w·,
No. 44– 9   To climb up by some other w·
Pan. 6– 4   never disappear in any other w·.
My. 152–15   or do I climb up some other w·?
    359–10   any other w· than through my

our
Mis. 215–18   infantile conception of our w· ;

out of the flesh
No. 33–26   show them that the w· out of the flesh,

paved the
My. 176– 6   the dear South paved the w·

perfect
'00. 14–16   perfect w·, or Golden Rule :

plain
Un. 9– 8   Jesus has made the w· plain,

pointing the
Mis. 327–23   the Stranger is pointing the w·,
No. 28–12   If Science is pointing the w·,

points the
'02. 6–24   metaphysics points the w·,

point the
Mis. 213– 7   point the w·, shorten the process,
    357–30   to help them and point the w·.
Ret. 85–19   God's finger to point the w·.

prepares the
My. 12–24   * God prepares the w· for

preparing the
My. 345–30   They are preparing the w· for us."

reveal "the
Mis. 308– 9   reveal "the w·,"— *John* 14 : 6.

right
Mis. 65–17   the right w· of treating disease?
My. 232– 6   The right w· wins the right

right of
My. 232– 6   wins the right of w·,

rugged
Mis. 398– 4   All the rugged w·.
Ret. 46–10   All the rugged w·.
Pul. 17– 9   All the rugged w·.
Hea. 19–24   along the rugged w·,
Po. 14– 8   All the rugged w·.
My. 201–24   All the rugged w·.

some
Mis. 236–26   in some w· or at some step
    300–19   liable, in some w·, to be printed
Ret. 1– 5   in some w· related to
    94– 4   At some period and in some w·
Un. 9– 6   some time and in some w·,

spiritual
'02. 10–20   finds the more spiritual w·,

that
My. 317–19   * wouldn't express it that w·."

their
Mis. 85–31   to learn their w· out of both
    265– 8   make mistakes and lose their w·.
    284–12   no danger of mistaking their w·.
    331– 3   committing their w· unto Him
    342– 4   their w· was material ;
    353–29   helping others, go their w·.
Ret. 16– 4   pushing their w· through the crowd
My. 355–24   their w· is onward,

way

the only
Mis. 60– 8   the only w· to destroy them ;
Ret. 73–17   This is the only w· whereby

thereto
'01. 35–18   Patient faith the w· thereto?

thine own
Mis. 328– 3   Make thine own w· ;

this
Mis. 347–15   One says, Go this w· ;
Ret. 24– 7   discovery came to pass in this w·.
Un. 9–10   but this w· is not the path of
My. 145–22   if in this w· I can serve
    360–21   in this w· God will bless

Thou hast
Po. 43–21   Just the w· Thou hast :

thy
Mis. 157– 6   He . . . will direct thy w·.
    157–22   "Commit thy w· unto— *Psal.* 37 : 5.
    268–32   "Commit thy w· unto— *Psal.* 37 : 5.
Pul. 53–13   * "Arise, go thy w· :— *Luke* 17 : 19.
Po. 29– 3   Pursue thy w·,
My. 170–23   Commit thy w· unto— *Psal.* 37 : 5.
    274–27   thy w· may be known— *Psal.* 67 : 2.

to escape
Mis. 105–11   showing us the w· to escape

to heaven
Mis. 268– 6   pointing the w· to heaven,
    344–27   point out the w· to heaven

to holiness
'01. 14–14   so hinder our w· to holiness.

treacherous
Po. 43–17   Rough or treacherous w·.

true
Ret. 94– 8   acknowledging the true w·,

Truth, is the
'02. 10–24   Truth, is the w·.

unfettered
Ret. 9–26   * her own unfettered w· !

unfolded the
My. 348–19   God unfolded the w·,

weary
Mis. 395–22   to shun my weary w·,
Po. 58– 7   to shun my weary w·,

wicked
Ret. 14–27   any wicked w· in me,— *Psal.* 139 : 24.
My. 33–11   any wicked w· in me,— *Psal.* 139 : 24.

'wildered
Po. 70–22   Shine on our 'wildered w·,

wisdom's
Po. 23–20   Guide him in wisdom's w· !

wise
Mis. 90–18   Break the yoke . . . in every wise w·.
My. 248–11   put an end to falsities in a wise w·

won the
My. 163– 4   won the w· and taught mankind

your
Mis. 117–31   Be sure that God *directs* your w· ;
My. 164–22   guiding, and guarding your w·

Mis. 39–25   *In what w· is a Christian Scientist an*
    64– 3   w· he made for mortals' escape.
    74–12   "the w·, the truth,— *John* 14 : 6.
    75– 2   Christ was "the w·;"— *John* 14 : 6.
    75– 3   Life and Truth were the w·
    96– 1   the w· of man's salvation
    132–15   * by the w·, from Mrs. Eddy, also."
    155–26   by w· of *The C· S· Journal*;
    323–22   The w· winds and widens
    359–23   The w· is absolute divine Science :
Un. 37– 1   declared himself "the w·'"— *John* 14 : 6.
    58–13   Christ as "the w·;"— *John* 14 : 6.
No. 7–11   and the w· out of it ;
No. 12–17   "the w·, the truth,— *John* 14 : 6.
'02. 2– 9   The Science . . . is on the w·,
    16–15   "I am the w·."— *John* 14 : 6.
Hea. 16–27   "I am the w·,— *John* 14 : 6.
My. 43–32   * The w· out of the wilderness
    72–28   * w· the Christian Scientists began
    81–20   * in a w· there was no mistaking.
    140– 3   a w· that they knew not ;— *Isa.* 42 : 16.
    257–16   "the w·, the truth,— *John* 14 : 6.
    292– 6   the w· pointed out,
    321– 3   * in a w· connected with your work,
    349–18   "the w·, the truth,— *John* 14 : 6.

wayfarer
Ret. 79– 9   signs for the w· in divine Science

waymarks
Mis. 213–15   so profit by these w·,
Ret. 27–11   valuable to me as w· of progress,

ways

and means
Mis. 66–17   God's perfect w· and means,
    98–11   in finding w· and means for
    153– 1   his material w· and means,

ways

and means
Mis. 204–17 human policy, w·, and means.
    212–13 human sense of w· and means
    215– 8 sense of God's w· and means,
    357– 3 w· and means of personal sense.
Ret. 52– 2 to find new w· and means
'01. 29– 5 providing w· and means for others.
My. 208–26 confidence in His w· and means
    253– 3 with the w· and means of the
God's
Mis. 102–17 God's w· are not ours.
    158– 3 God's w· are not as our ways ;
    215– 8 material sense of God's w·
Ret. 64–17 God's w· and works and thoughts
No. 21–18 because by it we lose God's w·
higher
Ret. 48–29 has led to higher w·, means, and
His
Mis. 361–32 His w· are not as our ways.
Rud. 10–26 acknowledge God in all His w·.
No. 18– 3 nor acknowledged God in all His w·.
My. 208–26 confidence in His w· and means
many
My. 84–28 * is notable in many w·.
mental
Pul. 15– 4 and expose evil's hidden mental w·
mighty
Un. 10–21 calculation of His mighty w·,
multitudinous
Ret. 50–10 shown me, in multitudinous w·,
of Christianity
Rud. 17–15 w· of Christianity have not changed.
of God
Ret. 31– 5 vindicating "the w· of God" — Job 40 : 19.
of living
My. 345–27 more etherealized w· of living.
other
'02. 10–29 in other w· than by walking
My. 277– 2 chapter sub-title
our
Mis. 158– 3 God's ways are not as our w· ;
    361–32 His ways are not as our w·.
self-destroying
Un. 55–16 self-destroying w· of error
social
My. 163–13 cannot show my love . . . in social w·
three
Mis. 230– 8 Three w· of wasting time,
Thy
Un. 5–28 parts of Thy w·," — see Job 26 : 14.
My. 229–27 Thy w· are not as ours.
thy
Mis. 175–32 remember God in all thy w·,
'01. 35– 1 In all thy w· acknowledge Him, — Prov. 3 : 6.
Peo. 12–12 acknowledge only God in all thy w·,
wisdom's
Ret. 90–25 walk steadfastly in wisdom's w·.
your
Mis. 236–14 follow God in all your w·,"

Mis. 78–14 * "w· that are vain"
    138– 5 wilderness or w· of the world.
    299–30 w·, means, and potency of Truth
My. 210–18 chapter sub-title

way-seeker
Pan. 12–19 w· gains and points the path.

Way-shower (see also Way-shower's)
Mis. 30–16 W· illustrated Life unconfined,
    162–19 He was the W·,
    206–28 understand and obey the W·,
    328–22 He . . . who follows the W·,
Man. 15–16 through Christ Jesus the W·
Ret. 26– 8 Our great W·, steadfast to the end
Un. 55– 9 He was the W·;
My. 4–10 how many are following the W·?
    19–25 Those words of our holy W·,
    140–22 God's W·, Christ,
    349–17 great W·, invested with glory,

Way-shower's
My. 161– 3 washing the W· feet

wayside
Mis. 99–32 Jesus taught by the w·,
    150–22 the w· is a sanctuary,
    163–10 and taught by the w·,
    337–26 by the w·, in humble homes,
    357–13 seeds of Truth fall by the w·,
No. 3–23 to sow by the w· for the way-weary,
Po. 47–16 Weary of sowing the w·
My. 185–12 by the w·, or in our homes.

wayward
Mis. 11–10 did not cease teaching the w· ones

way-weary
No. 3–23 to sow by the wayside for the w·,

weak
Mis. 227–15 w·, pitifully poor objects
    233–21 is a poor shift for the w· and worldly
    254–12 grows w· with wickedness
    262–18 strengthening the w·,
    288–10 A rash conclusion . . . is w· and wicked ;
    328–26 and strengthen the w·.
    345–15 * fit only for women and w· men ;"
    385–23 the flesh was w·, and doomed
Man. 55–15 this w· member shall not be
Pul. 4– 1 * "w· and infirm of purpose."
No. 44–17 w· hand outstretched to God.
'00. 10–20 individuals, w· provinces, or peoples.
'01. 2–11 may suit the w· or the worldly
    18– 4 w· criticisms and woeful warnings
Po. 48–18 the flesh was w·, and doomed
My. 287–12 poor shift for the w· and worldly.
    342–15 * not be understood that I mean w·,
    342–15 * for w· she was not.

weaken
Mis. 53–14 You only w· your power to heal
Hea. 13– 1 so w· both points of action ;

weakened
My. 227– 4 as one who never w· in his

weakens
'01. 15–10 The resistance to C. S. w·
My. 278–27 war w· power and must finally fall,

weakly
Po. 43–16 Beacon beams — athwart the w·,

weak-minded
Peo. 13–24 * fit only for women and w· men."

weakness
Mis. 10–21 their strength made perfect in w·,
    30–24 fossil of . . . w·, and superstition.
    64– 1 Jesus assumed . . . the w· of flesh,
    138–18 to know that human strength is w·,
    200–22 the touch of w·, pain, and
    206–13 scientific growth manifests no w·
    245–15 Their movements indicate fear and w·,
    252–13 sick thoughts are unreality and w· ;
    292–13 that brings to human w· might
    329– 4 a w·, or a — virtue?
    358–14 Human pride is human w·.
Un. 39–12 removes human w· by divine strength,
Rud. 9 8 will lead to w· in practice,
No. 45–10 indicates w·, fear, or malice ;
Po. 2–10 With all the strength of w·
My. 191– 7 Persecution is the w· of tyrants
    287– 8 giving to human w· strength,

weal
Mis. 65– 9 greater subject of human w·
Po. 3–11 Since first we met, in w· or woe
My. 36–28 * for the cause of human w·,
    213– 9 lurking foe to human w·,

wealth
Mis. 246– 8 to subserve the interests of w·,
    327–12 search for w· and fame.
Pul. 44–18 * chapter sub-title
No. 43–18 from mercenary motives, for w· and
'02. 17–21 to show man . . . the w· of love.
Hea. 16 7 w· and fame, or Truth and Love?
My. 84–18 * in numbers, w·, vigor,
    91–26 * even stranger is its increase in w·.
    252–28 allurements of w·, pride, or power ;
    265–29 w· should be governed by honesty,
    291–14 enfolded a w· of affection,

wealthy
Mis. ix– 7 among my . . . students few were w·.
Pul. 60–18 * gift of a w· Universalist
'02. 15–17 My husband, . . . was considered w·,
My. 97–18 * evidently w· congregation

weaned
'00. 11– 7 w· me from this love

weapon
Mis. 99–10 Fear is the w· in the hands of
Ret. 2–13 w· had been bestowed by

weapons
Mis. 139–10 w· of our warfare — II Cor. 10 : 4.
    204– 9 error yields up its w·
    351– 7 w· of the silent mental malpractice.
Pul. 84– 3 * with the w· of peace.

wear
Mis. 224–21 shall not w· upon our sensibilities ;
    303–16 If ever I w· out from serving
    340– 9 win and w· the crown of the faithful.
'00. 8–12 w· the purloined garment as his own,
My. 83–10 * Scientists frequently w· a small pin,
    339–23 only those . . . should w· sackcloth.

wearied

Pan.	13–25	Have I *w·* you with the mysticism
My.	196–21	lest ye be *w·* — *Heb.* 12 : 3.

weariness

Mis.	53– 8	*w·* and wickedness of mortal existence,
Man.	60–10	Amusement or idleness is *w·*.
Po.	35– 2	Beguile the lagging hours of *w·*

wearing

Po.	34–19	*W·* no earthly chain,

wearisome

Po.	32–20	comfort my soul all the *w·* day,
My.	189–19	fables flee and faith grows *w·*,

weary

Mis.	84–24	turn one, like a *w·* traveller, to
	85– 2	To the battle-worn and *w·*
	125–12	not stand waiting and *w·* ;
	144–18	great rock in a *w·* land :"— *Isa.* 32 : 2.
	153– 4	not *w·* in well doing."— *see Gal.* 6 : 9.
	155– 8	woo the *w·* wanderer to your door,
	159–26	*w·* wings sprung upward !
	208–14	to the *w·* and heavy-laden, rest.
	236– 7	*w·* with study to counsel wisely
	263–10	great rock in a *w·* land,"— *Isa.* 32 : 2.
	341–15	*w·* pilgrim, unloose the latchet of
	395–22	For joy, to shun my *w·* way,
Man.	60–11	rest the *w·* and heavy laden.
Ret.	33– 6	till I was *w·* of "scientific guessing,"
Pul.	14–15	*w·* wanderers, athirst in the desert
	20–19	great rock in a *w·* land."— *Isa.* 32 : 2.
	56–15	* hope and comfort to many *w·* souls.
Pan.	12–17	may run and not *w·*,
'02.	19–16	To the burdened and *w·*,
Hea.	2–10	* "I am *w·* of the world,
	2–11	* and the world is *w·* of me ;
	11– 8	*w·* of matter, it would catch the
Po.	vii–14	* *a balm to the w· heart.*
	34– 5	dear remembrance in a *w·* breast.
	41– 5	Where the *w·* and earth-stricken
	47–13	The *w·* of body and brain?
	47–14	*W·* of sobbing, like some tired
	47–16	*W·* of sowing the wayside
	58– 7	to shun my *w·* way,
My.	93–14	* rare lures for *w·* hearts,
	106–16	the winds would *w·*,
	150–13	never *w·* of struggling to
	182–27	rest their *w·* wings amid the
	254– 8	shall run and not be *w·*,
	355–24	their footsteps are not *w·* ;

weather

Mis.	198–31	suffered from inclement *w·*,
Pul.	49–16	brought here in warm *w·*,
	63–13	brought here in warm *w·*,
My.	275–20	Either my work, . . . or the *w·*,

weave

Mis.	99– 5	To *w·* one thread of Science
	228–18	to *w·* an existence fit for
	377– 2	to *w·* a web of words
Po.	53– 9	More softly warm and *w·*
My.	232– 4	waiting waves will *w·* for you

weaves

Mis.	390–15	The verdant grass it *w·* ;
Po.	55–16	The verdant grass it *w·* ;
My.	252– 6	*w·* webs that ensnare.

weaving

Mis.	329–15	*w·* the wavy grass,
My.	154–17	*w·* the new-old vesture

web

Mis.	145–27	woven . . . in the *w·* of history,
	377– 2	to weave a *w·* of words

webs

My.	232– 5	their winning *w·* of life
	252– 7	which weaves *w·* that ensnare.

Webster (*see also* Webster's)

Daniel

Mis.	345–18	Daniel *W·* said, "My heart has
Peo.	13–27	Daniel *W·* said : "My heart has

Mis.	68–21	According to *W·*, metaphysics is
Rud.	2– 1	definitions . . . as given by *W·*,
No.	9–27	according to *W·*, it is
Pan.	2–10	According to *W·* the word "pantheism"

Webster's

Pan.	2–12	*W· derivation* of the English word
'01.	3–10	*W·* definition of God,

wedded

Mis.	151–25	*w·* to the spiritual idea,
	276–22	*w·* to a purer, higher affection
	277– 1	is *w·* to their love,
	342–10	*w·* to a higher understanding
'00.	11– 7	*w·* me to spiritual music,
My.	269– 4	man *w·* to the Lamb,

wedding

'00.	15–19	a *w·* garment new and old,
My.	153–28	the *w·* of this Word to all

wedlock

Mis.	285–13	chapter sub-title
	297–19	voluntarily entered into *w·*,
My.	268–26	the Science of *w·*,

Wednesday

Man.	31–18	*W·* evening meetings.
	31–20	part of the *W·* evening services,
	47–23	at the *W·* evening meeting.
	90–11	on the first *W·* of December.
	96– 1	No *W·* Evening Lectures.
	96– 3	shall not appoint a lecture for *W·*
My.	79–24	* chapter sub-title
	134–21	* At the *W·* evening meeting

Wednesday Meetings

Man.	122– 1	heading

weds

Un.	17– 8	man thus *w·* himself with God,

weeds

Mis.	343–14	noxious *w·* of passion, malice, envy,
	343–20	*w·* of mortal mind are not always

week (*see also* week's)

Mis.	243–11	in less than one *w·*.
	350–14	convened in about one *w·*
Man.	90–12	will continue not over one *w·*.
Pul.	45–23	* *A w·* ago Judge Hanna withdrew
	60–13	* having remained over a *w·*
'00.	10–23	Only last *w·* I received a
'01.	11–18	and obeyed throughout the *w·*,
My.	25– 3	* special effort during the coming *w·*
	75– 4	* centre of the stage this *w·*.
	81–25	* fitting close to a memorable *w·*.
	82– 8	* crowding Boston the last *w·*
	97–26	* descended upon Boston . . . last *w·*
	97–30	* incidents witnessed during the *w·*

week-days

My.	90– 3	* Sundays or on *w·*

weekly

My.	152–31	sending to you *w·* flowers
	334– 9	* *w·* issue of the *C· S· Sentinel,*

week's

Mis.	135–14	Is it a cross to give one *w·* time

weeks (*see also* weeks')

Mis.	110–15	*W·* have passed into months,
	242–23	one ounce in two *w·*,
	243– 9	bandages to remain six *w·*,
	256–19	from one to two *w·* previous
	372– 8	In two *w·* from the date
	378– 4	in a few *w·* returned
Ret.	50– 7	lasting barely three *w·*.
'02.	15–21	Six *w·* I waited on God
My.	52–32	* *w·* lengthened into months ;
	66– 5	* During the past two *w·*
	74–28	* Within two *w·* we have had
	237– 3	in the *Sentinel* a few *w·* ago,

weeks'

Mis.	349– 5	included about . . . three *w·* time,

ween

Mis.	393– 6	Paints the limner's work, I *w·*,
Po.	51–11	Paints the limner's work, I *w·*,

weep

Mis.	170– 5	*w·* over the graves of their
	279– 6	and am too apt to *w·*
	279– 7	with those who *w·*,
Pul.	7–11	he would not *w·* over it,
'00.	8– 25	not Science for . . . the good to *w·*.
	13–16	promise to such as wait and *w·*.
Po.	67–13	Beside you they walk while you *w·*,

weepeth

Mis.	275– 8	where *w·* the faithful, stricken

weeping

Po.	9– 8	*w·* alone that the vision is fled,
My.	161–10	There shall be *w·* — *Luke* 13 : 28.

weigh

Mis.	47– 2	*w· over two hundred pounds*
	167–10	How much does he *w·*?
	280– 5	*w·* the thoughts and actions
	280–10	I would not *w·* you,
Ret.	71– 1	monuments which *w·* dust,
Pan.	14– 1	*w·* a sigh, and rise into

weighed

Mis.	5–28	*w·* down as is mortal thought
	280– 9	You have come to be *w·* ;
	280–10	nor have you *w·*.
	288– 7	and *w·* by spiritual Love,
	312– 3	*w·* in the scale of God
	365– 5	*w·* in the balances of God
Ret.	40–18	and *w·* twelve pounds.

wheat
My. 249–12 heat of hate burns the w·,
269–18 separating the tares from the w·.
316– 2 separated the tares from the w·,
wheels
Mis. 234– 3 clog the w· of progress.
235–22 start the w· of reason aright,
Rud. 17– 4 clogging the w· of progress
My. 145–20 keeps the w· revolving.
215–22 from clogging the w· of C. S.
288– 1 it starts the w· of right reason,
whence
Mis. 22– 6 W·, then, is it, if not from
23– 3 W· or what is the power back of
26–13 W· came the first seed,
26–14 W· came the infinitesimals,
37–19 mortal thought, w· cometh all evil.
66–17 w· to discern God's perfect ways
112– 3 not knowing w· they come,
116–14 tones w· come glad echoes
173–25 w·, then, is something besides Him
173–28 W·, then, is the atom or molecule
185–11 w· good flows into every avenue
218–12 w· to reason out God,
228– 6 standpoint w· to look upward;
233–31 w· we learn that sensation is not
235– 7 Mind w· sprang the universe.
289–31 w· they can choose only good.
316–26 w· they could have derived
324–30 w· he may hopefully look for
346–10 w· comes the evil?
387–23 W· joys supernal flow,
390– 2 W· are thy wooings, gentle June?
Un. 45–18 w· it telegraphs and telephones
Pul. 33–21 as to w· the stranger came
Rud. 11–23 w· emanate health, harmony
'00. 12–12 w· the Ephesian elders travelled
'02. 9–22 and knew not w· it came
Po. 6–18 W· joys supernal flow,
25– 2 W· the dewdrop is born,
55– 1 W· are thy wooings, gentle June?
My. 5–10 W·, then, came the creation of
62– 5 * W· did it come?
124–21 W· and whither?
180–31 the w· and why of the cosmos
256–22 and see w· they came
287–18 Mind w· springs the universe.
302– 7 corpse, w· mind has departed.
whenever
Mis. 11–20 w· opportunity occurs.
70–20 w· this word means the
138–24 but w· they are equal to the
169– 3 w· her thoughts had wandered
229– 3 w· there appear the circumstances
236– 8 counsel wisely w· giving advice
354–32 W· he soareth to fashion his nest,
383– 5 W· and wherever a church of C. S.
Man. 48– 3 But w· God calls a
80–17 W· a vacancy shall occur,
No. 8– 5 w· it can substitute censure.
1. 29–17 w· they return to the old home
99–13 * w· their form of religion
Whe Art Thou?
332–12 chapter sub-title Gen. 3:9.
ereas
is. 6–31 w·, in small families of one or two
34–13 w· spiritualism, so far as I
39–11 w· the Founder of genuine C. S.
47– 6 w·, substance means more than
62– 3 w·, the opposite image of man,
62–30 w·, "mind cure" rests on the notion
70–23 w· the body of the holy Spirit
0–20 w·, the spiritual sense of God
– 9 w· forecasting liberty and joy
–16 w·, they are by no means identical
4 W·, on March 20, 1895,
16 W·, The Massachusetts Metaphysical
5 W·, The material organization
W·, Other institutions for
W·, The fundamental principle for
W·, Mortals must learn to
w·, good is God ever-present,
w· the reverse is true in Science.
· Science reverses the testimony of
, evil *does*, according to belief,
the demonstration of God,
you may err in effort,
natter and human will,
od explains Himself in C. S.
erfect Love— *I John* 4:18.
ping a leader
discharged evidence of
sophy and so-called
l magnetism is the

whereas
My. 275–15 W· the fact that I am well
284–24 w· I do believe implicitly in
292–28 w· the human mind is a
whereby
Mis. 2– 1 w· we discern the power of
11–18 w· we love our friends;
17–20 w· man reflects the divine power
18–18 w· Father, Mother, and child are
28–18 w· he arose above the illusion of
29–29 w· matter is proven powerless
42–17 w· we meet the dear departed,
67–25 w· one expresses the sense of
79– 8 reflects all w· we can know God.
98– 2 w· to improve his present condition;
123–22 w· the just obtain a pardon for
127–21 condition w· to become blessed,
174–26 w· to gain heaven.
185–15 w· we can be saved,
194– 3 w· sin, sickness, . . . are destroyed;
202– 2 w· the sweet harmonies of C. S. are
252–15 w· any man can satisfy himself of
260–31 w· it may injure the race,
318– 3 wherein and w· the universal brotherhood
341–11 w· to arrive at the results of
342– 1 w· to enter into the joy of divine
364– 3 w· the sick are healed,
Man. 60–20 w· to exemplify our risen Lord.
Ret. 73–18 w· the false personality is laid off.
Un. 3–17 w· man is found in the image
8–18 same basis w· sickness is healed,
23–25 no sense w· to cognize evil.
55– 1 Jesus accepted the one fact w·
Rud. 8–22 w·, through will-power, sense may
11– 6 w· you learn that God is good,
No. 37–19 w· the work of Jesus would
Pan. 12–19 alterative agonies w· the way-seeker
'00. 5–15 w· to have one God,
'01. 7–14 w· we may consistently say,
10–22 w· good destroys evil,
16– 8 w· the demon of this world,
21–23 w· to benefit the race
25– 7 and w· is won the crown
34– 2 w· Christendom saves sinners,
'02. 6–16 w· the mortal concept and
8–24 w· man *is* Godlike.
Peo. 2–10 w· we learn that God, good,
3–27 w· we grow out of sin
9–25 w· we learn the great fact
My. 43– 6 * w· to order aright the affairs of
51–15 * w· to heal the sick
117–29 w· and wherein to show others
126–32 w· thought is *spiritualized*,
154–28 w· we are looking heavenward,
159–17 w· we reach our higher nature.
178– 5 w· the sick are healed
180– 1 w· man can prove God's love,
187– 9 w· to demonstrate the perfect man
232– 7 w· all our debts are paid,
238–18 w· the Science is reached
247– 4 w· man governed by his creator
254–26 w· man governed by his creator
267–27 w· soul is emancipate
277–16 w· wrong and injustice are righted
358– 8 w· the conflict against Truth
wherefor
Mis. vii–20 W·, have much to pay.
Un. 62–13 wherein and w· there is no evil.
wherefore
Mis. 9–25 w· our failure longer to relish
64–27 quite as possible to know w·
136–15 "W· come out from— *II Cor.* 6:17.
138–23 it is not so adapted . . . And w·?
326–31 "W· comest thou hither?"
351–22 w· it is hate instead of Love;
Chr. 53–25 Yet w· signalize the birth
'02. 7–28 called his disciples' . . . And w·?
10–19 W·, then, smite the reformer
Po. 34–15 Yet w· ask thy doom?
67– 9 w· the memory of dear ones
77– 6 Yet w· this Thy love?
My. 17– 4 "W· laying aside all— *I Pet.* 2:1.
17–14 "W· also it is contained— *I Pet.* 2:6.
189–30 W·, pray, the bell did toll?
190–30 w· vilify His prophets to-day
226–24 chapter sub-title
233– 5 Otherwise, w· the Lord's Prayer,
302–22 than others before me— and w·?
wherein
Mis. x– 2 life w· dwelleth peace,
9–10 W· is this conclusion relative to
10–23 w· old things pass away
11–18 w· and whereby we love our friends;
18–18 w· and whereby Father, Mother, and

weighed
Un. 29–21 w· or touched by physicality.
No. 18–13 when w· in the balance,
My. 291–16 w· in the scales of divinity,
weighing
Mis. 46–19 not w· equally with Him,
weighs
Mis. 119–16 w· mightily in the scale
293–12 w· in the scales of God
Rud. 9–18 w· against his healing power;
My. 277–18 Whatever w· in the eternal scale
weight
Mis. 46–17 to throw the w· of his thoughts
47– 3 *and carry about this w· daily?*
47–11 without consciousness of its w·?
255– 7 to throw the w· of thought and action
281–25 I felt the w· of this yesterday,
361–18 lay aside every w·,— *Heb.* 12:1.
372– 4 had not one feather's w·
Man. 59– 5 lose some w· in the scale of
Ret. 87–24 bear the w· of others' burdens,
95– 9 * For heavy is the w· of ill
No. 34–16 falls with its leaden w·
My. 146–30 He lays his whole w· of thought,
350–16 w· of anguish which they blindly
weights
Mis. 327–20 lay down a few of the heavy w·,
weighty
Mis. 227–11 to get their w· stuff into the
welcome
Mis. 18– 5 and w· these spiritual signs
206– 6 the Father and Mother's w·,
306– 7 * w· suggestions of events
321– 2 chants his w· over the cradle
Man. 59–15 The Leader's W·.
59–20 The Local Members' W·.
Ret. 6– 7 The needy were ever w·,
12– 2 Wake freedom's w·.
41– 2 contrasted with its present w·
Pul. 51–13 * w· others who have different
'01. 17– 9 and to w· him home.
'02. 2– 9 haste to meet and to w· it.
11– 7 awaits with warrant and w·,
20–25 good people w· Christian Scientists.
Po. 10– 3 We proffer thee warm w·
24–10 A wave of w· birth,
41–23 to w· the murmur it gave?
60–27 Wake freedom's w·,
My. 24– 8 * inspires you to w· all mankind
42–20 * affords me great pleasure to w·
52–12 * w· the fact of the spreading
72– 6 * open wide in w· to nobility.
74–27 * and as such they are w·.
154–23 I w· the means and methods,
170–12 *Beloved Brethren:*— W· home!
170–13 W· to Pleasant View,
257– 4 watchful shepherd shouts his w·
290–22 w· you where no arrow wounds
313–31 not w· in my father's house.
337– 5 We proffer thee warm w·
welcomed
Mis. 251– 8 has w· you to Concord
311– 3 Christian Scientists will be w·,
Pul. 51–22 * compromises have been w·.
'02. 1–20 be w. and sustained.
My. 86– 1 * is doubly w·.
99– 8 * is w· within our midst
173–20 my heart w· each and all.
188–22 heart of a Southron has w· me.
welcomes
Man. 59–16 w· to her seats in the church,
My 133– 2 w·, many pardons for the penitent.
346– 4 * w· it as another opportunity for
welcoming
Man. 59–14 w· STRANGERS.
My. 21–21 * w· their brethren from far and near,
66–25 * w· her children and giving
welding
Pul. 56–16 * W· Christianity and Science,
welfare
Mis. 152–14 for the w· of her children,
228– 4 whose w· thou hast promoted,
315–16 to look after the w· of his students,
Man. 45–11 strive to promote the w· of all
Ret. 72– 4 To disregard the w· of others
82–21 ease and w· of the workers.
90–22 w· and happiness of her children
Pul. 21–19 not indifferent to the w· of any one.
50– 1 * to promote the w· of
82–26 * upon which depends the w· of
My. 10–30 * their own individual w· is closely
10–31 * general w· of the Cause.

welfare
My. 11–13 * result in our w·.
280– 6 * solicitude for the w· of the nations
325– 3 * called to inquire of his w·
well
Mis. vii– 2 * To read it w·;
vii– 5 * thy w· made choice of friends
5– 1 This work w· done will elevate
9– 5 W· is it that the Shepherd of Israel
25–25 omniscience means as w·, all-science.
33–10 as w· as in the manhood of God,
33–28 for sickness, as w· as for sin,
36– 7 Beasts, as w· as men,
38–26 *to be healed by it and keep w·*
42–18 proves to have been w· done,
51– 2 physically as w· as spiritually,
54–17 *Must I study . . . in order to keep w·*
69–18 In one hour he was w·,
70– 9 belief, was removed, the man was w·.
71– 2 *when I am not entirely w· myself?*
72–23 as w· as the material universe,
84– 2 as w· as by speaking, the whole truth.
96–19 from sickness as w· as from sin.
110–21 We may w· unite in thanksgiving
111– 3 work, w· done, would dignify angels.
115–31 of your own as w· as of others' sins.
122–25 "W· done, good and— *Matt.* 25:23.
124–20 It is w· that C. S. has taken
130–21 should know w· whereof he speaks.
136–18 You can w· afford to give me up,
143–19 w· known physicians, teachers,
153– 4 not weary in w· doing."— *see Gal.* 6:9.
156– 8 It is w· at headquarters,
175– 6 may w· be likened to the
184– 7 in body as w· as in mind.
192–13 w· knowing the omnipotence of
216–14 "laying on of hands," as w·.— *Heb.* 6:2.
218–29 "Pretty w·, I thank you!"
219–23 and immortal Mind makes w·;
220– 6 "You are w·, and you know it;"
220–15 "I am w·, and I know it."
224– 4 W· may we feel wounded by our
226– 7 clergyman's son returned home— w·.
238–20 Let one's life answer w· these
241– 6 as w· as sin of every sort.
242–24 leaving the patient w·.
248–27 C. S. . . . made me w·,
249–11 w· known that I am not a spiritualist,
249–13 as w· as my intimate acquaintances.
252–20 physically, as w· as spiritually,
253–12 * chapter sub-title
255–23 for sickness, as w· as for sin,
265–24 Those who abide by them do w·.
269–27 w· knowing the willingness of
273–12 as w· as the better part of
273–31 more than one person can w· accomplish.
275– 7 it were w· to lift the veil
280–14 we imagine all is w· if we
283–19 as w· as its morals and Christianity.
284– 2 each one to do his own work w·,
288–21 as w· as thine own,
290–19 knew that this person was doing w·,
315–18 watch w· that they prove sound
326–24 W· might this heavenly messenger
333–12 in matter as w· as Spirit?
334– 5 Astrology is w· in its place,
344– 4 "Very w·," the teacher replied;
347–32 is w· paid by the umpire.
354–27 strength for a flight w· begun,
355– 7 the acme of "w· done;"— *Matt.* 25:21.
365–20 spiritual, as w· as physical, effects
378– 5 returned apparently w·,
380– 5 as w· as governs the universe,
Man. 28–17 perform the functions . . . w·.
32–20 They shall . . . be w· educated.
63–18 provided these rooms are w· located.
64– 1 shall be w· educated,
83–17 watch w· that they prove sound
90–18 lessons by a w· qualified teacher
Ret. 21–13 It is w· to know, dear reader,
24–15 discovery how to be w· myself,
33– 6 as it has been w· called.
34–12 all sickness, as w· as sin,
40–11 dressed herself, and was w·.
65–27 As w· expect to determine,
67–21 collective as w· as individual.
79– 1 against . . . the human race as w· as
81–14 so apparent as to be w· understood.
85– 2 doing their own work w·.
86– 9 Note w· the falsity of this
91– 5 utterance may w· be called
Un. 23– 9 How w· the Shakespearean tale
28– 9 As w· might you declare
Pul. 9– 5 tasks are done— w· done
9– 9 It was w· that the brother

well

Pul. 13–15 serpent of sin as w· as of sickness !
25– 2 * cooling . . . as w· as heating
36– 8 * Europe as w· as this country.
46–25 * as w· as looking into the
48– 1 * w· placed upon a terrace
48–29 * as w· as the hero who killed the
51–19 * is very w· known.
59–17 * w· adapted for its purpose,
61–16 * practical as w· as poetic,
62– 2 * w· and favorably known
62– 7 * economy of space, as w· as
63– 8 nourish trees as w· as souls,"
66–17 * w· suited to satisfy a taste
71–19 * It is w· known that Mrs. Eddy
72–18 * yet have been perfectly w·."
Rud. 1–12 misapprehension, as w· as definition.
15–20 w· assimilate what has been taught
No. v– 5 as w· as voluntary error.
3–17 to keep himself w· informed.
9–11 God will w· regenerate
19– 2 spiritual, as w· as physical,
28–15 I consider w· established.
28–16 present, as w· as the future,
42–28 Here a skeptic might w· ask
'00. 2–27 W·, all that is good.
12–23 It were w· if we had a St. Paul
'01. 7–19 as w· as infinite Person,
9–30 worketh w· and healeth quickly,
13– 9 not w· to maintain the position
13–10 w· that we take possession of
21– 2 understanding, and works as w·.
28–24 w· to know that even Christ
'02. 3–14 It is w· that our government,
Hea. 8– 7 sickness as w· as sin,
Peo. 2–28 nations as w· as individuals,
7– 3 on the body as w· as on history
10–10 It were w· if the sister States
10–16 divine as w· as human.
11– 6 disease as w· as sin ;
Po. vi–23 * *as w· as many poems*
27–20 Thy work is done, and w· :
My. v–10 * w· for earnest . . . Scientists to
24–28 * as w· as this can be done
30– 5 * w· over thirty thousand people
40–32 * as w· as by her teachings,
41–29 * for our sakes as w· as for her own ;
45– 3 * as w· as in the ultimate
46–25 * Bible and our textbook, as w· as
52– 6 * as w· as her instructions,
59– 9 * as w· as of healing,
62– 2 * "W· done, good and — *Matt.* 25 : 23.
66–15 * so w· situated for church purposes
69– 1 * church is unusually w· lighted,
75– 1 * we cannot w· withhold our
90–17 * readily grasped by sick or w·.
97– 5 * making the patient w·.
97– 6 * w· without the use of medicine.
98–26 * might w· be proud.
108– 2 succeeds as w· in healing his cases
124–13 "w· done" — *Matt.* 25 : 23.
134–11 work w· done should not be eclipsed
145–16 * "I am as w· as I ever was."
158–22 Most men and women talk w·,
162–21 "W· done, good and — *Matt.* 25 : 23.
180–21 in justice, as w· as in mercy,
187– 2 spiritually as w· as literally,
190–32 It were w· for the world if
202–13 "W· done, good and — *Matt.* 25 : 23.
207–21 "W· done, thou good and — *Matt.* 25 : 21.
215– 3 knew w· the priceless worth of
222–20 It is w· that thou canst unloose
225– 4 "W· done, good and — *Matt.* 25 : 23.
227–16 consider w· their ability to cope with
246– 7 must be w· educated
252– 9 you do to yourselves as w·,
256– 6 strict observance or note w·.
261–11 guarding and guiding w· the
264– 4 kind enough to speak w· of me
268–31 *man* meaning woman as w·,
275–15 Whereas the fact that I am w·
302–14 It is a fact w· understood
307–10 that word, as w· as other terms
318–20 He held himself w· in check
319–26 * These dates are very w· fixed
323– 1 * what Mr. Bates has so w· written
330–19 * as w· as by Wilmington newspapers
345–10 * "W·, electricity, engineering,
355–12 to religion as w· as to politics,

well-behaved

My. 93– 9 * the intelligent, and the w·.

well-being

Mis. 170–20 no more important to our w·
Rud. 12–20 requisite for the w· of man.
My. 81– 2 * air of w· and of prosperity

well-born

Pul. 48–26 * many another w· woman's.

well-bred

'01. 30–29 * honest, sensible, and w· man

well-conducted

My. 175–15 w· jail and state prison,

well-defined

My. 301–21 w· instances of the baneful

well-doing

My. 3– 5 demands w· in order to

well-dressed

My. 95–17 * w· body of people.
97–17 * w·, good-looking, eminently

well-earned

My. 47–20 * w· joy that is with us now.

well-equipped

My. 319– 9 and w· scholarship.

Wellesley College

Un. 6–20 though a graduate of W· C·,

well-established

Pul. 51–16 * will affect the w· methods.

well-informed

My. 309– 2 a w·, intellectual man,

welling

Mis. 1–12 w· up from infinite Truth
Ret. 80–19 w· up into unceasing spiritual
My. 186–11 w· up from the infinite

well-kept

Pul. 49–27 * to-day a strikingly w· estate
My. 277– 9 and sound, w· treaties.

well-known

Pul. 72–14 * a number of w· physicians.
My. 145–20 w· fact makes me the servant of

well-mannered

Mis. 275–28 The servants are w·,

well-meaning

Pul. 80–21 * caused an army of w· people
'01. 29–12 because w· people sometimes

well-nigh

My. v–25 * revealed God to w· countless
318– 2 w· constituted a new style of

well-to-do

My. 87– 8 * congenial, quietly happy, w·,
93– 8 * save the moderately w·,

well-tried

Mis. 200–25 calm of Paul's w· hope

wending

Mis. 323– 7 w· his way downward,

went

Mis. 30–28 "There w· up a mist — *Gen.* 2 : 6.
61–15 * I w· once to a place where
153– 6 w· forth before His people,
162–30 like him he w· forth, simple as
163– 3 he w· about doing good.
180–13 my heart w· out to God,
208–22 I w· astray : — *Psal.* 119 : 67.
242–30 if she w· without it twenty-four hours
279–17 They w· seven times around
327– 1 When I w· back into the house
370– 5 they w· away and took counsel
375–19 * I w· on to study each
Man. 17– 2 w· into deliberations over forming a
18– 8 little Church w· steadily on,
Ret. 8– 6 w· to her, beseeching her
8–21 w· to my mother, and once more
13–20 if I w· to Him in prayer,
16–13 Many pale cripples w· into
16–13 who w· out carrying them
19– 5 I w· with him to the South ;
38–23 while this w· on.
40– 8 I w· to the invalid's house.
89–10 they w· for liturgical worship,
93– 1 Jesus w· about doing good.
Pul. 6–19 * I w· with my husband,
6–20 * He w· out under the auspices
33–22 * or whither he w·
36–15 * w· to her peculiarly fatigued.
60– 3 * new order . . . w· into operation.
Hea. 11–22 as matter w· out and Mind came in
Peo. 13–21 his pure faith w· up through
My. 45–19 * Him who w· before you
76– 1 * it w· without saying that the
117– 3 "What w· ye out for — *Matt.* 11 : 8.
302–28 w· alone in my carriage
313–24 I never w· into a trance
320–25 * w· into matters of detail
343–22 * she w· on,

wept

Mis. 386–22 She that has w· o'er thee,
Ret. 9–12 Afterward I w·, and prayed
14–30 the oldest church-members w·.
Pul. 7–11 as he w· over Jerusalem !
Po. 50– 7 She that has w· o'er thee,
71–16 Ye who have w· fourscore
My. 119–13 Mary of old w· because

Wesley

Pul. 28–23 * Robertson, W·, Bowring,

West

My. 74– 2 * from abroad and from the far W·
193– 6 work for all, from East to W·,
241–13 * from a Christian Scientist in the W·,
323– 7 * by some minister in the far W·.

west

My. 63–28 * "from the w·, — *Psal.* 107 : 3.

Westerly, Rhode Island

Ret. 40– 5 Lyceum Club, at W·, R· I·.

Western and western

Mis. 275–26 wonder of the w· hemisphere.
276– 4 like all else, was purely W·
My. 74– 1 * w· sections of this country.
197–13 ready hands of our far W· students,

Western States

Pul. 89–23 * heading

Westminster Catechism

Ret. 10– 6 as with the W· C· ;

wet

Po. 27–18 with bright eye w·,
My. 326–16 where with w· eyes the Free Masons

whate'er

Mis. 392–10 W· thy mission, mountain
Po. 20–14 W· thy mission, mountain
28– 8 W· the gift of joy or woe,
79– 5 peace is thine, W· betide.

Whateley's Logic

My. 304– 8 book title

whatever (*see also* **whate'er**)

Mis. 8–19 W· purifies, sanctifies, and
10– 4 W· envy, hatred, revenge
10– 6 w· these try to do,
12–26 W· manifests aught else in its
26– 2 w· is of God, hath life
33– 2 W· is wrong will receive its
33–16 had no faith w· in the Science,
40–18 discord of w· sort.
71–21 W· is humanly conceived
71–30 W· is real is right and eternal ;
89–26 from itself, from w· is false.
102–24 W· seems material,
115–27 w· tends to impede progress.
119–16 w· or whoever opposes evil,
121–17 w· belittles, befogs, or belies
147–21 abhor w· is base or unworthy ;
183–13 w· is possible to God, is possible to
190–22 impersonal evil, or w· worketh ill.
198–29 w· seems to punish man for
199–17 w· denied and defied their
216–14 W· his *nom de plume* means,
228–21 W· man sees, feels, or
236–28 w· else may appear,
236–29 and at w· cost.
249– 5 drug had no effect upon me w·."
259– 3 W· appears to be law,
260–19 w· else seemeth to be intelligence
281–18 So, w· we meet that is hard
281–28 w· may come to you, remember the
288–32 W· intoxicates a man,
289– 5 in w· form it is made manifest.
290–10 since w· is false should disappear.
292–17 w· is unlike the risen, immortal Love ;
300–30 pays w· he is able to pay
309–19 w· is connected therewith,
328–23 W· obstructs the way,
329– 3 a satisfaction with w· is hers.
329–18 W· else droops, spring is gay :
334– 8 W· simulates power and Truth
348–19 I use no drugs w·,
367– 9 w· is wrongfully-minded will
367–28 would say that w· saves from sin,
374– 7 w· rebuked hypocrisy
Man. 43– 9 W· is requisite for either
Ret. 32– 5 learned that w· is loved materially,
47–10 C. S. shuns w· involves material
56– 5 W· diverges from the one divine Mind,
56–21 W· else claims to be mind,
59–15 W· errs is mortal,
65–18 to avoid w· follows the example of
Un. 22–16 W· exists must come from God,
22–19 W· cometh not from . . . Spirit,
24–25 W· matter thus affirms is
25–10 w· it appears to say of itself is
28–19 W· cannot be taken in by mortal mind
54–12 To admit that sin has any claim w·,
Pul. 21–16 shun w· would isolate us from
50–26 * and w· is likely to
57–13 * W· may be thought of the peculiar
57–14 * w· difference of opinion
65– 9 * w· attitude Rome may assume
73–23 * She placed no credit w· in the
Rud. 9–28 w· militates against health,
13– 4 W· saps, with human belief,
16–17 W· is said and written correctly
16–26 snatch at w· is progressive,
No. 7–22 draw no lines w· between
16– 5 w· He knows is made manifest,
24– 5 He is extension, of w· character.
27– 4 is in reality no claim w·.
37–25 w· is unlike God ;
45– 8 to ostracize w· uplifts mankind,
Pan. 10–27 W· promotes statuesque being,
11–22 w· strips off evil's disguise
14– 1 nature of w· is unlike good,
'00. 4–24 w· is real must proceed from
10–19 w· sways the sceptre of self
11– 9 w· turns mortals away from
14– 8 w· is spoken of in the Scriptures.
15– 1 you purchase, at w· price, a
'01. 13–21 conquers him, in w· direction.
22–27 receive no sense w· of it.
31–25 held fast to w· is good,
'02. 1–15 W· seems calculated to displace
9–30 W· enlarges man's facilities
Hea. 6–20 w· manifestation we see.
My. 4–31 W· is not divinely natural
12–22 W· needs to be done
52–21 * "W· is to be Mrs. Eddy's future
74–31 * W· opinions we may entertain
87–27 * w· one's special creed may be,
90– 7 * W· else it is, this faith is real
107–25 w· is entitled to a classification
128–27 w· the shaft aimed at you
128–31 evil suggestions, in w· guise,
154–30 take it in w· sense you may.
158–17 w· manifests love for God
180–12 no element w· of hypnotism
220– 1 W· changes come to this century
250–27 w· is done in this direction
271–24 * w· their religious beliefs,
277–18 W· weighs in the eternal scale
278–30 W· brings into human thought
285– 8 W· adorns Christianity
294–11 would rebuke w· accords not with
296– 4 w· hinders the Science of being.
299–12 w· portions of truth may be found
301–26 or affect . . . in any manner w·.
321–14 * that he has ever said anything w·

whatsoever

Mis. 54–23 not . . . to any disease w·,
66– 6 "W· a man soweth, — *Gal.* 6 : 7.
105–29 "W· a man soweth, — *Gal.* 6 : 7
119–31 w· ye would that men — *Matt*
128– 6 w· things are true, — *Phil.* 4
128– 7 w· things are honest, — *Phil*
128– 8 w· things are just, — *Phil.*
128– 8 w· things are pure, — *Ph*
128– 9 w· things are lovely, —
128– 9 w· things are of good
135– 1 marching under w·
146–18 "W· ye would th
235–28 w· ye would th
348– 4 w· a man sow
Man. 42–23 w· ye would
69–10 w· she ma
Ret. 87–20 "W· ye
94– 5 that w·
94– 7 w· se
94–10 con
94–19 w·
No. 31–28
32– 9
Hea. 5–2
My. 6– 5
41–1
266–

whe

Ret. 7
71–
My. 111–11
124–30

wherein

Mis.	27–13	natural science, w· no species ever
	46–29	w· man is perfect even as the Father,
	57–31	Mind that is God, w· man is
	108–19	w· evil seems as real as good,
	113– 2	w· is no darkness.
	121– 7	w· Spirit and matter, good and evil,
	123–24	w· sinners suffer for their own sins,
	124–21	w· to muse His praise,
	150–18	w·, . . . Scientists may worship
	153–16	w· violence covereth men as a
	155–18	and less w· to answer it
	182–27	w· man and his Maker are inseparable
	190– 6	w· the mortal evolves not the
	190– 8	w· man is coexistent with Mind,
	203–20	w· mortals gain severe views of
	227–21	w· calm, self-respected thoughts
	227–23	a life w· the mind can rest
	262– 2	w· it is permitted to enter,
	286–14	w· they neither marry nor are
	318– 3	w· and whereby the universal
	319– 1	w· the true sense of the unity of
	330– 6	w· no arrow wounds the dove
	354–24	w· all is controlled, not by man
	361–29	w· Principle and idea, God and man,
	362– 4	w· God and man are perfect,
Ret.	49– 8	hour has come w· the great need
Un.	21– 2	mental processes w· human thoughts
	42–26	w· the mortal does not develop the
	42–27	w· true manhood and womanhood
	51– 1	w· man is the reflection of
	62–13	an ideal w· . . . there is no evil.
No.	21–16	w· the human and divine mingle
	21–26	w· Principle heals and saves.
	25– 5	w· we were held ; — Rom. 7 : 6.
	30–20	light w· there is no darkness,
	36–22	w· there is no consciousness of
Pan.	7–20	w· theism seems meaningless,
'02.	2–21	w· Christ is Alpha and Omega,
	6–29	w· God is infinite Love,
	15–12	w· the connection between justice and
	17–16	w· joy is real and fadeless.
Peo.	11–11	w· man cooperates with . . . his Maker.
My.	6–15	temple w· to enter and pray.
	25–25	w· all vanity of victory disappears
	117–30	w· to show others the footsteps
	118– 6	w· the remedy is worse than the
	129–24	harmony w· the good man's heart
	154–28	w· . . . we are looking heavenward,
	187– 9	perfect path w· to walk,
	208–19	w· to gather in praise and prayer,
	234– 8	every hour w· to express this love
	239– 4	primitive proof, w· reason,
	247– 4	w· and whereby man
	254–25	w· and whereby man governed by
	267–26	w· and whereby soul is emancipate
	357– 5	w· matter has neither part nor portion,

whereof

Mis.	vii–19	W·, I've more to glory,
	21– 8	w· C. S. now bears testimony.
	66– 5	the genius w· is displayed in
	88–14	critic who knows w· he speaks.
	130–22	know well w· he speaks.
	132– 2	on a subject the substance w·
	139–24	wisdom w· a few persons
	154–14	even that vine w· our Father
	172–18	the evidences w· are taken
	195–16	premises w· are not to be found in
	251–15	w· our Master said :
	252–31	w· our Master said,
	296–31	but knew w· he speaks,
	350– 4	the workings w· were not
Man.	17–16	chief corner stone w· is,
	42–17	Christ w· the Scripture
	52–12	that w· he is accused
Un.	10–19	w· God is the Alpha and Omega,
	23–13	w· all are partakers,—Heb. 12 : 8.
	23–17	w· they are confessedly
Pul.	7– 4	w· this city is the capital.
Pan.	2– 4	who know w· they speak
'00.	12– 3	the spiritual import w·
	14–13	the name w· signifies
'01.	27–11	the basis w· cannot be traced to
	28– 6	w· our Master said,
My.	131– 9	the bread of heaven w·
	188–11	the Psalmist sang,
	244–15	w· David sang,
	285–24	w· they now accuse me.—Acts 24 : 13.

whereon

Mis.	128– 2	uncomfortable w· to repose.
	225–21	sofa w· lay the lad
	341–16	place w· thou standest
	395–17	The turf, w· I tread,
Man.	75–17	the land w· they stand,
Pul.	1–16	This spot w· thou troddest

whereon

Pul.	20– 1	land w· stands The First Church
'02.	14– 5	the land w· it stands.
Po.	44– 4	W· they may rest !
	58– 2	The turf, w· I tread,
My.	69– 8	* w· are placed inscriptions

whereout

Mis.	150–19	halls . . . wherein, as w·,

wheresoever

Pul.	21–24	but w· you recognize a
My.	19–31	W· this gospel shall be— Mark 14 : 9.

whereto

Mis.	397–19	w· God leadeth me.
Chr.	55– 2	w· their number corresponds.
Ret.	85–16	no position w· you do not
Pul.	19– 3	w· God leadeth me.
Po.	13– 7	w· God leadeth me.
My.	14– 1	"prosper in the thing w· — Isa. 55 : 11.

whereunto

Po.	35–11	Hushed in the heart w· none reply,
My.	201– 2	w· divine Love has called us

whereupon

Mis.	225– 9	w· the mother, . . . bore testimony to
My.	328–24	* w· application for license was

wherever

Mis.	256–26	W· law is, Mind is ;
	277–32	I rebuke it w· I see it.
	306– 3	* accompany the bell w· it goes.
	336–24	w· one ray of its effulgence
	383– 6	w· a church of C. S. is established,
Pul.	86–21	* contributors w· they may be,
Pan.	13–12	condemnation of all error, w· found.
My.	18–20	condemnation of all error, w· found.
	19–19	follow us in the sunlight w· we go ;
	81–28	* w· two or more of them are met
	185–11	w· thought, felt, spoken, or
	257–30	W· the child looks up in prayer,

wherewith

Mis.	9– 2	w· mortals become educated to
	10– 2	w· to obstruct life's joys
	19–18	w· to cover iniquity,
	104–32	w· to overcome all error.
	155–30	w· divine Love has entrusted us,
	176–28	divine energy w· we are armored
	380–21	evidence w· to satisfy the sick
Un.	34–10	summary of the whole matter, w· we
Pul.	2–13	of the house w·
	21– 3	love w· Christ loveth us ;
No.	39–19	love w· He loves us.
Hea.	3– 2	w· to heal both mind and body ;
	9–19	w· to make himself wicked.
My.	205– 4	liberty w· Christ hath— Gal. 5 : 1.
	212–11	w· to do evil ;
	212–13	w· to complete the sum total of sin.
	214–22	no monetary means left w· to

whether

Mis.	25–32	w· in philosphy, medicine, or
	48– 9	w· of ignorance of fanaticism,
	120– 9	w· of sin unto death,— Rom. 6 : 16.
	224–31	w· there is enough of a flatterer,
	239– 3	judge for yourself w· I can talk
	261–10	w· intentionally or ignorantly ;
	264–21	w· those be correct or incorrect.
	290–25	w· it be friend or foe,
Man.	110–10	w· of applicants, approvers, or
Ret.	82– 3	chord remains unchanged, w· we
Un.	44–17	w· expressive or not expressive
Pul.	7– 9	I wonder w·, were our dear Master
	66–25	* w· some of the pre-Christian ideas
No.	43– 6	w· stall-fed or famishing,
Pan.	14–20	w· in camp or in battle.
Hea.	0–17	w· that ideal is a flower or
Po.	68–22	w· near or afar.
My.	213–20	w· they lead you to God
	227–19	w· successful or not,
	342–13	* w· blue-gray or grayish brown,
	343– 7	w· my successor will be
	346–23	* as to w· she had in mind
	358–15	w· or not they shall publish

whichever

Mis.	221–28	w· might serve as the
My.	117– 4	W· it be, determines the

while

Mis.	xi– 8	W· no offering can liquidate
	2–32	W· we entertain decided views
	3–22	w· the supreme and perfect Mind,
	21– 6	w· on earth and in the flesh,
	26–11	even w· the Scripture declares
	42–23	w· the latter is real and
	49–12	w· acknowledged and notable
	66–20	and Truth be enthroned, w·
	70–26	w· our Lord would soon be rising
	103– 5	w· the other is eternal,

while

Mis.	103–32	*w·* his personality was on earth
	108–30	*w·* declaring that they have no
	110–20	*w·* leagues have lain between us.
	117–19	*w·* participating in the movements,
	126–13	ordeal refines *w·* it chastens.
	148– 1	*w·* he meditates evil against us
	155–10	*W·* pressing meekly on,
	162–12	*w·* the central point of his
	183–23	*w·* it shames human pride.
	184– 2	claiming that God is Spirit, *w·* man
	187– 8	*w·* discord, as seen in disease
	200– 9	*w·* God was the only substance,
	204–10	*w·* white-winged peace sings
	214– 2	*W·* Jesus' life was full of Love,
	215–31	*w·* the corn is in the blade,
	219–19	*w·* in the other he must change
	219–24	*w·* immortal Mind makes saints ;
	219–26	*w·* one person feels wickedly
	221–26	*w·* ten times five are not
	222– 5	*w·* injuring himself and others.
	222–30	*W·* the ways, means, and potency of
	223– 7	*w·* impure streams flow from
	223–17	*w·* doing unto others what
	224–30	*w·* it is a question in my mind,
	228–11	*w·* seeking to raise those barren
	238–29	*W·* I accord these evil-mongers
	240–17	*w·* the sturdy oak, with form
	252–13	*w·* healthy thoughts are reality
	256– 7	*W·* gratefully acknowledging the
	256–23	*w·* every quality of matter
	259–11	*w·* iniquity, too evil to
	259–25	*w·* error, or evil, is really
	263–29	*w·* they quote from other authors
	267–19	*w·* the left beats its way downward,
	267–29	*w·* disobedience to this divine Principle
	288–17	*w·* Science indicates that it *is not.*
	295–12	*W·* praising the Scotchman's
	302– 6	*w·* the perverter preserves in his own
	310–13	*W·* my affections plead for all
	324– 8	a little *w·*, and the music is dull,
	352–31	*w·* sickness must be covered with the
	363–11	*w·* the immortal modes of Mind
	368–26	But *w·* the best, perverted,
	369–10	*w·* we are strong in the unity of
	369–13	*w·* the leaders of materialistic
	375–12	* Years ago, *w·* in Italy,
	376–26	*w·* the lower lines of light kindled
	378– 1	*w·* the author of this work
Man.	47–24	*W·* members of this Church
	79– 8	*W·* the members of this Committee
Ret.	17– 1	*w·* visiting a family friend
	17– 5	*w·* I worship in deep sylvan spot,
	17–17	*W·* palm, bay, and laurel,
	18– 4	*W·* cactus a mellower glory receives
	38–23	*w·* this went on.
	49–12	*w·* in human growth
	65–21	*w·* it demonstrates the power of Christ
	68–11	One is false, *w·* the other is true.
	75– 7	*w·* appropriating my language and ideas,
	80–25	*w·* innocence strayeth yearningly.
	90– 5	*w·* he is serving another fold
Un.	6–25	*w·* the platoons of C. S. are
	11–27	*w·* ye say, There are yet four months,
	21– 3	mean *w·* accusing— *Rom. 2 : 15.*
	27–14	*w·* God is *egoistic,*
	46– 6	*w·* ours is man's man.
Pul.	7–21	*w·* their tabernacles crumble
	21–14	*W·* we entertain due respect
	28– 4	* *w·* the star of Bethlehem shines down
	29–20	* *w·* all these injunctions
	34– 5	* In 1866, *w·* living in Lynn, Mass.,
	44–11	* *W·* we all rejoice,
	48– 2	* *w·* they themselves are in
	50–24	* opposition . . . keeps up a *w·*,
	51–19	* *W·* it has done this, it may,
	67–21	* *w·* in many towns and villages
	79– 7	* *W·* we are not, ... devotees of
	81–22	* *w·* her own soul plays upon
	82–16	* *w·* the Jews themselves have
	83– 2	* *w·* we recklessly promise as lover
	84– 6	* *w·* side by side, equal partners in
	87–15	*w·* I fully appreciate your
Rud.	3– 1	*w·* mortals love to sin,
No.	3– 4	*w·* the trespassing error
	8–26	*w·* you walk on in equanimity,
	13–26	*w·* other parts of it have no
	19–16	*W·* material man and the
	20– 6	*w·* Truth is moulding a
	29–24	*w·* Truth walks triumphantly
	36– 7	even *w·* mortals believed it
	36–28	*w·* the divine and ideal Christ
	42–15	*W·* Science is engulfing error
	43–27	*w·* envy and hatred bark
Pan.	3– 1	*w·* pantheism suits not at all
	4–14	*w·* God is incapable of evil ;

while

'01.	14– 4	*w·* the Pharisee's self-righteousness
	24– 9	*w·* descanting on the virtues of
	29– 4	*w·* he was providing ways and means
'02.	1– 9	*w·* our branch churches are
	1–20	*W·* C. S., engaging the
	11–29	*w·* to-day Jew and Christian can
	15– 9	*w·* dependent on the income from
	20–23	*w·* gratefully appreciating the
Hea.	2– 5	*w·* it reasons with the storm,
	5– 2	*W·* admitting that God is omnipotent,
	12– 4	*W·* the matter-physician feels the
	13–26	*w·* it is supposed to cure
	20– 6	* vie with Gabriel, *w·* he sings,
Peo.	3–17	*w·* it inscribes on the thoughts
	6–12	* *w·* nature cures the disease.''
	11–19	*w·* the body, obedient to
Po.	v–10	* *was written w· the author*
	vii– 1	* *w· visiting a family friend*
	26– 8	*W·* Justice grasped the sword
	30–19	*W·* sacred song and loudest breath
	46–17	*W·* beauty fills each bar.
	62– 5	*w·* I worship in deep sylvan spot,
	63– 1	*W·* palm, bay, and laurel,
	63–12	*W·* cactus a mellower glory
	67–13	Beside you they walk *w·* you weep,
	70–18	The *w·* the glad stars sang
	78–14	O meekest of mourners, *w·* yet
My.	12–24	*w·* that which can be done
	38– 4	* *w·* we thank you and renew the
	51– 8	* *w·* we feel that she has not
	52– 2	* *w·* she had many obstacles
	52– 8	* *w·* we sincerely acknowledge
	52–11	* *w·* we realize the rapid growth,
	56–15	* For a *w·* it seemed that there
	61–13	* but after a *w·*, in the night,
	67–22	* *w·* vaster sums of money
	69–22	* *w·* in the basement is a
	70–14	* *w·* the chimes were being tested
	82– 6	* For a *w·* this morning it looked
	90–13	* *w·* health-seeking is the door
	94–20	* *W·* the dedicatory services
	149–29	*w·* those with a mighty rush,
	152–27	*w·* God, the divine Principle
	171–20	* *W·* on her regular afternoon drive
	186–22	*w·* they are yet speaking,— *Isa. 65 : 24.*
	194– 8	*w·* a silent, grand man or woman,
	204–27	*w·* returning good for evil,
	214–19	*w·* taking no remuneration for my
	220–10	even *w·* you render
	225– 2	*w·* the loyal at heart
	227–12	dies *w·* the others recover,
	234– 4	I cannot watch and pray *w·*
	246–19	*W·* revising "S. and H.
	282– 4	*W·* I admire the faith and friendship
	291–23	*W·* our nation's ensign of peace
	291–24	*w·* her reapers are strong,
	291–29	*w·* they work for their own country,
	306–29	*w·* I was his patient in Portland
	311– 3	*W·* I was living with Dr. Patterson
	312–19	*W·* on a business trip to Wilmington,
	320–20	* *w·* I was in your Primary class
	330–17	* *w·* on business in 1844,
	334–18	* *w·* being called unreal.
	334–22	* *w·* the Pharisee's self-righteousness
	335–15	* *W·* at Wilmington, N. C.,
	341–10	*w·* The bird of hope is singing
·	343–16	*w·* healing the sick.
	349– 5	*w·* disease is a mental state or error

whilst

My.	331–29	* *w·* recounting the kind attention

whine

Mis.	210– 7	Do men *w·* over a nest of serpents,

whining

Mis.	119– 5	and then *w·* over misfortune,

whirlwind

Mis.	51–23	* Shall, like a *w·*, scatter
Un.	10–25	God was not in the *w·*.
Po.	18–19	He rides on the *w·*

whisper

Mis.	119– 1	If malicious suggestions *w·* evil
	144–18	to *w·* our Master's promise,
Pan.	3– 8	to *w·*, "Solitude is sweet."
'02.	20– 6	*w·*, "No drunkards within,
Po.	10–14	List, brother ! angels *w·*
	66– 8	*w·* of one who sat by her side
My.	192–27	*w·* to you of the divine
	337–15	List, brother ! angels *w·*

whispered

Mis.	99–30	it is *w·*, "This is Science."
'02.	15–29	*w·* that name to my waiting hope
My.	62– 7	* *w·* : "Dear God, may I not

whisperers
 Mis. 368–21 these words . . . "*w*," and — *Rom.* 1 : 29.
whispering
 Mis. 269–30 heard the great Red Dragon *w*
 Ret. 9–21 * *w* woods, where dying thunders
 18– 6 nestling alder is *w* low,
 Po. 15–11 *w* voices are calling away
 63–15 nestling alder is *w* low,
whispers
 My. 128–10 and *w* to the breeze
whit
 My. 38–19 * not a *w* behind their elders,
Whitcomb
 E. Noyes
 Man. 102–15 Albert Metcalf and E. Noyes *W*
 Mr.
 My. 63– 2 * services of Mr. *W* as builder
 Mr. E. Noyes
 My. 16–19 * and Mr. E. Noyes *W*,
White, James T.
 Mis. 394–22 * signature
 395– 1 poem
 Po. 57– 8 * signature
white
 Mis. 124–22 adore the *w* Christ,
 212–22 and Love, the *w* Christ, is the
 238– 1 * helped 'niggers' kill the *w* folks !"
 313–19 field waves its *w* ensign,
 320–29 *w* stone in token of purity
 329– 7 taking up the *w* carpets
 398–19 *W* as wool, ere they depart,
 Chr. 53–38 now blends In seven-hued *w* !
 Ret. 32– 2 bearing on its *w* wings,
 46–25 *W* as wool, ere they depart,
 Un. 3–11 washed their robes *w*
 12– 1 fields are already *w* for the harvest ;
 51– 7 never make one hair *w* or black,
 Pul. 1– 5 promise clad in *w* raiment,
 17–24 *W* as wool, ere they depart
 25–22 * The floor is in *w* Italian mosaic,
 26– 3 * centre being of pure *w* light,
 26–23 * mosaic marble floor of *w*
 37– 8 * although her hair is *w*,
 42–15 * each of them wore a *w* satin badge
 42–22 * with a centre of *w* immortelles,
 42–27 * with ferns and pure *w* roses
 42–28 * large basket of *w* carnations
 76–11 * furniture frames are of *w* mahogany
 76–13 * upholstery is in *w* and gold
 77– 6 * plush casket with *w* silk linings.
 78–21 * Attached by a *w* ribbon to the
 78–23 * encased in a *w* satin-lined box
 82– 2 * brain for its great *w* throne.
 No. 41–17 *w* sanctuary will never admit such
 Peo. 9–10 *w* in the blood of the Lamb ;
 14– 6 smiling fountains, and *w* monuments.
 14– 9 * *w* fingers pointing upward."
 Po. 2–18 *w* waves kiss the murmuring rill
 14–23 *W* as wool, ere they depart,
 78– 3 Peace her *w* wings will spread
 My. 69–13 * pure *w* marble was used,
 83– 7 * tiny *w*, unmarked buttons,
 202– 1 May its *w* wings overshadow
 202– 2 overshadow this *w* temple
 259– 4 I have named it my *w* student.
white-haired
 My. 342– 3 * became aware of a *w* lady
 342– 7 * Older in years, *w* and frailer,
White Mountain Church
 My. 184– 7 chapter sub-title
White Mountain House
 My. 314–32 proprietor of the *W* *M* *H*,
White Mountains
 My. 184–11 built First Church . . . at the *W* *M*.
whiteness
 Mis. 393–24 To thy *w*, Cliff of Wight.
 Po. 52– 8 To thy *w*, Cliff of Wight.
white-robed
 Peo. 5–18 *w* thought points away from
Whiteside, Florence
 My. 323–14 * signature
white-winged
 Mis. 172– 9 *w* charity, brooding over all,
 204–10 *w* peace sings to the heart
 262–23 through this *w* messenger,
 331–12 *w* dove feeds her callow brood,
 369–21 *w* charity that heals
 396–22 wake a *w* angel throng
 Pul. 18– 6 wake a *w* angel throng

white-winged
 Po. 12– 6 wake a *w* angel throng
 24–21 Send us thy *w* dove.
 My. 275–26 *w* charity brooding over all,
whither
 Mis. 158–22 revelation of what, how, *w*.
 Man. 94– 2 the city *w* he is called
 Ret. 90– 7 towns *w* he sent his disciples ;
 Pul. 33–22 * or *w* he went
 '02. 2– 2 this daystar, and *w* it guides.
 9–22 whence it came nor *w* it tended,
 Po. 34– 6 But *w* wouldst thou rove,
 My. 124–21 Where art thou? Whence and *w* ?
 256–22 whence they came and *w* they tend.
 307–28 drifting *w* I knew not.
 350–11 poem
 350–23 *w* shall he flee?
whithersoever
 Mis. 327– 4 follow thee *w* thou goest."
Whiting
 Lilian
 Pul. 40– 5 * signature
 Miss
 Pul. 39–10 from my friend, Miss *W*,
Whittier
 Mr.
 Pul. 54–29 healed Mr. *W* with one visit,
 ————
 Pul. 28–24 * selections from *W* and Lowell,
 53–25 * *W*, grandest of mystic poets,
 My. 12–19 *W* mourned it as what
whoever
 Mis. 54– 7 That one, *w* it be,
 113–11 *W* is mentally manipulating
 119–16 whatever or *w* opposes evil,
 131– 1 *W* challenges the errors
 266– 6 *W* does this may represent
 283–30 *W* is honestly laboring to
 347–32 *w* hits this mark is well paid
 371–19 *W* desires to say,
 Pul. 75– 1 *W* in any age expresses
 Pan. 9–16 *W* demonstrates the highest
 My. 3–22 genuine, *w* did it.
Whole
 Mis. 16–21 God is a divine *W*, and *All*,
whole (noun)
 Mis. 102–14 God is not part, but the *w*.
 166–25 until the *w* shall be leavened
 171–24 *till the w was leavened. — Matt.* 13 : 33.
 252–19 to the *w* and not to a portion ;
 289–14 act as a *w* and per agreement.
 317–15 the *w* of the Scriptures
 Ret. 67– 3 not the *w* of error.
 Un. 6– 1 *w* is greater than its parts.
 Pul. 50–26 * No . . . holds the *w* of truth,
 Rud. 2–22 *Is healing the sick the w of Science?*
 No. 4– 7 the *w* of mortal existence,
 Pan. 2–16 * conceived of as a *w*,
 Hea. 19– 3 not in part, but as a *w* ;
 My. 165–17 portion of one stupendous *w*,
 236–11 Too much . . . spoils the *w*.
 269–12 * parts of one stupendous *w*,
whole (adj.)
 Mis. 11–13 my *w* duty to students.
 18–27 those of the *w* human family,
 38– 7 our *w* system of education,
 39–20 Truth to leaven the *w* lump.
 51–24 * *w* dark pile of human mockeries ;
 84– 2 by speaking, the *w* truth.
 96–22 It brings . . . a *w* salvation.
 98–12 helping the *w* human family ;
 167–22 dominion over the *w* earth ;
 175 4 until the *w* sense of being
 194–13 for the *w* human race.
 224–24 to cover the *w* world's evil,
 229–23 until the *w* human race
 265–19 the *w* line of reciprocal thought.
 268–15 His *w* inquiry and demonstration
 285–16 the *w* warfare of sensuality
 293–22 includes the *w* duty of man :
 330–30 grass, inhabiting the *w* earth,
 334–10 *w* fabrication is found to be a lie,
 341– 2 When will the *w* human race have
 370– 3 and be *w* !" — *Jas.* 12 : 13.
 Man. 44–26 God requires our *w* heart,
 Ret. 31–20 keep the *w* law, — *Jas.* 2 : 10.
 Un. 6– 4 the *w* human race will learn
 34– 8 *w* function of material sight
 34–10 summary of the *w* matter,
 36–10 This *w* subject is met and
 54– 9 In order to be *w*,
 Pul. 4– 8 and therefore *w* number,
 9–19 who, . . . is a very *w* man

whole (adj.)

Pul.	48–10 * coloring of the w· landscape
	53–14 * faith hath made thee w·."— Luke 17 : 19.
	53–16 * the w· law of human felicity
	54– 5 * And we are w· again.
	54–14 * w· transaction was in perfect obedience
	81–13 * spends her w· time helping others.
	84– 2 * shall subdue the w· earth
No.	15– 7 blessings for the w· human family.
	29–20 he is made w·.
'01.	1– 9 nearer the w· world's acceptance.
	32–21 is the w· duty of man.
'02.	12– 4 settles the w· question
Hea.	8–14 then it is willing to be made w·,
Peo.	5–27 * if the w· materia medica
	10–16 battles for man's w· rights,
	12–22 demonstrated . . . God's w· plan,
	14–13 put on the w· armor of Truth ;
My.	28–31 * changed the w· aspect of medicine
	59– 5 * should leaven the w· lump,
	80– 8 * they had been made w·,
	114–29 the w· lump of human thought
	132–30 whose w· head is sick
	132–31 and whose w· heart is faint ;
	146–30 his w· weight of thought,
	152– 6 faith hath made thee w·."— Matt. 9 : 22.
	153– 7 have come to fulfil the w· law.
	196–13 to bridle the w· body."— Jas. 3 : 2.
	208– 4 seem as if the w· import of C. S.
	208–20 prayer for the w· human family.
	269– 1 w· universe included in one infinite
	297–20 an inspiration to the w· field,
	329–22 * when the w· country is recognizing
	363–23 gist of the w· subject

(see also world)

wholeness

Un.	5– 4 understanding . . . the w· of Deity,

wholesome

Mis.	283–13 Any exception to the old w· rule,
	369–24 that w· but unattractive food.
Ret.	86– 1 energize w· spiritual warfare,
No.	42– 4 w· avowals of C. S.
My.	277– 8 by means of their w· tribunals,
	282–10 w· chastisements of Love,

whole-souled

Mis.	224–32 to offend a w· woman.

wholly

Mis.	14–28 therefore, w· problematical.
	16– 8 requisite to become w· Christlike,
	16–24 awakened consciousness is w· spiritual ;
	34–12 They are w· apart from it.
	37–26 Her time is w· devoted to
	46–28 thought has not yet w· attained unto
	53– 3 false claim can be w· dispelled.
	91–11 bond is w· spiritual and inviolate.
	140– 3 hold a w· material title.
	165– 7 a w· spiritual idea of God
	167– 6 He is w· symmetrical.
	171– 3 first effort . . . was not w· successful ;
	177–16 give yourselves w· and irrevocably
	197– 9 unless this be so, no man can be w·
	198– 1 w· governed by the one perfect Mind,
	295–20 not w· represented by one man.
	344–17 would place Soul w· inside of body,
Man.	92–10 C. S. heals the sick quickly and w·,
Ret.	37– 7 book is indeed w· original,
	78–15 w· Christlike and spiritual.
Un.	4–27 the vision of sin is w· excluded.
	5–23 w· or partially differ from them as to
	10– 2 w· separates my system from all others.
	23–21 anything so w· unlike Himself
	49–14 So long as . . . I cannot be w· good.
Pul.	28– 1 * designed to be w· typical of the
	69–18 * w· from the spiritual . . . standpoint.
Rud.	7–16 material evidence being w· false.
No.	23– 9 could not have been w· evil,
	36–10 w· opposed to the popular view
'00.	13–26 * seems not to have been w·
'01.	8–20 is he not w· spiritual?
Hea.	6–23 may be w· unknown to the
	11– 5 w· apart from the dream.
My.	5– 7 W· apart from this mortal dream,
	49– 4 * w· drawn over, as by
	53– 5 * that her duty was w· done,
	59–11 * accepted w· or in part
	84– 9 * until it be w· free from debt.
	130– 4 w· disloyal to the teachings
	134– 3 a heart w· in protest
	205–23 w· apart from human hypotheses,
	224–28 any literature as w· C. S.
	238–10 His language and meaning are w·
	293–23 regarded as w· contingent on
	315– 8 * being w· on his part ;

wholly

My.	349–31 W· hypothetical, inductive
	357– 1 w· apart from C. S.,
	357–16 on a w· spiritual foundation,

whoso

Mis.	65–30 "w· sheddeth man's— Gen. 9 : 6.
	335–30 w· departeth from divine Science,
Hea.	1– 8 w· builds on less than

whosoever

Mis.	52– 7 W· understands the power of
	195– 5 W· learns the letter of C. S.
	195– 7 w· hath the spirit without the
	211–22 "W· will save his life— Matt. 16 : 25.
	235–14 w· shall not be offended— Matt. 11 : 6.
	265–12 W· understands a single rule
	277– 7 W· proclaims Truth loudest,
	308– 4 W· looks to me personally
	337–13 W·. . . shall humble himself— Matt. 18 : 4.
	344–25 "W· shall not receive— Luke 18 : 17.
Chr.	55–23 w· shall do the will— Matt. 12 : 50.
	55–28 w· liveth and believeth— John 11 : 26.
Ret.	31–19 "W· shall keep the— Jas. 2 : 10.
	32– 7 w· will save his life— Matt. 16 : 25.
	38–28 W· learns the letter of this book,
	45–20 "W· shall smite thee— Matt. 5 : 39.
	63–18 W· covers iniquity
No.	13– 8 "W· liveth and believeth— John 11 : 26.
Pan.	9–12 "W· liveth and believeth— John 11 : 26.
'00.	9–22 W· attempts to ostracize C. S.
'01.	11–22 W· saith there is no sermon
	22– 2 w· demonstrates the truth of these
My.	180– 3 W· understands C. S.
	227–27 "W· shall smite thee— Matt. 5 : 39.
	229–17 w· doth not bear his cross,— Luke 14 : 27.

wicked

Mis.	19–14 and all the w· endeavors of
	187–32 by pagan religionists, by w· mortals
	191– 9 refers to a w· man as the devil :
	219–15 another feels w·.
	257– 5 wakes in a w· man.
	281–30 the w· shall not— Prov. 11 : 21.
	288–10 rash conclusion . . . is weak and w· ;
Ret.	14–27 if there be any w· way— Psal. 139 : 24.
Pul.	79–20 * a w· but witty writer
'00.	2–16 The w· idler earns little
	8–10 w· man has little real intelligence ;
	8–25 not Science for the w· to wallow
'01.	15–28 * your sinful, w· manner
Hea.	9–18 God never made a w· man ;
	9–20 wherewith to make himself w·.
My.	33–11 if there be any w· way— Psal. 139 : 24.
	128–26 the motive is not as w·,
	161– 1 hung around the necks of the w·.
	211– 5 they are . . . too ignorant, or too w·

wickedly

Mis.	219–12 mortals think w·
	219–13 and act w· :
	219–27 feels w· and acts w·,

wickedness

Mis.	53– 8 weariness and w· of mortal existence,
	116– 4 w· in high places."— Eph. 6 : 12.
	134–27 Spiritual w· is standing in high
	175–16 "the leaven of malice and w· ;— I Cor. 5 : 8.
	254–12 grows weak with w·
Pul.	13–10 is in proportion to its w·.
'01.	15–19 filling up the measure of w·
'02.	11–18 The world's w· gave our
My.	227– 5 because of another's w·

wide

Mis.	196–20 It opens w· the portals of salvation
	224–11 remember that the world is w· ;
	275–19 throw w· the gates of heaven.
	280–31 doors of animal magnetism open w·
Man.	45– 1 supplies within the w· channels of
Un.	7– 2 glorified in the w· extension of belief
	41–17 opening w· the portal from death into
Pul.	58–16 * main auditorium has w· galleries,
	78– 5 * nine inches w·,
My.	52–12 * spreading world w· of this great truth,
	72– 6 * gates of Boston are open w·
	88–15 * its accommodations are so w·,
	200–25 W· yawns the gap between this
	221–28 throwing the door w· open
	236–18 opens w· on the amplitude of liberty
	245– 3 w· demand for this universal

widely

Mis.	296– 1 this system of religion,— w· known ;
Pul.	28–13 * does not differ w· from that of any
My.	40–17 * more w· reassert its pristine
	85– 2 * in its w· international range,
	299–10 C. S. has been w· made known
	322–10 * correcting mistakes w· published
	357–20 open the way, w· and impartially,

widen
   Ret. 11–14 That *w·* in their course.
   Po. 60–11 That *w·* in their course.
   My. 291– 6 a uniting of breaches soon to *w·*,

widened
   Mis. 316–22 patching breaches *w·* the next hour ;

widening
   Mis. 322–27 laboring in its *w·* grooves

widens
   Mis. 265– 5 this divergence *w·*.
   323–22 way winds and *w·* in the valley ;

wider
   Mis. 132– 5 opening, even *w·* than before,
   227–17 *w·* aims of a life made honest :

wide-spreading
   My. 174– 4 *w·* elms and soft greensward

widest
   Ret. 82– 9 *w·* power and strongest growth
   Pul. 80–11 * the *w·* outlook.

widow
   My. 126–20 I . . . am no *w·*,— *Rev. 18: 7.*
   (see also **Eddy**)

widowhood
   My. 126–25 mourn over the *w·* of lust,

wield
   Pul. 83–15 * *w·* the ruthless sword of injustice.

wielded
   Ret. 54–23 salutary power which can be *w·*.

wielding
   Mis. 127–26 cannot avoid *w·* it if we reflect Him.

wife
   Mis. 90– 8 *Is it wrong for a w· to*
   143–22 husband and *w·* reckoned as one,
   225– 7 clergyman, his *w·* and child.
   236–16 solicitations of husband or *w·*
   275–10 bereft *w·* or husband,
   281–15 He replied to his *w·*,
   287–22 When asked by a *w·* or a husband
   289–23 nature has bestowed on a *w·*
   289–24 if the *w·* esteems not this
   306–20 * Mrs. Harrison, *w·* of the ex-President,
   339–22 Art thou a *w·*, and hast
   Man. 46– 4 spiritually adopted husband or *w·*.
   92–12 If both husband and *w·* are
   Ret. 1– 4 His *w·*, my great-grandmother,
   2– 7 Joseph Baker and his *w·*,
   4–23 The *w·* of Mark Baker was
   21– 7 had a *w·* and two children,
   Pul. 26–16 * healing of the *w·* of the donor.
   My. 59–22 * melodeon on which my *w·* played.
   314–20 for eloping with his *w·*,
   314–24 When this husband recovered his *w·*,
   314–27 the *w·* of this husband
   324–16 * Mr. Wiggin nor his estimable *w·*
   (see also **Eddy**)

Wiggin *(see also* **Wiggin's**)
  J. Henry
   My. 319–24 * call on the late J. Henry *W·* to
  Mr.
   My. 317– 5 * to the effect that Mr. *W·*
   317–11 I engaged Mr. *W·* so as to
   317–17 Mr. *W·* left my diction quite out of
   318– 3 every case where Mr. *W·* added words,
   318– 5 Mr. *W·* was not my proofreader
   318–16 I invited Mr. *W·* to visit one of my
   318–22 Mr. *W·* manifested more . . . agitation,
   318–30 "Now, Mr. *W·*," I said,
   319– 8 hold the late Mr. *W·* in loving,
   319–30 * as regards Mr. *W·*.
   320– 3 * Upon calling on Mr. *W·*,
   320–10 * Mr. *W·* spoke of "S. and H.
   320–15 * Mr. *W·* did not claim to be a
   320–20 * called on Mr. *W·* several times
   320–28 * I saw Mr. *W·* several times
   321– 6 * My recollections of Mr. *W·*
   321–11 * Mr. *W·* was an honest man
   322–14 * conversation I had with Mr. *W·*
   322–24 * Mr. *W·* kindly helped me
   323– 3 * Mr. *W·* gave me a pamphlet
   324– 3 * Mr. *W·* had somewhat of a thought of
   324–15 * sure that neither Mr. *W·* nor
   324–21 * Mr. *W·* regarded you as
   325– 5 Mr. *W·* was very much troubled
  Mr. and Mrs.
   My. 324–32 * Mr. and Mrs. *W·* frequently mentioned
  Mrs.
   My. 322–23 * Mrs. *W·* seemed inclined to banter me
  Rev. James Henry
   My. 52–20 years ago, the Rev. James Henry *W·*,
   52–30 * of the Rev. James Henry *W·*
   317– 3 * Rev. James *W·* of Boston,
   317–10 employed the Rev. James Henry *W·* to

Wiggin
  Rev. J. Henry
   My. 323–30 * home of the late Rev. J. Henry *W·*
  Rev. Mr.
   My. 319–14 * work . . . Rev. Mr. *W·* did for her,

   My. 322–16 * to dine with the *W·* family.

Wiggin's
  Mr. and Mrs.
   My. 324– 1 * in Mr. and Mrs. *W·* home.
  Rev. James H.
   My. 322–11 * the Rev. James H. *W·* work

Wight
   Mis. 392–18 poem
   393–24 To thy whiteness, Cliff of *W·*.
   Po. page 51 poem
   52– 8 To thy whiteness, Cliff of *W·*.

Wilbur, Miss
   My. 298– 8 I thank Miss *W·* and the

Wilbur's, Sibyl
   My. 297–30 have read Sibyl *W·* book,

wild
   Mis. 396– 1 The *w·* winds mutter, howl,
   Ret. 4–20 brooklets, beautiful *w·* flowers,
   17– 3 *W·* spirit of song,
   Peo. 13–18 to let loose the *w·* beasts
   Po. 1– 3 where the *w·* winds rest,
   47–16 sowing the wayside and *w·*,
   58–13 The *w·* winds mutter, howl,
   62– 1 *W·* spirit of song,

'wildered
   Po. 70–22 Shine on our *'w·* way,

wilderness
   Mis. 81–16 to go up into the *w·*,
   99–26 one crying in the *w·*,
   130–31 march out of the *w·*,
   138 - 5 to wander in the *w·*
   153– 7 they marched through the *w·* :
   246–23 heard crying in the *w·*,
   325–24 "provoke Him in the *w·*,— *Psal. 78: 40.*
   373–21 homelessness in a *w·*
   No. 9–21 a table in the *w·*'"— *Psal. 78: 19.*
   Pan. 15– 6 spread for us a table in the *w·*
   '00. 15–16 and fasts in the *w·*.
   Hea. 19–24 bearing . . . into the *w·*,
   My. 22–15 * forty years in the *w·*,
   43– 2 * unknown *w·* was before them,
   43– 3 * that *w·* must be conquered.
   43– 9 * During their sojourn in the *w·*
   43–32 * The way out of the *w·*
   47–25 * the *w·* of dogma and creed,
   50–26 * the little church in the *w·*
   162– 8 better than a *w·* of dullards
   182–25 May the wanderer in the *w·*
   252–20 an oasis in my *w·*.

wildernesses
   Mis. 142– 2 her *w·* to bud and blossom

wildfire
   My. 302–17 the word spread like *w·*.

wilful
   Mis. 293–18 inasmuch as *w·* transgression

wilfully
   Mis. 224–20 He who can *w·* attempt to injure

will
  caprice of
   Pul. 55– 1 * "Not in blind caprice of *w·*,
  creative
   Un. 19– 5 contrary to His creative *w·*,
  divine
   Mis. 141–22 the divine *w·* and the nobility of
  God's
   Pan. 13–16 till God's *w·* be witnessed
   My. 18–24 till God's *w·* be witnessed
   258–12 to know and to do God's *w·*,
  good
   Mis. 145–30 good *w·* toward men."— *Luke 2: 14.*
   162–13 good *w·*, love, teaching, and
   215–15 peace, and good *w·* toward men.
   369– 5 good *w·* toward men."— *Luke 2: 14.*
   Man. 45– 7 and good *w·* toward men ;
   Pul. 22– 1 peace and good *w·* towards men.
   41–25 * good *w·* toward men."— *Luke 2: 14.*
   No. 44–26 good *w·* toward men"— *Luke 2: 14.*
   Pan. 15–10 and good *w·* towards men.
   '02. 8–12 by love and good *w·* towards men.
   My. 4–20 Mind-power is good *w·* towards men.
   90–19 * good *w·* toward men."— *Luke 2: 14.*
   127–30 good *w·* toward men,"— *Luke 2: 14.*
   167–12 good *w·* toward men."— *Luke 2: 14.*
   167–18 peace, and good *w·* for yourselves,
   201– 6 love and good *w·* to man,
   210–16 peace, good *w·* towards men,

will

good
My. 262–28   letting good *w·* towards man,
    279–19   good *w·* toward men." — *Luke* 2 : 14.
    281– 9   good *w·* toward men." — *Luke* 2 : 14.
    282– 1   its purpose is good *w·* towards men.
    283–11   good *w·* toward men." — *Luke* 2 : 14.

His
Mis. 127–23   will do His *w·* even though
    208–12   to let His *w·* be done.
    208–15   do His *w·* or to let it be done
    213–29   *His w·* be done on earth
    334– 1   according to His *w·* — *Dan.* 4 : 35.
    386–18   Bowed to His *w·*.
Po.   50– 2   Bowed to His *w·*.
    79–20   doth His *w·* — His likeness still

his
Man. 28–12   according to his *w·*, — *Luke* 12 : 47.

his own
My. 132–15   "Of His own *w·* — *Jas.* 1 : 18.

human
    (*see* **human**)

intellect, and
Pan.   4– 3   to the reason, intellect, and *w·* of

iron
Ret.   5–14   strong intellect and an iron *w·*.

is capable
Pan.   4–13   *w·* is capable of use and of abuse,

last
My. 137–20   I have designated by my last *w·*,

lord's
Man. 28–11   knew his lord's *w·*, — *Luke* 12 : 47.

my
Mis. 212–20   "Not my *w·*, but Thine, — *Luke* 22 : 42.

no
Mis. 347–26   Those who know no *w·* but His
My. 336–15   * Mr. Glover had made no *w·*

of God
Mis. 185– 4   *w·* of God, or power of Spirit,

of his Father
Mis. 167–18   they who do the *w·* of his Father
No.   41– 8   to do the *w·* of his Father

of man
Mis. 180–23   nor of the *w·* of man, — *John* 1 : 13.
    181–17   nor of the *w·* of man, — *John* 1 : 13.
    182–17   "Nor of the *w·* of man." — *John* 1 : 13.

of my Father
Chr. 55–23   do the *w·* of my Father — *Matt.* 12 : 50.

of the Father
'01. 18–19   "the *w·* of the Father." — *see John* 5 : 30.

of the flesh
Mis. 180–23   nor of the *w·* of the flesh, — *John* 1 : 13.
    181–16   the *w·* of the flesh, — *John* 1 : 13.
    182–14   nor of the *w·* of the flesh." — *John* 1 : 13.

of the woman
Pul. 49–26   * the *w·* of the woman set at work,

reason and
Pan.   4– 8   reason and *w·* are properly classified
    4–11   reason and *w·* are human ;

stubborn
Mis. 398– 5   Thou wilt bind the stubborn *w·*,
Ret. 46–11   Thou wilt bind the stubborn *w·*,
Pul. 17–10   Thou wilt bind the stubborn *w·*,
No.   7–13   sinning sense, stubborn *w·*,
Po.   14– 9   Thou wilt bind the stubborn *w·*,

this
Rud.   9–11   this *w·* is an outcome of

Thy
Mis. 208– 1   chapter sub-title — *Matt.* 6 : 10.
    384– 9   Thy *w·* to know, and do.
Pul. 22– 7   Thy *w·* be done — *Matt.* 6 : 10.
Po.   36– 8   Thy *w·* to know, and do.
My. 281– 4   Thy *w·* be done — *Matt.* 6 : 10.

Mis. 265– 6   cannot regain, at *w·*, an upright
My. 10–21   * to contribute money against their *w·*
    160–12   truisms which can be buried at *w·* ;
    300– 6   both to *w·* and to do — *Phil.* 2 : 13.
    336–18   * he was unable to make a *w·*.

Williams, Mrs. Ella E.
My. 16–18   * Mrs. Ella E. *W·*, Second Reader ;

willing
Mis. xl– 9   the fervent heart and *w·* hand
    5– 6   *w·* to consecrate themselves
    22–27   he who is a *w·* sinner,
    118–17   *w·* to work alone with God
    118–18   *w·* to suffer patiently for
    189– 4   become *w·* to accept the
    208–14   *w·* to do His will
    269–26   are not *w·* to pay the price.
    335–19   *w·* participants in wrong,
    342–25   are *w·* to pay for error
    349–15   I was *w·*, and said so,
Man. 38–23   provided they are *w·*

willing
Ret. 14–15   I was *w·* to trust God,
    20–26   his stepfather was not *w·*
    49– 1   is *w·* to sacrifice all
    71–15   *w·* to be subjected to such
Un. 58–15   *w·* to test the full compass
Pul. 14–29   Many are *w·* to open the eyes of
    15– 2   not so *w·* to point out the
'00.   9– 6   the student is not *w·*
'01. 11–24   *w·* to hear a sermon from
    32–12   *w·* to renounce all for Him.
    35– 4   Are we *w·* to sacrifice self
    35– 5   *w·* to bare our bosom to the
'02. 17–17   It is wise to be *w·* to wait
Hea.   8–14   it is *w·* to be made whole,
    18– 6   *w·* to put new wine into
Po. 26–11   Lincoln's own Great *w·* heart
My. 21–17   * those who are *w·* to forego
    50–28   * were *w·* to labor for the Cause.
    61–25   * should be *w·* to let God work.
    124– 9   *w·* hands, and warm hearts,
    166–19   When we are *w·* to help
    209– 3   this *w·* and obedient church
    211–18   lend themselves as *w·* tools

willingly
Mis. 73– 6   doth not afflict *w·*." — *Lam.* 3 : 33.
    231– 8   *W·* — though I take no stock in
Ret. 90–16   mother never *w·* neglects
Pul. 44– 7   * I thought you would *w·* pause
Rud. 10–20   He afflicteth not *w·* the children
Hea. 18–13   it would *w·* adopt the new idea,
Peo. 12–27   not more *w·* than health ;
My. 40–10   * *w·* enter into the blessedness of
    43–11   * *w·* obedient to the voice of
    160–11   Most of us *w·* accept
    323–10   * nor *w·* leave any false impression.

willingness
Mis. 269–27   knowing the *w·* of mortals
    344–21   *w·* "to be absent — *II Cor.* 5 : 8.
My. 58–13   * *w·* of those who have contributed
    333–24   * assurance of his *w·* to die,

willow's
Po. 67–11   winds bow the tall *w·* head !

willowy
My. 150–15   sleeping amid *w·* banks

will-power
Mis.   4–24   very strong *w·* to heal,"
    4–27   there is no *w·* required,
    45– 2   This is not done by *w·*,
    281– 5   self-asserting mortal *w·*
Ret. 68–24   mortal thought and *w·*.
Un. 22–21   human intellect and *w·*.
Rud.   8–22   opens a way whereby, through *w·*,
My. 348– 3   electricity, magnetism, or *w·*,

wills
Mis. 208–16   Mortals obey their own *w·*,
    224–12   million different human *w·*,

Wilmington (*see also* **Wilmington's**)
N. C.
My. 176– 2   chapter sub-title
    197–24   chapter sub-title
    312–19   business trip to *W·*, N. C.,
    335– 1   * Died at *W·*, N. C.,
    335–15   * While at *W·*, N. C., in June, 1844,

North Carolina
Ret. 19– 7   He was in *W·*, North Carolina,

My. 312– 6   * took his bride to *W·*,
    330– 7   * locates Mrs. Eddy in *W·* in 1843,
    330– 9   * was not then a resident of *W·*.
    330–17   * was of Charleston, S. C., not of *W·*,
    330–20   * by *W·* newspapers of that year.
    331–20   * Major George W. Glover of *W·*
    332– 8   * friends at *W·* accept it as a tribute of
    332–18   * Christian Association at *W·*.
    333– 4   * records of St. John's Lodge, *W·*,
    333–32   * reports of unusual sickness in *W·*
    334–11   * her husband's demise at *W·*.

Wilmington Chronicle
My. 331–10   * *W· C·* of August 21, 1844,
    333–19   * The *W· C·* of July 3, 1844,

Wilmington (**N. C.**) *Chronicle*
My. 329–15   * taken from the *W· (N. C.) C·*

Wilmington (**N. C.**) *Despatch*
My. 329–12   * *W· (N. C.) D·*, October 24, 1903.

Wilmington's
My. 331– 5   * at the hands of *W·* best citizens,
    331–12   * by *W·* best men,

Wilson's, John
Ret. 2– 6   and in John *W·* sketches.

win

Mis.	122–25	neither . . . can *w·* high heaven,
	155– 8	*w·* the pilgrim and stranger
	289–26	she may *w·* a higher.
	340– 9	can you *w·* and wear the crown
	341–18	to *w·* the spiritual sense of good.
Ret.	13–16	to *w·* me from dreaded heresy.
	80–20	*w·* the golden scholarship of
Un.	55–11	that they may *w·* the prize.
'00.	9–24	no one can fight against God, and *w·*.
Hea.	10–24	*w·* or lose according to your plea.
My.	126–30	for with it *w·* we the race
	163– 4	to *w·* through meekness to might,
	188–25	As you work, the ages *w·* ;

wind

Mis.	144–16	hiding place from the *w·*, — *Isa.* 32 : 2.
	275–14	* "tempers the *w·* to the shorn lamb,"
Pul.	82– 3	* she comes like the south *w·*
No.	22– 1	every *w·* of doctrine." — *Eph.* 4 : 14.
	22–11	are reeds shaken by the *w·*.
'01.	29–20	waiting till the *w·* shifts.
Po.	25–18	*w·* Wreaths for the triumphs
	53–15	Where *w·* nor storm can numb
My.	117– 6	reed shaken with the *w·*," — *Matt.* 11 : 7.

wind-chests

Pul.	60–20	* containing pneumatic *w·*

winding-sheet

Peo.	5–15	wrapped in a pure *w·*,

window

Mis.	203– 6	From my tower *w·*, as I look
	324–10	from the *w·* of this dwelling
	355–30	rainbow seen from my *w·*
Ret.	90– 2	God's *w·* which lets in light,
Pul.	25–13	* the *w·* frames are of iron,
	26–26	* Before the great bay *w·*
	27–16	* The other rose *w·* represents the
	27–20	* great *w·* tells its pictorial story
	27–25	* *w·* in the auditorium represents
	27–30	* bay *w·*, composed of three separate
	39–13	* poem
	58–22	* a beautiful sunburst *w·*.
	78–25	* *w·* of J. C. Derby's jewelry store.
My.	178–23	entered the house through a *w·*

windows

Mis.	283–12	and break through *w·*
Pul.	24–28	* The *w·* of stained glass
	27– 8	* The *w·* are a remarkable feature
	27– 9	* There are no "memorial" *w·* ;
	27–12	* In the auditorium are two rose *w·*
	27–14	* with six small *w·* beneath,
	27–17	* Beneath are two small *w·*
	27–27	* In the gallery are *w·* representing
	27–29	* the *w·* are of still more unique
	49– 8	* Looking down from the *w·*
	58–20	* all the *w·* are of colored glass,
My.	131–27	the *w·* of heaven, — *Mal.* 3 : 10.
	132– 4	the *w·* of heaven, — *Mal.* 3 : 10.
	259– 3	pedestal between my bow *w·*,
	269–21	*w·* of heaven are sending forth
	269–27	the *w·* of heaven, — *Mal.* 3 : 10.

winds

Mis.	9–30	the path that *w·* upward
	23– 9	disease, death, *w·*, and waves,
	79– 5	swept clean by the *w·* of history.
	99–23	*w·* of time sweep clean the centuries,
	237–18	murmuring *w·* of their forest home.
	277– 3	Falsehood is on the wings of the *w·*,
	323–22	The way *w·* and widens
	330– 1	the *w·* make melody
	396– 1	wild *w·* mutter, howl, and moan,
	397–11	'Gainst which the *w·* and waves
Ret.	4–17	and wandering *w·* sigh low
Un.	11– 6	he commanded the *w·*,
Pul.	8– 3	Like the *w·* telling tales
	18–20	'Gainst which the *w·* and waves
Pan.	1– 6	the winter *w·* have come and gone ;
	1– 7	rushing *w·* of March have shrieked
'01.	19–18	*w·* and waves, which obeyed him
	29–19	and adverse *w·* are blowing,
	29–22	won for them by facing the *w·*.
Po.	1– 4	dweller where the wild *w·* rest,
	12–20	'Gainst which the *w·* and waves
	16–18	when the *w·* are all still.
	58–13	wild *w·* mutter, howl, and moan,
	67–11	*w·* bow the tall willow's head !
My.	106–16	the *w·* would weary,
	162–30	waves and *w·* beat in vain.
	226–12	commands the waves and the *w·*,

wine

and milk

Mis.	149– 2	buy *w·* and milk — *Isa.* 55 : 1.

bread and

Pul.	30–14	* symbols of bread and *w·*,

wine

drinking of

Mis.	170– 7	eating of bread and drinking of *w·*

inspiring

Mis.	369–27	We thirst for inspiring *w·*

is unsipped

Mis.	324– 9	music is dull, the *w·* is unsipped,

little

Mis.	243–25	"Take a little *w·* — see *I Tim.* 5 : 23.

new

Mis.	178– 7	He found that the new *w·*
No.	43–20	"new *w·* into old — *Matt.* 9 : 17.
Hea.	18– 6	put new *w·* into old bottles.
	18–12	new *w·* into old bottles.
	18–15	put the new *w·* into the

tempting

Mis.	9–20	tasted its tempting *w·*,

water into

Mis.	74–18	he turned the water into *w·* ;
	244–20	turn the water into *w·*,
Un.	11– 5	turned the water into *w·*,

without

Mis.	325– 7	"drunken without *w·*." — see *Isa* 29 : 9.

Mis.	144–27	*w·* poured into the cup of Christ.
	399–15	water, the bread, and the *w·*.
Chr.	55–12	pipe, and *w·*. — *Isa.* 5 : 12.
Hea.	18– 7	and the *w·* be spilled.
Po.	70– 7	Making its waters *w·*,
	75–22	water, the bread, and the *w·*.
My.	125–32	"drunk with the *w·* of — *Rev.* 17 : 2.

wine-cup

Mis.	121– 5	drank from their festal *w·*.

winepress

Mis.	301–31	trodden the *w·* alone ; — *Isa.* 63 : 3.
Un.	58– 6	"the *w·* alone." — *Isa.* 63 : 3.

wines

Mis.	278– 1	The *w·* of fornication, envy,

wing

Mis.	xii– 7	with strong *w·* to lift
	157–14	under the shadow of His *w·*.
	213–20	C. S. gives a fearless *w·*
	267–19	The bird whose right *w·*
	331–21	on upward *w·* to-night.
	387– 8	with Thy shelt'ring *w·*,
	389– 9	on upward *w·* to-night.
	389–18	shadow of His mighty *w·* ;
Chr.	53–57	no broken *w·*, no moan,
'01.	2–26	fearless *w·* and a sure reward.
Po.	4– 7	on upward *w·* tonight.
	4–17	shadow of His mighty *w·* ;
	6– 2	with Thy shelt'ring *w·*,
	18– 2	the eagle's proud *w·*,
	28–12	Give us the eagle's fearless *w·*,
	34– 7	Bird of the airy *w·*,
	53– 3	The bud, the leaf and *w·*

winged

Mis.	152– 7	thoughts *w·* with peace

wings

angel's

Mis.	388–22	To fold an angel's *w·* below ;
Po.	21–11	To fold an angel's *w·* below ;

both

Mis.	367–20	Both *w·* must be plumed for

chimerical

Ret.	70–11	chimerical *w·* to his imagination,

find

Mis.	86–30	find *w·* to reach the glory of

healing in its

'02.	9–10	with healing in its *w·*,

heaven-born

Mis.	374–14	pluck not their heaven-born *w·*.

her

Mis.	146– 2	with healing on her *w·*.
	331–13	nestles them under her *w·*,
	374–32	without *feathers* on her *w·*,

of divine Science

Ret.	88–28	to clip the *w·* of divine Science.

of joy

My.	192–26	My love can fly on *w·* of joy

of morning

Po.	2–16	On *w·* of morning gladly flit away,

of sense

Mis.	230–19	floating off on the *w·* of sense :

of the cherubim

My.	188–14	under the *w·* of the cherubim,

of the winds

Mis.	277– 3	Falsehood is on the *w·* of the winds,

of vanity

Hea.	11– 2	plucked from the *w·* of vanity.

our

Mis.	234– 3	We spread our *w·* in vain

protecting

Mis.	137–16	protecting *w·* of the mother-bird,

wings
  rustle of
    Mis. 306–23   we do not hear the rustle of *w'*,
  thy
    Po. page 34   poem
       34– 1   O for thy *w'*, sweet bird !
  tired
    Po. 16–12   The tired *w'* flitting through
  weary
    Mis. 159–26   many weary *w'* sprung upward !
    My. 182–27   rest their weary *w'* amid the
  white
    Ret. 32– 2   bearing on its white *w'*,
    Po. 78– 3   Peace her white *w'* will spread
    My. 202– 1   May its white *w'* overshadow this
  wisdom's
    Po. 23–15   soul, upborne on wisdom's *w'*,
  your
    My. 248–19   fold or falter your *w'*.

    Mis. 280– 6   not angels with *w'*, but messengers
    393– 4   Gives the artist's fancy *w'*.
    Po. 51– 9   Gives the artist's fancy *w'*.

winning
  Pul. 31–26   * *w'* in bearing and manner,
  My. 232– 4   weave for you their *w'* webs of life
    257–11   *w'* the heart of humanity with
    268–29   heart of humanity warming and *w'*.

winningly
  My. 248–11   to proclaim Truth so *w'*

wins
  Mis. 277–11   right *w'* the everlasting victory.
  My. 180–27   Take it up,— it *w'* the crown ;
    232– 6   right way *w'* the right of way,

winter (*see also* **winter's**)
  Mis. 239–11   upon the sidewalk one *w'* morning,
    332– 7   * long *w'* of our discontent,"
  Pul. 65–22   * one bitter *w'* day, a Roman soldier
    82– 9   * than *w'* could stop the coming of
  Pan. 1– 6   *w'* winds have come and gone ;
  Po. 16– 2   hopeful though *w'* appears.
  My. 153– 1   despite our *w'* snows.
    196–29   Over the glaciers of *w'*

winter's
  Mis. 329–29   stricken to the heart with *w'* snow,
  Po. 46– 4   Nor blasts of *w'* angry storm,
  My. 327–14   * last *w'* term of our Legislature,

wipe
  Ret. 86–12   *w'* the dust from his feet
  Un. 18–12   *w'* the tears from the eyes of My

wiped
  Po. 78–12   When to be *w'* away, Thou knowest
  My. 44– 4   * tears are being *w'* away,

wipes
  Mis. 325–26   *w'* off the dust from his feet
    327–32   *w'* away the blood stains,
    399– 2   Love *w'* your tears all away,
  Un. 57–27   divine Science *w'* away all tears.
  Po. 22– 9   bliss that *w'* the tears of time
    31–21   *w'* away the sting of death
    75– 9   Love *w'* your tears all away,
  My. 132–31   *w'* away the unavailing, tired tear,
    191–16   which *w'* away all tears.

wire
  My. 184–13   to *w'* an acknowledgment thereof
    281–21   * Will you do us the kindness to *w'*

wired
  My. 105–19   I was *w'* to attend the patient of

wireless
  '02. 11–13   a submarine cable, a *w'* telegraph,
  My. 110–14   *w'* telegraphy, navigation of the air ;
    259–12   I return my heart's *w'* love.

Wis. (State)
  (*see* **Milwaukee**)

wisdom (*see also* **wisdom's**)
  according to
    My. 291–10   zeal according to *w'*,
  all
    Pan. 4– 4   possesses all *w'*, goodness, and
  almighty
    Mis. 227–32   command of almighty *w'* ;
  and guidance
    My. 338–18   higher source for *w'* and guidance.
  and Love
    Mis. 321–29   a world of *w'* and Love
  and love
    Mis. 316–22   *w'* and love into sounding brass ;
    My. 303–29   need much humility, *w'*, and love
  and might
    Mis. 316–28   patterns of humility, *w'*, and might

wisdom
  and power
    Mis. 204–25   wonderful foresight, *w'*, and power ;
    Un. 14– 8   He should so gain *w'* and power
  and prosperity
    Pul. 2– 4   thy *w'* and prosperity — *I Kings* 10 : 7.
  and strength
    My. 164–27   unity is reserved *w'* and strength.
  and utility
    Mis. 60–26   power, *w'*, and utility of good ;
  aping the
    Mis. 61– 7   aping the *w'* and magnitude of
  beginning of
    Mis. 359–30   is the beginning of *w'*.
  divine
    Mis. 209– 4   the prerogative of divine *w'*,
    293– 6   unerring modes of divine *w'*.
    My. 5–32   Human will may . . . divine *w'*, **never.**
    215–32   his divine *w'* should temper human
  experience and
    My. 273–16   acquired by experience and *w'*,
  fair
    Pan. 3–17   * We court fair *w'*,
  far-seeing
    Mis. 254– 3   loving warning, the far-seeing *w'*,
  God is
    Un. 26–16   * God is *w'*, God is love.
  God's
    Mis. 362– 5   reason is at rest in God's *w'*,
    Un. 51–18   in the economy of God's *w'*
  has shown
    My. 22–20   * she has shown *w'*, faith, and
  His
    Mis. 114–26   His *w'* will test all mankind
    158– 4   His *w'* above ours.
  human
    (*see* **human**)
  immense
    Mis. 223–25   immense *w'* in the old proverb,
  infinite
    Mis. 18–11   These commands of infinite *w'*,
    Hea. 4–10   We ask infinite *w'* to possess our
  in human action
    Mis. 288–13   *W'* in human action begins with
  inspired
    No. 22–12   Compared with the inspired *w'*
  inspires
    Mis. 360– 1   Meekness, . . . inspires *w'*
  intelligence and
    My. 79–19   * intelligence and *w'* of the country
  is justified
    Mis. 374– 9   "*W'* is justified of — *Luke* 7 : 35.
    My. 228–22   "*w'* is justified of — *Matt.* 11 : 19.
  is unerring
    No. 8– 1   Father, whose *w'* is unerring
  is wedded
    Mis. 276–32   *W'* is wedded to their love,
  is won
    My. 205– 7   *W'* is won through faith,
  its
    Ret. 87– 5   its *w'* is as obvious in religion
    My. 84–10   * experience . . . has affirmed its *w'*.
  Jesus'
    Mis. 84– 1   Jesus' *w'* ofttimes was shown
  lack of
    My. 128–24   A lack of *w'* betrays Truth
  least
    Mis. 2– 4   who have the least *w'* or
  lengthens
    My. 146–10   "If *w'* lengthens my sum of years
    177–10   if *w'* lengthens my sum of years
  Love and
    Po. 44– 1   Then, O tender Love and *w'*,
    My. 223–28   divine Love and *w'* saith,
  manifold
    Mis. 363–18   His manifold *w'* shines through the
  my
    Mis. 335–18   Those who deny my *w'* or
  nor Science
    Mis. 359–16   but it is neither *w'* nor Science
  not infallible in
    Mis. 66– 1   is not infallible in *w'* ;
  of a serpent
    Mis. 210–11   *w'* of a serpent is to hide
  of God
    Mis. 210–12   *w'* of God, as revealed in C. S.,
    359–29   To ask *w'* of God, is the beginning
    My. 261– 5   elders, who seek *w'* of God,
  of his words
    My. 246–27   the *w'* of his words,
  of Mind-practice
    Ret. 78– 4   entire *w'* of Mind-practice.
  of Nicodemus
    My. 191– 1   *w'* of Nicodemus of old,
  of our forefathers
    '00. 10–18   *w'* of our forefathers is not

wisdom

of their elder
  My. 261– 4   *w·* of their elders, who seek
of the practitioner
  Man. 87– 6   left to the *w·* of the practitioner,
of the text
  Mis. 201– 1   entire *w·* of the text ;
of this decision
  Ret. 50–11   the *w·* of this decision ;
of withdrawing
  Mis. 326–21   Seeing the *w·* of withdrawing
order of
  Mis. 287–18   In the order of *w·*,
others'
  Ret. 71– 3   not the forager on others' *w·*
practical
  Man. 49–12   practical *w·* necessary in a sick room,
promotes
  My. 250– 5   promotes *w·*, quiets mad ambition,
requires
  Man. 77–19   God requires *w·*, economy,
requisite
  Ret. 79–20   *w·* requisite for teaching
same
  My. 162–19   same *w·* which spake thus
search after
  Mis. 364–13   It is not a search after *w·*,
  No. 21– 7   It was not a search after *w·* ;
set in
  Ret. 79–23   jewels of Love, set in *w·*.
speculative
  Mis. 361–22   subtlety of speculative *w·*
stature of
  Mis. 227–28   into the full stature of *w·*,
store of
  My. 253–23   I send with this a store of *w·*
stores of
  Mis. 165–29   secret stores of *w·* must be
supply the
  Pul. 15–17   and God will supply the *w·*
surprising
  Mis. 66– 5   surprising *w·* of these words
symbol of
  Mis. 191– 7   serpent became a symbol of *w·*.
temple of
  My. 60–14   * temple of "*w·*, Truth, and Love."
this
  Mis. 84– 4   This *w·*, which characterized his
to profit
  Mis. 359–28   give not the *w·* to profit by it.
true
  Mis. 139–26   like all true *w·*,
Truth and
  Mis. 391– 9   And learn that Truth and *w·*
  Po. 38– 8   And learn that Truth and *w·*
unerring
  Mis. 315–28   unerring *w·* and law of God,
  My. 44–29   * unerring *w·* of your leadership,
way of
  My. 356–21   chapter sub-title

  Mis. 139–24   at the *w·* whereof a few persons have
       303– 9   *w·* garrisons these strongholds of
       339–29   *w·* that might have blessed the past
       354– 9   *w·* is not "justified of— *Matt.* 11. 19.
       354–25   by *w·*, Truth, and Love.
       364–13   not a search after wisdom, it *is w·* :
       369–15   Metaphysical healing seeks a *w·* that
  No. 21– 8   not a search after wisdom ; it was *w·*,
  Pan. 14–17   give to our congress *w·*,
  Po. 77–10   Thou *w·*, Love, and Truth,
      79–16   Life is light, and *w·* might,
  My. 40 10   * *w·* that is from above— *Jas.* 3 : 17.
      42– 3   * her mouth with *w·* ;— *Prov.* 31 : 26.
      150–29   Then, if the *w·* you manifest
      227– 7   Charity is quite as rare as *w·*,
      228– 8   *w·* to "overcome evil with— *Rom.* 12 : 21.
      231–17   *w·* must govern charity,

wisdomless

  Mis. 30–23   the fossil of *w·* wit,

wisdom's

  Mis. 387–20   *w·* rod is given For faith to kiss,
  Ret. 11– 7   On learning's lore and *w·* might,
      90–24   walk steadfastly in *w·* ways.
  Po. 6–15   *w·* rod is given For faith to kiss,
      23–15   soul, upborne on *w·* wings,
      23–20   Guide him in *w·* way !
      27– 8   young year dawn with *w·* light
      43–15   Light with *w·* ray
      60– 3   On learning's lore and *w·* might,

wise

  Mis. 21–14   in no *w·* except by increase of
      73–13   a commandment to the *w·*.

wise

  Mis. 90–16   *w·* as serpents."— *Matt.* 10 : 16.
      90–17   Break the yoke . . . in every *w·* way.
      127–27   *W·* sayings and garrulous talk
      134– 2   "*w·* unto salvation" !— *II Tim.* 3 : 15.
      139–27   be regarded as greatly *w·*,
      167–25   *w·* and prudent,— *Luke* 10 : 21.
      170–14   right and *w·*, or wrong and foolish,
      209–22   To suffer for . . . is divinely *w·*.
      209–30   say . . . it is *w·* to cover iniquity
      210–11   *w·* as serpents — *Matt.* 10 : 16.
      215–32   a *w·* spiritual discernment
      252–30   *w·* man's spiritual dictionary ;
      276–16   The *w·* will have their lamps aglow,
      276–31   *w·* Christian Scientists stand
      281–16   * "It is *w·* to count the cost
      282–23   it is sometimes *w·* to do so,
      301–14   require only a word to be *w·* ;
      312– 1   *w·* enough to guard against
      319–17   chapter sub-title
      321– 1   *w·* men follow this guiding star ;
      332– 4   Infinitely just, merciful, and *w·*,
      342–22   *w·* virgins had no oil to spare,
      343– 1   make us *w·* unto salvation !
      344–26   shall in no *w·* enter— *Luke* 18 : 17.
      348–15   *w·* in his own conceit."— *Prov.* 26 : 5.
      363–29   the *w·* man's directory ;
      371–20   It is a *w·* saying that
      393–13   Students *w·*, he maketh now
  Man. 41– 8   The *w·* man saith,
  Ret. 22– 5   Writers less *w·* than the apostles
      24– 4   was in no *w·* connected with
      83– 3   The *w·* Christian Scientist will
  Un. 4–28   no *w·* men or women will
      6–20   No *w·* mother, though a graduate
      58–15   He was too *w·* not to be willing
  Pul. 15–13   If so, listen and be *w·*.
  No. 7– 2   to be *w·* and true rejoices every
      40– 8   sometimes *w·* to hide from
      45– 1   *w·* and prudent,— *Luke* 10 : 21.
  Pan. 9–14   What mortal to-day is *w·* enough
  '01. 19–13   notion that . . . is *w·* or efficient,
  '02. 2–14   *w·* builders will build on the
      17–17   *w·* to be willing to wait on God,
  Po. 51–18   Students *w·*, he maketh now
  My. vi–15   * *w·* and unerring counsellor.
      37–29   * its *w·* counsel and admonition.
      41– 5   * nor in any *w·* alter its effects.
      60– 4   * if Mrs. Eddy thought it *w·* to
      62–23   * appreciation of your *w·* counsel,
      93– 3   * they are in no *w·* at war with
      128–22   Therefore be *w·* and harmless,
      135– 2   The *w·* man has said,
      139–16   chapter sub-title
      149–14   * "I am *w·*, for I have conversed
      149–15   * conversed with many *w·* men,"
      150–28   *w·* as serpents,— *Matt.* 10 : 16.
      162– 7   A small group of *w·* thinkers
      179–25   in no *w·* affect C. S.
      205– 5   *w·* as serpents,— *Matt.* 10 : 16.
      223–26   chapter sub-title
      237–10   Hence, it were *w·* to accept only
      243–16   *w·* to remain in their own fields
      244–23   and your *w·*, faithful teachers
      248–10   to put an end to falsities in a *w·* way
      250– 1   chapter sub-title
      259–22   If wishing is *w·*, I send with this
      259–18   *w·* zeal, a lowly, triumphant trust,
      261–10   deceit or falsehood is never *w·*.
      263– 5   word to the *w·* is sufficient.
      273–13   I for one accept his *w·* deduction,
      285– 7   in all your *w·* endeavors
      291–19   was *w·*, brave, unselfed.
      292– 8   sanctify our nation's sorrow in this *w·*,
      339– 8   is specially requested to be *w·*
      362–20   * we rejoice . . . in your *w·*

wisely

  Mis. 117–16   work *w·*, in proportion as we love.
      236– 8   to counsel *w·* whenever
      247– 1   *w·* demand for man his
      332– 2   *W·* governing, informing the universe,
  No. 9–12   and separate *w·* and finally ;
  '00. 2–14   and gives it *w·* to the world.
  '01. 9–28   he speaketh *w·*,
  My. 3–17   for it acts and acts *w·*,
      6–13   dexterously and *w·* provided for
      148– 3   called to do your part *w·*
      201–16   mercifully forgive, *w·* ponder,
      240–15   for it acts and acts *w·*,
      286– 9   and should be, arbitrated *w·*, **fairly** ;
      304–24   naturalist and author, *w·* said :

Wisemen

  Mis. 164–11   To the vision of the *W·*,
      164–20   As the *W·* grew in the

wiser

Mis. 265– 4 or w· than somebody else,
281–17 * "It is w· to count the cost of
342–29 w· than the children of — Luke 16 : 8.
Pul. 1–12 w· by reason of its large lessons,
'02. 3–20 w· at the close than the beginning
17–18 and to be w· than serpents ;
My. 213–23 you will grow w· and better
281– 2 and awakened a w· want,
296–15 He is w· to-day, healthier and

wish

Mis. 69–28 w· to apply to him for information
126– 4 Truly, I half w· for society again ;
132–30 with the hope that you w· to be just.
211–17 you w· to save him from death.
262– 4 If you w· to brighten so pure a purpose,
296–26 a w· to promote female suffrage
344– 3 expressed the w· to become one of
391– 1 poem
Un. 15–25 they w· to bribe with prayers
Pul. 10–14 the w· to reign in hope's reality
58–29 * should she w· to make it a home
87–23 This w· stops not with my pen
'00. 2–29 not so successful as I could w·,
Hea. 7–23 I w· the age was up to his understanding
10–20 If you w· to be happy,
10–21 take the side you w· to carry,
Po. 3– 8 watch thy chair, and w· thee here ;
page 38 poem
My. 131–19 I w· to say briefly that
157–17 * expressed of Mrs. Eddy,
189– 1 warmest w· of men and angels.
244– 3 w· to share this opportunity
270–16 the father of their w·.
315–10 * happy home as one could w· for.
327–22 * did not w· to be "discourteous

wished

Mis. 98–23 * "consummation devoutly to be w·."
178–27 I w· to be excused from
223–27 * "If I w· to punish my enemy,
299–32 w· to handle them, does it justify
312– 1 w· I were wise enough to
Ret. 14–19 The minister then w· me to tell him
Un. 17–19 * consummation devoutly to be w·."
Pul. 41–20 * until all who w· had heard and seen ;
49–20 * she had long w· to get away
My. 181–16 * "a consummation devoutly to be w·"

wishes

Pul. 47–24 * when she w· to catch a glimpse of
My. 138– 7 carried on contrary to my w·.
263– 6 w· you all a happy Christmas,
358–23 Give my best w· and love to your

wishing

Po. 9–10 w· this earth more gifts from above,
My. 253–22 If w· is wise, I send with this a

wit

Mis. 15– 6 to w·, the redemption of — Rom. 8 : 23.
30–24 fossil of wisdomless w·,
95–22 to w·, the redemption of — Rom. 8 : 23.
117–11 * "there are w·, humor, and
182–10 to w·, the redemption of the body.
Peo. 10–26 to w·, the redemption of — Rom. 8 : 23.
My. 303–13 Mark Twain's w· was not wasted

witchcraft

Mis. 123– 7 superstition, lust, hypocrisy, w·.
211–11 class legislation, and Salem w·,
324–14 w·, variance, envy,

witch-grass

Mis. 343–22 reappear, like devastating w·,

withal

My. 261– 4 and profit them w· ?

withdraw

Mis. 49– 3 to w· before its close.
273– 7 I w· from an overwhelming prosperity.
Man. 51–12 shall either w· from the Church
Pul. 34–13 * requested those with her to w·,
'00. 9– 3 I sometimes w· that advice
My. 226–14 W· God, divine Principle, from
260– 5 matter would reverentially w·

withdrawal

My. 118–20 voluntary w· from society,

withdrawing

Mis. 278–29 I have been gradually w· from
326–21 Seeing the wisdom of w· from
'02. 3–12 our military forces w·,

withdrawn

Mis. 302–18 till this permission was w·,
Man. 38–11 but who have voluntarily w·,
My. 344–11 and then w· from it,

withdraws

Mis. 324–20 this mortal inmate w· ;

withdrew

Man. 38–17 Members who once W·.
Ret. 24–22 I then w· from society
Pul. 34–24 * Mrs. Eddy w· from the world
45–23 * Judge Hanna w· from the pastorate

withered

Mis. 357–16 Much . . . has w· away,
Un. 11–16 w· hand looks very real

withheld

Pul. 10–24 have not w· the timely shelter
My. 36–14 * or w· from open graves

withhold

Ret. 75– 7 Why w· my name,
My. 75– 1 * we cannot well w· our

withholds

Mis. 300–31 he who w· a slight equivalent

within

Mis. 12–32 to all w· the radius of our
21–10 kingdom of God is w· — Luke 17 : 21.
34–24 w· the realm of mortal thought
75–12 the infinite is not w· the finite ;
97– 7 that holds w· itself all evil.
114–18 resist the foe w· and without.
125–11 the reign of righteousness — w· him ;
125–29 w· the past few years :
128– 5 w· the limits of a letter.
137–14 w· the last few years.
143–22 w· about three months,
145–32 that my heart folds w· it,
154–18 reign of harmony already w· us.
156–10 heaven of Love w· your hearts.
169– 1 W· Bible pages she had found
173–16 Can the infinite be w· the finite?
174– 9 religious sentiment w· man.
174–24 Jesus said it is w· you,
227– 8 crime comes w· its jurisdiction.
251–18 kingdom of God is w· — Luke 17 : 21.
251–19 w· the present possibilities of
290– 3 found w· their precincts.
302–32 stay w· their own fields
324–13 W· this mortal mansion are
324–26 Finding no happiness w·,
368– 9 * Standeth God w· the shadow,
391– 5 Will find w· its portals
393– 9 w· the misty Mine of human thoughts,
399– 7 Cleanse the foul senses w· ;
Man. 45– 1 w· the wide channels of The
52– 8 w· ten days thereafter,
94– 2 can invite churches w· the city
Ret. 14–24 when the new light dawned w· me.
21– 5 Every means w· my power
80– 1 reign of harmony w· us,
80–18 warning will be w· him a spring,
86–11 "stranger that is w· thy — Deut. 5 : 14.
Un. 3–23 W· Himself is every embodiment of
6– 2 "the seed w· itself," — see Gen. 1 : 11.
28– 3 a reality w· the mortal body?
28– 8 dares define Soul as something w· man?
33–14 only matter w· the skull,
48– 1 a reason for the faith w·.
Pul. 2– 6 w·, the spirit of beauty dominates
2–21 and remain w· the walls
3– 7 kingdom of God is w· — Luke 17 : 21.
8– 9 Scientists, w· fourteen months,
10–30 May the kingdom of God w· you,
11– 8 find w· it home, and heaven.
30–27 * w· fifteen years it has grown to
45–13 * completion w· the year 1894
49–25 * w· one mile of the "Eton of
70–11 * w· a few years founded a sect
Rud. 6–16 * w· the last few years,
No. 30–21 not light holding darkness w· itself.
35–26 kingdom of God is w· — Luke 17 : 21.
Pan. 4–22 disquieted w· me? — Psal. 42 : 11.
13– 8 kingdom of God is w· — Luke 17 : 21.
'00. 1– 3 chinked w· the storied walls of
'01. 7–12 include w· this Mind the thoughts
24– 4 not without the mind, but w· it,
28– 5 the kingdom of heaven w· us
35– 9 the kingdom of heaven w· us
'02. 2–12 W· the last decade
8–27 the kingdom of heaven w· him.
20– 6 "No drunkards w·, no sorrow,
Hea. 4– 3 nor remain for a moment w· limits.
Po. 38– 4 Will find w· its portals
46– 3 W· life's summer bowers !
51–14 Work ill-done w· the misty
75–14 Cleanse the foul senses w· ;
My. 37– 3 * w· the sacred confines of this
49– 8 * sweeping the world w· a generation."
52–27 * W· a few months she has made
63–20 * But w· our sacred edifice
69–12 * Everywhere w· the building

within

My.
70–12   * The effect on all *w·* earshot
74– 4   * *w·* two or three days' ride,
74–28   * *W·* two weeks we have had here
76– 3   * Up to *w·* ten days
99– 9   * is welcomed *w·* our midst
118–28   consciousness of heaven *w·* us
145–17   *W·* the past year and two months,
155–19   heaven here, — heaven *w·* us,
160–13   a sapling *w·* rich soil
161–15   *w·* himself, *w·* his own consciousness,
164–12   and all *w·* the human heart
164–25   unfolds the thought most *w·* us
167– 5   suppositional world *w·* us
176– 9   pointing the path to heaven *w·* you,
181–22   *W·* those years it is estimated
191–20   I am not there, am not *w·*
193–28   *W·* its sacred walls may song
260–21   because of the heaven *w·* us.
265–24   kingdom of God is *w·* — *Luke* 17 : 21.
267–29   kingdom of God is *w·* — *Luke* 17 : 21.
267–29   *w·* man's spiritual understanding
276– 8   preference to remain *w·* doors
303–31   foretasting heaven *w·* us.
315–17   * made oath that the *w·* statement
339–23   have not the Christ, Truth, *w·* them
342– 1   *w·* the ample, richly furnished
348– 6   I sought this cause, not *w·*
348–10   the hope that was *w·* me.
356–14   *w·* the last five years

without

Mis.
x–11   *w·* due preparation.
7–30   *w·* any assistance.
9–11   hated thee *w·* a cause
14–23   proven . . . to be *w·* necessity.
28– 7   muscles cannot move *w·* mind.
30–11   *w·* pain, sin, or death.
42–29   *Can I be treated w· being present*
43– 3   *w·* even having seen the individual,
45–29   *w·* Him was not anything — *John* 1 : 3.
47–10   *w·* consciousness of its weight
51–20   *w·* your having to resort to
58–21   *W·* its theology there is no
59– 8   *w·* this Science there had better
62–16   *mind-cure claims to heal w· it ?*
67–28   *w·* his subjection to death,
90–26   *w·* this prerogative being conferred by
93–16   fear, . . . is *w·* divine authority.
93–26   *w·* repentance and reformation.
107–22   *W·* a sense of one's oft-repeated
107–29   *W·* a knowledge of his sins,
108– 8   a lie, being *w·* foundation
109–24   *w·* this the valuable sequence of
113–19   so that all are *w·* excuse.
114–18   resist the foe within and *w·*.
129– 4   to condemn his brother *w·* cause,
130–19   *w·* one single mistake,
144–13   *w·* pomp or pride,
149– 2   *w·* money — *Isa.* 55 : 1.
149– 3   and *w·* price." — *Isa.* 55 : 1.
154– 6   Your faith has not been *w·* works,
154–25   Pray *w·* ceasing.
158– 7   your speaking *w·* notes,
162–21   *w·* corporeality or finite mind.
165– 8   man, *w·* the fetters of the flesh,
173–17   Does an evil mind exist *w·* space
178– 8   not . . . *w·* bursting them,
193–25   *w·* this enlarged sense of the
195– 7   hath the spirit *w·* the letter,
210– 4   never healed a patient *w·* proving
216–28   * *phenomenon w· a noumenon*
216–20   * a grin *w·* a cat."
217– 3   effect *w·* a cause is inconceivable ;
218–23   tho "grin *w·* a cat ;"
227– 4   given up . . . *w·* friend
227– 5   given up . . . *w·* apologist.
228–25   *w·* questioning the reliability of
233– 1   *w·* knowing its fundamental Principle.
240–13   *w·* the assent of mind,
242– 8   reset certain dislocations *w·* the
242–30   if she went *w·* it twenty-four hours
244– 8   *w·* compliance to ordained conditions.
244–22   raised *w·* matter-agencies.
250–21   goodness *w·* activity and power.
259– 1   *w·* Him was not any thing — *John* 1 : 3.
261–27   *w·* apprehending the moral law
263–22   *w·* a full knowledge of the
263–28   *w·* credit, appreciation, or a
264– 7   *w·* the groundwork of right,
269–21   the body is *w·* action ;
279–15   from which we learn *w·* study.
280– 1   when the earth was *w·* form,
281–20   helplessness *w·* this understanding,
282– 8   *w·* their knowledge or consent?
282–21   to treat him *w·* his knowing it,
283– 6   *w·* his knowledge or consent,

without

Mis.
283–15   to treat another student *w·* his
283–22   *w·* incriminating the person
284– 8   may possess a zeal *w·* knowledge,
286– 3   marriage is not *w·* the law,
287–32   venturing on valor *w·* discretion,
295– 4   whom he quotes *w·* naming,
301– 2   *w·* the author's consent,
301–17   *w·* this word of warning
301–22   and read it publicly *w· my consent.*
302– 7   teaching the name *w·* the Spirit,
302– 8   the skeleton *w·* the heart,
302– 8   the form *w·* the comeliness,
302– 9   the sense *w·* the Science,
313–14   *w·* ill-humor or hyperbolic
319–20   *w·* one gift to me.
325– 7   "drunken *w·* wine." — see *Isa.* 29 : 9.
325–30   *w·* watchers and the doors unbarred !
334–16   *w·* one word of Truth in it.
340– 5   There is no excellence *w·* labor ;
344– 7   *w·* having mastered the sciences
356–30   "pray *w·* ceasing," — *I Thess.* 5 : 17.
357–11   *W·* the cross and healing,
359– 6   until you can cure *w·* it
367– 1   letter *w·* law, gospel, or
371– 4   wandering about *w·* a leader,
374–31   an angel is a woman *w· feathers*
380–18   could heal mentally, *w·* a sign
383– 8   In 1896 it goes *w·* saying,

Man.
17– 3   forming a church *w·* creeds,
27– 8   *w·* consulting with the full Board
28– 6   *W·* a proper system of
41– 8   but *w·* hard words.
43– 1   *w·* her or their consent
43–16   copyrighted works *w·* her permission,
48– 5   do it with love and *w·* fear.
49–24   *w·* previous injury or illness,
50– 9   *w·* the consent of the Board of Directors.
50–15   having the name *w·* the life of
53–11   *w·* her having requested the
53–13   unnecessarily and *w·* her consent,
59– 2   *w·* characterizing their origin
67– 9   *w·* her written consent.
67–15   *w·* having personally conferred
68– 6   *w·* the Directors' consent
70– 5   *w·* first consulting her on said
78–10   *w·* the written consent of the Pastor
82– 8   *w·* her knowledge or
82–11   *w·* the request of the advertiser,
85–21   shall not teach C. S. *w·*
86– 9   *W·* Teachers.
103– 7   *w·* the written consent of
104–10   *w·* the written consent of
105– 3   *w·* the written consent of
111–18   *w·* sufficient cause,

Chr.
53–39   *w·* birth and *w·* end,
55–20   *W·* father, *w·* mother, *w·* descent, — *Heb.* 7 : 3.

Ret.
14–11   I answered *w·* a tremor,
21– 3   *W·* my knowledge a guardian was
21– 5   employed . . . but *w·* success.
30–24   gained *w·* tasting this cup.
33– 9   *w·* receiving satisfaction.
41– 5   "*w·* money and *w·* price," — *Isa.* 55 : 1.
41– 6   *w·* an acknowledgment
44– 2   church, *w·* a creed,
44–26   *w·* a dissenting voice.
53–11   sheep that were *w·* shepherds,
54–12   *w·* bearing the fruits
54–14   admits Truth *w·* understanding it.
61–15   *w·* hope, and *w·* God — *Eph.* 2 : 12.
65–27   determine, *w·* a telescope,
71–10   *w·* the consent or knowledge
71–18   *w·* the permission of man
73– 4   *w·* materiality, *w·* finiteness
75– 1   book-borrowing *w·* credit
76– 5   Science *w·* trespassing,
85–17   Never forsake your post *w·*
86–21   No one can save himself *w·*
88–23   preach *w·* the consent of

Un.
2–28   *w·* having rightly improved
4– 2   *w·* a single taint of our
9– 9   all are *w·* excuse who
19–16   *w·* any actuality which
23–12   if ye be *w·* chastisement, — *Heb.* 12 : 8.
34– 8   cannot see *w·* matter ;
38– 8   is virtually *w·* existence.
40–23   which is . . . *w·* end,
49–22   Evil is *w·* Principle.
49–23   undemonstrable, *w·* proof.
56–26   Love which is *w·* dissimulation
57–10   *W·* it there is neither
58–17   yet *w·* sin." — *Heb.* 4 : 15.
60–22   *W·* Him, the universe would
60–22   Both *w·* and within,

Pul.
2– 6   "Faith *w·* works — *Jas.* 2 : 26.
9–29   "Faith *w·* works — *Jas.* 2 : 26.
44–26   * *w·* any special appeal,

without

Pul. 47–12 * w· receiving any real satisfaction.
64–17 * w· finding a clew :
70–10 * w· doubt one of the most
79–14 * w· seeing notices of
Rud. 9–21 w· a direct effort,
14– 9 w· remuneration, except the
14–13 She has never taught . . . w· several,
No. 7–24 w· reference to right or wrong
8–12 w· fear or doubt, knowing that God
15– 4 Reading my books, w· prejudice,
17–14 not w· an ever-present witness,
21–28 like a cloud w· rain,
35– 2 W· it, how poor the precedents of
35– 4 were C. S. w· the power to
40– 1 "Pray w· ceasing"— I Thess. 5 : 17.
41–16 W· question, the subtlest forms of
45– 3 St. Paul said that w· charity
Pan. 12–19 w· the alterative agonies
'01. 11–18 read each Sunday w· comment
11–22 saith there is no sermon w·
24– 3 argues that matter is not w· the
27–17 w· a Christian Scientist on earth,
34–27 man cannot live w· it ;
34–28 nor happiness w· godliness.
'02. 2– 4 w· clamor for distinction
7–14 without beginning and w· end,
15– 6 Healing . . . diseases w· charge,
15– 8 "w· money and w· price,"— Isa. 55 : 1.
16–13 w· which no man shall— Heb. 12 : 14.
18–24 faith w· proof loses its life,
Hea. 4–20 without beginning and w· end.
12–21 cannot shake the poor drug w· the
Peo. 2–24 Truth w· a lapse or error,
12–28 w· health there could be no heaven.
Po. 2– 9 never the sunshine w· a dark spot ;
42– 6 W· heart to define them,
My. v–17, 18 * "w· money and w· price."— Isa. 55 : 1.
3–10 sear leaves of faith w· works,
14–26 * carried on w· interruption
15– 8 w· the written consent of
29–30 * w· suffering the inconveniences of
30–23 * W· ostentation and quite voluntarily
31– 4 * "Just as I am, w· one plea ;"
40–28 * w· regrets and w· resistance,
41–11 * so receive judgment w· mercy ;
46– 6 * w· this spiritual significance
76– 1 * it went w· saying that the
76–18 * free of debt w· exception.
79–25 * w· a trace of fanaticism,
93– 2 * w· efforts at proselytizing ;
95–25 * w· faith in the things unseen.
97– 6 * w· the use of medicine.
105–24 restored by me w· material aid,
106– 4 and w· this proof of love
106–29 heals the sick w· drugs
107–13 can be swallowed w· harm
107–14 and w· appreciable effect.
108– 3 healing his cases w· drugs
128–23 w· the former the latter were
130–24 Borrowing from . . . w· credit,
138– 1 w· the help of others.
138– 6 suit was brought w· my knowledge
157– 9 * w· regard to class or creed,
158–19 letter w· the spirit is dead :
163–13 w· neglecting the sacred demands
178–16 if evil exists, it exists w· God.
195–28 unselfed love that builds w· hands,
197– 4 Attempt nothing w· God's help.
197– 6 glorious, w· spot or blemish.
203– 8 laws which are obeyed w· mutiny
204–15 Scientists to Practice w· Fees
213–18 wrong direction w· knowing it.
215– 4 bestowed w· money or price.
215– 9 w· having charity scholars,
215–28 first w·, and then with, provision
216– 2 live w· eating,
216–11 w· a cent to sustain it?
218–16 abstractions . . . w· their correlatives,
223– 3 w· previous appointment by letter.
224–18 one author w· quotation-marks,
228–30 It goes w· saying that
235– 2 w· using the word death,
244–18 do not enter w· a struggle
249– 1 w· harming any one
249–27 then w· reference to sex
263– 2 alone and w· His glory.
267– 7 w· Him was not any thing— John 1 : 3.
268–18 w· a living Divina.
301–28 w· the aid of mind.
302–16 But w· my consent, the use of
312– 9 * entirely w· money or friends.
312–15 * entirely w· means of support.
320–23 * w· any hesitation or restriction.
321–10 * w· any restriction.
334– 8 * The allegation . . . is w· foundation.

without

My. 339–30 w· the observance of a
340– 4 "Pray w· ceasing."— I Thess. 5 : 17.
341–26 * raining all day and was damp w·,
345–17 pellets w· any medication
(see also **beginning, Mind**)

withstood

Mis. 233–10 if not understood and w·,
Ret. 45–24 w· less the temptation of popularity
My. 249–11 Unless w·, the heat of hate burns

witless

Mis. 78–18 w· ventilation of false statements

witness

Mis. 46–22 beareth w· with our— Rom. 8 : 16.
54–10 they bear w· to this fact.
67–13 not bear false w· ;"— Exod. 20 : 16.
83– 3 w· to and perpetual idea of
218–19 beareth w· of things spiritual,
241–11 and w· the effects.
255–14 beareth w· with our— Rom. 8 : 16.
382–10 time and eternity bear w·
Man. 53–21 bear w· to the offense
Ret. 25–27 "If I bear w· of— John 5 : 31.
25–27 my w· is not true."— John 5 : 31.
67–17 lost for lack of w·.
Un. 7–15 can bear w· to these cures.
33– 8 "If I bear w· of— John 5 : 31.
33– 8 my w· is not true."— John 5 : 31.
36– 4 this lie was the false w·
Pul. 8–28 The children are destined to w·
No. 17–14 not without an ever-present w·,
Pan. 13– 1 w· more steadfastly to his
Po. 73–14 W· my presence and utter
My. 36–19 * bear w· to the abundance
192–23 to w· your prosperity,
270–23 I can appeal to Him as my w·
323–12 * living w· to Truth
340–11 as w· her schools,

witnessed

Pul. 84–14 * w· the completion of
Pan. 13–17 till God's will be w·
My. 18–25 till God's will be w·
30– 5 * who w· the opening.
42– 7 * "w· a good confession"— I Tim. 6 : 13.
79–14 * seldom w· anywhere
97–30 * incidents w· during the week
323–23 * we have so recently w·,

witnesses

Mis. 150–23 peopled with living w·
250–17 active w· to prove it,
321– 9 each recurring year w·
360–17 cloud of false w· ;
Ret. 25–22 senses are so many w· to
Un. 33–21 these w· for error,
33–24 two or three w·— Matt. 18 : 16.
'02. 10–25 martyrdom of God's best w·
16–22 self-defense against false w·,
My. 243–21 w· your fidelity
248–25 to you, my faithful w·.
347– 2 His two w·.

witnesseth

My. 191–15 w· a risen Saviour,

witnessing

My. 45– 6 * We are w· with joy

wittingly

Ret. 74– 8 afflicteth me not w· :

witty

Mis. 216–22 a w· or a happy hit at idealism,
Pul. 79–20 * a wicked but w· writer has said,

woe

Mis. 65–10 subject of human weal and w·
122– 2 "W· unto the world— Matt. 18 : 7.
122– 4 w· to that man by whom— Matt. 18 : 7.
250–28 want and w·, sickness and sorrow
279– 1 w· unto him, — Luke 17 : 1.
361–23 speculative wisdom and human w·.
388–23 And hover o'er the couch of w· ;
Ret. 31–13 ever-present relief from human w·.
Un. 15– 2 * "death into the world, and all our w·."
58–16 full compass of human w·,
Pul. 8– 7 Notwithstanding . . . the want and w·
12–12 W· to the inhabiters— Rev. 12 : 12.
No. 33–23 physical suffering and human w·.
34–26 Nameless w·, everlasting victories,
'02. 6–13 Here all human w· is seen to
Hea. 18–19 or claimed to reach that w· ;
Po. 3–11 Since first we met, in weal or w·
21–12 And hover o'er the couch of w· ;
28– 8 Whate'er the gift of joy or w·,
35– 6 binds to earth— infirmity of w· !
47–19 Evermore gathering in w·
My. 190– 2 bring the recompense of human w·,
283–15 sovereign remedies for all earth's w·.

woeful

Mis. 60– 7 *w·* unrealities of being,
'01. 18– 4 weak criticisms and *w·* warnings

woes

No. 30–13 God pities our *w·*
30–16 could not destroy our *w·* . . . if He
'02. 20– 7 glory of earth's *w·* is risen upon you,
Peo. 11–23 responsible for all the *w·* of
Po. 8– 6 Her bosom to fill with mortal *w·*.
41– 6 earth-stricken lay down their *w·*,

woke

Mis. 386–13 I *w·* to Life,
Ret. 12– 6 *W·* by her fancied feet.
Po. 49–19 I *w·* to Life,
61– 4 *W·* by her fancied feet.

wolf

Mis. 145–22 "The *w·* also shall — *Isa.* 11 : 6.
213–26 fleeth when he seeth the *w·* coming.
370–20 a *w·* in sheep's clothing

wolves

Mis. 294–18 *w·* in sheep's clothing
323–12 *w·* in sheep's clothing
My. 215–21 *w·* in sheep's clothing," — see *Matt.* 7 : 15.

woman (see also woman's)

acknowledged
Pul. 82–17 * have long acknowledged *w·* as
after
Pul. 14– 9 flood, after the *w·*, — *Rev.* 12 : 15.
as a chattel
Pul. 82–13 * they treated *w·* as a chattel,
at the sepulchre
My. 258– 9 To the *w·* at the sepulchre,
Babylonish
My. 125–29 The doom of the Babylonish *w·*,
126–24 The Babylonish *w·* is fallen,
behind the
Mis. 373– 3 placing the serpent behind the *w·*
373–10 out of his mouth, *behind* the *w·*,
born of a
Mis. 184– 8 The child born of a *w·*
Chr. 55–14 Man that is born of a *w·* — *Job.* 14 : 1.
certain
Mis. 166–22 leaven that a certain *w·* hid
climbed
Pul. 9–13 a *w·* climbed with feet and hands
drunken
My. 125–30 This *w·*, "drunken with — *Rev.* 17 : 6.
every
Mis. 232–22 Every man and every *w·*
good
My. 331–16 * the assailant of a good *w·* :
helped the
Pul. 14–11 earth helped the *w·*, — *Rev.* 12 : 16.
in travail
Mis. 253–16 metaphors, — of the *w·* in travail,
man and
(see **man**)
man meaning
My. 268–31 *man meaning w·* as well,
man or
(see **man**)
man or a
'01. 13– 1 a man or a *w·*, a place or a thing,
married
Man. 111– 5 If the applicant is a married *w·*
new
Mis. 253– 6 I am not enough the new *w·*
Pul. 79– 3 * chapter sub-title
81– 9 * chapter sub-title
84– 2 * "the new *w·*" shall subdue the
84– 8 * the new man with the new *w·*.
noble
My. 290– 9 beloved as this noble *w·*,
of the past
Pul. 81–10 * she is simply the *w·* of the past
of thirty
Pul. 32–21 * elastic bearing of a *w·* of thirty,
one
My. 239–15 *as one man and one w·*
324–28 * one *w·* under the sun who could
or a man
My. 343– 8 will be a *w·* or a man.
or child
Mis. 336–26 a better man, *w·*, or child.
Rud. 2– 3 * corporeal man, *w·*, or child ;
persecuted the
Pul. 13–28 he persecuted the *w·* — *Rev.* 12 : 13.
poor
Hea. 7–18 poor *w·* who dropped her mite
remarkable
Pul. 63–15 * made by a remarkable *w·*,
rich
Pul. 50– 1 * rich *w·* is using her money

woman

right of
No. 45–16 right of *w·* to fill the highest
sick
Ret. 40–11 sick *w·* rose from her bed,
suitable
Man. 100–27 a suitable *w·* shall be elected.
took
Mis. 171–23 which a *w· took*, — *Matt.* 13 : 33.
174–30 leaven which a *w·* took
true
Mis. 18–16 true man and true *w·*,
unworthy
My. 331–15 * hospitality to an unworthy *w·*
whole-souled
Mis. 224–32 *to* offend a whole-souled *w·*.
will help the
Pul. 14–22 the earth will help the *w·* ;
work of a
Pul. 55– 9 * should be the work of a *w·*
wroth with the
Hea. 10– 2 was wroth with the *w·*,

Mis. 100– 5 *w·*, "last at the cross,"
142–28 If as a *w·* I may not
175– 2 And *w·*, the spiritual idea,
244– 2 builded up the *w·*." — *Gen.* 2 : 21.
374–31 an angel is a *w·* without
Man. 29–21 shall be a man and a *w·*,
Ret. 26–23 *W·* must give it birth.
Un. 45– 4 as Truth and "the *w·*" — *Gen.* 3 : 15.
51–13 *What say you of w·?*
51–14 *W·* is the highest species of man,
Pul. 9–11 *W·*, true to her instinct,
27–23 * *w·* spoken of in the Apocalypse,
83– 8 * *W·* must not and will not
83–27 * *w·* clothed with the sun, — *Rev.* 12 : 1.
No. 45–13 *w·*, "last at the cross
46–10 *W·* should not be ordered to the rear,
Po. 39–12 *W·* — will watch to cleanse from dross
My. 5– 3 supposed . . . *w·* to be the outcome of
249–23 a man, rather than a *w·*,
262–15 of God and not of a *w·*.
277–23 *w·* would be armed with power
334–14 * *w·* whom he had in mind
(see also **Eddy**)

womanhood

Mis. 16– 6 grows into the manhood or *w·*
33–10 in the *w·* as well as in the manhood
166– 8 infancy, manhood, and *w·*
Un. 42–28 manhood and *w·* go forth
Hea. 10– 7 fell before the *w·* of God,
My. 12–30 in the settings of manhood and *w·*.
52– 7 * highest type of *w·*,
330–10 * whose *w·* and Christianity are
346–30 manhood and *w·* of God

woman's

Mis. 210–15 has faith in *w·* special adaptability
220–30 would be according to the *w·* belief ;
245–19 This is *w·* hour,
275– 3 even *w·* trembling, clinging faith
287–28 home, — which is *w·* world.
388–13 poem
Un. 57–12 felt the influence of the *w·* thought ;
Pul. 48–26 * as is many another well-born *w·*.
83– 1 * *w·* love and *w·* help
No. 45–19 This is *w·* hour,
'02. 3–23 *w·* thoughts . . . hallow the ring of state.
Po. page 21 poem
My. 258– 7 seems illuminated for *w·* hope

women (see also women's)

all
Un. 51–16 the generic term for all *w·* ;
American
Mis. 295– 1 certain references to American *w·*
296– 8 work and career of American *w·*,
and children
Pul. 45– 1 * *w·*, and children lent a helping hand,
64– 9 * Men, *w·*, and children contributed,
born of
My. 228–13 none greater had been born of *w·*,
committee of
Mis. 305– 1 * committee of *w·* representing each
devoted
My. 30–14 * devoted *w·* members,
leads
Mis. 295– 6 leads *w·* "along a gamut of isms
men and
(see **men**)
men or
Un. 5– 1 no wise men or *w·* will rudely
myriad of
Pul. 80–24 * myriad of *w·* more thoughtful

women

noble
Mis. 296–11 same category with noble *w·*
remarkable
Pul. 70–11 * most remarkable *w·* in America.
unmarried
Man. 111– 8 unmarried *w·* must sign "Miss."

Mis. 245–18 conclusion . . . that *w·* have no rights
345–15 * fit only for *w·* and weak men ;"
Man. 110–14 *W·* must sign "Miss" or "Mrs."
Pul. 80– 4 * religious sentiment in *w·*
82–18 * *w·* had few lawful claims
Peo. 13–23 * "Christianity is fit only for *w·* and

women's

Pul. 80– 9 * emphatically the *w·* paradise,
'00. 3–24 *w·* names contained this divine
My. 83–11 * laces of the *w·* frocks,

won

Mis. 33– 5 they lost, and he *w·*, heaven.
85–11 is not *w·* in a moment ;
109–32 your superiority to a delusion is *w·*.
120–13 mighty victory is yet to be *w·*,
131–32 perils past and victories *w·*.
147– 6 victory *w·* for time and eternity
319–24 object to be *w·* affords ample
358–32 a higher spiritual unity is *w·*,
362–27 Truth is *w·* through Science or
388–15 *w·* from vice, by virtue's smile,
Ret. 3–11 *w·* distinction in 1814
9–26 * And *w·*, through clouds, to Him,
30– 4 they have *w·* fields of battle
No. 25– 3 Having *w·* through great tribulation
'01. 10–24 victory over self, . . . is *w·*
14– 4 Publican's wail *w·* his humble desire,
25– 7 whereby is *w·* the crown
29–21 mother worked and *w·* for them
35–13 O the Master's glory *w·* thus,
Po. 21– 2 *w·* from vice, by virtue's smile,
22–20 peace is *w·*, and lost is vice :
26–12 Thy purpose hath been *w·* !
My. 62– 2 * and *w·* the reward,
112–28 *w·* its way into the palaces of
114–13 holiness is not yet *w·*.
136–15 *w·* a suit at law
163– 4 *w·* the way and taught mankind
205– 7 Wisdom is *w·* through faith,
273–22 is *w·* only by the spiritual
309–10 my father *w·* the suit.
334–22 wail *w·* his humble desire,
343–19 it *w·* converts from the first.

wonder

Mis. 69–22 though the *w·* was,
225– 9 the seventh modern *w·*,
275–26 Chicago is the *w·* of the
321–26 the great *w·* of the world,
337– 8 *W·* in heaven and on earth,
Un. 37–10 reveal this *w·* of being.
42–18 No *w·* "people were— *Matt.* 7 : 28.
Pul. 7– 9 I *w·* whether, were our
40– 3 * I *w·* how the seasons come
66–23 * may reasonably excite *w·*
83–27 * a great *w·* in heaven,— *Rev.* 12 : 1.
No. 37–13 to regard this *w·* of glory,
'01. 31–14 no vague, fruitless, inquiring *w·*.
'02. 5–15 human question and *w·*,
18– 8 only to mock, *w·*, and perish.
My. 31–20 * no *w·* that the first sight
43–29 * The world looks with *w·*
49– 2 * What *w·* that when these
82–11 * it was a matter of *w·*
92–12 * hardly more than a day's *w·*.
123– 3 they have become a *w·* !
323–28 * I *w·* if you will remember

wondered

Mis. 178–16 * *w·* what sort of people
278–13 *w·* at the Scriptural declaration

Wonderful

Mis. 161– 7 called *W·*, Counsellor,— *Isa.* 9 : 6.
164–18 called *W·*, Counsellor,— *Isa.* 9 : 6.
321– 5 called *W·*, Counsellor,— *Isa.* 9 : 6.
Un. 39–13 Messiah, whose name is *W·*.

wonderful

Mis. 70–28 those *w·* demonstrations of
162– 4 such *w·* spiritual import
164–15 a *w·* manifestation of Truth
167–27 Is he *w·* ?
175–31 done many *w·* works?
204–25 brings with it *w·* foresight,
290–17 * produced a *w·* illumination,
372–11 * pictures in your *w·* book
375–11 * *w·* new book you have given
Un. 1–10 characterized as *w·*.
5–26 this *w·* part of Truth

wonderful

Un. 17–15 *w·* utterances of him who
Pul. 32–10 * *w·* tumult in the air
'00. 15– 8 *w·* passage over a tear-filled sea of
'02. 16–21 sublime patience, *w·* works,
Hea. 3–20 *w·* works of our Master
My. 60–13 * corner-stone of this *w·* temple
60–28 * in this *w·* consummation.
70–22 * nothing more *w·* than the
85–12 * *w·* woman is a world power.
95–29 * such a *w·* demonstration of
98– 4 * *w·* growth of less than a score of
98–30 * has been a *w·* achievement,
193– 9 for His *w·* works— *Psal.* 107 : 8.
323–18 * your *w·* life and sacrifice

wonderfully

Pan. 10–16 *w·* broadened and brightened
My. 92–27 * Its growth has been *w·* rapid,
307–25 At first my case improved *w·*
342–21 It is growing *w·*.

wondering

Mis. 275–12 little ones, *w·*, huddle together,

wonderment

Mis. 234–22 grave *w·* to profound thinkers.
My. v– 7 * general *w·* and frequent comment,

wonders

Mis. 101– 4 He alone knows these *w·* who is
331– 4 tosses earth's mass of *w·* into
Pul. 52– 1 * *W·* will never cease.
My. 57–28 * "*W·* will never cease.
205–10 * His *w·* to perform ;

wonder-worker

Ret. 76–20 constitute the Mind-healer a *w·*,

wondrous

Mis. 214–12 closed— to the senses— that *w·* life,
Ret. 15–11 I declared Thy *w·* works."— *Psal.* 71 : 17.
Po. 31–11 veils the leaflet's *w·* birth

Wonolancet Club

My. 174– 6 courtesy extended . . . by the *W· C·*

wont

Ret. 13–20 as I was *w·* to do,

woo

Mis. 155– 8 *w·* the weary wanderer to your door,
Ret. 17– 5 And *w·*, while I worship
Po. 62– 5 And *w·*, while I worship

wood

Mis. 346–15 an image graven on *w·* or stone
Peo. 2–18 form its Deity out of . . . *w·* or stone.
13– 1 worshippers of *w·* and stone
My. 172– 1 * The *w·* of the head of the gavel
172– 5 * The *w·* in the handle was grown

woodland

Mis. 390–13 Through *w·*, grove, and dell ;
396– 2 To scare my *w·* walk,
Po. 8– 8 nymph and naiad from *w·* bower;
41–13 green sunny slopes of the *w·*
53– 6 On vale and *w·* deep ;
55–14 Through *w·*, grove, and dell ;
58–14 To scare my *w·* walk,

Woodlawn Ave., 5020

Mis. 157–20 Chicago,— 5020 *W· A·*,

woods

Ret. 9–21 * whispering *w·*, where dying thunders
Pul. 48–12 * *w·* that skirt the valley

woodwork

Pul. 58–17 * Scarcely any *w·* is to be found.
My. 68–32 * pews and principal *w·* are of

Woodworth, Mayor

Mis. 251– 8 Mayor *W·*, has welcomed you

wooed

Po. 34–13 Has *w·* some mystic spot,
My. 90– 3 * *w·* by no eloquence of orator or

wooings

Mis. 390– 2 Whence are thy *w·*, gentle June?
Po. 15–12 Their *w·* are soft as the vision
55– 1 Whence are thy *w·*, gentle June?

wool

Mis. 398–19 White as *w·*, ere they depart,
Ret. 46–25 White as *w·*, ere they depart,
Pul. 17–24 White as *w·*, ere they depart
Po. 14–23 White as *w·*, ere they depart,

woolen

My. 310–10 * workman in a Tilton *w·* mill.' '

Woolson

(see **Howe and Woolson Halls**)

Woolson Hall

My. 80–24 * *W· H·*, and Chickering Hall,

Wooten, Sheriff
  My. 328–18 * Sheriff *W·* issued licenses
Worcester
  Mis. 68–24 *W·* defines it as "the philosophy of
Word
dispensing the
  Mis. 172– 3 Dispensing the *W·* charitably,
divine
  Mis. 192–19 practicability of the divine *W·*,
  Pul. 73– 9 * meditated over His divine *W·*.
  No. 29–17 than to the divine *W·*.
echoing the
  My. 186–11 echoing the *W·* welling up
God's
  '01. 31–26 used faithfully God's *W·*,
  My. 352–22 hearers and the doers of God's *W·*.
His
  Mis. 151–22 spoken of you in His *W·*.
  159– 4 to elucidate His *W·*.
  170– 9 having rightly read His *W·*,
  My. 152–21 listen to His *W·* and serve no
immutable
  Mis. 72–11 The immutable *W·* saith,
inspired
  Man. 15– 4 the inspired *W·* of the Bible
  My. 238–17 *morale* of the inspired *W·*
interpreting the
  Mis. 364– 3 Interpreting the *W·* in the
is made flesh
  Mis. 182–29 When the *W·* is made flesh,
  Un. 39– 1 *W·"* is "made flesh"— *John* 1 : 14.
milk of the
  Mis. 15–30 on the milk of the *W·*,
  No. v–12 unadulterated milk of the *W·*,
must abide
  Mis. 270–19 the *W·* must abide in us,
of God
  Mis. 111–22 but the *W·* of God abideth.
  163–11 explained the *W·* of God,
  '01. 11–19 *W·* of God is a powerful preacher,
  34–15 bereft of the *W·* of God.
  My. 28–26 * when he preached the *W·* of God
of Truth
  No. 22–13 meaning of the *W·* of Truth,
original
  Mis. 188– 6 not the original *W·*,
power of the
  Mis. 398–23 Felt ye the power of the *W·*?
  Po. 75– 3 Felt ye the power of the *W·*?
practise the
  My. 238–12 little power to practise the *W·*.
revealed
  Mis. 315–30 to study His revealed *W·*,
signification of the
  No. 12–24 spiritual signification of the *W·*
Spirit and
  Ret. 76– 9 touched with the Spirit and *W·*
spirit and the
  My. 246–21 concurrence of the spirit and the *W·*
spoken
  Pul. 11– 4 *W·* spoken in this sacred temple
that is God
  Mis. 363–25 *W·* that *is* God, Spirit, and Truth.
  My. 184–28 Surely, the *W·* that is God must
this
  Mis. 363–25 This *W·* corrects the philosopher,
  My. 153–28 wedding of this *W·* to all human thought
Thy
  Man. 41–24 may Thy *W·* enrich the affections of
unspoken
  Mis. 302–17 *not* to leave the *W·* unspoken
was God
  Mis. 29–11 the *W·* was God."— *John* 1 : 1.
  Pan. 5– 4 "The *W·* was God ;"— *John* 1 : 1.
  My. 117–19 the *W·* was God"— *John* 1 ; 1,
was with God
  Mis. 29–11 "the *W·* was with God,— *John* 1 : 1.
  My. 117–18 the *W·* was with God,— *John* 1 : 1.

  Mis. 61–21 According to the *W·*, man is the
  116–22 doing, the *W·*— demonstrating Truth
  169– 7 misinterpretation of the *W·*,
  184– 6 The *W·* will be made flesh
  No. 45–24 Let the *W·* have free course
  Pan. 5– 5 made by Him,"— the *W·*.— *John* 1 : 3.
  My. 117–18 "In the beginning was the *W·*,— *John* 1 : 1.
  119–32 Christ, Truth, in the *W·*
  125–26 the bride (*W·*) is adorned,
  153–28 the *W·* and the wedding of this
  197–21 hope set before us in the *W·*

word
and deed
  Mis. 206–20 harmony in *w·* and deed,
  Ret. 79–22 temperate in thought, *w·*, and deed.
  My. 338–25 stands alone in *w·* and deed,

word
and deeds
  My. 350–27 ripe in prayer, in *w·*, and deeds.
and in deed
  My. 260–28 the Way, in *w·* and in deed,
and might
  Mis. 100– 8 *w·* and might of Truth
and works
  Man. 17–11 *w·* and works of our Master,
  My. 46–11 *w·* and works of our Master,
awe-filled
  No. 10– 2 I employ this awe-filled *w·*
Christian
  '01. 12–10 *w·* Christian was anciently an
death
  My. 235– 2 without using the *w·* death,
devil
  No. 23–17 moral sense of the *w· devil*,
  Hea. 6–27 *w· devil* comes from the Greek
each
  Mis. 338–28 * Speak truly, and each *w·* of thine
equivalent
  Rud. 1–13 In French the equivalent *w·* is
every
  Un. 33–25 every *w·* may be— *Matt.* 18 : 16.
  My. 78–30 * every *w·* of the exercises
fitly spoken
  Mis. 346–23 "A *w·* fitly spoken is like— *Prov.* 25 : 11.
from the Directors
  My. 20–22 * chapter sub-title
gave the
  Mis. 153–11 "the Lord gave the *w·* :— *Psal.* 68 : 11.
God
  Mis. 75–16 except where the *w· God* can be used
  Peo. 2– 8 gives another letter to the *w· God*
  My. 226– 3 substitute the *w·* God
"god"
  Pan. 2–13 His uncapitalized *w·* "god"
God's
  My. 47–25 * God's *w·* in the wilderness of
good
  Hea. 3–15 derived from the *w· good.*
grandeur of the
  Mis. 99–29 grandeur of the *w·*, the power of
her
  My. 52–26 * interest of the world to hear her *w·*
His
  Mis. 154–19 Abide in His *w·*, and it shall
  Chr. 53–41 The Way, the Truth, the Life— His *w·*
  My. 159–10 sent forth His *w·* to heal
his
  Mis. 262–26 Having his *w·*, you have little need of
  388–21 First at the tomb to hear his *w·* :
  Po. 21–10 First at the tomb to hear his *w·* :
in defence
  My. 264– 2 chapter sub-title
kind
  Mis. 127–20 kind *w·* spoken, at the right moment,
Latin
  Mis. 25–23 from the Latin *w·* meaning *all*,
Life
  Ret. 59– 6 *w· Life* never means that which is
limits with a
  My. 106–21 Mind calms and limits with a *w·*.
loud
  Mis. 298–26 * unable to speak a loud *w·*,"
  Ret. 16– 9 could not speak a loud *w·*,
Love
  Pul. 26–22 * on a . . . is the *w·* "Love."
meaning of a
  Un. 27– 2 meaning of a *w·* employed
milk of the
  My. 17– 6 sincere milk of the *w·*,— *I Pet.* 2 : 2.
mother
  Man. 65– 1 to drop the *w· mother*
my
  '00. 14– 2 and has kept my *w·*,— *Rev.* 3 : 8.
no
  Mis. 250– 9 No *w·* is more misconstrued ;
no idle
  Pul. 67– 7 * This is no idle *w·*,
offend not in
  My. 196–12 offend not in *w·*,— *Jas.* 3 : 2.
of God
  Mis. 191– 1 handling the *w·* of God— *II Cor.* 4 : 2.
  Pan. 6–12 contradicting the *w·* of God
  '01. 16–15 handling the *w·* of God deceitfully.
  My. 124– 2 handling the *w·* of God— *II Cor.* 4 : 2.
  240–19 according to the *w·* of God.
of might
  Mis. 388– 1 who gave that *w·* of might
  '02. 20–10 who gave that *w·* of might
  Po. 7– 1 who gave that *w·* of might
of mine
  Mis. 322–16 presence, or *w·* of mine,

word

of Scripture
Un. 23– 9　agrees with the *w·* of Scripture,
of their testimony
Pul. 12–10　*w·* of their testimony ;— *Rev.* 12 : 11.
of the Lord
Pul. 7–23　*w·* of the Lord endureth— *I Pet.* 1 : 25.
of Truth
Mis. 100–17　to grasp the *w·* of Truth,
334–16　without one *w·* of Truth
of truth
My. 132–16　with the *w·* of truth."— *Jas.* 1 : 18.
one
Pul. 53–10　* contained in the one *w·* — *faith.*
Po. 27– 5　One *w·*, receding year,
My. 178–26　not one *w·* in the book was
258–10　one *w·*, "Mary,"— *John* 20 : 16.
or work
Man. 54–20　either by *w·* or work,
"pantheism"
Pan. 2–10　*w·* "pantheism" is derived from
2–12　English *w·* "pantheism"
Person
'01. 5– 2　defined strictly by the *w·* Person,
person
Rud. 1–11　The *w· person* affords a large
personal
Rud. 1–16　Blackstone applies the *w· personal*
personality
Ret. 74– 3　meaning of the *w· personality,*
philosophical
Un. 27– 8　philosphical *w·*, signifying
popularity
'01. 26–16　shall the *w·* popularity be
Principle
My. 225–30　The *w·* Principle, when referring
reflection
Mis. 23–25　means by the *w· reflection.*
reiterates the
Mis. 25–20　as it reiterates the *w·*,
Science
Mis. 193–20　supplying the *w·* Science to
science
My. 307– 4　*w·* science was not used at all,
send out
Pul. 52– 2　* treasurer has to send out *w·*
sense of the
Un. 8–11　in our sense of the *w·*.
No. 32– 6　popular sense of the *w·*,
"son"
Mis. 180–26　the *w·* "son" is defined
Soul
Mis. 75–17　The *w· Soul* may sometimes
soul
Un. 30– 3　uses the *w· soul* for *sense.*
spoken
Mis. 316–16　*w·* spoken at this date.
thanks
Mis. 160– 3　in uttering the *w· thanks,*
that
Mis. 303–11　the fullest sense of that *w·* ;
388– 1　who gave that *w·* of might
Pul. 53–15　* "That *w·*, more than any other,
Rud. 2– 8　not a *person,* as that *w·* is used
'02. 20–10　who gave that *w·* of might
Po. 7– 1　who gave that *w·* of might
My. 307–10　After this I noticed he used that *w·*
this
Mis. 76–21　whenever this *w·* means the so-called
301–17　without this *w·* of warning in public,
Un. 51–15　this *w·* is the generic term for all
My. 226– 2　using this *w·* incorrectly,
thought or
Mis. 387–15　By thought or *w·* unkind,
Po. 6–10　By thought or *w·* unkind,
through the
Mis. 154–18　Through the *w·* that is spoken
through their
Mis. 29– 9　through their *w·*."— *John* 17 : 20.
My. 190–29　through their *w·*."— *John* 17 : 20.
Thy
Mis. 208–23　now have I kept Thy *w·*."— *Psal.* 119 : 67.
to the wise
Mis. 319–17　chapter sub-title
My. 139–16　chapter sub-title
223–26　chapter sub-title
263– 5　A *w·* to the wise is sufficient.
unspoken
No. 2–16　than the unspoken *w·*.
usage of the
My. 226– 4　an intelligent usage of the *w·*
use of the
My. 302–17　use of the *w·* spread like wildfire.
use the
Pul. 55–21　* if we may use the *w·*

word

was conveyed
My. 77–26　* *W·* was conveyed to them that
written
Mis. 316–15　have profited . . . from the written *w·*,

Mis. 193–20　a *w·* which the people are now
248–10　*w·* synonymous with devil.
249–28　What a *w·* !　I am in awe before it.
250–19　cast aside the *w·* as a sham
301–14　require only a *w·* to be wise ;
Ret. 25– 9　in a *w·*, C. S.
38–22　Not a *w·* had passed between us,
Pul. 35– 4　in a *w·*— C. S."
Rud. 2– 5　the *w·* stands for one of the three
Hea. 16–16　A *w·* about the five personal senses,
My. 6–21　*w·* which proceedeth out of the
57–30　* Treasurer has sent out *w·* that
235–30　commemorated in deed or in *w·*

words

added
My. 318– 3　where Mr. Wiggin added *w·*,
adopt the
Mis. 215–28　nor adopt the *w·*, that Jesus used
and actions
Mis. 220–10　sick man's thoughts, *w·*, and actions,
and classification
My. 224–18　thoughts, *w·*, and classification of
and the works
My. 148–30　*w·* and the works of our great Master.
and works
Mis. 21–11　all his *w·* and works.
120–30　immortality of his *w·* and works.
Ret. 44– 1　commemorate the *w·* and works
'02. 11–30　very basis of his *w·* and works.
My. 349–18　his *w·* and works illustrate
applicable
My. 19–30　These are applicable *w·* :
are inadequate
My. 197–10　*W·* are inadequate to express
are not vain
My. 128– 1　*w·* are not vain when the
behind
Mis. 160– 5　a mother's love behind *w·*
beyond
My. 63–22　* of awe and of reverence beyond *w·*,
combination of
'02. 16– 7　use of that combination of *w·*,
David's
Ret. 15– 7　I could say in David's *w·*,
English
Un. 27– 3　two English *w·*, often used as if
equivalent
Mis. 67–27　by equivalent *w·* in another,
exact
My. 322–30　* The exact *w·* I do not recall,
few
Mis. 77– 8　in those few *w·* of the apostle.
112–19　My few *w·* touched him ;
133– 4　to build a sentence of so few *w·*
137– 8　a few *w·* aside to your teacher.
'01. 32–19　explain in a few *w·* a good man.
My. 39–20　* a few *w·* of reminder and prophecy.
289–25　send a few *w·* of condolence,
360–13　settle this . . . amicably by a few *w·*,
following
Mis. 35–10　following *w·* of her husband,
My. 219–28　in the following *w·* :
for the wise
My. 250– 1　chapter sub-title
further
My. 42–11　* further *w·* of mine are unnecessary.
good
Mis. 233–18　Substituting good *w·* for a good life,
'01. 2–10　or to substitute good *w·* for
Greek
Pan. 2–11　two Greek *w·* meaning "all" and "god."
hard
Man. 41– 8　but without hard *w·*.
her
Pul. 82– 4　* her *w·* are smiles
her own
My. 334–16　* to quote her own *w·*.
his
Mis. 21–11　makes practical all his *w·*
29– 3　Do you believe his *w·*?
99–20　the immortality of his *w·*.
99–24　never bear into oblivion his *w·*.
120–30　the immortality of his *w·*
121– 1　his *w·* can never pass away :
163–14　His *w·* were articulated in
192–17　his *w·* reveal the great Principle
193– 6　His *w·* are unmistakable,
195–18　these are his *w·* :
216– 1　in your application of his *w·*

words

his
Mis. 245– 3   but we have his *w*,
344–24   His *w*, living in our hearts,
'01. 26– 6   supported it by his *w*
'02. 8–16   his *w* and his deeds,
11–30   basis of his *w* and works.
My. 246–27   the wisdom of his *w*,
349–18   his *w* and works illustrate

his own
My. 108–29   will close with his own *w* :

idle
Mis. 357– 2   no time for idle *w*,

immortal
Mis. 100– 2   His immortal *w* were articulated
My. 146–17   Yet his immortal *w*
277–20   the immortal *w* and deeds

in other
Mis. 14–27   in other *w*, a lie
36–16   in other *w*, the nature and
36–24   [in other *w*, mortal mind]
67– 5   in other *w*, thou shalt not
112– 1   in other *w*, the one evil
118– 2   in other *w*, the material senses,
186–17   in other *w*, the spiritual Principle
194–31   in other *w*, understand God
197–20   in other *w*, to
222–10   in other *w*, a moral idiot.
375–22   * In other *w*, the art is perfect.
Un. 33–10   In other *w* : matter testifies of
Pan. 5–21   in other *w*, we should not
'00. 14–23   in other *w*, he that toiled
'02. 9– 6   in other *w*, Let the world,
My. 179– 9   In other *w*, soul enters
239–24   in other *w*, a kind of man

Jesus'
Mis. 133–29   to the truth of Jesus' *w*.
149–30   in the faith of Jesus' *w* :
194–20   text explains Jesus' *w*,
'01. 13–13   and we verify Jesus' *w*,
My. 58–24   * verifying Jesus' *w*,
300–18   the summit of Jesus' *w*,

Jesus' own
Mis. 20– 3   aroma of Jesus' own *w*,

key
Pul. 47–19   * which are the key *w*

largest
No. 10– 6   largest *w* in the vocabulary

little need of
Mis. 262–27   little need of *w* of approval

loving
Mis. 292–22   by loving *w* and deeds.

Master's
Un. 44– 4   only repeat the Master's *w* :

may belie desire
No. 40–10   *W* may belie desire,

mere
My. 78–27   * No mere *w* can convey the

more than
Mis. 110–11   your example, more than *w*,
126–21   Works, more than *w*, should
250–22   affection is more than *w* :
Hea. 2– 2   works more than *w* ;
15–28   and works more than *w*,
My. 58–16   * speaks more than *w* can

Mother's Room
Pul. 42–17   * the *w*, "Mother's Room,"

my
Mis. 99–22   my *w* shall not — *Matt.* 24 : 35.
111–17   my *w* shall not — *Matt.* 24 : 35.
163–19   my *w* shall not — *Matt.* 24 : 35.
Ret. 92– 9   my *w* abide in you, — *John* 15 : 7.
Un. 9– 7   my *w* would not have been spoken.
My. 150–23   my *w* abide in you, — *John* 15 : 7.

no
Mis. 375–27   * no *w* can express,
Po. 8–18   love, that no *w* could speak

of cheer
My. 202–21   thank you for the *w* of cheer

of Christ
My. 105– 1   more than the *w* of Christ,

of commendation
Mis. 313– 1   chapter sub-title

of David
Mis. 196–23   and, in the *w* of David,

of encouragement
My. 62–24   * and *w* of encouragement

of God
Mis. 317–31   speaketh the *w* of God : — *John* 3 : 34.

of Jesus
Mis. 37–14   meaning of those *w* of Jesus,
198–10   with the *w* of Jesus :
My. 253–15   and these *w* of Jesus :

of Life
Mis. 337–27   taught . . . the *w* of Life.

words

of Mary Baker Eddy
My. 66–23   * *w* of Mary Baker Eddy will

of Mrs. Hemans
My. 185–26   with the *w* of Mrs. Hemans :

of my Master
Mis. 180–12   in the *w* of my Master,

of my uncle
My. 60– 6   * remember the *w* of my uncle,

of our Master
Mis. 83–17   In the *w* of our Master,
196–14   hence the *w* of our Master :
317–22   These *w* of our Master explain
Ret. 67–23   In the *w* of our Master,
No. 14–18   Hear the *w* of our Master :
'00. 5– 6   Here note the *w* of our Master
My. 147–27   in the *w* of our Master

of Paul
Hea. 18– 3   In the *w* of Paul,

of rejoicing
My. 63–17   * with *w* of rejoicing ;

of Samuel
Ret. 9–15   in the *w* of Samuel,

of Solomon
Mis. 281–29   remember the *w* of Solomon.

of St. John
Mis. 205–11   in the *w* of St. John,
'00. 15–22   In the *w* of St. John,

of St. Paul
Mis. 120– 6   In the *w* of St. Paul,
Pan. 13–22   in the *w* of St. Paul :
'00. 6– 4   In the *w* of St. Paul :
My. 151–15   And in the *w* of St. Paul,
153–20   in the *w* of St. Paul,
187–11   In the *w* of St. Paul :
202– 7   In the *w* of St. Paul :
258–13   in the *w* of St. Paul :
285–19   In the *w* of St. Paul,

of strange import
Mis. 275–13   *w* of strange import.

of the Book
My. 183–20   deaf hear the *w* of the Book,

of the judge
Pul. 46– 6   * *w* of the judge speak to the point,

of the Master
Un. 43–15   *w* of the Master in support of this
My. 114– 1   In the *w* of the Master,

of the prophet
Mis. 143–28   in the *w* of the prophet Isaiah :
308–15   In the *w* of the prophet,
Pul. 20–18   In the *w* of the prophet :

of the Psalmist
Mis. 153–11   In the *w* of the Psalmist,
Ret. 14–25   in the *w* of the Psalmist :
Pul. 10– 5   in the *w* of the Psalmist,

of the Scripture
My. 156– 3   to reply in *w* of the Scripture :
196– 7   in these *w* of the Scripture,

of Truth
Mis. 99–15   take not back the *w* of Truth.
320–22   *w* of Truth and Life.

of Wendell Phillips
Mis. 245–28   in the *w* of Wendell Phillips,

our
'02. 4–12   that our works be as worthy as our *w*.
Hea. 19–25   making our *w* golden rays

plain
Ret. 90–12   and gave in plain *w*,

power of
Pul. 26– 7   * beyond the power of *w* to depict.

redemptive
Mis. 331–16   redemptive *w* from a mother's lips

remarkable
No. 36–10   remarkable *w*, as wholly opposed to

sacred
Man. 60–17   sacred *w* of our beloved Master,

sense of
Mis. 67–26   expresses the sense of *w*

some
My. 306–31   Some *w* in these quotations

Soul-full
My. 201–10   Your Soul-full *w* and song

St. Paul's
Mis. 298– 3   St. Paul's *w* take in the situation :

such
Mis. 134– 5   To reiterate such *w* of apology as

suggestive
My. 50–22   * these simple but suggestive *w*,

symbolic
Ret. 42– 6   symbolic *w* on his office sign.

their
Ret. 76– 1   an author's ideas and their *w*.
'00. 13– 6   their *w* were brave and their
My. 125–15   History will record their *w*,

words

these
Mis.	66– 6	these *w·* of the New Testament :
	83–23	"These *w·* spake Jesus, — *John* 17 : 1.
	132–27	I read in your article these *w·* :
	298–12	These *w·* of St. Matthew
	317–22	These *w·* of our Master explain
	368–20	portrayed in these *w·* of the apostle,
Ret.	22– 9	summarized . . . in these *w·* :
	72– 8	portrays the result . . . in these *w·* :
Pan.	13– 6	according to Christ, in these *w·* :
'02.	5–18	in these *w·* : "God is Love." — *I John* 4 : 8.
	7–13	Use these *w·* to define God,
My.	161– 9	Hence these *w·* of Christ Jesus :
	196– 7	in these *w·* of the Scripture,
	206–18	May these *w·* of the Scriptures comfort
	253–15	and these *w·* of Jesus :
	360–15	subscribe these *w·* of love :

those
Mis.	100– 7	infinite meaning of those *w·*.
	132–30	those *w·* inspire me with
	169–32	those *w·* are salvation
	188–32	beheld the meaning of those *w·*
	195–11	the validity of those *w·*
No.	13–10	those *w·* were originally uttered,
My.	19–25	Those *w·* of our holy Way-shower,
	159– 4	those *w·* of our loved Lord,
	270–18	Those *w·* of our dear,

three
No.	30–11	God's law is in three *w·*,
My.	253–23	wisdom in three *w·* :

thy
My.	196–14	"By thy *w·* thou shalt — *Matt.* 12 : 37.

too deep for
Mis.	142–21	chords of feeling too deep for *w·*.

two
Mis.	263– 5	These two *w·* in Scripture
No.	17–21	could grasp these two *w·*
My.	257–26	Christmas gift, two *w·* enwrapped,

use the
Mis.	376– 3	* I use the *w·* *most authentic*

web of
Mis.	377– 3	to weave a web of *w·*

works and
Ret.	78–13	such works and *w·* becloud

your
My.	59–15	* your *w·* explaining the Scriptures,

Mis.	86–11	*Nothing* and *something* are *w·* which
	151– 2	In the *w·* of the loving disciple,
	161–14	prophet whose *w·* we have chosen
	192–13	*w·* of him who spake divinely,
	260–26	*W·* are not always the auxiliaries of
	262–10	however simple the *w·*,
	262–22	more grateful than *w·* can express,
	338– 5	proved to myself, not by "*w·*,"
	341– 6	then put thought into *w·*,
	341– 7	and *w·* into deeds ;
	373–31	presents not *w·* alone, but works,
Un.	43–16	*w·* which can never "pass — *Matt.* 5 : 18.
Pul.	5– 3	in the *w·* I use,
	42–23	* in letters of red were the *w·* :
Pan.	4–21	in the *w·* of the Hebrew singer,
'01.	34–28	In the *w·* of the Hebrew writers :
'02.	7–12	prefix to the *w· potence, presence,*
My.	vii–10	* Deeds, not *w·*, are the sound test
	29– 6	* *w·* of the Lord's Prayer !
	32–13	* *W·* by the Rev. Mary Baker Eddy.
	32–24	* *w·* by the Rev. Mary Baker Eddy,
	108–26	*w·* of the New York press
	172–15	In the *w·* of our great Master,
	197–15	*w·* are but the substitutes for
	270–15	*w·* of those who say that she
	290–25	*w·* of him who suffered and
	306–29	purporting to be Dr. Quimby's own *w·*,
	307– 1	read like *w·* that I said to him,
	323–18	* to tell you in *w·* all that your
	332– 5	* *w·* are indeed but a meagre tribute

wore
Pul.	42–15	* *w·* a white satin badge
My.	83– 6	* *w·* tiny white, unmarked buttons,

work (noun)

absorbed in the
Pul.	72–11	* much absorbed in the *w·*

accumulating
Ret.	44–13	because of accumulating *w·*
My.	276– 7	accumulating *w·* requires it,

actual
My.	86–14	* the actual *w·* was completed,

and career
Mis.	296– 7	unfamiliarity with the *w·* and career

applied for
Mis.	353–15	man who applied for *w·*,

work (noun)

at
Mis.	212–24	at *w·* in a wrong direction,
	230–10	and mere motion when at *w·*,
	257–12	so-called force, or law, at *w·*
	262–14	students, who are at *w·*
	276–27	or at *w·* erroneously,
	284– 7	the humanitarian at *w·*
	285–18	is still at *w·*, deep down in
	334–19	evil at *w·* in the name of good,
Pul.	33–17	* at *w·* in a field one day
'01.	20–17	individual knew what was at *w·*
Po.	67– 5	And thought be at *w·* with
My.	145–14	He remained at *w·*,
	200–21	Pale, sinful sense, at *w·*

begin with
My.	203– 9	begin wth *w·* and never stop

best
Mis.	273–26	I cannot do my best *w·* for
My.	108–23	designated as his best *w·*,
	108–25	best *w·* of a Christian Scientist.

bless the
My.	197–28	God will bless the *w·* of your

charity
Rud.	14–21	doing charity *w·* besides.

chosen
Ret.	42–13	untiring in his chosen *w·*.

Christian
Mis.	5– 7	to this Christian *w·*.
	242–16	department of Christian *w·*,

Christian Science
Ret.	88–18	another part of C. S. *w·*,
Rud.	13–26	to give all their time to C. S. *w·*,

church
Pul.	44–19	* chapter sub-title
My.	76–17	* in the support of their church *w·*,
	84– 1	* necessary expense of church *w·*,
	352– 7	* privileges . . . in this church *w·*.

College
Mis.	274– 8	outside of College *w·*,

commenced
Ret.	15–16	I accepted . . . and commenced *w·*.

commencing
My.	12–12	* and the date of commencing *w·*,

doing the
Mis.	266–11	doing the *w·* that nobody else can
'00.	8–19	when doing the *w·* that belongs to

done
My.	345–21	"The *w·* done by the surgeon is

earnest
My.	61–32	* earnest *w·* of our noble Board

editorial
Pul.	31–16	* resulting from editorial *w·*

extraordinary
My.	vi–10	* full credit for this extraordinary *w·*.

field of
My.	216–19	indicates another field of *w·*

God's
Mis.	317– 3	if you are doing God's *w·*.
My.	231–13	in order to help God's *w·*

good
'00.	3–12	love a good *w·* or good workers
My.	156– 9	to every good *w·*," — *II Cor.* 9 : 8.

gospel
Mis.	318–18	gospel *w·* of teaching C. S.,
Ret.	47–21	gospel *w·* of teaching C. S.,

gratutous
Rud.	14–12	in order to do gratutous *w·*.

great
Mis.	7–25	great *w·* already has been done,
	177–17	great *w·* of establishing the truth,
Ret.	55– 1	true sense of the great *w·*
Pul.	85– 6	* gratitude to her for her great *w·*,
'01.	11– 3	because of Jesus' great *w·* on earth,
My.	22–12	* to complete this great *w·*,
	321– 5	* accomplished this great *w·*.

greater
Mis.	7–25	greater *w·* yet remains to be done.

greatest
Mis.	358–25	greatest *w·* of the ages,

growth of the
Mis.	6–14	rapid growth of the *w·* shows.

hard
Mis.	230–15	have become such by hard *w·* ;
	234–14	to steal from others and avoid hard *w·* ;
	237–27	hero who did the hard *w·*,

healing
Man.	49– 2	endeavor to monopolize the healing *w·*

her
Mis.	62–21	her *w·* entitled "Mind-cure on a
Pul.	31– 5	* C. S., as they term her *w·*
	59–16	* were read from . . . her *w·*
My.	52–10	* to sustain her in her *w·*.
	52–23	* if only through her *w·*

His
Un.	14– 3	do His *w·* over again,

work (noun)

his
Mis.	92– 8	His *w·* is to replenish thought,
	212– 6	Jesus did his *w·*, and
	221–23	divorces his *w·* from Science.
	238–13	or his *w·* is utilized
Ret.	38–13	resumed his *w·* at the same time,
	86–20	carry his burden and do his *w·*,
Pul.	72–28	* Christ has told us to do his *w·*,
No.	41– 9	repeat his *w·* to the best advantage
'00.	3–28	improved on his *w·* of creation,
My.	291– 7	His *w·* began with heavy strokes,

his own
Mis.	284– 1	for each one to do his own *w·*

holds back
My.	84– 6	* holds back *w·* that would otherwise

holy
Man.	49– 5	privileged to enter into this holy *w·*,

ill-done
Mis.	393– 9	*W·* ill-done within the misty
Po.	51–14	*W·* ill-done within the misty

immortal
Mis.	237–27	immortal *w·*, of loosing the fetters

important
My.	241– 2	* to perform this important *w·*.

inspected the
My.	24–25	* have recently inspected the *w·*,
	145– 8	I inspected the *w·* every day,

is done
Ret.	33–13	the better the *w·* is done ;
Po.	27–20	Thy *w·* is done, and well :

its
Mis.	297– 7	bases its *w·* on ethical conditions
	308–21	little messenger has done its *w·*,
	359– 3	when it has done its *w·*,
My.	50–27	* few saw the grandeur of its *w·*
	245– 7	Law and order characterize its *w·*

James H. Wiggin's
My.	322–11	* Rev. James H. Wiggin's *w·*

limner's
Mis.	393– 6	Paints the limner's *w·*, I ween,
Po.	51–11	Paints the limner's *w·*, I ween,

literary
My.	320– 1	had done some literary *w·* for you

little
No.	9–18	first edition of this little *w·*

mental
Mis.	350–10	no advice given, no mental *w·*,

monstrous
Mis.	122– 9	such a monstrous *w·* ?

mosaic
Pul.	25– 6	* marble in mosaic *w·*,
	26– 9	* mosaic *w·*, with richly carved

most derided
No.	41– 7	Is it the *w·* most derided

most important
Ret.	37– 1	most important *w·*, S. and H.,

Mrs. Eddy's
Pul.	23– 6	* MRS. EDDY'S *W·* AND HER INFLUENCE

my
Mis.	29–19	first publication of my *w·*,
	300–26	from my *w·* S. and H.,
Ret.	27– 3	so laid the foundation of my *w·*
	38 2	could not go on with my *w·*.
	38– 4	and yet he stopped my *w·*.
Pul.	7– 1	speaking of my *w·*, said :
Rud.	7– 6	set forth in my *w·* S. and H.
No.	33– 5	if the Bible and my *w·* S. and H.
'01.	24–22	published my *w·* S. and H.,
My.	202–23	My *w·* is reflected light,
	275–19	Either my *w·*, the demands upon

needful
No.	1– 3	is a most needful *w·* ;

noble
Ret.	49–23	for her great and noble *w·*,

noblest
Mis.	294– 1	The noblest *w·* of God is man
Ret.	77– 3	* honest man's the noblest *w·* of God ;''
	77– 5	* honest God's the noblest *w·* of man.''

of a Reader
Man.	55–12	not to be fit for the *w·* of a Reader

of art
Mis.	372–17	* are truly a *w·* of art,

of a woman
Pul.	55– 9	* That it should be the *w·* of a woman

of Christianity
My.	30–25	* for the *w·* of Christianity.

of Christian Science
Man.	82–19	engaged in the *w·* of C. S.
Pul.	44– 9	* blessed onward *w·* of C. S.

of creation
'00.	3–28	improved on his *w·* of creation,

of healing
Mis.	7– 7	is necessary in this *w·* of healing.
	37–27	leaving to . . . the *w·* of healing ;
Ret.	54–22	*w·* of healing, in the Science of Mind,

work (noun)

of her life
Pul.	31–11	* familiarity with the *w·* of her life

of His hand
Mis.	152–10	o'er the *w·* of His hand.

of its erection
My.	23–28	* in the *w·* of its erection.

of Jesus
No.	37–19	whereby the *w·* of Jesus would

of moments
Mis.	68– 2	is not the *w·* of moments ;

of Mrs. Eddy
Pul.	28– 1	* typical of the *w·* of Mrs. Eddy.

of the church
My.	51–25	* very early *w·* of the church,

of the devil
My.	60– 9	* it is the *w·* of the devil.''

of the Lord
Chr.	55–12	*w·* of the Lord,— *Isa.* 5 : 12.

on this doctrine
Mis.	382– 5	my first *w·* on this doctrine,

on this subject
Ret.	35– 9	before a *w·* on this subject could be

our
Mis.	180–18	Let us do our *w·* ;
	215–14	Principle and object of our *w·*,
	216– 5	we must first have done our *w·*,
Hea.	5–23	to do our *w·* for us,

pioneer
Ret.	50–30	in the beginning of pioneer *w·*.
My.	148– 1	to do your pioneer *w·* in this city.

plaster
My.	68–26	* plaster *w·* for the great arches

present
Mis.	358–28	do their present *w·*, awaiting,

previous
Un.	14– 9	improve upon His own previous *w·*,

progress of the
My.	24–18	* progress of the *w·* on the extension

regarding the
My.	319–13	* her statement regarding the *w·*

relief
Pul.	26– 5	* richly panelled in relief *w·*.

religious
Pul.	36– 6	* foundation of her religious *w·*
	68– 9	* for the interests of her religious *w·*

result of the
My.	327–14	* This is the result of the *w·* done

scientific
Pul.	2–27	do this Christianly scientific *w·*

stupendous
Mis.	380–12	to begin this stupendous *w·* at once,

such a
My.	59–30	* has accomplished such a *w·* or

that
Mis.	35–26	the author of that *w·*,
	62–23	In that *w·* the author grapples with
My.	319–15	* what he himself thought of that *w·*

their
Mis.	120– 6	or repeat their *w·* in tears.
My.	66–20	* hurrying on with their *w·*
	177–23	direct their *w·* in truth,— *Isa.* 61 : 8.

their own
Mis.	317– 6	Scientists to do their own *w·* ;
Ret.	85– 3	doing their own *w·* well.
Un.	13– 5	doing their own *w·* in obedience to

this
Mis.	xi–27	in compiling this *w·*, I have
	4–18	periodical devoted to this *w·*
	5– 1	This *w·* well done will elevate
	7– 7	in this *w·* of healing.
	57– 8	This *w·* had been done ;
	378– 1	while the author of this *w·* was
Pul.	60– 7	* before coming into this *w·*,
My.	v–17	* this *w·* "without money"— *Isa.* 55 : 1.
	234–10	give me the holidays for this *w·*
	298–11	to publish and circulate this *w·*.

three days'
My.	214–11	three days' *w·* in the sepulchre

well done
My.	134–11	good achievements and *w·* well done

word or
Man.	54–20	either by word or *w·*,

would be accomplished
My.	61–15	* that the *w·* would be accomplished

years of
My.	22–20	* In these years of *w·* she has

your
Mis.	111– 3	your *w·*, well done, would dignify
My.	59– 1	* grandeur and magnitude of your *w·*
	194– 5	The letter of your *w·* dies,
	248– 3	satisfied with your *w·* :
	320– 6	* converse about you and your *w·*,
	320–26	* detail regarding your *w·*,
	321– 3	* connected with your *w·*,
	321–32	* their knowledge of your *w·*.

work (noun)
your
My.	322–30	* of you and your *w*.
	324– 2	* about you and your *w*,

Mis.	5– 3	devote our best energies to the *w*.
	15–13	is not the *w* of a moment.
	224–15	that human life is the *w*, the play,
	273– 7	where none other can do the *w*.
	273–31	The *w* is more than one person can
	274– 6	*w* that needs to be done,
Ret.	82–18	ample to supply many . . . with *w*.
Pul.	29– 6	* of whose *w* I shall venture to
	36– 3	* The *w* in the Metaphysical College
	49–26	* the will of the woman set at *w*,
Rud.	16–19	a *w* which I published in 1875
'01.	17–20	a difficult stage of the *w*,
My.	v–24	* an unparalleled record for a *w* of
	6–24	above the *w* of men's hands,
	12– 2	* *w* should be commenced as soon as
	12– 6	* those having the *w* in charge
	14–28	* rapidity with which the *w*
	16–15	* have the *w* directly in charge,
	42–26	* *w* that has been inaugurated by
	46–14	* *w* of true Christian Scientists.
	47–10	* After a *w* has been established,
	47–13	* labored unceasingly for the *w*
	61–21	* One feature about the *w*
	61–22	* admit that the *w* could be done,
	72–26	* paid in before the *w* was
	94–28	above the *w* of men's hands,
	105–25	*w* describing my system of healing.
	147–26	I have a *w* to do
	166–21	would be more irksome than *w*.
	216–20	*w* by which you can do much good
	242–18, 19	publication committee *w*, reading-room *w*,
	289– 1	All education is *w*.

work (verb)
Mis.	10– 6	"*w* together for good — *Rom.* 8 : 28.
	22– 9	must *w* for the discovery of
	39–29	when claiming to *w* with God
	52–24	should attempt to *w* out a rule
	52–27	*w* out the previous example,
	52–29	have the sum of being to *w* out,
	52–30	They must *w* out of this dream
	85–20	and *w* out his own salvation.
	116–28	never unready to *w* for God,
	117–16	reciprocate kindness and *w* wisely,
	118–17	being willing to *w* alone with God
	137–21	to *w* out individually and
	138– 2	sustain themselves and *w* for others.
	138– 9	For students to *w* together
	175–28	to *w* by means of both animal
	233–25	unwilling to *w* hard enough
	237–21	can only *w* out its own destruction ;
	271–10	take our magazine, *w* for it,
	273– 5	to *w* in other directions,
	283–24	*w* out his own problem
	288– 4	*w* out the greatest good to the
	303– 1	to *w* for the race ;
	333–18	to *w* out the problem of Mind,
	340– 6	the time to *w*, is *now*.
	340–21	they *w* on to the achievement of
	353–22	makes the machinery *w* rightly ;
	389– 3	the right to *w* and pray,
Ret.	38–10	Accordingly, I set to *w*,
	49–10	adapted to *w* this result ;
	55– 2	and *w* conscientiously.
	58– 3	with which to *w* out the problem
	88–21	to *w* in other vineyards
Un.	5– 5	*w* gradually and gently up
Pul.	69–13	* they can *w* a cure.
	69–22	* to *w* a cure the practitioner must
No.	2– 7	leaves you to *w* against that
	8–12	*w* out his own salvation,
	8–21	*w*, watch, and pray for
'00.	2–7, 8	"*W* — *w* — *w* — watch and pray."
	2–22	leave . . . to *w* for me."
	2–30	I *w* hard enough to be so."
	11–10	*w* together for good — *Rom.* 8 : 28.
Hea.	5–21	*w* out our own salvation,
	8–25	*w* to become Christians
	13– 2	taking . . . we should *w* at opposites
	19–22	But let us *w* more earnestly
Peo.	9–13	*w* out our own salvation,
Po.	21–17	the right to *w* and pray,
	39–15	*W* for our glorious cause!
My.	61–25	* be willing to let God *w*.
	63–15	* to *w* out the purposes of
	143–25	*w* together for good — *Rom.* 8 : 28.
	184– 6	wait upon Him and work righteousness.
	188–25	As you *w*, the ages win ;
	193– 5	to watch and *w* for all,
	195– 8	to love more, to *w* more,
	196–26	*W* and pray for it.
	196–28	*w* for their health and holiness.

work (verb)
My.	216–23	*w* in your own several localties,
	252–13	not *w* in the sunshine and run away
	252–14	*w* midst clouds of wrong,
	259–16	to think and *w* for others.
	291–29	*w* for their own country,
	300– 4	"*W* out your own salvation — *Phil.* 2 : 12.

worked
Mis.	365–17	*w* out a moral result ;
Ret.	52– 8	I have *w* to provide a
Pul.	33–20	* walked with him as he *w*,
	44– 3	* you have *w*, toiled, prayed
	51–12	* *w* in the mine of knowledge
'01.	29–21	*w* and won for them
My.	145–17	I have *w* even harder
	195– 6	new problems to be *w* out

worker (see also **worker's**)
Mis.	147–24	the pious *w*, the public-spirited
Ret.	52– 9	*w* in this vineyard of Truth.
	82–19	the prosperity of each *w* ;
'00.	2–10	the right thinker and *w*,
	2–25	intermediate *w* works at times.
	3– 4	The right thinker and *w*
	3–14	the best thinker and *w*
	3–19	the right thinker and *w*,
My.	225– 3	*w* in the spirit of Truth

worker's
'00.	3– 9	If the right thinker and *w* servitude

workers
Mis.	324– 1	converse with the watchers and *w*
Ret.	82–21	ease and welfare of the *w*.
	87– 9	settled and systematic *w*.
Pul.	8–23	youthful *w* were called "Busy Bees."
'00.	2–21	are my busiest *w* ;
	2–23	doom of such *w* will come,
	3–12	love a good work or good *w*
	3–12	are themselves *w* who appreciate a
	9–21	challenge the thinkers, . . . and *w*
My.	40– 9	* subsidence of criticism among *w*.
	50– 7	* little band of prayerful *w*.
	161–10	all ye *w* of iniquity.— *Luke* 13 : 27.

worketh
Mis.	118–26	divine Principle *w* with you,
	137–26	that *w* or maketh a lie.
	174–18	nothing that maketh or *w* a lie.
	190–22	impersonal evil, or whatever *w* ill.
	283–25	God *w* with him,
	366–14	nothing that *w* or maketh a lie
No.	15–26	"*w* or maketh a lie"— see *Rev.* 21 : 27.
'00.	10– 2	All that *w* good is
'01.	9–30	*w* well and healeth quickly,
	10–25	for God *w* with us,
	19– 4	He *w* with them to save sinners.
	28–22	all that *w* or maketh a lie.
My.	33–17	and *w* righteousness, — *Psal.* 15 : 2.
	228–24	and *w* righteousness, — *Psal.* 15 : 2.
	300– 6	God which *w* in you — *Phil.* 2 : 13.
	348–31	nothing that *w* ill can enter

working
Mis.	29–31	*w* up to those higher rules of Life
	44– 3	not *w* for emoluments,
	53– 4	suicide . . . is not *w* it out.
	70–27	*w*, . . . wonderful demonstrations
	87–17	*that no one there was *w* in Science,*
	197–31	*w* from no other Principle,
	263–17	*w* assiduously for our common Cause,
	280–16	*w* on one side and in Science.
	302–19	*w* faithfully for Christ's cause
	323– 9	*w* and watching for his coming.
	325–22	and seen *w* for it !
	343– 7	its cure, in *w* for God.
	368–25	*w* out the destinies of the
Man.	52–20	*W* Against the Cause.
	52–22	in *w* against the interests of
	72– 6	Christian Scientist *w* in the Field,
Ret.	49– 5	*w* out their periods of organization,
	49–16	loving unselfishly, *w* patiently
Pul.	5–29	palpably *w* in the sermons,
Rud.	v– 5	LOYAL STUDENTS, *w* AND WAITING
No.	2–18	*w* to mature what he has been taught.
	12– 2	*w* from a . . . Christian standpoint.
Pan.	1–12	mortals are hoping and *w*,
'00.	2–27	*w* when it is convenient."
'01.	10–25	*w* out our own salvation,
	28– 4	by praying, watching, and *w*
	30–24	*w* alone with God,
	35–16	And the *w* hitherto
Peo.	4– 1	*w* out our own salvation.
	7– 2	*w* out our own ideals,
My.	66–19	* Artisans and artists are *w*
	203– 9	begin with work and never stop *w*.
	213–16	*w* so subtly that we mistake its
	231– 5	liability of *w* in wrong directions.

working
My. 275–21   *W·* and praying for my dear friends'
    298– 7   distinguished all my *w·* years.

workingmen
My. 70–13   * *w·* stopped in the street

workings
Mis. 51– 8   the malicious *w·* of error
    108–19   evil and its subtle *w·*
    115– 5   culpable ignorance of the *w·* of
    290–13   its *w·* in the human heart.
    350– 4   *w·* whereof were not "terrible
My. 236–28   the *w·* of animal magnetism,

workman
Mis. 353–13   one day a *w·* in his mills,
Pul. 45–14   * predictions of *w·* and onlooker
My. 310– 9   * "a *w·* in a Tilton woolen mill."

workmen
Ret. 35–22   beneath the stroke of artless *w·*.
Pul. 50– 2   * the welfare of industrious *w·*,
My. 61–22   * as soon as the *w·* began to admit

work-rooms
My. 147–23   *w·* and a little hall,

works (noun)
accomplished the
Mis. 171–17   upon which are accomplished the *w·*
according to
'01. 10–29   faith according to *w·*.
and words
Ret. 78–13   such *w·* and words becloud the
beneficial
My. 99– 8   * good and beneficial *w·*,
copyrighted
Mis. 381– 1   copyrighted *w·* of Mrs. Eddy
Man. 43–16   Mary Baker Eddy's copyrighted *w·*
My. 130–23   Borrowing from my copyrighted *w·*,
dead
My. 128– 4   repentance from dead *w·*." — Heb. 6 : 1.
doing the
My. 28–20   * doing the *w·* which Jesus said
    245–20   doing the *w·* of primitive Christianity,
faith and
My. 103– 5   faith and *w·* demanded of man
faith by
Mis. 138–13   should he prove his faith by *w·*,
God's
My. 294–21   is shown him by God's *w·*
good
Mis. 203– 9   love, loyalty, and good *w·*.
    358– 1   Love impels good *w·*.
'00. 15–11   victory, faith, and good *w·*.
'01. 32– 9   Full of charity and good *w·*,
    34–23   understanding, and good *w·* ;
'02. 20– 9   thy unfaltering faith and good *w·*
My. 155– 6   abounding in love and good *w·*,
    191– 9   steadfast in love and good *w·*.
greater
Mis. 192–11   *greater w· than these — John* 14 : 12.
her
Mis. 35– 1   healing embodied in her *w·*.
My. vi–28   * for the publishing of her *w·* ;
    126–18   according to her *w·* : — *Rev.* 18 : 6.
his
Mis. 167–28   His *w·* thus prove him.
Man. 42– 9   By his *w·* he shall be judged,
My. 105– 6   prove one's faith by his *w·*.
    246–28   his *w·* are the same to-day as
    296–13   and his *w·* do follow him.
    305–25   simply how to do his *w·*.
illumined by
Mis. 338– 9   Faith illumined by *w·* ;
later
Pul. 83–21   * When we try to praise her later *w·*
marvellous
Mis. 199–23   Principle of these marvellous *w·*
mighty
My. 294– 8   not many mighty *w·* — *Matt.* 13 : 58.
Mrs. Eddy's
Mis. 35–13   * "Mrs. Eddy's *w·* are the outgrowths
my
Mis. 156–18   through the study of my *w·*
    214–22   even to understand my *w·*,
    247–11   departure in one of my *w·*
    249– 9   false report that . . . in my *w·*,
    300– 9   publish your copy of my *w·*,
    300–15   You literally publish my *w·*
    301–14   have read copies of my *w·*
    302–20   copying and reading my *w·*
    310– 2   is neither the intent of my *w·* nor
    318–21   the latest editions of my *w·*,
Chr. 57– 2   and keepeth my *w·* — *Rev.* 2 : 26.
Ret. 47–24   the latest editions of my *w·*,
'01. 27– 9   My *w·* are the first ever
Hea. 5–25   my faith by my *w·*." — *Jas.* 2 : 18.

works (noun)
my
My. 130– 8   to keep my *w·* from public recog
    130–21   quotations from my *w·* must hav
    285–18   and keepeth my *w·* — *Rev.* 2 : 26.
my published
Mis. x–27   in connection with my published
    89–24   will find . . . in my published *u*
of art
Mis. 375–13   * and their great *w·* of art
of Christ
Mis. 196–22   we shall do the *w·* of Christ,
of darkness
Rud. 4–24   extinguishes . . . the *w·* of dar
of masters
Mis. 372–14   *w·* of masters in France
of other authors
Ret. 75– 8   the *w·* of other authors?
of Satan
Mis. 68–16   to know that the *w·* of Satan
of the devil
No. 31–15   the *w·* of the devil" — *I John*
of the Spirit
Ret. 65– 4   the *w·* of the Spirit.
of Thy hands
Mis. 248– 7   the *w·* of Thy hands." — *Ps*
on science
Mis. 64–21   *W·* on science are profitable
on the subject
Mis. 382– 3   No *w·* on the subject of C.
other
Mis. 144–12   other *w·* written by the sar
Man. 34–13   and other *w·* by Mrs. Edd;
our
'02. 4–11   that our *w·* be as worthy
public
Mis. 335–16   In my public *w·*
published
Mis. 300– 3   Copying my published *w·*
My. 218–24   My published *w·* are teac
    321– 9   * as regards your publish
    321–15   * relations to your publis
repeats the
Mis. 25–20   repeats the *w·*, and man
scientific
Ret. 78–12   so-called scientific *w·*,
spurious
Mis. 80– 2   spurious *w·* on mental l
substitutes for
My. 197–16   are but the substitutes
that I do
Mis. 21– 9   "The *w·* that I do — *J*
    192–10   *the w· that I do — John*
    193–27   the *w·* that I do — *Joh*
    195–19   the *w·* that I do — *Jol*
    251–15   "The *w·* that I do — *J*
'02. 18–21   "The *w·* that I do — *J*
My. 221–22   the *w·* that I do — *Jo*
their
Mis. 243–19   their *w·* alone should
Pul. 57–17   * proved their faith l
'01. 33–17   they ask to be know!
    33–18   to be judged (if at al
My. 125–15   their *w·* will follow t
    127– 5   judged according to
    128–30   according to their *w*
these
No. 11–20   demonstrate what t
    41– 6   "For which of thes·
My. 103– 8   of this faith and th
    149– 1   To attain to these
those
'01. 27–12   be traced to some
My. 108–24   "For which of tho;
    227– 1   "For which of tho;
thy
'00. 15–24   I know thy *w·*, —
    15–25   thy patience, and
My. 3–12   by thy *w·*." — *see*
understanding, and
'01. 21– 2   Science, understa
voluminous
Ret. 76– 5   write voluminou;
ways and
Ret. 64–18   God's ways and
without
Mis. 154– 6   Your faith has r
Pul. 9–29   "Faith without
My. 3–10   sear leaves of fa
wonderful
Mis. 175–31   done many wor
'02. 16–21   sublime patien
Hea. 3–20   wonderful *w·* o
My. 193– 9   for His wonder
wondrous
Ret. 15–11   Thy wondrous *w·*

works (noun)
word and
  Man. 17–11 word and *w·* of our Master,
  My. 46–11 word and *w·* of our Master,
words and
  (see **words**)
words and the
  My. 148–30 words and the *w·* of our great Master.
your
  Mis. 299–13 * "Is it right to copy your *w·*
       301–20 "Is it right to copy your *w·*
  My. 148– 4 your faith be known by your *w·*.
       194–27 reward you according to your *w·*,
       320–15 * and the author of all your *w·*.
       320–23 * as the author of your *w·*
       321–25 * of the authorship of your *w·*

  Mis. 126–21 *W·*, more than words,
       311–23 *w·* I have written on C. S.
       373–31 presents not words alone, but *w·*,
  Hea. 2– 2 *w·* more than words ;
       15–27 and *w·* more than words,
  My. 70–21 * *w·* of both ancient and modern
       104–13 *w·* even more that the words of

orks (verb)
  Mis. 12–17 *w·* in the interest of both
       19–21 *w·* upon as high a basis
       48– 2 and avoid all that *w·* ill.
       117–24 *w·* somewhat in the dark ;
       220– 3 a good rule *w·* one way,
       238–12 reformer *w·* on unmentioned,
       288–10 this error *w·* out the results
       292–24 *w·* out the purposes of Love.
  Pul. 83–11 * with the certainty of . . . she *w·*,
  '00. 2–11 The right thinker *w·* ;
       2–25 intermediate worker *w·* at times.
  '02. 8–21 *w·* out the rule of
  My. 153–25 Principle of which *w·* intelligently
       292–17 *w·* unconsciously against the
       343– 3 * *w·* around a question

·ld (see also **world's**)
vancement of the
  Ret. 49– 2 advancement of the *w·* in Truth
vance the
  Mis. 366– 4 they would advance the *w·*.
inst the
  My. 134–2 constant battle against the *w·*,
over the
  Mis. 315– 9 Scientists, all over the *w·*,
  My. 30– 7 * Scientists from all over the *w·*,
       72–23 * members . . . all over the *w·*.
       73–14 * from all over the *w·*
       77– 9 * From all over the *w·*
       84–13 * Scientists all over the *w·*.
parts of the
  Pul. 68– 7 * from all parts of the *w·*,
  My. 47– 5 * from all parts of the *w·*,
       141–20 * from all parts of the *w·*.
he
  Mis. 37–14 "Go ye into all the *w·* — Mark 16 : 15.
       325–32 "Go ye into all the *w·* ;— Mark 16 : 15.
  o. 14–19 "Go ye into all the *w·*" !— Mark 16 : 15.
       41–20 "Go ye into all the *w·*, — Mark 16 : 15,
  y. 28–20 more than all the *w·*,
  y. 11– 7 * the one of all the *w·* who has
       47–00 * "Go ye into all the *w·*,— Mark 16 : 15.
       63–19 * all the *w·* was in some degree
       87–25 * if all the *w·* turned to the
       128–21 go into all the *w·*, preaching
       172–16 'Go ye into all the *w·*,' — Mark 16 : 15.
       271–15 * most discussed woman in all the *w·*.
       300–25 "Go ye into all the *w·*, — Mark 16 : 15.
er
       33–25 * spiritual form from another *w·*.
use of the
       325– 9 with the applause of the *w·* :
g with the
       1–12 before arguing with the *w·*
·d
       26–15 land is reached and the *w·* aroused,
·e
       169–16 and of the *w·* at large,
o the
       6– 3 and so come back to the *w·*
the
       29–24 * different status before the *w·* !
       64–10 * name an honored one before the *w·*.
       64–19 * standing of C. S. before the *w·*.
·
       39–22 * Gaze on the *w·* below.
·r
       6– 4 * to follow her to the brighter *w·*.
· to the
       28–29 * brought to the *w·* the spiritual

world
business
  My. 96– 6 * the social and business *w·*,
came to the
  My. 217–30 He came to the *w·* not to destroy
celestial
  Pan. 3–32 his man-face, the celestial *w·*.
challenge the
  Mis. 247– 9 I calmly challenge the *w·*
Christian
  My. 60–12 * What a change in the Christian *w·*!
       103 chapter sub-title
civilized
  Pul. 79–12 * every part of the civilized *w·*,
  My. 59–12 * accepted . . . in the civilized *w·*.
       90–25 * from all over the civilized *w·*,
       273– 9 * covers practically the civilized *w·*.
cleave to the
  Mis. 2– 7 to cleave to the *w·*, the flesh, and
come to the
  Un. 59– 2 why did the Messiah come to the *w·*,
conqueror of a
  '02. 19–15 happier than the conqueror of a *w·*.
contact with the
  Mis. 110– 9 not through contact with the *w·*.
  Pul. 36– 7 * to retire from . . . the *w·*.
       68–10 * to retire from . . . the *w·*.
convert the
  Mis. 279–28 are enough to convert the *w·*
doctrines of the
  My. 92– 3 * position in the doctrines of the *w·*
drops the
  Mis. 1–18 gathers fresh . . . and drops the *w·*.
end of the
  My. 44–13 * unto the end of the *w·*." — Matt. 28 : 20.
engirdle the
  My. 164–24 expansion that will engirdle the *w·*,
enlightening the
  '02. 2–18 enlightening the *w·* with the glory of
  My. 245–21 and enlightening the *w·*.
entire
  Mis. 154– 5 shelter to the entire *w·*.
  My. 31–13 * contributed from over the entire *w·*.
era of the
  My. 154–23 in our era of the *w·* I welcome
evil
  My. 297–12 gust of evil in this evil *w·*
explain to the
  My. 105–28 book which should explain to the *w·*
fills the
  Mis. 228–10 fills the *w·* with its fragrance,
floods the
  '02. 5– 8 floods the *w·* with the baptism of
forefront of the
  '02. 14–21 blazoned on the forefront of the *w·*
foundation of the
  My. 185–18 foundation of the *w·*," — Rev. 13 : 8.
friction of the
  Mis. 224–21 so genial that the friction of the *w·*
from the
  Hea. 6– 1 the more are we separated from the *w·* ;
given to the
  Mis. 165–30 reproduced and given to the *w·*,
       178–32 has been given to the *w·* to-day.
  '01. 26–29 What I have given to the *w·*
giveth
  Mis. 215– 6 not as the *w·* giveth,   John 14 : 27.
  My. 279– 4 not as the *w·* giveth, — John 14 : 27.
give to the
  Mis. 137–27 Then you can give to the *w·* the benefit
  Ret. 93–24 should give to the *w·* convincing proof of
glimpse of the
  Pul. 47–24 * wishes to catch a glimpse of the *w·*.
gross
  Po. 47– 7 Ever the gross *w·* above ;
has need
  Mis. 110– 4 the *w·* has need of you,
hidden from the
  Pul. 9–24 bounty hidden from the *w·*.
ideal
  Mis. 74–15 immortal sense of the ideal *w·*.
       217– 7 even the ideal *w·* whose cause is the
in general
  Mis. 291–14 and the *w·* in general ;
interest of the
  My. 52–26 * interest of the *w·* to hear her word
into the
  Un. 15– 2 * came "death into the *w·*,
       19–10 how could it have come into the *w·* ?
  Pan. 5–26 sickness, and death into the *w·*,
  '01. 21–22 not to bring death but life into the *w·*.
  '02. 6– 8 into the *w·* on the basis of a lie,
  My. 257–16 that cometh into the *w·*," — John 1 : 9.
is bereft
  Un. 51–10 In pantheism the *w·* is bereft of
is better
  My. 355–25 *w·* is better for this happy group

world
is far from ready
   Un. 6–16 *w·* is far from ready to
is slow
   Hea. 8–12 The *w·* is slow to perceive
is weary
   Hea. 2–10 * and the *w·* is weary of me ;
is wide
   Mis. 224–11 remember that the *w·* is wide ;
known to the
   My. 299– 8 * let them make it known to the *w·*,
         299–11 widely made known to the *w·*,
looks
   My. 43–29 * *w·* looks with wonder upon this
loved the
   Mis. 292– 6 Jesus, who so loved the *w·* that he
malice of the
   Hea. 2–20 beneath the malice of the *w·*.
material
     (*see* **material**)
more bright
   Mis. 397– 4 A *w·* more bright.
   Pul. 18–13 A *w·* more bright.
   Po. 12–13 A *w·* more bright.
my
   Mis. vii–17 My *w·* has sprung from Spirit,
new
   Ret. 27–29 led me into a new *w·* of light
nowhere in the
   My. 70–23 * Nowhere in the *w·* is there a
of flowers
   Mis. 390–10 The fairy-peopled *w·* of flowers,
   Po. 55–11 The fairy-peopled *w·* of flowers,
of glee
   My. 350–21 (The Stygian shadow of a *w·* of glee) ;
of letters
   Mis. 364– 5 paraphrase from the *w·* of letters.
of sense
   No. 34–15 upon whom the *w·* of sense falls
of wisdom
   Mis. 321–29 I have a *w·* of wisdom and Love to
old
   My. 72– 9 * titled aristocracy of the old *w·*
operative in the
   Pul. 35– 8 * a law as operative in the *w·* to-day
over
   My. 47–11 * people the *w·* over have been
overcome the
   Mis. 125– 7 enables him to overcome the *w·*,
   My. 132– 7 I have overcome the *w·*.''— *John* 16 : 33.
overcometh the
   Mis. 168– 2 and overcometh the *w·* !
parts of the
   My. 95– 7 * in different parts of the *w·*.
       96– 2 * Scientists from all parts of the *w*
       99–18 * coming from all parts of the *w·*,
physical
   Pul. 53–20 * dominion over the physical *w·*.
presented to the
   My. 40–24 * Mrs. Eddy, has presented to the *w·*
present to the
   '02. 14–17 with truths . . . to present to the *w·*.
proclaims to the
   My. 28–24 * proclaims to the *w·* that Jesus' gospel
real
   Pul. 80–27 * the invisible is the only real *w·*,
reform the
   No. 11–17 revolutionize and reform the *w·*,
rejoices
   '02. 3–18 *w·* rejoices with our sister nation
resistance of the
   Mis. 74–29 conquered the resistance of the *w·*.
retreat from the
   My. 117–29 I left . . . to *retreat* from the *w·*,
revolutionize the
   No. 33– 7 they would revolutionize the *w·*
rolling of a
   Mis. 174–12 to the rolling of a *w·*.
salvation of a
   Mis. 122– 7 salvation of a *w·* of sinners,
salvation of the
   Mis. 177–18 necessary to the salvation of the *w·*
saving the
   Man. 19– 5 saving the *w·* from sin and death ;
sink the
   Pul. 14–20 nor again sink the *w·* into the
sin of the
   '01. 9–18 the sin of the *w·* ;''— *John* 1 : 29.
sins of the
   Mis. 246– 3 covers the sins of the *w·*,
   Un. 56– 7 but the sins of the *w·*,
spiritual
   '01. 21–10 * many of the ideas about the spiritual *w·*
   My. 167– 5 separates us from the spiritual *w·*,
stand still
   My. 106–16 and the *w·* stand still.

world
suppositional
   My. 167– 5 suppositional *w·* within us
swept over the
   Pul. 52–22 * that swept over the *w·*
that
   My. 269– 7 to obtain that *w·*,— *Luke* 20 : 35.
this
   Mis. 155– 4 this *w·* that has nothing in Christ.
       190–29 serpent, liar, the god of this *w·*,
       190–31 god of this *w·* ;''— *II Cor.* 4 : 4.
       341–30 neither the cares of this *w·*
       342–28 children of this *w·*— *Luke* 16 : 8.
   Un. 52–19 self-destroying elements of this *w·*,
   Pul. 45– 4 * never be known in this *w·*.
       53–17 * felicity and power in this *w·*,
   '01. 16– 8 whereby the demon of this *w·*,
       16–14 *the god of this w·* ;
   My. 4–24 the prince of this *w·* that hath
throughout the
   Mis. 304– 8 * will pass . . . throughout the *w·*
       304–21 * its mission throughout the *w·*.
   Pul. 30–24 * Scientists throughout the *w·*
   My. 8–25 * Scientists from throughout the *w·*,
       21–13 * our Cause throughout the *w·*
     143–21 prospering throughout the *w·*
     191– 7 steadily throughout the *w·*.
to come
   Pul. 53–17 * salvation in the *w·* to come.
unfolded to the
   My. 207–13 * which you have unfolded to the *w·*,
unspotted from the
   Man. 31–10 themselves unspotted from the *w·*,
   Ret. 65–24 keeping man unspotted from the *w·*,
visible
   Mis. 363–19 shines through the visible *w·*
waiting
   Mis. 22–25 have proven to a waiting *w·*.
waken
   My. 356– 4 When will the *w·* waken to the
waken the
   '02. 17–13 should . . . awake and waken the *w·*.
waking up the
   Mis. 329–15 Spring passes . . . waking up the *w·* ;
was dark
   Ret. 23–10 The *w·* was dark.
was not worthy
   '01. 30– 3 *w·* was not worthy.''— *Heb.* 11 : 38.
watched over the
   '02. 15–24 stars watched over the *w·*,
watch over a
   My. 184–26 holding unwearied watch over a *w·*.
ways of the
   Mis. 138– 5 in the wilderness or ways of the *w·*.
weary of the
   Hea. 2–10 * ''I am weary of the *w·*,
well for the
   My. 191– 1 It were well for the *w·* if
whole
   Mis. 279–20 whole *w·* will feel the influence of
   '01. 19–28 The whole *w·* needs to know
       32–11 shield the whole *w·* in their hearts,
   My. v– 5 * attention of the whole *w·* is fixed on
       20– 1 throughout the whole *w·*,— *Mark* 14 : 9.
     115– 3 is circling the whole *w·*.
     229–16 help themselves and the whole *w·*,
withdrew from the
   Pul. 34–25 * withdrew from the *w·* to meditate,
woe unto the
   Mis. 122– 3 ''Woe unto the *w·*— *Matt.* 18 : 7.
woman's
   Mis. 287–29 home,— which is woman's *w·*.
wonder of the
   Mis. 321–26 during the great wonder of the *w·*,
would accept
   Hea. 18–13 tho *w·* would accept our sentiments ;

         ———
   Mis. 98–25 and call the *w·* to acknowledge its
     163– 2 the *w·*, the flesh, and the devil.
     169–19 most eminent divines of the *w·* have
     281– 7 I learned long ago that the *w·*
     290–21 When will the *w·* cease to judge of
     295–23 Nor is the *w·* ignorant of
     305– 3 * from each Republic in the *w·*,
     313–23 garner the supplies for a *w·*.
     316–29 patterns of humility, . . . for the *w·*.
     353–32 *w·* worship, pleasure seeking, and
   Man. 58–10 preach for this Church and the *w·*.
   Ret. 26–19 gave the *w·* a new date
       61–16 without God in the *w·*.'— *Eph.* 2 : 12.
       94– 3 we owe to ourselves and to the *w·*
   Pul. 39–11 * author of ''The *W·* Beautiful.''
       53–25 * Saviour of the *W·*.''
       73– 8 * secluded herself from the *w·*
       73–15 * His promises to her and to the *w·*.
       80– 7 * freest country in the *w·*

world

'00.	2–15	gives it wisely to the w.
'02.	9– 6	Let the w., popularity, pride, and
Hea.	2–20	why should the w. hate Jesus,
My.	7–19	* Christian Scientists of the w.,
	8– 9	* the best church in the w.,
	8–12	* in the best city in the w..
	33–29	w., and they that dwell— Psal. 24 : 1.
	36–27	* Christian Scientists of the w.,
	49– 8	* chance of sweeping the w.
	51– 2	* no one in the w. who could
	52–12	* spreading w. wide of this great
	53– 6	* send forth her book to the w.."
	70– 7	* any other denomination in the w.,
	71–17	* in the country— yes, in the w..
	71–19	* from any other church in the w..
	77– 4	* one of the largest in the w..
	79–14	* seldom witnessed anywhere in the w.
	79–17	* leading newspapers of the w..
	85–13	* this wonderful woman is a w. power.
	89– 7	* one of the largest organs in the w..
	89–25	* not to . . . but to the w. ;
	90–18	* w. is enormously richer for this
	91–28	* one of the finest . . . in the w.,
	104–17	of the utmost concern to the w.
	117– 1	the w. would not have lost
	122– 2	for one's self and for the w.
	132– 6	"In the w. ye shall have— John 16 : 33.
	150– 7	rendering the w. happier and
	178–26	If the w. were in ashes,
	183– 7	* will the w. have rest."
	184– 4	Since the w. was, men have
	253–12	w. hath not known Thee :— John 17 : 25.
	268–22	"the w., the flesh and the devil,"
	272–26	* plays so great a part in the w.
	300–22	make known his doctrine to the w.
	344–26	cannot force perfection on the w..

world-great

My.	269–20	world-wide, world-known, w..

world-imposed

'00.	10– 8	honest and a w. struggle.

world-known

My.	269–19	world-wide, w., world-great.

worldliness

Mis.	162–25	w., human pride, or self-will,
'02.	17– 1	selfishness, w., hatred, and

worldlings

'01.	28–26	not popular among the w.

worldly

Mis.	10–25	w. or material tendencies of
	212– 8	reminded . . . of their w. policy.
	233–21	poor shift for the weak and w.
	312–22	must have risen above w. schemes,
	327–11	to speculate in w. policy,
	354–29	genius inflated with w. desire.
Ret.	78–16	the adoption of a w. policy
	79–16	w. policy, pomp, and pride,
	79–19	quicksands of w. commotion,
'01.	2–12	may suit the weak or the w.
My.	203– 7	not clamorous for w. distinction.
	287–12	poor shift for the weak and w..

worldly-minded

Mis.	316–13	Until minds become less w.,

worldly-wise

Un.	46–19	as is still claimed by the w..

world's

Mis.	51–27	* sunshine of the w. new spring,
	84– 9	cost them . . . the w. temporary esteem;
	110–23	obvious that the w. acceptance
	224–24	to cover the whole w. evil,
	304–25	* w. progress toward liberty ;
	338–27	* Shall the w. famine feed ;
Pul.	vii–10	in the glass of the w. opinion.
	51–26	* cannot absorb the w. thought.
	79–27	* thought of the w. scientific leaders
	82–13	* conservators of the w. morals
'01.	1– 9	nearer the whole w. acceptance.
	16–14	St. Paul defines this w. god
'02.	11–18	The w. wickedness
	17–16	Who of the w. lovers ever found
	17–28	w. soft flattery or its frown.
Po.	23–10	Above the w. control?
My.	4– 4	w. nolens volens cannot enthrall
	31–19	* front rank of the w. houses
	124–11	w. arms outstretched to us,
	189–21	twilight of the w. pageantry,
	289–14	its loss and the w. loss,

worlds

Mis.	vii– 9	IF w. were formed by matter,
	26– 7	from the rolling of w.,
	184– 4	from the revolving of w. to the

worlds

Mis.	249–29	Over what w. on w. it hath range
	332– 1	kindling the stars, rolling the w.,

World's Congress Auxiliary

Mis.	312–11	President of the W. C. A.,

World's Exhibition

Mis.	304–14	* sent to the next W. E.,

World's Exposition

Mis.	304– 6	* coming W. E. at Chicago.

World's Fair

Mis.	321–26	wonder of the world, the W. F.,

World's Parliament of Religions

Pul.	4 –28	W. P. of R., held in Chicago,

world-wide

My.	269–19	Its harvest song is w.,
	271–19	* woman of w. renown

world-wish

Ret.	18– 1	Here the poet's w.,
Po.	63– 9	Here the poet's w.,

world-worshipper

'01.	30–30	The sensualist and w.

worm

Mis.	240–28	nothing but a loathsome w.

wormwood

My.	126– 3	would pour w. into the waters

worn

Mis.	295–30	w. the English crown
Pul.	50–21	* many who have w. off the novelty

wornout

Pan.	1–12	outgrown, w., or soiled garments

worry

Pul.	73– 2	* "Then why should we w. ourselves
My.	48–25	* discouragement of care and w.,

worse

Mis.	17–12	hygiene as w. than useless
	59– 9	in which the last state . . . is w. than
	138– 4	convention is w. than wasted, if
	230–20	and w. than waste its years.
	233–17	still w. in the eyes of Truth
	234–16	Empirical knowledge is w. than
	293–17	last error will be w. than the first
Ret.	63–23	Sin is w. than sickness.
Un.	49–20	* we make "the w. appear the better
Rud.	8–24	he makes morally w. the invalid
	9– 2	w. than the first."— Matt. 12 : 45.
No.	6– 1	makes the last . . . w. than the first.
	11–13	(w. still) by those who come falsely
	31– 8	and will multiply into w. forms,
Hea.	13–27	and that one is w. than the first ;
Peo.	6– 1	* all the w. for the fishes."
My.	118– 6	remedy is w. than the disease.
	231– 8	money, w. than wasted.
	245–15	Babel of confusion w. confounded,
	288–26	lest a w. thing come— John 5 : 14.

worship (noun)

Christian

Mis.	345–29	that it was a part of Christian w.
Un.	15–28	Surely this is no Christian w. !
My.	47–27	* opened an era of Christian w.

Christian Science

Mis.	149–29	first temple for C. S. w.
Ret.	51– 6	as a temple for C. S. w..

edifice of

Pul.	77– 1	* magnificent new edifice of w.

faith and

My.	59– 9	* a new system of faith and w.,

home for

My.	31–17	* The new home for w.

house of

Pul.	50–12	* erection of a visible house of w.
My.	182–20	dedicate this beautiful house of w.

houses of

My.	31–20	* the world's houses of w.,
	66–29	* many beautiful houses of w.

liturgical

Ret.	89–10	they went for liturgical w.,

meetings of

My.	53–10	* hold its meetings of w. in the

mode of

'01.	12– 1	mode of w. may be intangible,

my

'01.	12– 8	for me to believe, or for my w..

of God

Pul.	40–23	* dedicated to the w. of God.

of Spirit

My.	23–25	* which represents the w. of Spirit,

perfect

'00.	4–10	the perfect w. of one God.

worship (noun)
personal
Ret. 76–16 so far from being personal w',
Pul. 43–28 * that sort of personal w'
My. 116–13 and there is no personal w',
234– 6 personal w' which C. S. annuls.
place of
Mis. 325–31 Next he enters a place of w',
345–23 took their infants to a place of w'
places of
My. 91–28 * one of the finest places of w'
public
My. vi–13 * originated its form of public w',
real
My. 262–25 in mimicry of the real w'
reverence of
My. 98– 9 * enthusiasm and reverence of w'
sense of
My. 139–19 It was to turn your sense of w'
sensual
'00. 13–17 was devoted to a sensual w'.
solemn
'01. 15–29 * attending His solemn w'.
spiritual
My. 152–13 spiritual w', spiritual power.
sun
Pan. 8– 4 find expression in sun w',
Sunday
Mis. 314– 5 society formed for Sunday w',
thought and
Mis. 91–19 spiritual forms of thought and w'
true
Mis. 91– 2 as a type of the true w',
world
Mis. 353–32 world w', pleasure seeking, and

My. 187–23 w' of the only true God.
worship (verb)
Mis. 96–10 I w' that of which I can conceive,
96–15 divine Principle,— which I w';
96–16 so w' I God.''— see Acts 24 : 14.
106–23 How shall mankind w' the
123–30 who w' Him must w' Him spiritually,
124– 4 must w' Him in spirit.
152–17 those who w' in this tabernacle :
219– 9 they that w' Him — John 4 : 24.
219– 9 w' Him in spirit — John 4 : 24.
388–18 The right to w' deep and pure,
Ret. 2– 8 seeking "freedom to w' God ;"
9–18 * Is it not much that I may w' Him,
17– 5 I w' in deep sylvan spot,
Un. 15–22 devotees who w' not the good Deity,
31– 3 they that w' Him — John 4 : 24.
31– 3 w' Him in spirit — John 4 : 24.
Pan. 14– 6 w' in spirit and in truth ;
'00. 3–16 not apt to w' the pioneer
3–19 cannot w' him, for that would
'01. 7–24 The God whom all Christians . . . w'
Po. 21– 7 The right to w' deep and pure,
62– 5 I w' in deep sylvan spot,
My. 5–20 to w', not an unknown God,
26–21 throttle the lie that students w' me
151–20 * "Go forth, and w' God."
152–14 w' only Spirit and spiritually,
153–21 ye ignorantly w'." — Acts 17 : 23.
158–28 temple and all who w' therein
162–23 that in them Christians may w' God,
162–23 not that Christians may w' church
168– 2 Freedom to w' God according to
189– 8 You w' no distant deity,
192– 2 Ye w' Him whom ye serve.
192–14 the infinite Person whom we w',
195–25 an edifice in which to w'
270–32 they that w' Him — John 4 : 24.
270–32 w' Him in spirit — John 4 : 24.
285–26 so w' I the God — Acts 24 : 14.
341– 7 * "Freedom to w' God."
(see also **Father**)
worshiping (see also **worshipping**)
Po. 71– 5 Knelt w' at mammon's shrine.
worshipped
Mis. 333–24 worshippers of Baal w' the sun.
'00. 3–10 he is not thereby w'.
My. 20–19 * thousands who w'
55–29 * congregation w' in Copley Hall
worshipper
Mis. 152–20 meek in spirit the w' in truth,
Ret. 89–11 If one w' preached to
My. 163– 1 call the w' to seek the haven
worshippers
Mis. 178–17 * of what you were w'.
321–13 when the true w' — see John 4 : 23.
333–24 w' of Baal worshipped the sun.
No. 34–10 true w' shall worship — John 4 : 23.

worshippers
Peo. 13– 1 w' of wood and stone have a
13– 3 But the w' of a person have
My. 78– 5 * w' saw an imposing structure
85–23 * not merely for its thousands of w',
90– 3 * w', wooed by no eloquence
92–23 * or the thirty thousand w'
94– 8 * or the thirty thousand w'
100– 7 * thirty thousand w' were present
303–10 unscientific w' of a human being.
worshipping (see also **worshiping**)
My. 151–28 w' of matter in the name of
152– 2 w' person instead of
worst
Mis. 233– 4 the w' form of medicine.
237– 9 the w' of human passions
267– 5 w' enemies are the best friends
296–24 affinity for the w' forms of vice?
319–16 sinners of the w' sort.
368–27 perverted, . . . may become the w',
Peo. 2–17 the w' human qualities,
My. 165– 8 The best help the w' ;
190– 8 in healing the w' forms of
211–19 designs of their w' enemies,
335–17 * yellow fever of the w' type,
335–28 * yellow fever in its w' form,
worth
Mis. 4–22 the vastness of its w'
226–30 assassin of radical w' ;
273– 4 in proportion to its w'.
Chr. 53–27 rehearse the glorious w'
Pul. 84– 7 * all that is w' living for,
'00. 7–12 appreciated its w' as they did
'02. 17–24 conscious w' satisfies the
Hea. 20– 2 * speak the matchless w',
My. 166– 7 life is w' living and God takes care
203–10 All that is w' reckoning
215– 3 knew well the priceless w'
215–14 * teachings are w' much more
216–13 his truth not w' a cent.
258– 9 to all of holiest w'.
325– 8 * would never be w' what you
worthies
Mis. 246– 4 enlightenment of these w',
'01. 9– 6 The ancient w' caught glorious
worthily
My. 9–16 * desire that we may w' follow
202–14 rest w' on the builders of
worthiness
Mis. 154–10 God only waits for man's w'
My. 64–25 * and thus prove our w'
worthless
No. 27– 3 and the claim, being w',
worthy
Mis. 54– 9 whose lives are w' testimonials,
147–10 records w' to be borne heavenward?
157– 3 w' to suffer for Christ, Truth.
291–25 w' to suffer for righteousness,
Man. 39– 4 If, . . . they are found w',
39– 6 but if not found w'
69–19 is not w' of me." — Matt. 10 : 37.
80– 7 the vice-president . . . being found w'
Ret. 49– 7 accomplished the w' purpose
Un. 57–23 rejoiced that he was found w'
Pul. 48–27 * long list of w' ancestors
50– 3 * w' of his hire," — Luke 10 : 7.
'01. 30– 3 the world was not w'.'' — Heb. 11 : 38.
'02. 4–11 our works be as w' as our words.
My. 4– 8 is not w' of me." — Matt. 10 : 38.
24–27 * the structure is w' of our Cause
64–26 * w' members of The Mother Church
70–12 * The chimes . . . are w' of the dome.
92–10 * a portent w' of perhaps even
215–17 home for the poor w' student,
215–25 w' of his hire." — Luke 10 : 7.
233–25 is not w' of me — Matt. 10 : 38.
258– 4 Nothing is w' the name of
269– 6 shall be accounted w' — Luke 20 : 35.
358–19 a w' and charitable purpose.
would-be
Un. 17–14 the w' murderer of Truth.
wound
Mis. 215– 4 saying, "I w' to heal ;
244– 1 closed up the w' thereof,— see Gen. 2 : 21.
387–12 arrow that doth w' the dove
398– 6 W' the callous breast,
Ret. 46–12 W' the callous breast,
Pul. 17–11 W' the callous breast,
No. 44–20 healing balm . . . into every w'.
Po. 6– 7 arrow that doth w' the dove
14–10 W' the callous breast,
22–16 probe the w', then pour the balm
33–10 To kindly pass over a w',

wounded

Mis.	145–16	a *w·* sense of its own error,
	224– 5	'Well may we feel *w·* by
	258– 8	anointing the *w·* spirit with the
My.	257– 3	love that heals the *w·* heart.
	313–27	but I *w·* her pride

wounds

Mis.	209– 7	healest the *w·* of my people slightly
	275–15	binds up the *w·* of bleeding hearts,
	296–13	the *w·* of the broken-hearted,
	311–25	even as a surgeon who *w·* to heal.
	327–32	and kindly binds up their *w·*,
	330– 6	wherein no arrow *w·* the dove
Ret.	92– 4	*w·* he healed by Truth and Love.
Un.	55–15	false sense of . . . the *w·* it bears.
Po.	27–12	heal her *w·* too tenderly
My.	290–22	where no arrow *w·* the eagle

woven

Mis.	145–26	When the *hearts* . . . are *w·* together

wrapped

Peo.	5–14	*w·* in a pure winding-sheet,

wrapping

Mis.	326–14	*w·* their altars in ruins.

wraps

My.	69–24	* capacity of three thousand *w·*.

wrath

Mis.	41– 6	*w·* of man"— *Psal.* 76 : 10.
	324–15	emulation, hatred, *w·*, murder.
Man.	41– 9	turneth away *w·*."— *Prov.* 15 : 1.
Pul.	12–14	having great *w·*,— *Rev.* 12 : 12.
No.	7–17	*w·* of man cannot hide it from Him.
	8–13	make the *w·* of man to praise Him,
	33– 1	*w·* of man shall praise Him.
	35–11	not to appease the *w·* of God,
'02.	1–12	*w·* of man— *Psal.* 76 : 10.
	1–13	*w·* shalt Thou restrain."— *Psal.* 76 : 10.
Peo.	3– 8	*w·* of God, . . . false beliefs
My.	111– 2	*w·* of man— *Psal.* 76 : 10.
	151–10	*w·* of man— *Psal.* 76 : 10.
	151–11	*w·* shalt Thou restrain."— *Psal.* 76 : 10.
	196–10	slow to *w·*."— *Jas.* 1 : 19.
	207– 4	*w·* of men shall praise God,

wreath

Mis.	388–17	Affection's *w·*, a happy home ;
Po.	21– 6	Affection's *w·*, a happy home ;
	65–21	gathers a *w·* for his bier ;
My.	190– 2	falling upon the bridal *w·*

wreathed

Pul.	42–26	* The desk was *w·* with ferns

wreaths

Ret.	11–19	*w·* are twined round Plymouth Rock,
Peo.	14– 9	* are *w·* of immortelles,
Po.	25–19	*W·* for the triumphs o'er ill !
	60–16	*w·* are twined round Plymouth Rock,

wreck

Mis.	26– 1	survive the *w·* of time ;

wrecks

Mis.	280–30	by which so many *w·* are made.
No.	43–25	or reconstruct the *w·* of *"isms"*

wrench

Mis.	246– 7	to *w·* from man both human and

wrest

Un.	1– 7	*w·* . . . unto their own— *II Pet.* 3 : 16.

wrested

Mis.	171– 2	can never be *w·* from its

wrestle

Mis.	336– 4	your province to *w·* with error,
	392–15	to *w·* with the storms of time ;
Po.	20–19	to *w·* with the storms of time ;

wrestler

Mis.	385–18	Brave *w·*, lone.
Po.	48–12	Brave *w·*, lone.

wrestling

'02.	1–16	*w·* only with material observation,
Peo.	1–12	intellectual *w·* and collisions

wrestlings

Mis.	339–14	the strain of intellectual *w·*,
Ret.	57– 1	mighty *w·* with mortal beliefs,
No.	45–21	Drifting into intellectual *w·*,

wretched

Mis.	52–15	*w·* condition of human existence.

wriggles

Mis.	296–22	* *w·*'" itself into publicity

wrist-joint

Mis.	243– 8	In the case of sprain of the *w·*,

writ

Mis.	381–21	A *w·* of injunction was issued
Po.	22–12	'Tis *w·* on earth, on leaf and flower :

write

Mis.	106– 4	and if I could *w·* the history
	141–32	O recording angel ! *w·* :
	142–13	Let me *w·* to the donors,
	155–20	students, who *w·* such excellent letters
	155–24	cannot spare time to *w·* to God,
	157– 7	or caused my secretary to *w·*,
	157–26	*W·* me when you need me.
	271–10	*w·* for it, and read it.
	285–20	to *w·* briefly on marriage,
	379– 2	and *w·* at his desk.
	379–18	one could *w·* a sonnet.
Man.	71–21	shall not *w·* the Tenets of
Ret.	75–23	to *w·* out as his own the
	76– 4	student can *w·* voluminous works
No.	7–23	and *w·* the truth of C. S.
	39– 2	than we can *w·* or speak.
Pan.	11– 3	It caused St. Paul to *w·*,
	14– 4	Once more I *w·*,
'00.	13–30	bidden to *w·* the approval of
	15–23	may the angel . . . *w·* of this church :
'02.	2– 5	to *w·* truth first on the tablet
	3–17	learning to read and *w·*.
	15–15	dictation as to what I should *w·*,
	15–28	had led me to *w·* that book,
Po.	v–17	* *seated herself* . . . *and began to w·.*
	28– 3	to *w·* a deathless page
	32–12	inspires my pen as I *w·* ;
My.	59–25	* "Did Mrs. Eddy really *w·* S. and H.?
	105–27	urged me immediately to *w·*
	114–18	I could not *w·* these notes
	115– 4	I should blush to *w·* of "S. and H.
	214– 3	would *w·* your textbook on the
	258–32	To the children . . . I *w·* :
	324–19	* that he had helped you *w·* it.

writer

Mis.	71– 6	one *w·* thinks that he was
	290–18	I had not thought of the *w·*
	296–15	This *w·* classes C. S. with
Man.	43–26	the spirit in which the *w·*
Pul.	48– 5	* Mrs. Eddy took the *w·*
	67– 6	* by a great American *w·*.
	79–20	* wicked but witty *w·* has said,
My.	59– 2	* the *w·*, whom you will recall
	93– 1	* so far as the *w·* knows them,
	225– 9	the *w·* or the reader who does not
		(see also **Eddy***)*

writer's

(see **Eddy***)*

writers

Mis.	29–22	*w·* of chronic and acute diseases
	169–21	what the inspired *w·* left
	187–17	both *w·* and translators
Ret.	22–5	*W·* less wise than the apostles
'01.	28– 8	Of the ancient *w·* since
	34–29	words of the Hebrew *w·* :

writes

Mis.	8–21	Shakespeare *w·* : "Sweet are the
	24– 3	St. Paul *w·* : "For to be— *Rom.* 8 : 6.
	153–25	Sir Edwin Arnold, . . . *w·* :
	226–14	Shakespeare, . . . *w·* : — To thine own
	295– 3	Mr. Wakeman *w·* from London,
	317–30	St. John *w·* : "Whom God— *John* 3 : 34.
	373–23	and, as St. Mark *w·*,
Chr.	53–52	And *w·* the page.
Ret.	76– 5	if he *w·* honestly,
Un.	30–13	In his first epistle . . . Paul *w·* :
Pan.	12– 5	Lyman Abbott, D.D., *w·*,
'00.	13–14	*w·* of this church of Smyrna :
	13–25	Smith *w·* : "In this city the
'01.	21– 8	Rev. —— *w·* : "To the famous
	24–10	he *w·* : "I esteem my
	27– 3	My critic also *w·* :
	33– 6	Carlyle *w·* : "Quackery and dupery do
'02.	6–27	St. Paul *w·* : "For to be— *Rom.* 8 : 6.
	10–10	Rev. Hugh Black *w·* truly :
	16–12	St. Paul *w·* : "Follow peace— *Heb.* 12 : 14.
Hea.	1–15	A classic *w·*, — "At thirty, man
Peo.	6– 2	Dr. Benjamin Waterhouse *w·* :
	6– 4	Dr. Abercrombie, . . . *w·* :
My.	3– 7	St. John *w·* : "Blessed are they — *Rev.* 22 : 14.
	159–27	*w·*, "What is the essence of God?
	186– 3	that *w·* in living characters
	193–22	Carlyle *w·*, "Give a thing time ;
	194– 2	which Christianity *w·* in broad facts
	240– 6	An earnest student *w·* to me :
	272–28	* Mrs. Eddy *w·* very rarely for
	293–28	St. Paul *w·* : "For the law of— *Rom.* 8 : 2.
	299– 5	*w·* : "If they . . . have any truth

writing

Mis.	43–17	sad fact at this early w· is,
	88–12	reading, w·, extensive travel,
	239– 7	Lecturing, w·, preaching, teaching,
Ret.	36– 7	w· out my manuscripts for students
Pul.	35–12	* In w· of this experience,
'02.	15–22	name for the book I had been w·.
Po.	v–19	* asked her what she was w·,
My.	114–27	have been learning . . . since w· it.
	150– 7	* w· what deserves to be read ;
	225–10	used in w· about C. S.
	225–25	either in speaking or in w·,
	234– 3	w· or reading congratulations
	304–10	w· for the leading newspapers,
	312–29	My salary for w·
	322– 2	* when you were w· S. and H.,

writings

Mis.	x– 6	to collect my miscellaneous w·
	46–11	A reader of my w· would not
	291–16	by my thoughts and w·.
	300–20	printed as your original w·,
	301–12	w· of a few professed . . . Scientists.
	302–24	desist from further copying of my w·
	379–11	I inferred that his w· usually
	381–12	the author of her w· !
Man.	43–17	shall not plagiarize her w·.
	44– 2	His w· must show strict adherence to
	59– 3	w· of authors who think at random
	64– 7	other w· by this author ;
	75–10	and one's w· on ethics,
Ret.	75–10	and one's w· on ethics,
Pul.	37–12	* further w· on C. S.
	75– 5	my w·, teachings, and example
No.	3–25	Plagiarism from my w·
'01.	24–21	not read one line of Berkeley's w·
	25– 1	mysticism, so called, of my w·
	26–26	I have read little of their w·.
	28–11	Some of his w· have been
	34–11	and the canonical w· of the Fathers,
My.	vi– 8	* learned it from her and from her w· ;
	17–28	* extracts from Mrs. Eddy's w·
	18–31	* w· of the Rev. Mary Baker Eddy,
	48–19	* the Bible and her own w·,
	64–15	* In all her w·, through all the
	114–14	My first w· on C. S.
	120– 1	the sainted Revelator in his w·,
	120– 3	or elsewhere than in my w·,
	179– 2	the beginning of the gospel w·.
	270–20	My w· heal the sick,
	317–16	Calvin A. Frye copied my w·,
	338– 9	* her w· will fully corroborate

written

Mis.	x–11	were originally w· in haste,
	xi– 6	reproduction of what has been w·,
	98–26	Truly is it w· :
	121– 1	w· in a decaying language,
	142 7	W· on receipt of a beautiful
	144–12	w· by the same author,
	148–13	were w· at different dates,
	157– 7	I have w·, or caused my
	172–20	which law is w· on the heart,
	185–27	And so it is w·,— I Cor. 15 : 45.
	213– 3	All that I have w·, taught, or lived,
	286– 1	above prophecy, w· years ago,
	306–14	* a duplicate letter w·,
	311–23	works I have w· on C. S.
	315– 6	No copies . . . are allowed to be w·,
	316–15	have profited . . . from the w· word,
	317–14	by the study of what is w·.
	381–31	has been w· that "nobody can
	391– 2	W· to the Editor of the *Item*,
	399–19	W· on receiving a painting of
	395–15	W· in childhood, in a maple grove
	399–17	W· on laying the corner-stone of
Man.	3–10	were w· at different dates,
	27–18	the w· consent of said Board.
	28–24	shall be w· on the Church records.
	43– 6	No member shall use w· formulas,
	43–12	strengthen the faith by a w· text
	44– 1	spirit in which the writer has w·
	65–16	comply with any w· order,
	67– 9	without her w· consent.
	67–25	w· request of the Pastor
	71– 7	nor w· on applications
	78–10	without the w· consent
	79–14	for her w· approval.
	82– 9	knowledge or w· consent.
	87– 4	w· consent of the authority
	94–14	w· request of Mrs. Eddy,
	103– 7	without the w· consent
	104– 5	w· by Mary Baker Eddy
	104–10	without the w· consent
	105– 4	without the w· consent
	109–16	that names are legibly w·,
	110–12	must be plainly w·,
	110–13	names of each, w· in full.

written

Man.	110–16	All names must be w·
	111– 3	names must be w· in full.
Ret.	1–10	my grandmother said were w·
	17– 1	W· in youth, while visiting
	20–16	w· after this separation :
	27–10	until S. and H. was w·.
	27–27	its w· expression increases
	75–22	textbook w· by his teacher,
Un.	57–13	it is w· that he felt that
Pul.	30–12	* "confession of faith," w· by
	39–14	* [W· for the *Traveller*]
	43–15	* w· by Mrs. Eddy for the
	73–27	* which Mrs. Eddy had herself w·,
	74–10	* w· answer to the interrogatory,
Rud.	16–18	Whatever is said and w·
No.	42– 2	* things w· in the Scriptures,
'00.	13– 6	It is w· of this church
Peo.	13–25	* history of Christianity was w·,
Po.	v– 2	* w· at different periods
	v– 4	* They were not w· with a
	v–10	* w· while the author was
	vi– 6	* was w· for that occasion,
	vi–24	* poems w· in girlhood
	vi–28	* (w· in a maple grove),
	vi–29	* (w· while visiting a . . . friend
	3–15	W· many years ago.
	19– 6	W· in early years.
	33–20	W· in girlhood.
	35–15	W· more than sixty years ago
	59– 9	W· in girlhood,
My.	15– 9	without the w· consent
	31–29	* Hymn 161, w· by Mrs. Eddy,
	59–28	* before it was ever w·.
	114–32	either w· or indicated in
	124–20	w· in luminous letters,
	150– 6	* "Doing what deserves to be w·,
	151–10	Because it is w· :
	178–30	w· in A.D. 145,
	179–18	narratives had never been w·,
	179–26	contingent on nothing w·
	184–15	birch bark on which it was w·
	185–12	wherever thought, . . . or w·,
	189–28	gave expression to a poem w· in 1844,
	190–23	Bible was w· in order that
	217–23	w· in "S. and H. with Key to the
	225–31	should not be w· or used as a
	271– 8	learned the truth of what I had w·.
	285–27	which are w· in the law— *Acts 24 : 14.*
	292– 3	All good that ever was w·,
	306–29	w· while I was his patient
	317–19	dissented from what I had w·,
	323– 2	* with what Mr. Bates has so well w·
	323– 5	* he said he had w· in answer to
	354–26	* w· extemporaneously by Mrs. Eddy
	359–10	through my w· and published rules,
	359–20	* had been w· to Mrs. Augusta E. Stetson
	361–10	not w· to her since August 30, 1909.

wrong (noun)

actual		
Mis.	129– 9	an imaginary or an actual w·,
all		
'01.	14–26	To overcome all w·, it must
all that is		
Po.	33– 8	vanity, folly, and all that is w·
amplification of		
Mis.	261–11	every effect and amplification of w·
My.	288–24	every effect or amplification of w·
and injustice		
My.	277–16	whereby w· and injustice are righted
be robbed		
Pul.	84– 3	* Then shall w· be robbed of her
childhood's		
Mis.	238– 4	to contrast with that childhood's w·
clouds of		
My.	252–14	midst clouds of w·, injustice, envy,
commit		
Mis.	130– 7	how much better . . . than to commit w· ?
crouching		
Mis.	246–21	crouching w· that refused to
human		
Mis.	340–32	Human w·, sickness, sin, and
ignorant		
Mis.	300– 8	it is an ignorant w·.
iron heel of		
Pul.	82–30	* ceased to kiss the iron heel of w·.
is done		
Mis.	391–11	That when a w· is done us,
Po.	38–10	That when a w· is done us,
is thought		
'01.	14–23	W· is thought before it is acted ;
jubilant		
Po.	27–17	W· jubilant and right with
no		
Mis.	224–26	when no w· is meant,

wrong (noun)
nothingness of
  Mis. 267– 4 nothingness of *w·* and the supremacy of
or imperfection
  My. 41–17 * with sin, *w·*, or imperfection,
participants in
  Mis. 335–20 either willing participants in *w·*,
rebuke to
  Po. 23–14 A stern rebuke to *w·* !
recompense this
  Mis. 12– 7 God will recompense this *w·*,
right over
  My. 362– 5 in the victory of right over *w·*,
suffer from the
  Mis. 261– 9 suffer from the *w·* they commit,
unseen
  My. 211– 3 The unseen *w·* to individuals

  Mis. 13– 6 real wrongs (if *w·* can be real)
    33– 2 *w·* will receive its own reward.
  287–27 pleasanter to do right than *w·*
  368– 7 * *W·* forever on the throne.
  371–19 * "good right, and good *w·*,"
  '01. 14–27 *w·* has no divine authority ;
    31– 2 of truth, of right, and of *w·*.
  My. 117– 5 determines the right or the *w·* of
  252– 9 the *w·* you may commit must,
  283–16 *W·* may be a man's highest idea of
  306– 1 to lift the curtain on *w·*,

wrong (adj.)
  Mis. 19– 1 is unjust, — is *w·* and cruel.
    19– 3 hatred, malice, are always *w·*,
    32– 1 so succeed with his *w·* argument,
    49–17 can it be *w·*, sinful, or an error?
    59–11 Is it *w·* to pray for . . . the sick?
    67–22 *w·* practice discerned, disarmed, and
    80– 9 individual rights in a *w·* direction
    80–14 with a *w·* class of people.
    90– 8 Is it *w·* for a wife to
  117– 6 superinduced by the *w·* motive
  133–18 I hope I am not *w·* in
  170–14 *w·* and foolish, conceptions of God
  179–11 We are *w·* if our consciousness is
  190–26 *w·* power, or the lost sense,
  191–17 evils, apparent *w·* traits,
  212–25 If, . . . one is at work in a *w·*
  215–12 or start from *w·* motives.
  222– 8 conviction of his *w·* state of feeling
  240–25 teach them nothing that is *w·*.
  252– 9 *w·* thoughts are unreality
  263– 3 knowing that the *w·* motives are not
  279– 4 prevent the *w·* action?
  283–11 *w·* to burst open doors
  288–11 If the premise . . . is *w·*,
  351–17 never can place it in the *w·* hands
  365– 8 gets things *w·*, and is
  Ret. 57– 9 it is practice that is *w·*.
    81–17 arise from *w·* apprehension.
  Rud. 12– 6 *W·* thoughts and methods
  No. 7–24 right or *w·* personality
    18–20 If . . . the school gets things *w·*,
  Pan. 4–13 of right and *w·* action,
  Hea. 9– 6 on the *w·* side of the question.
    14–28 opposed to all that is *w·*,
  My. 146–25 in the right or in the *w·* direction.
  213–18 to drift in the *w·* direction
  223–18 superinduced by *w·* motives
  224–11 its right or its *w·* concept,
  231– 5 working in *w·* directions.
  241–22 * said that my statement was *w·*,

wrong (verb)
  Mis. 130–25 is to *w·* one of God's
wrong-doer
  Mis. 261–11 wrong will revert to the *w·*,
  My. 288–24 wrong will revert to the *w·* ;
wrong-doing
  Mis. 298– 3 Nothing is gained by *w·*.
wronged
  Mis. 12– 6 If you have been badly *w·*,
    12– 9 not fancy that you have been *w·*
  130– 7 how much better it is to be *w·*,
wrongfully
  Rud. 10– 9 beliefs, which govern mortals *w·*.
  My. 138–13 cruelly, unjustly, and *w·* accused.
wrongfully-minded
  Mis. 367– 9 whatever is *w·* will disappear

wrongly
  Mis. 357–26 If they have been taught *w·*,
  Un. 9–12 the centuries have *w·* reckoned.
    49– 7 sinner, *w·* named *man*.
  Peo. 3–21 begins *w·* to apprehend the infinite,
wrongs
done
  My. 160–32 *w·* done to others, are mill-stones
existing
  No. 9–18 existing *w·* of the nature referred to.
forgiving
  Mis. 107–12 forgetting self, forgiving *w·* and
of human life
  My. 6– 8 the *w·* of human life,
of mankind
  No. 40–18 but only the *w·* of mankind.
real
  Mis. 13– 6 real *w·* (if wrong can be real)
will redress
  Mis. 80–20 will redress *w·* and rectify injustice.

  Ret. 73–20 *w·* it, or terrifies people over it,
wrote
  Mis. 189–26 insomuch that St. Matthew *w·*,
  290–15 *w·* to me, naming the time of
  298– 1 The Hebrew bard *w·*,
  330–10 St. Paul *w·*, "Rejoice— *Phil.* 4 : 4.
  372–11 A mother *w·*, "Looking at the
  382–25 *w·* its constitution and bylaws,
  Ret. 1–12 *w·* a stray sonnet and an
    7– 5 *w·* of my brother as follows :
  27– 1 I *w·* also, at this period, comments
  32–12 the famous Spanish poet who *w·*,
  40–19 The mother afterwards *w·* to me,
  90–26 One of my students *w·* to me :
  Pul. 6–13 *w·* to me in 1894,
  31–20 * To a note which I *w·* her,
  54– 1 * Again, in a poem . . . he *w·* :
  '01. 29–29 students *w·* me, "quite quickly we
  My. v–20 * *w·* and published the C. S. textbook,
  vi–13 * *w·* its Church Manual and Tenets,
  19–15 * Mrs. Eddy *w·* as follows :
  52–21 * *w·* as follows : "Whatever is to be
  114–17 What I *w·* had a strange coincidence
  146–21 sure that what I *w·* is true,
  154–18 Carlyle *w·* : "Wouldst thou
  183– 6 what John Robinson *w·* in 1620
  215– 6 I *w·* "S. and H. with Key to the
  237– 5 What I *w·* on C. S.
  261–15 St. Paul *w·*, "When I— *I Cor.* 13 : 11.
  271– 4 When I *w·* "S. and H.
  304–11 I *w·* for the best magazines
  319– 6 he *w·* a kind little pamphlet,
  343–17 In 1875 I *w·* my book.
  343–28 I *w·* to each church in tenderness,
  359–26 * Mrs. Eddy *w·* to Mrs. Stetson
wroth
  Hea. 10– 2 dragon that was *w·* with the woman,
wrought
  Mis. 13– 8 *w·* out for me the law of
  24– 8 it *w·* my immediate recovery
  52–21 problem to be *w·* in divine Science.
  96– 2 salvation . . . as *w·* out by Jesus,
  110–19 our hands have *w·* steadfastly
  120–11 ye that have *w·* valiantly,
  187– 4 The great Metaphysician *w·*,
  201–21 so many proofs that he had *w·*
  237– 7 *w·* a change in the actions of men.
  333–26 believed . . . God *w·* through matter
  Ret. 24–20 divine Spirit had *w·* the miracle
  54– 2 some of the cures *w·* through
  92– 1 *w·* infinite results.
  Pul. 14–27 great benefit which Mind has *w·*.
  26–11 * richly *w·* oxidized silver lamps,
  34–21 divine Spirit had *w·* a miracle,"
  55– 3 * Not for show of power, was *w·*
  78– 3 * ever *w·* in this country.
  Rud. 3–18 He *w·* the cure of disease
  No. 18–23 have *w·* this moral result,
  33–17 and the good it *w·*.
  My. 164–19 has *w·* a resurrection among you,
  292– 4 that ever was written, taught, or *w·*
Wyclif
  '02. 16– 8 happy possessor of a copy of *W·*,
Wyclif's
  '02. 16– 2 brought to me *W·* translation of
  16– 6 *W·* use of that combination of

X, Y

X-rays
  Mis. 112– 6 Hypnotism, microbes, *X·*.

Yahwah (*see also* **Yawa**)
  '00. 3–23 the divine name *Y·*,
  3–26 *Y·*, misnamed Jehovah,

Yale College Athenæum

My. 172– 2   * taken from the old *Y· C· A·*,

Yawa (*see also* Yahwah)

Mis. 123–15   Babylonian *Y·*, or Jehovah,

yawns

My. 200–25   Wide *y·* the gap between

yea

Mis. 13– 6   *y·*, the real wrongs
15– 9   *y·*, the highest Christianization
23–27   *y·*, which manifests all His
63–19   *y·*, "that the Lord He is — *Deut.* 4 : 35.
66–28   *y·*, it is "the blind — *Matt.* 15 : 14.
73–20   *y·*, that all subjective states of
77– 5   *y·*, to *understand* those
104– 7   *y·*, the substance of God,
108– 7   *y·*, nothingness — of evil :
126– 2   *y·*, from darkness to daylight,
141–16   I believe, — *y·*, I understand,
149– 2   *y·*, come, buy wine — *Isa.* 55 : 1.
197–26   *y·*, that is divided against itself,
209– 6   *y·*, that healest the wounds
252–31   *y·*, it is the pearl priceless
333– 1   that sin — *y·*, selfhood
333– 7   falsity, *y·*, nothingness ;
336– 6   resort to stones and clubs, — *y·*,
357–32   *y·*, its foundation and superstructure.
Ret. 88–15   *y·*, its power to demonstrate
Pan. 12–18   *y·*, pass gently on without the
'01. 9–12   *Y·*, it is the healing power
15–29   * *Y·*, there is nothing else
17– 5   *y·*, quickly to return to divine Love,
18–21   *y·*, above the grandeur of
30–24   working alone with God, *y·*,
32–25   *y·*, all the way up to its
34–19   *y·*, which *knoweth no evil.*
'02. 6–15   *y·*, something that is not of God.
10–23   *y·*, from sin to holiness?
Peo. 3–12   *y·*, that make a mysterious God
5–20   *y·*, to the Principle that is God,
9– 5   *y·*, it is love leaving self
Po. 67–21   *Y·*, flowers of feeling may blossom
My. 139–21   *y·*, from the human to the divine.
248–17   *y·*, to the reality of God,
291–28   to think, to mourn, *y·*, to pray,
293–19   *y·*, the spirit and the flesh
299–20   *y·*, they understand it

year (*see also* year's)

about the

Mis. 285–14   It was about the *y·* 1875
378– 1   About the *y·* 1862,
'02. 18–28   downfall of . . . about the *y·* 325,
My. 105–19   About the *y·* 1869, I was wired to
315– 3   * About the *y·* 1874, Dr. Patterson,

ago

Mis. 178–15   * it was about a *y·* ago
Pul. 68–16   * in this city about a *y·* ago.
My. 11–14   * A *y·* ago she quietly alluded to
297–21   when he visited me a *y·* ago,

all of the

Mis. 131–19   was not in existence all of the *y·*.

another

Mis. 147– 3   Another *y·* has rolled on,
395–18   Ere autumn blanch another *y·*,
'02. 1– 1   another *y·* of God's loving providence
Po. 58– 3   Ere autumn blanch another *y·*,

brief

Ret. 19– 7   spared to me for only one brief *y·*.

by year

My. 266–23   have increased *y·* by year.

close of the

Pul. 45–12   * one month before the close of the *y·*
84–14   * close of the *y·*, Anno Domini 1894,

coming

My. 42– 6   * the President for the coming *y·*,

dawning

Po. 28– 5   Of truth, this dawning *y·* !

during the

Pul. 77– 9   * During the *y·* eighteen hundred and
78– 8   * During the *y·* 1894 a church
'02. 1– 7   during the *y·* ending June, 1902,

each

Mis. 159–17   grand collections once in each *y·*.
Man. 44–15   forwarded each *y·* to the Church
57– 5   first Friday in November of each *y·*.
60– 5   continued twelve months each *y·*.
61–14   in January and July of each *y·*,
93– 9   shall begin July 1 of each *y·*.
98–18   published each *y·* in a leading
Pul. 45–30   * elected each *y·* by the congregation.

ensuing

My. 39–13   list of officers for the ensuing *y·*
51–21   * pastorate for the ensuing *y·* ;

year

expiring

Po. 27–19   Thou fast expiring *y·*,

financial

Mis. 131–14   report of the first financial *y·*
131–28   After this financial *y·*, when you call

fixed the

My. 181–28   fixed the *y·* 1866 or 1867

illustrious

Po. 27–24   Illustrious *y·*, farewell !

last

Man. 76–14   expenditures for the last *y·*.
'00. 1– 9   last *y·* of the nineteenth century
My. 55–21   * during the last *y·* the hall was
57–22   * admitted during the last *y·*

lecture

Man. 93– 8   The lecture *y·* shall begin July 1

new

Pul. 1– 4   A new *y·* is a nursling,

next

My. 141–11   * would have been held next *y·*.

old

Pul. 1– 8   An old *y·* is time's adult,
Po. page 26   poem

once a

Mis. 159–23   Here I talk once a *y·*,

one

Man. 25–13   shall hold office for one *y·*,
26– 4   term of office . . . is one *y·* each,
26– 6   have served one *y·* or more,
39– 4   at the expiration of said one *y·*,
80–24   term of office . . . is one *y·* each,
80–26   Incumbents who have served one *y·*
My. 229–11   can acquire in one *y·* the

only a

Pul. 34– 2   * who lived only a *y·*.

over a

My. 301– 9   not seen Mrs. Stetson for over a *y·*,

past

Mis. 160–12   progress, the past *y·*, has been
239– 5   four day's vacation for the past *y·*,
Pul. 28–26   * For the past *y·* or two Judge Hanna,
My. 52– 2   * during the past *y·*.
145–17   Within the past *y·* and two months,

receding

Mis. 310–26   receding *y·* of religious jubilee,
321– 7   each receding *y·* sees the steady gain
Po. 27– 5   One word, receding *y·*,

recurring

Mis. 321– 9   each recurring *y·* witnesses the

returning

Mis. 330–21   With each returning *y·*, higher joys,

returnless

Pul. 1–14   Pass on, returnless *y·* !
Po. 26– 1   Pass on, returnless *y·* !

rolling

Po. 77– 1   God of the rolling *y·* !

same

Mis. 383– 4   took effect the same *y·*,
My. 49–29   * December 1 of the same *y·*,
51– 4   * May 26 of the same *y·*
57– 9   * annual meeting of the same *y·*
327– 5   they have the same *y·*,

some

Pul. 31–14   * It was during some *y·* in the

son of a

Mis. 180–28   month is called the son of a *y·*.

spent a

Ret. 6–20   later Albert spent a *y·* in

that

'00. 6–30   In that *y·* the C. S. textbook,
7– 2   From that *y·* the United States
My. 330–20   * newspapers of that *y·*.

third

Man. 26–12   Every third *y·* Readers shall
88–13   elected every third *y·*

this

Mis. 131–17   this *y·* of your firstfruits.
My. 20–29   * omit this *y·* the usual
21–18   * this *y·* will receive a greater
21–23   * very many of them this *y·*,
57–18   * admitted June 5 of this *y·*
199–18   This *y·*, standing on the verge
256– 7   This *y·*, my beloved Christian

throughout the

Man. 60– 3   Continued Throughout the *Y·*.

within the

Pul. 45–13   * completion within the *y·*

young

Po. 27– 8   will the young *y·* dawn with

Man. 64–14   In the *y·* eighteen hundred and
64–22   *y·* nineteen hundred and three

year
Ret. 15–13	In the y· 1878 I was called to
42– 4	at Lynn, . . . in the y· 1877.
Pul. 33– 4	* for a y· she heard her name
36– 1	* a y· after her founding of the
'00. 6–29	cites 1875 as the y· of the second
My. 22– 3	* In the y· 1902 our Leader
53–26	* y· ending December 7, 1885,
246–11	In the y· 1889, to gain a higher

yearly
Mis. 138– 3	time it takes y· to prepare for
Man. 68–12	rate of one thousand dollars y·
84– 8	shall teach but one class y·,
92–14	should teach y· one class.

yearn
Mis. 118–12	y· to forgive a mistake,
357– 7	y· to find living pastures

yearned
My. 164– 8	I have y· to express my thanks
214–24	which I y· to do,

yearning
Mis. 178– 5	a y· of the heart ;
Ret. 48– 2	but I was y· for retirement.
My. 135–12	my y· for more peace
137–18	and y· for more peace

yearningly
Ret. 80–25	while innocence strayeth y·.

yearnings
Mis. 386– 4	Where mortal y· come not,
Po. 49– 6	Where mortal y· come not,

yearns
Mis. 386–17	a hope that ever upward y·,
Ret. 90–20	What other heart y· with
Po. 50– 1	a hope that ever upward y·,

year's
Mis. 131–31	last y· records immortalized,
Man. 38–23	on one y· probation,

years (see also **years'**)

advancing
My. 135–13	for more peace in my advancing y·,
135–27	cheer my advancing y·.

afterward
Po. v–23	* Similar requests . . . y· afterward,

ago
Mis. 242–14	more difficult tasks fifteen y· ago.
248–23	Many y· ago my regular physician
286– 1	above prophecy, written y· ago,
375–11	* Y· ago, while in Italy,
Pul. 35– 9	* nineteen hundred y· ago.
36–20	* y· ago Mrs. Eddy removed from
53– 3	* nineteen hundred y· ago,
66– 5	* founded fifteen y· ago
67–15	* Founded twenty-five y· ago,
69– 2	* about three y· ago
69– 8	* some twelve y· ago,
72–13	* a number of y· ago
79–10	* starting fifteen y· ago,
85– 1	* nearly thirty y· ago
Rud. 8– 5	lion of six thousand y· ago ;
'01. 18– 6	the sneers forty y· ago
27–16	start thirty y· ago
Po. 3–15	Written many y· ago.
35–15	more than sixty y· ago
My. 10– 6	* externalized itself, ten y· ago,
22–14	* almost forty y· ago,
43–21	* Forty y· ago the Science of
50–29	* more than twenty-six y· ago,
52–20	* Eighteen y· ago, the Rev. . . . Wiggin,
55–31	* Twelve y· ago the twenty-first
59– 3	* nearly forty y· ago.
67–25	* begun nearly two years ago,
68–15	* built twelve y· ago,
70– 5	* only twelve y· ago,
72–29	* in Boston twelve y· ago
76–28	* twenty-seven y· ago was founded
85– 5	* Thirty y· ago it was comparatively
92–14	* it is but a few y· ago that
94–31	* But a few y· ago, men there were
104–28	learn of her who, thirty y· ago,
109–10	If nineteen hundred y· ago
181–21	Thirty y· ago (1866)
181–25	show that thirty y· ago
182– 1	Thirty y· ago Chicago
182– 4	Thirty y· ago at my request
237– 6	some twenty-five y· ago
313– 2	a silly song of y· ago.
322–15	* Thanksgiving Day twenty y· ago,
325–12	* Y· ago I offered my services
342– 9	* portraits of twenty y· ago,

allotted
My. 273– 7	* beyond the allotted y· of man,

years

all the
Man. 60–17	each day of all the y·.
My. 64–15	* all the y· of her leadership,

awaited the
My. 318–13	confidently awaited the y· to

beginning of
Un. 13–17	"without beginning of y· — see Heb. 7 : 3.

closing
Pul. 23–19	* closing y· of every century are

desired for
My. 40– 3	* She has desired for y· to

during the
Po. vi–24	* during the y· she resided in Lynn,

early
Mis. x–19	Timidity in early y· caused me,
Pul. 68– 2	* the church during its early y·,
Po. 19– 6	Written in early y·.

earthly
'01. 29–10	all the best of his earthly y·.

eight
Mis. 341–24	a little girl of eight y·,
Ret. 8– 3	when I was about eight y· old,
Pul. 33– 3	* When eight y· of age

eighteen
My. 52–20	* Eighteen y· ago, the Rev. . . . Wiggin,

1893
'00. 7– 8	in all the other 1893 y·.

eighty-seven
My. 272–25	* nearly eighty-seven y· of age,

eighty-six
My. 271–14	* lives at eighty-six y· of age

eleven
Pul. 72–16	* "And for the past eleven y·,"

few
Mis. 125–30	within the past few y· :
137–15	within the last few y·.
315–23	and for the first few y·,
Pul. 70–12	* She has within a few y·
Rud. 6–17	* within the last few y·,
My. 43–23	* A few y· later she
91–31	* After but a few y·,
92–14	* it is but a few y· ago that
94–31	* a few y· ago, men there were who

fifteen
Mis. 242–14	more difficult tasks fifteen y· ago.
Pul. 30–27	* within fifteen y· it has grown
66– 5	* was founded fifteen y· ago
79–10	* starting fifteen y· ago,
My. 309–28	* passed her first fifteen y· at

fifty
Un. 7– 1	in less than another fifty y·

first
My. 91–22	* during the first y· of

five
Ret. 36– 5	Five y· after . . . my first copyright,
44– 9	I had preached five y· before
Pul. 38– 2	* preached in other parishes for five y·
My. 356–15	within the last five y·

former
My. 141–17	* In former y·, the annual communion

forty
'01. 18– 6	the sneers forty y· ago
My. 22–14	* Since 1866, almost forty y· ago,
22–15	* almost forty y· in the wilderness,
37–14	* your obedience during forty y·
43–15	* forty y· before.
43–21	* Forty y· ago the Science of
59– 3	* nearly forty y· ago.
59– 8	* in less than forty y·
137–11	It is over forty y· that I have
174–22	For nearly forty y·
270–21	for the past forty y·
360–23	for forty y· in succession.

four
Mis. 349–23	preached four y·, . . . before I
Ret. 20– 8	about four y· of age,
Pul. 49–10	* "You have lived here only four y·,
49–13	"Four y· !" she ejaculated ;
My. 214–19	Four y· after my discovery of C. S.,

four hundred
Mis. 345– 3	four hundred y· before,

glide on
Mis. 110–25	increase rapidly as y· glide on.

goes on with
Mis. 15–14	and goes on with y· ;

gone by
My. 59–24	* In y· gone by I have been asked,

had passed
Mis. 386–19	" Y· had passed o'er thy broken
Po. 50– 3	" Y· had passed o'er thy broken

her
Mis. 39–12	all her y· in giving it birth.

impart
Po. 23– 3	A look that y· impart?

zeal
- *Mis.* 177–15   doff your lavender-kid *z·*,
-     284– 8   a *z·* without knowledge,
- *Ret.* 79–24   Restrain untempered *z·*.
- *My.* 85–14   * the *z·* and enthusiasm of
-     95–30   * religious faith and enlightened *z·*
-     97–22   * *z·* of its membership.
-     187– 1   faith, and Christian *z·*
-     259–18   an honest, wise *z·*,
-     291–10   *z·* according to wisdom,

zealots
- *Mis.* 335–22   is a fault of *z·*,

zealous
- *Mis.* 322–26   compensate your *z·* affection
- *Pul.* 84–27   * *z·* effort on the part of
- *My.* 213–12   more *z·* to do good,

zenith
- *Mis.* 320–24   the *z·* of Truth's domain,
- *Pul.* 36– 4   * very *z·* of its prosperity,
- *My.* 225– 4   rising to the *z·* of success,

zephyr
- *Mis.* 394– 2   'T is borne on the *z·*
- *Po.* 45– 1   'Tis borne on the *z·*

zephyrs
- *Ret.* 17– 3   midst the *z·* at play
- *Po.* 15– 1   soft sighing *z·*
-     62– 2   midst the *z·* at play

zest
- *Pul.* 45–24   * perhaps with an unusual *z·*,

Z

Zeus
- *My.* 159–26   *Z·*, the master of the gods,

Zion (*see also* **Zion's**)
- *Mis.* 126–28   this daughter of *Z·* :
-     146– 1   remember thee, and God's *Z·*,
-     150–14   loveth the gates of *Z·*.
-     154–12   the prosperity of His *Z·*.
-     369– 1   watchmen on the walls of *Z·*,
- *Pul.* 22–19   Then shall *Z·* have put on her
- *'01.* 35– 8   upon the hill-tops of *Z·*.
- *My.* 16–25   Behold, I lay in *Z·* — *Isa.* 28 : 16.
-     125–24   *Z·* must put on her beautiful
-     133– 8   church triumphant, and *Z·* be glorified.
-     171– 4   come to *Z·* with songs — *Isa.* 35 : 10.
-     184–24   prosperity of *Z·* is very precious
-     184–28   that saith unto *Z·*, — *Isa.* 52 : 7.
-     270–25   I love the prosperity of *Z·*,

Zion's
- *Mis.* 370– 9   sentinels of *Z·* watch-towers
- *My.* 3–11   in *Z·* waste places,

Zion's Herald
- *Mis.* 132–12   your communication to *Z· H·*,
-     242– 3   published in *Z· H·*.
- *My.* 97–15   * *Z· H·*, a rather bitter critic

zone
- *Chr.* 53– 1   circling on, from *z·* to *z·*,
- *'00.* 10–29   serving his country in that torrid *z·*

years

increasing
- *'01.* 29–16   parents' increasing *y·* and needs

intervening
- *Pul.* 85– 3   * during the intervening *y·*

its
- *Mis.* 230–21   and worse than waste its *y·*.
- *My.* 352– 9   * with its *y·* of tender ministry,

late
- *My.* 141– 8   * Of late *y·* members of the church

long
- *Mis.* 169– 8   the long *y·* of invalidism
- *Pul.* 84–26   * the result of long *y·* of untiring,
- *My.* 41–28   * through long *y·* of consecration

many
- *Mis.* 178– 2   my own sojourning for many *y·*,
-     248–23   Many *y·* ago my regular physician
-     300–24   I had for many *y·* been pastor,
- *Ret.* 5–18   who for many *y·* had resided in
- *'00.* 9–25   for many *y·* I have desired
-     15– 3   for many *y·* has been awaiting you.
- *'01.* 32–25   educated my thought many *y·*,
- *'02.* 15– 9   struggled on through many *y·* ;
- *Hea.* 14–23   waited many *y·* for a student to reach
- *Po.* 3–15   Written many *y·* ago.
- *My.* 42– 7   * one who has for many *y·*
-     91–19   * It has not been very many *y·* since
-     163–19   many *y·* of incessant labor
-     250–29   filled this sacred office many *y·*,
-     283–10   Many *y·* have I prayed and labored
-     286– 3   For many *y·* I have prayed
-     304–11   for many *y·* I wrote for the best
-     335–15   * for many *y·* after his death.

months or
- *Po.* 54– 1   It may be months or *y·*

nine
- *Pul.* 36– 3   * The work in . . . lasted nine *y·*,
-     63– 6   * taught the principles . . . for nine *y·*.
- *My.* v–19   * in 1875, after nine *y·* of arduous
-     314– 5   * During the following nine *y·*

nineteen hundred
- *Pul.* 35– 9   * nineteen hundred *y·* ago.
-     53– 3   * nineteen hundred *y·* ago,
- *My.* 109–10   If nineteen hundred *y·* ago

ninety-six
- *Mis.* 231– 6   had seen . . . ninety-six *y·*.

number of
- *Pul.* 79 13   * healed a number of *y·* ago
- *My.* 335–12   * a number of *y·* a resident

of toil
- *My.* 64– 6   * attainments and her *y·* of toil,

older in
- *My.* 342– 7   * Older in *y·*, white-haired and

one hundred
- *Pul.* 67–23   * exactly one hundred *y·*
- *Po.* 22– 5   One hundred *y·*, aflame with

oracle of
- *'02.* 17–27   this oracle of *y·* will put to flight

our
- *My.* 166–20   If all our *y·* were holidays,

recent
- *Mis.* 312–15   * has come in recent *y·*,
- *Po.* v– 4   * up to recent *y·*
- *My.* 83–29   * steady gains in recent *y·*.

riper
- *Mis.* 238– 5   the reverence of my riper *y·*

score of
- *Ret.* 2–10   more than a score of *y·*
- *My.* 98– 5   * less than a score of *y·*.

seven
- *Mis.* 348–18   once in about seven *y·*
- *'02.* 13– 5   During the last seven *y·*

several
- *Pul.* 36–20   * Several *y·* ago Mrs. Eddy
-     58– 6   * For several *y·* past
- *'01.* 29–27   I allowed them for several *y·*
- *My.* 134–29   * been familiar for several *y·*,
-     304–17   for several *y·* was the proprietor
-     309–12   For several *y·* father was

shadows of
- *My.* 184–19   which stays the shadows of *y·*.

sixteen
- *My.* 304– 9   At sixteen *y·* of age,

six thousand
- *Rud.* 8– 5   lion of six thousand *y·* ago ;

sixty
- *Pul.* 32–20   * some sixty *y·* of age,
- *Po.* 35–15   Written more than sixty *y·* ago

subsequent
- *My.* 304–20   and for ten subsequent *y·*

succeeding
- *My.* 177–18   but succeeding *y·* show

successive
- *Ret.* 40– 1   Through four successive *y·*
-     52– 1   many successive *y·* I have

years

sum of
- *My.* 146–10   "If wisdom lengthens my sum of *y·*
-     177–11   if wisdom lengthens my sum of *y·*

ten
- *Ret.* 10– 4   At ten *y·* of age I was
- *My.* 10– 6   * externalized itself, ten *y·* ago,
-     310–23   * Mary, a child ten *y·* old,

tender
- *Mis.* 254– 6   brooded . . . over their tender *y·*

that have passed
- *My.* 47–17   * over the *y·* that have passed
-     47–23   * *y·* that have passed since Mrs. Eddy

these
- *My.* 11– 9   * during these *y·* she has
-     22–20   * In these *y·* of work she has

thirty
- *Mis.* 161–19   when he was thirty *y·* of age ;
-     163– 4   had for thirty *y·* been preparing
-     341–25   vow of celibacy for thirty *y·*,
-     382– 8   has cost more than thirty *y·*
- *Pul.* vii– 4   during the ensuing thirty *y·*.
-     85– 1   * nearly thirty *y·* ago began to lay the
- *'01.* 27–16   could start thirty *y·* ago
- *My.* 70– 4   * organized only thirty *y·*
-     85– 5   * Thirty *y·* ago it was comparatively
-     104–28   thirty *y·* ago, was met with the
-     181–21   Thirty *y·* ago (1866) C. S. was discovered
-     181–25   thirty *y·* ago the death-rate was
-     182– 1   Thirty *y·* ago Chicago had few
-     182– 5   Thirty *y·* ago at my request
-     182– 7   a membership of thirty *y·*

three
- *Mis.* 120–24   once in three *y·* is perhaps as often
-     139– 2   three *y·* from this date ;
-     139– 3   to meet again in three *y·*.
-     163– 3   Three *y·* he went about doing good.
-     163–22   Only three *y·* a personal Saviour !
-     340–31   accepted no . . . for about three *y·*,
-     353–27   at about three *y·* of scientific age,
- *Man.* 25–14   but once in three *y·*.
-     54– 4   suspended for not less than three *y·*
-     55–16   three *y·* of exemplary character.
-     68– 2   member of this Church at least three *y·*
-     68– 5   to remain with Mrs. Eddy three *y·*
-     89–14   healing acceptably three *y·*,
-     89–22   healing successfully three *y·*
-     91–24   three *y·* beginning A.D. 1907 ;
-     94–17   shall not be less than three *y·*.
- *Ret.* 6–18   two or three *y·* no road law
-     24–22   withdrew from society about three *y·*,
- *Pul.* 53– 8   * three *y·* of his ministry on earth,
-     69– 2   * came to Baltimore about three *y·* ago
-     73– 8   * from the world for three *y·*
- *'00.* 7– 7   during the past three *y·*
- *My.* 98–20   * in a little less than three *y·*.
-     114–16   consulted no other . . . for about three *y·*.
-     246– 2   for three *y·* as practitioners
-     246– 8   practised C. S. three *y·*
-     250– 9   three *y·* of acceptable service
-     250 16   stipulating three *y·* as the term for
-     251–19   after three *y·* of good practice,
-     255– 9   removed every three *y·*,

three consecutive
- *Man.* 68–15   remain with her three consecutive *y·*,
-     91–25   are for three *consecutive y·*

tired
- *Peo.* 8– 8   for the sins of a few tired *y·*

to come
- *My.* 22–23   * In *y·* to come the moral and
-     56– 2   * adequate for *y·* to come.

twelve
- *Man.* 35– 1   Children when Twelve *Y·* Old.
-     35– 3   at the age of twelve *y·*,
-     54–18   not be received . . . for twelve *y·*.
- *Pul.* 60– 8   * some twelve *y·* ago,
- *My.* 55–31   * Twelve *y·* ago the twenty-first of
-     68–15   * built twelve *y·* ago,
-     70– 5   * its first church only twelve *y·* ago,
-     72–29   * in Boston twelve *y·* ago
-     169– 6   under twelve *y·* of age,
-     311–15   at twelve *y·* of age.

twenty
- *Mis.* 88–13   twenty *y·* in the pulpit,
-     242–23   having taken it twenty *y·* ;
- *Man.* 62–11   up to the age of twenty *y·*,
- *Ret.* 24– 7   During twenty *y·* prior to
- *Pul.* 38 7   * During these succeeding twenty *y·*
- *My.* 321–21   * twenty *y·* since I first saw you
-     321–29   * during the past twenty *y·*.
-     322–15   * Thanksgiving Day twenty *y·* ago,
-     342– 9   * portraits of twenty *y·* ago,

twenty-five
- *Pul.* 67–15   * Founded twenty-five *y·* ago,
- *My.* 100–11   * It is only twenty-five *y·*,
-     237– 6   some twenty-five *y·* ago

years
twenty-seven
My. 76–28 * which twenty-seven y· ago
twenty-six
My. 48–14 * and twenty-six y· later
50–29 * more than twenty-six y· ago,
two
Mis. 278–29 For two y· I have been gradually
375–14 * I spent two y· in Paris,
'00. 12–24 over two y·— he labored in the
My. 67–25 * begun nearly two y· ago,
181–31 first two y· of my discovery of
two and a half
Pul. 49–14 * only two and a half y·."
two consecutive
Ret. 6–27 for two consecutive y·.
two hundred
Pul. 26–27 * over two hundred y· old,
'01. 24–17 more than two hundred y· old.
working
My. 298–7 distinguished all my working y·.

Mis. ix–15 To preserve a long course of y·,
xi–25 through the dim corridors of y·,
35–1 Y· of practical proof,
110–16 and months into y·,
Pul. 23–20 * y· of more intense life,
Po. 67–20 change not with y·;
My. vi–18 * for y· the principal contributor to
181–22 Within those y· it is estimated
321–31 * who knew you y· before I did,

years'
Pul. 6–17 * ailment of seven y· standing.
My. 250–3 relative to a three y· term

yellow
Ret. 2–22 newspapers, y· with age.

yellow-fever and **yellow fever**
Ret. 19–8 y· raged in that city,
My. 312–8 * he died of y· f·.
312–20 suddenly seized with y· f·
335–17 * y· f· of the worst type,
335–27 * case was one of y· f·

yesterday
Mis. 281–25 I felt the weight of this y·,
Ret. 94–22 "the same y·,— *Heb.* 13: 8.
Un. 61–4 "the same y·,— *Heb.* 13: 8.
Pul. 40–22 * was y· dedicated to the
61–24 * Church . . . dedicated y·.
72–6 * called upon a few . . . y·
73–18 * When seen y· she emphasized
No. 31–7 than they did y·.
44–25 * "Heretics of y· are martyrs
'02. 4–21 statute for y·, and to-day,
5–3 tribal religions of y·
My. 29–10 * closing incident . . . y·
31–18 * opened . . . in Boston y·
65–7 * voted y· afternoon to raise
75–7 * Y· was a busy day
75–19 * Crowded as the hall was y·,
86–11 * present at the dedication y·
86–26 * attendance at the ceremonies y·
109–12 "the same y·,— *Heb.* 13: 8.
173–7 hospitality extended y·
173–13 would bring thousands here y·;
220–32 to-day than it did y·.
246–28 are the same to-day as y·
292–28 same y·, to-day, and forever;
296–16 healthier and happier, than y·.
328–18 * issued licenses y·

yet
Mis. 4–15 y· but little time has been
7–26 greater work y· remains to be done.
12–23 are y· to be uncovered
35–11 most concise, y· complete,
46–28 has not y· wholly attained unto
53–23 y· he found it difficult to
69–27 The man is living y·;
71–4 y· he saved many a drunkard
81–21 *or has not Truth y· reached the*
86–4 but it doth not y· appear.
105–7 y· this demonstration is the
120–13 mighty victory is y· to be won,
126–15 church is not y· quite sensible of
126–23 y· nothing circulates so rapidly:
130–6 Do we y· understand
139–5 such as you even y· have not
142–30 y· as friends we can
163–22 y· the foundations he laid
179–26 y· we look into matter and the earth
184–19 y· persists in evil,
190–13 needs y· to be learned.
194–8 y· should deny the validity
197–7 is not y· recognized.
212–32 had not y· drunk of his cup,

yet
Mis. 215–32 nor y· when it is in the ear;
222–24 for it is not y· known.
227–9 y· with malice aforethought
228–4 and y· not to avenge thyself,
236–25 Y·, notwithstanding one's
238–11 more than history has y· recorded.
238–17 Y· the good done, and the love that
243–5 not y· made surgery one of the
262–24 y· were our burdens heavy but for
270–22 y· follow him in healing.
273–18 not y· accomplished all the
280–9 y·, I would not weigh you,
286–17 y· this is possible in *Science,*
306–5 * motto has not y· been decided upon,
309–31 more than they have y· learned.
317–16 is y· assimilated spiritually
317–17 y· this assimilation is indispensable
360–2 Human lives are y· uncarved,
360–7 unpretentious y· colossal characters,
368–8 * Y· that scaffold sways the future,
377–4 y· so near and full of radiant relief
379–30 Y·, there remained the difficulty of
395–8 y· I trow, When sweet *rondeau*
396–9 Y· here, upon this faded sod,
Chr. 53–25 Y· wherefore signalize the birth
Ret. 18–12 Y·, dwellers in Eden,
21–22 awakening . . . is as y· imperfect;
26–27 know y· more of the nothingness of
31–20 y· offend in one point,— *Jas.* 2: 10.
38–4 y· he stopped my work.
67–8 and y· are separate from God.
78–4 student has not y· achieved the
80–4 y· it may seem severe.
80–9 * Y· they grind exceeding small;
82–1 y· their core is constantly
93–21 as y· this grandest verity has not
94–5 and y· contradicts divine Science
94–7 seems to be good, and y· errs,
Un. 6–26 are not y· thoroughly drilled
9–24 y· healing, as I teach it,
11–27 There are y· four months,
19–6 y· which He cannot avert.
21–5 y· each mortal is not two
21–7 y· they are not two but one,
29–25 I shall y· praise Him,— *Psal.* 42: 11.
33–7 y· we have it on divine authority:
34–15 y· put your finger on a burning
35–10 y·, strictly speaking, there is no
36–21 y· admit the reality of moral evil,
36–23 y· is not conscious of matter,
48–3 y· ask, and I will answer.
55–21 "Y· in my flesh— *Job.* 19: 26.
58–17 y· without sin."— *Heb.* 4: 15.
59–9 y· as "the Son of man— *John* 3: 13.
60–11 y· we descant upon sickness,
60–25 are y· in your sins."— *I Cor.* 15: 17.
62–4 y· God dies not,
Pul. 3–20 "Y· in my flesh— *Job* 19: 26.
7–7 Y· when I recall the past,
14–4 active y· unseen mental agencies
15–14 y· have given no warning.
32–20 * y· she had the coloring and the
38–26 * Y· each and all these movements,
44–11 * y· the mother in Israel, alone
49–10 * and y· from a barren waste
51–8 * y· they are to be numbered
59–2 * she has not y· visited her temple,
72–18 * y· have been perfectly well."
73–27 * no more complete and y· concise
83–6 * has not y· the moral strength
Rud. 8–19 y· is false to God and man,
14–17 y· will expect and require others to
No. 5–19 and y· is arrayed against being,
16–16 y· forever giving forth more light,
27–19 * "No man living hath y· seen man."
31–5 they are y· sick and sinful.
34–22 Life of Spirit is not y· discerned.
34–23 y· mounting to the throne of glory
35–19 and y· governs mankind.
Pan. 4–23 I shall y· praise Him,— *Psal.* 42: 11.
'01. 6–14 y· God must be One
7–29 and y· have believed."— *John* 20: 29.
9–18 y· Christ is rejected of men!
12–14 y· should not have charity,
14–2 and y· commit sin,
23–5 y· that God has an opposite
23–7 y· that evil exists and is real,
27–13 If any one as y· has healed
'02. 12–1 has not y· come;
15–2 y· I never lost my faith
18–21 Y· he said, "The works— *John* 14: 12.
19–2 Y· behold his love!
Peo. 8–16 y· we make more of matter,
10–28 y· that hour was a prophecy of
Po. vii–2 * *y·, even these are characterized*

yet
Po. 23–7 give those earnest eyes y· back
27–14 With traitors unvoiced y·?
27–16 ere they break in silence y·,
31–2 nor y· by nature sown,
34–15 Y· wherefore ask thy doom?
42–4 Y· there's one will be victor,
57–15 And y· I trow,
59–1 Y· here, upon this faded sod,
64–1 Y·, dwellers in Eden,
68–13 Y· stronger than these is the spell
74–4 Smile on me y·,
77–6 Y· wherefore this Thy love?
78–14 O meekest of mourners, while y·
My. v–1 * God of Hosts, be with us y·;
11–2 * we are as y· but imperfect
45–9 * Y· the upwards of thirty thousand
50–17 * "y· there was a feeling of trust
53–4 * y· not until the authoress
55–6 * y· the thought of obtaining
60–15 * I have y· the little Bible
69–17 * y· not a single pillar or post
75–27 * No church has ever y· been
80–9 * y· they were believed.
82–1 * Y· they all have the same
93–13 * y· it has rare lures for
97–7 * It has y· to be shown that
97–28 * Boston has not y· recovered
99–25 * and the end is not y·.
107–14 Y· the homœopathist administers
109–16 y· we may sometimes say
111–20 and y· the book itself be
114–7 y· reached the maximum
114–11 not y· uncovered to the gaze
114–13 is not y· won.
118–17 y· have believed."— *John* 20: 29.
121–10 y· yielding to the touch of
121–15 Y· peace is desirable,
134–13 imperative demand not y· met.
146–15 has not y· been reached.
146–16 Y· his immortal words
152–10 human race has not y· reached
186–22 while they are y· speaking,— *Isa.* 65: 24.
228–9 y· depart from Christ's teachings.
243–13 not y· had the privilege of
251–2 I cannot y· say.
273–11 y· have I not seen— *Psal* 37: 25.
292–3 more than history has y· recorded.
294–2 are y· in a large minority
302–23 Because C. S. is not y· popular,
323–7 * I have his little book y·.
331–28 * y· when we listen to Mrs. Glover
332–7 * y· it is all we can award:
334–20 and y· commit sin,
352–9 * y· we know that the real gratitude

yield
Mis. 46–3 "To whom ye y·— *Rom.* 6: 16.
120–7 to whom ye y·— *Rom.* 6: 16.
178–28 but will y· to circumstances.
182–31 sin, and death will y· to it,
184–16 y· to material sense, and lose his
190–26 must y· to the right sense,
221–28 y· the same product
236–11 and y· obedience to them
246–21 wrong that refused to y· its prey
345–9 * unless you y· your religion,"
346–18 "to whom ye y·— *Rom.* 6: 16.
395–24 The languid brooklets y· their sighs,
Ret. 23–4 y· to the irony of fate,
Un. 39–4 y· to holiness, health, and Life,
60–28 y· to His eternal presence,
64–13 must y· to despair,
No. 35–8 y· lovingly to the purpose of divine
'02. 13–10 y· this church a liberal income.
Hea. 18–2 y· to the government of God,
Po. 2–17 Y· to the sun's more genial,
46–12 And y· its beauty and perfume
58–9 languid brooklets y· their sighs,
67–22 y· earth the fragrance of goodness

yielded
Mis. 237–3 y· somewhat to the metaphysical
373–7 but, as usual, he finally y·.
Ret. 38–7 I y· to a constant conviction
57–14 would have y· to Science.
'01. 31–26 and y· up graciously

yielding
Mis. 12–20 danger of y· to temptation
107–20 three states . . . before y· error.
236–15 y· to constant solicitations of
'01. 20–1 y· to its aggressive features.
Hea. 11–6 physics are y· slowly to metaphysics;
Peo. 7–20 * If we carve it then on the y· stone
Po. 23–13 Y· a holy strength to right,
My. 121–11 y· to the touch of a finger.

yields
Mis. 37–23 appetite for alcohol y· to Science
84–30 y· a clearer and nearer sense of Life
204–9 error y· up its weapons
220–12 until the patient's mind y·,
339–15 if it y· not, grows stronger.
Ret. 18–12 earth y· you her tear,
49–1 which y· a large income,
Pul. 6–4 y· to the church established by
'00. 15–15 y· to sharp conviction
Peo. 2–6 y· its grosser elements,
Po. 64–1 earth y· you her tear,

yoke
Mis. 90–17 Break the y· of bondage in every
262–26 and renders the y· easy.

yon
Mis. 392–6 majestic oak, from y· high place
Po. 1–13 Proud from y· cloud-crowned
20–8 majestic oak, from y· high place

yonder
My. 222–12 hence to y· place;— *Matt.* 17: 20.

yore
Mis. 360–27 is heard as of y· saying
Pul. 7–5 To-day, as of y·, her laws
Po. 47–2 As sweetly they came of y·,
My. 110–8 and it shines as of y·,

York, Pa.
Pul. 88–27 * *Daily, Y·, P·.*

young
Mis. 49–1 A y· lady entered the College class
49–5 this y· lady had manifested
145–24 y· lion and the fatling— *Isa.* 11: 6.
201–28 y· man is awakened to bar his door
254–8 mother-bird tendeth her y·
390–24 Ne'er perish y·, like things of earth,
Ret. 7–7 * Albert Baker was a y· man
19–19 tender devotion to his y· bride
Un. 61–8 neither y· nor old,
Pul. 7–2 * "Had I y· blood in my veins,
Rud. 6–13 Langley, the y· American astronomer
Hea. 2–12 * too strong for y· Melanchthon."
Po. 8–20 thinking alone of a fair y· bride,
9–3 picturing alone a glad y· face,
27–8 will the y· year dawn with wisdom's
56–3 Ne'er perish y·, like things of earth,
66–12 but a y· heart and glad
My. 122–19 where the y· child lies,
149–14 When a y· man vainly boasted,
272–19 * chapter sub-title
273–11 "I have been y·,— *Psal.* 37: 25.
312–8 * He left his y· wife in a
330–31 tender devotion to his y· bride
335–30 * y· wife prayed incessantly

younger
My. 146–11 may then be even y· than now."
177–12 I shall then be even y·

youngest
Ret. 4–2 y· of whom was my father,
5–6 y· of my parents' six children
My. 309–17 Mark Baker was the y· of
310–9 my y· brother, George Sulliva

Young Men's Christian Asso
My. 332–17 * Y· M· C· A· at W

youth
Mis. ix–19 a y· that p
ix–21 fleeting
226–4 unbia
241–1 fai
324–6
Ret. 15–1
17
18
Pul. 3
Po.

youtl
Pul.

youwar
My. 216

Yule-fires
My. 256–23

Appendix A
Index to the Chapter Sub-titles and Headings of the Writings of Mary Baker Eddy
other than Science and Health
and to the Titles of the Poems

Index to the Chapter Sub-titles and Headings of the Writings of Mary Baker Eddy

other than Science and Health

and to the Titles of the Poems

Appendix B
Index to the Scriptural Quotations
in the Writings of Mary Baker Eddy
other than Science and Health

Index to the Scriptural Quotations

OLD TESTAMENT

Psalms
103 : 3
Mis. 184–13
320–18
Man. 47–17
Pul. 10– 6
Pan. 4–24
Peo. 12–13
My. 13–19
119–17
103 : 4
My. 13–20
103 : 5
My. 13–22
107 : 3
My. 63–27
107 : 8
My. 193– 8
118 : 22
Mis. 196–23
119 : 67
Mis. 208–21
121 : 2
Mis. 268–18
130 : 1
Mis. 211–13
My. 290–16
139 : 23
Ret. 14–25
My. 33– 9
139 : 24
Ret. 14–27
My. 33–11

Proverbs
3 : 5
Mis. 298– 1
'01. 34–29
3 : 6
'01. 34–30
My. 161–26
4 : 7
My. 60–18
11 : 21
Mis. 281–29
13 : 15
Mis. 261–14

Proverbs
15 : 1
Man. 41– 9
16 : 32
Mis. 223–25
My. 196–10
23 : 7
Mis. 70– 7
Peo. 3– 2
25 : 11
Mis. 346–23
26 : 4
Mis. 347– 1
'01. 11–26
26 : 5
Mis. 348–15
26 : 11
Mis. 353–31
27 : 19
Mis. 152– 3
203– 9
28 : 13
Mis. 213– 9
31 : 26
My. 42– 2

Ecclesiastes
1 : 9
Pul. 53– 4

Song
2 : 12
Mis. 329–24
2 : 15
My. 123–30
5 : 10
Ret. 23–19
23–20
5 : 16
Mis. 342–12
Ret. 23–19
'01. 6–30
6 : 10
Pul. 83–12

Isaiah
1 : 18
Mis. 59–19

Isaiah
2 : 4
Mis. xii– 6
5 : 12
Chr. 55–12
9 : 2
Chr. 55– 8
9 : 6
Mis. 161– 5
164–17
166–10
167–21
168–17
321– 3
321– 4
370–10
11 : 6
Mis. 145–22
26 : 3
My. 290–14
28 : 10
Mis. 32–10
28 : 16
My. 16–24
28 : 17
My. 16–28
29 : 9
Mis. 325– 7
32 : 2
Mis. 144–15
263– 9
Pul. 20–19
35 : 10
My. 171– 3
40 : 31
Mis. 364– 5
42 : 16
My. 140– 2
43 : 1
My. 193–27
45 : 5
Mis. 97–18
45 : 22
My. 282– 7
48 : 18
Mis. 268– 8

Isaiah
52 : 7
Ret. 45– 3
My. 184–26
53 : 1
Mis. 183–20
Un. 39– 9
53 : 3
Mis. 84–14
Un. 55– 4
53 : 5
Mis. 3–12
260– 2
Un. 55– 7
55 : 1
Mis. 148–29
Ret. 41– 5
'02. 15– 8
My. v–17
55 : 11
My. 13–32
58 : 11
Po. 71–22
59 : 1
Mis. 170–32
171– 1
59 : 14
Mis. 274–16
60 : 1
My. 183–26
60 : 19
My. 206–18
61 : 8
My. 177–23
63 : 3
Mis. 301–31
Un. 58– 6
65 : 24
My. 186–21

Jeremiah
6 : 14
Mis. 209– 6
My. 233–16
23 : 23
Mis. 103–32

Lamentations
3 : 33
Mis. 73– 5

Ezekiel
18 : 2
Mis. 72–12
18 : 3
Mis. 72–15
18 : 4
Mis. 75–27
Un. 28– 1
No. 28–25
18 : 20
Mis. 75–27
Un. 28– 1
No. 28–25
21 : 27
Mis. 80–22

Daniel
4 : 35
Mis. 334– 1
My. 200– 7

Micah
4 : 3
Mis. xii– 6
6 : 8
My. 283–23

Habakkuk
1 : 13
Un. 2– 1
My. 300– 1

Zechariah
4 : 6
My. 154–12

Malachi
3 : 10
My. 131–24
132– 3
269–26
3 : 11
My. 269–24

NEW TESTAMENT

Matthew
1 : 23
Mis. 103–28
331–27
My. 218– 8
3 : 3
Mis. 246–24
3 : 10
My. 296– 3
3 : 15
Mis. 91–10
380–22
Ret. 48–27
My. 140–21
162– 3
218– 3
357– 2
3 : 17
Mis. 206– 7
4 : 17
Un. 37– 6
My. 58–22
5 : 3
Mis. 325– 2
Ret. 26–26
5 : 7
My. 41–12
5 : 8
Mis. 15– 7
Pul. 35–10
5 : 9
My. 40–22
5 : 11
Mis. 8–22
8–29
'01. 3– 4
'02. 11–22
My. 104–29
191–13
316– 6
5 : 12
Mis. 8–25
'02. 11–24

Matthew
5 : 12
My. 6–11
270– 1
5 : 14
Mis. 323– 2
5 : 17
Mis. 261–18
261–20
'02. 5–23
My. 219–23
5 : 18
Un. 43–16
5 : 39
Ret. 45–20
My. 227–27
5 : 44
Mis. 9– 9
Ret. 29– 4
5 : 46
Pan. 9–24
5 : 48
Mis. 50–21
85–14
Pan. 9–11
11–30
'01. 8–15
6 : 5
Mis. 133–11
6 : 6
Mis. 133–14
133–25
133–26
6 : 9
My. 225–25
6 : 10
Mis. 174–25
208– 1
211–30
Man. 41–21
Pul. 22– 7
My. 281– 4

Matthew
6 : 13
My. 233– 6
6 : 23
Ret. 81–21
Un. 19–14
6 : 24
Mis. 89– 1
269– 6
Peo. 9–21
My. 138–16
356–22
6 : 25
Rud. 12–23
6 : 30
No. 26–25
6 : 31
Mis. 245– 3
6 : 32
Mis. 72–20
'02. 19–23
6 : 33
Mis. 270–14
Chr. 55–10
7 : 2
Mis. 298– 8
7 : 5
Mis. 355–21
7 : 6
Mis. 89–16
My. 227–23
7 : 12
Mis. 90–13
119–31
146–18
235–27
Man. 42–22
Ret. 87–20
My. 266– 8
7 : 14
'01. 28– 7
7 : 15
My. 215–20

Matthew
7 : 16
Mis. 27–16
7 : 20
Man. 49– 6
No. 15– 2
Pan. 10– 5
My. 233– 4
306–19
7 : 28
Mis. 189–26
Ret. 58–10
Un. 42–18
7 : 29
Mis. 189–27
Ret. 58–10
Un. 42–19
8 : 22
Mis. 129–13
169–30
Man. 60–18
Ret. 87– 1
'02. 9– 5
My. 353–25
8 : 25
Mis. 204– 4
'00. 7–26
8 : 29
'00. 9–11
'02. 10– 6
9 : 14
My. 339–18
9 : 17
No. 43–20
9 : 22
My. 152– 6
10 : 8
Mis. 37–14
325–32
Chr. 55–22
Ret. 36– 1
87–15
88– 5

Matthew
10 : 8
Ret. 88–10
Pul. 28– 7
28– 8
29–18
66–12
No. 14–19
22–18
41–21
My. 172–16
172–17
300–26
10 : 12
Mis. 282–14
10 : 13
My. 150–31
10 : 16
Mis. 90–16
210–10
My. 150–28
205– 5
10 : 17
'01. 10– 3
10 : 25
'01. 10– 4
28–23
10 : 26
Mis. 348–11
'01. 10– 6
10 : 34
Mis. 214– 4
'01. 31– 9
10 : 35
Mis. 214– 6
10 : 36
Mis. 214– 9
10 : 37
Man. 69–18
10 : 38
My. 4– 7
233–24
10 : 39
Mis. 327–25

Luke	John	John	John	Romans
18:8	**4:24**	**11:42**	**21:16**	**8:17**
'01. 12–11	Mis. 113– 4	My. 290–25	Mis. 397–21	Mis. 46–23
18:17	219– 8	**12:32**	Ret. page 46	255–15
Mis. 344–25	Un. 31– 1	Ret. 93– 8	Pul. 17– 1	**8:21**
20:14	31– 3	**13:7**	Po. page 14	Mis. 199– 9
Mis. 253–19	Rud. 4–21	Mis. 317–22	**21:22**	**8:23**
254–13	13–16	My. 246–25	Man. 60–19	Mis. 15– 5
20:35	'01. 3–15	251– 2	**Acts**	95–22
My. 269– 6	My. 25–21	**13:27**	**2:1**	Peo. 10–25
20:36	270–32	Mis. 57–11	Mis. 134–12	**8:28**
My. 269– 8	**4:32**	**13:34**	143–26	Mis. 10– 6
21:33	Mis. 170–16	Mis. 292– 4	My. 212–19	'00. 11–10
Mis. 99–21	My. 147–27	'02. 7–25	**3:6**	My. 143–25
111–17	**5:8**	18–16	Chr. 55–18	**8:31**
22:11	Mis. 370– 1	**14:6**	**7:60**	Mis. 150–21
My. 156–14	**5:14**	Mis. 74–12	'00. 14–27	Ret. 85–24
22:12	My. 288–25	75– 2	**10:34**	My. 143–27
My. 156–16	**5:25**	308– 9	My. 128– 9	151–15
22:42	Chr. 55– 6	Un. 37– 1	**10:38**	**11:36**
Mis. 212–20	**5:31**	37– 2	Mis. 355–22	Mis. 71–24
22:67	Ret. 25–27	55–10	**16:31**	**12:15**
Mis. 121–26	Un. 33– 8	55–11	Mis. 196–28	My. 192–23
22:68	**6:45**	55–12	**17:23**	**12:19**
Mis. 121–26	My. 230–26	55–13	My. 153–21	Mis. 130–15
23:2	**6:51**	58–13	**17:28**	**12:21**
No. 41– 5	My. 131–10	No. 12–17	Mis. 8– 5	Mis. 66–27
23:5	**6:53**	'02. 16–15	82–29	334–29
My. 104– 8	My. 156–22	Hea. 16–27	Ret. 93–17	My. 128–27
104–15	**6:63**	My. 257–14	Pul. 2–23	228– 8
222–18	My. 108– 9	349–18	Pan. 13–20	**13:7**
23:34	**6:70**	**14:12**	'02. 12–19	My. 202– 8
Un. 44– 4	Mis. 97– 8	Mis. 21– 9	No. 17– 7	**13:8**
My. 180–28	191– 9	192–10	My. 109–22	Rud. 14– 4
270–19	No. 22–24	193–27	**22:28**	My. 202–10
23:43	**7:12**	194–20	Peo. 10–13	**14:16**
Mis. 70–11	Hea. 3–19	195–18	**24:5**	Mis. 89–16
24:5	**7:46**	195–31	My. 104– 4	**14:22**
Un. 62–23	Mis. 269–11	196–25	104– 6	Ret. 94–18
24:6	Un. 17–16	251–15	104–12	**14:23**
Mis. 179– 1	**8:15**	'02. 18–21	106–22	Ret. 94–19
179–15	My. 364– 2	My. 221–22	**24:12**	
Un. 62–24	**8:32**	**14:15**	My. 285–21	**I Corinthians**
24:25	Mis. 241–22	'02. 17– 3	**24:13**	**1:31**
'02. 19– 6	'01. 10– 1	**14:19**	My. 285–23	Mis. 270–26
John	**8:44**	Mis. 179–32	**24:14**	**2:8**
1:1	Mis. 24–25	**14:27**	Mis. 96–15	Un. 56– 7
Mis. 29–11	83–18	My. 279– 3	My. 285–24	**2:9**
Pan. 5– 4	192– 5	**14:28**	**26:24**	Un. 28–22
My. 117–18	196–14	Pan. 8–20	Mis. 178–20	**2:16**
1:3	198–11	'01. 8– 8	**Romans**	My. 141–29
Mis. 45–28	257–20	**15:7**	**1:29**	**3:11**
259– 1	259– 5	Ret. 92– 8	Mis. 368–21	Mis. 365– 2
Pan. 5– 4	Ret. 67–24	My. 150–23	**2:15**	Un. 64– 8
My. 178–18	Un. 32–21	**15:8**	Un. 21– 2	No. 21–23
267– 7	Rud. 7–17	My. 202–28	**3:4**	**5:8**
1:4	7–20	**15:10**	Rud. 5– 3	Mis. 175–15
My. 154–12	No. 24–23	Mis. 118–15	**3:8**	**6:20**
154–13	32–16	**15:12**	Mis. 122–17	Man. 47–11
295– 6	Pan. 5–12	My. 187–28	298– 4	**8:5**
1:5	'00. 5– 8	**16:15**	335–29	Mis. 333–15
My. 110– 8	**8:51**	Mis. 205–11	**3:13**	Pan. 2–14
1:9	Mis. 76– 4	**16:24**	Mis. 368–21	**9:11**
My. 257–15	No. 31–27	'01. 19– 8	**6:16**	Mis. 38–10
1:12	My. 300–18	**16:28**	Mis. 46– 2	**10:18**
Mis. 180–21	**8:58**	Mis. 360–28	120– 7	Mis. 360–19
181–24	Mis. 189–14	**16:33**	346–17	**13:1**
182– 5	360–29	My. 132– 6	**6:23**	No. 45– 3
185–17	Chr. 55–15	**17:1**	Mis. 76–26	'01. 26–21
185–24	'01. 8–25	Mis. 83–23	**7:6**	**13:4**
1:13	**10:13**	**17:3**	No. 25– 4	No. 45– 4
Mis. 180–22	Mis. 213–25	Un. 4–23	**8:1**	My. 231–17
181–16	**10:16**	**17:11**	Mis. 188–12	260–23
182–14	Mis. 244–24	My. 253–16	My. 113–11	**13:5**
182–17	270–18	**17:20**	205– 1	No. 45– 5
1:14	Chr. 55–25	Mis. 29– 8	**8:2**	My. 19–22
Un. 39– 1	**10:27**	My. 190–28	Mis. 30–20	**13:6**
1:29	Mis. 151– 3	**17:25**	201–18	No. 45– 6
Mis. 121–23	213–21	My. 253–11	321–15	**13:11**
'01. 9–17	**10:28**	**18:11**	326– 2	Mis. 359– 8
2:19	Mis. 151– 4	Mis. 214– 1	'01. 9–10	My. 135– 2
Pul. 3– 5	213–23	214–14	'02. 9–11	261–15
3:2	**10:30**	214–16	My. 41–23	**13:12**
My. 191– 2	Mis. 37– 9	**19:24**	113–13	Mis. 359–10
3:6	Un. 46–13	Mis. 302– 5	272– 5	**14:40**
Ret. 26–22	'01. 8– 7	**20:13**	293–28	Mis. 310–16
3:13	'02. 12–15	'00. 7–20	**8:6**	**15:17**
Un. 59– 9	**10:32**	**20:16**	Mis. 24– 3	Un. 60–24
No. 36– 9	No. 41– 5	Mis. 179–29	'02. 6–27	**15:22**
3:34	My. 108–23	My. 258–10	**8:7**	Mis. 79–24
Mis. 317–30	227– 1	**20:17**	Mis. 36–24	**15:26**
4:23	**11:26**	Mis. 180–12	**8:10**	My. 300–15
Mis. 150–20	Chr. 55–28	**20:29**	Chr. 55–16	**15:45**
321–13	No. 13– 8	'01. 7–27	**8:16**	Mis. 185–27
Ret. 65–13	Pan. 9–12	My. 118–16	Mis. 46–22	188–31
No. 34– 9			255–14	189–13
My. 5–25				Un. 30–14

II Corinthians

2 : 16
Un. 43–13
3 : 17
My. 128–11
4 : 1
My. 123–32
4 : 2
Mis. 191– 1
My. 123–32
4 : 4
Mis. 190–31
4 : 18
Mis. 66–20
Un. 62– 6
5 : 1
Pul. 2–14
My. 188–13
192–29
194– 7
5 : 8
Mis. 344–21
My. 118–14
6 : 2
My. 12–17
6 : 14
Mis. 333–22
6 : 15
Mis. 333–23
6 : 17
Mis. 136–15
9 : 8
My. 156– 6
10 : 4
Mis. 139–10
10 : 5
Mis. 139–11
12 : 7
Un. 57–21
12 : 10
Mis. 199–11
200–21
201–20
201–20
201–23
13 : 11
Mis. 134–12
13 : 14
My. 19– 9

Galatians

2 : 20
Un. 61–20
5 : 1
My. 205– 3
5 : 22
My. 167– 4
6 : 2
Mis. 39–23
6 : 3
Pan. 10– 3
6 : 7
Mis. 66– 6
105–29
Pul. 7 22
No. 32– 9
Hea. 5–27
My. 6– 5
6 : 9
Mis. 153– 3

Ephesians

1 : 7
'01. 10–20
2 : 1
My. 133–14
2 : 12
Ret. 61–15
2 : 20
Ret. 15– 6
2 : 21
My. 24–14
3 : 20
My. 156– 5
4 : 5
Peo. 1– 1
5– 3
14–19
4 : 6
Pan. 13–22
'00. 4–30

Ephesians

4 : 14
No. 22– 1
5 : 8
My. 206–30
5 : 23
My. 108–29
6 : 12
Mis. 116– 4

Philippians

1 : 21
Mis. 84–19
2 : 5
Mis. 197–20
Ret. 76–17
Un. 4–19
2 : 12
My. 300– 4
2 : 13
My. 300– 5
3 : 12
Un. 43–24
43–25
3 : 13
Mis. 328–28
'00. 6– 4
3 : 14
'00. 6– 7
4 : 4
Mis. 330–11
4 : 5
Un. 5–20
4 : 7
No. 8– 7
4 : 8
Mis. 128– 6
4 : 9
Mis. 128–11

Colossians

1 : 12
My. 206–26
1 : 13
My. 206–28
3 : 1
Mis. 178–11
3 : 4
Mis. 76–27
3 : 9
Mis. 15–23
No. 27–21
27–22
Pan. 11– 3
Hea. 18– 4
3 : 10
Pan. 11– 4

I Thessalonians

5 : 17
Mis. 356–30
No. 39–28
My. 340– 4
5 : 21
My. 129– 2

I Timothy

1 : 5
My. 187–11
3 : 16
Chr. 53–61
Ret. 37–20
Un. 5–14
My. 109–24
124–28
5 : 23
Mis. 243–24
6 : 13
My. 42– 7

II Timothy

1 : 12
Ret. 54–16
My. 156– 4
156– 9
228–27
2 : 12
Mis. 157– 3
3 : 15
Mis. 134– 2
4 : 2
No. v– 3
4 : 7
Hea. 2–15

Hebrews

1 : 3
Mis. 26–25
4 : 15
Un. 58–16
6 : 1
My. 128– 3
6 : 2
Mis. 216–13
6 : 6
Un. 56– 8
7 : 3
Chr. 55–20
Un. 13–17
8 : 5
Mis. 44– 1
11 : 1
Mis. 27–30
175–11
Pan. 15– 8
My. 226–18
11 : 38
'01. 30– 3
12 : 1
Mis. 361–17
12 : 2
Mis. 361–20
Ret. 22–11
My. 258–13
349–16
12 : 3
Ret. 22– 9
My. 196–20
12 : 6
Mis. 18– 3
73– 4
125– 3
208–19
Ret. 80– 5
12 : 7
Un. 23–10
12 : 8
Un. 23–12
12 : 14
'02. 16–12
12 : 22
My. 46–28
12 : 23
My. 46–29
12 : 29
Mis. 326–14
13 : 1
'00. 14–14
13 : 3
Mis. 157–13
13 : 8
Ret. 94–22
Un. 61– 3
My. 109–12

James

1 : 17
Un. 14–17
1 : 18
My. 132–15
1 : 10
My. 196– 9
2 : 10
Ret. 31–19
2 : 18
Hea. 5–24
My. 3–12
2 : 26
Pul. 9–29
3 : 2
My. 190–12
3 : 9
Un. 60–13
3 : 10
Un. 60–15
3 : 11
Mis. 27–17
3 : 17
My. 40–19
3 : 18
My. 40–20
4 : 3
Mis. 51–30
No. 40– 1
Hea. 15–23
Peo. 9–17

James

4 : 8
Mis. 198–23
5 : 15
No. 41–25
My. 221–32

I Peter

1 : 4
My. 41–26
1 : 25
Pul. 7–22
2 : 1
My. 17– 4
2 : 2
My. 17– 6
2 : 3
My. 17– 8
2 : 4
My. 17– 0
2 : 5
My. 17–11
64–25
2 : 6
My. 17–14
2 : 9
My. 206–22
2 : 21
My. 196–16
2 : 23
My. 196–17
2 : 24
Un. 55– 6

II Peter

3 : 16
Un. 1– 4
1– 6

I John

2 : 16
Ret. 79–13
3 : 2
Mis. 196–22
Un. 41–19
3 : 8
No. 31–14
3 : 11
My. 187–14
4 : 1
Mis. 171–13
4 : 8
Mis. 96–14
125–19
150–24
'01. 3–16
'02. 5–18
8– 1
8– 7
My. 109–13
188–15
4 : 18
Mis. 229 27
229–27
Ret. 61–17
Un. 20–16
Peo. 6–15
5 : 21
Mis. 307–23

II John

1 : 1
Ret. 90–10

Revelation

1 : 8
Mis. 333–10
2 : 1
'00. 12– 3
2 : 4
'00. 12–17
15–23
2 : 5
'00. 12–19
2 : 6
'00. 13– 4
2 : 7
'00. 11–26
2 : 10
'00. 13–14
2 : 13
'00. 13–21
2 : 19
'00. 15–24

Revelation

2 : 26
Chr. 57– 1
My. 285–17
2 : 28
Chr. 57– 4
3 : 7
'00. 14–21
My. 153– 8
153– 9
3 : 8
'00. 14– 1
3 : 9
'00. 14– 3
3 : 11
'00. 14– 4
3 : 12
Mis. 153–19
Pul. 27–13
3 : 20
Chr. 55–26
6 : 1
Mis. 168–16
7 : 14
Mis. 358–16
10 : 2
My. 126– 8
12 : 1
Pul. 83–26
12 : 4
Hea. 10– 3
12 : 10
Mis. 191–26
Pul. 12– 5
'01. 33– 4
12 : 11
Pul. 12– 9
12 : 12
Pul. 12–11
12 : 13
Pul. 13–27
12 : 15
Pul. 14– 8
12 : 16
Pul. 14–10
13 : 8
My. 185–17
13 : 17
Mis. 113– 8
269–30
14 : 13
Un. 3– 6
17 : 2
My. 125–32
17 : 6
My. 125–30
18 : 2
My. 126–25
18 : 4
My. 126–14
18 : 5
My. 126–15
18 : 6
My. 126–17
18 : 7
My. 126–19
18 : 8
My. 126–20
19 : 6
Mis. 172–14
20 : 6
Mis. 2–20
20 : 7
Mis. 3–30
21 : 1
Mis. 21– 7
21 : 23
My. 206–20
21 : 25
Mis. 276–16
21 : 27
No. 15–26
22 : 2
Ret. 95– 1
95– 2
22 : 14
My. 3– 7
22 : 16
Chr. 55– 4
22 : 17
My. 153–27